Labels used in the dictionar

The following labels are used with words that express a particular attitude or are appropriate in a particular situation.
下列标识表示有关词汇反映特定态度或适用于特定场合。

approving expressions show that you feel approval or admiration, for example *feisty, petite.* 褒义词表示赞同或赞赏，如 feisty（坚决而据理力争的）、petite（娇小的）。

disapproving expressions show that you feel disapproval or contempt, for example *blinkered, newfangled.* 贬义词表示反对或藐视，如 blinkered（目光狭窄的；心胸隘窄的）、newfangled（新奇怪异的；时髦复杂的）。

figurative language is used in a non-literal or metaphorical way, as in *He didn't want to cast a shadow on* (= spoil) *their happiness.* 比喻指用比拟或隐喻方式表达，如：He didn't want to cast a shadow on (= spoil) their happiness.
他不想给他们的幸福蒙上阴影。

formal expressions are usually only used in serious or official language and would not be appropriate in normal everyday conversation. Examples are *admonish, besmirch.* 正式用语通常只用于庄重或正式场合，不宜用于日常会话中，如 admonish（告诫；警告）、besmirch（诋毁；败坏…的名声）。

humorous expressions are intended to be funny, for example *ignoramus, lurgy.* 幽默语目的是为了增加趣味，如 ignoramus（无知识的人）、lurgy（小恙；小病）。

informal expressions are used between friends or in a relaxed or unofficial situation. They are not appropriate for formal situations. Examples are *bonkers, dodgy.* 非正式用语用于朋友之间以及轻松或非正式场合，不宜用于正式场合，如 bonkers（疯狂；愚蠢透顶）、dodgy（狡诈的）。

have, as in *You're a great help,* … (= no help at all). 反语指说与表面意义相反的话，如：You're a great help, I must say! (= no help at all) 我得说，你可没少帮忙！（= 根本没帮忙）

literary language is used mainly in literature and imaginative writing, for example *aflame, halcyon.* 文学用语主要用于文学和创造性的写作中，如 aflame（在燃烧）、halcyon（平安幸福的）。

offensive expressions are used by some people to address or refer to people in a way that is very insulting, especially in connection with their race, religion, sex or disabilities, for example *half-caste, slut.* You should not use these words. 冒犯语指以侮辱的方式对人说话或提及某人，尤指与种族、宗教、性别或残疾等有关的问题，如 half-caste（混血儿）、slut（荡妇；邋遢女人）。这些词不应使用。

slang is very informal language, sometimes restricted to a particular group of people, for example people of the same age or those who have the same interests or do the same job. Examples are *dingbat, dosh.* 俚语指很不正式的用语，有时只限于某一特定群体，如同龄人、兴趣相同的人或同行，如 dingbat（笨蛋；蠢货；傻瓜）、dosh（钱）。

specialist language is used by people who specialize in particular subject areas, for example *accretion, adipose.* 专业术语指特定学科领域的人使用的专门词语，如 accretion（积聚层；堆积层；堆积或积聚过程）、adipose（身体组织用于贮存脂肪的）。

taboo expressions are likely to be thought by many people to be obscene or shocking. You should not use them. Examples are *bloody, shit.* 禁忌语指许多人认为猥亵或恶毒的用语，应该避免使用，如 bloody（该死）、shit（他妈的）。

The following labels show other restrictions on the use of words. 下列标识表明词汇使用的其他限制。

dialect describes expressions that are mainly used in particular regions of the British Isles, not including Ireland, Scotland or Wales, for example *beck, nowt.* 方言（dialect）指主要用于不包括爱尔兰、苏格兰或威尔士在内的不列颠群岛某些特定地区的词语，如 beck（小溪）、nowt（无；没有什么）。

old-fashioned expressions are passing out of current use, for example *balderdash, beanfeast.* 老式用法（old-fashioned）指逐渐过时的用语，如 balderdash（胡说）、beanfeast（聚会；喜庆）。

old use describes expressions that are no longer in current use, for example *ere, perchance.* 旧用法（old use）指现已不再使用的词语，如 ere（在…之前）、perchance（也许；可能）。

saying describes a well-known fixed or traditional phrase, such as a proverb, that is used to make a comment, give advice, etc., for example *actions speak louder than words.* 谚语、格言或警句（saying）指众所周知的固定说法或传统说法，用作评论、建议等，如 actions speak louder than words（行动比言语更为响亮）。

™ shows a trademark of a manufacturing company, for example *Band-Aid, Frisbee.* 表示生产厂家的商标，如 Band-Aid（邦迪牌创可贴）、Frisbee（弗里斯比飞盘）。

牛津高阶英汉双解词典

Oxford Advanced Learner's English-Chinese Dictionary

Ninth edition
第九版

原著 **A S Hornby**（霍恩比）

策划编辑 **Margaret Deuter**
Jennifer Bradbery
Joanna Turnbull

编辑 Leonie Hey
Suzanne Holloway

口语指南编辑 Mark Hancock

语音编辑 Michael Ashby

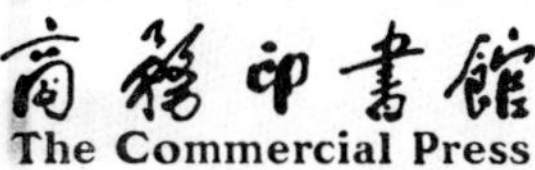

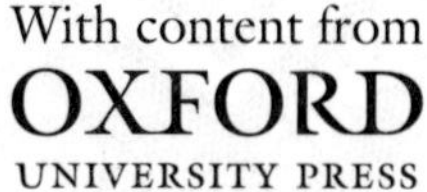

With content from
OXFORD
UNIVERSITY PRESS

English text originally published as Oxford Advanced Learner's Dictionary (Ninth Edition) by Oxford University Press, Great Clarendon Street, Oxford © Oxford University Press 2015

This English-Chinese edition published by The Commercial Press by arrangement with Oxford University Press (China) Ltd for distribution in the mainland of China only and not for export therefrom

本英汉双解版由牛津大学出版社授权商务印书馆出版，仅在中国大陆地区发行，不得出口到其他地区（包括中国香港、澳门和台湾）。

The Commercial Press has made some changes to the original work in order to make this edition more appropriate for readers in the mainland of China

商务印书馆对原书进行了个别修改，使其更符合中国读者的需要。

ISBN 978-7-100-15860-2

请注意识别

此扉页用含有商务印书馆注册商标的特制防伪纸印制，有这种扉页的《牛津高阶英汉双解词典》（第九版）是正版图书。

出版：商务印书馆
北京市王府井大街 36 号（邮政编码 100710）
牛津大学出版社（中国）有限公司
香港九龙湾宏远街 1 号一号九龙 39 楼
印制：中国
中国大陆地区总发行：商务印书馆
中国香港、澳门、台湾地区以及世界其他地区总发行：
牛津大学出版社（中国）有限公司

牛津高阶英汉双解词典

（第九版）

（简体汉字本）

出 版 前 言

本词典译自 *Oxford Advanced Learner's Dictionary*（《牛津高阶英语词典》）第9版，由商务印书馆和牛津大学出版社合作出版。

本词典共收单词、短语、义项185,000多条。其中新词新义近1,000条，具有鲜明的时代特色，如反映互联网的 live-stream（网络直播），以及反映全球文化交流融合的英语外来语，如来自中国的 guanxi（关系）、goji berry（枸杞；枸杞树）。本词典正文部分还增加了“情景表达”和“联想词”两类用法说明框，将词条内容和实际应用有机结合，进一步强化本词典的学习功能。此外，本词典附录部分增加“牛津口语指南”，介绍日常会话、口试、报告等常见口语场景中实用的口语技巧。词典后所附光盘包含 iSpeaker 程序，以音、视频和互动的形式提供发音、会话练习，并配有丰富的讲解和实例。加上现有的“牛津写作指南”和 iWriter 程序，本词典能满足读者学习英语的多种需求，是名副其实的“案头老师”。双解版译文力求准确规范，对增订内容的翻译严格把关，对旧版遗留问题加以更正，同时也对原文中存在的个别问题做了必要的修订。

从原编者霍恩比为词典赋予语言学习功能，到第九版编者将会话与写作功能融入学习型词典，这部词典在如何更好地满足读者需要方面从未停止探索和创新。今年适逢《牛津高阶英语词典》问世七十年，《牛津高阶英汉双解词典》引进出版三十年，我们欣喜地为读者奉上最新的第九版，感谢读者长期的支持，也期待读者的批评指正。

商务印书馆

二〇一八年三月

Contents 目录

inside front cover 前环衬 Abbreviations and symbols used in the dictionary 本词典使用的缩写和符号

Labels used in the dictionary 本词典使用的标识

iii Introduction by The Commercial Press (Simplified Chinese edition) 商务印书馆出版前言（简体汉字本）

vi Advisers of the English Edition 英文版顾问名单

vii Introduction by Oxford University Press (China) Ltd (Orthodox characters edition) 牛津大学出版社（中国）有限公司出版说明（繁体汉字本）

viii Advisory Board and Editorial Team of the English-Chinese Edition 英汉双解版顾问及编辑人员名单

ix Foreword 英文版序言（附译文）

xi Words from a Hornby Scholar 霍恩比奖学金学人的话（附译文）

xiii Key to dictionary entries 本词典词条说明

xx The Oxford 3000™ 牛津3000词汇表

xxiii The Academic Word List 学术词汇表

xxv Numbers 数字

1–2512 The Dictionary 词典正文

ST1–16 Oxford Speaking Tutor 牛津口语指南

WT1–52 Oxford Writing Tutor 牛津写作指南

V1–74 Visual Vocabulary Builder 图解词汇扩充

R1–80 Reference Section 参考信息

Reference Section Contents 参考信息目录

R1 Irregular verbs 不规则动词

R5 Verbs 动词

R13 Phrasal verbs 短语动词

R17 Nouns and adjectives 名词和形容词

R21 Collocation 词语搭配

R23 Idioms 习语

R25 More like this 同类词语学习

R30 Punctuation 标点符号用法

R34 Numbers 数字用法

R40 Geographical names 地名

R44 British and American English 英式英语和美式英语

R47 Pronunciation and phonetic symbols 读音和音标

R51 Detailed guide to the dictionary 本词典详细用法

R79 Acknowledgements 图片来源

Advisers of the English Edition
英文版顾问名单

Advisory Board 顾问小组

Prof Bas Aarts

Colin Campbell

Prof Vyv Evans

Danica Gondova

Tilly Harrison

Dr Amos Paran

Dr Robert Vanderplank

Consultants 特约顾问

Dr Maggie Charles
(Writing Tutor Consultant)

Prof Choong Bae Kim

Prof Paul Gunashekar

Prof Hirosada Iwasaki

Prof Masanori Toyota

Sally Wehmeier
(Chief Editor, 6th and 7th editions)

American English 美式英语顾问

Jamie Greene

Stephanie Hirschman

Karen Stern

Advisers on World English 世界各地英语顾问

Dr Modupe M Alimi (*West African*)

Tony Deverson (*New Zealand*)

Heather Fitzgerald (*Canadian*)

Prof Paul Gunashekar (*Indian*)

Megan Hall (*South African*)

Leah Kariuki (*East African*)

Dr Bruce Moore (*Australian*)

John Muitung'u (*East African*)

Joseph Noble (*South African*)

Advisers on scientific words 科技词汇顾问

Dr James Mendelssohn

Dr Geoffrey Neuss

出版说明（繁体汉字本）

牛津大学出版社于1948年出版了霍恩比（A S Hornby）编写的 *A Learner's Dictionary of Current English*，即《牛津高阶英语词典》(Oxford Advanced Learner's Dictionary）的第一版。此书开创了学习型词典的先河，出版后广受英语学子欢迎。据统计，至今超过1亿人使用过这本词典，影响极为深远。2018年是这本经典辞书问世七十周年，同时其最新第九版完成编译，推出英汉双解版。

为让《牛津高阶》与时并进，牛津大学出版社编辑部一直修订词典内容，并持续加入丰富实用的英语学习资料。第九版内容较上一版增加约15%。全文修订超过5,000项，另有近1,000全新的词汇和释义，例如crowdfunding、micropayment、ransomware、upcycle，还有源自汉语的guanxi（关系）等等。新版还广泛收录日渐通用的英语外来词，例如日语的shonen（少年漫画）和shojo（少女漫画），印度英语的mehndi（曼海蒂；人体彩绘术），以及中国人熟悉的goji berry（枸杞；枸杞树）等等。

修纂《牛津高阶英语词典》第九版之前，编辑按例对教师和学生作了广泛深入的意见调查，力求词典满足最普遍最迫切的学习需要。很多受访者表示，学英语最大的困难是"说"和"写"，再而是词汇不足。《牛津高阶》第九版为此新增提升口语能力的内容，包括书后的"牛津口语指南"和A-Z正文中的"情景表达"用法说明。另外，随书附送的DVD光碟包含iWriter和iSpeaker两个互动软件。iSpeaker收录"语音、练习、会话、口语考试"四个训练单元，让读者锻炼发音和会话技巧。其中的"口语考试"单元，乃参照主要的国际英语水平测试如IELTS、TOEFL、Cambridge English等口试部分常见的题型，编写出多项练习，并附应试技巧。iWriter则教授英语写作，跟词典中的"牛津写作指南"配合使用，涵盖议论文、报告、信件、评论等主要文体，从构思、起草、写作到检查，每个步骤都附详细说明，包含范文和常用词汇等，协助学生逐步实践各种文体的写作方法。

《牛津高阶》第九版其他主要的新内容还包括在A-Z正文中的"联想词"框，提示与词目意义相关的词语，启发读者学习更多词汇，触类旁通；于"参考信息"部分新增"同类词语学习"，分门别类列出具有相同特点的词语，帮助学习英语单词。

牛津词典编辑部经常收到读者查询，问题包罗万有，包括收词、释义、音标、拼写等等。为了解答这些问题，同时也让更多读者全面了解本书的学习功能，特别在参考信息末尾加录"本词典用法——词条使用详细说明"。在使用本词典前先仔细阅读一遍，查阅起来必定事半功倍。

第九版在保留并巩固学习功能之余，更注重语言实用技能；一方面让读者接触最鲜活地道的英语，准确理解词义，另一方面帮助读者学习更多词汇，训练英语"说"和"写"的技巧，提高沟通和应付考试的能力。

词典编辑工作繁复琐碎，疏漏之处在所难免，尚祈广大读者不吝指正为感。

牛津大学出版社（中国）有限公司

二〇一八年三月

Advisory Board and Editorial Team of the English-Chinese Edition
英汉双解版顾问及编辑人员名单

Foreword

The first edition of A. S. Hornby's dictionary, published by Oxford University Press in 1948, represented a great leap forward in the provision of suitable materials for learners of English as a foreign language. As a teacher, Hornby realized that although his students were used to decoding literary texts of a bygone age, when it came to communicating in the modern language, they needed more support than was available from the resources of the day. The dictionary that Hornby produced with his colleagues Wakefield and Gatenby was one of the ways in which he addressed this need. Besides simplified explanations and helpful illustrations to aid understanding, it supplied the information they needed to produce good English themselves: information on how to pronounce words and on how to use them in grammatically correct sentences, as well as good models of usage in examples.

In the intervening years, the *Oxford Advanced Learner's Dictionary* has changed, grown, and moved onto new media, but Hornby's principles continue to guide our work. This new edition is a rich resource for anyone who needs to communicate in English. "Express yourself" notes throughout the dictionary go beyond the single word to provide a bank of phrases for everyday situations, and the Speaking Tutor offers models, analysis, and tips on communicating at work, in exams, or in daily life, building on the resources for written English in the Writing Tutor and Language Banks. The digital versions of the dictionary offer the opportunity to watch, listen, and practise the spoken language interactively.

It is not just the dictionary that continues to pursue Hornby's aim of giving teachers and learners of English the tools to enable them to communicate, but also the Trust that he set up. The Hornby Trust ensures that standards of professionalism in TEFL continue to rise by offering teachers from around the world scholarships at British universities, where they can learn more about the teaching of English. Below, one recipient of a Hornby scholarship explains what this opportunity meant for him.

The legacy of A.S. Hornby lives on in the projects of the Trust and in this dictionary, and like the Scholars, we are proud to be associated with it.

Margaret Deuter
Managing Editor

英文版序言（译文）

牛津大学出版社于1948年出版了霍恩比编写的词典的第一版，为以英语为外语的学习者提供了合适的材料，代表该领域一个巨大的飞跃。作为教师，霍恩比认识到，尽管他的学生对于解读往昔的文学作品驾轻就熟，但一涉及用现代语言进行交流，他们当时能取得的相关学习材料却不敷使用。为弥补这一不足，霍恩比作了不少努力，其中一个成果就是他与同事韦克菲尔德 (Wakefield) 和盖滕比 (Gatenby) 编纂了这部词典。该词典释义简明扼要，配有帮助理解的插图，而且还提供了学习者表达规范英语所需的信息，包括如何读单词、如何将单词组成合乎语法的句子，以及通过示例示范正确的词语用法。

这些年来，《牛津高阶英语词典》(*Oxford Advanced Learner's Dictionary*) 经历了变化和成长，并且开始利用新媒体，但霍恩比的原则继续指导着我们的工作。这一新版为所有需要用英语交际的人提供了丰富的语料。贯穿整部词典的"情景表达"用法说明提供了超越单个词语的有用提示，汇集日常生活情境中的常用表达。除了继续保留上一版针对写作的"牛津写作指南"和"用语库"用法说明之外，新版增设了针对口语表达的"牛津口语指南"，提供了在工作、考试和日常生活中进行口头交流的范例、分析和技巧。本词典附赠的数字光盘提供了视、听和交互式口语练习的机会。

霍恩比致力于为英语教师和学习者提供能达至有效交流的工具，这不只是本词典，也是他设立的信托基金的不懈追求。霍恩比信托基金为来自全世界的教师提供在英国大学学习的奖学金，使他们有机会在英语教学领域深造，从而确保作为外语的英语教学的专业水准不断提升。下文中，一位霍恩比奖学金学人阐释了这个机会对他的意义。

霍恩比的精神在信托基金项目和这部词典中长存，跟那些霍恩比奖学金学人一样，我们很骄傲与他的精神密切相连。

Margaret Deuter
策划编辑

Words from a Hornby Scholar

After 10 years of English language teaching and teacher training in Cameroon, I was offered a unique opportunity through the Hornby scholarship to experience education outside my home country. The MA course onto which I enrolled at Warwick University in the UK was largely international with a good mix of very experienced and novice teachers. This offered me the opportunity not only to interact with my peers from a variety of language teaching and learning contexts, but also to develop better understanding of the theoretical and practical complexities of my profession and of the different strands of applied linguistics and ELT.

I came from a strongly transmission-based educational system, and the Hornby scholarship also exposed me to alternative forms of pedagogy which I was able to put into practice in my approach to teacher development back in Cameroon. While at Warwick, I was also able to apply my learning to developing a textbook series for English Language in Cameroonian French medium primary schools.

Returning to Cameroon after my MA studies, I played an even more active role both as policy maker in the Ministry of Basic Education and within the Cameroon English Language Teachers Association (CAMELTA). My research project on teaching and assessing writing in Cameroonian primary schools was further developed into an in-service training module which is now a requirement for teachers who have to mark end-of-primary-school certificate exams in some parts of the country. Networking with other 'Hornbies' from around the world has enabled me to tap into a vast reservoir of experience and while I am proud to have played an important part in the initiation of a Teacher Association research project within my community of practice, I cannot forget that this and other achievements at national and international level have been thanks to the good-will of a teacher who gave up his riches so that professionals like me can make a difference in their different contexts.

Dr Harry Kuchah Kuchah
University of Sheffield
Hornby Scholar 2006–7

霍恩比奖学金学人的话（译文）

我在喀麦隆从事英语教学和教师培训十年后，荣获霍恩比奖学金，由此得以在我的祖国之外体验教育，机会十分难得。我在英国华威大学修读了文学硕士课程。这一课程国际性很强，既有经验丰富的资深教师，也有初入行的教学新锐。这不仅给了我与来自各种不同语言教学背景的同侪进行交流的机会，也让我对教师职业在理论上和实践中的复杂性及应用语言学和英语教学的不同分支有了更好的理解。

我所在国家的教育制度是以传授知识为中心的，而霍恩比奖学金让我体验到不同的教学法，并得以在回到喀麦隆后将这些教学方法运用到我的教师培训工作中。在华威大学就读期间，我还运用所学知识开发了供喀麦隆法语小学使用的英语系列教材。

完成文学硕士的学业回到喀麦隆后，作为基础教育部的政策制定者，也作为喀麦隆英语教师协会的一员，我发挥了更加积极的作用。我的关于喀麦隆小学写作教学与评估研究项目发展成一个在职培训课程，现已成为我国部分地区小学结业证书考试的阅卷教师必须接受的培训项目。我与世界各地的“霍恩比学人”保持着联系，这使我能利用同侪积累的丰富经验。我在自己执教的社区内推动发起了一个教师协会的研究项目，在为这一努力成果感到自豪之时，我不会忘记，此项成就以及国家和国际层面上其他成就的取得皆仰赖一位教师的美好心愿，他献出了自己的财富，使得像我一样的专业人员在各自不同的环境里能够有所作为。

Dr Harry Kuchah Kuchah
谢菲尔德大学
2006–2007 霍恩比奖学金学人

Key to dictionary entries
本词典词条说明

Finding the word 查找单词

Information in the dictionary is given in **entries**, arranged in alphabetical order of **headwords. Compound words** are in separate entries, also arranged alphabetically. 本词典的词条按词目的字母顺序排列。复合词作独立词条列出，也按字母顺序排列。

headwords 词目

book·bind·er /ˈbʊkbaɪndə(r)/ *noun* a person whose job is fastening the pages of books together and putting covers on them 装订工人 ▶ **book·bind·ing** *noun* [U]

book·case /ˈbʊkkeɪs/ *noun* a piece of furniture with shelves for keeping books on 书架；书柜 ➲ VISUAL VOCAB PAGE V22

book club *noun* **1** an organization that sells books cheaply to its members 书友会（会员购书享受打折优惠） **2** = BOOK GROUP

entry 词条

Some headwords can have more than one part of speech. 有些词目会有两个或以上的词类。

blind·fold /ˈblaɪndfəʊld; *NAmE* -foʊld/ *noun, verb, adj., adv.*

headword and all possible parts of speech 词目及其词类

Squares show where the information on each part of speech begins. 方块标示每种词类信息的起始。

■ ***noun*** something that is put over sb's eyes so they cannot see 障眼物；眼罩

■ ***verb*** **~ sb** to cover sb's eyes with a piece of cloth or other covering so that they cannot see （用布等）蒙住…的眼睛： *The hostages were tied up and blindfolded.* 人质被捆绑起来并蒙上了眼睛。

■ ***adj., adv.*** (*BrE*) (*also* **blind·fold·ed** *BrE, NAmE*) with the eyes covered 被蒙住眼睛（的）： *The reporter was taken blindfold to a secret location.* 那位记者被蒙着眼睛带到了一处秘密的地方。 ◇ *I knew the way home blindfold* (= because it was so familiar). 我蒙着眼都能走到家。 ◇ *I could do that blindfold* (= very easily, with no problems). 我做这事易如反掌。

There are some words in English that have the same spelling as each other but different pronunciations. 英语中有些词拼法相同，但读音不同。

The small **homonym number** shows that this is the first of two headwords spelled *gill*. 同形异义词右上方的小号码表示同样拼作 gill 的词目中的第一个。

gill¹ /gɪl/ *noun* [usually pl.] one of the openings on the side of a fish's head that it breathes through 鳃 ➲ VISUAL VOCAB PAGE V12

IDM **to the 'gills** (*informal*) completely full （完全）满了，饱了；满满当当：*I was stuffed to the gills with chocolate cake.* 我吃巧克力蛋糕都撑到嗓子眼儿了。

gill² /dʒɪl/ *noun* a unit for measuring liquids. There are four gills in a pint. 及耳（液量单位，一品脱为四及耳）

Different pronunciation is given at each headword. 每个词目后给出不同的读音。

There are also some words in English that have more than one possible spelling, and both spellings are acceptable. Information about these words is given at the most frequent spelling. 英语中还有些词可能有两种或以上的拼法，而这些拼法都可接受。这类词的相关信息在使用频率最高的拼法下给出。

ban·is·ter (*also* **ban·nis·ter**) /ˈbænɪstə(r)/ *noun* (*BrE also* **ban·is·ters** [pl.]) the posts and rail which you can hold for support when going up or down stairs （楼梯的）栏杆，扶手：*to hold on to the banister/banisters* 紧抓住扶手 ➲ PICTURE AT STAIRCASE

banjo /ˈbændʒəʊ; *NAmE* ˈbændʒoʊ/ *noun* (*pl.* **-os**) a musical instrument like a GUITAR, with a long neck, a round body and four or more strings 班卓，班卓琴（拨弦乐器，长颈、圆身） ➲ VISUAL VOCAB PAGE V40

The variant spelling is given in brackets. 不同拼法在括号中给出。

At the entry for the less frequent spelling a cross-reference directs you to the main entry. 在使用频率较低的拼法词条中，以参见形式引向主词条。

ban·nis·ter = BANISTER

Irregular forms of verbs are treated in the same way. 不规则动词的各种形式以同样方式处理。

Some words that are **derivatives** of other words do not have their own entry in the dictionary because they can be easily understood from the meaning of the word from which they are derived (the root word). They are given in the same entry as the root word, in a specially marked section. 有些派生词在本词典中没有单独立目，因为从其源词（根词）很容易便可理解其含义。这些词置于根词词条内，以特定符号标示。

be·lated /bɪˈleɪtɪd/ *adj.* coming or happening late 迟来的；晚出现的： *a belated birthday present* 迟来的生日礼物 ▶ **be·lated·ly** *adv.*

The blue triangle shows where the derivative section starts. 蓝色三角形标示派生词部分的起始。

You can find **idioms** and **phrasal verbs** in separate sections, marked with special symbols. 习语和短语动词分别列出，以特定符号标示。

fetch /fetʃ/ *verb* **1** (*especially BrE*) to go to where sb/sth is and bring them/it back （去）拿来；（去）请来： **~ sb/sth** *to fetch help/a doctor* 去请人帮忙；去请医生 ◇ *The inhabitants have to walk a mile to fetch water.* 居民得走一英里路去取水。 ◇ *She's gone to fetch the kids from school.* 她去学校接孩子了。 ◇ **~ sb sth** *Could you fetch me my bag?* 你能帮我去取我的包吗？ **2 ~ sth** to be sold for a particular price 售得，卖得（某价） SYN **sell**: *The painting is expected to fetch $10 000 at auction.* 这幅画预计拍卖可得 10 000 美元。
IDM **fetch and ˈcarry (for sb)** to do a lot of little jobs for sb as if you were their servant （为某人）打杂，当听差，跑腿
PHR V **ˌfetch ˈup** (*informal, especially BrE*) to arrive somewhere without planning to 偶然来到；意外到达： *And then, a few years later, he somehow fetched up in Rome.* 后来，过了几年，他不知怎么到了罗马。

idioms section with symbol IDM (see pages R23–24) 符号 IDM 标示习语部分（见 R23–24 页）

phrasal verbs section with symbol PHR V (see pages R13–16) 符号 PHR V 标示短语动词部分（见 R13–16 页）

Wordfinder notes help you to find words that you don't know, or have forgotten. They suggest entries that you can look up to find vocabulary related to the headword. If those entries contain their own Wordfinder note or Collocations note, the word is shown in **bold**. 联想词信息框提示你不知道或遗忘的词，提供关联词条的查词线索。列出的词条中如果某词条本身包含联想词信息框或词语搭配用法说明，该单词会以粗体显示。

WORDFINDER 联想词： accommodation, deed, **house**, lease, let, **location**, mortgage, squat, tenant

For example, at the entry for **home**, the list of words includes **house**, where there is a Collocations note, and **location**, where there is another Wordfinder note with more words to do with describing an area. 比如，词条 home 的联想词信息框中，house 和 location 以粗体显示。查阅这两个词条可发现，house 条有词语搭配说明，location 条有联想词信息框，内含更多描述区域的词。

Finding the meaning 查找词义

Some words have very long entries. It is not usually necessary to read the whole entry from the beginning, if you already know something about the general meaning that you are looking for. 有些词条很长，如果你对所查词语的大意有所了解，通常不必从头到尾读完。

spin /spɪn/ *verb, noun*

■ ***verb*** (**spin·ning, spun, spun** /spʌn/)

• **TURN ROUND QUICKLY** 快速旋转 **1** [I, T] to turn round and round quickly; to make sth do this（使）快速旋转：(**+ adv./prep.**) *The plane was spinning out of control.* 飞机失去控制，进入尾旋状态。◇ *a spinning ice skater* 做旋转动作的溜冰者 ◇ *My head is spinning* (= I feel as if my head is going around and I can't balance). 我觉得天旋地转。◇ **~ (round/around)** *The dancers spun round and round.* 舞者不停地旋转。◇ **~ sth (round/around)** *to spin a ball/coin/wheel* 转动球 / 硬币 / 轮子 **2** [I, T] **~ (sb) round/around | + adv./prep.** to turn round quickly once; to make sb do this（使）急转身，猛转回头，急转弯：*He spun around to face her.* 他猛地回过身来，面对着她。

• **MAKE THREAD** 纺线 **3** [I, T] to make thread from wool, cotton, silk, etc. by twisting it 纺（线）；纺（纱）：*She sat by the window spinning.* 她坐在窗前纺线。◇ **~ sth** *to spin and knit wool* 纺毛线织毛活儿 ◇ **~ A into B** *spinning silk into thread* 把蚕丝纺成线 ◇ **~ B from A** *spinning thread from silk* 用蚕丝纺线

Short cuts show the context or general meaning. 义项提示给出语境或大意。

Meanings that are closely related share the same short cut. 相近词义收在同一义项提示内。

Understanding and using the word 理解和使用词汇

Words printed in larger type and with a 🔑 symbol are part of the **Oxford 3000** list of important words (see pages **xx–xxi**). Small keys indicate which parts of the entry are most important. 字体较大、标有钥匙符号 🔑 的单词是牛津3000词汇表中的重要单词（见 **xx–xxi** 页）。小钥匙符号标示词条中最重要的义项。

aban·doned 🔑 **AW** /əˈbændənd/ *adj.* **1** 🔑 left and no longer wanted, used or needed 被离弃的；被遗弃的；被抛弃的： *an abandoned car/house* 被抛弃的轿车；弃置的房子 ◇ *The child was found abandoned but unharmed.* 该弃儿被人们发现时安然无恙。 **2** (of people or their behaviour 人或行为) wild; not following accepted standards 放纵的；堕落的

Words from the Academic Word List are marked with **AW** (see pages **xxiii–xxiv**). 学术词汇表中的单词以符号 **AW** 标示（见 **xxiii–xxiv** 页）。

aard·vark /ˈɑːdvɑːk; *NAmE* ˈɑːrdvɑːrk/ *noun* an animal from southern Africa that has a long nose and tongue and that eats insects 土豚（非洲食蚁兽）

pronunciation, with American pronunciation where it is different (see pages **R47–50**) 读音：与英式读音不同的美式读音会标注出来（见 **R47–50** 页）

Stress marks show stress on compounds. 重音符号标出复合词的重读。

ˌbaby ˈgrand *noun* a small GRAND PIANO 小型卧式钢琴；小型三角钢琴

cling /klɪŋ/ *verb* (**clung**, **clung** /klʌŋ/) **1** [I] to hold on tightly to sb/sth 抓紧；紧握；紧抱： **~ to sb/sth** *survivors clinging to a raft* 紧紧抓住救生筏的幸存者 ◇ **~ on to sb/sth** *She clung on to her baby.* 她紧紧抱住她的婴儿。 ◇ **~ on** *Cling on tight!* 紧紧抓住！ ◇ **~ together** *They clung together, shivering with cold.* 他们紧紧地抱在一起，冷得直发抖。 ➲ SYNONYMS AT HOLD **2** [I] to stick to sth 粘住；附着： *a dress that clings* (= fits closely and shows the shape of your body) 紧身连衣裙 ◇ **~ to sth** *The wet shirt clung to his chest.* 湿衬衫紧贴在他的胸部。 ◇ *The smell of smoke still clung to her clothes.* 烟味仍附着在她的衣服上不散。 **3** [I] **~ (to sb)** (*usually disapproving*) to stay close to sb, especially because you need them emotionally（尤指情感上）依恋，依附： *After her mother's death, Sara clung to her aunt more than ever.* 萨拉在母亲去世后比以往任何时候都更依附于她的姨妈。

prepositions, adverbs and structures that can be used with this word 可与词目搭配的介词、副词和结构

examples of use in *italic type* 示例用斜体字标示。

Irregular forms of verbs, with their pronunciations. Irregular plurals of nouns are also shown. 不规则动词的形式及读音。亦给出不规则名词的复数形式。

label giving information about usage (see inside front cover) 用法说明标识（见前环衬）

hearty /ˈhɑːti; *NAmE* ˈhɑːrti/ *adj., noun*
■ ***adj.*** (**heart·ier, hearti·est**) **1** [usually before noun] showing friendly feelings for sb 亲切的；友好的：*a hearty welcome* 热情的欢迎 **2** (*sometimes disapproving*) loud, cheerful and full of energy 喧闹而活泼的；吵闹快活且精力充沛的：*a hearty and boisterous fellow* 活泼爱吵闹的家伙 ◇ *a hearty voice* 响亮的嗓子 **3** [only before noun] (of a meal or sb's APPETITE 饭菜或胃口) large; making you feel full 大的；丰盛的：*a hearty breakfast* 丰盛的早餐 ◇ *to have a hearty appetite* 胃口极好

comparatives and superlatives of adjectives 形容词的比较级和最高级

information on use of adjectives (see pages R19–20) 形容词用法说明（见 R19–20 页）

dock /dɒk; *NAmE* dɑːk/ *noun, verb*
■ ***noun*** **1** [C] a part of a port where ships are repaired, or where goods are put onto or taken off them 船坞；船埠；码头：*dock workers* 码头工人 ◇ *The ship was* ***in dock***. 船泊在船坞。 ➲ SEE ALSO DRY DOCK **2 docks** [pl.] a group of docks in a port and the buildings around them that are used for repairing ships, storing goods, etc. 港区 **3** [C] (*NAmE*) = JETTY **4** [C] (*NAmE*) a raised platform for loading vehicles or trains （供运货汽车或铁路货车装卸货物的）月台 **5** [C] the part of a court where the person who has been accused of a crime stands or sits during a trial （法庭的）被告席：*He's been* ***in the dock*** (= on trial for a crime) *several times already.* 他已受审多次。 ➲ COLLOCATIONS AT JUSTICE **6** [U] a wild plant of northern Europe with large thick leaves that can be rubbed on skin that has been stung by NETTLES to make it less painful 酸模（北欧阔叶野草，可用来揉擦被荨麻刺伤的皮肤以止痛）：*dock leaves* 酸模叶 **7** = DOCKING STATION
■ ***verb*** **1** [I, T] ~ (sth) if a ship **docks** or you **dock** a ship, it sails into a HARBOUR and stays there （使船）进港，停靠码头，进入船坞：*The ferry is expected to dock at 6.* 渡船预计在 6 点停靠码头。 **2** [I, T] ~ (sth) if two SPACECRAFT **dock**, or **are docked**, they are joined together in space （使航天器在外层空间）对接：*Next year, a technology module will be docked on the space station.* 明年将有一个技术舱与航天站对接。

fixed form of noun 名词的固定形式

information on different types of noun (see pages R17–19) 各类名词的说明（见 R17–19 页）

common phrase in **bold type** in example (see pages R21–22) 示例中用粗体标出常用短语（见 R21–22 页）

verb codes and frames (see pages R5–12) 动词代码和框架（见 R5–12 页）

word used in definition that is not in the **Oxford 3000** 释义中牛津 3000 词以外的词

Build your vocabulary 扩充词汇

The dictionary also contains a lot of information that will help you increase your vocabulary and use the language productively. **Language banks, Synonyms** and **Collocations** notes give useful vocabulary, especially for writing, and **Express yourself** notes help you find the right words in everyday situations. 本词典亦包括有助于扩充词汇和有效使用语言的各种信息。**用语库、同义词辨析和词语搭配**用法说明给出有用的词汇，尤其有益于写作。**情景表达**用法说明有助于找到适合日常情境的用语。

▼ EXPRESS YOURSELF 情景表达

Offering somebody something 主动提供某物

Particularly when you are the host, you may want to make polite offers to your guests. 尤其是作为主人招待宾客时，礼貌地主动提供某物或帮助可以这么说：

- *Would you like a magazine to read?* 您想看杂志吗？
- *Can I get you a coffee?* 我给你来杯咖啡好吗？
- *Can I offer you something to drink?* 我给你拿点喝的好吗？

sol·emn /ˈsɒləm; *NAmE* ˈsɑːləm/ *adj.* **1** (of a person 人) not happy or smiling 冷峻的；表情严肃的 SYN **serious**: *Her face grew solemn.* 她的脸显得严肃起来。◇ *a solemn expression* 冷峻的表情 OPP **cheerful** **2** done, said, etc. in a very serious and sincere way 庄严的；严正的；郑重的： ***a solemn oath/undertaking/vow, etc.*** 庄严的誓言、郑重的承诺、严肃的誓约等 **3** (of a religious ceremony or formal occasion 宗教仪式或正式场合) performed in a serious way 庄严的；隆重的： *a solemn ritual* 隆重的仪式 ➲ MORE LIKE THIS 20, page R27 ▶ **sol·emn·ly** *adv.*: *He nodded solemnly.* 他郑重地点了点头。◇ *She solemnly promised not to say a word to anyone about it.* 她郑重承诺不向任何人透露一个字。◇ *The choir walked solemnly past.* 唱诗班庄严地走过。

Special symbols show synonyms and opposites. 特殊符号表示同义词和反义词。

Cross references refer you to information in other parts of the dictionary, for example the MORE LIKE THIS pages that show you other words that behave in a similar way. 参见信息引导读者查阅本词典中其他部分的信息，比如**同类词语学习页 (MORE LIKE THIS)** 列出表现形式相似的其他词语。

The Oxford 3000™

The keywords of the **Oxford 3000** have been carefully selected by a group of language experts and experienced teachers as the words which should receive priority in vocabulary study because of their importance and usefulness. The selection is based on three criteria.

The words which occur most **frequently** in English are included, based on the information in the British National Corpus and the Oxford Corpus Collection. (A corpus is an electronically held collection of written or spoken texts, often consisting of hundreds of millions of words – for more information, visit the OALD website.) However, being frequent in the corpus alone is not enough for a word to qualify as a keyword: it may be that the word is used very frequently, but only in a narrowly defined area, such as newspapers or scientific articles. In order to avoid including these restricted words, we include as keywords only those words which are frequent across a **range** of different types of text. In other words, keywords are both frequent and used in a variety of contexts. In addition, the list includes some very important words which happen not to be used frequently, even though they are very **familiar** to most users of English. These include, for example, words for parts of the body, words used in travel, and words which are useful for explaining what you mean when you do not know the exact word for something. These words were identified by consulting a panel of over seventy experts in the fields of teaching and language study.

The words of the **Oxford 3000** are shown in the main section of the dictionary in larger print, and with a key symbol 🔑 immediately following. The most useful parts of the entries (particular parts of speech, meanings, phrasal verbs and idioms) are marked with a small key symbol. The entries for keywords often have extra information in the form of more examples of use, special notes explaining synonyms or related words, or helpful illustrations. This means that the keywords make an excellent starting point for expanding your vocabulary. With most keywords, there is far more to learn about them than the first meaning in the entry: often these words have many meanings, have a large family of words derived from them, or are used in a variety of patterns.

The list covers British and American English. Some basic phrases are also included. Proper names (names of people, places, etc. beginning with a capital letter) are not included in the list.

In order to make the definitions in this dictionary easy to understand, we have written them using the keywords of the **Oxford 3000**. All words used in normal definition text are keywords, or are on the list of language study terms, shown below. Numbers and proper names are also used in definitions. When it has been necessary to use a specialist term which is not in the **Oxford 3000**, the word is shown in SMALL CAPITALS. If you do not know the meaning of this word, look it up in the dictionary: it will help you to understand the definition that you are interested in, and will probably be a useful word to learn because it will be related to the original word you looked up.

For more information on the **Oxford 3000**, and to see the full list, visit the OALD website at **www.oxfordlearnersdictionaries.com**.

牛津3000词汇表

牛津3000核心词由一批语言专家和有经验的教师精心挑选而成，按重要性和实用性而选为词汇学习的重点，选词标准有三个。

第一是根据英国国家语料库和牛津语料库提供的资料，收录英语中最常用的词汇。（语料库指用电子方法汇集和保存的书面或口语文献，通常由数以亿万的词汇构成。有关语料库的详细信息，请访问《牛津高阶英语词典》(OALD) 网站。）不过，在语料库中出现频率高还不足以选进牛津3000词汇表中。有些词或许使用频率非常高，但只是在严格限定的范围内，如报章或科技文章中。为了避免收录这类受限词汇，本表只包括使用频率高且广泛用于各种不同文体的核心词。因此，核心词收录的第二个标准是既要使用频率高，又要能用于各种不同的语境。第三，词表中还包括一些对大多数英语使用者来说非常熟悉、但碰巧不太常用的重要词汇，如表示身体部位的词汇、旅行词汇和对释义非常有用的词汇。这些词汇均由教学和语言学习领域里70多位专家组成的专家咨询组确认。

牛津3000词汇表的词汇在本词典的主体部分用较大的字体显示，其后紧跟钥匙符 🔑。词条中最有用的部分（特定词类、词义、短语动词和习语）以小钥匙符标示。核心词词条通常有一些附加信息，如较多的用法实例、同义词和相关词特别注释或一些有用的插图，作为扩充词汇的基础。就多数核心词来说，要了解的远不止词条中的第一个含义。这些词常常具有多重含义，衍生出丰富的同族词，或用于各种句型中。

词汇表涵盖英式英语和美式英语，还包括一些基本短语。专有名词（以大写字母开头的人名、地名等）不包含在词汇表内。

为使本词典的释义易于理解，我们用牛津3000核心词来撰写释义，一般释义中使用的词汇均为牛津3000核心词或下页所列的语言学习术语词汇表中的词。数字和专有名词也用于释义中。必须使用牛津3000词汇表中未收录的专业术语时，术语会用小大写字母显示。要了解这些词的含义，可在本词典中查找，了解词义之余，因为与之前查找的词有关联，该词也很值得学习。

关于牛津3000词汇表的详细信息，以及下载该词汇表，请访问《牛津高阶英语词典》(OALD) 网站：
www.oxfordlearnersdictionaries.com。

Language study terms 语言学习术语

Knowing these words will be useful in your study of English and will also help you to use the *Oxford Advanced Learner's English-Chinese Dictionary* more effectively. It includes words to do with grammar, pronunciation and punctuation. 了解下列词汇有助于学习英语，并有助于更有效地使用本词典。这其中包括有关语法、读音和标点符号的词。

abbreviation *n.*
active *adj., n.*
adjective *n.*
adverb *n.*
apostrophe *n.*
article *n.*
auxiliary (*also* auxiliary verb) *n.*
bracket *n.*
clause *n.*
colon *n.*
comma *n.*
comparative *adj., n.*
compound *n., adj.*
conditional *adj., n.*
conjunction *n.*
consonant *n.*
contraction *n.*
countable *adj.*
continuous
➲ progressive
derivative *n.*
determiner *n.*
dialect *n.*
entry *n.*
exclamation *n.*
exclamation mark (*especially BrE*) (*NAmE usually* exclamation point) *n.*
figurative *adj.*
full stop *n.* (*BrE*)
gerund *n.*
hyphen *n.*
idiom *n.*
imperative *adj., n.*
indirect speech
➲ reported speech
infinitive *n.*
inverted commas
➲ quotation marks
ironic *adj.*
irregular *adj.*
literal *adj.*
literary *adj.*
modal *n.*
noun *n.*
object *n.*
ordinal *n.*
paragraph *n.*
parenthesis *n.*
part of speech (*also* word class) *n.*
participle *n.*
particle *n.*
passive *adj., n.*
perfect *adj.*
period *n.* (*NAmE*)
phrasal verb *n.*
plural *n., adj.*
possessive *adj., n.*
prefix *n.*
preposition *n.*
progressive (*also* continuous) *adj.*
pronoun *n.*
punctuation *n.*
question mark *n.*
question tag (*also* tag question) *n.*
quotation marks (*BrE also* inverted commas) *n.*
reflexive *adj.*
register *n.*
regular *adj.*
relative *adj.*
reported speech (*also* indirect speech) *n.*
saying *n.*
semicolon *n.*
simple *adj.*
singular *n., adj.*
slang *n.*
slash *n.*
subject *n.*
suffix *n.*
superlative *adj., n.*
syllable *n.*
taboo *adj.*
tag question
➲ question tag
tense *n.*
uncountable *adj.*
verb *n.*
vowel *n.*
word class
➲ part of speech

The Academic Word List:

A tool for vocabulary learning

Averil Coxhead
Victoria University of Wellington, New Zealand

You are holding a dictionary which contains many thousands of words. As a learner of English as a second or even third language, how can you decide which words you need to spend your valuable time on? One way you can do this is by looking at the frequency of words. That is, how often these words occur in your reading and listening material in English. What you read and listen to might depend on your purposes for learning English. If, for example, you want to study in an English-medium university, it will be important to focus on words that you will meet often at university.

How can this dictionary help you decide which words to learn for your studies? This dictionary includes words from the Academic Word List (AWL). The list was developed by analysing a corpus or body of academic written texts to find out which words occurred across a range of 28 subject areas (such as Biology, History, Marketing, and International Law) in four academic disciplines (Arts, Commerce, Law, and Science). These words were selected because of their range and frequency of occurrence. They are outside the first 2000 words of English. The AWL contains 570 word families and covers roughly 10% of a written academic text, which means that ten words in every 100 can be found in the list.

In this dictionary, you will find that words from the AWL are labelled AW. Words in the Oxford 3000 word list of general English are also highlighted. The AWL and the Oxford 3000 lists have some words in common because the AWL excludes the first 2000 words while the Oxford 3000 includes the first 2000 words and 1000 words more. Examples of some words that are shared include *abandon* and *academic*.

What are some other challenges for learners when it comes to academic vocabulary? First and foremost, it is important to know the meaning of a word and to recognise its meaning when the word is presented in context. Some words, such as 'require', carry roughly the same meaning in most contexts. Other words have developed very specific meanings depending on an area of study. An example is the word 'significant' which carries a particular meaning in statistical studies. You can use this dictionary to help you find out more about the meanings of words in context.

Another challenge is using tools such as this dictionary to enhance your understanding. The dictionary includes words that commonly occur with a target word, its pronunciation, and examples or sentences with the target word in it. All of this information can help you develop a fuller understanding of a word.

There is a saying which goes, 'If you don't use it, you'll lose it'. Make sure you try to use words, from the AWL for example, in your writing and speaking. That way you can get feedback and further develop your knowledge of these words. You also need useful strategies to cement your learning. If you find yourself looking up the same word more than once or you find specialised words for your studies, you may need to develop word cards or design a vocabulary notebook to help you learn.

If we think of language as a toolbox for life, this dictionary contains many useful tools for your learning. The AWL is a vocabulary tool that might help you prepare for your future studies.

You can find out more about the AWL on this website: **www.victoria.ac.nz/lals/staff/averil-coxhead.aspx**.

学术词汇表

词汇学习的工具

埃夫里尔·考克斯黑德
新西兰惠灵顿维多利亚大学

你手头的这本词典包含成千上万条词汇。作为以英语为第二甚至第三语言的学习者，你如何确定哪些词需要花费宝贵的时间来学习？方法之一是看词的频率，即这些词在你的英语阅读和听力材料中出现的频次。你所阅读和听的东西可能取决于你学习英语的目的。例如，如果想去用英语授课的大学学习，那么要紧的是重点学习在大学中将经常遇到的词汇。

如何借助本词典确定学习所需要的词汇？本词典收录学术词汇表（AWL）中的词汇。这个词汇表是通过分析语料库和大量学术文本、找出4个学术范畴（文学艺术、商业、法律和科学）中多达28个专业（如生物、历史、营销和国际法）中所出现的词汇。选取这些词汇是由于它们出现的广泛程度和频率。它们在最基本的2000个英语词汇以外。AWL包含570个词族，覆盖了学术文本约10%的内容，也就是说，每100个词中就有10个出现在本词汇表中。

在本词典中，AWL词汇以 AW 标示，牛津3000词汇表的常用英语词汇也特别标示出来。AWL和牛津3000词汇表中有些词相同，因为AWL不包括最基本的2000个英语词汇，而牛津3000词汇表除了最基本的2000个词外另行收录了1000个英语词汇。如abandon和academic在这两个词汇表中均可找到。

学习者在学术词汇方面还会遇到一些什么挑战呢？首先，重要的是要知道词的意思并识别它在上下文中的含义。有些词在大多数语境中的意思基本相同，如require。另外一些词在某一学科领域中有十分特定的含义，例如，significant在统计学中有其特定含义。本词典有助于进一步了解词汇在上下文中的意思。

另一挑战是利用本词典这一类的工具书加深理解。本词典列出经常与目标词连用的词语、目标词读音以及包含目标词的示例或例句。这些信息均有助于更充分地理解词语。

常言道，“不用则废”。在写作和口头表达中一定要尽可能地使用词汇，如AWL中的词汇，如此便可以获得反馈信息并进一步丰富词汇知识。还得有行之有效的策略以巩固所学知识。如果查阅同一个词超过一次或遇到学习中所需要的专门用语，也许就得制作单词卡片或设计生词本来帮助学习。

如果我们把语言看作生活的工具箱，那么本词典包含了许多有用的学习工具。AWL便是一种词汇工具，可帮助你为未来的学习做好准备。

要了解AWL的详细信息可登录以下网站：www.victoria.ac.nz/lals/staff/averil-coxhead.aspx。

Numbers 数字

10 000-foot view /ˌten ˈθaʊznd ˈfʊt ˈvjuː/ *noun* (*business* 商) a broad general view or description of a problem 概况；概述 SYN HELICOPTER VIEW, OVERVIEW: *Let me give you the 10 000-foot view.* 我来介绍一下大致情况。

1040 form /ˌten ˈfɔːti fɔːm; *NAmE* ˈfɔːrti fɔːrm/ *noun* (in the US) an official document in which you give details of the amount of money that you have earned so that the government can calculate how much tax you have to pay（美国）个人收入申报表

12 /twelv/ *noun* (in Britain) a label that is given to a film/movie to show that it can be watched legally only by people who are at least twelve years old; a film/movie that has this label（英国）12 岁可看影片（标签）: *I can take the kids too—it's a 12.* 我可以把孩子们也带去——这是供 12 岁以上的人观看的影片。

1471 /ˈwʌn fɔː sevn wʌn; *NAmE* fɔːr/ (in Britain) the telephone number you can use to find out the telephone number of the person who called you most recently, and the time the call was made（英国）用以查询最近一个来电号码和时间的电话号码

15 /ˌfɪfˈtiːn/ *noun* (in Britain) a label that is given to a film/movie to show that it can be watched legally only by people who are at least fifteen years old; a film/movie that has this label（英国）15 岁可看影片（标签）

18 /ˌeɪˈtiːn/ *noun* (in Britain) a label that is given to a film/movie to show that it can be watched legally only by people who are at least eighteen years old; a film/movie that has this label（英国）18 岁可看影片（标签）

18-wheeler /ˌeɪtiːn ˈwiːlə(r)/ *noun* (*NAmE*) a very large truck with nine wheels on each side * 18 轮大卡车

20/20 vision /ˌtwenti twenti ˈvɪʒn/ *noun* the ability to see perfectly without using glasses or CONTACT LENSES 标准视力；正常视力

2.1 /ˌtuː ˈwʌn/ *noun* the upper level of the second highest standard of degree given by a British or an Australian university（英国或澳大利亚大学的学位成绩）B 等 A 级 : *I got a 2.1.* 我获得 B 等 A 级。

2.2 /ˌtuː ˈtuː/ *noun* the lower level of the second highest standard of degree given by a British or an Australian university（英国或澳大利亚大学的学位成绩）B 等 B 级

24-hour clock /ˌtwenti fɔːr aʊə ˈklɒk; *NAmE* aʊər ˈklɑːk/ *noun* the system of using twenty four numbers to talk about the hours of the day, instead of dividing it into two units of twelve hours * 24 小时制

24/7 /ˌtwenti fɔː ˈsevən; *NAmE* fɔːr/ *adv.* (*informal*) twenty-four hours a day, seven days a week (used to mean 'all the time') 一周 7 天一天 24 小时；全时间 : *She's with me all the time—24/7.* 她白天黑夜都和我在一起。

3-D (also **three-D**) /ˌθriː ˈdiː/ *noun* [U] the quality of having, or appearing to have, length, width and depth 三维；立体 : *These glasses allow you to see the film in 3-D.* 这种眼镜可看立体影片。

3G /ˌθriː ˈdʒiː/ *abbr.* third generation (used to describe a level of performance for mobile/cell phones that makes it possible to move data to and from the Internet) * 3G；第三代移动通信 : *3G technology* * 3G 技术

35mm /ˌθɜːtifaɪv ˈmɪlimiːtə(r); *NAmE* ˌθɜːrti-/ *noun* the size of film that is usually used in cameras for taking photographs and making films/movies * 35 毫米胶片

360-degree feedback /ˈθriː hʌndrəd ən sɪksti dɪˈgriː ˈfiːdbæk/ (also **360-degree appraisal**) *noun* [U] (*business* 商) information provided by all the people that an employee deals with, used as a way of deciding how well the employee does their job（用于评估雇员绩效的）360 度反馈；360 度绩效考核：*360-degree feedback assessments* * 360 度绩效评估

4G /ˌfɔː ˈdʒiː; *NAmE* ˌfɔːr/ *abbr.* fourth generation (used to describe a level of performance for mobile/cell phones that makes it possible to move data to and from the Internet at high speed) * 4G；第四代移动通信：*a 4G phone* * 4G 手机 ◇ *4G technology* * 4G 技术

4×4 /ˌfɔː baɪ ˈfɔː; *NAmE* ˌfɔːr baɪ ˈfɔːr/ *noun* a vehicle with a system in which power is applied to all four wheels, making it easier to control 四轮驱动汽车

411 /ˌfɔː wʌn ˈwʌn; *NAmE* ˌfɔːr/ *noun* **1** [U] the telephone number of the service that you use in the US to find out a person's telephone number（美国）查号电话号码：*Call 411.* 拨 411 查号。**2 the 411** [sing.] (*NAmE, informal*) the true facts about a situation or the information you need 实情；需要了解的情况：*He'll give us the 411 on what to expect.* 他会就可能发生的情况向我们介绍的。

7/7 /ˌsevn ˈsevn/ *noun* (*BrE*) the abbreviation for the date 7 July, 2005, when several bomb attacks took place in London 七月七日（即 2005 年 7 月 7 日，那天伦敦遭到几次炸弹袭击）

the $64,000 question /ˌsɪksti fɔː ˌθaʊznd ˌdɒlə ˈkwestʃən; *NAmE* fɔːr, ˌdɑːlər/ *noun* (*informal*) the thing that people most want to know, or that is most important 人们最想知道的事；最重要的事：*It's a clever plan, but the sixty-four thousand dollar question is: will it work?* 这是个绝妙的计划，但最重要的是，行得通吗？

9/11 /ˌnaɪn ɪˈlevn/ *noun* the abbreviation for the date September 11, 2001, when terrorists flew planes into the Twin Towers in New York, the Pentagon in Washington, D.C., and a field in Pennsylvania, killing thousands of people 九一一（即 2001 年 9 月 11 日，那天恐怖分子驾驶飞机撞向纽约世贸大厦、华盛顿特区的五角大楼和宾夕法尼亚州野外，导致几千人死亡）

911 /ˌnaɪn wʌn ˈwʌn/ the telephone number used in the US to call the police, fire or ambulance services in an emergency 美国紧急求救电话号码：(*NAmE*) *Call 911.* 拨 911 报警。

99 /ˌnaɪnti ˈnaɪn/ *noun* (*BrE*) an ice cream in a cone with a stick of chocolate in the top 巧克力棒蛋卷冰淇淋

999 /ˌnaɪn naɪn ˈnaɪn/ the telephone number used in Britain to call the police, fire or ambulance services in an emergency 英国紧急求救电话号码：(*BrE*) *Dial 999.* 拨 999 报警。

Aa

A /eɪ/ *noun, symbol, abbr.*

■ ***noun*** (*also* **a**) (*pl.* **As, A's, a's** /eɪz/) **1** [C, U] the first letter of the English alphabet 英语字母表的第 1 个字母：*'Apple' begins with (an) A/'A'.* * apple 一词以字母 a 开头。 **2 A** [C, U] (*music* 音) the 6th note in the SCALE of C MAJOR * A 音（C 大调音阶的第六级音） **3** [C, U] the highest mark/grade that a student can get for a piece of work or course of study（学业成绩）第一等，优，甲：*She got (an) A in/for Biology.* 她生物科成绩得 A。◇ *He had* ***straight A's*** (= nothing but A's) *all through high school.* 他读中学时成绩全部是 A。 **4 A** [U] used to represent the first of two or more possibilities（表示两个或更多可能性中的）第一个：*Shall we go for plan A or plan B?* 我们采用第一方案还是第二方案？ **5 A** [U] used to represent a person, for example in an imagined situation or to hide their identity（代表一个假设的或不指名的人）甲：*Assume A knows B is guilty.* 假定甲知道乙有罪。 ➲ SEE ALSO A-FRAME, A LEVEL, A-ROAD

IDM **from A to B** from one place to another 从一地到另一地：*For me a car is just a means of getting from A to B.* 在我看来，汽车只不过是从一地到另一地的代步工具。 **from A to Z** including everything there is to know about sth 从头到尾；彻底地；完全：*He knew his subject from A to Z.* 他通晓自己的学科。

■ ***symbol*** **1** used in Britain before a number to refer to a particular important road * A 级公路，干线公路（英国公路代号，后接数字）：*the A34 to Newbury* 通往纽伯里的 A34 号（干线）公路 **2** used (but not in the US) before numbers which show standard METRIC sizes of paper（除美国外，用于数字前表示标准纸张尺寸）A…纸（尺寸）：*a sheet of* ***A4*** *paper* (= 297×210mm) 一张 A4 纸（= 297 毫米 × 210 毫米）◇ ***A3*** (= 420×297mm) * A3 纸（= 420 毫米 × 297 毫米）◇ ***A5*** (= 210×148mm) * A5 纸（= 210 毫米 × 148 毫米）

■ ***abbr.*** (in writing 书写形式) AMP 安，安培（电流单位）

a 🔑 /ə; *strong form* eɪ/ (*also* **an** /ən; *strong form* æn/) *indefinite article* **HELP** The form **a** is used before consonant sounds and the form **an** before vowel sounds. When saying abbreviations like 'FM' or 'UN', use **a** or **an** according to how the first letter is said. For example, **F** is a consonant, but begins with the sound /e/ and so you say: *an FM radio.* **U** is a vowel but begins with /j/ and so you say: *a UN declaration.* * a 用于辅音前，an 用于元音前。在 FM、UN 等缩略语前，用 a 还是用 an，需视首字母如何发音而定。如 F 是辅音字母，但其发音以 /e/ 开头，故应说：an FM radio。U 是元音字母，但其发音以 /j/ 开头，故应说：a UN declaration。 **1** 🔑 used before countable or singular nouns referring to people or things that have not already been mentioned（用于可数名词或单数名词前，表示未曾提到的）一（人、事、物）：*a man/horse/unit* 一个人；一匹马；一个单位 ◇ *an aunt/egg/hour/X-ray* 一位姑母；一枚鸡蛋；一小时；一张 X 光片 ◇ *I can only carry two at a time.* 我一次只能带两个。◇ *There's a visitor for you.* 有位客人找你。◇ *She's a friend of my father's* (= one of my father's friends). 她是我父亲的朋友。 **2** 🔑 used before uncountable nouns when these have an adjective in front of them, or phrase following them（用于前有形容词或后有短语的不可数名词前）：*a good knowledge of French* 精通法语 ◇ *a sadness that won't go away* 挥之不去的悲愁 **3** 🔑 any; every 任何一；每一：*A lion is a dangerous animal.* 狮子是猛兽。 **4** 🔑 used to show that sb/sth is a member of a group or profession（表示为某一群体或职业中的一员）：*Their new car's a BMW.* 他们的新轿车是辆宝马。◇ *She's a Buddhist.* 她是佛教徒。◇ *He's a teacher.* 他是教师。◇ *Is that a Monet* (= a painting by Monet)? 那是莫奈的画吗？ **5** used in front of two nouns that are seen as a single unit（用于视为一体的两个名词之前）：*a knife and fork* 一副刀叉 **6** used instead of *one* before some numbers（用于某些数字前，代替 one）：*A thousand people were there.* 那里有一千人。 **7** used when talking about prices, quantities and rates（用于价格、数量、比率等）一，每一 **SYN** **per**：*They cost 50p a kilo.* 这些东西一公斤 50 便士。◇ *I can type 50 words a minute.* 我每分钟能打 50 个单词。◇ *He was driving at 50 miles an hour.* 当时他正以每小时 50 英里的速度驾车。 **8** a person like sb 像（某人）的人；…式的人物：*She's a little Hitler.* 她是个小希特勒。 **9** used before sb's name to show that the speaker does not know the person（用于某人姓名前，表示说话者不认识此人）有个：*There's a Mrs Green to see you.* 有位格林太太要见你。 **10** used before the names of days of the week to talk about one particular day（用于一星期中某天的名称前，表示具体某一天）：*She died on a Tuesday.* 她是在某个星期二去世的。

a- /eɪ/ *prefix* (in nouns, adjectives and adverbs 构成名词、形容词和副词) not; without 非；不；无；没有：*atheist* 无神论者 ◇ *atypical* 非典型的 ◇ *asexually* 无性地 ➲ **MORE LIKE THIS** 6, page R25

A1 /ˌeɪ ˈwʌn/ *adj.* (*informal*) very good 很棒的；极好的：*The car was in A1 condition.* 汽车状况好极了。

A2 (level) /ˌeɪ ˈtuː levl/ *noun* [C, U] (until 2015) a British exam usually taken in Year 13 of school or college (= the final year) when students were aged 18. Students first studied a subject at AS level before taking an A2 exam. Together AS and A2 level exams formed the A-level qualification, which is needed for entrance to universities. * A2 证书考试（英国 2015 年以前的考试制度，中学生在 18 岁时参加，之前必须修完高级补充程度考试的同一门课，通过这两种考试才有资格入读大学）：*A2 exams* * A2 证书考试

AA /ˌeɪ ˈeɪ/ *abbr.* **1** (*usually* **the AA**) Automobile Association (a British organization which provides services for car owners) 汽车协会（英国一个为车主提供服务的组织） **2** ALCOHOLICS ANONYMOUS 匿名戒酒会

AAA /ˌeɪ eɪ ˈeɪ/ *abbr.* **1** /*especially NAmE* ˌtrɪpl ˈeɪ/ American Automobile Association (an American organization which provides services for car owners) 美国汽车协会（美国一个为车主提供服务的组织） **2** (in the UK) Amateur Athletic Association（英国）业余体育协会

A & E /ˌeɪ ənd ˈiː/ *abbr.* ACCIDENT AND EMERGENCY（医院）急诊室 ➲ **WORDFINDER NOTE AT HOSPITAL**

A & R /ˌeɪ ənd ˈɑː(r)/ *abbr.* artists and repertoire (the department in a record company that is responsible for finding new singers and bands and getting them to sign a contract with the company)（唱片公司的）艺人及音乐产品部

aard·vark /ˈɑːdvɑːk; *NAmE* ˈɑːrdvɑːrk/ *noun* an animal from southern Africa that has a long nose and tongue and that eats insects 土豚（非洲食蚁兽）

aargh /ɑː; *NAmE* ɑːr/ *exclamation* used to express fear, anger, or some other strong emotion（表示恐惧、愤怒等强烈情感）啊：*Aargh—get that cat off the table!* 啊，把那猫从桌上赶走！ ➲ **MORE LIKE THIS** 2, page R25

aback /əˈbæk/ *adv.*

IDM **be taken aˈback (by sb/sth)** to be shocked or surprised by sb/sth 被（…）吓了一跳；大吃一惊；震惊：*She was completely taken aback by his anger.* 他的愤怒把她吓了一大跳。 ➲ SEE ALSO TAKE SB ABACK at TAKE ➲ **SYNONYMS AT SURPRISE**

aba·cus /ˈæbəkəs/ *noun* (*pl.* **aba·cuses** /-kəsɪz/) a frame with small balls which slide along wires. It is used as a tool or toy for counting. 算盘

aba·lone /ˌæbəˈləʊni; *NAmE* -ˈloʊ-/ *noun* [C, U] a SHELLFISH that can be eaten and whose shell contains MOTHER-OF-PEARL 鲍鱼

aban·don 🔑 **AW** /əˈbændən/ *verb, noun*

■ ***verb*** **1** 🔑 to leave sb, especially sb you are responsible for, with no intention of returning（不顾责任、义务等）离弃，遗弃，抛弃：**~ sb** *The baby had been abandoned by its mother.* 这个婴儿被母亲遗弃了。◇ **~ sb to sth** *The study showed a deep fear among the elderly of being abandoned* to the care of strangers. 研究表明，老人十分害怕被丢给陌生人照管。 **2** to leave a thing or place, especially because it is impossible or dangerous to stay（不得已而）舍弃，丢弃，离开 SYN **leave**: **~ sth** *Snow forced many drivers to abandon their vehicles.* 大雪迫使许多驾驶者弃车步行。◇ *He gave the order to* ***abandon ship*** (= to leave the ship because it was sinking). 他下令弃船（因船快要沉没）。◇ **~ sth to sb/sth** *They had to abandon their lands to the invading forces.* 他们不得不舍弃土地，让侵略军占领。 **3** **~ sth** to stop doing sth, especially before it is finished; to stop having sth 中止；放弃；不再有：*They abandoned the match because of rain.* 因为下雨，他们中止了比赛。◇ *She abandoned hope of any reconciliation.* 她对和解已不再抱有希望。 **4** to stop supporting or helping sb; to stop believing in sth 停止（支持或帮助）；放弃（信念）：**~ sb** *The country abandoned its political leaders after the war.* 战后该国人民不再拥护他们的政治领袖。◇ **~ sth** *Critics accused him of abandoning his principles.* 批评者指责他背弃了自己的原则。 **5** **~ yourself to sth** (*literary*) to feel an emotion so strongly that you can feel nothing else 陷入，沉湎于（某种情感）：*He abandoned himself to despair.* 他陷入绝望。

■ ***noun*** [U] (*formal*) an uncontrolled way of behaving that shows that sb does not care what other people think 放任；放纵：*He signed cheques with careless abandon.* 他无所顾忌地乱开支票。 IDM SEE GAY *adj.*

aban·doned AW /əˈbændənd/ *adj.* **1** left and no longer wanted, used or needed 被离弃的；被遗弃的；被抛弃的：*an abandoned car/house* 被抛弃的轿车；弃置的房子 ◇ *The child was found abandoned but unharmed.* 该弃儿被人们发现时安然无恙。 **2** (of people or their behaviour 人或行为) wild; not following accepted standards 放纵的；堕落的

aban·don·ment AW /əˈbændənmənt/ *noun* [U] (*formal*) **1** the act of leaving a person, thing or place with no intention of returning 离弃；遗弃；抛弃 **2** the act of giving up an idea or stopping an activity with no intention of returning to it 放弃；中止：*the government's abandonment of its new economic policy* 政府对新经济政策的放弃

abase /əˈbeɪs/ *verb* **~ yourself** (*formal*) to act in a way that shows that you accept sb's power over you 表现卑微；卑躬屈节；屈从 ▶ **abase·ment** *noun* [U]

abashed /əˈbæʃt/ *adj.* [not before noun] embarrassed and ashamed because of sth that you have done 羞愧；窘迫；尴尬 OPP **unabashed**

abate /əˈbeɪt/ *verb* [I, T] (*formal*) to become less strong; to make sth less strong （使）减弱，减退，减轻，减少：*The storm showed no signs of abating.* 暴风雨没有减弱的迹象。◇ **~ sth** *Steps are to be taken to abate pollution.* 将会采取措施减少污染。 ▶ **abate·ment** *noun* [U]

ab·at·toir /ˈæbətwɑː(r)/ *noun* (*BrE*) = SLAUGHTERHOUSE

abaya /əˈbeɪjə; *NAmE* əˈbaɪjə/ *noun* a full-length piece of clothing worn over other clothes by Arab men or women 阿拉伯罩袍

abba /ˈʌbə/ (*also* **appa**) *noun* (*IndE*) (especially as a form of address 尤用于称呼) a father 阿爸；爸爸

ab·bess /ˈæbes/ *noun* a woman who is the head of a CONVENT 女修院院长

abbey /ˈæbi/ *noun* a large church together with a group of buildings in which MONKS or NUNS live or lived in the past （大）隐修院；（曾为大隐修院的）大教堂：*Westminster Abbey* 威斯敏斯特教堂 ◇ *a ruined abbey* 破败不堪的教堂

abbot /ˈæbət/ *noun* a man who is the head of a MONASTERY or an ABBEY 男修院院长

ab·bre·vi·ate /əˈbriːvieɪt/ *verb* [usually passive] **~ sth** (**to sth**) to make a word, phrase or name shorter by leaving out letters or using only the first letter of each word 缩略；把（词语、名称）缩写（成…） SYN **shorten**: *the Jet Propulsion Laboratory (usually abbreviated to JPL)* 喷气推进实验室（通常缩写成 JPL） ▶ **ab·bre·vi·ated** *adj.*: *Where appropriate, abbreviated forms are used.* 适当的地方用缩写形式。

ab·bre·vi·ation /əˌbriːviˈeɪʃn/ *noun* **1** [C] **~ (of/for sth)** a short form of a word, etc. 略语；缩写词；缩写形式：*What's the abbreviation for 'Saint'?* * Saint 的缩写形式是什么？ **2** [U] the process of abbreviating sth 缩略；缩写

ABC /ˌeɪ biː ˈsiː/ *noun, abbr.*

■ ***noun*** [sing.] (*BrE*) (*NAmE also* **ABCs** [pl.], **ABC's** [pl.]) **1** all the letters of the alphabet, especially as they are learnt by children 字母表（尤指儿童学习的全部字母）：*Do you know your ABC?* 你认识所有的字母吗？ **2** the basic facts about a subject （某学科的）基础知识，入门：*the ABC of gardening* 园艺入门 IDM SEE EASY *adj.*

■ ***abbr.*** **1** American Broadcasting Company (a large national American television company) 美国广播公司（美国一家全国性的大型电视广播公司） **2** Australian Broadcasting Corporation (the Australian national public broadcasting company) 澳大利亚广播公司

ABD /ˌeɪ biː ˈdiː/ *abbr.* (*NAmE*) all but dissertation (having completed all the work for a higher degree except the DISSERTATION) （课业修毕）仅差学位论文即可毕业；仅欠毕业论文：*ABD students may apply.* 仅欠毕业论文的学生可以申请。

ab·di·cate /ˈæbdɪkeɪt/ *verb* **1** [I, T] to give up the position of being king or queen 退位；逊位：*He abdicated in favour of his son.* 他把王位让给了儿子。◇ **~ sth** *She was forced to abdicate the throne of Spain.* 她被迫让出西班牙的王位。 ➲ WORDFINDER NOTE AT KING **2** [T] **~ responsibility/your responsibilities** to fail or refuse to perform a duty 失职；放弃职责 ▶ **ab·di·ca·tion** /ˌæbdɪˈkeɪʃn/ *noun* [U, C]

ab·do·men /ˈæbdəmən/ *noun* **1** the part of the body below the chest that contains the stomach, BOWELS, etc. 腹（部） **2** the end part of an insect's body that is attached to its THORAX （昆虫的）腹部 ➲ VISUAL VOCAB PAGE V13

ab·dom·inal /æbˈdɒmɪnl; *NAmE* -ˈdɑːm-/ *adj., noun*

■ ***adj.*** [only before noun] (*anatomy* 解) relating to or connected with the abdomen 腹部的：*abdominal pains* 腹痛

■ ***noun*** **abdominals** (*also informal* **abs**) [pl.] the muscles of the abdomen 腹肌

ab·duct /æbˈdʌkt/ *verb* **~ sb** to take sb away illegally, especially using force 诱拐；劫持；绑架 SYN **kidnap** ▶ **ab·duc·tion** /æbˈdʌkʃn/ *noun* [U, C]

ab·duct·ee /ˌæbdʌkˈtiː/ *noun* a person who has been abducted 被劫持者；被绑架者；肉票

ab·duct·or /æbˈdʌktə(r)/ *noun* **1** a person who abducts sb 劫持者；绑架者；绑匪 **2** (*also* **abˈductor muscle**) (*anatomy* 解) a muscle that moves a body part away from the middle of the body or from another part 展肌 ➲ COMPARE ADDUCTOR

abed /əˈbed/ *adv.* (*old use*) in bed 在床上

Aber·do·nian /ˌæbəˈdəʊniən; *NAmE* ˌæbərˈdoʊ-/ *noun* a person from Aberdeen in Scotland （苏格兰）阿伯丁人，阿伯丁居民 ▶ **Aber·do·nian** *adj.*

ab·er·rant /æˈberənt/ *adj.* (*formal*) not usual or not socially acceptable 违反常规的；反常的；异常的：*aberrant behaviour* 反常行为

ab·er·ra·tion /ˌæbəˈreɪʃn/ *noun* [C, U] (*formal*) a fact, an action or a way of behaving that is not usual, and that may be unacceptable 脱离常规；反常现象；异常行为

abet /əˈbet/ *verb* (**-tt-**) **~ sb** to help or encourage sb to do sth wrong 教唆；唆使；煽动；怂恿：*He was abetted in the deception by his wife.* 他行骗是受了妻子的怂恿。 IDM SEE AID *v.*

abey·ance /əˈbeɪəns/ *noun* [U]

IDM **in abeyance** (*formal*) not being used, or being stopped for a period of time 搁置；暂停使用；暂时中止

ABH /ˌeɪ biː ˈeɪtʃ/ *abbr.* (*BrE*, *law* 律) ACTUAL BODILY HARM 实际身体伤害（罪）

abhor /əbˈhɔː(r)/ *verb* (**-rr-**) (not used in the progressive tenses 不用于进行时) **~ sth** (*formal*) to hate sth, for example a way of behaving or thinking, especially for moral reasons （尤指因道德原因而）憎恨，厌恶，憎恶 **SYN** **detest, loathe**

ab·hor·rence /əbˈhɒrəns; *NAmE* -ˈhɔːr-; -ˈhɑːr-/ *noun* [U, sing.] (*formal*) a feeling of strong hatred, especially for moral reasons （尤指因道德原因的）憎恨，厌恶，憎恶

ab·hor·rent /əbˈhɒrənt; *NAmE* -ˈhɔːr-; -ˈhɑːr-/ *adj.* **~ (to sb)** (*formal*) causing hatred, especially for moral reasons （尤指因道德原因）令人憎恨的，令人厌恶的，令人憎恶的 **SYN** **repugnant**: *Racism is abhorrent to a civilized society.* 文明社会憎恶种族主义。

abide /əˈbaɪd/ *verb* (**abided**, **abided**) **HELP** In sense 2 **abode** is also used for the past tense and past participle. 作第 2 义时过去式和过去分词也用 abode。 **1** [T] **cannot/could not abide sb/sth** to dislike sb/sth so much that you hate having to be with or deal with them （十分厌恶而）不能容忍，无法容忍 **SYN** **bear, stand**: *I can't abide people with no sense of humour.* 我讨厌和没有幽默感的人打交道。◇ *He couldn't abide the thought of being cooped up in an office.* 一想到关在办公室里工作，他就觉得受不了。 **2** [I] **+ adv./prep.** (*old use* or *formal*) to stay or live in a place 逗留；停留；居留；居住: *May joy and peace abide in us all.* 愿我们大家都欢乐平安。

PHR V **aˈbide by sth** (*formal*) to accept and act according to a law, an agreement, etc. 遵守，遵循（法律、协议、协定等）: *You'll have to abide by the rules of the club.* 你必须遵守俱乐部的规定。◇ *We will abide by their decision.* 我们愿意遵从他们的决定。 ➲ **WORDFINDER NOTE AT LAW**

abid·ing /əˈbaɪdɪŋ/ *adj.* (*formal*) (of a feeling or belief 感情或信念) lasting for a long time and not changing 持久的；长久的；始终不渝的

abil·ity 🔑 /əˈbɪləti/ *noun* (*pl.* **-ies**) **1** 🔑 [sing.] **~ to do sth** the fact that sb/sth is able to do sth 能力: *The system has the ability to run more than one program at the same time.* 该系统能够同时运行一个以上的程序。◇ *Everyone has the right to good medical care regardless of their ability to pay.* 无论支付能力如何，每个人都有权得到良好的医疗保健。◇ *A gentle form of exercise will increase your ability to relax.* 和缓的运动锻炼会提高自我放松的能力。 **OPP** **inability** **2** 🔑 [C, U] a level of skill or intelligence 才能；本领；才智: *Almost everyone has some musical ability.* 几乎人人都有一些音乐才能。◇ *He was a man of extraordinary abilities.* 他才干卓著。◇ *students of mixed abilities* 能力参差不齐的学生 ◇ *A woman of her ability will easily find a job.* 有她那样才能的女子找工作不难。◇ *I try to do my job to the best of my ability* (= as well as I can). 我尽全力做好我的工作。

abi·ot·ic /ˌeɪbaɪˈɒtɪk; *NAmE* -ˈɑːtɪk/ *adj.* (*specialist*) not involving biology or living things 非生物的；与生物无关的: *abiotic processes* 非生物过程

ab·ject /ˈæbdʒekt/ *adj.* [usually before noun] (*formal*) **1** terrible and without hope 悲惨绝望的；凄惨的: ***abject poverty/misery/failure*** 赤贫；凄惨；惨败 **2** without any pride or respect for yourself 下贱的；卑躬屈节的；自卑的: *an abject apology* 低声下气的道歉 ▶ **ab·ject·ly** *adv.*

ab·jure /əbˈdʒʊə(r); *NAmE* əbˈdʒʊr/ *verb* **~ sth** (*formal*) to promise publicly that you will give up or reject a belief or a way of behaving 公开保证放弃，声明放弃（信念、行为、活动） **SYN** **renounce**

ab·la·tion /əˈbleɪʃn/ *noun* [U] (*geology* 地) the loss of material from a large mass of ice, snow or rock as a result of the action of the sun, wind or rain （冰、雪的）消融；冰消作用；（岩石的）磨蚀

ab·la·tive /ˈæblətɪv/ *noun* (*grammar* 语法) (in some languages 用于某些语言) the form that a noun, a pronoun or an adjective can take to show, for example, who or what sth is done by or where sth comes from （词的）夺格，离格 ➲ COMPARE ACCUSATIVE, DATIVE, GENITIVE, NOMINATIVE, VOCATIVE ▶ **ab·la·tive** *adj.*

ablaze /əˈbleɪz/ *adj.* [not before noun] **1** burning quickly and strongly 猛烈燃烧: *The whole building was soon ablaze.* 整栋大楼很快就熊熊燃烧起来。◇ *Cars and buses were **set ablaze** during the riot.* 暴乱中许多轿车和公共汽车被纵火焚烧。 **2** full of bright light or colours 闪耀；发光；明亮；色彩鲜艳: *There were lights still ablaze as they drove up to the house.* 他们驾车到屋前时，（屋内）灯火仍然通明。◇ **~ with sth** *The trees were ablaze with the colours of autumn.* 树木披上了绚丽的秋装。 **3** **~ (with sth)** full of strong emotion or excitement 充满激情的；情绪激动的: *He turned to her, his eyes ablaze with anger.* 他转过身来，怒目圆睁瞪着她。

able 🔑 /ˈeɪbl/ *adj.* **1** 🔑 **~ to do sth** (used as a modal verb 用作情态动词) to have the skill, intelligence, opportunity, etc. needed to do sth 能；能够: *You must be able to speak French for this job.* 干这项工作你得会说法语。◇ *A viral illness left her barely able to walk.* 一场病毒引起的疾病使她走路都十分困难。◇ *I didn't feel able to disagree with him.* 我觉得不能不同意他的意见。◇ *Will you be able to come?* 你能来吗？ **OPP** **unable** ➲ NOTE AT CAN[1] **2** (**abler** /ˈeɪblə(r)/, **ablest** /ˈeɪblɪst/) intelligent; good at sth 有才智的；有才能的；（某方面）擅长的: *the ablest student in the class* 班上最有才华的学生 ◇ *We aim to help the less able in society to lead an independent life.* 我们的宗旨是帮助社会上能力较弱的人独立生活。 ➲ SEE ALSO ABLY

> **WORD FAMILY**
> **able** *adj.* (≠ unable)
> **ably** *adv.*
> **ability** *noun* (≠ inability)
> **disabled** *adj.*
> **disability** *noun*

-able, **-ible** *suffix* (in adjectives 构成形容词) **1** that can or must be 可…的；能…的；应…的: *calculable* 可计算的 ◇ *taxable* 应纳税的 **2** having the quality of 具有…性质的: *fashionable* 时髦的 ◇ *comfortable* 舒适的 ◇ *changeable* 易变的 ▶ **-ability, -ibility** (in nouns 构成名词): *capability* 能力 ◇ *responsibility* 责任 **-ably, -ibly** (in adverbs 构成副词): *noticeably* 显著地 ◇ *incredibly* 令人难以置信 ➲ MORE LIKE THIS 7, page R25

ˌable-ˈbodied *adj.* physically healthy, fit and strong in contrast to sb who is weak or disabled 健康的；健壮的；体格健全的

ˌable ˈseaman *noun* a sailor of lower rank in the British navy （英国海军）一等水兵

ab·lu·tions /əˈbluːʃnz/ *noun* [pl.] (*formal* or *humorous*) the act of washing yourself 沐浴；净体（礼）；净手（礼）

ably /ˈeɪbli/ *adv.* skilfully and well 能干地: *We were ably assisted by a team of volunteers.* 我们得到一批志愿者的大力协助。 ➲ SEE ALSO ABLE (2)

ABM /ˌeɪ biː ˈem/ *abbr.* (*CanE*) automated banking machine 自动取款机 ➲ CASH MACHINE

ab·neg·ation /ˌæbnɪˈɡeɪʃn/ *noun* [U] (*formal*) the act of not allowing yourself to have sth that you want; the act of rejecting sth 克制；自制；拒绝；放弃

ab·nor·mal **AW** /æbˈnɔːml; *NAmE* -ˈnɔːrml/ *adj.* different from what is usual or expected, especially in a way that is worrying, harmful or not wanted 不正常的；反常的；变态的；畸形的: *abnormal levels of sugar in the blood* 血糖值不正常 ◇ *They thought his behaviour was abnormal.* 他们认为他行为反常。 **OPP** **normal** ▶ **ab·nor·mal·ly** **AW** /æbˈnɔːməli; *NAmE* -ˈnɔːrm-/ *adv.*: *abnormally high blood pressure* 异常高的血压

ab·nor·mal·ity /ˌæbnɔːˈmæləti; *NAmE* -nɔːrˈm-/ *noun* (*pl.* **-ies**) [C, U] a feature or characteristic in a person's body or behaviour that is not usual and may be harmful, worrying or cause illness （身体、行为等）异常，反常，变态，畸形: *abnormalities of the heart* 心脏异常 ◇ ***congenital/foetal abnormality*** 先天性 / 胎儿畸形

Abo /ˈæbəʊ; *NAmE* ˈæboʊ/ *noun* (*pl.* **-os**) (*AustralE*, *taboo*, *informal*) an extremely offensive word for an Aborigine （对澳大利亚土著的蔑称）土鬼，土包子

A

aboard /əˈbɔːd; *NAmE* əˈbɔːrd/ *adv., prep.* on or onto a ship, plane, bus or train 在（船、飞机、公共汽车、火车等）上；上（船、飞机、公共汽车、火车等） SYN **on board**: *We went aboard.* 我们上了船。◇ *He was already aboard the plane.* 他已经登机了。◇ *The plane crashed, killing all 157 passengers aboard.* 飞机坠毁，机上 157 名乘客全部遇难。◇ ***All aboard!*** (= the bus, boat, etc. is leaving soon) 请大家上车（或船等）！（表示马上就要开了）◇ ***Welcome aboard!*** (= used to welcome passengers or a person joining a new organization, etc.) 欢迎各位乘客！；欢迎加盟（新组织等）！

abode /əˈbəʊd; *NAmE* əˈboʊd/ *noun* [usually sing.] (*formal* or *humorous*) the place where sb lives 住所；家：*homeless people **of no fixed abode*** (= with no permanent home) 无家可归的人 ◇ *You are most welcome to my humble abode.* 竭诚欢迎光临寒舍。➲ SEE ALSO ABIDE (2), RIGHT OF ABODE

abol·ish /əˈbɒlɪʃ; *NAmE* əˈbɑːl-/ *verb* **~ sth** to officially end a law, a system or an institution 废除，废止（法律、制度、习俗等）：*This tax should be abolished.* 这种税应该取消。

abo·li·tion /ˌæbəˈlɪʃn/ *noun* [U] the ending of a law, a system or an institution （法律、制度、习俗等的）废除，废止：*the abolition of slavery* 奴隶制的废除

abo·li·tion·ist /ˌæbəˈlɪʃənɪst/ *noun* a person who is in favour of the abolition of sth 主张废除…的人

ˈA-bomb *noun* = ATOM BOMB

abom·in·able /əˈbɒmɪnəbl; *NAmE* əˈbɑːm-/ *adj.* extremely unpleasant and causing disgust 令人憎恶的；令人厌恶的；极其讨厌的 SYN **appalling**, **disgusting**: *The judge described the attack as an abominable crime.* 法官称那次袭击为令人发指的罪行。◇ *We were served the most abominable coffee.* 给我们喝的是最令人作呕的咖啡。▶ **abom·in·ably** /əˈbɒmɪnəbli; *NAmE* əˈbɑːm-/ *adv.*: *She treated him abominably.* 她待他极其恶劣。

Aˌbominable ˈSnowman *noun* = YETI

abom·in·ate /əˈbɒmɪneɪt; *NAmE* əˈbɑːm-/ *verb* (not used in the progressive tenses 不用于进行时) **~ sth/sb** (*formal*) to feel hatred or disgust for sth/sb 憎恨；憎恶；厌恶；极其讨厌

abom·in·ation /əˌbɒmɪˈneɪʃn; *NAmE* əˌbɑːm-/ *noun* (*formal*) a thing that causes disgust and hatred, or is considered extremely offensive 令人憎恨的事物；可恶的东西

abo·ri·ginal /ˌæbəˈrɪdʒənl/ *adj., noun*

■ ***adj.*** **1** (*usually* **Aboriginal**) relating to the original people living in Australia 澳大利亚土著的：*the issue of Aboriginal land rights* 澳大利亚土著土地权问题 **2** relating to the original people, animals, etc. of a place and to a period of time before Europeans arrived （欧洲人到来之前某地区的人、动物等）土著的，土生土长的：*the aboriginal peoples of Canada* 加拿大土著 ◇ *aboriginal art/culture* 土著艺术 / 文化

■ ***noun*** (*usually* **Aboriginal**) a member of a race of people who were the original people living in a country, especially Australia （尤指澳大利亚的）土著，土人 ➲ SEE ALSO KOORI

abo·ri·gine /ˌæbəˈrɪdʒəni/ *noun* **1** a member of a race of people who were the original people living in a country 原住民；土著；土人 **2** **Aborigine** a member of the race of people who were the original people of Australia 澳大利亚土著 ➲ SEE ALSO KOORI

abort /əˈbɔːt; *NAmE* əˈbɔːrt/ *verb* **1** [T] **~ sth** to end a PREGNANCY early in order to prevent a baby from developing and being born alive 使流产：*to **abort a child/pregnancy/foetus*** 终止妊娠；堕胎 **2** [I] (*specialist*) to give birth to a child or young animal too early for it to survive 流产；小产：*The virus can cause pregnant animals to abort.* 这种病毒可能导致怀孕动物流产。➲ SEE ALSO MISCARRY (1) **3** [I, T, often passive] to end or cause sth to end before it has been completed, especially because it is likely to fail （使）夭折，中止（尤指很可能失败的事情）：(*computing* 计) *If the wrong password is given the program aborts.* 如果键入错误的密码，程序即会中止。◇ **~ sth** *We had no option but to abort the mission.* 我们别无选择，只有取消这项任务。◇ *The plan was aborted at the last minute.* 计划在最后一刻取消了。

abor·tion /əˈbɔːʃn; *NAmE* əˈbɔːrʃn/ *noun* **1** [U] the deliberate ending of a PREGNANCY at an early stage 人工流产；堕胎；打胎：*to **support/oppose abortion*** 支持 / 反对堕胎 ◇ *a woman's right to abortion* 妇女做人工流产的权利 ◇ *abortion laws* 堕胎法 ◇ *I've always been anti-abortion.* 我一直反对堕胎。**2** [C] a medical operation to end a PREGNANCY at an early stage 人工流产手术；堕胎手术：*She decided to **have an abortion**.* 她决定做人工流产。SYN **termination** ➲ COMPARE MISCARRIAGE

abor·tion·ist /əˈbɔːʃənɪst; *NAmE* əˈbɔːrʃ-/ *noun* a person who performs abortions, especially illegally （尤指非法）为人堕胎者

abort·ive /əˈbɔːtɪv; *NAmE* əˈbɔːrtɪv/ *adj.* (*formal*) (of an action 行动) not successful; failed 不成功的；失败的 SYN **unsuccessful**: *an abortive military coup* 一次流产的军事政变 ◇ *abortive attempts to divert the course of the river* 河流改道不遂的尝试

abound /əˈbaʊnd/ *verb* [I] to exist in great numbers or quantities 大量存在；有许多：*Stories about his travels abound.* 有关他游历的故事多得很。

PHR V **aˈbound with/in sth** to have sth in great numbers or quantities 有大量；富于：*The lakes abound with fish.* 这些湖泊盛产鱼。➲ SEE ALSO ABUNDANCE, ABUNDANT

about /əˈbaʊt/ *adv., prep., adj.*

■ ***adv.*** **1** a little more or less than; a little before or after 大约；左右 SYN **approximately**: *It costs about $10.* 这大约要花 10 美元。◇ *They waited (for) about an hour.* 他们等了一小时左右。◇ *He arrived (at) about ten.* 他是十点钟左右到的。**2** nearly; very close to 将近；几乎：*I'm just about ready.* 我就要准备好了。◇ *This is about the best we can hope for.* 这差不多是我们所能希望的最好结果。**3** (*especially BrE*) in many directions; here and there 到处；处处；各处：*The children were rushing about in the garden.* 孩子们在花园里跑来跑去。**4** (*especially BrE*) in no particular order; in various places 凌乱地；四处；到处：*Her books were lying about on the floor.* 她的书在地板上东一本西一本地放着。**5** (*especially BrE*) doing nothing in particular 闲着；无所事事：*People were standing about in the road.* 人们在路上闲站着。**6** (*especially BrE*) able to be found in a place 在某地；附近；周围：*There was nobody about.* 附近没有人。◇ *There's a lot of flu about.* 这一带流感肆虐。**7** (*specialist* or *formal*) facing the opposite direction 向后转；掉转方向；掉头：*He brought the ship about.* 他掉转船头。➲ NOTE AT AROUND

IDM **that's about ˈall | that's about ˈit** used to say that you have finished telling sb about sth and there is nothing to add 我要说的就是这些；我的话完了：*'Anything else?' 'No, that's about it for now.'* "还有什么要说的吗？""没有了，现在我要说的就是这些。" ➲ MORE AT JUST *adv.*, OUT *adv.*

■ ***prep.*** **1** on the subject of sb/sth; in connection with sb/sth 关于；对于：*a book about flowers* 一本关于花卉的书 ◇ *Tell me **all about** it.* 把情况全部告诉我。◇ *What's she so angry about?* 她为什么生这么大的气？◇ *There's something strange about him.* 他有点怪。◇ *I don't know what you're **on about*** (= talking about). 我不懂你在谈什么。◇ *There's nothing you can do about it now.* 现在你对此毫无办法。**2** used to describe the purpose or an aspect of sth 目的是；为了；涉及…方面：*Movies are **all about** making money these days.* 当今电影只顾赚钱。◇ ***What was all that about?*** (= what was the reason for what has just happened?) 这到底是怎么回事？**3** busy with sth; doing sth 忙于；从事于：*Everywhere people were going about their daily business.* 无论哪里，人们都在忙着干日常工作。◇ ***And while you're about it…*** (= while you're doing that) 在你干这件事的同时，顺便… **4** (*especially BrE*) in many directions in a place; here and there 在…到处；在…各处：*We wandered about the town for an hour or so.* 我们在城里到处游逛了一个小时左右。◇ *He looked about the* room. 他在房间里四下看了看。 **5** (*especially BrE*) in various parts of a place; here and there 在…四处： *The papers were strewn about the room.* 房间里四处乱扔着文件。 **6** (*especially BrE*) next to a place or person; in the area mentioned 在…附近；在…地方： *She's somewhere about the office.* 她在办公室附近。 **7** (*literary*) surrounding sb/sth 围绕： *She wore a shawl about her shoulders.* 她披了一件披肩。

IDM **how/what about...?** **1** used when asking for information about sb/sth （询问消息）怎么样，如何： *How about Ruth? Have you heard from her?* 露丝怎么样了？你有她的消息吗？ ◇ *I'm having fish. What about you?* 我吃鱼，你呢？ **2** used to make a suggestion （提建议时说）怎么样，好吗： *How about going for a walk?* 去散散步怎么样？ ◇ (*especially NAmE*) *How about we go for a walk?* 我们去散散步怎么样？ ◇ *What about a break?* 休息一下如何？

■ ***adj.***

IDM **be about to do sth** to be close to doing sth; to be going to do sth very soon 即将，行将，正要（做某事）： *I was just about to ask you the same thing.* 我刚才正要问你同一件事情。 **not be about to do sth** to not be willing to do sth; to not intend to do sth 不愿，无意（做某事）： *I've never done any cooking and I'm not about to start now.* 我从来没有做过饭，也不想从现在开始做起来。

▼ LANGUAGE BANK 用语库

about

Saying what a text is about 描述文章的内容

- *The book* ***is about*** *homeless people in the cities.* 这本书写的是城市中无家可归的人们。
- *The report* ***deals with*** *the issue of homelessness in London.* 这篇报道是关于伦敦的无家可归问题。
- *The writer* ***discusses*** *the problems faced by homeless people.* 作者讨论了无家可归者面临的种种问题。
- *The article* ***presents an overview of*** *the issues surrounding homelessness.* 这篇文章概述了有关无家可归的种种问题。
- *The novel* ***explores*** *the theme of friendship among homeless people.* 这部小说探究了无家可归者之间的友谊这个主题。
- *The first chapter* ***examines*** *the relationship between homelessness and drug addiction.* 第一章考察了无家可归与吸毒成瘾之间的关系。
- *The paper* ***considers*** *the question of why so many young people become homeless.* 这篇论文论述了为何如此多的年轻人变得无家可归的问题。

a,bout-'turn (*BrE*) (*also* **a,bout-'face** *NAmE, BrE*) *noun* [sing.] a complete change of opinion, plan or behaviour （意见、计划、行为的）彻底改变： *The government did an about-turn over nuclear energy.* 政府对核能的态度来了个 180 度的大转变。

above /əˈbʌv/ *prep., adv., adj.*

■ ***prep.*** **1** at or to a higher place or position than sth/sb 在（或向）…上面： *The water came above our knees.* 水淹过了我们的膝盖。 ◇ *We were flying above the clouds.* 我们在云层上面飞行。 ◇ *the people in the apartment above mine* 我楼上那套公寓里的人们 ◇ *A captain in the navy ranks above a captain in the army.* 海军的 captain（上校）军衔比陆军的 captain（上尉）高。 ◇ *They finished the year six places above their local rivals.* 这一年结束，他们的排名比当地竞争对手超前六个名次。 **2** more than sth; greater in number, level or age than sb/sth （数目、数量、水平、年龄）超过，多于，大于： *Inflation is above 6%.* 通货膨胀超过 6%。 ◇ *Temperatures have been above average.* 气温一直比平均温度高。 ◇ *We cannot accept children above the age of 10.* 我们不能接受 10 岁以上的儿童。 **3** of greater importance or of higher quality than sb/sth （重要性、质量）超过，胜过： *I rate her above most other players of her age.* 我认为她优于大多数同龄参赛者。 **4** too good or too honest to do sth （因善良或诚实正直而）不至于，不屑于（做某事）： *She's not above lying when it suits her.* 她在适当时机还是会说谎的。 ◇ *He's above suspicion* (= he is completely trusted). 他无可置疑。 **5** (of a sound 声音) louder or clearer than another sound （音量或清晰度）超过（另一种声音）： *I couldn't hear her above the noise of the traffic.* 交通嘈杂，我听不见她的声音。

IDM **above 'all** most important of all; especially 最重要的是；尤其是： *Above all, keep in touch.* 最要紧的是保持联系。 ➲ LANGUAGE BANK AT EMPHASIS **a'bove yourself** (*disapproving*) having too high an opinion of yourself 自高自大；妄自尊大 ➲ MORE AT OVER *prep.*

■ ***adv.*** **1** at or to a higher place 在（或向）上面；在（或向）较高处： *Put it on the shelf above.* 把它放到上面的搁板上。 ◇ *Seen from above the cars looked tiny.* 从高处往下看，车辆显得很小。 ◇ *They were acting on instructions from above* (= from sb in a higher position of authority). 他们是在按照上级的指示办事。 **2** greater in number, level or age （数目、数量、水平、年龄）超过，更多，更大： *increases of 5% and above* 增加 5% 及以上 ◇ *A score of 70 or above will get you an 'A'.* * 70 分或以上就可以得"优"。 ◇ *children aged 12 and above* * 12 岁及 12 岁以上的孩子 **3** earlier in sth written or printed 上文；前文： *As was stated above...* 如上所述… ◇ *See above, page 97.* 见前文，第 97 页。

■ ***adj.*** [only before noun] mentioned or printed previously in a letter, book, etc. 前文述及的；上述的： *Please write to us at the above address.* 请按上述地址来函。 ▶ **the above** *noun* [sing.+sing./pl. v.]: *Please notify us if the above is not correct.* 如果上面所说的不正确，请通知我们。 ◇ *All the above* (= people mentioned above) *have passed the exam.* 以上各人都通过了考试。

▼ WHICH WORD? 词语辨析

above / over

- **Above** and **over** can both be used to describe a position higher than something. * above 和 over 均可表示位置高于…或在…上： *They built a new room above/over the garage.* 他们在车库上面加建了一个房间。 When you are talking about movement from one side of something to the other, you can only use **over**. 表示从某物的一边移至另一边只能用 over： *They jumped over the stream.* 他们跳过了小溪。 **Over** can also mean 'covering'. * over 亦可表示覆盖着： *He put a blanket over the sleeping child.* 他把毯子盖在睡着了的孩子身上。
- **Above** and **over** can also mean 'more than'. **Above** is used in relation to a minimum level or a fixed point. * above 和 over 亦可表示多于。above 与最低限度或某固定值关联： *2 000 feet above sea level* 海拔 2 000 英尺 ◇ *Temperatures will not rise above zero tonight.* 今天夜间的温度不会高于零度。 **Over** is used with numbers, ages, money and time. * over 与数目、年龄、金钱和时间连用： *He's over 50.* 他已年过半百。 ◇ *It costs over £100.* 这个花了 100 多英镑。 ◇ *We waited over 2 hours.* 我们等了两个多小时。

a,bove 'board *adj., adv.* legal and honest; in a legal and honest way 合法而坦诚（的）；开诚布公（的）；公开（的）： *Don't worry; the deal was completely above board.* 别担心，交易是完全合法的。 ORIGIN If card players keep their hands above the table (the board), other players can see what they are doing. 源于纸牌游戏。如果玩牌者将手放在桌上，其动作就会被其他玩牌者看得一清二楚。

a,bove-'mentioned *adj.* [only before noun] mentioned or named earlier in the same letter, book, etc. 前文述及的；上述的

a,bove-the-'fold *adj.* [only before noun] in a position where it is seen first, for example on the top half of the front page of a newspaper or in the part of a web page that you see first when you open it （报纸头版、网页等）居于上端的，位置明显的，第一眼看到的： *above-the-fold*

A

images 位置醒目的图像 ◇ *The company logo must be placed in an above-the-fold position.* 公司标志必须放在显眼的位置。➲ COMPARE BELOW-THE-FOLD **IDM** SEE FOLD *n.*

abra·ca·dabra /ˌæbrəkəˈdæbrə/ *exclamation* a word that people say when they do a magic trick, in order to make it successful （表演魔术、施魔法时所念的咒语）阿布拉卡达布拉

ab·rade /əˈbreɪd/ *verb* ~ **sth** (*specialist*) to rub the surface of sth, such as rock or skin, and damage it or make it rough 磨损（岩石等）；擦伤（皮肤等）

ab·ra·sion /əˈbreɪʒn/ *noun* (*specialist*) **1** [C] a damaged area of the skin where it has been rubbed against sth hard and rough （皮肤、表皮）擦伤处；（表层）磨损处：*He suffered cuts and abrasions to the face.* 他的脸上有许多伤口和擦伤。 **2** [U] damage to a surface caused by rubbing sth very hard against it 磨损；磨蚀：*Diamonds have extreme resistance to abrasion.* 钻石极抗磨损。

abra·sive /əˈbreɪsɪv/ *adj., noun*
▪ ***adj.*** **1** an **abrasive** substance is rough and can be used to clean a surface or to make it smooth 有研磨作用的；研磨的：*abrasive kitchen cleaners* 厨房擦洗去污剂 **2** (of a person or their manner 人或行为方式、态度) rude and unkind; acting in a way that may hurt other people's feelings 生硬粗暴的；粗鲁的；伤人感情的 ▶ **abra·sive·ly** *adv.* **abra·sive·ness** *noun* [U]
▪ ***noun*** a substance used for cleaning surfaces or for making them smooth （用来擦洗表面或使表面光滑的）磨料

abreast /əˈbrest/ *adv.* next to sb/sth and facing the same way 并列；并排；并肩：*cycling two abreast* 两人骑车并排而行 ◇ ~ **of sb/sth** *A police car **drew abreast** of us and signalled us to stop.* 一辆警车开过来与我们并行，示意我们停下来。
IDM **keep abreast of sth** to make sure that you know all the most recent facts about a subject 了解最新情况；跟上（某事物的发展）：*It is almost impossible to keep abreast of all the latest developments in computing.* 要跟上计算机领域所有最新的发展几乎不可能。

abridge /əˈbrɪdʒ/ *verb* ~ **sth** to make a book, play, etc. shorter by leaving parts out 删节，节略（书籍、剧本等） ▶ **abridged** *adj.*：*an **abridged edition/version*** 节本 **OPP** **unabridged** **abridge·ment** (*also* **abridg·ment**) *noun* [U, C]

abroad 🔑 /əˈbrɔːd/ *adv.* **1** 🔑 in or to a foreign country 在国外；到国外：*to **be/go/travel/live abroad*** 在外国；出国；到国外旅行；在外国居住 ◇ *She worked abroad for a year.* 她在国外工作了一年。◇ *imports of cheap food from abroad* 国外廉价食物的进口 ◇ *He was famous, both **at home and abroad*** (= in his own country and in other countries). 他享誉国内外。➲ WORDFINDER NOTE AT TOURIST **2** (*formal*) being talked about or felt by many people 广为流传：*There was news abroad that a change was coming.* 盛传即将有一个变动。 **3** (*old use*) outside; outdoors 在室外；到室外；户外

ab·ro·gate /ˈæbrəgeɪt/ *verb* ~ **sth** (*specialist*) to officially end a law, an agreement, etc. 废除，废止，撤销（法律、协议等） **SYN** **repeal** ▶ **ab·ro·ga·tion** /ˌæbrəˈgeɪʃn/ *noun* [U]

ab·rupt /əˈbrʌpt/ *adj.* **1** sudden and unexpected, often in an unpleasant way 突然的；意外的：*an **abrupt change/halt/departure*** 突然改变；骤然停顿；突然离去 **2** speaking or acting in a way that seems unfriendly and rude; not taking time to say more than is necessary （言语、行为）粗鲁的，莽撞的，唐突的；生硬的 **SYN** **brusque**, **curt**：*an abrupt manner* 唐突的举止 ◇ *She was very abrupt with me in our meeting.* 我们会面时，她跟我说话非常生硬。 ▶ **ab·rupt·ly** *adv.* **ab·rupt·ness** *noun* [U]

ABS /ˌeɪ biː ˈes/ *abbr.* anti-lock braking system 防抱死装置 ➲ SEE ALSO ANTI-LOCK

abs /æbz/ *noun* [pl.] (*informal*) = ABDOMINALS

ab·scess /ˈæbses/ *noun* a swollen and infected area on your skin or in your body, full of a thick yellowish liquid (called PUS) 脓肿

ab·scissa /æbˈsɪsə/ (*pl.* **ab·scissae** /-siː/ or **ab·scissas**) *noun* (*mathematics* 数) the COORDINATE that gives the distance along the horizontal AXIS 横坐标 ➲ COMPARE ORDINATE

ab·scond /əbˈskɒnd; *NAmE* əbˈskɑːnd/ *verb* **1** [I] ~ (**from sth**) to escape from a place that you are not allowed to leave without permission 逃走；逃遁 **2** [I] ~ (**with sth**) to leave secretly and take with you sth, especially money, that does not belong to you （携款）潜逃：*He absconded with the company funds.* 他卷走公司的资金潜逃了。

ab·seil /ˈæbseɪl/ (*BrE*) (*NAmE* **rap·pel**) *verb* [I] ~ (**down, off, etc. sth**) to go down a steep CLIFF or rock while attached to a rope, pushing against the slope or rock with your feet 绕绳下降（用绳缠绕着身体，双脚蹬陡坡或峭壁自己放绳下滑） ➲ VISUAL VOCAB PAGE V53 ▶ **ab·seil** (*BrE*) (*NAmE* **rap·pel**) *noun*

ab·sence 🔑 /ˈæbsəns/ *noun* **1** 🔑 [U, C] the fact of sb being away from a place where they are usually expected to be; the occasion or period of time when sb is away 缺席；不在：*The decision was made **in my absence*** (= while I was not there). 这个决定是我不在的时候作出的。 ◇ *We did not receive any news during his long absence.* 我们在他长期离开的时候没有得到一点消息。 ◇ ~ **from...** *absence from work* 缺勤 ◇ *repeated absences from school* 一再缺课 ➲ SEE ALSO LEAVE *n.* **2** 🔑 [U] the fact of sb/sth not existing or not being available; a lack of sth 不存在；缺乏：*The case was dismissed **in the absence of** any definite proof.* 此案因缺乏确凿证据而不予受理。 ◇ *the absence of any women on the board of directors* 董事会成员中没有女性的现象 **OPP** **presence**
IDM **ˌabsence makes the heart grow ˈfonder** (*saying*) used to say that when you are away from sb that you love, you love them even more 不相见，倍思念 ➲ MORE AT CONSPICUOUS

ab·sent 🔑 *adj., verb*
▪ ***adj.*** /ˈæbsənt/ **1** 🔑 ~ (**from...**) not in a place because of illness, etc. 缺席；不在：*to be absent from work* 缺勤 **OPP** **present** **2** 🔑 ~ (**from sth**) not present in sth 不存在；缺少：*Love was totally absent from his childhood.* 他童年时没有得到丝毫关爱。 **OPP** **present** **3** showing that you are not really looking at or thinking about what is happening around you 心不在焉的；出神的：*an absent expression* 心不在焉的神情 ➲ SEE ALSO ABSENTLY
▪ ***verb*** /æbˈsent/ ~ **yourself** (**from sth**) (*formal*) to not go to or be in a place where you are expected to be 缺席；不参加；不在：*He had absented himself from the office for the day.* 这一天他没有去办公室上班。

ab·sen·tee /ˌæbsənˈtiː/ *noun* a person who is not at a place where they were expected to be 缺席者；缺勤者；缺课者

ˌabsentee ˈballot (*NAmE*) (*BrE* **ˈpostal vote**) *noun* a vote in an election that you can send when you cannot be present 邮寄的选票；邮寄投票

ab·sen·tee·ism /ˌæbsənˈtiːɪzəm/ *noun* [U] the fact of being frequently away from work or school, especially without good reasons（经常性无故的）旷工，旷课 ➲ COMPARE PRESENTEEISM

ˌabsentee ˈlandlord *noun* a person who rents their property to sb, but does not live in it and rarely visits it 在外业主，在外地主（不在产业内居住也很少过来）

ab·sen·tia ➲ IN ABSENTIA

ab·sent·ly /ˈæbsəntli/ *adv.* in a way that shows you are not looking at or thinking about what is happening around you 心不在焉地；出神地：*He nodded absently, his attention absorbed by the screen.* 他全神注视着屏幕，心不在焉地点了点头。

ˌabsent-ˈminded *adj.* tending to forget things, perhaps because you are not thinking about what is around you, but about sth else 健忘的；心不在焉的 **SYN** **forgetful**

▸ ˌabsent-ˈminded·ly *adv.* ˌabsent-ˈminded·ness *noun* [U]

ab·sinthe /ˈæbsɪnθ/ *noun* [U, C] a very strong green alcoholic drink that tastes of ANISEED 苦艾酒（带茴香味的绿色烈性酒）

ab·so·lute /ˈæbsəluːt/ *adj., noun*

■ *adj.* **1** total and complete 完全的；全部的；绝对的：*a class for absolute beginners* 零起点班 ◇ *absolute confidence/trust/silence/truth* 充满信心；绝对信任；万籁俱寂；绝对真实 ◇ *'You're wrong,' she said with absolute certainty.* "你错了。" 她斩钉截铁地说。 **2** [only before noun] used, especially in spoken English, to give emphasis to what you are saying（口语中尤用以强调）道地的，确实的，十足的：*There's absolute rubbish on television tonight.* 今晚的电视节目简直糟糕透顶。 ◇ *He must earn an absolute fortune.* 他准是赚了一大笔钱。 **3** definite and without any doubt or confusion 肯定的；无疑的；明确的：*There was no absolute proof.* 没有确凿的证据。 ◇ *He taught us that the laws of physics were absolute.* 他教导我们说，物理定律是确实存在的。 ➲ SEE ALSO DECREE ABSOLUTE **4** (of a legal decision) final（法律判决）最终的：*The divorce became absolute last week.* 离婚在上周已成定局。 **5** not limited or restricted 不受限制的；不受约束的：***absolute power/authority*** 无上权力；绝对权威 ◇ *an **absolute ruler/monarchy*** (= one with no limit to their power) 独裁统治者；专制君主 **6** existing or measured independently and not in relation to sth else 独立的；绝对的：*Although prices are falling **in absolute terms**, energy is still expensive.* 尽管能源的绝对售价在下降，但仍然昂贵。 ◇ *Beauty cannot be measured by any absolute standard.* 美是不可能用任何绝对标准来衡量的。 ➲ COMPARE RELATIVE *adj.*

■ *noun* an idea or a principle that is believed to be true or valid in any circumstances 绝对（指思想或原理）：*Right and wrong are, for her, moral absolutes.* 她认为，是与非是道德上的绝对准则。

ab·so·lute·ly /ˈæbsəluːtli/ *adv.* **1** used to emphasize that sth is completely true（强调真实无误）绝对地，完全地：*You're absolutely right.* 你完全正确。 ◇ *He made it absolutely clear.* 他把此事讲得一清二楚。 **2** **absolutely no…, absolutely nothing** used to emphasize sth negative 绝对不；完全没有：*She did absolutely no work.* 她一点活儿也没有干。 ◇ *There's absolutely nothing more the doctors can do.* 医生的确再也无计可施了。 **3** used with adjectives or verbs that express strong feelings or extreme qualities to mean 'extremely' 极其：*I was absolutely furious with him.* 我被他气死了。 ◇ *She absolutely adores you.* 她极为崇拜你。 ◇ *He's an absolutely brilliant cook.* 他的厨艺精湛至极。 **4** /ˌæbsəˈluːtli/ used to emphasize that you agree with sb, or to give sb permission to do sth（强调同意或允许）当然，对极了：*'They could have told us, couldn't they?' 'Absolutely!'* "他们本来可以告诉我们的，不是吗？" "当然！" ◇ *'Can we leave a little early?' 'Absolutely!'* "我们可以早一点离开吗？" "完全可以！" **5** **absolutely not** used to emphasize that you strongly disagree with sb, or to refuse permission（强调坚决不同意或不允许）当然不，绝对不行：*'Was it any good?' 'No, absolutely not.'* "那有什么好处吗？" "绝对没有。"

ˌabsolute maˈjority *noun* more than half of the total number of votes or winning candidates 绝对多数（指超过半数的选票或竞选席位）

ˌabsolute ˈtemperature *noun* [U, C] temperature measured from absolute zero in degrees KELVIN 绝对温度

ˌabsolute ˈzero *noun* [U] the lowest temperature that is thought to be possible 绝对零度

ab·so·lu·tion /ˌæbsəˈluːʃn/ *noun* [U] (especially in the Christian Church 尤指基督教中的) a formal statement that a person is forgiven for what he or she has done wrong 赦罪；赦免；解罪

ab·so·lut·ism /ˈæbsəluːtɪzəm/ *noun* [U] **1** a political system in which a ruler or government has total power at all times 专制制度；专制政体 **2** belief in a political, religious or moral principle which is thought to be true in all circumstances（政治、宗教、道德上的）绝对主义，绝对论，绝对原则 ▸ **ab·so·lut·ist** *noun, adj.*

ab·solve /əbˈzɒlv; *NAmE* əbˈzɑːlv/ *verb* (*formal*) **1** ~ sb (of/from sth) to state formally that sb is not guilty or responsible for sth 宣告…无罪；判定…无责：*The court absolved him of all responsibility for the accident.* 法院判定他对该事故不负任何责任。 **2** ~ sb (from/of sth) to give ABSOLUTION to sb 赦免…的罪：*I absolve you from all your sins.* 我赦免你所有的罪过。

ab·sorb /əbˈzɔːb; -ˈsɔːb; *NAmE* -ˈzɔːrb; -ˈsɔːrb/ *verb*

• **LIQUID/GAS** 液体；气体 **1** to take in a liquid, gas or other substance from the surface or space around 吸收（液体、气体等）：~ sth *Plants absorb carbon dioxide from the air.* 植物吸收空气中的二氧化碳。 ◇ ~ **sth into sth** *The cream is easily absorbed into the skin.* 这种乳霜皮肤易吸收。 ➲ WORDFINDER NOTE AT LIQUID

• **MAKE PART OF STH LARGER** 使并入 **2** [often passive] to make sth smaller become part of sth larger 使并入；吞并；同化：~ **sth** *The country simply cannot absorb this influx of refugees.* 这个国家实在没有能力接纳这么多涌入的难民。 ◇ ~ **sth into sth** *The surrounding small towns have been absorbed into the city.* 四周的小城镇已并入这座城市。

• **INFORMATION** 信息 **3** ~ **sth** to take sth into the mind and learn or understand it 理解；掌握 SYN **take in**：*It's a lot of information to absorb all at once.* 要一下子消化这些资料，真是很多。

• **INTEREST SB** 引起兴趣 **4** ~ **sb** to interest sb very much so that they pay no attention to anything else 吸引全部注意力；使全神贯注 SYN **engross**：*This work had absorbed him for several years.* 这项工作曾使他沉迷了好几年。

• **HEAT/LIGHT/ENERGY** 热；光；能 **5** ~ **sth** to take in and keep heat, light, energy, etc. instead of reflecting it 吸收（热、光、能等）：*Black walls absorb a lot of heat during the day.* 黑色墙壁在白天吸收大量的热。

• **SHOCK/IMPACT** 震动；撞击 **6** ~ **sth** to reduce the effect of a blow, hit, etc. 减轻（打击、碰击等的）作用：*This tennis racket absorbs shock on impact.* 这款网球拍能减轻撞击所产生的剧烈震动。 ➲ SEE ALSO SHOCK ABSORBER

• **MONEY/TIME/CHANGES** 金钱；时间；变化 **7** ~ **sth** to use up a large supply of sth, especially money or time 耗费，耗去（大量金钱、时间等）：*The new proposals would absorb $80 billion of the federal budget.* 这些新提案将耗费 800 亿美元联邦政府预算。 **8** ~ **sth** to deal with changes, effects, costs, etc. 承受，承担，对付（变化、结果、费用等）：*The company is unable to absorb such huge losses.* 公司无法承受如此巨大的损失。

ab·sor·bance /əbˈzɔːbəns; -ˈsɔːb-; *NAmE* -ˈzɔːrb-; -ˈsɔːrb-/ *noun* (*physics* 物) the ability of a substance to absorb light（光）吸收度；吸光度

ab·sorbed /əbˈzɔːbd; -ˈsɔːbd; *NAmE* -ˈzɔːrbd; -ˈsɔːrbd/ *adj.* [not usually before noun] ~ **in sth/sb** very interested in sth/sb so that you are not paying attention to anything else 被…吸引住；专心致志；全神贯注：*She seemed totally absorbed in her book.* 她好像完全沉浸在书中。

ab·sorb·ent /əbˈzɔːbənt; -ˈsɔːb-; *NAmE* -ˈzɔːrb-; -ˈsɔːrb-/ *adj.* able to take in sth easily, especially liquid 易吸收（液体等）的：***absorbent paper/materials*** 吸水纸；吸收性材料 ▸ **ab·sorb·ency** /-ənsi/ *noun* [U]

ab·sorb·ing /əbˈzɔːbɪŋ; -ˈsɔːb-; *NAmE* -ˈzɔːrb-; -ˈsɔːrb-/ *adj.* interesting and enjoyable and holding your attention completely 十分吸引人的；引人入胜的；精彩的：*an absorbing book/game* 一本引人入胜的书；一个极有趣的游戏 ➲ SYNONYMS AT INTERESTING

ab·sorp·tion /əbˈzɔːpʃn; -ˈsɔːp-; *NAmE* -ˈzɔːrp-; -ˈsɔːrp-/ *noun* [U] **1** the process of a liquid, gas or other substance being taken in（液体、气体等的）吸收：*Vitamin D is necessary to aid the absorption of calcium from food.* 从食物中吸取钙需靠维生素 D 的帮助。 **2** the process of a smaller group, country, etc. becoming part of a larger group or country 并入；同化：*the absorption of immigrants into the host country* 移民融入移民国 **3** ~ (in sth)

A

the fact of sb being very interested in sth so that it takes all their attention 专心致志；全神贯注；着迷：*His work suffered because of his total absorption in sport.* 他痴迷于体育运动而影响了工作。

ab·stain /əb'steɪn/ *verb* [I] **1** ~ (**from sth**) to choose not to use a vote, either in favour of or against sth （投票时）弃权：*Ten people voted in favour, five against and two abstained.* 十人投票赞成，五人反对，两人弃权。 **2** ~ (**from sth**) to decide not to do or have sth, especially sth you like or enjoy, because it is bad for your health or considered morally wrong 戒；戒除：*to abstain from alcohol/sex/drugs* 戒酒；禁欲；戒毒 **3** ~ (**from sth**) (*IndE*) to stay away from sth 离开；回避：*The workers who abstained from work yesterday have been suspended.* 昨天旷工的工人被暂时停职。 ➲ SEE ALSO ABSTENTION, ABSTINENCE

ab·stain·er /əb'steɪnə(r)/ *noun* **1** a person who chooses not to vote either in favour of or against sth （投票）弃权者 **2** a person who never drinks alcohol 滴酒不沾的人

ab·ste·mi·ous /əb'sti:miəs/ *adj.* (*formal*) not allowing yourself to have much food or alcohol, or to do things that are enjoyable 饮食有度的；有节制的

ab·sten·tion /əb'stenʃn/ *noun* **1** [C, U] ~ (**from sth**) an act of choosing not to use a vote either in favour of or against sth 弃权（不投票）：*The voting was 15 in favour, 3 against and 2 abstentions.* 表决结果是 15 人赞成，3 人反对，2 人弃权。 **2** [U] (*formal*) the act of not allowing yourself to have or do sth enjoyable or sth that is considered bad 戒；戒除 ➲ SEE ALSO ABSTAIN

ab·stin·ence /'æbstɪnəns/ *noun* [U] ~ (**from sth**) (*formal*) the practice of not allowing yourself sth, especially food, alcoholic drinks or sex, for moral, religious or health reasons（因道德、宗教或健康原因对饮食、酒、色等的）节制；禁欲：*total abstinence from strong drink* 戒绝烈性酒 ➲ SEE ALSO ABSTAIN

ab·stin·ent /'æbstɪnənt/ *adj.* (*formal*) not allowing yourself sth, especially alcoholic drinks, for moral, religious or health reasons （因道德、宗教或健康原因对酒等）节制的；禁欲的

ab·stract AW *adj., noun, verb*

■ ***adj.*** /'æbstrækt/ **1** based on general ideas and not on any particular real person, thing or situation 抽象的（与个别情况相对）；纯理论的：***abstract knowledge/principles*** 理论知识；抽象原理 ◇ *The research shows that pre-school children are capable of thinking in abstract terms.* 研究显示，学前儿童具有抽象思维的能力。 ➲ COMPARE CONCRETE *adj.* **2** existing in thought or as an idea but not having a physical reality 抽象的（与具体经验相对）：*We may talk of beautiful things but beauty itself is abstract.* 我们尽可谈论美的事物，但美本身却是抽象的。 **3** (of art 艺术) not representing people or things in a realistic way, but expressing the artist's ideas about them 抽象（派）的 ➲ COMPARE FIGURATIVE (2), REPRESENTATIONAL (1) ▶ **ab·stract·ly** AW *adv.*

■ ***noun*** /'æbstrækt/ **1** an abstract work of art 抽象派艺术作品 **2** a short piece of writing containing the main ideas in a document （文献等的）摘要，概要 SYN **summary**

IDM **in the 'abstract** in a general way, without referring to a particular real person, thing or situation 抽象地；理论上

■ ***verb*** /æb'strækt/ **1** ~ **sth** (**from sth**) to remove sth from somewhere 把…抽象出；提取；抽取；分离：*She abstracted the main points from the argument.* 她提炼出论证的要点。 ◇ *a plan to abstract 8 million gallons of water from the river* 从这条河中抽取 800 万加仑水的计划 **2** ~ **sth** (*specialist*) to make a written summary of a book, etc. 写出（书等）的摘要

ab·stract·ed /æb'stræktɪd/ *adj.* (*formal*) thinking deeply about sth and not paying attention to what is around you 出神的；心神专注的 ▶ **ab·stract·ed·ly** *adv.*

,abstract ex'pressionism *noun* [U] a style and movement in abstract art that developed in New York in the middle of the 20th century and tries to express the feelings of the artist rather than showing a physical object 抽象表现主义（20 世纪中期源于纽约，旨在表现艺术家之情感而非现实形体） ▶ **,abstract ex'pressionist** *noun*：*abstract expressionists like Jackson Pollock* 抽象表现派画家如杰克逊・波洛克 **,abstract ex'pressionist** *adj.* [usually before noun]：*abstract expressionist art* 抽象表现主义艺术

ab·strac·tion AW /æb'strækʃn/ *noun* **1** [C, U] (*formal*) a general idea not based on any particular real person, thing or situation; the quality of being abstract 抽象概念；抽象 **2** [U] (*formal*) the state of thinking deeply about sth and not paying attention to what is around you 出神；心神专注 **3** [U, C] the action of removing sth from sth else; the process of being removed from sth else 提取；抽取；分离：*water abstraction from rivers* 从河流中抽取水

ab·strac·tion·ism /æb'strækʃnɪzəm/ *noun* [U] **1** (*specialist*) the principles and practices of ABSTRACT art 抽象（艺术）主义 **2** the expression of ideas in an abstract way （思想的）抽象表达；抽象主义创作 ▶ **ab·strac·tion·ist** *noun, adj.* [usually before noun]

,abstract 'noun *noun* (*grammar* 语法) a noun, for example *goodness* or *freedom*, that refers to an idea or a general quality, not to a physical object 抽象名词 ➲ COMPARE COMMON NOUN, PROPER NOUN

ab·struse /əb'stru:s; æb-/ *adj.* (*formal, often disapproving*) difficult to understand 难解的；深奥的：*an abstruse argument* 玄奥的论点

ab·surd /əb'sɜ:d; *NAmE* əb'sɜ:rd/ *adj.* **1** completely ridiculous; not logical and sensible 荒谬的；荒唐的；怪诞不经的 SYN **ridiculous**：*That uniform makes the guards look absurd.* 警卫们穿着那种制服看起来怪模怪样的。 ◇ *Of course it's not true, what an absurd idea.* 那当然不合乎事实，这个想法太荒唐了！ **2 the absurd** *noun* [sing.] things that are or that seem to be absurd 荒诞的事物；悖理的东西：*He has a good sense of the absurd.* 他对荒诞事物有较强的识别能力。 ▶ **ab·surd·ity** *noun* [U, C] (*pl.* **-ies**)：*It was only later that she could see the absurdity of the situation.* 直到后来她才看出了那种局面的荒唐。 **ab·surd·ly** *adv.* SYN **ridiculously**：*The paintings were sold for absurdly high prices.* 那些画以高得离谱的价格售出。

ab·surd·ism /əb'sɜ:dɪzəm; *NAmE* -'sɜ:rd-/ *noun* [U] the belief that humans exist in a world with no purpose or order 荒诞主义（认为人存在于无序宇宙之中） ▶ **ab·surd·ist** *noun* **ab·surd·ist** *adj.* [usually before noun]：*absurdist literature* 荒诞派文学

abun·dance /ə'bʌndəns/ *noun* [sing., U] ~ (**of sth**) (*formal*) a large quantity that is more than enough 大量；丰盛；充裕

IDM **in abundance** in large quantities 大量；丰盛；充裕：*Fruit and vegetables grew in abundance on the island.* 该岛盛产水果和蔬菜。

abun·dant /ə'bʌndənt/ *adj.* (*formal*) existing in large quantities; more than enough 大量的；丰盛的；充裕的 SYN **plentiful**：*Fish are abundant in the lake.* 湖里鱼很多。 ◇ *We have abundant evidence to prove his guilt.* 我们有充分的证据证明他有罪。

abun·dant·ly /ə'bʌndəntli/ *adv.* **1** ~ **clear** very clear 十分清楚；非常明白：*She made her wishes abundantly clear.* 她充分表明了她的意愿。 **2** in large quantities 大量地；丰盛地；充裕地：*Calcium is found most abundantly in milk.* 奶含钙最丰富。

abuse *noun, verb*

■ ***noun*** /ə'bju:s/ **1** [U, sing.] the use of sth in a way that is wrong or harmful 滥用；妄用 SYN **misuse**：***alcohol/drug/solvent abuse*** 酗酒；嗜毒；溶媒滥用 ◇ *The system of paying cash bonuses is* ***open to abuse*** (= might be used in the wrong way). 支付现金红利制度可能被人钻空子。 ◇ **~ of sth** *He was arrested on charges of corruption and* ***abuse of power.*** 他因被控贪污腐化和滥用职权而遭逮捕。 ◇ *What she did was an abuse of her position as manager.* 她的所

A

作所为是滥用经理职权。 ➲ WORDFINDER NOTE AT DRUG **2** 🔑 [U, pl.] unfair, cruel or violent treatment of sb 虐待：*child abuse* 虐待儿童 ◇ *sexual abuse* 性虐待 ◇ *reported abuses by the secret police* 已举报的秘密警察虐待行为 ◇ *She suffered years of physical abuse.* 她遭受了多年的肉体摧残。 **3** 🔑 [U] rude and offensive remarks, usually made when sb is very angry 辱骂；恶语 **SYN** **insult**：*to* ***scream/hurl/shout abuse*** 高声谩骂；破口大骂；大声辱骂 ◇ *a* ***stream/torrent of abuse*** 不断辱骂；劈头盖脸一通臭骂

■ ***verb*** /əˈbjuːz/ **1** 🔑 **~ sth** to make bad use of sth, or to use so much of sth that it harms your health 滥用：*to* ***abuse alcohol/drugs*** 酗酒；嗜毒 ◇ *He systematically abused his body with heroin and cocaine.* 他因吸食海洛因和可卡因一步一步地把身体搞垮了。 **2** 🔑 **~ sth** to use power or knowledge unfairly or wrongly 滥用，妄用（权力、所知所闻）：*She abused her position as principal by giving jobs to her friends.* 她滥用自己作为校长的职权，把工作安排给朋友们。 ◇ *He felt they had abused his trust by talking about him to the press* (= tricked him, although he had trusted them). 他觉得他们向新闻界透露有关他的情况是辜负了他的信任。 **3** 🔑 **~ sb/sth** to treat a person or an animal in a cruel or violent way, especially sexually 虐待；（尤指）性虐待；伤害：*All the children had been physically and emotionally abused.* 所有这些儿童的身心都受到了摧残。 ◇ *He had abused his own daughter.* 他曾奸污了自己的亲生女儿。 ◇ *The boy had been sexually abused.* 这个男孩曾遭受过性虐待。 **4** **~ sb** to make rude or offensive remarks to or about sb 辱骂；对…恶语相加；诋毁 **SYN** **insult**：*The referee had been threatened and abused.* 裁判遭到了恐吓和谩骂。 ➲ MORE LIKE THIS 21, page R27 ▶ **ab·user** *noun*：*a drug abuser* 嗜毒者 ◇ *a child abuser* 虐待儿童者

abu·sive /əˈbjuːsɪv/ *adj.* **1** (of speech or of a person 言语或人) rude and offensive; criticizing rudely and unfairly 辱骂的；恶语的；毁谤的：***abusive language/remarks*** 秽言恶语；恶言谩骂 ◇ *He became abusive when he was drunk.* 他喝醉时就满口脏话骂人了。 **2** (of behaviour 行为) involving violence 虐待的：*an abusive relationship* 虐待关系 ▶ **abu·sive·ly** *adv.*

abut /əˈbʌt/ *verb* (**-tt-**) [I, T] **~ (on/onto) sth** (*formal*) (of land or a building 土地或建筑物) to be next to sth or to have one side touching the side of sth 邻接；毗连；紧靠：*His land abuts onto a road.* 他的土地紧靠公路。

abys·mal /əˈbɪzməl/ *adj.* extremely bad or of a very low standard 极坏的；糟透的 **SYN** **terrible** ▶ **abys·mal·ly** *adv.*

abyss /əˈbɪs/ *noun* [usually sing.] (*formal* or *literary*) a very deep wide space or hole that seems to have no bottom 深渊：*Ahead of them was a gaping abyss.* 他们前面是一个巨大的深渊。 ◇ (*figurative*) *an* ***abyss of ignorance/despair/loneliness*** 无知到极点；彻底绝望；无尽的孤寂 ◇ (*figurative*) *The country is stepping back from the edge of an abyss.* 该国临渊而退。

AC /ˌeɪ ˈsiː/ *abbr.* **1** (*also* **ac**, **a/c**) (*especially NAmE*) AIR CONDITIONING 空气调节系统 **2** ALTERNATING CURRENT 交流；交流电流 ➲ COMPARE DIRECT CURRENT

a/c *abbr.* (in writing 书写形式) **1** ACCOUNT 账户 **2** AIR CONDITIONING 空气调节系统

aca·cia /əˈkeɪʃə/ (*also* **aˈcacia tree**) *noun* a tree with yellow or white flowers. There are several types of acacia tree, some of which produce a sticky liquid used in making glue. 金合欢树（有些种类的树汁用于制作黏胶）

aca·demia **AW** /ˌækəˈdiːmiə/ (*also formal* or *humorous* **aca·deme** /ˈækədiːm/) *noun* [U] the world of learning, teaching, research, etc. at universities, and the people involved in it 学术界

aca·dem·ic 🔑 **AW** /ˌækəˈdemɪk/ *adj.*, *noun*

■ ***adj.*** **1** 🔑 [usually before noun] connected with education, especially studying in schools and universities 学业的，教学的，学术的（尤指与学校教育有关）：*The students return in October for the start of the new academic year.* 学生于十月返校，开始新学年的学习。 ◇ *high/low academic standards* 高 / 低学术水平 ◇ *an academic career* 学术生涯 **2** 🔑 [usually before noun] involving a lot of reading and studying rather than practical or technical skills 学术性的（与实践性、技术性相对）：***academic subjects/qualifications*** 学科；学术资历 **3** 🔑 good at subjects involving a lot of reading and studying 学习良好的：*She wasn't very academic and hated school.* 她学习不怎么样，而且讨厌上学。 **4** not connected to a real or practical situation and therefore not important 纯理论的；空谈的；学究式的：*It is a purely academic question.* 这是一个纯理论问题。 ◇ *The whole thing's academic now—we can't win anyway.* 现在这一切都是纸上谈兵，反正我们赢不了。 ▶ **aca·dem·ic·al·ly** **AW** /-kli/ *adv.*：*You have to do well academically to get into medical school.* 你得学习成绩优良才能入读医学院。

■ ***noun*** a person who teaches and/or does research at a university or college 高等院校教师；高校科研人员

acad·em·ician /əˌkædəˈmɪʃn; *NAmE* ˌækədəˈmɪʃn/ *noun* a member of an ACADEMY (2) 院士；学会会员

ˌacademic ˈyear *noun* the period of the year during which students go to school or university 学年

acad·emy **AW** /əˈkædəmi/ *noun* (*pl.* **-ies**) **1** a school or college for special training 专科院校：*the Royal Academy of Music* 皇家音乐学院 ◇ *a* ***police/military academy*** 警官 / 军官学校 **2** (*usually* **Academy**) a type of official organization which aims to encourage and develop art, literature, science, etc.（艺术、文学、科学等的）研究院，学会：*the Royal Academy of Arts* 皇家艺术学会 **3** a SECONDARY SCHOOL in Scotland （苏格兰）中等学校，中学 **4** a private school in the US （美国）私立学校 **5** a SECONDARY SCHOOL in England which has a great deal of independence from local authority control （英格兰不受地方政府直接管辖的）国立中等学校，国立中学

Aˌcademy Aˈward™ (*also* **Oscar™**) *noun* one of the awards given every year by the US Academy of Motion Picture Arts and Sciences for achievement in the making of films/movies 学院奖，奥斯卡金像奖（美国电影艺术科学院颁发的年度电影成就奖）

Aca·dian /əˈkeɪdiən/ *noun* **1** a French-speaking Canadian from New Brunswick, and parts of Quebec near it, Nova Scotia or Prince Edward Island 阿卡迪亚人（操法语，居于加拿大新不伦瑞克省、邻近的魁北克省部分地区、新斯科舍省或爱德华王子岛省） **2** (in the US) a person from Louisiana whose family originally came from the French COLONY of Acadia in what is now Nova Scotia （美国路易斯安那州的）阿卡迪亚法国殖民地移民后裔

açai /əˈsaɪ; ˌæsaɪˈiː/ *noun* (*pl.* **açai**) a type of South American PALM TREE (= a straight tree with a mass of long leaves at the top), which produces small dark fruit that can be eaten or made into juice 阿萨伊（南美洲棕榈树，果实可食用或制成果汁）：*açai berries* 巴西莓

a cap·pella /ˌæ kəˈpelə; ˌɑː/ *adj.* (of music 音乐) for singing voices alone, without musical instruments 清唱的；无乐器伴奏的 ▶ **a cap·pella** *adv.*

ACAS /ˈeɪkæs/ *abbr.* (in Britain) Advisory, Conciliation and Arbitration Service (the organization that helps employers and employees settle disagreements) （英国）咨询调解与仲裁局（帮助雇主与雇员解决争议的机构）

ac·cede /əkˈsiːd/ *verb* [I] (*formal*) **1** **~ (to sth)** to agree to a request, proposal, etc. 同意（请求、建议等）：*He acceded to demands for his resignation.* 他同意要他辞职的要求。 **2** **~ (to sth)** to achieve a high position, especially to become king or queen 就任；就职；（尤指君主）即位：*Queen Victoria acceded to the throne in 1837.* 维多利亚女王于 1837 年即位。 ➲ SEE ALSO ACCESSION (1) ➲ WORDFINDER NOTE AT KING

ac·cel·er·ate /əkˈseləreɪt/ *verb* **1** [I, T] to happen or to make sth happen faster or earlier than expected （使）加速，加快：*Inflation continues to accelerate.* 通货膨胀不断加速。 ◇ **~ sth** *Exposure to the sun can accelerate the ageing process.* 暴露在日光下会加快老化过程。 **2** [I] (of a vehicle or person 车辆或人) to start to go faster 加速；加快：*The runners accelerated smoothly around the bend.*

A

赛跑运动员在转弯处顺势加速。 ◇ *The car accelerated to overtake me.* 那辆汽车加速超过了我。 ➲WORDFINDER NOTE AT CAR OPP **decelerate**

ac·cel·er·ation /əkˌseləˈreɪʃn/ *noun* **1** [U, sing.] ~ (**in sth**) an increase in how fast sth happens 加速；加快： *an acceleration in the rate of economic growth* 经济增长加速 **2** [U] the rate at which a vehicle increases speed （车辆）加速能力，加速的幅度： *a car with good acceleration* 加速性能良好的汽车 **3** [U] (*physics* 物) the rate at which the VELOCITY (= speed in a particular direction) of an object changes 加速度

ac·cel·er·ator /əkˈseləreɪtə(r)/ *noun* **1** (*also* **ˈgas pedal**) the PEDAL in a car or other vehicle that you press with your foot to control the speed of the engine （汽车等的）加速装置，油门 ➲COLLOCATIONS AT DRIVING ➲VISUAL VOCAB PAGE V56 **2** (*physics* 物) a machine for making ELEMENTARY PARTICLES move at high speeds （基本粒子）加速器

acˈcelerator board (*also* **acˈcelerator card**) *noun* (*computing* 计) a CIRCUIT BOARD that can be put into a small computer to increase the speed at which it processes information （计算机）加速板，加速卡

ac·cel·er·om·eter /əkˌseləˈrɒmɪtə(r); *NAmE* -ˈrɑːm-/ *noun* (*physics* 物) an instrument for measuring ACCELERATION 加速度计

ac·cent *noun, verb*

■*noun* /ˈæksent; -sənt/ **1** a way of pronouncing the words of a language that shows which country, area or social class a person comes from 口音；腔调；土音： *a northern/Dublin/Indian/Scottish accent* 北方 / 都柏林 / 印度 / 苏格兰口音 ◇ *a* ***strong/broad accent*** (= one that is very noticeable) 浓重的口音 ◇ *She spoke English* ***with an accent.*** 她说英语带有口音。 ➲COMPARE DIALECT ➲WORDFINDER NOTE AT LANGUAGE **2** the emphasis that you should give to part of a word when saying it 重音 SYN **stress**: *In 'today' the accent is on the second syllable.* * today 一词的重音在第二音节。 **3** a mark on a letter to show that it should be pronounced in a particular way 读音符号（标在字母上）： *Canapé has an accent on the 'e'.* * canapé 在 e 上面有尖音符号。 **4** [sing.] a special importance that is given to sth 着重点；强调 SYN **emphasis**: *In all our products* ***the accent is on*** *quality.* 我们的全部产品都强调质量。

■*verb* /ækˈsent/ ~ **sth** to emphasize a part of sth 着重；强调；突出

ac·cent·ed /ˈæksentɪd/ *adj.* **1** spoken with a foreign accent 带有异国口音的；带有他乡腔调的： *He spoke heavily accented English.* 他说英语带有浓重的异国口音。 **2** (*specialist*) spoken with particular emphasis 重读的： ***accented vowels/syllables*** 重读元音 / 音节 **3** (*specialist*) (of a letter of the alphabet 字母) written or printed with a special mark on it to show it should be pronounced in a particular way 带有特定读音符号的： ***accented characters*** 标有特定读音符号的字符

ac·cen·tu·ate /əkˈsentʃueɪt/ *verb* ~ **sth** to emphasize sth or make it more noticeable 着重；强调；使突出 ▶**ac·cen·tu·ation** /əkˌsentʃuˈeɪʃn/ *noun* [U]

ac·cept /əkˈsept/ *verb*

• **OFFER/INVITATION** 建议；邀请 **1** [I, T] to take willingly sth that is offered; to say 'yes' to an offer, invitation, etc. 收受；接受（建议、邀请等）： *He asked me to marry him and I accepted.* 他向我求婚，我答应了。 ◇ ~ **sth** *Please accept our sincere apologies.* 请接受我们真诚的歉意。 ◇ *It was pouring with rain so I accepted his offer of a lift.* 天正下着瓢泼大雨，所以我领了他的情，搭了他的便车。 ◇ *She's decided not to accept the job.* 她决定不接受这项工作。 ◇ ~ **sth from sb** *He is charged with accepting bribes from a firm of suppliers.* 他被控收受了一家供应商的贿赂。 ◇ ~ **sth for sth** *She said she'd accept $15 for it.* 她说她要 15 美元才卖。 OPP **refuse**[1]

• **RECEIVE AS SUITABLE** 认为合适而接受 **2** [T] to receive sth as suitable or good enough （认为合适或足够好而）接受： ~ **sth** *This machine only accepts coins.* 这台机器只收硬币。 ◇ *Will you accept a cheque?* 你收支票吗？ ◇ ~ **sth for sth** *My article has been accepted for publication.* 我的文章已被采用准备发表。

• **AGREE** 同意 **3** [T] to agree to or approve of sth 同意；认可： ~ **sth** *They accepted the court's decision.* 他们接受法院的判决。 ◇ *He accepted all the changes we proposed.* 他同意我们提出的全部修改方案。 ◇ ~ **sth from sb** *She won't accept advice from anyone.* 她不会接受任何人的忠告。 OPP **reject** ➲SYNONYMS AT AGREE

• **RESPONSIBILITY** 责任 **4** [T] ~ **sth** to admit that you are responsible or to blame for sth 承认，承担（责任等）： *He accepts full responsibility for what happened.* 他承认对发生的事负全部责任。 ◇ *You have to accept the consequences of your actions.* 你得对你的行为后果负责。

• **BELIEVE** 相信 **5** [T] to believe that sth is true 相信（某事属实）： ~ **sth** *I don't accept his version of events.* 我不相信他对事件的说法。 ◇ ~ **sth as sth** *Can we accept his account as the true version?* 我们能相信他说的是事实吗？ ◇ ~ **that…** *I accept that this will not be popular.* 我认为这是不会受欢迎的。 ◇ **it is accepted that…** *It is generally accepted that people are motivated by success.* 普遍认为，成功催人奋进。 ◇ **it is accepted to be, have, etc. sth** *The workforce is generally accepted to have the best conditions in Europe.* 这里工人的劳动环境公认是欧洲最好的。

• **DIFFICULT SITUATION** 困境 **6** [T] to continue in a difficult situation without complaining, because you realize that you cannot change it 容忍，忍受（困境等）： ~ **sth** *You just have to* ***accept the fact that*** *we're never going to be rich.* 你只得接受我们永远也富不起来这个事实。 ◇ *Nothing will change as long as the workers continue to accept these appalling conditions.* 只要工人继续容忍这种恶劣的劳动条件，情况就不会有任何改变。 ◇ ~ **sth as sth** *They accept the risks as part of the job.* 他们甘冒风险，把这当成工作的一部分。 ◇ ~ **that…** *He just refused to accept that his father was no longer there.* 他就是不肯接受他父亲已不在的现实。

• **WELCOME** 欢迎 **7** [T] to make sb feel welcome and part of a group 欢迎；接纳： ~ **sb** *It may take years to be completely accepted by the local community.* 也许需要多年方能被当地居民完全接纳。 ◇ ~ **sb into sth** *She had never been accepted into what was essentially a man's world.* 她从未被这个基本上属于男人的世界所接受。 ◇ ~ **sb as sth** *He never really accepted her as his own child.* 他一直没有真正接纳她为自己的女儿。 OPP **reject**

• **ALLOW SB TO JOIN** 准许加入 **8** [T] to allow sb to join an organization, attend an institution, use a service, etc. 接纳，接受（为成员、会员等）： ~ **sb** *The college he applied to has accepted him.* 他申请的那所学院录取了他。 ◇ ~ **sb into sth** *She was disappointed not to be accepted into the club.* 她没有获准加入俱乐部，感到失望。 ◇ ~ **sb as sth** *The landlord was willing to accept us as tenants.* 房东愿意把房子租给我们住。 ◇ ~ **sb to do sth** *She was accepted to study music.* 她获录取学习音乐。 OPP **reject**

ac·cept·able /əkˈseptəbl/ *adj.* **1** agreed or approved of by most people in a society （社会上）认同的，认可的： *Children must learn socially acceptable behaviour.* 儿童必须学会社会上认可的行为举止。 **2** that sb agrees is of a good enough standard or allowed 可接受的；令人满意的；可容许的： *For this course a pass in English at grade B is acceptable.* 英语成绩达到 B 级就可以学习这门课程。 ◇ *Air pollution in the city had reached four times the acceptable levels.* 这座城市的空气污染程度曾高达可接受标准的四倍。 ◇ ~ **to sb** *We want a political solution that is acceptable to all parties.* 我们需要一个各方都可接受的政治解决方案。 **3** not very good but good enough 还可以的；尚可的；差强人意的： *The food was acceptable, but no more.* 食物还可以，但说不上很好。 OPP **unacceptable** ▶**ac·cept·abil·ity** /əkˌseptəˈbɪləti/ *noun* [U] **ac·cept·ably** /-bli/ *adv.*

ac·cept·ance /əkˈseptəns/ *noun* **1** [U, C] the act of accepting a gift, an invitation, an offer, etc. 接受（礼物、邀请、建议等）： *Please confirm your acceptance of this offer in writing.* 请书面确认你接受这项建议。 ◇ *He made a short* ***acceptance speech/speech*** *of acceptance.* 他发表了简短的提名感言。 ◇ *Invitations have been sent out and 80 acceptances have already been received.* 请帖已经发出，目

前收到了 80 份接受邀请的回复。 **2** [U] the act of agreeing with sth and approving of it 同意；认可： *The new laws have **gained widespread acceptance**.* 新法律获得广泛赞同。 **3** [U] the process of allowing sb to join sth or be a member of a group 接纳，接受（为成员、会员等）： *Your acceptance into the insurance plan is guaranteed.* 你参加保险计划一事已有保证。 ◇ *Social acceptance is important for most young people.* 对大多数青年来说，为社会所接纳很重要。 **4** [U] willingness to accept an unpleasant or difficult situation 无怨接受（逆境、困境等）；逆来顺受： *acceptance of death/suffering* 接受死亡 / 苦难

ac·cess AW /ˈækses/ *noun, verb*

■ ***noun*** [U] **1** a way of entering or reaching a place 通道；通路；入径： *The police **gained access** through a broken window.* 警察从一扇破窗户钻了进去。 ◇ **~ to sth** *The only access to the farmhouse is across the fields.* 去那农舍的唯一通路是穿过田野。 ◇ *Disabled visitors are welcome; there is good wheelchair access to most facilities.* 欢迎残疾人参观，坐轮椅可以方便地到达多数设施。 ➲ COMPARE EGRESS **2** ~ **(to sth)** the opportunity or right to use sth or to see sb/sth（使用或见到的）机会，权利： *Students must **have access** to good resources.* 学生必须有机会使用好的资源。 ◇ *You need a password to **get access** to the computer system.* 使用这个计算机系统需要密码。 ◇ *access to confidential information* 接触机密情报的机会 ◇ *Journalists were **denied access** to the President.* 记者被挡住，无法见到总统。 ◇ *Many divorced fathers only have access to their children at weekends* (= they are allowed by law to see them only at weekends). 很多离婚父亲只有在周末才有权见自己的孩子。 ➲ COMPARE VISITATION (1) ➲ WORDFINDER NOTE AT WEB

■ ***verb*** **1** **~ sth** (*computing* 计) to open a computer file in order to get or add information 访问，存取（计算机文件） **2** **~ sth** (*formal*) to reach, enter or use sth 到达；进入；使用： *The loft can be accessed by a ladder.* 搭梯子可以上阁楼。

ˈaccess course *noun* (*BrE*) a course of education that prepares students without the usual qualifications, in order that they can study at university or college 高考资格补习班（为不具备所需条件者而设）

ac·cess·ible AW /əkˈsesəbl/ *adj.* **1** that can be reached, entered, used, seen, etc. 可到达的；可接近的；可进入的；可使用的；可见到的： *The remote desert area is accessible only by helicopter.* 只有乘直升机才能进入那偏远的荒漠地区。 ◇ **~ to sb** *These documents are not accessible to the public.* 公众无法看到这些文件。 **2** that can be reached, entered, used, etc. by sb who has problems walking 行动不便者可到达（或可进入、可使用等）的： *accessible toilets for wheelchair users* 供坐轮椅的人使用的无障碍厕所 **3** easy to understand 容易理解的；易懂的： *Her poetry is always very accessible.* 她的诗作总是非常通俗易懂。 ◇ **~ to sb** *a programme making science more accessible to young people* 一项使科学更容易为年轻人所了解的计划 **4** (of a person 人) easy to talk to and to get to know 易接近的；易相处的；易打交道的 OPP **inaccessible** ▸ **ac·ces·si·bil·ity** AW /əkˌsesəˈbɪləti/ *noun* [U]

ac·ces·sion /ækˈseʃn/ *noun* **1** [U] ~ **(to sth)** the act of becoming a ruler of a country（国家统治者的）就职，就任；（君主、帝王等的）登基，即位： *the accession of Queen Victoria to the throne* 维多利亚女王即位 ➲ SEE ALSO ACCEDE **2** [U] ~ **(to sth)** the act of becoming part of an international organization 正式加入（国际组织）： *the accession of new member states to the EU* 新成员国正式加入欧盟 ◇ *the new **accession states** of the EU* 正式加入欧盟的新成员国 **3** [C] (*specialist*) a thing that is added to a collection of objects, paintings, etc. in a library or museum（图书馆、博物馆的）新增项目，新增藏品，新增藏书

ac·ces·sor·ize (*BrE also* **-ise**) /əkˈsesəraɪz/ *verb* **~ sth** to add fashionable items or extra decorations to sth, especially to your clothes 加时髦配件于；加装饰物于；加搭配饰品于

ac·ces·sory /əkˈsesəri/ *noun, adj.*

■ ***noun*** (*pl.* **-ies**) **1** [usually pl.] an extra piece of equipment that is useful but not essential or that can be added to sth else as a decoration 附件；配件；附属物： *bicycle accessories* 自行车附件 ◇ *a range of furnishings and accessories for the home* 各种各样的家居装饰物及配件 **2** [usually pl.] a thing that you can wear or carry that matches your clothes, for example a belt or a bag （衣服的）配饰 ➲ VISUAL VOCAB PAGES V69-70 **3** (*law* 律) a person who helps sb to commit a crime or who knows about it and protects the person from the police 同谋；从犯；帮凶： *an **accessory before/after the fact*** (= before/after the crime was committed) 事前 / 事后从犯 ◇ **~ to sth** *He was charged with being an accessory to murder.* 他被控为谋杀罪的从犯。

■ ***adj.*** (*specialist*) not the most important when compared to others 辅助的；副的： *the accessory muscles of respiration* 副呼吸肌

ˈaccess provider *noun* = SERVICE PROVIDER

ˈaccess road *noun* a road used for driving into or out of a particular place（进出某处的）行车通道 ➲ COMPARE SLIP ROAD

ˈaccess time *noun* [U, C] (*computing* 计) the time taken to obtain data stored on a computer 存取时间（取出计算机中存储的数据所用的时间）

ac·ci·dent /ˈæksɪdənt/ *noun* **1** [C] an unpleasant event, especially in a vehicle, that happens unexpectedly and causes injury or damage（交通）事故；意外遭遇；不测事件： *a **car/road/traffic accident*** 车祸；公路事故；交通事故 ◇ *He was killed **in an accident**.* 他死于车祸。 ◇ *One in seven accidents is caused by sleepy drivers.* 每七次交通事故就有一次是驾驶员困倦造成的。 ◇ *The accident happened at 3 p.m.* 事故发生于下午 3 点钟。 ◇ *to **have an accident*** 出事故 ◇ *a **serious/minor accident*** 严重 / 轻微事故 ◇ *a **fatal accident*** (= in which sb is killed) 死亡事故 ◇ *accidents in the home* 家中发生的意外事件 ◇ *a **climbing/riding accident*** 登山 / 骑马意外 ◇ *Take out **accident insurance** before you go on your trip.* 你去旅行前要办理好意外保险。 ◇ *I didn't mean to break it—**it was an accident**.* 我不是故意打碎它的，这是个意外。

> **WORDFINDER** 联想词： ambulance, casualty, first aid, **hospital**, injure, paramedic, stretcher, victim, witness

2 [C, U] something that happens unexpectedly and is not planned in advance 意外；偶然的事： *Their early arrival was just an accident.* 他们早到仅仅是偶然而已。 ◇ ***It is no accident** that men fill most of the top jobs in nursing.* 男人担任护理中大多数最重要的工作绝非偶然。 ◇ *an **accident of birth/fate/history*** (= describing facts and events that are due to chance or circumstances) 出生 / 命运 / 历史的偶然性 ➲ SYNONYMS AT LUCK

IDM **ˌaccidents will ˈhappen** people say **accidents will happen** to tell sb who has had an accident, for example breaking sth, that it does not matter and they should not worry 出事是难免的 **by accident** in a way that is not planned or organized 偶然；意外地： *We met by accident at the airport.* 我们在机场不期而遇。 ◇ *Helen got into acting purely by accident.* 海伦当演员完全出于偶然。 OPP **deliberately, on purpose** ➲ MORE AT CHAPTER, WAIT *v.*

ac·ci·den·tal /ˌæksɪˈdentl/ *adj.* happening by chance; not planned 意外的；偶然的： *a verdict of accidental death* 意外死亡的裁决 ◇ *I didn't think our meeting was accidental—he must have known I would be there.* 我认为我们相遇不是偶然的，他肯定知道我要去那里。 ▸ **ac·ci·den·tal·ly** /-təli/ *adv.* : *As I turned around, I accidentally hit him in the face.* 我转身时不经意撞了他的脸。 ◇ *The damage couldn't have been caused accidentally.* 这次损毁不可能是偶然因素造成的。

ˌaccident and eˈmergency (*abbr.* **A & E**) (*BrE*) *noun* [U] (*NAmE* **eˈmergency room**) the part of a hospital where people who need urgent treatment are taken （医院）急诊室： *the hospital accident and emergency department* 医院的急诊部 ➲ SEE ALSO CASUALTY (3)

A

ˈ**accident-prone** *adj.* more likely to have accidents than other people （人）易出事故的

ac·claim /əˈkleɪm/ *verb, noun*

■ ***verb*** [usually passive] to praise or welcome sb/sth publicly 公开称誉某人 / 某事物（为…）；给予高度评价：**~ sb/sth** *a **highly/widely acclaimed** performance* 受到高度 / 广泛赞扬的演出 ◇ **~ sb/sth as sth** *The work was acclaimed as a masterpiece.* 该作品被誉为杰作。

■ ***noun*** [U] praise and approval for sb/sth, especially an artistic achievement （尤指对艺术成就的）称誉，高度评价：***international/popular/critical acclaim*** 国际上的 / 公众的 / 评论家的赞扬

ac·clam·ation /ˌækləˈmeɪʃn/ *noun* [U] **1** (*formal*) loud and enthusiastic approval or welcome 喝彩；欢呼；欢迎 **2** (*specialist*) the act of electing sb using a spoken not written vote （口头表决）拥护，赞成：*The decision was taken **by acclamation**.* 该决议是经口头表决而作出的。

ac·cli·mate /ˈækləmeɪt/ *verb* (*NAmE*) = ACCLIMATIZE ▶ **ac·cli·ma·tion** /ˌækləˈmeɪʃn/ *noun* [U]

ac·cli·ma·tize (*BrE also* **-ise**) /əˈklaɪmətaɪz/ (*NAmE also* **ac·cli·mate**) *verb* [I, T] to get used to a new place, situation or climate （使）习惯（新地方、新情况、新气候）；（使）服水土：**~ (to sth)** *Arrive two days early in order to acclimatize.* 提前两天到达以便适应新环境。 ◇ **~ yourself (to sth)** *She was fine once she had acclimatized herself to the cold.* 当她习惯了寒冷以后身体便好了起来。 ▶ **ac·cli·ma·tiza·tion, -isa·tion** /əˌklaɪmətaɪˈzeɪʃn; *NAmE* -təˈz-/ (*NAmE also* **ac·cli·ma·tion**) *noun* [U]

ac·col·ade /ˈækəleɪd; ˌækəˈleɪd/ *noun* (*formal*) praise or an award for an achievement that people admire 赞扬；表扬；奖励；荣誉

ac·com·mo·date AW /əˈkɒmədeɪt; *NAmE* əˈkɑːm-/ *verb* **1** [T] **~ sb** to provide sb with a room or place to sleep, live or sit 提供住宿（或膳宿、座位等）：*The hotel can accommodate up to 500 guests.* 这家旅馆可供 500 位旅客住宿。 **2** [T] **~ sb/sth** to provide enough space for sb/sth 容纳；提供空间：*Over 70 minutes of music can be accommodated on one CD.* 一张激光唱片可以容纳 70 多分钟的音乐。 **3** [T] **~ sth** (*formal*) to consider sth, such as sb's opinion or a fact, and be influenced by it when you are deciding what to do or explaining sth 考虑到；顾及：*Our proposal tries to accommodate the special needs of minority groups.* 我们的提案尽量照顾到少数群体的特殊需要。 **4** [T] **~ sb (with sth)** (*formal*) to help sb by doing what they want 帮忙；给…提供方便 SYN **oblige**：*I have accommodated the press a great deal, giving numerous interviews.* 我多次接受采访，已给了报界许多方便。 **5** [I, T] **~ (sth/yourself) to sth** (*formal*) to change your behaviour so that you can deal with a new situation better 顺应，适应（新情况）：*I needed to accommodate to the new schedule.* 我需要适应新的时间表。

ac·com·mo·dat·ing /əˈkɒmədeɪtɪŋ; *NAmE* əˈkɑːm-/ *adj.* (*formal*) willing to help and do things for other people 乐于助人的；与人方便的 SYN **obliging**

ac·com·mo·da·tion 🔑 AW /əˌkɒməˈdeɪʃn; *NAmE* əˌkɑːm-/ *noun* **1** 🔑 [U] (*BrE*) a place to live, work or stay in 住处；办公处；停留处：***rented/temporary/furnished accommodation*** 租的 / 临时的 / 有家具的住处 ◇ *Hotel accommodation is included in the price of your holiday.* 你度假的价钱包括旅馆住宿。 ◇ *The building plans include much needed new office accommodation.* 建筑规划包括紧缺的新办公用房在内。 ◇ *First-class accommodation is available on all flights.* 所有班机都备有一等舱位。 ➲ WORDFINDER NOTE AT HOME, HOTEL **2 accommodations** [pl.] (*NAmE*) somewhere to live or stay, often also providing food or other services 住宿；膳宿：*More and more travelers are looking for bed and breakfast accommodations in private homes.* 愈来愈多的旅行者在寻找提供住宿加早餐的民宿。 **3** [C, U] (*formal*) an agreement or arrangement between people or groups with different opinions which is acceptable to everyone; the process of reaching this agreement 和解；调解；调和：*They were forced to reach an accommodation with the rebels.* 他们被迫与叛乱分子达成调解协议。 ➲ MORE LIKE THIS 28, page R28

ac·com·pani·ment AW /əˈkʌmpənimənt/ *noun* **1** [C, U] **~ (to sth)** music that is played to support singing or another instrument （音乐）伴奏：*traditional songs with piano accompaniment* 用钢琴伴奏的传统歌曲 **2** [C] **~ (to sth)** something that you eat, drink or use together with sth else 佐餐物；伴随物：*The wine makes a good accompaniment to fish dishes.* 这种葡萄酒很适合作鱼菜的佐餐酒。 **3** [C] **~ (to sth)** (*formal*) something that happens at the same time as another thing 伴随发生的事情：*High blood pressure is a common accompaniment to this disease.* 这种病通常伴随有高血压。

IDM **to the accompaniment of sth 1** while a musical instrument is being played 在…的伴奏下：*They performed to the accompaniment of guitars.* 他们在吉他的伴奏下表演。 **2** while sth else is happening 在…发生时；伴随有；同时有：*She made her speech to the accompaniment of loud laughter.* 她的演讲不断引起哄堂大笑。

ac·com·pan·ist /əˈkʌmpənɪst/ *noun* a person who plays a musical instrument, especially a piano, while sb else plays or sings the main part of the music 伴奏者；（尤指）钢琴伴奏者

ac·com·pany 🔑 AW /əˈkʌmpəni/ *verb* (**ac·com·pan·ies, ac·com·pany·ing, ac·com·pan·ied, ac·com·pan·ied**) **1** 🔑 **~ sb** (*formal*) to travel or go somewhere with sb 陪同；陪伴：*His wife accompanied him on the trip.* 那次旅行他由妻子陪同。 **2** 🔑 **~ sth** to happen or appear with sth else 伴随；与…同时发生：*strong winds accompanied by heavy rain* 狂风夹着暴雨 ◇ *The curator of the exhibition also wrote the accompanying catalogue.* 展览的策划人还编写了介绍展览的目录。 **3 ~ sb (at/on sth)** to play a musical instrument, especially a piano, while sb else sings or plays the main tune （尤指用钢琴）为…伴奏：*The singer was accompanied on the piano by her sister.* 女歌手由她姐姐钢琴伴奏。

ac·com·plice /əˈkʌmplɪs; *NAmE* əˈkɑːm-/ *noun* a person who helps another to commit a crime or to do sth wrong 帮凶；共犯；同谋

ac·com·plish /əˈkʌmplɪʃ; *NAmE* əˈkɑːm-/ *verb* **~ sth** to succeed in doing or completing sth 完成 SYN **achieve**：*The first part of the plan has been safely accomplished.* 计划的第一部分已顺利完成。 ◇ *I don't feel I've accomplished very much today.* 我觉得我今天没干成多少事。 ◇ *That's it. **Mission accomplished*** (= we have done what we aimed to do). 就这样。大功告成。

ac·com·plished /əˈkʌmplɪʃt; *NAmE* əˈkɑːm-/ *adj.* very good at a particular thing; having a lot of skills 才华高的；技艺高超的；熟练的：*an accomplished artist/actor/chef* 技艺高超的艺术家 / 演员 / 厨师 ◇ *She was an elegant and accomplished woman.* 她是位优雅的才女。

ac·com·plish·ment /əˈkʌmplɪʃmənt; *NAmE* əˈkɑːm-/ *noun* **1** [C] an impressive thing that is done or achieved after a lot of work 成就；成绩 SYN **achievement**：*It was one of the President's greatest accomplishments.* 那是总统最大的成就之一。 **2** [C, U] a skill or special ability 才艺；技艺；专长：*Drawing and singing were among her many accomplishments.* 她多才多艺，能歌善画。 ◇ *a poet of rare accomplishment* 出类拔萃的诗人 **3** [U] (*formal*) the successful completing of sth 完成；成就：*Money will be crucial to the accomplishment of our objectives.* 要实现我们的目标，钱是至关重要的。

ac·cord /əˈkɔːd; *NAmE* əˈkɔːrd/ *noun, verb*

■ ***noun*** a formal agreement between two organizations, countries, etc. 协议；条约：*The two sides signed a **peace accord** last July.* 在刚过去的七月，双方签订了和平条约。 ➲ WORDFINDER NOTE AT ALLY

IDM **in accord (with sth/sb)** (*formal*) in agreement with 与…一致（或相符合）：*This action would not be in accord with our policy.* 这一行动不会符合我们的方针。 **of your own acˈcord** without being asked, forced or helped 自愿地；主动地：*He came back of his own accord.* 他主动回来了。 ◇ *The symptoms will clear up of their own accord.*

症状将会自行消失。 **with ˌone acˈcord** (*BrE, formal*) if people do sth **with one accord**, they do it at the same time, because they agree with each other 全体一致；一致地

■ ***verb*** (*formal*) [T] to give sb/sth authority, status or a particular type of treatment 给予，赠予，授予（权力、地位、某种待遇）： **~ sth to sb/sth** *Our society accords great importance to the family.* 我们的社会赋予家庭十分重要的地位。◇ **~ sb/sth sth** *Our society accords the family great importance.* 我们的社会赋予家庭十分重要的地位。

PHR V **acˈcord with sth** to agree with or match sth（与…）一致，符合，配合： *These results accord closely with our predictions.* 这些结果和我们的预测高度一致。

ac·cord·ance /əˈkɔːdns; *NAmE* əˈkɔːrdns/ *noun*

IDM **in accordance with sth** (*formal*) according to a rule or the way that sb says that sth should be done 依照；依据： *in accordance with legal requirements* 根据法律要求

ac·cord·ing·ly /əˈkɔːdɪŋli; *NAmE* əˈkɔːrd-/ *adv.* **1** in a way that is appropriate to what has been done or said in a particular situation 照着；相应地： *We have to discover his plans and act accordingly.* 我们得弄清楚他的计划，然后采取相应措施。 **2** (used especially at the beginning of a sentence 尤用于句首) for that reason 因此；所以 SYN **therefore**: *The cost of materials rose sharply last year. Accordingly, we were forced to increase our prices.* 去年材料成本大幅度提高，因此我们被迫加价。

ac·cord·ing to /əˈkɔːdɪŋ tə; *before vowels* tuː; *NAmE* əˈkɔːrdɪŋ/ *prep.* **1** as stated or reported by sb/sth 据（…所说）；按（…所报道）： *According to Mick, it's a great movie.* 据米克说，这是一部了不起的电影。◇ *You've been absent six times according to our records.* 根据我们的记录，你已经缺席六次了。➲ LANGUAGE BANK AT ILLUSTRATE **2** following, agreeing with or depending on sth 依照；按照；根据： *The work was done according to her instructions.* 这项工作是依照她的指示办的。◇ *Everything went **according to plan**.* 一切均按照计划进行。◇ *The salary will be fixed according to qualifications and experience.* 薪金将依资历和经验而定。 IDM SEE COAT *n.*

▼ LANGUAGE BANK 用语库

according to

Reporting someone's opinion 陈述某人的观点

- *Photography is, **according to** Vidal, the art form of untalented people.* 据维达尔所言，摄影是没有天赋的人的艺术形式。
- ***For** Vidal, photography is the art form of untalented people.* 对维达尔来说，摄影是没有天赋的人的艺术形式。
- *His **view is that** photography is not art but merely the mechanical reproduction of images.* 他的观点是摄影不是艺术，而只是机械地复制图像。
- *Smith **takes the view that** photography is both an art and a science.* 史密斯所持的观点是：摄影既是一门艺术也是一门科学。
- ***In** Brown's **view**, photography should be treated as a legitimate art in its own right.* 在布朗看来，摄影本身就应该被视为一种正当的艺术。
- *James **is of the opinion that** a good painter can always be a good photographer if he or she so decides.* 詹姆斯认为一个好的画家定能成为一个好的摄影师，只要他/她一心这样做。
- *Emerson **believed that** a photograph should only reflect what the human eye can see.* 埃默森认为照片应该只是反映人们肉眼所能见到的东西。

➲ LANGUAGE BANK AT ARGUE, OPINION

ac·cor·dion /əˈkɔːdiən; *NAmE* əˈkɔːrd-/ *noun* a musical instrument that you hold in both hands to produce sounds. You press the two ends together and pull them apart and press buttons and/or keys to produce the different notes. 手风琴 ➲ SEE ALSO PIANO ACCORDION

accordion 手风琴

concertina 六角形手风琴

ac·cost /əˈkɒst; *NAmE* əˈkɔːst; əˈkɑːst/ *verb* **~ sb** (*formal*) to go up to sb and speak to them, especially in a way that is rude or threatening （贸然）上前搭讪；（唐突地）走近谈话： *She was accosted in the street by a complete stranger.* 在街上，一个完全陌生的人贸然走到她跟前搭讪。

ac·count /əˈkaʊnt/ *noun, verb*

■ ***noun***

• **AT BANK** 银行 **1** (*abbr.* **a/c**) an arrangement that sb has with a bank, etc. to keep money there, take some out, etc. 账户： *I don't have a bank account.* 我没有银行账户。◇ *to have an **account at/with** a bank* 在银行有账户 ◇ *to **open/close an account*** 开户；销户 ◇ *What's your account number please?* 请问您的账号？◇ *I paid the cheque into my savings account.* 我把支票存入我的储蓄账户。◇ *a joint account* (= one in the name of more than one person) 联名账户 ➲ WORDFINDER NOTE AT BANK ➲ COLLOCATIONS AT FINANCE ➲ SEE ALSO BUDGET ACCOUNT, CHECKING ACCOUNT, CURRENT ACCOUNT, DEPOSIT ACCOUNT

• **BUSINESS RECORDS** 商业记录 **2** [usually pl.] a written record of money that is owed to a business and of money that has been paid by it 账目： *to do the accounts* 记账 ◇ *the accounts department* 会计部门 ➲ SEE ALSO EXPENSE ACCOUNT, PROFIT AND LOSS ACCOUNT

• **WITH SHOP/STORE** 商店 **3** (*BrE also* **ˈcredit account**) (*NAmE also* **ˈcharge account**) an arrangement with a shop/store or business to pay bills for goods or services at a later time, for example in regular amounts every month 赊销账；赊欠账；赊购： *Put it on my account please.* 请记在我的赊购账上。◇ *We have accounts with most of our suppliers.* 我们与大多数供应商都是实行赊购制。➲ SYNONYMS AT BILL

• **REGULAR CUSTOMER** 老主顾 **4** (*business* 商) a regular customer 老主顾： *The agency has lost several of its most important accounts.* 这家代理机构失去了几家最重要的老客户。

• **COMPUTING** 计算机技术 **5** an arrangement that sb has with a company that allows them to use the Internet, send and receive messages by email, etc. （互联网、电子邮件等的）账户，账号： *an Internet/email account* 互联网/电子邮件账户

• **DESCRIPTION** 描述 **6** a written or spoken description of sth that has happened 描述；叙述；报告： *She gave the police a full account of the incident.* 她向警方详尽地叙述了所发生的事情。➲ SYNONYMS AT REPORT **7** an explanation or a description of an idea, a theory or a process（对思想、理论、过程的）解释，说明，叙述： *the Biblical account of the creation of the world* 《圣经》对创世的叙述

IDM **by/from all accounts** according to what other people say 据说；根据报道： *I've never been there, but it's a lovely place, by all accounts.* 我从未去过那里，但据说是个美丽的地方。 **by your own account** according to what you say yourself 根据某人自己所说： *By his own account he had an unhappy childhood.* 据他自己说，他童年不快乐。 **give a good/poor acˈcount of yourself** (*BrE*) to do sth or perform well or badly, especially in a contest（尤指比赛中）表现好/不好，干得出色/差劲： *The team gave a good account of themselves in the match.* 这个队在比赛中表现出色。 **of no/little acˈcount** (*formal*) not important 不重要；无足轻重 **on account** if you buy sth or pay **on account**, you pay nothing or only a small amount immediately and the rest later 挂账；（先付小部分款额的）赊

A

账 **on sb's account** because of what you think sb wants 为了某人的缘故： *Please don't change your plans on my account.* 请别因为我而改变你的计划。 **on account of sb/sth** because of sb/sth 由于；因为： *She retired early on account of ill health.* 她体弱多病，所以提前退休。 ➲ LANGUAGE BANK AT BECAUSE **on no account | not on any account** (used to emphasize sth 用于强调) not for any reason 决不；绝对不： *On no account should the house be left unlocked.* 离开住宅时千万要锁门。 **on your own acˈcount 1** for yourself 为自己： *In 2012 Smith set up in business on his own account.* * 2012 年史密斯开始创业。 **2** because you want to and you have decided, not sb else 自愿地： *No one sent me. I am here on my own account.* 没有人派我，我自己来的。 **on this/that account** (*formal*) because of the particular thing that has been mentioned 由于这个 / 那个缘故： *Weather conditions were poor, but he did not delay his departure on that account.* 天气不好，但他并没有因此延期启程。 **put/turn sth to good acˈcount** (*formal*) to use sth in a good or helpful way 善用；利用 **take account of sth | take sth into account** to consider particular facts, circumstances, etc. when making a decision about sth 考虑到；顾及： *The company takes account of environmental issues wherever possible.* 这家公司总是尽量考虑到各方面的环境问题。 ◇ *Coursework is taken into account as well as exam results.* 除考试结果外，课程作业也要计入成绩。 ◇ *The defendant asked for a number of other offences to be taken into account.* 被告要求将其他一些犯罪行为一并考虑。 ➲ MORE AT BLOW *n.*, CALL *v.*, SETTLE *v.*

■ ***verb*** [usually passive] (*formal*) to have the opinion that sb/sth is a particular thing 认为是；视为： **~ sb/sth + adj.** *In English law a person is accounted innocent until they are proved guilty.* 按英格兰法律，一个人未经证实有罪之前被视为无罪。 ◇ **~ sb/sth + noun** *The event was accounted a success.* 人们认为这次活动是成功的。

IDM **there's no accounting for ˈtaste** (*saying*) used to say how difficult it is to understand why sb likes sb/sth that you do not like at all 人的爱憎好恶是无法解释的；人各有所好： *She thinks he's wonderful—oh well, there's no accounting for taste.* 她认为他了不起。嗯，算了，人各有所好嘛。

PHR V **acˈcount for sth 1** to be the explanation or cause of sth 是…的说明（或原因） **SYN** **explain**: *The poor weather may have accounted for the small crowd.* 天气不好可能是人来得少的原因。 ◇ *Oh well, that accounts for it* (= I understand now why it happened). 哎呀，原来是这么一回事。 **2** to give an explanation of sth 解释；说明 **SYN** **explain**: *How do you account for the show's success?* 你认为这次演出为何成功？ **3** to be a particular amount or part of sth （数量上、比例上）占： *The Japanese market accounts for 35% of the company's revenue.* 日本市场占该公司收入的 35%。 ➲ LANGUAGE BANK AT PROPORTION **acˈcount for sb/sth 1** to know where sb/sth is or what has happened to them, especially after an accident （尤指在事故之后）了解，查明： *All passengers have now been accounted for.* 现在所有乘客的情况均已查明。 **2** (*informal*) to defeat or destroy sb/sth 打败；破坏；摧毁；消灭： *Our anti-aircraft guns accounted for five enemy bombers.* 我们的高射炮击落了五架敌人的轰炸机。 **acˈcount for sth (to sb)** to give a record of how the money in your care has been spent 报账；出示经手款项的单据： *We have to account for every penny we spend on business trips.* 我们出公差所用的每一便士都得报清楚。

ac·count·able /əˈkaʊntəbl/ *adj.* [not usually before noun] responsible for your decisions or actions and expected to explain them when you are asked （对自己的决定、行为）负有责任，有说明义务： **~ to sb** *Politicians are ultimately accountable to the voters.* 从政者最终是向选民负责。 ◇ **~ for sth** *Someone must be **held accountable** for the killings.* 必须有人要对这些凶杀事件负责。 ▶ **ac·count·abil·ity** /əˌkaʊntəˈbɪləti/ *noun* [U] (*formal*)： *the accountability of a company's directors to the shareholders* 公司董事向股东所负之责

ac·count·ancy /əˈkaʊntənsi/ *noun* [U] the work or profession of an accountant 会计工作；会计职业

ac·count·ant /əˈkaʊntənt/ *noun* a person whose job is to keep or check financial accounts 会计；会计师 ➲ WORDFINDER NOTE AT BUSINESSMAN

acˈcount executive *noun* a business person, especially one working in advertising, who is responsible for dealing with one of the company's regular customers 客户经理（尤指在广告公司等中负责为指定长期客户提供服务）

ac·count·ing /əˈkaʊntɪŋ/ *noun* [U] the process or work of keeping financial accounts 会计： *a career in accounting* 会计职业 ◇ *accounting methods* 会计方法

acˌcounts ˈpayable *noun* [pl.] (*business* 商) money that is owed by a company （会计项目）应付款项，应付账款

acˌcounts reˈceivable *noun* [pl.] (*business* 商) money that is owed to a company （会计项目）应收款项，应收账款

ac·coutre·ments /əˈkuːtrəmənts/ (*US also* **ac·cou·ter·ments** /əˈkuːtərmənts/) *noun* [pl.] (*formal* or *humorous*) pieces of equipment that you need for a particular activity （某项活动所需的）装备，配备

ac·credit /əˈkredɪt/ *verb* **1** [usually passive] (*formal*) to believe that sb is responsible for doing or saying sth 把…归于；认为（某事为某人所说、所做）： **~ sth to sb** *The discovery of distillation is usually accredited to the Arabs of the 11th century.* 通常认为，蒸馏法是阿拉伯人在 11 世纪发明的。 ◇ **~ sb with sth** *The Arabs are usually accredited with the discovery of distillation.* 通常认为，阿拉伯人发明了蒸馏法。 **2** [usually passive] **~ sb to…** (*specialist*) to choose sb for an official position, especially as an AMBASSADOR 委任，委派（某人为大使等）： *He was accredited to Madrid.* 他被委任为驻马德里大使。 **3** **~ sth/sb** to officially approve sth/sb as being of an accepted quality or standard 正式认可： *Institutions that do not meet the standards will not be accredited for teacher training.* 没有达标的机构不会获得教师培训的资格。

ac·credit·ation /əˌkredɪˈteɪʃn/ *noun* [U] official approval given by an organization stating that sb/sth has achieved a required standard 达到标准；证明合格： *a letter of accreditation* 一份合格证明书

ac·credit·ed /əˈkredɪtɪd/ *adj.* [usually before noun] **1** (of a person 人) officially recognized as sth; with official permission to be sth 官方认可的；获正式承认的： *our accredited representative* 我们官方委任的代表 ◇ *Only accredited journalists were allowed entry.* 只有正式认可的记者才获准入内。 **2** officially approved as being of an accepted quality or standard 鉴定合格的；达到标准的： *a fully **accredited school/university/course*** 充分鉴定合格的学校 / 大学 / 课程

ac·cre·tion /əˈkriːʃn/ *noun* (*specialist* or *formal*) **1** [C] a layer of a substance or a piece of matter that is slowly added to sth 积聚层；堆积层 **2** [U] the process of new layers or matter being slowly added to sth 堆积，积聚（过程）

ac·crue /əˈkruː/ *verb* (*formal*) **1** [I] to increase over a period of time （逐渐）增长，增加： *Interest will accrue if you keep your money in a savings account.* 如果把钱存入储蓄账户，就会自然生息。 ◇ **~ (to sb) (from sth)** *economic benefits accruing to the country from tourism* 旅游业为该国带来的经济效益 **2** [T] **~ sth** to allow a sum of money or debts to grow over a period of time 积累（钱款或债务） **SYN** **accumulate**: *The firm had accrued debts of over $6m.* 该公司已积欠了 600 多万美元的债务。 ▶ **ac·crual** /əˈkruːəl/ *noun* [U, C]： *the accrual of interest* 利息积累

ac·cul·tur·ate /əˈkʌltʃəreɪt/ *verb* [I, T] **~ (sb) (to sth)** (*formal*) to learn to live successfully in a different culture; to help sb to do this （使）适应新的文化，融入…文化 ▶ **ac·cul·tur·ation** /əˌkʌltʃəˈreɪʃn/ *noun* [U]

ac·cu·mu·late **AW** /əˈkjuːmjəleɪt/ *verb* **1** [T] **~ sth** to gradually get more and more of sth over a period of time 积累；积聚 **SYN** **amass**: *I seem to have accumulated a lot* *of books.* 我好像已经收集了很多书。◇ *By investing wisely she accumulated a fortune.* 她投资精明，积累了一笔财富。➲ SYNONYMS AT COLLECT **2** [I] to gradually increase in number or quantity over a period of time （数量）逐渐增加；（数额）逐渐增长 SYN **build up**: *Debts began to accumulate.* 债务开始增加。➲ SYNONYMS AT COLLECT ▸ **ac·cu·mu·la·tion** AW /əˌkjuːmjəˈleɪʃn/ *noun* [U, C]: *the accumulation of wealth* 财富的积累 ◇ *an accumulation of toxic chemicals* 有毒化学物质的积聚

ac·cu·mu·la·tive /əˈkjuːmjələtɪv/ *adj.* (*formal*) growing by increasing gradually 累积的：*the accumulative effects of pollution* 污染的累积效应

ac·cu·mu·la·tor /əˈkjuːmjəleɪtə(r)/ *noun* **1** (*computing* 计) a section of a computer that is used for storing the results of what has been calculated 累加器 **2** (*BrE*) (*NAmE* **ˈstorage battery**) a large battery that you can fill with electrical power (= that you can RECHARGE) 蓄电池 **3** (*BrE*) a bet on a series of races or other events, where the money won or originally bet is placed on the next race, etc. 累计下注（每赢一次即押于下一轮赌博）

ac·cur·acy AW /ˈækjərəsi/ *noun* [U] the state of being exact or correct; the ability to do sth skilfully without making mistakes 准确（性）；精确（程度）：*They questioned the accuracy of the information in the file.* 他们怀疑档案中信息的准确性。◇ *She hits the ball with great accuracy.* 她击球十分准确。OPP **inaccuracy**

ac·cur·ate 🔑 AW /ˈækjərət/ *adj.* **1** 🔑 correct and true in every detail 正确无误的：*an accurate description/account/calculation* 准确的描述／叙述／计算 ◇ *accurate information/data* 正确无误的情报／资料 ◇ *Accurate records must be kept.* 必须保存准确的记录。**2** 🔑 able to give completely correct information or to do sth in an exact way 精确的；准确的：*a highly accurate electronic compass* 高度精确的电子罗盘仪 ◇ *accurate to within 3 mm* 精确得误差不超过 3 毫米 ◇ *My watch is not very accurate.* 我的表走得不太准。**3** 🔑 an **accurate** throw, shot, weapon, etc. hits or reaches the thing that it was aimed at 准确的（掷、射、击等） OPP **inaccurate** ▸ **ac·cur·ate·ly** 🔑 AW *adv.*: *The article accurately reflects public opinion.* 文章如实反映了公众的意见。◇ *You need to hit the ball accurately.* 你必须准确击球。

ac·cur·sed /əˈkɜːsɪd; *NAmE* -ˈkɜːrs-/ *adj.* (*old-fashioned*) having a CURSE (= a bad magic SPELL) on it 受诅咒的

ac·cus·ation /ˌækjuˈzeɪʃn/ *noun* [C, U] a statement saying that you think a person is guilty of doing sth wrong, especially of committing a crime; the fact of accusing sb 控告；起诉；告发；谴责：*I don't want to* **make an accusation** *until I have some proof.* 我要有一些证据以后才提出控告。◇ *There was a hint of accusation in her voice.* 她的语气暗含谴责。◇ **~ of sth** *accusations of corruption/cruelty/racism* 对贪污腐化／残暴行为／种族主义的控告 ◇ **~ against sb** *No one believed her wild accusations against her husband.* 无人相信她对她丈夫的无端指责。◇ **~ that…** *He denied the accusation that he had ignored the problems.* 他否认别人说他忽视这些问题的指控。

ac·cusa·tive /əˈkjuːzətɪv/ *noun* (*grammar* 语法) (in some languages 用于某些语言) the form of a noun, a pronoun or an adjective when it is the DIRECT OBJECT of a verb, or connected with the DIRECT OBJECT 宾格：*In the sentence, 'I saw him today', the word 'him' is* **in the accusative**. 在 I saw him today 一句中，him 一词为宾格。➲ COMPARE ABLATIVE, DATIVE, GENITIVE, NOMINATIVE, VOCATIVE ▸ **ac·cusa·tive** *adj.*

ac·cusa·tory /əˈkjuːzətəri; ˌækjuˈzeɪtəri; *NAmE* -tɔːri/ *adj.* (*formal*) suggesting that you think sb has done sth wrong 谴责的；指责的；控告的

ac·cuse 🔑 /əˈkjuːz/ *verb* **~ sb (of sth)** to say that sb has done sth wrong or is guilty of sth 控告；控诉；谴责：*to accuse sb of murder/theft* 控告某人谋杀／盗窃 ◇ *She accused him of lying.* 她指责他说谎。◇ *The government was accused of incompetence.* 政府被指责无能。◇ (*formal*) *They* **stand accused** *of crimes against humanity.* 他们被控危害人类罪。➲ WORDFINDER NOTE AT TRIAL ▸ **ac·cuser** *noun*

> **WORD FAMILY**
> accuse *verb*
> accusation *noun*
> accusing *adj.*
> accusatory *adj.*
> accused *noun*

the ac·cused /əˈkjuːzd/ *noun* (*pl.* **the ac·cused**) a person who is on trial for committing a crime （刑事）被告：*The accused was found innocent.* 被告被判定无罪。◇ *All the accused have pleaded guilty.* 所有被告都表示认罪。➲ COMPARE DEFENDANT

ac·cus·ing /əˈkjuːzɪŋ/ *adj.* showing that you think sb has done sth wrong 谴责的；指责的：*an* **accusing look/finger/tone** 谴责的目光；指责的手指；责备的语调 ◇ *Her accusing eyes were fixed on him.* 她用责备的眼光盯着他。▸ **ac·cus·ing·ly** *adv.*

ac·cus·tom /əˈkʌstəm/ *verb*
PHR V **acˈcustom yourself/sb to sth** to make yourself/sb familiar with sth or become used to it 使习惯于：*It took him a while to accustom himself to the idea.* 他过了一段时间才习惯这个想法。

ac·cus·tomed /əˈkʌstəmd/ *adj.* **1** (*rather formal*) familiar with sth and accepting it as normal or usual 习惯于 SYN **used to**: **~ to sth** *to* **become/get accustomed** *to sth* 习惯于某事物 ◇ *My eyes slowly* **grew accustomed** *to the dark.* 我的眼睛慢慢适应了黑暗。◇ **~ to doing sth** *She was a person accustomed to having eight hours' sleep a night.* 她是那种习惯每晚睡八个小时的人。**2** [usually before noun] (*formal*) usual 通常的；惯常的 SYN **habitual**: *He took his accustomed seat by the fire.* 他坐了炉火边惯常坐的座位。OPP **unaccustomed**

AC/DC /eɪ siː ˈdiː siː/ *adj.* (*slang*) = BISEXUAL

ace /eɪs/ *noun, adj., verb*
■ ***noun* 1** a PLAYING CARD with a large single symbol on it, which has either the highest or the lowest value in a particular card game * A 纸牌（亦称"爱司"）：*the ace of spades/hearts/diamonds/clubs* 黑桃／红心／方块／梅花 A ➲ WORDFINDER NOTE AT CARD ➲ VISUAL VOCAB PAGE V42 **2** (*informal*) a person who is very good at doing sth 擅长…的人；精于…的人：*a soccer/flying ace* 足球／飞行顶尖高手 ◇ *an ace marksman* 神枪手 **3** (in TENNIS 网球) a SERVE (= the first hit) that is so good that your opponent cannot reach the ball 发球得分；爱司球：*He served 20 aces in the match.* 他在这场比赛中发了 20 个爱司球。
IDM **an ace up your ˈsleeve** (*BrE*) (*NAmE* **an ace in the ˈhole**) (*informal*) a secret advantage, for example a piece of information or a skill, that you are ready to use if you need to 秘藏的王牌；撒手锏；锦囊妙计 **hold all the aces** to have all the advantages in a situation 占尽天时地利人和 **play your ˈace** to use your best argument, etc. in order to get an advantage in a situation 打出王牌；使出绝招 **within an ace of sth/of doing sth** (*BrE*) very close to sth 差一点儿；几乎：*We came within an ace of victory.* 我们差点儿赢了。
■ ***adj.*** (*informal*) very good 第一流的；极好的：*We had an ace time.* 我们过得真痛快。
■ ***verb*** **~ sth** (*informal, especially NAmE*) to be successful in sth 在…中获得成功：*He aced all his tests.* 他通过了对他的所有测试。

acer /ˈeɪsə(r)/ *noun* [C, U] a tree or plant that is often grown for its attractive leaves and bright autumn/fall colours 槭属植物，秋槭（常栽作风景树）

acerb·ic /əˈsɜːbɪk; *NAmE* əˈsɜːrb-/ *adj.* (*formal*) (of a person or what they say 人或言语) critical in a direct and rather cruel way 尖刻的；严厉的：*The letter was written in her usual acerbic style.* 这封信是用她惯常的尖刻语调写的。▸ **acerb·ity** /əˈsɜːbəti; *NAmE* əˈsɜːrb-/ *noun* [U]

acet·amino·phen /əˌsiːtəˈmɪnəfen/ (*NAmE*) (*BrE* **para·ceta·mol**) *noun* [U, C] a drug used to reduce pain and fever 对乙酰氨基酚；扑热息痛

acet·ate /ˈæsɪteɪt/ *noun* **1** [U] a chemical made from acetic acid, used in making plastics, etc. 醋酸盐；醋酸酯

A

2 [U] a chemical used to make FIBRES which are used to make clothes, etc. 醋酸纤维素 **3** [C] a transparent plastic sheet that you can write or print sth on and show on a screen using an OVERHEAD PROJECTOR 醋酸透明塑胶片；投影胶片

acet·ic acid /əˌsiːtɪk ˈæsɪd/ *noun* [U] the acid in VINEGAR that gives it its taste and smell 乙酸；醋酸

acet·one /ˈæsɪtəʊn; *NAmE* -toʊn/ *noun* [U] a clear liquid with a strong smell used for cleaning things, making paint thinner and producing various chemicals 丙酮

acetyl·ene /əˈsetəliːn/ (*also* **eth·yne**) *noun* [U] (*symb.* C_2H_2) a gas that burns with a very hot bright flame, used for cutting or joining metal 乙炔；电石气

ach /ɑːx/ *exclamation* (*ScotE*) used to express the fact that you are surprised, sorry, etc. （表示惊奇、遗憾等）啊

ach·cha /ʌˈtʃɑː/ *exclamation* (*IndE, informal*) **1** used to show that the speaker agrees with, accepts, understands, etc. sth （表示同意、接受、明白等）嗯，唔，噢：*Achcha! We'll meet at eight.* 好吧！我们八点钟见。 **2** used to express surprise, happiness, etc. （表示惊奇、高兴等）啊，哇，啊哈

ache /eɪk/ *verb, noun*

■ ***verb*** [I] **1** to feel a continuous dull pain 疼痛；隐痛 **SYN** **hurt**: *I'm aching all over.* 我周身疼痛。◇ **~ from sth** *Her eyes ached from lack of sleep.* 她的眼睛因睡眠不足而隐隐作痛。◇ (*figurative*) *It makes my heart ache* (= it makes me sad) *to see her suffer.* 看到她在受苦，我心里真难过。➲ SYNONYMS AT HURT **2** (*formal*) to have a strong desire for sb/sth or to do sth 渴望 **SYN** **long**: **~ for sb/sth** *I was aching for home.* 我很想回家。◇ **~ to do sth** *He ached to see her.* 他渴望见到她。

■ ***noun*** (often in compounds 常构成复合词) a continuous feeling of pain in a part of the body （身体某部位的）疼痛：*Mummy, I've got a tummy ache.* 妈妈，我肚子疼。◇ *Muscular **aches and pains** can be soothed by a relaxing massage.* 做放松按摩可以减轻肌肉疼痛。◇ (*figurative*) *an ache in my heart* (= a continuous sad feeling) 我心中的隐痛 ➲ SEE ALSO ACHY, BELLYACHE *n.*, HEARTACHE

achieve 🔑 **AW** /əˈtʃiːv/ *verb* **1** 🔑 [T] **~ sth** to succeed in reaching a particular goal, status or standard, especially by making an effort for a long time （凭长期努力）达到（某目标、地位、标准） **SYN** **attain**: *He had finally achieved success.* 他终于获得了成功。◇ *They could not achieve their target of less than 3% inflation.* 他们未能达到通货膨胀低于 3% 的目标。 **2** [T] **~ sth** to succeed in doing sth or causing sth to happen 完成 **SYN** **accomplish**: *I haven't achieved very much today.* 我今天没做成多少事。◇ *All you've achieved is to upset my parents.* 你唯一做到的就是使我的父母难过。 **3** [I] to be successful 成功：*Their background gives them little chance of achieving at school.* 他们的家庭背景使他们很难在学校获得成功。

▶ **achiev·able** **AW** *adj.* : *Profits of $20m look achievable.* * 2 000 万美元的利润看来是可以完成的。◇ *achievable goals* 可以达到的目标 **OPP** **unachievable**

achieve·ment 🔑 **AW** /əˈtʃiːvmənt/ *noun* **1** 🔑 [C] a thing that sb has done successfully, especially using their own effort and skill 成就；成绩；功绩：*the greatest scientific achievement of the decade* 这十年最伟大的科学成就 ◇ *It was a remarkable achievement for such a young player.* 如此年轻的选手有这样的成绩真是了不起。◇ *They were proud of their children's achievements.* 他们对孩子们的成绩感到自豪。 **2** 🔑 [U] the act or process of achieving sth 达到；完成：*the need to raise standards of achievement in education* 在教育中提高成绩标准的必要性 ◇ *Even a small success gives you **a sense of achievement*** (= a feeling of pride). 即便是小小的成功也给人一种成就感。 **3** [C] a reward that you can earn in some video games by completing a challenge or level 成就（电子游戏完成挑战或过关后得到的奖励）

achiever /əˈtʃiːvə(r)/ *noun* **1** a person who achieves a high level of success, especially in their career （尤指事业）成功者 **2** (after an adjective 用于形容词之后) a person who achieves the particular level of success that is stated 取得…成绩的人：*a low achiever* 成绩平庸的人

Achil·les heel /əˌkɪliːz ˈhiːl/ *noun* [sing.] a weak point or fault in sb's character, which can be attacked by other people 命门；死穴；致命弱点 ➲ MORE LIKE THIS 16, page R27 **ORIGIN** Named after the Greek hero **Achilles**. When he was a small child, his mother held him below the surface of the river Styx to protect him against any injury. She held him by his heel, which therefore was not touched by the water. Achilles died after being wounded by an arrow in the heel. 源自希腊神话英雄阿喀琉斯（Achilles）的故事。传说他年幼时，母亲把他浸在斯提克斯冥河中，使他刀枪不入。由于母亲提着他的脚踵，因此他的脚踵没有沾上河水。后来他因脚踵中箭身亡。

Achil·les ten·don /əˌkɪliːz ˈtendən/ (*also* **Achil·les**) *noun* the TENDON that connects the muscles at the back of the lower part of the leg to the heel 跟腱

ach·ing·ly /ˈeɪkɪŋli/ *adv.* (of qualities or feelings) very great and affecting you deeply （品质或情感）非常；极其；感人至深地：*an achingly beautiful song* 触人灵魂的妙曲

ach·kan /ˈʌʃkən/ *noun* a piece of men's clothing that reaches to the knees, with buttons down the front, worn in S Asia 爱客坎（南亚男子的开衫长款上衣）

achy /ˈeɪki/ *adj.* (*informal*) suffering from a continuous slight pain 隐痛不止的：*I feel all achy.* 我感到浑身酸痛。◇ *an achy back* 背痛

acid 🔑 /ˈæsɪd/ *noun, adj.*

■ ***noun*** **1** 🔑 [U, C] (*chemistry* 化) a chemical, usually a liquid, that contains HYDROGEN and has a pH of less than seven. The HYDROGEN can be replaced by a metal to form a salt. Acids are usually sour and can often burn holes in or damage things they touch. 酸 ➲ COMPARE ALKALI ➲ WORDFINDER NOTE AT CHEMISTRY ➲ SEE ALSO ACETIC ACID, AMINO ACID, ASCORBIC ACID, CITRIC ACID, HYDROCHLORIC ACID, LACTIC ACID, NITRIC ACID, NUCLEIC ACID, SULPHURIC ACID **2** [U] (*slang*) = LSD

■ ***adj.*** **1** (*specialist*) that contains acid or has the essential characteristics of an acid; that has a pH of less than seven 酸的；酸性的：*Rye is tolerant of poor, acid soils.* 黑麦耐贫瘠的酸性土壤。➲ COMPARE ALKALINE **2** that has a bitter sharp taste 酸的；酸味的 **SYN** **sour**: *acid fruit* 酸水果 ➲ SYNONYMS AT BITTER **3** (of a person's remarks 言辞) critical and unkind 尖刻的；尖酸的 **SYN** **sarcastic, cutting**: *an acid wit* 尖刻的俏皮话

ˈ**acid house** *noun* [U] a type of electronic music with a strong steady beat, often played at parties where some people take harmful drugs 迷幻豪斯音乐（节奏强烈、平稳的电子音乐，常在有人服用迷幻药的聚会上演奏）

acid·ic /əˈsɪdɪk/ *adj.* **1** very sour 很酸的：*Some fruit juices are very acidic.* 有些果汁酸得很。 **2** containing acid 酸性的：*acidic soil* 酸性土壤

acid·ify /əˈsɪdɪfaɪ/ *verb* (**acid·ifies, acid·ify·ing, acid·ified, acid·ified**) [I, T] **~ (sth)** (*specialist*) to become or make sth become an acid （使）变成酸，酸化

acid·ity /əˈsɪdəti/ *noun* [U] the state of having a sour taste or of containing acid 酸味；酸性

ˌ**acid** ˈ**jazz** *noun* [U] a type of dance music that combines JAZZ, FUNK, SOUL, and HIP HOP 迷幻爵士（结合爵士乐、放克乐、灵乐和嘻哈音乐成分的舞曲）

acid·ly /ˈæsɪdli/ *adv.* in an unpleasant or critical way 尖酸地；尖刻地：*'Thanks for nothing,' she said acidly.* "不用你费心。" 她挖苦地说。

ˌ**acid** ˈ**rain** *noun* [U] rain that contains harmful chemicals from factory gases and that damages trees, crops and buildings 酸雨；酸性降水 ➲ VISUAL VOCAB PAGE V7

ˌ**acid** ˈ**test** (*also* ˈ**litmus test** *especially in NAmE*) *noun* [sing.] a way of deciding whether sth is successful or true 决

定性考验；严峻的考验：*The acid test of a good driver is whether he or she remains calm in an emergency.* 在紧急情况下能否保持冷静是对好司机的严峻考验。

ackee (*also* **akee**) /'æki/ *noun* **1** [C] a type of tree that produces bright red fruit, originally from W Africa 阿开基木（原产于西非，结浅红色果实） **2** [U] the fruit from this tree, which is poisonous to eat unless it is completely RIPE 阿开基木果实（未完全成熟时有毒）

ac·know·ledge AW /ək'nɒlɪdʒ; *NAmE* ək'nɑːl-/ *verb*
- **ADMIT** 承认 **1** to accept that sth is true 承认（属实）：**~ sth** *She refuses to acknowledge the need for reform.* 她拒不承认改革的必要性。◇ *a generally acknowledged fact* 公认的事实 ◇ **~ that...** *I did not acknowledge that he had done anything wrong.* 我不认为他犯了什么错。◇ **~ sth to be, have, etc. sth** *It is generally acknowledged to be true.* 普遍认为那是真的。⇨ SYNONYMS AT ADMIT
- **ACCEPT STATUS** 承认地位 **2** to accept that sb/sth has a particular authority or status 承认（权威、地位） SYN **recognize**：**~ sb/sth** *The country acknowledged his claim to the throne.* 这个国家承认了他继承王位的权利。◇ **~ sb/sth as sth** *He is widely acknowledged as the best player in the world.* 普遍认为他是世界最佳球员。◇ **~ sb/sth to be, have, etc. sth** *He is widely acknowledged to be the best player in the world.* 普遍认为他是世界最佳球员。
- **REPLY TO LETTER** 复信 **3 ~ sth** to tell sb that you have received sth that they sent to you 告知收悉：*All applications will be acknowledged.* 所有的申请都将得到复函告知收悉。◇ *Please acknowledge receipt of this letter.* 信收到后请复函告知。
- **SMILE/WAVE** 微笑；挥手 **4 ~ sb/sth** to show that you have noticed sb/sth by smiling, waving, etc.（微笑、挥手等）致意：*I was standing right next to her, but she didn't even acknowledge me.* 我就站在她身边，可是她理都不理我。
- **EXPRESS THANKS** 表示感谢 **5 ~ sth** to publicly express thanks for help you have been given （公开）感谢：*I gratefully acknowledge financial support from several local businesses.* 我对几家本地企业的资助表示感谢。

ac·know·ledge·ment AW (*also* **ac·know·ledg·ment**) /ək'nɒlɪdʒmənt; *NAmE* ək'nɑːl-/ *noun* **1** [sing., U] an act of accepting that sth exists or is true, or that sth is there （对事实、现实、存在的）承认：*This report is an acknowledgement of the size of the problem.* 这个报告承认了问题的严重性。◇ *She gave me a smile of acknowledgement* (= showed that she had seen and recognized me). 她向我微笑打招呼。 **2** [C, U] an act or a statement expressing thanks to sb; something that is given to sb as thanks 感谢；谢礼：*The flowers were a small acknowledgement of your kindness.* 这些花聊表谢意，感谢你的好心帮助。◇ *I was sent a free copy* ***in acknowledgement of*** *my contribution.* 我收到一本赠刊，表示对我投稿的谢意。 **3** [C] a letter or an email saying that sth has been received 收件复函：*I didn't receive an acknowledgement of my application.* 我的申请没有得到复信告知收悉。 **4** [C, usually pl.] a statement, especially at the beginning of a book, in which the writer expresses thanks to the people who have helped （尤指作者在卷首的）致谢，鸣谢

ac,knowledgement of 'country (*also* **Acknowledgement of Country**) *noun* [sing., U] (in Australia) formal recognition of the traditional Aboriginal owners of the land at an event such as a conference or festival, and in Parliament （澳大利亚）土地声明（在公开场合如大会、庆典活动和议会上正式承认澳大利亚土著居民为传统意义上的土地所有者）

acme /'ækmi/ *noun* [usually sing.] (*formal*) the highest stage of development or the most excellent example of sth 顶峰；顶点；典范 SYN **height**

acne /'ækni/ *noun* [U] a skin condition, common among young people, that produces many PIMPLES (= spots), especially on the face and neck 痤疮；粉刺：*to suffer from/have acne* 患痤疮；长粉刺

aco·lyte /'ækəlaɪt/ *noun* **1** (*formal*) a person who follows and helps a leader 侍从；随员；助手 **2** (*specialist*) a person who helps a priest in some church ceremonies 辅祭；赞礼

acorn /'eɪkɔːn; *NAmE* -kɔːrn/ *noun* the small brown nut of the OAK tree, that grows in a base shaped like a cup 橡子；橡实 ⇨ VISUAL VOCAB PAGE V10 IDM SEE OAK

acous·tic /ə'kuːstɪk/ (*NAmE also* **acous·tic·al** /ə'kuːstɪkl/) *adj.* **1** related to sound or to the sense of hearing 声音的；音响的；听觉的 **2** [usually before noun] (of a musical instrument or performance 乐器或演奏) designed to make natural sound, not sound produced by electrical equipment 原声的；自然声的 ⇨ VISUAL VOCAB PAGE V40 ▶ **acous·tic·al·ly** /-kli/ *adv.*

acous·tics /ə'kuːstɪks/ *noun* **1** [pl.] (*also* **acoustic** [sing.]) the shape, design, etc. of a room or theatre that make it good or bad for carrying sound （房间、戏院的）传声效果，音响效果：*The acoustics of the new concert hall are excellent.* 新音乐厅的传声效果极佳。 **2** [U] the scientific study of sound 声学

ac·quaint /ə'kweɪnt/ *verb* **~ sb/yourself with sth** (*formal*) to make sb/yourself familiar with or aware of sth 使熟悉；使了解：*Please acquaint me with the facts of the case.* 请把这事的实情告诉我。◇ *You will first need to acquaint yourself with the filing system.* 你首先需要熟悉文件归档方法。

ac·quaint·ance /ə'kweɪntəns/ *noun* **1** [C] a person that you know but who is not a close friend 认识的人；泛泛之交；熟人：*Claire has a wide circle of* ***friends and acquaintances****.* 克莱尔交游很广。◇ *He's just a business acquaintance.* 他只是业务上认识的人。⇨ WORDFINDER NOTE AT FRIEND **2** [U, C] **~ (with sb)** (*formal*) slight friendship （与某人）认识，略有交情：*He hoped their acquaintance would develop further.* 他希望他们的交情会进一步发展。 **3** [U, C] **~ with sth** (*formal*) knowledge of sth （对某事物的）了解：*I had little acquaintance with modern poetry.* 我对现代诗所知甚少。

IDM **make sb's acquaintance | make the acquaintance of sb** (*formal*) to meet sb for the first time 与某人初次相见；结识某人：*I am delighted to make your acquaintance, Mrs Baker.* 贝克太太，我很高兴与您相识。◇ *I made the acquaintance of several musicians around that time.* 大约在那段时间，我结识了几位音乐家。 **of your ac'quaintance** (*formal*) that you know 所认识的；所了解的：*No one else of my acquaintance was as rich or successful.* 我所认识的人当中，其他人都没有如此富有或者成功。 **on first ac'quaintance** (*formal*) when you first meet sb 初次相见时：*Even on first acquaintance it was clear that he was not 'the right type'.* 初次见面就看出他显然不是"对路子的人"。⇨ MORE AT NOD *v.*

ac'quaintance rape *noun* [U, C] (*especially NAmE*) the crime of RAPING sb, committed by a person he or she knows 熟人强奸（罪）；约会强暴

ac·quaint·ance·ship /ə'kweɪntənsʃɪp/ *noun* [U, C, usually sing.] (*formal*) a slight friendship with sb or knowledge of sth 泛泛之交；认识；了解：*It was unfair to judge her on such a brief acquaintanceship.* 你刚认识她就对她作出评价，这是不公平的。

ac·quaint·ed /ə'kweɪntɪd/ *adj.* [not before noun] **1 ~ with sth** (*formal*) familiar with sth, having read, seen or experienced it 熟悉；了解：*The students are already acquainted with the work of Shakespeare.* 这些学生已经读过莎士比亚的著作。◇ *Employees should be fully acquainted with emergency procedures.* 雇员应当十分熟悉应急措施。 **2** not close friends with sb, but having met a few times before （与某人）相识，熟悉：*We got acquainted at the conference* (= met and started to get to know each other). 我们在那次会议上相识了。◇ **~ with sb** *I am well acquainted with her family.* 我和她家里的人很熟。

ac·qui·esce /,ækwi'es/ *verb* [I] **~ (in/to sth)** (*formal*) to accept sth without arguing, even if you do not really agree with it 默然接受；默认；默许；顺从：*Senior government figures must have acquiesced in the cover-up.* 政府高级官员必然已经默许掩盖真相。

A

ac·qui·es·cence /ˌækwiˈesns/ *noun* [U] (*formal*) the fact of being willing to do what sb wants and to accept their opinions, even if you are not sure that they are right 默然接受；默认；默许；顺从：*There was general acquiescence in the UN sanctions.* 普遍默认了联合国的制裁。▶ **ac·qui·es·cent** /-ˈesnt/ *adj.*

ac·quire 🔑 AW /əˈkwaɪə(r)/ *verb* (*formal*) **1** 🔑 ~ **sth** to gain sth by your own efforts, ability or behaviour（通过努力、能力、行为表现）获得，得到：*She has acquired a good knowledge of English.* 她英语已经学得很好。◇ *He has acquired a reputation for dishonesty.* 他得到了奸诈的名声。◇ *I have recently* ***acquired a taste*** *for olives.* 我最近开始喜欢吃橄榄了。 **2** 🔑 ~ **sth** to obtain sth by buying or being given it 购得；获得；得到：*The company has just acquired new premises.* 公司刚购得新办公楼。◇ *I've suddenly acquired a stepbrother.* 我突然有了一个继兄。

IDM **an acquired 'taste** a thing that you do not like much at first but gradually learn to like 养成的爱好：*Abstract art is an acquired taste.* 要慢慢培养才会欣赏抽象艺术。

ac·qui·si·tion AW /ˌækwɪˈzɪʃn/ *noun* **1** [U] the act of getting sth, especially knowledge, a skill, etc.（知识、技能等的）获得，得到：*theories of child language acquisition* 幼儿语言习得的理论 **2** [C] something that sb buys to add to what they already own, usually sth valuable（多指贵重的）购得物：*His latest acquisition is a racehorse.* 他最近购得一匹赛马。 **3** [C, U] (*business* 商) a company, piece of land, etc. bought by sb, especially another company; the act of buying it 购置物；收购的公司；购置的产业；购置；收购：*They have made acquisitions in several EU countries.* 他们在几个欧盟国家购买了一些产业。◇ *the acquisition of shares by employees* 雇员购股 ➲ WORDFINDER NOTE AT DEAL

ac·quisi·tive /əˈkwɪzətɪv/ *adj.* (*formal, disapproving*) wanting very much to buy or get new possessions 渴求获取财物的；贪婪的 ▶ **ac·quisi·tive·ness** *noun* [U]

ac·quit /əˈkwɪt/ *verb* (-tt-) **1** ~ **sb** (**of sth**) to decide and state officially in court that sb is not guilty of a crime 宣判无罪：*The jury acquitted him of murder.* 陪审团裁决他谋杀罪不成立。OPP **convict** **2** ~ **yourself well, badly, etc.** (*formal*) to perform or behave well, badly, etc. 表现好（或坏等）：*He acquitted himself brilliantly in the exams.* 他在考试中表现出色。➲ MORE LIKE THIS 36, page R29

ac·quit·tal /əˈkwɪtl/ *noun* [C, U] an official decision in court that a person is not guilty of a crime 宣告无罪；无罪的判决：*The case resulted in an acquittal.* 此案件最终作出无罪判决。◇ *The jury voted for acquittal.* 陪审团表决赞成判定无罪。OPP **conviction** ➲ COLLOCATIONS AT JUSTICE

acre /ˈeɪkə(r)/ *noun* a unit for measuring an area of land; 4 840 square yards or about 4 050 square metres 英亩（4 840 平方码，约为 4 050 平方米）：*3 000 acres of parkland* * 3 000 英亩开阔绿地 ◇ *a three-acre wood* 一片三英亩的林地 ◇ (*informal*) *Each house has acres of space around it* (= a lot of space). 每座房屋四周都有大量空地。

acre·age /ˈeɪkərɪdʒ/ *noun* [U, C] an area of land measured in acres 英亩数

acrid /ˈækrɪd/ *adj.* having a strong, bitter smell or taste that is unpleasant（气、味）辛辣的，难闻的，刺激的 SYN **pungent**：*acrid smoke from burning tyres* 燃烧轮胎产生的刺鼻气味 ➲ SYNONYMS AT BITTER

acri·mo·ni·ous /ˌækrɪˈməʊniəs; *NAmE* -ˈmoʊ-/ *adj.* (*formal*) (of an argument, etc. 争论等) angry and full of strong bitter feelings and words 尖刻的；讥讽的；激烈的 SYN **bitter**：*His parents went through an acrimonious divorce.* 他的父母在激烈争吵中离了婚。▶ **acri·mo·ni·ous·ly** *adv.*

acri·mony /ˈækrɪməni; *NAmE* -moʊni/ *noun* [U] (*formal*) angry bitter feelings or words（态度、言辞）尖刻，讥讽：*The dispute was settled without acrimony.* 没有唇枪舌剑，这场纠纷就解决了。

acro·bat /ˈækrəbæt/ *noun* an entertainer who performs difficult acts such as balancing on high ropes, especially at a CIRCUS 杂技演员

acro·bat·ic /ˌækrəˈbætɪk/ *adj.* involving or performing difficult acts or movements with the body 杂技的；杂技般的；杂技演员的：*acrobatic feats* 杂技表演 ◇ *an acrobatic dancer* 特技舞蹈演员 ▶ **acro·bat·ic·al·ly** /-kli/ *adv.*

acro·bat·ics /ˌækrəˈbætɪks/ *noun* [pl.] acrobatic acts and movements 杂技：*acrobatics on the high wire* 走钢丝杂技 ◇ (*figurative*) *vocal acrobatics* (= performing skilfully with the voice when singing) 高超的歌唱技巧

acro·nym /ˈækrənɪm/ *noun* a word formed from the first letters of the words that make up the name of sth, for example 'AIDS' is an acronym for 'acquired immune deficiency syndrome' 首字母缩略词（如 AIDS 是由 acquired immune deficiency syndrome 的首字母组成）

acrop·olis /əˈkrɒpəlɪs; *NAmE* əˈkrɑːp-/ *noun* (in an ancient Greek city) a castle, or an area that is designed to resist attack, especially one on top of a hill 卫城（古希腊城邦中的城堡或具有防卫性质的地区，多建于山顶）

across 🔑 /əˈkrɒs; *NAmE* əˈkrɔːs; əˈkrɑːs/ *adv.*, *prep.*

■ ***adv.*** HELP For the special uses of **across** in phrasal verbs, look at the entries for the verbs. For example **come across** is in the phrasal verb section at **come**. * across 在短语动词中的特殊用法见有关动词词条。如 come across 在词条 come 的短语动词部分。 **1** 🔑 from one side to the other side 从一边到另一边；横过；宽：*It's too wide. We can't swim across.* 这太宽了，我们游不过去。◇ *The yard measures about 50 feet across.* 庭院宽约 50 英尺。 **2** 🔑 in a particular direction towards or at sb/sth 从…的一边向…：*When my name was called, he looked across at me.* 当叫到我名字的时候，他从那边朝我看过来。 **3** 🔑 **across from** opposite 在对面；在对过：*There's a school just across from our house.* 有一所学校就在我们房子对面。 **4** (of an answer in a CROSSWORD 纵横字谜谜底) written from side to side 横写的：*I can't do 3 across.* 我猜不出第 3 格横写的谜底。

■ ***prep.*** **1** 🔑 from one side to the other side of sth 从…一边到另一边；横过：*He walked across the field.* 他走过田地。◇ *I drew a line across the page.* 我在这一页上画了一条横线。◇ *A grin spread across her face.* 她粲然一笑。◇ *Where's the nearest bridge across the river?* 过河最近的桥在哪儿？ **2** 🔑 on the other side of sth 在…对面；在…对过：*There's a bank right across the street.* 街对面就有一家银行。 **3** on or over a part of the body 在（身体某部位）上：*He hit him across the face.* 他打了他的脸。◇ *It's too tight across the back.* 背部太紧。 **4** in every part of a place, group of people, etc. 在…各处；遍及 SYN **throughout**：*Her family is scattered across the country.* 她的家人散居全国各地。◇ *This view is common across all sections of the community.* 该社区所有阶层的人普遍持有这种看法。

ac·ros·tic /əˈkrɒstɪk; *NAmE* -ˈkrɔːs-; -ˈkrɑːs-/ *noun* a poem or other piece of writing in which particular letters in each line, usually the first letters, can be read downwards to form a word or words 离合诗，离合诗体（各行的某些字母、通常是开头字母可组合成词）

acryla·mide /əˈkrɪləmaɪd/ *noun* [U, C] a substance used in various industrial processes. Acrylamide is also found in food that has been cooked at high temperatures, and may be a cause of cancer. 丙烯酰胺（工业用物质，也见于高温烹调的食物，可致癌）

acryl·ic /əˈkrɪlɪk/ *adj.*, *noun*

■ ***adj.*** made of a substance produced by chemical processes from a type of acid 丙烯酸的：***acrylic paints/fibres*** 丙烯酸涂料 / 纤维 ◇ *an acrylic sweater* 一件丙烯酸运动衫

■ ***noun*** **1** [U] a type of FIBRE produced by chemical processes, used to make clothes, etc. 丙烯酸纤维 **2** [C, usually pl.] a type of paint used by artists（画家用的）丙烯酸颜料

ACT™ /ˌeɪ siː ˈtiː/ *abbr.* American College Test (an exam that some HIGH SCHOOL students take before they go to college) 美国高等院校考试（一些高中生入读高等院校前参加的考试）

act 🔑 /ækt/ *noun, verb*

■*noun*

• **STH THAT SB DOES** 作为 **1** 🔑[C] a particular thing that sb does 行为；行动；所为： *a criminal act* 犯罪行为 ◇ **~ of sth** *an act of kindness* 善行 ◇ *acts of terrorism* 恐怖行动 ◇ **~ of sb** *The murder was the act of a psychopath.* 这次谋杀是精神变态者所为。 ➲ SYNONYMS AT ACTION

• **LAW** 法律 **2** 🔑[C] a law that has been passed by a parliament（议会通过的）法案，法令： *an Act of Congress* 国会法案 ◇ *the Care Act 2014* * 2014 年颁布的《照顾法》 ➲ WORDFINDER NOTE AT PARLIAMENT

• **PRETENDING** 假装 **3** 🔑[sing.] a way of behaving that is not sincere but is intended to have a particular effect on others 假装： *Don't take her seriously—it's all an act.* 别跟她认真，这全是假戏一场。 ◇ *You could tell she was just* ***putting on an act.*** 你可以看出，她是在装模作样。

• **IN PLAY/ENTERTAINMENT** 戏剧；娱乐 **4** [C] one of the main divisions of a play, an OPERA, etc.（戏剧、歌剧等的）一幕： *a play in five acts* 一出五幕剧 ◇ *The hero dies in Act 5, Scene 3.* 男主角在第 5 幕第 3 场死去。 ➲ WORDFINDER NOTE AT PLAY **5** [C] one of several short pieces of entertainment in a show 一段表演： *a* ***circus/comedy/magic act*** 马戏 / 喜剧 / 魔术表演 **6** [C] a performer or group of musicians 表演者；音乐人组合： *They were one of rock's most impressive live acts.* 他们是最富感染力的现场表演摇滚乐组合之一。

IDM **ˌact of 'God** (*law* 律) an event caused by natural forces beyond human control, such as a storm, a flood or an EARTHQUAKE 天灾；不可抗力（如风暴、洪水、地震） **be/get in on the act** (*informal*) to be/become involved in an activity that sb else has started, especially to get sth for yourself 参与；插一手 **do, perform, stage a disap'pearing/'vanishing act** (*informal*) to go away or be impossible to find when people need or want you 隐藏踪迹；潜踪隐迹 **get your 'act together** (*informal*) to organize yourself and your activities in a more effective way in order to achieve sth 集中精力： *He needs to get his act together if he's going to pass.* 要是他想合格，就必须集中精力。 **a ˌhard/ˌtough act to 'follow** a person who is so good or successful at sth that it will be difficult for anyone else coming after them to be as good or successful 令人望尘莫及的人 **in the act (of doing sth)** while you are doing sth 正在（做某事）；当场： *He was* ***caught in the act*** *of stealing a car.* 他偷汽车时被当场逮个正着。 ➲ MORE AT CLEAN *v.*, READ *v.*

■*verb*

• **DO STH** 做某事 **1** 🔑[I] to do sth for a particular purpose or in order to deal with a situation 做事；行动： *It is vital that we act to stop the destruction of the rainforests.* 至关紧要的是，我们应当采取行动制止破坏雨林。 ◇ *The girl's life was saved because the doctors acted so promptly.* 多亏医生行动迅速，女孩的生命得救了。 ◇ *He claims he acted in self-defence.* 他声称他是出于自卫。

• **BEHAVE** 行为 **2** 🔑[I] to behave in a particular way 表现得： **+ adv.** *John's been acting very strangely lately.* 近来约翰的行为怪得很。 ◇ **~ like sb/sth** *Stop acting like spoilt children!* 别再像惯坏的孩子那样胡闹了！ ◇ **~ as if/though...** *She was acting as if she'd seen a ghost.* 她的行为举止像是见到幽灵一般。 HELP In spoken English people often use **like** instead of **as if** or **as though** in this meaning, especially in *NAmE.* 口语中，尤其是美式英语中，常用 like 代替 as if 或 as though： *She was acting like she'd seen a ghost.* 她的行为举止像是见到幽灵一般。This is not considered correct in written *BrE.* 英式英语的书面语中，此用法被视为不正确。

• **PRETEND** 假装 **3** 🔑[I] to pretend by your behaviour to be a particular type of person 假装： **+ noun** *He's been acting the devoted husband all day.* 他整天装作模范丈夫的样子。 ◇ **+ adj.** *I decided to act dumb.* 我决定装傻。

• **PERFORM IN PLAY/MOVIE** 戏剧 / 电影表演 **4** 🔑[I, T] to perform a part in a play or film/movie 扮演（戏剧、电影中的角色）： *Have you ever acted?* 你演过戏吗？ ◇ *Most of the cast act well.* 这出戏大多数演员演得不错。 ◇ **~ sth** *Who's acting (the part of) Hamlet?* 谁演哈姆雷特（这个角色）？ ◇ *The play was well acted.* 这出戏演得不错。

• **PERFORM FUNCTION** 起作用 **5** [I] to perform a particular role or function 充当；起作用： **~ as sth** *Can you act as interpreter?* 你能担任口译员吗？ ◇ **~ like sth** *hormones in the brain that act like natural painkillers* 大脑中起着天然止痛药作用的激素

• **HAVE EFFECT** 有作用 **6** [I] **~ (on sth)** to have an effect on sth（对…）有作用，有影响： *Alcohol acts quickly on the brain.* 酒精对大脑迅速产生影响。 IDM SEE AGE *n.*, FOOL *n.*, OWN *v.*

PHR V **'act for/on behalf of sb** to be employed to deal with sb's affairs for them, for example by representing them in court（受雇）代表某人行事 **'act on/upon sth** to take action as a result of advice, information, etc. 根据（建议、信息等）行事： *Acting on information from a member of the public, the police raided the club.* 警察根据群众举报，突然搜查了这家俱乐部。 ◇ *Why didn't you act on her suggestion?* 你为什么没有按照她的建议去做呢？ **ˌact sth↔'out 1** to perform a ceremony or show how sth happened, as if performing a play 履行（仪式）；将…表演出来： *The ritual of the party conference is acted out in the same way every year.* 该党的大会程序年年照行如仪。 ◇ *The children started to act out the whole incident.* 孩子们开始表演整个事件。 **2** to act a part in a real situation 充当（真实情况中的角色）： *She acted out the role of the wronged lover.* 她扮作一个受冤枉的情人。 **ˌact 'up** (*informal*) **1** to behave badly 表现不好；捣乱： *The kids started acting up.* 孩子们开始调皮捣蛋起来。 **2** to not work as it should 出毛病： *How long has your ankle been acting up?* 你的脚踝受伤多久了？

act·ing /ˈæktɪŋ/ *noun, adj.*

■*noun* [U] the activity or profession of performing in plays, films/movies, etc.（戏剧、电影等中的）表演；演艺业

■*adj.* [only before noun] doing the work of another person for a short time 临时代理的 SYN **temporary**: *the acting manager* 代理经理

ac·tin·ium /ækˈtɪniəm/ *noun* [U] (*symb.* **Ac**) a chemical element. Actinium is a RADIOACTIVE metal. 锕（放射性化学元素）

ac·tion 🔑 /ˈækʃn/ *noun, verb*

■*noun*

• **WHAT SB DOES** 作为 **1** 🔑[U] the process of doing sth in order to make sth happen or to deal with a situation 行动；行为过程： *The time has come for action if these beautiful animals are to survive.* 若要使这些美丽的动物能生存下去，现在就要行动起来。 ◇ *Firefighters* ***took action*** *immediately to stop the blaze spreading.* 消防队员立即采取了行动制止大火蔓延。 ◇ *What is the best* ***course of action*** *in the circumstances?* 在这种情况下最佳行动方针是什么？ ◇ *She began to explain her* ***plan of action*** *to the group.* 她开始向小组讲解她的行动计划。 ➲ SEE ALSO DIRECT ACTION, INDUSTRIAL ACTION **2** 🔑[C] a thing that sb does 所做之事；行为： *Her quick action saved the child's life.* 她行动迅速，救了小孩的命。 ◇ *Each of us must take responsibility for our own actions.* 我们每个人都必须对自己的行为负责。 ➲ WORDFINDER NOTE AT BEHAVIOUR

• **LEGAL PROCESS** 诉讼程序 **3** 🔑[C, U] a legal process to stop a person or company from doing sth, or to make them pay for a mistake, etc. 诉讼；起诉： *A libel action is being brought against the magazine that published the article.* 刊登该文章的杂志将被起诉诽谤。 ◇ *He is considering taking legal action against the hospital.* 他正考虑起诉这家医院。

• **IN WAR** 战争 **4** 🔑[U] fighting in a battle or war 战斗；作战： *military action* 军事行动 ◇ *soldiers killed* ***in action*** 阵亡战士

• **IN STORY/PLAY** 故事；戏剧 **5** [U] the events in a story, play, etc.（故事、戏剧等中的）情节： *The action takes place in France.* 这个故事发生在法国。

• **EXCITING EVENTS** 激动人心的事 **6** 🔑[U] exciting events 激动人心的事： *I like films with plenty of action.* 我喜欢情节曲折离奇的影片。 ◇ *New York is* ***where the action is.*** 纽约是个热闹活跃的地方。

• **EFFECT** 作用 **7** [U] **~ of sth (on sth)** the effect that one substance or chemical has on another（一种物质或化学品对另一种所起的）作用： *the action of sunlight on the skin* 阳光对皮肤的作用

A

- **OF PART OF THE BODY** 身体部位 **8** [U, C] (*specialist*) the way a part of the body moves or functions（身体部位的）动作，功能： *a study of the action of the liver* 对肝功能的研究
- **OF MACHINE** 机器 **9** [sing.] the MECHANICAL parts of a piano, gun, clock, etc. or the way the parts move（钢琴、枪炮、钟表等的）机械装置，活动部件；（机械部件的）活动方式 ➲ SEE ALSO PUMP-ACTION

IDM **actions speak louder than 'words** (*saying*) what a person actually does means more than what they say they will do 行动胜于语言 **in 'action** if sb/sth is **in action**, they are doing the activity or work that is typical for them 在活动中；在运转： *Just press the button to see your favourite character in action.* 只要按一下按键就可以看到你最喜欢的角色表演。◇ *I've yet to see all the players in action.* 我还得看所有参赛者的实地比赛。 **into 'action** if you put an idea or a plan **into action**, you start making it happen or work 实行；实施： *The new plan for traffic control is being put into action on an experimental basis.* 新的交通管理方案正在试行。 **out of 'action** not able to work or be used because of injury or damage 不能工作；失去作用；停止运转： *Jon will be out of action for weeks with a broken leg.* 乔恩断了一条腿，将有几个星期不能工作。◇ *The photocopier is out of action today.* 复印机今天出故障了。 **a piece/slice of the 'action** (*informal*) a share or role in an interesting or exciting activity, especially in order to make money 插手，参与（尤指为了赚钱）： *Foreign firms will all want a piece of the action if the new airport goes ahead.* 要是新机场开始修建，外国公司都会来插一手捞好处。 ➲ MORE AT EVASIVE, SPRING *v.*, SWING *v.*

■ ***verb*** **~ sth** to make sure that sth is done or dealt with 务必做，确保处理（某事）： *Your request will be actioned.* 你的要求会处理的。

▼ SYNONYMS 同义词辨析

action

measure • step • act • move

These are all words for a thing that sb does. 以上各词均指行为、行动。

action a thing that sb does 指行动、动作： *Her quick action saved the child's life.* 她行动迅速，救了小孩的命。

measure an official action that is done in order to achieve a particular aim 指措施、方法： *Tougher measures against racism are needed.* 需要更强硬的反种族主义措施。

step one of a series of things that you do in order to achieve sth 指步骤、措施： *This was a first step towards a united Europe.* 这是向建立统一欧洲的目标迈出的第一步。

act a thing that sb does 指行为、行动、所为： *an act of kindness* 善行

ACTION OR ACT? 用 action 还是 act?

These two words have the same meaning but are used in different patterns. An **act** is usually followed by *of* and/or used with an adjective. **Action** is not usually used with *of* but is often used with *his, her, etc.* 这两个词意义相同，但用于不同的句型。act 后常跟 of，而且常与形容词连用。action 通常不与 of 连用，但常与 his、her 等词连用： *a heroic act of bravery* 英雄壮举 ◇ ~~*a heroic action of bravery*~~ ◇ *his heroic actions/acts during the war* 他在战争中的英雄壮举 **Action** often combines with *take* but **act** does not. * action 常与 take 搭配，act 则不能： ~~*We shall take whatever acts are necessary.*~~

move (used especially in journalism) an action that you do or need to do to achieve sth （尤用于新闻）指为达到某目标而采取或需要采取的行动： *They are waiting for the results of the opinion polls before deciding their next move.* 他们在等待民意测验的结果，然后再决定下一步行动。

PATTERNS

- to **take** action/measures/steps
- to **make** a step/move
- a **heroic/brave/daring** action/step/act/move

ac·tion·able /'ækʃənəbl/ *adj.* **1** giving sb a valid reason to bring a case to court 可予起诉的；可提起诉讼的 **2** that can be done or acted on 可执行的；可操作的： *The research is aimed at getting actionable solutions.* 这项研究旨在寻求可行的解决方案。

ac·tion·er /'ækʃənə(r)/ *noun* (*NAmE, informal*) = ACTION MOVIE

'action figure *noun* a DOLL representing a soldier or a character from a film/movie, TV show, etc.（仿影视等角色的）战士玩偶，人偶

'action film *noun* (*BrE*) = ACTION MOVIE

'action group *noun* (often as part of a name 常作名称的一部分) a group that is formed to work for social or political change（社会或政治改革的）行动小组： *the Child Poverty Action Group* 解除儿童贫困行动小组

'Action Man™ *noun* **1** a toy in the form of a soldier 机动人（一种玩具兵） **2** an active and aggressive man 积极进取的男子： *The illness damaged his Action Man image.* 这场病损害了他积极进取的形象。

'action movie (*BrE also* **'action film**) (*also NAmE, informal* **ac·tion·er**) *noun* a film/movie that has a lot of exciting action and adventure 动作影片

'action-packed *adj.* full of exciting events and activity 充满令人兴奋的活动的： *an action-packed weekend* 活动安排得满满的周末

'action point *noun* a suggestion for action that must be taken, especially one that is made in a meeting（尤指在会议上达成的）行动方案

,action 'replay *noun* (*BrE*) **1** (*NAmE* **,instant 'replay**) part of sth, for example a sports game on television, that is immediately repeated, often more slowly, so that you can see a goal or another exciting or important moment again（体育比赛等电视画面的）即时重放，慢镜头重放 **2** an event or a situation that repeats sth that has happened before（往事的）重演： *It was an action replay of the problems of his first marriage.* 这是他第一次婚姻问题的重演。

'action research *noun* [U] studies done to improve the working methods of people who do a particular job or activity, especially in education （尤指教育界为改进工作方法等而开展的）行动研究（法）

'action stations *noun* [pl.] the positions to which soldiers go to be ready for fighting 战斗岗位

ac·ti·vate /'æktɪveɪt/ *verb* **~ sth** to make sth such as a device or chemical process start working 使活动；激活；使活化： *The burglar alarm is activated by movement.* 这防盗警报器一动就会响。◇ *The gene is activated by a specific protein.* 这种基因由一种特异性蛋白激活。 ▶ **ac·ti·vation** /,æktɪ'veɪʃn/ *noun* [U]

ac·tive /'æktɪv/ *adj., noun*

■ ***adj.***

- **BUSY** 忙碌 **1** always busy doing things, especially physical activities （尤指体力上）忙碌的，活跃的： *Although he's nearly 80, he is still very active.* 尽管快 80 岁了，他还是十分活跃。 **OPP** **inactive**
- **TAKING PART** 参加 **2** involved in sth; making a determined effort and not leaving sth to happen by itself 积极的： *They were both politically active.* 他们两人在政治上都很积极。◇ ***active involvement/participation/support/resistance*** 积极参与 / 参加 / 支持 / 抵抗 ◇ *She takes an **active part** in school life.* 她积极参加学校活动。◇ *The parents were active in campaigning against cuts to the education budget.* 学生家长积极参加反对削减教育预算的活动。◇ *They took active steps to prevent the spread of the disease.* 他们采取积极措施，防止疾病蔓延。
- **DOING AN ACTIVITY** 活动 **3** doing sth regularly; functioning 定期进行的；起作用的： *sexually active teenagers*

有性生活的青少年 ◇ *animals that are active only at night* 仅在夜间活动的动物 ◇ *The virus is still active in the blood.* 这种病毒仍然在血液中起作用。◇ *an active volcano* (= likely to ERUPT) 活火山 OPP **inactive** ⊃ COMPARE DORMANT
• **LIVELY** 充满活力 **4** lively and full of ideas 活跃的；（思想上）充满活力的：*That child has a very active imagination.* 那个小孩想象力十分丰富。
• **CHEMICAL** 化学 **5** having or causing a chemical effect 起化学作用的；有效的：*What is the active ingredient in aspirin?* 什么是阿司匹林中的有效成分？OPP **inactive**
• **GRAMMAR** 语法 **6** connected with a verb whose subject is the person or thing that performs the action 主动语态的：*In 'He was driving the car', the verb is active.* 在 He was driving the car 一句中，动词是主动语态。⊃ COMPARE PASSIVE *adj.* ▶ **ac·tive·ly** *adv.*：*Your proposal is being actively considered.* 你的提议正得到认真考虑。◇ *She was actively looking for a job.* 她在积极找工作。
■ *noun* (*also* ˌ**active** ˈ**voice**) [sing.] the form of a verb in which the subject is the person or thing that performs the action 主动语态 ⊃ COMPARE PASSIVE *n.*

ˈ**active list** *noun* **1** a list of people that an organization may contact at any time, offering a service, providing information, or asking them to do sth 积极分子名单（可用于随时联系以便提供服务、信息或寻求帮助等）：*Please email us to be removed from our active list of blood donors.* 假如你想把自己的名字从献血积极分子名单中删去，请给我们发电子邮件。 **2** a list of officers or former officers connected to one of the armed forces who can be called for duty 服役名册（记录现役或退役军官）

ˌ**active** ˈ**service** (*NAmE also* ˌ**active** ˈ**duty**) *noun* [U] the work of a member of the armed forces, especially during a war 现役；（尤指）战时服役：*troops on active service* 现役部队

ac·tiv·ist /ˈæktɪvɪst/ *noun* a person who works to achieve political or social change, especially as a member of an organization with particular aims 积极分子；活跃分子：*gay activists* 争取男同性恋者权益的活动人士 ▶ **ac·tiv·ism** /ˈæktɪvɪzəm/ *noun* [U]

ac·tiv·ity /ækˈtɪvəti/ *noun* (*pl.* **-ies**) **1** [U] a situation in which sth is happening or a lot of things are being done 活动；热闹状况；活跃：*economic activity* 经济活动 ◇ *The streets were noisy and full of activity.* 街上熙熙攘攘，车水马龙。◇ *Muscles contract and relax during physical activity.* 身体活动时肌肉收缩放松。⊃ COMPARE INACTIVITY at INACTIVE **2** [C, usually pl.] a thing that you do for interest or pleasure, or in order to achieve a particular aim（为兴趣、娱乐或达到一定目的而进行的）活动：***leisure/outdoor/classroom activities*** 休闲 / 户外 / 课堂活动 ◇ *The club provides a wide variety of activities including tennis, swimming and squash.* 这家俱乐部的活动丰富多彩，诸如网球、游泳、壁球等。◇ ***illegal/criminal activities*** 不法 / 犯罪活动

actor /ˈæktə(r)/ *noun* a person who performs on the stage, on television or in films/movies, especially as a profession 演员 ⊃ **WORDFINDER NOTE** AT FILM

> **WORDFINDER** 联想词：audition, body double, cameo, cast, **play**, role, star, stuntman, understudy

⊃ **MORE LIKE THIS** 25, page R28

ˌ**actor-**ˈ**manager** *noun* an actor who is in charge of a theatre company and acts in the plays that they perform 演员兼剧团总监

ac·tress /ˈæktrəs/ *noun* a woman who performs on the stage, on television or in films/movies, especially as a profession 女演员 HELP Many women now prefer to be called **actors**, although when the context is not clear, **an actor** is usually understood to refer to a man. 虽然在上下文不明确时 actor 通常指男演员，但是现在很多女演员都喜欢被称为 actor。⊃ NOTE AT GENDER ⊃ **MORE LIKE THIS** 25, page R28

ac·tual /ˈæktʃuəl/ *adj.* [only before noun] **1** used to emphasize sth that is real or exists in fact 真实的；实际的：*What were his actual words?* 他的原话是什么？◇ *The actual cost was higher than we expected.* 实际成本比我们预计的要高。◇ *James looks younger than his wife but* ***in actual fact*** (= really) *he is five years older.* 詹姆斯看起来比他妻子年轻，但实际上他还大了五岁。 **2** used to emphasize the most important part of sth（强调事情最重要的部分）真正的，…本身：*The wedding preparations take weeks but the actual ceremony takes less than an hour.* 准备婚礼要几周，而婚礼仪式本身还不到一小时。

> ▼ **WHICH WORD?** 词语辨析
>
> **actual / current / present**
>
> • **Actual** does not mean **current** or **present**. It means 'real' or 'exact', and is often used in contrast with something that is not seen as real or exact. * actual 与 current 或 present 意义不同，其含义为真实的或确实的，常与不真实或不确实的事物形成对比：*I need the actual figures, not an estimate.* 我需要确切的数字，而不是估计。
> • **Present** means 'existing or happening now'. * present 意为现存、现行：*How long have you been in your present job?* 你干现在这工作多长时间了？
> • **Current** also means 'existing or happening now', but can suggest that the situation is temporary. * current 也指现存、现行，但含暂时之义：*The factory cannot continue its current level of production.* 这家工厂不能维持目前的生产水平。
> • **Actually** does not mean 'at the present time'. Use **currently**, **at present** or **at the moment** instead. * actually 无现在、目前之义，表示此义用 currently、at present 或 at the moment。
>
> ⊃ NOTE AT PRESENTLY

ˌ**actual** ˌ**bodily** ˈ**harm** *noun* [U] (*abbr.* **ABH**) (*BrE, law* 律) the crime of causing sb physical injury 实际身体伤害（罪）⊃ COMPARE GRIEVOUS BODILY HARM

ac·tu·al·ity /ˌæktʃuˈæləti/ *noun* (*pl.* **-ies**) (*formal*) **1** [U] the state of sth existing in reality 真实；实际：*The building looked as impressive* ***in actuality*** *as it did in photographs.* 这栋大楼外观雄伟，与照片中所见一模一样。 **2** [C, usually pl.] things that exist 真实情况；现实情况；事实 SYN **fact, reality**：*the grim actualities of prison life* 严酷的监狱生活现实

ac·tu·al·ize (*BrE also* **-ise**) /ˈæktʃuəlaɪz/ *verb* ~ **sth** to make sth real; to make sth happen 实现；使发生：*He finally actualized his dream.* 他最终实现了自己的梦想。

ac·tu·al·ly /ˈæktʃuəli/ *adv.* **1** used in speaking to emphasize a fact or a comment, or that sth is really true（在口语中用于强调事实）的确，真实地，事实上：*What did she actually say?* 她到底是怎么说的？◇ *It's not actually raining now.* 其实现在并没有下雨。◇ *That's the only reason I'm actually going.* 那是我确实要走的唯一理由。◇ *There are lots of people there who can actually help you.* 那里有很多人可以真正帮上你的忙。◇ *I didn't want to say anything without actually reading the letter first.* 在没有确确实实看过那封信之前我什么也不想说。 **2** used to show a contrast between what is true and what sb believes, and to show surprise about this contrast（表示想法与事实不一致因而惊奇）居然，竟然：*It was actually quite fun after all.* 这居然还很有趣。◇ *The food was not actually all that expensive.* 食物居然并不那么昂贵。◇ *Our turnover actually increased last year.* 去年我们的营业额竟然增加了。 **3** used to correct sb in a polite way（礼貌地纠正他人）实际上，事实上：*We're not American, actually. We're Canadian.* 实际上我们不是美国人。我们是加拿大人。◇ *Actually, it would be much more sensible to do it later.* 事实上，以后再办这件事可能要明智得多。◇ *They're not married, actually.* 他们实际上没有结婚。 **4** used to get sb's attention, to introduce a new topic or to say sth that sb may not like, in a polite way（礼貌地引起注意、转换话题、直言）确实，说实在的：*Actually, I'll* *be a bit late home.* 说真的，我回家会晚一点。◇ *Actually, I'm busy at the moment—can I call you back?* 说实在的，我这会儿正忙。我可以给你回电话吗？➲ NOTE AT ACTUAL

ac·tu·ary /ˈæktʃuəri; *NAmE* -eri/ *noun* (*pl.* **-ies**) a person whose job involves calculating insurance risks and payments for insurance companies by studying how frequently accidents, fires, deaths, etc. happen 精算师（研究事故、火灾、死亡等发生的频率，为保险公司计算保险风险和保险费）➲ WORDFINDER NOTE AT INSURANCE ▸ **ac·tu·ar·ial** /ˌæktʃuˈeəriəl; *NAmE* -ˈeriəl/ *adj.*

ac·tu·ate /ˈæktʃueɪt/ *verb* (*formal*) **1** ~ **sth** to make a machine or device start to work 开动（机器、装置等）SYN **activate** **2** [usually passive] ~ **sb** to make sb behave in a particular way 激励；驱使 SYN **motivate**: *He was actuated entirely by malice.* 他完全是出于恶意。

acu·ity /əˈkjuːəti/ *noun* [U] (*formal*) the ability to think, see or hear clearly（思维、视力、听力的）敏度，敏锐

acu·men /ˈækjəmən; əˈkjuːmən/ *noun* [U] the ability to understand and decide things quickly and well 精明；敏锐: ***business/commercial/financial acumen*** 生意上 / 商业上 / 理财上精明强干

acu·pres·sure /ˈækjupreʃə(r)/ (*also* **shi·atsu**) *noun* [U] a form of medical treatment, originally from East Asia, in which pressure is applied to particular parts of the body using the fingers 指针疗法（一种治疗方式，以手指按压身体特定部位）

acu·punc·ture /ˈækjupʌŋktʃə(r)/ *noun* [U] a Chinese method of treating pain and illness using special thin needles which are pushed into the skin in particular parts of the body 针刺疗法 ➲ WORDFINDER NOTE AT TREATMENT

acu·punc·tur·ist /ˈækjupʌŋktʃərɪst/ *noun* a person who is trained to perform acupuncture 针疗医师

acute /əˈkjuːt/ *adj.* **1** very serious or severe 十分严重的: *There is an acute shortage of water.* 水严重短缺。◇ *acute pain* 剧痛 ◇ *the world's acute environmental problems* 全球十分严重的环境问题 ◇ *Competition for jobs is acute.* 求职竞争非常激烈。 **2** an acute illness is one that has quickly become severe and dangerous（疾病）急性的: *acute appendicitis* 急性阑尾炎 OPP **chronic** ➲ WORDFINDER NOTE AT HEALTH **3** (of the senses 感官) very sensitive and well developed 灵敏的 SYN **keen**: *Dogs have an acute sense of smell.* 狗的嗅觉灵敏。 **4** intelligent and quick to notice and understand things 敏锐的；有洞察力的: *He is an acute observer of the social scene.* 他是个敏锐的社会现状观察者。◇ *Her judgement is acute.* 她的判断敏锐。 **5** (*geometry* 几何) (of an angle 角) less than 90° 锐角的 ▸ **acute·ness** *noun* [U]

aˌcute ˈaccent *noun* the mark placed over a vowel to show how it should be pronounced, as over the *e* in *fiancé* 尖音符号（标在元音上面）➲ COMPARE CIRCUMFLEX, GRAVE², TILDE, UMLAUT

aˌcute ˈangle *noun* an angle of less than 90° 锐角 ➲ PICTURE AT ANGLE ➲ COMPARE OBTUSE ANGLE, REFLEX ANGLE, RIGHT ANGLE

acute·ly /əˈkjuːtli/ *adv.* **1** ~ **aware/conscious** noticing or feeling sth very strongly 深深感觉到；强烈意识到: *I am acutely aware of the difficulties we face.* 我十分清楚我们面临的困难。 **2** (describing unpleasant feelings) very; very strongly（描述不快的感觉）极其，强烈地: *acutely embarrassed* 极其尴尬 **3** to a severe and dangerous degree 严重地；危险地: *acutely ill* 病重 OPP **chronically**

-acy ➲ -CY

acyc·lic /ˌeɪˈsaɪklɪk/ *adj.* **1** (*specialist*) not occurring in cycles 非周期的；非循环的 **2** (*chemistry* 化) (of a COMPOUND or MOLECULE 化合物或分子) containing no rings of atoms 无环的；非环状的

AD (*BrE*) (*NAmE also* **A.D.**) /ˌeɪ ˈdiː/ *abbr.* used in the Christian CALENDAR to show a particular number of years since the year when Christ was believed to have been born (from Latin 'Anno Domini') 公元（源自拉丁语 Anno Domini）: *in (the year) AD 55* 公元 55 年 ◇ *in 55 AD* 公元 55 年 ◇ *in the fifth century AD* 公元 5 世纪 ➲ COMPARE AH, BC, BCE, CE

ad 🔑 /æd/ *noun* (*informal*) = ADVERTISEMENT: *We put an ad in the local paper.* 我们在当地报纸上登了一则广告。◇ *an ad for a new chocolate bar* 新品种巧克力棒的广告 ➲ SYNONYMS AT ADVERTISEMENT ➲ SEE ALSO BANNER AD

adage /ˈædɪdʒ/ *noun* a well-known phrase expressing a general truth about people or the world 谚语；格言 SYN **saying**

ada·gio /əˈdɑːdʒiəʊ; *NAmE* -dʒioʊ/ *noun* (*pl.* **-os**) (*music* 音, *from Italian*) a piece of music to be played slowly 柔板 ▸ **ada·gio** *adj., adv.*

Adam /ˈædəm/ *noun* IDM ▸ SEE KNOW *v.*

ad·am·ant /ˈædəmənt/ *adj.* determined not to change your mind or to be persuaded about sth 坚决的；坚定不移的: *Eva was adamant that she would not come.* 伊娃坚决不来。 ▸ **ad·am·ant·ly** *adv.*: *His family were adamantly opposed to the marriage.* 他的家人坚决反对这门亲事。

ad·am·ant·ine /ˌædəˈmæntaɪn/ *adj.* (*literary*) very strong and impossible to break 坚韧的；刚劲的

ˌAdam's ˈapple *noun* the lump at the front of the throat that sticks out, particularly in men, and moves up and down when you swallow 喉结

adapt 🔑 AW /əˈdæpt/ *verb* **1** 🔑 [T] to change sth in order to make it suitable for a new use or situation 使适应，使适合（新用途、新情况）SYN **modify**: ~ **sth** *These styles can be adapted to suit individual tastes.* 这些式样可以修改，以适应个人不同爱好。◇ ~ **sth for sth** *Most of these tools have been specially adapted for use by disabled people.* 这些工具多数已经过特别改装，供残疾人使用。 **2** 🔑 [I, T] to change your behaviour in order to deal more successfully with a new situation 适应（新情况）SYN **adjust**: *It's amazing how soon you adapt.* 你这么快就适应了，真是令人惊奇。◇ *The organisms were forced to adapt in order to survive.* 生物被迫适应，以求生存。◇ ~ **to sth** *We have had to adapt quickly to the new system.* 我们不得不迅速适应了新制度。◇ *A large organization can be slow to adapt to change.* 大机构可能应变迟缓。◇ ~ **yourself to sth** *It took him a while to adapt himself to his new surroundings.* 他过了好一阵子才适应了新环境。 **3** 🔑 [T] ~ **sth** (**for sth**) (**from sth**) to change a book or play so that it can be made into a play, film/movie, television programme, etc. 改编；改写: *Three of her novels have been adapted for television.* 她的长篇小说中有三部已改编成电视节目。

adapt·able AW /əˈdæptəbl/ *adj.* (*approving*) able to change or be changed in order to deal successfully with new situations 有适应能力的；能适应的: *Older workers can be as adaptable and quick to learn as anyone else.* 较年长的工人的适应能力和学习速度有时并不亚于其他任何人。◇ *Successful businesses are highly adaptable to economic change.* 成功的企业对于经济变化的适应能力很强。 ▸ **adapt·abil·ity** AW /əˌdæptəˈbɪləti/ *noun* [U]

adap·ta·tion AW /ˌædæpˈteɪʃn/ (*also less frequent* **adap·tion** /əˈdæpʃn/) *noun* **1** [C] a film/movie, book or play that is based on a particular piece of work but that has been changed for a new situation 改编本；改写本: *a screen adaptation of Shakespeare's 'Macbeth'* 莎士比亚悲剧《麦克白》的电影改写本 **2** [U] the process of changing sth, for example your behaviour, to suit a new situation 适应: *the adaptation of desert species to the hot conditions* 沙漠物种对炎热环境的适应

adap·tive AW /əˈdæptɪv/ *adj.* (*specialist*) concerned with changing; able to change when necessary in order to deal with different situations 适应的；有适应能力的: *Adaptive learning systems offer students customized learning experiences according to their needs and capabilities.* 适应性学习系统根据学生的需要和能力为他们提供个性化的学习体验。

adap·tor (*also* **adap·ter**) /əˈdæptə(r)/ *noun* **1** a device for connecting pieces of electrical equipment that were not designed to fit together （电器设备的）转接器，适配器 **2** (*BrE*) a device for connecting more than one piece of equipment to the same SOCKET (= a place in the wall where equipment is connected to the electricity supply) （供多个设备连接电源的）多头插座，多功能插座

ADC /ˌeɪ diː ˈsiː/ *noun* AIDE-DE-CAMP （陆军或海军）副官，随从参谋

ADD /ˌeɪ diː ˈdiː/ *abbr.* ATTENTION DEFICIT DISORDER 注意障碍

add /æd/ *verb* **1** [T] to put sth together with sth else so as to increase the size, number, amount, etc. 增加；添加： **~ sth** *Next add the flour.* 接着加面粉。◇ *The juice contains no added sugar.* 这种果汁没有加糖。◇ *The plan has the added* (= extra) *advantage of bringing employment to rural areas.* 该计划还有一个优点，就是给农村地区带来了就业机会。◇ **~ sth to sth** *A new wing was added to the building.* 这栋大楼新添了一座配楼。◇ *Shall I add your name to the list?* 我可以把你的名字写进名单吗？ **2** [I, T] to put numbers or amounts together to get a total 加： **~ A to B** *Add 9 to the total.* 总数再加上 9。◇ **~ A and B together** *If you add all these amounts together you get a huge figure.* 你把这些数目加在一起就会得到一个巨额数字。 OPP **subtract** **3** [T] to say sth more; to make a further remark 补充说；继续说： **+ speech** *'And don't be late,' she added.* "还有别迟到。" 她补充说道。◇ **~ sth (to sth)** *I have nothing to add to my earlier statement.* 我对我早先说的话没有什么补充的。◇ **~ that...** *He added that they would return a week later.* 他接着说，他们一周以后会回来。 **4** [T] **~ sth (to sth)** to give a particular quality to an event, a situation, etc. 添加（特色）： *The suite will add a touch of class to your bedroom.* 这套家具会给你的卧室增添一些典雅气质。

IDM **add ˌinsult to ˈinjury** to make a bad relationship with sb worse by offending them even more 伤害之余又侮辱；（冒犯别人）令关系恶化 **ˈadded to this... | ˈadd to this...** used to introduce another fact that helps to emphasize a point you have already made 此外（还…）： *Add to this the excellent service and you can see why it's the most popular hotel on the island.* 这再加上优质服务，你就能明白为何这家旅馆在岛上最受欢迎。

PHR V **ˌadd sth↔ˈin** to include sth with sth else 把…加进去；包括： *Remember to add in the cost of drinks.* 记住把饮料费加进去。 **ˌadd sth↔ˈon (to sth)** to include or attach sth extra 附加；加上： *A service charge of 15% was added on to the bill.* 账单上附加了 15% 的服务费。 ➲ RELATED NOUN ADD-ON **ˈadd to sth** to increase sth in size, number, amount, etc. 使（数量）增加；使（规模）扩大： *The bad weather only added to our difficulties.* 恶劣的天气更增加了我们的困难。◇ *The house has been added to* (= new rooms, etc. have been built on to it) *from time to time.* 这座房子一次又一次地扩建。 **ˌadd ˈup** (*informal*) **1** (especially in negative sentences 尤用于否定句) to seem reasonable; to make sense 合乎情理；有道理： *His story just doesn't add up.* 他说的情况根本不合情理。 **2** (not used in the progressive tenses 不用于进行时) to increase by small amounts until there is a large total 积少成多： *When you're feeding a family of six the bills soon add up.* 你要养活一家六口，开支很快就大起来了。 **ˌadd ˈup | ˌadd sth↔ˈup** to calculate the total of two or more numbers or amounts 把…加起来： *The waiter can't add up.* 这个服务员不会算账。◇ *Add up all the money I owe you.* 把我欠你的钱全部加起来。 **ˌadd ˈup to sth 1** to make a total amount of sth 总共是；总计为： *The numbers add up to exactly 100.* 这些数字的总数恰好是 100。 **2** to lead to a particular result; to show sth 结果是；表示 SYN **amount to sth**: *These clues don't really add up to very much* (= give us very little information). 这些线索实际上说明不了什么问题。

ad·den·dum /əˈdendəm/ *noun* (*pl.* **ad·denda** /-də/) (*formal*) a section of extra information that is added to sth, especially to a book （尤指书籍的）补遗，补篇

adder /ˈædə(r)/ *noun* a small poisonous snake, often with diamond-shaped marks on its back. Adders are the only poisonous snakes in Britain. 蝰蛇（英国仅有的一种毒蛇，背部有菱形斑）

ad·dict /ˈædɪkt/ *noun* **1** a person who is unable to stop taking harmful drugs 吸毒成瘾的人；瘾君子： *a* ***heroin/drug/nicotine addict*** 吸食海洛因 / 毒品 / 尼古丁成瘾的人 ➲ WORDFINDER NOTE AT DRUG **2** a person who is very interested in sth and spends a lot of their free time on it 对…入迷的人： *a video game addict* 电子游戏迷

ad·dict·ed /əˈdɪktɪd/ *adj.* [not before noun] **1 ~ (to sth)** unable to stop taking harmful drugs, or using or doing sth as a habit 上瘾；成瘾；有瘾： *to become addicted to drugs/gambling* 吸毒成瘾；嗜赌 **2 ~ (to sth)** spending all your free time doing sth because you are so interested in it 入迷： *He's addicted to computer games.* 他迷上了电脑游戏。 ➲MORE LIKE THIS 31, page R28

ad·dic·tion /əˈdɪkʃn/ *noun* [U, C] the condition of being addicted to sth 瘾；入迷；嗜好： *cocaine addiction* 可卡因瘾 ◇ **~ to sth** *He is now fighting his addiction to alcohol.* 他现在正努力戒酒。 ➲COLLOCATIONS AT ILL

ad·dict·ive /əˈdɪktɪv/ *adj.* **1** if a drug is **addictive**, it makes people unable to stop taking it 使人上瘾的： *Heroin is highly addictive.* 海洛因很容易使人上瘾。 **2** if an activity or type of behaviour is **addictive**, people need to do it as often as possible because they enjoy it 使人入迷的： *I find jogging very addictive.* 我觉得慢跑锻炼很使人着迷。

ˈadd-in *noun* (*computing* 计) **1** a computer program that can be added to a larger program to allow it to do more things 附加程序；外加程序 **2** = EXPANSION CARD ▶ **ˈadd-in** *adj.* [only before noun]: *add-in software* 附加软件

add·ition /əˈdɪʃn/ *noun* **1** [U] the process of adding two or more numbers together to find their total 加；加法： *children learning addition and subtraction* 学习加减的儿童 OPP **subtraction** **2** [C] **~ (to sth)** a thing that is added to sth else 增加物；添加物： *the latest addition to our range of cars* 我们汽车系列新增加的款式 ◇ *an addition to the family* (= another child) 这家新添的一口人（又生了一个孩子） **3** [U] **~ (of sth)** the act of adding sth to sth else 增加；添加： *Pasta's basic ingredients are flour and water, sometimes* ***with the addition of*** *eggs or oil.* 意大利面制品的主要成分是面粉和水，有时加鸡蛋和食用油。 **4** (*NAmE*) (*BrE* **extension**) [C] **~ (to sth)** a new part that is added to a building （建筑物的）扩建部分，增建部分： *architects who specialize in home additions* 专门从事住宅扩建的建筑师 ➲LANGUAGE BANK ON NEXT PAGE

IDM **in addition (to sb/sth)** used when you want to mention another person or thing after sth else 除…以外（还）： *In addition to these arrangements, extra ambulances will be on duty until midnight.* 除了这些安排以外，另增救护车值班至午夜。◇ *There is, in addition, one further point to make.* 此外，还有一点要说。

add·ition·al /əˈdɪʃənl/ *adj.* more than was first mentioned or is usual 附加的；额外的；外加的 SYN **extra**: *additional resources/funds/security* 额外资源；附加基金；外加保安措施 ◇ *The government provided an additional £25 million to expand the service.* 政府另拨 2 500 万英镑用于扩展该服务。 ▶ **add·ition·al·ly** /-ʃənəli/ *adv.* SYN **in addition (to sb/sth)**: *Additionally, the bus service will run on Sundays, every two hours.* 此外，公共汽车将于星期天运行，每两小时一班。

addi·tive /ˈædətɪv/ *noun* a substance that is added in small amounts to sth, especially food, in order to improve it, give it colour, make it last longer, etc. （尤指食品的）添加剂，添加物： *food additives* 食品添加剂 ◇ *additive-free orange juice* 不含添加剂的橙汁 ◇ *chemical additives in petrol* 汽油中的化学添加剂 ➲COLLOCATIONS AT DIET

addle /ˈædl/ *verb* **~ sth** to make sb unable to think clearly; to confuse sb 使不能清晰地思考；使糊涂: *Being in love must have addled your brain.* 坠入爱河必已使你神魂颠倒。

▼ LANGUAGE BANK 用语库

addition

Adding another item 补充说明

- *Bilingual children do better in IQ tests than children who speak only one language.* ***In addition / What is more****, they seem to find it easier to learn third or even fourth languages.* 讲两种语言的儿童比只讲一种语言的儿童智商测试得分更高。此外 / 而且，讲两种语言的儿童似乎在学习第三种甚至第四种语言时觉得更容易。
- *Learning another language* ***not only*** *improves children's job prospects in later life,* ***but also*** *boosts their self-esteem.* 学习另一种语言不仅可以提升儿童未来的职业前景，而且可以增强他们的自尊心。
- *Teaching children a second language improves their job prospects in later life.* ***Other*** *benefits* ***include*** *increased self-esteem and greater tolerance of other cultures.* 教儿童第二语言可以提升他们未来的职业前景。此外，还可以使他们获得更强的自尊心、对其他文化更包容。
- ***Another / One further / One additional*** *reason for encouraging bilingual education is that it boosts children's self-esteem.* 另一个鼓励双语教育的原因是它能增强儿童的自尊心。
- *Studies suggest that bilingual children find it easier to learn additional languages. There is,* ***moreover****, increasing evidence that bilingual children perform better across a range of school subjects, not just foreign languages.* 研究表明，讲两种语言的儿童学习其他语言觉得更容易。此外，越来越多的证据表明，讲两种语言的儿童不仅在外语学习上，同时在其他各门学科的学习上都表现得更好。
- *His claim that children find bilingual education confusing is based on very little evidence.* ***Moreover****, the evidence he does provide is seriously flawed.* 他认为双语教育会使儿童感到迷惑的说法几乎是没有依据的。况且，他仅有的证据也是有严重缺陷的。
- *Research has shown that first-language development is not impeded by exposure to a second language.* ***Furthermore****, there is no evidence to support the claim that children find bilingual education confusing.* 研究已经表明，接触第二语言不会妨碍第一语言的发展。而且，没有证据支持双语教育使儿童感到迷惑这种说法。

'add-on *noun* a thing that is added to sth else 附加物；附加装置： *The company offers scuba-diving as an add-on to the basic holiday price.* 这家公司提供戴水肺潜水活动，费用不含在基本度假费用内。◇ *add-on software* (= added to a computer) 计算机附加软件

ad·dress 🔑 *noun, verb*

■ *noun* /ə'dres; *NAmE also* 'ædres/ **1** 🔑 [C] details of where sb lives or works and where letters, etc. can be sent 住址；地址；通信处： *What's your* ***name and address****?* 你的姓名、住址？◇ *I'll give you my address and phone number.* 我会告诉你我的地址和电话号码。◇ *Is that your* ***home address****?* 那是你的住址吗？◇ *Please note my* ***change of address****.* 请注意我的地址变了。◇ *Police found him at an address* (= a house or flat/apartment) *in West London.* 警方在伦敦西区一处住所里找到了他。◇ *people* ***of no fixed address*** (= with no permanent home) 没有固定居所的人 ➲ SEE ALSO FORWARDING ADDRESS **2** 🔑 [C] (*computing* 计) a series of words and symbols that tells you where you can find sth using a computer, for example on the Internet （互联网等的）地址： *What's your* ***email address****?* 你的电邮地址是什么？◇ *The project has a new* ***web address****.* 这个项目有个新的网址。➲ **WORDFINDER NOTE** AT MESSAGE **3** [C] a formal speech that is made in front of an audience 演说；演讲： *tonight's televised presidential address* 今晚总统的电视演讲 ➲ **SYNONYMS** AT SPEECH ➲ **COLLOCATIONS** AT VOTE **4** [U] **form/mode of ~** the correct title, etc. to use when you talk to sb 称呼

■ *verb* /ə'dres/ **1** 🔑 [usually passive] to write on an envelope, etc. the name and address of the person, company, etc. that you are sending it to by mail 写（收信人）姓名地址；致函： **~ sth** *The letter was correctly addressed, but delivered to the wrong house.* 信上的姓名地址写得都对，但被错投到另一家去了。◇ **~ sth to sb/sth** *Address your application to the Personnel Manager.* 把你的申请信寄给人事经理。➲ COMPARE READDRESS ➲ SEE ALSO SAE, SASE **2** to make a formal speech to a group of people 演说；演讲： *to address a meeting* 在会议上发表演讲 **3** (*formal*) to say sth directly to sb 向…说话： **~ sb** *I was surprised when he addressed me in English.* 他用英语跟我说话，我很诧异。◇ **~ sth to sb** *Any questions should be addressed to your teacher.* 任何问题都应该向你的老师求教。 **4 ~ sb (as sth)** to use a particular name or title for sb when you speak or write to them 称呼（某人）；冠以（某种称呼）： *The judge should be addressed as 'Your Honour'.* 对法官应该称"法官大人"。 **5** (*formal*) to think about a problem or a situation and decide how you are going to deal with it 设法解决；处理；对付： **~ sth** *Your essay does not address the real issues.* 你的论文没有论证实质问题。◇ **~ yourself to sth** *We must address ourselves to the problem of traffic pollution.* 我们必须设法解决交通污染问题。

ad·dress·able /ə'dresəbl/ *adj.* **1** (of a problem or situation 问题或情况) that can be addressed 可处理的；可解决的；可对付的： *Let's start with the more easily addressable issues.* 我们先从较容易处理的问题着手。 **2** (*computing* 计) (of a part of a computer system 计算机系统内) that is identified using its own address 可寻址的；可定址的： *addressable memory* 可寻址存储器

ad'dress bar *noun* a line near the top of a page on an Internet BROWSER where you can type in the address of a website or where the website address is displayed （互联网浏览器顶部的）地址栏，网址栏

ad'dress book *noun* **1** a book in which you keep addresses, phone numbers, etc. 通讯录；通讯簿 **2** a computer file where you store email and Internet addresses （计算机）通讯录

ad·dress·ee /ˌædre'siː/ *noun* a person that a letter, etc. is addressed to 收信人；收件人

ad·duce /ə'djuːs; *NAmE* ə'duːs/ *verb* [often passive] **~ sth** (*formal*) to provide evidence, reasons, facts, etc. in order to explain sth or to show that sth is true 引证，举出（证据、理由、事实等） **SYN** **cite**: *Several factors have been adduced to explain the fall in the birth rate.* 有几个因素已被援引来说明出生率降低的原因。

ad·duct·or /ə'dʌktə(r)/ (*also* **ad'ductor muscle**) *noun* (*anatomy* 解) a muscle that moves a body part towards the middle of the body or towards another part 收肌 ➲ COMPARE ABDUCTOR (2)

addy /'ædi/ (*pl.* **-ies**) *noun* (*informal*) an address 地址： *an email/IP addy* 电子邮件 / IP 地址

ad·en·oids /'ædənɔɪdz/ *noun* [pl.] pieces of soft TISSUE at the back of the nose and throat, that are part of the body's IMMUNE SYSTEM and that can swell up and cause breathing difficulties, especially in children 腺样体，增殖体（尤指小儿的咽扁桃体） ▶ **ad·en·oid·al** /ˌædə'nɔɪdl/ *adj.*

adept /ə'dept/ *adj.* **~ (at/in sth)** | **~ (at/in doing sth)** good at doing sth that is quite difficult 内行的；熟练的；擅长的 **SYN** **skilful** ▶ **adept** /'ædept/ *noun* **adept·ly** *adv.*

ad·equate 🔑 **AW** /'ædɪkwət/ *adj.* enough in quantity, or good enough in quality, for a particular purpose or need 足够的；合格的；合乎需要的： *an adequate supply of hot water* 热水供应充足 ◇ *The room was small but adequate.* 房间虽小但够用。◇ *There is a lack of adequate provision for disabled students.* 为残疾学生提供的服务不够。◇ *He didn't give an adequate answer to the question.* 他没有对这个问题作出令人满意的答复。◇ **~ for sth** *The space available is not adequate for our needs.* 现有的空间不能满足我们的需要。◇ **~ to do sth** *training that is adequate to meet the future needs of industry* 足以满足未来工业需要的培训 **OPP** **inadequate** ▶ **ad·equacy** **AW** /'ædɪkwəsi/ *noun* [U]: *The adequacy of the security arrangements has been questioned.* 有人质疑安全措施是

否充分。OPP inadequacy **ad·equate·ly** AW *adv.*：*Are you adequately insured?* 你买够保险了吗？ OPP inadequately

ADHD /ˌeɪ diː eɪtʃ 'diː/ *abbr.* ATTENTION DEFICIT HYPERACTIVITY DISORDER 注意缺陷障碍（伴多动）；儿童多动症

ad·here /əd'hɪə(r); *NAmE* əd'hɪr/ *verb* [I] ~ (**to sth**) (*formal*) to stick firmly to sth 黏附；附着：*Once in the bloodstream, the bacteria adhere to the surface of the red cells.* 细菌一进入血液里，就附着在红细胞表面上。

PHR V **ad'here to sth** (*formal*) to behave according to a particular law, rule, set of instructions, etc.; to follow a particular set of beliefs or a fixed way of doing sth 坚持，遵守，遵循（法律、规章、指示、信念等）：*For ten months he adhered to a strict no-fat low-salt diet.* 十个月来他严格坚持无脂肪少盐饮食。◇ *She adheres to teaching methods she learned over 30 years ago.* 她依循她 30 多年前所学的教学法教学。

ad·her·ence /əd'hɪərəns; *NAmE* əd'hɪr-/ *noun* [U] (*formal*) the fact of behaving according to a particular rule, etc., or of following a particular set of beliefs, or a fixed way of doing sth 坚持；遵守；遵循：*strict adherence to the rules* 严格遵守规章制度

ad·her·ent /əd'hɪərənt; *NAmE* əd'hɪr-/ *noun* (*formal*) a person who supports a political party or set of ideas（政党、思想的）拥护者，追随者，信徒 SYN **supporter**

ad·he·sion /əd'hiːʒn/ *noun* [U] (*specialist*) the ability to stick or become attached to sth 黏附（力）；黏着（力）

ad·he·sive /əd'hiːsɪv; -'hiːz-/ *noun, adj.*

■ ***noun*** [C, U] a substance that you use to make things stick together 黏合剂；黏着剂

■ ***adj.*** that can stick to sth 黏合的；黏附的；有附着力的 SYN **sticky**：*adhesive tape* 黏胶带 ➲ SEE ALSO SELF-ADHESIVE

ad hoc /ˌæd 'hɒk; *NAmE* 'hɑːk/ *adj.* (*from Latin*) arranged or happening when necessary and not planned in advance 临时安排的；特别的；专门的：*an ad hoc meeting to deal with the problem* 处理此问题的特别会议 ◇ *The meetings will be held **on an ad hoc basis**.* 会议将根据需要随时举行。▸ **ad hoc** *adv.*

ad hom·in·em /ˌæd 'hɒmɪnem; *NAmE* 'hɑːm-/ *adj., adv.* (*formal*) directed against a person's character rather than their argument 针对个人（而非理据）的：*an ad hominem attack* 人身攻击

adieu /ə'djuː; *NAmE* ə'duː/ *exclamation* (*from French*) (*old use* or *literary*) goodbye 再见：*I bid you adieu.* 向你道别。

Adi Granth /ˌɑːdɪ 'grʌnt/ *noun* = GURU GRANTH SAHIB

ad in·fin·itum /ˌæd ˌɪnfɪ'naɪtəm/ *adv.* (*from Latin*) without ever coming to an end; again and again 无止境地；无休止地：*You cannot stay here ad infinitum without paying rent.* 你不付房租就不能一直住在这里。◇ *The problem would be repeated ad infinitum.* 这个问题会一再出现。

adi·pose /'ædɪpəʊs; -z; *NAmE* -poʊ-/ *adj.* (*specialist*) (of body TISSUE 身体组织) used for storing fat 用于贮存脂肪的

ad·ja·cent AW /ə'dʒeɪsnt/ *adj.* (of an area, a building, a room, etc. 地区、建筑、房间等) next to or near sth 与…毗连的；邻近的：*The planes landed on adjacent runways.* 这些飞机在毗连的跑道上降落。◇ ~ **to sth** *Our farm land was adjacent to the river.* 我们的农田在河边。

aˌdjacent 'angle *noun* (*geometry* 几何) one of the two angles formed on the same side of a straight line when another line meets it 邻角

ad·jec·tive /'ædʒɪktɪv/ *noun* (*grammar* 语法) a word that describes a person or thing, for example *big*, *red* and *clever* in *a big house*, *red wine* and *a clever idea* 形容词 ▸ **ad·jec·tival** /ˌædʒek'taɪvl/ *adj.*：*an adjectival phrase* 形容词短语 **ad·jec·tival·ly** /-'taɪvəli/ *adv.*：*In 'bread knife', the word 'bread' is used adjectivally.* 在词组 bread knife 中，bread 用作形容词。

ad·join /ə'dʒɔɪn/ *verb* [T, I] ~ (**sth**) (*formal*) to be next to or joined to sth 紧挨；邻接；毗连：*A barn adjoins the farmhouse.* 一座谷仓紧靠着农舍。▸ **ad·join·ing** *adj.* [usually before noun]：*They stayed in adjoining rooms.* 他们住的房间紧挨着。◇ *We'll have more space if we knock down the adjoining wall* (= the wall between two rooms). 要是我们把这堵隔墙拆掉，就会有更大的空间。

ad·journ /ə'dʒɜːn; *NAmE* ə'dʒɜːrn/ *verb* [I, T, often passive] (*formal*) to stop a meeting or an official process, especially a trial, for a period of time 休庭；休会；延期：*The court adjourned for lunch.* 午餐时间法庭休庭。◇ ~ **sth** *The trial has been adjourned until next week.* 审判延期至下周。▸ **ad·journ·ment** *noun* [C, U]：*The judge granted us a short adjournment.* 法官允许我们暂时休庭。

PHR V **ad'journ to…** (*formal* or *humorous*) to go to another place, especially in order to relax（尤指为了休息放松）到别处，换地方

ad·judge /ə'dʒʌdʒ/ *verb* [usually passive] (*formal*) to make a decision about sb/sth based on the facts that are available 宣判；裁决；判定：~ **sth + adj.** *The company was adjudged bankrupt.* 该公司被宣判破产。◇ ~ **sth + noun** *The tour was adjudged a success.* 这次出行被认为是成功的。◇ **sth is adjudged to be, have, etc. sth** *The reforms were generally adjudged to have failed.* 人们普遍认为，改革已经失败。

ad·ju·di·cate /ə'dʒuːdɪkeɪt/ *verb* **1** [I, T] to make an official decision about who is right in a disagreement between two groups or organizations 判决，裁决（争执等）：~ (**on/upon/in sth**) *A special subcommittee adjudicates on planning applications.* 有一个特别小组委员会裁决规划申请项目。◇ ~ (**sth**) (**between A and B**) *Their purpose is to adjudicate disputes between employers and employees.* 他们的目的是裁决雇主与雇员之间的纠纷。 **2** [I] to be a judge in a competition （比赛中）裁判，评判：*Who is adjudicating at this year's contest?* 今年比赛谁当裁判？▸ **ad·ju·di·ca·tion** /əˌdʒuːdɪ'keɪʃn/ *noun* [U, C]：*The case was referred to a higher court for adjudication.* 该案件已提交上级法院裁决。 **ad·ju·di·ca·tor** *noun*：*You may refer your complaint to an independent adjudicator.* 你可以向独立裁判投诉。

ad·junct /'ædʒʌŋkt/ *noun* **1** (*grammar* 语法) an adverb or a phrase that adds meaning to the verb in a sentence or part of a sentence 附加语；修饰成分：*In 'She went home yesterday' and 'He ran away in a panic', 'yesterday' and 'in a panic' are adjuncts.* 在 She went home yesterday 和 He ran away in a panic 两句中，yesterday 和 in a panic 是修饰成分。 **2** (*formal*) a thing that is added or attached to sth larger or more important 附属物；附件：*The memory expansion cards are useful adjuncts to the computer.* 内存扩展卡是计算机很有用的附件。

ad·jure /ə'dʒʊə(r); *NAmE* ə'dʒʊr/ *verb* ~ **sb to do sth** (*formal*) to ask or to order sb to do sth 要求；命令：*He adjured them to tell the truth.* 他要求他们讲真话。

ad·just AW /ə'dʒʌst/ *verb* **1** [T] to change sth slightly to make it more suitable for a new set of conditions or to make it work better 调整；调节：~ **sth** *Watch out for sharp bends and adjust your speed accordingly.* 当心急转弯并相应调整车速。◇ *This button is for adjusting the volume.* 这个按钮是调节音量的。◇ ~ **sth to sth** *Adjust your language to the age of your audience.* 要根据听众的年龄使用相应的语言。 **2** [I, T] to get used to a new situation by changing the way you behave and/or think 适应；习惯 SYN **adapt**：*They'll be fine—they just need time to adjust.* 他们会好起来的，只是需要时间来适应。◇ ~ **to sth** *After a while his eyes adjusted to the dark.* 过了一会儿他的眼睛习惯了黑暗。◇ ~ **to doing sth** *It took her a while to adjust to living alone.* 她过了一段时间才适应独自生活。◇ ~ **yourself to sth** *You'll quickly adjust yourself to student life.* 你将很快适应学生生活。 **3** [T] ~ **sth** to move sth slightly so that it looks neater or feels more comfortable 整理：*He smoothed his hair and adjusted his tie.* 他捋平头发，整了整领带。➲ SEE ALSO WELL ADJUSTED

A

ad·just·able /əˈdʒʌstəbl/ *adj.* that can be moved to different positions or changed in shape or size 可调整的；可调节的：*adjustable seat belts* 可调节的安全带 ◊ *The height of the bicycle seat is adjustable.* 这辆自行车车座的高度可以调节。

adˌjustable ˈspanner (*BrE*) (*also* **ˈmonkey wrench** *NAmE, BrE*) *noun* a tool that can be adjusted to hold and turn things of different widths 活动扳手 ➲ VISUAL VOCAB PAGE V21 ➲ COMPARE SPANNER, WRENCH *n.* (1)

ad·just·ment AW /əˈdʒʌstmənt/ *noun* [C, U] **1** a small change made to sth in order to correct or improve it 调整；调节：*I've made a few adjustments to the design.* 我已对设计作了几处调整。◊ *Some adjustment of the lens may be necessary.* 可能需要调整一下镜头。 **2** a change in the way a person behaves or thinks （行为、思想的）调整，适应：*She went through a period of emotional adjustment after her marriage broke up.* 婚姻破裂后，她熬过了一段感情调整期。

ad·ju·tant /ˈædʒʊtənt/ *noun* an army officer who does office work and helps other officers 副官

ˌAdjutant ˈGeneral *noun* (*pl.* **Adjutants General**) **1** an officer of very high rank in the British army who is responsible for organization （英国陆军）副官长 **2** the officer of very high rank in the US army who is in charge of organization （美国陆军）官长，署长

ad-lib /ˌæd ˈlɪb/ *verb* (**-bb-**) [I, T] to say sth in a speech or a performance that you have not prepared or practised 即席讲话；即兴表演 SYN **improvise**：*She abandoned her script and began ad-libbing.* 她抛开脚本即兴表演起来。◊ **~ sth** *I lost my notes and had to ad-lib the whole speech.* 我把讲稿弄丢了，只好临时说了一通。 ▶ **ad lib** *noun*：*The speech was full of ad libs.* 讲话中满是即兴之词。 **ad lib** *adj.*：*an ad lib speech* 即兴演讲 **ad lib** *adv.*：*She delivered her lines ad lib.* 她的台词是即兴说出的。

adman /ˈædmæn/ *noun* (*pl.* **-men** /-men/) (*informal*) a person who works in advertising 广告人；广告从业人员

admin /ˈædmɪn/ *noun* [U] (*informal*) = ADMINISTRATION (1)：*a few admin problems* 一些行政问题 ◊ *She works in admin.* 她在行政部门工作。

ad·min·is·ter /ədˈmɪnɪstə(r)/ *verb* **1** [often passive] **~ sth** to manage and organize the affairs of a company, an organization, a country, etc. 管理（公司、组织、机构等）；治理（国家） SYN **manage**：*to administer a charity/fund/school* 管理一家慈善机构 / 一项基金 / 一所学校 ◊ *The pension funds are administered by commercial banks.* 养老基金由商业银行管理。 **2 ~ sth** to make sure that sth is done fairly and in the correct way 施行；执行：*to* ***administer justice/the law*** 司法；执法 ◊ *The questionnaire was administered by trained interviewers.* 问卷调查是由经过训练的采访人员负责执行的。 **3 ~ sth (to sb)** (*formal*) to give or to provide sth, especially in a formal way 给予；提供：*The teacher has the authority to administer punishment.* 老师有权处罚。 **4** [often passive] (*formal*) to give drugs, medicine, etc. to sb 给予，施用（药物等）：**~ sth** *Police believe his wife could not have administered the poison.* 警方认为他的妻子是不可能下毒的。◊ **~ sth to sb** *The dose was administered to the child intravenously.* 已给那孩子静脉注射了一剂药物。 ➲ WORDFINDER NOTE AT MEDICINE **5 ~ a kick, a punch, etc. (to sb/sth)** (*formal*) to kick or to hit sb/sth 踢；打：*He administered a severe blow to his opponent's head.* 他朝着对手的头部狠狠打了一拳。

ad·min·is·tra·tion AW /ədˌmɪnɪˈstreɪʃn/ *noun* **1** (*also informal* **admin**) [U] the activities that are done in order to plan, organize and run a business, school or other institution （企业、学校等的）管理，行政：*Administration costs are passed on to the customer.* 行政费用转嫁给了消费者。◊ *the day-to-day administration of a company* 公司的日常管理工作 ◊ *I work in the Sales Administration department.* 我在销售管理部门工作。 **2** [U] the process or act of organizing the way that sth is done 施行；执行：*the administration of justice* 司法 **3** [C] the people who plan, organize and run a business, an institution, etc. （企业、学校等的）管理部门，行政部门：*university administrations* 大学行政部门 **4** (*often* **Administration**) [C] the government of a country, especially the US （尤指美国）政府：*the Obama administration* 奥巴马政府 ◊ *Successive administrations have failed to solve the country's economic problems.* 一届又一届政府均未能解决这个国家的经济问题。 **5** [U] (*formal*) the act of giving a drug to sb （药物的）施用：*the administration of antibiotics* 施用抗生素 **6** [U] (*BrE, AustralE, law* 律) a situation in which the financial affairs of a business that cannot pay its debts are managed by an independent administrator 行政接管（公司破产时由独立管理人负责其运营）：*If it cannot find extra funds, the company will* ***go into administration.*** 如果公司筹不到额外资金就将进入行政接管程序。 ➲ COMPARE CHAPTER 11

ad·min·is·tra·tive AW /ədˈmɪnɪstrətɪv; *NAmE* -streɪtɪv/ *adj.* connected with organizing the work of a business or an institution 管理的；行政的：*an* ***administrative job/assistant/error*** 管理工作；行政助理；管理上的错误 ➲ WORDFINDER NOTE AT WORK ▶ **ad·min·is·tra·tive·ly** AW *adv.*

ad·min·is·tra·tor AW /ədˈmɪnɪstreɪtə(r)/ *noun* a person whose job is to manage and organize the public or business affairs of a company or an institution, or a person who works in an office dealing with records, accounts, etc. （公司、机构的）管理人员，行政人员：*a hospital administrator* 医院管理人员 ◊ *For an application form, please contact our administrator.* 请联系我们的行政人员索要申请表。

ad·mir·able /ˈædmərəbl/ *adj.* (*formal*) having qualities that you admire and respect 可钦佩的；值得赞赏的；令人羡慕的 SYN **commendable**：*Her dedication to her work was admirable.* 她对工作的奉献精神可钦可佩。◊ *He made his points with admirable clarity.* 他阐述观点明确，值得赞赏。 ▶ **ad·mir·ably** /-əbli/ *adv.*：*Joe coped admirably with a difficult situation.* 乔面对困境应付裕如。

ad·miral /ˈædmərəl/ *noun* an officer of very high rank in the navy 海军将官；海军上将；舰队司令：*The admiral visited the ships under his command.* 舰队司令视察了他所统率的军舰。◊ *Admiral Lord Nelson* 海军上将纳尔逊勋爵 ➲ WORDFINDER NOTE AT NAVY ➲ SEE ALSO REAR ADMIRAL, RED ADMIRAL

ˌAdmiral of the ˈFleet (*BrE*) (*US* **ˈFleet Admiral**) *noun* an admiral of the highest rank in the navy （英国）海军元帅；（美国）海军五星上将

the Ad·mir·alty /ˈædmərəlti/ *noun* [sing.+sing./pl. v.] (in Britain in the past) the government department controlling the navy （英国旧时）海军部

ad·mir·ation 🔑 /ˌædməˈreɪʃn/ *noun* [U] a feeling of respect and liking for sb/sth 钦佩；赞赏；羡慕：*to* ***watch/gaze in admiration*** 赞赏地观看 / 凝视着 ◊ **~ for sb/sth** *I have great admiration for her as a writer.* 我十分钦佩她这个作家。

ad·mire 🔑 /ədˈmaɪə(r)/ *verb* **1** 🔑 to respect sb for what they have done or to respect their qualities 钦佩；赞赏；仰慕：**~ sb/sth** *I really admire your enthusiasm.* 我确实钦佩你的热情。◊ *You have to* ***admire the way*** *he handled the situation.* 你不得不佩服他处理这个局面的手段。◊ **~ sb/sth for sth** *The school is widely admired for its excellent teaching.* 这所学校教学优秀，远近称誉。◊ **~ sb for doing sth** *I don't agree with her, but I admire her for sticking to her principles.* 我不同意她的意见，但是我赞赏她恪守原则。 **2** 🔑 **~ sth** to look at sth and think that it is attractive and/or impressive 欣赏：*He stood back to admire his handiwork.* 他退后几步欣赏他的手工制品。 ▶ **ad·mir·ing** *adj.*：*She was used to receiving admiring glances from men.* 她习惯了男人投来的赞赏目光。 **ad·mir·ing·ly** *adv.*

ad·mirer /ədˈmaɪərə(r)/ *noun* **1 ~ of sb/sth** a person who admires sb/sth, especially a well-known person or thing 钦佩者；赞赏者：*He is a great admirer of Picasso's early paintings.* 他十分赞赏毕加索的早期画作。 **2** a man who is attracted to a woman and admires her 追求者，爱慕者（指爱慕女人的男人）： *She never married but had many admirers.* 她从未结婚，不过追求者不少。

ad·mis·sible /ədˈmɪsəbl/ *adj.* that can be allowed or accepted, especially in court（尤指法庭）可接受的，受理的 OPP **inadmissible** ▸ **ad·mis·si·bil·ity** /ədˌmɪsəˈbɪləti/ *noun* [U]

ad·mis·sion /ədˈmɪʃn/ *noun* **1** [U, C] the act of accepting sb into an institution, organization, etc.; the right to enter a place or to join an institution or organization（机构、组织等的）准许加入，加入权，进入权： *Hospital admission is not necessary in most cases.* 大多数情况下，病人无须住院。◇ *Hospital admissions for asthma attacks have doubled.* 哮喘发作入院人次已成倍增加。◇ *the university* ***admissions policy/office*** 大学招生政策 / 招生办公室 ◇ *They tried to get into the club but were refused admission.* 他们试图进入俱乐部，但遭到了拒绝。◇ *She failed to* ***gain admission*** *to the university of her choice.* 她未被自己选择的大学录取。◇ **~ to sth** *countries applying for admission to the European Union* 申请加入欧洲联盟的国家 ◇ *Last admissions to the park are at 4 p.m.* 公园最晚的入园时间是下午 4 点。 **2** [C] a statement in which sb admits that sth is true, especially sth wrong or bad that they have done（尤指对过错、罪行的）承认，招认，招供： *He is a thief* ***by his own admission*** (= he has admitted it). 他自己供认是小偷。◇ **~ of sth** *an* ***admission of guilt/failure/defeat*** 承认有罪 / 失败 / 被击败 ◇ **~ that...** *The minister's resignation was an admission that she had lied.* 这位部长辞职等于承认她自己撒过谎。 **3** [U] the amount of money that you pay to go into a building or to an event 入场费；门票费： ***admission charges/prices*** 入场费 ◇ *£5 admission* 入场费 5 英镑 ◇ *What's the admission?* 门票多少钱？

admit /ədˈmɪt/ *verb* (**-tt-**)

• **ACCEPT TRUTH** 承认事实 **1** [I, T] **~ (to sb) (that...)** to agree, often unwillingly, that sth is true（常指勉强）承认 SYN **confess**: *It was a stupid thing to do, I admit.* 我承认，那次干的是件蠢事。◇ **+ speech** *'I'm very nervous,' she admitted reluctantly.* "我很紧张。"她勉强承认说。◇ **~ to sth** *Don't be afraid to admit to your mistakes.* 不要怕认错。◇ **~ to doing sth** *She admits to being strict with her children.* 她承认对自己的孩子很严厉。◇ **~ sth** *He admitted all his mistakes.* 他承认了全部错误。◇ *She stubbornly refuses to admit the truth.* 她顽固地拒不承认事实。◇ *Why don't you just* ***admit defeat*** (= recognize that you cannot do sth) *and let someone else try?* 你干吗不干脆承认自己不行，让别人来试试？◇ *Admit it! You were terrified!* 承认了吧！你吓坏了！◇ **~ (that)...** *They freely admit (that) they still have a lot to learn.* 他们坦率承认，他们要学的东西还很多。◇ ***You must admit that*** *it all sounds very strange.* 你必须承认这一切听起来很古怪。◇ **~ to sb that...** *I couldn't admit to my parents that I was finding the course difficult.* 我无法向父母实话实说，我觉得这门课程很难。◇ **be admitted that...** *It was generally admitted that the government had acted too quickly.* 普遍认为，政府行动过急。◇ **be admitted to be, have, etc. sth** *The appointment is now generally admitted to have been a mistake.* 现在公认那次任命是一个错误。

• **ACCEPT BLAME** 承认责任 **2** [I, T] to say that you have done sth wrong or illegal 承认（过错、罪行）；招认；招供 SYN **confess**: **~ to sth** *He refused to admit to the other charges.* 他拒不承认其他指控。◇ **~ to doing sth** *She admitted to having stolen the car.* 她供认偷了那辆轿车。◇ **~ sth** *She admitted theft.* 她招认了偷窃行为。◇ *He refused to admit his guilt.* 他拒不认罪。◇ **~ doing sth** *She admitted having driven the car without insurance.* 她供认驾驶了这辆没有保险的轿车。

• **ALLOW TO ENTER/JOIN** 准许进入 / 加入 **3** [T] (*formal*) to allow sb/sth to enter a place 准许…进入（某处）： **~ sb/sth** *Each ticket admits one adult.* 每张票只准许一位成人入场。◇ **~ sb/sth to/into sth** *You will not be admitted to the theatre after the performance has started.* 演出开始后不许进入剧场。◇ *The narrow windows admit little light into the room.* 窗户狭窄，只有少量光线可以照进房间。 **4** [T] (*formal*) to allow sb to become a member of a club, a school or an organization 准许…加入（俱乐部、组织）；接收（入学）： **~ sb** *The society admits all US citizens over 21.* 凡 21 岁以上的美国公民均可加入该社团。◇ **~ sb to/into sth** *Women were only admitted into the club last year.* 这家俱乐部去年才接纳女会员。

• **TO HOSPITAL** 医院 **5** [T, often passive] **~ sb to/into a hospital, an institution, etc.** (*formal*) to take sb to a hospital, or other institution where they can receive special care 接收入院（或收容所等）；收治： *Two crash victims were admitted to the local hospital.* 两位车祸受害者已送进当地医院。 ➲ **WORDFINDER NOTE** AT HOSPITAL ➲ **MORE LIKE THIS** 36, page R29

PHR V **adˈmit of sth** (*formal*) to show that sth is possible or probable as a solution, an explanation, etc. 容许，有…可能（指解决办法、解释等）

▼ **SYNONYMS 同义词辨析**

admit

acknowledge • recognize • concede • confess

These words all mean to agree, often unwillingly, that sth is true. 以上各词均含承认之义，常指不情愿地承认某事属实。

admit to agree, often unwillingly, that sth is true 指承认（常指不情愿地承认某事属实）： *It was a stupid thing to do, I admit.* 我承认，那次干的是件蠢事。

acknowledge (*rather formal*) to accept that sth exists, is true or has happened 指承认某事物存在或属实： *She refuses to acknowledge the need for reform.* 她拒不承认改革的必要性。

recognize to admit or be aware that sth exists or is true 指承认、意识到： *They recognized the need to take the problem seriously.* 他们认识到需要严肃对待这个问题。

concede (*rather formal*) to admit, often unwillingly, that sth is true or logical 指承认（常指不情愿地承认某事属实或合乎逻辑）： *He was forced to concede (that) there might be difficulties.* 他被迫承认可能有困难。

ADMIT OR CONCEDE? 用 admit 还是 concede?

When sb **admits** sth, they are usually agreeing that sth which is generally considered bad or wrong is true or has happened, especially when it relates to their own actions. When sb **concedes** sth, they are usually accepting, unwillingly, that a particular fact or statement is true or logical. * admit 通常指承认普遍认为不好或错误的事情属实或确实发生过，尤指与自己行为有关。concede 通常指勉强承认某事属实或某种说法合乎逻辑。

confess (*rather formal*) to admit sth that you feel ashamed or embarrassed about 指承认自己感到羞愧或尴尬的事： *She was reluctant to confess her ignorance.* 她不愿意承认自己无知。

PATTERNS

- to admit/acknowledge/recognize/concede/confess **that...**
- to admit/confess **to sth**
- to admit/concede/confess sth **to sb**
- to admit/acknowledge/recognize **the truth**
- to admit/confess your **mistakes/ignorance**

ad·mit·tance /ədˈmɪtns/ *noun* [U] (*formal*) the right to enter or the act of entering a building, an institution, etc.（建筑物、机构等的）进入权，进入： *Hundreds of people were unable to* ***gain admittance*** *to the hall.* 数以百计的人未能获准进入大厅。

ad·mit·ted·ly /ədˈmɪtɪdli/ *adv.* used, especially at the beginning of a sentence, when you are accepting that sth is true（尤用于句首）诚然，无可否认： *Admittedly, it is rather expensive but you don't need to use much.* 它的确很贵，但不需要用得很多。

ad·mix·ture /ədˈmɪkstʃə(r)/ *noun* (*formal*) **1** a mixture 混合；掺和： *an admixture of aggression and creativity* 进取精神和创意的结合 **2** something, especially a small amount of sth, that is mixed with sth else 掺入物：*a French-speaking region with an admixture of German speakers* 掺杂说德语的人的法语地区

ad·mon·ish /əd'mɒnɪʃ; *NAmE* -'mɑːn-/ *verb* (*formal*) **1 ~ sb (for sth/for doing sth) | + speech** to tell sb firmly that you do not approve of sth that they have done 责备；告诫；警告 **SYN reprove**：*She was admonished for chewing gum in class.* 她在课堂上嚼口香糖，受到了告诫。 **2 ~ sb (to do sth)** to strongly advise sb to do sth 力劝；忠告：*A warning voice admonished him not to let this happen.* 他耳边响起警钟，警告他别让这种事情发生。

ad·mon·ition /ˌædmə'nɪʃn/ (*also less frequent* **ad·mon·ish·ment** /əd'mɒnɪʃmənt; *NAmE* -'mɑːn-/) *noun* [C, U] (*formal*) a warning to sb about their behaviour 警告；告诫 ▶ **ad·moni·tory** /əd'mɒnɪtri; *NAmE* -'mɑːn-/ *adj.*

ad nau·seam /ˌæd 'nɔːziæm/ *adv.* (*from Latin*) if a person says or does sth **ad nauseam**, they say or do it again and again so that it becomes boring or annoying 令人厌烦地：*Sports commentators repeat the same phrases ad nauseam.* 体育解说员翻来覆去说着同样的词语，真叫人腻烦。

ado /ə'duː/ *noun*

IDM **without further/more ado** (*old-fashioned*) without delaying; immediately 毫不迟延；干脆；立即

adobe /ə'dəʊbi; *NAmE* ə'doʊbi/ *noun* [U] mud that is dried in the sun, mixed with STRAW and used as a building material （建筑用）黏土；黏土坯

ado·les·cence /ˌædə'lesns/ *noun* [U] the time in a person's life when he or she develops from a child into an adult 青春期；青春 **SYN puberty** ➲ COLLOCATIONS AT AGE

ado·les·cent /ˌædə'lesnt/ *noun* a young person who is developing from a child into an adult 青少年：*adolescents between the ages of 13 and 18 and the problems they face* * 13 至 18 岁的青少年以及他们面临的问题 ➲ WORDFINDER NOTE AT AGE, YOUNG ▶ **ado·les·cent** *adj.*：*adolescent boys/girls/experiences* 青春期的男孩 / 女孩 / 经历

Ado·nis /ə'dəʊnɪs; *NAmE* ə'doʊ-/ *noun* an extremely attractive young man 英俊青年 **ORIGIN** From the name of the beautiful young man in ancient Greek myths, who was loved by both Aphrodite and Persephone. He was killed by a wild boar but Zeus ordered that he should spend the winter months in the underworld with Persephone and the summer months with Aphrodite. 源自希腊神话中的美少年阿多尼斯之名，他同时为阿佛洛狄忒和珀耳塞福涅所爱。被野猪咬死后，宙斯命其在阴间和珀耳塞福涅一起度过冬季，和阿佛洛狄忒一起度过夏季。

adopt 🔑 /ə'dɒpt; *NAmE* ə'dɑːpt/ *verb*

• **CHILD** 小孩 **1** 🔑 [I, T] to take sb else's child into your family and become its legal parent(s) 收养；领养：*a campaign to encourage childless couples to adopt* 鼓励无子女夫妇领养孩子的运动 ◇ **~ sb** *to adopt a child* 领养孩子 ◇ *She was forced to have her baby adopted.* 她被迫把婴儿给人收养。 ➲ COMPARE FOSTER *v.* (2) ➲ COLLOCATIONS AT CHILD ➲ WORDFINDER NOTE AT FAMILY

• **METHOD** 方法 **2** 🔑 [T] **~ sth** to start to use a particular method or to show a particular attitude towards sb/sth 采用（某方法）；采取（某态度）：*All three teams adopted different approaches to the problem.* 三个队处理这个问题的方法各不相同。

• **SUGGESTION** 建议 **3** 🔑 [T] **~ sth** to formally accept a suggestion or policy by voting 正式通过，表决采纳（建议、政策等）：*to adopt a resolution* 通过一项决议 ◇ *The council is expected to adopt the new policy at its next meeting.* 委员会有望在下次会议上正式通过这项新政策。

• **NEW NAME/COUNTRY** 新名字 / 国家 **4** [T] **~ sth** to choose a new name, a country, a custom, etc. and begin to use it as your own 选用（名字等）；移居（某国）；承袭（风俗）：***to adopt a name/title/language*** 取名；袭用头衔；采用某语言 ◇ *Early Christians in Europe adopted many of the practices of the older, pagan religions.* 欧洲早期的基督教徒承袭了更古老的一些异教的许多习俗。

• **WAY OF BEHAVING** 行为方式 **5** [T] **sth** (*formal*) to use a particular manner, way of speaking, expression, etc. 采用（某种举止、说话方式等）：*He adopted an air of indifference.* 他摆出一副满不在乎的样子。

• **CANDIDATE** 候选人 **6** [T] **~ sb (as sth)** (*BrE, politics* 政) to choose sb as a candidate in an election or as a representative 选定，选举（某人为候选人或代表）：*She was adopted as parliamentary candidate for Wood Green.* 她被推举为伍德格林选区的议员候选人。

adopt·ed /ə'dɒptɪd; *NAmE* ə'dɑːp-/ *adj.* **1** an **adopted** child has legally become part of a family which is not the one in which he or she was born 收养的；领养的：*Danny is their adopted son.* 丹尼是他们的养子。 **2** an **adopted** country is one in which sb chooses to live although it is not the one they were born in 所选择居住的；移居的

adop·ter /ə'dɒptə(r); *NAmE* ə'dɑːp-/ *noun* **1** a person who adopts a child 收养者 **2** a person who starts using a new technology（新技术）采用者：***early/late adopters*** *of social media* 早期 / 后来使用社交媒体的人

adop·tion /ə'dɒpʃn; *NAmE* ə'dɑːpʃn/ *noun* **1** [U, C] the act of adopting a child 收养；领养：*She put the baby up for adoption.* 她提出要让人收养那个婴儿。 ➲ COLLOCATIONS AT CHILD **2** [U] the decision to start using sth such as an idea, a plan or a name（想法、计划、名字等的）采用：*the adoption of new technology* 新技术的采用 **3** [U, C] (*BrE, politics* 政) the act of choosing sb as a candidate for an election（候选人的）选定，推选，推举：*his adoption as the Labour candidate* 他被选定为工党候选人

adop·tive /ə'dɒptɪv; *NAmE* ə'dɑːp-/ *adj.* [usually before noun] an **adoptive** parent or family is one that has legally adopted a child 收养的；有收养关系的

ador·able /ə'dɔːrəbl/ *adj.* very attractive and easy to feel love for 可爱的；讨人喜爱的：*What an adorable child!* 多可爱的小孩呀！ ▶ **ador·ably** /-əbli/ *adv.*

ad·or·ation /ˌædə'reɪʃn/ *noun* [U] a feeling of great love or worship 热爱；爱慕；敬慕；崇拜：*He gazed at her with pure adoration.* 他一往情深地注视着她。 ◇ *The painting is called 'Adoration of the Infant Christ'.* 这幅画叫做《朝拜耶稣圣婴》。

adore /ə'dɔː(r)/ *verb* (not used in the progressive tenses 不用于进行时) **1 ~ sb** to love sb very much 热爱，爱慕（某人）：*It's obvious that she adores him.* 她显然深深地爱着他。 ➲ SYNONYMS AT LOVE **2** (*informal*) to like sth very much 喜爱，热爱（某事物）：**~ sth** *I simply adore his music!* 我简直太喜爱他的音乐了！ ◇ **~ doing sth** *She adores working with children.* 她热爱参与儿童工作。 ➲ SYNONYMS AT LIKE

ador·ing /ə'dɔːrɪŋ/ *adj.* [usually before noun] showing much love and admiration 热爱的；爱慕的；敬慕的；崇拜的 ▶ **ador·ing·ly** *adv.*

adorn /ə'dɔːn; *NAmE* ə'dɔːrn/ *verb* [often passive] (*formal*) to make sth/sb look more attractive by decorating it or them with sth 装饰；装扮：**~ sth/sb** *Gold rings adorned his fingers.* 他的手指上戴着几枚金戒指。 ◇ (*ironic*) *Graffiti adorned the walls.* 这些墙遭到乱画乱涂。 ◇ **~ sth/sb/yourself with sth** *The walls were adorned with paintings.* 墙上装饰了绘画。 ◇ *The children adorned themselves with flowers.* 孩子们佩戴着鲜花。 ▶ **adorn·ment** *noun* [U, C]：*A plain necklace was her only adornment.* 她身上的饰物就只有一串简单的项链。

ad·renal gland /ə'driːnl glænd/ *noun* either of the two small organs above the KIDNEYS that produce adrenaline and other HORMONES 肾上腺

adrena·line (*also* **adrena·lin**) /ə'drenəlɪn/ *noun* [U] a substance produced in the body when you are excited, afraid or angry. It makes the heart beat faster and increases your energy and ability to move quickly. 肾上腺素（能使心跳加速、精力充沛、行动迅速）：*The excitement at the start of a race can really* ***get the adrenaline***

flowing. 比赛起点的兴奋确实能使人热血沸腾。 ➲ WORDFINDER NOTE AT ADVENTURE

adrift /əˈdrɪft/ *adj.* [not before noun] **1** if a boat or a person in a boat is **adrift**, the boat is not tied to anything or is floating without being controlled by anyone 漂浮；漂流： *The survivors were adrift in a lifeboat for six days.* 幸存者在救生艇上漂流了六天。 **2** (of a person 人) feeling alone and without a direction or an aim in life 漫无目的；随波逐流；漂泊无依： *young people adrift in the big city* 在大城市四处漂泊的年轻人 **3** no longer attached or fixed in the right position 脱开；松开： *I nearly suffocated when the pipe on my breathing apparatus* ***came adrift.*** 我的呼吸器上的管子脱落时，我差一点窒息。 ◇ (*figurative*) *She had been* ***cut adrift*** *from everything she had known.* 她曾被迫与她熟悉的一切切断关系。 ◇ (*figurative*) *Our plans had gone badly adrift.* 我们的计划已严重受挫。 **4** ~ (**of sb/sth**) (*especially BrE*) (in sport 体育运动) behind the score or position of your opponents 分数落后；排名在后： *The team are now just six points adrift of the leaders.* 现在该队得分比领先的队只落后六分。

IDM **cast/set sb adrift** [usually passive] to leave sb to be carried away on a boat that is not being controlled by anyone 使漂流： (*figurative*) *Without language human beings are cast adrift.* 人无语言则茫然无依。

adroit /əˈdrɔɪt/ *adj.* (*formal*) skilful and clever, especially in dealing with people （尤指待人接物）精明的，干练的，机敏的 SYN **skilful**: *an adroit negotiator* 谈判老手 ▸ **adroit·ly** *adv.* **adroit·ness** *noun* [U]

ADSL /ˌeɪ diː es ˈel/ *abbr.* asymmetric digital subscriber line (a system for connecting a computer to the Internet using a telephone line) 不对称数字用户线（利用电话线上网）

ad·sorb /ədˈsɔːb; -ˈzɔːb; *NAmE* -ˈsɔːrb; -ˈzɔːrb/ *verb* ~ **sth** (*specialist*) if sth **adsorbs** a liquid, gas or other substance, it holds it on its surface 吸附（液体、气体等）： *The dye is adsorbed onto the fibre.* 染料已吸附在纤维上。

ADT /ˌeɪ diː ˈtiː/ *abbr.* ATLANTIC DAYLIGHT TIME 大西洋夏令时间

aduki /əˈduːki/ *noun* = ADZUKI

adu·la·tion /ˌædjuˈleɪʃn; *NAmE* ˌædʒəˈl-/ *noun* [U] (*formal*) admiration and praise, especially when this is greater than is necessary 称赞；吹捧；奉承 ▸ **adu·la·tory** /ˌædjuˈleɪtəri; *NAmE* ˈædʒələtɔːri/ *adj.*

adult 🔑 AW /ˈædʌlt; əˈdʌlt/ *noun, adj.*

■ ***noun*** **1** 🔑 a fully grown person who is legally responsible for their actions （法律上指能为自己的行为负责的）成年人 SYN **grown-up**²: *Children must be accompanied by an adult.* 儿童必须要有大人陪同。 ◇ *Why can't you two act like civilized adults?* 你们俩为什么就不能像有教养的成年人那样行事呢？ **2** 🔑 a fully grown animal 成年动物： *The fish return to the river as adults in order to breed.* 这种鱼长成以后回到河中产卵。

■ ***adj.*** **1** 🔑 fully grown or developed 成年的；发育成熟的： *preparing young people for adult life* 指导年轻人准备过成人生活 ◇ *the adult population* 成年人口 ◇ *adult monkeys* 长成的猴子 **2** behaving in an intelligent and responsible way; typical of what is expected of an adult （智力、思想、行为）成熟的，成人的 SYN **grown-up**¹: *When my parents split up, it was all very adult and open.* 我父母离异时，事情处理得很成熟、很开放。 **3** [only before noun] intended for adults only, because it is about sex or contains violence 仅限成人的（因有色情或暴力内容）： *an adult movie* 仅供成人观看的电影 ➲ SEE ALSO ADULTHOOD

ˌadult eduˈcation (*also* **conˌtinuing eduˈcation**) *noun* [U] education for adults that is available outside the formal education system, for example at evening classes 成人教育

adul·ter·ate /əˈdʌltəreɪt/ *verb* [often passive] ~ **sth** (**with sth**) to make food or drink less pure by adding another substance to it （在饮食中）掺杂，掺假 SYN **contaminate** ➲ SEE ALSO UNADULTERATED (2) ▸ **adul·ter·ation** /əˌdʌltəˈreɪʃn/ *noun* [U]

adul·ter·er /əˈdʌltərə(r)/ *noun* (*formal*) a person who commits adultery 通奸者；奸夫

adul·ter·ess /əˈdʌltərəs/ *noun* (*formal*) a woman who commits adultery 奸妇

adul·tery /əˈdʌltəri/ *noun* [U] sex between a married person and sb who is not their husband or wife 通奸： *He was accused of* ***committing adultery.*** 他被控通奸。 ▸ **adul·ter·ous** /əˈdʌltərəs/ *adj.*: *an adulterous relationship* 通奸关系

adult·hood AW /ˈædʌlthʊd; əˈdʌlt-/ *noun* [U] the state of being an adult 成年： *a child reaching adulthood* 已成年的孩子

ad·um·brate /ˈædəmbreɪt; *NAmE also* əˈdem-/ *verb* ~ **sth** (*formal*) to give a general idea or description of sth without details 概述；概括说明；勾画轮廓 SYN **outline**

ad·vance 🔑 /ədˈvɑːns; *NAmE* -ˈvæns/ *noun, verb, adj.*

■ ***noun***

• **FORWARD MOVEMENT** 向前移动 **1** 🔑 [C] the forward movement of a group of people, especially armed forces （尤指武装部队的）前进，行进： *We feared that an advance on the capital would soon follow.* 我们担心接下来会马上向首都推进。 ➲ COLLOCATIONS AT WAR

• **DEVELOPMENT** 发展 **2** 🔑 [C, U] ~ (**in sth**) progress or a development in a particular activity or area of understanding 进步；进展： *recent advances in medical science* 医学的最新进展 ◇ *We live in an age of rapid technological advance.* 我们生活在技术迅猛发展的时代。

• **MONEY** 金钱 **3** [C, usually sing.] money paid for work before it has been done or money paid earlier than expected 预付款： *They offered an advance of £5 000 after the signing of the contract.* 他们在合同签订后预付了 5 000 英镑。 ◇ *She asked for an advance on her salary.* 她要求预支薪金。

• **SEXUAL** 两性 **4** **advances** [pl.] attempts to start a sexual relationship with sb 勾引；求爱；追求： *He had* ***made advances*** *to one of his students.* 他曾追求过他的一个学生。

• **PRICE INCREASE** 涨价 **5** [C] ~ (**on sth**) (*business* 商) an increase in the price or value of sth （价格、价值的）上涨，提高： *Share prices showed significant advances.* 股票价格大幅上涨。

IDM **in advance** (**of sth**) **1** 🔑 before the time that is expected; before sth happens （时间上）在…前；预先；事先： *a week/month/year in advance* 提前一星期 / 一个月 / 一年 ◇ *It's cheaper if you book the tickets in advance.* 预订票要便宜一些。 ◇ *People were evacuated from the coastal regions in advance of the hurricane.* 飓风袭来之前，沿海地带的人已经撤离。 **2** more developed than sb/sth else （发展上）超前： *Galileo's ideas were well in advance of the age in which he lived.* 伽利略的思想远远超越了他所处的时代。

■ ***verb***

• **MOVE FORWARD** 向前移动 **1** 🔑 [I] to move forward towards sb/sth, often in order to attack or threaten them or it （为了进攻、威胁等）前进，行进： *The troops were finally given the order to advance.* 部队终于接到前进的命令。 ◇ *They had advanced 20 miles by nightfall.* 夜幕降临时，他们已推进了 20 英里。 ◇ *the advancing Allied troops* 节节挺进的盟军部队 ◇ ~ **on/towards sb/sth** *The mob advanced on us, shouting angrily.* 暴民愤怒地喊叫着向我们逼近。 ➲ COMPARE RETREAT *v.* (1)

• **DEVELOP** 发展 **2** 🔑 [I, T] if knowledge, technology, etc. **advances**, it develops and improves （知识、技术等）发展，进步： *Our knowledge of the disease has advanced considerably over recent years.* 近年来我们对这种疾病的了解深入多了。 ◇ ~ **sth** *This research has done much to advance our understanding of language learning.* 这项研究大大提高了我们对语言学习的认识。

• **HELP TO SUCCEED** 促进 **3** [T] to help sth to succeed 促进；推动 SYN **further**: *Studying for new qualifications is one way of advancing your career.* 为提高学历而进修是促进事业发展的一个办法。 ◇ *They worked together to advance the cause of democracy.* 他们合力推动民主事业。

A

• **MONEY** 金钱 **4** [T] to give sb money before the time it would usually be paid 预付： **~ sth to sb** *We are willing to advance the money to you.* 我们愿意预付款给你。◇ **~ sb sth** *We will advance you the money.* 我们将把款项预付给你。

• **SUGGEST** 建议 **5** [T] **~ sth** (*formal*) to suggest an idea, a theory, or a plan for other people to discuss 提出（想法、理论、计划） **SYN** **put forward**: *The article advances a new theory to explain changes in the climate.* 这篇文章提出了一个解释气候变化的新理论。

• **MAKE EARLIER** 提前 **6** [T] **~ sth** (*formal*) to change the time or date of an event so that it takes place earlier 提前；提早 **SYN** **bring forward**: *The date of the trial has been advanced by one week.* 审判日期提前了一星期。 **OPP** **postpone**

• **MOVE FORWARD** 向前移动 **7** [I, T] (*formal*) to move forward to a later part of sth; to move sth forward to a later part 向前推（至下一步）；（使）向前移动: *Users advance through the program by answering a series of questions.* 用户通过回答一系列问题，逐步完成整个程序。◇ **~ sth** *This button advances the hours and the red one advances the minutes in the display.* 在显示界面上，这个按键用来按小时快进，红色的那个键用来按分钟快进。

• **INCREASE** 增加 **8** [I] (*business* 商) (of prices, costs, etc. 价格、成本等) to increase in price or amount 上涨；增加: *Oil shares advanced amid economic recovery hopes.* 在一片经济复苏的希望中石油股票价格上涨。

■ ***adj.*** [only before noun] **1** done or given before sth is going to happen 预先的；事先的: *Please give us* ***advance warning*** *of any changes.* 如有变动，请事先通知我们。◇ *We need* ***advance notice*** *of the numbers involved.* 我们需要事先知道涉及的数量。◇ *No* ***advance booking*** *is necessary on most departures.* 大多数起程票无须预订。 **2 ~ party/team** a group of people who go somewhere first, before the main group 先遣队；先头部队

ad·vanced 🔑 /əd'vɑːnst; *NAmE* -'vænst/ *adj.* **1** 🔑 having the most modern and recently developed ideas, methods, etc. 先进的: *advanced technology* 先进技术 ◇ *advanced industrial societies* 先进的工业社会 **2** 🔑 (of a course of study 课程) at a high or difficult level 高级的；高等的: *There were only three of us on the advanced course.* 只有我们三人学高级课程。◇ *an advanced student of English* 高阶英语学生 **3** at a late stage of development (发展) 晚期的，后期的: *the advanced stages of the disease* 疾病晚期

IDM **of advanced 'years | sb's advanced 'age** used in polite expressions to describe sb as 'very old' 高龄；年事已高: *He was a man of advanced years.* 他年事已高。◇ (*humorous*) *Even at my advanced age I still know how to enjoy myself!* 我虽说是黄昏暮年，也还懂得如何找乐儿！

Ad,vanced 'Higher *noun* (in Scotland) an exam in a particular subject at a higher level than HIGHER, taken by some school students at the age of around 18 （苏格兰）学生高级进阶证书考试（应试年龄在 18 岁左右）

Ad'vanced Level *noun* = A LEVEL : *For this course, you need two GCE Advanced Level passes.* 要学习这个课程，需要通过普通教育证书两门学科的高级证书考试。

ad,vanced 'placement *noun* [U] (*abbr.* **AP**) an advanced course for high school students in the US by which students can gain college CREDITS before they actually go to college 先修课程，进阶课程（美国中学生在上大学前所修习以获得大学学分的课程）

ad'vance guard (*also* **ad'vanced guard**) *noun* [C+sing./pl. v.] a group of soldiers who go somewhere to make preparations before other soldiers arrive 先遣部队

ad·vance·ment /əd'vɑːnsmənt; *NAmE* -'væns-/ *noun* (*formal*) **1** [U, C] the process of helping sth to make progress or succeed; the progress that is made 促进；推动；发展；前进: *the* ***advancement of knowledge/education/science*** 知识 / 教育 / 科学的发展 **2** [U] progress in a job, social class, etc. （工作、社会阶级等的）提升，晋升: *There are good opportunities for advancement if you have the right skills.* 如果有合适的技能，就有很好的晋升机会。

ad·van·cing /əd'vɑːnsɪŋ; *NAmE* -'væns-/ *adj.* **~ years/age** used as a polite way of referring to the fact of time passing and of sb growing older 年事渐高: *She is still very active, in spite of her advancing years.* 她尽管年事渐高，仍然十分活跃。

ad·van·tage 🔑 /əd'vɑːntɪdʒ; *NAmE* -'væn-/ *noun, verb*

■ ***noun*** [C, U] **1** 🔑 a thing that helps you to be better or more successful than other people 有利条件；有利因素；优势: *a* ***big/great/definite advantage*** 大的 / 很大的 / 确定的优势 ◇ *an unfair advantage* (= sth that benefits you, but not your opponents) 不公平的有利因素（指有利于自己、但并不有利于对手）◇ *She* ***had the advantage of*** *a good education.* 她具有受过良好教育的有利条件。 ◇ *You will* ***be at an advantage*** (= have an advantage) *in the interview if you have thought about the questions in advance.* 如果你预先考虑过面试中提出的问题，就会处于优势。◇ **~ over sb** *Being tall gave him an advantage over the other players.* 他个子高，比其他运动员有利。 **OPP** **disadvantage** **2** 🔑 a quality of sth that makes it better or more useful 优点: *A small car* ***has the*** *added* ***advantage of*** *being cheaper to run.* 小型轿车还有一个优点是养护成本比较便宜。 ◇ *One advantage of/One of the advantages of living in the country is the fresh air.* 在乡下居住的一个好处就是空气清新。◇ *Each of these systems has its advantages and disadvantages.* 这些系统各有其优缺点。 **OPP** **disadvantage** **3** [U] (in TENNIS 网球) the first point scored after a score of 40–40（局末平分后）占先；优势分: *Advantage Murray.* 穆雷占先。

IDM **be/work to your ad'vantage** to give you an advantage; to change a situation in a way that gives you an advantage 对…有利: *It would be to your advantage to attend this meeting.* 参加这次会议会对你有利。◇ *Eventually, the new regulations will work to our advantage.* 新规章制度最终将对我们有利。 **take ad'vantage of sth/sb** **1** 🔑 to make use of sth well; to make use of an opportunity 利用；利用（机会）: *She took advantage of the children's absence to tidy their rooms.* 她趁孩子们不在时收拾了他们的房间。◇ *We* ***took full advantage of*** *the hotel facilities.* 我们充分享用了旅馆设施。 **2** 🔑 to make use of sb/sth in a way that is unfair or dishonest 欺骗；占…的便宜 **SYN** **exploit**: *He took advantage of my generosity* (= for example, by taking more than I had intended to give). 他利用我的慷慨占了便宜。 **to (good/best) ad'vantage** in a way that shows the best of sb/sth （十分 / 最）有效地，出色地；使优点突出: *The photograph showed him to advantage.* 他在这张照片中照得挺不错的。 **turn sth to your ad'vantage** to use or change a bad situation so that it helps you 使转为有利；变（不利）为有利；利用

■ ***verb*** **~ sb** (*formal*) to put sb in a better position than other people or than they were in before 使处于有利地位；有利于；有助于

ad·van·taged /əd'vɑːntɪdʒd; *NAmE* -'væn-/ *adj.* being in a good social or financial situation （在社会上或经济上）处于优越地位的: *We aim to improve opportunities for the less advantaged in society.* 我们的宗旨是为社会地位比较低下的人增加机会。 **OPP** **disadvantaged**

ad·van·ta·geous /,ædvən'teɪdʒəs/ *adj.* **~ (to sb)** good or useful in a particular situation 有利的；有好处的 **SYN** **beneficial**: *A free trade agreement would be advantageous to both countries.* 自由贸易协定对两国都会有利。 **OPP** **disadvantageous** ▶ **ad·van·ta·geous·ly** *adv.*

ad·vent /'ædvent/ *noun* **1** [sing.] **the ~ of sth/sb** the coming of an important event, person, invention, etc. （重要事件、人物、发明等的）出现，到来: *the advent of new technology* 新技术的出现 **2 Advent** [U] (in the Christian religion) the period of approximately four weeks before Christmas （基督教）降临节，将临节（圣诞节前的四个星期左右）

'Advent calendar *noun* a piece of stiff paper with a picture and 24 small doors with numbers on. Children open a door each day during Advent and find a picture or a piece of chocolate behind each one. 基督降临历（硬纸制成的儿童日历，上有门形开口，里面有图片或巧克力）

ad·ven·ti·tious /ˌædvenˈtɪʃəs/ *adj.* (*formal*) happening by accident; not planned 偶然发生的；非计划中的

ad·ven·ture /ədˈventʃə(r)/ *noun* **1** [C] an unusual, exciting or dangerous experience, journey or series of events 冒险；冒险经历；奇遇：*her adventures travelling in Africa* 她在非洲旅行时的冒险经历 ◇ *When you're a child, life is one big adventure.* 孩提时代的生活充满新奇刺激。◇ *adventure stories* 历险故事 **2** [U] excitement and the willingness to take risks, try new ideas, etc. 冒险的刺激；大胆开拓：*a* ***sense/spirit of adventure*** 冒险意识 / 精神

> **WORDFINDER** 联想词：adrenaline, attempt, challenge, enthusiasm, escapade, **explore**, excitement, kick, thrill

adˈventure game *noun* a type of computer game in which you play a part in an adventure （电脑）涉险游戏，冒险游戏

adˌventure ˈplayground *noun* (*BrE*) an area where children can play, with large structures, ropes, etc. for climbing on 奇遇游乐场，冒险乐园（有大型结构、绳子等，供儿童玩耍攀登）

ad·ven·turer /ədˈventʃərə(r)/ *noun* **1** (*old-fashioned*) a person who enjoys exciting new experiences, especially going to unusual places 冒险者；冒险家 **2** (*often disapproving*) a person who is willing to take risks or act in a dishonest way in order to gain money or power 投机分子

ad·ven·ture·some /ədˈventʃəsəm; *NAmE* -tʃərs-/ *adj.* (*NAmE*) = ADVENTUROUS (1)

ad·ven·tur·ess /ədˈventʃəres/ *noun* **1** (*old-fashioned*) a woman who enjoys exciting new experiences, especially going to unusual places 女冒险家 **2** (*often disapproving*) a woman who is willing to take risks or act in a dishonest way in order to gain money or power 女投机分子

ad·ven·tur·ism /ədˈventʃərɪzəm/ *noun* [U] (*disapproving*) a willingness to take risks in business or politics in order to gain sth for yourself （企业、政治等方面）冒险主义

ad·ven·tur·ous /ədˈventʃərəs/ *adj.* **1** (*NAmE also* **ad·ven·ture·some**) (of a person 人) willing to take risks and try new ideas; enjoying being in new, exciting situations 有冒险精神的；大胆开拓的：*For the more adventurous tourists, there are trips into the mountains with a local guide.* 对更愿猎奇探险的旅游者，有本地向导带领进山游览。◇ *Many teachers would like to be more adventurous and creative.* 许多教师愿意更加进取，更富创造性。 **2** including new and interesting things, methods and ideas （指事物、方法、思想）新奇的：*The menu contained traditional favourites as well as more adventurous dishes.* 这份菜单有受欢迎的传统菜，也有较为新奇的菜肴。 **3** full of new, exciting or dangerous experiences 充满新鲜事物的；刺激不断的；惊险的：*an* ***adventurous trip/lifestyle*** 惊险的旅行；充满刺激的生活方式 OPP **unadventurous** ▶ **ad·ven·tur·ous·ly** *adv.*

ad·verb /ˈædvɜːb; *NAmE* -vɜːrb/ *noun* (*grammar* 语法) a word that adds more information about place, time, manner, cause or degree to a verb, an adjective, a phrase or another adverb 副词：*In 'speak kindly', 'incredibly deep', 'just in time' and 'too quickly', 'kindly', 'incredibly', 'just' and 'too' are all adverbs.* 在 speak kindly、incredibly deep、just in time 和 too quickly 四个短语中，kindly、incredibly、just 和 too 都是副词。 ➲ SEE ALSO SENTENCE ADVERB ▶ **ad·ver·bial** /ædˈvɜːbiəl; *NAmE* -ˈvɜːrb-/ *adj.*：*'Very quickly indeed' is an adverbial phrase.* * very quickly indeed 是副词短语。

adˌverbial ˈparticle *noun* (*grammar* 语法) an adverb used especially after a verb to show position, direction of movement, etc. 副词小词，副词小品词（尤用于动词后，表示位置、运动方向等）：*In 'come back', 'break down' and 'fall off', 'back', 'down' and 'off' are all adverbial particles.* 在 come back、break down 和 fall off 中，back、down 和 off 都是副词小词。

ad·ver·sar·ial /ˌædvəˈseəriəl; *NAmE* -vərˈseriəl/ *adj.* (*formal* or *specialist*) (especially of political or legal systems 尤指政治或法律制度) involving people who are in opposition and who make attacks on each other 对立的；敌对的：*the adversarial nature of the two-party system* 两党制的对抗本质 ◇ *an adversarial system of justice* 诉讼抗辩制

ad·ver·sary /ˈædvəsəri; *NAmE* -vərseri/ *noun* (*pl.* **-ies**) (*formal*) a person that sb is opposed to and competing with in an argument or a battle （辩论、战斗中的）敌手，对手 SYN **opponent**

ad·verse /ˈædvɜːs; ədˈvɜːs; *NAmE* -vɜːrs/ *adj.* [usually before noun] negative and unpleasant; not likely to produce a good result 不利的；有害的；反面的：***adverse change/circumstances/weather conditions*** 不利的变动；逆境；恶劣天气 ◇ *Lack of money will have an* ***adverse effect*** *on our research programme.* 缺少资金将对我们的研究计划有不利影响。 ◇ *They have attracted strong adverse criticism.* 他们已招致强烈非难。 ◇ *This drug is known to have adverse side effects.* 众所周知，这种药具有不良副作用。▶ **ad·verse·ly** *adv.*：*Her health was* ***adversely affected*** *by the climate.* 那种气候损害了她的健康。

ad·ver·sity /ədˈvɜːsəti; *NAmE* -ˈvɜːrs-/ *noun* [U, C] (*pl.* **-ies**) (*formal*) a difficult or unpleasant situation 困境；逆境：*courage* ***in the face of adversity*** 面对逆境的勇气 ◇ *He overcame many personal adversities.* 多次身处逆境，他都挺了过来。

ad·vert /ˈædvɜːt; *NAmE* -vɜːrt/ *noun* (*BrE, informal*) = ADVERTISEMENT (1), (2)：*the adverts on television* 电视广告 ◇ *When the adverts came on I got up to put the kettle on.* 电视播放广告时，我起身去烧了壶水。 ➲ SYNONYMS AT ADVERTISEMENT

ad·ver·tise /ˈædvətaɪz; *NAmE* -vərt-/ *verb* **1** [I, T] to tell the public about a product or a service in order to encourage people to buy or to use it 做广告；登广告：*If you want to attract more customers, try advertising in the local paper.* 如果你要吸引更多顾客，就试试在当地报纸登广告。 ◇ **~ sth (as sth)** *The cruise was advertised as the 'journey of a lifetime'.* 这次航行被宣传为"终生难得的旅行"。

> **WORDFINDER** 联想词：cold-calling, leaflet, mailing, mailshot, marketing, poster, product placement, prospectus, publicize

2 [I, T] to let people know that sth is going to happen, or that a job is available by giving details about it in a newspaper, on a notice in a public place, on the Internet, etc. （在报纸、公共场所公告牌、互联网等上）公布，征聘：**~ (for sb/sth)** *We are currently advertising for a new sales manager.* 目前我们公开征聘一位新的销售经理。 ◇ **~ sth** *We advertised the concert quite widely.* 我们为这次音乐会作了相当广泛的宣传。 **3** [T] **~ sth** to show or tell sth about yourself to other people 展现，宣传（自己的事） SYN **publicize**：*I wouldn't advertise the fact that you don't have a work permit.* 我不会向外声张你没有工作许可证这件事。

ad·ver·tise·ment /ədˈvɜːtɪsmənt; *NAmE* ˌædvərˈtaɪz-/ *noun* **1** [C] (*also informal* **ad**) (*also BrE, informal* **ad·vert**) **~ (for sth)** a notice, picture or film telling people about a product, job or service 广告；启事：*Put an advertisement in the local paper to sell your car.* 在当地报纸登一则广告来出售你的汽车。 ➲ SEE ALSO CLASSIFIED ADVERTISEMENTS ➲ SYNONYMS ON NEXT PAGE **2** [C] (*BrE also* **ad·vert**) **~ for sth** an example of sth that shows its good qualities 广告（样）品：*Dirty streets and homelessness are no advertisement for a prosperous society.* 肮脏的街道和无家可归现象绝不是繁荣社会的景象。 **3** [U] the act of advertising sth and making it public 广告活动；广告宣传

ad·ver·tiser /ˈædvətaɪzə(r); *NAmE* -vərt-/ *noun* a person or company that advertises 广告商；广告人员；广告公司；登广告者

A

▼ SYNONYMS 同义词辨析

advertisement

publicity • ad • commercial • promotion • trailer

These are all words for a notice, picture or film/movie telling people about a product, job or service. 以上各词均指广告、启事。

advertisement a notice, picture or film/movie telling people about a product, job or service; an example of sth that shows its good qualities; the act of advertising sth and making it public 指广告、宣传的实例、广告活动或广告宣传： *Put an advertisement in the local paper to sell your car.* 在当地报纸登一则广告来出售你的汽车。◇ *Dirty streets are no advertisement for a prosperous society.* 肮脏的街道绝不是繁荣社会的景象。

publicity [U] the business of attracting the attention of the public to sb/sth such as a company, book, film/movie, film/movie star or product; the things that are done to attract attention 指宣传业、广告宣传工作或传播工作： *She works in publicity.* 她从事宣传工作。◇ *There has been a lot of advance publicity for her new film.* 她的新电影尚未上映即大加宣传。

ad, advert (*informal*) a notice, picture or film/movie telling people about a product, job or service 指广告、启事： *We put an ad in the local paper.* 我们在当地报纸上刊登了一则广告。◇ *an ad for a new chocolate bar* 新品种巧克力棒的广告

commercial an advertisement on television or on the radio 指电视或电台播放的广告

promotion a set of advertisements for a particular product or service; activities done in order to increase the sales of a product or service 指广告宣传、促销活动： *a special promotion of local products* 当地产品的特别促销活动◇ *She works in sales and promotion.* 她从事销售和推广工作。

trailer (*especially BrE*) a series of short scenes from a film/movie or television programme, shown in advance to advertise it 指电影或电视节目的预告片

PATTERNS

- (a/an) advertisement/publicity/ad/commercial/promotion/trailer **for** sth
- a **TV/television/radio/cinema** advertisement/ad/commercial/promotion
- to **run/show** a(n) advertisement/ad/commercial/trailer

ad·ver·tis·ing 🔑 /ˈædvətaɪzɪŋ; *NAmE* -vərt-/ *noun* [U] the activity and industry of advertising things to people on television, in newspapers, on the Internet, etc. 广告活动；广告业；做广告： *A good **advertising campaign** will increase our sales.* 良好的广告宣传活动会增加我们的销售量。◇ *Cigarette advertising has been banned.* 香烟广告已遭禁止。◇ ***radio/TV advertising*** 广播 / 电视广告 ◇ *Val works for an **advertising agency*** (= a company that designs advertisements). 瓦尔为一家广告公司工作。◇ *a career in advertising* 广告职业

ad·ver·tor·ial /ˌædvəˈtɔːriəl; *NAmE* -vərˈt-/ *noun* an advertisement that is designed to look like an article in the newspaper or magazine in which it appears 社论式广告

ad·vice 🔑 /ədˈvaɪs/ *noun* [U] ~ (**on sth**) an opinion or a suggestion about what sb should do in a particular situation 劝告；忠告；建议；意见： *advice on road safety* 有关道路安全的建议 ◇ *They **give advice** to people with HIV and AIDS.* 他们向艾滋病病毒携带者和艾滋病患者提供咨询。◇ ***Ask** your **teacher's advice**/**Ask** your **teacher for advice** on how to prepare for the exam.* 向你的老师咨询一下如何准备考试。◇ *We were advised to **seek legal advice**.* 有人劝我们找律师咨询。◇ *Let me give you **a piece of advice**.* 让我给你一个忠告。◇ *A **word of advice**. Don't wear that dress.* 一句忠告：别穿那件连衣裙。◇ ***Take my advice**. Don't do it.* 听我的劝告，别干这件事。◇ *I chose it **on his advice**.* 我这是照他的建议选择的。 ➲ MORE LIKE THIS 28, page R28

▼ EXPRESS YOURSELF 情景表达

Giving somebody advice 提出建议

There are a number of tactful ways of telling people what you think they should do. 给别人提建议时有一些较为得体的表达方式：

- ***If I were you,** I'd wait.* 如果我是你，我会等等看。
- ***I think you should/ought to** see a doctor.* 我觉得你该去看看医生。
- ***Why don't you/Why not/Could you maybe** ask Tom to help?* 你为什么不 / 你或许可以找汤姆帮忙？
- ***If you want my advice/If you want to know what I think,** I'd say it's better to tell him.* 如果你想听我的建议 / 如果你想知道我的想法，我认为最好还是告诉他。
- ***I'd advise you to** sell it now.* 我劝你现在就卖掉它。

adˈvice column (*NAmE*) (*BrE also* **ˈagony column**) *noun* part of a newspaper or magazine in which sb gives advice to readers who have sent letters about their personal problems （报纸或杂志的）答问专栏

adˈvice columnist (*NAmE*) (*BrE* **ˈagony aunt/uncle**) *noun* a person who writes in a newspaper or magazine giving advice in reply to people's letters about their personal problems （报纸或杂志的）答问专栏作者

ad·vis·able /ədˈvaɪzəbl/ *adj.* [not usually before noun] sensible and a good idea in order to achieve sth 明智；可取： *Early booking is advisable.* 预订宜早。◇ **~ to do sth** *It is advisable to book early.* 预订宜早。 OPP **inadvisable**
▶ **ad·vis·abil·ity** /ədˌvaɪzəˈbɪləti/ *noun* [U]

ad·vise 🔑 /ədˈvaɪz/ *verb* **1** 🔑 [I, T] to tell sb what you think they should do in a particular situation 劝告；忠告；建议： **~ (sb) against sth/against doing sth** *I would **strongly advise** against going out on your own.* 我要极力奉劝你别单独外出。◇ **~ sb** *Her mother was away and couldn't advise her.* 她的母亲不在身边，无法劝她。◇ **~ sth** *I'd advise extreme caution.* 我建议要慎之又慎。◇ **+ speech** *'Get there early,' she advised (them).* "早点儿到那里。"她嘱咐（他们）说。◇ **~ sb to do sth** *Police are advising people to stay at home.* 警方告诫民众要留在家里。◇ *I'd advise you not to tell him.* 我劝你别告诉他。◇ **~ that...** *They advise that a passport be carried with you at all times.* 他们建议护照要随时带在身边。◇ (*BrE also*) *They advise that a passport should be carried with you at all times.* 他们建议护照要随时带在身边。◇ **it is advised that...** *It is strongly advised that you take out insurance.* 奉劝你务必办理保险。◇ **~ doing sth** *I'd advise buying your tickets well in advance if you want to travel in August.* 要是想在八月份去旅行，我建议及早购票。 ➲ SEE ALSO ILL-ADVISED, WELL ADVISED ➲ SYNONYMS AT RECOMMEND **2** 🔑 [I, T] to give sb help and information on a subject that you know a lot about 出主意；提出建议；提供咨询： **~ (sb) on/about sth/about doing sth** *We employ an expert to advise on new technology.* 我们聘用了一位专家担任新技术顾问。◇ *She advises the government on environmental issues.* 她是政府的环境问题顾问。◇ **~ (sb) what, which, whether, etc....** *The pharmacist will advise which medicines are safe to take.* 药剂师会建议服用哪些药才安全。◇ *Your lawyer can advise you whether to take any action.* 你的律师可以告诉你是否起诉。 **3** [T] (*formal*) to officially tell sb sth 通知；正式告知 SYN **inform**： **~ sb of sth** *Please advise us of any change of address.* 如地址有变，敬请告知。◇ **~ sb when, where, how, etc....** *I will contact you later to advise you when to come.* 稍后我会与你联系，通知你何时前来。◇ **~ sb that...** *I regret to advise you that the course is now full.* 我很遗憾地通知您，本课程已满额。

ad·vised·ly /ədˈvaɪzədli/ *adv.* (*formal*) if you say that you are using a word **advisedly**, you mean that you have

A

thought carefully before choosing it 经过认真思考；经过深思熟虑

ad·vise·ment /əd'vaɪzmənt/ *noun* [U] (*NAmE, formal*) advice 劝告；忠告；建议；意见：*the University Advisement Center* 大学咨询中心

IDM **take sth under ad'visement** (*formal*) to think carefully about sth before making a decision about it 对某事作周密考虑；深思熟虑：*The judge has taken the matter under advisement.* 法官已经周密考虑这一事情。

ad·viser (*also* **ad·visor**) /əd'vaɪzə(r)/ *noun* a person who gives advice, especially sb who knows a lot about a particular subject 顾问；忠告者；提供意见者：*a financial adviser* 财务顾问 ◇ ~ **(to sb) (on sth)** *a special adviser to the President on education* 总统的教育特别顾问

ad·vis·ory /əd'vaɪzəri/ *adj., noun*
■ *adj.* having the role of giving professional advice 顾问的；咨询的：*an* ***advisory committee/body/service*** 顾问委员会 / 咨询机构 / 服务 ◇ *He acted in an advisory capacity only.* 他仅以顾问身份工作。
■ *noun* (*pl.* **-ies**) (*especially NAmE*) an official warning that sth bad is going to happen 警报：*a tornado advisory* 龙卷风警报

ad·vo·cacy AW /'ædvəkəsi/ *noun* [U] **1** ~ **(of sth)** (*formal*) the giving of public support to an idea, a course of action or a belief （对某思想、行动方针、信念的）拥护，支持，提倡 **2** (*specialist*) the work of lawyers who speak about cases in court （律师）出庭辩护；律师的工作

'advocacy group *noun* (*NAmE*) a group of people who work together to achieve sth, especially by putting pressure on the government, etc., usually on behalf of people who are unable to speak for themselves 倡议团体；吁请团；请愿团体：*an advocacy group for the rights of the mentally ill* 代表精神病患者的维权团体 ➲ COMPARE INTEREST GROUP, PRESSURE GROUP

ad·vo·cate AW *verb, noun*
■ *verb* /'ædvəkeɪt/ (*formal*) to support sth publicly 拥护；支持；提倡：~ **sth** *The group does not advocate the use of violence.* 该团体不支持使用暴力。◇ ~ **(sb) doing sth** *Many experts advocate rewarding your child for good behaviour.* 很多专家主张对小孩的良好表现加以奖励。◇ ~ **that…** *The report advocated that all buildings be fitted with smoke detectors.* 报告主张所有的建筑物都应安装烟雾报警器。◇ (*BrE also*) *The report advocated that all buildings should be fitted with smoke detectors.* 报告主张所有的建筑物都应安装烟雾报警器。➲ SYNONYMS AT RECOMMEND
■ *noun* /'ædvəkət/ **1** a person who supports or speaks in favour of sb or of a public plan or action 拥护者；支持者；提倡者：~ **(for sth/sb)** *an advocate for hospital workers* 医院工作人员的支持者 ◇ ~ **(of sth/sb)** *a staunch advocate of free speech* 言论自由的坚定拥护者 ➲ SEE ALSO DEVIL'S ADVOCATE **2** a person who defends sb in court 辩护律师；出庭辩护人 **3** (in Scotland) a lawyer who has the right to argue cases in higher courts （苏格兰）出庭律师，辩护律师，大律师 ➲ NOTE AT LAWYER ➲ MORE LIKE THIS 21, page R27

ad·ware (*BrE*) /'ædweə(r); *NAmE* -wer/ *noun* [U] a type of software that automatically displays or DOWNLOADS advertisements on a computer screen, SMARTPHONE, etc. when a user is online 广告软件（上网时会自动播放或下载广告）：*My computer keeps getting infected with unwanted adware.* 我的电脑老是感染讨厌的广告软件。➲ COMPARE MALWARE, SPYWARE

adze (*NAmE also* **adz**) /ædz/ *noun* a heavy tool with a curved blade at RIGHT ANGLES to the handle, used for cutting or shaping large pieces of wood 锛子（削平木料用的平头斧）

ad·zuki /əd'zuːki/ (*also* **ad'zuki bean, aduki**) *noun* a type of small round dark red BEAN that you can eat 赤豆；红豆

aegis /'iːdʒɪs/ *noun*

IDM **under the aegis of sb/sth** (*formal*) with the protection or support of a particular organization or person 在…保护（或支持）下

ae·olian (*especially US* **eo·lian**) /iː'əʊliən; *NAmE* iː'oʊ-/ *adj.* (*specialist*) connected with or caused by the action of the wind 风的；风成的

aeon (*BrE*) (*also* **eon** *NAmE, BrE*) /'iːən/ *noun* **1** (*formal*) an extremely long period of time; thousands of years 极漫长的时期；千万年 **2** (*geology* 地) a major division of time, divided into ERAS 宙（地质学上的年代分期，下分代）：*aeons of geological history* 数以亿万年计的地质史

aer·ate /'eəreɪt; *NAmE* 'er-/ *verb* **1** ~ **sth** to make it possible for air to become mixed with soil, water, etc. 使（土壤、水等）透气：*Earthworms do the important job of aerating the soil.* 蚯蚓干着使土壤透气的重要工作。**2** ~ **sth** to add a gas, especially CARBON DIOXIDE, to a liquid under pressure 充二氧化碳于，充气于（液体）：*aerated water* 汽水 ▸ **aer·ation** /eə'reɪʃn; *NAmE* e'reɪ-/ *noun* [U]

aer·ial /'eəriəl; *NAmE* 'er-/ *noun, adj.*
■ *noun* (*especially BrE*) (*also* **an·tenna** *NAmE, BrE*) a piece of equipment made of wire or long straight pieces of metal for receiving or sending radio and television signals 天线 ➲ VISUAL VOCAB PAGES V18, V56
■ *adj.* **1** from a plane 从飞机上的：***aerial attacks/bombardment/photography*** 空中攻击 / 轰炸 / 摄影 ◇ *an aerial view of Palm Island* 棕榈岛鸟瞰图 **2** in the air; existing above the ground 空中的；空气中的；地表以上的：*The banyan tree has aerial roots.* 榕树有气生根。

aerie (*NAmE*) = EYRIE

aero- /'eərəʊ; *NAmE* 'eroʊ/ *combining form* (in nouns, adjectives and adverbs 构成名词、形容词和副词) connected with air or aircraft 空气的；空中的；飞行器的：*aerodynamic* 空气动力的 ◇ *aerospace* 航空航天工业

aero·bat·ics /ˌeərə'bætɪks; *NAmE* ˌerə-/ *noun* [U+sing./pl. v.] exciting and skilful movements performed in an aircraft, such as flying upside down, especially in front of an audience 特技飞行 ▸ **aero·batic** *adj.*：*an aerobatic display* 特技飞行表演 ➲ VISUAL VOCAB PAGE V57

aer·obic /eə'rəʊbɪk; *NAmE* e'roʊ-/ *adj.* **1** (*biology* 生) needing OXYGEN 需氧的；好氧的：*aerobic bacteria* 好氧细菌 **2** (of physical exercise 健身活动) especially designed to improve the function of the heart and lungs 有氧的；增强心肺功能的 OPP **anaerobic**

aer·obics /eə'rəʊbɪks; *NAmE* e'roʊ-/ *noun* [U] physical exercises intended to make the heart and lungs stronger, often done in classes, with music 有氧运动（经常分班伴随音乐进行的增强心肺功能的健身活动）：*to do aerobics* 做有氧运动

aero·drome /'eərədrəʊm; *NAmE* 'erədroʊm/ (*BrE*) (*US* **air·drome**) *noun* (*old-fashioned*) a small airport 小型飞机场

aero·dy·nam·ics /ˌeərəʊdaɪ'næmɪks; *NAmE* ˌeroʊ-/ *noun* **1** [pl.] the qualities of an object that affect the way it moves through the air 空气动力（特性）：*Research has focused on improving the car's aerodynamics.* 研究的重点是改善轿车的流线型。**2** [U] the science that deals with how objects move through air 空气动力学 ▸ **aero·dy·nam·ic** /-mɪk/ *adj.*：*the car's aerodynamic shape* (= making it able to move faster) 汽车的流线型 **aero·dy·nam·ic·al·ly** /-kli/ *adv.*

aero·foil /'eərəfɔɪl; *NAmE* 'er-/ (*BrE*) (*NAmE* **air·foil**) *noun* the basic curved structure of an aircraft's wing that helps to lift it into the air 翼型（指机翼在空气中运动时能产生升力的型面）

aero·gramme (*NAmE also* **aero·gram**) /'eərəgræm; *NAmE* 'erə-/ (*also* **'air letter** *NAmE, BrE*) *noun* a sheet of light paper that can be folded and sent by air as a letter 航空邮简（一张薄纸折成，作航空信寄出）

aero·naut /'eərənɔːt; *NAmE* 'erə-/ *noun* a traveller in a HOT-AIR BALLOON or AIRSHIP 热气球（或飞艇）乘客

aero·naut·ics /ˌeərə'nɔːtɪks; *NAmE* ˌerə-/ *noun* [U] the science or practice of building and flying aircraft 航空

A

学；飞行学；飞行术 ▶ **aero·naut·ic·al** /-ˈnɔːtɪkl/ *adj.* : *an aeronautical engineer* 航空工程师

aero·plane /ˈeərəpleɪn; *NAmE* ˈerə-/ (*BrE*) (*also* **air·plane** *especially in NAmE*) (*also* **plane** *BrE, NAmE*) *noun* a flying vehicle with wings and one or more engines 飞机 ➲ VISUAL VOCAB PAGE V57

aero·sol /ˈeərəsɒl; *NAmE* ˈerəsɔːl; ˈerəsɑːl/ *noun* a metal container in which a liquid such as paint or HAIRSPRAY is kept under pressure and released as a spray（喷油漆、头发定型剂等的）喷雾器，雾化器：*ozone-friendly aerosols* 不损害臭氧层的气雾剂 ◇ *an* ***aerosol can/spray*** 喷雾罐；气雾喷雾器 ➲ VISUAL VOCAB PAGE V36

aero·space /ˈeərəʊspeɪs; *NAmE* ˈeroʊ-/ *noun* [U] the industry of building aircraft, vehicles and equipment to be sent into space 航空航天工业：*jobs in aerospace and defence* 航天与国防工作 ◇ *the aerospace industry* 航空航天工业

aero·stat /ˈeərəstæt; *NAmE* ˈerə-/ *noun* (*specialist*) an aircraft such as an AIRSHIP or HOT-AIR BALLOON that is filled with a gas（充注热空气的）浮空器，飞行器（如飞艇、热气球）

aes·thete (*NAmE also* **es·thete**) /ˈiːsθiːt; ˈes-; *NAmE* ˈes-/ *noun* (*formal, sometimes disapproving*) a person who has a love and understanding of art and beautiful things 审美家

aes·thet·ic (*NAmE also* **es·thet·ic**) /iːsˈθetɪk; es-; *NAmE* es-/ *adj., noun*

■ ***adj.*** **1** concerned with beauty and art and the understanding of beautiful things 审美的；有审美观点的；美学的：*an aesthetic appreciation of the landscape* 用审美的眼光欣赏风景 ◇ *The works of art are judged on purely aesthetic grounds.* 评判艺术作品依据的是纯粹的美学标准。◇ *The benefits of conservation are both financial and aesthetic.* 保护自然环境既促进经济又增加美感。 **2** made in an artistic way and beautiful to look at 美的；艺术的：*Their furniture was more aesthetic than functional.* 他们的家具美观多于实用。 ▶ **aes·thet·ic·al·ly** (*NAmE also* **es-**) /-kli/ *adv.* : *aesthetically pleasing colour combinations* 赏心悦目的色彩搭配

■ ***noun*** **1** [C] the aesthetic qualities and ideas of sth 美感；审美观：*The students debated the aesthetic of the poems.* 学生就这些诗的美展开了辩论。 **2 aesthetics** [U] the branch of philosophy that studies the principles of beauty, especially in art 美学 ▶ **aes·theti·cism** (*NAmE also* **es-**) /iːsˈθetɪsɪzəm; es-; *NAmE* es-/ *noun* [U]

aeti·ology (*BrE*) (*NAmE* **eti·ology**) /ˌiːtiˈɒlədʒi; *NAmE* -ˈɑːl-/ *noun* [U] (*medical* 医) the scientific study of the causes of disease 病原学；病因学（说）

AFAIK *abbr.* (*informal*) (especially in TEXT MESSAGES, emails, etc.) as far as I know 据我所知（全写为 as far as I know，尤用于短信、电邮等）

afar /əˈfɑː(r)/ *adv.*

IDM **from a'far** (*literary*) from a long distance away 从远处：*He loved her from afar* (= did not tell her he loved her). 他暗恋着她。

afara /əˈfɑːrə/ *noun* **1** (*also* **limba**) [C] a tall tree that grows in W Africa（西非）榄仁树 **2** (*also* **limba**) [U] the wood from this tree, often used for making furniture 榄仁木（常用于制作家具） **3** [C] (*WAfrE*) a bridge, usually made of wood 桥；（通常指）木桥

AFC /ˌeɪ ef ˈsiː/ *abbr.* **1** (*BrE*) Association Football Club 足球俱乐部；足球联合会：*Leeds United AFC* 利兹联队足球俱乐部 **2** (*NAmE*) (in the US) the American Football Conference (one of the two groups of teams in the National Football League) 美国橄榄球联合会（美国国家橄榄球大联盟下两大联合会之一） **3** (*BrE*) Air Force Cross (an award given to members of the AIR FORCE, for being brave when flying rather than when fighting the enemy) 空军十字勋章（奖励飞行而非作战的英勇表现） **4** (*specialist*) automatic frequency control (a system which allows radios and televisions to continue to receive the same signal) 自动频率控制

af·fable /ˈæfəbl/ *adj.* pleasant, friendly and easy to talk to 和蔼可亲的；平易近人的 SYN **genial** ▶ **af·fa·bil·ity** /ˌæfəˈbɪləti/ *noun* [U] **af·fably** *adv.*

af·fair 🔑 /əˈfeə(r); *NAmE* əˈfer/ *noun*

• PUBLIC/POLITICAL ACTIVITIES 公共 / 政治活动 **1** 🔑 **affairs** [pl.] events that are of public interest or political importance 公共事务；政治事务：***world/international/business affairs*** 世界 / 国际 / 商业事务 ◇ *an expert on foreign affairs* (= political events in other countries) 外事专家 ◇ *affairs of state* 国务 ➲ SEE ALSO CURRENT AFFAIRS

• EVENT 事件 **2** 🔑 [C, usually sing.] an event that people are talking about or describing in a particular way 事件；事情：*The newspapers exaggerated the whole affair wildly.* 报章毫无根据地夸大了整个事件。◇ *The debate was a pretty disappointing affair.* 那次辩论使人颇感失望。◇ *She wanted the celebration to be a simple* ***family affair***. 她希望庆祝活动仅限于家人参加。

• RELATIONSHIP 关系 **3** 🔑 [C] a sexual relationship between two people, usually when one or both of them are married to sb else（尤指已婚男女的）私通，风流韵事：*She* ***is having an affair*** *with her boss.* 她跟老板有暧昧关系。➲ SEE ALSO LOVE AFFAIR (1) ➲ WORDFINDER NOTE AT LOVE

• PRIVATE BUSINESS 私人业务 **4** 🔑 **affairs** [pl.] matters connected with a person's private business and financial situation 私人业务：*I looked after my father's financial affairs.* 我照管父亲的财务。◇ *She wanted to* ***put her affairs in order*** *before she died.* 她想在去世前把自己的事务安排妥当。 **5** [sing.] a thing that sb is responsible for (and that other people should not be concerned with) 个人的事 SYN **business**：*How I spend my money is my affair.* 我如何用钱是我自己的事。

• OBJECT 物品 **6** [C] (*old-fashioned*) (with an adjective 与形容词连用) an object that is unusual or difficult to describe 不寻常之物；难描述的东西：*Her hat was an amazing affair with feathers and a huge brim.* 她的帽子嵌着羽毛，帽檐很宽，真是件奇物。IDM SEE STATE *n.*

af·faire /əˈfeə(r); *NAmE* əˈfer/ *noun* (*from French, literary*) a love affair 风流韵事

▼ **WHICH WORD?** 词语辨析

affect / effect

- **affect** *verb* = 'to have an influence on sb/sth' * affect 动词 = 影响某人 / 某事：*Does television affect children's behaviour?* 电视对孩子的行为有影响吗？ It is not a noun. 该词不作名词。
- **effect** *noun* = 'result, influence' * effect 名词 = 作用；影响：*Does television have an effect on children's behaviour?* 电视对孩子的行为有影响吗？
- **effect** *verb* is quite rare and formal and means 'to achieve or produce' * effect 作动词罕见且正式，意为实现、产生：*They hope to effect a reconciliation.* 他们希望实现和解。

af·fect 🔑 AW /əˈfekt/ *verb* **1** 🔑 [often passive] **~ sb/sth** to produce a change in sb/sth 影响：*How will these changes affect us?* 这些变化对我们会有什么影响？◇ *Your opinion will not affect my decision.* 你的意见不会影响我的决定。◇ *The south of the country was worst affected by the drought.* 该国南方旱情最严重。 **2** 🔑 [often passive] **~ sb/sth** (of a disease 疾病) to attack sb or a part of the body; to make sb become ill/sick 侵袭；使感染：*The condition affects one in five women.* 每五个妇女就有一个人患有这种病。◇ *Rub the cream into the affected areas.* 把乳膏揉进患处。 **3 ~ sb** [often passive] to make sb have strong feelings of sadness, pity, etc.（感情上）深深打动；使悲伤（或怜悯等）：*They were deeply affected by the news of her death.* 她死亡的消息使他们唏嘘不已。 **4 ~ (to do) sth** (*formal*) to pretend to be feeling or thinking sth 假装：*She affected a calmness she did not feel.* 她强装镇静。 **5 ~ sth** (*formal, disapproving*) to use or wear sth that is intended to impress other people 炫耀；做作地使用（或穿戴） SYN put on: *I wish he wouldn't affect that ridiculous accent.* 但愿他别故意装出那种可笑的腔调。

af·fect·ation /ˌæfekˈteɪʃn/ *noun* [C, U] behaviour or an action that is not natural or sincere and that is often intended to impress other people 假装；做作；装模作样：*His little affectations irritated her.* 他的装腔作势令她不快。◇ *Kay has no affectation at all.* 凯一点也不做作。◇ *He raised his eyebrows with an affectation of surprise* (= pretending to be surprised). 他扬起双眉装出一副惊奇的样子。

af·fect·ed /əˈfektɪd/ *adj.* (of a person or their behaviour 人或行为) not natural or sincere 假装的；做作的：*an affected laugh/smile* 假笑；不自然的微笑 **OPP unaffected** ▸ **af·fect·ed·ly** *adv.*

af·fect·ing /əˈfektɪŋ/ *adj.* (*formal*) producing strong feelings of sadness and sympathy 深深打动人的；感动人的；激起怜悯的

af·fec·tion /əˈfekʃn/ *noun* **1** [U, sing.] the feeling of liking or loving sb/sth very much and caring about them 喜爱；钟爱：*Children need lots of love and affection.* 孩子需要多多疼爱和关怀。◇ *He didn't* **show** *his wife any* **affection**. 他没有向妻子表示一点爱。◇ *She was held in deep affection by all her students.* 她的学生都十分爱戴她。◇ ~ **for sb/sth** *Mr Darcy's affection for his sister* 达西先生对他妹妹的关爱之情 ◇ *I have a great affection for New York.* 我很喜欢纽约。 ➲ COLLOCATIONS AT MARRIAGE **2 affections** [pl.] (*formal* or *literary*) a person's feelings of love 爱情：*Anne had two men trying to win her affections.* 安妮有两个男人追求。

af·fec·tion·ate /əˈfekʃənət/ *adj.* showing caring feelings and love for sb 表示关爱的 **SYN loving**: *He is very affectionate towards his children.* 他非常关爱他的孩子。◇ *an affectionate kiss* 亲昵的一吻 ▸ **af·fec·tion·ate·ly** *adv.*: *William was affectionately known as Billy.* 威廉的昵称为比利。

af·fect·ive AW /əˈfektɪv/ *adj.* (*specialist*) connected with emotions and attitudes 感情的；情感的：*affective disorders* 情感障碍 ▸ **af·fect·ive·ly** AW *adv.*

af·fi·da·vit /ˌæfəˈdeɪvɪt/ *noun* (*law* 律) a written statement that you swear is true, and that can be used as evidence in court 宣誓书；宣誓陈述书

af·fili·ate *verb, noun*

■ ***verb*** /əˈfɪlieɪt/ **1** [T, usually passive] ~ **sb/sth** (**with/to sb/sth**) to link a group, a company or an organization very closely with another, larger one 使隶属，使并入（较大的团体、公司、组织）：*The hospital is affiliated with the local university.* 这家医院附属于当地大学。◇ *The group is not affiliated to any political party.* 该团体不隶属任何政党。 **2** [T, I] ~ (**yourself**) (**with sb/sth**) to join, to be connected with, or to work for an organization 加入；与…有关；为…工作：*The majority of people questioned affiliated themselves with a religious group.* 接受询问的人大多数都加入了宗教团体。

■ ***noun*** /əˈfɪliət/ a company, an organization, etc. that is connected with or controlled by another, larger one 附属机构；分支机构；分公司；分会

af·fili·ated /əˈfɪlieɪtɪd/ *adj.* [only before noun] closely connected to or controlled by a group or an organization 隶属的：*All affiliated members can vote.* 所有隶属成员都有投票权。◇ *a government-affiliated institute* 一家隶属于政府的研究所 **OPP unaffiliated**

af·fili·ation /əˌfɪliˈeɪʃn/ *noun* [U, C] (*formal*) **1** a person's connection with a political party, religion, etc. （与政党、宗教等的）隶属关系：*He was arrested because of his political affiliation.* 他因所属政党的关系而被捕。 **2** one group or organization's official connection with another 隶属；从属

af·fin·ity /əˈfɪnəti/ *noun* (*pl.* **-ies**) (*formal*) **1** [sing.] ~ (**for/with sb/sth**) | ~ (**between A and B**) a strong feeling that you understand sb/sth and like them or it 喜好；喜爱 **SYN rapport**: *Sam was born in the country and had a deep affinity with nature.* 萨姆在乡下出生，特别喜爱大自然。 **2** [U, C] ~ (**with sb/sth**) | ~ (**between A and B**) a close relationship between two people or things that have similar qualities, structures or features 密切的关系；类同：*There is a close affinity between Italian and Spanish.* 意大利语和西班牙语关系密切。

afˈfinity card *noun* a CREDIT CARD printed with the name of an organization, for example a charity, which receives a small amount of money each time the card is used 认同卡（印有某机构名称的信用卡，持卡人每次使用此卡，该机构均可获得回馈金）

afˈfinity group *noun* (*especially NAmE*) a group of people who share the same interest or purpose （有共同利益或目的的）亲和团体

af·firm /əˈfɜːm; *NAmE* əˈfɜːrm/ *verb* (*formal*) to state firmly or publicly that sth is true or that you support sth strongly 申明；断言；肯定属实 **SYN confirm**: ~ **sth** *Both sides affirmed their commitment to the ceasefire.* 双方均申明同意停火。◇ ~ **that**... *I can affirm that no one will lose their job.* 我可以肯定，谁都不会丢掉工作。 ▸ **af·firm·ation** /ˌæfəˈmeɪʃn; *NAmE* ˌæfərˈm-/ *noun* [U, C]: *She nodded in affirmation.* 她肯定地点了点头。

af·firma·tive /əˈfɜːmətɪv; *NAmE* əˈfɜːrm-/ *adj., noun*

■ ***adj.*** (*formal*) an **affirmative** word or reply means 'yes' or expresses agreement 肯定的；同意的 **OPP negative** ▸ **af·firma·tive·ly** *adv.*: *90% voted affirmatively.* * 90% 投票赞成。

■ ***noun*** (*formal*) a word or statement that means 'yes'; an agreement or a CONFIRMATION 肯定；同意：*She answered* **in the affirmative** (= said 'yes'). 她作出了肯定的答复。 **OPP negative**

afˌfirmative ˈaction (*especially NAmE*) (*BrE usually* **ˌpositive disˌcriminˈation**) *noun* [U] the practice or policy of making sure that a particular number of jobs, etc. are given to people from groups that are often treated unfairly because of their race, sex, etc. 积极区别对待政策（对因种族、性别等原因遭歧视的群体在就业等方面给予特别照顾） ➲ COMPARE REVERSE DISCRIMINATION

affix *verb, noun*

■ ***verb*** /əˈfɪks/ [often passive] ~ **sth** (**to sth**) (*formal*) to stick or attach sth to sth else 粘上；贴上；附上：*The label should be firmly affixed to the package.* 这张标签应该牢牢地贴在包裹上。

■ ***noun*** /ˈæfɪks/ (*grammar* 语法) a letter or group of letters added to the beginning or end of a word to change its meaning. The PREFIX *un-* in *unhappy* and the SUFFIX *-less* in *careless* are both affixes. 词缀（unhappy 中的 un-和 careless 中的 -less 都是词缀）

af·flict /əˈflɪkt/ *verb* [often passive] (*formal*) to affect sb/sth in an unpleasant or harmful way 折磨；使痛苦：~ **sb/sth** *Aid will be sent to the afflicted areas.* 将向受灾地区提供援助。◇ **be afflicted with sth** *About 40% of the country's population is afflicted with the disease.* 全国 40% 左右的人口患有这种疾病。

af·flic·tion /əˈflɪkʃn/ *noun* [U, C] (*formal*) pain and suffering or sth that causes it 折磨；痛苦

af·flu·ent /ˈæfluənt/ *adj.* (*formal*) having a lot of money and a good standard of living 富裕的 **SYN prosperous, wealthy**: *affluent Western countries* 富裕的西方国家 ◇ *a very affluent neighbourhood* 富人区 ➲ SYNONYMS AT RICH ▸ **af·flu·ence** /ˈæfluəns/ *noun* [U] **SYN prosperity**

af·ford /əˈfɔːd; *NAmE* əˈfɔːrd/ *verb* **1** [no passive] (usually used with *can, could* or *be able to*, especially in negative sentences or questions 通常与 can、could 或 be able to 连用，尤用于否定句或疑问句) to have enough money or time to be able to buy or to do sth 买得起；（有时间）做，能做：~ **sth** *Can we afford a new car?* 我们买得起一辆新车吗？◇ *None of them could afford £50 for a ticket.* 他们中没有哪个拿得出 50 英镑买一张票。◇ *She felt she couldn't afford any more time off work.* 她觉得再也抽不出时间歇班了。◇ ~ **to do sth** *We can't afford to go abroad this summer.* 今年夏天我们没有足够的钱去国外。◇

She never took a taxi, even though she could afford to. 尽管她坐得起出租汽车，但她从来不坐。◇ **~ sth to do sth** *He couldn't afford the money to go on the trip.* 这次旅行他钱不够。 ➲ WORDFINDER NOTE AT MONEY **2** [no passive] (usually used with *can* or *could*, especially in negative sentences and questions 通常与 can 或 could 连用，尤用于否定句或疑问句) if you say that you **can't afford** to do sth, you mean that you should not do it because it will cause problems for you if you do 承担得起（后果）：**~ to do sth** *We cannot afford to ignore this warning.* 我们对这个警告绝不能等闲视之。◇ (*formal*) *They could* **ill afford** *to lose any more staff.* 他们再也不能损失员工了。◇ **~ sth** *We cannot afford any more delays.* 我们不能再有任何耽搁了。 **3** (*formal*) to provide sb with sth 提供；给予： **~ sth** *The tree affords some shelter from the sun.* 这棵树可以挡一挡太阳。◇ **~ sb sth** *The programme affords young people the chance to gain work experience.* 这项计划给年轻人提供了获得工作经验的机会。 ➲ MORE LIKE THIS 26, page R28 ▶ **af·ford·abil·ity** /əˌfɔːdəˈbɪləti; *NAmE* əˌfɔːrd-/ *noun* [U] **af·ford·able** /əˈfɔːdəbl; *NAmE* əˈfɔːrd-/ *adj.* : *affordable prices/housing* 付得起的价格；买得起的住宅 OPP **unaffordable** ➲ SYNONYMS AT CHEAP **af·ford·ably** *adv.* : *affordably priced apartments* 经济型公寓住宅

af·for·est·ation /əˌfɒrɪˈsteɪʃn; *NAmE* əˌfɔːr-; əˌfɑːr-/ *noun* [U] (*specialist*) the process of planting areas of land with trees in order to form a forest 人工造林；（无林地）造林 ➲ COMPARE DEFORESTATION ▶ **af·for·est** /əˈfɒrɪst; *NAmE* əˈfɔːr-; əˈfɑːr-/ *verb* [usually passive] **~ sth**

af·fray /əˈfreɪ/ *noun* [C, usually sing., U] (*law* 律) a fight or violent behaviour in a public place （在公共场所）斗殴，闹事

af·fri·cate /ˈæfrɪkət/ *noun* (*phonetics* 语音) a speech sound that is made up of a PLOSIVE followed immediately by a FRICATIVE, for example /tʃ/ and /dʒ/ in *chair* and *jar* 塞擦音

af·front /əˈfrʌnt/ *noun, verb*

- *noun* [usually sing.] **~ (to sb/sth)** a remark or an action that insults or offends sb/sth 侮辱；冒犯
- *verb* [usually passive] **~ sb/sth** (*formal*) to insult or offend sb 侮辱；冒犯： *He hoped they would not feel affronted if they were not invited.* 他希望如果他们没有获得邀请也不要感到受辱。◇ *an affronted expression* 受到冒犯的表情

Afghan hound /ˌæfgæn ˈhaʊnd/ *noun* a tall dog with long soft hair and a pointed nose 阿富汗猎狗

afi·cion·ado /əˌfɪʃəˈnɑːdəʊ; *NAmE* -doʊ/ *noun* (*pl.* **-os**) a person who likes a particular sport, activity or subject very much and knows a lot about it 酷爱…者；…迷

afield /əˈfiːld/ *adv.*

IDM **far/farther/further a'field** far away from home; to or in places that are not near 远离家乡；去远处；在远方： *You can hire a car if you want to explore further afield.* 假如你想逛更远的地方，可以租辆汽车。◇ *Journalists came* **from as far afield as** *China.* 新闻记者有的来自遥远的中国。

AFK *abbr.* (*informal*) (usually in emails, messages on online GAMING websites, etc.) away from the keyboard 暂离键盘，暂时离开（全写为 away from the keyboard，通常用于电邮、网上通信等）： *He's going to be AFK for a few days so won't be able to work on the project.* 他要暂时离开几天，所以这个项目的工作他做不了。

aflame /əˈfleɪm/ *adj.* [not before noun] (*literary*) **1** burning; on fire 在燃烧 SYN **ablaze**: *The whole building was soon aflame.* 整栋大楼很快就燃烧起来。 **2** full of bright colours and lights 五彩缤纷 SYN **ablaze**: *The woods were aflame with autumn colours.* 秋林斑斓绚丽。 **3** showing excitement or embarrassment 激动；窘迫： ***eyes/cheeks aflame*** 两眼闪光；两颊绯红

AFL-CIO /ˌeɪ ef el siː aɪ ˈəʊ; *NAmE* ˈoʊ/ *abbr.* American Federation of Labor and Congress of Industrial Organizations (an organization of trade/labor unions) 劳联 – 产联，美国劳工联合会 – 产业工会联合会（美国工会的一个联合组织）

afloat /əˈfləʊt; *NAmE* əˈfloʊt/ *adj.* [not before noun] **1** floating on water （在水上）漂浮： *Somehow we kept the boat afloat.* 我们想办法使船没有下沉。 **2** (of a business, etc. 企业等) having enough money to pay debts; able to survive 有偿债能力；能维持下去： *They will have to borrow £10 million next year, just to* **stay afloat**. 明年他们得举债 1 000 万英镑才能维持下去。 ➲ MORE LIKE THIS 31, page R28

afoot /əˈfʊt/ *adj.* [not before noun] being planned; happening 计划中；进行中： *There are plans afoot to increase taxation.* 正在拟订增税方案。◇ *Changes were afoot.* 各种变革正在进行之中。

afore·men·tioned /əˌfɔːˈmenʃənd; *NAmE* əˌfɔːrˈm-/ (*also* **afore·said** /əˈfɔːsed; *NAmE* əˈfɔːrsed/) (*also* **said**) *adj.* [only before noun] (*formal* or *law* 律) mentioned before, in an earlier sentence 前面提到的；上述的： *The aforementioned person was seen acting suspiciously.* 有人看见前面提到的那个人行动可疑。

afore·thought /əˈfɔːθɔːt; *NAmE* əˈfɔːrθ-/ *adj.* IDM SEE MALICE

a for·ti·ori /ˌeɪ fɔːtiˈɔːraɪ; *NAmE* ˌfɔːrt-/ *adv.* (*formal* or *law* 律, *from Latin*) for or with an even stronger reason 更有理由；理由更充分

afoul /əˈfaʊl/ *adv.* (*NAmE*)

IDM **run a'foul of sth** to do sth that is not allowed by a law or rule, or to do sth that people in authority disapprove of （与法律、规章、当权者等）相抵触，有冲突： *to run afoul of the law* 违犯法律

afraid /əˈfreɪd/ *adj.* [not before noun] **1** feeling fear; frightened because you think that you might be hurt or suffer 害怕，畏惧（可能受伤害、受苦）： *Don't be afraid.* 别怕。◇ **~ of sb/sth** *It's all over. There's nothing to be afraid of now.* 一切都结束了。现在没有什么可怕的了。◇ *Are you afraid of spiders?* 你怕蜘蛛吗？◇ **~ of doing sth** *I started to feel afraid of going out alone at night.* 我开始害怕夜间单独外出了。◇ **~ to do sth** *She was afraid to open the door.* 她不敢开门。 **2** worried about what might happen 担心（会发生某事）： **~ of doing sth** *She was afraid of upsetting her parents.* 她担心会使她父母不安。◇ **~ to do sth** *Don't be afraid to ask if you don't understand.* 你要是不懂，尽管问好了。◇ **~ (that...)** *We were afraid (that) we were going to capsize the boat.* 我们担心会把船弄翻。 **3 ~ for sb/sth** worried or frightened that sth unpleasant, dangerous, etc. will happen to a particular person or thing 担心，生怕（将发生不快、不幸或危险的事）： *I'm not afraid for me, but for the baby.* 我担心的不是自己，而是婴儿。◇ *They had already fired three people and he was afraid for his job.* 他们已经解雇了三人，所以他为他的工作担忧。 ➲ MORE LIKE THIS 31, page R28

IDM **I'm afraid** used as a polite way of telling sb sth that is unpleasant or disappointing, or that you are sorry about （礼貌地说出令人不快、失望或感到遗憾的事）我怕，恐怕，很遗憾，对不起： *I can't help you, I'm afraid.* 对不起，我帮不了你的忙。◇ *I'm afraid we can't come.* 很遗憾，我们来不了。◇ *I'm afraid that it's not finished yet.* 此事恐怕还没有完。◇ *He's no better,* ***I'm afraid to say.*** 我很抱歉地说，他一点也不见好转。◇ *'Is there any left?' '****I'm afraid not.****'* "还有剩的没有？" "恐怕没有。" ◇ *'Will it hurt?' '****I'm afraid so.****'* "那痛不痛？" "恐怕会痛。"

ˈA-frame (*also* **ˌA-frame ˈhouse**) *noun* (*especially NAmE*) a house with very steep sides that meet at the top in the shape of the letter A * A 形房屋

ˈA-frame tent *noun* = RIDGE TENT

afresh /əˈfreʃ/ *adv.* (*formal*) again, especially from the beginning or with new ideas 从头；重新；另行： *It was a chance to* **start afresh**. 这是个重新开始的机会。

Af·ri·can /ˈæfrɪkən/ *adj., noun*

- *adj.* of or connected with Africa 非洲的
- *noun* a person from Africa, especially a black person 非洲人（尤指黑人）

ˌ**African Aˈmerican** *noun* a person from America who is a member of a race of people who have dark skin, originally from Africa 非裔美国人 ▶ ˌ**African Aˈmerican** *adj.*

ˌ**African Caˈnadian** *noun* a Canadian citizen whose family was originally from Africa 非裔加拿大人 ▶ **African Canadian** *adj.*

ˌ**African reˈnaissance** *noun* [sing.] a period of time when Africa will experience great development in its economy and culture. Some people believe that this started at the end of the 20th century. 非洲复兴（非洲在经济和文化方面将出现巨大发展的时期，有人认为这一趋势始于 20 世纪末）

Af·ri·kaans /ˌæfrɪˈkɑːns/ *noun* [U] a language that has developed from Dutch, spoken in South Africa 阿非利堪斯语；南非荷兰语

▼ **SYNONYMS 同义词辨析**

afraid

frightened • scared • terrified • alarmed • paranoid

These words all describe feeling or showing fear. 以上各词均形容害怕。

afraid [not before noun] feeling fear; worried that sth bad might happen 指害怕、担心不幸的事可能发生： *There's nothing to be afraid of.* 没有什么要害怕的。◇ *Aren't you afraid (that) you'll fall?* 你不怕会跌倒吗？

frightened feeling fear; worried that sth bad might happen 指害怕、担心不幸的事可能发生： *a frightened child* 受惊的孩子 ◇ *She was frightened that the glass would break.* 她担心玻璃会破碎。

scared (*rather informal*) feeling fear; worried that sth bad might happen 指害怕、担心不幸的事可能发生： *The thieves got scared and ran away.* 小偷慌张起来，都跑掉了。

AFRAID, FRIGHTENED OR SCARED? 用 afraid、frightened 还是 scared?

Scared is more informal, more common in speech, and often describes small fears. **Afraid** cannot come before a noun. It can only take the preposition *of*, not *about*. If you are **afraid/frightened/scared of** sb/sth/doing sth or **afraid/frightened/scared to** do sth, you think you are in danger of being hurt or suffering in some way. If you are **frightened/scared about** sth/doing sth, it is less a fear for your personal safety and more a worry that sth unpleasant might happen. * scared 较非正式，较常用于日常谈话中，常指有些害怕。afraid 不用于名词前，只能与介词 of 而非 about 连用。be afraid/frightened/scared of sb/sth/doing sth 或 be afraid/frightened/scared to do sth 均指担心受到伤害或遭受痛苦。be frightened/scared about sth/doing sth 较少指担心个人安全，更多的是指害怕不快的事情发生。

terrified very frightened 指恐惧、很害怕： *I was terrified (that) she wouldn't come.* 我很害怕她不来。◇ *She looked at him with wide, terrified eyes.* 她看着他，双目圆睁，充满恐惧。

alarmed afraid that sth dangerous or unpleasant might happen 指担心危险或不快的事情发生： *She was alarmed at the prospect of travelling alone.* 她一想到独自旅行的情景就害怕。

paranoid (*rather informal*) afraid or suspicious of other people and believing that they are trying to harm you, in a way that is not reasonable 指多疑、不合情理地恐惧： *You're just being paranoid.* 你只是在疑神疑鬼。

PATTERNS

- afraid/frightened/scared **of** spiders, etc.
- frightened/scared/paranoid **about** ...
- afraid/frightened/scared/terrified **that** ...
- afraid/frightened/scared **to** open the door, etc.
- **Don't be** afraid/frightened/scared/alarmed.

Af·ri·kaner /ˌæfrɪˈkɑːnə(r)/ *noun* a person from South Africa, usually of Dutch origin, whose first language is Afrikaans 阿非利堪人（以南非荷兰语为第一语言的南非人，常为荷兰裔）

Afro /ˈæfrəʊ; *NAmE* ˈæfroʊ/ *noun* (*pl.* **-os**) a HAIRSTYLE sometimes worn by black people and popular in the 1970s, in which the hair forms a round mass of tight curls 非洲式发型（20 世纪 70 年代流行的某些黑人的圆形紧密鬈发）

Afro- /ˈæfrəʊ; *NAmE* ˈæfroʊ/ *combining form* (in nouns and adjectives 构成名词和形容词) African 非洲人；非洲（人）的： *Afro-Asian* 亚非的

Afro·beat /ˈæfrəʊbiːt; *NAmE* ˈæfroʊ-/ *noun* [U] a type of music that combines traditional Nigerian rhythms and singing styles with JAZZ and FUNK 非洲节拍乐（将传统尼日利亚节奏及歌唱风格与爵士乐、放克乐相融合）

ˌ**Afro-Caribˈbean** *noun* a person who comes, or whose family comes, from the Caribbean and who is a member of a group of people with dark skin who originally came from Africa 加勒比海黑人 ▶ ˌ**Afro-Caribˈbean** *adj.*

aft /ɑːft; *NAmE* æft/ *adv.* (*specialist*) in, near or towards the back of a ship or an aircraft 在（或向）船尾；在（或向）机尾 ▶ **aft** *adj.* ➲ COMPARE FORE *adv.* (1)

after 🔑 /ˈɑːftə(r); *NAmE* ˈæf-/ *prep., conj., adv., adj.*

■ ***prep.*** **1** 🔑 later than sth; following sth in time （时间）在…后： *We'll leave after lunch.* 我们将在午饭后动身。◇ *They arrived* ***shortly after*** *5.* 他们是在 5 点钟刚过到达的。◇ ***Not long after that*** *he resigned.* 那以后不久他就辞职了。◇ *Let's meet* ***the day after tomorrow/the week after next.*** 咱们后天 / 下下周再见。◇ *After winning the prize she became famous overnight.* 她获奖后一夜之间成名了。◇ *After an hour I went home* (= when an hour had passed). 一小时之后我回家了。◇ (*NAmE*) *It's ten after seven in the morning* (= 7.10 a.m.). 现在是早上七点十分。 **2** 🔑 **... after...** used to show that sth happens many times or continuously （表示反复不断或一个接着一个）： *day after day of hot weather* 日复一日的炎热天气 ◇ *I've told you time after time not to do that.* 我一再告诉过你不要干那件事。➲ SEE ALSO ONE AFTER ANOTHER/THE OTHER at ONE **3** 🔑 behind sb when they have left; following sb 跟随；追赶；在（某人）后面： *Shut the door after you.* 随手关门。◇ *I'm always having to clean up after the children* (= clean the place after they have left it dirty and untidy). 孩子们离开以后，我总得打扫一番。◇ *He ran after her with the book.* 他拿着那本书在后面追赶她。◇ *She was left staring after him.* 她目不转睛地望着他离去的背影。 **4** 🔑 next to and following sb/sth in order or importance （按顺序、重要性）在…后面，仅次于： *Your name comes after mine in the list.* 在名单上你的名字在我的后面。◇ *He's the tallest, after Richard.* 除了理查德，他的个子最高。◇ ***After you*** (= Please go first). 请先走。◇ ***After you with the paper*** (= Can I have it next?). 报纸你看完了给我看。 **5** 🔑 in contrast to sth 与…对照；与…对比： *It was pleasantly cool in the house after the sticky heat outside.* 与户外的湿热相比，屋里真是凉爽惬意。 **6** 🔑 as a result of or because of sth that has happened 鉴于；由于： *I'll never forgive him after what he said.* 由于他说了那些话，我永远也不会原谅他。 **7** despite sth; although sth has happened 尽管；虽然： *I can't believe she'd do that, not after all I've done for her.* 在我为她做了这一切之后，我无法相信她会那样做。 **8** trying to find or catch sb/sth 寻找；追捕： *The police are after him.* 警方正在追捕他。◇ *He's after a job at our place.* 他到我们这儿找工作。 **9** about sb/sth 关于： *She asked after you* (= how you were). 她问候你。 **10** in the style of sb/sth; following the example of sb/sth 模仿；依照： *a painting after Goya* 一幅仿戈雅的画 ◇ *We named the baby 'Ena' after her grandmother.* 我们以婴儿祖母的名字给婴儿取名"埃娜"。 **11 after-** (in adjectives 构成形容词) happening or done later than the time or event mentioned …后的： *after-hours drinking* (= after closing time) 打烊时间以后饮酒 ◇ *an after-school club* 课外活动俱乐部 ◇ *after-dinner mints* 餐后薄荷糖

IDM ˌafter ˈall 1 ⚷ despite what has been said or expected 毕竟；终归：*So you made it after all!* 你毕竟成功了！ 2 ⚷ used when you are explaining sth, or giving a reason （解释或说明理由）别忘了，到底：*He should have paid. He suggested it, after all.* 他本来就应该付款，反正他自己也这么提出。 **be after doing sth** (*IrishE*) 1 to be going to do sth soon; to be intending to do sth soon 正要做某事；打算就要做某事 2 to have just done sth 刚做了某事

■ ***conj.*** ⚷ at a time later than sth; when sth has finished 在…以后：*I'll call you after I've spoken to them.* 我和他们谈了以后就给你打电话。◇ *Several years after they'd split up they met again by chance in Paris.* 他们分手几年以后在巴黎又偶然相遇。

■ ***adv.*** ⚷ later in time; afterwards 后来；以后：*That was in 1996. **Soon after**, I heard that he'd died.* 那是在 1996 年。不久以后我听说他死了。◇ *I could come next week, or the week after.* 我可能下周来，或者再下下周。◇ *And they all **lived happily ever after**.* 从此以后他们都过着幸福的生活。

■ ***adj.*** [only before noun] (*old use*) following; later 后来的；以后的：*in after years* 在以后的岁月中

after·birth /ˈɑːftəbɜːθ; *NAmE* ˈæftərbɜːrθ/ *noun* (*usually* **the afterbirth**) [sing.] the material that comes out of a woman or female animal's body after a baby has been born, and which was necessary to feed and protect the baby 胞衣；胎衣 SYN **placenta**

after·burn·er /ˈɑːftəbɜːnə(r); *NAmE* ˈæftərbɜːrnər/ *noun* (*specialist*) a device for increasing the power of a JET ENGINE （喷气发动机的）加力燃烧室，复燃室，补燃室

after·care /ˈɑːftəkeə(r); *NAmE* ˈæftərker/ *noun* [U] 1 care or treatment given to a person who has just left hospital, prison, etc. （病人出院后的）护理，治疗；（犯人出狱后的）安置，事后处理：*aftercare services* 出院后护理服务 2 (*BrE*) service and advice that is offered by some companies to customers who have bought a car, WASHING MACHINE, etc. 售后服务

ˈ**after-effect** *noun* [usually pl.] the **after-effects** of a drug, an illness or an unpleasant event are the feelings that you experience later as a result of it （药物的）后效应，后作用；（疾病、不快事情的）后遗症，不良后果

after·glow /ˈɑːftəgləʊ; *NAmE* ˈæftərgloʊ/ *noun* [usually sing.] (*literary*) 1 the light that is left in the sky after the sun has set （日落后的）余晖，落照，晚霞 2 a pleasant feeling after a good experience 美好的回忆

after·life /ˈɑːftəlaɪf; *NAmE* ˈæftərl-/ *noun* [sing.] a life that some people believe exists after death 阴世；死后（灵魂的）生活

after·math /ˈɑːftəmæθ; -mɑːθ; *NAmE* ˈæftərmæθ/ *noun* [usually sing.] the situation that exists as a result of an important (and usually unpleasant) event, especially a war, an accident, etc. （战争、事故、不快事情的）后果，创伤：*A lot of rebuilding took place **in the aftermath of** the war.* 战后进行了大量的重建工作。◇ *the assassination of the Prime Minister and its immediate aftermath* 暗杀首相及其直接后果

after·noon ⚷ /ˌɑːftəˈnuːn; *NAmE* ˌæftərˈn-/ *noun* [U, C] the part of the day from 12 midday until about 6 o'clock 下午（中午 12 点至下午 6 点左右）：***this/yesterday/tomorrow afternoon*** 今天 / 昨天 / 明天下午 ◇ ***In the afternoon** they went shopping.* 他们下午去购物了。◇ *She studies art two afternoons a week.* 她每周两个下午学习美术。◇ *Are you ready for this afternoon's meeting?* 今天下午的会议你准备好了没有？◇ *The baby always has an afternoon nap.* 婴儿午后总要睡一会儿。◇ *Come over on Sunday afternoon.* 星期天下午过来。◇ *Where were you **on the afternoon of** May 21?* * 5 月 21 日下午你在哪里？ ➲ SEE ALSO GOOD AFTERNOON

after·noons /ˌɑːftəˈnuːnz; *NAmE* ˌæftərˈn-/ *adv.* during the afternoon every day 每天下午：*Afternoons he works at home.* 每天下午他在家里工作。

af·ters /ˈɑːftəz; *NAmE* ˈæftərz/ *noun* [U] (*BrE, informal*) a sweet dish that you eat at the end of a meal （正餐最后一道菜）甜食，后盘：*fruit salad for afters* 作为正餐后盘的水果色拉 ➲ SEE ALSO DESSERT, PUDDING, SWEET *n.*

ˌ**after-ˌsales ˈservice** *noun* [U] the fact of providing help to customers after they have bought a product, usually involving doing repairs that are needed or giving advice on how to use the product 售后服务

after·shave /ˈɑːftəʃeɪv; *NAmE* ˈæftərʃ-/ *noun* [U, C] a liquid with a pleasant smell that men sometimes put on their faces after they shave （男人剃须后抹的）润肤液；须后水

after·shock /ˈɑːftəʃɒk; *NAmE* ˈæftərʃɑːk/ *noun* a small EARTHQUAKE that happens after a bigger one （地震后的）余震

after·taste /ˈɑːftəteɪst; *NAmE* ˈæftərt-/ *noun* [sing.] a taste (usually an unpleasant one) that stays in your mouth after you have eaten or drunk sth （饮食留在口中不快的）回味，余味，苦味

after·thought /ˈɑːftəθɔːt; *NAmE* ˈæftərθ-/ *noun* [usually sing.] a thing that is thought of, said or added later, and is often not carefully planned 事后想法，事后添加的事物（常未经周密考虑）：*They only invited Jack and Sarah **as an afterthought**.* 他们后来才想到邀请杰克和萨拉。

after·wards ⚷ /ˈɑːftəwədz; *NAmE* ˈæftərwərdz/ (*especially BrE*) (*NAmE usually* **after·ward**) *adv.* at a later time; after an event that has already been mentioned 以后；后来：*Afterwards she was sorry for what she'd said.* 后来她后悔说了那些话。◇ *Let's go out now and eat afterwards.* 咱们现在出去，然后再吃饭。◇ *Shortly afterwards he met her again.* 不久之后，他又遇到了她。

after·word /ˈɑːftəwɜːd; *NAmE* ˈæftərwɜːrd/ *noun* a section at the end of a book that says sth about the main text, and may be written by a different author 后记；跋 ➲ COMPARE FOREWORD

ag /æx; ʌx/ *exclamation* (*SAfrE*) used when you are reacting to sth that has been said, or when you are angry or irritated by sth （对他人的话作出反应或表示生气、恼怒）唔，啊，哎呀：*Ag, don't worry about it.* 哦，别担心。◇ *Ag, no man!* 嘿，不行！

Aga™ /ˈɑːgə/ *noun* (*BrE*) a type of British cooker/stove made of solid iron that is also used for heating. 'Aga saga' is a humorous name for a novel about the lives of British middle-class women, because Agas are very popular with this group. 雅家炉（铁制，用于烹饪和取暖。"雅家炉小说"趣指描写英国中产阶级妇女生活的小说，因她们喜用此炉而得名）

again ⚷ /əˈgen; əˈgeɪn/ *adv.* 1 ⚷ one more time; on another occasion 再一次；又一次：*Could you say it again, please?* 请再说一遍好吗？◇ *When will I see you again?* 我何时能再见到你？◇ *This must never happen again.* 这种事再也不能发生了。◇ ***Once again** (= as had happened several times before), the train was late.* 火车又晚点了。◇ *I've told you **again and again** (= many times) not to do that.* 我一再告诉过你别干那种事。◇ *I'll have to write it **all over again** (= again from the beginning).* 我得从头再写一遍。 2 ⚷ showing that sb/sth is in the same place or state that they were in originally 返回原处；复原：*He was glad to be home again.* 他很高兴又回到家了。◇ *She spends two hours a day getting to work and **back again**.* 她每天上班来回要花两小时。◇ *You'll soon feel well again.* 你很快就会康复的。 3 added to an amount that is already there 增加；多：*The cost is about **half as much again** as it was two years ago.* 现在的价格比两年前提高约一半。◇ *I'd like **the same again** (= the same amount or the same thing).* 我想再来一份同样的。 4 used to show that a comment or fact is connected with what you have just said 再说；其次：*And again, we must think of the cost.* 再说，我们必须考虑成本。 5 **then/there ~** used to introduce a fact or an opinion that contrasts with what you have just said （引出相对照的事实或看法）再说，另一方面：*We might buy it but then again we might not.* 我们可能买，不过也可能不买。 6 used when you ask sb to tell you sth or repeat sth that you think they have told you already 请再说一遍: *What was the name again?* 叫什么名字，再说一遍好不好？ IDM SEE NOW *adv.*, SAME *pron.*, TIME *n.*

against /əˈgenst; əˈgeɪnst/ *prep.* HELP For the special uses of **against** in phrasal verbs, look at the entries for the verbs. For example **count against sb** is in the phrasal verb section at **count**. * against 在短语动词中的特殊用法见有关动词词条。如 count against sb 在词条 count 的短语动词部分。 **1** opposing or disagreeing with sb/sth 反对；与…相反；逆；违反: *the fight against terrorism* 反对恐怖主义的斗争 ◇ *We're playing against the league champions next week.* 下周我们要和联赛冠军队比赛。◇ *We were rowing against the current.* 我们划船逆流而上。◇ *That's against the law.* 那是违法的。◇ *She was forced to marry against her will.* 她被迫违背自己的心愿嫁了人。◇ *Are you for or against the death penalty?* 你赞成还是反对死刑？ ◇ *She is against seeing* (= does not want to see) *him.* 她不想见他。◇ *I'd advise you against doing that.* 我劝你别做那事。 **2** not to the advantage or favour of sb/sth 对…不利: *The evidence is against him.* 证据对他不利。◇ *Her age is against her.* 她的年龄对她不利。 ➲ COMPARE FOR *prep.* (7) **3** close to, touching or hitting sb/sth 紧靠；倚；碰；撞: *Put the piano there, against the wall.* 把钢琴放在那儿，紧靠着墙。◇ *The rain beat against the windows.* 雨点击打着窗户。 **4** in order to prevent sth from happening or to reduce the damage caused by sth 以防: *an injection against rabies* 狂犬病预防注射 ◇ *They took precautions against fire.* 他们采取了防火措施。◇ *Are we insured against theft?* 我们保了盗窃险没有？ **5** with sth in the background, as a contrast 以…为背景；衬托: *His red clothes stood out clearly against the snow.* 他的红衣服在白雪中格外显眼。◇ (*figurative*) *The love story unfolds against a background of civil war.* 这爱情故事以内战为背景展开。 **6** used when you are comparing two things 和…相比: *You must weigh the benefits against the cost.* 你一定要权衡利益与成本二者的得失。◇ *Check your receipts against the statement.* 核对你的收据与结算单是否相符。◇ *What's the rate of exchange against the dollar?* 与美元的兑换率是多少？ IDM SEE AS *conj.*, STACKED

agape /əˈgeɪp/ *adj.* [not before noun] (*formal*) if a person's mouth is **agape**, it is wide open, especially because they are surprised or shocked （嘴巴因吃惊等）大张着

agar /ˈeɪgɑː(r)/ (*also* ˌagar-ˈagar) *noun* [U] a substance like jelly, used by scientists for growing CULTURES 琼脂；洋菜

agate /ˈægət/ *noun* [U, C] a hard stone with bands or areas of colour, used in jewellery 玛瑙

agave /əˈgeɪvi; -ˈgɑːv-; *NAmE* əˈgɑːvi/ *noun* a plant that grows in hot dry areas of N and S America, with sharp points on the leaves and tall groups of flowers 龙舌兰（生长在南北美洲热带干旱地区）

ag·bada /ægˈbɑːdə/ *noun* a long ROBE (= long piece of clothing) worn by men in some parts of W Africa （西非）男式长袍

age /eɪdʒ/ *noun, verb*

■***noun*** **1** [C, U] the number of years that a person has lived or a thing has existed 年龄: *He left school **at the age of** 18.* 他 18 岁读完中学。◇ *She needs more friends of her own age.* 她需要更多的同龄朋友。◇ *children from 5–10 **years of age*** * 5 至 10 岁的儿童 ◇ *Young people of all ages go there to meet.* 不同年龄的年轻人都去那里聚会。◇ *When I was your age I was already married.* 我在你这个年纪时已经结婚了。◇ *He started playing the piano **at an early age**.* 他幼年开始弹钢琴。 ◇ *All ages admitted.* 不限年龄均可入内。◇ *Children **over the age of** 12 must pay full fare.* * 12 岁以上儿童须购全票。◇ *She was beginning to **feel her age*** (= feel that she was getting old). 她开始感到自己上年纪了。 ◇ *He was tall **for his age*** (= taller than you would expect, considering his age). 以他的年龄，他算高个子。◇ *There's a big **age gap** between them* (= a big difference in their ages). 他们的年龄相差很大。◇ *ways of calculating the age of the earth* 计算地球年龄的方法

WORDFINDER 联想词: adolescent, elderly, generation, infant, juvenile, middle-aged, minor, teenage, **young**

2 [U, C] a particular period of a person's life 年龄段: *middle age* 中年 ◇ *15 is an awkward age.* * 15 岁是个尴尬的年纪。 ◇ *He died of old age.* 他终其天年。 ➲ SEE ALSO THIRD AGE **3** [C] a particular period of history （历史上的）时代，时期: *the nuclear age* 核时代 ◇ *the age of the computer* 计算机时代 ➲ SEE ALSO BRONZE AGE, IRON AGE,

▼**COLLOCATIONS** 词语搭配

The ages of life 年龄段

Childhood/youth 童年 / 青年时期

- **be born and raised/bred** in Oxford; **be born** into a wealthy/middle-class family 在牛津出生并长大；在富裕 / 中产家庭出生
- **have** a happy/an unhappy/a tough childhood 有幸福 / 不幸 / 艰苦的童年
- **grow up** in a musical family/in an orphanage/on a farm 成长于音乐之家 / 孤儿院 / 农场
- **be/grow up** an only child (= with no brothers or sisters) 是独生子
- **reach/hit/enter/go through** adolescence/puberty 进入 / 经历青春期
- **be in** your teens/early twenties/mid-twenties/late twenties 十几岁；二十出头；二十五岁左右；将近三十岁
- **undergo/experience** physical/psychological changes 经历生理 / 心理变化
- **give in to/succumb to/resist** peer pressure 屈服于 / 顶住同辈的压力
- **assert** your independence/individuality 维护独立 / 个性

Adulthood 成年

- **leave** school/university/home 中学 / 大学毕业；离家
- **go out to** work (at sixteen) （16 岁）投身工作
- **get/find** a job/partner 找到工作 / 伴侣
- **be/get** engaged/married 订婚；结婚
- **have/get** a wife/husband/mortgage/steady job 有妻子 / 丈夫 / 按揭贷款 / 稳定的工作
- **settle down and have** kids/children/a family 安定下来并生儿育女
- **begin/start/launch/build** a career (in politics/science/the music industry) 开始（政治 / 科学 / 音乐）职业生涯
- **prove (to be)/represent/mark/reach** a turning point in your life/career 最终成为 / 代表 / 标志 / 达到某人人生 / 某人职业生涯的转折点
- **reach/be well into/settle into** middle age 进入 / 安度中年
- **have/suffer/go through** a midlife crisis 经历中年危机
- **take/consider** early retirement 提前退休；考虑提前退休
- **approach/announce/enjoy** your retirement 临近 / 宣布 / 享受退休

Old age 老年

- **have/see/spend time with** your grandchildren 有孙辈；与孙辈共度时光
- **take up/pursue/develop** a hobby 开始 / 追求 / 培养一种爱好
- **get/receive/draw/collect/live on** a pension 得到 / 提取 / 领取退休金；靠退休金生活
- **approach/save for/die from** old age 临近晚年；存钱养老；老死
- **live to** a ripe old age 高寿
- **reach** the grand old age of 102/23 (*often ironic*) 活到 102 / 23 岁高龄（常作反语）
- **be/become/be getting/be going** senile (*often ironic*) 变得衰老（常作反语）
- **die (peacefully)/pass away** in your sleep/after a brief illness 在睡梦中 / 患病不久（平静地）离开人世

A

NEW AGE, STONE AGE **4** [U] the state of being old 老年；陈年；破旧；老化：*Wine improves **with age**.* 陈酒味浓。◇ *The jacket was showing signs of age.* 这件夹克已露出破旧的痕迹。◇ *the wisdom that comes with age* 随着年龄而增加的智慧 **5** **ages** [pl.] (*also* **an age** [sing.]) (*informal, especially BrE*) a very long time 很长时间：*I waited for **ages**.* 我等了好长时间。◇ *It'll probably **take ages** to find a parking space.* 大概得老半天才能找到停车位。◇ *Carlos left **ages ago**.* 卡洛斯老早就离开了。◇ *It's been **an age** since we've seen them.* 我们有很长一段时间没有见到他们了。 **6** [C] (*geology* 地) a length of time which is a division of an EPOCH 期

IDM ˌ**be/ˌact your ˈage** to behave in a way that is suitable for sb of your age and not as though you were much younger 行为和年龄相称；举止不再有孩子气 ˌ**come of ˈage 1** when a person **comes of age**, they reach the age when they have an adult's legal rights and responsibilities 成年；达到法定年龄 ➲ SEE ALSO COMING OF AGE **2** if sth **comes of age**, it reaches the stage of development at which people accept and value it 成熟；发达 ˌ**look your ˈage** to seem as old as you really are and not younger or older 容貌与年龄相当 ˌ**under ˈage** not legally old enough to do a particular thing 未到法定年龄：*It is illegal to sell cigarettes to children who are under age.* 售香烟给未到法定年龄的孩子是非法的。➲ SEE ALSO UNDERAGE ➲ MORE AT ADVANCED, CERTAIN *adj.*, DAY, FEEL *v.*, GRAND *adj.*, RIPE

■ *verb* (**ag·ing, aged, aged**) HELP In *BrE* the present participle can also be spelled **age·ing**. 英式英语中，现在分词也可拼作 ageing。 **1** [I] to become older 变老：*As he aged, his memory got worse.* 他随着年事增高，记忆力就变差了。◇ *The population is aging* (= more people are living longer). 人口正在老龄化。 **2** [T] to make sb/sth look, feel or seem older 使显老；使变老；使苍老：**~ sb** *The shock has aged her.* 这次打击让她显得苍老了。◇ **~ sth** *Exposure to the sun ages the skin.* 太阳暴晒会使皮肤衰老。 **3** [I, T] to develop in flavour over a period of time; to allow sth to do this （使）成熟，变陈 SYN **mature**：*The cheese is left to age for at least a year.* 这种奶酪至少要搁一年才成熟。◇ **~ sth** *The wine is aged in oak casks.* 这种酒是用栎木酒桶放陈的。

-age *suffix* (in nouns 构成名词) **1** the action or result of （表示动作或结果）：*breakage* 破损 **2** a state or condition of （表示状态或状况）：*bondage* 奴役 **3** a set or group of （表示一套或一组）：*baggage* 行李 **4** an amount of （表示数量）：*mileage* 英里数 **5** the cost of （表示费用）：*postage* 邮费 **6** a place where （表示地方）：*anchorage* 泊地 ➲ MORE LIKE THIS 7, page R25

aged *adj.* **1** /eɪdʒd/ [not before noun] of the age of …岁：*They have two children aged six and nine.* 他们有两个小孩，一个六岁，一个九岁。◇ *volunteers aged between 25 and 40* * 25 至 40 岁的志愿者 **2** /ˈeɪdʒɪd/ (*formal*) very old 年迈的：*my aged aunt* 我年迈的婶婶 ➲ SYNONYMS AT OLD **3 the aged** /ˈeɪdʒɪd/ *noun* [pl.] very old people （统称）老人：*services for the sick and the aged* 为病人和老人提供的服务 ➲ MORE LIKE THIS 22, page R27

ˈ**age group** (*also less frequent* ˈ**age bracket**) *noun* people of a similar age or within a particular range of ages 年龄组；年龄段：*men in the older age group* 较年长组别的男子 ◇ *education for the 16–18 age group* * 16 至 18 岁年龄段的教育 ◇ *Which age bracket are you? (Please tick the box).* 你在哪个年龄段？（请在方格中打钩。）

age·ing (*BrE*) (*also* **aging** *NAmE, BrE*) /ˈeɪdʒɪŋ/ *noun, adj.*

■ *noun* [U] the process of growing old 变老；苍老；变旧；老化：*signs of ageing* 变老的迹象

■ *adj.* [usually before noun] becoming older and usually less useful, safe, healthy, etc. 变老的；老朽的；变旧的；老化的：*ageing equipment* 老化的设备 ◇ *an ageing rock star* 日益年迈的摇滚乐歌星

age·ism (*NAmE also* **agism**) /ˈeɪdʒɪzəm/ *noun* [U] unfair treatment of people because they are considered too old 对老年人的歧视；年龄歧视 ▸ **age·ist** *adj.* **age·ist** *noun*

age·less /ˈeɪdʒləs/ *adj.* (*literary*) **1** never looking old or never seeming to grow old 青春永驻的；永不显老的 SYN **timeless**：*Her beauty appeared ageless.* 她的美似乎不随时间改变。 **2** existing for ever; impossible to give an age to 永恒的 SYN **timeless**：*the ageless mystery of the universe* 宇宙永恒之谜

ˈ**age limit** *noun* the oldest or youngest age at which you are allowed to do sth 年龄限制：*the **upper/lower age limit*** 年龄上限 / 下限

ˈ**age-mate** *noun* a person of the same age or belonging to the same age group 同龄人；年龄相仿的人：*The toddlers participated in playgroups with age-mates.* 刚学会走路的孩子参加同年龄组的游戏班。

agency /ˈeɪdʒənsi/ *noun* (*pl.* **-ies**) **1** a business or an organization that provides a particular service especially on behalf of other businesses or organizations 服务机构；（尤指）代理机构，经销机构：*an **advertising/employment agency*** 广告公司；职业介绍所 ◇ *You can book at your local **travel agency**.* 你可以在当地的旅行社预订。◇ *international **aid agencies** caring for refugees* 国际援助难民事务所 ➲ SEE ALSO DATING AGENCY, NEWS AGENCY, PRESS AGENCY **2** (*especially NAmE*) a government department that provides a particular service（政府的）专门机构：*the Central Intelligence Agency (CIA)*（美国）中央情报局

IDM **through the agency of** (*formal*) as a result of the action of sb/sth 由于…的作用

agenda /əˈdʒendə/ *noun* **1** a list of items to be discussed at a meeting（会议的）议程表，议事日程：*The next item **on the agenda** is the publicity budget.* 议程表上的下一项是宣传预算。➲ WORDFINDER NOTE AT MEETING **2** a plan of things to be done, or problems to be addressed （待办事项或待解决问题的）计划，方案：*This is an ambitious agenda that will take time to implement.* 这是个宏大的计划，实施起来需要时间。◇ *For the government, education is now **at the top of the agenda*** (= most important). 对政府来说，教育是当务之急。◇ *Newspapers have been accused of trying to **set the agenda** for the government* (= decide what is important). 人们指责报章企图替政府决定政务的轻重缓急。◇ *In our company, quality is **high on the agenda**.* 我们公司高度重视质量。 **3** the intention behind what sb says or does, that is often secret （隐秘的）意图，目的：*The artist is letting **his own agenda** affect what was meant to be a community project.* 这本是个集体项目，可这个艺术家在其中掺入了自己的意图。➲ SEE ALSO HIDDEN AGENDA

▼ **WHICH WORD?** 词语辨析

agenda / diary / schedule / timetable

- A book with a space for each day where you write down things that you have to do in the future is called a **diary** or a **datebook** (*NAmE*) (not an *agenda*). You may also have a **calendar** on your desk or hanging up in your room, where you write down your appointments. A **diary** or a **journal** is also the record that some people keep of what has happened during the day. 记事簿用 diary 或 datebook（美式英语），不用 agenda。记录约会等事宜也可用台历或挂历 (calendar)。diary 或 journal 亦指日记、日志：*The Diary of Anne Frank*《安妮日记》
- In *BrE* your **schedule** is a plan that lists all the work that you have to do and when you must do each thing and a **timetable** is a list showing the fixed times at which events will happen. 在英式英语中，schedule 指工作计划、日程安排，timetable 指时间表、时刻表：*a bus/train timetable* 公共汽车 / 火车时刻表 In *NAmE* these are both called a **schedule**. 在美式英语中，上述两种含义均用 schedule。

agent /ˈeɪdʒənt/ *noun* **1** a person whose job is to act for, or manage the affairs of, other people in business, politics, etc.（企业、政治等的）代理人，经纪

人： *an insurance agent* 保险经纪人 ◇ *Our agent in New York deals with all US sales.* 我们在纽约的代理商经办在整个美国的销售。 ➲ WORDFINDER NOTE AT BUSINESSMAN, COMPANY ➲ SEE ALSO ESTATE AGENT, LAND AGENT, TRAVEL AGENT **2** a person whose job is to arrange work for an actor, musician, sports player, etc. or to find sb who will publish a writer's work （演员、音乐家、运动员、作家等的）代理人，经纪人： *a **theatrical/literary agent*** 戏剧演出经纪人；文稿（出版）代理人 ➲ SEE ALSO PRESS AGENT **3** = SECRET AGENT ： *an enemy agent* 敌方特务 ➲ SEE ALSO DOUBLE AGENT, SPECIAL AGENT **4** (*formal*) a person or thing that has an important effect on a situation 原动力，动因（指对事态起重要作用的人、事物）： *The charity has been an agent for social change.* 这个慈善机构一直推动社会变革。 **5** (*specialist*) a chemical or a substance that produces an effect or a change or is used for a particular purpose （化学）剂： ***cleaning/oxidizing agents*** 清洁剂；氧化剂 **6** (*grammar* 语法) the person or thing that does an action (expressed as the subject of an active verb, or in a 'by' phrase with a passive verb) 施事者；施动者；行为主体 ➲ COMPARE PATIENT *n.* (3) ➲ SEE ALSO FREE AGENT

ˌagent ˈgeneral *noun* (*pl.* **agents general**) the representative of an Australian state or Canadian PROVINCE in a foreign country （澳大利亚州或加拿大省的）驻外代表

agent pro·voca·teur /ˌæʒɒ̃ prəˌvɒkəˈtɜː(r); *NAmE* ˌɑːʒɑ̃ː proʊˌvɑːkəˈtɜːr/ (*also* **pro·voca·teur**) *noun* (*pl.* **agents pro·voca·teurs** /ˌæʒɒ̃ prəˌvɒkəˈtɜː(r); *NAmE* ˌɑːʒɑ̃ː proʊˌvɑːkəˈtɜːr/) (*from French*) a person who is employed by a government to encourage people in political groups to do sth illegal so that they can be arrested（受雇于政府，怂恿某些政治团体人士犯法以便将之逮捕的）密探，坐探

ˌage of conˈsent *noun* [sing.] the age at which sb is legally old enough to agree to have a sexual relationship 同意年龄，承诺年龄（可发生性关系的法定年龄）

ˌage-ˈold *adj.* [usually before noun] having existed for a very long time 古老的；已存在很久的： *an **age-old custom/problem*** 古老的风俗；由来已久的问题

ˈage-set *noun* (*EAfrE*) a group of boys or men of a similar age （男孩或男子的）同龄组

ag·glom·er·ate *verb, noun, adj.* (*specialist*)
■ ***verb*** /əˈglɒməreɪt; *NAmE* əˈglɑːm-/ [I, T] to form into a mass or group; to collect things and form them into a mass or group （使）成团，聚结： *These small particles agglomerate together to form larger clusters.* 这些颗粒聚结形成较大的团。◇ **~ sth** *They agglomerated many small pieces of research into a single large study.* 他们把许多小的研究课题汇集成一个大项目。
■ ***noun*** /əˈglɒmərət; *NAmE* əˈglɑːm-/ a mass or collection of things 大团；聚结物： *a multimedia agglomerate* (= group of companies) 一个多媒体集团
■ ***adj.*** /əˈglɒmərət; *NAmE* əˈglɑːm-/ formed into a mass or group 成团的；聚结的

ag·glom·er·ation /əˌglɒməˈreɪʃn; *NAmE* əˌglɑːm-/ *noun* [C, U] (*specialist*) a group of things put together in no particular order or arrangement （杂乱聚集的）团，块，堆；聚集

ag·glu·tin·ative /əˈgluːtɪnətɪv/ *adj.* (*linguistics* 语言) = SYNTHETIC (2)

ag·grand·ize·ment (*BrE also* **-ise·ment**) /əˈgrændɪzmənt/ *noun* [U] (*formal, disapproving*) an increase in the power or importance of a person or country （个人、国家权力或重要性的）扩大，增加，提高： *Her sole aim is personal aggrandizement.* 她唯一的目的就是扩大个人权势。

ag·gra·vate /ˈægrəveɪt/ *verb* **1 ~ sth** to make an illness or a bad or unpleasant situation worse 使严重；使恶化 SYN **worsen**： *Pollution can aggravate asthma.* 污染会使哮喘加重。◇ *Military intervention will only aggravate the conflict even further.* 军事介入只会使冲突加剧。 **2 ~ sb** (*informal*) to annoy sb, especially deliberately （尤指故意地）激怒，惹恼 SYN **irritate** ▸ **ag·gra·vat·ing** *adj.* **ag·gra·va·tion** /ˌægrəˈveɪʃn/ *noun* [U, C]： *I don't need all this aggravation at work.* 我工作时可不想有这么多烦人的事。◇ *The drug may cause an aggravation of the condition.* 这种药可能导致病情恶化。

ag·gra·vat·ed /ˈægrəveɪtɪd/ *adj.* [only before noun] (*law* 律) an **aggravated** crime involves further unnecessary violence or unpleasant behaviour （罪行）严重的，加重的

ag·gre·gate AW *noun, adj., verb*
■ ***noun*** /ˈægrɪgət/ **1** [C] a total number or amount made up of smaller amounts that are collected together 总数；合计 **2** [U, C] (*specialist*) sand or broken stone that is used to make concrete or for building roads, etc. （可制成混凝土或修路等用的）集料，骨料
IDM **in** (**the**) **ˈaggregate** (*formal*) added together as a total or single amount 总共；作为总体 **on ˈaggregate** (*BrE, sport* 体育) when the scores of a number of games are added together （各次比赛相加的）总分： *They won 4–2 on aggregate.* 他们以总分 4:2 获胜。
■ ***adj.*** /ˈægrɪgət/ [only before noun] (*economics* 经 or *sport* 体育) made up of several amounts that are added together to form a total number 总数的；总计的： ***aggregate demand/investment/turnover*** 总需求；总投资；总成交量 ◇ (*BrE*) *an aggregate win over their rivals* 以总分战胜他们的对手
■ ***verb*** /ˈægrɪgeɪt/ [usually passive] **~ sth** (**with sth**) (*formal* or *specialist*) to put together different items, amounts, etc. into a single group or total 总计；合计： *The scores were aggregated with the first round totals to decide the winner.* 此次得分与第一轮所得总分合计决出优胜者。 ▸ **ag·gre·ga·tion** AW /ˌægrɪˈgeɪʃn/ *noun* [U, C]： *the aggregation of data* 数据聚合

ag·gre·ga·tor /ˈægrɪgeɪtə(r)/ *noun* (*computing* 计) an Internet company that collects information about other companies' products and services and puts it on a single website 信息汇集公司（汇集互联网其他公司的产品和服务信息并在单独的网站上发布）： *a news aggregator* 新闻汇总机构

ag·gres·sion /əˈgreʃn/ *noun* [U] **1** feelings of anger and hatred that may result in threatening or violent behaviour 好斗情绪；攻击性： *The research shows that computer games may cause aggression.* 研究显示，电脑游戏可能引起好斗情绪。 **2** a violent attack or threats by one person against another person or by one country against another country 侵犯；挑衅；侵略： *unprovoked military aggression* 无端军事侵犯 ➲ WORDFINDER NOTE AT CONFLICT

ag·gres·sive /əˈgresɪv/ *adj.* **1** angry, and behaving in a threatening way; ready to attack 好斗的；挑衅的；侵略的；富于攻击性的： *He gets aggressive when he's drunk.* 他喝醉了就喜欢寻衅滋事。◇ *a dangerous aggressive dog* 一条危险的恶犬 **2** acting with force and determination in order to succeed 气势汹汹的；声势浩大的；志在必得的： *an aggressive advertising campaign* 一场声势浩大的广告宣传活动 ◇ *A good salesperson has to be aggressive in today's competitive market.* 在当今竞争激烈的市场上，好的销售员应该有进取精神。 ▸ **ag·gres·sive·ly** *adv.*： *'What do you want?' he demanded aggressively.* "你想怎么样？" 他挑衅地问道。◇ *aggressively marketed products* 极力推销的产品 **ag·gres·sive·ness** *noun* [U]

ag·gres·sor /əˈgresə(r)/ *noun* a person, country, etc. that attacks first 侵略者；挑衅者

ag·grieved /əˈgriːvd/ *adj.* **1 ~** (**at/by sth**) feeling that you have been treated unfairly 愤愤不平的；感到受委屈的 **2** (*law* 律) suffering unfair or illegal treatment and making a complaint 受害的；受委屈的： *the aggrieved party* (= person) *in the case* 案件中的受害方

aggro /ˈægrəʊ; *NAmE* ˈægroʊ/ *noun* [U] (*BrE, informal*) **1** violent aggressive behaviour 暴力侵犯行为；闹事；寻衅： *Don't give me any aggro or I'll call the police.* 不要对我动粗，不然我就叫警察。 **2** problems and difficulties that are annoying 烦恼；麻烦： *I had a lot of aggro at the bank.* 我在银行遇到了很多麻烦。

A

aghast /ə'ɡɑːst; *NAmE* ə'ɡæst/ *adj.* [not before noun] filled with horror and surprise when you see or hear sth 惊恐；惊骇 SYN **horrified**: *Erica looked at him aghast.* 埃里卡惊恐地望着他。◇ ~ **at sth** *He stood aghast at the sight of so much blood.* 他看见这么多血，吓得目瞪口呆。

agile /'ædʒaɪl; *NAmE* 'ædʒl/ *adj.* **1** able to move quickly and easily（动作）敏捷的，灵活的 SYN **nimble** **2** able to think quickly and in an intelligent way （思维）机敏的，机灵的：*an agile mind/brain* 敏捷的思维 ▶ **agil·ity** /ə'dʒɪləti/ *noun* [U]: *He had the agility of a man half his age.* 他的敏捷赶得上岁数比他小一半的人。

aging, agism = AGEING, AGEISM

agi·tate /'ædʒɪteɪt/ *verb* **1** [I, T] to argue strongly for sth you want, especially for changes in a law, in social conditions, etc.（尤指为法律、社会状况的改变而）激烈争论，鼓动，煽动 SYN **campaign**: ~ (**for/against sth**) *political groups agitating for social change* 鼓吹社会变革的政治团体 ◇ ~ **to do sth** *Her family are agitating to have her transferred to a prison in the UK.* 她的家人正多方游说把她转到英国监狱。**2** [T] ~ **sb** to make sb feel angry, anxious or nervous 激怒；使不安；使烦乱 **3** [T] ~ **sth** (*specialist*) to make sth, especially a liquid, move around by stirring or shaking it 搅动，摇动（液体等）

agi·tated /'ædʒɪteɪtɪd/ *adj.* showing in your behaviour that you are anxious and nervous 焦虑不安的；激动的：*Calm down! Don't get so agitated.* 冷静下来！别那么激动。

agi·ta·tion /ˌædʒɪ'teɪʃn/ *noun* **1** [U] worry and anxiety that you show by behaving in a nervous way 焦虑不安；忧虑；烦乱：*Dot arrived in a state of great agitation.* 多特到达时十分焦虑不安。**2** [U] ~ (**for/against sth**) public protest in order to achieve political change 骚动；煽动；鼓动：*widespread agitation for social reform* 要求社会改革的大骚动 **3** [C] (*IndE*) a public meeting or march at which people show that they are protesting against or supporting sth 公众集会；游行示威：*The situation has provoked agitations all over the region.* 这种状况已经在整个地区引发了民众示威。◇ *Protesters are expected to launch an agitation over the issue.* 预计反对者要就这个问题发动一次游行示威。**4** [U] (*specialist*) the act of stirring or shaking a liquid （液体的）搅拌，摇动

agi·ta·tor /'ædʒɪteɪtə(r)/ *noun* (*disapproving*) a person who tries to persuade people to take part in political protest （政治上的）煽动者，鼓动者

agit·prop /'ædʒɪtprɒp; *NAmE* -prɑːp/ *noun* [U] the use of art, films/movies, music, etc. to spread LEFT-WING political ideas （利用影视等艺术形式对左翼政见的）宣传鼓动

aglow /ə'ɡləʊ; *NAmE* ə'ɡloʊ/ *adj.* [not before noun] (*literary*) shining with warmth and colour or happiness 光照融融；发红光

AGM /ˌeɪ dʒiː 'em/ *abbr.* (*BrE*) annual general meeting (an important meeting which the members of an organization hold once a year in order to elect officers, discuss past and future activities and examine the accounts) 年会；年度大会 ➲ WORDFINDER NOTE AT CLUB, MEETING

ag·nos·tic /æɡ'nɒstɪk; *NAmE* -'nɑːs-/ *noun, adj.*
■ *noun* a person who believes that it is not possible to know whether God exists or not 不可知论者（认为上帝存在与否是不可知的） ➲ COMPARE ATHEIST
■ *adj.* **1** (*religion* 宗) holding or showing the belief that it is not possible to know whether God exists or not 不可知论的 **2** not having a strong opinion about an activity or topic 没有强烈意见的；无可无不可的：*I'm largely agnostic on this issue as I know so little about it.* 对于这个问题，我没什么意见，因为我对此所知甚少。**3** (*computing* 计) (often in compounds 常构成复合词) (used about computer HARDWARE or software) able to be used with many different types of computer systems, software or OPERATING SYSTEMS (= sets of programs that control the way computers work and run other programs) （计算机硬件或软件）兼容…的，不限…的：*Now that the services are platform-agnostic, they can be accessed by far more users.* 由于这些服务不限平台，因此更多的用户可以使用了。▶ **ag·nos·ti·cism** /æɡ'nɒstɪsɪzəm; *NAmE* -'nɑːs-/ *noun* [U]

ago /ə'ɡəʊ; *NAmE* ə'ɡoʊ/ *adv.* used in expressions of time with the simple past tense to show how far in the past sth happened（与动词的一般过去时连用）以前：*two weeks/months/years ago* 两周 / 两月 / 两年以前 ◇ *The letter came a few days ago.* 这封信是几天前寄来的。◇ *She was here just a minute ago.* 刚才她还在这儿。◇ *a short/long time ago* 不久 / 很久以前 ◇ *How long ago did you buy it?* 这东西你是多久以前买的？◇ *It was on TV not (so) long ago.* 电视不（很）久以前播出了这个节目。◇ *He stopped working some time ago* (= quite a long time ago). 好久以前他就不工作了。◇ *They're getting married? It's not that long ago* (= it's only a short time ago) *that they met!* 他们要结婚啦？他们刚认识不久嘛！

agog /ə'ɡɒɡ; *NAmE* ə'ɡɑːɡ/ *adj.* [not before noun] excited and very interested to find out sth 兴奋期待；急于了解

ag·on·ize (*BrE also* **-ise**) /'æɡənaɪz/ *verb* [I] ~ (**over/about sth**) to spend a long time thinking and worrying about a difficult situation or problem 苦苦思索；焦虑不已：*I spent days agonizing over whether to take the job or not.* 我用了好些天苦苦思考是否接受这个工作。

ag·on·ized (*BrE also* **-ised**) /'æɡənaɪzd/ *adj.* suffering or expressing severe pain or anxiety 十分痛苦的；很焦虑的：*agonized cries* 痛苦不堪的叫声

ag·on·iz·ing (*BrE also* **-is·ing**) /'æɡənaɪzɪŋ/ *adj.* causing great pain, anxiety or difficulty 使人十分痛苦的；令人焦虑不安的；带来巨大困难的：*his father's agonizing death* 他父亲极度痛苦的死 ◇ *It was the most agonizing decision of her life.* 这是她一生中最难作的决定。

ag·on·iz·ing·ly (*BrE also* **-is·ing·ly**) /'æɡənaɪzɪŋli/ *adv.* used meaning 'extremely' to emphasize sth negative（强调反面事物）极其：*an agonizingly slow process* 极其缓慢的过程

agony /'æɡəni/ *noun* (*pl.* **-ies**) [U, C] extreme physical or mental pain（精神或肉体的）极度痛苦：*Jack collapsed* **in agony** *on the floor.* 杰克十分痛苦地瘫倒在地板上。◇ *It was agony not knowing where the children were.* 孩子们下落不明真让人揪心。◇ *She waited in an agony of suspense.* 她提心吊胆地等待着。◇ *The worst agonies of the war were now beginning.* 战争最深重的苦难现在开始了。◇ *Tell me now! Don't* **prolong the agony** (= make it last longer). 现在就告诉我吧！别再让我心急如焚。IDM SEE PILE *v.*

'agony aunt (*BrE*) (*NAmE* **ad'vice columnist**) *noun* a person who writes in a newspaper or magazine giving advice in reply to people's letters about their personal problems （报纸或杂志的）答问专栏作者 ➲ COMPARE AGONY UNCLE

'agony column (*BrE*) (*NAmE* **ad'vice column**) *noun* part of a newspaper or magazine in which sb gives advice to readers who have sent letters about their personal problems（报纸或杂志中为读者个人疑难问题提供咨询的）答问专栏

'agony uncle *noun* (*BrE*) (*NAmE* **ad'vice columnist**) a man who writes in a newspaper or magazine giving advice in reply to people's letters about their personal problems （报纸或杂志的）答问专栏男作者 ➲ COMPARE AGONY AUNT

agora /'æɡɒrə; *NAmE* 'æɡərə/ *noun* (*pl.* **agorae** /-riː/ or **agoras**) in ancient Greece, an open space used for markets and public meetings （古希腊的）广场，露天集市，露天聚会场所

agora·pho·bia /ˌæɡərə'fəʊbiə; *NAmE* -'foʊ-/ *noun* [U] (*specialist*) a fear of being in public places where there are many other people 广场恐怖（症）；公共场所恐惧（症） ➲ COMPARE CLAUSTROPHOBIA

agora·pho·bic /ˌæɡərə'fəʊbɪk; *NAmE* -'foʊ-/ *noun* a person who suffers from agoraphobia 广场恐怖症患者；公共场所恐惧症患者 ▶ **agora·pho·bic** *adj.*

agrar·ian /əˈɡreəriən; *NAmE* əˈɡrer-/ *adj.* [usually before noun] (*specialist*) connected with farming and the use of land for farming 农业的；土地的；耕地的

aˌgrarian revoˈlution *noun* [sing.] (*often* **the Agrarian Revolution**) a period when farming in a country changes completely as a result of new methods or a change in who owns the land 农业革命；土地革命

▼ **EXPRESS YOURSELF** 情景表达

Agreeing 表示赞同

In a discussion, people may say certain things which you want to support. (In addition, before you make a negative comment, you may want to say first that there are points that you agree with.) 在讨论中可以对某些观点表示支持（另外，在说出负面评价前也可以先对某些观点表示赞同）：

- ***Yes, that's true.*** 对，的确如此。
- ***That's right.*** *On the other hand, there are some drawbacks to the plan...* 没错，但另一方面，这个计划也有一些弊端…
- ***Exactly.*** 一点不错。
- ***Absolutely.*** 对极了。
- ***Definitely.*** 当然。
- ***Yes, I suppose/guess so.*** 是的，我想是这样。
- ***I agree.*** *It's definitely the best idea.* 我同意。这绝对是最好的主意。
- ***I think you're right.*** *We should listen to what they have to say.* 我想你是对的。我们应该听听他们有什么话要说。
- *Sue* ***is absolutely right.*** *It's too early to make a decision now.* 休绝对正确。现在就做决定太早了。
- ***I would go along with the idea*** *that we should change the logo.* 我赞成更改徽标这个想法。
- ***We are in agreement on*** *the best way to proceed, but we need to discuss the timing.* (*formal*) 我们就如何推进的最佳方式达成了一致，但还需要讨论时机问题。

agree 🔑 /əˈɡriː/ *verb*

• **SHARE OPINION** 同意 **1** 🔑 [I, T] to have the same opinion as sb; to say that you have the same opinion 同意；赞成：*When he said that, I had to agree.* 他说了那话，我只好同意。◇ **+ speech** *'That's true', she agreed.* "是这样的。"她赞同道。◇ **~ (with sb) (about/on sth)** *He agreed with them about the need for change.* 他同意他们需要变革的意见。◇ **~ with sth** *I agree with her analysis of the situation.* 我赞成她对形势的分析。◇ **~ (that)...** *We agreed (that) the proposal was a good one.* 我们一致认为这个建议不错。◇ *'It's terrible.' 'I couldn't agree more!'* (= I completely agree) "太糟糕了。""可不是嘛！" **OPP** **disagree** **2** 🔑 [T] if people **are agreed** or sth **is agreed**, everyone has the same opinion about sth （对…）取得一致意见，一致同意：**be agreed (on/about sth)** *Are we all agreed on this?* 我们在这个问题上是不是全体意见一致？◇ **be agreed (that...)** *It was agreed (that) we should hold another meeting.* 大家一致同意我们应该再开一次会。

• **SAY YES** 应允 **3** 🔑 [I, T] to say 'yes'; to say that you will do what sb wants or that you will allow sth to happen 应允；答应；同意：*I asked for a pay rise and she agreed.* 我要求提高工资，她答应了。◇ **~ to sth** *Do you think he'll agree to their proposal?* 你认为他会同意他们的建议吗？◇ **~ (that)...** *She agreed (that) I could go early.* 她允许我早走。◇ **~ to do sth** *She agreed to let me go early.* 她容许我早走。

• **DECIDE** 决定 **4** 🔑 [I, T] to decide with sb else to do sth or to have sth 商定；约定：**~ on sth** *Can we agree on a date?* 我们能否约定一个日期？◇ **~ sth** *They met at the agreed time.* 他们在约定的时间见面了。◇ *Can we agree a price?* 我们可不可以商定一个价格？◇ *They left at ten, as agreed.* 他们按照约好的时间在十点钟离去。◇ **~ to do sth** *We agreed to meet on Thursday.* 我们约定在星期四见面。◇ **~ what, where, etc....** *We couldn't agree what to do.* 关于应该怎么办我们各执己见。➲ **MORE LIKE THIS** 26, page R28

• **ACCEPT** 认可 **5** [T] **~ sth** to officially accept a plan, request, etc. 批准，认可（计划、要求等）**SYN** **approve**：*Next year's budget has been agreed.* 明年的预算已获批准。

• **BE THE SAME** 相符 **6** [I] to be the same as sth （与…）相符，一致 **SYN** **tally**：*The figures do not agree.* 这些数字不相符。◇ **~ with sth** *Your account of the accident does not agree with hers.* 你对事故的叙述与她的叙述不一致。**OPP** **disagree**

• **GRAMMAR** 语法 **7** [I] **~ (with sth)** to match a word or phrase in NUMBER, GENDER or PERSON（在数、性或人称上与…）一致：*In 'Tom likes jazz', the singular verb 'likes' agrees with the subject 'Tom'.* 在 Tom likes jazz 一句中，动词单数形式 likes 与主语 Tom 一致。

IDM **aˌgree to ˈdiffer** if two people **agree to differ**, they accept that they have different opinions about sth, but they decide not to discuss it any longer 同意各自保留不同意见

PHR V **not aˈgree with sb** (of food 食物) to make you feel ill/sick 使难受；不适合；不相宜：*I love strawberries, but they don't agree with me.* 我喜欢草莓，但吃了以后不舒服。

▼ **SYNONYMS** 同义词辨析

agree

accept • approve • go along with sb/sth • consent

These words all mean to say that you will do what sb wants or that you will allow sth to happen. 以上各词均含答应、同意之义。

agree to say that you will do what sb wants or that you will allow sth to happen 指答应、容许：*He agreed to let me go early.* 他容许我早走。

accept to be satisfied with sth that has been done, decided or suggested 指同意、接受、认可：*They accepted the court's decision.* 他们接受法院的判决。

approve to officially agree to a plan, suggestion or request 指批准、正式通过（计划、建议或要求）：*The committee unanimously approved the plan.* 委员会一致通过了计划。

go along with sb/sth (*rather informal*) to agree to sth that sb else has decided; to agree with sb else's ideas 指赞同某事，同意某人的观点：*She just goes along with everything he suggests.* 他的一切建议她都赞同。

consent (*rather formal*) to agree to sth or give your permission for sth 指同意、准许、允许：*She finally consented to answer our questions.* 她最终同意回答我们的问题。

PATTERNS

- to agree/consent **to** sth
- to agree/consent **to do sth**
- to agree to/accept/approve/go along with/consent to a **plan/proposal**
- to agree to/accept/approve a **request**

agree·able /əˈɡriːəbl/ *adj.* (*formal*) **1** pleasant and easy to like 愉悦的；讨人喜欢的；宜人的：*We spent a most agreeable day together.* 我们在一起度过了非常愉快的一天。◇ *He seemed extremely agreeable.* 他似乎特别招人喜欢。**OPP** **disagreeable** **2** [not before noun] **~ (to sth)** willing to do sth or allow sth 欣然同意：*Do you think they will be agreeable to our proposal?* 你认为他们会爽快同意我们的提议吗？**3** **~ (to sb)** able to be accepted by sb 可以接受的；适合的：*The deal must be agreeable to both sides.* 处理方法必须是双方都可以接受的。

agree·ably /əˈɡriːəbli/ *adv.* (*formal*) in a pleasant, nice way 愉悦地；令人愉快地；惬意地：*an agreeably warm day* 暖洋洋的一天 ◇ *They were agreeably surprised by the quality of the food.* 他们对食物的质量感到又惊又喜。

agree·ment 🔑 /əˈɡriːmənt/ *noun* **1** 🔑 [C] an arrangement, a promise or a contract made with sb 协定；协议；契约：*an international peace agreement* 国际和平协定

◇ *The agreement* (= the document recording the agreement) *was signed during a meeting at the UN.* 这个协定是在联合国的一次会议上签订的。◇ **~ with sb** *They have a free trade agreement with Australia.* 他们与澳大利亚签有自由贸易协定。◇ **~ between A and B** *An* ***agreement*** *was finally* ***reached*** *between management and employees.* 劳资双方终于达成了协议。◇ **~ to do sth** *They had made a verbal agreement to sell.* 他们达成了口头售货协定。◇ *They had an agreement never to talk about work at home.* 他们约定在家中绝不谈工作。 ➲ WORDFINDER NOTE AT DOCUMENT, PEACE ➲ SEE ALSO GENTLEMAN'S AGREEMENT, PRENUPTIAL AGREEMENT **2** [U] the state of sharing the same opinion or feeling （意见或看法）一致: *The two sides failed to* ***reach agreement****.* 双方未能取得一致意见。◇ **in ~** *Are we in agreement about the price?* 对这个价格我们是否意见一致？ OPP **disagreement** **3** [U] the fact of sb approving of sth and allowing it to happen 应允；同意: *You'll have to get your parents' agreement if you want to go on the trip.* 你要想去旅行就必须征得你父母的同意。 **4** [U] **~ (with sth)** (*grammar* 语法) (of words in a phrase 短语中的单词) the state of having the same NUMBER, GENDER or PERSON （在数、性或人称方面的）一致 SYN **concord**: *In the sentence 'They live in the country', the plural form of the verb 'live' is* ***in agreement with*** *the plural subject 'they'.* 在 They live in the country 一句中，动词复数形式 live 与复数主语 they 一致。

agri- ➲ AGRO-

agri·busi·ness /ˈæɡrɪbɪznəs/ *noun* [U, C] (*specialist*) an industry concerned with the production and sale of farm products, especially involving large companies 农业综合经营；农业综合企业

agri·cul·tur·al·ist /ˌæɡrɪˈkʌltʃərəlɪst/ *noun* an expert in agriculture who gives advice to farmers 农学家；农业技术员；农艺师

agri·cul·ture /ˈæɡrɪkʌltʃə(r)/ *noun* [U] the science or practice of farming 农业；农学；农艺: *The number of people employed in agriculture has fallen in the last decade.* 过去十年，农业从业人数已经下降。 ➲ COLLOCATIONS AT TOWN ▶ **agri·cul·tural** /ˌæɡrɪˈkʌltʃərəl/ *adj.*: *agricultural policy/land/production/development* 农业政策 / 用地 / 生产 / 发展

agri·tour·ism /ˈæɡrɪtʊərɪzəm; -tɔːr-; *NAmE* -tʊr-/ *noun* [U] holidays/vacations in which tourists visiting a country stay with local people who live in the countryside 农业旅游；农家乐旅游

agro- /ˈæɡrəʊ; *NAmE* ˈæɡroʊ/ (*also* **agri-** /ˈæɡrɪ/) *combining form* (in nouns, adjectives and adverbs 构成名词、形容词和副词) connected with farming 农业；农业的…: *agro-industry* 农用工业 ◇ *agriculture* 农业

agro·chem·ical /ˌæɡrəʊˈkemɪkl; *NAmE* ˌæɡroʊ-/ *noun* any chemical used in farming, especially for killing insects or for making plants grow better 农药

ˌagro-ˈindustry *noun* [U] industry connected with farming 农用工业 ▶ **ˌagro-inˈdustrial** *adj.*

agrono·mist /əˈɡrɒnəmɪst; *NAmE* əˈɡrɑːn-/ *noun* a scientist who studies the relationship between crops and the environment 农学家 ▶ **agron·omy** *noun* [U]

aground /əˈɡraʊnd/ *adv.* if a ship **runs/goes aground**, it touches the ground in shallow water and cannot move （船）搁浅 ▶ **aground** *adj.* [not before noun]

ague /ˈeɪɡjuː/ *noun* [U] (*old-fashioned*) a disease such as MALARIA that causes fever and SHIVERING (= shaking of the body) 疟疾（等使人发热后寒战的疾病）

AH (*BrE*) (*US also* **A.H.**) /ˌeɪ ˈeɪtʃ/ *abbr.* used in the Muslim CALENDAR to show a particular number of years since the year when Muhammad left Mecca in AD 622 (from Latin 'Anno Hegirae') 伊斯兰教纪元，希吉来历（从公元 622 年起算）: *a Koran dated 556 AH* 希吉来历 556 年的一部《古兰经》 ➲ COMPARE AD, BC, BCE, CE (2)

ah /ɑː/ *exclamation* used to express surprise, pleasure, admiration or sympathy, or when you disagree with sb （表示惊奇、高兴、赞赏、同情或不同意）啊: *Ah, there you are!* 啊，你原来在这儿！◇ *Ah, this coffee is good.* 啊，这咖啡真好。◇ *Ah well, better luck next time.* 好啦好啦，祝你下次运气好一些。◇ *Ah, but that may not be true.* 不过嘛，那可能不是真的。 ➲ MORE LIKE THIS 2, page R25

aha /ɑːˈhɑː/ *exclamation* used when you are expressing pleasure that you have understood sth or found sth out （表示了解或发现某事物的喜悦）啊哈: *Aha! So that's where I left it!* 啊哈！原来我把它丢在那儿了！ ➲ MORE LIKE THIS 2, page R25

aˈha moment *noun* [usually sing.] a moment where you suddenly understand sth, realize sth important, have a good idea, or find the answer to a problem 顿悟时刻；突然开窍: *I had an aha moment and suddenly knew what to do.* 我突然福至心灵，知道该怎么做了。

ahchoo /ɑːˈtʃuː; əˈtʃuː/ *exclamation* = ATISHOO

ahead /əˈhed/ *adv.* HELP For the special uses of **ahead** in phrasal verbs, look at the entries for the verbs. For example **press ahead (with sth)** is in the phrasal verb section at **press**. * ahead 在短语动词中的特殊用法见有关动词词条。如 press ahead (with sth) 在词条 press 的短语动词部分。 **1** further forward in space or time; in front （时间、空间）向前，在前面: *I'll run ahead and warn them.* 我要跑在前头，警告他们。◇ *The road ahead was blocked.* 前面的路被封了。◇ *We've got a lot of hard work ahead.* 我们往后还有很多艰苦工作要做。◇ *This will create problems in the months ahead.* 在以后的几个月中这个就要出问题。◇ *He was looking straight ahead* (= straight forward, in front of him). 他径直往前看去。 **2** earlier 提前；预先；提早 SYN **in advance**: *The party was planned weeks ahead.* 聚会提前几个星期就已筹划好了。 **3** winning; further advanced 占优势；领先: *Our team was ahead by six points.* 我们队领先六分。◇ *You need to work hard to keep ahead.* 你要努力才能保持领先优势。

aˈhead of *prep.* **1** further forward in space or time than sb/sth; in front of sb/sth （时间、空间）在…前面: *Two boys were ahead of us.* 有两个男孩在我们前面。◇ *Ahead of us lay ten days of intensive training.* 我们将要进行十天的强化训练。 **2** earlier than sb/sth 早于: *I finished several days ahead of the deadline.* 我是在最后期限的前几天完成的。 **3** further advanced than sb/sth; in front of sb, for example in a race or competition 领先: *She was always* ***well ahead*** *of the rest of the class.* 她总是遥遥领先班上的同学。◇ *His ideas were way* ***ahead of their time*** (= very new and so not widely understood or accepted). 他的思想远远超越了他们那个时代。

ahem /əˈhem; əˈhəm/ *exclamation* used in writing to show the sound of a short cough made by sb who is trying to get attention or to say sth that is difficult or embarrassing （书写用语，表示引起注意或难以启齿时发出的短促咳嗽声）呃哼: *Ahem, can I make a suggestion?* 呃哼，我可以提个建议吗？ ➲ MORE LIKE THIS 2, page R25

ahis·tor·ic·al /ˌeɪhɪˈstɒrɪkl; *NAmE* -ˈstɔːr-; -ˈstɑːr-/ *adj.* (*formal*) not showing any knowledge of history or of what has happened before 非历史的；没有历史背景的；不顾史实的

-aholic /əˈhɒlɪk; *NAmE* əˈhɔːl-; əˈhɑːl-/ *suffix* (in nouns 构成名词) liking sth very much and unable to stop doing or using it 嗜好…的；对…成瘾的: *a shopaholic* 购物成癖的人 ◇ *a chocaholic* 嗜食巧克力的人

ahoy /əˈhɔɪ/ *exclamation* used by people in boats to attract attention （船上的人用以引起注意）啊呵: *Ahoy there!* 啊呵！◇ *Ship ahoy!* (= there is a ship in sight) 啊，一条船！

AI /ˌeɪ ˈaɪ/ *abbr.* **1** ARTIFICIAL INSEMINATION 人工授精: *AID or artificial insemination by a donor* 供精人工授精 **2** ARTIFICIAL INTELLIGENCE 人工智能

aid AW /eɪd/ *noun, verb*

■ **noun** **1** [U] money, food, etc. that is sent to help countries in difficult situations 援助；救援物资；援助款项: ***economic/humanitarian/emergency aid*** 经济 / 人道主义 / 紧急援助 ◇ *An extra £10 million in* ***foreign aid***

A

has been promised. 额外的 1 000 万英镑外国援助款项已得到保证。◇ *aid agencies* (= organizations that provide help) 救援机构 ◇ *medical aid programmes* 医疗援助计划 ➲ COLLOCATIONS AT INTERNATIONAL ➲ SEE ALSO FINANCIAL AID, LEGAL AID **2** 🔑 [U] help that you need to perform a particular task （完成某工作所需的）帮助，助手，辅助物： *He was breathing only* ***with the aid of*** *a ventilator.* 他只能靠呼吸器呼吸。◇ *This job would be impossible* ***without the aid of*** *a computer.* 这项工作不用计算机是不行的。 **3** [U] (*formal*) help that is given to a person 帮助；援助： *One of the staff saw he was in difficulty and* ***came to his aid*** (= helped him). 一名工作人员见他有困难，便过来帮忙。 ➲ SEE ALSO FIRST AID **4** [C] an object, a machine, etc. that you use to help you do sth 辅助设备： *a hearing aid* 助听器 ◇ *Photos make useful teaching aids.* 照片可以成为有用的教具。

IDM **in aid of sth/sb** 🔑 (*BrE*) in order to help sb/sth 为了帮助某人 / 某事物： *collecting money in aid of charity* 为资助慈善事业的募捐 **what's... in aid of?** (*BrE*) used to ask why sth is happening …究竟是为什么（发生）；…是做什么用的： *What's all this crying in aid of?* 这样大哭大叫究竟是为什么？

■ ***verb*** 🔑 [I, T] (*formal*) to help sb/sth to do sth, especially by making it easier 帮助；援助 SYN **assist**: **~ (sb/sth) in sth/in doing sth** *The new test should aid in the early detection of the disease.* 新的化验应该有助于早早检查出这种疾病。◇ **~ sb (to do sth)** *This feature is designed to aid inexperienced users.* 这个特色装置是为帮助没有经验的用户而设计的。◇ **~ sth** *Aided by heat and strong winds, the fire quickly spread.* 借助高温和大风，火势迅速蔓延。◇ *They were accused of aiding his escape.* 他们被控帮助他逃跑。◇ **~ sb/sth in sth/in doing sth** *They were accused of aiding him in his escape.* 他们被控帮助他逃跑。◇ **~ sb (with sth)** *Words will be displayed around the room to aid students with spelling.* 单词会张贴在室内各处以帮助学生学习拼写。

IDM **ˌaid and aˈbet** (*law* 律) to help sb to do sth illegal or wrong 帮助和教唆： *She stands accused of aiding and abetting the crime.* 她被控帮助和教唆犯罪。

aide /eɪd/ *noun* a person who helps another person, especially a politician, in their job （尤指从政者的）助手： *White House aides* 白宫助理

aide-de-camp /ˌeɪd də ˈkɒ̃; *NAmE* ˈkæmp/ *noun* (*pl.* **aides-de-camp** /ˌeɪd də ˈkɒ̃; *NAmE* ˈkæmp/) (*abbr.* **ADC**) an officer in the army or navy who helps a more senior officer （陆军或海军）副官，随从参谋

aide-memoire /ˌeɪd memˈwɑː(r)/ *noun* (*from French*) (*pl.* **aides-memoire**, **aides-memoires** /ˌeɪd memˈwɑː(r)/) a thing, especially a book or document, that helps you to remember sth 帮助记忆的东西（尤指书、文档）

AIDS (*BrE usually* **Aids**) /eɪdz/ *noun* [U] the abbreviation for 'Acquired Immune Deficiency Syndrome' (an illness which attacks the body's ability to resist infection and which usually causes death) 艾滋病（全写为 Acquired Immune Deficiency Syndrome，获得性免疫缺陷综合征）： *AIDS research/education/victims* 艾滋病研究 / 教育 / 患者 ◇ *He developed* ***full-blown AIDS*** *five years after contracting HIV.* 他感染艾滋病病毒五年以后，患上了完全型艾滋病。

ai·kido /aɪˈkiːdəʊ; *NAmE* -doʊ/ *noun* [U] (*from Japanese*) a Japanese system of fighting in which you hold and throw your opponent 合气道（以擒、摔为主的一种日本武术）

ail /eɪl/ *verb* **1 ~ sth** (*formal*) to cause problems for sb/sth 困扰；干扰；使麻烦： *They discussed the problems ailing the steel industry.* 他们讨论了困扰钢铁工业的问题。 **2 ~ sb** (*old use*) to make sb ill/sick 使患病；使不适： *What is ailing you?* 你哪里不舒服？

ail·eron /ˈeɪlərɒn; *NAmE* -rɑːn/ *noun* (*specialist*) a part of the wing of a plane that moves up and down to control the plane's balance （飞机的）副翼 ➲ VISUAL VOCAB PAGE V57

ail·ing /ˈeɪlɪŋ/ *adj.* (*formal*) **1** ill/sick and not improving 有病的；体弱的： *She looked after her ailing father.* 她照顾她有病的父亲。 **2** (of a business, government, etc. 企业、政府等) having problems and getting weaker 处境困难的；每况愈下的： *measures to help the ailing economy* 改善经济不景气的措施

ail·ment /ˈeɪlmənt/ *noun* an illness that is not very serious 轻病；小恙： ***childhood/common/minor ailments*** 儿童期 / 常见 / 轻微小病 ➲ SYNONYMS AT DISEASE

aim 🔑 /eɪm/ *noun, verb*

■ ***noun*** **1** 🔑 [C] the purpose of doing sth; what sb is trying to achieve 目的；目标： *the aims of the lesson* 本课教学目标 ◇ *She went to London* ***with the aim of*** *finding a job.* 她去伦敦是为了找工作。◇ *Our main aim is to increase sales in Europe.* 我们的主要目标是增加在欧洲的销售量。◇ *Bob's one aim in life is to earn a lot of money.* 鲍勃唯一的人生目标就是挣很多的钱。◇ *Teamwork is required in order to* ***achieve these aims.*** 要达到这些目标需要齐心协力。◇ *She set out the company's* ***aims and objectives*** *in her speech.* 她在讲话中提出了公司的各项目标。 ➲ SYNONYMS AT PURPOSE **2** [U] the action or skill of pointing a weapon at sb/sth 瞄准： *Her aim was good and she hit the lion with her first shot.* 她瞄得准，第一枪就打中了狮子。◇ *The gunman* ***took aim*** (= pointed his weapon) *and fired.* 持枪歹徒瞄准后就射击了。

IDM **take ˈaim at sb/sth** (*NAmE*) to direct your criticism at sb/sth 把目标对准某人（或某事物）；把批评的矛头指向某人（或某事物）

■ ***verb*** **1** 🔑 [I, T] to try or plan to achieve sth 力求达到；力争做到： *He has always* ***aimed high*** (= tried to achieve a lot). 他总是心气很高。◇ **~ for sth** *We should aim for a bigger share of the market.* 我们应该以更大的市场份额为目标。◇ **~ at sth** *The government is aiming at a 50% reduction in unemployment.* 政府正着力将失业人数减少 50%。◇ **~ to do sth** *They are aiming to reduce unemployment by 50%.* 他们正力求使失业人数减少 50%。◇ *We aim to be there around six.* 我们设法六点钟左右到那里。◇ **~ at doing sth** *They're aiming at training everybody by the end of the year.* 他们力求在年底前让人人得到培训。 **2** 🔑 [T] **be aimed at sth/at doing sth** to have sth as an aim 目的是；旨在： *These measures are aimed at preventing violent crime.* 这些措施旨在防止暴力犯罪。 **3** 🔑 [I, T] to point or direct a weapon, a shot, a kick, etc. at sb/sth 瞄准；对准： **~ at sb/sth** *I was aiming at the tree but hit the car by mistake.* 我对准树射击，不料误中了汽车。◇ **~ for sb/sth** *Aim for the middle of the target.* 瞄准靶心。◇ **~ sth (at sb/sth)** *The gun was aimed at her head.* 枪瞄准了她的头。 **4** 🔑 [T, usually passive] **~ sth at sb** to say or do sth that is intended to influence or affect a particular person or group 针对；对象是： *The book is aimed at very young children.* 这本书的读者对象是幼童。◇ *My criticism wasn't aimed at you.* 我的批评不是针对你的。

aim·less /ˈeɪmləs/ *adj.* having no direction or plan 没有方向的；无目标的；无计划的： *My life seemed aimless.* 我的生活似乎没有目标。 ▶ **aim·less·ly** *adv.*: *He drifted aimlessly from one job to another.* 他漫无目的地换了一份又一份工作。 **aim·less·ness** *noun* [U]

ain't /eɪnt/ *short form* (*non-standard* or *humorous*) **1** am not/is not/are not 不是： *Things ain't what they used to be.* 现在情况不比从前了。 **2** has not/have not 没有： *I ain't got no money.* 我没有钱。◇ *You ain't seen nothing yet.* 你还什么都没有看到呢。 ➲ MORE LIKE THIS 5, page R25

IDM **if it ain't ˌbroke, don't ˈfix it** (*informal*) used to say that if sth works well enough, it should not be changed 未损勿修；能用莫换

air 🔑 /eə(r); *NAmE* er/ *noun, verb*

■ ***noun***

• GAS 气体 **1** 🔑 [U] the mixture of gases that surrounds the earth and that we breathe 空气： *air pollution* 空气污染 ◇ *Let's go out for some* ***fresh air.*** 咱们出去呼吸点新鲜空气。◇ *I need to put some air in my tyres.* 我需要给我的轮胎打些气。◇ *currents of warm air* 暖气流

• SPACE 空间 **2** 🔑 [U] (*usually* **the air**) the space above the ground or that is around things 空中；天空： *I kicked the ball high* ***in/into the air.*** 我把球高高地踢到空中。◇ *Spicy smells wafted* ***through the air.*** 空中飘来一阵阵浓烈的气

A

味。◇ *Music filled the night air.* 乐声荡漾在夜空中。 ➲ SEE ALSO OPEN AIR

• FOR PLANES 飞机 **3** [U] the space above the earth where planes fly（飞行的）空中，天空：*It only takes three hours* ***by air*** (= in a plane). 乘飞机只要三个小时。◇ ***air travel/traffic*** 航空旅行；空中交通 ◇ *The temple was clearly visible from the air.* 从空中看去，那座庙宇清晰可辨。◇ *A surprise air attack* (= from aircraft) *was launched at night.* 夜间突然发起了空袭。

• IMPRESSION 印象 **4** [sing.] the particular feeling or impression that is given by sb/sth; the way sb does sth 感觉；印象；神态：*The room had an air of luxury.* 房间具有豪华的气派。◇ *She looked at him with a defiant air.* 她用蔑视的神情望着他。

• TUNE 曲调 **5** [C] (*old-fashioned*) (often used in the title of a piece of music 常用于乐曲名) a tune 曲调：*Bach's Air on a G string* 巴赫《G 弦上的咏叹调》

• BEHAVIOUR 行为 **6 airs** [pl.] (*disapproving*) a way of behaving that shows that sb thinks that they are more important, etc. than they really are 摆架子；装腔作势：*I hate the way she* ***puts on airs****.* 我不喜欢她那装腔作势的样子。

IDM **ˌairs and ˈgraces** (*BrE, disapproving*) a way of behaving that shows that sb thinks that they are more important, etc. than they really are 摆架子；装腔作势 SYN **air** **float/walk on ˈair** to feel very happy 欢天喜地；得意扬扬 **in the ˈair** felt by a number of people to exist or to be happening 在传播中；流行；可感觉到：*There's romance in the air.* 有种浪漫的气氛。 **ˌon/ˌoff (the) ˈair** broadcasting or not broadcasting on television or radio（电视、广播）正在 / 停止播送：*We will be back on air tomorrow morning at 7.* 明天早上 7 点本节目再见。◇ *The programme was taken off the air over the summer.* 这个节目在夏季停播。 **up in the ˈair** not yet decided 悬而未决：*Our travel plans are still up in the air.* 我们的旅行计划尚未决定。 ➲ MORE AT BREATH, CASTLE, CLEAR *v.*, NOSE *n.*, PLUCK *v.*, THIN *adj.*

■ ***verb***

• CLOTHES 衣服 **1** [T, I] ~ (**sth**) to put clothing, etc. in a place that is warm or has plenty of air so that it dries completely and smells fresh; to be left to dry somewhere 晾；晾干：*Air the sheets well.* 把这些床单好好晾晒一下。◇ *Leave the towels out to air.* 把毛巾拿出去晾干。

• A ROOM 房间 **2** [T, I] ~ (**sth**) (*BrE*) (*NAmE* **ˌair (sth) ˈout**) to allow fresh air into a room or a building; to be filled with fresh air（使）通风，透风：*The rooms had all been cleaned and aired.* 所有的房间都已打扫干净并且通了风。

• OPINIONS 意见 **3** [T] ~ **sth** to express your opinions publicly 公开表达 SYN **voice**：*The weekly meeting enables employees to* ***air their grievances****.* 周会可以让雇员诉说他们的委屈。

• RADIO/TV PROGRAMME 广播 / 电视节目 **4** [T, I] ~ (**sth**) to broadcast a programme on the radio or on television; to be broadcast 播出；播送：*The show will be aired next Tuesday night.* 这个节目将在下周二夜间播出。◇ *The program aired last week.* 该节目已于上周播出。 ➲ WORDFINDER NOTE AT RADIO ➲ COLLOCATIONS AT TELEVISION

PHR V **ˌair ˈout** | **ˌair sth↔ˈout** (*NAmE*) = AIR (2)

ˌair ˈambulance *noun* (*especially BrE*) an aircraft, especially a HELICOPTER, with special equipment, used for taking sick or injured people to a hospital, especially in cases where a road vehicle cannot get through or cannot make the journey quickly enough 救护机；（尤指）救护直升机 ➲ COMPARE MEDEVAC

air·bag /ˈeəbæɡ; *NAmE* ˈerb-/ *noun* a safety device in a car that fills with air if there is an accident, to protect the people in the car 安全气囊（遇车祸时充气保护车内的人）

air·base /ˈeəbeɪs; *NAmE* ˈerb-/ *noun* a place where military aircraft fly from and are kept, and where some staff live 空军基地；航空基地

air·bed /ˈeəbed; *NAmE* ˈerb-/ (*BrE*) (*also* **ˈair bed** *NAmE*, **ˈair mattress** *NAmE, BrE*) *noun* a large plastic or rubber bag that can be filled with air and used as a bed 充气床垫 ➲ VISUAL VOCAB PAGE V24

air·borne /ˈeəbɔːn; *NAmE* ˈerbɔːrn/ *adj.* **1** [not before noun] (of a plane or passengers 飞机或乘客) in the air 在空中：*Do not leave your seat until the plane is airborne.* 飞机升空时不要离开座位。 **2** [only before noun] carried through the air 空气传播的：***airborne seeds/viruses*** 空气传播的种子 / 病毒 ➲ COMPARE WATERBORNE **3** [only before noun] (of soldiers 士兵) trained to jump out of aircraft onto enemy land in order to fight 空降的：*an airborne division* 空降师

ˈair brake *noun* a BRAKE in a vehicle that is worked by air pressure（车辆的）空气制动

ˈair bridge (*BrE*) (*NAmE* **Jet·way™**) *noun* a piece of equipment like a bridge that can be moved and put against the door of an aircraft, so people can get on and off 旅客登机（活动）桥

air·brush /ˈeəbrʌʃ; *NAmE* ˈerb-/ *noun, verb*

■ ***noun*** an artist's tool for spraying paint onto a surface, that works by air pressure（绘画等用的）气笔，喷枪

■ ***verb*** to paint sth with an airbrush; to change a detail in a photograph with an airbrush 用喷枪喷绘；用气笔修改（照片）：**~ sth** *an airbrushed photograph of a model* 用气笔修改过的模特儿照片 ◇ **~ sth out** *Somebody had been airbrushed out of the picture.* 画面上有个人用气笔给抹掉了。

Air·bus™ /ˈeəbʌs; *NAmE* ˈerb-/ *noun* an aircraft designed to carry a large number of passengers 空中客车（一种大型客机）

ˌair chief ˈmarshal *noun* an officer of very high rank in the British AIR FORCE（英国）空军上将：*Air Chief Marshal Sir Robin Hall* 空军上将罗宾·霍尔爵士

ˌair ˈcommodore *noun* an officer of high rank in the British AIR FORCE（英国）空军准将：*Air Commodore Peter Shaw* 空军准将彼得·肖

ˈair conditioner *noun* a machine that cools and dries air 空调机；空调设备

ˈair conditioning (*also* **ˈair con**) *noun* [U] (*abbr.* **AC**, **a/c**) a system that cools and dries the air in a building or car 空气调节系统 ▸ **ˈair-con·di·tioned** *adj.*：*air-conditioned offices* 装有空调的办公室

ˈair-cooled *adj.* made cool by a current of air 风冷的；空冷的

ˈair corridor *noun* an area in the sky that aircraft must stay inside when they fly over a country（飞机飞越外国领空时获准使用的）空中走廊

ˈair cover *noun* [U] protection which aircraft give to soldiers and military vehicles on the land or sea 空中掩护

air·craft 🔑 /ˈeəkrɑːft; *NAmE* ˈerkræft/ *noun* (*pl.* **air·craft**) any vehicle that can fly and carry goods or passengers 飞机；航空器：***fighter/transport/military aircraft*** 战斗机；运输机；军用飞机 ➲ VISUAL VOCAB PAGES V57-58 ➲ SEE ALSO LIGHT AIRCRAFT

> **WORDFINDER** 联想词：bomber, drone, fighter, helicopter, jet, jump jet, parachute, pilot, warplane

ˈaircraft carrier *noun* a large ship that carries aircraft which use it as a base to land on and take off from 航空母舰 ➲ WORDFINDER NOTE AT NAVY

air·craft·man /ˈeəkrɑːftmən; *NAmE* ˈerkræft-/, **air·craft·woman** /ˈeəkrɑːftwʊmən; *NAmE* ˈerkræft-/ *noun* (*pl.* **-men** /-mən/, **-women** /-wɪmɪn/) the lowest rank in the British AIR FORCE 空军士兵（英国空军最低军阶）：*Aircraftman John Green* 空军士兵约翰·格林

air·crew /ˈeəkruː; *NAmE* ˈerk-/ *noun* [C+sing./pl. v.] the pilot and other people who fly a plane, especially in the air force（尤指空军的）机组人员，空勤人员，空勤组

ˈair-dash *verb* [I] (*IndE*) to fly somewhere in a plane without much time for preparation 空中急赶（突然或匆匆

乘机前往）：*He air-dashed to Delhi when he heard the news.* 他听到消息后匆忙飞往德里。

air·drome /ˈeədrəʊm; *NAmE* ˈerdroʊm/ (*US*) (*BrE* **aero·drome**) *noun* (*old-fashioned*) a small airport 小型飞机场

air·drop /ˈeədrɒp; *NAmE* ˈerdrɑːp/ *noun* the act of dropping supplies, soldiers, etc. from an aircraft by PARACHUTE 空投；空降：*The UN has begun making airdrops of food to refugees.* 联合国已开始向难民空投食物。▶ **air·drop** *verb* (**-pp-**) **~ sth**

air·fare /ˈeəfeə(r); *NAmE* ˈerfer/ *noun* the money that you pay to travel by plane 机票费用；飞机票价：*Take advantage of low-season airfares.* 利用淡季飞机票价。

air·field /ˈeəfiːld; *NAmE* ˈerf-/ *noun* an area of flat ground where military or private planes can take off and land 飞机场

air·flow /ˈeəfləʊ; *NAmE* ˈerfloʊ/ *noun* [U] the flow of air around a moving aircraft or vehicle （运行中的飞机或汽车周围的）气流

air·foil /ˈeəfɔɪl; *NAmE* ˈerf-/ (*NAmE*) (*BrE* **aero·foil**) *noun* the basic curved structure of an aircraft's wing that helps to lift it into the air 翼型（指机翼在空气中运动时能产生升力的曲线型面）

ˈ**air force** *noun* [C+sing./pl. v.] the part of a country's armed forces that fights using aircraft 空军：*the US Air Force* 美国空军 ◇ *air-force officers* 空军军官 ➲ COLLOCATIONS AT WAR

ˌ**Air Force** ˈ**One** *noun* the name given to a special aircraft in the US AIR FORCE when the US President is using it 空军一号（美国总统的专用座机）

air·freight /ˈeəfreɪt; *NAmE* ˈerf-/ *noun* [U] goods that are transported by aircraft; the system of transporting goods by aircraft 空运的货物；空中货运 ▶ **air·freight** *verb* **~ sth**

ˈ**air freshener** *noun* [C, U] a substance or device for making a place smell more pleasant 空气清新剂；空气清新机；空气净化器

ˈ**air guitar** *noun* [U, C] used to refer to the actions of a person playing an imaginary electric GUITAR, especially while listening to rock music 虚拟吉他（尤指听摇滚乐时佯装弹吉他的动作）：*Whenever he hears this music, he starts playing air guitar.* 每当听到这首乐曲，他便开始做出弹吉他的样子。

ˈ**air·gun** /ˈeəgʌn; *NAmE* ˈer-/ (*also* ˈ**air rifle**) *noun* a gun that uses air pressure to fire small metal balls (called PELLETS) 气枪

air·head /ˈeəhed; *NAmE* ˈerh-/ *noun* (*informal, disapproving*) a stupid person 笨蛋；傻瓜：*She's a total airhead!* 她完全是个大傻瓜！▶ **air·head·ed** *adj.*

ˈ**air hostess** *noun* (*BrE, old-fashioned*) a female FLIGHT ATTENDANT （客机上的）女乘务员；空中小姐

air·ily /ˈeərəli; *NAmE* ˈer-/ *adv.* (*formal*) in a way that shows that you are not worried or that you are not treating sth as serious 无忧无虑地；无所谓地

air·ing /ˈeərɪŋ; *NAmE* ˈerɪŋ/ *noun* [sing.] **1** the expression or discussion of opinions in front of a group of people （意见等的）公开发表，公开讨论：*an opportunity to give your views an airing* 公开发表你观点的一次机会 ◇ *The subject got a thorough airing in the British press.* 这个问题在英国新闻界得到了充分讨论。**2** the act of allowing warm air to make clothes, beds, etc. fresh and dry 晾；晾晒；透风

ˈ**airing cupboard** *noun* (*BrE*) a warm cupboard in which clean sheets, clothes, etc. are put to make sure they are completely dry （烘干衣物的）烘柜 ➲ MORE LIKE THIS 9, page R26

ˈ**air kiss** *noun* a way of saying hello or goodbye to sb by kissing them near the side of their face but not actually touching them （见面或道别时的）撮唇示吻 ▶ ˈ**air-kiss** *verb* [T, I] **~ (sb/sth)**

air·less /ˈeələs; *NAmE* ˈerl-/ *adj.* not having any fresh or moving air or wind, and therefore unpleasant 没有新鲜空气的；没有一丝风的；空气沉闷的：*a stuffy, airless room* 空气沉闷不通风的房间 ◇ *The night was hot and airless.* 夜晚很热，没有一丝风。

ˈ**air letter** *noun* = AEROGRAMME

air·lift /ˈeəlɪft; *NAmE* ˈerl-/ *noun, verb*

■ *noun* an operation to take people, soldiers, food, etc. to or from an area by aircraft, especially in an emergency or when roads are closed or dangerous 空运；空投 ➲ COMPARE SEALIFT

■ *verb* **~ sb/sth** to take sb/sth to or from an area by aircraft, especially in an emergency or when roads are closed or dangerous 空运，空投（人员或物资）：*Two casualties were **airlifted to safety**.* 两名伤员已空运到安全地区。

air·line /ˈeəlaɪn; *NAmE* ˈerl-/ *noun* [C+sing./pl. v.] a company that provides regular flights to take passengers and goods to different places 航空公司：*international airlines* 国际航空公司 ◇ *an airline pilot* 航空公司飞行员 ➲ COLLOCATIONS AT TRAVEL

air·liner /ˈeəlaɪnə(r); *NAmE* ˈerl-/ *noun* a large plane that carries passengers 大型客机；班机

air·lock /ˈeəlɒk; *NAmE* ˈerlɑːk/ *noun* **1** a small room with a tightly closed door at each end, which you go through to reach another area at a different air pressure, for example on a SPACECRAFT or SUBMARINE （航天器或潜艇等的）气闸舱，气密过渡舱 **2** a bubble of air that blocks the flow of liquid in a PUMP or pipe 气塞

air·mail /ˈeəmeɪl; *NAmE* ˈerm-/ *noun* [U] the system of sending letters, etc. by air 航空邮递：*Send it airmail/by airmail.* 将它空邮寄出。

air·man /ˈeəmən; *NAmE* ˈerm-/, **air·woman** /ˈeəwʊmən; *NAmE* ˈerw-/ *noun* (*pl.* **-men** /-mən/, **-women** /-wɪmɪn/) **1** a member of the British AIR FORCE, especially one below the rank of an officer （英国尤指军阶比军官低的）空军人员 **2** a member of one of the lowest ranks in the US AIR FORCE （美国空军军阶最低的）空军士兵：*Airman Brines* 空军士兵布赖恩斯

ˈ**air marshal** *noun* **1** an officer of very high rank in the British AIR FORCE （英国）空军中将：*Air Marshal Gordon Black* 空军中将戈登·布莱克 **2** (*also* ˈ**sky marshal**) an armed guard, especially a government official, who travels on a plane with the passengers in order to protect the plane from TERRORISTS 空中反恐武装警卫

ˈ**air mattress** (*especially NAmE*) (*also* **air·bed** *BrE*, **air bed** *NAmE*) *noun* a large plastic or rubber bag that can be filled with air and used as a bed 充气床垫 ➲ VISUAL VOCAB PAGE V24

ˈ**Air Miles™** *noun* [pl.] points that you collect by buying plane tickets and other products, which you can then use to pay for air travel 飞行里程积分（可用来充抵机票费用）

ˈ**air pistol** *noun* a small gun that uses air pressure to fire small metal balls (called PELLETS) 气手枪

air·plane /ˈeəpleɪn; *NAmE* ˈerp-/ *noun* (*especially NAmE*) = PLANE (1)：*They arrived in Belgium **by airplane**.* 他们乘飞机到达比利时。◇ *an **airplane crash/flight*** 飞机坠毁 / 飞行 ◇ *a **commercial/jet/military airplane*** 商用 / 喷气 / 军用飞机

air·play /ˈeəpleɪ; *NAmE* ˈerp-/ *noun* [U] time that is spent broadcasting a particular record, performer, or type of music on the radio（唱片、歌手或某种音乐等的）电台播放时间：*The band is starting to get a lot of airplay.* 这支乐队的歌曲已开始在电台热播。

ˈ**air pocket** *noun* **1** a closed area that becomes filled with air 气窝 **2** an area of low air pressure that makes a plane suddenly drop while flying 气阱，气穴（使飞机突然下降的低气压区）

air·port /ˈeəpɔːt; *NAmE* ˈerpɔːrt/ *noun* a place where planes land and take off and that has buildings for passengers to wait in 航空站；航空港；机场： *Gatwick Airport* 盖特威克机场 ◇ *waiting in the airport lounge* 在机场候机厅等候

WORDFINDER 联想词： baggage reclaim, board, check-in, gate, immigration, lounge, passport, security, terminal

ˌairport ˈfiction *noun* [U] novels that are popular and easy to read, often bought by people at airports 机场小说（常指在机场购买的通俗消遣读物）

ˈair power *noun* [U] military forces involving aircraft 空军实力

ˈair pump *noun* a piece of equipment for sending air into or out of sth 抽气泵；抽气机

ˈair quality *noun* [U] the degree to which the air is clean and free from pollution 空气质量

ˈair quotes *noun* [pl.] imaginary quotation marks made in the air with your fingers when you are speaking, to show that you are using a word or phrase in an unusual way, especially when it is not an expression you would usually use yourself 手势引号（用双手手指比画的引号，用以表示所用词语非常规意义）

ˈair rage *noun* [U] a situation in which a passenger on a plane becomes violent or aggressive, usually because of stress or anxiety related to flying 空怒（飞机乘客出现的暴力或好斗倾向，通常与飞行产生的压力或焦虑有关）

ˈair raid *noun* an attack by a number of aircraft dropping many bombs on a place 空袭： *The family was killed in an air raid.* 这家人在一次空袭中遇难。 ◇ *an* ***air-raid shelter/warning*** 防空洞；空袭警报

ˈair rifle *noun* = AIRGUN

ˌair-sea ˈrescue *noun* [C, U] the process of rescuing people from the sea using aircraft （使用飞机的）海空救援

air·ship /ˈeəʃɪp; *NAmE* ˈerʃɪp/ *noun* a large aircraft without wings, filled with a gas which is lighter than air, and driven by engines 飞艇；飞船 ➲ VISUAL VOCAB PAGE V58

ˈair show *noun* a show at which people can watch aircraft flying 航空表演；飞行表演

air·sick /ˈeəsɪk; *NAmE* ˈersɪk/ *adj.* [not usually before noun] feeling ill/sick when you are travelling on an aircraft 晕机 ▶ **air·sick·ness** *noun* [U]

air·space /ˈeəspeɪs; *NAmE* ˈers-/ *noun* [U] the part of the sky where planes fly, usually the part above a particular country that is legally controlled by that country 领空；（某国的）空域： *The jet entered Chinese airspace without permission.* 那架喷气式飞机未经许可闯入中国领空。

air·speed /ˈeəspiːd; *NAmE* ˈer-/ *noun* the speed of an aircraft relative to the air through which it is moving （飞机的）空速 ➲ COMPARE GROUND SPEED

air·stream /ˈeəstriːm; *NAmE* ˈer-/ *noun* a movement of air, especially a strong one （尤指强烈的）气流

ˈair strike *noun* an attack made by aircraft 空中打击；空袭

air·strip /ˈeəstrɪp; *NAmE* ˈers-/ (*also* **ˈlanding strip**) *noun* a narrow piece of cleared land that an aircraft can land on 简易机场；简易跑道

ˈair support *noun* [U] help which aircraft give to soldiers and military vehicles on the land or sea 空中支援

ˈair terminal *noun* **1** a building at an airport that provides services for passengers travelling by plane （机场）航站楼，候机大楼 **2** (*BrE*) an office in a city from which passengers can catch buses to the airport 城市中心民航班车站

air·tight /ˈeətaɪt; *NAmE* ˈert-/ *adj.* not allowing air to get in or out 密封的；不透气的： *Store the cake in an airtight container.* 把蛋糕存放在密封容器里。 ◇ (*figurative*) *an airtight alibi* (= one that cannot be proved to be false) 无懈可击的不在犯罪现场的证据

air·time /ˈeətaɪm; *NAmE* ˈert-/ *noun* [U] **1** the amount of time that is given to a particular subject on radio or television （广播或电视节目的）播放时间 **2** the amount of time that is paid for when you are using a mobile/cell phone 空中通话时长（移动电话计费的通话时间）

ˌair-to-ˈair *adj.* [usually before noun] from one aircraft to another while they are both flying 空对空的： *an air-to-air missile* 空对空导弹

ˌair-to-ˈground *adj.* [usually before noun] directed or operating from an aircraft to the surface of the land 空对地的；从飞机对地面的： *air-to-ground weapons* 空对地武器

ˌair-to-ˈsurface *adj.* [usually before noun] moving or passing from a flying aircraft to the surface of the sea or land 空对面的；空地（舰）的： *air-to-surface missiles* 空地（舰）导弹

ˌair traffic conˈtrol *noun* [U] **1** the activity of giving instructions by radio to pilots of aircraft so that they know when and where to take off or land 空中交通管制；空管 **2** the group of people or the organization that provides an air traffic control service 空中交通管制人员（或管制站）： *The pilot was given clearance to land by air traffic control.* 飞行员得到空中交通管制站发出的着陆许可。

ˌair traffic conˈtroller *noun* a person whose job is to give instructions by radio to pilots of aircraft so that they know when and where to take off or land 空中交通管制员；航空调度员

ˌair vice-ˈmarshal *noun* an officer of very high rank in the British AIR FORCE （英国）空军少将： *Air Vice-Marshal Andrew Burns* 空军少将安德鲁•伯恩斯

air·waves /ˈeəweɪvz; *NAmE* ˈerw-/ *noun* [pl.] radio waves that are used in broadcasting radio and television （广播、电视使用的）无线电波；波段： *More and more TV and radio stations are crowding the airwaves.* 愈来愈多的电视台和广播电台使无线电波段愈来愈拥挤。 ◇ *A well-known voice came* ***over the airwaves.*** 电波传来了一个大家熟悉的声音。

air·way /ˈeəweɪ; *NAmE* ˈerweɪ/ *noun* **1** (*medical* 医) the passage from the nose and throat to the lungs, through which you breathe 气道 **2** (often used in names of AIRLINES 常用于航空公司名称) a route regularly used by planes （飞机的）固定航线；航路： *British Airways* 英国航空公司

air·worthy /ˈeəwɜːði; *NAmE* ˈerwɜːrði/ *adj.* (of aircraft 飞行器) safe to fly 适航的 ▶ **air·worthi·ness** *noun* [U]

airy /ˈeəri; *NAmE* ˈeri/ *adj.* (**air·ier**, **airi·est**) **1** with plenty of fresh air because there is a lot of space 通风的；空气流通的： *The office was light and airy.* 办公室又明亮又通风。 **2** (*formal*) acting or done in a way that shows that you are not worried or that you are not treating sth as serious 无忧无虑的；无所谓的；漫不经心的： *He dismissed her with an airy wave.* 他随意一挥手就把她打发走了。 ➲ SEE ALSO AIRILY **3** (*formal, disapproving*) not serious or practical 轻率的；不切实际的： ***airy promises/speculation*** 轻率的诺言；无端猜测

ˌairy-ˈfairy *adj.* (*BrE, informal, disapproving*) not clear or practical 模糊的；不现实的；不切实际的 ➲ MORE LIKE THIS 11, page R26

aisle /aɪl/ *noun* a passage between rows of seats in a church, theatre, train, etc., or between rows of shelves in a supermarket （教堂、戏院、火车等座位间或超市货架间的）走道，过道： *an aisle seat* (= in a plane or train) （飞机或火车上）紧靠过道的座位 ◇ *Coffee and tea are in the next aisle.* 下一个走道处有咖啡和茶。 ➲ COMPARE

GANGWAY (1) ➲ WORDFINDER NOTE AT TRAIN

IDM **go/walk down the 'aisle** (*informal*) to get married 结婚 ➲ MORE AT ROLL *v.*

aitch /eɪtʃ/ *noun* the letter H written as a word 字母 H: *He spoke with a cockney accent and* ***dropped his aitches*** (= did not pronounce the letter H at the start of words). 他带伦敦东区的口音，总是漏发词首的 h 音。

aiyo /aɪ'jəʊ; *NAmE* -'joʊ/ (*also* **ai·aiyo**) *exclamation* (*IndE*) used to show that you are surprised or upset（表示吃惊或沮丧）哎呦: *Aiyo, what terrible news!* 哎呦，真是个坏消息！◇ *Aiyo, that hurts!* 哎呦，好疼！

ajar /ə'dʒɑː(r)/ *adj.* [not before noun] (of a door 门) slightly open 半开；微启: *I'll leave the door ajar.* 我会让门半开着。

aka /ˌeɪ keɪ 'eɪ/ *abbr.* also known as 又名；亦称: *Antonio Fratelli, aka 'Big Tony'* 安东尼奥·弗拉泰利，又名"大托尼"

akimbo /ə'kɪmbəʊ; *NAmE* -boʊ/ *adv.*

IDM **(with) arms a'kimbo** with your hands on your hips and your elbows pointing away from your body 双手叉腰

akin /ə'kɪn/ *adj.* **~ to sth** (*formal*) similar to 相似的；类似的: *What he felt was more akin to pity than love.* 他感受到的更像怜悯，而不是爱。

-al *suffix* **1** (in adjectives 构成形容词) connected with 与…有关的: *magical* 魔术的 ◇ *verbal* 言语的 ➲ SEE ALSO -ALLY **2** (in nouns 构成名词) a process or state of（表示过程或状态）: *survival* 幸存 ➲ **MORE LIKE THIS** 7, page R25

à la /'ɑː lɑː/ *prep.* (*from French*) in the same style as sb/sth else 按照…方式；仿照: *a new band that sings à la Beatles* 模仿披头士乐队唱歌的一支新乐队

ala·bas·ter /'æləbɑːstə(r); *NAmE* -bæs-/ *noun* [U] a type of white stone that is often used to make statues and decorative objects 雪花石膏（常用于雕塑和装饰品）: *an alabaster tomb* 雪花石膏墓 ◇ (*literary*) *her pale, alabaster* (= white and smooth) *skin* 她白净光滑的皮肤

à la carte /ˌɑː lɑː 'kɑːt; *NAmE* 'kɑːrt/ *adj., adv.* (*from French*) if food in a restaurant is **à la carte**, or if you eat **à la carte**, you choose from a list of dishes that have separate prices, rather than having a complete meal at a fixed price 按菜单点菜（与套餐相对）➲ WORDFINDER NOTE AT RESTAURANT

alack /ə'læk/ *exclamation* (*old use* or *humorous*) used to show you are sad or sorry（表示悲伤或遗憾）哎呀，唉: ***Alas and alack****, we had missed our bus.* 唉，完了，我们没赶上公共汽车。

alac·rity /ə'lækrəti/ *noun* [U] (*formal*) great willingness or enthusiasm 欣然同意；十分乐意: *They accepted the offer with alacrity.* 他们欣然接受了建议。

A,laddin's 'cave *noun* a place where there are many wonderful objects 阿拉丁的藏宝洞；宝库

à la mode /ˌɑː lɑː 'məʊd; *NAmE* 'moʊd/ *adj., adv.* (*from French*) **1** [not before noun] (*old-fashioned*) fashionable; in the latest fashion 流行；时髦 **2** [after noun] (*NAmE*) served with ice cream 加有冰淇淋的: *apple pie à la mode* 苹果馅饼加冰淇淋

alarm /ə'lɑːm; *NAmE* ə'lɑːrm/ *noun, verb*

■ *noun* **1** [U] fear and anxiety that sb feels when sth dangerous or unpleasant might happen 惊恐；惊慌；恐慌: *'What have you done?' Ellie cried* ***in alarm.*** "你干了些什么？"埃利惊恐地喊道。◇ *I felt a growing sense of alarm when he did not return that night.* 那天夜里他没有回家，我越来越感到恐慌。◇ *The doctor said there was no* ***cause for alarm.*** 医生说不必惊慌。➲ SYNONYMS AT FEAR **2** [C, usually sing.] a loud noise or a signal that warns people of danger or of a problem 警报: *She decided to* ***sound the alarm*** (= warn people that the situation was dangerous). 她决定发出警报。◇ *I hammered on all the doors to* ***raise the alarm.*** 我敲打所有的门让大家警觉。➲ SEE ALSO FALSE ALARM **3** [C] a device that warns people of a particular danger 警报器: *a burglar/fire/smoke alarm* 防盗/防火/烟雾警报器 ◇ *The cat* ***set off the alarm*** (= made it start ringing). 猫碰响了警铃。◇ *A car* ***alarm went off*** *in the middle of the night* (= started ringing). 半夜里一辆汽车的警报器突然响了起来。**4** [C] a ringing sound or a tune played by a clock or your phone after you have set it to play at a particular time to wake you up（时钟或手机的）闹铃: *The* ***alarm went off*** *at 7 o'clock.* 闹铃在 7 点钟响了。

IDM **a'larm bells ring/start ringing** if you say that **alarm bells are ringing**, you mean that people are starting to feel worried and suspicious 警钟敲响；发出危险信号

■ *verb* **1** **~ sb** to make sb anxious or afraid 使惊恐；使害怕；使担心 **SYN** **worry**: *The captain knew there was an engine fault but didn't want to alarm the passengers.* 船长知道一台发动机出了故障，不过他不想惊动乘客。➲ SYNONYMS AT FRIGHTEN **2** **~ sth** to fit sth such as a door with a device that warns people when sb is trying to enter illegally 给（门等）安装警报器

a'larm call *noun* **1** a telephone call which is intended to wake you up 催醒电话；叫醒电话: *Could I have an alarm call at 5.30 tomorrow, please?* 请在明天早晨 5:30 打电话叫醒我好吗？**2** a cry of warning made by a bird or animal（鸟兽遇险时发出的）报警鸣叫；告警声

a'larm clock *noun* a clock that you can set to ring a bell, etc. at a particular time and wake you up 闹钟: *I set the alarm clock for 7 o'clock.* 我把闹钟定在 7 点钟闹响。➲ PICTURE AT CLOCK ➲ SEE ALSO ALARM *n.* (4)

alarmed /ə'lɑːmd; *NAmE* ə'lɑːrmd/ *adj.* **1** **~ (at/by sth)** anxious or afraid that sth dangerous or unpleasant might happen 担心；害怕: *She was alarmed at the prospect of travelling alone.* 她一想到独自旅行的情景就害怕。➲ SYNONYMS AT AFRAID **2** [not before noun] protected by an alarm 有警报装置: *This door is alarmed.* 这扇门安装了警报器。

alarm·ing /ə'lɑːmɪŋ; *NAmE* ə'lɑːrm-/ *adj.* causing worry and fear 使人惊恐的；令人惊慌的；引起恐慌的: *an alarming increase in crime* 犯罪活动骇人的增加 ◇ *The rainforests are disappearing* ***at an alarming rate.*** 雨林正以惊人的速度消失。▶ **alarm·ing·ly** *adv.*: *Prices have risen alarmingly.* 价格涨得吓人。

alarm·ist /ə'lɑːmɪst; *NAmE* ə'lɑːrm-/ *adj.* (*disapproving*) causing unnecessary fear and anxiety 危言耸听的；骇人的: *A spokesperson for the food industry said the TV programme was alarmist.* 食品行业的一位发言人说这个电视节目危言耸听。▶ **alarm·ist** *noun*

alas /ə'læs/ *exclamation* (*old use* or *literary*) used to show you are sad or sorry（表示悲伤或遗憾）哎呀，唉: *For many people, alas, hunger is part of everyday life.* 唉，对很多人来说，挨饿是家常便饭。

al·ba·tross /'ælbətrɒs; *NAmE* -trɔːs; -trɑːs/ *noun* **1** a very large white bird with long wings that lives in the Pacific and Southern Oceans 信天翁（白色长翼大海鸟，生活于太平洋和南大洋）➲ VISUAL VOCAB PAGE V12 **2** [usually sing.] (*formal*) a thing that causes problems or prevents you from doing sth 惹麻烦的事；苦恼；障碍

al·beit **AW** /ˌɔːl'biːɪt/ *conj.* (*formal*) although 尽管；虽然: *He finally agreed, albeit reluctantly, to help us.* 尽管勉强，他最后还是同意帮助我们。

al·bin·ism /'ælbɪnɪzəm/ *noun* [U] (*specialist*) the condition of being an albino 白化病

al·bino /æl'biːnəʊ; *NAmE* -'baɪnoʊ/ *noun* (*pl.* **-os**) a person or an animal that is born with no PIGMENT (= colour) in the hair or skin, which are white, or in the eyes, which are pink 患白化病的人（或动物）▶ **al·bino** *adj.* [only before noun]

Al·bion /'ælbiən/ *noun* [U] (*literary*) an ancient name for Britain or England 阿尔比恩（古时用以指不列颠或英格兰）

album /'ælbəm/ *noun* **1** a book in which you keep photographs, stamps, etc. 相册；影集；集邮簿；集物簿册: *a photo album* 相册 ◇ *an online album* (= a website where

A

you can store and view photographs) 网上相册（可存储和观看照片的网站） ➲ VISUAL VOCAB PAGE V45 **2** a collection of pieces of music released as a single item, usually on a CD or on the Internet （唱片、盒式磁带或网上的）音乐专辑，歌曲专辑： *the band's latest album* 这个乐队的最新专辑 ◇ *an online album* (= an album that you can listen to on the Internet) 网上专辑 ➲ COLLOCATIONS AT MUSIC ➲ COMPARE SINGLE *n.* (2)

al·bu·men /ˈælbjʊmɪn; *NAmE* ælˈbjuːmən/ *noun* [U] (*specialist*) the clear inside part of an egg that is white when cooked 蛋白；蛋清 SYN **white** ➲ COMPARE YOLK

Al·ca·traz /ˈælkətræz/ *noun* a small US island near San Francisco where there is a former prison 阿尔卡特拉斯岛（旧金山附近的美属小岛，有一旧时的监狱）： *The clinic felt like Alcatraz. There was no escape.* 那家诊所令人感觉像四面环水的监牢，无路可逃。

al·chem·ist /ˈælkəmɪst/ *noun* a person who studied alchemy 炼金术士

al·chemy /ˈælkəmi/ *noun* [U] **1** a form of chemistry studied in the Middle Ages which involved trying to discover how to change ordinary metals into gold 炼金术（见于中世纪，企图把普通金属炼成黄金） **2** (*literary*) a mysterious power or magic that can change things （改变事物的）神秘力量，魔力

al·cher·inga /ˌæltʃəˈrɪŋɡə/ (*also* **Dream·time**) *noun* [U] according to some Australian Aboriginals, the time when the first people were created （澳大利亚土著神话中的）世界发端，梦想期，梦幻时代

al·co·hol 🔑 /ˈælkəhɒl; *NAmE* -hɔːl; -hɑːl/ *noun* [U] **1** 🔑 drinks such as beer, wine, etc. that can make people drunk 含酒精饮料；酒： *He never drinks alcohol.* 他从来不喝酒。 ◇ *alcohol abuse* 酗酒 ➲ COLLOCATIONS AT DIET **2** 🔑 the clear liquid that is found in drinks such as beer, wine, etc. and is used in medicines, cleaning products, etc. 酒精；乙醇： *Wine contains about 10% alcohol.* 葡萄酒含有约 10% 的酒精。 ◇ *levels of alcohol in the blood* 血液中酒精含量 ◇ *He pleaded guilty to driving with excess alcohol.* 他对过量饮酒后驾车一事表示服罪。 ◇ ***low-alcohol*** *beer* 酒精度低的啤酒 ◇ ***alcohol-free*** *beer* 不含酒精的啤酒

al·co·hol·ic 🔑 /ˌælkəˈhɒlɪk; *NAmE* -ˈhɔːl-; -ˈhɑːl-/ *adj.*, *noun*

■ ***adj.*** **1** 🔑 connected with or containing alcohol 酒精的；含酒精的： *alcoholic drinks* 含酒精的饮料 OPP **non-alcoholic** ➲ SEE ALSO SOFT DRINK **2** caused by drinking alcohol 饮酒引起的： *The guests left in an alcoholic haze.* 客人们醉醺醺地离去了。

■ ***noun*** 🔑 a person who regularly drinks too much alcohol and cannot easily stop drinking, so that it has become an illness 酒精中毒者；嗜酒如命者；酒鬼 ➲ SEE ALSO LUSH *n.*

Alco,holics A'nonymous *noun* [U] (*abbr.* **AA**) an international organization, begun in Chicago in 1935, for people who are trying to stop drinking alcohol. They have meetings to help each other. 匿名戒酒会（1935 年成立于芝加哥的国际组织，成员不用全名）

al·co·hol·ism /ˈælkəhɒlɪzəm; *NAmE* -hɔːl-; -hɑːl-/ *noun* [U] the medical condition caused by drinking too much alcohol regularly 酒精中毒

al·co·pop /ˈælkəʊpɒp; *NAmE* -koʊpɑːp/ *noun* (*BrE*) a sweet FIZZY (= with bubbles) drink that contains alcohol 泡泡甜酒 ➲ MORE LIKE THIS 1, page R25

al·cove /ˈælkəʊv; *NAmE* -koʊv/ *noun* an area in a room that is formed by part of a wall being built farther back than the rest of the wall 壁凹，凹室，壁龛（房内墙壁凹进空间）： *The bookcase fits neatly into the alcove.* 书架正好放得进壁凹。

al dente /ˌæl ˈdenteɪ; -ti/ *adj.* (*from Italian*) (of cooked food, especially PASTA 尤指意大利面等煮过的食物) firm, but not hard, when bitten 筋道的；有韧性耐咀嚼的；有嚼劲的 ▸ **al dente** *adv.*

alder /ˈɔːldə(r)/ *noun* a tree like a BIRCH that grows in northern countries, usually in wet ground 桤木（多见于北方国家潮湿地区）

al·der·man /ˈɔːldəmən; *NAmE* -dərm-/ *noun* (*pl.* **-men** /-mən/) **1** (in England and Wales in the past) a senior member of a town, BOROUGH or county council, below the rank of a MAYOR, chosen by other members of the council （旧时英格兰和威尔士的）高级市政官（职位低于市长） **2** (*feminine* **al·der·woman**, *pl.* **-women** /-wɪmɪn/) (in the US, Canada and Australia) an elected member of a town or city council （美国、加拿大、澳大利亚的）市政委员会委员： *Alderman Tim Evans* 市政委员会委员蒂姆 • 埃文斯

ale /eɪl/ *noun* **1** [U, C] a type of beer, usually sold in bottles or cans. There are several kinds of ale. 麦芽啤酒： ***brown/pale ale*** 棕色 / 淡色麦芽啤酒 **2** [C] a glass, bottle or can of ale 一杯（或一瓶、一罐）麦芽啤酒： *Two light ales please.* 请来两杯淡麦芽啤酒。 **3** [U] (*old-fashioned*) beer generally （泛指）啤酒 ➲ SEE ALSO BROWN ALE, GINGER ALE, REAL ALE

alec, aleck ➲ SMART ALEC

ale·house /ˈeɪlhaʊs/ *noun* (*old-fashioned*, *BrE*) a place where people used to drink beer 啤酒店；酒馆

alert /əˈlɜːt; *NAmE* əˈlɜːrt/ *adj.*, *verb*, *noun*

■ ***adj.*** **1** able to think quickly; quick to notice things 警觉的；警惕的；戒备的： *Suddenly he found himself awake and fully alert.* 突然他发觉自己醒了过来，而且高度警觉。 ◇ *Two alert scientists spotted the mistake.* 两个警觉的科学家发现了这个错误。 **2 ~ to sth** aware of sth, especially a problem or danger 意识到，注意到（问题或危险）： *We must be alert to the possibility of danger.* 我们必须认识到危险发生的可能性。 ▸ **alert·ly** *adv.* **alert·ness** *noun* [U]

■ ***verb*** [often passive] **1 ~ sb (to do sth) | ~ sb (that)...** to warn sb about a dangerous or urgent situation 向…报警；使警觉；使警惕；使戒备： *Neighbours quickly alerted the emergency services.* 邻居很快向应急服务机构报了警。 ◇ *Alerted by a noise downstairs, he sat up and turned on the light.* 楼下的响声使他警觉，他坐起来打开灯。 **2 ~ sb to sth** to make sb aware of sth 使意识到；使认识到： *They had been alerted to the possibility of further price rises.* 他们已意识到价格可能继续上涨。

■ ***noun*** **1** [sing., U] a situation in which people are watching for danger and ready to deal with it 警戒；戒备；警惕： *Police are warning the public to* ***be on the alert for*** *suspicious packages.* 警方警告公众要警惕可疑包裹。 ◇ *More than 5 000 troops have been placed* ***on (full) alert.*** * 5 000 多名士兵已处于（全面）戒备状态。 **2** [C] a warning of danger or of a problem 警报： ***a bomb/fire alert*** 炸弹 / 火警警报 ➲ WORDFINDER NOTE AT ATTACK ➲ SEE ALSO RED ALERT

A level /ˈeɪ levl/ (*also* **ad'vanced level**) *noun* [C, U] a British exam taken in a particular subject, usually in the final year of school at the age of 18 高级证书考试（英国中学单科考试，通常在毕业年级进行）： *You need three A levels to get onto this university course.* 你要学习这门大学课程，就需要通过三科高级证书考试。 ◇ *What A levels are you doing?* 你在准备哪些科目的高级证书考试？ ◇ *I'm doing maths A level.* 我在准备数学高级证书考试。 ◇ *two A level passes/two passes at A level* 两门高级证书考试及格 ➲ COMPARE AS (LEVEL), GCE, GCSE, NVQ

alex·an·drine /ˌælɪɡˈzɑːndrɪn; -aɪn; *NAmE* -ˈzæn-/ *adj.* (*specialist*) (of lines of poetry 诗行) containing six IAMBIC FEET 亚历山大诗体的；含六音步抑扬格的 ▸ **alex·an·drine** *noun*

al·fal·fa /ælˈfælfə/ *noun* [U] a plant with small divided leaves and purple flowers, grown as food for farm animals and as a salad vegetable 紫（花）苜蓿；苜蓿

al fresco /æl ˈfreskəʊ; *NAmE* -koʊ/ *adj.*, *adv.* (*from Italian*) outdoors 在户外的： *an al fresco lunch party* 户外午餐会 ◇ *eating al fresco* 在户外用餐

algae /ˈældʒiː; ˈælɡiː/ *noun* [U, pl.] very simple plants, such as SEAWEED, that have no real leaves, STEMS or roots, and that grow in or near water 藻类；海藻 HELP The singular of **algae** is **alga** /ˈælɡə/ but this is a specialist term used only in scientific writing. * algae 的单数形式是 alga，但 alga 是专业术语，仅用于科学语境的书面语中。 ▶ **algal** /ˈælɡəl/ *adj.* [only before noun]: ***algal blooms/growth*** 藻华；藻类生长

al·ge·bra /ˈældʒɪbrə/ *noun* [U] a type of mathematics in which letters and symbols are used to represent quantities 代数学 ➲ WORDFINDER NOTE AT MATHS ▶ **al·ge·bra·ic** /ˌældʒɪˈbreɪɪk/ *adj.*

al·go·rithm /ˈælɡərɪðəm/ *noun* (*computing* 计) a set of rules that must be followed when solving a particular problem 算法；计算程序

al·haja /ælˈhædʒə/ *noun* (*WAfrE*) a woman who is a Muslim and has completed a religious journey to Mecca (often used as a title) 哈娅（去麦加完成了正朝功课的穆斯林女子，常用作称谓） ➲ COMPARE ALHAJI

al·haji /ælˈhædʒi/ *noun* (*WAfrE*) a man who is a Muslim and has completed a religious journey to Mecca (often used as a title) 哈吉（去麦加完成了正朝功课的穆斯林男子，常用作称谓） ➲ COMPARE ALHAJA

-alia /ˈeɪliə/ *suffix* (in plural nouns 构成复数名词) items connected with the particular area of activity or interest mentioned （与某活动或兴趣范围）有关的物品： *kitchenalia* 厨房用品

alias /ˈeɪliəs/ *adv., noun*

■***adv.*** used when a person, especially a criminal or an actor, is known by two names （罪犯、演员等）又名，亦名，别名，化名： *Mick Clark, alias Sid Brown* 米克·克拉克，又名锡德·布朗 ◇ *Hercule Poirot, alias David Suchet* (= David Suchet plays the part of Hercule Poirot) 赫尔克里·波洛，由大卫·苏切特扮演 ◇ *David Suchet, alias Hercule Poirot of the famous TV series* 大卫·苏切特，即著名电视连续剧中的赫尔克里·波洛

■***noun*** **1** a false or different name, especially one that is used by a criminal （尤指罪犯所用的）化名，别名： *He checked into the hotel under an alias.* 他用化名登记住进旅馆。 **2** (*computing* 计) a name that can be used instead of the actual name for a file, Internet address, etc. （档案、互联网地址等用的）别名，假名

alibi /ˈæləbaɪ/ *noun* **1** evidence that proves that a person was in another place at the time of a crime and so could not have committed it 不在犯罪现场证明： *The suspects all had alibis for the day of the robbery.* 嫌疑人均有证据证明抢劫当天不在犯罪现场。 **2** an excuse for sth that you have done wrong 借口；托辞

Alice band /ˈælɪs bænd/ *noun* (*BrE*) a band which holds your hair back away from your face, but lets it hang freely at the back 发箍

Alice in Wonder·land /ˌælɪs ɪn ˈwʌndəlænd; *NAmE* -dərl-/ *noun* [U] used to describe a situation that is very strange, in which things happen that do not make any sense and are the opposite of what you would expect （事情悖理且与想象的截然相反的）怪异局面： *The country's economic system is pure Alice in Wonderland.* 这个国家的经济制度实属匪夷所思。 ▶ **Alice-in-Wonderland** *adj.* [only before noun]: *I felt I was in an Alice-in-Wonderland world.* 我感觉就像置身于奇幻世界之中。 ➲ MORE LIKE THIS 17, page R27 ORIGIN From the title of a children's story by Lewis Carroll. 源自刘易斯·卡罗尔所著的儿童小说《艾丽丝漫游奇境记》。

alien /ˈeɪliən/ *adj., noun*

■***adj.*** **1 ~ (to sb/sth)** strange and frightening; different from what you are used to 陌生的；不熟悉 SYN **hostile**: *an alien environment* 陌生的环境 ◇ *In a world that had suddenly become alien and dangerous, he was her only security.* 在一个突然变得陌生而危险的世界里，他是她唯一的守护神。 **2** (*often disapproving*) from another country or society; foreign 外国的；异域的： *an alien culture* 异族文化 **3** (*disapproving*) not usual or acceptable 不相容；相抵触；格格不入： **~ to sb/sth** *The idea is alien to our religion.* 这种思想与我们的宗教不相容。 ◇ *Cruelty was quite alien to him.* 他绝无残忍之心。 **4** connected with creatures from another world 外星的： *alien beings from outer space* 外星人

■***noun*** **1** (*NAmE also* ˌ**non-ˈcitizen**) (*law* 律 or *specialist*) a person who is not a citizen of the country in which they live or work 外国人；外侨： *an illegal alien* 非法外侨 ➲ COMPARE RESIDENT ALIEN **2** a creature from another world 外星生物： *aliens from outer space* 外星人

alien·ate /ˈeɪliəneɪt/ *verb* **1 ~ sb** to make sb less friendly or sympathetic towards you 使疏远；使不友好；离间： *His comments have alienated a lot of young voters.* 他的评论使许多年轻选民离他而去。 **2 ~ sb (from sth/sb)** to make sb feel that they do not belong in a particular group 使（与某群体）格格不入；使疏远： *Very talented children may feel alienated from the others in their class.* 天才出众的孩子可能觉得与班上的同学格格不入。 ▶ **alien·ation** /ˌeɪliəˈneɪʃn/ *noun* [U]: *The new policy resulted in the alienation of many voters.* 新政策导致许多选民疏远了。 ◇ *Many immigrants suffer from a sense of alienation.* 许多移民因感到不容于社会而苦恼。

alight /əˈlaɪt/ *adj., verb*

■***adj.*** [not before noun] **1** on fire 燃烧；着火： *A cigarette* ***set*** *the dry grass* ***alight***. 一支香烟把干草点燃了。 ◇ *Her dress* ***caught alight*** *in the fire.* 她的衣服让火烧着了。 **2** (*formal*) (of faces or eyes 脸或眼) showing a feeling of happiness or excitement 容光焕发；兴奋 IDM SEE WORLD

■***verb*** (*formal* or *literary*) **1** [I] **~ (in/on/upon sth)** (of a bird or an insect 鸟或昆虫) to land in or on sth after flying to it 降落；飞落 SYN **land** **2** [I] **~ (from sth)** to get out of a bus, a train or other vehicle 从（公共汽车、火车等）下来 SYN **get off**: *Do not alight from a moving bus.* 公共汽车行驶时不要下车。

PHR V **aˈlight on/upon sth** to think of, find or notice sth, especially by chance （尤指偶然地）想到，发现，注意到： *Eventually, we alighted on the idea of seeking sponsorship.* 最后我们偶然想到了寻求赞助。 ◇ *Her eyes suddenly alighted on the bundle of documents.* 她的目光突然落到了这捆文件上。

align /əˈlaɪn/ *verb* **1** [I, T] **~ (sth) (with sth)** to arrange sth in the correct position, or to be in the correct position, in relation to sth else, especially in a straight line 排列整齐；使对齐；（尤指）成一直线： *Make sure the shelf is aligned with the top of the cupboard.* 务必使搁架与橱柜顶端对齐。 ◇ *The top and bottom line of each column on the page should align.* 版面每栏的头一行和末一行要对齐。 **2** [T] **~ sth (with/to sth)** to change sth slightly so that it is in the correct relationship to sth else 使一致： *Domestic prices have been aligned with those in world markets.* 国内价格已调整到与世界市场一致。 ➲ MORE LIKE THIS 20, page R27

PHR V **aˈlign yourself with sb/sth** to publicly support an organization, a set of opinions or a person that you agree with 公开支持（某组织、意见、人）

align·ment /əˈlaɪnmənt/ *noun* [U, C] **1** arrangement in a straight line 排成直线： *A bone in my spine was* ***out of alignment***. 我的脊椎骨有一节脱位。 **2** political support given to one country or group by another （国家、团体间的）结盟： *Japan's alignment with the West* 日本与西方国家的结盟

alike /əˈlaɪk/ *adj., adv.*

■***adj.*** [not before noun] very similar 相像；十分相似： *My sister and I do not look alike.* 我和妹妹外貌不相像。 ➲ COMPARE UNLIKE *adj.* ➲ MORE LIKE THIS 31, page R28

■***adv.*** **1** in a very similar way 十分相像地；很相似地： *They tried to treat all their children alike.* 他们尽量对自己的孩子一视同仁。 **2** used after you have referred to two people or groups, to mean 'both' or 'equally' 两者都；同样地： *Good management benefits employers and employees alike.* 良好的管理对雇主和雇员同样有利。 IDM SEE GREAT *adj.*, SHARE *v.*

ali·men·tary canal /ˌælɪmentəri kəˈnæl/ *noun* the passage in the body that carries food from the mouth to the ANUS 消化道

ali·mony /ˈælɪməni; *NAmE* -moʊni/ *noun* [U] (*especially NAmE*) the money that a court orders sb to pay regularly to their former wife or husband when the marriage is ended（离婚后一方给另一方的）生活费，扶养费 ➲ COMPARE MAINTENANCE (3), PALIMONY

'A-line *adj.* (of a skirt or dress 裙子或连衣裙) wider at the bottom than at the top 呈 A 字型的；宽下摆的

ali·quot /'ælɪkwɒt; *NAmE* -kwɑːt/ *noun* **1** (*specialist*) a small amount of sth that is taken from a larger amount, especially when it is taken in order to do chemical tests on it（尤指化学实验的）试样 **2** (*mathematics* 数) a quantity which can be exactly divided into another 整除数

'A-list *adj.* [usually before noun] used to describe the group of people who are considered to be the most famous, successful or important 第一等的；最出名（或成功、重要）的： *He only invited **A-list celebrities** to his parties.* 他只邀请头等名流参加他的聚会。 ➲ COMPARE B-LIST ▶ **'A-lister** *noun*： *A-lister Cameron Diaz* 一线明星卡梅隆 • 迪亚兹

alive /ə'laɪv/ *adj.* [not before noun] **1** living; not dead 活着；在世： *We don't know whether he's alive or dead.* 我们不知道他是死是活。 ◇ *Is your mother **still alive**?* 你的母亲还健在吗？ ◇ *Doctors **kept** the baby **alive** for six weeks.* 医生使婴儿活了六周。 ◇ *I was glad to hear you're **alive and well**.* 听说你健在我很高兴。 ◇ *She had to steal food just to **stay alive**.* 她得偷食物才不至于饿死。 ◇ *He was **buried alive** in the earthquake.* 地震把他活埋了。 **2** ~ (**with sth**) full of emotion, excitement, activity, etc. 情绪饱满；激动兴奋；有生气；有活力： *Ed was alive with happiness.* 埃德高兴得眉飞色舞。 **3** continuing to exist 继续存在： *to **keep** a tradition **alive*** 继承传统 **4** ~ **with sth** full of living or moving things 充满（活的或动的东西）： *The pool was alive with goldfish.* 池塘里满是游来游去的金鱼。 **5** ~ **to sth** aware of sth; knowing sth exists and is important 意识到；认识到；注意到： *to be alive to the dangers/facts/possibilities* 意识到危险；认识到事实；注意到可能 ➲ MORE LIKE THIS 31, page R28

IDM **a,live and 'kicking** very active, healthy or popular 充满活力；活蹦乱跳；生气勃勃；流行 **bring sth a'live** to make sth interesting 使有趣： *The pictures bring the book alive.* 图片使得这本书生动有趣。 **come a'live 1** (of a subject or an event 主题或活动) to become interesting and exciting 引起兴趣；生动起来 SYN **come to life**： *The game came alive in the second half.* 比赛在下半场变得有看头了。 **2** (of a place 地方) to become busy and full of activity 热闹起来；活跃起来 SYN **come to life**： *The city starts to come alive after dark.* 这座城市天黑以后便热闹起来。 **3** (of a person 人) to show interest in sth and become excited about it 兴致勃勃；有精神起来： *She came alive as she talked about her job.* 她一谈到她的工作精神就来了。 ➲ MORE AT EAT

al·kali /'ælkəlaɪ/ *noun* [C, U] (*chemistry* 化) a chemical substance that reacts with acids to form a salt and gives a SOLUTION with a pH of more than seven when it is dissolved in water 碱 ➲ COMPARE ACID *n.* (1)

al·ka·line /'ælkəlaɪn/ *adj.* **1** (*chemistry* 化) having the nature of an alkali 碱性的 **2** (*specialist*) containing alkali 含碱的： *alkaline soil* 碱性土壤 ➲ COMPARE ACID *adj.* (1)

al·ka·lin·ity /,ælkə'lɪnəti/ *noun* [U] the state of being or containing an ALKALI 碱度；碱性

al·kal·oid /'ælkəlɔɪd/ *noun* (*biology* 生 or *medical* 医) a poisonous substance found in some plants. There are many different alkaloids and some are used as the basis for drugs. 生物碱

al·kane /'ælkeɪn/ *noun* (*chemistry* 化) any of a series of COMPOUNDS that contain CARBON and HYDROGEN 烷烃： *Methane and propane are alkanes.* 甲烷和丙烷是烷烃。

Alka-Seltzer™ /,ælkə 'seltsə(r)/ *noun* [C, U] a medicine that you mix with water to make a drink that helps with INDIGESTION 我可舒适（一种水溶性胃药片）

al·kene /'ælkiːn/ *noun* (*chemistry* 化) any of a series of gases that contain HYDROGEN and CARBON and that have a double BOND (= force of attraction) between two of the CARBON atoms 烯；烯烃

all /ɔːl/ *det., pron., adv.*

■ *det.* **1** (used with plural nouns. The noun may have *the, this, that, my, her, his,* etc. in front of it, or a number. 与复数名词连用。名词前可用 the、this、that、my、her、his 等，也可用数词。) the whole number of 所有；全部；全体；一切： *All horses are animals, but not all animals are horses.* 所有的马都是动物，但并不是所有的动物都是马。 ◇ *Cars were coming from all directions* (= every direction). 汽车从四面八方驶来。 ◇ *All the people you invited are coming.* 你邀请的人都会来。 ◇ *All my plants have died.* 我的花草全死光了。 ◇ *All five men are hard workers.* 五个人全都工作努力。 **2** (used with uncountable nouns. The noun may have *the, this, that, my, her, his,* etc. in front of it. 与不可数名词连用。名词前可用 the、this、that、my、her、his 等。) the whole amount of 所有；全部；一切： *All wood tends to shrink.* 所有的木头都会收缩。 ◇ *You've had all the fun and I've had all the hard work.* 享受都是你得，苦活儿都是我做。 ◇ *All this mail must be answered.* 所有这些信件都必须回复。 ◇ *He has lost all his money.* 他失去了所有的钱。 **3** used with singular nouns showing sth has been happening for a whole period of time（与单数名词连用，表示某事在某段时间内持续发生）全部的，整个的： *He's worked hard all year.* 他一年到头都在辛勤劳动。 ◇ *She was unemployed for all that time.* 那段时间她一直失业。 **4** the greatest possible 极度；尽量： *In all honesty* (= being as honest as I can), *I can't agree.* 说实在的，我不能同意。 **5** consisting or appearing to consist of one thing only 唯一；全是；仅仅： *The magazine was all advertisements.* 这份杂志全是广告。 ◇ *She was **all smiles*** (= smiling a lot). 她笑容满面。 **6** any whatever 无论什么；任何： *He denied all knowledge of the crime.* 他矢口否认对这桩罪案知情。

IDM **and all 'that (jazz, rubbish, stuff, etc.)** (*informal*) and other similar things 以及诸如此类的： *I'm bored by history—dates and battles and all that stuff.* 我厌烦历史，尽是些年代啦战争啦什么的。 **not all that good, well, etc.** not particularly good, well, etc. 不那么好；不很好： *He doesn't sing all that well.* 他唱得并不特别好。 **not as bad(ly), etc. as all 'that** not as much as has been suggested 并非那么坏（等）： *They're not as rich as all that.* 他们并不是那么富有。 ◇ *We didn't play particularly well, but we didn't do as badly as all that.* 我们打得不是特别好，但也不是那么差。 **of 'all people, things, etc.** (*informal*) used to express surprise because sb/sth seems the least likely person, example, etc. 在所有的…当中偏偏： *I didn't think you, of all people, would become a vegetarian.* 我真没有想到，在所有的人当中偏偏你会成为素食者。 **of 'all the...** (*informal*) used to express anger（表示生气）真是，真气人： *I've locked myself out. Of all the stupid things to do!* 我把自己锁在门外了，真是蠢得很！ ➲ MORE AT FOR *prep.*

■ *pron.* **1** the whole number or amount 所有；全部；全体；一切： *All of the food has gone.* 食物全光了。 ◇ *They've eaten all of it.* 他们全吃光了。 ◇ *They've eaten it all.* 他们吃得一点也没剩。 ◇ *I invited some of my colleagues but not all.* 我邀请了一些同事，并不是所有的。 ◇ *Not all of them were invited.* 他们当中并不是人人都受到邀请。 ◇ *All of them enjoyed the party.* 他们都喜欢那次聚会。 ◇ *They all enjoyed it.* 他们都喜欢。 ◇ *His last movie was best of all.* 他最近的那部电影是他所有电影中最好的一部。 **2** (followed by a relative clause, often without *that* 后接常不带 that 的关系从句) the only thing; everything 唯一的事物；所有的事物；一切： *All I want is peace and quiet.* 我只要和平安宁。 ◇ *It was all that I had.* 那就是我拥有的一切。 ➲ NOTE AT ALTOGETHER

IDM **all in 'all** when everything is considered 从各方面考虑；总的说来： *All in all it had been a great success.* 总的说来，那是个巨大的成功。 **all in 'one** having two or more uses, functions, etc. 多功能；多用途： *It's a corkscrew and bottle-opener all in one.* 这是一物多用，既是瓶塞钻，又是开瓶器。 **and 'all 1** also; included; in addition 而且；还；包括： *She jumped into the river, clothes and all* (= with her clothes on). 她连衣服也没脱就跳进河中。

2 (*informal*) as well; too 也：*'I'm freezing.' 'Yeah, me and all.'* "我都快冻僵了。" "对，我也是。" (**not**) **at all** 🔑 in any way; to any degree 一点也（不）；完全（不）：*I didn't enjoy it at all.* 我一点也不喜欢。 **in all** as a total 总共；共计 SYN **altogether**：*There were twelve of us in all for dinner.* 我们一共十二人吃饭。◊ *That's £25.40 in all.* 总计 25.40 英镑。 **ˌnot at ˈall** 🔑 used as a polite reply to an expression of thanks （回答道谢的客套语）不用谢，哪儿的话：*'Thanks very much for your help.' 'Not at all, it was a pleasure.'* "多谢你帮了忙。" "别客气，不用谢。" **your ˈall** everything you have 所有的一切：*They gave their all* (= fought and died) *in the war.* 他们在战争中英勇牺牲，献出了一切。 ➲ MORE AT ABOVE *prep.*, AFTER *prep.*, END *v.*, END *n.*, FOR *prep.*, SIDE *n.*

■*adv.* **1** 🔑 completely 完全：*She was dressed all in white.* 她穿得一身白。◊ *He lives all alone.* 他索居独处。◊ *The coffee went all over my skirt.* 咖啡溅了我一裙子。 **2** (*informal*) very 很；十分；非常：*She was all excited.* 她非常激动。◊ *Now don't get all upset about it.* 别再为那件事那么难过了。 **3** **~ too...** used to show that sth is more than you would like 太；过分：*I'm all too aware of the problems.* 我实在太明白这些问题了。◊ *The end of the trip came all too soon.* 这次旅行结束得未免太快了。 **4** (in sports and games 体育运动、比赛、游戏) to each side 每方；各：*The score was four all.* 比分是四平。

IDM **all aˈlong** all the time; from the beginning 一直；始终：*I realized it was in my pocket all along.* 我发觉它一直就在我口袋里。 **all aˈround** (*NAmE*) ➲ ALL ROUND **all the better, harder, etc.** so much better, harder, etc. 更好（或努力等）：*We'll have to work all the harder with two people off sick.* 有两个人病了没上班，所以我们得加把劲干。 **all but 1** almost 几乎；差不多：*The party was all but over when we arrived.* 我们到的时候，聚会都快要结束了。◊ *It was all but impossible to read his writing.* 他的笔迹几乎没法辨认。 **2** everything or everyone except sth/sb 除…外全部：*All but one of the plates were damaged.* 除去一只，盘子全打碎了。 **all ˈin 1** physically tired 疲劳；疲惫 SYN **exhausted**：*At the end of the race he felt all in.* 他在赛跑结束时感到筋疲力尽。 **2** (*BrE*) including everything 全部包括在内；总共：*The trip cost £750 all in.* 旅行总共花了 750 英镑。 ➲ SEE ALSO ALL-IN **all of sth** (*often ironic*) used to emphasize an amount, a size, etc. usually when it is very small （强调数量、体积等，而实际上通常很小）足足：*It must be all of 100 metres to the car!* 走到车那里一定足足有 100 米呀！ **all ˈover 1** everywhere 到处；处处：*We looked all over for the ring.* 我们到处找那枚戒指。 **2** (*informal*) what you would expect of the person mentioned 正如所提到的人那样；十分像；十足：*That sounds like my sister all over.* 这听起来很像我的妹妹。 **all ˈround** (*BrE*) (*NAmE* **all aˈround**) **1** in every way; in all respects 在各方面；全面：*a good performance all round* 从各方面看来都精彩的演出 **2** for each person 给每个人：*She bought drinks all round.* 她给每个人都买了饮料。 **ˌall ˈthere** (*informal*) having a healthy mind; thinking clearly 心理健全；头脑清醒：*He behaves very oddly at times—I don't think he's quite all there.* 他有时候怪里怪气的，我觉得他脑筋不大正常。 **be all about sb/sth** used to say what the most important aspect of sth is 最重要的是；主要的是：*It's all about money these days.* 如今谈的就是钱。 **be all for sth/for doing sth** (*informal*) to believe strongly that sth should be done 坚信某事应完成；完全赞成：*They're all for saving money where they can.* 他们想尽一切办法省钱。 **be all ˈover sb** (*informal, often disapproving*) to show a lot of affection for or enthusiasm about sb 向某人献殷勤；讨好某人；谄媚：*He was all over her at the party.* 他在聚会上向她大献殷勤。 **be all ˈthat** (*US, informal*) to be very attractive or impressive 魅力十足；美丽动人；十分出色：*He thinks he's all that.* 他觉得自己颇有魅力。 **be all up** (**with sb**) (*old-fashioned, informal*) to be the end for sb （某人）完蛋了：*It looks as though it's all up with us now* (= we are ruined, have no further chances, etc.). 看来我们现在全完蛋了。

all- /ɔːl/ *combining form* (in adjectives and adverbs 构成形容词和副词) **1** completely 全部；完全；十足：*an all-British cast* 清一色的英国演员阵容 ◊ *an all-inclusive price* 全部包括在内的价格 **2** in the highest degree 最高程度；最：*all-important* 极重要的 ◊ *all-powerful* 有无上权力的

ˌall-ˈaction *adj.* [only before noun] having a lot of exciting events 充满打斗动作的；全动感的：*an all-action movie* 动作影片

Allah /ˈælə/ *noun* the name of God among Muslims 安拉，真主（穆斯林信奉的神）

ˌall-Aˈmerican *adj.* **1** having good qualities that people think are typically American 具有典型美国人优良素质的；典型美国人的：*a clean-cut all-American boy* 外表整洁的典型美国男孩 **2** (of a sports player 运动员) chosen as one of the best players in the US （被选为）全美最佳的

ˌall-aˈround (*NAmE*) (*BrE* **ˌall-ˈround**) *adj.* [only before noun] **1** including many different subjects, skills, etc. 全面的；多方面的 **2** (of a person 人) with a wide range of skills or abilities 全能的；多才多艺的

allay /əˈleɪ/ *verb* **~ sth** (*formal*) to make sth, especially a feeling, less strong 减轻（尤指情绪）：*to allay fears/concern/suspicion* 减轻恐惧；减轻忧虑；减少怀疑

the ˈAll Blacks *noun* [pl.] the RUGBY UNION team of New Zealand 全黑队（指新西兰国家橄榄球队）

ˌall-Caˈnadian *adj.* **1** chosen as one of the best in, or representing the whole of, Canada, for example in sports （被选为）全加拿大最佳的；代表加拿大的 **2** having qualities that people think are typically Canadian 具有典型加拿大人素质的；典型加拿大人的

the ˌall-ˈclear *noun* [sing.] **1** a signal (often a sound) which shows that a place or situation is no longer dangerous 解除警报；警报解除信号 **2** if a doctor gives sb **the all-clear**, they tell the person that he/she does not have any health problems 没有疾病；完全健康 **3** permission to do sth 准许；许可：*The ship was given the all-clear to sail.* 这艘船获得了航行许可。

ˌall-ˈcomers *noun* [pl.] anyone who wants to take part in an activity or a competition 所有申请者；所有想参加者

ˌall-conˈsum·ing *adj.* (of an interest 兴趣) taking up all of your time or energy 耗尽时间（或精力）的；全身心投入的；令人着迷的：*an all-consuming love of jazz* 对爵士乐的迷恋

ˈall-day *adj.* [only before noun] continuing or available for the whole day 整整一天的；全天的：*an all-day meeting* 持续一天的会议 ◊ *The cafe serves an all-day breakfast.* 这家小餐馆供应全日早餐。

al·le·ga·tion /ˌæləˈɡeɪʃn/ *noun* a public statement that is made without giving proof, accusing sb of doing sth that is wrong or illegal （无证据的）说法，指控 SYN **accusation**：*to* ***investigate/deny/withdraw an allegation*** 调查 / 否认 / 撤回指控 ◊ **~ of sth** *Several newspapers* ***made allegations*** *of corruption in the city's police department.* 有几家报纸声称该市警察局腐败。◊ **~ (of sth) against sb** *allegations of dishonesty against him* 关于他不诚实的多种说法 ◊ **~ about sb/sth** *The committee has made serious allegations about interference in its work.* 委员会严厉谴责对其工作的干涉。◊ **~ that...** *an allegation that he had been dishonest* 一种关于他不诚实的说法 ➲ SYNONYMS AT CLAIM

al·lege /əˈledʒ/ *verb* [often passive] (*formal*) to state sth as a fact but without giving proof （未提出证据）断言，指称，声称：**~ (that)...** *The prosecution alleges* (*that*) *she was driving carelessly.* 控方指控她粗心驾驶。◊ **it is alleged (that)...** *It is alleged that he mistreated the prisoners.* 据称他虐待犯人。◊ **be alleged to be, have, etc. sth** *He is alleged to have mistreated the prisoners.* 他被指控虐待犯人。◊ **~ sth** *This procedure should be followed in cases where dishonesty has been alleged.* 指控欺诈的案件应遵循本诉讼程序。 ▶ **al·leged** *adj.* [only before noun] (*formal*)：*the* ***alleged*** *attacker/victim/killer* (= that sb says is one) 据称的袭击者 / 受害者 / 杀人凶手 ◊ *the* ***alleged*** *attack/offence/incident* (= that sb says has happened) 据称的袭击 / 罪行 / 事件 **al·leged·ly** /əˈledʒɪdli/ *adv.*：*crimes*

A

allegedly committed during the war 据说是战争期间所犯的罪行

al·le·giance /ə'li:dʒəns/ *noun* [U, C] a person's continued support for a political party, religion, ruler, etc. (对政党、宗教、统治者的)忠诚，效忠，拥戴: *to **switch/transfer/change allegiance*** 转变/转移/改变拥戴对象 ◇ ***an oath/a vow/a statement of allegiance*** 效忠宣誓/誓约/声明 ◇ *People of various party allegiances joined the campaign.* 各个不同政党的拥护者都参加了这次活动。 ◇ **~ (to sb/sth)** *to **pledge/swear allegiance*** 宣誓；发誓 ◇ *He affirmed his allegiance to the president.* 他坚称自己拥戴总统。

al·le·gory /'æləgəri; *NAmE* -gɔ:ri/ *noun* [C, U] (*pl.* **-ies**) a story, play, picture, etc. in which each character or event is a symbol representing an idea or a quality, such as truth, evil, death, etc.; the use of such symbols 寓言；讽喻；寓言体；讽喻法: *a political allegory* 政治讽喻 ◇ *the poet's use of allegory* 诗人的讽喻手法 ➲ SEE ALSO FABLE (1) ▶ **al·le·gor·ic·al** /,ælə'gɒrɪkl; *NAmE* -'gɔ:r-/ *adj.*: *an **allegorical figure/novel*** 寓言人物；讽喻小说 **al·le·gor·ic·al·ly** *adv.*

al·legro /ə'legrəʊ; *NAmE* -groʊ/ *noun* (*pl.* **-os**) (*music* 音, *from Italian*) a piece of music to be played in a fast and lively manner 快板 ▶ **al·legro** *adj., adv.*

al·lele /ə'li:l/ *noun* (*biology* 生) one of two or more possible forms of a GENE that are found at the same place on a CHROMOSOME 等位基因

al·le·luia /,ælɪ'lu:jə/ *noun, exclamation* = HALLELUJAH

,all-em'brac·ing *adj.* (*formal*) including everything 无所不包的；概括一切的

,all-en'compass·ing *adj.* (*formal*) including everything 包罗万象的；总括的

Allen key™ /'ælən ki:/ (*BrE*) (*NAmE* **'Allen wrench™**) *noun* a small tool used for turning an Allen screw™ 艾伦螺钉扳手；六角螺钉小扳手 ➲ PICTURE AT KEY

'Allen screw™ *noun* a screw with a hole that has six sides 艾伦螺钉，六角螺钉(顶端有六角形孔)

al·ler·gen /'ælədʒən; *NAmE* 'ælərdʒən/ *noun* a substance that causes an allergy 变应原，过敏原(能引起变态反应或过敏的物质)

al·ler·gic /ə'lɜ:dʒɪk; *NAmE* ə'lɜ:rdʒɪk/ *adj.* **1** **~ (to sth)** having an allergy to sth (对…)变态反应的，变应的，过敏的: *I like cats but unfortunately I'm allergic to them.* 我喜欢猫，但遗憾的是我对猫过敏。 **2** caused by an allergy 变态反应性的；变应性的；过敏性的: *an **allergic reaction/rash*** 过敏性反应/皮疹 **3** [not before noun] **~ to sth** (*informal, humorous*) having a strong dislike of sth/sb 对…十分反感；厌恶: *You could see he was allergic to housework.* 你可以看出他很讨厌做家务。

al·lergy /'ælədʒi; *NAmE* 'ælərdʒi/ *noun* (*pl.* **-ies**) **~ (to sth)** a medical condition that causes you to react badly or feel ill/sick when you eat or touch a particular substance 变态反应；过敏反应: *I have an allergy to animal hair.* 我对动物毛过敏。

al·le·vi·ate /ə'li:vieɪt/ *verb* **~ sth** to make sth less severe 减轻；缓和；缓解 **SYN** **ease**: *to alleviate suffering* 减轻苦难 ◇ *A number of measures were taken to alleviate the problem.* 采取了一系列措施缓解这个问题。 ▶ **al·le·vi·ation** /ə,li:vi'eɪʃn/ *noun* [U]

alley /'æli/ *noun* **1** (*also* **al·ley·way** /'æliweɪ/) a narrow passage behind or between buildings (建筑群中间或后面的)小街，小巷，胡同: *a **narrow/dark alley*** 狭窄的/黑暗的小巷 ➲ VISUAL VOCAB PAGE V3 ➲ SEE ALSO BLIND ALLEY, BOWLING ALLEY **2** (*NAmE*) (*BrE* **tram·lines**) (*informal*) the pair of parallel lines on a TENNIS or BADMINTON COURT that mark the extra area that is used when four people are playing (网球或羽毛球球场两侧的)双打边线

IDM **(right) up your 'alley** (*NAmE*) (*especially BrE* **(right) up your 'street**) (*informal*) very suitable for you because it is sth that you know a lot about or are very interested in (正)适合你；(正)和你对口

'alley cat *noun* a cat that lives on the streets 流浪猫；(街上的)野猫

al·li·ance /ə'laɪəns/ *noun* **1** an agreement between countries, political parties, etc. to work together in order to achieve sth that they all want (国家、政党等的)结盟，联盟，同盟: *to **form/make an alliance*** 结成/缔结同盟 ◇ **~ with sb/sth** *The Social Democrats are now **in alliance with** the Greens.* 社会民主党现在与绿党结成联盟。 ◇ **~ between A and B** *an alliance between education and business to develop the use of technology in schools* 为在学校中加强技术应用而结成的校企联盟 **2** a group of people, political parties, etc. who work together in order to achieve sth that they all want 结盟团体；联盟: *The Green Alliance was formed to campaign against environmental damage.* 成立绿色联盟是为了开展反对破坏环境的运动。

al·lied 🔑 *adj.* **1** /'ælaɪd/ (*often* **Allied**) [only before noun] connected with countries that unite to fight a war together, especially the countries that fought together against Germany in the First and Second World Wars (国与国协同作战)结盟的，联盟的；(第一次世界大战期间)协约国的；(第二次世界大战期间)同盟国的: *Italy joined the war on the Allied side in 1915.* * 1915 年，意大利加入协约国参战。 ◇ ***allied forces/troops*** 盟军；盟军部队 **2** /ə'laɪd; 'ælaɪd/ (*formal*) (of two or more things) similar or existing together; connected with sth (两个或以上事物)类似的；共存的；有关联的: *medicine, nursing, physiotherapy and other allied professions* 医药、护理、理疗以及其他相关专业 ◇ **~ to/with sth** *In this job you will need social skills allied with technical knowledge.* 这项工作需要社交能力和专业知识。 ➲ SEE ALSO ALLY

al·li·ga·tor /'ælɪgeɪtə(r)/ *noun* a large REPTILE similar to a CROCODILE, with a long tail, hard skin and very big JAWS, that lives in rivers and lakes in N and S America and China 钝吻鳄

'alligator clip *noun* (*especially NAmE*) = CROCODILE CLIP

,all-im'port·ant *adj.* extremely important 极重要的

,all-'in *adj.* [only before noun] (*BrE*) including the cost of all parts of sth 包括所有费用的 **SYN** **inclusive**: *an all-in price of £500 with no extras to pay* 共 500 英镑、无需支付额外费用的全包价格 **IDM** SEE ALL *adv.*

,all-in'clusive *adj.* including everything or everyone 包括一切的；无所不包的: *Our trips are all-inclusive—there are no hidden costs.* 我们的旅行费用全包，没有任何隐含性费用。

,all-in-'one *adj.* [only before noun] able to do the work of two or more things that are usually separate 多用途的；多功能的；几合一的: *an all-in-one shampoo and conditioner* 二合一洗发护发剂 ▶ **,all-in-'one** *noun*: *We sell printers and scanners, and all-in-ones that combine the two.* 我们出售打印机、扫描仪，以及打印扫描二合一设备。

al·lit·er·ation /ə,lɪtə'reɪʃn/ *noun* [U] (*specialist*) the use of the same letter or sound at the beginning of words that are close together, as in *sing a song of sixpence* 头韵，头韵法(相连单词的开头使用同样的字母或语音) ➲ SEE ALSO ASSONANCE ➲ WORDFINDER NOTE AT IMAGE ▶ **al·lit·era·tive** /ə'lɪtrətɪv; *NAmE* ə'lɪtəreɪtɪv/ *adj.*

al·lium /'æliəm/ *noun* (*specialist*) any plant that belongs to the same group as onions and GARLIC 葱属植物

,all-'night *adj.* [only before noun] **1** (of a place 地方) open through the night 通宵开放的；通宵服务的: *an all-night cafe* 通宵营业的咖啡馆 **2** (of an activity 活动) continuing through the night 通宵的: *an all-night party* 通宵聚会

,all-'nighter *noun* (*informal*) a time when you stay awake all night studying or at a party 通宵学习；开通宵夜车

al·lo·cate **AW** /'æləkeɪt/ *verb* to give sth officially to sb/sth for a particular purpose 拨…(给)；划…(归)；分配…(给): **~ sth (for sth)** *A large sum has been allocated for buying new books for the library.* 已划拨了一大笔款子

给图书馆购买新书。◇ **~ sth (to sb/sth)** *They intend to allocate more places to mature students this year.* 今年他们打算给成人学生提供更多的名额。◇ *More resources are being allocated to the project.* 正在调拨更多的资源给这个项目。◇ **~ sb/sth sth** *The project is being allocated more resources.* 这个项目正获得更多的资源。◇ **~ sth to do sth** *Millions have been allocated to improve students' performance.* 为促进学生学业已经划拨数百万款项。

al·lo·ca·tion AW /ˌæləˈkeɪʃn/ *noun* **1** [C] an amount of money, space, etc. that is given to sb for a particular purpose 划拨的款项；拨给的场地；分配的东西 **2** [U] the act of giving sth to sb for a particular purpose 划；拨；分配：*the allocation of food to those who need it most* 分配食物给最需要的人

allo·morph /ˈæləmɔːf; *NAmE* -mɔːrf/ *noun* (*linguistics* 语言) one possible form of a particular MORPHEME. The forms /s/, /z/ and /ɪz/ in *cats*, *dogs* and *horses* are allomorphs of the plural ending *s*. 语素变体（如 cats、dogs、horses 中的 /s/、/z/ 和 /ɪz/ 是复数词尾 s 的变体）

allo·phone /ˈæləfəʊn; *NAmE* -foʊn/ *noun* **1** (*phonetics* 语音) a sound that is slightly different from another sound, although both sounds belong to the same PHONEME and the difference does not affect meaning. For example, the /l/ at the beginning of *little* is different from the /l/ at the end. 音位变体，同位音（同一音位有不同发音，如 little 中的第一个 /l/ 与结尾的 /l/ 发音不同） **2** (*CanE*) a person who comes to live in Canada, especially Quebec, from another country, whose first language is neither French nor English（尤指魁北克省）母语既非法语也非英语的加拿大人 ▶ **allo·phone** *adj.*：*Within French-speaking Quebec, anglophone, allophone and Aboriginal minorities also exist.* 在魁北克的法语区，也居住着讲英语的人、讲英法以外语言的人，以及少数族裔的原住民。

ˌall-or-ˈnothing *adj.* used to describe two extreme situations which are the only possible ones（只可能出现两种极端局面）全赢或全输的：*an all-or-nothing decision* (= one which could either be very good or very bad) 孤注一掷的决定

allo·saurus /ˌæləˈsɔːrəs/ *noun* a type of large DINOSAUR 异龙（大型恐龙）

allot /əˈlɒt; *NAmE* əˈlɑːt/ *verb* (**-tt-**) to give time, money, tasks, etc. to sb/sth as a share of what is available 分配，配给（时间、钱财等）；分派（任务等）：**~ sth** *I completed the test within the* ***time allotted****.* 我在限定的时间内完成了测试。◇ **~ sth to sb/sth** *How much money has been allotted to us?* 我们分到了多少拨款？◇ **~ sb/sth sth** *How much money have we been allotted?* 我们分到了多少拨款？ ➲ MORE LIKE THIS 36, page R29

al·lot·ment /əˈlɒtmənt; *NAmE* əˈlɑːt-/ *noun* **1** [C] (*BrE*) a small area of land in a town which a person can rent in order to grow fruit and vegetables on it（城镇内租用的）私家菜地 **2** [C, U] (*formal*) an amount of sth that sb is given or allowed to have; the process of giving sth to sb 分配物；分配量；份额；分配：*Water allotments to farmers were cut back in the drought.* 在干旱时期配给农民的水量减少。◇ *the allotment of shares to company employees* 公司雇员股票分配

allo·trope /ˈælətrəʊp; *NAmE* -troʊp/ *noun* (*chemistry* 化) one of the different forms in which a chemical element exists. For example, diamond and GRAPHITE are allotropes of CARBON. 同素异形体

ˌall-ˈout *adj.* [only before noun] using or involving every possible effort and done in a very determined way 全力以赴的：*all-out war* 全面战争 ◇ *an all-out attack on the opposition* 向对方的全面进攻 ▶ **ˌall ˈout** *adv.*：*We're going all out to win.* 我们竭尽全力争取胜利。

ˈall-over *adj.* [only before noun] covering the whole of sth 遍布表面的：*an all-over tan* 全身晒黑的皮肤

allow 🔑 /əˈlaʊ/ *verb*
• **LET SB/STH DO STH** 允许 **1** 🔑 to let sb/sth do sth; to let sth happen or be done 允许；准许：**~ sb to do sth** *His parents won't allow him to stay out late.* 他的父母不会允许他在外待到很晚。◇ *He* ***is not allowed to*** *stay out late.* 他不可以在外待到很晚。◇ *They shouldn't be allowed to get away with it.* 不应就此放过他们。◇ **~ sth to do sth** *He allowed his mind to wander.* 他听任自己的思绪信马由缰。◇ **~ yourself to do sth** *She won't allow herself to be dictated to.* 她不会听人摆布的。◇ **~ sth** *Smoking is not allowed in the hall.* 大厅内不准吸烟。 **2** 🔑 **~ sb/yourself sth** to let sb have sth 给予：*You're allowed an hour to complete the test.* 你们有一个小时的时间来完成这次测验。◇ *I'm not allowed visitors.* 我不可以接见来访者。 **3** 🔑 [usually passive] to let sb/sth go into, through, out of, etc. a place 允许进入（或出去、通过）：**~ sth** *No dogs allowed* (= you cannot bring them in). 不准携狗入内。◇ **~ sb/sth + adv./prep.** *The prisoners are* ***allowed out*** *of their cells for two hours a day.* 囚犯每天可以放风两小时。◇ *The crowd parted to* ***allow her through****.* 人群向两旁闪开让她通过。◇ *You won't be* ***allowed up*** (= out of bed) *for several days.* 你将有几天不能下床。 ➲ WORDFINDER NOTE AT FREEDOM
• **MAKE POSSIBLE** 使可能 **4** 🔑 **~ sth** to make sth possible 使可能：*A ramp allows easy access for wheelchairs.* 坡道便于轮椅进出。 ➲ LANGUAGE BANK AT PROCESS[1]
• **TIME/MONEY/FOOD, ETC.** 时间；金钱；食物 **5** 🔑 **~ sth (for sb/sth)** to make sure that you have enough of sth for a particular purpose（为某目的）留出，给出：*You need to allow three metres of fabric for the dress.* 这身衣服你需要用三米布料。
• **ACCEPT/ADMIT** 接受；承认 **6** (*formal*) to accept or admit sth; to agree that sth is true or correct 接受；承认；同意（某事属实或正确）：**~ sth** *The judge allowed my claim.* 法官接受了我的诉讼请求。◇ (= in a court of law) *'Objection!' 'I'll allow it.'* "反对！" "反对无效。" ◇ **~ that…** *He refuses to allow that such a situation could arise.* 他拒不承认这种情况可能发生。◇ **~ sb sth** *She was very helpful when my mother was ill—I'll allow you that.* 我母亲生病时她帮了很大的忙，我同意你说的这一点。 ➲ COMPARE DISALLOW

IDM **allow ˈme** used to offer help politely（礼貌地表示主动帮忙）让我来 ➲ MORE AT REIN *n.*

PHR V **alˈlow for sb/sth** 🔑 to consider or include sb/sth when calculating sth 考虑到；把…计算在内：*It will take about an hour to get there, allowing for traffic delays.* 考虑到交通阻塞，到那里大约需要一小时。◇ *All these factors must be allowed for.* 所有这些因素都必须估计进去。 **alˈlow of sth** (*formal*) to make sth possible 容许；使有可能：*The facts allow of only one explanation.* 这些事实只可能有一种解释。

al·low·able /əˈlaʊəbl/ *adj.* **1** that is allowed, especially by law or by a set of rules（法律、规章等）允许的，承认的，容许的 **2** (*BrE, specialist*) **allowable** amounts of money are amounts that you do not have to pay tax on 可免税的（钱款部分）

al·low·ance /əˈlaʊəns/ *noun* **1** an amount of money that is given to sb regularly or for a particular purpose 津贴；补贴；补助：*an allowance of $20 a day* 每天 20 美元补贴 ◇ *a* ***clothing/living/travel allowance*** 服装 / 生活 / 交通补贴 ◇ *Do you get an allowance for clothing?* 你有服装补贴吗？ ➲ SEE ALSO ATTENDANCE ALLOWANCE **2** the amount of sth that is allowed in a particular situation 限额；定量：*a baggage allowance of 20 kilos* 行李限重 20 公斤 **3** (*BrE, specialist*) an amount of money that can be earned or received before you start paying tax 免税额：*personal tax allowances* 直接税免税额 **4** (*especially NAmE*) = POCKET MONEY

IDM **make allowance(s) for sth** to consider sth, for example when you are making a decision or planning sth 考虑到，估计到（如在制订决策或计划时）：*The budget made allowance for inflation.* 预算考虑到了通货膨胀。◇ *The plan makes no allowance for people working at different rates.* 这个计划没有把人们工作速度不同考虑在内。 **make allowances (for sb)** to allow sb to behave in a way that you would not usually accept, because of a problem or because there is a special reason 体谅；谅解：*You have to make allowances for him because he's tired.* 你得体谅他，因为他累了。

A

alloy *noun, verb*

- ***noun*** /ˈælɔɪ/ [C, U] a metal that is formed by mixing two types of metal together, or by mixing metal with another substance 合金： *Brass is an alloy of copper and zinc.* 黄铜是铜锌合金。
- ***verb*** /əˈlɔɪ/ **~ sth (with sth)** (*specialist*) to mix one metal with another, especially one of lower value 把…铸成合金（尤指掺入一种价值较低的金属）

ˌall-ˈparty *adj.* [usually before noun] involving all political parties 所有政党的；各党派的；跨党派的： *all-party support* 各党派的支持

ˌall-points ˈbulletin *noun* (*abbr.* **APB**) (*US*) a radio message sent to every officer of a police force, giving details of people who are suspected of a crime, of stolen vehicles, etc. 全面警戒通告（警方无线电联络信息，通告嫌犯特征、失窃详情等）

ˌall-ˈpowerful *adj.* having complete power 有无上权力的；拥有全权的： *the all-powerful secret police* 权力无限的秘密警察

ˌall-ˈpurpose *adj.* [only before noun] having many different uses; able to be used in many situations 多用途的；通用的

ˌall-purpose ˈflour (*NAmE*) (*BrE* **ˌplain ˈflour**) *noun* [U] flour that does not contain BAKING POWDER（不含发酵粉的）普通面粉 ➲ COMPARE SELF-RISING FLOUR

all ˈright 🔑 (*also non-standard or informal* **al·right**) *adj. adv., exclamation*

- ***adj., adv.*** **1** 🔑 acceptable; in an acceptable manner 可接受（的）；满意（的） SYN **OK**： *Is the coffee all right?* 这咖啡还满意吗？ ◇ *Are you getting along all right in your new job?* 你的新工作顺利吗？ ◇ *'They're off to Spain next week.' 'It's* ***all right for some,*** *isn't it?'* (= some people are lucky) "他们下周去西班牙。" "有些人就是幸运，是不是？" **2** 🔑 safe and well 安全健康（的）；平安无恙（的） SYN **OK**： *I hope the children are all right.* 我希望孩子们平安无事。 ◇ *Do you feel all right?* 你感觉还好吗？ ➲ SYNONYMS AT WELL **3** 🔑 only just good enough 尚可；还算可以 SYN **OK**： *Your work is all right but I'm sure you could do better.* 你的工作还算可以，但我相信你可以干得更好。 **4** 🔑 that can be allowed 可允许（的）；可以（的） SYN **OK**： *Are you sure it's all right for me to leave early?* 你确定我早点离开没问题吗？ **5** (*informal*) used to emphasize that there is no doubt about sth （加强语气）无疑，确实： *'Are you sure it's her?' 'Oh, it's her all right.'* "你肯定是她吗？" "哦，确实是她。"

IDM **I'm all ˈright, Jack** (*BrE, informal*) used by or about sb who is happy with their own life and does not care about other people's problems 我没事就好，好在我没事（别人的事我是不管的） **it'll be all ˌright on the ˈnight** (*saying*) used to say that a performance, an event, etc. will be successful even if the preparations for it have not gone well（演出、活动等）到时候自会成功的；车到山前必有路 ➲ MORE AT BIT

- ***exclamation*** **1** 🔑 used to check that sb agrees or understands （确保对方同意或理解）如何，是不是 SYN **OK**： *We've got to get up early, all right?* 我们得早起，可以吧？ **2** 🔑 used to say that you agree （表示同意）好，行，可以 SYN **OK**： *'Can you do it?' 'Oh, all right.'* "你能干好这件事吗？" "噢，能。" **3** 🔑 used when accepting thanks for help or a favour, or when sb says they are sorry （回答对方的感谢或道歉）不要紧，没什么 SYN **OK**： *'I'm really sorry.' 'That's all right, don't worry.'* "实在对不起。" "没事，不打紧。" **4** 🔑 used to get sb's attention （引起注意）哎 SYN **OK**： *All right class, turn to page 20.* 好啦，同学们，翻到第 20 页。 **5** (*BrE, informal*) used to say hello （打招呼）你好： *'All right, Bill.' 'All right.'* "你好，比尔。" "你好。" **6 you're all right** (*BrE, informal*) used to refuse an offer or invitation, especially one that you think is unreasonable or not very good 不用啦（表示拒绝，尤其认为不合理或不太好的提议或邀请）： *'Could I interest you in our special offer?' 'No, you're all right, mate.'* "您要不要考虑一下我们的特价商品呢？" "不用啦，伙计。"

ˌall-ˈround (*BrE*) (*NAmE* **ˌall-aˈround**) *adj.* [only before noun] **1** including many different subjects, skills, etc. 全面的，多方面的： *an all-round education* 培养全面发展的教育 **2** (of a person 人) with a wide range of skills or abilities 全能的；多才多艺的： *She's a good all-round player.* 她是个优秀的全能选手。 ➲ MORE LIKE THIS 32, page R28

ˌall-ˈrounder *noun* (*BrE*) a person who has many different skills and abilities 多才多艺者；全才；通才

ˌAll ˈSaints' Day *noun* a Christian festival in honour of the SAINTS, held on 1 November 万圣节，诸圣日（基督教节日，11 月 1 日）

ˌall-ˈsinging, ˌall-ˈdancing *adj.* [only before noun] (*BrE, informal*) (of a machine or system 机器或系统) having a lot of advanced technical features and therefore able to perform many different functions 先进的；多功能的

ˌAll ˈSouls' Day *noun* a Christian festival in honour of the dead, held on 2 November 万灵节，追思节（基督教节日，11 月 2 日）

all·spice /ˈɔːlspaɪs/ *noun* [U] the dried BERRIES of a tree from the West Indies, used in cooking as a spice 多香果（西印度群岛多香果的果干，用作调味香料）

ˈall-star *adj.* [only before noun] including many famous actors, players, etc. 全明星（或演员、运动员等）组成的： *an all-star cast* 全明星阵容

ˌall-terrain ˈboard *noun* = MOUNTAINBOARD

ˌall-terrain ˈvehicle *noun* = ATV

ˌall-ˈticket *adj.* [usually before noun] for which tickets need to be obtained in advance 需预先购票的： *an all-ticket match* 全部凭票入场的比赛

ˈall-time *adj.* [only before noun] (used when you are comparing things or saying how good or bad sth is) of any time（用于比较或表示好坏程度）空前的，创纪录的，一向的： *one of the all-time great players* 历来最杰出的选手之一 ◇ *my all-time favourite song* 我一直喜爱的歌曲 ◇ *Unemployment reached an all-time record of 3 million.* 失业人数高达 300 万的创纪录数字。 ◇ *Profits are at an* ***all-time high/low.*** 利润空前地高 / 低。

al·lude /əˈluːd/ *verb*

PHR V **alˈlude to sb/sth** (*formal*) to mention sth in an indirect way 间接提到；暗指；影射 ➲ SEE ALSO ALLUSION

al·lure /əˈlʊə(r); *NAmE* əˈlʊr/ *noun* [U] (*formal*) the quality of being attractive and exciting 诱惑力；引诱力；吸引力： *sexual allure* 性诱惑 ◇ *the allure of the big city* 大城市的吸引力

al·lur·ing /əˈlʊərɪŋ; *NAmE* əˈlʊrɪŋ/ *adj.* attractive and exciting in a mysterious way 诱人的；迷人的；有吸引力的： *an alluring smile* 迷人的微笑 ▶ **al·lur·ing·ly** *adv.*

al·lu·sion /əˈluːʒn/ *noun* [C, U] **~ (to sb/sth)** (*formal*) something that is said or written that refers to or mentions another person or subject in an indirect way (= alludes to it) 暗指；引喻；典故： *His statement was seen as an allusion to the recent drug-related killings.* 他的声明被视为暗指最近与毒品有关的多起凶杀案。 ◇ *Her poetry is full of obscure literary allusion.* 她的诗随处可见晦涩的文学典故。

al·lu·sive /əˈluːsɪv/ *adj.* (*formal*) containing allusions 间接提到的；暗指的；影射的；含典故的： *an allusive style of writing* 引经据典的写作风格

al·lu·vial /əˈluːviəl/ *adj.* [usually before noun] (*geology* 地) made of sand and earth that is left by rivers or floods （河流、洪水）冲积的

al·lu·vium /əˈluːviəm/ *noun* [U] (*geology* 地) sand and earth that is left by rivers or floods 冲积层；冲积物

ˌall-ˈweather *adj.* [usually before noun] suitable for all types of weather 适合各种气候的；全天候的： *an all-weather football pitch* 全天候足球场

ˌall-wheel ˈdrive *noun* (*especially NAmE*) = FOUR-WHEEL DRIVE

A

ally 🔑 *noun, verb*

WORD FAMILY
ally *verb, noun*
allied *adj.*
alliance *noun*

■ ***noun*** /ˈælaɪ/ (*pl.* **-ies**) **1** 🔑 [C] a country that has agreed to help and support another country, especially in case of a war（尤指战时的）同盟国

WORDFINDER 联想词：accord, bilateral, cross-border, diplomat, embassy, **international**, rapprochement, relationship, treaty

2 🔑 [C] a person who helps and supports sb who is in a difficult situation, especially a politician（尤指从政者的）盟友，支持者：*a close ally and friend of the prime minister* 首相的一个亲密盟友兼伙伴 ◇ *her most powerful political ally* 她最有权势的政治盟友 **3 the Allies** [pl.] the group of countries including Britain and the US that fought together in the First and Second World Wars（第一次世界大战中的）协约国；（第二次世界大战中的）同盟国

■ ***verb*** 🔑 /əˈlaɪ/ (**al·lies, ally·ing, al·lied, al·lied**) [T, I] **~ (yourself) with sb/sth** to give your support to another group or country 与…结盟：*The prince allied himself with the Scots.* 王子与苏格兰人结盟。

-ally *suffix* (makes adverbs from adjectives that end in *-al* 以 -al 结尾的形容词加 ly 构成副词)：*magically* 有魔力地 ◇ *sensationally* 轰动地

alma mater /ˌælmə ˈmɑːtə(r); ˈmeɪtə(r)/ (*also* **Alma Mater**) *noun* [sing.] (*especially NAmE*) the school, college or university that sb went to 母校

al·manac (*also less frequent* **al·man·ack**) /ˈɔːlmənæk; ˈæl-/ *noun* **1** a book that is published every year giving information for that year about a particular subject or activity 年鉴 **2** a book that gives information about the sun, moon, times of the TIDES (= the rise and fall of the sea level), etc. for each day of the year 历书；年历

al·mighty /ɔːlˈmaɪti/ *adj.* **1** (in prayers 祈祷时说) having complete power 全能的：*Almighty God, have mercy on us.* 全能的上主，请垂怜我们。 **2** [only before noun] (*informal*) very great or severe 极大的；十分严重的：*an **almighty** bang/crash/roar* 砰的 / 哗啦 / 轰的一声巨响 **3** (*taboo, offensive*) used in the expressions shown in the example, to express surprise or anger（表示惊奇或愤怒）全能的，有无限权力的：*Christ/God Almighty! What the hell do you think you are doing?* 全能的基督 / 上帝！你认为你究竟在干什么？ **4 the Almighty** *noun* [sing.] God 全能者（指上帝）

al·mirah /ælˈmaɪrə/ *noun* (*IndE*) a piece of furniture for storing clothes, valuable items, etc. in, that stands on the floor 立柜（存放衣服、贵重物品等）

al·mond /ˈɑːmənd/ *noun* the flat pale sweet nut of the **almond tree** used in cooking and to make almond oil 扁桃仁（扁桃树的果仁）：*ground almonds* 扁桃仁粉 ◇ ***blanched almonds*** (= with their skins removed) 去皮扁桃仁 ◇ *almond paste* 扁桃仁糊 ◇ *almond eyes* (= eyes shaped like almonds) 杏眼 ➲ VISUAL VOCAB PAGE V35

al·most 🔑 /ˈɔːlməʊst; *NAmE* -moʊst/ *adv.* not quite 几乎；差不多 SYN **nearly**：*I like almost all of them.* 我差不多所有的都喜欢。 ◇ *It's a mistake they almost always make.* 这是他们几乎总要犯的错误。 ◇ *The story is almost certainly false.* 这个陈述差不多肯定是虚假的。 ◇ *It's almost time to go.* 是差不多该走的时候了。 ◇ *Dinner's almost ready.* 饭就要做好了。 ◇ *He slipped and almost fell.* 他滑了一下，险些跌倒。 ◇ *Their house is almost opposite ours.* 他们的房子几乎正对着我们的房子。 ◇ *They'll eat almost anything.* 他们几乎什么都吃。 ◇ *Almost no one* (= hardly anyone) *believed him.* 几乎没人相信他的话。

alms /ɑːmz/ *noun* [pl.] (*old-fashioned*) money, clothes and food that are given to poor people 施舍物；救济金

alms·house /ˈɑːmzhaʊs/ *noun* (in the past in Britain) a house owned by a charity where poor people (usually the old) lived without paying rent（英国旧时的）救济院，贫民所

aloe /ˈæləʊ; *NAmE* ˈæloʊ/ *noun* a tropical plant with thick leaves that have sharp points and that contain a lot of water. The juice of some types of aloe is used in medicine and COSMETICS. 芦荟（有些品种的汁液可用于制药和化妆品）

aloe vera /ˌæləʊ ˈvɪərə; *NAmE* ˌæloʊ ˈvɪrə/ *noun* **1** [U] a substance that comes from a type of aloe, used in products such as skin creams 芦荟汁（用于生产护肤霜等） **2** [C] the aloe that this substance comes from 真芦荟

aloft /əˈlɒft; *NAmE* əˈlɔːft/ *adv.* (*formal*) high in the air 在高空中

aloha /əˈləʊhə; *NAmE* əˈloʊhə/ *exclamation* a Hawaiian word meaning 'love', used to say hello or goodbye 你好，再见（夏威夷语意为"爱"）

▼ **WHICH WORD?** 词语辨析

almost / nearly / practically

These three words have similar meanings and are used frequently with the following words. 上述三个近义词常与下列词语连用：

almost ~	nearly ~	practically ~
certainly	(numbers)	all
all	all	every
every	always	no
entirely	every	nothing
impossible	finished	impossible
empty	died	anything

- They are used in positive sentences. 三词均用于肯定句：*She almost/nearly/practically missed her train.* 她差点儿误了火车。 They can be used before words like *all, every* and *everybody*. 三词均可用于 all、every、everybody 等词前：*Nearly all the students have bikes.* 几乎所有学生都有自行车。 ◇ *I've got practically every CD they've made.* 他们灌制的每张激光唱片我几乎都有。 **Practically** is used more in spoken than in written English. **Nearly** is the most common with numbers. * practically 多用于口语，少用于书面语。nearly 最常与数字连用：*There were nearly 200 people at the meeting.* 与会者有近 200 人。 They can also be used in negative sentences but it is more common to make a positive sentence with **only just**. 三词亦可用于否定句，但是用 only just 构成肯定句更常见：*We only just got there in time.* (or 或：*We almost/nearly didn't get there in time.*) 我们险些未能及时赶到那儿。
- **Almost** and **practically** can be used before words like *any, anybody, anything*, etc. * almost 和 practically 均可用于 any、anybody、anything 等词前：*I'll eat almost anything.* 我几乎吃什么都行。 You can also use them before *no, nobody, never*, etc. but it is much more common to use **hardly** or **scarcely** with *any, anybody, ever*, etc. 这两个词亦可用于 no、nobody、never 等词前，但是这类情况更常用 hardly 或 scarcely 与 any、anybody、ever 等词搭配：*She's hardly ever in.* (or 或：*She's almost never in.*) 她几乎从来不在家。
- **Almost** can be used when you are saying that one thing is similar to another. 表示某物与另一物相似可用 almost：*The boat looked almost like a toy.* 这船看上去简直像个玩具。
- In *BrE* you can use *very* and *so* before **nearly**. 在英式英语中，nearly 前可用 very 和 so：*He was very nearly caught.* 他差点儿被抓住。

➲ NOTE AT HARDLY

A

aˈloha shirt *noun* = HAWAIIAN SHIRT

alone /əˈləʊn; *NAmE* əˈloʊn/ *adj.* [not before noun] *adv.* **1** without any other people 独自：*I don't like going out alone at night.* 我不喜欢夜晚单独外出。◇ *He lives alone.* 他独居独处。◇ *Finally the two of us were* ***alone together***. 最后只有我们两人在一起。◇ *She was sitting* ***all alone*** *in the hall.* 她一个人坐在大厅里。◇ *Tom is* ***not alone in*** *finding Rick hard to work with.* 并不只是汤姆一人认为里克难以共事。 **2** without the help of other people or things 独力；单独：*It's hard bringing up children alone.* 一个人独力抚养孩子是艰难的。◇ *The assassin said he had acted alone.* 暗杀者声称他当时单独行动。 **3** lonely and unhappy or without any friends 孤苦伶仃；无依无靠；孤独；寂寞：*Carol felt all alone in the world.* 卡罗尔感到自己在世界上无依无靠。◇ *I've been so alone since you went away.* 你走了以后我一直很寂寞。 **4** used after a noun or pronoun to show that the person or thing mentioned is the only one（用于名词或代词后）唯一，只有：*You can't blame anyone else; you alone made the decision.* 你不能责怪任何人，是你一人做的决定。 **5** used after a noun or pronoun to emphasize one particular thing（用于名词或代词后以加强语气）仅仅，单，只：*The shoes alone cost £200.* 仅鞋子一项就花了 200 英镑。 ➲ MORE LIKE THIS 31, page R28

IDM **go it aˈlone** to do sth without help from anyone 独力；独自干；单干：*Andrew decided to go it alone and start his own business.* 安德鲁决定独力开办自己的企业。 **leave/let sb alone** to stop annoying sb or trying to get their attention 不打扰；不惊动：*She's asked to be left alone but the press photographers follow her everywhere.* 她要求别打扰她，但是摄影记者到处都跟着她。 **leave/let sth alone** to stop touching, changing, or moving sth 不碰；不变动；不移动：*I've told you before—leave my things alone!* 我告诉过你，别碰我的东西！ **let alone** used after a statement to emphasize that because the first thing is not true or possible, the next thing cannot be true or possible either 更不用说：*There isn't enough room for us, let alone any guests.* 连我们都没有足够的空间，更不用说客人了。 **stand aˈlone 1** to be independent or not connected with other people, organizations or ideas 单独；独立：*These islands are too small to stand alone as independent states.* 这些岛屿太小，不能成为独立的国家。 **2** to be not near other objects or buildings 孤零零地矗立：*The arch once stood alone at the entrance to the castle.* 拱门曾经孤零零地矗立在城堡的入口处。 ➲ MORE AT TIME *n.*

▼ **WHICH WORD? 词语辨析**

alone / lonely / lone

- **Alone**, and **on your own/by yourself** (which are less formal and are the normal phrases used in spoken English), describe a person or thing that is separate from others. They do not mean that the person is unhappy. * alone 和较非正式、常用于口语的 on your own、by yourself 均指独自，但无孤独之义：*I like being alone in the house.* 我喜欢独自一人待在家里。◇ *I'm going to London by myself next week.* 我准备下星期一个人去伦敦。◇ *I want to finish this on my own* (= without anyone's help). 我想独自完成这项工作。
- **Lone/solitary/single** mean that there is only one person or thing there; **lone** and **solitary** may sometimes suggest that the speaker thinks the person involved is lonely. * lone、solitary、single 意为单独；lone 和 solitary 有时可能暗示说话者认为谈及的人孤单：*a lone jogger in the park* 在公园里独自慢跑的一个人 ◇ *long, solitary walks* 独自一人长途行走
- **Lonely** (*NAmE* also **lonesome**) means that you are alone and sad. * lonely（美式英语亦作 lonesome）意为孤寂：*a lonely child* 孤寂的孩子 ◇ *Sam was very lonely when he first moved to New York.* 萨姆刚搬到纽约时非常寂寞。 It can also describe places or activities that make you feel lonely. * lonely 还可描述使人感到孤寂的地方或活动：*a lonely house* 一座冷清的房子

along /əˈlɒŋ; *NAmE* əˈlɔːŋ; əˈlɑːŋ/ *prep.*, *adv.*

■ *prep.* **1** from one end to or towards the other end of sth 沿着；顺着：*They walked slowly along the road.* 他们沿公路慢慢走。◇ *I looked along the shelves for the book I needed.* 我在书架上一格一格地找我需要的那本书。 **2** in a line that follows the side of sth long 靠着…边：*Houses had been built along both sides of the river.* 沿河两岸已盖起了房屋。 **3** at a particular point on or beside sth long 沿着…的某处（或旁边）：*You'll find his office just along the corridor.* 沿着走廊你就可以找到他的办公室。

■ *adv.* HELP For the special uses of **along** in phrasal verbs, look at the entries for the verbs. For example **get along with sb** is in the phrasal verb section at **get**. * along 在短语动词中的特殊用法见有关动词词条。如 get along with sb 在词条 get 的短语动词部分。 **1** forward 向前：*I was just walking along singing to myself.* 我独自唱着歌向前走去。◇ *He pointed out various landmarks as we drove along.* 我们驱车前行时，他指给我们看各种各样的地标。 **2** with sb（与某人）一道，一起：*We're going for a swim. Why don't you come along?* 我们要去游泳。你干吗不一起去？◇ *I'll be along* (= I'll join you) *in a few minutes.* 过一会儿我就来。 **3** towards a better state or position 越来越（好）：*The book's coming along nicely.* 这本书愈来愈好看了。

IDM **along with sb/sth** in addition to sb/sth; in the same way as sb/sth 除…以外（还）；与…同样地：*She lost her job when the factory closed, along with hundreds of others.* 工厂倒闭时，她和其他几百人一样失去了工作。

along·side /əˌlɒŋˈsaɪd; *NAmE* əˌlɔːŋ-; əˌlɑːŋ-/ *prep.* **1** next to or at the side of sth 在…旁边；沿着…的边：*A police car pulled up alongside us.* 一辆警车在我们旁边停了下来。 **2** together with or at the same time as sth/sb 与…一起；与…同时：*Traditional beliefs still flourish alongside a modern urban lifestyle.* 现代城市生活方式盛行的同时，传统信念仍然广泛流行。 ▸ **along·side** *adv.*：*Nick caught up with me and rode alongside.* 尼克赶上了我，跟我并骑前进。

aloo (*also* **alu**) /ˈæluː/ *noun* [U] (*IndE*) potatoes 土豆

aloof /əˈluːf/ *adj.* [not usually before noun] not friendly or interested in other people 冷漠；冷淡 SYN **distant**, **remote** ▸ **aloof·ness** *noun* [U]

IDM **keep/hold (yourself) aloof | remain/stand aloof** to not become involved in sth; to show no interest in people 不参与；远离；无动于衷；漠不关心：*The Emperor kept himself aloof from the people.* 这个皇帝对人民漠不关心。

alo·pe·cia /ˌæləˈpiːʃə/ *noun* [U] (*medical* 医) loss of hair from the head and body, often caused by illness 脱发，秃发（常因疾病而起）

aloud /əˈlaʊd/ *adv.* **1** in a voice that other people can hear 出声地：*The teacher listened to the children* ***reading aloud***. 老师听着孩子们朗读。◇ *He read the letter aloud to us.* 他把信念给我们听。◇ *'What am I going to do?' she wondered aloud.* "我怎么办呢？" 她疑惑地说。 ➲ NOTE AT LOUD **2** in a loud voice 大声地：*She cried aloud in protest.* 她大声抗议。 IDM SEE THINK *v.*

al·paca /ælˈpækə/ *noun* **1** [C] a S American animal that is related to the LLAMA and has long hair 羊驼（南美长毛动物） **2** [U] a type of soft wool or cloth made from the hair of the alpaca, used especially for making expensive clothes 羊驼毛；羊驼呢：*an alpaca coat* 羊驼毛外衣

alpha /ˈælfə/ *noun* **1** the first letter of the Greek alphabet (Α, α) 希腊字母表的第 1 个字母 **2** = ALPHA VERSION

al·pha·bet /ˈælfəbet/ *noun* a set of letters or symbols in a fixed order used for writing a language（一种语言的）字母表，全部字母 ORIGIN From *alpha* and *beta*, the first two letters of the Greek alphabet. 源自希腊字母表的头两个字母 alpha 和 beta。 ➲ WORDFINDER NOTE AT LANGUAGE

A

▼ BRITISH/AMERICAN 英式 / 美式英语

already / just / yet

- **Already** and **yet** are usually used with the present perfect tense, but in *NAmE* they can also be used with the simple past tense. * already 和 yet 通常与现在完成时连用，但在美式英语中还可与简单过去时连用：*I already did it.* 我已经完成了。◇ *Did you eat yet?* 你吃饭了吗？
- However, this is much more common in spoken than in written English and some Americans do not consider it acceptable, even in speech. The present perfect is more common in *NAmE* and almost always used in *BrE*. 不过，此用法多见于口语，而且有些美国人认为，即使在口语中此用法也不可取。在美式英语中较常用现在完成时，在英式英语中则几乎总是用现在完成时表示：*I've already done it.* 我已经完成了。◇ *Have you eaten yet?* 你吃饭了吗？
- **Just** is mostly used with the perfect tenses in *BrE* and with the simple past in *NAmE*. * just 在英式英语中多与完成时连用，在美式英语中则多与一般过去时连用：(*BrE*) *I've just had some bad news.* ◇ (*NAmE*) *I just got some bad news.* 我刚得到个坏消息。

al·pha·bet·ic /ˌælfəˈbetɪk/ (*also* **al·pha·bet·ic·al**) *adj.* (of a written or printed character 手写或印刷字符) being one of the letters of the alphabet, rather than a number or other symbol (属于) 字母的 ➲ COMPARE NON-ALPHABETIC

al·pha·bet·ic·al 🔑 /ˌælfəˈbetɪkl/ *adj.* **1** 🔑 according to the correct order of the letters of the alphabet 按字母 (表) 顺序的：*The names on the list are* ***in alphabetical order****.* 名单上的名字是按字母顺序排列的。➲ WORDFINDER NOTE AT DICTIONARY **2** = ALPHABETIC ▶ **al·pha·bet·ic·al·ly** 🔑 /-kli/ *adv.*：***arranged/listed/stored alphabetically*** 按字母顺序安排 / 列表 / 存储

al·pha·bet·ize (*BrE also* **-ise**) /ˈælfəbətaɪz/ *verb* ~ **sth** to arrange a list of words in alphabetical order 按字母顺序排列

ˌalphabet ˈsoup *noun* [U] **1** (*informal*) language that is extremely difficult to understand, especially because it contains many symbols or abbreviations (因含有许多符号或缩略语等而极难懂的) 代号语言 **2** soup that contains PASTA in the shape of letters 字母汤 (汤里含有字母形面食)

ˌalpha ˈmale *noun* **1** [usually sing.] the man or male animal in a particular group who has the most power 老大 (某一群体中最有权力的男子或雄性动物)：*The alpha male was a large black wolf.* 老大是一只大黑狼。**2** a man who tends to take control in social and professional situations 大男子主义者；控制欲强的男性：*Most alpha males need to control the women in their lives.* 多数大男子主义者需要控制他们生活中的女性。

alpha·numer·ic /ˌælfənjuːˈmerɪk; *NAmE* -nuːˈm-/ (*also* **alpha·numer·ic·al** /-ɪkl/) *adj.* containing both letters and numbers 含有字母和数字的；字母与数字并用的：*an alphanumeric code* 含字母和数字的代码

ˈalpha particle *noun* (*specialist*) the NUCLEUS of a HELIUM atom; a PARTICLE with a positive electrical charge, that is produced in a nuclear reaction * α 粒子

ˈalpha test *noun* (*specialist*) a test done by a company on a new product that they are developing * α 测试 (公司试验其正在开发的新产品) ➲ COMPARE BETA TEST ▶ **ˈalpha-test** *verb* ~ **sth**

ˈalpha version *noun* [usually sing.] (*also* **alpha**) a version of a product, especially computer software, that is not yet ready for the public to buy or use, and that is tested by the company that is developing it (尤指计算机软件等新产品开发过程中的) α 版，预览版 ➲ COMPARE BETA VERSION

al·pine /ˈælpaɪn/ *adj.*, *noun*

■ ***adj.*** existing in or connected with high mountains, especially the Alps in Central Europe 高山的；(尤指中欧) 阿尔卑斯山的

■ ***noun*** any plant that grows best on mountains 高山植物

al·pi·nist /ˈælpɪnɪst/ *noun* a person who climbs high mountains as a sport, especially in the Alps 登高山者 (尤指阿尔卑斯山) ▶ **al·pi·nism** /ˈælpɪnɪzəm/ *noun* [U]

al·ready 🔑 /ɔːlˈredi/ *adv.* **1** 🔑 before now or before a particular time in the past 已经；早已：*'Lunch?' 'No thanks, I've already eaten.'* "午餐？" "不，谢谢，我已吃过了。" ◇ *We got there early but Mike had already left.* 我们提早到了那里，但是迈克已经离开了。**2** 🔑 used to express surprise that sth has happened so soon or so early (表示惊奇) 已经，都：*Is it 10 o'clock already?* 都 10 点钟了？◇ *You're not leaving already, are you?* 你不是这就走？**3** 🔑 used to emphasize that a situation or problem exists (强调情况或问题存在) 已经：*I'm already late.* 我已经迟到了。◇ *There are far too many people already. We can't take any more.* 已经有太多的人了。我们再也接待不了啦。
IDM SEE ENOUGH *pron.*

al·right /ɔːlˈraɪt/ *adv.* (*informal*) = ALL RIGHT HELP Some people consider that this form should not be used in formal writing. 有人认为正式书面语中不应该用此形式。

Al·sa·tian /ælˈseɪʃn/ (*BrE*) (*also* ˌ**German ˈshepherd** *NAmE*, *BrE*) *noun* a large dog, often trained to help the police, to guard buildings or (especially in the US) to help blind people find their way 德国牧羊犬 (常训练成警犬，看家护院，尤其在美国用作导盲犬)

▼ WHICH WORD? 词语辨析

also / as well / too

- **Also** is more formal than **as well** and **too**, and it usually comes before the main verb or after *be*. * also 比 as well 和 too 正式，通常置于主要动词之前或 be 之后：*I went to New York last year, and I also spent some time in Washington.* 我去年去了纽约，还在华盛顿待了些时间。In *BrE* it is not usually used at the end of a sentence. **Too** is much more common in spoken and informal English. It is usually used at the end of a sentence. 在英式英语中，also 通常不置于句末。too 则多用于非正式的口语，且通常置于句末：*'I'm going home now.' 'I'll come too.'* "现在我要回家了。" "我也一起走。" In *BrE* **as well** is used like **too**, but in *NAmE* it sounds formal or old-fashioned. 在英式英语中，as well 的用法同 too，但在美式英语中，as well 显得正式或过时。
- When you want to add a second negative point in a negative sentence, use **not…either**. 在否定句中要增加一个否定成分可用 not ... either：*She hasn't phoned and she hasn't written either.* 她没来过电话，也没有写信。If you are adding a negative point to a positive one, you can use **not… as well/too**. 在肯定句中要增加一个否定成分可用 not ... as well / too：*You can have a burger, but you can't have fries as well.* 你可以吃汉堡包，但不可以同时又吃炸薯条。

also 🔑 /ˈɔːlsəʊ; *NAmE* ˈɔːlsoʊ/ *adv.* (not used with negative verbs 不与否定动词连用) in addition; too 而且；此外；也；同样：*She's fluent in French and German. She also speaks a little Italian.* 她的法语和德语讲得流利，也会说一点意大利语。◇ *rubella,* ***also known as*** *German measles* * rubella (风疹)，亦称 German measles ◇ *I didn't like it that much. Also, it was much too expensive.* 我并不怎么喜欢它，再说它太贵了。◇ *Jake's father had also been a doctor* (= both Jake and his father were doctors). 杰克的父亲也做过医生。◇ *She was* ***not only*** *intelligent* ***but also*** *very musical.* 她不仅聪明，而且极具音乐天分。➲ LANGUAGE BANK AT ADDITION

A

ˈ**also-ran** *noun* a person who is not successful, especially in a competition or an election 失败者；（尤指竞赛或竞选的）失利者

altar /ˈɔːltə(r)/ *noun* a holy table in a church or TEMPLE（教堂、庙宇的）圣坛，祭坛，祭台：*the high altar* (= the most important one in a particular church) 教堂正祭台

IDM **at/on the altar of sth** (*formal*) because of sth that you think is worth suffering for 因为，为了（值得为之受苦的事物）： *He was willing to sacrifice his happiness on the altar of fame.* 为了名声，他心甘情愿牺牲幸福。

ˈ**altar boy** *noun* a boy who helps the priest in church services, especially in the Roman Catholic church 辅祭（宗教礼仪中的辅助男童，尤见于天主教）

al·tar·piece /ˈɔːltəpiːs; *NAmE* -tərp-/ *noun* a painting or other piece of art located near the ALTAR in a church 祭坛画（教堂祭坛附近的装饰性艺术品）

alter AW /ˈɔːltə(r)/ *verb* **1** [I, T] to become different; to make sb/sth different （使）改变，更改，改动： *Prices did not alter significantly during 2014.* * 2014 年间，价格没有大的变化。 ◇ *He had altered so much I scarcely recognized him.* 他变化大得我几乎认不出来了。 ◇ **~ sb/sth** *It doesn't alter the way I feel.* 这并没有改变我的感受。 ◇ *Nothing can* ***alter the fact that*** *we are to blame.* 错在我们，这是无法改变的事实。 ◇ *The landscape has been radically altered, severely damaging wildlife.* 地貌彻底改变，严重损害了野生生物。 **2** [T] **~ sth** to make changes to a piece of clothing so that it will fit you better 修改（衣服使更合身） ▶ **al·ter·able** AW *adj.* (*formal*) OPP **unalterable**

al·ter·ation AW /ˌɔːltəˈreɪʃn/ *noun* **1** [C] a change to sth that makes it different 改变；变化： ***major/minor alterations*** 大 / 小改变 ◇ **~ to sth** *They are making some alterations to the house.* 他们正在对这栋房子做一些改动。 ◇ **~ in sth** *an alteration in the baby's heartbeat* 这婴儿心搏的变化 **2** [U] the act of making a change to sth 改变；更改；改动： *The dress will not need much alteration.* 这件衣服不需大改。

al·ter·ca·tion /ˌɔːltəˈkeɪʃn; *NAmE* -tərˈk-/ *noun* [C, U] (*formal*) a noisy argument or disagreement 争论；争辩；争吵

alter ego /ˌæltər ˈiːɡəʊ; ˌɔːl-; *NAmE* ˈiːɡoʊ/ *noun* (*pl.* **alter egos**) (*from Latin*) **1** a person whose personality is different from your own but who shows or acts as another side of your personality 第二自我： *Superman's alter ego was Clark Kent.* 超人的第二自我是克拉克 • 肯特。 **2** a close friend who is very like yourself 至交；知己；挚友

al·ter·nate AW *adj.*, *verb*, *noun*

■ ***adj.*** /ɔːlˈtɜːnət; *NAmE* ˈɔːltərnət/ [usually before noun] **1** (of two things 两事物) happening or following one after the other regularly 交替的；轮流的： *alternate layers of fruit and cream* 水果层和奶油层相间 **2** if sth happens on **alternate** days, nights, etc. it happens on one day, etc. but not on the next 间隔的；每隔（…天等）的： *John has to work on alternate Sundays.* 约翰每隔一周就有一个星期日得上班。 **3** (*especially NAmE*) = ALTERNATIVE (1) ▶ **al·ter·nate·ly** *adv.* : *He felt alternately hot and cold.* 他感到忽冷忽热。

■ ***verb*** /ˈɔːltəneɪt; *NAmE* -tərn-/ **1** [T] to make things or people follow one after the other in a repeated pattern 使交替；使轮流： **~ A and B** *Alternate cubes of meat and slices of red pepper.* 交替放置肉丁和红辣椒片。 ◇ **~ A with B** *Alternate cubes of meat with slices of red pepper.* 交替放置肉丁和红辣椒片。 **2** [I] (of things or people 事物或人) to follow one after the other in a repeated pattern 交替；轮流： *alternating dark and pale stripes* 深浅条纹相间 ◇ **~ with sth** *Dark stripes alternate with pale ones.* 深浅条纹相间。 **3** [I] **~ between A and B** to keep changing from one thing to another and back again 交替： *Her mood alternated between happiness and despair.* 她的心情一会儿高兴一会儿绝望。 ▶ **al·ter·na·tion** /ˌɔːltəˈneɪʃn; *NAmE* -tərˈn-/ *noun* [U, C]： *the alternation of day and night* 日夜交替

■ ***noun*** /ˈɔːltənət; *NAmE* ˈɔːltərnət/ (*NAmE*) a person who does a job for sb who is away 代替者；代理人；候补者 ➲ MORE LIKE THIS 21, page R27

alˌternate ˈangles (*also* ˈ**Z angles**) *noun* [pl.] (*geometry* 几何) equal angles formed on opposite sides of a line that crosses two parallel lines, in the position of the inner angles of a Z （内）错角 ➲ PICTURE AT ANGLE ➲ COMPARE CORRESPONDING ANGLES

ˌ**alternating ˈcurrent** *noun* [U, C] (*abbr.* **AC**) an electric current that changes its direction at regular intervals many times a second 交流；交流电流 ➲ COMPARE DIRECT CURRENT

al·ter·na·tive AW /ɔːlˈtɜːnətɪv; *NAmE* -ˈtɜːrn-/ *noun*, *adj.*

■ ***noun*** a thing that you can choose to do or have out of two or more possibilities 可供选择的事物： *We can agree to their terms or else pull out of the deal completely: those are the two alternatives.* 我们要么同意他们的条款，要么彻底退出交易。二者选其一。 ◇ *We had* ***no alternative but to*** *fire Gibson.* 我们别无他法，只有辞退吉布森。 ◇ *There is a vegetarian alternative on the menu every day.* 每天的菜单上另有素食餐点。 ➲ SYNONYMS AT OPTION

■ ***adj.*** [only before noun] **1** (*also* **al·ter·nate** *especially in NAmE*) that can be used instead of sth else 可供替代的： *an alternative method of doing sth* 做某事的其他方法 ◇ *Do you have an alternative solution?* 你有没有别的解决办法？ **2** different from the usual or traditional way in which sth is done 非传统的；另类的： ***alternative comedy/lifestyles/values*** 非传统喜剧 / 生活方式 / 价值观 ◇ ***alternative energy*** (= electricity or power that is produced using the energy from the sun, wind, water, etc.) 替代能源（指太阳能、风能、水能等）

alˌternative ˈfuel *noun* [C, U] fuel that can be used instead of FOSSIL FUELS such as coal and oil, and instead of nuclear fuel 代用燃料，替代燃料（可代替化石燃料或核燃料）

al·ter·na·tive·ly AW /ɔːlˈtɜːnətɪvli; *NAmE* -ˈtɜːrn-/ *adv.* used to introduce a suggestion that is a second choice or possibility （引出第二种选择或可能的建议）要不，或者： *The agency will make travel arrangements for you. Alternatively, you can organize your own transport.* 旅行社将为你安排旅行，或者你也可以自行安排交通工具。

alˌternative ˈmedicine *noun* [C, U] any type of treatment that does not use the usual scientific methods of Western medicine, for example one using plants instead of artificial drugs 另类医疗，替代疗法（不用西医通常使用的科学方法，而使用其他方法，如用草药代替人造药物） ➲ WORDFINDER NOTE AT TREATMENT

alˌternative ˈvote *noun* (*BrE*) [sing.] a system that allows people to choose candidates for an election in order of preference. All first preferences are counted, and if no candidate achieves a majority, the candidate with the fewest votes is removed from the process and each vote for that candidate is transferred to each person's second preference. This process is repeated until one candidate achieves the majority. 选择性投票制（按选民喜好排序计票的选举制度，先依照票上第一选择计票，如无候选人获得多数票，则得票最少的候选人出局，然后将其得票根据选民的第二选择分配给余下候选人，以此类推，直到有候选人获得多数票为止）

al·ter·na·tor /ˈɔːltəneɪtə(r); *NAmE* -tərn-/ *noun* a device, used especially in a car, that produces an ALTERNATING CURRENT （尤指汽车上的）交流发电机

al·though (*US also, informal* **altho**) /ɔːlˈðəʊ; *NAmE* ɔːlˈðoʊ/ *conj.* **1** used for introducing a statement that makes the main statement in a sentence seem surprising 虽然；尽管；即使 SYN **though**： *Although the sun was shining, it wasn't very warm.* 尽管太阳高照，却不很暖和。 ◇ *Although small, the kitchen is well designed.* 厨房虽小，但设计巧妙。 ➲ LANGUAGE BANK AT HOWEVER **2** used to mean 'but' or 'however' when you are commenting on a statement 不过；然而： *I felt he was wrong, although I*

A

didn't say so at the time. 我觉得他错了，不过我当时没有说出来。

▼ **WHICH WORD? 词语辨析**

although / even though / though

- You can use these words to show contrast between two clauses or two sentences. **Though** is used more in spoken than in written English. You can use **although, even though** and **though** at the beginning of a sentence or clause that has a verb. Notice where the commas go. 在两个从句或句子之间可用上述词表示对比。though 多用于口语，although、even though 和 though 可用于句首或带有动词的从句开头。注意逗号的位置： *Although/Even though/Though everyone played well, we lost the game.* 尽管每个人都打得不错，我们还是输了。◇ *We lost the game, although/even though/though everyone played well.* 我们输了，尽管每个人都打得不错。
- You cannot use **even** on its own at the beginning of a sentence or clause instead of **although, even though** or **though**. * even 不能单独置于句首或从句开头以代替 although、even though 或 though： ~~*Even everyone played well, we lost the game.*~~

al·tim·eter /ˈæltɪmiːtə(r); *NAmE* ælˈtɪmətər/ *noun* an instrument for showing height above sea level, used especially in an aircraft （尤指用于航空器中的）测高仪，高度表

al·ti·tude /ˈæltɪtjuːd; *NAmE* -tuːd/ *noun* **1** [C, usually sing.] the height above sea level 海拔；海拔高度；高程： *We are flying **at an altitude of** 6 000 metres.* 我们的飞行高度是 6 000 米。◇ *The plane made a dive to a lower altitude.* 飞机俯冲到较低高度。 **2** [C, usually pl., U] a place that is high above sea level （海拔高的）高处，高地： *Snow leopards live **at high altitudes**.* 雪豹生活在海拔高的地区。◇ *The athletes trained **at altitude** in Mexico City.* 田径运动员在海拔高的墨西哥城受训。 ➲ WORDFINDER NOTE AT MOUNTAIN

ˈaltitude sickness *noun* [U] illness caused by a lack of OXYGEN, because of being very high above sea level, for example on a mountain 高山病，高原病（由缺氧引起）

Alt key (*also* **ALT key**) /ˈɔːlt kiː/ *noun* a key on a computer keyboard which you press while pressing other keys, in order to change their function （计算机键盘上的）替换键，功能扩展键

alto /ˈæltəʊ; *NAmE* ˈæltoʊ/ *noun, adj.*
▪ *noun* (*pl.* **-os**) **1** (*also* **con·tralto**) [C] a singing voice with a lower range than that of a SOPRANO; a person with an alto voice 女低音；女低音声部 **2** [sing.] a musical part that is written for an alto voice 中音声部 ➲ COMPARE BARITONE, BASS[1] *n.* (2), (3), COUNTERTENOR, TENOR *n.* (1), (2)
▪ *adj.* [only before noun] (of a musical instrument 乐器) with the second highest range of notes in its group 中音的： *an alto saxophone* 中音萨克斯管 ➲ COMPARE SOPRANO *adj.*, TENOR *adj.*

al·together 🔑 /ˌɔːltəˈgeðə(r)/ *adv., noun*
▪ *adv.* **1** 🔑 (used to emphasize sth) completely; in every way （用以强调）完全，全部： *The train went slower and slower until it stopped altogether.* 火车愈来愈慢，最后完全停了。◇ *I don't altogether agree with you.* 我不完全同意你的意见。◇ *I am **not altogether** happy* (= I am very unhappy) *about the decision.* 我对这个决定很不满意。◇ *It was an altogether different situation.* 这完全是另外一种情况。 **2** 🔑 used to give a total number or amount （表示总数或总额）总共，一共： *You owe me £68 altogether.* 你一共欠我 68 英镑。 **3** 🔑 used to introduce a summary when you have mentioned a number of different things 总之；总而言之： *The food was good and we loved the music. Altogether it was a great evening.* 吃的不错，音乐我们也喜欢。总之，那天晚上过得非常愉快。
▪ *noun*
IDM **in the altoˈgether** (*old-fashioned, informal*) without any clothes on 一丝不挂；赤身裸体

▼ **WHICH WORD? 词语辨析**

altogether / all together

- **Altogether** and **all together** do not mean the same thing. **Altogether** means 'in total' or (in *BrE*) 'completely'. * altogether 和 all together 含义不同。altogether 指总共或完全地（英式英语）： *We have invited fifty people altogether.* 我们共邀请了五十人。◇ *I am not altogether convinced by this argument.* 我不完全信服这一论点。
- **All together** means 'all in one place' or 'all at once'. * all together 指全部在同一地方或同一时间： *Can you put your books all together in this box?* 你能把你的书都放进这个箱子里吗？◇ *Let's sing 'Happy Birthday'. All together now!* 咱们来唱"生日快乐"。现在一起唱！

al·tru·ism /ˈæltruɪzəm/ *noun* [U] (*formal*) the fact of caring about the needs and happiness of other people more than your own 利他主义；利他；无私 ▸ **al·tru·is·tic** /ˌæltruˈɪstɪk/ *adj.* : *altruistic behaviour* 利他行为

alu = ALOO

alum /ˈæləm/ *noun* [U] a substance formed from ALUMINIUM/ALUMINUM and another metal, used, for example, to prepare leather and to change the colour of things 明矾，白矾（用于制革、印染等）

alu·mina /əˈluːmɪnə/ *noun* [U] (*specialist*) a white substance found in many types of rock, especially CLAY 矾土

alu·min·ium /ˌæljəˈmɪniəm; ˌælə-/ (*BrE*) (*NAmE* **alu·mi·num** /əˈluːmɪnəm/) *noun* [U] (*symb.* **Al**) a chemical element. Aluminium is a light, silver-grey metal used for making pans, etc. 铝： *aluminium saucepans/window frames* 铝锅；铝窗框 ◇ ***aluminium foil*** (= for example, for wrapping food in) 铝箔（如用于包裹食物）

alumna /əˈlʌmnə/ *noun* (*pl.* **alum·nae** /-niː/) (*formal, especially NAmE*) a former woman student of a school, college or university 女校友；女毕业生

alumni /əˈlʌmnaɪ/ *noun* [pl.] (*especially NAmE*) the former male and female students of a school, college or university （统称）校友，毕业生： *Harvard Alumni Association* 哈佛大学校友会

alum·nus /əˈlʌmnəs/ *noun* (*pl.* **alumni** /əˈlʌmnaɪ/) (*formal, especially NAmE*) a former male student of a school, college or university 男校友；男毕业生

al·veo·lar /ælˈviːələ(r); ˌælviˈəʊlə(r); *NAmE* ælˈviːələr/ *noun* (*phonetics* 语音) a speech sound made with the tongue touching the part of the mouth behind the upper front teeth, for example /t/ and /d/ in *tie* and *die* 齿龈音 ▸ **al·veo·lar** *adj.*

al·veo·lus /ælˈviːələs; *BrE also* ˌælviˈəʊləs/ *noun* (*pl.* **al·veoli** /ælˈviːəlaɪ; *BrE also* ˌælviˈəʊlaɪ; *BrE also* -liː/) (*anatomy* 解) one of the many small spaces in each lung where gases can pass into or out of the blood 肺泡

al·ways 🔑 /ˈɔːlweɪz/ *adv.* **1** 🔑 at all times; on every occasion 总是；每次都是： *There's always somebody at home in the evenings.* 晚上总有人在家。◇ *Always lock your car.* 每次都要把汽车锁上。◇ *She always arrives at 7.30.* 她每次都是 7:30 到。◇ *The children always seem to be hungry.* 孩子们永远都好像肚子饿。◇ *We're not always this busy!* 我们并不总是这么忙！ **2** 🔑 for a long time; since you can remember 一直；一贯： *Pat has always loved gardening.* 帕特一直喜爱园艺。◇ *This is the way we've always done it.* 我们一直是这样干的。◇ *This painting is very good—Ellie always was very good at art* (= so it is not very surprising). 这幅画很好 —— 埃利一直擅长绘画。

A

◇ *Did you always want to be an actor?* 你以前一直想当演员吗？ **3** 🔑 for all future time （将）永远： *I'll always love you.* 我将永远爱你。 **4** 🔑 if you say a person is **always doing** sth, or sth is **always happening**, you mean that they do it, or it happens, very often, and that this is annoying （讨厌地）老是，一再： *She's always criticizing me.* 她老是批评我。 ◇ *That phone's always ringing.* 那个电话总是响个不停。 **5 can/could always..., there's always...** used to suggest a possible course of action （建议可能的行动）总还，总还有： *If it doesn't fit, you can always take it back.* 要是它不合适，你总还可以把它退回去嘛。 ◇ *If he can't help, there's always John.* 如果他帮不上忙，总还有约翰呢。

IDM as 'always 🔑 as usually happens or is expected 和往常一样；和料想的一样 **SYN as usual**： *As always, Polly was late for school.* 波莉和往常一样，上学又迟到了。 ➲ MORE AT ONCE *adv.*

Alz·heim·er's dis·ease /ˈæltshaɪməz dɪziːz; *NAmE* -ərz/ (*also* **Alz·heim·er's**) *noun* [U] a serious disease, especially affecting older people, that prevents the brain from functioning normally and causes loss of memory, loss of ability to speak clearly, etc. 阿尔茨海默病 ➲ COMPARE SENILE DEMENTIA

AM /ˌeɪ ˈem/ *noun, abbr.*

▪ ***noun*** the abbreviation for 'Assembly Member' (a person who has been elected to represent an area of Wales in the Welsh Assembly, the parliament for Wales) 议员（全写为 Assembly Member，威尔士议会成员）： *Peter Black AM* 彼得·布莱克议员 ◇ *Labour AMs* 工党议员

▪ ***abbr.*** amplitude modulation (one of the main methods of broadcasting sound by radio) 调幅；振幅调制

am /əm; *strong form* æm/ ➲ BE *v.*

a.m. 🔑 (*NAmE also* **A.M.**) /ˌeɪ ˈem/ *abbr.* between midnight and midday (from Latin 'ante meridiem') 午夜至正午，上午，午前（源自拉丁语 ante meridiem）： *It starts at 10 a.m.* 上午 10 点开始。 ➲ COMPARE P.M.

amah /ˈɑːmə/ *noun* (in S or E Asia) a woman employed by a family to clean, care for children, etc. 阿嬷（东亚或南亚国家的女佣、保姆或奶妈）

amal·gam /əˈmælgəm/ *noun* **1** [C, usually sing.] ~ (**of sth**) (*formal*) a mixture or combination of things 混合物；综合体： *The film script is an amalgam of all three books.* 这个电影脚本由三本书合成。 **2** [U] (*specialist*) a mixture of MERCURY and another metal, used especially to fill holes in teeth 汞齐（尤用于补牙）

amal·gam·ate /əˈmælgəmeɪt/ *verb* ~ (**sth**) (**with/into sth**) **1** [I, T] if two organizations **amalgamate** or **are amalgamated**, they join together to form one large organization （使）合并，联合 **SYN merge**： *A number of colleges have amalgamated to form the new university.* 一些学院联合组成了这所新大学。 ◇ **~ with/into sth** *The company has now amalgamated with another local firm.* 这家公司现在已与当地另一家公司合并了。 ◇ **~ sth** *They decided to amalgamate the two schools.* 他们决定将两所学校合并。 ◇ **~ sth with/into sth** *The two companies were amalgamated into one.* 这两家公司合并成一家公司。 **2** [T] **~ sth (into/with sth)** to put two or more things together so that they form one 使混合；使合并 **SYN merge**： *This information will be amalgamated with information obtained earlier.* 这个信息要与早先得到的信息综合在一起。 ▶ **amal·gam·ation** /əˌmælgəˈmeɪʃn/ *noun* [U, C]： *the amalgamation of small farms into larger units* 小农场合并成大农场

amanu·en·sis /əˌmænjuˈensɪs/ *noun* (*pl.* **amanu·en·ses** /-siːz/) (*formal*) **1** a person who writes down your words when you cannot write, for example if you are injured and have an exam 代笔人；抄写员 **2** an assistant, especially one who writes or types for sb 助手；（尤指）秘书

amar·yl·lis /ˌæməˈrɪlɪs/ *noun* [C, U] a tall white, pink or red flower shaped like a TRUMPET 朱顶兰（喇叭状白色、粉红色或红色高茎花）

amasi /əˈmɑːsi/ (*also* **maas**) *noun* [U] (*SAfrE*) sour milk 酸牛奶

amass /əˈmæs/ *verb* **~ sth** to collect sth, especially in large quantities （尤指大量）积累，积聚 **SYN accumulate**： *He amassed a fortune from silver mining.* 他靠开采银矿积累了一笔财富。 ➲ SYNONYMS AT COLLECT

ama·teur /ˈæmətə(r); -tʃə(r)/ *noun, adj.*

▪ ***noun*** **1** a person who takes part in a sport or other activity for enjoyment, not as a job 业余爱好者；业余运动员： *The tournament is open to both amateurs and professionals.* 这次锦标赛业余选手和职业选手均可参加。 **2** (*usually disapproving*) a person who is not skilled 生手；外行： *This work was done by a bunch of amateurs!* 这项工作是一伙外行干的！ **OPP professional** ▶ **ama·teur·ism** /ˈæmətərɪzəm; -tʃə-/ *noun* [U]： *New rules on amateurism allow payment for promotional work.* 新的业余条例规定，做促销工作可获得报酬。

▪ ***adj.*** **1** [usually before noun] doing sth for enjoyment or interest, not as a job 业余爱好的： *an amateur photographer* 业余摄影爱好者 **2** [usually before noun] done for enjoyment, not as a job 业余的： *amateur athletics* 业余田径运动 **3** (*usually disapproving*) = AMATEURISH **OPP professional**

ˌamateur draˈmatics *noun* [U] (*BrE*) the activity of producing and acting in plays for the theatre, by people who do it for enjoyment, not as a job 玩票；业余戏剧爱好活动

ama·teur·ish /ˈæmətərɪʃ; -tʃə-/ (*also* **ama·teur**) *adj.* (*usually disapproving*) not done or made well or with skill 外行的；生手的；业余的： *Detectives described the burglary as 'crude and amateurish'.* 侦探称这次入室盗窃是拙劣的生手干的。 **OPP professional**

ama·tory /ˈæmətəri; *NAmE* -tɔːri/ *adj.* [only before noun] (*formal* or *humorous*) relating to or connected with sexual desire or activity 性欲的；性爱的： *his amatory exploits* 他的风流韵事

amaze 🔑 /əˈmeɪz/ *verb* to surprise sb very much 使惊奇；使惊愕；使惊诧： **~ sb** *Just the size of the place amazed her.* 仅仅地方之大就使她十分惊奇。 ◇ **~ sb what, how, etc.... *It never ceases to amaze me*** *what some people will do for money.* 有些人为了钱什么都干得出来，这一直使我惊愕不已。 ◇ ***What amazes me is*** *how long she managed to hide it from us.* 使我惊诧的是，她竟然能把这件事瞒了我们这么久。 ◇ **it amazes sb that...** *It amazed her that he could be so calm at such a time.* 在这个时候他还能如此冷静，真让她感到惊讶。 ◇ **it amazes sb to see, find, learn, etc....** *It amazes me to think what we have achieved this year.* 想想我们今年取得的成绩，真令我惊讶。 ➲ SYNONYMS AT SURPRISE

amazed 🔑 /əˈmeɪzd/ *adj.* very surprised 大为惊奇： *an amazed silence* 惊愕得无语 ◇ **~ at sb/sth** *I was amazed at her knowledge of French literature.* 她的法国文学知识之丰富使我大为惊奇。 ◇ **~ by sb/sth** *We were amazed by his generosity.* 他的慷慨令我们喜出望外。 ◇ **~ (that)...** *I was banging so loudly I'm amazed (that) they didn't hear me.* 我把门敲得砰砰响。真奇怪，他们居然没有听见。 ◇ **~ how...** *She was amazed how little he had changed.* 她惊讶的是他竟然没怎么改变。 ◇ **~ to see, find, learn, etc.** *We were amazed to find that no one was hurt.* 我们很惊异地发现竟没有人受伤。

amaze·ment /əˈmeɪzmənt/ *noun* [U] a feeling of great surprise 惊奇；惊愕；惊诧： ***To my amazement,*** *he remembered me.* 使我大为惊奇的是他还记得我。 ◇ *She looked at him **in amazement**.* 她惊愕地望着他。

amaz·ing 🔑 /əˈmeɪzɪŋ/ *adj.* very surprising, especially in a way that makes you feel pleasure or admiration 令人大为惊奇的；（尤指）令人惊喜（或惊羡、惊叹）的 **SYN astounding, incredible**： *an amazing achievement/discovery/success/performance* 惊人的成就 / 发现 / 成功 / 表演 ◇ *That's amazing, isn't it?* 真是令人惊叹，是不是？ ◇ ***It's amazing*** *how quickly people adapt.* 人适应环境的速度之快真是惊人。 ▶ **amaz·ing·ly** *adv.*： *Amazingly, no one* *noticed.* 令人惊奇的是，竟没有人注意到。◇ *The meal was amazingly cheap.* 这餐饭便宜得出奇。

Amazon /ˈæməzən; *NAmE also* -zɑːn/ *noun* **1** (in ancient Greek stories) a woman from a group of female WARRIORS (= soldiers) （古希腊神话中的）亚马孙族女战士 **2 amazon** (*literary*) a tall strong woman 高大强悍的女人

am·bas·sador /æmˈbæsədə(r)/ *noun* an official who lives in a foreign country as the senior representative there of his or her own country 大使；使节；代表： *the British Ambassador to Italy/in Rome* 英国驻意大利 / 罗马大使 ◇ *a former ambassador to the UN* 前任驻联合国代表 ◇ (*figurative*) *The best ambassadors for the sport are the players.* 这种运动最好的大使就是运动员。 ▶ **am·bas·sador·ial** /æmˌbæsəˈdɔːriəl/ *adj.*

amber /ˈæmbə(r)/ *noun* [U] **1** a hard clear yellowish-brown substance, used in making decorative objects or jewellery 琥珀： *amber beads* 琥珀珠子 **2** a yellowish-brown colour 琥珀色；黄褐色： *The traffic lights were on amber.* 交通信号黄灯亮了。 ▶ **amber** *adj.*

ˌamber ˈfluid (*also* **ˌamber ˈliquid**) *noun* [U] (*AustralE, informal*) beer 啤酒

am·ber·gris /ˈæmbəgriːs; -grɪs; *NAmE* ˈæmbər-/ *noun* [U] a substance that is used in making some PERFUMES. It is produced naturally by a type of WHALE. 龙涎香（抹香鲸分泌物，用以制香水）

ambi- /ˈæmbi/ *prefix* (in nouns, adjectives and adverbs 构成名词、形容词和副词) referring to both of two 二者（都）： *ambidextrous* 左右手都灵巧的 ◇ *ambivalent* 矛盾情绪的

ambi·dex·trous /ˌæmbiˈdekstrəs/ *adj.* able to use the left hand or the right hand equally well 左右手都灵巧的；左右开弓的

am·bi·ence (*also* **am·bi·ance**) /ˈæmbiəns/ *noun* [sing.] the character and atmosphere of a place 环境；气氛；格调： *the relaxed ambience of the city* 这座城市轻松的氛围

am·bi·ent /ˈæmbiənt/ *adj.* **1** [only before noun] (*specialist*) relating to the surrounding area; on all sides 周围环境的；周围的： ***ambient temperature/light/conditions*** 周围的温度 / 光线 / 环境 **2** (especially of music 尤指音乐) creating a relaxed atmosphere 产生轻松氛围的： *a compilation of ambient electronic music* 氛围电子音乐选辑 ◇ *soft, ambient lighting* 轻松柔和的照明

am·bi·gu·ity **AW** /ˌæmbɪˈgjuːəti/ *noun* (*pl.* **-ies**) **1** [U] the state of having more than one possible meaning 歧义；一语多义： *Write clear definitions in order to avoid ambiguity.* 释义要写清楚以免产生歧义。 **2** [C] a word or statement that can be understood in more than one way 模棱两可的词；含混不清的语句： *There were several inconsistencies and ambiguities in her speech.* 她的发言有几处前后不一致和含混不清。 **3** [U, C] the state of being difficult to understand or explain because of involving many different aspects 模棱两可；不明确： *You must understand the ambiguity of my position.* 你必须理解我处的位置不明确。

am·bigu·ous **AW** /æmˈbɪgjuəs/ *adj.* **1** that can be understood in more than one way; having different meanings 模棱两可的；含混不清的；多义的： *an **ambiguous word/term/statement*** 模棱两可的词 / 用语 / 说法 ◇ *Her account was deliberately ambiguous.* 她的陈述故意含混不清。 **2** not clearly stated or defined 不明确的： *His role has always been ambiguous.* 他的角色一直不明确。 **OPP** **unambiguous** ▶ **am·bigu·ous·ly** *adv.* ： *an ambiguously worded agreement* 措辞含混的协议

ambit /ˈæmbɪt/ *noun* [sing.] (*formal*) the range of the authority or influence of sth （权力、影响的）范围，界限： *This case falls clearly **within the ambit of** the 2001 act.* 这件案子显然属于 2001 年法案的适用范围。

am·bi·tion 🔑 /æmˈbɪʃn/ *noun* **1** 🔑 [C] something that you want to do or achieve very much 追求的目标；夙愿： *It had been her **lifelong ambition**.* 这是她终生追求的目标。 ◇ ***political/literary/sporting ambitions*** 政治抱负；文学夙愿；运动目标 ◇ **~ of being/doing sth** *She never **achieved her ambition** of becoming a famous writer.* 她一直未能实现当名作家的夙愿。 ◇ **~ to be/do sth** *His burning ambition was to study medicine.* 他梦寐以求的是学医。 **2** 🔑 [U] the desire or determination to be successful, rich, powerful, etc. 野心；雄心；志向；抱负： *motivated by personal ambition* 为个人野心所驱使 ◇ *She was intelligent but suffered from a lack of ambition.* 她很聪明，但却缺乏远大志向。

am·bi·tious /æmˈbɪʃəs/ *adj.* **1** determined to be successful, rich, powerful, etc. 有野心的；有雄心的： *a fiercely ambitious young manager* 雄心勃勃的年轻经理 ◇ *They were very ambitious for their children* (= they wanted them to be successful). 他们望子成龙心切。 **2** needing a lot of effort, money or time to succeed 费力的；耗资的；耗时的： *the government's ambitious plans for social reform* 政府耗资巨大的社会改革计划 **OPP** **unambitious** ▶ **am·bi·tious·ly** *adv.*

am·biva·lent /æmˈbɪvələnt/ *adj.* **~ (about/towards sb/sth)** having or showing both good and bad feelings about sb/sth （喜忧参半、好坏参半等）矛盾情绪的： *She seems to feel ambivalent about her new job.* 她似乎对她的新工作喜忧参半。 ◇ *He has an ambivalent attitude towards her.* 他对她怀着矛盾的心情。 ▶ **am·biva·lence** *noun* [U, sing.]: **~ (about/towards sb/sth)** *Many people feel some ambivalence towards television and its effect on our lives.* 很多人以矛盾的态度对待电视及其对生活的影响。 **am·biva·lent·ly** *adv.*

amble /ˈæmbl/ *verb* [I] **+ adv./prep.** to walk at a slow relaxed speed 缓行；漫步 **SYN** **stroll**： *We ambled down to the beach.* 我们漫步向海滩走去。

am·bro·sia /æmˈbrəʊziə; *NAmE* -ˈbroʊ-/ *noun* [U] **1** (in ancient Greek and Roman stories 古希腊和古罗马神话) the food of the gods 神的食物；神肴；仙馐 **2** (*literary*) something that is very pleasant to eat 美味佳肴；珍馐 **3** (*NAmE*) a sweet dish of fruit and cream, often with COCONUT (2), eaten at the end of a meal, often at THANKSGIVING 奶油水果甜点（原料中常有椰子，常在感恩节期间吃）

am·bu·lance 🔑 /ˈæmbjələns/ *noun* a vehicle with special equipment, used for taking sick or injured people to a hospital 救护车： *the ambulance service* 救护车服务 ◇ *ambulance staff* 救护车全体人员 ◇ *Call an ambulance!* 叫救护车！ ➲ WORDFINDER NOTE AT ACCIDENT

ˈambulance chaser *noun* (*informal, disapproving, especially NAmE*) a lawyer who earns money by encouraging people who have been in an accident to make claims in court 怂恿事故受害者提出索赔诉讼的律师

am·bu·la·tory /ˈæmbjələtəri; *NAmE* -tɔːri/ *adj.* (*formal*) **1** related to or adapted for walking （适用于）步行的： *an ambulatory corridor* 回廊 **2** that is not fixed in one place and can move around easily 非固定的；可移动的；流动的 **SYN** **mobile**： *an ambulatory care service* 流动护理服务

am·bush /ˈæmbʊʃ/ *noun, verb*

■ ***noun*** [C, U] the act of hiding and waiting for sb and then making a surprise attack on them 伏击；埋伏： *Two soldiers were killed in a terrorist ambush.* 两名士兵遭到恐怖分子伏击而死亡。 ◇ *They were **lying in ambush**, waiting for the aid convoy.* 他们埋伏起来，等着袭击援助车队。

■ ***verb*** **~ sb/sth** to make a surprise attack on sb/sth from a hidden position 伏击： *The guerrillas ambushed them near the bridge.* 游击队员在大桥附近伏击了他们。 ◇ (*figurative*) *She was ambushed by reporters.* 记者突然一拥而上采访她。

ameba, ameb·ic (*US*) = AMOEBA, AMOEBIC

ameli·or·ate /əˈmiːliəreɪt/ *verb* **~ sth** (*formal*) to make sth better 改善；改进；改良： *Steps have been taken to ameliorate the situation.* 已经采取措施以改善局面。 ▶ **ameli·or·ation** /əˌmiːliəˈreɪʃn/ *noun* [U]

amen /ɑːˈmen; eɪˈmen/ (*also* **Amen**) *exclamation, noun* a word used at the end of prayers and HYMNS, meaning 'may it be so' 阿门（用于祈祷或圣歌结束时，表示诚心所

愿）： *We ask this through our Lord, Amen.* 奉主之名而求，阿门。◇ *Amen to that* (= I certainly agree with that). 我当然同意那个意见。

amen·able /əˈmiːnəbl/ *adj.* **1** (of people 人) easy to control; willing to be influenced by sb/sth 顺从的；顺服的：*They had three very amenable children.* 他们有三个很听话的孩子。◇ **~ to sth** *He seemed most amenable to my idea.* 他似乎对我言听计从。 **2 ~ to sth** (*formal*) that you can treat in a particular way 可用某种方式处理的：*'Hamlet' is the least amenable of all Shakespeare's plays to being summarized.* 在莎士比亚所有的戏剧中，《哈姆雷特》最难概括。

amend **AW** /əˈmend/ *verb* **~ sth** to change a law, document, statement, etc. slightly in order to correct a mistake or to improve it 修正，修订（法律、文件、声明等）：*He asked to see the amended version.* 他要求看修订本。

amend·ment **AW** /əˈmendmənt/ *noun* **1** [C, U] a small change or improvement that is made to a law or a document; the process of changing a law or a document（法律、文件的）改动，修正案，修改，修订：*to* ***introduce/propose/table an amendment*** (= to suggest it) 提出一项修正案 ◇ *Parliament passed the bill without further amendment.* 议会未作进一步修改便通过了议案。◇ **~ to sth** *She made several minor amendments to her essay.* 她对自己的论文作了几处小的修改。 **2 Amendment** [C] a statement of a change to the CONSTITUTION of the US（美国的）宪法修正案：*The 19th Amendment gave women the right to vote.* 第 19 条宪法修正案赋予妇女选举权。

amends /əˈmendz/ *noun* [pl.]

IDM **make amends (to sb) (for sth/for doing sth)** to do sth for sb in order to show that you are sorry for sth wrong or unfair that you have done（因某事向某人）赔偿，补偿，赔不是；将功补（过） **SYN** **make up for sth** ➲ WORDFINDER NOTE AT SORRY

amen·ity /əˈmiːnəti; *NAmE* əˈmenəti/ *noun* [usually pl.] (*pl.* **-ies**) a feature that makes a place pleasant, comfortable or easy to live in 生活福利设施；便利设施：*The campsite is close to all* ***local amenities.*** 营地紧靠当地所有的便利设施。◇ *Many of the houses lacked even* ***basic amenities*** (= baths, showers, hot water, etc.). 很多房屋甚至缺少基本的生活设施。 ➲ WORDFINDER NOTE AT CITY

amen·or·rhoea (*BrE*) (*NAmE* **amen·or·rhea**) /əˌmenəˈriːə; *NAmE* eɪˌmen-/ *noun* [U] (*medical* 医) a condition in which an adult woman does not MENSTRUATE (= there is no flow of blood from her WOMB every month) 闭经

Amer·asian /ˌæməˈreɪʃn; -ˈreɪʒn/ *noun* a person with one Asian parent and one parent from the US 美亚混血儿（父母一方为亚洲人，一方为美国人） ▶ **Amer·asian** *adj.*

Ameri·can /əˈmerɪkən/ *noun, adj.*

▪ ***noun*** **1** a person from America, especially the US 美洲人；（尤指）美国人 ➲ SEE ALSO AFRICAN AMERICAN, NATIVE AMERICAN **2** (*also* **Aˈmerican English**) the English language as spoken in the US 美国英语

▪ ***adj.*** of or connected with N or S America, especially the US 美洲的；（尤指）美国的：*I'm American.* 我是美国人。◇ *American culture/tourists* 美国文化 / 游客

IDM **as Aˌmerican as apple ˈpie** used to say that sth is typical of America 典型美国式的；地道美国式的

Ameri·cana /əˌmerɪˈkɑːnə/ *noun* [pl.] things connected with the US that are thought to be typical of it 典型美国事物

Aˌmerican ˈbreakfast *noun* a large breakfast which can include CEREAL and cooked food, such as eggs with HAM 美式早餐（量大，包括麦片粥、蛋、火腿等） ➲ SEE ALSO ENGLISH BREAKFAST, CONTINENTAL BREAKFAST

Aˌmerican ˈcheese *noun* [U] (*US*) a kind of orange cheese that is usually sold in thin slices wrapped in plastic 美式奶酪（橙色，通常切片用塑料包装出售）

the Aˌmerican ˈdream *noun* [sing.] the belief that America offers the opportunity to everyone of a good and successful life achieved through hard work 美国梦（相信只要经过努力不懈的奋斗便能在美国获得更好生活的信仰）

the Aˌmerican ˈeagle *noun* a bird with a white head and white tail feathers that is the national symbol of the US 白头雕（美国的象征）

Aˌmerican ˈfootball (*BrE*) (*NAmE* **foot·ball**) *noun* [U] a game played by two teams of 11 players, using an OVAL ball which players kick, throw, or carry. Teams try to put the ball over the other team's line. 美式足球，美式橄榄球（双方队员各 11 人，球呈椭圆形，球员可足踢、手传或持球奔跑，球越过对方得分线得分） ➲ VISUAL VOCAB PAGE V48

Aˌmerican ˈIndian *noun* = NATIVE AMERICAN

Ameri·can·ism /əˈmerɪkənɪzəm/ *noun* **1** [C] a word, phrase or spelling that is typical of American English, used in another variety of English 美式英语；美式说法 **2** [U] the essential quality of being American 美国特色；美洲特色

Ameri·can·ize (*BrE also* **-ise**) /əˈmerɪkənaɪz/ *verb* **~ sb/sth** to make sb/sth American in character 使美国化 ▶ **Ameri·can·iza·tion, -isa·tion** /əˌmerəkənaɪˈzeɪʃn; *NAmE* -nəˈz-/ *noun* [U]

the Aˈmerican League *noun* (in the US) one of the two organizations for professional BASEBALL 美国职业棒球联盟 ➲ SEE ALSO NATIONAL LEAGUE

Aˌmerican ˈplan *noun* [U] = FULL BOARD

▼ **MORE ABOUT ...** 补充说明

America

- The continent of **America** is divided into **North America** and **South America**. The narrow region joining North and South America is **Central America.** 美洲 (America) 大陆划分为北美洲 (North America) 和南美洲 (South America)，连接两地的地峡为中美洲 (Central America)。
- **North America**, which is a geographical term, consists of the **United States of America**, **Canada** and **Mexico.** **Latin America**, a cultural term, refers to the non-English speaking countries of Central and South America, where mainly Portuguese and Spanish are spoken. Mexico is part of Latin America. 北美洲 (North America) 是地理称谓，由美国 (United States of America)、加拿大 (Canada) 和墨西哥 (Mexico) 组成。拉丁美洲 (Latin America) 是文化称谓，指中美洲和南美洲的非英语国家，那里主要说葡萄牙语和西班牙语。墨西哥是拉丁美洲的一部分。
- The **United States of America** is usually shortened to the **USA**, the **US**, the **States** or simply **America**. * the United States of America（美国）通常简称为 the USA、the US、the States 或干脆叫 America： *the US President* 美国总统 ◇ *Have you ever been to the States?* 你去过美国吗？◇ *She emigrated to America in 1995.* 她 1995 年移民美国。 Many people from other parts of the continent dislike this use of **America** to mean just the US, but it is very common. 虽然在美洲大陆其他地方，许多人不喜欢用 America 指美国，但此用法非常普遍。
- **American** is usually used to talk about somebody or something from the United States of America. * American 通常指美国的人或事物： *Do you have an American passport?* 你有美国护照吗？◇ *American football* 美式足球 ◇ *I'm not American, I'm Canadian.* 我不是美国人，我是加拿大人。 **Latin American** and **South American** are used to refer to other parts of the continent. * Latin American（拉丁美洲的；拉丁美洲人）和 South American（南美洲的；南美洲人）指美洲大陆的其他部分： *Latin American dance music* 拉丁美洲舞曲 ◇ *Quite a lot of South Americans study here.* 相当多的南美洲人在这里学习。

ameri·cium /ˌæməˈrɪsiəm; -ˈrɪʃi-/ *noun* [U] (*symb.* **Am**) a chemical element. Americium is a RADIOACTIVE metal. 镅（放射性化学元素）

Amer·in·dian /ˌæməˈrɪndiən/ *noun* (*old-fashioned*) = NATIVE AMERICAN

ameth·yst /ˈæməθɪst/ *noun* [C, U] a purple SEMI-PRECIOUS stone, used in making jewellery 紫水晶；紫晶： *an amethyst ring* 紫水晶戒指

ami·able /ˈeɪmiəbl/ *adj.* pleasant; friendly and easy to like 和蔼可亲的；亲切友好的 **SYN agreeable**： *an amiable tone of voice* 亲切的声调 ◇ *Her parents seemed very amiable.* 她的父母好像很和蔼可亲。 ▶ **ami·abil·ity** /ˌeɪmiəˈbɪləti/ *noun* [U] **ami·ably** *adv.*： *'That's fine,' he replied amiably.* "那很好。"他亲切友好地回答道。

am·ic·able /ˈæmɪkəbl/ *adj.* done or achieved in a polite or friendly way and without arguing 心平气和的；友善的： *an amicable relationship* 和睦的关系 ◇ *An amicable settlement was reached.* 已达成和解。 ▶ **am·ic·ably** *adv.*

amid /əˈmɪd/ (*also* **mid**, **amidst** /əˈmɪdst/) *prep.* (*formal*) **1** in the middle of or during sth, especially sth that causes excitement or fear 在…过程中；在…中： *He finished his speech amid tremendous applause.* 他在雷鸣般的掌声中结束了演讲。◇ *The firm collapsed amid allegations of fraud.* 该公司在一片指控其诈骗的声音中倒闭了。 **2** surrounded by sth 在…中；四周是： *The hotel was in a beautiful position amid lemon groves.* 旅馆位于柠檬树丛之中，优美宜人。

amid·ships /əˈmɪdʃɪps/ *adv.* (*specialist*) in or near the middle part of a ship 在（或靠近）船体中部

amino acid /əˌmiːnəʊ ˈæsɪd; *NAmE* -noʊ/ *noun* (*chemistry* 化) any of the substances that combine to form the basic structure of PROTEINS 氨基酸

amir = EMIR

the Amish /ˈɑːmɪʃ; *BrE also* ˈæmɪʃ/ *noun* [pl.] the members of a strict religious group in N America. The Amish live a simple farming life and reject some forms of modern technology. 阿曼门诺派（北美洲戒律严谨的宗教团体，其成员过简朴的农耕生活，拒绝使用某些现代技术） ▶ **Amish** *adj.*

amiss /əˈmɪs/ *adj., adv.*

■ *adj.* [not before noun] wrong; not as it should be 不对；不正常： *She sensed something was amiss and called the police.* 她觉得有点不对头，就叫了警察。

■ *adv.*

IDM **not come/go aˈmiss** (*BrE*) to be useful or pleasant in a particular situation 并非不称心；并非不顺当： *A little luck wouldn't go amiss right now!* 此刻若交点好运就好了。 **take sth aˈmiss** (*BrE*) to feel offended by sth, perhaps because you have understood it in the wrong way 见怪： *Would she take it amiss if I offered to help?* 我要是提出帮助，她会不会见怪？

amity /ˈæməti/ *noun* [U] (*formal*) a friendly relationship between people or countries 和睦；友好

amma /ˈʌmɑː/ *noun* (*IndE*) (especially as a form of address 尤用作称谓) a mother 阿妈；妈妈

am·meter /ˈæmiːtə(r)/ *noun* an instrument for measuring the strength of an electric current 安培计；电流表

ammo /ˈæməʊ; *NAmE* ˈæmoʊ/ *noun* [U] (*old-fashioned, informal*) = AMMUNITION

am·mo·nia /əˈməʊniə; *NAmE* əˈmoʊ-/ *noun* [U] (*symb.* NH_3) a gas with a strong smell; a clear liquid containing ammonia, used as a cleaning substance 氨；氨水

am·mon·ite /ˈæmənaɪt/ *noun* a FOSSIL of a simple sea creature which no longer exists, and which was related to SNAILS 菊石（已灭绝的头足动物，与螺近缘）

am·mo·nium /əˈməʊniəm; *NAmE* əˈmoʊ-/ *noun* [U] (*chemistry* 化) an ION made from AMMONIA containing NITROGEN and HYDROGEN together with another element 铵

am·mu·ni·tion /ˌæmjuˈnɪʃn/ *noun* [U] **1** a supply of bullets, etc. to be fired from guns 弹药 **2** information that can be used against another person in an argument （辩论中可攻击对方的）把柄，证据： *The letter gave her all the ammunition she needed.* 这封信给了她所需的一切有力证据。

am·nesia /æmˈniːziə; *NAmE* -ˈniːʒə/ *noun* [U] a medical condition in which sb partly or completely loses their memory 遗忘（症）；记忆缺失 ▶ **am·nesiac** /æmˈniːziæk; *NAmE* -ˈniːʒ-/ *noun*： *This new discovery helps amnesiacs keep their memory.* 这项新发现有助于遗忘症患者保持记忆。

am·nesty /ˈæmnəsti/ *noun* (*pl.* **-ies**) **1** [C, usually sing., U] an official statement that allows people who have been put in prison for crimes against the state to go free （对政治犯的）赦免，大赦： *The president granted a general amnesty for all political prisoners.* 总统大赦了所有的政治犯。 **2** [C, usually sing.] a period of time during which people can admit to a crime or give up weapons without being punished 赦免期（此期间交代罪行或交出武器可获赦免）： *2 000 knives have been handed in during the month-long amnesty.* 在为期一个月的赦免期中交出的刀有2 000把。

ˌAmnesty Interˈnational *noun* an international human rights organization that works to help people who have been put in prison for their beliefs or race and not because they have committed a crime. It also works to prevent TORTURE and CAPITAL PUNISHMENT (= punishment by death). 大赦国际；国际特赦组织

am·nio·cen·tesis /ˌæmniəʊsenˈtiːsɪs; *NAmE* -nioʊ-/ *noun* [U, sing.] a medical test that involves taking some liquid from a pregnant woman's WOMB in order to find out if the baby has particular illnesses or health problems 羊膜腔穿刺术（经孕妇腹壁吸出液体检查胎儿健康状况）

am·ni·ot·ic fluid /ˌæmniɒtɪk ˈfluːɪd; *NAmE* -ɑːtɪk/ *noun* [U] the liquid that surrounds a baby inside the mother's WOMB 羊水

amn't /ˈæmənt/ *short form* (*ScotE, IrishE, non-standard*) am not 不是

amoeba (*US also* **ameba**) /əˈmiːbə/ *noun* (*pl.* **amoe·bas** or **amoe·bae** /-biː/) a very small living creature that consists of only one cell 阿米巴，变形虫（单细胞生物）

amoeb·ic (*US also* **ameb·ic**) /əˈmiːbɪk/ *adj.* related to or similar to an amoeba 变形虫的；变形虫状的

aˌmoebic ˈdysentery (*US also* **aˌmebic ˈdysentery**) *noun* [U] an infection of the INTESTINE caused by a type of amoeba 阿米巴痢疾

amok /əˈmɒk; *NAmE* əˈmɑːk/ *adv.*

IDM **run amok** to suddenly become very angry or excited and start behaving violently, especially in a public place （尤指在公共场所）发狂，狂暴，疯狂

among /əˈmʌŋ/ (*also* **amongst** /əˈmʌŋst/) *prep.* **1** surrounded by sb/sth; in the middle of sb/sth 在…中；周围是： *a house among the trees* 树林中的一座房子 ◇ *They strolled among the crowds.* 他们在人群中信步而行。 ◇ *I found the letter amongst his papers.* 我在他的文件中找到这封信。◇ *It's OK, you're among friends now.* 没事，周围都是自己人。 **2** being included or happening in groups of things or people 在（其）中；…之一： *A British*

ammonite 菊石

woman was among the survivors. 幸存者中有一位英国妇女。◇ He was among the last to leave. 他是最晚离开的人之一。◇ This attitude is common among the under-25s. 这种态度在 25 岁以下的人群中很普遍。◇ 'What was wrong with the job?' 'Well, the pay wasn't good, **among other things.**' "这份工作有什么不好吗？" "嗯，别的不说，工资就不怎么样。" ◇ Discuss it **among yourselves** (= with each other) first. 你们自己先讨论一下。 **3** used when you are dividing or choosing sth, and three or more people or things are involved 在（三者或以上）中（分配或选择）: They divided the money up among their three children. 他们把钱分给了他们的三个孩子。

amoral /ˌeɪˈmɒrəl; NAmE -ˈmɔːr-/ adj. not following any moral rules and not caring about right and wrong 不关道德的；不遵守道德准则的 ➲ COMPARE IMMORAL, MORAL adj. ▶ **amor·al·ity** /ˌeɪməˈræləti/ noun [U]

am·or·ous /ˈæmərəs/ adj. showing sexual desire and love towards sb 示爱的；含情脉脉的: Mary rejected Tony's amorous advances. 玛丽拒绝了托尼的挑逗。 ▶ **am·or·ous·ly** adv.

amorph·ous /əˈmɔːfəs; NAmE -ˈmɔːrf-/ adj. [usually before noun] (formal) having no definite shape, form or structure 无固定形状的；不规则的；无组织的 SYN **shapeless**: an amorphous mass of cells with no identity at all 没有任何特征的杂乱一团的细胞

amort·ize (BrE also **-ise**) /əˈmɔːtaɪz; NAmE ˈæmərtaɪz/ verb **~ sth** (business 商) to pay back a debt by making small regular payments over a period of time 分期偿还，摊还（债款） ▶ **amort·iza·tion**, **-isa·tion** /əˌmɔːtaɪˈzeɪʃn; NAmE ˌæmərtəˈz-/ noun [U, C]

amount /əˈmaʊnt/ noun, verb

■ noun [C, U] **1** a sum of money 金额: The insurance company will refund any amount due to you. 保险公司将赔偿你应得的所有款项。◇ You will receive a bill for the full amount. 你将收到一张全额的账单。 **2** **~ (of sth)** (used especially with uncountable nouns 尤与不可数名词连用) a quantity of sth 数量；数额: an amount of time/money/information 一段时间；一笔钱；一些信息 ◇ We've had an enormous amount of help from people. 我们得到了人们的大力帮助。◇ The server is designed to store huge amounts of data. 该服务器是为存储大量数据设计的。

IDM **any amount of sth** a large quantity of sth 大量: There's been any amount of research into the subject. 对这个课题已进行了大量研究。 **no amount of sth** used for saying that sth will have no effect 即使再多（或再大）（也不）: No amount of encouragement would make him jump into the pool. 再怎样鼓励，他也不肯往游泳池里跳。

■ verb

PHRV **aˈmount to sth** **1** to add up to sth; to make sth as a total 总计；共计: His earnings are said to amount to £300 000 per annum. 据说他每年挣的钱多达 30 万英镑。◇ They gave me some help in the beginning but it **did not amount to much** (= they did not give me much help). 起初他们给了我一些帮助，但帮助不大。 **2** to be equal to or the same as sth 等于；相当于: Her answer amounted to a complete refusal. 她的答复等于完全拒绝。◇ Their actions amount to a breach of contract. 他们的行为已属违反合同。◇ It'll cost a lot—well, take a lot of time, but it **amounts to the same thing.** 会花很多，哦，得花大量时间，不过反正都是一回事。

amour /əˈmʊə(r); NAmE əˈmʊr/ noun (old-fashioned, from French) a love affair, especially a secret one （尤指秘密的）恋情；风流韵事

amp /æmp/ noun **1** (also **am·pere** /ˈæmpeə(r); NAmE ˈæmpɪr; -per/) (abbr. **A**) the unit for measuring electric current 安，安培（电流单位）: a 13 amp fuse/plug * 13 安保险丝 / 插头 **2** (informal) = AMPLIFIER

amped /æmpt/ (also ˌ**amped ˈup**) adj. (NAmE, informal) excited, especially because of an event 兴奋的；激动的: an amped audience of hardcore fans 狂热的铁杆支持者观众 ◇ I get pretty amped up before I compete. 在比赛之前我激动得热血沸腾。

am·per·age /ˈæmpərɪdʒ/ noun [U] (specialist) the strength of an electric current, measured in amps （电流强度）安培数

am·per·sand /ˈæmpəsænd; NAmE -pərs-/ noun the symbol &, used to mean 'and' * &（表示 and 的符号）: She works for Bond & Green. 她在邦德－格林公司工作。

am·phet·amine /æmˈfetəmiːn/ noun [C, U] a drug that makes you feel excited and full of energy. Amphetamines are sometimes taken illegally. 苯丙胺（中枢兴奋药）；安非他明

am·phib·ian /æmˈfɪbiən/ noun any animal that can live both on land and in water. Amphibians have cold blood and skin without SCALES. FROGS, TOADS and NEWTS are all amphibians. 两栖动物 ➲ COLLOCATIONS AT LIFE ➲ VISUAL VOCAB PAGE V13 ➲ COMPARE REPTILE

am·phibi·ous /æmˈfɪbiəs/ adj. **1** able to live both on land and in water （生物）水陆两栖的 **2** (of military operations 军事行动) involving soldiers landing at a place from the sea 两栖作战的；登陆的 **3** suitable for use on land or water 水陆两用的: amphibious vehicles 水陆两用车辆

amphi·theatre (especially US **-ter**) /ˈæmfɪθɪətə(r); NAmE -θiːətər/ noun **1** a round building without a roof and with rows of seats that rise in steps around an open space. Amphitheatres were used especially in ancient Greece and Rome for public entertainments. （尤指古希腊和古罗马的）圆形露天剧场，圆形露天竞技场 ➲ VISUAL VOCAB PAGE V15 **2** a room, hall or theatre with rows of seats that rise in steps 阶梯式座位大厅（或剧场、室） **3** (specialist) an open space that is surrounded by high sloping land 圆形凹地

am·phora /ˈæmfərə; NAmE also æmˈfɔːrə/ noun (pl. **am·phorae** /ˈæmfəriː; NAmE æmˈfɔːriː/ or **am·phoras**) a tall ancient Greek or Roman container with two handles and a narrow neck （古希腊或古罗马的）双耳细颈瓶

ampi·cil·lin /ˌæmpɪˈsɪlɪn/ noun [U] a form of PENICILLIN that is used to treat certain infections 氨苄青霉素；氨苄西林

ample /ˈæmpl/ adj. **1** enough or more than enough 足够的；丰裕的: ample opportunity/evidence/space/proof 充分的机会；足够的证据；宽敞的空间；充足的证明 ◇ There was ample time to get to the airport. 有足够的时间到达机场。◇ Ample free parking is available. 有宽敞的免费停车场。➲ SEE ALSO PLENTY adv. (1) **2** (of a person's figure 人的体形) large, often in an attractive way 丰满的；硕大的: an ample bosom 丰满的胸部 ▶ **amply** /ˈæmpli/ adv.: His efforts were amply rewarded. 他的努力得到了丰厚的回报。

amp·li·fier /ˈæmplɪfaɪə(r)/ (also informal **amp**) noun an electrical device or piece of equipment that makes sounds or radio signals louder 放大器；扩音器；扬声器: a 25 watt amplifier 一台 25 瓦扩音器 ➲ VISUAL VOCAB PAGE V40

amp·lify /ˈæmplɪfaɪ/ verb (**amp·li·fies**, **amp·li·fy·ing**, **amp·li·fied**, **amp·li·fied**) **1** [T] **~ sth** to increase sth in strength, especially sound 放大，增强（声音等）: to amplify a guitar/an electric current/a signal 放大吉他声音；增强电流 / 信号 **2** [I, T] (formal) to add details to a story, statement, etc. 阐发，充实（故事、事情、陈述等）: She refused to amplify further. 她拒绝提供详情。◇ **~ sth** You may need to amplify this point. 你可能需要对这一点进一步予以说明。 ▶ **amp·li·fi·ca·tion** /ˌæmplɪfɪˈkeɪʃn/ noun [U]: electronic amplification 电子放大 ◇ That comment needs some amplification. 这个评论有待充实。

amp·li·tude /ˈæmplɪtjuːd; NAmE -tuːd/ noun [U, C] (physics 物) the greatest distance that a wave, especially a sound or radio wave, VIBRATES (= moves up and down) （声波、无线电波等的）振幅 ➲ WORDFINDER NOTE AT PHYSICS ➲ PICTURE AT WAVELENGTH

amply adv. ➲ AMPLE

A

am·poule (*US also* **am·pule**) /ˈæmpuːl; *NAmE also* -pjuːl/ *noun* a small container, usually made of glass, containing a drug that will be used for an INJECTION 安瓿（装针剂的小玻璃瓶）

am·pu·tate /ˈæmpjuteɪt/ *verb* [T, I] ~ (**sth**) to cut off sb's arm, leg, finger or toe in a medical operation （用外科手术）切断；截（肢）：*He had to have both legs amputated.* 他不得不截掉双腿。◇ *They may have to amputate.* 他们可能不得不施行截肢手术。 ➲ WORDFINDER NOTE AT OPERATION ➲ COLLOCATIONS AT INJURY ▶ **am·pu·ta·tion** /ˌæmpjuˈteɪʃn/ *noun* [U, C]

am·pu·tee /ˌæmpjuˈtiː/ *noun* a person who has had an arm or a leg amputated 被截肢者

amu·let /ˈæmjʊlət/ *noun* a piece of jewellery that some people wear because they think it protects them from bad luck, illness, etc. 护身符，驱邪物（为祛邪防病等佩戴的珠宝） ➲WORDFINDER NOTE AT LUCK

amuse /əˈmjuːz/ *verb* **1** to make sb laugh or smile 逗笑；逗乐：**~ sb** *My funny drawings amused the kids.* 我的滑稽图画把孩子们逗乐了。◇ *This will amuse you.* 这个会逗你笑的。◇ **it amuses sb to do sth** *It amused him to think that they were probably talking about him at that very moment.* 想到就在这会儿他们大概正在谈论他，他不禁笑了起来。 **2** to make time pass pleasantly for sb/yourself （提供）消遣；（使）娱乐 SYN **entertain**：**~ sb** *She suggested several ideas to help Laura amuse the twins.* 她给劳拉出了一些主意，好逗这对双胞胎开心。◇ **~ yourself** *I'm sure I'll be able to amuse myself for a few hours.* 我肯定几个小时都会自得其乐。

amused /əˈmjuːzd/ *adj.* thinking that sb/sth is funny, so that you smile or laugh 被逗乐的；觉得好笑的：*There was an amused look on the President's face.* 总统面带愉悦的神情。◇ *Janet was* **not amused** (= she was annoyed or angry). 珍妮特感到不悦。◇ **~ at/by sth** *We were all amused at his stories.* 我们都被他的故事逗笑了。◇ **~ to see, find, learn, etc.** *He was amused to see how seriously she took the game.* 他看见她玩这个游戏十分认真的样子，觉得好笑。

IDM **keep sb aˈmused** to give sb interesting things to do, or to entertain them so that they do not become bored 使某人快乐；使某人消遣：*Playing with water can keep children amused for hours.* 嬉水可以使孩子们玩好几个小时都不烦。

amuse·ment /əˈmjuːzmənt/ *noun* **1** [U] the feeling that you have when sth is funny or amusing, or it entertains you 可笑；愉悦；娱乐：*She could not hide her amusement at the way he was dancing.* 她见他跳舞的姿势，不禁笑出声来。◇ ***To my amusement** he couldn't get the door open.* 使我感到好笑的是，他竟然打不开门。◇ *Her eyes twinkled **with amusement**.* 她的眼睛闪耀着愉悦的光芒。 **2** [C, usually pl.] a game, an activity, etc. that provides entertainment and pleasure 娱乐活动；游戏；消遣活动：*traditional seaside amusements including boats, go-karts and a funfair* 包括乘船、微型赛车和露天游乐场的传统海滨娱乐活动

aˈmusement arcade (*BrE*) (*also* **ar·cade** *NAmE, BrE*) *noun* an indoor place where you can play games on machines which you use coins to operate 游戏机厅；电动游乐场

aˈmusement park *noun* a large park which has a lot of things that you can ride and play on and many different activities to enjoy 游乐场；娱乐园

amus·ing /əˈmjuːzɪŋ/ *adj.* funny and enjoyable 逗人笑的；有乐趣的；好笑的：*an amusing story/game/incident* 逗人笑的故事 / 游戏 / 事件 ◇ *I didn't find the joke at all amusing.* 我认为这笑话一点也不可笑。 ➲ SYNONYMS AT FUNNY ▶ **amus·ing·ly** *adv.*

amyg·dala /əˈmɪɡdələ/ *noun* (*pl.* **amyg·da·lae** /əˈmɪɡdəliː/) (*anatomy* 解) either of two areas in the brain that are linked to memory, the emotions and the sense of smell 杏仁核，杏仁体（大脑中的两个区域之一，与记忆、情绪及嗅觉有关）

amy·lase /ˈæmɪleɪz; *NAmE* ˈæməleɪs/ *noun* [U] (*chemistry* 化) an ENZYME (= a substance that helps a chemical change to take place) that allows the body to change some substances into simple sugars 淀粉酶

an *indefinite article* ➲A

-an, -ana ➲-IAN, -IANA

ana·bol·ic ster·oid /ˌænəbɒlɪk ˈsterɔɪd; ˈstɪə-; *NAmE* ˌænəbɑːlɪk ˈster-; ˈstɪr-/ *noun* an artificial HORMONE (= a chemical substance) that increases the size of the muscles. It is sometimes taken illegally by people who play sports. 同化激素类药，合成代谢类固醇（人工合成激素，能增大肌肉，有时被运动员违禁使用） ➲ SEE ALSO STEROID

an·achron·ism /əˈnækrənɪzəm/ *noun* **1** a person, a custom or an idea that seems old-fashioned and does not belong to the present 过时的人（或风俗、思想）：*The monarchy is seen by many people as an anachronism in the modern world.* 很多人认为君主制在现代世界不合时宜。 **2** something that is placed, for example in a book or play, in the wrong period of history 弄错年代；时代错误 ▶ **ana·chron·is·tic** /əˌnækrəˈnɪstɪk/ *adj.*

ana·conda /ˌænəˈkɒndə; *NAmE* -ˈkɑːn-/ *noun* a large S American snake of the BOA family, that crushes other animals to death before eating them 水蚺（南美洲蟒蛇）

an·aemia (*BrE*) (*NAmE* **an·e·mia**) /əˈniːmiə/ *noun* [U] a medical condition in which sb has too few red cells in their blood, making them look pale and feel weak 贫血（症）

an·aemic (*BrE*) (*NAmE* **an·emic**) /əˈniːmɪk/ *adj.* **1** suffering from anaemia 贫血的；患贫血症的：*She looks anaemic.* 她看来像是有贫血症。 **2** weak and not having much effect 衰弱无力的；无生气的 SYN **feeble**：*an anaemic performance* 一场有气无力的表演

an·aer·obic /ˌæneəˈrəʊbɪk; *NAmE* ˌæneˈroʊ-/ *adj.* **1** (*biology* 生) not needing OXYGEN 厌氧的：*anaerobic bacteria* 厌氧细菌 **2** (of physical exercise 身体锻炼) not especially designed to improve the function of the heart and lungs 无氧的（不专为改善心肺功能） OPP **aerobic**

an·aes·the·sia /ˌænəsˈθiːziə/ (*especially US* **an·es·the·sia** /ˌænəsˈθiːʒə/) *noun* [U] **1** the use of anaesthetics during medical operations 麻醉 **2** (*specialist*) the state of being unable to feel anything, especially pain 感觉缺失；麻木

an·aes·the·sio·logist (*especially US* **an·es·the·sio·logist**) /ˌænəsˌθiːziˈɒlədʒɪst; *NAmE* -ˈɑːlə-/ *noun* a doctor who studies the use of anaesthetics 麻醉师

an·aes·thet·ic (*especially US* **an·es·thet·ic**) /ˌænəsˈθetɪk/ *noun, adj.*

■ ***noun*** [U, C] a drug that makes a person or an animal unable to feel anything, especially pain, either in the whole body or in a part of the body 麻醉药；麻醉剂：*How long will I **be under anaesthetic**?* 我会处于麻醉状态多长时间？◇ *They gave him a **general anaesthetic*** (= one that makes you become unconscious). 他们对他施行了全身麻醉。◇ *(a) **local anaesthetic*** (= one that affects only a part of the body) 局部麻醉 ➲ WORDFINDER NOTE AT DENTIST, OPERATION

■ ***adj.*** [only before noun] containing a substance that makes a person or an animal unable to feel pain in all or part of the body 麻醉的：*an **anaesthetic drug/spray*** 麻醉药；麻醉喷剂

an·aes·the·tist (*especially US* **an·es·the·tist**) /əˈniːsθətɪst/ *noun* a person who is trained to give anaesthetics to patients 麻醉师

an·aes·the·tize (*BrE also* **-ise**) (*especially US* **an·es·the·tize**) /əˈniːsθətaɪz/ *verb* **~ sb** to make a person unable to feel pain, etc., especially by giving them an anaesthetic before a medical operation 使麻醉；使麻木

A

ana·gram /ˈænəɡræm/ *noun* a word or phrase that is made by arranging the letters of another word or phrase in a different order 相同字母异序词：*An anagram of 'Elvis' is 'lives'.* * lives 是 Elvis 的一个异序词。

anal /ˈeɪnl/ *adj.* **1** connected with or located near the ANUS 肛门的：*the anal region* 肛区 **2** (*also* **ˌanal-reˈtentive**) (*disapproving*) caring too much about small details and about how things are organized 挑剔枝节的；专注小事的 ▶ **anal·ly** /-nəli/ *adv.*

an·al·gesia /ˌænəlˈdʒiːziə; *NAmE* -ʒə/ *noun* [U] (*medical* 医) the loss of the ability to feel pain while still conscious 镇痛；痛觉缺失

an·al·gesic /ˌænəlˈdʒiːzɪk/ *noun* (*medical* 医) a substance that reduces pain 止痛药；镇痛剂 SYN **painkiller**: *Aspirin is a mild analgesic.* 阿司匹林是药性平和的止痛药。 ▶ **an·al·gesic** *adj.* : **analgesic drugs/effects** 止痛药；止痛效果

analo·gous AW /əˈnæləɡəs/ *adj.* (*formal*) ~ (**to/with sth**) similar in some way to another thing or situation and therefore able to be compared with it 相似的；类似的：*Sleep has often been thought of as being in some way analogous to death.* 人们常常认为睡眠在某种意义上来说类似死亡。

ana·logue (*BrE*) (*NAmE* **ana·log**) /ˈænəlɒɡ; *NAmE* -lɔːɡ; -lɑːɡ/ *adj., noun*

■ ***adj.*** (*specialist*) **1** (of an electronic process 电子处理方法) using a continuously changing range of physical quantities to measure or store data 模拟的：*an* ***analogue circuit/computer/signal*** 模拟线路 / 计算机 / 信号 **2** (*BrE also* **ana·log**) (of a clock or watch 钟表) showing the time using hands on a DIAL and not with a display of numbers 指针式的 ➲ COMPARE DIGITAL *adj.* (2)

■ ***noun*** (*formal* or *specialist*) a thing that is similar to another thing 相似物；类似事情：*Scientists are attempting to compare features of extinct animals with living analogues.* 科学家正试图把已灭绝动物的特征与现存类似动物的相比较。

ana·logy AW /əˈnælədʒi/ *noun* (*pl.* **-ies**) **1** [C] a comparison of one thing with another thing that has similar features; a feature that is similar 类比；比拟；相似之处：~ (**between A and B**) *The teacher* ***drew an analogy*** *between the human heart and a pump.* 老师打了个比喻，把人的心脏比作水泵。◇ ~ (**with sth**) *There are no analogies with any previous legal cases.* 以往的法律案件没有哪一宗可与此案类比。 **2** [U] the process of comparing one thing with another thing that has similar features in order to explain it 类推；比拟：*learning* ***by analogy*** 用类推法学习

an·al·pha·bet·ic /ˌænælfəˈbetɪk/ *adj.* **1** (*specialist*) completely unable to read or write 全文盲的；完全不懂读写的 **2** = NON-ALPHABETIC **3** (*linguistics* 语言) representing sounds with signs made of several parts rather than by single letters or symbols 非拼音的；非字母的

ˌanal-reˈtentive *adj.* (*disapproving*) = ANAL (2)

ana·lyse 🔑 AW (*BrE*) (*NAmE* **ana·lyze**) /ˈænəlaɪz/ *verb* **1** 🔑 to examine the nature or structure of sth, especially by separating it into its parts, in order to understand or explain it 分析：~ **sth** *The job involves gathering and analysing data.* 这项工作包括收集和分析资料。◇ *He tried to analyse his feelings.* 他试图分析自己的感情。◇ ~ **what, how, etc....** *We need to analyse what went wrong.* 我们需要分析是什么出了差错。 ➲ SYNONYMS AT EXAMINE **2** ~ **sb** = PSYCHOANALYSE

an·aly·sis 🔑 AW /əˈnæləsɪs/ *noun* (*pl.* **an·aly·ses** /-siːz/) **1** 🔑 [U, C] the detailed study or examination of sth in order to understand more about it; the result of the study （对事物的）分析，分析结果：*statistical analysis* 统计分析 ◇ *The book is an analysis of poverty and its causes.* 这本书分析了贫困及其原因。 **2** 🔑 [U, C] a careful examination of a substance in order to find out what it consists of （对物质成分的）分析：*The blood samples are sent to the laboratory* ***for analysis.*** 血样要送往实验室进行分析。◇ *You can ask for a chemical analysis of your tap water.* 你可以要求给你的自来水做化学分析。 **3** [U] = PSYCHOANALYSIS : *In analysis the individual resolves difficult emotional conflicts.* 在心理分析治疗法中，个人可以化解严重的情感冲突。 ➲ WORDFINDER NOTE AT SCIENCE

IDM **in the ˌfinal/ˌlast aˈnalysis** used to say what is most important after everything has been discussed, or considered 归根结底；总之：*In the final analysis, it's a matter of personal choice.* 归根结底，这是个人的选择。

ana·lyst AW /ˈænəlɪst/ *noun* **1** a person whose job involves examining facts or materials in order to give an opinion on them 分析者；化验员：*a political/food analyst* 政治分析家；食物化验员 ◇ *City analysts forecast huge profits this year.* 伦敦金融分析家预测今年的利润非常丰厚。 ➲ SEE ALSO SYSTEMS ANALYST **2** = PSYCHOANALYST

ana·lyt·ic AW /ˌænəˈlɪtɪk/ *adj.* **1** = ANALYTICAL **2** (*also* **isol·at·ing**) (*linguistics* 语言) (of languages 语言) using word order rather than word endings to show the functions of words in a sentence 分析的，分析型的（用词序而非词尾显示词在句中的功能） ➲ COMPARE SYNTHETIC *adj.* (2), AGGLUTINATIVE

ana·lyt·ic·al AW /ˌænəˈlɪtɪkl/ (*also* **ana·lyt·ic**) *adj.* **1** using a logical method of thinking about sth in order to understand it, especially by looking at all the parts separately 分析的；解析的；分析性的：*She has a clear analytical mind.* 她头脑清醒，善于分析。◇ *an analytic approach to the problem* 用分析方法处理这个问题 **2** using scientific analysis in order to find out about sth （科学）分析的：*analytical methods of research* 分析研究法 ▶ **ana·lyt·ic·al·ly** AW /-kli/ *adv.*

ana·lyt·ics /ˌænəˈlɪtɪks/ *noun* [U] a thorough analysis of data using a model, usually performed by a computer; information resulting from this analysis（通常通过计算机利用模型所做的）数据分析；数据分析结果：*web/business analytics* 网站 / 商业数据分析

ana·lyze AW (*NAmE*) = ANALYSE

ana·paest /ˈænəpiːst; -pest/ (*BrE*) (*NAmE* **ana·pest** /ˈænəpest/) *noun* (*specialist*) a unit of sound in poetry consisting of two weak or short syllables followed by one strong or long syllable 抑抑扬格（诗歌中由两轻一重或两短一长音节组成的音步） ▶ **ana·paes·tic** (*BrE*) (*NAmE* **ana·pes·tic**) /ˌænəˈpiːstɪk; -ˈpestɪk; *NAmE* ˌænəˈpestɪk/ *adj.*

anaphor /ˈænəfə(r); -fɔː(r)/ *noun* (*grammar* 语法) a word or phrase that refers back to an earlier word or phrase. For example, in the phrase 'My mother said she was leaving', 'she' is used as an anaphor for 'my mother'. 照应语，回指语（返指上文中的词或词组）

anaph·ora /əˈnæfərə/ *noun* [U] the use of a word that refers to or replaces another word used earlier in a sentence, for example the use of 'does' in the sentence 'I disagree and so does John' 逆向照应（下文的词返指或代替上文的词） ▶ **ana·phor·ic** /ˌænəˈfɒrɪk; *NAmE* -ˈfɔːr-; -ˈfɑːr-/ *adj.*

ana·phyl·axis /ˌænəfɪˈlæksɪs/ *noun* [U, C] (*pl.* **ana·phyl·axes** /ˌænəfɪˈlæksiːz/) (*medical* 医) an extreme ALLERGIC reaction to sth that you eat or touch 过敏反应 ▶ **ana·phyl·ac·tic** /ˌænəfɪˈlæktɪk/ *adj.* : *anaphylactic shock* 过敏性休克

an·arch·ism /ˈænəkɪzəm; *NAmE* ˈænərk-/ *noun* [U] the political belief that laws and governments are not necessary 无政府主义

an·arch·ist /ˈænəkɪst; *NAmE* ˈænərk-/ *noun* a person who believes that laws and governments are not necessary 无政府主义者 ▶ **an·arch·is·tic** /ˌænəˈkɪstɪk; *NAmE* ˌænərˈk-/ *adj.*

an·archy /ˈænəki; *NAmE* ˈænərki/ *noun* [U] a situation in a country, an organization, etc. in which there is no government, order or control 无政府状态；混乱；无法无天：*The overthrow of the military regime was followed by a period of anarchy.* 军事统治政权被推翻以后，接着是

一段时期的无政府状态。◇ *There was complete anarchy in the classroom when their usual teacher was away.* 任课老师不在时，班上一片混乱。 ▶ **an·arch·ic** /əˈnɑːkɪk; *NAmE* əˈnɑːrkɪk/ (*also less frequent* **an·arch·ic·al** /-kl/) *adj.*

anath·ema /əˈnæθəmə/ *noun* [U, C, usually sing.] (*formal*) a thing or an idea which you hate because it is the opposite of what you believe 可憎的事物；可恶的想法：*Racial prejudice is (an) anathema to me.* 对我来说，种族歧视非常可恶。

anato·mist /əˈnætəmɪst/ *noun* a scientist who studies anatomy 解剖学家

anat·omy /əˈnætəmi/ *noun* (*pl.* **-ies**) **1** [U] the scientific study of the structure of human or animal bodies 解剖学 **2** [C, U] the structure of an animal or a plant （动植物的）结构，解剖：*the anatomy of the horse* 马的身体构造 ◇ *human anatomy* 人体解剖 **3** [C] (*humorous*) a person's body 人体：*Various parts of his anatomy were clearly visible.* 他身体的各个部位都清晰可见。 **4** [C] (*formal*) an examination of what sth is like or why it happens 剖析；解析：*an anatomy of the current recession* 对当前经济衰退的剖析 ▶ **ana·tom·ical** /ˌænəˈtɒmɪkl; *NAmE* -ˈtɑːm-/ *adj.*：*anatomical diagrams* 解剖示意图 **ana·tom·ic·al·ly** /-kli/ *adv.*

ANC /ˌeɪ en ˈsiː/ *abbr.* African National Congress (= a political party in South Africa) 非洲人国民大会（南非政党）

-ance, **-ence** *suffix* (in nouns 构成名词) the action or state of（表示行动或状况）：*assistance* 帮助 ◇ *confidence* 信心 ➲ MORE LIKE THIS 7, page R25

an·ces·tor /ˈænsestə(r)/ *noun* **1** a person in your family who lived a long time ago 祖宗；祖先 SYN **forebear**：*His ancestors had come to America from Ireland.* 他的祖先从爱尔兰来到美国。 ➲ WORDFINDER NOTE AT RELATION **2** an animal that lived in the past which a modern animal has developed from （动物的）原始种型：*a reptile that was the common ancestor of lizards and turtles* 作为蜥蜴和龟的共同原种的一种爬行动物 **3** an early form of a machine which later became more developed（机器的）原型 SYN **forerunner**：*The ancestor of the modern bicycle was called a penny-farthing.* 现代自行车的原型称作 penny-farthing（一种前轮大后轮小的自行车）。 ➲ COMPARE DESCENDANT ▶ **an·ces·tral** /ænˈsestrəl/ *adj.*：*her ancestral home* (= that had belonged to her ancestors) 她的祖居

an·ces·try /ˈænsestri/ *noun* [C, usually sing., U] (*pl.* **-ies**) the family or the race of people that you come from（统称）祖宗，祖先；列祖列宗：*to have Scottish ancestry* 祖籍苏格兰 ◇ *He was able to trace his ancestry back over 1 000 years.* 他可追祖溯宗至 1 000 多年以前。

anchor 锚

an·chor /ˈæŋkə(r)/ *noun, verb*

■ *noun* **1** [C, U] a heavy metal object that is attached to a rope or chain and dropped over the side of a ship or boat to keep it in one place 锚：*to* ***drop anchor*** 抛锚 ◇ *The ship lay* ***at anchor*** *two miles off the rocky coast.* 船在离岩岸两英里处抛锚停泊。 ◇ *We* ***weighed anchor*** (= pulled it out of the water). 我们起锚。 **2** [C] a person or thing that gives sb a feeling of safety 给以安全感的人（或物）；精神支柱；顶梁柱：*the anchor of the family* 全家的顶梁柱 **3** [C] (*especially NAmE*) = ANCHORMAN, ANCHORWOMAN ➲ MORE LIKE THIS 25, page R28

■ *verb* **1** [I, T] ~ (sth) to let an anchor down from a boat or ship in order to prevent it from moving away 抛锚；下锚：*We anchored off the coast of Spain.* 我们在西班牙沿海抛锚停泊。 **2** [T] ~ **sth** to fix sth firmly in position so that it cannot move 使固定；扣牢；系牢：*Make sure the table is securely anchored.* 务必要把桌子固定好。 **3** [T, usually passive] ~ **sb/sth** (**in/to sth**) to firmly base sth on sth else 使扎根；使基于：*Her novels are anchored in everyday experience.* 她的小说取材自日常生活经验。 **4** [I, T] ~ (**sth**) (*especially NAmE*) to be the person who introduces reports or reads the news on television or radio 主持（电视、广播节目）：*She anchored the evening news for seven years.* 她主持了七年晚间新闻报道。

an·chor·age /ˈæŋkərɪdʒ/ *noun* [C, U] **1** a place where ships or boats can anchor （船的）锚（泊）地 **2** a place where sth can be fastened to sth else 固定处；扣牢处；系牢点：*anchorage points for a baby's car seat* 汽车安全座椅的固定点

an·chor·man /ˈæŋkəmæn; *NAmE* -kərm-/, **an·chor·woman** /ˈæŋkəwʊmən; *NAmE* -kərw-/ *noun* (*pl.* **-men** /-men/, **-women** /-wɪmɪn/) (*also* **an·chor** *especially in NAmE*) a man or woman who presents a live radio or television programme and introduces reports by other people（电台、电视现场直播的）节目主持人 ➲ MORE LIKE THIS 25, page R28

an·chovy /ˈæntʃəvi; *NAmE* -tʃoʊvi/ *noun* [C, U] (*pl.* **-ies**) a small fish with a strong salty flavour 鳀（咸水小鱼）：*a pizza topped with cheese and anchovies* 奶酪鳀鱼比萨饼

an·cient 🔑 /ˈeɪnʃənt/ *adj.* **1** 🔑 belonging to a period of history that is thousands of years in the past 古代的：***ancient history/civilization*** 古代史；古代文明 ◇ *ancient Greece* 古希腊 OPP **modern** **2** 🔑 very old; having existed for a very long time 古老的；很老的：*an ancient oak tree* 古橡树 ◇ *ancient monuments* 古迹 ◇ (*humorous*) *He's ancient—he must be at least fifty!* 他老得很了，肯定至少有五十岁！ **3 the ancients** *noun* [pl.] the people who lived in ancient times, especially the Egyptians, Greeks and Romans（尤指古埃及、古希腊和古罗马的）古代人 ▶ **an·cient·ly** *adv.* (*formal*)：*the area where the market was anciently held* (= in ancient times) 古代集市所在地

an·cil·lary /ænˈsɪləri; *NAmE* ˈænsəleri/ *adj.* ~ (**to sth**) **1** providing necessary support to the main work or activities of an organization 辅助的；补充的 SYN **auxiliary**：***ancillary staff/services/equipment*** 辅助人员 / 服务设施 / 设备 ◇ ***ancillary workers*** *in the health service such as cooks and cleaners* 公共医疗部门中诸如厨师和清洁工之类的辅助人员 **2** in addition to sth else but not as important 附属的；附加的：*ancillary rights* 附属权利

-ancy, **-ency** *suffix* (in nouns 构成名词) the state or quality of（表示状况或性质）：*expectancy* 期待 ◇ *complacency* 自满

and 🔑 /ənd; ən; *BrE also* n; *strong form* ænd/ *conj.* (used to connect words or parts of sentences 用于连接单词或句中并列部分) **1** 🔑 also; in addition to 和；与；又；而：*bread and butter* 涂黄油的面包 ◇ *a table, two chairs and a desk* 一张桌子、两把椅子和一张办公桌 ◇ *Sue and I left early.* 我和休早离开了。 ◇ *Do it slowly and carefully.* 要慢慢仔细地做。 ◇ *Can he read and write?* 他能读会写吗？ ◇ *I cooked lunch. And I made a cake.* (= you are emphasizing how much you have done) 我做了午饭，还做了一个蛋糕。 HELP When **and** is used in common phrases connecting two things or people that are closely linked, the determiner is not usually repeated before the second: *a knife and fork* ◇ *my father and mother*, but: *a knife and a spoon* ◇ *my father and my uncle.* 如果 and 在一般短语中连接两个联系密切的人或事物，第二个单词前的限定词通常省略：a knife and fork、my father and mother，而 a knife and a spoon、my father and my uncle 则不省略。 **2** 🔑 added to 加；加上 SYN **plus**[1]：*5 and 5 makes 10.* * 5 加 5 等于 10。 ◇ *What's 47 and 16?* * 47 加 16 得多少？ HELP When numbers (but not dates) are spoken, **and** is used between the hundreds and the figures that follow:

A

2 264—two thousand, two hundred **and** *sixty-four*, but: *1964—nineteen sixty-four*. 口语中说数字时（日期除外），and 用于百位数与紧跟的数之间：2 264 说 two thousand, two hundred and sixty-four，但 1964 年只说 nineteen sixty-four。 **3** then; following this 然后；接着：*She came in and took her coat off.* 她进来后脱了外衣。 **4** **go, come, try, stay, etc.** ~ used before a verb instead of *to*, to show purpose （用于动词前代替 to，表示目的）…为了：*Go and get me a pen please.* 请你去给我拿支钢笔来。◇ *I'll come and see you soon.* 我很快就会来看你。◇ *We stopped and bought some bread.* 我们停下来买了一些面包。 HELP In this structure **try** can only be used in the infinitive or to tell somebody what to do. 在此结构中，try 只能用于不定式或祈使句：*Try and finish quickly.* 尽快完成。 **5** used to introduce a comment or a question （引出说话或提问）那么，于是：*'We talked for hours.' 'And what did you decide?'* "我们谈了好几小时。" "那么你们作出了什么决定？" **6** as a result （表示结果）结果是；那么；就：*Miss another class and you'll fail.* 你再缺一次课就会不及格。 **7** used between repeated words to show that sth is repeated or continuing （连接相同的词，表示反复或连续）接连，又，愈来愈：*He tried and tried but without success.* 他反复尝试，但没有成功。◇ *The pain got worse and worse.* 疼痛越来越厉害了。 **8** used between repeated words to show that there are important differences between things or people of the same kind. （连接相同的词，强调差别）与…不同，各有不同：*I like city life but there are cities and cities.* 我喜欢城市生活，但城市之间也有差异。 ➲ SEE ALSO AND/OR

an·dante /æn'dænteɪ/ *noun* (*music* 音, *from Italian*) a piece of music to be played fairly slowly 行板（速度稍缓） ▸ **an·dante** *adv., adj.*

and/or *conj.* (*informal*) used when you say that two situations exist together, or as an alternative to each other 和（或）；以及（或者）；和 / 或：*There is no help for those with lots of luggage and/or small children.* 对于行李多而且（或者）有小孩的人一点帮助都没有。

an·dro·gen /'ændrədʒən/ *noun* (*biology* 生) a male sex HORMONE, for example TESTOSTERONE 雄激素

an·drogy·nous /æn'drɒdʒənəs; *NAmE* -'drɑːdʒ-/ *adj.* having both male and female characteristics; looking neither strongly male nor strongly female 雌雄同体的；兼具两性的

Android™ /'ændrɔɪd/ *noun* [U] a type of OPERATING SYSTEM, designed for mobile devices, which controls the way the device works and runs APPS (= programs designed to do particular jobs)（移动设备的）安卓操作系统：*I've downloaded dozens of apps on my Android phone.* 我在我的安卓手机里下载了很多应用程序。

an·droid /'ændrɔɪd/ *noun* a ROBOT that looks like a real person 人形机器人

an·ec·dotal /ˌænɪk'dəʊtl; *NAmE* -'doʊtl/ *adj.* based on anecdotes and possibly not true or accurate 逸事的；趣闻的；传闻的：*anecdotal evidence* 传闻的证据 ▸ **an·ec·dot·al·ly** /-təli/ *adv.*：*This reaction has been reported anecdotally by a number of patients.* 一些患者据称有这种反应。

an·ec·dote /'ænɪkdəʊt; *NAmE* -doʊt/ *noun* [C, U] **1** a short, interesting or amusing story about a real person or event 逸事；趣闻：*amusing anecdotes about his brief career as an actor* 关于他短暂演员生涯的趣闻逸事 **2** a personal account of an event 传闻：*This research is based on anecdote, not fact.* 这项研究的根据是传闻，而非事实。

an·emia, **an·emic** (*NAmE*) = ANAEMIA, ANAEMIC

an·emom·eter /ˌænɪ'mɒmɪtə(r); *NAmE* -'mɑːm-/ (*also* **'wind gauge**) *noun* an instrument for measuring the speed of the wind or of a current of gas 风速计；风速表

anem·one /ə'neməni/ *noun* a small plant with white, red, blue or purple flowers that are shaped like cups and have dark centres 银莲花，风花（开杯形有黑心的白、红、蓝、紫花） ➲ SEE ALSO SEA ANEMONE

an·es·the·sia, **an·es·the·sio·logist**, **an·es·thet·ic**, **an·es·the·tist**, **an·es·the·tize** (*NAmE*) = ANAESTHESIA, ANAESTHESIOLOGIST, ANAESTHETIC, ANAESTHETIST, ANAESTHETIZE

an·eur·ysm /'ænjərɪzəm/ *noun* (*medical* 医) an area of extreme swelling on the wall of an ARTERY 动脉瘤

anew /ə'njuː; *NAmE* ə'nuː/ *adv.* (*formal*) if sb does sth **anew**, they do it again from the beginning or do it in a different way 重新；再：*They started life anew in Canada.* 他们在加拿大开始新生活。

angel /'eɪndʒl/ *noun* **1** a spirit who is believed to be a servant of God, and is sent by God to deliver a message or perform a task. Angels are often shown dressed in white, with wings. 天使 ➲ SEE ALSO GUARDIAN ANGEL **2** a person who is very good and kind; a child who behaves well 安琪儿（指善良的人或可爱的小孩）；善人：*John* **is no angel**, *believe me* (= he does not behave well). 相信我，约翰绝非善良之辈。 **3** (*informal*) used when you are talking to sb and you are grateful to them 大好人（感激某人时所说）：*Thanks Dad,* **you're an angel**. 谢谢爸爸，你是个大好人。◇ **Be an angel** *and make me a cup of coffee.* 行行好，给我冲杯咖啡。 IDM SEE FOOL *n.*

Angel·eno (*also* **Angel·ino**) /ˌændʒə'liːnəʊ; *NAmE* -'liːnoʊ/ *noun* (*pl.* **-os**) (*informal*) a person who lives in Los Angeles 洛杉矶人

angel·fish /'eɪndʒlfɪʃ/ *noun* (*pl.* **angel·fish** or **angel·fishes**) a type of brightly coloured FRESHWATER or SALTWATER fish with a thin deep body and long FINS 神仙鱼

'angel food cake *noun* [U, C] (*NAmE*) a light cake made with the white part of eggs and without fat, often baked in a ring shape 天使蛋糕，安琪儿蛋糕（用蛋白等做成的脱脂松软蛋糕，常为环状）

an·gel·ic /æn'dʒelɪk/ *adj.* good, kind or beautiful; like an angel 善良的；美丽的；天使般的：*an angelic smile* 天使般的微笑 ▸ **an·gel·ic·al·ly** /-kli/ *adv.*

an·gel·ica /æn'dʒelɪkə/ *noun* [U] pieces of a plant with a sweet smell, that have been boiled in sugar and are used to decorate cakes 白芷（糖渍可作甜点配饰）

an·gelus /'ændʒələs/ (*also* **the Angelus**) *noun* [sing.] (in the Roman Catholic Church 天主教) prayers said in the morning, at midday and in the evening; a bell rung when it is time for these prayers 三钟经（于晨、午、晚颂念）；三钟经的鸣钟

anger /'æŋɡə(r)/ *noun, verb*

■ ***noun*** [U] the strong feeling that you have when sth has happened that you think is bad and unfair 怒；怒火；怒气：*Jan slammed her fist on the desk* **in anger**. 简气愤地捶打桌子。◇ *the growing anger and frustration of young unemployed people* 年轻失业者日益增长的愤怒和沮丧◇ **~ at sb/sth** *He was filled with anger at the way he had been treated.* 他因遭受如此待遇而怒火满腔。

■ ***verb*** [often passive] **~ sb** to make sb angry 使发怒；激怒：*The question clearly angered him.* 这个问题显然激怒了他。

an·gina /æn'dʒaɪnə/ (*medical* 医 **an·gina pec·toris** /ænˌdʒaɪnə 'pektərɪs/) *noun* [U] severe pain in the chest caused by a low supply of blood to the heart during exercise because the ARTERIES are partly blocked 心绞痛

angio·plasty /'ændʒiəʊplæsti; *NAmE* 'ændʒioʊ-/ *noun* [C, U] (*pl.* **-ies**) (*medical* 医) a medical operation to repair or open a blocked BLOOD VESSEL, especially either of the two ARTERIES that supply blood to the heart 血管成形术（修复或打开栓塞的冠状动脉血管等）

angle /'æŋɡl/ *noun, verb*

■ ***noun*** **1** the space between two lines or surfaces that join, measured in degrees 角：*a 45° angle* * 45° 角 ➲ SEE ALSO ACUTE ANGLE, ADJACENT ANGLE, CORRESPONDING ANGLES, OBTUSE ANGLE, RIGHT ANGLE, WIDE-ANGLE LENS **2** the direction that sth is leaning or pointing in when it is not in a vertical or horizontal line 斜角；

角度：*The tower of Pisa leans **at an angle**.* 比萨斜塔塔身倾斜。◇ *The plane was coming in at a steep angle.* 飞机当时正俯冲降落。◇ *His hair was sticking up at all angles.* 他的头发都竖了起来，乱蓬蓬的。 **3** a position from which you look at sth 角度：*The photo was taken from an unusual angle.* 这张照片是从不寻常的角度拍摄的。 **4** a particular way of presenting or thinking about a situation, problem, etc. 观点；立场；角度：*We need a new angle for our next advertising campaign.* 我们需要从一个新的角度去展开下一次广告活动。◇ *You can look at the issue from many different angles.* 你可以从很多不同的角度看这个问题。◇ *The article concentrates on the human angle* (= the part that concerns people's emotions) *of the story.* 这篇文章集中讨论了故事中人的情感问题。

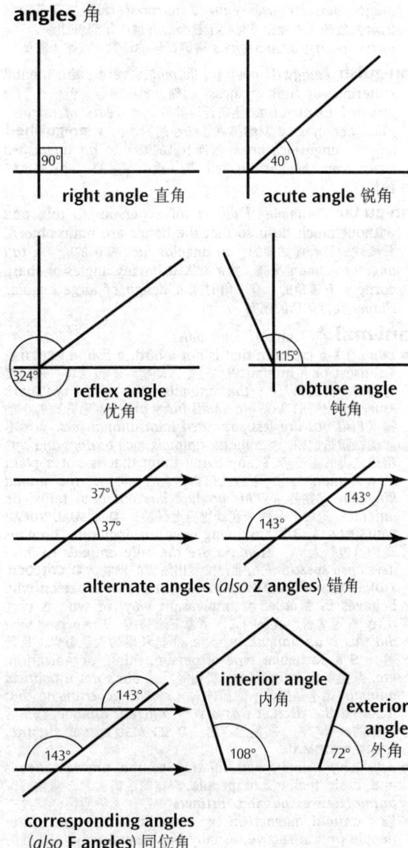

■ ***verb*** **1** [T] ~ **sth** to move or place sth so that it is not straight or not directly facing sb/sth 斜移；斜置：*He angled his chair so that he could sit and watch her.* 他斜移了椅子，以便坐着观察她。 **2** [T] ~ **sth** to present information, a report, etc. based on a particular way of thinking or for a particular audience 以（某角度）报道；以（某观点）提供信息：*The programme is angled towards younger viewers.* 这个节目的对象是较年轻的观众。 **3** (*usually* **go angling**) [I] to catch fish with a line and a hook 垂钓；钓鱼

PHR V **'angle for sth** to try to get a particular reaction or response from sb, without directly asking for what you want 转弯抹角地打听；博取：*She was angling for sympathy.* 她有意博取同情。

'angle bracket *noun* [usually pl.] one of a pair of marks, < >, used around words or figures to separate them from the surrounding text 尖角括号

ang·ler /ˈæŋɡlə(r)/ *noun* a person who catches fish (= goes angling) as a hobby 垂钓者 ➲ COMPARE FISHERMAN

An·gli·can /ˈæŋɡlɪkən/ *noun* a member of the Church of England or of a Church connected with it in another country 圣公会教徒 ▸ **An·gli·can** *adj.*：*the Anglican Church* 圣公会

An·gli·cism /ˈæŋɡlɪsɪzəm/ *noun* a word or phrase from the English language that is used in another language 英式用语，英式说法（指从英语中借用的词语）：*Many French people try to avoid Anglicisms such as 'weekend' and 'shopping'.* 很多法国人尽量避免使用 weekend 和 shopping 之类的英式用语。

an·gli·cize (*BrE also* **-ise**) /ˈæŋɡlɪsaɪz/ *verb* ~ **sb/sth** to make sb/sth English in character 使英语化；使英国化：*Gutmann anglicized his name to Goodman.* * Gutmann 把他的名字改为英语化的 Goodman。

an·gling /ˈæŋɡlɪŋ/ *noun* [U] the art or sport of catching fish with a FISHING ROD, usually in rivers and lakes rather than in the sea 垂钓

Anglo- /ˈæŋɡləʊ; *NAmE* ˈæŋɡloʊ/ *combining form* (in nouns and adjectives 构成名词和形容词) English or British 英格兰的；英国的：*Anglo-American* 英美的 ◇ *Anglophile* 亲英者 ◇ *Anglo-Indian* 英印的

ˌAnglo-ˈCatholic *noun* a member of the part of the Church of England that is most similar to the Roman Catholic Church in its beliefs and practices 英国国教高派教会教徒（英国圣公会内一派的教徒，信仰与礼仪与天主教最相似）

anglo·mania /ˌæŋɡləʊˈmeɪniə; *NAmE* ˌæŋɡloʊ-/ *noun* [U] extremely strong admiration for England or English customs 英格兰狂（对英格兰或英格兰习俗的迷恋）

ˌAnglo-ˈNorman *noun* [U] a form of Norman French spoken in England in the MIDDLE AGES 盎格鲁－诺曼语，英格兰法语（指中世纪英格兰人讲的诺曼法语）

Anglo·phile /ˈæŋɡləʊfaɪl; *NAmE* ˈæŋɡloʊ-/ *noun* a person who is not British but who likes Britain or British things very much 亲英者；崇英者

Anglo·pho·bia /ˌæŋɡləʊˈfəʊbiə; *NAmE* ˌæŋɡloʊˈfoʊbiə/ *noun* [U] hatred or fear of England or Britain 仇英；恐英 ▸ **Anglo·phobe** /ˈæŋɡləʊfəʊb; *NAmE* ˈæŋɡloʊfoʊb/ *noun*：*Her father was an Anglophobe.* 她父亲是个仇英分子。 **Anglo·phobic** /ˌæŋɡləʊˈfəʊbɪk; *NAmE* ˌæŋɡloʊˈfoʊbɪk/ *adj.*

anglo·phone /ˈæŋɡləʊfəʊn; *NAmE* -oʊfoʊn/ *noun* a person who speaks English, especially in countries where English is not the only language that is spoken 讲英语的人（尤指在英语非唯一语言的国家） ▸ **anglo·phone** *adj.*：*anglophone communities* 英语社区

ˌAnglo-ˈSaxon *noun* **1** [C] a person whose ANCESTORS were English 盎格鲁－撒克逊人（英格兰血统的人） **2** [C] an English person of the period before the Norman Conquest（诺曼征服以前的）英国人 **3** [U] the Old English language 盎格鲁－撒克逊语；古英语 ▸ **ˌAnglo-ˈSaxon** *adj.*：*Anglo-Saxon kings* 盎格鲁－撒克逊诸王

the Anglo·sphere /ˈæŋɡləʊsfɪə(r); *NAmE* ˈæŋɡloʊsfɪr/ *noun* [sing.] the group of countries where English is the main language 英语文化圈

an·gora /æŋˈɡɔːrə/ *noun* **1** [C] a breed of cat, GOAT or RABBIT that has long soft hair 安哥拉猫（或山羊、兔） **2** [U] a type of soft wool or cloth made from the hair of the angora GOAT or RABBIT 安哥拉山羊毛线（织物）；安哥拉兔毛线（织物）：*an angora sweater* 安哥拉羊毛套衫

An·gos·tura™ /ˌæŋɡəˈstjʊərə; NAmE -ˈstʊrə/ (*also* ˌ**Angos·tura ˈbitters**) *noun* [U] a bitter liquid, flavoured with the BARK of a tropical tree, that is used to give flavour to alcoholic drinks 安格斯托拉树树皮汁，苦精（用以调酒）

▼ **SYNONYMS 同义词辨析**

angry

mad • indignant • cross • irate

These words all describe people feeling and/or showing anger. 以上各词均形容人愤怒和/或发怒。

angry feeling or showing anger 指愤怒、发怒：*Please don't be angry with me.* 请别生我的气。◇ *Thousands of angry demonstrators filled the square.* 广场上聚满了成千上万的愤怒示威者。

mad [not before noun] (*informal, especially NAmE*) angry 指愤怒或发怒：*He got mad and walked out.* 他大动肝火，愤然离去。◇ *She's mad at me for being late.* 我迟到了，她非常生气。NOTE **Mad** is the usual word for 'angry' in informal American English. In British English, the phrase 'go mad' means 'very angry'. 在非正式的美式英语中，mad 为表示愤怒或发怒 (angry) 的常用词。在英式英语中，短语 go mad 表示非常气愤：*Dad'll go mad when he sees what you've done.* 父亲看到你的所作所为会非常气愤。'Go mad' can also mean 'go crazy' or 'get very excited'. * go mad 也可指发疯、发狂或激动起来。

indignant feeling or showing anger and surprise because you think that you or sb else has been treated unfairly 指因遭遇或见到不公平的事而愤慨、愤怒：*She was very indignant at the way she had been treated.* 她对自己受到的待遇大为光火。

cross (*especially BrE, rather informal*) rather angry or annoyed 指十分愤怒、恼怒：*I was quite cross with him for being late.* 我因他迟到而十分生气。NOTE This word is often used by or to children. 该词常为儿童用语或对儿童的用语。

irate very angry 指极其愤怒的、暴怒的：*irate customers* 愤怒的顾客 ◇ *an irate letter* 言辞激愤的信 NOTE **Irate** is not usually followed by a preposition. * irate 后通常不跟介词：~~*She was irate with me/about it.*~~

PATTERNS

- angry/mad/indignant/cross **about/at** sth
- angry/cross **with** sb (for doing sth)
- angry/mad/indignant/cross **that** ...
- to **get** angry/mad/cross
- to **make sb** angry/mad/cross

angry 🔑 /ˈæŋɡri/ *adj.* (**an·grier**, **an·gri·est**) HELP You can also use **more angry** and **most angry**. 亦可用 more angry 和 most angry。 **1** 🔑 having strong feelings about sth that you dislike very much or about an unfair situation 发怒的；愤怒的；生气的：*Her behaviour really **made me angry**.* 她的行为确实令我恼火。◇ *Thousands of angry demonstrators filled the square.* 广场上聚满了成千上万的愤怒示威者。◇ *The comments provoked an angry response from union leaders.* 这些评论激起了工会领导人的愤怒。◇ **~ with/at sb** *Please don't **be angry** with me. It wasn't my fault.* 请别冲着我发脾气，不是我的错。◇ **~ with/at sb about/for sth** *I was very angry with myself for making such a stupid mistake.* 我很生自己的气，竟犯了这样愚蠢的错误。◇ **~ at/about/over sth** *He felt angry at the injustice of the situation.* 他对这种不公的现象感到愤愤不平。◇ *The passengers grew angry about the delay.* 延误使乘客气愤起来。 **2** (of a wound 伤口) red and infected 红肿的；感染的；发炎的 **3** (*literary*) (of the sea or the sky 海或天空) dark and STORMY 狂风暴雨的；波涛汹涌的；天昏地暗的 ▸ **an·grily** 🔑 /-əli/ *adv.*：*Some senators reacted angrily to the President's remarks.* 一些参议员对总统的言辞感到愤怒，反应强烈。◇ *He swore angrily.* 他愤然咒骂。

angst /æŋst/ *noun* [U] (*from German*) a feeling of anxiety and worry about a situation, or about your life （对形势、事态、生活的）忧虑，焦虑：*songs full of teenage angst* 充满青少年焦虑的歌曲

ˈ**angst-ridden** *adj.* having feelings of angst 忧虑的；焦虑的：*a generation of angst-ridden adolescents* 焦虑躁动的青少年一代

ang·strom /ˈæŋstrəm/ *noun* (*chemistry* 化，*physics* 物) a very small unit of length, equal to 1×10^{-10} metre, used for measuring WAVELENGTHS and the distance between atoms 埃（长度单位，等于 10^{-10} 米，用于量度波长和原子间的距离）

angsty /ˈæŋsti/ *adj.* having or showing feelings of angst 忧虑的；焦虑的：*Stefan plays the role of a rebellious, angsty outsider who joins a terrorist cell.* 斯蒂芬扮演的角色叛逆、焦躁、不见容于社会，并加入了恐怖组织。◇ *angsty poetry/drama/lyrics* 格调忧郁的诗歌/戏剧/歌词

an·guish /ˈæŋɡwɪʃ/ *noun* [U] (*formal*) severe pain, mental suffering or unhappiness 剧痛；极度痛苦；苦恼：*He groaned in anguish.* 他痛苦地呻吟。◇ *Tears of anguish filled her eyes.* 她双眸噙满了伤心的泪水。▸ **an·guished** *adj.*：*anguished cries* 痛苦不堪的喊声 ◇ *an anguished letter from her prison cell* 她从狱中寄来的一封悲痛欲绝的信

an·gu·lar /ˈæŋɡjələ(r)/ *adj.* **1** (of a person 人) thin and without much flesh so that the bones are noticeable 瘦骨嶙峋的；骨瘦如柴的：*an angular face* 瘦削的脸 ◇ *a tall angular woman* 又高又瘦的女人 **2** having angles or sharp corners 有棱角的；有尖角的：*a design of large angular shapes* 大棱角形的图案

ani·mal 🔑 /ˈænɪml/ *noun, adj.*

■ ***noun*** **1** 🔑 a creature that is not a bird, a fish, a REPTILE, an insect or a human 兽；牲畜；动物（不包括鸟、鱼、爬行动物、昆虫和人）：*the animals and birds of South America* 南美的鸟兽 ◇ *a small furry animal* 毛茸茸的小动物 ◇ *Fish oils are less saturated than animal fats.* 鱼油不如动物脂肪饱和。◇ *domestic animals such as dogs and cats* 狗猫之类的家畜 **2** 🔑 any living thing that is not a plant or a human 动物（不包括植物和人的生物）：*the animal kingdom* 动物界 ◇ *This product has not been tested on animals.* 这种产品尚未在动物身上试验。➲ VISUAL VOCAB PAGES V12-13 **3** 🔑 any living creature, including humans 动物（包括人）：*Humans are the only animals to have developed speech.* 人是唯一发展出语言的动物。➲ COLLOCATIONS AT LIFE ➲ COMPARE VEGETABLE (1) **4** a person who behaves in a cruel or unpleasant way, or who is very dirty 衣冠禽兽；残暴的人；卑鄙下流的人：*The person who did this is an animal, a brute.* 干这种事的人是畜生，是野兽。 **5** a particular type of person, thing, organization, etc. 某类型的人（或事物、机构等）：*She's not a political animal.* 她不是搞政治的那种人。◇ *The government that followed the election was a very different animal.* 选举后产生的政府与前一届截然不同。➲ SEE ALSO DUMB ANIMAL, HIGHER ANIMALS

■ ***adj.*** [only before noun] relating to the physical needs and basic feelings of people 肉体的；肉欲的；情欲的：***animal desires/passion/instincts*** 兽欲；肉欲激情；情欲本能 ◇ ***animal magnetism*** (= a quality in sb that other people find attractive, usually in a sexual way) 对异性的吸引力

ˌ**animal conˈtrol officer** *noun* (*NAmE, formal*) a person whose job is to catch animals that are walking freely in the streets and do not seem to have a home 流浪动物管理员 ➲ COMPARE DOGCATCHER

ˌ**animal ˈhusbandry** *noun* [U] (*specialist*) farming that involves keeping animals to produce food 畜牧业

ˌ**animal ˈrights** *noun* [pl.] the rights of animals to be treated well, for example by not being hunted or used for medical research 动物权益（指获得善待，如不能猎杀或用于医学研究）：*His research work was attacked by **animal rights activists**.* 他的研究受到了动物权益维护者的抨击。

an·im·ate *verb, adj.*

■ ***verb*** /ˈænɪmeɪt/ **1 ~ sth** to make sth more lively or full of energy 使具活力；使生气勃勃：*A smile suddenly animated her face.* 她嫣然一笑，立显容光焕发。 **2** [usually passive] **~ sth** to make models, toys, etc. seem to move in a film/movie by rapidly showing slightly different pictures of them in a series, one after another 把…制作成动画片

■ ***adj.*** /ˈænɪmət/ (*formal*) living; having life 有生命的；有活力的；有生气的：*animate beings* 生物 OPP **inanimate**

ani·mated /ˈænɪmeɪtɪd/ *adj.* **1** full of interest and energy 兴致勃勃的；活跃的；生气勃勃的 SYN **lively**：*an **animated discussion/conversation*** 热烈的讨论；兴致勃勃的交谈 ◇ *Her face suddenly became animated.* 她的表情突然变得生动起来。 **2** (of pictures, drawings, etc. in a film/movie 电影的画面、图画等) made to look as if they are moving 栩栩如生的；（似）能活动的：***animated cartoons/graphics/models*** 动画片；活动图形 / 模型 ▶ **ani·mated·ly** *adv.*：*People were talking animatedly.* 人们热烈地交谈着。

an·ima·teur /ˌænɪməˈtɜː(r)/ *noun* (*from French*) a person whose job is to organize or encourage artistic or social projects and activities （艺术或社会活动的）发起人，倡导者

ani·ma·tion /ˌænɪˈmeɪʃn/ *noun* **1** [U] energy and enthusiasm in the way you look, behave or speak 生气；活力；富有生命力：*His face was drained of all colour and animation.* 他面如死灰。 ➲ SEE ALSO SUSPENDED ANIMATION **2** [U] the process of making films/movies, videos and computer games in which drawings or models of people and animals seem to move（电影、录像、电脑游戏的）动画制作：***computer/cartoon animation*** 电脑动画 / 动画片制作 ➲ WORDFINDER NOTE AT SOFTWARE **3** [C] a film/movie in which drawings of people and animals seem to move 动画片：*The electronic dictionary included some animations.* 这个电子词典中有一些动画片。

ani·ma·tor /ˈænɪmeɪtə(r)/ *noun* a person who makes animated films 动画片制作者；动画片绘制者

anima·tron·ics /ˌænɪməˈtrɒnɪks; *NAmE* -ˈtrɑːn-/ *noun* [U] the process of making and operating ROBOTS that look like real people or animals, used in films/movies and other types of entertainment 电子动画制作技术（电影等制作中机器人或动物的制造和操作） ▶ **anima·tron·ic** *adj.*

anime /ˈænɪmeɪ; ˈænɪmə/ *noun* [U] Japanese film/movie and television ANIMATION, often with a SCIENCE FICTION subject 日本动画片（常以科幻为主题）

ani·mism /ˈænɪmɪzəm/ *noun* [U] **1** the belief that plants, objects and natural things such as the weather have a living soul 泛灵论；万物有灵论 **2** belief in a power that organizes and controls the universe 神力主宰论（认为有某种力量掌管宇宙） ▶ **ani·mist** /ˈænɪmɪst/ *noun* **ani·mis·tic** /ˌænɪˈmɪstɪk/ *adj.*

ani·mos·ity /ˌænɪˈmɒsəti; *NAmE* -ˈmɑːs-/ *noun* [U, C] (*pl.* **-ies**) a strong feeling of opposition, anger or hatred 仇恨；愤怒；敌意；憎恶 SYN **hostility**：**~ (toward(s) sb/sth)** *He felt no animosity towards his critics.* 他对批评他的人并不心怀怨恨。 ◇ **~ (between A and B)** *personal animosities between members of the two groups* 两个集团成员之间的私仇

ani·mus /ˈænɪməs/ *noun* [U, sing.] **~ (against sb/sth)** (*formal*) a strong feeling of opposition, anger or hatred 仇恨；愤怒；敌意

anion /ˈænaɪən/ *noun* (*chemistry* 化, *physics* 物) an ION with a negative electrical CHARGE 负离子；阴离子 ➲ COMPARE CATION

anise /ˈænɪs/ *noun* [U] a plant with seeds that have a strong sweet smell and taste 茴芹

ani·seed /ˈænəsiːd/ *noun* [U] the dried seeds of the anise plant, used to give flavour to alcoholic drinks and sweets/candy 茴芹籽（用于为酒精饮料及糖果提味）

ankh /æŋk/ *noun* an object or design like a cross but with a LOOP instead of the top arm, sometimes worn as jewellery. The ankh was used in ancient Egypt as the symbol of life. 安可（顶部为环状结构的"十"字，古埃及用以象征生命）

ankh 安可

ankle 🔑 /ˈæŋkl/ *noun* the joint connecting the foot to the leg 踝；踝关节：*to **sprain/break your ankle*** 扭伤 / 折断踝关节 ◇ *My ankles have swollen.* 我的两个脚腕子都肿了。 ◇ *We found ourselves **ankle-deep** in water* (= the water came up to our ankles). 水淹到了我们的脚踝。 ◇ ***ankle boots*** (= that cover the ankle) 及踝短筒靴 ➲ VISUAL VOCAB PAGE V64

ˈankle sock (*BrE*) (*US* **ank·let**) *noun* a type of very short sock 套袜，船袜（只及踝关节处）：*a girl in a blue dress and ankle socks* 身穿蓝色连衣裙和船袜的女孩

ank·let /ˈæŋklət/ *noun* **1** a piece of jewellery worn around the ankle 脚镯；踝环 **2** (*US*) (*BrE* **ˈankle sock**) a type of very short sock 套袜，船袜（只及踝关节处）

an·ky·lo·saur /ˈæŋkɪləsɔː(r)/ *noun* a type of plant-eating DINOSAUR covered with hard plates made of bone for protection 甲龙（食草恐龙，全身披甲）

anna /ˈʌnə/ *noun* (*IndE*) **1** an older brother 哥哥；兄长 **2** the leader of a group of young people who go around together and sometimes cause trouble 小混混头儿；（青少年帮派的）老大

annals /ˈænlz/ *noun* [pl.] **1** an official record of events or activities year by year; historical records 编年史；历史记载：*His deeds went down **in the annals of** British history.* 他的事迹已载入英国史册。 **2** used in the title of academic JOURNALS（用于学术杂志的名称）年报，年鉴：*Annals of Science, vol. viii*《科学年报》卷八

an·neal /əˈniːl/ *verb* **~ sth** (*specialist*) to heat metal or glass and allow it to cool slowly, in order to make it stronger or softer 给（金属或玻璃）退火

annex /əˈneks/ *verb* **~ sth** (*formal*) to take control of a country, region, etc., especially by force 强占，并吞（国家、地区等） SYN **occupy**：*Germany annexed Austria in 1938.* * 1938 年德国吞并了奥地利。 ▶ **an·nex·ation** /ˌænekˈseɪʃn/ *noun* [U, C]

an·nexe (*BrE*) (*also* **annex** *NAmE, BrE*) /ˈæneks/ *noun* **1** a building that is added to, or is near, a larger one and that provides extra living or work space 附属建筑物；附加建筑物：*Our rooms were in the annexe.* 我们的房间在附属建筑物里。 **2** (*formal*) an extra section of a document （文件的）附件，附录 SYN **appendix**

an·ni·hi·late /əˈnaɪəleɪt/ *verb* **1 ~ sb/sth/yourself** to destroy sb/sth completely 消灭；歼灭；毁灭：*The human race has enough weapons to annihilate itself.* 人类有足够的武器灭绝自己。 **2 ~ sb/sth** to defeat sb/sth completely 彻底击败：*She annihilated her opponent, who failed to win a single game.* 她大获全胜，对方连一局也没有赢。 ▶ **an·ni·hi·la·tion** /əˌnaɪəˈleɪʃn/ *noun* [U]：*the annihilation of the whole human race* 全人类的毁灭

an·ni·ver·sary 🔑 /ˌænɪˈvɜːsəri; *NAmE* -ˈvɜːrs-/ *noun* (*pl.* **-ies**) a date that is an exact number of years after the

A

date of an important or special event 周年纪念日： *on the anniversary of his wife's death* 在他妻子去世的周年忌日 ◇ *to celebrate your **wedding anniversary*** 庆祝结婚纪念日 ◇ *the theatre's 25th anniversary celebrations* 剧院 25 周年庆祝活动 ➲ WORDFINDER NOTE AT CELEBRATE ➲ COLLOCATIONS AT MARRIAGE

an·no·tate /ˈænəteɪt/ *verb* **~ sth** to add notes to a book or text, giving explanations or comments 给…作注解（或评注） ▸ **an·no·ta·tion** /ˌænəˈteɪʃn/ *noun* [C, U]: *It will be published with annotations and an index.* 这本书出版时将附有注释和索引。 **an·no·tated** *adj.*： *an annotated edition* 附有注解的版本

an·nounce /əˈnaʊns/ *verb* **1** to tell people sth officially, especially about a decision, plans, etc. 宣布，宣告（决定、计划等）： **~ sth** *They haven't formally announced their engagement yet.* 他们还没有正式宣布订婚。 ◇ (*figurative*) *A ring at the doorbell announced Jack's arrival.* 门铃一响就知道杰克驾到。 ◇ **~ that…** *We are pleased to announce that all five candidates were successful.* 我们高兴地宣布，五位候选人全都当选了。 ◇ **it is announced that…** *It was announced that new speed restrictions would be introduced.* 据宣布，将有新的限速规定出台。 ◇ **~ sth to sb** *The government yesterday announced to the media plans to create a million new jobs.* 政府昨天向媒体宣布了创造一百万个新工作的计划。 HELP You cannot 'announce somebody something'. 不能说 announce somebody something: ~~*They announced us their decision.*~~ ➲ SYNONYMS AT DECLARE **2** to give information about sth in a public place, especially through a LOUDSPEAKER （尤指通过广播）通知： **~ sth** *Has our flight been announced yet?* 广播通知了我们的航班没有？ ◇ **+ speech** *'Now boarding flight 897, destination Seattle,' the loudspeaker announced.* "飞往西雅图的 897 次航班现在开始登机。"广播通知说。 ◇ **~ that…** *They announced that the flight would be delayed.* 广播通知，该航班将晚点。 **3** to say sth in a loud and/or serious way 声称；宣称： **+ speech** *'I've given up smoking,' she announced.* "我戒烟了。"她郑重其事地说。 ◇ **~ that…** *She announced that she'd given up smoking.* 她宣称已戒烟。 ➲ SYNONYMS AT DECLARE **4** **~ yourself/sb** to tell sb your name or sb else's name when you or they arrive at a place 宣布（某人）到达；通报…的到来： *Would you announce the guests as they arrive?* (= call out their names, for example at a formal party) 客人到达时请你通报他们的姓名好吗？ **5** **~ sth** to introduce, or to give information about, a programme on the radio or television （在广播或电视中）播音，广播 ➲ WORDFINDER NOTE AT RADIO

an·nounce·ment /əˈnaʊnsmənt/ *noun* **1** [C] a spoken or written statement that informs people about sth （一项）公告，布告，通告： *to **make an announcement*** 发表公告 ◇ *Today's announcement of a peace agreement came after weeks of discussion.* 经过几周的讨论之后，今天公布了和平协议。 ◇ *Announcements of births, marriages and deaths appear in some newspapers.* 有些报纸刊登出生、结婚、死亡通告。 ➲ SYNONYMS AT STATEMENT **2** [U] the act of publicly informing people about sth （指行动）宣布，宣告： *Announcement of the verdict was accompanied by shouts and cheers.* 在一片喊叫和欢呼声中宣布了正式判决。

an·noun·cer /əˈnaʊnsə(r)/ *noun* **1** a person who introduces, or gives information about, programmes on the radio or television （广播、电视的）广播员，播音员，节目主持人 ➲ SEE ALSO HOST *n.* (3), PRESENTER (1) **2** a person who gives information about sth in a station, an airport, etc., especially through a LOUDSPEAKER （车站、机场等的）广播员，播音员

annoy /əˈnɔɪ/ *verb* **1** to make sb slightly angry 使恼怒；使生气 SYN **irritate**： **~ sb** *His constant joking was beginning to annoy her.* 他不停地开玩笑，已开始惹她生气。 ◇ **it annoys sb when…** *It really annoys me when people forget to say thank you.* 有人连谢谢都忘记说时我确实感到不愉快。 ◇ **~ sb to do sth** *It annoys me to see him getting ahead of me.* 我看见他领先于我就心里不痛快。 **2** **~ sb** to make sb uncomfortable or unable to relax 打扰；骚扰 SYN **bother**： *He swatted a fly that was annoying him.* 他猛力拍打一只搅得他心烦的苍蝇。

an·noy·ance /əˈnɔɪəns/ *noun* **1** [U] the feeling of being slightly angry 恼怒；生气；烦恼 SYN **irritation**： *He could not conceal his annoyance at being interrupted.* 他因受扰而难掩怒色。 ◇ ***Much to our annoyance**, they decided not to come after all.* 他们最终决定不来，使我们很生气。 ◇ *She stamped her foot **in annoyance**.* 她气得直跺脚。 **2** [C] something that makes you slightly angry 使人烦恼的事；令人生气的事物： *The delay is now shorter but still an annnoyance.* 延迟的时间现在变短了，但还是让人厌烦。

annoy·ed /əˈnɔɪd/ *adj.* [not usually before noun] slightly angry 恼怒；生气；烦恼 SYN **irritated**： **~ (with sb) (at/about sth)** *He was beginning to get very annoyed with me about my carelessness.* 因为我粗心大意，他已开始恼火了。 ◇ *I was **annoyed with myself** for giving in so easily.* 我气自己那么轻易就让步了。 ◇ *I bet she was annoyed at having to write it out again.* 我敢说她对不得不重写一遍感到恼火。 ◇ **~ that…** *I was annoyed that they hadn't turned up.* 我恼怒的是他们一直没有露面。 ◇ **~ to find, see, etc.** *He was annoyed to find himself going red.* 他因为发觉自己脸红而懊恼。

annoy·ing /əˈnɔɪɪŋ/ *adj.* making sb feel slightly angry 使恼怒的；使生气的；使烦恼的 SYN **irritating**: *This interruption is very annoying.* 这样打岔令人讨厌。 ◇ *Her most annoying habit was eating with her mouth open.* 她最让人讨厌的习惯就是张着嘴吃东西。 ▸ **an·noy·ing·ly** *adv.*

an·nual AW /ˈænjuəl/ *adj., noun*
■ *adj.* [usually before noun] **1** happening or done once every year 每年的；一年一次的；年度的： *an **annual meeting/event/report*** 年会；一年一度的大事；年度报告 **2** relating to a period of one year 一年的： *an **annual income/subscription/budget*** 年收入；年度订阅费；年度预算 ◇ *an average annual growth rate of 8%* 平均 8% 的年增长率 ◇ *annual rainfall* 年降雨量 ➲ COMPARE BIANNUAL
■ *noun* **1** a book, especially one for children, that is published once a year, with the same title each time, but different contents 年刊；年报；年鉴 **2** any plant that grows and dies within one year or season 一年生植物；一季生植物 ➲ COMPARE BIENNIAL *n.*, PERENNIAL *n.*

an·nu·al·ized (*BrE also* **-ised**) /ˈænjuəlaɪzd/ *adj.* (*specialist*) calculated for a period of a year but based on the amounts for a shorter period 按年度计算的；折算成为年度总额的

an·nu·al·ly AW /ˈænjuəli/ *adv.* once a year 一年一次地： *The exhibition is held annually.* 这个展览每年举行一次。

an·nu·ity /əˈnjuːəti; *NAmE* -ˈnuː-/ *noun* (*pl.* **-ies**) **1** a fixed amount of money paid to sb each year, usually for the rest of their life 年金（常为养老金） **2** a type of insurance that pays a fixed amount of money to sb each year 年金保险 ➲ WORDFINDER NOTE AT INSURANCE

annul /əˈnʌl/ *verb* (**-ll-**) **~ sth** to state officially that sth is no longer legally valid 废除；取消；宣告无效： *Their marriage was annulled after just six months.* 他们的婚姻仅过半年就宣告取消。 ▸ **an·nul·ment** *noun* [C, U]

an·nu·lar /ˈænjələ(r)/ *adj.* (*specialist*) shaped like a ring 环状的

the An·nun·ci·ation /əˌnʌnsiˈeɪʃn/ *noun* [sing.] (in the Christian religion) the occasion when Mary was told that she was to be the mother of Christ, celebrated on 25 March （基督教）圣母领报，天使报喜（马利亚被告知将做基督的母亲）；圣母领报节，天使报喜节（3 月 25 日）

anode /ˈænəʊd; *NAmE* ˈænoʊd/ *noun* (*specialist*) the ELECTRODE in an electrical device where OXIDATION occurs; the positive electrode in an ELECTROLYTIC cell and the negative electrode in a battery 阳极；（电解池的）正极；（原电池的）负极 ➲ COMPARE CATHODE

ano·dize (*BrE also* **-ise**) /ˈænədaɪz/ *verb* **~ sth** to cover a metal, especially ALUMINIUM/ALUMINUM, with a layer

A

of OXIDE in order to protect it 对（铝等金属）作阳极氧化；阳极处理

ano·dyne /ˈænədaɪn/ *adj.* (*formal*) unlikely to cause disagreement or offend anyone; not expressing strong opinions 不得罪人的；温和的 **SYN** **bland**

anoint /əˈnɔɪnt/ *verb* **~ sb/sth (with sth)** to put oil or water on sb's head as part of a religious ceremony 傅，涂（圣油、圣水）: *The priest anointed her with oil.* 神父为她傅油。

anom·al·ous /əˈnɒmələs; *NAmE* -ˈnɑːm-/ *adj.* (*formal*) different from what is normal or expected 异常的；反常的 ▶ **anom·al·ous·ly** *adv.*

anom·aly /əˈnɒməli; *NAmE* əˈnɑːm-/ *noun* (*pl.* **-ies**) **~ (in sth)** a thing, situation, etc. that is different from what is normal or expected 异常事物；反常现象: *the many anomalies in the tax system* 税制中的许多破格现象 ◇ *the apparent anomaly that those who produced the wealth, the workers, were the poorest* 创造财富的工人最贫穷这一明显不正常现象

an·omie (*also* **anomy**) /ˈænəmi/ *noun* [U] (*formal*) a lack of social or moral standards 失范，无规范状态（社会准则或价值观的崩溃）

anon /əˈnɒn; *NAmE* əˈnɑːn/ *adv.* (*old-fashioned* or *literary*) soon 不久；很快: *See you anon.* 再见。

anon. /əˈnɒn; *NAmE* əˈnɑːn/ *abbr.* anonymous (1) (= used to describe a poem, piece of music, etc. when it is not known who wrote it) （诗、乐曲等）佚名的

ano·nym·ity /ˌænəˈnɪməti/ *noun* [U] **1** the state of remaining unknown to most other people 匿名；不知姓名；名字不公开: *Names of people in the book were changed to preserve anonymity.* 为了姓名保密，书中的人用的都是化名。 ◇ *the anonymity of the city* (= where people do not know each other) 城市中的人互不相识的现象 ◇ (*especially NAmE*) *He agreed to give an interview* ***on condition of anonymity*** (= if his name was not mentioned). 他同意在不披露姓名的条件下接受采访。 **2** the state of not having any unusual or interesting features 无特色；无个性特征: *the anonymity of the hotel decor* 这家旅馆毫无特色的装饰风格

an·onym·ize (*BrE also* **-ise**) /əˈnɒnɪmaɪz; *NAmE* əˈnɑːn-/ *verb* **1 ~ sth** (*specialist*) if you **anonymize** a test result, especially a medical test result, you remove any information that shows who it belongs to 隐匿（实验结果）的对象信息；使匿名化 **2 ~ sth** (*computing* 计) if you **anonymize** data that is sent or received over the Internet, you remove any information that identifies which particular computer that data originally came from 匿名化处理（经网络发送或接收的数据信息） ▶ **an·onym·iza·tion** *noun* [U]

an·onym·ous /əˈnɒnɪməs; *NAmE* əˈnɑːn-/ *adj.* **1** (of a person 人) with a name that is not known or that is not made public 不知姓名的；名字不公开的: *an anonymous donor* 不知姓名的捐赠者 ◇ *The money was donated by a local businessman who wishes to* ***remain anonymous.*** 这笔款子是当地一位不愿透露姓名的企业家捐赠的。 **2** written, given, made, etc. by sb who does not want their name to be known or made public 匿名的；不具名的: *an anonymous letter* 匿名信 **3** without any unusual or interesting features 没有特色的: *long stretches of dull and anonymous countryside* 大片大片千篇一律、枯燥平淡的乡村 ▶ **an·onym·ous·ly** *adv.*

aˌnonymous FTˈP *noun* [U] (*computing* 计) a system that allows anybody to DOWNLOAD files from the Internet without having to give their name 匿名文件传送协议

ano·rak /ˈænəræk/ *noun* **1** (*especially BrE*) a short coat with a HOOD that is worn as protection against rain, wind and cold 带帽防寒短上衣 ➲ VISUAL VOCAB PAGE V66 **2** (*BrE, informal*) a person who spends a lot of time learning facts or collecting things that most other people think are boring 怪僻的搜集者（花大量时间了解或收集别人大多认为无聊的东西）

an·or·exia /ˌænəˈreksiə/ (*also* **an·or·exia ner·vosa** /ˌænəˌreksiə nɜːˈvəʊsə; *NAmE* nɜːrˈvoʊsə/) *noun* [U] an emotional DISORDER, especially affecting young women, in which there is an ABNORMAL fear of being fat, causing the person to stop eating, leading to dangerous weight loss （尤指年轻女子害怕肥胖而引起的）厌食，食欲缺乏，神经性厌食 ➲ WORDFINDER NOTE AT CONDITION ➲ COLLOCATIONS AT DIET ➲ COMPARE BULIMIA

an·or·exic /ˌænəˈreksɪk/ *noun* a person who is suffering from anorexia 厌食者；食欲缺乏者 ▶ **an·or·exic** *adj.*: *She's anorexic.* 她是厌食症患者。

an·other 🔑 /əˈnʌðə(r)/ *det., pron.* **1** 🔑 one more; an extra thing or person 又一；再一；另一（事物或人）: *Would you like another drink?* 还想喝一杯吗？ ◇ *'Finished?' 'No, I've got another three questions to do.'* "做完了？" "没有，我还有三个问题要解答。" ◇ *We've still got another* (= a further) *forty miles to go.* 我们还要走四十英里。 ◇ *'It's a bill.' 'Oh no, not another!'* "这是账单。" "哦，别又来一张！" ◇ *I got another of those calls yesterday.* 昨天我又接了一个那样的电话。 **HELP** **Another** can be followed by a singular noun, by **of** and a plural noun, or by a number and a plural noun. * another 后可接单数名词、of 加复数名词或数字加复数名词。 ➲ COMPARE OTHER ➲ LANGUAGE BANK AT ADDITION **2** 🔑 different; a different person or thing 另一；不同的（人或事物）: *Let's do it another time.* 咱们下次再办这件事吧。 ◇ *We need another computer* (= a new one). 我们还需要一台电脑。 ◇ *We can try that—but whether it'll work is* ***another matter.*** 我们可以试试看，但行不行则是另一回事。 ◇ *The room's too small. Let's see if they've got* ***another one.*** 这房间太小。咱们看看他们有没有另一间。 ◇ *I don't like this room. I'm going to ask for another.* 我不喜欢这个房间。我打算另要一间。 **3** a person or thing of a very similar type 类似的（人或事物）: *She's going to be another Madonna* (= as famous as her). 她就要变得跟麦当娜一般出名了。 ◇ *There'll never be another like him.* 不会再有像他那样的人物了。 ➲ SEE ALSO ONE ANOTHER

IDM **of one kind, sort, etc. or aˈnother** used when you are referring to various types of a thing, without saying exactly what you mean 各种不同的: *We've all got problems of one kind or another.* 我们都有这样那样的问题。 ➲ MORE AT ONE

A. N. Other /ˌeɪ en ˈʌðə(r)/ *noun* [sing.] a person whose name is not known or not yet decided, for example in a list of players in a team （名单中）未指名者，某人，待定人选

an·swer 🔑 /ˈɑːnsə(r); *NAmE* ˈæn-/ *noun, verb*

■ ***noun*** **1** 🔑 something that you say, write or do to react to a question or situation 答复；回答: *I rang the bell, but there was no answer.* 我按了门铃，但没有人应门。 ◇ **~ to sth** *I can't easily* ***give an answer*** *to your question.* 你的问题我难以回答。 ◇ *Have you had an answer to your letter?* 你那封信有回音没有？ ◇ *As if* ***in answer to*** *our prayers, she offered to lend us £10 000.* 好像祈祷很灵验似的，她提出借给我们 1 万英镑。 ◇ *She had no answer to the accusations.* 她对控告无以为答。 **2** 🔑 something that you write or say in reply to a question in a test, an exam, an exercise, etc.; the correct reply to a question in a test, etc. （试题、练习等的）答案，正确答案: *Write your answers on the sheet provided.* 在所发的答题纸上写下答案。 ◇ *Do you know the answer* (= the right one) *to question 12?* 你知道第 12 题的正确答案吗？ **3** 🔑 a solution to a problem （问题的）解决办法，答案: *There is no easy answer.* 没有容易的解决办法。 ◇ *This could be the answer to all our problems.* 这可能就是我们全部问题的解决办法。 ◇ *The obvious answer would be to cancel the party.* 明摆着的解决方法是取消聚会。 **4** a person or thing from one place that may be thought to be as good as a famous person or thing from another place 足以媲美的人；堪称相当的事物: *The new theme park will be Britain's answer to Disneyland.* 英国新的主题乐园可与迪士尼乐园媲美。 ➲ MORE LIKE THIS 20, page R27

A

IDM **have/know all the 'answers** (*informal, often disapproving*) to be confident that you know sth, especially when you actually do not （自以为）全懂，什么都精通：*He thinks he knows all the answers.* 他自以为什么都知道。
➲ MORE AT NO *exclamation*

■ *verb* **1** [I, T] to say, write or do sth as a reaction to a question or situation 答复；回答 SYN **reply**: *I repeated the question, but she didn't answer.* 我把问题重复了一遍，但是她仍没有回答。 ◇ ~ **sth** *You haven't* **answered my question.** 你没有回答我的问题。 ◇ *to* **answer a letter/an advertisement** 复信；对广告作出反应 ◇ *to* **answer the phone** (= to pick up the phone when it rings) 接电话 ◇ *to* **answer the door** (= to open the door when sb knocks/rings) 应门（铃）声开门 ◇ *My* **prayers have been answered** (= I have got what I wanted). 我的祈祷应验了。 ◇ *He refused to answer the charges against him.* 他拒绝就对他的指控进行答辩。 ◇ ~ (**sb**) *Come on, answer me! Where were you?* 快点，回答我！你到哪儿去了？ ◇ *He answered me with a smile.* 他对我报以微笑。 ◇ **+ speech** *'I'd prefer to walk,' she answered.* "我宁愿步行。" 她答道。 ◇ **~ sb + speech** *'I'd prefer to walk,' she answered him.* "我宁愿步行。" 她回答他道。 ◇ ~ (**sb**) **that...** *She answered that she would prefer to walk.* 她回答说她宁愿步行。 ◇ **~ sb sth** *Answer me this: how did they know we were here?* 回答我这个问题：他们怎么知道我们在这儿？ **2** [T] **~ sth** (*formal*) to be suitable for sth; to match sth 适合；符合；比得上；相配： *Does this answer your requirements?* 这个符合你的要求吗？

IDM **answer to the name of sth** (especially of a pet animal 尤指宠物) to be called sth 名叫；叫作 ➲ MORE AT DESCRIPTION

PHR V **,answer 'back** to defend yourself against criticism 为自己辩护；答辩： *He was given the chance to answer back in a radio interview.* 在一次广播访谈中他得到了辩白的机会。 **,answer 'back** | **,answer sb 'back** to speak rudely to sb in authority, especially when they are criticizing you or telling you to do sth 顶嘴；回嘴；还嘴： *Don't answer back!* 别回嘴！ ◇ *Stop answering your mother back!* 不准和母亲顶嘴！ **'answer for sth 1** to accept responsibility or blame for sth 对…负责；因…受到谴责： *You will have to answer for your behaviour one day.* 总有一天你要为你的行为承担责任。 ◇ *This government* **has a lot to answer for** (= is responsible for a lot of bad things). 这届政府对很多坏事都有责任。 **2** to promise that sb has a particular quality or can be relied on to do sth 担保，保证（某人的品质等）： *I can answer for her honesty.* 我可以担保她为人诚实。 **'answer for sb** (usually in negative sentences 通常用于否定句) to say that sb else will do sth or have a particular opinion 代表…讲话；代表…的意见： *I agree, but I can't answer for my colleagues.* 我同意，但是我不能代表我同事们的意见。 **'answer to sb** (**for sth**) to have to explain your actions or decisions to sb 向某人（为某事）负责： *All sales clerks answer to the store manager.* 所有售货员都向商店经理负责。

> ▼ **WHICH WORD?** 词语辨析
>
> **answer / reply**
>
> Verbs 动词
>
> - **Answer** and **reply** are the most common verbs used for speaking or writing as a reaction to a question, letter, etc. * answer 和 reply 为口语或书面语中表示回答问题、复信等最通用的动词。
> - Note that you **answer** a person, question or letter, not *answer to* them, but you **reply to** somebody or something. 表示回答或回复时，answer 后不用 to，宾语可以是人，也可以是问题或信，而 reply 后要用 to： *I'm writing to answer your questions.* 特此函复贵方提问。 ◇ *I'm writing to reply to your questions.* 特此函复贵方提问。 ◇ ~~*I'm writing to answer to your questions.*~~
> - **Answer** can be used with or without an object. * answer 既可带宾语，也可不带宾语： *I haven't answered her email yet.* 我还没有回复她的电邮。 ◇ *I knocked on the door but nobody answered.* 我敲了门，但无人应答。 **Reply** is often used with the actual words spoken. * reply 常带直接引语： *'I won't let you down,' he replied.* "我不会让你失望的。" 他回答说。
> - **Respond** is less common and more formal. * respond 较少用，且较正式： *The directors were unwilling to respond to questions.* 董事们不愿意回答问题。
> - You can only **answer** a door or a phone. 应门或接电话只能用 answer。
>
> ➲ SEE ALSO REJOIN[2], RETORT, GET BACK TO SB
>
> Nouns 名词
>
> - Note the phrases **in answer to** and **in reply to**. 注意 in answer to 和 in reply to 的用法： *I'm writing in answer to your letter.* 特此函复。
>
> ➲ SEE ALSO RESPONSE, REJOINDER, RETORT

an·swer·able /ˈɑːnsərəbl; *NAmE* ˈæn-/ *adj.* **1** [not before noun] **~ to sb** (**for sth**) having to explain your actions to sb in authority over you 向某人（对某事）负责： *She was a free agent, answerable to no one for her behaviour.* 她不归任何人管，我行我素。 **2** [not before noun] **~** (**for sth**) responsible for sth and ready to accept punishment or criticism for it （为某事）承担责任，承担后果： *Ministers must be made answerable for their decisions.* 各部长必须对所做的决定承担责任。 **3** (of a question 问题) that can be answered 可答复的

'answering machine (*BrE also* **an·swer·phone**) *noun* a machine that you connect to your telephone to answer your calls and record any message left by the person calling 电话答录机： *I called several times, but only got the answering machine.* 我打了几次电话，但只有电话答录机答话。 ➲ **MORE LIKE THIS** 9, page R26

an·swer·phone /ˈɑːnsəfəʊn; *NAmE* ˈænsərfoʊn/ *noun* (*BrE*) = ANSWERING MACHINE： *She left her name and number on his answerphone.* 她把自己的姓名和电话号码留在他的电话答录机上。

ant /ænt/ *noun* a small insect that lives in highly organized groups. There are many types of ant. 蚂蚁： *an ants' nest* 蚁窝 ◇ *an ant colony* 蚁群 ➲ **VISUAL VOCAB** PAGE V13 ➲ SEE ALSO ANTHILL

IDM **have 'ants in your pants** (*informal*) to be very excited or impatient about sth and unable to stay still 焦躁不安；坐立不安

-ant, -ent *suffix* **1** (in adjectives 构成形容词) that is or does sth 是…的；做…的： *significant* 有意义的 ◇ *different* 不同的 **2** (in nouns 构成名词) a person or thing that …人；…事物： *inhabitant* 居民 ◇ *deterrent* 威慑因素 ➲ **MORE LIKE THIS** 7, page R25

ant·acid /æntˈæsɪd/ *noun* a medicine that prevents or corrects ACIDITY, especially in the stomach 抗酸药；解酸药

an·tag·on·ism /ænˈtæɡənɪzəm/ *noun* [U, pl.] **~** (**to/toward(s) sb/sth**) | **~** (**between A and B**) feelings of hatred and opposition 对立情绪；对抗情绪；敌对；敌意 SYN **hostility**: *The antagonism he felt towards his old enemy was still very strong.* 他对宿敌的仇恨仍然十分强烈。 ◇ *the racial antagonisms in society* 社会上的种族对立情绪

an·tag·on·ist /ænˈtæɡənɪst/ *noun* (*formal*) a person who strongly opposes sb/sth 对立者；对抗者；对手；敌人 SYN **opponent**

an·tag·on·is·tic /ænˌtæɡəˈnɪstɪk/ *adj.* **~** (**to/toward(s) sb/sth**) (*formal*) showing or feeling opposition 对立情绪的；对抗的；敌对的；敌意的 SYN **hostile** ▸ **an·tag·on·is·tic·al·ly** /-kli/ *adv.*

an·tag·on·ize (*BrE also* **-ise**) /ænˈtæɡənaɪz/ *verb* **~ sb** to do sth to make sb angry with you 使对立；使生气： *Not wishing to antagonize her further, he said no more.* 他不愿惹她更生气，便不再说话。

the Ant·arc·tic /ænˈtɑːktɪk; *NAmE* -ˈtɑːrk-/ *noun* [sing.] the regions of the world around the South Pole 南极地区

A

▶ **Ant·arc·tic** *adj.* [only before noun]: *Antarctic explorers* 南极探险家 ➲ COMPARE ARCTIC *adj.*

the An,tarctic 'Circle *noun* [sing.] the line of LATITUDE 66° 33′ South 南极圈 ➲ COMPARE ARCTIC CIRCLE

ante /'ænti/ *noun* [sing.]
IDM **raise/up the 'ante** to increase the level of sth, especially demands or sums of money 提高要求；增加金额

ante- /'ænti/ *prefix* (in nouns, adjectives and verbs 构成名词、形容词和动词) before; in front of 在…前；在…前面：*anteroom* 前厅 ◇ *antenatal* 产前的 ◇ *antedate* 早于 ➲ COMPARE POST-, PRE- ➲ MORE LIKE THIS 6, page R25

ant·eat·er /'ænti:tə(r)/ *noun* an animal with a long nose and tongue that eats ANTS 食蚁兽

ante·bellum /,ænti'beləm/ *adj.* [only before noun] (*formal*) connected with the years before a war, especially the American Civil War 战前岁月的；（尤指）美国内战前的：*the laws of the antebellum American South* 内战前美国南方的法律

ante·ce·dent /,æntɪ'si:dnt/ *noun, adj.*
■ ***noun*** **1** [C] (*formal*) a thing or an event that exists or comes before another, and may have influenced it 前事；前情 **2 antecedents** [pl.] (*formal*) the people in sb's family who lived a long time ago 祖先；先人 **SYN** **ancestor**, **forebear** **3** [C] (*grammar* 语法) a word or phrase to which the following word, especially a pronoun, refers 先行词；先行语：*In 'He grabbed the ball and threw it in the air', 'ball' is the antecedent of 'it'.* 在 He grabbed the ball and threw it in the air 一句中，ball 是 it 的先行词。
■ ***adj.*** (*formal*) previous 先前的：*antecedent events* 先前的事件

ante·cham·ber /'æntitʃeɪmbə(r)/ *noun* (*formal*) = ANTEROOM

ante·date /,ænti'deɪt/ *verb* **~ sth** = PREDATE

ante·di·lu·vian /,æntidɪ'lu:viən/ *adj.* (*formal* or *humorous*) very old-fashioned 早已过时的；十分老式的

ante·lope /'æntɪləʊp; *NAmE* -loʊp/ *noun* (*pl.* **ante·lope** or **ante·lopes**) an African or Asian animal like a DEER, that runs very fast. There are many types of antelope. 羚；羚类动物

ante·natal /,ænti'neɪtl/ (*BrE*) (*also* **pre·natal** *NAmE, BrE*) *adj.* [only before noun] relating to the medical care given to pregnant women 产前的：***antenatal care/classes/screening*** 产前保健 / 学习班 / 检查 ◇ *an **antenatal clinic*** 产前检查诊所 ➲ COMPARE POSTNATAL ➲ WORDFINDER NOTE AT PREGNANT ➲ MORE LIKE THIS 32, page R28

an·tenna /æn'tenə/ *noun* **1** (*pl.* **an·ten·nae** /-ni:/) either of the two long thin parts on the heads of some insects and some animals that live in shells, used to feel and touch things with 触角；第二触角；大触角 **SYN** **feeler**: (*figurative*) *The minister was praised for his acute political antennae* (= ability to understand complicated political situations). 这位部长以政治触觉敏锐而为人称道。➲ VISUAL VOCAB PAGE V13 **2** (*pl.* **an·ten·nas** or **an·ten·nae**) (*especially NAmE*) (*BrE usually* **aer·ial**) a piece of equipment made of wire or long straight pieces of metal for receiving or sending radio and television signals 天线：*radio antennas* 收音机天线 ➲ VISUAL VOCAB PAGES V18, V56

an·ter·ior /æn'tɪəriə(r); *NAmE* -'tɪr-/ *adj.* [only before noun] (*specialist*) (of a part of the body 身体部位) at or near the front 前部的；前面的 **OPP** **posterior**

ante·room /'æntiru:m; -rʊm/ (*also formal* **ante·cham·ber**) *noun* a room where people can wait before entering a larger room, especially in an important public building （尤指重要公共建筑的）前厅，接待室

an·them /'ænθəm/ *noun* **1** a song that has a special importance for a country, an organization or a particular group of people, and is sung on special occasions 国歌；（组织或群体的）社歌，团歌：*The European anthem was played at the opening and closing ceremonies.* 欧洲颂歌在开幕式和闭幕式上演奏。➲ SEE ALSO NATIONAL ANTHEM **2** a short religious song for a CHOIR (= a group of singers), often with an organ （宗教）颂歌（常由管风琴伴奏）

an·them·ic /æn'θi:mɪk/ *adj.* (*formal*) (of a piece of music 乐曲) that makes you feel happy and enthusiastic 欢乐的；激发热情的

an·ther /'ænθə(r)/ *noun* (*biology* 生) the part of a flower at the top of a STAMEN that produces POLLEN 花药（花的雄蕊顶端产生花粉的部分）➲ VISUAL VOCAB PAGE V11

ant·hill /'ænthɪl/ *noun* a pile of earth formed by ANTS over their nests 蚁冢；蚁垤

an·tholo·gize (*BrE also* **-ise**) /æn'θɒlədʒaɪz; *NAmE* -'θɑ:l-/ *verb* **~ sb/sth** to include a writer or piece of writing in an anthology 把（作者或作品）收入选集

an·thol·ogy /æn'θɒlədʒi; *NAmE* -'θɑ:l-/ *noun* (*pl.* **-ies**) a collection of poems, stories, etc. that have been written by different people and published together in a book （不同作家作品的）选集

an·thra·cite /'ænθrəsaɪt/ *noun* [U] a very hard type of coal that burns slowly without producing a lot of smoke or flames 无烟煤

an·thrax /'ænθræks/ *noun* [U] a serious disease that affects sheep and cows and sometimes people, and can cause death 炭疽（牛羊疾病，人偶得，可致命）

an·thro·po- /'ænθrəpəʊ; *NAmE* -poʊ/ *combining form* (in nouns, adjectives and adverbs 构成名词、形容词和副词) connected with humans 人的；人类的：*anthropology* 人类学

an·thro·po·cen·tric /,ænθrəpə'sentrɪk/ *adj.* believing that humans are more important than anything else 人类中心论的；人本位的 ▶ **an·thro·po·cen·trism** /,ænθrəpə'sentrɪzəm/ *noun* [U]

an·thro·poid /'ænθrəpɔɪd/ *adj., noun* (*specialist*)
■ ***adj.*** (of an APE 猿) looking like a human 类人的；似人的
■ ***noun*** any type of APE that is similar to a human 类人猿

an·thro·polo·gist /,ænθrə'pɒlədʒɪst; *NAmE* -'pɑ:l-/ *noun* a person who studies anthropology 人类学家

an·thro·pol·ogy /,ænθrə'pɒlədʒi; *NAmE* -'pɑ:l-/ *noun* [U] the study of the human race, especially of its origins, development, customs and beliefs 人类学 ▶ **an·thro·po·logic·al** /,ænθrəpə'lɒdʒɪkl; *NAmE* -'lɑ:dʒ-/ *adj.*

an·thro·po·morph·ic /,ænθrəpə'mɔ:fɪk; *NAmE* -'mɔ:rf-/ *adj.* (of beliefs or ideas 信念或思想) treating gods, animals or objects as if they had human qualities 人格化的；拟人化的 ▶ **an·thro·po·morph·ism** /,ænθrəpə'mɔ:fɪzəm; *NAmE* -'mɔ:rf-/ *noun* [U]

anti /'ænti/ *prep.* (*informal*) if sb is **anti** sb/sth, they do not like or agree with that person or thing 反对 ➲ COMPARE PRO *prep.*

anti- 🔑 /'ænti/ *prefix* (in nouns and adjectives 构成名词和形容词) **1** 🔑 opposed to; against 反；反对：*anti-tank weapons* 反坦克武器 ◇ *antisocial* 反社会 ➲ COMPARE PRO- **2** 🔑 the opposite of 对立；对立面：*anti-hero* 反英雄 ◇ *anticlimax* 扫兴的结局 **3** 🔑 preventing 防；防止：*antifreeze* 防冻剂 ➲ MORE LIKE THIS 6, page R25

,anti-'aircraft *adj.* [only before noun] designed to destroy enemy aircraft 防空的：***anti-aircraft fire/guns/missiles*** 防空火力；高射炮；防空导弹

anti·bac·ter·ial /,æntibæk'tɪəriəl; *NAmE* -'tɪriəl/ *adj.* that kills bacteria 抗菌的；灭菌的：*antibacterial treatments* 抗菌处理

anti·bi·ot·ic /,æntibaɪ'ɒtɪk; *NAmE* -'ɑ:tɪk/ *noun* [usually pl.] a substance, for example PENICILLIN, that can destroy or prevent the growth of bacteria and cure infections 抗菌素，抗生素（如青霉素）：*The doctor put her on antibiotics* (= told her to take them). 医生要她服用抗生素。

A

▶ **anti·bi·ot·ic** *adj.*：*an antibiotic drug* 抗生素 ◇ *effective antibiotic treatment* 有效的抗生素治疗

anti·body /ˈæntibɒdi; *NAmE* -bɑːdi/ *noun* (*pl.* **-ies**) a substance that the body produces in the blood to fight disease, or as a reaction when certain substances are put into the body 抗体（血液中抵抗疾病或当某些物质进入身体时产生反应的物质）

ˌanti-ˈchoice *adj.* (*NAmE*, *disapproving*) against giving women the right to have an ABORTION 反对自由堕胎的 ➲ COMPARE PRO-CHOICE

Anti·christ /ˈæntikraɪst/ (*usually* **the Antichrist**) *noun* [sing.] (in Christianity 基督教) the DEVIL; Christ's greatest enemy 敌基督（指基督的大敌魔王）

an·tici·pate 🔑 AW /ænˈtɪsɪpeɪt/ *verb* **1** 🔑 to expect sth 预料；预期：**~ sth** *We don't anticipate any major problems.* 我们预料不会出现什么大问题。◇ *Our anticipated arrival time is 8.30.* 我们预计抵达的时间是 8:30。◇ *The eagerly anticipated movie will be released next month.* 那部观众翘首企盼的电影将于下月上映。◇ **~ doing sth** *They anticipate moving to bigger premises by the end of the year.* 他们预期年底前迁入较大的经营场址。◇ **~ sth doing sth** *I don't anticipate it being a problem.* 我不认为它会成为一个问题。◇ **~ that…** *We anticipate that sales will rise next year.* 我们预料明年销售量将会增加。◇ **it is anticipated that…** *It is anticipated that inflation will stabilize at 3%.* 据预测，通货膨胀将稳定在 3%。➲ COMPARE UNANTICIPATED **2** 🔑 to see what might happen in the future and take action to prepare for it 预见，预计（并做准备）：**~ sth** *We need someone who can anticipate and respond to changes in the fashion industry.* 我们需要一个能预见时装业变化并做出应对的人。◇ **~ what, how, that, etc.…** *Try and anticipate what the interviewers will ask.* 尽量设想面试主持者会提出什么问题。**3 ~ (doing) sth | ~ (sth doing) sth** to think with pleasure and excitement about sth that is going to happen 期盼；期望：*We eagerly anticipated the day we would leave school.* 我们迫切地期盼着毕业离校的那一天。◇ *The more I anticipated arriving somewhere, the more disappointed I was.* 我越期盼在某方面有所成就，就越失望。**4 ~ sb (doing sth)** (*formal*) to do sth before it can be done by sb else 先于…做；早于…行动 SYN **forestall**：*When Scott reached the South Pole he found that Amundsen had anticipated him.* 斯科特到达南极时发现阿蒙森已到过那里。▶ **an·tici·pa·tory** /ænˌtɪsɪˈpeɪtəri; *NAmE* ænˈtɪsəpətɔːri/ *adj.* (*formal*)：*a fast anticipatory movement by the goalkeeper* 守门员的快速预判动作

an·tici·pa·tion AW /ænˌtɪsɪˈpeɪʃn/ *noun* [U] **1** the fact of seeing that sth might happen in the future and perhaps doing sth about it now 预料；预期；预见；预计：*He bought extra food* ***in anticipation of*** *more people coming than he'd invited.* 他预料来的客人会比邀请的多，就多买了食物。**2** a feeling of excitement about sth (usually sth good) that is going to happen 期盼；期望：***happy/eager/excited anticipation*** 愉快的 / 殷切的 / 激动的期盼 ◇ *The courtroom was filled with anticipation.* 法庭上人们满怀期望的心情。

anti·cler·ic·al /ˌæntiˈklerɪkl/ *adj.* opposed to priests and their influence in political life 反教权主义的：*anticlerical movements in the seventeenth century* 十七世纪的反教权主义运动 ▶ **anti·cler·ic·al·ism** /-ɪzəm/ *noun* [U]

anti·cli·max /ˌæntiˈklaɪmæks/ *noun* [C, U] a situation that is disappointing because it happens at the end of sth that was much more exciting, or because it is not as exciting as you expected 扫兴的结局；扫兴：*Travelling in Europe was something of an anticlimax after the years he'd spent in Africa.* 他在非洲生活了多年，到欧洲旅行真是有点太平淡了。◇ *a* ***sense/feeling of anticlimax*** 扫兴感 ➲ COMPARE CLIMAX *n.* ▶ **anti·cli·mac·tic** /ˌæntiklaɪˈmæktɪk/ *adj.*

anti·cline /ˈæntiklaɪn/ *noun* (*geology* 地) an area of ground where layers of rock in the earth's surface have been folded into a curve that is higher in the middle than at the ends 背斜（指地球表面岩层叠起成弧状、中间高于边缘的区域）➲ COMPARE SYNCLINE

anti·clock·wise /ˌæntiˈklɒkwaɪz; *NAmE* -ˈklɑːk-/ (*BrE*) (*NAmE* **coun·ter·clock·wise**) *adv.*, *adj.* in the opposite direction to the movement of the hands of a clock 逆时针方向（的）：*Turn the key anticlockwise/in an anticlockwise direction.* 朝逆时针方向转动钥匙。OPP **clockwise**

anti·coagu·lant /ˌæntikəʊˈægjələnt; *NAmE* -koʊ-/ *noun* (*medical* 医) a substance that stops the blood from becoming thick and forming CLOTS 抗凝（血）剂

antics /ˈæntɪks/ *noun* [pl.] **1** behaviour which is silly and funny in a way that people usually like 滑稽可笑的举止：*The bank staff got up to all sorts of antics to raise money for charity.* 银行职员使出各种可笑的招数为慈善事业筹款。**2** behaviour which is ridiculous or dangerous 荒唐行为；危险举动

anti·cyc·lone /ˌæntiˈsaɪkləʊn; *NAmE* -kloʊn/ *noun* an area of high air pressure that produces calm weather conditions with clear skies 反气旋（天气晴朗平静）➲ COMPARE DEPRESSION (5)

anti·depres·sant /ˌæntidɪˈpresnt/ *noun* a drug used to treat the illness DEPRESSION 抗抑郁药；抗抑郁剂 ▶ **anti·depres·sant** *adj.* [only before noun]: *antidepressant drugs* 抗抑郁药

anti·dote /ˈæntidəʊt; *NAmE* -doʊt/ *noun* **1 ~ (to sth)** a substance that controls the effects of a poison or disease 解毒药；解毒剂：*There is no known antidote to the poison.* 这种毒的解药尚未发现。**2 ~ (to sth)** anything that takes away the effects of sth unpleasant 消除不快的事物；矫正方法：*A Mediterranean cruise was the perfect antidote to a long cold winter.* 到地中海航游是度过漫长寒冬的绝妙办法。

anti·freeze /ˈæntifriːz/ *noun* [U] a chemical that is added to the water in the RADIATOR of cars and other vehicles to stop it from freezing 防冻剂，抗凝剂（加入车辆散热器的水中以防冻结）

anti·gen /ˈæntɪdʒən/ *noun* (*medical* 医) a substance that enters the body and starts a process that can cause disease. The body then usually produces ANTIBODIES to fight the antigens. 抗原（能激发人体产生抗体）

anti·glob·al·iza·tion (*BrE also* **-isa·tion**) /ˌæntiˌgləʊbəlaɪˈzeɪʃn; *NAmE* -ˌgloʊbələˈz-/ *noun* [U] opposition to the increase in the power of large international companies and institutions because of the bad effects on the economies of individual countries, especially poorer ones 反全球化：*antiglobalization protests at the G8 summit* 八国峰会时的反全球化抗议 ◇ *the antiglobalization movement* 反全球化运动

anti·grav·ity /ˌæntiˈgrævɪti/ *noun* [U] (*physics* 物) an imaginary force that works against GRAVITY 反重力；反引力

ˈanti-hero *noun* the main character in a story, but one who does not have the qualities of a typical hero, and is either more like an ordinary person or morally bad 反英雄（故事中不按传统主角品格塑造的主人公）➲ WORDFINDER NOTE AT CHARACTER

anti·his·ta·mine /ˌæntiˈhɪstəmiːn/ *noun* [C, U] a drug used to treat ALLERGIES, especially HAY FEVER 抗组胺药（抗枯草热等过敏反应）：***antihistamine cream/injections/shots*** 抗组胺乳膏 / 注射

ˌanti-inˈflam·ma·tory *adj.* (of a drug 药) used to reduce INFLAMMATION 消炎的；抗炎的 ▶ **anti-inflam·ma·tory** *noun* (*pl.* **-ies**)

ˈanti-lock *adj.* [only before noun] **anti-lock** BRAKES stop the wheels of a vehicle locking if you have to stop suddenly, and so make the vehicle easier to control 防抱死的：*an anti-lock braking system or ABS* 防抱死装置

anti·mat·ter /ˈæntimætə(r)/ *noun* [U] (*physics* 物) matter that is made up of antiparticles 反物质（由反粒子组成）

A

an·tim·ony /ˈæntɪməni; *NAmE* -moʊni/ *noun* [U] (*symb.* **Sb**) a chemical element. Antimony is a silver-white metal that breaks easily, used especially in making ALLOYS. 锑

anti·oxi·dant /ˌæntiˈɒksɪdənt; *NAmE* -ˈɑːks-/ *noun* **1** (*biology* 生) a substance such as VITAMIN C or E that removes dangerous MOLECULES, etc., such as FREE RADICALS from the body 抗氧剂（如维生素 C 或 E，可消除体内的有害分子等，如消除自由基） **2** (*chemistry* 化) a substance that helps prevent OXIDATION, especially one used to help prevent stored food products from going bad（尤用于食物保鲜的）抗氧化剂

anti·par·ticle /ˈæntipɑːtɪkl; *NAmE* -pɑːrt-/ *noun* (*physics* 物) a very small part of an atom that has the same mass as a normal PARTICLE but the opposite electrical CHARGE 反粒子（与基本粒子质量相同，但电荷相反） ➲ **WORDFINDER NOTE AT ATOM**

anti·pasto /ˌæntiˈpæstəʊ; *NAmE* -oʊ/ *noun* (*pl.* **anti·pasti** /-ti/) (in Italian cooking 意大利烹饪) a small amount of food that you eat before the main part of a meal 开胃菜；开胃食物 **SYN** **appetizer, starter**

an·tip·athy /ænˈtɪpəθi/ *noun* [U, C, usually sing.] (*pl.* **-ies**) ~ **(between A and B)** | ~ **(to/toward(s) sb/sth)** (*formal*) a strong feeling of dislike 厌恶；反感 **SYN** **hostility**: ***personal/mutual antipathy*** 个人 / 相互反感 ◇ ***a growing antipathy*** *towards the idea* 对这个想法越来越强烈的反感 ▶ **anti·path·et·ic** /ˌæntɪpəˈθetɪk/ *adj.*： ~ **(to sb/sth)** *antipathetic to change* 厌恶变革

ˌ**anti-personˈnel** *adj.* [only before noun] (of weapons 武器) designed to kill or injure people, not to destroy buildings or vehicles, etc. 专门用于杀伤人的；杀伤性的

anti·per·spir·ant /ˌæntiˈpɜːspərənt; *NAmE* -ˈpɜːrs-/ *noun* [U, C] a substance that people use, especially under their arms, to prevent or reduce sweat 止汗剂 ➲ SEE ALSO DEODORANT

the An·tipo·des /ænˈtɪpədiːz/ *noun* [pl.] a way of referring to Australia and New Zealand, often used in a humorous way 澳大利亚和新西兰，澳新（常为幽默说法） ▶ **An·tipo·dean** /ˌæntɪpəˈdiːən/ *adj.*

anti·pro·ton /ˈæntiprəʊtɒn; *NAmE* -proʊtɑːn/ *noun* (*physics* 物) a PARTICLE that has the same mass as a PROTON, but a negative electrical CHARGE 反质子（与质子质量相同，但电荷相反）

anti·quar·ian /ˌæntɪˈkweəriən; *NAmE* -ˈkwer-/ *adj.*, *noun*

■ ***adj.*** [usually before noun] connected with the study, collection or sale of valuable old objects, especially books（尤指书籍）古文物的，古文物研究（或收藏、经营）的

■ ***noun*** (*also less frequent* **anti·quary** /ˈæntɪkwəri; *NAmE* -kweri/) a person who studies, collects or sells old and valuable objects 古文物研究者（或收藏家、经营者）

anti·quark /ˈæntikwɑːk; *NAmE* -kwɑːrk/ *noun* (*physics* 物) the ANTIPARTICLE of a QUARK 反夸克

anti·quated /ˈæntɪkweɪtɪd/ *adj.* (*usually disapproving*) (of things or ideas 事物或思想) old-fashioned and no longer suitable for modern conditions 过时的；陈旧的 **SYN** **outdated**

an·tique /ænˈtiːk/ *adj.*, *noun*

■ ***adj.*** [usually before noun] (of furniture, jewellery, etc. 家具、珠宝等) old and often valuable 古老的；古董的： *an antique mahogany desk* 古红木办公桌

■ ***noun*** an object such as a piece of furniture that is old and often valuable 文物；古物；古董；古玩： *Priceless antiques were destroyed in the fire.* 价值连城的古董在大火中焚毁。◇ *an antique shop* (= one that sells antiques) 古玩店 ◇ *an antique dealer/antiques dealer* (= a person who sells antiques) 古董商

an·tiquity /ænˈtɪkwəti/ *noun* (*pl.* **-ies**) **1** [U] the ancient past, especially the times of the Greeks and Romans 古代（尤指古希腊和古罗马时期）： *The statue was brought to Rome* ***in antiquity***. 这座雕像是古时运到罗马的。 **2** [U] the state of being very old or ancient 古老；古： *A number of the monuments are of considerable antiquity.* 有些历史遗迹相当古老。 **3** [C, usually pl.] an object from ancient times 文物；古物；古董；古迹： *Egyptian/Roman antiquities* 埃及 / 罗马古物

anti·retro·viral /ˌæntiˌretrəʊˈvaɪrəl; *NAmE* -troʊ-/ *adj.* (*medical* 医) designed to stop viruses such as HIV damaging the body 抗逆转录病毒的；抗反转录病毒的： *antiretroviral drugs* 抗逆转录病毒药物

ˌ**anti-ˈroll bar** *noun* a metal bar that is part of a car's SUSPENSION, which stops the car from leaning too much when it goes around corners（汽车悬架的）横向平衡杆，防倾斜杆

anti-Semitism /ˌænti ˈsemətɪzəm/ *noun* [U] hatred of Jews; unfair treatment of Jews 反犹太（主义）；排犹（主义） ➲ **COLLOCATIONS AT RACE** ▶ **anti-Semitic** /ˌænti səˈmɪtɪk/ *adj.*： *anti-Semitic propaganda* 反犹宣传 **anti-Semite** /ˌænti ˈsiːmaɪt/ *noun*： *He was a notorious anti-Semite.* 他是臭名昭著的反犹主义者。

anti·sep·tic /ˌæntiˈseptɪk/ *noun, adj.*

■ ***noun*** [C, U] a substance that helps to prevent infection in wounds by killing bacteria 防腐剂；抗菌剂 **SYN** **disinfectant**

■ ***adj.*** **1** able to prevent infection 防腐的；抗菌的： ***antiseptic cream/lotion/wipes*** 防腐乳膏 / 洗液 / 擦剂 **2** very clean and free from bacteria 无菌的；消过毒的 **SYN** **sterile**: *Cover the burn with an antiseptic dressing.* 在烧伤处包上无菌敷料。

anti·social /ˌæntiˈsəʊʃl; *NAmE* -ˈsoʊʃl/ *adj.* **1** harmful or annoying to other people, or to society in general 反社会的；危害社会的；令人讨厌的： *antisocial behaviour* 反社会行为 **2** not wanting to spend time with other people 不合群的；孤僻的： *They'll think you're being antisocial if you don't go.* 要是你不去，他们就会认为你不合群。 ➲ COMPARE SOCIABLE

ˌ**anti-ˈtank** *adj.* [only before noun] (of weapons 武器) for use against enemy tanks 反坦克的： *anti-tank missiles/mines* 反坦克导弹 / 地雷

an·tith·esis /ænˈtɪθəsɪs/ *noun* [usually sing.] (*pl.* **an·tith·eses** /ænˈtɪθəsiːz/) (*formal*) **1** the opposite of sth 对立（面）；对照： *Love is the antithesis of selfishness.* 爱是自私的对立面。 ◇ *Students finishing their education at 16 is* ***the very antithesis of*** *what society needs.* * 16 岁停止学业的学生恰恰无法满足社会的需要。 **2** a contrast between two things（二者间的）对比，对照： *There is an antithesis between the needs of the state and the needs of the people.* 政府的需要和人民的需要这二者存在着对立。 ▶ **an·ti·thet·ic·al** /ˌæntɪˈθetɪkl/ *adj.* ~ **(to sth)**

anti·trust /ˌæntiˈtrʌst/ *adj.* [only before noun] (of laws 法律) preventing companies or groups of companies from controlling prices unfairly 反托拉斯的；反垄断的

anti·viral /ˌæntiˈvaɪrəl/ *adj.* (of a drug 药) used to treat infectious diseases caused by a virus 抗病毒的

anti·virus /ˈæntivaɪrəs/ *adj.* (*computing* 计) designed to find and destroy computer viruses 防病毒的；杀毒的： *antivirus software* 防病毒软件

ant·ler /ˈæntlə(r)/ *noun* [usually pl.] one of the two horns that grow on the head of male DEER 鹿角 ➲ **VISUAL VOCAB PAGE V12**

ant·onym /ˈæntənɪm/ *noun* (*specialist*) a word that means the opposite of another word 反义词 **SYN** **opposite**: *'Old' has two possible antonyms: 'young' and 'new'.* * old 的反义词可能有两个：young 和 new。 ➲ COMPARE SYNONYM

antsy /ˈæntsi/ *adj.* (*NAmE, informal*) impatient; not able to keep still 烦躁的；坐立不安的

anus /ˈeɪnəs/ *noun* (*anatomy* 解) the opening in a person's bottom through which solid waste leaves the body 肛门 ➲ **VISUAL VOCAB PAGE V64** ➲ SEE ALSO ANAL (1)

A

anvil /ˈænvɪl/ *noun* an iron block on which a BLACKSMITH puts hot pieces of metal before shaping them with a HAMMER 铁砧

anx·iety /æŋˈzaɪəti/ *noun* (*pl.* **-ies**) **1** [U] ~ (**about/over sth**) the state of feeling nervous or worried that sth bad is going to happen 焦虑；忧虑：*acute/intense/deep anxiety* 非常 / 极度 / 深深的忧虑 ◇ *Some hospital patients experience high levels of anxiety.* 有些住院病人十分焦虑不安。 **2** [C] a worry or fear about sth 担心；忧虑；害怕：*If you're worried about your health, share your anxieties with your doctor.* 你要是担心自己的健康，就把忧虑告诉医生吧。 **3** [U] a strong feeling of wanting to do sth or of wanting sth to happen 渴望：**~ to do sth** *the candidate's anxiety to win the vote* 候选人对选举胜利的渴望 ◇ **~ for sth** *the people's anxiety for the war to end* 人民对结束战争的渴望

anx·ious /ˈæŋkʃəs/ *adj.* **1** feeling worried or nervous 焦虑；忧虑；担心：**~ (about sth)** *He seemed anxious about the meeting.* 他似乎对这次会议忧心忡忡。 ◇ **~ (for sb)** *Parents are naturally anxious for their children.* 父母自然为儿女担心。 ➲ SYNONYMS AT WORRIED **2** causing anxiety; showing anxiety 令人焦虑的；流露出忧虑的：*There were a few anxious moments in the baseball game.* 那场棒球赛中有些时刻令人焦虑不安。◇ *an anxious look/face/expression* 忧虑的目光 / 面容 / 表情 **3** wanting sth very much 渴望；非常希望：**~ to do sth** *She was anxious to finish school and get a job.* 她渴望毕业，然后找一份工作。◇ *He was* **anxious not to** *be misunderstood.* 他希望不被人误解。◇ **~ for sth** *There are plenty of graduates anxious for work.* 有大量毕业生渴求工作。 ◇ **~ for sb to do sth** *I'm anxious for her to do as little as possible.* 我盼她尽量少干。◇ **~ that…** *She was anxious that he should meet her father.* 她盼望他见她父亲。 ▶ **anx·ious·ly** *adv.*：*to ask/look/wait anxiously* 忧虑地问 / 瞧 / 等待 ◇ *Residents are anxiously awaiting a decision.* 居民焦虑地等待决定。

any /ˈeni/ *det., pron., adv.*

■ *det.* **1** used with uncountable or plural nouns in negative sentences and questions, after *if* or *whether*, and after some verbs such as *prevent, ban, forbid*, etc. to refer to an amount or a number of sth, however large or small（与不可数或复数名词连用，用于否定句和疑问句，也用于 if 或 whether 之后，或紧接某些动词如 prevent、ban、forbid 等）任何的，任一的：*I didn't eat any meat.* 我一点儿肉也没吃。◇ *Are there any stamps?* 有邮票吗？◇ *I've got hardly any money.* 我几乎不名一文。◇ *You can't go out without any shoes.* 你不能不穿鞋就出门。◇ *He forbids any talking in class.* 他严禁课堂上讲话。◇ *She asked if we had any questions.* 她问我们有没有问题。 HELP In positive sentences **some** is usually used instead of **any**. 在肯定句中通常用 some 不用 any：*I've got some paper if you want it.* 你需要纸吗？我这儿有。It is also used in questions that expect a positive answer. * some 还用于预期得到肯定回答的问句中：*Would you like some milk in your tea?* 茶里加点奶吗？ **2** used with singular countable nouns to refer to one of a number of things or people, when it does not matter which one（与单数可数名词连用）任一：*Take any book you like.* 你喜欢哪本书就拿哪本。 ◇ *Any colour will do.* 什么颜色都行。◇ *Any teacher will tell you that students learn at different rates.* 任何老师都知道学生学习有快有慢。➲ SEE ALSO IN ANY CASE at CASE *n.*, IN ANY EVENT at EVENT, AT ANY RATE at RATE *n.* **3 not just ~ sb/sth** used to show that sb/sth is special 非一般的；不寻常的：*It isn't just any day—it's my birthday!* 今天不是一般的日子，是我的生日！

■ *pron.* **1** used in negative sentences and in questions and after *if* or *whether* to refer to an amount or a number, however large or small（用于否定和疑问句中或 if、whether 后）任何数量，任一数额：*We need some more paint; there isn't any left.* 我们还需要一些油漆，已经用光了。◇ *I need some stamps. Are there any in your bag?* 我需要一些邮票。你包里有吗？ ◇ *Please let me know how many people are coming, if any.* 如果有人要来的话，请告诉我有多少。◇ *She spent hardly any of the money.* 这钱她几乎一点儿都没花。◇ *He returned home without any of the others.* 仅他一人回到了家。 HELP In positive sentences **some** is usually used instead of **any**. It is also used in questions that expect a positive reply. 在肯定句中通常用 some 而非 any。some 还用于预期得到肯定回答的问句中：*I've got plenty of paper—would you like some?* 我的纸够多的了，你要点儿吗？ **2** one or more of a number of people or things, especially when it does not matter which 任一；任何一些：*I'll take any you don't want.* 你不要的我拿走。◇ *'Which colour do you want?' 'Any of them will do.'* "你要哪种颜色？" "随便哪种都行。"

IDM **sb isn't having any (of it)** (*informal*) somebody is not interested or does not agree 某人不感兴趣；某人不同意：*I suggested sharing the cost, but he wasn't having any of it.* 我提议分担费用，可是他不同意。

■ *adv.* **1** used to emphasize an adjective or adverb in negative sentences or questions, meaning 'at all'（用于否定句或疑问句中，加强形容词或副词的语气）一点儿也（不），完全（不），丝毫：*He wasn't any good at French.* 他的法语糟透了。◇ *I can't run any faster.* 我不能跑得更快了。◇ *Is your father feeling any better?* 你父亲身体好些了吗？ ◇ *I don't want any more.* 我不再要了。◇ *If you don't tell them, nobody will be* **any the wiser** (= they will not find out about it). 如果你不告诉他们，谁也不会察觉。 **2** (*NAmE, informal*) used at the end of a negative sentence to mean 'at all'（用于否定句末）根本（不）：*That won't hurt you any.* 那根本不会伤害你。

any·body /ˈenibɒdi; *NAmE* -bɑːdi; -bʌdi/ *pron.* = ANYONE：*Is there anybody who can help me?* 有人能帮我吗？ ◇ *Anybody can use the pool—you don't need to be a member.* 任何人都可使用这个游泳池，不必是会员。 ◇ *She wasn't anybody before she got that job.* 她在获得那个职位之前不过是个无名之辈。

any·how /ˈenihaʊ/ *adv.* **1** = ANYWAY **2** in a careless way; not arranged in an order 随便地；杂乱无章地：*She piled the papers in a heap on her desk, just anyhow.* 她把文件在桌上随便搁成一堆。

any 'more (*BrE*) (*also* **any·more** *NAmE, BrE*) *adv.* often used at the end of negative sentences and at the end of questions, to mean 'any longer'（常用于否定句和疑问句句末）再也（不），（不）再：*She doesn't live here any more.* 她已经不在这里住了。◇ *Why doesn't he speak to me any more?* 他为啥不再理我了？ ◇ *Now she won't have to go out to work any more.* 现在她不必再出去工作了。 HELP Do not use 'no more' with this meaning. 不能用 no more 表示此义：~~*She doesn't live here no more.*~~

any·one /ˈeniwʌn/ (*also* **any·body**) *pron.* **1** used instead of *someone* in negative sentences and in questions after *if/whether*, and after verbs such as *prevent, forbid, avoid*, etc.（用于否定句、疑问句，也用于 if 或 whether 之后，或紧接 prevent、forbid、avoid 等动词，代替 someone）任何人：*Is anyone there?* 有人吗？◇ *Does anyone else want to come?* 还有人想来吗？ ◇ *Did anyone see you?* 有没有人见到了你？ ◇ *Hardly anyone came.* 几乎没有人来。◇ *I forbid anyone to touch that clock.* 我不准任何人碰那台钟。 HELP The difference between **anyone** and **someone** is the same as the difference between **any** and **some**. Look at the notes there. * anyone 和 someone 的区别与 any 和 some 的区别相同。参看该两词条下的注解。 **2** any person at all; it does not matter who 随便哪个人：*Anybody can see that it's wrong.* 随便哪个人都可以看出这是错的。◇ *The exercises are so simple that almost anyone can do them.* 练习十分简单，几乎谁都会做。 **3** (in negative sentences 用于否定句) an important person 重要人物：*She wasn't anyone before she got that job.* 她在获得那个职位之前不过是个无名之辈。

any·place /ˈenipleɪs/ *adv.* (*NAmE*) = ANYWHERE

any·thing /ˈeniθɪŋ/ *pron.* **1** used instead of *something* in negative sentences and in questions; after *if/whether*; and after verbs such as *prevent, ban, avoid*, etc.（用于否定句、疑问句，也用于 if 或 whether 之后，或紧接 prevent、ban、avoid 等动词，代替 something）任何东西，任何事物：*Would you like anything else?* 你要点别的什么吗？ ◇ *There's never anything worth watching on TV.* 电视上根本没有什么值得看的节目。◇ *If you remember* *anything at all, please let us know.* 如果你记得点儿什么请告诉我们。◇ *We hope to prevent anything unpleasant from happening.* 我们希望防止任何不愉快的事发生。 HELP The difference between **anything** and **something** is the same as the difference between **any** and **some**. Look at the notes there. * anything 和 something 的区别与 any 和 some 的区别相同。参看该两词条下的注解。 **2** any thing at all, when it does not matter which 随便哪个东西；随便什么事物： *I'm so hungry, I'll eat anything.* 我饿慌了，随便吃什么都行。 **3** any thing of importance 重要东西；重要事物： *Is there anything* (= any truth) *in these rumours?* 这些传闻中有没有真实的东西？

IDM **anything but** definitely not 决不；根本不： *The hotel was anything but cheap.* 这家旅馆根本不便宜。◇ *It wasn't cheap. Anything but.* 它不便宜。绝对不。 **anything like sb/sth** (*informal*) (used in questions and negative statements 用于疑问句和否定陈述) similar to sb/sth 和…相像；与…相似： *He isn't anything like my first boss.* 他完全不像我的第一个老板。 **as happy, quick, etc. as anything** (*informal*) very happy, quick, etc. 非常幸福（或迅速等）： *I felt as pleased as anything.* 我感到无比高兴。 **like 'anything** (*BrE, informal*) very much 非常；像什么似的： *They're always slagging me off like anything.* 他们经常把我骂得狗血淋头。 **not anything like as good, much, etc.** used to emphasize that sth is not as good, not enough, etc. 根本不，无论如何都不（好、够等）： *The book wasn't anything like as good as her first one.* 这本书远远不如她的处女作。 **not for 'anything** (*informal*) definitely not 决不；根本不： *I wouldn't give it up for anything.* 我决不放弃。 **or anything** (*informal*) or another thing of a similar type 或其他什么类似的： *If you want to call a meeting or anything, just let me know.* 要是你想召集个会议什么的，就请告诉我。

'any time (*BrE*) (*also* **any·time** *NAmE, BrE*) *adv.* at a time that is not fixed 在任何时候；随便什么时候： *Call me any time.* 随时给我打电话。

IDM **,anytime 'soon** (*especially NAmE*) used in negative sentences and questions to refer to the near future （用于否定句和疑问句）即将，马上： *Will she be back anytime soon?* 她会马上回来吗？

Any·town /ˈenitaʊn/ *noun* [U] (*NAmE*) a way of referring to a typical small town in the US （美国）任一代表性小镇： *Let's say you run a store in Anytown, USA.* 比方说，你在美国小镇经营一家店。

any·way /ˈeniweɪ/ (*also* **any·how**) (*also NAmE, informal* **any·ways**) *adv.* **1** used when adding sth to support an idea or argument 而且；加之；反正 SYN **besides**： *It's too expensive and anyway the colour doesn't suit you.* 这个太贵，而且颜色也不适合你。◇ *It's too late now, anyway.* 反正现在已经太迟了。 **2** despite sth; even so 尽管；即使这样： *The water was cold but I took a shower anyway.* 水很冷，不过我还是冲了个淋浴。 ◇ *I'm afraid we can't come, but thanks for the invitation anyway.* 恐怕我们来不了，不过还是感谢邀请。 **3** used when changing the subject of a conversation, ending the conversation or returning to a subject （转换话题、结束谈话或回到原话题时说）不过，总之，反正： *Anyway, let's forget about that for the moment.* 总之，眼下别想这事。◇ *Anyway, I'd better go now—I'll see you tomorrow.* 不过我还是走吧，明天见。 **4** used to correct or slightly change what you have said （纠正或略微改变说过的话）至少： *She works in a bank. She did when I last saw her, anyway.* 她在银行工作。至少我上次见到她时是这样。

any·where /ˈeniweə(r); *NAmE* -wer/ (*NAmE also* **any·place**) *adv.* **1** used in negative sentences and in questions instead of *somewhere* （用于否定句和疑问句，代替 somewhere）在任何地方： *I can't see it anywhere.* 我哪儿也见不到它。◇ *Did you go anywhere interesting?* 你去过什么有趣的地方吗？ ◇ *Many of these animals are not found anywhere else.* 这些动物中有很多是其他地方没有的。◇ *He's never been anywhere outside Britain.* 他从来没有去过英国以外的任何地方。 HELP The difference between **anywhere** and **somewhere** is the same as the difference between **any** and **some**. Look at the notes there. * anywhere 和 somewhere 的区别与 any 和 some 的区别相同。参看该两词条下的注解。 **2** in, at or to any place, when it does not matter where 在（或去）任何地方；随便哪个地方： *Put the box down anywhere.* 把箱子随便放在哪儿都可以。◇ *An accident can happen anywhere.* 任何地方都可能发生事故。
▸ **any·where** *pron.*： *I don't have anywhere to stay.* 我没有可以待的地方。◇ *Do you know anywhere I can buy a second-hand computer?* 你知道我在哪儿可以买到二手计算机吗？

AOB /ˌeɪ əʊ ˈbiː; *NAmE* oʊ/ *abbr.* any other business (the things that are discussed at the end of an official meeting that are not on the AGENDA) 其他事项（正式会议末尾所讨论的未列入议程的事项）

A-OK /ˌeɪ əʊ ˈkeɪ; *NAmE* ˌeɪ oʊ ˈkeɪ/ *adj.* [not before noun] (*NAmE, informal*) in good condition; in an acceptable manner 状况良好；过得去；还好： *Everything's A-OK now.* 现在一切都妥帖了。 ▸ **A-OK** *adv.*： *The party went off A-OK.* 聚会进行得还顺利。

aorta /eɪˈɔːtə; *NAmE* eɪˈɔːrtə/ *noun* (*anatomy* 解) the main ARTERY that carries blood from the heart to the rest of the body once it has passed through the LUNGS 主动脉

Ao·tea·roa /aʊˌteɪəˈrəʊə; *NAmE* -ˈroʊə/ *noun* (*NZE*) the Maori name for New Zealand, usually translated as 'the land of the long white cloud' 新西兰（毛利语，意为"白云绵绵之地"）

apace /əˈpeɪs/ *adv.* (*formal*) at a fast speed; quickly 高速地；迅速地： *to* ***continue/grow/proceed/develop apace*** 保持高速；迅速生长；进展迅速；高速发展

Apa·che /əˈpætʃi/ *noun* (*pl.* **Apa·che** or **Apa·ches**) a member of a Native American people, many of whom live in the south-western US 阿帕切人（美洲土著，多居于美国西南部）

apart /əˈpɑːt; *NAmE* əˈpɑːrt/ *adv.* **1** separated by a distance, of space or time （指空间或时间）相隔，相距： *The two houses stood 500 metres apart.* 两座房子相距500米。◇ *Their birthdays are only three days apart.* 他们的生日仅隔三日。◇ (*figurative*) *The two sides in the talks are still a long way apart* (= are far from reaching an agreement). 谈判双方的意见仍相去甚远。 **2** not together; separate or separately 不在一起；分离；分开： *We're living apart now.* 我们现在不住在一起。◇ *Over the years, Rosie and I had* ***drifted apart***. 多年以来，我和罗西早已疏远。◇ *She keeps herself apart from other people.* 她与其他人保持距离。◇ *I can't* ***tell*** *the twins* ***apart*** (= see the difference between them). 我分不出这一对双胞胎中谁是谁。 **3** into pieces 成碎片： *The whole thing just* ***came apart*** *in my hands.* 这整件东西偏偏在我手里破裂了。◇ *We had to* ***take*** *the engine* ***apart***. 我们不得不拆卸了引擎。◇ *When his wife died, his world* ***fell apart***. 他在妻子去世后万念俱灰。 **4** used to say that sb/sth is not included in what you are talking about （指所说的不包括在内）除外： *Victoria apart, not one of them seems suitable for the job.* 除了维多利亚，看来他们谁也不适合这个工作。 IDM SEE JOKE *v.*, POLE *n.*, RIP *v.*, WORLD

a'part from (*also* **a'side from** *especially in NAmE*) *prep.* **1** except for 除了…外（都）；要不是： *I've finished apart from the last question.* 除了最后一道题，我全做完了。 ⮊ LANGUAGE BANK AT EXCEPT **2** in addition to; as well as 除了…外（还）；此外；加之： *Apart from their house in London, they also have a villa in Spain.* 他们在伦敦有一座房子，此外在西班牙还有一座别墅。◇ *It was a difficult time. Apart from everything else, we had financial problems.* 当时是困难时期。别的且不说，我们财政上就有问题。 ◇ *You've got to help. Apart from anything else you're my brother.* 你得帮忙。别的不说，你总归是我兄弟。 ⮊ NOTE AT BESIDE

apart·heid /əˈpɑːtaɪt; əˈpɑːteɪt; *NAmE* əˈpɑːrtaɪt; əˈpɑːrteɪt/ *noun* [U] the former political system in South Africa in which only white people had full political rights and other people, especially black people, were forced to live away from white people, go to separate schools, etc. 种族隔离（前南非政府推行的政策）

A

apart·ment /əˈpɑːtmənt; *NAmE* əˈpɑːrt-/ *noun* **1** (*especially NAmE*) a set of rooms for living in, usually on one floor of a building （通常指在同一楼层的）公寓套房 ➲ COLLOCATIONS AT HOUSE ➲ COMPARE CONDOMINIUM, FLAT *n.* (1) **2** a set of rooms used for a holiday/vacation （度假用的）公寓套房： *self-catering holiday apartments* 可自己开伙的度假套房 **3** [usually pl.] (*BrE*) a room in a house, especially a large or famous house （尤指巨屋、名宅的）房间： *You can visit the whole palace except for the private apartments.* 整座宫殿除内殿外均可参观。

aˈpartment block (*BrE*) (*NAmE* **aˈpartment building**) *noun* a large building with flats/apartments on each floor 公寓大楼 ➲ VISUAL VOCAB PAGE V16

aˈpartment house *noun* (*US*) a small apartment block （小的）公寓楼

apa·thet·ic /ˌæpəˈθetɪk/ *adj.* showing no interest or enthusiasm 冷漠；淡漠；无动于衷： *The illness made her apathetic and unwilling to meet people.* 疾病使她心情低落，不愿见人。 ▶ **apa·thet·ic·al·ly** /ˌæpəˈθetɪkli/ *adv.*

ap·athy /ˈæpəθi/ *noun* [U] the feeling of not being interested in or enthusiastic about something, or things in general 冷漠；淡漠： *There is **widespread apathy** among the electorate.* 选民普遍态度冷淡。

apato·saurus /əˌpætəˈsɔːrəs/ (*also* **bron·to·saurus**) *noun* a very large DINOSAUR with a long neck and tail 谬龙（长颈长尾的巨型恐龙）

APB /ˌeɪ piː ˈbiː/ *abbr.* (*NAmE*) ALL-POINTS BULLETIN 全面警戒通告

ape /eɪp/ *noun, verb*

■ ***noun*** a large animal like a MONKEY, with no tail. There are different types of ape. 类人猿： *the great apes* (= for example, ORANG-UTANS or CHIMPANZEES) 类人猿（如猩猩、黑猩猩）

IDM **go ˈape/ˈapeshit** (*slang, especially NAmE*) to become extremely angry or excited 暴跳如雷；激动异常

■ ***verb*** **1** **~ sb/sth** (*BrE, disapproving*) to do sth in the same way as sb else, especially when it is not done very well （尤指笨拙地）模仿，学…的样子 SYN **imitate**： *For years the British film industry merely aped Hollywood.* 多年来，英国电影业一味模仿好莱坞。 **2** **~ sb/sth** (*especially NAmE*) to copy the way sb else behaves or talks, in order to make fun of them （为了取笑）学…的样，模仿 SYN **mimic**： *We used to ape the teacher's southern accent.* 我们过去常模仿老师的南方口音。

ape·man /ˈeɪpmæn/ *noun* (*pl.* **-men** /-men/) a large animal, half way between an APE and a human, thought to have existed before modern humans developed 猿人

aperi·tif /əˌperəˈtiːf/ *noun* a drink, usually one containing alcohol, that people sometimes have just before a meal （餐前）开胃酒

aper·ture /ˈæpətʃə(r); *NAmE also* -tʃʊr/ *noun* **1** (*formal*) a small opening in sth 小孔；缝隙 **2** (*specialist*) an opening that allows light to reach a LENS, especially in cameras （尤指摄影机等的光圈）孔径： *For flash photography, set the aperture at f.5.6.* 用闪光照相，要把光圈孔径定为 5.6。

ape·shit /ˈeɪpʃɪt/ *noun*

IDM **go ˈapeshit** ➲ APE *n.*

Apex /ˈeɪpeks/ (*also* **APEX**) *abbr.* Advanced Purchase Excursion (a system that offers cheaper travel tickets when they are bought in advance) 预付款旅游票优惠

apex /ˈeɪpeks/ *noun* [usually sing.] (*pl.* **apexes**) the top or highest part of sth 顶点；最高点： *the apex of the roof/triangle* 房顶；三角形的顶点 ◇ (*figurative*) *At 37, she'd reached the apex of her career.* 她在 37 岁时达到了事业的巅峰。

apha·sia /əˈfeɪziə/ *noun* [U] (*medical* 医) the loss of the ability to understand or produce speech, because of brain damage 失语（症）

aphid /ˈeɪfɪd/ *noun* a very small insect that is harmful to plants. There are several types of aphid, including, for example, GREENFLY. 蚜虫

aph·or·ism /ˈæfərɪzəm/ *noun* (*formal*) a short phrase that says sth true or wise 格言；警句 ▶ **aph·or·is·tic** /ˌæfəˈrɪstɪk/ *adj.*

aph·ro·dis·iac /ˌæfrəˈdɪziæk/ *noun* a food or drug that is said to give people a strong desire to have sex 春药；激发性欲的食物 ▶ **aph·ro·dis·iac** *adj.*： *the aphrodisiac qualities of ginseng* 人参的催欲功效

api·ary /ˈeɪpiəri; *NAmE* -ieri/ *noun* (*pl.* **-ies**) a place where BEES are kept 养蜂场

apiece /əˈpiːs/ *adv.* (used after a noun or number 用于名词或数字后) having, costing or measuring a particular amount each 每人；每个；各： *Sterling and Walcott scored a goal apiece.* 斯特林和沃尔科特各进一球。 ◇ *The largest stones weigh over five tonnes apiece.* 最大的石头每块重五吨以上。

aplenty /əˈplenti/ *adv., adj.* [after noun] (*formal*) in large amounts, especially more than is needed 大量；充裕；绰绰有余

aplomb /əˈplɒm; *NAmE* əˈplɑːm/ *noun* [U] (*formal*) if sb does sth **with aplomb**, they do it in a confident and successful way, often in a difficult situation 镇定；沉着；泰然自若： *with **considerable/great/remarkable aplomb*** 相当的／十分的／非凡的镇定 ◇ *He delivered the speech with his **usual aplomb**.* 他以惯常的沉着语气作了演讲。

ap·noea (*BrE*) (*NAmE* **ap·nea**) /æpˈniːə/ *noun* [U] (*medical* 医) a condition in which sb stops breathing temporarily, especially while they are sleeping （睡眠）呼吸暂停

apoca·lypse /əˈpɒkəlɪps; *NAmE* əˈpɑːk-/ *noun* **1** [sing., U] the destruction of the world 世界毁灭： *Civilization is on the brink of apocalypse.* 文明已濒临毁灭的边缘。 **2 the Apocalypse** [sing.] the end of the world, as described in the Bible （《圣经》所述的）末世 **3** [sing.] a situation causing very serious damage and destruction 大动乱；大灾变： *an environmental apocalypse* 环境大灾变

apoca·lyp·tic /əˌpɒkəˈlɪptɪk; *NAmE* əˌpɑːk-/ *adj.* **1** describing very serious damage and destruction in past or future events 描述（历史）大动乱的；预示（未来）大灾变的： *an apocalyptic view of history* 对历史极其悲观的观点 ◇ *apocalyptic warnings of the end of society* 对社会末日骇人听闻的预警 **2** like the end of the world 似末世的；像世界末日的： *an apocalyptic scene* 末世景象

apoc·rypha /əˈpɒkrɪfə; *NAmE* əˈpɑːk-/ *noun* [sing. or pl. v.] **1** Christian religious texts that are related to the Bible but not officially considered to be part of it 外典，旁经（没有列入正典《圣经》的经籍） **2** writings which are not considered to be genuine 赝文；伪书

apoc·ryph·al /əˈpɒkrɪfl; *NAmE* əˈpɑːk-/ *adj.* (of a story 传说) well known, but probably not true 流传甚广但不足为凭的；虚构的： *Most of the stories about him are apocryphal.* 关于他的传闻多属虚构。

apo·gee /ˈæpədʒiː/ *noun* [sing.] **1** (*formal*) the highest point of sth, where it is greatest or most successful 顶峰；顶点；最高点 **2** (*astronomy* 天) the point in the ORBIT of the moon, a planet or other object in space when it is furthest from the planet, for example the earth, around which it turns 远地点（绕地运动的天体在轨道上离地球或其他行星的最远点） ➲ COMPARE PERIGEE

apol·it·ical /ˌeɪpəˈlɪtɪkl/ *adj.* **1** (of a person 人) not interested in politics; not thinking politics are important 不关心政治的；不重视政治的 **2** not connected with a political party 与政党无关的

apolo·get·ic /əˌpɒləˈdʒetɪk; *NAmE* əˌpɑːl-/ *adj.* feeling or showing that you are sorry for doing sth wrong or for causing a problem 道歉的；谢罪的；愧疚的： *'Sorry,' she said, with an apologetic smile.* "对不起。"她说，歉然一笑。 ◇ **~ about/for sth** *They were very apologetic about the trouble they'd caused.* 他们对所惹的麻烦深感愧疚。 ▶ **apolo·get·ic·al·ly** /əˌpɒləˈdʒetɪkli; *NAmE* əˌpɑːl-/ *adv.*：

'I'm sorry I'm late,' he murmured apologetically. "对不起，我迟到了。" 他小声道歉说。

apo·lo·gia /ˌæpəˈləʊdʒiə; *NAmE* -ˈloʊ-/ *noun* (*formal*) a formal written defence of your own or sb else's actions or opinions 书面辩解；辩解书；辩解文：*His book was seen as an apologia for the war.* 他的著作被视为是对这场战争的辩护。

apolo·gist /əˈpɒlədʒɪst; *NAmE* əˈpɑːl-/ *noun* ~ (**for sb/sth**) a person who tries to explain and defend sth, especially a political system or religious ideas（尤指政治或宗教方面的）辩护者，辩解者

apolo·gize (*BrE also* **-ise**) /əˈpɒlədʒaɪz; *NAmE* əˈpɑːl-/ *verb* [I] ~ (**to sb**) (**for sth**) to say that you are sorry for doing sth wrong or causing a problem 道歉；谢罪：*Why should I apologize?* 我为什么要道歉？◇ *Go and apologize to her.* 去给她赔不是。◇ *We apologize for the late departure of this flight.* 本航班起飞延误，谨致歉意。➲ WORDFINDER NOTE AT SORRY ➲ EXPRESS YOURSELF AT SORRY

apol·ogy /əˈpɒlədʒi; *NAmE* əˈpɑːl-/ *noun* (*pl.* **-ies**) **1** [C, U] ~ (**to sb**) (**for sth**) a word or statement saying sorry for sth that has been done wrong or that causes a problem 道歉；谢罪：*to **offer/make/demand/accept an apology*** 主动道歉；致歉；要求 / 接受道歉 ◇ *You **owe him an apology** for what you said.* 你要为你所说的话向他道歉。◇ *We should like to offer our apologies for the delay to your flight today.* 今天航班误点，敬请原谅。◇ *We received a letter of apology.* 我们收到了一封道歉信。**2** [C, usually pl.] information that you cannot go to a meeting or must leave early（因不能赴会或提前离会的）致歉：*The meeting started with apologies* (= the names of people who said they could not go to the meeting). 会议一开始就宣布了请假缺席者的名单。◇ (*formal*) *She **made her apologies** and left early.* 她致歉后就提前离开了。➲ WORDFINDER NOTE AT MEETING

IDM **make no aˈpology/aˈpologies for sth** if you say that you **make no apology/apologies for** sth, you mean that you do not feel that you have said or done anything wrong（对某事）无可道歉，无错可认

apo·plec·tic /ˌæpəˈplektɪk/ *adj.* **1** very angry 大怒的；十分生气的：*He was apoplectic with rage at the decision.* 他对这个决定异常愤怒。**2** (*old-fashioned*) connected with apoplexy 中风的：*an **apoplectic attack/fit*** 中风的发作

apo·plexy /ˈæpəpleksi/ *noun* [U] (*old-fashioned*) the sudden loss of the ability to feel or move, normally caused by an injury in the brain 中风；（脑）卒中 SYN **stroke**

aporia /əˈpɔːriə/ *noun* (*specialist*) a situation in which two or more parts of a theory or argument do not agree, meaning that the theory or argument cannot be true（理论或论据的）自相矛盾，不成立

apos·tate /əˈpɒsteɪt; *NAmE* əˈpɑːs-/ *noun* (*formal*) a person who has rejected their religious or political beliefs 叛教者；脱党者；变节者 ▶ **apos·tasy** /əˈpɒstəsi; *NAmE* əˈpɑːs-/ *noun* [U]

a pos·teri·ori /ˌeɪ ˌpɒsteriˈɔːraɪ; *NAmE* ˌpɑːs-/ *adj., adv.* (*from Latin, formal*) analysing sth by starting from known facts and then thinking about the possible causes of the facts, for example saying 'Look, the streets are wet so it must have been raining.' 从事实推断原因；由果及因 ➲ COMPARE A PRIORI

apos·tle /əˈpɒsl; *NAmE* əˈpɑːsl/ *noun* **1 Apostle** any one of the twelve men that Christ chose to tell people about him and his teachings 宗徒，使徒（耶稣十二门徒之一）**2** ~ (**of sth**) (*formal*) a person who strongly believes in a policy or an idea and tries to make other people believe in it（政策或思想的）倡导者，鼓吹者：*an apostle of free enterprise* 自由企业的鼓吹者

apos·tolic /ˌæpəˈstɒlɪk; *NAmE* -ˈstɑːlɪk/ *adj.* (*specialist*) **1** connected with the Apostles or their teaching 宗徒的；使徒的；传自宗徒的 **2** connected with the Pope or Popes, who are considered to have had authority passed down to them from Christ's Apostles 罗马教皇的；宗座的

apos·tro·phe /əˈpɒstrəfi; *NAmE* əˈpɑːs-/ *noun* **1** the mark (') used to show that one or more letters or numbers have been left out, as in *she's* for *she is* and *'63* for *1963* 撇号；省字符 **2** the mark (') used before or after the letter 's' to show that sth belongs to sb, as in *Sam's watch* and *the horses' tails* 撇号；所有格符号 **3** the mark (') used before the letter 's' to show the plural of a letter or number, as in *How many 3's are there in 9?* and *There are two m's in 'comma'.* 撇号；复数符号

apos·tro·phize (*BrE also* **-ise**) /əˈpɒstrəfaɪz; *NAmE* əˈpɑːs-/ *verb* **1** (*specialist*) ~ **sb** to address what you are saying, or a poem, a speech in a play, etc. to a particular person 对…述说；向…诵诗（或台词等）**2** ~ **sth** to add apostrophes to a piece of writing 给…加撇号

apoth·ecary /əˈpɒθəkəri; *NAmE* əˈpɑːθəkeri/ *noun* (*pl.* **-ies**) a person who made and sold medicines in the past（旧时制药兼售药的）药剂师，药商

apothe·osis /əˌpɒθiˈəʊsɪs; *NAmE* əˌpɑːθiˈoʊ-/ *noun* [usually sing.] (*pl.* **apothe·oses** /-siːz/) (*formal*) **1** the highest or most perfect development of sth 鼎盛时期；发展顶峰；完美阶段 **2** the best time in sb's life or career（人生或事业的）巅峰 **3** a formal statement that a person has become a god（指人）擢升为神，尊奉为神，神化：*the apotheosis of a Roman emperor* 擢升罗马皇帝为神

app /æp/ *noun* **1** a piece of software that you can download to a device such as a SMARTPHONE or TABLET (4), for example to look up information or to play a game（下载到智能手机或平板电脑等设备上使用的）应用软件：*Have you got the dictionary app on your phone?* 你的手机上有这个词典的应用软件吗？**2** APPLICATION (5) 应用程序；应用软件

appa /ˈʌpə/ *noun* (*IndE*) = ABBA

appal (*BrE*) (*NAmE* **ap·pall**) /əˈpɔːl/ *verb* (**-ll-**) to shock sb very much 使大为震惊；使惊骇 SYN **horrify**：~ **sb** *The brutality of the crime has appalled the public.* 罪行之残暴使公众大为震惊。◇ *The idea of sharing a room appalled her.* 合住一个房间的想法吓着了她。◇ **it appals sb that…/to do sth** *It appalled me that they could simply ignore the problem.* 他们竟然对这个问题置之不理，令我非常诧异。➲ MORE LIKE THIS 36, page R29

ap·palled /əˈpɔːld/ *adj.* feeling or showing horror or disgust at sth unpleasant or wrong 感到惊骇的；表示憎恶的 SYN **horrified**：*an **appalled expression/silence*** 惊恐的表情；吓得说不出话 ◇ *We watched appalled as the child ran in front of the car.* 小孩在汽车前面跑过，我们看得心惊胆战。◇ ~ **at sth** *They were appalled at the waste of recyclable material.* 他们憎恶浪费可回收材料。

ap·pal·ling /əˈpɔːlɪŋ/ *adj.* **1** (*NAmE, formal* or *BrE*) shocking; extremely bad 令人震惊的；使人惊骇的；极为恶劣的：*The prisoners were living in appalling conditions.* 囚犯的居住条件极为恶劣。**2** (*informal*) very bad 糟糕的；很不像话的：*The bus service is appalling now.* 现在公共汽车服务很差。▶ **ap·pal·ling·ly** *adv.*：***appallingly bad/difficult*** 极差；极为困难 ◇ *The essay was appallingly written.* 这文章写得一塌糊涂。

app·ar·at /ˌæpəˈrɑːt/ *noun* [usually sing.] the system of officials, offices, etc. that a government, especially a Communist government, uses to run a country（尤指共产党的）政府体制

ap·par·at·chik /ˌæpəˈrɑːtʃɪk/ *noun* (*from Russian, disapproving* or *humorous*) an official in a large political organization（大政治机构的）官员：*party apparatchiks* 党的官员

ap·par·atus /ˌæpəˈreɪtəs; *NAmE* -ˈrætəs/ *noun* (*pl.* **ap·par·atuses**) **1** [U] the tools or other pieces of equipment that are needed for a particular activity or task 仪器；器械；装置：*a piece of laboratory apparatus* 一件实验室仪器 ◇ *Firefighters needed breathing apparatus to enter the burning house.* 消防队员需要呼吸器以便进入燃烧的大楼。

A

➲ SYNONYMS AT EQUIPMENT **2** [C, usually sing.] the structure of a system or an organization, particularly that of a political party or a government（尤指政党或政府的）机构，组织，机关：*the power of the state apparatus* 国家机关的权力 **3** [C, usually sing.] (*specialist*) a system of organs in the body 器官：*the sensory apparatus* 感觉器官

ap·parel /əˈpærəl/ *noun* [U] **1** (*especially NAmE*) clothing, when it is being sold in shops/stores（商店出售的）衣服，服装：*The store sells women's and children's apparel.* 这家商店出售女装和童装。 **2** (*old-fashioned* or *formal*) clothes, particularly those worn on a formal occasion（尤指正式场合穿的）衣服，服装：*lords and ladies in fine apparel* 衣着漂亮的贵族和贵妇

ap·par·ent 🔑 AW /əˈpærənt/ *adj.* **1** 🔑 [not usually before noun] easy to see or understand 显而易见；明白易懂；显然 SYN **obvious**：*Their devotion was apparent.* 他们的忠诚显而易见。◇ *Then, **for no apparent reason**, the train suddenly stopped.* 接着，不知什么原因，火车突然停了下来。◇ ~ **(from sth) (that…)** *It was apparent from her face that she was really upset.* 从面容上一眼就可以看出她确实心绪烦乱。◇ ~ **(to sb) (that…)** *It soon **became apparent** to everyone that he couldn't sing.* 很快大家就看出来他不会唱歌。➲ SYNONYMS AT CLEAR ➲ LANGUAGE BANK AT ILLUSTRATE **2** 🔑 [usually before noun] that seems to be real or true but may not be 貌似的；表面上的；未必真实的 SYN **seeming**：*My parents were concerned at my apparent lack of enthusiasm for school.* 我看来对上学不感兴趣，使父母担心。➲ SEE ALSO APPEAR

ap·par·ent·ly 🔑 AW /əˈpærəntli/ *adv.* according to what you have heard or read; according to the way sth appears 可见；看来；显然：*Apparently they are getting divorced soon.* 看样子，他们很快就要离婚。◇ *I thought she had retired, but apparently she hasn't.* 我原以为她退休了，但显然她还没有退。◇ *He paused, apparently lost in thought.* 他停顿下来，显然陷入了沉思。

ap·par·ition /ˌæpəˈrɪʃn/ *noun* a GHOST or an image of a person who is dead（人死后的）鬼，鬼魂，幽灵

ap·peal 🔑 /əˈpiːl/ *noun, verb*

■ ***noun*** **1** 🔑 [C, U] a formal request to a court or to sb in authority for a judgement or a decision to be changed 上诉；申诉：(*BrE*) *to lodge an appeal* 提出上诉 ◇ (*NAmE*) *to file an appeal* 提出上诉 ◇ (*BrE*) *an appeal court/judge* 上诉法庭 / 法官 ◇ (*NAmE*) *an appeals court/judge* 上诉法庭 / 法官 ◇ ~ **against sth** *an appeal against the 3-match ban* 不服禁赛 3 场令的申诉 ➲ WORDFINDER NOTE AT TRIAL ➲ COLLOCATIONS AT JUSTICE ➲ SEE ALSO COURT OF APPEAL **2** 🔑 [U] a quality that makes sb/sth attractive or interesting 吸引力；感染力；魅力：***mass/wide/popular appeal*** 对大众的 / 广泛的 / 普遍的吸引力 ◇ *The Beatles have never really **lost their appeal**.* 披头士乐队的感染力经久不衰。◇ *The prospect of living in a city **holds little appeal** for me.* 住在城市里的机会对我没有什么吸引力。➲ SEE ALSO SEX APPEAL **3** 🔑 [C, U] an urgent and deeply felt request for money, help or information, especially one made by a charity or by the police（尤指慈善机构或警方的）呼吁，吁请，恳求：*a look of silent appeal* 默默恳求的目光 ◇ ~ **(to sb) (for sth)** *to launch a TV appeal for donations to the charity* 通过电视呼吁为该慈善事业捐赠 ◇ *The child's mother made an emotional appeal on TV for his return.* 孩子的母亲在电视上恳切地要求儿子回家。◇ ~ **to sb to do sth** *The police made an appeal to the public to remain calm.* 警方吁请公众保持镇静。➲ WORDFINDER NOTE AT CHARITY **4** [C] ~ **to sth** an indirect suggestion that any good, fair or reasonable person would act in a particular way 启发；打动：*I relied on an appeal to his finer feelings.* 我寄望能唤起他的爱心。

■ ***verb*** **1** 🔑 [I] ~ **(to sb/sth) (against sth)** to make a formal request to a court or to sb in authority for a judgment or a decision to be changed 上诉；申诉：*He said he would appeal after being found guilty on four counts of murder.* 法庭判决他犯有四项谋杀罪，他表示要上诉。◇ *The company is appealing against the ruling.* 公司正对判决提出申诉。HELP In North American English, the form **appeal (sth) (to sb/sth)** is usually used, without a preposition. 美式英语通常用 appeal (sth) (to sb/sth)，不加介词：*The company has ten days to appeal the decision to the tribunal.* 这家公司可在十天内就该决定向裁判所提出上诉。 **2** 🔑 [I] to attract or interest sb 有吸引力；有感染力；引起兴趣：*The prospect of a long wait in the rain did not appeal.* 想到要在雨中久等使人扫兴。◇ ~ **to sb** *The design has to appeal to all ages and social groups.* 设计得要雅俗共赏，老幼皆宜。 **3** 🔑 [I] to make a serious and urgent request 呼吁；吁请；恳求：*I am appealing* (= asking for money) *on behalf of the famine victims.* 我代表饥民吁请捐款。◇ ~ **(to sb) (for sth)** *Community leaders appealed for calm* (= urged people to remain calm). 社区领导们呼吁保持冷静。◇ *Police have appealed for witnesses to come forward.* 警方呼吁证人挺身而出。◇ ~ **to sb to do sth** *Organizers appealed to the crowd not to panic.* 组织者呼吁人群不要惊慌。 **4** [I] ~ **(to sth)** to try to persuade sb to do sth by suggesting that it is a fair, reasonable or honest thing to do 启发；劝说；打动：*They needed to appeal to his sense of justice.* 他们需要激发他的正义感。

apˈpeal court *noun* **1** = COURT OF APPEAL **2 Apˈpeals Court** (*US*) = COURT OF APPEAL (3)

ap·peal·ing /əˈpiːlɪŋ/ *adj.* **1** attractive or interesting 有吸引力的；有感染力的；令人感兴趣的：*Spending the holidays in Britain wasn't a prospect that I found particularly appealing.* 在英国度假对我并不特别有吸引力。 OPP **unappealing 2** showing that you want people to help you or to show you pity or sympathy 恳求的；可怜的；希望同情的：*'Would you really help?' he said with an appealing look.* "你真的愿意帮忙吗？" 他恳求道。▸ **ap·peal·ing·ly** *adv.*：*The dog looked up at her appealingly.* 狗可怜巴巴地抬头望着她。

ap·pear 🔑 /əˈpɪə(r); *NAmE* əˈpɪr/ *verb*

• **LOOK/SEEM** 看来；好像 **1** 🔑 *linking verb* (not used in the progressive tenses 不用于进行时) to give the impression of being or doing sth 显得；看来；似乎 SYN **seem**：+ **adj.** *She didn't appear at all surprised at the news.* 她听到这消息时一点也没有显得吃惊。◇ ***It appears** unlikely that interest rates will fall further.* 看来利率不大会再降低。◇ + **noun** *He appears a perfectly normal person.* 他看上去完全是个正常的人。◇ ~ **to do sth** *She appeared to be in her late thirties.* 看样子她快四十岁了。◇ *They appeared not to know what was happening.* 他们似乎不知道正在发生的事。◇ *There appears to have been a mistake.* 看来一直有一个差错。◇ **it appears (that)**… *It appears that there has been a mistake.* 看来一直有一个差错。◇ ***It would appear that** this was a major problem.* 看来这是个主要问题。➲ LANGUAGE BANK AT PERHAPS ➲ MORE LIKE THIS 26, page R28

• **BE SEEN** 出现 **2** 🔑 [I] to start to be seen 出现；呈现；显露：*Three days later a rash appeared.* 三天后出现了皮疹。◇ + **adv./prep.** *A bus appeared around the corner.* 一辆公共汽车出现在拐角处。◇ *Smoke appeared on the horizon.* 地平线上升起了烟雾。

• **BEGIN TO EXIST** 起源；出现 **3** 🔑 [I] (+ **adv./prep.**) to begin to exist or be known or used for the first time 起源；出现；首次使用：*When did mammals appear on the earth?* 地球上的哺乳动物起源于何时？◇ *This problem first appeared in the inner cities.* 这个问题最初在内城区出现。

• **OF BOOK/PROGRAMME** 书；节目 **4** [I] (+ **adv./prep.**) to be published or broadcast 出版；广播：*His new book will be appearing in the spring.* 他的新书将于春季出版。◇ *It was too late to prevent the story from appearing in the national newspapers.* 要阻止全国性报纸刊登这件事情已为时太晚。

• **IN MOVIE/PLAY** 电影；戏剧 **5** [I] (+ **adv./prep.**) to take part in a film/movie, play, television programme, etc. 演出：*He has appeared in over 60 movies.* 他参演了 60 多部电影。◇ *She regularly appears on TV.* 她经常在电视上露面。◇ *Next month he will be appearing as Obama in a new play on Broadway.* 下月他将在百老汇上演的一出新戏中扮演奥巴马。

• **ARRIVE** 到达 **6** [I] (+ **adv./prep.**) to arrive at a place 抵达；来到：*By ten o'clock Lee still hadn't appeared.* 到十点钟李仍然没有露面。

• **BE WRITTEN/MENTIONED** 记载；提及 **7** [I] (+ **adv./prep.**) to be written or mentioned somewhere 记载；提及：*Your name will appear at the front of the book.* 你的名字将出现在书的封面上。

• IN COURT 法庭 **8** [I] (+ **adv./prep.**) to be present in court in order to give evidence or answer a charge 出庭（作证或答辩）；应诉：*A man will appear in court today charged with the murder.* 一个被控犯谋杀罪的男人今天将出庭受审。◇ *She appeared on six charges of theft.* 她因被控犯有六项盗窃罪而出庭受审。◇ *He has been asked to appear as a witness for the defence.* 他已被传唤出庭为被告作证。 **9** [I] **~ for/on behalf of sb** to act as sb's lawyer in court （作为律师）出庭；出庭当…的律师：*James Gilbert is the lawyer appearing for the defendant.* 詹姆斯·吉尔伯特作为被告的辩护律师出庭。➲ COMPARE DISAPPEAR ➲ SEE ALSO APPARENT

ap·pear·ance /ə'pɪərəns; NAmE ə'pɪr-/ *noun*

• WAY STH LOOKS/SEEMS 外观 **1** [C, U] the way that sb/sth looks on the outside; what sb/sth seems to be 外貌；外观；外表：*the **physical/outward/external appearance** of sth* 某物的外观 ◇ *She had never been greatly concerned about her appearance.* 她从来不怎么注重外貌。◇ *The dog was similar in general appearance to a spaniel.* 这条狗总的来看像西班牙猎狗。◇ *He **gave every appearance of*** (= seemed very much to be) *enjoying himself.* 他处处表现得很快活。◇ *Judging by appearances can be misleading.* 单凭外表判断可能出错。◇ ***To all appearances*** (= as far as people could tell) *he was dead.* 从一切迹象来看，他已经死了。◇ *When she lost all her money, she was determined to **keep up appearances*** (= hide the true situation and pretend that everything was going well). 她把钱全亏光时，决意佯装若无其事。

• SB/STH ARRIVING 到达 **2** [C, usually sing.] the fact of sb/sth arriving, especially when it is not expected （尤指突然的）抵达，到来：*The sudden appearance of a security guard caused them to drop the money and run.* 保安人员突然出现，他们丢下钱就跑了。◇ *I don't want to go to the party, but I suppose I'd better **put in an appearance*** (= go there for a short time). 我不想去参加这个聚会，不过我认为最好还是去露个面。 **3** [C, usually sing.] the moment at which sth begins to exist or starts to be seen or used 起源；出现；首次使用：*the early appearance of daffodils in spring* 春来早开的水仙 ◇ *the appearance of organic vegetables in the supermarkets* 有机蔬菜在超市出售

• IN PUBLIC 公开 **4** [C] an act of appearing in public, especially as a performer, politician, etc., or in court 公开露面；演出；出庭：*The Dutch player will make his first appearance for Liverpool this Saturday.* 这名荷兰球员将于本星期六在利物浦队中首次亮相。◇ *The singer's first public appearance was at the age of eight.* 这位歌手八岁时初次登台演出。◇ *the defendant's appearance in court* 被告出庭

• BEING PUBLISHED/BROADCAST 出版；广播 **5** [C, usually sing.] an act of being published or broadcast 出版；广播：*the appearance of claims about the minister's private life in the press* 关于这位大臣私生活的说法见诸报端

ap·pease /ə'pi:z/ *verb* (*formal, usually disapproving*) **1 ~ sb** to make sb calmer or less angry by giving them what they want 安抚；抚慰：*The move was widely seen as an attempt to appease critics of the regime.* 普遍认为，这一举措是试图安抚批评政权的人。 **2 ~ sb/sth** to give a country what it wants in order to avoid war 绥靖（满足另一国的要求以避免战争） ▶ **ap·pease·ment** *noun* [U]：*a policy of appeasement* 绥靖政策

ap·pel·lant /ə'pelənt/ *noun* (*law* 律) a person who appeals against a decision made in court 上诉人

ap·pel·late court /ə'pelət kɔ:t; NAmE kɔ:rt/ *noun* (*specialist*) a court in which people can appeal against decisions made in other courts of law 上诉法庭

ap·pel·la·tion /,æpə'leɪʃn/ *noun* (*formal*) a name or title 名称；称呼；称号

ap·pel·la·tive /ə'pelətɪv/ *adj., noun*

■ ***adj.*** (*formal*) relating to the giving of a name 命名的；称谓的；称呼的

■ ***noun*** (*specialist*) a common noun that is used to address a person or thing, for example 'mother' or 'doctor' 称呼词（可作呼语的名词）

ap·pend AW /ə'pend/ *verb* **~ sth (to sth)** (*formal*) to add sth to the end of a piece of writing （在文章后面）附加，增补：*Footnotes have been appended to the document.* 该文件附加了脚注。

ap·pend·age /ə'pendɪdʒ/ *noun* (*formal*) a smaller or less important part of sth larger 附加物；附属物

ap·pend·ec·tomy /,æpen'dektəmi/ *noun* [C, U] (*pl.* **-ies**) (*medical* 医) the removal of the APPENDIX by SURGERY 阑尾切除术

ap·pen·di·citis /ə,pendə'saɪtɪs/ *noun* [U] a painful swelling of the appendix that can be very serious 阑尾炎

ap·pen·dix AW /ə'pendɪks/ *noun* (*pl.* **ap·pen·di·ces** /-dɪsi:z/ or **ap·pen·dixes** /ə'pendɪksɪz/) **1** a small bag of TISSUE that is attached to the large INTESTINE. In humans, the appendix has no clear function. 阑尾：*He had to have his appendix out* (= removed). 他不得不切除了阑尾。➲ VISUAL VOCAB PAGE V64 **2** a section giving extra information at the end of a book or document （书、文件的）附录：*Full details are given in Appendix 3.* 详见附录 3。

ap·per·tain /,æpə'teɪn; NAmE -pər't-/ *verb*

PHR V **apper'tain to sb/sth** (*formal*) to belong or refer to sb/sth 属于；涉及；关系到：*rights appertaining to the property* 产权 ◇ *These figures appertain to last year's sales.* 这些数字指的是去年的销售额。

ap·pe·tite /'æpɪtaɪt/ *noun* **1** [U, C, usually sing.] physical desire for food 食欲；胃口：*He suffered from headaches and **loss of appetite**.* 他头痛，而且食欲不振。◇ *The walk gave me a good appetite.* 散步使我胃口大开。◇ *Don't **spoil your appetite** by eating between meals.* 不要在两餐之间吃东西，以免影响胃口。 **2** [C] a strong desire for sth 强烈欲望：*sexual appetites* 性欲 ◇ *The preview was intended to **whet your appetite*** (= make you want more). 预告是为了吊胃口。◇ **~ for sth** *The public have an insatiable appetite for scandal.* 公众对丑事总是喜闻乐道。

ap·pet·izer (*BrE also* **-iser**) /'æpɪtaɪzə(r)/ *noun* a small amount of food or a drink that you have before a meal （餐前的）开胃品，开胃饮料

ap·pe·tiz·ing (*BrE also* **-is·ing**) /'æpɪtaɪzɪŋ/ *adj.* (of food, etc. 食物等) that smells or looks attractive; making you feel hungry or thirsty 开胃的；引起食欲的；使渴的 OPP **unappetizing**

ap·plaud /ə'plɔ:d/ *verb* **1** [I, T] to show your approval of sb/sth by clapping your hands 鼓掌：*He started to applaud and the others joined in.* 他开始鼓掌，其他人也跟着鼓起掌来。◇ **~ sb** *They rose to applaud the speaker.* 他们起立向演讲者鼓掌。◇ *She was applauded as she came on stage.* 她上台时人们向她鼓掌。 **2** [T] (*formal*) to express praise for sb/sth because you approve of them or it 称赞；赞许；赞赏：**~ sth** *We applaud her decision.* 我们称赞她的决定。◇ *His efforts to improve the situation are to be applauded.* 他为改善状况所作的努力应该受到赞许。◇ **~ sb (for sth)** *I applaud her for having the courage to refuse.* 我赞赏她敢于拒绝。

ap·plause /ə'plɔ:z/ *noun* [U] the noise made by a group of people clapping their hands and sometimes shouting to show their approval or enjoyment 鼓掌；喝彩：*Give her a big **round of applause**!* 为她热烈鼓掌！◇ *The audience broke into rapturous applause.* 听众中爆发出一片欢呼喝彩声。

apple /'æpl/ *noun* a round fruit with shiny red or green skin and firm white flesh 苹果：*Peel and core the apples.* 将这些苹果削皮、去核儿。◇ *an apple pie* 苹果馅饼 ◇ *apple sauce* 苹果沙司 ◇ *a garden with three apple trees* 有三棵苹果树的花园 ➲ VISUAL VOCAB PAGE V32 ➲ SEE ALSO ADAM'S APPLE, BIG APPLE, COOKING APPLE, CRAB APPLE, EATING APPLE, TOFFEE APPLE

IDM **the apple doesn't fall/never falls far from the 'tree** (*saying, especially NAmE*) a child usually behaves in a similar way to his or her parent(s) 有什么样的父母就有什

A

么样的儿女；上行下效 **the ˌapple of sb's ˈeye** a person or thing that is loved more than any other 心肝宝贝；掌上明珠 **ˌapples and ˈoranges** (*especially NAmE*) used to describe a situation in which two people or things are completely different from each other 苹果橘子两码事；截然不同：*They really are apples and oranges.* 他们确实是迥然不同。◇ *They are both great but* ***you can't compare apples and oranges.*** 他们俩都很棒，但是截然不同，无法比较。➲ MORE AT AMERICAN *adj.*, ROTTEN *adj.*

ˈapple cart *noun* IDM SEE UPSET *v.*

ˌapple ˈpie *noun* **1** [C, U] apples baked in a dish with PASTRY on the bottom, sides and top 苹果派；苹果馅饼：*a slice of apple pie* 一片苹果馅饼 **2** [U] (*NAmE*) used to represent an idea of perfect home life and comfort 完美的家庭生活；温馨舒适：*Who could argue against motherhood and apple pie?* 谁会反对母性与家庭的温馨呢？IDM SEE AMERICAN *adj.*

ap·pli·ance /əˈplaɪəns/ *noun* a machine that is designed to do a particular thing in the home, such as preparing food, heating or cleaning（家用）电器，器具：***electrical/household appliances*** 电器；家用器具 ◇ *They sell a wide range of* ***domestic appliances****—washing machines, dishwashers and so on.* 他们出售各种家用电器，如洗衣机、洗碗机等等。➲ WORDFINDER NOTE AT STORE ➲ VISUAL VOCAB PAGE V26

ap·plic·able /əˈplɪkəbl; ˈæplɪkəbl/ *adj.* [not usually before noun] that can be said to be true in the case of sb/sth 适用；合适 SYN **relevant**: *Give details of children where applicable* (= if you have any). 如有子女请提供详情。◇ **~ to sb/sth** *Much of the form was not applicable* (= did not apply) *to me.* 表格中很多部分不适用于我。▶ **ap·plic·abil·ity** /əˌplɪkəˈbɪləti; ˌæplɪk-/ *noun* [U]: *The new approach had wide applicability to all sorts of different problems.* 新方法广泛适用于解决各种各样的问题。

ap·pli·cant /ˈæplɪkənt/ *noun* **~ (for sth)** a person who makes a formal request for sth (= applies for it), especially for a job, a place at a college or university, etc. 申请人（尤指求职、进高等学校等）：*There were over 500 applicants for the job.* 有 500 多人申请这份工作。

ap·pli·ca·tion /ˌæplɪˈkeɪʃn/ *noun*

• **FOR JOB/COURSE** 求职；办手续 **1** [C, U] a formal (often written) request for sth, such as a job, permission to do sth or a place at a college or university 申请；请求；申请书；申请表：*a planning/passport application* 规划 / 护照申请 ◇ *an* ***application form*** (= a piece of paper on which to apply for sth) 申请表 ◇ **~ for sth/to do sth** *an application for membership/a loan/a licence* 会籍 / 贷款 / 执照申请 ◇ **~ to sb (for sth/to do sth)** *His application to the court for bail has been refused.* 他向法庭申请保释遭到拒绝。◇ *Further information is available* ***on application*** *to the principal.* 详情可致函校长索取。➲ COLLOCATIONS AT JOB

• **PRACTICAL USE** 实用 **2** [U, C] **~ (of sth) (to sth)** the practical use of sth, especially a theory, discovery, etc.（尤指理论、发现等的）应用，运用：*the application of new technology to teaching* 新技术在教学上的应用 ◇ *The invention would have a wide range of applications in industry.* 这项发明在工业中会有广泛用途。

• **OF PAINT/CREAM** 油漆；乳剂 **3** [C, U] an act of putting or spreading sth, such as paint or medical creams, onto sth else 涂抹；敷用；施用：*It took three applications of paint to cover the graffiti.* 刷了三道油漆才盖住了涂鸦。◇ *lotion for external application only* (= to be put on the skin, not swallowed) 仅限外部敷用的乳液

• **OF RULE/LAW** 规章；法律 **4** [U] the act of making a rule, etc. operate or become effective 运用；生效：*strict application of the law* 法律的严格执行

• **COMPUTING** 计算机技术 **5** [C] (*abbr.* **app**) a program designed to do a particular job; a piece of software 应用程序；应用软件：*a database application* 数据库应用软件 ➲ WORDFINDER NOTE AT SOFTWARE ➲ VISUAL VOCAB PAGE V74 ➲ SEE ALSO KILLER APPLICATION

• **HARD WORK** 勤奋 **6** [U] (*formal*) determination to work hard at sth; great effort 勤奋；努力：*Success as a writer demands great application.* 作家要成功就得悉力以赴。

ap·pli·ca·tor /ˈæplɪkeɪtə(r)/ *noun* a small tool that is used to put a substance onto a surface, or to put sth into an object 敷抹器；充填器：*Use the applicator to apply cream to the affected area.* 用涂药器把药膏抹在患处。➲ VISUAL VOCAB PAGE V65

ap·plied /əˈplaɪd/ *adj.* [usually before noun] (especially of a subject of study 尤指学科) used in a practical way; not THEORETICAL 应用的；实用的：*applied mathematics* (= as used by engineers, etc.) 应用数学 ➲ COMPARE PURE (6)

apˌplied linˈguistics *noun* [U] the scientific study of language as it relates to practical problems, in areas such as teaching and dealing with speech problems 应用语言学

ap·pli·qué /əˈpliːkeɪ; *NAmE* ˌæpləˈkeɪ/ *noun* [U] a type of NEEDLEWORK in which small pieces of cloth are sewn or stuck in a pattern onto a larger piece（织物的）缝饰，嵌花，贴花 ▶ **ap·pli·quéd** *adj.*

apply /əˈplaɪ/ *verb* (**ap·plies**, **ap·ply·ing**, **ap·plied**, **ap·plied**)

• **FOR JOB/COURSE** 求职；办手续 **1** [I, T] to make a formal request, usually in writing, for sth such as a job, a place at college, university, etc.（通常以书面形式）申请，请求：*You should* ***apply in person/by letter.*** 你应该当面 / 写信申请。◇ **~ for sth** *to apply for a job/passport/grant* 申请工作 / 护照 / 拨款 ◇ **~ to sb/sth (for sth)** *to apply to a company/university* 向公司 / 大学申请 ◇ **~ to do sth** *He has applied to join the army.* 他已报名参军。➲ WORDFINDER NOTE AT EMPLOY

WORDFINDER 联想词：appoint, candidate, CV, experience, interview, job description, qualification, reference, shortlist

• **USE** 用 **2** [T] to use sth or make sth work in a particular situation 使用；应用：**~ sth** *to apply economic sanctions/political pressure* 采取经济制裁；施加政治压力 ◇ **~ sth to sth** *The new technology was applied to farming.* 这项新技术已应用于农业。

• **PAINT/CREAM** 油漆；乳剂 **3** [T] **~ sth (to sth)** to put or spread sth such as paint, cream, etc. onto a surface 涂；敷；施：*Apply the cream sparingly to your face and neck.* 把乳霜薄薄地抹在脸和脖子上。

• **BE RELEVANT** 有关 **4** [I, T] (not used in the progressive tenses 不用于进行时) to concern or relate to sb/sth 有关；涉及：*Special conditions apply if you are under 18.* * 18 岁以下者按特殊情况处理。◇ **~ to sb/sth** *What I am saying applies only to some of you.* 我所说的只涉及你们中的一些人。◇ **~ sth to sb/sth** *The word 'unexciting' could never be applied to her novels.* "乏味"这个词绝对和她的小说沾不上边儿。

• **WORK HARD** 勤奋 **5** [T] to work at sth or study sth very hard 勤奋工作；努力学习：**~ yourself** *You would pass your exams if you applied yourself.* 努力学习就会通过考试。◇ **~ yourself/sth to sth/to doing sth** *We applied our minds to finding a solution to our problem.* 我们绞尽脑汁寻求解决问题的办法。

• **PRESS HARD** 用力压 **6** [T] to press on sth hard with your hand, foot, etc. to make sth work or have an effect on sth 手压；脚踩：**~ sth** *to apply the brakes* (*of a vehicle*) 踩刹车 ◇ **~ sth to sth** *Pressure applied to the wound will stop the bleeding.* 压住伤口可以止血。

ap·point /əˈpɔɪnt/ *verb* **1** to choose sb for a job or position of responsibility 任命；委任：**~ sb** *They have appointed a new head teacher at my son's school.* 我儿子读书的学校任命了一位新校长。◇ **~ sb to sth** *She has recently been appointed to the committee.* 她最近获委任为委员会成员。◇ **~ sb + noun | ~ sb as sth** *They appointed him (as) captain of the English team.* 他们任命他为英格兰队队长。◇ **~ sb to do sth** *A lawyer was appointed to represent the child.* 一名律师被指定为这个孩子的代理人。➲ WORDFINDER NOTE AT APPLY, EMPLOY **2** [usually passive] **~ sth** (*formal*) to arrange or decide on a time or place for doing sth 安排，确定（时间、地点）：*A date for the meeting is still to be appointed.* 会议日期尚待确定。◇

A

Everyone was assembled at the ***appointed time.*** 全体人员均按规定时间召集到场。

ap·point·ee /əˌpɔɪnˈtiː/ *noun* a person who has been chosen for a job or position of responsibility 被任命者；被委任者：*the new appointee to the post* 新委任此职务者

ap·point·ment /əˈpɔɪntmənt/ *noun* **1** [C] a formal arrangement to meet or visit sb at a particular time, especially for a reason connected with their work 约会；预约；约定：*I've got a* ***dental appointment*** *at 3 o'clock.* 我约了下午 3 点看牙医。◇ *to make/keep an appointment* 预约；守约 ◇ *Viewing is* ***by appointment only*** (= only at a time that has been arranged in advance). 参观必须预约。◇ **~ with sb** *an appointment with my lawyer* 与我的律师的约定 ◇ **~ for sth** *an appointment for a blood test* 验血预约 ◇ **~ for sb to do sth** *She* ***made an appointment*** *for her son to see the doctor.* 她为儿子约定了看医生的时间。**2** [C, U] **~ (as/to sth)** the act of choosing a person for a job or position of responsibility; the fact of being chosen for a job, etc. 任命；委任：*her recent appointment to the post* 她新近获此职位的任命 ◇ *his appointment as principal* 他担任校长的任命 **3** [C] a job or position of responsibility 职务；职位：*a permanent/first appointment* 固定职位；第一次任职 ➲ SYNONYMS AT JOB

ap·por·tion /əˈpɔːʃn; *NAmE* əˈpɔːrʃn/ *verb* (*formal*) to divide sth among people; to give a share of sth to sb 分配；分摊；分派：**~ sth** *The programme gives the facts but does not* ***apportion blame.*** 这个节目只摆出事实，并不评论谁是谁非。◇ **~ sth among/between/to sb** *They apportioned the land among members of the family.* 他们把土地分给了家中各人。▶ **ap·por·tion·ment** *noun* [U, sing.] (*formal*)：*The apportionment of seats in the House of Representatives is based on the population of each state.* 众议院的席位是根据各州的人口分配的。

ap·po·site /ˈæpəzɪt/ *adj.* **~ (to sth)** (*formal*) very appropriate for a particular situation or in relation to sth 很合适；很恰当

ap·pos·ition /ˌæpəˈzɪʃn/ *noun* [U] (*grammar* 语法) the use of a noun phrase immediately after another noun phrase that refers to the same person or thing 同位：*In the phrase 'Paris, the capital of France', 'the capital of France' is* ***in apposition to*** *'Paris'.* 在短语 Paris, the capital of France 中，the capital of France 是 Paris 的同位语。

ap·prais·al /əˈpreɪzl/ *noun* [C, U] **1** a judgement of the value, performance or nature of sb/sth 评价；估价；估计；鉴定：*He had read many detailed critical appraisals of her work.* 他读了许多详细评论她的作品的文章。◇ *She was honest in her appraisal of her team's chances.* 她对自己队的获胜机会做了客观评价。**2** (*BrE*) a meeting in which an employee discusses with their manager how well they have been doing their job; the system of holding such meetings（上司对雇员的）工作鉴定会；工作表现评估：*I have my appraisal today.* 我今天与上司见面讨论我的工作表现。◇ ***staff/performance appraisal*** 员工 / 工作表现评估

ap·praise /əˈpreɪz/ *verb* **1 ~ sb/sth** (*formal*) to consider or examine sb/sth and form an opinion about them or it 估量；估价：*an* ***appraising glance/look*** 打量的一瞥 / 目光 ◇ *His eyes coolly appraised the young woman before him.* 他双眼冷静地打量着面前的年轻女子。◇ *She stepped back to appraise her workmanship.* 她退后一步，看看她的作品是否完美。**2 ~ sb** to make a formal judgement about the value of a person's work, usually after a discussion with them about it（对某人的工作）作出评价：*Managers must appraise all staff.* 经理必须对全体员工作出评价。

ap·praisee /əˌpreɪˈziː/ *noun* (in an appraisal meeting or system) the person who is being judged on how well they are doing their job 被评估人

ap·prais·er /əˈpreɪzə(r)/ *noun* **1** (*NAmE*) a person whose job is to examine a building and say how much it is worth（房地产）估价师 **2** a person who makes a formal judgement about the value of a person's work, usually after discussion with them about it（工作业绩的）评估人

ap·pre·ciable AW /əˈpriːʃəbl/ *adj.* large enough to be noticed or thought important（大得）可以觉察到的，足以认为重要的；可观的 SYN **considerable**：*The new regulations will not make an appreciable difference to most people.* 新的规定对大多数人将无大影响。◇ *an* ***appreciable effect/increase/amount*** 可观的效果 / 增长 / 数量 ▶ **ap·pre·ciably** AW /-əbli/ *adv.*：*The risk of infection is appreciably higher among children.* 受到感染的危险在儿童中要高得多。

ap·preci·ate AW /əˈpriːʃieɪt/ *verb* **1** [T] (not used in the progressive tenses 不用于进行时) **~ sb/sth** to recognize the good qualities of sb/sth 欣赏；赏识；重视：*You can't really appreciate foreign literature in translation.* 看翻译作品不能真正欣赏到外国文学原著的美妙之处。◇ *His talents are not* ***fully appreciated*** *in that company.* 他的才干在那家公司未受到充分赏识。◇ *Her family doesn't appreciate her.* 她的家人不重视她。**2** [T] (not usually used in the progressive tenses 通常不用于进行时) to be grateful for sth that sb has done; to welcome sth 感激；感谢；欢迎：**~ sth** *I'd appreciate some help.* 如果有人帮忙我将非常感激。◇ *Your support is greatly appreciated.* 十分感谢你的支持。◇ *Thanks for coming. I* ***appreciate it.*** 谢谢光临。无任欢迎。◇ ***I would appreciate it if*** *you paid in cash.* 假如你支付现金的话，我会不胜感激。◇ **~ doing sth** *I don't appreciate being treated like a second-class citizen.* 我不愿被人当作二等公民。◇ **~ sb doing sth** *We would appreciate you letting us know of any problems.* 如有任何问题，请告诉我们。➲ EXPRESS YOURSELF AT THANK **3** [T] (not used in the progressive tenses 不用于进行时) to understand that sth is true 理解；意识到；领会 SYN **realize**：**~ sth** *What I failed to appreciate was the distance between the two cities.* 我没有意识到这两座城市间的距离。◇ **~ how, what, etc....** *I don't think you appreciate how expensive it will be.* 我想你不了解它会有多昂贵。◇ **~ that...** *We didn't* ***fully appreciate*** *that he was seriously ill.* 我们没有充分认识到他的病情很严重。**4** [I] to increase in value over a period of time 增值；升值：*Their investments have appreciated over the years.* 他们的投资这些年来已经增值。OPP **depreciate**

ap·pre·ci·ation AW /əˌpriːʃiˈeɪʃn/ *noun* **1** [U] pleasure that you have when you recognize and enjoy the good qualities of sb/sth 欣赏：*She shows little appreciation of good music.* 她感受不到美好音乐的妙处。◇ *The crowd murmured* ***in appreciation.*** 人群低声赞叹着。**2** [U, sing.] **~ of sth** a full or sympathetic understanding of sth, such as a situation or a problem, and of what it involves 理解；体谅；同情：*I had no appreciation of the problems they faced.* 我没有体谅到他们所面临的困难。**3** [U] **~ (of/for sth)** the feeling of being grateful for sth 感激；感谢：*Please accept this gift* ***in appreciation of*** *all you've done for us.* 承蒙鼎力相助，不胜感激，谨备薄礼，敬请笑纳。**4** [U, sing.] **~ (in sth)** increase in value over a period of time 增值；升值 OPP **depreciation** **5** [C] **~ (of sth)** (*formal*) a piece of writing or a speech in which the strengths and weaknesses of sb/sth, especially an artist or a work of art, are discussed and judged（尤指艺术方面的）鉴定，评价，评估

ap·pre·cia·tive /əˈpriːʃətɪv/ *adj.* **1 ~ (of sth)** feeling or showing that you are grateful for sth 感激的；感谢的：*The company was very appreciative of my efforts.* 公司对我的努力十分赞赏。**2** showing pleasure or enjoyment 欣赏的；赏识的：*an* ***appreciative audience/smile*** 有欣赏力的观众；会意的微笑 ◇ ***appreciative laughter/comments*** 赞赏的笑声 / 议论 ▶ **ap·pre·cia·tive·ly** *adv.*

ap·pre·hend /ˌæprɪˈhend/ *verb* (*formal*) **1 ~ sb** (of the police 警方) to catch sb and arrest them 逮捕；拘押 **2 ~ sth** (*old-fashioned*) to understand or recognize sth 理解；认识到；领会

ap·pre·hen·sion /ˌæprɪˈhenʃn/ *noun* **1** [U, C] worry or fear that sth unpleasant may happen 忧虑；担心；疑惧；恐惧 SYN **anxiety**：*There is growing apprehension that fighting will begin again.* 人们愈来愈担心会重开战火。◇

A

He watched the election results ***with some apprehension.*** 他不无忧虑地观察选举结果。 **2** [U] (*formal*) the act of capturing or arresting sb, usually by the police 逮捕；拘押

ap·pre·hen·sive /ˌæprɪˈhensɪv/ *adj.* worried or frightened that sth unpleasant may happen 忧虑的；担心的；疑惧的；恐惧的： *an* ***apprehensive face/glance/look*** 忧虑的面容 / 一瞥 / 目光 ◇ **~ about/of sth** *I was a little apprehensive about the effects of what I had said.* 我有点担忧我说的话所带来的影响。◇ *You have no reason to be apprehensive of the future.* 你不必忧虑未来。◇ **~ that…** *She was deeply apprehensive that something might go wrong.* 她很担心可能要出什么差错。 ▸ **ap·pre·hen·sive·ly** *adv.*

ap·pren·tice /əˈprentɪs/ *noun, verb*

■ ***noun*** a young person who works for an employer for a fixed period of time in order to learn the particular skills needed in their job 学徒；徒弟： *an apprentice electrician/chef* 电工 / 厨师学徒 ➲ WORDFINDER NOTE AT TRAINING

■ ***verb*** [usually passive] **~ sb (to sb) (as sth)** (*old-fashioned*) to make sb an apprentice 使某人当（某人的）学徒

ap·pren·tice·ship /əˈprentɪʃɪp/ *noun* [C, U] a period of time working as an apprentice; a job as an apprentice 学徒期；学徒工作： *She was in the second year of her apprenticeship as a carpenter.* 她当木工学徒已是第二年了。 ◇ *He had* ***served his apprenticeship*** *as a plumber.* 他当过管子工学徒。

ap·prise /əˈpraɪz/ *verb* **~ sb of sth** (*formal*) to tell or inform sb of sth 通知；告知

ap·proach 🔑 AW /əˈprəʊtʃ; *NAmE* əˈproʊtʃ/ *verb, noun*

■ ***verb***

• **MOVE NEAR** 接近 **1** 🔑 [I, T] to come near to sb/sth in distance or time （在距离或时间上）靠近，接近： *We heard the sound of an approaching car/a car approaching.* 我们听见一辆汽车驶近的声音。◇ *Winter is approaching.* 冬天就要来临。 ◇ **~ sb/sth** *As you approach the town, you'll see the college on the left.* 快到市镇时就可以看见左边的学院。

• **OFFER/ASK** 建议；要求 **2** 🔑 [T] to speak to sb about sth, especially to ask them for sth or to offer to do sth 接洽；建议；要求： **~ sb** *We have been approached by a number of companies that are interested in our product.* 一些对我们的产品感兴趣的公司已和我们接洽。◇ *I'd like to ask his opinion but I find him difficult to approach* (= not easy to talk to in a friendly way). 我想征求他的意见，但发现很难和他谈得拢。 ◇ **~ sb for sth/about (doing) sth** *She approached the bank for a loan.* 她向银行要求贷款。

• **AMOUNT/QUALITY** 数量；质量 **3** 🔑 [T] **~ sth** to come close to sth in amount, level or quality （在数额、水平或质量上）接近： *profits approaching 30 million dollars* 接近 3 000 万美元的利润 ◇ *Few writers approach his richness of language.* 他语言之丰富很少有作家能望其项背。

• **PROBLEM/TASK** 问题；任务 **4** 🔑 [T] **~ sth** to start dealing with a problem, task, etc. in a particular way 着手处理；对付： *What's the best way of approaching this problem?* 处理这个问题的最佳方式是什么？

■ ***noun***

• **TO PROBLEM/TASK** 问题；任务 **1** 🔑 [C] a way of dealing with sb/sth; a way of doing or thinking about sth such as a problem or a task （待人接物或思考问题的）方式，方法，态度： *She took the wrong approach in her dealings with them.* 她和他们打交道的方式错了。 ◇ **~ to sth** *The school has decided to adopt a different approach to discipline.* 学校决定采取另外一种方式解决纪律问题。 ➲ WORDFINDER NOTE AT BEHAVIOUR

• **MOVEMENT NEARER** 接近 **2** 🔑 [sing.] movement nearer to sb/sth in distance or time （在距离或时间上的）靠近，接近： *She hadn't heard his approach and jumped as the door opened.* 她没有听见他走近的声音，所以门开时吓了一跳。 ◇ *the approach of spring* 春天的来临

• **OFFER/REQUEST** 建议；要求 **3** [C] the act of speaking to sb about sth, especially when making an offer or a request 接洽；建议；要求： *The club has* ***made an approach*** *to a local company for sponsorship.* 俱乐部已向当地一家公司寻求赞助。 ◇ *She resented his persistent approaches.* 她对他没完没了的纠缠极为反感。

• **PATH/ROAD** 小径；道路 **4** [C] a path, road, etc. that leads to a place 通路；路径；道路： *All the approaches to the palace were guarded by troops.* 通往宫殿的所有道路都有军队守卫。 ◇ *a new approach road to the port* 去港口的一条新通路

• **OF AIRCRAFT** 飞机 **5** [C] the part of an aircraft's flight immediately before landing 进场；进场着陆： *to begin the final approach to the runway* 开始进入跑道着陆

• **STH SIMILAR** 相似事物 **6** [sing.] a thing that is like sth else that is mentioned 相似（或近似）的事物： *That's the* ***nearest approach*** *to an apology you'll get from him.* 那是他所能作出的最似歉意的表示。 IDM SEE CARROT

ap·proach·able AW /əˈprəʊtʃəbl; *NAmE* əˈproʊtʃ-/ *adj.* **1** friendly and easy to talk to; easy to understand 和蔼可亲的；易理解的： *Despite being a big star, she's very approachable.* 她虽然是个大明星，却非常平易近人。 ◇ *an approachable piece of music* 浅显易懂的乐曲 OPP **unapproachable** **2** [not before noun] that can be reached by a particular route or from a particular direction 可接近的；能达到的： *The summit was approachable only from the south.* 只有从南面才能到达山顶。

ap·pro·ba·tion /ˌæprəˈbeɪʃn/ *noun* [U] (*formal*) approval or agreement 认可；批准

ap·pro·pri·acy AW /əˈprəʊpriəsi; *NAmE* əˈproʊ-/ *noun* [U] **1** the extent to which sth is suitable or acceptable 适合性；恰当性 **2** (*linguistics* 语言) the extent to which a word or phrase sounds correct and natural in relation to the situation it is used in （词语等的）得体；恰当用词

ap·pro·pri·ate 🔑 AW *adj., verb*

■ /əˈprəʊpriət; *NAmE* əˈproʊ-/ ***adj.*** 🔑 suitable, acceptable or correct for the particular circumstances 合适的；恰当的： *an appropriate response/measure/method* 恰如其分的反应；恰当的措施 / 方法 ◇ *Now that the problem has been identified, appropriate action can be taken.* 现在既已找出问题的症结，即可采取适当行动。◇ *Is now an appropriate time to make a speech?* 现在发表演讲是不是时候？◇ *Please debit my Mastercard/Visa/American Express card* (***delete as appropriate***) (= cross out the options that do not apply). 请在我的万事达 / 维萨 / 美国运通信用卡（删除不适用者）账户中扣除。 ◇ **~ for sth** *Jeans are not appropriate for a formal party.* 正式聚会上穿牛仔裤不合适。 ◇ **~ to sth** *The book was written in a style appropriate to the age of the children.* 这本书的文体适合儿童阅读。 OPP **inappropriate** ▸ **ap·pro·pri·ate·ly** AW *adv.* : *The government has been accused of not responding appropriately to the needs of the homeless.* 政府未采取恰当的措施以应无家可归者的需要，为此已受到谴责。 ◇ *The chain of volcanoes is known,* ***appropriately enough,*** *as the 'Ring of Fire'.* 人们把这火山链很恰当地称作"火环"。 **ap·pro·pri·ate·ness** AW *noun* [U]

■ ***verb*** /əˈprəʊprieɪt; *NAmE* əˈproʊ-/ (*formal*) **1** **~ sth** to take sth, sb's ideas, etc. for your own use, especially illegally or without permission 盗用；挪用；占用；侵吞： *He was accused of appropriating club funds.* 他被控盗用俱乐部资金。 ◇ *Some of the opposition party's policies have been appropriated by the government.* 反对党的一些政策已被政府照搬照用。 **2** **~ sth (for sth)** to take or give sth, especially money for a particular purpose 拨（专款等）： *Five million dollars have been appropriated for research into the disease.* 已拨款五百万美元用于这种疾病的研究。 ➲ COMPARE MISAPPROPRIATE

ap·pro·pri·ation /əˌprəʊpriˈeɪʃn; *NAmE* əˌproʊ-/ *noun* **1** [U, sing.] (*formal* or *law* 律) the act of taking sth that belongs to sb else, especially without permission 擅自调用；挪用；占用；侵吞： *dishonest appropriation of property* 以欺骗的手法侵吞财产 ➲ COMPARE MISAPPROPRIATION at MISAPPROPRIATE **2** [U, sing.] (*formal*) the act of keeping or saving money for a particular purpose 拨（专）款： *a meeting to discuss the appropriation of funds* 讨论拨款的会议 **3** [C] (*formal*) a sum of money to be used for a particular purpose, especially by a government or company （尤指政府、公司的）所拨款项，专款： *an appropriation of £20 000 for payment of debts* 用于还债的 2 万英镑拨款

ap·prov·al /əˈpruːvl/ *noun* **1** [U] the feeling that sb/sth is good or acceptable; a positive opinion of sb/sth 赞成；同意： *She desperately wanted to win her father's approval.* 她急不可待地想赢得她父亲的赞同。◇ *Do the plans* ***meet with your approval?*** 这些计划你赞成吗？◇ *Several people nodded* ***in approval.*** 好几个人点头表示同意。 OPP **disapproval** **2** [U, C] agreement to, or permission for sth, especially a plan or request 批准，通过，认可（计划、要求等）： *The plan will be submitted to the committee for official approval.* 该计划将送交委员会正式批准。◇ ***parliamentary/congressional/government approval*** 议会的 / 国会的 / 政府的批准 ◇ *Senior management have given their* ***seal of approval*** (= formal approval) *to the plans.* 高层管理部门已经正式批准这些计划。◇ *I can't agree to anything without my partner's approval.* 没有合伙人的认可我什么也不能答应。◇ *planning approvals* （建筑）规划的批准 ◇ *The proposal is* ***subject to approval*** *by the shareholders* (= they need to agree to it). 这项建议须得到股东的批准。◇ **~ (for sth) (from sb)** *They* ***required/received approval*** *for the proposal from the shareholders.* 他们要求 / 获得股东对这项提议的批准。 **3** [U] if you buy goods or if goods are sold **on approval**, you can use them for a time without paying, until you decide if you want to buy them or not （商品）试用，包退包换

ap·prove /əˈpruːv/ *verb* **1** [I] to think that sb/sth is good, acceptable or suitable 赞成；同意： *I told my mother I wanted to leave school but she didn't approve.* 我告诉母亲我不想继续上学，但是母亲不同意。◇ **~ of sb/sth** *Do you approve of my idea?* 你同意我的想法吗？◇ **~ of sb doing sth** *She doesn't approve of me leaving school this year.* 她不同意我今年毕业。◇ (*formal*) **~ of sb's doing sth** *She doesn't approve of my leaving school this year.* 她不同意我今年毕业。 OPP **disapprove** **2** [T] **~ sth** to officially agree to a plan, request, etc. 批准，通过（计划、要求等）： *The committee unanimously approved the plan.* 委员会一致通过了计划。 ➲ SYNONYMS AT AGREE **3** [T, often passive] **~ sth** to say that sth is good enough to be used or is correct 认可；核准： *The course is approved by the Department for Education.* 课程已获教育部核准。

apˈproved school *noun* (*BrE*) a school where young people who had committed crimes were sent in the past （旧时的）少年犯教养院，少年感化院

ap·prov·ing /əˈpruːvɪŋ/ *adj.* showing that you believe that sb/sth is good or acceptable 赞成的；同意的： *He gave me an approving nod.* 他向我点头表示同意。 OPP **disapproving** ▶ **ap·prov·ing·ly** *adv.* : *She looked at him approvingly and smiled.* 她面带微笑赞许地望着他。

approx *abbr.* (in writing 书写形式) APPROXIMATE, APPROXIMATELY 大约；大概；约莫： *Contents: approx 6 000 beads* 内容物：约 6 000 颗珠子

ap·proxi·mant /əˈprɒksɪmənt; *NAmE* əˈprɑːks-/ *noun* **1** (*phonetics* 语音) a speech sound made by bringing the parts of the mouth that produce speech close together but not actually touching, for example /r/ and /w/ in *right* and *wet* in many accents of English 近似音；无擦通音；无摩擦延续音 **2** (*mathematics* 数) an answer to a problem in mathematics that is a close estimate of the solution of the problem 逼近式

ap·proxi·mate AW *adj., verb*

■ ***adj.*** /əˈprɒksɪmət; *NAmE* əˈprɑːk-/ almost correct or accurate, but not completely so 大约的；近似的；接近的： *an* ***approximate number/total/cost*** 约数；概算总额；约计成本 ◇ *The cost given is only approximate.* 所列成本仅系约计。◇ *Use these figures as an approximate guide in your calculations.* 计算时把这些数字作为近似参考数值。 OPP **exact**

■ ***verb*** /əˈprɒksɪmeɪt; *NAmE* əˈprɑːk-/ (*formal*) **1** [T, I] to be similar or close to sth in nature, quality, amount, etc., but not exactly the same 近似；接近： **~ sth** *The animals were reared in conditions which approximated the wild as closely as possible.* 这些动物是在尽量近似自然的环境下饲养的。◇ *The total cost will approximate £15 billion.* 总费用将近 150 亿英镑。◇ **~ to sth** *His story approximates to the facts that we already know.* 他的陈述和我们已掌握的事实接近。 **2** [T] **~ sth** to calculate or estimate sth fairly accurately 近似计算；概略估算： *a formula for approximating the weight of a horse* 估算一匹马重量的公式 ➲ MORE LIKE THIS 21, page R27

▼ **VOCABULARY BUILDING 词汇扩充**

Ways of saying approximately 表示"大约"的方式

- The flight takes **approximately** three hours. 飞行大约需要三小时。
- The tickets cost **about** £20 each. 票每张约 20 英镑。
- The repairs will cost $200, **give or take** a few dollars. 修理费要花 200 美元，出入不过几美元。
- How much will it cost, **more or less**? 这个大概得花多少钱？
- We are expecting thirty **or so** people to come. 我们预计会来三十人左右。
- She must be 25 **or thereabouts**. 她肯定在 25 岁上下。
- Profits have fallen by **roughly** 15%. 利润下降了大约 15%。
- You can expect to earn **round about** £40,000 a year. 你可望一年赚 4 万英镑左右。
- The price is **somewhere around** $800. 价格在 800 美元上下。
- She earns **somewhere in the region of** £25,000. 她大约挣 25 000 英镑。

All these words and phrases are used in both speaking and writing; **about** is the most common and **approximately** the most formal. 上述各词和短语在口语和书面语中均可使用，about 最常用，approximately 最正式。

ap·proxi·mate·ly AW /əˈprɒksɪmətli; *NAmE* əˈprɑːk-/ *adv.* used to show that sth is almost, but not completely, accurate or correct 大概；大约；约莫： *The journey took approximately seven hours.* 旅程大约花了七个小时。

ap·proxi·ma·tion AW /əˌprɒksɪˈmeɪʃn; *NAmE* əˌprɑːk-/ *noun* **1** an estimate of a number or an amount that is almost correct, but not exact 近似值；粗略估算： *That's just an approximation, you understand.* 你知道那仅仅是近似值。 **2** **~ (of/to sth)** a thing that is similar to sth else, but is not exactly the same 类似事物： *Our results should be a good approximation of the true state of affairs.* 我们的结果应该和实际情况相当接近。

ap·pur·ten·ance /əˈpɜːtɪnəns; *NAmE* əˈpɜːrt-/ *noun* [usually pl.] (*formal* or *humorous*) a thing that forms a part of sth larger or more important 附属物；附加物

APR /ˌeɪ piː ˈɑː(r)/ *noun* [sing.] the abbreviation for 'annual percentage rate' (the amount of interest a bank charges on money that it lends, calculated for a period of a year) 年度百分比利率（全写为 annual percentage rate，指银行贷款年百分率）： *a rate of 26.4% APR* 贷款年利率 26.4%

après-ski /ˌæpreɪ ˈskiː/ *noun* [U] (*from French*) social activities and entertainments that take place in hotels and restaurants after a day's SKIING （一整天）滑雪后的社交娱乐（在旅馆、餐厅举行）

apri·cot /ˈeɪprɪkɒt; *NAmE* ˈæprɪkɑːt/ *noun* **1** [C] a round fruit with yellow or orange skin and a large seed inside 杏；杏子： *dried apricots* 杏干 **2** [U] a yellowish-orange colour 杏黄色 ▶ **apri·cot** *adj.* : *The room was painted apricot and white.* 房间漆成了杏黄色和白色。

April /ˈeɪprəl/ *noun* [U, C] (*abbr.* **Apr.**) the fourth month of the year, between March and May 四月： *She was born in April.* 她是四月出生的。◇ (*BrE*) *The meeting is on the fifth of April/April the fifth.* 会议日期是四月五日。◇ (*NAmE*) *The meeting is on April fifth.* 会议日期是四月五日。◇ *We went to Japan last April.* 去年四月我们去了日本。◇ *I arrived at the end of April.* 我是四月底到达的。◇

last April's election 去年四月的选举 ◇ *April showers* (= light rain that falls in the spring) 四月的阵雨 ◇ *an April wedding* 四月的婚礼

ˌApril ˈFool *noun* **1** a trick that is traditionally played on sb on 1 April (called **April Fool's Day** or **All Fools' Day**) 在愚人节开的玩笑 **2** a person who has a trick played on them on April Fool's Day 愚人节被愚弄的人

a pri·ori /ˌeɪ praɪˈɔːraɪ/ *adj., adv.* (*from Latin, formal*) using facts or principles that are known to be true in order to decide what the probable effects or results of sth will be, for example saying 'They haven't eaten anything all day so they must be hungry.' 从事实推断结果；由因及果 ➲ COMPARE A POSTERIORI

ap·ron /ˈeɪprən/ *noun* **1** a piece of clothing worn over the front of the body, from the chest or the waist down, and tied around the waist. Aprons are worn over other clothes to keep them clean, for example when cooking. 围裙 ➲ COMPARE PINAFORE (2) **2** (*specialist*) an area with a hard surface at an airport, where aircraft are turned around, loaded, etc. (机场的）停机坪 **3** (*also* **ˈapron stage**) (*specialist*) (in a theatre 剧院) the part of the stage that is in front of the curtain 台唇（舞台幕前的部分）

IDM **(tied to) sb's apron strings** (too much under) the influence and control of sb（过分受）某人的影响（或控制）: *The British prime minister is too apt to cling to Washington's apron strings.* 英国首相对华府过于唯命是从。

apro·pos /ˌæprəˈpəʊ; *NAmE* -ˈpoʊ/ (*also* **apro·pos of**) *prep.* concerning or related to sb/sth 关于；至于：*Apropos (of) what you were just saying...* 至于你刚才所说的…

apse /æps/ *noun* a small area in a church, often in the shape of a SEMICIRCLE and usually at the east end of the building（教堂东端的）半圆形壁龛

apt /æpt/ *adj.* **1** suitable or appropriate in the circumstances 恰当的；适当的：*a particularly* ***apt description/name/comment*** 特别恰当的描述／名字／评论 **2** likely or having a natural tendency to do sth 易于…；有…倾向：**~ to be...** *apt to be forgetful/careless* 健忘；常常粗心大意 ◇ **~ to do sth** *Babies are apt to put objects into their mouths.* 婴儿爱把东西往嘴里塞。 **3 ~ pupil** a person who has a natural ability to learn and understand 天资聪颖的人 ▸ **aptly** *adv.*：*the aptly named Grand Hotel* 名副其实的大饭店 **apt·ness** *noun* [U]

ap·ti·tude /ˈæptɪtjuːd; *NAmE* -tuːd/ *noun* [U, C] natural ability or skill at doing sth 天资；天生的才能；天赋 SYN **talent**: *an aptitude test* (= one designed to show whether sb has the natural ability for a particular job or course of education) 能力倾向测验 ◇ **~ for sth** *She showed a natural aptitude for the work.* 她表现出了做这工作的天赋。◇ **~ for doing sth** *His aptitude for dealing with children got him the job.* 他善于和儿童打交道的本事使他得到了这份工作。

aqua /ˈækwə/ *noun* [U] **1** water (used especially on the labels on packages of food, drinks, medicines, etc. in order to show how much water they contain) 水（尤用于表示食物、饮料、药物等的水含量） **2** a bluish-green colour 湖绿色

aqua·culture /ˈækwəkʌltʃə(r)/ *noun* [U] the growing of plants in water for food 水产养殖（业）

aqua·lung (*US also* **Aqua·lung™**) /ˈækwəlʌŋ/ *noun* a piece of breathing equipment that a DIVER wears on his/her back when swimming underwater 轻便潜水器；水肺

aqua·mar·ine /ˌækwəməˈriːn/ *noun* **1** [C, U] a pale greenish-blue SEMI-PRECIOUS stone 海蓝宝石 **2** [U] a pale greenish-blue colour 海蓝色；浅蓝色 ▸ **aqua·mar·ine** *adj.*：*an aquamarine sea* 蓝色的大海

aqua·plane /ˈækwəpleɪn/ *verb, noun*

■ *verb* **1** (*BrE*) (*NAmE* **hydro·plane**) [I] (of a motor vehicle 机动车辆) to slide out of control on a wet road 在潮湿路面上打滑失控 **2** [I] to stand on a board that is pulled along on water behind a SPEEDBOAT in the sport of aquaplaning 滑水

■ *noun* a board that sb stands on in the sport of aquaplaning 滑水板

aqua·plan·ing /ˈækwəpleɪnɪŋ/ *noun* [U] **1** the sport of being pulled along on a board behind a SPEEDBOAT on water（快艇牵引）滑水板运动 **2** (*BrE*) (*NAmE* **hydro·plan·ing**) the fact of a motor vehicle sliding on a wet surface, so that it is out of control（机动车辆在潮湿路面上的）打滑

aquar·ium /əˈkweəriəm; *NAmE* əˈkwer-/ *noun* (*pl.* **aquar·iums** or **aqua·ria** /-riə/) **1** a large glass container in which fish and other water creatures and plants are kept 养鱼缸；水族玻璃槽 **2** a building where people can go to see fish and other water creatures 水族馆

Aquar·ius /əˈkweəriəs; *NAmE* əˈkwer-/ *noun* **1** [U] (*also* **the ˈWater Bearer, the ˈWater Carrier**) the 11th sign of the ZODIAC 黄道第十一宫；宝瓶宫；宝瓶（星）座 **2** [sing.] a person born when the sun is in this sign, that is between 21 January and 19 February 属宝瓶座的人（约出生于 1 月 21 日至 2 月 19 日） ▸ **Aquar·ian** /əˈkweəriən; *NAmE* əˈkwer-/ *noun, adj.*

aqua·robics /ˌækwəˈrəʊbɪks; *NAmE* -ˈroʊ-/ *noun* [U] physical exercises that you do in water, often done in classes 水中有氧操（常为分班组练习） ➲ COMPARE AEROBICS

aqua·tic /əˈkwætɪk/ *adj.* [usually before noun] **1** growing or living in, on or near water 水生的；水栖的：***aquatic plants/life/ecosystems*** 水生植物／动植物／生态系统 **2** connected with water 水的；水中的；水上的：*aquatic sports* 水上运动

aquat·ics /əˈkwætɪks; əˈkwɒ-; *NAmE* əˈkwɑː-/ *noun* [pl.] sports that are done on or in water, for example sailing and WATERSKIING 水上运动 SYN **water sports**

aqua·tint /ˈækwətɪnt/ *noun* [U, C] (*specialist*) a method of producing a picture using acid on a metal plate; a picture produced using this method 飞尘腐蚀法；飞尘腐蚀版画

aque·duct /ˈækwɪdʌkt/ *noun* a structure for carrying water, usually one built like a bridge across a valley or low ground 渡槽；高架渠 ➲ VISUAL VOCAB PAGE V14

aque·ous /ˈeɪkwiəs/ *adj.* (*specialist*) containing water; like water 水的；含水的；水状的

ˌaqueous ˈhumour (*US* **ˌaqueous ˈhumor**) *noun* [U] (*anatomy* 解) the clear liquid inside the front part of the eye 房水，眼房水（眼球的水状液） ➲ COMPARE VITREOUS HUMOUR

aqui·fer /ˈækwɪfə(r)/ *noun* (*geology* 地) a layer of rock or soil that can absorb and hold water（岩石或土壤的）含水层

aquil·ine /ˈækwɪlaɪn/ *adj.* (*formal*) a person with an **aquiline nose** or **aquiline features** has a nose that is thin and curved, similar to the BEAK of an EAGLE 钩状的；鹰喙状的

Arab /ˈærəb/ *noun, adj.*

■ *noun* **1** a person from the Middle East or N Africa, whose ANCESTORS lived in the Arabian Peninsula 阿拉伯人 **2** a type of horse originally from Arabia 阿拉伯马

■ *adj.* of or connected with Arabia or Arabs 阿拉伯的；阿拉伯人的：*Arab countries* 阿拉伯诸国

ar·ab·esque /ˌærəˈbesk/ *noun* **1** [C] (in BALLET 芭蕾舞) a position in which the dancer balances on one leg with the other leg lifted and stretched out behind parallel to the ground 阿拉贝斯克舞姿，迎风展翅（一脚着地，一条腿向后平伸） **2** [C, U] (in art 艺术) a type of design where lines wind around each other 阿拉伯花饰（互相交织的曲线图案）

Ara·bian /əˈreɪbiən/ *adj.* of or connected with Arabia 阿拉伯的 HELP **Arabian** is used to describe places. * Arabian 用以描述地方：*the Arabian peninsula* 阿拉伯半岛 The people are **Arabs** and the adjective to describe them is

Arab. * Arabs 表示人，其形容词为 Arab：*Arab children* 阿拉伯儿童 The language is **Arabic**. * Arabic 指语言：*Arabic script* 阿拉伯文字

Arab·ic /ˈærəbɪk/ *noun, adj.*
▪ ***noun*** [U] the language of the Arabs 阿拉伯语
▪ ***adj.*** of or connected with the literature and language of Arab people 阿拉伯文学的；阿拉伯语的：*Arabic poetry* 阿拉伯诗歌

ˌArabic ˈnumeral *noun* any of the symbols 0, 1, 2, 3, 4, etc. used for writing numbers in many countries 阿拉伯数字 ➲ COMPARE ROMAN NUMERAL

ar·able /ˈærəbl/ *adj.* connected with growing crops such as WHEAT 耕作的；可耕的：***arable farming/farms/crops*** 耕作农业 / 农场 / 庄稼 ◇ ***arable land/fields*** (= used or suitable for growing crops) 可耕地；可耕田 ➲ **WORDFINDER NOTE** AT FARM

arach·nid /əˈræknɪd/ *noun* (*specialist*) any small creature of the class that includes spiders, SCORPIONS, MITES and TICKS 蛛形纲动物（包括蜘蛛、蝎子、螨和蜱） ➲ **VISUAL VOCAB** PAGE V13 ➲ COMPARE INSECT

arach·no·pho·bia /əˌræknəˈfəʊbiə; *NAmE* -ˈfoʊ-/ *noun* [U] an extreme fear of spiders 蜘蛛恐惧症

Aran /ˈærən/ *adj.* [only before noun] (*especially BrE*) (of knitted clothing 针织服饰) with a traditional pattern of lines and diamond shapes made by raised STITCHES 阿伦式的（有凸线和菱形图案）：*an Aran sweater* 阿伦式针织套衫

ar·bi·ter /ˈɑːbɪtə(r); *NAmE* ˈɑːrb-/ *noun* **~ (of sth)** (*formal*) a person with the power or influence to make judgements and decide what will be done or accepted 仲裁人；公断人；裁决人；权威人士：*The law is the final arbiter of what is considered obscene.* 何谓猥亵最终由法律裁决。◇ ***an arbiter of taste/style/fashion*** 鉴赏 / 款式 / 时装权威

ar·bi·trage /ˈɑːbɪtrɑːʒ; -trɪdʒ; *NAmE* ˈɑːrbətrɑːʒ/ *noun* [U] (*business* 商) the practice of buying sth (for example, shares or foreign money) in one place and selling it in another place where the price is higher 套汇；套购；套利 ▸ **ar·bi·tra·geur** /ˌɑːbɪtrɑːˈʒɜː(r); *NAmE* ˌɑːrbətrɑːˈʒɜːr/ (*also* **ar·bi·trager** /ˈɑːbɪtrɪdʒə(r); *NAmE* ˈɑːrbətrɑːʒər/) *noun*

ar·bi·trary **AW** /ˈɑːbɪtrəri; ˈɑːbɪtri; *NAmE* ˈɑːrbətreri/ *adj.* **1** (of an action, a decision, a rule, etc. 行动、决定、规章等) not seeming to be based on a reason, system or plan and sometimes seeming unfair 任意的；武断的；随心所欲的：*The choice of players for the team seemed completely arbitrary.* 看来这个队的队员完全是随意选定的。◇ *He makes unpredictable, arbitrary decisions.* 他做的决定难以预料，主观武断。 **2** (*formal*) using power without restriction and without considering other people 专横的；专制的：*the arbitrary powers of officials* 官员的专制权力 ▸ **ar·bi·trar·ily** **AW** /ˌɑːbɪˈtrerəli; ˈɑːbɪtrəli; *NAmE* ˌɑːrbəˈt-/ *adv.*：*The leaders of the groups were chosen arbitrarily.* 这些团体的领导人是任意挑选的。 **ar·bi·trari·ness** **AW** *noun* [U]

ar·bi·trate /ˈɑːbɪtreɪt; *NAmE* ˈɑːrb-/ *verb* [I, T] to officially settle an argument or a disagreement between two people or groups 仲裁；公断：**~ (in/on) (sth)** *to arbitrate in a dispute* 对一场纠纷进行仲裁 ◇ **~ between A and B** *A committee was created to arbitrate between management and the unions.* 已成立一个委员会在资方与工会之间进行仲裁。

ar·bi·tra·tion /ˌɑːbɪˈtreɪʃn; *NAmE* ˌɑːrb-/ *noun* [U] the official process of settling an argument or a disagreement by sb who is not involved 仲裁；公断：*Both sides in the dispute have agreed to* ***go to arbitration.*** 争执双方已同意提请仲裁。

ar·bi·tra·tor /ˈɑːbɪtreɪtə(r); *NAmE* ˈɑːrb-/ *noun* a person who is chosen to settle a disagreement 仲裁人；公断人

ar·bor·eal /ɑːˈbɔːriəl; *NAmE* ɑːrˈb-/ *adj.* (*specialist*) relating to trees; living in trees 乔木的；林栖的

ar·bor·etum /ˌɑːbəˈriːtəm; *NAmE* ˌɑːrb-/ *noun* (*pl.* **ar·bor·etums** or **ar·bor·eta** /-tə/) a garden where many different types of tree are grown, for people to look at or for scientific study（供观赏、科研的）树木园，植物园

ar·bori·cul·ture /ˈɑːbərɪkʌltʃə(r); *NAmE* ˈɑːrb-/ *noun* [U] the study or practice of growing trees and SHRUBS 树木栽培研究；树木栽培 ▸ **ar·bori·cul·tural** /ˌɑːbərɪˈkʌltʃərəl; *NAmE* ˌɑːrb-/ *adj.*：*an arboricultural specialist* 树木栽培专家 **ar·bori·cul·tur·ist** *noun*

ar·bor·ist /ˈɑːbərɪst; *NAmE* ˈɑːrb-/ *noun* (*formal*) = TREE SURGEON

ar·bour (*US* **arbor**) /ˈɑːbə(r); *NAmE* ˈɑːrb-/ *noun* a shelter in a garden/yard for people to sit under, made by growing climbing plants over a frame（花园、院子中由藤蔓在架子上攀缘而成的）棚架，凉棚

arc /ɑːk; *NAmE* ɑːrk/ *noun, verb*
▪ ***noun*** **1** (*geometry* 几何) part of a circle or a curved line 弧 ➲ PICTURE AT CIRCLE **2** a curved shape 弧形：*the arc of a rainbow* 彩虹的弧形 ◇ *The beach swept around in an arc.* 海滩呈弧形伸展开来。 **3** (*specialist*) an electric current passing across a space between two TERMINALS 电弧 ➲ SEE ALSO ARC LAMP
▪ ***verb*** (**arc·ing** /ˈɑːkɪŋ; *NAmE* ˈɑːrk-/, **arced**, **arced** /ɑːkt; *NAmE* ɑːrkt/) (*specialist*) **1** [I] to move in the shape of an arc 作弧形运动 **2** [I] to form an electric arc 形成电弧

ar·cade /ɑːˈkeɪd; *NAmE* ɑːrˈk-/ *noun* **1** a covered passage with ARCHES along the side of a row of buildings (usually a row of shops/stores) 拱廊，拱廊通道（常指一排商店门前的带顶走道） **2** a covered passage between streets, with shops/stores on either side 拱廊商店街（设于两街之间，两侧均有商店） ➲ **VISUAL VOCAB** PAGE V3 **3** (*also* **ˈshopping arcade**) (*both BrE*) a large building with a number of shops/stores in it 商场；购物中心；商业中心 ➲ COMPARE SHOPPING MALL **4** (*BrE also* **aˈmusement arcade**) a place where you can play games on machines which you use coins to operate 游戏机厅；电动游乐场：*arcade games* 游戏机室游戏

Ar·ca·dia /ɑːˈkeɪdiə; *NAmE* ɑːrˈk-/ *noun* [sing.] a part of southern Greece used in poetry and stories to represent an idea of perfect country life 阿卡迪亚（希腊南部地区，在诗歌和小说中常用来指代世外桃源）

Ar·ca·dian /ɑːˈkeɪdiən; *NAmE* ɑːrˈk-/ *adj.* of or connected with Arcadia or an idea of perfect country life 阿卡迪亚的；世外桃源式的

ar·ca·na /ɑːˈkeɪnə; *NAmE* ɑːrˈk-/ *noun* **1** [pl.] things that are secret or mysterious 秘密事件；神秘事物 **2** [sing.] either of the two groups of cards in a TAROT PACK/DECK, the **major arcana** and the **minor arcana** 阿卡纳牌（塔罗牌中的两组牌之一，分大阿卡纳和小阿卡纳）

ar·cane /ɑːˈkeɪn; *NAmE* ɑːrˈk-/ *adj.* (*formal*) secret and mysterious and therefore difficult to understand 神秘的；晦涩难懂的

arch /ɑːtʃ; *NAmE* ɑːrtʃ/ *noun, verb, adj.*
▪ ***noun*** **1** a curved structure that supports the weight of sth above it, such as a bridge or the upper part of a building 拱（支撑如桥梁或房屋上部的弧形结构） **2** a structure with a curved top that is supported by straight sides, sometimes forming an entrance or built as a MONUMENT 拱门：*Go through the arch and follow the path.* 穿过拱门沿小径往前走。◇ *Marble Arch is a famous London landmark.* 大理石拱门是伦敦著名的地标。➲ **VISUAL VOCAB** PAGE V14 **3** the raised part of the foot formed by a curved section of bones 足背；足弓 ➲ **VISUAL VOCAB** PAGE V64 **4** anything that forms a curved shape at the top 拱形；拱形物：*the delicate arch of her eyebrows* 她那弯弯的柳眉 ➲ SEE ALSO ARCHED
▪ ***verb*** **1** [T, I] **~ (sth)** if you **arch** part of your body, or if it **arches**, it moves and forms a curved shape （使）成弓形：*The cat arched its back and hissed.* 猫弓起背发出嘶嘶声。 **2** [I] to be in a curved line or shape across or over sth 呈拱形覆盖；呈弧形横跨：*Tall trees arched over the path.* 大树呈拱形遮阴了小道。
▪ ***adj.*** [usually before noun] (*often disapproving*) seeming amused because you know more about a situation than

other people 调皮的；淘气的： *an arch tone of voice* 调皮的语气 ▸ **arch·ly** *adv.*：*'Guess what?' she said archly.* "猜猜看？"她调皮地说道。

arch- /ˌɑːtʃ; *NAmE* ɑːrtʃ/ *combining form* (in nouns 构成名词) main; most important or most extreme 主要的；最重要的；极端的： *archbishop* 大主教 ◇ *arch-enemy* 主要敌人

archae·olo·gist (*NAmE also* **arche·olo·gist**) /ˌɑːkiˈɒlədʒɪst; *NAmE* ˌɑːrkiˈɑːl-/ *noun* a person who studies archaeology 考古学家

archae·ology (*NAmE also* **arche·ology**) /ˌɑːkiˈɒlədʒi; *NAmE* ˌɑːrkiˈɑːl-/ *noun* [U] the study of cultures of the past, and of periods of history by examining the remains of buildings and objects found in the ground 考古学 ➲ SEE ALSO INDUSTRIAL ARCHAEOLOGY ▸ **arch·aeo·logic·al** (*NAmE also* **arch·eo·logic·al**) /ˌɑːkiəˈlɒdʒɪkl; *NAmE* ˌɑːrkiəˈlɑːdʒ-/ *adj.*：*archaeological excavations/evidence* 考古发掘/实证

archae·op·teryx /ˌɑːkiˈɒptərɪks; *NAmE* ˌɑːrkiˈɑːptərɪks/ *noun* the oldest known bird, which existed about 150 million years ago 始祖鸟（约 1.5 亿年前存在）

ar·chaic /ɑːˈkeɪɪk; *NAmE* ɑːrˈk-/ *adj.* **1** old and no longer used 古体的；已不通用的： *'Thou art' is an archaic form of 'you are'.* * thou art 是 you are 的古体。 **2** very old-fashioned 早已过时的；陈旧的 **SYN** **outdated**: *The system is archaic and unfair and needs changing.* 这个制度早已过时而且不公平，需要改变。 **3** from a much earlier or ancient period of history 古代的；早期的： *archaic art* 古代艺术

archa·ism /ˈɑːkeɪɪzəm; *NAmE* ˈɑːrk-/ *noun* (*specialist*) a very old word or phrase that is no longer used 古词；古语

arch·an·gel /ˈɑːkeɪndʒl; *NAmE* ˈɑːrk-/ *noun* an ANGEL of the highest rank 总领天使；天使长；大天使： *the Archangel Gabriel* 大天使加百列

arch·bishop /ˌɑːtʃˈbɪʃəp; *NAmE* ˌɑːrtʃ-/ *noun* a BISHOP of the highest rank, responsible for all the churches in a large area 大主教；总主教： *the Archbishop of Canterbury* (= the head of the Church of England) 坎特伯雷大主教（即英国国教会领袖）

arch·bish·op·ric /ˌɑːtʃˈbɪʃəprɪk; *NAmE* ˌɑːrtʃ-/ *noun* **1** the position of an archbishop 大主教职位 **2** the district for which an archbishop is responsible 大主教区

arch·deacon /ˌɑːtʃˈdiːkən; *NAmE* ˌɑːrtʃ-/ *noun* a priest just below the rank of BISHOP, especially in the Anglican Church（尤指圣公会的）会吏长

arch·dio·cese /ˌɑːtʃˈdaɪəsɪs; *NAmE* ˌɑːrtʃ-/ *noun* a district under the care of an ARCHBISHOP 大主教区

arch·duch·ess /ˌɑːtʃˈdʌtʃəs; *NAmE* ˌɑːrtʃ-/ *noun* (in the past) the wife of an archduke or a daughter of the EMPEROR of Austria 大公夫人；女大公（旧时奥地利公主）

arch·duke /ˌɑːtʃˈdjuːk; *NAmE* ˌɑːrtʃˈduːk/ *noun* (in the past) a son of the EMPEROR of Austria 大公（旧时奥地利皇太子）：*Archduke Franz Ferdinand* 弗兰茨·斐迪南大公 ➲ COMPARE GRAND DUKE

arched /ɑːtʃt; *NAmE* ɑːrtʃt/ *adj.* in the shape of an ARCH 拱形的；弧形的： *a chair with an arched back* 有拱形靠背的椅子

ˌarch-ˈenemy *noun* a person's main enemy 主要敌人；大敌；死敌

arche·olo·gist, **arche·ology** (*NAmE*) = ARCHAEOLOGIST, ARCHAEOLOGY

arch·er /ˈɑːtʃə(r); *NAmE* ˈɑːrtʃ-/ *noun* a person who shoots with a BOW² and arrows 弓箭手；射箭运动员 ➲ VISUAL VOCAB PAGE V44

arch·ery /ˈɑːtʃəri; *NAmE* ˈɑːrtʃ-/ *noun* [U] the art or sport of shooting arrows with a BOW² 射箭术；射箭运动 ➲ VISUAL VOCAB PAGE V44

arche·typal /ˌɑːkiˈtaɪpl; *NAmE* ˌɑːrki-/ *adj.* having all the important qualities that make sb/sth a typical example of a particular kind of person or thing 典型的： *The Beatles were the archetypal pop group.* 披头士乐队是典型的流行乐队。

arche·type /ˈɑːkitaɪp/ *noun* (*formal*) the most typical or perfect example of a particular kind of person or thing 典型： *She is the archetype of an American movie star.* 她是典型的美国影星。

archi·pel·ago /ˌɑːkɪˈpeləɡəʊ; *NAmE* ˌɑːrkɪˈpeləɡoʊ/ *noun* (*pl.* **-os** or **-oes**) a group of islands and the sea surrounding them 群岛；列岛

archi·tect /ˈɑːkɪtekt; *NAmE* ˈɑːrk-/ *noun* **1** a person whose job is designing buildings 建筑师 **2** a person who is responsible for planning or creating an idea, an event or a situation 设计师；缔造者；创造者： *He was one of the principal architects of the revolution.* 他是那次革命的主要发动者之一。 ◇ *Jones was the architect of the team's first goal.* 琼斯策动球队攻入第一球。

archi·tec·ton·ic /ˌɑːkɪtekˈtɒnɪk; *NAmE* ˌɑːrkɪtekˈtɑːnɪk/ *adj.* (*specialist*) of or connected with architecture or architects 建筑（学）的；建筑师的

archi·tec·tural /ˌɑːkɪˈtektʃərəl; *NAmE* ˌɑːrk-/ *adj.* connected with architecture 建筑学的；建筑方面的： *architectural features* 建筑特色 ▸ **archi·tec·tur·al·ly** *adv.*：*The house is of little interest architecturally.* 这座房子建筑方面平淡无奇。

archi·tec·ture /ˈɑːkɪtektʃə(r); *NAmE* ˈɑːrk-/ *noun* **1** [U] the art and study of designing buildings 建筑学： *to study architecture* 学习建筑学 **2** [U] the design or style of a building or buildings 建筑设计；建筑风格： *the architecture of the eighteenth century* 十八世纪的建筑风格 ◇ *modern architecture* 现代建筑设计 ➲ VISUAL VOCAB PAGE V14 **3** [C, U] (*computing* 计) the design and structure of a computer system 体系结构；（总体、层次）结构，架构

archi·trave /ˈɑːkɪtreɪv; *NAmE* ˈɑːrk-/ *noun* (*specialist*) the frame around a door or window（门、窗的）框缘

arch·ive /ˈɑːkaɪv; *NAmE* ˈɑːrk-/ *noun, verb*

■ ***noun*** (*also* **archives** [pl.]) a collection of historical documents or records of a government, a family, a place or an organization; the place where these records are stored 档案；档案馆；档案室： *the National Sound Archive* 国家音响档案馆 ◇ *archive film* 档案胶片 ◇ *The BBC's archives are bulging with material.* 英国广播公司的档案库材料极其丰富。

■ ***verb*** **1** **~ sth** to put or store a document or other material in an archive 把…存档；把…归档 **2** **~ sth** (*computing* 计) to move information that is not often needed to a different disk, tape or other computer to store it 将（不常用信息）存档

arch·iv·ist /ˈɑːkɪvɪst; *NAmE* ˈɑːrk-/ *noun* a person whose job is to develop and manage an archive 档案保管员

ˌarch-ˈrival *noun* a person's main opponent 主要竞争对手；主要敌手

arch·way /ˈɑːtʃweɪ; *NAmE* ˈɑːrtʃ-/ *noun* a passage or an entrance with an ARCH over it 拱道；拱门： *We went through a stone archway into the courtyard.* 我们穿过石拱门进入院子。

ˈarc lamp (*also* **ˈarc light**) *noun* a lamp that gives very bright light that is produced by an electric ARC 弧光灯

Arc·tic /ˈɑːktɪk; *NAmE* ˈɑːrk-/ *adj., noun*

■ ***adj.*** **1** [only before noun] related to or happening in the regions around the North Pole 北极的；北极地区的： *Arctic explorers* 北极探险者 ➲ COMPARE ANTARCTIC **2** **arctic** extremely cold 极冷的；严寒的： *TV pictures showed the arctic conditions.* 电视画面显示了严寒的环境。

■ ***noun*** [sing.] **the Arctic** the regions of the world around the North Pole 北极；北极地区

the ˌArctic ˈCircle *noun* [sing.] the line of LATITUDE 66°33′ North 北极圈 ➲ COMPARE ANTARCTIC CIRCLE

A

ar·dent /'ɑːdnt; NAmE 'ɑːrdnt/ adj. [usually before noun] very enthusiastic and showing strong feelings about sth/sb 热烈的；激情的 SYN **passionate**: *an ardent supporter of European unity* 欧洲一体化的热烈支持者 ▸ **ar·dent·ly** adv.

ar·dour (*especially US* **ardor**) /'ɑːdə(r); NAmE 'ɑːrdər/ noun [U] (*formal*) very strong feelings of enthusiasm or love 激情；热情 SYN **passion**

ar·du·ous /'ɑːdjuəs; -dʒu-; NAmE 'ɑːrdʒuəs/ adj. involving a lot of effort and energy, especially over a period of time 艰苦的；艰难的：*an arduous journey across the Andes* 翻越安第斯山脉的艰苦之行 ◇ *The work was arduous.* 这项工作很艰巨。▸ **ar·du·ous·ly** adv.

are¹ /ə(r); *strong form* ɑː(r)/ ➲ BE v.

are² /eə(r); ɑː(r); NAmE er/ noun a unit for measuring an area of land; 100 square metres 公亩（等于 100 平方米）

area 🔑 AW /'eəriə; NAmE 'eriə/ noun
- PART OF PLACE 地区 **1** [C] part of a place, town, etc., or a region of a country or the world（地方、城市、国家、世界的）地区，地域：*mountainous/desert areas* 山区；荒漠地域 ◇ *rural/urban/inner-city areas* 农村 / 城市地区；内城区 ◇ *There is heavy traffic in the downtown area tonight.* 今夜商业闹市区交通繁忙。◇ *She knows the* ***local area*** *very well.* 她非常了解这地区的情况。◇ *John is the London area manager.* 约翰是伦敦地区经理。◇ *Wreckage from the plane was scattered over a* ***wide area.*** 飞机失事残骸散落在一个广阔地域。◇ *The farm and* ***surrounding area*** *were flooded.* 农场和周围地区遭洪水淹没。➲ SEE ALSO CATCHMENT AREA, CONSERVATION AREA, DEVELOPMENT AREA, NO-GO AREA **2** [C] a part of a room, building or particular space that is used for a special purpose（房间、建筑物、处所划为某用途的）地方，场地，区：*the hotel reception area* 旅馆接待处 ◇ *a play/parking/dining area* 游戏场地；停车场；用餐处 ➲ SYNONYMS AT PLACE ➲ SEE ALSO REST AREA, SERVICE AREA
- PARTICULAR PLACE 部位 **3** [C] a particular place on an object（物体上的）区，部位：*Move the cursor to a blank area of the computer screen.* 把光标移至电脑屏幕的空区。◇ *The tumour had not spread to other areas of the body.* 肿瘤尚未扩散到身体其他部位。
- SUBJECT/ACTIVITY 学科；活动 **4** [C] ~ (**of sth**) a particular subject or activity, or an aspect of it 领域；方面：*the areas of training and development* 训练和发展方面 ◇ *Finance is Mark's area.* 财务是马克负责的范围。◇ *The big* ***growth area*** *of recent years has been in health clubs.* 健身俱乐部是近年来发展迅速的领域。➲ SEE ALSO GREY AREA
- MEASUREMENT 量度 **5** [C, U] the amount of space covered by a flat surface or piece of land, described as a measurement 面积：*the area of a triangle* 三角形的面积 ◇ *The room is 12 square metres in area.* 这个房间面积是 12 平方米。
- FOOTBALL 足球 **6 the area** (*BrE*) [sing.] (in football (SOCCER) 足球) = PENALTY AREA：*He shot from just outside the area.* 他就在禁区外边拔脚射门。

'area code noun the numbers for a particular area or city, which you use when you are making a telephone call from outside the local area（电话的）地区代码，区号 ➲ COMPARE DIALLING CODE ➲ WORDFINDER NOTE AT CALL

arena /ə'riːnə/ noun **1** a place with a flat open area in the middle and seats around it where people can watch sports and entertainment 圆形运动场；圆形剧场：*a concert at Wembley Arena* 在温布利体育馆举行的音乐会 **2** (*formal*) an area of activity that concerns the public, especially one where there is a lot of opposition between different groups or countries 斗争场所；竞争舞台；活动场所：*the* ***political/international arena*** 政治 / 国际舞台

aren't /ɑːnt; NAmE ɑːrnt/ *short form* **1** are not **2** (in questions 用于疑问句) am not：*Aren't I clever?* 难道我不聪明吗？

areola /ə'riːələ/ noun (*pl.* **areo·lae** /-liː/) (*anatomy* 解) the round area of skin around the NIPPLE 乳晕

argon /'ɑːɡɒn; NAmE 'ɑːrɡɑːn/ noun [U] (*symb.* **Ar**) a chemical element. Argon is a gas that does not react with anything and is used in electric lights. 氩

argot /'ɑːɡəʊ; NAmE 'ɑːrɡət; -ɡoʊ/ noun [sing., U] (*from French*) words and phrases that are used by a particular group of people and not easily understood by others 行话；暗语；黑话；切口 SYN **jargon**

ar·gu·able /'ɑːɡjuəbl; NAmE 'ɑːrɡ-/ adj. (*formal*) **1** that you can give good reasons for 可论证的；有论据的：***It is arguable that*** *giving too much detail may actually be confusing.* 过分详细反而使人糊涂，这种说法是有道理的。**2** not certain; that you do not accept without question 无把握的；可疑的 SYN **debatable**: *It is arguable whether the case should have ever gone to trial* (= perhaps it should not have). 这个案件原本是否应该审理还是个问题。

ar·gu·ably /'ɑːɡjuəbli; NAmE 'ɑːrɡ-/ adv. used (often before a comparative or superlative adjective) when you are stating an opinion that you believe you could give reasons to support（常用于形容词比较级或最高级前）可论证地，按理：*He is arguably the best actor of his generation.* 按理他是他那一代中最优秀的演员。

▼ LANGUAGE BANK 用语库

argue

Verbs for reporting an opinion 陈述观点的动词

- *Some critics* ***argue*** *that Picasso remained a great master all his life.* 一些评论家认为毕加索毕生都是一位大师。
- *Others* ***maintain*** *that there is a significant deterioration in quality in his post-war work.* 其他人坚称他战后的作品质量明显下降。
- *Picasso himself* ***claimed*** *that good art is created, but great art is stolen.* 毕加索自己声称，好的艺术是创造出来的，伟大的艺术却是偷来的。
- ***As*** *Smith* ***has noted****, Picasso borrowed imagery from African art.* 正如史密斯所述，毕加索借用了非洲艺术的意象。
- ***As*** *the author* ***points out****, Picasso borrowed imagery from African art.* 正如作者指出的那样，毕加索借用了非洲艺术的意象。
- *The writer* ***challenges the notion that*** *Picasso's sculpture was secondary to his painting.* 作者对这种观点表示质疑，即毕加索的雕塑不及他的绘画。
- ***It has been suggested that*** *Picasso's painting was influenced by jazz music.* 据说毕加索的绘画受到爵士乐的影响。

➲ LANGUAGE BANK AT ABOUT, ACCORDING TO

argue 🔑 /'ɑːɡjuː; NAmE 'ɑːrɡ-/ verb **1** [I] to speak angrily to sb because you disagree with them 争论；争吵；争辩：*My brothers are always arguing.* 我的兄弟们总是争论不休。◇ ~ (**with sb**) (**about/over sth**) *We're always arguing with each other about money.* 我们总是为钱吵嘴。◇ ~ **with sb** *I don't want to argue with you—just do it!* 我不想和你争辩，干吧！ **2** [I, T] to give reasons why you think that sth is right/wrong, true/not true, etc., especially to persuade people that you are right 论证；说理；争辩：~ **for/against sth/doing sth** *They argued for the right to strike.* 他们据理力争罢工权利。◇ ~ **sth** *She argued the case for bringing back the death penalty.* 她为恢复死刑的主张提供论据。◇ *He was too tired to* ***argue the point*** (= discuss the matter). 他太倦了，不想讨论这个问题。◇ *a well-argued article* 凿凿有据的文章 ◇ ~ **that...** *He argued that they needed more time to finish the project.* 他提出理由说明他们需要更多的时间来完成该项目。◇ ***It could be argued that*** *laws are made by and for men.* 法律由人并为人制定的这一点颇有道理。➲ LANGUAGE BANK AT NEVERTHELESS, PERHAPS **3** [T] ~ **sth** (*formal*) to show clearly that sth exists or is true 证明；表明：*These latest developments argue a change in government policy.* 最近的事态发展表明政府改变了政策。

IDM ˌ**argue the** ˈ**toss** (*BrE, informal*) to continue to disagree about a decision, especially when it is too late to

A

change it or it is not very important （对决定）徒然反对，作无谓的争执

PHR V ˌ**argue sb** ˈ**into/**ˈ**out of doing sth** to persuade sb to do/not do sth by giving them reasons 说服（某人）做 / 不做（某事）： *They argued him into withdrawing his complaint.* 他们说服他撤回了投诉。 ˈ**argue with sth** (usually used in negative sentences 通常用于否定句) (*informal*) to disagree with a statement 不同意（说法）；不承认（表述）： *He's a really successful man—you can't argue with that.* 他是一个真正成功的人，你不得不承认这个事实。

ar·gu·ment /ˈɑːgjumənt; *NAmE* ˈɑːrg-/ *noun* **1** [C, U] a conversation or discussion in which two or more people disagree, often angrily 争论；争吵；争辩；辩论： *to* ***win/lose an argument*** 辩论赢了 / 输了 ◇ *After some heated argument a decision was finally taken.* 激烈辩论以后终于做出了决定。 ◇ **~ (with sb) (about/over sth)** *We had* ***an argument*** *with the waiter about the bill.* 我们和服务员就账单发生了争吵。 ◇ **~ with sb** *She got into an argument with the teacher.* 她和老师争论了起来。 **2** [C] a reason or set of reasons that sb uses to show that sth is true or correct 论据；理由；论点： *Her main argument was a moral one.* 她的主要论据是道德上的。 ◇ **~ for/against sth** *There are strong* ***arguments for and against*** *euthanasia.* 对安乐死支持和反对的人都有强而有力的论据。 ◇ **~ that...** *His argument was that public spending must be reduced.* 他的论点是公共开支必须缩减。 **3** [U] **~ (about sth)** the act of disagreeing in a conversation or discussion using a reason or set of reasons 辩论： *Let's assume* ***for the sake of argument*** (= in order to discuss the problem) *that we can't start till March.* 为方便讨论起见，先假定我们要到三月份才能开始。 ➲ WORDFINDER NOTE AT DEBATE

ar·gu·men·ta·tion /ˌɑːgjumənˈteɪʃn; *NAmE* ˌɑːrg-/ *noun* [U] logical arguments used to support a theory, an action or an idea 推论；论证；论据

ar·gu·men·ta·tive /ˌɑːgjuˈmentətɪv; *NAmE* ˌɑːrg-/ *adj.* a person who is **argumentative** likes arguing or often starts arguing 好争论的；爱辩论的

argy-bargy /ˌɑːdʒi ˈbɑːdʒi; *NAmE* ˌɑːrdʒi ˈbɑːrdʒi/ *noun* [U, C] (*pl.* **argy-bargies**) (*BrE, informal*) noisy disagreement 争吵；拌嘴；吵闹；抬杠 ➲ MORE LIKE THIS 11, page R26

ar·gyle /ɑːˈgaɪl; *NAmE* ˈɑːrgaɪl/ *noun* [U] a knitted pattern of diamond shapes on a plain background, especially on a sweater or on socks （套衫、袜子等上的）菱形花纹，菱形图案

aria /ˈɑːriə/ *noun* a song for one voice, especially in an OPERA or ORATORIO （尤指歌剧或清唱剧中的）咏叹调 ➲ WORDFINDER NOTE AT OPERA

-arian *suffix* (in nouns and adjectives 构成名词和形容词) believing in; practising 相信…的；实行…的： *humanitarian* 人道主义的 ◇ *disciplinarian* 严格执行纪律者 ➲ MORE LIKE THIS 7, page R25

arid /ˈærɪd/ *adj.* **1** (of land or a climate 土地或气候) having little or no rain; very dry 干旱的；干燥的： *arid and semi-arid deserts* 干旱和半干旱的沙漠 ➲ WORDFINDER NOTE AT CLIMATE **2** (*formal*) with nothing new or interesting in it 枯燥的；乏味的；毫无新意的： *an arid discussion* 枯燥的讨论 ▶ **arid·ity** /əˈrɪdəti/ *noun* [U]

Aries /ˈeəriːz; *NAmE* ˈeriːz/ *noun* **1** [U] the first sign of the ZODIAC, the RAM 黄道第一宫；白羊宫；白羊（星）座 **2** [sing.] a person born when the sun is in this sign, that is between 21 March and 20 April 属白羊座的人（约出生于3 月 21 日至 4 月 20 日）

aright /əˈraɪt/ *adv.* (*old-fashioned*) correctly 正确地；对

arise /əˈraɪz/ *verb* (**arose** /əˈrəʊz; *NAmE* əˈroʊz/, **arisen** /əˈrɪzn/) **1** [I] (*rather formal*) (especially of a problem or a difficult situation 尤指问题或困境) to happen; to start to exist 发生；产生；出现 SYN **occur**： *A new crisis has arisen.* 新危机已经出现。 ◇ *We keep them informed of any changes as they arise.* 如有任何变化，我们随时通知他们。 ◇ *Children should be disciplined* ***when the need arises*** (= when it is necessary). 必要时孩子应该受到管教。 ◇ *A storm arose during the night.* 夜间暴风雨大作。 **2** [I] **~ (out of/from sth)** (*rather formal*) to happen as a result of a particular situation （由…）引起；（因…）产生： *injuries arising out of a road accident* 道路交通事故造成的伤害 ◇ *Emotional or mental problems can arise from a physical cause.* 身体上的原因可以引起情绪或精神上的问题。 ◇ *Are there any* ***matters arising*** *from the minutes of the last meeting?* 根据上次会议记录，有没有什么新情况出现？ **3** [I] (*formal*) to begin to exist or develop 出现；产生；发展： *Several new industries arose in the town.* 城里出现了好几种新行业。 **4** [I] (*old use* or *literary*) to get out of bed; to stand up 起床；起立；起身： *He arose at dawn.* 他黎明即起。 **5** [I] **~ (against sb/sth)** (*old use*) to come together to protest about sth or to fight for sth 群起反对；奋起斗争： *The peasants arose against their masters.* 农民奋起反对奴役他们的人。 **6** [I] (*literary*) (of a mountain, a tall building, etc. 山、高大建筑物等) to become visible gradually as you move towards it （随着人走近而）逐渐显现

ar·is·toc·racy /ˌærɪˈstɒkrəsi; *NAmE* -ˈstɑːk-/ *noun* [C+sing./pl. v.] (*pl.* **-ies**) (in some countries) people born in the highest social class, who have special titles （某些国家的）贵族 SYN **nobility**： *members of the aristocracy* 贵族成员

ar·is·to·crat /ˈærɪstəkræt; *NAmE* əˈrɪst-/ *noun* a member of the aristocracy （一个）贵族 ➲ COMPARE COMMONER

ar·is·to·crat·ic /ˌærɪstəˈkrætɪk; *NAmE* əˌrɪstə-/ *adj.* belonging to or typical of the ARISTOCRACY 贵族的 SYN **noble**： ***an aristocratic name/family/lifestyle*** 贵族姓氏 / 家庭 / 生活方式

Ar·is·to·tel·ian /ˌærɪstəˈtiːliən/ *adj.* connected with Aristotle or his philosophy 亚里士多德（哲学）的

arith·met·ic /əˈrɪθmətɪk/ *noun* [U] **1** the type of mathematics that deals with the adding, multiplying, etc. of numbers 算术： *He's not very good at arithmetic.* 他不太擅长算术。 **2** sums involving the adding, multiplying, etc. of numbers 算术运算；四则运算： *a quick bit of* ***mental arithmetic*** (= sums you do in your head, without writing anything down) 快速心算 ◇ *I think there's something wrong with your arithmetic.* 我认为你的计算有错。 ➲ WORDFINDER NOTE AT MATHS

arith·met·ic·al /ˌærɪθˈmetɪkl/ (*also* **arith·met·ic**) *adj.* relating to arithmetic 算术的： *an arithmetical calculation* 算术运算 ▶ **arith·met·ic·al·ly** /-kli/ *adv.*

arithˌmetic ˈ**mean** *noun* (*mathematics* 数) = MEAN

arithˌmetic proˈ**gression** (*also* **arithˌmetic** ˈ**series**) *noun* a series of numbers that decrease or increase by the same amount each time, for example 2, 4, 6, 8 算术数列，等差数列（如 2、4、6、8） ➲ COMPARE GEOMETRIC PROGRESSION

the ark /ɑːk; *NAmE* ɑːrk/ (*also* ˌ**Noah's** ˈ**ark**) *noun* [sing.] (in the Bible《圣经》) a large boat which Noah built to save his family and two of every type of animal from the flood 方舟，诺亚方舟（诺亚为家人及一对对各种动物避洪水所造的大船）

IDM **out of the** ˈ**ark** | **sth went out with the** ˈ**ark** (*BrE, informal*) if sb says that an object or a custom is **out of the ark** or **went out with the ark**, they think that it is very old-fashioned 极古老；十分陈旧；过时

arm /ɑːm; *NAmE* ɑːrm/ *noun, verb*

■ ***noun*** ➲ SEE ALSO ARMS

• **PART OF BODY** 身体部位 **1** either of the two long parts that stick out from the top of the body and connect the shoulders to the hands 臂；手臂；上肢： *He escaped with only a broken arm.* 他得以逃生，只是断了一条胳膊。 ◇ *She threw her arms around his neck.* 她张开双臂搂住他的脖子。 ◇ *The officer grabbed him* ***by the arm*** (= grabbed his arm). 警察抓住了他的手臂。 ◇ *She touched him gently* ***on the arm.*** 她轻轻地碰了碰他的胳膊。 ◇ *He held the dirty rag* ***at arm's length*** (= as far away from his body as possible). 他拎着脏抹布，身子离得远远的。 ◇ *They walked along* ***arm in arm*** (= with the arm of one person linked with the arm of the other). 他们臂挽着臂一路走着。◇ *She cradled the child* ***in her arms***. 她怀抱着小孩。◇ *They fell asleep* ***in each other's arms*** (= holding each other). 他们互相搂抱着睡着了。◇ *He was carrying a number of files* ***under his arm*** (= between his arm and his body). 他腋下挟着一些卷宗。◇ *He walked in with a tall blonde* ***on his arm*** (= next to him and holding his arm). 他挎着一个高个子金发女郎走了进来。➲ COLLOCATIONS AT PHYSICAL ➲ VISUAL VOCAB PAGE V64

- **OF CLOTHING** 衣服 **2** the part of a piece of clothing that covers the arm 袖子 SYN **sleeve**
- **OF CHAIR** 椅子 **3** the part of a chair, etc. on which you rest your arms 扶手 ➲ VISUAL VOCAB PAGES V22, V71
- **OF MACHINERY** 机器 **4** a long narrow part of an object or a piece of machinery, especially one that moves 臂状物（尤指可移动的物体部分或机器部件）: *a robotic arm* 机械臂
- **OF WATER/LAND** 水；陆地 **5** a long narrow piece of water or land that is joined to a larger area 狭长港湾；（连接较大地区的）狭长地带：*A small bridge spans the arm of the river.* 一座小桥横跨河湾。
- **OF ORGANIZATION** 组织机构 **6** [usually sing.] ~ (**of sth**) a section of a large organization that deals with one particular activity 分部；职能部门 SYN **wing**: *the research arm of the company* 公司的科研部门

IDM **cost/pay an ˌarm and a ˈleg** (*informal*) to cost/pay a lot of money （使）花一大笔钱 **keep sb at arm's length** to avoid having a close relationship with sb 与某人保持距离；不亲近某人：*He keeps all his clients at arm's length.* 他不与任何委托人过分亲密。➲ MORE AT AKIMBO, BABE, BEAR *v.*, CHANCE *v.*, FOLD *v.*, LONG *adj.*, OPEN *adj.*, RIGHT *adj.*, SHOT *n.*, TWIST *v.*

■ ***verb*** **1** [I, T] to provide weapons for yourself/sb in order to fight a battle or a war 武装；装备；备战：*The country was arming against the enemy.* 这个国家正在备战迎击敌人。◇ **~ yourself/sb** (**with sth**) *The men armed themselves with sticks and stones.* 这些人以棍棒和石块作为武器。◇ (*figurative*) *She had armed herself for the meeting with all the latest statistics.* 为了这次会议，她准备了所有最新统计资料。➲ SEE ALSO ARMED **2** [T] **~ sth** to make a bomb, etc. ready to explode 使（炸弹等）随时爆炸 ➲ COMPARE DISARM ➲ SEE ALSO ARMED

ar·mada /ɑːˈmɑːdə; *NAmE* ɑːrˈm-/ *noun* a large group of armed ships sailing together （大型）舰队：*The Spanish Armada was sent to attack England in 1588.* * 1588 年西班牙无敌舰队被派遣进攻英国。◇ (*figurative*) *a vast armada of football fans* 一大群足球迷

ar·ma·dillo /ˌɑːməˈdɪləʊ; *NAmE* ˌɑːrməˈdɪloʊ/ *noun* (*pl.* **-os**) an American animal with a hard shell made of pieces of bone 犰狳（美洲动物，体表覆盖甲胄状原骨质板）

Ar·ma·ged·don /ˌɑːməˈgedn; *NAmE* ˌɑːrm-/ *noun* [sing., U] **1** (in the Bible 《圣经》) a battle between good and evil at the end of the world 世界末日的善恶大决战 **2** a terrible war that could destroy the world （足以毁灭世界的）大决战

ar·ma·ment /ˈɑːməmənt; *NAmE* ˈɑːrm-/ *noun* **1** [C, usually pl.] weapons, especially large guns, bombs, tanks, etc. 军备；武器：*the armaments industry* 军火工业 **2** [U] the process of increasing the amount of weapons an army or a country has, especially to prepare for war 武装；战备 ➲ COMPARE DISARMAMENT

arma·ture /ˈɑːmətʃə(r); *NAmE* ˈɑːrm-/ *noun* (*specialist*) a frame that is covered to make a figure （塑像的）骨架，模架：*The figures are made from clay over a wire armature.* 这些塑像是将黏土贴在金属丝骨架上制成的。

arm·band /ˈɑːmbænd; *NAmE* ˈɑːrm-/ *noun* **1** a cloth band worn around the arm as a sign of sth, for example that sb has an official position 臂章；袖章：*The stewards all wore armbands.* 乘务员都戴了臂章。◇ *Many people at the funeral service were wearing black armbands.* 葬礼上许多人戴着黑纱。 **2** either of two plastic rings that can be filled with air and worn around the arms by sb who is learning to swim （学游泳时用的可充气）臂圈 ➲ WORDFINDER NOTE AT SWIM

ˈarm candy *noun* [U] (*informal*) a beautiful woman that a man takes with him when he goes to a public event in order to impress other people （男子参加社交活动时所带的）挂臂美女

arm·chair *noun, adj.*

■ ***noun*** /ˈɑːmtʃeə(r); ɑːmˈtʃeə(r); *NAmE* ˈɑːrmtʃer; ɑːrmˈtʃer/ a comfortable chair with sides on which you can rest your arms 扶手椅：*to sit in an armchair* 坐在扶手椅上 ➲ VISUAL VOCAB PAGE V22

■ ***adj.*** /ˈɑːmtʃeə(r); *NAmE* ˈɑːrmtʃer/ [only before noun] knowing about a subject through books and television, rather than by doing it for yourself 书本知识的；只说而没有行动的：*an* ***armchair critic/traveller*** 不切实际的批评家；端坐家中的神游旅行者

armed /ɑːmd; *NAmE* ɑːrmd/ *adj.* **1** involving the use of weapons 使用武器的；用武力的：*an armed robbery* 持械抢劫 ◇ *an international* ***armed conflict*** (= a war) 国际武装冲突 OPP **unarmed** **2** carrying a weapon, especially a gun 携带武器的；持枪的；荷枪实弹的：*The man is armed and dangerous.* 这个男子有枪，是个危险分子。◇ *armed guards* 武装警卫 ◇ *Police were* ***heavily armed***. 警察全副武装。◇ **~ with a gun, etc.** *He was armed with a rifle.* 他配有一支步枪。OPP **unarmed** **3** **~** (**with sth**) knowing sth or carrying sth that you need in order to help you to perform a task 备有所需的：*He was armed with all the facts.* 他备有所需的全部事实材料。

IDM **ˌarmed to the ˈteeth** having many weapons 武装到牙齿；全副武装

the ˌarmed ˈforces (*also* **the ˌarmed ˈservices**) *noun* [pl.] a country's army, navy and AIR FORCE （一国的）武装部队，武装力量

arm·ful /ˈɑːmfʊl; *NAmE* ˈɑːrm-/ *noun* a quantity that you can carry in one or both arms 单臂（或双臂）一抱的量；一抱

arm·hole /ˈɑːmhəʊl; *NAmE* ˈɑːrmhoʊl/ *noun* the place in a coat, shirt, dress, etc. that your arm goes through 袖孔

ar·mis·tice /ˈɑːmɪstɪs; *NAmE* ˈɑːrm-/ *noun* [sing.] a formal agreement during a war to stop fighting and discuss making peace 休战；停战；休战条约；停战协定 SYN **ceasefire** ➲ WORDFINDER NOTE AT PEACE

arm·lock /ˈɑːmlɒk; *NAmE* ˈɑːrmlɑːk/ *noun* (in WRESTLING 摔跤运动) a way of holding an opponent's arm so that they cannot move 锁臂：*He had him in an armlock.* 他锁住了对手的手臂。

ar·moire /ɑːmˈwɑː(r); *NAmE* ɑːrmˈwɑːr/ *noun* (*from French*) a cupboard with drawers or shelves underneath, especially one that has a lot of decoration （常指华丽或精致的）大衣橱，大橱柜

ar·mor·ial /ɑːˈmɔːriəl; *NAmE* ɑːrˈm-/ *adj.* connected with HERALDRY 纹章的

ar·mour (*especially US* **armor**) /ˈɑːmə(r); *NAmE* ˈɑːrm-/ *noun* [U] **1** special metal clothing that soldiers wore in the past to protect their bodies while fighting 盔甲；甲胄：*a suit of armour* 一副盔甲 ◇ (*figurative*) *Monkeys do not have any kind of protective armour and use their brains to solve problems.* 猴子没有任何防身的盔甲，就动脑筋解决问题。 **2** metal covers that protect ships and military vehicles such as tanks （军舰、坦克等的）装甲，防弹钢板 **3** (*specialist*) military vehicles used in war 装甲部队；装甲车辆：*an attack by infantry and armour* 步兵和装甲兵的进攻 IDM SEE CHINK *n.*, KNIGHT *n.*

ar·moured (*especially US* **ar·mored**) /ˈɑːməd; *NAmE* ˈɑːrmərd/ *adj.* **1** (especially of a military vehicle 尤指军用交通工具) protected by metal covers 有装甲的：*The cruiser was heavily armoured.* 这艘巡洋舰有坚固的装甲。◇ *an armoured car* 装甲车 **2** using armoured vehicles 使用装甲交通工具的：*an armoured division* 装甲师

A

ˌarmoured personˈnel carrier (*especially US* **ˌarmored personˈnel carrier**) *noun* a military vehicle used to transport soldiers 装甲运兵车

ar·mour·er (*especially US* **ar·mor·er**) /ˈɑːmərə(r); *NAmE* ˈɑːrm-/ *noun* a person who makes or repairs weapons and armour 军械制造师；军械维修工；军械工

ˌarmour-ˈplated (*especially US* **armor-**) *adj.* (of vehicles 交通工具) covered with sheets of metal to provide protection against bullets, etc. 有装甲的；由装甲钢板覆盖的

ar·moury (*especially US* **ar·mory**) /ˈɑːməri; *NAmE* ˈɑːrm-/ *noun* (*pl.* **-ies**) **1** a place where weapons and armour are kept 军械库 SYN **arsenal** **2** (in the US or Canada) a building which is the HEADQUARTERS for training people who are not professional soldiers, for example the National Guard （美国或加拿大国民卫队等的）总部大楼 **3** (*formal*) the things that sb has available to help them achieve sth 锦囊；宝库：*Doctors have an armoury of drugs available.* 医生都备有各种各样的药物。**4** all the weapons and military equipment that a country has （一国的）军事装备：*Britain's nuclear armoury* 英国的核武器装备

arm·pit /ˈɑːmpɪt; *NAmE* ˈɑːrm-/ (*also NAmE, informal* **pit**) *noun* the part of the body under the arm where it joins the shoulder 腋；腋窝 ➲ VISUAL VOCAB PAGE V64 ➲ SEE ALSO UNDERARM

IDM **the ˈarmpit of sth** (*informal, especially NAmE*) the most unpleasant or ugly place in a country or region 肮脏的角落；龌龊的地方：*The city has been called the armpit of America.* 这座城市被称为美国最令人厌恶的地方。

arm·rest /ˈɑːmrest; *NAmE* ˈɑːrm-/ *noun* the part of some types of seat, especially in planes or cars, which supports your arm （飞机、汽车等座位的）靠手，扶手

arms 🔑 /ɑːmz; *NAmE* ɑːrmz/ *noun* [pl.] **1** 🔑 (*formal*) weapons, especially as used by the army, navy, etc. 兵器；武器：*arms and ammunition* 兵器和弹药 ◊ *Police officers in the UK do not usually* **carry arms**. 英国警察通常不携带武器。➲ WORDFINDER NOTE AT CONFLICT ➲ SEE ALSO FIREARM, SMALL ARMS **2** = COAT OF ARMS：*the King's Arms* (= used as the name of a pub) 国王盾形徽章（酒吧名）

IDM **be under ˈarms** (*formal*) to have weapons and be ready to fight in a war 处于备战状态；严阵以待；枕戈待旦 **lay down your ˈarms** (*formal*) to stop fighting 放下武器；停止作战 **take up arms (against sb)** (*formal*) to prepare to fight 拿起武器；准备战斗 **(be) up in ˈarms (about/over sth)** (*informal*) (of a group of people 一群人) to be very angry about sth and ready to protest strongly about it 极力反对；强烈抗议 ➲ MORE AT BEAR *v.*, PRESENT *v.*

ˈarms control *noun* [U] international agreements to destroy weapons or limit the number of weapons that countries have 军备控制

ˈarms race *noun* [sing.] a situation in which countries compete to get the most and best weapons 军备竞赛

ˈarm-twisting *noun* [U] (*informal*) the use of a lot of pressure or even physical force to persuade sb to do sth 强迫；施加压力

ˈarm-wrestling *noun* [U] a competition to find out which of two people is the stronger, in which they try to force each other's arm down onto a table 扳手腕；比腕力

army 🔑 /ˈɑːmi; *NAmE* ˈɑːrmi/ *noun* (*pl.* **-ies**) **1** 🔑 [C+sing./pl. v.] a large organized group of soldiers who are trained to fight on land 陆上作战军队；陆军部队：*The two opposing armies faced each other across the battlefield.* 敌对两军在战场上严阵对峙。➲ WORDFINDER NOTE AT CONFLICT

WORDFINDER 联想词：artillery, battalion, command, defend, invade, officer, regiment, tactics, weapon

2 🔑 **the army** [sing.+sing./pl. v.] the part of a country's armed forces that fights on land （一国的）陆军：*Her husband is in the army.* 她的丈夫在陆军服役。◊ *After leaving school, Mike* **went into the army**. 迈克中学毕业后参加了陆军。◊ *an army officer* 陆军军官 ➲ COLLOCATIONS AT WAR **3** [C+sing./pl. v.] a large number of people or things, especially when they are organized in some way or involved in a particular activity 大批；大群：*an army of advisers/volunteers* 一大批顾问；志愿者大军 ◊ *An army of ants marched across the path.* 一大群蚂蚁浩浩荡荡地穿过小径。

ˌarmy ˈsurplus *noun* [U] clothing and equipment that the army no longer needs and is sold to the public （可公开出售的）剩余军用物资

ar·nica /ˈɑːnɪkə; *NAmE* ˈɑːrn-/ *noun* [U] a natural medicine made from a plant, used to treat BRUISES (= marks that appear on the skin after sb has fallen, been hit, etc.) 山金车酊（用于治疗挫伤等的天然药物）

ˈA-road *noun* (in Britain) a road that is less important than a MOTORWAY, but wider and straighter than a B-ROAD （英国）干线公路，A 级公路（略次于高速公路，但较 B 级公路宽直）

aroma /əˈrəʊmə; *NAmE* əˈroʊmə/ *noun* a pleasant, noticeable smell 芳香；香味：*the aroma of fresh coffee* 新鲜咖啡的香味

aroma·ther·apy /əˌrəʊməˈθerəpi; *NAmE* əˌroʊmə-/ *noun* [U] the use of natural oils that smell sweet for controlling pain or for rubbing into the body during MASSAGE 芳香疗法（用天然芳香油镇痛或按摩时揉入体内）▸ **aroma·ther·ap·ist** *noun*

aro·mat·ic /ˌærəˈmætɪk/ *adj.* having a pleasant noticeable smell 芳香的；有香味的 SYN **fragrant**：*aromatic oils/herbs* 芳香油；芳香草

arose PAST TENSE OF ARISE

around 🔑 /əˈraʊnd/ *adv.*, *prep.*

■ *adv.* HELP For the special uses of **around** in phrasal verbs, look at the entries for the verbs. For example **come around to sth** is in the phrasal verb section at **come**. * around 在短语动词中的特殊用法见有关动词词条。如 come around to sth 在词条 come 的短语动词部分。**1** 🔑 approximately 大约：*He arrived around five o'clock.* 他大约是五点钟到的。◊ *The cost would be somewhere around £1 500.* 费用要在 1 500 英镑上下。**2** 🔑 on every side; surrounding sb/sth 周围；四周：*I could hear laughter all around.* 我可以听见周围的笑声。◊ *a yard with a fence* **all around** 四周围着栅栏的院子 **3** 🔑 (*especially NAmE*) (*BrE usually* **round**) moving in a circle 围绕；环绕：*How do you make the wheels go around?* 你怎样使这些轮子转动起来？**4** 🔑 (*especially NAmE*) (*BrE usually* **round**) measured in a circle

▼ WHICH WORD? 词语辨析

around / round / about

- **Around** and **round** can often be used with the same meaning in *BrE*, though **around** is more formal. 在英式英语中，around 和 round 近义，不过 around 较正式：*The earth goes round/around the sun.* 地球绕着太阳转。◊ *They live round/around the corner.* 他们住在附近。◊ *We travelled round/around India.* 我们在印度各地旅行。◊ *She turned round/around when I came in.* 我进来时她转过身来。In *NAmE* only **around** can be used in these meanings. 在美式英语中，表示上述意思只能用 around。
- **Around, round** and **about** can also sometimes be used with the same meaning in *BrE*. 在英式英语中，有时 around、round 和 about 的含义相同：*The kids were running around/round/about outside.* 孩子们在外面跑来跑去。◊ *I've been waiting around/round/about to see her all day.* 为了要见到她，我等了一整天。In *NAmE* only **around** can be used in these meanings. **About** or **around** can be used in both *BrE* and *NAmE* to mean 'approximately'. 在美式英语中，表示上述意思只能用 around。在英式英语和美式英语中，about 或 around 均可表示大约：*We left around/about 8 o'clock.* 我们在 8 点钟左右离开了。

以圆周计算： *an old tree that was at least ten feet around* 合抱至少十英尺的古树 **5** in or to many places 到处；向各处： *We were all running around trying to get ready in time.* 我们东奔西跑，望能按时准备就绪。◇ *This is our new office—Kay will show you around.* 这是我们的新办公室，凯会带你参观一下。◇ *There were papers lying around all over the floor.* 地板上四处散乱着文件。 **6** used to describe activities that have no real purpose 闲散地；无目的地： *There were several young people sitting around looking bored.* 有几个年轻人闲坐着，一副无聊的样子。 **7** present in a place; available 出现；现有；可用： *There was more money around in those days.* 那年头比现在富裕。◇ *I knocked but there was no one around.* 我敲了门，但是没有人应门。◇ *Digital television has been around for some time now.* 数字电视已经面市一段时间了。 **8** active and well known in a sport, profession, etc.（体育运动、专业等中）走红的，活跃的： *a new tennis champion who could be around for a long time* 可能会走红很长时期的新网球冠军 ◇ *She's been around as a film director since the 1980s.* 自 20 世纪 80 年代以来她一直是活跃在影坛的著名导演。 **9** (*especially NAmE*) (*BrE usually* **round**) in a circle or curve to face another way or the opposite way 转弯；掉转；掉头： *She turned the car around and drove off.* 她把轿车掉头开走了。◇ *They looked around when he called.* 他呼喊时他们回头张望。 ➲ SEE ALSO ABOUT *adv.*, ROUND *adv.*

IDM **have been around** to have gained knowledge and experience of the world 阅历世事；饱经世故

■ ***prep.*** (*especially NAmE*) (*BrE usually* **round**) **1** surrounding sb/sth; on each side of sth 围绕；环绕： *The house is built around a central courtyard.* 这房子是围绕着中央的庭院而建的。◇ *He put his arms around her.* 他搂着她。 **2** on, to or from the other side of sb/sth 在那边；到那边；从那边： *Our house is just around the corner.* 过了拐角就是我们的房子。◇ *The bus came around the bend.* 公共汽车从拐弯处驶来。◇ *There must be a way around the problem.* 肯定有解决这个问题的办法。 **3** in a circle 绕着： *They walked around the lake.* 他们绕着湖边行走。 **4** in or to many places in an area 到处；向各处： *They walked around the town looking for a place to eat.* 他们在城里到处寻找吃饭的地方。 **5** to fit in with particular people, ideas, etc. 同…一致；适合；符合： *I can't arrange everything around your timetable!* 我不可能事事都按着你的时刻表安排！

a͵round-the-ˈclock *adj.* = ROUND-THE-CLOCK

arouse /əˈraʊz/ *verb* **1** **~ sth** to make sb have a particular feeling or attitude 激起，引起（感情、态度）： ***to arouse sb's interest/curiosity/anger*** 引起某人的兴趣 / 好奇心 / 怒气 ◇ *Her strange behaviour aroused our suspicions.* 她的古怪行为引起了我们的怀疑。 **2** **~ sb** to make sb feel sexually excited 激起性欲 SYN **excite** **3** **~ sb** to make you feel more active and want to start doing sth 使行动起来；激发： *The whole community was aroused by the crime.* 这个罪行使整个社会行动起来。 **4** **~ sb (from sth)** (*formal*) to wake sb from sleep 唤醒 ➲ SEE ALSO ROUSE ▸ **arousal** /əˈraʊzl/ *noun* [U]: ***emotional/sexual arousal*** 情绪激动；性冲动

ar·peg·gio /ɑːˈpedʒiəʊ; *NAmE* ɑːrˈpedʒioʊ/ *noun* (*pl.* **-os**) (*music* 音, *from Italian*) the notes of a CHORD played quickly one after the other 琶音（快速连续弹出和弦的音符）

arr. *abbr.* **1** (in writing 书写形式) arrives; arrival 抵达；到达： *arr. London 06.00* 早晨 6 点抵达伦敦 ➲ COMPARE DEP. **2** (*music* 音) (in writing 书写形式) arranged by 由…改编： *Handel, arr. Mozart* 莫扎特改编的亨德尔的乐曲

ar·raign /əˈreɪn/ *verb* [usually passive] **~ sb (for sth)** (*law* 律) to bring sb to court in order to formally accuse them of a crime 提讯；提审；控告： *He was arraigned for murder.* 他因谋杀罪而被提讯。◇ *He was arraigned on a charge of murder.* 他以谋杀罪名而受到提审。 ▸ **ar·raign·ment** *noun* [C, U]

ar·range /əˈreɪndʒ/ *verb* **1** [T, I] to plan or organize sth in advance 安排；筹备： **~ sth** *The party was arranged quickly.* 聚会很快就安排好了。◇ *She arranged a loan with the bank.* 她和银行商定了一项贷款。 ◇ *Can I arrange an appointment for Monday?* 我可以安排星期一约见吗？ ◇ *We met at six,* ***as arranged.*** 我们按时在六点钟碰面。 ◇ **~ how, where, etc....** *We've still got to arrange how to get to the airport.* 我们还得安排如何去机场。◇ **~ to do sth** *Have you arranged to meet him?* 你安排好去见他了吗？ ◇ **~ that...** *I've arranged that we can borrow their car.* 我已经说好了，我们可以借用他们的车。 ◇ **~ for sth (to do sth)** *We arranged for a car to collect us from the airport.* 我们安排了一辆轿车到机场接我们。◇ **~ with sb (about sth)** *I've arranged with the neighbours about feeding the cat while we are away.* 我们外出期间给猫喂食的事，我已和邻居安排妥了。 ➲ MORE LIKE THIS 26, page R28 **2** [T] **~ sth** to put sth in a particular order; to make sth neat or attractive 整理；排列；布置： *The books are arranged alphabetically by author.* 这些书是按作者姓名字母顺序排列的。◇ *I must arrange my financial affairs and make a will.* 我必须把我的财务安排好，并立下遗嘱。 ◇ *She arranged the flowers in a vase.* 她用花瓶把花插好。 **3** [T] **~ sth (for sth)** to write or change a piece of music so that it is suitable for a particular instrument or voice 谱写，改编（乐曲）： *He arranged traditional folk songs for the piano.* 他把传统民歌改编成钢琴曲。

ar͵ranged ˈmarriage *noun* [C, U] a marriage in which the parents choose the husband or wife for their child 包办婚姻

ar·range·ment /əˈreɪndʒmənt/ *noun* **1** [C, usually pl.] a plan or preparation that you make so that sth can happen 安排；筹备： *travel arrangements* 旅行安排 ◇ **~ for sth** *I'll* ***make arrangements*** *for you to be met at the airport.* 我会安排人到机场接你。 **2** [C, usually pl.] the way things are done or organized 安排方式；布置： *She's happy with her unusual living arrangements.* 她对自己不同寻常的生活安排方式感到很得意。 ◇ *new security arrangements* 新保安措施 ◇ *There are special arrangements for people working overseas.* 对赴海外工作的人员有特别安排。 **3** [C, U] an agreement that you make with sb that you can both accept 商定；约定： *We can* ***come to an arrangement*** *over the price.* 我们可以就价格问题达成一项协议。◇ **~ between A and B** *an arrangement between the school and the parents* 学校和家长的一项约定 ◇ **~ with sb (to do sth)** *Guided tours are available* ***by prior arrangement*** *with the museum.* 经事先预约，博物馆可提供导览服务。◇ **~ that...** *They had an arrangement that the children would spend two weeks with each parent.* 他们商定，孩子们与父方母方各住两个星期。 **4** [C, U] a group of things that are organized or placed in a particular order or position; the act of placing things in a particular order 整理好的东西；整理；排列；布置： *plans of the possible seating arrangements* 几种可行的座次安排方案 ◇ *the art of flower arrangement* 插花艺术 **5** [C, U] a piece of music that has been changed, for example for another instrument to play 改编乐曲

ar·ran·ger /əˈreɪndʒə/ *noun* **1** a person who arranges music that has been written by sb different 编曲者 **2** a person who arranges things 筹备者；安排者： *arrangers of care services for the elderly* 安排照料老人的筹划者

ar·rant /ˈærənt/ *adj.* [only before noun] (*old-fashioned*) used to emphasize how bad sth/sb is （强调有多坏）十足的，坏透的： *arrant nonsense* 一派胡言

array /əˈreɪ/ *noun, verb*

■ ***noun*** **1** [usually sing.] a group or collection of things or people, often one that is large or impressive 大堆；大群；大量： *a vast array of bottles of different shapes and sizes* 一大批形状大小不一的瓶子 ◇ *a dazzling array of talent* 耀眼的大批天才 **2** (*computing* 计) a way of organizing and storing related data in a computer memory 数组；阵列 **3** (*specialist*) a set of numbers, signs or values arranged in rows and columns 数组；阵列

■ ***verb*** [usually passive] (*formal*) **1** **~ sth** to arrange a group of things in a pleasing way or so that they are in order 布置；排列： *Jars of all shapes and sizes were arrayed on the shelves.* 在搁架上整齐地排列着大大小小各式各样的

罐子。 **2 ~ sb** (*specialist*) to arrange soldiers in a position from which they are ready to attack 配置（兵力）

array·ed /əˈreɪd/ *adj.* [not before noun] **~ (in sth)** (*literary*) dressed in a particular way, especially in beautiful clothes 穿戴（尤指漂亮衣服）： *She was arrayed in a black velvet gown.* 她穿着一件黑色天鹅绒长礼服。

ar·rears /əˈrɪəz; *NAmE* əˈrɪrz/ *noun* [pl.] money that sb owes that they have not paid at the right time 逾期欠款： ***rent/mortgage/tax arrears*** 拖欠租金 / 按揭贷款 / 税款

IDM **be in arrears | get/fall into arrears** to be late in paying money that you owe 到期未付；拖欠： *We're two months in arrears with the rent.* 我们拖欠了两个月的租金。 **in arrears** if money or a person is paid **in arrears** for work, the money is paid after the work has been done 后付；拖欠；拖延

ar·rest /əˈrest/ *verb, noun*

■ ***verb*** **1** [T, often passive] if the police **arrest** sb, the person is taken to a POLICE STATION and kept there because the police believe they may be guilty of a crime 逮捕；拘留： **~ sb** *A man has been arrested in connection with the robbery.* 一名男子因与这桩抢劫案有关已被逮捕。 ◇ **~ sb for sth** *She was arrested for drug-related offences.* 她因涉嫌毒品犯罪而被捕。 ◇ **~ sb for doing sth** *You could get arrested for doing that.* 你干那种事可能要遭逮捕。 ➲ WORDFINDER NOTE AT POLICE ➲ COLLOCATIONS AT JUSTICE **2** [T] **~ sth** (*formal*) to stop a process or a development 阻止；中止： *They failed to arrest the company's decline.* 他们未能阻止公司的衰落。 **3** [T] **~ sth** (*formal*) to make sb notice sth and pay attention to it 吸引（注意）： *An unusual noise **arrested his attention**.* 一阵不寻常的嘈杂声引起了他的注意。 **4** [I] (*medical* 医) if sb **arrests**, their heart stops beating 心跳停止： *He arrested on the way to the hospital.* 他在送医院途中停止了心跳。

■ ***noun*** [C, U] **1** the act of arresting sb 逮捕；拘捕： *The police made several arrests.* 警方逮捕了好几人。 ◇ *She was **under arrest** on suspicion of murder.* 她因涉嫌谋杀而被逮捕。 ◇ *Opposition leaders were put under **house arrest*** (= not allowed to leave their houses). 反对党领袖遭软禁。 ➲ SEE ALSO CITIZEN'S ARREST **2** an act of sth stopping or being interrupted 停止；中止： *He died after suffering a **cardiac arrest*** (= when his heart suddenly stopped). 他死于心脏停搏。

ar,restable ˈoffence *noun* (*law* 律) an offence for which sb can be arrested without a WARRANT from a judge 构成逮捕的罪行；应予逮捕的罪行

ar·rest·ing /əˈrestɪŋ/ *adj.* (*formal*) attracting a lot of attention; very attractive 引人注意的；很有吸引力的

ar·rival /əˈraɪvl/ *noun* **1** [U, C] an act of coming or being brought to a place 到达；抵达： *Guests receive dinner **on/upon arrival** at the hotel.* 旅客一到旅馆即可就餐。 ◇ *We apologize for the late arrival of the train.* 我们为火车误点表示歉意。 ◇ *the arrival of the mail in the morning* 上午送达的邮件 ◇ *daily arrivals of refugees* 每天到来的难民 ◇ *There are 120 **arrivals and departures** every day.* 每天有 120 次航班离港和抵港。 **OPP** **departure** **2** [C] a person or thing that comes to a place 到达者；抵达物： *The first arrivals at the concert got the best seats.* 最早来到音乐会的人坐上了最好的座位。 ◇ ***early/late/new arrivals*** 早到 / 晚到 / 新到者 ◇ *We're expecting **a new arrival*** (= a baby) *in the family soon.* 我们家很快就会添一个新生儿。 **3** [U] the time when a new technology or idea is introduced （新技术、新思想的）引进，采用，推行： *the arrival of pay TV* 收费电视的引进 **IDM** SEE DEAD *adj.*

ar·rive /əˈraɪv/ *verb* **1** [I] (*abbr.* **arr.**) to get to a place, especially at the end of a journey 到达；抵达： *I'll wait until they arrive.* 我会一直等到他们来。 ◇ *I was pleased to hear you arrived home safely.* 听说你平安到家我很高兴。 ◇ *to **arrive early/late** for a meeting* 开会早到 / 迟到 ◇ *The police arrived to arrest him.* 警察赶来逮捕了他。 ◇ **~ at/in/on...** *She'll arrive in New York at noon.* 她将在正午抵达纽约。 ◇ *The train arrived at the station 20 minutes late.* 火车迟了 20 分钟到站。 ◇ *By the time I **arrived on the scene**, it was all over.* 我来到现场时，一切都已结束。 ◇ *We didn't arrive back at the hotel until very late.* 我们很晚才回到了旅馆。 **2** [I] (of things 东西) to be brought to sb 送达；寄到： *A letter arrived for you this morning.* 今天上午来了一封给你的信。 ◇ *Send your application to arrive by 31 October.* 申请信要在 10 月 31 日前寄到。 ◇ *We waited an hour for our lunch to arrive.* 我们等午饭等了一小时。 ◇ *The new product will arrive on supermarket shelves* (= be available) *early next year.* 明年初该新产品就会在超市上架。 **3** [I] (of an event or a moment 事件或时刻) to happen or to come, especially when you have been waiting for it 发生；到来： *The wedding day finally arrived.* 婚礼这一天终于到来。 ◇ *The baby arrived* (= was born) *early.* 婴儿早早地出生了。

IDM **sb has arˈrived** (*informal*) somebody has become successful 某人成功了： *He knew he had arrived when he was shortlisted for the Man Booker prize.* 入围曼布克小说奖后，他知道自己成功了。

PHR V **arˈrive at sth** to decide on or find sth, especially after discussion and thought 达成（协议）；作出（决议等）；得出（结论等） **SYN** **reach**: ***to arrive at an agreement/a decision/a conclusion*** 达成协议；作出决定；得出结论 ◇ *to arrive at the truth* 找到真理

ar·riv·iste /ˌæriːˈviːst/ *noun* (*from French, disapproving*) a person who is determined to be accepted as a member of a social group, etc. to which they do not really belong 攀龙附凤的人

ar·ro·gance /ˈærəɡəns/ *noun* [U] the behaviour of a person when they feel that they are more important than other people, so that they are rude to them or do not consider them 傲慢；自大

ar·ro·gant /ˈærəɡənt/ *adj.* behaving in a proud, unpleasant way, showing little thought for other people 傲慢的；自大的 ▸ **ar·ro·gant·ly** *adv.*

ar·ro·gate /ˈærəɡeɪt/ *verb* **~ sth (to yourself)** (*formal*) to claim or take sth that you have no right to 妄称；擅取： *I do not arrogate to myself the right to decide.* 我不擅自决定。

arrow /ˈærəʊ; *NAmE* ˈæroʊ/ *noun* **1** a thin stick with a sharp point at one end, which is shot from a BOW² 箭： *a **bow and arrow*** 弓箭 ◇ *to **fire/shoot an arrow*** 射箭 ◇ *The road continues as straight as an arrow.* 公路笔直延伸。 ➲ VISUAL VOCAB PAGE V44 **2** a mark or sign like an arrow (→), used to show direction or position 箭号；箭头： *Follow the arrows.* 顺着箭头指示方向走。 ◇ *Use the arrow keys to move the cursor.* 用键盘上的箭头键移动光标。

ar·row·head /ˈærəʊhed; *NAmE* ˈæroʊ-/ *noun* the sharp pointed end of an arrow 箭头；箭镞

ar·row·root /ˈærəʊruːt; *NAmE* ˈæroʊ-/ *noun* [U] a plant whose roots can be cooked and eaten or made into a type of flour, used especially to make sauces thick; the flour itself 竹芋（根状茎可食用或用于烹饪，使调味汁变稠）；竹芋粉

ar·royo /əˈrɔɪəʊ; *NAmE* -oʊ/ *noun* (*pl.* **-os**) (*from Spanish*) a narrow channel with steep sides cut by a river in a desert region （沙漠地区的）旱谷，干谷

arse /ɑːs; *NAmE* ɑːrs/ *noun, verb*

■ ***noun*** (*BrE, taboo, slang*) **1** (*NAmE* **ass**) the part of the body that you sit on; your bottom 屁股；腚： *Get off your arse!* (= stop sitting around doing nothing) 别闲坐着！ **2** (usually following an adjective 通常置于形容词后) a stupid person 笨蛋；傻瓜 ➲ SEE ALSO SMART-ARSE

IDM **My arse!** (*taboo, slang*) used by some people to show they do not believe what sb has said 我才不信这屁话 **work your ˈarse off** (*taboo, slang*) to work very hard 拼命干 ➲ MORE AT KISS *v.*, KNOW *v.*, LICK *v.*, PAIN *n.*

■ ***verb***

IDM **can't be ˈarsed (to do sth)** (*BrE, taboo, slang*) to not want to do sth because it is too much trouble 不愿（做麻烦事）： *I was supposed to do some work this weekend but I couldn't be arsed.* 这个周末我本应该干点事，不过我不愿去找那个麻烦。

PHR V ˌ**arse aˈbout/aˈround** (*BrE, taboo, slang*) to waste time by behaving in a silly way 鬼混；闲混

arse·hole /ˈɑːshəʊl; *NAmE* ˈɑːrshoʊl/ (*BrE*) (*NAmE* **ass·hole**) *noun* (*taboo, slang*) **1** the ANUS 屁眼；肛门 **2** a stupid or unpleasant person 笨蛋；讨厌鬼：*What an arsehole!* 真蠢得出奇！

ˈ**arse-licker** (*BrE*) (*NAmE* ˈ**ass-licker**) *noun* (*taboo, slang*) a person who is too friendly to sb in authority and is always ready to do what they want 马屁精 ▸ ˈ**arse-licking** (*BrE*) (*NAmE* ˈ**ass-licking**) *noun* [U]

ar·senal /ˈɑːsənl; *NAmE* ˈɑːrs-/ *noun* **1** a collection of weapons such as guns and EXPLOSIVES （统称）武器：*Britain's nuclear arsenal* 英国的核武器 **2** a building where military weapons and EXPLOSIVES are made or stored 兵工厂；武器库；军火库

ar·senic /ˈɑːsnɪk; *NAmE* ˈɑːrs-/ *noun* [U] (*symb.* **As**) a chemical element. Arsenic is an extremely poisonous white powder. 砷

arsey /ˈɑːsi; *NAmE* ˈɑːrsi/ *adj.* (*AustralE, informal*) very lucky 交鸿运的；运气十足的

arson /ˈɑːsn; *NAmE* ˈɑːrsn/ *noun* [U] the crime of deliberately setting fire to sth, especially a building 纵火（罪）；放火（罪）：*to carry out an **arson attack*** 进行纵火袭击 ➲ COLLOCATIONS AT CRIME

ar·son·ist /ˈɑːsənɪst; *NAmE* ˈɑːrs-/ *noun* a person who commits the crime of arson 纵火犯；放火犯

art 🔑 /ɑːt; *NAmE* ɑːrt/ *noun, verb*

■ ***noun*** **1** 🔑 [U] the use of the imagination to express ideas or feelings, particularly in painting, drawing or SCULPTURE 艺术，美术（尤指绘画、雕刻、雕塑）：*modern/contemporary/American art* 现代／当代／美国艺术 ◇ *an **art critic/historian/lover*** 艺术批评家／史家／爱好者 ◇ *Can we call television art?* 我们能把电视称作艺术吗？ ◇ *stolen **works of art*** 被盗艺术品 ◇ *Her performance displayed great art.* 她的表演展现了精湛的技艺。 ➲ SEE ALSO CLIP ART, FINE ART **2** 🔑 [U] examples of objects such as paintings, drawings or SCULPTURES 艺术品；美术作品：*an **art gallery/exhibition*** 美术馆；美术展览 ◇ *a collection of art and antiques* 一批收藏的艺术品和古董 ➲ WORDFINDER NOTE AT PAINTING **3** 🔑 [U] the skill of creating objects such as paintings and drawings, especially when you study it 艺术技巧：*She's good at art and design.* 她擅长美术和设计。 ◇ *an **art teacher/student/college/class*** 美术教师／学生／学院／班 **4** 🔑 **the arts** [pl.] art, music, theatre, literature, etc. when you think of them as a group （统称）艺术：*lottery funding for the arts* 为艺术筹集资金的彩票 ➲ SEE ALSO PERFORMING ARTS **5** [C] a type of VISUAL or performing art 表演艺术：*Dance is a very theatrical art.* 舞蹈是非常讲究舞台感的一种艺术。 **6** 🔑 [C, usually pl.] the subjects you can study at school or university that are not scientific, such as languages, history or literature 人文科学，文科（如语言、历史、文学）：*an arts degree* 文科学位 ➲ COMPARE SCIENCE (3) **7** [C, U] an ability or a skill that you can develop with training and practice 技能；技术；技巧：*a therapist trained in the art of healing* 接受过治疗技术训练的治疗员 ◇ *Letter-writing is a lost art nowadays.* 当今尺牍是一种已消失的技巧。 ◇

▼ **COLLOCATIONS** 词语搭配

Fine arts 美术

Creating art 艺术创作

- **make** a work of art/a drawing/a sketch/a sculpture/a statue/engravings/etchings/prints 创作艺术品；绘画；画素描；创作雕塑／雕像／雕版印刷品／蚀刻画／版画
- **do** an oil painting/a self-portrait/a line drawing/a rough sketch 画油画／自画像／线条画／草图
- **create** a work of art/an artwork/paintings and sculptures 创作一件艺术品／绘画和雕塑
- **produce** paintings/portraits/oil sketches/his most celebrated work/a series of prints 创作绘画／肖像画／油画速写／他最知名的作品／一组版画
- **paint** a picture/landscape/portrait/mural/in oils/in watercolours/(*especially US*) in watercolors/on canvas 画画／风景画／肖像画／壁画／油画／水彩画；在画布上画
- **draw** a picture/a portrait/a cartoon/a sketch/a line/a figure/the human form/in charcoal/in ink 画画／肖像／漫画／素描／线条／形体／人形／木炭画／墨水画
- **sketch** a preliminary drawing/a figure/a shape 勾勒草图／形体／图形
- **carve** a figure/an image/a sculpture/an altarpiece/reliefs/a block of wood 雕刻形体／形象／雕塑／祭坛雕塑／浮雕／一块木头
- **sculpt** a portrait bust/a statue/an abstract figure 雕刻半身像／塑像／抽象形体
- **etch** a line/a pattern/a design/a name into the glass 蚀刻线条／图案／图样／名字在玻璃杯上
- **mix** colours/(*especially US*) colors/pigments/paints 调色；调颜料
- **add/apply** thin/thick layers of paint/colour/(*especially US*) color/pigment 加上薄薄／厚厚几层颜料
- **use** oil pastels/charcoal/acrylic paint/a can of spray paint 使用油画棒／木炭笔／丙烯酸颜料／一罐喷雾颜料
- **work in** bronze/ceramics/stone/oils/pastels/watercolour/a wide variety of media 用青铜／陶瓷／石头／油彩／蜡笔／水彩／各种各样的材料制作艺术品

Describing art 描述艺术

- **paint/depict** a female figure/a biblical scene/a pastoral landscape/a domestic interior 画／描绘女性形体／与《圣经》有关的场景／田园风光／家庭室内场景
- **depict/illustrate** a traditional/mythological/historical/religious theme 描绘／阐释传统的／神话的／历史的／宗教的主题
- **create** an abstract composition/a richly textured surface/a distorted perspective 设计抽象的艺术构图／丰富的层次／视觉扭曲效果
- **paint** dark/rich/skin/flesh tones 用颜料绘成深色／浓重的颜色／肤色／肉色
- **use** broad brush strokes/loose brushwork/vibrant colours/a limited palette/simple geometric forms 用粗笔线条／散漫的笔法／鲜艳的颜色／有限的色调／简单的几何图形
- **develop/adopt/paint** in a stylized manner/an abstract style 用非写实手法／抽象方式阐明／采用／描绘

Showing and selling art 艺术品展示及销售

- **commission** an altarpiece/a bronze bust of sb/a portrait/a religious work/an artist to paint sth 委托创作一幅祭坛画／一座某人的半身铜像／一幅肖像画／一件宗教艺术品；委托艺术家为某物作画
- **frame** a painting/portrait 给一幅画／肖像画镶框
- **hang** art/a picture/a painting 悬挂艺术品／图画／画作
- **display/exhibit** modern art/sb's work/a collection/original artwork/drawings/sculptures/a piece 陈列／展出现代艺术品／某人的作品／收藏品／艺术真品／图画／雕塑／一件艺术品
- **be displayed/hung** in a gallery/museum 在美术馆／博物馆展出
- **install/place** a sculpture in/at/on sth 在某处安放一座雕塑
- **erect/unveil** a bronze/marble/life-size statue 竖立／揭幕一座铜像／大理石像／与真人一样大的雕像
- **hold/host/mount/open/curate/see** an exhibition (*especially BrE*)/(*NAmE usually*) an exhibit 举办／主持／筹办／举行／组织／观看展览
- **be/go on** (*BrE*) exhibition/(*NAmE*) exhibit 参展
- **feature/promote/showcase** a conceptual artist/contemporary works 重点介绍／宣传／展示一位概念派艺术家／当代作品
- **collect** African art/modern British paintings/Japanese prints 收藏非洲艺术品／现代英国绘画／日本版画
- **restore/preserve** a fresco/great works of art 修复／保护湿壁画／伟大的艺术品

Appearing confident at interviews is ***quite an art*** (= rather difficult). 面试时表现出充满信心是一门很高的艺术。 IDM SEE FINE *adj.*

■ ***verb*** **thou art** (*old use*) used to mean 'you are', when talking to one person （即 you are，对一人讲话时用）

art deco /ˌɑːt ˈdekəʊ; *NAmE* ˌɑːrt ˈdekoʊ/ (*also* **Art Deco**) *noun* [U] a popular style of decorative art in the 1920s and 1930s that has GEOMETRIC shapes with clear outlines and bright strong colours 装饰派艺术（流行于 20 世纪 20 至 30 年代，呈几何图形，线条清晰，色彩鲜明）

ˈart director *noun* **1** the person who is responsible for the pictures, photos, etc. in a magazine （杂志的）美术编辑 **2** the person who is responsible for the SETS and PROPS when a film/movie is being made （电影的）布景师，美术指导

arte·fact (*also* **ar·ti·fact** *especially in NAmE*) /ˈɑːtɪfækt; *NAmE* ˈɑːrt-/ *noun* (*specialist*) an object that is made by a person, especially sth of historical or cultural interest 人工制品，手工艺品（尤指有历史或文化价值的）

ar·terio·scler·osis /ɑːˌtɪəriəʊskləˈrəʊsɪs; *NAmE* ɑːrˌtɪrioʊskləˈroʊsɪs/ *noun* [U] (*medical* 医) a condition in which the walls of the arteries become thick and hard, making it difficult for blood to flow 动脉硬化

ar·tery /ˈɑːtəri; *NAmE* ˈɑːrt-/ *noun* (*pl.* **-ies**) **1** any of the tubes that carry blood from the heart to other parts of the body 动脉: *blocked arteries* 堵塞的动脉 ➲ COLLOCATIONS AT ILL ➲ COMPARE VEIN ➲ SEE ALSO CORONARY ARTERY **2** a large and important road, river, railway/railroad line, etc. 干线（指主要公路、河流、铁路线等）▶ **ar·ter·ial** /ɑːˈtɪəriəl; *NAmE* ɑːrˈtɪr-/ *adj.* [only before noun]: ***arterial blood/disease*** 动脉血；动脉病变 ◇ *an* ***arterial road*** 干线公路

ar·te·sian well /ɑːˌtiːziən ˈwel; *NAmE* ɑːrˌtiːʒn/ *noun* a hole made in the ground through which water rises to the surface by natural pressure 自流井

ˈart form *noun* **1** [C] a particular type of artistic activity 艺术形式: *The short story is a difficult art form to master.* 短篇小说是一种很难掌握的艺术形式。 **2** [sing.] an activity that sb does very well and gives them the opportunity to show imagination 擅长且可发挥想象力的活动: *She has elevated the dinner party into an art form.* 她把宴会办得犹如一种艺术。

art·ful /ˈɑːtfl; *NAmE* ˈɑːrtfl/ *adj.* [usually before noun] **1** (*disapproving*) clever at getting what you want, sometimes by not telling the truth 施展巧计的；取巧的 SYN **crafty** **2** (of things or actions 事物或行动) designed or done in a clever way 精巧的；巧妙的 ▶ **art·ful·ly** /-fəli/ *adv.*

ˈart gallery (*also* **gal·lery**) *noun* a building where paintings and other works of art are shown to the public 美术馆；艺术展览馆

ˌart ˈhistory *noun* [U] the study of the history of painting, SCULPTURE, etc. 艺术史

ˈart-house *adj.* [only before noun] **art-house** films/movies are usually made by small companies and are not usually seen by a wide audience （电影）实验性的，不公开放映的

arth·ri·tic /ɑːˈθrɪtɪk; *NAmE* ɑːrˈθ-/ *adj.* suffering from or caused by arthritis 患关节炎的；关节炎引起的: ***arthritic hands/pain*** 患关节炎的手；关节炎引起的疼痛

arth·ritis /ɑːˈθraɪtɪs; *NAmE* ɑːrˈθ-/ *noun* [U] a disease that causes pain and swelling in one or more joints of the body 关节炎 ➲ SEE ALSO OSTEOARTHRITIS, RHEUMATOID ARTHRITIS

arthro·pod /ˈɑːθrəpɒd; *NAmE* ˈɑːrθrəpɑːd/ *noun* (*biology* 生) an INVERTEBRATE animal such as an insect, spider, or CRAB, that has its SKELETON on the outside of its body and has joints on its legs 节肢动物

Ar·thur·ian /ɑːˈθjʊəriən; *NAmE* ɑːrˈθʊr-/ *adj.* connected with the stories about Arthur, a king of ancient Britain, his Knights of the Round Table and COURT at Camelot 亚瑟王（及骑士和朝臣）故事的: *Arthurian legends* 亚瑟王传奇故事

ar·ti·choke /ˈɑːtɪtʃəʊk; *NAmE* ˈɑːrtətʃoʊk/ *noun* [C, U] **1** (*also* **ˌglobe ˈarti·choke**) a round vegetable with a lot of thick green leaves. The bottom part of the leaves and the inside of the artichoke can be eaten when cooked. 朝鲜蓟，洋蓟，球蓟（圆形蔬菜，绿色厚叶基部及茎内部均可食用） ➲ VISUAL VOCAB PAGE V33 **2** = JERUSALEM ARTICHOKE

art·icle 🔑 /ˈɑːtɪkl; *NAmE* ˈɑːrt-/ *noun* **1** 🔑 **~ (on/about sth)** a piece of writing about a particular subject in a newspaper or magazine （报刊上的）文章，论文，报道: *Have you seen that article about young fashion designers?* 你见到了关于年轻时装设计师的那篇文章没有？ ➲ SEE ALSO LEADING ARTICLE ➲ WORDFINDER NOTE AT NEWSPAPER **2** 🔑 (*law* 律) a separate item in an agreement or a contract （协议、契约的）条款，项: *Article 10 of the European Convention guarantees free speech.* 《欧洲公约》第 10 条保障言论自由。 **3** 🔑 (*formal*) a particular item or separate thing, especially one of a set 物件，物品（尤指整套中的一件） SYN **item**: *articles of clothing* 衣物 ◇ *toilet articles such as soap and shampoo* 诸如肥皂和洗发水之类的梳妆用品 ◇ *The articles found in the car helped the police to identify the body.* 在汽车上发现的物品有助于警方辨认死者身份。 **4** (*grammar* 语法) the words *a* and *an* (**the indefinite article**) or *the* (**the definite article**) 冠词（a 和 an 为不定冠词，the 为定冠词）

art·icled /ˈɑːtɪkld; *NAmE* ˈɑːrt-/ *adj.* (*BrE*) employed by a group of lawyers, ARCHITECTS or ACCOUNTANTS while training to become qualified 签约给（律师、建筑师、会计师）当实习生的: *an articled clerk* (= sb who is training to be a SOLICITOR) 见习律师 ◇ *She* ***was articled to*** *a firm of solicitors.* 她与律师事务所签了约当见习律师。

ˌarticle of ˈfaith *noun* (*pl.* **articles of faith**) something you believe very strongly, as if it were a religious belief 信条；信念

ar·ticu·late *verb, adj.*

■ ***verb*** /ɑːˈtɪkjuleɪt; *NAmE* ɑːrˈt-/ **1** [T] **~ sth (to sb)** (*formal*) to express or explain your thoughts or feelings clearly in words 明确表达；清楚说明: *She struggled to articulate her thoughts.* 她竭力表明她的想法。 **2** [I, T] to speak, pronounce or play sth in a clear way 口齿清楚；清晰吐（词）；清晰发（音）: *He was too drunk to articulate properly.* 他醉得连话都说不清楚。 ◇ **~ sth** *Every note was carefully articulated.* 每个音都唱得很认真、很清楚。 **3** [I] **~ (with sth)** (*formal*) to be related to sth so that together the two parts form a whole 与…合成整体: *These courses are designed to articulate with university degrees.* 这些课程旨在与大学学位接轨。 **4** [I, T] (*specialist*) to be joined to sth else by a joint, so that movement is possible; to join sth in this way 用关节连接；链合；铰接: **~ (with sth)** *bones that articulate with others* 与其他骨骼以关节相连的骨骼 ◇ **~ sth** *a robot with articulated limbs* 关节型四肢机器人

■ ***adj.*** /ɑːˈtɪkjələt; *NAmE* ɑːrˈt-/ **1** (of a person 人) good at expressing ideas or feelings clearly in words 善于表达的 **2** (of speech 说话) clearly expressed or pronounced 口齿清楚的；发音清晰的: *All we could hear were loud sobs, but no articulate words.* 我们听到的只是大声啜泣，没有清楚的话语。 OPP **inarticulate** ➲ MORE LIKE THIS 21, page R27 ▶ **ar·ticu·late·ly** *adv.*

ar·ticu·lated /ɑːˈtɪkjuleɪtɪd; *NAmE* ɑːrˈt-/ *adj.* (of a vehicle 车辆) with two or more sections joined together in a way that makes it easier to turn corners 铰接的: *an articulated lorry/truck* 铰接式卡车 ➲ VISUAL VOCAB PAGE V62 ➲ SEE ALSO TRACTOR-TRAILER

ar·ticu·la·tion /ɑːˌtɪkjuˈleɪʃn; *NAmE* ɑːrˌt-/ *noun* **1** [U] (*formal*) the expression of an idea or a feeling in words （思想感情的）表达: *the articulation of his theory* 他的理论的表述 **2** [U] (*formal*) the act of making sounds in speech or music 说话；吐词；发音: *The singer worked hard on the* *clear articulation of every note.* 歌手苦练把每一个音都唱得清晰。 **3** [U, C, usually sing.] (*specialist*) a joint or connection that allows movement 关节；关节连接；铰接式接头

ar·ti·fact (*especially NAmE*) = ARTEFACT

ar·ti·fice /ˈɑːtɪfɪs; *NAmE* ˈɑːrt-/ *noun* [U, C] (*formal*) the clever use of tricks to cheat sb 诡计；奸计 **SYN** **cunning**

▼ **SYNONYMS 同义词辨析**

artificial

synthetic • false • man-made • fake • imitation

These words all describe things that are not real, or not naturally produced or grown. 以上各词均指假的、非天然的、人造的。

artificial made or produced to copy sth natural; not real 指人工的、人造的、假的： *artificial flowers* 假花 ◇ *artificial light* 人造光

synthetic made by combining chemical substances rather than being produced naturally by plants or animals 指人工合成的： *synthetic drugs* 合成药物 ◇ *shoes with synthetic soles* 合成鞋底的鞋

false not natural 指非天然的、非天生的、假的： *false teeth* 假牙 ◇ *a false beard* 假胡子

man-made made by people; not natural 指人造的、非天然的： *man-made fibres such as nylon* 尼龙之类的人造纤维

fake made to look like sth else; not real 指伪造的、冒充的、假的： *a fake-fur jacket* 一件人造毛皮的短上衣

imitation [only before noun] made to look like sth else; not real 指仿制的、人造的、假的： *She would never wear imitation pearls.* 她绝不会戴假珍珠。

PATTERNS
- artificial/synthetic/man-made **fabrics/fibres/materials/products**
- artificial/synthetic/fake/imitation **fur/leather**
- artificial/synthetic/false/fake/imitation **diamonds/pearls**

ar·ti·fi·cial 🔑 /ˌɑːtɪˈfɪʃl; *NAmE* ˌɑːrt-/ *adj.* **1** 🔑 made or produced to copy sth natural; not real 人工的；人造的；假的： *an* ***artificial limb/flower/sweetener/fertilizer*** 假肢；假花；人造甜味剂；化肥 ◇ ***artificial lighting/light*** 人工照明；人造光 **2** 🔑 created by people; not happening naturally 人为的；非自然的： *A job interview is a very artificial situation.* 求职面试是一个相当不自然的场面。 ◇ *the artificial barriers of race, class and gender* 种族、阶级、性别的人为障碍 **3** 🔑 not what it appears to be 虚假的；假装的 **SYN** **fake**： *artificial emotion* 假装的情感 ▶ **ar·ti·fi·ci·al·ity** /ˌɑːtɪˌfɪʃiˈæləti; *NAmE* ˌɑːrt-/ *noun* [U] **ar·ti·fi·cial·ly** 🔑 /ˌɑːtɪˈfɪʃəli; *NAmE* ˌɑːrt-/ *adv.*： *artificially created lakes* 人工湖泊 ◇ *artificially low prices* 人为压低的价格

ˌartificial inseminˈnation *noun* [U] (*abbr.* **AI**) the process of making a woman or female animal pregnant by an artificial method of putting male SPERM inside her, and not by sexual activity 人工授精： *artificial insemination by a donor, abbreviated to 'AID'* 供精人工授精（缩写为 AID）

ˌartificial inˈtelligence *noun* [U] (*abbr.* **AI**) (*computing* 计) an area of study concerned with making computers copy intelligent human behaviour 人工智能

ˌartificial ˈlanguage *noun* a language invented for international communication or for use with computers （为国际交流目的的）人造语言；（用于计算机的）人工语言

ˌartificial respiˈration (*BrE also* **ˌartificial ventiˈlation**) *noun* [U] the process of helping a person who has stopped breathing begin to breathe again, usually by blowing into their mouth or nose 人工呼吸 ➲ COMPARE MOUTH-TO-MOUTH RESUSCITATION

ar·til·lery /ɑːˈtɪləri; *NAmE* ɑːrˈt-/ *noun* **1** [U] large, heavy guns which are often moved on wheels （统称）火炮： *The town is under heavy artillery fire.* 该市镇处于密集的炮火之下。 **2 the artillery** [sing.] the section of an army trained to use these guns 炮兵部队 ➲ WORDFINDER NOTE AT ARMY

ar·ti·san /ˌɑːtɪˈzæn; *NAmE* ˈɑːrtəzn/ *noun, adj.*

■ ***noun*** (*formal*) a person who does skilled work, making things with their hands 工匠；手艺人 **SYN** **craftsman**

■ ***adj.*** [only before noun] (*also* **ar·ti·san·al** /ɑːˈtɪzənl; *NAmE* ɑːrˈtiː-/) **1** relating to an artisan, or typical of an artisan's work 手工的；手工艺的： *an artisan bakery* 一家手工面包店 ◇ *artisanal skills* 手工技能 **2** (of food and drink) made in a traditional way with high-quality ingredients （食品和饮料）手工制作的，传统工艺精制的： *artisan bread* 手工面包

art·ist 🔑 /ˈɑːtɪst; *NAmE* ˈɑːrt-/ *noun* **1** 🔑 a person who creates works of art, especially paintings or drawings 艺术家；（尤指）画家： *an exhibition of work by contemporary British artists* 当代英国画家作品展 ◇ *a graphic artist* 平面造型艺术家 ◇ *a make-up artist* 化妆师 ◇ *Police have issued an artist's impression of her attacker.* 警方公布了袭击她的人的模拟像。 ◇ (*figurative*) *Whoever made this cake is a real artist.* 制作这个蛋糕的人真是个艺术大师。 ➲ COLLOCATIONS AT ART **2** 🔑 (*also* **ar·tiste** /ɑːˈtiːst; *NAmE* ɑːrˈt-/) a professional entertainer such as a singer, a dancer or an actor 专业演员；艺人： ***a recording/solo artist*** 音像录制艺术师；单人表演演员

ar·tis·tic 🔑 /ɑːˈtɪstɪk; *NAmE* ɑːrˈt-/ *adj.* **1** 🔑 connected with art or artists 艺术的；艺术家的： *the artistic works of the period* 该时期的艺术品 ◇ *a work of great artistic merit* 艺术价值很高的作品 ◇ *the artistic director of the theatre* 戏剧艺术总监 **2** 🔑 showing a natural skill in or enjoyment of art, especially being able to paint or draw well 有艺术天赋的；（尤指）有美术才能的： ***artistic abilities/achievements/skills/talent*** 艺术才能 / 成就 / 技巧 / 天才 ◇ *She comes from a very artistic family.* 她出身于艺术世家。 **3** 🔑 done with skill and imagination; attractive or beautiful 有艺术性的；精美的： *an artistic arrangement of dried flowers* 富有艺术性的干花插花 **IDM** SEE LICENCE ▶ **ar·tis·tic·al·ly** 🔑 /ɑːˈtɪstɪkli; *NAmE* ɑːrˈt-/ *adv.*

arˌtistic diˈrector *noun* the person in charge of deciding which plays, OPERAS, etc. a theatre company will perform, and the general artistic policy of the company （剧团）艺术总监 ➲ WORDFINDER NOTE AT THEATRE

art·is·try /ˈɑːtɪstri; *NAmE* ˈɑːrt-/ *noun* [U] the skill of an artist 艺术技巧： *He played the piece with effortless artistry.* 他游刃有余地演奏了这首乐曲。

art·less /ˈɑːtləs; *NAmE* ˈɑːrt-/ *adj.* (*formal*) **1** simple, natural and honest 天真的；直率的： *the artless sincerity of a young child* 幼童的天真烂漫 **2** made without skill or art 缺乏艺术性的；拙劣的

art nou·veau /ˌɑː(t) nuːˈvəʊ; *NAmE* ˌɑːr(t) nuːˈvoʊ/ (*also* **Art Nouveau**) *noun* [U] a style of decorative art and ARCHITECTURE popular in Europe and the US at the end of the 19th century and beginning of the 20th century that uses complicated designs and curved patterns based on natural shapes like leaves and flowers 新艺术（19 世纪末 20 世纪初流行于欧洲和美国的装饰艺术和建筑风格，采用基于花、叶等自然形状的复杂设计和曲线图案）

ˌarts and ˈcrafts *noun* [pl.] activities that need both artistic and practical skills, such as making cloth, jewellery and POTTERY 手工艺

artsy /ˈɑːtsi; *NAmE* ˈɑːrtsi/ (*NAmE*) (*also* **arty**) *adj.* (*informal, usually disapproving*) seeming or wanting to be very artistic or interested in the arts 附庸风雅的；似乎爱好艺术的

artsy-fartsy /ˌɑːtsi ˈfɑːtsi; *NAmE* ˌɑːrtsi ˈfɑːrtsi/ (*especially NAmE*) (*BrE* **arty-farty**) *adj.* (*informal, disapproving*) connected with, or having an interest in, the arts 附庸风雅的

A

ˌ**art 'therapy** *noun* [U] a type of PSYCHOTHERAPY in which you are encouraged to express yourself using art materials 艺术治疗（通过艺术形式表达自我以达到治疗效果的心理疗法）

art·work /ˈɑːtwɜːk; *NAmE* ˈɑːrtwɜːrk/ *noun* **1** [U] photographs and pictures prepared for books, magazines, etc.（书刊等上的）插图，图片 **2** [C] a work of art, especially one in a museum （尤指博物馆里的）艺术作品

arty /ˈɑːti; *NAmE* ˈɑːrti/ (*BrE*) (*NAmE* **artsy**) *adj.* (*informal, usually disapproving*) seeming or wanting to be very artistic or interested in the arts 附庸风雅的；似乎爱好艺术的：*She hangs out with the arty types she met at drama school.* 她和一些在戏剧学校认识的附庸风雅的朋友常混在一起。

arty-farty /ˌɑːti ˈfɑːti; *NAmE* ˌɑːrti ˈfɑːrti/ (*BrE*) (*especially NAmE* ˌ**artsy-'fartsy**) *adj.* (*informal, disapproving*) connected with, or having an interest in, the arts 附庸风雅的：*I expect he's out with his arty-farty friends.* 我想他去会他那帮玩艺术的朋友了。

aru·gula /æˈruːgjʊlə/ (*NAmE*) (*BrE* **rocket**) *noun* [U] a plant with long green leaves that have a strong flavour and are eaten raw in salads 大蒜芥；芝麻菜；紫花南芥

arum lily /ˈeərəm lɪli; *NAmE* ˈerəm/ *noun* (*especially BrE*) (*NAmE usually* **calla lily**) an African plant with large white PETAL 马蹄莲；水芋；海芋

arvo /ˈɑːvəʊ; *NAmE* ˈɑːrvoʊ/ *noun* (*pl.* **-os**) (*AustralE, NZE, informal*) afternoon 下午；午后：*See you this arvo!* 下午见！

-ary *suffix* (in adjectives and nouns 构成形容词和名词) connected with 与…有关（的）：*planetary* 行星的 ◇ *budgetary* 预算的 ➲ MORE LIKE THIS 7, page R25

Aryan /ˈeəriən; *NAmE* ˈer-/ *noun* **1** a member of the group of people that went to S Asia in around 1500 BC 雅利安人（公元前 1500 年前后到南亚） **2** a person who spoke any of the languages of the Indo-European group 讲印欧系语言的人 **3** (especially according to the ideas of the German Nazi party) a member of a Caucasian, not Jewish, race of people, especially one with fair hair and blue eyes 属于雅利安人种的人（尤指德国纳粹党认为的非犹太民族白种人） ▶ **Aryan** *adj.*

AS ➲ AS (LEVEL)

as 🔑 /əz; *strong form* æz/ *prep., adv., conj.*

▪ ***prep.*** **1** 🔑 used to describe sb/sth appearing to be sb/sth else 像；如同：*They were all dressed as clowns.* 他们都打扮成小丑。◇ *The bomb was disguised as a package.* 炸弹伪装成一个包裹。 **2** 🔑 used to describe the fact that sb/sth has a particular job or function 作为；当作：*She works as a courier.* 她的职业是导游。 ◇ *Treat me as a friend.* 要把我当作朋友。◇ *I respect him as a doctor.* 我尊敬他这个医生。◇ *You can use that glass as a vase.* 你可以把那个玻璃杯当作花瓶用。◇ *The news came as a shock.* 消息传来，令人震惊。◇ *She had been there often as a child* (= when she was a child). 她小时候常去那里。

▪ ***adv.*** **1** 🔑 **as… as…** used when you are comparing two people or things, or two situations （比较时用）像…一样，如同：*You're as tall as your father.* 你和你父亲一样高。 ◇ *He was as white as a sheet.* 他面无血色。 ◇ *She doesn't play as well as her sister.* 她演奏得不如她姐姐。◇ *I haven't known him as long as you* (= as you have known him). 我认识他的时间没有你长。◇ *He doesn't earn as much as me.* 他挣的钱比我少。◇ *He doesn't earn as much as I do.* 他挣的钱比我少。◇ *It's not as hard as I thought.* 这没有我想象的那么困难。◇ *Run as fast as you can.* 你尽量快跑。◇ *We'd like it as soon as possible.* 我们希望越快越好。 **2** 🔑 used to say that sth happens in the same way （指事情以同样的方式发生）和…一样：*As always, he said little.* 他和平时一样，少言寡语。◇ *The 'h' in honest is silent, as in 'hour'.* * honest 中的 h 与 hour 中的 h 一样都不发音。

▪ ***conj.*** **1** 🔑 while sth else is happening 当…时；随着：*He sat watching her as she got ready.* 他一直坐着看她准备停当。◇ *As she grew older she gained in confidence.* 随着年龄的增长她的信心增强了。➲ LANGUAGE BANK AT PROCESS[1] **2** 🔑 in the way in which 照…方式：*They did as I had asked.* 他们是按照我的要求做的。◇ *Leave the papers as they are.* 别去动那些文件。◇ *She lost it, just as I said she would.* 我就说了吧，她把它弄丢了。 **3** 🔑 used to state the reason for sth 因为；由于：*As you were out, I left a message.* 你不在，所以我留了一张字条儿。◇ *She may need some help as she's new.* 她是新来的，可能需要一些帮助。 **4** used to make a comment or to add information about what you have just said 正如；如同：*As you know, Julia is leaving soon.* 你是知道的，朱莉娅马上要离开了。◇ *She's very tall, as is her mother.* 她个子很高，和她母亲一样。 **5** used to say that in spite of sth being true, what follows is also true 尽管；虽然；即使 SYN **though**: *Happy as they were, there was something missing.* 尽管他们很快乐，但总缺少点什么。◇ *Try as he might* (= however hard he tried), *he couldn't open the door.* 他想尽了办法也没能打开门。

IDM **as against sth** in contrast with sth 与…相对照；和…相比较：*They got 27% of the vote as against 32% at the last election.* 这次选举他们得了 27% 的票，而上次他们得了 32%。 ˌ**as and 'when** used to say that sth may happen at some time in the future, but only when sth else has happened（用于在特定条件下才会发生的事情）将来…时，到时候：*We'll decide on the team as and when we qualify.* 将来我们具备了条件时就会决定成立这个队。 ◇ *I'll tell you more as and when* (= as soon as I can). 我一有可能就会告诉你更多情况。 **as for sb/sth** 🔑 used to start talking about sb/sth 至于；关于 SYN **regarding**: *As for Jo, she's doing fine.* 至于乔，她现在日子过得不错。 ◇ *As for food for the party, that's all being taken care of.* 关于聚会要用的食物，都在置办当中。 **as from…/as of…** used to show the time or date from which sth starts （指起始时间或日期）自…起：*Our phone number is changing as from May 12.* 我们的电话号码自 5 月 12 日起更改。 **as if/as though** 🔑 in a way that suggests sth 似乎；好像；仿佛：*He behaved as if nothing had happened.* 他表现得若无其事。◇ *It sounds as though you had a good time.* 听起来你好像过得挺愉快。◇ *It's my birthday. As if you didn't know!* 今天是我的生日。你好像不知道似的！ ◇ *'Don't say anything.' 'As if I would!'* (= surely you do not expect me to) "什么也别说。" "我才不会说呢！" ˌ**as it 'is** considering the present situation; as things are 照现状：*We were hoping to finish it by next week—as it is, it may be the week after.* 我们本希望在下周完成，看样子可能要下下周才行。◇

▼ WHICH WORD? 词语辨析

as / like

You can use both **as** and **like** to say that things are similar. * as 和 like 均可表示相似。

- **Like** is a preposition and is used before nouns and pronouns. * like 为介词，置于名词和代词前：*He has blue eyes like me.* 他和我一样有双蓝眼睛。
- **As** is a conjunction and an adverb and is used before a clause, another adverb or a clause beginning with a preposition. * as 为连词和副词，置于从句、另一副词或以介词引导的从句前：*She enjoys all kinds of music, as I do.* 她和我一样什么音乐都喜欢。◇ *Repeat these five steps, as in the last exercise.* 照前面的练习一样，重复这五个步骤。
- In informal English **like** is frequently used as a conjunction or an adverb instead of **as**. 在非正式英语中，like 常常代替 as，用作连词或副词：*Nobody understands him like I do.* 谁都不像我那么了解他。◇ *I don't want to upset him again like before.* 我不愿意再像过去那样使他扫兴。 It is also used instead of **as if**. * like 亦可用以代替 as if：*It looks like we're going to be late.* 看来我们要迟到了。 These uses of **like** are common but are not considered correct in formal written English. * like 的这类用法很常见，但在规范的书面语中被视为不正确。

You will find more help on the use of **as** and **like** in the entries for particular verbs, such as *act, behave*, etc. 关于 as 和 like 的其他用法，参见 act、behave 等动词词条。

I can't help—I've got too much to do as it is (= already). 我帮不了忙，我已经有太多的工作了。 **as it 'were** used when a speaker is giving his or her own impression of a situation or expressing sth in a particular way 可以说；在一定程度上： *Teachers must put the brakes on, as it were, when they notice students looking puzzled.* 当老师发现学生神色茫然时，就应该在一定程度上放慢速度。 **as to sth | as regards sth** used when you are referring to sth 关于；至于： *As to tax, that will be deducted from your salary.* 至于税款，将从你薪水中扣除。 **as you 'do** used as a comment on sth that you have just said （对刚说过的话的评论）： *He smiled and I smiled back. As you do.* 他微笑，我也报以微笑。正所谓礼尚往来。 ➲ MORE AT WELL *adv.*, YET *adv.*

ASA /ˌeɪ es ˈeɪ/ *abbr.* **1** Advertising Standards Authority (an organization in Britain that controls the standard of advertising) （英国）广告标准局 **2** American Standards Association (used especially to show the speed of film) 美国标准协会（尤用于额定胶片感光度）： *a 400 ASA film* 美国标准 400 度胶片

asap /ˌeɪ es eɪ ˈpiː/ *abbr.* as soon as possible 尽快

as·bes·tos /æsˈbestəs/ *noun* [U] a soft grey mineral that does not burn, used especially in the past in building as a protection against fire or to prevent heat loss 石棉

as·bes·tosis /ˌæsbesˈtəʊsɪs; *NAmE* -ˈtoʊ-/ *noun* [U] a disease of the lungs caused by breathing in asbestos dust 石棉沉着病，石棉肺（因吸入石棉粉尘引起的肺病）

ASBO /ˈæzbəʊ; *NAmE* -boʊ/ *noun* the abbreviation for 'antisocial behaviour order' (in the UK, an order made by a court which says that sb must stop behaving in a harmful or annoying way to other people) 反社会行为令（全写为 antisocial behaviour order，由英国法院发出的对伤害或骚扰他人行为的禁令）

as·cend /əˈsend/ *verb* [I, T] (*formal*) to rise; to go up; to climb up 上升；升高；登高： *The path started to ascend more steeply.* 小径开始陡峭而上。 ◇ *The air became colder as we ascended.* 我们越往上攀登，空气就越冷。 ◇ *The results, ranked* ***in ascending order*** (= from the lowest to the highest) *are as follows:* 结果按由低到高的顺序排列如下： ◇ **~ from sth** *Mist ascended from the valley.* 薄雾从山谷升起。 ◇ **~ to sth** (*figurative*) *He ascended to the peak of sporting achievement.* 他达到了运动成就的顶峰。 ◇ **~ sth** *Her heart was thumping as she ascended the stairs.* 她上楼梯时，心怦怦跳个不停。 ◇ (*figurative*) *to ascend the throne* (= become king or queen) 登基 OPP **descend**

as·cend·ancy (*also* **as·cend·ency**) /əˈsendənsi/ *noun* [U] **~ (over sb/sth)** (*formal*) the position of having power or influence over sb/sth 支配地位；优势；影响： ***moral/political/intellectual ascendancy*** 道德影响；政治支配地位；智力优势 ◇ *The opposition party was* ***in the ascendancy*** (= gaining control). 反对党已渐占优势。

as·cend·ant (*also* **as·cend·ent**) /əˈsendənt/ (*also* **ˈrising sign**) *noun* the sign of the ZODIAC that is on the eastern HORIZON at the time and location of an event, particularly a birth （诞生时的）上升星座： *I'm a Capricorn but my ascendant is Leo.* 我是摩羯座，但我的上升星座是狮子座。

IDM **in the ascendant** (*formal*) being or becoming more powerful or popular （权力、影响等）越来越大；日益受欢迎

as·cen·sion /əˈsenʃn/ *noun* [sing.] **1 the Ascension** (in the Christian religion 基督教) the journey of Jesus from the earth into heaven 耶稣升天 **2** (*formal*) the act of moving up or of reaching a high position 上升；升高；登上： *her ascension to the throne* 她的登基

Asˈcension Day *noun* (in the Christian religion 基督教) the 40th day after Easter when Christians remember when Jesus left the earth and went into heaven 耶稣升天节（复活节后的第 40 天）

as·cent /əˈsent/ *noun* **1** [C, usually sing.] the act of climbing or moving up; an upward journey 上升；升高；登高： *the first ascent of Mount Kilimanjaro* 首次攀登乞力马扎罗山 ◇ *The cart began its gradual ascent up the hill.* 运货马车开始缓缓上山。 ◇ *The rocket steepened its ascent.* 火箭飞速升空。 OPP **descent** **2** [C, usually sing.] an upward path or slope 上坡；上坡路： *At the other side of the valley was a steep ascent to the top of the hill.* 山谷的那边是直达山顶的陡坡。 OPP **descent** **3** [U] (*formal*) the process of moving forward to a better position or of making progress 前进；提高；进步： *man's ascent to civilization* 人类向文明的进化 ➲ MORE LIKE THIS 20, page R27

as·cer·tain /ˌæsəˈteɪn; *NAmE* ˌæsərˈt-/ *verb* (*formal*) to find out the true or correct information about sth 查明；弄清： **~ sth** *It can be difficult to ascertain the facts.* 可能难以查明事实真相。 ◇ **~ that…** *I ascertained that the driver was not badly hurt.* 我已查清，驾驶员伤势不重。 ◇ **it is ascertained that…** ***It should be ascertained that*** *the plans comply with the law.* 须要弄清楚，这些计划要合法。 ◇ **~ what, whether, etc.…** *The police are trying to ascertain what really happened.* 警方正设法查清到底发生了什么事。 ◇ *Could you ascertain whether she will be coming to the meeting?* 请你弄清楚她来不来开会好吗？ ◇ **it is ascertained what, whether, etc.…** ***It must be ascertained*** *if the land is still owned by the government.* 必须确定这块土地是否仍属于政府所有。 ▶ **as·cer·tain·able** /ˌæsəˈteɪnəbl; *NAmE* ˌæsərˈt-/ *adj.* **as·cer·tain·ment** /ˌæsəˈteɪnmənt; *NAmE* ˌæsərˈt-/ *noun* [U]

as·cet·ic /əˈsetɪk/ *adj.* [usually before noun] not allowing yourself physical pleasures, especially for religious reasons; related to a simple and strict way of living 过清苦生活的；（尤指）苦行的；禁欲的： *The monks lived a very ascetic life.* 僧侣过着很清苦的生活。 ▶ **as·cet·ic** *noun*： *monks, hermits and ascetics* 僧侣、隐士和苦行者 **as·ceti·cism** /əˈsetɪsɪzəm/ *noun* [U]

ASCII /ˈæski/ *noun* [U] (*computing* 计) the abbreviation for 'American Standard Code for Information Interchange' (a standard code used so that data can be moved between computers that use different programs) 美国信息交换用标准代码（全写为 American Standard Code for Information Interchange，使用不同程序的计算机可互相传送数据的一种标准码）

as·cor·bic acid /əsˌkɔːbɪk ˈæsɪd; *NAmE* -ˌkɔːrb-/ *noun* [U] = VITAMIN C

ascot /ˈæskɒt; *NAmE* ˈæskɑːt/ *noun* (*NAmE*) = CRAVAT

ascribe /əˈskraɪb/ *verb*

PHRV **aˈscribe sth to sb** to consider or state that a book, etc. was written by a particular person 认为…是（某人）所写 SYN **attribute**： *This play is usually ascribed to Shakespeare.* 通常认为这部剧是莎士比亚所写。 **aˈscribe sth to sb/sth** (*formal*) **1** to consider that sth is caused by a particular thing or person 把…归因于；认为…是由于： *He ascribed his failure to bad luck.* 他认为自己的失败是运气不好。 **2** to consider that sb/sth has or should have a particular quality 认为…具有 SYN **attribute**： *We ascribe great importance to these policies.* 我们认为这些政策十分重要。 ▶ **ascrib·able** *adj.*： **~ to sb/sth** *Their success is ascribable to the quality of their goods.* 他们的成功在于商品的质量。 **ascrip·tion** /əˈskrɪpʃn/ *noun* [U, C]： **~ (to sb/sth)** *the ascription of meaning to objects and events* 事物所赋有的内涵

ASEAN /ˈæsiæn/ *abbr.* Association of Southeast Asian Nations 东盟；东南亚国家联盟

asep·tic /ˌeɪˈseptɪk/ *adj.* (*medical* 医) free from harmful bacteria 无（病）菌的 OPP **septic**

asex·ual /ˌeɪˈsekʃuəl/ *adj.* **1** (*specialist*) not involving sex; not having sexual organs 无性的；无性器官的： *asexual reproduction* 无性生殖 **2** not having sexual qualities; not interested in sex 性缺乏的；性冷淡的： *the tendency to see old people as asexual* 认为老年人性缺乏的倾向 ▶ **asex·ual·ly** *adv.*： *to reproduce asexually* 无性生殖

ash /æʃ/ *noun* **1** [U] the grey or black powder that is left after sth, especially TOBACCO, wood or coal, has burnt 灰；灰烬： *cigarette ash* 香烟灰 ◇ *black volcanic ash* 黑色

火山灰 **2 ashes** [pl.] what is left after sth has been destroyed by burning 灰烬；废墟：*The town was reduced to ashes in the fighting.* 这座城镇在战斗中化为灰烬。◇ *the glowing ashes of the campfire* 营火剩下的灼热余烬 ◇ (*figurative*) *The party had risen, like a phoenix, from the ashes of electoral disaster.* 该党像长生鸟一样，从选举惨败的灰烬中重新崛起。 **3 ashes** [pl.] the powder that is left after a dead person's body has been CREMATED (= burned) 骨灰：*She wanted her ashes to be scattered at sea.* 她希望自己的骨灰撒向大海。 ➲ WORDFINDER NOTE AT DIE **4** [C, U] (*also* ˈ**ash tree**) a forest tree with grey BARK 梣；白蜡树 ➲ VISUAL VOCAB PAGE V10 ➲ SEE ALSO MOUNTAIN ASH **5** [U] the hard pale wood of the ash tree 梣木 **6** (*specialist*) the letter æ, used in Old English, and as a PHONETIC symbol to represent the vowel sound in *cat* * æ（古英语的一个字母，也为音标，表示如 cat 一词中的元音） IDM SEE SACKCLOTH

▼ **WHICH WORD? 词语辨析**

ashamed / embarrassed

- You feel **ashamed** when you feel guilty because of something wrong that you have deliberately done. 因明知故犯而感到羞愧用 ashamed：*You should be ashamed of treating your daughter like that.* 你这样对待自己的女儿应该感到羞愧。Do not use **ashamed** when you are talking about something that is not very serious or important. 不很严重或不很重要的事情不要用 ashamed：*I am sorry that I forgot to buy the milk.* 对不起，我忘了买牛奶。◇ ~~*I am ashamed that I forgot to buy the milk.*~~
- You feel **embarrassed** when you have made a mistake or done something stupid or feel awkward in front of other people. 犯了错误、干了傻事或在他人面前感到难为情用 embarrassed：*I was embarrassed about forgetting his name.* 我把他的名字忘了，感到尴尬。

ashamed 🔑 /əˈʃeɪmd/ *adj.* [not before noun] **1** feeling shame or embarrassment about sb/sth or because of sth you have done 惭愧；羞愧；尴尬：**~ of sth** *She was deeply ashamed of her behaviour at the party.* 她对自己在聚会上的行为深感羞愧。◇ *Mental illness is* ***nothing to be ashamed of.*** 不必因精神病而感到羞愧。◇ **~ of sb** *His daughter looked such a mess that he was ashamed of her.* 他为女儿一副邋遢的样子感到羞惭。◇ **~ of yourself** *You should be ashamed of yourself for telling such lies.* 你扯这种谎应该感到羞耻。◇ **~ that…** *I feel almost ashamed that I've been so lucky.* 真有点不好意思，我太幸运了。◇ **~ to be sth** *The football riots made me ashamed to be English.* 足球骚乱事件使我身为英国人汗颜得无地自容。➲ WORDFINDER NOTE AT SORRY **2** **~ to do sth** unwilling to do sth because of shame or embarrassment 因惭愧而不情愿；因尴尬而勉强：*I'm* ***ashamed to say*** *that I lied to her.* 我真不好意思说我向她撒了谎。◇ *I cried at the end and I'm not ashamed to admit it.* 最后我哭了，我并不耻于承认哭过。
➲ MORE LIKE THIS 31, page R28

ˌ**ash ˈblonde** *adj., noun*
■ ***adj.*** (*also* ˌ**ash ˈblond**) **1** (of hair 头发) very pale blonde in colour 淡褐色的 **2** (of a person 人) having ash blonde hair 头发淡褐色的
■ ***noun*** a woman with hair that is ash blonde in colour 头发淡褐色的女子 ➲ SEE ALSO BLONDE *n.*

ashen /ˈæʃn/ *adj.* (usually of sb's face 通常指脸) very pale; without colour because of illness or fear 面色苍白的；没有血色的：*They listened ashen-faced to the news.* 他们听着消息时面如死灰。◇ *His face was ashen and wet with sweat.* 他面如土色，汗如雨下。

Ash·ken·azi /ˌæʃkəˈnɑːzi/ *noun* (*pl.* **Ash·ken·azim** /-ɪm/) a Jew whose ANCESTORS came from central or eastern Europe（德系）犹太人（祖先居住在欧洲中部或东部） ➲ COMPARE SEPHARDI

ashore /əˈʃɔː(r)/ *adv.* towards, onto or on land, having come from an area of water such as the sea or a river 向（或在）岸上；向（或在）陆地：*to* ***come/go ashore*** 上岸 ◇ *a drowned body found washed ashore on the beach* 冲到海滩上被人发现的一具溺水者尸体 ◇ *The cruise included several days ashore.* 这次航行包括几天陆上行程。

ash·ram /ˈæʃrəm/ *noun* a place where Hindus who wish to live away from society live together as a group; a place where other Hindus go for a short time to say prayers before returning to society（印度教徒的）静修处，隐修处

ash·tray /ˈæʃtreɪ/ *noun* a container into which people who smoke put ASH, cigarette ends, etc. 烟灰缸

ˌ**Ash ˈWednesday** *noun* [U, C] the first day of Lent 圣灰星期三（基督教四旬期首日） ➲ SEE ALSO SHROVE TUESDAY

Asia Minor /ˌeɪʃə ˈmaɪnə(r)/ *noun* [sing.] the western PENINSULA of Asia, which now forms most of Turkey 小亚细亚（亚洲西部半岛，现构成土耳其大部分国土）

Asian /ˈeɪʃn; ˈeɪʒn/ *noun, adj.*
■ ***noun*** a person from Asia, or whose family originally came from Asia 亚洲人：*British Asians* 英籍亚裔人 HELP In *BrE* **Asian** is used especially to refer to people from India, Pakistan and Bangladesh. In *NAmE* it is used especially to refer to people from the Far East. 英式英语中，Asian 尤指印度人、巴基斯坦人和孟加拉人。美式英语中，Asian 尤指远东人。
■ ***adj.*** of or connected with Asia 亚洲的：*Asian music* 亚洲音乐

ˌ**Asian Aˈmerican** *noun* a person from America whose family come from Asia, especially E Asia 亚裔美国人；（尤指）东亚裔美国人 ▶ ˌ**Asian-Aˈmerican** *adj.*

Asi·at·ic /ˌeɪʃiˈætɪk; ˌeɪʒi-/ *adj.* (*specialist*) of or connected with Asia 亚洲的：*the Asiatic tropics* 亚洲热带

ˈ**A-side** *noun* the side of a pop record that was considered more likely to be successful（流行唱片的）A 面（常收录主打歌曲） ➲ COMPARE B-SIDE

aside 🔑 /əˈsaɪd/ *adv., noun*
■ ***adv.*** **1** to one side; out of the way 到旁边；在旁边：*She pulled the curtain aside.* 她把窗帘拉向一边。◇ ***Stand aside*** *and let these people pass.* 闪开，让这些人过去。◇ *He* ***took me aside*** (= away from a group of people) *to give me some advice.* 他把我拉到一旁，给我出主意。◇ (*figurative*) ***Leaving aside*** (= not considering at this stage) *the cost of the scheme, let us examine its benefits.* 方案的费用暂且不理，咱们来审查方案的好处。◇ *All our protests were* ***brushed aside*** (= ignored). 我们的一切抗议均被置之不理。**2** to be used later 留；存：*We* ***set aside*** *some money for repairs.* 我们存了一些钱作为修理费用。**3** used after nouns to say that except for one thing, sth is true（用于名词后）除…以外：*Money worries aside, things are going well.* 除了钱令人发愁外，事情进展顺利。
■ ***noun*** **1** (in the theatre 戏剧) something that a character in a play says to the audience, but which the other characters on stage are not intended to hear 旁白 **2** a remark, often made in a low voice, which is not intended to be heard by everyone present 低声说的话 **3** a remark that is not directly connected with the main subject that is being discussed 离题话：*I mention it only as an aside.* 我只是顺便提及。

aˈside from 🔑 *prep.* (*especially NAmE*) = APART FROM：*Aside from a few scratches, I'm OK.* 除了几处擦伤外，我安然无恙。➲ LANGUAGE BANK AT EXCEPT

as·in·ine /ˈæsɪnaɪn/ *adj.* (*formal*) stupid or silly 愚蠢的；笨的 SYN ridiculous

ask 🔑 /ɑːsk; *NAmE* æsk/ *verb, noun*
■ ***verb***
• **QUESTION** 问题 **1** [I, T] to say or write sth in the form of a question, in order to get information 问；询问：*How old are you—if you don't mind me/my asking?* 要是你

不介意我提问，你多大年纪了？ ◇ **~ about sb/sth** *He asked about her family.* 他询问了她的家庭情况。 ◇ **~ sth** *Can I **ask a question**?* 我能提个问题吗？ ◇ *Did you ask the price?* 你问了价钱没有？ ◇ **+ speech** *'Where are you going?' she asked.* "你去哪里？" 她问道。 ◇ **~ sb + speech** *'Are you sure?' he asked her.* "你有把握吗？" 他问她。 ◇ **~ sb sth** *She asked the students their names.* 她问了学生们的姓名。 ◇ *I often **get asked** that!* 我常常被问到那件事！ ◇ **~ sb (about sth)** *The interviewer asked me about my future plans.* 采访者问了我的未来计划。 ◇ **~ where, what, etc....** *He asked where I lived.* 他问我住在哪里。 ◇ **~ sb where, what, etc....** *I had to ask the teacher what to do next.* 我不得不问老师下一步做什么。 ◇ *I was asked if/whether I could drive.* 有人问我会不会开车。 HELP You cannot say 'ask to sb'. 不能说 ask to sb： ~~*I asked to my friend what had happened.*~~

• **REQUEST** 请求 **2** [T] to tell sb that you would like them to do sth or that you would like sth to happen 要求；请求： **~ sb to do sth** *All the students were asked to complete a questionnaire.* 全体学生都被要求填一份调查表。 ◇ *Eric asked me to marry him.* 埃里克求我嫁给他。 ◇ **~ whether, what, etc....** *I asked whether they could change my ticket.* 我问他们是否可以给我换票。 ◇ **~ sb whether, what, etc....** *She asked me if I would give her English lessons.* 她问我愿不愿意给她上英语课。 ◇ **~ that...** (*formal*) *She asked that she be kept informed of developments.* 她要求继续向她报告事态发展情况。 ◇ (*BrE also*) *She asked that she should be kept informed.* 她要求继续向她报告有关情况。 ➲ EXPRESS YOURSELF AT HELP **3** [I, T] to say that you would like sb to give you sth 请求，恳求（给予）；征求： **~ for sth** *to ask for a job/a drink/an explanation* 求职；要一杯饮料；要求解释 ◇ *I am writing to ask for some information about courses.* 我写信是想了解关于课程的情况。 ◇ **~ sth** *Why don't you ask his advice?* 你为什么不征询他的意见？ ◇ **~ sb for sth** *Why don't you ask him for his advice?* 你为什么不征求他的意见？ ◇ **~ sth of sb** *Can I ask a favour of you?* 我能请你帮个忙吗？ ◇ **~ sb sth** *Can I ask you a favour?* 我能请你帮个忙吗？ ➲ EXPRESS YOURSELF AT PLEASE

• **PERMISSION** 准许 **4** [T] to request permission to do sth 请求允许；要求准许： **~ to do sth** *Did you ask to use the car?* 你是提出想用这辆车吗？ ◇ *I asked to see the manager.* 我要求见经理。 ◇ **~ if, whether, etc....** *I'll ask if it's all right to park here.* 我会问是否可以在这里停车。 ◇ **~ sb if, whether, etc....** *She asked her boss whether she could have the day off.* 她问老板可不可以让她休一天假。

• **INVITE** 邀请 **5** [T] to invite sb 请；邀请： **~ sb (+ adv./prep.)** *They've asked me to dinner.* 他们已邀请我吃饭。 ◇ *I didn't ask them in* (= to come into the house). 我没有请他们进屋。 ◇ *We must ask the neighbours round* (= to our house). 我们得请邻居到家里来。 ◇ **~ sb to do sth** *She's asked him to come to the party.* 她已邀请他来参加聚会。 ➲ EXPRESS YOURSELF AT INVITE

• **MONEY** 钱 **6** [T] **~ sth (for sth)** to request a particular amount of money for sth that you are selling 要价；索价： *He's asking £2 000 for the car.* 这辆轿车他要价 2 000 英镑。

• **EXPECT/DEMAND** 期望；要求 **7** [T] to expect or demand sth 期望；要求： **~ sth** *I know I'm asking a great deal.* 我知道我的要求很高。 ◇ **~ sth of sb** *You're asking too much of him.* 你对他要求过分了。 ◇ **~ sth to do sth** *I know it's asking a lot to expect them to win again.* 我知道期望他们再次获胜未免要求太高了。 ➲ SYNONYMS AT DEMAND

IDM **'ask for it** (*informal*) to deserve sth bad that happens to you or that sb does to you 罪有应得；自讨苦吃；自找麻烦 **be 'asking for trouble | be 'asking for it** (*informal*) to behave in a way that is very likely to result in trouble 要自找麻烦；要自讨苦吃 **,don't 'ask** (*informal*) if you say **don't ask** to sb, you mean that you do not want to reply to their question, because it would be awkward, embarrassing, etc. 不问为好；还是别问的好 **,don't ask 'me** (*informal*) if you say **don't ask me**, you mean that you do not know the answer to a question and are annoyed you have been asked （不知答案并表示恼怒时说）别问我 **for the 'asking** if you can have sth **for the asking**, it is very easy for you to get it if you ask for it 只需要求，一经索取（便可获得）： *The job is yours for the asking.* 只要开口，这份工作就是你的了。 **I 'ask you** (*informal*) if you say **I ask you**, you are expressing disapproval, shock or anger about sth/sb （表示不赞成、震惊或气愤）请问，真是，这还了得 **if you ask 'me** (*informal*) in my personal opinion 我认为；依我说： *Their marriage was a mistake, if you ask me.* 依我看，他们的婚姻是个错误。

PHR V **'ask after sb** (*BrE*) to say that you would like to know how sb is, what they are doing, etc. 问候；问好： *He always asks after you in his letters.* 他在信中常问你好。 **,ask a'round** to speak to a number of different people in order to try and get some information 四处打听；多方询问： *I don't know of any vacancies in the company but I'll ask around.* 我不知道公司有没有空缺，不过我会打听打听。 **,ask sb 'back** (*especially BrE*) to invite sb to come back to your house when you are both out together 邀请（一起外出的人）回到家里来： *I hoped he wouldn't ask me back.* 我本不希望他会邀请我回到他家去。 **'ask for sb/sth** to say that you want to speak to sb or be directed to a place 说要找（某人）；问到（某处）的路： *When you arrive, ask for Jane.* 你到达后找简。 **,ask sb 'out** to invite sb to go out with you, especially as a way of starting a romantic relationship 邀请外出（尤指男女交往约会之始）： *He's too shy to ask her out.* 他太腼腆，不好意思约她外出。

▼ **SYNONYMS** 同义词辨析

ask

enquire • demand

These words all mean to say or write sth in the form of a question, in order to get information. 以上各词均含口头或书面询问之义。

ask to say or write sth in the form of a question, in order to get information 指口头或书面提问、询问： *'Where are you going?' she asked.* "你去哪？" 她问道。 ◇ *She asked the students their names.* 她问了学生的姓名。 ◇ *Can I ask a question?* 我能提个问题吗？

enquire/inquire (*rather formal*) to ask sb for information 指询问、查询： *I called the station to enquire about train times.* 我打电话到车站询问了火车时刻。

demand to ask a question very firmly 指严正地问、质问： *'And where have you been?' he demanded angrily.* "那你去了哪里？" 他怒气冲冲地质问道。

PATTERNS

- to ask/enquire **about/after** sb/sth
- to ask/enquire/demand sth **of** sb
- to ask/enquire/demand **what/who/how**, etc.
- to ask/enquire **politely**
- to ask/enquire/demand **angrily**

■ *noun*

IDM **a big 'ask** (*informal*) a difficult thing to achieve or deal with 难以做到的事情；棘手的事： *Beating the world champions is certainly a big ask for the team.* 这个队要打败世界冠军当然难度很大。

askance /əˈskæns/ *adv.*

IDM **look askance (at sb/sth) | look (at sb/sth) askance** to look at or react to sb/sth with suspicion or doubt, or in a critical way （怀疑或不满地）斜眼看，瞟

ask·ari /əˈskɑːri/ *noun* (*EAfrE*) a person who is employed to guard a building, valuable things, etc.; a SECURITY GUARD 保安；警卫

askew /əˈskjuː/ *adv., adj.* [not before noun] not in a straight or level position 歪；斜 SYN **crooked**： *His glasses had been knocked askew by the blow.* 他的眼镜一下子被打歪了。 ◇ *Her hat was slightly askew.* 她的帽子戴得有点歪。

'asking price *noun* the price that sb wants to sell sth for 要价；索价 ➲ COMPARE SELLING PRICE ➲ MORE LIKE THIS 9, page R26

A

aslant /ə'slɑːnt; *NAmE* ə'slænt/ *adv.* not exactly vertical or horizontal; at an angle 倾斜地；歪斜地： *The picture hung aslant.* 照片挂歪了。

asleep /ə'sliːp/ *adj.* [not before noun] sleeping 睡着： *The baby was **sound asleep** (= sleeping deeply) upstairs.* 婴儿在楼上睡得很香。◇ *I waited until they were all **fast asleep** (= sleeping deeply).* 我一直等到他们都进入了梦乡。◇ *He was so exhausted that he **fell asleep** at his desk.* 他太累了，竟伏在书桌上睡着了。◇ *She was still **half asleep** (= not fully awake) when she arrived at work.* 她到了上班地点时仍然睡眼惺忪。◇ *The police found him asleep in a garage.* 警察发现他在车库里睡着了。 OPP **awake** ➲ MORE LIKE THIS 31, page R28

AS (level) /eɪ 'es levl/ *noun* [C, U] Advanced Subsidiary (level); a British exam usually taken in Year 12 or Year 13 of school or college (= the final year or the year before it) covering half the material of an A-level qualification 高级补充程度考试（英国中学通常在 12 年级或 13 年级举行的考试，涵盖高级证书考试一半的内容）： *AS exams* 高级补充程度考试 ◇ *She's **doing an AS (level)** in French.* 她正为参加高级补充程度考试学习法语。◇ *More than 20 subjects are on offer **at AS level** at our college.* 本校提供 20 多门高级补充程度考试学科。

asp /æsp/ *noun* **1** a small poisonous snake found in SW Europe 小毒蛇（见于欧洲西南部） **2** a general name for various types of small poisonous snake found in N Africa 角蝰（见于北非的小毒蛇）

as·para·gus /ə'spærəgəs/ *noun* [U] a plant whose young green or white STEMS are cooked and eaten as a vegetable 芦笋；龙须菜 ➲ VISUAL VOCAB PAGE V33

as·par·tame /ə'spɑːteɪm; *NAmE* 'æspɑːrteɪm/ *noun* [U] a sweet substance used instead of sugar in drinks and food products, especially ones for people who are trying to lose weight 阿斯巴甜代糖（常用作减肥食品、饮料的人造甜味添加剂）

as·pect AW /'æspekt/ *noun* **1** [C] a particular part or feature of a situation, an idea, a problem, etc.; a way in which it may be considered 方面；层面： *The book aims to cover all aspects of city life.* 这本书旨在涵盖城市生活的各个方面。◇ *the most important aspect of the debate* 这场辩论最重要的方面 ◇ *She felt she had looked at the problem from every aspect.* 她觉得她已从各个角度去考虑了这个问题。◇ *This was one aspect of her character he hadn't seen before.* 这是他过去没有了解到的她的性格的一个方面。 **2** [sing., U] (*formal*) the appearance of a place, a situation or a person 样子；外观；外表： *Events began to take on a more sinister aspect.* 事情开始呈现较为不祥的征兆。 **3** [C, usually sing.] (*formal*) the direction in which a building, window, piece of land, etc. faces; the side of a building that faces a particular direction 朝向；方位 SYN **orientation** **4** [U, C] (*grammar* 语法) the form of a verb that shows, for example, whether the action happens once or repeatedly, is completed or still continuing （动词的）体（如表示动作等发生一次或多次、已完成或正在进行） ➲ SEE ALSO PERFECT *adj.* (7), PROGRESSIVE *adj.* (3)

aspen /'æspən/ *noun* a type of POPLAR tree, with leaves that move even when there is very little wind （美洲）颤杨，大齿杨；（欧洲）山杨

Asperger's syndrome /'æspɜːgəz sɪndrəʊm; *NAmE* 'æspərgərz sɪndroʊm/ *noun* [U] a mild type of AUTISM (= a mental condition in which a person finds it very difficult to communicate or form relationships with others) 阿斯珀格综合征，亚斯伯格症候群（一种轻度自闭症）

as·per·gill·osis /ˌæspədʒɪ'ləʊsɪs; *NAmE* ˌæspərdʒɪ'loʊsɪs/ *noun* [U] a serious condition in which parts of the body, usually the lungs, become infected by FUNGI 曲霉病（由真菌引起的肺部感染）

as·per·ity /æ'sperəti/ *noun* [U] (*formal*) the fact of being rough or severe, especially in the way you speak to or treat sb （尤指语言、态度）粗暴，严厉 SYN **harshness**

as·per·sions /ə'spɜːʃnz; *NAmE* ə'spɜːrʒnz/ *noun* [pl.] (*formal*) critical or unpleasant remarks or judgements 批评意见；非难；中伤： *I wouldn't want to **cast aspersions on** your honesty.* 我可不想批评你的诚信。

as·phalt /'æsfælt; *NAmE* -fɔːlt/ *noun* [U] a thick black sticky substance used especially for making the surface of roads 沥青；柏油

as·phyxia /æs'fɪksiə; əs'f-/ *noun* [U] (*specialist*) the state of being unable to breathe, causing death or loss of CONSCIOUSNESS 窒息

as·phyxi·ate /əs'fɪksieɪt/ *verb* ~ **sb** to make sb become unconscious or die by preventing them from breathing 使窒息；闷死 SYN **suffocate** ▶ **as·phyxi·ation** /əsˌfɪksi'eɪʃn/ *noun* [U]

aspic /'æspɪk/ *noun* [U] clear jelly which food can be put into when it is being served cold 肉冻： *chicken breast **in aspic*** 鸡脯冻

as·pi·dis·tra /ˌæspɪ'dɪstrə/ *noun* a plant with broad green pointed leaves, often grown indoors 蜘蛛抱蛋（常为室内盆栽植物，绿叶宽而尖）

as·pir·ant /ə'spaɪərənt; 'æspərənt/ *noun* ~ **(to/for sth)** (*formal*) a person with a strong desire to achieve a position of importance or to win a competition 有抱负的人；有雄心壮志的人： *aspirants to the title of world champion* 有志夺取世界冠军的人 ▶ **as·pir·ant** *adj.* [only before noun] = ASPIRING

as·pir·ate *noun, verb*

■ ***noun*** /'æspərət/ (*phonetics* 语音) the sound /h/, as in *house* * h 音；送气音： *The word 'hour' is pronounced without an initial aspirate.* * hour 的首字母 h 不发送气音。

■ ***verb*** /'æspəreɪt/ **1** ~ **sth** (*medical* 医) to remove liquid from a person's body with a machine （用吸引机）抽吸（体腔中的液体） **2** ~ **sth** (*phonetics* 语音) to pronounce sth with an 'h' sound or with a breath 发 h 音；发送气音

as·pir·ation /ˌæspə'reɪʃn/ *noun* **1** [C, usually pl., U] a strong desire to have or do sth 渴望；抱负；志向： *I didn't realize you had political aspirations.* 我没有意识到你有政治上的抱负。◇ ~ **to do sth** *He has never had any aspiration to earn a lot of money.* 他从未企求赚很多钱。◇ ~ **for sth** *What changes are needed to meet women's aspirations for employment?* 需要什么样的改革才能满足女性对就业的渴望呢？ **2** [U] (*phonetics* 语音) the action of pronouncing a word with a /h/ sound, as in *house* 发送气音；送气

as·pir·ation·al /ˌæspə'reɪʃənl/ *adj.* wanting very much to achieve success in your career or to improve your social status and standard of living 渴望成功的；一心想提高社会地位和生活水平的

as·pire /ə'spaɪə(r)/ *verb* [I, T] to have a strong desire to achieve or to become sth 渴望（成就）；有志（成为）： ~ **(to sth)** *She aspired to a scientific career.* 她有志于科学事业。◇ ~ **to be/do sth** *He aspired to be their next leader.* 他渴望成为他们的下一届领导人。

as·pirin /'æsprɪn; 'æspərɪn/ *noun* [U, C] (*pl.* **as·pirin** or **as·pir·ins**) a drug used to reduce pain, fever and INFLAMMATION 阿司匹林（镇痛解热消炎药）： *Do you have any aspirin?* 你有阿司匹林吗？◇ *Take two aspirin(s) for a headache.* 头痛服两片阿司匹林。

as·pir·ing /ə'spaɪərɪŋ/ (*also less frequent* **as·pir·ant**) *adj.* [only before noun] **1** wanting to start the career or activity that is mentioned 渴望从事…的；有志成为…的： *Aspiring musicians need hours of practice every day.* 想当音乐家就要每天练好几个小时。 **2** wanting to be successful in life 有抱负的；有志向的： *He came from an aspiring working-class background.* 他出身于有抱负的工人阶级家庭。 ➲ MORE LIKE THIS 32, page R28

ass /æs/ *noun* **1** (*NAmE*) (*BrE* **arse**) (*taboo, slang*) the part of the body that you sit on; your bottom 屁股；腚 **2** (*BrE, informal*) a stupid person 蠢人；笨蛋 SYN **fool**: *Don't be such an ass!* 别那么傻头傻脑的！◇ ***I made an ass of myself** at the meeting—standing up and then forgetting the question.* 我在会议上出了个大洋相，站起来却忘了要问的问题。 **3** (*BrE, old use*) a DONKEY 驴

IDM **get your 'ass in gear | move your 'ass** (*slang, especially NAmE*) a rude way of telling sb to hurry 别磨磨蹭蹭的；赶快 **get your ˌass over/in 'here, etc.** (*slang, especially NAmE*) a rude way of telling sb to come here, etc. 滚过来（或进来等） ➲ MORE AT BLOW *v.*, COVER *v.*, KICK *v.*, KISS *v.*, PAIN *n.*

as·sa·gai = ASSEGAI

as·sail /əˈseɪl/ *verb* (*formal*) **1 ~ sb/sth** to attack sb/sth violently, either physically or with words 攻击；袭击；抨击： *He was assailed with fierce blows to the head.* 他的头遭到猛烈殴打。◇ *The proposal was assailed by the opposition party.* 提案遭到反对党的抨击。◇ (*figurative*) *A vile smell assailed my nostrils.* 一股恶臭十分刺鼻。 **2** [usually passive] **~ sb** to disturb or upset sb severely 困扰；使苦恼： *to* ***be assailed by worries/doubts/fears*** 为焦虑 / 疑虑 / 担心所困扰

as·sail·ant /əˈseɪlənt/ *noun* (*formal*) a person who attacks sb, especially physically 攻击者；行凶者 SYN **attacker**

as·sas·sin /əˈsæsɪn; *NAmE* -sn/ *noun* a person who murders sb important or famous, for money or for political reasons （为金钱或政治目的的）暗杀者，行刺者

as·sas·sin·ate /əˈsæsmeɪt; *NAmE* -sən-/ *verb* [often passive] **~ sb** to murder an important or famous person, especially for political reasons（尤为政治目的）暗杀，行刺： *The prime minister was assassinated by extremists.* 首相遭极端分子暗杀。◇ *a plot to assassinate the president* 刺杀总统的阴谋 ➲ WORDFINDER NOTE AT ATTACK ▶ **as·sas·sin·ation** /əˌsæsɪˈneɪʃn; *NAmE* -səˈn-/ *noun* [U, C]: *The president survived a number of assassination attempts.* 总统在数次暗杀企图中幸免于难。◇ *the assassination of John F. Kennedy* 暗杀约翰 • F. 肯尼迪

as·sault /əˈsɔːlt/ *noun, verb*

■ ***noun*** **1** [U, C] the crime of attacking sb physically 侵犯他人身体（罪）；侵犯人身罪： *Both men were charged with assault.* 两人均被控侵犯他人身体罪。◇ *sexual assaults* 性侵犯（指强奸、猥亵） ◇ **~ on/upon sb** *A significant number of* ***indecent assaults*** *on women go unreported.* 大量的猥亵妇女罪没有被举报。 ➲ COLLOCATIONS AT CRIME **2** [C] **~ (on/upon/against sb/sth)** (by an army, etc. 军队等) the act of attacking a building, an area, etc. in order to take control of it 攻击；突击；袭击 SYN **attack**: *An assault on the capital was launched in the early hours of the morning.* 凌晨时分向首都发起了攻击。 **3** [C] **~ (on/upon sth)** the act of trying to achieve sth that is difficult or dangerous （向困难或危险事物发起的）冲击： *The government has mounted a new assault on unemployment.* 政府向失业发起新的攻势。◇ *Three people died during an assault on the mountain* (= while trying to climb it). 登山过程中有三人死亡。 **4** [C] an act of criticizing sb/sth severely 抨击 SYN **attack**: *The suggested closures* ***came under assault*** *from all parties.* 关闭机构的建议受到各方严厉批评。◇ **~ on/upon/against sb/sth** *The paper's assault on the president was totally unjustified.* 这份报纸对总统的攻击纯属无稽之谈。

■ ***verb*** **1 ~ sb** to attack sb violently, especially when this is a crime 猛烈攻击，袭击，侵犯（尤指构成罪）： *He has been charged with assaulting a police officer.* 他被控袭击警察。◇ *Four women have been* ***sexually assaulted*** *in the area recently.* 近来这个地区有四名妇女遭到性侵犯。 **2 ~ sth** (*formal*) to affect your senses in a way that is very unpleasant or uncomfortable 使（感官）难受： *Loud rock music assaulted our ears.* 喧闹的摇滚乐直往我们耳朵里钻。

asˌsault and 'battery *noun* [U] (*law* 律) the crime of threatening to harm sb and then attacking them physically 企图伤害罪和殴击罪

as'sault course (*BrE*) (*NAmE* **'obstacle course**) *noun* an area of land with many objects that are difficult to climb, jump over or go through, which is used, especially by soldiers, for improving physical skills and strength 近战训练场；障碍场

assay /əˈseɪ/ *noun* [C, U] (*specialist*) the testing of metals and chemicals for quality, often to see how pure they are 含量测定 ▶ **assay** *verb* **~ sth**

as·se·gai (*also* **as·sa·gai**) /ˈæsəgaɪ/ *noun* **1** a weapon consisting of a long stick with a sharp metal point on the end, used mainly in southern Africa （多为南非部落所用的）长矛，标枪 **2** a South African tree which produces hard wood （南非的）山茱萸树

as·sem·blage /əˈsemblɪdʒ/ *noun* (*formal* or *specialist*) a collection of things; a group of people （人、物的）聚集，集聚： *Tropical rainforests have the most varied assemblage of plants in the world.* 热带雨林聚集了世界上种类最繁多的植物。

as·sem·ble AW /əˈsembl/ *verb* **1** [I, T] to come together as a group; to bring people or things together as a group 聚集；集合；收集： *All the students were asked to assemble in the main hall.* 全体学生接到通知到大礼堂集合。◇ *She then addressed the* ***assembled company*** (= all the people there). 接着她向全体集合者讲话。 ◇ **~ sth** *to assemble evidence/data* 收集证据 / 数据 ◇ *The manager has assembled a world-class team.* 经理组建了一个世界一流的团队。 **2** [T] **~ sth** to fit together all the separate parts of sth, for example a piece of furniture 装配；组装： *The shelves are easy to assemble.* 搁架容易装配。 OPP **disassemble** ➲ SYNONYMS AT BUILD

as·sem·bler /əˈsemblə(r)/ *noun* **1** a person who assembles a machine or its parts 装配工 **2** (*computing* 计) a program for changing instructions into MACHINE CODE 汇编程序，汇编器，组译器（将指令转变为机器码） **3** (*computing* 计) = ASSEMBLY LANGUAGE

Asˌsemblies of 'God *noun* [pl.] the largest Pentecostal Church in the US (= one that emphasizes the gifts of the Holy Spirit, such as the power to heal people who are ill/sick) 神召会（美国规模最大的五旬节教派，强调医治等神恩）

as·sem·bly AW /əˈsembli/ *noun* (*pl.* **-ies**) **1** (*also* **Assembly**) [C] a group of people who have been elected to meet together regularly and make decisions or laws for a particular region or country 立法机构；会议；议会： ***state/legislative/federal/local assemblies*** 州众议院；立法会议；联邦 / 地方议会 ◇ *Power has been handed over to provincial and regional assemblies.* 权力已移交给省和地区议会。◇ *The national assembly has voted to adopt the budget.* 国民议会已表决通过预算。◇ *the California Assembly* 美国加利福尼亚州众议院 ◇ *the UN General Assembly* 联合国大会 **2** [U, C] the meeting together of a group of people for a particular purpose; a group of people who meet together for a particular purpose 集会；（统称）集会者： *They were fighting for freedom of speech and freedom of assembly.* 他们为言论自由和集会自由而斗争。◇ *He was to address a public assembly on the issue.* 他要对公众集会发表演说谈论这个问题。◇ *an* ***assembly point*** (= a place where people have been asked to meet) 集会地点 **3** [C, U] a meeting of the teachers and students in a school, usually at the start of the day, to give information, discuss school events or say prayers together （全校师生的）晨会，朝会 **4** [U] the process of putting together the parts of sth such as a vehicle or piece of furniture 装配；组装；总成： *Putting the bookcase together should be a simple assembly job.* 组装书橱应该是个简单的装配活。◇ *a car assembly plant* 汽车装配厂

as'sembly language *noun* [C, U] (*also* **as·sem·bler**) (*computing* 计) the language in which a program is written before it is changed into MACHINE CODE 汇编语言；组合语言

as'sembly line *noun* = PRODUCTION LINE : *workers on the assembly line* 装配线上的工人 ➲ WORDFINDER NOTE AT FACTORY

as·sem·bly·man /əˈsemblimən/, **as·sem·bly·wo·man** /əˈsembliwʊmən/ *noun* (*pl.* **-men** /-mən/, **-women** /-wɪmɪn/) a person who is an elected representative in a state assembly in the US （美国）州众议院议员 ➲ MORE LIKE THIS 25, page R28

as'sembly room *noun* [usually pl.] (*especially BrE*) a public room or building in which meetings and social events are held（供会议、社交活动等用的）礼堂

as·sent /ə'sent/ *noun, verb*

■ ***noun*** [U] **~ (to sth)** (*formal*) official agreement to or approval of sth 同意；赞成：*The director has **given her assent to** the proposals.* 负责人已表示同意提案。◇ *He nodded (his) assent.* 他点头同意了。◇ *There were murmurs of both assent and dissent from the crowd.* 人群议论纷纷，赞成和反对的都有。◇ *The bill passed in Parliament has now **received** (the) **Royal Assent*** (= been approved by the king/queen). 议会通过的法案已获御准。

■ ***verb*** [I] **~ (to sth)** | **(+ speech)** (*formal*) to agree to a request, an idea or a suggestion 同意，赞成（要求、想法或建议）：*Nobody would assent to the terms they proposed.* 谁也不会同意他们提出的条件。

as·sert /ə'sɜːt; *NAmE* ə'sɜːrt/ *verb* **1** to state clearly and firmly that sth is true 明确肯定；断言：**~ that...** *She continued to assert that she was innocent.* 她仍然坚称自己无辜。◇ **~ sth** *She continued to assert her innocence.* 她仍然坚称自己无辜。◇ **+ speech** *'That is wrong,' he asserted.* "那是错的。"他断言道。◇ **it is asserted that...** *It is commonly asserted that older people prefer to receive care from family members.* 人们普遍确认，老年人更愿意由家人照顾。 **2 ~ yourself** to behave in a confident and determined way so that other people pay attention to your opinions 坚持自己的主张；表现坚定 **3 ~ sth** to make other people recognize your right or authority to do sth, by behaving firmly and confidently 维护自己的权利（或权威）：*to **assert your independence/rights*** 维护你的独立 / 权利 ◇ *I was determined to **assert** my **authority** from the beginning.* 我决心一开始就维护我的权威。 **4 ~ itself** to start to have an effect 生效；起作用：*Good sense asserted itself.* 明智服人。

as·ser·tion /ə'sɜːʃn; *NAmE* ə'sɜːrʃn/ *noun* **1** [C] a statement saying that you strongly believe sth to be true 认定；断言 **SYN claim**：*He was correct in his assertion that the minister had been lying.* 他认定部长说谎，事实果然如此。◇ *Do you have any evidence to support your assertions?* 你的断言是否有真凭实据？ ➲ SYNONYMS AT CLAIM **2** [U, C] the act of stating, using or claiming sth strongly 声称；使用；主张：*the assertion of his authority* 对他权威的维护 ◇ *The demonstration was an assertion of the right to peaceful protest.* 这次示威游行行使了和平抗议权。

as·sert·ive /ə'sɜːtɪv; *NAmE* ə'sɜːrtɪv/ *adj.* expressing opinions or desires strongly and with confidence, so that people take notice 坚定自信的；坚决主张的：*You should try and be more assertive.* 你应该努力坚定信心。◇ *assertive behaviour* 坚定自信的行为 **OPP submissive** ▶ **as·sert·ive·ly** *adv.* **as·sert·ive·ness** *noun* [U]：*an assertiveness training course* 建立自信心训练班

as·sess AW /ə'ses/ *verb* **1** to make a judgement about the nature or quality of sb/sth 评估，评定（性质、质量）：**~ sb/sth** *It's difficult to assess the effects of these changes.* 这些变化带来的效果难以评估。◇ *to assess a patient's needs* 判定病人的需要 ◇ **~ sb/sth as sth** *The young men were assessed as either safe or unsafe drivers.* 这些年轻人被评定为谨慎驾驶员和不谨慎驾驶员两类。◇ *I'd assess your chances as low.* 我估计你的机会不大。◇ **~ whether, how, etc....** *The committee assesses whether a building is worth preserving.* 该委员会评定一栋建筑物是否值得保存。◇ *We are trying to assess how well the system works.* 我们正设法评估这个系统运行得是否顺畅。 **2** to calculate the amount or value of sth 估算，估定，核定（数量、价值）**SYN estimate**：**~ sth** *They have assessed the amount of compensation to be paid.* 他们已经核定赔偿额。◇ **~ sth at sth** *Damage to the building was assessed at £40 000.* 该建筑物的损失估定为 4 万英镑。 ▶ **as·sess·able** AW *adj.*

as·sess·ment AW /ə'sesmənt/ *noun* **1** [C] an opinion or a judgement about sb/sth that has been thought about very carefully 看法；评价 **SYN evaluation**：*a detailed assessment of the risks involved* 对涉及的风险所作的详细判断 ◇ *his assessment of the situation* 他对形势的看法 **2** [U] the act of judging or forming an opinion about sb/sth 评定；核定；判定：*written exams and other forms of assessment* 笔试及其他形式的考核 ◇ *Objective assessment of the severity of the problem was difficult.* 难以客观判定该问题的严重性。 ➲ SEE ALSO CONTINUOUS ASSESSMENT **3** [C] an amount that has been calculated and that must be paid 核定的付款额：*a tax assessment* 税款核定额

a'ssessment centre (*BrE*) (*NAmE* **a'ssessment center**) *noun* (*business* 商) an event where people applying for a job are given a number of tests and interviews to find out what their strengths and weaknesses are; the place where this happens 求职评估；求职评估中心：*After the first interview you may be asked back for an assessment centre.* 第一次面试之后可能要求你回来接受求职评估。

as·ses·sor /ə'sesə(r)/ *noun* **1** an expert in a particular subject who is asked by a court or other official group to give advice（法庭或官方团体的）顾问 **2** a person who calculates the value or cost of sth or the amount of money to be paid（财产、费用等的）估价员：*an **insurance/tax assessor*** 保险估价员；估税员 **3** a person who judges how well sb has done in an exam, a competition, etc.（考试、比赛等的）考核人，评判员：*College lecturers acted as external assessors of the exam results.* 学院讲师是考试成绩的校外考核人。

asset /'æset/ *noun* **1** a person or thing that is valuable or useful to sb/sth 有价值的人（或事物）；有用的人（或事物）：*In his job, patience is an invaluable asset.* 他干的这份工作，耐心是无价之宝。◇ **~ to sb/sth** *She'll be an asset to the team.* 她将是这个队的骨干。 **2** [usually pl.] a thing of value, especially property, that a person or company owns, which can be used or sold to pay debts 资产；财产：*the net **asset value** of the company* 公司的资产净值 ◇ *Her assets include shares in the company and a house in France.* 她的财产包括公司的股份和在法国的一座房子。◇ ***asset sales/management*** 资产销售 / 管理 ◇ ***financial/capital assets*** 金融 / 资本资产 ➲ COMPARE LIABILITY ➲ WORDFINDER NOTE AT INVEST

'asset-stripping *noun* [U] (*business* 商, *usually disapproving*) the practice of buying a company which is in financial difficulties at a low price and then selling everything that it owns in order to make a profit 资产倒卖，资产拆卖（以低价购进公司，再将其资产出售，以获取利润）

ass·hole /'æshəʊl; *NAmE* -hoʊl/ (*NAmE*) (*BrE* **arse·hole**) *noun* (*taboo, slang*) **1** the ANUS 屁眼；肛门 **2** a stupid or unpleasant person 笨蛋；讨厌鬼

as·sidu·ous /ə'sɪdjuəs; *NAmE* -dʒuəs/ *adj.* (*formal*) working very hard and taking great care that everything is done as well as it can be 兢兢业业的；勤勤恳恳的 **SYN diligent** ▶ **as·si·du·ity** /ˌæsɪ'djuːəti/ *noun* [U] **as·sidu·ous·ly** *adv.*

as·sign AW /ə'saɪn/ *verb* **1** to give sb sth that they can use, or some work or responsibility 分配（某物）；分派，布置（工作、任务等）：**~ sth (to sb)** *The two large classrooms have been assigned to us.* 这两间大教室分配给了我们。◇ *The teacher assigned a different task to each of the children.* 老师给每个孩子都布置了不同的作业。◇ **~ sb sth** *We have been assigned the two large classrooms.* 我们分得了这两间大教室。◇ *The teacher assigned each of the children a different task.* 老师给每个孩子都布置了不同的作业。 **2** to provide a person for a particular task or position 指定；指派：**~ sb (to sth/as sth)** *They've assigned their best man to the job.* 他们指派了最优秀的人承担这项工作。◇ **~ sb to do sth** *British forces have been assigned to help with peacekeeping.* 英国军队被派遣协助维持和平。 **3** [usually passive] **~ sb to sb/sth** to send a person to work under the authority of sb or in a particular group 委派；派遣：*I was assigned to B platoon.* 我被派到 B 排工作。 **4** to say that sth has a particular value or function, or happens at a particular time or place 确定（价值、功能、时间、地点）：**~ sth to sth** *Assign a different colour to each different type of information.* 给每类信息分别确定一种颜色。◇ **~ sth sth** *The painting cannot be assigned an exact date.* 这幅画的年代确定不了。 **5 ~ sth to sb** (*law* 律) to say that your property or rights now belong to sb else 转让，让与（财产、权利）： *The agreement assigns copyright to the publisher.* 协议规定将版权转让给出版商。

as·sig·na·tion /ˌæsɪɡˈneɪʃn/ *noun* (*formal* or *humorous*) a meeting, especially a secret one, often with a lover 幽会；约会

as·sign·ment AW /əˈsaɪnmənt/ *noun* **1** [C, U] a task or piece of work that sb is given to do, usually as part of their job or studies （分派的）工作，任务： *You will need to complete three written assignments per semester.* 你每学期要完成三个书面作业。◇ *She is in Greece on an assignment for one of the Sunday newspapers.* 她在希腊为一家星期日报执行一项任务。◇ *one of our reporters* ***on assignment*** *in China* 我们派驻中国的一名记者 ◇ *I had set myself a tough assignment.* 我给自己定了一项艰巨任务。 **2** [U] the act of giving sth to sb; the act of giving sb a particular task （工作等的）分派，布置： *his assignment to other duties in the same company* 他在同一公司内担任的其他职务

as·simi·late /əˈsɪməleɪt/ *verb* **1** [T] **~ sth** to fully understand an idea or some information so that you are able to use it yourself 透彻理解；消化；吸收： *The committee will need time to assimilate this report.* 委员会需要时间来吃透这个报告。 **2** [I, T] to become, or allow sb to become, a part of a country or community rather than remaining in a separate group （使）同化，融入： **~ (into/to sth)** *New arrivals find it hard to assimilate.* 新来者感到难以融入当地社会。◇ **~ sb (into/to sth)** *Immigrants have been successfully assimilated into the community.* 外来移民顺利地融入当地社会。 **3** [T, often passive] **~ sth into/to sth** to make an idea, a person's attitude, etc. fit into sth or be acceptable 使吸收，使接受（想法、态度等）： *These changes were gradually assimilated into everyday life.* 这些改变逐渐渗进了日常生活。

as·simi·la·tion /əˌsɪməˈleɪʃn/ *noun* **1** [U] the act of assimilating sb or sth, or being assimilated 吸收；接受： *the rapid assimilation of new ideas* 对新思想的迅速吸收 ◇ *his assimilation into the community* 他融入社区 **2** [U, C] (*phonetics* 语音) the act of making two sounds in speech that are next to each other more similar to each other in certain ways, for example the pronunciation of the /t/ in *football* as a /p/; an example of this process 同化（使相邻的两个音发音接近，如 football 中 /t/ 同化为 /p/）；同化现象

as·sist 🔑 AW /əˈsɪst/ *verb, noun*

■ ***verb*** (*formal*) **1** 🔑 [I, T] to help sb to do sth 帮助；协助；援助： *Anyone willing to assist can contact this number.* 凡愿协助者可拨此号码联系。◇ **~ in/with sth** *We are looking for people who would be willing to assist in the group's work.* 我们正寻找愿意协助该团体工作的人。◇ **~ sb** *We'll do all we can to assist you.* 我们会尽量帮你。◇ *The play was directed by Mike Johnson, assisted by Sharon Gale.* 该剧由迈克・约翰逊导演，沙伦・盖尔为助理导演。◇ **~ sb in doing sth** *We will assist you in finding somewhere to live.* 我们将帮你找个住的地方。◇ **~ sb in/with sth** *Two men are* ***assisting the police with their enquiries*** (= are being questioned by the police). 有两个人正配合警方接受询问。◇ **~ sb to do sth** *a course to assist adults to return to the labour market* 成人重返劳工市场的辅导班 **2** 🔑 [T] **~ sth** to help sth to happen more easily 促进： *activities that will assist the decision-making process* 促进决策进程的活动

■ ***noun*** **1** an action in ICE HOCKEY, football/SOCCER, etc. in which a player passes the ball in a way that helps another player on the same team to score a goal （冰球、足球等运动中的）助攻： *He had/made ten assists.* 他有十次助攻。 **2** an action in BASEBALL in which a player throws the ball to another member of the team who gets an opponent out either by stepping onto the base before the runner reaches it, or by touching the runner with the ball before he or she reaches the base （棒球运动中的）助杀

as·sist·ance 🔑 AW /əˈsɪstəns/ *noun* [U] (*formal*) help or support 帮助；援助；支持： ***technical/economic/military assistance*** 技术 / 经济 / 军事援助 ◇ ***financial assistance*** *for people on low incomes* 给低收入者的经济援助 ◇ ***Can I be of any assistance?*** 我能帮上忙吗？ ◇ *Despite his cries, no one* ***came to his assistance.*** 尽管他喊叫，却没有人来帮助他。◇ *He can walk only* ***with the assistance of*** *crutches.* 他只能靠拐杖走路。◇ **~ with sth** *She offered me practical assistance with my research.* 她给我的研究提供了实实在在的援助。◇ **~ in doing sth/to do sth** *The company provides advice and assistance in finding work.* 公司提供就业咨询和帮助。

as·sist·ant 🔑 AW /əˈsɪstənt/ *noun, adj.*

■ ***noun*** **1** 🔑 a person who helps or supports sb, usually in their job 助理；助手： *My assistant will now demonstrate the machine in action.* 现在我的助手将演示机器运转情况。◇ *a senior research assistant* 高级研究助理 ➲ SEE ALSO PERSONAL ASSISTANT, TEACHING ASSISTANT **2** 🔑 (*especially BrE*) = SALES CLERK, SHOP ASSISTANT : *an assistant in a department store* 一名百货公司售货员 ➲ WORDFINDER NOTE AT SHOP **3** (*BrE*) a student at university or college who spends time in a foreign country teaching his or her own language in a school 助教（在国外留学的大学生，教授本国语）

■ ***adj.*** 🔑 [only before noun] (*abbr.* **Asst**) (often in titles 常用于头衔) having a rank below that of a senior person and helping them in their work 助理的；副的： *the assistant manager* 协理 ◇ *Assistant Chief Constable Owen* 助理警察局长欧文 ◇ *Assistant Attorney General William Weld* 助理总检察长威廉・韦尔德

asˌsistant proˈfessor *noun* (in the US and Canada) a teacher at a college or university who has a rank just below the rank of an ASSOCIATE PROFESSOR （美国和加拿大的）助理教授（职位比副教授低一级）

asˌsistant refeˈree (*also* **referee's assistant**) *noun* (in football (SOCCER) 足球) the official name for a LINESMAN (= an official who helps the REFEREE, for example in deciding whether or where a ball has passed outside the field of play) 助理裁判（边线裁判员的正式名称）

as·sis·tant·ship /əˈsɪstəntʃɪp/ *noun* **1** (*BrE*) the position of being an ASSISTANT (3) 助手职位；助理职位 **2** (*NAmE*) a paid position for a GRADUATE student that involves some teaching or research （研究生的）助教金职位，助研金职位

asˌsisted ˈliving *noun* [U] accommodation for people who need help, for example with tasks like washing and dressing themselves 赡养院；安养照护： *assisted living apartments* 赡养公寓

asˌsisted ˈsuicide *noun* [U] the act of a person killing himself/herself with the help of sb such as a doctor, especially because he/she is suffering from a disease that has no cure （假医生等他人之手的）辅助自杀，协助自杀

as·sizes /əˈsaɪzɪz/ *noun* [pl.] a court in the past which travelled to each county of England and Wales （英格兰和威尔士旧时的）巡回法庭 ▶ **as·size** *adj.* [only before noun]: *the assize court* 巡回审判法庭

ˈass-kicking *adj.* = KICK-ASS

ˈass-licker (*NAmE*) (*BrE* **ˈarse-licker**) *noun* (*taboo, slang*) a person who is too friendly to sb in authority and is always ready to do what they want 马屁精 ▶ **ˈass-licking** (*NAmE*) (*BrE* **ˈarse-licking**) *noun* [U]

Assoc. *abbr.* (in writing 书写形式) ASSOCIATION 协会；社团；联盟

as·so·ci·ate 🔑 *verb, adj., noun*

■ ***verb*** /əˈsəʊʃieɪt; -sieɪt; *NAmE* əˈsoʊ-/ **1** 🔑 [T] **~ sb/sth (with sb/sth)** to make a connection between people or things in your mind 联想；联系： *I always associate the smell of baking with my childhood.* 一闻到烘烤食物的味道，我就想起了童年。◇ *He is closely associated in the public mind with horror movies.* 在公众的心目中，他总是和恐怖电影紧密联系在一起。 **2** [I] **~ with sb** to spend time with sb, especially a person or people that sb else does not approve of 交往；（尤指）混在一起 SYN **mix**: *I don't like* *you associating with those people.* 我不喜欢你和那些人混在一起。 **3** [T] **~ yourself with sth** (*formal*) to show that you support or agree with sth 表明支持；表示同意： *I associate myself with the Prime Minister's remarks* (= I agree with them). 我赞同首相所言。 **OPP dissociate**

■ ***adj.*** /əˈsəʊʃiət; -siət; *NAmE* əˈsoʊ-/ [only before noun] **1** (often in titles 常用于头衔) of a lower rank; having fewer rights in a particular profession or organization 非正式的；准的；副的： *associate membership of the European Union* 欧洲联盟的非正式会员身份 ◇ *an* ***associate member/director/editor*** 准会员；副导演；副主编 **2** joined to or connected with a profession or an organization 联合的；有关联的： *an associate company in Japan* 在日本的一家联营公司

■ ***noun*** /əˈsəʊʃiət; *NAmE* əˈsoʊ-/ **1** a person that you work with, do business with or spend a lot of time with 同事；伙伴： *business associates* 业务伙伴 **2** (*also* **Associate**) an ASSOCIATE (1) member 准会员 **3 Associate** (*US*) a person who has an Associate's degree (= one that is given after completing two years of study at a junior college) 准学士（获得两年制高校学位）

as·so·ci·ated 🔑 /əˈsəʊʃieɪtɪd; -sieɪt-; *NAmE* əˈsoʊ-/ *adj.* **1** 🔑 if one thing is **associated with** another, the two things are connected because they happen together or one thing causes the other 有关联的；相关的 **SYN connected**： *the risks associated with taking drugs* 与吸毒有关的危险 ◇ *Salaries and associated costs have risen substantially.* 薪金与相关费用大大增加。 **2** 🔑 if a person is **associated with** an organization, etc. they support it 有联系的： *He no longer wished to be associated with the party's policy on education.* 他不再愿意认同该党的教育方针。 **3 Associated** used in the name of a business company that is made up of a number of smaller companies （用于联合企业的名称）联合的： *Associated Newspapers* 联合报业

asˌsociate proˈfessor *noun* (in the US and Canada) a teacher at a college or university who has a rank just below the rank of a professor （美国和加拿大的）副教授（职位比教授低一级）

as·so·ci·ation 🔑 /əˌsəʊʃiˈeɪʃn; -siˈeɪ-; *NAmE* əˌsoʊ-/ *noun* **1** 🔑 [C+sing./pl. v.] (*abbr.* **Assoc.**) an official group of people who have joined together for a particular purpose 协会；社团；联盟 **SYN organization**： *Do you belong to any professional or trade associations?* 你参加了专业学会或行业协会没有？ ◇ *the Football Association* 足球协会 ◇ *a residents' association* 居民联合会 ➲ SEE ALSO HOUSING ASSOCIATION **2** 🔑 [C, U] **~ (with sb/sth)** a connection or relationship between people or organizations 联合；合伙；关联；交往： *his alleged association with terrorist groups* 他被指称的与恐怖组织的关联 ◇ *They have maintained a close association with a college in the US.* 他们和美国一所学院保持了密切联系。 ◇ *The book was published* ***in association with*** (= together with) *English Heritage.* 这本书是与英国文化遗产保护协会联合出版的。 ◇ *She became famous through her association with the group of poets.* 她通过与这些诗人交往而成名。 **3** 🔑 [C, usually pl.] an idea or a memory that is suggested by sb/sth; a mental connection between ideas 联想；联系： *The seaside had all sorts of pleasant associations with childhood holidays for me.* 海滨使我联想起童年假期的各种愉快情景。 ◇ *The cat soon made the association between human beings and food.* 这只猫很快就把人类与食物联系起来。 **4** 🔑 [C] a connection between things where one is caused by the other 因果关系： *a proven association between passive smoking and cancer* 已被证实的被动吸烟与癌症之间的因果关系

Asˌsociation ˈfootball *noun* [U] (*BrE, formal*) = FOOTBALL (1)

as·so·cia·tive /əˈsəʊʃiətɪv; *NAmE* əˈsoʊ-/ *adj.* **1** relating to the association of ideas or things 联想的 **2** (*mathematics* 数) giving the same result no matter what order the parts of a calculation are done, for example (a × b) × c = a × (b × c) 结合的

as·son·ance /ˈæsənəns/ *noun* [U] (*specialist*) the effect created when two syllables in words that are close together have the same vowel sound, but different consonants, or the same consonants but different vowels, for example, *sonnet* and *porridge* or *cold* and *killed* 准押韵，半谐韵，半谐音（靠得很近的单词中有两个音节元音相同而辅音不同，或辅音相同而元音不同） ➲ SEE ALSO ALLITERATION

as·sort·ed /əˈsɔːtɪd; *NAmE* əˈsɔːrtəd/ *adj.* of various different sorts 各种各样的；混杂的；什锦的： *The meat is served with salad or assorted vegetables.* 端上的肉配有色拉或什锦蔬菜。 ◇ *The jumper comes in assorted colours.* 各种颜色的针织套衫一应俱全。

as·sort·ment /əˈsɔːtmənt; *NAmE* əˈsɔːrt-/ *noun* [usually sing.] a collection of different things or of different types of the same thing 各种各样 **SYN mixture**： *a wide assortment of gifts to choose from* 各式各样可供挑选的礼品 ◇ *He was dressed in an odd assortment of clothes.* 他穿着奇装异服。

Asst (*also* **Asst.** *especially in NAmE*) *abbr.* (in writing 书写形式) ASSISTANT 助理的；副的： *Asst Manager* 协理

as·suage /əˈsweɪdʒ/ *verb* **~ sth** (*formal*) to make an unpleasant feeling less severe 缓和，减轻（不快）

as·sume 🔑 **AW** /əˈsjuːm; *NAmE* əˈsuːm/ *verb* **1** 🔑 to think or accept that sth is true but without having proof of it 假定；假设；认为： **~ (that)...** ***It is reasonable to assume*** *(that) the economy will continue to improve.* 认为经济将继续好转是有道理的。 ◇ ***Let us assume*** *for a moment that the plan succeeds.* 咱们暂时假设计划成功。 ◇ *She would, he assumed, be home at the usual time.* 他认为，她会在通常时间回到家的。 ◇ **it is assumed (that)...** *It is generally assumed that stress is caused by too much work.* 普遍认为，紧张是工作过重所致。 ◇ **~ sth** *Don't always* ***assume the worst*** (= that sth bad has happened). 别总往最坏处想。 ◇ *In this example we have assumed a unit price of $10.* 在这个例子中，我们已假定单价为 10 美元。 ◇ **~ sb/sth to be/have sth** *I had assumed him to be a Belgian.* 我本以为他是比利时人。 **2 ~ sth** (*formal*) to take or begin to have power or responsibility 承担（责任）；就（职）；取得（权力）： *Rebel forces have assumed control of the capital.* 反叛武装力量已控制了首都。 ◇ *The court assumed responsibility for the girl's welfare.* 法庭承担了保障这个女孩福利的责任。 **3 ~ sth** (*formal*) to begin to have a particular quality or appearance 呈现（外观、样子）；显露（特征） **SYN take on**： *This matter has assumed considerable importance.* 这件事看来相当重要。 ◇ *In the story the god assumes the form of an eagle.* 在这个故事中神以鹰的形象出现。 **4 ~ sth** (*formal*) to pretend to have a particular feeling or quality 装出；假装 **SYN put on**： *He assumed an air of concern.* 他装出关心的样子。

as·sumed **AW** /əˈsjuːmd; *NAmE* əˈsuːmd/ *adj.* [only before noun] that you suppose to be true or to exist 假定的；假设的： *the assumed differences between the two states* 两种状况的假定区别

asˌsumed ˈname *noun* a name that sb uses that is not their real name 化名 **SYN pseudonym**： *He was living* ***under an assumed name.*** 他过着隐姓埋名的生活。

as·sum·ing **AW** /əˈsjuːmɪŋ; *NAmE* əˈsuːmɪŋ/ *conj.* **~ (that)** used to suppose that sth is true so that you can talk about what the results might be 假设…为真；假如： *Assuming (that) he's still alive, how old would he be now?* 假定他还活着，现在有多大年纪了？ ◇ *I hope to go to college next year,* ***always assuming*** *I pass my exams.* 我希望明年上大学，当然是在我通过考试的前提下。

as·sump·tion **AW** /əˈsʌmpʃn/ *noun* **1** [C] a belief or feeling that sth is true or that sth will happen, although there is no proof 假定；假设： *an* ***underlying/implicit assumption*** 暗含的假定 ◇ *We need to challenge some of the basic assumptions of Western philosophy.* 我们有必要向西方哲学的某些基本假设提出质疑。 ◇ *We are working* ***on the assumption that*** *everyone invited will turn up.* 我们假定了每一个人都会应邀出席并正就此作出安排。 ◇ *It was impossible to* ***make assumptions about*** *people's reactions.* 臆断人们的反应是不可能的。 ◇ *His actions were based on a false assumption.* 他的行为基于错误的设想。 **2** [C, U] **~ of sth** (*formal*) the act of taking or beginning to have power or responsibility（责任的）承担；担任；（权力的）获得：*their assumption of power/control* 他们权力 / 控制的取得

as·sur·ance AW /əˈʃʊərəns; -ˈʃɔːr-; *NAmE* əˈʃʊr-/ *noun* **1** [C] a statement that sth will certainly be true or will certainly happen, particularly when there has been doubt about it 保证；担保 SYN **guarantee, promise**: *They called for assurances that the government is committed to its education policy.* 他们要求政府保证切实执行其教育方针。◇ *Unemployment seems to be rising, despite repeated* ***assurances to the contrary.*** 尽管反复担保减少失业，失业率看来却在上升。 **2** (*also* ˌ**self-asˈsurance**) [U] belief in your own abilities or strengths 自信 SYN **confidence**: *There was an air of easy assurance and calm about him.* 他表现出从容自信和冷静。 **3** [U] (*BrE*) a type of insurance in which money is paid out when sb dies or after an agreed period of time 人寿保险：*a life assurance company* 人寿保险公司 ➲ SEE ALSO QUALITY ASSURANCE

as·sure AW /əˈʃʊə(r); əˈʃɔː(r); *NAmE* əˈʃʊr/ *verb* **1** to tell sb that sth is definitely true or is definitely going to happen, especially when they have doubts about it 使确信；向…保证：**~ sb (that)**... *You think I did it deliberately, but I assure you (that) I did not.* 你认为这是我故意干的，不过我向你保证不是的。◇ *We were assured that everything possible was being done.* 我们得到保证说，正在尽一切努力。◇ *She's perfectly safe,* ***I can assure you.*** 我可以向你保证，她绝对安全。◇ **~ sb (of sth)** *We assured him of our support.* 我们向他保证给予支持。◇ **~ sb + speech** *'He'll come back,' Susan assured her.* "他会回来的。"苏珊安慰她道。 **2** (*formal*) to make yourself certain about sth 弄清；查明：**~ yourself of sth** *He assured himself of her safety.* 他确定她是安全的。◇ **~ yourself that**... *She assured herself that the letter was still in the drawer.* 她查清楚信仍然在抽屉里。 **3** to make sth certain to happen 确保；使确定 SYN **guarantee**: **~ sth** *Victory would assure a place in the finals.* 胜利将确保能参加决赛。◇ **~ sb sth** *Victory would assure them a place in the finals.* 获胜后他们就能参加决赛。 **4 ~ sth** (*BrE*) to INSURE sth, especially against sb's death 保险（尤指人寿险）：*What is the sum assured?* 人寿保险额是多少？ IDM SEE REST *v.*

as·sured AW /əˈʃʊəd; əˈʃɔːd; *NAmE* əˈʃʊrd/ *adj.* **1** (*also* ˌ**self-asˈsured**) confident in yourself and your abilities 自信的；有把握的：*He spoke in a calm, assured voice.* 他冷静自信地说。 **2** certain to happen 必将发生的；确定的 SYN **guaranteed**: *Success seemed assured.* 看来已必胜无疑。 **3 ~ of sth** (of a person 人) certain to get sth 肯定得到：*You are assured of a warm welcome at this hotel.* 你在这家旅馆肯定会受到热情欢迎。

as·sured·ly AW /əˈʃʊərədli; əˈʃɔːr-; *NAmE* əˈʃʊr-/ *adv.* (*formal*) certainly; definitely 肯定地；一定地

AST /ˌeɪ es ˈtiː/ *abbr.* ATLANTIC STANDARD TIME 大西洋标准时间

as·ta·tine /ˈæstətiːn/ *noun* [U] (*symb.* **At**) a chemical element. Astatine is a RADIOACTIVE element which is found in small amounts in nature, and is produced artificially for use in medicine. 砹（放射性化学元素）

aster /ˈæstə(r)/ *noun* a garden plant that has pink, purple, blue or white flowers with many long narrow PETALS 紫菀（园艺植物）

as·ter·isk /ˈæstərɪsk/ *noun* the symbol (*) placed next to a particular word or phrase to make people notice it or to show that more information is given in another place 星号（置于词语旁以引起注意或另有注释）：*I've placed an asterisk next to the tasks I want you to do first.* 我在要你优先处理的工作旁标了星号。 ▶ **as·ter·isk** *verb*：**~ sth** *I've asterisked the tasks I want you to do first.* 我在要你优先处理的工作旁标了星号。

astern /əˈstɜːn; *NAmE* əˈstɜːrn/ *adv.* (*specialist*) **1** in, at or towards the back part of a ship or boat 在船尾；向船尾 **2** if a ship or boat is moving **astern**, it is moving backwards （指船）向后

as·ter·oid /ˈæstərɔɪd/ *noun* any one of the many small planets that go around the sun 小行星 ➲ WORDFINDER NOTE AT UNIVERSE

asthma /ˈæsmə; *NAmE* ˈæzmə/ *noun* [U] a medical condition of the chest that makes breathing difficult 哮病；哮喘：*a severe asthma attack* 哮喘严重发作

asth·mat·ic /æsˈmætɪk; *NAmE* æzˈmætɪk/ *noun* a person who suffers from asthma 气喘患者；哮喘患者 ▶ **asth·mat·ic** *adj.*：*asthmatic patients* 哮喘患者 ◇ *an asthmatic attack* 哮喘发作

astig·ma·tism /əˈstɪɡmətɪzəm/ *noun* [U] (*medical* 医) a fault in the shape of a person's eye that prevents them from seeing clearly 散光

as·ton·ish /əˈstɒnɪʃ; *NAmE* əˈstɑːn-/ *verb* to surprise sb very much 使十分惊讶；使大为惊奇；使吃惊 SYN **amaze** ➲ SYNONYMS AT SURPRISE: **~ sb** *The news astonished everyone.* 这消息使大家十分惊讶。◇ *She astonished us by saying she was leaving.* 她说她要离开，令我们大为惊讶。◇ **it astonishes sb (that)**... *It astonishes me (that) he could be so thoughtless.* 我真没有料到他会如此轻率。

as·ton·ished /əˈstɒnɪʃt; *NAmE* əˈstɑːn-/ *adj.* very surprised 感到十分惊讶；吃惊 SYN **amazed**: *The helicopter landed before our astonished eyes.* 直升机就降落在我们眼前，令人十分惊讶。◇ **~ at/by sth/sb** *My parents looked astonished at my news.* 我的父母听到我的消息后显得十分惊讶。◇ **~ (that)**... *She seemed astonished (that) I had never been to Paris.* 我从未去过巴黎，这似乎使她大为惊奇。◇ **~ to find/hear/learn/see**... *He was astonished to learn he'd won the competition.* 他听说他比赛赢了，感到很惊讶。

as·ton·ish·ing /əˈstɒnɪʃɪŋ; *NAmE* əˈstɑːn-/ *adj.* very surprising; difficult to believe 令人十分惊讶的；使人大为惊奇的；难以置信的 SYN **amazing**: *She ran 100m in an astonishing 10.6 seconds.* 她以 10.6 秒的惊人速度跑完了 100 米。◇ *I find it absolutely astonishing that you didn't like it.* 你不喜欢它，我感到难以置信。 ▶ **as·ton·ish·ing·ly** *adv.*：*Jack took the news astonishingly well.* 杰克对这个消息表现得出奇地冷静。◇ *Astonishingly, a crowd of several thousands turned out to hear him.* 令人十分惊异的是有几千人来听他讲话。

as·ton·ish·ment /əˈstɒnɪʃmənt; *NAmE* əˈstɑːn-/ *noun* [U] a feeling of very great surprise 大为惊奇；惊诧 SYN **amazement**: ***To my utter astonishment,*** *she remembered my name.* 她竟记得我的名字，使我万分惊讶。◇ *He stared* ***in astonishment*** *at the stranger.* 他惊愕地盯着那陌生人。

as·tound /əˈstaʊnd/ *verb* **~ sb** to surprise or shock sb very much 使震惊；使大惊 SYN **astonish**: *His arrogance astounded her.* 他的傲慢使她震惊。◇ *She was astounded by his arrogance.* 他的傲慢使她震惊。 ➲ NOTE AT SURPRISE

as·tound·ed /əˈstaʊndɪd/ *adj.* very surprised or shocked by sth, because it seems very unlikely 感到震惊的；大吃一惊的 SYN **astonished**: *an astounded expression* 大吃一惊的表情 ◇ *How can you say that? I'm absolutely astounded.* 你怎么能说出那种话？我感到大为震惊。◇ **~ at/by sth** *She looked astounded at the news.* 她听到那消息时显得震惊。◇ **~ (that)**... *The doctors were astounded (that) he survived.* 医生们十分惊愕的是他竟活过来了。◇ **~ to find/hear/learn/see**... *I was astounded to see her appear from the house.* 我看见她从房子里出来，大吃一惊。

as·tound·ing /əˈstaʊndɪŋ/ *adj.* so surprising that it is difficult to believe 令人震惊的；使大吃一惊的 SYN **astonishing**: *There was an astounding 20% increase in sales.* 销售量惊人地增加了 20%。 ▶ **as·tound·ing·ly** *adv.*

as·tra·khan /ˌæstrəˈkæn; *NAmE* ˈæstrəkən/ *noun* [U] a type of black tightly-curled cloth made from the wool of a particular type of young sheep, used especially for making coats and hats; a type of cloth that is made to look like this 阿斯特拉罕羔羊毛织物；仿阿斯特拉罕羔羊毛织物

as·tral /ˈæstrəl/ *adj.* [only before noun] **1** (*specialist*) connected with the stars 星的：*astral navigation* 星际航行 **2** connected with the spiritual rather than the physical

A

world of existence 精神世界的：*the astral plane* 精神世界层面

astray /əˈstreɪ/ *adv.*

IDM **go aˈstray 1** to become lost; to be stolen 丢失；被盗：*Several letters went astray or were not delivered.* 有几封信丢失或未投递。◇ *We locked up our valuables so they would not go astray.* 我们把贵重物品锁了起来以免被盗。**2** to go in the wrong direction or to have the wrong result 走错方向；误入歧途：*Fortunately the gunman's shots went astray.* 幸好持枪歹徒把子弹打偏了。◇ *Jack's parents thought the other boys might* ***lead him astray*** (= make him do things that are wrong). 杰克的父母认为，其他的男孩可能会把他引入歧途。

astride /əˈstraɪd/ *prep., adv.*
▪ ***prep.*** with one leg on each side of sth 跨（或骑）在…上：*to sit* ***astride a horse/bike/chair*** 骑马 / 自行车；跨坐在椅子上 ◇ (*figurative*) *a town astride the river* 跨河的城镇
▪ ***adv.* 1** with legs or feet wide apart 叉开两腿 **2** with one leg on each side 跨着；骑着

astrin·gent /əˈstrɪndʒənt/ *adj., noun*
▪ ***adj.* 1** (*specialist*) (of a liquid or cream 液体或乳剂) able to make the skin feel less OILY or to stop the loss of blood from a cut（能使皮肤或伤口）收敛的 **2** (*formal*) critical in a severe or clever way 尖刻的；辛辣的：***astringent writers/comments*** 尖刻的作家 / 话 **3** (*formal*) (of a taste or smell 味道或气味) slightly bitter but fresh 微苦而清新的：*the astringent taste of lemon juice* 柠檬汁微苦却清新的味道 ▶ **astrin·gency** /-ənsi/ *noun* [U]
▪ ***noun*** a liquid or cream used in COSMETICS or medicine to make the skin less OILY or to stop the loss of blood from a cut（用于化妆品或药物中的）收敛剂，收敛药

astro- /ˈæstrəʊ; *NAmE* ˈæstroʊ/ *combining form* (in nouns, adjectives and adverbs 构成名词、形容词和副词) connected with the stars or outer space 星（的）；天体（的）；外层空间（的）；宇宙空间（的）：*astronaut* 宇航员 ◇ *astrophysics* 天体物理学

astro·labe /ˈæstrəleɪb/ *noun* (*astronomy* 天) a device used in the past for measuring the distances of stars, planets etc. and for calculating the position of a ship 星盘，等高仪（旧时用于测量天体距离或计算船只位置）

as·trol·oger /əˈstrɒlədʒə(r); *NAmE* əˈstrɑːl-/ *noun* a person who uses astrology to tell people about their character, about what might happen to them in the future, etc. 占星家

as·trol·ogy /əˈstrɒlədʒi; *NAmE* əˈstrɑːl-/ *noun* [U] the study of the positions of the stars and the movements of the planets in the belief that they influence human affairs 占星术；占星学 ▶ **astro·logic·al** /ˌæstrəˈlɒdʒɪkl; *NAmE* -ˈlɑːdʒ-/ *adj.*：*astrological influences* 占星术的影响

astro·naut /ˈæstrənɔːt/ *noun* a person whose job involves travelling and working in a SPACECRAFT 宇航员；航天员 ➲ WORDFINDER NOTE AT SPACE

as·tron·omer /əˈstrɒnəmə(r); *NAmE* əˈstrɑːn-/ *noun* a scientist who studies astronomy 天文学家

astro·nom·ic·al /ˌæstrəˈnɒmɪkl; *NAmE* -ˈnɑːm-/ *adj.* **1** connected with ASTRONOMY 天文学的；天文的：*astronomical observations* 天文观测 **2** (*also* **astro·nom·ic**) (*informal*) (of an amount, a price, etc. 数量、价格等) very large 极其巨大的：*the astronomical price of land for building* 建筑用地的惊人价格 ◇ *The figures are astronomical.* 这些都是天文数字。▶ **astro·nom·ic·al·ly** /-kli/ *adv.*：*Interest rates are astronomically high.* 利率极高。

astroˌnomical ˈunit *noun* (*abbr.* **AU**) (*astronomy* 天) a unit of measurement equal to 149.6 million kilometres, which is the distance from the centre of the earth to the sun 天文单位（即地球中心与太阳的距离，约合 1.496 亿公里）

as·tron·omy /əˈstrɒnəmi; *NAmE* əˈstrɑːn-/ *noun* [U] the scientific study of the sun, moon, stars, planets, etc. 天文学 ➲ WORDFINDER NOTE AT UNIVERSE

astro·phys·ics /ˌæstrəʊˈfɪzɪks; *NAmE* ˌæstroʊ-/ *noun* [U] the scientific study of the physical and chemical structure of the stars, planets, etc. 天体物理（学）▶ **astro·physi·cist** /-ˈfɪzɪsɪst/ *noun*

Astro·Turf™ /ˈæstrəʊtɜːf; *NAmE* ˈæstroʊtɜːrf/ *noun* [U] an artificial surface that looks like grass, for playing sports on 阿斯特罗人造草皮

ˈA student *noun* (*especially NAmE*) a student who gets or is likely to get the highest marks/grades in his/her work or exams 学业成绩得 A 者；优等生

as·tute /əˈstjuːt; *NAmE* əˈstuːt/ *adj.* very clever and quick at seeing what to do in a particular situation, especially how to get an advantage 精明的；狡猾的 SYN **shrewd**：***an astute businessman/politician/observer*** 精明的商人；狡猾的政客；敏锐的观察家 ◇ *It was an astute move to sell the shares then.* 那时出售股份是精明之举。▶ **as·tute·ly** *adv.* **as·tute·ness** *noun* [U]

asun·der /əˈsʌndə(r)/ *adv.* (*old-fashioned* or *literary*) into pieces; apart 碎；散：*families* ***rent/torn asunder*** *by the revolution* 这场革命所拆散的家庭

asy·lee /əsaɪˈliː/ *noun* a person who has asked for or has been given protection by a foreign government after leaving their own country, usually because they were in danger for political reasons（政治）避难者：*a political asylee* 政治避难者

asy·lum /əˈsaɪləm/ *noun* **1** (*also formal* **poˌlitical aˈsylum**) [U] protection that a government gives to people who have left their own country, usually because they were in danger for political reasons（政治）庇护，避难：***to seek/apply for/be granted asylum*** 寻求 / 申请 / 获准政治避难 ◇ *There was a nationwide debate on whether the asylum laws should be changed.* 对是否应该修改政治避难法展开了一场全国性的大辩论。**2** [C] (*old use*) a hospital where people who were mentally ill could be cared for, often for a long time 精神病院

aˈsylum seeker *noun* a person who has been forced to leave their own country because they are in danger and who arrives in another country asking to be allowed to stay there 寻求避难者；寻求庇护的移民 ➲ COLLOCATIONS AT RACE

asym·met·ric /ˌeɪsɪˈmetrɪk/ (*also* **asym·met·ric·al** /ˌeɪsɪˈmetrɪkl/) *adj.* **1** having two sides or parts that are not the same in size or shape 不对称的：*Most people's faces are asymmetric.* 大多数人的脸不对称。OPP **symmetrical 2** (*specialist*) not equal, for example in the way each side or part behaves 不对等的：*Linguists are studying the asymmetric use of Creole by parents and children* (= parents use one language and children reply in another). 语言学家正在研究父母和孩子使用克里奥尔混合语时的不对等现象（即父母使用一种语言而孩子用另一种语言回答）。▶ **asym·met·ric·al·ly** /-ɪkli/ *adv.* **asym·met·ry** /ˌeɪˈsɪmətri/ *noun* [C, U]

asymˌmetric ˈbars (*BrE*) (*NAmE* **unˌeven ˈbars**) *noun* [pl.] two bars on posts of different heights that are used by women for doing GYMNASTIC exercises on 高低杠（女子体操器械）

asymp·tom·at·ic /ˌeɪsɪmptəˈmætɪk/ *adj.* (*medical* 医) (of a person or illness 人或疾病) having no SYMPTOMS 无症状的

asyn·chron·ous /eɪˈsɪŋkrənəs/ *adj.* (*formal*) (of two or more objects or events 两个或多个物体或事情) not existing or happening at the same time 不同时存在（或发生）的；非共时的 ▶ **asyn·chron·ous·ly** *adv.*

at /ət; *strong form* æt/ *prep.* **1** used to say where sth/sb is or where sth happens 在（某处）：*at the corner of the street* 在街角 ◇ *We changed at Crewe.* 我们在克鲁换的车。◇ *They arrived late at the airport.* 他们晚到了机场。◇ *At the roundabout take the third exit.* 在环岛处走第三个出口。◇ *I'll be at home all morning.* 我一上午都在家。◇ *She's* *at Tom's* (= at Tom's house). 她在汤姆家中。◇ *I met her at the hospital.* 我在医院遇见了她。◇ *How many people were there at the concert?* 音乐会上有多少人？ **2** used to say where sb works or studies 在（表示学习或工作地点）： *He's been at the bank longer than anyone else.* 他在银行工作的时间比任何人都长。◇ *She's at Yale* (= Yale University). 她在耶鲁大学。 **3** used to say when sth happens 在（某时间或时刻）： *We left at 2 o'clock.* 我们在两点钟离开的。◇ *at the end of the week* 在周末 ◇ *We woke at dawn.* 我们在黎明醒来。◇ *I didn't know at the time of writing* (= when I wrote). 我写的时候并不知道。◇ *At night you can see the stars.* 夜晚可以看见星星。◇ (*BrE*) *What are you doing at the weekend?* 你打算周末干什么？ **4** used to state the age at which sb does sth 在…岁时： *She got married at 25.* 她 25 岁结婚。◇ *He left school at the age of 16.* 他 16 岁中学毕业。 **5** in the direction of or towards sb/sth 向；朝： *What are you looking at?* 你在看什么？◇ *He pointed a gun at her.* 他把枪口对着她。◇ *Somebody threw paint at the prime minister.* 有人朝首相泼油漆。 **6** used after a verb to show that sb tries to do sth, or partly does sth, but does not succeed or complete it（用于动词后，涉及未做成或未做完的事）： *He clutched wildly at the rope as he fell.* 他坠落时拼命想抓住绳子。◇ *She nibbled at a sandwich* (= ate only small bits of it). 她一小口一小口地吃三明治。 **7** used to state the distance away from sth 在…远；从相隔…远的地方： *I held it at arm's length.* 我伸直胳膊拿着它。◇ *Can you read a car number plate at fifty metres?* 在五十米远处你能看清汽车牌吗？ **8** used to show the situation sb/sth is in, what sb is doing or what is happening 处于…状态： *The country is now at war.* 这个国家正在打仗。◇ *I felt at a disadvantage.* 我觉得处于不利地位。◇ *I think Mr Harris is at lunch.* 我想哈里斯先生正在吃午饭。 **9** used to show a rate, speed, etc.（用于速度、比率等）以，达： *He was driving at 70 mph.* 他以每小时 70 英里的速度驾车行驶。◇ *The noise came at two-minute intervals* (= once every two minutes). 每两分钟传来一次响声。◇ *Prices start at $1 000.* 起价 1 000 美元。 **10** **~ sb's/sth's best/worst, etc.** used to say that sb/sth is as good, bad, etc. as they can be 处于最佳（或最差等）状态；在全盛（或谷底等）时期： *This was Murray at his best.* 这是穆雷的最佳表现。◇ *The garden's at its most beautiful in June.* 六月的花园最美丽。 **11** used with adjectives to show how well sb does sth（与形容词连用，表示能力）在…方面： *I'm* ***good at*** *French.* 我的法语很好。◇ *She's hopeless at managing people.* 她对人事管理一窍不通。 **12** used with adjectives to show the cause of sth（与形容词连用）因为，由于，对…： *They were impatient at the delay.* 他们对拖延不耐烦了。◇ *She was delighted at the result.* 她对这个结果感到高兴。 **13** (*formal*) in response to sth 应…（而）；响应；回答： *They attended the dinner at the chairman's invitation.* 他们应董事长之邀出席了宴会。 **14** (*NAmE*) used when giving a telephone number （提供电话号码时用）： *You can reach me at 637-2335, extension 354.* 你可以打 637-2335 这个电话号码，转分机 354 与我联系。 **15** (*computing* 计) the symbol (@) used in email addresses （用于电子邮箱地址中的符号 @）

IDM **at that** used when you are giving an extra piece of information （提供额外信息时）而且还： *He managed to buy a car after all—and a nice one at that.* 他终于设法买了一辆小轿车，而且还挺不错的。 **be 'at it again** to be doing sth, especially sth bad 正在做某事（尤指坏事）： *Look at all that graffiti—those kids have been at it again.* 瞧，那么多涂鸦，又是那些孩子干的好事。 **ˌwhere it's 'at** (*informal*) a place or an activity that is very popular or fashionable 盛大活动（场合）；流行活动（地方）： *Judging by the crowds waiting to get in, this seems to be where it's at.* 从等待入场的人群来看，这好像是个盛大活动。

at·av·is·tic /ˌætəˈvɪstɪk/ *adj.* (*formal*) related to the attitudes and behaviour of the first humans 返祖性的： *an* ***atavistic urge/instinct/fear*** 返祖倾向 / 本能；原始畏惧

ataxia /əˈtæksiə/ (*also* **ataxy** /əˈtæksi/) *noun* [U] (*medical* 医) the loss of full control of the body's movements 共济失调，运动失调（表现为动作不稳、不协调） ▶ **ataxic** *adj.*

ate PAST TENSE OF EAT

-ate *suffix* **1** (in adjectives 构成形容词) full of or having the quality of 充满…的；有…性质的： *passionate* 充满热情的 ◇ *Italianate* 意大利风格的 **2** (in verbs 构成动词) to give the thing or quality mentioned to 赋予某物；给予…性质： *hyphenate* 用连字符连接 ◇ *activate* 使活动 **3** (in nouns 构成名词) the status or function of （表示地位或职能）： *a doctorate* 博士学位 **4** (in nouns 构成名词) a group with the status or function of（表示有地位或职能的群体）： *the electorate* 全体选民 **5** (*chemistry* 化) (in nouns 构成名词) a salt formed by the action of a particular acid（酸作用形成的）盐： *sulphate* 硫酸盐

'A-team *noun* [usually sing.] **1** the best sports team in a school, club, etc.（学校等的）最佳运动队，甲队 **2** a group of the best workers, soldiers, etc. （工人、士兵等的）精英小组

atel·ier /əˈtelieɪ; *NAmE* ˌætlˈjeɪ/ *noun* a room or building in which an artist works （艺术家的）工作室，制作室 **SYN** studio

atem·poral /ˌeɪˈtempərəl/ *adj.* (*formal*) existing or considered without relation to time 非时间的；不受时间影响的

athe·ism /ˈeɪθiɪzəm/ *noun* [U] the belief that God does not exist 无神论 **OPP** **theism** ▶ **athe·is·tic** /ˌeɪθiˈɪstɪk/ *adj.*

athe·ist /ˈeɪθiɪst/ *noun* a person who believes that God does not exist 无神论者 ➲ COMPARE AGNOSTIC *n.*

ath·lete /ˈæθliːt/ *noun* **1** a person who competes in sports 运动员： *Olympic athletes* 奥运会运动员 **2** (*BrE*) a person who competes in sports such as running and jumping 田径运动员 **3** a person who is good at sports and physical exercise 擅长运动的人；健儿： *She is a natural athlete.* 她是个天生的运动健将。 ➲ WORDFINDER NOTE AT SPORT

ˌathlete's 'foot *noun* [U] an infectious skin disease that affects the feet, especially between the toes 脚癣

ath·let·ic /æθˈletɪk/ *adj.* **1** physically strong, fit and active 健壮的： *an* ***athletic figure/build*** 健壮的体形 / 体格 ◇ *a tall, slim athletic girl* 修长健美的姑娘 **2** [only before noun] (*BrE*) connected with sports such as running, jumping and throwing (= athletics) 体育运动的；田径运动的： *an* ***athletic club/coach*** 运动员俱乐部 / 教练 ▶ **ath·let·ical·ly** /-ɪkli/ *adv.* **ath·leti·cism** /æθˈletɪsɪzəm/ *noun* [U]: *She moved with great athleticism about the court.* 她在球场上矫健地奔跑活动。

ath·let·ics /æθˈletɪks/ *noun* [U] **1** (*BrE*) (*NAmE* **ˌtrack and 'field**) sports such as running and jumping that people compete in 田径运动 ➲ VISUAL VOCAB PAGE V50 **2** (*NAmE*) any sports that people compete in 体育运动： *students involved in all forms of college athletics* 参加各种大学体育运动的学生 ➲ MORE LIKE THIS 29, page R28

ath'letic shoe *noun* (*NAmE*) = TENNIS SHOE

athˌletic sup'porter *noun* (*especially NAmE*) = JOCKSTRAP

at-'home *noun, adj.*

■ ***noun*** (*old-fashioned*) a party in sb's home 家中聚会： *We're having an at-home—can you come?* 我们要在家中聚会，你能来吗？

■ ***adj.* ˌat-'home** [only before noun] **1** done or taking place at home 在家里进行（或发生）的： *an at-home job* 一份在家里做的工作 **2** (of a parent 父亲或母亲) staying at home rather than going out to work 在家的；不外出工作的： *at-home dads* 家庭全职爸爸

-athon /əθən; *NAmE* əθɑːn/ *suffix* (in nouns 构成名词) an event in which a particular activity is done for a very long time, especially one organized to raise money for charity 持续时间很长的活动（尤指为慈善事业募捐）： *a swimathon* 马拉松式游泳

athwart /əˈθwɔːt; *NAmE* əˈθwɔːrt/ *prep.* (*literary* or *formal*) **1** across; from one side to the other 横跨于： *They put a table athwart the doorway.* 他们把桌子横放在门口。 **2** not

agreeing with; opposite to 与…不一致；与…相反： *His statement ran athwart what was previously said.* 他讲的话与先前所说的相抵触。

-ation ➲ -ION

atish·oo /əˈtɪʃuː/ (*BrE*) (*also* **ah·choo** *NAmE, BrE*) *exclamation* the word for the sound people make when they SNEEZE 阿嚏（指喷嚏声） ➲ MORE LIKE THIS 2, page R25

-ative *suffix* (in adjectives 构成形容词) doing or tending to do sth 做…的；有…倾向的： *illustrative* 解说性的 ◇ *talkative* 爱说话的 ▸ **-atively** *suffix* (in adverbs 构成副词)： *creatively* 有创造性地

At,lantic 'Daylight Time *noun* [U] (*abbr.* **ADT**) the time used in summer in an area that includes the east of Canada, Puerto Rico and the Virgin Islands, that is three hours behind UTC 大西洋夏令时间（加拿大东部、波多黎各、美属维尔京群岛的夏季时间，比协调世界时晚三个小时）

At,lantic 'Standard Time *noun* [U] (*abbr.* **AST**) (*also* **At'lantic time**) the time used in winter in an area that includes the east of Canada, Puerto Rico and the Virgin Islands, that is four hours behind UTC 大西洋标准时间（加拿大东部、波多黎各、美属维尔京群岛的冬季时间，比协调世界时晚四个小时）

At·lan·tis /ætˈlæntɪs/ *noun* [U] (in stories 传说) an island full of beauty and wealth, that was said to have been covered by the sea and lost. There are many stories about people's attempts to find it. 亚特兰蒂斯，大西岛（一座美丽富饶的海岛，据说已沉入海底消失）

atlas /ˈætləs/ *noun* a book of maps 地图册；地图集： *a world atlas* 世界地图册 ◇ *a road atlas of Europe* 欧洲交通地图册

ATM /ˌeɪ tiː ˈem/ *noun* the abbreviation for 'automated teller machine' 自动柜员机，自动取款机（全写为 automated teller machine） ➲ CASH MACHINE

,AT'M card (*US*) (*BrE* **'cash card**) *noun* a plastic card used to get money from a CASH MACHINE (= a machine in or outside a bank) 现金卡；自动取款卡 ➲ COMPARE CREDIT CARD, DEBIT CARD

at·mos·phere 🔑 /ˈætməsfɪə(r); *NAmE* -fɪr/ *noun* **1** 🔑 **the atmosphere** [sing.] the mixture of gases that surrounds the earth （围绕地球的）大气，大气圈，大气层： *the upper atmosphere* 高层大气 ◇ *pollution of the atmosphere* 大气污染 **2** 🔑 [C] a mixture of gases that surrounds another planet or a star （围绕其他天体的）气体： *Saturn's atmosphere* 土星的大气 **3** 🔑 [C] the air in a room or in a confined space; the air around a place （房间、封闭空间或某处的）空气： *a smoky/stuffy atmosphere* 烟雾弥漫的 / 闷热的空气 ◇ *These plants love warm, humid atmospheres.* 这些植物喜欢温暖潮湿的空气。 **4** 🔑 [C, sing., U] the feeling or mood that you have in a particular place or situation; a feeling between two people or in a group of people 气氛；氛围： *a party atmosphere* 聚会的气氛 ◇ *The hotel offers a friendly atmosphere and personal service.* 这家旅馆提供个人服务，使客人感到宾至如归。 ◇ *Use music and lighting to create a romantic atmosphere.* 用音乐和照明创造一种浪漫的气氛。 ◇ *There was an atmosphere of mutual trust between them.* 他们之间以前有一种相互信任的气氛。 ◇ *The children grew up in an atmosphere of violence and insecurity.* 这些孩子在暴力和无安全感的环境中长大。 ◇ *The old house is full of atmosphere* (= it's very interesting). 这座老房子情趣盎然。 **IDM** SEE HEAVY *adj.*

at·mos·pher·ic /ˌætməsˈferɪk/ *adj.* **1** [only before noun] related to the earth's atmosphere 大气的；大气层的： ***atmospheric pollution/conditions/pressure*** 大气污染 / 状况 / 压力 **2** creating an exciting or emotional mood 令人激动的；使人动感情的： *atmospheric music* 有感染力的音乐

at·mos·pher·ics /ˌætməsˈferɪks; *NAmE also* -ˈfɪr-/ *noun* [pl.] **1** qualities in sth that create a particular atmosphere 气氛特征 **2** noises that sometimes interrupt a radio broadcast 天电；大气噪声

atoll /ˈætɒl; *NAmE* ˈætɔːl; -tɑːl/ *noun* an island made of CORAL and shaped like a ring with a lake of sea water (called a LAGOON) in the middle 环礁

atom 🔑 /ˈætəm/ *noun* the smallest PARTICLE (1) of a chemical element that can exist 原子： *the splitting of the atom* 原子的分裂 ◇ *Two atoms of hydrogen combine with one atom of oxygen to form a molecule of water.* 两个氢原子和一个氧原子结合组成一个水分子。 ➲ WORDFINDER NOTE AT PHYSICS

> **WORDFINDER** 联想词： antiparticle, electron, ion, neutron, nucleus, particle, positron, proton, valency

'atom bomb (*also* **'A-bomb**) *noun* a bomb that explodes using the energy that is produced when an atom or atoms are split 原子弹

atom·ic /əˈtɒmɪk; *NAmE* əˈtɑːmɪk/ *adj.* [usually before noun] **1** connected with atoms or an atom 原子的；与原子有关的： *atomic structure* 原子结构 **2** related to the energy that is produced when atoms are split; related to weapons that use this energy 原子能的；原子武器的： ***atomic energy/power*** 原子能 / 动力 ◇ *the atomic bomb* 原子弹

a,tomic 'clock *noun* an extremely accurate clock that uses the movement of atoms or MOLECULES to measure time 原子钟（利用原子或分子运动计时，精确度极高）

atom·ic·ity /ˌætəmˈɪsɪti/ *noun* (*chemistry* 化) the number of atoms in one MOLECULE of a substance 化合价

a,tomic 'mass *noun* (*chemistry* 化) = RELATIVE ATOMIC MASS

a,tomic 'number *noun* (*chemistry* 化) the number of PROTONS in the NUCLEUS (= centre) of an atom, which is characteristic of a chemical element. Elements are placed in the PERIODIC TABLE according to their atomic numbers. 原子序数（指原子在元素周期表中的序号）

a,tomic 'theory *noun* (*chemistry* 化, *physics* 物) the theory that all elements are made up of small PARTICLES called atoms which are made up of a central NUCLEUS surrounded by moving ELECTRONS 原子论

a,tomic 'weight *noun* (*chemistry* 化) = RELATIVE ATOMIC MASS

atom·ism /ˈætəmɪzəm/ *noun* [U] (*specialist*) the idea of analysing sth by separating it into its different parts 原子论（借助各个组成部分来分析整体） ➲ COMPARE HOLISM (1) ▸ **atom·is·tic** /ˌætəˈmɪstɪk/ *adj.*

atom·ize (*BrE also* **-ise**) /ˈætəmaɪz/ *verb* ~ **sth** to reduce sth to atoms or very small pieces 使分裂成原子；使粉碎；使成微粒；使雾化

atom·izer (*BrE also* **-iser**) /ˈætəmaɪzə(r)/ *noun* a container that forces a liquid such as water or paint out as a very fine spray 雾化器；喷雾器

atonal /eɪˈtəʊnl; *NAmE* eɪˈtoʊnl/ *adj.* (of a piece of music 乐曲) not written in any particular KEY 无调的 **OPP** **tonal** ▸ **aton·al·ity** /ˌeɪtəʊˈnæləti; *NAmE* ˌeɪtoʊˈn-/ *noun* [U]

atone /əˈtəʊn; *NAmE* əˈtoʊn/ *verb* [I] ~ (**for sth**) (*formal*) to act in a way that shows you are sorry for doing sth wrong in the past 赎（罪）；弥补（过错） **SYN** **make amends**： *to atone for a crime* 赎罪 ▸ **atone·ment** *noun* [U]： *to make atonement for his sins* 赎他的罪过 ◇ *Yom Kippur, the Jewish day of atonement* 犹太教的赎罪日

atop /əˈtɒp; *NAmE* əˈtɑːp/ *prep.* (*especially NAmE*) (*old-fashioned or literary* in *BrE* 英式英语中为老式用法或文学用语) on top of; at the top of 在…顶上： *a flag high atop a pole* 高挂在旗杆顶端的旗子 ◇ *a scoop of ice cream atop a slice of apple pie* 一片苹果馅饼上面的一勺冰淇淋

atopic /eɪˈtɒpɪk; *NAmE* -ˈtɑːp-/ *adj.* (*medical* 医) relating to a form of ALLERGY where there is a reaction in a part of the body that does not have direct contact with the thing causing the ALLERGY 特应性的，异位的（指过敏部位并非直接接触过敏原）

-ator *suffix* (in nouns 构成名词) a person or thing that does sth 做…的人（或事物）: *creator* 创造者 ◇ *percolator* 咖啡渗滤器

A to Z /ˌeɪ tə ˈzed; *NAmE* ˌeɪ tə ˈziː/ *noun* [sing.] **1** (*BrE*) a book containing street maps of all the areas of a large city（标明各街道位置的）城市地图册 **2** a book containing all the information you need about a subject or place 指南大全: *an A to Z of needlework* 女红大全

ATP /ˌeɪ tiː ˈpiː/ *abbr.* (*BrE*) the abbreviation for 'automatic train protection' (a system for automatically stopping a train if the driver does not stop or go slower when a signal tells him/her to) 列车自动保护系统（全写为 automatic train protection）

ˌat-ˈrisk *adj.* [only before noun] (of a person or group 人或群体) in danger of being attacked or hurt, especially in their own home（尤指居家时）处于危险中的，可能遭受伤害的: *Social services keep lists of* ***at-risk children.*** 社工组织保留有在家里可能遭受伤害的孩子名单。

at·rium /ˈeɪtriəm/ *noun* (*pl.* **atria** /ˈeɪtriə/) **1** a large high space, usually with a glass roof, in the centre of a modern building（现代建筑物中央通常带有玻璃屋顶的）中庭，中厅 **2** an open space in the centre of an ancient Roman VILLA (= a large house)（古罗马大宅的）天井 **3** (*anatomy* 解) either of the two upper spaces in the heart that are used in the first stage of sending the blood around the body 心房 **SYN** **auricle**

atro·cious /əˈtrəʊʃəs; *NAmE* əˈtroʊ-/ *adj.* **1** very bad or unpleasant 糟透的；十分讨厌的 **SYN** **terrible**: *She speaks French with an atrocious accent.* 她讲的法语带有很难听的口音。◇ *Isn't the weather atrocious?* 天气不是糟透了吗？ **2** very cruel and shocking 残暴的；残忍的；凶恶的: *atrocious acts of brutality* 残暴的兽行 ▶ **atro·cious·ly** *adv.*

atro·city /əˈtrɒsəti; *NAmE* əˈtrɑːs-/ *noun* [C, usually pl., U] (*pl.* **-ies**) a cruel and violent act, especially in a war（尤指战争中的）残暴行为

at·ro·phy /ˈætrəfi/ *noun, verb*

■ ***noun*** [U] (*medical* 医) the condition of losing flesh, muscle, strength, etc. in a part of the body because it does not have enough blood 萎缩: (*figurative, formal*) *The cultural life of the country will sink into atrophy unless more writers and artists emerge.* 如果没有更多的作家和艺术家出现，这个国家的文化生活将衰退。

■ ***verb*** (**at·ro·phies**, **at·ro·phy·ing**, **at·ro·phied**, **at·ro·phied**) [I] if a part of the body **atrophies**, it becomes weak because it is not used or because it does not have enough blood 萎缩；衰退: *patients whose muscles have atrophied* 肌萎缩症患者 ◇ (*figurative*) *Memory can atrophy through lack of use.* 记忆力不常使用就会衰退。 ▶ **at·ro·phied** *adj.*: *atrophied muscles* 萎缩的肌肉 ◇ *atrophied religious values* 淡化的宗教价值观念

at·ta·boy /ˈætəbɔɪ/ *exclamation* (*informal, especially NAmE*) used when you want to encourage sb or show your admiration of them, especially a boy or man（对男性表示鼓励或钦佩）好样的 ➲ SEE ALSO ATTAGIRL

at·tach 🔑 **AW** /əˈtætʃ/ *verb* **1** 🔑 [T] to fasten or join one thing to another 把…固定，把…附（在…上）: **~ sth** *I attach a copy of my notes for your information.* 我附上笔记一份供你参考。◇ *I attach a copy of the spreadsheet* (= send it with an email). 我随电子邮件附上电子表格一份。◇ **~ sth to sth** *Attach the coupon to the front of your letter.* 把优惠券附在信的正面。◇ (*figurative*) *They have attached a number of conditions to the agreement* (= said that the conditions must be part of the agreement). 他们在协议上附加了一些条件。 ➲ COMPARE DETACH **2** 🔑 [T] **~ importance, significance, value, weight, etc. (to sth)** to believe that sth is important or worth thinking about 认为有重要性（或意义、价值、分量等）；重视: *I attach great importance to this research.* 我认为这项研究十分重要。 **3** [T] **~ yourself to sb** to join sb for a time, sometimes when you are not welcome or have not been invited（有时不受欢迎或未受邀请而）参加，和…在一起，缠着: *He attached himself to me at the party and I couldn't get rid of him.* 在聚会上他老是缠着我，我简直无法摆脱他。 **4** [I, T] (*formal*) to be connected with sb/sth; to connect sth to sth（使）与…有联系；与…有关联: **~ to sb/sth** *No one is suggesting that any health risks attach to this product.* 没有人指出这个产品可能会危害健康。◇ *No blame attaches to you.* 你一点责任也没有。◇ **~ sth to sb/sth** *This does not attach any blame to you.* 这事你一点责任也没有。

at·taché /əˈtæʃeɪ; *NAmE* ˌætəˈʃeɪ/ *noun* a person who works at an EMBASSY, usually with a special responsibility for a particular area of activity（使馆的）专员，随员: *a cultural attaché* 文化专员

atˈtaché case *noun* a small hard flat case used for carrying business documents 公文包 ➲ VISUAL VOCAB PAGE V69 ➲ COMPARE BRIEFCASE

at·tached 🔑 **AW** /əˈtætʃt/ *adj.* **1** 🔑 **~ (to sb/sth)** full of affection for sb/sth 依恋；爱慕: *I've never seen two people so attached to each other.* 我从未见过两个人如此形影不离。◇ *We've grown very attached to this house.* 我们变得非常喜欢这座房子。 ➲ COMPARE UNATTACHED **2** 🔑 [not before noun] **~ to sth** working for or forming part of an organization 附属于；为…工作: *The research unit is attached to the university.* 这个研究单位附属于大学。 **3** 🔑 **~ (to sth)** joined to sth 所附的: *Please complete the attached application form.* 请填写所附申请表。

at·tach·ment **AW** /əˈtætʃmənt/ *noun* **1** [C, U] a strong feeling of affection for sb/sth 依恋；爱慕: *a child's strong attachment to its parents* 孩子对父母的强烈依恋 **2** [C, U] belief in and support for an idea or a set of values 信念；信仰；忠诚；拥护: *the popular attachment to democratic government* 对民主政府的普遍拥护 **3** [C] a tool that you can fix onto a machine, to make it do another job（机器的）附件，附加装置，附属物: *an electric drill with a range of different attachments* 配有各种附件的电钻 **4** [U, C] the act of joining one thing to another; a thing that joins two things together 连接；连接物: *All cars built since 1981 have points for the attachment of safety restraints.* 自 1981 年起生产的轿车都有安全保护装置的接口。◇ *They discussed the attachment of new conditions to the peace plans.* 他们讨论把新条件加入到和平计划中去。◇ *They had to check the strength of the seat attachments to the floor of the plane.* 他们需要检查座椅与飞机舱面连接部位的强度。 **5** [U, C] (*BrE*) a short time spent working with an organization such as a hospital, school or part of the armed forces 暂时隶属于（某医院、学校、部队等）；短期在…工作: *She's* ***on attachment*** *to the local hospital.* 她暂时在当地医院工作。◇ *a 4-month training attachment* 为期 4 个月的培训 **6** [C] (*computing* 计) a document that you send to sb using email（用电子邮件发送的）附件 ➲ WORDFINDER NOTE AT MESSAGE ➲ COLLOCATIONS AT EMAIL

at·tack 🔑 /əˈtæk/ *noun, verb*

■ ***noun***

• **VIOLENCE** 暴力 **1** 🔑 [C, U] **~ (on sb)** an act of using violence to try to hurt or kill sb 袭击；攻击: *a series of racist attacks* 一连串的种族袭击行为

• **IN WAR** 战争 **2** 🔑 [C, U] **~ (on sb/sth)** an act of trying to kill or injure the enemy in war, using weapons such as guns and bombs（在战争中使用武器的）进攻，攻击: *to* ***launch/make/mount an attack*** 发起 / 进行攻击；发动进攻 ◇ *The patrol came* ***under attack*** *from all sides.* 巡逻队受到四面八方的攻击。 ➲ COLLOCATIONS AT WAR ➲ SEE ALSO COUNTER-ATTACK *n.*

> **WORDFINDER** 联想词: alert, assassinate, campaign, execute, extremist, hijack, hostage, kidnap, terrorism

• **CRITICISM** 批评 **3** 🔑 [C, U] **~ (on sb/sth)** strong criticism of sb/sth in speech or in writing（口头或书面的）抨击，非难: *a scathing attack on the government's policies* 对政府政策的猛烈抨击 ◇ *The school has come* ***under attack*** *for failing to encourage bright pupils.* 这所学校因未能鼓励聪

明学生而受到非难。

- **ACTION TO STOP STH** 制止 **4** [C] ~ **(on sth)** an action that you take to try to stop or change sth that you feel is bad 抑制；打击；处理： *to launch* ***an all-out attack on*** *poverty/unemployment* 全力抑制贫穷 / 失业
- **OF ILLNESS** 疾病 **5** [C] a sudden, short period of illness, usually severe, especially an illness that you have often（尤指常发疾病的）发作，侵袭： *to suffer an asthma attack* 哮喘发作 ◇ *an acute attack of food poisoning* 急性食物中毒 ◇ *a panic attack* 一阵恐慌 ◇ (*figurative*) *an attack of the giggles* 一阵咯咯傻笑 ➲ SEE ALSO HEART ATTACK
- **OF EMOTION** 情感 **6** [C] a sudden period of feeling an emotion such as fear（情感的）一阵突发： *an attack of nerves* 突然紧张不安
- **DAMAGE** 损害 **7** [U, C] the action of sth such as an insect, or a disease, that causes damage to sth/sb（病虫等的）损害，伤害： *The roof timbers were affected by rot and insect attack.* 屋顶的木料已经腐朽并遭虫蛀。
- **IN SPORT** 体育运动 **8** [sing.] (*BrE*) (*NAmE* **of·fense**) the players in a team whose job is to try to score goals or points 进攻队员： *Germany's attack has been weakened by the loss of some key players through injury.* 德国队几名主力队员因伤不能上场，削弱了进攻力量。 ➲ COMPARE DEFENCE (7) **9** [C, U] the actions that players take to try to score a goal or win the game （队员等的）进攻： *a sustained attack on the Arsenal goal* 向阿森纳队球门的持续进攻

■ ***verb***

- **USE VIOLENCE** 使用暴力 **1** [I, T, often passive] to use violence to try to hurt or kill sb 袭击；攻击： *Most dogs will not attack unless provoked.* 大多数的狗受到挑衅才会攻击。 ◇ **~ sb** *A woman was attacked and robbed by a gang of youths.* 一名妇女遭到一伙年轻人袭击和抢劫。 ◇ **~ sb with sth** *The man attacked him with a knife.* 那个男人持刀向他行凶。
- **IN WAR** 战争 **2** [I, T] to use weapons, such as guns and bombs against an enemy in a war, etc.（在战争等中使用武器）进攻，攻击： *The guerrillas attack at night.* 游击队在夜间发动袭击。 ◇ **~ sb/sth** *At dawn the army attacked the town.* 军队在拂晓时向这座城镇发动攻击。 ➲ WORDFINDER NOTE AT CONFLICT
- **CRITICIZE** 批评 **3** [T] to criticize sb/sth severely 抨击；非难： **~ sb/sth** *a newspaper article attacking the England football manager* 报纸上的一篇抨击英格兰足球队主教练的文章 ◇ **~ sb/sth for sth/for doing sth** *She has been attacked for ignoring her own party members.* 她因漠视本党党员而受到非难。
- **DAMAGE** 损害 **4** [T] **~ sth** to have a harmful effect on sth 侵袭；损害： *a disease that attacks the brain* 侵袭大脑的疾病 ◇ *The vines were attacked by mildew.* 葡萄藤受到了霉菌的侵害。
- **DO STH WITH ENERGY** 奋力做 **5** [T] **~ sth** to deal with sth with a lot of energy and determination 奋力处理；全力对付： *Let's attack one problem at a time.* 咱们每次全力处理一个问题。
- **IN SPORT** 体育运动 **6** [I] to go forward in a game in order to try to score goals or points 进攻 ➲ COMPARE DEFEND (3): *Spain attacked more in the second half and deserved a goal.* 西班牙队在下半场加强攻势，攻进了一球。

at'tack dog *noun* **1** a dog that has been trained to attack people or other animals （经过训练的）攻击犬 **2** (*disapproving*) a person who often makes strong personal attacks on other people in public 言辞激烈的人身攻击者；疯狗： *His image has changed from statesman to attack dog.* 他的形象从政治家变成了见人就咬的恶狗。

at·tack·er /əˈtækə(r)/ *noun* a person who attacks sb 攻击者；袭击者；进攻者： *She didn't really see her attacker.* 她没有看清楚袭击她的人。

at·ta·girl /ˈætəgɜːl; *NAmE* -gɜːrl/ *exclamation* (*informal, especially NAmE*) used when you want to encourage a girl or woman, or show your admiration of them（对女性表示鼓励或钦佩）好样的 ➲ SEE ALSO ATTABOY

at·tain AW /əˈteɪn/ *verb* (*formal*) **1 ~ sth** to succeed in getting sth, usually after a lot of effort （通常经过努力）获得，得到： *Most of our students attained five 'A' grades in their exams.* 我们多数学生的考试成绩是五个优。 **2 ~ sth** to reach a particular age, level or condition 达到（某年龄、水平、状况）： *The cheetah can attain speeds of up to 97 kph.* 猎豹的奔跑速度可达 97 千米每小时。

at·tain·able AW /əˈteɪnəbl/ *adj.* that you can achieve 可达到的；可获得的： ***attainable goals/objectives/targets*** 可达到的目标 ◇ *This standard is easily attainable by most students.* 这个标准大多数学生都容易达到。 OPP **unattainable**

at·tain·ment AW /əˈteɪnmənt/ *noun* (*formal*) **1** [C, usually pl.] (*BrE*) something that you achieved 成就；造诣： *a young woman of impressive educational attainments* 一位学业成就斐然的年轻女子 **2** [U] success in achieving sth 达到；获得： *The attainment of his ambitions was still a dream.* 他要实现的抱负仍然是一个梦想。 ◇ *attainment targets* (= for example in education) 学业成绩目标

attar /ˈætə(r)/ (*also* **otto**) *noun* [U] an ESSENTIAL OIL usually made from ROSE PETALS（从玫瑰花瓣等中提取的）精油；玫瑰油

at·tempt /əˈtempt/ *noun, verb*

■ ***noun*** **1** [C, U] an act of trying to do sth, especially sth difficult, often with no success 企图；试图；尝试： *I passed my driving test* ***at the first attempt.*** 我考汽车驾驶执照时一次就通过了。 ◇ **~ to do sth** *Two factories were closed* ***in an attempt*** *to cut costs.* 为削减费用，关闭了两家工厂。 ◇ *They* ***made no attempt*** *to escape.* 他们没有企图逃跑。 ◇ **~ at sth/at doing sth** *The couple made an unsuccessful attempt at a compromise.* 这对夫妇试图和解但未成功。 **2** [C] ~ **(on sb/sb's life)** an act of trying to kill sb 杀人企图： *Someone has* ***made an attempt on*** *the President's* ***life.*** 有人企图刺杀总统。 **3** [C] ~ **(on sth)** an effort to do better than sth, such as a very good performance in sport（为超越某事物的）尝试，努力： *his attempt on the world land speed record* 他为创造陆上速度世界纪录所作的尝试 ➲ WORDFINDER NOTE AT ADVENTURE

■ ***verb*** to make an effort or try to do sth, especially sth difficult 努力；尝试；试图： **~ to do sth** *I will attempt to answer all your questions.* 我将努力回答你的全部问题。 ◇ *Do not attempt to repair this yourself.* 不要试图自己修理这个东西。 ◇ **~ sth** *The prisoners attempted an escape, but failed.* 囚犯企图逃跑，但失败了。 ➲ MORE LIKE THIS 26, page R28

at·tempted /əˈtemptɪd/ *adj.* [only before noun] (of a crime, etc. 犯罪等) that sb has tried to do but without success 未遂的： ***attempted rape/murder/robbery*** 强奸 / 谋杀 / 抢劫未遂

at·tend /əˈtend/ *verb* **1** [I, T] (*rather formal*) to be present at an event 出席；参加： *We'd like as many people as possible to attend.* 我们希望出席的人越多越好。 ◇ **~ sth** *The meeting was attended by 90% of shareholders.* * 90% 的股东出席了会议。 ◇ *to attend a wedding/funeral* 参加婚礼 / 葬礼 **2** [T, I] **~ sth** (*formal*) to go regularly to a place 经常去，定期去（某处）： *Our children attend the same school.* 我们的孩子上同一所学校。 ◇ *How many people attend church every Sunday?* 每个星期天有多少人去教堂？ ◇ *Your dentist will ask you to attend for regular check-ups.* 你的牙医会让你定期去检查。 **3** [I] ~ **(to sb/sth)** (*formal*) to pay attention to what sb is saying or to what you are doing 注意；专心： *She hadn't been attending during the lesson.* 上课时她一直不专心。 **4** [T] **~ sth** (*formal*) to happen at the same time as sth 伴随发生： *She dislikes the loss of privacy that attends TV celebrity.* 她不喜欢成为电视名人后随之失去个人隐私。 **5** [T] **~ sb** (*formal*) to be with sb and help them 随同；陪同： *The President was attended by several members of his staff.* 总统有几名幕僚随从。

PHR V **at'tend to sb/sth** to deal with sb/sth; to take care of sb/sth 处理；对付；照料；关怀： *I have some urgent business to attend to.* 我有一些急事要处理。 ◇ *A nurse attended to his needs constantly.* 有一位护士经常照料他的需要。 ◇ (*BrE, formal*) *Are you being attended to, Sir?* (= for example, in a shop) 先生，有人接待你吗？

at·tend·ance /ə'tendəns/ *noun* **1** [U, C] the act of being present at a place, for example at school 出席；参加；上学；到场：*Attendance at these lectures is not compulsory.* 这些课不是硬性规定要听的。◇ *Teachers must keep a record of students' attendances.* 老师必须记录学生的出勤情况。 **2** [C, U] the number of people present at an organized event 出席人数：***high/low/falling/poor attendances*** 出席的人数多 / 少 / 下降 / 很少 ◇ *There was an attendance of 42 at the meeting.* 有 42 人参加了会议。

IDM **be in at'tendance** (*formal*) to be present at a special event 出席（特别活动）：*Several heads of state were in attendance at the funeral.* 有几位国家元首出席了葬礼。 **be in at'tendance (on sb)** (*formal*) to be with or near sb in order to help them if necessary 陪侍；随侍（某人）左右；服侍：*He always has at least two bodyguards in attendance.* 他总有至少两名保镖护卫。 **take at'tendance** (*NAmE*) to check who is present and who is not present at a place and to mark this information on a list of names 点名 ➲ MORE AT DANCE *v.*

at'tendance allowance *noun* [U] the money that a very sick or disabled older person receives from the government in Britain if they need sb to care for them nearly all the time 护理津贴（英国政府发给全日需要照料的病残老年人）

at·tend·ant /ə'tendənt/ *noun, adj.*

■ ***noun*** **1** a person whose job is to serve or help people in a public place 服务员；侍者：***a cloakroom/parking/museum attendant*** 衣帽间 / 停车服务员；博物馆接待员 ➲ SEE ALSO FLIGHT ATTENDANT **2** a person who takes care of and lives or travels with an important person or a sick or disabled person（要人的）侍从，随从；（病人的）护理者

■ ***adj.*** [usually before noun] (*formal*) closely connected with sth that has just been mentioned 伴随的；随之而来的：***attendant problems/risks/circumstances*** 随之而来的问题 / 风险 / 情况 ◇ **~ upon sth** *We had all the usual problems attendant upon starting a new business.* 我们遇到了创业时通常会出现的所有问题。

at·tend·ee /ˌæten'diː/ *noun* a person who attends a meeting, etc. 出席者；在场者

at·tend·er /ə'tendə(r)/ (*especially BrE*) (*NAmE usually* **at·tend·ee**) *noun* a person who goes to a place or an event, often on a regular basis（常指经常的）出席者：*She's a regular attender at evening classes.* 她按时上夜校学习。

at·ten·tion 🔑 /ə'tenʃn/ *noun, exclamation*

■ ***noun***

• **LISTENING/LOOKING CAREFULLY** 注意听 / 看 **1** 🔑 [U] the act of listening to, looking at or thinking about sth/sb carefully 注意；专心；留心；注意力：*the report's attention to detail* 报告对细节的注意 ◇ *He turned his attention back to the road again.* 他把注意力转回到道路上。◇ *Small children have a very short* ***attention span.*** 幼儿的注意力持续时间很短。◇ *Please* ***pay attention*** (= listen carefully) *to what I am saying.* 请注意听我讲的话。◇ *Don't* ***pay any attention*** *to what they say* (= don't think that it is important). 别在意他们所说的话。◇ *She tried to* ***attract*** *the waiter's* ***attention.*** 她试图引起服务员的注意。◇ *I tried not to* ***draw attention to*** (= make people notice) *the weak points in my argument.* 我尽量使人察觉不到我论证中的弱点。◇ *An article in the newspaper* ***caught my attention.*** 报纸上一篇文章引起了我的注意。◇ *I couldn't give the programme my* ***undivided attention.*** 我不能专心一意地关注这个方案。◇ (*formal*) *It* ***has come to my attention*** (= I have been informed) *that…* 我已获悉… ◇ (*formal*) *He* ***called*** (*their*) ***attention*** *to the fact that many files were missing.* 他提请他们注意许多档案已经遗失这一事实。◇ (*formal*) *Can I have your attention please?* 请注意听我讲话好吗？ ➲ LANGUAGE BANK AT EMPHASIS

• **INTEREST** 兴趣 **2** 🔑 [U] interest that people show in sb/sth 兴趣；关注：*Films with big stars always* ***attract*** *great* ***attention.*** 有大明星演出的电影总是引起很大的关注。◇ *As the youngest child, she was always* ***the centre of attention.*** 身为幼女，她一直是大家关注的中心。 **3** [C, usually pl.] things that sb does to try to please you or to show their interest in you 殷勤；关心：*She tried to escape the unwanted attentions of her former boyfriend.* 她尽量避开她前男友多余的殷勤。

• **TREATMENT** 处理 **4** 🔑 [U] special care, action or treatment 特别照料（或行动、处理）：*She was in need of medical attention.* 她需要治疗。◇ *The roof needs attention* (= needs to be repaired). 房顶需要修理了。◇ ***for the attention of…*** (= written on the envelope of an official letter to say who should deal with it) 由…办理（正式信件信封上的用语）

• **SOLDIERS** 士兵 **5** [U] the position soldiers take when they stand very straight with their feet together and their arms at their sides 立正姿势：*to* ***stand at/to attention*** 立正站着；立正 ➲ COMPARE (STAND) AT EASE at EASE *n.*

■ ***exclamation*** **1** used for asking people to listen to sth that is being announced 注意：*Attention, please! Passengers for flight KL412 are requested to go to gate 21 immediately.* 请注意！请 KL412 航班的乘客立即到 21 号登机口登机。 **2** used for ordering soldiers to stand to attention 立正

at'tention deficit disorder (*also* **atˌtention ˌdeficit hyperac'tivity disorder**) *noun* [U] (*abbr.* **ADD**, **ADHD**) a medical condition, especially in children, that makes it difficult for them to pay attention to what they are doing, to stay still for long and to learn things 注意（缺陷）障碍（伴多动）；儿童多动症

at·ten·tive /ə'tentɪv/ *adj.* **1** listening or watching carefully and with interest 注意的；专心的；留心的：*an attentive audience* 聚精会神的听众 **2** helpful; making sure that people have what they need 关心的；肯帮忙的：*The hotel staff are friendly and attentive.* 旅馆人员友好而且照顾周到。◇ **~ to sb/sth** *Ministers should be more attentive to the needs of families.* 部长们应该更关怀家庭的需求。 ▶ **at·ten·tive·ly** *adv.* **at·ten·tive·ness** *noun* [U] **OPP** **inattentive**

at·tenu·ate /ə'tenjueɪt/ *verb* **~ sth** (*formal*) to make sth weaker or less effective 使减弱；使降低效力：*The drug attenuates the effects of the virus.* 这药能减轻病毒的作用。 ▶ **at·tenu·ation** /əˌtenju'eɪʃn/ *noun* [U]

at·tenu·ated /ə'tenjueɪtɪd/ *adj.* (*formal*) **1** made weaker or less effective 减弱的：*an attenuated form of the virus* 毒性已衰减的病毒 **2** (of a person 人) very thin 消瘦的

at·tenu·ator /ə'tenjueɪtə(r)/ *noun* (*specialist*) a device consisting of a number of RESISTORS which reduce the strength of a radio sound or signal（信号）衰减器

at·test /ə'test/ *verb* (*formal*) **1** [I, T] **~ (to sth) | ~ (that…) | ~ (sth)** to show or prove that sth is true 证实；是…的证据 **SYN** **bear/give witness (to sth)**: *Contemporary accounts attest to his courage and determination.* 当时的报道证实了他的勇气和决心。 **2** [T] **~ (sth) | ~ (that…)** to state that you believe that sth is true or genuine, for example in court 作证，证明（如在法庭上）：*to attest a will* 就遗嘱作见证 ◇ *The signature was attested by two witnesses.* 这个签名有两名见证人。

attic /'ætɪk/ *noun* a room or space just below the roof of a house, often used for storing things（紧靠屋顶的）阁楼，顶楼：*furniture stored in the attic* 存放在阁楼的家具 ◇ *an attic bedroom* 顶楼卧室 ➲ COMPARE GARRET, LOFT *n.* (1)

at·tire /ə'taɪə(r)/ *noun* [U] (*formal*) clothes 服装；衣服：*dressed in formal evening attire* 穿着晚礼服

at·tired /ə'taɪəd; *NAmE* ə'taɪərd/ *adj.* [not before noun] (*formal* or *literary*) dressed in a particular way 穿着…衣服

at·ti·tude 🔑 **AW** /'ætɪtjuːd; *NAmE* 'ætɪtuːd/ *noun* **1** 🔑 [C] the way that you think and feel about sb/sth; the way that you behave towards sb/sth that shows how you think and feel 态度；看法：**~ (to/towards/about/on sb/sth)** *social attitudes to/towards/about/on education* 社会对教育的看法 ◇ *the government's attitude towards single parents* 政府对单亲的看法 ◇ *to* ***have a good/bad/positive/negative attitude towards sb/sth*** 对某人（或事物）持好

的 / 坏的 / 肯定的 / 否定的态度 ◇ *Youth is simply an **attitude of mind**.* 青春仅仅是心态问题。◇ *If you want to pass your exams you'd better change your attitude!* 你若想通过考试就最好改变你的态度！ ◇ *You're taking a pretty selfish attitude over this, aren't you?* 你对这个问题的看法相当自私，对不对？◇ *A lot of drivers have a serious **attitude problem*** (= they do not behave in a way that is acceptable to other people). 许多驾车者有严重的态度问题。➲ WORDFINDER NOTE AT BEHAVIOUR **2** [U] confident, sometimes aggressive behaviour that shows you do not care about other people's opinions and that you want to do things in an individual way 我行我素的做派： *a band **with attitude*** 一味只顾自我陶醉的乐队 ◇ *You'd better get rid of that attitude and shape up, young man.* 年轻人，你最好改掉那种态度，学学好。**3** [C] (*formal*) a position of the body 姿势： *Her hands were folded in an attitude of prayer.* 她双手合拢摆成祈祷姿势。IDM SEE STRIKE *v.*

at·ti·tu·din·al /ˌætɪ'tjuːdɪnl; *NAmE* -'tuː-/ *adj.* (*formal*) related to the attitudes that people have 态度上的

attn (*also* **attn.** *especially in NAmE*) *abbr.* (*business* 商) (in writing 书写形式) for the attention of 由…办理；收件人为： *Sales Dept, attn C Biggs* 销售部，由 C. 比格斯收 ➲ SEE ALSO FAO

at·tor·ney /ə'tɜːni; *NAmE* ə'tɜːrni/ *noun* **1** (*especially US*) a lawyer, especially one who can act for sb in court 律师（尤指代表当事人出庭者） ➲ NOTE AT LAWYER ➲ SEE ALSO DISTRICT ATTORNEY **2** a person who is given the power to act on behalf of another in business or legal matters （业务或法律事务上的）代理人： *She was made her father's attorney when he became ill.* 她在父亲生病时代理父亲的事务。➲ SEE ALSO POWER OF ATTORNEY

atˌtorney 'general *noun* (*pl.* **attorneys general** or **attorney generals**) **1** the most senior legal officer in some countries or states, for example the UK or Canada, who advises the government or head of state on legal matters （英国、加拿大等国家的）总检察长，首席检察官 **2 the Atˌtorney 'General** the head of the US Department of Justice and a member of the President's cabinet (= a group of senior politicians who advise the President) （美国的）司法部长

at·tract /ə'trækt/ *verb* **1** [usually passive] if you are **attracted** by sth, it interests you and makes you want it; if you are **attracted** by sb, you like or admire them 吸引；使喜爱；引起…的好感（或爱慕）： **~ sb** *I had always been attracted by the idea of working abroad.* 我总是向往去国外工作。◇ **~ sb to sb/sth** *What first attracted me to her was her sense of humour.* 她首先吸引我的是她的幽默感。 **2** **~ sb/sth (to sth)** to make sb/sth come somewhere or take part in sth 招引： *The warm damp air attracts a lot of mosquitoes.* 温暖潮湿的空气招来了大量蚊子。◇ *The exhibition has attracted thousands of visitors.* 展览吸引了成千上万的参观者。**3** **~ sth** to make people have a particular reaction 引起（反应）： *This proposal has **attracted a lot of interest**.* 这个提案引起了人们很大的兴趣。◇ *His comments were bound to **attract criticism**.* 他的评论必然会招致批评。◇ *She tried to **attract the attention** of the waiter.* 她试图引起服务员的注意。 **4** (*physics* 物) if a MAGNET or GRAVITY **attracts** sth, it makes it move towards it 吸引 OPP **repel** IDM SEE OPPOSITE *n.*

at·tract·ant /ə'træktənt/ *noun* (*specialist*) a substance that attracts sth, especially an animal （对动物等的）诱食剂，引诱剂： *This type of trap uses no bait or other attractant.* 这种陷阱不用诱饵或其他引诱剂。

at·trac·tion /ə'trækʃn/ *noun* **1** [sing., U] a feeling of liking sb, especially sexually （尤指两性间的）爱慕，吸引： *She felt an immediate attraction for him.* 她立即对他产生了爱慕之情。◇ *Sexual attraction is a large part of falling in love.* 堕入爱河很大程度是由于性吸引。 **2** [C] an interesting or enjoyable place to go or thing to do 向往的地方；有吸引力的事： *Buckingham Palace is a major **tourist attraction**.* 白金汉宫是重要的旅游胜地。 ◇ *The **main attraction** at Giverny is Monet's garden.* 吉维尼主要的景点是莫奈花园。 **3** [C, U] a feature, quality or person that makes sth seem interesting and enjoyable, and worth having or doing 有吸引力的特征（或品质、人）： *I can't see the attraction of sitting on a beach all day.* 我看不出整天坐在海滩上有什么乐趣。 ◇ *City life holds little attraction for me.* 我对城市生活不感兴趣。◇ *She is the star attraction of the show.* 她是这个节目中耀眼的明星。 **4** [U] (*physics* 物) a force that pulls things towards each other 吸引（力）： ***gravitational/magnetic attraction*** 地心引力；磁力 ➲ COMPARE REPULSION

at·tract·ive /ə'træktɪv/ *adj.* **1** (of a person 人) pleasant to look at, especially in a sexual way 性感的；妩媚的；英俊的；诱人的： *an attractive woman* 妩媚的女人 ◇ *I like John but I don't **find him attractive** physically.* 我喜欢约翰，不过我认为他长得并不英俊。➲ SYNONYMS AT BEAUTIFUL **2** (of a thing or a place 物或地方) pleasant 吸引人的；令人愉快的： *a big house with an attractive garden* 带有美丽花园的一所巨宅 ◇ *That's one of the less attractive aspects of her personality.* 那是她个性中不太讨人喜欢的一面。 **3** having features or qualities that make sth seem interesting and worth having （事物）有吸引力的；诱人的 SYN **appealing**： *an attractive offer/proposition* 诱人的提议 OPP **unattractive** ▸ **at·tract·ive·ly** *adv.*： *The room is arranged very attractively.* 这个房间布置得十分宜人。◇ *attractively priced hotel rooms* 价格诱人的旅馆房间 **at·tract·ive·ness** *noun* [U]: *the attractiveness of travelling abroad* 国外旅游的吸引力

at·trib·ut·able AW /ə'trɪbjətəbl/ *adj.* [not before noun] **~ to sb/sth** probably caused by the thing mentioned 可归因于；可能由于： *Their illnesses are attributable to a poor diet.* 他们的病可能是不良饮食所致。

at·tri·bute AW *verb, noun*

■ ***verb*** /ə'trɪbjuːt/ **1 ~ sth to sth** to say or believe that sth is the result of a particular thing 把…归因于；认为…是由于： *She attributes her success to hard work and a little luck.* 她认为她的成功来自勤劳和一点运气。 **2** to say or believe that sb is responsible for doing sth, especially for saying, writing or painting sth 认为是…所为（或说、写、作）： **~ sth** *The committee refused to **attribute blame** without further information.* 如果没有进一步的情况，委员会拒绝归罪于任何人。◇ **~ sth to sb** *This play is usually attributed to Shakespeare.* 人们通常认为这部戏剧是莎士比亚所写。 ▸ **at·tri·bu·tion** AW /ˌætrɪ'bjuːʃn/ *noun* [U]: *The attribution of this painting to Rembrandt has never been questioned.* 这幅画是伦勃朗所作从未有人怀疑。

■ ***noun*** /'ætrɪbjuːt/ a quality or feature of sb/sth 属性；性质；特征： *Patience is one of the most important attributes in a teacher.* 耐心是教师最重要的品质之一。

at·tribu·tive /ə'trɪbjətɪv/ *adj.* (*grammar* 语法) (of adjectives or nouns 形容词或名词) used before a noun to describe it （用于所修饰的名词前）定语的： *In 'the blue sky' and 'a family business', 'blue' and 'family' are attributive.* 在 the blue sky 和 a family business 中，blue 和 family 是定语。➲ COMPARE PREDICATIVE ▸ **at·tribu·tive·ly** *adv.*： *Some adjectives can only be used attributively.* 有些形容词只能用作定语。

at·tri·tion /ə'trɪʃn/ *noun* [U] (*formal*) **1** a process of making sb/sth, especially your enemy, weaker by repeatedly attacking them or creating problems for them （尤指给敌人造成的）削弱，消耗： *It was a **war of attrition**.* 这是一场消耗战。 **2** (*especially NAmE*) (*BrE also* ˌ**natural 'wastage**) the process of reducing the number of people who are employed by an organization by, for example, not replacing people who leave their jobs 自然减员

at·tuned /ə'tjuːnd; *NAmE* ə'tuːnd/ *adj.* [not before noun] **~ (to sb/sth)** familiar with sb/sth so that you can understand or recognize them or it and act in an appropriate way 熟悉；适应；习惯： *She wasn't yet attuned to her baby's needs.* 她还没有熟悉她宝宝的需求。

ATV /ˌeɪ tiː 'viː/ *noun* (*especially NAmE*) the abbreviation for 'all-terrain vehicle' (a small open vehicle with one seat and four wheels with very thick tyres, designed especially for use on rough ground without roads) 全地形车（全写为 all-terrain vehicle） ➲ SEE ALSO QUAD BIKE

atyp·ical /ˌeɪˈtɪpɪkl/ *adj.* not typical or usual 非典型的；反常的：*atypical behaviour* 反常行为 OPP **typical**

AU /ˌeɪ ˈjuː/ *abbr.* ASTRONOMICAL UNIT 天文单位

au·ber·gine /ˈəʊbəʒiːn; *NAmE* ˈoʊbərʒiːn/ (*BrE*) (*NAmE* **egg·plant**) *noun* [C, U] a vegetable with shiny dark purple skin and soft white flesh 茄子 ➲ VISUAL VOCAB PAGE V33

au·burn /ˈɔːbən; *NAmE* ˈɔːbərn/ *adj.* (of hair 毛发) reddish-brown in colour 红褐色的 ➲ WORDFINDER NOTE AT BLONDE ▸ **au·burn** *noun* [U]: *the rich auburn of her hair* 她头发的深红褐色

auc·tion /ˈɔːkʃn; ˈɒk-; *NAmE* ˈɔːk-/ *noun, verb*

■ ***noun*** [C, U] a public event at which things are sold to the person who offers the most money for them 拍卖：*an auction of paintings* 绘画拍卖会 ◇ *The house is **up for auction*** (= will be sold at an auction). 这所房子将被拍卖。◇ *A classic Rolls-Royce fetched* (= was sold for) ***£25 000 at auction.*** 一辆古典式劳斯莱斯轿车拍得 25 000 英镑。◇ *an Internet auction site* 互联网拍卖网站

■ ***verb*** [usually passive] **~ sth** to sell sth at an auction 拍卖：*The costumes from the movie are to be auctioned for charity.* 这部电影用过的服装将用于慈善拍卖。

PHR V **ˌauction sth↔ˈoff** to sell sth at an auction, especially sth that is no longer needed or wanted 拍卖掉（尤指不再需要的物品）：*The Army is auctioning off a lot of surplus equipment.* 陆军正在把大量剩余设备拍卖掉。

auc·tion·eer /ˌɔːkʃəˈnɪə(r); ˌɒk-; *NAmE* ˌɔːkʃəˈnɪr/ *noun* a person whose job is to direct an auction and sell the goods 拍卖人；拍卖商

ˈauction house *noun* a company that sells things in auctions 拍卖行

ˈauction room *noun* a building in which auctions are held 拍卖厅

au·da·cious /ɔːˈdeɪʃəs/ *adj.* (*formal*) willing to take risks or to do sth shocking 敢于冒险的；大胆的 SYN **daring**: *an audacious decision* 大胆的决定 ▸ **au·da·cious·ly** *adv.*

au·da·city /ɔːˈdæsəti/ *noun* [U] brave but rude or shocking behaviour 鲁莽；大胆无礼 SYN **nerve**: *He **had the audacity to** say I was too fat.* 他竟敢说我太肥胖。

aud·ible /ˈɔːdəbl/ *adj.* that can be heard clearly 听得见的：*Her voice was **barely audible** above the noise.* 一片嘈杂，她的声音只能勉强听得见。OPP **inaudible** ▸ **audi·bil·ity** /ˌɔːdəˈbɪləti/ *noun* [U] **aud·ibly** /-əbli/ *adv.*

audi·ence 🔑 /ˈɔːdiəns/ *noun* **1** 🔑 [C+sing./pl. v.] the group of people who have gathered to watch or listen to sth (a play, concert, sb speaking, etc.)（戏剧、音乐会或演讲等的）观众，听众：*The audience was/were clapping for 10 minutes.* 观众鼓掌 10 分钟。◇ *an audience of 10 000* * 1 万名观众 ◇ *The debate was televised in front of a **live audience**.* 这场辩论当着现场观众的面进行电视直播。➲ WORDFINDER NOTE AT CONCERT **2** 🔑 [C] a number of people or a particular group of people who watch, read or listen to the same thing （同一事物的）观众，读者，听众：*An audience of millions watched the wedding on TV.* 几百万观众在电视上观看了婚礼。◇ ***TV/cinema/movie audiences*** 电视 / 电影院 / 电影观众 ◇ *His book reached an even wider audience when it was made into a movie.* 他的书被搬上银幕后赢得了更广大的观众。◇ *The **target audience** for this advertisement was mainly teenagers.* 这个广告的对象主要是十几岁的青少年观众。 **3** [C] a formal meeting with an important person（与要人的）会见；觐见；进见：*an audience with the Pope* 觐见教皇 ➲ SYNONYMS AT INTERVIEW

audio /ˈɔːdiəʊ; *NAmE* ˈɔːdioʊ/ *adj.* [only before noun] connected with sound that is recorded 声音的；录音的：*audio and video cassettes* 盒式录音带和录像带 ▸ **audio** *noun* [U]

audio- /ˈɔːdiəʊ; *NAmE* ˈɔːdioʊ/ *combining form* (in nouns, adjectives and adverbs 构成名词、形容词和副词) connected with hearing or sound 音的；声的；听的：*audiovisual* 视听的

audio·book /ˈɔːdiəʊbʊk; *NAmE* ˈɔːdioʊ-/ *noun* a reading of a book, especially a novel, recorded on a CD, etc. 有声书；有声读物 ➲ COMPARE E-BOOK

ˈaudio guide *noun* a small device, usually with HEADPHONES, that visitors to a museum, gallery, city, etc. can hold in their hand and use to listen to recorded information while they are walking around 导览机；语音导览机：*The museum provides free audio guides.* 博物馆提供免费的导览机。

audi·ology /ˌɔːdiˈɒlədʒi; *NAmE* -ˈɑːl-/ *noun* [U] the science and medicine that deals with the sense of hearing 听力（医）学 ▸ **audi·ologist** *noun*

audi·om·etry /ˌɔːdiˈɒmətri; *NAmE* -ˈɑːm-/ *noun* [U] (*specialist*) the measurement of how good a person's sense of hearing is 测听（法）；听力测量

ˈaudio tape *noun* [U] MAGNETIC tape on which sound can be recorded 录音带

audiovisual /ˌɔːdiəʊˈvɪʒuəl; *NAmE* ˌɔːdioʊ-/ *adj.* (*abbr.* **AV**) using both sound and pictures 视听的：*audiovisual aids for the classroom* 课堂视听教具

audit /ˈɔːdɪt/ *noun, verb*

■ ***noun*** [C, U] **1** an official examination of business and financial records to see that they are true and correct 审计；稽核：*an annual audit* 年度审计 ◇ *a tax audit* 税项审计 **2** an official examination of the quality or standard of sth（质量或标准的）审查，检查 ➲ SEE ALSO GREEN AUDIT

■ ***verb*** **1 ~ sth** to officially examine the financial accounts of a company 审计；稽核 **2 ~ sth** (*NAmE*) to attend a course at college or university but without taking any exams or receiving credit 旁听（大学课程）

the ˈAudit Commission *noun* [sing.] (in Britain) an organization that checks that public money is being spent in the best way by local governments and other public services （英国）审计署

au·di·tion /ɔːˈdɪʃn/ *noun, verb*

■ ***noun*** a short performance given by an actor, a singer, etc., so that sb can decide whether they are suitable to act in a play, sing in a concert, etc. （拟进行表演者的）试演，试唱，试音 ➲ WORDFINDER NOTE AT ACTOR

■ ***verb*** **1** [I] **~ (for sth)** to take part in an audition 试演；试唱；试音：*She was auditioning for the role of Lady Macbeth.* 她试演了麦克白夫人的角色。 **2** [T] **~ sb (for sth)** to watch, listen to and judge sb at an audition 对（某人）面试；让（某人）试演（或试唱、试音）：*We auditioned over 200 children for the part.* 我们为这个角色面试了 200 多名儿童。

audit·or /ˈɔːdɪtə(r)/ *noun* **1** a person who officially examines the business and financial records of a company 审计员；稽核员 ➲ WORDFINDER NOTE AT BUSINESSMAN **2** (*NAmE*) a person who attends a college course, but without having to take exams and without receiving credit （大学课程的）旁听生

audi·tor·ium /ˌɔːdɪˈtɔːriəm/ *noun* (*pl.* **audi·tor·iums** or **audi·toria** /-riə/) **1** the part of a theatre, concert hall, etc. in which the audience sits（剧院、音乐厅等的）听众席，观众席 ➲ WORDFINDER NOTE AT THEATRE **2** (*especially NAmE*) a large building or room in which public meetings, concerts, etc. are held 礼堂；会堂 ➲ WORDFINDER NOTE AT CONCERT

audi·tory /ˈɔːdətri; *NAmE* -tɔːri/ *adj.* (*specialist*) connected with hearing 听的；听觉的：*auditory stimuli* 听觉刺激

ˈaudit trail *noun* the detailed record of information on paper or on a computer that can be examined to prove what happened, for example what pieces of business were done and what decisions were made 审计轨迹（指用来进行审查的详细记录）

au fait /ˌəʊ ˈfeɪ; *NAmE* ˌoʊ/ *adj.* [not before noun] **~ (with sth)** (*from French*) completely familiar with sth 完全熟悉：*I'm*

A

new here so I'm not completely au fait with the system. 我初来乍到，所以对这个系统还不完全熟悉。

auger /ˈɔːɡə(r)/ *noun* a tool for making holes in wood, that looks like a large CORKSCREW 木螺钻；螺旋钻（用于木材钻孔）

aught /ɔːt/ *pron.* (*old use*) anything 任何事物

aug·ment /ɔːɡˈment/ *verb* ~ **sth** (*formal*) to increase the amount, value, size, etc. of sth 增加；提高；扩大 ▸ **aug·men·ta·tion** /ˌɔːɡmenˈteɪʃn/ *noun* [U, C]

aug·men·ta·tive /ˌɔːɡˈmentətɪv/ *adj.* (*linguistics* 语言) (of an AFFIX or a word using an affix 词缀或含词缀词) increasing a quality expressed in the original word, especially by meaning 'a large one of its kind' 增义的，增强词义的（尤指表示巨大）

aug,mented re'ality *noun* [U] a technology that combines computer-generated images on a screen with the real object or scene that you are looking at 增强现实技术，AR 技术（将电脑生成图像与真实物体或场景相结合）：*the potential use of augmented reality for crime-scene visualization* 增强现实技术对于犯罪现场重现的潜在用途

augur /ˈɔːɡə(r)/ *verb* [I] ~ **well/badly** (*formal*) to be a sign that sth will be successful or not successful in the future 主（吉或凶）；是…的预兆 **SYN** **bode**: *Conflicts among the various groups do not augur well for the future of the peace talks.* 各派之间的冲突对和平谈判不是一个好兆头。

au·gury /ˈɔːɡjʊri/ *noun* (*pl.* **-ies**) (*literary*) a sign of what will happen in the future 预兆；征兆 **SYN** **omen**

Au·gust 🔑 /ˈɔːɡəst/ *noun* [U, C] (*abbr.* **Aug.**) the 8th month of the year, between July and September 八月：(*BrE*) *August Bank Holiday* (= a public holiday on the last Monday in August in Britain) 八月银行假日（英国公共假日，八月最后一个星期一） **HELP** To see how **August** is used, look at the examples at **April**. * August 的用法见词条 April 下的示例。

au·gust /ɔːˈɡʌst/ *adj.* [usually before noun] (*formal*) impressive, making you feel respect 威严的；庄严的

Au·gust·an /ɔːˈɡʌstən/ *adj.* **1** connected with or happening during the time of the Roman EMPEROR Augustus（古罗马帝国皇帝）奥古斯都的；奥古斯都时代的 **2** connected with English literature of the 17th and 18th centuries that was written in a style that was considered CLASSICAL 奥古斯都时代文学的（指 17、18 世纪的英国文学）；英国古典文学的

auk /ɔːk/ *noun* a northern bird with short narrow wings that lives near the sea 海雀（北方海鸟，翅短窄）

auld lang syne /ˌɔːld læŋ ˈsaɪn/ *noun* an old Scottish song expressing feelings of friendship, traditionally sung at midnight on New Year's Eve《美好往昔》，《友谊地久天长》（苏格兰古老民歌，按传统在新年前夜唱起）

au nat·urel /ˌəʊ nætjuˈrel; *NAmE* ˌoʊ/ *adj.*, *adv.* [not before noun] (*from French*) in a natural way 自然：*The fish is served au naturel, uncooked and with nothing added.* 这条鱼是生吃的，未经蒸煮，也没加任何调味品。

aunt 🔑 /ɑːnt; *NAmE* ænt/ *noun* **1** the sister of your father or mother; the wife of your uncle 姑母；姨母；伯母；婶母；舅母：*Aunt Alice* 艾丽斯姨母 ◇ *My aunt lives in Canada.* 我的姑母住在加拿大。 **2** (*informal*) used by children, with a first name, to address a woman who is a friend of their parents（儿语）阿姨 ➲ SEE ALSO AGONY AUNT

aun·tie (*also* **aunty**) /ˈɑːnti; *NAmE* ˈænti/ *noun* (*informal*) aunt 姑母；姨母；伯母；舅母；阿姨；婶婶：*Auntie Mary* 玛丽婶婶

Aunt Sally /ˌɑːnt ˈsæli; *NAmE* ˌænt/ *noun* **1** (*BrE*) a game in which people throw balls at a model of a person to win prizes 萨莉大婶投掷游戏（用球投掷一人头模型赢奖） **2** a person or thing that a lot of people criticize 遭众人批评的人（或事物）：*The foreign minister has become everybody's favourite Aunt Sally.* 外交部长已成为众矢之的。 ➲ MORE LIKE THIS 18, page R27

au pair /ˌəʊ ˈpeə(r); *NAmE* ˌoʊ ˈper/ *noun* a young person, usually a woman, who lives with a family in a foreign country in order to learn the language. An au pair helps in the house and takes care of children and receives a small wage. 互惠（女）生（住国外家庭，以劳动换取食宿并学习语言）

aura /ˈɔːrə/ *noun* ~ (**of sth**) a feeling or particular quality that is very noticeable and seems to surround a person or place 气氛；氛围；气质：*She always has an aura of confidence.* 她总是满有信心的样子。

aural /ˈɔːrəl/ *adj.* (*specialist*) connected with hearing and listening 听觉的；听的：*aural and visual images* 视听图像 ◇ *aural comprehension tests* 听力理解测验 ▸ **aur·al·ly** /-əli/ *adv.*

aure·ate /ˈɔːriət/ *adj.* (*formal*) **1** decorated in a complicated way 华丽的：*an aureate style of writing* 华丽的文风 **2** made of gold or of the colour of gold 金的；金（黄）色的 **SYN** **golden**

aure·ole /ˈɔːriəʊl; *NAmE* -oʊl/ *noun* (*literary*) a circle of light 光环；光轮

au re·voir /ˌəʊ rəˈvwɑː(r); *NAmE* ˌoʊ/ *exclamation* (*from French*) goodbye (until we meet again) 再见

aur·icle /ˈɔːrɪkl/ *noun* (*anatomy* 解) **1** either of the two upper spaces in the heart used to send blood around the body 心耳 **SYN** **atrium** ➲ COMPARE VENTRICLE (1) **2** the outer part of the ear 耳郭；耳廓

aur·ora aus·tra·lis /ɔːˌrɔːrə ɒsˈtrɑːlɪs; ɔːsˈt-; *NAmE* ɔːsˈt-/ *noun* [sing.] = SOUTHERN LIGHTS

aur·ora bor·ealis /ɔːˌrɔːrə ˌbɔːriˈeɪlɪs/ *noun* [sing.] = NORTHERN LIGHTS

aus·pices /ˈɔːspɪsɪz/ *noun* [pl.]

IDM **under the auspices of sb/sth** with the help, support or protection of sb/sth 在…帮助（或支持、保护）下：*The community centre was set up under the auspices of a government initiative.* 在政府的大力支持下，社区中心建成了。

aus·pi·cious /ɔːˈspɪʃəs/ *adj.* (*formal*) showing signs that sth is likely to be successful in the future 吉利的；吉祥的 **SYN** **promising**: *an auspicious start to the new school year* 新学年的开门红 **OPP** **inauspicious** ▸ **aus·pi·cious·ly** *adv.*

Aus·sie (*also* **Oz·zie**) /ˈɒzi; *NAmE* ˈɔːzi/ *noun* (*informal*) a person from Australia 澳大利亚人 ▸ **Aus·sie** *adj.*

aus·tere /ɒˈstɪə(r); ɔːˈst-; *NAmE* ɔːˈstɪr/ *adj.* **1** simple and plain; without any decorations 朴素的；简陋的；无华饰的：*her austere bedroom with its simple narrow bed* 她那仅有一张窄床的简陋卧室 **2** (of a person 人) strict and serious in appearance and behaviour 严肃的；严厉的：*My father was a distant, austere man.* 我父亲是个难以接近的严肃的人。 **3** allowing nothing that gives pleasure; not comfortable 苦行的；禁欲的：*the monks' austere way of life* 僧侣的苦行生活方式 ▸ **aus·tere·ly** *adv.*

aus·ter·ity /ɒˈsterəti; ɔːˈster-; *NAmE* ɔːˈster-/ *noun* (*pl.* **-ies**) **1** [U] a situation when people do not have much money to spend because there are bad economic conditions（经济的）紧缩；严格节制消费：*War was followed by many years of austerity.* 紧随战争的是多年的经济紧缩。 **2** [U] the quality of being austere 苦行；禁欲：*the austerity of the monks' life* 僧侣的禁欲生活 **3** [C, usually pl.] something that is part of an austere way of life 艰苦；朴素：*the austerities of wartime Europe* 战时欧洲的艰苦生活

aus·tral /ˈɒstrəl; ˈɔːs-; *NAmE* ˈɔːs-/ *adj.* (*specialist*) relating to the south 南的；南方的；南部的

Austra·la·sia /ˌɒstrəˈleɪʃə; -ˈleɪʒə; ˌɔːstrə-; *NAmE* ˌɔːstrə-/ *noun* the region including Australia, New Zealand and the islands of the SW Pacific 澳大拉西亚（包括澳大利亚、新西兰及太平洋西南岛屿） ▸ **Austra·la·sian** *adj.*, *noun*

A

Australia Day /ɒˈstreɪliə deɪ; *NAmE* ɔːˈstreɪljə; ɑːˈs-/ *noun* a national public holiday in Australia on 26 January, when people remember the founding of New South Wales on that date in 1788 澳大利亚日（1 月 26 日，澳大利亚国庆日，纪念 1788 年新南威尔士州成立）

Aus·tra·lian /ɒˈstreɪliən; ɔːˈstreɪ-; *NAmE* ɔːˈstreɪ-/ *adj.*, *noun*
■ ***adj.*** of or connected with Australia 澳大利亚的
■ ***noun*** a person from Australia 澳大利亚人

Auˌstralian ˈRules (*also* **Australian ˌRules ˈfootball**) *noun* [U] an Australian game, played by two teams of 18 players, using an OVAL ball, which may be kicked, carried or hit with the hand 澳大利亚式橄榄球（两队各 18 人参赛，球呈椭圆形，可以足踢、抱传或以手击球）

Austro- /ˈɒstrəʊ; *NAmE* ˈɔːstroʊ/ *combining form* (in nouns and adjectives 构成名词和形容词) Austrian 奥地利（的）；奥地利人（的）：*the Austro-Hungarian border* 奥匈边境

aut·archy (*also* **aut·arky**) /ˈɔːtɑːki; *NAmE* ˈɔːtɑːrki/ *noun* (*pl.* **-ies**) **1** [U, C] = AUTOCRACY **2** [U] (*economics* 经) economic independence 经济独立；自给自足 ▶ **aut·arch·ic** (*also* **aut·ark·ic**) /ɔːˈtɑːkɪk; *NAmE* -ˈtɑːrk-/ *adj.*

au·teur /əʊˈtɜː(r); ɔːˈt-; *NAmE* oʊˈt-/ *noun* a film/movie director who plays such an important part in making their films/movies that they are considered to be the author 主创导演；导演作者 ORIGIN From the French word *auteur*, meaning author. 源自法语 auteur，意为"作者"。

au·then·tic /ɔːˈθentɪk/ *adj.* **1** known to be real and genuine and not a copy 真正的；真品的；真迹的：*I don't know if the painting is authentic.* 我不知道这幅画是不是真迹。OPP **inauthentic** **2** true and accurate 真实的；真正的：*an authentic account of life in the desert* 对沙漠生活的真实描述 ◇ *the authentic voice of young black Americans* 年轻美国黑人的真实呼声 OPP **inauthentic** **3** made to be exactly the same as the original 逼真的：*an authentic model of the ancient town* 古城的仿真模型 ▶ **au·then·tic·al·ly** /-kli/ *adv.*：*authentically flavoured Mexican dishes* 地道的墨西哥风味菜肴

au·then·ti·cate /ɔːˈθentɪkeɪt/ *verb* to prove that sth is genuine, real or true 证明…是真实的；证实：**~ sth** *The letter has been authenticated by handwriting experts.* 这封信已由笔迹专家证明是真的。◇ **~ sth as sth** *Experts have authenticated the writing as that of Byron himself.* 专家鉴定这字迹是拜伦的亲笔。▶ **au·then·ti·ca·tion** /ɔːˌθentɪˈkeɪʃn/ *noun* [U]

au·then·ti·city /ˌɔːθenˈtɪsəti/ *noun* [U] the quality of being genuine or true 真实性；确实性

author 🔑 AW /ˈɔːθə(r)/ *noun*, *verb*
■ ***noun*** **1** 🔑 a person who writes books or the person who wrote a particular book 著者；作者；作家：*Who is your favourite author?* 你最喜欢哪位作家？◇ *He is the author of three books on art.* 他写了三本艺术专著。◇ *best-selling author Paul Theroux* 畅销书作家保罗·泰鲁 ◇ *Who's the author?* 作者是谁？ ➲ WORDFINDER NOTE AT WRITE ➲ COLLOCATIONS AT LITERATURE **2** the person who creates or starts sth, especially a plan or an idea（尤指计划或思想的）创造者，发起人：*As the author of the proposal I cannot agree with you.* 我作为提案的发起人，不能同意你的意见。
■ ***verb*** **~ sth** (*formal*) to be the author of a book, report, etc. 著作；写作；编写

author·ess /ˈɔːθəres/ *noun* (*old-fashioned*) a woman author 女著者；女作者；女作家

au·thor·ial /ɔːˈθɔːriəl/ *adj.* [usually before noun] (*specialist*) coming from or connected with the author of sth 著者的；作者的；作家的

author·ing /ˈɔːθərɪŋ/ *noun* [U] (*computing* 计) creating computer programs without using programming language, for use in MULTIMEDIA products 著作 ➲ WORDFINDER NOTE AT SOFTWARE

au·thori·tar·ian /ɔːˌθɒrɪˈteəriən; *NAmE* əˌθɔːrəˈter-; əˌθɑːr-/ *adj.* believing that people should obey authority and rules, even when these are unfair, and even if it means that they lose their personal freedom 威权主义的；专制的：*an authoritarian regime/government/state* 威权主义的政体 / 政府 / 国家 ▶ **au·thori·tar·ian** *noun*：*Father was a strict authoritarian.* 父亲是个严厉的专制主义者。**au·thori·tar·ian·ism** *noun* [U]

au·thori·ta·tive AW /ɔːˈθɒrətətɪv; *NAmE* əˈθɔːrəteɪtɪv; əˈθɑːr-/ *adj.* **1** showing that you expect people to obey and respect you 命令式的；专断的；权威式的：*an authoritative tone of voice* 命令式的口气 **2** that you can trust and respect as true and correct 权威性的：*the most authoritative book on the subject* 这个学科最具权威的著作 ▶ **au·thori·ta·tive·ly** *adv.*

au·thor·ity 🔑 AW /ɔːˈθɒrəti; *NAmE* əˈθɔːr-; əˈθɑːr-/ *noun* (*pl.* **-ies**)
• **POWER** 权力 **1** 🔑 [U] the power to give orders to people 权力；威权；当权（地位）：*in a position of authority* 当权 ◇ *She now* ***has authority over*** *the people who used to be her bosses.* 她现在管辖着过去是她上司的那些人。◇ *Nothing will be done because no one* ***in authority*** (= who has a position of power) *takes the matter seriously.* 什么也办不了，因为掌权的谁也不认真对待这个问题。**2** 🔑 [U] **~ (to do sth)** the power or right to do sth 权；职权：*Only the Board has the authority to approve the budget.* 只有董事会有权批准预算。
• **PERMISSION** 准许 **3** 🔑 [U] official permission to do sth 批准；授权：*It was done without the principal's authority.* 做这件事未经校长批准。◇ *We acted* ***under the authority of*** *the UN.* 我们是经联合国授权行动的。
• **ORGANIZATION** 组织机构 **4** 🔑 [C, usually pl.] the people or an organization who have the power to make decisions or who have a particular area of responsibility in a country or region 当局；官方；当权者：*The health authorities are investigating the problem.* 卫生当局正在调查这个问题。◇ *I have to report this to the authorities.* 我得向官方报告此事。➲ SEE ALSO LOCAL AUTHORITY
• **KNOWLEDGE** 知识 **5** 🔑 [U] the power to influence people because they respect your knowledge or official position 权威；威信；影响力：*He spoke* ***with authority*** *on the topic.* 他就这个课题发表权威意见。
• **EXPERT** 专家 **6** [C] **~ (on sth)** a person with special knowledge 专家；学术权威；泰斗 SYN **specialist**：*She's an authority on criminal law.* 她是刑法专家。

IDM **have sth on good auˈthority** to be able to believe sth because you trust the person who gave you the information 有可靠的根据

au·thor·iza·tion (*BrE also* **-isa·tion**) /ˌɔːθəraɪˈzeɪʃn; *NAmE* -rəˈz-/ *noun* **1** [U, C] official permission or power to do sth; the act of giving permission 批准；授权：*You may not enter the security area without authorization.* 未经批准不得进入警戒地区。◇ *Who gave the authorization to release the data?* 谁授权公开这些资料的？ **2** [C] a document that gives sb official permission to do sth 批准书；授权书：*Can I see your authorization?* 我能看你的授权书吗？

au·thor·ize (*BrE also* **-ise**) /ˈɔːθəraɪz/ *verb* [often passive] to give official permission for sth, or for sb to do sth 批准；授权：**~ sth** *I can authorize payments up to £5 000.* 我有权批准的付款限额为 5 000 英镑。◇ *an authorized biography* 经授权的传记 ◇ **~ sb to do sth** *I have authorized him to act for me while I am away.* 我已授权他在我外出时代理我的职务。◇ *The soldiers were authorized to shoot at will.* 士兵得到允许可以随意开枪。➲ SEE ALSO UNAUTHORIZED

ˌAuthorized ˈVersion *noun* [sing.] an English version of the Bible that was translated in 1611 on the instructions of King James I of England 《圣经》钦定英译本（英王詹姆斯一世于 1611 年颁行）

author·ship AW /ˈɔːθəʃɪp; *NAmE* ˈɔːθərʃɪp/ *noun* [U] **1** the identity of the person who wrote sth, especially a book（尤指书的）作者，作者身份：*The authorship of the poem is unknown.* 这首诗的作者不详。**2** the activity or fact of writing a book 写作；著述

A

aut·ism /'ɔːtɪzəm/ *noun* [U] a mental condition in which a person finds it very difficult to communicate or form relationships with others 自闭症；孤独症 ➲ WORDFINDER NOTE AT CONDITION ▶ **aut·is·tic** /ɔː'tɪstɪk/ *adj.*：*autistic behaviour/children* 自闭症行为 / 儿童

auto /'ɔːtəʊ; NAmE 'ɔːtoʊ/ *noun* (*pl.* **-os**) (*NAmE*) a car 汽车：*the auto industry* 汽车工业

auto- /'ɔːtəʊ; NAmE 'ɔːtoʊ/ (*also* **aut-**) *combining form* (in nouns, adjectives and adverbs 构成名词、形容词和副词) **1** of or by yourself 自己（的）；本身（的）：*autobiography* 自传 **2** by itself without a person to operate it 由本身（的）；无人操作（的）：*automatic* 自动的

auto·biog·raphy /ˌɔːtəbaɪ'ɒɡrəfi; NAmE -'ɑːɡ-/ *noun* [C, U] (*pl.* **-ies**) the story of a person's life, written by that person; this type of writing 自传；自传体写作 ➲ COMPARE BIOGRAPHY ▶ **auto·bio·graph·ic·al** /ˌɔːtəˌbaɪə'ɡræfɪkl/ *adj.*：*an autobiographical novel* (= one that contains many of the writer's own experiences) 自传体小说

'auto bra *noun* (*NAmE*) = BRA (2)

auto·clave /'ɔːtəʊkleɪv; 'ɔːtəkleɪv; NAmE 'ɔːtoʊkleɪv/ *noun* a strong closed container, used for processes that involve high temperatures or pressure 高压釜，加压釜（用于强热高压工序的密封坚固容器）

auto·com·plete /ˌɔːtəʊkəm'pliːt; NAmE ˌɔːtoʊ-/ *noun* [U] a piece of software that completes a word, address, etc. when you have typed the first few letters so that you do not have to type it in full 自动补全软件（根据用户输入的前几个字母将单词、地址等自动补充完整）➲ COMPARE AUTOFILL ▶ **auto·com·plete** *verb* [T, I] ~ (**sth**)：*When you enter the first few letters of a name from your address book, the field will autocomplete.* 输入通讯录中人名的前几个字母，字段会自动补全。◇ *The program will autocomplete your address each time you begin to type it.* 每次开始输入地址，这个程序会自动将地址补全。

au·toc·racy /ɔː'tɒkrəsi; NAmE ɔː'tɑːk-/ *noun* (*pl.* **-ies**) (*also* **aut·archy**) **1** [U] a system of government of a country in which one person has complete power 独裁政体；专制制度 **2** [C] a country that is ruled by one person who has complete power 独裁国家；专制国家

auto·crat /'ɔːtəkræt/ *noun* **1** a ruler who has complete power 独裁者；专制统治者；专制君主 SYN **despot** **2** a person who expects to be obeyed by other people and does not care about their opinions or feelings 专横的人；独断专行的人 ▶ **auto·crat·ic** /ˌɔːtə'krætɪk/ *adj.*：*an autocratic manager* 独断专行的经理 **auto·crat·ic·al·ly** /-kli/ *adv.*

auto·cross /'ɔːtəʊkrɒs; NAmE 'ɔːtoʊkrɔːs; 'ɔːtoʊkrɑːs/ *noun* [U] a form of motor racing in which cars are driven over rough ground 汽车越野赛 ➲ COMPARE RALLYCROSS

Auto·cue™ /'ɔːtəʊkjuː; NAmE 'ɔːtoʊ-/ (*BrE*) (*also* **tele·prompt·er** *NAmE, BrE*) *noun* a device used by people who are speaking in public, especially on television, which displays the words that they have to say 电子提词器，自动提示器（尤用于电视广播时向说话人提示讲词）

auto·didact /'ɔːtəʊdɪdækt; NAmE 'ɔːtoʊ-/ *noun* (*formal*) a person who has taught himself or herself sth rather than having lessons 自学者；自修者 ▶ **auto·didac·tic** /ˌɔːtəʊdɪ'dæktɪk; NAmE ˌɔːtoʊ-/ *adj.*

ˌauto-e'rotic *adj.* relating to the practice of sb getting sexual excitement from their own body 自慰的

ˌauto-ex'posure *noun* **1** [C] part of a camera that automatically adjusts the amount of light that reaches the film（照相机的）自动曝光装置 **2** [U] the ability of a camera to do this（照相机的）自动曝光

auto·fill /'ɔːtəʊfɪl; NAmE 'ɔːtoʊ-/ *noun* [U] a piece of software that remembers information and uses it to fill in data in an online form so that you do not have to type it again 自动填充软件（可记忆信息并自动填入在线表格）：*I often use autofill to enter delivery information for online purchases.* 网购时我经常使用自动填充功能输入送递信息。➲ COMPARE AUTOCOMPLETE

auto·focus /ˌɔːtəʊ'fəʊkəs; NAmE ˌɔːtoʊ'foʊkəs/ *noun* **1** [C] part of a camera that automatically adjusts itself, so that the picture will be clear（照相机的）自动聚焦装置 **2** [U] the ability of a camera to do this（照相机的）自动聚焦，自（动）调焦

auto·genic /ˌɔːtəʊ'dʒenɪk; ˌɔːtə'dʒenɪk; NAmE ˌɔːtoʊ'dʒenɪk/ *adj.* (*formal*) created by or from the thing itself 自生的；自体的

ˌautogenic 'training *noun* [U] a way of relaxing and dealing with stress using positive thoughts and mental exercises 自生训练（利用积极思维和心理训练缓解压力）

auto·graph /'ɔːtəɡrɑːf; NAmE -ɡræf/ *noun, verb*

■ ***noun*** a famous person's signature, especially when sb asks them to write it（名人的）亲笔签名：*Could I have your autograph?* 我能请你签个名吗？

■ ***verb*** **~ sth** (of a famous person 名人) to sign your name on sth for sb to keep（在…上）签名：*The whole team has autographed a football, which will be used as a prize.* 全体队员在一个足球上签了名，用作奖品。

auto·immune /ˌɔːtəʊɪ'mjuːn; NAmE ˌɔːtoʊ-/ *adj.* [only before noun] (*medical* 医) an **autoimmune** disease or medical condition is one that is caused by substances that usually prevent illness 自身免疫的；自体免疫的

auto·magic·al·ly /ˌɔːtəʊ'mædʒɪkli; NAmE ˌɔːtoʊ-/ *adv.* (*informal*) (used especially about a certain kind of computer process that does not need a person to operate it) happening in such a clever way that it seems impossible to understand how it works（尤用于无需人工操作的电脑程序）以不可思议的自动方式：*The audio automagically downloads to your MP3 player.* 音频奇迹般地自动下载到你的 MP3 播放器上。ORIGIN From **automatically** and **magically**. 源自 automatically 和 magically。

auto·maker /'ɔːtəʊmeɪkə(r); NAmE 'ɔːtoʊ-/ *noun* (*NAmE*) a company that makes cars 汽车制造商

auto·mat /'ɔːtəmæt/ *noun* (*US*) in the past, a restaurant in which food and drink were bought from machines 自动餐馆（旧时用自动售卖机供应食物的餐馆）

auto·mate AW /'ɔːtəmeɪt/ *verb* [usually passive] **~ sth** to use machines and computers instead of people to do a job or task 使自动化：*The entire manufacturing process has been automated.* 整个生产过程已自动化。◇ *The factory is now **fully automated**.* 这家工厂现在是全自动化。

ˌautomated 'teller machine *noun* (*abbr.* **ATM**) = CASH MACHINE

auto·mat·ic 🔑 AW /ˌɔːtə'mætɪk/ *adj., noun*

■ ***adj.*** **1** 🔑 (of a machine, device, etc. 机器、装置等) having controls that work without needing a person to operate them 自动的：*automatic doors* 自动门 ◇ *a **fully automatic** driverless train* 全自动无人驾驶列车 ◇ *automatic transmission* (= in a car, etc.)（汽车等内的）自动变速器 ◇ *an automatic rifle* (= one that continues to fire as long as the TRIGGER is pressed) 自动步枪 **2** 🔑 done or happening without thinking 无意识的；不假思索的 SYN **instinctive**：*Breathing is an automatic function of the body.* 呼吸是一种无意识的功能。◇ *My reaction was automatic.* 我的反应是不由自主的。 **3** 🔑 always happening as a result of a particular action or situation 必然的；当然的：*A fine for this offence is automatic.* 这种违法行为当然要罚款。▶ **auto·mat·ic·al·ly** 🔑 AW /-kli/ *adv.*：*The heating switches off automatically.* 该供暖系统可自动关闭。◇ *I turned left automatically without thinking.* 我不假思索地向左转弯。◇ *You will automatically get free dental treatment if you are under 18.* * 18 岁以下的人一律免费得到牙科治疗。

■ ***noun*** **1** a gun that can fire bullets continuously as long as the TRIGGER is pressed 自动步枪 **2** (*BrE*) a car with a system of gears that operates without direct action from the driver 自动变速汽车；自动换挡汽车 ➲ COMPARE STICK SHIFT

ˌ**automatic 'pilot** (*also* **auto·pilot**) *noun* [C, U] a device in an aircraft or a ship that keeps it on a fixed course without the need for a person to control it （飞机的）自动驾驶仪；（船的）自动操舵装置

IDM **be on ˌautomatic 'pilot** to do sth without thinking because you have done the same thing many times before 习惯性地做；机械性地做：*I got up and dressed on automatic pilot.* 我习惯性地起床穿衣。

ˌ**automatic trans'mission** *noun* [U, C] a system in a vehicle that changes the gears for the driver automatically （机动车的）自动变速器

ˌ**automatic 'writing** *noun* [U] writing which is believed to have been done in an unconscious state or under a SUPERNATURAL influence （无意识状态或在超自然力影响下的）自书动作

auto·ma·tion **AW** /ˌɔːtə'meɪʃn/ *noun* [U] the use of machines to do work that was previously done by people 自动化：*Automation meant the loss of many factory jobs.* 自动化意味着许多工厂工人失业。

au·toma·tism /ɔː'tɒmətɪzəm; *NAmE* ɔː'tɑːm-/ *noun* [U] (*art* 美术) a method of painting that avoids conscious thought and allows a free flow of ideas 自动主义（避免意识思维、任凭想象力自由发挥的绘画方法）

au·toma·ton /ɔː'tɒmətən; *NAmE* ɔː'tɑːm-/ *noun* (*pl.* **au·toma·tons** or **au·tom·ata** /-tə/) **1** a person who behaves like a machine, without thinking or feeling anything 不动脑筋机械行事的人 **SYN** **robot** **2** a machine that moves without human control; a small ROBOT 自动机；小型机器人

auto·mo·bile /'ɔːtəməbiːl/ *noun* (*NAmE*) a car 汽车：*the automobile industry* 汽车工业 ◇ *an automobile accident* 车祸

auto·mo·tive /ˌɔːtə'məʊtɪv; *NAmE* -'moʊ-/ *adj.* (*formal*) [usually before noun] connected with vehicles that are driven by engines 汽车的；机动车的：*the automotive industry* 汽车工业

auto·nom·ic ner·vous sys·tem /ˌɔːtənɒmɪk 'nɜːvəs sɪstəm; *NAmE* ˌɔːtənɑːmɪk 'nɜːrvəs/ *noun* the part of your NERVOUS SYSTEM that controls processes which are unconscious, for example the process of your heart beating 自主神经系统，植物性神经系统（控制心跳等无意识运动）

au·tono·mous /ɔː'tɒnəməs; *NAmE* ɔː'tɑːn-/ *adj.* **1** (of a country, a region or an organization 国家、地区、组织) able to govern itself or control its own affairs 自治的；有自治权的 **SYN** **independent**：*an* ***autonomous republic/state/province*** 自治共和国 / 州 / 省 **2** (of a person 人) able to do things and make decisions without help from anyone else 自主的；有自主权的 ▶ **au·tono·mous·ly** *adv.*

au·ton·omy /ɔː'tɒnəmi; *NAmE* ɔː'tɑːn-/ *noun* [U] (*formal*) **1** the freedom for a country, a region or an organization to govern itself independently 自治；自治权 **SYN** **independence**：*a campaign in Wales for greater autonomy* 威尔士争取更大自治权的运动 **2** the ability to act and make decisions without being controlled by anyone else 自主；自主权：*giving individuals greater autonomy in their own lives* 给个人在生活中更大的自主权

auto·pilot /'ɔːtəʊpaɪlət; *NAmE* 'ɔːtoʊ-/ *noun* = AUTOMATIC PILOT

aut·opsy /'ɔːtɒpsi; *NAmE* 'ɔːtɑːpsi/ *noun* (*pl.* **-ies**) an official examination of a dead body by a doctor in order to discover the cause of death 验尸；尸体解剖 **SYN** **post-mortem**：*an autopsy report* 验尸报告 ◇ *to perform an autopsy* 进行尸体剖验

'**auto racing** *noun* [U] (*NAmE*) = MOTOR RACING

'**auto-rickshaw** *noun* a covered motor vehicle with three wheels, a driver's seat in front and a seat for passengers at the back, used especially in some Asian countries 机动三轮拉客车，机动黄包车，摩的（主要在亚洲国家）

auto·save /'ɔːtəʊseɪv; *NAmE* 'ɔːtoʊ-/ *noun* [sing.] (*computing* 计) the fact that changes to a document are saved automatically as you work 自动保存；自动存储；自动存档 ▶ **auto·save** *verb* ~ sth

auto·sug·ges·tion /ˌɔːtəʊsə'dʒestʃən; *NAmE* ˌɔːtoʊ-; -səɡ'dʒ-/ *noun* [U] (*psychology* 心) a process that makes you believe sth or act in a particular way according to ideas that come from within yourself without you realizing it 自我暗示

au·tumn 🔑 /'ɔːtəm/ (*especially BrE*) (*NAmE usually* **fall**) *noun* [U, C] the season of the year between summer and winter, when leaves change colour and the weather becomes colder 秋天；秋季：*in the autumn of 2010* 在 2010 年秋季 ◇ *in* ***early/late autumn*** 初秋；晚秋 ◇ *the autumn term* (= for example at a school or college in Britain) 秋季学期 ◇ ***autumn colours/leaves*** 秋色；秋叶 ◇ *It's been a very mild autumn this year.* 今年秋天一直很暖和。 ➲ MORE LIKE THIS 20, page R27

au·tum·nal /ɔː'tʌmnəl/ *adj.* [usually before noun] like or connected with autumn 秋天的；秋季的：*autumnal colours* 秋天的色彩

aux·il·iary /ɔːɡ'zɪliəri/ *adj.*, *noun*

■ ***adj.*** **1** (of workers 工人) giving help or support to the main group of workers 辅助的 **SYN** **ancillary**：***auxiliary nurses/workers/services*** 助理护士；辅助工 / 服务 **2** (*specialist*) (of a piece of equipment 设备) used if there is a problem with the main piece of equipment 备用的

■ ***noun*** (*pl.* **-ies**) **1** (*also* **auˌxiliary 'verb**) (*grammar* 语法) a verb such as *be*, *do* and *have* used with main verbs to show tense, etc. and to form questions and negatives 助动词 **2** a worker who gives help or support to the main group of workers 辅助工；辅助人员：*nursing auxiliaries* 护理辅助人员

auxin /'ɔːksɪn/ *noun* [U] a HORMONE found in plants （植物）生长素

AV /ˌeɪ 'viː/ *abbr.* AUDIOVISUAL 视听的

avail /ə'veɪl/ *noun*, *verb*

■ ***noun***

IDM **to little/no a'vail** (*formal*) with little or no success 没有什么效果；不成功：*The doctors tried everything to keep him alive but to no avail.* 医生千方百计想使他活下来，但无济于事。 **of little/no a'vail** (*formal*) of little or no use 没有什么用处；没有用：*Your ability to argue is of little avail if the facts are wrong.* 如果论据是错的，你的辩才也就没有什么用了。

■ ***verb*** **1** [T] ~ sb (sth) | ~ sth (*formal* or *old-fashioned*) to be helpful or useful to sb 有帮助；有益；有用 **2** [T, I] (*IndE*, *non-standard*) to make use of sth, especially an opportunity or offer 利用（尤指机会、提议等）：**~ sth** *To avail all these benefits, just register online.* 要想得到所有这些好处，就在线注册吧。 ◇ **~ of sth** *Why not avail of our special offers?* 为什么不利用我们的特别优惠呢？

PHR V **a'vail yourself of sth** (*formal*) to make use of sth, especially an opportunity or offer 利用（尤指机会、提议等）：*Guests are encouraged to avail themselves of the full range of hotel facilities.* 旅馆鼓励旅客充分利用各种设施。

avail·able 🔑 **AW** /ə'veɪləbl/ *adj.* **1** 🔑 that you can get, buy or find 可获得的；可购得的；可找到的：*available resources/facilities* 可利用的资源 / 设备 ◇ ***readily/freely/publicly/generally available*** 可以容易 / 免费 / 让公众 / 普遍得到的 ◇ *Tickets are available free of charge from the school.* 学校有免费票。 ◇ *When will the information be* ***made available****?* 何时才可以了解到情况？ ◇ *Further information is available on request.* 详情备索。 ◇ *This was the only room available.* 这是唯一可用的房间。 ◇ *We'll send you a copy as soon as it* ***becomes available****.* 一有货我们就会给你寄一本去。 ◇ *Every available doctor was called to the scene.* 所有能找到的医生都被召集到了现场。 **2** 🔑 (of a person 人) free to see or talk to people 有空的：*Will she be available this afternoon?* 今天下午她有空吗？ ◇ *The director was not available for comment.* 主管没有时间发表意见。 ▶ **avail·abil·ity** **AW** /əˌveɪlə'bɪləti/ *noun* [U]: *the* *availability of cheap flights* 有廉价机票出售 ◇ (*BrE*) *This offer is* **subject to availability**. 优惠至此产品售完为止。

ava·lanche /ˈævəlɑːnʃ; *NAmE* ˈævəlæntʃ/ (*NAmE also* **snow·slide**) *noun* a mass of snow, ice and rock that falls down the side of a mountain 雪崩；山崩；崩塌：*alpine villages destroyed in an avalanche* 在一场雪崩中被摧毁的高山村庄 ◇ (*figurative*) *We received an avalanche of letters in reply to our advertisement.* 我们在登出广告后收到了雪片般飞来的大批答复信件。➲ WORDFINDER NOTE AT DISASTER, SNOW

avant- /ˈævɒ̃; *NAmE* ˈævɑ̃ː/ *combining form* (used especially with types of popular music 尤用于各类流行音乐) in a style that is modern and very different from what has been done before 前卫的：*experimental music like avant-rock* 前卫摇滚乐之类的实验音乐 ◇ *avant-jazz* 前卫爵士乐 ◇ *avant-pop* 前卫流行乐

the avant-garde /ˌævɒ̃ ˈɡɑːd; *NAmE* ˌævɑ̃ː ˈɡɑːrd/ *noun* (*from French*) **1** [sing.] new and very modern ideas in art, music or literature that are sometimes surprising or shocking（艺术、音乐或文学方面的）前卫派思想 **2** [sing.+ sing./pl. v.] a group of artists, etc. who introduce new and very modern ideas 前卫派（艺术家等）▸ **avant-garde** *adj.*

avar·ice /ˈævərɪs/ *noun* [U] (*formal*) extreme desire for wealth （对钱财的）贪婪，贪心，贪得无厌 SYN **greed** ▸ **avar·icious** /ˌævəˈrɪʃəs/ *adj.*

ava·tar /ˈævətɑː(r)/ *noun* **1** (in Hinduism and Buddhism) a god appearing in a physical form 化身（印度教和佛教中化作人形或兽形的神） **2** a picture of a person or an animal that represents a particular computer user, on a computer screen, especially in a computer game or on SOCIAL MEDIA （尤指电脑游戏或社交媒体中的）用户头像

Ave. (*NAmE also* **Av.**) *abbr.* (used in written addresses) AVENUE （用于书写地址）大街：*Fifth Ave.* 第五大街

avenge /əˈvendʒ/ *verb* (*formal*) to punish or hurt sb in return for sth bad or wrong that they have done to you, your family or friends 报（某事）之仇；向（某人）报仇：**~ sth** *He promised to avenge his father's murder.* 他发誓要报杀父之仇。◇ **~ yourself on sb** *She was determined to avenge herself on the man who had betrayed her.* 她决心向那个负心男人报仇。▸ **aven·ger** *noun*

▼ GRAMMAR POINT 语法说明

avenge / revenge

Avenge is a verb; **revenge** is (usually) a noun. * avenge 为动词，revenge 通常作名词。

- People **avenge** something or **avenge** themselves **on** somebody. 报某事之仇用 avenge something，向某人报仇用 avenge oneself on somebody：*She vowed to avenge her brother's death.* 她发誓要为哥哥之死报仇。◇ *He later avenged himself on his wife's killers.* 他后来向杀害他妻子的人报了仇。You **take revenge on** a person. 报复某人用 take revenge on。
- In more formal or literary English, **revenge** can also be a verb. People **revenge** themselves **on** somebody or **are revenged on** them (with the same meaning). 在较正式或文学用语中，revenge 亦可作动词。revenge oneself on somebody 或 be revenged on somebody 意思相同，均表示向某人报仇：*He was later revenged on his wife's killers.* 他后来向杀害他妻子的人报了仇。You cannot **revenge** something. 不能说 revenge something：~~*She vowed to revenge her brother's death.*~~

av·enue /ˈævənjuː; *NAmE* -nuː/ *noun* **1** (*abbr.* **Ave.**, **Av.**) a street in a town or city （城镇的）大街：*a hotel on Fifth Avenue* 第五大街上的一家旅馆 **2** a wide straight road with trees on both sides, especially one leading to a big house 林荫道（尤指通往大住宅者） **3** a choice or way of making progress towards sth 选择；途径；手段：*Several avenues are open to us.* 有几个办法可以供我们选择。◇ *We will explore every avenue until we find an answer.* 我们会探索一切途径，直到找到答案为止。

aver /əˈvɜː(r)/ *verb* (**-rr-**) **~ that…** | **~ sth** | **+ speech** (*formal*) to state firmly and strongly that sth is true 断言；确认 SYN **assert, declare**：*She averred that she had never seen the man before.* 她斩钉截铁地说以前从未见过这个男人。

aver·age 🔑 /ˈævərɪdʒ/ *adj., noun, verb*

■ *adj.* **1** 🔑 [only before noun] calculated by adding several amounts together, finding a total, and dividing the total by the number of amounts 平均的：*an* ***average rate/cost/price*** 平均费率 / 成本 / 价格 ◇ *Average earnings are around £20 000 per annum.* 年平均收入约为 2 万英镑。◇ *at an average speed of 100 miles per hour* 以平均每小时 100 英里的速度 **2** 🔑 typical or normal 典型的；正常的：*40 hours is a fairly average working week for most people.* 对大多数人来说，一周工作 40 小时是相当正常的。◇ *children of* ***above/below average*** *intelligence* 高于 / 低于一般智力的儿童 ◇ *£20 for dinner is about average.* 花 20 英镑吃正餐算是价格一般。 **3** 🔑 ordinary; not special 普通的；平常的；一般的：*I was just an average sort of student.* 我只是一个普通的学生。▸ **aver·age·ly** *adv.*：*He was attractive and averagely intelligent.* 他讨人喜欢，智力一般。

■ *noun* [C, U] **1** 🔑 the result of adding several amounts together, finding a total, and dividing the total by the number of amounts 平均数：*The average of 4, 5 and 9 is 6.* * 4、5、9 三个数的平均数是 6。◇ *Parents spend* ***an average of*** *$220 a year on toys.* 父母为孩子买玩具的花费每年平均为 220 美元。◇ *If I get an A on this essay, that will bring my average* (= average mark/grade) *up to a B+.* 如果我的这篇论文得 A，我的平均成绩就会提高到 B+。➲ SEE ALSO GRADE POINT AVERAGE **2** 🔑 a level which is usual 平均水平；一般水准：*Temperatures are* ***above/below average*** *for the time of year.* 温度高于 / 低于此时的年平均温度。◇ *400 people a year die of this disease* ***on average***. 平均每年有 400 人死于这种疾病。◇ *Class sizes in the school are below* ***the national average***. 这所学校班上的人数少于全国平均数。IDM SEE LAW

■ *verb* **1 ~ sth** [no passive] to be equal to a particular amount as an average 平均为：*Economic growth is expected to average 2% next year.* 明年经济增长预计平均可达 2%。◇ *Drivers in London can expect to average about 12 miles per hour* (= to have that as their average speed). 估计伦敦的驾车者平均时速为 12 英里。 **2 ~ sth** to calculate the average of sth 计算出…的平均数：*Earnings are averaged over the whole period.* 所计算的是整个时期的平均收入。

PHR V **ˌaverage ˈout (at sth)** to result in an average amount over a period of time or when several things are considered 平均数为：*The cost should average out at about £6 per person.* 费用应该是平均每人约 6 英镑。◇ *Sometimes I pay, sometimes he pays—it seems to average out* (= result in us paying the same amount). 有时我付钱，有时他付钱，看来两相持平。 **ˌaverage sth↔ˈout (at sth)** to calculate the average of sth 计算出…的平均数

averse /əˈvɜːs; *NAmE* əˈvɜːrs/ *adj.* [not before noun] **1 not ~ to sth/to doing sth** liking sth or wanting to do sth; not opposed to doing sth 喜欢；想做；不反对做：*I mentioned it to Kate and she wasn't averse to the idea.* 我向凯特提起这个想法，她不反对。 **2 ~ to sth/to doing sth** (*formal*) not liking sth or wanting to do sth; opposed to doing sth 不喜欢；不想做；反对做：*He was averse to any change.* 他反对任何改变。

aver·sion /əˈvɜːʃn; *NAmE* əˈvɜːrʒn/ *noun* [C, U] a strong feeling of not liking sb/sth 厌恶；憎恶：*a strong aversion* 深深厌恶 ◇ **~ to sb/sth** *He had an aversion to getting up early.* 他十分讨厌早起。

aˈversion therapy *noun* [U] a way of helping sb to lose a bad habit, by making the habit seem to be associated with an effect that is not pleasant 厌恶疗法（通过令人不愉快的刺激，使接受治疗者避免不良行为）

avert /əˈvɜːt; *NAmE* əˈvɜːrt/ *verb* **1 ~ sth** to prevent sth bad or dangerous from happening 防止，避免（危险、坏

事）：*A disaster was narrowly averted.* 及时防止了一场灾难。◇ *He did his best to avert suspicion.* 他尽量避嫌。**2 ~ your eyes/gaze/face (from sth)** to turn your eyes, etc. away from sth that you do not want to see 转移目光；背过脸：*She averted her eyes from the terrible scene in front of her.* 她背过脸，不去看面前可怕的场面。

avian /ˈeɪviən/ *adj.* [usually before noun] (*specialist*) of or connected with birds 鸟（类）的；关于鸟（类）的

ˈavian flu *noun* [U] (*formal*) = BIRD FLU

avi·ary /ˈeɪviəri; *NAmE* ˈeɪvieri/ *noun* (*pl.* **-ies**) a large CAGE or building for keeping birds in, for example in a ZOO 大鸟笼，鸟舍（如动物园内的）

avi·ation /ˌeɪviˈeɪʃn/ *noun* [U] the designing, building and flying of aircraft 航空制造业；航空；飞行：***civil/military aviation*** 民用 / 军用航空 ◇ ***the aviation business/industry*** 航空业

avi·ator /ˈeɪvieɪtə(r)/ *noun* (*old-fashioned*) a person who flies an aircraft 飞行员；飞机驾驶员

avid /ˈævɪd/ *adj.* **1** [usually before noun] very enthusiastic about sth (often a hobby) 热衷的；酷爱的 SYN **keen**: *an **avid reader/collector*** 酷爱阅读 / 收藏的人 ◇ *She **has taken an avid interest in** the project* (= she is extremely interested in it). 她对这个项目入了迷。**2 ~ for sth** wanting to get sth very much 渴望的；渴求的：*He was avid for more information.* 他渴望知道更多信息。▶ **avid·ity** /əˈvɪdəti/ *noun* [U] **avid·ly** *adv.*：*She reads avidly.* 她如饥如渴地阅读。

avi·on·ics /ˌeɪviˈɒnɪks; *NAmE* -ˈɑːn-/ *noun* **1** [U] the science of ELECTRONICS when used in designing and making aircraft 航空电子学 **2** [pl.] the electronic devices in an aircraft or a SPACECRAFT 航空（或航天）电子设备 ▶ **avi·on·ic** *adj.*

avo·cado /ˌævəˈkɑːdəʊ; *NAmE* -ˈkɑːdoʊ/ *noun* (*pl.* **-os**) (*BrE also* **ˌavocado ˈpear**) a tropical fruit with hard, dark green skin, soft, light green flesh and a large seed inside. Avocados are not sweet and are sometimes eaten at the beginning of a meal. 油梨，鳄梨（热带水果，皮硬呈深绿色，肉软呈浅绿色，核大）➲ VISUAL VOCAB PAGE V32

avo·ca·tion /ˌævəʊˈkeɪʃn; *NAmE* ˌævoʊ-/ *noun* (*formal*) a hobby or other activity that you do for interest and enjoyment 业余爱好

avo·cet /ˈævəset/ *noun* a bird that lives on or near water, with long legs and black and white feathers 反嘴鹬（腿长、羽毛黑白相间的涉禽）

avoid 🔑 /əˈvɔɪd/ *verb* **1** 🔑 to prevent sth bad from happening 避免；防止：**~ sth** *The accident could have been avoided.* 这个事故本来是可以避免的。◇ *They **narrowly avoided** defeat.* 他们险些被击败了。◇ *The name was changed to avoid confusion with another firm.* 改名是为了避免和另一家公司混淆。◇ **~ doing sth** *They built a wall to avoid soil being washed away.* 他们建了一堵墙防止土壤流失。**2** 🔑 to keep away from sb/sth; to try not to do sth 回避；避开；躲避：**~ sb/sth** *He's been avoiding me all week.* 整整一个星期他一直在回避我。◇ *She kept avoiding my eyes* (= avoided looking at me). 她总是躲避我的目光。◇ *I left early to avoid the rush hour.* 我早早动身以避开交通高峰时刻。◇ **~ doing sth** *I've been avoiding getting down to work all day.* 我一整天都故意拖着不去工作。◇ *You should avoid mentioning his divorce.* 你应该避免提及他离婚的事。➲ MORE LIKE THIS 27, page R28 **3** 🔑 **~ sth** to prevent yourself from hitting sth 避免撞到（某物）：*The car swerved to avoid a cat.* 汽车猛急转弯以免轧到一只猫。

IDM **avoid sb/sth like the ˈplague** (*informal*) to try very hard not to meet sb, do sth, etc. 像避瘟疫似的躲着某人（或某事物）；尽量避开某人（或某事物）➲ MORE AT TRAP *n.*

avoid·able /əˈvɔɪdəbl/ *adj.* that can be prevented 可以避免的：*Many deaths from heart disease are actually avoidable.* 许多因心脏病造成的死亡实际上是可以避免的。OPP **unavoidable**

avoid·ance /əˈvɔɪdəns/ *noun* [U] **~ (of sth)** not doing sth; preventing sth from existing or happening 避免；防止；回避；避开：*A person's health improves with the avoidance of stress.* 一个人只要别有压力，健康状况就会改善。➲ SEE ALSO TAX AVOIDANCE

avoir·du·pois /ˌævədəˈpɔɪz; ˌævwɑːdjuːˈpwɑː; *NAmE* ˌævərdəˈpɔɪz/ *noun* [U] the system of weights based on the pound 常衡（以磅为基本单位的衡制）

avow /əˈvaʊ/ *verb* **~ that...** | **~ sth** | **+ speech** (*formal*) to say firmly and often publicly what your opinion is, what you think is true, etc. 声明；公开宣称：*An aide avowed that the President had known nothing of the deals.* 一位助理声明，总统对那些交易毫不知情。▶ **avow·al** /əˈvaʊəl/ *noun* (*formal*)：*an avowal of love* 公开示爱

avowed /əˈvaʊd/ *adj.* [only before noun] (*formal*) that has been admitted or stated in public 公开承认的；公开宣称的：*an avowed atheist* 公开宣称的无神论者 ◇ *an **avowed aim/intention/objective/purpose*** 公开宣称的宗旨 / 意图 / 目标 / 目的 ▶ **avow·ed·ly** /əˈvaʊɪdli/ *adv.*

avun·cu·lar /əˈvʌŋkjələ(r)/ *adj.* (*formal*) behaving in a kind and friendly way towards young people, similar to the way a kind uncle treats his nieces or nephews 像伯伯（或叔叔）似的；长辈风范的；慈爱的

aw /ɔː/ *exclamation* (*especially NAmE*) used to express disapproval, protest or sympathy （表示不满、抗议或同情等）呀：*Aw, come on, Andy!* 呀，行啦，安迪！➲ MORE LIKE THIS 2, page R25

await /əˈweɪt/ *verb* (*formal*) **1 ~ sb/sth** to wait for sb/sth 等候；等待；期待：*He is in custody **awaiting trial**.* 他正被拘留候审。◇ *Her latest novel is eagerly awaited.* 人们正急切地期待着她的最新小说。**2 ~ sb** to be going to happen to sb 将发生在，将降临到（某人头上）：*A warm welcome awaits all our guests.* 我们的客人都将受到热烈欢迎。

awake 🔑 /əˈweɪk/ *adj.*, *verb*

■ ***adj.*** 🔑 [not before noun] not asleep (especially immediately before or after sleeping) 醒着（尤指入睡前或刚醒时）：*to be **half/fully awake*** 半睡半醒；睡意全无 ◇ *to be **wide awake*** (= fully awake) 毫无睡意 ◇ *I was still awake when he came to bed.* 他就寝时我还没有入睡。◇ *The noise was **keeping** everyone **awake**.* 喧闹声吵得大家都睡不着。◇ *I was finding it hard to **stay awake**.* 我已困得难熬。◇ *He **lies awake** at night worrying about his job.* 他担心他的工作，夜晚躺在床上睡不着。◇ *She was awake* (= not unconscious) *during the operation on her leg.* 给她的腿动手术时她一直醒着。➲ MORE LIKE THIS 31, page R28

■ ***verb*** (**awoke** /əˈwəʊk; *NAmE* əˈwoʊk/, **awoken** /əˈwəʊkən; *NAmE* əˈwoʊkən/) (*formal*) **1** [I, T] to wake up; to make sb

▼ **WHICH WORD?** 词语辨析

awake / awaken / wake up / waken

- **Wake (up)** is the most common of these verbs. It can mean somebody has finished sleeping 上述动词中 wake (up) 最常用，可表示睡醒：*What time do you usually wake up?* 你通常什么时候醒来？ or that somebody or something has disturbed your sleep. 亦指弄醒、唤醒：*The children woke me up.* 孩子们把我吵醒了。◇ *I was woken (up) by the telephone.* 电话铃声把我吵醒了。
- The verb **awake** is usually only used in writing and in the past tense **awoke**. 动词 awake 通常只用于书面语，而且用过去时 awoke：*She awoke to a day of brilliant sunshine.* 她醒来时是阳光灿烂的一天。**Waken** and **awaken** are much more formal. **Awaken** is used especially in literature. * waken 和 awaken 要正式得多。awaken 尤用于文学作品：*The Prince awakened Sleeping Beauty with a kiss.* 王子的吻唤醒了睡美人。
- **Awake** is also an adjective. * awake 亦作形容词：*I was awake half the night worrying.* 我忧心忡忡，半宿不能成眠。◇ *Is the baby awake yet?* 宝宝醒来了吗？ **Waking** is not used in this way. * waking 不能这样用。

➲ SEE ALSO ASLEEP, SLEEP *verb*

wake up（使）醒来： ~ (sb) (from/to sth) *I awoke from a deep sleep.* 我从沉睡中醒来。◇ ~ **to do sth** *He awoke to find her gone.* 他醒来发现她已经走了。◇ ~ **sb** *Her voice awoke the sleeping child.* 她的声音惊醒了睡着的小孩。 **2** [I, T] ~ (sth) if an emotion **awakes** or sth **awakes** an emotion, you start to feel that emotion 唤起；被唤起： *His speech is bound to awake old fears and hostilities.* 他的发言必然要激起昔日的恐惧和敌对情绪。

PHR V **a'wake to sth** to become aware of sth and its possible effects or results 察觉到；意识到；醒悟到： *It took her some time to awake to the dangers of her situation.* 过了一些时间她才意识到她处境的危险。 ➲ COMPARE WAKE *v.*

awaken /ə'weɪkən/ *verb* (*formal*) **1** [I, T, often passive] to wake up; to make sb wake up （使）醒来： ~ (sb) (from/to sth) *She awakened to the sound of birds singing.* 她醒来听到鸟的叫声。◇ ~ **to do sth** *We awakened to find the others gone.* 我们醒来发现其他人已经走了。◇ ~ **sb** *He was awakened at dawn by the sound of crying.* 黎明时他被哭喊声吵醒。 ➲ NOTE AT AWAKE **2** [I, T] ~ (sth) if an emotion **awakens** or sth **awakens** an emotion, you start to feel that emotion 唤起；被唤起： *The dream awakened terrible memories.* 这个梦唤起了可怕的往事。

PHR V **a'waken (sb) to sth** to become aware or to make sb aware of sth and its possible effects or results （使）察觉到，意识到，醒悟到： *I gradually awakened to the realization that our marriage was over.* 我逐渐意识到我们的婚姻结束了。 ➲ COMPARE WAKEN

awaken·ing /ə'weɪkənɪŋ/ *noun* **1** [C, usually sing.] an occasion when you realize sth or become aware of sth 醒悟；觉醒： *If they had expected a warm welcome, they were in for a* ***rude awakening*** (= they would soon realize that it would not be warm). 要是他们以为会受到热烈欢迎，他们很快就会醒悟并非如此。 **2** [C, U] the act of beginning to understand or feel sth; the act of sth starting or sb waking 认识；感到；开始出现（或苏醒）： *sexual awakening* 性欲的萌动 ◇ *the awakening of interest in the environment* 对环境产生的兴趣

award 🔑 /ə'wɔːd; *NAmE* ə'wɔːrd/ *noun, verb*

▪ ***noun*** **1** 🔑 [C] (often in names of particular awards 常用于奖项名称) a prize such as money, etc. for sth that sb has done 奖；奖品；奖金；奖状： *He was nominated for the best actor award.* 他获得最佳男演员奖提名。◇ *an* ***award presentation/ceremony*** 颁奖；颁奖仪式 ◇ *the Housing Design Award* 住宅设计奖 ◇ ~ **for sth** *to win/receive/get an award for sth* 因某事赢得/得到/获得奖项 ➲ SEE ALSO ACADEMY AWARD™ **2** [C] an increase in the amount of money sb earns （收入的）增加额： *an annual pay award* 年工资增加额 **3** [C, U] the amount of money that a court decides should be given to sb who has won a case; the decision to give this money （赔偿）裁定额；（赔偿）裁决： *an award of £600 000 in libel damages* * 60 万英镑的诽谤损害赔偿 **4** [U] the official decision to give sth (such as a DIPLOMA) to sb （毕业证书等的）授予： *Satisfactory completion of the course will lead to the award of the Diploma of Social Work.* 完成此课程合格者将获得社会福利工作文凭。 **5** [C] (*BrE*) money that students get to help pay for living costs while they study or do research 奖学金；助学金

▪ ***verb*** 🔑 [T] to make an official decision to give sth to sb as a payment, prize, etc. 授予；给予奖励；判给： ~ **sth (to sb)** *The judges awarded equal points to both finalists.* 裁判判定决赛双方得分相等。◇ ~ **(sb) sth** *The judges awarded both finalists equal points.* 裁判判定决赛双方得分相等。◇ *He was awarded damages of £50 000.* 他判得损害赔偿金 5 万英镑。

award·ee /əˌwɔː'diː; *NAmE* əˌwɔːr'diː/ *noun* a person who is awarded sth, such as a prize 受奖者；获奖者

a'ward-winning *adj.* [only before noun] having won a prize 获奖的： *the award-winning TV drama* 获奖电视剧

aware 🔑 **AW** /ə'weə(r); *NAmE* ə'wer/ *adj.* **1** 🔑 [not before noun] knowing or realizing sth 知道；意识到；明白： *As you're aware, this is not a new problem.* 正如你所了解的，这不是一个新问题。◇ ***As far as I'm aware,*** *nobody has done anything about it.* 据我所知，尚无人对此采取任何措施。◇ ***acutely/painfully*** (= very) ***aware*** 深切地/痛苦地认识到 ◇ ~ **of sth** *I don't think people are really aware of just how much it costs.* 我认为人们并不真正明白这要花多少钱。◇ *He was* ***well aware*** *of the problem.* 他很清楚这个问题。◇ *Everybody should* ***be made aware of*** *the risks involved.* 应该让人人都知道所涉及的风险。◇ ~ **that...** *Were you aware that something was wrong?* 你有没有意识到已经出了问题？ **2** 🔑 [not before noun] noticing that sth is present, or that sth is happening 察觉到；发觉；发现： ~ **of sb/sth** *She slipped away without him being aware of it.* 她悄悄离开，没有让他发觉。◇ *They suddenly became aware of people looking at them.* 他们突然意识到有些人在瞧着他们。◇ ~ **that...** *I was aware that she was trembling.* 我察觉到她在发抖。 **3** (used with an adverb 与副词连用) interested in and knowing about sth, and thinking it is important 对…有兴趣的；有…意识的： *Young people are very environmentally aware.* 年轻人的环保意识很强。 **OPP** **unaware**

aware·ness **AW** /ə'weənəs; *NAmE* ə'wer-/ *noun* [U, sing.] ~ (of sth) | ~ (that...) knowing sth; knowing that sth exists and is important; being interested in sth 知道；认识；意识；兴趣： *an awareness of the importance of eating a healthy diet* 对健康饮食重要性的认识 ◇ *There was an almost complete* ***lack of awareness*** *of the issues involved.* 对有关问题几乎是一无所知。◇ *It is important that students* ***develop an awareness of*** *how the Internet can be used.* 重要的是学生逐渐懂得如何使用互联网。◇ *to* ***raise/heighten/increase*** *public* ***awareness*** *of sth* 加强/提高/增强公众对某事物的意识 ◇ ***a greater/a growing/an increasing awareness*** *of sth* 对某事物更大的/日益增长的/愈来愈大的兴趣 ◇ *environmental awareness* (= knowing that looking after the environment is important) 环境意识 ◇ *Energy Awareness Week* （节约）能源意识周 ◇ *There seems to be a general awareness that this is not the solution.* 似乎人们已普遍认识到这不是解决问题的办法。

awash /ə'wɒʃ; *NAmE* ə'wɔːʃ; ə'wɑːʃ/ *adj.* [not before noun] **1** ~ (with water) covered with water 被淹没；被漫过；被水覆盖 **2** ~ **with sth** having sth in large quantities 充满： *The city is awash with drugs.* 这座城市毒品泛滥。

away 🔑 /ə'weɪ/ *adv.* **HELP** For the special uses of **away** in phrasal verbs, look at the entries for the verbs. For example **get away with sth** is in the phrasal verb section at **get**. * away 在短语动词中的特殊用法见有关动词词条。如 get away with sth 在词条 get 的短语动词部分。 **1** 🔑 to or at a distance from sb/sth in space or time （时间或空间上）离开（某距离），在（某距离）处： *The beach is a mile away.* 海滩在一英里外。◇ *Christmas is still months away.* 离圣诞节还有几个月。◇ ~ **from sb/sth** *The station is a few minutes' walk away from here.* 车站离这里有步行几分钟的路程。 **2** 🔑 to a different place or in a different direction 去别处；朝另一个方向： *Go away!* 走开！◇ *Put your toys away.* 把你的玩具收拾起来。◇ *The bright light made her look away.* 强光使她把视线转向别处。 **3** 🔑 not present 不在；离开 **SYN** **absent**： *There were ten children away yesterday.* 昨天有十个孩子缺席。◇ *Sorry, he's away.* 对不起，他不在。◇ ~ **from sb/sth** *She was away from work for a week.* 她有一个星期没来上班。 **4** used after verbs to say that sth is done continuously or with a lot of energy （用于动词后）持续地，劲头十足地： *She was still writing away furiously when the bell went.* 铃声响时她还在不停地写着。◇ *They were soon chatting away like old friends.* 他们很快就像老朋友一样聊起天来。 **5** until disappearing completely 直到完全消失： *The water boiled away.* 水烧干了。◇ *The music faded away.* 乐声逐渐消失。◇ *They danced the night away* (= all night). 他们跳舞跳了一个通宵。 **6** (*sport* 体育) at the opponent's ground or STADIUM 在客场： *Chelsea are playing away this Saturday.* 本周六切尔西队要在客场比赛。 **HELP** **Away** is also used as an adjective in this context. 在这一语境下，away 也可用作形容词： *an* ***away match/game*** 客场比赛 ➲ COMPARE HOME *adj.* (4)

IDM **away with...** (*literary*) used to say that you would like to be rid of sb/sth 让（某人或事物）消失吧： *Away with all these rules and regulations!* 让所有这些规章制度见鬼去

吧！ ➲ MORE AT COBWEB, DANCE *v.*, FAR *adv.*, RIGHT *adv.*, STRAIGHT *adv.*

away·day /əˈweɪdeɪ/ *noun* (*BrE, business* 商) a day that a group of workers spend together away from their usual place of work in order to discuss ideas or plans （不在工作场所的）外出研讨日： *The management are having an awayday to discuss strategy.* 管理层今天外出商议策略。◇ *We talked about it at the awayday.* 我们外出开会那天说起过这事。

awe /ɔː/ *noun, verb*

■ ***noun*** [U] feelings of respect and slight fear; feelings of being very impressed by sth/sb 敬畏；惊叹： *awe and respect* 敬畏和尊敬 ◇ *awe and wonder* 敬畏和惊奇 ◇ *He speaks of her* ***with awe.*** 他谈到她时肃然起敬。◇ *'It's magnificent,' she whispered* ***in awe.*** "真是壮丽。" 她小声地惊叹道。

IDM **be/stand in ˈawe of sb/sth** to admire sb/sth and be slightly frightened of them/it 对…敬畏；对…望而生畏： *While Diana was in awe of her grandfather, she adored her grandmother.* 黛安娜敬畏她的祖父，但深爱她的祖母。

■ ***verb*** **~ sb** [usually passive] (*formal*) to fill sb with awe 使敬畏；使惊叹： *She seemed awed by the presence of so many famous people.* 见到这么多名人出席，似乎令她惊叹不已。 ▶ **awed** *adj.*： *We watched in awed silence.* 我们敬畏地默然观看着。

ˈawe-inspir·ing *adj.* impressive; making you feel respect and admiration 令人惊叹的；使人敬佩的；令人敬慕的： *The building was awe-inspiring in size and design.* 这座建筑的规模和设计气势宏伟。

awe·some /ˈɔːsəm/ *adj.* **1** very impressive or very difficult and perhaps rather frightening 令人惊叹的；使人惊惧的；很困难的；难得吓人的： *an awesome sight* 惊人的奇观 ◇ *awesome beauty/power* 天仙之美；惊人能量 ◇ *They had an awesome task ahead.* 他们面前有十分艰巨的任务。 **2** (*especially NAmE, informal*) very good, enjoyable, etc. 很好的（或极好玩的等）： *I just bought this awesome new CD!* 我刚买了这张特棒的新 CD！ ◇ *Wow! That's totally awesome!* 哇！真是棒极了！ ➲ SYNONYMS AT GREAT ▶ **awe·some·ly** *adv.*： *awesomely beautiful* 极其美丽

awe·struck /ˈɔːstrʌk/ *adj.* (*literary*) feeling very impressed by sth 惊叹的： *People were awestruck by the pictures the satellite sent back to Earth.* 人们对人造卫星传送回地球的图片叹为观止。

awful 🔑 /ˈɔːfl/ *adj., adv.*

■ ***adj.*** **1** 🔑 (*informal*) very bad or unpleasant 很坏的；极讨厌的： *That's an awful colour.* 那颜色难看得很。◇ *'They didn't even offer to pay.' 'Oh that's awful.'* "他们甚至不主动付钱。" "哦，那真不像话。" ◇ *It's awful, isn't it?* 糟糕透了，不是吗？ ◇ *The weather last summer was awful.* 刚过去的夏季天气真坏。 ◇ *I feel awful about forgetting her birthday.* 我忘了她的生日，感到很过意不去。◇ ***to look/feel awful*** (= to look/feel ill) 面带病容；感到很不舒服 ◇ *There's an awful smell in here.* 这里有股很难闻的味道。◇ *The awful thing is, it was my fault.* 糟糕的是，这是我的过失。 ➲ NOTE AT TERRIBLE **2** 🔑 (*informal*) used to emphasize sth, especially that there is a large amount or too much of sth 非常的；很多的；过多的： *It's going to cost* ***an awful lot of*** *money.* 这要花非常多的钱。◇ *There's not an awful lot of room.* 没有很多的空间。 ◇ *I feel an awful lot better than I did yesterday.* 我觉得身体比昨天好得多了。◇ (*BrE*) *I had an awful job persuading him to come* (= it was very difficult). 说服他来真是费劲死了。 **3** 🔑 very shocking 骇人听闻的；可怕的 SYN **terrible**： *the awful horrors of war* 骇人听闻的战争恐怖情形 ▶ **aw·ful·ness** *noun* [U]： *the sheer awfulness of the situation* 糟透了的情况

■ ***adv.*** (*informal, non-standard, especially NAmE*) very; extremely 非常；极其： *Clint is awful smart.* 克林特机灵极了。

aw·ful·ly 🔑 /ˈɔːfli/ *adv.* very; extremely 非常；极其 SYN **terribly**： *I'm awfully sorry about that problem the other day.* 我对前几天的那个问题感到非常遗憾。

awhile /əˈwaɪl/ *adv.* (*formal* or *literary*) for a short time 片刻；一会儿

awk·ward 🔑 /ˈɔːkwəd; *NAmE* -wərd/ *adj.* **1** 🔑 making you feel embarrassed 令人尴尬的；使人难堪的： *There was an awkward silence.* 一阵令人尴尬的沉默。 **2** 🔑 difficult to deal with 难对付的；难处理的 SYN **difficult**： *Don't ask awkward questions.* 不要问难答的问题。◇ *You've put me in an awkward position.* 你使得我狼狈不堪。◇ *an awkward customer* (= a person who is difficult to deal with) 难对付的家伙 ◇ *Please don't be awkward about letting him come.* 关于让他来这事请你不要作梗。 **3** 🔑 not convenient 不方便的 SYN **inconvenient**： *Have I come at an awkward time?* 我来得不是时候吧？ **4** 🔑 difficult or dangerous because of its shape or design （因形状、设计而）产生困难的，危险的： *This box is very awkward for one person to carry.* 这只箱子一个人很不好搬。 **5** 🔑 not moving in an easy way; not comfortable （动作）笨拙的；不舒适的： *He tried to dance, but he was too clumsy and awkward.* 他试着跳舞，但是太笨拙，太别扭。◇ *I must have slept in an awkward position—I'm aching all over.* 我肯定是睡姿不当，搞得全身疼痛。 ▶ **awk·ward·ly** 🔑 *adv.*： *'I'm sorry,' he said awkwardly.* "对不起。" 他局促不安地说。 ◇ *She fell awkwardly and broke her ankle.* 她笨重地摔了一跤，摔断了踝关节。 ◇ *an awkwardly shaped room* 形状别扭的房间 **awk·ward·ness** *noun* [U]： *She laughed to cover up her feeling of awkwardness.* 她用笑声掩饰她的难堪。

awl /ɔːl/ *noun* a small pointed tool used for making holes, especially in leather （尤指钻皮革的）钻子，锥子

awn·ing /ˈɔːnɪŋ/ *noun* a sheet of strong cloth that stretches out from above a door or window to keep off the sun or rain（门窗上面的）遮阳篷，雨篷 ➲ VISUAL VOCAB PAGE V3

awoke PAST TENSE OF AWAKE

awoken PAST PART. OF AWAKE

AWOL /ˈeɪwɒl; *NAmE* ˈeɪwɔːl/ *abbr.* absent without leave (used especially in the armed forces when sb has left their group without permission) 擅离职守，无故离队，开小差（尤用于军队）： *He's* ***gone AWOL*** *from his base.* 他从基地开了小差。 ◇ (*humorous*) *The guitarist went AWOL in the middle of the recording.* 在录音过程当中吉他手溜走了。

awry /əˈraɪ/ *adv., adj.* **1** if sth **goes awry**, it does not happen in the way that was planned 出错；出岔子： *All my plans for the party had gone awry.* 我的聚会计划全乱了套。 **2** not in the right position 歪；斜 SYN **untidy**： *She rushed out, her hair awry.* 她披头散发冲了出来。

axe /æks/ *noun, verb*

■ ***noun*** (*especially BrE*) (*US usually* **ax**) **1** a tool with a wooden handle and a heavy metal blade, used for chopping wood, cutting down trees, etc. 斧 ➲ SEE ALSO BATTLEAXE, ICE AXE, PICKAXE **2 the axe** [sing.] (*informal*) (often used in newspapers 常用于报刊中) if sb gets **the axe**, they lose their job; if an institution or a project gets **the axe**, it is closed or stopped, usually because of a lack of money （遭）解雇；倒闭；被停业： *Up to 300 workers* ***are facing the axe*** *at a struggling Merseyside firm.* 默西赛德的一家艰苦挣扎的公司有多达 300 名工人面临被解雇。◇ *Patients are delighted their local hospital has been saved from the axe.* 病人高兴的是当地医院得以免遭关闭。

IDM **ˌhave an ˈaxe to grind** to have private reasons for being involved in sth or for arguing for a particular cause 有私心；有个人打算： *She had no axe to grind and was only acting out of concern for their safety.* 她毫无私心，这样做只是出于对他们安全的担忧。

■ ***verb*** (*BrE*) (*US* **ax**) [often passive] **1 ~ sth** (*informal*) (often used in newspapers 常用于报刊中) to get rid of a service, system, etc. or to reduce the money spent on it by a large amount 精简（机构等）；大量削减（经费等）： *Other less profitable services are to be axed later this year.* 其他盈利较少的服务预计今年稍晚将被大量削减。 **2 ~ sb** (*informal*) (often used in newspapers 常用于报刊中) to remove sb from their job 解雇；开除： *Jones has been*

A

axed from the team. 琼斯已被开除出队。 **3 ~ sb** to kill sb with an axe 用斧把…砍死

axe 斧

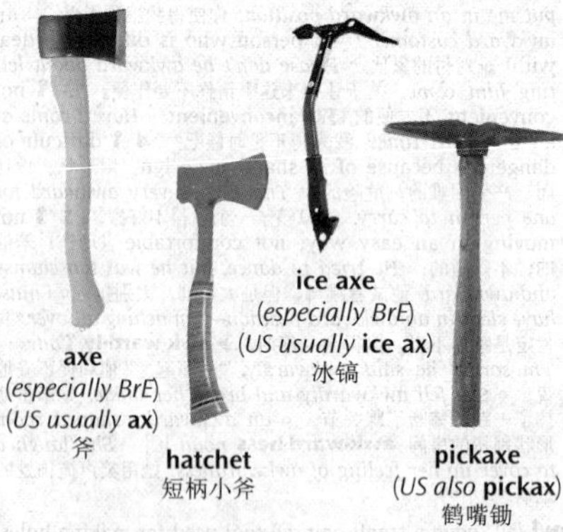

axel /ˈæksl/ *noun* a jump in SKATING in which you jump from the front outside edge of one foot, turn in the air, and land on the outside edge of your other foot 阿克塞尔跳，前外跳（滑冰运动中以一脚前外刃起跳空中旋转后以另一脚外刃落冰）

axe·man /ˈæksmən/ (*especially BrE*) (*NAmE usually* **axman**) (*pl.* **-men**) *noun* (*informal*) a man who attacks other people with an axe 用斧砍人的人

axial /ˈæksiəl/ *adj.* of or related to an AXIS 轴的；轴线的：*an axial road* 轴路

axiom /ˈæksiəm/ *noun* (*formal*) a rule or principle that most people believe to be true 公理

axio·mat·ic /ˌæksiəˈmætɪk/ *adj.* [not usually before noun] (*formal*) true in such an obvious way that you do not need to prove it 公理；不证自明 **SYN** **self-evident**：*It is axiomatic that life is not always easy.* 生活并不总是一帆风顺，这是明摆着的事实。 ▶ **axio·mat·ic·al·ly** *adv.*

axis /ˈæksɪs/ *noun* (*pl.* **axes** /ˈæksiːz/) **1** an imaginary line through the centre of an object, around which the object turns 轴（旋转物体假想的中心线）：*Mars takes longer to revolve on its axis than the Earth.* 火星自转一周的时间比地球长。 **2** (*specialist*) a fixed line against which the positions of points are measured, especially points on a GRAPH 坐标轴：*the* ***vertical/horizontal axis*** 纵 / 横坐标轴 **3** (*geometry* 几何) a line that divides a shape into two equal parts 对称中心线（将物体平分为二）：*an axis of symmetry* 对称轴 ◇ *The axis of a circle is its diameter.* 圆的对称中心线就是其直径。 **4** [usually sing.] (*formal*) an agreement or ALLIANCE between two or more countries 轴心

axis 对称中心线

axis 轴
axis of symmetry 对称轴
vertical axis 纵轴
horizontal axis 横轴

（国与国之间的协议或联盟）：*the Franco-German axis* 法德轴心

axle /ˈæksl/ *noun* a long straight piece of metal that connects a pair of wheels on a vehicle 车轴：***the front/rear axle*** 前 / 后车轴

axman (*US*) = AXEMAN

axon /ˈæksɒn; *NAmE* ˈæksɑːn/ *noun* (*biology* 生) the long thin part of a nerve cell along which signals are sent to other cells 轴突（神经细胞长的突起，将信号传递到其他细胞） ➲ COMPARE DENDRITE

ayah /ˈaɪə/ *noun* (*IndE*) **1** a woman whose job is caring for children, doing domestic work, etc.（照看孩子、做家务等的）女佣，阿嬷 **2** a person whose job is caring for sb who is ill/sick （照料病人的）护理员，看护人员

aya·tol·lah /ˌaɪəˈtɒlə; *NAmE* -ˈtoʊlə/ *noun* a religious leader of Shiite Muslims in Iran 阿亚图拉（伊朗伊斯兰教什叶派宗教领袖）

aye /aɪ/ *exclamation* (*old use* or *dialect*) **1** yes 是；对：*'Did you see what happened?' 'Oh aye, I was there.'* "你看见了发生的事吗？""啊，是的，我在场。" **2** always; still 总是；仍然

ayes /aɪz/ *noun* [pl.] the total number of people voting 'yes' in a formal debate, for example in a parliament（议会等辩论中的）赞成票总数：*The ayes have it* (= more people have voted for sth than against it). 投票赞成的人占多数。 **OPP** **noes** ➲ WORDFINDER NOTE AT DEBATE

Ayur·vedic medi·cine /ˌɑːjʊəˌveɪdɪk ˈmedsn; ˈmedɪsn; *NAmE* ˌɑːjʊr-/ *noun* [U] (*also* **Ayur·veda**, **ayur·veda** /ˌɑːjʊəˈveɪdə; -ˈviːdə; *NAmE* ˌɑːjʊrˈveɪdə/) a type of traditional Hindu medicine that treats illnesses using a combination of foods, HERBS and breathing exercises 阿育吠陀医学（结合食物、草药和呼吸运动治疗疾病的印度教传统医学）

aza·lea /əˈzeɪliə/ *noun* a plant or bush with large flowers that may be pink, purple, white or yellow, grown in a pot or in a garden 杜鹃；映山红

azi·muth /ˈæzɪməθ/ *noun* (*astronomy* 天) an angle related to a distance around the earth's HORIZON, used to find out the position of a star, planet, etc. 方位角，地平经度（用以找出恒星、行星等的方位）

AZT™ /ˌeɪ zed ˈtiː; *NAmE* ziː/ *noun* [U] a drug that is used to treat AIDS 齐多夫定（用于治疗艾滋病的药）

azure /ˈæʒə(r); *BrE also* ˈæzjʊə(r)/ *adj.* bright blue in colour like the sky 天蓝色的；蔚蓝色的 ▶ **azure** *noun* [U]

Bb

B

B /biː/ *noun, symbol*

■ ***noun*** (*also* **b**) (*pl.* **Bs, B's, b's** /biːz/) **1** [C, U] the second letter of the English alphabet 英语字母表的第 2 个字母: *'Butter' begins with (a) B/'B'.* * butter 一词以字母 b 开头。 **2 B** [C, U] (*music* 音) the 7th note in the SCALE of C MAJOR * B 音（C 大调的第 7 音或音符） **3 B** [C, U] the second highest mark/grade that a student can get for a piece of work （学业成绩）第二等，良： *She got (a) B in/for History.* 她的历史科成绩是 B。 **4 B** [U] used to represent the second of two or more possibilities （表示两个或两个以上可能性中的）第二个: *Shall we go for plan A or plan B?* 我们选用第一方案还是第二方案？ **5 B** [U] used to represent a person, for example in an imagined situation or to hide their identity （假设的或不指出姓名身份的第二人）乙，乙某： *Let's pretend A meets B in the park.* 假设甲某和乙某在公园里相遇。 ➲ SEE ALSO B-ROAD IDM SEE A *n.*

■ ***symbol*** used in Britain before a number to refer to a particular secondary road * B 级公路（英国公路代号，后接数字）： *the B1224 to York* 通往约克的 B1224 号公路

b. *abbr.* (in writing 书写形式) born 出生： *Emily Clifton, b. 1800* 埃米莉·克利夫顿，1800 年生

B2B /ˌbiː tə ˈbiː/ *abbr.* BUSINESS-TO-BUSINESS 企业对企业

B2C /ˌbiː tə ˈsiː/ *abbr.* BUSINESS-TO-CONSUMER 企业对消费者；商家对顾客

BA (*BrE*) (*NAmE usually* **B.A.**) /ˌbiː ˈeɪ/ *noun* the abbreviation for 'Bachelor of Arts' (a first university degree in an ARTS subject) 文学士（全写为 Bachelor of Arts，大学文科的初级学位）： *to **be/have/do a BA*** 是文学士；有文学士学位；攻读文学士 ◇ (*BrE*) *Darren Green BA* 文学士达伦·格林

baa /bɑː/ *noun* the sound made by sheep or LAMBS （羊叫声）咩 ▶ **baa** *verb* [I] (**baa·ing, baaed, baa'd**) ➲ MORE LIKE THIS 4, page R25

baba /ˈbɑːbɑː/ *noun* **1** a small cake, often with RUM poured over it （常浇有朗姆酒的）松软小蛋糕；婆婆蛋糕 **2** (*IndE, EAfrE*) a father (often also used as a title or form of address for any older man, showing respect) 阿爸，前辈（常用作对年长男子的敬称） **3** (*IndE*) a holy man 圣洁的人；圣人 **4** (*IndE*) (used especially as a form of address 尤用作称呼) a small child 宝宝；小孩子

Bab·bitt /ˈbæbɪt/ *noun* (*NAmE*) a person who is satisfied with a narrow set of values and thinks mainly about possessions and making money 巴比特式人物（满足于一套狭隘的价值观、只关心财富和赚钱） ORIGIN From the name of the main character in the novel *Babbitt* by Sinclair Lewis. 源自辛克莱·刘易斯的小说《巴比特》中主人公的名字。

bab·ble /ˈbæbl/ *noun, verb*

■ ***noun*** [sing.] **1** the sound of many people speaking at the same time 嘈杂的人声： *a babble of voices* 人声嘈杂 **2** talking that is confused or silly and is difficult to understand 含混不清的话；胡言乱语： *I can't listen to his constant babble.* 我听不得他那没完没了的瞎扯。 **3** the sounds a baby makes before beginning to say actual words （幼儿）咿呀学语声 ➲ SEE ALSO PSYCHOBABBLE

■ ***verb*** **1** [I, T] ~ (**away/on**) (**sth**) to talk quickly in a way that is difficult to understand 含混不清地说；嘀里嘟噜地说： *They were all babbling away in a foreign language.* 他们都叽里咕噜地说着外语。 ◇ *I realized I was babbling like an idiot.* 我意识到我像个傻瓜一样在胡言乱语。 **2** [I] to make the sound of water flowing over rocks, like a stream （水流过石块）潺潺作响： *a babbling brook* 潺潺的小溪

babby /ˈbæbi/ *noun* (*pl.* **-ies**) (*BrE, dialect*) a baby 婴儿

babe /beɪb/ *noun* **1** (*old use*) a baby 婴儿 **2** (*slang*) a word used to address a young woman, or your wife, husband or lover, usually expressing affection but sometimes considered offensive if used by a man to a woman he does not know 宝贝儿，心肝儿（对年轻女子或爱人的昵称。男子用以称呼不相识的女子则有冒犯之嫌）： *What're you doing tonight, babe?* 你今晚做什么，宝贝儿？ **3** (*informal*) an attractive young woman 有魅力的年轻女子

IDM **a ˌbabe in ˈarms** (*old-fashioned*) a very small baby that cannot yet walk 襁褓中的婴儿 ➲ MORE AT MOUTH *n.*

babel /ˈbeɪbl/ *noun* [sing.] (*formal*) the sound of many voices talking at one time, especially when more than one language is being spoken 嘈杂声（尤指讲多种语言） ORIGIN From the Bible story in which God punished the people who were trying to build a tower to reach heaven (the **tower of Babel**) by making them unable to understand each others' languages. 源自《圣经》故事。世人拟建造通天的巴别塔 (the tower of Babel)，上帝为惩罚他们而使他们无法理解彼此的语言。

ˈbabe magnet *noun* (*slang, especially NAmE*) a man or something that a man owns that is considered to be attractive to women 宝贝磁铁（指吸引女性的男子或男性物品）： *Bob's such a babe magnet.* 鲍勃真是个吸引异性的万人迷。 ◇ *A sports car like that is a complete babe magnet.* 那样的跑车绝对吸引女性。

ˌbabes in the ˈwood *noun* [pl.] innocent people who are easily tricked or harmed 幼稚易受骗的人；易受伤害的人 ORIGIN From a children's story about a boy and a girl who are left alone in a wood where they die and a bird covers them with leaves. 源自童话，一双男女孩童被弃于森林中。孩子死后，一只鸟衔来树叶将其掩埋。

ba·boon /bəˈbuːn; *NAmE* bæˈb-/ *noun* a large African or Asian MONKEY with a long face like a dog's 狒狒

babu /ˈbɑːbuː/ *noun* (*IndE*) a person who works in an office 办公室职员；白领

ba·bushka /bəˈbʊʃkə; ˈbæbʊʃkə/ *noun* (*from Russian*) **1** a Russian old woman or grandmother （俄罗斯）老太婆，祖母，外婆 **2** a traditional Russian woman's HEADSCARF, tied under the chin 婆婆头巾（传统俄罗斯头巾，在颏下打结）

baby 🔑 /ˈbeɪbi/ *noun, adj., verb*

■ ***noun*** (*pl.* **-ies**) **1** 🔑 a very young child or animal 婴儿；动物幼崽： *The baby's crying!* 婴儿在哭！ ◇ *a newborn baby* 新生儿 ◇ *My sister's **expecting a baby*** (= she is pregnant). 我姐姐怀孕了。 ◇ *She **had a baby** last year.* 她去年生了个孩子。 ◇ *a baby boy/girl* 男婴；女婴 ◇ *baby food/clothes* 婴儿食品 / 服装 ◇ *a baby monkey/blackbird* 幼猴；黑鹂雏 ➲ COLLOCATIONS AT CHILD

WORDFINDER 联想词： **birth, child,** dummy, feed, incubator, nappy, pram, premature, teethe

2 (*informal*) the youngest member of a family or group （家庭或团体中）最年幼的成员： *He's the baby of the team.* 他在队里年纪最小。 **3** (*disapproving*) a person who behaves like a young child and is easily upset 幼稚的人；孩子气的人： *Stop crying and don't be such a baby.* 别哭了，别这么孩子气。 **4** (*slang, especially NAmE*) a word used to address sb, especially your wife, husband or lover, in a way that expresses affection but that can be offensive if used by a man to a woman he does not know 宝贝儿，心肝儿（尤用于对爱人的昵称。男子用以称呼不相识的女子则有冒犯之嫌）

IDM **be your/sb's baby** (*informal*) to be a plan or project that sb is responsible for and cares about because they have created it （计划或项目）就像某人的孩子一样（因亲自制订而尽心负责） **leave sb holding the ˈbaby** (*informal*) to suddenly make sb responsible for sth important that is really your responsibility （突然）把重大责任推给某人： *He changed to another job and we were left holding the baby.* 他换了工作，把活儿甩给我们。 **throw the baby out with the ˈbathwater** (*informal*) to lose sth that you want at the same time as you are trying to get rid of sth that you do not want 把婴儿和洗澡水一起倒掉（丢弃不想要的东西的同时失去宝贵的东西） ➲ MORE AT CANDY, SLEEP *v.*

■ ***adj.*** [only before noun] **baby** vegetables are a very small version of particular vegetables, or are vegetables that are picked when they are very small （蔬菜）小型的，幼嫩的： *baby carrots* 小胡萝卜

■ *verb* (**ba·bies**, **baby·ing**, **ba·bied**, **ba·bied**) ~ **sb** to treat sb with too much care, as if they were a baby 婴儿般对待；百般呵护

ˌ**baby ˈblue** *adj.* very pale blue in colour 婴儿蓝的；淡蓝色的 ▸ ˌ**baby ˈblue** *noun* [U] ➲ MORE LIKE THIS 15, page R26

ˈ**baby blues** *noun* [pl.] (*informal*) a depressed feeling that some women get after the birth of a baby 产后抑郁 SYN **postnatal depression**

ˈ**baby boom** *noun* a period when many more babies are born than usual 生育高峰（期）

ˈ**baby boomer** (*NAmE also* **boom·er**) *noun* a person born during a baby boom, especially after the Second World War （尤指第二次世界大战后）生育高峰期出生的人

ˈ**baby bouncer** *noun* (*BrE*) a type of seat that hangs from pieces of ELASTIC, in which a baby can sit and BOUNCE up and down 婴儿蹦蹦椅

ˈ**baby buggy** *noun* **1** (*BrE*) = BUGGY (2) **2** (*old-fashioned, NAmE*) = BABY CARRIAGE

ˈ**baby bump** *noun* the round shape of a woman's stomach when she is pregnant 孕肚（孕妇腹部的隆起）

ˈ**baby carriage** (*NAmE*) (*also* **baby buggy**) (*BrE* **pram**) *noun* a small vehicle on four wheels for a baby to go out in, pushed by a person on foot 婴儿车 ➲ PICTURE AT PUSHCHAIR

baby·daddy /ˈbeɪbidædi/ (*also* **baby·father**) *noun* (*informal*) the father of a child, who is not married to or in a relationship with the child's mother 未婚爸爸（与孩子生母无婚姻或恋爱关系）

ˌ**baby-ˈdoll** *adj.* used to describe a style of women's dress or NIGHTDRESS that is short with a high waist and is similar to the type of dress traditionally worn by DOLLS （女子的连衣裙或睡袍）娃娃装式的

ˈ**baby-faced** *adj.* with a face that looks young and innocent 长着稚气的脸的；娃娃脸的

ˈ**baby fat** (*NAmE*) (*BrE* ˈ**puppy fat**) *noun* [U] fat on a child's body that disappears as the child grows older 婴儿肥（长大后消失）

baby·father /ˈbeɪbifɑːθə(r)/ *noun* ➲ BABYDADDY

ˌ**baby ˈgrand** *noun* a small GRAND PIANO 小型卧式钢琴；小型三角钢琴

Baby·gro™ /ˈbeɪbirəʊ; *NAmE* -groʊ/ *noun* (*pl.* **-os**) (*BrE*) a piece of clothing for babies, usually covering the whole body except the head and hands, made of a type of cloth that stretches easily （弹性）婴儿连身服 ➲ COMPARE ONESIES™

ba·by·hood /ˈbeɪbihʊd/ *noun* [U] the period of your life when you are a baby 婴儿期

baby·ish /ˈbeɪbiɪʃ/ *adj.* (*usually disapproving*) typical of or suitable for a baby 婴儿的；婴儿般的；稚气的

baby·mama /ˈbeɪbimæmə/ (*also* **baby·mother** /ˈbeɪbimʌθə(r)/) *noun* (*informal*) the mother of a child, who is not married to or in a relationship with the child's father 未婚妈妈（与孩子生父无婚姻或恋爱关系）

ˈ**baby shower** *noun* (*especially NAmE*) a party given for a woman who is going to have a baby, at which her friends give her presents for the baby （为即将分娩的女子举办的）新生儿送礼会，产前派对

baby·sit /ˈbeɪbisɪt/ *verb* (**baby·sit·ting**, **baby·sat**, **baby·sat**) (*especially NAmE* **sit**) [I, T] to take care of babies or children for a short time while their parents are out 代人临时照看小孩；当临时保姆： ~ (**for sb**) *She regularly babysits for us.* 她定期来为我们照看小孩。 ◇ ~ **sb** *He's babysitting the neighbour's children.* 他在帮邻居临时照看小孩。 ▸ **baby·sit·ting** *noun* [U]

baby·sit·ter /ˈbeɪbisɪtə(r)/ (*also* **sit·ter** *especially in NAmE*) *noun* a person who takes care of babies or children while their parents are away from home and is usually paid to do this 临时保姆；代人临时照看小孩的人： *I can't find a babysitter for tonight.* 我找不到人今天晚上帮我看小孩。 ➲ SEE ALSO CHILDMINDER

ˈ**baby step** *noun* [usually pl.] a small act or measure, usually at the start of a long or difficult process （大行动初期采取的）小幅度行动，温和措施： *The president is taking baby steps in the direction of reform.* 总统正朝改革的方向迈出谨慎的步子。

ˈ**baby talk** *noun* [U] the words or sounds a baby says when it is learning to talk; the special language adults sometimes use when talking to babies 牙牙学语（声）；（成人对婴儿所用的）模仿儿语

ˈ**baby tooth** (*BrE also* ˈ**milk tooth**) *noun* any of the first set of teeth in young children that drop out and are replaced by others 乳牙

ˈ**baby walker** (*BrE*) (*NAmE* **walk·er**) *noun* a frame with wheels and a HARNESS that you can put a baby in so that it is supported and can walk on its own around a room （幼儿）学步车

bac·ca·laur·eate /ˌbækəˈlɔːriət/ *noun* **1** the last SECONDARY SCHOOL exam in France and some other countries, and in some international schools （法国等国家以及一些国际学校的）中学毕业会考： ***to sit/take/pass/fail your baccalaureate*** 参加 / 通过 / 未通过中学毕业会考 ➲ SEE ALSO INTERNATIONAL BACCALAUREATE™ **2** (in the US) a religious service or talk for students who have completed HIGH SCHOOL or college （美国为中学或大学毕业生举行的）宗教礼仪，布道

bac·carat /ˈbækərɑː/ *noun* [U] a card game in which players hold two or three cards each and bet on whose cards will have the highest number left over when their value is divided by ten 巴卡拉纸牌游戏，百家乐（玩牌者手持两张或三张纸牌，赌谁的点数被十除后余数最大）

bac·chan·al·ian /ˌbækəˈneɪliən/ *adj.* (*formal*) (of a party, etc. 聚会等) wild and involving large amounts of alcohol 纵酒狂欢的 ORIGIN From the name of the Greek god **Bacchus** (also called Dionysus), the god of wine and wild enjoyment. 源自希腊酒神与狂欢之神巴克斯 (Bacchus) 的名字。

baccy /ˈbæki/ *noun* [U] (*BrE, informal*) TOBACCO 烟草

bach /bætʃ/ *noun* (*NZE*) a small holiday house 度假小屋

bach·elor /ˈbætʃələ(r)/ *noun* **1** a man who has never been married 未婚男子；单身汉： *an eligible bachelor* (= one that many people want to marry, especially because he is rich) 合意单身男子（常因富有而为理想对象） ◇ *a **confirmed bachelor*** (= a person who does not intend to marry; often used in newspapers to refer to a HOMOSEXUAL man) 信守独身主义的单身汉（报章上常用来指同性恋男子） ➲ COMPARE SPINSTER **2** (*usually* **Bachelor**) a person who has a Bachelor's degree (= a first university degree) 学士： *a **Bachelor of Arts/Engineering/Science*** 文学士；工程学士；理学士 ➲ SEE ALSO BA, BEd, BSc **3** (*CanE*) = BACHELOR APARTMENT

ˈ**bachelor apartment** *noun* a small flat/apartment suitable for a person living alone 单身套房；单身公寓房

ba·chelor·ette /ˌbætʃələˈret/ *noun* (*NAmE*) a young woman who is not married 单身女子；单身女郎

ˈ**bachelor girl** *noun* an independent young woman who is not married 独立生活的年轻女子；单身女子

bach·elor·hood /ˈbætʃələhʊd; *NAmE* -lərh-/ *noun* [U] the time in a man's life before he is married 男子的未婚时期

ˈ**bachelor pad** *noun* a house or flat/apartment in which a man who is not married enjoys a lifestyle without family responsibilities 单身男子的窝；单身男子公寓；单身汉公寓

B

ˈ**bachelor party** (*NAmE*) (*BrE* ˈ**stag night**, *also* ˈ**stag party** *NAmE, BrE*) *noun* a party that a man has with his male friends just before he gets married, often the night before 男子婚前聚会（常在结婚前一夜举行，招待男性朋友）

ba·cil·lus /bəˈsɪləs/ *noun* (*pl.* **ba·cilli** /bəˈsɪlaɪ/) a type of bacteria. There are several types of bacillus, some of which cause disease. 杆菌（有些可致病）

back /bæk/ *noun, adj., adv., verb*

■ ***noun***

• **PART OF BODY** 身体部位 **1** the part of the human body that is on the opposite side to the chest, between the neck and the tops of the legs; the part of an animal's body that CORRESPONDS to this （人体或动物的）背部，背；腰背: *Do you sleep on your back or your front?* 你睡觉是仰着还是趴着？ ◇ *He stood with his back to the door.* 他背对着门站着。◇ *They had their hands tied behind their backs.* 他们双手被反剪起来。◇ *back pain* 背痛 ◇ *a back massage* 背部按摩 ◇ *A small boy rode on the elephant's back.* 一个小男孩骑在大象背上。 ➲ COLLOCATIONS AT PHYSICAL ➲ VISUAL VOCAB PAGE V64 ➲ SEE ALSO BAREBACK, HORSEBACK *n.* **2** the row of bones in the middle of the back 脊柱；脊梁骨 SYN **backbone, spine**: *She broke her back in a riding accident.* 她在一次骑马事故中摔断了脊梁骨。◇ *He* ***put his back out*** (= DISLOCATED sth in his back) *lifting the crates.* 他搬大木箱时脊椎脱了臼。

• **PART FURTHEST FROM FRONT** 后部 **3** [usually sing.] ~ (**of sth**) the part or area of sth that is furthest from the front 后部；后面；末尾: *We could only get seats* ***at the back*** (= of the room). 我们只能找到后排的座位。◇ *I found some old photos at the back of the drawer.* 我从抽屉尽里头找到一些旧照片。◇ *He was shot in the back of the knee.* 他被子弹击中了腘窝。◇ *The house has three bedrooms at the front and two* ***at the back***. 房屋正面有三间卧室，后面两间。◇ (*BrE*) *There's room for three people* ***in the back***. 后排的空间可容三人。◇ (*NAmE*) *There's room for three people* ***in back*** (= of a car, etc.). 后排的空间可容三人。◇ (*BrE*) *Come* ***round the back*** (= to the area behind the house) *and I'll show you the garden.* 到房子后面来，我带你看看花园。 ➲ SEE ALSO HARDBACK, PAPERBACK, SHORT BACK AND SIDES

• **OF PIECE OF PAPER** 纸张 **4** [usually sing.] ~ (**of sth**) the part of a piece of paper, etc. that is on the opposite side to the one that has information or the most important information on it （文件等的）背面: *Write your name on the back of the cheque.* 把你的名字写在支票背面。

• **OF BOOK** 书刊 **5** [usually sing.] ~ (**of sth**) the last few pages of a book, etc. （书等的）最后几页，末尾: *The television guide is at the back of the paper.* 电视节目指南在报纸的末尾。

• **OF CHAIR** 椅子 **6** the part of a chair, etc. against which you lean your back （椅子等的）靠背 ➲ VISUAL VOCAB PAGE V22

▼ **WHICH WORD?** 词语辨析

at the back / at the rear / behind

• **At the back** and **at the rear** have a similar meaning, but **at the rear** is used more in formal or official language. * at the back 和 at the rear 意义相近，但 at the rear 多用于正式或官方语言： *What's that at the back of the fridge?* 冰箱尽里头那东西是什么？ ◇ *Smoking is only allowed at the rear of the aircraft.* 只有飞机后舱允许抽烟。 It is more usual to talk about the **back door** of a house but the **rear exit** of an aircraft or public building. If something is **behind** something else it is near to the back of it but not part of it. 指房子的后门较常用 back door，但飞机或公共建筑的后门较常用 rear exit。behind 指在后面，但不是其中的部分。 Compare 比较： *Our room was at the back of the hotel.* 我们的房间在旅馆靠后面的地方。 and 和： *There's a lovely wood just behind our hotel.* 在我们旅馆的后面就有一片美丽的树林。

• **-BACKED** 靠背… **7** (in adjectives 构成形容词) used to describe furniture that has the type of back mentioned （家具）…靠背的: *a high-backed sofa* 高靠背沙发

• **IN SPORT** 体育运动 **8** (in some sports 某些体育运动) a player whose main role is to defend their team's goal 后卫 ➲ COMPARE FORWARD *n.* ➲ SEE ALSO FULL BACK, HALF BACK

IDM **at/in the back of your mind** if a thought, etc. is **at the back of your mind**, you are aware of it but it is not what you are mainly thinking about 在潜意识里；依稀记得 **the ˌback of beˈyond** (*informal*) a place that is a long way from other houses, towns, etc. 偏僻地方；边远地区 **ˌback to ˈback 1** if two people stand **back to back**, they stand with their backs facing or touching each other 背靠背；背对背 ➲ SEE ALSO BACK-TO-BACK **2** if two or more things happen **back to back**, they happen one after the other 接连地；接二连三 **ˌback to ˈfront** (*BrE*) (*NAmE* **back·wards**) if you put on a piece of clothing **back to front**, you make a mistake and put the back where the front should be （衣服）前后颠倒（或前后穿反）: *I think you've got that sweater on back to front.* 我觉得你把毛衣前后穿反了。 ➲ COMPARE INSIDE OUT at INSIDE *n.* **be glad, etc. to see the back of sb/sth** (*informal, especially BrE*) to be happy that you will not have to deal with or see sb/sth again because you do not like them or it 庆幸终于摆脱（不喜欢的人或事物）: *Was I pleased to see the back of her!* 真高兴不会再见到她了！ **behind sb's ˈback** without sb's knowledge or permission 背着某人；背地里；私下: *Have you been talking about me behind my back?* 你们是不是在背后说我的闲话？ ◇ *They went ahead and sold it behind my back.* 他们径自背着我把它卖了。 ➲ COMPARE TO SB'S FACE at FACE *n.* **be on sb's ˈback** (*informal*) to keep asking or telling sb to do sth that they do not want to do, in a way that they find annoying 缠磨；烦扰 **break the ˈback of sth** to finish the largest or most important part of a task 完成（任务等的）主要部分 **get/put sb's ˈback up** (*informal*) to annoy sb 惹恼: *That sort of attitude really gets my back up!* 那种态度实在叫我恼火！ **get off sb's ˈback** (*informal*) to stop annoying sb, for example by criticizing them, or asking them to do sth 不再烦扰某人（如停止批评或缠磨等）: *Just get off my back, will you!* 请别烦我了好吗！ **have (got) sb's ˈback** (*NAmE, informal*) to protect and support sb 保护，支持（某人）: *Don't worry, I've got your back.* 别担心，我支持你。 **have your ˌback to the ˈwall** (*informal*) to be in a difficult situation in which you are forced to do sth but are unable to make the choices that you would like 处于背水一战的境地；没有退路 **off the ˌback of a ˈlorry** (*BrE, informal, humorous*) goods that **fell off the back of a lorry** were probably stolen. People say or accept that they came 'off the back of a lorry' to avoid saying or asking where they really came from. （指货物等）来路不明 **on the back of sth** as a result of an achievement or a success 由于（某项成就）: *The profits growth came on the back of a 26 per cent rise in sales.* 利润增长来自 26% 的销售额增长。 **(flat) on your back** (*informal*) in bed because you are ill/sick 因病卧床；卧病: *She's been flat on her back for over a week now.* 她卧病有一个多星期了。 ◇ (*figurative*) *The UK market was flat on its back* (= business was very bad). （当时）英国的市场十分不景气。 **put your ˈback into sth** to use a lot of effort and energy on a particular task 全力以赴 **turn your back** to turn so that you are facing in the opposite direction 扭头；转身 **turn your back on sb/sth 1** to move so that you are standing or sitting with your back facing sb/sth 转身背对某人（或某物）: *When on stage, try not to turn your back on the audience.* 在舞台上尽量不要背对观众。 **2** to reject sb/sth that you have previously been connected with 背弃；抛弃: *She turned her back on them when they needed her.* 他们需要她的时候，她却背弃了他们。 ➲ MORE AT COVER *v.*, EYE *n.*, KNOW *v.*, PAT *n.*, PAT *v.*, PUSH *v.*, ROD, SCRATCH *v.*, SHIRT, STAB *n.*, STAB *v.*, STRAW, WATER *n.*

■ ***adj.*** [only before noun]

• **AWAY FROM FRONT** 后面 **1** located behind or at the back of sth 背后的；后面的；后部的: *We were sitting in the* *back row.* 我们坐在后排。◇ *back teeth* 臼齿 ◇ *a back room* (= one at the back of a building) 后室（位于建筑物后部）◇ *the back page of a newspaper* 报纸最末一页 ➲ COMPARE FRONT *adj.*

- **FROM PAST** 过去 **2** of or from a past time 过去的；旧时的： *a back number of the magazine* 一份过期杂志
- **OWED** 拖欠 **3** owed for a time in the past 到期未付的；拖欠的： *back pay/taxes/rent* 欠薪；欠税；欠租金
- **PHONETICS** 语音 **4** (*phonetics* 语音) (of a vowel 元音) produced with the back of the tongue in a higher position than the front, for example /ɑː/ in English 舌后的，后位性的（舌高点位于口腔后部发音） ➲ COMPARE CENTRAL, FRONT *adj.*

IDM **on the back 'burner** (*informal*) (of an idea, a plan, etc. 主意、计划等) left for the present time, to be done or considered later 暂时搁置 ➲ SEE ALSO BACK-BURNER ➲ COMPARE ON THE FRONT BURNER at FRONT *adj.*

■ ***adv.*** HELP For the special uses of **back** in phrasal verbs, look at the entries for the verbs. For example **pay sb back** is in the phrasal verb section at **pay**. * back 在短语动词中的特殊用法见有关动词词条。如 pay sb back 在词条 pay 的短语动词部分。

- **AWAY FROM FRONT** 后面 **1** 🔑 away from the front or centre; behind you 向后；在后；在背面： *I stepped back to let them pass.* 我退后一步给他们让路。◇ *Sit back and relax.* 靠椅背坐好，放松放松。◇ *You've combed your hair back.* 你把头发往后梳了。◇ *He turned and looked back.* 他转身向后望。◇ *She fell back towards the end of the race.* 赛跑快结束时她落后了。OPP **forward**
- **AT A DISTANCE** 距离 **2** 🔑 at a distance away from sth （与某物）有距离： *The barriers kept the crowd back.* 障碍物拦住了人群。◇ *Stand back and give me some room.* 站远点儿，给我腾出些地方。
- **UNDER CONTROL** 受控制 **3** 🔑 under control; prevented from being expressed or coming out 控制住；忍住： *He could no longer hold back his tears.* 他再也无法控制住眼泪。
- **AS BEFORE** 像先前 **4** 🔑 to or into the place, condition, situation or activity where sb/sth was before 回原处；恢复原状： *Put the book back on the shelf.* 把书放回书架上。◇ *Please give me my ball back.* 请把我的球还给我。◇ *He'll be back on Monday.* 他星期一会回来。◇ *It takes me an hour to walk **there and back**.* 我步行往返要花一个小时。◇ *Could you go back to the beginning of the story?* 你能不能回到故事的开头？◇ *She woke up briefly and then went back to sleep.* 她醒了片刻又睡了。◇ *We were right **back where we started**, only this time without any money.* 我们回到了起点，只是这次一点钱也没有。
- **IN PAST** 过去 **5** 🔑 in or into the past; ago 以前： *The village has a history going back to the Middle Ages.* 这个村子的历史可追溯至中世纪。◇ *She left **back in November**.* 她十一月已经离开了。◇ *That was a few years back.* 那是几年以前的事。
- **AT A PREVIOUS PLACE** 在原处 **6** 🔑 at a place previously left or mentioned 在曾去过（或提到过）的地方；在前面： *We should have turned left five kilometres back.* 我们在五公里之前就该左拐的。◇ *Back at home, her parents were worried.* 在家中，她的父母很担心。◇ *I can't wait to get back home.* 我急不可待想赶回家。
- **IN RETURN** 回应 **7** 🔑 in return or reply 回报；回答： *If he kicks me, I'll kick him back.* 他要是踢我，我就踢他。◇ *Could you call back later, please?* 请稍后再打电话来好吗？

IDM **,back and 'forth** 🔑 from one place to another and back again repeatedly 反复来回： *ferries sailing back and forth between the islands* 往返于岛屿之间的渡船 **,back in the 'day** in the past 过去；从前；旧时： *My dad's always talking about how great everything was back in the day.* 我爸爸总是讲过去的一切如何如何的好。**,back in the 'days** at a particular time in the past 在过去的某个时候： *I was a fan back in the days when the band wasn't yet famous.* 在这个乐队还没出名的时候，我就是他们的歌迷。**back of sth** (*NAmE, informal*) behind sth 在某物的背后（或背面）： *the houses back of the church* 位于教堂后面的房屋 ➲ MORE AT EARTH *n.*, SQUARE *n.*

■ ***verb***

- **MOVE BACKWARDS** 后退 **1** 🔑 [I, T] to move or make sth move backwards （使）后退，倒退： **+ adv./prep.** *He backed against the wall, terrified.* 他退到墙边，惊恐万分。◇ **~ sth + adv./prep.** *If you can't drive in forwards, try backing it in.* 若不能开车正面驶入，不妨倒车进去。➲ COMPARE REVERSE *v.*
- **SUPPORT** 支持 **2** 🔑 [T] **~ sb/sth** to give help or support to sb/sth 帮助；支持： *Her parents backed her in her choice of career.* 她父母支持她的职业选择。◇ *Doctors have backed plans to raise the tax on cigarettes.* 医生们对提高烟草税计划给予了支持。◇ *The programme of economic reform is backed* (= given financial support) *by foreign aid.* 经济改革计划得到外资援助。◇ *a United Nations-backed peace plan* 得到联合国支持的和平计划
- **BET MONEY** 下赌注 **3** [T] **~ sth** to bet money on a horse in a race, a team in a competition, etc. 下赌注于（赛马、参赛队伍等）： *I backed the winner and won fifty pounds.* 我押对了赌注，赢了五十英镑。
- **MUSIC** 音乐 **4** [T] **~ sth** to play or sing music that supports the main singer or instrument 为…伴奏；为…伴唱 ➲ SEE ALSO BACKING
- **COVER BACK** 覆盖背面 **5** [T] **~ sth (with sth)** [usually passive] to cover the back of sth in order to support or protect it （用某物）在…背后加固，给…加背衬
- **BE BEHIND** 在后面 **6** [T, usually passive] **~ sth** to be located behind sth 位于（某物）的后面；在…后面： *The house is backed by fields.* 房子的后面是田野。

IDM **,back the wrong 'horse** (*BrE*) to support sb/sth that is not successful 下错赌注（支持了失败的一方或事情）

PHR V **,back a'way (from sb/sth)** to move away backwards from sb/sth that is frightening or unpleasant; to avoid doing sth that is unpleasant 躲避（可怕或讨厌的人或事物）；避免（做讨厌的事）；退避 **,back 'down (on/from sth)** (*NAmE also* **,back 'off**) to take back a demand, an opinion, etc. that other people are strongly opposed to; to admit defeat 放弃（别人强烈反对的要求、主张等）；认输： *She refused to back down on a point of principle.* 她在一个原则问题上拒绝让步。**,back 'off 1** to move backwards in order to get away from sb/sth frightening or unpleasant 退缩，退却（以躲避可怕或讨厌的人或事物）： *As the riot police approached, the crowd backed off.* 随着防暴警察逼近，人群往后退却了。**2** to stop threatening, criticizing or annoying sb 停止威胁（或批评、骚扰）： *Back off! There's no need to yell at me.* 走开点！没必要对我大喊大叫。◇ *The press have agreed to back off and leave the couple alone.* 新闻界同意退让，不再搅扰这对夫妇。**,back 'off (from sth)** to choose not to take action, in order to avoid a difficult situation 放弃（采取行动）；退让： *The government backed off from a confrontation.* 政府放弃对抗。**,back 'onto sth** (of a building 建筑物) to have sth directly behind it 背向；背靠： *Our house backs onto the river.* 我们的房子背向河流。**,back 'out (of sth)** to decide that you are no longer going to take part in sth that has been agreed 退出；撤手： *He lost confidence and backed out of the deal at the last minute.* 他失去了信心，在最后一刻退出了协议。**,back 'up** | **,back sth↔'up** to move backwards, especially in a vehicle 后退；倒（车）： *You can back up another two feet or so.* 你可以再退两英尺左右。◇ *I backed the car up to the door.* 我把车倒到门前。**,back sb/sth↔'up 1** 🔑 to support sb/sth; to say that what sb says, etc. is true 支持；证实（某人所言）： *I'll back you up if they don't believe you.* 如果他们不相信你，我会为你作证。◇ *The writer doesn't back up his opinions with examples.* 作者没用实例印证他的看法。**2** 🔑 to provide support for sb/sth 支持；支援： *two doctors backed up by a team of nurses* 由一组护士辅助的两名医生 ◇ *The rebels backed up their demands with threats.* 反叛者以恐吓手段要挟。➲ RELATED NOUN BACKUP **,back sth↔'up** (*computing* 计) to prepare a second copy of a file, program, etc. that can be used if the main one fails or needs extra support 给（文件、程序等）做备份；备份 ➲ RELATED NOUN BACKUP

back·ache /ˈbækeɪk/ *noun* [U, C] a continuous pain in the back 背痛；腰痛： (*BrE*) *to have backache/a backache* 背痛 ◇ (*NAmE*) *to have a backache* 背痛

B

ˌback ˈalley *noun* a narrow passage behind or between buildings 后巷；夹道

ˌback-ˈalley *adj.* [only before noun] happening or done secretly, often illegally（非法）秘密发生的，秘密进行的；偷偷摸摸的：*a back-alley abortion* 非法秘密堕胎

back·beat /ˈbækbiːt/ *noun* (*music* 音) a strong emphasis on one or two of the beats that are not normally emphasized, used especially in JAZZ and rock music 基调强节奏（尤见于爵士乐和摇滚乐）

ˌback ˈbench *noun* [usually pl.] (in the House of Commons in Britain, and in certain other parliaments) any of the seats for Members of Parliament who do not have senior positions in the government or the other parties（英国下院及其他某些国家议会的）后座议员席，普通议员席：*He resigned as Home Secretary and returned to the back benches.* 他辞去了内政大臣的职务，回到后座议员席。◇ *back-bench MPs* 下院普通议员 ➲ COMPARE FRONT BENCH

back·bench·er /ˌbækˈbentʃə(r)/ *noun* (in the House of Commons in Britain and in certain other parliaments) a member who sits in the rows of seats at the back, and who does not have an important position in the government or the Opposition（英国和其他某些国家议会的）后座议员，普通议员，后排议员 ➲ COMPARE FRONTBENCHER

back·bit·ing /ˈbækbaɪtɪŋ/ *noun* [U] unpleasant and unkind talk about sb who is not present 背后中伤；背后诽谤

back·board /ˈbækbɔːd; *NAmE* -bɔːrd/ *noun* the board behind the BASKET in the game of BASKETBALL（篮球）篮板

back·bone /ˈbækbəʊn; *NAmE* -boʊn/ *noun* **1** [C] the row of small bones that are connected together down the middle of the back 脊梁骨；脊柱 **SYN** **spine** ➲ VISUAL VOCAB PAGE V64 **2** [sing.] the most important part of a system, an organization, etc. that gives it support and strength 支柱；骨干；基础：*Agriculture forms the backbone of the rural economy.* 农业是农村经济的基础。 **3** [U] the strength of character that you need to do sth difficult 毅力；骨气：*He doesn't have the backbone to face the truth.* 他没有面对现实的勇气。

ˈback-breaking *adj.* (of physical work 体力劳动) very hard and tiring 艰苦繁重的；累死人的 ➲ MORE LIKE THIS 10, page R26

ˌback-ˈburner *verb* **~ sth** (*informal, especially NAmE*) to leave an idea or a plan for a time, to be done or considered later 搁置；稍后处理 ➲ COMPARE ON THE BACK BURNER at BACK *adj.*

ˈback button *noun* a small area on a computer screen that you click on or tap to return to the previous screen or page（计算机屏幕上的）后退按钮，返回按钮

ˈback catalogue (*NAmE also* **ˈback catalog**) *noun* all the recorded music previously produced by a musician（音乐家的）先期录音全辑：*The entire Beatles' back catalogue has been put online.* 披头士的全套作品都已经放到网上。

back·channel /ˈbæktʃænl/ *noun* **1** a secret or unusual way of passing information to other people（传递消息的）秘密渠道，特殊途径 **2** (*linguistics* 语言) a sound or sign that sb makes to show that they are listening to the person who is talking to them 言语反馈示意，反输，附应（以声音或示意作为对说话人的反馈）

back·chat /ˈbæktʃæt/ (*BrE*) (*NAmE* **ˈback talk**) *noun* [U] (*informal*) a way of answering that shows no respect for sb in authority 顶嘴

back·cloth /ˈbækklɒθ; *NAmE* -klɔːθ; -klɑːθ/ *noun* (*BrE*) = BACKDROP

back·comb /ˈbækkəʊm; *NAmE* -koʊm/ (*BrE*) (*NAmE* **tease**) *verb* **~ sth** to COMB your hair in the opposite direction to the way it grows so that it looks thicker 反梳（头发）使之蓬起

ˌback ˈcopy *noun* (*BrE*) = BACK ISSUE

back·coun·try /ˈbækkʌntri/ *noun* [U] (*NAmE*) an area away from roads and towns, especially in the mountains（山中等）偏僻地区，偏远地区

back·court /ˈbækkɔːt; *NAmE* -kɔːrt/ *noun* **1** (in TENNIS, BASKETBALL, etc. 网球、篮球等) the area at either end of the COURT 后场 **2** (in BASKETBALL 篮球) the players who form the defence 防守队员 **3** (*ScotE*) an area surrounded by walls but with no roof at the back of a building 后院

back·crawl /ˈbækkrɔːl/ *noun* [U, sing.] (*BrE*) = BACKSTROKE

back·date /ˌbækˈdeɪt/ *verb* **1 ~ sth** to write a date on a cheque or other document that is earlier than the actual date 倒填日期（在支票等上签写比实际较早的日期）➲ COMPARE POST-DATE (1) **2 ~ sth** (*BrE*) to make sth, especially a payment, take effect from an earlier date 使（付款等）在较早的日期开始生效：*Postal workers are getting a 5.2% pay rise, backdated to February.* 邮政员工的工资将提高 5.2%，追溯至二月份起算。

ˌback ˈdoor *noun* the door at the back or side of a building 后门；边门

IDM **by/through the back door** in an unfair or indirect way 走后门：*He used his friends to help him get into the civil service by the back door.* 他利用朋友帮他开后门当上了公务员。

ˌback-ˈdoor *adj.* [only before noun] using indirect or secret means in order to achieve sth 后门的；不正当的

back·draught (*also* **back·draft**) /ˈbækdrɑːft; *NAmE* -dræft/ *noun* **1** a current of air that flows backwards down a CHIMNEY, pipe, etc.（烟囱、管道等的）倒烟，倒灌风 **2** an explosion caused by more OXYGEN being supplied to a fire, for example by a door being opened（给火焰供氧过多引起的）回火爆炸

back·drop /ˈbækdrɒp; *NAmE* -drɑːp/ (*BrE also* **back·cloth**) *noun* **1** a painted piece of cloth that is hung behind the stage in a theatre as part of the SCENERY（舞台的）背景幕布 ➲ WORDFINDER NOTE AT STAGE **2** everything that can be seen around an event that is taking place, but which is not part of that event（事件发生时）周围陪衬景物：*The mountains provided a dramatic backdrop for our picnic.* 群山如画，给我们的野餐平添景色。 **3** the general conditions in which an event takes place, which sometimes help to explain that event（事态或活动的）背景：*It was* ***against this backdrop*** *of racial tension that the civil war began.* 这场内战肇端于种族之间的紧张状态。

ˌback ˈend *noun* (*especially BrE*) **1** the end of a period or process（时段或过程的）结束，结尾：*the back end of last year* 去年年终 **2** the part of sth which is behind the part that you can see（物体的）后端，背面 **3** (*informal*) a person's bottom (= the part they sit on) 屁股

ˈback-end *adj.* [only before noun] **1** relating to the end of a period or process 结束的；结尾的 **2** (*computing* 计) (of a device or program 设备或程序) not used directly by a user, but used by a program or computer 后端的，后台的（指不归用户直接使用，而由程序或电脑使用）➲ COMPARE FRONT-END

back·er /ˈbækə(r)/ *noun* a person or company that gives support to sb/sth, especially financial support 支持者；资助者；赞助人

back·field /ˈbækfiːld/ *noun* [sing., U] **1** (in AMERICAN FOOTBALL 美式足球) the area of play behind the line of SCRIMMAGE 后场（争球线后面的区域） **2** the players who play in or around this area 守卫队员

back·fill /ˈbækfɪl/ *verb* **~ sth** to fill a hole with the material that has been dug out of it 回填（用挖出的材料重新填回洞穴）

back·fire /ˌbækˈfaɪə(r)/ *verb* **1** [I] **~ (on sb)** to have the opposite effect to the one intended, with bad or dangerous results 产生事与愿违的不良（或危险）后果：*Unfortunately the plan backfired.* 不幸的是，计划产生了

适得其反的结果。 **2** [I] (of an engine or a vehicle 发动机或车辆) to make a sudden noise like an explosion 逆火；回火 ➲ COMPARE MISFIRE

back·flip /ˈbækflɪp/ *noun* if sb does a **backflip**, they turn their body over backwards in the air and land on their feet again 后空翻

ˈback-formation *noun* [U, C] (*linguistics* 语言) a word formed by removing or changing the end of a word that already exists. For example, *commentate* is a back-formation from *commentator*. 逆构词法（将已存在的词通过去除或改变其后缀构成新词。如 commentate 由 commentator 一词逆构而成）

back·gam·mon /ˈbækgæmən; ˌbækˈgæmən/ *noun* [U] a game for two people played on a board marked with long thin triangles. Players throw DICE and move pieces around the board. 十五子棋戏（棋盘上有楔形小区，两人玩，掷骰子决定走棋步数） ➲ VISUAL VOCAB PAGE V43

back·ground /ˈbækgraʊnd/ *noun*
- **FAMILY/EDUCATION, ETC.** 家庭、教育等 **1** [C] the details of a person's family, education, experience, etc. 出身背景；学历；经历： *a person's **family/social/cultural/educational/class background*** 一个人的出身 / 社会 / 文化 / 教育 / 阶级背景 ◇ *The job would suit someone with a business background.* 这项工作适合有商务经验的人。
- **PAST** 过去 **2** [C, usually sing., U] the circumstances or past events that help explain why sth is how it is; information about these（事态发展等的）背景： *the historical background to the war* 这场战争的历史背景 ◇ ***background information/knowledge*** 背景资料 / 知识 ◇ *The elections are taking place **against a background of** violence.* 选举正在暴乱的情况下进行。 ◇ *Can you give me more background on the company?* 你能给我多提供一些这家公司的背景资料吗？
- **OF PICTURE/PHOTO** 图画；照片 **3** [C, usually sing.] the part of a picture, photograph or view behind the main objects, people, etc. 后景；背景： *a photograph with trees **in the background*** 以树木为远景的照片 ➲ COMPARE FOREGROUND *n.* (1) ➲ SYNONYMS AT ENVIRONMENT ➲ WORDFINDER NOTE AT PAINTING ➲ EXPRESS YOURSELF AT DESCRIBE
- **LESS IMPORTANT POSITION** 次要位置 **4** [sing.] a position in which people are not paying attention to sb/sth or not as much attention as they are paying to sb/sth else 不显眼的位置；幕后： *He prefers to remain **in the background** and let his assistant talk to the press.* 他喜欢待在幕后，让他的助理向新闻界发布消息。 ◇ *A piano tinkled gently **in the background.*** 背景是悠扬的钢琴声。 ◇ ***background music*** 背景音乐 ◇ *There was a lot of **background noise*** (= that you could hear, but were not listening to). 背景噪音很多。 ➲ COMPARE FOREGROUND *n.* (2)
- **COLOUR UNDER STH** 底色 **5** [C, usually sing.] a colour or design on which sth is painted, drawn, etc. 底色；底花；底子： *The name of the company is written in red on a white background.* 公司的名称是用白底红字写的。

IDM **in the ˈbackground** (*computing* 计) (of a computer program 计算机程序) not being used at the present time and appearing on the screen behind programs that are being used 在后台；背景的 ➲ COMPARE IN THE FOREGROUND at FOREGROUND *n.* ➲ MORE AT MERGE

back·hand /ˈbækhænd/ *noun* [usually sing.] (in TENNIS, etc. 网球等) a stroke played with the back of the hand turned in the direction towards which the ball is hit 反手；反手击球： *He has a good backhand* (= he can make good backhand strokes). 他的反手击球很棒。 ◇ *a **backhand volley/drive*** 反手截击 / 抽球 ➲ COMPARE FOREHAND

back·han·ded /ˌbækˈhændɪd/ *adj.* having a meaning that is not directly or clearly expressed, or that is not intended 间接的；拐弯抹角的；有言外之意的

IDM **a ˌbackhanded ˈcompliment** (*NAmE also* **ˌleft-handed ˈcompliment**) a remark that seems to express admiration but could also be understood as an insult 隐含讥讽的恭维

back·hand·er /ˈbækhændə(r)/ *noun* (*BrE, informal*) a secret and illegal payment made to sb in exchange for a favour 贿赂 SYN **bribe**

ˌback-ˈheel *verb* ~ **sth** to kick a ball using the heel 用脚跟踢（球）： *He back-heeled the ball towards goal.* 他用脚跟将球踢向球门。 ▶ **ˌback-ˈheel** *noun*

back·hoe /ˈbækhəʊ; *NAmE* -hoʊ/ *noun* a large vehicle with machinery for digging, used in building roads, etc. 反铲；反铲挖土机

back·ing /ˈbækɪŋ/ *noun* **1** [U] help 帮助；协助 SYN **support**: *financial backing* 资助 ◇ *The police gave the proposals their full backing.* 警方对这些提案给予全力支持。 **2** [U, C] material attached to the back of sth in order to protect it or make it stronger 背衬 **3** [U, C, usually sing.] (especially in pop music) music that accompanies the main singer or tune （尤指流行音乐的）伴唱，伴奏： *a **backing group/singer/track*** 伴奏乐团；伴唱歌手；伴奏歌曲

ˌback ˈissue (*BrE also* **ˌback ˈcopy**, **ˌback ˈnumber**) *noun* a copy of a newspaper or magazine from a date in the past 过期的报纸（或杂志）

back·lash /ˈbæklæʃ/ *noun* [sing.] ~ **(against sth)** | ~ **(from sb)** a strong negative reaction by a large number of people, for example to sth that has recently changed in society （对社会变动等的）强烈抵制，集体反对： *The government is facing an angry backlash from voters over the new tax.* 政府正面临选民对新税项的强烈反对。

back·less /ˈbækləs/ *adj.* (of a dress 连衣裙) not covering most of the back 露背的

back·light /ˈbæklaɪt/ *noun, verb*
- *noun* [U] light from behind sth in a photograph or painting （照片或绘画的）背景光
- *verb* (**back·lit**, **back·lit** or **back·lighted**, **back·lighted**) ~ **sth** to shine light on sth from behind 从背后照亮；背景照明；给…打背景灯 ▶ **back·lit** *adj.*: *a backlit photograph* 有背景光的照片

back·link /ˈbæklɪŋk/ *noun* a link on a WEB PAGE (= a document that is connected to the World Wide Web) to another website （网页上的）反向链接 ➲ COMPARE HYPERLINK ▶ **back·link** *verb*

back·list /ˈbæklɪst/ *noun* the list of books that have been published by a company in the past and are still available （出版商的）存书目录

back·log /ˈbæklɒg; *NAmE* -lɔːg; -lɑːg/ *noun* a quantity of work that should have been done already, but has not yet been done 积压的工作

back·lot /ˈbæklɒt; *NAmE* -lɑːt/ *noun* an outdoor area in a film/movie studio, where pieces of SCENERY are made and some scenes are filmed （电影制片厂的）外景场地

back·mark·er /ˈbækmɑːkə(r); *NAmE* -mɑːrk-/ *noun* (*BrE*) the person, horse, etc. who is in last position in a race （赛跑、赛马等）最后一名，末位

back·most /ˈbækməʊst; *NAmE* -moʊst/ *adj.* [usually before noun] furthest back 最后面的： *the backmost teeth* 最里面的牙齿

ˌback ˈnumber *noun* (*BrE*) = BACK ISSUE

ˌback ˈoffice *noun* (*business* 商) the part of a business company which does not deal directly with the public 后勤部门

back·pack /ˈbækpæk/ *noun, verb*
- *noun* **1** (*BrE also* **ruck·sack**) a large bag, often supported on a light metal frame, carried on the back and used especially by people who go climbing or walking （尤指登山者或远足者使用的）背包，旅行包 ➲ VISUAL VOCAB PAGE V69 **2** a piece of equipment that is carried on the back 背负式设备： *a weed-sprayer backpack* 背负式喷雾除草器
- *verb* [I] (*usually* **go backpacking**) to travel on holiday/vacation carrying your equipment and clothes in a backpack 背包旅行： *They went backpacking in Spain*

last year. 他们去年背着背包在西班牙旅行。 ➲ WORDFINDER NOTE AT TOURIST ▸ **back·pack·er** *noun*

ˌback ˈpassage *noun* (*BrE*) a polite way of referring to sb's RECTUM (= the part of the body where solid waste leaves the body) （委婉语）直肠

ˌback-ˈpedal *verb* (**-ll-**, *NAmE* **-l-**) **1** [I] ~ (**on sth**) to change an earlier statement or opinion; to not do sth that you promised to do 收回（意见等）；（立场）软化；出尔反尔： *The protests have forced the government to back-pedal on the new tax.* 抗议活动已迫使政府撤销新的税目。 **2** [I] to PEDAL backwards on a bicycle; to walk or run backwards 倒踩自行车的脚蹬；倒走；倒跑 ➲ WORDFINDER NOTE AT CYCLING

back·plane /ˈbækpleɪn/ *noun* (*computing* 计) a CIRCUIT BOARD that other devices can be connected to 底板，背板（可接其他装置的电路板）

ˈback-projec·tion *noun* **1** [U] the process of shining an image onto the back of a screen 反投影；背投影 **2** [C] an image that has been shone onto the back of a screen 背投影像

back·rest /ˈbækrest/ *noun* part of a seat that supports sb's back 靠背

ˌback ˈroom *noun* a room at the back of a building, away from the entrance, often where secret activities take place 后室；密室

ˈback-room boys *noun* [pl.] (*BrE, informal*) people who do important work for a person or an organization but who are not well known themselves 默默无闻地从事重要工作的人；无名功臣

back·scratch·ing /ˈbækskrætʃɪŋ/ *noun* [U] (*informal, often disapproving*) the fact of giving sb help in return for help that they have given you, often in connection with sth that might be illegal 互开方便之门，互相利用（常指从事非法活动）

ˌback ˈseat *noun* a seat at the back of a vehicle （车辆的）后座

IDM **take a back seat** to allow sb else to play a more active and important role in a particular situation than you do 允许他人领先；甘愿居于人下；退居幕后

ˌback-seat ˈdriver *noun* (*disapproving*) **1** a passenger in a vehicle who keeps giving advice to the driver about how he or she should drive 对驾驶者指手画脚的乘客 **2** a person who wants to be in control of sth that is not really their responsibility 企图越权者

back·sheesh = BAKSHEESH

back·shift /ˈbækʃɪft/ *noun* [U] (*linguistics* 语言) the changing of a tense when reporting what sb said, for example when reporting the words 'What *are* you doing?' as 'He asked me what I *was* doing'. （转成间接引语时的）时态后移

back·side /ˈbæksaɪd/ *noun* (*informal*) the part of the body that you sit on 屁股 SYN **behind, bottom**: *Get up off your backside and do some work!* 起来干点活儿吧！ IDM SEE PAIN *n.*

back·slap·ping /ˈbækslæpɪŋ/ *noun* [U] loud and enthusiastic behaviour when people are praising each other for sth good they have done （热情的）互相祝贺，互相打气 ▸ **back·slap·ping** *adj.* [only before noun]: *backslapping tributes* 互勉的话

back·slash /ˈbækslæʃ/ *noun* a mark (\ ), used in computer commands 反斜线（计算机符号） ➲ COMPARE FORWARD SLASH

back·slid·ing /ˈbækslaɪdɪŋ/ *noun* [U] the situation when sb fails to do sth that they agreed to do and returns to their former bad behaviour 倒退；故态复萌

back·space /ˈbækspeɪs/ *noun, verb*

■ **noun** the key on the keyboard of a computer or other device that removes the last letter that you typed （电脑等设备的）回格键，回删键 ➲ WORDFINDER NOTE AT KEYBOARD

■ **verb** [I] to use the backspace key on the keyboard of a computer or other device 回格；回退；回删

back·spin /ˈbækspɪn/ *noun* [U] a backward spinning movement of a ball that has been hit, which makes it go less far than it normally would （球的）回旋，下旋

ˈback·stabbing *noun* [U] the action of criticizing sb when they are not there, while pretending to be their friend at other times 背后中伤；暗箭伤人

back·stage /ˌbækˈsteɪdʒ/ *adv.* **1** in the part of a theatre where the actors and artists get ready and wait to perform 在后台： *After the show, we were allowed to go backstage to meet the cast.* 表演结束之后，我们获准到后台和演员们见面。 **2** away from the attention of the public; in secret 私下；秘密地： *I'd like to know what really goes on backstage in government.* 我想知道政府在幕后究竟干些什么。 ▸ **back·stage** *adj.*

back·stairs /ˈbæksteəz; *NAmE* -sterz/ *noun, adj.*

■ **noun** [pl.] stairs at the back or side of a building, sometimes used by servants 后楼梯，侧楼梯（有时供仆人用）

■ **adj.** secret or dishonest 背地里的；暗中的： *backstairs deals between politicians* 政客之间的幕后交易

back·stitch /ˈbækstɪtʃ/ *noun* [U, C] a method of sewing in which each STITCH begins at the middle of the previous one 回式针脚缝法；倒缝

back·story /ˈbækstɔːri/ *noun* (*pl.* **-ies**) [C, U] **1** the things that are supposed to have happened to the characters in a film/movie, novel, etc., before the film/movie, etc. starts （电影、小说等的）幕后故事，故事背景： *The film spends too long establishing the characters' backstories.* 这部电影对人物的背景故事着墨太多。 **2** (especially in journalism 尤用于新闻业) the background to a news story 新闻报道的背景： *First, some backstory:…* 首先讲一些背景资料：…

back·street /ˈbækstriːt/ *noun, adj.*

■ **noun** a small quiet street, usually in a poor part of a town or city, away from main roads 偏僻街道，小巷（常位于贫民区）

■ **adj.** [only before noun] acting or happening secretly, often dishonestly or illegally 秘密的；偷偷摸摸的；暗地里的： *backstreet dealers* 非法交易者 ◇ *backstreet abortions* 非法堕胎

back·stroke /ˈbækstrəʊk; *NAmE* -stroʊk/ (*BrE also* **back·crawl**) *noun* [U, sing.] a style of swimming in which you lie on your back 仰泳： *Can you do (the) backstroke?* 你会仰泳吗？ ◇ *He won the 100 metres backstroke* (= the race). 他获得 100 米仰泳比赛冠军。 ➲ VISUAL VOCAB PAGE V48

back·swing /ˈbækswɪŋ/ *noun* (*sport* 体育) the backwards movement of your arm or arms before you hit the ball （击球前）向后摆臂动作

ˈback talk (*NAmE*) (*BrE* **back·chat**) *noun* [U] (*informal*) a way of answering that shows no respect for sb in authority 顶嘴

ˌback-to-ˈback *noun* (*BrE*) a house in a row of houses that share walls with the houses on each side and behind 连背排房（侧面和背面与其他房屋相连接）： *back-to-backs built for the poor in the 19th century* * 19 世纪为贫民建造的连背排房

back·track /ˈbæktræk/ *verb* **1** [I] to go back along the same route that you have just come along 原路返回；折回；折返 **2** [I] to change an earlier statement, opinion or promise because of pressure from sb/sth （屈于压力而）改变声明（或主张），出尔反尔；退缩

back·up /ˈbækʌp/ *noun* [U, C] **1** extra help or support that you can get if necessary 增援；后援： *The police had backup from the army.* 警方得到了军方的增援。 ◇ *We can use him as a backup if one of the other players drops out.* 如果有参赛者退出，我们可以用他作为替补。 ◇ *a backup power supply* 备用电源 **2** (*computing* 计) a copy of a file, etc. that can be used if the original is lost or damaged （文件等的）备份：*Always make a backup of your work.* 所有文件都须备份。◇ *a backup copy* 备份文件 ➲ SEE ALSO BACK STH↔UP at BACK *v.*

ˈ**backup light** (*NAmE*) (*BrE* **reˈversing light**) *noun* a white light at the back of a vehicle that comes on when the vehicle moves backwards 倒车灯

back·ward /ˈbækwəd; *NAmE* -wərd/ *adj.*, *adv.*

■ *adj.* **1** [only before noun] directed or moving towards the back 向后的；朝后的：*She strode past him **without a backward glance**.* 她大步从他身边走过，都没有回头瞧他一眼。**2** moving in a direction that means that no progress is being made 倒退的；反向的 SYN **retrograde**: *She felt that going back to live in her home town would be a backward step.* 她觉得回到家乡生活就是没出息。**3** having made less progress than normal; developing slowly 落后的；进步缓慢的：*a backward part of the country, with no paved roads and no electricity* 该国的一个落后地区，没有铺设马路也没有电力 ◇ *a backward child* 迟钝儿童 ◇ (*BrE, informal*) *She's not **backward in coming forward*** (= she's not shy). 她勇敢地站出来。➲ COMPARE FORWARD *adj.*

■ *adv.* (*NAmE*) = BACKWARDS

ˌ**backward ˈclasses** *noun* [pl.] (in India) the people in a CASTE (= division of society) or community who are recommended by each state authority for special help in education and employment 落后阶层，落后种姓（印度各邦当局建议在教育和就业方面给予优惠）

ˈ**backward-looking** *adj.* (*disapproving*) opposed to progress or change 反进步（或变革）的；滞后的；落后的

back·ward·ness /ˈbækwədnəs; *NAmE* -wərd-/ *noun* [U] the state of having made less progress than normal 落后状况

back·wards /ˈbækwədz; *NAmE* -wərdz/ (*also* **back·ward** *especially in NAmE*) *adv.* **1** towards a place or position that is behind 向后：*I lost my balance and fell backwards.* 我没有站稳，仰面摔倒。◇ *He took a step backwards.* 他退后一步。OPP **forward 2** in the opposite direction to the usual one 朝反方向；倒着：*'Ambulance' is written backwards so you can read it in the mirror.* * ambulance 是倒着写的，以便在镜中认读。◇ *In the movie they take a journey backwards through time.* 影片中的人作逆时光旅行。**3** towards a worse state 每况愈下地：*I felt that going to live with my parents would be a step backwards.* 我觉得回去和我父母一同生活会更糟。OPP **forward 4** (*NAmE*) (*BrE* ˌ**back to ˈfront**) if you put on a piece of clothing **backwards**, you make a mistake and put the back where the front should be （衣服）前后颠倒（或前后穿反）

IDM ˌ**backward(s) and ˈforward(s)** from one place or position to another and back again many times 来来回回：*She rocked backwards and forwards on her chair.* 她坐在摇椅上前后摇晃着。**bend/lean over ˈbackwards (to do sth)** to make a great effort, especially in order to be helpful or fair 尽力；竭力：*I've bent over backwards to help him.* 我已尽最大努力帮助他。➲ MORE AT KNOW *v.*

ˌ**backwards comˈpatible** (*also* ˌ**backward comˈpatible**) *adj.* (*computing* 计) able to be used with systems, machines or programs which are older 向后兼容的；兼容旧系统（或机器、程序）的

back·wash /ˈbækwɒʃ; *NAmE* -wɔːʃ; -wɑːʃ/ *noun* [sing., U] **1** the unpleasant result of an event 恶果；余波；不良后果 **2** waves caused by a boat moving through water; the movement of water back into the sea after a wave has hit the beach （行船激起的）反流，尾流；（海浪拍击岸边后的）退浪

back·water /ˈbækwɔːtə(r)/ *noun* **1** a part of a river away from the main part, where the water only moves slowly （河流的）滞水，壅水，回水 **2** (*often disapproving*) a place that is away from the places where most things happen, and is therefore not affected by events, progress, new ideas, etc. 与世隔绝的地区；落后地区：***a sleepy/quiet/rural backwater*** 沉寂的 / 宁静的 / 乡下的落后地区

back·woods /ˈbækwʊdz/ *noun* [pl.] a place that is away from any big towns and from the influence of modern life 边远落后地区

back·woods·man /ˈbækwʊdzmən/ *noun* (*pl.* **-men** /-mən/) (*NAmE*) a person who lives in a region far from towns where not many people live, especially one who does not have much education or good manners （尤指没有文化或粗野的）边远地区的乡下人

back·yard /ˌbækˈjɑːd; *NAmE* -ˈjɑːrd/ *noun* **1** (*BrE*) an area with a hard surface behind a house, often surrounded by a wall （屋后常有围墙的）后院 **2** (*NAmE*) the whole area behind and belonging to a house, including an area of grass and the garden （包括草坪和花园的）屋后附属地带：*a backyard barbecue* 后院烤肉野宴 ➲ SEE ALSO YARD

IDM **in your (own) backyard** in or near the place where you live or work 在自己生活（或工作）的地方附近；在自己的后院：*The residents didn't want a new factory in their backyard.* 居民不希望在自己家附近建新工厂。◇ *The party leader is facing opposition in his own backyard* (= from his own members). 该党领导面临着党内人士的反对。➲ SEE ALSO NIMBY

bacon /ˈbeɪkən/ *noun* [U] meat from the back or sides of a pig that has been CURED (= preserved using salt or smoke), usually served in thin slices 咸猪肉；熏猪肉：*a rasher of bacon* 一片咸猪肉 ◇ *bacon and eggs* 咸肉和鸡蛋 ◇ ***smoked/unsmoked bacon*** 熏制 / 未熏制的猪肉 ➲ COMPARE GAMMON, HAM *n.* (1), PORK (1) IDM SEE HOME *adv.*, SAVE *v.*

bac·teria /bækˈtɪəriə; *NAmE* -ˈtɪr-/ *noun* [pl.] (*sing.* **bac·ter·ium** /-iəm/) the simplest and smallest forms of life. Bacteria exist in large numbers in air, water and soil, and also in living and dead creatures and plants, and are often a cause of disease. 细菌 ➲ WORDFINDER NOTE AT DISEASE ➲ COLLOCATIONS AT LIFE ➲ MORE LIKE THIS 30, page R28 ▸ **bac·ter·ial** /-riəl/ *adj.*: ***bacterial infections/growth*** 细菌感染 / 生长

bac·teri·ology /bækˌtɪəriˈɒlədʒi; *NAmE* -ˌtɪriˈɑːl-/ *noun* [U] the scientific study of bacteria 细菌学 ▸ **bac·terio·logic·al** /bækˌtɪəriəˈlɒdʒɪkl; *NAmE* -ˌtɪriəˈlɑːdʒ-/ *adj.* **bac·teri·olo·gist** *noun*

bad /bæd/ *adj.*, *noun*, *adv.*

■ *adj.* (**worse** /wɜːs; *NAmE* wɜːrs/, **worst** /wɜːst; *NAmE* wɜːrst/)

• **UNPLEASANT** 令人不快 **1** unpleasant; full of problems 令人不快的；问题成堆的；坏的：*bad news/weather/dreams/habits* 坏消息；坏天气；噩梦；恶习 ◇ *I'm having a really bad day.* 我今天倒霉透了。◇ *It was the worst experience of her life.* 那是她一生中最糟糕的经历。◇ *Smoking gives you bad breath.* 吸烟会导致口臭。◇ *Things are **bad enough** without our own guns shelling us.* 本来情况就够糟的了，偏偏我们自己的大炮又向我们开起火来。

• **POOR QUALITY** 劣质 **2** of poor quality; below an acceptable standard 质量差的；不合格的：*bad conditions/driving* 恶劣的情况；拙劣的驾驶技术 ◇ *a bad copy/diet* 不清晰的复印本；劣质饮食 ◇ *I thought it was a very bad article.* 我以为那是一篇很低劣的文章。◇ *This isn't as bad as I thought.* 这没我原来所想的那么差。◇ *That's not a bad idea.* 那个主意不错。

• **NOT GOOD AT STH** 不擅长 **3** **~ at sth/at doing sth** (of a person 人) not able to do sth well or in an acceptable way 拙于；不擅；不善于 SYN **poor**: *a bad teacher* 不称职的教师 ◇ *You're a bad liar!* 你连说谎都不会！◇ *He's a bad loser* (= he complains when he loses a game). 他是个输不起的人。◇ *She is so bad at keeping secrets.* 她一点都不会保守秘密。

• **SERIOUS** 严重 **4** serious; severe 严重的；剧烈的：*You're heading for a bad attack of sunburn.* 你会被严重晒伤的。◇ *The engagement was a bad mistake.* 这婚约是个大错。◇ *My headache is getting worse.* 我头痛越来越厉害了。

• **NOT APPROPRIATE** 不合适 **5** [only before noun] not appropriate in a particular situation 不适合的；不适当

的：*I know that this is a bad time to ask for help.* 我知道在这时候要求帮助不合适。◇ *He now realized that it had been a bad decision on his part.* 他现在意识到是他作了一个不恰当的决定。

- **WICKED** 邪恶 **6** morally unacceptable 不道德的；邪恶的：*The hero gets to shoot all the bad guys.* 主人公结果射杀了所有的坏蛋。◇ *He said I must have done something bad to deserve it.* 他说我肯定是罪有应得。
- **CHILDREN** 儿童 **7** [usually before noun] (especially of children 尤指儿童) not behaving well 顽皮的；不乖的 SYN **naughty**: *Have you been a bad boy?* 你调皮了吗？
- **HARMFUL** 有害 **8** [not before noun] **~ for sb/sth** harmful; causing or likely to cause damage 有害；招致损害：*Those shoes are bad for her feet.* 那双鞋会伤她的脚。◇ *Weather like this is bad for business.* 这种天气不利于做买卖。
- **PAINFUL** 疼痛 **9** [usually before noun] (of parts of the body 身体部位) not healthy; painful 有病的；疼痛的：*I've got a bad back.* 我背部疼痛。
- **FOOD** 食物 **10** not safe to eat because it has decayed 变质的；腐烂的：*Put the meat in the fridge so it doesn't go bad.* 把肉放进冰箱里，免得坏了。
- **TEMPER/MOOD** 脾气；情绪 **11 ~ temper/mood** the state of feeling annoyed or angry 发脾气；坏情绪；恼怒：*It put me in a bad mood for the rest of the day.* 那事让我整天再也没了好心情。
- **GUILTY/SORRY** 愧疚；遗憾 **12 feel ~** to feel guilty or sorry about sth 感到愧疚（或遗憾）：*She felt bad about leaving him.* 她因离开他而感到歉疚。◇ *Why should I want to make you feel bad?* 我干吗要让你难过呢？
- **ILL/SICK** 有病；不舒服 **13 feel/look ~** to feel or look ill/sick 觉得不舒服；感到有病；面有病容；气色不好：*I'm afraid I'm feeling pretty bad.* 很抱歉，我觉得很不舒服。
- **EXCELLENT** 极好 **14** (**bad·der**, **bad·dest**) (*slang, especially NAmE*) good; excellent 顶呱呱的；没治

IDM HELP Most idioms containing **bad** are at the entries for the nouns and verbs in the idioms, for example **be bad news (for sb/sth)** is at **news**. 大多数含 bad 的习语，都可在该等习语中的名词及动词相关词条找到，如 be bad news (for sb/sth) 在词条 news 下。 **can't be bad** (*informal*) used to try to persuade sb to agree that sth is good（劝导时说）没有什么不好：*You'll save fifty dollars, which can't be bad, can it?* 你会省下五十美元，这没什么不好，对吧？ **have got it 'bad** (*informal, humorous*) to be very much in love 热恋着；在热恋中：*You're not seeing him again tonight, are you? That's five times this week—you've got it bad!* 你今天晚上不再和他见面了，是吧？这个星期都约会了五次，你们热恋了！ **not 'bad** (*informal*) quite good; better than you expected 不错；比预料的好：*'How are you?' 'Not too bad.'* "你怎么样？" "还不错。" ◇ *That wasn't bad for a first attempt.* 第一次尝试，还算不错。 **too bad** (*informal*) **1** (*ironic*) used to say 'bad luck' or 'it's a shame' when you do not really mean it（等于说"倒霉"或"可惜"，实际上并无同情之意）：*If sometimes they're the wrong decisions, too bad.* 如果有时决定错了，那可是太不幸了。 **2** a shame; a pity 遗憾；可惜：*Too bad every day can't be as good as this.* 可惜并不是每一天都像今天这么好。 **3** (*old-fashioned*) annoying 令人生气的；恼人的：*Really, it was too bad of you to be so late.* 你来得这么晚实在不像话。

▪ ***noun* the bad** [U] bad people, things, or events 坏人；坏事（物）：*You will always have the bad as well as the good in the world.* 人生在世总是有苦有甜。

IDM **,go to the 'bad** (*old-fashioned*) to begin behaving in an immoral way 堕落：*I hate to see you going to the bad.* 我不愿看到你堕落。 **'my bad** (*NAmE, informal*) used when you are admitting that sth is your fault or that you have made a mistake 是我的错；我错了：*I'm sorry—my bad.* 对不起，我错了。 **take the ,bad with the 'good** to accept the bad aspects of sth as well as the good ones 接受人生的甘苦（或事物的好与坏） **to the 'bad** (*BrE*) used to say that sb now has a particular amount less money than they did before 亏损：*After the sale they were £300 to the bad.* 这笔买卖使他们亏损了 300 英镑。

▪ ***adv.*** (*NAmE, informal*) badly 很；非常：*She wanted it real bad.* 她确实很想得到它。◇ *Are you hurt bad?* 你伤得重吗？

badam /bʌˈdɑːm; *NAmE* ˈbɑːdɑːm/ *noun* [C] (*IndE*) an ALMOND 扁桃仁；巴旦木

bad·ass /ˈbædæs/ *adj.* (*NAmE, informal*) (of a person 人) tough and aggressive 粗野蛮横的 ▸ **bad·ass** *noun*

'bad boy *noun* (*informal*) a man who behaves badly, especially in a particular area of activity 坏小子（尤指在某领域操守欠佳的男子）：*He used to be known as the bad boy of Hollywood.* 他曾经是好莱坞有名的坏小子。

,bad 'breath *noun* [U] breath that smells unpleasant 难闻的呼气；口臭 SYN **halitosis**: *Have I got bad breath?* 我有口臭吗？

,bad 'debt *noun* [C, U] a debt that is unlikely to be paid 坏账；呆账；倒账

baddy /ˈbædi/ *noun* (*pl.* **-ies**) (*informal*) a bad or evil character in a film/movie, book, play, etc.（电影、书、戏剧等中的）坏人，恶棍：*As usual, the cops get the baddies in the end.* 跟平常一样，警察最后把坏人都抓起来了。 OPP **goody** ➲ WORDFINDER NOTE AT CHARACTER

bade PAST TENSE OF BID[2]

badge /bædʒ/ *noun* **1** a small piece of metal or plastic, with a design or words on it, that a person wears to show that they belong to an organization, support sth, have achieved sth, have a particular rank, etc. 徽章；奖章：*She wore a badge saying 'Vote for Coates'.* 她戴着一枚徽章，上面写着"投科茨一票"。◇ *All employees have to wear name badges.* 所有员工均须佩戴名牌。 ➲ VISUAL VOCAB PAGE V70 ➲ COMPARE BUTTON *n.* (4) **2** (*BrE*) (*NAmE* **patch**) a piece of material that you sew onto clothes as part of a uniform（制服上的）标记，标识：*the school badge* 校徽 **3** a small piece of metal that you carry or wear to prove who you are, used, for example, by police officers 证章；警徽：*He pulled out a badge and said he was a cop.* 他拿出证章，说他是警察。 **4** (*formal*) something that shows that a particular quality is present 标记；象征：*His gun was a badge of power for him.* 他的枪对他而言是权力的标志。

badger /ˈbædʒə(r)/ *noun, verb*

▪ ***noun*** an animal with grey fur and wide black and white lines on its head. Badgers are NOCTURNAL (= active

---

▼ **VOCABULARY BUILDING** 词汇扩充

Bad and very bad

Instead of saying that something is **bad** or **very bad**, try to use more precise and interesting adjectives to describe things. 表示不好或糟糕，除了用 bad 或 very bad 外，尽量用更贴切、更有意思的形容词来描述：

- an **unpleasant**/a **foul**/a **disgusting** smell 令人不快的／难闻的／恶心的气味
- **appalling**/**dreadful**/**severe** weather 糟透的／十分恶劣的／非常恶劣的天气
- an **unpleasant**/a **frightening**/a **traumatic** experience 不愉快的／可怕的／痛苦难忘的经历
- **poor**/**weak** eyesight 视力差
- a **terrible**/**serious**/**horrific** accident 重大的／严重的／可怕的事故
- a **wicked**/an **evil**/an **immoral** person 恶毒的／邪恶的／道德败坏的人
- an **awkward**/an **embarrassing**/a **difficult** situation 令人尴尬的／使人难堪的／艰难的处境
- We were working in **difficult**/**appalling** conditions. 我们在艰苦的／恶劣的条件下工作。

To refer to your health, you can say 谈及身体状况可说：*I feel* ***unwell***/***sick***/***terrible***. 我感到不舒服／恶心／难受极了。◇ *I don't feel (**very**) **well**.* 我感到不（太）舒服。

In conversation, words like **terrible**, **horrible**, **awful** and **dreadful** can be used in most situations to mean 'very bad'. 在口语中，terrible、horrible、awful、dreadful 等词在多数情况下均可表示糟糕。

B

mostly at night) and live in holes in the ground. 獾（挖洞居住，夜间活动）
■ ***verb*** to put pressure on sb by repeatedly asking them questions or asking them to do sth 纠缠，烦扰（反复提出问题或要求） SYN **pester**: **~ sb (into doing sth)** *I finally badgered him into coming with us.* 我终于磨着他和我们一起来了。◇ **~ sb about sth** *Reporters constantly badger her about her private life.* 记者经常纠缠着打听她的私生活。◇ **~ sb to do sth** *His daughter was always badgering him to let her join the club.* 他女儿老缠着他让她加入俱乐部。

ˌbad ˈhair day *noun* (*informal*) a day on which everything seems to go wrong 很不顺利的一天；倒霉的一天

bad·in·age /ˈbædɪnɑːʒ; *NAmE* ˌbædənˈɑːʒ/ *noun* [U] (*from French, literary*) friendly joking between people 开玩笑；打趣 SYN **banter**

bad·lands /ˈbædlændz/ *noun* [pl.] **1** large areas of land that have been farmed too much with the result that plants will not grow there （耕作过度的）劣地，恶地 **2 the Badlands** a large area of land in the western US where plants will not grow 巴德兰兹地区（美国西部一处贫瘠地带）

ˌbad ˈlanguage *noun* [U] words that many people find offensive 脏话；冒犯人（或咒骂人）的话 SYN **swear words**

badly /ˈbædli/ *adv.* (**worse**, **worst**) **1** not skilfully or not carefully 拙劣地；差；不认真仔细：*to play/sing badly* 表演/唱得不好 ◇ *badly designed/organized* 设计/组织得很差 OPP **well 2** not successfully 不成功地；受挫：*Things have been **going badly**.* 事情进展得不顺利。◇ *I **did badly*** (= was not successful) *in my exams.* 我考得不好。OPP **well 3** not in an acceptable way 未能令人满意：*to behave/sleep badly* 表现差；睡得不好 ◇ *badly paid/treated* 报酬低微；受虐待 ◇ *The kids took the dog's death very badly* (= they were very unhappy). 孩子们对狗的死感到很难过。OPP **well 4** in a way that makes people get a bad opinion about sth 给人坏的印象；负面地：*The economic crisis reflects badly on the government's policies.* 经济危机反映出政府政策不如人意的一面。◇ *She's only trying to help, so don't **think badly of** her.* 她只是想帮忙，所以别把她想得太坏。OPP **well 5** used to emphasize how much you want, need, etc. sb/sth 很；非常：*The building is **badly in need of** repair.* 这栋楼急需维修。◇ *They wanted to win so badly.* 他们求胜心切。◇ *I miss her badly.* 我十分想念她。**6** used to emphasize how serious a situation or an event is 严重地；厉害地：***badly damaged/injured/hurt*** 损坏/伤势/伤害严重 ◇ *The country has been badly affected by recession.* 该国受到经济衰退的严重影响。◇ *Everything's **gone badly wrong**!* 一切都糟透了！

badly ˈoff *adj.* (**worse off**, **worst off**) **1** not having much money 穷困的；拮据的 SYN **poor**: *We aren't too badly off but we can't afford a house like that.* 我们并不是一文不名，但我们负担不起那样的房子。OPP **well off 2** not in a good situation 境况不佳的：*I've got quite a big room so I'm not too badly off.* 我有一间蛮大的屋子，所以住得还不坏。OPP **well off**

IDM **be badly ˈoff for sth** (*BrE*) to not have enough of sth 某物短少；缺乏某物

bad·mash /bʌdˈmɑːʃ/ *noun* (*IndE*) a dishonest man 不诚实的男子；恶汉；流氓

bad·min·ton /ˈbædmɪntən/ *noun* [U] a game like TENNIS played by two or four people, usually indoors. Players hit a small light kind of ball, originally with feathers around it (= a SHUTTLECOCK) across a high net using a RACKET. 羽毛球运动 ➲ VISUAL VOCAB PAGE V48

ˈbad-mouth *verb* **~ sb** (*informal*) to say unpleasant things about sb 说（人）坏话：*No one wants to employ somebody who bad-mouths their former employer.* 没有人愿意雇用说前雇主坏话的人。

bad·ness /ˈbædnəs/ *noun* [U] the fact of being morally bad 道德败坏：*There was not a hint of badness in him.* 他道德十分高尚。

ˌbad-ˈtempered *adj.* often angry; in an angry mood 易怒的；爱发脾气的：*She gets very bad-tempered when she's tired.* 她累的时候就很爱发脾气。

Ba·fana Ba·fana /bəˌfɑːnə bəˈfɑːnə/ *noun* (*SAfrE*) a popular name for the South African national men's football (SOCCER) team 南非小子（南非国家男子足球队的俗称）

baf·fle /ˈbæfl/ *verb, noun*
■ ***verb*** to confuse sb completely; to be too difficult or strange for sb to understand or explain 使困惑；难住：**~ sb** *His behaviour baffles me.* 他的行为使我难以琢磨。◇ **be baffled (as to) why, how, where, etc....** *I'm baffled as to why she hasn't called.* 我不明白她为什么还没打电话。◇ *I'm baffled why she hasn't called.* 我不明白她为什么还没打电话。▶ **baffle·ment** *noun* [U]: *His reaction was one of bafflement.* 他的反应是迷惑不解。**baf·fling** *adj.*
■ ***noun*** (*specialist*) a screen used to control or prevent the flow of sound, light or liquid （控制声、光、液体等流动的）隔板，挡板，反射板

BAFTA /ˈbæftə/ *abbr., noun*
■ ***abbr.*** British Academy of Film and Television Arts 英国电影电视艺术学院
■ ***noun*** an award presented by the British Academy of Film and Television Arts 英国电影电视艺术学院奖：*He won a BAFTA for the role.* 他凭借这个角色获得英国电影电视艺术学院奖。

bag /bæg/ *noun, verb*
■ ***noun***
• **CONTAINER** 容器 **1** [C] (often in compounds 常构成复合词) a container made of paper or plastic, that opens at the top, used especially in shops/stores （尤指商店用的）纸袋，塑料袋：*a **plastic/polythene/paper bag*** 塑料袋；聚乙烯袋；纸袋 ◇ *a **laundry/mail bag*** 洗衣袋；邮袋 ◇ *a black plastic **rubbish/garbage bag*** 一个黑色塑料垃圾袋 **2** [C] a strong container made from cloth, plastic, leather, etc., usually with one or two handles, used to carry things in when shopping or travelling 手提包；旅行袋：*a shopping bag* 购物袋 ◇ *a make-up bag* 化妆包 ◇ *He's upstairs unpacking his bags.* 他在楼上打开他的旅行袋取出东西。◇ *She opened her bag* (= her HANDBAG) *and took out her comb.* 她打开手提包，取出梳子。➲ VISUAL VOCAB PAGE V69 ➲ SEE ALSO AIRBAG, BEANBAG, BUMBAG, GOODY BAG, PUNCHBAG, SANDBAG *n.*, TEABAG
• **AMOUNT** 数量 **3** [C] **~ (of sth)** the amount contained in a bag 一袋（的量）：*She ate a bag of chips.* 她吃了一袋炸土豆条。➲ VISUAL VOCAB PAGE V36 ➲ SEE ALSO MIXED BAG, RAGBAG **4 bags** [U, pl.] **~ (of sth)** (*BrE, informal*) a large amount or a large number of sth 大量；很多：*Get in! There's bags of room.* 进来吧！地方很空。
• **UNDER EYES** 眼下方 **5 bags** [pl.] dark circles or loose folds of skin under the eyes, as a result of getting old or lack of sleep 黑眼圈；眼袋
• **UNPLEASANT WOMAN** 讨厌的女人 **6** [C] (*informal, especially BrE*) an insulting word for an unpleasant or bad-tempered older woman 丑妇，泼妇（指讨厌或坏脾气的年长女人） ➲ SEE ALSO RATBAG, SCUMBAG, WINDBAG
• **BIRDS/ANIMALS** 鸟；动物 **7** [C, usually sing.] all the birds, animals, etc. shot or caught on one occasion （一次）猎获物 HELP There are many other compounds ending in **bag**. You will find them at their place in the alphabet. 以 bag 结尾的复合词还有很多，可在各字母中的适当位置查到。

IDM **ˌbag and ˈbaggage** with all your possessions, especially secretly or suddenly （尤指秘密地或突然地）携带全部财产：*He threw her out onto the street, bag and baggage.* 他突然把她连人带东西一股脑儿扔到大街上。**a ˌbag of ˈbones** (*informal*) a very thin person or animal 瘦骨嶙峋的人（或动物）；皮包骨 **be in the ˈbag** (*informal*) if sth is **in the bag**, it is almost certain to be won or achieved 十拿九稳；稳操胜券 **leave sb holding the ˈbag** (*NAmE, informal*) to suddenly make sb responsible for sth important, such as finishing a difficult job, that is really your responsibility 突然把重担推给某人 **(not) sb's ˈbag** (*informal*) (not) sth that you are interested in or good at （非）爱好，特长： *Poetry isn't really my bag.* 我其实并不擅长诗歌。 ➲ MORE AT CAT, NERVE *n.*, PACK *v.*, TRICK *n.*

■ *verb* (-gg-)

• PUT INTO BAGS 装进袋子 **1** ~ sth (up) to put sth into bags 把…装进袋子： *The fruit is washed, sorted and bagged at the farm.* 水果在农场洗净、分拣并装袋。

• CATCH ANIMAL 捕猎动物 **2** ~ sth (*informal*) to catch or kill an animal 捕获，猎杀（动物）

• IN SPORT 体育运动 **3** ~ sth (*informal*) to score a goal, point, etc. 得分： *Harkin bagged two goals in last night's win.* 在昨晚获胜的那场比赛中哈金射进两球。

• CLAIM STH 声称拥有 **4** ~ sth (*informal*) to claim sth as yours before sb else claims it; to take sth before sb else can get it 抢占；占有： *Sally had managed to bag the two best seats.* 萨莉抢到了那两个最好的位子。 ◇ *Quick, bag that table over there!* 快点占住那边的桌子！

• CRITICIZE SB/STH 批评 **5** ~ sb/sth (*AustralE, NZE, informal*) to criticize sb/sth 批评；挑剔；指责

• DECIDE NOT TO DO STH 决定不做 **6** ~ sth (*NAmE, informal*) to decide not to do sth because you think it will not be successful or because you think it will be better to do it later（认为不会成功或以后做会更好而）放弃，取消： *They decided to bag the trip because they were short of cash.* 因为缺钱，他们决定取消这次旅行。

IDM **bags (I)...** (*BrE*) (*NAmE* **'dibs on...**) (*informal*) used to claim sth as yours before sb else can claim it …是我的；我要求…： *Bags I sit in the front seat!* 我一定要坐前面的位子！

baga·telle /ˌbægəˈtel/ *noun* **1** [U] a game played on a board with small balls that you try to hit into holes 小型台球 **2** [C, usually sing.] (*literary*) a small and unimportant thing or amount 琐事；无足轻重的事；微量： *It cost a mere bagatelle.* 这个只花了一点钱。

bagel /ˈbeɪɡl/ *noun* a hard bread roll shaped like a ring 百吉圈（硬面包）

bag·gage 🔑 /ˈbæɡɪdʒ/ *noun* [U] **1** 🔑 (*especially NAmE*) = LUGGAGE： *excess baggage* (= weighing more than the limit allowed on a plane) 超重行李（超出乘飞机所允许的重量） ◇ *baggage handlers* (= people employed to load and unload baggage at airports) （机场）行李员 ◇ (*NAmE*) *We loaded our baggage into the car.* 我们把行李装上了汽车。 ➲ COLLOCATIONS AT TRAVEL **2** the beliefs and attitudes that sb has as a result of their past experiences （因阅历而形成的）信仰，看法： *She was carrying a lot of* ***emotional baggage.*** 她背负着很多感情债。 IDM SEE BAG *n.*

▼ WHICH WORD? 词语辨析

baggage / luggage

- **Luggage** is the usual word in *BrE*, but **baggage** is also used, especially in the context of the bags and cases that passengers take on a flight. In *NAmE* **baggage** is usually used. 英式英语常用 luggage，但也用 baggage，尤指旅客乘飞机时所带的行李。美式英语通常用 baggage。
- Both these words are uncountable nouns. 两者均为不可数名词： *Do you have a lot of luggage?* 你的行李多吗？ ◇ *Two pieces of luggage have gone missing.* 有两件行李丢失了。 ◇ *Never leave baggage unattended.* 切勿丢下行李不管。

'baggage car (*NAmE*) (*BrE* **'luggage van**) *noun* a coach/car on a train for carrying passengers' luggage （火车的）行李车厢

'baggage reclaim (*BrE*) (*NAmE* **'baggage claim**) *noun* [U] the place at an airport where you get your suitcases, etc. again after you have flown （机场）行李提取处 ➲ WORDFINDER NOTE AT AIRPORT

Bag·gie™ /ˈbæɡi/ *noun* (*NAmE*) a small bag made of clear plastic that is used for storing SANDWICHES, etc. 巴吉袋（用于包三明治等的透明小塑料袋）

baggy /ˈbæɡi/ *adj.* (**bag·gier**, **bag·gi·est**) (of clothes 衣服) fitting loosely 宽松的： *a baggy T-shirt* 宽松的 T 恤衫 OPP **tight**

bagh /bɑːɡ/ *noun* (*IndE*) a large garden or piece of land on which fruit trees are grown 大果园

'bag lady *noun* a woman who has no home and who walks around carrying her possessions with her （携带行囊露宿街头的）流浪女人

'bag lunch *noun* (*NAmE*) a meal of SANDWICHES, fruit, etc. that you take to school, work, etc. in a bag 自备袋装午餐 ➲ COMPARE BOX LUNCH, PACKED LUNCH

bag·pipes /ˈbæɡpaɪps/ (*also* **pipes**) *noun* [pl.] (*NAmE also* **bag·pipe** [sing.]) a musical instrument played especially in Scotland. The player blows air into a bag held under the arm and then slowly forces the air out through pipes to produce a noise. 风笛 ➲ PICTURE AT PIPE ▶ **bag·pipe** *adj.*： *bagpipe music* 风笛乐

ba·guette /bæˈɡet/ *noun* **1** (*also* ˌ**French 'loaf**, ˌ**French 'stick**) a LOAF of white bread in the shape of a long thick stick that is crisp on the outside and soft inside （法国）脆皮白面包棒 **2** a small baguette or part of one that is filled with food and eaten as a SANDWICH 脆皮夹馅面包棒；三明治小面包棒： *a cheese baguette* 奶酪夹心小面包棒

bah /bɑː/ *exclamation* used to show a sound that people make to express disapproval （表示不赞成的声音） ➲ MORE LIKE THIS 2, page R25

Baha'i (*also* **Bahai**) /bɑːˈhɑːi; bəˈhaɪ/ *noun* [U] a religion that teaches that all people and religions are the same, and that there should be peace 巴哈教（其教义为人类一体，宗教同源，倡导和平）

Ba·hasa In·do·nesia /bəˌhɑːsə ɪndəˈniːʒə/ *noun* [U] the official language of Indonesia 印尼语（指该国官方语言）

Ba·hasa Ma·lay·sia /bəˌhɑːsə məˈleɪʒə/ *noun* [U] the official language of Malaysia 马来语（指该国官方语言）

bail /beɪl/ *noun, verb*

■ *noun* **1** [U] money that sb agrees to pay if a person accused of a crime does not appear at their trial. When bail has been arranged, the accused person is allowed to go free until the trial. 保释金；保释： *Can anyone* ***put up bail*** *for you?* 有人保释你吗？ ◇ *She was released on £2 000 bail.* 她以 2 000 英镑获得保释。 ◇ *Bail was set at $1 million.* 保释金定为 100 万美元。 ◇ *He committed another offence while he was out* ***on bail*** (= after bail had been agreed). 他在取保候审期间又犯罪了。 ◇ *The judge* ***granted/refused bail.*** 法官准予 / 不准保释。 ◇ *She* ***jumped/skipped bail*** (= did not appear at her trial). 她弃保潜逃（未如期到庭受审）。 ➲ COLLOCATIONS AT JUSTICE **2** [C, usually pl.] (in CRICKET 板球) either of the two small pieces of wood on top of each set of three wooden posts (called STUMPS) 三柱门上的横木

■ *verb* **1** [T] ~ sb (to do sth) to release sb on bail 允许保释（某人）： *He was* ***bailed to appear*** *in court on 15 March.* 他获得保释，定于 3 月 15 日到庭应诉。 **2** [I] (*NAmE, informal*) to leave a place, especially quickly （尤指迅速地）离开： *Sorry, I really have to bail.* 对不起，我真得赶紧走了。 **3** [T] ~ sb (up) (*AustralE, NZE, informal*) to approach sb and talk to them, often when they do not want this 与…搭讪（尤指对方不愿意）

PHR V ˌ**bail 'out (of sth)** (*BrE also* ˌ**bale 'out (of sth)**) **1** to jump out of a plane that is going to crash （从即将坠毁的飞机上）跳伞 **2** to escape from a situation that you no longer want to be involved in 逃避，摆脱（不想再牵连其中的情况）： *I'd understand if you wanted to bail out of this relationship.* 如果你想从这种关系中摆脱出来，我可以理解。 ˌ**bail 'out** | ˌ**bail (sth)↔'out** (*BrE also* ˌ**bale 'out**, ˌ**bale (sth)↔'out**) to empty water from sth by lifting it out with your hand or a container （从…中）往外舀水： *He had to stop rowing to bail water out of the boat.* 他不得不停止划船，把船里的水舀出去。 ◇ *The boat*

B

will sink unless we bail out. 我们若不排水，船就要沉。
ˌ**bail sb↔ˈout** to pay sb's bail for them 保释（某人）
ˌ**bail sb↔ˈout** (**of sth**) (*BrE also* ˌ**bale sb↔ˈout** (**of sth**)) to rescue sb from a difficult situation 帮助（某人）脱离困境：*The government had to bail the company out of financial difficulty.* 政府只得帮助该公司渡过财政难关。◇ *Ryan's late goal bailed out his team.* 瑞安在比赛临近结束时攻入一球，拯救了他的球队。➲ SYNONYMS AT SAVE

bai·ley /ˈbeɪli/ *noun* the open area of a castle, inside the outer wall（城堡外廓内的）堡场

bail·iff /ˈbeɪlɪf/ *noun* **1** (*BrE*) a law officer whose job is to take the possessions and property of people who cannot pay their debts 执达员；执达官 **2** (*BrE*) a person employed to manage land or a large farm for sb else 庄园主管家 **3** (*NAmE*) an official who keeps order in court, takes people to their seats, watches prisoners, etc. 法警

bail·out /ˈbeɪlaʊt/ *noun* an act of giving money to a company, a foreign country, etc. that has very serious financial problems 紧急财政援助

bain-marie /ˌbæn məˈriː/ *noun* (*from French*) a pan of hot water in which a bowl of food is cooked or warmed slowly 热水炖锅；热水蒸锅；双层保温锅

bairn /beən; *NAmE* bern/ *noun* (*ScotE, NEngE*) a child 小孩

bait /beɪt/ *noun, verb*

■ ***noun*** [U, C] **1** food put on a hook to catch fish or in nets, traps, etc. to catch animals or birds 鱼饵；诱饵：*The fish took the bait.* 鱼咬了钓饵。➲ WORDFINDER NOTE AT FISHING **2** a person or thing that is used to catch sb or to attract them, for example to make them do what you want 用作诱饵的人（或物）

■ ***verb*** **1** ~ **sth** (**with sth**) to place food on a hook, in a trap, etc. in order to attract or catch an animal 下诱饵；在（鱼钩上、陷阱中等）放诱饵：*He baited the trap with a piece of meat.* 他在陷阱中放了一片肉做诱饵。 **2** ~ **sb** to deliberately try to make sb angry by making cruel or insulting remarks （故意以侮辱性言语）激怒 **3** **-baiting** (in compound nouns 构成复合名词) the activity of attacking a wild animal with dogs 纵犬袭击（野兽）：*bear-baiting* 纵犬斗熊

ˌ**bait-and-ˈswitch** *noun* [C, usually sing.] a selling method where advertisements for low-priced products are used to attract customers, who are then persuaded to buy sth more expensive 诱售法（以廉价商品招徕，再兜售较高价商品）

baize /beɪz/ *noun* [U] a type of thick cloth made of wool that is usually green, used especially for covering card tables and BILLIARD, SNOOKER or POOL tables 台面呢（通常绿色，尤用作牌桌、台球台面的衬垫）

ba·jil·lion /bəˈdʒɪljən/ *noun* (*informal*) an extremely large number 极大的数目；天文数字：*My inbox contained a bajillion emails when I came back from my holiday.* 我度假回来，收件箱里堆积了无数封电邮。

bake 🔑 /beɪk/ *verb, noun*

■ ***verb*** **1** 🔑 [T, I] to cook food in an oven without extra fat or liquid; to be cooked in this way （在烤炉里）烘烤；焙：~ (**sth**) *baked apples* 烤苹果 ◇ *the delicious smell of baking bread* 烤制面包的香味 ◇ ~ **sth for sb** *I'm baking a birthday cake for Alex.* 我在给亚历克斯烤生日蛋糕。◇ ~ **sb sth** *I'm baking Alex a cake.* 我在给亚历克斯烤蛋糕。 ➲ COLLOCATIONS AT COOKING ➲ VISUAL VOCAB PAGE V28 **2** [I, T] to become or to make sth become hard by heating （将某物）烤硬：*The bricks are left in the kiln to bake.* 砖坯放在窑里烧。◇ ~ **sth** (+ **adj.**) *The sun had baked the ground hard.* 太阳把地面晒硬了。 **3** [I] (*informal*) to be or become very hot （变得）灼热，炎热：*We sat baking in the sun.* 我们坐在太阳底下晒得热死了。 ➲ SEE ALSO HALF-BAKED

■ ***noun*** **1** a dish consisting of mixed ingredients that is cooked in the oven 烘烤食品：*a pasta/vegetable bake* 烤意大利面；烤蔬菜 **2** (*NAmE*) a social event at which a specific food is cooked and eaten 烧烤聚餐会

baked Al·aska /ˌbeɪkt əˈlæskə/ *noun* [C, U] a DESSERT made of cake and ice cream covered in MERINGUE and cooked quickly in a very hot oven 烤脆皮冰淇淋蛋糕，火焰冰淇淋（将蛋糕冰淇淋裹上蛋糖，放入高温烤箱烤制）

baked ˈbeans *noun* [pl.] **1** (*especially BrE*) small white BEANS cooked in a tomato sauce and usually sold in cans 番茄酱烘豆（常制成罐头） **2** (*NAmE*) = BOSTON BAKED BEANS

ˌ**baked poˈtato** (*also* ˌ**jacket poˈtato**) *noun* a potato cooked in its skin in an oven （带皮）烤土豆：*a baked potato and beans* 一份烤土豆加烘豆

bake·house /ˈbeɪkhaʊs/ *noun* (*old-fashioned*) a building or an area where bread is made 面包作坊；面包房

Bake·lite™ /ˈbeɪkəlaɪt; *NAmE also* ˈbeɪkl-/ *noun* [U] a type of hard plastic used in the past for electrical equipment, etc. 酚醛塑料；电木；胶木

baker /ˈbeɪkə(r)/ *noun* **1** a person whose job is baking and selling bread and cakes 面包（糕饼）师傅；面包店老板 **2** **baker's** (*pl.* **bakers**) (*BrE*) a shop that sells bread and cakes 面包店：*I'm just going to the baker's.* 我正要去面包店。 ➲ MORE LIKE THIS 34, page R29

ˌ**baker's ˈdozen** *noun* [sing.] (*old-fashioned*) a group of thirteen (= one more than a dozen, which is twelve) 十三 **ORIGIN** This phrase comes from bakers' old custom of adding one extra loaf to an order of a dozen. 源自旧时面包店老板的惯常做法，即给购买十二条面包的顾客免费多送一条。

bakery /ˈbeɪkəri/ *noun* (*pl.* **-ies**) (*NAmE also* **bake·shop**) a place where bread and cakes are made and/or sold 面包（糕饼）店；面包（糕饼）烘房；面包厂

ˈ**bake sale** *noun* (*NAmE*) an event at which cakes, etc. are baked and sold to make money, usually for a school or charity 烤饼义卖（为学校或慈善事业等募集资金）

bake·shop /ˈbeɪkʃɒp; *NAmE* -ʃɑːp/ *noun* (*NAmE*) = BAKERY

bake·ware /ˈbeɪkweə(r); *NAmE* -wer/ *noun* [U] tins and other containers used for baking 烘焙用具

bak·ing /ˈbeɪkɪŋ/ *noun, adj.*

■ ***noun*** [U] the process of cooking using dry heat in an oven 烤制；烘焙：*a **baking dish/tin*** 烤盘；烤模

■ ***adj.*** (*also* ˌ**baking ˈhot**) (*informal*) extremely hot 灼热的；炽热的

ˈ**baking flour** *noun* [U] (*US*) = SELF-RISING FLOUR

ˈ**baking powder** *noun* [U] a mixture of powders that are used to make cakes rise and become light as they are baked 发酵粉 ➲ MORE LIKE THIS 9, page R26

ˈ**baking sheet** (*BrE also* ˈ**baking tray**, *NAmE also* ˈ**cookie sheet**) *noun* a small sheet of metal used for baking food on （小片）烘烤板，烤盘

ˈ**baking soda** *noun* [U] = SODIUM BICARBONATE

bak·kie /ˈbʌki/ *noun* (*SAfrE*) a motor vehicle with low sides and no roof at the back, used for transporting goods or people, or as a car （无后盖的）小型轻便客货车 ➲ COMPARE PICKUP *n.* (1)

bak·sheesh (*also* **back·sheesh**) /ˌbækˈʃiːʃ/ *noun* [U] (*informal*) (in some Asian countries) a small amount of money that is given as a gift to poor people, or given to sb to thank them or to persuade them to help you （一些亚洲国家中的）施舍，小费，小额贿赂

bala·clava /ˌbæləˈklɑːvə/ (*also* ˌ**balaclava ˈhelmet**) *noun* (*especially BrE*) a type of hat made of wool that covers most of the head, neck and face 巴拉克拉瓦盔式帽，巴拉克拉瓦羊毛头罩（裹住头、颈和脸的大部分）

bala·fon /ˈbæləfɒn; *NAmE* -fɑːn/ *noun* a large type of XYLOPHONE (= a musical instrument with rows of wooden bars that you hit) that is used in W African music 巴拉风；西非大木琴

bala·laika /ˌbæləˈlaɪkə/ *noun* a musical instrument like a GUITAR with a body shaped like a triangle and two, three, or four strings, popular especially in Russia 巴拉莱卡琴（俄罗斯拨弦乐器，腹呈三角形，可有二弦、三弦或四弦）➲ VISUAL VOCAB PAGE V40

bal·ance 🔑 /ˈbæləns/ *noun, verb*

■ *noun*

• **EQUAL AMOUNTS** 等量 **1** 🔑 [U, sing.] a situation in which different things exist in equal, correct or good amounts 均衡；平衡；均势：*This newspaper maintains a good balance in its presentation of different opinions.* 这份报纸不偏不倚地报道不同的意见。◇ *Tourists often disturb the delicate balance of nature on the island.* 观光客常常干扰岛上脆弱的自然生态平衡。◇ *His wife's death disturbed the* ***balance of his mind.*** 妻子的离世使他心神不宁。◇ **~ between A and B** *Try to keep a balance between work and relaxation.* 尽量保持工作与休闲均衡。➲ SEE ALSO IMBALANCE

• **OF BODY** 身体 **2** 🔑 [U] the ability to keep steady with an equal amount of weight on each side of the body 平衡能力：*Athletes need a good sense of balance.* 运动员要有良好的平衡感。◇ *I struggled to* ***keep my balance*** *on my new skates.* 我穿着新溜冰鞋，努力保持平衡。◇ *She cycled round the corner,* ***lost her balance*** *and fell off.* 她骑车拐弯时失去平衡，摔了下来。

• **MONEY** 钱 **3** 🔑 [C, usually sing.] the amount that is left after taking numbers or money away from a total 余额：*to check your* ***bank balance*** (= to find out how much money there is in your account) 核对银行结存 **4** 🔑 [C, usually sing.] an amount of money still owed after some payment has been made 结欠：*The balance of $500 must be paid within 90 days.* * 500 美元结欠款必须于 90 天之内付清。➲ WORDFINDER NOTE AT BANK

• **INSTRUMENT FOR WEIGHING** 秤 **5** [C] an instrument for weighing things, with a bar that is supported in the middle and has dishes hanging from each end 天平；秤

IDM **(on) the balance of ˈevidence/probaˈbility** (*formal*) (considering) the evidence on both sides of an argument, to find the most likely reason for or result of sth （从）总的来说；（考虑）正反两方面；权衡双方证据 **(be/hang) in the ˈbalance** if the future of sth/sb, or the result of sth is/hangs **in the balance**, it is uncertain （前途）不明朗；（结果）未定，悬而未决：*The long-term future of the space programme hangs in the balance.* 航天计划的长远前景尚未明朗。 **(catch/throw sb) off ˈbalance 1** to make sb/sth unsteady and in danger of falling 使失去平衡（而有跌落危险）：*I was thrown off balance by the sudden gust of wind.* 突如其来的一阵风差点儿把我吹倒。 **2** to make sb surprised and no longer calm 使（毫无准备而）不知所措：*The senator was clearly caught off balance by the unexpected question.* 参议员显然因这意想不到的问题而乱了阵脚。 **on ˈbalance** after considering all the information 总的来说：*On balance, the company has had a successful year.* 总的来说，公司这一年业绩很好。➲ MORE AT REDRESS *v.*, STRIKE *v.*, SWING *v.*, TIP *v.*

■ *verb*

• **KEEP STEADY** 保持平衡 **1** 🔑 [I, T] to put your body or sth else into a position where it is steady and does not fall 使（在某物上）保持平衡；立稳：**~ (on sth)** *How long can you balance on one leg?* 你单腿能站多久？◇ **~ sth (on sth)** *The television was precariously balanced on top of a pile of books.* 电视机放在一堆书上面，不稳当。◇ *She balanced the cup on her knee.* 她把杯子在膝盖上放稳。

• **BE/KEEP EQUAL** （使）相等 **2** 🔑 [I, T] to be equal in value, amount, etc. to sth else that has the opposite effect 相抵；抵消 SYN **offset**：**~ out** *The good and bad effects of any decision will usually balance out.* 任何决策的效果往往利弊互见。◇ **~ sth (out)** *This year's profits will balance out our previous losses.* 本年度的赢利将可弥补我们之前的亏损。◇ *His lack of experience was balanced by a willingness to learn.* 他的好学弥补了他经验的不足。 **3** 🔑 [T] **~ A with/and B** to give equal importance to two contrasting things or parts of sth 同等重视（相对的两个事物或方面）：*She tries to balance home life and career.* 她力图兼顾家庭生活和事业。

• **COMPARE** 比较 **4** [T] **~ A against B** to compare the relative importance of two contrasting things 比较（两个相对的事物）；权衡重要性：*The cost of obtaining legal advice needs to be balanced against its benefits.* 法律咨询的费用与其效益需权衡一下。

• **MONEY** 钱 **5** [T] **~ sth** (*finance* 财) to show that in an account the total money spent is equal to the total money received; to calculate the difference between the two totals 结平（账目） **6** [I] (of an account) to have an equal amount of money spent and money received （账目）收支平衡：*I tried to work out why the books wouldn't balance.* 我想要弄清这些账目收支为什么不平衡。

ˈbalance beam *noun* (*NAmE*) = BEAM (3)

bal·anced /ˈbælənst/ *adj.* [usually before noun] (*approving*) keeping or showing a balance so that different things or different parts of sth exist in equal or correct amounts 保持（或显示）平衡的：*The programme presented a balanced view of the two sides of the conflict.* 节目公平地反映了冲突双方的情况。◇ *a balanced diet* (= one with the quantity and variety of food needed for good health) 均衡饮食

ˌbalance of ˈpayments *noun* [sing.] the difference between the amount a country pays for imports and the amount it receives for exports in a particular period of time 国际收支差额（一国在某时期的进出口差额）

ˌbalance of ˈpower *noun* [sing.] **1** a situation in which political or military strength is divided between two countries or groups of countries （国际政治或军事的）均势 ➲ COLLOCATIONS AT INTERNATIONAL **2** the power held by a small group which can give its support to either of two larger and equally strong groups 举足轻重的力量（两个较大团体势力均衡时，小团体所具有的可改变均势的力量）

ˌbalance of ˈtrade (*also* **ˈtrade balance**) *noun* [sing.] the difference in value between imports and exports 国际贸易差额：*a balance-of-trade deficit* (= when a country spends more on imports than it earns from exports) 国际贸易逆差

ˈbalance sheet *noun* (*finance* 财) a written statement showing the amount of money and property that a company has and listing what has been received and paid out 资产负债表；决算表；资金平衡表

ˈbalancing act *noun* [usually sing.] a process in which sb tries to please two or more people or groups who want different things 平衡各方权益的行动：*The UN must perform a delicate balancing act between the different sides in the conflict.* 联合国必须在冲突各方之间担任公正的协调工作。

bal·cony /ˈbælkəni/ *noun* (*pl.* **-ies**) **1** a platform that is built on the upstairs outside wall of a building, with a wall or rail around it. You can get out onto a balcony from an upstairs room. 阳台 ➲ VISUAL VOCAB PAGE V18 **2** an area of seats upstairs in a theatre （剧院的）楼厅，楼座 ➲ SEE ALSO CIRCLE *n.* (4), FIRST BALCONY ➲ WORDFINDER NOTE AT THEATRE

bald /bɔːld/ *adj.* **1** having little or no hair on the head 秃顶的；秃头的：*He started* ***going bald*** *in his twenties.* 他二十几岁便开始谢顶。➲ VISUAL VOCAB PAGE V65 **2** without any of the usual hair, marks, etc. covering the skin or surface of sth 无毛的；无茸毛的；光秃的：*Our dog has a bald patch on its leg.* 我们的狗腿上脱了一片毛。◇ *a bald tyre* (= a tyre whose surface has become smooth) 磨平了的轮胎 **3** without any extra explanation or detail to help you understand or accept what is being said 不加赘述的；简单的；赤裸裸的：*The bald fact is that we don't need you any longer.* 事实很简单，我们不再需要你了。◇ *The letter was a bald statement of our legal position.* 那封信直截了当地说出我们的法律立场。➲ SEE ALSO BALDLY ▶ **bald·ness** *noun* [U]

IDM **(as) bald as a coot** (*BrE, informal*) completely bald 光秃秃 ➲ MORE LIKE THIS 14, page R26

B

ˌbald ˈeagle *noun* a N American BIRD OF PREY (= a bird that kills other creatures for food) with a white head and white tail feathers. It is used as a symbol of the US. 白头雕，白头鹫（北美猛禽，头尾羽毛呈白色，是美国的象征）

bal·der·dash /ˈbɔːldədæʃ; *NAmE* -dərd-/ *noun* [U] (*old-fashioned*) nonsense 胡说；废话

ˌbald-ˈfaced *adj.* (*disapproving, especially NAmE*) making no attempt to hide your dishonest behaviour 赤裸裸的；公然的；厚颜无耻的 **SYN** **barefaced, blatant**: *bald-faced lies* 赤裸裸的谎话

bald·ing /ˈbɔːldɪŋ/ *adj.* starting to lose the hair on your head 开始脱发的；变秃的： *a short balding man with glasses* 一个戴眼镜的有些秃顶的小个子男人

bald·ly /ˈbɔːldli/ *adv.* in a few words with nothing extra or unnecessary 直截了当地；不加赘述地： *'You're lying,' he said baldly.* "你撒谎。"他直截了当地说。

baldy (*also* **baldie**) /ˈbɔːldi/ *noun* (*pl.* **-ies**) (*informal, offensive*) a person who has no hair or almost no hair on their head 秃头；秃子

bale /beɪl/ *noun, verb*

■ ***noun*** a large amount of a light material pressed tightly together and tied up 大包，大捆（轻物品）： ***bales of hay/straw/cotton/wool*** 大捆大捆的干草 / 稻草 / 棉花 / 羊毛

■ ***verb*** **1** ~ **sth** to make sth into bales 将…打成大包（或大捆）： *The waste paper is baled, then sent for recycling.* 废纸被打成大包，然后送去回收再利用。 **2** ~ **sb (to do sth)** (*BrE*) = BAIL

PHR V **ˌbale ˈout | ˌbale sth↔ˈout | ˌbale sb↔ˈout** (*BrE*) = BAIL OUT (OF STH), BAIL OUT, BAIL SB↔OUT (OF STH)

bale·ful /ˈbeɪlfl/ *adj.* (*literary*) threatening to do sth evil or to hurt sb 威吓的；吓唬的： *a baleful look/influence* 凶恶的外表 / 势力 ▶ **bale·ful·ly** /ˈbeɪlfəli/ *adv.*

baler /ˈbeɪlə(r)/ *noun* a machine for making paper, cotton, HAY, etc. into bales 打包机；压捆机

balk (*especially NAmE*) = BAULK

Bal·kan·ize (*BrE also* **-ise**) /ˈbɔːlkənaɪz; *BrE also* ˈbɒl-/ *verb* ~ **sth** to divide a region into smaller regions which are unfriendly or aggressive towards each other 使巴尔干化（将某地区分裂成敌对区域） ▶ **Bal·kan·iza·tion, -isa·tion** /ˌbɔːlkənaɪˈzeɪʃn; *BrE also* ˌbɒl-; *NAmE* ˌbɔːlkənəˈzeɪʃn/ *noun* [U]

the Bal·kans /ˈbɔːlkənz; *BrE also* ˈbɒl-/ *noun* [pl.] a region of SE Europe, including the countries to the south of the rivers Sava and Danube 巴尔干（位于欧洲东南部，包括萨瓦河和多瑙河以南诸国） ▶ **Bal·kan** *adj.*： *the Balkan Peninsula* 巴尔干半岛

balky /ˈbɔːlki; ˈbɔːki/ *adj.* (*NAmE*) (of a person or machine 人或机器) refusing or failing to do what you want them to do 倔强的；不听使唤的

ball 🔑 /bɔːl/ *noun, verb*

■ ***noun*** **1** 🔑 a round object used for throwing, hitting or kicking in games and sports 球： *a* ***golf/tennis/cricket ball*** 高尔夫球；网球；板球 ◇ *Bounce the ball and try and hit it over the net.* 让球反弹起来，然后试着把它打过网。 ➲ VISUAL VOCAB PAGE V48 **2** 🔑 a round object or a thing that has been formed into a round shape 球状物： *The sun was a huge ball of fire low on the horizon.* 落在地平线上的太阳像个大火球。 ◇ *a ball of string* 一团线 ◇ *Some animals roll themselves into a ball for protection.* 有些动物会蜷缩成一团来保护自己。 **3** a kick, hit or throw of the ball in some sports 踢出（或击出、投出）的一球： *He sent over a high ball.* 他投了一个高球。 **4** (in BASEBALL 棒球) a throw by the PITCHER that is outside the STRIKE ZONE (= the area between the BATTER's upper arms and knees) （投手投出的）坏球 **5** ~ **of the foot/hand** the part underneath the big toe or the thumb 大脚趾球；拇指球；鱼际；跖球 ➲ VISUAL VOCAB PAGE V64 **6** [usually pl.] (*taboo, informal*) a TESTICLE 睾丸 ➲ SEE ALSO BALLS *n.* (4) **7** a large formal party with dancing （大型正式的）舞会

IDM **a ˌball and ˈchain** a problem that prevents you from doing what you would like to do 羁绊；障碍 **the ball is in your/sb's ˈcourt** it is your/sb's responsibility to take action next （球已经丢给你了）下一步就看你的了： *They've offered me the job, so the ball's in my court now.* 他们已答应把那份工作给我，下一步就看我怎么办了。 **a ˌball of ˈfire** (*informal*) a person who is full of energy and enthusiasm 充满活力和热情的人；生龙活虎的人；朝气蓬勃的人 **get/set/start/keep the ball ˈrolling** to make sth start happening; to make sure that sth continues to happen 开始某事；继续某事 **have a ˈball** (*informal*) to enjoy yourself a lot 狂欢；玩得痛快 **have something/a lot on the ˈball** (*US, informal*) to be capable of doing a job very well; to be intelligent 有能耐；有才智 **(be) on the ˈball** to be aware of and understand what is happening and able to react quickly 敏锐；机警： *The new publicity manager is really on the ball.* 新任宣传部经理的确精明干练。 **pick up/take the ˌball and ˈrun with it** (*especially NAmE*) to develop an idea or plan that already exists 采纳（想法）并发扬光大；接手并发展（计划）： *It's up to the private sector to take the ball and run with it.* 该轮到私营部门接手并发展它了。 **play ˈball (with sb)** **1** (*NAmE*) to play with a ball 玩球；耍球： *Chris was in the park playing ball with the kids.* 克里斯在公园里和孩子们一起玩球。 **2** (*informal*) to be willing to work with other people in a helpful way, especially so that sb can get what they want （和某人）合作 **the whole ball of ˈwax** (*NAmE, informal*) the whole thing; everything 整个；全部；一切： *I panicked, I cried—the whole ball of wax.* 我惊慌失措，我大喊大叫，所有的反应都做齐了。 ➲ MORE AT CARRY, DROP *v.*, EYE *n.*

■ ***verb*** **1** [I, T] to form sth or be formed into the shape of a ball 做成球状；使成团块： ~ **(into sth)** *Her hands balled into fists.* 她双手攥拳。 ◇ ~ **sth (into sth)** *My hands were balled into fists.* 我双手攥成拳头。 **2** [T] ~ **sb** (*NAmE, taboo, slang*) (of a man) to have sex with a woman 和（女性）交媾

bal·lad /ˈbæləd/ *noun* **1** a song or poem that tells a story 叙事诗；民歌；民谣： *a medieval ballad about a knight and a lady* 一首关于骑士和贵族小姐的中世纪谣曲 **2** a slow song about love （节奏缓慢的）情歌： *Her latest single is a ballad.* 她的最新单曲是一首情歌。 ➲ COLLOCATIONS AT MUSIC

bal·lad·eer /ˌbæləˈdɪə(r); *NAmE* -ˈdɪr/ *noun* a person who sings or writes ballads 叙事曲演唱者（或编写者）；叙事诗作者

ball-and-socket joint 球窝关节

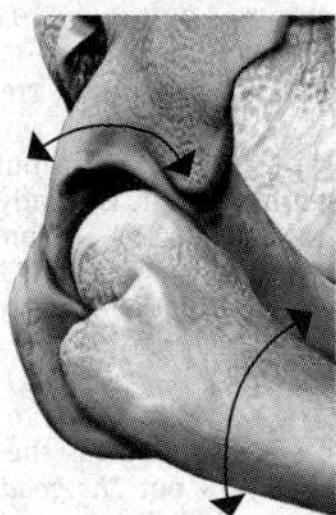

ˌball-and-ˈsocket joint *noun* (*anatomy* 解) a joint such as the hip joint at the top of the leg, in which a ball-shaped part moves inside a curved hollow part 球窝关节；杵臼关节

bal·last /ˈbæləst/ *noun* [U] **1** heavy material placed in a ship or HOT-AIR BALLOON to make it heavier and keep it steady （船中保持平衡的）压舱物；（热气球的）镇重物 **2** a layer of stones that makes a strong base on which a road, railway/railroad, etc. can be built （用作公路或铁路路基的）道砟

ball bearing 滚珠轴承

ˌball ˈbearing *noun* a ring of small metal balls used in a machine to enable the parts to turn smoothly; one of these small metal balls 球轴承；滚珠轴承；滚珠

ball·boy /ˈbɔːlbɔɪ/ *noun* a boy who picks up the balls for the players in a TENNIS match （网球赛中替球手捡球的）球童 ➲ SEE ALSO BALLGIRL

ˈball-breaker *noun* (*informal*) a sexually aggressive woman who destroys men's confidence （性欲旺盛，使男子甘拜下风的）女魔 ▸ **ˈball-breaking** *adj.*

ball·cock /ˈbɔːlkɒk; *NAmE* -kɑːk/ *noun* a device with a floating ball that controls the amount of water going into a container, for example the water tank of a toilet 浮球旋塞；浮球阀

bal·ler·ina /ˌbæləˈriːnə/ *noun* a female dancer in BALLET 芭蕾舞女演员 ➲ SEE ALSO PRIMA BALLERINA

bal·let /ˈbæleɪ/ *noun* **1** [U] a style of dancing that tells a dramatic story with music but no talking or singing 芭蕾舞：*She wants to be a **ballet dancer**.* 她想当芭蕾舞演员。◇ *ballet shoes* 芭蕾舞鞋 ➲ **WORDFINDER NOTE** AT DANCE **2** [C] a story or work of art performed by a group of ballet dancers 芭蕾舞剧：*'Swan Lake' is one of the great classical ballets.*《天鹅湖》是一部伟大的古典芭蕾舞剧。**3** [C+sing./pl. v.] a group of dancers who work and perform ballet together 芭蕾舞团：*members of the Royal Ballet* 皇家芭蕾舞团成员

bal·let·ic /bæˈletɪk/ *adj.* (*formal, approving*) smooth and elegant, like a movement or a dancer in ballet （动作）舒展优雅的，芭蕾舞风格的

ˈball game *noun* **1** any game played with a ball 球类运动 **2** (*NAmE*) a game of BASEBALL 棒球比赛：*Are you going to the ball game?* 你去看棒球赛吗？

IDM **a (whole) different/new ˈball game** (*informal*) a completely different kind of situation 截然不同的新局面

ball·girl /ˈbɔːlɡɜːl; *NAmE* -ɡɜːrl/ *noun* a girl who picks up the balls for the players in a TENNIS match （网球赛中替球手捡球的）女球童 ➲ SEE ALSO BALLBOY

ball·hawk /ˈbɔːlhɔːk/ *noun* (*US, informal*) a player who is good at getting or catching balls, especially in AMERICAN FOOTBALL, BASEBALL or BASKETBALL （尤指美式足球、棒球或篮球中的）争球能手

ˈball hockey *noun* [U] (*CanE*) a version of ICE HOCKEY played on a hard surface without ice, and with a ball instead of a PUCK 旱地曲棍球；旱地冰球

bal·lis·tic /bəˈlɪstɪk/ *adj.* connected with ballistics 弹道（学）的；发射的

IDM **go balˈlistic** (*informal*) to become very angry 大怒；暴怒：*He went ballistic when I told him.* 我告诉他时他勃然大怒。

balˌlistic ˈmissile *noun* a MISSILE that is fired into the air at a particular speed and angle in order to fall in the right place 弹道导弹

bal·lis·tics /bəˈlɪstɪks/ *noun* [U] the scientific study of things that are shot or fired through the air, such as bullets and MISSILES 弹道学；发射学 ➲ **MORE LIKE THIS** 29, page R28

bal·loon /bəˈluːn/ *noun, verb*

■ ***noun*** **1** a small bag made of very thin rubber that becomes larger and rounder when you fill it with air or gas. Balloons are brightly coloured and used as decorations or toys. 气球：***to blow up/burst/pop a balloon*** 吹起气球；使气球爆裂 ➲ COMPARE TRIAL BALLOON **2** (*also* **hot-ˈair balloon**) a large balloon made of strong material that is filled with hot air or gas to make it rise in the air, usually carrying a BASKET for passengers 热气球 ➲ **VISUAL VOCAB** PAGE V58

IDM **when the balˈloon goes up** (*BrE, informal*) when the trouble that you are expecting begins 意料中的麻烦出现时；（不出所料）出乱子时 ➲ MORE AT LEAD²

■ ***verb*** **1** [I] **~ (out/up)** to suddenly swell out or get bigger （突然）膨胀，涨大：*Her skirt ballooned out in the wind.* 她的裙子让风吹得鼓起来了。**2** [I] (*usually* **go ballooning**) to travel in a HOT-AIR BALLOON as a sport or for entertainment 乘热气球飞行

bal·loon·ist /bəˈluːnɪst/ *noun* a person who travels in a balloon as a sport 乘气球飞行者

balˈloon whisk *noun* a WHISK that you hold in your hand, made of thin pieces of curved wire 气球形手动搅拌器，打蛋器（用弧状细金属丝制成）

bal·lot /ˈbælət/ *noun, verb*

■ ***noun*** **1** [U, C] the system of voting in writing and usually in secret; an occasion on which a vote is held （无记名）投票选举；投票表决：*The chairperson is chosen by **secret ballot**.* 主席是通过无记名投票选举产生的。◇ *The union cannot call a strike unless it **holds a ballot** of members.* 工会未经会员投票表决不得发动罢工。➲ **SYNONYMS** AT ELECTION ➲ **COLLOCATIONS** AT VOTE **2** (*BrE also* **ˈballot paper**) [C] the piece of paper on which sb marks who they are voting for 选票：*What percentage of eligible voters **cast their ballots**?* 合资格选民的投票率是多少？**3 the ballot** [sing.] the total number of votes in an election （选举中的）投票总数：*She won 58.8% of the ballot.* 她赢得了投票总数的 58.8%。➲ SEE ALSO POLL *n.* (3) ➲ **WORDFINDER NOTE** AT UNION

■ ***verb*** **1** [T] **~ sb (on sth)** to ask sb to vote in writing and secretly about sth 要求某人（对某事）无记名投票 SYN **poll**：*The union balloted its members on the proposed changes.* 工会要求会员对所提议的变革进行无记名投票。**2** [I] to vote secretly about sth 进行无记名投票：*The workers balloted for a strike.* 工人对是否罢工进行无记名投票表决。

ˈballot box *noun* **1** [C] a box in which people put their ballots after voting 投票箱 **2 the ballot box** [sing.] the system of voting in an election 投票选举制：*The people make their wishes known through the ballot box.* 人们以投票方式表达他们的愿望。

ˈballot paper *noun* (*BrE*) = BALLOT (2)

ball·park /ˈbɔːlpɑːk; *NAmE* -pɑːrk/ *noun* **1** [C] (*especially NAmE*) a place where BASEBALL is played 棒球场 **2** [sing.] an area or a range within which an amount is likely to be correct or within which sth can be measured （数额的）变动范围；可量范围：*The offers for the contract were **all in the same ballpark**.* 就此合同的开价均在同一范围内。◇ *If you said five million you'd be **in the ballpark**.* 如果你说的是五百万，那就差不多了。◇ *Give me a **ballpark figure*** (= a number that is approximately right). 给我个大致的数字。

ball·point /ˈbɔːlpɔɪnt/ (*also* **ˌballpoint ˈpen**) *noun* a pen with a very small metal ball at its point, that rolls ink onto the paper 圆珠笔；原子笔 ➲ **VISUAL VOCAB** PAGE V71 ➲ COMPARE BIRO™

ball·room /ˈbɔːlruːm; -rʊm/ *noun* a very large room used for dancing on formal occasions 舞厅 ➲ COMPARE DANCE HALL ➲ **WORDFINDER NOTE** AT DANCE

ˌballroom ˈdancing *noun* [U] a type of dancing done with a partner and using particular fixed steps and

B

movements to particular types of music such as the WALTZ 交际舞；交谊舞

balls /bɔːlz/ *noun, verb*

■***noun*** (*taboo, slang*) **1** [U] (*BrE*) nonsense 胡说；废话：*That's a load of balls!* 那是一派胡言！ **2** [pl.] courage 勇气：*She's got balls, I'll say that for her.* 我敢说她有胆量。◇ *It took a lot of balls to do that.* 那么做需要很大的勇气。 **3** **Balls!** (*BrE*) ***exclamation*** used as a swear word when you are disagreeing with sth, or when you are angry about sth（粗俗话，表示不同意或恼怒） HELP Less offensive ways to express this are 'Nonsense!', 'Rubbish!' or 'Come off it!' 较温和的用语是 Nonsense!、Rubbish! 或 Come off it!。 **4** [pl.] TESTICLES 睾丸

IDM **go 'balls out** (*taboo, slang*) to do sth in a very determined or extreme way, especially when it means taking risks 豁出去；拼命干：*The team went balls out in the final.* 决赛时这个队拼得很凶。

■***verb***

PHR V **,balls sth↔'up** (*BrE, taboo, slang*) to spoil sth; to do sth very badly 把…搞糟；弄得一塌糊涂 ⊃ RELATED NOUN BALLS-UP HELP A more polite way of saying this is **foul sth up, mess sth up**, or **bungle sth**. 较礼貌的说法是 foul sth up、mess sth up 或 bungle sth。

'balls-out *adj.* (*taboo, slang*) very determined or extreme 很坚决的；十分极端的：*a balls-out attack* 猛烈攻击 ◇ *It's a balls-out shoot-'em-up action movie.* 那是一部火爆枪战动作片。

'balls-up *noun* (*BrE, taboo, slang*) something that has been done very badly 混乱；一团糟：*I made a real balls-up of my exams.* 我考试考得一塌糊涂。

ballsy /'bɔːlzi/ *adj.* (*informal, especially NAmE*) showing a lot of courage and determination 有胆量的；有决心的；有种的：*She is one ballsy lady!* 她是个敢作敢为的女子！

bally·hoo /,bæli'huː; *NAmE* 'bælihuː/ *noun* [U] (*informal, disapproving*) unnecessary noise and excitement 大吹大擂；喧嚣

balm /bɑːm/ *noun* [U, C, usually sing.] **1** (*also* **bal·sam**) oil with a pleasant smell that is obtained from some types of trees and plants, used in the past to help heal wounds, for example 香脂油（昔日用于疗伤等） **2** a liquid, cream, etc. that has a pleasant smell and is used to make wounds less painful or skin softer 镇痛软膏；护肤膏；香液：*lip balm* 润唇膏 **3** (*literary*) something that makes you feel calm or relaxed 令人感到安慰（或镇定）的事物

balmy /'bɑːmi/ *adj.* (*approving*) (of the air, weather, etc. 空气、天气等) warm and pleasant 温暖惬意的 SYN **mild**：*a balmy summer evening* 清爽宜人的夏夜 ⊃ MORE LIKE THIS 20, page R27

ba·lo·ney /bə'ləʊni; *NAmE* -'loʊ-/ *noun* [U] **1** (*informal, especially NAmE*) nonsense; lies 胡说；谎话：*Don't give me that baloney!* 别对我讲那些鬼话！ **2** (*NAmE*) = BOLOGNA

balsa /'bɔːlsə/ (*also* **'balsa wood**) *noun* [U] the light wood of the tropical American **balsa tree**, used especially for making models 热带美洲轻木（尤用于制作模型）

bal·sam /'bɔːlsəm/ *noun* **1** [U, C] = BALM (1) **2** [C] any plant or tree from which BALM is obtained 产香脂的花草（或树）

bal·sam·ic vin·egar /bɔː,sæmɪk 'vɪnɪɡə(r)/ *noun* [U] a dark sweet Italian VINEGAR, stored in BARRELS (= round wooden containers) to give it flavour 香脂醋，意大利黑醋（黑色，味甜，贮存于木桶中以酿制出香味）

balti /'bɔːlti; 'bɒlti; *NAmE* 'bɑːlti/ *noun* [C, U] a type of meat or vegetable dish cooked in Pakistani style, usually served in a round metal pan which gives its name to the dish 巴尔蒂锅菜（一种巴基斯坦式菜肴，通常用圆形平底锅盛放）

Bal·tic /'bɔːltɪk/ *adj.* relating to the Baltic Sea in northern Europe and the countries surrounding it 波罗的海的；波罗的海各国的：*the Baltic republics of Estonia, Latvia and Lithuania* 爱沙尼亚、拉脱维亚和立陶宛诸波罗的海共和国

bal·us·ter /'bæləstə(r)/ *noun* any of the short posts that form a balustrade 栏杆柱

bal·us·trade /,bælə'streɪd/ *noun* a row of posts, joined together at the top, built along the edge of a BALCONY, bridge, etc. to prevent people from falling off, or as a decoration（阳台、桥等的）栏杆

bam /bæm/ *exclamation* (*informal*) **1** used to represent the sound of a sudden loud hit or a gun being fired（表示突然的重击声或枪声）嘭，砰：*She pointed the gun at him and—bam!* 她把枪对着他，然后 —— 砰！ **2** used to show that sth happens very suddenly （表示突然）蓦地：*I saw him yesterday and—bam!—I realized I was still in love with him.* 我昨天见到他，突然间，我意识到我还爱着他。

bam·boo /,bæm'buː/ *noun* [C, U] (*pl.* **-oos**) a tall plant that is a member of the grass family and has hard hollow STEMS that are used for making furniture, poles, etc. 竹；竹子：*a bamboo grove* 竹林 ◇ *a bamboo chair* 竹椅 ◇ *bamboo shoots* (= young bamboo plants that can be eaten) 竹笋 ⊃ VISUAL VOCAB PAGE V11

bam·boo·zle /bæm'buːzl/ *verb* ~ **sb** (*informal*) to confuse sb, especially by tricking them 迷惑；（尤指）哄骗，欺骗

ban /bæn/ *verb, noun*

■***verb*** (**-nn-**) **1** ~ **sth** to decide or say officially that sth is not allowed 明令禁止；取缔 SYN **prohibit**：*Chemical weapons are banned internationally.* 国际上禁止使用化学武器。 **2** [usually passive] to order sb not to do sth, go somewhere, etc., especially officially 禁止（某人）做某事（或去某处等）：~ **sb from sth** *He was banned from the meeting.* 他被取消了出席会议的资格。 ◇ ~ **sb from doing sth** *She's been banned from leaving Greece while the allegations are investigated.* 在对那些指控进行调查期间，禁止她离开希腊。 ◇ (*BrE*) *He was banned from driving for six months.* 他被禁止驾驶六个月。

■***noun*** ~ (**on sth**) an official rule that says that sth is not allowed 禁令：*There is to be a total ban on smoking in the office.* 办公室将彻底禁止吸烟。◇ *to* ***impose/lift a ban*** 颁布 / 解除禁令

banal /bə'nɑːl; *NAmE also* 'beɪnl/ *adj.* (*disapproving*) very ordinary and containing nothing that is interesting or important 平庸的；平淡乏味的；无关紧要的；陈腐的

ban·al·ity /bə'næləti/ *noun* (*pl.* **-ies**) [U, C] (*disapproving*) the quality of being banal; things, remarks, etc. that are banal 平庸；平淡乏味；陈腐的事物；陈词滥调：*the banality of modern city life* 现代城市生活的单调乏味 ◇ *They exchanged banalities for a couple of minutes.* 他们彼此客套了几分钟。

ba·nana /bə'nɑːnə; *NAmE* bə'nænə/ *noun* a long curved fruit with a thick yellow skin and soft flesh, that grows on trees in hot countries 香蕉：*a bunch of bananas* 一串香蕉 ⊃ VISUAL VOCAB PAGE V33

IDM **go ba'nanas** (*slang*) to become angry, crazy or silly 发怒；发疯；犯傻

ba'nana belt *noun* (*NAmE, informal*) a region where the weather is warm 香蕉带（指气候温暖地带）

ba,nana re'public *noun* (*disapproving, offensive*) a poor country with a weak government, that depends on foreign money 香蕉共和国（政府无能、依赖外援的贫穷国家）

ba'nana skin *noun* (*BrE, informal*) something that could cause difficulty or embarrassment, especially to sb in a public position 造成麻烦（或使人当众出丑）的事物

ba,nana 'split *noun* a cold DESSERT (= a sweet dish) made from a BANANA that is cut in half along its length and filled with ice cream, nuts, etc. 香蕉圣代，香蕉船（将香蕉纵向剖开，加进冰淇淋、果仁等做成的甜食冷盘）

band /bænd/ *noun, verb*

■*noun*

• GROUP OF MUSICIANS 乐队 **1** [C+sing./pl. v.] a small group of musicians who play popular music together, often with a singer or singers 流行音乐乐队： *a rock/jazz band* 摇滚 / 爵士乐队 ◇ *She's a singer with a band.* 她是一个乐队的歌手。 ➲SEE ALSO BOY BAND, GIRL BAND ➲WORDFINDER NOTE AT DANCE **2** [C+sing./pl. v.] a group of musicians who play BRASS and PERCUSSION instruments 管乐队；鼓号乐队： *a military band* 军乐队 ➲SEE ALSO BRASS BAND, MARCHING BAND, ONE-MAN BAND

• GROUP OF PEOPLE 人群 **3** [C+sing./pl. v.] a group of people who do sth together or who have the same ideas 一伙人；一帮人： *a band of outlaws* 一帮歹徒 ◇ *He persuaded a small band of volunteers to help.* 他劝服了一小批志愿者来帮忙。

• STRIP OF MATERIAL/COLOUR 带子；颜色带 **4** [C] a thin flat strip or circle of any material that is put around things, for example to hold them together or to make them stronger 带；箍： *She always ties her hair back in a band.* 她总是用一条带子把头发扎在后面。 ◇ *All babies in the hospital have name bands on their wrists.* 医院里所有新生儿手腕上都套着写有名字的手环。 ◇ *She wore a simple band of gold* (= a ring) *on her finger.* 她戴着一枚净面的金戒指。 ➲VISUAL VOCAB PAGE V70 ➲SEE ALSO ARMBAND, HAIRBAND, HATBAND, RUBBER BAND, SWEATBAND, WAISTBAND **5** [C] a strip of colour or material on sth that is different from what is around it 条纹；条饰： *a white plate with a blue band around the edge* 带蓝边的白盘子 ➲WORDFINDER NOTE AT PATTERN

• OF RADIO WAVES 无线电波 **6** (*also* **wave·band**) [C] a range of radio waves 频带；波段： *Short-wave radio uses the 20–50-metre band.* 短波收音机用的波段是 20–50 米。

• RANGE 范围 **7** [C] a range of numbers, ages, prices, etc. within which people or things are counted or measured （数目、年龄、价格等的）范围，段： *the 25–35 age band* * 25–35 岁的年龄段 ◇ *tax bands* 税收等级

■*verb*

• WITH COLOUR/MATERIAL 色彩；材料 **1** [usually passive] to put a band of a different colour or material around sth 加彩条（或嵌条等）： **be banded (+ adj.)** *Many insects are banded black and yellow.* 很多昆虫有黑色和黄色的条纹。

• PUT INTO RANGE 划分范围 **2** [usually passive] (*BrE*) to organize sth into bands of price, income, etc. （将价格、收入等）划分档次，分等级： **be banded** *Tax is banded according to income.* 赋税是按收入划分等级的。

PHR V **,band to'gether** to form a group in order to achieve sth 联合；携手： *Local people banded together to fight the drug dealers.* 当地人齐心协力打击毒品贩子。

ban·dage /'bændɪdʒ/ *noun, verb*

■*noun* a strip of cloth used for tying around a part of the body that has been hurt in order to protect or support it 绷带 ➲WORDFINDER NOTE AT HURT

■*verb* ~ **sth/sb (up)** to wrap a bandage around a part of the body in order to protect it because it is injured 用绷带包扎 ➲COLLOCATIONS AT INJURY

'Band-Aid™ *noun* (*especially NAmE*) **1** (*BrE also* **plas·ter, 'sticking plaster**) [C, U] material that can be stuck to the skin to protect a small wound or cut; a piece of this 膏药；创可贴；护创胶布 **2** (*disapproving*) a temporary solution to a problem that does not really solve it at all 权宜之计

ban·dana (*also* **ban·danna**) /bæn'dænə/ *noun* a piece of brightly coloured cloth worn around the neck or head 色彩鲜艳的围巾（或头巾）

B and B (*also* **B & B, b and b, b & b**) /,bi: ən 'bi:/ *abbr.* (*informal, especially BrE*) BED AND BREAKFAST 住宿加（次日）早餐；提供住宿加早餐的旅馆

'band council *noun* (*CanE*) a local form of Aboriginal government in Canada, consisting of an elected chief and COUNCILLORS 社议会（加拿大土著的地方政府，由一名酋长和数名社议员组成）

ban·deau /'bændəʊ; *NAmE* -doʊ/ *noun* **1** a narrow band worn around the head to hold the hair in place 束发带 **2** a piece of women's clothing that is tied around the body to cover the breasts 管状胸罩；狭带式胸罩： *a bandeau bikini top* 管状比基尼上装

bandh /bʌnd/ *noun* (*IndE*) a general strike 总罢工

bandi·coot /'bændɪku:t/ *noun* **1** a small Australasian animal with a long nose and long tail, which eats mainly insects 袋狸（澳大拉西亚长鼻长尾小动物，主食昆虫） **2** (*also* **,bandicoot 'rat**) an Asian RAT 袋狸鼠

band·ing /'bændɪŋ/ *noun* [U] (*BrE*) = STREAMING (1)

ban·dit /'bændɪt/ *noun* a member of an armed group of thieves who attack travellers 土匪

ban·dito /bæn'di:təʊ; *NAmE* -toʊ/ (*also* **ban·dido** /-dəʊ; *NAmE* -doʊ/) *noun* (*NAmE, from Spanish*) (*pl.* **-os**) a Mexican BANDIT 墨西哥土匪

ban·dit·ry /'bændɪtri/ *noun* [U] (*formal*) acts of stealing and violence by bandits 土匪行为（或活动）

band·leader /'bændli:də(r)/ *noun* a player who is in charge of a band, especially a JAZZ band （尤指爵士乐的）乐队领队

band·mas·ter /'bændmɑ:stə(r); *NAmE* -mæs-/ *noun* a person who CONDUCTS a military band or a BRASS BAND 军乐队（或管乐队）指挥

bando·bast /'bʌndəbʌst/ (*also* **bundo·bast, bundo·bust**) *noun* [U, C, usually sing.] (*IndE*) preparation or an arrangement for dealing with sth 准备；安排： *The police bandobast was very effective.* 警方的安排十分奏效。

ban·do·lier (*also* **ban·do·leer**) /,bændə'lɪə(r); *NAmE* -'lɪr/ *noun* a belt made for carrying bullets and worn over the shoulder （斜挎肩上的）子弹带

bands·man /'bændzmən/ *noun* (*pl.* **-men** /-mən/) a musician who plays in a military band or a BRASS BAND 军乐队（或管乐队）队员

band·stand /'bændstænd/ *noun* a covered platform outdoors, where musicians, especially a BRASS or military band, can stand and play （室外有篷的）乐队演奏台

band·wagon /'bændwægən/ *noun* [usually sing.] an activity that more and more people are becoming involved in 风靡的活动；时尚： *The World Cup bandwagon is starting to roll.* 世界杯足球赛热潮即将涌起。

IDM **climb/jump on the 'bandwagon** (*informal, disapproving*) to join others in doing sth that is becoming fashionable because you hope to become popular or successful yourself 赶时髦；追随潮流： *politicians eager to jump on the environmental bandwagon* 急于随大溜加入环保行列的政客们 ORIGIN In the US, political PARADES often included a band on a wagon. Political leaders would join them in the hope of winning popular support. 源自美国的政治宣传游行，常有乐队彩车随行。政治领袖参与游行希望赢得民众支持。

band·width /'bændwɪdθ/ *noun* [C, U] (*computing* 计) **1** a band of FREQUENCIES used for sending electronic signals 带宽；频宽 **2** a measurement of the amount of information that a particular computer network or Internet connection can send in a particular time. It is often measured in BITS per second. 带宽值，频宽值（计算机网络或互联网接口一定时间内传送信息量的量度，按每秒传送的比特数计）

bandy /'bændi/ *adj., verb, noun*

■*adj.* (of the legs 双腿) curving, with the knees wide apart 向外弯曲的；罗圈的： *to be bandy-legged* 有罗圈腿

■*verb* (**ban·dies, bandy·ing, ban·died, ban·died**)

IDM **bandy 'words (with sb)** (*old-fashioned*) to argue with sb or speak rudely to them （与…）争吵，发生口角

PHR V **,bandy sth↔a'bout/a'round** [usually passive] if a name, a word, a story, etc., is **bandied about/around**, it is mentioned frequently by many people 传播；散布： *His name was being bandied about as a future prime minister.* 人们纷纷传说他是未来的首相。

B

■ *noun* [U] a game similar to hockey, played on a field or on ice with a ball and large curved sticks 班迪球（一种类似曲棍球的运动）

bane /beɪn/ *noun* [sing.] **the ~ of sb/sth** something that causes trouble and makes people unhappy 造成困扰（或不快）的事物：*The neighbours' kids are the **bane of my life**.* 街坊邻居的孩子们让我生活得很不安宁。

bane·ful /ˈbeɪnfl/ *adj.* (*literary*) evil or causing evil 邪恶的；引起灾祸的

bang /bæŋ/ *verb, noun, adv., exclamation*

■ *verb* **1** [I, T] to hit sth in a way that makes a loud noise 猛敲；砸：**~ on sth** *She banged on the door angrily.* 她愤怒地砰砰打门。◇ **~ sth** (**with sth**) *The baby was banging the table with his spoon.* 婴孩用调羹敲打着桌子。➲ SYNONYMS AT HIT **2** [I, T] to close sth or to be closed with a loud noise （把…）砰地关上 SYN **slam**：*A window was banging somewhere* (= opening and closing noisily). 什么地方有扇窗户在砰砰的开开关关。◇ **+ adj.** *The door banged shut behind her.* 她出去时把门砰的一声关上了。◇ **~ sth** *Don't bang the door when you go out!* 出去时别那么砰一声地关门！ **3** [T] **~ sth + adv./prep.** to put sth somewhere suddenly and violently 猛摔；砰地一扔 SYN **slam**：*He banged the money down on the counter.* 他把钱往柜台上砰地一掷。◇ *She banged saucepans around irritably.* 她暴躁地把锅摔来摔去。 **4** [T] **~ sth** (**+ adv./prep.**) to hit sth, especially a part of the body, against sth by accident 碰撞；磕 SYN **bump**：*She tripped and banged her knee on the desk.* 她绊了一跤，膝盖磕在桌子上。 **5** [T] **~ sb** (*taboo, slang*) (of a man 男性) to have sex with a woman 和（女性）性交 IDM SEE DRUM *n.*, HEAD *n.*

PHR V ˌ**bang aˈbout/aˈround** to move around noisily 乒乓作响地来来去去：*We could hear the kids banging around upstairs.* 我们能听到孩子们在楼上咚咚地跑来跑去。 ˌ**bang ˈinto sth** to crash into or hit sth by mistake （不小心）撞着某物：*I banged into a chair and hurt my leg.* 我撞到椅子上，碰伤了腿。 ˌ**bang ˈon** (**about sth**) (*BrE, informal*) to talk a lot about sth in a boring way 唠叨；絮叨 SYN **go on**：*He keeps banging on about his new job.* 他没完没了地唠叨他那份新工作。 ˌ**bang sb↔ˈup** (*BrE, informal*) to put sb in prison 使某人锒铛入狱；把某人收监 ˌ**bang sth↔ˈup** (*NAmE, informal*) to damage or injure sth 毁坏；损害

■ *noun* **1** [C] a sudden loud noise 突然的巨响：*The door swung shut with a bang.* 门砰的一声关上了。◇ *Suddenly there was a loud bang and a puff of smoke.* 突然一声巨响，喷出了一股烟。➲ SEE ALSO BIG BANG **2** [C] a sudden painful blow on a part of the body （对身体部位的）猛撞，猛敲，猛击：*a bang on the head* 头被撞击 **3 bangs** [pl.] (*NAmE*) (*BrE* **fringe**) the front part of sb's hair that is cut so that it hangs over their FOREHEAD 额前短发；刘海儿 ➲ VISUAL VOCAB PAGE V65 **4** [U] = BHANG **5** [C] (*informal, computing* 计) the symbol (!) 叹号

IDM ˌ**bang for your ˈbuck** (*especially NAmE, informal*) if you get more, better, etc. **bang for your buck**, you get better value for the money you spend or the effort you put in to sth 钱花得合算；所作的努力值得 **with a ˈbang** (*informal*) **1** very successfully 很成功：*The party went with a bang.* 聚会十分圆满。 **2** in a way that everyone notices; with a powerful effect 引人注目；有强烈影响：*The team won their last four games, ending the season with a bang.* 该队赢了最后四场比赛，给本赛季画了一个亮丽的句号。➲ MORE AT EARTH *n.*

■ *adv.* (*informal, especially BrE*) exactly; completely 正好；完全地：*Our computers are **bang up to date**.* 我们的电脑是最先进的。◇ *My estimate was bang on target.* 我的估计完全准确。◇ *You're bang on time, as usual.* 你像往常一样，非常准时。➲ SEE ALSO SLAP *adv.*

IDM **bang goes sth** (*BrE, informal*) used when you say that sth you hoped to have or achieve is no longer possible （希望等）破灭：*Bang went my hopes of promotion.* 我晋升的希望破灭了。 **go ˈbang** (*informal*) to burst or explode with a loud noise; to make a sudden loud noise 爆；爆炸；发出巨响：*A balloon suddenly went bang.* 一只气球突然砰的一声爆了。➲ MORE AT RIGHT *n.*

■ *exclamation* used to show the sound of sth loud, like a gun （表示枪声等巨响）砰：*'Bang, bang, you're dead!' shouted the little boy.* "砰！砰！你死了！"小男孩喊道。

ˌ**banged ˈup** *adj.* (*NAmE, informal*) injured or damaged 受伤的；损坏的：*Two days after the accident she still looked pretty banged up.* 事故过去两天后她看上去伤势仍然很重。➲ COMPARE BANG SB↔UP, BANG STH↔UP at BANG *v.*

bang·er /ˈbæŋə(r)/ *noun* (*BrE, informal*) **1** a SAUSAGE 香肠：*bangers and mash* 香肠和土豆泥 **2** (*NAmE* **beat·er**) an old car that is in bad condition 破旧的汽车 **3** a FIREWORK that makes a loud noise when it explodes 爆竹；鞭炮

Bangla /ˈbʌŋlɜː/ *noun* [U] **1** the Bengali language 孟加拉语 **2** Bangladesh 孟加拉国

ban·gle /ˈbæŋgl/ *noun* a piece of jewellery in the form of a large ring of gold, silver, etc. worn loosely around the wrist 手镯 ➲ VISUAL VOCAB PAGE V70

ˈ**bang-up** *adj.* (*NAmE, informal*) very good 挺好的；很棒的

bania /ˈbʌnjə/ *noun* (*IndE*) **1** a person who sells things 商人 **2** (*disapproving*) a person who is interested in making money 财迷；贪财的人

ban·ish /ˈbænɪʃ/ *verb* **1** [usually passive] **~ sb** (**from…**) (**to…**) to order sb to leave a place, especially a country, as a punishment 放逐；流放；把（某人）驱逐出境 SYN **exile**：*He was banished to Australia, where he died five years later.* 他被流放到澳大利亚，五年后在那里去世。◇ *The children were banished from the dining room.* 孩子们被赶出餐室。 **2 ~ sb/sth** (**from sth**) to make sb/sth go away; to get rid of sb/sth 赶走；驱除：*The sight of food banished all other thoughts from my mind.* 看到吃的，我别的什么都忘记了。

ban·ish·ment /ˈbænɪʃmənt/ *noun* [U] the punishment of being sent away from a place, especially from a country 放逐；流放；驱逐出境

ban·is·ter (*also* **ban·nis·ter**) /ˈbænɪstə(r)/ *noun* (*BrE also* **ban·is·ters** [pl.]) the posts and rail which you can hold for support when going up or down stairs （楼梯的）栏杆，扶手：*to hold on to the banister/banisters* 紧抓住扶手 ➲ PICTURE AT STAIRCASE

banjo /ˈbændʒəʊ; *NAmE* ˈbændʒoʊ/ *noun* (*pl.* **-os**) a musical instrument like a GUITAR, with a long neck, a round body and four or more strings 班卓，班卓琴（拨弦乐器，长颈、圆身）➲ VISUAL VOCAB PAGE V40

bank 🔑 /bæŋk/ *noun, verb*

■ *noun*

• **FOR MONEY** 金钱 **1** 🔑 an organization that provides various financial services, for example keeping or lending money 银行：*My salary is paid directly into my bank.* 我的工资直接打到我的银行。◇ *I need to go to the bank* (= the local office of a bank). 我得去趟银行。◇ *a bank loan* 银行贷款 ◇ *a bank manager* 银行经理 ➲ WORDFINDER NOTE AT MONEY ➲ COLLOCATIONS AT FINANCE ➲ SEE ALSO INVESTMENT BANK, MERCHANT BANK

> **WORDFINDER** 联想词：account, balance, credit, debit, deposit, interest, **loan**, statement, withdrawal

• **IN GAMBLING** 赌博 **2** a supply of money or things that are used as money in some games, especially those in which gambling is involved （尤指赌博中的）筹码；赌本

• **STH COLLECTED/STORED** 收集 / 贮存物 **3** an amount of sth that is collected; a place where sth is stored ready for use 库存；库：*a bank of knowledge* 知识宝库 ◇ *a **blood/sperm bank*** 血库；精子库 ➲ SEE ALSO DATABANK

• **OF RIVER/CANAL** 河；水道 **4** 🔑 the side of a river, CANAL, etc. and the land near it 岸；河畔：*He jumped in and swam to the opposite bank.* 他跳下水，游到对岸。◇ *It's on the north bank of the Thames.* 它位于泰晤士河北岸。◇ *a house on the banks of the River Severn* (= on land near the river) 塞文河畔的一所房子

• **SLOPE** 斜坡 **5** a raised area of ground that slopes at the sides, often at the edge of sth or dividing sth 斜坡；垄；埂：*There were low banks of earth between the rice fields.* 稻田之间有低矮的田埂。◇ *The girls ran down the steep grassy bank.* 女孩子们沿长满青草的陡坡跑下去。 **6** an artificial slope built at the side of a road, so that cars can drive fast around bends （路面拐弯处为方便车辆快速行驶而筑起的）边坡

• **OF CLOUD/SNOW, ETC.** 云、雪等 **7** a mass of cloud, snow, etc., especially one formed by the wind （尤指风吹到一起的）积云，积雪：*The sun disappeared behind a bank of clouds.* 太阳消失在一大片云后面。

• **OF MACHINES, ETC.** 机器等 **8** a row or series of similar objects, especially machines 一排，一系列（同类物品，尤指机器）：*a bank of lights/switches/computers* 一排灯 / 开关 / 计算机

IDM **not ˌbreak the ˈbank** (*informal, humorous*) if you say sth **won't break the bank**, you mean that it won't cost a lot of money, or more than you can afford 花费不太大；支付得起 ➲ MORE AT LAUGH *v.*

■ ***verb***

• **MONEY** 钱 **1** [T] **~ sth** to put money into a bank account 把（钱）存入银行：*She is believed to have banked* (= been paid) *£10 million in two years.* 据信她两年内在银行存了 1 000 万英镑。 **2** [I] **~ (with/at...)** to have an account with a particular bank （在某银行）开账户，存款：*The family had banked with Coutts for generations.* 那家几代人都在库茨银行存钱。

• **OF PLANE** 飞机 **3** [I] to travel with one side higher than the other when turning （转弯时）倾斜飞行：*The plane banked steeply to the left.* 飞机向左作高度倾斜飞行。

• **FORM PILES** 堆积 **4** [T] **~ sth (up)** to form sth into piles 堆积（某物）：*They banked the earth (up) into a mound.* 他们把土堆成了一个土丘。

• **A FIRE** 炉火 **5** [T] **~ sth (up)** to pile coal, etc. on a fire so that the fire burns slowly for a long time （用煤等）封炉火：*The fire was banked up as high as if it were midwinter.* 炉火被封得很厚实，好像是在隆冬。

PHR V **ˈbank on sb/sth** to rely on sb/sth 依靠；指望：*I'm banking on your help.* 我还得靠你帮助呢。◇ *'I'm sure he'll help.' '**Don't bank on it** (= it is not likely to happen).'* "我相信他会帮忙的。" "那可不见得。" ◇ **bank on sb/sth to do sth** *I'm banking on you to help me.* 我还得靠你帮忙呢。◇ **bank on sb/sth doing sth** *I was banking on getting something to eat on the train.* 我指望在火车上能找到吃的。 **ˌbank ˈup** to form into piles, especially because of the wind 堆积（尤指由于风吹）：*The snow had banked up against the wall.* 雪靠墙堆积起来了。

bank·able /ˈbæŋkəbl/ *adj.* (*informal*) likely to make money for sb 可赚钱的；可赢利的：*The movie's success has made her one of the world's most bankable stars.* 这部影片的成功使她成了世界上最有身价的明星之一。

ˈbank account *noun* an arrangement that you have with a bank that allows you to keep your money there, to pay in or take out money, etc. 银行账户：*to **open/close a bank account*** 开立 / 结清银行账户

ˈbank balance *noun* the amount of money that sb has in their bank account at a particular time 银行存款余额；银行结存

ˈbank card *noun* **1** (*also* **ˈbanker's card**) (*both BrE*) a plastic card provided by your bank that may be used as a DEBIT CARD or to get money from your account out of a machine 支票保付卡；取款机提款卡 **2** (*NAmE*) a credit card provided by your bank, that can also be used as a DEBIT CARD and to get money from your account out of a machine 银行信用卡；取款机提款卡

ˈbank draft (*also* **ˈbanker's draft**) *noun* a cheque paid by a bank to another bank or to a particular person or organization 银行汇票

bank·er /ˈbæŋkə(r)/ *noun* **1** a person who owns a bank or has an important job at a bank 银行老板（或要员）；银行家：*a merchant banker* 投资银行家 **2** a person who is in charge of the money in particular games （某些赌博游戏中的）庄家

ˌbanker's ˈorder *noun* (*BrE*) an instruction to your bank to pay money to sb directly from your bank account 付款委托，自动转账委托（让银行直接从账户付款） ➲ COMPARE STANDING ORDER

ˌbank ˈholiday (*BrE*) *noun* a public holiday, for example Christmas Day, New Year's Day, etc. 银行假日（公共假日，如圣诞节、元旦等）：*Bank Holiday Monday* 银行假日星期一 ◇ *a bank holiday weekend* (= a weekend followed by a Monday which is a holiday) 银行假日周末（之后的星期一为假日的大周末） ➲ COMPARE LEGAL HOLIDAY, PUBLIC HOLIDAY ➲ SEE ALSO HOLIDAY *n.* (3)

bank·ing /ˈbæŋkɪŋ/ *noun* [U] the business activity of banks 银行业：*She's thinking about a career in banking.* 她正在考虑从事银行业。

bank·note /ˈbæŋknəʊt; *NAmE* -noʊt/ *noun* (*especially BrE*) = NOTE (6)：*forged* (= illegally copied) *banknotes* 伪钞

ˈbank rate *noun* the rate of interest charged by a bank for lending money, which is fixed by a central bank in a country 银行利率；银行贴现率

bank·roll /ˈbæŋkrəʊl; *NAmE* -roʊl/ *verb, noun*

■ ***verb*** **~ sb/sth** (*informal, especially NAmE*) to support sb/sth by giving money 资助；提供资金给 **SYN** **finance**：*They claimed his campaign had been bankrolled with drug money.* 他们声称他的竞选活动是由贩毒资金支持的。

■ ***noun*** (*especially NAmE*) a supply of money 资金：*He is the candidate with the biggest campaign bankroll.* 他是竞选资金最雄厚的候选人。

bank·rupt /ˈbæŋkrʌpt/ *adj., noun, verb*

■ ***adj.*** **1** without enough money to pay what you owe 破产；倒闭 **SYN** **insolvent**：*They **went bankrupt** in 2009.* 他们于 2009 年破产。◇ *The company was **declared bankrupt** in the High Court.* 那家公司经高等法院宣告破产了。 ➲ WORDFINDER NOTE AT MONEY **2 ~ (of sth)** (*formal, disapproving*) completely lacking in anything that has value 完全缺乏（有价值的东西）：*a government bankrupt of new ideas* 完全缺乏新观念的政府 ◇ *a society that is morally bankrupt* 道德沦丧的社会

■ ***noun*** (*law* 律) a person who has been judged by a court to be unable to pay his or her debts （经法院判决的）破产者

■ ***verb*** **~ sb** to make sb bankrupt 使破产：*The company was almost bankrupted by legal costs.* 这家公司为律师费用所累几乎破产。

bank·rupt·cy /ˈbæŋkrʌptsi/ *noun* [U, C] (*pl.* **-ies**) the state of being bankrupt 破产 **SYN** **insolvency**：*The company **filed for bankruptcy*** (= asked to be officially bankrupt) *in 2009.* 这家公司于 2009 年提交了破产申请。◇ ***moral/political bankruptcy*** 道德的沦丧；政治的破产 ◇ *There could be further bankruptcies among small farmers.* 小农场主中可能还会有人破产。 ➲ COLLOCATIONS AT BUSINESS

ˈbank statement (*also* **state·ment**) *noun* a printed record of all the money paid into and out of a customer's bank account within a particular period 银行结单（某时期内存户存取款项的清单）

ban·ner /ˈbænə(r)/ *noun* a long piece of cloth with a message on it that is carried between two poles or hung in a public place to show support for sth 横幅；旗幡：*Protesters carried a banner reading 'Save our Wildlife'.* 抗议者打着"救救我们的野生生物"字样的横幅。 ➲ VISUAL VOCAB PAGE V3

ˈbanner ad *noun* an advertisement across the top or bottom or down the side of a page on the Internet （互联网上的）通栏广告，横幅广告；网幅广告

ˌbanner ˈheadline *noun* a line of words printed in large letters across the front page of a newspaper （报纸头版的）通栏大标题

ˌbanner ˈyear *noun* (*NAmE*) a year in which sth is especially successful 辉煌的一年

ban·nis·ter = BANISTER

banns /bænz/ *noun* [pl.] a public statement in church that two people intend to marry each other （教堂里的）结婚预告

ban·offi pie (*also* **ban·offee pie**) /bəˌnɒfi ˈpaɪ; *NAmE* bəˌnɔːfi; -ˌnɑːf-/ *noun* a sweet food made with TOFFEE, BANANAS and cream 香蕉太妃派（用乳脂糖、香蕉和奶油制成）

ban·quet /ˈbæŋkwɪt/ *noun* **1** a formal meal for a large number of people, usually for a special occasion, at which speeches are often made 宴会；盛宴：*a state banquet in honour of the visiting President* 为来访总统举办的国宴 **2** a large impressive meal 筵席

ban·quet·ing /ˈbæŋkwɪtɪŋ/ *adj.* connected with banquets 宴会的：*a banqueting hall* 宴会厅

ban·quette /bæŋˈket/ *noun* a long soft seat along a wall in a restaurant, etc. （饭店内等沿墙的）长软座，长沙发

ban·shee /bænˈʃiː; ˈbænʃiː/ *noun* (in Irish stories) a female spirit who gives a long sad cry as a warning to people that sb in their family is going to die soon 猜女（爱尔兰传说中以哀嚎预报死讯的女妖）

ban·tam /ˈbæntəm/ *noun* a type of small chicken 矮脚鸡

ban·tam·weight /ˈbæntəmweɪt/ *noun* a BOXER weighing between 51 and 53.5 kilograms, or a WRESTLER who weighs between 52 and 57 kilograms, heavier than a FLYWEIGHT 最轻量级拳击运动员（体重为 51 到 53.5 公斤）；次轻量级摔跤运动员（体重为 52 到 57 公斤）：*a bantamweight champion* 最轻量级拳击冠军

ban·ter /ˈbæntə(r)/ *noun, verb*

■ *noun* [U] friendly remarks and jokes （善意的）玩笑，打趣：*He enjoyed exchanging banter with the customers.* 他喜欢和顾客开玩笑。

■ *verb* [I] ~ (with sb) to joke with sb （和某人）开玩笑；逗乐：*He bantered with reporters and posed for photographers.* 他和记者们打趣，并摆姿势让摄影师拍照。

ban·ter·ing /ˈbæntərɪŋ/ *adj.* (of a way of talking 讲话方式) amusing and friendly 风趣的；诙谐的：*There was a friendly, bantering tone in his voice.* 他的声音里流露着友好诙谐的语调。

ban·yan /ˈbænjən/ (*also* **ˈbanyan tree**) *noun* a S Asian tree with structures that grow down from the branches to the ground and then grow into new roots and TRUNKS 榕树（见于南亚，树枝上有气根伸入土壤，变成新的树干）

bao·bab /ˈbeɪəʊbæb; *NAmE* ˈbeɪoʊ-/ *noun* a short thick tree, found especially in Africa and Australia, that lives for many years 猴面包树（尤见于非洲和澳大利亚，生命力强）

bap /bæp/ *noun* (*BrE*) a round flat bread roll 圆面包 ➲ SEE ALSO BUN (2)

bap·tism /ˈbæptɪzəm/ *noun* a Christian ceremony in which a few drops of water are poured on sb or they are covered with water, to welcome them into the Christian Church and often to name them （基督教的）洗礼，浸礼 ➲ COMPARE CHRISTENING

IDM **a ˌbaptism of ˈfire** a difficult introduction to a new job or activity 重大的考验；战火的洗礼

bap·tis·mal /bæpˈtɪzməl/ *adj.* [only before noun] connected with baptism 洗礼的；浸礼的：*a* ***baptismal service/ceremony*** 洗礼仪式

Bap·tist /ˈbæptɪst/ *noun* a member of a Christian Protestant Church that believes that baptism should take place when a person is old enough to understand what it means, and not as a baby 浸礼会教徒 ▶ **Bap·tist** *adj.* [usually before noun]：*a Baptist church* 浸礼会教派

bap·tize (*BrE also* **-ise**) /bæpˈtaɪz/ *verb* [usually passive] ~ sb (+ noun) to give sb BAPTISM 授洗；付洗；施洗：*She was baptized Mary.* 她受洗时取名为玛丽。◇ *I was baptized a Catholic.* 我领洗成为天主教徒。➲ SEE ALSO CHRISTEN (1)

Bapu /ˈbɑːpuː/ *noun* (*IndE*) **1** (used especially as a form of address 尤用作称呼) a father 父亲；爸爸 **2** a name by which Mahatma Gandhi is referred to, showing affection 巴普（对圣雄甘地的爱称）

bars 吧台；条；棒

bar 吧台

sandwich bar 三明治店

five-bar gate 五根横木的栅门

bars on a window 窗条

bar of chocolate 巧克力块

bar of soap 肥皂块

barcode 条码

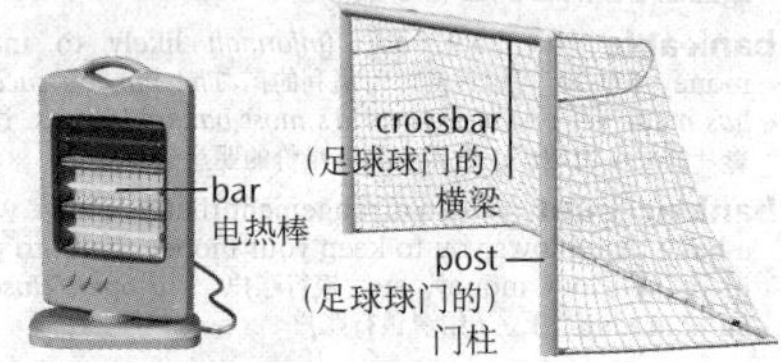

bars on an electric fire 电取暖器的电热棒

crossbar 横梁

bar of music 乐谱的小节

bar 🔑 /bɑː(r)/ *noun, verb, prep.*

■ *noun*

• **FOR DRINKS/FOOD** 饮食 **1** 🔑 [C] a place where you can buy and drink alcoholic and other drinks 酒吧：*We met at a bar called the Flamingo.* 我们在一家名为"火烈鸟"的酒吧相遇。◇ *the island's only* ***licensed bar*** (= one that is allowed to sell alcoholic drinks) 岛上唯一有酒类销售许可证的酒吧 ◇ *a cocktail bar* 鸡尾酒酒吧 ◇ (*BrE*) *I found David in the* *bar of the Red Lion* (= a room in a pub where drinks are served). 我在"红狮"酒吧找到了戴维。 ➲SEE ALSO BARROOM, LOUNGE BAR, MINIBAR, PUBLIC BAR, SALOON (2) **2** [C] a long wide wooden surface where drinks, etc. are served （出售饮料等的）柜台；吧台： *She was sitting at the bar.* 她坐在吧台那里。 ◇ *It was so crowded I couldn't get to the bar.* 人太多了，我无法挤到吧台那儿。 **3** [C] (especially in compounds 尤用于构成复合词) a place in which a particular kind of food or drink is the main thing that is served （专售某类饮食的）小吃店，小馆子： *a sandwich bar* 三明治店 ◇ *a coffee bar* 小咖啡馆 ➲SEE ALSO OXYGEN BAR, SNACK BAR, WINE BAR

• **OF CHOCOLATE/SOAP** 巧克力；肥皂 **4** [C] a piece of sth with straight sides （长方形）条，块： ***a bar of chocolate/ soap*** 一条巧克力 / 肥皂 ◇ *candy bars* 糖棒

• **OF METAL/WOOD** 金属；木材 **5** [C] a long straight piece of metal or wood. Bars are often used to stop sb from getting through a space. 长条，棒，栏杆（常用作护栏）： *He smashed the window with an iron bar.* 他用铁棒敲碎了窗户。 ◇ *All the ground floor windows were fitted with bars.* 底层所有的窗户都装了铁栅。 ◇ *a five-bar gate* (= one made with five horizontal bars of wood) 用五根横木条钉成的栅门 ➲VISUAL VOCAB PAGE V50 ➲SEE ALSO BULL BARS, ROLL BAR, SPACE BAR, TOW BAR

• **IN COMPUTING** 计算机技术 **6** a long narrow area, usually at the top or side of a computer screen, that contains links or PULL-DOWN (2) menus or displays information about the website or program that you are using （电脑屏幕上的）状态栏，工具栏，导航条 ➲SEE ALSO ADDRESS BAR, MENU BAR, NAVIGATION BAR, SCROLL BAR, TITLE BAR

• **IN SPORTS** 体育运动 **7 the bar** [sing.] the CROSSBAR of a goal （球门的）横梁： *His shot hit the bar.* 他射门击中球门的横梁。

• **OF COLOUR/LIGHT** 颜色；光 **8** [C] a band of colour or light 条；带： *Bars of sunlight slanted down from the tall narrow windows.* 一道道阳光从高高的狭窄窗口斜射下来。

• **THAT PREVENTS STH** 障碍 **9** [C, usually sing.] ~ (**to sth**) a thing that stops sb from doing sth 障碍；羁绊： *At that time being a woman was a bar to promotion in most professions.* 那时在大多数职业中，身为女性就是晋升的障碍。 ➲SEE ALSO COLOUR BAR

• **IN MUSIC** 音乐 **10** (*BrE*) (*NAmE also* **meas·ure**) [C] one of the short sections of equal length that a piece of music is divided into, and the notes that are in it （乐谱的）小节： *four beats to the bar* 每小节四拍 ◇ *the opening bars of a piece of music* 乐曲开头的几个小节 ➲PICTURE AT MUSIC

• **LAW** 法律 **11 the Bar** [sing.] (*BrE*) the profession of BARRISTER (= a lawyer in a higher court) 大律师职业（可出席高等法庭）： *to **be called to the Bar*** (= allowed to work as a qualified BARRISTER) 获得大律师资格 **12 the Bar** [sing.] (*NAmE*) the profession of any kind of lawyer 律师职业

▼**VOCABULARY BUILDING** 词汇扩充

A bar of ...

If you want to describe a whole unit of a particular substance, or a group of things that are normally together, for example when you buy them, you need to use the correct word. 指一件或一组东西（如购物时）须用恰当的量词。

- a **bar** of soap/chocolate; a candy **bar** 一条肥皂 / 巧克力；糖果棒
- a **block** of ice/stone/wood 一大块冰 / 石头 / 木头
- a **bolt**/**roll**/**length** of fabric 一匹 / 一卷 / 一段织物
- an ice/a sugar **cube** 一块冰块 / 方糖
- a **loaf** of bread 一条面包
- a **roll** of film/carpet 一卷胶片 / 地毯
- a **slab** of marble/concrete 大理石板；混凝土板
- a **stick** of gum 一条口香糖
- a **bunch** of bananas/grapes 一串香蕉 / 葡萄
- a **bunch**/**bouquet** of flowers 一束花
- a **bundle** of sticks 一捆枝条
- a **set**/**bunch** of keys 一套 / 一串钥匙
- a **set** of chairs/glasses/clothes/guitar strings 一套椅子 / 玻璃杯 / 衣服；一副吉他弦

• **MEASUREMENT** 度量 **13** a unit for measuring the pressure of the atmosphere, equal to a hundred thousand NEWTONS per square metre 巴（气压单位，等于 100 000 牛顿 / 平方米） ➲SEE ALSO MILLIBAR

• **IN ELECTRIC FIRE** 电热炉 **14** [C] a piece of metal with wire wrapped around it that becomes red and hot when electricity is passed through it 电热棒

IDM **not have a 'bar of sth** (*AustralE, NZE, informal*) to have nothing to do with sth 与（某事）无关；与（某事）毫不相干；不沾手： *If he tries to sell you his car, don't have a bar of it.* 他若是想要把车卖给你，你可别去理他。 **be,hind 'bars** (*informal*) in prison 蹲班房；被监禁；坐牢： *The murderer is now safely behind bars.* 杀人犯现在被关在监狱里，不会再造成危险了。 **set the 'bar** to set a standard of quality or performance 设定标准： *The show really sets the bar for artistic invention.* 这场演出真正为艺术创新设立了标杆。 ➲MORE AT LOWER[1] *v.*, RAISE *v.*

■ ***verb*** (**-rr-**)

• **CLOSE WITH BARS** 用铁条等封住 **1** [usually passive] ~ **sth** to close sth with a bar or bars （用铁条或木条）封，堵： *All the doors and windows were barred.* 所有的门、窗都加上了铁条。

• **BLOCK** 阻挡 **2** ~ **sth** to block a road, path, etc. so that nobody can pass 阻挡；拦住： *Two police officers were barring her exit.* 两名警察挡着她的出路。 ◇ *We found our way barred by rocks.* 我们发现大石块挡住了我们的路。

• **PREVENT** 阻止 **3** ~ **sb** (**from sth/from doing sth**) to ban or prevent sb from doing sth 禁止，阻止（某人做某事）： *The players are barred from drinking alcohol the night before a match.* 运动员在参赛前夜不得喝酒。 IDM SEE HOLD *n.* ➲MORE LIKE THIS 36, page R29

■ ***prep.*** (*especially BrE*) except for sb/sth 除…外： *The students all attended, bar two who were ill.* 除了两人生病，所有的学生都到了。 ◇ *It's the best result we've ever had, **bar none*** (= none was better). 这是我们所取得的前所未有的好成绩。 IDM SEE SHOUTING

bar·aza /bəˈrɑːzə/ *noun* (*EAfrE*) a public meeting that is held in order to discuss important matters affecting the community 社区集会；公共集会

barb /bɑːb; *NAmE* bɑːrb/ *noun* **1** the point of an arrow or a hook that is curved backwards to make it difficult to pull out （箭、钩的）倒钩，倒刺 **2** a remark that is meant to hurt sb's feelings 挖苦（或伤人、带刺）的话 ➲SEE ALSO BARBED

bar·bar·ian /bɑːˈbeəriən; *NAmE* bɑːrˈber-/ *noun* **1** (in ancient times 古代) a member of a people who did not belong to one of the great CIVILIZATIONS (Greek, Roman, Christian) 野蛮人（指非希腊人、非罗马人及非基督徒）： *barbarian invasions of the fifth century* 五世纪时野蛮人的入侵 **2** a person who behaves very badly and has no respect for art, education, etc. 没有文化的人；粗野的人

bar·bar·ic /bɑːˈbærɪk; *NAmE* bɑːrˈb-/ *adj.* **1** cruel and violent and not as expected from people who are educated and respect each other 残暴的；野蛮的；没有文化的： *a **barbaric act/custom/ritual*** 野蛮的行为 / 习俗 / 仪式 ◇ *The way these animals are killed is barbaric.* 宰杀这些动物的手段很残忍。 **2** connected with BARBARIANS 野蛮人的；原始部落人的 ▶ **bar·bar·ic·al·ly** /-kli/ *adv.*

bar·bar·ism /ˈbɑːbərɪzəm; *NAmE* ˈbɑːrb-/ *noun* [U] **1** a state of not having any education, respect for art, etc. 野蛮；未开化；不文明 **2** cruel or violent behaviour 残暴的行为；残酷： *the barbarism of war* 战争的残酷

bar·bar·ity /bɑːˈbærəti; *NAmE* bɑːrˈb-/ *noun* (*pl.* **-ies**) [U, C] behaviour that deliberately causes extreme pain or suffering to others 暴行；残忍

bar·bar·ous /ˈbɑːbərəs; *NAmE* ˈbɑːrb-/ *adj.* (*formal*) **1** extremely cruel and shocking 残酷的；极其残忍的： *the barbarous treatment of these prisoners of war* 对这些战犯的残酷待遇 **2** showing a lack of education and good manners 缺乏教养的；粗野的 ▶ **bar·bar·ous·ly** *adv.*

B

bar·be·cue /ˈbɑːbɪkjuː; *NAmE* ˈbɑːrb-/ *noun, verb*
■ ***noun*** (*abbr.* **BBQ**) (*also informal* **bar·bie** *BrE, AustralE*) **1** a metal frame for cooking food on over an open fire outdoors （户外烧烤用的）烤架：*I put another steak on the barbecue.* 我在烤架上又放了一块肉排。◇ *a barbecue sausage* (= cooked in this way) 烤香肠 ➲ VISUAL VOCAB PAGES V20, V28 **2** an outdoor meal or party when food is cooked in this way 户外烧烤：*Let's have a barbecue!* 我们来一次户外烧烤吧！➲ COMPARE COOKOUT
■ ***verb*** [T, I] ~ (sth) to cook food on a barbecue （在烤架上）烧烤 ➲ COMPARE BROIL (1)

ˌbarbecue ˈsauce *noun* [C, U] a spicy sauce served with food that has been cooked on a barbecue 烤肉酱

ˈbarbecue stopper *noun* (*AustralE, informal*) a topic of conversation that is very interesting, often one on which people have different views 热点话题（常具争议性）：*Work-life balance is a barbecue stopper for Australians.* 工作与生活两不误是澳大利亚人的一个热点话题。

barbed /bɑːbd; *NAmE* bɑːrbd/ *adj.* **1** (of an ARROW or a hook 箭或钩) having a point that is curved backwards (called a BARB) 有倒钩的 **2** (of a remark or comment 说话或评论) meant to hurt sb's feelings 挖苦的；伤人的；带刺的

barbed wire 带刺铁丝网

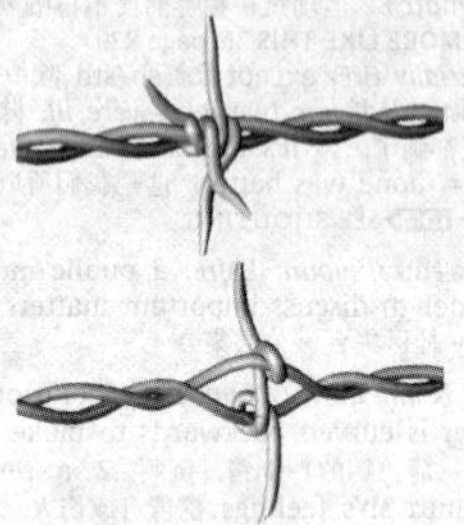

ˌbarbed ˈwire *noun* [U] strong wire with short sharp points on it, used especially for fences 带刺铁丝网（尤用作围栏）：*a barbed wire fence* 带刺铁丝网围栏

bar·bell /ˈbɑːbel; *NAmE* ˈbɑːrbel/ *noun* a long metal bar with weights at each end, used in the sport of WEIGHT-LIFTING and for exercise 杠铃（举重器械）➲ VISUAL VOCAB PAGE V46

bar·ber /ˈbɑːbə(r); *NAmE* ˈbɑːrb-/ *noun* **1** a person whose job is to cut men's hair and sometimes to shave them （为男子理发、修面的）理发师 **2** (*also* **barber's**) (*both BrE*) (*pl.* **bar·bers**) a shop where men can have their hair cut （男子）理发店 ➲ COMPARE HAIRDRESSER ➲ MORE LIKE THIS 34, page R29

bar·ber·shop /ˈbɑːbəʃɒp; *NAmE* ˈbɑːrbərʃɑːp/ *noun* **1** (*especially NAmE*) (*BrE usually* **barber's**) [C] a place where a barber works 理发店 **2** [U] a type of light music for four parts sung by men, without instruments 理发店四重唱（一种无乐器伴奏的男声四重唱）：*a barbershop quartet* 男声四重唱

ˌbarber's ˈpole *noun* a pole painted with a SPIRAL of red and white that is traditionally hung outside a barber's shop 转花筒（挂在理发店外的红白两色旋转彩柱，为理发店传统标志）

bar·bie /ˈbɑːbi; *NAmE* ˈbɑːrbi/ *noun* (*BrE, AustralE, informal*) = BARBECUE

ˈBarbie doll™ (*also* **Barbie**) *noun* **1** a DOLL that looks like an attractive young woman 芭比娃娃 **2** (*informal*) a woman who is sexually attractive, especially one who is thought to be stupid or boring 芭比女郎（尤指愚蠢或俗气的性感女子）

ˌbar ˈbilliards *noun* [U] (*BrE*) a game played on a small table, in which you try to hit balls into holes without knocking down the small wooden objects that stand in front of the holes 酒吧台球（小型台球游戏，须击球入洞，不得撞倒洞口障碍木块）

bar·bit·ur·ate /bɑːˈbɪtʃʊrət; *NAmE* bɑːrˈb-/ *noun* a powerful drug that makes you feel calm and relaxed or puts you to sleep. There are several types of barbiturate. 巴比土酸盐，巴比妥酸盐（用于镇静、催眠等）

Bar·bour™ /ˈbɑːbə(r); *NAmE* ˈbɑːrbər/ *noun* a type of coat, usually dark green, made of special cotton with WAX on it that protects against rain and wind 巴伯风雨衣（通常为深绿色，用蜡棉布制成）

ˈbar chart (*also* **ˈbar graph**) *noun* a diagram that uses lines or narrow RECTANGLES (= bars) of different heights (but equal widths) to show different amounts, so that they can be compared 条形图，柱形图（以不同长度的条形表示不同数量以作比较）➲ COMPARE HISTOGRAM

bar·code /ˈbɑːkəʊd; *NAmE* ˈbɑːrkoʊd/ *noun* a pattern of thick and thin lines that is printed on things you buy. It contains information that a computer can read. 条码 ➲ PICTURE AT BAR

bard /bɑːd; *NAmE* bɑːrd/ *noun* (*literary*) a person who writes poems 诗人

bare /beə(r); *NAmE* ber/ *adj., verb, adv.*
■ ***adj.*** (**barer, bar·est**) **1** not covered by any clothes 裸体的；裸露的：*She likes to walk around in* ***bare feet****.* 她喜欢光着脚走来走去。➲ SEE ALSO BAREFOOT **2** (of trees or countryside 树木或村野) not covered with leaves; without plants or trees （树木）光秃秃的；（土地）荒芜的：*the bare branches of winter trees* 冬天树木光秃秃的枝桠 ◇ *a bare mountainside* 光秃秃的山坡 **3** (of surfaces 表面) not covered with or protected by anything 无遮盖的；没有保护的：*bare wooden floorboards* 未铺地毯的木地板 ◇ *Bare wires were sticking out of the cable.* 电缆露出了裸线。◇ *The walls were bare except for a clock.* 墙上除了一只挂钟什么也没有。**4** (of a room, cupboard, etc. 房间、柜子等) empty 空的：*The fridge was completely bare.* 电冰箱里什么也没有。◇ *bare shelves* 空荡荡的架子 **5** [only before noun] just enough; the most basic or simple 仅够的；最基本的；最简单的：*The family was short of even the* ***bare necessities*** *of life.* 那家人甚至没有最起码的生活所需。◇ *We only had the* ***bare essentials*** *in the way of equipment.* 我们只有最基本的设备。◇ *He did the* ***bare minimum*** *of work but still passed the exam.* 他只下了最少的功夫，却仍然通过了考试。◇ *She gave me only the bare facts of the case.* 她只给我介绍了这个案件的一些基本资料。◇ *It was the barest hint of a smile.* 那是一个几乎不露一丝痕迹的笑。➲ NOTE AT NAKED, PLAIN ▶ **bare·ness** *noun* [U]
IDM **the bare ˈbones (of sth)** the basic facts 梗概；概要：*the bare bones of the story* 故事梗概 **with your bare ˈhands** without weapons or tools 赤手空拳；徒手：*He was capable of killing a man with his bare hands.* 他赤手空拳就能取人性命。**lay sth ˈbare** (*formal*) to show sth that was covered or to make sth known that was secret 暴露；揭露：*Every aspect of their private lives has been laid bare.* 他们的私生活全面曝光了。➲ MORE AT CUPBOARD
■ ***verb*** ~ sth to remove the covering from sth, especially from part of the body 揭开；脱（衣服）：*She was paid several thousand dollars to* ***bare all*** (= take all her clothes off) *for the magazine.* 她为那本杂志拍裸照获得数千美元报酬。
IDM **bare your ˈsoul (to sb)** to tell sb your deepest and most private feelings （向某人）打开心扉，倾诉衷肠 **bare your ˈteeth** to show your teeth in an aggressive and threatening way （凶狠地）龇牙咧嘴：*The dog bared its teeth and growled.* 那条狗龇牙咧嘴地低吼。
■ ***adv.*** (*BrE, slang*) very 很；非常：*The party on Saturday was bare good!* 星期六的聚会棒极了！

bare·back /ˈbeəbæk; *NAmE* ˈberb-/ *adj., adv.* on a horse without a SADDLE （骑马）不用马鞍（的）： *a bareback rider* 不用马鞍的骑手 ◇ *riding bareback* 不用马鞍骑马

bare·faced /ˈbeəfeɪst; *NAmE* ˈberf-/ *adj.* [only before noun] (*disapproving*) showing that you do not care about offending sb or about behaving badly 厚颜无耻的；公然的；露骨的 SYN **bald-faced**, **blatant**： *a barefaced lie* 无耻的谎言 ◇ *barefaced cheek* 厚颜无耻

bare·foot /ˈbeəfʊt; *NAmE* ˈberf-/ (*also less frequent* **bare·foot·ed**) *adj., adv.* not wearing anything on your feet 赤脚（的）： *poor children going barefoot in the street* 光着脚在街头行走的穷孩子

bare·head·ed /ˌbeəˈhedɪd; *NAmE* ˌberˈh-/ *adj., adv.* not wearing anything to cover your head 头上不戴东西（的）；光着头（的）

ˌbare-ˈknuckle (*also* **ˌbare-ˈknuckled**) *adj.* [only before noun] (of a BOXER or BOXING match 拳击手或拳击比赛) without gloves 不戴拳击手套的

bare·ly /ˈbeəli; *NAmE* ˈberli/ *adv.* **1** in a way that is just possible but only with difficulty 仅仅；刚刚；勉强可能： *The music was barely audible.* 音乐声勉强能听见。 ◇ *She was barely able to stand.* 她勉强能站立。 ◇ *We barely had time to catch the train.* 我们差点没赶上火车。 **2** in a way that almost does not happen or exist 几乎不；几乎没有： *She barely acknowledged his presence.* 她只略微向他打了个招呼。 ◇ *There was barely any smell.* 几乎没有什么气味。 **3** just; certainly not more than (a particular amount, age, time, etc.) 刚好；不超过（某个数量、年龄、时间等）： *Barely 50% of the population voted.* 仅有 50% 的人口投票。 ◇ *He was barely 20 years old and already running his own company.* 他只有 20 岁，却已经营起自己的公司了。 ◇ *They arrived barely a minute later.* 过了不到一分钟他们就到了。 **4** only a very short time before 刚才；刚刚： *I had barely started speaking when he interrupted me.* 我刚刚开始讲话，他便打断了我。 ➲ NOTE AT HARDLY

barf /bɑːf; *NAmE* bɑːrf/ *verb* [I] (*especially NAmE, informal*) to VOMIT 呕吐 ▶ **barf** *noun* [U]

bar·fly /ˈbɑːflaɪ; *NAmE* ˈbɑːr-/ *noun* (*pl.* **-ies**) (*informal*) a person who spends a lot of time drinking in bars 吧虫；酒吧常客

bar·gain 🔑 /ˈbɑːɡən; *NAmE* ˈbɑːrɡən/ *noun, verb*

■ *noun* **1** 🔑 a thing bought for less than the usual price 减价品；便宜货： *I picked up a few good bargains in the sale.* 我在减价期间买了几样挺不错的便宜货。 ◇ *The car was a bargain at that price.* 那辆车的价格真便宜。 ◇ *bargain prices* 廉价 ➲ COLLOCATIONS AT SHOPPING **2** ~ (**with sb**) an agreement between two or more people or groups, to do sth for each other 协议；交易： *He and his partner had **made a bargain** to tell each other everything.* 他和他的合伙人约定，要互通信息，毫无保留。 ◇ *I've done what I promised and I expect you to **keep your side of the bargain*** (= do what you agreed in return). 我已经履约，希望你也能遵守协议。 ◇ *Finally the two sides **struck a bargain*** (= reached an agreement). 双方最终达成了协议。

IDM **into the ˈbargain** (*BrE*) (*NAmE* **in the ˈbargain**) (used to emphasize an extra piece of information 强调额外的信息) also; as well 另外；而且；也： *Volunteers learn a lot and enjoy themselves into the bargain.* 志愿者在学到很多东西的同时还能得到乐趣。 ➲ MORE AT HARD *adj.*, STRIKE *v.*

■ *verb* [I] to discuss prices, conditions, etc. with sb in order to reach an agreement that is acceptable （与某人就某事）讨价还价，商讨条件 SYN **negotiate**： ~ (**with sb**) (**about/over/for sth**) *In the market dealers were bargaining with growers over the price of coffee.* 在市场上商人正和种植者就咖啡的价格进行商谈。 ◇ *He said he wasn't prepared to bargain.* 他说他不愿讨价还价。

PHR V **ˌbargain sth↔aˈway** to give sth away and not get sth of equal value in return 做亏本交易；贱卖： *They felt that their leaders had bargained away their freedom.* 他们认为他们的领导人拿他们的自由做了交易。 **ˈbargain for/on sth** (usually in negative sentences 通常用于否定句) to expect sth to happen and be prepared for it 预料到；料想到： *We hadn't bargained for this sudden change in the weather.* 我们没有预料到这样的天气突变。 ◇ *When he agreed to answer a few questions, **he got more than he bargained for*** (= he got more questions, or more difficult ones, than he had expected). 他同意回答几个问题，但结果却是始料未及。 ◇ **bargain for/on doing sth** *I didn't bargain on finding them here as well.* 我没想到还会在这里遇到他们。 ◇ **bargain for/on sb/sth doing sth** *I hadn't bargained on them being here.* 我没想到他们会在这里。

ˌbargain ˈbasement *noun* a part of a large shop/store, usually in the floor below street level, where goods are sold at reduced prices （商场的）地下减价商品部： *bargain-basement prices* 减价部的价格

ˈbargain hunter *noun* a person who is looking for goods that are good value for money, usually because they are being sold at prices that are lower than usual 减价品搜寻者；专买便宜货者 ▶ **ˈbargain hunting** *noun* [U]

bar·gain·ing /ˈbɑːɡənɪŋ; *NAmE* ˈbɑːrɡ-/ *noun* [U] discussion of prices, conditions, etc. with the aim of reaching an agreement that is acceptable 讨价还价；商谈；商讨 SYN **negotiation**： *After much **hard bargaining** we reached an agreement.* 经过一番艰难的讨价还价，我们达成了协议。 ◇ *wage bargaining* 有关工资的谈判 ◇ *Exporters are in a strong **bargaining position** at the moment.* 目前出口商在洽谈中处于有利地位。 ➲ SEE ALSO COLLECTIVE BARGAINING, PLEA BARGAINING

ˈbargaining chip (*BrE also* **ˈbargaining counter**) *noun* a fact or a thing that a person or a group of people can use to get an advantage for themselves when they are trying to reach an agreement with another group 讨价还价的筹码；谈判中的有利条件

ˈbargaining power *noun* [U] the amount of control a person or group has when trying to reach an agreement with another group in a business or political situation （谈判中一方的）讨价还价的能力

barge /bɑːdʒ; *NAmE* bɑːrdʒ/ *noun, verb*

■ *noun* a large boat with a flat bottom, used for carrying goods and people on CANALS and rivers 驳船（运河、河流上运载客货的大型平底船）

■ *verb* [I, T] + **adv./prep.** to move in an awkward way, pushing people out of the way or crashing into them 冲撞；乱闯 SYN **push**： *He barged past me to get to the bar.* 他硬从我的身边向吧台挤过去。 ◇ *They **barged their way** through the crowds.* 他们横冲直撞地挤过人群。

PHR V **ˌbarge ˈin** (**on sb/sth**) to enter a place or join a group of people, rudely interrupting what sb else is doing or saying 闯入；插嘴；打岔： *I hope you don't mind me barging in like this.* 希望你不介意我如此冒昧打岔。 ◇ *He barged in on us while we were having a meeting.* 我们正在开会，他闯了进来。

barge·board /ˈbɑːdʒbɔːd; *NAmE* ˈbɑːrdʒbɔːrd/ *noun* a board that is fixed to the end of a roof to hide the ends of the wooden roof BEAMS 封檐板

bar·gee /bɑːˈdʒiː; *NAmE* bɑːrˈdʒiː/ *noun* a person who controls or works on a BARGE 驳船船长；驳船船员

barge·pole /ˈbɑːdʒpəʊl; *NAmE* ˈbɑːrdʒpoʊl/ *noun* IDM SEE TOUCH *v.*

ˈbar graph *noun* = BAR CHART

ˈbar-hop *verb* [I] (**-pp-**) (*NAmE, informal*) to drink in a series of bars in a single day or evening 逐吧买醉（一天或一夜之中从一家酒吧喝到另一家）

bar·is·ta /bæˈriːstə; -ˈrɪs-/ *noun* a person who works in a COFFEE BAR 小咖啡厅服务生

bari·tone /ˈbærɪtəʊn; *NAmE* -toʊn/ *noun* **1** a man's singing voice with a range between TENOR and BASS[1]; a man with a baritone voice 男中音；男中音歌手 **2** a musical instrument that is second lowest in PITCH in its family 上低音号 ▶ **bari·tone** *adj.* ➲ COMPARE ALTO *n.*, BASS[1] *n.*, TENOR *n.*

B

bar·ium /ˈbeəriəm; *NAmE* ˈber-/ *noun* [U] (*symb.* **Ba**) a chemical element. Barium is a soft silver-white metal. 钡

ˌbarium ˈmeal *noun* a substance containing barium that a doctor gives sb to swallow before an X-RAY because it makes organs in the body easier to see 钡餐（X 光造影剂）

bark /bɑːk; *NAmE* bɑːrk/ *noun, verb*

■ *noun* [U, C] **1** the outer covering of a tree 树皮 ➲ VISUAL VOCAB PAGE V10 **2** the short loud sound made by dogs and some other animals （狗等的）吠声，嗥叫声 **3** a short loud sound made by a gun or a voice 枪声；短促响亮的人声：*a bark of laughter* 一声大笑

IDM **sb's bark is worse than their bite** (*informal*) used to say that sb is not really as angry or as aggressive as they sound 嘴硬心软；说话强硬，其实并不伤人；貌似凶狠

■ *verb* **1** [I] ~ (**at sb/sth**) when a dog **barks**, it makes a short loud sound （狗）吠叫：*The dog suddenly started barking at us.* 那条狗突然开始对我们汪汪叫。 **2** [T] to give orders, ask questions, etc. in a loud, unfriendly way 厉声发令；厉声质问：~ **out sth** *She barked out an order.* 她厉声命令。◇ ~ **sth** (**at sb**) *He barked questions at her.* 他厉声质问她。◇ **+ speech** *'Who are you?' he barked.* "你是谁？"他厉声质问道。 **3** [T] ~ **sth** (*BrE*) to rub the skin off your knee, etc. by falling or by knocking against sth 擦破（或蹭掉）…的皮 SYN **graze**

IDM **be barking up the wrong ˈtree** (*informal*) to have the wrong idea about how to get or achieve sth 把方法搞错（或想偏）；走错路线：*You're barking up the wrong tree if you're expecting us to lend you any money.* 你要是指望我们借钱给你，你是走错庙门了。➲ MORE AT DOG *n.*

bark·er /ˈbɑːkə(r); *NAmE* ˈbɑːrk-/ *noun* a person who stands outside a place where there is entertainment and shouts to people to go in （在娱乐场所门外）大声招徕顾客者，拉客者

ˌbarking ˈmad (*also* **bark·ing**) *adj.* (*BrE, informal*) completely crazy 疯狂透顶的；完全发疯的

bar·ley /ˈbɑːli; *NAmE* ˈbɑːrli/ *noun* [U] a plant grown for its grain that is used for making food, beer and WHISKY; the grains of this plant （皮）大麦；大麦粒 ➲ VISUAL VOCAB PAGE V35

ˈbarley sugar *noun* [U] a hard clear sweet/candy made from boiled sugar 大麦糖；麦芽糖

ˈbarley water *noun* [U, C] (*BrE*) a drink made by boiling BARLEY in water. It is usually flavoured with orange or lemon. 大麦茶（常以柑橘或柠檬调味）：*lemon barley water* 柠檬大麦茶

ˌbarley ˈwine *noun* [U] a strong English beer 大麦啤酒（英格兰啤酒，酒精度高）

ˈbar line *noun* (*music* 音) a vertical line used in written music to mark a division between BARS/MEASURES 小节线

bar·maid /ˈbɑːmeɪd; *NAmE* ˈbɑːrm-/ (*BrE*) (*NAmE* **bar·tend·er**) *noun* a woman who works in a bar, serving drinks 酒吧女招待

bar·man /ˈbɑːmən; *NAmE* ˈbɑːrmən/ *noun* (*pl.* **-men** /-mən/) (*especially BrE*) (*NAmE usually* **bar·tend·er**) a man who works in a bar, serving drinks 酒吧男招待；酒吧男侍

bar mitz·vah /ˌbɑː ˈmɪtsvə; *NAmE* ˌbɑːr/ *noun* **1** a ceremony and celebration for a Jewish boy who has reached the age of 13, at which he accepts the religious responsibilities of an adult 受诫礼（为年满 13 岁的犹太男孩举行的成人仪式） **2** the boy who is celebrating this occasion 行受诫礼的犹太男孩 ➲ COMPARE BAT MITZVAH

barmy /ˈbɑːmi; *NAmE* ˈbɑːrmi/ *adj.* (*BrE, informal*) slightly crazy 傻乎乎的；疯疯癫癫的

barn /bɑːn; *NAmE* bɑːrn/ *noun* **1** a large farm building for storing grain or keeping animals in 谷仓；畜棚；仓房：*a hay barn* 干草棚 ◇ *They live in a converted barn* (= a barn that has been turned into a house). 他们住在由谷仓改成的房子里。➲ WORDFINDER NOTE AT FARM ➲ VISUAL VOCAB PAGES V3, V15 ➲ SEE ALSO DUTCH BARN **2** a large plain ugly building 简陋的大建筑物：*They live in a great barn of a house.* 他们住在一所简陋的大房子里。 **3** (*NAmE*) a building in which buses, trucks, etc. are kept when not being used （公共汽车、卡车等的）车库

IDM **close, etc. the barn door after the horse has eˈscaped** (*NAmE*) (*BrE* **close, etc. the stable door after the horse has ˈbolted**) to try to prevent or avoid loss or damage when it is already too late to do so 马跑了才去关厩门；贼走关门，为时已晚

bar·nacle /ˈbɑːnəkl; *NAmE* ˈbɑːrn-/ *noun* a small SHELLFISH that attaches itself to objects underwater, for example to rocks and the bottoms of ships 藤壶（小甲壳动物，附着于水下岩石或船底等）

Bar·nardo's /bəˈnɑːdəʊz; *NAmE* bərˈnɑːrdoʊz/ *noun* a British charity that helps children with social, physical and mental problems 巴纳多基金会（英国慈善机构，向有社交、身体和智力问题的儿童提供帮助） ORIGIN From Dr Thomas Barnardo, who opened a home for poor children without parents in London in 1870. 源自托马斯・巴纳多医生 (Dr Thomas Barnardo)，他于 1870 年在伦敦设立了一所孤儿院。

ˈbarn dance *noun* an informal social event at which people dance traditional COUNTRY DANCES 谷仓舞会（跳乡村舞的非正式社交聚会）

bar·net /ˈbɑːnɪt; *NAmE* ˈbɑːrn-/ *noun* (*BrE, slang*) a person's hair 头发

bar·ney /ˈbɑːni; *NAmE* ˈbɑːrni/ *noun* (*BrE, informal*) an argument 斗嘴

ˈbarn owl *noun* a BIRD OF PREY (= a bird that kills other creatures for food) of the OWL family, that often makes its nest in BARNS and other buildings 仓鸮（常筑巢于谷仓等的猫头鹰） ➲ VISUAL VOCAB PAGE V12

barn·storm /ˈbɑːnstɔːm; *NAmE* ˈbɑːrnstɔːrm/ *verb* [I, T] ~ (**sth**) (*especially NAmE*) to travel quickly through an area making political speeches, or getting a lot of attention for your organization, ideas, etc. 作巡回政治演说（或宣传、游说等）：*He barnstormed across the southern states in an attempt to woo the voters.* 他在南方各州作巡回演说，企图拉选票。

barn·storm·ing /ˈbɑːnstɔːmɪŋ; *NAmE* ˈbɑːrnstɔːrmɪŋ/ *adj.* [only before noun] a **barnstorming** performance or show of skill in a sports game, etc. is one that people find very exciting to watch （演出、比赛等）令人兴奋的，激烈的，精彩的

barn·yard /ˈbɑːnjɑːd; *NAmE* ˈbɑːrnjɑːrd/ *noun* an area on a farm that is surrounded by farm buildings 仓院（农场仓房围着的空地）

bar·om·eter /bəˈrɒmɪtə(r); *NAmE* -ˈrɑːm-/ *noun* **1** an instrument for measuring air pressure to show when the weather will change 气压计；气压表；晴雨表：*The barometer is falling* (= showing that it will probably rain). 气压在下降（表示可能要下雨）。 **2** something that shows the changes that are happening in an economic, social or political situation （显示经济、社会、政治变化的）晴雨表，标志，指标：*Infant mortality is a reliable barometer of socio-economic conditions.* 婴儿死亡率是社会经济状况的可靠指标。▶ **baro·metric** /ˌbærəˈmetrɪk/ *adj.*：*barometric pressure* 大气压

baron /ˈbærən/ *noun* **1** a NOBLEMAN of the lowest rank. In Britain, barons use the title *Lord*; in other countries they use the title *Baron*. 男爵（贵族中的最末一等。英国男爵头衔为 Lord，其他国家为 Baron） **2** a person who owns or controls a large part of a particular industry 工商业巨头：*a press baron* 报业大王 ◇ *drug barons* 毒枭

bar·on·ess /ˈbærənəs; *NAmE* ˌbærəˈnes/ *noun* **1** a woman who has the same rank as a baron. In Britain, baronesses use the title *Lady* or *Baroness*. 女男爵（英国女男爵头衔为 Lady 或 Baroness）：*Baroness Thatcher* 撒切尔女男爵 **2** the wife of a baron 男爵夫人

bar·onet /ˈbærənət/ *noun* (*abbr.* **Bart**, **Bt**) (in Britain) a man who has the lowest rank of honour that can be passed from a father to his son when he dies. Baronets use the title *Sir*. 准男爵（英国爵位的最低一级，称号世袭。头衔为 Sir）➲ COMPARE KNIGHT *n.* (2)

bar·on·et·cy /ˈbærənətsi/ *noun* (*pl.* **-ies**) the rank or position of a baronet 准男爵爵位

bar·on·ial /bəˈrəʊniəl; *NAmE* -ˈroʊ-/ *adj.* [usually before noun] connected with or typical of a BARON 男爵的；有男爵特色的；豪华的：*a baronial hall* 豪华的大厅

bar·ony /ˈbærəni/ *noun* (*pl.* **-ies**) **1** the rank or position of a BARON 男爵爵位 **2** an area of land that is owned and controlled by a BARON 男爵领地

bar·oque /bəˈrɒk; *NAmE* bəˈroʊk/ (*also* **Baroque**) *adj.* [usually before noun] used to describe European ARCHITECTURE, art and music of the 17th and early 18th centuries that has a grand and highly decorated style 巴罗克风格的（17 至 18 世纪早期流行于欧洲，气势雄伟、装饰华丽的特色反映在建筑、绘画和音乐等艺术上）：***baroque churches/music*** 巴罗克风格教堂 / 音乐 ◇ *the baroque period* 巴罗克风格流行时期 ▶ **bar·oque** (*also* **Baroque**) *noun* [sing.]: *paintings representative of the baroque* 典型的巴罗克风格绘画

barque /bɑːk; *NAmE* bɑːrk/ *noun* a sailing ship with three or more MASTS (= posts that support the sails) 三桅（或多桅）帆船

bar·rack /ˈbærək/ *verb* **1** [I, T] ~ (**sb**) (*BrE*) to shout criticism at players in a game, speakers at a meeting, performers, etc. 喝倒彩；起哄；发出嘘声 **2** [I, T] ~ (**for**) **sb** (*AustralE, NZE*) to shout encouragement to a person or team that you support 给（所支持的人或队）加油；喝彩助威 ▶ **bar·rack·ing** *noun* [U]

bar·racks /ˈbærəks/ *noun* [C+sing./pl. v.] (*pl.* **bar·racks**) **1** a large building or group of buildings for soldiers to live in 营房；兵营：*an army barracks* 一座兵营 ◇ *The troops were ordered **back to barracks**.* 士兵们被命令返回营房。**2** any large ugly building or buildings（一所或一群）简陋的大房子 ▶ **bar·rack** *adj.* [only before noun]: *a barrack unit* 一处兵营（单位）

bar·ra·cuda /ˌbærəˈkjuːdə; *NAmE* -ˈkuːdə/ *noun* a large aggressive fish with sharp teeth that lives in warm seas 舒（掠食性鱼类，生活于温暖海域）

bar·rage /ˈbærɑːʒ; *NAmE* bəˈrɑːʒ/ *noun* **1** [C, usually sing.] the continuous firing of a large number of guns in a particular direction, especially to protect soldiers while they are attacking or moving towards the enemy 火力网；弹幕射击；（尤指）掩护炮火 **2** [sing.] ~ (**of sth**) a large number of sth, such as questions or comments, that are directed at sb very quickly, one after the other, often in an aggressive way 接二连三的一大堆（质问或指责等）：***a barrage of questions/criticisms/complaints*** 连珠炮似的问题 / 批评 / 抱怨 **3** /*NAmE* ˈbɑːrɪdʒ/ [C] a wall or barrier built across a river to store water, prevent a flood, etc. 堰；水坝；拦河坝

ˈbarrage balloon *noun* a large BALLOON that floats in the air and is held in place by cables, used in the past to make the progress of enemy aircraft more difficult 拦截气球（旧时防空用）

bar·ra·mundi /ˌbærəˈmʌndi/ *noun* (*pl.* **bar·ra·mundi**) a large fish found in rivers in Australia and SE Asia 尖吻鲈（见于澳大利亚和东南亚河流）

bar·rel /ˈbærəl/ *noun, verb*

■ ***noun*** **1** a large round container, usually made of wood or metal, with flat ends and, usually, curved sides 桶：*a **beer/wine barrel*** 啤酒桶；葡萄酒桶 **2** the contents of or the amount contained in a barrel; a unit of measurement in the oil industry equal to between 120 and 159 litres 一桶（的量）；桶（石油计量单位，相当于 120 到 159 升）：*They got through two barrels of beer.* 他们喝了两桶啤酒。◇ *Oil prices fell to $9 a barrel.* 石油价格降到了每桶 9 美元。**3** the part of a gun like a tube through which the bullets are fired 枪管

IDM **a barrel of ˈlaughs** (*informal, often ironic*) very amusing; a lot of fun 很有趣；开心；快乐：*Life hasn't exactly been a barrel of laughs lately.* 最近生活并不十分令人开心。**(get/have sb) over a barrel** (*informal*) (to put/have sb) in a situation in which they must accept or do what you want（使某人）听从摆布，处于被动地位：*They've got us over a barrel. Either we agree to their terms or we lose the money.* 他们让我们别无选择。我们要么答应他们的条件，要么损失这笔钱。➲ MORE AT LOCK *n.*, SCRAPE *v.*, SHOOT *v.*

■ ***verb*** (**-ll-**, *NAmE* **-l-**) [I] **+ adv./prep.** (*NAmE, informal*) to move very fast in a particular direction, especially in a way that you cannot control（无法控制地）高速行进，飞驰：*He came barreling down the hill and smashed into a phone booth.* 他沿山坡飞驰下来，撞进了一个电话亭。

ˌbarrel-ˈchested *adj.* (of a man 男子) having a large rounded chest 胸肌发达的；胸围宽大的

ˈbarrel organ *noun* a musical instrument that is played by turning a handle, usually played in the streets for money 手摇风琴（街头卖艺常用）➲ SEE ALSO ORGAN GRINDER

bar·ren /ˈbærən/ *adj.* **1** (of land or soil 土地或土壤) not good enough for plants to grow on it 贫瘠的；不毛的：*a barren desert* 不毛的沙漠 ◇ *a barren landscape* (= one that is empty, with few plants) 寸草不生的荒凉景色 ➲ WORDFINDER NOTE AT LANDSCAPE **2** (of plants or trees 花草树木) not producing fruit or seeds 不结果实的 SYN **infertile 3** (*old-fashioned* or *formal*) (of women or female animals 女人或雌性动物) not able to produce children or young animals 不育的；不孕的 SYN **infertile 4** [usually before noun] not producing anything useful or successful 无益的；无效果的：*The team will come through this **barren patch** and start to win again.* 这个队将会在经历这段低潮时期之后再创佳绩。▶ **bar·ren·ness** /ˈbærənnəs/ *noun* [U]

bar·rette /bæˈret/ (*NAmE*) (*BrE* **hair·slide**, **slide**) *noun* a small decorative piece of metal or plastic used by women for holding their hair in place（装饰性）小发夹

bar·ri·cade /ˌbærɪˈkeɪd/ *noun, verb*

■ ***noun*** a line of objects placed across a road, etc. to stop people from getting past 路障；街垒：*The police stormed the barricades the demonstrators had put up.* 警察冲破了示威者筑起的街垒。

■ ***verb*** ~ **sth** to defend or block sth by building a barricade 设路障防护；阻挡：*They barricaded all the doors and windows.* 他们用障碍物堵住了所有的门窗。

PHR V **barriˌcade yourself ˈin/inˈside** (**sth**) to build a barricade in front of you in order to prevent anyone from coming in 躲在…里：*He had barricaded himself in his room.* 他把自己关在房间里。

bar·rier /ˈbæriə(r)/ *noun* **1** an object like a fence that prevents people from moving forward from one place to another 屏障；障碍物：*The crowd had to stand behind barriers.* 人群只好站在障碍物后面。◇ *Show your ticket at the barrier.* 请在验票处出示车票。➲ SEE ALSO CRASH BARRIER **2** a problem, rule or situation that prevents sb from doing sth, or that makes sth impossible 障碍；阻力；关卡：*the removal of trade barriers* 贸易壁垒的消除 ◇ ~ **to sth** *Lack of confidence is a psychological barrier to success.* 缺乏信心是阻碍成功的心理因素。➲ COLLOCATIONS AT INTERNATIONAL **3** something that exists between one thing or person and another and keeps them separate 分界线；隔阂；障碍：*The Yangtze River is a natural barrier to the north-east.* 长江是东北面的一道天然屏障。◇ *the **language barrier*** (= when people cannot communicate because they do not speak the same language) 语言隔阂（因语言不通而无法交流）◇ ~ **between A and B** *There was no real barrier between reality and fantasy in his mind.* 在他的头脑中，现实与幻想之间没有真正的界线。◇ ~ **against sth** *Ozone is the earth's barrier against ultra-violet radiation.* 臭氧是地球防止紫外线辐射的屏障。**4** a particular amount, level or number that it is difficult to get past 难以逾越的数量

B

（或水平、数目）；关口： *the first player whose earnings passed the $10 million barrier* 第一位收入超过 1 000 万美元大关的运动员

'barrier method *noun* a method of avoiding becoming pregnant by stopping the SPERM from reaching the egg, for example by using a CONDOM 屏障避孕法（使用避孕套等）

ˌbarrier 'reef *noun* a line of rock and CORAL in the sea, often not far from land 堡礁（近海岸的珊瑚礁）

bar·ring /'bɑːrɪŋ/ *prep.* except for; unless there is/are 除了；除非： *Barring accidents, we should arrive on time.* 除非有意外情况，我们应可按时到达。

bar·rio /'bæriəʊ; *NAmE* 'bɑːrioʊ/ *noun* (*from Spanish*) (*pl.* **-os**) **1** a district of a city in Spain or in another Spanish-speaking country（西班牙或西班牙语国家的）区 **2** (*US*) a district of a city in the US where a lot of Spanish-speaking people live（美国城市中说西班牙语的人聚居的）西语区

bar·ris·ter /'bærɪstə(r)/ *noun* a lawyer in Britain who has the right to argue cases in the higher courts of law 出庭律师，大律师，辩护律师（在英国有资格出席高等法庭进行辩护） ➲ NOTE AT LAWYER

bar·room /'bɑːruːm; -rʊm/ *noun* a room in which alcoholic drinks are served at a bar 酒吧间： *a topic much discussed in barrooms across the country* 全国各地酒吧间议论纷纷的话题 ◇ *a barroom brawl* 酒吧间的斗殴

bar·row /'bærəʊ; *NAmE* -roʊ/ *noun* **1** (*BrE*) a small open vehicle with two wheels from which fruit, vegetables, etc. are sold in the street 两轮流动售货车（售卖水果、蔬菜等） **2** a large pile of earth built over a place where people were buried in ancient times 古坟；古冢 **3** = WHEELBARROW

'barrow boy *noun* (*BrE*) a man or boy who sells things from a barrow in the street 街头推车售货男子（或男孩）；街头推车小贩

'bar stool *noun* a tall seat for customers at a bar to sit on 酒吧高脚凳

Bart /bɑːt; *NAmE* bɑːrt/ *abbr.* BARONET 准男爵

bar·tend·er /'bɑːtendə(r); *NAmE* 'bɑːrt-/ *noun* (*especially NAmE*) **1** (*BrE also* **bar·maid**) a woman who works in a bar, serving drinks 酒吧女招待 **2** = BARMAN

bar·ter /'bɑːtə(r); *NAmE* 'bɑːrt-/ *verb* [I, T] to exchange goods, property, services, etc. for other goods, etc. without using money（同某人）以物易物；以财产（或劳务等）作交换： **~ (with sb) (for sth)** *The prisoners tried to barter with the guards for items like writing paper and books.* 囚犯们试着从看守那里换得信纸和书之类的东西。 ◇ **~ sth (for sth)** *The local people bartered wheat for tools.* 当地人用小麦换取工具。 ▸ **bar·ter** *noun* [U]: *The islanders use a system of barter instead of money.* 岛上的居民采用以物易物的交易方式，而不是用货币。

basal /'beɪsl/ *adj.* (*specialist*) forming or belonging to a bottom layer or base 底层的；基部的；基底的： *basal cells of the skin* 皮肤基底细胞

bas·alt /'bæsɔːlt; *NAmE* bə'sɔːlt/ *noun* [U] a type of dark rock that comes from VOLCANOES 玄武岩（深色的火山岩）

base 🔑 /beɪs/ *noun, verb, adj.*

■ ***noun***

• **LOWEST PART** 底部 **1** 🔑 [C, usually sing.] the lowest part of sth, especially the part or surface on which it rests or stands 根基；基底；底座： *the base of a column/glass* 柱基；玻璃杯底座 ◇ *a pain at the base of the spine* 脊柱末端的疼痛 ◇ *The lamp has a heavy base.* 这盏灯的底座很沉。 ➲ VISUAL VOCAB PAGE V24 ➲ SYNONYMS AT BOTTOM

• **ORIGINAL IDEA/SITUATION** 根源思想 / 状况 **2** 🔑 [C] an idea, a fact, a situation, etc. from which sth is developed 根据；出发点 SYN **basis**: *She used her family's history as a base for her novel.* 她以她的家族史作为小说的素材。 ◇ *His arguments have a sound economic base.* 他的论点有充分的经济上的根据。 ➲ SYNONYMS AT BASIS

• **OF SUPPORT/INCOME/POWER** 支持；收入；力量 **3** [C, usually sing.] the people, activity, etc. from which sb/sth gets most of their support, income, power, etc.（支持、收入、力量等的）来源，源泉，基础： *These policies have a broad base of support.* 这些政策得到广泛支持。 ◇ *an economy with a solid* ***manufacturing base*** 以制造业为坚实基础的经济体 ➲ SEE ALSO CUSTOMER BASE, POWER BASE **4** (*especially NAmE*) (*BrE usually* **basic**) **~ pay/salary/wage** the pay that you get before anything extra is added 基本工资： *All we got was base pay—we didn't reach profitability levels to award a bonus.* 我们只拿到了基本工资，因为没有达到可发奖金的盈利水平。

• **FIRST/MAIN SUBSTANCE** 首要 / 主要材料 **5** [C, usually sing.] the first or main part of a substance to which other things are added 混合物的首要（或主要）成分： *a drink with a rum base* 主要成分为朗姆酒的饮料 ◇ *Put some moisturizer on as a base before applying your make-up.* 化妆前先搽些润肤霜打底。

• **MAIN PLACE** 主要地方 **6** 🔑 [C] the main place where you live or stay or where a business operates from 据点；总部；大本营： *I spend a lot of time in Britain but Paris is still my base.* 我有很多时间在英国度过，但主要还是居住在巴黎。 ◇ *The town is an ideal base for touring the area.* 这个镇子是在这一地区旅游观光的理想据点。 ◇ *The company has its base in New York, and branch offices all over the world.* 公司总部设在纽约，分支遍及全世界。

• **OF ARMY, NAVY, ETC.** 陆军、海军等 **7** 🔑 [C, U] a place where an army, a navy, etc. operates from 基地： ***a military/naval base*** 军事 / 海军基地 ◇ ***an air base*** 空军基地 ◇ *After the attack, they returned to base.* 他们发动攻击之后返回了基地。 ➲ WORDFINDER NOTE AT NAVY

• **CHEMISTRY** 化学 **8** [C] a chemical substance, for example an ALKALI, that can combine with an acid to form a salt 碱

• **MATHEMATICS** 数学 **9** [C, usually sing.] a number on which a system of counting and expressing numbers is built up, for example 10 in the DECIMAL system and 2 in the BINARY system 基数（如十进制的 10 和二进制的 2）

• **IN BASEBALL/ROUNDERS** 棒球；圆场棒球 **10** [C] one of the four positions that a player must reach in order to score points 垒 ➲ SEE ALSO DATABASE

IDM **off base** (*NAmE, informal*) completely wrong about sth 完全错误： *If that's what you think, you're way off base.* 你如果那么想就全错了。 ➲ MORE AT COVER *v.*, FIRST BASE, TOUCH *v.*

■ ***verb*** 🔑 [usually passive] **~ sb/sth/yourself in...** to use a particular city, town, etc. as the main place for a business, holiday/vacation, etc. 以…为据点（或大本营等）；把（总部等）设在： *They decided to base the new company in York.* 他们决定将新成立的公司总部设在约克。 ◇ *We're going to base ourselves in Tokyo and make trips from there.* 我们将以东京为据点到各地旅行。

PHR V **'base sth on/upon sth** 🔑 to use an idea, a fact, a situation, etc. as the point from which sth can be developed 以…为基础（或根据）： *What are you basing this theory on?* 你这理论的根据是什么？ ➲ SEE ALSO BASED

■ ***adj.*** (**baser**, **bas·est**) (*formal*) not having moral principles or rules 卑鄙的；不道德的： *He acted from base motives.* 他的行动动机卑鄙。 ▸ **base·ly** *adv.*

base·ball /'beɪsbɔːl/ *noun* **1** [U] a game played especially in the US by two teams of nine players, using a BAT (1) and ball. Each player tries to hit the ball and then run around four BASES before the other team can return the ball. 棒球运动： *a baseball bat/team/stadium* 棒球球棒 / 球队 / 球场 ◇ *a pair of baseball boots* 一双棒球靴 ➲ COMPARE ROUNDERS ➲ VISUAL VOCAB PAGE V47 **2** [C] the ball used in this game 棒球

'baseball cap *noun* a cap with a long PEAK (= a curved part sticking out in front), originally worn by BASEBALL players 棒球帽（有长鸭舌） ➲ VISUAL VOCAB PAGE V70

base·board /'beɪsbɔːd; *NAmE* -bɔːrd/ (*NAmE*) (*BrE* **'skirting board**, **skirt·ing**) *noun* [C, U] a narrow piece of wood that is fixed along the bottom of the walls in a house 踢脚板；裙脚

ˈ**base camp** *noun* a camp where people start their journey when climbing high mountains 登山大本营

based /beɪst/ *adj.* [not before noun] **1** ~ (**on sth**) if one thing is **based** on another, it uses it or is developed from it （以某事）为基础（或根据）：*The movie is based on a real-life incident.* 这部电影以真实事件为蓝本。◇ *The report is based on figures from six different European cities.* 报告的依据是欧洲六个不同城市的数据。 **2** (also in compounds 亦构成复合词) if a person or business is **based** in a particular place, that is where they live or work, or where the work of the business is done 在…居住（或工作）；基地（或总部）在…：*We're based in Chicago.* 我们住在芝加哥。◇ *a Chicago-based company* 总部设在芝加哥的公司 **3** **-based** (in compounds 构成复合词) containing sth as an important part or feature 以…为重要部分（或特征）；以…为主：*lead-based paints* 铅基涂料 ◇ *a class-based society* 以阶级为特征的社会 ➲ SEE ALSO BROAD-BASED

ˈ**base form** *noun* (*grammar* 语法) the basic form of a word to which endings can usually be added, for example *wall* is the base form of *walls* and *walled*. The base form is the form in which words in the dictionary are usually shown. （词的）基础形式；派生词基础形式

ˈ**base jumping** (*also* **BASE jumping**) *noun* [U] the sport of jumping with a PARACHUTE from a high place such as a building or a bridge 高处跳伞（从建筑物、大桥等高处乘降落伞跳下） ▸ ˈ**base jumper** *noun*

base·less /ˈbeɪsləs/ *adj.* (*formal*) not supported by good reasons or facts 无根据的；无缘无故的 SYN **unfounded**: *The rumours were completely baseless.* 那些谣传毫无根据。

base·line /ˈbeɪslaɪn/ *noun* [usually sing.] **1** (*sport* 体育) a line marking each end of the COURT in TENNIS or the edge of the area where a player can run in BASEBALL （网球场的）底线；（棒球场的）垒线 **2** (*specialist*) a line or measurement that is used as a starting point when comparing facts （用于比较的）基准，基线：*The figures for 2014 were used as a baseline for the study.* 这项研究以 2014 年的数据为基准。

base·man /ˈbeɪsmæn/ *noun* (*pl.* **-men** /-mən/) (in BASEBALL 棒球) a player who defends first, second or third base 守垒员；垒手

base·ment /ˈbeɪsmənt/ *noun* a room or rooms in a building, partly or completely below the level of the ground 地下室：*Kitchen goods are sold in the basement.* 厨房用具在地下室出售。◇ *a **basement flat/apartment*** 设在地下室的一套房间 ➲ VISUAL VOCAB PAGE V18 ➲ SEE ALSO BARGAIN BASEMENT

ˌ**base ˈmetal** *noun* a metal, for example iron or LEAD², that is not a PRECIOUS METAL such as gold 贱金属

ˈ**base rate** *noun* (*finance* 财) a rate of interest, set by a central bank, that banks in Britain use when calculating the amount of interest that they charge on money they lend 基本利率（英国各银行使用的贷款利率，由中央银行规定） ➲ COMPARE PRIME RATE

bases **1** PL. OF BASIS **2** PL. OF BASE

bash /bæʃ/ *verb, noun*

■ ***verb*** (*informal*) **1** [T, I] to hit sb/sth very hard 猛击；猛撞：**~ sb/sth** *He bashed her over the head with a hammer.* 他用锤子猛击她的头部。◇ **~ into sb/sth** *I braked too late and bashed into the car in front.* 我刹车太晚，撞上了前面的车。 ➲ SYNONYMS AT HIT **2** [T] **~ sb/sth** to criticize sb/sth strongly 严厉批评：*Bashing politicians is normal practice in the press.* 严厉批判政治人物乃是新闻界常事。◇ *a liberal-bashing administration* 打击自由主义的政府 ➲ SEE ALSO BASHING

PHR V ˌ**bash aˈway** (**on/at sth**) | ˌ**bash ˈon** (**with sth**) (*BrE, informal*) to continue working hard at sth 持续努力；持之以恒：*He sat bashing away at his essay all day.* 他一整天都坐着不停地写文章。◇ *We'll never get finished at this rate. We'd better bash on.* 以这种速度我们永远也完成不了。我们最好加把劲。 ˌ**bash sth↔ˈdown/ˈin** (*informal*) to destroy sth by hitting it very hard and often 不断猛击使之毁坏：*The police bashed the door down.* 警察使劲把门撞倒了。◇ *I'll bash your head in if you do that again.* 如果你再那么做，我就砸扁你的脑袋。 ˌ**bash sth↔ˈout** (*informal*) to produce sth quickly and in large quantities, but not of very good quality 大量粗制滥造 SYN **knock out**: *She bashed out about four books a year.* 她一年大概炮制出四本书。 ˌ**bash sb ˈup** (*BrE, informal*) to attack sb violently 猛击某人

■ ***noun*** (*informal*) **1** a hard hit 猛击；重击：*He gave Mike a bash on the nose.* 他照着迈克的鼻子狠狠地给了一下。 **2** a large party or celebration 盛大的聚会；盛典：*a birthday bash* 生日庆典

IDM **have a bash** (**at sth**) (*BrE, informal*) to try to do sth, especially when you are not sure if you will succeed 尝试做（没有把握的事）：*I'm not sure I'll be any good but I'll have a bash.* 我不敢保证我能帮上什么忙，但我会试试。

bash·ful /ˈbæʃfl/ *adj.* shy and easily embarrassed 羞怯的；忸怩的 ▸ **bash·ful·ly** /-fəli/ *adv.*: *She smiled bashfully.* 她忸怩地笑了笑。 **bash·ful·ness** *noun* [U]

bash·ing /ˈbæʃɪŋ/ *noun* [U, C] (often in compounds 常构成复合词) **1** (used especially in newspapers 尤用于报章) very strong criticism of a person or group 猛烈抨击；严厉批评：*union-bashing* 对工会的猛烈抨击 **2** a physical attack, or a series of attacks, on a person or group of people （对某人或群体的）殴打，接连打击：*gay-bashing* (= attacking HOMOSEXUALS) 对同性恋者的攻击 ◇ *to give sb a bashing* 痛打某人

BASIC /ˈbeɪsɪk/ *noun* [U] a simple language, using familiar English words, for writing computer programs * BASIC 语言，初学者通用符号指令码（一种使用一般英语词汇的简单计算机编程语言）

basic /ˈbeɪsɪk/ *adj.* **1** forming the part of sth that is most necessary and from which other things develop 基本的；基础的：*basic information/facts/ideas* 基本信息 / 事实 / 思想 ◇ *the basic principles of law* 法律的基本原则 ◇ **~ to sth** *Drums are basic to African music.* 鼓是非洲音乐的基本乐器。 **2** of the simplest kind or at the simplest level 最简单的；初级的；初步的：*The campsite provided only basic facilities.* 野营地只提供最基本的设施。◇ *My knowledge of French is pretty basic.* 我的法语学得很粗浅。 **3** [only before noun] necessary and important to all people 必需的；基本需要的：*basic human rights* 基本人权 ◇ *the cost of basic foods* 基本食粮的费用 **4** (*especially BrE*) (*NAmE usually* **base**) before anything extra is added 基本的；没有附加成分的：*The **basic pay** of the average worker has risen by 3 per cent.* 工人的平均基本工资上升了 3%。

ba·sic·ally /ˈbeɪsɪkli/ *adv.* **1** in the most important ways, without considering things that are less important 大体上；基本上 SYN **essentially**: *Yes, that's basically correct.* 对，基本正确。◇ *The two approaches are basically very similar.* 两种方法其实差不多。◇ *There have been some problems but basically it's a good system.* 虽然出现过一些问题，但这基本上仍不失为一个好系统。 **2** used when you are giving your opinion or stating what is important about a situation 总的说来；从根本上说：*Basically, there's not a lot we can do about it.* 总的说来，我们能做的有限。◇ *He basically just sits there and does nothing all day.* 他根本就是一天到晚坐在那儿无所事事。◇ *And that's it, basically.* 说穿了，就是这么回事。

ˌ**Basic ˈEnglish** *noun* [U] a set of 850 carefully chosen words of English, used for international communication 基本英语（简化国际通用语，共有 850 个词语）

basics /ˈbeɪsɪks/ *noun* [pl.] **1** ~ (**of sth**) the most important and necessary facts, skills, ideas, etc. from which other things develop 基本因素（或原理、原则、规律等）：*the basics of computer programming* 计算机编程概要 **2** the simplest and most important things that people need in a particular situation 基本设施；基本需要：*Some schools lack money for basics like books and pencils.* 有些学校缺少资金购买书本、铅笔之类的基本用具。

B

IDM **go/get back to 'basics** to think about the simple or most important ideas within a subject or an activity instead of new ideas or complicated details 回归本原；返璞归真

basil /'bæzl; *NAmE also* 'beɪzl/ *noun* [U] a plant with shiny green leaves that smell sweet and are used in cooking as a HERB 罗勒（叶子碧绿芳香，用于烹调） ➲ VISUAL VOCAB PAGE V35

ba·sil·ica /bə'zɪlɪkə/ *noun* a large church or hall with a curved end and two rows of columns inside 巴西利卡，会堂（一端呈半圆形，内设两排廊柱）

basi·lisk /'bæzɪlɪsk/ *noun* (in ancient stories) a creature like a snake, which can kill people by looking at them or breathing on them 蛇怪，巴兹里斯克蛇（古代传说中目光或气息可致人死亡的怪物）

basin /'beɪsn/ *noun* **1** (*especially BrE*) = WASHBASIN **2** a large round bowl for holding liquids or (in British English) for preparing foods in; the amount of liquid, etc. in a basin 盆；（英式英语）调菜盆；一盆（的量）：*a pudding basin* 布丁盆 **3** an area of land around a large river with streams running down into it 流域：*the Amazon Basin* 亚马孙河流域 **4** (*specialist*) a place where the earth's surface is lower than in other areas of the world 盆地；凹地；海盆：*the Pacific Basin* 太平洋海盆 **5** a sheltered area of water providing a safe HARBOUR for boats 港池；内港；内湾；船坞：*a yacht basin* 停放游艇的内港

basis 🔑 /'beɪsɪs/ *noun* (*pl.* **bases** /'beɪsiːz/) **1** 🔑 [sing.] the reason why people take a particular action 原因；缘由：*She was chosen for the job* ***on the basis of*** *her qualifications.* 她因资历适合而获选中担任这项工作。◇ *Some movies have been banned* ***on the basis that*** *they are too violent.* 有些影片因暴力镜头过多而被查禁。➲ SYNONYMS AT REASON **2** 🔑 [sing.] the way things are organized or arranged 基准；准则；方式：*on a* ***regular/permanent/part-time/temporary basis*** 以定期 / 永久 / 兼职 / 临时性的方式 ◇ *on a* ***daily/day-to-day/weekly basis*** 按每天 / 每周一次的标准 **3** 🔑 [C, usually sing., U] the important facts, ideas or events that support sth and that it can develop from 基础；要素；基点：*The basis of a good marriage is trust.* 美满婚姻的基础是信赖。◇ ***This article will form the basis for our discussion.*** 这篇文章将作为我们讨论的基点。◇ *The theory seems to have no basis in fact.* 这一理论似乎没有事实根据。

> ▼ **SYNONYMS 同义词辨析**
>
> **basis**
>
> **foundation • base**
>
> These are all words for the ideas or facts that sth is based on. 以上各词均指基础、根据。
>
> **basis** [usually sing.] a principle, an idea or a fact that supports sth and that it can develop from 指基础、要素、基点：*This article will form the basis for our discussion.* 这篇文章将作为我们讨论的基点。
>
> **foundation** [C, U] a principle, an idea or a fact that supports sth and that it develops from 指基本原理、基础、根据：*Respect and friendship provide a solid foundation for marriage.* 尊重和友爱是婚姻的牢固基础。◇ *The rumour is totally without foundation* (= is not based on any facts). 这谣传毫无事实根据。
>
> **BASIS OR FOUNDATION?** 用 basis 还是 foundation?
>
> **Foundation** is often used to talk about larger or more important things than **basis**. 与 basis 相比，foundation 常用以指更大、更重要的事物：*He laid the foundations of Japan's modern economy.* 他奠定了日本现代经济的基础。◇ *These figures formed the basis of their pay claim.* 这些数字是他们要求提高工资的根据。
>
> **base** [usually sing.] an idea, a fact or a situation from which sth is developed 指根据、出发点：*His arguments have a sound economic base.* 他的论点在经济上有充分的根据。
>
> **PATTERNS**
>
> - a/the basis/foundation/base **for**/**of** sth
> - a **secure**/**solid**/**sound**/**strong**/**weak** basis/foundation/base
> - to **form** the basis/foundation/base of sth
> - to **be without** basis/foundation

bask /bɑːsk; *NAmE* bæsk/ *verb* [I] ~ (**in sth**) to enjoy sitting or lying in the heat or light of sth, especially the sun 晒太阳；取暖：*We sat basking in the warm sunshine.* 我们坐着享受温暖的阳光。

PHR V **'bask in sth** to enjoy the good feelings that you have when other people praise or admire you, or when they give you a lot of attention 沉浸，沐浴（在赞美、关注等中）：*He had always basked in his parents' attention.* 他一直沉浸在父母的呵护中。◇ *I never minded* ***basking in*** *my wife's* ***reflected glory*** (= enjoying the praise, attention, etc. she got). 妻子的荣耀惠及于我，我并不觉得有什么不好意思。

baskets 篮；篓；筐

shopping basket 购物篮　**washing basket** 洗衣筐　**clothes basket** (*BrE*) **hamper** (*NAmE*) 脏衣篮

picnic basket (*BrE also* **hamper**) 野餐篮子　**hanging basket** 吊篮　**waste-paper basket** (*BrE*) **wastebasket** (*NAmE*) 废纸篓

bas·ket /'bɑːskɪt; *NAmE* 'bæs-/ *noun* **1** a container for holding or carrying things. Baskets are made of thin strips of material that bends and twists easily, for example plastic, wire or WICKER. 篮；篓；筐：*a* ***shopping basket*** 购物篮 ◇ *a* ***picnic basket*** 野餐篮子 ◇ *a* ***clothes/laundry basket*** (= in which dirty clothes are put before being washed)（存放待洗衣服的）脏衣篮 ◇ *a* ***wicker/wire basket*** 柳条筐；铁丝筐 ◇ *a* ***cat/dog basket*** (= in which a cat or dog sleeps or is carried around) 猫篮；狗篮 ➲ VISUAL VOCAB PAGE V58 ➲ SEE ALSO WASTE-PAPER BASKET **2** the amount contained in a basket 一篮，一筐，一篓（的量）：*a basket of fruit* 一筐水果 **3** (*also* **cart**, **'shopping cart** *both especially NAmE*) a facility on a website that records the items that you select to buy（网站上的）购物篮，购物车：*Click to drop items into your shopping basket.* 点击将商品放入购物车。**4** the net and the metal ring it hangs from, high up at each end of a BASKETBALL COURT; a point that is scored by throwing the ball through this net（篮球运动的）篮；投篮得分：*to make/shoot a basket* 投球得分 / 入篮 ➲ VISUAL VOCAB PAGE V47 **5** (*economics* 经) a number of different goods or CURRENCIES 一组（不同的物品或货币）：*the value of the rupee against a basket of currencies* 卢比对各种货币的比值 IDM SEE EGG *n.*

B

bas·ket·ball /ˈbɑːskɪtbɔːl; *NAmE* ˈbæs-/ *noun* **1** [U] a game played by two teams of five players, using a large ball which players try to throw into a high net hanging from a ring 篮球运动： *a **basketball game/coach/team*** 篮球比赛 / 教练 / 球队 ➲ VISUAL VOCAB PAGE V47 **2** [C] the ball used in this game 篮球

ˈ**basket case** *noun* (*informal*) **1** a country or an organization whose economic situation is very bad 经济状况极差的国家（或机构） **2** a person who is slightly crazy and who has problems dealing with situations 精神失常的人；无适应能力的人

basket·work /ˈbɑːskɪtwɜːk; *NAmE* ˈbæskɪtwɜːrk/ *noun* [U] **1** material twisted together in the style of a basket 篮状编制物 **2** the craft of making baskets, etc. 编篮工艺；编制工艺

bas·mati /bæsˈmæti; bæz-/ (*also* **bas,mati ˈrice**) *noun* [U] a type of rice with long grains and a delicate flavour 巴斯马蒂香米；印度香米

bas mitzvah /ˌbæs ˈmɪtsvə/ *noun* = BAT MITZVAH

Basque /bɑːsk; bæsk; *NAmE* bæsk/ *noun, adj.*
■ ***noun*** **1** [C] a person who was born in the Basque country 巴斯克人 **2** [U] the language of the people living in the Basque country of France and Spain 巴斯克语（指法国和西班牙的巴斯克地区居民的语言）
■ ***adj.*** connected with these people or their language 巴斯克人的；巴斯克语的

basque /bɑːsk; bæsk; *NAmE* bæsk/ *noun* a piece of women's underwear that covers the body from just under the arms to the tops of the legs 巴斯克衫（自臂部以下至腿根处的女子内衣）

bas-relief /ˌbæs rɪˈliːf/ *noun* [U, C] (*specialist*) a form of SCULPTURE in which the shapes are cut so that they are slightly raised from the background; a SCULPTURE made in this way 浅浮雕；浅浮雕品

bass[1] /beɪs/ *noun, adj.* ➲ SEE ALSO BASS[2]
■ ***noun*** **1** [U] the lowest tone or part in music, for instruments or voices （音乐、乐器、声乐等的）低音，低音部： *He always plays his stereo with the bass turned right up.* 他放立体声音响时总把低音调得很大。◇ *He sings bass.* 他唱低音。◇ *a pounding bass line* 深沉有力的低音 ➲ COMPARE TREBLE *n.* ➲ SEE ALSO DRUM AND BASS **2** [C] a man's singing voice with a low range; a man with a bass voice 男低音；男低音歌手 ➲ COMPARE ALTO *n.*, BARITONE, TENOR *n.* **3** [sing.] a musical part that is written for a bass voice （乐曲的）低音部 **4** (*also* ˌ**bass guiˈtar**) [C] an electric GUITAR that plays very low notes 低音电吉他；电贝司： *a **bass player*** 低音电吉他手 ◇ ***bass and drums*** 低音电吉他和鼓的合奏 ◇ *Eilís Phillips on* (= playing) *bass* 由艾利斯·菲利普斯演奏低音电吉他 **5** [C] = DOUBLE BASS
■ ***adj.*** [only before noun] low in tone 低音的；低声调的： *a bass voice* 低音部 ◇ *the **bass clef*** (= the symbol in music showing that the notes following it are low) 低音谱号 ➲ PICTURE AT MUSIC ➲ COMPARE TREBLE *adj.*

bass[2] /bæs/ *noun* [C, U] (*pl.* **bass**) a sea or FRESHWATER fish that is used for food 鲈（包括多种食用海鱼和淡水鱼） ➲ SEE ALSO BASS[1]

bass drum /ˌbeɪs ˈdrʌm/ *noun* a large drum that makes a very low sound, used in ORCHESTRAS （管弦乐队用的）大鼓，低音鼓 ➲ VISUAL VOCAB PAGE V37

bas·set /ˈbæsɪt/ (*also* ˈ**basset hound**) *noun* a dog with short legs, a long body and long ears 短腿猎犬

bas·sinet /ˌbæsɪˈnet/ (*especially NAmE*) (*BrE usually* **Moses basket**) *noun* a small bed for a baby, that looks like a BASKET 婴儿摇篮；摇篮式婴儿床

bass·ist /ˈbeɪsɪst/ *noun* a person who plays the BASS GUITAR or the DOUBLE BASS 电贝司手；低音提琴手

bas·soon /bəˈsuːn/ *noun* a musical instrument of the WOODWIND group. It is shaped like a large wooden tube with a double REED that you blow into, and produces notes with a low sound. 大管；巴松 ➲ VISUAL VOCAB PAGE V38

bas·soon·ist /bəˈsuːnɪst/ *noun* a person who plays the bassoon 大管（巴松）演奏者

bas·tard /ˈbɑːstəd; ˈbæs-; *NAmE* ˈbæstərd/ *noun* **1** (*taboo, slang*) used to insult sb, especially a man, who has been rude, unpleasant or cruel 杂种；浑蛋；恶棍： *He's a real bastard.* 他是个十足的恶棍。◇ *You bastard! You've made her cry.* 你这个浑蛋！你把她弄哭了。 **2** (*BrE, slang*) a word that some people use about or to sb, especially a man, who they feel very jealous of or sorry for （认为别人走运或不幸时说）家伙，可怜虫： *What a lucky bastard!* 真是个走运的家伙！◇ *You poor bastard!* 你这个可怜虫！ **3** (*BrE, slang*) used about sth that causes difficulties or problems 讨厌的事物；麻烦事： *It's a bastard of a problem.* 那是个挺麻烦的问题。 **4** (*old-fashioned, disapproving*) a person whose parents were not married to each other when he or she was born 私生子

bas·tard·ize (*BrE also* **-ise**) /ˈbɑːstədaɪz; ˈbæs-; *NAmE* ˈbæstərd-/ *verb* **~ sth** (*formal*) to copy sth, but change parts of it so that it is not as good as the original 拙劣地仿造；假冒

baste /beɪst/ *verb* **1 ~ sth** to pour liquid fat or juices over meat, etc. while it is cooking （烹调时往肉等上）浇卤汁 **2 ~ sth** to sew pieces of cloth together temporarily with long loose STITCHES 用长针脚缝；绗缝；粗缝 ➲ WORDFINDER NOTE AT SEW

ˈ**basting brush** *noun* a brush used for brushing liquid fat or juices over meat, etc. while it is cooking （烹调肉类等用的）涂油刷，烤肉刷 ➲ VISUAL VOCAB PAGE V27

bas·tion /ˈbæstiən/ *noun* **1** (*formal*) a group of people or a system that protects a way of life or a belief when it seems that it may disappear 堡垒；捍卫者： *a bastion of male privilege* 大男子主义的堡垒 ◇ *a bastion of freedom* 捍卫自由的堡垒 **2** a place that military forces are defending 堡垒；防御工事

bat /bæt/ *noun, verb*
■ ***noun*** **1** a piece of wood with a handle, made in various shapes and sizes, and used for hitting the ball in games such as BASEBALL, CRICKET and TABLE TENNIS 球棒；球拍；球板： *a **baseball/cricket bat*** 棒球球棒；板球球板 ➲ VISUAL VOCAB PAGES V47, V49 ➲ COMPARE RACKET (3) **2** an animal like a mouse with wings, that flies and feeds at night (= it is NOCTURNAL). There are many types of bat. 蝙蝠 ➲ VISUAL VOCAB PAGE V12 ➲ SEE ALSO FRUIT BAT, OLD BAT, VAMPIRE BAT

IDM **like a bat out of ˈhell** (*informal*) very fast 疾速地；迅速地 **off your own ˈbat** (*BrE, informal*) if you do sth **off your own bat**, it is your own idea and you do it without help or encouragement from anyone else 自觉地；主动地 ➲ MORE AT BLIND *adj.*, RIGHT *adv.*
■ ***verb*** (**-tt-**) **1** [I, T] **~ (sth)** to hit a ball with a bat, especially in a game of BASEBALL or CRICKET 用球板击球，用球棒击球（尤指板球或棒球运动）： *He bats very well.* 他擅长击球。◇ *Who's batting first for the Orioles?* 金莺队谁第一个出场击球？ **2** [T] **~ sth + adv./prep.** to hit sth small that is flying through the air 挥打，拍打（空中飞舞的小东西）： *He batted the wasp away.* 他把那只黄蜂赶跑了。

IDM ˌ**bat your ˈeyes/ˈeyelashes** to open and close your eyes quickly, in a way that is supposed to be attractive 眉目传情；挤眉弄眼 **bat a ˈthousand** (*NAmE, informal*) to be very successful 非常成功；大获全胜 **go to ˈbat for sb** (*NAmE, informal*) to give sb help and support 帮助（或支持）某人 **not bat an ˈeyelid** (*BrE*) (*NAmE* **not bat an ˈeye**) (*informal*) to show no surprise or embarrassment when sth unusual happens 不动声色；面不改色；眼睛都不眨一下： *She didn't bat an eyelid when I told her my news.* 我把我最近的事告诉她时，她一点也不为所动。

PHR V ˌ**bat sth↔aˈround** (*informal*) to discuss whether an idea or a plan is good or not, before deciding what to do 详细讨论（想法、计划等）的可行性： *It's just an idea we've been batting around.* 这只不过是我们一直在讨论的一种想法。

B

batch /bætʃ/ *noun, verb*
▪ ***noun*** **1** a number of people or things that are dealt with as a group 一批：*Each summer a new batch of students tries to find work.* 每年夏天都有新的一批学生要找工作。◇ *We deliver the goods **in batches**.* 我们分批交付货物。 **2** an amount of food, medicine, etc. produced at one time（食物、药物等的）一批生产的量：*a batch of cookies* 一批曲奇饼 **3** (*computing* 计) a set of jobs that are processed together on a computer 批；批量：*to process a batch job* 处理一批作业 ◇ ***a batch file/program*** 批处理文件 / 程序
▪ ***verb*** [T, I] ~ (sth) to put things into groups in order to deal with them 分批处理：*The service will be improved by batching and sorting enquiries.* 分批、分类处理查询将会提高服务质量。

batch·mate /ˈbætʃmeɪt/ *noun* (*IndE*) a person who is or was in the same year group as you at school or college 同年级同学（或同窗）；同届同学（或同窗）

ˌbatch ˈprocessing *noun* [U] (*computing* 计) a way of running a group of programs at the same time, usually automatically 批处理

bated /ˈbeɪtɪd/ *adj.*
IDM **with bated ˈbreath** (*formal*) feeling very anxious or excited 焦虑；兴奋：*We waited with bated breath for the winner to be announced.* 我们屏住呼吸等待宣布冠军是谁。

bath 🔑 /bɑːθ; *NAmE* bæθ/ *noun, verb*
▪ ***noun*** (*pl.* **baths** /bɑːðz; *NAmE* bæðz/) **1** 🔑 [C] (*BrE*) (*also* **bath·tub**, *informal* **tub** *NAmE, BrE*) a large, long container that you put water in and then get into to wash your whole body 浴缸；浴盆 ➲ VISUAL VOCAB PAGE V25 ➲ SEE ALSO BIRDBATH **2** 🔑 [C] the water in a bath/BATHTUB, ready to use 浴缸的水：*a long soak in a hot bath* 一次长时间的热水浴 ◇ *Please **run a bath** for me* (= fill the bath with water). 请给我把浴缸放满水。 **3** 🔑 [C] an act of washing your whole body by sitting or lying in water 洗澡；洗浴：*I think I'll **have a bath** and go to bed.* 我想洗个澡，然后睡觉。◇ (*especially NAmE*) *to **take a bath*** 洗澡 ➲ SEE ALSO BUBBLE BATH **4 baths** [pl.] (*old-fashioned, BrE*) a public building where you can go to swim 游泳池 ➲ SEE ALSO SWIMMING BATH, SWIMMING POOL **5** [C, usually pl.] a public place where people went in the past to wash or have a bath（旧时的）公共浴室，澡堂：*Roman villas and baths* 罗马别墅和浴室 ➲ SEE ALSO TURKISH BATH **6** [C] (*specialist*) a container with a liquid such as water or a DYE in it, in which sth is washed or placed for a period of time. Baths are used in industrial, chemical and medical processes. 浴器，浴锅，染缸（工业、化学以及医学加工处理用） ➲ SEE ALSO BLOODBATH
IDM **take a ˈbath** (*NAmE*) to lose money on a business agreement（在交易中）蒙受经济损失
▪ ***verb*** (*BrE*) (*NAmE* **bathe**) **1** [T] **~ sb** to give a bath to sb 给…洗澡：*It's your turn to bath the baby.* 轮到你给婴儿洗澡了。 **2** [I] (*old-fashioned*) to have a bath 洗澡

▼ **WHICH WORD?** 词语辨析

bath / bathe / swim / sunbathe

- When you wash yourself you can say that you **bath** (*BrE*) or **bathe** (*NAmE*), but it is much more common to say **have a bath** (*BrE*) or **take a bath** (*NAmE*). 自己洗澡可用 bath（英式英语）或 bathe（美式英语），但一般说 have a bath（英式英语）或 take a bath（美式英语）。
- You can also **bath** (*BrE*) or **bathe** (*NAmE*) another person, for example a baby. 给别人（如婴儿）洗澡亦可用 bath（英式英语）或 bathe（美式英语）。
- You **bathe** a part of your body, especially to clean a wound. 洗身体某部位（尤指清洗伤口）用 bathe。
- When you go swimming it is old-fashioned to say that you **bathe**, and you cannot say that you *bath* or *take a bath*. It is more common to use **swim**, **go for a swim**, **have a swim** or **go swimming**. 游泳旧时说 bathe，但不能说 bath 或 take a bath。较通用的说法为 swim、go for a swim、have a swim 或 go swimming：*Let's go for a quick swim in the pool.* 咱们去游泳池游会儿泳吧。◇ *She goes swimming every morning before breakfast.* 她每天早饭前去游泳。 What you wear for this activity is usually called a **swimsuit** or **swimming trunks**. 游泳时穿的衣服通常叫做 swimsuit（游泳衣）或 swimming trunks（游泳裤）。
- When you lie in the sun in order to go brown you **sunbathe**. 沐日光浴为 sunbathe。

ˌbath ˈchair *noun* a special chair with wheels, used in the past for moving a person who was sick or old 巴斯轮椅（旧时用来推病人或老人）

bathe /beɪð/ *verb, noun*
▪ ***verb*** **1** [T] **~ sth** to wash sth with water, especially a part of your body 用水清洗（尤指身体部位）：*Bathe the wound and apply a clean dressing.* 清洗伤口，再用洁净敷料包扎。 **2** [T, I] ~ (sb) (*NAmE*) = BATH：*Have you bathed the baby yet?* 你给婴儿洗澡了吗？◇ *I bathe every day.* 我每天洗澡。 ➲ NOTE AT BATH **3** [I] (*old-fashioned*) to go swimming in the sea, a river, etc. for enjoyment（到海、河等中）游泳消遣 ➲ SEE ALSO SUNBATHE **4** [T] **~ sth (in sth)** (*literary*) to fill or cover sth with light（以光线）撒满，覆盖；使沐浴（在光线里）：*The moon bathed the countryside in a silver light.* 月光下的乡村沐浴在一片银辉之中。
▪ ***noun*** [sing.] (*BrE, formal*) an act of swimming in the sea, a river, etc.（在海、河等中的）游泳：*to go for a bathe* 去游泳

bathed /beɪðd/ *adj.* **1 ~ in sth** (*literary*) covered with light 被（光线）覆盖；沐浴着（光线）：*The castle was bathed in moonlight.* 城堡沐浴在月光里。 **2 ~ in sth** wet because covered with sweat or tears 汗流浃背；泪流满面：*I was so nervous that I was bathed in perspiration.* 我紧张得浑身是汗。

bather /ˈbeɪðə(r)/ *noun* **1** [C] (*BrE*) a person who is swimming in the sea, a river, etc.（在海、河等中）游泳的人 **2 bathers** [pl.] (*AustralE*) = SWIMMING COSTUME, SWIMMING TRUNKS

bath·house /ˈbɑːθhaʊs; *NAmE* ˈbæθ-/ *noun* **1** a public building in which there are baths, steam rooms, etc. 澡堂；公共浴室 **2** (*NAmE*) a building in which you change your clothes for swimming（游泳处的）更衣室

bath·ing /ˈbeɪðɪŋ/ *noun* [U] (*BrE*) the activity of going into the sea, a river, etc. to swim（到海、河等中的）游泳，畅游：*facilities for bathing and boating* 游泳和划船设施 ◇ *a safe bathing beach* 一处可以安全游泳的海滩

ˈbathing cap (*especially NAmE*) (*BrE also* **ˈswimming cap**, **ˈswimming hat**) *noun* a soft rubber or plastic cap that fits closely over your head to keep your hair dry while you are swimming 游泳帽

ˈbathing costume *noun* (*BrE, old-fashioned*) = SWIMSUIT

ˈbathing machine *noun* a shelter with wheels that people in the past went into to put swimming clothes on. It was then pulled to the edge of the sea so they could swim from it.（旧时可推到海边的）活动更衣室，游泳更衣车

ˈbathing suit *noun* (*NAmE* or *old-fashioned*) = SWIMSUIT

ˈbath mat *noun* **1** a piece of material that you put beside the bath/BATHTUB to stand on when you get out 浴室脚垫（放在浴缸旁） ➲ VISUAL VOCAB PAGE V25 **2** a piece of rubber that you put on the bottom of the bath/BATHTUB so that you do not slip 浴缸防滑垫（放在浴缸里）

bathos /ˈbeɪθɒs; *NAmE* -θɑːs/ *noun* [U] (*formal*) (in writing or speech 写作或演讲) a sudden change, that is not always intended, from a serious subject or feeling to sth that is silly or not important 突降（严肃的内容突然变得荒谬，常非出自本意）

bath·robe /ˈbɑːθrəʊb; *NAmE* ˈbæθroʊb/ (*also* **robe**) *noun* **1** a loose piece of clothing worn before and after taking a bath 浴衣；浴袍 ➲ VISUAL VOCAB PAGE V25 **2** (*NAmE*) (*BrE* ˈ**dressing gown**) a long loose piece of clothing, usually with a belt, worn indoors over night clothes, for example when you first get out of bed 晨衣，晨袍（起床后套于睡衣外在室内穿的宽松长罩衫，通常有束带） ➲ VISUAL VOCAB PAGE V68

bath·room /ˈbɑːθruːm; -rʊm; *NAmE* ˈbæθ-/ *noun* **1** a room in which there is a bath/BATHTUB, a WASHBASIN and often a toilet 浴室：*Go and wash your hands in the bathroom.* 到盥洗室洗手去。➲ VISUAL VOCAB PAGE V25 **2** (*NAmE*) a room in which there is a toilet, a SINK and sometimes a bath/BATHTUB or shower 洗手间；卫生间：*I have to* ***go to the bathroom*** (= use the toilet). 我得上洗手间。◇ *Where's the bathroom?* (= for example in a restaurant) 卫生间在哪里？◇ *We were allowed to stop occasionally for bathroom breaks.* 我们获准偶尔停下来上趟洗手间。➲ NOTE AT TOILET

bath·tub /ˈbɑːθtʌb; *NAmE* ˈbæθ-/ (*also informal* **tub**) (*both especially NAmE*) (*BrE also* **bath**) *noun* a large, long container that you put water in and then get into to wash your whole body 浴缸；浴盆 ➲ VISUAL VOCAB PAGE V25

bath·water /ˈbɑːθwɔːtə(r); *NAmE* ˈbæθwɔːtər; -wɑːt-/ *noun* [U] water in a bath/BATHTUB 洗澡水 IDM SEE BABY *n.*

batik /bəˈtiːk/ *noun* [U, C] a method of printing patterns on cloth using WAX (= a solid substance made from fat or oil) on the parts that will not have any colour; a piece of cloth printed in this way 巴蒂克印花法；蜡防印花法；蜡染；蜡防印花布

bat·man /ˈbætmən/ *noun* (*pl.* **-men** /-mən/) (*BrE*) the personal servant of an officer in the armed forces 勤务兵；传令兵

bat mitzvah /ˌbæt ˈmɪtsvə/ (*also* ˌ**bas** ˈ**mitzvah**) *noun* **1** a ceremony and celebration that is held for a Jewish girl between the ages of 12 and 14 at which she accepts the religious responsibilities of an adult 受诫礼（为 12 至 14 岁的犹太女孩举行的成人仪式） **2** the girl who is celebrating this occasion 行受诫礼的犹太女孩 ➲ COMPARE BAR MITZVAH

baton /ˈbætɒn; -tɔ̃; *NAmE* bəˈtɑːn/ *noun* **1** (*also* **trun·cheon**) (*both especially BrE*) (*NAmE usually* **night·stick**) a short thick stick that police officers carry as a weapon 警棍：*a* ***baton charge*** (= one made by police carrying batons, to force a crowd back) 持警棍驱击 **2** a thin light stick used by the person (called a CONDUCTOR) who is in control of an ORCHESTRA, etc. （乐队）指挥棒 **3** a short light stick that one member of a team in a RELAY race passes to the next person to run 接力棒：*to* ***pass/hand over the baton*** 交接力棒 ◇ (*figurative*) *The President* ***handed over the baton*** (= passed responsibility) *to his successor.* 总统把权杖传给了他的继任者。 **4** a long stick that is held and thrown in the air by a person marching in front of a band, or by a MAJORETTE （行进中军乐队领队的）指挥杖

ˈ**baton round** *noun* (*BrE*) a rubber or plastic bullet that is fired to control a crowd that has become violent 橡胶子弹，塑料子弹（镇压暴乱等用）

bats·man /ˈbætsmən/ *noun* (*pl.* **-men** /-mən/) (in CRICKET 板球) the player who is hitting the ball 击球手 ➲ VISUAL VOCAB PAGE V47

bat·tal·ion /bəˈtæliən/ *noun* **1** (*BrE*) a large group of soldiers that form part of a BRIGADE （军队的）营 ➲ WORDFINDER NOTE AT ARMY **2** (*formal*) a large group of people, especially an organized group with a particular purpose （有组织的）队伍：*a battalion of supporters* 由支持者组成的队伍

bat·ten /ˈbætn/ *noun, verb*

■ ***noun*** (*specialist*) a long strip of wood that is used to keep other building materials in place on a wall or roof 挂瓦条，压条，板条（用于固定其他建筑材料）

■ ***verb***

IDM ˌ**batten down the** ˈ**hatches** **1** to prepare yourself for a period of difficulty or trouble 做好迎接困难的准备 **2** (on a ship 船上) to firmly shut all the entrances to the lower part, especially because a storm is expected （风暴来临前）封住底舱口

PHR V ˌ**batten sth**↔ˈ**down** to fix sth firmly in position with strips of wood 用木板固定某物：*He was busy battening down all the shutters and doors.* 他正忙着用板条钉牢所有的百叶窗和门。 ˈ**batten on sb** (*BrE, disapproving, formal*) to live well by using other people's money, etc. 靠（别人的钱等）享福；损人肥己

bat·ter /ˈbætə(r)/ *verb, noun*

■ ***verb*** [I, T, often passive] to hit sb/sth hard many times, especially in a way that causes serious damage 连续猛击；殴打：**~ at/on sth** *She battered at the door with her fists.* 她用双拳不断地擂门。◇ **~ sb** *He had been badly battered about the head and face.* 他被打得鼻青脸肿。◇ *Her killer had* ***battered*** *her* ***to death.*** 凶手把她殴打致死。◇ **~ sth** *Severe winds have been battering the north coast.* 狂风一直在北海岸肆虐。➲ SYNONYMS AT BEAT

PHR V ˌ**batter sth**↔ˈ**down** to hit sth hard many times until it breaks or comes down （以连续重击）砸毁，砸倒

■ ***noun*** **1** [U, C] a mixture of eggs, milk and flour used in cooking to cover food such as fish or chicken before you fry it, or to make PANCAKES 面糊（煎料） **2** [U, C] (*NAmE*) a mixture of eggs, milk, flour, etc. used for making cakes 面糊（用于做糕饼） **3** [C] (*NAmE*) (in BASEBALL 棒球) the player who is hitting the ball 击球手；击球员 ➲ VISUAL VOCAB PAGE V47

bat·tered /ˈbætəd; *NAmE* -tərd/ *adj.* **1** old, used a lot, and not in very good condition 破旧不堪的：*a battered old car* 一辆破旧的老爷车 **2** [usually before noun] attacked violently and injured; attacked and badly damaged by weapons or by bad weather 受到严重虐待的；受到（炮火、恶劣天气）重创的：***battered women/children*** 受虐待的妇女 / 儿童 ◇ *The child had suffered what has become known as 'battered baby syndrome.'* 那孩子患的是后来人称“受虐儿童综合征”的疾病。◇ *Rockets and shells continued to hit the battered port.* 火箭和炮弹继续袭击已遭重创的港口。

bat·ter·ing /ˈbætərɪŋ/ *noun* [U, sing.] a violent attack that injures or damages sb/sth 殴打；猛击：*wife battering* 对妻子的暴力行为 ◇ (*figurative*) *The film* ***took a battering*** *from critics in the US.* 该影片在美国遭遇到批评家的猛烈抨击。

ˈ**battering ram** *noun* a long, heavy piece of wood used in war in the past for breaking down doors and walls （旧时的圆木）攻城锤

bat·tery /ˈbætri; -təri/ *noun* (*pl.* **-ies**) **1** [C] a device that is placed inside a car engine, clock, radio, etc. and that produces the electricity that makes it work 电池：*to replace the batteries* 更换电池 ◇ *a rechargeable battery* 充电电池 ◇ ***battery-powered/-operated*** 用电池驱动的 ◇ *a car battery* 汽车蓄电池 ◇ *The battery is flat* (= it is no longer producing electricity). 电池没电了。➲ WORDFINDER NOTE AT ELECTRICITY **2** [C] **~ (of sth)** a large number of things or people of the same type 一系列；一批；一群：*He faced a battery of questions.* 他面临一连串的问题。◇ *a battery of reporters* 一大批记者 **3** [C] (*specialist*) a number of large guns that are used together 排炮 **4** [C] (*BrE*) (often used as an adjective 常用作形容词) a large number of small CAGES that are joined together and are used for keeping chickens, etc. in on a farm 层架式鸡笼；层架式饲养笼：*a battery hen* 层架式养鸡笼养的母鸡 ◇ *battery eggs* 层架式养鸡场所产的蛋 ➲ COMPARE FREE-RANGE **5** [U] (*law* 律) the crime of attacking sb physically 殴打罪 ➲ SEE ALSO ASSAULT AND BATTERY IDM SEE RECHARGE

ˈ**battery farm** *noun* (*BrE*) a farm where large numbers of chickens or other animals are kept in very small CAGES or crowded conditions 密集式养鸡场（或牲畜饲养

场） ➲ COMPARE FACTORY FARM, FREE-RANGE ▶ **'battery farming** *noun* [U]

B

bat·tle 🔑 /'bætl/ *noun, verb*

■ ***noun*** **1** 🔑 [C, U] a fight between armies, ships or planes, especially during a war; a violent fight between groups of people 战役；战斗；搏斗： *the battle of Waterloo* 滑铁卢战役 ◇ *to be killed* ***in battle*** 阵亡 ◇ *a gun battle* 枪战 ➲ SEE ALSO PITCHED BATTLE **2** 🔑 [C] ~ **(with sb) (for sth)** a competition, an argument or a struggle between people or groups of people trying to win power or control 较量；争论；斗争： *a legal battle for compensation* 要求赔偿的法律斗争 ◇ *a battle with an insurance company* 同一家保险公司的争执 ◇ *a* ***battle of wits*** (= when each side uses their ability to think quickly to try to win) 智斗 ◇ *a* ***battle of wills*** (= when each side is very determined to win) 意志的较量 ➲ SYNONYMS AT CAMPAIGN **3** 🔑 [C, usually sing.] a determined effort that sb makes to solve a difficult problem or succeed in a difficult situation 奋斗；斗争： ~ **(against sth)** *her long battle against cancer* 她同癌症的长期斗争 ◇ *to fight an uphill battle against prejudice* 同偏见作艰苦斗争 ◇ ~ **(for sth)** *a battle for survival* 一场生死斗 ◇ ~ **(with sth)** *his battle with alcoholism* 他戒酒的斗争

IDM **the battle lines are 'drawn** used to say that people or groups have shown which side they intend to support in an argument or contest that is going to begin 战线已经划清（指争战之际各拥一方形成对垒之势） **do 'battle (with sb) (over sth)** to fight or argue with sb （同某人就某事）进行斗争（或辩论） **half the 'battle** the most important or difficult part of achieving sth （完成某事的）关键；最艰难的阶段 ➲ MORE AT FIGHT *v.*, JOIN *v.*

■ ***verb*** [I, T] to try very hard to achieve sth difficult or to deal with sth unpleasant or dangerous 搏斗；奋斗；斗争： *Both teams battled hard.* 两队拼得很厉害。 ◇ *I had to battle hard just to stay afloat.* 我得用力挣扎才能勉强浮住。 ◇ ~ **with/against sb/sth (for sth)** *She's still battling with a knee injury.* 她还在同膝部的伤痛作斗争。 ◇ ~ **for sth** *The two leaders are battling for control of the government.* 两位领导人在争夺政府的主导权。 ◇ ~ **it out** *The two sides will battle it out in the final next week.* 双方将于下周决赛中决一胜负。 ◇ ~ **sth** *He battled cancer for four years.* 他同癌症斗争了四年。

battle·axe (*BrE*) (*US also* **battle·ax**) /'bætlæks/ *noun* **1** (*informal, disapproving*) an aggressive and unpleasant older woman 悍妇；母老虎 **2** a heavy AXE with a long handle, used in the past as a weapon （旧时的）战斧

battle·cruiser /'bætlkruːzə(r)/ *noun* a large fast ship used in war in the past, faster and lighter than a BATTLESHIP 战列巡洋舰（旧时作战用，比战列舰快而轻）

'battle cry *noun* **1** a shout that soldiers used to give in battle to encourage their own army or to frighten the enemy （战斗中的）呐喊助威，喊杀声 **2** a word or phrase used by a group of people who work together for a particular purpose, especially a political one （尤指政治的）战斗口号，口号

battle·dress /'bætldres/ *noun* [U] (*BrE*) the uniform that soldiers wear for training and when they go to fight 战地服装

'battle fatigue *noun* [U] = COMBAT FATIGUE

'battle fatigues *noun* [pl.] = COMBAT FATIGUES

battle·field /'bætlfiːld/ (*also* **battle·ground** /'bætlgraʊnd/) *noun* **1** a place where a battle is being fought or has been fought 战场 **2** a subject that people feel strongly about and argue about 争论主题；斗争领域

'battle-hardened *adj.* (of soldiers) having experience of war and therefore effective at fighting battles 久经沙场的；身经百战的

battle·ments /'bætlmənts/ *noun* [pl.] a low wall around the top of a castle with spaces in it that people inside could shoot through 城垛；雉堞 ➲ VISUAL VOCAB PAGE V15

'battle-scarred *adj.* a person or place that is **battle-scarred** has been in a war or fight and shows the signs of injury or damage 伤痕累累的；满目疮痍的

battle·ship /'bætlʃɪp/ *noun* a very large ship used in war, with big guns and heavy ARMOUR (= metal plates that cover the ship to protect it) 战列舰

batty /'bæti/ *adj.* (*informal, especially BrE*) (of people or ideas 人或思想) slightly crazy, in a harmless way 疯疯癫癫的；古怪的 ➲ SYNONYMS AT MAD

bau·ble /'bɔːbl/ *noun* **1** a piece of jewellery that is cheap and has little artistic value 花哨的廉价首饰 **2** (*BrE*) a decoration for a Christmas tree in the shape of a ball 圣诞树装饰球

baud /bɔːd/ *noun* (*computing* 计) a unit for measuring the speed at which electronic signals and information are sent from one computer to another 波特（信号、信息传输速率单位）

Bau·haus /'baʊhaʊs/ *noun* [U] (*from German*) a style and movement in German ARCHITECTURE and design in the early 20th century that was influenced by the methods and materials used in industry and placed emphasis on how things would be used 包豪斯建筑学派（20 世纪初德国建筑和设计的风格、流派，受工业界方法和材料的影响，强调实用功能）

baulk (*BrE*) (*NAmE usually* **balk**) /bɔːk/ *verb* **1** [I] ~ **(at sth)** to be unwilling to do sth or become involved in sth because it is difficult, dangerous, etc. 畏缩；回避： *Many parents may baulk at the idea of paying $100 for a pair of shoes.* 许多父母可能不愿出 100 美元买一双鞋。 **2** [I] ~ **(at sth)** (of a horse 马) to stop suddenly and refuse to jump a fence, etc. 逡巡不前；突然拒绝前行（如跳越障碍物等） **3** [T] ~ **sb (of sth)** [usually passive] (*formal*) to prevent sb from getting sth or doing sth 阻止；阻碍： *She looked like a lion baulked of its prey.* 她看上去像一头吃不到猎物的狮子。

baux·ite /'bɔːksaɪt/ *noun* [U] a soft mineral from which ALUMINIUM/ALUMINUM is obtained 铝土矿；铝土

bawd /bɔːd/ *noun* (*old use*) a woman who was in charge of a BROTHEL (= a house where men pay to have sex) 妓院女老板；鸨母

bawdy /'bɔːdi/ *adj.* (**bawd·ier**, **bawd·iest**) (*old-fashioned*) (of songs, plays, etc. 歌曲、戏剧等) loud, and dealing with sex in an amusing way 喧闹并猥亵作乐的；说黄色笑话的

bawl /bɔːl/ *verb* **1** [I, T] to shout loudly, especially in an unpleasant or angry way 大喊；怒吼： ~ **(at sb)** *She bawled at him in front of everyone.* 她当着大家的面冲他大喊大叫。 ◇ ~ **(out) sth (at sb)** *He sat in his office bawling orders at his secretary.* 他坐在办公室里，对秘书厉声发号施令。 ◇ ~ **speech (+ out)** *'Get in here now!' she bawled out.* "马上进来！"她嚷道。 **2** [I, T] **(+ speech)** to cry loudly, especially in an unpleasant and annoying way 号哭： *A child was bawling in the next room.* 隔壁有个孩子在大声哭闹。 ◇ *He was* ***bawling his eyes out*** (= crying very loudly). 他正号啕大哭。

PHR V **,bawl sb↔'out** (*informal*) to speak angrily to sb because they have done sth wrong 大声训斥： *The teacher bawled him out for being late.* 老师因他迟到而把他训斥了一顿。

bay 🔑 /beɪ/ *noun, verb, adj.*

■ ***noun*** **1** 🔑 [C] a part of the sea, or of a large lake, partly surrounded by a wide curve of the land （海或湖的）湾： *the Bay of Bengal* 孟加拉湾 ◇ *Hudson Bay* 哈得孙湾 ◇ *a magnificent view across the bay* 海湾一带的壮观景象 ➲ VISUAL VOCAB PAGE V5 **2** [C] a marked section of ground either inside or outside a building, for example for a vehicle to park in, for storing things, etc. 分隔间（户外或室内的，用以停放车辆、存放货物等）： *a* ***parking/loading bay*** 停车位；装货区 ◇ *Put the equipment in No 3 bay.* 把设备放在 3 号仓房。 ➲ SEE ALSO SICKBAY **3** [C] a curved area of a room or building that sticks out from the rest of the building （建筑物的）突出结构 **4** [C] a horse of a dark brown colour 深棕色马；栗色马： *He was* *riding a big bay.* 他骑着一匹高大的栗色马。 **5** [C] a deep noise, especially the noise made by dogs when hunting (尤指猎犬捕猎时的) 低沉吠声 **6** (*also* ˈ**sweet bay**) [C] = BAY TREE **7** [U] a HERB used to give flavour to food, made of the leaves of the BAY TREE 月桂 (用作香料) ➲ VISUAL VOCAB PAGE V35

IDM **at ˈbay** when an animal that is being hunted is **at bay**, it must turn and face the dogs and HUNTERS because it is impossible to escape from them (猎物) 被围困, 被迫作困兽之斗 **hold/keep sb/sth at ˈbay** to prevent an enemy from coming close or a problem from having a bad effect 不让 (敌人) 接近; 防止 (问题) 恶化 SYN **ward off**: *I'm trying to keep my creditors at bay.* 我在竭力避开债主。 ◇ *Charlotte bit her lip to hold the tears at bay.* 夏洛特咬住嘴唇不让眼泪流出来。

■*verb* **1** [I] (of a dog or WOLF 狗或狼) to make a long deep sound, especially while hunting (尤指捕猎时) 发出长嗥, 低沉地吠叫 SYN **howl**: *a pack of baying hounds* 一群不断吠叫着的猎犬 **2** [I] ~ (**for sth**) (usually used in the progressive tenses 通常用于进行时) to demand sth in a loud and angry way 厉声强要: *The referee's decision left the crowd* ***baying for blood*** (= threatening violence towards him). 裁判的裁决引起群众怒吼着要暴力相向。

■*adj.* (of a horse 马) dark brown in colour 深棕色的; 栗色的: *a bay mare* 一匹栗色的母马

ˈbay leaf *noun* the dried leaf of the BAY TREE that is used in cooking as a HERB 月桂叶 (干叶常作香料)

bay·onet *noun, verb*

■*noun* /ˈbeɪənət/ a long, sharp knife that is fastened onto the end of a RIFLE and used as a weapon in battle 枪刺; 刺刀

■*verb* /ˈbeɪənət; ˌbeɪəˈnet/ ~ **sb** to push a bayonet into sb in order to kill them 用刺刀刺

bayou /ˈbaɪuː/ *noun* a branch of a river in the southern US that moves very slowly and has many plants growing in it (美国南部的) 长沼, 牛轭湖

ˈbay tree (*also* **bay**) *noun* a small tree with dark green leaves with a sweet smell that are used in cooking 月桂树, 甜月桂 (叶子可作香料) ➲ SEE ALSO BAY LEAF

ˌbay ˈwindow *noun* a large window, usually with glass on three sides, that sticks out from the outside wall of a house 凸窗 ➲ VISUAL VOCAB PAGE V18

ba·zaar /bəˈzɑː(r)/ *noun* **1** (in some Eastern countries) a street or an area of a town where there are many small shops (某些东方国家的) 集市 **2** (in Britain, the US, etc.) a sale of goods, often items made by hand, to raise money for a charity or for people who need help (英、美等国的) 义卖

ba·zooka /bəˈzuːkə/ *noun* a long gun, shaped like a tube, which is held on the shoulder and used to fire ROCKETS at military vehicles (反坦克) 巴祖卡火箭筒

ba·zoom /bəˈzuːm/ *noun* [usually pl.] (*informal, especially NAmE*) a woman's breast (女人的) 乳房, 奶子

BBC /ˌbiː biː ˈsiː/ *abbr.* British Broadcasting Corporation (a national organization which broadcasts television and radio programmes and which is paid for by the public and not by advertising) 英国广播公司: *The news is on BBC One at 6.* 新闻在英国广播公司电视一台 6 点钟播出。 ◇ *BBC Radio 4* 英国广播公司广播四台

the ˌBBC World ˈService *noun* [sing.] a department of the BBC which broadcasts programmes, including news programmes, in English and many other languages to other countries 英国广播公司环球广播部

BBQ *abbr.* BARBECUE 户外烧烤

BBS /ˌbiː ˌbiː ˈes/ *noun* [C, U] (*computing* 计) bulletin board system (a system which allows a group of people to leave messages which the others in the group can read and reply to) 公告板系统; 留言板系统; 电子布告栏系统

BC (*BrE*) (*US* **B.C.**) /ˌbiː ˈsiː/ *abbr.* before Christ (used in the Christian CALENDAR to show a particular number of years before the year when Christ is believed to have been born) 公元前: *in (the year) 2000 BC* 在公元前 2000 年 ◇ *the third century BC* 公元前 3 世纪 ➲ COMPARE AD, AH, BCE, CE

bcc /ˌbiː siː ˈsiː/ *abbr., verb*

■*abbr.* blind carbon copy (to) (used on emails or business letters to show that a copy is being sent to another person whose name and address cannot be seen by the other person or people who receive it) 密件抄送, 密送 (全写为 blind carbon copy (to))

■*verb* (**bcc's**, **bcc'ing**, **bcc'ed**, **bcc'ed** /ˌbiː siː ˈsiːd/) (*informal*) to send a copy of a letter or email to another person whose name and email address cannot be seen by the other people who receive it 密件抄送; 密送: ~ **sb** (**sth**) | ~ **sth** (**to sb**) *Send an email to the head of finance and bcc me.* 给财务主管发一封电邮并密送给我。 ◇ *That company keeps bcc'ing promotional emails to me.* 那家公司不断把促销电邮密送给我。 ◇ ~ **sb on sth** *He now bcc'ed his boss on every email he sent to difficult clients.* 他现在给难缠客户每发一封电邮就密送给他老板一份。

BCE /ˌbiː siː ˈiː/ (*also* **B.C.E.** *especially in NAmE*) *abbr.* before the Common Era (before the birth of Christ, when the Christian CALENDAR starts counting years. BCE can be used to give dates in the same way as BC.) 公元前 (用于表示年份, 用法与 BC 同): *in (the year) 2000 BCE* 在公元前 2000 年 ◇ *the third century BCE* 公元前三世纪 ➲ COMPARE AD, AH, BC, CE

be 🔑 /bi; *strong form* biː/ *verb, auxiliary verb* ➲ IRREGULAR VERBS at page R4

■*verb* **1** 🔑 *linking verb* **there is/are + noun** to exist; to be present 有; 存在: *Is there a God?* 上帝存在吗? ◇ *Once upon a time there was a princess...* 从前有一位公主… ◇ *I tried phoning but there was no answer.* 我试打过电话, 但没人接。 ◇ *There's a bank down the road.* 沿马路不远有一家银行。 ◇ *Was there a pool at the hotel?* 宾馆里有游泳池吗? **2** 🔑 [I] **+ adv./prep.** to be located; to be in a place 位于; 在 (某处): *The town is three miles away.* 镇子距此地三英里远。 ◇ *If you're looking for your file, it's on the table.* 你要找的文件在桌子上。 ◇ *Mary's upstairs.* 玛丽在楼上。 **3** 🔑 [I] **+ adv./prep.** to happen at a time or in a place (在某时或某地) 发生: *The party is on Friday evening.* 聚会定于周五晚上举行。 ◇ *The meetings are always in the main conference room.* 会议总是在主会议室进行。 **4** 🔑 [I] **+ adv./prep.** to remain in a place 留在 (某地); 逗留: *She has been in her room for hours.* 她已经在她的房间里待了几个小时了。 ◇ *They're here till Christmas.* 他们将在这里一直住到圣诞节。 **5** 🔑 [I] **+ adv./prep.** to attend an event; to be present in a place 出席; 到场: *I'll be at the party.* 我将出席聚会。 ◇ *He'll be here soon* (= will arrive soon). 他很快就会到达。 **6** 🔑 [I] (only used in the perfect tenses 仅用于完成时) **+ adv./prep.** to visit or call 前往; 造访; 访问: *I've never been to Spain.* 我从未去过西班牙。 ◇ *He had been abroad many times.* 他曾多次出国。 ◇ (*BrE*) *Has the postman been yet?* 邮递员来过了吗? HELP In *NAmE*, **come** is used instead. 在美式英语中用 come 代替: *Has the mailman come yet?* 邮递员来过了吗? **7** 🔑 [I] ~ **from...** used to say where sb was born or where their home is 出生于 (某地); 来自…; 是 (某地的) 人: *She's from Italy.* 她是意大利人。 **8** 🔑 *linking verb* used when you are naming people or things, describing them or giving more information about them (提供名称或信息时用): **+ noun** *Today is Monday.* 今天是星期一。 ◇ *'Who is that?' 'It's my brother.'* "那个人是谁?" "是我哥哥。" ◇ *She's a great beauty.* 她是个大美人。 ◇ *Susan is a doctor.* 苏珊是医生。 ◇ *He wants to be* (= become) *a pilot when he grows up.* 他想长大后当飞行员。 ◇ **+ adj.** *It's beautiful!* 美呀! ◇ *Life is unfair.* 人生没有公平。 ◇ *He is ten years old.* 他十岁了。 ◇ *'How are you?' 'I'm very well, thanks.'* "你好吗?" "我很好, 谢谢。" ◇ *Be quick!* 快点! ◇ ~ (**that**)... ***The fact is*** (*that*) *we don't have enough money.* 事实是我们没有那么多钱。 ◇ ~ **doing sth** *The problem is getting it all done in the time available.* 问题是要在现有的时间内把它全部完成。 ◇ ~ **to do sth** *The problem is to get it all done in the time available.* 问题是要在现有的时间内把它全部完成。 **9** 🔑 *linking verb* **it is/was** used when you are describing a situation or saying what you think about it （描述情况或表达想法时用）： **+ adj.** *It was really hot in the sauna.* 桑拿浴的确很热。◇ *It's strange how she never comes to see us any more.* 奇怪，她怎么再也不来看我们了。◇ *He thinks it's clever to make fun of people.* 他觉得拿别人开玩笑显得聪明。◇ **+ noun** *It would be a shame if you lost it.* 你要是把它丢了就太可惜了。◇ *It's going to be a great match.* 这将是一场了不起的比赛。 **10** *linking verb* **it is/was** used to talk about time （用于表达时间）： **+ noun** *It's two thirty.* 现在是两点三十。◇ **+ adj.** *It was late at night when we finally arrived.* 我们最后到达时已是深夜。 **11** *linking verb* **+ noun** used to say what sth is made of （表示所用的材料）： *Is your jacket real leather?* 你的夹克是真皮的吗？ **12** *linking verb* [I] used to say who sth belongs to or who it is intended for （表示某物所属）： **~ mine, yours, etc.** *The money's not yours, it's John's.* 这钱不是你的，是约翰的。◇ **~ for me, you, etc.** *This package is for you.* 这个包裹是给你的。 **13** *linking verb* **+ noun** to cost 花费；值： *'How much is that dress?' 'Eighty dollars.'* "那条连衣裙多少钱？" "八十美元。" **14** *linking verb* **+ noun** to be equal to 等于；等同： *Three and three is six.* 三加三等于六。◇ *How much is a thousand pounds in euros?* 一千英镑合多少欧元？ ◇ *Let x be the sum of a and b.* 设 x 为 a 加 b 之和。◇ *London is not England* (= do not think that all of England is like London). 伦敦并不等于英格兰（不要以为整个英格兰都像伦敦）。 **15** *linking verb* **~ everything, nothing, etc.** (**to sb**) used to say how important sth is to sb （表示对某人的重要性）： *Money isn't everything* (= it is not the only important thing). 金钱不是一切（不是唯一重要的东西）。◇ *A thousand dollars is nothing to somebody as rich as he is.* 一千美元对于像他这么富有的人来说算不上什么。

IDM **HELP** Most idioms containing **be** are at the entries for the nouns and adjectives in the idioms, for example **be the death of sb** is at **death**. 大多数含 be 的习语，都可在该等习语中的名词及形容词相关词条找到，如 be the death of sb 在词条 death 下。 **the ˌbe-all and ˈend-all (of sth)** (*informal*) the most important part; all that matters 最重要的部分；最要紧的事： *Her career is the be-all and end-all of her existence.* 她的事业是她生活中至关重要的事。 **as/that was** as sb/sth used to be called 像以往所称呼的；作为曾用名： *Jill Davis that was* (= before her marriage) （婚前）姓名为吉尔·戴维斯 ◇ *the Soviet Union, as was* 旧称苏联 **(he, she, etc. has) been and ˈdone sth** (*BrE, informal*) used to show that you are surprised and annoyed by sth that sb has done （表示吃惊和恼怒）： *Someone's been and parked in front of the entrance!* 有人居然把车停在大门口！ ➲ SEE ALSO GO AND DO STH **if it wasn't/weren't for…** used to say that sb/sth stopped sb/sth from happening 若不是（某人 / 某事）；幸亏： *If it weren't for you, I wouldn't be alive today.* 如果不是你，我早就死了。 **ˌleave/ˌlet sb/sth ˈbe** to leave sb/sth alone without disturbing them or it 随…去；不打扰某人 / 某事物： *Leave her be, she obviously doesn't want to talk about it.* 别烦她了，她显然不想谈论这事。◇ *Let the poor dog be* (= don't annoy it). 别逗弄那条可怜的狗了。 **-to-be** (in compounds 构成复合词) future 将来： *his bride-to-be* 他的未婚妻 ◇ *mothers-to-be* (= pregnant women) 准妈妈 **sth ˌis what it ˈis** (*informal*) used to show that you accept that sth negative cannot be changed 事已至此（表示接受无法改变的负面事情）： *I never imagined that our company share prices would fall so low, but it is what it is.* 我从没想到我们公司的股价会跌到这么低，但事已至此，又能如何？

■ ***auxiliary verb*** **1** used with a past participle to form the passive （与过去分词连用构成被动语态）： *He was killed in the war.* 他死于这场战争。◇ *Where were they made?* 这些东西是在哪里制造的？ ◇ *The house was still being built.* 房子还在建造中。◇ *You will be told what to do.* 会有人告诉你该干什么的。 **2** used with a present participle to form progressive tenses （与现在分词连用构成进行时）： *I am studying Chinese.* 我正在学中文。◇ *I'll be seeing him soon.* 我很快就要见到他了。◇ *What have you been doing this week?* 你这个星期都在做些什么？ ◇ *I'm always being criticized.* 我总是受到批评。 **3** used to make QUESTION TAGS (= short questions added to the end of statements) （用于反意疑问句）： *You're not hungry, are you?* 你不饿，对吧？ ◇ *Ben's coming, isn't he?* 本要来，是不是？ ◇ *The old theatre was pulled down, wasn't it?* 老戏院被拆了，对不？ **4** used to avoid repeating the full form of a verb in the passive or a progressive tense （在被动语态或进行时中代替重复的动词完整形式）： *Karen wasn't beaten in any of her games, but all the others were.* 卡伦没有输掉任何一场比赛，但所有其他人都输过。◇ *'Are you coming with us?' 'No, I'm not.'* "你和我们一起去吗？" "不，我不了。" **5** **~ to do sth** used to say what must or should be done （表示必须或应该）： *I am to call them once I reach the airport.* 我一到机场就得给他们打电话。◇ *You are to report this to the police.* 你应该报警。◇ *What is to be done about this problem?* 该如何处理这个问题？ **6** **~ to do sth** used to say what is arranged to happen （表示已安排好要做的事）： *They are to be married in June.* 他们计划于六月份结婚。 **7** **~ to do sth** used to say what happened later （表示后来发生的事）： *He was to regret that decision for the rest of his life* (= he did regret it). 他终生都会后悔作出了那一决定。 **8** **~ not, never, etc. to be done** used to say what could not or did not happen （表示不会或没有发生时用）： *Anna was nowhere to be found* (= we could not find her anywhere). 我们到处都找不到安娜。◇ *He was never to see his wife again* (= although he did not know it would be so at the time, he did not see her again). 他注定再也见不到他的妻子了。◇ *She wanted to write a successful novel, but* ***it was not to be*** (= it turned out never to happen). 她曾想写一部成功的小说，但从未如愿。 **9** **if sb/it were to do sth… | were sb/it to do sth…** (*formal*) used to express a condition （表述条件）： *If we were to offer you more money, would you stay?* 假如我们给你加钱，你愿意留下吗？ ◇ *Were we to offer you more money, would you stay?* 假如我们给你加钱，你愿意留下吗？

be- /bɪ/ *prefix* **1** (in verbs 构成动词) to make or treat sb/sth as 使…变成；把…当作： *Don't belittle his achievements* (= say they are not important). 不要贬低他的成就。◇ *An older girl befriended me.* 一个年纪大些的女孩对我很友善。 **2** (in adjectives ending in *-ed* 构成以 -ed 结尾的形容词) wearing or covered with 穿着；戴着；裹着： *heavily bejewelled fingers* 戴满珠宝的手指 ◇ *bespattered with mud* 溅满污泥 **3** (in verbs and adjectives ending in *-ed* 构成以 -ed 结尾的动词和形容词) to cause sth to be 使；使成为： *The ship was becalmed* (= there was no wind so it could not move). 帆船因无风而停航。◇ *The rebels besieged the fort.* 叛乱者包围了城堡。 **4** used to turn INTRANSITIVE verbs (= without an object) into TRANSITIVE verbs (= with an object) （与不及物动词结合，构成及物动词）： *She is always bemoaning her lot.* 她总是怪命不好。 ➲ MORE LIKE THIS 6, page R25

beach /biːtʃ/ *noun, verb*

■ ***noun*** an area of sand or small stones (called SHINGLE), beside the sea or a lake 海滩；沙滩；海滨；湖滨： *tourists sunbathing on the beach* 在海滩上沐浴着阳光的游客 ◇ *a* ***sandy/pebble/shingle beach*** 细沙 / 卵石 / 砾石海滩 ◇ *a beach bar* 海滨酒吧 ➲ SYNONYMS AT COAST ➲ WORDFINDER NOTE AT COAST, SEA ➲ VISUAL VOCAB PAGE V5

■ ***verb*** [T, I] **~ (sth)** to come or bring sth out of the water and onto the beach （使）上岸；把…拖上岸： *He beached the boat and lifted the boy onto the shore.* 他把小船拖上岸，把男孩抱到海岸上。◇ *a beached whale* (= one that has become stuck on land and cannot get back into the water) 搁浅在海滩上的鲸

ˈbeach ball *noun* a large, light, coloured plastic ball that people play games with on the beach 沙滩球

ˈbeach buggy (*also* **ˈdune buggy**) *noun* a small car used for driving on sand 沙滩车

beach·comb·er /ˈbiːtʃkəʊmə(r); *NAmE* -koʊm-/ *noun* a person who walks along beaches collecting interesting or valuable things, either for pleasure or to sell 海滩拾荒者（或寻宝的人）

beach·front /ˈbiːtʃfrʌnt/ (*often* **the beachfront**) *noun* [sing.] (*especially NAmE*) the part of a town facing the beach

滨海区；滨湖区；滨水区：*beachfront hotels/apartments* 海滨旅馆 / 公寓

beach·head /ˈbiːtʃhed/ *noun* a strong position on a beach from which an army that has just landed prepares to go forward and attack （军队的）滩头堡，滩头阵地 ➲ SEE ALSO BRIDGEHEAD (1)

ˌbeach ˈvolleyball *noun* [U] a form of VOLLEYBALL played on sand by teams of two players 沙滩排球

beach·wear /ˈbiːtʃweə(r); *NAmE* -wer/ *noun* [U] (used especially in shops/stores 尤用于商店) clothes for wearing on the beach 沙滩服装

bea·con /ˈbiːkən/ *noun* **1** a light that is placed somewhere to guide vehicles and warn them of danger （指引车船等的）灯标，灯塔，立标：*a navigation beacon* 航标灯 ◇ (*figurative*) *He was **a beacon of hope** for the younger generation.* 他是年轻一代的希望之灯。 ➲ SEE ALSO BELISHA BEACON **2** a radio station whose signal helps ships and aircraft to find their position （导航）无线电信标台 **3** (in the past) a fire lit on top of a hill as a signal （旧时）烽火

bead /biːd/ *noun* **1** [C] a small piece of glass, wood, etc. with a hole through it, that can be put on a string with others of the same type and worn as jewellery, etc. （有孔的）珠子：*a necklace of wooden beads* 一条木珠项链 ◇ *A bead curtain separated the two rooms.* 一挂珠帘子把两个房间分开。 ➲ VISUAL VOCAB PAGE V70 ➲ SEE ALSO WORRY BEADS **2 beads** [pl.] a ROSARY （天主教徒念经时用的）数珠，念珠 **3** [C] a small drop of liquid （液体的）小滴：*There were beads of sweat on his forehead.* 他的额头上挂满汗珠。

IDM **draw/get a ˈbead on sb/sth** (*especially NAmE*) to aim carefully at sb/sth before shooting a gun （射击前）瞄准

bead·ed /ˈbiːdɪd/ *adj.* **1** decorated with beads 饰以珠子的：*a beaded dress* 缀着珠子的连衣裙 **2 ~ with sth** with small drops of a liquid on it 带着小滴液体的：*His face was beaded with sweat.* 他脸上挂着汗珠子。

bead·ing /ˈbiːdɪŋ/ *noun* [U] **1** a strip of wood, stone or plastic with a pattern on it, used for decorating walls, doors and furniture 串珠状缘饰 **2** beads that are sewn together and used as a decoration on clothes （衣服上的）串珠饰

beady /ˈbiːdi/ *adj.* (of eyes 眼睛) small, round and bright; watching everything closely or with suspicion 小圆珠般且亮晶晶的；机警的：(*BrE*) *I shall certainly **keep a beady eye** on his behaviour.* 我一定会时刻睁大眼睛提防他的行为。

ˌbeady-ˈeyed *adj.* (*informal*) watching carefully and noticing every small detail 机警地盯着的；目光锐利的

bea·gle /ˈbiːɡl/ *noun* a small dog with short legs, used in hunting 小猎兔狗

beak 🔑 /biːk/ *noun* **1** 🔑 the hard pointed or curved outer part of a bird's mouth 鸟喙 **SYN** **bill**: *The gull held the fish in its beak.* 海鸥嘴里叼着鱼。 ➲ VISUAL VOCAB PAGE V12 **2** (*humorous*) a person's nose, especially when it is large and/or pointed 鹰钩鼻；尖鼻；鼻子 **3** (*old-fashioned, BrE, slang*) a person in a position of authority, especially a judge 掌权者；（尤指）法官

beaked /biːkt/ *adj.* (usually in compounds 通常构成复合词) having a beak, or the type of beak mentioned 有…喙的：*flat-beaked* 扁平喙的 ➲ MORE LIKE THIS 8, page R25

bea·ker /ˈbiːkə(r)/ *noun* **1** (*BrE*) a plastic or paper cup, often without a handle, used for drinking from （常指无柄的）塑料杯，纸杯 ➲ VISUAL VOCAB PAGES V23, V25 **2** (*BrE*) the amount contained in a beaker 一杯（的量）：*a beaker of coffee* 一杯咖啡 **3** a glass cup with straight sides and a lip, used in chemistry, for example for measuring liquids 烧杯 ➲ VISUAL VOCAB PAGE V72

beam /biːm/ *noun, verb*

■ *noun* **1** a line of light, electric waves or PARTICLES 光线；（电波的）波束；（粒子的）束：*narrow **beams of light/sunlight*** 一丝丝的光线 / 阳光 ◇ *the beam of a torch/flashlight* 手电筒光柱 ◇ *a laser/electron beam* 激光束；电子束 ◇ (*BrE*) *The car's headlights were on **full beam*** (= shining as brightly as possible and not directed downwards). 那辆汽车大开着前灯。◇ (*NAmE*) *a car with its **high beams** on* 前灯大开着的汽车 **2** a long piece of wood, metal, etc. used to support weight, especially as part of the roof in a building 梁：*The cottage had exposed oak beams.* 小屋的橡木梁裸露着。 **3** (*especially BrE*) (*NAmE usually* **ˈbalance beam**) a wooden bar that is used in the sport of GYMNASTICS for people to move and balance on 平衡木 **4** a wide and happy smile 笑容；眉开眼笑：*a beam of satisfaction* 满意的笑容 ➲ WORDFINDER NOTE AT EXPRESSION

IDM **off ˈbeam** (*informal*) not correct; wrong 不正确；错误：*Your calculation is way off beam.* 你的计算完全错误。

■ *verb* **1** [I, T, no passive] to have a big happy smile on your face 笑容满面；眉开眼笑：**~ (at sb)** *He beamed at the journalists.* 他笑容满面地面对记者。◇ **~ (with sth)** *She was positively beaming with pleasure.* 她的确喜不自胜。◇ **~ sth (at sb)** *The barman beamed a warm smile at her.* 酒吧侍者对她热情地微笑。 ◇ *'I'd love to come,' she beamed* (= said with a large smile). "我很乐意来。"她满面笑容地说。 **2** [T] **+ adv./prep.** to send radio or television signals over long distances using electronic equipment 发射（电波）；播送：*Live pictures of the ceremony were beamed around the world.* 典礼的实况经电视直播传到世界各地。 **3** [I] **+ adv./prep.** to produce a stream of light and/or heat 照射；发光；发热：*The morning sun beamed down on us.* 早上的太阳照射着我们。◇ *Light beamed through a hole in the curtain.* 光线透过窗帘上的一个孔照射进来。 **IDM** SEE EAR

PHR V **ˌbeam sb ˈdown/ˈup** (in SCIENCE FICTION stories) to transport sb to or from a SPACESHIP using special electronic equipment 发送某人下来 / 上去（用特殊的电子设备将人运送至太空飞船或从太空飞船运送至其他地方）

ORIGIN From the American television series *Star Trek*. 源自美国电视剧《星际迷航》。

beamed /biːmd/ *adj.* having beams of wood 有木梁的：*a high beamed ceiling* 木梁高高支撑着的天花板

bean /biːn/ *noun, verb*

■ *noun* **1** a seed, or POD containing seeds, of a climbing plant, eaten as a vegetable. There are several types of bean and the plants that they grow on are also called beans. 豆；菜豆；豆荚；豆科植物：*broad beans* 蚕豆 ◇ *runner beans* 红花菜豆 ◇ *beans* (= BAKED BEANS) *on toast* 面包片加烘豆 ➲ VISUAL VOCAB PAGE V34 **2** (usually in compounds 通常构成复合词) a seed from a coffee plant, or some other plants （咖啡树或其他某些植物的）籽实：***coffee/cocoa beans*** 咖啡豆；可可豆 ➲ SEE ALSO JELLY BEAN

IDM **full of ˈbeans/ˈlife** (of a person 人) having a lot of energy 精力充沛 **not have a ˈbean** (*BrE, informal*) to have no money 没钱；不名一文 ➲ MORE AT HILL, KNOW *v.*, SPILL *v.*

■ *verb* **~ sb** (*NAmE, informal*) to hit sb on the head 击中（某人）头部：*I got beaned by a rock someone threw.* 我的头被扔出的石头砸中了。

bean·bag /ˈbiːnbæɡ/ *noun* **1** a very large bag made of cloth and filled with small pieces of plastic, used for sitting on 豆袋坐垫（内填碎塑料） **2** a small bag made of cloth filled with beans or small pieces of plastic and used as a ball 豆子袋（内填豆粒或碎塑料的小布袋，当作球玩）

ˈbean counter *noun* (*informal, disapproving*) a person who works with money, for example as an ACCOUNTANT and who wants to keep strict control of how much money a company spends 精打细算的账房先生；"铁公鸡"会计

ˈbean curd *noun* [U] = TOFU

bean·feast /ˈbiːnfiːst/ *noun* (*old-fashioned, BrE*) a party or celebration 聚会；喜庆

beanie /ˈbiːni/ *noun* a small, round close-fitting hat 无檐小便帽 ➲ VISUAL VOCAB PAGE V70

B

beano /ˈbiːnəʊ; *NAmE* -noʊ/ *noun* (*pl.* **-os**) (*old-fashioned, BrE, informal*) a party 招待会；聚会；宴会

bean·pole /ˈbiːnpəʊl; *NAmE* -poʊl/ *noun* (*informal, usually disapproving*) a tall thin person 瘦高个子

ˈ**bean sprouts** *noun* [pl.] BEAN seeds that are just beginning to grow, often eaten raw 豆芽 ➲ VISUAL VOCAB PAGE V34

bean·stalk /ˈbiːnstɔːk/ *noun* the tall fast-growing STEM of a BEAN plant 豆茎

bear /beə(r); *NAmE* ber/ *verb, noun*

■ *verb* (**bore** /bɔː(r)/, **borne** /bɔːn; *NAmE* bɔːrn/)

• ACCEPT/DEAL WITH 承受；应付 **1** [T] (used with *can/could* in negative sentences and questions 在否定句和疑问句中与 can / could 连用) to be able to accept and deal with sth unpleasant 承受；忍受 SYN **stand**: **~ sth** *The pain was almost more than he could bear.* 这种痛苦几乎使他无法忍受。◇ *She* ***couldn't bear the thought of*** *losing him.* 失去他的情景她想都不敢想。◇ **~ doing sth** *I can't bear having cats in the house.* 家里有猫我可受不了。◇ *He can't bear being laughed at.* 他无法忍受遭人嘲笑。◇ **~ to do sth** *He can't bear to be laughed at.* 他无法忍受遭人嘲笑。◇ **~ sb doing sth** *I can't bear you doing that.* 我无法忍受你做那种事。➲ SYNONYMS AT HATE

• NOT BE SUITABLE 不合适 **2** [T] **not ~** to not be suitable for sth 不适于某事（或做某事）: **~ sth** *Her later work* ***does not bear comparison*** *with her earlier novels* (= because it is not nearly as good). 她后期的作品比不上她早期的小说。◇ *The plan* ***won't bear*** *close* ***inspection*** (= it will be found to be unacceptable when carefully examined). 这项计划经不起推敲。◇ **~ doing sth** *The joke* ***doesn't bear repeating*** (= because it is not funny or may offend people). 这个笑话不可说第二遍（因为不好笑或可能得罪人）。◇ *His sufferings* ***don't bear thinking about*** (= because they are so terrible). 他遭受的苦难不堪回首。

• BE RESPONSIBLE FOR STH 负责 **3** [T] **~ sth** (*formal*) to take responsibility for sth 承担责任: *She* ***bore the responsibility*** *for most of the changes.* 她对大多数变革负责。◇ *Do parents have to* ***bear the*** *whole* ***cost*** *of tuition fees?* 父母是否应当负担全部学费？◇ *You shouldn't have to* ***bear the blame*** *for other people's mistakes.* 你本不必代人受过。

• NEGATIVE FEELING 坏心情 **4** [T] to have a feeling, especially a negative feeling心怀（感情，尤指坏心情）: **~ sth (against/towards sb)** *He* ***bears no resentment*** *towards them.* 他对他们毫无怨恨。◇ *He's* ***borne a grudge*** *against me ever since that day.* 从那一天起他便对我怀恨在心。◇ **~ sb sth** *He's* ***borne me a grudge*** *ever since that day.* 从那一天起他便对我怀恨在心。◇ *She* ***bore him no ill will.*** 她对他没有恶意。

• SUPPORT WEIGHT 支撑重量 **5** [T] **~ sth** to support the weight of sb/sth 支撑，承受（重量）: *The ice is too thin to bear your weight.* 冰太薄，承受不住你的重量。

• SHOW 显示 **6** [T] **~ sth** (*formal*) to show sth; to carry sth so that it can be seen 显示；带有: *The document bore her signature.* 文件上有她的签字。◇ *He was badly wounded in the war and still bears the scars.* 他在战争中负了重伤，现在还留有伤疤。◇ *She* ***bears little resemblance to*** (= is not much like) *her mother.* 她很不像她的母亲。◇ *The title of the essay* ***bore little relation to*** (= was not much connected with) *the contents.* 这篇文章的题目与内容很不相符。

• NAME 名称 **7** [T] **~ sth** (*formal*) to have a particular name 有（某个名称）: *a family that bore an ancient and honoured name* 名门世家

• CARRY 携带 **8** [T] **~ sb/sth** (*old-fashioned* or *formal*) to carry sb/sth, especially while moving 携带: *three kings bearing gifts* 三个带着礼品的国王

• YOURSELF 自身 **9** [T] **~ yourself well, etc.** (*formal*) to move, behave or act in a particular way 举止；表现: *He bears himself* (= stands, walks, etc.) *proudly, like a soldier.* 他昂首阔步，像个军人。◇ *She bore herself with dignity throughout the funeral.* 整个葬礼过程中她都保持着尊严。

• CHILD 孩子 **10** [T] (*formal*) to give birth to a child 生（孩子）: **~ sth** *She was not able to bear children.* 她不能生育。◇ **~ sb sth** *She had borne him six sons.* 她为他生了六个儿子。

• OF TREES/PLANTS 树木花草 **11** [T] **~ sth** (*formal*) to produce flowers or fruit 开（花）；结（果实）

• TURN 转向 **12** [I] **~ (to the) left, north, etc.** to go or turn in the direction mentioned 转向（左或北等）: *When you get to the fork in the road, bear right.* 走到岔道时向右拐。

IDM **bear ˈarms** (*old use*) to be a soldier; to fight 当兵；打仗 **bear ˈfruit** to have a successful result 成功；取得成果 **bear ˈhard, ˈheavily, seˈverely, etc. on sb** (*formal*) to be a cause of difficulty or suffering to sb 使为难；使受苦；压迫: *Taxation bears heavily on us all.* 赋税给我们大家带来沉重的负担。 **be borne ˈin on sb** (*formal, especially BrE*) to be realized by sb, especially after a period of time（逐渐被某人）认识到: *It was gradually borne in on us that defeat was inevitable.* 我们逐渐认识到，失败是不可避免的。 **bring sth to bear (on sb/sth)** (*formal*) to use energy, pressure, influence, etc. to try to achieve sth or make sb do sth 把精力用于；对…施加压力（或影响等）: *We must bring all our energies to bear upon the task.* 我们必须全力以赴不辱使命。◇ ***Pressure was brought to bear on us to finish the work on time.*** 我们得按时完成工作，没有回旋余地。➲ MORE AT BRUNT, CROSS *n.*, GRIN *v.*, MIND *n.*, WITNESS *n.*

PHR V ˌ**bear ˈdown on sb/sth 1** (*BrE*) to move quickly towards sb/sth in a determined or threatening way 冲向；咄咄逼近 **2** (*especially NAmE*) to press on sb/sth 施加压力于；压住: *Bear down on it with all your strength so it doesn't move.* 用全力压住它，别让它动弹。 ˈ**bear on sth** (*formal*) to relate to sth 和（某事物）有关；涉及 SYN **affect**: *These are matters that bear on the welfare of the community.* 这些是关系到整个社群的福祉的事情。 ˌ**bear sb/sth↔ˈout** (*especially BrE*) to show that sb is right or that sth is true 证实；为…作证: *The other witnesses will bear me out.* 其他证人将给我作证。◇ *The other witnesses will bear out what I say.* 其他证人将会证实我的话。 ˌ**bear ˈup (against/under sth)** to remain as cheerful as possible during a difficult time 保持振作；承受；挺住: *He's bearing up well under the strain of losing his job.* 他坚强地顶住了失业的压力。◇ *'How are you?' 'Bearing up.'* "你怎么样了？""还挺得住。" ˈ**bear with sb/sth** to be patient with sb/sth 耐心对待；容忍: *She's under a lot of strain. Just bear with her.* 她承受着很大的压力。对她容忍一下。◇ *If you will bear with me* (= be patient and listen to me) *a little longer, I'll answer your question.* 你如果能耐心点听我把话说完，我会回答你的问题的。

■ *noun* **1** a heavy wild animal with thick fur and sharp CLAWS (= pointed parts on the ends of its feet). There are many types of bear. 熊: *a black bear* 黑熊 ➲ SEE ALSO GRIZZLY BEAR, POLAR BEAR, TEDDY BEAR **2** (*finance* 财) a person who sells shares in a company, etc., hoping to buy them back later at a lower price（在证券市场等）卖空的人 ➲ COMPARE BULL (3) ➲ SEE ALSO BEARISH

IDM **like a bear with a sore ˈhead** (*informal*) bad-tempered or in a bad-tempered way 急性子；脾气暴躁

bear·able /ˈbeərəbl; *NAmE* ˈber-/ *adj.* a person or thing that is **bearable** can be accepted or dealt with 可忍受的；能应付的: *She was the only thing that made life bearable.* 只因有了她，生活才可以过得下去。 OPP **unbearable**

beard /bɪəd; *NAmE* bɪrd/ *noun, verb*

■ *noun* [C, U] hair that grows on the chin and cheeks of a man's face; similar hair that grows on some animals（人的）胡须，络腮胡子；（动物的）颔毛，须: *He has decided to grow a beard and a moustache.* 他已经决定留起胡子。◇ *a week's growth of beard* 一星期未刮的胡子 ◇ *a goat's beard* 山羊的胡子 ➲ COLLOCATIONS AT PHYSICAL ➲ VISUAL VOCAB PAGE V65 ➲ COMPARE MOUSTACHE ▶ **beard·ed** *adj.*: *a bearded face/man* 有胡子的脸 / 男子

■ *verb*

IDM **to beard the lion in his ˈden** to go to see an important or powerful person to tell them that you disagree with them, that you want sth, etc. 进狮穴捋狮须（敢于触犯有权势者）

beardie /ˈbɪədi; *NAmE* ˈbɪrdi/ *noun* (*BrE, informal*) a man with a beard, espeially one that you think lacks style 蓄须的男子；大胡子

bear·er /ˈbeərə(r); *NAmE* ˈber-/ *noun* **1** a person whose job is to carry sth, especially at a ceremony（尤指在仪式中）持…者，抬…者： *coffin bearers* 扶灵者 ➲ SEE ALSO PALL-BEARER, RING BEARER, STANDARD-BEARER, STRETCHER-BEARER **2** a person who brings a message, a letter, etc. 传达消息者；送信人： *I'm sorry to be the bearer of bad news.* 很遗憾我带来了坏消息。 **3** (*formal*) a person who has sth with them or is the official owner of sth, such as a document 持有者；正式持有人；持票人： *A pass will allow the bearer to enter the building.* 持有通行证者方可进入这栋大楼。 **4** a person who has knowledge of sth, such as an idea or a tradition, and makes sure that it is not forgotten, by teaching others about it（观念、传统等的）传授者，传播者

ˈ**bear hug** *noun* an act of showing affection for sb by holding them very tightly and strongly in your arms 紧紧的（或热烈的）拥抱；熊抱

bear·ing /ˈbeərɪŋ; *NAmE* ˈber-/ *noun* **1** [U] **~ on sth** the way in which sth is related to sth or influences it 关系；影响： *Recent events had no bearing on our decision.* 近期的事件与我们的决定没有关系。 ◇ *Regular exercise has a direct bearing on fitness and health.* 经常性锻炼对于身体健康有直接影响。 **2** [sing.] the way in which you stand, walk or behave 姿态；举止： *Her whole bearing was alert.* 她整个人保持着戒备状态。 **3** [C] (*specialist*) a direction measured from a fixed point using a COMPASS（用罗盘测定的）方位 **4** [C] (*specialist*) a part of a machine that supports a moving part, especially one that is turning（机器的）支座；（尤指）轴承 ➲ SEE ALSO BALL BEARING

IDM **get/find/take your ˈbearings** to make yourself familiar with your surroundings in order to find out where you are or to feel comfortable in a place 判明方位；弄清自己所处的地位；熟悉环境 **lose your ˈbearings** to become lost or confused 迷失方向；陷入困惑

bear·ish /ˈbeərɪʃ; *NAmE* ˈber-/ *adj.* (*finance* 财) showing or expecting a fall in the prices of shares 熊市的；（证券市场）看跌的： *a bearish market* 跌市 ◇ *Japanese banks remain bearish.* 日本银行继续看跌。 ➲ COMPARE BULLISH (2)

ˈ**bear market** *noun* (*finance* 财) a period during which people are selling shares, etc. rather than buying, because they expect the prices to fall 熊市（预期价格下跌而售出股票的一段时期） ➲ COMPARE BULL MARKET

bear·skin /ˈbeəskɪn; *NAmE* ˈbers-/ *noun* **1** the skin and fur of a BEAR 熊皮： *a bearskin rug* 熊皮地毯 **2** a tall hat of black fur worn for special ceremonies by some British soldiers 熊皮高帽；英国禁卫军帽

beast /biːst/ *noun* **1** (*old-fashioned* or *formal*) an animal, especially one that is large or dangerous, or one that is unusual（尤指大型或凶猛、独特的）动物，兽： ***wild/savage/ferocious beasts*** 野兽；猛兽 ◇ ***mythical beasts*** *such as unicorns and dragons* 独角兽和龙之类的神话动物 **2** a person who is cruel and whose behaviour is uncontrolled 性情凶残的人；行为粗暴的人 SYN **animal** **3** (*informal, often humorous*) an unpleasant person or thing 讨厌的人（或事物）： *The maths exam was a real beast.* 数学考试实在令人讨厌。 **4** (*informal*) a thing of a particular kind（某种）东西 SYN **animal**: *His new guitar is a very expensive beast.* 他的新吉他贵得吓人。

beast·ly /ˈbiːstli/ *adj.* (*old-fashioned, BrE, informal*) unpleasant 恶劣的；讨厌的；令人厌恶的 SYN **horrible, nasty** ▸ **beast·li·ness** *noun* [U]

ˌ**beast of ˈburden** *noun* an animal used for heavy work such as carrying or pulling things 役畜；牲口；驮兽

beat 🔑 /biːt/ *verb, noun, adj.*

■ *verb* (**beat, beaten** /ˈbiːtn/)

• **IN GAME** 比赛 **1** 🔑 [T] **~ sb (at sth)** to defeat sb in a game or competition（在比赛或竞争中）赢，打败（某人）： *He beat me at chess.* 他下棋赢了我。 ◇ *Their recent wins have proved they're still **the ones to beat*** (= the most difficult team to beat). 他们最近的胜利已证明，他们仍然是最难打败的队。

• **CONTROL** 控制 **2** 🔑 [T] **~ sth** (*informal*) to get control of sth 控制： *The government's main aim is to beat inflation.* 政府的主要目标是抑制通货膨胀。

• **BE TOO DIFFICULT** 太难 **3** 🔑 [T] (*informal*) to be too difficult for sb 难倒 SYN **defeat**: **~ sb** *a problem that beats even the experts* 连专家都难以解决的问题 ◇ **~ sb why, how, etc....** ***It beats me*** (= I don't know) *why he did it.* 我弄不懂他为什么这样做。 ◇ ***What beats me*** *is how it was done so quickly* (= I don't understand how). 使我困惑不解的是，这事怎么这么快就完成了。

• **BE BETTER** 更好 **4** 🔑 [T] **~ sth** (*rather informal*) to do or be better than sth 比…更好；赛过；胜过： ***Nothing beats*** *home cooking.* 什么也比不上家里做的好吃。 ◇ ***You can't beat*** *Italian shoes.* 意大利鞋是无与伦比的。 ◇ *They want to **beat the speed record*** (= go faster than anyone before). 他们想打破这一速度纪录。

• **AVOID** 避免 **5** [T] **~ sth** (*informal*) to avoid sth 避免；逃避： *If we go early we should beat the traffic.* 我们早点出发应该就可以避开交通拥挤。 ◇ *We were up and off early to **beat the heat**.* 我们很早就起床出发了，趁天还没热。

• **HIT** 击打 **6** 🔑 [I, T] to hit sb/sth many times, usually very hard 敲打；锤砸： **+ adv./prep.** *Somebody was beating at the door.* 有人在打门。 ◇ *Hailstones beat against the*

▼ **SYNONYMS 同义词辨析**

beat

batter • pound • lash • hammer

These words all mean to hit sb/sth many times, especially hard. 以上各词均含多次击打之义，尤指用力打。

beat to hit sb/sth a lot of times, especially very hard 指反复敲打、使劲锤砸： *Someone was beating at the door.* 有人在打门。 ◇ *A young man was found beaten to death last night.* 昨天夜里有人发现一名小伙子被打死了。 ◇ *At that time, children were often beaten for quite minor offences* (= as a punishment). 那时候孩子们常常因为很小的过错而挨打。

batter to hit sb/sth hard a lot of times, especially in way that causes serious injury or damage 指连续猛击，尤指造成伤害或破坏： *He had been badly battered around the head and face.* 他被打得鼻青脸肿。 ◇ *Severe winds have been battering the coast.* 狂风一直在海岸肆虐。

pound to hit sb/sth hard a lot of times, especially in a way that makes a lot of noise 指连续猛击，尤指发出砰砰的撞击声： *Heavy rain pounded on the roof.* 暴雨砰砰地砸在屋顶上。

lash to hit sb/sth with a lot of force 指猛击、狠打： *The rain lashed at the window.* 雨点猛烈地打在窗户上。 NOTE The subject of **lash** is often *rain, wind, hail, sea* or *waves*. * lash 的主语常为 rain、wind、hail、sea 或 waves。

hammer to hit sb/sth hard a lot of times, in a way that is noisy or violent 指大声、猛烈地反复敲打、连续击打： *He hammered the door with his fists.* 他不断地用拳头擂门。

POUND OR HAMMER? 用 pound 还是 hammer?

There is not much difference in meaning between these two, but to **pound** is sometimes a steadier action. To **hammer** can be more violent and it is often used figuratively. 这两个词意思差别不大，但 pound 有时指较匀速而稳定地击打；hammer 更猛烈，且常用作比喻。

PATTERNS

- to beat/batter/pound/lash/hammer sb/sth **with** sth
- to beat/batter/pound/lash/hammer **against** sth
- to beat/batter/pound/hammer **on** sth
- to beat/batter/hammer sth **down**
- the **rain/wind/sea** beats/batters/pounds/lashes (at) sth

window. 冰雹不断地砸在窗户上。◇ **~ sth** *Someone was beating a drum.* 有人在敲鼓。◇ **~ sth + adv./prep.** *She was beating dust out of the carpet* (= removing dust from the carpet by beating it). 她正在拍掉地毯上的灰尘。◇ **~ sb** *At that time children were regularly beaten for quite minor offences* (= a punishment). 那时候孩子们常常因为很小的过错而挨打。◇ **~ sb + adv./prep.** *An elderly man was found* ***beaten to death.*** 有人发现一名老翁被打死了。◇ **~ sb + adj.** *They beat him unconscious* (= hit him until he became unconscious). 他们把他打得不省人事。

- **OF HEART/DRUMS/WINGS** 心脏；鼓；翅膀 **7** [I, T] to make, or cause sth to make, a regular sound or movement （使）规律作响，做规律性运动：*She's alive—her* ***heart is still beating.*** 她没死，她的心还在跳动。◇ *We heard the* ***drums beating.*** 我们听到击鼓声。◇ *The bird was* ***beating its wings*** (= moving them up and down) *frantically.* 鸟儿没命地扑着翅膀。
- **MIX** 搅拌 **8** [T] to mix sth with short quick movements with a fork, etc. （用叉等）快速搅拌，打：**~ sth (up)** *Beat the eggs up to a frothy consistency.* 把鸡蛋打成黏稠泡沫状。◇ **~ A and B together** *Beat the flour and milk together.* 把面粉和牛奶搅拌在一起。
- **SHAPE METAL** 使金属成形 **9** [T] to change the shape of sth, especially metal, by hitting it with a hammer , etc. 把（金属等）锤成；敲打（成…）：**~ sth (out) (into sth)** *beaten silver* 银箔 ◇ *The gold is beaten out into thin strips.* 金子被锤成了薄薄的长条。◇ **~ sth + adj.** *The metal had been beaten flat.* 那块金属被锤平了。
- **MAKE PATH** 开辟路径 **10** [T] **~ sth (through, across, along, etc. sth)** to make a path, etc. by walking somewhere or by pressing branches down and walking over them 踏出，踩出（道路）：*a well-beaten track* (= one that has been worn hard by much use) 经过很多人踏出来的路 ◇ *The hunters beat a path through the undergrowth.* 猎人们在灌木丛中踩出了一条小径。

IDM **beat about the 'bush** (*BrE*) (*NAmE* **beat around the 'bush**) to talk about sth for a long time without coming to the main point 拐弯抹角地讲话；绕圈子：*Stop beating about the bush and tell me what you want.* 别绕来绕去了，告诉我你想要什么吧。 **beat sb at their own 'game** to defeat or do better than sb in an activity which they have chosen or in which they think they are strong 赢某人的看家本领；打败某人的强项 **beat your 'brains out** (*informal, especially NAmE*) to think very hard about sth for a long time 绞尽脑汁；反复推敲 **beat your 'breast** to show that you feel sorry about sth that you have done, especially in public and in an exaggerated way 捶胸顿足（尤指对自己的作为刻意表示悲伤或愧疚） **beat the 'clock** to finish a task, race, etc. before a particular time 提前完成任务（或跑到终点等） **'beat it** (*slang*) (usually used in orders 通常用于命令) to go away immediately 滚开；立即走开：*This is private land, so beat it!* 这里是私人土地，滚开！ **beat a path to sb's 'door** if a lot of people **beat a path to sb's door**, they are all interested in sth that person has to sell, or can do or tell them 使门庭若市；蜂拥而至；使成注意焦点：*Top theatrical agents are beating a path to the teenager's door.* 顶尖级演员经纪正纷纷把目光投向那个青少年。 **beat the 'rap** (*NAmE, slang*) to escape without being punished 逃脱惩罚 **beat a (hasty) re'treat** to go away or back quickly, especially to avoid sth unpleasant （仓促）逃走；（慌忙）撤退 **beat 'time (to sth)** to mark or follow the rhythm of music, by waving a stick, tapping your foot, etc. （随着音乐）打拍子：*She beat time with her fingers.* 她用手指打拍子。 **beat sb to the 'punch** (*informal*) to get or do sth before sb else can 抢先下手；抢在前面 **can you beat that/it!** (*informal*) used to express surprise or anger 难以置信；太不像话 **if you can't beat them, 'join them** (*saying*) if you cannot defeat sb or be as successful as they are, then it is more sensible to join them in what they are doing and perhaps get some advantage for yourself by doing so 打不赢，就投靠 **,off the ,beaten 'track** far away from other people, houses, etc. 远离闹市；偏远：*They live miles off the beaten track.* 他们住在偏远地带。 **a rod/stick to 'beat sb with** a fact, an argument, etc. that is used in order to blame or punish sb 用以责备或惩罚某人的事实依据（或把柄等） **take some 'beating** to be difficult to beat 难以超越：*That score is going to take some beating.* 那一得分将很难超过。◇ *For sheer luxury, this hotel takes some beating.* 单看豪华的程度，这家旅馆是难以超越的。➲ MORE AT BLACK *adj.*, DAYLIGHTS, DRUM *n.*, HELL

PHR V **,beat sth↔'down** to hit a door, etc. many times until it breaks open 砸开，砸破（门等） **,beat 'down (on sb/sth)** if the sun **beats down**, it shines with great heat （阳光）强烈照射，晒 **,beat sb/sth 'down (to sth)** to persuade sb to reduce the price at which they are selling sth 说服某人降价；杀价：*He wanted $8 000 for the car but I beat him down to $6 000.* 他那辆汽车要价 8 000 美元，但我压到了 6 000 美元。◇ *I beat down the price to $6 000.* 我把价杀到了 6 000 美元。 **,beat 'off** (*NAmE, taboo, slang*) to MASTURBATE 手淫 **,beat sb/sth↔'off** to force sb/sth back or away by fighting 击退；驱走：*The attacker was beaten off.* 袭击者被击退了。◇ *She beat off a challenge to her leadership.* 她击退了对她的领导地位的质疑。 **'beat on sb** = BEAT UP ON SB **,beat sth↔'out** **1** to produce a rhythm by hitting sth many times 敲打出节奏 **2** to put a fire out by beating 扑打灭（火）：*We beat the flames out.* 我们把火扑打灭了。 **3** to remove sth by hitting it with a HAMMER, etc. 敲掉；锤平：*They can beat out the dent in the car's wing.* 他们能把汽车挡泥板上的凹痕敲平。 **,beat sth 'out of sb** to hit sb until they tell you what you want to know 殴打某人逼其说出 **'beat sb out of sth** (*NAmE, informal*) to cheat sb by taking sth from them （从某人）骗取，骗得：*Her brother beat her out of $200.* 她哥哥骗走了她 200 美元。 **'beat sb to sth/… | ,beat sb 'to it** to get somewhere or do sth before sb else 抢先；捷足先登：*She beat me to the top of the hill.* 她比我先到达山顶。◇ *I was about to take the last cake, but he beat me to it.* 我正要拿那最后一块蛋糕，却给他抢先一步。 **,beat sb↔'up** to hit or kick sb hard, many times 痛殴；毒打：*He was badly beaten up by a gang of thugs.* 他被一帮暴徒打得遍体鳞伤。 **,beat 'up on sb** (*also* **'beat on sb**) (*NAmE*) to blame sb too much for sth 过分责备：*Don't beat up on Paul, he tried his best.* 不要过分责备保罗，他已经尽力了。 **,beat yourself 'up (about/over sth)** (*also* **,beat 'up on yourself (about/over sth)**) (*NAmE, informal*) to blame yourself too much for sth （为某事）过分自责：*Look, there's no need to beat yourself up over this.* 听我说，没有必要为此过分自责。

■ ***noun***

- **OF DRUMS/HEART/WINGS** 鼓；心脏；翅膀 **1** [C] a single blow to sth, such as a drum, or a movement of sth, such as your heart; the sound that this makes （鼓的）一击；（翅的）一振；（心脏等的）跳动；击鼓声；振翅声；跳动声：*several loud beats on the drum* 几下隆隆鼓声 ◇ (*figurative*) *His heart missed a beat when he saw her.* 他在见到她的一刹那心跳顿了一下。 **2** [sing.] a series of regular blows to sth, such as a drum; the sound that this makes 有规律的敲击（声）：*the steady beat of the drums* 有节奏的敲鼓声 ➲ SEE ALSO HEARTBEAT
- **RHYTHM** 节奏 **3** [C] the main rhythm, or a unit of rhythm, in a piece of music, a poem, etc. （音乐、诗歌等的）主节奏，节拍：*This type of music has a strong beat to it.* 这种音乐节奏感很强。◇ *The piece has four beats to the bar.* 这首曲子每小节四拍。 ➲ **WORDFINDER NOTE** AT SING
- **OF POLICE OFFICER** 警察 **4** [C, usually sing.] the area that a police officer walks around regularly and which he or she is responsible for （警察）巡逻地段：*More police officers out* ***on the beat*** *may help to cut crime.* 增加巡逻的警察可能有助于减少罪行。 **IDM** SEE HEART, MARCH *v.*, WALK *v.*

■ ***adj.*** [not before noun] (*informal*) = DEAD BEAT

beat·box /'bi:tbɒks; *NAmE* -bɑ:ks/ *noun, verb*

■ ***noun*** **1** [C] (*informal*) an electronic machine that produces drum sounds 电子鼓 **2** [C] (*informal*) a radio, CD player, etc. that can be carried around and is used for playing loud music 播放重音乐的收音机（或 CD 播放机等）；重音乐播放机 **3** (*also* **beat·boxer**) [C] a person who uses the voice to make sounds like a drum to create the beat in HIP HOP （嘻哈音乐的）节奏口技表演者，口技说唱者 **4** [U] music that is created using sounds made with the human voice 人声敲击乐；节奏口技

B

■ ***verb*** [I] to imitate the sound of a drum with the voice 人声模仿鼓声；表演节奏口技

beat·box·ing /ˈbiːtbɒksɪŋ; *NAmE* -bɑːks-/ *noun* [U] the use of the human voice to create the beat in HIP HOP （嘻哈音乐的）节奏口技：*an amazing beatboxing performance* 令人惊叹的节奏口技表演

ˌbeaten-ˈup *adj.* = BEAT-UP

beat·er /ˈbiːtə(r)/ *noun* **1** (often in compounds 常构成复合词) a tool used for beating things 拍打器；搅拌器：*a carpet beater* 地毯拍子 ◇ *an egg beater* 打蛋器 **2** a person employed to drive birds and animals out of bushes, etc., into the open, so they can be shot for sport 驱猎物者（受雇将鸟兽从树丛中赶到开阔地供人射猎） **3 -beater** (in compounds 构成复合词) a person who hits someone 打…的人：*a wife-beater* 殴打妻子的人 **4** (*NAmE*) (*BrE* **bang·er**) (*informal*) an old car that is in bad condition 破旧的汽车 ➲ SEE ALSO WORLD-BEATER

the ˈbeat generation *noun* [sing.] a group of young people in the 1950s and early 1960s who rejected the way most people lived in society, wanted to express themselves freely, and liked modern JAZZ 垮掉的一代（指 20 世纪 50 年代和 60 年代初期拒绝主流生活方式、追求个性自我表现、喜爱现代爵士乐的一批年轻人）

bea·tif·ic /ˌbiːəˈtɪfɪk/ *adj.* (*formal*) showing great joy and peace 快乐安详的；幸福的：*a **beatific smile/expression*** 幸福的微笑 / 表情

be·atify /biˈætɪfaɪ/ *verb* (**be·ati·fies, be·ati·fy·ing, be·ati·fied, be·ati·fied**) **~ sb** (of the Pope 教皇) to give a dead person a special honour by stating officially that he/she is very holy 为（逝者）行宣福礼 ➲ COMPARE BLESS *v.*, CANONIZE ▶ **be·ati·fi·ca·tion** /biˌætɪfɪˈkeɪʃn/ *noun* [C, U]

beat·ing /ˈbiːtɪŋ/ *noun* **1** [C] an act of hitting sb hard and repeatedly, as a punishment or in a fight 狠打；揍；笞打：*to give sb a beating* 把某人揍一顿 **2** [C] (*informal*) a very heavy defeat 惨败；严重受挫：*The team has **taken** a few **beatings** this season.* 本赛季该队已经几次严重受挫。**3** [U] a series of regular blows to sth such as a drum, or movements of sth, such as your heart; the sound that this makes 有规律的敲打（声）；有节奏的运动（声）：*He could hear the beating of his own heart.* 他听得到自己的心跳。◇ *the **beating of drums/wings*** 敲鼓声；翅膀的拍打声

IDM **take some ˈbeating** (*BrE*) to be difficult to do or be better than 难以超越：*As a place to live, Oxford takes some beating.* 就居住环境而论，牛津市是个难得的好地方。

the Be·ati·tudes /biˈætɪtjuːd; *NAmE* -tuːd/ *noun* [pl.] (in the Bible 《圣经》) the eight statements made by Christ about people who are BLESSED 八福，真福八端（耶稣的山中圣训）

beat·nik /ˈbiːtnɪk/ *noun* a young person in the 1950s and early 1960s who rejected the way of life of ordinary society and showed this by behaving and dressing in a different way from most people “垮掉的一代”的一员（20 世纪 50 年代及 60 年代初摈弃传统生活与衣着的年轻人）

ˌbeat-ˈup (*also* **ˌbeaten-ˈup**) *adj.* [usually before noun] (*informal*) old and damaged 破旧的；破损的：*a beat-up old truck* 破旧的老卡车

beau /bəʊ; *NAmE* boʊ/ *noun* (*pl.* **beaux** or **beaus** /bəʊz; *NAmE* boʊz/) (*old-fashioned*) a woman's male lover or friend （女性的）男友，情郎

beau·coup /ˈbəʊkuː; *NAmE* ˈboʊ-/ *det.* (*US, informal, from French*) many or a lot 很多的：*You can spend beaucoup bucks* (= a lot of money) *on software.* 买软件会花掉很多钱。

the Beau·fort scale /ˈbəʊfət skeɪl; *NAmE* ˈboʊfərt/ *noun* [sing.] a range of numbers used for measuring how strongly the wind is blowing. The lowest number 0 means that there is no wind and the highest number 12 means that there is a HURRICANE (= a violent storm with very strong winds). 蒲福风级，蒲福风力等级（按风力大小分为 0 至 12 级）：*The storm measured 10 **on the Beaufort scale**.* 这次风暴按蒲福风级测量为 10 级。
ORIGIN From Sir Francis Beaufort, the English admiral who invented it. 源自发明此方法的英格兰海军上将弗朗西斯·蒲福爵士 (Sir Francis Beaufort)。

Beau·jo·lais /ˈbəʊʒəleɪ; *NAmE* ˌboʊʒəˈleɪ/ *noun* (*pl.* **Beau·jo·lais**) [C, U] a light wine, usually red, from the Beaujolais district of France 博若莱葡萄酒（通常为红色，醇度低，产于法国博若莱地区）

beaut /bjuːt/ *noun, adj., exclamation*
■ ***noun*** (*NAmE, AustralE, NZE, informal*) an excellent or beautiful person or thing 出众的人（或事物）；美人；美好的东西
■ ***adj., exclamation*** (*AustralE, informal*) excellent; very good 极好的；很棒的

beaut·eous /ˈbjuːtiəs/ *adj.* (*literary*) beautiful 美丽的；美好的

beaut·ician /bjuːˈtɪʃn/ *noun* a person, usually a woman, whose job is to give beauty treatments to the face and body 美容师

beau·ti·ful 🔑 /ˈbjuːtɪfl/ *adj.* **1** 🔑 having beauty; pleasing to the senses or to the mind 美丽的；美好的：*a beautiful woman/face/baby/voice/poem/smell/evening* 漂亮的女人 / 面孔 / 婴儿；美妙的声音 / 诗歌 / 香味 / 夜晚 ◇ *beautiful countryside/weather/music* 美丽的乡村；美好的天气；美妙的音乐 ➲ SYNONYMS ON NEXT PAGE **2** 🔑 very good or skilful 很好的；出色的；巧妙的：*What beautiful timing!* 时间把握得正好！

beau·ti·ful·ly 🔑 /ˈbjuːtɪfli/ *adv.* **1** 🔑 in a beautiful way 美好地；美妙地；漂亮地：*She sings beautifully.* 她唱歌很动听。◇ *a beautifully decorated house* 装潢典雅的房子 **2** 🔑 very well; in a pleasing way 很好；令人满意地：*It's all working out beautifully.* 一切进展都很顺利。

beaut·ify /ˈbjuːtɪfaɪ/ *verb* (**beau·ti·fies, beau·ti·fy·ing, beau·ti·fied, beau·ti·fied**) **~ sb/sth** to make sb/sth beautiful or more beautiful 美化；使更美丽

beauty 🔑 /ˈbjuːti/ *noun* (*pl.* **-ies**) **1** 🔑 [U] the quality of being pleasing to the senses or to the mind 美；美丽：*the **beauty of** the sunset/of poetry/of his singing* 落日 / 诗作 / 他的歌声之美 ◇ *a woman of great beauty* 大美人 ◇ *The woods were designated an **area of outstanding natural beauty**.* 这片森林被划定为超级自然美景区。◇ ***beauty products/treatment*** (= intended to make a person more beautiful) 美容产品；美容 **2** [C] a person or thing that is beautiful 美人；美好的东西：*She had been a beauty in her day.* 她年轻时是个美人。 **3** [C] an excellent example of its type 极好的榜样；典型的例子：*That last goal was a beauty!* 最后进的一球真绝！ **4** [C] a pleasing feature 好处；优点 SYN **advantage**：*One of the beauties of living here is that it's so peaceful.* 在这里生活的好处之一是安宁。◇ *The project will require very little work to start up; **that's the beauty of it**.* 这项工程几乎不需要启动工作，好就好在这里。

IDM **beauty is in the eye of the ˈbeholder** (*saying*) people all have different ideas about what is beautiful 情人眼里出西施；对美的判别因人而异 **beauty is only skin-ˈdeep** (*saying*) how a person looks is less important than their character 美貌不过一张皮；貌美不如心灵美

ˌBeauty and the ˈBeast *noun* **1** a traditional story about a young girl who saves a large ugly creature from a magic SPELL by her love. He becomes a HANDSOME prince and they get married. 美女与野兽（传说中少女用爱拯救丑陋的野兽使之摆脱魔法变成英俊王子，然后两人结婚） **2** (*informal, humorous*) two people of whom one is much more attractive than the other 美女与野兽（指相貌差别很大的两个人）

ˈbeauty contest *noun* (*BrE*) **1** a competition to choose the most beautiful from a group of women 选美比赛 ➲ COMPARE PAGEANT (2) **2** (*US* **ˌbeauty paˈrade**) an occasion on which several competing companies or people try to persuade sb to use their services “选美式”竞争（指互相竞争的公司或个人为说服某人采用其服务而举行的展示活动）

B

ˈ**beauty mark** *noun* (*NAmE*) = BEAUTY SPOT (2)

ˈ**beauty queen** *noun* a woman who is judged to be the most beautiful in a BEAUTY CONTEST 选美比赛冠军；选美王后

ˈ**beauty salon** (*also* ˈ**beauty parlour**) (*US also* ˈ**beauty shop**) *noun* a place where you can pay for treatment to your face, hair, nails, etc., which is intended to make you more beautiful 美容院

ˈ**beauty school** *noun* (*NAmE*) a place that trains people to cut hair, take care of nails, etc. as a job 美容学校

ˈ**beauty sleep** *noun* [U] (*humorous*) enough sleep at night to make sure that you look and feel healthy and beautiful 美容觉（夜间睡足以保持健康美丽）

▼ SYNONYMS 同义词辨析

beautiful

pretty • handsome • attractive • lovely • good-looking • gorgeous

These words all describe people who are pleasant to look at. 以上各词均形容人好看。

beautiful (especially of a woman or girl) very pleasant to look at （尤指女子或女孩）漂亮的，美丽的： *She looked stunningly beautiful that night.* 她那天晚上美极了。

pretty (especially of a girl or woman) pleasant to look at （尤指女孩或女子）漂亮的，俊俏的： *She's got a very pretty face.* 她有一张非常俏丽的脸。NOTE **Pretty** is used most often to talk about girls. When it is used to talk about a woman, it usually suggests that she is like a girl, with small, delicate features. * pretty 多形容女孩。如果形容女子，通常表示这女子像女孩一样小巧玲珑。

handsome (of a man) pleasant to look at; (of a woman) pleasant to look at, with large strong features rather than small delicate ones 指（男子）英俊的，漂亮的；（女子）健美的： *He was described as* ***'tall, dark and handsome'***. 他被描述为"高大黝黑、相貌堂堂"。

attractive (of a person) pleasant to look at, especially in a sexual way 指（人）性感的、妩媚的、俊朗的、迷人的： *She's a very attractive woman.* 她是个非常迷人的女子。

lovely (of a person) beautiful; very attractive 指（人）美丽的、迷人的： *She looked particularly lovely that night.* 她那天晚上特别妩媚动人。NOTE When you describe sb as **lovely**, you are usually showing that you also have a strong feeling of affection for them. 用 lovely 形容人时，通常表示说话者很喜欢这个人。

good-looking (of a person) pleasant to look at, often in a sexual way 指（人）好看的、漂亮的、性感的： *She arrived with a very good-looking man.* 她和一个非常英俊的男人一起到来。

gorgeous (*informal*) (of a person) extremely attractive, especially in a sexual way 指（人）非常漂亮的、美丽动人的、性感的： *You look gorgeous!* 你美极了！

ATTRACTIVE OR GOOD-LOOKING? 用 attractive 还是 good-looking?

If you describe sb as **attractive** you often also mean that they have a pleasant personality as well as being pleasant to look at; **good-looking** just describes sb's physical appearance. 用 attractive 形容人时，常常还表示这人不仅长得漂亮，性格也很可爱，而 good-looking 只指人的长相好看。

PATTERNS

- a(n) beautiful/pretty/handsome/attractive/lovely/good-looking/gorgeous **girl/woman**
- a(n) beautiful/handsome/attractive/good-looking/gorgeous **boy/man**
- a(n) beautiful/pretty/handsome/attractive/lovely/good-looking **face**

ˈ**beauty spot** *noun* **1** (*BrE*) a place in the countryside which is famous because it is beautiful 风景点；名胜 **2** (*NAmE also* ˈ**beauty mark**) a small dark spot on a woman's face, which used to be thought to make her more beautiful 美人痣；美人斑

beaux PL. OF BEAU

bea·ver /ˈbiːvə(r)/ *noun, verb*

■ ***noun*** **1** [C] an animal with a wide flat tail and strong teeth. Beavers live in water and on land and can build DAMS (= barriers across rivers), made of pieces of wood and mud. It is an official symbol of Canada. 河狸（生活在水边，会筑坝，是加拿大的象征） ➲ VISUAL VOCAB PAGE V12 ➲ SEE ALSO EAGER BEAVER **2** [U] the fur of the beaver, used in making hats and clothes 河狸毛皮（用以制作衣帽） **3** [C] (*taboo, slang, especially NAmE*) the area around a woman's sex organs 女子阴部

■ ***verb***

PHR V ˌ**beaver aˈway (at sth)** (*informal*) to work very hard at sth 忙于（某事）；勤奋工作： *He's been beavering away at the accounts all morning.* 他一上午都忙于做账。

bebop /ˈbiːbɒp; *NAmE* -bɑːp/ (*also* **bop**) *noun* [U] a type of JAZZ with complicated rhythms 比博普，博普（一种节奏复杂的爵士乐）

be·calmed /bɪˈkɑːmd/ *adj.* (of a ship with a sail 帆船) unable to move because there is no wind （因无风而）不能航行的

be·came PAST TENSE OF BECOME

be·cause 🔑 /bɪˈkɒz; -ˈkʌz; *NAmE* -ˈkɔːz; -ˈkʌz/ *conj.* for the reason that 因为： *I did it because he told me to.* 是他吩咐我才做的。◊ *Just because I don't complain, people think I'm satisfied.* 就因为我不发牢骚，大家便以为我满意了。➲ EXPRESS YOURSELF AT WHY ▶ **because of** 🔑 *prep.* : *They are here because of us.* 他们是因为我们来这里的。◊ *He walked slowly because of his bad leg.* 他因为腿不方便而行走缓慢。◊ *Because of his wife('s) being there, I said nothing about it.* 他的妻子在场，我便没提及这事。

▼ LANGUAGE BANK 用语库

because of

Explaining reasons 解释原因

- *The number of people with diabetes is growing, partly* ***because of*** *an increase in levels of obesity.* 患糖尿病的人数不断上升，部分原因是肥胖人数增加。
- *The number of overweight children has increased dramatically in recent years, largely* ***as a result of*** *changes in diet and lifestyle.* 近年来肥胖儿童的数量急剧上升，很大程度上是由饮食和生活方式的改变引起的。
- *The increase in childhood obesity is largely* ***due to***/ ***the result of*** *changes in lifestyle and diet over the last twenty years.* 肥胖儿童人数的增多主要是过去二十年来饮食和生活方式的改变所致。
- *Many obese children are bullied at school* ***on account of*** *their weight.* 许多肥胖儿童因为其体重问题在学校受到欺负。
- *Part of the problem with treating childhood obesity* ***stems from*** *the fact that parents do not always recognize that their children are obese.* 治疗肥胖儿童的困难部分源自父母有时并不认为自己的孩子肥胖。
- *Childhood obesity may be* ***caused by*** *genetic factors, as well as environmental ones.* 儿童肥胖既可能由环境因素引起，也可能是遗传因素所致。

➲ LANGUAGE BANK AT CAUSE, CONSEQUENTLY, THEREFORE

béch·amel /ˈbeɪʃəmel/ (*also* ˌ**béchamel ˈsauce**) *noun* [U] a thick sauce made with milk, flour and butter 贝夏美调味白汁（用牛奶、面粉和黄油调制而成） SYN **white sauce**

beck /bek/ *noun* (*BrE, dialect*) a small river 小溪 SYN **stream**

B

IDM **at sb's ˌbeck and ˈcall** always ready to obey sb's orders 随时待命： *Don't expect to have me at your beck and call.* 休想随意摆布我。

beckon /ˈbekən/ *verb* **1** [I, T] to give sb a signal using your finger or hand, especially to tell them to move nearer or to follow you 招手示意；举手召唤 **SYN** **signal**：**~ to sb (to do sth)** *He beckoned to the waiter to bring the bill.* 他招手示意服务生把账单送过来。◇ **~ sb (+ adv./prep.)** *He beckoned her over with a wave.* 他挥手让她过去。◇ *The boss beckoned him into her office.* 老板招手示意他进她的办公室。◇ **~ sb to do sth** *She beckoned him to come and join them.* 她打手势要他来加入他们的活动。**2** [I, T] to appear very attractive to sb 吸引；诱惑： *The clear blue sea beckoned.* 清澈蔚蓝的大海令人向往。◇ **~ sb** *The prospect of a month without work was beckoning her.* 一个月的闲暇时光令她神往。**3** [I] to be sth that is likely to happen or will possibly happen to sb in the future 很可能发生（或出现）： *For many kids leaving college the prospect of unemployment beckons.* 许多刚踏出大学校门的孩子可能会面临失业。

be·come 🔑 /bɪˈkʌm/ *verb* (**be·came** /bɪˈkeɪm/, **be·come**) **1** 🔑 *linking verb* to start to be sth 开始变得；变成；成为： **+ adj.** *It was becoming more and more difficult to live on his salary.* 他越来越难以靠他的工资维持生计了。◇ *It soon became apparent that no one was going to come.* 很快就很清楚，没人会来。◇ *She was becoming confused.* 她开始糊涂了。◇ **+ noun** *She became queen in 1952.* 她于 1952 年成为女王。◇ *The bill will become law next year.* 该议案将于明年成为法律。**2** [T, no passive] (not used in the progressive tenses 不用于进行时) **~ sb** (*formal*) to be suitable for sb 适合（某人）；（与…）相称： *Such behaviour did not become her.* 这种举止与她的身份不相称。**3** [T, no passive] (not used in the progressive tenses 不用于进行时) **~ sb** (*formal*) to look attractive on sb 使（人）显得漂亮；使好看 **SYN** **suit**： *Short hair really becomes you.* 你理短发很好看。

IDM **what became, has become, will become of sb/sth?** used to ask what has happened or what will happen to sb/sth （遭遇）如何；（结果）怎么样： *What became of that student who used to live with you?* 以前和你住在一起的那个学生后来怎么样了？◇ *I dread to think what will become of them if they lose their home.* 我不敢设想他们如果无家可归将会怎么样。

▼ **WHICH WORD?** 词语辨析

become / get / go / turn

These verbs are used frequently with the following adjectives. 这些动词常与下列形容词连用：

become ~	get ~	go ~	turn ~
involved	used to	wrong	blue
clear	better	right	sour
accustomed	worse	bad	bad
pregnant	pregnant	white	red
extinct	tired	crazy	cold
famous	angry	bald	
ill	dark	blind	

- **Become** is more formal than **get**. Both describe changes in people's emotional or physical state, or natural or social changes. * become 较 get 正式。两者均指人的感情、身体状况、自然或社会发生变化。
- **Go** is usually used for negative changes. * go 常用于负面变化。
- **Go** and **turn** are both used for changes of colour. * go 和 turn 均用以指颜色发生变化。
- **Turn** is also used for changes in the weather. * turn 亦用于天气的变化。

be·com·ing /bɪˈkʌmɪŋ/ *adj.* (*formal*) **1** (of clothes, etc. 衣服等) making the person wearing them look more attractive 相配的；合身的 **SYN** **flattering** **2** suitable or appropriate for sb or their situation 合适的；与…相称的 **SYN** **fitting**： *It was not very becoming behaviour for a teacher.* 这种举止与一个教师的身份不太相称。**OPP** **unbecoming**

bec·que·rel /ˈbekərel/ *noun* (*abbr.* **Bq**) (*physics* 物) a unit for measuring RADIOACTIVITY 贝可勒尔，贝可（放射性活度单位）

BEd (*also* **B.Ed.** *especially in NAmE*) /ˌbiː ˈed/ *noun* the abbreviation for 'Bachelor of Education' (a first university degree in education) 教育学学士（全写为 Bachelor of Education，大学教育学的初级学位）：(*BrE*) *Sarah Wells BEd* 教育学学士萨拉・韦尔斯

bed 🔑 /bed/ *noun, verb*

■ *noun*

• **FURNITURE** 家具 **1** 🔑 [C, U] a piece of furniture for sleeping on 床： *a **single/double bed*** 一张单人 / 双人床 ◇ *She **lay on the bed*** (= on top of the covers). 她躺在床上（指没盖被子）。◇ *He **lay in bed*** (= under the covers). 他躺在床上（指盖着被子）。◇ *I'm tired—I'm **going to bed**.* 我累了，我要睡觉了。◇ *It's **time for bed*** (= time to go to sleep). 该是睡觉的时候了。◇ *I'll just **put the kids to bed**.* 我这就安排孩子们去睡觉。◇ *He likes to have a mug of cocoa before bed* (= before going to bed). 他睡前喜欢喝一大杯可可。◇ *to **get into/out of bed*** 就寝；起床 ◇ *to **make the bed*** (= arrange the covers in a tidy way) 铺床 ◇ *Could you give me a bed for the night* (= somewhere to sleep)? 今晚你能给我弄个睡的地方吗？◇ *There's a shortage of hospital beds* (= not enough room for patients to be admitted). 医院床位短缺。◇ *He has been **confined to bed** with flu for the past couple of days.* 他因患流感，已经几天未下床了。➲ VISUAL VOCAB PAGE V24 ➲ SEE ALSO AIRBED, CAMP BED, SOFA BED, TWIN BED, WATERBED

• **OF RIVER/LAKE/SEA** 河；湖；海 **2** 🔑 [C] the bottom of a river, the sea, etc. （河）床；（海等的）底： *the ocean bed* 海洋底 ◇ *oyster beds* (= an area in the sea where there are many OYSTERS) 牡蛎层

• **FOR FLOWERS/VEGETABLES** 花卉；蔬菜 **3** [C] an area of ground in a garden/yard or park for growing flowers, vegetables, etc. 花坛；苗圃；菜园： *flower beds* 花坛 ➲ SEE ALSO SEEDBED

• **BOTTOM LAYER** 底层 **4** [C] **~ of sth** a layer of sth that other things lie or rest on 底层；基；基座： *grilled chicken, served on a bed of rice* 烤鸡盖饭 ◇ *The blocks should be laid on a bed of concrete.* 石块应该固定在混凝土基座上。

• **GEOLOGY** 地质学 **5** [C] a layer of CLAY, rock, etc. in the ground （地下由黏土、岩石等构成的）地层 ➲ SEE ALSO BEDROCK (2)

IDM **(not) a bed of ˈroses** (not) an easy or a pleasant situation （并非）轻松的境况，令人愉快的情况： *Their life together hasn't exactly been a bed of roses.* 他们在一起的生活并不十分幸福。**get out of bed on the wrong side** (*BrE*) (*NAmE* **get up on the wrong side of the bed**) to be bad-tempered for the whole day for no particular reason （无缘由地）一起床就整天情绪不好 **go to bed with sb** (*informal*) to have sex with sb 与（某人）上床 **in bed** used to refer to sexual activity （指性行为）： *What's he like in bed?* 他的床上功夫怎么样？◇ *I caught them in bed together* (= having sex). 我撞见他们睡在一起。**you've made your bed and you must ˈlie in/on it** (*saying*) you must accept the results of your actions 自己承担后果 **take to your ˈbed** to go to bed and stay there because you are ill/sick （因病）卧床；卧病 ➲ MORE AT DIE *v.*, WET *v.*

■ *verb* (**-dd-**) **1 ~ sth (in sth)** to fix sth firmly in sth 把…固定在： *The bricks were bedded in sand to improve drainage.* 砖块铺在沙里，以增加透水性。◇ *Make sure that you bed the roots firmly in the soil.* 一定要使根部牢牢地扎在土壤里。**2 ~ sb** (*old-fashioned*) to have sex with sb 与（某人）发生性关系

PHR V **ˌbed ˈdown** to sleep in a place where you do not usually sleep 换个地方睡觉： *You have my room and I'll bed down in the living room.* 你用我的房间，我睡客厅。

B

ˌ**bed and ˈboard** *noun* [U] (*BrE*) a room to sleep in and food 食宿；连吃带住

ˌ**bed and ˈbreakfast** *noun* (*abbr.* **B and B**, **B & B**) **1** [U] (*BrE*) a service that provides a room to sleep in and a meal the next morning in private houses and small hotels 住宿加（次日）早餐；床位加早餐：*Do you do bed and breakfast?* 你们提供住宿加早餐的服务吗？◇ *Bed and breakfast costs £50 a night.* 住宿加次日早餐每晚合 50 英镑。➲ COMPARE EUROPEAN PLAN, FULL BOARD, HALF BOARD **2** [C] a place that provides this service 提供住宿加早餐的旅馆：*There were several good bed and breakfasts in the area.* 这个地区有几家不错的提供住宿加早餐的旅馆。

be·dazzle /bɪˈdæzl/ *verb* [usually passive] **~ sb** to impress sb very much with intelligence, beauty, etc. 深深打动；使着迷；使眼花缭乱：*He was so bedazzled by her looks that he couldn't speak.* 她的美貌令他说不出话来。
▶ **be·dazzle·ment** /bɪˈdæzlmənt/ *noun* [U]

bed·bug /ˈbedbʌg/ *noun* a small flat insect that lives especially in beds, where it bites people and sucks their blood 臭虫；床虱

bed·cham·ber /ˈbedtʃeɪmbə(r)/ *noun* (*old use*) a bedroom 卧室：*the royal bedchamber* 国王的卧室

bed·clothes /ˈbedkləʊðz; *NAmE* -kloʊðz/ (*BrE also* **bed·covers** /ˈbedkʌvəz; *NAmE* ˈbedkʌvərz/) *noun* [pl.] the sheets and other covers that you put on a bed 床上用品；寝具；铺盖

bed·cover /ˈbedkʌvə(r)/ *noun* **1** = BEDSPREAD **2** (*BrE*) **bedcovers** = BEDCLOTHES

bed·ding /ˈbedɪŋ/ *noun* [U] **1** the sheets and covers that you put on a bed, often also the MATTRESS and the PILLOWS 寝具；铺盖 ➲ VISUAL VOCAB PAGE V24 **2** STRAW, etc. for animals to sleep on （给动物歇息的）垫草

ˈ**bedding plant** *noun* a plant that is planted out in a garden bed, usually just before it gets flowers. It usually grows and dies within one year. 开花前种在花坛里的植物；花坛植物

beddy-byes /ˈbedi baɪz/ (*BrE*) (*NAmE* **ˈbeddy-bye**) *noun* [U] a child's word for bed, used when talking about the time sb goes to bed （儿语）床床，困困床：*Time for beddy-byes.* 该上床床睡觉了。

be·deck /bɪˈdek/ *verb* [usually passive] **~ sth/sb (with/in sth)** (*literary*) to decorate sth/sb with flowers, flags, PRECIOUS STONES, etc. （用花、旗子、珠宝等）装饰，打扮

be·devil /bɪˈdevl/ *verb* (**-ll-**, *especially US* **-l-**) **~ sb/sth** (*formal*) to cause a lot of problems for sb/sth over a long period of time 长期搅扰 **SYN** **beset**：*The expedition was bedevilled by bad weather.* 探险队深受恶劣天气的困扰。

bed·fel·low /ˈbedfeləʊ; *NAmE* -feloʊ/ *noun* a person or thing that is connected with or related to another, often in a way that you would not expect （常指意外的）伙伴，同伴，相伴之物：***strange/unlikely bedfellows*** 奇怪的伙伴；本未想到会成为伙伴的人

bed·head /ˈbedhed/ *noun* the part of the bed that is at the end, behind the head of the person sleeping on it 床头

bed·jacket /ˈbeddʒækɪt/ *noun* a short jacket worn when sitting up in bed 床上用短上衣（坐起时披）

bed·lam /ˈbedləm/ *noun* [U] a scene full of noise and confusion 混乱嘈杂的场面 **SYN** **chaos**：*It was **bedlam** at our house on the morning of the wedding.* 婚礼的那天早上，我们家闹哄哄的。

ˈ**bed linen** *noun* [U] sheets and PILLOWCASES for a bed 床单及枕套；床上用品

Bed·ouin /ˈbedum/ *noun* (*pl.* **Bed·ouin**) a member of an Arab people that traditionally lives in tents in the desert 贝都因人（阿拉伯人，传统上生活在沙漠里，住帐篷）

bed·pan /ˈbedpæn/ *noun* a container used as a toilet by a person who is too ill/sick to get out of bed （卧床病人用的）便盆

bed·post /ˈbedpəʊst; *NAmE* -poʊst/ *noun* one of the four vertical supports at the corners of a bed (especially an old type of bed with a wooden or metal frame) （四帷柱床的）床柱 ➲ VISUAL VOCAB PAGE V24

be·drag·gled /bɪˈdrægld/ *adj.* made wet, dirty or untidy by rain, mud, etc. 弄湿的；给泥水弄脏的；不整洁的：***bedraggled hair/clothes*** 湿漉漉的头发；满是泥污的衣服

bed·rid·den /ˈbedrɪdn/ *adj.* having to stay in bed all the time because you are sick, injured or old 长期卧床的

bed·rock /ˈbedrɒk; *NAmE* -rɑːk/ *noun* **1** [sing.] a strong base for sth, especially the facts or the principles on which it is based 牢固基础；基本事实；基本原则：*The poor suburbs traditionally **formed the bedrock of** the party's support.* 传统上说，该党的根基在贫穷的郊区。◇ *Honesty is the bedrock of any healthy relationship.* 诚实是维持一切良好关系的基本原则。**2** [U] the solid rock in the ground below the loose soil and sand 基岩（松软的沙、土层下的岩石）

bed·roll /ˈbedrəʊl; *NAmE* -roʊl/ *noun* (*especially NAmE*) a thick piece of material or a SLEEPING BAG that you can roll up for carrying and use for sleeping on or in, for example when you are camping 铺盖，睡袋（露营等用）

bed·room 🔑 /ˈbedruːm; -rʊm/ *noun, adj.*
■ ***noun*** **1** a room for sleeping in 卧室：*the spare bedroom* 备用卧室 ◇ *a hotel with 20 bedrooms* 有 20 个房间的旅馆 ◇ *This is the **master bedroom*** (= the main bedroom of the house). 这是主卧室。**2 -bedroomed** having the number of bedrooms mentioned 有…个卧室的：*a three-bedroomed house* 有三个卧室的房子
■ ***adj.*** [only before noun] used as a way of referring to sexual activity 房事的；男女性爱的：*the bedroom scenes in the movie* 电影中的床上戏

ˈ**bedroom community** (*also* ˈ**bedroom suburb**) (*both NAmE*) (*BrE* ˈ**dormitory town**) *noun* a town that people live in and from where they travel to work in a bigger town or city 郊外住宅区

bed·side /ˈbedsaɪd/ *noun* [usually sing.] the area beside a bed 床边：*His mother has been **at his bedside** throughout his illness.* 在他生病期间，他母亲一直守候在他床边。◇ *a bedside lamp* 床头灯

ˌ**bedside ˈmanner** *noun* [sing.] the way in which a doctor or other person talks to sb who is ill/sick （医护人员等）对待病人的态度

ˌ**bedside ˈtable** (*especially BrE*) (*NAmE usually* **night·stand**, ˈ**night table**) *noun* a small table beside a bed 床头小几；床头柜 ➲ VISUAL VOCAB PAGE V24

bed·sit /ˈbedsɪt/ (*also* **bed·sit·ter** /ˈbedsɪtə(r)/) (*also formal* ˌ**bedˈsitting room**) *noun* (*all BrE*) a room that a person rents and uses for both living and sleeping in 起居兼卧室两用租间 ➲ COLLOCATIONS AT HOUSE

bed·sore /ˈbedsɔː(r)/ *noun* a painful and sometimes infected place on a person's skin, caused by lying in bed for a long time 褥疮

bed·spread /ˈbedspred/ (*also* **bed·cover**) (*NAmE also* **spread**) *noun* an attractive cover put on top of all the sheets and covers on a bed 床罩 ➲ VISUAL VOCAB PAGE V24

bed·stead /ˈbedsted/ *noun* the wooden or metal frame of an old-fashioned type of bed （旧式）床架

bed·time /ˈbedtaɪm/ *noun* [U, C] the time when sb usually goes to bed 就寝时间：*It's way past your bedtime.* 你早该睡觉了。◇ *Will you read me a bedtime story?* 给我读个睡前故事好吗？

ˈ**bed-wetting** *noun* [U] the problem of URINATING in bed, usually by children while they are asleep 尿床

bee /biː/ *noun* **1** a black and yellow flying insect that can sting. Bees live in large groups and make HONEY (= a sweet sticky substance that is good to eat). 蜜蜂：

a swarm of bees 一群蜜蜂 ◇ *a bee sting* 蜜蜂蜇伤 ◇ *Bees were buzzing in the clover.* 蜜蜂在三叶草丛中嗡嗡作响。 ➲ SEE ALSO BEEHIVE, BEESWAX, BUMBLEBEE, QUEEN BEE (1) **2** (*NAmE*) a meeting in a group where people combine work, competition and pleasure（集工作、竞赛、娱乐为一体的）聚会： *a sewing bee* 缝纫友谊赛 ➲ SEE ALSO SPELLING BEE

IDM **the ˌbee's ˈknees** (*informal*) an excellent person or thing 出类拔萃的人（或物）： *She thinks she's the bee's knees* (= she has a very high opinion of herself). 她自以为很了不起。 **have a ˈbee in your bonnet (about sth)** (*informal*) to think or talk about sth all the time and to think that it is very important（认为某事很重要而）念念不忘，老是提起 ➲ MORE AT BIRD *n.*, BUSY *adj.*

the Beeb /biːb/ *noun* [sing.] an informal name for the BBC 英国广播公司（非正式名称）

beech /biːtʃ/ *noun* **1** [U, C] (*also* **ˈbeech tree** [C]) a tall forest tree with smooth grey BARK, shiny leaves and small nuts 山毛榉： *forests planted with beech* 山毛榉林 ◇ *beech hedges* 山毛榉树篱 ◇ *The great beeches towered up towards the sky.* 一棵棵山毛榉高耸入云。 ➲ VISUAL VOCAB PAGE V10 ➲ SEE ALSO COPPER BEECH **2** (*also* **ˈbeech·wood** /ˈbiːtʃwʊd/) [U] the wood of the beech tree 山毛榉木材

beef 🔑 /biːf/ *noun, verb*

■ ***noun*** **1** 🔑 [U] meat that comes from a cow 牛肉： ***roast/minced beef*** 烤牛肉；碎牛肉 ◇ *beef and dairy cattle* 菜牛和奶牛 ➲ SEE ALSO CORNED BEEF **2** [C] (*informal*) a complaint 抱怨；牢骚： *What's his latest beef?* 他最近在抱怨什么？

■ ***verb*** [I] ~ **(about sb/sth)** (*informal*) to complain a lot about sb/sth 老是抱怨；大发牢骚

PHR V **ˌbeef sth↔ˈup** (*informal*) to make sth bigger, better, more interesting, etc. 使更大（或更好、更有意思等）

beef·bur·ger /ˈbiːfbɜːɡə(r); *NAmE* -bɜːrɡ-/ *noun* (*BrE*) = HAMBURGER (1)

beef·cake /ˈbiːfkeɪk/ *noun* [U] (*slang*) attractive men with big muscles, especially those that appear in magazines（尤指杂志中健壮性感的）肌肉男

beef·eater /ˈbiːfiːtə(r)/ *noun* a guard who dresses in a traditional uniform at the Tower of London 伦敦塔卫兵（穿传统制服）

beef·steak /ˈbiːfsteɪk/ *noun* [C, U] = STEAK (1)

ˌbeef ˈtea *noun* [U] (*BrE*) a hot drink made by boiling beef in water. It used to be given to people who were sick. 牛肉茶，牛肉汤（旧时给病人喝）

ˌbeef toˈmato (*also* **ˌbeefsteak toˈmato** *especially in NAmE*) *noun* a type of large tomato 牛肉番茄，牛茄（一种大个儿番茄）

beefy /ˈbiːfi/ *adj.* (**beef·ier**, **beefi·est**) (*informal*) (of a person or their body 人或人体) big or fat 高大的；肥胖的： ***beefy men/arms/thighs*** 粗壮的人 / 胳膊 / 大腿

bee·hive /ˈbiːhaɪv/ *noun* **1** = HIVE (1) **2** a HAIRSTYLE for women, with the hair piled high on top of the head 蜂窝状发型

bee·keep·er /ˈbiːkiːpə(r)/ *noun* a person who owns and takes care of BEES 养蜂人 ▸ **bee·keep·ing** *noun* [U]

bee·line /ˈbiːlaɪn/ *noun*

IDM **make a ˈbeeline for sth/sb** (*informal*) to go straight towards sth/sb as quickly as you can 直奔某物；径直奔向某人

Be·el·ze·bub /bɪˈelzɪbʌb/ *noun* a name for the DEVIL 别西卜（魔鬼的名字）

been /biːn; bɪn; *NAmE* bɪn/ ➲ BE *v.* ➲ SEE ALSO GO *v.*

ˈbeen-to *noun* (*WAfrE*) a person who returns to his or her home in Africa after studying, working, etc. in a foreign country. People are often identified as **been-tos** because they have a different accent.（非洲操异国口音的）学成归来者，海归人

beep /biːp/ *noun, verb*

■ ***noun*** a short high sound such as that made by a car horn or by electronic equipment（汽车喇叭或电子设备发出的）嘟嘟声，哔哔声

■ ***verb*** **1** [I] (of an electronic machine 电子机器) to make a short high sound 发出哔哔声；发出嘟嘟声： *The microwave beeps to let you know when it has finished.* 微波炉烹饪完毕时会发出哔哔声提醒你。 ➲ MORE LIKE THIS 3, page R25 **2** [I, T] when a car horn, etc. **beeps** or when you **beep** it, it makes a short noise（使汽车喇叭等）发出嘟嘟声： *The car behind started beeping at us.* 后面的汽车开始对我们鸣喇叭。 ◇ **~ sth** *He beeped his horn at the cyclist.* 他对骑自行车的人按喇叭。 **3** (*NAmE*) (*BrE* **bleep**) [T] **~ sb** to call sb on their beeper 打（某人）的传呼机；给（某人）打传呼

beep·er /ˈbiːpə(r)/ *noun* (*especially NAmE*) = BLEEPER

beer 🔑 /bɪə(r); *NAmE* bɪr/ *noun* **1** 🔑 [U, C] an alcoholic drink made from MALT and flavoured with HOPS. There are many types of beer. 啤酒： ***a barrel/bottle/glass of beer*** 一桶 / 一瓶 / 一杯啤酒 ◇ *beers brewed in Germany* 德国酿造的啤酒 ◇ *a beer glass* 啤酒杯 ◇ *Are you a beer drinker?* 你经常喝啤酒吗？ **2** 🔑 [C] a glass, bottle or can of beer 一杯（或一瓶、一罐）啤酒： *Shall we have a beer?* 我们来杯啤酒吧？ ➲ SEE ALSO GINGER BEER, GUEST BEER, KEG BEER, ROOT BEER, SMALL BEER

ˈbeer belly (*also* **ˈbeer gut**) *noun* (*informal*) a man's very fat stomach, caused by drinking a lot of beer over a long period 啤酒肚

ˈbeer cellar *noun* **1** a room for storing beer below a pub or bar（酒馆的）酒窖 **2** a pub or bar that is underground or partly underground（半）地下酒馆

ˈbeer garden *noun* an outdoor area at a pub or bar with tables and chairs 啤酒花园（酒馆的露天摊位）

ˈbeer goggles *noun* [pl.] (*informal*) you say that sb is wearing **beer goggles** when they have drunk too much alcohol and are attracted to sb that they would not usually find attractive 啤酒眼镜（wear beer goggles 表示饮酒过量后会觉得相貌平平者很有吸引力）： *He must have been wearing beer goggles when he was flirting with that awful woman!* 他跟那个丑女调情时一定是酒喝多了！

ˈbeer mat *noun* (*BrE*) a small piece of cardboard that you put under a glass, usually in a bar, etc. in order to protect the surface below 啤酒杯垫子

beery /ˈbɪəri; *NAmE* ˈbɪri/ *adj.* smelling of beer; influenced by the drinking of beer 啤酒味的；喝啤酒所致的

bees·wax /ˈbiːzwæks/ *noun* [U] a yellow sticky substance that is produced by BEES and is used especially for making CANDLES and polish for wood 蜂蜡；黄蜡

beet /biːt/ *noun* [C, U] **1** a plant with a root that is used as a vegetable, especially for feeding animals or making sugar 甜菜；糖萝卜 ➲ SEE ALSO SUGAR BEET **2** (*NAmE*) (*BrE* **beet·root**) a plant with a round dark red root that is cooked and eaten as a vegetable 甜菜；甜菜根 ➲ VISUAL VOCAB PAGE V34

bee·tle /ˈbiːtl/ *noun, verb*

■ ***noun*** an insect, often large and black, with a hard case on its back, covering its wings. There are several types of beetle. 甲虫 ➲ VISUAL VOCAB PAGE V13 ➲ SEE ALSO DEATH-WATCH BEETLE

■ ***verb*** [I] **+ adv./prep.** (*BrE, informal*) to move somewhere quickly 快速移动 SYN **scurry**: *I last saw him beetling off down the road.* 我上次见到他时，他正快步沿路而去。

beet·root /ˈbiːtruːt/ (*BrE*) (*NAmE* **beet**) *noun* [U, C] a plant with a round dark red root that is cooked and eaten as a vegetable 甜菜；甜菜根 ➲ VISUAL VOCAB PAGE V34

be·fall /bɪˈfɔːl/ *verb* (**be·fell** /bɪˈfel/, **be·fallen** /bɪˈfɔːlən/) **sth befalls sb** (used only in the third person 仅用于第三人称) (*literary*) (of sth unpleasant 令人不快的事) to happen to sb 降临到（某人）头上；发生在（某人）身上：*They were unaware of the fate that was to befall them.* 他们并不知道即将降临到他们头上的厄运。

befit /bɪˈfɪt/ *verb* (**-tt-**) **sth befits sb** (used only in the third person and in participles 仅用于第三人称和分词) (*formal*) to be suitable and good enough for sb/sth 适合；对…相称：*It was a lavish reception* ***as befitted*** *a visitor of her status.* 这场铺张的招待可算得正适合她这种身份的来访者。◇ *He lived in the style befitting a gentleman.* 他过的是一种与绅士相称的生活。

befog /bɪˈfɒg; *NAmE* -ˈfɑːg/ *verb* **sth befogs sb/sth** (used only in the third person 仅用于第三人称) to make sb confused 使迷惑；使困惑：*Her brain was befogged by lack of sleep.* 她因缺乏睡眠而头脑昏沉。

be·fore /bɪˈfɔː(r)/ *prep., conj., adv.*

■***prep.*** **1** earlier than sb/sth 在…以前：*before lunch* 午餐前 ◇ *the day before yesterday* 前天 ◇ *The year before last he won a gold medal, and the year before that he won a silver.* 他前年得了一枚金牌，大前年得了一枚银牌。◇ *She's lived there since before the war.* 她从战前起就一直住在那里。◇ *He arrived before me.* 他比我先到。◇ *She became a lawyer as her father had before her.* 像她父亲先前一样，她成了一名律师。◇ *Leave your keys at reception before departure.* 离开前请把钥匙留在服务台。◇ *Something ought to have been done before now.* 先前就该采取措施了。◇ *We'll know* ***before long*** (= soon). 我们很快就会知道了。◇ *Turn left just before* (= before you reach) *the bank.* 在快到银行时向左拐。 **2** (*rather formal*) used to say that sb/sth is in a position in front of sb/sth 在…面前（或前面）：*They knelt before the throne.* 他们跪在御座前。◇ *Before you is a list of the points we have to discuss.* 放在你面前的是一份我们所要讨论的要点清单。 ⊃ COMPARE BEHIND *prep.* **3** used to say that sb/sth is ahead of sb/sth in an order or arrangement（次序或排列）在前面：*Your name is before mine on the list.* 名单上你的名字在我之前。◇ *He puts his work before everything* (= regards it as more important than anything else). 他一切以工作为重。 **4** used to say that sth is facing sb in the future（表示面临或临近）：*The task before us is a daunting one.* 我们所面临的任务令人生畏。◇ *The whole summer lay before me.* 整个夏季正等待着我。 **5** in the presence of sb who is listening, watching, etc. 当面：*He was brought before the judge.* 他被带上法庭。◇ *She said it before witnesses.* 她当着证人的面讲出这事。◇ *They had the advantage of playing before their home crowd.* 他们有在主场观众面前比赛的优势。 **6** (*formal*) used to say how sb reacts when they have to face sb/sth（表示面对某人、某事时的反应）：*They retreated before the enemy.* 面对敌人，他们撤退了。

■***conj.*** **1** earlier than the time when 在…以前：*Do it before you forget.* 尽早动手，免得忘了。◇ *Did she leave a message before she went?* 她走之前留言了吗？ **2** until 到…为止；到…之前：*It may be many years before the situation improves.* 这种状况或许要过很多年才能得到改善。◇ *It was some time before I realized the truth.* 过了很长一段时间我才悟出真相。 **3** used to warn or threaten sb that sth bad could happen 以免；不然：*Put that away before it gets broken.* 把它收好，免得打碎了。 **4** (*formal*) rather than（宁可…而）不愿：*I'd die before I apologized!* 我宁愿死也不道歉！

■***adv.*** at an earlier time; in the past; already 以前；过去；已经：*You should have told me so before.* 你早该告诉我的。◇ *It had been fine the week before* (= the previous week). 前一个星期天气很好。◇ *That had happened long before* (= a long time earlier). 那是很早以前的事了。◇ *I think we've met before.* 我觉得我们以前见过面。

be·fore·hand /bɪˈfɔːhænd; *NAmE* -ˈfɔːrh-/ *adv.* earlier; before sth else happens or is done 预先；事先：*two weeks/three days/a few hours beforehand* 提前两星期 / 三天 / 几小时 ◇ *I wish we'd known about it beforehand.* 要是我们预先知道这事就好了。

be·friend /bɪˈfrend/ *verb* [usually passive] **~ sb** to become a friend of sb, especially sb who needs your help（尤指和需要帮助者）做朋友；友善相待：*Shortly after my arrival at the school, I was befriended by an older girl.* 我到学校后不久便得到了一位年龄较大的女孩友善对待。

be·fud·dled /bɪˈfʌdld/ *adj.* confused and unable to think normally 迷糊的；糊涂的：*He was befuddled by drink.* 他喝得迷迷糊糊的。

beg /beg/ *verb* (**-gg-**) **1** [I, T] to ask sb for sth especially in an anxious way because you want or need it very much 恳求；祈求；哀求：**~ (for sth)** *He wants to see them beg for mercy.* 他想亲眼看看他们求饶。◇ **~ sb (for sth)** *They begged him for help.* 他们向他求援。◇ **~ sth (of/from sb)** *She begged permission to leave.* 她请求允许她离开。◇ *I managed to beg a lift from a passing motorist.* 我设法求得一位开车路过的人让我搭车。◇ **~ (sb) + speech** *'Give me one more chance,' he begged (her).* "再给我一次机会吧。"他恳求（她）道。◇ **~ sb to do sth** *She begged him not to go.* 她求他别离开。◇ **~ to do sth** *He begged to be told the truth.* 他请求把真相告诉他。◇ **~ that...** (*formal*) *She begged that she be allowed to go.* 她请求让她离开。◇ (*BrE also*) *She begged that she should be allowed to go.* 她请求让她离开。◇ **~ of sb** (*formal*) *Don't leave me here, I beg of you!* 别把我扔在这儿，求求你！ ⊃ MORE LIKE THIS 26, page R28 **2** [I, T] to ask sb for money, food, etc., especially in the street 乞讨；行乞：*London is full of homeless people begging in the streets.* 伦敦的街头到处都是无家可归的乞丐。◇ *a begging letter* (= one that asks sb for money)（要钱的）求援信 ◇ **~ for sth (from sb)** *The children were begging for food.* 那些孩子正在讨饭。◇ **~ sth (from sb)** *We managed to beg a meal from the cafe owner.* 我们设法向咖啡馆老板讨了一顿饭。 ⊃ WORDFINDER NOTE AT POOR **3** [I] if a dog **begs**, it sits on its back legs with its front legs in the air, waiting to be given sth（狗蹲坐在后腿上将前腿抬起）等食物 ⊃ MORE LIKE THIS 36, page R29

IDM **beg ˈleave to do sth** (*formal*) to ask sb for permission to do sth 请求准许做某事 **be going ˈbegging** (*BrE, informal*) if sth **is going begging**, it is available because nobody else wants it 无人问津；没人要 **beg sb's ˈpardon** (*formal, especially BrE*) to ask sb to forgive you for sth you have said or done 请人原谅；向人道歉 **beg the ˈquestion** **1** to make sb want to ask a question that has not yet been answered 令人置疑；引起疑问：*All of which begs the question as to who will fund the project.* 所有这一切都令人想到究竟由谁来投资该工程的问题。 **2** to talk about sth as if it were definitely true, even though it might not be 想当然：*These assumptions beg the question that children learn languages more easily than adults.* 这些假设想当然地认为儿童比成年人学习语言容易。 **I beg to differ** used to say politely that you do not agree with sth that has just been said 很抱歉，我不敢苟同 **I beg your pardon** **1** (*formal*) used to tell sb that you are sorry for sth you have said or done 请原谅；对不起：*I beg your pardon, I thought that was my coat.* 对不起，我还以为那是我的外衣呢。 **2** used to ask sb to repeat what they have just said because you did not hear（未听清楚）请再说一遍：*'It's on Duke Street.' 'I beg your pardon.' 'Duke Street.'* "在公爵大街上。" "请再说一遍。" "公爵大街。" **3** (*BrE*) used to tell sb that you are offended by what they have just said or by the way that they have said it（感到被冒犯时说）：*'Just go away.' 'I beg your pardon!'* "走开。" "你再说一遍！"

PHR V **ˌbeg ˈoff** to say that you are unable to do sth that you have agreed to do 推辞（已答应做的事）；反悔：*He's always begging off at the last minute.* 他总是在最后一分钟反悔。

begad /bɪˈgæd/ *exclamation* (*old use*) used to express surprise or for emphasis（表示惊奇或强调）天哪，的确呀

began PAST TENSE OF BEGIN

beget /bɪˈget/ *verb* (**be·get·ting**, **begot**, **begot** /bɪˈgɒt; *NAmE* bɪˈgɑːt/) HELP In sense 1 **begat** /bɪˈgæt/ is used for the past tense, and **be·got·ten** /bɪˈgɒtn; *NAmE* -ˈgɑːtn/ is used for the past participle. 第 1 义的过去式用 begat，过去分词用 begotten。 **1** (old use, for example in the Bible 旧用法，如《圣经》中) **~ sb** to become the father of a child 成为…之父：*Isaac begat Jacob.* 以撒生了雅各。 **2** **~ sth** (*formal or old-fashioned*) to make sth happen 引发；导致：*Violence begets violence.* 暴力招致暴力。 ▶ **be·get·ter** *noun*

beg·gar /ˈbeɡə(r)/ *noun, verb*

■ ***noun* 1** a person who lives by asking people for money or food 乞丐；叫花子 **2** (*BrE, informal*) used with an adjective to describe sb in a particular way （与形容词连用）家伙：*Aren't you dressed yet, you lazy beggar?* 你这个懒虫还没穿好衣服吗？

IDM ˌ**beggars can't be ˈchoosers** (*saying*) people say **beggars can't be choosers** when there is no choice and sb must be satisfied with what is available 要饭就不能嫌馊；给什么就得要什么 ➲ MORE AT WISH *n.*

■ ***verb* ~ sb/sth/yourself** to make sb/sth very poor 使贫穷；使匮乏：*Why should I beggar myself for you?* 我为什么要为你受穷？

IDM **beggar beˈlief/deˈscription** to be too extreme, shocking, etc. to believe/describe 难以相信；无法形容：*It beggars belief how things could have got this bad.* 真是难以置信，情况怎么会恶化到这种地步。

beg·gar·ly /ˈbeɡəli; *NAmE* -ɡərli/ *adj.* (*literary*) very small in amount 微量的；少得可怜的

ˈ**begging bowl** *noun* a bowl held out by sb asking for food or money 讨饭碗；讨钱钵；乞钵：(*figurative*) *He is taking round the begging bowl on behalf of the party's campaign fund.* 他为筹集该党的竞选资金而四处求助。

begin /bɪˈɡɪn/ *verb* (**be·gin·ning**, **began** /bɪˈɡæn/, **begun** /bɪˈɡʌn/) **1** [I, T] to start doing sth; to do the first part of sth 开始；启动：*Shall I begin?* 我可以开始了吗？◇ **~ at/with sth** *Let's begin at page 9.* 咱们从第 9 页开始。◇ **~ by doing sth** *She began by thanking us all for coming.* 她首先对我们大家的到来表示感谢。◇ **~ sth** *We began work on the project in May.* 我们于五月份启动这个项目。◇ *I began* (= started reading) *this novel last month and I still haven't finished it.* 我上月就开始读这本小说，到现在还没读完。◇ **~ sth at/with sth** *He always begins his lessons with a warm-up exercise.* 他讲课前总是先让学生做预备练习题。◇ **~ sth as sth** *He began his political career as a student* (= when he was a student). 他从当学生时起就开始了他的政治生涯。◇ **~ to do sth** *I began to feel dizzy.* 我开始感到头晕目眩。◇ *At last the guests began to arrive.* 客人们终于陆续到达了。◇ *She began to cry.* 她哭了起来。◇ *It was beginning to snow.* 开始下雪了。◇ *I was beginning to think you'd never come.* 我都开始以为你不会来了。◇ **~ doing sth** *Everyone began talking at once.* 大家立刻开始谈了起来。◇ *When will you begin recruiting?* 你们何时开始招募人员？ ➲ SYNONYMS AT START ➲ LANGUAGE BANK AT FIRST **2** [I] to start to happen or exist, especially from a particular time 起始；开始存在（或进行）：*When does the concert begin?* 音乐会什么时间开始？◇ *Work on the new bridge is due to begin in September.* 新桥定于九月份动工。◇ *The evening began well.* 晚会开始得很顺利。**3** [I] **~ as sth** to be sth first, before becoming sth else 起初是；本来是：*He began as an actor, before starting to direct films.* 他先是当演员，后来开始执导影片。◇ *What began as a minor scuffle turned into a full-scale riot.* 最初的小冲突演变成了大规模的暴乱。**4** [I] to have sth as the first part or the point where sth starts （从…）开始；（以…）为起点：*Where does Europe end and Asia begin?* 欧洲和亚洲的交界处在哪里？◇ **~ with sth** *Use 'an' before words beginning with a vowel.* 在以元音开始的词之前使用 an。◇ *'I'm thinking of a country in Asia.' 'What does it begin with* (= what is the first letter)?' "我想的是一个亚洲国家。" "它的首字母是什么？" ◇ *Each chapter begins with a quotation.* 每一章的开头都有一条引语。◇ **~ at…** *The path begins at Livingston village.* 这条小路始于利文斯顿村。**5** [T] **+ speech** to start speaking 开始讲话：*'Ladies and gentlemen,' he began, 'welcome to the Town Hall.'* 他开始讲话："女士们、先生们，欢迎光临市政厅。" **6** [I, T] to start or make sth start for the first time 创始；创办：*The school began in 1920, with only ten pupils.* 这所学校创建于 1920 年，当时只有十名学生。◇ **~ sth** *He began a new magazine on post-war architecture.* 他创办了一份专论战后建筑的新杂志。**7** [T] **not ~ to do sth** to make no attempt to do sth or have no chance of doing sth 不想；绝不能：***I can't begin to*** *thank you enough.* 我说不尽对你的感激。◇ *He didn't even begin to understand my problem.* 他甚至没有弄明白我的问题。

IDM **to beˈgin with 1** at first 起初；开始：*I found it tiring to begin with but I soon got used to it.* 我起初觉得很累，但不久便适应了。◇ *We'll go slowly to begin with.* 我们开始时会慢慢来的。**2** used to introduce the first point you want to make 首先；第一点：*'What was it you didn't like?' 'Well, to begin with, our room was far too small.'* "你不喜欢的是什么呢？" "嗯，首先是，我们的屋子太小了。" ➲ MORE AT CHARITY

▼ **WHICH WORD? 词语辨析**

begin / start

- There is not much difference in meaning between **begin** and **start**, though **start** is more common in spoken English. * begin 和 start 的含义差别不大，不过 start 较常用于口语：*What time does the concert start/begin?* 音乐会什么时候开场？◇ *She started/began working here three months ago.* 她三个月前开始在这儿工作。 **Begin** is often used when you are describing a series of events. * begin 常用以指一系列事情的开始：*The story begins on the island of Corfu.* 故事从科孚岛上开始。 **Start**, but not **begin**, can also mean 'to start a journey', 'to start something happening' or 'to start a machine working'. * start 亦含出发、使发生、使（机器）运转之义，begin 不含此义：*We'll need to start at 7.00.* 我们需要在 7 点钟出发。◇ *Who do you think started the fire?* 你看是谁点的火？◇ *The car won't start.* 汽车发动不起来。
- You can use either an infinitive or a form with *-ing* after **begin** and **start**, with no difference in meaning. * begin 和 start 之后接动词不定式或 -ing 形式均可，在意义上无差别：*I didn't start worrying/to worry until she was 2 hours late.* 她晚了两小时还没到，我才开始担忧起来。
- After the forms **beginning** and **starting**, the *-ing* form of the verb is not normally used. * beginning 和 starting 之后一般不用动词的 -ing 形式：*It's starting/beginning to rain.* 开始下雨了。◇ ~~*It's starting/beginning raining.*~~

be·gin·ner /bɪˈɡɪnə(r)/ *noun* a person who is starting to learn sth and cannot do it very well yet 新手；初学者：*She's in the beginners' class.* 她在初级班。

beˌ**ginner's ˈluck** *noun* [U] good luck or unexpected success when you start to do sth new 新手的好运；生手的意外成功

be·gin·ning /bɪˈɡɪnɪŋ/ *noun* **1** [C, usually sing.] **~ (of sth)** the time when sth starts; the first part of an event, a story, etc. 开头；开端；开始部分：*We're going to Japan* ***at the beginning of*** *July.* 我们七月初要去日本。◇ *She's been working there* ***since the beginning of*** *last summer.* 她自从去年夏初起就一直在那里工作。◇ *We missed the beginning of the movie.* 我们错过了电影的开头部分。◇ *Let's start again* ***from the beginning.*** 让我们再从头开始。◇ *The birth of their first child* ***marked the beginning of*** *a new era in their married life.* 第一个孩子的出世使他们的婚姻生活开始了一个新阶段。◇ *I've read the whole book* ***from beginning to end*** *and still can't understand it.* 我把整本书从头到尾看了一遍，但还是没看懂。 HELP **At the beginning (of)** is used for the time and place when something begins. **In the beginning** means 'at first' and suggests a contrast with a later situation. * at the beginning (of)表示开始的时间和起点。in the beginning 意思相当于 at first，与后来相对：***at the beginning of*** *the week/year/story/movie/game* 一周 / 一年 / 故事 / 电影 / 游戏的开始 ◇ ***In the beginning,*** *we just tried to keep everything very simple. Later on, …* 一开始，我们尽量把所有事情简单化，但后来… **2 beginnings** [pl.] the first or early ideas, signs or stages of sth 原始思想；前兆；初级阶段：*Did democracy have its beginnings in ancient Greece?* 民主制度发端于古希腊吗？◇ *He built up his multimillion-pound music business* ***from small beginnings.*** 他从小本生意起步，逐步建立起了数百万英镑的音乐企业。

IDM **the beginning of the ˈend** the first sign of sth ending 结束的前兆；结局的开始

B

be·gone /bɪˈɡɒn; *NAmE* -ˈɡɔːn; -ˈɡɑːn/ *exclamation* (*old use*) a way of telling sb to go away immediately 走开；滚开

be·go·nia /bɪˈɡəʊniə; *NAmE* -ˈɡoʊ-/ *noun* a plant with large shiny flowers that may be pink, red, yellow or white, grown indoors or in a garden 秋海棠

be·gorra /bɪˈɡɒrə; *NAmE* bɪˈɡɔːrə; -ˈɡɑːr-/ *exclamation* (*IrishE, old-fashioned*) used to express surprise（表示惊奇）天哪，哎呀

begot PAST TENSE OF BEGET

be·got·ten PAST PART. OF BEGET

be·grudge /bɪˈɡrʌdʒ/ *verb* (often used in negative sentences 常用于否定句) **1** to feel unhappy that sb has sth because you do not think that they deserve it 嫉妒；对（某人所享有的）感到不满：**~ sb sth** *You surely don't begrudge him his happiness.* 你该不是嫉妒他的幸福吧。◇ **~ sb doing sth** *I don't begrudge her being so successful.* 我并没有因她如此成功而怏怏不乐。 **2** to feel unhappy about having to do, pay or give sth 勉强做；不乐意地做（或付出）：**~ sth** *I begrudge every second I spent trying to help him.* 我为了帮助他而花掉的每一秒钟都令我不痛快。◇ **~ doing sth** *They begrudge paying so much money for a second-rate service.* 花这么多的钱，却得到二流的服务，这使他们十分不快。

be·grudg·ing·ly /bɪˈɡrʌdʒɪŋli/ *adv.* = GRUDGINGLY

be·guile /bɪˈɡaɪl/ *verb* (*formal*) **1 ~ sb (into doing sth)** to trick sb into doing sth, especially by being nice to them 哄骗（某人做某事）；诱骗：*She beguiled them into believing her version of events.* 她哄骗他们相信了她叙述的事情。 **2 ~ sb** to attract or interest sb 吸引（某人）；使感兴趣：*He was beguiled by her beauty.* 他为她的美丽所倾倒。

be·guil·ing /bɪˈɡaɪlɪŋ/ *adj.* (*formal*) attractive and interesting but sometimes mysterious or trying to trick you 迷人的；诱人的；诱骗的；难以琢磨的：*beguiling advertisements* 富有诱惑力的广告 ◇ *Her beauty was beguiling.* 她的美有种蛊惑力。▶ **be·guil·ing·ly** *adv.*

begum /ˈbeɪɡəm/ *noun* a title of respect used for a Muslim woman of high rank and for a married Muslim woman（对穆斯林贵妇或已婚妇女的尊称）贵夫人：*Begum Zia* 齐亚夫人

begun PAST PART. OF BEGIN

be·half 🔑 AW /bɪˈhɑːf; *NAmE* bɪˈhæf/ *noun*
IDM **in behalf of sb | in sb's behalf** 🔑 (*US*) in order to help sb 为帮助某人：*We collected money in behalf of the homeless.* 我们为帮助无家可归者而募捐。 **on behalf of sb | on sb's behalf 1** 🔑 as the representative of sb or instead of them 代表（或代替）某人：*On behalf of the department I would like to thank you all.* 我谨代表全系感谢大家。◇ *Mr Knight cannot be here, so his wife will accept the prize on his behalf.* 奈特先生不能来，因此由他的夫人代他领奖。 **2** 🔑 in order to help sb 为帮助某人：*They campaigned on behalf of asylum seekers.* 他们为政治难民发起运动。 **3** because of sb; for sb 因为某人；为了某人：*Don't worry on my behalf.* 别为我担心。

be·have 🔑 /bɪˈheɪv/ *verb* **1** 🔑 [I] **+ adv./prep.** to do things in a particular way 表现 SYN **act**: *The doctor behaved very unprofessionally.* 那位医生的做法违反职业道德。◇ *They behaved very badly towards their guests.* 他们对客人们很不礼貌。◇ *He behaved like a true gentleman.* 他的行为像个真正的绅士。◇ *She behaved with great dignity.* 她显得很尊贵。◇ *He* ***behaved as if/though*** *nothing had happened.* 他显得像是什么都没发生过。◇ *They behave differently when you're not around.* 你不在时他们就是另一副面孔。 HELP In spoken English people often use **like** instead of **as if** or **as though**, especially in *NAmE*. 英语口语中，尤其是美式英语，常用 like 代替 as if 或 as though: *He behaved like nothing had happened.* 他显得像是什么都没发生过。This is not considered correct in written *BrE*. 英式英语书面语中，此用法被视为不正确。 **2** 🔑 [I, T] to do things in a way that people think is correct or polite 表现得体；有礼貌：*Will you kids just behave!* 孩子们，规矩点！◇ *She doesn't know how to behave in public.* 她在公共场合举止无措。◇ **~ yourself** *I want you to behave yourselves while I'm away.* 我不在时你们要乖乖的。OPP **misbehave** **3** 🔑 **-behaved** (in adjectives 构成形容词) behaving in the way mentioned 表现得…的：***well-/badly behaved*** *children* 表现好 / 差的孩子 **4** [I] **+ adv./prep.** (*specialist*) to naturally react, move, etc. in a particular way 作某种自然反应（或变化等）：*a study of how metals behave under pressure* 对于金属受压反应的研究 IDM SEE OWN *v.*

be·hav·iour 🔑 (*especially US* **be·hav·ior**) /bɪˈheɪvjə(r)/ *noun* **1** 🔑 [U] the way that sb behaves, especially towards other people 行为；举止；态度：***good/bad behaviour*** 良好 / 恶劣行为 ◇ ***social/sexual/criminal behaviour*** 社会 / 性 / 犯罪行为 ◇ *His behaviour towards her was becoming more and more aggressive.* 他对待她的态度越来越蛮横。

WORDFINDER 联想词：action, approach, attitude, conform, eccentric, etiquette, habit, manner, morality

2 🔑 [U, C] the way a person, an animal, a plant, a chemical, etc. behaves or functions in a particular situation（人、动植物、化学品等的）表现方式，活动方式：*the behaviour of dolphins/chromosomes* 海豚 / 染色体的习性 ◇ *studying human and animal behaviour* 研究人类和动物的行为模式 ◇ (*specialist*) *to study learned behaviours* 研究习得行为 ▶ **be·hav·iour·al** (*especially US* **be·hav·ior·al** /-jərəl/) *adj.*: *children with behavioural difficulties* 有行为问题的儿童 ◇ *behavioural science* (= the study of human behaviour) 行为科学 **be·hav·iour·al·ly** (*especially US* **be·hav·ior·al·ly**) *adv.*

IDM **be on your best be'haviour** to behave in the most polite way you can 尽量表现得体

be·hav·iour·ism (*especially US* **be·hav·ior·ism**) /bɪˈheɪvjərɪzəm/ *noun* [U] (*psychology* 心) the theory that all human behaviour is learnt by adapting to outside conditions and that learning is not influenced by thoughts and feelings 行为主义 ▶ **be·hav·iour·ist** (*especially US* **be·hav·ior·ist**) /-jərɪst/ *noun*

be·head /bɪˈhed/ *verb* [usually passive] **~ sb** to cut off sb's head, especially as a punishment 斩首（尤指刑罚）SYN **decapitate**

be·held PAST TENSE, PAST PART. OF BEHOLD

be·he·moth /bɪˈhiːmɒθ; ˈbiːhɪmɒθ; *NAmE* -mɔːθ/ *noun* (*formal*) something that is very big and powerful, especially a company or organization 超级公司（或机构）：*a multinational corporate behemoth* 巨型跨国公司

be·hest /bɪˈhest/ *noun* [sing.]
IDM **at sb's be'hest** (*old use* or *formal*) because sb has ordered or requested it 受某人的吩咐（或要求）

be·hind 🔑 /bɪˈhaɪnd/ *prep., adv., noun*
■ ***prep.* 1** 🔑 at or towards the back of sb/sth, and often hidden by it or them 在（或向）…的后面；在（或向）…的背面：*Who's the girl standing behind Jan?* 站在简身后的女孩是谁？◇ *Stay close behind me.* 紧跟在我后面。◇ *a small street behind the station* 车站后面的小街 ◇ *She glanced behind her.* 她扭头朝背后扫了一眼。◇ *Don't forget to lock the door behind you* (= when you leave). 出门时记着把门锁上。◇ *The sun disappeared behind the clouds.* 太阳消失在云层里。 ➲ NOTE AT BACK ➲ COMPARE IN FRONT OF at FRONT *n.* **2** 🔑 making less progress than sb/sth 落后于：*He's behind the rest of the class in reading.* 他的阅读能力不及班上其他人。◇ *We're* ***behind schedule*** (= late). 我们的工作进度落后了。 **3** 🔑 giving support to or approval of sb/sth 支持；赞成：*She knew that, whatever she decided, her family was right behind her.* 她知道，无论她作出什么决定，她的家人肯定会支持她的。 **4** responsible for starting or developing sth 是…产生（或发展）的原因：*What's behind that happy smile* (= what is causing it)? 为什么会笑得那么开心？◇ *He was the man behind the plan to build a new hospital.* 他就是策划建立新医院的人。 **5** used to say that sth is in sb's past 成为（某人的）过去：*The accident is behind you now, so try to forget it.* 这次意外已经过去了，把它忘掉吧。◇ *She has*

ten years' useful experience behind her. 她有十年非常实用的经验。

■ ***adv.*** **1** at or towards the back of sb/sth; further back 在（或向）后面；在后面较远处：*She rode off down the road with the dog running behind.* 她骑车沿路而去，狗跟在后面奔跑着。◇ *The others are a long way behind.* 其余的人远远地落在后面。◇ *He was shot from behind as he ran away.* 他逃跑时后背中了弹。◇ *I had fallen so far behind that it seemed pointless trying to catch up.* 我落后太多，似乎追赶下去也毫无意义。 **2** in the place where sb/sth is or was 留在原地：*I was told to* ***stay behind*** *after school* (= remain in school). 我被告知放学后留下。◇ *This bag was* ***left behind*** *after the class.* 这个书包是有人下课后落下的。 **3** late in paying money or completing work 拖欠；积压（工作）：~ (**with sth**) *She's* ***fallen behind*** *with the payments.* 她尚未付款。◇ ~ (**in sth**) *He was terribly behind in his work.* 他积压了大量工作。

■ ***noun*** (*informal*) a person's bottom. People often say 'behind' to avoid saying 'bottom'. 腚（义同 bottom，委婉说法） SYN **backside**: *The dog bit him on his behind.* 狗咬了他的腚。

be·hind·hand /bɪˈhaɪndhænd/ *adj.* [not before noun] ~ (**with/in sth**) late in doing sth or in paying money that is owed 拖欠；拖拉：*They were behindhand in settling their debts.* 他们没有及时还清债务。

be·hold /bɪˈhəʊld; *NAmE* bɪˈhoʊld/ *verb* (**be·held** /bɪˈheld/, **be·held**) ~ **sb/sth** (*old use* or *literary*) to look at or see sb/sth 看；看见：*Her face was a joy to behold.* 她的容貌十分悦目。◇ *They beheld a bright star shining in the sky.* 他们看到了一颗明亮的星在天空中闪闪发光。 IDM SEE LO

be·holden /bɪˈhəʊldən; *NAmE* -ˈhoʊld-/ *adj.* ~ **to sb** (**for sth**) (*formal*) owing sth to sb because of sth that they have done for you （因受恩惠而心存）感激，感谢；欠人情：*She didn't like to be beholden to anyone.* 她不愿欠任何人的情。

be·hold·er /bɪˈhəʊldə(r); *NAmE* -ˈhoʊld-/ *noun* IDM SEE BEAUTY

be·hove /bɪˈhəʊv; *NAmE* bɪˈhoʊv/ (*BrE*) (*NAmE* **be·hoove** /bɪˈhuːv/) *verb*

IDM **it behoves sb to do sth** (*formal*) it is right or necessary for sb to do sth （对某人来说）理应，应当，有必要：*It behoves us to study these findings carefully.* 我们理应认真研究这些发现。

beige /beɪʒ/ *adj.* light yellowish-brown in colour 浅褐色的；米黄色的 ▶ **beige** *noun* [U]

being /ˈbiːɪŋ/ *noun* **1** [U] existence 存在；生存：*The Irish Free State* ***came into being*** *in 1922.* 爱尔兰自由邦成立于 1922 年。◇ *A new era was* ***brought into being*** *by the war.* 那场战争带来了一个新的时代。 ⊃ SEE ALSO WELL-BEING **2** [C] a living creature 生物：*human beings* 人 ◇ *a strange being from another planet* 来自另一星球的奇怪生物 **3** [U] (*formal*) your mind and all of your feelings 思想感情；身心：*I hated him with my whole being.* 我从心底憎恨他。 ⊃ SEE ALSO BE

be·jew·elled (*BrE*) (*US* **be·jew·eled**) /bɪˈdʒuːəld/ *adj.* (*literary*) decorated with PRECIOUS STONES; wearing jewellery 饰以珠宝的；佩戴珠宝的

bel /bel/ *noun* (*specialist*) a measurement of sound equal to 10 DECIBELS 贝尔，贝（声音计量单位，等于 10 分贝）

be·la·bour (*especially US* **be·la·bor**) /bɪˈleɪbə(r)/ *verb*

IDM **belabour the ˈpoint** (*formal*) to repeat an idea, argument, etc. many times to emphasize it, especially when it has already been mentioned or understood 一再强调观点（或论点等）

be·lated /bɪˈleɪtɪd/ *adj.* coming or happening late 迟来的；晚出现的：*a belated birthday present* 迟来的生日礼物 ▶ **be·lated·ly** *adv.*

belay /ˈbiːleɪ; bɪˈleɪ/ *verb* [I, T] ~ (**sth/sb**) (*specialist*) (in climbing 攀缘) to attach a rope to a rock, etc.; to make a person safe while climbing by attaching a rope to the person and to a rock, etc. 把（绳索）固定在岩石等上；把（攀岩者）用绳索拴在岩石等上

bel canto /ˌbel ˈkæntəʊ; *NAmE* -toʊ/ *noun* [U] (*music* 音, *from Italian*) a style of OPERA or opera singing in the 19th century in which producing a beautiful tone was considered very important 美声唱法（19 世纪歌剧艺术或演唱风格）

belch /beltʃ/ *verb* **1** [I] to let air come up noisily from your stomach and out through your mouth 打嗝 SYN **burp**: *He wiped his hand across his mouth, then belched loudly.* 他用手抹了抹嘴，然后打了个响亮的饱嗝。 **2** [I, T] ~ (**out/forth**) (**sth**) to send out large amounts of smoke, flames, etc.; to come out of sth in large amounts （大量）喷出，吐出 SYN **spew** ▶ **belch** *noun*: *He sat back and gave a loud belch.* 他靠到椅背上，大声打了个嗝。

be·lea·guered /bɪˈliːɡəd; *NAmE* -ɡərd/ *adj.* **1** (*formal*) experiencing a lot of criticism and difficulties 饱受批评的；处于困境的：*The beleaguered party leader was forced to resign.* 那位饱受指责的党领导人被迫辞职。 **2** surrounded by an enemy 受到围困（或围攻）的：*supplies for the beleaguered city* 给受围困城市的补给品

bel·fry /ˈbelfri/ *noun* (*pl.* **-ies**) a tower in which bells hang, especially as part of a church （尤指教堂的）钟楼，钟塔

belie /bɪˈlaɪ/ *verb* (**be·lies**, **be·ly·ing**, **be·lied**, **be·lied**) (*formal*) **1** ~ **sth** to give a false impression of sb/sth 掩饰；遮掩；给人以假象：*Her energy and youthful good looks belie her 65 years.* 她的活力与年轻美貌使人看不出她有 65 岁了。 **2** ~ **sth** to show that sth cannot be true or correct 显示（某事）不正确；证明（某事）错误：*Government claims that there is no poverty are belied by the number of homeless people on the streets.* 大街上那些无家可归者证明政府所声称的没有贫困的说法是谎言。

be·lief /bɪˈliːf/ *noun* **1** [U] ~ (**in sth/sb**) a strong feeling that sth/sb exists or is true; confidence that sth/sb is good or right 相信；信心：*I admire his passionate belief in what he is doing.* 我佩服他对自己的工作所抱的坚定信心。◇ *belief in God/democracy* 对上帝 / 民主的笃信 **2** [sing., U] ~ (**that…**) an opinion about sth; sth that you think is true 看法；信念：*She acted* ***in the belief that*** *she was doing good.* 她这么做是因为她认定自己是在做好事。◇ ***Contrary to popular belief*** (= in spite of what people may think), *he was not responsible for the tragedy.* 与大家的看法相反，他对这桩悲剧没有责任。◇ *There is a general belief that things will soon get better.* 大家普遍认为情况很快就会好转。 **3** [C, usually pl.] something that you believe, especially as part of your religion 信仰；宗教信仰：***religious/political beliefs*** 宗教 / 政治信仰 ⊃ COMPARE DISBELIEF, UNBELIEF

IDM **beyond beˈlief** (in a way that is) too great, difficult, etc. to be believed 令人难以置信：*Dissatisfaction with the government has grown beyond belief.* 对政府的不满已经达到令人难以置信的程度。◇ *icy air that was cold beyond belief* 冷得令人无法相信的冰冷空气 ⊃ MORE AT BEGGAR *v.*, BEST *n.*

be·liev·able /bɪˈliːvəbl/ *adj.* that can be believed 可相信的；可信任的 SYN **plausible**: *Her explanation certainly sounded believable.* 她的解释听起来的确可信。◇ *a play with believable characters* 剧中人物真实可信的戏剧 OPP **unbelievable**

be·lieve /bɪˈliːv/ *verb* (not used in the progressive tenses 不用于进行时)

• **FEEL CERTAIN** 相信 **1** [T] to feel certain that sth is true or that sb is telling you the truth 相信；认为真实：~ **sb** *I don't believe you!* 我不相信你的话！◇ *The man claimed to be a social worker and the old woman believed him.* 那个男人自称是社会福利工作者，老妇人信以为真。◇ *Believe me, she's not right for you.* 相信我，她不适合你。◇ ~ **sth** *I believed his lies for years.* 我很多年都对他的谎话信以为真。◇ *I find that* ***hard to believe.*** 我对此感到难以相信。◇ ***Don't believe a word of it*** (= don't believe any part of what sb is saying). 一点也不要相信那些话。◇ ~ (**that**)… *People used to believe (that) the earth was flat.* 人们一度认为地球是平的。◇ *He refused to believe (that) his son was*

B

involved in drugs. 他不愿相信他的儿子沾染毒品。◇ ***I do believe you're right*** (= I think sth is true, even though it is surprising). 我的确相信你是对的。

• **THINK POSSIBLE** 认为有可能 **2** [I, T] to think that sth is true or possible, although you are not completely certain 把（某事）当真；认为有可能：*'Where does she come from?' 'Spain, I believe.'* "她是哪里人？""我想是西班牙人。" ◇ *'Does he still work there?' '**I believe so/not.**'* "他还在那里工作吗？""我想是 / 不是。" ◇ **~ (that)...** *Police believe (that) the man may be armed.* 警方认为那个人可能携有武器。◇ **it is believed (that)...** *It is believed that the couple have left the country.* 据信那对夫妇已经离开了这个国家。◇ **~ sb/sth to be, have, etc. sth** *The vases are believed to be worth over $20 000 each.* 那些花瓶据估计每个价值都超过 2 万美元。◇ **~ sb/sth + adj.** *Three sailors are missing, believed drowned.* 有三位船员失踪，相信是淹死了。➲ SYNONYMS AT THINK

• **HAVE OPINION** 认定 **3** [T] **~ (that)...** to have the opinion that sth is right or true 认定；看作：*The party believes (that) education is the most important issue facing the government.* 该党把教育视为政府面临的最重要的问题。➲ LANGUAGE BANK AT ACCORDING TO, OPINION

• **BE SURPRISED/ANNOYED** 吃惊；恼怒 **4** [T] **don't/can't ~** used to say that you are surprised or annoyed at sth（表示对某事吃惊或恼怒）：**~ (that)...** *She couldn't believe (that) it was all happening again.* 她简直无法相信整件事又在重演。◇ **~ how, what, etc....** *I can't believe how much better I feel.* 真想不到我觉得好多了。

• **RELIGION** 宗教 **5** [I] to have a religious faith 有宗教信仰：*The god appears only to those who believe.* 信神则神在。

IDM **believe it or 'not** (*informal*) used to introduce information that is true but that may surprise people 信不信由你：*Believe it or not, he asked me to marry him!* 信不信由你，他向我求婚了！ **believe (you) 'me** (*informal*) used to emphasize that you strongly believe what you are saying 我敢保证：*You haven't heard the last of this, believe you me!* 我敢保证你没听说过最新的消息。 **don't you be'lieve it!** (*informal*) used to tell sb that sth is definitely not true 绝对不正确（不可相信） **I don't be'lieve it!** (*informal*) used to say that you are surprised or annoyed about sth （表示吃惊或恼怒）我简直无法相信：*I don't believe it! What are you doing here?* 我简直无法相信！你在这里干什么？ **if you believe that, you'll believe 'anything** (*informal*) used to say that you think sb is stupid if they believe that sth is true 你要是连这都相信，还有什么不信的 **make believe (that...)** to pretend that sth is true 假装 ➲ RELATED NOUN MAKE-BELIEVE **not believe your 'ears/'eyes** (*informal*) to be very surprised at sth you hear/see 不相信自己的耳朵（或眼睛）；对所闻（或所见）非常吃惊：*I couldn't believe my eyes when she walked in.* 她走进来时我简直不相信自己的眼睛。 **seeing is be'lieving** (*saying*) used to say that sb will have to believe that sth is true when they see it, although they do not think it is true now 眼见为实；百闻不如一见 **would you be'lieve (it)?** (*informal*) used to show that you are surprised and annoyed about sth （表示惊讶或气愤）你能相信吗：*And, would you believe, he didn't even apologize!* 而且，可气的是，他连个道歉都没有！ **you/you'd better be'lieve it!** (*informal*) used to tell sb that sth is definitely true 当然没错；千真万确 ➲ MORE AT GIVE *v.*

PHR V **be'lieve in sb/sth** to feel certain that sb/sth exists 相信某人（或事物）的存在：*Do you believe in God?* 你相信有上帝吗？ **be'lieve in sb** to feel that you can trust sb and/or that they will be successful 信赖；信任；相信某人会成功：*They need a leader they can believe in.* 他们需要一个可以信赖的领导。➲ SYNONYMS AT TRUST **be'lieve in sth** to think that sth is good, right or acceptable 认为某事好（或对、可接受）：**believe in doing sth** *I don't believe in hitting children.* 我不赞成打孩子。 **be'lieve sth of sb** to think that sb is capable of sth 相信某人能干出某事：*Are you sure he was lying? I can't believe that of him.* 你确信他在说谎吗？我不相信他会干这种事。

be·liever /bɪ'liːvə(r)/ *noun* a person who believes in the existence or truth of sth, especially sb who believes in a god or religious faith 信徒 OPP **unbeliever**

IDM **be a (great/firm) believer in sth** to believe strongly that sth is good, important or valuable 坚信（或极力推崇）某事物的人

Be·li·sha bea·con /bəˌliːʃə 'biːkən/ *noun* (in Britain) a post with an orange flashing light on top marking a place where cars must stop to allow people to cross the road 人行横道指示灯柱（英国，上有标示人行横道的橘黄色闪光灯）

be·lit·tle /bɪ'lɪtl/ *verb* **~ sb/sth** to make sb or the things that sb does seem unimportant 贬低；小看：*She felt her husband constantly belittled her achievements.* 她觉得她的丈夫时常贬低她的成就。

bell /bel/ *noun* **1** a hollow metal object, often shaped like a cup, that makes a ringing sound when hit by a small piece of metal inside it; the sound that it makes 铃（声）；钟（声）；钟状物：*A peal of church bells rang out in the distance.* 远处响起了一阵教堂的钟声。◇ *a bicycle bell* 自行车铃铛 ◇ *His voice came down the line **as clear as a bell**.* 他的声音如铃声般清脆地从听筒里传出来。◇ *the bell of a trumpet* (= the bell-shaped part at the end of it) 小号的喇叭口 ◇ *a bell-shaped flower* 喇叭形花朵 ➲ VISUAL VOCAB PAGE V37 **2** an electrical device which makes a ringing sound when a button on it is pushed; the sound that it makes, used as a signal or a warning 电铃（声）：***Ring the bell** to see if they're in.* 按按门铃，看他们在不在家。◇ *The **bell's ringing**!* 打铃了！◇ *The bell went for the end of the lesson.* 下课的铃声响了。◇ *An **alarm bell** went off.* 警钟响了。◇ (*figurative*) ***Warning bells** started ringing in her head as she sensed that something was wrong.* 当她意识到有差错时，头脑中便敲了警钟。

IDM **give sb a 'bell** (*BrE, informal*) to call sb by telephone 打电话给某人 ➲ MORE AT ALARM *n.*, PULL *v.*, RING² *v.*, SOUND *adj.*

bella·donna /ˌbelə'dɒnə; *NAmE* -'dɑːnə/ *noun* [U] **1** = DEADLY NIGHTSHADE **2** a poisonous drug made from DEADLY NIGHTSHADE 颠茄制剂

'bell-bottoms *noun* [pl.] trousers/pants with legs that become very wide below the knee 喇叭裤

bell·boy /'belbɔɪ/ (*especially NAmE*) (*NAmE also* **bell·hop**) *noun* a person whose job is to carry people's cases to their rooms in a hotel （旅馆的）行李员

'bell curve *noun* (*mathematics* 数) a line on a GRAPH that rises to a high round curve in the middle, showing NORMAL DISTRIBUTION 钟形曲线

belle /bel/ *noun* (*old-fashioned*) a beautiful woman; the most beautiful woman in a particular place 美女；（某地）最美的女人

belles-lettres /ˌbel 'letrə/ *noun* [U+sing./pl. v.] (*from French, old-fashioned*) studies or writings on the subject of literature or art, contrasted with those on technical or scientific subjects 纯文学，美文学，美文（指有别于科技题材的文学或艺术研究或作品）

bell·hop /'belhɒp; *NAmE* -hɑːp/ *noun* (*NAmE*) = BELLBOY

bel·li·cose /'belɪkəʊs; -kəʊz; *NAmE* -koʊs; -koʊz/ *adj.* (*formal*) having or showing a desire to argue or fight 好争辩的；好斗的；好战的 SYN **aggressive, warlike** ▸ **bel·li·cos·ity** /ˌbelɪ'kɒsəti; *NAmE* -'kɑːs-/ *noun* [U]

-bellied ➲ BELLY *n.* (3)

bel·liger·ent /bə'lɪdʒərənt/ *adj.*, *noun*

■ *adj.* **1** unfriendly and aggressive 好斗的；寻衅的；挑衅的 SYN **hostile**：*a belligerent attitude* 寻衅的态度 **2** [only before noun] (*formal*) (of a country 国家) fighting a war 参战的；交战的：***the belligerent countries/states/nations*** 交战各国 ▸ **bel·liger·ence** /-əns/ *noun* [U] **bel·liger·ent·ly** *adv.*

■ *noun* (*formal*) a country or group that is fighting a war 交战国；交战团体

ˈbell jar *noun* a tall round glass cover, used by scientists 钟形玻璃罩（科学家使用）

bel·low /ˈbeləʊ; *NAmE* -loʊ/ *verb* **1** [I, T] to shout in a loud deep voice, especially because you are angry 大声吼叫；怒吼 **SYN** **yell**: **~ (at sb)** *They bellowed at her to stop.* 他们吼叫着让她停下。◇ **~ sth (at sb)** *The coach bellowed instructions from the sidelines.* 教练在场边大声发号施令。◇ **+ speech** *'Get over here!' he bellowed.* "给我过来！"他吼道。➲ SYNONYMS AT SHOUT **2** [I] when a large animal such as a BULL **bellows**, it makes a loud deep sound （公牛等）吼叫 ▶ **bel·low** *noun*: *to let out a bellow of rage/pain* 发出怒吼；疼痛地叫喊

bellows 风箱

bel·lows /ˈbeləʊz; *NAmE* -loʊz/ *noun* (*pl.* **bel·lows**) [C+sing./pl. v.] a piece of equipment for blowing air into or through sth. Bellows are used for making a fire burn better or for producing sound in some types of musical instruments. 风箱；吹风器: *a pair of bellows* (= a small bellows with two handles to be pushed together) 手用吹风器（俗称皮老虎）

ˈbell pepper (*NAmE*) (*BrE* **pep·per**) (*also* **ˌsweet ˈpepper** *BrE, NAmE*) *noun* a hollow fruit, usually red, green or yellow, eaten as a vegetable either raw or cooked 甜椒；柿子椒；灯笼椒 ➲ VISUAL VOCAB PAGE V34

ˈbell pull *noun* a rope or handle that you pull to make a bell ring, for example to make sb in another room hear you 拉铃索；拉铃手柄

ˈbell push *noun* (*BrE*) a button that you press to make an electric bell ring 电铃按钮

ˈbell-ringer (*also* **ringer**) *noun* a person who rings church bells as a hobby （教堂的）业余敲钟人 ▶ **ˈbell-ringing** *noun* [U] ➲ SEE ALSO CAMPANOLOGIST, CAMPANOLOGY

ˌbells and ˈwhistles *noun* [pl.] (*computing* 计) attractive extra features 华丽的点缀

bell·wether /ˈbelweðə(r)/ *noun* [usually sing.] something that is used as a sign of what will happen in the future 征兆；前导: *University campuses are often the bellwether of change.* 大学校园往往引领变革的新潮。

belly /ˈbeli/ *noun, verb*

▪ *noun* (*pl.* **-ies**) **1** the part of the body below the chest 腹部；肚子 **SYN** **stomach, gut**: *They crawled along on their bellies.* 他们匍匐前进。➲ SEE ALSO BEER BELLY, POT BELLY at POT-BELLIED **2** (*literary*) the round or curved part of an object （物体的）圆形或凸起部分: *the belly of a ship* 船腹 ➲ VISUAL VOCAB PAGE V38 **3 -bellied** (in adjectives 构成形容词) having the type of belly mentioned 腹部…形的: *swollen-bellied* 腹部肿胀的 ◇ *round-bellied* 肚子圆圆的 ➲ MORE LIKE THIS 8, page R25

IDM **go belly ˈup** (*informal*) to fail completely 彻底失败；垮掉；完蛋: *Last year the business went belly up after one of the partners resigned.* 去年一位合伙人退出后，这家企业就垮掉了。

▪ *verb* (**bel·lies, belly·ing, bel·lied, bel·lied**) [I] **~ (out)** (especially of sails 尤指船帆) to fill with air and become rounder 胀满；鼓起

belly·ache /ˈbelieɪk/ *noun, verb*

▪ *noun* [C, U] (*informal*) a pain in the stomach 肚子疼: *I've got (a) bellyache.* 我肚子疼。

▪ *verb* [I] (*informal*) to complain a lot about sth in an annoying or unreasonable way 无端地大发牢骚

ˈbelly button *noun* (*informal*) = NAVEL

ˈbelly dance *noun* a dance, originally from the Middle East, in which a woman moves her belly and hips around 肚皮舞（起源于中东地区，跳舞女郎扭动肚皮和臀部）▶ **ˈbelly dancer** *noun* **ˈbelly dancing** *noun* [U]

belly·flop /ˈbeliflɒp; *NAmE* -flɑːp/ *noun* (*informal*) a bad DIVE into water, in which the front of the body hits the water flat 肚皮跳（跳水时肚子先落水）

belly·ful /ˈbelifʊl/ *noun*

IDM **have had a ˈbellyful of sb/sth** (*informal*) to have had more than enough of sb/sth, so that you cannot deal with any more 受够了某人 / 某事物: *I've had a bellyful of your moaning.* 我已经听够了你的抱怨了。

ˈbelly laugh *noun* (*informal*) a deep loud laugh 捧腹大笑

be·long 🔑 /bɪˈlɒŋ; *NAmE* -ˈlɔːŋ/ *verb* (not used in the progressive tenses 不用于进行时) **1** 🔑 [I] **+ adv./prep.** to be in the right or suitable place 应在（某处）: *Where do these plates belong* (= where are they kept)? 这些盘子该放在哪里？ ◇ *Are you sure these documents belong together?* 你肯定这些文件应放在一起吗？ **2** 🔑 [I] to feel comfortable and happy in a particular situation or with a particular group of people 适应；合得来: *I don't feel as if I belong here.* 我在这里感觉格格不入。▶ **be·long·ing** *noun* [U]: *to feel a sense of belonging* 有一种归属感

PHR V **beˈlong to sb** **1** 🔑 to be owned by sb 属于某人；归某人所有: *Who does this watch belong to?* 这块表是谁的？ ◇ *The islands belong to Spain.* 这些岛屿隶属西班牙。 **2** an event, a competition, etc. that **belongs to** sb is one in which they are the most successful or popular （事件、比赛等中某人）获胜，最受欢迎: *British actors did well at the award ceremony, but the evening belonged to the Americans.* 英国演员在颁奖仪式上表现很好，但整个晚上却是美国人大出风头。 **beˈlong to sth** **1** 🔑 to be a member of a club, an organization, etc. 是（俱乐部、组织等）的成员: *Have you ever belonged to a political party?* 你加入过什么政党吗？ **2** 🔑 to be part of a particular group, type, or system 是（某族类或纲目）的一部分；属于: *Lions and tigers belong to the cat family.* 狮子和老虎属于猫科。

be·long·ings /bɪˈlɒŋɪŋz; *NAmE* -ˈlɔːŋ-/ *noun* [pl.] the things that you own which can be moved, for example not land or buildings 动产；财物 **SYN** **possessions**: *insurance of property and personal belongings* 不动产和个人财物保险 ◇ *She packed her few belongings in a bag and left.* 她把她的几件东西装进包里便离开了。➲ SYNONYMS AT THING

be·loved *adj., noun*

▪ *adj.* (*formal*) **1** /bɪˈlʌvd/ **~ by/of sb** loved very much by sb; very popular with sb 钟爱的；深受喜爱的: *the deep purple flowers so beloved by artists* 受艺术家青睐的深紫色花 **2** /bɪˈlʌvɪd/ [only before noun] loved very much 深爱的；亲爱的: *in memory of our dearly beloved son, John* 为纪念我们的爱子约翰 ➲ MORE LIKE THIS 22, page R27

▪ *noun* /bɪˈlʌvɪd/ (*old use* or *literary*) a person who is loved very much by sb 心爱的人: *It was a gift from her beloved.* 那是她心爱的人送的礼物。

below 🔑 /bɪˈləʊ; *NAmE* bɪˈloʊ/ *prep., adv.*

▪ *prep.* **1** 🔑 at or to a lower level or position than sb/sth 在（或到）…下面: *He dived below the surface of the water.* 他潜入了水中。◇ *Please do not write below this line.* 请不要在这条线下面书写。◇ *Skirts will be worn below* (= long enough to cover) *the knee.* 穿裙子要过膝。 **2** 🔑 of a lower amount or standard than sb/sth （数量）少于；（标准）低于: *The temperatures remained below freezing all day.* 气温一整天都保持在冰点以下。◇ *Her work was well below average for the class.* 她的功课远在班上的中等水平以下。 **3** 🔑 of a lower rank or of less importance than sb/sth （级别、重要性）低于: *A police sergeant is below an inspector.* 巡佐的级别低于巡官。

▪ *adv.* **1** 🔑 at or to a lower level, position or place 在（或到）下面: *They live on the floor below.* 他们住在下一层楼。◇ *I could still see the airport buildings far below.*

B

我还能远远地看到下方的机场建筑。◇ *See below* (= at the bottom of the page) *for references.* 见本页末参考资料。◇ *The passengers who felt seasick stayed below* (= on a lower DECK). 晕船的乘客待在下层客舱。**2** (of a temperature 温度) lower than zero 零度以下: *The thermometer had dropped to a record 40 below* (= –40 degrees). 温度计降到了零下 40 度的纪录。 **3** at a lower rank 下级: *This ruling applies to the ranks of Inspector and below.* 这项规定适用于巡官及以下人员。

beˌlow-the-ˈfold *adj.* not in a position where it is seen first, for example on the bottom part of a newspaper page or web page（报纸版面、网页等）居于下端的，位置不明显的，第一眼看不到的: *below-the-fold links* 网页下端的链接 ◇ *That story would have been better in a less prominent, below-the-fold position.* 那则报道如果刊登在不那么醒目的页底位置效果本可以更好。➲ COMPARE ABOVE-THE-FOLD IDM SEE FOLD *n.*

belt /belt/ *noun, verb*

■ ***noun*** **1** a long narrow piece of leather, cloth, etc. that you wear around the waist 腰带；皮带: *to* ***do up/fasten/ tighten a belt*** 系上 / 扎牢 / 扎紧腰带 ◇ *a belt buckle* 腰带扣 ➲ VISUAL VOCAB PAGE V68 ➲ SEE ALSO BLACK BELT, LIFE-BELT, SEAT BELT, SUSPENDER BELT **2** a continuous band of material that moves round and is used to carry things along or to drive machinery 传送带；传动带 ➲ SEE ALSO CONVEYOR BELT, FAN BELT **3** an area with particular characteristics or where a particular group of people live 地带；地区: *the country's* ***corn/industrial belt*** 这个国家的产粮区 / 工业区 ◇ *We live in the* ***commuter belt.*** 我们住在通勤者居住带。◇ *a belt of rain moving across the country* 横穿这个国家的降雨带 ➲ SEE ALSO GREEN BELT **4** (*informal*) an act of hitting sth/sb hard 狠打；猛击: *She gave the ball a terrific belt.* 她猛击了一下球。

IDM **below the ˈbelt** (of a remark 说话) unfair or cruel 不公正的；伤人的: *That was distinctly below the belt!* 那显然是不公正的！ **ˌbelt and ˈbraces** (*informal*) taking more actions than are really necessary to make sure that sth succeeds or works as it should 双管齐下；多重保障: *a belt-and-braces policy* 稳妥可靠的政策 ➲ MORE LIKE THIS 13, page R26 **have sth under your ˈbelt** (*informal*) to have already achieved or obtained sth 已经获得某物: *She already has a couple of good wins under her belt.* 她已大胜两场。➲ MORE AT TIGHTEN

■ ***verb*** **1 ~ sb/sth** (*informal*) to hit sb/sth hard 猛击；狠打: *He belted the ball right out of the park.* 他用力一击，球径直飞出了球场外。◇ *I'll belt you if you do that again.* 你要是再这样，我就揍你。 **2** [I] **+ adv./prep.** (*informal, BrE*) to move very fast 飞奔；飞驰 SYN **tear**[1]: *A truck came belting up behind us.* 一辆货车从我们后方飞驰而来。 **3** [T] **~ sth** to fasten a belt around sth 用带子系住: *The dress was belted at the waist.* 那件连衣裙的裙腰束着条带子。

PHR V **ˌbelt sth↔ˈout** (*informal*) to sing a song or play music loudly 高声唱歌（或奏乐） **ˌbelt ˈup** (*BrE*) **1** (*NAmE* **ˌbuckle ˈup**) (*informal*) to fasten your SEAT BELT (= a belt worn by a passenger in a vehicle) 系上安全带 **2** (*informal*) used to tell sb rudely to be quiet 住口；闭嘴 SYN **shut up**: *Just belt up, will you!* 你安静点行不行！

belt·ed /ˈbeltɪd/ *adj.* with a belt around it 系着带子的: *a belted jacket* 有腰带的夹克

belt·way /ˈbeltweɪ/ *noun* (*US*) a RING ROAD, especially the one around Washington DC（尤指环绕华盛顿特区的）环行路，环路

be·luga /bəˈluːɡə/ (*pl.* **be·luga** or **be·lugas**) *noun* **1** [C] a type of small WHALE 白鲸 **2** [C] a type of large fish that lives in rivers and lakes in eastern Europe 欧洲鳇，欧鳇（大型鲟鱼） **3** (*also* **beˌluga ˈcaviar**) [U] a type of CAVIAR (= fish eggs), from a beluga 鲟鱼鱼子酱

be·moan /bɪˈməʊn; *NAmE* bɪˈmoʊn/ *verb* **~ sth** (*formal*) to complain or say that you are not happy about sth 哀怨；悲叹: *They sat bemoaning the fact that no one would give them a chance.* 他们坐在那里，埋怨别人不肯给他们一个机会。

be·mused /bɪˈmjuːzd/ *adj.* showing that you are confused and unable to think clearly 困惑的；茫然的 SYN **bewildered**: *a* ***bemused expression/smile*** 困惑不解的表情 / 微笑 ▸ **be·muse** *verb* **~ sb** **be·mus·ed·ly** /bɪˈmjuːzɪdli/ *adv.*

bench /bentʃ/ *noun* **1** [C] a long seat for two or more people, usually made of wood（木制）长凳，长椅: *a park bench* 公园长椅 ➲ VISUAL VOCAB PAGE V20 **2 the bench** [sing.] (*law* 律) a judge in court or the seat where he/she sits; the position of being a judge or MAGISTRATE 法官；法官席位；法官（或裁判官）的职位: *His lawyer turned to address the bench.* 他的律师转身对法官讲话。◇ *She has recently been appointed to the bench.* 她最近当上了法官。 **3** [C, usually pl.] (in the British parliament) a seat where a particular group of politicians sit（英国议会的）议员席: *There was cheering from the Opposition benches.* 反对党议员席那边响起了欢呼声。➲ SEE ALSO BACK BENCH, FRONT BENCH **4 the bench** [sing.] (*sport* 体育) the seats where players sit when they are not playing in the game（场边的）运动员休息区: *the substitutes' bench* 替补队员席 **5** [C] = WORKBENCH: *a carpenter's bench* 木工的工作台

bench·mark /ˈbentʃmɑːk; *NAmE* -mɑːrk/ *noun, verb*

■ ***noun*** something that can be measured and used as a standard that other things can be compared with 基准: *Tests at the age of seven provide a benchmark against which the child's progress at school can be measured.* 七岁时进行的测试为孩子在学校中的学习发展提供了一个测量基准。

■ ***verb* ~ sth (against sth)** to judge the quality of sth in relation to that of other similar things 以（某事物）为标准评估（某事物）: *Projects are assessed and benchmarked against the targets.* 以这些目标作为对项目进行评估和检测的基准。

ˈbench press *noun* an exercise in which you lie on a raised surface with your feet on the floor and raise a weight with both arms 仰卧推举

bench·warm·er /ˈbentʃwɔːmə(r); *NAmE* -wɔːrm-/ *noun* (*NAmE, informal*) a sports player who is not chosen to play in a particular game, but is available if their team needs them（运动队的）板凳队员，替补队员 SYN **substitute**

bend /bend/ *verb, noun*

■ ***verb*** (**bent, bent** /bent/) **1** [I, T] (especially of sb's body or head 尤指人的身体或头部) to lean, or make sth lean, in a particular direction（使）倾斜，偏向: *He bent and kissed her.* 他低下头吻了她。◇ **+ adv./prep.** *fields of poppies bending in the wind* 一畦畦随风摇摆的罂粟 ◇ *His dark head bent over her.* 他那黑色的头向她弯去。◇ *She bent forward to pick up the newspaper.* 她弯腰去捡报纸。◇ *Slowly bend from the waist and bring your head down to your knees.* 慢慢弯下腰，把头低垂到膝部。◇ **~ sth (+ adv./ prep.)** *He bent his head and kissed her.* 他低下头吻了她。◇ *She was bent over her desk writing a letter.* 她正伏案写信。 **2** [T, I] **~ (sth)** if you **bend** your arm, leg, etc. or if it **bends**, you move it so that it is no longer straight（使四肢等）弯曲: *Bend your knees, keeping your back straight.* 膝盖弯曲，背部挺直。◇ *Lie flat and let your knees bend.* 平躺曲膝。 **3** [T] **~ sth** to force sth that was straight into an angle or a curve 把…弄弯（或折起）: *Mark the pipe where you want to bend it.* 在管子上把要弄弯的地方做个记号。◇ *The knives were bent out of shape.* 那些刀已经弯曲变形了。◇ *He bent the wire into the shape of a square.* 他把铁丝折成正方形。 **4** [I, T] to change direction to form a curve or an angle; to make sth change direction in this way（使）拐弯，弯曲: *The road bent sharply to the right.* 路向右急拐。◇ **~ sth** *Glass and water both bend light.* 玻璃和水都折光。

IDM **bend sb's ˈear (about sth)** (*informal*) to talk to sb a lot about sth, especially about a problem that you have 向某人唠叨诉说（尤指自己的难处） **bend your ˈmind/ˈefforts to sth** (*formal*) to think very hard about or put a lot of effort into one particular thing 致力于某事；专心致志 **bend the ˈtruth** to say sth that is not completely true 扭曲事理；歪曲事实 **on bended ˈknee(s)** if you ask for sth **on bended knee(s)**, you ask for it in a very anxious and/or HUMBLE way 下跪（请求…）；央求；苦苦哀求 ➲ MORE AT BACKWARDS, RULE *n.*

PHR V **'bend sb to sth** (*formal*) to force or persuade sb to do what you want or to accept your opinions 迫使；说服：*He manipulates people and tries to* ***bend them to his will*** (= make them do what he wants). 他能左右民众，让大家跟随他的意志。

▪ ***noun*** **1** [C] a curve or turn, especially in a road or river（尤指道路或河流的）拐弯，弯道：*a sharp bend in the road* 道路的急拐弯 ➲ WORDFINDER NOTE AT RIVER ➲ SEE ALSO HAIRPIN BEND **2** **the bends** [pl.] severe pain and difficulty in breathing experienced by a DIVER who comes back to the surface of the water too quickly（潜水员过快浮出水面造成的）减压病

IDM **round the 'bend/'twist** (*NAmE* **around the bend**) (*informal*) crazy 疯狂：*She's gone completely round the bend.* 她完全疯了。◇ *The kids have been* ***driving me round the bend*** *today* (= annoying me very much). 孩子们今天快把我气疯了。

bend·er /'bendə(r)/ *noun* (*slang*) a period of drinking a lot of alcohol or taking a lot of drugs （一段时间）狂饮作乐，大量吸毒：*to go on a bender* 纵酒作乐

bendy /'bendi/ *adj.* (*BrE, informal*) **1** that can be bent easily 易弯曲的；易折的 SYN **flexible** **2** with many bends 多弯道的：*a bendy road* 迂回的道路

'bendy bus *noun* (*BrE, informal*) a long bus that bends in the middle so that it can turn corners more easily 铰接式公共汽车；多节巴士

be·neath /bɪ'ni:θ/ *prep.* (*formal*) **1** in or to a lower position than sb/sth; under sb/sth 在（或往）…下面；在（或往）…下方：*They found the body buried beneath a pile of leaves.* 他们发现尸体被埋在一堆树叶下面。◇ *The boat sank beneath the waves.* 小船被大浪吞没了。**2** not good enough for sb（对某人来说）不够好：*He considers such jobs beneath him.* 他觉得这些工作有失他的身份。◇ *They thought she had married beneath her* (= married a man of lower social status). 他们认为她下嫁了（嫁给了地位比她低的人）。▸ **be·neath** *adv.*：*Her careful make-up hid the signs of age beneath.* 她精心的化妆掩盖了她年龄的痕迹。

Bene·dic·tine /ˌbenɪ'dɪktɪn/ *noun* a member of a Christian group of MONKS or NUNS following the rules of St Benedict 本笃会修士（或修女） ▸ **Bene·dic·tine** *adj.*：*a Benedictine monastery* 本笃会隐修院

bene·dic·tion /ˌbenɪ'dɪkʃn/ *noun* [C, U] (*formal*) a Christian prayer of BLESSING（基督教的）祝福，祝祷

bene·fac·tion /ˌbenɪ'fækʃn/ *noun* (*formal*) a gift, usually of money, that is given to a person or an organization in order to do good 捐赠；捐款

bene·fac·tor /'benɪfæktə(r)/ *noun* (*formal*) a person who gives money or other help to a person or an organization such as a school or charity 施主；捐款人；赞助人

bene·fice /'benɪfɪs/ *noun* the paid position of a Christian priest in charge of a PARISH（教区牧师等的）有俸圣职

be·nefi·cent /bɪ'nefɪsnt/ *adj.* (*formal*) giving help; showing kindness 有裨益的；行善的；慈善的 SYN **generous** ▸ **be·nefi·cence** /bɪ'nefɪsns/ *noun* [U]

bene·fi·cial AW /ˌbenɪ'fɪʃl/ *adj.* ~ (**to sth/sb**) (*formal*) improving a situation; having a helpful or useful effect 有利的；有裨益的；有用的 SYN **advantageous, favourable**：*A good diet is beneficial to health.* 良好的饮食有益于健康。OPP **detrimental** ▸ **bene·fi·cial·ly** *adv.*

bene·fi·ciary AW /ˌbenɪ'fɪʃəri; *NAmE* -'fɪʃieri/ *noun* (*pl.* **-ies**) **1** ~ (**of sth**) a person who gains as a result of sth 受益者；受惠人：*Who will be the main beneficiary of the cuts in income tax?* 削减所得税的主要受益者将是谁？**2** ~ (**of sth**) a person who receives money or property when sb dies 遗产继承人

bene·fit AW /'benɪfɪt/ *noun, verb*

▪ ***noun*** **1** [U, C] an advantage that sth gives you; a helpful and useful effect that sth has 优势；益处；成效：*I've* ***had the benefit of*** *a good education.* 我得益于受过良好教育。◇ *The new regulations will be* ***of benefit to*** *everyone concerned.* 新规章将使所有有关人员受益。◇ *It will be* ***to your benefit*** *to arrive early.* 早到将会对你有利。◇ *He couldn't see the benefit of arguing any longer.* 他看不出再争论下去有什么好处。◇ *the benefits of modern medicine* 现代医学的助益 ◇ *It was good to see her finally* ***reaping the benefits*** (= enjoying the results) *of all her hard work.* 看到她终于得享辛勤劳动的成果令人欣慰。➲ SEE ALSO COST-BENEFIT, FRINGE BENEFIT **2** [C, usually pl., U] (*BrE*) money provided by the government to people who need financial help because they are unemployed, ill/sick, etc. 福利费（政府对失业者、病人等提供的补助金）：*The aim is to help people who are* ***on benefits*** (= receiving benefits) *to find jobs.* 目的是帮助领福利金的人找到工作。◇ *You may be eligible to receive benefits.* 你也许有资格领取福利金。◇ *The number of people claiming unemployment benefit fell last month.* 上个月申请领取失业救济金的人数下降了。➲ SEE ALSO CHILD BENEFIT, HOUSING BENEFIT, SICKNESS BENEFIT ➲ WORDFINDER NOTE AT POOR **3** [C, usually pl.] an advantage that you get from a company in addition to the money that you earn（公司发的）福利，奖金：*Private health insurance is offered as part of the employees' benefits package.* 私人医疗保险是提供给员工的一整套福利的其中一项。➲ SEE ALSO FRINGE BENEFIT **4** [C, usually pl.] money from an insurance company（保险公司发的）给付，保险金：*The insurance plan will provide substantial cash benefits to your family in case of your death.* 投保人一旦死亡，该项保险将支付给其家属相当可观的保险金。**5** [C] an event such as a performance, a dinner, etc., organized in order to raise money for a particular person or charity 慈善（或公益）活动：*a* ***benefit match/concert*** 义赛；慈善音乐会 ➲ WORDFINDER NOTE AT CHARITY

IDM **for sb's benefit** especially in order to help or be useful to sb 为帮助某人；为某人的利益：*I have typed out some lecture notes for the benefit of those people who were absent last week.* 我帮上星期缺席的人打印了些课堂笔记。◇ *Don't go to any trouble for my benefit!* 别为我费功夫！**give sb the ˌbenefit of the 'doubt** to accept that sb has told the truth or has not done sth wrong because you cannot prove that they have not told the truth/have done sth wrong（在证据不足的情况下）假定某人说实话，假定某人没有错

▪ ***verb*** (**-t-** or **-tt-**) **1** [T] ~ **sb** to be useful to sb or improve their life in some way 对（某人）有用；使受益：*We should spend the money on something that will benefit everyone.* 我们应该把这笔钱花在大家都能得益的事上。**2** [I] ~ (**from/by sth**) to be in a better position because of sth 得益于；得利于：*Who exactly* ***stands to benefit*** *from these changes?* 到底是谁会从这些变革中直接获益？

Bene·lux /'benɪlʌks/ *noun* [U] a name for Belgium, the Netherlands and Luxembourg, when they are thought of as a group 比荷卢（比利时、荷兰、卢森堡三国并提时的简称）

be·nevo·lent /bə'nevələnt/ *adj.* **1** (*formal*) (especially of people in authority 尤指当权者) kind, helpful and generous 慈善的；行善的；乐善好施的：*a benevolent smile/attitude* 和蔼的笑容 / 态度 ◇ *belief in the existence of a benevolent god* 对于存在仁慈的神的笃信 OPP **malevolent** **2** used in the names of some organizations that give help and money to people in need（用于慈善机构名称）：*the RAF Benevolent Fund* 英国皇家空军慈善基金（组织） ▸ **be·nevo·lence** /bə'nevələns/ *noun* [U] **be·nevo·lent·ly** *adv.*

Ben·gali /beŋ'gɔ:li; *NAmE* -'gɑ:li/ *noun* **1** [C] a person from Bangladesh or West Bengal in eastern India 孟加拉国人；（印度东部的）西孟加拉邦人 **2** [U] the language of people from Bangladesh or West Bengal in eastern India 孟加拉语 ▸ **Ben·gali** *adj.*

be·night·ed /bɪ'naɪtɪd/ *adj.* (*old-fashioned*) **1** (of people 人) without understanding 愚昧无知的 **2** (of places 地方) without the benefits of modern life 落后的；未开发的

B

be·nign /bɪˈnaɪn/ *adj.* **1** (*formal*) (of people 人) kind and gentle; not hurting anybody 善良的；和善的；慈祥的 **2** not causing damage or harm 无害的：*environmentally benign cleaning products* 对环境无害的清洁产品 **3** (*medical* 医) (of TUMOURS growing in the body 体内生长的肿瘤) not dangerous or likely to cause death 良性的 OPP **malignant** ▶ **be·nign·ly** *adv.*：*He smiled benignly.* 他露出了和蔼的笑容。

bent /bent/ *adj., noun* ➲ SEE ALSO BEND *v.*
■ *adj.* **1** not straight 弯曲的：*a piece of bent wire* 一段弯曲的金属丝 ◇ *Do this exercise with your knees bent* (= not with your legs straight). 做这个动作要双膝弯曲。➲ PICTURE AT CURVED **2** (of a person 人) not able to stand up straight, usually as a result of being old or ill/sick（因年老或生病）驼背的，弯腰的：*a small bent old woman* 一个矮小驼背的老太太 ◇ *He was* **bent double** *with laughter.* 他笑弯了腰。 **3** (*BrE, informal*) (of a person in authority 当权者) dishonest 不诚实的；不正派的
IDM ▶ **ˈbent on sth/on doing sth** determined to do sth (usually sth bad) 决心要做，一心想做（通常指坏事）：*She seems bent on making life difficult for me.* 她似乎铁了心要和我过不去。➲ SEE ALSO HELL-BENT **get bent out of ˈshape (about/over sth)** (*NAmE, informal*) to become angry, anxious or upset （为某事）生气，焦虑，烦躁：*Don't get bent out of shape about it. It was just a mistake!* 不要为这事烦恼了，那只是一个错误而已！
■ *noun* [usually sing.] **~ (for sth)** a natural skill or interest in sth（某方面的）天赋，爱好：*She has a bent for mathematics.* 她有数学天赋。

bent·wood /ˈbentwʊd/ *noun* [U] wood that is artificially shaped for making furniture 曲木（经处理用于做家具）：*bentwood chairs* 曲木椅

ben·zene /ˈbenziːn/ *noun* [U] a clear liquid obtained from PETROLEUM and COAL TAR, used in making plastics and many chemical products 苯

be·queath /bɪˈkwiːð/ *verb* (*formal*) **1** to say in a WILL that you want sb to have your property, money, etc. after you die（在遗嘱中）把…遗赠给 SYN **leave**：**~ sth (to sb)** *He bequeathed his entire estate* (= all his money and property) *to his daughter.* 他把全部财产遗赠给他的女儿。◇ **~ sb sth** *He bequeathed his daughter his entire estate.* 他把全部财产遗赠给他的女儿。 **2 ~ sth (to sb) | ~ sb sth** to leave the results of your work, knowledge, etc. for other people to use or deal with, especially after you have died（尤指死后）将（工作成果、知识等）留下（给后人享用或处理）

be·quest /bɪˈkwest/ *noun* (*formal*) money or property that you ask to be given to a particular person when you die 遗产；遗赠：*He left a bequest to each of his grandchildren.* 他给他的孙子孙女每人留下一笔遗产。

be·rate /bɪˈreɪt/ *verb* **~ sb/yourself** (*formal*) to criticize or speak angrily to sb because you do not approve of sth they have done 痛斥；严厉指责

be·reave /bɪˈriːv/ *verb* **be bereaved** if sb **is bereaved**, a relative or close friend has just died 丧失亲友：*The ceremony was an ordeal for those who had been recently bereaved.* 这个仪式对于那些新近丧失亲友的人来说是一种折磨。

be·reaved /bɪˈriːvd/ *adj.* (*formal*) **1** having lost a relative or close friend who has recently died 丧失亲友的：*recently bereaved families* 刚刚痛失亲人的家庭 **2 the bereaved** *noun* (*pl.* **the bereaved**) a person who is bereaved 死者的亲友：*an organization offering counselling for the bereaved* 为死者亲友提供辅导的组织

be·reave·ment /bɪˈriːvmənt/ *noun* **1** [U] the state of having lost a relative or close friend because they have died 丧失亲人；丧亲之痛：*the pain of an emotional crisis such as divorce or bereavement* 诸如离婚或痛失亲人等的情感危机的痛苦 **2** [C] the death of a relative or close friend 亲友的丧亡：*A family bereavement meant that he could not attend the conference.* 他家里有人去世了，所以不能出席会议。

be·reft /bɪˈreft/ *adj.* [not before noun] (*formal*) **1 ~ of sth** completely lacking sth; having lost sth 完全没有，丧失，失去（某物）：*bereft of ideas/hope* 无计可施；失去希望 **2** (of a person 人) sad and lonely because you have lost sth 感到失落：*He was utterly bereft when his wife died.* 他的妻子去世时，他十分凄凉。

beret /ˈbereɪ; *NAmE* bəˈreɪ/ *noun* a round flat cap made out of soft cloth 贝雷帽（扁圆无檐）➲ VISUAL VOCAB PAGE V70

berg /bɜːg; *NAmE* bɜːrg/ *noun* (*SAfrE*) **1** a mountain or group of mountains 山；群山；山脉 **2 the Berg** [sing.] the Drakensberg, a group of tall mountains in South Africa（南非）德拉肯斯山脉

ber·ga·mot /ˈbɜːgəmɒt; *NAmE* ˈbɜːrgəmɑːt/ *noun* [U] **1** (*also* **ˈbergamot oil**) oil from the skin of a small orange 香柠檬精油 **2** a type of HERB 香柠檬香草；香柠檬草药

berg·schrund /ˈbɜːgʃrʊnd; *NAmE* ˈbɜːrkʃrʊnt/ *noun* (*geology* 地) a deep crack formed where a GLACIER (= a large moving mass of ice) meets the side of a mountain 冰后隙（山侧面的冰川边沿裂隙）

beri·beri /ˌberiˈberi/ *noun* [U] a disease that affects the nerves and heart, caused by a lack of VITAMIN B 脚气病

berk /bɜːk; *NAmE* bɜːrk/ *noun* (*old-fashioned, BrE, slang*) a stupid person 傻瓜；蠢人 SYN **idiot**

ber·ke·lium /bɜːˈkiːliəm; ˈbɜːkliəm; *NAmE* ˈbɜːrkliəm/ *noun* [U] (*symb.* **Bk**) a chemical element. Berkelium is a RADIOACTIVE metal that is produced artificially from AMERICIUM and HELIUM. 锫（放射性元素）

Ber·lin·er /ˌbɜːˈlɪnə(r); *NAmE* ˌbɜːr-/ *adj.* (*BrE*) (of a newspaper) printed on pages measuring 470mm by 315mm, smaller than a BROADSHEET and larger than a TABLOID 柏林型版式的（纸张规格为 470 毫米× 315 毫米）

berm /bɜːm; *NAmE* bɜːrm/ *noun* (*specialist*) **1** an area of ground at the side of a road; a raised area of ground at the side of a river or CANAL 护坡道；护道；岸堤 **2** a narrow raised area of sand formed on a beach by the waves coming in from the sea 滩沿，后滨阶地（海浪淘沙淤积而成）

Bermuda shorts /bəˌmjuːdə ˈʃɔːts; *NAmE* bərˌmjuːdə ˈʃɔːrts/ (*also* **Ber·mu·das** /bəˈmjuːdəz; *NAmE* bərˈm-/) *noun* [pl.] SHORTS (= short trousers/pants) that come down to just above the knee 百慕大短裤（长及膝部）：*a pair of Bermudas* 一条百慕大短裤

the Berˌmuda ˈTriangle *noun* [sing.] an area in the Atlantic Ocean between Bermuda, Florida and Puerto Rico where a large number of ships and aircraft are believed to have disappeared in a mysterious way 百慕大三角（大西洋中位于百慕大、佛罗里达州和波多黎各之间的海域，已有许多船只、飞机在此神秘地失踪）：*This area of town is known as the Bermuda Triangle because drinkers can disappear into the pubs and clubs and be lost to the world.* 城里的这一地区称作"百慕大三角"，因为酒徒进入这里的酒吧和夜总会后就可能消失得无影无踪。

berry /ˈberi/ *noun* (*pl.* **-ies**) (often in compounds 常构成复合词) a small fruit that grows on a bush. There are several types of berry, some of which can be eaten. 浆果；莓：*Birds feed on nuts and berries in the winter.* 鸟类靠坚果和浆果过冬。◇ *blackberries/raspberries* 黑莓；覆盆子 ➲ VISUAL VOCAB PAGES V10, V33

ber·serk /bəˈzɜːk; -ˈsɜːk; *NAmE* bərˈzɜːrk; -ˈsɜːrk/ *adj.* [not usually before noun] (*informal*) **1** very angry, often in a violent or uncontrolled way 盛怒；暴跳如雷：*He went berserk when he found out where I'd been.* 他弄清楚我去过哪儿后勃然大怒。 **2** very excited 极为激动；兴奋不已；发狂：*People were going berserk with excitement.* 人们兴奋得发狂了。

berth /bɜːθ; *NAmE* bɜːrθ/ *noun, verb*
■ *noun* **1** a place to sleep on a ship or train, or in a CARAVAN/CAMPER（船或火车等的）卧铺，舱位，铺位

SYN **bunk 2** a place where a ship or boat can stop and stay, usually in a HARBOUR （船的）泊位，锚地 IDM SEE WIDE *adj.*

■*verb* [T, I] ~ (**sth**) to put a ship in a berth or keep it there; to sail into a berth （使船）停泊：*The ship is berthed at Southampton.* 船停泊在南安普敦。

beryl /ˈberəl/ *noun* [U] a transparent pale green, blue or yellow SEMI-PRECIOUS stone, used in making jewellery 绿柱石

beryl·lium /bəˈrɪliəm/ *noun* [U] (*symb.* **Be**) a chemical element. Beryllium is a hard grey metal found mainly in the mineral BERYL. 铍

besan /ˈbeɪsʌn/ *noun* [U] = GRAM FLOUR

be·seech /bɪˈsiːtʃ/ *verb* (**be·sought**, **be·sought** /bɪˈsɔːt/ or **be·seeched**, **be·seeched**) ~ **sb** (**to do sth**) (*formal*) to ask sb for sth in an anxious way because you want or need it very much 恳求；哀求；乞求 SYN **implore, beg**：*Let him go, I beseech you!* 求求你让他走吧！

be·seech·ing /bɪˈsiːtʃɪŋ/ *adj.* [only before noun] (*formal*) (of a look, tone of voice, etc. 眼神、语调等) showing that you want sth very much 恳求的；哀求的；乞求的 ▸ **be·seech·ing·ly** *adv.*

beset /bɪˈset/ *verb* (**be·set·ting**, **beset**, **beset**) [usually passive] (*formal*) to affect sb/sth in an unpleasant or harmful way 困扰；威胁：*The team was beset by injury all season.* 这个队整个赛季都因队员受伤而受困扰。◇ *It's one of the most difficult problems besetting our modern way of life.* 那是困扰我们现代生活方式的一个最棘手的问题。

be·side /bɪˈsaɪd/ *prep.* **1** next to or at the side of sb/sth 在旁边（或附近）：*He sat beside her all night.* 整个晚上他都坐在她的身边。◇ *a mill beside a stream* 小溪旁的磨房 **2** compared with sb/sth 与…相比：*My painting looks childish beside yours.* 同你的相比，我的画显得很幼稚。

IDM **be beside the ˈpoint** to not be important or closely related to the main thing you are talking about 无关紧要；离题；不相关：*Yes, I know it was an accident, but that's beside the point.* 是的，我知道那是个事故，可是这无关紧要。 **beˈside yourself** (**with sth**) unable to control yourself because of the strength of emotion you are feeling （因情绪）失去自制力；失常：*He was beside himself with rage when I told him what I had done.* 我告诉他我做了什么事，他快气疯了。

▼**WHICH WORD?** 词语辨析

beside / besides

- The preposition **beside** usually means 'next to something/somebody' or 'at the side of something/somebody'. 介词 beside 通常表示靠近、在旁边：*Sit here beside me.* 坐到我旁边来。 The preposition **besides** means 'in addition to something'. 介词 besides 表示除…之外（还）：*What other sports do you play besides hockey?* 除了玩曲棍球你还做哪些运动？ Do not use **beside** with this meaning. 此义不用 beside。
- The adverb **besides** is not usually used on its own with the same meaning as the preposition. It is mainly used to give another reason or argument for something. * besides 作副词单独使用时通常与作介词时的含义不同，主要用以提出另一理由或论据：*I don't think I'll come on Saturday. I have a lot of work to do. Besides, I don't really like parties.* 我想我星期六不会来。我有好多事要做。再说，我不太喜欢社交聚会。◇ ~~*She likes football. Besides, she likes tennis and basketball.*~~

be·sides /bɪˈsaɪdz/ *prep., adv.*

■*prep.* in addition to sb/sth; apart from sb/sth 除…之外（还）：*We have lots of things in common besides music.* 除了音乐，我们还有很多共通点。◇ *Besides working as a doctor, he also writes novels in his spare time.* 除了当医生之外，他在业余时间还写小说。◇ *I've got no family besides my parents.* 除了父母外，我没有其他亲人。 ➲ LANGUAGE BANK AT EXCEPT ➲ NOTE AT BESIDE

▼**WHICH WORD?** 词语辨析

besides / apart from / except

- The preposition **besides** means 'in addition to'. * besides 作介词表示除…之外（还）：*What other sports do you like besides football?* 除足球外你还喜欢哪些运动？ You use **except** when you mention the only thing that is not included in a statement. 指仅有某事物不包括在内用 except：*I like all sports except football.* 除足球外我喜欢所有的运动。 You can use **apart from** with both these meanings. 上述两种含义均可用 apart from：*What other sports do you like apart from football?* 除足球外你还喜欢哪些运动？◇ *I like all sports apart from football.* 除足球外我喜欢所有的运动。

■*adv.* **1** used for making an extra comment that adds to what you have just said 而且；再说：*I don't really want to go. Besides, it's too late now.* 我并不真的想去，而且现在太晚了。 ➲ LANGUAGE BANK AT ADDITION ➲ NOTE AT BESIDE **2** in addition; also 此外；以及；也：*discounts on televisions, stereos and much more besides* 电视、立体声音响设备以及很多其他货品的折扣

be·siege /bɪˈsiːdʒ/ *verb* **1** ~ **sth** to surround a building, city, etc. with soldiers until the people inside are forced to let you in 围困；包围 SYN **lay siege to**：*Paris was besieged for four months and forced to surrender.* 巴黎被围困了四个月后被迫投降。◇ (*figurative*) *Fans besieged the box office to try and get tickets for the concert.* 歌迷们围着售票处，试图买到音乐会的票。 **2** [usually passive] ~ **sb/sth** (especially of sth unpleasant or annoying 尤指令人不快或烦恼的事) to surround sb/sth in large numbers 团团围住：*The actress was besieged by reporters at the airport.* 那位女演员在机场被记者团团围住。 **3** ~ **sb** (**with sth**) to send so many letters, ask so many questions, etc. that it is difficult for sb to deal with them all （用大量的信件、提问等）使某人应接不暇：*The radio station was besieged with calls from angry listeners.* 广播电台疲于应付愤怒的听众打来的电话。

be·smirch /bɪˈsmɜːtʃ; *NAmE* bɪˈsmɜːrtʃ/ *verb* ~ **sb/sth** (*formal*) to damage the opinion that people have of sb/sth 诋毁；败坏…的名声 SYN **sully**

besom /ˈbiːzəm/ *noun* a brush for sweeping floors, made from sticks tied onto a long handle （长柄）扫帚

be·sot·ted /bɪˈsɒtɪd; *NAmE* -ˈsɑːt-/ *adj.* ~ (**by/with sb/sth**) loving sb/sth so much that you do not behave in a sensible way （对某人、某物）爱得发狂的，痴迷的：*He is completely besotted with his new girlfriend.* 他对他的新女友一片痴心。

be·sought PAST TENSE, PAST PART. OF BESEECH

be·spat·ter /bɪˈspætə(r)/ *verb* ~ **sth** (*literary*) to accidentally cover sth with small drops of water or other liquid 溅洒；溅污

be·speak /bɪˈspiːk/ *verb* (**be·spoke** /bɪˈspəʊk; *NAmE* bɪˈspoʊk/, **be·spoken** /-ˈspəʊkən; *NAmE* -ˈspoʊ-/) ~ **sth** (*literary*) to show or suggest sth 展现；显示：*His style of dressing bespoke great self-confidence.* 他的衣着风格显得十分自信。

be·spec·tacled /bɪˈspektəkld/ *adj.* (*formal*) wearing SPECTACLES 戴眼镜的

be·spoke /bɪˈspəʊk; *NAmE* bɪˈspoʊk/ *adj.* [usually before noun] (*especially BrE, formal*) **1** (*NAmE usually* **ˌcustom-ˈmade**) (of a product 产品) made specially, according to the needs of an individual customer 定做的 SYN **tailor-made**：*bespoke software* 定制的软件 ◇ *a bespoke suit* 一套定做的衣服 **2** making products specially, according to the needs of an individual customer 专做订货的：*a bespoke tailor* 做定做衣服的裁缝

B

bes·sie /'besi/ *noun, adj.* (*BrE, informal*) = BEZZIE

best /best/ *adj., adv., noun, verb*

■ ***adj.*** (superlative of *good* * good 的最高级) **1** of the most excellent type or quality 最好的；最出色的；最优秀的：*That's the best movie I've ever seen!* 那是我看过的最棒的电影！◇ *She was one of the best tennis players of her generation.* 她是同辈中最出色的网球运动员之一。◇ *Is that your best suit?* 那是你最漂亮的一套衣服吗？◇ *They've been* ***best friends*** (= closest friends) *since they were children.* 他们从孩提时起就是最要好的朋友。◇ *the company's* ***best-ever*** *results* 公司有史以来最大的成就 ◇ *We want the kids to have the* ***best possible*** *education.* 我们想让孩子们接受尽可能最好的教育。 **2** most enjoyable; happiest 最愉快的；最幸福的：*Those were the best years of my life.* 那些年是我一生最幸福的时光。 **3** most suitable or appropriate 最合适的；最恰当的：*What's the best way to cook steak?* 牛排怎么做最好？◇ *The best thing to do would be to apologize.* 最恰当的做法应该是道歉。◇ *He's the best man for the job.* 他是担任这项工作的最佳人选。◇ ***It's best*** *if you go now.* 你最好现在就走。◇ *I'm not in the best position to advise you.* 给你提建议，我不是很适合。

IDM HELP Idioms containing **best** *adj.* are at the entries for the nouns and verbs in the idioms, for example **on your best behaviour** is at **behaviour**. 含形容词 best 的习语，都可在该等习语中的名词及动词相关词条找到，如 on your best behaviour 在词条 behaviour 下。

■ ***adv.*** (superlative of *well*, often used in adjectives * well 的最高级，常用于构成形容词) **1** most; to the greatest extent 最；最高程度地：*Which one do you like best?* 你最喜欢哪一个？◇ *Well-drained soil suits the plant best.* 排水性好的土壤最适合于这种植物。◇ *her* ***best-known*** *poem* 她的最有名的诗 **2** in the most excellent way; to the highest standard 最出色地；最高标准地：*He works best in the mornings.* 他早上工作效率最高。◇ *Britain's* ***best-dressed*** *woman* 英国最佳穿戴女士 ◇ *The beaches are beautiful, but,* ***best of all****, there are very few tourists.* 这些海滩很美，最妙的是游客稀少。 **3** in the most suitable or appropriate way 最适合地；最恰当地：*Painting is best done in daylight.* 作画的最佳时间是白天。◇ *Do as you* ***think best*** (= what you think is the most suitable thing to do). 你觉得怎么好，就怎么办吧。

IDM **as ˌbest you ˈcan** not perfectly but as well as you are able 尽可能；尽力：*We'll manage as best we can.* 我们将尽力处理。

■ ***noun*** [sing.] (*usually* **the best**) **1** the most excellent thing or person 最好的事物（或人）：*We all want the best for our children.* 我们都想给孩子提供最好的条件。◇ *They only buy the best.* 他们只买最好的。◇ *They're all good players, but she's the best of all.* 他们都是优秀运动员，而她更是其中的佼佼者。◇ *We're* ***the best of friends*** (= very close friends). 我们是至交。 **2** the highest standard that sb/sth can reach （人或事物所能达到的）最高标准：*She always brings out the best in people.* 她总是让人表现出最优秀的品质。◇ *The town* ***looks its best*** (= is most attractive) *in the spring.* 这个小镇在春天景色最美。◇ *Don't worry about the exam—just* ***do your best****.* 别担心考试，尽你的最大努力吧。◇ *The roses are* ***past their best*** *now.* 这些玫瑰花已开败了。◇ *I don't really feel* ***at my best*** *today.* 我今天状态不佳。 **3** something that is as close as possible to what you need or want 最合乎要求的事物：*Fifty pounds is the best I can offer you.* 我顶多出五十英镑。◇ *The best we can hope for in the game is a draw.* 我们至多能希望比赛打成平局。 **4** the highest standard that a particular person has reached, especially in a sport （个人的）最高水平，最高纪录：*a lifetime best of 12.0 seconds* * 12.0 秒的毕生最好成绩 ➲ SEE ALSO PERSONAL BEST

IDM **all the ˈbest** (*informal*) used when you are saying goodbye to sb or ending a letter, to give sb your good wishes （告别用语或书信结语）祝一切顺利，万事如意 **at ˈbest** used for saying what is the best opinion you can have of sb/sth, or the best thing that can happen, when the situation is bad （表达最正面的看法或恶劣状况下可能出现的最好转机）充其量：*Their response to the proposal was, at best, cool.* 他们对提议的反应充其量只能说是漠然置之。◇ *We can't arrive before Friday at best.* 我们无论如何星期五之前也到不了。 **be (all) for the ˈbest** used to say that although sth appears bad or unpleasant now, it will be good in the end 结局总会好的：*I don't want you to leave, but perhaps it's for the best.* 我并不想让你走，但也许还是走的好。 **the best of a bad ˈbunch** (*BrE also* **the best of a bad ˈlot**) (*informal*) a person or thing that is a little better than the rest of a group, although none are very good 一群（或堆）坏的里较好者；矮子中的将军 **the best of ˈthree, ˈfive, etc.** (especially in games and sports 尤指游戏和体育比赛) up to three, five, etc. games played to decide who wins, the winner being the person who wins most of them 三局两胜（或五局三胜等） **the best that money can ˈbuy** the very best 佳品；精品；极品：*We make sure our clients get the best that money can buy.* 我们确保客户买到最好的产品。 **do, mean, etc. sth for the ˈbest** to do or say sth in order to achieve a good result or to help sb 为美好的目的；出于好意：*I just don't know what to do for the best.* 我就是弄不清做什么才好。◇ *I'm sorry if my advice offended you—I meant it for the best.* 如果我的建议冒犯了你，我很抱歉。但我原本是出于好意。 **have/get the ˈbest of sth** to gain more advantage from sth than sb else 获胜；胜过；占上风：*I thought you had the best of that discussion.* 我以为你在那场讨论中占了上风。 **make the best of sth/it | make the best of things | make the best of a bad job** to accept a bad or difficult situation and do as well as you can 尽力而为 **to the best of your ˈknowledge/beˈlief** as far as you know 据某人所知（或了解）：*He never made a will, to the best of my knowledge.* 据我所知，他从未立过遗嘱。 **with the ˈbest (of them)** as well as anyone 不亚于任何人；不比任何人差：*He'll be out there, dancing with the best of them.* 他将出现在舞池中，跳得不亚于任何人。 ➲ MORE AT BUNCH *n.*, HOPE *v.*, LUCK *n.*, SUNDAY

■ ***verb*** [usually passive] **~ sb** (*formal*) to defeat or be more successful than sb 打败；胜过

ˌbest-beˈfore date *noun* (*BrE*) a date printed on a container or package, advising you to use food or drink before this date as it will not be of such good quality after that 最佳食用期限，最佳保质期，保存期限（见于食物或饮料包装） ➲ COMPARE SELL-BY DATE

bes·tial /'bestiəl; *NAmE* 'bestʃəl/ *adj.* (*formal*) cruel and disgusting; of or like a BEAST 凶残的；野兽的；野兽般的；兽性的：***bestial acts/cruelty/noises*** 毫无人性的行为 / 残忍；野兽般的喧闹声

bes·ti·al·ity /ˌbesti'æləti; *NAmE* ˌbestʃi-/ *noun* [U] **1** (*specialist*) sexual activity between a human and an animal 兽交；兽奸 **2** (*formal*) cruel or disgusting behaviour 兽行

bes·tiary /'bestiəri; *NAmE* -eri/ *noun* (*pl.* **-ies**) a collection of descriptions of, or stories about, various types of animal, especially one written in the Middle Ages （尤指中世纪的）动物寓言集

bestie /'besti/ *noun* (*informal*) a person's best friend 最要好的朋友；死党：*It was fun hanging out with my bestie.* 那时候跟好友一起出去玩真开心。 ◇ **be besties with sb** *Hank is besties with Sarah.* 汉克跟萨拉是死党。

be·stir /bɪ'stɜː(r)/ *verb* (**-rr-**) **~ yourself** (*formal* or *humorous*) to start doing things after a period during which you have been doing nothing 发奋；振作起来 SYN rouse

ˌbest ˈman *noun* [sing.] a male friend or relative of the BRIDEGROOM at a wedding, who helps him during the wedding ceremony 男傧相；伴郎 ➲ COMPARE BRIDESMAID ➲ WORDFINDER NOTE AT WEDDING

be·stow /bɪ'stəʊ; *NAmE* bɪ'stoʊ/ *verb* **~ sth (on/upon sb)** (*formal*) to give sth to sb, especially to show how much they are respected （将…）给予，授予，献给：*It was a title bestowed upon him by the king.* 那是国王赐给他的头衔。

ˌbest ˈpractice *noun* [U, C] a way of doing sth that is seen as a very good example of how it should be done and can be copied by other companies or organizations（公司或机构的）最佳实践，最佳做法

be·stride /bɪˈstraɪd/ *verb* ~ **sth** (*literary*) to sit with one leg on either side of sth 跨坐；骑：*He bestrode his horse.* 他骑上马。

best·sell·er /ˌbestˈselə(r)/ *noun* a product, usually a book, which is bought by large numbers of people 畅销品；畅销书：*the bestseller list* 畅销书榜 ▸ **best·sell·ing** *adj.*：*a* ***bestselling novel/author*** 畅销小说；畅销书作者

be·suit·ed /bɪˈsuːtɪd; *BrE also* -ˈsjuːt-/ *adj.* (*formal*) wearing a suit 身着套装的：*besuited businessmen* 身着套装的商界人员

bet 🔑 /bet/ *verb, noun*

■ ***verb*** (**bet·ting, bet, bet**) **1** 🔑 [I, T] to risk money on a race or an event by trying to predict the result 下赌注（于）；用…打赌：*You have to be over 16 to bet.* 赌博者年龄不得低于 16 岁。◇ **~ on/against (sb/sth doing) sth** *I wouldn't bet on them winning the next election.* 下一次选举我不会赌他们赢。◇ **~ sth (on sth)** *He bet $2 000 on the final score of the game.* 他下 2 000 美元赌比赛的最后比分。◇ **~ (sb) (sth) (that…)** *She bet me £20 that I wouldn't do it.* 她和我打 20 英镑的赌，说我不会那么做。➲ SEE ALSO BETTING, GAMBLE *v.* ➲ **WORDFINDER NOTE** AT GAMBLING **2** 🔑 [T] (*informal*) used to say that you are almost certain that sth is true or that sth will happen 敢说；八成儿：**~ (that)…** *I bet (that) we're too late.* 我们八成儿太晚了。◇ *You can bet (that) the moment I sit down, the phone will ring.* 几乎可以肯定，我一坐下，电话铃就会响起来。◇ **~ sb (that)…** *I'll bet you (that) he knows all about it.* 我敢说他了解一切。➲ **MORE LIKE THIS** 33, page R28

IDM **I/I'll bet!** (*informal*) **1** used to show that you can understand what sb is feeling, describing, etc.（表示理解）有同感，当然：*'I nearly died when he told me.' 'I bet!'* "他告诉我时，我差一点死掉了。" "肯定是这样！" **2** used to tell sb that you do not believe what they have just said（表示不相信对方的话）：*'I'm going to tell her what I think of her.' 'Yeah, I bet!'* "我要告诉她我对她的看法。" "谅你不敢！" **I wouldn't ˈbet on it | don't ˈbet on it** (*informal*) used to say that you do not think that sth is very likely 不大可能：*'She'll soon get used to the idea.' 'I wouldn't bet on it.'* "她很快就会接受这种看法的。" "很难说。" **ˌyou ˈbet!** (*informal*) used instead of 'yes' to emphasize that sb has guessed sth correctly or made a good suggestion 的确；当然：*'Are you nervous?' 'You bet!'* "你紧张吗？" "这还用说！" **you can bet your ˈlife/your bottom ˈdollar (on sth/(that)…)** (*informal*) used to say that you are certain that sth will happen 肯定；毫无疑问：*You can bet your bottom dollar that he'll be late.* 他肯定会迟到。 **bet the farm/ranch on sth** (*NAmE, informal*) to risk everything you have on an investment, a bet, etc. 赌上全部身家：*The company bet the farm on the new marketing model, only to find that it wasn't successful.* 公司把全部身家都赌在了新的营销模式上，结果却并不成功。

■ ***noun*** **1** 🔑 an arrangement to risk money, etc. on the result of a particular event; the money that you risk in this way 打赌；赌注：*to win/lose a bet* 赢 / 输一场赌 ◇ **~ on sth** *We've got a bet on who's going to arrive first.* 我们打了个赌，看谁先到。◇ *He had a bet on the horses.* 他在那些马上下了赌注。◇ *They all put a bet on the race.* 他们都对比赛下了赌注。◇ *I hear you're taking bets on whether she'll marry him.* 我听说你在拿她是否会嫁给他的事和人打赌。◇ *I did it* ***for a bet*** (= because sb had agreed to pay me money if I did). 我是为了打赌才这么干的。◇ *'Liverpool are bound to win.'* ***'Do you want a bet?'*** (= I disagree with you, I don't think they will.) "利物浦必胜。" "你敢打赌吗？" **2** (*informal*) an opinion about what is likely to happen or to have happened 预计；估计：*My bet is that they've been held up in traffic.* 我估计他们是堵车了。

IDM **all bets are ˈoff** used to say that if a particular event happens then your current forecast, agreement, etc. will no longer apply（某事发生则）结局难料：*We expect shares to rise unless the economy slows down again, in which case all bets are off.* 我们预计股票会涨，除非经济再次下滑。如果真是那样的话，结局就难料了。 **the/your best bet** (*informal*) used to tell sb what is the best action for them to take to get the result they want 最好的办法：*If you want to get around London fast, the Underground is your best bet.* 如果你想在伦敦四处转转而又不费时间，最好是乘地铁。 **a ˌgood/ˌsafe ˈbet** something that is likely to happen, to succeed or to be suitable 很可能发生的事；有望成功的事；合适的东西：*Clothes are a safe bet as a present for a teenager.* 衣服适合作为送给十几岁孩子的礼物。➲ MORE AT HEDGE *v.*

beta /ˈbiːtə; *NAmE* ˈbeɪtə/ *noun* **1** the second letter of the Greek alphabet (Β, β) 希腊字母表的第 2 个字母 **2** = BETA VERSION

ˈbeta blocker *noun* a drug used to control heart rhythm, treat severe chest pain and reduce high blood pressure * β阻滞药（用以控制心率、治疗严重胸部疼痛和降低血压）

ˌbeta-ˈcarotene *noun* [U] a substance found in carrots and other plants, which is needed by humans * β 胡萝卜素

ˈbeta decay *noun* [U] (*physics* 物) the breaking up of an atom in which an ELECTRON is given off * β 衰变（指原子分裂并释放出一个电子）

be·take /bɪˈteɪk/ *verb* (**be·took** /-ˈtʊk/, **be·taken** /-ˈteɪkən/) **~ yourself + adv./prep.** (*literary*) to go somewhere 前往，去（某处）：*He betook himself to his room.* 他进了自己的房间。

ˈbeta particle (*also* **ˈbeta ray**) *noun* (*physics* 物) a fast-moving ELECTRON that is produced when some RADIOACTIVE substances decay * β 粒子；贝塔粒子

ˈbeta test *noun* a test on a new product, done by sb who does not work for the company that is developing the product * β 测试（外部对公司新产品的测试）➲ COMPARE ALPHA TEST ▸ **ˈbeta-test** *verb* **~ sth**

ˈbeta version (*also* **beta**) *noun* [usually sing.] a version of a product, especially computer software, that is almost ready for the public to buy or use, and that is tested by people who do not work for the company that is developing it（尤指计算机软件等新产品上市前的）β 版，测试版 ➲ **WORDFINDER NOTE** AT SOFTWARE

betel /ˈbiːtl/ *noun* [U] the leaves of a climbing plant, also called betel, chewed by people in Asia 槟榔叶

ˈbetel nut *noun* the slightly bitter nut of a tropical Asian PALM, that is cut into small pieces, wrapped in betel leaves, and chewed 槟榔果

bête noire /ˌbet ˈnwɑː(r)/ *noun* (*pl.* **bêtes noires** /ˌbet ˈnwɑː(r); *NAmE also* ˈnwɑːrz/) (*from French*) a person or thing that particularly annoys you and that you do not like 特别讨厌的人（或事物）

be·tide /bɪˈtaɪd/ *verb* IDM SEE WOE

be·token /bɪˈtəʊkən; *NAmE* -ˈtoʊ-/ *verb* **~ sth** (*literary*) to be a sign of sth 预示；表示：*a clear blue sky betokening a fine day* 预示着好天气的晴朗蓝天

be·tray /bɪˈtreɪ/ *verb* **1** to give information about sb/sth to an enemy 出卖；泄露（机密）：**~ sb/sth** *He was offered money to betray his colleagues.* 有人收买他出卖他的同事。◇ **~ sb/sth to sb** *For years they had been betraying state secrets to Russia.* 他们多年来一直向俄罗斯泄露国家机密。 **2 ~ sb/sth** to hurt sb who trusts you, especially by not being loyal or faithful to them 辜负；对…不忠：*She felt betrayed when she found out the truth about him.* 她发现他的真实情况时，感到受了欺骗。◇ *She* ***betrayed his trust*** *over and over again.* 她一次又一次地辜负了他的信任。◇ *I have never known her to* ***betray a confidence*** (= tell other people sth that should be kept secret). 我从未听说过她泄露秘密。➲ **SYNONYMS** AT CHEAT **3 ~ sth** to ignore your principles or beliefs in order to achieve sth or gain an advantage for yourself 背叛（原则或信仰）：*He has been accused of betraying his former socialist ideals.* 有人指责他背弃了他先前的社会主义理想。 **4** to tell sb or make them aware of a piece of information, a

B

feeling, etc., usually without meaning to （无意中）泄露信息，流露情感 **SYN** **give away**: **~ sth** *His voice betrayed the worry he was trying to hide.* 他的声音掩盖不了内心的担忧。◇ **~ yourself** *She was terrified of saying something that would make her betray herself* (= show her feelings or who she was). 她害怕说话时露了自己的底。

be·tray·al /bɪˈtreɪəl/ *noun* [U, C] the act of betraying sb/sth or the fact of being betrayed （被）背叛，出卖：*a sense/a feeling/an act of betrayal* 被出卖的感觉；背叛行为 ◇ *I saw her actions as a betrayal of my trust.* 我认为她的所作所为辜负了我的信任。◇ *the many disappointments and betrayals in his life* 他一生中遭受的诸多失望与背叛

be·troth·al /bɪˈtrəʊðl; *NAmE* -ˈtroʊ-/ *noun* **~ (to sb)** (*formal* or *old-fashioned*) an agreement to marry sb 婚约；订婚 **SYN** **engagement**

be·trothed /bɪˈtrəʊðd; *NAmE* -ˈtroʊ-/ *adj.* (*formal* or *old-fashioned*) **1 ~ (to sb)** having promised to marry sb 订了婚的 **SYN** **engaged** **2 sb's betrothed** *noun* [sing.] the person that sb has promised to marry 已订婚的人；未婚妻（或夫）

bet·ter /ˈbetə(r)/ *adj., adv., noun, verb*

■ ***adj.*** (comparative of *good* * good 的比较级) **1** of a higher standard or less poor quality; not as bad as sth else 较好的；更好的：*We're hoping for better weather tomorrow.* 我们希望明天天气转好。◇ *Her work is getting* ***better and better****.* 她的工作干得越来越好了。◇ *He is in a much better mood than usual.* 他的情绪比平时好多了。◇ *The meal couldn't have been better.* 这顿饭再好吃不过了。◇ *There's nothing better than a long soak in a hot bath.* 没有什么比好好地泡个热水澡更舒服的了。◇ *If you can only exercise once a week, that's* ***better than nothing*** (= better than taking no exercise at all). 即便是一个星期锻炼一次，也比完全不锻炼好。**2** more able or skilled 能力更强的；更熟练的：*She's far better at science than her brother.* 她在理科方面比她的弟弟强得多。**3** more suitable or appropriate 更合适的；更恰当的：*Can you think of a better word than 'nice'?* 你能找到一个比 nice 更合适的字眼吗？◇ *It would be better for him to talk to his parents about his problems.* 他把自己的问题同父母谈谈会比较好。◇ ***You'd be better*** *going by bus.* 你坐公共汽车去会更好些。**4** less ill/sick or unhappy （病势）好转的，见轻的；舒畅些的：*She's a lot better today.* 她今天好多了。◇ *His leg was getting better.* 他的腿在渐渐恢复。◇ *You'll feel* ***all the better for*** *a good night's sleep.* 你晚上睡个好觉就会感觉好得多。**5** fully recovered after an illness; in good health again 痊愈；恢复健康：*Don't go back to work until you are better.* 身体康复之前，不要回去工作。➲ SEE ALSO WELL *adj.* (1)

IDM **HELP** Most idioms containing **better** are at the entries for the nouns and verbs in the idioms, for example **better luck next time** is at **luck**. 大多数含 better 的习语，都可在该等习语中的名词及动词相关词条找到，如 better luck next time 在词条 luck 下。**little/no better than** almost or just the same as; almost or just as bad as 同…（几乎）一样；和…（几乎）一样坏：*The path was no better than a sheep track.* 那条小路简直就像是给羊群踏出来的。**that's (much) ˈbetter 1** used to give support to sb who has been upset and is trying to become calmer （安慰他人时说）很好，这就对了：*Dry your eyes now. That's better.* 把眼泪擦干。这就对了。**2** used to praise sb who has made an effort to improve （称赞努力加以改进的人）很好：*That's much better—you played the right notes this time.* 很好，你这次把音弹准了。**the ˌbigger, ˌsmaller, ˌfaster, ˌslower, etc. the ˈbetter** used to say that sth should be as big, small, etc. as possible 越大（或小、快、慢等）越好：*I love giving parties, the bigger the better.* 我喜欢开派对，越盛大越好。➲ MORE AT DISCRETION, HEAD *n.*, PART *n.*, PREVENTION

■ ***adv.*** (comparative of *well* * well 的比较级) **1** in a more excellent or pleasant way; not as badly 更好；更愉快；不那么差：*She sings much better than I do.* 她唱歌比我好得多。◇ *Sound travels better in water than in air.* 声音在水中比在空气中传播得快。◇ *People are better educated now.* 现在人们教育程度更高了。**2** more; to a greater degree 更；较大程度地：*You'll like her when you know her better.* 你对她了解得多一点就会喜欢她。◇ *A cup of tea? There's nothing I'd like better!* 一杯茶吗？那最好不过了！◇ *Fit people are better able to cope with stress.* 健康的人较能应付压力。**3** used to suggest that sth would be a suitable or appropriate thing to do 更妥；更恰当：*The money could be better spent on more urgent cases.* 这笔钱用于较紧迫的事情也许会好些。◇ *Some things are better left unsaid.* 有些事还是不提为好。◇ *You'd* ***do better to*** *tell her everything before she finds out from someone else.* 你把一切都告诉她才是上策，免得她从别人口中听到。

IDM **HELP** Most idioms containing **better** are at the entries for the nouns, adjectives and verbs in the idioms, for example **better the devil you know** is at **devil**. 大多数含 better 的习语，都可在该等习语中的名词、形容词及动词相关词条找到，如 better the devil you know 在词条 devil 下。**be better ˈoff** to have more money 有较多钱；比较宽裕：*Families will be better off under the new law.* 新法律会使家庭经济宽裕一些。◇ *Her promotion means she's $100 a week better off.* 她的晋升意味着她每星期多挣 100 美元。**OPP** **be worse off** **(than sb/sth) be better off (doing sth)** used to say that sb is/would be happier or more satisfied if they were in a particular position or did a particular thing （在某情况下或因做某事）更幸福，更满意：*She's better off without him.* 没有他，她活得更幸福。◇ *The weather was so bad we'd have been better off staying at home.* 天气非常恶劣，我们还不如待在家里舒服。**had better/best (do sth)** used to tell sb what you think they should do （告诉别人应该做的事）应该，最好：*You'd better go to the doctor about your cough.* 你最好去找医生看看你的咳嗽。◇ *We'd better leave now or we'll miss the bus.* 我们最好现在就走，不然就赶不上公共汽车了。◇ *You'd better not do that again.* 你最好别再这样做了。◇ *'I'll give you back the money tomorrow.' 'You'd better!'* (= as a threat) "我明天会还你钱。""那样最好！"◇ *If you think it is going to be easy, you'd best think again.* 如果你认为那会很容易，你最好再想想。➲ NOTE AT SHOULD

■ ***noun*** **1** [sing., U] something that is better 更好的事物；较好者：*the better of the two books* 两本书中较好的一本 ◇ *I expected better of him* (= I thought he would have behaved better). 我本以为他会表现得好一些。**2 your betters** [pl.] (*old-fashioned*) people who are more intelligent or more important than you 更有才智者；更重要的人

IDM **for ˌbetter or (for) ˈworse** used to say that sth cannot be changed, whether the result is good or bad 不论好坏；不管是福是祸；不管怎样 **get the better of sb/sth** to defeat sb/sth or gain an advantage 挫败…；占上风：*No one can get the better of her in an argument.* 辩论起来没人能辩过她。◇ *She always gets the better of an argument.* 她在争辩中总是占上风。◇ *His curiosity got the better of him* (= he didn't intend to ask questions, but he wanted to know so badly that he did). 好奇心使得他不禁要问。**so much the ˈbetter/ˈworse** used to say that sth is even better/worse 那就更好了 / 更糟了：*We don't actually need it on Tuesday, but if it arrives by then, so much the better.* 实际上我们星期二并不需要它，但如果那时能到就更好。➲ MORE AT CHANGE *n.*, ELDER *n.*, THINK *v.*

■ ***verb*** **1** [often passive] **~ sth** to be better or do sth better than sb/sth else 胜过；超过：*The work he produced early in his career has never really been bettered.* 他后来没出过什么作品能真正比得上他的早期作品。**2 ~ yourself** to improve your social position through education, a better job, etc. （通过教育、更好的工作等）改进社会地位，上进：*Thousands of Victorian workers joined educational associations in an attempt to better themselves.* 维多利亚时代成千上万名工人加入了各种教育协会，以求上进。

ˌbetter ˈhalf *noun* = OTHER HALF

bet·ter·ment /ˈbetəmənt; *NAmE* ˈbetərm-/ *noun* [U] (*formal*) the process of becoming or making sth/sb better 改进；改善；改良 **SYN** **improvement**

bet·ting /ˈbetɪŋ/ *noun* [U] the act of risking money, etc. on the unknown result of an event 打赌；赌钱：*illegal betting* 非法赌博 ➲ SEE ALSO SPREAD BETTING

IDM **what's the betting...? | the betting is that...** (*informal*) it seems likely that... 很可能；大概会：*What's the betting that he gets his own way?* 你认为他可能会自行其是吗？◇ *The betting is that he'll get his own way.* 他很可能会自行其是。

ˈ**betting shop** *noun* (*BrE*) a shop where you can bet on horse races and other competitions 赌马店；彩票经销点 ➲ MORE LIKE THIS 9, page R26

be·tween /bɪˈtwiːn/ *prep., adv.*

■ *prep.* **1** in or into the space separating two or more points, objects, people, etc. （空间上）在…中间，介于…之间：*Q comes between P and R in the English alphabet.* 英语字母表中，Q 在 P 和 R 之间。◇ *I sat down between Jo and Diana.* 我在乔和黛安娜中间坐下。◇ *Switzerland lies between France, Germany, Austria and Italy.* 瑞士位于法国、德国、奥地利和意大利之间。◇ *The paper had fallen down between the desk and the wall.* 那张纸掉在桌子和墙壁之间的缝隙里。◇ (*figurative*) *My job is somewhere between a secretary and a personal assistant.* 我的工作介于秘书和私人助理之间。 **2** in the period of time that separates two days, years, events, etc. （时间上）在…之间，在…中间：*It's cheaper between 6 p.m. and 8 a.m.* 下午 6 点到早晨 8 点间价钱较便宜。◇ *Don't eat between meals.* 正餐之间不要吃零食。◇ *Children must attend school between the ages of 5 and 16.* * 5 到 16 岁的孩子必须上学。◇ *Many changes took place between the two world wars.* 两次世界大战之间发生了很多变化。 **3** at some point along a scale from one amount, weight, distance, etc. to another （数量、重量、距离等）介于…之间：*It weighed between nine and ten kilos.* 重量在九到十公斤之间。◇ *The temperature remained between 25°C and 30°C all week.* 整个星期气温都保持在 25 到 30 摄氏度之间。 **4** (of a line 界线) separating one place from another 分隔着；在…之间：*the border between Sweden and Norway* 瑞典和挪威之间的边界 **5** from one place to another 从（一地）到（另一地）；往返于：*We fly between Rome and Paris twice daily.* 我们每天有两次航班往返于罗马和巴黎之间。 **6** used to show a connection or relationship （表示联系或关系）：*a difference/distinction/contrast between two things* 两事物之间的差异 / 区别 / 对比 ◇ *a link between unemployment and crime* 失业与犯罪之间的关联 ◇ *There's a lot of bad feeling between them.* 他们彼此间芥蒂颇多。◇ *I had to choose between the two jobs.* 我得在两份工作之间作出选择。 **7** shared by two or more people or things 合用；共享：*We ate a pizza between us.* 我们合吃了一张比萨饼。◇ *This is just* **between you and me/between ourselves** (= it is a secret). 这事只限我们两人知道。 **8** by putting together the efforts or actions of two or more people or groups 通过共同努力；一起：*We ought to be able to manage it between us.* 我们齐心协力应该能把这事办妥。 **9 ~ doing sth** used to show that several activities are involved （同时进行几项活动时用）：*Between working full-time and taking care of the kids, he didn't have much time for hobbies.* 他一边全职工作一边又要照顾孩子，所以抽不出很多时间搞业余爱好。

■ *adv.* (*usually* **in between**) in the space or period of time separating two or more points, objects, etc. or two dates, events, etc. （空间或时间上）在中间，当中：*The house was near a park but there was a road in between.* 房子在一处公园附近，但两者之间隔着一条马路。◇ *I see her most weekends but not very often in between.* 我周末大多都能见到她，但平时不常见到。 IDM SEE BETWIXT

be·twixt /bɪˈtwɪkst/ *adv., prep.* (*literary* or *old use*) between 在…之间（或中间）

IDM **beˌtwixt and beˈtween** (*old-fashioned*) in a middle position; neither one thing nor the other 居中；非此非彼

bevel /ˈbevl/ *noun* **1** a sloping edge or surface, for example at the side of a picture frame or sheet of glass 斜边；斜面 **2** a tool for making sloping edges on wood or stone 斜角规

bevelled (*especially US* **beveled**)
斜面的

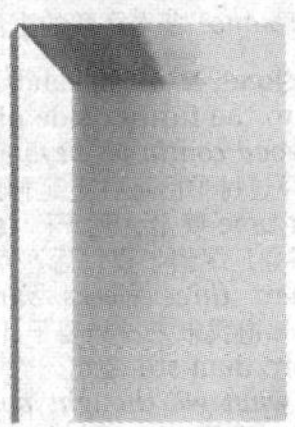

bev·elled (*especially US* **bev·eled**) /ˈbevld/ *adj.* [usually before noun] having a sloping edge or surface 斜边的；斜面的

bev·er·age /ˈbevərɪdʒ/ *noun* (*formal*) any type of drink except water （除水以外的）饮料：*laws governing the sale of alcoholic beverages* 控制酒类销售的法规

bevvy /ˈbevi/ *noun* (*pl.* **-ies**) (*BrE*, *informal*) an alcoholic drink, especially beer 酒；啤酒：*We went out for a few bevvies last night.* 我们昨晚出去喝了几杯。

bevy /ˈbevi/ *noun* [sing.] (*informal*) a large group of people or things of the same kind （同类人或东西的）一群，一批，一堆：*a bevy of beauties* (= beautiful young women) 一群美丽的姑娘

be·wail /bɪˈweɪl/ *verb* **~ sth** (*formal* or *humorous*) to express great sadness about sth 悲悼；哀叹；为…感到悲恸

be·ware /bɪˈweə(r); *NAmE* -ˈwer/ *verb* [I, T] (used only in infinitives and in orders 仅用于不定式和命令) if you tell sb to **beware**, you are warning them that sb/sth is dangerous and that they should be careful 当心；小心；提防：**~ of sb/sth** *Motorists have been warned to beware of icy roads.* 已经提醒开车的人当心冰封的路面。◇ **~ (of) doing sth** *Beware of saying anything that might reveal where you live.* 说话时谨防透露你的住址。◇ **~ sb/sth** *It's a great place for swimming, but beware dangerous currents.* 那是个游泳的好去处，但要当心危险的水流。

be·wigged /bɪˈwɪgd/ *adj.* (*formal*) (of a person 人) wearing a WIG 戴假发的

be·wil·der /bɪˈwɪldə(r)/ *verb* [usually passive] **~ sb** to confuse sb 使迷惑；使糊涂：*She was totally bewildered by his sudden change of mood.* 他的情绪突变搞得她全然不知所措。 ▸ **be·wil·dered** *adj.*：*He turned around, with a bewildered look on his face.* 他转过身来，满脸困惑。

be·wil·der·ing /bɪˈwɪldərɪŋ/ *adj.* making you feel confused because there are too many things to choose from or because sth is difficult to understand 令人困惑的；使人糊涂的 SYN **confusing**：*a bewildering array/range* 令人眼花缭乱的摆设 / 种类 ◇ *There is a bewildering variety of software available.* 各种可供挑选的软件使人目不暇接。 ▸ **be·wil·der·ing·ly** *adv.*：*All the houses looked bewilderingly similar.* 所有的房屋都一样，使人难以分辨。

be·wil·der·ment /bɪˈwɪldəmənt; *NAmE* -dərm-/ *noun* [U] a feeling of being completely confused 迷惘；困惑；迷乱 SYN **confusion**：*to look/stare in bewilderment* 迷惑地看着 / 盯着

be·witch /bɪˈwɪtʃ/ *verb* **1** [often passive] **~ sb** to attract or impress sb so much that they cannot think in a sensible way 迷住；迷惑：*He was completely bewitched by her beauty.* 他完全被她的美貌迷住了。 **2 ~ sb** to put a magic SPELL on sb 施魔法于；使中魔法 SYN **enchant**

B

be·witch·ing /bɪˈwɪtʃɪŋ/ *adj.* so beautiful or interesting that you cannot think about anything else 迷人的；令人沉醉的：*a bewitching girl/smile* 迷人的女孩 / 微笑 ◇ *a bewitching performance* 令人陶醉的表演

be·yond /bɪˈjɒnd; *NAmE* bɪˈjɑːnd/ *prep., adv.*
■ ***prep.*** **1** on or to the further side of sth 在（或向）…较远的一边：*The road continues beyond the village up into the hills.* 那条路经过村子后又往上延伸到群山中。**2** later than a particular time 晚于；迟于：*It won't go on beyond midnight.* 这事不会延续到午夜以后。◇ *I know what I'll be doing for the next three weeks but I haven't thought beyond that.* 我知道我未来三周要干什么，但再往后我还没有想过。**3** more than sth 超出；除…之外：*Our success was far beyond what we thought possible.* 我们的成功远远超出了我们的估计范围。◇ *She's got nothing beyond her state pension.* 除了政府发的养老金外，她什么都没有。**4** used to say that sth is not possible（表示不可能）：*The bicycle was beyond repair* (= is too badly damaged to repair). 自行车已损坏得无法修理。◇ *The situation is beyond our control.* 我们已无法控制这一局面。**5** too far or too advanced for sb/sth 超出…之外；非…所能及：*The handle was just beyond my reach.* 我差一点儿才够得着把手。◇ *The exercise was beyond the abilities of most of the class.* 这个练习超出了班上大多数学生的能力。
IDM **be beyond sb** (*informal*) to be impossible for sb to imagine, understand or do 使人无法想象（或理解、做等）：*It's beyond me why she wants to marry Jeff.* 我无法理解她为什么要嫁给杰夫。
■ ***adv.*** on the other side; further on 在另一边；在（或向）更远处；以远：*Snowdon and the mountains beyond were covered in snow.* 斯诺登山及其以远的山脉都被积雪覆盖着。◇ *The immediate future is clear, but it's hard to tell what lies beyond.* 不久的将来已经明朗，但更往后就很难说了。◇ *the year 2016 and beyond* * 2016 年及以后 IDM SEE BACK *n.*, DOUBT *n.*

bez·el /ˈbezl/ *noun* (*specialist*) a ring with a long narrow cut around the inside, used to hold sth in place, such as the cover of a watch or mobile/cell phone （手表、手机等的）嵌玻璃凹槽，镶嵌板外圈

bez·zie (*also* **bezzy**) (*pl.* **-ies**) /ˈbezi/ (*also* **bessie**) *noun* (*BrE, informal*) a person's closest friend 密友 ▶ **bez·zie** *adj.*：*She's my bezzie pal.* 她是我的闺蜜。

BF (*also* **bf**) /ˌbiː ˈef/ *abbr.* (*informal*) (especially in TEXT MESSAGES, emails, etc.) boyfriend; best friend 男朋友，最好的朋友（全写分别为 boyfriend 和 best friend，尤用于短信、电邮等）

BFN /ˌbiː ef ˈen/ *abbr.* (*informal*) (especially in TEXT MESSAGES, emails, etc.) bye for now 再见（全写为 bye for now，尤用于短信、电邮等）

Bhag·wan /bʌɡˈwɑːn/ *noun* (*IndE*) **1** God 神：*'May Bhagwan bless you,' he said.* "愿神保佑你。"他说。**2** a title for a GURU or a god in the form of a man 巴关（对古鲁或神的化身的称呼）：*Bhagwan Rajneesh* 拉吉尼希巴关大人

bhai /baɪ/ *noun* (*IndE*) **1** a brother 哥哥；弟弟 **2** used as a polite form of address to a man; in western India, often added to the first or last name （对男子的礼貌称呼；在西印度，常缀于名或姓）：*Suresh Bhai* 苏雷什兄弟 ◇ *Gandhi Bhai* 甘地先生

bhaji /ˈbɑːdʒi/ (*also* **bha·jia** /ˈbɑːdʒiə/) *noun* (*pl.* **bhajis, bha·jia**) **1** [C] a spicy S Asian food consisting of vegetables fried in BATTER (= a mixture of flour and liquid) 巴吉（南亚食品，将蔬菜放入面糊后油炸而成） **2** [U] a S Asian dish of spicy fried vegetables 南亚油炸辣菜

bhang (*also* **bang**) /bæŋ/ *noun* [U] the leaves and flower tops of the CANNABIS plant, used as a drug 大麻的叶和花穗（用作麻醉品）

bhangra /ˈbɑːŋɡrə/ *noun* [U] a type of dance music that combines traditional Punjabi music from India and Pakistan with Western pop music 彭戈拉（融合了印度和巴基斯坦的旁遮普乐和西方流行乐的舞蹈音乐）

Bha·rata·na·tyam /ˌbʌrətəˈnɑːtjəm/ *noun* [U] a CLASSICAL dance form from southern India 婆罗多舞（一种印度南部的古典舞）

bha·van /ˈbʌvən/ *noun* (*IndE*) a building made or used for a special purpose, for example for meetings or concerts （用于集会、音乐会等的）厅，馆，府

bhindi /ˈbɪndi/ *noun* (*pl.* **bhindi** or **bhindis**) [C, U] (*IndE*) = OKRA

bi /baɪ/ *adj.* (*informal*) = BISEXUAL (1)

bi- /baɪ/ *combining form* (in nouns and adjectives 构成名词和形容词) two; twice; double 二；两次；两倍；双：*bilingual* 双语的 ◇ *bicentenary* 两百周年 HELP **Bi-** with a period of time can mean either 'happening twice' in that period of time, or 'happening once in every two' periods. * bi- 和某个时期结合可表示在该时期内发生两次，或每两个时期发生一次。

bi·an·nual /baɪˈænjuəl/ *adj.* [only before noun] happening twice a year 一年两度的 ➲ COMPARE ANNUAL *adj.* ➲ SEE ALSO BIENNIAL *adj.*

bias AW /ˈbaɪəs/ *noun, verb*
■ ***noun*** **1** [U, C, usually sing.] a strong feeling in favour of or against one group of people, or one side in an argument, often not based on fair judgement 偏见；偏心；偏向：*accusations of political bias in news programmes* (= that reports are unfair and show favour to one political party) 对新闻报道中政治倾向性的指责 ◇ *Employers must consider all candidates impartially and without bias.* 雇主必须公平而毫无成见地考虑所有求职者。◇ *Some institutions still have a strong bias against women.* 有些机构仍然对女性持有很大偏见。 ➲ WORDFINDER NOTE AT EQUAL ➲ COLLOCATIONS AT RACE **2** [C, usually sing.] an interest in one thing more than others; a special ability 偏爱；特殊能力：*The course has a strong practical bias.* 这个课程偏重实用。**3** [U, C] the fact that the results of research or an experiment are not accurate because a particular factor has not been considered when collecting the information （研究或实验结果的）偏倚，偏差：*If a response rate is low, the risk of bias in the findings will be greater.* 如果回应率低，调查结果出现偏差的风险会增加。**4** [U, sing.] the **bias** of a piece of cloth is an edge cut DIAGONALLY across the threads 斜裁：*The skirt is cut on the bias.* 这条裙子是斜裁的。
■ ***verb*** (**-s-** or **-ss-**) **1** ~ **sb/sth (towards/against/in favour of sb/sth)** to unfairly influence sb's opinions or decisions 使有偏见；使偏心；使偏向 SYN **prejudice**：*The newspapers have biased people against her.* 报章使人们对她产生了偏见。**2** ~ **sth** to have an effect on the results of research or an experiment so that they do not show the real situation 影响（研究或实验结果）以致产生偏差：*The experiment contained an error which could bias the results.* 这项实验有一个错误，可能导致结果出现偏差。

ˈbias-cut *adj.* (of cloth or of an item of clothing 布料或衣物) cut across the natural direction of the lines in the cloth 斜裁的；斜切的

biased AW (*also* **biassed**) /ˈbaɪəst/ *adj.* **1** ~ **(toward(s)/against/in favour of sb/sth)** having a tendency to show favour towards or against one group of people or one opinion for personal reasons; making unfair judgements 有偏见的；倾向性的；片面的：*biased information/sources/press reports* 片面的信息 / 消息来源 / 新闻报道 ◇ *a biased jury/witness* 有成见的陪审团 / 证人 OPP **unbiased** **2** ~ **toward(s) sth/sb** having a particular interest in one thing more than others 偏重；偏向：*a school biased towards music and art* 一所偏重音乐和艺术的学校

bi·ath·lon /baɪˈæθlən/ *noun* a sporting event that combines CROSS-COUNTRY SKIING and RIFLE shooting 现代冬季两项（越野滑雪和步枪射击） ➲ COMPARE DECATHLON, HEPTATHLON, PENTATHLON, TRIATHLON

bib /bɪb/ *noun* **1** a piece of cloth or plastic that you put under a baby's chin to protect its clothes while it is eating 围嘴；围兜 **2** (*especially BrE*) a piece of cloth or plastic with a number or special colours on it that people wear on their chests and backs when they are taking part in a sport, so that people know who they are （运动员佩戴的）号码布，彩色身份标记

IDM **your best bib and 'tucker** (*humorous*) your best clothes that you only wear on special occasions （个人）最漂亮的衣服

bible /'baɪbl/ *noun* **1 the Bible** [sing.] the holy book of the Christian religion, consisting of the Old Testament and the New Testament 基督教的《圣经》（包括《旧约》和《新约》） **2 the Bible** [sing.] the holy book of the Jewish religion, consisting of the Torah (or Law), the PROPHETS and the Writings 犹太教的《圣经》（包括《律法书》、《先知书》以及《圣录》） **3** [C] a copy of the holy book of the Christian or Jewish religion 一册（基督教或犹太教的）《圣经》 **4** [C] a book containing important information on a subject, that you refer to very often 权威著作（或参考书）：*the stamp-collector's bible* 集邮者的宝典

'Bible-bashing (*also* **'Bible-thumping**) *noun* [U] (*informal, disapproving*) the act of teaching or talking about the Bible in public in a very enthusiastic or aggressive way 对《圣经》的狂热宣讲 ▶ **'Bible-basher** (*also* **'Bible-thumper**) *noun*

the 'Bible Belt *noun* [sing.] an area of the southern and middle western US where people have strong and strict Christian beliefs 《圣经》地带（指美国南部和中西部有着较强基督教信仰基础的地区）

bib·lical (*also* **Biblical**) /'bɪblɪkl/ *adj.* **1** connected with the Bible; in the Bible 有关《圣经》的；《圣经》中的：***biblical scholarship/times/scenes*** 与《圣经》有关的研究 / 时代 / 场景 ◇ ***biblical stories/passages*** 《圣经》故事 / 章节 **2** very great; on a large scale 宏大的；大规模的：*a thunderstorm* ***of biblical proportions*** 特大雷暴

IDM **know sb in the 'biblical sense** (*humorous*) to have had sex with sb 与某人发生过性关系：*He had known her—but not in the biblical sense.* 他认识她，但未有过肌肤之亲。

biblio- /'bɪbliəʊ; *NAmE* -lioʊ/ *combining form* (in nouns, adjectives and adverbs 构成名词、形容词和副词) connected with books （有关）书的：*bibliophile* 爱书者

bibli·og·raphy /ˌbɪbli'ɒɡrəfi; *NAmE* -'ɑːɡ-/ *noun* (*pl.* **-ies**) **1** [C] a list of books or articles about a particular subject or by a particular author; the list of books, etc. that have been used by sb writing an article, etc. （某一专题或作家的）书目，索引；参考书目 **2** [U] the study of the history of books and their production 目录学；文献学；书志学 ▶ **bibli·og·raph·er** /-'ɒɡrəfə(r); *NAmE* -'ɑːɡ-/ *noun* **bib·lio·graph·ic·al** /ˌbɪbliə'ɡræfɪkl/ (*also* **bib·lio·graph·ic**) *adj.*

bib·lio·phile /'bɪbliəfaɪl/*noun* (*formal*) a person who loves or collects books 爱书者；藏书家

'bib overalls *noun* [pl.] (*NAmE*) = OVERALLS (3)

bibu·lous /'bɪbjələs/ *adj.* (*old-fashioned* or *humorous*) liking to drink too much alcohol 爱喝酒的；嗜酒的

bi·cam·eral /ˌbaɪ'kæmərəl/ *adj.* (*specialist*) (of a parliament 议会) having two main parts, such as the Senate and the House of Representatives in the US, and the House of Commons and the House of Lords in Britain 两院制的（如美国的参议院和众议院，英国的下议院和上议院）

bi·carb /'baɪkɑːb; *NAmE* -kɑːrb/ *noun* [U] (*informal*) = SODIUM BICARBONATE

bi·car·bon·ate /ˌbaɪ'kɑːbənət; *NAmE* -'kɑːrb-/ *noun* [U] (*chemistry* 化) a salt made from CARBONIC ACID containing CARBON, HYDROGEN and OXYGEN together with another element 碳酸氢盐

biˌcarbonate of 'soda *noun* [U] = SODIUM BICARBONATE

bi·cen·ten·ary /ˌbaɪsen'tiːnəri; *NAmE* -'ten-/ *noun* (*pl.* **-ies**) (*BrE*) (*especially NAmE* **bi·cen·ten·nial**) the year, or the day, when you celebrate an important event that happened exactly 200 years earlier * 200 周年；200 周年纪念日 ▶ **bi·cen·ten·ary** *adj.* [only before noun]: *bicentenary celebrations* * 200 周年庆典

bi·cen·ten·nial /ˌbaɪsen'teniəl/ (*NAmE*) (*BrE* **bi·cen·ten·ary**) *noun* the year, or the day, when you celebrate an important event that happened exactly 200 years earlier * 200 周年；200 周年纪念日 ▶ **bi·cen·ten·nial** *adj.* [only before noun] (*especially NAmE*)：*bicentennial celebrations* * 200 周年庆典

bi·ceps /'baɪseps/ *noun* (*pl.* **bi·ceps**) the main muscle at the front of the top part of the arm 二头肌（上臂前侧的主要肌肉） ➲ COMPARE TRICEPS

bicker /'bɪkə(r)/ *verb* [I] ~ (**about/over sth**) to argue about things that are not important （为小事）斗嘴，争吵 SYN **squabble**：*The children are always bickering about something or other.* 孩子们有事没事总是在争吵。▶ **bicker·ing** *noun* [U]

bicky (*also* **bikky**) /'bɪki/ *noun* (*pl.* **-ies**) (*informal*) a biscuit 饼干

IDM **big 'bickies** (*AustralE, NZE, informal*) a large sum of money 一大笔钱

bi·coast·al /ˌbaɪ'kəʊstl; *NAmE* -'koʊstl/ *adj.* (*NAmE*) involving people and places on both the east and west coasts of the US （美国）东西海岸的

bi·cycle 🔑 /'baɪsɪkl/ *noun, verb*

■ ***noun*** 🔑 (*also informal* **bike**) a road vehicle with two wheels that you ride by pushing the PEDALS with your feet 自行车；脚踏车：*He got on his bicycle and rode off.* 他骑上自行车走了。◇ *We went for a* ***bicycle ride*** *on Sunday.* 我们星期天骑自行车兜风了。➲ VISUAL VOCAB PAGES V9, V55

■ ***verb*** [I] (+ **adv./prep.**) (*old-fashioned*) to go somewhere on a bicycle 骑自行车 ➲ COMPARE BIKE *v.*, CYCLE *v.*

'bicycle clip *noun* one of the two bands that people wear around their ankles when they are riding a bicycle to stop their trousers/pants getting caught in the chain 裤管夹（骑自行车时用）

'bicycle lane (*also informal* **'bike lane**) (*both NAmE*) (*BrE* **'cycle lane**) *noun* a part of a road that only bicycles are allowed to use 自行车车道 ➲ VISUAL VOCAB PAGE V3

bi·cyc·list /'baɪsɪklɪst/ *noun* (*old-fashioned* in British English, *formal* in North American English 英式英语中属过时用语，美式英语中属正式用语) a person who rides a bicycle 骑自行车者 ➲ COMPARE CYCLIST

bid[1] 🔑 /bɪd/ *verb, noun* ➲ SEE ALSO BID[2]

■ ***verb*** (**bid·ding, bid, bid**) **1** 🔑 [I, T] to offer to pay a particular price for sth, especially at an AUCTION 出（价）；（尤指拍卖中）喊价：~ **(sth) (for sth)** *I bid £2 000 for the painting.* 我出 2 000 英镑买这幅画。◇ ~ **(against sb)** *We wanted to buy the chairs but another couple were bidding against us.* 我们想买下那几把椅子，但另一对夫妇在同我们较劲出价。 **2** 🔑 [I] ~ **(for sth)** | (*NAmE also*) ~ **(on sth)** | ~ **(to do sth)** to offer to do work or provide a service for a particular price, in competition with other companies, etc. 投标 SYN **tender**：*A French firm will be bidding for the contract.* 一家法国公司将投标争取这项合同。➲ WORDFINDER NOTE AT DEAL **3** [T] ~ **to do sth** (used especially in newspapers 尤用于报章) to try to do, get or achieve sth 努力争取；企图获得 SYN **attempt**：*The team is bidding to retain its place in the league.* 这个队正争取保住它在联赛中的位置。 **4** [T, I] ~ **(sth)** (in some card games) to say how many points you expect to win （某些牌戏中）叫牌；叫出的点数：*She bid four hearts.* 她叫四红桃。

IDM **what am I 'bid?** used by an AUCTIONEER when he or she is selling sth （拍卖人用语）诸位愿出多少钱：*What am I bid for this vase?* 诸位愿给这个花瓶出多少钱？

■ ***noun*** **1** 🔑 ~ **(for sth)** an offer by a person or a company to pay a particular amount of money for sth （买方的）出价：*Granada mounted a hostile* ***takeover bid*** *for Forte.* 格兰纳达公司向福特公司出价进行敌意收购。◇ *At the auction* (= a public sale where things are sold to the person who

B

offers the most), *the highest bid for the picture was £200.* 拍卖会上，这幅画的最高出价为 200 英镑。◇ *Any more bids?* 还有谁出更高的价吗？ **2** ~ **(for sth)** | *(NAmE also)* ~ **(on sth)** an offer to do work or provide a service for a particular price, in competition with other companies, etc. 投标 SYN **tender**: *The company submitted a bid for the contract to clean the hospital.* 该公司投标承包这所医院的清洁工作。 **3** (used especially in newspapers 尤用于报章) an effort to do sth or to obtain sth 努力争取： **~ for sth** *a bid for power* 权力之争 ◇ **~ to do sth** *a desperate bid to escape from his attackers* 竭力躲避攻击他的人 **4** (in some card games 某些牌戏中) a statement of the number of points a player thinks he or she will win 叫牌；叫出的点数

bid² /bɪd/ *verb* ➲ SEE ALSO BID¹ (**bid·ding, bade** /beɪd; bæd/, **bidden** /ˈbɪdn/ or **bid·ding, bid, bid**) **1** ~ **(sb) good morning, farewell, etc.** *(formal)* to say 'good morning', etc. to sb 向（某人）问候、道别等： *I bade farewell to all the friends I had made in Paris.* 我告别了我在巴黎结交的所有朋友。◇ *I bade all my friends farewell.* 我告别了所有的朋友。 **2** ~ **sb (do sth)** *(old use* or *literary)* to tell sb to do sth 告诉（某人做某事）；吩咐： *He bade me come closer.* 他让我靠近些。

bid·dable /ˈbɪdəbl/ *adj.* *(formal, especially BrE)* (of people 人) willing to obey and to do what they are told to 顺从的；听话的

bid·der /ˈbɪdə(r)/ *noun* **1** a person or group that offers to pay an amount of money to buy sth 出价者： *It went to the highest bidder* (= the person who offered the most money). 出价最高者得之。 **2** a person or group that offers to do sth or to provide sth for a particular amount of money, in competition with others 投标者： *There were six bidders for the catering contract.* 投标承办酒席的有六家公司。

bid·ding /ˈbɪdɪŋ/ *noun* [U] **1** the act of offering prices, especially at an AUCTION （尤指拍卖中的）出价，喊价： *There was fast bidding between private collectors and dealers.* 私人收藏家和交易商急速竞相喊价。◇ *Several companies remained **in the bidding**.* 有几家公司仍在竞价。 **2** the act of offering to do sth or to provide sth for a particular price 投标： *competitive bidding for the contract* 这一合同的竞标 **3** (in some card games 某些牌戏中) the process of stating the number of points that players think they will win 叫牌 **4** *(old-fashioned* or *formal)* what sb asks or orders you to do 请求；吩咐；命令： ***to do sb's bidding*** (= to obey sb) 服从某人

biddy /ˈbɪdi/ *noun* *(pl.* **-ies**) *(informal, disapproving)* an old woman, especially an annoying one （尤指令人厌烦的）老太婆

bide /baɪd/ *verb* [I] *(old use)* = ABIDE

IDM **bide your ˈtime** to wait for the right time to do sth 等待时机

bidet /ˈbiːdeɪ; *NAmE* bɪˈdeɪ/ *noun* a low bowl in the bathroom, usually with taps/faucets, that you fill with water and sit on to wash your bottom 坐浴盆 ➲ VISUAL VOCAB PAGE V25

bi·di·rec·tion·al /ˌbaɪdəˈrekʃənl; -dɪ-; -daɪ-/ *adj.* *(specialist)* functioning in two directions 双向的

bi·en·nial /baɪˈeniəl/ *adj., noun*

■ *adj.* [usually before noun] happening once every two years 两年一次的： *a biennial convention* 两年召开一次的大会 ▸ **bi·en·ni·al·ly** *adv.* ➲ SEE ALSO ANNUAL *adj.*, BIANNUAL

■ *noun* any plant that lives for two years, producing flowers in the second year 两年生植物（第二年开花） ➲ COMPARE ANNUAL *n.*, PERENNIAL *n.*

bier /bɪə(r); *NAmE* bɪr/ *noun* a frame on which the dead body or the COFFIN is placed or carried at a funeral 停尸架；棺材架

biff /bɪf/ *verb* ~ **sb** *(old-fashioned, informal)* to hit sb hard with your FIST （用拳头）狠打，猛击： *He biffed me on the nose.* 他一拳砸在我鼻子上。 ▸ **biff** *noun*

bi·focals /ˌbaɪˈfəʊklz; *NAmE* -ˈfoʊ-/ *noun* [pl.] a pair of glasses with each LENS made in two parts. The upper part is for looking at things at a distance, and the lower part is for looking at things that are close to you. 双光眼镜（上半片为看远，下半片为看近） ➲ COMPARE VARIFOCALS ▸ **bi·focal** *adj.* [only before noun]

bi·fur·cate /ˈbaɪfəkeɪt; *NAmE* -fərk-/ *verb* [I] *(formal)* (of roads, rivers, etc. 路、河等) to divide into two separate parts 分叉；分支 ▸ **bi·fur·ca·tion** /ˌbaɪfəˈkeɪʃn; *NAmE* -fərˈk-/ *noun* [C, U]

big /bɪg/ *adj., adv., verb* ➲ SEE ALSO BIGS

■ *adj.* (**big·ger, big·gest**)

• **LARGE** 大 **1** large in size, degree, amount, etc. （体积、程度、数量等）大的，巨大的： *a big man/house/increase* 高大的男人；大房子；大幅度增长 ◇ *This shirt isn't big enough.* 这件衬衣不够大。 ◇ *It's the world's biggest computer company.* 它是全球最大的计算机公司。◇ *(informal) He had this **great big** grin on his face.* 他乐开了花。◇ *They were earning big money.* 他们在赚大钱。◇ *The news came as a big blow.* 那消息犹如晴天霹雳。

• **OLDER** 年龄较大 **2** *(informal)* older 年龄较大的： *my big brother* 我哥哥 ◇ *You're a big girl now.* 你现在已长成大姑娘了。

• **IMPORTANT** 重大 **3** [only before noun] *(rather informal)* important; serious 重大的；严重的： *a big decision* 重大决定 ◇ *Tonight is the biggest match of his career.* 今晚是他职业生涯中最重要的比赛。 ◇ *You are making a big mistake.* 你正在犯一个严重的错误。 ◇ *She took the stage for her **big moment**.* 她把这一阶段视为她的重要历程。◇ *(informal) Do you really think we can take on the **big boys*** (= compete with the most powerful people)? 你真的认为我们能与那些大人物抗衡？

• **AMBITIOUS** 有雄心 **4** *(informal)* (of a plan 计划) needing a lot of effort, money or time to succeed 庞大的；宏大的： *They're full of big ideas.* 他们满怀勃勃雄心。

• **POPULAR** 受欢迎 **5** *(informal)* popular with the public; successful 大受欢迎的；成功的： *Orange is the big colour*

▼ **WHICH WORD?** 词语辨析

big / large / great

These adjectives are frequently used with the following nouns. 这些形容词常常与下列名词连用：

big ~	large ~	great ~
man	numbers	success
house	part	majority
car	area	interest
boy	room	importance
dog	company	difficulty
smile	eyes	problem
problem	family	pleasure
surprise	volume	beauty
question	population	artist
difference	problem	surprise

• **Large** is more formal than **big** and should be used in writing unless it is in an informal style. It is not usually used to describe people, except to avoid saying 'fat'. * large 较 big 正式，应该用于书面语，但非正式语体除外。该词通常不用来形容人，除非是为了避免使用 fat （胖）。

• **Great** often suggests quality and not just size. Note also the phrases. * great 不仅指大，还常含伟大之意。另注意下列短语的用法： *a large amount of* 大量 ◇ *a large number of* 许多 ◇ *a large quantity of* 大量 ◇ *a great deal of* 大量 ◇ *in great detail* 非常详细 ◇ *a person of great age* 年长者

this year. 橘黄色是今年的流行色。◇ **~ in...** *The band's very big in Japan.* 这个乐队在日本很走红。

- **ENTHUSIASTIC** 热衷 **6** (*informal*) enthusiastic about sb/sth 热衷于…的；狂热的： *I'm a big fan of hers.* 我是她的狂热追随者。
- **DOING STH A LOT** 大量做 **7** doing sth often or to a large degree 经常（或大量）做某事的： *a big eater/drinker/spender* 食量大的 / 有酒量的 / 花钱手大的人
- **GENEROUS** 慷慨 **8** **~ of sb** (*usually ironic*) kind or generous 大方的；慷慨的： *He gave me an extra five pounds for two hours' work. I thought 'That's big of you'.* 我做两小时的工作他多给我五英镑。我心想"您真大方"。➲ MORE LIKE THIS 35, page R29

▶ **big·ness** *noun* [U]

IDM **be/get too big for your 'boots** to be/become too proud of yourself; to behave as if you are more important than you really are 自视过高；妄自尊大 **a ˌbig 'cheese** (*informal, humorous*) an important and powerful person, especially in an organization 大人物；要员 **ˌbig 'deal!** (*informal, ironic*) used to say that you are not impressed by sth 没什么了不起： *So he earns more than me. Big deal!* 他不就是比我多赚点钱，有什么了不起的！ **the big enchi'lada** (*NAmE, informal, humorous*) the most important person or thing 首要人物（或事物） **a big fish (in a small pond)** an important person (in a small community) （小圈子里的）大人物 **a ˌbig girl's 'blouse** (*BrE, informal*) a weak man, who is not brave or confident 懦弱的男人；胆小没自信的男人 **a big noise/shot/name** an important person 大人物；要人 **the big 'picture** (*informal*) the situation as a whole 整个局面；大局： *Right now forget the details and take a look at the big picture.* 现在别管细节问题，先通观全局。 **the big 'stick** (*informal*) the use or threat of force or power 大棒政策（以武力或权力相威胁）： *The authorities used quiet persuasion instead of the big stick.* 当权者平心静气地劝说，而不是施加压力。 **the Big Three, Four, etc.** the three, four, etc. most important countries, people, companies, etc. 三（或四等）强；前三个（或四个等）首要的国家（或人物、公司等）： *She works for one of the Big Six.* 她为六巨头之一工作。 **give sb/get a big 'hand** to show your approval of sb by clapping your hands; to be APPLAUDED in this way 给某人 / 受到鼓掌喝彩： *Ladies and gentlemen, let's give a big hand to our special guests tonight.* 女士们、先生们，让我们以热烈的掌声欢迎今晚的特邀嘉宾。 **have a big 'mouth** **1** to be bad at keeping secrets 嘴不严；爱泄露秘密 **2** to talk too much, especially about your own abilities and achievements 多嘴；吹牛；自吹自擂 **me and my big 'mouth** (*informal*) used when you realize that you have said sth that you should not have said 我真多嘴；真不该说出来 **no big 'deal** (*informal*) used to say that sth is not important or not a problem 没什么大不了；无所谓；没关系： *If I don't win it's no big deal.* 我输了也没关系。➲ MORE AT EYE *n.*, FISH *n.*, THING, WAY *n.*

■ ***adv.*** (*informal*) in an impressive way 大大；给人印象深地： *We need to think big.* 我们应该考虑干一番大事。

IDM **go over 'big (with sb)** (*informal*) to make a good impression on sb; to be successful （给某人）留下好印象；成功： *This story went over big with my kids.* 这个故事我的孩子们非常喜欢。 **make it 'big** (*informal*) to be very successful 获得成功： *He's hoping to make it big on TV.* 他正想成为电视明星。➲ MORE AT HIT *v.*

■ ***verb*** (-gg-)

PHR V **ˌbig sb/sth↔'up** (*BrE, slang*) to praise or recommend sb/sth strongly 高度赞扬；极力推荐： *He's been bigging up the CD on his radio show.* 他在电台广播节目中一直极力推荐这张 CD。

bigam·ist /ˈbɪɡəmɪst/ *noun* a person who commits the crime of bigamy 犯重婚罪者

big·amy /ˈbɪɡəmi/ *noun* [U] the crime of marrying sb when you are still legally married to sb else 重婚罪 ➲ COMPARE MONOGAMY (1), POLYGAMY ▶ **big·am·ous** /ˈbɪɡəməs/ *adj.*： *a bigamous relationship* 重婚关系

the ˌBig 'Apple *noun* [sing.] (*informal*) New York City 纽约市

the ˌBig Bad 'Wolf *noun* [sing.] (*informal*) a dangerous and frightening enemy "大坏狼"；凶险的敌人 **ORIGIN** From the wolf in several children's stories and the song *Who's Afraid of the Big Bad Wolf?* 源自几个童话故事中的狼以及儿歌"谁怕大坏狼？"

ˈbig band *noun* a large group of musicians playing JAZZ or dance music （演奏爵士乐或舞曲的）大乐队： *the big-band sound* 大乐队风格

ˌBig 'Bang *noun* [sing.] (*usually* **the Big Bang**) the single large explosion that some scientists suggest created the universe （宇宙的）创世大爆炸

ˌbig 'box (*also* **ˌbig-box 'store**) *noun* (*NAmE, informal*) a very large shop/store, built on one level and located outside a town, which sells goods at low prices 大卖场（指位于市郊的单层大超市，货品售价低廉）： *When a big-box store opens, smaller retailers often go out of business.* 大卖场一开业，往往零售小店就关门歇业。◇ *Efforts were made to limit big-box expansion.* 在限制大卖场的扩张上已做出了一些努力。

ˌBig 'Brother *noun* [sing.] a leader, a person in authority or a government that tries to control people's behaviour and thoughts, but pretends to act for their benefit 老大哥（意欲控制人们思想行为的虚伪领导者） **ORIGIN** From George Orwell's novel *Nineteen Eighty-Four*, in which the leader of the government, **Big Brother**, had total control over the people. The slogan 'Big Brother is watching you' reminded people that he knew everything they did. 源自乔治·奥威尔的小说《一九八四》。书中的政府头目"老大哥"(Big Brother) 彻底控制着人民。"老大哥在看着你"这一标语提醒人们注意，他知道他们所做的一切。

ˌbig 'bucks *noun* [pl.] (*especially NAmE, informal*) a large amount of money 一大笔钱

ˌbig 'business *noun* [U] **1** large companies that have a lot of power, considered as a group （统称）大企业： *links between politics and big business* 政治和大企业之间的联系 **2** something that has become important because people are willing to spend a lot of money on it 大生意： *Health and fitness have become big business.* 保健已经成为大生意。

ˌbig 'cat *noun* any large wild animal of the cat family. LIONS, TIGERS and LEOPARDS are all big cats. 大型猫科动物（如狮、虎和豹）

ˌBig 'Chief *noun* (*informal*) the person in charge of a business or other organization 总经理；主管；一把手

ˌbig 'data *noun* [U, pl.] (*computing* 计) sets of information that are too large or too complex to handle, analyse or use with standard methods 大数据： *Customer intelligence is created from big data analysis, so customers benefit from more personalized experiences.* 通过大数据分析编集客户情报，客户可因此获得更切合个人需要的体验而受益。

ˌbig 'dipper *noun* **1** (*old-fashioned, BrE*) a small train at an AMUSEMENT PARK, which goes very quickly up and down a steep track and around bends （游乐场的）云霄飞车，过山车 ➲ SEE ALSO ROLLER COASTER (1) **2 the ˌBig 'Dipper** (*NAmE*) (*BrE* **the Plough**) [sing.] a group of seven bright stars that can only be seen from the northern half of the world 北斗七星；大熊星座

ˌbig 'end *noun* (in a car engine) the end of a connecting ROD that fits around the CRANKSHAFT （汽车引擎中带动曲轴的）连杆大头

Big·foot /ˈbɪɡfʊt/ *noun* (*pl.* **Big·feet**) (*also* **Sas·quatch**) a large creature covered with hair like an APE, which some people believe lives in western N America （据信出没于北美西部的）大脚野人，大脚怪

ˌbig 'game *noun* [U] large wild animals that people hunt for sport, for example ELEPHANTS and LIONS 大猎物（如大象和狮子）

big·gie /ˈbɪɡi/ *noun* (*informal*) an important thing, person or event 重要的人（或事物）；大事；大人物

ˌbig ˈgovernment *noun* [U] (*disapproving*) a type of government that has a lot of control over people's lives and the economy （对人民生活、经济等控制严厉的）大政府

ˌbig ˈgun *noun* (*informal*) a person who has a lot of power or influence 大人物；有影响力的人物

ˌbig ˈhair *noun* [U] (*informal*) hair in a style that makes a large shape around the head 蜂窝头，爆炸头（一种发型）

ˌbig-ˈheaded *adj.* (*informal, disapproving*) having a very high opinion of how important and clever you are; too proud 自负的；傲慢的 ▸ **big-head** *noun*

ˌbig-ˈhearted *adj.* very kind; generous 善良的；慷慨的

ˌbig ˈhitter *noun* (*informal*) a person who is successful and has a lot of influence 大人物；大腕；大亨： *They've appointed one of the industry's big hitters to the board.* 他们委任了行内的一位重量级人物为董事会成员。

bight /baɪt/ *noun* a long curved part of a coast or river 海湾；河湾： *the Great Australian Bight* 大澳大利亚湾

ˈbig league *noun* (*NAmE*) **1** [C] a group of teams in a professional sport, especially BASEBALL, that play at the highest level 大联盟（棒球等职业运动的一流水平运动队组织） **2 the big league** [sing.] (*informal*) a very successful and important group 一流水平的团体；星级团体；佼佼者： *Over the past year, the company has joined the big league.* 过去一年中，公司已跻身一流之列。

ˈbig-league *adj.* (*NAmE*) **1** connected with sports teams that are in a big league 大联盟运动队的 **2** very important and successful 一流水平的；出色的

ˌBig Man on ˈCampus *noun* (*abbr.* **BMOC**) (*NAmE, informal*) a successful popular male student at a college or university 校园大人物（大学里成功而受欢迎的男生）

ˈbig mouth *noun* (*informal*) a person who talks a lot, especially about him- or herself, and who cannot keep secrets 大嘴巴（多嘴、自吹且不能保守秘密的人） ▸ **ˈbig-mouthed** *adj.*

bigot /ˈbɪɡət/ *noun* a person who has very strong, unreasonable beliefs or opinions about race, religion or politics and who will not listen to or accept the opinions of anyone who disagrees （种族、宗教或政治的）顽固盲从者，偏执者： *a **religious/racial bigot*** 宗教 / 种族的偏执者

big·ot·ed /ˈbɪɡətɪd/ *adj.* showing strong, unreasonable beliefs or opinions and a refusal to change them 顽固盲从的；偏执的

big·ot·ry /ˈbɪɡətri/ *noun* [U] the state of feeling, or the act of expressing, strong, unreasonable beliefs or opinions 顽固盲从；偏执

bigs /bɪɡz/ *noun* [pl.] (*NAmE, informal*) **1 the bigs** the major league in a professional sport （职业体育运动）大联盟 **2** large companies with a lot of money and influence 各大公司： *software bigs* 软件业诸巨头 ◇ *the Internet travel bigs* 经营在线旅行服务的各大公司

the ˌbig ˈscreen *noun* [sing.] the cinema (when contrasted with television) 大银幕；电影： *The movie hits the big screen in July.* 这部电影于七月份在影院上映。 ◇ *her first big-screen success* 她在影坛的初次成功

the ˌbig ˈsmoke (*also* **the Smoke**) *noun* [sing.] (*BrE, informal*) London, or another large city 伦敦；大城市

ˌbig ˈtent *noun* a group or philosophy that accepts and includes individuals and organizations that have a wide variety of opinions or styles "大帐篷"（指兼容并蓄的团体或理念） **SYN** **broad church**: *The movement soon became a big tent under which many campaign groups gathered.* 这场运动很快便集结了五花八门的运动团体。

ˈbig-ticket *adj.* [only before noun] costing a lot of money 高价的： *big-ticket items* 高价项目

ˈbig time *noun, adv.* (*informal*)
■ ***noun* the big time** great success in a profession, especially the entertainment business （尤指在娱乐行业的）巨大成功，大红大紫： *a bit-part actor who finally **made/hit the big time*** 一位终于走红的小角色演员 ➲ COMPARE SMALL-TIME
■ ***adv.*** on a large scale; to a great extent 大范围地；很大程度地： *This time they've messed up big time!* 这一次他们把事情搞得糟透了！

ˌbig ˈtoe *noun* the largest toe on a person's foot 大脚趾 ➲ VISUAL VOCAB PAGE V64

ˌbig ˈtop (*usually* **the big top**) *noun* the large tent in which a CIRCUS gives performances （马戏团演出用的）大帐篷

ˌbig ˈwheel *noun* **1** (*usually* **the Big Wheel**) (*BrE*) (*also* **Fer·ris wheel** *NAmE, BrE*) a large wheel which stands in a vertical position at an AMUSEMENT PARK, with seats hanging at its edge for people to ride in （游乐场的）大转轮，摩天轮 **2** (*NAmE, informal*) an important person in a company or an organization 要人；大亨

big·wig /ˈbɪɡwɪɡ/ *noun* (*informal*) an important person 要人；大人物： *She had to entertain some boring local bigwigs.* 她不得不款待当地一些无聊的大人物。

bijou /ˈbiːʒuː/ *adj.* [only before noun] (*BrE, sometimes ironic*) (of a building or a garden 建筑或花园) small but attractive and fashionable 小巧玲珑的；小而别致的： *The house was terribly small and cramped, but the agent described it as a bijou residence.* 房子十分狭小拥挤，但经纪人却把它说成是小巧别致的住宅。

bike 🔑 /baɪk/ *noun, verb*
■ ***noun*** (*informal*) **1** a bicycle 自行车；脚踏车： *She got on her bike and rode off.* 她骑上自行车走了。 ◇ *I usually go to work **by bike**.* 我通常骑自行车上班。 ➲ VISUAL VOCAB PAGE V55 ➲ SEE ALSO MOUNTAIN BIKE, PUSHBIKE, QUAD BIKE **2** a motorcycle 摩托车
IDM **on your bike!** (*BrE, informal*) a rude way of telling sb to go away 走开；滚开
■ ***verb*** **1** [I] (+ **adv./prep.**) (*informal*) to go somewhere on a bicycle or motorcycle 骑自行车（或摩托车）；骑车： *My dad bikes to work every day.* 我爸爸每天骑车上班。 **2** [T] **~ sth** (+ **adv./prep.**) (*informal*) to send sth to sb by motorcycle 骑摩托车递送： *I'll bike the contract over to you this afternoon.* 今天下午我骑摩托车把合同给你送过去。 ▸ **bik·ing** *noun* [U]: *The activities on offer include sailing and **mountain biking**.* 提供的活动项目有帆船运动和山地骑车。 ➲ COMPARE BICYCLE *v.*, CYCLE *v.*

ˈbike lane *noun* (*NAmE, informal*) = BICYCLE LANE

biker /ˈbaɪkə(r)/ *noun* **1** a person who rides a motorcycle, usually as a member of a large group 骑摩托车的人（常为大团伙成员） **2** a person who rides a bicycle, especially a MOUNTAIN BIKE 骑自行车的人（尤指骑山地自行车者）

bikie /ˈbaɪki/ *noun* (*AustralE, NZE, informal*) a member of a group of people who ride motorcycles 摩托车队成员

bi·kini /bɪˈkiːni/ *noun* a piece of clothing in two pieces that women wear for swimming and lying in the sun 比基尼泳装

biˈkini line *noun* the area of skin around the bottom half of a BIKINI and the hair that grows there, which some women remove 比基尼线（指比基尼泳裤边缘外露的一圈皮肤和阴毛）

bikky = BICKY

bi·la·bial /ˌbaɪˈleɪbiəl/ *noun* (*phonetics* 语音) a speech sound made by using both lips, such as /b/, /p/ and /m/ in *buy*, *pie* and *my* 双唇音 ▸ **bi·la·bial** *adj.*

bi·lat·eral /ˌbaɪˈlætərəl/ *adj.* **1** involving two groups of people or two countries 双方的；双边的： ***bilateral relations/agreements/trade/talks*** 双边关系 / 协议 / 贸易 / 谈判 ➲ WORDFINDER NOTE AT ALLY **2** (*medical* 医)

involving both of two parts or sides of the body or brain （身体部位）双侧的，对称的；（大脑）两半球的 ▶ **bi·lat·eral·ly** *adv.* ➲ COMPARE MULTILATERAL, TRILATERAL, UNILATERAL

bil·berry /ˈbɪlbəri; *NAmE* -beri/ (*also* **whortle·berry**) *noun* (*pl.* **-ies**) a small dark blue BERRY that grows on bushes on hills and in woods in northern Europe and can be eaten. The bush is also called a bilberry. 欧洲越橘（指植物或浆果，浆果深蓝色，可食）➲ COMPARE BLUEBERRY

bilby /ˈbɪlbi/ *noun* (*pl.* **-ies**) a small Australasian animal with a long nose, a long tail and big ears 兔耳袋狸（生活于澳大拉西亚）

bile /baɪl/ *noun* [U] **1** the greenish brown liquid with a bitter unpleasant taste that is produced by the LIVER to help the body to deal with the fats we eat, and that can come into your mouth when you VOMIT with an empty stomach 胆汁 **2** (*formal*) anger or hatred 愤怒；憎恨：*The critic's review of the play was just a paragraph of bile.* 那位批评家对这部戏剧的评论不过是在发泄怒气。

ˈbile duct *noun* the tube that carries bile from the LIVER and the GALL BLADDER to the DUODENUM 胆管 ➲ VISUAL VOCAB PAGE V64

bilge /bɪldʒ/ *noun* **1** [C] (*also* **bilges** [pl.]) the almost flat part of the bottom of a boat or a ship, inside or outside 舭；底舱 **2** (*also* **ˈbilge water**) [U] dirty water that collects in a ship's bilge 底舱污水

bil·har·zia /bɪlˈhɑːtsiə; *NAmE* -ˈhɑːrt-/ *noun* [U] a serious disease, common in parts of Africa and S America, caused by small WORMS that get into the blood 血吸虫病（常见于非洲和南美洲的某些地区）

bil·iary /ˈbɪliəri; *NAmE* -eri/ *adj.* (*medical* 医) relating to BILE or to the BILE DUCT 胆汁的；胆管的

bi·lin·gual /ˌbaɪˈlɪŋɡwəl/ *adj.* **1** able to speak two languages equally well 会说两种语言的：*She is bilingual in English and Punjabi.* 她会说英语和旁遮普语。**2** using two languages; written in two languages 用两种语言（写）的：***bilingual education/communities*** 双语教育 / 社群 ◇ *a bilingual dictionary* 双语词典 ▶ **bi·lin·gual** *noun*：*Welsh/English bilinguals* 会说威尔士语和英语两种语言的人 ➲ COMPARE MONOLINGUAL, MULTILINGUAL

bili·ous /ˈbɪliəs/ *adj.* **1** feeling as if you might VOMIT soon 恶心的；想呕吐的 **2** (of colours, usually green or yellow 颜色，通常指绿色或黄色) creating an unpleasant effect 刺眼的；花哨的；难看的：*a bilious green dress* 一条绿得扎眼的连衣裙 **3** (*formal*) bad-tempered; full of anger 脾气坏的；易怒的

bili·ru·bin /ˌbɪlɪˈruːbɪn/ *noun* [U] (*medical* 医) an orange substance produced in the LIVER 胆红素

bilk /bɪlk/ *verb* (*informal, especially NAmE*) **~ sb (out of sth) | ~ sth (from sb)** to cheat sb, especially by taking money from them 欺骗；诈骗（钱财）：*a conman who bilked investors out of millions of dollars* 诈取投资者几百万美元的骗子

bill 🔑 /bɪl/ *noun, verb*

■ ***noun***

• **FOR PAYMENT** 付款 **1** 🔑 a document that shows how much you owe sb for goods or services 账单：*the* ***telephone/electricity/gas bill*** 电话费 / 电费 / 煤气费账单 ◇ *We* ***ran up a*** *massive hotel* ***bill***. 我们累积了大笔的旅馆费。◇ *She always* ***pays*** *her* ***bills*** *on time.* 她总是按时支付账单。◇ *The bills are piling up* (= there are more and more that have still not been paid). 账单越积越多。➲ COLLOCATIONS AT FINANCE **2** 🔑 (*especially BrE*) (*NAmE usually* **check**) a piece of paper that shows how much you have to pay for the food and drinks that you have had in a restaurant （餐馆的）账单：*Let's ask for the bill.* 我们结账吧。➲ COLLOCATIONS AT RESTAURANT

• **MONEY** 货币 **3** 🔑 (*NAmE*) (*BrE* **note**) (*also* **bank·note** *especially in BrE*) a piece of paper money 纸币；钞票：*a ten-dollar bill* 一张十美元的钞票

• **IN PARLIAMENT** 议会 **4** 🔑 a written suggestion for a new law that is presented to a country's parliament so that its members can discuss it （提交议会讨论的）议案，法案：*to* ***introduce/approve/reject a bill*** 提出 / 通过 / 否决一项议案 ◇ *the Education Reform Bill* 教育改革法案 ➲ WORDFINDER NOTE AT PARLIAMENT

• **AT THEATRE, ETC.** 剧院等 **5** a programme of entertainment at a theatre, etc. （剧院等的）节目单：*a horror* ***double bill*** (= two horror films/movies shown one after the other) 双场恐怖片节目单 ◇ ***Topping the bill*** (= the most important performer) *is Paul Simon.* 领衔演出的是保罗·西蒙。

• **ADVERTISEMENT** 广告 **6** a notice in a public place to advertise an event 海报；招贴；广告 SYN **poster** ➲ SEE ALSO HANDBILL

• **OF BIRDS** 鸟 **7** the hard pointed or curved outer part of a bird's mouth 鸟嘴；喙 SYN **beak** ➲ VISUAL VOCAB PAGE V12 **8 -billed** (in adjectives 构成形容词) having the type of bill mentioned 有…形喙的：*long-billed waders* 长嘴涉禽 ➲ MORE LIKE THIS 8, page R25

• **ON HAT** 帽子 **9** (*also* **visor**) (*both NAmE*) (*BrE* **peak**) the stiff front part of a cap that sticks out above your eyes 帽舌；帽檐 ➲ VISUAL VOCAB PAGE V70 ➲ SEE ALSO OLD BILL

IDM **fill/fit the ˈbill** to be what is needed in a particular situation or for a particular purpose 符合要求；合格：*On paper, several of the applicants fit the bill.* 从书面材料看，有几位申请人符合条件。➲ MORE AT CLEAN *adj.*, FOOT *v.*

■ ***verb***

• **ASK FOR PAYMENT** 要求付款 **1 ~ sb (for sth)** to send sb a bill for sth 开账单，发账单（要求付款）：*Please bill me for the books.* 请就所购的书给我开列账单。

• **ADVERTISE** 做广告 **2** [usually passive] **~ sb/sth as sth** to advertise or describe sb/sth in a particular way 把（某人或事物）宣传为…：*He was billed as the new Tom Cruise.*

▼ **SYNONYMS** 同义词辨析

bill

account • invoice • check

These are all words for a record of how much you owe for goods or services you have bought or used. 以上各词均指账单、账目。

bill a list of goods that you have bought or services that you have used, showing how much you owe; the price or cost of sth 指账单：*the gas bill* 煤气费账单

account an arrangement with a shop/store or business to pay bills for goods or services at a later time, for example in regular amounts every month 指赊销账、赊欠账、赊购：*Put it on my account please.* 请记在我的赊购账上。

invoice (*rather formal*) a bill for goods that sb has bought or work that has been done for sb 指发票、发货或服务费用清单：*The builders sent an invoice for £250.* 营造商发出了一张 250 英镑的发票。

BILL OR INVOICE? 用 bill 还是 invoice?

You would get a **bill** in a restaurant, bar or hotel; from a company that supplies you with gas, electricity, etc.; or from sb whose property you have damaged. An **invoice** is for goods supplied or work done as agreed between a customer and supplier. * bill 指餐馆、酒吧、旅馆、煤气公司、电力公司等开出的账单或财产所有者开出的索赔清单。invoice 指客户与供应商约定的供货或服务费用清单。

check (*NAmE*) a piece of paper that shows how much you have to pay for the food and drinks that you have had in a restaurant 指餐馆的账单：*Can I have the check, please?* 请给我结账。NOTE In British English the usual word for this is **bill**. 此义英式英语中常用 bill。

PATTERNS

• the bill/invoice/check **for** sth
• to **pay/settle** a(n) bill/account/invoice/check
• to **put sth on** the/sb's bill/account/invoice/check

他被宣传为新汤姆·克鲁斯。 **3** [usually passive] **~ sb/sth to do sth** to advertise that sb/sth will do sth 宣布…将做某事： *She was billed to speak on 'China—Yesterday and Today'.* 海报上说她要发表题为"中国 —— 昨天和今天"的演讲。

IDM **bill and 'coo** (*old-fashioned, informal*) if two people who are in love **bill and coo**, they kiss and speak in a loving way to each other 卿卿我我；情话绵绵

billa·bong /ˈbɪləbɒŋ; *NAmE* -bɔːŋ/ *noun* (in Australia) a lake that is formed when a river floods （澳大利亚河水泛滥形成的）死水潭

bill·board /ˈbɪlbɔːd; *NAmE* -bɔːrd/ (*especially NAmE*) (*BrE also* **hoard·ing**) *noun* a large board on the outside of a building or at the side of the road, used for putting advertisements on 大幅广告牌 ➲ VISUAL VOCAB PAGE V3

bil·let /ˈbɪlɪt/ *noun, verb*

■ *noun* a place, often in a private house, where soldiers live temporarily 部队临时营舍（常设在民宅里）

■ *verb* [T, usually passive] **+ adv./prep.** to send soldiers to live somewhere temporarily, especially in private houses during a war 部队临时设营（常在民宅里）

bill·fold /ˈbɪlfəʊld; *NAmE* -foʊld/ *noun* (*NAmE*) = WALLET (1)

bill·hook /ˈbɪlhʊk/ *noun* a tool with a long handle and a curved blade, used for cutting the small branches off trees 长柄钩镰（修剪树枝用）

bil·liards /ˈbɪliədz; *NAmE* ˈbɪljərdz/ *noun* [U] a game for two people played with CUES (= long sticks) and three balls on a long table covered with green cloth. Players try to hit the balls against each other and into pockets at the edge of the table. （三球落袋式）台球： *a game of billiards* 一局台球赛 ➲ COMPARE POOL *n.*, SNOOKER *n.* ▸ **bil·liard** *adj.* [only before noun]: *a billiard cue* 台球球杆

bill·ing /ˈbɪlɪŋ/ *noun* **1** [U] the position, especially an important one, that sb is advertised or described as having in a show, etc. （演员表上的）排名；演员名次： *to have* ***top/star billing*** 领衔主演 **2** [U] the act of preparing and sending bills to customers 开具账单 **3** [C, usually pl.] the total amount of business that a company does in a particular period of time 营业额： *billings around $7 million* * 700 万美元左右的营业额

bil·lion 🔑 /ˈbɪljən/ *number* (*plural verb* 复数动词) **1** 🔑 (*abbr.* **bn**) 1 000 000 000; one thousand million 十亿： *Worldwide sales reached 2.5 billion.* 全球销售额达到了 25 亿。 ◇ *half a billion dollars* 五亿美元 ◇ *They have spent billions on the problem* (= billions of dollars, etc.). 他们花了几十亿解决这个问题。 HELP You say **a, one, two, several, etc. billion** without a final 's' on 'billion'. **Billions (of…)** can be used if there is no number or quantity before it. Always use a plural verb with **billion** or **billions**, except when an amount of money is mentioned. 说 a, one, two, several, etc. billion 时，billion 后面不加 s。若前面没有数目或数量，可用 billions (of...)。除非指金额，billion 和 billions 均用复数动词： *Two billion (people) worldwide are expected to watch the game.* 预计全世界将有 20 亿人观看这场比赛。 ◇ *Two billion (dollars) was withdrawn from the account.* 从该账户提取了 20 亿美元。There are more examples of how to use numbers at the entry for **hundred**. 更多数词用法示例见 hundred 条。 **2** 🔑 **a billion** or **billions (of…)** (*informal*) a very large amount 数以十亿计；大量： *Our immune systems are killing billions of germs right now.* 我们的免疫系统正在杀死数以十亿计的细菌。 **3** (*old-fashioned, BrE*) 1 000 000 000 000; one million million 一万亿 SYN **trillion**

bil·lion·aire /ˌbɪljəˈneə(r); *NAmE* -ˈner/ *noun* an extremely rich person, who has at least a thousand million pounds, dollars, etc. in money or property 巨富；亿万富翁

ˌbill of ˈcosts *noun* (*pl.* **bills of costs**) (*BrE, law* 律) a list of the charges and expenses that sb must pay to a lawyer or to sb who has won a legal case 诉讼费用清单

ˌbill of exˈchange *noun* (*pl.* **bills of exchange**) (*business* 商) a written order to pay a sum of money to a particular person on a particular date 汇票

ˌbill of ˈfare *noun* (*pl.* **bills of fare**) (*old-fashioned*) a list of the food that can be ordered in a restaurant （餐馆的）菜单，菜谱 SYN **menu**

bill of lad·ing /ˌbɪl əv ˈleɪdɪŋ/ *noun* (*pl.* **bills of lad·ing**) (*business* 商) a list giving details of the goods that a ship, etc. is carrying 提单；提货单

ˌbill of ˈrights *noun* [sing.] a written statement of the basic rights of the citizens of a country 权利宣言；人权宣言

ˌbill of ˈsale *noun* (*pl.* **bills of sale**) (*business* 商) an official document showing that sth has been bought 转让契据；卖据

bil·low /ˈbɪləʊ; *NAmE* -loʊ/ *verb, noun*

■ *verb* **1** [I] (of a sail, skirt, etc. 船帆、裙子等) to fill with air and swell out 鼓起： *The curtains billowed in the breeze.* 微风吹得窗帘鼓了起来。 **2** [I] if smoke, cloud, etc. **billows**, it rises and moves in a large mass （烟雾等）涌出，大量冒出： *A great cloud of smoke billowed out of the chimney.* 滚滚浓烟从烟囱中喷涌而出。

■ *noun* [usually pl.] a moving mass or cloud of smoke, steam, etc. like a wave 波涛般的浓烟（或蒸汽等）

billy /ˈbɪli/ *noun* (*pl.* **-ies**) (*also* **billy·can** /ˈbɪlikæn/) (*both BrE*) a metal can with a lid and a handle used for boiling water or for cooking when you are camping 带盖金属罐（有柄，露营时烧水或煮东西用）

ˈbilly club *noun* (*NAmE*) a short wooden stick used as a weapon by police officers （木制）警棍

ˈbilly goat *noun* a male GOAT 公山羊 ➲ COMPARE NANNY GOAT

bil·tong /ˈbɪltɒŋ; ˈbəl-; *NAmE* ˈbɪltɔːŋ/ *noun* [U] (*SAfrE*) raw dry meat that is eaten in small pieces. Biltong is preserved by being treated with salt. （盐卤）生肉干，干肉条

bim·ble /ˈbɪmbl/ *verb, noun* (*BrE, informal*)

■ *verb* [I] **+ adv./prep.** to walk or travel without hurrying 漫步；溜达；悠闲地旅行： *We spent the morning bimbling around the market.* 我们一上午都在市场里闲逛。 ◇ *I bimbled into town.* 我慢悠悠地溜达进城。

■ *noun* [usually sing.] a slow, relaxed walk or journey 漫步；溜达；悠闲旅行： *We were enjoying a pleasant bimble in the country.* 我们当时漫步乡间，十分惬意。

bimbo /ˈbɪmbəʊ; *NAmE* -boʊ/ *noun* (*pl.* **-os**) (*informal, disapproving*) a young person, usually a woman, who is sexually attractive but not very intelligent 傻乎乎的性感青年（通常为女子）： *He's going out with an empty-headed bimbo half his age.* 他正在和一个年龄比他小一半的傻里傻气的性感女子谈恋爱。

bi·month·ly /ˌbaɪˈmʌnθli/ *adj., adv.* produced or happening every two months or twice each month 两月一次（的）；一月两次（的）

bin 🔑 /bɪn/ *noun, verb*

■ *noun* **1** 🔑 a container that you put waste in 垃圾箱： *a rubbish bin* 垃圾箱 ➲ SEE ALSO DUSTBIN, WASTE BIN **2** a large container, usually with a lid, for storing things in （有盖）大容器，箱，柜： *a bread bin* 面包箱

■ *verb* (-nn-) **~ sth** (*BrE, informal*) to throw sth away 扔掉；丢弃： *Do you need to keep these letters or shall we bin them?* 你需要保存这些信件吗，还是干脆把它们扔掉？

bin·ary /ˈbaɪnəri/ *adj.* **1** (*computing* 计, *mathematics* 数) using only 0 and 1 as a system of numbers 二进制的（用 0 和 1 记数）： *the* ***binary system*** 二进制 ◇ *binary arithmetic* 二进制算术 **2** (*specialist*) based on only two numbers; consisting of two parts 仅基于两个数字的；二元的；由两部分组成的： ***binary code/numbers*** 二进制代码 / 数字 ▸ **bin·ary** *noun* [U]: *The computer performs calculations in binary and converts the results to decimal.* 计算机以二进制数运算，然后把运算结果转换为十进制数。

'bin bag *noun* (*BrE, informal*) a large plastic bag for putting rubbish/garbage in 塑料垃圾袋；塑胶垃圾袋

bind /baɪnd/ *verb, noun*
■ *verb* (**bound, bound** /baʊnd/)
• TIE WITH ROPE/CLOTH 捆绑 **1** [T] (*formal*) to tie sb/sth with rope, string, etc. so that they/it cannot move or are held together firmly 捆绑；系：**~ sb/sth to sth** *She was bound to a chair.* 她被捆在一把椅子上。◇ **~ sb/sth together** *They bound his hands together.* 他们把他的双手绑在一起。◇ **~ sb/sth** *He was left* ***bound and gagged*** (= tied up and with a piece of cloth tied over his mouth). 他被捆了起来并用布封住了嘴。**2** [T] **~ sth (up)** (*formal*) to tie a long thin piece of cloth around sth （用长布条）缠绕：*She bound up his wounds.* 她把他的伤口包扎好。
• UNITE 结合 **3** [T] to unite people, organizations, etc. so that they live or work together more happily or effectively （使）联合在一起，结合：**~ A (and B) (together)** *Organizations such as schools and clubs bind a community together.* 诸如学校、俱乐部等机构使社区成为一个整体。◇ **~ A to B** *She thought that having his child would bind him to her forever.* 她以为生了他的孩子就会永远把他拴住。
• MAKE SB DO STH 驱使 **4** [T, usually passive] to force sb to do sth by making them promise to do it or by making it their duty to do it 约束；迫使：**~ sb (to sth)** *He had been bound to secrecy* (= made to promise not to tell people about sth). 他被迫保守秘密。◇ **~ sb to do sth** *The agreement binds her to repay the debt within six months.* 根据协议，她必须在六个月内还清债务。➲ SEE ALSO BINDING *adj.*, BOUND *adj.* (2)
• STICK TOGETHER 黏合 **5** [I, T] to stick together or to make things stick together in a solid mass （使）黏合，凝结：**~ (together)** *Add an egg yolk to make the mixture bind.* 加个蛋黄使混合料凝结。◇ **~ sth (together)** *Add an egg yolk to bind the mixture together.* 加个蛋黄使混合料凝结在一起。
• BOOK 书籍 **6** [T, usually passive] **~ sth (in sth)** to fasten the pages of a book together and put them inside a cover 装订：*two volumes bound in leather* 两卷皮面装帧的书
• SEW EDGE 缝边 **7** [T, often passive] **~ sth (with sth)** to sew a piece of material to the edge of sth to decorate it or to make it stronger 给…镶边；缝牢…的边：*The blankets were bound with satin.* 那些毯子是用缎子包边的。➲ WORDFINDER NOTE AT SEW IDM SEE HAND *n.*
PHR V **,bind sb 'over** [usually passive] **1** (*NAmE, law* 律) to give sb BAIL while they are waiting to go to trial 允许某人保释候审：*He was bound over for trial.* 他获准了保释候审。**2** (*BrE, law* 律) to give sb a formal warning that if they break the law again they will be punished 令某人具结保证（不再违法）：*She was* ***bound over to keep the peace*** *for a year.* 她被责令具保一年内不再闹事。
■ *noun* [sing.] (*BrE, informal*) an annoying situation that is often difficult to avoid 窘境 ➲ SEE ALSO DOUBLE BIND
IDM **in a 'bind** (*especially NAmE*) in a difficult situation that you do not know how to get out of 陷于困境；进退维谷

bin·daas /'bɪndɑːs/ *adj.* (*IndE, informal*) independent and seeming to have no worries or responsibilities 无忧无虑的；轻松自如的：*a bindaas girl* 无忧无虑的女孩 ◇ *a bindaas attitude* 悠然自得的态度

bind·er /'baɪndə(r)/ *noun* **1** [C] a hard cover for holding sheets of paper, magazines, etc. together 活页夹：*a ring binder* 活页夹 ➲ VISUAL VOCAB PAGE V71 **2** [C] a person or machine that puts covers on books 装订工；装订机 **3** [C, U] a substance that makes things stick or mix together in a solid form 黏合剂；黏结剂 **4** [C] a machine that fastens WHEAT into bunches after it has been cut （谷物）割捆机

bindi /'bɪndi/ *noun* a decorative mark worn in the middle of the FOREHEAD, usually by Hindu women （印度教妇女等的）眉心红点，眉心饰记

bind·ing /'baɪndɪŋ/ *adj., noun*
■ *adj.* **~ (on/upon sb)** that must be obeyed because it is accepted in law 必须遵守的；有法律约束力的：*a binding* ***promise/agreement/contract*** 有约束力的承诺 / 协议 / 合同 ➲ WORDFINDER NOTE AT DOCUMENT
■ *noun* **1** [C, U] the cover that holds the pages of a book together （书籍的）封皮 **2** [C, U] cloth that is fastened to the edge of sth to protect or decorate it 镶边；绲边 **3** [C] a device on a SKI that holds the heel and toe of your boot in place and releases the boot automatically if you fall （滑雪板的）滑雪鞋固定装置 ➲ VISUAL VOCAB PAGE V52

'binding theory *noun* ➲ GOVERNMENT AND BINDING THEORY

bind·weed /'baɪndwiːd/ *noun* [U] a wild plant that twists itself around other plants 旋花类植物

binge /bɪndʒ/ *noun, verb*
■ *noun* (*informal*) a short period of time when sb does too much of a particular activity, especially eating or drinking alcohol （短时间的）狂热活动，寻欢作乐，大吃大喝：*to go on a binge* 饮酒作乐 ◇ *binge drinking* 狂喝滥饮 ◇ *One of the symptoms is* ***binge eating.*** 症状之一是饮食无度。
■ *verb* (**binge·ing** or **bin·ging**, **binged**, **binged**) [I] **~ (on sth)** to eat or drink too much, especially without being able to control yourself 大吃大喝；狂欢作乐：*When she's depressed she binges on chocolate.* 她心情不好的时候就大嚼巧克力。➲ WORDFINDER NOTE AT EAT

bingo /'bɪŋɡəʊ; *NAmE* -ɡoʊ/ *noun, exclamation*
■ *noun* [U] a game in which each player has a card with numbers on. Numbers are called out in no particular order and the first player whose numbers are all called out, or who has a line of numbers called out, wins a prize. 宾戈游戏（玩者均持有一张数字卡，第一个凑齐庄家喊出的全部或一组数字者胜出）：*to play bingo* 玩宾戈游戏 ◇ *a bingo hall* 宾戈游戏厅
■ *exclamation* (*informal*) used to express pleasure and/or surprise because you have found sth that you were looking for, or done sth that you were trying to do （事情如愿时说）好，瞧：*The computer program searches, and bingo! We've got a match.* 电脑程序在搜索，瞧！找到匹配的了。

'bingo wings *noun* [pl.] (*BrE, informal, humorous*) long folds of loose skin and fat that hang down from the upper arms, especially of older people 宾果翼，蝴蝶臂，蝴蝶袖（尤指较年长的人上臂松弛下垂的部分）

binky /'bɪŋki/ *noun* (*pl.* **-ies**) (*informal*) **1 Binky™** = DUMMY (5) **2** a small child's favourite SOFT TOY or BLANKET (= a cover, used especially on beds to keep people warm) 宾基（幼儿喜爱的一种毛绒玩具或毯子）

'bin liner *noun* (*BrE*) a plastic bag that is placed inside a container for holding waste 垃圾箱衬袋；垃圾袋

bin·man /'bɪnmæn/ *noun* (*pl.* **-men** /-men/) (*BrE, informal*) = DUSTMAN

bin·ocu·lar /bɪ'nɒkjələ(r); *NAmE* bɪ'nɑːkjələr/ *adj.* (*specialist*) using two eyes to see 双目并用的；双眼的：*binocular vision* 双眼视力

binoculars 双筒望远镜 **telescope** 望远镜

bin·ocu·lars /bɪ'nɒkjələz; *NAmE* bɪ'nɑːkjələrz/ (*also specialist* **'field glasses**) *noun* [pl.] an instrument, like two small TELESCOPES fixed together, that makes objects that are far away seem nearer when you look through it 双筒望远镜：*a pair of binoculars* 一副双筒望远镜 ◇ *We looked at the birds through binoculars.* 我们用双筒望远镜观鸟。

bi·no·mial /baɪˈnəʊmiəl; *NAmE* -ˈnoʊ-/ *noun* **1** (*mathematics* 数) an expression that has two groups of numbers or letters, joined by the sign + or – 二项式 **2** (*linguistics* 语言) a pair of nouns joined by a word like 'and', where the order of the nouns is always the same, for example 'knife and fork' 双名词组（由 and 连接的一对名词，两个名词的前后顺序不变，如 knife and fork） ▶ **bi·no·mial** *adj.*

bint /bɪnt/ *noun* (*BrE, slang*) an offensive way of referring to a woman （含冒犯意）娘们儿，雌儿： *a posh bint* 时髦娘们儿

bio- /ˈbaɪəʊ; *NAmE* ˈbaɪoʊ/ *combining form* (in nouns, adjectives and adverbs 构成名词、形容词和副词) connected with living things or human life 生物的；人生的： *biodegradable* 可生物降解的 ◇ *biography* 传记

bio·bank /ˈbaɪəʊbæŋk; *NAmE* ˈbaɪoʊ-/ *noun* a large collection of samples of TISSUE (= a group of cells that form the different parts of humans, animals and plants) and data connected with medicine or biology, brought together for research 生物样本库；生物数据库

bio·break /ˈbaɪəʊbreɪk; *NAmE* ˈbaɪoʊ-/ *noun* a short period of time when you leave your computer or a meeting in order to go to the toilet/bathroom 方便时间（离开电脑或会议去洗手间的时间）： *I need to take a biobreak.* 我得去方便一下。

bio·chem·ist /ˌbaɪəʊˈkemɪst; *NAmE* ˌbaɪoʊ-/ *noun* a scientist who studies biochemistry 生（物）化学家

bio·chem·is·try /ˌbaɪəʊˈkemɪstri; *NAmE* ˌbaɪoʊ-/ *noun* **1** [U] the scientific study of the chemistry of living things 生物化学 **2** [U, C] the chemical structure and behaviour of a living thing 生物的化学结构和特性 ▶ **bio·chem·ical** /ˌbaɪəʊˈkemɪkl; *NAmE* ˌbaɪoʊ-/ *adj.*

bio·con·ver·sion /ˌbaɪəʊkənˈvɜːʃn; *NAmE* ˌbaɪoʊkənˈvɜːrʒn; -ˈvɜːrʃn/ *noun* [U] the process of using living ORGANISMS to change one chemical COMPOUND (2) or form of energy into another 生物转化（利用活体生物将一种化合物或能量形式转化成另一类别）

bio·data /ˈbaɪəʊdeɪtə; *NAmE* ˈbaɪoʊ-; -dætə/ *noun* **1** [U, pl.] information about a person and about what they have done in their life 个人简历 **2** [C] (*IndE*) = CURRICULUM VITAE

bio·defence (*NAmE* **bio·defense**) /ˌbaɪəʊdɪˈfens; *NAmE* ˌbaɪoʊ-/ *noun* [U] measures taken to protect people against an attack using BIOLOGICAL WEAPONS (= weapons of war that spread disease) 生物防御（为应对生物武器对人的袭击而采取的防护措施）

bio·degrad·able /ˌbaɪəʊdɪˈɡreɪdəbl; *NAmE* ˌbaɪoʊ-/ *adj.* a substance or chemical that is **biodegradable** can be changed to a harmless natural state by the action of bacteria, and will therefore not damage the environment 可生物降解的 OPP **non-biodegradable** ➲ COLLOCATIONS AT ENVIRONMENT

bio·de·grade /ˌbaɪəʊdɪˈɡreɪd; *NAmE* ˌbaɪoʊ-/ *verb* [I] (of a substance or chemical 物质或化学品) to change back to a harmless natural state by the action of bacteria 生物降解

bio·diesel /ˈbaɪəʊdiːzl; *NAmE* ˈbaɪoʊ-/ *noun* [U] a type of fuel made from plant or animal material and used in DIESEL engines 生物柴油

bio·di·ver·sity /ˌbaɪəʊdaɪˈvɜːsəti; *NAmE* ˌbaɪoʊdaɪˈvɜːrs-/ (*also less frequent* **ˌbioˌlogical diˈversity**) *noun* [U] the existence of a large number of different kinds of animals and plants which make a balanced environment 生物多样性（大量各种生物的共存以维持生态环境平衡） ➲ WORDFINDER NOTE AT GREEN ➲ COLLOCATIONS AT ENVIRONMENT

bio·energy /ˌbaɪəʊˈenədʒi; *NAmE* ˌbaɪoʊ-/ *noun* [U] a type of energy produced using ORGANIC substances that can be replaced naturally, such as wood or vegetable oil 生物质能；生物能源： *The plant crops will be used for sustainable bioenergy.* 农作物将用来提供可持续的生物质能。

bio·engin·eer·ing /ˌbaɪəʊˌendʒɪˈnɪərɪŋ; *NAmE* ˌbaɪoʊˌendʒɪˈnɪrɪŋ/ *noun* [U] the use of engineering methods to solve medical problems, for example the use of artificial arms and legs 生物工程（指利用工程方法解决医学问题，如使用义肢等）

bio·etha·nol /ˌbaɪəʊˈeθənɒl; *NAmE* ˌbaɪoʊˈeθənɔːl; -nɑːl/ *noun* [U] a type of alcohol, produced from SUGAR CANE (= the plant from which sugar is made), MAIZE/CORN, etc., that is used as an alternative to petrol/gas 生物乙醇（产自甘蔗、玉米等，用作汽油替代品）

bio·eth·ics /ˌbaɪəʊˈeθɪks; *NAmE* ˌbaɪoʊ-/ *noun* [U] (*specialist*) the moral principles that influence research in medicine and biology 生命伦理学，生物伦理学（影响医学和生物学研究的道德准则）

bio·feed·back /ˌbaɪəʊˈfiːdbæk; *NAmE* ˌbaɪoʊ-/ *noun* [U] (*specialist*) the use of electronic equipment to record and display activity in the body that is not usually under your conscious control, for example your heart rate, so that you can learn to control that activity 生物反馈（指利用电子仪器监测心跳等身体状况，以便加以控制）

bio·fuel /ˈbaɪəʊfjuːəl; *NAmE* ˈbaɪoʊ-/ *noun* [C, U] fuel made from plant or animal sources and used in engines 生物燃料： *biofuels made from sugar cane and sugar beet* 用甘蔗和甜菜制成的生物燃料

bio·gas /ˈbaɪəʊɡæs; *NAmE* ˈbaɪoʊ-/ *noun* [U] gas, especially METHANE, that is produced by dead plants and that can be burned to produce heat 沼气（由植物残体产生的甲烷等可燃气体）

biog·raph·er /baɪˈɒɡrəfə(r); *NAmE* -ˈɑːɡ-/ *noun* a person who writes the story of another person's life 传记作家

biog·raphy /baɪˈɒɡrəfi; *NAmE* -ˈɑːɡ-/ *noun* [C, U] (*pl.* **-ies**) the story of a person's life written by sb else; this type of writing 传记；传记作品： *Boswell's biography of Johnson* 博斯韦尔写的约翰逊传 ➲ COMPARE AUTOBIOGRAPHY ➲ WORDFINDER NOTE AT BOOK ▶ **bio·graph·ic·al** /ˌbaɪəˈɡræfɪkl/ *adj.*

bio·hazard /ˈbaɪəʊhæzəd; *NAmE* ˈbaɪoʊhæzərd/ *noun* a risk to human health or to the environment, from a BIOLOGICAL source （生物源对人体或环境造成的）生物危害

bio·logic·al /ˌbaɪəˈlɒdʒɪkl; *NAmE* -ˈlɑːdʒ-/ *adj.* **1** connected with the science of biology 生物学的： *the biological sciences* 生物科学 **2** connected with the processes that take place within living things 生物的；与生命过程有关的： *the biological effects of radiation* 辐射对生物体的影响 ◇ *the **biological control** of pests* (= using living ORGANISMS to destroy them, not chemicals) 对害虫的生物防治（用生物方法而非化学药剂来消灭它们） ◇ *a child's **biological parents*** (= natural parents, not the people who adopted him/her) 孩子的亲生父母 **3** (of washing powder, etc. 洗衣粉等) using ENZYMES (= chemical substances that are found in plants and animals) to get clothes, etc. clean 加酶的： *biological and non-biological powders* 加酶和不加酶的洗衣粉 ▶ **bio·logic·al·ly** /-kli/ *adv.*

ˌbioˌlogical ˈclock *noun* (*specialist*) a natural system in living things that controls regular physical activities such as sleeping 生物钟；生理钟： (*figurative*) *At 35, Kate's biological clock was ticking* (= she was beginning to think that she would soon be too old to have children). 到 35 岁时，凯特的生物钟开始滴答作响（开始觉得很快就会年龄大得不宜生育了）。

ˌbioˌlogical diˈversity *noun* [U] = BIODIVERSITY

ˌbioˌlogical ˈwarfare (*also* **ˌgerm ˈwarfare**) *noun* [U] the use of weapons of war that spread disease 生物战；细菌战

ˌbioˌlogical ˈweapon *noun* a weapon of war that spreads disease 生物武器 ➲ COMPARE CHEMICAL WEAPON

biolo·gist /baɪˈɒlədʒɪst; *NAmE* -ˈɑːl-/ *noun* a scientist who studies biology 生物学家

biol·ogy /baɪˈɒlədʒi; *NAmE* -ˈɑːl-/ *noun* [U] **1** the scientific study of the life and structure of plants and animals 生物学: *a degree in biology* 生物学学位 ➲ COMPARE BOTANY, ZOOLOGY

WORDFINDER 联想词: **biotechnology, breed**, cell, chromosome, DNA, gene, mutation, organism, protein

2 the way in which the body and cells of a living thing behave 生理: *How far is human nature determined by biology?* 人性在多大程度上是由其生理因素决定的? ◇ *the biology of marine animals* 海洋动物的生理习性

bio·lu·min·es·cence /ˌbaɪəuluːmɪˈnesns; *NAmE* ˌbaɪoʊ-/ *noun* [U] (*biology* 生) the natural production of light by living creatures such as GLOW-WORMS 生物发光

bio·mass /ˈbaɪəumæs; *NAmE* ˈbaɪoʊ-/ *noun* [U, sing.] (*specialist*) **1** the total quantity or MASS (= weight) of plants and animals in a particular area or volume 生物量（单位面积或体积中所含的生物个体总量或其总质量）**2** natural materials from living or recently dead plants, trees and animals, used as fuel and in industrial production, especially in the generation of electricity 生物质（活着的或刚死去的动植物的天然腐化物质，用于燃料或工业生产，尤其是发电）: *biomass crops* 生物质农作物 ➲ COMPARE FOSSIL FUEL

biome /ˈbaɪəum; *NAmE* ˈbaɪoʊm/ *noun* (*biology* 生) the characteristic plants and animals that exist in a particular type of environment, for example in a forest or desert 生物群系（特定环境条件的典型植物和动物群落）

bio·mech·an·ics /ˌbaɪəuməˈkænɪks; *NAmE* ˌbaɪoʊ-/ *noun* [U] the scientific study of the physical movement and structure of living creatures 生物力学

bio·med·ical /ˌbaɪəuˈmedɪkl; *NAmE* ˌbaɪoʊ-/ *adj.* [usually before noun] relating to how biology affects medicine 生物医学的

bio·metric /ˌbaɪəuˈmetrɪk; *NAmE* ˌbaɪoʊ-/ *adj.* [usually before noun] using measurements of human features, such as fingers or eyes, in order to identify people 生物统计的

bi·onic /baɪˈɒnɪk; *NAmE* -ˈɑːnɪk/ *adj.* having parts of the body that are electronic, and therefore able to do things that are not possible for normal humans （因体内有电子装置）能力超人的

bio·phys·ics /ˌbaɪəuˈfɪzɪks; *NAmE* ˌbaɪoʊ-/ *noun* [U] the science that uses the laws and methods of physics to study biology 生物物理学

bio·pic /ˈbaɪəupɪk; *NAmE* ˈbaɪoʊ-/ *noun* a film/movie about the life of a particular person 传记片

bi·opsy /ˈbaɪɒpsi; *NAmE* -ɑːpsi/ *noun* (*pl.* **-ies**) the removal and examination of TISSUE from the body of sb who is ill/sick, in order to find out more about their disease 活组织检查（从身体取下细胞或组织进行检验）➲ WORDFINDER NOTE AT EXAMINE

bio·rhythm /ˈbaɪəurɪðəm; *NAmE* ˈbaɪoʊ-/ *noun* [usually pl.] the changing pattern of how physical processes happen in the body, that some people believe affects human behaviour 生物节律（指体内生物过程的变化模式，据信对行为有影响）

bio·sci·ence /ˌbaɪəuˈsaɪəns; *NAmE* ˌbaɪoʊ-/ *noun* [C, U] any of the LIFE SCIENCES (= sciences concerned with studying humans, animals or plants) 生物科学; 生命科学

bio·se·cur·ity /ˌbaɪəusɪˈkjʊərəti; *NAmE* ˌbaɪoʊsəˈkjʊr-/ *noun* [U] the activities involved in preventing the spread of animal and plant diseases from one area to another 生物安全保障; 生物防疫

bio·sphere /ˈbaɪəusfɪə(r); *NAmE* ˈbaɪoʊsfɪr/ *noun* [sing.] (*specialist*) the part of the earth's surface and atmosphere in which plants and animals can live 生物圈

bio·tech·nol·ogy /ˌbaɪəutekˈnɒlədʒi; *NAmE* ˌbaɪoʊtekˈnɑːl-/ (*also informal* **bio·tech** /ˈbaɪəutek; *NAmE* ˈbaɪoʊ-/) *noun* [U] the use of living cells and bacteria in industrial

▼**COLLOCATIONS** 词语搭配

Biotechnology 生物技术

Arguments for GM crops 支持转基因作物的理由

- **face/suffer from/alleviate** food shortages 面临 / 遭受 / 缓解食物短缺
- **begin/do/conduct** field trials of GM crops 开始 / 进行 / 实施转基因作物的田间试验
- **grow/develop** GM crops/seeds/plants/foods 种植 / 研发转基因作物 / 种子 / 植物 / 食物
- **improve/increase** food security/crop yields 提高 / 增加食品安全 / 粮食产量
- **label** food that contains GMOs (= genetically modified organisms) 给含有转基因生物的食物贴上标签
- **fund/invest in** genetic engineering/research 资助 / 投资基因工程 / 研究
- **promote/support/be in favour of** GM food/GM crops/genetic engineering 推广 / 支持 / 赞同转基因食物 / 转基因作物 / 基因工程
- **embrace** biotechnology/GM technology 欣然接受生物技术 / 转基因技术

Arguments against GM crops 反对转基因作物的理由

- **oppose/be against** GM technology/food/crops/trials 反对转基因技术 / 食品 / 作物 / 试验
- **call for/introduce/impose** a ban on genetic modification/a moratorium on the release of GMOs 呼吁 / 开始实施 / 强行禁止基因改造 / 暂停转基因生物上市
- **ban/prohibit/outlaw** the use of pesticides/chemical fertilizers/GMOs/so-called 'Frankenfoods' 明令禁止使用杀虫剂 / 化肥 / 转基因生物 / 所谓的"弗兰肯斯坦食物"
- **stop/halt/wreck/destroy** GM crop trials 停止 / 中止 / 破坏转基因作物试验
- **promote/support/be in favour of** organic farming 促进 / 支持 / 赞成有机农业

Arguments for biotechnology in medicine 支持生物医学技术的理由

- **grow/obtain/harvest** human organs/stem cells from human embryos 从人类胚胎中培育 / 获取 / 采集人类器官 / 干细胞
- **transplant** organs/genes/tissue/cells (into mice/animals/embryos) 移植器官 / 基因 / 组织 / 细胞（给老鼠 / 动物 / 胚胎）
- **use** biotechnology/gene therapy to treat/repair/cure sth 应用生物技术 / 基因疗法来治疗 / 修复 / 治愈某种疾病
- **fund/invest in/promote/support/be in favour of** (embryonic) stem cell research 资助 / 投资于 / 促进 / 支持 / 赞同（胚胎）干细胞研究
- **successfully clone/succeed in cloning** a sheep/a human embryo/a human being 成功克隆羊 / 人类胚胎 / 人

Arguments against biotechnology in medicine 反对生物医学技术的理由

- **create/produce** 'designer babies' 制造"定制婴儿"
- **consider/explore/address** the ethical issues raised by/related to/surrounding sth 研究 / 探究 / 论及由…引起 / 与…相关的伦理问题
- **oppose/be against** human cloning/stem cell research 反对人体克隆 / 干细胞研究
- **call for/introduce/impose** a ban on human cloning/a moratorium on xenotransplantation 呼吁 / 开始实施 / 强行禁止人类克隆 / 暂停异种移植
- **ban/prohibit/outlaw** human cloning/stem cell research/xenotransplantation 明令禁止人类克隆 / 干细胞研究 / 异种移植

and scientific processes 生物技术 ➲ WORDFINDER NOTE AT BIOLOGY ▶ **bio·tech·no·logic·al** /ˌbaɪəʊteknəˈlɒdʒɪkl; *NAmE* ˌbaɪoʊteknəˈlɑːdʒɪkl/ *adj.*: *biotechnological research* 生物科技研究

bi·ot·ic /baɪˈɒtɪk; *NAmE* baɪˈɑːtɪk/ *adj.* (*biology* 生) of or related to living things 生物的；生命的

bio·type /ˈbaɪəʊtaɪp; *NAmE* ˈbaɪoʊ-/ *noun* (*biology* 生) a group of living things with exactly the same combination of GENES 生物型（基因组合完全相同的一组生物）

bi·par·tisan /ˌbaɪpɑːtɪˈzæn; *NAmE* ˌbaɪˈpɑːrtɪzn/ *adj.* involving two political parties 两党的；涉及两党的：*a bipartisan policy* 两党都支持的政策

bi·par·tite /baɪˈpɑːtaɪt; *NAmE* -ˈpɑːrt-/ *adj.* (*specialist*) involving or made up of two separate parts 有两个部分的；两部分组成的

biped /ˈbaɪped/ *noun* (*specialist*) any creature with two feet 两足动物 ➲ COMPARE QUADRUPED

bi·pedal /ˌbaɪˈpiːdl; *NAmE also* -ˈpedl/ *adj.* (*specialist*) (of animals 动物) using only two legs for walking 双足行走的；两腿行走的

bi·plane /ˈbaɪpleɪn/ *noun* an early type of plane with two sets of wings, one above the other （早期的）双翼飞机 ➲ VISUAL VOCAB PAGE V58 ➲ COMPARE MONOPLANE

bi·polar /ˌbaɪˈpəʊlə(r); *NAmE* -ˈpoʊlər/ (*also* ˌ**manic-deˈpressive**) *adj.* (*psychology* 心) suffering from or connected with bipolar disorder 双相型障碍的；躁狂抑郁性精神病的 ▶ **bi·polar** (*also* ˌ**manic-deˈpressive**) *noun*

ˌ**biˌpolar disˈorder** (*also* ˌ**biˌpolar afˌfective disˈorder**) *noun* [U, C] (*also old-fashioned* ˌ**manic deˈpression** [U]) (*psychology* 心) a mental illness causing sb to change suddenly from being extremely depressed to being extremely happy 双相型障碍；躁狂抑郁性精神病 ➲ WORDFINDER NOTE AT CONDITION

bi·racial /ˌbaɪˈreɪʃl/ *adj.* (*NAmE*) = MIXED-RACE

birch /bɜːtʃ; *NAmE* bɜːrtʃ/ *noun* **1** [C, U] (*also* ˈ**birch tree** [C]) a tree with smooth BARK and thin branches, that grows in northern countries 桦树；白桦树 ➲ SEE ALSO SILVER BIRCH **2** (*also* **birch·wood** /ˈbɜːtʃwʊd; *NAmE* ˈbɜːrtʃ-/) [U] the hard pale wood of the birch tree 桦木 **3 the birch** [sing.] the practice of hitting sb with a bunch of birch sticks, as a punishment 用桦木条抽打（作为惩罚）

bird 🔑 /bɜːd; *NAmE* bɜːrd/ *noun, verb*

■ ***noun*** **1** 🔑 a creature that is covered with feathers and has two wings and two legs. Most birds can fly. 鸟；禽：*a bird's nest with two eggs in it* 内有两只鸟蛋的鸟窝 ◇ *a species of bird* 一种鸟 ◇ *The area has a wealth of bird life.* 这个地区栖息着大量的鸟。➲ COLLOCATIONS AT LIFE ➲ VISUAL VOCAB PAGE V12 ➲ SEE ALSO GAME BIRD, SEABIRD, SONGBIRD, WATERBIRD **2** (*old-fashioned, BrE, slang, sometimes offensive*) a way of referring to a young woman 姑娘；妞 ➲ SEE ALSO DOLLY BIRD **3** (*informal*) a person of a particular type, especially sb who is strange or unusual in some way 某类人；（尤指）古怪的人，不寻常的人：*a wise old bird* 处世老练的人 ◇ *She is that rare bird: a politician with a social conscience.* 她是这么一种少见的人：有社会良知的政治家。

IDM **be (strictly) for the birds** (*informal*) to not be important or practical 不重要；不实际 **the bird has ˈflown** the wanted person has escaped 要抓的人逃掉了 **a bird in the ˈhand is worth two in the ˈbush** (*saying*) it is better to keep sth that you already have than to risk losing it by trying to get much more 一鸟在手胜过双鸟在林（满足于现有的总比因过分追求而失去一切好） **the birds and the ˈbees** (*humorous*) the basic facts about sex, especially as told to children （尤指跟儿童讲的）性的基本知识 **a** ˌ**bird's-ˌeye ˈview (of sth)** a view of sth from a high position looking down 鸟瞰；俯视 **birds of a ˈfeather (flock toˈgether)** (*saying*) people of the same sort (are found together) 同类的人（聚在一起）；物以类聚 **give sb/get the ˈbird** (*informal*) **1** (*BrE*) to shout at sb as a sign of disapproval; to be shouted at （被）喝倒彩 **2** (*NAmE*) to make a rude sign at sb with your middle finger; to have this sign made at you 向某人竖起中指（表示侮辱）；受到竖中指的侮辱 ➲ MORE AT EARLY *adj.*, KILL *v.*, LITTLE *adj.*

■ ***verb*** [I, T] (*NAmE, informal*) ~ (**sth**) to go BIRDWATCHING 去观鸟

bird·bath /ˈbɜːdbɑːθ; *NAmE* ˈbɜːrdbæθ/ *noun* a bowl filled with water for birds to wash in and drink from, usually in a garden/yard 鸟盆（通常置于园中，供鸟儿洗澡和饮水）

bird·brain /ˈbɜːdbreɪn; *NAmE* ˈbɜːrd-/ *noun* (*especially NAmE*) a stupid person 愚笨的人；傻瓜

bird·cage /ˈbɜːdkeɪdʒ; *NAmE* ˈbɜːrd-/ *noun* a CAGE in which birds are kept, usually one in a house 鸟笼

ˈ**bird dog** *noun* (*NAmE, informal*) **1** a dog used in hunting to bring back birds that have been shot 猎鸟犬（狩猎时用以捡回击落的鸟） **2** a person whose job involves searching for good players for a sports team （运动队的）星探

bird·er /ˈbɜːdə(r); *NAmE* ˈbɜːrdər/ (*informal*) = BIRDWATCHER ➲ COMPARE ORNITHOLOGIST

ˈ**bird feeder** *noun* a container or platform in a garden in/on which people put food for birds （放在花园里的）鸟食槽，鸟食盒

ˈ**bird flu** (*also* ˈ**chicken flu**) (*also formal* ˈ**avian flu**) *noun* [U] a serious illness that affects birds, especially chickens, that can be spread from birds to humans and that can cause death 禽流感（鸟类传染病，可感染人类并导致死亡）：*Ten new cases of bird flu were reported yesterday.* 昨天新增十例禽流感病例报告。

bir·die /ˈbɜːdi; *NAmE* ˈbɜːrdi/ *noun* **1** (*informal*) a child's word for a little bird 小鸟（儿语） **2** (in GOLF 高尔夫球) a score of one stroke less than PAR (= the standard score for a hole) 小鸟击（比标准杆少一杆入洞） ➲ COMPARE BOGEY (4), EAGLE (2) **3** (*NAmE*) = SHUTTLECOCK

bird·ing /ˈbɜːdɪŋ; *NAmE* ˈbɜːrd-/ (*informal*) = BIRDWATCHING

ˌ**bird of ˈparadise** *noun* (*pl.* **birds of paradise**) a bird with very bright feathers, found mainly in New Guinea 极乐鸟，风鸟，天堂鸟（羽毛鲜艳，主要分布于新几内亚）

ˌ**bird of ˈpassage** *noun* (*pl.* **birds of passage**) **1** a bird that travels regularly from one part of the world to another at different seasons of the year 候鸟 **2** a person who passes through a place without staying there long 过客

ˌ**bird of ˈprey** *noun* (*pl.* **birds of prey**) a bird that hunts and kills other creatures for food. EAGLES, HAWKS and OWLS are all birds of prey. 猛禽（捕食其他动物的鸟，如鹰、隼和猫头鹰） ➲ VISUAL VOCAB PAGE V12

bird·seed /ˈbɜːdsiːd; *NAmE* ˈbɜːrd-/ *noun* [U] special seeds for feeding birds 鸟食种籽

bird·song /ˈbɜːdsɒŋ; *NAmE* ˈbɜːrdsɔːŋ/ *noun* [U] the musical sounds made by birds （婉转动听的）鸟鸣

ˈ**bird strike** *noun* an occasion when a bird hits an aircraft 鸟撞击飞机事故；鸟击

ˈ**bird table** *noun* (*BrE*) a wooden platform in a garden/yard on which people put food for birds 鸟食平台（花园中供人们投放鸟食的木板台） ➲ VISUAL VOCAB PAGE V20

bird·watch·er /ˈbɜːdwɒtʃə(r); *NAmE* ˈbɜːrdwɑːtʃər/ (*also informal* **bird·er**) *noun* a person who watches birds in their natural environment and identifies different breeds, as a hobby 观鸟者（在自然环境中观察并鉴定鸟类，作为一种爱好） ➲ COMPARE ORNITHOLOGIST ▶ **bird·watch·ing** (*also informal* **bird·ing**) *noun* [U]

bi·retta /bɪˈretə/ *noun* a square cap worn by Roman Catholic priests （天主教神职人员所戴的）四角帽，礼节帽，方形帽

biri·ani, biri·yani = BIRYANI

Biro™ /ˈbaɪrəʊ; *NAmE* ˈbaɪroʊ/ *noun* (*pl.* **-os**) (*BrE*) a plastic pen with a metal ball at the top that rolls ink onto the paper 伯罗圆珠笔 ➲ VISUAL VOCAB PAGE V71 ➲ COMPARE BALLPOINT

birth /bɜːθ; *NAmE* bɜːrθ/ *noun* **1** [U, C] the time when a baby is born; the process of being born 出生；诞生；分娩：*The baby weighed three kilos **at birth**.* 婴儿出生时体重为三公斤。◇ *John was present at the birth of both his children.* 约翰的两个孩子出生时他均在场。◇ *It was a difficult birth.* 那是一次难产。◇ *a **hospital/home birth*** 在医院里 / 家中的分娩 ◇ *Mark has been blind **from birth**.* 马克先天失明。◇ *Please state your **date and place of birth**.* 请列明你的出生日期和地点。➲ WORDFINDER NOTE AT BABY ➲ COLLOCATIONS AT CHILD

WORDFINDER 联想词：breech birth, caesarean, contraction, deliver, induce, labour, midwife, obstetrics, umbilical cord

2 [sing.] the beginning of a new situation, idea, place, etc. 创始；起源：*the birth of a new society in South Africa* 南非一个新社会的诞生 **3** [U] a person's origin or the social position of their family 出身；门第：*Anne was French **by birth** but lived most of her life in Italy.* 安妮在血统上是法国人，但一生大部分时间住在意大利。◇ *a woman of noble birth* 出身贵族的女子

IDM **give 'birth (to sb/sth)** to produce a baby or young animal 生孩子；产崽：*She died shortly after giving birth.* 她生下孩子后不久便死了。◇ *Mary gave birth to a healthy baby girl.* 玛丽生了个健康的女婴。◇ (*figurative*) *It was the study of history that gave birth to the social sciences.* 对历史的研究孕育了社会科学。

'birth certificate *noun* an official document that shows when and where a person was born 出生证明（书）

'birth control *noun* [U] the practice of controlling the number of children a person has, using various methods of CONTRACEPTION 节育：*a reliable method of birth control* 可靠的节育措施

birth·day /ˈbɜːθdeɪ; *NAmE* ˈbɜːrθ-/ *noun* the day in each year which is the same date as the one on which you were born 生日：*Happy Birthday!* 生日快乐！◇ *Oliver's 13th birthday* 奥利弗的 13 岁生日 ◇ *a **birthday card/party/present*** 生日贺卡 / 聚会 / 礼物 ➲ WORDFINDER NOTE AT CELEBRATE

IDM **in your 'birthday suit** (*humorous*) not wearing any clothes 光着身子；裸体

birth·ing /ˈbɜːθɪŋ; *NAmE* ˈbɜːrθ-/ *noun* [U] the action or process of giving birth 分娩；生产：*a birthing pool* 分娩池

birth·mark /ˈbɜːθmɑːk; *NAmE* ˈbɜːrθmɑːrk/ *noun* a red or brown mark on a person's skin that has been there since they were born 胎记；胎痣

'birth mother *noun* the woman who gave birth to a child who has been adopted （被领养的孩子的）生母

'birth partner *noun* a person whom a woman chooses to be with her when she is giving birth to a baby （产妇挑选的）分娩陪护，陪产者

birth·place /ˈbɜːθpleɪs; *NAmE* ˈbɜːrθ-/ *noun* **1** the house or area where a person was born, especially a famous person （尤指名人的）出生时的住宅，出生地 **2** the place where sth first happened 发源地；发祥地：*Hawaii was the birthplace of surfing.* 夏威夷是冲浪运动的发源地。

'birth rate *noun* the number of births every year for every 1 000 people in the population of a place 出生率（某地区每年每 1 000 人中的出生数目）：*a **low/high birth rate*** 低 / 高出生率

birth·right /ˈbɜːθraɪt; *NAmE* ˈbɜːrθraɪt/ *noun* (*formal*) a thing that sb has a right to because of the family or country they were born in, or because it is a basic right of all humans 与生俱来的权利（或所有物）；基本人权：*The property is the birthright of the eldest child.* 年龄最大的孩子享有财产的继承权。◇ *Education is every child's birthright.* 接受教育是每个孩子的基本权利。

birth·stone /ˈbɜːθstəʊn; *NAmE* ˈbɜːrθstoʊn/ *noun* a SEMI-PRECIOUS stone that is associated with the month of sb's birth or their sign of the ZODIAC 诞生石（表示出生月份或星座的半宝石）

birth·weight /ˈbɜːθweɪt; *NAmE* ˈbɜːrθ-/ *noun* [U, C] the recorded weight of a baby when it is born （婴儿的）出生体重

biry·ani (*also* **biri·ani, biri·yani**) /ˌbɪriˈɑːni/ *noun* [U, C] a S Asian dish made from rice with meat, fish or vegetables 比尔亚尼饭（南亚的一种肉饭、鱼肉饭或菜饭）：*chicken biryani* 比尔亚尼鸡肉饭

bis /bɪs/ *adv.* (*music* 音) (used as an instruction 指示语) again 重复

bis·cuit /ˈbɪskɪt/ *noun* **1** [C] (*BrE*) a small flat dry cake for one person, usually sweet, and baked until crisp 饼干：*a packet of chocolate biscuits* 一包巧克力饼干 ◇ *a selection of cheese biscuits* 各种乳酪饼干 ➲ COMPARE COOKIE (1) ➲ SEE ALSO DIGESTIVE BISCUIT, DOG BISCUIT **2** [C] (*NAmE*) a soft bread roll, often eaten with GRAVY 松饼（食用时常佐以肉汁） **3** [U] a pale yellowish-brown colour 淡黄褐色 ➲ MORE LIKE THIS 20, page R27

IDM **take the 'biscuit** (*BrE*) (*also* **take the 'cake** *NAmE, BrE*) (*informal*) to be the most surprising, annoying, etc. thing that has happened or that sb has done 空前惊人；极其讨厌：*You've done some stupid things before, but this really takes the biscuit!* 你以前确也干过些蠢事，但这一次实在蠢到了极点！

bi·sect /baɪˈsekt/ *verb* ~ **sth** (*specialist*) to divide sth into two equal parts 对半分；二等分

bi·sex·ual /ˌbaɪˈsekʃuəl/ *adj., noun*

■ ***adj.*** **1** (*also informal* **bi**) sexually attracted to both men and women 双性恋的 **2** (*biology* 生) having both male and female sexual organs 有两性生殖器官的；两性的；雌雄同体的 ▶ **bi·sexu·al·ity** /ˌbaɪˌsekʃuˈæləti/ *noun* [U]

■ ***noun*** a person who is bisexual 双性恋者 ➲ COMPARE HETEROSEXUAL, HOMOSEXUAL

bishop /ˈbɪʃəp/ *noun* **1** a senior priest in charge of the work of the Church in a city or district 主教：*the Bishop of Oxford* 牛津区主教 ◇ *Bishop Pritchard* 普里查德主教 ➲ SEE ALSO ARCHBISHOP **2** a piece used in the game of CHESS that is shaped like a bishop's hat and can move any number of squares in a DIAGONAL line （国际象棋中的）象 ➲ VISUAL VOCAB PAGE V42

bish·op·ric /ˈbɪʃəprɪk/ *noun* **1** the position of a bishop 主教职位 **2** the district for which a bishop is responsible 主教的辖区 SYN **diocese**

bis·muth /ˈbɪzməθ/ *noun* [U] (*symb.* **Bi**) a chemical element. Bismuth is a reddish-white metal that breaks easily and is used in medicine. 铋（用于医学）

bison /ˈbaɪsn/ *noun* (*pl.* **bison**) a large wild animal of the cow family that is covered with hair. There are two types of bison, the N American (also called BUFFALO) and the European. 野牛（分北美野牛和欧洲野牛两类）：*a herd of bison* 一群野牛

bisque /bɪsk; biːsk/ *noun* [U, C] a thick soup, especially one made from SHELLFISH （尤指虾、蟹、贝类海鲜做的）浓汤：*lobster bisque* 龙虾浓汤 ➲ SEE ALSO CHOWDER

bis·tro /ˈbiːstrəʊ; *NAmE* -stroʊ/ *noun* (*pl.* **-os**) a small informal restaurant 小餐馆；小酒馆

bit /bɪt/ *noun*

• SMALL AMOUNT 小量 **1** **a bit** [sing.] (used as an adverb 用作副词) (*especially BrE*) rather 有点儿；稍微 SYN **a little**：*These trousers are a bit tight.* 这条裤子有点紧。◇ *'Are you tired?' 'Yes, I am a bit.'* "你累了吗？" "是的，有点。" ◇ *It costs a bit more than I wanted to spend.* 比我预计的消费高了一点。◇ *I can lend you fifty pounds, if you want. That should help a bit.* 如果你需要，我可以借给你五十英镑。那应该有些帮助。 **2** **a bit** [sing.] (*especially BrE*) a short time or distance 稍顷；短距离： *Wait a bit!* 等会儿！◇ *Can you move up a bit?* 你请挪过去点儿好吗？◇ *Greg thought for a bit before answering.* 格雷格略微思考了一下才回答。 **3** [C] **~ of sth** (*especially BrE*) a small amount or piece of sth 小量；小块： *some useful bits of information* 一些有用的零星信息 ◇ *With **a bit of luck**, we'll be there by 12.* 如果顺利点，我们将于 12 点钟赶到那里。◇ *I've got a bit of shopping to do.* 我要买点东西。◇ *a bit of cake* 一小块饼 ◇ *bits of grass/paper* 些许的草；纸屑

• PART OF STH 部分 **4** [C] (*especially BrE*) a part of sth larger （事物的）一部分，一段： *The best bit of the holiday was seeing the Grand Canyon.* 假期中最精彩的片段是参观大峡谷。◇ *The school play was a huge success—the audience roared with laughter at all the funny bits.* 学校的演出获得了巨大成功，所有的滑稽片段都令观众哄堂大笑。

• LARGE AMOUNT 大量 **5** [sing.] **a ~** (**of sth**) (*informal, especially BrE*) a large amount 大量： *'How much does he earn?' **'Quite a bit!'*** "他有多少收入？" "挺多的！" ◇ *The new system will **take a bit of** getting used to* (= it will take a long time to get used to). 适应新系统将需花很多时间。

• COMPUTING 计算机技术 **6** [C] the smallest unit of information used by a computer 比特，二进制位，位（计算机的最小信息单位）

• FOR HORSE 马 **7** [C] a metal bar that is put in a horse's mouth so that the rider can control it 嚼子

• TOOL 工具 **8** [C] a tool or part of a tool for DRILLING (= making) holes 钻头；刀头；钎头 ➲ VISUAL VOCAB PAGE V21 ➲ SEE ALSO DRILL *n.* (1)

• MONEY 钱 **9** [C] (*NAmE, informal*) an amount of money equal to 12½ cents * 12.5 分；一角二分半

• SEXUAL ORGANS 生殖器官 **10 bits** [pl.] (*BrE, informal*) a person's sexual organs （人的）生殖器 ➲ SEE ALSO BITE, BIT, BITTEN

IDM **be in 'bits** (*BrE, informal*) to be very sad or worried 非常难过（或焦虑）： *Inside I'm in bits because I miss him so much.* 我内心非常难受，因为太想念他了。 **the (whole)... bit** (*informal, disapproving*) behaviour or ideas that are typical of a particular group, type of person or activity （某团体、某类人或活动的）典型行为，特有观念： *She couldn't accept the whole drug-culture bit.* 她无法接受这种毒品文化。 **bit by 'bit** a piece at a time; gradually 一点一点地；逐渐地： *He assembled the model aircraft bit by bit.* 他把飞机模型一点一点地组装起来。◇ *Bit by bit memories of the night came back to me.* 我渐渐回忆起了那晚的点点滴滴。 **a bit 'much** (*informal*) not fair or not reasonable 过分；不应当；不合理： *It's a bit much calling me at three in the morning.* 凌晨三点钟打电话给我，太过分了。 **a bit of a...** (*informal, especially BrE*) used when talking about unpleasant or negative things or ideas, to mean 'rather a...' （谈及负面事情时用）有点儿： *We may have a bit of a problem on our hands.* 我们手头的问题可能有点棘手。◇ *The rail strike is a bit of a pain.* 这次铁路罢工有点头痛。 **a bit of all 'right** (*BrE, slang*) a person that you think is sexually attractive 有魅力的人；性感的人 **a bit of 'rough** (*BrE, slang*) a person of a low social class who has a sexual relationship with sb of a higher class （与社会地位较高者有性关系的）草根情人 **a bit on the 'side** (*BrE, slang*) the boyfriend or girlfriend of sb who is already married or in a steady sexual relationship with sb else 婚外情人；第三者 **ˌbits and 'pieces/'bobs** (*BrE, informal*) small objects or items of various kinds 零七碎八；零星物品： *She stuffed all her bits and pieces into a bag and left.* 她把她零零碎碎的东西都塞进了一只包里就走了。 **do your 'bit** (*informal*) to do your share of a task 干分内的事： *We can finish this job on time if everyone does their bit.* 要是每个人都尽职，我们就能按时完成这项工作。 **every bit as good, bad, etc.** (**as sb/sth**) just as good, bad, etc.; equally good, bad, etc. （和某人、某事物）同样好、同样坏等： *Rome is every bit as beautiful as Paris.* 罗马和巴黎一样美丽。 **get the bit between your teeth** (*informal*) to become very enthusiastic about sth that you have started to do so that you are unlikely to stop until you have finished 果断地做某事；义无反顾 **not a 'bit | not one** (**little**) **'bit** not at all; not in any way 一点也不；毫不： *'Are you cold?' 'Not a bit.'* "你冷吗？" "一点不冷。" ◇ *It's not a bit of use* (= there's no point in) *complaining.* 抱怨毫无意义。◇ *I don't like that idea one bit.* 我根本不喜欢那个主意。 **not a 'bit of it!** (*informal, BrE*) used for saying that sth that you had expected to happen did not happen （预计要发生的事）根本不是那样，压根儿没有发生： *You'd think she'd be tired after the journey but not a bit of it!* 你以为她旅行之后会疲劳，根本没那回事！ **to bits 1** into small pieces 成为碎片；变成小块： *The book fell to bits in my hands.* 那本书在我手中成了碎片。◇ *She took the engine to bits, then carefully put it together again.* 她把发动机拆开，又再仔细装好。 **2** (*informal*) very much 非常；十分： *I love my kids to bits.* 我非常爱我的孩子。◇ *She was **thrilled to bits** when I said I'd come.* 我说我会来，她高兴坏了。 ➲ MORE AT BLIND *adj.*, CHAMP *v.*

▼ BRITISH/AMERICAN 英式 / 美式英语

a bit / a little

- In *BrE* it is common to use **a bit** to mean 'slightly' or 'to a small extent'. 英式英语常用 a bit 表示稍微、有点儿： *These shoes are a bit tight.* 这鞋有点儿紧。◇ *I'll be a bit later home tomorrow.* 明天我要晚点儿回家。◇ *Can you turn the volume up a bit?* 你能把音量开大点儿吗？
- It is more common in *NAmE* to say **a little**, or (*informal*) **a little bit**. You can also use these phrases in *BrE*. 美式英语较常用 a little 或 a little bit（非正式），英式英语亦可以这样说： *These shoes are a little bit too tight.* 这鞋有点儿紧。◇ *I'll be a little later home tomorrow.* 明天我要晚点儿回家。◇ *Can you turn the volume up a little bit?* 你能把音量开大点儿吗？

---

bitch /bɪtʃ/ *noun, verb*

■ *noun* **1** [C] a female dog 母狗： *a greyhound bitch* 母灵缇 **2** [C] (*slang, disapproving*) an offensive way of referring to a woman, especially an unpleasant one 泼妇；讨厌的女人： *You stupid little bitch!* 你这个愚蠢的小悍妇！◇ *She can be a real bitch.* 她撒起泼来可真不得了。 **3** [sing.] (*slang*) a thing that causes problems or difficulties 棘手的事；难办的事： ***Life's a bitch.*** 人生真受罪。 **4** [sing.] **~** (**about sb/sth**) (*informal*) a complaint about sb/sth or a conversation in which you complain about them 怨言；牢骚： *We've been having a bitch about our boss.* 我们一直对老板牢骚满腹。 ➲ SEE ALSO SON OF A BITCH

■ *verb* [I] **~** (**about sb/sth**) (*informal*) to make unkind and critical remarks about sb/sth, especially when they are not there 挖苦；（尤指背后）说坏话

bitch·in' (*also* **bitch·ing**) /ˈbɪtʃɪn/ *adj.* (*slang, especially NAmE*) very good 很好的；很棒的

bitchy /ˈbɪtʃi/ *adj.* (*informal*) (**bitch·ier**, **bitchi·est**) saying unpleasant and unkind things about other people 说人坏话的；出言不逊的： *bitchy remarks* 刻薄的话 ▸ **bitchi·ness** *noun* [U]

bit·coin /ˈbɪtkɔɪn/ *noun* (*abbr.* **BTC**) **1** [U] a system of electronic money, used for buying and selling online and without the need for a central bank 比特币（电子货币系统，用于在线交易） **2** [C] a unit of the bitcoin electronic system of money 比特币（货币单位）

bite /baɪt/ *verb, noun*

■ *verb* (**bit** /bɪt/, **bit·ten** /ˈbɪtn/)

• USE TEETH 用牙齿 **1** [I, T] to use your teeth to cut into or through sth 咬： *Does your dog bite?* 你的狗咬人吗？◇ *Come here! I won't bite!* (= you don't need to be afraid) 过来吧！我不会咬人的！◇ **~ into/through sth** *She bit into a ripe juicy pear.* 她咬了一口熟透多汁的梨。◇ **~ sb/sth** *She was bitten by the family dog.* 她被家里的狗咬伤了。◇ *Stop biting your nails!* 别咬指甲了！◇ **~ off sth/sth off** *He bit off a large chunk of bread./He bit a large chunk of bread off.* 他咬下了一大块面包。

• OF INSECT/SNAKE 昆虫；蛇 **2** [I, T] to wound sb by

making a small hole or mark in their skin 叮；蜇；咬：*Most European spiders don't bite.* 大多数欧洲蜘蛛不咬人。◇ **~ sb** *We were badly bitten by mosquitoes.* 我们被蚊子叮得不行。

• **OF FISH** 鱼 **3** [I] if a fish **bites**, it takes food from the hook of a FISHING LINE and may get caught 咬饵；上钩 ➲ WORDFINDER NOTE AT FISHING

• **HAVE EFFECT** 产生影响 **4** [I] to have an unpleasant effect 产生不良影响：*The recession is beginning to bite.* 经济衰退开始产生不良影响。

IDM **be bitten by sth** to develop a strong interest in or enthusiasm for sth 对某事物着迷；热衷于某事物：*He's been* ***bitten by the travel bug.*** 他迷上了旅游。 **bite the 'bullet** (*informal*) to start to deal with an unpleasant or difficult situation which cannot be avoided 硬着头皮对付不愉快的（或艰难的）情况；咬紧牙关应付 **ORIGIN** From the custom of giving soldiers a bullet to bite on during a medical operation without anaesthetic. 源自战地手术习惯。战士们在无麻醉剂的情况下咬住子弹接受手术。 **bite the 'dust** (*informal*) **1** to fail, or to be defeated or destroyed 失败；被打败；被摧毁：*Thousands of small businesses bite the dust every year.* 每年有数以千计的小企业倒闭。 **2** (*humorous*) to die 死 **bite the hand that 'feeds you** to harm sb who has helped you or supported you 伤害恩人；恩将仇报 **bite your 'lip** to stop yourself from saying sth or from showing an emotion 忍住话；抑制情感的流露 **bite off more than you can 'chew** to try to do too much, or sth that is too difficult 想一口吃成胖子；不自量力 **bite your 'tongue** to stop yourself from saying sth that might upset sb or cause an argument, although you want to speak 隐忍不言（避免祸从口出）：*I didn't believe her explanation but I bit my tongue.* 我不相信她的解释，但我忍着没有说出来。 ➲ MORE AT HAIR, HEAD *n.*, ONCE *adv.*

PHR V **,bite 'back (at sb/sth)** to react angrily, especially when sb has criticized or harmed you 反击；反驳 **,bite sth↔'back** to stop yourself from saying sth or from showing your feelings 忍住不说出某事；不流露情感：*She bit back her anger.* 她按捺住怒火。 **,bite 'into sth** to cut into the surface of sth 咬（或切、陷等）入某物：*The horses' hooves bit deep into the soft earth.* 马蹄深深地陷进了松软的土里。

▪ ***noun***

• **USING TEETH** 用牙齿 **1** 🔑 [C] an act of biting 咬：*The dog gave me a playful bite.* 狗闹着玩地咬了我一下。 **2** [C, usually sing.] the way the upper and lower teeth fit together（上、下牙的）咬合；啮合：*He has to wear a brace to correct his bite.* 他得戴上牙箍来矫正牙齿的咬合。

• **FOOD** 食物 **3** 🔑 [C] a small piece of food that you can bite from a larger piece （咬下的）一口：*She took a couple of bites of the sandwich.* 她吃了两口三明治。◇ *He didn't eat a bite of his dinner* (= he ate nothing). 他一口饭也没吃。 **4 a ~ (to eat)** [sing.] (*informal*) a small amount of food; a small meal 少量食物；简单的一餐：*How about a bite of lunch?* 简单吃点午饭好吗？◇ *We just have time for* ***a bite to eat*** *before the movie.* 电影开演之前，我们只够时间匆匆吃一点东西。

• **OF INSECT/ANIMAL** 昆虫；动物 **5** 🔑 [C] a wound made by an animal or insect 咬伤；叮伤；蜇伤：*Dog bites can get infected.* 狗咬的伤口会感染。◇ *a mosquito/snake bite* 蚊子叮咬；蛇咬伤

• **STRONG TASTE** 浓郁的味道 **6** [U] a pleasant strong taste 浓香：*Cheese will add extra bite to any pasta dish.* 干酪会增加面食的香味。

• **COLD** 冷 **7** [sing.] a sharp cold feeling 寒冷；凛冽：*There's a bite in the air tonight.* 今晚寒气刺骨。

• **POWERFUL EFFECT** 强烈影响 **8** [U] a quality that makes sth effective or powerful 影响力；感染力：*The performance had no bite to it.* 这次演出毫无感染力。

• **OF FISH** 鱼 **9** [C] the act of a fish biting food on a hook 咬饵；上钩 ➲ SEE ALSO FROSTBITE, LOVE BITE, SOUND BITE

IDM **a bite at/of the 'cherry** (*BrE*) an opportunity to do sth 做某事的机会（或时机）：*They were eager for a second bite of the cherry.* 他们渴望能得到第二次机会。 ➲ MORE AT BARK *n.*

'bite-sized (*also* **'bite-size**) *adj.* [usually before noun] **1** small enough to put into the mouth and eat 一口能吃下的；小块的：*Cut the meat into bite-sized pieces.* 把肉切成小块。 **2** (*informal*) very small or short 很小的；很短的：*The exams are taken in bite-size chunks over two years.* 这些考试零零碎碎，得两年才考完。

bit·ing /'baɪtɪŋ/ *adj.* **1** (of a wind 风) very cold and unpleasant 刺骨的；凛冽的 **2** (of remarks 说话) cruel and critical 刻薄的；辛辣的：***biting sarcasm/wit*** 尖酸刻薄的讽刺 / 俏皮话 ▸ **bit·ing·ly** *adv.*

bit·map /'bɪtmæp/ *noun* (*computing* 计) a way in which an image is stored with a fixed number of BITS (= units of information) for each unit of the image 位图 ▸ **bit·map** *verb* (**-pp-**) **~ sth**

bi·tonal /,baɪ'təʊnl; *NAmE* -'toʊ-/ *adj.* (*music* 音) having parts in two different KEYS sounding together 双调性的；二重调性的 ▸ **bi·ton·al·ity** /,baɪtəʊ'næləti; *NAmE* -toʊ-/ *noun* [U]

'bit part *noun* a small part in a film/movie （电影中的）小角色

'bit player *noun* **1** an actor with a small part in a film/movie 小角色；小演员 **2** a person or an organization that is involved in a situation but does not have an important role and has little influence 无足轻重的人（或组织）

bit·stream /'bɪtstriːm/ *noun* (*computing* 计) a flow of data in BINARY form 位流；比特流

bit·ten PAST PART. OF BITE

bit·ter 🔑 /'bɪtə(r)/ *adj.*, *noun*

▪ ***adj.*** **HELP** **more bitter** and **most bitter** are the usual comparative and superlative forms, but **bitterest** can also be used. * more bitter 和 most bitter 是常用的比较级和最高级形式，但也可以用 bitterest。 **1** 🔑 (of arguments, disagreements, etc. 争论、分歧等) very serious and unpleasant, with a lot of anger and hatred involved 激烈而不愉快的；充满愤怒与仇恨的：*a long and bitter dispute* 漫长而激烈的争论 **2** 🔑 (of people 人) feeling angry and unhappy because you feel that you have been treated unfairly 愤愤不平的：*She is very bitter about losing her job.* 她丢掉了工作，心里很不服气。 **3** 🔑 [usually before noun] making you feel very unhappy; caused by great unhappiness 令人不快的；使人悲痛的；由痛苦引起的：*to* ***weep/shed bitter tears*** 伤心落泪 ◇ *Losing the match was* ***a bitter disappointment*** *for the team.* 输掉这场比赛对这个队来说是一件伤心失望的事。◇ *I've learnt from* ***bitter experience*** *not to trust what he says.* 我已从痛苦的经验中得到了教训，不要相信他的话。 **4** 🔑 (of food, etc. 食物等) having a strong, unpleasant taste; not sweet 味苦的：*Black coffee leaves a bitter taste in the mouth.* 不加牛奶的咖啡在嘴里留下苦味。 ➲ COMPARE SWEET *adj.* ➲ WORDFINDER NOTE AT TASTE **5** 🔑 (of weather conditions 天气) extremely cold and unpleasant 严寒的：*bitter cold* 严寒 ◇ *a bitter wind* 刺骨寒风 ◇ *It's really bitter out today.* 今天户外的确很冷。 ▸ **bit·ter·ness** *noun* [U]：*The pay cut caused bitterness among the staff.* 降低工资使职员们十分愤懑。◇ *The flowers of the hop plant add bitterness to the beer.* 忽布花可增加啤酒的苦味。

IDM **a bitter 'pill (for sb) (to swallow)** a fact or an event that is unpleasant and difficult to accept 严酷的现实；（难以咽下的）苦果 **to/until the bitter 'end** continuing until you have done everything you can, or until sth is completely finished, despite difficulties and problems （不怕艰苦）坚持到底，奋斗到底：*They were prepared to fight to the bitter end for their rights.* 他们甘愿为自己的权利斗争到底。

▪ ***noun*** **1** (*BrE*) [U, C] a type of beer with a dark colour and a strong bitter taste, that is very popular in Britain 苦啤酒（在英国很受欢迎）：*A pint of bitter, please.* 请来一品脱苦啤酒。 ➲ COMPARE MILD *n.* **2 bitters** [U+sing./pl. v.] a strong bitter alcoholic liquid that is made from plants and added to other alcoholic drinks to give flavour 苦酒原汁（从植物中提取的苦酒精液体，可增加其他酒精饮料的味道）： *gin with a dash of bitters* 掺了少量苦酒汁的杜松子酒

▼ SYNONYMS 同义词辨析

bitter

pungent • sour • acrid • sharp • acid

These words all describe a strong, unpleasant taste or smell. 以上各词均形容味道或气味强烈、令人不适。

bitter (of a taste or smell) strong and usually unpleasant; (of food or drink) having a bitter taste 指（味道或气味）强烈的、令人不适的，（食物或饮料）味苦的

pungent (of a smell or taste) strong and usually unpleasant; (of food or smoke) having a pungent smell or taste 指（气味或味道）强烈的、令人不适的，（食物）味苦的，（烟）呛人的、刺鼻的： *the pungent smell of burning rubber* 烧橡胶的刺鼻气味

sour (of a taste) bitter like the taste of a lemon or of fruit that is not ripe; (of food or drink) having a sour taste 指（味道）酸的，（食物或饮料）有酸味的： *Too much pulp produces a sour wine.* 过多的果肉会让酒变酸。

acrid (of a smell or taste) strong and unpleasant; (of smoke) having an acrid smell 指（气味或味道）刺激的、难闻的，（烟）呛人的、刺鼻的： *acrid smoke from burning tyres* 燃烧轮胎产生的熏烟

sharp (of a taste or smell) strong and slightly bitter; (of food or drink) having a sharp taste 指（味道或气味）强烈而略苦的、刺鼻的，（食物或饮料）味苦的、辛辣的： *The cheese has a distinctively sharp taste.* 这奶酪味道很冲。

acid (of a taste or smell) bitter, like the taste of a lemon or of fruit that is not ripe; (of food or drink) having an acid taste 指（味道）酸的，（气味）有刺激性的，（食物或饮料）有酸味的

WHICH WORD? 词语辨析

A **bitter** taste is usually unpleasant, but some people enjoy the bitter flavour of coffee or chocolate. No other word can describe this flavour. A **sharp** or **pungent** flavour is more strong than unpleasant, especially when describing cheese. **Sharp**, **sour** and **acid** all describe the taste of a lemon or a fruit that is not ripe. An **acrid** smell is strong and unpleasant, especially the smell of smoke or burning, but not the smell of food.

* bitter 指味道通常为苦的、令人不快的，有人却喜欢咖啡或巧克力的苦味。没有其他词可用来形容这种味道。sharp 或 pungent 主要强调味道强烈而非令人不快，在描述奶酪的味道时尤其如此。sharp、sour 和 acid 均形容柠檬或未熟水果的酸味。acrid 指气味强烈而令人不快，尤指烟味或燃烧产生的气味，但不用来形容食物的气味。

PATTERNS

- a(n) bitter/pungent/sour/acrid/sharp/acid **taste/flavour**
- a(n) bitter/pungent/acrid/sharp/acid **smell/odour**
- a(n) bitter/sour/sharp/acid **fruit**
- pungent/sharp **cheese**
- pungent/acrid **smoke**

ˌbitter ˈlemon *noun* [U, C] (*BrE*) a FIZZY drink (= with bubbles) that tastes of lemon and is slightly bitter 苦柠檬（发泡饮料）

bit·ter·ly /ˈbɪtəli; *NAmE* -tərli/ *adv.* **1** in a way that shows feelings of sadness or anger 伤心地；愤怒地： *She wept bitterly.* 她哭得很伤心。◇ *They complained bitterly.* 他们气愤地抱怨。◇ *The development was bitterly opposed by the local community.* 这一开发项目遭到了当地社区的愤怒抵制。 **2** (describing unpleasant or sad feelings 形容不快或伤痛) extremely 极其；非常： *bitterly disappointed/ashamed* 极其失望 / 羞愧 **3** ~ **cold** very cold 非常寒冷；严寒

bit·tern /ˈbɪtən; *NAmE* -tərn/ *noun* a European bird of the HERON family, that lives on wet ground and has a loud call 麻鸦（沼泽鸟，鸣声响亮）

bitter·sweet /ˌbɪtəˈswiːt; *NAmE* ˌbɪtərˈswiːt/ *adj.* (*BrE*) **1** bringing pleasure mixed with sadness 甜中有苦的；既有欢乐又有悲伤的： *bittersweet memories* 悲喜交集的回忆 **2** (of tastes or smells 味道或气味) bitter and sweet at the same time 又苦又甜的

bitty /ˈbɪti/ *adj.* (*BrE, informal*) (**bit·tier**, **bit·ti·est**) made up of many small separate parts, which do not seem to fit together well 零散的；支离破碎的

bitu·men /ˈbɪtʃəmən; *NAmE* bəˈtuːmən; -ˈtjuː-/ *noun* [U] **1** a black sticky substance obtained from oil, used for covering roads or roofs 沥青 **2** (*AustralE, informal*) the surface of a road that is covered with TAR 沥青路面；柏油路面： *a kilometre and a half of bitumen* 一公里半的柏油路面

bi·tu·min·ous /bɪˈtjuːmɪnəs; *NAmE* bəˈtuː-/ *adj.* containing bitumen 含沥青的；沥青的

bit·zer /ˈbɪtsə(r)/ *noun* (*AustralE, NZE, informal*) **1** a thing that is made from parts that originally did not belong together 拼凑的东西；杂烩 **2** a dog that is a mixture of different breeds 杂种狗；混种狗 SYN **mongrel**

bi·valve /ˈbaɪvælv/ *noun* (*specialist*) any SHELLFISH with a shell in two parts, for example a MUSSEL 双壳（类）软体动物（如贻贝） ⊃ COMPARE MOLLUSC

biv·ouac /ˈbɪvuæk/ *noun, verb*

■ ***noun*** a temporary camp or shelter, without a tent, that is made and used especially by people climbing mountains or by soldiers 临时营地，军事野营（无帐篷）

■ ***verb*** (**-ck-**) [I] to spend the night in a bivouac 临时露营；野营

bivvy /ˈbɪvi/ *noun, verb*

■ ***noun*** (*pl.* **biv·vies**) a tent or temporary shelter 帐篷；临时遮蔽处

■ ***verb*** (**biv·vies**, **bivvy·ing**, **biv·vied**, **biv·vied**) [I] to sleep in a tent or temporary shelter 睡帐篷；睡在临时遮蔽处

the biz /bɪz/ *noun* [sing.] (*informal*) a particular type of business, especially one connected with entertainment 生意；（尤指）娱乐业： *people in the music biz* 音乐圈的人

IDM **be the ˈbiz** (*informal*) to be very good 非常棒

bi·zarre /bɪˈzɑː(r)/ *adj.* very strange or unusual 极其怪诞的；异乎寻常的 SYN **weird**: *a bizarre situation/incident/story* 稀奇古怪的局势 / 事件 / 故事 ◇ *bizarre behaviour* 古怪的行为 ▸ **bi·zarre·ly** *adv.*: *bizarrely dressed* 穿着奇装异服

blab /blæb/ *verb* (**-bb-**) [I, T] ~ (**to sb**) (**about sth**) | ~ (**sth**) (**to sb**) (*informal*) to tell sb information that should be kept secret （向某人）透露秘密，告密： *Someone must have blabbed to the police.* 一定有人向警方告密了。

blab·ber /ˈblæbə(r)/ *verb* [I] ~ (**on**) (**about sth**) (*informal*) to talk in a way that other people think is silly and annoying 说蠢话；胡扯；瞎说： *What was she blabbering on about this time?* 她这会儿又在瞎扯些什么？

blab·ber·mouth /ˈblæbəmaʊθ; *NAmE* -bərm-/ *noun* (*informal, disapproving*) a person who tells secrets because they talk too much 多嘴多舌的人；碎嘴子

black /blæk/ *adj., noun, verb*

■ ***adj.*** (**black·er**, **black·est**)

• **COLOUR** 颜色 **1** having the very darkest colour, like coal or the sky at night 黑的；黑色的： *a shiny black car* 发亮的黑汽车 ◇ *black storm clouds* 带来暴风雨的乌云

• **WITH NO LIGHT** 无光线 **2** without light; completely dark 黑暗的；漆黑的： *a black night* 漆黑的夜晚

• **PEOPLE** 人 **3** (*also* **Black**) belonging to a race of people who have dark skin; connected with black people 黑色人种的；黑人的： *a black woman writer* 一位黑人女作家 ◇ *black culture* 黑人文化 HELP **Black** is the word most widely used and generally accepted in Britain. In the US the currently accepted term is **African American**. * black 在英国广为使用和接受。在美国目前为人所接受的词是 African American。

- **TEA/COFFEE** 茶；咖啡 **4** without milk 不加牛奶的：*Two black coffees, please.* 请来两杯不加牛奶的咖啡。➲ COMPARE WHITE *adj.*
- **DIRTY** 肮脏 **5** very dirty; covered with dirt 很脏的；布满污垢的：*chimneys black with smoke* 满布烟尘的烟囱 ◇ *Go and wash your hands; they're absolutely black!* 洗洗手去，你的手脏极了！
- **ANGRY** 愤怒 **6** full of anger or hatred 愤怒的；仇恨的：*She's been in a really black mood all day.* 她一整天都心情很坏。◇ *Rory shot her a black look.* 罗里愤怒地瞪了她一眼。
- **DEPRESSING** 令人沮丧 **7** without hope; very depressing 无希望的；令人沮丧的：*The future looks pretty black.* 前景看来很暗淡。◇ *It's been another black day for the north-east with the announcement of further job losses.* 东北部又经历了一个黑色的日子，当地公布的失业人数再度上升。
- **EVIL** 邪恶 **8** (*literary*) evil or immoral 邪恶的；不道德的：*black deeds/lies* 邪恶行为；昧良心的谎言
- **HUMOUR** 幽默 **9** dealing with unpleasant or terrible things, such as murder, in a humorous way 黑色的（以幽默的方式对待讨厌的或可怕的事物，如凶杀）：*'Good place to bury the bodies,' she joked with* ***black humour***. "真是个掩埋尸体的风水宝地。"她以黑色幽默打趣道。◇ *The play is a* ***black comedy***. 那是个黑色喜剧。➲ SEE ALSO BLACKLY

▶ **black·ness** *noun* [U, sing.]: *She peered out into the blackness of the night.* 她凝视着外面黑沉沉的夜色。

IDM **(beat sb) black and 'blue** (to hit sb until they are) covered with BRUISES (= blue, brown or purple marks on the body) （把某人打得）青一块紫一块，伤痕累累 ➲ MORE LIKE THIS 13, page R26 **not as black as he/she/it is 'painted** not as bad as people say he/she/it is 不像别人说的那么坏：*He's not very friendly, but he's not as black as he's painted.* 他不太友善，但也不像别人说的那么坏。➲ MORE AT POT *n.*

■ ***noun***

- **COLOUR** 颜色 **1** [U] the very darkest colour, like night or coal 黑色：*the black of the night sky* 夜空的漆黑 ◇ *Everyone at the funeral was dressed in black.* 参加葬礼的人都身着黑服。
- **PEOPLE** 人 **2** (*also* **Black**) [C, usually pl.] a member of a race of people who have dark skin 黑色人种的人；黑人 HELP In this meaning **black** is more common in the plural. It can sound offensive in the singular. Instead, you can use the adjective ('a black man/woman') or, in the US, **African American**. * black 在此义中常以复数形式出现。单数形式可能使人感到冒犯。但可用作形容词 (a black man/woman)，或者，在美国可说 African American。

IDM **be in the 'black** to have money, for example in your bank account 有盈余；有结余 ➲ COMPARE BE IN THE RED at RED *n.* **ˌblack and 'white** having no colours except black, white and shades of grey (in photographs, on television, etc.) （照片、电视等）黑白的：*a film made in black and white* 黑白电影 ◇ *black-and-white photos* 黑白照片 **in black and white** in writing or in print 白纸黑字；书写的；印刷的：*I never thought they'd put it in black and white on the front page.* 我从未想到他们会在头版把它登出来。**(in) black and white** in a way that makes people or things seem completely bad or good, or completely right or wrong 黑白分明（好坏、是非等清楚的）：*It's a complex issue, but he only sees it in black and white.* 那是个复杂的问题，但他却只用非此即彼的眼光来看待。◇ *This is not a black-and-white decision* (= where the difference between two choices is completely clear). 这不是个非此即彼的决定。

■ ***verb*** **1** ~ **sth/sb** (*BrE*) to refuse to deal with goods or to do business with sb as a political protest 抵制；拒绝处理（货物）；拒绝同（某人）做生意 SYN **boycott**: *The unions have blacked all imports from the country.* 工会拒绝处理从这个国家进口的所有货物。 **2** ~ **sth** to make sth black 使变黑；染黑；涂黑 SYN **blacken**

PHR V **ˌblack 'out** to become unconscious for a short time 暂时失去知觉；昏厥 SYN **faint**: *The driver had probably blacked out at the wheel.* 司机很可能在开车时昏厥了。➲ RELATED NOUN BLACKOUT (5) **ˌblack sth↔'out 1** to make a place dark by turning off lights, covering windows, etc. 使（某处）变黑暗：*A power failure blacked out the city last night.* 昨晚停电造成整个城市一片漆黑。◇ *a house with blacked out windows* 窗户被遮住不透光的房子 ➲ RELATED NOUN BLACKOUT (1) **2** to prevent sth such as a piece of writing or a television broadcast from being read or seen 涂掉（文章）；截断（电视广播）；封锁（新闻）：*Some lines of the document have been blacked out for security reasons.* 为安全起见，这份文件的一些句子被涂掉了。

black·amoor /ˈblækəmɔː(r)/ *noun* (*old use, taboo*) an offensive word for a black person（含冒犯意）黑人；黑鬼

the ˌblack 'arts *noun* [pl.] = BLACK MAGIC

black·ball /ˈblækbɔːl/ *verb* ~ **sb** to prevent sb from joining a club or a group by voting against them 投票反对（某人加入俱乐部或团体）

ˌblack 'belt *noun* **1** a belt that you can earn in a sport such as JUDO or KARATE which shows that you have reached a very high standard （柔道、空手道等运动中显示已达到很高水平的）黑腰带 **2** a person who has gained a black belt 黑带级选手

Black·Berry™ /ˈblækbəri; *NAmE* -beri/ *noun* (*pl.* **-ies**) a type of SMARTPHONE or TABLET (4) 黑莓手机；黑莓平板电脑：*Check your emails via your BlackBerry.* 用黑莓手机查收邮件。

black·berry /ˈblækbəri; *NAmE* -beri/ (*pl.* **-ies**) (*BrE also* **bram·ble**) *noun* a small soft black fruit that grows on a bush with THORNS in gardens/yards or in the countryside. The bush is also called a blackberry/bramble. 黑莓（浆果）；黑莓（有刺灌木）：*blackberry and apple pie* 黑莓苹果馅饼 ➲ VISUAL VOCAB PAGE V33

black·berry·ing /ˈblækbəriɪŋ; *NAmE* -beriɪŋ/ *noun* [U] the act of picking blackberries 采集黑莓：*Shall we go blackberrying?* 我们去采黑莓好不好？

black·bird /ˈblækbɜːd; *NAmE* -bɜːrd/ *noun* **1** a European bird: the male is black with a yellow beak and the female is brown with a brown beak 乌鸫（见于欧洲，雄鸟黑羽黄喙，雌鸟棕色） **2** a black N American bird, larger than the European blackbird, related to the STARLING 拟鹂（见于北美洲）

black·board /ˈblækbɔːd; *NAmE* -bɔːrd/ (*also* **chalk·board** *especially in NAmE*) *noun* a large board with a smooth black or dark green surface that teachers write on with a piece of CHALK 黑板：*to write on the blackboard* 在黑板上写字 ➲ COMPARE WHITEBOARD (1)

ˌblack 'box *noun* **1** (*also* **'flight recorder**) a small machine in a plane that records all the details of each flight and is useful for finding out the cause of an accident 黑匣子；黑盒；飞行记录仪 **2** [usually sing.] (*informal*) a complicated piece of equipment, usually electronic, that you know produces particular results, but that you do not completely understand 黑箱（常为电子的复杂仪器，内部结构不详）

ˌblack 'cab *noun* (*BrE*) a traditional type of taxi in London and some other British cities. Its driver is licensed by the city to stop and pick up passengers in the street. 黑色出租车（伦敦等英国城市的市区老牌出租车）：*a queue of black cabs at the station* 车站前的一溜老牌黑色出租车

the 'Black Country *noun* [sing.] an area in the West Midlands of England where there used to be a lot of heavy industry 黑乡（在英格兰西米德兰兹，原为重工业地带）

black·cur·rant /ˌblækˈkʌrənt; ˈblækkʌrənt; *NAmE* -kɜːr-/ *noun* a small black BERRY that grows in bunches on a garden bush and can be eaten 黑茶藨子；黑加仑子：*blackcurrant jam* 黑茶藨子酱 ◇ *a blackcurrant bush* 黑茶藨子灌木

B

the ˌBlack ˈDeath *noun* [sing.] the name used for the very serious infectious disease, (called BUBONIC PLAGUE), which killed millions of people in Europe and Asia in the 14th century 黑死病（14 世纪蔓延于欧亚的鼠疫）

ˌblack ˈdiamond *noun* **1** [C] (*BrE, informal*) a lump of coal 煤块 **2** [U, C] a dark form of diamond 黑金刚石；黑钻石 **3** [C] (*NAmE*) a slope that is difficult to SKI down 黑钻石坡道（难以下滑的陡坡）： *a black diamond run* 黑钻石滑道

the ˌblack eˈconomy (*BrE*) (*NAmE* **the ˌunderground eˈconomy**) *noun* [sing.] business activity or work that is done without the knowledge of the government or other officials so that people avoid paying tax on the money they earn 黑市经济；黑市经营；地下经济活动

ˌblack emˈpowerment (*also* **ˌblack ecoˌnomic emˈpowerment**) *noun* [U] in southern Africa, a policy which aims to give black people the chance to earn more money, own more property, etc., and have a greater role in the economy than they did before 黑人赋权（非洲南部政策，旨在给黑人提供机会增加收入并拥有财产等，以及参与更多经济活动）

black·en /ˈblækən/ *verb* **1** [T, I] **~ (sth)** to make sth black; to become black （使）变黑： *Their faces were blackened with soot.* 他们满脸煤灰。◇ *Smoke had blackened the walls.* 烟把墙壁都熏黑了。 **2** [T] **~ sb's name/reputation/character** to say unpleasant things that give people a bad opinion of sb 抹黑；丑化；败坏…的名誉： *He accused the newspaper of trying to blacken his name.* 他指责报纸企图败坏他的名声。

ˌBlack ˈEnglish *noun* [U] any of various forms of English spoken by black people, especially a form spoken in US cities （尤指美国城市中的）黑人英语

ˌblack ˈeye *noun* an area of dark skin (called a BRUISE), that can form around sb's eye when they receive a blow on it （被打成的）青肿眼眶

black·face /ˈblækfeɪs/ *noun* **1** [C] a type of sheep with a black face 黑面羊；黑脸羊 **2** [U] a dark substance used by actors to make their skin look dark （演员用）黑油彩，黑脸化装品

ˌblack ˈflag *noun* **1** a black flag used in motor racing to stop a driver who has done sth wrong 黑旗（赛车中用以示意犯规车手停车） **2** a flag with a SKULL AND CROSSBONES on it 海盗旗（上有骷髅和交叉的股骨图形）

black·fly /ˈblækflaɪ/ *noun* (*pl.* **black·fly** or **black·flies**) **1** a small black or dark green insect that damages plants 黑蚜虫，深绿色蚜虫（侵害植物） **2** (*also* **ˈblack fly**) a small black fly that sucks blood from humans and animals 蚋（吸血）

Black·foot /ˈblækfʊt/ *noun* (*pl.* **Black·feet** /ˈblækfiːt/ or **Black·foot**) a member of a Native American people, many of whom live in the US state of Montana and in Alberta in Canada 黑脚族人，黑脚人（美洲土著，很多居于美国蒙大拿州和加拿大艾伯塔省）

ˌBlack ˈFriday *noun* [U] (in the US) the day after THANKSGIVING, the first day of traditional Christmas shopping, when stores have special offers to attract consumers 黑色星期五（感恩节翌日，美国传统圣诞购物季的第一天，商店推出特价优惠吸引消费者）

ˌblack ˈgold *noun* [U] (*especially NAmE, informal*) oil 黑金子；石油

black·guard /ˈblæɡɑːd; *NAmE* ˈblækɡɑːrd/ *noun* (*old-fashioned, BrE*) a man who is dishonest and has no sense of what is right and what is wrong 无赖；恶棍

black·head /ˈblækhed/ *noun* a small spot on the skin, often on the face, with a black top 黑头粉刺（常长在面部）

ˌblack ˈhole *noun* an area in space that nothing, not even light, can escape from, because GRAVITY (= the force that pulls objects in space towards each other) is so strong there 黑洞（宇宙中包括光线在内的任何东西都无法逃逸的强引力区域）： (*figurative*) *The company viewed the venture as a financial black hole* (= it would use a lot of the company's money with no real result). 公司认为该项投资是财政上的一个黑洞。

ˌblack ˈice *noun* [U] ice in a thin layer on the surface of a road 黑冰，薄冰（路面上很薄的冰层）

black·jack /ˈblækdʒæk/ *noun* **1** (*BrE also* **pon·toon**) [U] a card game in which players try to collect cards with a total value of 21 and no more * 21 点纸牌游戏（玩者力争取得 21 点的总点数） **2** [C] (*especially NAmE*) a type of CLUB used as a weapon, especially a metal pipe covered with leather （包革）金属棍棒，金属警棍

black·leg /ˈblækleg/ *noun* (*BrE, disapproving*) a person who continues to work when the people they work with are on strike; a person who is employed to work instead of those who are on strike 破坏罢工者，工贼（罢工时继续工作或受雇顶替罢工者工作） ➲ COMPARE STRIKEBREAKER ➲ SEE ALSO SCAB (4)

ˌblack ˈlight *noun* [U] ULTRAVIOLET or INFRARED RAYS, which cannot be seen 不可见光，黑光（指紫外线和红外线）

black·list /ˈblæklɪst/ *noun, verb*

■ ***noun*** a list of the names of people, companies, products or countries that an organization or a government considers unacceptable and that must be avoided 黑名单

■ ***verb*** **~ sb/sth** to put the name of a person, a company, a product or a country on a blacklist 将…列入黑名单： *She was blacklisted by all the major Hollywood studios because of her political views.* 由于她的政见，所有好莱坞大制片公司都拒绝用她。

ˌblack ˈlung *noun* [U] (*especially NAmE*) a lung disease caused by breathing in coal dust over a long period of time 黑肺病，煤肺病，炭肺病（长期吸入煤尘引起）

black·ly /ˈblækli/ *adv.* **~ comic/funny/humorous/satirical** dealing with unpleasant or terrible things, such as murder, in a humorous way 以黑色幽默方式： *The movie takes a blackly humorous look at death.* 这影片以黑色幽默视角看待死亡。

ˌblack ˈmagic *noun* [U] (*also* **the black ˈarts** [pl.]) a type of magic which is believed to use the power of the DEVIL in order to do evil 魔法；妖术；巫术

black·mail /ˈblækmeɪl/ *noun, verb*

■ ***noun*** [U] **1** the crime of demanding money from a person by threatening to tell sb else a secret about them 勒索；敲诈 **2** the act of putting pressure on a person or a group to do sth they do not want to do, for example by making threats or by making them feel guilty 胁迫；威胁；恐吓： ***emotional/moral blackmail*** 情感上 / 道德上胁迫

■ ***verb*** to force sb to give you money or do sth for you by threatening them, for example by saying you will tell people a secret about them 勒索；敲诈；要挟；胁迫： **~ sb** *She blackmailed him for years by threatening to tell the newspapers about their affair.* 她以向报界公开他们的私情要挟了他很多年。◇ **~ sb into doing sth** *The President said he wouldn't be blackmailed into agreeing to the terrorists' demands.* 总统说他不会因受恐怖分子的威胁而答应他们的要求。

black·mail·er /ˈblækmeɪlə(r)/ *noun* a person who commits blackmail 勒索者；敲诈者

Black Maria /ˌblæk məˈraɪə/ *noun* (*old-fashioned, informal*) a police van that was used in the past for transporting prisoners in （旧时）囚车

ˌblack ˈmark *noun* (*BrE*) a note, either in writing on an official record, or in sb's mind, of sth you have done or said that makes people think badly of you （记录在案的或留在别人印象中的）污点： *She earned a black mark for opposing company policy.* 她因反对公司政策而得到考绩不良的评语。◇ *The public scandal was a black mark against him.* 那条尽人皆知的丑闻成了他的一个污点。

ˌ**black ˈmarket** *noun* [usually sing.] an illegal form of trade in which foreign money, or goods that are difficult to obtain, are bought and sold 黑市（交易）：*to buy or sell goods **on the black market*** 从事黑市买卖 ◇ *a flourishing black market in foreign currency* 猖獗的外币黑市交易

ˌ**black marke'teer** *noun* a person who sells goods on the black market 在黑市出售商品者；黑市商人

ˌ**black ˈmass** *noun* a ceremony in which people worship the DEVIL 黑弥撒（崇拜撒旦）

ˌ**Black ˈMuslim** *noun* a member of a group of black people, especially in the US, who follow the religion of Islam and want a separate black society 黑人穆斯林（尤指美国信仰伊斯兰教且致力于建立黑人社会的组织及其成员）

black·out /ˈblækaʊt/ *noun* **1** a period when there is no light as a result of an electrical power failure 断电；停电 **2** a situation when the government or the police will not allow any news or information on a particular subject to be given to the public 新闻封锁 **3** [usually sing.] a period of time during a war when all lights must be put out or covered at night, so that they cannot be seen by an enemy attacking by air 灯火管制（期） **4** [usually pl.] (*BrE*) a covering for windows that stops light being seen from outside, or light from outside from coming into a room 不透光窗罩（或窗帘） **5** a temporary loss of CONSCIOUSNESS, sight or memory 一时性黑蒙；眼前昏黑；短时失忆：*She had a blackout and couldn't remember anything about the accident.* 她一时失忆，那场事故怎么也想不起来了。

ˌ**black ˈpepper** *noun* [U] a black powder made from dried BERRIES (called PEPPERCORNS), used to give a spicy flavour to food 黑胡椒粉：*salt and freshly ground black pepper* 盐和新研磨的黑胡椒粉

ˌ**Black ˈPower** *noun* [U] a movement supporting rights and political power for black people 黑人民权运动

ˌ**black ˈpudding** (*BrE*) (*NAmE* **ˈblood sausage**) (*also* ˌ**blood ˈpudding** *BrE, NAmE*) *noun* [U, C] a type of large dark SAUSAGE made from pig's blood, fat and grain 黑香肠，血肠（用猪血、油脂和谷粒制成）

ˌ**Black ˈRod** *noun* [U] an official who takes part in the opening ceremony of the British parliament （英国议会开幕仪式上的）黑杖侍卫，黑杖礼仪官

ˌ**black ˈsheep** *noun* [usually sing.] a person who is different from the rest of their family or another group, and who is considered bad or embarrassing 有辱家族的人；害群之马：*the black sheep of the family* 家族败类

black·shirt (*also* **Black·shirt**) /ˈblækʃɜːt; *NAmE* -ʃɜːrt/ *noun* a member of a FASCIST organization, especially in the 1920s and 30s 黑衫党成员（尤指 20 世纪 20 和 30 年代的法西斯组织成员）

black·smith /ˈblæksmɪθ/ (*also* **smith**) *noun* a person whose job is to make and repair things made of iron, especially HORSESHOES 铁匠（尤指打马蹄铁者）➲ COMPARE FARRIER

ˈ**black spot** *noun* (*BrE*) a place, a situation or an event that is a problem or that causes a lot of problems 事故多发区；问题成堆的状况；（问题）焦点：*an environmental black spot* 环境污染严重的地区 ◇ *That corner is a notorious accident black spot* (= a lot of accidents happen there). 那个拐弯处是有名的事故多发区。

black·thorn /ˈblækθɔːn; *NAmE* -θɔːrn/ *noun* [U] a bush with THORNS with black branches, white flowers and sour purple fruit called SLOES 黑刺李（多刺灌木，开白花，结紫色酸果）

ˌ**black ˈtie** *noun* a black BOW TIE worn with a DINNER JACKET （晚礼服佩戴的）黑领结 ▸ ˌ**black ˈtie** *adj.*：*The party is black tie* (= dinner jackets should be worn). 聚会要求穿礼服。◇ *a black-tie dinner* 要求穿晚礼服的宴会

black·top /ˈblæktɒp; *NAmE* -tɑːp/ *noun* (*NAmE*) = TARMAC™ (1)

ˌ**black ˈwidow** *noun* a poisonous American spider. The female black widow often eats the male. 黑寡妇毒蛛（美洲蜘蛛，雌蛛常吃掉雄蛛）

blad·der /ˈblædə(r)/ *noun* **1** an organ that is shaped like a bag in which liquid waste (= URINE) collects before it is passed out of the body 膀胱 ➲ SEE ALSO GALL BLADDER ➲ VISUAL VOCAB PAGE V64 **2** a bag made of rubber, leather, etc. that can be filled with air or liquid, such as the one inside a football 皮囊，气囊（如球胆）

blad·dered /ˈblædəd; *NAmE* ˈblædərd/ *adj.* [not before noun] (*BrE, slang*) drunk 喝醉

blades 刀身；刀刃；刀片；桨叶；叶片

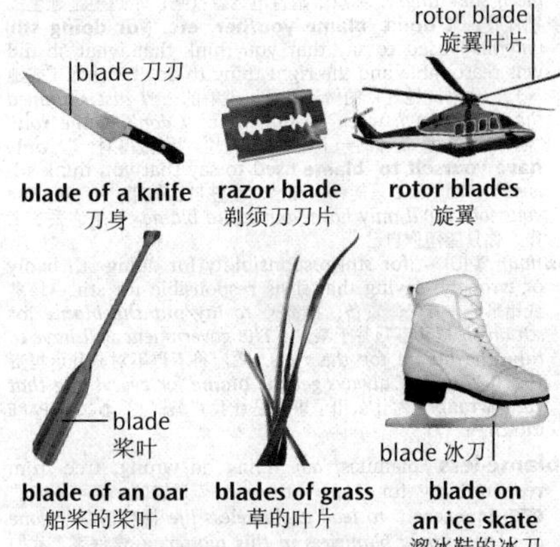

blade 🔑 /bleɪd/ *noun* **1** 🔑 the flat part of a knife, tool or machine, which has a sharp edge or edges for cutting 刀身；刀片；刀刃 ➲ VISUAL VOCAB PAGES V21, V23, V25, V27 ➲ SEE ALSO RAZOR BLADE, SWITCHBLADE **2** one of the flat parts that turn around in an engine or on a HELICOPTER （机器上旋转的）叶片；桨叶：*the blades of a propeller* 螺旋桨叶 ◇ *rotor blades on a helicopter* 直升机的旋翼 ➲ VISUAL VOCAB PAGE V57 **3** the flat wide part of an OAR (= one of the long poles that are used to ROW[1] a boat) that goes in the water （船桨的）桨叶，桨身 ➲ VISUAL VOCAB PAGE V60 **4** a single flat leaf of grass （草的）叶片 **5** the flat metal part on the bottom of an ICE SKATE （溜冰鞋的）冰刀 ➲ SEE ALSO SHOULDER BLADE

blad·ing /ˈbleɪdɪŋ/ *noun* [U] the sport of moving on ROLLERBLADES 轮滑；直排轮溜冰运动；滚轴溜冰

blag /blæg/ *verb* (**-gg-**) **~ sth** (*BrE, informal*) to persuade sb to give you sth, or to let you do sth, by talking to them in a clever or amusing way 哄…；哄得：*I blagged some tickets for the game.* 我骗到了这场比赛的几张门票。◇ *We **blagged our way** into the reception by saying that we were from the press.* 我们自称记者混进了招待会。

blah /blɑː/ *noun, adj.*

▪ ***noun*** [U] (*informal*) people say **blah, blah, blah**, when they do not want to give the exact words that sb has said or written because they think they are not important or are boring （觉得厌烦不想重复别人的话时说）：*They said, 'Come in, sit down, blah, blah, blah, sign here'.* 他们说："进来，坐下，干这个，干那个，在这里签字。"

▪ ***adj.*** (*NAmE, informal*) **1** not interesting 乏味的：*The movie was pretty blah.* 那场电影真没意思。 **2** not feeling well; feeling slightly unhappy 不舒服；闷闷不乐

B

blame /bleɪm/ *verb, noun*

■ *verb* to think or say that sb/sth is responsible for sth bad 把…归咎于；责怪；指责：**~ sb/sth (for sth)** *She doesn't blame anyone for her father's death.* 她没把她父亲的死归罪于任何人。◇ *A dropped cigarette is being blamed for the fire.* 一根乱扔的烟被认为是这场火灾的肇因。◇ **~ sth on sb/sth** *Police are blaming the accident on dangerous driving.* 警方把事故原因归咎于危险驾驶。

IDM **be to blame (for sth)** to be responsible for sth bad 对（坏事）负有责任：*If anyone's to blame, it's me.* 如果有人该承担责任，那就是我。◇ *Which driver was to blame for the accident?* 哪个司机是此次事故的肇事者？ **don't blame 'me** (*informal*) used to advise sb not to do sth, when you think they will do it despite your advice（劝阻别人时说）别怪我：*Call her if you like, but don't blame me if she's angry.* 你想给她打电话就打吧，不过要是她生气别怪我。 **I don't 'blame you/her, etc. (for doing sth)** (*informal*) used to say that you think that what sb did was reasonable and the right thing to do 我不怪你（或她等）；你（或她等）的做法是可以理解的：*'I just slammed the phone down when he said that.' 'I don't blame you!'* "他一说那话我就啪的一下挂了电话。" "你做得对！" **only have yourself to 'blame** used to say that you think sth is sb's own fault 只能怪你自己；是你自己的错：*If you lose your job, you'll only have yourself to blame.* 如果你丢了工作，你只能怪你自己。

■ *noun* [U] **~ (for sth)** responsibility for doing sth badly or wrongly; saying that sb is responsible for sth（坏事或错事的）责任；责备；指责：*to* ***lay/put the blame*** *for sth on sb* 把某事归咎于某人 ◇ *The government will have* ***to take the blame*** *for the riots.* 政府将不得不对骚乱承担责任。◇ *Why do I always* ***get the blame*** *for everything that goes wrong?* 为什么出了事总是让我背黑锅？ ➲ COMPARE CREDIT *n.* (7)

blame·less /ˈbleɪmləs/ *adj.* doing no wrong; free from responsibility for doing sth bad 无过错的；无可指责的 SYN **innocent**：*to lead a blameless life* 活得清白 ◇ *None of us is entirely blameless in this matter.* 在这件事上我们没有一个人是完全没有责任的。 ▸ **blame·less·ly** *adv.*

blame·worthy /ˈbleɪmwɜːði; *NAmE* -wɜːrði/ *adj.* (*formal*) deserving disapproval and criticism; responsible for doing sth wrong 该受指责的；（对坏事）负有责任的

blanch /blɑːntʃ; *NAmE* blæntʃ/ *verb* **1** [I] **~ (at sth)** (*formal*) to become pale because you are shocked or frightened（受惊吓）脸发白 **2** [T] **~ sth** to prepare food, especially vegetables, by putting it into boiling water for a short time 焯（把蔬菜等放在沸水中略微一煮）

blanc·mange /bləˈmɒnʒ; *NAmE* -ˈmɑːnʒ/ *noun* [C, U] (*BrE*) a cold DESSERT (= a sweet dish) that looks like jelly, made with milk and flavoured with fruit 果味牛奶冻

bland /blænd/ *adj.* (**bland·er**, **bland·est**) **1** with little colour, excitement or interest; without anything to attract attention 平淡的；乏味的 SYN **nondescript**：*bland background music* 毫无情调的背景音乐 **2** not having a strong or interesting taste 清淡的；无滋味的：*a rather bland diet of soup, fish and bread* 汤、鱼和面包的清淡饮食 ➲ WORDFINDER NOTE AT TASTE **3** showing no strong emotions or excitement; not saying anything very interesting 沉稳的；无动于衷的；讲话枯燥的：*a bland smile* 淡然一笑 ◇ *After the meeting, a bland statement was issued.* 会后发布了一条乏味的声明。 ▸ **bland·ly** *adv.* **bland·ness** *noun* [U]

bland·ish·ments /ˈblændɪʃmənts/ *noun* [pl.] (*formal*) pleasant things that you say to sb or do for them to try to persuade them to do sth（因有所求而）说的好话（或做的好事），讨人欢心

blank /blæŋk/ *adj., noun, verb*

■ *adj.* **1** empty, with nothing written, printed or recorded on it 空白的：*Sign your name in the blank space below.* 把名字签在下面的空白处。◇ *a blank CD* 空白光盘 ◇ *Write on one side of the paper and leave the other side blank.* 写在纸的一面，把另一面空出来。◇ *She turned to a blank page in her notebook.* 她翻开笔记本的一张空白页。 **2** (of a wall or screen 墙壁或屏幕) empty; with no pictures, marks or decoration 空的；无图画（或标记、装饰）的：*blank whitewashed walls* 光秃秃的白灰墙 ◇ *Suddenly the screen* ***went blank.*** 屏幕突然变成一片空白。 **3** showing no feeling, understanding or interest 没表情的；不理解的；不感兴趣的：*She stared at me with a blank expression on her face.* 她一脸木然地盯着我。◇ *Steve* ***looked blank*** *and said he had no idea what I was talking about.* 史蒂夫显得很迷惑，说他不知道我在说什么。◇ *Suddenly* ***my mind went blank*** (= I could not remember anything). 我脑子里突然一片空白。 **4** [only before noun] (of negative things 否定的事情) complete and total 完全的；彻底的：*a* ***blank refusal/denial*** 断然拒绝 / 否认 ➲ SEE ALSO POINT-BLANK ▸ **blank·ly** *adv.*：*She stared blankly into space, not knowing what to say next.* 她两眼发直，不知道下面该说什么。 **blank·ness** *noun* [U]

■ *noun* **1** [C] an empty space on a printed form or document for you to write answers, information, etc. in（文件等的）空白处，空格：*Please* ***fill in the blanks.*** 请在空白处填写。◇ *If you can't answer the question, leave a blank.* 如果回答不了问题，就空着它。 **2** [sing.] a state of not being able to remember anything（记忆中的）空白，遗忘：*My* ***mind was a blank*** *and I couldn't remember her name.* 我脑子里一片空白，记不起她的名字了。 **3** [C] (*also* ˌ**blank ˈcartridge**) a CARTRIDGE in a gun that contains an EXPLOSIVE but no bullet 空弹：*The troops fired blanks in the air.* 部队向天放空弹。 IDM SEE DRAW *v.*

■ *verb* **1** [T] **~ sb** (*BrE, informal*) to ignore sb completely 毫不理睬（某人）：*I saw her on the bus this morning, but she totally blanked me.* 我今天早晨在公共汽车上见到她，但她连一眼都没瞧我。 **2** [I] (*NAmE*) to be suddenly unable to remember or think of sth 突然忘掉；突然思路模糊：*I knew the answer, but I totally blanked during the test.* 我本来知道答案，但考试时我什么都忘了。

PHR V ˌ**blank ˈout** to suddenly become empty 突然变空：*The screen blanked out.* 屏幕突然变成一片空白。 ˌ**blank sth↔ˈout 1** to cover sth completely so that it cannot be seen 掩盖；遮盖：*All the names in the letter had been blanked out.* 信中所有的名字都已涂掉。 **2** to deliberately forget sth unpleasant 刻意忘记；抹去记忆：*She had tried to blank out the whole experience.* 她曾试图把全部经历从记忆中抹去。

ˌ**blank ˈcall** *noun* (*IndE*) a telephone call made by a person who does not give their name and who wants to threaten, annoy or worry sb（威胁或骚扰的）匿名电话

ˌ**blank ˈcheque** (*BrE*) (*NAmE* ˌ**blank ˈcheck**) *noun* **1** a cheque that is signed but which does not have the amount of money to be paid written on it 空白支票，空额支票（已签名但未填金额） **2** permission or authority to do sth that is necessary in a particular situation（特定情况下的）自由行动权：*The President was* ***given a blank check*** *by Congress to continue the war.* 国会授予总统全权可继续这场战争。

blan·ket /ˈblæŋkɪt/ *noun, adj., verb*

■ *noun* **1** a large cover, often made of wool, used especially on beds to keep people warm 毯子；毛毯 ➲ VISUAL VOCAB PAGE V24 ➲ SEE ALSO ELECTRIC BLANKET **2** [usually sing.] **~ of sth** a thick layer or covering of sth 厚层；厚的覆盖层：*a* ***blanket of fog/snow/cloud*** 厚厚的一层雾 / 雪 / 云 ◇ (*figurative*) *The trial was conducted under a blanket of secrecy.* 审讯在高度保密下进行。 ➲ SEE ALSO WET BLANKET

■ *adj.* [only before noun] including or affecting all possible cases, situations or people 包括所有情形（或人员）的；总括的；综合的：*a* ***blanket ban*** *on tobacco advertising* 烟草广告的全面取缔 ◇ *a blanket refusal* 完全拒绝

■ *verb* [often passive] **~ sth** (*formal*) to cover sth completely with a thick layer 以厚层覆盖：*The ground was soon blanketed with snow.* 地面很快铺上了一层厚厚的积雪。

ˈ**blanket bath** *noun* (*BrE*) an act of washing the whole of sb's body when they cannot get out of bed because they are sick, injured or old（为伤病或年老者所做的）卧床浴，卧床全身擦浴

ˌblank ˈverse *noun* [U] (*specialist*) poetry that has a regular rhythm, usually with ten syllables and five stresses in each line, but which does not RHYME 无韵诗（不押韵的抑扬五音步诗行，常为每行十个音节）➲ COMPARE FREE VERSE

blare /bleə(r); *NAmE* bler/ *verb, noun*

■ ***verb*** [I, T] to make a loud unpleasant noise 发出响亮而刺耳的声音：*police cars with lights flashing and sirens blaring* 警灯闪烁、警笛刺耳的警车 ◇ **~ out** *Music blared out from the open window.* 喧闹的音乐从敞开的窗口传出。◇ **~ sth (out)** *The radio was blaring (out) rock music.* 收音机在高声播放着嘈杂的摇滚乐。

■ ***noun*** [sing.] a loud unpleasant noise 响亮刺耳的声音：*the blare of car horns* 汽车喇叭的刺耳声

blar·ney /ˈblɑːni; *NAmE* ˈblɑːrni/ *noun* [U] (*informal*) talk that is friendly and amusing but probably not true, and which may be used to persuade or trick you 花言巧语；谄媚 ORIGIN From **Blarney**, a castle in Ireland where there is a stone which is said to have magic powers: anyone who kisses the 'Blarney Stone' is given the gift of speaking persuasively ('the gift of the gab'). 源自爱尔兰的布拉尼城堡(Blarney)，那里有一块布拉尼石。相传此石具有魔力，吻了可变得能言善辩。

blasé /ˈblɑːzeɪ; *NAmE* blɑːˈzeɪ/ *adj.* **~ (about sth)** not impressed, excited or worried about sth, because you have seen or experienced it many times before （对某事物）不稀罕，认为司空见惯

blas·pheme /blæsˈfiːm/ *verb* [I, T] **~ (sb/sth)** to speak about God or the holy things of a particular religion in an offensive way; to swear using the names of God or holy things 亵渎（上帝或神明）▶ **blas·phemer** *noun*

blas·phemy /ˈblæsfəmi/ *noun* (*pl.* **-ies**) [U, C] behaviour or language that insults or shows a lack of respect for God or religion 亵渎上帝（或神明）的言行 ▶ **blas·phem·ous** /ˈblæsfəməs/ *adj.*：*Many people found the film blasphemous.* 很多人觉得那部电影亵渎了神灵。**blas·phem·ous·ly** *adv.*

blast /blɑːst; *NAmE* blæst/ *noun, verb, exclamation*

■ ***noun***

• **EXPLOSION** 爆炸 **1** [C] an explosion or a powerful movement of air caused by an explosion 爆炸；（爆炸引起的）气浪，冲击波：*a bomb blast* 炸弹爆炸 ◇ *27 schoolchildren were injured in the blast.* * 27 名学龄儿童在爆炸中受了伤。

• **OF AIR** 空气 **2** [C] a sudden strong movement of air 突如其来的强劲气流：*A blast of hot air hit us as we stepped off the plane.* 我们下飞机时，一股热浪向我们袭来。◇ *the wind's icy blasts* 凛冽的狂风

• **LOUD NOISE** 大声 **3** [C] a sudden loud noise, especially one made by a musical instrument that you blow, or by a whistle or a car horn （吹奏乐器、哨子、汽车喇叭等突然发出的）响声，吹奏声，轰鸣：*three short blasts on the ship's siren* 船上三次短促的汽笛声

• **CRITICISM** 批评 **4** [C] (used especially in newspapers 尤用于报章) strong criticism 严厉的批评；激烈的抨击：*Blast for prison governors in judge's report.* 法官报告中对典狱长猛烈抨击

• **FUN** 欢乐 **5** [sing.] (*informal*) a very enjoyable experience that is a lot of fun 热闹的聚会；狂欢：*The party was a blast.* 聚会非常热闹。◇ *We had a blast at the party.* 我们在聚会上玩得很开心。

• **EMAIL** 电子邮件 **6** [C] (*NAmE, informal*) a piece of advertising or information that is sent to a large number of people at the same time by email 群发的电子邮件广告（或信息）

IDM **a ˌblast from the ˈpast** (*informal*) a person or thing from your past that you see, hear, meet, etc. again in the present （现在又看见、听到、遇到等的）故人，往事，旧物 **(at) full ˈblast** with the greatest possible volume or power 最大音量地；最大马力地：*She had the car stereo on at full blast.* 她把汽车音响开到了最大音量。

■ ***verb***

• **EXPLODE** 爆炸 **1** [T, I] **~ (sth) (+ adv./prep.)** to violently destroy or break sth into pieces, using EXPLOSIVES （用炸药）炸毁，把…炸成碎片；爆破：*They blasted a huge crater in the runway.* 他们在飞机跑道上炸了一个大坑。◇ *They had to blast a tunnel through the mountain.* 他们得炸出一条穿山隧道。◇ *All the windows were blasted inwards with the force of the explosion.* 爆炸的震动力把所有窗户都震碎到屋里。◇ *The jumbo jet was blasted out of the sky.* 那架巨型喷气式飞机在空中被炸成碎片。◇ *Danger! Blasting in Progress!* 危险！爆破进行中！

• **MAKE LOUD NOISE** 发出高声 **2** [I, T] to make a loud unpleasant noise, especially music 发出刺耳的高音，轰鸣（尤指音乐）：**~ (out)** *Music suddenly blasted out from the speakers.* 喇叭中突然响起了轰鸣的音乐。◇ **~ sth (out)** *The radio blasted out rock music at full volume.* 收音机以最大音量播放摇滚乐。

• **CRITICIZE** 批评 **3** [T] **~ sb/sth (for sth/for doing sth)** (*informal*) to criticize sb/sth severely 严厉批评；猛烈抨击：*The movie was blasted by all the critics.* 这部影片受到了所有评论家的严厉抨击。

• **HIT/KICK/SHOOT** 打；踢；击 **4** [T] **~ sb/sth (+ adv./prep.)** (*informal*) to hit, kick or shoot sb/sth with a lot of force 狠打；猛踢；猛击：*He blasted the ball past the goalie.* 他飞脚将球踢过了守门员。◇ *He blasted (= shot) the policeman right between the eyes.* 他对着那个警察的眉心开了一枪。

• **AIR/WATER** 空气；水 **5** [T] **~ sb/sth (+ adv./prep.)** to direct air, water, etc. at sb/sth with a lot of force 向…猛吹；（用水）向…喷射：*Police blasted the demonstrators with water cannons.* 警察用高压水炮喷射示威者。

• **DESTROY WITH DISEASE, ETC.** 使毁于疾病等 **6** [T, usually passive] **~ sth** to destroy sth such as a plant with disease, cold, heat, etc. 使（植物等）毁于疾病（或寒冷、酷热等）：*Their whole crop had been blasted by a late frost.* 一场晚霜把他们的庄稼全毁了。

PHR V **ˌblast aˈway** if a gun or sb using a gun **blasts away**, the gun fires continuously and loudly 连续高声地射击 **ˌblast ˈoff** (of SPACECRAFT 宇宙飞船) to leave the ground 发射升空 SYN **lift off, take off** ➲ RELATED NOUN BLAST-OFF

■ ***exclamation*** (*informal, especially BrE*) people sometimes say **Blast!** when they are annoyed about sth （恼怒时说）该死，倒霉：*Oh blast! The car won't start.* 真该死！车子发动不了。

blast·ed /ˈblɑːstɪd; *NAmE* ˈblæs-/ *adj.* [only before noun] (*informal*) used when you are very annoyed about sth （十分恼火时说）该死的，可恶的：*Make your own blasted coffee!* 你自己煮那该死的咖啡吧！

ˈblast furnace *noun* a large structure like an oven in which iron ORE (= rock containing iron) is melted in order to take out the metal （炼铁的）高炉，鼓风炉

ˈblast-off *noun* [U] the moment when a SPACECRAFT leaves the ground （宇宙飞船的）发射，升空

bla·tant /ˈbleɪtnt/ *adj.* (*disapproving*) (of actions that are considered bad 坏的行为) done in an obvious and open way without caring if people are shocked 明目张胆的；公然的 SYN **flagrant**：*a blatant attempt to buy votes* 公然的贿选企图 ◇ *It was a blatant lie.* 那是个赤裸裸的谎言。▶ **bla·tant·ly** *adv.*：*a blatantly unfair decision* 明显不公正的裁决 ◇ *He just blatantly lied about it.* 他简直是睁着眼睛说瞎话。

blather /ˈblæðə(r)/ (*also* **bleth·er**) *verb* [I] **~ (on) (about sth)** (*informal*) to talk continuously about things that are silly or unimportant 喋喋不休地胡说；唠叨 ▶ **blather** (*also* **blether**) *noun* [U]

blax·ploit·ation /ˌblæksplɔɪˈteɪʃn/ *noun* [U] the use of black people in films/movies, especially in a way which shows them in fixed ways that are different from real life 黑人利用（尤指在电影中黑人形象模式化且脱离现实）

blaze /bleɪz/ *verb, noun*

■ ***verb*** **1** [I] to burn brightly and strongly 熊熊燃烧：*A huge fire was blazing in the fireplace.* 壁炉中火烧得正旺。◇ *Within minutes the whole building was blazing.* 不消几分钟整个大楼便成了一片火海。◇ *He rushed back into the*

B

blazing house. 他又冲进了燃烧着的房子。 **2** [I] to shine brightly 闪耀；发亮光： *The sun blazed down from a clear blue sky.* 耀眼的阳光从清澈蔚蓝的天空中照射下来。 ◇ *The garden blazed with colour.* 花园里姹紫嫣红。 **3** [I] **~ (with sth)** (*formal*) if sb's eyes **blaze**, they look extremely angry 怒视；（怒火）燃烧： *Her eyes were blazing with fury.* 她的双眼燃烧着怒火。 **4** (*also* **blazon**) [T, usually passive] **~ sth (across/all over sth)** to make news or information widely known by telling people about it in a way they are sure to notice 大肆宣扬： *The story was blazed all over the daily papers.* 那个传闻被各家报纸炒得沸沸扬扬。 **5** [I] **~ (away)** if a gun or sb using a gun **blazes**, the gun fires continuously 连续射击： *In the distance machine guns were blazing.* 机关枪在远处不停地射击。

IDM **blaze a 'trail** to be the first to do or to discover sth that others follow 作开路先锋；领先： *The department is blazing a trail in the field of laser surgery.* 这个部门正在为激光外科学领域开辟一条新路。 ➲ COMPARE TRAILBLAZER ➲ MORE AT GUN *n.*

PHR V **ˌblaze 'up 1** to suddenly start burning very strongly （突然）熊熊燃烧起来 **2** to suddenly become very angry 突然动怒

■ ***noun*** **1** [C] (used especially in newspapers 尤用于报章) a very large fire, especially a dangerous one 烈火；火灾： *Five people died in the blaze.* 火灾中有五人丧生。 **2** [sing.] strong bright flames in a fire 火焰： *Dry wood makes a good blaze.* 干木柴烧得旺。 **3** [sing.] **a ~ of sth** a very bright show of lights or colour; an impressive or noticeable show of sth （光或色彩等的）展现： *The gardens are a blaze of colour.* 花园里姹紫嫣红。 ◇ *a blaze of lights in the city centre* 市中心通明的灯火 ◇ *the bright blaze of the sun* 太阳的光辉 ◇ *a blaze of glory* 荣耀 ◇ *They got married in a blaze of publicity.* 他们结婚的事受到了传媒的广泛关注。 **4** [sing.] **(a) ~ of sth** a sudden show of very strong feeling （感情的）迸发；发泄： ***a blaze of anger/passion/hate*** 怒火 / 激情 / 仇恨的迸发 **5** [C, usually sing.] a white mark on an animal's face 动物面部的白斑

IDM **what/where/who the 'blazes...?** (*old-fashioned, informal*) used to emphasize that you are annoyed and surprised, to avoid using the word 'hell' （委婉语，烦恼和惊奇时说，与 hell 同义）： *What the blazes have you done?* 你到底搞的什么名堂？ **like blazes** (*old-fashioned, informal*) very hard; very fast 猛烈地；迅速地

blazer /ˈbleɪzə(r)/ *noun* a jacket, not worn with matching trousers/pants, often showing the colours or BADGE of a club, school, team, etc. （常带有俱乐部、学校、运动队等的颜色或徽章的）夹克

blaz·ing /ˈbleɪzɪŋ/ *adj.* [only before noun] **1** (*also* **ˌblazing 'hot**) extremely hot 酷热的；炽热的： *blazing heat* 十分炎热 ◇ *a blazing hot day* 大热天 **2** extremely angry or full of strong emotion 极其愤怒的；感情强烈的： *She had a **blazing row** with Eddie and stormed out of the house.* 她和埃迪大吵一架后怒气冲冲地夺门而出。

blazon /ˈbleɪzn/ *verb* **1** [usually passive] **~ sth (on/across/over sth)** = EMBLAZON： *He had the word 'Cool' blazoned across his chest.* 他的胸前饰有 Cool 的字样。 **2** = BLAZE (4)

bleach /bliːtʃ/ *verb, noun*

■ ***verb*** [I, T] to become white or pale by a chemical process or by the effect of light from the sun; to make sth white or pale in this way （使）变白，漂白，晒白，退色： *bones of animals bleaching in the sun* 在阳光中变白的动物骸骨 ◇ **~ sth** *His hair **was bleached by the sun**.* 他的头发被太阳晒得发白。 ◇ *bleached cotton/paper* 漂白棉；漂白纸 ◇ **~ sth + adj.** *She bleached her hair blonde.* 她把头发染成了金黄色。

■ ***noun*** [U, C] a chemical that is used to make sth become white or pale and as a DISINFECTANT (= to prevent infection from spreading) 漂白剂

bleach·ers /ˈbliːtʃəz; *NAmE* -tʃərz/ *noun* [pl.] (*NAmE*) rows of seats at a sports ground that are cheaper and not covered by a roof （运动场的）露天座位，露天看台 ▶ **bleach·er** *adj.* [only before noun]: *bleacher seats* 露天看台座位

bleak /bliːk/ *adj.* (**bleak·er, bleak·est**) **1** (of a situation 状况) not encouraging or giving any reason to have hope 不乐观的；无望的；暗淡的： *a **bleak outlook/prospect*** 暗淡的前景 / 前途 ◇ ***The future looks bleak** for the fishing industry.* 渔业前景暗淡。 ◇ *The medical prognosis was bleak.* 医疗预后不良。 **2** (of the weather 天气) cold and unpleasant 阴冷的： *a bleak winter's day* 一个阴冷的冬日 **3** (of a place 地方) exposed, empty, or with no pleasant features 无遮掩的；荒凉的；索然无味的： *a **bleak landscape/hillside/moor*** 荒芜的景色 / 山坡 / 野地 ◇ *bleak concrete housing* 索然乏味的混凝土住宅 ▶ **bleak·ly** *adv.*： *'There seems no hope,' she said bleakly.* "好像没希望了。"她黯然地说。 ◇ *bleakly lit corridors* 光线很暗的走廊 **bleak·ness** *noun* [U]

bleari·ly /ˈblɪərəli; *NAmE* ˈblɪr-/ *adv.* with bleary eyes; in a tired way 睡眼惺忪地；困乏地： *'I was asleep,' she explained blearily.* "我睡着了。"她懒洋洋地解释说。

bleary /ˈblɪəri; *NAmE* ˈblɪri/ *adj.* (of eyes 眼睛) not able to see clearly, especially because you are tired （因疲倦等）视力模糊的，看不清的： *She had bleary red eyes from lack of sleep.* 她由于缺乏睡眠而双眼昏花，布满血丝。

ˌbleary-'eyed *adj.* with bleary eyes and seeming tired 困倦而视线模糊的： *He appeared at breakfast bleary-eyed and with a hangover.* 他吃早餐时两眼迷糊，宿醉未醒。

bleat /bliːt/ *verb* **1** [I] to make the sound that sheep and GOATS make 咩咩叫 **2** [I, T] **~ (on) (about sth) | ~ that... | + speech** to speak in a weak or complaining voice 以微弱的声音说话；抱怨： *'But I've only just got here,' he bleated feebly.* "可我刚刚才到这里呢。"他小声抱怨说。 ▶ **bleat** *noun*： *The lamb gave a faint bleat.* 羊羔轻轻地咩了一声。 **bleat·ing** *noun* [U, C]: *the distant bleating of sheep* 远处的羊叫声

bleed /bliːd/ *verb* (**bled, bled** /bled/) **1** [I] to lose blood, especially from a wound or an injury 流血；失血： *My finger's bleeding.* 我的手指出血了。 ◇ *She slowly **bled to death**.* 她慢慢地失血死去。 ◇ *He was bleeding from a gash on his head.* 他头上的伤口在出血。 ➲ WORDFINDER NOTE AT HURT **2** [T] **~ sb** (in the past) to take blood from sb as a way of treating disease （旧时）给（某人）放血 **3** [T] **~ sb (for sth)** (*informal*) to force sb to pay a lot of money over a period of time 长期榨取（某人的钱）： *My ex-wife is bleeding me for every penny I have.* 我的前妻不断地榨取我的每一分钱。 **4** [T] **~ sth** to remove air or liquid from sth so that it works correctly 放掉气体或水（以使某物运行正常）；抽干 **5** [I] **~ (into sth)** to spread from one area of sth to another area 散开；渗开： *Keep the paint fairly dry so that the colours don't bleed into each other.* 涂料尽量干一些，以免颜色相互渗透。

IDM **bleed sb 'dry** (*disapproving*) to take away all sb's money 榨取某人所有的钱；把某人榨干： *The big corporations are bleeding some of these small countries dry.* 一些大企业正在把这些小国榨干。 ➲ MORE AT HEART

bleed·er /ˈbliːdə(r)/ *noun* (*old-fashioned, BrE, informal*) a rude way of referring to a person 吸血鬼；浑蛋

bleed·ing /ˈbliːdɪŋ/ *adj., noun*

■ ***adj.*** [only before noun] (*BrE, slang*) = BLOODY[1]

■ ***noun*** [U] the process of losing blood from the body 流血；失血： *Press firmly on the wound to stop the bleeding.* 用力压住伤口止血。

ˌbleeding 'edge *noun* [sing.] **the ~ (of sth)** (*computing* 计) technology that is so advanced that there may be problems when you use it 前沿技术（可能有潜在问题或风险）： *They were working at the bleeding edge of chip design.* 他们正在研发芯片设计的前沿技术。 ➲ COMPARE CUTTING EDGE

ˌbleeding 'heart *noun* (*disapproving*) a person who is too kind and sympathetic towards people that other people think do not deserve kindness 过于善良的人；滥好人： *a bleeding-heart liberal* 一个心肠太软的自由主义者

bleep /bliːp/ *noun, verb*

■ ***noun*** a short high sound made by a piece of electronic equipment （电子仪器发出的）短促响亮的声音，哔哔声

■ ***verb*** **1** [I] to make a short high electronic sound 发出短促响亮的声音；发哔哔声：*The microwave will bleep when your meal is ready.* 烹调结束时，微波炉会发出哔哔的声音。 **2** (*BrE*) (*NAmE* **beep**) [T] **~ sb** to call sb on their bleeper 打（某人）的传呼机；给（某人）打传呼：*Please bleep the doctor on duty immediately.* 请立即打值班医生的传呼机。 **3** [T] **~ sth (out)** to broadcast a short high electronic sound in place of a SWEAR WORD on a television or radio show, so that people will not be offended （电视或广播节目中）用哔哔声覆盖（脏话） ➲ MORE LIKE THIS 3, page R25

bleep·er /ˈbliːpə(r)/ (*NAmE* **beep·er**) *noun* a small electronic device that you carry around with you and that lets you know when sb is trying to contact you, by making a sound 寻呼机；BP 机

blem·ish /ˈblemɪʃ/ *noun, verb*

■ ***noun*** a mark on the skin or on an object that spoils it and makes it look less beautiful or perfect 斑点；疤痕；瑕疵：*make-up to cover blemishes* 遮盖霜 ◇ (*figurative*) *His reputation is without a blemish.* 他的名誉可说是白璧无瑕。

■ ***verb*** [usually passive] **~ sth** (*formal*) to spoil sth that is beautiful or perfect in all other ways 破坏…的完美；玷污

blench /blentʃ/ *verb* [I] (*BrE, formal*) to react to sth in a way that shows you are frightened （因惊吓而）退缩；惊悸

blend /blend/ *verb, noun*

■ ***verb*** **1** [T] to mix two or more substances together 使混合；掺和：**~ A with B** *Blend the flour with the milk to make a smooth paste.* 把面粉和牛奶调成均匀的面糊。◇ **~ A and B (together)** *Blend together the eggs, sugar and flour.* 把鸡蛋、糖和面粉掺到一起。 ➲ SYNONYMS AT MIX **2** [I] to form a mixture with sth （和某物）混合；融合：**~ with sth** *Oil does not blend with water.* 油不融于水。◇ **~ (together)** *Oil and water do not blend.* 油与水不相融。 **3** [I, T] to combine with sth in an attractive or effective way; to combine sth in this way （使）调和，协调，融合：**~ (sth) (together)** *The old and new buildings blend together perfectly.* 新旧建筑物相映成趣。◇ **~ sth (and/with sth)** *Their music blends traditional and modern styles.* 他们的音乐融合了传统和现代风格。 **4** [T, usually passive] **~ sth** to produce sth by mixing different types together 调制；配制：***blended whisky/tea*** 调配的威士忌 / 茶 **IDM** SEE WOODWORK

PHR V ˌ**blend ˈin (with sth/sb)** if sth **blends in**, it is similar to its surroundings or matches its surroundings （与环境）和谐，协调：*Choose curtains that blend in with your decor.* 挑选和装饰格调一致的窗帘。◇ *The thieves soon blended in with the crowd and got away.* 窃贼很快混入人群逃跑了。 ˌ**blend sth↔ˈin** (in cooking 烹饪) to add another substance and mix it in with the others 调入：*Beat the butter and sugar; then blend in the egg.* 把黄油和糖打好，然后调入鸡蛋。 ˌ**blend ˈinto sth** to look so similar to the background that it is difficult for you to see it separately 融合到（背景）中：*He blended into the crowd.* 他消失在人群中。

■ ***noun*** **1** a mixture of different types of the same thing （同一事物中不同类型的）混合品，混合物：*a blend of tea* 调制茶 **2** [usually sing.] a pleasant or useful combination of different things （不同事物的）和谐结合，融合：*a blend of youth and experience* 年轻而且有经验

ˌ**blended ˈfamily** *noun* (*especially NAmE*) a family that consists of two people and their children from their own relationship and from previous ones 混合家庭（成员包括夫妇、其子女及其各自过去关系中所生的子女）

ˌ**blended ˈlearning** *noun* [U] a way of studying a subject that combines being taught in class with the use of different technologies, including learning over the Internet 混合式学习（将课堂学习与互联网学习等技术相结合）：*Blended learning is a cost-effective way of delivering training.* 混合式学习是一种划算的培训方式。

blend·er /ˈblendə(r)/ (*BrE also* **li·quid·izer**) *noun* an electric machine for mixing soft food or liquid （电动）食物搅拌器 ➲ VISUAL VOCAB PAGE V26

bless /bles/ *verb, exclamation*

■ ***verb*** (**blessed, blessed** /blest/) **1 ~ sb/sth** to ask God to protect sb/sth 求上帝降福；祝福：*They brought the children to Jesus and he blessed them.* 他们把孩子带到耶稣跟前，耶稣祝福了他们。◇ *God bless you!* 愿上帝保佑你！ **2 ~ sth** to make sth holy by saying a prayer over it 祝圣：*The priest blessed the bread and wine.* 神父祝圣了面包和葡萄酒。 **3 ~ sb/sth** (*formal*) to call God holy; to praise God 称颂上帝；赞美上帝：*We bless your holy name, O Lord.* 主啊，我们颂扬您的圣名。 **4 ~ sb/sth** (*old-fashioned, informal*) used to express surprise （表示惊奇）：*Bless my soul! Here comes Bill!* 我的天哪！比尔来了！ ◇ *'Where's Joe?' 'I'm blessed if I know!'* (= I don't know) "乔在哪儿？" "我要是知道才怪呢！"

IDM **be blessed with sth/sb** to have sth good such as ability, great happiness, etc. 赋有（能力等）；享有（幸福等）：*She's blessed with excellent health.* 她身体很好，是一种福气。 ◇ *We're blessed with five lovely grandchildren.* 我们很有福气，有五个可爱的孙子孙女。 ˈ**bless you** said to sb after they have SNEEZED （别人打喷嚏时说） ˈ**bless you, her, him, etc.** (*informal*) used to show that you are pleased with sb, especially because of sth they have done （表示满意或感谢）：*Sarah, bless her, had made a cup of tea.* 真得感谢萨拉，她给沏了一杯茶。 ➲ MORE AT GOD

■ ***exclamation*** (*BrE, sometimes humorous*) used to show affection towards sb because of sth they have done （对他人所做之事表示喜爱）哎呀，太好啦，太谢谢了：*'He bought us all a present.' 'Oh, bless!'* "他给我们都买了一件礼物。" "啊，太好了！"

blessed /ˈblesɪd/ *adj.* **1 Blessed** holy 神圣的：*the Blessed Virgin Mary* 荣福童贞马利亚 **2** (in religious language) lucky （宗教用语）有福的：*Blessed are the poor.* 神贫的人是有福的。 **3** [only before noun] enjoyable in a way that gives you a sense of peace or a feeling of freedom from anxiety or pain 愉快安宁的；无忧无虑的：*a moment of blessed calm* 片刻愉快的宁静 **4** [only before noun] (*old-fashioned, informal*) used to express mild anger （表示愠怒）：*I can't see a blessed thing without my glasses.* 我不戴眼镜根本看不清什么东西。 ▸ **bless·ed·ly** *adv.*：*The kitchen was warm and blessedly familiar.* 厨房又温暖又亲切温馨。 **bless·ed·ness** *noun* [U]

bless·ing /ˈblesɪŋ/ *noun* **1** [usually sing.] God's help and protection, or a prayer asking for this 上帝的恩宠；祝福；祝颂：*to pray for God's blessing* 祈求上帝降福 ◇ *The bishop said the blessing.* 主教祝福（会众）。 ➲ COLLOCATIONS AT RELIGION **2** [usually sing.] approval of or permission for sth 赞同；许可：*The government* ***gave its blessing to*** *the new plans.* 政府已批准这些新计划。 ◇ *He went* ***with his parents' blessing.*** 他是得到父母的同意去的。 **3** something that is good or helpful 好事；有益之事：*Lack of traffic is one of the blessings of country life.* 往来车辆少是乡村生活的一大好处。 ◇ ***It's a blessing*** *that nobody was in the house at the time.* 幸好当时屋子里没人。 ➲ SEE ALSO MIXED BLESSING

IDM **a blessing in disˈguise** something that seems to be a problem at first, but that has good results in the end 因祸得福；祸中有福 ➲ MORE AT COUNT *v.*

blether /ˈbleðə(r)/ *verb, noun* = BLATHER

blew PAST TENSE OF BLOW

blight /blaɪt/ *verb, noun*

■ ***verb*** **~ sth** to spoil or damage sth, especially by causing a lot of problems 损害；妨害；贻害：*His career has been blighted by injuries.* 他的事业不断受到伤病的困扰。 ◇ *an area blighted by unemployment* 饱受失业之苦的地区

■ ***noun*** **1** [U, C] any disease that kills plants, especially crops （农作物等的）疫病：*potato blight* 马铃薯疫病 ➲ WORDFINDER NOTE AT CROP **2** [sing., U] **~ (on sb/sth)** something that has a bad effect on a situation, a person's life or the environment （对局势、生活或环境）有害的事物，不利因素： *His death **cast a blight on** the whole of that year.* 他的死使那一整年都处在阴影之中。 ◇ ***urban blight*** (= areas in a city that are ugly or not cared for well) 城市里环境脏、乱、差的地区

blight·er /ˈblaɪtə(r)/ *noun* (*old-fashioned, BrE, informal*) a way of referring to a person (usually a man) that you either find unpleasant or that you feel some sympathy for 讨厌的（或可怜的）家伙（通常指男性）

Blighty /ˈblaɪti/ *noun* [U] (*BrE*) a name for Britain or England, used especially by soldiers in the First and Second World Wars, and now sometimes used in a humorous way 英国，英格兰（第一次和第二次世界大战期间英国士兵用语，现含诙谐意味）

bli·mey /ˈblaɪmi/ (*also* **ˌcor ˈbli·mey**) *exclamation* (*BrE, informal, slang*) used to express surprise or anger （表示惊奇或生气）： *Blimey, it's hot today.* 哎呀，今天真热。

blimp /blɪmp/ *noun* **1** (*especially NAmE*) a small AIRSHIP (= an aircraft without wings) 软式飞艇 **2** (*also* **ˌColonel ˈBlimp**) (*old-fashioned, BrE, disapproving*) an older person, especially an old army officer, with very old-fashioned political opinions 政见保守的老人（尤指年长的军官） ▸ **blimp·ish** *adj.*

blind /blaɪnd/ *adj., verb, noun, adv.*

■ ***adj.*** (**blind·er**, **blind·est**) **1** not able to see 瞎的；失明的： *Doctors think he will go blind.* 医生们认为他会失明。 ◇ *blind and partially sighted people* 盲人和弱视者 ◇ *One of her parents is blind.* 她的父母有一个是盲人。 **2 the blind** *noun* [pl.] people who are blind 盲人： *recorded books for the blind* 为盲人制作的录音书 ◇ *guide dogs for the blind* 导盲犬 ➲ MORE LIKE THIS 24, page R28 **3 ~ (to sth)** not noticing or realizing sth （对某事）视而不见的，未察觉的： *She is blind to her husband's faults.* 她对丈夫的过错毫无察觉。 ◇ *I must have been blind not to realize the danger we were in.* 当时我一定是眼瞎了，竟然没有意识到我们所处的危险。 **4** [usually before noun] (of strong feelings 强烈的感觉) seeming to be unreasonable, and accepted without question; seeming to be out of control 盲目接受的；不能自制的： ***blind faith/obedience*** 盲目的信念；盲从 ◇ *It was a moment of **blind panic**.* 当时一阵莫名的惊慌。 **5** [usually before noun] (of a situation or an event 局势或事情) that cannot be controlled by reason 无理性的： *blind chance* 盲目的偶然性 ◇ *the blind force of nature* 无法抵挡的自然力 **6** that a driver in a car cannot see, or cannot see around 汽车司机看不见的；隐蔽的： *a blind driveway* 视线有盲区的车道 ◇ ***a blind bend/corner*** 隐蔽的弯道 / 拐角 ▸ **blind·ness** *noun* [U]: ***total/temporary/partial blindness*** 全盲；暂时性失明；半盲 ➲ SEE ALSO BLINDLY

IDM **(as) blind as a ˈbat** (*humorous*) not able to see well 视力不佳 ➲ MORE LIKE THIS 14, page R26 **the blind leading the ˈblind** a situation in which people with almost no experience or knowledge give advice to others who also have no experience or knowledge 盲人教盲人；盲人引导瞎子 **not a blind bit/the blindest bit of...** (*BrE, informal*) not any 丝毫没有： *He didn't **take a blind bit of notice** of me* (= he ignored me). 他压根儿没理睬我。 ◇ *It won't **make the blindest bit of difference*** (= it will make no difference at all). 那根本不会有什么分别的。 **turn a blind ˈeye (to sth)** to pretend not to notice sth bad that is happening, so you do not have to do anything about it （对某事）佯装不见，睁一只眼闭一只眼 ➲ MORE AT LOVE *n.*

■ ***verb*** **1 ~ sb** to permanently destroy sb's ability to see 使变瞎；使失明： *She was blinded in the explosion.* 她在那场爆炸中双目失明了。 **2 ~ sb/sth** to make it difficult for sb to see for a short time 使眼花；使目眩： *When she went outside she was temporarily blinded by the sun.* 走出户外时，她一时被阳光照得眼睛昏花。 **3 ~ sb (to sth)** to make sb no longer able to think clearly or behave in a sensible way 使思维混沌；使失去判断力： *His sense of loyalty blinded him to the truth.* 他的赤诚忠心使他看不清真相。

IDM **blind sb with ˈscience** to confuse sb by using technical or complicated language that they do not understand 用术语（或深奥的言语）使某人困惑 ➲ MORE AT EFF

■ ***noun*** **1** (*NAmE also* **shade**, **ˈwindow shade**) [C] a covering for a window, especially one made of a roll of cloth that is fixed at the top of the window and can be pulled up and down 窗帘；（尤指）卷帘 ➲ SEE ALSO VENETIAN BLIND **2** [sing.] something people say or do to hide the truth about sth in order to trick other people 用以蒙蔽人的言行；借口；托辞；幌子

■ ***adv.*** (in connection with flying 有关飞行) without being able to see; using instruments only 视线受阻地；仅靠仪表操纵地；盲目地

IDM **blind ˈdrunk** extremely drunk 烂醉如泥 ➲ MORE AT ROB, SWEAR

▼ **WHICH WORD?** 词语辨析

blind / blindly

- There are two adverbs that come from the adjective **blind**. **Blindly** means 'not being able to see what you are doing' or 'not thinking about something'. The adverb **blind** is mainly used in the context of flying and means 'without being able to see', 'using instruments only'. 形容词 blind 有两个副词。blindly 表示没有看清楚或盲目，副词 blind 主要用于指飞行时的黑蒙、单凭仪器导航。

ˌblind ˈalley *noun* a way of doing sth that seems useful at first, but does not produce useful results, like following a path that suddenly stops 行不通的方法；死胡同

ˌblind ˈdate *noun* a meeting between two people who have not met each other before. The meeting is sometimes organized by their friends because they want them to develop a romantic relationship. （有时由第三方安排的）男女初次约会

blind·er /ˈblaɪndə(r)/ *noun* **1** [C, usually sing.] (*BrE, informal*) something which is excellent, especially in sport （尤指体育运动中的）出色之举，精彩表现： *a blinder of a game* 比赛中的精彩表现 **2 blinders** [pl.] (*NAmE*) = BLINKERS

blind·fold /ˈblaɪndfəʊld; *NAmE* -foʊld/ *noun, verb, adj., adv.*

■ ***noun*** something that is put over sb's eyes so they cannot see 障眼物；眼罩

■ ***verb*** **~ sb** to cover sb's eyes with a piece of cloth or other covering so that they cannot see （用布等）蒙住…的眼睛： *The hostages were tied up and blindfolded.* 人质被捆绑起来并蒙上了眼睛。

■ ***adj., adv.*** (*BrE*) (*also* **blind·fold·ed** *BrE, NAmE*) with the eyes covered 被蒙住眼睛（的）： *The reporter was taken blindfold to a secret location.* 那位记者被蒙着眼睛带到了一处秘密的地方。 ◇ *I knew the way home blindfold* (= because it was so familiar). 我蒙着眼都能走到家。 ◇ *I could do that blindfold* (= very easily, with no problems). 我做这事易如反掌。

blind·ing /ˈblaɪndɪŋ/ *adj.* [usually before noun] **1** very bright; so strong that you cannot see 雪亮的；刺眼的；使人视线模糊的： *a blinding flash of light* 令人目眩的闪光 ◇ (*figurative*) *a blinding* (= very bad) *headache* 使人两眼昏花的头痛 **2** (*BrE, informal*) very good or enjoyable 绝妙的；精彩的

blind·ing·ly /ˈblaɪndɪŋli/ *adv.* very; extremely 很；极其： *The reason is **blindingly obvious**.* 原因十分明显。 ◇ *The latest computers can work at a **blindingly fast** speed.* 最新的计算机能达到极高的运行速度。

blind·ly /ˈblaɪndli/ *adv.* **1** without being able to see what you are doing 摸黑地；在黑暗中： *She groped blindly for the light switch in the dark room.* 她在黑暗的房间里摸索电灯开关。 **2** without thinking about what you are doing 不加思考地；盲目地： *He wanted to decide* *for himself instead of blindly following his parents' advice.* 他想自己拿主意，而不是盲目听从他父母的意见。➲ NOTE AT BLIND

ˌblind man's 'buff (*NAmE also* **ˌblind man's 'bluff**) *noun* [U] a children's game in which a player whose eyes are covered with a piece of cloth tries to catch and identify the other players 捉迷藏（游戏）

'blind side *noun* a direction in which sb cannot see very much, especially approaching danger （尤指接近危险时）看不清的一侧，未加防备的一侧

blind·side /ˈblaɪndsaɪd/ *verb* (*NAmE*) **1** **~ sb** to attack sb from the direction where they cannot see you coming 攻其不备；出其不意地袭击 **2** [usually passive] **~ sb** to give sb an unpleasant surprise 使遭受意外的打击：*Just when it seemed life was going well, she was blindsided by a devastating illness.* 正当生活似乎一帆风顺的时候，她突然得了一场重病。

'blind spot *noun* **1** an area that sb cannot see, especially an area of the road when they are driving a car 视线盲区（尤指车辆驾驶员看不见的路段） **2** if sb has a **blind spot** about sth, they ignore it or they are unwilling or unable to understand it 无视；没有认识 **3** the part of the RETINA in the eye that is not sensitive to light （视网膜的）盲点 **4** an area where a radio signal cannot be received （无线电）盲区，静区

ˌblind 'test *noun* a way of deciding which product out of a number of competing products is the best or most popular, or how a new product compares with others. People are asked to try the different products and to say which ones they prefer, but they are not told the names of the products. 盲测（比较产品质量或受欢迎程度，参加者不知道产品名称）

ˌblind 'trust *noun* a type of TRUST that takes care of sb's investments, without the person knowing how their money is being invested. It is used by politicians, for example, so that their private business does not influence their political decisions. 全权信托，保密委托（信托人对投资方式不知情，如从政者为避免私人生意影响其政策决定而采用）

bling /blɪŋ/ (*also* **ˌbling-'bling**) *noun* [U] (*informal*) expensive shiny jewellery and bright fashionable clothes worn in order to attract attention to yourself 闪亮风潮的穿戴 ▸ **bling** (*also* **ˌbling-'bling**) *adj.*：*women with big hair and bling jewellery* 梳着爆炸头、穿金戴银的女人 ◇ *bling culture/lifestyles* 穿戴奢华的文化 / 生活方式

blini /ˈblɪni; ˈbliːni/ (*also* **blinis**) *noun* [pl.] (*sing.* **blin**) small Russian PANCAKES (= thin flat round cakes), served with SOUR CREAM 俄式薄煎饼，荞麦薄烤饼（佐以酸奶油）

blink /blɪŋk/ *verb, noun*

■ *verb* **1** [I, T] **~ (sth)** when you **blink** or **blink your eyes** or **your eyes blink**, you shut and open your eyes quickly 眨眼睛：*He blinked in the bright sunlight.* 他在强烈的阳光下直眨眼睛。◇ *I'll be back* ***before you can blink*** (= very quickly). 我眨眼工夫就回来。◇ *When I told him the news he* ***didn't even blink*** (= showed no surprise at all). 我把那个消息告诉他时，他眼都没眨一下。➲ COMPARE WINK *v.* **2** [I] to shine with an unsteady light; to flash on and off 闪烁：*Suddenly a warning light blinked.* 突然有一盏警告灯开始闪亮。

PHR V **ˌblink sth↔a'way/'back** to try to control tears or clear your eyes by blinking 眨眼以控制泪水（或挤掉脏东西）：*She bravely blinked back her tears.* 她勇敢地抑制住了泪水。

■ *noun* [usually sing.] the act of shutting and opening your eyes very quickly 眨眼睛

IDM **in the blink of an 'eye** very quickly; in a short time 眨眼的工夫；很快 **on the 'blink** (*informal*) (of a machine 机器) no longer working correctly 失灵；出毛病

blink·er /ˈblɪŋkə(r)/ *noun* **1** [C] (*informal*) = INDICATOR (3), TURN SIGNAL **2** **blinkers** (*NAmE also* **blind·ers**) [pl.] pieces of leather that are placed at the side of a horse's eyes to stop it from looking sideways 马眼罩：(*figurative*) *We need to have a fresh look at the plan, without blinkers* (= we need to consider every aspect of it). 我们应该用新的眼光全面地考虑这个计划。

blink·ered /ˈblɪŋkəd; *NAmE* -kərd/ *adj.* (*disapproving*) not aware of every aspect of a situation; not willing to accept different ideas about sth 目光狭窄的；心胸隘窄的 SYN **narrow-minded**：***a blinkered policy/attitude/approach*** 褊狭的政策 / 态度 / 方法

blink·ing /ˈblɪŋkɪŋ/ *adj., adv.* (*BrE, old-fashioned, informal*) a mild swear word that some people use when they are annoyed, to avoid saying 'bloody' （委婉语，与 bloody 同义）讨厌，可恶：*Shut the blinking door!* 关上那扇该死的门！

blip /blɪp/ *noun* **1** a change in a process or situation, usually when it gets worse for a short time before it gets better; a temporary problem 变故；暂时性问题：*a temporary blip* 暂时的麻烦 **2** a short high sound made by an electronic device （电子装置发出的）短促尖声 **3** a small flashing point of light on a RADAR screen, representing an object 目标标志（雷达屏幕上代表目标的光点）

bliss /blɪs/ *noun, verb*

■ *noun* [U] extreme happiness 极乐：***married/wedded/domestic bliss*** 婚后的 / 家庭的幸福 ◇ *My idea of bliss is a month in the Bahamas.* 我认为最大的幸福就是在巴哈马群岛住上一个月。◇ *Swimming on a hot day is* ***sheer bliss.*** 热天游泳是天大的乐事。IDM SEE IGNORANCE

■ *verb*

PHR V **ˌbliss 'out** (*also* **be ˌblissed 'out**) to reach a state of perfect happiness, when you are not aware of anything else 欣喜若狂；乐不可支

bliss·ful /ˈblɪsfl/ *adj.* extremely happy; showing happiness 极乐的；幸福的：*We spent three blissful weeks away from work.* 我们无忧无虑地度了三个星期的假。◇ *a blissful smile* 欣喜的笑容 ◇ *We preferred to remain in* ***blissful ignorance*** *of* (= not to know) *what was going on.* 我们乐得对正在发生的事情一无所知。➲ SYNONYMS AT HAPPY ▸ **bliss·ful·ly** /-fəli/ *adv.*：*blissfully happy* 极其幸福 ◇ ***blissfully ignorant/unaware*** 乐得无知 / 不知情

'B-list *adj.* [usually before noun] used to describe the group of people who are considered to be fairly famous, successful or important, but not as much as the A-LIST people 第二等的；比较出名（或成功、重要）的：*a TV chat show full of* ***B-list celebrities*** 由众多二流人物参加的电视访谈节目

blis·ter /ˈblɪstə(r)/ *noun, verb*

■ *noun* **1** a swelling on the surface of the skin that is filled with liquid and is caused, for example, by rubbing or burning （皮肤上摩擦或烫等引起的）水疱，疱 ➲ SEE ALSO FEVER BLISTER **2** a similar swelling, filled with air or liquid, on metal, painted wood or another surface （金属、油漆过的木头或其他表面上的）泡，气泡，水泡

■ *verb* **1** [I, T] to form blisters; to make sth form blisters （使）起疱，起泡：*His skin was beginning to blister.* 他的皮肤开始起疱。◇ **~ sth** *Her face had been blistered by the sun.* 她的脸让太阳晒起水疱了。 **2** [I, T] **~ (sth)** when a surface **blisters** or sth **blisters** it, it swells and cracks （使表皮等）涨破，爆裂 **3** [T] **~ sb** (*NAmE*) to criticize sb strongly 猛烈抨击；严厉批评 ▸ **blis·tered** *adj.*：*cracked and blistered skin* 开裂起疱的皮肤 ◇ *blistered paintwork* 起泡的漆面

blis·ter·ing /ˈblɪstərɪŋ/ *adj.* [usually before noun] **1** (describing actions in sport) done very fast or with great energy （描述体育动作）迅速的，劲头十足的：*The runners set off at a blistering pace.* 赛跑运动员如脱缰野马般起跑了。 **2** extremely hot in a way that is uncomfortable 酷热的 SYN **baking**：*a blistering July day* 七月的一个大热天 ◇ *blistering heat* 酷热 **3** very critical 言辞激烈的；尖刻的：*a blistering attack* 激烈的抨击 ▸ **blis·ter·ing·ly** *adv.*

B

'blister pack (*also* **'bubble pack**) *noun* a pack in which small goods, such as tablets, are sold, with each individual item in its own separate plastic or FOIL section on a piece of card （药片等的）吸塑包装 ➲ VISUAL VOCAB PAGE V36

blithe /blaɪð/ *adj.* [usually before noun] **1** (*disapproving*) showing you do not care or are not anxious about what you are doing 不在意的；漫不经心的： *He drove with blithe disregard for the rules of the road.* 他开车时全然不顾交通法规。 **2** (*literary*) happy; not anxious 快乐的；无忧无虑的： *a blithe and carefree girl* 快乐无忧的女孩 ▶ **blithe·ly** *adv.* : *He was blithely unaware of the trouble he'd caused.* 他漫不经心，丝毫没有察觉他惹的麻烦。 ◇ *'It'll be easy,' she said blithely.* "那很容易。"她不在乎地说。

blith·er·ing /ˈblɪðərɪŋ/ *adj.* [only before noun] (*old-fashioned, BrE, informal*) complete 完全的；全部的： *He was a* ***blithering idiot.*** 他是个十足的傻瓜。

BLitt (*NAmE* **B.Litt**) /ˌbiː ˈlɪt/ *noun* the abbreviation for 'Bachelor of Letters' or 'Bachelor of Literature' (a university degree in an ARTS subject that may be a first or second degree) 文学学士（全写为 Bachelor of Letters 或 Bachelor of Literature，大学文科的初级或二级学位）

blitz /blɪts/ *noun, verb*
■ ***noun*** **1** [C, usually sing.] something which is done with a lot of energy 集中力量的行动；闪击式行动： *an* ***advertising/a media blitz*** (= a lot of information about sth on television, in newspapers, etc.) 集中火力的广告 / 媒体宣传 **2** [C, usually sing.] a sudden attack 突袭；闪电战： *Five shops were damaged in a firebomb blitz.* 在一次燃烧弹袭击中有五家店铺被烧毁。 ◇ **~ on sth** (*figurative*) *a blitz on passengers who avoid paying fares* 对逃票乘客的突袭检查 ◇ (*figurative*) *I've had a blitz on the house* (= cleaned it very thoroughly). 我彻底打扫了房子。 **3 the Blitz** [sing.] the German air attacks on the United Kingdom in 1940–1 * 1940 至 1941 年德国对英国的空袭
■ ***verb*** **1** [T] **~ sth** to attack or damage a city by dropping a large number of bombs on it in a short time 用闪电战空袭（或毁坏） **2** [T, I] (of food) to mix or cut into smaller pieces using an electric mixing machine （用电动搅拌机将食物）搅拌，打碎： *Blitz the strawberries to a purée in a food processor.* 用食物加工机将草莓打成酱。 ◇ *Blitz until smooth and creamy.* 用搅拌器搅打至柔滑细腻。

blitz·krieg /ˈblɪtskriːɡ/ *noun* (*from German*) a sudden military attack intended to win a quick victory 闪电战；闪击战

bliz·zard /ˈblɪzəd; *NAmE* -zərd/ *noun* **1** a SNOWSTORM with very strong winds 暴风雪；雪暴： *blizzard conditions* 暴风雪天气 ◇ *a* ***raging/howling blizzard*** 猛烈的 / 怒吼着的暴风雪 ➲ WORDFINDER NOTE AT SNOW ➲ COLLOCATIONS AT WEATHER **2** a large quantity of things that may seem to be attacking you 大批侵扰性的事物；大量的负担： *a blizzard of documents* 一大堆棘手的文件

bloat /bləʊt; *NAmE* bloʊt/ *verb* [T, I] **~ sth** to swell or make sth swell, especially in an unpleasant way （使）膨胀，肿胀： *Her features had been bloated by years of drinking.* 她酗酒多年，已变得面部浮肿。

bloat·ed /ˈbləʊtɪd; *NAmE* ˈbloʊ-/ *adj.* **1** full of liquid or gas and therefore bigger than normal, in a way that is unpleasant 膨胀的；肿胀的；臃肿的： *a bloated body floating in the canal* 运河里一具发胀的浮尸 ◇ (*figurative*) *a bloated organization* (= with too many people in it) 臃肿的机构 **2** full of food and feeling uncomfortable 饮食过度的；胃胀的： *I felt bloated after the huge meal they'd served.* 吃过他们提供的大餐后，我觉得肚子胀得很。

bloat·er /ˈbləʊtə(r); *NAmE* ˈbloʊ-/ *noun* (*BrE*) a HERRING (a type of fish) that has been left in salt water and then smoked 腌熏鲱鱼

blob /blɒb; *NAmE* blɑːb/ *noun* a small amount or drop of sth, especially a liquid; a small area of colour （尤指液体的）一点，一滴；（颜色的）一小片，斑点： *a blob of ink* 一滴墨水 ◇ *a pink blob* 粉红色斑点

bloc /blɒk; *NAmE* blɑːk/ *noun* a group of countries that work closely together because they have similar political interests （政治利益一致的）国家集团 ➲ COLLOCATIONS AT INTERNATIONAL ➲ SEE ALSO EN BLOC

block 🔑 /blɒk; *NAmE* blɑːk/ *noun, verb*
■ ***noun***
• **SOLID MATERIAL** 固体 **1** 🔑 [C] a large piece of a solid material that is square or RECTANGULAR in shape and usually has flat sides （方形或长方形）大块；立方体；长方体： *a block of ice/concrete/stone* 一方冰 / 混凝土 / 石头 ◇ *a chopping block* (= for cutting food on) 砧板 ➲ SEE ALSO BREEZE BLOCK, BUILDING BLOCK, CINDER BLOCK
• **BUILDING** 建筑 **2** 🔑 [C] (*BrE*) a tall building that contains flats or offices; buildings that form part of a school, hospital, etc. which are used for a particular purpose （公寓、办公、教学、医院等）大楼；（成组建筑中的）一栋楼房： *a tower block* 高层建筑 ◇ *a block of flats* 公寓大楼 ◇ *an office block* 办公大楼 ◇ *the university's science block* 这所大学的理科大楼 ➲ VISUAL VOCAB PAGE V16 ➲ SYNONYMS AT BUILDING
• **STREETS** 街道 **3** 🔑 [C] a group of buildings with streets on all sides 街道围成的楼群；街区： *She took the dog for a walk around the block.* 她带着狗绕街区散步。 **4** 🔑 [C] (*NAmE*) the length of one side of a piece of land or group of buildings, from the place where one street crosses it to the next （两条街道之间的）一段街区： *His apartment is three blocks away from the police station.* 他住在和警察局相隔三个街区的公寓里。
• **AREA OF LAND** 一片土地 **5** [C] (*especially NAmE*) a large area of land 一大片土地 **6** [C] (*AustralE*) an area of land for building a house on 房基地；宅基地
• **AMOUNT** 数量 **7** [C] a quantity of sth or an amount of time that is considered as a single unit （东西的）一批，一组；（时间的）一段： *a block of shares* 一大宗股份 ◇ *a block of text in a document* 文件中的一段文字 ◇ (*BrE*) *The theatre gives discounts for* ***block bookings*** (= a large number of tickets bought at the same time). 该剧院给团体票打折。 ◇ *The three-hour class is divided into four blocks of 45 minutes each.* 三小时的课分成四节，每节 45 分钟。
• **THAT STOPS PROGRESS** 形成阻碍 **8** [C, usually sing.] something that makes movement or progress difficult or impossible 障碍物；阻碍；妨害 SYN **obstacle**: *Lack of training acts as a block to progress in a career.* 缺乏训练会妨碍事业的发展。 ➲ SEE ALSO ROADBLOCK, STUMBLING BLOCK, WRITER'S BLOCK
• **IN SPORT** 体育运动 **9** [C] a movement that stops another player from going forward 阻挡；拦截 **10 the blocks** [pl.] = STARTING BLOCKS
• **FOR PUNISHMENT** 刑罚 **11 the block** [sing.] (in the past) the piece of wood on which a person's head was cut off as a punishment （旧时斩首用的）垫头木

IDM **go on the 'block** to be sold, especially at an AUCTION (= a sale in which items are sold to the person who offers the most money) 被拿去卖；推上拍卖场 **have been around the 'block (a few times)** (*informal*) to have a lot of experience 经验丰富；见多识广 **put/lay your head/neck on the block** to risk losing your job, damaging your reputation, etc. by doing or saying sth 冒（失业、损失名誉等）的险 ➲ MORE AT CHIP *n.*, KNOCK *v.*, NEW

■ ***verb*** **1** 🔑 **~ sth** to stop sth from moving or flowing through a pipe, a passage, a road, etc. by putting sth in it or across it 堵塞；阻塞： *After today's heavy snow, many roads are still blocked.* 今天下过大雪，很多道路仍然堵塞。 ◇ *a blocked sink* 堵塞了的洗涤槽 **2** 🔑 **~ the/sb's way, exit, view, etc.** to stop sb from going somewhere or seeing sth by standing in front of them or in their way 堵住（某人的路等）；挡住（某人的视线等）： *One of the guards moved to block her path.* 一名守卫走过去挡住她的路。 ◇ *An ugly new building blocked the view from the window.* 一座难看的大楼把窗外的景物遮住了。 **3** 🔑 **~ sth** to prevent sth from happening, developing or making progress 妨碍；阻碍： *The proposed merger has been* *blocked by the government.* 建议中的合并计划遇到了政府的阻力。 **4 ~ sth** to stop a ball, blow, etc. from reaching somewhere by moving in front of it 拦截，挡住（球、打击等）： *His shot was blocked by the goalie.* 他起脚射门，球被守门员拦住了。

PHR V ˌ**block sb/sth↔ˈin** to prevent a car from being able to be driven away by parking too close to it（紧挨着停靠车辆）把另一辆车堵住 ˌ**block sth↔ˈin** to draw or paint sth roughly, without showing any detail 画（某物）的草图： *I have blocked in the shapes of the larger buildings.* 我勾出了较大型建筑的轮廓。 ˌ**block sth↔ˈoff** to close a road or an opening by placing a barrier at one end or in front of it（用路障）封锁，堵住 ˌ**block sth↔ˈout 1** to stop light or noise from coming in 挡住，遮住（光线或声音）： *Black clouds blocked out the sun.* 乌云遮住了太阳。 **2** to stop yourself from thinking about or remembering sth unpleasant 忘掉，抹去（不愉快的事）： *Over the years she had tried to block out that part of her life.* 多年来她努力想把她生命中的那一段经历从记忆中抹去。 ˌ**block sth↔ˈup** to completely fill a hole or an opening and so prevent anything from passing through it 塞住，封住（孔、洞）： *One door had been blocked up.* 一扇门被封死了。 ◇ *My nose is blocked up.* 我的鼻子塞了。

block·ade /blɒˈkeɪd; *NAmE* blɑːˈk-/ *noun, verb*

■ ***noun* 1** the action of surrounding or closing a place, especially a port, in order to stop people or goods from coming in or out（尤指对港口的）包围，封锁： *a naval blockade* 海上封锁 ◇ ***to impose/lift a blockade*** 实行 / 解除封锁 ◇ *an economic blockade* (= stopping goods from entering or leaving a country) 经济封锁 **2** a barrier that stops people or vehicles from entering or leaving a place 障碍物；屏障： *The police set up blockades on highways leading out of the city.* 警察在出城的公路上设了路障。

■ ***verb* ~ sth** to surround a place, especially a port, in order to stop people or goods from coming in or out 包围，封锁（尤指港口）

block·age /ˈblɒkɪdʒ; *NAmE* ˈblɑːk-/ *noun* **1** a thing that blocks flow or movement, for example of a liquid in a narrow place 造成阻塞的东西；阻塞物 **SYN obstruction**： *a blockage in an artery/a pipe/a drain* 动脉 / 管道 / 排水沟堵塞物 **2** the state of being blocked 堵塞；阻塞： ***to cause/clear the blockage*** 引起 / 疏通阻塞

block and tackle 滑轮组

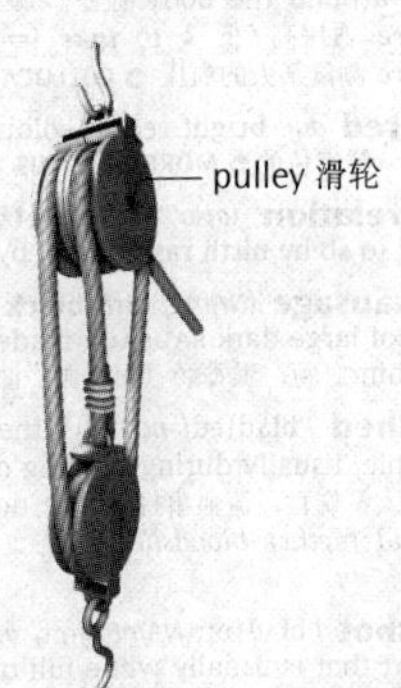

ˌ**block and ˈtackle** *noun* [sing.] a piece of equipment for lifting heavy objects, which works by a system of ropes and PULLEYS (= small wheels around which the ropes are stretched) 滑轮组；滑车组

block·bust·er /ˈblɒkbʌstə(r); *NAmE* ˈblɑːk-/ *noun* (*informal*) something very successful, especially a very successful book or film/movie 一鸣惊人的事物；（尤指）非常成功的书（或电影）： *a Hollywood blockbuster* 一部好莱坞大片 ➲ WORDFINDER NOTE AT BOOK ▶ **block·bust·ing** *adj.*： *a blockbusting performance* 引起轰动的演出

ˌ**block ˈcapitals** (*also* ˌ**block ˈletters**) *noun* [pl.] separate capital letters 正体大写字母： *Please fill out the form in block capitals.* 请用正体大写字母填写表格。

block·head /ˈblɒkhed; *NAmE* ˈblɑːk-/ *noun* (*informal*) a very stupid person 愚蠢的人；傻瓜

block·house /ˈblɒkhaʊs; *NAmE* ˈblɑːk-/ *noun* **1** a strong concrete shelter used by soldiers, for example during a battle 碉堡 **2** (*NAmE*) a house made of LOGS (= thick pieces of wood) 木屋

ˌ**block ˈvote** *noun* a voting system in which each person who votes represents a number of people 集体投票（投票人代表着一批人的投票制度）

blog /blɒɡ; *NAmE* blɑːɡ/ *noun, verb*

■ ***noun*** (*also less frequent* **web·log**) a website where a person writes regularly about recent events or topics that interest them, usually with photos and links to other websites that they find interesting 博客；网志 ➲ WORDFINDER NOTE AT WEB ➲ COLLOCATIONS AT EMAIL

■ ***verb*** (**-gg-**) [I, T] to keep a blog; to write sth in a blog 写博客；写网志： *I will be blogging from the convention all week.* 整个一星期我都会写博客对大会进行报道。 ◇ *Here are some reactions to the story I blogged this morning.* 下面是对我今天上午所写博客文章的一些回应。 ➲ MORE LIKE THIS 36, page R29 ▶ **blog·ger** *noun* **blog·ging** *noun* [U] **bloggy** *adj.* (*informal*)： *The article is quite bloggy, with lots of opinions rather than facts.* 这是颇为典型的博客文章，观点远多于事实。

blog·gable /ˈblɒɡəbl; *NAmE* ˈblɑːɡ-/ *adj.* interesting enough to be a topic for a blog 可作博客话题的；可写博客的： *The film gave me a whole range of bloggable ideas.* 这部电影给了我各种写博客的点子。

blogo·sphere /ˈblɒɡəsfɪə(r); *NAmE* ˈblɑːɡəsfɪr/ *noun* (*usually* **the blogosphere**) [sing.] (*informal*) all the personal websites that exist on the Internet, viewed as a network of people communicating with each other 博客圈；博客世界： *It's one of the top stories in the blogosphere.* 那件事是博客圈热门的话题之一。 ◇ *the growing influence of the political blogosphere* 政治博客世界与日俱增的影响力

blog·roll /ˈblɒɡrəʊl; *NAmE* ˈblɑːɡroʊl/ *noun* (*computing* 计) a list on a website of links to other websites that the website owner thinks are useful or interesting 友情链接；博客链接

bloke /bləʊk; *NAmE* bloʊk/ *noun* (*BrE, informal*) a man 男人；家伙： *He seemed like a nice bloke.* 他看上去像个好人。

bloke·ish (*also* **blok·ish**) /ˈbləʊkɪʃ; *NAmE* ˈbloʊk-/ *adj.* (*BrE, informal*) behaving in a way that is supposed to be typical of men, especially men enjoying themselves in a group 举止豪爽的，爷儿们般的（尤指喜欢成伙作乐）

blonde 🔑 /blɒnd; *NAmE* blɑːnd/ *adj., noun*

■ ***adj.*** (*also* **blond**) **HELP** In British English it is usual to spell this word **blonde** when writing about a woman or girl and **blond** when writing about a man or boy, although the spelling **blonde** is sometimes used for men and boys too. In American English the spelling **blond** is often preferred for either sex. **Blonde** may be used to describe a woman's hair, but it is sometimes considered offensive to refer to a woman as 'a blonde' because hair colour should not define what a person is like. 英式英语中通常用 blonde 描述女性，blond 描述男性，不过，blonde 有时也用于男性。美式英语中描述男女都倾向于用 blond。blonde 可用以描述女性的头发，但用 a blonde 来指代女性有时被认为是不礼貌的，因为头发颜色并不代表整个人。 **1** 🔑 (of hair 头发) pale gold in colour 金黄色的 **2** 🔑 (of a person 人) having blonde hair 头发金黄的： *a small, blond boy* 一个金发小男孩

WORDFINDER 联想词： auburn, dark, fair, ginger, grey, jet black, mousy, redhead, sandy

■ ***noun*** 🔑 (*sometimes offensive*) a woman with hair that is pale gold in colour 金发女郎： *Is she a natural blonde* (= Is her hair naturally blonde)? 她的头发原本就是金黄色吗？ ➲ COMPARE BRUNETTE, REDHEAD

blood /blʌd/ *noun, verb*

■ *noun* **1** [U] the red liquid that flows through the bodies of humans and animals 血： *He lost a lot of blood in the accident.* 他在那场事故中流了很多血。◇ *Blood was pouring out of a cut on her head.* 血不断地从她头上的伤口中涌出。◇ *to* ***give blood*** (= to have blood taken from you so that it can be used in the medical treatment of other people) 献血 ◇ *to* ***draw blood*** (= to wound a person so that they lose blood) 放血（伤人以致流血）◇ *a* ***blood cell/sample*** 血细胞；血样 **2 -blooded** (in adjectives 构成形容词) having the type of blood mentioned 有…类型的血的： *cold-blooded reptiles* 冷血爬行动物 ➲ SEE ALSO BLUE-BLOODED, HOT-BLOODED, RED-BLOODED ➲ MORE LIKE THIS 8, page R25 **3** [U] (*formal*) family origins 血统；家世： *She is of noble blood.* 她有贵族血统。 **4** [C] (*old-fashioned, BrE*) a rich and fashionable man 纨绔子弟；花花公子

IDM **bad 'blood (between A and B)** (*old-fashioned*) feelings of hatred or strong dislike （甲、乙之间的）仇恨，厌恶 **be after/out for sb's 'blood** (*informal, often humorous*) to be angry with sb and want to hurt or punish them 恨不得伤害（或惩罚）某人；恨不得放某人的血 **be/run in your 'blood** to be a natural part of your character and of the character of other members of your family 是与生俱来的（或遗传的）特性 **blood is thicker than 'water** (*saying*) family relationships are stronger than any others 血浓于水；亲属关系最牢靠 **sb's 'blood is up** (*BrE*) somebody is very angry and ready to argue or fight 怒气冲天；怒从心上来；怒不可遏 **blood, sweat and 'tears** very hard work; a lot of effort 血汗；艰苦奋斗 **have sb's 'blood on your hands** to be responsible for sb's death 对某人的死亡罪责难逃： *a dictator with the blood of thousands on his hands* 手上沾满千万人鲜血的独裁者 **like getting blood out of/from a 'stone** almost impossible to obtain 水中捞月；缘木求鱼： *Getting an apology from him was like getting blood from a stone.* 让他道歉几乎是不可能的。 **make sb's 'blood boil** to make sb extremely angry 使某人怒不可遏 **make sb's blood run cold** to make sb very frightened or fill them with horror 使某人不寒而栗（或毛骨悚然） **new/fresh 'blood** new members or employees, especially young ones, with new ideas or ways of doing things 新成员（尤指年轻、有新思想或方法的）；新生力量；新鲜血液 ➲ MORE AT COLD *adj.*, FLESH *n.*, FREEZE *v.*, SPILL *v.*, SPIT *v.*, STIR *v.*, SWEAT *v.*

■ *verb* **~ sb** (*BrE*) to give sb their first experience of an activity 让（新人）初试

'blood bank *noun* a place where blood is kept for use in hospitals, etc. 血库

blood·bath /'blʌdbɑːθ; *NAmE* -bæθ/ *noun* [sing.] a situation in which many people are killed violently 大屠杀 SYN **massacre**

'blood brother *noun* a man who has promised to treat another man as his brother, usually in a ceremony in which their blood is mixed together （尤指歃血为盟的）结义兄弟；血盟兄弟

'blood clot (*also* **clot**) *noun* a lump that is formed when blood dries or becomes thicker 血凝块；血块： *a blood clot on the brain* 大脑中的血块

'blood count *noun* the number of red and white cells in sb's blood; a medical test to count these 血细胞总数；血细胞计数

'blood-curdling *adj.* (of a sound or a story 声音或故事) filling you with horror; extremely frightening 使人毛骨悚然的；极为可怕的： *a* ***blood-curdling scream/story*** 令人不寒而栗的尖叫 / 故事

'blood diamond *noun* = CONFLICT DIAMOND

'blood donor *noun* a person who gives some of his or her blood to be used in the medical treatment of other people 献血者；捐血者

'blood group (*also* **'blood type** *especially in NAmE*) *noun* any of the different types that human blood is separated into for medical purposes 血型： (*BrE*) *What blood group are you?* 你是什么血型？◇ (*NAmE*) *What blood type do you have?* 你是什么血型？◇ *blood group/type O* * O 型血

'blood heat *noun* [U] the normal temperature of a human body 血温；人体正常的温度

blood·hound /'blʌdhaʊnd/ *noun* a large dog with a very good sense of smell, used to follow or look for people 大警犬（嗅觉十分灵敏，常用于追踪人）

blood·ied /'blʌdid/ *adj.* covered in blood 血染的；有血的： *his bruised and bloodied nose* 他沾满血的青肿的鼻子

blood·less /'blʌdləs/ *adj.* **1** without any killing 不流血的；和平的： *a* ***bloodless coup/revolution*** 不流血的政变 / 革命 **2** (of a person or a part of the body 人或身体部位) very pale 苍白的；无血色的： *bloodless lips* 没有血色的双唇 **3** lacking human emotion 无情的；冷酷的 SYN **cold, unemotional**

blood·let·ting /'blʌdletɪŋ/ *noun* [U] **1** (*formal*) the killing or wounding of people 杀戮；伤害 SYN **bloodshed 2** a medical treatment used in the past in which some of a patient's blood was removed 放血疗法

blood·line /'blʌdlaɪn/ *noun* (*specialist*) the set of ANCESTORS of a person or an animal 世系；血统；（动物的）种系

blood·lust /'blʌdlʌst/ *noun* [U] a strong desire to kill or be violent 杀戮欲；暴力欲

'blood money *noun* [U] (*disapproving*) **1** money paid to a person who is hired to murder sb （付给受雇杀人者的）血腥钱 **2** money paid to the family of a murdered person （付给被杀害者家属的）赎罪金

'blood orange *noun* a type of orange with red flesh 血橙（果肉红色）

'blood poisoning *noun* an illness where the blood becomes infected with harmful bacteria 败血病

'blood pressure *noun* [U] the pressure of blood as it travels around the body 血压： *to have* ***high/low blood pressure*** 血压高 / 低 ◇ *to* ***take*** (= measure) ***sb's blood pressure*** 测量某人的血压 ➲ COLLOCATIONS AT DIET

,blood-'red *adj.* bright red in colour, like fresh blood 血红色的；鲜红色的 ➲ MORE LIKE THIS 15, page R26

'blood relation (*also* **'blood relative**) *noun* a person related to sb by birth rather than by marriage 血亲；骨肉

'blood sausage (*NAmE*) (*BrE* **,black 'pudding**) *noun* [U, C] a type of large dark SAUSAGE made from pig's blood, fat and grain 血肠，黑香肠（用猪血、油脂和谷粒制成）

blood·shed /'blʌdʃed/ *noun* [U] the killing or wounding of people, usually during fighting or a war （战斗或战争中的）人员伤亡，流血事件： *The two sides called a truce to avoid further bloodshed.* 双方宣布休战，以免再有人员伤亡。

blood·shot /'blʌdʃɒt; *NAmE* -ʃɑːt/ *adj.* (of eyes 眼睛) with the part that is usually white full of red lines because of lack of sleep, etc. 布满血丝的

'blood sport *noun* [usually pl.] a sport in which animals or birds are killed 血腥运动

blood·stain /'blʌdsteɪn/ *noun* a mark or spot of blood on sth 血迹；血污 ▶ **blood·stained** *adj.* : *a bloodstained shirt* 血迹斑斑的衬衫

blood·stock /'blʌdstɒk; *NAmE* -stɑːk/ *noun* [U] horses of pure breed, bred especially for racing （为赛马特地培育的）纯种马

blood·stream /'blʌdstriːm/ *noun* [sing.] the blood flowing through the body 体内循环的血液；血流： *They injected* *the drug directly into her bloodstream.* 他们把药物直接注射到她的血液里。

blood·sucker /ˈblʌdsʌkə(r)/ *noun* **1** an animal or insect that sucks blood from people or animals 吸血动物 **2** (*informal, disapproving*) a person who takes advantage of other people in order to gain financial benefit 敲诈勒索者；吸血鬼 ▸ **blood·suck·ing** /ˈblʌdsʌkɪŋ/ *adj.* [only before noun]: *bloodsucking insects* 吸血昆虫 ◇ (*disapproving*) *bloodsucking lawyers* 敲诈勒索的律师

ˌ**blood ˈsugar** *noun* [U] the amount of GLUCOSE in your blood 血糖

ˈ**blood test** *noun* an examination of a small amount of your blood by doctors in order to make judgements about your medical condition 验血

blood·thirsty /ˈblʌdθɜːsti; *NAmE* -θɜːrsti/ *adj.* **1** wanting to kill or wound; enjoying seeing or hearing about killing and violence 嗜杀成性的；喜好看（或听）凶杀与暴力的 **2** (of a book, film/movie, etc. 书、电影等) describing or showing killing and violence 描写（或表现）凶杀与暴力的

ˈ**blood transfusion** (*also* **transfusion**) *noun* [C, U] the process of putting new blood into the body of a person or an animal 输血: *He was given a blood transfusion.* 他接受了输血。

ˈ**blood type** *noun* (*especially NAmE*) = BLOOD GROUP

ˈ**blood vessel** *noun* any of the tubes through which blood flows through the body 血管 ➲ SEE ALSO ARTERY (1), CAPILLARY, VEIN (1)

bloody[1] /ˈblʌdi/ *adj.* [only before noun] *adv.* ➲ SEE ALSO BLOODY[2] (*BrE, taboo, slang*) a swear word that many people find offensive that is used to emphasize a comment or an angry statement （用以加强语气；很多人认为含冒犯意）: *Don't be such a bloody fool.* 别像个大傻瓜似的。◇ *That was a bloody good meal!* 那顿饭真他妈丰盛！◇ *What bloody awful weather!* 多么糟糕透顶的天气！◇ *She did bloody well to win that race.* 她非常出色地赢了那场赛跑。◇ *He doesn't bloody care about anybody else.* 他根本不关心别人。◇ *'Will you apologize?' 'Not bloody likely!'* (= Certainly not!) "你会道歉吗？" "没门儿。"

IDM **bloody well** (*BrE, informal, taboo*) used to emphasize an angry statement or an order （强调气愤的话或命令）: *You can bloody well keep your job—I don't want it!* 你就继续干你那份臭工作吧，我才不稀罕呢！

bloody[2] /ˈblʌdi/ *adj.* ➲ SEE ALSO BLOODY[1] (**blood·ier, bloodi·est**) **1** involving a lot of violence and killing 嗜杀的；血腥的；残暴的: *a bloody battle* 一场血战 ◇ *The terrorists have halted their bloody campaign of violence.* 恐怖分子已经停止了他们凶残的暴力活动。 **2** covered with blood; BLEEDING 血淋淋的；流血的: *to give sb a bloody nose* (= in a fight) 把某人打得鼻孔流血 ▸ **blood·ily** *adv.*
IDM SEE SCREAM *v.*

Bloody Mary /ˌblʌdi ˈmeəri; *NAmE* ˈmeri/ *noun* (*pl.* **Bloody Marys**) an alcoholic drink made by mixing VODKA with tomato juice 红玛丽鸡尾酒，血腥玛丽（用伏特加酒加番茄汁调制而成）

ˌ**bloody-ˈminded** *adj.* (*informal*) behaving in a way that makes things difficult for other people; refusing to be helpful 和别人过不去的；故意不合作的 ▸ ˌ**bloody-ˈminded·ness** *noun* [U]

bloom /bluːm/ *noun, verb*
■ *noun* **1** (*formal* or *specialist*) [C] a flower (usually one on a plant that people admire for its flowers) （常指供观赏的）花: *the exotic blooms of the orchid* 奇异的兰花 **2** [sing., U] a healthy fresh appearance 健康有精神的面貌: *the bloom in her cheeks* 她面颊上的红润光泽
IDM **in (full) bloom** (of trees, plants, gardens, etc. 树木、花草、园子等) with the flowers fully open 鲜花盛开
■ *verb* **1** [I] to produce flowers 开花 SYN **flower**: *Most roses will begin to bloom from late May.* 大多数玫瑰从五月末开始开花。 **2** [I] to become healthy, happy or confident 变得健康（或快活、自信） SYN **blossom**: *The children had bloomed during their stay on the farm.* 孩子们在农场期间健康活泼有生气。

bloom·er /ˈbluːmə(r)/ *noun* (*old-fashioned, BrE, informal*) a mistake 错误

bloom·ers /ˈbluːməz; *NAmE* -ərz/ *noun* [pl.] **1** (*informal*) an old-fashioned piece of women's underwear like long loose UNDERPANTS （旧时妇女穿的）宽松长内裤 **2** short loose trousers/pants that fit tightly at the knee, worn in the past by women for games, riding bicycles, etc. （旧时妇女骑自行车等穿的）短灯笼裤: *a pair of bloomers* 一条短灯笼裤

bloom·ing /ˈbluːmɪŋ; ˈblʊm-/ *adj.* [only before noun] *adv.* (*BrE, informal*) a mild swear word, used to emphasize a comment or a statement, especially an angry one （气愤等时用以加强语气）: *What blooming awful weather!* 多糟糕的天气！

bloop /bluːp/ *verb* [I] (*NAmE, informal*) to make a mistake 出错

bloop·er /ˈbluːpə(r)/ *noun* (*especially NAmE*) an embarrassing mistake that you make in public 当众出的洋相；出丑

blos·som /ˈblɒsəm; *NAmE* ˈblɑːs-/ *noun, verb*
■ *noun* [C, U] a flower or a mass of flowers, especially on a fruit tree or bush （尤指果树或灌木的）花朵，花簇: *cherry/orange/apple blossom* 樱桃花；橘子花；苹果花 ◇ *The trees are* **in blossom**. 树上鲜花盛开。 ➲ VISUAL VOCAB PAGE V10
■ *verb* **1** [I] (of a tree or bush 树或灌木) to produce blossom 开花 **2** [I] to become more healthy, confident or successful 变得更加健康（或自信、成功）: *She has visibly blossomed over the last few months.* 她近几个月以来身体明显好多了。◇ **~ into sth** *Their friendship blossomed into love.* 他们的友谊发展成了爱情。

blot /blɒt; *NAmE* blɑːt/ *verb, noun*
■ *verb* (**-tt-**) **1 ~ sth (up)** to remove liquid from a surface by pressing soft paper or cloth on it （用软纸或布）吸干液体 **2 ~ sth** to make a spot or spots of ink fall on paper 把墨水溅到（纸上）
IDM **blot your ˈcopybook** (*old-fashioned, informal*) to do sth to spoil the opinion that other people have of you 做出有损形象的事；玷污名誉
PHR V ˌ**blot sth↔ˈout 1** to cover or hide sth completely 遮住；掩盖；隐藏: *Clouds blotted out the sun.* 云遮住了太阳。 **2** to deliberately try to forget an unpleasant memory or thought 有意地忘记（不愉快的记忆或想法）；抹去: *He tried to blot out the image of Helen's sad face.* 他尽量不去想海伦的那张忧伤的脸。
■ *noun* **1** a spot or dirty mark on sth, made by ink, etc. 污点；墨渍 ➲ SYNONYMS AT MARK **2 ~ (on sth)** something that spoils the opinion that other people have of you, or your happiness 有损形象（或幸福）的事情；污点: *Her involvement in the fraud has left a serious blot on her character.* 她卷入了这桩欺诈案，在她的品格上留下了一个很大的污点。
IDM **a blot on the ˈlandscape** an object, especially an ugly building, that spoils the beauty of a place 影响景观的物体（尤指丑陋建筑物）

blotch /blɒtʃ; *NAmE* blɑːtʃ/ *noun* a mark, usually not regular in shape, on skin, plants, material, etc. （皮肤、植物、物体等上面不规则的）斑点，污点: *He had come out in* (= become covered in) *dark red blotches.* 他身上长出了一块块深红色的斑。

blotchy /ˈblɒtʃi; *NAmE* ˈblɑː-/ (*also* **blotched**) *adj.* covered in blotches 有斑点的；有污点的: *her blotchy and swollen face* 她的布满斑点的浮肿的脸

blot·ter /ˈblɒtə(r); *NAmE* ˈblɑːt-/ *noun* **1** a large piece of blotting paper in a cover with a stiff back which is kept on a desk 吸墨纸板；吸墨用具 **2** (*NAmE*) the record of arrests in a police district （警察管区的）拘捕记录

B

'**blotting paper** *noun* [U] soft thick paper used for drying ink after you have written sth on a piece of paper 吸墨纸

blotto /'blɒtəʊ; *NAmE* 'blɑːtoʊ/ *adj.* [not before noun] (*old-fashioned, informal*) very drunk 烂醉如泥

blouse /blaʊz; *NAmE* blaʊs/ *noun* a piece of clothing like a shirt, worn by women （女式）短上衣，衬衫 ➲ VISUAL VOCAB PAGE V66 IDM SEE BIG *adj.*

blouson /'bluːzɒn; *NAmE* 'blaʊsɑːn/ *noun* a short loose jacket that is gathered together at the waist 束腰短上衣

blo·vi·ate /'bləʊvieɪt; *NAmE* 'bloʊ-/ *verb* [I] (*NAmE, informal, disapproving*) to talk or write in a way that shows that you think you know a lot and have sth important to say, when in fact you do not know much and have nothing important to say （空泛地）高谈阔论；夸夸其谈

blow 🔑 /bləʊ; *NAmE* bloʊ/ *verb, noun, exclamation*

■ *verb* (**blew** /bluː/, **blown** /bləʊn; *NAmE* bloʊn/) HELP In sense 14 **blowed** is used for the past participle. 作第 14 义时过去分词用 blowed。

• **FROM MOUTH** 口 **1** 🔑 [I, T] to send out air from the mouth 吹： **+ adv./prep.** *You're not blowing hard enough!* 你没有用劲吹！ ◇ *The policeman asked me to blow into the breathalyser.* 警察要我对着呼气酒精含量探测器吹气。 ◇ **~ sth + adv./prep.** *He drew on his cigarette and blew out a stream of smoke.* 他含着烟卷吸了一口，接着吐出一股烟。

• **OF WIND** 风 **2** 🔑 [I, T] (**+ adv./prep.**) when the wind or a current of air **blows**, it is moving; when **it blows**, the wind is blowing 刮；吹： *A cold wind blew from the east.* 东边吹来一股冷风。 ◇ *It was blowing hard.* 刮着大风。 ◇ *It was* **blowing a gale** (= there was a strong wind). 狂风大作。

• **MOVE WITH WIND/BREATH** 风 / 口吹动 **3** 🔑 [I, T] to be moved by the wind, sb's breath, etc.; to move sth in this way （被）刮动，吹动： **+ adv./prep.** *My hat blew off.* 我的帽子被风吹走了。 ◇ **+ adj.** *The door blew open.* 门被风吹开了。 ◇ **~ sb/sth + adv./prep.** *I was almost blown over by the wind.* 我被风刮得快倒了。 ◇ *She blew the dust off the book.* 她吹掉了书上的灰尘。 ◇ *The ship was blown onto the rocks.* 强风使船撞上了礁石。 ◇ **~ sth + adj.** *The wind blew the door shut.* 风把门吹关上了。

• **WHISTLE/INSTRUMENT** 哨子；乐器 **4** 🔑 [T, I] **~ (sth)** if you **blow** a whistle, musical instrument, etc. or if a whistle, etc. **blows**, you produce a sound by blowing into the whistle, etc. 吹，吹奏（哨子、乐器等）；（哨子、乐器等）吹奏出音： *The referee blew his whistle.* 裁判吹响了哨子。 ◇ *the sound of trumpets blowing* 吹喇叭的声音

• **YOUR NOSE** 鼻 **5** 🔑 [T] **~ your nose** to clear your nose by blowing strongly through it into a TISSUE or HANDKERCHIEF 擤（鼻子）

• **A KISS** 吻 **6** [T] **~ (sb) a kiss** to kiss your hand and then pretend to blow the kiss towards sb （向某人）送飞吻

• **SHAPE STH** 使成形 **7** [T] **~ sth** to make or shape sth by blowing 吹出（某物）；把（某物）吹出形状： *to blow smoke rings* 吐烟圈 ◇ *to* **blow bubbles** (= for example, by blowing onto a thin layer of water mixed with soap) 吹泡泡 ◇ *to* **blow glass** (= to send a current of air into melted glass to shape it) 吹制玻璃器皿

• **ELECTRICITY** 电 **8** [I, T] **~ (sth)** if a FUSE **blows** or you **blow** a FUSE, the electricity stops flowing suddenly because the FUSE (= a thin wire) has melted because the current was too strong （使保险丝）熔化，烧断

• **TYRE** 轮胎 **9** [I, T] to break open or apart, especially because of pressure from inside; to make a tyre break in this way 破裂；爆裂；爆胎： *The car spun out of control when a tyre blew.* 车胎爆了一个，车随后失去了控制。 ◇ *The truck blew a tyre and lurched off the road.* 这辆卡车爆了一个胎，斜冲出了公路。

• **WITH EXPLOSIVES** 炸药 **10** [T] **~ sth** to break sth open with EXPLOSIVES 炸开： *The safe had been blown by the thieves.* 保险柜被窃贼炸开了。

• **SECRET** 秘密 **11** [T] **~ sth** (*informal*) to make known sth that was secret 泄露；暴露： *One mistake could* **blow your cover** (= make your real name, job, intentions, etc. known). 一不小心就会让你暴露身份。

• **MONEY** 钱 **12** [T] **~ sth (on sth)** (*informal*) to spend or waste a lot of money on sth （在某事物上）花大钱，挥霍： *He inherited over a million dollars and blew it all on drink and gambling.* 他继承了一百多万美元，全部挥霍在饮酒和赌博上了。

• **OPPORTUNITY** 机会 **13** [T] **~ sth** (*informal*) to waste an opportunity 浪费（机会）： *She* **blew her chances** *by arriving late for the interview.* 她面试时迟到，结果错过了机会。 ◇ *You had your chance and you* **blew it**. 你本来有机会，却没有抓住。

• **EXCLAMATION** 感叹 **14** [T] **~ sb/sth** (*BrE, informal*) used to show that you are annoyed, surprised or do not care about sth （表示生气、吃惊或不在乎）： *Blow it! We've missed the bus.* 真该死！我们错过了公交车。 ◇ *Well, blow me down! I never thought I'd see you again.* 啊，天哪！我以为再也见不到你了。 ◇ ***I'm blowed if** I'm going to* (= I certainly will not) *let him treat you like that.* 我绝不会允许他那么对待你。 ◇ *Let's take a taxi and blow* (= never mind) *the expense.* 我们乘出租车吧，别在意费用。

• **LEAVE SUDDENLY** 突然离开 **15** [T, I] **~ (sth)** (*NAmE, slang*) to leave a place suddenly 突然离开（某地）： *Let's blow this joint.* 咱们马上离开这家酒吧。

IDM **blow your/sb's 'brains out** to kill yourself/sb by shooting yourself/them in the head 枪击头部自杀 / 杀人 **blow 'chunks** (*NAmE, slang*) to VOMIT 呕；呕吐 **blow a 'fuse** (*informal*) to get very angry 大怒；暴跳如雷 **blow the 'gaff (on sb/sth)** (*BrE, informal*) to tell sth secret, especially by mistake （尤指因大意）泄露秘密 **blow hot and 'cold (about sth)** (*informal*) to change your opinion about sth often 拿不定主意；出尔反尔 **blow sb/sth out of the 'water** (*informal*) **1** to destroy sb/sth completely 彻底摧毁；毁灭 **2** to show that sb/sth is not good by being very much better than it/them （以更加优异者）表明…不好，显得…差得多： *I like my old phone, but this new model blows it out of the water.* 我喜欢我的旧手机，但这个新款比它强多了。 **blow 'smoke (up sb's ass)** (*taboo, NAmE, slang*) to try to trick sb or lie to sb, particularly by saying sth is better than it really is 吹牛皮；说大话蒙人 **blow your 'mind** (*informal*) to produce a very strong pleasant or shocking feeling 使某人兴奋（或吃惊）： *Wait till you hear this. It'll blow your mind.* 等着听听这个吧。它会让你大感意外的。 ➲ SEE ALSO MIND-BLOWING **blow your own 'trumpet** (*especially BrE*) (*NAmE usually* **blow/toot your own 'horn**) (*informal*) to praise your own abilities and achievements 自吹自擂 SYN **boast** ORIGIN This phrase refers to the custom of announcing important guests by blowing a horn. 这个短语源自吹号宣布贵宾到达的习俗。 **blow your 'top** (*NAmE also* **blow your 'stack**) (*informal*) to get very angry 大怒；暴跳如雷 **blow up in sb's 'face** if a plan, etc. **blows up in your face**, it goes wrong in a way that causes you damage, embarrassment, etc. 事情失败，害了自己 **blow the 'whistle on sb/sth** (*informal*) to tell sb in authority about sth wrong or illegal that sb is doing 告发 ➲ SEE ALSO WHISTLE-BLOWER IDM SEE COBWEB, ILL *adj.*, KINGDOM, LARK *n.*, LID, PUFF *v.*, SOCK *n.*, WAY *n.*

PHR V ˌ**blow sth↔a'part** **1** to completely destroy sth in an explosion 炸毁；炸掉 **2** to show that an idea is completely false 推翻（观点）；表明…是错误的： *What we discovered blew apart all our preconceptions about this fascinating species.* 我们的发现将我们对这一奇妙物种的先入之见全盘推翻了。 ˌ**blow sb↔a'way** (*informal, especially NAmE*) **1** to kill sb by shooting them 枪杀某人 **2** to impress sb a lot or to make them very happy 给某人留下深刻印象；使某人很高兴 **3** to defeat sb easily 轻易击败某人 ˌ**blow 'in** | ˌ**blow 'into sth** (*informal*) to arrive or enter a place suddenly 突然来到；突然进入： *Look who's just blown in!* 看，谁来了！ ◇ *Have you heard who's blown into town?* 你听说谁突然来了吗？ ˌ**blow 'off** (*BrE, informal*) a rude way of saying 'BREAK WIND' (= release gas through your bottom) （粗俗语）放屁 ˌ**blow sb↔'off** (*NAmE*) to deliberately not meet sb when you said you would; to end a romantic relationship with sb （故意）失约；结束与…的恋爱关系 ˌ**blow sth↔'off** (*NAmE*) to deliberately not do sth that you said you would （故意）推脱，逃避： *He looks for any excuse he can to blow* *off work.* 他寻找任何可能的借口来逃避工作。 **ˌblow ˈout 1** if a flame, etc. **blows out**, it is put out by the wind, etc. 被（风等）吹灭；熄灭：*Somebody opened the door and the candle blew out.* 有人打开了门，蜡烛就被吹灭了。 **2** if an oil or gas WELL **blows out**, it sends out gas suddenly and with force （油井或气井）喷气；井喷 ➲ RELATED NOUN BLOWOUT **ˌblow itself ˈout** when a storm **blows itself out**, it finally loses its force （风暴等）平息，减弱 **ˌblow sb↔ˈout** (*NAmE, informal*) to defeat sb easily 轻易击败某人 **ˌblow sth↔ˈout** 🔑 to put out a flame, etc. by blowing 吹灭（火焰等） **ˌblow ˈover** to go away without having a serious effect 刮过去了，平静下来（未造成严重影响）：*The storm blew over in the night.* 风暴在夜间平息了。◇ *The scandal will soon blow over.* 流言蜚语很快就会烟消云散的。 **ˌblow ˈup 1** 🔑 to explode; to be destroyed by an explosion 爆炸；被炸毁：*The bomb blew up.* 炸弹爆炸了。◇ *A police officer was killed when his car blew up.* 一名警察在其汽车爆炸时遇难。 ➲ SYNONYMS AT EXPLODE **2** to start suddenly and with force 爆发：*A storm was blowing up.* 暴风雨大作。◇ *A crisis has blown up over the President's latest speech.* 总统最近的讲话引发了一场危机。 **ˌblow sth↔ˈup 1** to destroy sth by an explosion 炸毁：*The police station was blown up by terrorists.* 警察局被恐怖分子炸毁了。 ➲ SYNONYMS AT EXPLODE **2** 🔑 to fill sth with air or gas so that it becomes firm 给（某物）充气：*The tyres on my bike need blowing up.* 我的自行车该打气了。 **3** to make a photograph bigger 放大（照片） SYN **enlarge** ➲ RELATED NOUN BLOW-UP **4** to make sth seem more important, better, worse, etc. than it really is 夸大；夸张：*The whole affair was **blown up out of all proportion**.* 整个事件被渲染得太过了。 **ˌblow ˈup (at sb)** (*informal*) to get angry with sb （对某人）发火，动怒 SYN **lose your temper**：*I'm sorry I blew up at you.* 对不起，我对你发脾气了。 ➲ RELATED NOUN BLOW-UP

■ ***noun* 1** 🔑 a hard hit with the hand, a weapon, etc. （用手、武器等的）猛击：*She received a severe blow on the head.* 她头上挨了重重的一击。◇ *He was knocked out by a single blow to the head.* 他头上只被打了一下便昏过去了。◇ *The two men were **exchanging blows**.* 那两个人在相互厮打。◇ *He **landed a blow** on Hill's nose.* 他对着希尔的鼻子来了一拳。 **2** 🔑 **~ (to sb/sth)** a sudden event which has damaging effects on sb/sth, causing sadness or disappointment 打击；挫折：*Losing his job **came as a** terrible **blow to** him.* 失业给他造成了沉重的打击。◇ *It was a shattering blow to her pride.* 那事彻底摧毁了她的自尊心。 ➲ SEE ALSO BODY BLOW **3** 🔑 the action of blowing 吹：*Give your nose a good blow* (= clear it completely). 把你的鼻子擤干净。

IDM **a ˌblow-by-ˌblow acˈcount, deˈscription, etc. (of sth)** (*informal*) a description of an event which gives you all the details in the order in which they happen 原原本本的描述等 **come to ˈblows (over sth)** to start fighting because of sth （因某事）动武，打起架来 **soften/cushion the ˈblow** to make sth that is unpleasant seem less unpleasant and easier to accept 缓解；缓和 ➲ MORE AT DEAL *v.*, STRIKE *v.*

■ ***exclamation*** (*old-fashioned, BrE*) used to show that you are annoyed about sth （表示厌烦）：*Blow! I completely forgot it.* 哎呀！我给忘得一干二净了。

blow·back /ˈbləʊbæk; *NAmE* ˈbloʊbæk/ *noun* [U, C] **1** (*specialist*) a process in which gases expand or travel in a direction that is opposite to the usual one 反吹；回吹；逆吹：*blowback gas* 回膛气体 ◇ *Blowback may be caused by a defective mechanism.* 气体后泄可能是由机械结构缺陷引起的。 **2** (*especially NAmE*) the results of a political action or situation that are not what was intended or wanted 违背初衷的结果：*The policy has led to blowback.* 这项政策结果适得其反。◇ *The war created a ferocious blowback.* 这场战争激起了强烈的反冲效应。

ˈblow-dry *verb* **~ sth** to dry hair with a HAIRDRYER and shape it into a particular style 吹发（用吹风机吹干头发并使之成型） ▸ **ˈblow-dry** *noun*：*a cut and blow-dry* 剪发及吹干

blow·er /ˈbləʊə(r); *NAmE* ˈbloʊ-/ *noun* **1** [C] a device that produces a current of air 吹风机；送风机：*a hot-air blower* 热风机 **2 the blower** [sing.] (*old-fashioned, BrE, informal*) the telephone 电话 ➲ SEE ALSO WHISTLE-BLOWER

blow·fly /ˈbləʊflaɪ; *NAmE* ˈbloʊ-/ *noun* (*pl.* **blow·flies**) a large fly that lays its eggs on meat and other food 丽蝇（在肉等食物上产卵）

blow·hard /ˈbləʊhɑːd; *NAmE* ˈbloʊhɑːrd/ *noun* (*NAmE, informal, disapproving*) a person who talks too proudly about sth they own or sth they have done 吹牛大王；自吹自擂的人

blow·hole /ˈbləʊhəʊl; *NAmE* ˈbloʊhoʊl/ *noun* **1** a hole in the top of a WHALE's head through which it breathes （鲸头顶的）呼吸孔 ➲ VISUAL VOCAB PAGE V12 **2** a hole in a large area of ice, through which SEALS, etc. breathe （供海豹等呼吸的）冰窟窿

blowie /ˈbləʊi; *NAmE* ˈbloʊi/ *noun* (*AustralE, NZE, informal*) a BLOWFLY 丽蝇

ˈblow-in *noun* (*AustralE, informal*) a person who has recently arrived somewhere 刚到的人；新来的人

ˈblow job *noun* (*taboo, slang*) the act of touching a man's PENIS with the tongue and lips to give sexual pleasure （对阴茎的）口淫，口交 SYN **fellatio**

blow·lamp /ˈbləʊlæmp; *NAmE* ˈbloʊ-/ (*BrE*) (*NAmE* **ˈblow-torch, torch**) *noun* a tool for directing a very hot flame onto part of a surface, for example to remove paint 喷灯

blown PAST PART. OF BLOW

blow·out /ˈbləʊaʊt; *NAmE* ˈbloʊ-/ *noun* **1** an occasion when a tyre suddenly bursts on a vehicle while it is moving （机动车行驶过程中的）爆胎 SYN **puncture**：*to have a blowout* 车胎爆裂 **2** [usually sing.] (*informal*) a large meal at which people eat too much 大餐；盛宴：*a four-course blowout* 有四道菜的大餐 **3** (*NAmE, informal*) a large party or social occasion 盛大聚会；交谊会：*We're going to have a huge blowout for Valentine's Day.* 情人节时我们会举办一场盛大聚会。 **4** (*NAmE, informal*) an easy victory 轻易的胜利：*The game was a blowout, 8–1.* 这场比赛赢得易如反掌，结果是 8 比 1。 **5** a sudden escape of oil or gas from an OIL WELL 井喷

blow·pipe /ˈbləʊpaɪp; *NAmE* ˈbloʊ-/ *noun* **1** a weapon consisting of a long tube through which an arrow is blown 吹箭筒 **2** a long tube for blowing glass into a particular shape （吹制玻璃器皿的）吹管

blowsy (*also* **blowzy**) /ˈblaʊzi/ *adj.* (*BrE, informal, disapproving*) a woman who is **blowsy** is big and fat and looks untidy （女人）肥硕邋遢的

blow·torch /ˈbləʊtɔːtʃ; *NAmE* ˈbloʊtɔːrtʃ/ (*also* **torch**) (*both NAmE*) (*BrE* **blow·lamp**) *noun* a tool for directing a very hot flame onto part of a surface, for example to remove paint 喷灯

ˈblow-up *noun* **1** an ENLARGEMENT of a photograph, picture or design 照片（或图画、图案等）的放大：*Can you do me a blow-up of his face?* 你能帮我把他的脸部放大吗？ **2** (*NAmE*) an occasion when sb suddenly becomes angry 发脾气；发怒

BLT /ˌbiː el ˈtiː/ *noun* the abbreviation for 'bacon, lettuce and tomato' (used to refer to a SANDWICH filled with this) 熏猪肉、生菜加番茄三明治（全写为 bacon, lettuce and tomato）：*I'll have a BLT with extra mayonnaise.* 我要一个熏肉、生菜加番茄三明治，多加蛋黄酱。

blub /blʌb/ *verb* (**-bb-**) [I] (*BrE, informal*) to cry 哭

blub·ber /ˈblʌbə(r)/ *noun, verb*

■ ***noun*** [U] the fat of WHALES and other sea animals 鲸脂；海兽脂

■ ***verb*** [I, T] (**+ speech**) (*informal, disapproving*) to cry noisily 大声哭：*There he sat, blubbering like a baby.* 他坐在那里像个婴儿似的大哭。

bludge /blʌdʒ/ *verb, noun* (*AustralE, NZE, informal*)

■ ***verb* 1** [I] to not do any work and live from what other

people give you 不劳动而靠别人维持生活；吃现成饭 **2** [T] **~ sth** to ask sb for sth especially because you cannot or do not want to pay for it yourself 乞讨；讨要 **SYN** **cadge, scrounge**: *The girls bludged smokes.* 那些女孩子要烟抽。
■ ***noun*** an easy job 轻松的工作

bludg·eon /ˈblʌdʒən/ *verb* **1 ~ sb** to hit sb several times with a heavy object 用重器连击（某人） **2 ~ sb (into sth/into doing sth)** to force sb to do sth, especially by arguing with them （尤指通过争辩）迫使…: *They tried to bludgeon me into joining their protest.* 他们试图强迫我和他们一同抗议。

bludger /ˈblʌdʒə(r)/ *noun* (*AustralE, NZE, informal*) **1** a lazy person 懒货；懒骨头 **2** a person who asks other people for sth because they cannot or do not want to pay for it 吃现成饭的人 **SYN** **scrounger**

blue /bluː/ *adj., noun*
■ ***adj.*** (**bluer, blu·est**) **1** having the colour of a clear sky or the sea/ocean on a clear day 蓝色的；天蓝色的；蔚蓝色的: *piercing blue eyes* 锐利的蓝眼睛 ◇ *a blue shirt* 蓝色衬衫 **2** (of a person or part of the body 人或身体部位) looking slightly blue in colour because the person is cold or cannot breathe easily （由于冷或呼吸困难）发青的，青紫的: *Her hands were blue with cold.* 她的双手冻得发青。 **3** (*informal*) sad 忧郁的；悲伤的 **SYN** **depressed**: *He'd been feeling blue all week.* 他整个星期都郁郁不乐。 **4** films/movies, jokes or stories that are **blue** are about sex （电影、玩笑或故事）色情的，黄色的: *a blue movie* 色情片 **5** (*politics* 政) (of an area in the US) having more people who vote for the DEMOCRATIC candidate than the REPUBLICAN one （美国地区）蓝色的（支持民主党候选人多于支持共和党候选人）: *blue states/counties* 蓝州；蓝县 **OPP** **red** ➲ SEE ALSO TRUE-BLUE ▶ **blue·ness** *noun* [U, sing.]: *the blueness of the water* 蔚蓝色的水面
IDM **do sth till you are blue in the ˈface** (*informal*) to try to do sth as hard and as long as you possibly can but without success 徒然拼命地干；徒劳无功: *You can argue till you're blue in the face, but you won't change my mind.* 你可以费尽口舌，但改变不了我的主意。 ➲ MORE AT BLACK *adj.*, DEVIL, ONCE *adv.*, SCREAM *v.*
■ ***noun*** ➲ SEE ALSO BLUES **1** [C, U] the colour of a clear sky or the sea/ocean on a clear day 蓝色；天蓝色；蔚蓝色: ***bright/dark/light/pale blue*** 明亮的 / 深 / 浅 / 淡蓝色 ◇ *The room was decorated in vibrant blues and yellows.* 房间饰以鲜亮的蓝色和黄色。 ◇ *She was dressed in blue.* 她身着蓝色服装。 **2** [C] (*BrE*) a person who has played a particular sport for Oxford or Cambridge University; a title given to them 蓝色荣誉者（牛津或剑桥大学的校队运动员）；蓝色荣誉的头衔 **3** [C] (*AustralE, NZE, informal*) a mistake 错误；失误 **4** [C] (*AustralE, NZE, informal*) a name for a person with red hair 红发人 **5** [C] (*AustralE, NZE, informal*) a fight 打架；打斗；斗殴
IDM **out of the ˈblue** unexpectedly; without warning 出乎意料；突然；晴天霹雳: *The decision came out of the blue.* 这个决定来得很突然。 ➲ MORE AT BOLT *n.*, BOY *n.*

ˌblue ˈbaby *noun* a baby whose skin is slightly blue at birth because there is sth wrong with its heart 青紫婴儿（因先天性心脏损害而在出生时皮肤发青）

blue·bell /ˈbluːbel/ *noun* **1** a garden or wild flower with a short STEM and small blue or white flowers shaped like bells 蓝钟花；风铃草 ➲ VISUAL VOCAB PAGE V11 **2** (*ScotE*) = HAREBELL

blue·berry /ˈbluːbəri; *NAmE* -beri/ *noun* (*pl.* **-ies**) a dark blue BERRY that grows on bushes in N America and can be eaten 越橘蓝色浆果，蓝莓（产于北美，可食） ➲ COMPARE BILBERRY

blue·bird /ˈbluːbɜːd; *NAmE* -bɜːrd/ *noun* a small N American bird with blue feathers on its back or head 蓝鸲（北美小鸟，背及头有蓝色羽毛）

ˌblue-ˈblooded *adj.* from a royal or NOBLE family 出身皇族（或贵族）的 ▶ **ˌblue ˈblood** *noun* [U]

blue book *noun* **1** (*US*) a book with a blue cover used by students for writing the answers to examination questions in （考试用）蓝皮答题卷 **2** (*NAmE*) a book that lists the prices that people should expect to pay for used cars 二手车参考价目册

blue·bot·tle /ˈbluːbɒtl; *NAmE* -bɑːtl/ *noun* a large fly with a blue body 青蝇；绿头蝇

ˌblue ˈcheese *noun* [U, C] cheese with lines of blue MOULD in it 蓝纹奶酪（有霉菌引起的斑纹）

ˌblue-ˈchip *adj.* [only before noun] (*finance* 财) a **blue-chip** investment is thought to be safe and likely to make a profit （投资）稳妥可靠的；蓝筹的: *blue-chip companies* 蓝筹公司

ˌblue-ˈcollar *adj.* [only before noun] connected with people who do physical work in industry 从事体力劳动的；蓝领的: ***blue-collar workers/voters/votes*** 蓝领工人 / 选民 / 选票 ➲ COMPARE PINK-COLLAR, WHITE-COLLAR

ˌblue ˈcrane *noun* a type of CRANE (= a large bird with long legs and a long neck) that has blue-grey feathers. It is the national bird of South Africa. 蓝（蓑羽）鹤（南非国鸟）

ˌblue-eyed ˈboy *noun* [usually sing.] (*BrE, informal, often disapproving*) a person treated with special favour by sb 宠儿: *He's the manager's blue-eyed boy.* 他备受经理的青睐。

ˌblue ˈflag *noun* **1** (*BrE*) a blue flag used in motor racing to show that a driver who is much further ahead is trying to pass 蓝旗（赛车中用以示意后方有领先车手试图超车） **2** an award given to beaches in Europe that are clean and safe （为欧洲清洁安全的海滩颁发的）"蓝旗"奖

ˌblue ˈfunk *noun* [sing.] (*old-fashioned, informal*) = FUNK (2)

blue·grass /ˈbluːɡrɑːs; *NAmE* -ɡræs/ *noun* [U] a type of traditional American country music played on GUITARS and BANJOS 蓝草音乐（美国传统乡村音乐，用吉他和班卓琴演奏）

ˌblue ˈhelmet *noun* a member of a United Nations force that is trying to prevent war or violence in a place 蓝盔；联合国维和部队成员

blue·jay /ˈbluːdʒeɪ/ *noun* a large N American bird with blue feathers on its back and a row of feathers (called a CREST) standing up on its head 蓝松鸦，冠蓝鸦（北美大鸟，背部羽毛蓝色，头部有羽冠）

ˈblue jeans *noun* [pl.] (*especially NAmE*) trousers/pants made of blue DENIM 蓝色牛仔裤

ˈblue law *noun* [usually pl.] (in the US) a law that bans business and certain other activities, such as sports, on Sundays 蓝色法规（美国法规，禁止星期天从事商业和体育运动等活动）

ˌblue-on-ˈblue *adj.* [only before noun] (*BrE*) in a war, used to describe an accident or attack in which people are hit by a bomb or weapon that is fired by their own side （战争中）误伤己方的 ➲ COMPARE FRIENDLY FIRE

ˌblue ˈpages *noun* [pl.] (in the US) the blue pages in a TELEPHONE DIRECTORY that give a list of government departments and their telephone numbers （美国列出政府部门及电话号码的）电话蓝页

blue·print /ˈbluːprɪnt/ *noun* **1** a PHOTOGRAPHIC print of a plan for a building or a machine, with white lines on a blue background （建筑、机器等的）蓝图 **2 ~ (for sth)** a plan which shows what can be achieved and how it can be achieved 行动方案；计划蓝图: *a blueprint for the privatization of health care* 医疗保健私有化方案 **3** (*specialist*) the pattern in every living cell, which decides how the plant, animal or person will develop and what it will look like （生物细胞的）模型，型板: *DNA carries* ***the genetic blueprint*** *which tells any organism how to build itself.* 脱氧核糖核酸带有决定有机体形成方式的遗传型板。

blue riband /ˌbluː ˈrɪbənd/ (*BrE*) (*also* **ˌblue ˈribbon** *NAmE, BrE*) *noun* an honour (sometimes in the form of a blue

RIBBON) given to the winner of the first prize in a competition 冠军荣誉，优胜者称号（有时以蓝绶带形式授予冠军得主）：*a blue-riband event* (= a very important one) 重大事件

blues /bluːz/ *noun* **1** (*often* **the blues**) [U] a type of slow sad music with strong rhythms, developed by African American musicians in the southern US 布鲁斯音乐，蓝调（源于美国南部黑人，节奏感强、缓慢忧郁）：*a blues band/singer* 布鲁斯乐队 / 歌手 **2** [C] (*pl.* **blues**) a blues song 布鲁斯歌曲；蓝调歌曲 **3 the blues** [pl.] (*informal*) feelings of sadness 忧郁；悲伤；沮丧：*the Monday morning blues* 星期一早晨的郁闷情绪 ➲ SEE ALSO BABY BLUES

ˌ**blue-ˈsky** *adj.* [only before noun] involving new and interesting ideas for things which are not yet possible or practical 新颖而未可行的；未能付诸实行的：*The government has been doing some **blue-sky thinking** on how to improve school standards.* 就如何提高学校的水平，政府仍然在作一些漫无边际的构想。

blue·stock·ing /ˈbluːstɒkɪŋ; *NAmE* -stɑːk-/ *noun* (*old-fashioned, sometimes disapproving*) a well-educated woman who is more interested in ideas and studying than in traditionally FEMININE things 才女（受过相当教育，不喜欢传统女性生活）

bluesy /ˈbluːzi/ *adj.* having the slow strong rhythms and sad mood of blues music 布鲁斯音乐的；有布鲁斯音乐情调的；蓝调的：*a bluesy sound/voice* 布鲁斯音乐风格 / 歌声

ˈ**blue tit** *noun* a small European bird of the TIT family, with a blue head, wings and tail and yellow parts underneath 蓝山雀（欧洲小山雀，头顶、两翼及尾部呈蓝色，胸腹部黄色）

Blue·tooth™ /ˈbluːtuːθ/ *noun* [U] a radio technology that makes it possible for mobile/cell phones, computers and other electronic devices to be linked over short distances, without needing to be connected by wires 蓝牙（用于手机、计算机等电子设备的短距离无线连接技术）：*Bluetooth-enabled devices* 蓝牙设备

ˌ**blue ˈwhale** *noun* a type of WHALE that is the largest known living animal 蓝鲸

bluff /blʌf/ *verb, noun, adj.*

■ ***verb*** [I, T] ~ (sth) to try to make sb believe that you will do sth that you do not really intend to do, or that you know sth that you do not really know 虚张声势；唬人；吹牛：*I don't think he'll shoot—I think he's just bluffing.* 我认为他不会开枪，我想他不过是在吓唬人。

IDM ˌ**bluff it ˈout** to get out of a difficult situation by continuing to tell lies, especially when people suspect you are not being honest （受到怀疑后）继续蒙混过关，靠说谎摆脱困境

PHR V ˈ**bluff sb into doing sth** to make sb do sth by tricking them, especially by pretending you have more experience, knowledge, etc. than you really have 靠吹牛哄人… ˌ**bluff your way ˈin/ˈout/ˈthrough** | ˌ**bluff your way ˈinto/ˈout of/ˈthrough sth** to succeed in dealing with a difficult situation by making other people believe sth which is not true 蒙混过关：*She successfully bluffed her way through the interview.* 她胡乱吹嘘，成功地通过了面试。

■ ***noun*** **1** [U, C] an attempt to trick sb by making them believe that you will do sth when you really have no intention of doing it, or that you know sth when you do not, in fact, know it 虚张声势的做法；唬人：*It was just a game of bluff.* 那只不过是唬人的把戏。◇ *He said he would resign if he didn't get more money, but it was only a bluff.* 他说如果不给他加薪他就辞职，但那不过是虚张声势而已。➲ SEE ALSO DOUBLE BLUFF **2** [C] a steep CLIFF or slope, especially by the sea or a river （尤指海边或河边的）峭壁，陡岸 IDM SEE CALL *v.*

■ ***adj.*** (of people or their manner 人或态度) very direct and cheerful, with good intentions, although not always very polite 直率豪爽的（尽管有时不够礼貌）：*Beneath his bluff exterior he was a sensitive man.* 他外表大大咧咧，但其实是个敏感的人。

blu·ish /ˈbluːɪʃ/ *adj.* fairly blue in colour 带蓝色的；有点蓝的：*a bluish-green carpet* 绿中带蓝的地毯

blun·der /ˈblʌndə(r)/ *noun, verb*

■ ***noun*** a stupid or careless mistake 愚蠢（或粗心）的错误：*to make a terrible blunder* 犯大错 ◇ *a series of political blunders* 一连串政治失误

■ ***verb*** [I] to make a stupid or careless mistake 犯愚蠢的（或粗心的）错误：*The government had blundered in its handling of the affair.* 政府在这件事的处理上犯了大错。

PHR V ˌ**blunder aˈbout, aˈround, etc.** to move around in an awkward way, knocking into things, as if you cannot see where you are going 跌跌撞撞 ˌ**blunder ˈinto sth 1** to knock into sth because you are awkward or are not able to see （因笨拙或看不见）撞上某物 **2** to find yourself in a difficult or unpleasant situation by accident 无意中陷入（困境）；偶然遇到（尴尬事） ˌ**blunder ˈon** to continue doing sth in a careless or stupid way 一再粗心（或荒唐）地做某事；一错再错

blun·der·buss /ˈblʌndəbʌs; *NAmE* -dərb-/ *noun* an old type of gun with a wide end （老式）大口径枪；喇叭枪

blunt /blʌnt/ *adj., verb*

■ ***adj.*** (**blunt·er, blunt·est**) **1** without a sharp edge or point 不锋利的；钝的：*a blunt knife* 钝刀子 ◇ *This pencil's blunt!* 这支铅笔不尖了！◇ *The police said he had been hit with a **blunt instrument**.* 警方说他遭到了钝器袭击。OPP sharp **2** (of a person or remark 人或话语) very direct; saying exactly what you think without trying to be polite 嘴直的；直言的：*She has a reputation for blunt speaking.* 她说话出了名地直截了当。◇ *To be blunt, your work is appalling.* 坦率地说，你的活干得糟透了。➲ SYNONYMS AT HONEST ▶ **blunt·ness** *noun* [U]

■ ***verb*** **1 ~ sth** to make sth weaker or less effective 使减弱；使降低效应：*Age hadn't blunted his passion for adventure.* 岁月没有冲淡他的冒险激情。**2 ~ sth** to make a point or an edge less sharp 使（尖端、刃）变钝

blunt·ly /ˈblʌntli/ *adv.* in a very direct way, without trying to be polite or kind 直言地；单刀直入地：***To put it bluntly**, I want a divorce.* 坦白地说，我要离婚。◇ *'Is she dead?' he asked bluntly.* "她死了吗？"他冲口而出。

blur /blɜː(r)/ *noun, verb*

■ ***noun*** [usually sing.] **1** a shape that you cannot see clearly, often because it is moving too fast （移动的）模糊形状：*His arm was a rapid blur of movement as he struck.* 他出击时胳膊快速一晃，令人眼花缭乱。◇ *Everything is a blur when I take my glasses off.* 我摘掉眼镜什么都变得模糊不清。**2** something that you cannot remember clearly 模糊的记忆：*The events of that day were just a blur.* 那天发生的事只剩一片模糊的记忆。

■ ***verb*** (-rr-) **1** [I, T] if the shape or outline of sth **blurs**, or if sth **blurs** it, it becomes less clear and sharp （使）变得模糊不清：*The writing blurred and danced before his eyes.* 字迹变得一片模糊，在他眼前晃动。◇ **~ sth** *The mist blurred the edges of the buildings.* 建筑群在薄雾中若隐若现。**2** [T, I] ~ (sth) if sth **blurs** your eyes or vision, or your eyes or vision **blur**, you cannot see things clearly （使）视线模糊；（使）看不清：*Tears blurred her eyes.* 泪水模糊了她的视线。**3** [I, T] to become or make sth become difficult to distinguish clearly （使）难以区分：*The differences between art and life seem to have blurred.* 艺术和生活之间的差别似乎已变得模糊不清。◇ **~ sth** *She tends to **blur the distinction** between her friends and her colleagues.* 她往往将朋友和同事混淆起来。

Blu-ray /ˈbluː reɪ/ *noun* [U] technology that uses a blue LASER (= a very strong line of light) to record and play large amounts of high quality data on a type of DVD 蓝光（用蓝色激光刻录并播放大容量高品质资料的光盘技术）：*These high definition movies are all out on Blu-ray.* 这些高清晰度影片全部以蓝光技术推出。

ˈ**Blu-ray Disc™** *noun* (*abbr.* **BD, BD-ROM**) a type of DVD on which large amounts of data can be stored, used especially to play high quality video 蓝光光盘，蓝光光碟（尤用以播放高品质影像）

B

blurb /blɜːb; *NAmE* blɜːrb/ *noun* a short description of a book, a new product, etc., written by the people who have produced it, that is intended to attract your attention and make you want to buy it （书的）宣传语；（生产商等的）产品推介

blurred /blɜːd; *NAmE* blɜːrd/ *adj.* **1** not clear; without a clear outline or shape 模糊不清的：*She suffered from dizziness and blurred vision.* 她饱受头晕目眩之苦。◇ *a* ***blurred image/picture*** 模糊的图像 / 照片 **2** difficult to remember clearly 记不清的：*blurred memories* 模糊的记忆 **3** difficult to distinguish, so that differences are not clear 难以区分的；模棱两可的：***blurred distinctions/boundaries*** 含混不清的区别 / 界线

blurry /ˈblɜːri/ *adj.* (*informal*) without a clear outline; not clear 模糊不清的：*blurry, distorted photographs* 模糊走样的照片 ◇ (*figurative*) *a blurry policy* 不明确的政策

blurt /blɜːt; *NAmE* blɜːrt/ *verb* **~ sth** (**out**) | **~ that…** | **~ what, how, etc….** | **+ speech** to say sth suddenly and without thinking carefully enough 脱口而出：*She blurted it out before I could stop her.* 我还没来得及制止，她已脱口而出。➲ SYNONYMS AT CALL

blush /blʌʃ/ *verb, noun*

▪ ***verb*** **1** [I] to become red in the face because you are embarrassed or ashamed （因尴尬或害羞）脸红，涨红了脸 **SYN go red**：**~ (with sth) (at sth)** *to blush with embarrassment/shame* 尴尬 / 羞愧得面颊绯红 ◇ *She blushed furiously at the memory of the conversation.* 她一想起那次谈话就气得满脸通红。◇ **+ adj./noun** *He blushed scarlet at the thought.* 他想起那事便面红耳赤。 **2** [T] **~ to do sth** to be ashamed or embarrassed about sth （因某事）羞愧，尴尬：*I blush to admit it, but I quite like her music.* 不好意思，但我得承认我很喜欢她的音乐。

▪ ***noun*** **1** [C] the red colour that spreads over your face when you are embarrassed or ashamed （因难堪、羞愧）面部泛起的红晕：*She felt a warm blush rise to her cheeks.* 她感到双颊热辣辣的。◇ *He turned away to hide his blushes.* 他转过身去，不让人看见他脸红。 **2** [U, C] (*NAmE*) = BLUSHER **IDM** SEE SPARE *v.*

blush·er /ˈblʌʃə(r)/ (*NAmE also* **blush**) *noun* [U, C] a coloured cream or powder that some people put on their cheeks to give them more colour 胭脂 ➲ WORDFINDER NOTE AT MAKE-UP ➲ VISUAL VOCAB PAGE V65

blus·ter /ˈblʌstə(r)/ *verb* **1** [T, I] **~ (sth)** | **+ speech** to talk in an aggressive or threatening way, but with little effect 气势汹汹地说话，咄咄逼人，威吓（但效果不大）：*'I don't know what you're talking about,' he blustered.* "我不知道你到底在说什么！"他气势汹汹地说。◇ *a blustering bully* 咄咄逼人的恶霸 **2** [I] (of the wind 风) to blow violently 狂吹；咆哮 ▶ **blus·ter** *noun* [U]：*I wasn't frightened by what he said—it was all bluster.* 我没有被他的话吓倒，那不过是在吓唬人。

blus·tery /ˈblʌstəri/ *adj.* (of weather 天气) with strong winds 狂风大作的：***blustery winds/conditions*** 狂风；大风天气 ◇ *The day was cold and blustery.* 日间天气寒冷，狂风呼啸。

Blu-tack™ /ˈbluː tæk/ *noun* [U] a blue sticky material used to attach paper to walls 蓝丁胶

Blvd. *abbr.* (used in written addresses 用于书写地址) BOULEVARD 要道；大街

BMI /ˌbiː em ˈaɪ/ *abbr.* BODY MASS INDEX 体重指数

BMOC /ˌbiː em əʊ ˈsiː; *NAmE* oʊ/ *abbr.* (*US*) BIG MAN ON CAMPUS 校园大人物（大学里成功而受欢迎的男生）

ˈB-movie (*also* **ˈB-picture**) *noun* a film/movie which is made cheaply and is not considered to be of high quality 二流电影；劣质电影：*a B-movie actress* 一个二流电影女演员

BMus (*NAmE* **B.Mus**) /ˌbiː ˈmʌz/ *noun* the abbreviation for 'Bachelor of Music' (a university degree in music that is usually a first degree) 音乐学士（全写为 Bachelor of Music，通常为大学音乐专业的初级学位）

BMX /ˌbiː em ˈeks/ *noun* **1** [C] a strong bicycle which can be used for riding on rough ground 小轮车；越野自行车 **2** (*also* **BMXing**) [U] the sport of racing BMX bicycles on rough ground 小轮车越野赛

bn *abbr.* (*BrE*) (in writing 书写形式) BILLION 十亿

the BNP /ˌbiː en ˈpiː/ *abbr.* the British National Party (a small British political party on the extreme right) 英国国家党（极右派小政党）

BO /ˌbiː ˈəʊ; *NAmE* ˈoʊ/ *noun* [U] the abbreviation for 'body odour' (an unpleasant smell from a person's body, especially of sweat) 汗臭，体臭（全写为 body odour）：*She's got BO.* 她有狐臭。

boa /ˈbəʊə; *NAmE* ˈboʊə/ *noun* **1** = BOA CONSTRICTOR **2** = FEATHER BOA

boa constrictor /ˈbəʊə kənstrɪktə(r); *NAmE* ˈboʊə/ (*also* **boa**) *noun* a large S American snake that kills animals for food by winding its long body around them and crushing them 巨蚺（南美蟒，捕食时把猎物缢死）

boar /bɔː(r)/ *noun* (*pl.* **boar** or **boars**) **1** (*also* ˌ**wild ˈboar**) a wild pig 野猪 **2** a male pig that has not been CASTRATED 未阉的公猪 ➲ COMPARE HOG *n.*, SOW[2]

board 🔑 /bɔːd; *NAmE* bɔːrd/ *noun, verb*

▪ ***noun***

• **PIECE OF WOOD, ETC.** 木板等 **1** 🔑 [C, U] a long thin piece of strong hard material, especially wood, used, for example, for making floors, building walls and roofs and making boats 板；（尤指）木板：*He had ripped up the carpet, leaving only the bare boards.* 他用力扯去了地毯，只剩下裸露的地板。➲ SEE ALSO CHIPBOARD, FLOORBOARD, HARDBOARD, SKIRTING BOARD **2** 🔑 [C] (especially in compounds 尤用于构成复合词) a piece of wood, or other strong material, that is used for a special purpose …用木板（或板材）：*a blackboard* 黑板 ◇ *I'll write it up on the board.* 我会把它写在黑板上。◇ (*BrE*) *a noticeboard* 布告牌 ◇ (*NAmE*) *a bulletin board* 布告牌 ◇ *The exam results went up on the board.* 考试成绩张贴在布告牌上。◇ *a diving board* 跳水板 ◇ *She jumped off the top board.* 她从高层跳板上跳了下来。◇ *a chessboard* 棋盘 ◇ *He removed the figure from the board.* 他从黑板上抹去了那个数字。➲ SEE ALSO MESSAGE BOARD

• **IN WATER SPORTS** 水上运动 **3** [C] = BODYBOARD, SAILBOARD, SURFBOARD

• **GROUP OF PEOPLE** 班子 **4** 🔑 [C+sing./pl. v.] a group of people who have power to make decisions and control a company or other organization （公司或其他机构的）董事会，委员会，理事会：*She has a seat on the board of directors.* 她是董事会成员。◇ *The board is/are unhappy about falling sales.* 董事会对销售额下降感到不满。◇ *members of the board* 董事会成员 ◇ *discussions at board level* 董事会讨论 ◇ *the* ***academic board*** (= for example, of a British university) 高等学校教务委员会 ◇ (*NAmE*) *the* ***Board of Education*** (= a group of elected officials who are in charge of all the public schools in a particular area) 管理地方公立学校的教育委员会

• **ORGANIZATION** 机构 **5** [C] used in the name of some organizations （用于机构名称）：*the Welsh Tourist Board* (= responsible for giving tourist information) 威尔士旅游局

• **MEALS** 膳食 **6** [U] the meals that are provided when you stay in a hotel, GUEST HOUSE, etc.; what you pay for the meals （旅馆、招待所等提供的）伙食，膳食；膳食费用：*He pays £90 a week board and lodging.* 他每周的膳宿花费为 90 英镑。➲ SEE ALSO BED AND BOARD, FULL BOARD, HALF BOARD

• **EXAMS** 考试 **7 boards** [pl.] (*old-fashioned, US*) exams that you take when you apply to go to college in the US （美国大学的）入学考试

• **IN THEATRE** 剧院 **8 the boards** [pl.] (*old-fashioned, informal*) the stage in a theatre 舞台：*His play is on the boards on Broadway.* 他的戏剧搬上了百老汇的舞台。◇ *She's treading the boards* (= working as an actress). 她当上了演员。

• ICE HOCKEY 冰球运动 **9 the boards** [pl.] (*NAmE*) the low wooden wall surrounding the area where a game of ICE HOCKEY is played（冰球场周围的）界墙：*The puck went wide, hitting the boards.* 冰球击偏了，打在了界墙上。
HELP There are many other compounds ending in **board**. You will find them at their place in the alphabet. 以 board 结尾的复合词还有很多，可在各字母中的适当位置查到。

IDM **a,cross the 'board** involving everyone or everything in a company, an industry, etc. 全体；整体；全面：*The industry needs more investment across the board.* 这一行业需要全面增加投资。◇ *an across-the-board wage increase* 全体人员的加薪 **,go by the 'board** (of plans or principles 计划或原则) to be rejected or ignored; to be no longer possible 被废弃；被忽视：*All her efforts to be polite went by the board and she started to shout.* 她力图保持和颜悦色的一切努力都白费了，于是她开始大喊大叫。**on 'board** 🔑 **1** on or in a ship, an aircraft or a train 在船上（或飞机上、火车上）SYN **aboard**: *Have the passengers gone on board yet?* 乘客们登机了吗？**2** giving your support to an idea or a project 支持：*We must get more sponsors on board.* 我们必须得到更多赞助商的支持。◇ *You need to bring the whole staff on board.* 你需要取得全体员工的支持。**take sth on 'board** to accept and understand an idea or a suggestion 采纳，接纳（主意、建议）：*I told her what I thought, but she didn't take my advice on board.* 我把我的想法告诉了她，可她没有听取我的建议。➲ MORE AT SWEEP *v.*

■ *verb*

• GET ON PLANE/SHIP, ETC. 上飞机 / 船等 **1** 🔑 [I, T] (*formal*) to get on a ship, train, plane, bus, etc. 上船（或火车、飞机、公共汽车等）：*Passengers are waiting to board.* 乘客们正在候机。◇ **~ sth** *The ship was boarded by customs officials.* 海关官员登上了这艘船。**2** 🔑 [I] **be boarding** when a plane or ship **is boarding**, it is ready for passengers to get on 让乘客登机（或上船等）：*Flight BA193 for Paris is now boarding at Gate 37.* 乘 BA193 航班飞往巴黎的乘客请于 37 号登机口登机。➲ WORDFINDER NOTE AT AIRPORT

• LIVE SOMEWHERE 住宿 **3** [I] **~ at…/with sb** to live and take meals in sb's home, in return for payment 付费（在某人家里）膳宿：*She always had one or two students boarding with her.* 她的家总有一两名寄宿学生。**4** [I] to live at a school during the school year （在学校）寄宿

PHR V **,board sb 'out** (*BrE*) to arrange for sb to live somewhere away from their place of work, school, etc. in return for payment 把（某人）安排在外膳宿 **,board sth↔'up** to cover a window, door, etc. with wooden boards 用木板封住（门窗等）

board·er /ˈbɔːdə(r); *NAmE* ˈbɔːrd-/ *noun* (*especially BrE*) **1** a child who lives at school and goes home for the holidays 在学校寄宿的学生；寄宿生：*boarders and day pupils* 寄宿生和走读生 **2** a person who pays money to live in a room in sb else's house 付费寄住者；寄膳宿者 SYN **lodger**

'board game *noun* any game played on a board, often using DICE and small pieces that are moved around 棋类游戏

board·ing /ˈbɔːdɪŋ; *NAmE* ˈbɔːrd-/ *noun* [U] **1** long pieces of wood that are put together to make a wall, etc. （做墙等的）木板；板材 **2** the arrangement by which school students live at their school, going home during the holidays （学生的）寄宿：*boarding fees* 寄宿费用

'boarding card (*BrE*) (*also* **'boarding pass** *NAmE, BrE*) *noun* a card that you show before you get on a plane or boat 登机卡；登船卡

'boarding house *noun* a private house where people can pay for accommodation and meals 提供膳宿的私人住宅

'boarding kennel *noun* [usually pl.] a place where people can leave their dogs to be taken care of when they go on holiday/vacation 狗的临时寄养所 ➲ SEE ALSO KENNEL (2)

'boarding school *noun* a school where children can live during the school year 寄宿学校 ➲ COMPARE DAY SCHOOL (1) ➲ MORE LIKE THIS 9, page R26

board·room /ˈbɔːdruːm; -rʊm; *NAmE* ˈbɔːrd-/ *noun* a room in which the meetings of the board of a company (= the group of people who control it) are held 董事会会议室：*a boardroom row* 董事会会议上的争吵

board·sail·ing /ˈbɔːdseɪlɪŋ; *NAmE* ˈbɔːrd-/ *noun* [U] = WINDSURFING

board·walk /ˈbɔːdwɔːk; *NAmE* ˈbɔːrd-/ *noun* (*especially NAmE*) a path made of wooden boards, especially on a beach or near water 木板人行道（尤指海滩或岸边的）

boast /bəʊst; *NAmE* boʊst/ *verb, noun*

■ *verb* **1** [I, T] to talk with too much pride about sth that you have or can do 自夸；自吹自擂：*I don't want to boast, but I can actually speak six languages.* 不是我吹嘘，我确实能讲六种语言。◇ **~ about sth** *She is always boasting about how wonderful her children are.* 她总是夸耀她的孩子多么出色。◇ **~ of sth** *He openly boasted of his skill as a burglar.* 他公然炫耀他的盗窃手法。◇ **~ that…** *Sam boasted that she could beat anyone at poker.* 萨姆吹嘘说打扑克牌谁都不是她的对手。◇ **+ speech** *'I won!' she boasted.* "我赢了！"她夸口道。**2** [T] (not used in the progressive tenses 不用于进行时) **~ sth** to have sth that is impressive and that you can be proud of 有（值得自豪的东西）：*The hotel also boasts two swimming pools and a golf course.* 那家酒店还有两个游泳池和一个高尔夫球场。

■ *noun* **~ (that…)** (*often disapproving*) something that a person talks about in a very proud way, often to seem more important or clever 夸耀；夸口：*Despite his boasts that his children were brilliant, neither of them went to college.* 尽管他夸赞他的两个孩子聪明，他们却都没念上大学。◇ *It was her* **proud boast** *that she had never missed a day's work because of illness.* 她引以自豪的是她从未因病而耽误过一天工作。

boast·ful /ˈbəʊstfl; *NAmE* ˈboʊstfl/ *adj.* (*disapproving*) talking about yourself in a very proud way 自吹自擂的；自夸的：*I tried to emphasize my good points without sounding boastful.* 我在强调自己的优点时尽量不让人觉得我是在自我吹嘘。

boat 🔑 /bəʊt; *NAmE* boʊt/ *noun* **1** 🔑 a vehicle (smaller than a ship) that travels on water, moved by OARS, sails or a motor 小船；汽艇；舟：*a* **rowing/sailing boat** 划艇；帆船 ◇ *a fishing boat* 渔船 ◇ *You can take a* **boat trip** *along the coast.* 你可以乘船沿海岸旅游一趟。➲ SEE ALSO CANAL BOAT, LIFEBOAT, MOTORBOAT, POWERBOAT, SPEEDBOAT, STEAMBOAT **2** 🔑 any ship （泛指）船：*'How are you going to France?' 'We're going* **by boat** *(= by* FERRY*).'* "你们怎么去法国？""我们乘船去。" ➲ VISUAL VOCAB PAGES V59-61 ➲ SEE ALSO GRAVY BOAT, SAUCE BOAT

IDM **be in the same 'boat** to be in the same difficult situation 处于同样的困境 ➲ MORE AT BURN *v.*, FLOAT *v.*, MISS *v.*, PUSH *v.*, ROCK *v.*

boat·er /ˈbəʊtə(r); *NAmE* ˈboʊt-/ *noun* a hard STRAW hat with a flat top 平顶硬草帽 ➲ VISUAL VOCAB PAGE V70

boat·hook /ˈbəʊthʊk; *NAmE* ˈboʊt-/ *noun* a long pole with a hook at one end, used for pulling or pushing boats 撑篙钩杆（一端有钩，用于推拉船只）

boat·house /ˈbəʊthaʊs; *NAmE* ˈboʊt-/ *noun* a building beside a river or lake for keeping a boat in 船库

boat·ing /ˈbəʊtɪŋ; *NAmE* ˈboʊtɪŋ/ *noun* [U] the activity of using a small boat for pleasure 划船（运动或消遣）：*to go boating* 去划船 ◇ *Local activities include walking, boating and golf.* 当地的活动包括散步、划船以及打高尔夫球。

boat·man /ˈbəʊtmən; *NAmE* ˈboʊt-/ *noun* (*pl.* **-men** /-mən/) a man who earns money from small boats, either by carrying passengers or goods on them, or by renting them out 靠小船营生的人；摆渡者；小船出租人

'boat people *noun* [pl.] people who escape from their own country in small boats to try to find safety in another country 船民（乘小船逃到他国的难民）

boat·swain /'bəʊsn; *NAmE* 'boʊ-/ *noun* = BOSUN

'boat train *noun* a train that takes passengers to or from a place where a boat arrives or leaves 港口联运列车；港口接驳列车

boat·yard /'bəʊtjɑːd; *NAmE* 'boʊtjɑːrd/ *noun* a place where boats are built, repaired or kept 造船厂；修船厂；船坞

Bob /bɒb; *NAmE* bɑːb/ *noun*

IDM **Bob's your 'uncle** (*BrE, informal*) used to say how easy and quick it is to do a particular task 易如反掌：*Press here and Bob's your uncle! It's disappeared.* 按一下这里就成了！消失了。

bob /bɒb; *NAmE* bɑːb/ *verb, noun*

■ *verb* (**-bb-**) **1** [I, T] to move or make sth move quickly up and down, especially in water （使在水中）上下快速移动，摆动：**~ up and down** *Tiny boats bobbed up and down in the harbour.* 小船在港湾中颠簸。◇ **~ sth (up and down)** *She bobbed her head nervously.* 她紧张地不断点头。**2** [T] **~ sth** to cut sb's hair so that it is the same length all the way around 把（头发）剪成短头发 ➲ MORE LIKE THIS 36, page R29

PHR V **,bob 'up** to come to the surface suddenly （突然）冒出：*The dark head of a seal bobbed up a few yards away.* 在几码远处一只海豹的黑脑袋猛地钻出水面。

■ *noun* **1** a quick movement down and up of your head and body 快速的点头（或鞠躬）：*a bob of the head* 点头 **2** a style of a woman's hair in which it is cut the same length all the way around （女式）齐短发型：*She wears her hair in a bob.* 她留齐短发。➲ VISUAL VOCAB PAGE V65 **3** (*pl.* **bob**) (*informal*) an old British coin, the SHILLING, worth 12 old pence 先令（英国旧制硬币，等于 12 旧便士）：*That'll cost a few bob* (= a lot of money). 那东西很值钱。**4** = BOBSLEIGH IDM SEE BIT

bobbed /bɒbd; *NAmE* bɑːbd/ *adj.* (of hair 头发) cut so that it hangs loosely to the level of the chin all around the back and sides 齐而短的

bob·ber /'bɒbə(r); *NAmE* 'bɑːb-/ *noun* **1** a floating object used in fishing to hold the hook at the right depth （钓鱼用的）浮子，浮标 **2** (*BrE*) a person who rides on a BOBSLEIGH 乘大雪橇的人

bob·bin /'bɒbɪn; *NAmE* 'bɑːbɪn/ *noun* a small device on which you wind thread, used, for example, in a sewing machine 线轴；绕线筒

bob·ble /'bɒbl; *NAmE* 'bɑːbl/ *noun, verb*

■ *noun* **1** (*BrE*) a small, soft ball, usually made of wool, that is used especially for decorating clothes 小绒球，小羊毛球（尤用作衣服缀饰）SYN **pom-pom**：*a woolly hat with a bobble on top* 帽顶带一只小绒球的羊毛帽子 ➲ VISUAL VOCAB PAGE V70 **2** a piece of elastic with a small ball or other decoration on it, used to tie hair back 装饰发圈（带有小球或其他饰物）

■ *verb* (*informal*) **1** [I] **+ adv./prep.** to move along the ground with small BOUNCES 弹跳着向前移动：*The ball somehow bobbled into the net.* 球不知怎么在地上弹了几下钻入网窝。**2** [T] **~ sth** (*NAmE*) to drop a ball or to fail to stop it 漏球；漏接球；没有停住球：*She tried to catch the ball but bobbled it.* 她想要接球，但没有接住。**3** [I] (*BrE, informal*) (of a piece of clothing, especially one made of wool 衣服，尤指毛料的) to become covered in very small balls of FIBRE 起绒线球

bobby /'bɒbi; *NAmE* 'bɑːbi/ *noun* (*pl.* **-ies**) (*old-fashioned, BrE, informal*) a police officer 警察 ORIGIN Named after Sir Robert Peel, the politician who created London's police force in the 19th century. **Bobby** is a familiar form of 'Robert'. 源自罗伯特·皮尔爵士的名字。他于 19 世纪创建了伦敦的警察队伍。Bobby 是 Robert 的昵称。

,bobby-'dazzler *noun* (*old-fashioned, BrE, informal*) an excellent or very special person or thing 出色的人（或事物）；与众不同的人（或事物）

'bobby pin (*NAmE*) (*BrE* **hair·grip**, **grip**, **kirby grip**) *noun* a small thin piece of metal or plastic folded in the middle, used by women for holding their hair in place 发夹 ➲ COMPARE HAIRPIN

'bobby socks *noun* [pl.] short white socks worn with a dress or skirt, especially by girls and young women in the US in the 1940s and 50s （20 世纪 40 和 50 年代美国少女和年轻妇女爱穿的）白色短袜

bob·cat /'bɒbkæt; *NAmE* 'bɑːb-/ *noun* a N American wild cat 短尾猫，红猫（北美野猫）

bobs /bɒbz; *NAmE* bɑːbz/ *noun* [pl.] IDM SEE BIT

bob·sleigh /'bɒbsleɪ; *NAmE* 'bɑːb-/ (*BrE*) (*NAmE* **bob·sled** /'bɒbsled; *NAmE* 'bɑːb-/) (*also* **bob**) *noun* a racing SLEDGE (= a vehicle for two or more people that slides over snow) 大雪橇（供两人或以上比赛用）➲ VISUAL VOCAB PAGE V52

bob·tail /'bɒbteɪl; *NAmE* 'bɑːbteɪl/ *noun* **1** a dog, cat or horse with a tail that has been cut short 短尾狗（或猫、马）**2** a tail that has been cut short 截短的尾巴；短尾

bod /bɒd; *NAmE* bɑːd/ *noun* (*informal*) **1** (*BrE*) a person 人：*She's a bit of an odd bod* (= rather strange). 她是个相当古怪的人。**2** a person's body 人体；身体：*He's got a great bod.* 他是个大块头。

boda boda /,bəʊdə 'bəʊdə; *NAmE* ,boʊdə 'boʊdə/ *noun* (*EAfrE*) (in some countries) a type of motorcycle or bicycle with a space for a passenger or for carrying goods, often used as a taxi 波达波达（东非一些国家常用作出租车的摩托车或自行车）：*boys on boda bodas riding on Kampala's streets* 坎帕拉街头开摩的的男孩

bo·da·cious /bəʊ'deɪʃəs; *NAmE* boʊ-/ *adj.* (*informal, especially NAmE*) **1** excellent; extremely good 出色的；非凡的；非常棒的 **2** willing to take risks or to do sth shocking 敢于冒险的；大胆的 SYN **audacious**

bode /bəʊd; *NAmE* boʊd/ *verb*

IDM **bode 'well/'ill (for sb/sth)** (*formal*) to be a good/bad sign for sb/sth （对某人／某事）是吉兆，是凶兆 SYN **augur**：*These figures do not bode well for the company's future.* 这些数据对于公司的前景不是个好兆头。

bodge /bɒdʒ; *NAmE* bɑːdʒ/ *verb* **~ sth (up/together)** (*BrE, informal*) to make or repair sth in a way that is not as good as it should be 粗制滥造；拙劣地修补

Bodhi·sat·tva /,bɒdɪ'sɑːtvə; *NAmE* ,boʊd-/ *noun* (in Mahayana Buddhism 大乘佛教) a person who is able to reach NIRVANA (= a state of peace and happiness) but who delays doing this because of the suffering of other humans 菩提萨埵；菩萨

bodh·rán /'baʊrɑːn; *NAmE* 'bɔːr-/ *noun* (*IrishE*) a shallow Irish drum that you hold sideways in your hand and play with a short wooden stick 宝思兰鼓（爱尔兰小鼓）

bod·ice /'bɒdɪs; *NAmE* 'bɑːdɪs/ *noun* the top part of a woman's dress, above the waist 连衣裙上身

'bodice-ripper *noun* (*informal*) a romantic novel or film/movie with a lot of sex in it, which is set in the past （以旧时生活为背景的）性爱小说（或电影）

bod·ily /'bɒdɪli; *NAmE* 'bɑːd-/ *adj., adv.*

■ *adj.* [only before noun] connected with the human body 人体的；身体的：*bodily functions/changes/needs* 身体的机能／变化／需要 ◇ *bodily fluids* 体液 ◇ *bodily harm* (= physical injury) 对身体的伤害

■ *adv.* **1** by moving the whole of sb's body; by force 移动全身地；用力地：*The force of the blast hurled us bodily to the ground.* 爆炸的力量把我们震落在地上。◇ *He lifted her bodily into the air.* 他把她整个人举到空中。**2** in one piece; completely 整个地；完全地：*The monument was moved bodily to a new site.* 整个纪念碑被迁到了新的地点。

bod·kin /'bɒdkɪn; *NAmE* 'bɑːd-/ *noun* a thick needle with no point 粗钝的缝针；大眼粗针；锥子

body /ˈbɒdi; *NAmE* ˈbɑːdi/ *noun* (*pl.* **-ies**)
- **OF PERSON/ANIMAL** 人；动物 **1** [C] the whole physical structure of a human or an animal 身体；躯体：*a **human/female/male/naked body*** 人 / 女性 / 男性 / 赤裸的身体 ◇ *parts of the body* 身体的部位 ◇ *His whole body was trembling.* 他浑身发抖。◇ ***body fat/weight/temperature/size/heat*** 身体的脂肪；体重；体温；身材；体热 **2** [C] the main part of a body not including the head, or not including the head, arms and legs 躯干：*She had injuries to her head and body.* 她的头上和身上都有伤。◇ *He has a large body, but thin legs.* 他身宽腿细。 **3** [C] the body of a dead person or animal 尸体；死尸：*a dead body* 一具尸体 ◇ *The family of the missing girl has been called in by the police to identify the body.* 失踪女孩的家人已被警察叫来认尸。
- **MAIN PART** 主体 **4** [sing.] **the ~ of sth** the main part of sth, especially a building, a vehicle or a book, an article, etc.（尤指建筑、车辆或书、文章等的）主体，主要部分：*the body of a plane* (= the central part where the seats are) 飞机机身 ◇ *the **main body** of the text* 课文的正文
- **GROUP OF PEOPLE** 集体 **5** [C+sing./pl. v.] a group of people who work or act together, often for an official purpose, or who are connected in some other way 团体；社团；群体：*a **regulatory** /**an advisory** /**a review body*** 监管 / 咨询 / 评审机构 ◇ *The governing body of the school is/are concerned about discipline.* 学校的管理部门很重视纪律问题。◇ *recognized professional bodies such as the Law Association* 诸如律师公会之类的获得承认的专业团体 ◇ *An independent body has been set up to investigate the affair.* 已成立了一个独立机构调查这件事。◇ *A large body of people will be affected by the tax cuts.* 将有一大批人受到减税的影响。◇ *The protesters marched **in a body** (= all together) to the White House.* 抗议者集体游行到白宫。◇ *a meeting of representatives of the student body and teaching staff* 全体学生和教师代表大会
- **LARGE AMOUNT** 大量 **6** [C] **~ of sth** a large amount or collection of sth 大量；大批；大堆：*a vast **body of** evidence/information/research* 大量证据 / 信息 / 研究 ◇ *large bodies of water* (= lakes or seas) 大片水域 ◇ *There is a powerful body of opinion against the ruling.* 裁决引起一片哗然。
- **OBJECT** 物体 **7** [C] (*formal*) an object 物体：***heavenly bodies*** (= stars, planets, etc.) 天体（恒星、行星等）◇ *an operation to remove a **foreign body*** (= sth that would not usually be there) *from a wound* 清除伤口异物的手术
- **OF DRINK/HAIR** 饮料；头发 **8** [U] the full strong flavour of alcoholic drinks or the thick healthy quality of sb's hair（酒的）浓香，香醇；（头发的）浓密：*a wine with plenty of body* 浓郁香醇的葡萄酒 ◇ *Regular use of conditioner is supposed to give your hair more body.* 据信经常使用护发素能使头发更浓密。
- **-BODIED** 有…躯体、浓郁味道等 **9** (in adjectives 构成形容词) having the type of body mentioned 有…的身体（或浓郁味道等）的：*full-bodied red wines* 醇厚的红葡萄酒 ◇ *soft-bodied insects* 软体昆虫 ➲ SEE ALSO **ABLE-BODIED** ➲ **MORE LIKE THIS** 8, page R25
- **CLOTHING** 衣服 **10** [C] (*BrE*) (*NAmE* **body·suit**) a piece of clothing which fits tightly over a woman's upper body and bottom, usually fastening between the legs 女紧身衣（通常止于大腿根）

IDM **body and ˈsoul** with all your energy 竭尽全力；全心全意：*She committed herself body and soul to fighting for the cause.* 她全心全意为这一事业而奋斗。 **keep body and ˈsoul together** to stay alive with just enough of the food, clothing, etc. that you need 勉强糊口；生活拮据 SYN **survive**：*They barely have enough money to keep body and soul together.* 他们仅有活命的钱。 ➲ MORE AT **BONE** *n.*, **DEAD** *adj.*, **SELL** *v.*

ˈbody armour (*especially US* **ˈbody armor**) *noun* [U] clothing worn by the police, etc. to protect themselves 防弹服，胸甲，防弹背心（警察等穿）

ˈbody bag *noun* a bag for carrying a dead body in, for example in a war 运尸袋

ˈbody blow *noun* something which has damaging effects on sb/sth, creating problems or causing severe disappointment 严重打击；挫折

body·board /ˈbɒdibɔːd; *NAmE* ˈbɑːdibɔːrd/ *noun* a short light type of SURFBOARD that you ride lying on your front 俯伏冲浪板；趴板 ▶ **body·board·ing** *noun* [U] ➲ **VISUAL VOCAB PAGE V54**

body·build·ing /ˈbɒdibɪldɪŋ; *NAmE* ˈbɑːdi-/ *noun* [U] the activity of doing regular exercises in order to make your muscles bigger and stronger 健身 ▶ **body·build·er** *noun*

ˈbody check *noun* (in ICE HOCKEY 冰球) an attempt to prevent a player's movement by blocking them with your shoulder or hip （用肩或臀的）身体阻截，身体阻挡

ˈbody clock *noun* the natural tendency that your body has to need sleep, food, etc. at particular times of the day （人体）生物钟

ˈbody double *noun* a person who takes part in a film/movie in place of an actor when the scene involves being naked, or using special or dangerous skills 替身演员 ➲ **WORDFINDER NOTE AT ACTOR**

body·guard /ˈbɒdigɑːd; *NAmE* ˈbɑːdigɑːrd/ *noun* [C+sing./pl. v.] a person or a group of people who are employed to protect sb 保镖，警卫（队）：*The President's bodyguard is/are armed.* 总统的护卫人员携带着武器。

ˈbody language *noun* [U] the process of communicating what you are feeling or thinking by the way you place and move your body rather than by words 身势语，肢体语言（通过姿势等表露思想感情）

ˈbody mass index *noun* (*abbr.* **BMI**) an approximate measure of whether sb weighs too much or too little, calculated by dividing their weight in kilograms by their height in metres squared 体重指数；身体质量指数

▼ **VOCABULARY BUILDING** 词汇扩充

Actions expressing emotions 表达情感的动作

Often parts of the body are closely linked to particular verbs. The combination of the verb and part of the body expresses an emotion or attitude. 身体部位常与某些动词紧密相连，搭配运用可反映特定的情感或态度。

action	part of body	you are…
bite	lips	nervous
clench	fist	angry, aggressive
click	fingers	trying to remember sth
click	tongue	annoyed
drum/tap	fingers	impatient
hang	head	ashamed
lick	lips	anticipating sth good, nervous
nod	head	agreeing
purse	lips	disapproving
raise	eyebrows	enquiring, surprised
scratch	head	puzzled
shake	head	disagreeing
shrug	shoulders	doubtful, indifferent
stamp	foot	angry
wrinkle	nose	feeling dislike or distaste
wrinkle	forehead	puzzled

For example 比如：*She bit her lip nervously.* 她紧张地咬嘴唇。◇ *He scratched his head and looked thoughtful.* 他挠着头显出一副深思的样子。◇ *I wrinkled my nose in disgust.* 我厌恶地皱起鼻子。◇ *She raised questioning eyebrows.* 她扬起眉毛表示怀疑。

B

ˈbody odour (*US* **ˈbody odor**) *noun* [U] (*abbr.* **BO**) an unpleasant smell from a person's body, especially of sweat 汗臭；体臭

ˈbody piercing (*also* **pier·cing**) *noun* [C] **1** [U] the making of holes in parts of the body in order to wear a ring, etc. as a decoration 穿体装饰： *tattooing and body piercing* 文身和穿体装饰 **2** [C] a hole made in a part of the body so that a ring, etc. can be worn （身体部位为戴首饰打的）孔，洞眼： *She had a nose stud and multiple ear piercings.* 她戴着一个鼻钉，还打了多个耳洞。

the ˌbody ˈpolitic *noun* [sing.] (*formal*) all the people of a particular nation considered as an organized political group 全体人民，国家（被视为政治集体）

ˈbody-popping *noun* [U] a way of dancing in which you make stiff movements like a ROBOT 机械舞（动作如机器人般僵硬的舞蹈风格）

ˈbody scanner *noun* an electronic machine, used at an airport, a prison, etc., that produces a picture of a person's body through their clothes on a screen so that illegal drugs or weapons can be found 人体扫描仪，全身扫描仪（用于机场、监狱等场所的安检仪器）

ˈbody search *noun* a search of a person's body, for example by the police or by a customs official, for drugs, weapons, etc. 搜身

ˈbody shop *noun* **1** the part of a car factory where the main bodies of the cars are made （汽车厂）车身制造车间 **2** a place where repairs are made to the main bodies of cars （汽车）车身维修厂

body·snatch·er /ˈbɒdisnætʃə(r); *NAmE* ˈbɑːdi-/ *noun* a person who stole bodies from GRAVEYARDS in the past, especially to sell for medical experiments （旧时为出售尸体供医学实验等的）墓地盗尸人

ˈbody stocking *noun* a piece of clothing that fits closely over the whole body from the neck to the ankles, often including the arms, worn for example by dancers 连裤紧身衣（常有袖）

body·suit /ˈbɒdisuːt; *BrE also* -sjuːt; *NAmE* ˈbɑːdisuːt/ **1** (*NAmE*) (*BrE* **body**) *noun* a piece of clothing which fits tightly over a woman's upper body and bottom, usually fastening between the legs 女紧身衣（通常止于大腿根） **2** a piece of clothing that fits closely over the body, including the arms and legs, worn by men and women for sports （运动时穿的）紧身衣裤

ˈbody swerve *noun* a sudden movement that you make to the side when running to avoid crashing into sb/sth （奔跑过程中为避免冲撞的）突然侧身

ˈbody warmer *noun* (*BrE*) a thick warm jacket without sleeves that you wear outdoors （户外穿的）无袖厚夹克 ➲ VISUAL VOCAB PAGE V66

body·work /ˈbɒdiwɜːk; *NAmE* ˈbɑːdiwɜːrk/ *noun* [U] the main outside structure of a vehicle, usually made of painted metal 车辆等的外壳，车身（通常为喷漆金属）

Boer /bɔː(r)/ *noun* **1** a South African whose family originally came from the Netherlands 布尔人（即荷裔南非人）： *the Boer War* (= the war between the Boers and the British, 1899–1902) 布尔战争（1899 至 1902 年间布尔人与英国人的战争） ➲ SEE ALSO AFRIKANER **2 boer** (*SAfrE*) a farmer 农民；农夫 **3 boer** (*SAfrE, disapproving*) used to refer to a member of the police or the army, especially in the past （旧时用以指）警察，当兵的

boere·wors /ˈbʊrəvɔːs; ˈbʊ-; *NAmE* -vɔːrs/ *noun* [U] (*SAfrE*) a spicy SAUSAGE that is prepared in a long piece and sold usually wound into a COIL (= a series of circles) 南非农夫香肠（盘起来出售的长条香肠）

bof·fin /ˈbɒfɪn; *NAmE* ˈbɑːfən/ *noun* (*BrE, informal*) a scientist, especially one doing research （尤指从事研究工作的）科学家，研究员

bog /bɒɡ; *NAmE* bɑːɡ; bɔːɡ/ *noun, verb*

■ ***noun*** **1** [C, U] (an area of) wet soft ground, formed of decaying plants 沼泽（地区）： *a peat bog* 泥炭沼 ➲ SEE ALSO BOGGY **2** [C] (*BrE, slang*) a toilet/bathroom 厕所；浴室： *Have you got any **bog roll** (= toilet paper)?* 你带卫生纸了吗？

■ ***verb*** **(-gg-)**

PHR V **ˌbog sth/sb ˈdown (in sth)** [usually passive] **1** to make sth sink into mud or wet ground 使某人/某物陷进烂泥（或泥沼）： *The tank became bogged down in mud.* 坦克陷入了烂泥中。 **2** to prevent sb from making progress in an activity 使停滞不前： *We mustn't get **bogged down** in details.* 我们一定不能因细节问题而拖慢进度。 **ˌbog ˈoff** (*BrE, taboo, slang*) only used in orders, to tell sb to go away （只用于命令）走开： *Bog off, I'm trying to sleep!* 走开，我要睡觉！

bogan /ˈbəʊɡən; *NAmE* ˈboʊ-/ *noun* (*AustralE, NZE, informal*) (*disapproving*) a rude or socially unacceptable person 粗人；怪人

bogey /ˈbəʊɡi; *NAmE* ˈboʊɡi/ *noun* **1** (*also* **bogy**) a thing that causes fear, often without reason （无缘无故）使人害怕的事物 **2** (*also* **bogy**) (*both BrE*) (*NAmE* **boo·ger**) (*informal*) a piece of dried MUCUS from inside your nose （干结的）鼻屎 **3** (*also* **bogy**) = BOGEYMAN **4** (in GOLF 高尔夫球) a score of one stroke over PAR (= the standard score for a hole) 柏忌（超出标准杆一杆） ➲ COMPARE BIRDIE (2), EAGLE (2)

bo·gey·man (*also* **bogy·man**) /ˈbəʊɡimæn; *NAmE* ˈboʊɡi-/ *noun* (*also* **bogey, bogy**) (*NAmE also* **boo·gey·man**) (*pl.* **-men**) an imaginary evil spirit that is used to frighten children （用以吓唬小孩的）鬼怪： *The bogeyman's coming!* 妖怪来了！

bog·gle /ˈbɒɡl; *NAmE* ˈbɑːɡl/ *verb* [I] **~ (at sth)** (*informal*) to be slow to do or accept sth because you are surprised or shocked by it （因吃惊而）不知所措，犹豫不决： *Even I boggle at the idea of spending so much money.* 一想到要花这么多钱，连我都有点犹豫。

IDM **sth boggles the ˈmind** (*also* **the mind ˈboggles**) (*informal*) if sth **boggles the mind** or **the mind boggles** at it, it is so unusual that people find it hard to imagine or accept 使人无法想象；使人难以接受： *The vastness of space really boggles the mind.* 太空之辽阔的确使人难以想象。◇ *'He says he's married to his cats!' 'The mind boggles!'* "他说他和他的那些猫结婚了！""难以置信！" ➲ COMPARE MIND-BOGGLING

boggy /ˈbɒɡi; *NAmE* ˈbɑːɡi; ˈbɔːɡi/ *adj.* (**bog·gier, bog·gi·est**) (of land 土地) soft and wet, like a BOG 松软潮湿的；沼泽般的： *boggy ground* 松软潮湿的地面

bogie /ˈbəʊɡi; *NAmE* ˈboʊɡi/ *noun* **1** (*especially BrE*) a frame with four or six wheels that forms part of a railway carriage/railroad car. The main body of the carriage/car usually rests on two bogies, one at each end. （轨道车辆）转向架 **2** (*IndE*) a railway carriage/railroad car （火车的）客车厢

BOGOF /ˈbɒɡɒf; *NAmE* ˈbɑːɡɑːf/ *abbr.* (*BrE, informal*) buy one, get one free (a type of special offer used in shops/stores) 买一送一： *BOGOF offers and bargains* 买一送一的优惠与便宜货

ˌbog-ˈstandard *adj.* (*BrE, informal*) ordinary; with no special features 普通的；一般的 SYN **average**

bogus /ˈbəʊɡəs; *NAmE* ˈboʊ-/ *adj.* pretending to be real or genuine 假的；伪造的 SYN **false**： *a bogus doctor/contract* 冒牌医生；伪造的合同 ◇ *bogus claims of injury by workers* 工人们虚报受伤情况索赔

bogy, bogy·man = BOGEY, BOGEYMAN

bo·he·mian /bəʊˈhiːmiən; *NAmE* boʊˈh-/ *noun* a person, often sb who is involved with the arts, who lives in a very informal way without following accepted rules of behaviour 行为举止不拘泥成规者；放荡不羁的艺术家 ▸ **bo·he·mian** *adj.*： *a **bohemian** existence/lifestyle* 放荡不羁的生活/生活方式

boho /ˈbəʊhəʊ; *NAmE* ˈboʊhoʊ/ (*also* ˈ**boho chic**) *noun* [U] a style of women's fashion that was popular at the beginning of the 21st century. It included loose tops, long skirts, wide belts and boots. 波西米亚风格（流行于 21 世纪初的女性着装风格，包括宽松上衣、长裙、宽腰带和靴子）

boh·rium /ˈbɔːriəm/ *noun* [U] (*symb.* **Bh**) a RADIOACTIVE chemical element. Bohrium is produced when atoms COLLIDE (= crash into each other). 铍（放射性化学元素）

boil /bɔɪl/ *verb, noun*

■ ***verb*** **1** [I, T] when a liquid **boils** or when you **boil** it, it is heated to the point where it forms bubbles and turns to steam or VAPOUR （使）沸腾；煮沸；烧开：*The water was bubbling and boiling away.* 水在咕嘟咕嘟地沸腾着。◇ **~ sth** *Boil plenty of salted water, then add the spaghetti.* 把足量的盐水烧开，再放入意大利面条。➲ VISUAL VOCAB PAGE V28 **2** [I, T] when a KETTLE, pan, etc. **boils** or when you **boil** a KETTLE, etc., it is heated until the water inside it **boils** （把壶、锅等里面的水）烧开：(*BrE*) *The kettle's boiling.* 壶开了。◇ **~ sth** *I'll boil the kettle and make some tea.* 我来烧壶开水泡点茶。◇ **+ adj.** *She left the gas on by mistake and the pan* ***boiled dry*** (= the water boiled until there was none left). 她忘了关煤气，结果把锅烧干了。 **3** [I, T] to cook or wash sth in boiling water; to be cooked or washed in boiling water 用沸水煮（或烫洗）；被煮（或烫洗）：*She put some potatoes on to boil.* 她煮了些土豆。◇ **~ sth** *boiled carrots/cabbage* 水煮胡萝卜 / 卷心菜 ◇ *to boil an egg for sb* 给某人煮个鸡蛋 ◇ **~ sb sth** *to boil sb an egg* 给某人煮个鸡蛋 ➲ COLLOCATIONS AT COOKING **4** [I] **~ (with sth)** if you **boil** with anger, etc. or anger, etc. **boils** inside you, you are very angry 怒火中烧；异常气愤：*He was boiling with rage.* 他怒不可遏。

IDM SEE BLOOD *n.*, WATCH *v.*

PHR V ˌ**boil** ˈ**down** | ˌ**boil sth**↔ˈ**down** to be reduced or to reduce sth by boiling （使）煮浓，熬浓 ˌ**boil sth** ˈ**down (to sth)** to make sth, especially information, shorter by leaving out the parts that are not important 概括；归纳；压缩：*The original speech I had written got boiled down to about ten minutes.* 我写的演讲原稿被压缩到了大约十分钟。 ˌ**boil** ˈ**down to sth** (not used in the progressive tenses 不用于进行时) (of a situation, problem, etc. 局势、问题等) to have sth as a main or basic part 归结为；基本问题是：*In the end,* ***what it all boils down to*** *is money, or the lack of it.* 问题的症结是钱，或者说是缺钱。 ˌ**boil** ˈ**over** **1** (of liquid 液体) to boil and flow over the side of a pan, etc. 煮溢；潽出 **2** (*informal*) to become very angry 怒火中烧；大怒 **3** (of a situation, an emotion, etc. 局势、情绪等) to change into sth more dangerous or violent 恶化；爆发 **SYN** **explode**：*Racial tension finally boiled over in the inner city riots.* 种族间的紧张状态最终演化成了内城区的暴乱。 ˌ**boil** ˈ**up** if a situation or an emotion **boils up**, it becomes dangerous, worrying, etc. （局势、情绪等）进入危急关头，令人担忧：*I could feel anger boiling up inside me.* 我感到怒火中烧。 ˌ**boil sth**↔ˈ**up** to heat a liquid or some food until it boils 把（液体或食物）烧开

■ ***noun*** **1** [sing.] a period of boiling; the point at which liquid boils 沸腾；沸点：(*BrE*) ***Bring the soup to the boil****, then allow it to simmer for five minutes.* 把汤煮开，然后文火煮五分钟。◇ (*NAmE*) ***Bring the soup to a boil.*** 把汤煮开。 **2** [C] a painful infected swelling under the skin which is full of a thick yellow liquid (called PUS) 疖；皮下脓肿；黄水疮

IDM **off the** ˈ**boil** (*BrE*) less good than before 不如以前：*The second series of the show really went off the boil.* 节目的续集的确逊色一些。 **on the** ˈ**boil** very active 十分活跃；如火如荼：*We have several projects all on the boil at once.* 我们热火朝天地同时上马了几个项目。

ˌ**boiled** ˈ**sweet** (*BrE*) (*NAmE* ˌ**hard** ˈ**candy**) *noun* a hard sweet/candy made from boiled sugar, often with fruit flavours 硬糖（常加水果味）

boil·er /ˈbɔɪlə(r)/ (*also* **fur·nace** *especially in NAmE*) *noun* a container in which water is heated to provide hot water and heating in a building or to produce steam in an engine 锅炉；汽锅

boiler·maker /ˈbɔɪləmeɪkə(r); *NAmE* -lərm-/ *noun* **1** a person or company that makes boilers 锅炉制造工（或公司） **2** (*NAmE*) a person who makes and repairs metal objects for industry 金属制造维修工 **3** (*NAmE*) a drink of WHISKY followed immediately by a glass of beer 加啤威士忌（指饮下威士忌后立刻饮一杯啤酒）

boil·er·plate /ˈbɔɪləpleɪt; *NAmE* -lər-/ *noun* [C, U] (*NAmE*) a standard form of words that can be used as a model for writing parts of a business document, legal agreement, etc. （可供模仿的）样板文件，文件范例

ˈ**boiler room** *noun* **1** a room in a building or ship containing the boiler 锅炉房；锅炉间 **2** (*NAmE*) a room or office used by people using telephones to sell sth, especially shares, in an aggressive or a dishonest way 电话交易所，电话推销室（以硬性或欺骗性手段推销证券等的场所）

ˈ**boiler suit** *noun* (*especially BrE*) (*NAmE usually* **cov·er·alls**) a piece of clothing like trousers/pants and a jacket in one piece, worn for doing dirty work 连衫裤工作服 ➲ COMPARE OVERALL *n.* (2)

boil·ing /ˈbɔɪlɪŋ/ (*also* ˌ**boiling** ˈ**hot**) *adj.* very hot 炽热的；很热的 **SYN** **baking**：*You must be boiling in that sweater!* 你穿着那件毛衣一定很热！◇ *a boiling hot day* 酷热的一天 **OPP** **freezing**

ˈ**boiling point** *noun* [U, C] **1** the temperature at which a liquid starts to boil 沸点 **2** the point at which a person becomes very angry, or a situation is likely to become violent 极度愤怒；（某种状态的）爆发点：*Racial tension has* ***reached boiling point****.* 种族间的紧张状态已达到一触即发的程度。

bois·ter·ous /ˈbɔɪstərəs/ *adj.* (of people, animals or behaviour 人、动物或行为) noisy and full of life and energy 热闹的；充满活力的；活蹦乱跳的：*It was a challenge, keeping ten boisterous seven-year-olds amused.* 要逗着十个好动的七岁孩子玩真是一种挑战。 ▸ **bois·ter·ous·ly** *adv.*

bok choy /ˌbɒk ˈtʃɔɪ; *NAmE* ˌbɑːk/ (*NAmE*) (*BrE* **pak choi**) *noun* [U] a type of CHINESE CABBAGE with long dark green leaves and thick white STEMS 白菜；小白菜

bold /bəʊld; *NAmE* boʊld/ *adj., noun*

■ ***adj.*** (**bold·er**, **bold·est**) **1** (of people or behaviour 人或举止) brave and confident; not afraid to say what you feel or to take risks 大胆自信的；敢于表白情感的；敢于冒险的：*It was a bold move on their part to open a business in France.* 在法国开业是他们的一个大胆举动。◇ *The wine made him bold enough to approach her.* 他趁着酒劲，鼓足勇气上前和她说话。 **2** (of shape, colour, lines, etc. 形状、颜色、线条等) that can be easily seen; having a strong clear appearance 明显的；轮廓突出的：*the bold outline of a mountain against the sky* 天空映衬下的山的清晰轮廓 ◇ *She paints with bold strokes of the brush.* 她的绘画笔锋遒劲。 **3** (*specialist*) (of printed words or letters 印刷字或字符) in a thick, dark TYPE 粗体的；黑体的：*Highlight the important words in bold type.* 用黑体突出重要词语。◇ *bold lettering* 黑字体 ▸ **bold·ly** *adv.* **bold·ness** *noun* [U]

IDM **be/make so bold (as to do sth)** (*formal*) used especially when politely asking a question or making a suggestion which you hope will not offend anyone (although it may criticize them slightly) （谦辞，表示自己轻率说话）不揣冒昧，恕我无礼；擅自；胆敢：*If I may be so bold as to suggest that he made a mistake in his calculations...* 恕我冒昧说，他的计算有个错误… **(as) bold as** ˈ**brass** (*informal*) without showing any respect, shame or fear 放肆的；厚颜无耻的；胆大妄为的 ➲ MORE LIKE THIS 14, page R26

■ ***noun*** (*also* **bold·face** /ˈbəʊldfeɪs; *NAmE* ˈboʊld-/) [U] (*specialist*) thick, dark TYPE used for printing words or letters 黑体；粗体：*Headwords are printed* ***in bold****.* 首词用黑体印刷。

B

bole /bəʊl; *NAmE* boʊl/ *noun* the main STEM of a tree 树干 SYN **trunk**

bol·ero /bəˈleərəʊ; *NAmE* bəˈleroʊ/ *noun* (*pl.* **-os**) **1** a traditional Spanish dance; a piece of music for this dance 波列罗舞（一种传统的西班牙舞）；波列罗舞曲 **2** /bəˈleərəʊ; *BrE also* ˈbɒlərəʊ; *NAmE* bəˈleroʊ/ a women's short jacket that is not fastened at the front 波蕾若外套（前胸敞开的女短上衣）

bol·etus /bəˈliːtəs/ (*also* **bol·ete** /bəˈliːt/) *noun* [C, U] a MUSHROOM with small round holes under the top part. Some types of boletus can be eaten. 牛肝菌属真菌（有些种类可食用）

boll /bəʊl; *NAmE* boʊl/ *noun* the part of the cotton plant that contains the seeds 棉铃

bol·lard /ˈbɒlɑːd; *NAmE* ˈbɑːlərd/ *noun* **1** (*BrE*) a short thick post that is used to stop vehicles from going on to a road or part of a road（阻止车辆开到某段路上的）路桩 ➲ VISUAL VOCAB PAGE V3 **2** a short thick post on a ship, or on land close to water, to which a ship's rope may be tied（甲板或岸边的）带缆桩，系船桩

bol·lock·ing /ˈbɒləkɪŋ; *NAmE* ˈbɑːl-/ *noun* (*BrE, taboo*) an occasion when sb tells you that they are very angry with you, often by shouting at you 训斥；臭骂：*to give sb a bollocking* 把某人臭骂一通 ◇ *to get a bollocking* 挨了一顿臭骂 HELP There are more polite ways to express this, for example **to give sb/to get a rocket**, or **to tear a strip off sb**. 较礼貌的说法有 to give sb / to get a rocket，或 to tear a strip off sb 等。

bol·locks /ˈbɒləks; *NAmE* ˈbɑːl-/ *noun* (*BrE, taboo, slang*) **1** [U] nonsense 胡说；废话：*You're talking a load of bollocks!* 你这是一派胡言！ **2** [pl.] a man's TESTICLES 睾丸 **3 Bollocks!** *exclamation* used as a swear word when sb is disagreeing with sth, or when they are angry about sth（粗俗话，表示不赞同或气愤）：*Bollocks! He never said that!* 胡说！他从没那么说过！

ˈboll weevil *noun* an insect that damages cotton plants 墨西哥棉铃象（棉花害虫）

Bol·ly·wood /ˈbɒliwʊd; *NAmE* ˈbɑːl-/ *noun* [U] (*informal*) used to refer to the Hindi film/movie industry, which is mainly based in the Indian city of Mumbai (formerly called Bombay) 宝莱坞（指主要集中于孟买的印度电影业）

bol·ogna /bəˈləʊnjə; bəˈlɒnjə; *NAmE* -ˈloʊ-/ (*also* **ba·lo·ney**) *noun* [U] (*NAmE*) a type of SAUSAGE that is put in SANDWICHES, made of a mixture of meats 博洛尼亚大红肠（用各种肉混合制成）

bolo tie /ˈbəʊləʊ taɪ; *NAmE* ˈboʊloʊ/ *noun* (*NAmE*) a string worn around the neck and fastened with a decorative CLASP or bar 波罗领带（用饰物或搭扣系的线编领带）

Bol·shevik /ˈbɒlʃɪvɪk; *NAmE* ˈboʊl-/ *noun* a member of the group in Russia that took control after the 1917 Revolution 布尔什维克 ▶ **Bol·shevik** *adj.* **Bol·shevism** /ˈbɒlʃɪvɪzəm; *NAmE* ˈboʊl-/ *noun* [U]

bol·shie (*also* **bol·shy**) /ˈbɒlʃi; *NAmE* ˈboʊl-/ *adj.* (*BrE, informal, disapproving*) (of a person 人) creating difficulties or arguments deliberately, and refusing to be helpful 找茬儿的；不给人方便的

bol·ster /ˈbəʊlstə(r); *NAmE* ˈboʊl-/ *verb, noun*

■ *verb* to improve sth or make it stronger 改善；加强：**~ sth** *to* ***bolster sb's confidence/courage/morale*** 增强某人的信心 / 勇气 / 士气 ◇ **~ sth up** *Falling interest rates may help to bolster up the economy.* 利率下降可能有助于刺激经济。

■ *noun* a long thick PILLOW that is placed across the top of a bed under the other pillows 垫枕（长而厚）

bolt /bəʊlt; *NAmE* boʊlt/ *noun, verb, adv.*

■ *noun* **1** a long, narrow piece of metal that you slide across the inside of a door or window in order to lock it（门窗的）闩，插销 **2** a piece of metal like a screw without a point which is used with a circle of metal (= a NUT) to fasten things together 螺栓：*nuts and bolts* 螺帽和螺栓 ➲ VISUAL VOCAB PAGE V21 **3 ~ of lightning** a sudden flash of LIGHTNING in the sky, appearing as a line 闪电 **4** a short heavy arrow shot from a CROSSBOW 弩箭 **5** a long piece of cloth wound in a roll around a piece of cardboard 一匹（布）

bolts 插销；螺栓；弩箭

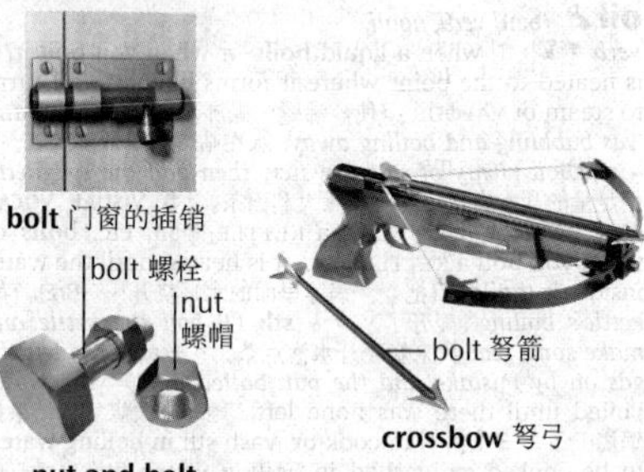

IDM **a ˌbolt from the ˈblue** an event or a piece of news which is sudden and unexpected; a complete surprise 突如其来的事件（或消息）；晴天霹雳：*Her dismissal came as a bolt from the blue.* 她被解雇简直就是晴天霹雳。 **make a ˈbolt for sth | make a ˈbolt for it** to run away very fast, in order to escape 迅速逃跑；溜走 ➲ MORE AT NUT *n.*, SHOOT *v.*

■ *verb* **1** [T, I] **~ (sth)** to fasten sth such as a door or window by sliding a bolt across; to be able to be fastened in this way 用插销闩上；能被闩上：*Don't forget to bolt the door.* 别忘了闩门。◇ *The gate bolts on the inside.* 大门在里面上闩。 **2** [T] to fasten things together with a bolt 用螺栓把（甲和乙）固定在一起：**~ A to B** *The vice is bolted to the workbench.* 这虎钳是用螺栓固定在工作台上的。◇ **~ A and B together** *The various parts of the car are then bolted together.* 然后汽车的各种部件便用螺栓装配在一起。 **3** [I] if an animal, especially a horse, **bolts**, it suddenly runs away because it is frightened（马等受惊）脱缰 **4** [I] (+ **adv./prep.**) (of a person 人) to run away, especially in order to escape 跑开；（尤指）逃跑：*When he saw the police arrive, he bolted down an alley.* 他看见警察来了，便从小巷逃走了。 **5** [T] **~ sth (down)** to eat sth very quickly 狼吞虎咽：*Don't bolt your food!* 吃饭不能狼吞虎咽！ **6** (*NAmE*) [T, I] **~ (sth)** to stop supporting a particular group or political party 停止支持（某团体或政党）：*Many Democrats bolted the party to vote Republican.* 很多民主党人放弃本党，转而投共和党的票。 **7** [I] (of a plant, especially a vegetable 植物，尤指蔬菜) to grow too quickly and start producing seeds and so become less good to eat 过早结实（因而食用价值降低） IDM SEE STABLE DOOR

■ *adv.*

IDM **sit/stand bolt ˈupright** to sit or stand with your back straight 背部笔挺地坐 / 站；坐 / 站得笔直

ˈbolt-action *adj.* (of a gun 枪) having a back part that is opened by turning a BOLT and sliding it back 手动栓式枪机的；有枪栓的

bolt·hole /ˈbəʊlthəʊl; *NAmE* ˈboʊlthoʊl/ *noun* (*BrE*) a place that you can escape to, for example when you are in a difficult situation 匿身处；躲避困境之地

ˈbolt-on *adj.* [only before noun] able to be easily added to a machine, etc. to make it able to do sth new 易安装的；贴附式的

bolus /ˈbəʊləs; *NAmE* ˈboʊləs/ *noun* **1** (*medical* 医) a single amount of a drug that is given at one time（单次给药的）剂量 SYN **dose** **2** (*specialist*) a small round mass of substance, especially chewed food that is swallowed 小团；小丸；（尤指咀嚼后吞咽的）食团

boma /ˈbəʊmə; *NAmE* ˈboʊ-/ *noun* (*EAfrE, SAfrE*) (in wild country) an area surrounded by a fence, often made of sticks, used to protect animals or people （野外的）围栏防护场地

bomb /bɒm; *NAmE* bɑːm/ *noun, verb*

■*noun* **1** [C] a weapon designed to explode at a particular time or when it is dropped or thrown 炸弹：*a bomb attack/blast/explosion* 轰炸；炸弹爆炸 ◇ *a* **bomb** *goes off/explodes* 炸弹爆炸 ◇ *extensive bomb damage* 轰炸造成的巨大破坏 ◇ *Hundreds of bombs were dropped on the city.* 几百枚炸弹投到了这座城市。 ➲ SEE ALSO DIRTY BOMB **2 the bomb** [sing.] nuclear weapons (ATOMIC or HYDROGEN bombs) 核武器；核弹：*countries which have the bomb* 拥有核武器的国家 **3 a bomb** [sing.] (*BrE, informal*) a lot of money 很多钱：*That dress must have cost a bomb!* 那条连衣裙花费不菲吧！ **4 a bomb** [sing.] (*NAmE, informal*) a complete failure 彻底的失败：*The musical was a complete bomb on Broadway.* 那出音乐剧在百老汇的演出完全失败。 **5** [C] (*NAmE*) (in AMERICAN FOOTBALL 美式足球) a long forward throw of the ball 长传 **6** [C] (*NAmE*) a container in which a liquid such as paint or insect poison is kept under pressure and released as a spray or as FOAM 气溶胶弹式容器（油漆、杀虫剂等液体加压贮存可喷出）：*a bug bomb* (= used for killing insects) 喷雾杀虫剂 ➲ MORE LIKE THIS 20, page R27

IDM **be the ˈbomb** (*NAmE*) to be very good; to be the best 很好；最佳：*Check out the new website. It's the bomb!* 看一看这新网站。简直是太棒了！ **go down a ˈbomb | go (like) a ˈbomb** (*BrE*) to be very successful 十分成功：*Our performance went down a bomb.* 我们的演出获得了巨大成功。◇ *The party was really going (like) a bomb.* 聚会办得非常成功。 **go like a ˈbomb** (*BrE*) (of a vehicle 车辆等) to go very fast 飞驰

■*verb* **1** [T] ~ **sth** to attack sb/sth by leaving a bomb in a place or by dropping bombs from a plane 轰炸；对…投炸弹：*Terrorists bombed several army barracks.* 恐怖分子轰炸了几处兵营。◇ *The city was heavily bombed in the war.* 这座城市在战争中遭到了猛烈轰炸。 **2** [I] + **adv./prep.** (*BrE, informal*) to move very fast, especially in a vehicle, in a particular direction 快速移动，疾行（尤指乘车）：*They were bombing down the road at about 80 miles an hour.* 他们正以大约一小时 80 英里的速度沿路飞驰。 **3** [T, I] ~ **(sth)** (*NAmE, informal*) to fail a test or an exam very badly （考试）惨败：*The exam was impossible! I definitely bombed it.* 考试太难了！我肯定考砸了。 **4** [I] (*informal*) (of a play, show, etc. 戏剧、演出等) to fail very badly 大败；票房极差；不卖座：*His latest musical bombed and lost thousands of dollars.* 他最近的一部音乐剧演砸了，赔了几千美元。

PHR V **be ˌbombed ˈout 1** if you are **bombed out**, your home is destroyed by bombs （家园）被炸毁；被炸得无家可归 **2** if a building is **bombed out**, it has been destroyed by bombs （建筑）被炸毁

ˈbomb alert *noun* (*BrE*) = BOMB SCARE

bom·bard /bɒmˈbɑːd; *NAmE* bɑːmˈbɑːrd/ *verb* **1** ~ **sb/sth (with sth)** to attack a place by firing large guns at it or dropping bombs on it continuously 轰炸；轰击 **2** ~ **sb/sth (with sth)** to attack sb with a lot of questions, criticisms, etc. or by giving them too much information 大量提问；大肆抨击；提供过多信息：*We have been bombarded with letters of complaint.* 我们接二连三收到了大批的投诉信件。 ▸ **bom·bard·ment** *noun* [U, C]: *The city came under heavy bombardment.* 那座城市受到猛烈轰炸。

bom·bard·ier /ˌbɒmbəˈdɪə(r); *NAmE* ˌbɑːmbərˈdɪr/ *noun* **1** the person on a military plane in the US AIR FORCE who is responsible for aiming and dropping bombs （美国空军的）投弹手 **2** a member of a low rank in the Royal Artillery (= a part of the British army that uses large guns) （英国皇家炮兵的）下士

bom·bast /ˈbɒmbæst; *NAmE* ˈbɑːm-/ *noun* [U] (*formal*) words which sound important but have little meaning, used to impress people 华而不实的言辞；大话 ▸ **bombas·tic** /bɒmˈbæstɪk; *NAmE* bɑːm-/ *adj.*: *a bombastic speaker* 大放厥词的演说家

Bombay mix /ˌbɒmbeɪ ˈmɪks; *NAmE* ˌbɑːm-/ *noun* [U] an Indian food consisting of LENTILS, PEANUTS and spices, eaten as a SNACK 兵豆花生香味什锦（印度小吃）

ˈbomb bay *noun* a part of an aircraft in which bombs are held and from which they can be dropped （飞机的）炸弹舱

ˈbomb disposal *noun* [U] the job of removing or exploding bombs in order to make an area safe 未爆弹处理：*a* **bomb disposal expert/squad/team** 拆弹专家 / 小组

bombed /bɒmd; *NAmE* bɑːmd/ *adj.* [not before noun] (*informal*) extremely drunk 烂醉如泥

bomb·er /ˈbɒmə(r); *NAmE* ˈbɑːm-/ *noun* **1** a plane that carries and drops bombs 轰炸机 ➲ WORDFINDER NOTE AT AIRCRAFT **2** a person who puts a bomb somewhere illegally 非法放置炸弹者

ˈbomber jacket *noun* a short jacket that fits tightly around the waist and fastens with a ZIP/ZIPPER 紧腰短夹克

bomb·ing /ˈbɒmɪŋ; *NAmE* ˈbɑːm-/ *noun* [C, U] an occasion when a bomb is dropped or left somewhere; the act of doing this 炸弹投掷（或安放）：*recent bombings in major cities* 近期发生在大城市的投放炸弹事件 ◇ *enemy bombing* 敌机轰炸

bom·bora /bɒmˈbɔːrə; *NAmE* bɑːm-/ *noun* (*AustralE*) **1** a wave which forms over an underwater rock, sometimes producing a dangerous area of water 潜浪（遇暗礁形成，可造成危险的碎浪水域） **2** an area of rock underwater 暗礁水域

bomb·proof /ˈbɒmpruːf; *NAmE* ˈbɑːm-/ *adj.* strong enough to give protection against an attack by a bomb 防炸弹的

ˈbomb scare (*also* **ˈbomb threat** *especially in NAmE*) (*BrE also* **ˈbomb alert**) *noun* an occasion when sb says that they have put a bomb somewhere and everyone has to leave the area 炸弹恐吓（声称在某处放置炸弹，所有人都得撤离）

bomb·shell /ˈbɒmʃel; *NAmE* ˈbɑːm-/ *noun* [usually sing.] (*informal*) **1** an event or a piece of news which is unexpected and usually unpleasant 出乎意料的事情，意外消息（常指不幸）：*The news of his death came as a bombshell.* 他去世的消息令人震惊。◇ *She* **dropped a bombshell** *at the meeting and announced that she was leaving.* 她在会上宣布了令人吃惊的消息，说她将要离开。 **2 a blond(e) bombshell** a very attractive woman with blonde hair 金发美女

ˈbomb site *noun* an area where all the buildings have been destroyed by bombs 轰炸后的废墟

bona fide /ˌbəʊnə ˈfaɪdi; *NAmE* ˌboʊnə/ *adj.* [usually before noun] (*from Latin*) genuine, real or legal; not false 真诚的；真实的；合法的：*a bona fide reason* 真正原因 ◇ *Is it a bona fide, reputable organization?* 这是不是个合法的、值得信赖的机构？

bona fides /ˌbəʊnə ˈfaɪdiːz; *NAmE* ˌboʊnə/ *noun* [pl.] (*from Latin*) evidence that sb is who they say that they are; evidence that sb/sth is honest 真诚；信誉

bon·anza /bəˈnænzə/ *noun* [sing.] **1** a situation in which people can make a lot of money or be very successful 发财（或成功）的机遇：*a cash bonanza for investors* 投资者的赚钱机会 ◇ *a bonanza year for the computer industry* 计算机业兴旺发达的一年 **2** a situation where there is a large amount of sth pleasant 兴盛；繁荣：*the usual bonanza of sport in the summer* 夏季总有许多好看的赛事

B

bon·bon /ˈbɒnbɒn; *NAmE* ˈbɑːnbɑːn/ *noun* a sweet/candy, especially one with a soft centre （尤指软夹心的）糖果

bonce /bɒns; *NAmE* bɑːns/ *noun* (*BrE, informal*) a person's head 人头

bond AW /bɒnd; *NAmE* bɑːnd/ *noun, verb*

■ *noun*

• STRONG CONNECTION 牢固的联系 **1** [C] ~ (**between A and B**) something that forms a connection between people or groups, such as a feeling of friendship or shared ideas and experiences 纽带；联系；关系；契合：*A bond of friendship had been forged between them.* 他们之间形成了友谊的纽带。◇ *The agreement strengthened the bonds between the two countries.* 该协定加强了两国间的联系。◇ *the special bond between mother and child* 母子间的独特关系 ➲ WORDFINDER NOTE AT FRIEND

• MONEY 钱 **2** [C] an agreement by a government or a company to pay you interest on the money you have lent; a document containing this agreement 债券；公债 ➲ SEE ALSO JUNK BOND ➲ WORDFINDER NOTE AT INVEST **3** [U] (*law* 律, *especially NAmE*) a sum of money that is paid as BAIL 保释金：*He was released on $5 000 bond.* 他以 5 000 美元取保释放。**4** [C] (*also* ˈ**mortgage bond**) (*SAfrE*) a legal agreement by which a bank lends you money to buy a house, etc. which you pay back over many years; the sum of money that is lent 按揭贷款协议；按揭贷款：*to pay off a bond* 偿清按揭贷款 ◇ *We had to take out a second bond on the property.* 我们得申请第二按揭以购买这个房产。◇ *bond rates* (= of interest) 按揭贷款利率

• ROPES/CHAINS 绳索；链条 **5 bonds** [pl.] (*formal*) the ropes or chains keeping sb prisoner; anything that stops you from being free to do what you want 捆绑犯人的绳索（或镣铐）；羁绊；桎梏：*to release sb from their bonds* 给某人脱去枷锁 ◇ *the* ***bonds of oppression/injustice*** 压迫 / 不公正的枷锁

• LEGAL AGREEMENT 法律协定 **6** [C] (*formal*) a legal written agreement or promise 书面的法律协定（或承诺）：*We entered into a solemn bond.* 我们缔结了一项庄严的协定。

• JOIN 结合 **7** [C] the way in which two things are joined together 连接；结合：*a firm bond between the two surfaces* 两个面之间的牢固接合

• CHEMISTRY 化学 **8** [C] the way in which atoms are held together in a chemical COMPOUND 键合；键 IDM SEE WORD *n.*

■ *verb*

• JOIN FIRMLY 牢固地结合 **1** [T, I] to join two things firmly together; to join firmly to sth else 使牢固结合；把…紧紧地连接到：**~ sth** *This new glue bonds a variety of surfaces in seconds.* 这种新型胶水可迅速粘牢各种材质的面板。◇ **~ (A) to B** *It cannot be used to bond wood to metal.* 这不能把木料粘贴在金属上。◇ **~ (A and B) together** *The atoms bond together to form a molecule.* 原子结合形成分子。

• DEVELOP RELATIONSHIP 发展关系 **2** [I, T] ~ (**with sb**) to develop or create a relationship of trust with sb 增强（与某人的）信任关系；建立（与某人的）互信关系：*Mothers who are depressed sometimes fail to bond with their children.* 患抑郁症的母亲有时无法和孩子建立亲子关系。

bond·age /ˈbɒndɪdʒ; *NAmE* ˈbɑːn-/ *noun* [U] **1** (*old-fashioned* or *formal*) the state of being a SLAVE or prisoner 奴役；束缚 SYN **slavery**: (*figurative*) *women's liberation from the bondage of domestic life* 女性从家庭生活束缚中的解脱 **2** the practice of being tied with ropes, chains, etc. in order to gain sexual pleasure （以捆绑寻求性快感的）性虐待癖

ˌ**bonded** ˈ**labour** (*especially US* ˌ**bonded** ˈ**labor**) *noun* [U] forced work for an employer for a fixed time without being paid, often as a way of paying a debt 债役劳动；抵押劳动：*Many of the immigrants are used as bonded labour.* 移民中有很多人被用作债役劳工。▶ ˌ**bonded** ˈ**labourer** (*especially US* ˌ**bonded** ˈ**laborer**) *noun*

ˌ**bonded** ˈ**warehouse** *noun* a government building where imported goods are stored until tax has been paid on them 保税仓库

bond·ing AW /ˈbɒndɪŋ; *NAmE* ˈbɑːn-/ *noun* [U] **1** the process of forming a special relationship with sb or with a group of people 人与人之间的关系（或联结）：*mother-child bonding* 母子亲情 ◇ *male bonding* 男性的情谊 **2** (*chemistry* 化) the process of atoms joining together 原子的结合；键合：*hydrogen bonding* 氢键结合

bone 🔑 /bəʊn; *NAmE* boʊn/ *noun, verb*

■ *noun* **1** 🔑 [C] any of the hard parts that form the SKELETON of the body of a human or an animal 骨头；骨：*He survived the accident with no broken bones.* 他在事故中幸免于难，没有骨折。◇ *This fish has a lot of bones in it.* 这种鱼多刺。**2** [U] the hard substance that bones are made of 骨质：*knives with bone handles* 有骨质手把的刀子 **3 -boned** (in adjectives 构成形容词) having bones of the type mentioned 有…样的骨头的：*fine-boned* 骨架小的

IDM **a bone of conˈtention** a subject which causes disagreement and arguments between people 争执所在 **close to the ˈbone** (*informal*) (of a remark, joke, story, etc. 话语、玩笑、故事等) so honest or clearly expressed that it is likely to cause offence to some people 过于直率 **cut, pare, etc. sth to the ˈbone** to reduce sth, such as costs, as much as you possibly can 尽量削减（开支等） **have a ˈbone to pick with sb** (*informal*) to be angry with sb about sth and want to discuss it with them 对某人生气，想与之解决；有理由反对（或恼恨）某人 **make no bones about (doing) sth** (*informal*) to be honest and open about sth; to not hesitate to do sth 开诚布公；毫不犹疑：*She made no bones about telling him exactly what she thought of him.* 她毫无保留地把对他的看法照直告诉了他。**not have a… bone in your body** (*informal*) to have none of the quality mentioned 毫无…的素质：*She was honest and hard-working, and didn't have an unkind bone in her body.* 她诚实勤劳，身上没有一点儿不好的品质。**throw sb a ˈbone** to give sb a small part of what they want as a way of showing that you want to help them, without offering them the main thing they want 施以小惠（以示助人，却不满足主要的要求）；丢给某人一块骨头 **to the ˈbone** affecting you very strongly 影响极强地；深刻地：*His threats chilled her to the bone.* 他的威胁使她不寒而栗。➲ MORE AT BAG *n.*, BARE *adj.*, FEEL *v.*, FINGER *n.*, FLESH *n.*, SKIN *n.*

■ *verb* **~ sth** to take the bones out of fish or meat 挑鱼刺；剔骨头

PHR V ˌ**bone ˈup on sth** (*informal*) to try to learn about sth or to remind yourself of what you already know about it 钻研学习；复习：*She had boned up on the city's history before the visit.* 她在前往这个城市之前先对它的历史研究了一番。

ˌ**bone ˈchina** *noun* [U] thin delicate CHINA made of CLAY mixed with crushed bone; cups, plates, etc. made of this 骨质瓷，骨质瓷器（用瓷土与骨灰混合烧制成）

ˌ**bone ˈdry** *adj.* [not usually before noun] completely dry 完全干燥

bone·head /ˈbəʊnhed; *NAmE* ˈboʊn-/ *noun* (*informal*) a stupid person 笨蛋；傻瓜

ˌ**bone ˈidle** *adj.* (*old-fashioned, BrE, informal*) very lazy 懒透了的

bone·less /ˈbəʊnləs; *NAmE* ˈboʊn-/ *adj.* (of meat or fish 肉或鱼) without any bones 无骨的；去骨的：*boneless chicken breasts* 去骨鸡胸肉

ˈ**bone marrow** (*also* **mar·row**) *noun* [U] a soft substance that fills the hollow parts of bones 骨髓：*a bone marrow transplant* 骨髓移植

bone·meal /ˈbəʊnmiːl; *NAmE* ˈboʊn-/ *noun* [U] a substance made from crushed animal bones which is used to make soil richer （用作肥料的）骨粉

boner /ˈbəʊnə(r); *NAmE* ˈboʊn-/ *noun* (*NAmE, informal*) **1** (*taboo*) an ERECTION of the PENIS （阴茎的）勃起 **2** an embarrassing mistake 令人尴尬的错误

bone·shaker /ˈbəʊnʃeɪkə(r); *NAmE* ˈboʊn-/ *noun* (*BrE, informal*) **1** an old vehicle that is in bad condition 破旧的车 **2** an old type of bicycle without rubber tyres （旧时的）无胎自行车，硬轮自行车

bon·fire /ˈbɒnfaɪə(r); *NAmE* ˈbɑːn-/ *noun* a large outdoor fire for burning waste or as part of a celebration （在室外为焚烧垃圾或为庆祝而燃起的）大火堆，篝火

ˈ**Bonfire Night** (*also* ˌ**Guy** ˈ**Fawkes night**) *noun* [U, C] the night of 5 November, when there is a tradition in Britain that people light bonfires and have FIREWORKS to celebrate the failure of the plan in 1605 to destroy the parliament buildings with EXPLOSIVES 篝火之夜（11 月 5 日夜晚，英国人借以庆祝 1605 年炸毁议会大厦的阴谋失败）

bong /bɒŋ; *NAmE* bɑːŋ/ *noun* **1** the sound made by a large bell （大钟发出的）噹噹声： *the bongs of Big Ben* 大本钟的噹噹声 **2** a long pipe for smoking CANNABIS and other drugs, which passes the smoke through a container of water 烟枪；水烟斗

bongo /ˈbɒŋgəʊ; *NAmE* ˈbɑːŋgoʊ; ˈbɔːŋgoʊ/ (*pl.* **-os**) (*also* ˈ**bongo drum**) *noun* a small drum, usually one of a pair, that you play with your fingers 邦戈鼓（用手指扣击的小手鼓，通常成对）

bon·homie /ˈbɒnəmi; *NAmE* ˌbɑːnəˈmiː/ *noun* [U] (*from French, formal*) a feeling of cheerful friendship 欢快友好的感觉；欢乐的友情

bonk /bɒŋk; *NAmE* bɑːŋk/ *noun, verb*

■ ***noun*** (*BrE, informal*) **1** [sing.] an act of having sex with sb 性交 **2** [C] the act of hitting sb on the head or of hitting your head on sth 拍头；撞头

■ ***verb*** (*BrE, informal*) **1** [T, I] ~ (**sb**) to have sex with sb （和某人）性交： *He's been bonking one of his students.* 他同他的一名学生一直有性关系。 **2** [T] ~ **sth** to hit sb lightly on the head or to hit yourself by mistake 轻击（或拍某人的头）；（不小心）碰撞： *I bonked my head on the doorway.* 我没留意在门口碰了一下头。

bonk·buster /ˈbɒŋkbʌstə(r); *NAmE* ˈbɑːŋk-/ *noun* (*BrE, informal*) a type of popular novel in which there is a lot of sex or romantic love 情色小说；言情小说

bonk·ers /ˈbɒŋkəz; *NAmE* ˈbɑːŋkərz/ *adj.* [not before noun] (*informal*) completely crazy and silly 疯狂；愚蠢透顶： *I'll go bonkers if I have to wait any longer.* 如果再等下去，我非发疯不可。 IDM SEE RAVING *adv.*

bon mot /ˌbɒn ˈməʊ; *NAmE* ˌbɑːn ˈmoʊ; ˌbɔːn ˈmoʊ/ *noun* (*pl.* **bons mots** /ˌbɒn ˈməʊ; *NAmE* ˌbɑːn ˈmoʊ; ˌbɔːn ˈmoʊ/) (*from French, formal*) a funny and clever remark 妙语；诙谐的话

bon·net /ˈbɒnɪt; *NAmE* ˈbɑːnət/ *noun* **1** a hat tied with strings under the chin, worn by babies and, especially in the past, by women （带子系于下巴的）童帽，旧式女帽 **2** (*BrE*) (*NAmE* **hood**) the metal part over the front of a vehicle, usually covering the engine （车辆的）引擎盖 ➲ COLLOCATIONS AT DRIVING ➲ VISUAL VOCAB PAGE V56 IDM SEE BEE

bonny (*also* **bonnie**) /ˈbɒni; *NAmE* ˈbɑːni/ *adj.* (**bon·nier, bon·ni·est**) (*dialect, especially ScotE*) very pretty; attractive 十分漂亮的；有魅力的： ***a bonny baby/lass*** 漂亮的婴儿 / 姑娘

bon·sai /ˈbɒnsaɪ; *NAmE* ˈbɑːn-/ *noun* (*pl.* **bon·sai**) **1** [C] a small tree that is grown in a pot and prevented from reaching its normal size 盆景 **2** [U] the Japanese art of growing bonsai 日本盆栽艺术

bon·sella /bɒnˈselə; *NAmE* bɑːn-/ *noun* (*SAfrE, informal*) something that you receive as a present or reward, especially money 礼物；奖品；（尤指）礼金，奖金

bonus /ˈbəʊnəs; *NAmE* ˈboʊ-/ *noun* (*pl.* **-es**) **1** an extra amount of money that is added to a payment, especially to sb's wages or salary as a reward 奖金；红利： *a £100 Christmas bonus* * 100 英镑圣诞节奖金 ◇ *productivity bonuses* 生产奖金 ◇ *the row over bankers' bonuses* 关于银行家红利的严重分歧 ➲ WORDFINDER NOTE AT PAY ➲ SEE ALSO NO-CLAIMS BONUS **2** [usually sing.] anything pleasant that is extra and more or better than you were expecting 意外收获： *Being able to walk to work is an* ***added bonus*** *of the new job.* 能够步行去上班是这份新工作额外的好处。

bon viv·ant /ˌbɒ̃ viːˈvɒ̃; *NAmE* ˌbɑːn viːˈvɑːnt/ (*also* **bon viv·eur** /ˌbɒ̃ viːˈvɜː(r); *NAmE* ˌbɑːn viːˈvɜːr/) *noun* (*from French*) a person who enjoys going out with friends and eating good food, drinking good wine, etc. 喜欢吃喝玩乐的人 HELP The plural forms can be **bon vivants** or **bons vivants**; **bon viveurs** or **bons viveurs** but the pronunciation is the same as the singular. 复数形式可以是 bon vivants 或 bons vivants，bon viveurs 或 bons viveurs，其读音与单数形式相同。

bon voy·age /ˌbɒn vɔɪˈɑːʒ; *NAmE* ˌbɑːn/ *exclamation* (*from French*) said to sb who is leaving on a journey, to wish them a good journey 一路平安；旅途愉快

bony /ˈbəʊni; *NAmE* ˈboʊni/ *adj.* (**boni·er, boni·est**) **1** (of a person or part of the body 人或人体部位) very thin so that the bones can be seen under the skin 瘦骨嶙峋的 **2** (of fish 鱼) full of small bones 多刺的 **3** consisting of or like bone 由骨骼组成的；类似骨头的

bon·zer /ˈbɒnzə(r); *NAmE* ˈbɑːn-/ *adj.* (*AustralE, NZE, informal*) excellent 极好的；很棒的

boo /buː/ *exclamation, noun, verb*

■ ***exclamation, noun* 1** a sound that people make to show that they do not like an actor, speaker, etc. （对演员、讲话者等表示不满）嘘： *'Boo!' they shouted, 'Get off!'* "去！"他们大声喊道，"滚下去！" ◇ *The speech was greeted with loud boos from the audience.* 演讲引来观众一片嘘声。 **2** people shout **Boo!** when they want to surprise or frighten sb （惊吓他人的声音）乒 IDM SEE SAY *v.* ➲ MORE LIKE THIS 2, page R25

■ ***verb*** [I, T] to show that you do not like a person, performance, idea, etc. by shouting 'boo' 发嘘声；喝倒彩： *The audience booed as she started her speech.* 她一开始讲话，听众便发出一阵嘘声。 ◇ ~ **sb** *He was* ***booed off the stage.*** 他在一片倒彩声中退下舞台。

boob /buːb/ *noun, verb*

■ ***noun* 1** (*slang*) a woman's breast （女人的）乳房 **2** (*BrE, informal*) a stupid mistake 愚蠢的错误： *I made a bit of a boob deleting that file.* 我犯了个愚蠢的错误，把那份文件删除了。 **3** (*NAmE*) a stupid person 傻瓜；蠢货

■ ***verb*** [I] (*informal*) to make a stupid mistake 犯愚蠢的错误

ˈ**boo-boo** *noun* **1** (*informal*) a stupid mistake 愚蠢的错误： *I think I've made a boo-boo.* 我想我犯了个愚蠢的错误。 **2** (*NAmE*) a child's word for a small cut or injury （儿童用语）小伤口，轻伤

ˈ**boob tube** *noun* (*informal*) **1** (*BrE*) (*NAmE* ˈ**tube top**) a piece of women's clothing that is made of cloth that stretches and covers the chest （女人的）紧身平口胸衣 **2** (*NAmE, disapproving*) the television 电视机

bonsai 盆景

B

booby /ˈbuːbi/ *noun* (*pl.* **-ies**) **1** (*informal*) a stupid person 笨蛋；傻瓜：*Don't be such a booby!* 不要那么傻！ **2** [usually pl.] (*informal*) a word for a woman's breast, used especially by children （女人的）乳房（多见于儿童用语） **3** a large tropical bird with brightly coloured feet that lives near the sea 鲣鸟（大型热带海鸟）

ˈ**booby prize** *noun* a prize that is given as a joke to the person who is last in a competition 末名奖（作为玩笑赠予比赛中最后一名） ➲ COMPARE WOODEN SPOON

ˈ**booby trap** *noun* **1** a hidden bomb that explodes when the object that it is connected to is touched 饵雷；诡雷 **2** a hidden device that is meant as a joke to surprise sb, for example an object placed above a door so that it will fall on the first person who opens the door （为开玩笑而设下的）陷阱

ˈ**booby-trap** *verb* (**-pp-**) **~ sth** to place a booby trap in or on sth 设陷阱于；布置机关于；设饵雷于

boof·head /ˈbuːfhed/ *noun* (*AustralE, informal*) a stupid person 笨蛋；傻瓜

boo·ger /ˈbuːɡə(r)/ (*NAmE*) (*BrE* **bogey, bogy**) *noun* (*informal*) a piece of dried MUCUS from inside your nose （干结的）鼻屎

boo·gey·man /ˈbuːɡimæn/ *noun* (*NAmE*) = BOGEYMAN

boo·gie /ˈbuːɡi; *NAmE* ˈbʊɡi/ *noun, verb*

■ *noun* (*also* ˌ**boogie-ˈwoogie** /-ˈwuːɡi; *NAmE* -ˈwʊɡi/) [U] a type of blues music played on the piano, with a fast strong rhythm 布吉乐（布鲁斯钢琴乐，节奏快而强）

■ *verb* [I] (*informal*) to dance to fast pop music 随着快节奏的流行音乐跳舞

ˈ**boogie board** *noun* a small board used for riding on waves in a lying position 趴板（卧式小型冲浪板）

boo·hoo /ˈbuːhuː; ˌbuːˈhuː/ *exclamation* used in written English to show the sound of sb crying （书面语，表示哭声）呜呜 ➲ MORE LIKE THIS 3, page R25

book 🔑 /bʊk/ *noun, verb*

■ *noun*

• PRINTED WORK 印刷品 **1** 🔑 [C] a set of printed pages that are fastened inside a cover so that you can turn them and read them 书；书籍：*a pile of books* 一摞书 ◇ *hardback/paperback books* 精装书；平装书 **2** 🔑 [C] a written work published in printed or electronic form 印刷（或电子）出版物；著作：*a book by Stephen King* 斯蒂芬·金写的书 ◇ *a book about/on wildlife* 有关野生生物的书 ◇ *reference/children's/library books* 参考书；儿童读物；馆藏书籍 ➲ WORDFINDER NOTE AT WRITE ➲ COLLOCATIONS AT LITERATURE

> WORDFINDER 联想词：biography, blockbuster, **character**, editor, narrator, novel, **plot**, publish, title

• FOR WRITING IN 书写用 **3** 🔑 [C] a set of sheets of paper that are fastened together inside a cover and used for writing in 本子；簿子：*an exercise book* 练习本 ◇ *a notebook* 笔记本 ➲ SEE ALSO ADDRESS BOOK

• OF STAMPS/TICKETS/MATCHES, ETC. 邮票、票券、火柴等 **4** 🔑 [C] a set of things that are fastened together like a book 装订成册的一套东西：*a book of stamps/tickets/matches* 一封邮票；一本票券；一纸板火柴 ◇ *a chequebook* 支票簿

• ACCOUNTS 账目 **5 the books** [pl.] the written records of the financial affairs a business （企业的）账簿 SYN **accounts**: *to do the books* (= to check the accounts) 查账

• SECTION OF BIBLE, ETC. 《圣经》等的卷、部 **6** [C] a section of a large written work （长篇作品的）篇，卷，部：*the books of the Bible* 《圣经》中各卷

• FOR BETTING 赌博用 **7** [C] (*BrE*) a record of bets made on whether sth will happen, sb will win a race, etc. 赌注记录

IDM **be in sb's good/bad ˈbooks** (*informal*) used to say that sb is pleased/annoyed with you 令某人喜欢／厌烦：*I'm in her good books at the moment because I cleared up the kitchen.* 她现在对我有好感，因为我把厨房清理干净了。 **bring sb to ˈbook** (**for sth**) (*formal, especially BrE*) to punish sb for doing sth wrong and make them explain their behaviour （为某事）惩罚某人并要求作出解释 **by the ˈbook** following rules and instructions in a very strict way 循规蹈矩；严格遵守章法：*She always does everything by the book.* 她总是照章行事。 **in my ˈbook** (*informal*) used when you are giving your opinion （发表意见时说）：*That's cheating in my book.* 依我看那是欺骗。 (**be**) **on sb's ˈbooks** (to be) on an organization's list, for example of people who are available for a particular type of work （在某机构）登记备用的：*We have very few nurses on our books at the moment.* 目前在我们这里登记备用的护士很少。 ◇ *Most of the houses on our books are in the north of the city.* 我们手头的房子大多数在城北。 **throw the ˈbook at sb** (*informal*) to punish sb who has committed an offence as severely as possible 从严惩处（罪犯） ➲ MORE AT CLOSE¹ *v.*, CLOSED, COOK *v.*, HISTORY, JUDGE *v.*, LEAF *n.*, OPEN *adj.*, READ *v.*, SUIT *v.*, TRICK *n.*

■ *verb* **1** 🔑 [I, T] to arrange to have or use sth on a particular date in the future; to buy a ticket in advance 预约；预订：*Book early to avoid disappointment.* 及早预约，以免向隅。 ◇ **~ sth** *She booked a flight to Chicago.* 她订了张去芝加哥的机票。 ◇ *The performance is **booked up*** (= there are no more tickets available). 演出票订完了。 ◇ *I'm sorry—we're **fully booked**.* 对不起，客满了。 ◇ (*BrE*) *I'd like to book a table for two for 8 o'clock tonight.* 我想订一张今晚 8 点钟的二人餐桌。 HELP In American English **book** is not used if you do not have to pay in advance; instead use **make a reservation**. 美式英语中，不必预付款时不用 book，而用 make a reservation：*I'd like to make a reservation for 8 o'clock tonight.* 我想预订今晚 8 点钟的位子。 ➲ COMPARE RESERVE *v.* (1) ➲ WORDFINDER NOTE AT HOTEL **2** 🔑 [T] to arrange for sb to have a seat on a plane, etc. 给（某人）预订飞机等座位：**~ sb + adv./prep.** *I've booked you on the 10 o'clock flight.* 我给你订了 10 点钟的飞机票。 ◇ **~ sb sth** (**+ adv./prep.**) *I've booked you a room at the Park Hotel.* 我已在百乐酒店为你订了一个房间。 **3** [T] **~ sb/sth** (**for sth**) to arrange for a singer, etc. to perform on a particular date 和（歌手等）预约演出日期：*We've booked a band for the wedding reception.* 我们已经为婚宴预约了乐队。 **4** [T] **~ sb** (**for sth**) (*informal*) to write down sb's name and address because they have committed a crime or an offence 立案（控告某人）：*He was booked for possession of cocaine.* 他因藏有可卡因而被立案审查。 **5** [T] **~ sb** (*BrE*) (of a REFEREE 裁判) to write down in an official book the name of a player who has broken the rules of the game 记名警告（犯规运动员）

PHR V ˌ**book ˈin/ˈinto sth** (*BrE*) to arrive at a hotel, etc. and arrange to stay there 到（旅馆等）办理入住手续：*I got in at ten and booked straight into a hotel.* 我十点钟到达后直接到一家旅馆办理了住宿手续。 ˌ**book sb ˈin/ˈinto sth** to arrange for sb to have a room at a hotel, etc. 为某人预订（旅馆房间等）

book·able /ˈbʊkəbl/ *adj.* **1** tickets, etc. that are **bookable** can be ordered in advance 可预订的 **2** (*BrE*) if an offence in football (SOCCER) is **bookable**, the name of the player responsible can be written down in a book by the REFEREE as a punishment （足球队员犯规）可记名警告的 **3** (*NAmE*) if a crime is a **bookable** offence, the person responsible can be arrested 够拘捕条件的

book·bind·er /ˈbʊkbaɪndə(r)/ *noun* a person whose job is fastening the pages of books together and putting covers on them 装订工人 ▶ **book·bind·ing** *noun* [U]

book·case /ˈbʊkkeɪs/ *noun* a piece of furniture with shelves for keeping books on 书架；书柜 ➲ VISUAL VOCAB PAGE V22

ˈ**book club** *noun* **1** an organization that sells books cheaply to its members 书友会（会员购书享受打折优惠） **2** = BOOK GROUP

book·end /ˈbʊkend/ *noun* [usually pl.] one of a pair of objects used to keep a row of books standing up 书挡

'book group (*also* **'book club**, **'reading group**) *noun* a group of people who meet together regularly to discuss a book they have all read 读书小组；读书会；读书俱乐部

bookie /ˈbʊki/ *noun* (*informal*) = BOOKMAKER

book·ing /ˈbʊkɪŋ/ *noun* **1** [C, U] (*especially BrE*) an arrangement that you make in advance to buy a ticket to travel somewhere, go to the theatre, etc. 预订： *a **booking form/hall/clerk*** 订票表；售票厅；售票员 ◇ *Can I make a **booking** for Friday?* 我可以订星期五的票吗？ ◇ ***Early booking** is recommended.* 请提早订票。 ◇ ***No advance booking** is necessary.* 无须提前订票。 ◇ *We can't take any more bookings.* 我们不能再接受订票了。 ➲ COMPARE RESERVATION (1) **2** [C] an arrangement for sb to perform at a theatre, in a concert, etc. （登台等的）预约，约定 **3** [C] (*BrE*) (in football (SOCCER) 足球) an act of the REFEREE writing a player's name in a book, as a punishment because an offence has been committed （对犯规者的）记名警告

'booking office *noun* (*BrE*) a place where you can buy tickets, at a train or bus station or at a theatre （车站、剧院等的）售票处 ➲ **MORE LIKE THIS** 9, page R26

book·ish /ˈbʊkɪʃ/ *adj.* (*often disapproving*) interested in reading and studying, rather than in more active or practical things 书呆子气的；学究似的

book·keep·er /ˈbʊkkiːpə(r)/ *noun* a person whose job is to keep an accurate record of the accounts of a business 簿记员 ▶ **book·keep·ing** *noun* [U]

'book learning *noun* [U] knowledge from books or study rather than from experience 书本知识，学堂知识（有别于实践经验）

book·let /ˈbʊklət/ *noun* a small thin book with a paper cover that contains information about a particular subject 小册子

book·maker /ˈbʊkmeɪkə(r)/ (*also informal* **bookie**) (*also BrE, formal* **'turf accountant**) *noun* a person whose job is to take bets on the result of horse races, etc. and pay out money to people who win （赛马等）赌注登记人 ▶ **book·mak·ing** *noun* [U]

book·mark /ˈbʊkmɑːk; *NAmE* -mɑːrk/ *noun* **1** a strip of paper, etc. that you put between the pages of a book when you finish reading so that you can easily find the place again 书签 **2** (*computing* 计) a record of the address of a file, a page on the Internet, etc. that enables you to find it quickly （电子文件、网页等的）书签 ➲ COMPARE FAVOURITE *n.* (3) ➲ **WORDFINDER NOTE** AT WEBSITE ▶ **book·mark** *verb* : **~ sth** *Do you want to bookmark this site?* 你想把这个网站加入书签吗？

book·mobile /ˈbʊkməbiːl/ (*NAmE*) (*BrE* **,mobile 'library**) *noun* a van/truck that contains a library and travels from place to place so that people in different places can borrow books 流动图书馆；图书馆车

book·plate /ˈbʊkpleɪt/ *noun* a decorative piece of paper that is stuck in a book to show the name of the person who owns it 藏书者标签（贴在书中）

book·sel·ler /ˈbʊkselə(r)/ *noun* a person whose job is selling books 书商

book·shelf /ˈbʊkʃelf/ *noun* (*pl.* **book·shelves** /ˈbʊkʃelvz/) a shelf that you keep books on 书架

book·shop /ˈbʊkʃɒp; *NAmE* -ʃɑːp/ (*especially BrE*) (*NAmE usually* **book·store** /ˈbʊkstɔː(r)/) *noun* a shop/store that sells books 书店

'book-smart *adj.* (*NAmE, becoming old-fashioned, often disapproving*) having a lot of academic knowledge learned from books and studying, but not necessarily knowing much about people and living in the real world 书本知识丰富的；书呆子的： *He's book-smart but he's got no common sense.* 他学究气十足，但缺乏常识。 ➲ COMPARE STREET-SMART

book·stall /ˈbʊkstɔːl/ (*especially BrE*) (*NAmE usually* **newsstand**) *noun* a small shop/store that is open at the front, where you can buy books, newspapers or magazines, for example at a station or an airport 书亭；书摊

'book token *noun* (*BrE*) a card, usually given as a gift, that you can exchange for books of a particular value 购书（代金）券

book·worm /ˈbʊkwɜːm; *NAmE* -wɜːrm/ *noun* a person who likes reading very much 极爱读书的人；书迷；书呆子

Bool·ean /ˈbuːliən/ *adj.* (*mathematics* 数, *computing* 计) connected with a system, used especially in COMPUTING and ELECTRONICS, that uses only the numbers 1 (to show sth is true) and 0 (to show sth is false) 布尔逻辑体系的（分别以 1 和 0 代指是和非）

,Boolean 'operator *noun* (*computing* 计) a symbol or word such as 'or' or 'and', used in computer programs and searches to show what is or is not included 布尔运算符（计算机程序或搜索中 or 或 and 等表示"包括"或"排除"的符号或词）

boom /buːm/ *noun, verb*

■ ***noun***

• **IN BUSINESS/ECONOMY** 商业；经济 **1** a sudden increase in trade and economic activity; a period of wealth and success （贸易和经济活动的）激增，繁荣： *Living standards improved rapidly during the post-war boom.* 在战后那段繁荣昌盛的时期里，生活水平得到了迅速提高。 ◇ **~ in sth** *a boom in car sales* 汽车销售额的剧增 ◇ *a **boom year** (for trade, exports, etc.)* （贸易、出口等）兴盛的一年 ◇ *a **property/housing boom*** 房地产的迅速发展 ◇ *a chaotic period of **boom and bust*** 经济繁荣与经济萧条交替出现的混乱时期 ➲ **WORDFINDER NOTE** AT TRADE, TREND ➲ **COLLOCATIONS** AT ECONOMY ➲ COMPARE SLUMP *n.* ➲ SEE ALSO BABY BOOM

• **POPULAR PERIOD** 风靡期 **2** [usually sing.] a period when sth such as a sport or a type of music suddenly becomes very popular and successful （某种体育运动、音乐等）突然风靡的时期： *The only way to satisfy the golf boom was to build more courses.* 满足这场高尔夫球热的唯一途径是增建球场。

• **ON BOAT** 船 **3** a long pole that the bottom of a sail is attached to and that you move to change the position of the sail 帆桁 ➲ **VISUAL VOCAB** PAGE V61

• **SOUND** 声音 **4** [usually sing.] a loud deep sound 深沉的响声： *the distant boom of the guns* 远处隆隆的炮声 ➲ SEE ALSO SONIC BOOM

• **IN RIVER/HARBOUR** 河；港口 **5** a floating barrier that is placed across a river or the entrance to a HARBOUR to prevent ships or other objects from coming in or going out 水栅

• **FOR MICROPHONE** 麦克风 **6** a long pole that carries a MICROPHONE or other equipment 吊杆；支架

■ ***verb***

• **MAKE LOUD SOUND** 发出巨响 **1** [I] to make a loud deep sound 轰鸣；轰响： *Outside, thunder boomed and crashed.* 外面雷声隆隆，霹雳炸响。 **2** [T, I] to say sth in a loud deep voice 以低沉有力的声音说话： **+ speech** *'Get out of my sight!' he boomed.* "别让我再见到你！"他低沉而有力地说。 ◇ **~ (out)** *A voice boomed out from the darkness.* 黑暗中传来低沉有力的嗓音。 ◇ *He had a **booming voice**.* 他的嗓音低沉有力。

• **OF BUSINESS/ECONOMY** 商业；经济 **3** [I] to have a period of rapid growth; to become bigger, more successful, etc. 迅速发展；激增；繁荣昌盛： *By the 1980s, the computer industry was booming.* 到 20 世纪 80 年代时，计算机行业迅猛发展。 ◇ *Business is booming!* 生意兴隆！

'boom box *noun* (*especially NAmE*) = GHETTO BLASTER

boom·burb /ˈbuːmbɜːb; *NAmE* -bɜːrb/ *noun* (*NAmE*) an area of a city that is outside the centre and that is quickly becoming larger as many people move there （人口快速增长的）市郊住宅区

boom·er /ˈbuːmə(r)/ *noun* **1** (*NAmE*) = BABY BOOMER **2** a large male KANGAROO 大雄袋鼠

boomerang 回力镖

boom·er·ang /ˈbuːməræŋ/ *noun, verb*

■ ***noun*** a curved flat piece of wood that you throw and that can fly in a circle and come back to you. Boomerangs were first used by Australian Aborigines as weapons when they were hunting. 回力镖，飞去来器（澳大利亚土著人最先用于狩猎）

■ ***verb*** [I] if a plan **boomerangs** on sb, it hurts them instead of the person it was intended to hurt （计划等）令人反受其害 SYN **backfire**

ˈ**boomerang kid** (*also* ˈ**boomerang child**) *noun* (*informal*) an adult child who returns home to live with his or her parents after being away for some time （成年子女离家一段时间后回家与父母同住的）还巢儿，回巢族

ˈ**boom town** *noun* a town that has become rich and successful because trade and industry has developed there （由于贸易和工业而）发达的城市

boon /buːn/ *noun* ~ (**to/for sb**) something that is very helpful and makes life easier for you 非常有用的东西；益处： *The new software will prove a boon to Internet users.* 这种新软件将会对互联网用户大有益处。

ˌ**boon comˈpanion** *noun* (*literary*) a very good friend 密友

boon·docks /ˈbuːndɒks; *NAmE* -dɑːks/ (*also* **boon·ies**) *noun* [pl.] (*NAmE, informal, disapproving*) an area far away from cities or towns 偏僻地区

boon·dog·gle /ˈbuːndɒɡl; *NAmE* -dɑːɡl; -dɔːɡl/ *noun* (*NAmE, informal*) a piece of work that is unnecessary and that wastes time and/or money 毫无意义的工作（或事情）；浪费时间金钱的工作（或事情）

boor /bʊə(r); bɔː(r); *NAmE* bʊr/ *noun* (*old-fashioned*) a rude unpleasant person 粗鲁讨厌的人；粗野的人

boor·ish /ˈbʊərɪʃ; ˈbɔːr-; *NAmE* ˈbʊr-/ *adj.* (of people and their behaviour 人及其行为) very unpleasant and rude 粗鲁讨厌的；粗野的

boost /buːst/ *verb, noun*

■ ***verb*** **1** ~ **sth** to make sth increase, or become better or more successful 使增长；使兴旺： *to boost exports/profits* 增加出口；提高利润 ◇ *The movie helped boost her screen career.* 那部电影有助于她的银幕生涯的发展。 ◇ *to* ***boost sb's confidence/morale*** 增强某人的信心 / 士气 ◇ *Getting that job did a lot to* ***boost his ego*** (= make him feel more confident). 得到那份工作使他信心倍增。 **2** ~ **sth** (*NAmE, informal, becoming old-fashioned*) to steal sth 偷窃

■ ***noun*** [usually sing.] **1** something that helps or encourages sb/sth 帮助；激励： *a* ***great/tremendous/welcome boost*** 很大的 / 极大的 / 令人欣喜的激励 ◇ *The tax cuts will give a much needed boost to the economy.* 减税将给经济带来迫切需要的推动力。 ◇ *Winning the competition was a wonderful boost for her morale.* 赢得那场比赛使她士气大振。 **2** an increase in sth 增长；提高： *a boost in car sales* 汽车销售额的增长 **3** an increase in power in an engine or a piece of electrical equipment （发动机或电气设备的）功率增大 **4** (*especially NAmE*) an act of pushing sb up from behind （从后面的）向上一推，一举： *He gave her a boost over the fence.* 他推了她一把，帮她翻过围墙。

boost·er /ˈbuːstə(r)/ *noun* **1** (*also* ˈ**booster rocket**) a ROCKET that gives a SPACECRAFT extra power when it leaves the earth, or that makes a MISSILE go further 助推器 **2** a device that gives extra power to a piece of electrical equipment （电器的）升压机，升压器 **3** an extra small amount of a drug that is given to increase the effect of one given earlier, for example to protect you from a disease for longer 加强剂量： *a tetanus booster* 破伤风加强剂 **4** a thing that helps, encourages or improves sb/sth 帮助（或激励、改善）…的事物： *a* ***morale/confidence booster*** 士气 / 信心的激励 **5** (*especially NAmE*) a person who gives their support to sb/sth, especially in politics （尤指政治上的）支持者，拥护者： *a meeting of Republican boosters* 共和党支持者的会议

ˈ**booster seat** *noun* a seat that you put on a car seat, or on a chair at a table, so that a small child can sit higher 幼儿加高座椅，幼儿加高坐垫（可放在车座或椅子上）

boot 🔑 /buːt/ *noun, verb*

■ ***noun*** **1** 🔑 a strong shoe that covers the foot and ankle and often the lower part of the leg 靴子： (*BrE*) *walking boots* 便靴 ◇ (*NAmE*) *hiking boots* 旅行靴 ◇ *a pair of black leather boots* 一双黑皮靴 ◇ *cowboy boots* 牛仔靴 ➲ VISUAL VOCAB PAGE V69 ➲ SEE ALSO DESERT BOOT, FOOTBALL BOOT, WELLINGTON **2** (*BrE*) (*NAmE* **trunk**) the space at the back of a car that you put bags, cases, etc. in （汽车后部的）行李厢： *I'll put the luggage in the boot.* 我去把行李放进后车厢。 ➲ VISUAL VOCAB PAGE V56 ➲ SEE ALSO CAR BOOT SALE **3** [usually sing.] (*informal*) a quick hard kick 猛踢： *He gave the ball a tremendous boot.* 他抽起脚猛踢了一下球。 **4** (*NAmE*) = DENVER BOOT

IDM **be given the ˈboot** | **get the ˈboot** (*informal*) to be told that you must leave your job or that a relationship you are having with sb is over 被解雇；被抛弃；（和某人的关系）被解除 **the boot is on the other ˈfoot** (*BrE*) (*NAmE* **the shoe is on the other ˈfoot**) used to say that a situation has changed so that sb now has power or authority over the person who used to have power or authority over them 情况正好相反；宾主易位 **put/stick the ˈboot in** (*BrE, informal*) **1** to kick sb very hard, especially when they are on the ground 猛踢（尤指倒地的人） **2** to attack sb by criticizing them when they are in a difficult situation 乘人之危抨击（某人） **to boot** (*old-fashioned* or *humorous*) used to add a comment to sth that you have said （用作附带评述）而且，另外，加之： *He was a vegetarian, and a fussy one to boot.* 他是个素食主义者，而且过于讲究。 ➲ MORE AT BIG *adj.*, FILL *v.*, LICK *v.*, TOUGH *adj.*

■ ***verb*** **1** [T] ~ **sth + adv./prep.** to kick sb/sth hard with your foot 猛踢： *He booted the ball clear of the goal.* 他一个大脚把球踢离了球门。 **2** [I, T] ~ (**sth**) (**up**) (*computing* 计) to prepare a computer for use by loading its OPERATING SYSTEM; to be prepared in this way 装入操作系统；启动（计算机） **3** [T] **be/get booted** (*NAmE, informal*) if you or your car is **booted**, a piece of equipment is fixed to the car's wheel so that you cannot drive it away, usually because the car is illegally parked 在（通常为非法停放的汽车）车轮上装制动装置 ➲ SEE ALSO CLAMP *v.*

PHR V ˌ**boot sb** ↔ **out** (**of sth**) (*informal*) to force sb to leave a place or job 赶走；解雇 SYN **throw out**

boot·boy /ˈbuːtbɔɪ/ *noun* (*BrE*) **1** (*informal*) a violent young man, especially one with very short hair and heavy boots （尤指蓄短发穿厚重靴子的）凶暴小青年 **2** in the past, a boy employed to clean boots and shoes （旧时的）擦鞋男童

ˈ**boot camp** *noun* **1** a training camp for new members of the armed forces, where they have to work hard 新兵训练营 **2** a type of prison for young criminals where there is strict discipline （青少年犯的）改造营 **3** a short course of very hard physical training 短期高强度体能训练： *I joined a boot camp to get fit.* 我参加了体能短训营进行健身。 ◇ (*figurative*) *You can cram for the exam at a one-week boot camp.* 你可以参加为期一周的集训课以全力备考。

'**boot-cut** *adj.* [usually before noun] **boot-cut** trousers/pants are slightly wider at the bottom of the legs where the material goes over the feet or shoes （裤子）裤脚套鞋面的，盖没脚面的

bootee (*also* **bootie**) /buːˈtiː/ *noun* **1** a baby's sock, worn instead of shoes 编织婴儿鞋；编织婴儿袜： *a pair of bootees* 一双当鞋穿的编织婴儿袜 **2** a woman's short boot 短筒女靴

ˌ**boot-ˈfaced** *adj.* (*BrE, informal*) looking very serious, angry or annoyed 表情严肃的；怒容满面的： *The boot-faced security guard wouldn't let us in.* 保安板着脸不让我们进去。

booth /buːð; *NAmE* buːθ/ *noun* **1** a small confined place where you can do sth privately, for example make a telephone call, or vote 不受干扰的划定空间（如电话亭、投票间等）： *a phone booth* 电话亭 ◇ *a polling/voting booth* 投票间 ◇ *an information/a ticket booth* 问询处；售票亭 ➲ SEE ALSO PHOTO BOOTH, TOLLBOOTH **2** a small tent or temporary structure at a market, an exhibition or a FAIRGROUND, where you can buy things, get information or watch sth 临时货摊（或放映棚等） **3** a place to sit in a restaurant which consists of two long seats with a table between them （餐馆中的）火车座，卡座

'**booth capturing** *noun* [U] (*IndE*) a practice carried out by members of a political party during an election, that involves staying in a POLLING BOOTH for long periods of time, stopping people who are registered to vote entering, and voting in their place in order to give the party an unfair advantage 占领投票亭（选举时某政党成员占据投票亭以阻止登记选民入内并代替他们投票，从而为本党赢得不公平的优势）

ˌ**Boot ˈHill** *noun* [U] (*US, informal, humorous*) (in the Wild West) a place where people are buried 靴丘（美国西大荒地区的坟地）

bootie *noun* = BOOTEE

boot·lace /ˈbuːtleɪs/ *noun* [usually pl.] a long thin piece of leather or string used to fasten boots or shoes 鞋带

boot·leg /ˈbuːtleg/ *adj., verb*
■ ***adj.*** [only before noun] made and sold illegally 非法制造贩卖的： *a bootleg CD* (= for example, one recorded illegally at a concert) 一张非法录制的 CD ➲ SEE ALSO PIRATE *n.* (2) ▸ **boot·leg** *noun*： *a bootleg of the concert* 非法录制的音乐会唱片
■ ***verb*** (**-gg-**) **~ sth** to make or sell goods, especially alcohol, illegally 非法生产或销售（商品，尤指酒） ▸ **boot·leg·ger** *noun* **boot·leg·ging** *noun* [U]

boot·lick·er /ˈbuːtlɪkə(r)/ *noun* (*informal, disapproving*) a person who is too friendly to sb in authority and is always ready to do what they want 马屁精 ▸ **boot·lick·ing** /ˈbuːtlɪkɪŋ/ *noun* [U]

boot·strap /ˈbuːtstræp/ *noun*
IDM ▸ **pull/drag yourself up by your (own) ˈbootstraps** (*informal*) to improve your situation yourself, without help from other people 自力更生

booty /ˈbuːti/ (*pl.* **-ies**) *noun* **1** [U] valuable things that are stolen, especially by soldiers in a time of war 赃物；掠夺物；战利品 SYN **loot** **2** [U] (*informal*) valuable things that sb wins, buys or obtains （赢得、购买、得到的）贵重物品： *When we got home from our day's shopping, we laid all our booty out on the floor.* 我们购物一天回到家里，把搜罗到的好东西都摊开摆在地板上。 **3** [C] (*informal, especially NAmE*) the part of the body that you sit on 屁股 SYN **buttocks**： *to shake your booty* (= to dance with great energy) 扭屁股（指用力跳舞）

boo·ty·li·cious /ˌbuːtɪˈlɪʃəs/ *adj.* (*informal, especially NAmE*) sexually attractive 性感的

'**boo word** *noun* (*BrE, informal*) a word or expression for sth that people dislike or disapprove of 引发嘘声的词；令人反感的说法： *Elitism has become a boo word in education.* 精英主义在教育领域已经成为不受欢迎的字眼。

booze /buːz/ *noun, verb*
■ ***noun*** [U] (*informal*) alcoholic drink 酒精饮料
■ ***verb*** [I] (*informal*) (usually used in the progressive tenses 通常用于进行时) to drink alcohol, especially in large quantities 喝酒；（尤指）狂饮： *He's out boozing with his mates.* 他和他的朋友们喝酒去了。

'**booze cruise** *noun* (*informal, humorous*) **1** (*BrE*) a short trip by FERRY from Britain to France or Belgium in order to buy alcohol or cigarettes cheaply 烟酒扫货游（指从英国乘船去法国或比利时买便宜的烟酒）： *to go on a booze cruise* 作烟酒扫货游 **2** (*especially NAmE*) a social occasion when people travel on a ship or boat and enjoy themselves by drinking alcohol, eating and dancing 游艇酒会游

boozer /ˈbuːzə(r)/ *noun* (*informal*) **1** (*BrE*) a pub 酒吧 **2** a person who drinks a lot of alcohol 豪饮者；酒鬼

'**booze-up** *noun* (*BrE, informal*) an occasion when people drink a lot of alcohol 狂饮作乐

boozy /ˈbuːzi/ *adj.* (*informal*) liking to drink a lot of alcohol; involving a lot of alcoholic drink 嗜酒的；豪饮的： *one of my boozy friends* 我的一位酒友 ◇ *a boozy lunch* 午间聚饮

bop /bɒp; *NAmE* bɑːp/ *noun, verb*
■ ***noun*** **1** [C] (*BrE, informal*) a dance to pop music; a social event at which people dance to pop music 博普舞，博普舞会（伴以流行音乐） **2** [U] = BEBOP
■ ***verb*** (**-pp-**) (*informal*) **1** [I] (*BrE*) to dance to pop music 跳博普舞 **2** [T] **~ sb** to hit sb lightly 轻打（某人）

bor·age /ˈbɒrɪdʒ; *NAmE* ˈbɔːrɪdʒ; ˈbɑːrɪdʒ/ *noun* [U] a Mediterranean plant with blue flowers that are shaped like stars, and leaves covered with small hairs. Borage leaves are eaten raw as a salad vegetable. 玻璃苣（地中海植物，开星形蓝花，叶子多绒毛，可作色拉菜生食）

borax /ˈbɔːræks/ *noun* [U] a white mineral, usually in powder form, used in making glass and as an ANTISEPTIC (= a substance that helps to prevent infection in wounds) 硼砂（作玻璃成分或用以给伤口消毒）

bor·dello /bɔːˈdeləʊ; *NAmE* bɔːrˈdeloʊ/ *noun* (*pl.* **-os**) (*especially NAmE*) = BROTHEL

bor·der 🔑 /ˈbɔːdə(r); *NAmE* ˈbɔːrd-/ *noun, verb*
■ ***noun*** **1** 🔑 the line that divides two countries or areas; the land near this line 国界；边界；边疆；边界地区： *a national park on the border between Kenya and Tanzania* 位于肯尼亚和坦桑尼亚边界的国家公园 ◇ *Denmark's border with Germany* 丹麦和德国的国界线 ◇ *in the US, near the Canadian border* 在美国，接近加拿大边界 ◇ *Nevada's northern border* 内华达州的北部边界 ◇ *to cross the border* 穿越边界 ◇ *to flee* ***across/over the border*** 穿越边境逃亡 ◇ ***border guards/controls*** 边防警卫；边境管制 ◇ *a* ***border dispute/incident*** 边界争端 / 事件 ◇ *a* ***border town/state*** 位于边疆的城镇 / 州 ◇ (*figurative*) *It is difficult to define the border between love and friendship.* 爱情和友情之间的界线难以划清。 ➲ WORDFINDER NOTE AT TOURIST ➲ COLLOCATIONS AT INTERNATIONAL **2** 🔑 a strip around the edge of sth such as a picture or a piece of cloth 镶边；包边： *a pillowcase with a lace border* 有花边的枕套 ➲ PICTURE AT EDGE **3** (in a garden 花园) a strip of soil which is planted with flowers, along the edge of the grass （草坪边等的）狭长花坛 ➲ VISUAL VOCAB PAGE V20
■ ***verb*** **1** **~ sth** (of a country or an area 国家或地区) to share a border with another country or area 和…毗邻；与…接壤： *the countries bordering the Baltic* 波罗的海沿岸国家 **2** **~ sth** to form a line along or around the edge of sth 沿…的边；环绕…；给…镶边： *Meadows bordered the path to the woods.* 通往树林的小径两边都是草坪。 ◇ *The large garden is bordered by a stream.* 大花园紧临着一条小溪。

PHR V ▸ '**border on sth** **1** to come very close to being sth, especially a strong or unpleasant emotion or quality 濒于；近乎： *She felt an anxiety bordering on hysteria.* 她感觉到一种近乎歇斯底里的焦虑。 **2** to be next to sth 挨着；接壤： *areas bordering on the Black Sea* 黑海沿岸地区

▼ SYNONYMS 同义词辨析

border

boundary • frontier

These are all words for a line that marks the edge of sth and separates it from other areas or things. 以上各词均指边界、分界线。

border the line that separates two countries or areas; the land near this line 指国界、边界、边疆、边界地区： *a national park on the border between Kenya and Tanzania* 位于肯尼亚和坦桑尼亚边界的国家公园

boundary a line that marks the edges of an area of land and separates it from other areas 指边界、界限、分界线： *The fence marked the boundary between my property and hers.* 那道篱笆曾是我和她的房产之间的地界。

frontier (*BrE*) the line that separates two countries or areas; the land near this line 指国界、边界、边疆、边境： *The river formed the frontier between the land of the Saxons and that of the Danes.* 这条河曾是撒克逊人与古斯堪的纳维亚人土地的分界线。

WHICH WORD? 词语辨析

The point where you cross from one country to another is usually called the **border**. In British English it can also be called the **frontier**, but this is often in a context of wildness, danger and uncertainty. 国界线通常叫 border；英式英语亦可叫 frontier，但 frontier 常与荒芜、危险和不确定联系在一起： *The rebels control the frontier and the surrounding area.* 叛乱分子控制了边疆地区。 The line on a map that shows the border of a country can be called the **boundary** but 'boundary' is not used when you cross from one country to another. 地图上标示的国界线可叫 boundary，但穿越国界不用 boundary： *After the war the national boundaries were redrawn.* 战后重新划定了国界。 ◇ ~~*Thousands of immigrants cross the boundary every day.*~~ **Boundary** can also be a physical line between two places, for example between property belonging to two different people, marked by a fence or wall. * boundary 亦可指两地间的分界线，如用篱笆或墙隔开的分属于不同的两个人的土地分界线： *the boundary fence/wall between the properties* 分隔两所房子的篱笆 / 墙

PATTERNS

- **across/along/on/over** a/the border/boundary/frontier
- **at** the boundary/frontier
- the border/boundary/frontier **with** a place
- the **northern/southern/eastern/western** border/boundary/frontier
- a **national/common/disputed** border/boundary/frontier

Border 'collie *noun* a medium-sized black and white dog, often used as a SHEEPDOG 边境牧羊犬（毛黑白相间）

bor·der·land /ˈbɔːdəlænd; *NAmE* ˈbɔːrdər-/ *noun* **1** [C] an area of land close to a border between two countries 边疆；边境 **2** [sing.] an area between two qualities, ideas or subjects that has features of both but is not clearly one or the other （介乎两种品质、思想或学科等之间的）边缘领域： *the murky borderland between history and myth* 历史与神话之间的边缘领域

bor·der·line /ˈbɔːdəlaɪn; *NAmE* ˈbɔːrdər-/ *adj., noun*

■ *adj.* not clearly belonging to a particular condition or group; not clearly acceptable 所属不清的；两可之间的；临界的： *In* ***borderline cases*** *teachers will take the final decision, based on the student's previous work.* 在难以定夺的情况下，教师将根据学生先前的作业作出最终评分。 ◇ *a* ***borderline pass/fail*** *in an exam* 考试得分刚刚在及格线上 / 下

■ *noun* the division between two qualities or conditions 两种品质（或状况）之间的分界线： *This biography sometimes crosses the borderline between fact and fiction.* 这部传记有时混淆了事实和虚构。

bore 🔑 /bɔː(r)/ *verb, noun* ➲ SEE ALSO BEAR *v.*, BORE *v.*, BORNE

■ *verb* **1** 🔑 [T] to make sb feel bored, especially by talking too much （尤指因啰嗦）使厌烦： **~ sb** *I'm not boring you, am I?* 我没有让你厌烦吧，是不是？ ◇ **~ sb with sth** *Has he been boring you with his stories about his trip?* 他是不是用他旅游的见闻在烦你？ **2** [I, T] to make a long deep hole with a tool or by digging 钻，凿，挖（长而深的洞）： **~ into/through sth** *The drill is strong enough to bore through solid rock.* 这把钻足以钻透坚固的岩石。 ◇ **~ sth (in/through sth)** *to bore a hole in sth* 在某物体上挖个洞 **3** [I] **~ into sb/sth** (of eyes 眼睛) to stare in a way that makes sb feel uncomfortable 盯着看： *His blue eyes seemed to bore into her.* 他的一双蓝眼睛似乎要穿透她。

■ *noun* **1** [C] a person who is very boring, usually because they talk too much （常因话多）令人厌烦的人 **2** [sing.] a situation or thing that is boring or that annoys you 烦人的状况（或事情）： *It's such a bore having to stay late this evening.* 今天晚上得熬夜了，真是烦人。 **3** [C] (*also* **gauge** *especially in NAmE*) the hollow inside of a tube, such as a pipe or a gun; the width of the hole （管道、枪炮等的）孔，内径，口径；膛径： *a tube with a wide/narrow bore* 内径宽 / 窄的管子 ◇ *a twelve-bore shotgun* 一支十二口径猎枪 **4** [C] a strong, high wave that rushes along a river from the sea at particular times of the year （海水涌入江河的）涌潮，激潮 **5** [C] (*also* **bore·hole**) a deep hole made in the ground, especially to find water or oil （尤指找水或石油的）探孔，钻孔 IDM SEE CRASH *v.*

bored 🔑 /bɔːd; *NAmE* bɔːrd/ *adj.* feeling tired and impatient because you have lost interest in sb/sth or because you have nothing to do （对某人 / 事物）厌倦的；烦闷的： *There was a bored expression on her face.* 她脸上有一种厌倦的表情。 ◇ **~ with/of sb/sth | ~ with/of doing sth** *The children quickly* ***got bored*** *with staying indoors.* 孩子们在屋子里很快就待不住了。

IDM **bored 'stiff | bored to 'death/'tears | bored out of your 'mind** (*informal*) extremely bored 厌烦透了的；极其厌倦的 ➲ MORE AT WITLESS

bore·dom /ˈbɔːdəm; *NAmE* ˈbɔːrdəm/ *noun* [U] the state of feeling bored; the quality of being very boring 厌烦；厌倦；无聊： *I started to eat too much out of sheer boredom.* 由于实在闲极无聊，我开始无节制地大吃起来。 ◇ *Television helps to relieve the boredom of the long winter evenings.* 电视有助于打发漫长无聊的冬夜。

bore·hole /ˈbɔːhəʊl; *NAmE* ˈbɔːrhoʊl/ *noun* = BORE (5)

bore·well /ˈbɔːwel; *NAmE* ˈbɔːrwel/ *noun* (*IndE*) a pipe that is put into a hole that has been BORED in the ground, and used with a PUMP in order to get water from under the ground 孔式水井；泵压水井

bor·ing 🔑 /ˈbɔːrɪŋ/ *adj.* not interesting; making you feel tired and impatient 没趣的；令人厌倦（或厌烦）的： *a boring man* 惹人烦的人 ◇ *a boring job/book/evening* 无聊的工作 / 书 / 夜晚 ▶ **bor·ing·ly** *adv.* ： *boringly normal* 平淡无味

born 🔑 /bɔːn; *NAmE* bɔːrn/ *verb, adj.*

■ *verb* **be born** (used only in the passive, without *by* 仅用于被动语态，不用 by) **1** 🔑 (*abbr.* **b.**) to come out of your mother's body at the beginning of your life 出生；出世： *I was born in 1976.* 我生于 1976 年。 ◇ *She was born with a weak heart.* 她生来就有一个衰弱的心脏。 ◇ **~ into sth** *She was born into a very musical family.* 她生于音乐之家。 ◇ **~ of/to sb** *He was born of/to German parents.* 他的生身父母是德国人。 ◇ **+ adj.** *Her brother was* ***born blind***

(= was blind when he was born). 她的哥哥先天性失明。◇ **+ noun** *John Wayne was born Marion Michael Morrison* (= that was his name at birth). 约翰·韦恩出生时取名马里恩·迈克尔·莫里森。➲ COLLOCATIONS AT AGE **2** 🔑 (of an idea, an organization, a feeling, etc. 思想、机构、感情等) to start to exist 出现；形成；成立： *the city where the protest movement was born* 抗议运动发源的城市 ◇ **~ (out) of sth** *She acted with a courage born (out) of desperation.* 绝望驱使她鼓起勇气，作出行动。 **3 -born** (in compounds 构成复合词) born in the order, way, place, etc. mentioned 以…的顺序（或方式、地点等）出生的： *firstborn* 第一个孩子 ◇ *nobly born* 出身贵族 ◇ *French-born* 法国出生的 ➲ SEE ALSO NEWBORN

IDM **be 'born to be/do sth** to have sth as your DESTINY (= what is certain to happen to you) from birth 注定会成为；注定要做： *He was born to be a great composer.* 他是个天生的伟大作曲家。 **,born and 'bred** born and having grown up in a particular place with a particular background and education （在某地）出生长大；受过…熏陶： *He was born and bred in Boston.* 他生于波士顿，长于波士顿。◇ *I'm a Londoner, born and bred.* 我是个土生土长的伦敦人。➲ MORE LIKE THIS 13, page R26 **born with a silver 'spoon in your mouth** (*saying*) having rich parents 生于富裕之家；出身富裕 **in all my born 'days** (*old-fashioned, informal*) used when you are very surprised at sth you have never heard or seen before （表示惊讶）这辈子（未听说，未见）： *I've never heard such nonsense in all my born days.* 我这辈子还从没听说过此等废话呢。 **not be born 'yesterday** (*informal*) used to say that you are not stupid enough to believe what sb is telling you （表示自己并不傻，不会轻信别人的话）： *Oh yeah? I wasn't born yesterday, you know.* 是吗？我可不是三岁的小孩子，你知道的。 **there's one born every 'minute** (*saying*) used to say that sb is very stupid 总有那种傻瓜 ➲ MORE AT KNOW *v.*, MANNER, WAY *n.*

▪ ***adj.*** [only before noun] having a natural ability or skill for a particular activity or job 天生（有某方面才能）的： *a* ***born*** *athlete/writer/leader* 天生的运动员 / 作家 / 领袖 ◇ *a* ***born*** *loser* (= a person who always loses or is unsuccessful) 永远的失败者

,born-a'gain *adj.* [usually before noun] having come to have a strong belief in a particular religion (especially EVANGELICAL Christianity) or idea, and wanting other people to have the same belief （宗教等信仰上）再生的；（尤指基督教徒）重生的： *a born-again Christian* 皈依基督教的人 ◇ *a born-again vegetarian* 开始信仰素食的人

▼ **SYNONYMS** 同义词辨析

boring

dull • tedious

These words all describe a subject, activity, person or place that is not interesting or exciting. 以上各词均形容话题、活动、人或地方等没意思、乏味。

boring not interesting; making you feel tired and impatient 指没有趣味的、令人厌倦或厌烦的： *He's such a boring man!* 他那人无趣得很！◇ *She found her job very boring.* 她觉得自己的工作很无聊。

dull not interesting or exciting 指枯燥无味的、沉闷的： *Life in a small town could be deadly dull.* 小城镇的生活可能会非常没意思。

tedious lasting or taking too long and not interesting, so that you feel bored and impatient 指冗长的、单调乏味的、令人厌烦的： *The journey soon became tedious.* 那次旅行不久就变得乏味起来。

PATTERNS

- to be boring/dull/tedious **for** sb
- boring/dull/tedious **subjects/books**
- boring/dull/tedious **jobs/work/games**
- a boring/dull **place/man/woman/person**
- **deadly** boring/dull

borne /bɔːn; *NAmE* bɔːrn/ **1** PAST PART. OF BEAR **2 -borne** (in adjectives 构成形容词) carried by 由…携带的： *water-borne diseases* 由水传染的疾病

boron /ˈbɔːrɒn; *NAmE* -rɑːn/ *noun* [U] (*symb.* **B**) a chemical element. Boron is a solid substance used in making steel ALLOYS and parts for nuclear REACTORS. 硼

bor·ough /ˈbʌrə; *NAmE* ˈbɜːroʊ/ *noun* a town or part of a city that has its own local government 自治市镇；（城市）行政区： *the London borough of Westminster* 伦敦的威斯敏斯特自治市 ◇ *The Bronx is one of the five boroughs of New York.* 布朗克斯是纽约市的五个行政区之一。◇ *a borough council* 自治镇政务会

bor·row 🔑 /ˈbɒrəʊ; *NAmE* ˈbɑːroʊ; ˈbɔːr-/ *verb* **1** 🔑 [T] to take and use sth that belongs to sb else, and return it to them at a later time 借；借用： **~ sth** *Can I borrow your umbrella?* 借你的伞用一下行吗？◇ **~ sth from sb/sth** *Members can borrow up to ten books from the library at any one time.* 会员在图书馆每次最多可借十本书。◇ **~ sth off sb** (*BrE, informal*) *I borrowed the DVD off my brother.* 我从我哥哥那里借了这张 DVD。➲ COMPARE LEND (1) **2** 🔑 [T, I] to take money from a person or bank and agree to pay it back to them at a later time 借入（款项）；（向…）借贷： *She borrowed £2 000 from her parents.* 她向她的父母借了 2 000 英镑。◇ **~ (from sb/sth)** *I don't like to borrow from friends.* 我不喜欢向朋友借钱。◇ **~ sth off sb** (*informal*) *I had to borrow the money off a friend.* 我不得不向一个朋友开口借这笔钱。➲ COMPARE LEND (2) **3** [I, T] to take words, ideas, etc. from another language, person, etc. and use them, as your own 引用，借用（思想、言语等）： **~ (from sb/sth)** *The author borrows heavily from Henry James.* 那位作家大量引用亨利·詹姆斯的作品。◇ **~ sth (from sb/sth)** *Some musical terms are borrowed from Italian.* 某些音乐术语是从意大利语引入的。

IDM **be (living) on borrowed 'time 1** to still be alive after the time when you were expected to die 活过寿限；大限已近 **2** to be doing sth that other people are likely to soon stop you from doing 做很快就会遭到制止的事；好景不长

▼ **WHICH WORD?** 词语辨析

borrow / lend

- These two words are often confused. You **borrow** something from someone else, while they **lend** it to you. 这两个词常被混淆，借入用 borrow，借出用 lend： *Can I borrow your pen?* 我可以借用你的钢笔吗？◇ *Can I borrow a pen from you?* 我可以借用你的钢笔吗？◇ *Here, I'll lend you my pen.* 喏，我把钢笔借给你。

bor·row·er /ˈbɒrəʊə(r); *NAmE* ˈbɑːroʊər; ˈbɔːr-/ *noun* a person or an organization that borrows money, especially from a bank 借款人；借方 ➲ COMPARE LENDER

bor·row·ing /ˈbɒrəʊɪŋ; *NAmE* ˈbɑːroʊɪŋ; ˈbɔːr-/ *noun* **1** [C, U] the money that a company, an organization or a person borrows; the act of borrowing money 借款；贷款；借贷： *an attempt to reduce bank borrowings* 减少向银行借贷的努力 ◇ *High interest rates help to keep borrowing down.* 高利率有助于控制借贷。➲ COLLOCATIONS AT ECONOMY **2** [C] a word, a phrase or an idea that sb has taken from another person's work or from another language and used in their own 借用的言语（或思想等）

borscht /bɔːʃt; *NAmE* bɔːrʃt/ (*BrE also* **borsch** /bɔːʃ; *NAmE* bɔːrʃ/) *noun* [U] a Russian or Polish soup made from BEETROOT (= a dark red root vegetable) （俄罗斯或波兰）甜菜汤；罗宋汤

B

bor·stal /ˈbɔːstl; *NAmE* ˈbɔːrstl/ *noun* [C, U] (in Britain in the past) a type of prison for young criminals （英国旧时的）青少年犯教养院 ➲ SEE ALSO YOUTH CUSTODY

bor·zoi /ˈbɔːzɔɪ; *NAmE* ˈbɔːr-/ *noun* a large Russian dog with soft white hair 俄罗斯灵㹴

bos·ber·aad /ˈbɒsbərɑːt; *NAmE* ˈbɔːs-; ˈbɑːs-/ *noun* (*SAfrE*) a meeting of business leaders, politicians, etc. at a place that is a long way from a town, in order to discuss important matters （商界领袖、政治家等参加，远离市区的）重大会议，战略会议

bosom /ˈbʊzəm/ *noun* **1** [C] a woman's chest or breasts 女人的胸部（或乳房）： *her ample bosom* 她丰满的乳房 ◇ *She pressed him to her bosom.* 她紧紧地把他抱在胸前。 **2** [C] the part of a piece of clothing that covers a woman's bosom 女衣胸部（或胸襟）： *a rose pinned to her bosom* 别在她胸襟上的一朵玫瑰 **3 the ~ of sth** [sing.] a situation in which you are with people who love and protect you 和爱护自己的人在一起的情形；在…的怀抱中： *to live in the bosom of your family* 生活在家庭的温暖怀抱中

ˌbosom ˈfriend (*NAmE also* **ˌbosom ˈbuddy**) *noun* a very close friend 密友；知己

bos·omy /ˈbʊzəmi/ *adj.* (*old-fashioned, informal*) (of a woman 女人) having large breasts 乳房发达的；胸部丰满的

boss 🔑 /bɒs; *NAmE* bɔːs; bɑːs/ *noun, verb, adj.*

▪ ***noun*** **1** 🔑 a person who is in charge of other people at work and tells them what to do 老板；工头；领班： *I'll ask my boss if I can have the day off.* 我要问一下老板我能不能请一天假。 ◇ *I like being **my own boss*** (= working for myself and making my own decisions). 我喜欢自己做老板，自己拿主意。 ◇ *Who's the boss* (= who's in control) *in this house?* 这个家里谁说了算？ **2** 🔑 (*informal*) a person who is in charge of a large organization 总经理；领导： *the new boss at IBM* * IBM 公司的新领导 ◇ *Hospital bosses protested at the decision.* 医院领导们抗议这一决定。 IDM SEE SHOW *v.*

▪ ***verb*** **~ sb (about/around)** to tell sb what to do in an aggressive and/or annoying way 对（某人）发号施令： *I'm sick of you bossing me around!* 我讨厌你对我指手画脚。

▪ ***adj.*** (*especially NAmE, slang*) very good 很好的

bossa nova /ˌbɒsə ˈnəʊvə; *NAmE* ˌbɑːsə ˈnoʊvə; ˌbɔːsə ˈnoʊvə/ *noun* [U, C] a style of Brazilian popular music, popular in the 1960s 巴萨诺瓦（20 世纪 60 年代广受欢迎的一种巴西流行乐）

bossy /ˈbɒsi; *NAmE* ˈbɔːsi; ˈbɑːsi/ *adj.* (*disapproving*) (**boss·ier, bossi·est**) always telling people what to do 好指挥人的；专横的 ▸ **boss·ily** *adv.* **bossi·ness** *noun* [U]

bossy·boots /ˈbɒsibuːts; *NAmE* ˈbɔːs-/ *noun* (*pl.* **bossy·boots**) (*BrE, informal, disapproving*) a person who always tells people what they should do 爱支使人的人；颐指气使的人

ˌBoston baked ˈbeans (*also* **baked ˈbeans**) *noun* [pl.] (*NAmE*) small white beans baked with pork and brown sugar or MOLASSES (= a dark, sweet, thick liquid obtained from sugar) （加猪肉和红糖或糖浆制的）波士顿烤豆

bo·sun (*also* **bo'sun, boat·swain**) /ˈbəʊsn; *NAmE* ˈboʊ-/ *noun* an officer on a ship whose job is to take care of the equipment and the people who work on the ship 水手长

bot /bɒt; *NAmE* bɑːt/ *noun* (*computing* 计) a computer program that performs a particular task many times 网上机器人；自动程序

bo·tan·ic·al /bəˈtænɪkl/ *adj.* connected with the science of botany 植物学的

boˌtanical ˈgarden (*also* **boˌtanic ˈgarden**) *noun* [usually pl.] a park where plants, trees and flowers are grown for scientific study 植物园

bot·an·ist /ˈbɒtənɪst; *NAmE* ˈbɑːt-/ *noun* a scientist who studies botany 植物学家

bot·any /ˈbɒtəni; *NAmE* ˈbɑːt-/ *noun* [U] the scientific study of plants and their structure 植物学 ➲ COMPARE BIOLOGY, ZOOLOGY

botch /bɒtʃ; *NAmE* bɑːtʃ/ *verb, noun*

▪ ***verb*** **~ sth (up)** (*informal*) to spoil sth by doing it badly 笨拙地弄糟（某事物）： *He completely botched up the interview.* 他面试表现得糟透了。 ◇ *The work they did on the house was a **botched job**.* 他们整修房子做得一塌糊涂。

▪ ***noun*** (*also* **ˈbotch-up**) (*BrE, informal*) a piece of work or a job that has been done badly 拙劣的工作；粗制滥造的活儿： *I've made a real botch of the decorating.* 我的装潢工作做得实在是糟糕。

both 🔑 /bəʊθ; *NAmE* boʊθ/ *det., pron.* **1** 🔑 used with plural nouns to mean 'the two' or 'the one as well as the other' （与复数名词连用）两个，两个都： *Both women were French.* 两名妇女都是法国人。 ◇ *Both the women were French.* 两名妇女都是法国人。 ◇ *Both of the women were French.* 两名妇女都是法国人。 ◇ *I talked to the women. Both of them were French/They were both French.* 我和两位妇女交谈了，她们都是法国人。 ◇ *I liked them both.* 他俩我都喜欢。 ◇ *We were both tired.* 咱俩都累了。 ◇ *Both of us were tired.* 咱俩都累了。 ◇ *We have both seen the movie.* 我们俩都看过这部电影。 ◇ *I have two sisters. Both of them live in London/They both live in London.* 我有两个姐妹，她俩都住在伦敦。 ◇ *Both (my) sisters live in London.* 我的两个姐妹都住在伦敦。 **2** 🔑 **both… and…** not only… but also… 不仅…而且…；…和…都： *Both his mother and his father will be there.* 他父母二人都要去那里。 ◇ *For this job you will need a good knowledge of both Italian and Spanish.* 担任这项工作需要精通意大利语和西班牙语。 ➲ LANGUAGE BANK AT SIMILARLY

bother 🔑 /ˈbɒðə(r); *NAmE* ˈbɑːð-/ *verb, noun, exclamation*

▪ ***verb*** **1** 🔑 [I, T] (often used in negative sentences and questions 常用于否定句和疑问句) to spend time and/or energy doing sth 花费时间精力（做某事）： *'Shall I wait?' 'No, don't bother'.* "要我等一下吗？""不，别费事了。" ◇ *I don't know why I bother! Nobody ever listens!* 我不知道我干吗要浪费时间！根本没人听！ ◇ **~ with/about sth** *It's not worth bothering with* (= using) *an umbrella—the car's just outside.* 不必打伞，汽车就停在外面。 ◇ *I don't know why you bother with that crowd* (= why you spend time with them). 我弄不懂你为什么和那伙人浪费时间。 ◇ **~ to do sth** *He didn't even bother to let me know he was coming.* 他甚至连通知都没通知我他要来。 ◇ **~ doing sth** *Why bother asking if you're not really interested?* 如果你不是真的感兴趣，干吗费口舌打听呢？ **2** 🔑 [T] to annoy, worry or upset sb; to cause sb trouble or pain 使（某人）烦恼（或担忧、不安）；给（某人）造成麻烦（或痛苦）： **~ sb** *The thing that bothers me is…* 让我感到不安的是… ◇ *That sprained ankle is still bothering her* (= hurting). 她那扭伤的脚踝还在隐隐作痛。 ◇ *'I'm sorry he was so rude to you.' 'It doesn't bother me.'* "对不起，他对你太没礼貌。""没关系。" ◇ **~ sb with sth** *I don't want to bother her with my problems at the moment.* 我此刻不想让她为我的事操心。 ◇ **~ sb that…** *Does it bother you that she earns more than you?* 她比你挣的钱多，你是不是觉得不自在？ ◇ **it bothers sb to do sth** *It bothers me to think of her alone in that big house.* 想到她孤零零地待在那所大房子里，我便坐立不安。 **3** 🔑 [T] to interrupt sb; to talk to sb when they do not want to talk to you 打扰；搭话烦扰： **~ sb** *Stop bothering me when I'm working.* 我工作时别来烦我。 ◇ *Let me know if he bothers you again.* 他要是再搅扰你，就告诉我。 ◇ ***Sorry to bother you**, but there's a call for you on line two.* 很抱歉打扰你一下，二号线有你的电话。

IDM **be bothered (about sb/sth)** 🔑 (*informal, especially BrE*) to think that sb/sth is important 认为（某人或某事）重要；关心（某人或某事）： *I'm not bothered about what he thinks.* 我不在乎他怎么想。 ◇ *'Where shall we eat?' 'I'm not bothered.'* (= I don't mind where we go.) "我们去

哪里吃饭？”“随便。” **can't be bothered (to do sth)** used to say that you do not want to spend time and/or energy doing sth （表示不想花时间精力做某事）: *I should really do some work this weekend but I can't be bothered.* 我这个周末真该做点事了，可我懒得做。◇ *All this has happened because you couldn't be bothered to give me the message.* 就是因为你嫌麻烦没通知我，才出了这事。 **not bother yourself/your head with/about sth** (*especially BrE*) to not spend time/effort on sth, because it is not important or you are not interested in it 不为某事花费时间（或精力）；不操心 ➲ MORE AT HOT *adj.*

■ ***noun*** **1** [U] trouble or difficulty 麻烦；困难: *You seem to have got yourself into a* ***spot of bother.*** 你似乎惹上了点麻烦。◇ *I don't want to* ***put you to any bother*** (= cause you any trouble). 我不想给你添乱子。◇ ***Don't go to the bother*** *of tidying up on my account* (= don't make the effort to do it). 别为了我费事整理一番。◇ *'Thanks for your help!' 'It was no bother.'* "多谢你的帮助！" "没什么。" ◇ *Call them and save yourself the bother of going round.* 给他们打个电话就免得你亲自去了。 **2 a bother** [sing.] an annoying situation, thing or person 令人烦恼的情况（或事物、人） **SYN** **nuisance**: *I hope I haven't been a bother.* 希望我没烦扰你。

■ ***exclamation*** (*BrE, informal*) used to express the fact that you are annoyed about sth/sb （表示对某事或某人烦恼）: *Bother! I've left my wallet at home.* 真烦人！我把钱包落在家里了。◇ *Oh, bother him! He's never around when you need him.* 哎呀，他可真讨厌！需要他的时候从来都找不到他。

both·er·ation /ˌbɒðəˈreɪʃn; *NAmE* ˌbɑːð-/ *exclamation* (*old-fashioned, informal*) a word that people use to show that they are annoyed 讨厌；烦人

both·er·some /ˈbɒðəsəm; *NAmE* ˈbɑːðərsəm/ *adj.* (*old-fashioned*) causing trouble or difficulty 引起麻烦的；困扰人的 **SYN** **annoying**

bothy /ˈbɒθi; *NAmE* ˈbɔːθi/ *noun* (*pl.* **-ies**) a small building in Scotland for farm workers to live in or for people to shelter in （苏格兰供农场工人居住或供人栖身的）茅屋，棚屋

bot·net /ˈbɒtnet; *NAmE* ˈbɑːt-/ *noun* (*computing* 计) a group of computers that are controlled by MALWARE (= software such as a virus that the users do not know about or want) 僵尸网络（指受恶意软件控制的计算机群）

Bo·tox™ /ˈbəʊtɒks; *NAmE* ˈboʊtɑːks/ *noun* [U] a substance that makes muscles relax. It is sometimes INJECTED into the skin around sb's eyes to remove lines and make the skin look younger. 保妥适注射液，肉毒杆菌素（可用于除皱） ▶ **Bo·tox** *verb* **~ sb/sth** [usually passive]: *Do you think she's been Botoxed?* 你认为她用过肉毒素除皱吗？

bot·tle /ˈbɒtl; *NAmE* ˈbɑːtl/ *noun, verb*

■ ***noun*** **1** [C] a glass or plastic container, usually round with straight sides and a narrow neck, used especially for storing liquids （细颈）瓶子: ***a wine/beer/milk bottle*** 酒瓶；啤酒瓶；奶瓶 ◇ *Put the top back on the bottle.* 把瓶盖盖上。 ➲ VISUAL VOCAB PAGE V36 **2** [C] (*also* **bottle·ful** /-fʊl/) the amount contained in a bottle 一瓶（的量）: *He drank a whole bottle of wine.* 他喝了整整一瓶酒。 **3 the bottle** [sing.] (*informal*) alcoholic drink 酒: *After his wife died, he really* ***hit the bottle*** (= started drinking heavily). 他妻子死后，他就酗酒了。 **4** [C, usually sing.] a bottle used to give milk to a baby; the milk from such a bottle (used instead of mother's milk) （婴儿）奶瓶；奶瓶里的奶（非母乳）: *It's time for her bottle.* 该给她用奶瓶喂奶了。 **5** [U] (*BrE, informal*) courage or confidence, for example to do sth that is dangerous or unpleasant 勇气；信心 **SYN** **nerve**: *It took a lot of bottle to do that.* 那样做需要很大的勇气。

■ ***verb*** **1 ~ sth** to put a liquid into a bottle 把（液体）装入瓶中: *The wines are bottled after three years.* 那些酒是在三年之后装瓶的。 **2 ~ sth** to put fruit or vegetables into glass containers in order to preserve them 把（水果或蔬菜等）装入玻璃瓶储存 ▶ **bot·tled** *adj.*: ***bottled beer/water/pickles*** 瓶装啤酒 / 水 / 腌菜 ◇ ***bottled gas*** (= sold in metal containers for use in heating and cooking) 瓶装液化气

IDM **ˈbottle it** (*BrE, informal*) to not do sth, or not finish sth, because you are frightened 不敢做；（中途）放弃，退缩

PHR V **ˌbottle ˈout (of sth/doing sth)** (*BrE, informal*) to not do sth that you had intended to do because you are too frightened （因恐惧而）放弃原计划 **ˌbottle sth↔ˈup** to not allow other people to see that you are unhappy, angry, etc., especially when this happens over a long period of time 长时间掩饰，遏制，隐瞒（不快等）: *Try not to bottle up your emotions.* 尽量不要压抑自己的情感。

ˈbottle bank *noun* (*BrE*) a large container in a public place where people can leave their empty bottles so that the glass can be used again (= RECYCLED); a public place with several of these containers 玻璃瓶回收箱；玻璃瓶回收点 ➲ VISUAL VOCAB PAGE V9

ˌbottle ˈblonde (*also* **ˌbottle ˈblond**) *adj.* (*disapproving*) (of hair 头发) artificially coloured blonde 染成金色的 ▶ **ˌbottle ˈblonde** *noun*: *She's a bottle blonde.* 她的金发是染的。

ˈbottle-feed *verb* [T, I] **~ (sb)** to feed a baby with artificial milk from a bottle 用奶瓶喂（婴儿） ➲ COMPARE BREAST-FEED

ˌbottle-ˈgreen *adj.* (*especially BrE*) dark green in colour 深绿色的: *a bottle-green coat* 一件深绿色的大衣 ▶ **ˌbottle ˈgreen** *noun* [U] ➲ **MORE LIKE THIS** 15, page R26

bottle·neck /ˈbɒtlnek; *NAmE* ˈbɑːtl-/ *noun* **1** a narrow or busy section of road where the traffic often gets slower and stops 瓶颈路段（常引起交通阻塞） **2** anything that delays development or progress, particularly in business or industry （尤指工商业发展的）瓶颈，阻碍，障碍 **SYN** **logjam**

ˈbottle opener *noun* a small tool for opening bottles with metal tops, for example beer bottles 开瓶器 ➲ VISUAL VOCAB PAGE V27

ˈbottle party *noun* (*BrE*) a party to which the people who have been invited are asked to bring a bottle, usually of wine 自带酒水聚会

ˈbottle store (*also* **ˈbottle shop**) *noun* (*AustralE, NZE, SAfrE*) a shop/store that sells a variety of alcoholic drinks in bottles, cans, etc. to take away 瓶装酒销售店；酒铺 ➲ COMPARE OFF-LICENCE

bot·tom /ˈbɒtəm; *NAmE* ˈbɑːtəm/ *noun, adj., verb*

■ ***noun***

• **LOWEST PART** 底部 **1** [C, usually sing.] **~ (of sth)** the lowest part of sth 底部；最下部: *Footnotes are given at the bottom of each page.* 脚注附于每页的下端。◇ *I waited for them at the bottom of the hill.* 我在山脚下等候他们。◇ *The book I want is right at the bottom* (= of the pile). 我想要的书就压在（那堆书的）最下面。 **OPP** **top** **2** [C, usually sing.] **~ (of sth)** the part of sth that faces downwards and is not usually seen （朝下的）底，底面: *The manufacturer's name is on the bottom of the plate.* 厂家的名称在盘子底面。

• **OF CONTAINER** 容器 **3** [C, usually sing.] **~ (of sth)** the lowest surface on the inside of a container （容器内的）底: *I found some coins at the bottom of my bag.* 我在我的手提包底找到了几枚硬币。

• **OF RIVER/POOL** 河；池 **4** [sing.] the ground below the water in a lake, river, swimming pool, etc. （湖、河、游泳池等的）底；水底: *He dived in and hit his head on the bottom.* 他跳进水里，头撞到了池底。

• **END OF STH** 尾端 **5 the ~ (of sth)** [sing.] (*especially BrE*) the part of sth that is furthest from you, your house, etc. …尽头: *I went to the school at the bottom of our street.* 我在我们街尾的学校上学。◇ *There was a stream at the bottom of the garden.* 花园尽头有一条小溪。

• **LOWEST POSITION** 最末位置 **6** [sing.] **~ (of sth)** the lowest position in a class, on a list, etc.; a person, team, etc. that is in this position （班级、名单等的）最末位置；排名最后的人（或团队等）: *a battle between the teams at* the bottom of the league 联盟排名最后的几个队之间的较量 ◇ *You have to be prepared to start at the bottom and work your way up.* 你得准备好从最基层干起，努力向上。◇ *I was always bottom of the class in math.* 我的数学成绩总是班上最后一名。**OPP top**

• **PART OF BODY** 身体部位 **7** [C] (*especially BrE*) the part of the body that you sit on 屁股；臀部 **SYN backside, behind**

• **CLOTHING** 衣服 **8** [C, usually pl.] the lower part of a set of clothes that consists of two pieces 套装的裙（或裤）：*a pair of pyjama/tracksuit bottoms* 一条睡裤 / 运动裤 ◇ *a bikini bottom* 比基尼泳装的短裤 ➲ COMPARE TOP *n.* (6)

• **OF SHIP** 船 **9** [C] the lower part of a ship that is below the surface of the water （吃水线以下的）船底，船身 **SYN hull**

• **-BOTTOMED** 有…底 **10** (in adjectives 构成形容词) having the type of bottom mentioned 有…底的：*a flat-bottomed boat* 平底船

IDM at bottom used to say what sb/sth is really like 归根结底；本质上；实际上：*Their offer to help was at bottom self-centred.* 他们提出要帮忙，这其实还是他们为自己考虑。**be/lie at the bottom of sth** to be the original cause of sth, especially sth unpleasant 是某事的根源（或起因、导火线） **the bottom drops/falls out (of sth)** people stop buying or using the products of a particular industry （某行业）产品滞销；销量暴跌：*The bottom has fallen out of the travel market.* 旅游市场出现了萧条局面。**bottoms 'up!** (*informal*) used to express good wishes when drinking alcohol, or to tell sb to finish their drink 干杯 **get to the bottom of sth** to find out the real cause of sth, especially sth unpleasant 找到起因；挖出祸根 ➲ MORE AT HEAP *n.*, HEART, PILE *n.*, RACE *n.*, SCRAPE *v.*, TOP *n.*, TOUCH *v.*

▼ **SYNONYMS** 同义词辨析

bottom

base • foundation • foot

These are all words for the lowest part of sth. 以上各词均指底部、最下部。

bottom [usually sing.] the lowest part of sth 指底部、最下部：*Footnotes are given at the bottom of each page.* 脚注附于每页的下端。◇ *I waited for them at the bottom of the hill.* 我在山脚下等他们。

base [usually sing.] the lowest part of sth, especially the part or surface on which it rests or stands 指根基、基底、底座：*The lamp has a heavy base.* 这台灯的底座很沉。

foundation [usually pl.] a layer of bricks, concrete, etc. that forms the solid underground base of a building 指地基、房基、基础：*to lay the foundations of the new school* 给新校舍打地基

foot [sing.] the lowest part of sth 指最下部、底部：*At the foot of the stairs she turned to face him.* 她在楼梯底转过身来面对着他。

BOTTOM OR FOOT? 用 bottom 还是 foot?

Foot is used to talk about a limited number of things: it is used most often with *tree, hill/mountain, steps/stairs* and *page*. **Bottom** can be used to talk about a much wider range of things, including those mentioned above for **foot**. **Foot** is generally used in more literary contexts. * foot 用于有限的一些事物，最常与 tree、hill/mountain、steps/stairs 和 page 等连用。bottom 适用的范围要广得多，其中也包括上面提到的与 foot 搭配的词。foot 一般用于文学性较强的语境中。

PATTERNS

• **at/near/towards** the bottom/base/foot of sth
• **on** the bottom/base of sth
• (a) **firm/solid/strong** base/foundation(s)

■ *adj.* [only before noun] in the lowest, last or furthest place or position 底部的；最后的；尽头的：*the bottom line (on a page)* （一页的）最末一行 ◇ *your bottom lip* 下嘴唇 ◇ *the bottom step (of a flight of stairs)* （楼梯的）最低一级 ◇ *on the bottom shelf* 在架子底层 ◇ *Put your clothes in the bottom drawer.* 把你的衣服放在最下面的抽屉里。◇ *Their house is at the bottom end of Bury Road* (= the end furthest from where you enter the road). 他们的房子位于贝里路的尽头。◇ *in the bottom right-hand corner of the page* 在这一页的右下角 ◇ *the bottom end of the price range* 最低价位 ◇ *to go up a hill in bottom gear* 用低挡爬山 ◇ *We came* **bottom** (= got the worst result) *with 12 points.* 我们以 12 分垫底儿。**IDM** SEE BET *v.*

■ *verb*

PHR V ˌbottom 'out (of prices, a bad situation, etc. 价格、恶劣局势等) to stop getting worse 降到最低点；停止恶化：*The recession is finally beginning to show signs of bottoming out.* 经济衰退终于出现了走出谷底的迹象。

ˌbottom 'drawer *noun* (*BrE*) items for the house collected by a woman, especially in the past, in preparation for her marriage (and often kept in a drawer) （尤指旧时）女子为结婚而存储的物品，压箱钱财 ➲ COMPARE HOPE CHEST

'bottom feeder *noun* **1** (*NAmE, informal*) a person who earns money by taking advantage of bad things that happen to other people or by using things that other people throw away 乘人之危谋利的人；利用他人丢弃物为生的人；拾荒者 **2** a fish that feeds at the bottom of a river, lake or the sea 底栖鱼

bot·tom·less /'bɒtəmləs; *NAmE* 'bɑːt-/ *adj.* (*formal*) very deep; seeming to have no bottom or limit 很深的；深不可测的；深不见底的

IDM a bottomless 'pit (of sth) a thing or situation which seems to have no limits or seems never to end 无限度事物；无休止的状况；无底洞：*There isn't a bottomless pit of money for public spending.* 公共开支并非用之不尽的。◇ *the bottomless pit of his sorrow* 他无尽的悲哀

ˌbottom 'line *noun* **1 the bottom line** [sing.] the most important thing that you have to consider or accept; the essential point in a discussion, etc. 要旨；基本论点；底线：*The bottom line is that we have to make a decision today.* 底线是，我们今天必须作出决定。**2** (*business* 商) [C] the amount of money that is a profit or a loss after everything has been calculated 最终赢利（或亏损）；损益表底线：*The bottom line for 2014 was a pre-tax profit of £85 million.* * 2014 年最终获得税前利润 8 500 万英镑。

ˌbottom-'up *adj.* (of a plan, project, etc. 计划、项目等) starting with details and then later moving on to more general principles 自下而上的；从点到面的：*a bottom-up approach to tackling the problem* 处理这个问题的自下而上的方法 ➲ COMPARE TOP-DOWN (1)

botu·lin /'bɒtjulɪn; *NAmE* 'bɑːtjə-/ *noun* [U] the poisonous substance in the bacteria that cause BOTULISM 肉毒杆菌毒素

botu·lism /'bɒtjulɪzəm; *NAmE* 'bɑːtʃə-/ *noun* [U] a serious illness caused by bacteria in badly preserved food 肉毒中毒（由加工食品中的杆菌引起）

bou·doir /'buːdwɑː(r)/ *noun* (*old-fashioned*) a woman's small private room or bedroom 闺房；女子卧室

bouf·fant /'buːfɒ̃; *NAmE* buː'fɑːnt/ *adj.* (of a person's hair 头发) in a style that raises it up and back from the head in a high round shape （往后梳）蓬松式的

bou·gain·vil·lea (*also* **bou·gain·vil·laea**) /ˌbuːgən'vɪliə/ *noun* a tropical climbing plant with red, purple, white or pink flowers 叶子花，九重葛（热带攀缘植物，开红、紫、白或粉色花）

bough /baʊ/ *noun* (*formal* or *literary*) a large branch of a tree 大树枝

bought PAST TENSE, PAST PART. OF BUY

bouil·la·baisse /ˈbuːjəbeɪs/ *noun* [U] (*from French*) a spicy fish soup from the south of France 普罗旺斯鱼汤；法式鱼羹

bouil·lon /ˈbuːjɒn; -jɔ̃; *NAmE* -jɑːn/ *noun* [U, C] (*from French*) a liquid made by boiling meat or vegetables in water, used for making clear soups or sauces （用作清汤或调味的）肉汤，菜汤

boul·der /ˈbəʊldə(r); *NAmE* ˈboʊl-/ *noun* a very large rock which has been shaped by water or the weather （受水或天气侵蚀而成的）巨石；漂砾 ➲ VISUAL VOCAB PAGE V5

boul·der·ing /ˈbəʊldərɪŋ; *NAmE* ˈboʊl-/ *noun* [U] the sport or activity of climbing on large rocks 攀岩（运动）

boule (*also* **boules**) /buːl/ *noun* [U] a French game in which players take turns to roll metal balls as near as possible to a small ball 法式滚球戏（游戏者依次将金属球滚至靠近靶球）

boule·vard /ˈbuːləvɑːd; *NAmE* ˈbʊləvɑːrd/ *noun* **1** a wide city street, often with trees on either side （市区的）林荫大道 **2** (*abbr.* **Blvd.**) (*NAmE*) a wide main road (often used in the name of streets) （常用作街道名称）要道，大街：*Sunset Boulevard* 日落大道

bounce /baʊns/ *verb, noun*

■ *verb*

• MOVE OFF SURFACE 离开表面 **1** [I, T] if sth **bounces** or you **bounce** it, it moves quickly away from a surface it has just hit or you make it do this （使）弹起，弹跳；反射：*The ball bounced twice before he could reach it.* 球弹跳两次他才接到。◇ **~ off sth** *Short sound waves bounce off even small objects.* 短声波即使遇到小物体都会产生回音。◇ *The light bounced off the river and dazzled her.* 河面上银波粼粼，令她目眩。◇ **~ sth (against/on/off sth)** *She bounced the ball against the wall.* 她对着墙打球。

• MOVE UP AND DOWN 上下移动 **2** [I] **~ (up and down) (on sth)** (of a person 人) to jump up and down on sth （在…上）跳动，蹦：*She bounced up and down excitedly on the bed.* 她兴奋地在床上蹦蹦跳跳。 **3** [T] **~ sb (up and down) (on sth)** to move a child up and down while he or she is sitting on your knee in order to entertain him or her 把（小孩）放在膝上颠着玩 **4** [I, T] **~ (sth) (up and down)** to move up and down; to move sth up and down （使）上下晃动：*Her hair bounced as she walked.* 她走起路来头发上下晃动。 **5** [I] **+ adv./prep.** to move up and down in a particular direction （朝某个方向）颠簸行进：*The bus bounced down the hill.* 公共汽车颠簸着开下山去。

• MOVE WITH ENERGY 有活力地走动 **6** [I] **+ adv./prep.** (of a person 人) to move somewhere in a lively and cheerful way 活泼兴奋地走，蹦蹦跳跳地去（到某处）：*He bounced across the room to greet them.* 他兴奋地冲过房间去迎接他们。

• CHEQUE 支票 **7** [I, T] **~ (sth)** (*informal*) if a cheque **bounces**, or a bank **bounces** it, the bank refuses to accept it because there is not enough money in the bank account to pay it （支票等）被拒付退回；拒付，退回（支票等）

• IDEAS 主意 **8** [T] **~ ideas (off sb)/(around)** to tell sb your ideas in order to find out what they think about them （向某人）试探地透露（主意）：*He bounced ideas off colleagues everywhere he went.* 他在同事中逢人便试探地大讲他的想法。

• COMPUTING 计算机技术 **9** [I, T] **~ (sth) (back)** if an email **bounces** or the system **bounces** it, it returns to the person who sent it because the system cannot deliver it （电子邮件）被退回；退回（电子邮件）

• MAKE SB LEAVE 使离开 **10** [T] **~ sb (from sth)** (*informal, especially NAmE*) to force sb to leave a job, team, place, etc. 解雇；开除；撵走；逐出：*He was soon bounced from the post.* 他不久被解职。

IDM **be ˈbouncing off the walls** (*informal*) to be so full of energy or so excited that you cannot keep still 精力充沛得待不住；激动得难以平静

PHR V **ˌbounce ˈback** to become healthy, successful or confident again after being ill/sick or having difficulties 恢复健康（或信心等）；重整旗鼓 SYN **recover**: *He's had a lot of problems, but he always seems to bounce back pretty quickly.* 他遭遇过很多挫折，但他似乎总能很快地振作起来。 **ˌbounce ˈback (from sth)** (*business* 商) (of prices, shares, etc. 价格、股票等) to return to their previous high level or value after a period of difficulty 回升；反弹；上扬：*The airline's shares have bounced back from two days of heavy losses.* 航空公司的股票狂跌两天后已经反弹回来。 **ˌbounce sb ˈinto sth** (*BrE*) to make sb do sth without giving them enough time to think about it 追逼（或催逼）别人做某事

■ *noun*

• MOVEMENT 动作 **1** [C] the action of bouncing 弹跳；跳动：*one bounce of the ball* 球的一次弹起 ◇ (*NAmE*) *a bounce* (= increase) *in popularity* 声望的增加 **2** [U] the ability to bounce or to make sth bounce 弹性；反弹力：*There's not much bounce left in these balls.* 这些球已没有多少弹性了。◇ *Players complained about the uneven bounce of the tennis court.* 运动员抱怨说网球场的反弹力不均匀。

• ENERGY 精力 **3** [U, C] the energy that a person has 活力；精力：*All her old bounce was back.* 她完全恢复了以往的活力。◇ *There was a bounce to his step.* 他的步伐矫健有力。

• OF HAIR 头发 **4** [U] the quality in a person's hair that shows that it is in good condition and means that it does not lie flat 富有弹性；蓬松：*thin fine hair, lacking in bounce* 没有弹性、稀疏纤细的头发

IDM **on the ˈbounce** (*BrE, informal*) one after the other, without anything else coming between 接连；连续；相继：*We've won six matches on the bounce.* 我们已经六连胜。

boun·cer /ˈbaʊnsə(r)/ *noun* **1** a person employed to stand at the entrance to a club, pub, etc. to stop people who are not wanted from going in, and to throw out people who are causing trouble inside （俱乐部、酒店等的）门卫 **2** (in CRICKET 板球) a ball thrown very fast that rises high after it hits the ground 弹得很高的快球 **3** (*NAmE*) (*BrE* **ˌbouncy ˈcastle**) a plastic castle or other shape which is filled with air and which children can jump and play on 充气欢乐堡（儿童游戏用的塑料城堡）

ˈbounce rate *noun* (*specialist*) the number of people who visit a particular website but only view one page, expressed as a PERCENTAGE of all the people who visit the site 跳出率，跳离率，弹出率（只访问一个网页的访问量占网站总访问量的比率）

boun·cing /ˈbaʊnsɪŋ/ *adj.* **~ (with sth)** healthy and full of energy 健壮的；茁壮的：*a bouncing baby boy* 茁壮的男婴

bouncy /ˈbaʊnsi/ *adj.* (**boun·cier, boun·ci·est**) **1** that bounces well or that has the ability to make sth bounce 弹性好的；有反弹力的：*a very bouncy ball* 弹性很好的球 ◇ *his bouncy blond curls* 他富有弹性的金色鬈发 **2** lively and full of energy 生气勃勃的；精神饱满的

ˌbouncy ˈcastle (*BrE*) (*NAmE* **bouncer, inˌflatable ˈbouncer**) *noun* a plastic castle or other shape which is filled with air and which children can jump and play on 充气欢乐堡（儿童游戏用的塑料城堡）

bound 🔑 /baʊnd/ *adj., verb, noun* ➲ SEE ALSO BIND *v.*

■ *adj.* [not before noun] **1** 🔑 **~ to do/be sth** certain or likely to happen, or to do or be sth 一定会；很可能会：*There are bound to be changes when the new system is introduced.* 引进新系统后一定会发生变化。◇ *It's bound to be sunny again tomorrow.* 明天肯定又是阳光灿烂。◇ *You've done so much work—you're bound to pass the exam.* 你下了这么大功夫，考试准能及格。◇ *It was bound to happen sooner or later* (= we should have expected it). 这事迟早都是要发生的。◇ *You're bound to be nervous the first time* (= it's easy to understand). 第一次总是会紧张的。➲ SYNONYMS AT CERTAIN **2** forced to do sth by law, duty or a particular situation 受（法律、义务或情况）约束（必须做某事）；有义务（做某事）：**~ by sth** *We are not bound by the decision.* 我们不受该决定的约束。◇ *You are bound by the contract to pay before the end of the month.* 按照合同规定，你必须在月底前付款。 **~ (by sth) to do sth**：(*formal*) *I am* **bound to say** *I disagree with you on*

B

this point. 我觉得有必要指出，在这一点上我不同意你的观点。 **3** (in compounds 构成复合词) prevented from going somewhere or from working normally by the conditions mentioned 因…受阻（或不能正常工作）： *Strike-bound travellers face long delays.* 因罢工滞留的旅客要耽搁很长时间。◇ *fogbound airports* 因雾不能正常作业的机场 **4** (also in compounds 亦构成复合词) travelling, or ready to travel, in a particular direction or to a particular place 正旅行去（某地）；准备前往（某地）： *homeward bound* (= going home) 在回家途中 ◇ *Paris-bound* 前往巴黎的 ◇ ***northbound/southbound/eastbound/westbound*** 向北 / 向南 / 向东 / 向西行进的 ◇ **~ for...** *a plane bound for Dublin* 开往都柏林的飞机

IDM **be bound 'up in sth** very busy with sth; very interested or involved in sth 忙于某事；热衷于某事： *He's too bound up in his work to have much time for his children.* 他工作太忙，没有很多时间陪孩子们。 **bound and de'termined** (*NAmE*) very determined to do sth 矢志不渝；下定决心 **be bound to'gether by/in sth** to be closely connected 因…（或在…方面）密切联系： *communities bound together by customs and traditions* 因习俗和传统而结合在一起的社区 **bound 'up with sth** closely connected with sth 和某事密切相关： *From that moment my life became inextricably bound up with hers.* 从那一刻起，我的一生就和她结下不解之缘。 **'I'll be bound** (*old-fashioned, BrE, informal*) I feel sure 我敢肯定 ➲ MORE AT HONOUR *n.*

■ ***verb*** **1** [I] **+ adv./prep.** to run with long steps, especially in an enthusiastic way 跳跃着跑： *The dogs bounded ahead.* 那些狗在前面蹦蹦跳跳地跑。 **2** [T, usually passive] **~ sth** (*formal*) to form the edge or limit of an area 形成…的边界（或界限）： *The field was bounded on the left by a wood.* 那片地左边依傍着一片树林。

■ ***noun*** (*formal*) a high or long jump 蹦跳；跳跃 ➲ SEE ALSO BOUNDS **IDM** SEE LEAP *n.*

bound·ary /ˈbaʊndri/ *noun* (*pl.* **-ies**) **1** a real or imagined line that marks the limits or edges of sth and separates it from other things or places; a dividing line 边界；界限；分界线： *national boundaries* 国界 ◇ (*BrE*) *county boundaries* 郡界 ◇ ***boundary changes/disputes*** 边界变化 / 争端 ◇ *The fence marks the boundary between my property and hers.* 那道篱笆是我和她的住宅之间的分界。◇ *Scientists continue to* ***push back the boundaries*** *of human knowledge.* 科学家不断扩大人类知识的范围。 ◇ *the boundary between acceptable and unacceptable behaviour* 可接受和不可接受的行为之间的分界线 ➲ SYNONYMS AT BORDER **2** (in CRICKET 板球) a hit of the ball that crosses the boundary of the playing area and scores extra points 使球越过边界线的击球（得加分）

bound·en /ˈbaʊndən/ *adj.*

IDM **a/your bounden 'duty** (*old-fashioned, formal*) something that you feel you must do; a responsibility which cannot be ignored 应尽的义务；不可推卸的责任

bound·er /ˈbaʊndə(r)/ *noun* (*old-fashioned, informal*) a man who behaves badly and cannot be trusted 缺德的人；无赖

bound·less /ˈbaʊndləs/ *adj.* without limits; seeming to have no end 无限的；无止境的 **SYN** **infinite**

bounds /baʊndz/ *noun* [pl.] the accepted or furthest limits of sth 限制范围；极限： ***beyond/outside/within the bounds of*** *decency* 没体统；有体统 ◇ *Public spending must be kept within reasonable bounds.* 公共开支必须控制在合理的范围内。◇ *It was not* ***beyond the bounds of possibility*** *that they would meet again one day.* 他们有一天会再度相遇，这不是没有可能。 ◇ *His enthusiasm* ***knew no bounds*** (= was very great). 他有无限热情。

IDM **out of 'bounds 1** (in some sports 某些体育运动) outside the area of play which is allowed 出界；界外： *His shot went out of bounds.* 他的球出界了。 **2** (*NAmE*) not reasonable or acceptable 不合理的；令人无法接受的： *His demands were out of bounds.* 他的要求不合理。 **out of 'bounds (to/for sb)** (*especially BrE*) if a place is **out of bounds**, people are not allowed to go there 不准进入；禁止入内 ➲ SEE ALSO OFF-LIMITS (1) ➲ MORE AT LEAP *n.*

boun·teous /ˈbaʊntiəs/ *adj.* (*formal* or *literary*) giving very generously 十分慷慨的；非常大方的

boun·ti·ful /ˈbaʊntɪfl/ *adj.* (*formal* or *literary*) **1** in large quantities; large 大量的；巨大的： *a bountiful supply of food* 富足的食物供应 **2** giving generously 慷慨的；大方的 **SYN** **generous**： *belief in a bountiful god* 对慷慨的神的信仰

bounty /ˈbaʊnti/ *noun* (*pl.* **-ies**) **1** [U, C] (*literary*) generous actions; sth provided in large quantities 慷慨之举；大量给予之物 **2** [C] money given as a reward 奖金；赏金： *a bounty hunter* (= sb who catches criminals or kills people for a reward) 为得到赏金而抓捕罪犯或去杀人的人

bou·quet /buˈkeɪ/ *noun* **1** [C] a bunch of flowers arranged in an attractive way so that it can be carried in a ceremony or presented as a gift 花束： *The little girl presented the princess with a large* ***bouquet of flowers.*** 那小女孩向公主献上了一大束鲜花。 **2** [C, U] the pleasant smell of a type of food or drink, especially of wine （尤指酒的）香味，芬芳

bou·quet garni /ˌbuːkeɪ ɡɑːˈniː; *NAmE also* ɡɑːrˈniː; *also* boʊˌkeɪ/ *noun* (*pl.* **bou·quets gar·nis** /ˌbuːkeɪ ɡɑːˈniː; *NAmE also* ɡɑːrˈniː; *also* boʊˌkeɪ/) (*from French*) a bunch of different HERBS in a small bag, used in cooking to give extra flavour to food 香料束，香料袋（有各种香草，用于烹调食物）

bour·bon /ˈbɜːbən; *NAmE* ˈbɜːrbən/ *noun* **1** [U, C] a type of American WHISKY made with CORN (MAIZE) and RYE 波旁威士忌酒（产于美国，用玉米和黑麦酿制） **2** [C] a glass of bourbon 一杯波旁威士忌

bour·geois /ˈbʊəʒwɑː; ˌbʊəˈʒwɑː; *NAmE* ˌbʊrˈʒ-; ˈbʊrʒ-/ *adj.* **1** belonging to the middle class 中产阶级的： *a traditional bourgeois family* 一个传统的中产阶级家庭 ➲ SEE ALSO PETIT BOURGEOIS **2** (*disapproving*) interested mainly in possessions and social status and supporting traditional values 追求名利且平庸的；世俗的： ***bourgeois attitudes/tastes*** 世俗的态度 / 趣味 ◇ *They've become very bourgeois since they got married.* 他们结婚后变得十分庸俗。 **3** (*politics* 政) supporting the interests of CAPITALISM 资产阶级的；资本家的： *bourgeois ideology* 资产阶级意识形态 ▶ **bour·geois** *noun* (*pl.* **bour·geois**)

the bour·geoisie /ˌbʊəʒwɑːˈziː; *NAmE* ˌbʊrʒ-/ *noun* [sing.+ sing./pl. v.] **1** the middle classes in society 中产阶级： *the rise of the bourgeoisie in the nineteenth century* 十九世纪中产阶级的兴起 **2** (*politics* 政) the CAPITALIST class 资产阶级；资本家阶级： *the proletariat and the bourgeoisie* 无产阶级和资产阶级

Bourke /bɜːk; *NAmE* bɜːrk/ *noun*

IDM **back of Bourke** (*AustralE*) (in) the country, a long way from the coast and towns; in the OUTBACK （在）乡村，远离海滨和城镇；在内地 **ORIGIN** From the name of the town Bourke in New South Wales. 源自新南威尔士伯克镇。

bourse /bʊəs; *NAmE* bʊrs/ *noun* (*from French*) a STOCK EXCHANGE, especially the one in Paris （尤指巴黎的）证券交易所

bout /baʊt/ *noun* **1** a short period of great activity; a short period during which there is a lot of a particular thing, usually sth unpleasant 一阵；一场；（尤指坏事的）一通，一次： *a drinking bout* 狂饮一通 ◇ **~ of sth/of doing sth** *the latest bout of inflation* 最近一波通货膨胀 **2 ~ (of sth)** an attack or period of illness （疾病的）发作；发病期： *a severe bout of flu/coughing* 流感 / 咳嗽的猛烈发作 ◇ *He suffered occasional bouts of depression.* 他有时会犯抑郁症。 ◇ **~ (with sth)** (*NAmE*) *a bout with the flu* 流感发作期 **3** a BOXING or WRESTLING match 拳击（或摔跤）比赛

bou·tique /buːˈtiːk/ *noun, adj.*

■ ***noun*** a small shop/store that sells fashionable clothes or expensive gifts 时装店；精品店

■ ***adj.*** [only before noun] (of a business) small and offering products or services of a high quality to a small number of customers （商店）精品的，提供专门服务的（针对小量的顾客）：*a boutique hotel that offers an escape from the outside world* 让人远离尘世喧嚣的精品酒店 ◇ *a boutique investment bank* 精品投资银行

bou·ton·nière /ˌbuːtɒnˈjeə(r); *NAmE* ˌbuːtnˈɪr; -tənˈjer/ (*NAmE, from French*) (*BrE* **but·ton·hole**) *noun* a flower that is worn in the BUTTONHOLE of a coat or jacket 佩戴在扣眼上的花

bou·zou·ki /buˈzuːki/ *noun* a Greek musical instrument with strings that are played with the fingers 布祖基琴（希腊弦乐器）

bo·vine /ˈbəʊvaɪn; *NAmE* ˈboʊ-/ *adj.* [usually before noun] **1** (*specialist*) connected with cows 牛的；与牛有关的：*bovine diseases* 牛病 **2** (*disapproving*) (of a person 人) stupid and slow 愚笨的；反应迟钝的

bow 船头；鞠躬

bow of a boat 船头　**take a bow** 鞠躬答谢

bow¹ /baʊ/ *verb, noun* ➲ SEE ALSO BOW²

■ ***verb* 1** [I] to move your head or the top half of your body forwards and downwards as a sign of respect or to say hello or goodbye 鞠躬；点头：~ **(to/before sb/sth)** *He bowed low to the assembled crowd.* 他向集结的人群深深地鞠了一躬。◇ ~ **down (to/before sb/sth)** *The people all bowed down before the Emperor.* 全体给皇帝鞠躬。 **2** [T] ~ **your head** to move your head forwards and downwards 低（头）；垂（首）：*She bowed her head in shame.* 她羞愧地低下了头。◇ *They stood in silence with their heads bowed.* 他们默默地垂头而立。 **3** [I, T] to bend or make sth bend （使）弯曲：**(+ adv./prep)** *The pines bowed in the wind.* 松树被风吹弯了。◇ ~ **sth (+ adv./prep)** *Their backs were bowed under the weight of their packs.* 沉重的背包压弯了他们的脊背。

IDM ˌ**bow and ˈscrape** (*disapproving*) to be too polite to an important person in order to gain their approval 卑躬屈膝；点头哈腰

PHR V ˌ**bow ˈdown to sb/sth** (*disapproving*) to allow sb/sth to tell you what to do 屈从于人；听任摆布 ˌ**bow ˈout (of sth)** to stop taking part in an activity, especially one in which you have been successful in the past 退出，告别（尤指一度成功的事业）：*She has finally decided it's time to bow out of international tennis.* 她最终认定是退出世界网坛的时候了。ˈ**bow to sth** to agree unwillingly to do sth because other people want you to 屈从于：*They finally bowed to pressure from the public.* 他们终于在公众的压力下让步了。◇ *She **bowed to the inevitable*** (= accepted a situation in which she had no choice) *and resigned.* 她迫于无奈，只得辞职。

■ ***noun* 1** the act of bending your head or the upper part of your body forward in order to say hello or goodbye to sb or to show respect 鞠躬；弯腰行礼 **2** (*also* **bows** [pl.]) the front part of a boat or ship 船头；艏 ➲ VISUAL VOCAB PAGE V59 ➲ COMPARE STERN *n.*

IDM **take a/your ˈbow** (of a performer 演员) to bow to the audience as they are APPLAUDING you 谢幕；鞠躬答谢 ➲ MORE AT SHOT *n.*

bow² /bəʊ; *NAmE* boʊ/ *noun, verb* ➲ SEE ALSO BOW¹

■ ***noun* 1** a weapon used for shooting arrows, consisting of a long curved piece of wood or metal with a tight string joining its ends 弓：*He was armed with a **bow and arrow**.* 他佩带着弓箭。➲ VISUAL VOCAB PAGE V44 **2** a knot with two LOOPS and two loose ends which is used for decoration on clothes, in hair, etc. or for tying shoes 蝴蝶结：*to tie your shoelaces in a bow* 把鞋带打成蝴蝶结 ◇ *Her hair was tied back in a neat bow.* 她的头发扎在脑后打了个整齐的蝴蝶结。➲ PICTURE AT KNOT **3** a long thin piece of wood with thin string stretched along it, used for playing musical instruments such as the VIOLIN 琴弓 ➲ VISUAL VOCAB PAGE V38 IDM SEE STRING *n.*

■ ***verb*** [I, T] ~ **(sth)** to use a bow² (3) to play a musical instrument that has strings 用琴弓拉奏（弦乐器）

bows 弓；蝴蝶结；琴弓

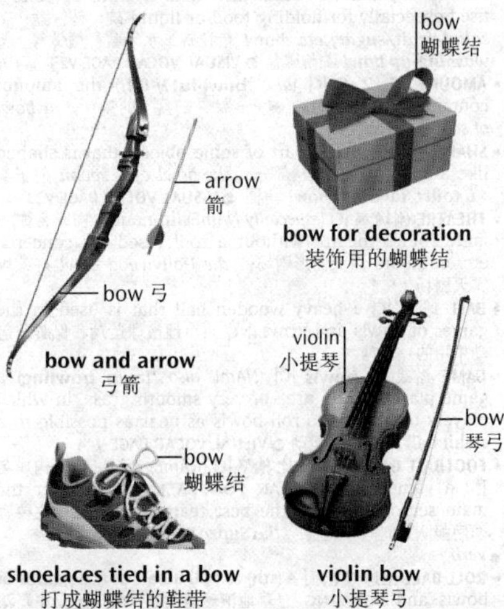

bow for decoration 装饰用的蝴蝶结　**bow and arrow** 弓箭　**shoelaces tied in a bow** 打成蝴蝶结的鞋带　**violin bow** 小提琴弓

bowd·ler·ize (*BrE also* **-ise**) /ˈbaʊdləraɪz/ *verb* ~ **sth** (*usually disapproving*) to remove the parts of a book, play, etc. that you think are likely to shock or offend people 删改（认为书或戏剧等中有伤风化或有冒犯性的部分）；鲍德勒化 SYN **expurgate** ORIGIN Named after Dr Thomas **Bowdler**, who in 1818 produced a version of Shakespeare from which he had taken out all the material which he considered not suitable for family use. 源自托马斯·鲍德勒博士 (Dr Thomas Bowdler) 的名字。他于 1818 年出版了莎士比亚戏剧的改写本，删掉了他认为不适合家庭阅读的内容。

bowel /ˈbaʊəl/ *noun* **1** [C, usually pl.] the tube along which food passes after it has been through the stomach, especially the end where waste is collected before it is passed out of the body 肠：(*medical* 医) *to **empty/move/open your bowels*** (= to pass solid waste out of the body) 解大便 ◇ *bowel cancer/cancer of the bowel* 肠癌 **2 the bowels of sth** [pl.] (*literary*) the part that is deepest inside sth 内部最深处：*A rumble came from **the bowels of the earth*** (= deep underground). 从地下深处传来隆隆的响声。

ˈ**bowel movement** (*also* **movement**) *noun* (*medical* 医) an act of emptying waste material from the bowels; the waste material that is emptied 解大便；粪便

bower /ˈbaʊə(r)/ *noun* (*literary*) a pleasant place in the shade under trees or climbing plants in a wood or garden/yard 树荫处；阴凉处

bower·bird /ˈbaʊəbɜːd; *NAmE* ˈbaʊərbɜːrd/ *noun* a bird found in Australia, the male of which decorates a place with shells, feathers, etc. to attract females 园丁鸟（见于澳大利亚，雄鸟构筑凉亭状物求偶）

bow·fin /ˈbəʊfɪn; *NAmE* ˈboʊ-/ *noun* (*pl.* **bow·fin** or **bow·fins**) an American fish with a large head that can survive for a long time out of water 弓鳍鱼（产于美洲，头大，耐旱）

bow·ie knife /ˈbəʊi naɪf; *NAmE* ˈboʊi/ *noun* a large heavy knife with a long blade, used in hunting 长刃猎刀

bowl /bəʊl; *NAmE* boʊl/ *noun, verb*

■ *noun*

• CONTAINER 容器 **1** [C] (especially in compounds 尤用于构成复合词) a deep round dish with a wide open top, used especially for holding food or liquid 碗；钵；盆：*a* ***salad/fruit/sugar, etc. bowl*** 色拉碗、水果盆、糖钵等 ◇ *a* ***washing-up bowl*** 洗碗碟盆 ➲ VISUAL VOCAB PAGE V23

• AMOUNT 量 **2** [C] (*also* **bowl·ful** /-fʊl/) the amount contained in a bowl 一碗，一钵，一盆（的量）：*a bowl of soup* 一碗汤

• SHAPE 形状 **3** [C] the part of some objects that is shaped like a bowl 物体的碗状部分：*the bowl of a spoon* 勺子头 ◇ *a* ***toilet/lavatory bowl*** 马桶 ➲ VISUAL VOCAB PAGE V23

• THEATRE 剧场 **4** [C] (*especially NAmE*) (in names 构成名称) a large round theatre without a roof, used for concerts, etc. outdoors 露天圆形剧场：*the Hollywood Bowl* 好莱坞露天剧场

• BALL 球 **5** [C] a heavy wooden ball that is used in the games of bowls and BOWLING （草地滚球运动和保龄球运动中用的）木球

• GAME 游戏 **6 bowls** [U] (*NAmE also* **ˈlawn bowling**) a game played on an area of very smooth grass, in which players take turns to roll bowls as near as possible to a small ball 草地滚球运动 ➲ VISUAL VOCAB PAGE V44

• FOOTBALL GAME 橄榄球比赛 **7** [C] (*NAmE*) (in names 构成名称) a game of AMERICAN FOOTBALL played after the main season between the best teams （美式足球主要赛季后强队之间的）碗赛：*the Super Bowl* 超级碗季后赛

■ *verb*

• ROLL BALL 滚球 **1** [I, T] ~ (**sth**) to roll a ball in the games of bowls and BOWLING （草地滚球运动或保龄球运动中）滚球，投球

• IN CRICKET 板球 **2** [I, T] ~ (**sth**) to throw a ball to the BATSMAN (= the person who hits the ball) 把（球）投给击球员 ➲ SYNONYMS AT THROW **3** [T] ~ **sb** (**out**) to make the BATSMAN have to leave the field by throwing a ball that hits the WICKET 击掉三柱门的横木使（击球员）杀出局；破门使（击球员）出局

• MOVE QUICKLY 迅速移动 **4** [I] + **adv./prep.** to move quickly in a particular direction, especially in a vehicle （向某处）迅速移动；（尤指）快速行驶：*Soon we were bowling along the country roads.* 我们不久便在乡村的公路上疾驰了。

PHR V **ˌbowl sb ˈover 1** to run into sb and knock them down 把某人撞倒 **2** to surprise or impress sb a lot 使某人惊叹；让某人印象深刻

bow legs /ˌbəʊ ˈlegz; *NAmE* ˌboʊ/ *noun* [pl.] legs that curve out at the knees 弓形腿；罗圈腿 ▶ **bow-legged** /ˌbəʊ ˈlegɪd; *NAmE* ˌboʊ/ *adj.*

bowl·er /ˈbəʊlə(r); *NAmE* ˈboʊ-/ *noun* **1** (in CRICKET 板球) a player who throws the ball towards the BATSMAN 投球手 **2** (*also* **ˌbowler ˈhat**) (*both especially BrE*) (*NAmE usually* **derby**) a hard black hat with a curved BRIM and round top, worn, for example, in the past by men in business in Britain 常礼帽（英国旧时商人等戴） ➲ VISUAL VOCAB PAGE V70

bow·line¹ /ˈbaʊlaɪn/ *noun* a rope that attaches one side of a sail to the BOW¹ of a boat 帆脚索；张帆绳

bow·line² /ˈbəʊlɪn; *NAmE* ˈboʊlən/ *noun* a type of knot, used for making a LOOP at the end of a rope 单套结；称人结

bowl·ing /ˈbəʊlɪŋ; *NAmE* ˈboʊ-/ *noun* [U] a game in which players roll heavy balls (called BOWLS) along a special track towards a group of PINS (= bottle-shaped objects) and try to knock over as many of them as possible 保龄球运动 ➲ COMPARE BOWL *n.* (6) ➲ VISUAL VOCAB PAGE V44

ˈbowling alley *noun* a building or part of a building where people can go bowling 保龄球场 ➲ MORE LIKE THIS 9, page R26

ˈbowling green *noun* an area of grass that has been cut short on which the game of BOWLS is played 草地滚球场 ➲ VISUAL VOCAB PAGE V44

bow·man /ˈbəʊmən; *NAmE* ˈboʊ-/ *noun* (*pl.* **-men** /-mən/) (*old-fashioned*) = ARCHER

bow·ser /ˈbaʊzə(r)/ *noun* (*especially BrE*) a container, often on wheels, used for holding liquids such as water or fuel, often because the normal supply is not available （临时）加水车；（应急）加油车

bow·sprit /ˈbəʊsprɪt; *NAmE* ˈboʊ-/ *noun* a thick pole that sticks forward at the front of a ship 船头斜桁

bow·string /ˈbəʊstrɪŋ; *NAmE* ˈboʊ-/ *noun* the string on a BOW² (1) which is pulled back to shoot arrows 弓弦

bow tie /ˌbəʊ ˈtaɪ; *NAmE* ˌboʊ/ *noun* a man's tie that is tied in the shape of a BOW² (2) and that does not hang down 蝶形领结 ➲ VISUAL VOCAB PAGE V66

bow-wow /ˈbaʊ waʊ/ *noun* a child's word for a dog 汪汪（儿语，指狗）

box /bɒks; *NAmE* bɑːks/ *noun, verb*

■ *noun*

• CONTAINER 容器 **1** [C] (especially in compounds 尤用于构成复合词) a container made of wood, cardboard, metal, etc. with a flat stiff base and sides and often a lid, used especially for holding solid things 盒；箱；匣：*She kept all the letters in a box.* 她把信件都保存在一个盒子里。◇ *a money box* 钱匣 ◇ *cardboard boxes* 纸板箱 ◇ *a toolbox* 工具箱 ◇ *a matchbox* 火柴盒 ➲ VISUAL VOCAB PAGE V36 **2** [C] a box and its contents 一盒，一箱（东西）：*a* ***box of chocolates/matches*** 一盒巧克力 / 火柴 ➲ VISUAL VOCAB PAGE V36

• IN THEATRE/COURT 剧院；法庭 **3** [C] a small area in a theatre or court separated off from where other people sit （剧院中的）包厢；（法庭中的）专席：*a box at the opera* 歌剧院的包厢 ◇ *the* ***witness/jury box*** 证人席；陪审团席

• SHELTER 遮蔽处 **4** [C] a small shelter used for a particular purpose 小亭；岗亭：*a* ***sentry/signal box*** 岗亭；铁路信号所 ◇ (*BrE*) *a telephone box* 电话亭 ◇ *I called him from the phone box on the corner.* 我在拐角处的电话亭打电话给他。

• SHAPE 形状 **5** [C] a small square or RECTANGLE drawn on a page or computer screen for people to put information in 方框；长方格：*Put a cross in the appropriate box.* 在适当的方格里打叉号。◇ *to* ***tick/check a box*** 在方格里画钩

• TELEVISION 电视 **6 the box** [sing.] (*informal, especially BrE*) the television 电视：*What's on the box tonight?* 今晚有什么电视节目？

• ON ROAD 道路 **7** [C] (*BrE*) = BOX JUNCTION：*Only traffic turning right may enter the box.* 只允许右拐的车辆进入交叉路口黄格区。

• IN SPORT 体育运动 **8** [C] an area on a sports field that is marked by lines and used for a particular purpose 运动场上以线标出的特定区域：(*BrE*) *He was fouled in the box* (= the penalty box). 有人在禁区对他犯规。

• FOR MAIL 邮递 **9** [C] = BOX NUMBER ➲ SEE ALSO PO BOX

• PROTECTION 保护 **10** [C] (*BrE*) a piece of plastic that a man wears over his sex organs to protect them while he is playing a sport, especially CRICKET （运动员的）下体护身

• TREE/WOOD 树木 **11** [C, U] a small EVERGREEN tree or bush with thick dark leaves, used especially for garden HEDGES 黄杨（常绿，尤用作花园树篱） **12** (*also* **box·wood**) [U] the hard wood of this bush 黄杨木

IDM **give sb a box on the ˈears** (*old-fashioned*) to hit sb with your hand on the side of their head as a punishment 打某人耳光 ➲ MORE AT THINK *v.*, TICK *v.*, TRICK *n.*

■ *verb*

• FIGHT 击打 **1** [I, T] ~ (**sb**) to fight sb in the sport of BOXING （拳击运动中）击打（某人）

B

• PUT IN CONTAINER 装入容器 **2** [T] ~ **sth (up)** to put sth in a box 把（某物）装箱（或盒、匣）

IDM **box 'clever** (*BrE, informal*) to act in a clever way to get what you want, sometimes tricking sb 巧妙地得到想要的东西（有时蒙骗人） **box sb's 'ears** (*old-fashioned*) to hit sb with your hand on the side of their head as a punishment 打某人耳光

PHR V **,box sb/sth 'in 1** to prevent sb/sth from being able to move by surrounding them with people, vehicles, etc. 围困；拦挡：*Someone had parked behind us and boxed us in.* 有人把车停在我们后面，困住了我们。 **2** [usually passive] (of a situation 处境) to prevent sb from doing what they want by creating unnecessary problems 阻挡；阻碍：*She felt boxed in by all their petty rules.* 她觉得被他们的琐碎规章束缚住了手脚。

box·car /ˈbɒkskɑː(r); *NAmE* ˈbɑːks-/ *noun* (*especially NAmE*) a closed coach/car on a train, with a sliding door, used for carrying goods （铁路）棚车，闷子车，货车车厢

boxed /bɒkst; *NAmE* bɑːkst/ *adj.* put and/or sold in a box 盒装的；整盒出售的：*a boxed set of original recordings* 一套盒装原声录音带

boxer /ˈbɒksə(r); *NAmE* ˈbɑːk-/ *noun* **1** a person who boxes, especially as a job 拳击手；拳击运动员：*a **professional/amateur/heavyweight boxer*** 职业 / 业余 / 重量级拳击运动员 **2** a large dog with smooth hair, a short flat nose and a tail that has often been cut very short 拳师狗

Bo·xer·cise™ /ˈbɒksəsaɪz; *NAmE* ˈbɑːksər-/ *noun* [U] (*BrE*) a form of exercise that uses movements and equipment used in BOXING 健身拳击运动

'boxer shorts (*also* **boxers**) (*NAmE also* **shorts**) *noun* [pl.] men's UNDERPANTS similar to the SHORTS worn by boxers 男用平脚短内裤（类似拳击短裤）：*a pair of boxer shorts* 一条男用平脚短内裤

box·ful /ˈbɒksfʊl; *NAmE* ˈbɑːksfʊl/ *noun* a full box (of sth) 一盒，一箱（的量）

box·ing /ˈbɒksɪŋ; *NAmE* ˈbɑːks-/ *noun* [U] a sport in which two people fight each other with their hands, while wearing very large thick gloves (called **boxing gloves**) 拳击（运动）：*a **boxing champion/match*** 拳击冠军 / 比赛 ◇ *heavyweight boxing* 重量级拳击 ➲ VISUAL VOCAB PAGE V52

'Boxing Day *noun* [U, C] (*BrE*) the first day after Christmas Day that is not a Sunday. Boxing Day is an official holiday in Britain and some other countries. 节礼日（圣诞节后的第一个工作日，英国和其他一些国家定为假日）

'box junction (*also* **box**) *noun* (*BrE*) a place where two roads cross or join, marked with a pattern of yellow lines to show that vehicles must not stop in that area 交叉路口黄格区（车辆不得停留）

'box kite *noun* a KITE in the shape of a long box which is open at both ends （两端开口的）箱形风筝

'box lunch *noun* (*NAmE*) a meal of SANDWICHES, fruit, etc. that you take to school, work, etc. in a box 自备的盒装午餐；便当 ➲ COMPARE BAG LUNCH, PACKED LUNCH

'box number (*also* **box**) *noun* a number used as an address, especially one given in newspaper advertisements to which replies can be sent 信箱号码（报章广告常用）

'box office *noun* the place at a theatre, cinema/movie theater, etc. where the tickets are sold 售票处；票房：*The movie has been a huge **box-office success*** (= many people have been to see it). 那部电影十分卖座。 ➲ WORDFINDER NOTE AT THEATRE ➲ COLLOCATIONS AT CINEMA

'box room *noun* (*BrE*) a small room in a house for storing things in 贮藏室

'box score *noun* (*NAmE*) the results of a BASEBALL game or other sporting event shown in the form of rows and columns which include details of each player's performance （棒球等运动的）得分记录表，个人技术统计表

'box seat *noun*

IDM **in the 'box seat** (*AustralE, NZE, informal*) in a position in which you have an advantage 处于有利地位

box·wood /ˈbɒkswʊd; *NAmE* ˈbɑːks-/ *noun* [U] = BOX (12)

boxy /ˈbɒksi; *NAmE* ˈbɑːksi/ *adj.* having a square shape 箱状的；四四方方的：*a boxy car* 厢式汽车

boy 🔑 /bɔɪ/ *noun, exclamation*

■ ***noun*** **1** 🔑 [C] a male child or a young male person 男孩；男青年：*a **little/small/young boy*** 小男孩；小伙子 ◇ *I used to play here as a boy.* 我小时候常在这里玩。◇ *The older boys at school used to tease him.* 学校里大一些的男生过去常常取笑他。◇ *Now she's a teenager, she's starting to be interested in boys.* 她现在已经是个十几岁的姑娘了，开始对男孩子感兴趣。 ➲ SEE ALSO OLD BOY, TOY BOY **2** 🔑 [C] a young son 年少的儿子：*They have two boys and a girl.* 他们有两个儿子和一个女儿。◇ *Her eldest boy is at college.* 她的长子在上大学。 **3** [C] (in compounds; offensive when used of an older man 构成复合词；用于年长的男子时含冒犯意) a boy or young man who does a particular job 做某工作的男孩（或小伙子）；伙计：*a delivery boy* 报童 ➲ SEE ALSO BARROW BOY **4** [C] a way of talking about sb who comes from a particular place, etc. （指称某地等的人）：*He's a **local boy**.* 他是本地人。◇ *a **city/country boy*** 城里 / 乡下来的人 **5 the boys** [pl.] (*informal*) a group of male friends who often go out together 一帮男伙伴：*a night out with the boys* 和弟兄们一同消遣的一夜 **6 our boys** [pl.] a way of talking with affection about your country's soldiers （对本国士兵的昵称）兵哥哥们，小伙子们 **7** [C] (*NAmE, taboo*) used as an offensive way of addressing a black man, especially in the past （尤为旧时不礼貌地称呼黑人男子用）黑仔，小子

IDM **the boys in 'blue** (*informal*) the police 警察 **,boys ,will be 'boys** (*saying*) you should not be surprised when boys or men behave in a noisy or rough way as this is part of typical male behaviour 男孩子总归是男孩子（不必为男孩或男子的吵闹粗野大惊小怪） ➲ MORE AT JOB, MAN *n.*, WORK *n.*

■ ***exclamation*** (*informal, especially NAmE*) used to express feelings of surprise, pleasure, pain, etc. （表示惊奇、高兴、痛苦等）：*Boy, it sure is hot!* 嗬，真够辣的！◇ *Oh boy! That's great!* 哇！真了不起！

'boy band *noun* a group of attractive young men who sing pop music and dance, and who are especially popular with young people 男孩乐队；男孩组合

boy·cott /ˈbɔɪkɒt; *NAmE* -kɑːt/ *verb, noun*

■ ***verb*** ~ **sth** to refuse to buy, use or take part in sth as a way of protesting 拒绝购买（或使用、参加）；抵制：*We are asking people to boycott goods from companies that use child labour.* 我们正呼吁大家抵制雇用童工的公司的产品。

■ ***noun*** an act of boycotting sb/sth （对某事物的）抵制：~ **(of sth)** *a trade boycott of British goods* 对英国货品的贸易抵制 ◇ ~ **(on sth)** *a boycott on the use of tropical wood* 拒绝使用热带木材

boyf /bɔɪf/ *noun* (*BrE, informal*) a boyfriend 男友

boy·friend 🔑 /ˈbɔɪfrend/ *noun* a man or boy that sb has a romantic or sexual relationship with 男朋友

boy·hood /ˈbɔɪhʊd/ *noun* [U] (*becoming old-fashioned*) the time in a man's life when he is a boy （男子的）孩童期，青少年时代：***boyhood days/memories/friends*** 童年时代 / 回忆；儿时的朋友

boy·ish /ˈbɔɪɪʃ/ *adj.* (*approving*) looking or behaving like a boy, in a way that is attractive （长相或举止）像男孩的，顽皮可爱的：***boyish charm/enthusiasm*** 男孩般的魅力 / 热心 ◇ *her slim boyish figure* 她那男孩子般修长的体形 ▸ **boy·ish·ly** *adv.*

boyo /ˈbɔɪəʊ; *NAmE* ˈbɔɪoʊ/ *noun* (*informal*) (*WelshE*) used for addressing a boy or a man （用以称呼男孩或男子）小家伙，小伙子

B

ˌ**boy ˈracer** *noun* (*BrE, informal, disapproving*) a man, especially a young man, who drives his car too fast and without care 飙车者（尤指年轻男子）

ˌ**Boy ˈScout** *noun* (*US* or *old-fashioned*) a boy who is a member of the SCOUTS 童子军

boy·sen·berry /ˈbɔɪznbəri; *NAmE* -beri/ *noun* (*pl.* **-ies**) a large red fruit like a BLACKBERRY. The bush it grows on is also called a boysenberry. 博伊森莓，博伊森莓树（果大，暗红黑色）

ˈ**boy shorts** *noun* [pl.] a piece of women's underwear that covers the body from the hips to the top of the legs 平脚女内裤；女用平口裤

ˈ**boy toy** *noun* (*NAmE, informal*) **1** (*BrE* ˈ**toy boy**) (*humorous*) a male lover who is much younger than his partner 小男友；小白脸 **2** (*disapproving*) a young woman who is happy to be considered only for her sexual attraction and not for her character or intelligence 女玩偶，花瓶（甘愿以貌取悦男人）

ˌ**boy ˈwonder** *noun* (*informal, humorous*) a boy or young man who is extremely good at sth （指男孩或年轻男子）神童，天才

bozo /ˈbəʊzəʊ; *NAmE* ˈboʊzoʊ/ *noun* (*pl.* **-os**) (*informal, especially NAmE*) a stupid person 傻瓜；笨蛋

BPhil (*NAmE* **B.Phil**) /ˌbiː ˈfɪl/ *noun* the abbreviation for 'Bachelor of Philosophy' (a university degree in philosophy that is usually a second degree) 哲学学士（全写为 Bachelor of Philosophy，通常是大学的第二个学位）

bpi /ˌbiː piː ˈaɪ/ *abbr.* (*computing* 计) bits per inch (a measure of the amount of data that can fit onto a tape or disk) 每英寸位数，每英寸比特数（磁带或磁盘的数据容量标准）

ˈ**B-picture** *noun* = B-MOVIE

bps /ˌbiː piː ˈes/ *abbr.* (*computing* 计) bits per second (a measure of the speed at which data is sent or received) 位每秒，比特每秒，每秒位元数（数据收发速度的量度标准）

Bq *abbr.* (in writing 书写形式) = BECQUEREL

Br. *abbr.* (in writing 书写形式) British 英国的

bra /brɑː/ *noun* **1** (*also formal* **brassière**) a piece of women's underwear worn to cover and support the breasts 胸罩；文胸 **2** (*also* ˈ**car bra**, ˈ**auto bra**) a tightly fitting cover that is put over the front end of a car to protect it, sometimes made of a material that absorbs the waves from police RADAR equipment, so that it is more difficult to tell if a driver is going too fast （汽车前部的）活动罩，车头罩

braai /braɪ/ *noun, verb* (*SAfrE*)

■ *noun* **1** (*also* **braai·vleis**) a social event at which food is cooked outdoors over an open fire 露天烧烤餐会：*We're having a braai at our place next Saturday.* 下个星期六我们家要搞一场露天烧烤。◇ *a bring-and-braai* (= everyone brings their own meat) 自带肉食的露天烧烤餐会 **2** the surface or piece of equipment where the fire is made 烧烤位；烧烤炉

■ *verb* (**braais**, **braai·ing**, **braaied**, **braaied**) [T, I] ~ (**sth**) to cook food over an open fire, especially as part of a social event （聚会等时）露天烧烤 ➲ COMPARE BARBECUE

braai·vleis /ˈbraɪfleɪs/ *noun* (*SAfrE*) **1** [C] = BRAAI (1) **2** [U] meat that is cooked over an open fire （露天烧烤的）烤肉

brace /breɪs/ *noun, verb*

■ *noun* **1** [C] a device that holds things firmly together or holds and supports them in position 箍子；夹子；支架：*a neck brace* (= worn to support the neck after an injury) 矫治用的颈箍 **2** [C] (*NAmE* **braces** [pl.]) a metal device that people, especially children, wear inside the mouth to help their teeth grow straight （儿童）牙箍 **3 braces** (*BrE*) (*NAmE* **sus·pend·ers**) [pl.] long narrow pieces of cloth, leather, etc. for holding trousers/pants up. They are fastened to the top of the trousers/pants at the front and back and passed over the shoulders. 吊裤带；背带：*a pair of braces* 一副吊裤带 ➲ VISUAL VOCAB PAGE V66 **4** (*NAmE*) (*BrE* **cal·li·per**) [C, usually pl.] a metal support for weak or injured legs 双脚规形夹（支撑无力或受伤的腿的金属支架） **5** [C] either of the two marks, { }, used to show that the words, etc. between them are connected 大括弧；大括号 ➲ COMPARE BRACKET *n.* (1) **6** [C] (*pl.* **brace**) a pair of birds or animals that have been killed in hunting 猎获的一对鸟（或兽） IDM SEE BELT *n.*

■ *verb* **1** ~ **sb/yourself** (**for sth**) | ~ **sb/yourself** (**to do sth**) to prepare sb/yourself for sth difficult or unpleasant that is going to happen （为困难或坏事）使做准备；使防备：*UN troops are braced for more violence.* 联合国部队准备应付更多的暴行。◇ *They are bracing themselves for a long legal battle.* 他们在为漫长的法律诉讼做准备。 **2** ~ **sth/yourself** (**against sth**) to press your body or part of your body firmly against sth in order to stop yourself from falling 使（身体或身体部位）顶住，抵住（以免跌倒等）：*They braced themselves against the wind.* 他们顶着大风站稳。 **3** ~ **sth** to contract the muscles in your body or part of your body before doing sth that is physically difficult （做费劲的事之前）绷紧肌肉：*He stood with his legs and shoulders braced, ready to lift the weights.* 他绷紧腿和肩膀站着，准备举起杠铃。 **4** ~ **sth** (*specialist*) to make sth stronger or more solid by supporting it with sth 加强；加固：*The roof was braced by lengths of timber.* 屋顶用几根木头支撑固定住了。

brace·let /ˈbreɪslət/ *noun* a piece of jewellery worn around the wrist or arm 手镯；手链；臂镯 ➲ VISUAL VOCAB PAGE V70

bracer /ˈbreɪsə(r)/ *noun* a drink, usually alcoholic, which is intended to give strength to the person who drinks it 用于提神（或壮胆）的饮料；晨酒

bra·chio·pod /ˈbrækiəpɒd; *NAmE* -pɑːd/ *noun* (*biology* 生) a shellfish that has two joined shells and uses small TENTACLES (= long thin parts) to find food 腕足动物

bra·chio·saurus /ˌbrækiəˈsɔːrəs/ *noun* a very large DINOSAUR whose front legs were much longer than its back legs 腕龙（大型恐龙，前肢长于后肢）

brac·ing /ˈbreɪsɪŋ/ *adj.* (especially of weather 尤指天气) making you feel full of energy because it is cold 凉爽宜人的；令人精神焕发的：*bracing sea air* 清新宜人的海风

bracken /ˈbrækən/ *noun* [U] a wild plant with large leaves that grows thickly on hills and in woods and turns brown in the autumn/fall 欧洲蕨（叶大，秋季干枯）

bracket /ˈbrækɪt/ *noun, verb*

■ *noun* **1** (*also* ˈ**round bracket**) (*both BrE*) (*also* **par·en·thesis** *NAmE* or *formal*) [usually pl.] either of a pair of marks, ( ), placed around extra information in a piece of writing or part of a problem in mathematics 括号：*Publication dates are given* **in brackets** *after each title.* 出版日期括于书名后面。◇ *Add the numbers in brackets first.* 先把括号里的数字加起来。 ➲ SEE ALSO ANGLE BRACKET ➲ COMPARE BRACE *n.* (5) **2** (*NAmE*) (*especially BrE* ˌ**square** ˈ**bracket**) [usually pl.] either of a pair of marks, [ ], placed at the beginning and end of extra information in a text, especially comments made by an editor 方括号 **3 price, age, income, etc.** ~ prices, etc. within a particular range （价格、年龄、收入等的）组级，等级：*people in the lower income bracket* 低收入等级的人们 ◇ *Most of the houses are out of our price bracket.* 大多数房子都超出我们的价格范围。◇ *the 30–34 age bracket* (= people aged between 30 and 34) * 30-34 岁的年龄组 **4** a piece of wood, metal or plastic fixed to the wall to support a shelf, lamp, etc. （固定在墙上的）托架，支架

■ *verb* **1** ~ **sth** to put words, information, etc. between brackets 用括弧括上 **2** ~ **A and B** (**together**) | ~ **A** (**together**) **with B** [often passive] to consider people or things to be similar or connected in some way 把…等同考虑；把…相提并论：*It is unfair to bracket together those* *who cannot work with those who will not.* 把不能工作的人和不愿工作的人等同看待是不公平的。

brack·ish /ˈbrækɪʃ/ *adj.* (of water 水) salty in an unpleasant way 咸的；太咸的： ***brackish lakes/lagoons/marshes*** 咸水湖 / 潟湖 / 沼泽

brad /bræd/ *noun* a small thin nail with a small head and a flat tip 角钉；平头钉

brad·awl /ˈbrædɔːl/ *noun* a small pointed tool used for making holes 打眼钻；锥钻 ➲ VISUAL VOCAB PAGE V21

brae /breɪ/ *noun* (*ScotE*) (often in place names 常用于地名) a steep slope or hill 陡坡

brag /bræɡ/ *verb, noun*

▪***verb*** [I, T] (**-gg-**) ~ (**to sb**) (**about/of sth**) | ~ **that...** | + **speech** (*disapproving*) to talk too proudly about sth you own or sth you have done 吹嘘；自吹自擂 **SYN boast**: *He bragged to his friends about the crime.* 他向朋友炫耀那桩罪行。

▪***noun*** [U] a card game which is a simple form of POKER 勃莱格牌戏（简化的扑克牌戏）

brag·ga·docio /ˌbræɡəˈdəʊtʃiəʊ; *NAmE* -ˈdoʊtʃioʊ/ *noun* [U] (*literary, from Italian*) behaviour that seems too proud or confident 傲慢；自负

brag·gart /ˈbræɡət; *NAmE* -ɡərt/ *noun* (*old-fashioned*) a person who brags 吹牛大王；自吹自擂者

ˈ**bragging rights** *noun* [pl.] (*informal*) if you say that a person, a team, an organization, etc. has bragging rights, you mean that they have achieved a good result or are better or more successful than their rivals at that time 炫耀的权利；吹嘘的资格；狂傲资本

Brah·man /ˈbrɑːmən/ (*also* **Brah·min**) *noun* a Hindu who belongs to the CASTE (= division of society) that is considered the highest, originally that of priests 婆罗门（印度教种姓制度中最高阶层成员，原为僧侣级）

Brah·min /ˈbrɑːmɪn/ *noun* **1** = BRAHMAN **2** (*NAmE*) a person who is rich and has a lot of influence in society, especially sb from New England whose family belongs to the highest social class （尤指来自新英格兰某些高贵家族的）要人，名士，巨头： *a Boston Brahmin* 波士顿的上层人物

braid /breɪd/ *noun, verb*

▪***noun*** **1** [U] thin coloured rope that is used to decorate furniture and military uniforms （装饰家具和军装的）彩色穗带： *The general's uniform was trimmed with gold braid.* 将军的制服饰有金色穗带。 **2** (*especially NAmE*) (*BrE also* **plait**) [C] a long piece of sth, especially hair, that is divided into three parts and twisted together 辫状物；发辫；辫子： *She wears her hair in braids.* 她梳着发辫。 ➲ VISUAL VOCAB PAGE V65

▪***verb*** ~ **sth** (*especially NAmE*) (*BrE also* **plait**) to twist three or more long pieces of hair, rope, etc. together to make one long piece 将（头发、绳子等）编成辫： *She'd braided her hair.* 她梳着发辫。

Braille /breɪl/ (*also* **braille**) *noun* [U] a system of printing for blind people in which the letters of the alphabet and the numbers are printed as raised dots that can be read by touching them 布拉耶盲文（凸点符号）

brain 🔑 /breɪn/ *noun, verb*

▪***noun***

• **IN HEAD** 头 **1** 🔑 [C] the organ inside the head that controls movement, thought, memory and feeling 脑： *damage to the brain* 脑部损伤 ◇ *brain cells* 脑细胞 ◇ *She died of a brain tumour.* 她死于脑瘤。 ◇ *a device to measure brain activity during sleep* 检测睡眠时脑部活动的仪器 ➲ VISUAL VOCAB PAGE V64

• **FOOD** 食物 **2 brains** [pl.] the brain of an animal, eaten as food （供食用的）动物脑髓： *sheep's brains* 羊脑

• **INTELLIGENCE** 智力 **3** 🔑 [U, C, usually pl.] the ability to learn quickly and think about things in a logical and intelligent way 智力；脑力；逻辑思维能力： *It doesn't take much brain to work out that both stories can't be true.* 不必费多大脑筋就知道，两种说法不可能都是真的。 ◇ *Teachers spotted that he had a good brain at an early age.* 老师们发现他小时候就很聪颖。 ◇ *You need brains as well as brawn (= intelligence as well as strength) to do this job.* 这项工作既需要脑力又需要体力。 ➲ SEE ALSO NO-BRAINER

• **INTELLIGENT PERSON** 聪明人 **4** [C, usually pl.] (*informal*) an intelligent person 聪明的人；有智慧的人： *one of the best scientific brains in the country* 国家最优秀的科技人才之一 **5 the brains** [sing.] the most intelligent person in a particular group; the person who is responsible for thinking of and organizing sth （群体中）最聪明的人；策划组织者： *He's always been the brains of the family.* 这家人数他聪明。 ◇ *The band's drummer is **the brains behind** their latest venture.* 这位乐队鼓手是他们最近一次活动的策划人。

IDM have sth on the brain (*informal*) to think about sth all the time, especially in a way that is annoying 某事萦绕心头；过分热衷： *He has sex on the brain.* 他脑子里想的全是性。 ➲ MORE AT BEAT *v.*, BLOW *v.*, CUDGEL *v.*, PICK *v.*, RACK *v.*

▪***verb*** ~ **sb/sth/yourself** (*informal*) to kill a person or an animal by hitting them very hard on the head 猛击…的脑袋致死： *I nearly brained myself on that low beam.* 那根低横梁差点儿把我撞死。

brain·box /ˈbreɪnbɒks; *NAmE* -bɑːks/ *noun* (*BrE, informal*) a person who is very intelligent 脑瓜灵的人

ˈ**brain candy** *noun* [U] popular entertainment in the form of a film, TV programme, etc., that does not improve your knowledge or make you think seriously about a subject or issue 头脑糖果，脑轻松（指不能让人增长知识或严肃思考的电影、电视节目等大众娱乐方式）： *Chick-lit novels have been dismissed as brain candy.* 鸡仔小说已被贬斥为头脑糖果，不受待见。

brain·child /ˈbreɪntʃaɪld/ *noun* [sing.] an idea or invention of one person or a small group of people （个人或小群体的）主意，发明

ˈ**brain damage** *noun* [U] permanent damage to the brain caused by illness or an accident （疾病、事故导致的）脑损伤 ▸ ˈ**brain-damaged** *adj.*

ˈ**brain-dead** *adj.* **1** suffering from serious damage to the brain and needing machines to stay alive 脑死亡的 **2** (*humorous*) very stupid and boring; not intelligent 愚笨的；愚不可耐的

ˈ**brain death** *noun* [U] very serious damage to the brain that cannot be cured. A person who is suffering from brain death needs machines to keep them alive, even though their heart is still beating. 脑死亡（脑功能永久丧失，尽管心脏仍然跳动）

ˈ**brain drain** *noun* [sing.] (*informal*) the movement of highly skilled and qualified people to a country where they can work in better conditions and earn more money （国家的）人才流失

brain·iac /ˈbreɪniæk/ *noun* (*NAmE, informal*) a very intelligent person 超天才 **ORIGIN** From the name of a character in the *Superman* stories. 源自"超人"系列故事中的人名。

brain·less /ˈbreɪnləs/ *adj.* stupid; not able to think or talk in an intelligent way 愚蠢的；无头脑的

brain·power /ˈbreɪnpaʊə(r)/ *noun* [U] the ability to think; intelligence 智能；智力

brain·stem /ˈbreɪnstem/ *noun* (*anatomy* 解) the central part of the brain, which continues downwards to form the SPINAL CORD 脑干

brain·storm /ˈbreɪnstɔːm; *NAmE* -stɔːrm/ *noun* [sing.] **1** (*BrE*) a sudden inability to think clearly which causes unusual behaviour 脑猝变（突然神志不清）： *She had a brainstorm in the exam and didn't answer a single question.* 她考试时脑子里突然一片混乱，一个题也没答。 **2** (*NAmE*) = BRAINWAVE (1)

brain·storm·ing /ˈbreɪnstɔːmɪŋ; *NAmE* -stɔːrm-/ *noun* [U] a way of making a group of people all think about sth at the same time, often in order to solve a problem or to create good ideas 集思广益：*a brainstorming session* 一个集思广益的讨论会 ➲ WORDFINDER NOTE AT MEETING ▸ **brain·storm** *verb* [T, I]: ~ (**sth**) *Brainstorm as many ideas as possible.* 大家尽量献计。

ˈ**brain surgery** *noun* [U]
IDM **it's not ˈbrain surgery** (*informal*) used to emphasize that sth is easy to do or understand （强调容易完成或理解）这又不是大脑开刀 SYN **rocket science**: *Look, this isn't brain surgery we're doing here.* 听着，我们在这儿做的事又不像大脑开刀那么难。

ˈ**brain-teaser** *noun* a problem that is difficult but fun to solve 有趣的难题

brain·wash /ˈbreɪnwɒʃ; *NAmE* -wɔːʃ; -wɑːʃ/ *verb* to force sb to accept your ideas or beliefs, for example by repeating the same thing many times or by preventing the person from thinking clearly 给（某人）洗脑；强制说服：~ **sb** *The group is accused of brainwashing its young members.* 那个团体被指控对年轻成员洗脑。◇ ~ **sb into doing sth** *Women have been brainwashed into thinking that they must go out to work in order to fulfil themselves.* 妇女们被反复灌输的思想是：她们必须出去工作才能实现自己的价值。▸ **brain·wash·ing** *noun* [U]: *the victims of brainwashing and torture* 饱受洗脑和肉体折磨的人

brain·wave /ˈbreɪnweɪv/ *noun* **1** (*NAmE also* **brain·storm**) a sudden good idea 灵感；妙计：*I've had a brainwave!* 我灵机一动，想出了个主意来。**2** an electrical signal in the brain 脑电波

brainy /ˈbreɪni/ *adj.* (*informal*) (**brain·ier, braini·est**) very intelligent 十分聪明的

braise /breɪz/ *verb* ~ **sth** to cook meat or vegetables very slowly with a little liquid in a closed container 焖：*braising steak* (= that is suitable for braising) 供焖烧的肉排

brak /bræk/ *adj.* (*SAfrE*) (of water or soil) salty or containing ALKALI （水或土壤）有盐分的，含碱的

brake /breɪk/ *noun, verb*
■ ***noun*** **1** a device for slowing or stopping a vehicle 刹车；制动器；车闸：*to* **put/slam on the brakes** 踩 / 猛踩刹车 ◇ *the brake pedal* 刹车踏板 ➲ COLLOCATIONS AT DRIVING ➲ VISUAL VOCAB PAGES V55, V56 ➲ SEE ALSO AIR BRAKE, DISC BRAKE, FOOTBRAKE, HANDBRAKE **2** ~ (**on sth**) a thing that stops sth or makes it difficult 阻力；障碍：*High interest rates are a brake on the economy.* 高利率阻碍了经济发展。IDM SEE JAM *v.*
■ ***verb*** [I, T] to go slower or make a vehicle go slower using the brake 用闸减速；刹（车）：*The car braked and swerved.* 那辆车减慢车速并来了个急转弯。◇ *The truck* **braked to a halt.** 那辆卡车刹住了。◇ *You don't need to brake at every bend.* 没必要一遇到拐弯就刹车。◇ *She had to brake hard to avoid running into the car in front.* 她不得不猛踩刹车，以免撞上前面的车。◇ ~ **sth** *He braked the car and pulled in to the side of the road.* 他减缓车速，然后开到路边。➲ WORDFINDER NOTE AT CAR

ˈ**brake fluid** *noun* [U] liquid used in BRAKES to make the different parts move smoothly 刹车油；制动液

ˈ**brake light** (*NAmE also* ˈ**stop light**) *noun* a red light on the back of a vehicle that comes on when the brakes are used 刹车指示灯，制动灯（在车尾）

ˈ**brake pad** *noun* a thin block that presses onto the disc in a DISC BRAKE in a vehicle, in order to stop the vehicle （汽车盘式制动器上的）制动垫块

bram·ble /ˈbræmbl/ *noun* **1** (*especially BrE*) a wild bush with THORNS on which BLACKBERRIES grow 黑莓灌木 **2** (*BrE*) = BLACKBERRY

bran /bræn/ *noun* [U] the outer covering of grain which is left when the grain is made into flour 糠；麸皮

branch 🔑 /brɑːntʃ; *NAmE* bræntʃ/ *noun, verb*
■ ***noun***
• **OF TREE** 树 **1** 🔑 a part of a tree that grows out from the main STEM and on which leaves, flowers and fruit grow 树枝 ➲ VISUAL VOCAB PAGE V10
• **OF COMPANY** 公司 **2** 🔑 a local office or shop/store belonging to a large company or organization 分支；分部；分行；分店：*The bank has branches all over the country.* 那家银行在全国各地设有分行。◇ *Our New York branch is dealing with the matter.* 我们的纽约分部正在处理这件事。
• **OF GOVERNMENT** 政府 **3** 🔑 a part of a government or other large organization that deals with one particular aspect of its work 政府部门；分支机构 SYN **department**: *the anti-terrorist branch* 反恐部门
• **OF KNOWLEDGE** 知识 **4** 🔑 a division of an area of knowledge or a group of languages （学科及语言的）分支：*the branch of computer science known as 'artificial intelligence'* 计算机科学中的所谓"人工智能"分科
• **OF RIVER/ROAD** 河；路 **5** a smaller or less important part of a river, road, railway/railroad, etc. that leads away from the main part 支流；支路；支线：*a branch of the Rhine* 莱茵河的支流 ◇ *a* **branch line** (= a small line off a main railway line, often in country areas) 铁路支线
• **OF FAMILY** 家庭 **6** a group of members of a family who all have the same ANCESTORS 家族分支：*My uncle's branch of the family emigrated to Canada.* 我们家族中我叔父的这一支移居到了加拿大。IDM SEE ROOT *n.* ➲ WORDFINDER NOTE AT RELATION
■ ***verb*** [I] to divide into two or more parts, especially smaller or less important parts 分开；分岔：*The accident happened where the road branches.* 事故发生在岔道处。

PHR V ˌ**branch ˈoff 1** (of a road or river 路或河) to be joined to another road or river but lead in a different direction 分岔：*Just after the lake, the path branches off to the right.* 小路在经过湖后右边有一岔道。**2** (of a person 人) to leave a road or path and travel in a different direction 改道；转道 ˌ**branch ˈout** (**into sth**) to start to do an activity that you have not done before, especially in your work or business 涉足（新工作）；拓展（新业务）SYN **diversify**: *The company branched out into selling insurance.* 该公司开展了保险销售业务。◇ *I decided to* **branch out on my own.** 我决定自己开业。

brand 🔑 /brænd/ *noun, verb*
■ ***noun* 1** 🔑 a type of product made by a particular company 品牌：*Which brand of toothpaste do you use?* 你用什么牌子的牙膏？◇ (*BrE*) *You pay less for the supermarket's* **own brand.** 超市自有品牌的东西要便宜些。◇ (*NAmE*) *You pay less for the* **store brand.** 商店品牌的东西要便宜些。◇ **brand loyalty** (= the tendency of customers to continue buying the same brand) 品牌忠诚（顾客购买同一牌子商品的倾向）◇ *Champagne houses owe their success to* **brand image.** 香槟公司的成功在于他们的品牌形象。◇ *the* **leading brand** *of detergent* 一流品牌的洗涤剂 ➲ SEE ALSO OWN-BRAND **2** a particular type or kind of sth 类型：*an unorthodox brand of humour* 别具一格的幽默 **3** a mark made with a piece of hot metal, especially on farm animals to show who owns them 烙印（尤指农场牲畜身上表示所属的印记）
■ ***verb*** [often passive] **1** to describe sb/sth as being sth bad or unpleasant, especially unfairly （尤指不公正地）丑化（某人），败坏（某人）名声：~ **sb/sth as sth** *They were branded as liars and cheats.* 他们被说成是说谎者和骗子。◇ ~ **sb/sth + noun/adj.** *The newspapers branded her a hypocrite.* 报章污蔑她是伪君子。**2** ~ **sth** (**with sth**) to mark an animal with a BRAND *n.* (3) to show who owns it 给（牲畜）打烙印

brand·ed /ˈbrændɪd/ *adj.* [only before noun] (of a product 产品) made by a well-known company and having that company's name on it 名牌的：***branded drugs/goods/products*** 名牌药 / 商品 / 产品

brand·ing /ˈbrændɪŋ/ *noun* [U] the activity of giving a particular name and image to goods and services so that people will be attracted to them and want to buy them 品牌创建

ˈ**branding iron** *noun* a metal tool that is heated and used to BRAND farm animals （给农场牲畜打烙印的）烙铁

B

bran·dish /ˈbrændɪʃ/ *verb* **~ sth** to hold or wave sth, especially a weapon, in an aggressive or excited way 挑衅地挥舞，激动地挥舞（尤指武器）

ˈ**brand name** (*also* ˈ**trade name**) *noun* the name given to a product by the company that produces it 品牌名称

ˌ**brand ˈnew** *adj.* completely new 全新的；崭新的：*a brand new computer* 全新的计算机 ◇ *She bought her car brand new.* 她买的汽车是全新的。

brandy /ˈbrændi/ *noun* (*pl.* **-ies**) **1** [U, C] a strong alcoholic drink made from wine 白兰地（酒） **2** [C] a glass of brandy 一杯白兰地

ˌ**brandy ˈbutter** *noun* [U] a very thick sweet sauce made with butter, sugar and brandy, often eaten with CHRISTMAS PUDDING 白兰地黄油（用黄油、糖和白兰地酒调制而成，常配圣诞布丁食用）

ˈ**brandy snap** *noun* (*especially BrE*) a thin crisp biscuit/cookie in the shape of a tube, flavoured with GINGER and often filled with cream 姜味薄脆卷心饼，白兰地小脆饼（常带奶油夹心）

ˈ**bran tub** *noun* (*BrE*) a container that holds prizes hidden in BRAN, paper, etc., which children have to find as a game 摸彩桶（内有藏在麸皮、纸等中的奖品，供儿童游戏用）

brash /bræʃ/ *adj.* (*disapproving*) **1** confident in an aggressive way 盛气凌人的；自以为是的：*Beneath his brash exterior, he's still a little boy inside.* 他外表盛气凌人，内心里还是个孩子。 **2** (of things and places 东西、地方) too bright or too noisy in a way that is not attractive 耀眼的；嘈杂的 ▸ **brash·ly** *adv.* **brash·ness** *noun* [U]

brass /brɑːs; *NAmE* bræs/ *noun*
- **METAL** 金属 **1** [U] a bright yellow metal made by mixing COPPER and ZINC; objects made of brass 黄铜；黄铜制品：*solid **brass fittings/door** handles* 纯黄铜配件 / 门把手 ◇ *a **brass plate*** (= a sign outside a building giving the name and profession of the person who works there) 黄铜门牌（刻有姓名和职业） ◇ *to **clean/polish the brass*** 擦净 / 擦亮黄铜器
- **MUSICAL INSTRUMENTS** 乐器 **2** [U+sing./pl. v.] the musical instruments made of metal, such as TRUMPETS or FRENCH HORNS, that form a band or section of an ORCHESTRA; the people who play them（管弦乐团的）铜管乐器，铜管乐器组：*music for piano, strings and brass* 钢琴、弦乐器和铜管乐器的合奏乐曲 ➲ COMPARE PERCUSSION, STRING *n.* (5), (6), WIND INSTRUMENT, WOODWIND ➲ VISUAL VOCAB PAGE V37
- **FOR A HORSE** 马用 **3** [C] (*BrE*) a decorated piece of brass used as a decorative object, especially a round flat piece attached to a horse's HARNESS 黄铜饰品（尤指马挽具上的黄铜圆片）
- **IN CHURCH** 教堂 **4** [C] (*especially BrE*) a flat piece of brass with words or a picture on it, fixed to the floor or wall of a church in memory of sb who has died 黄铜纪念牌（钉在教堂的地上或墙上以纪念死者，上面刻有文字或雕像） ➲ SEE ALSO BRASS RUBBING
- **IMPORTANT PEOPLE** 要人 **5** (*especially NAmE*) (*also informal* ˌ**top ˈbrass**) [U+sing./pl. v.] the people who are in the most important positions in a company, an organization, etc.（公司、机构等的）最高负责人，要员，头目
- **MONEY** 钱 **6** [U] (*old-fashioned, BrE, informal*) money 钱 ➲ SEE ALSO BRASSY

IDM ˌ**brass ˈmonkeys** | ˌ**brass ˈmonkey weather** (*BrE, slang*) if you say that it is **brass monkeys** or **brass monkey weather**, you mean that it is very cold weather 极冷的天气；天寒地冻 ˌ**brass ˈneck/ˈnerve** (*BrE, informal*) a combination of confidence and lack of respect 自以为是；傲慢无理：*I didn't think she would have the brass neck to do that.* 我本以为她不会胆大妄为的。 **the** ˌ**brass ˈring** (*NAmE, informal*) the opportunity to be successful; success that you have worked hard to get 成功的机遇；获胜良机；（来之不易的）成功：*The girls' outdoor track team has **grabbed the brass ring** seven times.* 女子室外径赛运动队已经七次夺冠。 **ORIGIN** From the custom of giving a free ride to any child who grabbed one of the rings hanging around the side of a merry-go-round at a fairground. 源自一种习俗，孩子只要抓住露天游乐场旋转木马边悬挂的铜环，就可以免费骑木马一次。 (**get down to**) **brass ˈtacks** (*informal*) (to start to consider) the basic facts or practical details of sth（开始考虑）基本事实，具体问题 ➲ MORE AT BOLD *adj.*, MUCK *n.*

ˌ**brass ˈband** *noun* [C+sing./pl. v.] a group of musicians who play brass instruments 铜管乐队

ˌ**brassed ˈoff** *adj.* (*BrE, slang*) annoyed 恼怒的；厌烦的 **SYN** **fed up**

bras·serie /ˈbræsəri; *NAmE* ˌbræsəˈriː/ *noun* a type of restaurant, often one in a French style that is not very expensive 法式（廉价）餐馆

bras·sica /ˈbræsɪkə/ *noun* a plant of a type that includes CABBAGE, RAPE and MUSTARD 芥属植物（包括甘蓝、油菜及芥菜类）

brass·ière /ˈbræziə(r); *NAmE* brəˈzɪr/ *noun* (*formal*) = BRA (1)

ˌ**brass ˈknuckles** *noun* [pl.] (*NAmE*) = KNUCKLEDUSTER

ˈ**brass rubbing** *noun* [U, C] the art of rubbing a soft pencil or CHALK on a piece of paper placed over a BRASS in a church; the pattern you get by doing this（在教堂黄铜纪念牌上拓印图文的）拓印；拓印的图文

brassy /ˈbrɑːsi; *NAmE* ˈbræsi/ *adj.* **1** (*sometimes disapproving*) (of music 音乐) loud and unpleasant 声高刺耳的；喧闹的；嘈杂的 **2** (*informal, disapproving*) (of a woman 女人) dressing in a way that makes her sexual attraction obvious, but without style 衣着花里胡哨的：*the brassy blonde behind the bar* 酒吧吧台后面的花哨金发女郎 **3** like BRASS (1) in colour; too yellow and bright 黄铜色的；黄得耀眼的 **4** (*NAmE, informal*) saying what you think, without caring about other people 直截了当的；过于直率的

brat /bræt/ *noun* (*informal, disapproving*) a person, especially a child, who behaves badly 没有规矩的人；（尤指）顽童：*a **spoiled/spoilt brat*** 被宠坏了的顽皮孩子 ▸ **bratty** /ˈbræti/ *adj.*：*a bratty kid* 一个刁蛮小子

the ˈ**brat pack** *noun* [usually sing.] a group of famous young people, especially film/movie actors, who sometimes behave badly 新星帮（少年得志、有时行为不端的一群电影明星等）

bra·vado /brəˈvɑːdəʊ; *NAmE* -doʊ/ *noun* [U] a confident way of behaving that is intended to impress people, sometimes as a way of hiding a lack of confidence 逞能；逞强；（有时）虚张声势：*an act of sheer bravado* 纯属逞能的举动

brave 🔑 /breɪv/ *adj.*, *verb*, *noun*

■ ***adj.*** (**braver**, **brav·est**) **1** 🔑 (of a person 人) willing to do things which are difficult, dangerous or painful; not afraid 勇敢的；无畏的 **SYN** **courageous**：*brave men and women* 英勇无畏的男女 ◇ *Be brave!* 勇敢一些！ ◇ *I wasn't brave enough to tell her what I thought of her.* 我当时没有勇气告诉她我对她的看法。 **2** 🔑 (of an action 行为) requiring or showing courage 需要勇气的；表现勇敢的：*a brave decision* 有勇气的决定 ◇ *She died after a brave fight against cancer.* 她在同癌症进行了顽强的搏斗之后死去了。 ◇ *He felt homesick, but made a brave attempt to appear cheerful.* 他很想家，但却竭力表现得很高兴。 **3** **~ new** (*sometimes ironic*) new in an impressive way 新颖的；崭新的：*a vision of a brave new Britain* 令人叹为观止的新英国远景 ▸ **brave·ly** *adv.* **bravery** /ˈbreɪvəri/ *noun* [U] **SYN** **courage**：*an award for outstanding bravery* 杰出英勇奖 ◇ *acts of skill and bravery* 有勇有谋的行为

IDM (**a**) ˌ**brave new ˈworld** a situation or society that changes in a way that is meant to improve people's lives but is often a source of extra problems 美好的新世界（本欲改善人们的生活，实则带来预料不到的问题）：*the brave new world of technology* 科技进步的美好新世界 **put on a brave ˈface** | **put a brave ˈface on sth** to pretend that you feel confident and happy when you do not 强装自信快乐；佯装满不在乎

■ *verb* ~ **sb/sth** to have to deal with sth difficult or unpleasant in order to achieve sth 勇敢面对；冒（风险）；经受（困难）： *He did not feel up to braving the journalists at the airport.* 他怯于在机场直接面对记者。◇ *Over a thousand people* ***braved the elements*** (= went outside in spite of the bad weather) *to attend the march.* 一千多人不顾天气恶劣参加了游行。

■ *noun* **1 the brave** [pl.] people who are brave 勇敢的人： *America, the land of the free and the home of the brave* 美国，自由者的土地、勇士的家园 **2** [C] (*old-fashioned*) a Native American WARRIOR 美洲印第安武士

bravo /ˌbrɑːˈvəʊ; *NAmE* -ˈvoʊ/ *exclamation* (*becoming old-fashioned*) people say **Bravo!** at the end of sth they have enjoyed, such as a play at the theatre （喝彩声、叫好声）好哇

bra·vura /brəˈvjʊərə; *NAmE* -ˈvjʊrə/ *noun* [U] (*formal*) great skill and enthusiasm in doing sth artistic 精湛技艺： *a bravura performance* 出色的演出

braw /brɔː/ *adj.* (*ScotE*) fine 好的；不错的： *braw lads and bonny lasses* 俊男靓女 ◇ *It was a braw day.* 那天天气挺好。

brawl /brɔːl/ *noun, verb*

■ *noun* a noisy and violent fight involving a group of people, usually in a public place 喧闹；斗殴；闹事： *a drunken brawl* 酒后闹事 ➲ SYNONYMS AT FIGHT

■ *verb* [I] to take part in a noisy and violent fight, usually in a public place 打斗；闹事： *They were arrested for brawling in the street.* 他们因在街上打斗而遭到拘捕。 ▶ **brawl·er** *noun*

brawn /brɔːn/ *noun* [U] **1** physical strength 体力： *In this job you need brains as well as brawn.* 这项工作耗神又耗力。 **2** (*BrE*) (*NAmE* **head·cheese**) meat made from the head of a pig or CALF that has been boiled and pressed into a container, served cold in thin slices （罐装）猪头肉，牛犊头肉

brawny /ˈbrɔːni/ *adj.* (*informal*) having strong muscles 健壮的；肌肉发达的 SYN **burly**： *He was a great brawny brute of a man.* 他是个魁梧壮实、冷酷无情的人。

bray /breɪ/ *verb* **1** [I] when a DONKEY **brays**, it makes a loud unpleasant sound （驴子）嘶叫 **2** [I] (of a person 人) to talk or laugh in a loud unpleasant voice 以刺耳的高声讲话（或笑）： *He brayed with laughter.* 他刺耳地大笑。◇ *a braying voice* 刺耳的声音 ▶ **bray** *noun*

bra·zen /ˈbreɪzn/ *adj., verb*

■ *adj.* **1** (*disapproving*) open and without shame, usually about sth that people find shocking 厚颜无耻的 SYN **shameless**： *She had become brazen about the whole affair.* 她对整件事已经不感到羞耻了。◇ *his brazen admission that he was cheating* 他恬不知耻地承认自己作弊 **2** made of, or the colour of, BRASS (1) 黄铜制的；黄铜色的 ▶ **brazen·ly** *adv.* ： *She had brazenly admitted allowing him back into the house.* 她恬不知耻地承认了让他回到屋里的事。 **brazen·ness** *noun* [U]

■ *verb*

IDM ˌ**brazen it ˈout** to behave as if you are not ashamed or embarrassed about sth even though you should be 厚着脸皮： *Now that everyone knew the truth, the only thing to do was to brazen it out.* 既然大家都知道真相了，只好硬着头皮撑过去。

bra·zier /ˈbreɪziə(r)/ *noun* a large metal container that holds a fire and is used to keep people warm when they are outside （金属）火盆

bra·zil /brəˈzɪl/ (*also* **braˈzil nut**) *noun* the curved nut of a large S American tree. It has a hard shell with three sides. 巴西坚果 ➲ VISUAL VOCAB PAGE V35

Bra·zil·ian /brəˈzɪliən/ *adj., noun*

■ *adj.* from or connected with Brazil 巴西的

■ *noun* a person from Brazil 巴西人

Braˌzilian ˈwax *noun* a style of removing a woman's PUBIC hair using WAX, in which almost all the hair is removed with only a very small central strip remaining 巴西蜜蜡脱毛（一种女子阴部脱毛方式）

BRB /ˌbiː ɑː ˈbiː; *NAmE* ɑːr/ *abbr.* (*informal*) (especially in emails, messages sent using an INSTANT MESSAGING service, etc.) be right back (when you have to leave your computer, etc. for a short time) 马上回来（全写为 be right back，尤用于电邮、即时消息等）

breach /briːtʃ/ *noun, verb*

■ *noun* (*formal*) **1** [C, U] ~ **of sth** a failure to do sth that must be done by law （对法规等的）违背，违犯： *a* ***breach of contract/copyright/warranty*** 违约；侵犯版权；违反保证 ◇ *They are* ***in breach of*** *Article 119.* 他们违犯了第 119 条。◇ (*BrE*) (*a*) ***breach of the peace*** (= the crime of behaving in a noisy or violent way in public) 扰乱治安 **2** [C, U] ~ **of sth** an action that breaks an agreement to behave in a particular way 破坏；辜负： *a* ***breach of confidence/trust*** 泄密；背信 ◇ *a breach of security* (= when sth that is normally protected is no longer secure) 破坏安全 **3** [C] a break in a relationship between people or countries （关系）中断，终止： *a breach in Franco-German relations* 法德关系的破裂 **4** [C] an opening that is created during a military attack or by strong winds or seas 突破口；缺口；窟窿： *They escaped through a breach in the wire fence.* 他们从铁丝网上的一个缺口逃走了。 IDM SEE STEP *v.*

■ *verb* (*formal*) **1** ~ **sth** to not keep to an agreement or not keep a promise 违反；违背 SYN **break**： *The government is accused of breaching the terms of the treaty.* 政府被控违反条约中的规定。 **2** ~ **sth** to make a hole in a wall, fence, etc. so that sb/sth can go through it 在…上打开缺口： *The dam had been breached.* 大坝决口了。

bread /bred/ *noun* [U] **1** a type of food made from flour, water and usually YEAST mixed together and baked 面包： ***a loaf/slice/piece of bread*** 一条 / 一片 / 一块面包 ◇ ***white/brown/wholemeal bread*** 白 / 黑 / 全麦面包 ➲ SEE ALSO CRISPBREAD, FRENCH BREAD, GINGERBREAD **2** (*old-fashioned, slang*) money 钱

IDM **take the bread out of sb's ˈmouth** to take away sb's job so that they are no longer able to earn enough money to live 剥夺某人的生计；砸某人的饭碗 ➲ MORE AT DAILY *adj.*, HALF *det.*, KNOW *v.*, SLICED BREAD

ˌ**bread and ˈbutter** *noun* [U] **1** slices of bread that have been spread with butter 黄油面包片： *a piece of bread and butter* 一块黄油面包 **2** (*informal*) a person or company's main source of income （某人或公司的）主要收入来源

ˌ**bread-and-ˈbutter** *adj.* [only before noun] basic; very important 基本的；很重要的： *Employment and taxation are the bread-and-butter issues of politics.* 就业和征税是很重要的政治问题。

ˌ**bread-and-butter ˈpudding** *noun* [U, C] a DESSERT (= sweet dish) consisting of layers of bread with butter on, cooked with dried fruit in a mixture of eggs and milk 面包黄油布丁，面包奶油布丁（黄油面包层加干果在鸡蛋牛奶中烘焙而成）

bread·bas·ket /ˈbredbɑːskɪt; *NAmE* -bæs-/ *noun* [sing.] the part of a country or region that produces large amounts of food, especially grain, for the rest of the country or region 粮仓（指一国或地区的粮食生产基地，尤指谷物生产基地）

ˈ**bread bin** (*BrE*) (*NAmE* **bread·box** /ˈbredbɒks; *NAmE* -bɑːks/) *noun* a wooden, metal or plastic container for keeping bread in so that it stays fresh 面包箱（存放面包用）

bread·board /ˈbredbɔːd; *NAmE* -bɔːrd/ *noun* a flat board used for cutting bread on 切面包板

bread·crumbs /ˈbredkrʌmz/ *noun* [pl.] **1** very small pieces of bread that can be used in cooking 面包屑 **2** (*also* **breadcrumb trail** [C]) a series of links displayed at the top of a web page, indicating the path to that page 面包屑导航（网页上方指向该页面的路径链接信息）

bread·ed /'bredɪd/ *adj.* covered in breadcrumbs 裹着面包屑的

bread·fruit /'bredfruːt/ *noun* [C, U] (*pl.* **bread·fruit**) a large tropical fruit with a thick skin, that tastes and feels like bread when it is cooked. It grows on a tree which is called a **breadfruit tree.** 面包果（皮厚个大，煮熟似面包）

bread·line /'bredlaɪn/ *noun* **1** [sing.] the lowest level of income on which it is possible to live 只能勉强维持生计的收入水平；贫困线： *Many people without jobs are living* ***on the breadline*** (= are very poor). 很多没工作的人生活十分贫苦。 **2** [C] (*NAmE*) (in the past) a line of people waiting to receive free food （旧时）等待领取救济食品的队伍

ˌbread 'roll *noun* = ROLL (3)

bread·stick /'bredstɪk/ *noun* **1** a long thin piece of bread, which is dry like a biscuit 棍子面包；面包棒 **2** a piece of fresh bread, baked in the shape of a small stick 小棍状烤面包

breadth /bredθ/ *noun* [U, C] **1** the distance or measurement from one side to the other; how broad or wide sth is 宽度 SYN **width**: *She estimated the breadth of the lake to be 500 metres.* 她估计湖面大约有 500 米宽。 ➲ COMPARE LENGTH (1) **2** a wide range (of knowledge, interests, etc.) （知识、兴趣等）广泛： *He was surprised at her breadth of reading.* 他对于她的博览群书感到惊讶。 ◇ *The curriculum needs breadth and balance.* 课程设置应该内容广泛而且均衡。 ◇ *a new political leader whose* ***breadth of vision*** (= willingness to accept new ideas) *can persuade others to change* 一位能凭远见卓识说服他人做出改变的新政治领袖 IDM SEE LENGTH

'bread tree (*also* **'bread palm**) *noun* a large plant found in tropical and southern Africa whose thick main STEM can be made into a type of flour 面包棕榈（产于非洲南部，树干可制成面粉）

bread·win·ner /'bredwɪnə(r)/ *noun* a person who supports their family with the money they earn 挣钱养家的人

break 🔑 /breɪk/ *verb, noun*

■ *verb* (**broke** /brəʊk; *NAmE* broʊk/, **broken** /'brəʊkən; *NAmE* 'broʊ-/)

• **IN PIECES** 破碎 **1** 🔑 [I, T] to be damaged and separated into two or more parts , as a result of force; to damage sth in this way （使）破，裂，碎： *All the windows broke with the force of the blast.* 爆炸的巨大力量震碎了所有的窗户。 ◇ **~ in/into sth** *She dropped the plate and it* ***broke into pieces.*** 她把盘子掉在地上打碎了。 ◇ **~ sth** *to break a cup/window* 打破杯子 / 窗户 ◇ *She fell off a ladder and broke her arm.* 她从梯子上掉下来，摔断了胳膊。 ◇ **~ sth in/into sth** *He* ***broke*** *the chocolate* ***in two.*** 他把那块巧克力一分为二。 ➲ COLLOCATIONS AT INJURY

• **STOP WORKING** 停止运转 **2** 🔑 [I, T] to stop working as a result of being damaged; to damage sth and stop it from working 弄坏；损坏；坏掉： *My watch has broken.* 我的表坏了。 ◇ **~ sth** *I think I've broken the washing machine.* 我可能把洗衣机弄坏了。

• **SKIN** 皮肤 **3** [T] **~ sth** to cut the surface of the skin and make it BLEED 弄破；使流血： *The dog bit me but didn't break the skin.* 那条狗咬了我，但没咬破皮肤。

• **LAW/PROMISE** 法律；承诺 **4** 🔑 [T] **~ sth** to do sth that is against the law; to not keep a promise, etc. 违犯；背弃： *to break the law/rules/conditions* 违反法律 / 规章 / 所定条件 ◇ *to break an agreement/a contract/a promise/your word* 违反协议 / 合同 / 允诺；食言 ◇ *to break an appointment* (= not to come to it) 失约 ◇ *He was breaking the speed limit* (= travelling faster than the law allows). 他违章超速驾驶。

• **STOP FOR SHORT TIME** 暂停 **5** 🔑 [I, T] to stop doing sth for a while, especially when it is time to eat or have a drink 稍停；暂停： **~ (for sth)** *Let's break for lunch.* 我们休息一会儿，吃午饭。 ◇ **~ sth** *a broken night's sleep* (= a night during which you often wake up) 夜间时时醒来的睡眠 ◇ (*especially BrE*) *We* ***broke our journey*** *in Oxford* (= stopped in Oxford on the way to the place we were going to). 我们途中在牛津停留了一下。

• **END STH** 中断 **6** [T] **~ sth** to interrupt sth so that it ends suddenly 打断；中断： *She* ***broke the silence*** *by coughing.* 她的咳嗽声打破了寂静。 ◇ *A tree* ***broke his fall*** (= stopped him as he was falling). 他坠落时一棵树挡住了他。 ◇ *The phone rang and broke my train of thought.* 电话铃响起来，打断了我的思路。 **7** [T] **~ sth** to make sth end by using force or strong action 强行终止；破坏： *an attempt to break the year-long siege* 试图冲破长达一年的围困 ◇ *Management has not succeeded in* ***breaking the strike.*** 资方未能使罢工终止。 **8** [T] **~ sth** to end a connection with sth or a relationship with sb 终止，断绝（关系、联系）： *He broke all ties with his parents.* 他断绝了与父母的一切关系。

• **ESCAPE** 逃跑 **9** [I] **~ free** (**from sb/sth**) (of a person or an object 人或物体) to get away from or out of a position in which they are stuck or trapped 逃脱；挣脱： *He finally managed to break free from his attacker.* 他终于设法逃脱了袭击他的人。

• **DESTROY, BE DESTROYED** 毁坏；被毁坏 **10** [T, I] **~ (sb/sth)** to destroy sth or make sb/sth weaker; to become weak or be destroyed （被）摧毁，削弱： *to break sb's morale/resistance/resolve/spirit* 瓦解某人的士气 / 抵抗 / 决心 / 精神 ◇ *The government was determined to break the power of the trade unions.* 政府决心削弱工会的力量。 ◇ *The scandal broke him* (= ruined his reputation and destroyed his confidence). 这桩丑闻把他毁了。 ◇ *She broke under questioning* (= was no longer able to bear it) *and confessed to everything.* 她经不住盘问，招认了一切。

• **MAKE SB FEEL BAD** 使难过 **11** [T] **~ sb** to make sb feel so sad, lonely, etc. that they cannot live a normal life 使心碎；使十分悲伤；使孤寂： *The death of his wife broke him completely.* 妻子的死使他悲痛欲绝。

• **OF WEATHER** 天气 **12** [I] to change suddenly, usually after a period when it has been fine （常指好天气）突变

• **SHOW OPENING** 露出缝隙 **13** [I] to show an opening 露出缝隙；散开： *The clouds broke and the sun came out.* 云开日出。

▼ **VOCABULARY BUILDING** 词汇扩充

Words that mean 'break' 表示弄碎、破碎的词

burst 爆裂；胀破	*The balloon hit a tree and burst.* 气球碰到树就爆了。
crack 破裂；裂开	*The ice started to crack.* 冰开始裂了。
crumble （使）破碎，成碎屑	*Crumble the cheese into a bowl.* 将干酪弄碎放进碗里。
cut 切开；割断；剪断	*Now cut the wire in two.* 现在将电线剪成两段。
fracture （使）断裂，折断	*He fell and fractured his hip.* 他跌了一跤摔裂了髋骨。
shatter （使）破裂，碎裂	*The vase hit the floor and shattered.* 花瓶掉在地板上摔了个粉碎。
smash （哗啦一声）打碎，破碎	*Vandals had smashed two windows.* 故意破坏公物者打碎了两扇窗户。
snap （咔嚓一声）断裂，绷断	*I snapped the pencil in half.* 我啪的一声将铅笔折成两段。
split 撕裂；裂开	*The bag had split open on the way home.* 在回家的路上袋子裂开了。
tear 撕裂；扯破	*She tore the letter into pieces.* 她把信撕碎了。

All these verbs, except **cut**, can be used with or without an object. 除 cut 外，上述动词带不带宾语均可。

- **OF DAY/DAWN/STORM** 白天；黎明；风暴 **14** [I] when the day or DAWN or a storm **breaks**, it begins 开始；（风暴）发作：*Dawn was breaking when they finally left.* 他们终于离开时正是破晓时分。➲ SEE ALSO DAYBREAK
- **OF NEWS** 消息 **15** [I] if a piece of news **breaks**, it becomes known 透露；传开：*There was a public outcry when the scandal broke.* 丑闻一传开，舆论一片哗然。◇ ***breaking news*** (= news that is arriving about events that have just happened) 突发性新闻 **16** [T] **~ it/the news to sb** to be the first to tell sb some bad news （第一个将坏消息向某人）公布，透露，说出：*Who's going to break it to her?* 由谁来把这事告诉她呢？◇ *I'm sorry to be the one to break the news to you.* 我很难过，这消息得由我来告诉你。
- **OF VOICE** 嗓音 **17** [I] if sb's voice **breaks**, it changes its tone because of emotion （因激动）变调：*Her voice broke as she told us the dreadful news.* 她告诉我们这可怕的消息时，声音都变了。**18** [I] when a boy's voice **breaks**, it becomes permanently deeper at about the age of 13 or 14 （指男孩在 13 或 14 岁时嗓音）变粗，变低
- **A RECORD** 纪录 **19** 🔑 [T] **~ a record** to do sth better, faster, etc. than anyone has ever done it before 打破（纪录）：*She had broken the world 100 metres record.* 她打破了 100 米世界纪录。◇ *The movie broke all box-office records.* 这部影片打破了所有的票房纪录。
- **OF WAVES** 波浪 **20** [I] when waves **break**, they fall and are dissolved into FOAM, usually near land 拍岸；进溅：*the sound of waves breaking on the beach* 浪涛拍岸的声音 ◇ *The sea was breaking over the wrecked ship.* 海浪冲刷着破船的残骸。
- **STH SECRET** 秘密 **21** [T] **~ a code/cipher** to find the meaning of sth secret 破译；破解：*to break a code* 破译密码
- **MONEY** 钱 **22** [T] **~ sth** (*especially NAmE*) to change a BANKNOTE for coins 把…换成零钱；找开：*Can you break a twenty-dollar bill?* 可以给我找开二十美元的钞票吗？

IDM **HELP** Idioms containing **break** are at the entries for the nouns and adjectives in the idioms, for example **break sb's heart** is at **heart**. 含 break 的习语，都可在该等习语中的名词及形容词相关词条找到，如 break sb's heart 在词条 heart 下。

PHR V ˌ**break aˈway (from sb/sth) 1** to escape suddenly from sb who is holding you or keeping you prisoner 突然挣脱；逃脱：*The prisoner broke away from his guards.* 犯人挣脱了看守。**2** to leave a political party, state, etc., especially to form a new one 脱离，背叛（政党、国家等，尤指为了组建新的）：*The people of the province wished to break away and form a new state.* 该省人民希望分离成立一个新国家。➲ RELATED NOUN BREAKAWAY (1) **3** to move away from a crowd or group, especially in a race （尤指速度竞赛）甩掉：*She broke away from the pack and opened up a two-second lead.* 她甩开所有其他赛跑者，以两秒领先。

ˌ**break ˈdown 1** 🔑 (of a machine or vehicle 机器或车辆) to stop working because of a fault 出故障；坏掉：*The telephone system has broken down.* 电话系统瘫痪了。◇ *We (= the car) broke down on the freeway.* 我们的车在高速公路上抛锚了。➲ RELATED NOUN BREAKDOWN (1) **2** 🔑 to fail 失败：*Negotiations between the two sides have broken down.* 双方谈判失败了。➲ RELATED NOUN BREAKDOWN (2) **3** to become very bad 被搞垮；垮掉：*Her health broke down under the pressure of work.* 她因工作压力身体垮掉了。➲ SEE ALSO NERVOUS BREAKDOWN **4** 🔑 to lose control of your feelings and start crying 情不自禁地哭起来：*He broke down and wept when he heard the news.* 听到这个消息，他不禁失声痛哭。**5** to divide into parts to be analysed 划分（以便分析）：*Expenditure on the project breaks down as follows: wages $10m, plant $4m, raw materials $5m.* 这项工程的支出费用分项列明如下：工资 1 000 万美元，设备 400 万美元，原料 500 万美元。➲ RELATED NOUN BREAKDOWN (3) ➲ LANGUAGE BANK AT ILLUSTRATE ˌ**break sth↔ˈdown 1** 🔑 to make sth fall down, open, etc. by hitting it hard 打倒，砸破（某物）：*Firefighters had to break the door down to reach the people trapped inside.* 消防队员不得不破门而入，解救困在里面的人。**2** to destroy sth or make it disappear, especially a particular feeling or attitude that sb has 破坏，消除（尤指某种感情或态度）：*to break down resistance/opposition* 瓦解抵抗 / 反对 ◇ *to break down sb's reserve/shyness* 驱除某人的矜持 / 胆怯 ◇ *Attempts must be made to break down the barriers of fear and hostility which divide the two communities.* 必须设法消除造成这两个团体不和的恐惧和敌意。**3** to divide sth into parts in order to analyse it or make it easier to do 把…分类；划分：*Break your expenditure down into bills, food and other.* 把支出费用按账单、食物及其他分类列明。◇ *Each lesson is broken down into several units.* 每一课都分成几个单元。➲ RELATED NOUN BREAKDOWN (3) **4** to make a substance separate into parts or change into a different form in a chemical process 使分解（为）；使变化（成）：*Sugar and starch are broken down in the stomach.* 糖和淀粉在胃里被分解。➲ RELATED NOUN BREAKDOWN (4)

ˈ**break for sth** to suddenly run towards sth when you are trying to escape （试图逃脱时）突然冲向；向…挣脱：*She had to hold him back as he tried to break for the door.* 他试图向门口逃去，她只好拉住他。

ˌ**break ˈin** 🔑 to enter a building by force 强行进入；破门而入：*Burglars had broken in while we were away.* 我们不在家时，窃贼闯进屋里了。➲ RELATED NOUN BREAK-IN ˌ**break sb/sth ˈin 1** to train sb/sth in sth new that they must do 训练某人 / 某物；培训：*to break in new recruits* 训练新人 ◇ *The young horse was not yet broken in* (= trained to carry a rider). 那匹刚长成的马还没被驯服。**2** to wear sth, especially new shoes, until they become comfortable 把…穿得合身，使舒适自如（尤指新鞋）ˌ**break ˈin (on sth)** to interrupt or disturb sth 打断；搅扰：*She longed to break in on their conversation but didn't want to appear rude.* 她很想打断他们的谈话，但又不愿显得粗鲁。◇ **+ speech** *'I didn't do it!' she broke in.* "不是我干的！"她插嘴说。

ˌ**break ˈinto sth 1** 🔑 to enter a building by force; to open a car, etc. by force 强行闯入；撬开（汽车等）：*We had our car broken into last week.* 我们的车上周被撬了。➲ RELATED NOUN BREAK-IN **2** to begin laughing, singing, etc. suddenly 突然开始（笑、唱等）：*As the President's car drew up, the crowd broke into loud applause.* 总统的座驾停下时，人群中爆发出热烈的掌声。**3** to suddenly start running; to start running faster than before 突然开始（跑）；开始快跑：*He broke into a run when he saw the police.* 他看见警察，撒腿就跑。◇ *Her horse broke into a trot.* 她的马突然开始加速小跑。**4** (*BrE*) to use a BANKNOTE of high value to buy sth that costs less 找开（大面值钞票买小额商品）：*I had to break into a £20 note to pay the bus fare.* 我只好找开一张 20 英镑的钞票买公交车票。**5** to open and use sth that has been kept for an emergency 启用（应急备用品）：*They had to break into the emergency food supplies.* 他们不得不动用应急食物。**6** to be successful when you get involved in sth 成功参与；顺利打入：*The company is having difficulty breaking into new markets.* 该公司在打入新市场时遇到困难。

ˌ**break ˈoff 1** 🔑 to become separated from sth as a result of force 断开；折断：*The back section of the plane had broken off.* 飞机尾部脱落了。**2** to stop speaking or stop doing sth for a time 停顿；中断：*He broke off in the middle of a sentence.* 他一句话说了一半就不说了。ˌ**break sth↔ˈoff** 🔑 **1** to separate sth, using force 使折断：*She broke off a piece of chocolate and gave it to me.* 她掰了一块巧克力给我。**2** 🔑 to end sth suddenly 突然终止：*Britain threatened to break off diplomatic relations.* 英国威胁说要断绝外交关系。◇ *They've broken off their engagement.* 他们突然解除了婚约。

ˌ**break ˈout** 🔑 (of war, fighting or other unpleasant events 战争、打斗等不愉快事件) to start suddenly 突然开始；爆发：*They had escaped to America shortly before war broke out in 1939.* * 1939 年战争爆发前不久他们逃到了美国。◇ *Fighting had broken out between rival groups of fans.* 双方球迷发生了打斗。◇ *Fire broke out during the night.* 夜间突然发生了火灾。➲ RELATED NOUN OUTBREAK ˌ**break ˈout (of sth)** to escape from a place or situation 逃离（某地）；摆脱（某状况）：*Several prisoners broke out of the jail.* 几名囚犯越狱了。◇ *She needed to break out of her daily routine and do something exciting.* 她需要从日常事务中解脱出来，找点有意思的事做。➲ RELATED NOUN

B

BREAKOUT ˌ**break 'out in sth** to suddenly become covered in sth 突然布满某物: *Her face broke out in a rash.* 她脸上突然长出一片红疹。◇ *He broke out in a cold sweat* (= for example, through fear). 他突然冒出一身冷汗。

ˌ**break 'through** to make new and important discoveries 有新的重大发现；突破: *Scientists think they are beginning to break through in the fight against cancer.* 科学家认为他们在对抗癌症的研究中开始有所突破。➲ RELATED NOUN BREAKTHROUGH ˌ**break 'through | ˌbreak 'through sth 1** to make a way through sth using force 冲破；突破: *Demonstrators broke through the police cordon.* 示威群众冲破了警方的警戒线。**2** (of the sun or moon 太阳或月亮) to appear from behind clouds 从云层后露出: *The sun broke through at last in the afternoon.* 下午太阳终于拨云而出。ˌ**break 'through sth** to succeed in dealing with an attitude that sb has and the difficulties it creates 克服；战胜 SYN **overcome**: *He had finally managed to break through her reserve.* 他终于设法消除了她的拘谨。

ˌ**break 'up 1** 🔑 to separate into smaller pieces 粉碎；破碎: *The ship broke up on the rocks.* 船触礁撞碎了。**2** 🔑 to come to an end 结束: *Their marriage has broken up.* 他们的婚姻已经破裂。➲ RELATED NOUN BREAK-UP **3** to go away in different directions 散开；解散: *The meeting broke up at eleven o'clock.* 会议在十一点散会。**4** (*especially BrE*) to begin the holidays when school closes at the end of a term （学校）期终放假: *When do you break up for Christmas?* 你们什么时候放假过圣诞节？ **5** (*BrE*) to become very weak 变得虚弱；垮掉: *He was breaking up under the strain.* 过度的劳累使他快要垮了。**6** (*NAmE*) to laugh very hard 捧腹大笑: *Woody Allen makes me just break up.* 伍迪·艾伦令我几乎笑破肚皮。**7** when a person who is talking on a mobile/cell phone **breaks up**, you can no longer hear them clearly because the signal has been interrupted （打移动电话的人）声音不清（因信号受干扰） ˌ**break sb↔'up** (*especially NAmE*) to make sb feel upset 使烦恼；使不安: *The thought of hurting her just breaks me up.* 一想到要伤害她我就感到不安。 ˌ**break sth↔'up 1** 🔑 to make sth separate into smaller pieces; to divide sth into smaller parts 拆开；打散: *The ship was broken up for scrap metal.* 船被拆解成为废铁。◇ *Sentences can be broken up into clauses.* 句子可以分成从句。**2** to end a relationship, a company, etc. 结束（关系）；关闭（公司）: *They decided to break up the partnership.* 他们决定拆伙。➲ RELATED NOUN BREAK-UP **3** to make people leave sth or stop doing sth, especially by using force （尤指用武力）迫使放弃（某事）: *Police were called in to break up the fight.* 有人叫来了警察制止打斗。ˌ**break 'up (with sb)** 🔑 to end a relationship with sb （同某人）绝交: *She's just broken up with her boyfriend.* 她刚刚和男朋友分手。➲ RELATED NOUN BREAK-UP

'**break with sth** to end a connection with sth 和某事终止关联；破除: *to* ***break with tradition/old habits/the past*** 摒弃传统 / 旧习惯 / 过去

■ ***noun***

• **SHORT STOP/PAUSE** 暂停；间歇 **1** 🔑 [C] a short period of time when you stop what you are doing and rest, eat, etc. 间歇；休息: *a* ***coffee/lunch/tea break*** 用咖啡 / 午饭 / 茶的休息时间 ◇ *Let's* ***take a break.*** 咱们休息会儿吧。◇ *a break for lunch* 午餐休息 ◇ *She worked all day without a break.* 她接连工作了一整天。➲ SYNONYMS AT REST **2** (*also* '**break time**) (*both BrE*) (*NAmE* **re·cess**) [U] a period of time between lessons at school 课间休息: *Come and see me at break.* 课间休息时来见我。**3** 🔑 [C] a pause or period of time when sth stops before starting again 间断；暂停: *a break in my daily routine* 我日常生活中的一段小插曲 ◇ *She wanted to take a* ***career break*** *in order to have children.* 她想暂时放下工作，去生孩子。 **4** 🔑 [C] a pause for advertisements in the middle of a television or radio programme （电视或电台节目的）插播广告的间隙: *More news after the break.* 广告后继续报道新闻。

• **HOLIDAY/VACATION** 假期 **5** 🔑 [C] a short holiday/vacation 短期休假: *We had a weekend break in New York.* 我们在纽约度过了一个周末假日。◇ *a well-earned break* 应得的休假 ➲ WORDFINDER NOTE AT HOLIDAY

• **CHANGE IN SITUATION** 状况改变 **6** [sing.] the moment when a situation or a relationship that has existed for a time changes, ends or is interrupted （持续一段时间的状况或关系的）改变，终止，中断: **~ (with sb/sth)** *He needed to make a complete break with the past.* 他得与过去彻底告别。◇ *a* ***break with tradition/convention*** (= a change from what is accepted, in sth such as art, behaviour, etc.) 突破传统；破除习俗 ◇ **~ (in sth)** *a* ***break in the weather*** (= a change from one type of weather to a different one) 天气的转变 ◇ *a break in diplomatic relations* 外交关系的中断

• **OPENING/SPACE** 缝隙；空间 **7** [C] **~ (in sth)** a space or an opening between two or more things 间隔；缝隙: *We could see the moon through a break in the clouds.* 我们能从云缝里看到月亮。

• **OPPORTUNITY** 机遇 **8** [C] (*informal*) an opportunity to do sth, usually to get sth that you want or to achieve success 机会；机遇: *I got my* ***lucky break*** *when I won a 'Young Journalist of the Year' competition.* 我时来运转，在"年度最佳青年记者"竞赛中取胜。 ◇ *We've had a few bad breaks* (= pieces of bad luck) *along the way.* 我们一路上遭遇了几次厄运。

• **OF BONE** 骨骼 **9** [C] a place where sth, especially a bone in your body, has broken 破裂；骨折: *The X-ray showed there was no break in his leg.* * X 光照片显示他的腿没有骨折。

• **IN TENNIS** 网球 **10** (*also* **break of 'serve**) [C] a win in a game in which your opponent is SERVING 破发: *It was her second break in the set.* 这是本盘比赛中她第二次破掉对手的发球局。◇ ***break point*** (= a situation in which, if you win the next point, you win the game) 破对方发球局的破发点

• **IN BILLIARDS/SNOOKER** 台球；斯诺克 **11** [C] a series of successful shots by one player; the number of points scored in a series of successful shots 单杆；单杆得分: *He's put together a magnificent break.* 他这杆球打得很不错。◇ *a 147 break* (= the highest possible break in SNOOKER) 单杆 147 分（斯诺克中的单杆最高得分）

IDM **break of 'day/'dawn** (*literary*) the moment in the early hours of the morning when it begins to get light 破晓；黎明 **give me a 'break!** (*informal*) used when sb wants sb else to stop doing or saying sth that is annoying, or to stop saying sth that is not true 别烦我了；别胡说了 **give sb a 'break** (*informal*) to give sb a chance; to not judge sb too severely 给某人一次机会；不苛求某人: *Give the lad a break—it's only his second day on the job.* 别苛求这小伙子，他上工才第二天。 **make a 'break for sth/for it** to run towards sth in order to try and escape 向某处逃窜；试图逃跑: *He suddenly leapt up and made a break for the door.* 他突然一跃而起，向门口逃窜。◇ *They decided to make a break for it* (= to try and escape) *that night.* 他们决定那天晚上逃跑。➲ MORE AT CLEAN *adj.*

break·able /'breɪkəbl/ *adj.* likely to break; easily broken 会碎的；易碎的

break·age /'breɪkɪdʒ/ *noun* **1** [C, usually pl.] an object that has been broken 破碎物品: *The last time we moved house there were very few breakages.* 我们上次搬家时几乎没有什么物品破损。 **2** [U, C] the act of breaking sth 毁坏；损坏: *Wrap it up carefully to protect against breakage.* 把它包好，以免破损。

break·away /'breɪkəweɪ/ *adj., noun*

■ ***adj.*** [only before noun] (of a political group, an organization, or a part of a country 政治团体、组织、国家的一部分) having separated from a larger group or country 已分离的；已脱离的；已独立的: *a* ***breakaway faction/group/section*** 脱离原组织的派系 / 集体 / 部分 ◇ *a breakaway republic* 一个已经独立的共和国

■ ***noun*** [sing.] **1** an occasion when members of a political party or an organization leave it in order to form a new party, etc. 脱离；独立 **2** a change from an accepted style 对（公认风格的）改变: *a breakaway from his earlier singing style* 对他以往演唱风格的改变

break·beat /'breɪkbiːt/ *noun* **1** [C] a series of drum beats that are repeated to form the rhythm of a piece of dance music 碎拍（组成舞曲节奏的一系列鼓点） **2** [U] dance music, for example HIP HOP, that uses breakbeats 碎拍舞曲（如嘻哈音乐）

break·bone fever /ˈbreɪkbəʊn fiːvə(r); *NAmE* -boʊn/ *noun* [U] = DENGUE

break·dan·cing /ˈbreɪkdɑːnsɪŋ; *NAmE* -dæn-/ *noun* [U] a style of dancing with ACROBATIC movements, often performed in the street 霹雳舞（掺入杂技动作，常在街头表演） ▸ **break·dance** *verb* [I] **break·dan·cer** *noun*

break·down /ˈbreɪkdaʊn/ *noun* **1** [C] an occasion when a vehicle or machine stops working （车辆或机器的）故障，损坏： *a breakdown on the motorway* 在高速公路上出的故障 ◇ *a breakdown recovery service* 车辆抢修服务 **2** [C, U] a failure of a relationship, discussion or system （关系）破裂；（讨论、系统）失败： *the breakdown of a marriage* 婚姻破裂 ◇ *marriage breakdown* 婚姻破裂 ◇ *a breakdown in communications* 通信中断 ◇ *The breakdown of the negotiations was not unexpected.* 谈判的失败是预料之中的事。 ◇ *the breakdown of law and order* 治安陷入瘫痪 **3** [C, usually sing.] detailed information that you get by studying a set of figures 数字细目；分类： *First, let's look at a breakdown of the costs.* 我们首先看一下成本的详细数字。 **4** [U] (*specialist*) the breaking of a substance into the parts of which it is made 分解： *the breakdown of proteins in the digestive system* 蛋白质在消化系统中的分解 **5** [C] = NERVOUS BREAKDOWN： *She's still recovering from her breakdown.* 她精神崩溃后还在恢复中。

ˈbreakdown lane (*US*) (*BrE* ˌ**hard ˈshoulder**) *noun* a strip of ground with a hard surface beside a major road such as a MOTORWAY or INTERSTATE where vehicles can stop in an emergency 硬路肩（在高速公路旁，可供紧急停车）

ˈbreakdown truck (*BrE*) (*also* ˈ**tow truck** *NAmE, BrE*) *noun* a truck that is used for taking cars away to be repaired when they have had a breakdown （把故障车辆送去修理的）救险车 ➲ VISUAL VOCAB PAGE V62

break·er /ˈbreɪkə(r)/ *noun* a large wave covered with white bubbles that is moving towards land 拍岸的白浪 ➲ SEE ALSO CIRCUIT BREAKER, ICEBREAKER (1), LAWBREAKER, RECORD-BREAKER, STRIKE-BREAKER, TIEBREAKER

ˈbreak-even *noun* [U] (*business* 商) a time when a company or piece of business earns just enough money to pay for its costs 收支相抵： *The company expects to reach break-even next year.* 公司预期明年达到盈亏平衡。 ➲ SEE ALSO EVEN *adj.* (3)

break·fast 🔑 /ˈbrekfəst/ *noun, verb*

■ ***noun*** 🔑 [C, U] the first meal of the day 早餐；早饭： *a **big/hearty/light breakfast*** 量大的／丰盛的／量少的早餐 ◇ (*especially BrE*) *a cooked breakfast* 热食早餐 ◇ *Do you want bacon and eggs **for breakfast**?* 你早饭要吃熏咸肉和鸡蛋吗？ ◇ *They were having breakfast when I arrived.* 我到达时他们正在吃早饭。 ◇ *She doesn't eat much breakfast.* 她早饭吃得不多。 ➲ SEE ALSO BED AND BREAKFAST, CONTINENTAL BREAKFAST, ENGLISH BREAKFAST, POWER BREAKFAST, WEDDING BREAKFAST IDM SEE DOG *n.*

■ ***verb*** [I] ~ (**on sth**) (*formal*) to eat breakfast 吃早饭；用早餐

ˈbreak-in *noun* an entry into a building using force, usually to steal sth 破门而入；闯入；入室偷窃

ˌ**breaking and ˈentering** *noun* [U] (*NAmE* or *old-fashioned*) the crime of entering a building illegally and using force 破门侵入（罪）

ˈbreaking point (*also* ˈ**break point**) *noun* [U] the time when problems become so great that a person, an organization or a system can no longer deal with them （问题难以遏制的）顶点，极限： *to **be at/to reach breaking point*** 处于／达到极限 ◇ *to be stretched to breaking point* 已抻至极限

break·neck /ˈbreɪknek/ *adj.* [only before noun] very fast and dangerous 飞速惊险的： *to drive, etc. **at breakneck speed*** 亡命飞车等

break·out /ˈbreɪkaʊt/ *noun, adj.*

■ ***noun*** an escape from prison, usually by a group of prisoners （常指集体的）越狱： *a mass breakout from a top security prison* 从防守高度严密的监狱的集体越狱

■ ***adj.*** [only before noun] **1** (*NAmE, informal*) suddenly extremely popular and successful; establishing sb's reputation 一炮走红的；扬名的： *a breakout hit/movie* 一炮走红的唱片／电影 **2** taking place separately from the main meeting with a smaller number of people 分组会议的： *a **breakout session** before the plenary* （全体会议前的）分组会议 ◇ *a **breakout group** on ethical issues* 讨论道德问题的小组 ➲ WORDFINDER NOTE AT MEETING

ˈbreak point *noun* **1** (*specialist*) the point where sth, especially a computer program, is interrupted （尤指计算机程序的）断点，中断点 **2** ˌ**break ˈpoint** (especially in TENNIS 尤指网球) a point that the person who is SERVING must win in order not to lose a game 破发点；破对方发球局的末点 **3** = BREAKING POINT

break·through /ˈbreɪkθruː/ *noun, adj.*

■ ***noun*** an important development that may lead to an agreement or achievement 重大进展；突破： *to **make/achieve a breakthrough*** 取得突破性进展 ◇ *a significant breakthrough in negotiations* 谈判中的重大突破 ◇ *a major breakthrough in cancer research* 癌症研究中的重要突破

■ ***adj.*** [only before noun] in which a performer or type of product is successful for the first time, when it is likely to be even more successful in the future 突破性的： *It was a breakthrough album for the band.* 这是该乐队的成名专辑。 ◇ *breakthrough technology/products* 突破性技术／产品

ˈbreak time *noun* [U] (*BrE*) = BREAK (2)

ˈbreak-up *noun* **1** [C, usually sing., U] the ending of a relationship or an association （关系、联系、交往的）破裂，中断： *a marital break-up* 婚姻破裂 **2** [C] the division of a large organization or country into smaller parts （组织、国家的）拆分，分裂，分离

break·water /ˈbreɪkwɔːtə(r)/ *noun* a wall built out into the sea to protect the SHORE or HARBOUR from the force of the waves 防波堤

bream /briːm/ *noun* (*pl.* **bream**) a FRESHWATER or sea fish that is used for food 欧鳊（食用淡水鱼）；海鲷

breast 🔑 /brest/ *noun, verb*

■ ***noun***

• **PART OF BODY** 身体部位 **1** 🔑 [C] either of the two round soft parts at the front of a woman's body that produce milk when she has had a baby （女子的）乳房： *She put the baby to her breast.* 她开始给婴儿哺乳。 ◇ *breast cancer* 乳腺癌 ◇ *breast milk* 母乳 **2** 🔑 [C] the similar, smaller part on a man's body, which does not produce milk （男子的）退化乳房 **3** [C] (*literary*) the top part of the front of your body, below your neck 胸部；胸脯 SYN **chest**： *He cradled the child against his breast.* 他把孩子抱在怀里。

• **CLOTHING** 衣服 **4** [C] the part of a piece of clothing that covers your chest 前胸部分： *A row of medals was pinned to the breast of his coat.* 他的外套胸前别着一排勋章。

• **OF BIRD** 鸟 **5** [C] the front part of a bird's body （鸟的）胸部： *breast feathers* 胸部羽毛 ◇ *The robin has a red breast.* 知更鸟的胸部为红色。

• **MEAT** 肉 **6** [C, U] meat from the front part of the body of a bird or an animal （鸟或动物的）胸脯肉： ***chicken/turkey breasts*** 鸡／火鸡胸脯肉 ◇ ***breast of lamb*** 羊羔胸脯肉

• **-BREASTED** 有…胸脯 **7** (in adjectives 构成形容词) having the type of chest or breasts mentioned 胸脯（或乳房）…的： *a **small-breasted/full-breasted** woman* 乳房小／丰满的女子 ◇ *bare-breasted* 裸胸 ◇ *the yellow-breasted male of the species* 这个物种中有黄色胸部的雄性 ➲ SEE ALSO DOUBLE-BREASTED, SINGLE-BREASTED

• **HEART** 心 **8** [C] (*literary*) the part of the body where the feelings and emotions are thought to be 心窝；情感： *a troubled breast* 忧虑的心情 ➲ SEE ALSO CHIMNEY BREAST IDM SEE BEAT *v.*, CLEAN *adj.*

■ ***verb*** (*formal*) **1** ~ **sth** to reach the top of a hill, etc. 登上…的顶部： *As they breasted the ridge, they saw the valley and lake before them.* 他们到达山脊时山谷和湖泊尽收眼底。 **2** ~ **sth** to push through sth, touching it with your chest 挺胸从…中挤过： *He strode into the ocean, breasting the waves.* 他挺胸顶着波浪大步走进海里。

breast·bone /ˈbrestbəʊn; *NAmE* -boʊn/ *noun* the long flat bone in the chest that the seven top pairs of RIBS are connected to 胸骨 **SYN** **sternum** ➲ VISUAL VOCAB PAGE V64

breast·feed /ˈbrestfiːd/ *verb* (**breast·fed**, **breast·fed** /-fed/) [I, T] ~ (**sb**) when a woman **breastfeeds**, she feeds her baby with milk from her breasts 用母乳喂养；哺乳 ➲ COMPARE BOTTLE-FEED, NURSE *v.* (6)

breast·plate /ˈbrestpleɪt/ *noun* a piece of ARMOUR worn by soldiers in the past to protect the upper front part of the body （古时士兵护胸的）胸铠

ˌ**breast ˈpocket** *noun* a pocket on a shirt, or on the outside or inside of the part of a jacket that covers the chest （衣服）胸袋 ➲ VISUAL VOCAB PAGE V68

ˈ**breast pump** *noun* a device for getting milk from a woman's breasts, so that her baby can be fed later from a bottle 吸奶器；吸乳器

breast·stroke /ˈbreststrəʊk; *NAmE* -stroʊk/ *noun* [U, sing.] a style of swimming that you do on your front, moving your arms and legs away from your body and then back towards it in a circle 蛙泳 ➲ VISUAL VOCAB PAGE V48

breath /breθ/ *noun* **1** [U] the air that you take into your lungs and send out again 呼吸的空气： *His breath smelt of garlic.* 他呼出的气中有大蒜味。 ◇ *bad breath* (= that smells bad) 口臭 ◇ *We had to stop for breath before we got to the top.* 我们不得不喘口气，然后再登山顶。 ◇ *She was very* ***short of breath*** (= had difficulty breathing). 她呼吸很困难。 **2** [C] an amount of air that enters the lungs at one time 一次吸入的空气： *to take a deep breath* 深深吸一口气 ◇ *He recited the whole poem in one breath.* 他一口气背出了整首诗。 **3** [sing.] ~ **of sth** (*formal*) a small amount of sth; slight evidence of sth 微量；迹象： *a* ***breath of suspicion/scandal*** 一丝怀疑；丑闻的嫌疑 **4** [sing.] **a ~ of air/wind** (*literary*) a slight movement of air （空气的）微微流动，拂动

IDM **a breath of (fresh) ˈair** clean air breathed in after being indoors or in a dirty atmosphere 新鲜空气；透气： *We'll get a breath of fresh air at lunchtime.* 我们午餐时出去透透气。 **a breath of fresh ˈair** a person, thing or place that is new and different and therefore interesting and exciting 令人耳目一新的人（或事物、地方） **the breath of ˈlife to/for sb** (*literary*) an essential part of a person's existence 某人生存的必需品 **get your ˈbreath (again/back)** (*BrE*) (*also* **catch your ˈbreath** *NAmE, BrE*) to breathe normally again after running or doing some tiring exercise 恢复正常呼吸 **hold your ˈbreath 1** to stop breathing for a short time 闭气；屏气： *Hold your breath and count to ten.* 屏住呼吸，数到十。 **2** to be anxious while you are waiting for sth that you are worried about 屏息以待；焦虑地等待： *He held his breath while the results were read out.* 宣读结果时，他屏住了呼吸。 **3** (*informal*) people say **don't hold your breath!** to emphasize that sth will take a long time or may not happen 别眼巴巴等着；有你等的： *She said she'd do it this week, but don't hold your breath!* 她说她这个星期要干，不过你可别眼巴巴干等！ **in the same ˈbreath** immediately after saying sth that suggests the opposite intention or meaning 但紧接着，但同时（意味着与前一段意图或意思相反）： *He praised my work and in the same breath told me I would have to leave.* 他称赞了一番我的工作，但紧接着却对我说不得不辞退我。 **his/her last/dying ˈbreath** the last moment of a person's life 最后一口气；临终；临死 **out of ˈbreath** having difficulty breathing after exercise （运动后）喘不上气，透不过气来： *We were out of breath after only five minutes.* 我们五分钟后便气喘吁吁了。 **say sth, speak, etc. under your ˈbreath** to say sth quietly so that people cannot hear 小声地，轻声地（说）： *'Rubbish!' he murmured under his breath.* "胡说！"他悄悄地小声说。 **take sb's ˈbreath away** to be very surprising or beautiful 令人惊叹；让人叹绝： *My first view of the island from the air took my breath away.* 我第一次从空中看到这个岛时，叹赏不已。 ➲ MORE AT BATED, CATCH *v.*, DRAW *v.*, SAVE *v.*, WASTE *v.*

breath·able /ˈbriːðəbl/ *adj.* (*specialist*) (of material used in making clothes 衣料) allowing air to pass through 透气的： *Breathable, waterproof clothing is essential for most outdoor sports.* 大多数户外运动服必须透气且防水。

breath·alyse (*BrE*) (*NAmE* **breath·alyze**) /ˈbreθəlaɪz/ *verb* [usually passive] ~ **sb** to check how much alcohol a driver has drunk by making him or her breathe into a breathalyser 检测（驾驶者）的呼气酒精含量： *Both drivers were breathalysed at the scene of the accident.* 两方司机均在事故现场接受了呼气酒精检测。

breath·alyser (*BrE*) (*NAmE* **Breath·alyzer™**) /ˈbreθəlaɪzə(r)/ *noun* a device used by the police to measure the amount of alcohol in a driver's breath 呼气酒精含量探测器 ➲ MORE LIKE THIS 1, page R25

breathe /briːð/ *verb*
• **AIR/BREATH** 空气；呼吸 **1** [I, T] to take air into your lungs and send it out again through your nose or mouth 呼吸： *He breathed deeply before speaking again.* 他深深吸一口气，然后继续说下去。 ◇ *The air was so cold we could hardly breathe.* 空气非常寒冷，我们难以呼吸。 ◇ *She was beginning to breathe more easily.* 她呼吸开始较为顺畅了。 ◇ **~ sth** *Most people don't realize that they are breathing polluted air.* 大多数人没有意识到自己正呼吸着污染了的空气。 **2** [T] **~ sth (+ adv./prep.)** to send air, smoke or a particular smell out of your mouth 呼出： *He came up close, breathing alcohol fumes all over me.* 他走过来靠近我，喷得我满身酒气。
• **SAY QUIETLY** 低声说 **3** [T] **~ sth** | **+ speech** (*literary*) to say sth quietly 低声说： *'I'm over here,' she breathed.* "我在这儿呢。"她轻声说。
• **OF WINE** 酒 **4** [I] if you allow wine to **breathe**, you open the bottle and let air get in before you drink it （打开瓶盖，让酒）通气飘香
• **OF CLOTH/SKIN** 布料；皮肤 **5** [I] if cloth, leather, skin, etc. can **breathe**, air can move around or through it 透气： *Cotton clothing allows your skin to breathe.* 棉织品能使皮肤透气。
• **FEELING/QUALITY** 感觉；品质 **6** [T] **~ sth** (*formal*) to be full of a particular feeling or quality 充满，散发（某种感情或品质）： *Her performance breathed wit and charm.* 她的表演灵巧迷人。

IDM **breathe (easily/freely) again** to feel calm again after sth unpleasant or frightening has ended 平静下来；松一口气 **breathe down sb's ˈneck** (*informal*) to watch closely what sb is doing in a way that makes them feel anxious and/or annoyed 紧盯着某人看；看得某人发毛（或心烦）；监视 ˌ**breathe (new) ˈlife into sth** to improve sth by introducing new ideas and making people more interested in it （给某事物）带来起色，注入活力 **breathe your ˈlast** (*literary*) to die 气绝（身亡）；断气 ➲ MORE AT EASY *adv.*, LIVE[1]

PHR V ˌ**breathe ˈin** to take air into your lungs through your nose or mouth 吸气 **SYN** **inhale** ˌ**breathe sth↔ˈin** to take air, smoke, etc. into your lungs through your nose or mouth 吸入（气体）： *His illness is a result of breathing in paint fumes over many years.* 他的病是多年吸入油漆气体引起的。 ˌ**breathe ˈout** to send air out of your lungs through your nose or mouth 呼气 **SYN** **exhale** ˌ**breathe sth↔ˈout** to send air, smoke, etc. out of your lungs through your nose or mouth 呼出（气体）： *Humans take in oxygen and breathe out carbon dioxide.* 人吸入氧气，呼出二氧化碳。

breather /ˈbriːðə(r)/ *noun* (*informal*) a short pause for rest or to relax 短暂的休息： *to* ***take/have a breather*** 歇一下 ◇ *Tell me when you need a breather.* 你需要休息时就告诉我。 ◇ *a five-minute breather* 休息五分钟 ➲ SEE ALSO HEAVY BREATHER

breath·ing /ˈbriːðɪŋ/ *noun* [U] the action of taking air into the lungs and sending it out again 呼吸： *Her breathing became steady and she fell asleep.* 她的呼吸变得均匀，然后睡着了。 ◇ *Deep breathing exercises will help you relax.* 深呼吸运动有助于放松自己。 ◇ *Heavy* (= loud) *breathing was all I could hear.* 我所能听到的只有沉重的呼吸声。

ˈbreathing space *noun* [C, U] a short rest in the middle of a period of mental or physical effort 短暂休息；喘息时间 ➲ SYNONYMS AT REST ➲ MORE LIKE THIS 9, page R26

breath·less /ˈbreθləs/ *adj.* **1** having difficulty in breathing; making it difficult for sb to breathe （使）气喘吁吁的，上气不接下气的： *He arrived breathless at the top of the stairs.* 他爬上楼梯顶时气喘吁吁的。◇ *They maintained a breathless* (= very fast) *pace for half an hour.* 他们疾走了半小时。 **2** (*formal*) experiencing, or making sb experience, a strong emotional reaction （使人）屏息的，目瞪口呆的： *the breathless excitement of seeing each other again* 再次相见时无比的兴奋 ◇ **~ with sth** *breathless with terror* 吓得目瞪口呆 **3** (*formal*) with no air or wind 令人窒息的；无风的： *the breathless heat of a summer afternoon* 夏日午后的闷热 ▶ **breath·less·ly** *adv.* **breath·less·ness** *noun* [U]

breath·tak·ing /ˈbreθteɪkɪŋ/ *adj.* **1** very exciting or impressive (usually in a pleasant way) 激动人心的；令人赞叹的： *a breathtaking view of the mountains* 群山的壮丽景色 ◇ *The scene was one of breathtaking beauty.* 美妙的景色令人叹为观止。 **2** very surprising 惊人的： *He spoke with breathtaking arrogance.* 他说话时的傲慢态度令人咋舌。 ▶ **breath·tak·ing·ly** *adv.* : *a breathtakingly expensive diamond* 昂贵得惊人的钻石

ˈbreath test *noun* a test used by the police to show the amount of alcohol in a driver's breath （警察对驾驶者的）呼气酒精含量检测

breathy /ˈbreθi/ *adj.* speaking or singing with a noticeable sound of breathing （讲话或唱歌时）带呼吸声的

bred PAST TENSE, PAST PART. OF BREED

breech /briːtʃ/ *noun* the part of a gun at the back where the bullets are loaded 枪炮的后膛

ˈbreech birth (*also* **ˌbreech deˈlivery**) *noun* a birth in which the baby's bottom or feet come out of the mother first 臀位分娩 ➲ WORDFINDER NOTE AT BIRTH

breeches /ˈbrɪtʃɪz/ *noun* [pl.] short trousers/pants fastened just below the knee （裤脚束于膝下的）半长裤，马裤： *a pair of breeches* 一条半长裤 ◇ *riding breeches* 马裤

breed 🔑 /briːd/ *verb, noun*

■ ***verb*** (**bred, bred** /bred/) **1** 🔑 [I] (of animals 动物) to have sex and produce young 交配繁殖： *Many animals breed only at certain times of the year.* 很多动物只在一年的某个时候交配繁殖。 ➲ SEE ALSO INTERBREED **2** 🔑 [T] **~ sth (for/as sth)** to keep animals or plants in order to produce young ones in a controlled way 饲养，培育（动植物）： *The rabbits are bred for their long coats.* 饲养兔子是为了获取它们的长毛。 ➲ COLLOCATIONS AT FARMING ➲ SEE ALSO CROSS-BREED, PURE-BRED, THOROUGHBRED **3** [T] **~ sth** to be the cause of sth 孕育；导致： *Nothing breeds success like success.* 一事成功，万事亨通。 **4** [T, usually passive] **~ sth into sb** to educate sb in a particular way as they are growing up 以…方式教育；使养成： *Fear of failure was bred into him at an early age.* 他从小就养成了对失败的恐惧。 ➲ SEE ALSO WELL BRED **IDM** SEE BORN *v.*, FAMILIARITY

■ ***noun*** **1** 🔑 a particular type of animal that has been developed by people in a controlled way, especially a type of dog, cat or farm animal 品种（尤指人工培育的狗、猫或牲畜）： *Labradors and other large breeds of dog* 拉布拉多及其他大型犬 ◇ *a breed of cattle/sheep* 某个品种的牛／羊 ◇ *rare breeds* 稀有品种 ➲ WORDFINDER NOTE AT BIOLOGY

WORDFINDER 联想词： class, classification, genus, hybrid, kingdom, order, phylum, species, taxonomy

2 [usually sing.] a type of person （人的）类型，种类： *He represents a new breed of politician.* 他代表着新一类的政治家。◇ *Players as skilful as this are **a rare breed**.* 如此有技巧的演奏者很少见。

breed·er /ˈbriːdə(r)/ *noun* a person who breeds animals 饲养员： *a dog/horse/cattle, etc. **breeder*** 饲养狗、马、牛等的人

breed·ing /ˈbriːdɪŋ/ *noun* [U] **1** the keeping of animals in order to breed from them （为繁殖的）饲养： *the breeding of horses* 马的饲养 **2** the producing of young animals, plants, etc. （动植物的）生育，繁殖： *the breeding season* 繁殖季节 **3** the family or social background that is thought to result in good manners 教养： *a sign of good breeding* 良好教养的体现

ˈbreeding ground *noun* **1** [usually pl.] a place where wild animals go to produce their young （野生动物的）繁殖地 **2 ~ (for sth)** [usually sing.] a place where sth, especially sth bad, is able to develop （尤指坏事物的）滋生地： *This area of the city has become a breeding ground for violent crime.* 这片市区已成为暴力犯罪的滋生地。 ➲ MORE LIKE THIS 9, page R26

breeze /briːz/ *noun, verb*

■ ***noun*** **1** [C] a light wind 微风；和风： *a sea breeze* 柔和的海风 ◇ *The flowers were gently swaying **in the breeze**.* 花儿在微风中轻轻舞动。◇ *A light breeze was blowing.* 轻风习习。 ➲ WORDFINDER NOTE AT WIND[1] ➲ COLLOCATIONS AT WEATHER **2** [sing.] (*informal*) a thing that is easy to do 轻而易举的事： *It was a breeze.* 这事不费吹灰之力。 **IDM** SEE SHOOT *v.*

■ ***verb*** [I] **+ adv./prep.** (*informal*) to move in a cheerful and confident way in a particular direction 轻盈而自信地走： *She just breezed in and asked me to help.* 她一阵风似的飘然进来，要求我帮她。

PHR V **ˌbreeze ˈthrough sth** (*informal*) to do sth successfully and easily 轻易通过；轻松完成： *He breezed through the tests.* 他轻松顺利地通过了这些测试。

ˈbreeze block (*BrE*) (*NAmE* **ˈcinder block**) *noun* a light building block, made of sand, coal ASHES and CEMENT 煤灰砖（用砂、煤灰和水泥制成）

breeze·way /ˈbriːzweɪ/ *noun* (*NAmE*) an outside passage with a roof and open sides between two separate parts of a building （建筑物两部分之间的）有顶通道，有顶过道

breezy /ˈbriːzi/ *adj.* (**breez·ier, breezi·est**) **1** with the wind blowing quite strongly 通风良好的；有微风的： *It was a bright, breezy day.* 那天和风丽日。◇ *the breezy east coast* 微风吹拂的东海岸 **2** having or showing a cheerful and relaxed manner 轻松愉快的： *You're very bright and breezy today!* 你今天精神焕发！ ▶ **breez·ily** /ˈbriːzɪli/ *adv.* : *'Hi folks,' he said breezily.* "嗨，诸位。"他快活地说。 **breezi·ness** /ˈbriːzinəs/ *noun* [U]

breth·ren /ˈbreðrən/ *noun* [pl.] (*old-fashioned*) **1** used to talk to people in church or to talk about the members of a male religious group （称呼教友或男修会等的成员）弟兄们： *Let us pray, brethren.* 请众同祷。 **2** people who are part of the same society as yourself 同一组织等的成员；同道；同仁： *We should do all we can to help our less fortunate brethren.* 我们应当尽力帮助那些不幸的兄弟姐妹。

Bre·ton /ˈbretən/ *noun, adj.*

■ ***noun*** **1** [U] the Celtic language of Brittany in NW France （法国西北部）布列塔尼语 **2** [C] a person who was born in Brittany or who lives in Brittany （法国）布列塔尼人

■ ***adj.*** connected with Brittany or its language or culture 布列塔尼（文化）的；布列塔尼语的

breve /briːv/ *noun* (*music* 音) a note that lasts as long as eight CROTCHETS/QUARTER NOTES and that is rarely used in modern music 二全音符（现已罕用）

brev·ity **AW** /ˈbrevəti/ *noun* [U] (*formal*) **1** the quality of using few words when speaking or writing 简洁；简练 **SYN** **conciseness**: *The report is a masterpiece of brevity.* 那份报告是言简意赅的典范。 **2** the fact of lasting a short time 短暂： *the brevity of human life* 人生之短暂 ➲ SEE ALSO BRIEF *n.*

brew /bruː/ *verb, noun*

■ ***verb*** **1** [T, I] **~ sth** to make beer 酿制（啤酒）: *This beer is brewed in the Czech Republic.* 这种啤酒是在捷克共和国酿造的。 **2** [T] **~ sth** to make a hot drink of tea or coffee 沏（茶）；煮（咖啡）: *freshly brewed coffee* 刚刚煮好的咖啡 **3** [I] (*especially BrE*) (of tea or coffee 茶或咖啡) to be mixed with hot water and become ready to drink 冲泡；沏: *Always let tea brew for a few minutes.* 每次都要让茶泡上几分钟。 **4** [I] **~ (up)** (usually used in the progressive tenses 通常用于进行时) if sth unpleasant **is brewing** or **brewing up**, it seems likely to happen soon （不愉快的事）即将来临，酝酿

PHR V **ˌbrew ˈup | ˌbrew sth↔ˈup** (*BrE, informal*) to make a hot drink, especially tea 冲泡；沏: *Whose turn is it to brew up?* 该谁煮咖啡了？ ➲ RELATED NOUN BREW-UP

■ ***noun*** **1** [C, U] a type of beer, especially one made in a particular place （尤指某地酿造的）啤酒: *I thought I'd try the local brew.* 我想我还是尝尝本地的啤酒。 ◇ *home brew* (= beer made at home) 家酿啤酒 **2** [C, usually sing.] (*BrE, informal*) an amount of tea made at one time （茶）一次的冲泡量: *I'll make a fresh brew.* 我来重新沏壶茶。 ◇ *Let's have a brew.* 我们来泡杯茶喝吧。 **3** [C, usually sing.] a mixture of different ideas, events, etc. （不同思想、事件等的）交融，混合: *The movie is a potent brew of adventure, sex and comedy.* 这部影片将历险、性爱和喜剧有机地糅和在一起。 ◇ *His music is* ***a heady brew*** (= a powerful mixture) *of heavy metal and punk.* 他的音乐是重金属乐和朋克摇滚乐的强节奏混合体。

IDM **a witch's/an evil ˈbrew** (*BrE, informal*) an unpleasant drink that is a mixture of different things 难喝的混合饮料

brew·er /ˈbruːə(r)/ *noun* a person or company that makes beer 酿造啤酒者；啤酒公司

brew·ery /ˈbruːəri/ *noun* (*pl.* **-ies**) a factory where beer is made; a company that makes beer 啤酒厂；啤酒公司

brew·house /ˈbruːhaʊs/ *noun* a factory where beer is made 啤酒厂 **SYN** **brewery**

ˈbrew-up *noun* (*BrE, informal*) an act of making tea 沏茶: *We always have a brew-up at 11 o'clock.* 我们总是在 11 点沏茶。

briar (*also* **brier**) /ˈbraɪə(r)/ *noun* **1** a wild bush with THORNS, especially a wild ROSE bush 多刺野灌木；（尤指）野蔷薇丛 **2** a bush with a hard root that is used for making TOBACCO pipes; a tobacco pipe made from this root 欧石楠（其坚硬根部可制烟斗）；（用欧石楠根制的）烟斗

bribe /braɪb/ *noun, verb*

■ ***noun*** a sum of money or sth valuable that you give or offer to sb to persuade them to help you, especially by doing sth dishonest 贿赂: *It was alleged that he had* ***taken bribes*** *while in office.* 他被指在任时收受贿赂。◇ *She had been offered a $50 000 bribe to drop the charges.* 有人用 5 万美元贿赂她，要她撤回控告。 ➲ COLLOCATIONS AT CRIME

■ ***verb*** to give sb money or sth valuable in order to persuade them to help you, especially by doing sth dishonest 向（某人）行贿；贿赂: **~ sb (with sth)** *They bribed the guards with cigarettes.* 他们用香烟贿赂看守。◇ **~ sb into doing sth** *She was bribed into handing over secret information.* 她被收买交出了机密。◇ **~ sb to do sth** *She bribed him to sign the certificate.* 她贿赂他签署了这张证明。◇ **~ your way...** *He managed to* ***bribe his way*** *onto the ship.* 他设法行贿混上了船。

brib·ery /ˈbraɪbəri/ *noun* [U] the giving or taking of bribes 行贿；受贿；贿赂: *She was arrested on bribery charges.* 她因被控贿赂罪而遭逮捕。 ◇ *allegations of* ***bribery and corruption*** 有关贿赂和贪污的指控

bric-a-brac /ˈbrɪk ə bræk/ *noun* [U] ORNAMENTS and other small decorative objects of little value （不值钱的）小装饰品，小摆设: *market stalls selling cheap bric-a-brac* 集市上出售廉价小摆设的货摊

brick 🔑 /brɪk/ *noun, verb*

■ ***noun*** **1** 🔑 [C, U] baked CLAY used for building walls, houses and other buildings; an individual block of this 砖；砖块: *The school is built of brick.* 那所学校是用砖建造的。◇ *a pile of bricks* 一摞砖 ◇ *a brick wall* 砖墙 ➲ SEE ALSO RED-BRICK (1) ➲ VISUAL VOCAB PAGE V18 **2** [C] a plastic or wooden block, used as a toy for young children to build things with 积木 **3** [C, usually sing.] (*old-fashioned, BrE, informal*) a friend that you can rely on when you need help 可靠的朋友

IDM **be up against a brick ˈwall** to be unable to make any progress because there is a difficulty that stops you 遇到难以逾越的障碍 **make bricks without ˈstraw** (*BrE*) to try to work without the necessary material, money, information, etc. 做无米之炊 ➲ MORE AT CAT, DROP *v.*, HEAD *n.*, TON

■ ***verb***

PHR V **ˌbrick sth↔ˈin/ˈup** to fill an opening in a wall with bricks 用砖堵住（或砌住）墙上的洞: *The windows had been bricked up.* 那些窗户用砖堵住了。

brick·bat /ˈbrɪkbæt/ *noun* [usually pl.] an insulting remark made in public 公开辱骂；当众侮辱

brick·lay·er /ˈbrɪkleɪə(r)/ (*also BrE, informal* **brickie**) *noun* a person whose job is to build walls, etc. with bricks 砌砖工；瓦工 ▸ **brick·lay·ing** *noun* [U]

ˌbricks and ˈmortar *noun* **1** [U, pl.] buildings, when you are thinking of them in connection with how much they cost to build or how much they are worth; housing, when it is considered as an investment 房地产；（作为投资的）房产: *People invested in bricks and mortar.* 人们过去投资房产。 **2** [C] a business that operates from a shop/store or a building that customers visit, rather than only online 实体店；实体企业: *They translated a bricks and mortar to the Web.* 他们把实体店转为网店。 ◇ *bricks-and-mortar businesses* 实体企业 ◇ (*NAmE also*) *brick-and-mortar businesses* 实体企业

brick·work /ˈbrɪkwɜːk; *NAmE* -wɜːrk/ *noun* **1** [U] the bricks in a wall, building, etc. （建筑物等的）砖结构: *Plaster had fallen away in places, exposing the brickwork.* 有些地方的灰泥脱落了，露出了砖。 **2** **brick·works** [C] (*pl.* **brick·works**) (*BrE*) a place where bricks are made 砖厂；砖窑

bri·dal /ˈbraɪdl/ *adj.* [only before noun] connected with a bride or a wedding 新娘的；婚礼的: *a bridal gown* 新娘的礼服 ◇ *the* ***bridal party*** (= the bride and the bridegroom and the people helping them at their wedding, sometimes used to refer only to the bride and those helping her) 新人（或单指新娘）及协助其婚礼的人 ◇ *a* ***bridal suite*** (= a set of rooms in a hotel for a couple who have just got married) 宾馆的新婚套间 ◇ (*NAmE*) *a* ***bridal shower*** (= a party for a woman who will get married soon) 女子新婚前的送礼会

bride /braɪd/ *noun* a woman on her wedding day, or just before or just after it 新娘；即将（或刚刚）结婚的女子: *a toast to the* ***bride and groom*** 向新娘新郎祝酒 ◇ *He introduced his new bride.* 他介绍了他的新娘。 ➲ WORDFINDER NOTE AT WEDDING

bride·groom /ˈbraɪdgruːm/ (*also* **groom**) *noun* a man on his wedding day, or just before or just after it 新郎；即将（或刚刚）结婚的男子

brides·maid /ˈbraɪdzmeɪd/ *noun* a young woman or girl who helps a BRIDE before and during the marriage ceremony 女傧相；伴娘 ➲ COMPARE BEST MAN, PAGEBOY (1)

bridge 🔑 /brɪdʒ/ *noun, verb*

■ ***noun***

• **OVER ROAD/RIVER** 路 / 河上方 **1** 🔑 [C] a structure that is built over a road, railway/railroad, river, etc. so that people or vehicles can cross from one side to the other 桥: *We crossed the bridge over the River Windrush.* 我们穿过了温德拉什河上的桥。 ➲ VISUAL VOCAB PAGES V3, V14 ➲ SEE ALSO SUSPENSION BRIDGE, SWING BRIDGE

• **CONNECTION** 联系 **2** 🔑 [C] a thing that provides a connection or contact between two different things 起联系作用的事物；桥梁；纽带: *Cultural exchanges are a way of* *building bridges between countries.* 文化交流是各国之间建立联系的纽带。

- **OF SHIP** 船 **3** [C, usually sing.] (*usually* **the bridge**) the part of a ship where the captain and other officers stand when they are controlling and steering the ship （舰船的）驾驶台；船桥；舰桥 ➲ VISUAL VOCAB PAGE V59
- **CARD GAME** 纸牌游戏 **4** [U] a card game for two pairs of players who have to predict how many cards they will win. They score points if they succeed in winning that number of cards and lose points if they fail. 桥牌 ➲ SEE ALSO CONTRACT BRIDGE
- **OF NOSE** 鼻 **5 the ~ of sb's nose** [sing.] the hard part at the top of the nose, between the eyes 鼻梁 ➲ VISUAL VOCAB PAGE V64
- **OF GLASSES** 眼镜 **6** [C] the part of a pair of glasses that rests on your nose 鼻梁架
- **OF GUITAR/VIOLIN** 吉他；小提琴 **7** [C] a small piece of wood on a GUITAR, VIOLIN, etc. over which the strings are stretched 琴马 ➲ VISUAL VOCAB PAGE V40
- **FALSE TEETH** 假牙 **8** [C] a false tooth or false teeth, held permanently in place by being fastened to natural teeth on either side （固定的）假牙；齿桥 IDM SEE BURN *v.*, CROSS *v.*, WATER *n.*

■ ***verb*** **~ sth** to build or form a bridge over sth 在…上架桥：*The valley was originally bridged by the Romans.* 那条峡谷上的桥最初是古罗马人修建的。◇ *A plank of wood bridged the stream.* 溪上架了一条木板桥。

IDM **bridge the 'gap/'gulf/di'vide (between A and B)** to reduce or get rid of the differences that exist between two things or groups of people 消除（甲、乙间的）隔阂 / 鸿沟 / 分歧

bridges 桥；鼻梁；鼻梁架；琴马

bridge over a river 河上的桥 **bridge of the nose** 鼻梁

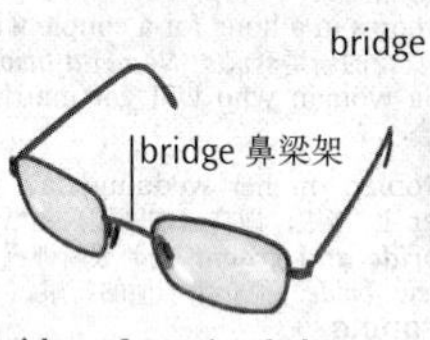

bridge of a pair of glasses 眼镜的鼻梁架 **bridge of a violin** 小提琴的琴马

'bridge-building *noun* [U] activities intended to make relations between two groups, countries, etc. friendlier 友好往来；友善活动

bridge·head /'brɪdʒhed/ *noun* **1** a strong position that an army has captured in enemy land, from which it can go forward or attack the enemy 桥头堡（部队在敌占区内夺取的据点） **2** [usually sing.] a good position from which to make progress （进一步前进的）立足点，据点

bridge·work /'brɪdʒwɜːk; *NAmE* -wɜːrk/ *noun* [U] **1** artificial teeth and the parts that keep them in place in the mouth （假牙的）齿桥；桥托（牙） **2** the work of making these teeth or putting them in place 齿桥制作；镶齿桥

'bridging loan (*BrE*) (*NAmE* **'bridge loan**) *noun* an amount of money that a bank lends you for a short time, especially so that you can buy a new house while you are waiting to sell your old one 过渡性贷款（常在卖掉旧房前作买新房之用）

bri·die /'braɪdi/ *noun* (*ScotE*) a small PIE containing meat 肉馅饼

bridle /'braɪdl/ *noun, verb*

■ ***noun*** a set of leather bands, attached to REINS, which is put around a horse's head and used for controlling it 马勒；马笼头 ➲ WORDFINDER NOTE AT HORSE

■ ***verb*** **1** [T] **~ sth** to put a bridle on a horse 给（马）套笼头 **2** [I] **~ (at sth)** (*literary*) to show that you are annoyed and/or offended at sth, especially by moving your head up and backwards in a proud way （尤指傲慢地昂首对…）表示恼怒，表示不快：*She bridled at the suggestion that she was lying.* 她对暗示她在说谎的言论嗤之以鼻。

'bridle path (*BrE also* **bridle·way** /'braɪdlweɪ/) *noun* a rough path that is suitable for people riding horses or walking, but not for cars 马道；步行道

Brie /briː/ *noun* [U, C] a type of soft French cheese 布里干酪（一种松软的法国奶酪）

brief 🔑 AW /briːf/ *adj., noun, verb*

■ ***adj.*** **(brief·er, brief·est)** **1** 🔑 lasting only a short time; short 短时间的；短暂的：*a brief visit/meeting/conversation* 短时间的访问 / 会议 / 交谈 ◇ *a brief pause/silence* 暂时停顿 / 沉默 ◇ *Mozart's life was brief.* 莫扎特的一生很短暂。 **2** 🔑 using few words 简洁的；简单的：*a brief description/summary/account* 简明扼要的描述 / 总结 / 叙述 ◇ *Please* ***be brief*** (= say what you want to say quickly). 请简明扼要。 **3** (of clothes 衣服) short and not covering much of the body 过短的；暴露身体的：*a brief skirt* 超短裙 ➲ SEE ALSO BREVITY, BRIEFLY

IDM **in brief** in a few words, without details 简言之；一言以蔽之：*In brief, the meeting was a disaster.* 总之，那会议糟透了。◇ *Now the rest of the news in brief.* 现在简要报道其他新闻。

■ ***noun*** ➲ SEE ALSO BRIEFS **1** (*BrE*) the instructions that a person is given explaining what their job is and what their duties are 任务简介；指示：*It wasn't part of his brief to speak to the press.* 交付他的任务不包括向新闻界发言。◇ *I was* ***given the brief*** *of reorganizing the department.* 我被分派去改组这个部门。◇ ***to stick to your brief*** (= to only do what you are asked to do) 仅做分内的事 ◇ *to* ***prepare/produce a brief*** *for sb* 给某人准备 / 制订指示 **2** (*BrE, law* 律) a legal case that is given to a lawyer to argue in court; a piece of work for a BARRISTER （向出庭律师提供的）诉讼摘要；委托辩护 **3** (*NAmE, law* 律) a written summary of the facts that support one side of a legal case, that will be presented to a court 辩护状 **4** (*BrE, informal*) a SOLICITOR or a defence lawyer 事务律师；辩护律师：*I want to see my brief.* 我想见我的律师。 **5** (*especially NAmE*) = BRIEFING (2)：*Officials are pushing for this target to be included in the next presidential brief.* 官员正敦促在下一次总统的简报中一定要包括这个目标。

IDM **hold no brief for sb/sth** (*formal*) to not support or be in favour of sb/sth 不支持，不赞成（某人或某事）；不为…辩护：*I hold no brief for either side in this war.* 这次战争的双方我都不支持。

■ ***verb*** **1** to give sb information about sth so that they are prepared to deal with it 给（某人）指示；向（某人）介绍情况：**~ sb** *I expect to be kept fully briefed at all times.* 我希望随时向我报告所有情况。◇ **~ sb on/about sth** *The officer briefed her on what to expect.* 军官简要向她说了一下可能遇到的情况。 ➲ COMPARE DEBRIEF **2 ~ sb (to do sth)** (*BrE, law* 律) to give a lawyer, especially a BARRISTER, the main facts of a legal case so that it can be argued in court 向（出庭律师）提供诉讼摘要

brief·case /'briːfkeɪs/ *noun* a flat case used for carrying papers and documents 公文包；公事包 ➲ VISUAL VOCAB PAGE V69 ➲ COMPARE ATTACHÉ CASE

brief·ing AW /'briːfɪŋ/ *noun* **1** [C] a meeting in which people are given instructions or information 传达指示会；情况介绍会：*a press briefing* 新闻发布会 ➲ COMPARE DEBRIEFING at DEBRIEF **2** (*also* **brief** *especially in NAmE*)

[C, U] the detailed instructions or information that are given at such a meeting 详细指示；详情介绍： *Captain Trent gave his men a full briefing.* 特伦特队长给了他的下属详细的指示。 ◇ *a **briefing session/paper*** 任务发布会 / 文件

brief·ly 🔑 AW /ˈbriːfli/ *adv.* **1** 🔑 for a short time 短暂地；暂时地： *He had spoken to Emma **only briefly**.* 他和埃玛只讲了短短的几句话。 **2** 🔑 in few words 简短地；简要地： *Briefly, the argument is as follows…* 简言之，理由如下… ◇ *Let me tell you briefly what happened.* 我来大致给你讲一下发生的事情吧。

briefs /briːfs/ *noun* [pl.] men's UNDERPANTS or women's KNICKERS（男子或女子的）内裤： *a pair of briefs* 一条内裤

brier = BRIAR

Brig. *abbr.* (in writing 书写形式) BRIGADIER 陆军准将

brig /brɪɡ/ *noun* **1** a ship with two MASTS (= posts that support the sails) and square sails 横帆双桅船 **2** (*NAmE*) a prison, especially one on a WARSHIP（尤指军舰上的）禁闭室

bri·gade /brɪˈɡeɪd/ *noun* **1** a large group of soldiers that forms a unit of an army 旅（陆军编制单位） **2** [usually sing.] (*often disapproving*) used, always with a word or phrase in front of it, to describe a group of people who share the same opinions or are similar in some other way（主张相同或其他某方面相似的）伙，帮，派： *the anti-smoking brigade* 反吸烟派 ➲ SEE ALSO FIRE BRIGADE IDM ➤ SEE HEAVY *adj.*

briga·dier /ˌbrɪɡəˈdɪə(r); *NAmE* -ˈdɪr/ *noun* (*abbr.* **Brig.**) an officer of high rank in the British army（英国陆军）准将，旅长： *Brigadier Michael Swift* 迈克尔 • 斯威夫特准将

ˌbrigadier ˈgeneral *noun* an officer of high rank in the US army, AIR FORCE or MARINES（美国陆军、空军或海军陆战队）准将

brig·and /ˈbrɪɡənd/ *noun* (*old-fashioned*) a member of a group of criminals that steals from people, especially one that attacks travellers 盗贼；强盗 SYN **bandit**

bright 🔑 /braɪt/ *adj., adv., noun*

■ ***adj.*** (**bright·er**, **bright·est**) **1** 🔑 full of light; shining strongly 光线充足的；明亮的： ***bright light/sunshine*** 明亮的光线；明媚的阳光 ◇ *a bright room* 明亮的屋子 ◇ *Her eyes were bright with tears.* 她的双眼泪光闪闪。 ◇ *a bright morning* (= with the sun shining) 阳光灿烂的早晨 **2** 🔑 (of a colour 颜色) strong and easy to see 鲜艳夺目的： *I like bright colours.* 我喜欢艳丽的色彩。 ◇ *a bright yellow dress* 鲜黄色的连衣裙 ◇ *Jack's face turned **bright red**.* 杰克的脸变得通红。 **3** 🔑 cheerful and lively 快活而生气勃勃的： *His eyes were bright and excited.* 他目光发亮，兴奋不已。 ◇ *She gave me a bright smile.* 她对我粲然一笑。 ◇ *Why are you so **bright and cheerful** today?* 你今天怎么这么高兴？ ◇ *His face was **bright with** excitement.* 他兴奋得满脸放光。 **4** 🔑 intelligent; quick to learn 聪明的；悟性强的： *the brightest pupil in the class* 班里最聪明的学生 ◇ *Do you have any **bright ideas** (= clever ideas)?* 你有何高见？ ➲ SYNONYMS AT INTELLIGENT **5** giving reason to believe that good things will happen; likely to be successful 有希望的；大有可能成功的： *This young musician has a **bright future**.* 这位年轻的音乐家前途无量。 ◇ *Prospects for the coming year look bright.* 来年的前景一片光明。 ◇ *a bright start to the week* 本周的良好开端 ▶ **bright·ly** 🔑 *adv.* : *a brightly lit room* 亮堂的屋子 ◇ *'Hi!' she called brightly.* "嗨！"她轻快地招呼道。 **bright·ness** *noun* [U]

IDM **bright and ˈearly** very early in the morning 大清早： *You're up bright and early today!* 你今天起得很早啊！ **(as) bright as a ˈbutton** (*BrE, informal*) intelligent and quick to understand 机灵的；聪颖的 ➲ MORE LIKE THIS 14, page R26 **the bright ˈlights** the excitement of city life 城市生活的多姿多彩： *Although he grew up in the country, he's always had a taste for the bright lights.* 尽管他是在农村长大的，他始终对城市的五光十色情有独钟。 **a bright ˈspark** (*BrE, informal, often ironic*) a lively and intelligent person, especially sb young 活泼机灵的人（尤指年轻人）： *Some bright spark (= stupid person) left the tap running all night.* 不知是哪个聪明人让自来水流了一夜。 **a/the ˈbright spot** a good or pleasant part of sth that is unpleasant or bad in all other ways（不幸或逆境中的）可喜部分，闪光点： *The win last week was the only bright spot in their last ten games.* 上周的胜利是他们最近十场比赛中唯一振奋人心的一次。 **look on the ˈbright side** to be cheerful or positive about a bad situation, for example by thinking only of the advantages and not the disadvantages（对坏情况）持乐观态度，看到光明的一面

■ ***adv.*** (**bright·er**, **bright·est**) (*literary*) (usually with the verbs *burn* and *shine* 通常与动词 burn、shine 连用) brightly 光亮地；明亮地： *The stars were shining bright.* 星光闪烁。

■ ***noun*** **brights** [pl.] (*NAmE*) the HEADLIGHTS on a vehicle set to a position in which they are shining as brightly as possible and not directed downwards（车辆的）前大灯，头灯

▼ **SYNONYMS 同义词辨析**

bright

brilliant • vivid • vibrant

These words all describe things that are shining or full of light or colours that are strong and easy to see. 以上各词均形容事物明亮、光线充足、鲜艳夺目。

bright full of light; shining strongly; (of colours) strong and easy to see 指光线充足的、明亮的、色彩鲜明的： *a bright yellow dress* 鲜黄色的连衣裙

brilliant very bright 指明亮的、鲜艳的： *The sky was a brilliant blue.* 天空一片蔚蓝。

vivid (*approving*) (of colours) bright and strong 指（颜色）耀眼的、鲜艳的、醒目的： *His eyes were a vivid green.* 他的眼睛碧绿。

vibrant (*approving*) (of colours) bright and strong 指（颜色）耀眼的、鲜艳的、醒目的： *The room was decorated in vibrant blues and greens.* 那房间以鲜艳的蓝绿两色装饰。

VIVID OR VIBRANT? 用 vivid 还是 vibrant?

These two words are very similar, but **vivid** emphasizes how bright a colour is, while **vibrant** suggests a more lively and exciting colour or combination of colours. 这两个词非常相似，但 vivid 强调颜色鲜艳明亮，而 vibrant 则指色彩或颜色组合活泼而富生气。

PATTERNS

- bright/brilliant/vivid/vibrant **colours**
- bright/brilliant **light/sunlight/sunshine/eyes**

bright·en /ˈbraɪtn/ *verb* **1** [I, T] to become or make sth lighter or brighter in colour（使）明亮，色彩鲜艳： *In the distance, the sky was beginning to brighten.* 远方的天空开始泛白。 ◇ **~ sth** *a shampoo to brighten and condition your hair* 有亮泽兼护发效果的洗发剂 **2** [I, T] to become, feel or look happier; to make sb look happier（使）快活起来： *Her eyes brightened.* 她的眼睛亮了起来。 ◇ **~ up** *He brightened up at their words of encouragement.* 听到他们鼓励的话，他高兴起来。 ◇ **~ sth (up)** *A smile brightened her face.* 她的脸上露出了灿烂的笑容。 **3** [T, I] **~ (sth) (up)** to become or make sth become more pleasant or enjoyable; to bring hope（使）增添乐趣，有希望： *A personal letter will usually brighten up a person's day.* 一封私人来信往往就能使人一天心情愉快。 **4** [T] **~ sth (up)** to make sth look more brightly coloured and attractive 使更艳丽；使更美丽： *Fresh flowers will brighten up any room in the house.* 鲜花会使屋里的任何房间都亮丽生色。 **5** [I] **~ (up)** (of the weather 天气) to improve and become brighter 放晴： *According to the forecast, it should brighten up later.* 根据天气预报，晚一点天应该会转晴。

ˌbright-ˈeyed (*also* **ˌbright-eyed and ˌbushy-ˈtailed** *informal*) *adj.* (of a person 人) full of interest and enthusiasm 兴致勃勃的；精神奋发的

B

ˌbright young ˈthing *noun* an enthusiastic and intelligent young person who wants to be successful in their career 聪明的有志青年 ORIGIN From the name used in the 1920s for rich young people whose behaviour was considered shocking. 源自 20 世纪 20 年代对放荡不羁的年轻富人的称呼。

brill /brɪl/ *adj.* (*BrE, informal*) very good 很好的；很棒的

bril·liant /ˈbrɪliənt/ *adj.* **1** extremely clever or impressive 巧妙的；使人印象深的： *What a brilliant idea!* 真是个绝妙的主意！ ◇ *a brilliant performance/invention* 出色的表演；杰出的发明 **2** very successful 很成功的： *a brilliant career* 一帆风顺的事业 ◇ *The play was a brilliant success.* 那个剧获得了巨大成功。 **3** very intelligent or skilful 聪颖的；技艺高的： *a brilliant young scientist* 一位才华横溢的青年科学家 ◇ *She has one of the most brilliant minds in the country.* 她是全国最有才气的人之一。 ➲ SYNONYMS AT INTELLIGENT **4** (of light or colours 光线或色彩) very bright 明亮的；鲜艳的： *brilliant sunshine* 明媚的阳光 ◇ *brilliant blue eyes* 湛蓝的眼睛 ➲ SYNONYMS AT BRIGHT **5** (*BrE, informal*) very good; excellent 很好的；杰出的： *'How was it?' 'Brilliant!'* "怎么样？" "棒极了！" ◇ *Thanks. You've been brilliant* (= very helpful). 多谢。你帮大忙了。 ➲ SYNONYMS AT GREAT ▶ **bril·liance** /ˈbrɪliəns/ *noun* [U] **bril·li·ant·ly** *adv.* : *The plan worked brilliantly.* 计划实施得十分顺利。 ◇ *It was brilliantly sunny.* 阳光明媚。

bril·lian·tine /ˈbrɪliəntiːn/ *noun* [U] oil used in the past to make men's hair shiny （旧时）男用润发油

brim /brɪm/ *noun, verb*

■ *noun* **1** the top edge of a cup, bowl, glass, etc. （杯、碗等容器的）边，边沿： *two wine glasses, filled to the brim* 两只斟满的酒杯 **2** the flat edge around the bottom of a hat that sticks out 帽檐 ➲ VISUAL VOCAB PAGE V70 **3 -brimmed** (in adjectives 构成形容词) having the type of brim mentioned 有…边的： *a wide-brimmed hat* 宽檐帽

■ *verb* (**-mm-**) [I] to be full of sth; to fill sth （使）满，盛满： *Tears brimmed in her eyes.* 她热泪盈眶。 ◇ **~ with sth** *Her eyes brimmed with tears.* 她热泪盈眶。 ◇ *The team were brimming with confidence before the game.* 该队在赛前信心十足。

PHR V **ˌbrim ˈover (with sth)** (of a cup, container, etc. 杯、容器等) to be so full of a liquid that it flows over the edge 盛满（…）；满溢 SYN **overflow**: (*figurative*) *Her heart was brimming over with happiness.* 她心中洋溢着幸福。

brim·ful /ˈbrɪmfʊl/ *adj.* **~ of sth** completely full of sth 装满…的；充盈的： *She's certainly brimful of energy.* 她的确精力充沛。 ◇ *a jug brimful of cream* 一满罐奶油

brim·stone /ˈbrɪmstəʊn; *NAmE* -stoʊn/ *noun* (*old use*) the chemical element SULPHUR 硫黄

brin·dle /ˈbrɪndl/ (*also* **brin·dled** /ˈbrɪndld/) *adj.* (of dogs, cats and cows 狗、猫、牛) brown with bands or marks of another colour 棕色间杂其他花纹（或斑点）的

brine /braɪn/ *noun* [U] very salty water, used especially for preserving food 盐水（常用于腌制食物） ➲ SEE ALSO BRINY

bring /brɪŋ/ *verb* (**brought, brought** /brɔːt/)

• **COME WITH SB/STH** 带来 **1** to come to a place with sb/sth 带…到某处；带来；取来： **~ sb/sth (with you)** *Don't forget to bring your books with you.* 别忘了把书带来。 ◇ **~ sb/sth to sth** *She brought her boyfriend to the party.* 她带着男朋友去参加聚会。 ◇ **~ sth for sb** *Bring a present for Helen.* 给海伦带件礼物来。 ◇ **~ sb sth** *Bring Helen a present.* 给海伦带件礼物来。

• **PROVIDE** 提供 **2** to provide sb/sth with sth 提供；供给： **~ sb/sth sth** *His writing brings him $10 000 a year.* 写作每年为他赚 1 万美元。 ◇ **~ sth to sb/sth** *The team's new manager brings ten years' experience to the job.* 该队的新经理到任时已有十年的相关经验。

• **CAUSE** 导致 **3** **~ sth** to cause sth 导致；引起： *The revolution brought many changes.* 这场革命导致很多变化。 ◇ *The news* **brought tears to his eyes** (= made him cry). 这个消息使他不禁流下泪来。 ◇ *Retirement usually* **brings with it** *a massive drop in income.* 收入通常随着退休而大大减少。 **4** **~ sb/sth + adv./prep.** to cause sb/sth to be in a particular condition or place 使处于某种状况；使到某地： *to* **bring** *a meeting* **to an end** 结束会议 ◇ **Bring** *the water* **to the boil**. 把水烧开。 ◇ *The article brought her into conflict with the authorities.* 这篇文章使她与当局发生冲突。 ◇ *Hello Simon! What brings you here?* 你好，西蒙！什么风把你吹来了？

• **MAKE SB/STH MOVE** 移动 **5** to make sb/sth move in a particular direction or way 使朝（某方向或按某方式）移动： **~ sb/sth + adv./prep.** *The judge brought his hammer down on the table.* 法官在桌子上敲下他的木槌。 ◇ **~ sb/sth running** *Her cries brought the neighbours running* (= made them run to her). 邻居们听到她的叫喊声便纷纷赶来。

• **ACCUSATION** 指控 **6** **~ sth (against sb)** to officially accuse sb of a crime 起诉： *to* **bring a charge/a legal action/an accusation** *against sb* 控告某人；对某人起诉；控告某人

• **FORCE YOURSELF** 强迫自己 **7** **~ yourself to do sth** to force yourself to do sth 强迫自己做某事： *She could not bring herself to tell him the news.* 她难以开口把这个消息告诉他。 ➲ MORE LIKE THIS 33, page R28

IDM HELP Idioms containing **bring** are at the entries for the nouns and adjectives in the idioms, for example **bring sb/sth to heel** is at **heel**. 含 bring 的习语，都可在该等习语中的名词及形容词相关词条找到，如 bring sb / sth to heel 在词条 heel 下。

PHR V **ˌbring sth↔aˈbout** to make sth happen 导致；引起 SYN **cause**: *What brought about the change in his attitude?* 是什么使他改变了态度？ ➲ LANGUAGE BANK AT CAUSE

ˌbring sb aˈround (*NAmE*) = BRING SB ROUND **ˌbring sth aˈround to sth** (*NAmE*) = BRING STH ROUND TO STH

ˌbring sb/sth↔ˈback to return sb/sth 把…送回；归还： *Please bring back all library books by the end of the week.* 请在周末前把图书馆的书全部归还。 ◇ *He brought me back* (= gave me a ride home) *in his car.* 他用车把我送回家。 **ˌbring sth↔ˈback** **1** to make sb remember sth or think about it again 使回忆起；使想起： *The photographs brought back many pleasant memories.* 那些照片给人带来很多美好的回忆。 **2** to make sth that existed before be introduced again 恢复；重新使用 SYN **reintroduce**: *Most people are against bringing back the death penalty.* 大多数人反对恢复死刑。 **ˌbring sb sth↔ˈback | ˌbring sth↔ˈback (for sb)** to return with sth for sb （给…）带回： *What did you bring the kids back from Italy?* 你从意大利给孩子们带了什么回来？ ◇ *I brought a T-shirt back for Mark.* 我给马克带回来一件 T 恤衫。

ˈbring sb/sth before sb (*formal*) to present sb/sth for discussion or judgement 将…提交讨论（或审判等）： *The matter will be brought before the committee.* 这件事将交给委员会讨论。 ◇ *He was brought before the court and found guilty.* 他被送交法庭审判，并被裁定有罪。

ˌbring sb↔ˈdown **1** to make sb lose power or be defeated 打垮；击败： *The scandal may bring down the government.* 那件丑闻可能使政府垮台。 **2** (in sports 体育运动) to make sb fall over 使跌倒： *He was brought down in the penalty area.* 他在禁区被撂倒。 **ˌbring sth↔ˈdown** **1** to reduce sth 减少；降低： *We aim to bring down prices on all our computers.* 我们打算降低我们所有计算机的价格。 **2** to land an aircraft 使（飞机）着陆： *The pilot managed to bring the plane down in a field.* 飞行员设法将飞机降落在一处田里。 **3** to make an aircraft fall out of the sky 击落： *Twelve enemy fighters had been brought down.* 有十二架敌方的战斗机被击落。 **4** to make an animal or a bird fall down or fall out of the sky by killing or wounding it 打倒（动物）；打落（鸟）： *He brought down the bear with a single shot.* 他一枪就撂倒了那头熊。

ˌbring sb/sth↔ˈforth (*old use* or *formal*) to give birth to sb; to produce sth 生产；产出： *She brought forth a son.* 她生了个儿子。 ◇ *trees bringing forth fruit* 结果实的树木

ˌbring sth↔ˈforward **1** to move sth to an earlier date or time 将（…的日期或时间）提前： *The meeting has been brought forward from 10 May to 3 May.* 会议已由 5

月 10 号提前到 5 月 3 号。 **2** to suggest sth for discussion 提议；提出讨论： *Please bring the matter forward at the next meeting.* 请将这事在下次会议上提出。 **3** to move a total sum from the bottom of one page or column of numbers to the top of the next 把账目转入次页；承前页： *A credit balance of $50 was brought forward from his September account.* * 50 美元的贷方余额是从他九月份的账上转来的。

ˌbring sb↔ˈin 1 to ask sb to do a particular job or to be involved in sth 请…做；让…参与： *Local residents were angry at not being brought in on* (= asked for their opinion about) *the new housing proposal.* 新的住房方案未征求当地居民的意见，对此他们感到愤怒。 ◇ **bring sb in to do sth** *Experts were brought in to advise the government.* 政府请来专家们出谋划策。 **2** (of the police 警方) to bring sb to a police station in order to ask them questions or arrest them 将（某人）带到警察局讯问；逮捕： *Two men were brought in for questioning.* 有两名男子被带到警察局进行讯问。 **ˌbring sb/sth↔ˈin 1** to introduce a new law 提出（新法案）： *They want to bring in a bill to limit arms exports.* 他们想提出一项限制武器出口的议案。 **2** to attract sb/sth to a place or business 吸引；引入： *We need to bring in a lot more new business.* 我们得吸引更多的新业务。 **3** to give a decision in court 宣布，作出（裁决）： *The jury brought in a verdict of guilty.* 陪审团作出裁决宣判有罪。 **ˌbring sb ˈin sth | ˌbring ˈin sth** to make or earn a particular amount of money 赚得；挣： *His freelance work brings him in about $20 000 a year.* 他做自由职业每年大约赚 2 万美元。 ◇ *How much does she bring in now?* 她现在挣多少钱？

ˌbring sth↔ˈoff to succeed in doing sth difficult 完成，做完（艰难的工作） **SYN** **pull sth↔off**： *It was a difficult task but we brought it off.* 那是一项艰难的工作，但我们还是完成了。 ◇ *The goalie brought off a superb save.* 守门员作出了一次精彩的扑救。

ˌbring sb↔ˈon to help sb develop or improve while they are learning to do sth 帮助（学习者）进步；促使提高 **ˌbring sth↔ˈon 1** to make sth develop, usually sth unpleasant 使发展，导致（通常指坏事） **SYN** **cause**： *He was suffering from stress brought on by overwork.* 他正苦于超负荷工作带来的压力。 **2** to make crops, fruit, etc. grow well 促使（作物、水果等）成长 **ˈbring sth on yourself/sb** to be responsible for sth unpleasant that happens to you/sb 使（自己 / 他人）遭受…： *I have no sympathy—you brought it all on yourself.* 我根本不同情你，这都怪你自己。

ˌbring sb↔ˈout (*BrE*) to make people go on strike 使罢工 **ˌbring sb ˈout of himself, herself, etc.** to help sb to feel more confident 使更加自信： *She's a shy girl who needs friends to bring her out of herself.* 她是个腼腆的女孩，需要朋友帮助她克服羞怯心理。 **ˌbring sth↔ˈout 1** 🔑 to make sth appear 使显现；使表现出： *A crisis brings out the best in her.* 这场危机让她的才能得到最大发挥。 **2** to make sth easy to see or understand 使显出；阐明： *That dress really brings out the colour of your eyes.* 那件衣服果真能衬托出你眼睛的颜色。 **3** 🔑 to produce sth; to publish sth 生产；出版： *The band have just brought out their second album.* 这个乐队刚刚推出了他们的第二张专辑。 **ˌbring sb ˈout in sth** to make sb's skin be covered in spots, etc. 使（某人的）皮肤长出（斑点等）： *The heat brought him out in a rash.* 炎热的天气使他浑身长满了痱子。

ˌbring sb ˈround (*BrE*) (*NAmE* **ˌbring sb aˈround**) (*also* **ˌbring sb ˈto**) to make sb who is unconscious become conscious again 使苏醒 **ˌbring sb ˈround (to...)** (*BrE*) (*NAmE* **ˌbring sb aˈround**) to bring sb to sb's house 带某人串门： *Bring the family round one evening. We'd love to meet them.* 哪天晚上带全家人来坐坐吧，我们很想见见他们。 **ˌbring sb ˈround (to sth)** (*BrE*) (*NAmE* **ˌbring sb aˈround**) to persuade sb to agree to sth 说服某人同意（某事）： *He didn't like the plan at first, but we managed to bring him round.* 他起初并不喜欢这个计划，但我们最终使他回心转意了。 **ˌbring sth ˈround to sth** (*BrE*) (*NAmE* **ˌbring sth aˈround to sth**) to direct a conversation to a particular subject 将（话题）导向…

ˌbring sb ˈto = BRING SB ROUND

ˌbring A and B toˈgether to help two people or groups to end a disagreement 使双方言和；使双方和好：

The loss of their son brought the two of them together. 丧子使他们两人重归于好。

ˌbring sb↔ˈup 1 🔑 [often passive] to care for a child, teaching him or her how to behave, etc. 抚养；养育；教养 **SYN** **raise**： *She brought up five children.* 她抚育了五个孩子。 ◇ *He was brought up by his aunt.* 他是由姨妈带大的。 ◇ *a **well/badly brought up** child* 有教养 / 缺乏教养的孩子 ◇ **bring sb up to do sth** *They were brought up to* (= taught as children to) *respect authority.* 他们从小就被教导尊敬权威。 ◇ **+ noun** *I was brought up a Catholic.* 我从小就受教养成为天主教徒。 ➲ RELATED NOUN UPBRINGING **2** (*law* 律) to make sb appear for trial 使出庭受审；传讯： *He was brought up on a charge of drunken driving.* 他因酒后开车而受到传讯。 **ˌbring sth↔ˈup 1** 🔑 to mention a subject or start to talk about it 提出（讨论等） **SYN** **raise**： *Bring it up at the meeting.* 请将此事在会议上提出。 **2** to VOMIT 呕吐： *to bring up your lunch* 把午饭吐出来 **3** to make sth appear on a computer screen 使显示在计算机屏幕上；调出： *Click with the right mouse button to bring up a new menu.* 单击鼠标的右键，调出一个新选单。 **ˌbring sb ˈup against sth** to force sb to know about sth and have to deal with it （使）面临，面对： *Working in the slums brought her up against the realities of poverty.* 在贫民窟工作使她直面了解贫困的现实。

ˌbring-and-ˈbuy sale *noun* (*BrE*) a sale, usually for charity, at which people bring things for sale and buy those brought by others （捐献物品）义卖

brin·jal /ˈbrɪndʒl/ *noun* [C, U] (*IndE, SAfrE*) an AUBERGINE/EGGPLANT (= a vegetable with shiny dark purple skin and soft white flesh) 茄子

brink /brɪŋk/ *noun* [sing.] **1 the ~ (of sth)** if you are on the brink of sth, you are almost in a very new, dangerous or exciting situation （新的、危险的，或令人兴奋的处境的）边缘，初始状态： *on the **brink of** collapse/war/death/disaster* 濒于崩溃 / 战争 / 死亡 / 灾难 ◇ *Scientists are on the brink of making a major new discovery.* 科学家很快就会有新的重大发现。 ◇ *He's pulled the company **back from the brink*** (= he has saved it from disaster). 他使公司起死回生。 **2** (*literary*) the extreme edge of land, for example at the top of a CLIFF or by a river （峭壁、河岸等的）边沿，边缘： *the brink of the precipice* 悬崖边缘 **IDM** SEE TEETER

brink·man·ship /ˈbrɪŋkmənʃɪp/ (*NAmE also* **brinks·man·ship** /ˈbrɪŋks-/) *noun* [U] the activity, especially in politics, of getting into a situation that could be very dangerous in order to frighten people and make them do what you want 边缘政策（刻意进入极其危险的处境，以恐吓并驯服人民）

briny /ˈbraɪni/ *adj.* (of water 水) containing a lot of salt 多盐分的；很咸的 **SYN** **salty** ➲ SEE ALSO BRINE

brio /ˈbriːəʊ; *NAmE* ˈbriːoʊ/ *noun* [U] (*formal*) enthusiasm and individual style 热情活泼

bri·oche /briˈɒʃ; *NAmE* briˈoʊʃ/ *noun* [C, U] a type of sweet bread made from flour, eggs and butter, usually in the shape of a small bread roll 黄油鸡蛋圆面包

bri·quette /brɪˈket/ *noun* a small hard block made from coal dust and used as fuel 煤砖；煤球；煤饼

brisk /brɪsk/ *adj.* (**brisk·er**, **brisk·est**) **1** quick; busy 快的；敏捷的；忙碌的： *a brisk walk* 轻盈的步履 ◇ *to set off at a brisk pace* 以轻快的步伐上路 ◇ *Ice-cream vendors were doing a brisk trade* (= selling a lot of ice cream). 冰淇淋小贩的生意很红火。 **2** (of a person, their voice or manner 人、嗓音或举止) practical and confident; showing a desire to get things done quickly 现实自信的；麻利的： *His tone became brisk and businesslike.* 他的语气变得自信干练而务实。 **3** (of wind and the weather 风和天气) cold but pleasantly fresh 凉爽的；清新的： *a **brisk** wind/breeze* 凉爽的风；微风 ▶ **brisk·ly** *adv.* **brisk·ness** *noun* [U]

bris·ket /ˈbrɪskɪt/ *noun* [U] meat that comes from the chest of an animal, especially a cow （牛等的）胸腩肉

B

bris·tle /ˈbrɪsl/ *noun, verb*

■ ***noun*** **1** a short stiff hair 短而硬的毛发；刚毛： *the bristles on his chin* 他下巴上的胡茬子 **2** one of the short stiff hairs or wires in a brush 刷子毛

■ ***verb*** **1** [I] ~ **(with sth) (at sth)** to suddenly become very annoyed or offended at what sb says or does （对某人的言行）大为恼怒；被激怒： *His lies made her bristle with rage.* 他的谎话使她火冒三丈。 **2** [I] (of an animal's fur 动物的毛) to stand up on the back and neck because the animal is frightened or angry （背部或颈部的毛因惊吓或发怒）竖起，耸起 ➲ MORE LIKE THIS 20, page R27

PHR V **ˈbristle with sth** to contain a large number of sth 装满；充斥着： *The whole subject bristles with problems.* 整个事情问题成堆。

brist·ly /ˈbrɪsli/ *adj.* like or full of bristles; rough 刚毛似的；布满刚毛的；粗糙的： ***a bristly chin/moustache*** 长满胡茬子的下巴；短而硬的小胡子

bris·tols /ˈbrɪstlz/ *noun* [pl.] (*BrE, slang*) a woman's breasts （女人的）乳房，奶子

Brit /brɪt/ *noun* (*informal*) a British person 英国人 ➲ NOTE AT BRITISH

Brit·ain /ˈbrɪtn/ *noun* [sing.] the island containing England, Scotland and Wales 不列颠（包括英格兰、苏格兰及威尔士） ➲ SEE ALSO GREAT BRITAIN, UNITED KINGDOM

Bri·tan·nia /brɪˈtæniə/ *noun* [sing.] a figure of a woman used as a symbol of Britain. She is usually shown sitting down wearing a HELMET and holding a SHIELD and a TRIDENT (= a long weapon with three points). 不列颠尼亚（英国的拟人化称呼，以头戴钢盔手持盾牌及三叉戟的女子为象征）

Bri·tan·nic /brɪˈtænɪk/ *adj.* (*old-fashioned, formal*) (used mainly in names or titles 主要用于名称或头衔) relating to Britain or the British Empire 不列颠的；英国的；大英帝国的： *her Britannic Majesty* (= the Queen) 英国女王陛下

Brit·ish /ˈbrɪtɪʃ/ *adj.* **1** (*abbr.* **Br.**) connected with the United Kingdom of Great Britain and Northern Ireland or the people who live there （大不列颠及北爱尔兰）联合王国的；英国的；英国人的： *the British Government* 英国政府 ◇ *He was born in France but his parents are British.* 他生在法国，但父母是英国人。 ◇ *British-based/British-born/British-made* 以英国为基地的；英国出生的；英国制造的 **2 the British** *noun* [pl.] the people of the United Kingdom 联合王国人民；（统称）英国人 ▸ **Brit·ish·ness** *noun* [U]

▼ MORE ABOUT ... 补充说明

the British

- There is no singular noun which is commonly used to refer to a person from Britain. Instead the adjective **British** is used. 英语中没有指英国人的通用单数名词，一般用形容词 British： *She's British.* 她是英国人。◇ *The British have a very odd sense of humour.* 英国人的幽默感很奇特。The adjective **English** refers only to people from England, not the rest of the United Kingdom. 形容词 English 只指英格兰人，不包括英国其他地方的人。
- The noun **Briton** is used mainly in newspapers. 名词 Briton 主要用于报刊： *The survivors of the avalanche included 12 Britons.* 雪崩的幸存者中有 12 名英国人。It also describes the early inhabitants of Britain. 该词亦指英国早期居民： *the ancient Britons* 古代不列颠人 **Brit** is informal. **Britisher** is now very old-fashioned. * Brit 是非正式用语。Britisher 现已非常过时。

➲ NOTE AT SCOTTISH

the ˌBritish ˈCouncil *noun* [sing.] an organization that represents British culture in other countries and develops closer cultural relations with them 英国文化协会（设立于英国以外的国家，旨在加强文化交流）

ˌBritish ˈEnglish *noun* [U] the English language as spoken in Britain and certain other countries 英式英语

Brit·ish·er /ˈbrɪtɪʃə(r)/ *noun* (*old-fashioned, NAmE, informal*) a person from Britain 英国人

the ˌBritish ˈLions *noun* [pl.] a RUGBY team of the best players from England, Ireland, Scotland and Wales that plays abroad 英国雄狮队（由英格兰、爱尔兰、苏格兰和威尔士的一流橄榄球员组成）

ˌBritish ˌoverseas ˈterritory *noun* (*BrE*) an area that is not part of the United Kingdom but in which the British government is responsible for defence and relations with other countries 英国海外领地

ˌBritish ˈSummer Time *noun* [U] (*abbr.* **BST**) the time used in the UK in summer that is one hour ahead of GMT 英国夏令时间（比格林尼治平时早一个小时）

Briton /ˈbrɪtn/ *noun* (*formal*) a person from Britain 英国人： *the ancient Britons* 古英国人 ◇ *the first Briton to walk in space* 第一个在太空行走的英国人 ➲ NOTE AT BRITISH

brit·tle /ˈbrɪtl/ *adj.* **1** hard but easily broken 硬但易碎的；脆性的： ***brittle bones/nails*** 易折的骨骼 / 指甲 **2** a **brittle** mood or state of mind is one that appears to be happy or strong but is actually nervous and easily damaged 脆弱的： *a brittle temperament* 脆弱的性情 **3** (of a sound 声音) hard and sharp in an unpleasant way 尖厉的；刺耳的： *a brittle laugh* 尖厉的笑声 ▸ **brittle·ness** *noun* [U]

ˌbrittle ˈbone disease *noun* [U] (*medical* 医) **1** a rare disease in which sb's bones break extremely easily 成骨不全；脆骨病 **2** = OSTEOPOROSIS

bro /brəʊ; *NAmE* broʊ/ *noun* (*pl.* **bros**) (*informal*) **1** a brother 兄（或弟） **2** (*especially NAmE*) a friendly way of addressing a male person （对男子的友好称呼）哥们儿，伙计： *Thanks, bro!* 谢谢你，老兄！

broach /brəʊtʃ; *NAmE* broʊtʃ/ *verb* ~ **sth (to/with sb)** to begin talking about a subject that is difficult to discuss, especially because it is embarrassing or because people disagree about it 开始谈论，引入（尤指令人尴尬或有异议的话题）： *She was dreading having to* ***broach the subject*** *of money to her father.* 她正在为不得不向父亲提出钱的事犯愁。

ˈB-road *noun* (in Britain) a road that is less important than an A-ROAD and usually joins small towns and villages （英国）B 级公路（次于 A 级公路，通常连接小城镇及村落）

broad 🔑 /brɔːd/ *adj., noun*

WORD FAMILY
broad *adj.*
broadly *adv.*
broaden *verb*
breadth *noun*

■ ***adj.*** **(broad·er, broad·est)**

• WIDE 宽阔 **1** 🔑 wide 宽阔的；广阔的： *a broad street/avenue/river* 宽广的街道 / 林荫道 / 河流 ◇ *broad shoulders* 宽肩 ◇ *He is tall, broad and muscular.* 他身高体宽，肌肉发达。 ◇ ***a broad smile/grin*** (= one in which your mouth is stretched very wide because you are very pleased or amused) 咧嘴笑 OPP **narrow** **2** used after a measurement of distance to show how wide sth is …宽（用于表示距离的量度之后）： *two metres broad and one metre high* 两米宽，一米高

• WIDE RANGE 广泛 **3** including a great variety of people or things 涉及各种各样的人（或事物）的；广泛的： *a broad range of products* 各种各样的产品 ◇ *a broad spectrum of interests* 广泛的兴趣 ◇ *There is broad support for the government's policies.* 政府的政策得到了广泛的支持。 ◇ *She* ***took a broad view*** *of the duties of being a teacher* (= she believed her duties included a wide range of things). 她认为教师的职责范围很广。 OPP **narrow**

• GENERAL 概括 **4** 🔑 [only before noun] general; not detailed 概括的；一般的；不具体的： *the broad outline of a proposal* 提案的纲要 ◇ *The negotiators were in broad agreement on the main issues.* 谈判代表们在主要问题上的意见大致相同。 ◇ *She's a feminist, in the* ***broadest sense of the word***. 广义而言，她算是个女权主义者。 ◇ ***In broad terms***, *the paper argues that each country should develop* *its own policy.* 从大体上说，这份报纸认为各国的政策应由自己制定。

• LAND/WATER 陆地；水 **5** covering a wide area 开阔的；辽阔的：*a broad expanse of water* 一片辽阔的水域

• ACCENT 口音 **6** if sb has a **broad accent**, you can hear very easily which area they come from 口音重的；乡音浓的 SYN **strong**

• HINT 暗示 **7** if sb gives a **broad hint**, they make it very clear what they are thinking or what they want 明确的；明显的

• HUMOUR 幽默 **8** (*NAmE*) dealing with sex in an amusing way 粗俗滑稽的；以肉欲作笑料的：*The movie mixes broad humor with romance.* 那部电影把粗俗幽默和浪漫故事结合在一起。 ➲NOTE AT WIDE

IDM **a broad 'church** (*BrE*) an organization that accepts a wide range of opinions 广纳众议的机构 SYN **big tent** **(in) broad 'daylight** (in) the clear light of day, when it is easy to see 光天化日（之下）：*The robbery occurred in broad daylight, in a crowded street.* 抢劫就发生在光天化日之下的一条熙熙攘攘的街道上。 **it's as ˌbroad as it's 'long** (*BrE, informal*) it makes no real difference which of two possible choices you make 两种选择都一样 ➲MORE AT PAINT *v.*

■*noun* (*old-fashioned, NAmE, slang*) an offensive way of referring to a woman （对女人的粗俗称呼）婆娘

broad·band /ˈbrɔːdbænd/ *noun* [U] **1** (*specialist*) signals that use a wide range of FREQUENCIES 宽（谱）带 ➲ COMPARE NARROWBAND **2** a way of connecting a computer to the Internet, which allows you to receive information, including pictures, etc., very quickly （互联网的）宽带：*plans to provide rural areas with fast broadband* 为农村地区提供高速宽带的计划 ➲ COLLOCATIONS AT EMAIL

ˌbroad-ˈbased (*also* **ˌbroadly-ˈbased**) *adj.* based on a wide variety of people, things or ideas; not limited 有广泛基础的；无限制的

ˌbroad ˈbean (*BrE*) (*NAmE usually* **ˈfava bean**) *noun* a type of round, pale green BEAN. Several broad beans grow together inside a fat POD. 蚕豆

ˌbroad-ˈbrush *adj.* [only before noun] dealing with a subject or problem in a general way rather than considering details 粗线条的；不考虑细节的：*a broad-brush approach* 粗线条的处理方法

broad·cast /ˈbrɔːdkɑːst; *NAmE* -kæst/ *verb, noun*

■*verb* (**broad·cast, broad·cast**) **1** [T, I] ~ (**sth**) to send out programmes on television or radio 播送（电视或无线电节目）；广播：*The concert will be* ***broadcast live*** (= at the same time as it takes place) *tomorrow evening.* 明晚的音乐会将现场直播。 ◊ *They began broadcasting in 1922.* 他们于 1922 年开播。 ➲COLLOCATIONS AT TELEVISION **2** [T] ~ **sth** to tell a lot of people about sth 散布，传播（信息等）：*I don't like to* ***broadcast the fact*** *that my father owns the company.* 我不想宣扬这家公司为我父亲所有。

■*noun* a radio or television programme 广播节目；电视节目：(*BrE*) *a party political broadcast* (= for example, before an election) 政党政治广播节目 ◊ *We watched a* ***live broadcast*** *of the speech* (= one shown at the same time as the speech was made). 我们观看了那场演说的现场直播。

broad·cast·er /ˈbrɔːdkɑːstə(r); *NAmE* -kæst-/ *noun* **1** a person whose job is presenting or talking on television or radio programmes 广播员；（电视或电台的）节目主持人 **2** a company that sends out television or radio programmes 电视台；广播公司

broad·cast·ing /ˈbrɔːdkɑːstɪŋ; *NAmE* -kæst-/ *noun* [U] the business of making and sending out radio and television programmes （无线电和电视的）节目制作和播放；广播：*to work in broadcasting* 从事广播工作 ◊ *the British Broadcasting Corporation* (= the BBC) 英国广播公司

broad·en /ˈbrɔːdn/ *verb* **1** [I] to become wider 变宽；变阔：*Her smile broadened.* 她笑得更加灿烂了。 **2** [T, I] ~ (**sth**) to affect or make sth affect more people or things （使）扩大影响：*a promise to broaden access to higher education* 拓宽高等教育渠道的承诺 ◊ *The party needs to broaden its appeal to voters.* 该党需要进一步吸引选民。 **3** [T] ~ **sth** to increase your experience, knowledge, etc. 增长（经验、知识等）：*Few would disagree that travel* ***broadens the mind*** (= helps you to understand other people's customs, etc.). 旅游有助于开阔眼界，很少有人会不同意这一点。 ◊ *Spending a year working in the city helped to* ***broaden his horizons.*** 在城市工作的一年拓宽了他的视野。

PHR V **ˌbroaden ˈout** (of a road, river, etc. 路、河等) to become wider 变宽；变阔 SYN **widen**

the ˈbroad jump *noun* [sing.] (*NAmE*) = LONG JUMP

broad·leaved /ˈbrɔːdliːvd/ (*also less frequent* **broad·leaf** /ˈbrɔːdliːf/) *adj.* (*specialist*) (of plants 植物) having broad flat leaves 阔叶的

broad·ly /ˈbrɔːdli/ *adv.* **1** generally, without considering details 大体上；基本上；不考虑细节地：***Broadly speaking, I agree with you.*** 我大体上赞同你的意见。 ◊ ***broadly similar/comparable/equivalent/consistent*** 大致相似 / 相当 / 相等 / 一致 **2** if you smile **broadly**, you smile with your mouth stretched very wide because you are very pleased or amused 咧开嘴（笑）的；开心（笑）的

ˌbroad-ˈminded *adj.* willing to listen to other people's opinions and accept behaviour that is different from your own 愿意听取他人意见的；胸怀宽阔的；有气量的 SYN **tolerant** OPP **narrow-minded** ► **ˌbroad-ˈminded·ness** *noun* [U]

broad·ness /ˈbrɔːdnəs/ *noun* [U] the quality of being broad 宽阔；宽广；辽阔

broad·scale /ˈbrɔːdskeɪl/ *adj.* on a large scale 大规模的；大范围的：*The broadscale cutting down of trees is damaging the environment.* 对树木的大规模砍伐正在破坏环境。

broad·sheet /ˈbrɔːdʃiːt/ *noun* **1** a newspaper printed on a large size of paper, generally considered more serious than smaller newspapers 大幅报纸（一般比小幅报纸内容严肃） ➲ COMPARE TABLOID (1) **2** a large piece of paper printed on one side only with information or an advertisement 单面全版大幅信息（或广告）

broad·side /ˈbrɔːdsaɪd/ *noun, adv., verb*

■*noun* an aggressive attack in words, whether written or spoken （书面或口头的）猛烈抨击：*The prime minister* ***fired a broadside*** *at his critics.* 首相对批评他的人进行了猛烈反击。

■*adv.* with one side facing sth 一侧对着某物 SYN **sideways**：*The car skidded and crashed broadside into another car.* 汽车打滑，车身撞上了另一辆车。 ◊ (*BrE*) *The boat swung* ***broadside on*** *to the current of the river.* 小船打转以舷侧冲入河水的洪流。

■*verb* ~ **sth** (*NAmE*) to crash into the side of sth 撞上（某物的）侧面：*The driver ran a stop light and broadsided the truck.* 司机闯红灯，撞上了卡车的一侧。

ˌbroad-ˈspectrum *adj.* [only before noun] (*specialist*) (of a drug or chemical 药物或化学品) effective against a large variety of bacteria, insects, etc. 广谱的；效用广泛的

broad·sword /ˈbrɔːdsɔːd; *NAmE* -sɔːrd/ *noun* a large SWORD with a broad flat blade 大砍刀；阔剑

Broad·way /ˈbrɔːdweɪ/ *noun* [U] a street in New York City where there are many theatres, sometimes used to refer to the US theatre industry in general 百老汇（美国纽约市戏院集中的一条大街）；（美国的）戏剧业：*a Broadway musical* 百老汇音乐剧 ◊ *The play opened* ***on Broadway*** *in 2013.* 该剧于 2013 年在百老汇首演。 ➲ SEE ALSO OFF-BROADWAY

bro·cade /brəˈkeɪd/ *noun* [U, C] a type of thick heavy cloth with a raised pattern made especially from gold or silver silk thread 织锦缎；（尤指用金银线织出凸纹的）厚织物

bro·caded /brəˈkeɪdɪd/ *adj.* [usually before noun] made of or decorated with brocade 用锦缎制作（或装饰）的；织锦缎的

Broca's area /ˈbrəʊkəz eəriə; *NAmE* ˈbroʊkəz eriə/ *noun* (*anatomy* 解) an area in the front part of the brain connected with speech 布罗卡区（大脑前部控制语言表达的区域）

broc·coli /ˈbrɒkəli; *NAmE* ˈbrɑːk-/ *noun* [U] a vegetable with a thick green STEM and several dark green or purple flower heads 青花菜；绿菜花；西兰花 ➲ VISUAL VOCAB PAGE V33

bro·chette /brɒˈʃet; *NAmE* broʊ-/ *noun* (*from French*) **1** [C, U] a dish consisting of pieces of food cooked on a thin stick over a fire 串烤肉（用扦子明火烤制） **2** [C] one of the sticks used for cooking food in this way 烤肉扦

bro·chure /ˈbrəʊʃə(r); *NAmE* broʊˈʃʊr/ *noun* a small magazine or book containing pictures and information about sth or advertising sth 资料（或广告）手册：*a travel brochure* 旅游手册

bro·derie ang·laise /ˌbrəʊdəri ˈɒŋɡleɪz; *NAmE* ˌbroʊdəri ˈɑːŋɡleɪz/ *noun* [U] (*from French*) decoration with sewing on fine white cloth; the cloth decorated in this way 英格兰刺绣；细白布绣饰；英格兰刺绣品

broer /ˈbruːə(r)/ *noun* (*SAfrE, informal*) **1** a brother 哥哥；弟弟 **2** (used of a boy or man) a friend （称男孩或男子）朋友，哥们儿 **3** a friendly form of address that is used by one boy or man to another 老兄；老弟：*How's it going, my broer?* 怎么样了，老兄？

brogue /brəʊɡ; *NAmE* broʊɡ/ *noun* **1** [usually pl.] a strong shoe which usually has a pattern in the leather （粗革）拷花皮鞋：*a pair of brogues* 一双拷花皮鞋 ➲ VISUAL VOCAB PAGE V69 **2** [usually sing.] the accent that sb has when they are speaking, especially the accent of Irish or Scottish speakers of English 口音；（尤指讲英语的爱尔兰或苏格兰人的）土腔

broil /brɔɪl/ *verb* **1** [T] ~ **sth** (*NAmE*) to cook meat or fish under direct heat or over heat on metal bars 烤，焙（肉或鱼）：*broiled chicken* 烤鸡 ➲ COMPARE BARBECUE *v.*, GRILL *v.* **2** [I, T] ~ (**sb**) to become or make sb become very hot （使）变得灼热，受炙热：*They lay broiling in the sun.* 他们躺在太阳底下几乎要晒熟了。

broil·er /ˈbrɔɪlə(r)/ *noun* **1** (*also* **ˈbroiler chicken**) (*especially NAmE*) a young chicken suitable for broiling or ROASTING （适于烤焙的）嫩鸡 **2** (*NAmE*) the part inside the oven of a cooker/stove that directs heat downwards to cook food that is placed underneath it （烤炉内的）烘烤器 ➲ COMPARE GRILL *n.* (1)

broke /brəʊk; *NAmE* broʊk/ *adj.* [not before noun] (*informal*) having no money 没钱；囊中羞涩；破产：*I'm always broke by the end of the month.* 我总是一到月底就没钱花了。◇ *During the recession thousands of small businesses* ***went broke*** (= had to stop doing business). 经济衰退期间成千上万家小企业被迫关门了。◇ ***flat/stony broke*** (= completely broke) 彻底破产 ➲ SEE ALSO BREAK *v.*

IDM **go for ˈbroke** (*informal*) to risk everything in one determined effort to do sth 孤注一掷 ➲ MORE AT AIN'T

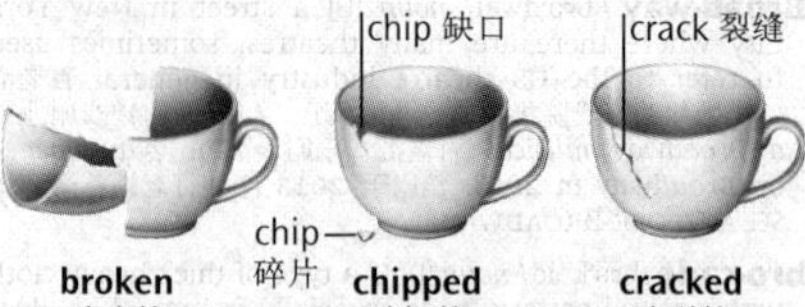

broken 破碎的 **chipped** 破损的 **cracked** 破裂的

broken 🔑 /ˈbrəʊkən; *NAmE* ˈbroʊ-/ *adj.*
- **DAMAGED** 受损 **1** 🔑 that has been damaged or injured; no longer whole or working correctly 破损的；伤残的；残缺的；出了毛病的：*a broken window/plate* 破碎的窗玻璃 / 盘子 ◇ *a broken leg/arm* 断了的腿 / 臂 ◇ *pieces of broken glass* 玻璃碎片 ◇ *How did this dish* ***get broken?*** 这个盘子是怎么打破的？◇ *The TV's broken.* 电视机坏了。➲ SEE ALSO BROKEN HEART
- **RELATIONSHIP** 关系 **2** 🔑 [usually before noun] ended or destroyed 终止了的；破坏了的：***a broken marriage/engagement*** 破裂的婚姻；解除了的婚约 ➲ SEE ALSO BROKEN HOME
- **PROMISE/AGREEMENT** 诺言；协定 **3** 🔑 [usually before noun] not kept 被违背的；未履行的
- **NOT CONTINUOUS** 不连续 **4** 🔑 [usually before noun] not continuous; disturbed or interrupted 不连续的；间断的；被打扰的：*a night of broken sleep* 睡得不踏实的一夜 ◇ *a single broken white line across the road* 横穿马路的一条断断续续的白线
- **PERSON** 人 **5** [only before noun] made weak and tired by illness or difficulties 衰弱的；精疲力竭的：*He was a broken man after the failure of his business.* 生意失败后他变得心灰意懒。
- **LANGUAGE** 语言 **6** [only before noun] (of a language that is not your own 非母语) spoken slowly and with a lot of mistakes; not FLUENT 说得结结巴巴的；不流利的：*to speak in broken English* 说着一口结结巴巴的英语
- **GROUND** 地面 **7** having a rough surface 凹凸不平的；坎坷的：*an area of broken, rocky ground* 崎岖、多岩石的地区 ➲ SEE ALSO BREAK, BROKE, BROKEN

ˌbroken-ˈdown *adj.* [usually before noun] in a very bad condition; not working correctly; very tired and sick 状况很差的；出故障的；衰弱的：*a broken-down old car/horse* 出了毛病的旧车；衰老的马

ˌbroken ˈheart *noun* a feeling of great sadness, especially when sb you love has died or left you 破碎的心；哀恸：*No one ever died of a broken heart.* 从来没有人因为过度悲伤而死。► **ˌbroken-ˈhearted** *adj.*：*He was broken-hearted when his wife died.* 他的妻子去世，他伤心极了。➲ COMPARE HEARTBROKEN

ˌbroken ˈhome *noun* a family in which the parents are divorced or separated 破裂的家庭；父母离异（或分居）的家庭：*She comes from a broken home.* 她生长于一个破碎的家庭。

broken·ly /ˈbrəʊkənli; *NAmE* ˈbroʊ-/ *adv.* (*formal*) (of sb's manner of speaking 讲话方式) in phrases that are very short or not complete, with a lot of pauses; not FLUENTLY 结结巴巴地；不流利地

broker /ˈbrəʊkə(r); *NAmE* ˈbroʊ-/ *noun, verb*
- *noun* **1** a person who buys and sells things for other people 经纪人；掮客：*an insurance broker* 保险经纪人 **2** = STOCKBROKER ➲ SEE ALSO HONEST BROKER, PAWNBROKER, POWER BROKER
- *verb* ~ **sth** to arrange the details of an agreement, especially between different countries 安排，协商（协议的细节，尤指在两国间）：*a peace plan brokered by the UN* 由联合国出面协商的和平计划 ➲ WORDFINDER NOTE AT DEAL

broker·age /ˈbrəʊkərɪdʒ; *NAmE* ˈbroʊ-/ *noun* [U] **1** the business of being a broker 经纪业务：***a brokerage firm/house*** 经纪公司 **2** an amount of money charged by a broker for work that he/she does 经纪人佣金（或回扣）

ˈbroker-dealer *noun* (*finance* 财) a person who works on the Stock Exchange buying shares from and selling shares to BROKERS and the public （证券交易所的）经纪经销商，综合证券商 ➲ COMPARE JOBBER

brolly /ˈbrɒli; *NAmE* ˈbrɑːli/ *noun* (*pl.* **-ies**) (*BrE, informal*) = UMBRELLA (1)

bro·mance /brəʊˈmæns; ˈbrəʊmæns; *NAmE* ˈbroʊmæns/ *noun* (*informal*) a very close friendship between two men 兄弟情谊（男人之间的亲密友好关系） ORIGIN From **brother** and **romance**. 源自 brother 和 romance。➲ MORE LIKE THIS 1, page R25

brom·ide /ˈbrəʊmaɪd; *NAmE* ˈbroʊ-/ *noun* [C, U] a chemical which contains BROMINE, used, especially in the past, to make people feel calm 溴化物（旧时尤用作镇静剂）

brom·ine /ˈbrəʊmiːn; *NAmE* ˈbroʊ-/ *noun* [U] (*symb.* **Br**) a chemical element. Bromine is a dark red poisonous liquid and has a very strong unpleasant smell. It is mainly found in the form of salts in sea water. 溴（富集于海水）

bron·chial /ˈbrɒŋkiəl; *NAmE* ˈbrɑːŋ-/ *adj.* [usually before noun] (*medical* 医) of or affecting the two main branches of the WINDPIPE (called **bronchial tubes**) leading to the lungs 支气管的：*bronchial pneumonia* 支气管肺炎 ➲ VISUAL VOCAB PAGE V64

bron·chitis /brɒŋˈkaɪtɪs; *NAmE* brɑːŋ-/ *noun* [U] an illness that affects the bronchial tubes leading to the lungs 支气管炎：*He was suffering from chronic bronchitis.* 他患有慢性支气管炎。▸ **bron·chit·ic** /brɒŋˈkɪtɪk; *NAmE* brɑːŋ-/ *adj.*：*a bronchitic cough* 支气管炎引起的咳嗽

bron·chus /ˈbrɒŋkəs; *NAmE* ˈbrɑːŋ-/ *noun* (*pl.* **bron·chi** /ˈbrɒŋkaɪ; *NAmE* ˈbrɑːŋ-/) (*anatomy* 解) any one of the system of tubes which make up the main branches of the WINDPIPE through which air passes in and out of the lungs 支气管

bronco /ˈbrɒŋkəʊ; *NAmE* ˈbrɑːŋkoʊ/ *noun* (*pl.* **-os**) a wild horse of the western US 布朗科马；（美国西部的）野马：*a bucking bronco in the rodeo* 牛仔竞技表演中一匹弓背跳跃的野马

bron·to·saurus /ˌbrɒntəˈsɔːrəs; *NAmE* ˌbrɑːn-/ *noun* = APATOSAURUS

Bronx cheer /ˌbrɒŋks ˈtʃɪə(r); *NAmE* ˌbrɑːŋks ˈtʃɪr/ *noun* (*NAmE, informal*) = RASPBERRY (2)

bronze /brɒnz; *NAmE* brɑːnz/ *noun, adj.*

▪ ***noun*** **1** [U] a dark reddish-brown metal made by mixing COPPER and tin 青铜：*a bronze statue* 青铜像 ◇ *a figure cast in bronze* 一尊青铜铸像 **2** [U] a dark reddish-brown colour, like bronze 深红褐色；青铜色 **3** [C] a work of art made of bronze, for example a statue 青铜艺术品 **4** [C, U] = BRONZE MEDAL

▪ ***adj.*** dark reddish-brown in colour 深红棕色的；青铜色的：*bronze skin* 古铜色的皮肤

the ˈBronze Age *noun* [sing.] the period in history between the Stone Age and the Iron Age when people used tools and weapons made of bronze 青铜时代；青铜器时代

bronzed /brɒnzd; *NAmE* brɑːnzd/ *adj.* having skin that has been turned brown in an attractive way by the sun 古铜色的（太阳晒的健康肤色） SYN **tanned**

ˌbronze ˈmedal (*also* **bronze**) *noun* [C, U] a MEDAL given as third prize in a competition or race 铜牌；铜质奖章：*an Olympic bronze medal winner* 奥林匹克铜牌得主 ◇ *She won (a) bronze at the Olympics.* 她在奥林匹克运动会上赢得了一枚铜牌。➲ COMPARE GOLD MEDAL, SILVER MEDAL ▸ **ˌbronze ˈmedallist** (*BrE*) (*NAmE* **ˌbronze ˈmedalist**) *noun*：*She's an Olympic bronze medallist.* 她是奥林匹克铜牌得主。

brooch /brəʊtʃ; *NAmE* broʊtʃ/ (*especially BrE*) (*NAmE usually* **pin**) *noun* a piece of jewellery with a pin on the back of it, that can be fastened to your clothes 饰针；胸针；领针 ➲ VISUAL VOCAB PAGE V70

brood /bruːd/ *verb, noun*

▪ ***verb*** **1** [I] ~ (**over/on/about sth**) to think a lot about sth that makes you annoyed, anxious or upset 焦虑，忧思（使人厌烦、担忧或不安的事）：*You're not still brooding over what he said, are you?* 你不是还在为他的话闷闷不乐吧？ **2** [I, T] ~ (**sth**) if a bird **broods**, or **broods** its eggs, it sits on the eggs in order to HATCH them (= make the young come out of them) 孵（蛋）

▪ ***noun*** [C+sing./pl. v.] **1** all the young birds or creatures that a mother produces at one time （一次孵或生的）一窝鸟，一窝动物 SYN **clutch** **2** (*humorous*) a large family of children 一大家孩子

brood·ing /ˈbruːdɪŋ/ *adj.* (*literary*) sad and mysterious or threatening 幽怨的；忧思的；森然的；险恶的：*dark, brooding eyes* 一双乌黑幽怨的眼睛 ◇ *a brooding silence* 森然的寂静 ◇ *Ireland's brooding landscape* 爱尔兰的险要地形

ˈbrood mare *noun* a female horse kept for breeding 传种母马

broody /ˈbruːdi/ *adj.* **1** (of a woman 女人) wanting very much to have a baby 急于生孩子的：*I reached the age of 27 and suddenly started to feel broody.* 到 27 岁时，我突然产生了很想要个孩子的念头。 **2** (of a female bird 雌禽) wanting to lay eggs and sit on them 要抱窝的：*a broody hen* 要抱窝的母鸡 **3** quiet and thinking about sth because you are unhappy or disappointed 闷闷不乐的；郁郁寡欢的 ▸ **broodi·ness** *noun* [U]

brook /brʊk/ *noun, verb*

▪ ***noun*** a small river 溪；小河；小川

▪ ***verb*** **not brook sth/not brook sb doing sth/brook no...** (*formal*) to not allow sth 不允许（某事）：*The tone in his voice brooked no argument.* 他的话里带着不容争辩的语气。

broom /bruːm/ *noun* **1** [C] a brush on the end of a long handle, used for sweeping floors 扫把；扫帚 ➲ VISUAL VOCAB PAGE V21 **2** [U] a wild bush with small yellow flowers 金雀花（野生，开小黄花） IDM SEE NEW

ˈbroom cupboard *noun* (*BrE*) **1** a large built-in cupboard used for keeping cleaning equipment, etc. in 清洁用具壁橱 **2** (*often humorous*) a very small room 狭小的房间：*I couldn't afford more than a broom cupboard to set up office in.* 我的钱也就够搞一间鸡窝大的办公室。

broom·stick /ˈbruːmstɪk/ *noun* a broom with a long handle and small thin sticks at the end, or the handle of a broom. In stories WITCHES (= women with evil magic powers) ride through the air on broomsticks. 长柄扫帚；扫帚柄（传说中女巫用以飞行）

Bros (*also* **Bros.** *especially in NAmE*) *abbr.* (used in the name of a company) Brothers （用于公司名称）兄弟：*Warner Bros.* 华纳兄弟娱乐公司

broth /brɒθ; *NAmE* brɑːθ; brɔːθ/ *noun* [U, C] thick soup made by boiling meat or fish and vegetables in water （加入蔬菜的）肉汤，鱼汤：*chicken broth* 鸡汤 ➲ SEE ALSO SCOTCH BROTH IDM SEE COOK *n.*

brothel /ˈbrɒθl; *NAmE* ˈbrɑːθl; ˈbrɔːθl/ (*also* **bor·dello** *especially in NAmE*) *noun* a house where people pay to have sex with PROSTITUTES 妓院

ˈbrothel creepers *noun* [pl.] (*BrE, informal*) SUEDE shoes with thick soft SOLES, popular in the 1950s （流行于 20 世纪 50 年代的）绒面革厚软底鞋

brother 🔑 /ˈbrʌðə(r)/ *noun, exclamation*

▪ ***noun***

• **IN FAMILY** 家庭 **1** a boy or man who has the same mother and father as another person 哥哥；弟弟：*We're brothers.* 我们是亲兄弟。 ◇ *He's my brother.* 他是我哥哥（或弟弟）。 ◇ *an* ***older/younger brother*** 哥哥；弟弟 ◇ *a* ***twin brother*** 孪生哥哥（或弟弟） ◇ *Does she have any* ***brothers and sisters****?* 她有兄弟姐妹吗？ ◇ *Edward was the youngest of the Kennedy brothers.* 爱德华是肯尼迪弟兄中最小的一个。 ◇ *He was like a brother to me* (= very close). 他如同我的亲兄弟一样。 ➲ SEE ALSO HALF-BROTHER, STEP-BROTHER

• **OTHER MEN** 其他男性 **2** (*pl.* **brothers** or *old-fashioned* **brethren**) used for talking to or talking about other male members of an organization or other men who have the same ideas, purpose, etc. as yourself （称男性的共事者或同道）同事，弟兄，伙伴：*We must work together, brothers!* 我们必须携手工作，伙计们！ ◇ *He was greatly respected by his brother officers.* 他非常受军官同僚的敬重。 ◇ *We must support our weaker brethren.* 我们必须支持弱势的同胞。

• IN RELIGIOUS GROUP 宗教团体 **3** (*also* **Brother**) (*pl.* **brethren** or **brothers**) a male member of a religious group, especially a MONK（同一宗教团体的男性）教友；（尤指）修士： *Brother Luke* 卢克修士 ◇ *The Brethren meet regularly for prayer.* 兄弟教会成员定期聚集祈祷。
• FORM OF ADDRESS 称呼 **4** (*NAmE, informal*) used by black people as a form of address for a black man（黑人对黑人男子的称呼）
• AT COLLEGE/UNIVERSITY 大学 **5** (in the US) a member of a FRATERNITY (= a club for a group of male students at a college or university)（美国）大学生联谊会成员
■ *exclamation* (*old-fashioned, especially NAmE*) used to express the fact that you are annoyed or surprised（表示生气或吃惊）： *Oh brother!* 天哪！

brother·hood /ˈbrʌðəhʊd; *NAmE* -ðərh-/ *noun* **1** [U] friendship and understanding between people 友谊与谅解；手足情谊： *to live in peace and brotherhood* 生活在和平互爱中 **2** [C+sing./pl. v.] an organization formed for a particular purpose, especially a religious society or political organization 宗教（或政治等）组织 **3** [U] the relationship of brothers 兄弟关系： *the ties of brotherhood* 兄弟情义

ˈ**brother-in-law** (*pl.* **brothers-in-law**) *noun* the brother of your husband or wife; your sister's or brother's husband; the husband of your husband or wife's sister 配偶的哥哥（或弟弟）；姐夫；妹夫；配偶的姐夫（或妹夫） ➲ COMPARE SISTER-IN-LAW

brother·ly /ˈbrʌðəli; *NAmE* -ðərli/ *adj.* [usually before noun] showing feelings of affection and kindness that you would expect a brother to show 兄弟的；兄弟般的；亲切友好的： ***brotherly love/advice*** 兄弟间的爱；亲切的劝告 ◇ *He gave her a brotherly kiss on the cheek.* 他像兄长一样吻了她的面颊。

brougham /ˈbruːəm/ *noun* a type of CARRIAGE used in the past, which had a closed roof and four wheels and was pulled by one horse（旧时的）四轮单马马车

brought PAST TENSE, PAST PART. OF BRING IDM SEE LOW *adj.*

brou·haha /ˈbruːhɑːhɑː/ *noun* [U, sing.] (*old-fashioned, informal*) noisy excitement or complaints about sth 喧闹；喧哗；起哄

brow /braʊ/ *noun* **1** (*literary*) the part of the face above the eyes and below the hair 额头 SYN **forehead**: *The nurse mopped his fevered brow.* 护士擦拭了他发烫的前额。 ◇ *Her* ***brow furrowed*** *in concentration.* 她眉头紧锁全神贯注。 **2** [usually pl.] = EYEBROW : *One dark brow rose in surprise.* 一道乌黑的眉毛惊奇地挑起。 **3** [usually sing.] the top part of a hill 山脊；坡顶： *The path disappeared over the brow of the hill.* 小径过山顶后消失了。 ➲ SEE ALSO HIGHBROW, LOWBROW, MIDDLEBROW IDM SEE KNIT *v.*

brow·beat /ˈbraʊbiːt/ *verb* (**brow·beat**, **brow·beat·en** /ˈbraʊbiːtn/) ~ **sb** (**into doing sth**) to frighten or threaten sb in order to make them do sth 恫吓；威逼 SYN **intimidate**: *They were browbeaten into accepting the offer.* 他们被威逼接受了提议。

brown 🔑 /braʊn/ *adj., noun, verb*
■ *adj.* (**brown·er**, **brown·est**) **1** 🔑 having the colour of earth or coffee 棕色的；褐色的： *brown eyes* 褐色的眼睛 ◇ *brown bread* 黑面包 ◇ *dark brown shoe polish* 深棕色鞋油 ◇ *a package wrapped in brown paper* 用牛皮纸包扎的包裹 **2** 🔑 having skin that is naturally brown or has been made brown by the sun（皮肤）棕色的，被晒黑的：(*BrE*) *I don't go brown very easily.* 我不容易晒黑。 ◇ *After the summer in Spain, the children were* ***brown as berries.*** 在西班牙度过了一个夏天之后，孩子们晒得黝黑。
IDM **in a brown ˈstudy** (*old-fashioned, BrE*) thinking deeply so that you do not notice what is happening around you 出神；沉思默想（以致没注意到周围情况）
■ *noun* 🔑 [U, C] the colour of earth or coffee 棕色；褐色： *leaves of various shades of brown* 深浅不一的棕色叶子 ◇ *Brown doesn't* (= brown clothes do not) *suit you.* 你不适合穿棕色衣服。
■ *verb* [I, T] to become brown; to make sth brown （使）变成棕色；成褐色： *Heat the butter until it browns.* 把黄油加热，使之呈棕色。 ◇ *The grass was browning in patches.* 草地一片片地变成褐色。 ◇ ~ **sth** *Brown the onions before adding the meat.* 把洋葱炒成褐色，然后放进肉。
IDM ˌ**browned ˈoff** (**with sb/sth**) (*BrE, informal*) bored, unhappy and/or annoyed（对某人）厌倦，不快，烦恼 SYN **fed up**: *By now the passengers were getting browned off with the delay.* 此时乘客们对延误已开始感到不满。

ˌ**brown ˈale** *noun* (*BrE*) **1** [U, C] a type of mild sweet dark beer sold in bottles 棕色淡啤酒（瓶装出售） **2** [C] a bottle or glass of brown ale 一瓶（或一杯）棕色淡啤酒

ˈ**brown-bag** *verb* (**-gg-**) ~ **it** (*NAmE, informal*) to bring your lunch with you to work or school, usually in a brown paper bag 自带（午餐，常用棕色纸袋）： *My kids have been brown-bagging it this week.* 我几个孩子这个星期都是自带午餐上学。

ˌ**brown ˈdwarf** *noun* (*astronomy* 天) an object in space that is between a large planet and a small star in size, and produces heat 棕矮星（体积在大行星和小星体之间，产生热）

brown·field /ˈbraʊnfiːld/ *adj.* [only before noun] used to describe an area of land in a city that was used by industry or for offices in the past and that may now be cleared for new building development 棕色地带（待重新开发的城市用地）： *a brownfield site* 城市棕色地带工地

ˈ**brown goods** *noun* [pl.] small electrical items such as televisions, radios, music and video equipment 黑色家电（如电视、收音机、视频设备等） ➲ COMPARE WHITE GOODS

Brown·ian motion /ˈbraʊniən məʊʃn; *NAmE* moʊʃn/ *noun* [U] (*physics* 物) the movement without any regular pattern made by very small pieces of matter in a liquid or gas 布朗运动（流体中悬浮颗粒所做的不规则运动）

brownie /ˈbraʊni/ *noun* **1** [C] a thick soft flat cake made with chocolate and sometimes nuts and served in small squares 巧克力方块蛋糕（有时放有坚果）： *a fudge brownie* 一块巧克力软糖糕 **2 the Brownies** [pl.] a branch of the SCOUT ASSOCIATION for girls between the ages of seven and ten or eleven 幼女童军（由 7 到 10 或 11 岁的女孩组成）： *to join the Brownies* 加入幼女童军 **3** [C] **Brownie** (*BrE also* ˈ**Brownie Guide**) a member of the Brownies （一个）幼女童军 ➲ COMPARE CUB (2), (3), GUIDE *n.* (6), SCOUT *n.* (1), (2)

ˈ**brownie point** *noun* [usually pl.] (*informal*) if sb does sth to earn **brownie points**, they do it to make sb in authority have a good opinion of them 讨好上级所得的好印象；拍马屁得分 ORIGIN The Brownies is a club for young girls who are not yet old enough to be Guides. They are awarded points for good behaviour and achievements. 源自幼女童军 (the Brownies)。该俱乐部是为年龄不够参加女童子军的女孩设立的，表现好或成绩好的女孩奖以分数鼓励。

brown·ish /ˈbraʊnɪʃ/ (*also less frequent* **browny** /ˈbraʊni/) *adj.* fairly brown in colour 带棕色的；近棕色的： *You can't see in this light, but my new coat is a sort of brownish colour.* 这种光线下你看不清楚，其实我的新外衣带棕色。

ˈ**brown-nose** *verb* [I, T] (*informal, disapproving*) to treat sb in authority with special respect in order to make them approve of you or treat you better 谄媚；拍马屁

ˈ**brown-out** *noun* (*especially NAmE*) a period of time when the amount of electrical power that is supplied to an area is reduced 电力减弱；电压降低

ˌ**brown ˈrat** (*also* ˌ**common ˈrat**, ˌ**Norway ˈrat**) *noun* a common type of RAT 褐家鼠

ˌ**brown ˈrice** *noun* [U] rice that is light brown because it has not had all of its outside part removed 糙米

ˌ**brown ˈsauce** *noun* [U] **1** (*BrE*) a sauce made with VINEGAR and spices, sold in bottles（用醋、调味品等制

成、瓶装出售的）棕色调味料 **2** (*NAmE*) a sauce made with fat and flour, cooked until it becomes brown （将脂油和面粉煮至呈棕色后制成的）棕色沙司

brown·stone /ˈbraʊnstəʊn; *NAmE* -stoʊn/ *noun* (*NAmE*) a house built of, or with a front made of, a type of reddish-brown stone, which is also called brownstone 褐砂石；用褐砂石建筑或饰面的房屋： *New York brownstones* 纽约的褐砂石房屋

ˌbrown ˈsugar *noun* [U] sugar that has a brown colour and has only been partly REFINED 红糖；黄糖

browse /braʊz/ *verb* **1** [I, T] to look at a lot of things in a shop/store rather than looking for one particular thing （在商店里）随便看看： *You are welcome to come in and browse.* 欢迎您光临本店随便看看。 ◇ **~ sth** *She browsed the shelves for something interesting to read.* 她浏览着书架，想找本有趣的书看。 **2** [I, T] **~ (through) sth** to look through the pages of a book, newspaper, etc. without reading everything 浏览；翻阅： *I found the article while I was browsing through some old magazines.* 我在翻阅一些旧杂志时找到了这篇文章。 **3** [I, T] **~ (sth)** (*computing* 计) to look for or to look at information on a computer, especially on the Internet or a specific website （在计算机，尤指互联网上）搜寻信息，浏览信息 ➲ WORDFINDER NOTE AT WEB **4** [I] **~ (on sth)** (of cows, GOATS, etc. 牛、羊等) to eat leaves, etc. that are growing high up 吃（绿叶等高处的植物） ▸ **browse** *noun* [sing.]: *The gift shop is well worth a browse.* 这家礼品店很值得一看。

browser /ˈbraʊzə(r)/ *noun* **1** (*computing* 计) a program that lets you look at or read documents on the World Wide Web 浏览器；浏览程序： *a web browser* 互联网浏览器 ➲ COLLOCATIONS AT EMAIL ➲ VISUAL VOCAB PAGE V74 **2** a person who looks through books, magazines, etc. or at things for sale, but may not seriously intend to buy anything 浏览图书报刊者；逛商店的人

brrr /bər/ *exclamation* a sound that people make to show that they are very cold （表示感觉寒冷）呵，哦： *Brrr, it's freezing here.* 呵，这儿真冷啊。 ➲ MORE LIKE THIS 3, page R25

bru·cel·losis /ˌbruːsəˈləʊsɪs; *NAmE* -ˈloʊs-/ *noun* [U] a disease caused by bacteria that affects cows and that can cause fever in humans 布鲁菌病，布氏菌病（由细菌引起的牛类疾病，人类感染可引起发烧）

bruise /bruːz/ *noun, verb*

■ ***noun*** **1** a blue, brown or purple mark that appears on the skin after sb has fallen, been hit, etc. 青肿；瘀伤；碰伤： *to be covered in bruises* 浑身青肿 ◇ *cuts and bruises* 伤口和瘀伤 ➲ SYNONYMS AT INJURE **2** a mark on a fruit or vegetable where it is damaged （水果或蔬菜的）碰伤，伤痕

■ ***verb*** **1** [I, T] to develop a bruise, or make a bruise or bruises appear on the skin of sb/sth （使）出现伤痕；撞伤；擦伤： *Strawberries bruise easily.* 草莓容易碰伤。 ◇ **~ sth** *She had slipped and badly bruised her face.* 她滑了一跤，摔得鼻青脸肿。 ➲ SYNONYMS AT INJURE ➲ WORDFINDER NOTE AT HURT ➲ COLLOCATIONS AT INJURY **2** [T, usually passive] **~ sb** to affect sb badly and make them feel unhappy and less confident 打击；挫伤： *They had been badly bruised by the defeat.* 失败使他们的自信心大为受挫。 ▸ **bruised** *adj.*: *He suffered badly bruised ribs in the crash.* 他在事故中肋骨被严重撞伤。 ◇ *bruised fruit* 碰伤的水果 ◇ *a bruised ego* 受伤的自尊心 **bruis·ing** *noun* [U]: *She suffered severe bruising, but no bones were broken.* 她挫伤严重，但骨骼完好。 ◇ *internal bruising* 内伤 ➲ SEE ALSO BRUISING

bruiser /ˈbruːzə(r)/ *noun* (*informal*) a large strong aggressive man 好勇斗狠的彪形大汉

bruis·ing /ˈbruːzɪŋ/ *adj.* difficult and unpleasant, making you feel tired or weak 艰难讨厌的；繁重麻烦的： *a* ***bruising*** *meeting/experience* 令人厌烦的会议；艰辛的经历

bruit /bruːt/ *verb* **~ sth (about)** (*formal*) to spread a piece of news widely 传播，散播（信息）： *This rumour has been bruited about for years.* 这个谣言已传播多年了。

Brum·mie /ˈbrʌmi/ *noun* (*BrE, informal*) a person from the city of Birmingham in England （英格兰）伯明翰人 ▸ **Brum·mie** *adj.*: *a Brummie accent* 伯明翰口音

brunch /brʌntʃ/ *noun* [C, U] a meal that you eat in the late morning as a combination of breakfast and lunch 早午餐（早午两餐并作一餐） ➲ MORE LIKE THIS 1, page R25

bru·nette /bruːˈnet/ *noun* (*sometimes offensive*) a white-skinned woman with dark brown hair 深褐色头发的白人女子 ➲ COMPARE BLONDE *n.*, REDHEAD

brunt /brʌnt/ *noun*

IDM **bear, take, etc. the ˈbrunt of sth** to receive the main force of sth unpleasant 承受某事的主要压力；首当其冲： *Schools will bear the brunt of cuts in government spending.* 政府削减开支，学校将首当其冲受到影响。

brus·chetta /bruˈsketə/ *noun* [U] (*from Italian*) an Italian dish consisting of pieces of warm bread covered with oil and chopped raw tomatoes （意大利）番茄涂油面包片： *a first course of bruschetta* 番茄涂油面包片作为第一道菜

brush /brʌʃ/ *noun, verb*

■ ***noun*** **1** [C] an object made of short stiff hairs (called BRISTLES) or wires set in a block of wood or plastic, usually attached to a handle. Brushes are used for many different jobs, such as cleaning, painting and tidying your hair. 刷子；毛刷；画笔： *a paintbrush* 画笔 ◇ *a hairbrush* 发刷 ◇ *a toothbrush* 牙刷 ◇ *brush strokes* (= the marks left by a brush when painting) 画笔的笔触 ◇ *a dustpan and brush* 簸箕和刷子 ◇ *Apply the paint with a fine brush.* 用细画笔涂颜料。 ➲ VISUAL VOCAB PAGES V21, V65 **2** [sing.] an act of brushing 刷： *to give your teeth a good brush* 好好刷一刷牙 **3** [sing.] a light touch made in passing sth/sb 轻擦；掠过： *the brush of his lips on her cheek* 他的嘴唇在她脸上的轻轻一碰 **4** [C] **~ with sb/sth** a short unfriendly meeting with sb; an occasion when you nearly experience sth unpleasant 小冲突；稍有不快的场合： *She had a nasty brush with her boss this morning.* 她今天早晨和老板闹得挺别扭的。 ◇ *In his job he's had frequent brushes with death.* 他在工作中常常与死神擦肩而过。 ◇ *a brush with the law* 轻微的触犯法律 **5** [U] land covered by small trees or bushes 灌木丛： *a brush fire* 灌木丛火 **6** [C] the tail of a FOX 狐狸尾巴 IDM SEE DAFT, PAINT *v.*, TAR *v.*

■ ***verb*** **1** [T] to clean, polish, or make smooth with a brush （用刷子）刷净，刷亮，刷平顺： **~ sth** *to brush your hair/teeth/shoes* 刷头发；刷牙；刷鞋 ◇ **~ sth + adj.** *A tiled floor is easy to brush clean.* 瓷砖地板容易打扫干净。 **2** [T] to put sth, for example oil, milk or egg, on sth using a brush （用刷子）抹，涂： **~ A with B** *Brush the pastry with beaten egg.* 用刷子把打匀的鸡蛋抹在油酥面团上。 ◇ **~ B over, on, etc. A** *Brush beaten egg over the pastry.* 用刷子把打匀的鸡蛋抹在油酥面团上。 **3** [T] **~ sth + adv./prep.** to remove sth from a surface with a brush or with your hand （用刷子或手）拂，掸，擦掉： *He brushed the dirt off his jacket.* 他拂掉衣服上的灰尘。 ◇ *She brushed the fly away.* 她挥手赶走了苍蝇。 **4** [I, T] to touch sb/sth lightly while moving close to them/it 轻擦，掠过（某人／某物）： **~ against/by/past sb/sth** *She brushed past him.* 她和他擦肩而过。 ◇ *His hand accidentally brushed against hers.* 他的手无意之中碰了一下她的手。 ◇ **~ sth** *The leaves brushed her cheek.* 叶子轻拂着她的面颊。 ◇ **~ sth with sth** *He brushed her lips with his.* 他轻轻地吻了一下她的嘴唇。

PHR V **ˌbrush sb/sth↔aˈside** to ignore sb/sth; to treat sb/sth as unimportant 不理会某人／某物；漠视 SYN dismiss: *He brushed aside my fears.* 他不理会我的恐惧。 **ˌbrush sb/yourself ˈdown** (*BrE*) = BRUSH SB/YOURSELF OFF **ˌbrush sth↔ˈdown** to clean sth by brushing it 刷干净： *to brush a coat/horse down* 把外套／马刷干净 **ˌbrush ˈoff** to be removed by brushing 被刷掉；被拂去： *Mud brushes off easily when it is dry.* 泥巴干了容易刷掉。 **ˌbrush sb↔ˈoff** to rudely ignore sb or refuse to listen to them 不理睬某人；打发： *She brushed him off impatiently.* 她不耐烦地把他打发走了。 ➲ RELATED NOUN BRUSH-OFF **ˌbrush sb/yourself ˈoff** (*BrE* **ˌbrush**

sb/yourself 'down) to make sb/yourself tidy, especially after you have fallen, by brushing your clothes, etc. with your hands 掸净某人 / 自己，拂去衣服上的灰尘（尤指跌倒后） **,brush sth↔'up | ,brush 'up on sth** to quickly improve a skill, especially when you have not used it for a time 快速提高；重温（生疏了的技术等）：*I must brush up on my Spanish before I go to Seville.* 我去塞维利亚之前一定得好好温习我的西班牙语。

'brush-off *noun* [sing.] (*informal*) rude or unfriendly behaviour that shows that a person is not interested in sb 漠视；不理睬：*Paul asked Tara out to dinner but she gave him the* ***brush-off***. 保罗邀请塔拉外出吃饭，但遭到拒绝。

brush·wood /ˈbrʌʃwʊd/ *noun* [U] small broken or dead branches of trees, often used to make fires （常指当柴火用的）断树枝，枯树枝

brush·work /ˈbrʌʃwɜːk; *NAmE* -wɜːrk/ *noun* [U] the particular way in which an artist uses a brush to paint （画家的）笔触，画法 ➲ COLLOCATIONS AT ART

brusque /bruːsk; brʊsk; *NAmE* brʌsk/ *adj.* using very few words and sounding rude 寡言而无礼的 SYN **abrupt, curt**: *The doctor spoke in a brusque tone.* 医生不客气地简单说了几个字。 ▶ **brusque·ly** *adv.*: *'What's your name?' he asked brusquely.* "你叫什么名字？"他唐突地问道。 **brusque·ness** *noun* [U]

Brus·sels sprout /ˌbrʌslz ˈspraʊt/ (*also* **Brussel sprout, sprout**) *noun* a small round green vegetable like a very small CABBAGE 汤菜；抱子甘蓝 ➲ VISUAL VOCAB PAGE V33

bru·tal /ˈbruːtl/ *adj.* **1** violent and cruel 残暴的；兽性的：*a brutal attack/murder/rape/killing* 野蛮的攻击 / 谋杀 / 强奸 / 杀害 **2** direct and clear about sth unpleasant; not thinking of people's feelings 直截了当的；冷酷的：*With brutal honesty she told him she did not love him.* 她冷酷地直接告诉他，她不爱他。 ▶ **bru·tal·ity** /bruːˈtæləti/ *noun* [U, C] (*pl.* **-ies**): *police brutality* 警察的粗暴 ◇ *the brutalities of war* 战争的残酷 **bru·tal·ly** /-təli/ *adv.*: *He was brutally assaulted.* 他遭到毒打。 ◇ *Let me be brutally frank about this.* 让我把这件事无情地挑明说吧。

bru·tal·ism /ˈbruːtəlɪzəm/ *noun* [U] (*architecture* 建, *sometimes disapproving*) a style of architecture used especially in the 1950s and 60s which uses large concrete blocks, steel, etc., and is sometimes considered ugly and unpleasant 粗野主义，野性主义，粗犷主义（尤见于 20 世纪 50 和 60 年代的建筑风格，采用大块混凝土板、钢筋等，有时被认为粗陋欠雅） ▶ **bru·tal·ist** /ˈbruːtəlɪst/ *adj., noun*

bru·tal·ize (*BrE also* **-ise**) /ˈbruːtəlaɪz/ *verb* **1** [usually passive] **~ sb** to make sb unable to feel normal human emotions such as pity 使丧失人类情感；使变残忍：*soldiers brutalized by war* 在战争中变得残酷无情的士兵 **2 ~ sb** to treat sb in a cruel or violent way 残酷对待

brute /bruːt/ *noun, adj.*

■ ***noun*** **1** (*sometimes humorous*) a man who treats people in an unkind, cruel way 残酷的人；暴君：*His father was a drunken brute.* 他父亲是个蛮横的醉鬼。 ◇ *You've forgotten my birthday again, you brute!* 你又忘了我的生日了，你这个没良心的！ **2** a large strong animal 大野兽；牲畜 **3** a thing which is awkward and unpleasant 笨重难看的东西；麻烦事

■ ***adj.*** [only before noun] **1** involving physical strength only and not thought or intelligence 蛮干不动脑筋的：*brute force/strength* 暴力；蛮劲 **2** basic and unpleasant 根本而令人不快的；赤裸裸的：*the brute facts of inequality* 赤裸裸的不平等事实

bru·tish /ˈbruːtɪʃ/ *adj.* unkind and violent and not showing thought or intelligence 残忍的；粗野的；蛮横的 ▶ **bru·tish·ness** *noun* [U]

BS[1] (*NAmE also* **B.S.**) /ˌbiː ˈes/ *abbr.* **1** (*NAmE*) = BSc **2** (*BrE*) Bachelor of Surgery (a university degree in medicine) 外科学士（大学医学学位）

BS[2] /ˌbiː ˈes/ *abbr.* **1** British Standard (used on labels, etc. showing a number given by the British Standards Institution which controls the quality of products) 英国标准（写在商品标签上，表明英国标准协会的规格编号）：*produced to BS4353* 按英国标准规格编号 4353 生产的 **2** (*US, taboo, slang*) BULLSHIT 胡说；狗屁：*That guy's full of BS.* 那家伙满嘴喷粪。

BSc /ˌbiː es ˈsiː/ (*BrE*) (*NAmE* **B.S.**, **BS**) *noun* the abbreviation for 'Bachelor of Science' (a first university degree in science) 理学士（全写为 Bachelor of Science，大学理科初级学位）：(*BrE*) *to be/have/do a BSc in Zoology* 是 / 有 / 攻读动物学理学士（学位） ◇ (*BrE*) *Jill Ayres BSc* 理学士吉尔·艾尔斯

BSE /ˌbiː es ˈiː/ (*also informal* **,mad 'cow disease**) *noun* [U] the abbreviation for 'bovine spongiform encephalopathy' (a brain disease of cows that causes death) 牛海绵状脑病，疯牛病（全写为 bovine spongiform encephalopathy，导致牛死亡的脑病）

BSI /ˌbiː es ˈaɪ/ *abbr.* the British Standards Institution (the organization that decides the standard sizes for goods produced in Britain, and tests the safety of electrical goods, children's toys, etc.) 英国标准协会（负责制定英国国内产品的规格标准并对电器商品、儿童玩具等进行安全检测）

'B-side *noun* the side of a pop record that was considered less likely to be successful （流行唱片的）B 面（常收录非主打歌曲） ➲ COMPARE A-SIDE

BST /ˌbiː es ˈtiː/ *abbr.* BRITISH SUMMER TIME 英国夏令时间（全写为 British Summer Time）

BTEC /ˈbiːtek/ *noun* used to refer to any of a large group of British qualifications that can be taken in many different subjects at several levels (the abbreviation for 'Business and Technology Education Council') 商业与技术教育委员会（全写为 Business and Technology Education Council，BTEC 在英国代表多个学科的不同程度资格）：*a BTEC Higher National Diploma in Public Service Studies* * BTEC 公共服务科高等国家证书

BTW *abbr.* used in writing to mean 'by the way' （书写形式）顺便提一句

bub·ble 🔑 /ˈbʌbl/ *noun, verb*

■ ***noun*** **1** 🔑 a ball of air or gas in a liquid, or a ball of air inside a solid substance such as glass 泡；气泡：*champagne bubbles* 香槟酒的泡沫 ◇ *a bubble of oxygen* 氧气泡 ◇ *blowing bubbles into water through a straw* 用吸管在水里吹泡泡 ➲ PICTURE AT FROTH ➲ SEE ALSO SPEECH BUBBLE **2** 🔑 a round ball of liquid, containing air, produced by soap and water 肥皂泡：*The children like to have bubbles in their bath.* 孩子们喜欢浴盆里有肥皂泡。 **3** a small amount of a feeling that sb wants to express （欲表达的）一点感情：*a* ***bubble of laughter/hope/enthusiasm*** 一点笑声 / 希望 / 热心 **4** a good or lucky situation that is unlikely to last long （很可能持续不长的）好景，好运；泡沫：*Economists warned of a stock-market bubble.* 经济学家警告说股市有泡沫。

IDM **the bubble 'bursts** there is a sudden end to a good or lucky situation （好事或好运）突然告吹，成为泡影；泡沫破灭：*When the bubble finally burst, hundreds of people lost their jobs.* 当泡沫最终破灭时，有几百人丢了饭碗。 ➲ MORE AT BURST *v.*

■ ***verb*** **1** [I] to form bubbles 起泡；冒泡：*The water in the pan was beginning to bubble.* 锅里的水开始冒泡。 ◇ *Add the white wine and let it* ***bubble up***. 加入白葡萄酒，让它产生泡沫。 **2** [I] (+ **adv./prep.**) to make a bubbling sound, especially when moving in the direction mentioned （移动时）发出冒泡的声音：*I could hear the soup bubbling away.* 我能听到汤在咕嘟咕嘟地响。 ◇ *A stream came bubbling between the stones.* 一条小溪沿着石缝汩汩地流过来。 **3** [I] **~ (over) with sth** to be full of a particular feeling 洋溢着（某种感情）：*She was bubbling over with excitement.* 她兴奋不已。 **4** [I] **+ adv./prep.** (of a feeling 感情) to be felt strongly by a person; to be present in a situation 被强烈感受；充溢；存在：*Laughter bubbled up inside him.* 他忍不住心中窃笑。◇ *the anger that bubbled beneath the surface* 内心潜涌着的愤怒

PHR V ˌ**bubble ˈunder** (*especially BrE*) (*NAmE usually* ˌ**bubble under the ˈradar**) (*informal*) to be likely to be very successful or popular soon 即将成功；快要出名：*Here are two records that are bubbling under.* 这两张唱片将会走红。

ˌ**bubble and ˈsqueak** *noun* [U] a type of British food made from cold cooked potatoes and CABBAGE that are mixed together and fried 卷心菜煎土豆（英国菜）

ˈ**bubble bath** *noun* **1** [U] a liquid soap that smells pleasant and makes a lot of bubbles when it is added to bath water 泡沫浴液 **2** [C] a bath with bubble bath in the water 泡沫浴

bubble·gum /ˈbʌblɡʌm/ *noun, adj.*
■ *noun* [U] a type of CHEWING GUM that can be blown into bubbles 泡泡糖
■ *adj.* [only before noun] simple in style, not serious and liked mainly by young people "泡泡糖"的（简单随意，主要为年轻人所喜欢）：*This album is pure bubblegum pop.* 这张专辑纯粹是"泡泡糖"流行音乐。

bubble·jet printer /ˈbʌbldʒet prɪntə(r)/ *noun* a type of printer that uses bubbles of air to blow small dots of ink in order to form letters, numbers, etc. on paper 喷墨打印机

ˈ**bubble pack** *noun* = BLISTER PACK

bubble ˈtea *noun* [U, C] a drink from East Asia made from cold tea mixed with milk, FLAVOURINGS, etc., which also contains small sweet balls that look like bubbles and are made from TAPIOCA 珍珠奶茶

ˈ**bubble wrap** (*NAmE* ˈ**BubbleWrap™**) *noun* [U] a sheet of plastic which has lots of small raised parts filled with air, used for protecting things that are being carried or sent by post/mail 气泡膜包装；泡塑包装； 气泡垫

bubb·ly /ˈbʌbli/ *adj.* (**bub·blier, bub·bli·est**) *noun*
■ *adj.* **1** full of bubbles 充满气泡的；多泡沫的 **2** (*informal*) (of a person 人) always cheerful, friendly and enthusiastic 快活热情的
■ *noun* [U] (*informal*) = CHAMPAGNE

bu·bon·ic plague /bjuːˌbɒnɪk ˈpleɪɡ; *NAmE* -ˌbɑːnɪk/ (*also* **the plague**) *noun* [U] a disease spread by RATS that causes fever, swellings on the body and usually death 腺鼠疫

buc·can·eer /ˌbʌkəˈnɪə(r); *NAmE* -ˈnɪr/ *noun* **1** (in the past) a sailor who attacked ships at sea and stole from them （旧时）海盗 **SYN** **pirate** **2** (especially in business 尤指商业) a person who achieves success in a skilful but not always honest way 投机取巧者

bucc·an·eer·ing /ˌbʌkəˈnɪərɪŋ; *NAmE* -ˈnɪrɪŋ/ *adj.* enjoying taking risks, especially in business 爱冒险的，大胆的（尤指经商方面）：*Virgin's buccaneering founder, Richard Branson* 维珍公司富有冒险精神的创始人理查德·布兰森

buck /bʌk/ *noun, verb*
■ *noun* **1** [C] (*informal*) a US, an Australian or a New Zealand dollar; a South African RAND; an Indian RUPEE （一）美元；（一）澳元；（一）新西兰元；（一）南非兰特；（一）印度卢比：*They cost ten bucks.* 这些值十元钱。◇ *We're talking* ***big bucks*** (= a lot of money) *here.* 我们这当儿谈的可是大买卖。**2** [C] a male DEER, HARE or RABBIT (also called a **buck rabbit**) 雄鹿；公兔 ➲ COMPARE DOE, HART, STAG **3** [C] (*pl.* **buck**) (*SAfrE*) a DEER, whether male or female 鹿（不论雌雄）：*a herd of buck* 一群鹿 **4** [C] (*old-fashioned, informal*) a young man 小伙子 **5 the buck** [sing.] used in some expressions to refer to the responsibility or blame for sth （用于某些表达方式）责任，过失：*It was my decision.* ***The buck stops here*** (= nobody else can be blamed). 那是我的决定，不要追究别人了。◇ *I was tempted to* ***pass the buck*** (= make sb else responsible). 我很想把责任推给别人。 **ORIGIN** From **buck**, an object which in a poker game is placed in front of the player whose turn it is to deal. 源自 buck（培克），扑克牌游戏中的庄家标志。

IDM **make a fast/quick buck** (*informal, often disapproving*) to earn money quickly and easily 轻易地赚钱 ➲ MORE AT BANG *n.*, MILLION
■ *verb* **1** [I] (of a horse 马) to jump with the two back feet or all four feet off the ground 尥起后蹄跳跃；弓背四蹄跳起 **2** [I] to move up and down suddenly or in a way that is not controlled 猛然震荡；猛烈颠簸：*The boat bucked and heaved beneath them.* 小船在他们脚下猛烈颠簸着。 **3** [T] ~ **sth** (*informal*) to resist or oppose sth 抵制；反抗：*One or two companies have managed to* ***buck the trend*** *of the recession.* 有一两家公司顶住了经济滑坡的势头。◇ *He admired her willingness to* ***buck the system*** (= oppose authority or rules). 他赞赏她反抗现存体制的主动性。

IDM **buck your iˈdeas up** (*BrE, informal*) to start behaving in a more acceptable way, so that work gets done better, etc. 振作起来

PHR V ˌ**buck ˈup** (*informal*) **1** (often in orders 常用于命令) to become more cheerful 振作 **SYN** **cheer up**：*Buck up, kid! It's not the end of the game.* 年轻人，振作起来！比赛还未结束呢。 **2 buck up!** (*old-fashioned*) used to tell sb to hurry 快点；赶快 **SYN** **hurry** ˌ**buck sb ˈup** (*BrE, informal*) to make sb more cheerful 使某人振作 **SYN** **cheer up**：*The good news bucked us all up.* 好消息使我们全都为之振奋。

bucket /ˈbʌkɪt/ *noun, verb*
■ *noun* **1** (*NAmE also* **pail**) [C] an open container with a handle, used for carrying or holding liquids, sand, etc. （有提梁的）桶：*a plastic bucket* 塑料桶 ◇ (*BrE*) *They were playing on the beach with their* ***buckets and spades.*** 他们带着桶和铲子在沙滩上玩。 ➲ VISUAL VOCAB PAGE V21 **2** [C] a large container that is part of a CRANE or DIGGER and is used for lifting things 吊桶；水斗；（挖掘机的）铲斗 **3** (*also* **bucket·ful** /-fʊl/) (*NAmE also* **pail, pail·ful**) [C] the amount contained in a bucket 一桶（的量）：*two buckets/bucketfuls of water* 两桶水 ◇ *They used to drink tea* ***by the bucket/bucketful*** (= in large quantities). 他们过去喝很多茶。 **4 buckets** [pl.] (*informal*) a large amount 大量：*To succeed in show business, you need buckets of confidence.* 要想在演艺界干出名堂，就得有十足的信心。 ◇ *We* ***wept buckets.*** 我们泪如泉涌。 ◇ *He was* ***sweating buckets*** *by the end of the race.* 跑到终点时他汗流浃背。 ◇ *The rain was coming down* ***in buckets*** (= it was raining very heavily). 下着瓢泼大雨。 **IDM** SEE DROP *n.*, KICK *v.*
■ *verb*

PHR V ˈ**bucket down** (*BrE, informal*) to rain heavily 下大雨 **SYN** **pour**：*It's bucketing down.* 大雨倾盆。

ˈ**bucket list** *noun* a list of things that you want to do before you die 人生愿望清单：*Travelling to India has been on my bucket list for years.* 去印度旅行多年来一直是我的人生愿望之一。

ˈ**bucket seat** *noun* a seat with a curved back for one person, especially in a car （尤指汽车上的）凹背单人座位

buck·eye /ˈbʌkaɪ/ *noun* **1** a N American tree that has bright red or white flowers and produces nuts 鹿眼树，七叶树（产于北美洲） **2** an orange and brown BUTTERFLY with large spots on its wings that look like eyes （橙棕杂色的）眼形斑翅蝴蝶 **3 Buckeye** (*US, informal*) a person from the US state of Ohio 俄亥俄州人

ˌ**Buck ˈHouse** *noun* (*BrE, often ironic*) an informal name for Buckingham Palace 巴克宫（白金汉宫的俗称）：*We stayed at Tom's place. It isn't exactly Buck House, but it's comfortable enough.* 我们待在汤姆那里。那并不是白金汉宫，但足够舒适了。

Buck·ing·ham Pal·ace /ˌbʌkɪŋəm ˈpæləs/ *noun* **1** the official home of the British royal family in London 白金汉宫（在伦敦的英国王室宫邸） **2** the British royal family or the people who advise them 英国王室；英国王室幕僚：*Buckingham Palace refused to comment.* 英国王室拒绝发表评论。

B

buckle /ˈbʌkl/ *verb, noun*
■ *verb* **1** [T, I] to fasten sth or be fastened with a buckle （使）搭扣扣住： **~ (sth)** *She buckled her belt.* 她扣上了腰带。◇ **~ (sth on/up)** *He buckled on his sword.* 他把剑扣好。◇ *These shoes buckle at the side.* 这双鞋从侧边系带。 **2** [I, T] to become crushed or bent under a weight or force; to crush or bend sth in this way （被）压垮，压弯： *The steel frames began to buckle under the strain.* 钢架在重压下开始变形。 ◇ (*figurative*) *A weaker man would have buckled under the pressure.* 意志薄弱的人在这种压力下可能就垮了。◇ **~ sth** *The crash buckled the front of my car.* 我的汽车前部被撞扁了。 **3** [I] when your knees or legs **buckle** or when you **buckle** at the knees, your knees become weak and you start to fall 双腿发软
PHR V ˌ**buckle ˈdown (to sth)** (*informal*) to start to do sth seriously 开始认真做；努力干： *I'd better buckle down to those reports.* 我最好认真静下来努力完成那些报告。 ˌ**buckle ˈup** (*NAmE*) (*BrE* ˌ**belt ˈup**) (*informal*) to fasten your SEAT BELT (= a belt worn by a passenger in a vehicle) 系上安全带
■ *noun* a piece of metal or plastic used for joining the ends of a belt or for fastening a part of a bag, shoe, etc. （皮带等的）搭扣，锁扣 ➲ VISUAL VOCAB PAGES V68, V69

Buck·ley's /ˈbʌkliz/ *noun*
IDM **not have Buckley's (chance)** (*AustralE, NZE, informal*) used to suggest that sb has little or no hope of achieving a particular aim 希望（或机会）渺茫

buck ˈnaked *adj.* (*NAmE, informal*) (of a person 人) not wearing any clothes at all 一丝不挂的；赤裸裸的

buck·ram /ˈbʌkrəm/ *noun* [U] a type of stiff cloth made especially from cotton or LINEN, used in the past for covering books and for making clothes stiffer （旧时用作书皮或衣服衬里的）硬棉布，硬麻布，硬衬布

ˌ**Buck's ˈFizz** (*BrE*) (*NAmE* **mi·mosa**) *noun* [U, C] an alcoholic drink made by mixing SPARKLING white wine (= with bubbles) with orange juice 巴克泡腾酒（发泡白葡萄酒与橙汁混合而成）

buck·shot /ˈbʌkʃɒt; *NAmE* -ʃɑːt/ *noun* [U] balls of LEAD² that are fired from a SHOTGUN （猎枪用的）铅弹

buck·skin /ˈbʌkskɪn/ *noun* [U] soft leather made from the skin of DEER or GOATS, used for making gloves, bags, etc. 鹿皮革；羊皮革

ˌ**buck ˈteeth** *noun* [pl.] top teeth that stick forward 龅牙 ▸ ˌ**buck-ˈtoothed** *adj.*

buck·wheat /ˈbʌkwiːt/ *noun* [U] small dark seed that is grown as food for animals and for making flour 荞麦

bu·col·ic /bjuːˈkɒlɪk; *NAmE* -ˈkɑːlɪk/ *adj.* (*literary*) connected with the countryside or country life 乡村的；乡村生活的；田园的

bud /bʌd/ *noun, verb*
■ *noun* **1** a small lump that grows on a plant and from which a flower, leaf or STEM develops 芽；苞；花蕾： *the first buds appearing in spring* 春天的初芽 ◇ *The tree is* **in bud** *already.* 树已发芽。 ➲ COLLOCATIONS AT LIFE ➲ VISUAL VOCAB PAGE V10 **2** a flower or leaf that is not fully open 半开的花；未长大的叶 ➲ VISUAL VOCAB PAGE V11 **3** (*NAmE, informal*) = BUDDY： *Listen, bud, enough of the wisecracks, OK?* 听着，老兄，别再说俏皮话了行不行？ ➲ SEE ALSO COTTON BUD, ROSEBUD, TASTE BUD IDM SEE NIP *v.*
■ *verb* [I] to produce buds 发芽

Bud·dha /ˈbʊdə/ *noun* **1** (*also* **the Buddha**) [sing.] the person on whose teachings the Buddhist religion is based 佛陀（佛教创始人） **2** [C] a statue or picture of the Buddha 佛像 **3** [C] a person who has achieved ENLIGHTENMENT (= spiritual knowledge) in Buddhism 佛，觉者（佛教中觉行圆满的人）

Bud·dhism /ˈbʊdɪzəm/ *noun* [U] an Asian religion based on the teaching of Siddhartha Gautama (or Buddha) 佛教 ▸ **Bud·dhist** /ˈbʊdɪst/ *noun*： *a devout Buddhist* 虔诚的佛教徒 **Bud·dhist** /ˈbʊdɪst/ *adj.* [usually before noun]： *a* **Buddhist monk/temple** 佛教僧侣 / 寺庙

bud·ding /ˈbʌdɪŋ/ *adj.* [only before noun] beginning to develop or become successful 开始发展的；崭露头角的： *a* **budding artist/writer** 一位艺术界 / 文坛新秀 ◇ *our budding romance* 我们刚刚发展起来的恋爱关系

bud·dleia /ˈbʌdliə/ *noun* [C, U] a bush with purple or white flowers that grow in groups 醉鱼草

buddy /ˈbʌdi/ *noun, verb*
■ *noun* (*pl.* **-ies**) **1** (*NAmE also* **bud**) (*informal*) a friend 朋友；同伴： *an old college buddy of mine* 我的一位老校友 ➲ WORDFINDER NOTE AT FRIEND **2** (*also* **bud**) (*both NAmE, informal*) used to speak to a man you do not know （称呼不认识的男子）老兄，喂： *'Where to, buddy?' the driver asked.* "去哪儿，老兄？"司机问道。 **3** (*especially NAmE*) a partner who does an activity with you so that you can help each other 搭档；伙伴： *The school uses a* **buddy system** *to pair newcomers with older students.* 学校采用结伴制让每个新生跟一较大的学生结伴以获得照顾。
■ *verb* (**bud·dies, buddy·ing, bud·died, bud·died**)
PHR V ˌ**buddy ˈup (to/with sb)** (*NAmE*) **1** (*BrE* ˌ**pal ˈup (with sb)**) (*informal*) to become friendly with sb 成为（某人的）朋友： *You and your neighbour might want to buddy up to make the trip more enjoyable.* 你同你的邻居或许应该结伴旅游，热闹一点。 **2** to become friendly with sb in order to get an advantage for yourself （为谋私利）亲近（某人），（和某人）结交

ˈ**buddy movie** *noun* (*informal*) a film/movie in which there is a close friendship between two people 伙伴电影（两角色之间关系密切）

budge /bʌdʒ/ *verb* (usually used in negative sentences 通常用于否定句) (*rather informal*) **1** [I, T] to move slightly; to make sth/sb move slightly （使）轻微移动，挪动： *She pushed at the door but it wouldn't budge.* 她推了推门，门却一动不动。◇ *The dog refused to budge.* 狗不肯动弹。◇ **~ sth** *I heaved with all my might but still couldn't budge it.* 我用尽全力也没把它拽动。 **2** [I, T] to change your opinion about sth; to make sb change their opinion （使）改变主意，改变观点： *He* **won't budge an inch** *on the issue.* 在这一点上他丝毫不肯让步。◇ **~ sb** *He was not to be budged on the issue.* 在这一点上他不会让步。
PHR V ˌ**budge ˈup** (*BrE, informal*) to move, so that there is room for other people 让开；挪开 SYN **move over**： *Budge up a bit!* 闪开点！

budg·eri·gar /ˈbʌdʒərigɑː(r)/ *noun* (*also informal* **budgie**) a small bird of the PARROT family, often kept in a CAGE as a pet 虎皮鹦鹉

budget /ˈbʌdʒɪt/ *noun, verb, adj.*
■ *noun* **1** [C, U] the money that is available to a person or an organization and a plan of how it will be spent over a period of time 预算： *a* **monthly/an annual/a family budget** 每月 / 年度 / 家庭预算 ◇ *the* **education/defence budget** (= the amount of money that can be spent on this) 教育 / 国防预算 ◇ *an advertising budget of $2 million* 预计 200 万美元的广告费 ◇ *a big-budget movie* 一部巨额预算的电影 ◇ *We decorated the house* **on a tight budget** (= without much money to spend). 我们俭省地装修了房子。◇ *The work was finished on time and* **within budget** (= did not cost more money than was planned). 工作按时完成且未超出预算。 ◇ *They went* **over budget** (= spent too much money). 他们超出了预算。◇ *budget cuts* 预算削减 ➲ COLLOCATIONS AT BUSINESS, FINANCE **2** (*BrE also* **Budget**) [C, usually sing.] an official statement by the government of a country's income from taxes, etc. and how it will be spent 政府的年度预算： *tax cuts in this year's budget* 本年度政府预算中的税收削减 ◇ *a budget deficit* (= when the government spends more money than it earns) 政府预算赤字 ➲ COLLOCATIONS AT ECONOMY
■ *verb* [I, T] to be careful about the amount of money you spend; to plan to spend an amount of money for a particular purpose 谨慎花钱；把…编入预算： *If we budget carefully we'll be able to afford the trip.* 我们精打细算一点，就能够负担这次旅行。◇ **~ for sth** *I've budgeted for two new members of staff.* 我已经把两名新职员名额编入预算。

◇ ~ sth (for sth) *Ten million francs has been budgeted for the project.* 为该工程已编制了一千万法郎的预算。 ◇ ~ sth (at sth) *The project has been budgeted at ten million francs.* 该工程已制订一千万法郎的预算。 ➲ SYNONYMS AT SAVE ▶ **budget·ing** *noun* [U]

■ ***adj.*** [only before noun] (used in advertising, etc. 用于广告等) low in price 价格低廉的；花钱少的： *a* ***budget flight/hotel*** 便宜的航班 / 旅馆 ➲ SYNONYMS AT CHEAP

'budget account *noun* (*BrE*) an arrangement with a shop/store or company to pay your bills in fixed regular amounts and not as one large payment 预算账户（作定期付账之用）

budget·ary /ˈbʌdʒɪtəri; *NAmE* -teri/ *adj.* connected with a budget 预算的： ***budgetary control/policies/reform*** 预算控制 / 政策 / 改革 ➲ SYNONYMS AT ECONOMIC

budgie /ˈbʌdʒi/ *noun* (*informal*) = BUDGERIGAR

buff /bʌf/ *noun, adj., verb*

■ ***noun*** **1** [C] (used in compounds 用于构成复合词) a person who is very interested in a particular subject or activity and knows a lot about it 爱好者；行家里手： *an opera buff* 歌剧爱好者 **2** [U] a pale yellow-brown colour 浅黄褐色 SYN **beige** **3** [U] soft strong yellowish-brown leather 坚韧的黄褐色软皮革 ➲ SEE ALSO BLIND MAN'S BUFF

IDM **in the 'buff** (*informal*) wearing no clothes 一丝不挂；赤裸 SYN **naked**

■ ***adj.*** **1** pale yellow-brown in colour 浅黄褐色的 SYN **beige**： *a buff envelope* 浅黄褐色信封 **2** (*slang*) physically fit and attractive with big muscles 健美（或健壮）而肌肉发达的

■ ***verb*** ~ sth (up) to polish sth with a soft cloth 用软布擦亮

PHR V **,buff 'up | ,buff yourself 'up** (*slang*) to make yourself more attractive, especially by exercising in order to make your muscles bigger 练健美；使更健美： *He buffed up to take the role of the commando captain.* 他为饰演这个突击队队长的角色练出了一身肌肉。 **,buff sb/sth 'up** (*informal*) to work on sb/sth to make them/it seem more attractive or impressive 提升…的形象： *The team will have to buff up their tarnished image.* 这支队伍必须改善其受损的形象。

buf·falo /ˈbʌfələʊ; *NAmE* -loʊ/ *noun* (*pl.* **buf·falo** or **buf·faloes**) **1** a large animal of the cow family. There are two types of buffalo, the African and the Asian, which has wide, curved horns. 水牛（分非洲水牛和亚洲水牛两种） ➲ SEE ALSO WATER BUFFALO **2** = BISON

buf·fer /ˈbʌfə(r)/ *noun, verb*

■ ***noun*** **1** a thing or person that reduces a shock or protects sb/sth against difficulties 缓冲物；起缓冲作用的人： ~ (**against sth**) *Support from family and friends acts as a buffer against stress.* 家庭和朋友的支持有助于减缓压力。 ◇ ~ (**between sth and sth**) *She often had to act as a buffer between father and son.* 她常常不得不在父子之间扮演调解人角色。 ◇ *a* ***buffer state*** (= a small country between two powerful states that helps keep peace between them) 缓冲国（两大国之间有助于维持和平的小国家） ◇ *a* ***buffer zone*** (= an area of land between two opposing armies or countries) 缓冲区（两敌对军队或国家之间的地区） **2** (*BrE*) one of two round metal devices on the front or end of a train, or at the end of a railway/railroad track, that reduce the shock if the train hits sth （火车头尾或轨道末端的）减震器，缓冲器 **3** (*computing* 计) an area in a computer's memory where data can be stored for a short time 缓存区；缓冲存储区；缓冲器 **4** (*also* **old 'buffer**) (*old-fashioned, BrE*) a silly old man 愚蠢老头 IDM SEE HIT *v.*

■ ***verb*** **1** ~ sth to reduce the harmful effects of sth 减少，减缓（伤害）： *to buffer the effects of stress on health* 减少压力对健康的影响 **2** ~ sb (**against sth**) to protect sb from sth 保护；使不受…的侵害： *They tried to buffer themselves against problems and uncertainties.* 他们尽力保护自己免受困难和不确定因素的影响。 **3** ~ sth (*computing* 计) (of a computer 计算机) to hold data for a short time before using it 缓冲存储；缓存

buf·fet¹ /ˈbʊfeɪ; ˈbʌfeɪ; *NAmE* bəˈfeɪ/ *noun* ➲ SEE ALSO BUFFET² **1** a meal at which people serve themselves from a table and then stand or sit somewhere else to eat 自助餐： *a* ***buffet lunch/supper*** 自助午餐 / 晚餐 ◇ *Dinner will be a cold buffet, not a sit-down meal.* 主餐是自助冷食，不是坐着等服务员送来的那种。 **2** a place, for example in a train or bus station, where you can buy food and drinks to eat or drink there, or to take away （火车）饮食柜台；（车站）快餐部 **3** (*BrE*) = BUFFET CAR **4** (*especially NAmE*) = SIDEBOARD

buf·fet² /ˈbʌfɪt/ *verb* ➲ SEE ALSO BUFFET¹ [often passive] ~ **sb/sth** to knock or push sb/sth roughly from side to side 打来打去；推来搡去： *to be buffeted by the wind* 被风吹得左右摇摆 ◇ (*figurative, formal*) *The nation had been buffeted by a wave of strikes.* 罢工浪潮使这个国家受到了重创。 ➲ WORDFINDER NOTE AT WIND¹ ▶ **buf·fet·ing** *noun* [U, C, usually sing.]

buffet car /ˈbʊfeɪ kɑː(r); ˈbʌfeɪ; *NAmE* bəˈfeɪ/ (*also* **buffet**) *noun* (*BrE*) the part of a train where you can buy sth to eat and drink （火车）餐车 ➲ WORDFINDER NOTE AT TRAIN

buf·foon /bəˈfuːn/ *noun* (*old-fashioned*) a person who does silly but amusing things 小丑；滑稽可笑的人 ▶ **buf·foon·ery** /-əri/ *noun* [U]

bug /bʌɡ/ *noun, verb*

■ ***noun*** **1** [C] (*especially NAmE*) any small insect 小昆虫；虫子 **2** [C] (*informal*) an infectious illness that is usually fairly mild 轻微的传染病；小病： *a flu bug* 流感 ◇ *There's a stomach* ***bug going round*** (= people are catching it from each other). 现在流行一种肠胃传染病。 ◇ *I picked up a bug in the office.* 我在办公室被传染了疾病。 ➲ SYNONYMS AT DISEASE ➲ COLLOCATIONS AT ILL **3** (*usually* **the ... bug**) [sing.] (*informal*) an enthusiastic interest in sth such as a sport or a hobby 热衷；着迷： *the travel bug* 旅游狂热 ◇ *She was never interested in fitness before but now* ***she's been bitten by the bug.*** 她以前从来不在乎健身，现在她却着了迷。 **4** [C] (*informal*) a small hidden device for listening to other people's conversations 窃听器 **5** [C] a fault in a machine, especially in a computer system or program （机器，尤指计算机的）故障，程序错误，缺陷；隐错

■ ***verb*** (**-gg-**) **1** ~ **sth** to put a special device (= a bug) somewhere in order to listen secretly to other people's conversations 在（某处）装窃听器；窃听（谈话）： *They bugged her hotel room.* 他们在她的旅馆房间里装了窃听器。 ◇ *They were bugging his telephone conversations.* 他们在窃听他的电话交谈。 ◇ *a* ***bugging device*** 窃听器 **2** ~ **sb** (*informal*) to annoy or irritate sb 使烦恼；使恼怒： *Stop bugging me!* 别烦我了！ ◇ *It's something that's been bugging me a lot recently.* 那事使我最近一直大伤脑筋。 ➲ MORE LIKE THIS 36, page R29

IDM **,bug the 'hell/'crap/'shit out of sb** (*taboo, slang*) to annoy sb very much 使十分烦恼；使恼怒： *The song just bugs the hell out of me.* 这首歌真他妈的烦死我了。

PHR V **bug 'off!** (*NAmE, informal*) a rude way of telling sb to go away 滚开 **,bug 'out** (*informal*) **1** (*NAmE*) (especially of sb's eyes) to be wide open and stick out （尤指眼睛）瞪圆了： *Their eyes were bugging out of their heads when they saw it.* 他们看到它时眼珠都要瞪掉了。 **2** (*NAmE, AustralE*) to leave a place or situation, especially because it is becoming dangerous （尤指危险来临之时）撤离，逃生： *We should bug out now before it's too late.* 我们现在就应该撤离，以免为时太晚。 **3** (*NAmE*) to become too frightened to do sth 惊呆了： *Susan started to bug out when she heard a noise in the bushes.* 苏珊听到灌木丛中的声音时吓呆了。

bug·a·boo /ˈbʌɡəbuː/ *noun* (*NAmE, informal*) a thing that people are afraid of 恐怖的东西

bug·bear /ˈbʌɡbeə(r); *NAmE* -ber/ *noun* (*especially BrE*) a thing that annoys people and that they worry about 使人烦恼担忧的事；牵挂： *Inflation is the government's main bugbear.* 通货膨胀是政府最头痛的问题。

'bug-eyed *adj.* (*informal*) having eyes that stick out 眼睛凸出的

bug·ger /ˈbʌɡə(r)/ *noun, verb*

■ ***noun*** (*BrE, taboo, slang*) **1** an offensive word used to insult sb, especially a man, and to show anger or dislike（侮辱性称呼，尤用于男子）家伙；浑蛋；坏蛋：*Come here, you little bugger!* 过来，你这个小浑蛋！◇ *You stupid bugger! You could have run me over!* 蠢货！你差点儿碾死我！ **2** used to refer to a person, especially a man, that you like or feel sympathy for （表示亲昵或同情，尤用于男子）小伙子；老头儿；汉子：*Poor bugger! His wife left him last week.* 可怜的家伙！他妻子上周离开了他。◇ *He's a tough old bugger.* 他是个铁汉子。 **3** [usually sing.] a thing that is difficult or causes problems 难题；麻烦的事：*This door's a bugger to open.* 这扇门很难打开。◇ *Question 6 is a real bugger.* 第 6 题真难。 IDM SEE SILLY *adj.*

■ ***verb*** **1** [I, T] (*BrE, taboo, slang*) used as a swear word when sb is annoyed about sth or to show that they do not care about sth at all （生气或不在乎时说）该死，妈的，去它的：*Bugger! I've left my keys at home.* 妈的！我把钥匙忘在家里了。◇ **~ sth** *Bugger it! I've burnt the toast.* 该死！我把面包烤煳了。◇ *Oh, bugger the cost! Let's get it anyway.* 嗨，管它多贵！咱们还是买了吧。 **2** [T] **~ sth** (*BrE, taboo, slang*) to break or ruin sth 毁坏：*I think I've buggered the computer.* 我想我把计算机搞坏了。 **3** [T] **~ sb** (*taboo* or *law* 律) to have ANAL sex with sb 鸡奸（某人）

IDM **ˌbugger ˈme** (*BrE, taboo, slang*) used to express surprise （表示惊奇）好家伙；哎呀：*Bugger me! Did you see that?* 好家伙！你看见了吗？

PHR V **ˌbugger aˈbout/aˈround** (*BrE, taboo, slang*) to waste time by behaving in a silly way or with no clear purpose 闲混；胡闹：*Stop buggering about and get back to work.* 别瞎混了，回去干活吧。 HELP A more polite, informal way of saying this is **mess about** (*BrE*) or **mess around** (*NAmE, BrE*). 较礼貌和非正式的说法是 mess about（英式英语）或 mess around （美式、英式英语）。 **ˌbugger sb aˈbout/aˈround** (*BrE, taboo, slang*) to treat sb in a way that is deliberately not helpful to them or wastes their time 难为某人；故意浪费某人的时间：*I'm sick of being buggered about by the company.* 那家公司就跟我拖着，我真是受够了。 HELP A more polite, informal way of saying this is **mess sb about/around.** 较礼貌和非正式的说法是 mess sb about/around。 **ˌbugger ˈoff** (*BrE, taboo, slang*) (often used in orders 常用于命令) to go away 走开：*Bugger off and leave me alone.* 走开，别管我。◇ *Where is everyone? They've all buggered off.* 大家都在哪儿呀？他们都走了。 **ˌbugger sth↔ˈup** (*BrE, taboo, slang*) to do sth badly or spoil sth 弄糟；破坏；糟蹋：*I buggered up the exam.* 我考试考砸了。◇ *Sorry for buggering up your plans.* 对不起，打乱了你的计划。 HELP A more polite, informal way of saying this is **foul sth up, mess sth up** or **bungle sth.** 较礼貌和非正式的说法是 foul sth up、mess sth up 或 bungle sth。

ˌbugger ˈall *noun* [U] (*BrE, taboo, slang*) nothing at all; none at all 什么也没有；屁都没有：*There's bugger all on TV tonight.* 今晚电视屁也没有。◇ *Well, she was bugger all help* (= no help at all). 咳，她帮个屁忙。

bug·gered /ˈbʌɡəd; *NAmE* -ɡərd/ *adj.* [not before noun] (*BrE, taboo, slang*) **1** very tired 累得要死；筋疲力尽 **2** broken or ruined 毁坏；坏掉：*Oh no, the TV's buggered.* 哎呀！电视机坏了。

IDM **I'll be buggered** (*BrE, taboo, slang*) used to express great surprise （表示吃惊）：*Well, I'll be buggered! Look who's here.* 嘀，老天爷！看是谁在这儿。 **I'm ˈbuggered if…** (*BrE, taboo, slang*) used to say that you do not know sth or to refuse to do sth （表示不知道或拒绝做某事）：*'What's this meeting all about?' 'I'm buggered if I know.'* "这次开的是什么会？" "我要是知道才怪呢。" ◇ *Well I'm buggered if I'm going to help her after what she said to me.* 哼，她对我说那种话，我再也不会帮她了。

bug·gery /ˈbʌɡəri/ *noun* [U] (*BrE, taboo, slang* or *law* 律) ANAL sex 鸡奸

Bug·gins' turn /ˈbʌɡɪnz tɜːn; ˈbʌɡɪnzɪz; *NAmE* tɜːrn/ *noun* [U] (*BrE, informal*) used to refer to the way in which it sometimes seems that people get jobs or are promoted not because they are good at what they do, but because they have been doing it for longer than anybody else 论资排辈；轮流坐庄

buggy /ˈbʌɡi/ *noun* (*pl.* **-ies**) **1** (*BrE*) (*NAmE* **cart**) a small car, often without a roof or doors, used for a particular purpose （常指无顶无门的）专用小汽车：***a garden/golf buggy*** 花园 / 高尔夫球场小汽车 ➲ SEE ALSO BEACH BUGGY **2** (*BrE also* **ˈbaby buggy**) (*NAmE* **stroll·er**) a type of light folding chair on wheels in which a baby or small child is pushed along 婴儿车；童车 ➲ COMPARE PUSHCHAIR **3** a light CARRIAGE for one or two people, pulled by one horse （由一匹马拉的单座或双座）轻便马车

bugle /ˈbjuːɡl/ *noun* a musical instrument like a small TRUMPET, used in the army for giving signals 军号

bu·gler /ˈbjuːɡlə(r)/ *noun* a person who plays the bugle 司号兵；号手

bui·bui /ˈbʊibʊi/ *noun* (*EAfrE*) an item of clothing worn by some Muslim women, consisting of a long black dress and a piece of black cloth that covers the head showing only the face or eyes 布依布依（一些穆斯林妇女穿戴的黑长袍和只露出脸或眼睛的头巾）

build 🔑 /bɪld/ *verb, noun*

■ ***verb*** (**built, built** /bɪlt/) **1** 🔑 [T, I] to make sth, especially a building, by putting parts together 建筑；建造：**~ (sth)** *They have permission to build 200 new houses.* 他们得到建 200 座新房的许可。◇ *Robins build nests almost anywhere.* 知更鸟几乎可随处筑巢。◇ *They're going to build on the site of the old power station.* 他们要在老发电站那里盖房子。◇ **~ sth of/in/from sth** *a house built of stone* 用石头建造的房子 ◇ **~ sth for sb** *They had a house built for them.* 他们让人给他们建了一栋房子。◇ **~ sb sth** *David built us a shed in the back yard.* 戴维帮我们在后院搭了个棚子。 ➲ MORE LIKE THIS 33, page R28 **2** 🔑 [T] **~ sth** to create or develop sth 创建；开发：*She's built a new career for herself.* 她为自己开辟了一条新的谋生之路。◇ *We want to build a better life.* 我们想创造更美好的生活。◇ *This information will help us build a picture of his attacker.* 这条信息将有助于描画出袭击他的人的相貌。 **3** [I] (of a feeling 感觉) to become gradually stronger 逐渐增强：*The tension and excitement built gradually all day.* 整个一天中，紧张与兴奋的气氛越来越浓。 IDM SEE CASTLE, ROME ➲ MORE LIKE THIS 20, page R27

PHR V **ˌbuild sth aˈround sth** [usually passive] to create sth, using sth else as a basis 在…基础上创作：*The story is built around a group of high school dropouts.* 故事围绕着一群辍学的中学生展开。 **ˌbuild sth↔ˈin | ˌbuild sth ˈinto sth** [often passive] **1** to make sth a permanent part of a larger structure 把…建造在（较大的建筑物）里；使…固定于：*We're having new wardrobes built in.* 我们的新衣橱是嵌入式的。◇ *The pipes were built into the concrete.* 管子已固定在混凝土里。 **2** to make sth a permanent part of a system, plan, etc. 使…成为（体系、计划等的）组成部分：*A certain amount of flexibility is built into the system.* 该体系加入了一定的灵活性。 ➲ SEE ALSO BUILT-IN **ˈbuild on sth** to use sth as a basis for further progress 在…的基础上发展：*This study builds on earlier work.* 这项研究是在以往工作的基础上进行的。 **ˈbuild sth on sth** [usually passive] to base sth on sth 把…作为…的基础：*an argument built on sound logic* 建立在严密的逻辑基础上的论点 **ˌbuild sth↔ˈon | ˌbuild sth ˈonto sth** to add sth (for example, an extra room) to an existing structure by building 在（已有建筑物上）增建某物：*They've built an extension on.* 他们进行了一项扩建。◇ *The new wing was built onto the hospital last year.* 医院的新翼楼是去年增建的。 **ˌbuild ˈup (to sth)** 🔑 to become greater, more powerful or larger in number 加大；加强；增多：*All the pressure built up and he was off work for weeks with stress.* 各方面的压力越来越大，他因负荷太重有好几个星期没上班。◇ *The music builds up to a rousing climax.* 音乐逐渐达到了令人振奋的高潮。 ➲ RELATED NOUN BUILD-UP (1) **ˌbuild ˈup to sth | ˌbuild yourself ˈup to sth** to prepare for a particular moment or event 为…作准备：*Build yourself up to peak performance on the day of the exam.* 好好准备在考试那天发挥出最高水平。 ➲ RELATED NOUN BUILD-UP (2) **ˌbuild sb/sth ˈup** [usually passive] to give a very positive and enthusiastic description of sb/sth, often exaggerating your claims 吹捧；鼓吹：*The play was built up to be a masterpiece but I found it very disappointing.* 那部戏被捧为杰作，可我却大失所望。➲ RELATED NOUN BUILD-UP (3) ˌ**build sb/yourself**↔ˈ**up** to make sb/yourself healthier or stronger 增强…的体质；使更加强壮：*You need more protein to build you up.* 你需要更多蛋白质以增强体质。ˌ**build sth**↔ˈ**up 1** to create or develop sth 创建；开发：*She's built up a very successful business.* 她创办了一家非常成功的企业。◇ *These finds help us* ***build up a picture*** *of life in the Middle Ages.* 这些发现有助于建构中世纪的生活画面。◇ *I am anxious not to* ***build up false hopes*** (= to encourage people to hope for too much). 我非常在意不要让大家期望过高。**2** to make sth higher or stronger than it was before 增高；加强

▼ **SYNONYMS** 同义词辨析

build

construct • assemble • erect • put sth up

These words all mean to make sth, especially by putting different parts together. 以上各词均含制造、建造之义。

build to make sth, especially a building, by putting parts together 指制造、建造、修建（尤指房屋）：*a house built of stone* 用石头建造的房子 ◇ *They're going to build on the site of the old power station.* 他们要在老发电站那里盖房子。

construct [often passive] (*rather formal*) to build sth such as a road, building or machine 指修建、建造（公路、房屋、机器等）

assemble (*rather formal*) to fit together all the separate parts of sth such as a piece of furniture or a machine 指装配、组装（家具、机器等）：*The cupboard is easy to assemble.* 这个橱柜容易组装。

erect (*formal*) to build sth; to put sth in position and make it stand upright 指建立、建造、安装、竖立、搭起：*Police had to erect barriers to keep crowds back.* 警察只得设立路障来阻截人群。

put sth up to build sth or place sth somewhere 指修建、建立、设立、设置：*They're putting up new hotels in order to boost tourism in the area.* 他们正在盖新旅馆以促进该地区的旅游业。

PATTERNS

- to build/construct/erect/put up a **house/wall**
- to build/construct/erect/put up some **shelves**
- to build/construct/erect/put up a **barrier/fence/shelter**
- to build/construct/assemble a(n) **engine/machine**
- to build/construct a **road/railway/railroad/tunnel**
- to erect/put up a **tent/statue/monument**

■ ***noun*** [U, C, usually sing.] the shape and size of the human body 体形；体格；身材：*a man of average build* 中等身材的人

build·er /ˈbɪldə(r)/ *noun* **1** a person or company whose job is to build or repair houses or other buildings 建筑工人；建筑公司；营造商 **2** (usually in compounds 通常构成复合词) a person or thing that builds, creates or develops sth 建筑者；创建者；开发者：*a shipbuilder* 造船工人 ◇ *a confidence builder* 令人增强信心的事物 ➲ SEE ALSO BODY-BUILDER at BODYBUILDING

ˈ**builders' merchant** *noun* a person or shop that supplies materials to the building trade 建材商；建材商店

build·ing /ˈbɪldɪŋ/ *noun* **1** [C] a structure such as a house or school that has a roof and walls 建筑物；房子；楼房：*tall/old/historic buildings* 高大 / 老 / 有历史意义的建筑物 ➲ COLLOCATIONS AT DECORATE ➲ VISUAL VOCAB PAGE V15 **2** [U] the process and work of building 建筑；建筑业：*the building of the school* 学校的修建 ◇ *There's building work going on next door.* 邻居正大兴土木。◇ *the building trade* 建筑业 ◇ ***building materials/costs/regulations*** 建筑材料 / 费用 / 规章

ˈ**building block** *noun* **1** [C] a piece of wood or plastic used as a toy for children to build things with 积木；塑料积木 ➲ VISUAL VOCAB PAGE V41 **2 building blocks** [pl.] parts that are joined together in order to make a large thing exist 组成部分；构成要素：*Single words are the building blocks of language.* 单词是语言结构的基本单位。

ˈ**building site** (*especially BrE*) (*NAmE usually* **conˈstruction site**) *noun* an area of land where sth is being built 建筑工地

ˈ**building society** *noun* (*BrE*) (*US* ˌ**savings and ˈloan association**) an organization like a bank that lends money to people who want to buy a house. People also save money with a building society. 房屋互助协会（提供住房贷款及储蓄服务）

ˈ**build-up** *noun* **1** [sing., U] an increase in the amount of sth over a period of time 逐步的增长：*a steady build-up of traffic in the evenings* 晚间逐渐繁忙的交通 **2** [C, usually sing.] ~ (**to sth**) the time before an important event, when people are preparing for it（重要事情的）准备期，准备过程：*the build-up to the President's visit* 总统访问前的准备工作 **3** [C, usually sing.] a very positive and enthusiastic description of sth that is going to happen, that is intended to make people excited about it 宣扬；鼓吹：*The media have given the show a huge build-up.* 传媒为这次演出大力造势。

▼ **SYNONYMS** 同义词辨析

building

property • premises • complex • structure • block

These are all words for a structure such as a house, office block or factory that has a roof and four walls. 以上各词均指建筑物、房屋、楼房。

building a structure such as a house, office block or factory that has a roof and four walls 指建筑物、房屋、楼房

property a building or buildings and the surrounding land; land and buildings 指房屋及院落、庄园、房地产：*We have a buyer who would like to view the property.* 我们有一买主想看看这房产。◇ *The price of property has risen enormously.* 房地产的价格大幅上升了。**NOTE** This word is often used when talking about buying/selling houses or other buildings and land. 谈及买卖房屋或房地产时常用该词。

premises [pl.] the building or buildings and surrounding land that a business owns or uses 指企业拥有或使用的建筑及附属场地、营业场所：*The company is looking for larger premises.* 这家公司正在寻找更大的营业场所。

complex a group of buildings of a similar type together in one place 指类型相似的建筑群：*a leisure complex* 休闲活动中心

structure a thing that is made of several parts, especially a building 指结构体、建筑物：*The pier is a wooden structure.* 这个码头是木结构建筑。

block (*BrE*) a tall building that contains flats or offices; a building that forms part of a school, hospital, etc. and is used for a particular purpose 指公寓、办公大楼或学校、医院等作特定用途的大楼：*a block of flats* 公寓大楼 ◇ *the school's science block* 这所学校的理科大楼

PATTERNS

- a(n) **commercial/industrial/residential** building/property/premises/complex/block
- an **apartment** building/complex/block
- a/the **school** building/premises
- to **build** a property/complex/structure/block
- to **put up** a building/property/structure/block
- to **demolish/pull down** a building/property/complex/structure/block

B

built /bɪlt/ *combining form* (after adverbs and in compound adjectives 用于副词后，或构成复合形容词) made in the particular way that is mentioned …建成的；…造的：*a newly built station* 新建的车站 ◇ *American-built cars* 美国制造的汽车 ➲ SEE ALSO PURPOSE-BUILT, WELL BUILT

ˌ**built-ˈin** (*also less frequent* ˌ**in-ˈbuilt**) *adj.* [only before noun] included as part of sth and not separate from it 是…的组成部分的；嵌入式的；内置的：*built-in cupboards* 壁橱 ➲ COMPARE INBUILT

ˌ**built-ˈup** *adj.* [usually before noun] (*especially BrE*) (of an area of land 地区) covered in buildings, roads, etc. 建筑物密集的：*to reduce the speed limit in built-up areas* 在楼房林立的地区降低最高限速

bulb /bʌlb/ *noun* **1** (*also* ˈ**light bulb**) the glass part that fits into an electric lamp, etc. to give light when it is switched on 电灯泡：*a halogen bulb* 卤素灯泡 ◇ *a room lit by bare bulbs* (= with no decorative cover) 只有光秃秃的电灯泡照明的屋子（无灯罩、灯饰） ➲ VISUAL VOCAB PAGE V22 **2** the round underground part of some plants, shaped like an onion, that grows into a new plant every year （植物）鳞茎 ➲ VISUAL VOCAB PAGE V11 **3** an object shaped like a bulb, for example the end of a THERMOMETER 鳞茎状物（如温度计的球部）

bulb·ous /ˈbʌlbəs/ *adj.* shaped like a bulb; round and fat in an ugly way 鳞茎状的；圆胖难看的：*a bulbous red nose* 蒜头红鼻子

bul·gar (*also* **bul·gur**) /ˈbʌlɡə(r)/ (*also* ˈ**bulgar wheat**) *noun* [U] a type of food consisting of grains of WHEAT that are boiled then dried 干小麦，燕谷麦（将小麦煮后烘干）

bulge /bʌldʒ/ *verb, noun*

■ *verb* **1** [I] ~ (**with sth**) (usually used in the progressive tenses 通常用于进行时) to be completely full (of sth) 充满，塞满：*Her pockets were bulging with presents.* 她的口袋里装满了礼物。◇ *a bulging briefcase* 鼓鼓囊囊的公文包 **2** [I] to stick out from sth in a round shape 凸出；鼓胀：*His eyes bulged.* 他双眼凸出。 IDM SEE SEAM

■ *noun* **1** a lump that sticks out from sth in a round shape 鼓起；凸起：*the bulge of a gun in his pocket* 他衣袋里鼓起一把枪的模样 **2** (*informal*) fat on the body that sticks out in a round shape （身体的）肥胖部位：*That skirt's too tight. It shows all your bulges.* 那条裙子太紧了，把你的发胖部位全显出来了。 **3** a sudden temporary increase in the amount of sth 一时的激增；暴涨：*After the war there was a bulge in the birth rate.* 战后出生率一度激增。

bul·ging /ˈbʌldʒɪŋ/ *adj.* that sticks out from sth in a round shape 鼓起的；隆起的：*bulging eyes* 凸出的眼睛

bu·limia /buˈlɪmiə; -ˈliːmiə; *BrE also* bju-/ (*also* **bulimia nervosa** /buˌlɪmiə nɜːˈvəʊsə; *NAmE* nɜːrˈvoʊsə/) *noun* [U] an emotional DISORDER in which a person repeatedly eats too much and then forces him- or herself to VOMIT 神经性贪食 ➲ COLLOCATIONS AT DIET ➲ COMPARE ANOREXIA ► **bu·lim·ic** /buˈlɪmɪk; -ˈliːmɪk; bju-/ *adj., noun*

bulk AW /bʌlk/ *noun, verb*

■ *noun* **1** [sing.] **the** ~ (**of sth**) the main part of sth; most of sth 主体；大部分：*The bulk of the population lives in cities.* 大多数人口居住在城市里。 **2** [U] the (large) size or quantity of sth （大）体积；大（量）：*Despite its bulk and weight, the car is extremely fast.* 尽管这辆车大而且重，速度却非常快。 ◇ *a* ***bulk order*** (= one for a large number of similar items) 一份大额订单 ◇ ***bulk buying*** (= buying in large amounts, often at a reduced price) （常指以低价）大量购买 ◇ *It's cheaper to buy* ***in bulk.*** 大批购买便宜些。 **3** [sing.] the weight or shape of sb/sth large 巨大的体重（或重量、形状、身体等）：*She heaved her bulk out of the chair.* 她挪动庞大的躯体，费力地从椅子里站起来。

■ *verb*

IDM **bulk ˈlarge** (*BrE, formal*) to be the most important part of sth 是最重要部分

PHR V ˌ**bulk sth↔ˈout/ˈup** to make sth bigger, thicker or heavier 使加大（或加厚、加重）

bulk·head /ˈbʌlkhed/ *noun* (*specialist*) a wall that divides a ship or an aircraft into separate parts （船的）舱壁；（飞机的）隔框

bulky AW /ˈbʌlki/ *adj.* (**bulk·ier, bulki·est**) **1** (of a thing 东西) large and difficult to move or carry 庞大的；笨重的：*Bulky items will be collected separately.* 大件物品将分开收集。 **2** (of a person 人) tall and heavy 大块头的；高大肥胖的：*The bulky figure of Inspector Jones appeared at the door.* 琼斯督察的壮硕身躯出现在门口。

bull /bʊl/ *noun* **1** [C] the male of any animal in the cow family 公牛：*a bull neck* (= a short thick neck like a bull's) （公牛般的）短粗脖子 ➲ COMPARE BULLOCK, COW *n.* (1), OX, STEER *n.* (2) **2** [C] the male of the ELEPHANT, WHALE and some other large animals 雄的（象、鲸等）大动物 ➲ COMPARE COW *n.* (2) **3** [C] (*finance* 财) a person who buys shares in a company, hoping to sell them soon afterwards at a higher price （预期证券价格上升的）买空者，多头 ➲ COMPARE BEAR *n.* (2) **4** [C] an official order or statement from the POPE (= the head of the Roman Catholic Church) 教皇诏书；教皇训谕：*a papal bull* 教皇训谕 **5** [U] (*slang*) = BULLSHIT：*That's a load of bull!* 那是胡说八道！ **6** [C] = BULLSEYE ➲ SEE ALSO COCK AND BULL STORY

IDM **a bull in a ˈchina shop** a person who is careless, or who moves or acts in a rough or awkward way, in a place or situation where skill and care are needed （不顾环境）笨拙莽撞的人，冒失鬼 **take the bull by the ˈhorns** to face a difficult or dangerous situation directly and with courage 勇敢面对困境（或险境） ➲ MORE AT SHOOT *v.*, WAVE *v.*

ˈ**bull bars** *noun* [pl.] (*BrE*) a set of strong metal bars fixed to the front of a large vehicle to protect it from damage （大汽车前端的）保险杠

bull·dog /ˈbʊldɒɡ; *NAmE* -dɔːɡ/ *noun* a short strong dog with a large head, a short flat nose and a short thick neck 斗牛狗，牛头犬（头大鼻短平、脖子短粗）

ˈ**Bulldog clip™** *noun* (*BrE*) a metal device for holding papers together 弹簧金属纸夹 ➲ VISUAL VOCAB PAGE V71

bull·doze /ˈbʊldəʊz; *NAmE* -doʊz/ *verb* **1** [T] ~ **sth** to destroy buildings, trees, etc. with a bulldozer （用推土机）推倒，铲平：*The trees are being bulldozed to make way for a new superstore.* 那片树正被推土机铲除，以兴建一家新超市。 **2** [I, T] to force your way somewhere; to force sth somewhere （使）强行通过：**+ adv./prep.** *Rooney bulldozed through to score.* 鲁尼强行突破得分。◇ **~ sth + adv./prep.** *They bulldozed the tax through Parliament.* 他们强行使税收提案在议会通过。◇ *He* ***bulldozed his way*** *to victory.* 他一路上过关斩将，取得了最后胜利。 **3** [T] **~ sb** (**into doing sth**) to force sb to do sth 强迫（某人做某事） SYN **railroad**：*They bulldozed him into selling.* 他们胁迫他卖出。

bull·dozer /ˈbʊldəʊzə(r); *NAmE* -doʊz-/ *noun* a powerful vehicle with a broad steel blade in front, used for moving earth or knocking down buildings 推土机 ➲ VISUAL VOCAB PAGE V63

bull·dyke (*also* **bull·dike**) /ˈbʊldaɪk/ *noun* (*offensive*) a LESBIAN who is thought to look very male or to act in a typically male way 女公牛（指女子同性恋中偏男性化者）

bul·let 🔑 /ˈbʊlɪt/ *noun* a small metal object that is fired from a gun 子弹；弹丸：*bullet wounds* 枪伤 ◇ *There were bullet holes in the door.* 门上有弹孔。◇ *He was killed by a bullet in the head.* 他头部中弹死亡。 ➲ SEE ALSO MAGIC BULLET, PLASTIC BULLET, RUBBER BULLET IDM SEE BITE *v.*

bul·let·ed /ˈbʊlɪtɪd/ *adj.* (of a list, text, etc.) containing items that each have a square, a diamond or a circle (= a bullet point) in front of them to show that they are important; a bulleted item on a list has a square, a diamond or a circle in front of it to show that it is important （清单、文本等）包含重要项目的；（清单事项）带项目符号的（以示重要）

bul·letin /ˈbʊlətɪn/ *noun* **1** a short news report on the radio or television （电台或电视台的）新闻简报 ➲ WORDFINDER NOTE AT RADIO **2** an official statement about sth important 公告；布告：*a bulletin on the President's health* 关于总统健康的公告 **3** a printed report that gives news about an organization or a group （机构或组织的）简报

ˈ**bulletin board** *noun* **1** (*NAmE*) (*BrE* **no·tice·board**) (*also* **board** *BrE, NAmE*) a board for putting notices on 告示牌；布告板 ➲ VISUAL VOCAB PAGE V71 **2** (*computing* 计) a place on a computer network where any user can write or read messages 公告板；布告栏

ˈ**bullet point** *noun* an item in a list in a document, that is printed with a square, diamond or circle in front of it in order to show that it is important. The square, etc. is also called a bullet point. 点句重要项目（文件中列举时用正方形、菱形等点句符开始）；点句符；项目符号

bul·let·proof /ˈbʊlɪtpruːf/ *adj.* that can stop bullets from passing through it 防弹的：*a bulletproof vest* 防弹背心

ˈ**bullet train** *noun* (*informal*) a Japanese train that carries passengers at high speeds （日本载客的）高速列车，子弹列车

bull·fight /ˈbʊlfaɪt/ *noun* a traditional public entertainment, popular especially in Spain, in which BULLS are fought and usually killed （尤指盛行于西班牙的）斗牛表演 ▶ **bull·fight·er** *noun* **bull·fight·ing** *noun* [U] ➲ SEE ALSO MATADOR

bull·finch /ˈbʊlfɪntʃ/ *noun* a small European bird of the FINCH family, with a strong curved beak and a pink breast 红腹灰雀

bull·frog /ˈbʊlfrɒg; *NAmE* -frɔːg; -frɑːg/ *noun* a large American FROG with a loud CROAK （美洲）牛蛙

bull·head·ed /ˌbʊlˈhedɪd/ *adj.* (*NAmE*) unwilling to change your opinion about sth, in a way that other people think is annoying and unreasonable 固执的；死心眼儿的 SYN **obstinate, stubborn** ▶ **bull·head·ed·ness** *noun* [U]

bull·horn /ˈbʊlhɔːn; *NAmE* -hɔːrn/ (*NAmE*) (*BrE* **loud·hail·er**) *noun* an electronic device, shaped like a horn, with a MICROPHONE at one end, that you speak into in order to make your voice louder so that it can be heard at a distance 电子喇叭；扩音器 ➲ COMPARE MEGAPHONE

bul·lion /ˈbʊliən/ *noun* [U] gold or silver in large amounts or in the form of bars 大量的金（或银）；金（或银）条：*gold bullion* 金条

bull·ish /ˈbʊlɪʃ/ *adj.* **1** feeling confident and positive about the future 对未来有信心的；积极乐观的：*in a bullish mood* 满怀希望 **2** (*finance* 财) causing, or connected with, an increase in the price of shares （对股票价格）看涨的；牛市的：*a bullish market* 牛市 ➲ COMPARE BEARISH

ˈ**bull market** *noun* (*finance* 财) a period during which share prices are rising and people are buying shares 牛市（股票价格上升、股民纷纷购买股票的时期） ➲ COMPARE BEAR MARKET

ˌ**bull ˈmastiff** *noun* a large strong dog with short smooth hair 斗牛獒

bul·lock /ˈbʊlək/ *noun* a young BULL (= a male cow) that has been CASTRATED (= had part of its sex organs removed) 阉小公牛 ➲ COMPARE OX (1), STEER *n.* (2)

bull·pen /ˈbʊlpen/ *noun* (*NAmE*) **1** the part of a BASEBALL field where players practise PITCHING (= throwing) before the game 牛棚（棒球投手上场前的热身区域） **2** extra PITCHERS (= players who throw the ball) in a BASEBALL team who are used, if necessary, to replace the usual pitchers 替补投手：*The team's bullpen is solid this year.* 今年该队的替补投手实力不错。 **3** a type of large office which is OPEN-PLAN (= it does not have walls dividing the office area) 敞开式办公室 **4** a room where prisoners wait before they go into the court for their trial （嫌犯）候审室

bull·ring /ˈbʊlrɪŋ/ *noun* the large round area, like an outdoor theatre, where BULLFIGHTS take place 斗牛场

bull·rush = BULRUSH

ˈ**bull session** *noun* (*NAmE, informal*) an occasion when people meet and talk in an informal way 闲谈；聊天

bulls·eye /ˈbʊlzaɪ/ (*also* **bull**) *noun* [usually sing.] the centre of the target that you shoot or throw at in shooting, ARCHERY or DARTS; a shot or throw that hits this 靶心；鹄的；命中靶心：*He scored a bullseye.* 他命中了靶心。 ➲ VISUAL VOCAB PAGE V44

bull·shit /ˈbʊlʃɪt/ *noun, verb*

■ ***noun*** [U] (*taboo, slang*) (*also informal* **bull**) (*abbr. US* **BS**) nonsense 胡说；狗屁：*That's just bullshit.* 那纯粹是胡说。

■ ***verb*** (**-tt-**) [I, T] (*taboo, slang*) to say things that are not true, especially in order to trick sb 胡说（尤指哄骗）：*She's just bullshitting.* 她不过是在瞎扯。 ◇ **~ sb** *Don't try to bullshit me!* 休想哄我！ ▶ **bull·shit·ter** *noun*

ˌ**bull ˈterrier** *noun* a strong dog with short hair, a thick neck and a long nose 斗牛㹴狗（毛短脖子粗、身体壮实） ➲ SEE ALSO PIT BULL TERRIER

bully /ˈbʊli/ *noun, verb, exclamation*

■ ***noun*** (*pl.* **-ies**) a person who uses their strength or power to frighten or hurt weaker people 仗势欺人者；横行霸道者：*the school bully* 学校里的恶霸学生

■ ***verb*** (**bul·lies, bully·ing, bul·lied, bul·lied**) to frighten or hurt a weaker person; to use your strength or power to make sb do sth 恐吓；伤害；胁迫：**~ sb** *My son is being bullied at school.* 我儿子在学校里受欺负。 ◇ **~ sb into sth/into doing sth** *I won't be bullied into signing anything.* 我绝不会屈服于压力签署任何东西。 ▶ **bully·ing** *noun* [U]：*Bullying is a problem in many schools.* 很多学校都出现学生仗势作恶的问题。 ◇ *He refused to give in to bullying and threats.* 他拒不向恐吓威逼势力让步。 ◇ *bullying behaviour/tactics* 霸道行为 / 手段 ➲ COLLOCATIONS AT EDUCATION

■ ***exclamation***

IDM **bully for you, etc.** (*informal*) used to show that you do not think that what sb has said or done is very impressive 没什么了不起：*He's got a job in New York? Well, bully for him!* 他在纽约找到了份工作？哼，那没什么了不起！

ˈ**bully boy** *noun* (*BrE, informal*) an aggressive violent man 流氓；恶霸：*The group have frequently used bully-boy tactics.* 那个团伙常常耍流氓。

ˈ**bully pulpit** *noun* [sing.] (*NAmE*) a position of authority that gives sb the opportunity to speak in public about an issue 名望讲坛（能提供机会阐明自己观点的重要公职）

bul·rush (*also* **bull·rush**) /ˈbʊlrʌʃ/ *noun* a tall plant with long narrow leaves and a long brown head of flowers, that grows in or near water 藨草；宽叶香蒲；灯芯草 ➲ VISUAL VOCAB PAGE V11

bul·wark /ˈbʊlwək; *NAmE* -wɜːrk/ *noun* **1** [usually sing.] **~ (against sth)** (*formal*) a person or thing that protects or defends sth 保护者，防御者（指人或事物）：*a bulwark against extremism* 坚决反对极端主义的人 **2** [C] a wall built as a defence 堡垒；防御工事 **3** [usually pl.] the part of a ship's side that is above the level of the DECK （船的）舷墙

bum /bʌm/ *noun, verb, adj.*

■ ***noun*** (*informal*) **1** (*BrE*) the part of the body that you sit on 屁股 SYN **backside, behind, bottom** **2** (*especially NAmE*) a person who has no home or job and who asks other people for money or food 流浪乞丐；无业游民：*a beach bum* (= sb who spends all their time on the beach, without having a job) 海滨流浪汉 **3** a lazy person who does nothing for other people or for society 懒汉；游手好闲者：*He's nothing but a no-good bum!* 他不过是个没用的懒汉。

B

IDM **bums on 'seats** (*BrE, informal*) used to refer to the number of people who attend a show, talk, etc., especially when emphasizing the need or desire to attract a large number 观众（或听众）的数量大（尤用于强调吸引大量观众的需要或愿望）：*They're not bothered about attracting the right audience—they just want bums on seats.* 他们不在乎观众是什么样的人，只求卖座。 **give sb/get the ˌbum's 'rush** (*informal, especially NAmE*) to force sb/be forced to leave a place quickly 赶走某人；被撵走：*He was soon given the bum's rush from the club.* 他很快从俱乐部里被撵了出来。

■ ***verb*** (-mm-) **1 ~ sth (off sb)** (*informal*) to get sth from sb by asking 提出要；乞讨 **SYN** **cadge**: *Can I bum a cigarette off you?* 给我一根烟好吗？ **2 ~ sb (out)** (*NAmE, informal*) to make sb feel upset or disappointed 使不安；使灰心

PHR V **ˌbum a'round/a'bout** (*informal*) to travel around or spend your time with no particular plans （漫无目的地）闲荡，漫游：*He bummed around the world for a year.* 他在世界各地漫游了一年。

■ ***adj.*** [only before noun] (*informal*) of bad quality; wrong or useless 劣质的；错误的；没用的：*He didn't play one bum note.* 他一个音也没奏错。◇ *a* ***bum deal*** (= a situation where you do not get what you deserve or have paid for) 不合算的交易

bum·bag /ˈbʌmbæg/ (*BrE*) (*NAmE* **'fanny pack**) *noun* (*informal*) a small bag attached to a belt and worn around the waist, to keep money, etc. in （围在腰间，放钱物的）腰包 ➲ VISUAL VOCAB PAGE V69

bum·ble /ˈbʌmbl/ *verb* [I] **+ adv./prep.** to act or move in an awkward or confused way 笨手笨脚；跌跌撞撞：*I could hear him bumbling around in the kitchen.* 我听得见他在厨房里瞎折腾。

bumble·bee /ˈbʌmblbiː/ *noun* a large BEE covered with small hairs that makes a loud noise as it flies 熊蜂；大黄蜂 ➲ VISUAL VOCAB PAGE V13

bum·bling /ˈbʌmblɪŋ/ *adj.* [only before noun] behaving in an awkward confused way, often making careless mistakes 笨手笨脚的（常马虎出错）

bumf (*also* **bumph**) /bʌmf/ *noun* [U] (*BrE, informal*) written information, especially advertisements, official documents, forms, etc., that seem boring or unnecessary 乏味（或多余）的书面材料（尤指广告、公文、表格等）：*He threw away my letter, thinking it was just more election bumf.* 他扔掉我的信，以为那不过又是些选举传单。

bum·fluff /ˈbʌmflʌf/ *noun* [U] (*informal*) the soft hair that grows on the upper lip and chin of a boy, as his beard begins to grow （男孩开始长胡子时上唇的）茸毛，小胡子

bum·mer /ˈbʌmə(r)/ *noun* **a bummer** [sing.] (*informal*) a disappointing or unpleasant situation 失望（或不愉快）的局面：*It's a real bummer that she can't come.* 她不能来，实在令人失望。

bump /bʌmp/ *verb, noun*

■ ***verb*** **1** [I] to hit sb/sth by accident （无意地）碰，撞：**~ into sb/sth** *In the dark I bumped into a chair.* 我在黑暗中撞上了一把椅子。◇ **~ against sb/sth** *The car bumped against the kerb.* 汽车撞上了路缘。 ➲ SYNONYMS AT HIT **2** [T] **~ sth (against/on sth)** to hit sth, especially a part of your body, against or on sth （尤指身体部位）碰上，撞上：*Be careful not to bump your head on the beam when you stand up.* 当心站起来时头别撞了横梁。 **3** [I, T] to move across a rough surface 颠簸行进：**+ adv./prep.** *The jeep bumped along the dirt track.* 吉普车在土路上颠簸着行驶。◇ **~ sth + adv./prep.** *The car* ***bumped its way*** *slowly down the drive.* 汽车沿车道缓慢地颠簸行进。 **4** [T] **~ sb + adv./prep.** to move sb from one group or position to another; to remove sb from a group 把（某人）掉换到（另一群体或位置）；调出，开除出（某群体）：*The airline apologized and bumped us up to first class.* 航空公司道歉后把我们掉换到头等舱。◇ *If you are bumped off an airline because of overbooking, you are entitled to compensation.* 假如机票超售而不能登机，你有权获得赔偿。◇ *The coach told him he had been bumped from the crew.* 教练通知他已被调出赛艇队。

PHR V **ˌbump 'into sb** (*informal*) to meet sb by chance 碰见；偶然遇见 **ˌbump sb↔'off** (*informal*) to murder sb 谋杀；杀害 **ˌbump sth↔'up** (*informal*) to increase or raise sth 增加；提高 **ˌbump 'up against sth** to experience a problem or factor that you did not expect 突然碰到；遭遇：*We kept bumping up against inflexible regulations.* 我们不断遇到僵化的管理条例。

■ ***noun*** **1** [C] the action or sound of sth hitting a hard surface 碰撞（声）；撞击（声）：*He fell to the ground* ***with a bump****.* 他砰的一声摔倒在地上。◇ *We could hear loud bumps from upstairs where the children were playing.* 我们能听到孩子们在楼上嬉戏的乒乓声。 **2** [C] a swelling on the body, often caused by a blow 肿块（常因击打所致） **SYN** **lump**: *She was covered in bumps and bruises.* 她全身青肿，伤痕累累。◇ *How did you get that bump on your forehead?* 你额头上怎么起了个包？ **3** [C] a part of a flat surface that is not even, but raised above the rest of it 隆起；凸块：*a bump in the road* 路面上的凸块 ➲ SEE ALSO BUMPY (1) **4** [C] a slight accident in which your vehicle hits sth 轻微撞车事故 **5 the bumps** [pl.] (*BrE*) (on a child's birthday) the act of lifting the child in the air and then putting them down on the ground, once for every year of their age 生日举放仪式（在孩子生日时将其举高后再放在地上的仪式，举放次数与年龄相等）：*We gave her the bumps.* 我们给她举行了生日举放仪式。 **IDM** SEE EARTH *n.*, THING

bump·er /ˈbʌmpə(r)/ *noun, adj.*

■ ***noun*** a bar fixed to the front and back of a car, etc. to reduce the effect if it hits anything （汽车头尾的）保险杠：*a* ***bumper sticker*** (= a sign that people stick on the bumper of their cars with a message on it) 贴在保险杠上的小标语 ◇ *The cars were* ***bumper to bumper*** *on the road to the coast* (= so close that their bumpers were nearly touching). 车辆一辆紧接一辆把通往海岸的马路挤得水泄不通。 ➲ VISUAL VOCAB PAGE V56

■ ***adj.*** [only before noun] (*approving*) unusually large; producing an unusually large amount 异常大的；丰盛的：*a bumper issue* (= of a magazine, etc.) （期刊的）特大号 ◇ *a* ***bumper crop/harvest/season/year*** 丰收；丰收季节；丰收年

'bumper car (*especially NAmE*) (*BrE also* **dodgem**, **'dodgem car**) *noun* one of the small electric cars that you drive in THE DODGEMS 碰碰车

bumph = BUMF

bump·kin /ˈbʌmpkɪn/ *noun* = COUNTRY BUMPKIN

bump·tious /ˈbʌmpʃəs/ *adj.* (*disapproving*) showing that you think that you are very important; often giving your opinions in a loud, confident and annoying way 傲慢的；自以为了不起的；骄横的

bumpy /ˈbʌmpi/ *adj.* (**bump·ier**, **bumpi·est**) **1** (of a surface 平面) not even; with a lot of bumps 不平的；多凸块的：*a bumpy road/track* 崎岖不平的道路 / 小道 ◇ *bumpy ground* 高低不平的地面 **2** (of a journey 行程) uncomfortable with a lot of sudden unpleasant movements caused by the road surface, weather conditions, etc. 颠簸的：*a* ***bumpy ride/flight*** 颠簸的行车 / 飞行

IDM **have/give sb a bumpy 'ride** to have a difficult time; to make a situation difficult for sb （使）处境艰难

bun /bʌn/ *noun* **1** [C] a small round sweet cake 小圆甜蛋糕；小圆甜饼：*an iced bun* 加糖霜的小圆蛋糕 ➲ SEE ALSO HOT CROSS BUN **2** [C] a small round flat bread roll 圆面包：*a hamburger bun* 一个用来夹汉堡饼的面包 ➲ COMPARE ROLL *n.* (3) **3** [C] long hair that has been twisted into a round shape and is worn on top or at the back of the head 圆发髻：*She wore her hair in a bun.* 她盘了个发髻。 ➲ VISUAL VOCAB PAGE V65 **4 buns** [pl.] (*slang, especially NAmE*) the two sides of a person's bottom 屁股

IDM **have a 'bun in the oven** (*informal, humorous*) to be pregnant 大肚子；怀孕

bunch /bʌntʃ/ *noun, verb*

■ ***noun*** **1** [C] **~ of sth** a number of things of the same type which are growing or fastened together 串；束；扎：*a bunch of bananas, grapes, etc.* 一把香蕉、一串葡萄等 ◇ *a bunch of keys* 一串钥匙 ◇ *She picked me a **bunch of flowers**.* 她给我采了一束鲜花。 ➲ VISUAL VOCAB PAGE V32 **2** [sing.] **a ~ (of sth)** (*informal, especially NAmE*) a large amount of sth; a large number of things or people 大量；大批：*I have **a whole bunch of** stuff to do this morning.* 我今天上午有一大堆活儿。 **3** [sing.] (*informal*) a group of people 群体：*The people that I work with are a great bunch.* 和我一起工作的那些人很不错。 **4 bunches** [pl.] (*BrE*) long hair that is divided in two and tied at each side of the head （扎在头两侧的）发辫：*She wore her hair in bunches.* 她梳着两条辫子。 ➲ VISUAL VOCAB PAGE V65

IDM **the best/pick of the 'bunch** the best out of a group of people or things 出类拔萃的人（或事物）；精英；精品 ➲ MORE AT BEST *n.*

■ ***verb*** [I, T] to become tight or to form tight folds; to make sth do this （使）变紧，成皱褶：*His muscles bunched under his shirt.* 他衬衫下面的肌肉紧绷绷的。 ◇ **~ (sth) up** *Her skirt had bunched up round her waist.* 她的裙子在腰际成皱褶收拢。 ◇ **~ sth** *His forehead was bunched in a frown.* 他皱紧眉头。

PHR V **ˌbunch 'up/to'gether | ˌbunch sb/sth 'up/to'gether** to move closer and form into a group; to make people or things do this （使）集中，聚拢：*The sheep bunched together as soon as they saw the dog.* 那些绵羊一见到狗就挤作一团。

bun·dle /ˈbʌndl/ *noun, verb*

■ ***noun*** **1** [C] a number of things tied or wrapped together; sth that is wrapped up （一）捆，包，扎：***a bundle of rags/papers/firewood*** 一捆碎布 / 报纸 / 木柴 ◇ *She held her little bundle* (= her baby) *tightly in her arms.* 她怀中紧紧地抱着襁褓中的婴儿。 **2** [C] a number of things that belong, or are sold together 一批（同类事物或出售的货品）：*a bundle of ideas* 一套想法 ◇ *a bundle of graphics packages for your PC* 一批个人电脑图形软件包 **3** [sing.] **a ~ of laughs, fun, etc.** (*informal*) a person or thing that makes you laugh 风趣的人；笑料：*He wasn't exactly a bundle of laughs* (= a happy person to be with) *last night.* 他昨晚有点让人扫兴。 ➲ SEE ALSO BUNDLE OF JOY **4 a bundle** [sing.] (*informal*) a large amount of money 一大笔钱：*That car must have cost a bundle.* 那部车一定价格不菲。

IDM **not go a bundle on sb/sth** (*BrE, informal*) to not like sb/sth very much 不十分喜欢某人 / 某事物 ➲ MORE AT DROP *v.*, NERVE *n.*

■ ***verb*** **1** [T] **~ sb + adv./prep.** to push or send sb somewhere quickly and not carefully 匆匆送走；推搡；赶：*They bundled her into the back of a car.* 他们把她塞进了车后座。 ◇ *He was bundled off to boarding school.* 他被匆匆送到了寄宿学校。 **2** [I] **+ adv./prep.** to move somewhere quickly in a group （成群地）匆忙赶往：*We bundled out onto the street.* 我们大伙急忙跑到街上。 **3** [T] **~ sth (with sth)** to supply extra equipment, especially software when selling a new computer, at no extra cost 额外免费提供（设备等）；（尤指出售计算机时）赠送软件：*A further nine applications are bundled with the system.* 该系统免费附送九套应用软件。

PHR V **ˌbundle sth↔'up | ˌbundle sth↔to'gether** to make or tie sth into a bundle 捆扎；把…打包：*He bundled up the dirty clothes and stuffed them into the bag.* 他把脏衣服捆起来塞进袋子。 ◇ *The papers were all bundled together, ready to be thrown out.* 报纸全部捆好，准备扔掉。 **ˌbundle sb 'up (in sth)** to put warm clothes or coverings on sb 使穿暖和（或盖被子等）：*I bundled her up in a blanket and gave her a hot drink.* 我给她裹了条毯子，又给了她一杯热饮。

ˌbundle of 'joy *noun* (*informal, humorous, sometimes ironic*) a baby son or daughter 幸福襁褓（指婴儿）：*Here are the latest pictures of our little bundle of joy.* 这些是我们的小淘气包的最新照片。

bundo·bast (*also* **bundo·bust**) /ˈbʌndəbæst; -bʌst/ *noun* [U, C, usually sing.] (*IndE*) = BANDOBAST

bun·fight /ˈbʌnfaɪt/ *noun* (*BrE, informal*) **1** an impressive or important party or other social event 隆重的聚会；重要聚会；重大场合 **2** an angry argument or discussion 争吵；争论

bung /bʌŋ/ *verb, noun, adj.*

■ ***verb*** **~ sth + adv./prep.** (*BrE, informal*) to put or throw sth somewhere, carelessly and quickly 扔；丢：*Bung this in the bin, can you?* 你可以把它扔进垃圾箱里吗？

PHR V **ˌbung sth 'up (with sth)** [usually passive] to block sth 堵塞；塞住：*My nose is all bunged up.* 我的鼻子全堵了。 ◇ *The drains are bunged up with dead leaves.* 排水沟被枯树叶堵住了。

■ ***noun*** **1** a round piece of wood, rubber, etc. used for closing the hole in a container such as a BARREL or JAR （桶、罐、广口瓶的）塞子，盖子 **2** (*BrE, informal*) an amount of money that is given to sb to persuade them to do sth illegal 贿款；贿金；贿赂

■ ***adj.*** (*AustralE, NZE, informal*) broken 破损的；破坏了的

bun·ga·low /ˈbʌŋɡələʊ; *NAmE* -loʊ/ *noun* **1** (*BrE*) a house built all on one level, without stairs 平房 ➲ VISUAL VOCAB PAGE V16 ➲ COMPARE RANCH HOUSE (2) **2** (in some Asian countries) a large house, sometimes on more than one level, that is not joined to another house on either side （某些亚洲国家的）平房，独座房屋

bun·gee /ˈbʌndʒi/ *noun* **1** a long rope which can stretch, that people tie to their feet when they do bungee jumping 蹦极；蹦极索 ➲ VISUAL VOCAB PAGE V54 **2** (*also* **'bungee cord**) a thick ELASTIC rope with a hook at each end that can be used to hold packages together, keep things in position, etc. （两端带钩子的）弹力绳索

'bungee jumping *noun* [U] a sport in which a person jumps from a high place, such as a bridge or a CLIFF, with a bungee tied to their feet 蹦极跳，高空弹跳（体育运动，用弹力长绳捆脚从高空跳下）：*to go bungee jumping* 去蹦极 ➲ VISUAL VOCAB PAGE V54 ▶ **'bun·gee jump** *noun*：*to do a bungee jump* 玩蹦极跳

bun·gle /ˈbʌŋɡl/ *verb, noun*

■ ***verb*** [T, I] **~ (sth)** to do sth badly or without skill; to fail at sth 笨拙地做；失败 **SYN** **botch**: *They bungled the job.* 他们把活儿搞糟了。 ◇ *a **bungled robbery/raid/attempt*** 未遂的抢劫 / 袭击 / 尝试 ▶ **bun·gler** /ˈbʌŋɡlə(r)/ *noun* **bun·gling** *adj.* [only before noun]：*bungling incompetence* 笨拙无能

■ ***noun*** [usually sing.] something that is done badly and that causes problems 搞糟了的事情；失误：*Their pay was late because of a computer bungle.* 由于计算机出错，他们的工资晚发了。

bun·ion /ˈbʌnjən/ *noun* a painful swelling on the foot, usually on the big toe 脚部的肿块；（通常指）拇囊炎

bunk /bʌŋk/ *noun, verb*

■ ***noun*** **1** [C] a narrow bed that is fixed to a wall, especially on a ship or train （尤指船或火车的）卧铺 **2** [C] (*also* **'bunk bed**) one of two beds that are fixed together, one above the other, especially for children （尤指儿童的）双层床，架子床；上铺；下铺 ➲ VISUAL VOCAB PAGE V24 **3** [U] (*old-fashioned, informal*) nonsense 瞎话；胡话 **SYN** **bunkum**

IDM **do a 'bunk** (*BrE, informal*) to run away from a place without telling anyone 溜走；悄悄离开

■ ***verb***

PHR V **ˌbunk 'off | ˌbunk off 'school/'work** (*BrE, informal*) to stay away from school or work when you should be there; to leave school or work early 逃学；旷工；早退 **SYN** **skive, play truant**

bun·ker /ˈbʌŋkə(r)/ *noun, verb*

■ ***noun*** **1** a strongly built shelter for soldiers or guns, usually underground 地堡；掩体：***a concrete/underground/secret bunker*** 混凝土 / 地下 / 秘密掩体 **2** a container for storing coal, especially on a ship or outside a house 煤舱；煤箱：*a coal bunker* 煤箱 **3** (*also especially NAmE* **'sand trap, trap**) a small area filled with sand on a GOLF COURSE （高尔夫球场上的）沙坑 ➲ VISUAL VOCAB PAGE V44

B

■ *verb* **be bunkered** (in GOLF 高尔夫球) to have hit your ball into a bunker (and therefore to be in a difficult position) 把球击入了沙坑（因而处境艰难）

bunk·house /ˈbʌŋkhaʊs/ *noun* a building for workers to sleep in 工棚；简易工人宿舍

bun·kum /ˈbʌŋkəm/ *noun* [U] (*old-fashioned, informal*) nonsense 废话；瞎话 SYN **bunk**

bunny /ˈbʌni/ *noun* (*pl.* **-ies**) (*also* ˈ**bunny rabbit**) **1** a child's word for a RABBIT（儿语）兔子 **2** a person who enjoys a particular activity or who is in a particular mood（某项活动的）爱好者；处于某种情绪中的人：*gym/beach/snow bunnies* 健身 / 沙滩 / 冰雪爱好者 ◇ *an angry bunny* 发怒的人 IDM SEE HAPPY

ˈ**bunny-hop** *noun* a small jump forward in a CROUCHING position 兔子跳；蹲跳 ▶ ˈ**bunny-hop** *verb* (**-pp-**) [I]

ˈ**bunny slope** (*NAmE*) (*BrE* ˈ**nursery slope**) *noun* a slope that is not very steep and is used by people who are learning to SKI（初学滑雪者使用的）平缓坡地

Bun·sen burn·er /ˌbʌnsn ˈbɜːnə(r); *NAmE* ˈbɜːrn-/ *noun* an instrument used in scientific work that produces a hot gas flame 本生灯（科学实验用煤气灯）➲ VISUAL VOCAB PAGE V72

bunt /bʌnt/ *verb* [T, I] ~ (**sth**) (*NAmE*) (in BASEBALL 棒球) to deliberately hit the ball only a short distance 触击 ▶ **bunt** *noun*

bunt·ing /ˈbʌntɪŋ/ *noun* **1** [U] coloured flags or paper used for decorating streets and buildings in celebrations（装饰街道、房屋等的）彩旗，彩纸 **2** [C] a small bird related to the FINCH and SPARROW families. There are several types of bunting. 鹀：*a corn/reed/snow bunting* 黍鹀；芦鹀；雪鹀

bun·yip /ˈbʌnjɪp/ *noun* (*AustralE*) (in stories) a MONSTER that lives in or near water 本耶普（传说中的沼泽湖泊地区怪兽）

buoy /bɔɪ; *NAmE also* ˈbuːi/ *noun, verb*

■ *noun* an object which floats on the sea or a river to mark the places where it is dangerous and where it is safe for boats to go 浮标；航标 ➲ SEE ALSO LIFEBUOY

■ *verb* [usually passive] **1** ~ **sb** (**up**) to make sb feel cheerful or confident 鼓舞；鼓励：*Buoyed by their win yesterday the team feel confident of further success.* 在昨天的胜利鼓舞下，该队有信心再次获胜。**2** ~ **sb/sth** (**up**) to keep sb/sth floating on water 使漂浮；使浮起 **3** ~ **sth** (**up**) to keep prices at a high or acceptable level 使（价格）上浮；使（价格）维持于较高水平

buoy·ant /ˈbɔɪənt; *NAmE also* ˈbuːjənt/ *adj.* **1** (of prices, business activity, etc. 价格、商业活动等) tending to increase or stay at a high level, usually showing financial success 看涨的；保持高价的；繁荣的：*a* ***buoyant economy/market*** 繁荣的经济 / 市场 ◇ ***buoyant sales/prices*** 上升的销售额 / 价格 ◇ *a buoyant demand for homes* 越来越大的住房需求 **2** cheerful and feeling sure that things will be successful 愉快而充满信心的；乐观的：*They were all in buoyant mood.* 他们都很乐观。**3** floating, able to float or able to keep things floating 漂浮的；能够漂起的；有浮力的：*The boat bobbed like a cork on the waves: light and buoyant.* 小船在大浪中犹如软木塞：轻轻漂来漂去。◇ *Salt water is more buoyant than fresh water.* 盐水比淡水浮力大。▶ **buoy·ancy** /ˈbɔɪənsi; *NAmE also* ˈbuːjənsi/ *noun* [U]：*the buoyancy of the market* 市场的活跃 ◇ *a mood of buoyancy* 轻松愉快的心情 ◇ *a buoyancy aid* (= sth to help you float) 助浮物

bup·pie (*also* **buppy**) /ˈbʌpi/ (*pl.* **-ies**) *noun* (*SAfrE, informal*) a black person who is a YUPPIE 黑人雅皮士；黑人雅痞

bur = BURR (3)

Bur·berry™ /ˈbɜːbəri; *NAmE* ˈbɜːrberi/ *noun* (*pl.* **-ies**) a type of RAINCOAT 博柏利雨衣

bur·ble /ˈbɜːbl; *NAmE* ˈbɜːrbl/ *verb* **1** [I, T] ~ (**on**) (**about sth**) | **+ speech** (*disapproving*) to speak in a confused or silly way that is difficult to hear or understand 语无伦次地讲；说蠢话：*What's he burbling about?* 他在嘟囔些啥？**2** [I] to make the gentle sound of a stream flowing over stones 汩汩作响

burbs /bɜːbz; *NAmE* bɜːrbz/ *noun* **the burbs** [pl.] (*NAmE, informal*) = SUBURBS

bur·den /ˈbɜːdn; *NAmE* ˈbɜːrdn/ *noun, verb*

■ *noun* **1** the ~ (**of sth**) | a ~ (**on/to sb**) a duty, responsibility, etc. that causes worry, difficulty or hard work（义务、责任等的）重担，负担：*to* ***bear/carry/ease/reduce/share the burden*** 承受 / 担负 / 减轻 / 减少 / 分担重担 ◇ *The main burden of caring for old people falls on the state.* 国家担负起了照料老人的大部分责任。◇ *the heavy tax burden on working people* 加在劳动者头上的重税 ◇ *I don't want to become a burden to my children when I'm old.* 我不想在年老的时候成为孩子们的累赘。**2** (*formal*) a heavy load that is difficult to carry 重担；重负 ➲ SEE ALSO BEAST OF BURDEN

■ *verb* **1** ~ **sb/yourself** (**with sth**) to give sb a duty, responsibility, etc. that causes worry, difficulty or hard work（使）担负（沉重或艰难的任务、职责等）：*They have burdened themselves with a high mortgage.* 他们负担了一笔很高的按揭借款。◇ *I don't want to burden you with my worries.* 我不想让你为我的烦恼操心。◇ *to be burdened by high taxation* 不堪重税负荷 OPP **unburden** **2** **be burdened with sth** to be carrying sth heavy 负重：*She got off the bus, burdened with two heavy suitcases.* 她提着两只沉重的手提箱下了公共汽车。

the ˌburden of ˈproof *noun* [sing.] (*law* 律) the task or responsibility of proving that sth is true 举证责任；证明责任

bur·den·some /ˈbɜːdnsəm; *NAmE* ˈbɜːrd-/ *adj.* (*formal*) causing worry, difficulty or hard work 负担沉重的；难以承担的；繁重的 SYN **onerous**

bur·dock /ˈbɜːdɒk; *NAmE* ˈbɜːrdɑːk/ *noun* [U] a plant with flowers that become PRICKLY and stick to passing animals 牛蒡（植物）

bur·eau /ˈbjʊərəʊ; *NAmE* ˈbjʊroʊ/ *noun* (*pl.* **bur·eaux** or **bur·eaus** /-rəʊz; *NAmE* -roʊz/) **1** (*BrE*) a desk with drawers and usually a top that opens down to make a table to write on（附抽屉及活动写字台的）书桌 **2** (*NAmE*) = CHEST OF DRAWERS **3** an office or organization that provides information on a particular subject（提供某方面信息的）办事处，办公室，机构：*an employment bureau* 职业介绍所 **4** (in the US) a government department or part of a government department（美国政府部门）局，处，科：*the Federal Bureau of Investigation* 联邦调查局

bur·eau·cracy /bjʊəˈrɒkrəsi; *NAmE* bjʊˈrɑːk-/ *noun* (*pl.* **-ies**) **1** [U] (*often disapproving*) the system of official rules and ways of doing things that a government or an organization has, especially when these seem to be too complicated 官僚主义；官僚作风：***unnecessary/excessive bureaucracy*** 不必要的官僚式繁文缛节；过分的官僚作风 **2** [U, C] a system of government in which there are a large number of state officials who are not elected; a country with such a system 官僚体制；实行官僚体制的国家：*the power of the state bureaucracy* 国家官僚体制的权力 ◇ *living in a modern bureaucracy* 生活在一个现代官僚体制中

bur·eau·crat /ˈbjʊərəkræt; *NAmE* ˈbjʊr-/ *noun* (*often disapproving*) an official working in an organization or a government department, especially one who follows the rules of the department too strictly 官僚主义者；官僚

bur·eau·crat·ic /ˌbjʊərəˈkrætɪk; *NAmE* ˌbjʊr-/ *adj.* (*often disapproving*) connected with a bureaucracy or bureaucrats and involving complicated official rules which may seem unnecessary 官僚的；官僚主义的：***bureaucratic power/control/procedures/organizations*** 官僚权力 / 管理 / 程序 / 组织 ◇ *The report revealed a great deal of bureaucratic inefficiency.* 报道大量揭示了官僚体制的无能。▶ **bur·eau·crat·ic·al·ly** /-ɪkli/ *adv.*

B

bur·eau de change /ˌbjʊərəʊ də ˈʃɑːnʒ; *NAmE* ˌbjʊroʊ/ *noun* (*pl.* **bur·eaux de change** /ˌbjʊərəʊ də ˈʃɑːnʒ; *NAmE* ˌbjʊroʊ/) (*from French*) an office at a hotel, in an airport, etc., where you can exchange money from one country for that from another 外币兑换处；外币兑换所

bur·ette (*US also* **buret**) /bjuˈret/ *noun* a glass tube with measurements on it and a tap/faucet at one end, used, for example, in chemical experiments for measuring out amounts of a liquid 滴定管；量管 ➲ VISUAL VOCAB PAGE V72

burg /bɜːɡ; *NAmE* bɜːrɡ/ *noun* (*NAmE, informal*) a town or city 镇；市；城

bur·geon /ˈbɜːdʒən; *NAmE* ˈbɜːrdʒən/ *verb* [I] (*formal*) to begin to grow or develop rapidly 激增；迅速发展 ▸ **bur·geon·ing** *adj.*： *a burgeoning population* 急剧增长的人口 ◇ *burgeoning demand* 迅速增加的需求

bur·ger /ˈbɜːɡə(r); *NAmE* ˈbɜːrɡ-/ *noun* **1** = HAMBURGER **2 -bur·ger** (in compounds 构成复合词) finely chopped fish, vegetables, nuts, etc. made into flat round shapes like HAMBURGERS （汉堡牛肉式的）鱼松饼，菜末饼，果仁饼： *a spicy beanburger* 香辣豆蓉饼 ➲ SEE ALSO CHEESEBURGER, VEGGIE BURGER

burgh /ˈbʌrə/ *noun* (*old-fashioned* or *ScotE*) a town or part of a city that has its own local government 自治市；（城市的）自治区

bur·gher /ˈbɜːɡə(r); *NAmE* ˈbɜːrɡ-/ *noun* (*old use* or *humorous*) a citizen of a particular town （某市的）市民

burg·lar /ˈbɜːɡlə(r); *NAmE* ˈbɜːrɡ-/ *noun* a person who enters a building illegally in order to steal 破门盗贼；入室窃贼

ˈburglar alarm *noun* an electronic device, often fixed to a wall, that rings a loud bell if sb tries to enter a building by force 防盗铃 ➲ VISUAL VOCAB PAGE V18

burg·lary /ˈbɜːɡləri; *NAmE* ˈbɜːrɡ-/ *noun* [U, C] (*pl.* **-ies**) the crime of entering a building illegally and stealing things from it 入室偷盗罪 SYN **housebreaking**: *The youth was charged with three counts of burglary.* 那个年轻人被控犯有三次入室盗窃罪。◇ *a rise in the number of burglaries committed in the area* 该地区盗窃案例数目的上升 ➲ COMPARE ROBBERY, THEFT

bur·gle /ˈbɜːɡl; *NAmE* ˈbɜːrɡl/ (*BrE*) (*NAmE* **burg·lar·ize** /ˈbɜːɡləraɪz; *NAmE* ˈbɜːrɡ-/) *verb* **~ sb/sth** to enter a building illegally, usually using force, and steal from it 入室盗窃： *We were burgled while we were away* (= our house was burgled). 我们外出时家里失窃了。◇ *The house next door was burgled.* 邻居家被盗了。 ➲ COLLOCATIONS AT CRIME

bur·goo /bɜːˈɡuː; *NAmE* bɜːrˈɡuː/ *noun* (*pl.* **-oos**) (*NAmE*) **1** [U] a type of thick soup, especially one eaten outdoors （常在野餐时喝的）杂烩汤 **2** [C] an event at which burgoo is eaten outdoors 杂烩汤野餐

bur·gundy /ˈbɜːɡəndi; *NAmE* ˈbɜːrɡ-/ *noun* **1 Burgundy** [U, C] (*pl.* **-ies**) a red or white wine from the Burgundy area of eastern France 勃艮第葡萄酒（产于法国东部的勃艮第地区，有红葡萄酒和白葡萄酒） **2** [U] a dark red colour 深红色 ▸ **bur·gundy** *adj.*： *a burgundy leather briefcase* 深红色的皮革公文包

bur·ial /ˈberiəl/ *noun* [U, C] the act or ceremony of burying a dead body 埋葬；葬礼： *a* ***burial place/mound/site*** 安葬地；坟头；坟地 ◇ *Her body was sent home for burial.* 她的尸骨已运回家乡安葬。◇ *His family insisted he should be given a proper burial.* 他的家人坚持应该为他举行得体的葬礼。

ˈburial ground *noun* a place where dead bodies are buried, especially an ancient place （尤指古老的）墓地，坟地

burka (*also* **burkha**, **burqa**) /ˈbʊəkə; ˈbɜːkə; *NAmE* ˈbɜːrkə/ *noun* a long loose piece of clothing that covers the whole body, including the head and face, worn by some Muslim women 布尔卡（一些穆斯林妇女穿的一种蒙面长袍）

bur·lap /ˈbɜːlæp; *NAmE* ˈbɜːrl-/ *noun* [U] (*NAmE*) = HESSIAN

bur·lesque /bɜːˈlesk; *NAmE* bɜːrˈl-/ *noun* **1** [C] a performance or piece of writing which tries to make sth look ridiculous by representing it in a humorous way 滑稽讽刺表演（或作品） SYN **parody**: *a burlesque of literary life* 对文学生活的戏谑 **2** [U] a type of entertainment involving humorous acts, singing, dancing, etc. and often including STRIPTEASE 滑稽娱乐（常有脱衣舞表演） ▸ **bur·lesque** *adj.* [usually before noun]

burly /ˈbɜːli; *NAmE* ˈbɜːrli/ *adj.* (**bur·lier**, **bur·li·est**) (of a man or a man's body 男人或男人身体) big, strong and heavy 高大强壮的；魁梧的 SYN **brawny**

burn 🔑 /bɜːn; *NAmE* bɜːrn/ *verb, noun*

■ *verb* (**burnt**, **burnt** /bɜːnt; *NAmE* bɜːrnt/ or **burned**, **burned** /bɜːnd; *NAmE* bɜːrnd/)

• FIRE 火 **1** 🔑 [I] to produce flames and heat 燃烧；烧： *A welcoming fire was burning in the fireplace.* 壁炉里燃烧着暖融融的炉火。◇ *Fires were burning all over the city.* 全城处处燃烧着大火。 **2** 🔑 [I] (used especially in the progressive tenses 尤用于进行时) to be on fire 着火；烧着： *By nightfall the whole city was burning.* 到黄昏时，全城已是一片火海。◇ *Two children were rescued from the burning car.* 两名儿童从燃烧着的车中被救了出来。◇ *The smell of burning rubber filled the air.* 空气中弥漫着橡胶燃烧的气味。 **3** 🔑 [T, I] to destroy, damage, injure or kill sb/sth by fire; to be destroyed, etc. by fire （使）烧毁，烧坏，烧伤，烧死： **~ (sb/sth)** *to burn waste paper/dead leaves* 焚烧废纸／枯树叶 ◇ *All his belongings were burnt in the fire.* 他所有的财物都在大火中付之一炬。◇ *The cigarette burned a hole in the carpet.* 香烟把地毯烧了个洞。◇ *The house was* ***burnt to the ground*** (= completely destroyed). 那座房子彻底焚毁了。◇ *The house* ***burned to the ground.***

▼ SYNONYMS 同义词辨析

burn

char • scald • scorch • singe

These words all mean to damage, injure, destroy or kill sb/sth with heat or fire. 以上各词均含因高温或火导致损坏、损伤、毁灭之义。

burn to damage, injure, destroy or kill sb/sth with fire, heat or acid; to be damaged, etc. by fire, heat or acid 指烧（或灼）坏、烧（或灼）伤、烧（或灼）死： *She burned all his letters.* 她把他的信全部付之一炬。◇ *The house* ***burned down*** *in 1995.* 那所房子在 1995 年烧毁了。

char [usually passive] to make sth black by burning it; to become black by burning 指（使）烧黑、烧焦： *The bodies had been charred beyond recognition.* 这些尸体已烧焦，无法辨认。

scald to burn part of your body with very hot liquid or steam 指被高温液体或气体烫伤

scorch to burn and slightly damage a surface by making it too hot 指把物体表面烫坏、烧煳、烤焦： *I scorched my dress when I was ironing it.* 我把自己的连衣裙熨焦了。

singe to burn the surface of sth slightly, usually by mistake; to be burnt in this way 尤指不小心把物体表面烤焦、烫煳： *He singed his hair as he tried to light his cigarette.* 他点烟时把头发给燎了。

SCORCH OR SINGE? 用 scorch 还是 singe?

Things are **scorched** by heat or fire. Things can only be **singed** by fire or a flame. * scorch 指高温烫坏或火烧煳；singe 仅指火或火舌烧焦。

PATTERNS

- to burn/scald **yourself/your hand**
- to burn/scorch/singe your **hair/clothes**
- burnt out/charred/scorched **remains/ruins/buildings**

B

房子被大火夷为平地。◇ *Ten people **burned to death** in the hotel fire.* 旅馆火灾中有十人被烧死。◇ **~ sb/sth + adj.** *His greatest fear is of being **burnt alive**.* 他最怕的是被活活烧死。

• **FUEL** 燃料 **4** [T, I] ~ (**sth**) if you **burn** a fuel, or a fuel **burns**, it produces heat, light or energy （使燃料）燃烧：*a furnace that burns gas/oil/coke* 煤气 / 煤油 / 焦炭熔炉 ◇ (*figurative*) *Some people burn calories* (= use food to produce energy) *faster than others.* 有些人热量消耗得比其他人快。◇ *Which fuel burns most efficiently?* 哪种燃料燃烧效果最佳？

• **FOOD** 食物 **5** [I, T] if food **burns**, or if you **burn** it, it is spoiled because it gets too hot （使）烧焦，烧煳：*I can smell something burning in the kitchen.* 我闻到厨房里有东西烧焦了。◇ **~ sth** *Sorry—I burnt the toast.* 抱歉，我把面包烤煳了。

• **SUN/HEAT/ACID** 太阳；热；酸 **6** [I, T] to be damaged or injured by the sun, heat, acid, etc.; to damage or injure sb/sth in this way （使）晒伤，烫伤，烧伤：*My skin burns easily* (= in the sun). 我的皮肤容易晒伤。◇ **~ sb** *I got badly burned by the sun yesterday.* 我昨天严重晒伤。◇ **~ sth** *The soup's hot. Don't burn your mouth.* 汤很热，别烫了嘴。◇ **~ yourself** *I burned myself on the stove.* 我被炉子烫了。

• **OF PART OF BODY** 身体部位 **7** [I] if part of your body **burns** or **is burning**, it feels very hot and painful 火辣辣地痛；发烫：*Your forehead's burning. Have you got a fever?* 你的前额很烫，你发烧了吗？ ◇ *Her cheeks burned with embarrassment.* 她羞得面颊发烫。➲ SYNONYMS AT HURT

• **OF A LIGHT** 灯 **8** [I] to produce light 发光；发亮：*Lights were burning upstairs, but no one answered the door.* 楼上亮着灯，但叫门没人回应。

• **FEEL EMOTION/DESIRE** 有情感 / 热望 **9** [I, T] (*literary*) to feel a very strong emotion or desire 有强烈的情感；渴望：**~ with sth** *to be burning with rage/ambition/love* 满怀强烈的仇恨 / 远大的抱负 / 炽热的爱 ◇ **~ to do sth** *He was burning to go climbing again.* 他渴望再去爬山。

• **GO FAST** 走得快 **10** [I] + **adv./prep.** (*informal*) to move very fast in a particular direction 向…迅速移动：*The car was burning down the road.* 汽车沿着公路疾驰而去。

• **MAKE ANGRY** 使生气 **11** [T] ~ **sb** (*NAmE, informal*) to make sb very angry 激怒；使大怒：*So you did it just to burn me?* 这么说，你那样做只是为了气我？

• **CD, DVD** 光盘、数字影碟 **12** [T, I] ~ (**sth**) (**to sth**) to put information onto a CD or DVD 刻录（光盘或数字影碟）

IDM **burn your 'bridges** (*BrE also* **burn your 'boats**) to do sth that makes it impossible to return to the previous situation later 不留退路；破釜沉舟；背水而战：*Think carefully before you resign—you don't want to burn your bridges.* 辞职前要三思，你得给自己留条退路。 **burn the candle at both 'ends** to become very tired by trying to do too many things and going to bed late and getting up early 过度劳累；起早贪黑而疲惫不堪 **burn your 'fingers | get your 'fingers burnt** to suffer as a result of doing sth without realizing the possible bad results, especially in business （尤指生意上）没有先见之明而蒙受损失，因不慎而吃亏：*He got his fingers badly burnt dabbling in the stock market.* 他糊里糊涂地进入股票市场，结果赔了老本。 **burn a 'hole in your pocket** if money **burns a hole in your pocket**, you want to spend it as soon as you have it 一有（钱）就想花；花钱没有节制 **burn the midnight 'oil** to study or work until late at night 挑灯夜战；熬夜 **burn 'rubber** (*informal*) to drive very fast 飞车 **burn sth to a 'cinder/'crisp** to cook sth for too long or with too much heat, so that it becomes badly burnt 把某物烧焦（或烧煳） ➲ MORE AT EAR, FEEL *v.*, MONEY

PHR V ˌ**burn a'way** | ˌ**burn sth↔a'way** to disappear as a result of burning; to make sth do this （使）烧掉，烧光：*Half the candle had burnt away.* 那根蜡烛烧掉了一半。◇ *The clothing on his back got burnt away in the fire.* 他背部的衣服在大火中烧掉了。 ˌ**burn 'down** if a fire **burns down**, it becomes weaker and has smaller flames （火势）减弱 ˌ**burn 'down** | ˌ**burn sth↔'down** to be destroyed, or to destroy sth, by fire （被）焚毁：*The house burned down in 1895.* 那房子在 1895 年烧毁了。 ˌ**burn sth↔'off 1** to remove sth by burning 烧掉；烧除：*Burn off the old paint before repainting the door.* 先把门上的旧漆烧掉，再刷新油漆。 **2** to use energy by doing exercise （通过锻炼等）消耗能量：*This workout helps you to burn off fat and tone muscles.* 这项锻炼有助于消耗脂肪，使肌肉强健。 ˌ**burn 'out** | ˌ**burn itself 'out** (of a fire 火) to stop burning because there is nothing more to burn 烧尽；熄灭：*The fire had burnt (itself) out before the fire engines arrived.* 救火车到达之前火就熄灭了。 ˌ**burn 'out** | ˌ**burn sth↔'out** to stop working or to make sth stop working because it gets too hot or is used too much （因过热或使用过多）出故障：*The clutch has burnt out.* 离合器因过热而失灵了。 ˌ**burn 'out** | ˌ**burn yourself/sb 'out** to become extremely tired or sick by working too hard over a period of time 耗尽体力；积劳成疾；累垮：*If he doesn't stop working so hard, he'll burn himself out.* 他要是继续这样拼命工作，就会把自己累垮。◇ *By the age of 25 she was completely burned out and retired from the sport.* 她到 25 岁时就已体力耗尽，退出了体坛。 ➲ RELATED NOUN BURNOUT (1) ˌ**burn sth 'out** [usually passive] to destroy sth completely by fire so that only the outer frame remains 把…烧成空架子：*The hotel was completely burnt out.* 旅馆被烧得只剩一片废墟。◇ *the burnt-out wreck of a car* 汽车烧毁后的残骸 ˌ**burn 'up 1** to be destroyed by heat 被烧毁；被烧掉：*The spacecraft burned up as it entered the earth's atmosphere.* 宇宙飞船进入地球大气层时被烧毁。 **2** (usually used in the progressive tenses 通常用于进行时) (*informal*) to have a high temperature 发烧；体温高：*You're burning up—have you seen a doctor?* 你发烧了，你看过医生吗？ **3** (of a fire 火) to burn more strongly and with larger flames 烧得更旺；火势加大 ˌ**burn sb 'up** (*NAmE, informal*) to make sb very angry 激怒；使大怒：*The way he treats me really burns me up.* 他这样对待我真使我恼火。 ˌ**burn sth↔'up 1** to get rid of or destroy sth by burning 焚毁；烧掉：*The fire burned up 1 500 acres of farmland.* 大火烧掉了 1 500 英亩农田。 **2** to use CALORIES or energy by doing exercise （通过锻炼）消耗热能：*Which burns up more calories—swimming or cycling?* 游泳和骑车，哪种运动消耗热量大？

■ ***noun***

• **INJURY** 伤 **1** [C] an injury or a mark caused by fire, heat or acid 烧伤；烫伤；灼伤；烧（或烫、灼）的痕迹：***minor/severe/third-degree burns*** 轻度 / 重度 / 三度烧伤 ◇ *cigarette burns on the furniture* 烟头在家具上烫出的痕迹 ◇ *burn marks* 烙印 ◇ *a specialist burns unit in a hospital* 医院的烧伤专科

• **IN MUSCLES** 肌肉 **2 the burn** [sing.] the feeling that you get in your muscles when you have done a lot of exercise 酸痛感

• **RIVER** 河流 **3** [C] (*ScotE*) a small river 小河；溪流 SYN **stream** IDM SEE SLOW *adj.*

burn·er /'bɜːnə(r); *NAmE* 'bɜːrn-/ *noun* **1** the part of a cooker/stove, etc. that produces a flame 煤气头；煤气灶火圈；炉膛 ➲ VISUAL VOCAB PAGE V26 **2** a large, solid, metal piece of equipment for burning wood or coal, used for heating a room （取暖用的）炉子：*a wood burner* 烧木柴的炉子 ➲ SEE ALSO BUNSEN BURNER IDM SEE BACK *adj.*, FRONT *adj.*

burn·ing /'bɜːnɪŋ; *NAmE* 'bɜːrn-/ *adj.*, *adv.*

■ ***adj.*** [only before noun] **1** (of feelings, etc. 感情等) very strong; extreme 强烈的；极度的：*a **burning desire** to win* 取胜的迫切愿望 ◇ *He's always had a **burning ambition** to start his own business.* 他总是雄心勃勃地想自己创业。 **2 a ~ issue/question** a very important and urgent problem 重大迫切的问题；当务之急 **3** (of pain, etc. 疼痛等) very strong and giving a feeling of burning 强烈的；火辣辣的 ➲ SYNONYMS AT PAINFUL **4** very hot; looking and feeling very hot 炽热的；（看似或感觉）热辣辣的：*the burning sun* 灼热的太阳 ◇ *her burning face* 她的热辣辣的脸 **5 ~ eyes** (*literary*) eyes that seem to be staring at you very hard 紧盯着看的眼睛；热切的目光

■ ***adv.*** **burning hot** very hot 灼热地

bur·nish /'bɜːnɪʃ; *NAmE* 'bɜːrnɪʃ/ *verb* **~ sth** (*formal*) to polish metal until it is smooth and shiny 磨光，擦亮（金

属） ▶ **bur·nished** *adj.* [usually before noun]: ***burnished gold/copper*** 擦得锃亮的金器 / 铜器

bur·nous (*NAmE usually* **bur·noose**) /bɜːˈnuːs; *NAmE* bɜːrˈn-/ *noun* a long loose item of outer clothing with a HOOD (= covering for the head), worn by Arabs 布尔努斯袍（阿拉伯人穿的带风帽长外衣）

burn·out /ˈbɜːnaʊt; *NAmE* ˈbɜːrn-/ *noun* [C, U] **1** the state of being extremely tired or ill, either physically or mentally, because you have worked too hard 精疲力竭；过度劳累 **2** the point at which a ROCKET has used all of its fuel and has no more power （火箭）熄火点，燃烧终止

ˈ**Burns Night** *noun* [U, C] the evening of 25 January when Scottish people celebrate the birthday of the Scottish POET, Robert Burns, with traditional Scottish music, WHISKY and dishes such as HAGGIS 彭斯之夜（1 月 25 日，苏格兰人民纪念苏格兰诗人罗伯特•彭斯诞辰的节日）

burnt 🔑 /bɜːnt; *NAmE* bɜːrnt/ *adj.* damaged or injured by burning 烧坏的；烧伤的；烫伤的；灼伤的：*burnt toast* 烤焦了的面包片 ◇ *Your hand looks badly burnt.* 你的手似乎烧伤很重。

ˌ**burnt ˈochre** (*NAmE* ˌ**burnt ˈocher**) *noun* [U] **1** a deep yellow-brown colour 焦赭色；赤土色 **2** a yellow-brown PIGMENT, used in art 烧赭石（颜料）

ˌ**burnt ˈoffering** *noun* **1** something (usually an animal) that is burnt in a religious ceremony as a gift offered to a god 燔祭品（宗教仪式上焚烧祭神的动物等） **2** (*BrE, humorous*) food that has been badly burnt by accident 烧焦的食物

ˌ**burnt-ˈout** (*also* ˌ**burned-ˈout**) *adj.* **1** destroyed or badly damaged by fire 烧毁的；烧坏的：*a burnt-out car* 烧毁的汽车 **2** feeling as if you have done sth for too long and need to have a rest 精疲力竭的；疲乏的：*I'm feeling burnt-out at work—I need a holiday.* 我觉得工作得太累了，我需要休假。

ˌ**burnt siˈenna** *noun* [U] **1** a deep red-brown colour 熟褐色；赭褐色 **2** a deep red-brown PIGMENT, used in art 煅黄土（颜料）

ˌ**burnt ˈumber** *noun* [U] **1** a dark brown colour 深赭色；深褐色 **2** a dark brown PIGMENT, used in art 烧棕土（颜料）

burp /bɜːp; *NAmE* bɜːrp/ *verb* (*informal*) **1** [I] to let out air from the stomach through the mouth, making a noise 打嗝 **SYN** **belch** **2** [T] **~ sb** to make a baby bring up air from the stomach, especially by rubbing or PATTING its back 使（婴儿）打嗝（尤指通过抚摩或轻拍背部） ▶ **burp** *noun*

burqa *noun* = BURKA

burr /bɜː(r)/ *noun* **1** [usually sing.] a strong pronunciation of the 'r' sound, typical of some accents in English; an accent with this type of pronunciation 小舌 r 音，颤音 r，带浓重 r 音的口音（某些英语方言中的典型发音）：*She speaks with a soft West Country burr.* 她说话带有一种西部地区浓重 r 的口音。 **2** [usually sing.] the soft regular noise made by parts of a machine moving quickly （机器部件快速运转时有规律的）呼呼声 **SYN** **whir** **3** (*also* **bur**) [C] the seed container of some plants which is covered in very small hooks that stick to clothes or fur （某些植物）带芒刺的小果实

bur·rito /bʊˈriːtəʊ; *NAmE* -toʊ/ *noun* (*pl.* **-os**) (*from Spanish*) a Mexican dish consisting of a TORTILLA filled with meat or BEANS （墨西哥）肉馅（或豆馅）玉米粉圆饼

burro /ˈbʊrəʊ; *NAmE* ˈbɜːroʊ/ *noun* (*pl.* **-os**) (*NAmE, from Spanish*) a small DONKEY 小驴

bur·row /ˈbʌrəʊ; *NAmE* ˈbɜːroʊ/ *verb, noun*
■ *verb* **1** [I, T] to make a hole or a tunnel in the ground by digging 挖掘（洞或洞穴通道）；挖洞 **SYN** **dig**: (**+ adv./prep.**) *Earthworms burrow deep into the soil.* 蚯蚓钻土很深。◇ **~ sth + adv./prep.** *The rodent* ***burrowed its way*** *into the sand.* 这只鼠掘洞钻进沙里。 **2** [I, T] to press yourself close to sb or under sth 偎依；（使…）钻到（…下面）：**+ adv./prep.** *He burrowed down beneath the blankets.* 他钻到毯子下面。◇ **~ sth + adv./prep.** *She burrowed her face into his chest.* 她把脸埋进他的怀里。 **3** [I] **+ adv./prep.** to search for sth under or among things （在…里面或下面）搜寻：*She burrowed in the drawer for a pair of socks.* 她在抽屉里翻找一双袜子。◇ *He was afraid that they would burrow into his past.* 他担心他们会追查他的过去。
■ ***noun*** a hole or tunnel in the ground made by animals such as RABBITS for them to live in （动物的）洞穴，洞穴通道

bursa /ˈbɜːsə; *NAmE* ˈbɜːrsə/ *noun* (*pl.* **bur·sae** /-siː/ or **bur·sas**) (*anatomy* 解) a part inside the body like a bag or sleeve, which is filled with liquid, especially around a joint so that it can work smoothly 囊；黏液囊

bur·sar /ˈbɜːsə(r); *NAmE* ˈbɜːrs-/ *noun* (*especially BrE*) a person whose job is to manage the financial affairs of a school or college （学校或大学的）财务主管

bur·sary /ˈbɜːsəri; *NAmE* ˈbɜːrs-/ *noun* (*pl.* **-ies**) (*especially BrE*) an amount of money that is given to sb so that they can study, usually at a college or university （通常指大学的）奖学金 **SYN** **grant, scholarship**

bur·sitis /ˌbɜːˈsaɪtɪs; *NAmE* ˌbɜːr-/ *noun* [U] (*medical* 医) a condition in which a bursa becomes swollen and sore 滑囊炎

burst 🔑 /bɜːst; *NAmE* bɜːrst/ *verb, noun*
■ *verb* (**burst, burst**) **1** 🔑 [I, T] to break open or apart, especially because of pressure from inside; to make sth break in this way （使）爆裂，胀开：*That balloon will burst if you blow it up any more.* 你再给气球充气，它就要爆了。◇ *The dam burst under the weight of water.* 大坝在水的巨大压力下溃决了。◇ *Shells were bursting* (= exploding) *all around us.* 炮弹在我们四周爆炸。◇ (*figurative*) *He felt he would burst with anger and shame.* 他恼羞成怒，都要气炸了。◇ *a burst pipe* 爆裂的管子 ◇ **~ sth** *Don't burst that balloon!* 别把那气球弄爆了！◇ *The river* ***burst its banks*** *and flooded nearby towns.* 那条河决堤淹没了附近的城镇。➲ SYNONYMS AT EXPLODE **2** 🔑 [I] **+ adv./prep.** to go or move somewhere suddenly with great force; to come from somewhere suddenly 猛冲；突然出现：*He burst into the room without knocking.* 他没敲门就闯进了屋子。◇ *The sun burst through the clouds.* 太阳破云而出。◇ *The words burst from her in an angry rush.* 她破口说出了那一大堆气话。 **3** [I] **be bursting** (**with sth**) to be very full of sth; to be very full and almost breaking open 爆满；涨满：*The roads are bursting with cars.* 车辆把那些道路挤满了。◇ *to* ***be bursting with ideas/enthusiasm/pride*** 满怀想法 / 热情 / 骄傲 ◇ *The hall was filled to* ***bursting point.*** 大厅里挤满了人。◇ *The hall was* ***full to bursting.*** 大厅里挤满了人。◇ (*informal*) ***I'm bursting*** (*for a pee*)! (= I need to use the toilet right now.) 我（被尿）憋坏了！
IDM **be bursting to do sth** to want to do sth so much that you can hardly stop yourself 急于（或迫切想）做某事：*She was bursting to tell him the good news.* 她急不可待要把好消息告诉他。 ˌ**burst sb's ˈbubble** to bring an end to sb's hopes, happiness, etc. 使某人希望破灭；毁掉某人的幸福 ˌ**burst ˈopen** | ˌ**burst** (**sth**) ˈ**open** to open suddenly or violently; to make sth open in this way （使）猛然打开：*The door burst open.* 门突然开了。◇ *Firefighters burst the door open and rescued them.* 消防队员撞开门，把他们救了出来。➲ MORE AT BUBBLE *n.*, SEAM
PHR V ˌ**burst ˈin** to enter a room or building suddenly and noisily 闯进；突然破门而入 ˌ**burst ˈin on sb/sth** to interrupt sb/sth by entering a place suddenly and noisily 突然闯进而打断（或扰乱）：*He burst in on the meeting.* 他闯进来打断了会议。 ˈ**burst into sth** 🔑 to start producing sth suddenly and with great force 突然爆发：*The aircraft crashed and* ***burst into flames*** (= suddenly began to burn). 飞机坠毁后猛烈燃烧起来。◇ *She* ***burst into tears*** (= suddenly began to cry). 她突然大哭起来。 ˈ**burst on/onto sth** to appear somewhere suddenly in a way that is very noticeable 突然在…出现；突然显现：*A major new talent has* ***burst onto the*** *literary scene.* 文坛突然冒出一位重要的新秀。 ˌ**burst ˈout 1** to speak suddenly, loudly

B

and with strong feeling 突然激动地喊叫： + **speech** *'For heavens' sake!' he burst out.* "天哪！"他大叫一声。 ➲ RELATED NOUN OUTBURST ➲ SYNONYMS AT CALL **2** to begin doing sth suddenly 突然开始（做某事）： **burst out doing sth** *Karen **burst out laughing**.* 卡伦突然大笑起来。

■ ***noun*** **1** a short period of a particular activity or strong emotion that often starts suddenly 突发；猝发；迸发；爆破： *a sudden **burst of activity/energy/anger/enthusiasm*** 活动/能量/怒火/热情的迸发 ◇ *Her breath was coming **in short bursts**.* 她的呼吸急迫短促。◇ *I tend to work **in bursts**.* 我的工作劲头往往是一阵一阵的。◇ *spontaneous bursts of applause* 自发的阵阵掌声 **2** an occasion when sth bursts; the hole left where sth has burst 爆裂；裂口： *a burst in a water pipe* 水管上的裂缝 **3** a short series of shots from a gun 一阵短促的射击： *frequent bursts of machine-gun fire* 机枪的频频扫射

bursty /'bɜːsti; *NAmE* 'bɜːrsti/ *adj.* (**burst·ier**, **bursti·est**) **1** (*specialist*) used to describe data that is sent in small, sudden groups of signals 突发式数据的；集送数据的；脉冲数据的： *a bursty connection* 突发式连接 ◇ *bursty Internet traffic* 突发性网络拥塞 **2** (*informal*) occurring at intervals, for short periods of time 阵发性的；间歇的

bur·ton /'bɜːtn; *NAmE* 'bɜːrtn/ *noun*

IDM **gone for a 'burton** (*old-fashioned, BrE, informal*) lost or destroyed 失踪；毁坏了

bury /'beri/ *verb* (**bur·ies**, **bury·ing**, **bur·ied**, **bur·ied**)
• **DEAD PERSON** 死人 **1** ~ **sb/sth** to place a dead body in a grave 埋葬；安葬： *He was buried in Highgate Cemetery.* 他被安葬在海格特墓地。◇ (*figurative*) *Their ambitions were finally **dead and buried**.* 他们的雄心壮志最终给埋葬了。 **2** ~ **sb** (*old-fashioned*) to lose sb by death 丧失（某人）： *She's 85 and has buried three husbands.* 她 85 岁了，三度丧夫。
• **HIDE IN GROUND** 埋藏 **3** ~ **sth** to hide sth in the ground 把（某物）掩藏在地下；埋藏： *buried treasure* 埋藏的财宝 ◇ *The dog had buried its bone in the garden.* 狗把骨头埋在花园里。
• **COVER** 覆盖 **4** [often passive] to cover sb/sth with soil, rocks, leaves, etc. （以土、石、树叶等）覆盖： ~ **sb/sth** *The house was buried under ten feet of snow.* 房子被埋在十英尺厚的积雪中。◇ ~ **sb/sth** + **adj.** *The miners were **buried alive** when the tunnel collapsed.* 坑道塌方，矿工都被活埋。 **5** ~ **sth** to cover sth so that it cannot be seen 遮盖；掩盖： *Your letter got buried under a pile of papers.* 你的信被压在一堆文件底下。◇ *He buried his face in his hands and wept.* 他双手掩面而泣。
• **HIDE FEELING** 掩藏感情 **6** ~ **sth** to ignore or hide a feeling, a mistake, etc. 不顾，掩藏（感情、错误等）： *She had learnt to bury her feelings.* 她已经学会了感情不外露。
• **PUT DEEPLY INTO STH** 插入 **7** ~ **sth** (**in sth**) to put sth deeply into sth else 使陷入，把…插入（某物）： *He walked slowly, his hands buried in his pockets.* 他双手插在口袋里缓步而行。◇ *She always has her head buried in a book.* 她总是埋头读书。

IDM ˌ**bury the 'hatchet** | ˌ**bury your 'differences** to stop being unfriendly and become friends again 消除隔阂（重归于好） ➲ MORE AT HEAD *n.*

PHR V '**bury yourself in sth** **1** to give all your attention to sth 专心致志于某事： *Since she left, he's buried himself in his work.* 自从她走后，他全心扑在工作上。 **2** to go to or be in a place where you will not meet many people 隐居： *She buried herself in the country to write a book.* 她隐居乡间写书。

bus /bʌs/ *noun, verb*

■ ***noun*** (*pl.* **buses**, *US also* **busses**) **1** a large road vehicle that carries passengers, especially one that travels along a fixed route and stops regularly to let people get on and off 公共汽车；巴士： *Shall we walk or go **by bus**?* 我们步行呢，还是坐公共汽车？◇ *A regular bus service connects the train station with the town centre.* 火车站和市中心之间有定时班车。◇ ***a bus company/driver*** 公共汽车公司/司机 ◇ *a school bus* 校车 ➲ VISUAL VOCAB PAGE V62 ➲ COMPARE COACH *n.* ➲ SEE ALSO BUS LANE, BUS SHELTER, BUS STATION, BUS STOP, MINIBUS, TROLLEYBUS **2** (*computing* 计) a set of wires that carries information from one part of a computer system to another （计算机系统的）总线

IDM **throw sb under the bus** (*especially NAmE, informal*) to make sb else suffer in order to save yourself or gain an advantage for yourself （为了自救或私利而）使别人受苦，拿某人当牺牲品： *Plenty of my co-workers are satisfied to throw everyone else under the bus as long as they keep their wages.* 我的许多同事只要能保住自己的工资，而不惜牺牲其他所有人的利益。

■ ***verb*** (**-s-** or **-ss-**) **1** ~ **sb** (**from/to...**) to transport sb by bus 用公共汽车运送： *We were bussed from the airport to our hotel.* 公共汽车把我们从机场送到旅馆。 **2** ~ **sb** (in the US) to transport young people by bus to another area so that students of different races can be educated together 用校车送（学生往外区就读，使不同种族的学生一起受教育） **3** ~ **sth** (*NAmE*) to take the dirty plates, etc. off the tables in a restaurant, as a job （在餐厅里）收（盘子），清理（桌子）

bus·boy /'bʌsbɔɪ/ *noun* (*NAmE*) a person who works in a restaurant and whose job is to clear the dirty dishes, etc. 餐厅勤杂工（负责收餐具、抹桌子等）

busby /'bʌzbi/ *noun* (*pl.* **-ies**) a tall fur hat worn by some British soldiers for special ceremonies （英国士兵在特别场合戴的）毛皮高顶帽

bush /bʊʃ/ *noun* **1** [C] a plant that grows thickly with several hard STEMS coming up from the root 灌木： *a rose bush* 玫瑰丛 ◇ *holly bushes* 冬青树丛 ➲ COMPARE TREE **2** [C] a thing that looks like a bush, especially an area of thick hair or fur 灌木状的东西（尤指浓密的毛发或皮毛） **3** (*often* **the bush**) [U] an area of wild land that has not been cleared, especially in Africa and Australia; in New Zealand an area where the forest has not been cleared （尤指非洲和澳大利亚的）荒野；（新西兰未被砍伐的）林区 IDM SEE BEAT *v.*, BIRD *n.*

bush·baby /'bʊʃbeɪbi/ *noun* (*pl.* **-ies**) a small African animal with large eyes, which lives in trees 灌丛婴猴（生活于非洲丛林）

bushed /bʊʃt/ *adj.* [not before noun] (*informal*) very tired 疲乏不堪 SYN **exhausted**

bushel /'bʊʃl/ *noun* **1** [C] a unit for measuring grain and fruit (equal in volume to 8 gallons) 蒲式耳（谷物和水果的容量单位，相当于 8 加仑） **2** **bushels** [pl.] ~ (**of sth**) (*NAmE, informal*) a large amount of sth 大量；很多 IDM SEE HIDE *v.*

'**bush fire** *noun* a fire in a large area of rough open ground, especially one that spreads quickly 野火；山林大火

bush·fowl /'bʊʃfaʊl/ *noun* [C, U] (*pl.* **bush·fowl** or **bush·fowls**) (*WAfrE*) a bird with a large body and brown and white feathers that walks a lot on the ground and is often used for food 鹧鸪

bu·shido /'bʊʃiːdəʊ; bʊ'ʃiːdəʊ; *NAmE* -doʊ/ *noun* [U] (*from Japanese*) the system of honour and morals of the Japanese SAMURAI 武士道

'**bush-league** *adj.* (*NAmE, informal*) of very low quality 质量低劣的；次等的

Bush·man /'bʊʃmən/ *noun* (*pl.* **-men** /-mən/) **1** a member of one of the races of people from southern Africa who live and hunt in the African BUSH 布须曼人（非洲南部土著民族） **2** **bushman** a person who lives, works or travels in the Australian BUSH 布须曼人（在澳大利亚灌木地带居住、流动、工作的人）

bush·meat /'bʊʃmiːt/ *noun* [U] the meat of African wild animals used as food （非洲）野味

bush·ran·ger /'bʊʃreɪndʒə(r)/ *noun* (*AustralE, NZE*) (in the past) an OUTLAW (= a person who has done sth illegal and is hiding to avoid being caught) who lives in the bush (= areas of wild land far away from large towns) 绿林好汉（旧时的丛林逃犯）

ˈbush rat *noun* [C, U] (*pl.* **bush rat** or **bush rats**) (in W Africa) a type of large RODENT similar to a RAT that is found in wild areas and used for food 蹊鼠（产于西非，可食用）

ˌbush ˈtelegraph *noun* [U, sing.] (*informal, humorous*) the process by which information and news are passed quickly from person to person （信息等的）迅速传播，迅速散播

bush·whack /ˈbʊʃwæk/ *verb* **1** (*NAmE, AustralE, NZE*) [I] to live or travel in wild country 在野外生活（或旅行） **2** (*NAmE, AustralE, NZE*) [I] + **adv./prep.** to cut your way through bushes, plants, etc. in wild country 在丛林（或植物丛等）中开路：*We had to bushwhack through undergrowth.* 我们只好在灌木丛中劈开一条路。 **3** (*NAmE*) [T] **~ sb** to attack sb very suddenly from a hidden position 伏击 SYN **ambush** **4** (*NAmE*) [I] to fight as a GUERRILLA 游击作战；打游击战 ▸ **bush·whacking** *noun* [U]

bush·whack·er /ˈbʊʃwækə(r)/ *noun* **1** (*NAmE, AustralE, NZE*) a person who lives or travels in an area of wild country 荒野居民；荒野旅行者 **2** (*NAmE*) a person who fights in a GUERRILLA war 游击队员

bushy /bʊʃi/ *adj.* (**bush·ier, bushi·est**) **1** (of hair or fur 毛发或毛皮) growing thickly 浓密的：*a* ***bushy beard/tail*** 密匝匝的胡子；毛茸茸的尾巴 ◇ *bushy eyebrows* 浓密的眉毛 **2** (of plants 植物) growing thickly, with a lot of leaves 茂密的；多叶的

ˌbushy-ˈtailed *adj.* ⊃ BRIGHT-EYED

busily ⊃ BUSY *adj.*

busi·ness 🔑 /ˈbɪznəs/ *noun*
• **TRADE** 贸易 **1** 🔑 [U] the activity of making, buying, selling or supplying goods or services for money 商业；买卖；生意 SYN **commerce, trade**：*business contacts/affairs/interests* 商业联系 / 事务 / 利益；企业权益 ◇ *a business investment* 商业投资 ◇ *It's been a pleasure to* ***do business with*** *you.* 和你做买卖很愉快。◇ *She has set up* ***in business*** *as a hairdresser.* 她已经开店当理发师。 ◇ *When he left school, he* ***went into business*** *with his brother.* 他毕业后和他哥哥去经商了。◇ *She works in the computer business.* 她从事电脑业。 ⊃ WORDFINDER NOTE AT TRADE ⊃ SEE ALSO AGRIBUSINESS, BIG BUSINESS, SHOW BUSINESS
• **WORK** 工作 **2** 🔑 [U] work that is part of your job 商务；公事：*Is the trip to Rome* ***business or pleasure****?* 这次去罗马是公干还是游玩？ ◇ *a business lunch* 商务午餐 ◇ *He's away* ***on business.*** 他出差去了。 **3** 🔑 [U] the amount of work done by a company, etc.; the rate or quality of this work 营业额；贸易额：*Business was bad.* 生意不景气。◇ *Business was booming.* 生意兴隆。◇ *Her job was to drum up (= increase) business.* 她的工作是提高营业额。 ◇ *How's business?* 生意如何？

▼ **COLLOCATIONS** 词语搭配

Business 商业

Running a business 经营企业

- **buy/acquire/own/sell** a company/firm/franchise 收购 / 获得 / 拥有 / 出售公司 / 商行 / 特许经销权
- **set up/establish/start/start up/launch** a business/company 创办企业 / 公司
- **run/operate** a business/company/franchise 经营企业 / 公司 / 专卖店
- **head/run** a firm/department/team 管理公司 / 部门 / 团队
- **make/secure/win/block** a deal 达成 / 阻止一笔交易
- **expand/grow/build** the business 扩展业务
- **boost/increase** investment/spending/sales/turnover/earnings/exports/trade 增加投资 / 支出 / 销售量 / 营业额 / 收入 / 出口 / 贸易
- **increase/expand** production/output/sales 增加产量 / 输出量 / 销售量
- **boost/maximize** production/productivity/efficiency/income/revenue/profit/profitability 使产量 / 生产力 / 效率 / 收入 / 收益 / 利润 / 收益增加 / 最大化
- **achieve/maintain/sustain** growth/profitability 实现 / 维持 / 保持增长 / 收益
- **cut/reduce/bring down/lower/slash** costs/prices 削减成本 / 价格
- **announce/impose/make** cuts/cutbacks宣布 / 强制实行 / 实施削减

Sales and marketing 销售和市场营销

- **break into/enter/capture/dominate** the market 打入 / 进入 / 占领 / 控制市场
- **gain/grab/take/win/boost/lose** market share 取得 / 夺取 / 得到 / 赢得 / 增加 / 丢失市场份额
- **find/build/create** a market for sth 为某物找到 / 建立 / 开创市场
- **start/launch** an advertising/a marketing campaign 发起广告 / 营销宣传活动
- **develop/launch/promote** a product/website 开发 / 推出 / 推销产品 / 网站
- **create/generate** demand for your product 为产品创造需求
- **attract/get/retain/help** customers/clients 吸引 / 赢得 / 留住 / 帮助顾客 / 客户
- **drive/generate/boost/increase** demand/sales 刺激 / 创造 / 提高 / 增加需求 / 销售量
- **beat/keep ahead of/out-think/outperform** the competition 打败 / 领先于 / 智胜 / 胜过竞争对手
- **meet/reach/exceed/miss** sales targets 完成 / 达到 / 超过 / 未达到销售目标

Finance 财务

- **draw up/set/present/agree/approve** a budget 起草 / 制订 / 提出 / 批准预算
- **keep to/balance/cut/reduce/slash** the budget 执行 / 平衡 / 削减 / 大幅削减预算
- **be/come in below/under/over/within** budget 未超出 / 超出预算；在预算之内
- **generate** income/revenue/profit/funds/business 产生收益 / 利润 / 资金 / 营业额
- **fund/finance** a campaign/a venture/an expansion/spending/a deficit 为活动 / 商业项目 / 扩张 / 开支 / 赤字提供资金
- **provide/raise/allocate** capital/funds 提供 / 筹集 / 分配资金
- **attract/encourage** investment/investors 吸引 / 鼓励投资 / 投资者
- **recover/recoup** costs/losses/an investment 收回成本 / 亏损 / 投资
- **get/obtain/offer sb/grant sb** credit/a loan 获得 / 为某人提供 / 准予某人贷款
- **apply for/raise/secure/arrange/provide** finance 申请 / 筹集 / 获得 / 安排 / 提供资金

Failure 失败；不成功

- **lose** business/trade/customers/sales/revenue 失去生意 / 买卖 / 顾客 / 销量 / 收益
- **accumulate/accrue/incur/run up** debts 累积 / 积累 / 招致 / 积欠债务
- **suffer/sustain** enormous/heavy/serious losses 蒙受惨重损失
- **face** cuts/a deficit/redundancy/bankruptcy 面临削减 / 赤字 / 裁员 / 破产
- **file for/** (*NAmE*) **enter/avoid/escape** bankruptcy 申请 / 避免 / 幸免破产
- (*BrE*) **go into** administration/liquidation 进入行政接管 / 清算
- **liquidate/wind up** a company 清算 / 关闭公司
- **survive/weather** a recession/downturn 艰难渡过萧条期 / 衰退期
- **propose/seek/block/oppose** a merger 提出 / 寻求 / 阻止 / 反对合并
- **launch/make/accept/defeat** a takeover bid 发起 / 进行 / 接受 / 阻止收购投标

B

- **COMPANY** 公司 **4** [C] a commercial organization such as a company, shop/store or factory 商业机构；企业；公司；商店；工厂： *to* ***have/start/run a business*** 拥有 / 开办 / 经营企业 ◇ *business premises* 商务场址 ◇ *She works in the family business.* 她在家族的企业工作。◇ *They've got a small catering business.* 他们做餐饮小生意。➲ WORDFINDER NOTE AT COMPANY
- **RESPONSIBILITY** 职责 **5** [U] something that concerns a particular person or organization 归（某人或某机构）管的事；职责： *It is the business of the police to protect the community.* 警察的职责是保护社会。◇ *I shall* ***make it my business*** *to find out who is responsible.* 我要亲自查出是谁的责任。◇ *My private life is* ***none of your business*** (= does not concern you). 我的私生活与你无关。◇ *It's* ***no business of yours*** *who I invite to the party.* 你无权过问我邀请谁参加聚会。
- **IMPORTANT MATTERS** 要事 **6** [U] important matters that need to be dealt with or discussed （需要处理或讨论的）重要事情，要点： *the main business of the meeting* 会议的主要议题 ◇ *He has some* ***unfinished business*** *to deal with.* 他还要处理一些尚未了结的事务。
- **EVENT** 事情 **7** [sing.] (usually with an adjective 通常与形容词连用) a matter, an event or a situation 事情；事件；状况： *That plane crash was a terrible business.* 那次飞机坠毁是十分可怕的事。◇ *I found the whole business very depressing.* 我觉得整件事令人沮丧。◇ *The business of the missing tickets hasn't been sorted out.* 遗失票这件事还没解决呢。
- **BEING A CUSTOMER** 消费 **8** (*especially NAmE*) (*also BrE, formal* **cus·tom**) [U] the fact of a person or people buying goods or services at a shop/store or business （顾客对商店的）惠顾，光顾： *We're grateful for your business.* 感谢您光顾本店。

IDM **any other 'business** the things that are discussed at the end of an official meeting that do not appear on the AGENDA （会议结束前）议程以外的议题： *I think we've finished item four. Now is there any other business?* 我想我们已经讨论完第四项。还有其他要讨论的吗？ ➲ SEE ALSO AOB **be in 'business** (*informal*) to have everything that you need in order to be able to start sth immediately 准备就绪： *All we need is a car and we'll be in business.* 我们所需要的只是一辆车，然后我们就准备就绪了。 **be the 'business** (*informal*) to be very good 很好 **business as 'usual** a way of saying that things will continue as normal despite a difficult situation （尽管处境困难）一切照常，不受干扰 **ˌbusiness is 'business** a way of saying that financial and commercial matters are the important things to consider and you should not be influenced by friendship, etc. 公事公办 **get down to 'business** to start dealing with the matter that needs to be dealt with , or doing the work that needs to be done 着手处理正事；开始认真工作 **go about your 'business** to do the things that you normally do 忙自己的事；做通常做的事： *streets filled with people going about their daily business* 挤满为日常生活奔忙的人的街道 **have no business doing sth | have no business to do sth** to have no right to do sth 无权做某事： *You have no business being here.* 你无权待在这里。 **like 'nobody's business** (*BrE, informal*) very much, very fast, very well, etc. 非常；很多；很快；很好： *I've been working like nobody's business to get it finished in time.* 为按时完成任务，我一直在快马加鞭地工作。 **not be in the business of doing sth** not to be intending to do sth (which it would be surprising for you to do) 无意做某事： *I'm not in the business of getting other people to do my work for me.* 我无意让别人替我工作。 **out of 'business** having stopped operating as a business because there is no more money or work available 停业；歇业： *The new regulations will* ***put*** *many small businesses* ***out of business.*** 新法规将使很多小企业关闭。◇ *Some travel companies will probably* ***go out of business*** *this summer.* 今年夏天一些旅游公司很可能歇业。 ➲ MORE AT MEAN *v.*, MIND *v.*, PLY *v.*

'business administration *noun* [U] the study of how to manage a business 工商管理学： *a master's degree in business administration* (= an MBA) 工商管理学硕士学位

'business card (*also* **card**) *noun* a small card printed with sb's name and details of their job and company （业务）名片 ➲ COMPARE VISITING CARD

ˌbusiness 'casual *noun* [U] a style of dressing in which people who work in business wear clothes that are suitable for their profession but less formal than traditional business clothes 商务休闲装；商务便装

'business class (*BrE also* **'club class**) *noun* [U] the part of a plane where passengers have a high level of comfort and service, designed for people travelling on business, and less expensive than first class （飞机上的）公务舱，商务舱 ▶ **'business class** (*BrE also* **'club class**) *adv.*： *I always fly business class.* 我总是乘坐商务舱旅行。

the 'business end *noun* [sing.] ~ (**of sth**) (*informal*) the end of a tool or weapon which performs its main function （工具或武器）行使主要功能的一端，使用的一头

'business hours *noun* [pl.] the hours in a day that a shop/store or company is open 营业时间；办公时间

busi·ness·like /ˈbɪznəslaɪk/ *adj.* (of a person 人) working in an efficient and organized way and not wasting time or thinking about personal things 效率高的；井然有序的；工作认真而有条理的： *She adopted a brisk businesslike tone.* 她用一种公务口吻，说话干脆利落。

busi·ness·man /ˈbɪznəsmæn; -mən/, **busi·ness·woman** /ˈbɪznəswʊmən/ *noun* (*pl.* **-men** /-men; -mən/, **-women** /-wɪmɪn/) **1** a person who works in business, especially at a high level （尤指上层）商界人员；企业家

> **WORDFINDER** 联想词： accountant, agent, auditor, CEO, chairman, consultant, entrepreneur, executive, manager

2 a person who is skilful in business and financial matters 商界能手；善做生意的人： *I should have got a better price for the car, but I'm not much of a businessman.* 那辆车我本应卖个更好的价钱，但我不大会做生意。 ➲ NOTE AT GENDER ➲ MORE LIKE THIS 25, page R28

'business park *noun* an area of land that is specially designed for offices and small factories 工商业园区

'business person *noun* a person who works in business, especially at a high level （尤指高层的）商界人士；实业家 ➲ MORE LIKE THIS 25, page R28

'business school *noun* a part of a college or university that teaches business, often to GRADUATES (= people who already have a first degree) （大学里针对毕业生的）工商学院

'business studies *noun* [U+sing./pl. v.] the study of subjects connected with money and managing a business 企业管理研究；商学： *a degree in business studies* 企业管理学位

ˌbusiness-to-'business *adj.* [usually before noun] (*abbr.* **B2B**) done between one business and another rather than between a business and its ordinary customers 企业对企业的

ˌbusiness-to-con'sumer (*also* **ˌbusiness-to-'customer**) *adj.* [usually before noun] (*abbr.* **B2C**) used to describe the selling of products, services or information to consumers over the Internet （互联网销售）企业对消费者的，商家对顾客的 ➲ COMPARE BUSINESS-TO-BUSINESS

bus·ing (*NAmE*) = BUSSING

busk /bʌsk/ *verb* [I] to perform music in a public place and ask for money from people passing by 街头卖艺 ▶ **busk·er** *noun* ➲ VISUAL VOCAB PAGE V3 **busk·ing** *noun* [U]

'bus lane *noun* a part of a road that only buses are allowed to use 公共汽车专用道

bus·load /ˈbʌsləʊd; *NAmE* -loʊd/ *noun* (*especially NAmE*) a large group of people on a bus 公共汽车上一大车的人

bus·man's holi·day /ˌbʌsmənz ˈhɒlɪdeɪ; ˈhɒlɪdi; *NAmE* ˈhɑːlɪdeɪ/ *noun* [sing.] a holiday that is spent doing the same thing that you do at work 如常工作的假日

'bus pass *noun* **1** a ticket that allows you to travel on any bus within a particular area for a fixed period of time 公交月票（凭此票可在特定时间内在某一地区乘坐任何公共汽车） **2** a ticket that allows people from particular groups (for example, students or old people) to travel free or at a reduced cost 免费巴士票，乘车优惠票（为学生、老人等而设）：(*BrE, humorous*) *I'm not old enough for my bus pass yet!* 我还不到领取免费乘车票的年龄。

'bus shelter *noun* a structure with a roof where people can stand while they are waiting for a bus 公共汽车候车亭

buss·ing (*NAmE also* **bus·ing**) /'bʌsɪŋ/ *noun* [U] (in the US) a system of transporting young people by bus to another area so that students of different races can be educated together （美国）校车接送制度（用校车接送学生去其他校区上学，让不同种族的学生一同受教育）

'bus station *noun* the place in a town or city where buses (especially to or from other towns) leave and arrive 公共汽车站；（尤指）长途汽车站

'bus stop *noun* a place at the side of a road that is marked with a sign, where buses stop 公共汽车停靠站 ➲ VISUAL VOCAB PAGE V3

bust /bʌst/ *verb, noun, adj.*

■ ***verb*** (**bust**, **bust** or **bust·ed**, **bust·ed**) (*informal*) **1 ~ sth** to break sth 打破；摔碎：*I bust my camera.* 我把照相机摔坏了。◇ *The lights are busted.* 灯泡被砸碎了。◇ *Come out, or I'll bust the door down!* 出来，不然我就砸门了！ **2 ~ sb/sth** (**for sth**) (of the police 警方) to suddenly enter a place and search it or arrest sb 突击搜查（或搜捕）：*He's been busted for drugs.* 他因涉嫌毒品而遭到拘捕。 **3 ~ sb** (*especially NAmE*) to make sb lower in military rank as a punishment （使）降级，降低军阶 SYN **demote**

IDM **bust a 'gut** (**doing sth/to do sth**) (*informal*) to make a great effort to do sth 努力（做某事） **... or 'bust** (*informal*) used to say that you will try very hard to get somewhere or achieve sth （表示将全力以赴）：*For him it's the Olympics or bust.* 他将竭尽全力参加奥运会。

PHR V **,bust 'up** (*informal*) (of a couple, friends, partners, etc. 夫妻、朋友、合伙人等) to have an argument and separate 吵翻；分手 SYN **break up** (**with sb**)：*They bust up after five years of marriage.* 他们结婚五年后离异了。➲ RELATED NOUN BUST-UP **,bust sth↔'up** (*informal*) to make sth end by disturbing or ruining it 断送；毁灭 SYN **break sth up**：*It was his drinking that bust up his marriage.* 是他的酗酒葬送了他的婚姻。

■ ***noun*** **1** a stone or metal model of a person's head, shoulders and chest （石或金属的）半身像 **2** (used especially when talking about clothes or measurements) a woman's breasts or the measurement around the breasts and back （尤指衣服或尺寸）女子的胸部，胸围：*What is your bust measurement, Madam?* 您的胸围是多少，太太？ **3** a period of economic difficulty in which people and businesses struggle to survive 经济萧条期；经济不景气：*a boom and bust cycle* 经济的盛衰周期 **4** (*informal*) an unexpected visit made by the police in order to arrest people for doing sth illegal （警方的）突击搜捕，突击搜查：*a drug bust* 突击搜查毒品 **5** (*NAmE*) a thing that is not good 蹩脚的东西；没价值的事物：*As a show it was a bust.* 作为一场演出，那可不怎么样。

■ ***adj.*** [not usually before noun] (*informal*) **1** (*BrE*) broken 破碎；毁坏：*My watch is bust.* 我的表坏了。 **2** (of a person or business 个人或企业) failed because of a lack of money 破产 SYN **bankrupt**：*We're bust!* 我们破产了！◇ *We lost our money when the travel company* ***went bust***. 旅行社破产，我们的钱都赔了进去。

bus·tard /'bʌstəd; *NAmE* 'bʌstərd/ *noun* a large European bird that can run fast 鸨（见于欧洲，奔跑速度快）

busted /'bʌstɪd/ *adj.* [not before noun] (*NAmE, informal*) caught in the act of doing sth wrong and likely to be punished 被当场逮住：*You are so busted!* 你被当场逮住了！

bus·tee /'bʌstiː/ *noun* (*IndE*) an area in or near a town that is very poor and where the houses, often made of pieces of wood, metal and cardboard, are in bad condition 贫民窟；棚户区

bus·ter /'bʌstə(r)/ *noun* **1** (*NAmE, informal*) used to speak to a man you do not like （称呼不喜欢的男子）：*Get lost, buster!* 走开，小子！ **2** (usually in compounds; often used in newspapers 通常构成复合词；常用于报章) a person or thing that stops or gets rid of sth 遏制者；破坏者：*crime-busters* 打击犯罪活动的人

bus·tier /'bʌstieɪ/ *noun* a woman's tight top which does not cover the arms or shoulders （露臂肩的）紧身女胸衣

bus·tle /'bʌsl/ *verb, noun*

■ ***verb*** [I, T] to move around in a busy way or to hurry sb in a particular direction 四下忙碌；催促（某人向某方向）：**+ adv./prep.** *She bustled around in the kitchen.* 她在厨房里忙得团团转。◇ **~ sb + adv./prep.** *The nurse bustled us out of the room.* 护士催促我们离开房间。

■ ***noun*** **1** [U] busy and noisy activity 忙乱嘈杂；喧闹：*the* ***hustle and bustle*** *of city life* 都市生活的喧闹繁忙 **2** [C] a frame that was worn under a skirt by women in the past in order to hold the skirt out at the back （旧时女子用的）裙撑

bust·ling /'bʌslɪŋ/ *adj.* full of people moving about in a busy way 繁忙的；熙熙攘攘的：*a bustling city* 熙熙攘攘的城市 ◇ **~ with sth** *The market was bustling with life.* 市场一片蓬勃。

'bust-up *noun* (*informal, especially BrE*) **1** a bad argument or very angry disagreement 激烈的争吵；愤怒的争执 SYN **row²**：*Sue and Tony had a bust-up and aren't speaking to each other.* 休和托尼大吵了一架，现在谁也不理谁。 **2** the end of a relationship 关系的结束；破裂 SYN **break-up**：*the final bust-up of their marriage* 他们的婚姻的最终破裂

busty /'bʌsti/ *adj.* (*informal*) (of a woman 女子) having large breasts 胸部丰满的

bus·way /'bʌsweɪ/ *noun* (*BrE*) a road or section of a road that can only be used by buses, especially one with special tracks for guiding the buses 公共汽车专用道；公交专用道

busy 🔑 /'bɪzi/ *adj., verb*

■ ***adj.*** (**busier**, **busi·est**)

• DOING STH 做事情 **1** 🔑 having a lot to do; perhaps not free to do sth else because you are working on sth 忙碌的；无暇的：*Are you busy tonight?* 你今晚忙吗？◇ *I'm afraid the doctor is busy at the moment. Can he call you back?* 恐怕医生现在没空。让他给你回话行吗？◇ *I'll be too busy to come to the meeting.* 我会很忙，不能到会。◇ *The principal is a very busy woman.* 校长她可是个大忙人。◇ *She was always too busy to listen.* 她总是很忙，无暇听我说话。◇ *a very busy life* 繁忙的生活 ◇ **~ with sth/sb** *Kate's busy with her homework.* 凯特正忙着做家庭作业。 **2** 🔑 **~** (**doing sth**) spending a lot of time on sth 忙于（做某事）：*James is busy practising for the school concert.* 詹姆斯正忙着为学校音乐会排练。◇ *Let's get busy with the clearing up.* 我们开始清理吧。

• PLACE 地方 **3** 🔑 full of people, activity, vehicles, etc. 人来车往的；熙熙攘攘的：*a busy main road* 熙熙攘攘的大街 ◇ *Victoria is one of London's busiest stations.* 维多利亚站是伦敦最繁忙的车站之一。

• PERIOD OF TIME 一段时间 **4** 🔑 full of work and activity 工作忙的；充满活动的：*Have you had a busy day?* 你今天忙了一天吗？◇ *This is one of the busiest times of the year for the department.* 这是部门里一年中最忙的时间。

• TELEPHONE 电话 **5** 🔑 (*especially NAmE*) being used 正被占用的；占线的 SYN **engaged**：*The line is busy—I'll try again later.* 电话占线，我过会儿再打。◇ *the busy signal* 忙音 ➲ COLLOCATIONS AT PHONE

• PATTERN/DESIGN 图案；图样 **6** too full of small details 杂乱的；纷繁的；令人眼花缭乱的

▶ **busily** *adv.*：*He was busily engaged repairing his bike.* 他正忙着修他的自行车。

IDM **as busy as a 'bee** very busy 忙得不可开交 ➲ MORE LIKE THIS 14, page R26 **keep yourself 'busy** to find enough things to do 不让自己闲着：*Since she retired she's kept herself very busy.* 自从退休后，她一直没闲着。

■ *verb* (**busies**, **busy·ing**, **busied**, **busied**) to fill your time doing an activity or a task 忙着做某事：**~ yourself (with sth)** *She busied herself with the preparations for the party.* 她忙于准备晚会。◇ **~ yourself (in/with) doing sth** *While we talked, Bill busied himself fixing lunch.* 我们谈话时，比尔忙着做午饭。

busy·body /ˈbɪzibɒdi; *NAmE* -bɑːdi/ *noun* (*pl.* **-ies**) (*disapproving*) a person who is too interested in what other people are doing 好事的人：*He's an interfering old busybody!* 他老爱管闲事！

busy Lizzie /ˌbɪzi ˈlɪzi/ *noun* a small plant with a lot of red, pink or white flowers, often grown indoors or in gardens 非洲凤仙花

busy·work /ˈbɪziwɜːk; *NAmE* -wɜːrk/ *noun* [U] (*NAmE*) work that is given to sb to keep them busy, without really being useful 消磨时间的工作

but /bət; *strong form* bʌt/ *conj., prep., adv., noun*

■ *conj.* **1** used to introduce a word or phrase that contrasts with what was said before 而；相反：*I got it wrong. It wasn't the red one but the blue one.* 我弄错了。不是红的那个，是蓝的那个。◇ *His mother won't be there, but his father might.* 他母亲不会去那里，但他父亲也许会去。◇ *It isn't that he lied exactly, but he does tend to exaggerate.* 他不见得是真的说谎，但他的确是有意夸大。**2** however; despite this 然而；尽管如此：*I'd asked everybody but only two people came.* 每个人我都请了，却只来了两个人。◇ *By the end of the day we were tired but happy.* 一天结束时，我们很累，但很高兴。➲ LANGUAGE BANK AT NEVERTHELESS **3** used when you are saying sorry about sth （表示歉意时说）：*I'm sorry but I can't stay any longer.* 很抱歉，我不能再待下去了。**4** used to introduce a statement that shows that you are surprised or annoyed, or that you disagree （引出下文，表示吃惊、生气或不同意）：*But that's not possible!* 但那是不可能的！◇ *'Here's the money I owe you.' 'But that's not right—it was only £10.'* "这是我欠你的钱。" "但这不对呀，我只借了 10 英镑给你。" **5** except 除…外；只有：*I had no choice but to sign the contract.* 我别无选择，只好签了合同。**6** used before repeating a word in order to emphasize it（重复字词前用，加强语气）：*Nothing, but nothing would make him change his mind.* 没有什么，绝对没有什么会使他改变主意。**7** (*literary*) used to emphasize that sth is always true （强调一贯真实）：*She never passed her old home but she thought of the happy years she had spent there* (= she always thought of them). 她每次经过自己的旧居，都会想起在那里度过的幸福岁月。

IDM **but for** **1** if it were not for 倘若没有；若非；要不是：*He would have played but for a knee injury.* 他要不是膝部有伤的话，就上场了。**2** except for （表示不包括在内）除了…外：*The square was empty but for a couple of cabs.* 除了几辆出租汽车外，广场上空空如也。**but then (again)** **1** however; on the other hand 然而；另一方面：*He might agree. But then again he might have a completely different opinion.* 他可能同意，但也可能会意见完全相反。**2** used before a statement that explains or gives a reason for what has just been said （引出解释或原因）：*She speaks very good Italian. But then she did live in Rome for a year* (= so it's not surprising). 她的意大利语讲得很流利。不过她毕竟在罗马生活过一年。**you cannot/could not but...** (*formal*) used to show that everything else is impossible except the thing that you are saying 只有；除…之外别无可能：*What could he do but forgive her?* (= that was the only thing possible) 他不原谅她又能怎么办？

■ *prep.* except; apart from 除了；除…之外：*We've had nothing but trouble with this car.* 我们这辆车净出毛病。◇ *The problem is anything but easy.* 这个问题一点也不简单。◇ *Who but Rosa could think of something like that?* 除了罗莎，谁会想得到那种事？◇ *Everyone was there but him.* 除他之外，大家都在。◇ *I came* **last but one** *in the race* (= I wasn't last but next to last). 我赛跑得了倒数第二名。◇ *Take the first turning but one* (= not the first one but the one after it). 在第二个拐弯处转弯。

■ *adv.* only 只有；仅仅：*I don't think we'll manage it. Still, we can but try.* 我想我们应付不了这事。但不妨试试。◇ *There were a lot of famous people there: Lady Gaga and Hugh Jackman, to name but two.* 那里有很多名人，就提两个名字吧，有嘎嘎小姐和休·杰克曼。

■ *noun* /bʌt/ [usually pl.] a reason that sb gives for not doing sth or not agreeing 借口；托辞：*'Let us have no buts,' he said firmly. 'You are coming.'* "别找借口了。"他坚定地说，"你得来。" ◇ *With so many* **ifs and buts**, *it is easier to wait and see.* 有这么多托辞，还是静观其变吧。

bu·tane /ˈbjuːteɪn/ *noun* [U] a gas produced from PETROLEUM, used in liquid form as a fuel for cooking etc. 丁烷

butch /bʊtʃ/ *adj.* (*informal*) **1** (of a woman 女子) behaving or dressing like a man （举止或衣着）男子般的，男性化的 ➲ COMPARE FEMME **2** (of a man 男子) big, and often behaving in an aggressive way 高大的；（常指）趾高气扬的

butcher /ˈbʊtʃə(r)/ *noun, verb*

■ *noun* **1** a person whose job is cutting up and selling meat in a shop/store or killing animals for this purpose 屠夫；肉贩 **2** **butcher's** (*pl.* **butchers**) a shop/store that sells meat 肉店；肉铺：*He owns the butcher's in the main street.* 他在大街上开了一家肉铺。➲ MORE LIKE THIS 34, page R29 **3** a person who kills people in a cruel and violent way 刽子手

IDM **have/take a 'butcher's** (*BrE, slang*) to have a look at sth 观看 **ORIGIN** From rhyming slang, in which **butcher's hook** stands for 'look'. 源自同韵俚语，其中的 butcher's hook 代表 look。

■ *verb* **1** **~ sb** to kill people in a very cruel and violent way 屠杀；杀戮 **2** **~ sth** to kill animals and cut them up for use as meat 屠宰；宰杀 **3** **~ sth** (*especially NAmE*) to spoil sth by doing it very badly 弄砸；糟蹋：*The script was good, but those guys butchered it.* 剧本很好，但让那帮家伙给演砸了。

'butcher block *noun* [U] (*NAmE*) a material used for surfaces in kitchens, especially those that you work on 厨房面板；（尤指）案板，砧板

'butcher's block *noun* a thick block of wood on which a butcher cuts meat, also used in kitchens as a surface for cutting food on （肉贩的）砧板，肉墩子；（厨房）案板，砧板

butch·ery /ˈbʊtʃəri/ *noun* [U] **1** cruel, violent and unnecessary killing 残杀；杀戮 **2** the work of preparing meat to be sold 屠宰工作

but·ler /ˈbʌtlə(r)/ *noun* the main male servant in a large house 男管家

butt /bʌt/ *verb, noun*

■ *verb* **1** **~ sb/sth** to hit or push sb/sth hard with your head （人）用头顶撞 **2** **~ sb/sth** if an animal **butts** sb/sth, it hits them or it hard with its horns and head （动物）用头（或角）顶

PHR V **,butt 'in (on sb/sth)** **1** to interrupt a conversation rudely 插嘴；打断说话：*How can I explain if you keep butting in?* 你一直插嘴，我还怎么解释？◇ **+ speech** *'Is that normal?' Josie butted in.* "那是正常的吗？"乔西插了一句。**2** (*informal*) to become involved in a situation that does not concern you 插手；干涉 **SYN** **interfere**：*I didn't ask you to butt in on my private business.* 我没请你干预我的私事。**,butt 'out** (*informal, especially NAmE*) used to tell sb rudely to go away or to stop INTERFERING in sth that does not concern them 走开；别管闲事：*Butt out, Neil! This is none of your business.* 不许插手，尼尔！这不关你的事。

■ *noun* **1** the thick end of a weapon or tool （武器或工具的）粗大的一端：*a rifle butt* 步枪的枪托 **2** the part of a cigarette or CIGAR that is left after it has been smoked 烟蒂；烟头 **3** (*BrE*) a large round container for storing or collecting liquids （盛液体的）大桶：*a water butt* 集雨桶 **4** (*informal, especially NAmE*) the part of the body that you sit on 屁股 **SYN** **buttocks**：*Get off your butt and do some work!* 起来干点活儿吧！◇ *Get your butt over here!* (= Come here!) 过来！**5** the act of hitting sb with your head （头的）顶撞：*a butt from his head* 被他的头撞的一下 ➲ SEE ALSO HEADBUTT

B

IDM **be the butt of sth** to be the person or thing that other people often joke about or criticize 受到嘲讽（或批评）；是笑柄（或话柄等） **SYN** **target**: *She was the butt of some very unkind jokes.* 她受到了刻薄的嘲弄。 ➲ MORE AT PAIN *n.*

butte /bjuːt/ *noun* (*especially NAmE*) a hill that is flat on top and is separate from other high ground 地垛（顶部平坦的小丘、高地）

but·ter 🔑 /ˈbʌtə(r)/ *noun, verb*

■ ***noun*** 🔑 [U] a soft yellow food made from cream, used in cooking and for spreading on bread 黄油；奶油： *Fry the onions in butter.* 用黄油炒洋葱。 ➲ SEE ALSO BREAD AND BUTTER, PEANUT BUTTER

IDM **butter wouldn't melt (in sb's ˈmouth)** (*informal*) used to say that sb seems to be innocent, kind, etc. when they are not really 假装一副老实样；装作天真无邪 ➲ MORE AT KNIFE *n.*

■ ***verb*** **~ sth** to spread butter on sth 涂黄油于： *She buttered four thick slices of bread.* 她用黄油涂了四片厚面包。

IDM SEE KNOW *v.*

PHR V **ˌbutter sb↔ˈup** (*informal*) to say nice things to sb so that they will help you or give you sth 以甜言蜜语巴结某人；奉承；拍马屁

ˈbutter bean *noun* a large pale yellow BEAN. Butter beans are often sold dried. 利马豆

but·ter·cream /ˈbʌtəkriːm; *NAmE* -tərk-/ *noun* [U] a soft mixture of butter and sugar, used inside and on top of cakes 黄油乳脂（用黄油和糖调制而成，用于糕点）

but·ter·cup /ˈbʌtəkʌp; *NAmE* -tərk-/ *noun* a wild plant with small shiny yellow flowers that are shaped like cups 毛茛（野生植物，开杯状有光泽的小黄花） ➲ VISUAL VOCAB PAGE V11

but·ter·fat /ˈbʌtəfæt; *NAmE* ˈbʌtər-/ *noun* [U] the natural fat contained in milk and milk products 乳脂

but·ter·fin·gers /ˈbʌtəfɪŋɡəz; *NAmE* ˈbʌtərfɪŋɡərz/ *noun* [sing.] (*informal*) a person who often drops things 黄油手（常掉落东西的人）

but·ter·fly /ˈbʌtəflaɪ; *NAmE* -tərf-/ *noun* (*pl.* **-ies**) **1** [C] a flying insect with a long thin body and four large, usually brightly coloured, wings 蝴蝶： *butterflies and moths* 蝴蝶和蛾 ◇ *She's like a butterfly. She flits in and out of people's lives.* 她像一只蝴蝶，在人们的生活中穿梭。 ➲ VISUAL VOCAB PAGE V13 **2** [U] a swimming stroke in which you swim on your front and lift both arms forward at the same time while your legs move up and down together 蝶泳： *She was third in the 200m butterfly* (= a swimming race). 她得了 200 米蝶泳比赛的第三名。 ➲ VISUAL VOCAB PAGE V48

IDM **have ˈbutterflies (in your stomach)** (*informal*) to have a nervous feeling in your stomach before doing sth（做某事前）心慌，紧张

ˈbutter knife *noun* a knife that has a flat blade with a round end, used for spreading butter on bread 黄油刀

but·ter·milk /ˈbʌtəmɪlk; *NAmE* -tərm-/ *noun* [U] the liquid that remains after butter has been separated from milk, used in cooking or as a drink 脱脂乳；白脱牛奶

but·ter·nut /ˈbʌtənʌt; *NAmE* ˈbʌtər-/ *noun* a N American tree grown as a decoration and for its wood 灰胡桃树（北美观赏树，木材可用）

ˌbut·ter·nut ˈsquash *noun* [C, U] a long vegetable that grows on the ground, has a hard yellow skin and orange flesh and is fatter at one end than the other 冬南瓜

but·ter·scotch /ˈbʌtəskɒtʃ; *NAmE* ˈbʌtərskɑːtʃ/ *noun* [U] **1** a type of hard pale brown sweet/candy made by boiling butter and brown sugar together 奶油硬糖（用奶油和黄糖熬制） **2** (*especially NAmE*) a sauce flavoured with butterscotch, used for pouring on ice cream, etc. 奶油硬糖汁（用于浇在冰淇淋等上）

but·tery /ˈbʌtəri/ *adj.* like, containing or covered with butter 黄油般的；含黄油的；以黄油覆盖的

but·tock /ˈbʌtək/ *noun* [usually pl.] either of the two round soft parts at the top of a person's legs 屁股的一边；臀部 ➲ VISUAL VOCAB PAGE V64

but·ton 🔑 /ˈbʌtn/ *noun, verb*

■ ***noun*** **1** 🔑 a small round piece of metal, plastic, etc. that is sewn onto a piece of clothing and used for fastening two parts together 纽扣；扣子： (*BrE*) *to* ***do up/undo your buttons*** 系上 / 解开扣子 ◇ (*NAmE*) *to* ***button/unbutton your buttons*** 系上 / 解开扣子 ◇ *to sew on a button* 缝上扣子 ◇ *shirt buttons* 衬衫的纽扣 ➲ VISUAL VOCAB PAGE V68 **2** 🔑 a small part of a machine that you press to make it work（机器的）按钮： *the* ***play/stop/rewind button*** 播放键；停止键；倒带键 ◇ *Adam pressed a button and waited for the lift.* 亚当按了一个按钮，然后等着乘坐电梯。 ◇ *Choose 'printer' from the menu and click with the right mouse button.* 从菜单上选取"打印机"，然后点击鼠标右键。 ◇ *The windows slide down* ***at the touch of a button***. 按一下开关，窗玻璃便降下来。 ➲ PICTURE AT HANDLE ➲ SEE ALSO PUSH-BUTTON **3** a small area on a computer screen that you click on to make it do sth（电脑屏幕上的）按键： *Click on the back button to go back to the previous screen.* 点击返回键，回到上一页。 **4** (*especially NAmE*) a BADGE, especially one with a message printed on it（尤指印有信息的）徽章 ➲ VISUAL VOCAB PAGE V70 ➲ SEE ALSO BELLY BUTTON

IDM **on the ˈbutton** (*informal, especially NAmE*) **1** at exactly the right time or at the exact time mentioned 准时；正好： *We arrived at 4 o'clock on the button.* 我们在 4 点钟准时到达。 **2** exactly right 精确；准确；确切： *You're on the button there!* 那让你说中了！ **ˌpush all the (right) ˈbuttons** (*also* **ˌpress all the (right) ˈbuttons** *especially in BrE*) (*informal*) to do exactly the right things to please sb 做得面面俱到以讨好人： *a new satirical comedy show that pushes all the right buttons* 一出新的极尽搞笑之能事的讽刺喜剧 **ˌpush sb's ˈbuttons** (*also* **ˌpress sb's ˈbuttons** *especially in BrE*) (*informal*) to make sb react in either a positive or a negative way 使有所反应（无论是积极或消极的）： *I've known him for years, but I still don't know what pushes his buttons.* 我已认识他多年，可还是摸不透他的脾气。 ➲ MORE AT BRIGHT *adj.*

■ ***verb*** **1** [T] **~ sth (up)** to fasten sth with buttons 扣…的纽扣： *She hurriedly buttoned (up) her blouse.* 她急忙扣好衬衫。 **2** [I] **~ (up)** to be fastened with buttons 用纽扣扣上： *The dress buttons (up) at the back.* 这件连衣裙是从后背系扣的。

IDM **ˈbutton it!** (*BrE, informal*) used to tell sb rudely to be quiet 闭嘴；住口

ˌbutton-ˈdown *adj.* a **button-down** COLLAR, shirt, etc. has the ends of the COLLAR fastened to the shirt with buttons （领尖）用纽扣系（在衬衫上）的 ➲ VISUAL VOCAB PAGE V68

ˌbuttoned-ˈup *adj.* (*informal, especially BrE*) not expressing your emotions openly 沉默寡言的；嘴紧的

but·ton·hole /ˈbʌtnhəʊl; *NAmE* -hoʊl/ *noun, verb*

■ ***noun*** **1** a hole on a piece of clothing for a button to be put through 纽扣孔；扣眼 ➲ VISUAL VOCAB PAGE V68 **2** (*BrE*) (*NAmE* **bou·ton·nière**) a flower that is worn in the buttonhole of a coat or jacket 佩戴在扣眼上的花

■ ***verb*** **~ sb** (*informal*) to make sb stop and listen to you, especially when they do not want to 勉强（某人）停下来听

ˈbutton lift (*also* **Poma™**) *noun* a machine with poles which pulls people up the mountain on their SKIS 上山牵引机（用吊杆拉滑雪者上山）

ˌbutton ˈmushroom *noun* a small young MUSHROOM used in cooking （食用）小蘑菇

but·tress /ˈbʌtrəs/ *noun, verb*

■ ***noun*** a stone or brick structure that supports a wall 扶壁；支墩

■ ***verb*** **~ sb/sth** (*formal*) to support or give strength to sb/sth 支持；给…以力量： *The sharp increase in crime seems*

B

to buttress the argument for more police officers on the street. 犯罪率急剧上升似乎支持了街上增加巡警的论点。

butt 'ugly *adj.* (*NAmE, informal*) (especially of a person) extremely unpleasant to look at （尤指人）极其丑陋的，奇丑无比的

butty /'bʌti/ *noun* (*pl.* **-ies**) **1** (*BrE, informal*) a SANDWICH 三明治： *a jam butty* 果酱三明治 **2** (*WelshE, informal*) a friend; a person that you work with 朋友；伙伴

buxom /'bʌksəm/ *adj.* (of a woman 女子) large in an attractive way, and with large breasts 丰盈的；乳房丰满的

buy /baɪ/ *verb, noun*

■ ***verb*** (**bought, bought** /bɔːt/)

• **WITH MONEY** 用钱 **1** [T, I] to obtain sth by paying money for it 买；购买： **~ (sth)** *Where did you buy that dress?* 那件连衣裙你是在哪里买的？ ◇ *If you're thinking of getting a new car, now is a good time to buy.* 你要是想买辆新车的话，现在正是时候。 ◇ **~ sth from sb** *I bought it from a friend for £10.* 这是我从朋友那里花 10 英镑买来的。 ◇ **~ sb sth** *He bought me a new coat.* 他给我买了一件新外套。 ◇ **~ sth for sb** *He bought a new coat for me.* 他给我买了一件新外套。 ◇ **~ sth + adv.** *I bought my car second-hand.* 我买了一辆二手车。 OPP **sell** ➲ WORDFINDER NOTE AT SHOP ➲ MORE LIKE THIS 33, page R28

WORDFINDER 联想词： discount, loyalty card, purchase, receipt, reduction, refund, short-change, store card, voucher

2 [T] **~ sth** (of money 钱) to be enough to pay for sth 够支付： *He gave his children the best education that money can buy.* 他让孩子们接受花钱能买到的最好的教育。 ◇ *Five pounds doesn't buy much nowadays.* 如今五英镑买不到多少东西了。 **3** [T] **~ sb** to persuade sb to do sth dishonest in return for money 买通；收买；贿赂 SYN **bribe**： *He can't be bought* (= he's too honest to accept money in this way). 他是收买不了的。

• **OBTAIN** 获得 **4** [T, usually passive] **~ sth** to obtain sth by losing sth else of great value 付出极大的代价而获得： *Her fame was bought at the expense of her marriage.* 她出了名，却牺牲了她的婚姻。

• **BELIEVE** 相信 **5** [T] **~ sth** (*informal*) to believe that sth is true, especially sth that is not very likely 相信（尤指不大可能的事）： *You could say you were ill but I don't think they'd buy it* (= accept the explanation). 你可以称病，但我想他们不会相信的。

IDM **(have) 'bought it** (*informal*) to be killed, especially in an accident or a war 被杀死；（尤指）在事故中丧生，阵亡 **buy the 'farm** (*NAmE, informal*) to die 死；死亡 **buy 'time** to do sth in order to delay an event, a decision, etc. 拖延时间 ➲ MORE AT BEST *n.*, PIG *n.*, PUP

PHR V **,buy sth↔'in** (*BrE*) to buy sth in large quantities 大量购买 **,buy 'into sth 1** to buy shares in a company, especially in order to gain some control over it 购买公司股份（尤指为取得部分控制权） **2** (*informal*) to believe sth, especially an idea that many other people believe in 信从（尤指随大溜）： *She had never bought into the idea that to be attractive you have to be thin.* 她从不随大溜认为要想有魅力，就得瘦身。 ➲ RELATED NOUN BUY-IN **,buy sb↔'off** to pay sb money, especially dishonestly, to prevent them from doing sth you do not want them to do 收买，贿赂（某人不干某事） **,buy sb↔'out 1** to pay sb for their share in a business, usually in order to get total control of it for yourself 买断…的股份；买下…的全部股权 ➲ RELATED NOUN BUYOUT **2** to pay money so that sb can leave an organization, especially the army, before the end of an agreed period （为提前退役、离职等）支付补偿金 **,buy sth↔'up** to buy all or as much as possible of sth 全部（或尽量）买下某物；收购： *Developers are buying up all the land on the island.* 开发商们要把岛上的全部土地都买尽了。

■ ***noun* 1 a good, better, etc. ~** a thing that is worth the money that you pay for it 合算的商品： *That jacket was a really good buy.* 那件夹克确实买得很划算。 ◇ *Best buys this week are carrots and cabbages.* 这个星期最便宜的是胡萝卜和卷心菜。 **2** something that is bought or that is for sale; the act of buying sth 买进（或出售）的东西；购买： *Computer games are a popular buy this Christmas.* 这个圣诞节电脑游戏很畅销。

buyer /'baɪə(r)/ *noun* **1** a person who buys sth, especially sth expensive （尤指贵重物品的）买主；买方： *Have you found a buyer for your house?* 你的房子找到买主了吗？ ➲ COMPARE PURCHASER OPP **seller, vendor 2** a person whose job is to choose goods that will be sold in a large shop/store 采购员

IDM **a ,buyer's 'market** a situation in which there is a lot of a particular item for sale, so that prices are low and people buying have a choice 买方市场

,buyer's re'morse *noun* [U] (*NAmE*) the feeling of disappointment sb has after they have bought sth when they think they have made a mistake 买主的懊悔（购物后感到后悔的情绪）

'buy-in *noun* [U] (*business* 商) the fact of accepting a policy or change because you agree with it （对政策或变更的）认可，接受： *If you want to make major changes you need buy-in from everyone in the organization.* 如果想进行重大变革，就需要得到机构中所有人的认可。 ◇ *You need to win people's buy-in.* 你需要赢得人们的支持。 ➲ SEE ALSO BUY INTO STH at BUY

buy·out /'baɪaʊt/ *noun* a situation in which a person or group gains control of a company by buying all or most of its shares 控制股权收购： *a management buyout* 管理层购买控制性股权

buzz /bʌz/ *verb, noun*

■ ***verb* 1** [I] (of a BEE 蜜蜂) to make a continuous low sound 发出嗡嗡声： *Bees buzzed lazily among the flowers.* 蜜蜂在花丛中懒洋洋地嗡嗡作响。 **2** [I] to make a sound like a BEE buzzing 发出蜂鸣声： *The doorbell buzzed loudly.* 门铃蜂鸣声大作。 ◇ *My ears were buzzing* (= were filled with a continuous sound). 我耳鸣了。 ➲ MORE LIKE THIS 3, page R25 **3** [I] to be full of excitement, activity, etc. 充满兴奋（或活动等）： *New York buzzes from dawn to dusk.* 纽约从早到晚都熙熙攘攘的。 ◇ *My head was still buzzing after the day's events.* 一天的活动结束后，我头脑中还是闹哄哄的。 ◇ **~ with sth** *The place was buzzing with journalists.* 那个地方被记者搞得闹哄哄的。 **4** [I, T] **~ (sth) (for sb/sth)** to call sb to come by pressing a BUZZER 用蜂鸣器（发信号）： *The doctor buzzed for the next patient to come in.* 医生按蜂鸣器叫下一个病人进来。 **5** [T] **~ sb/sth** (*informal*) to fly very close to sb/sth, especially as a warning or threat 飞近（尤指作为警告或威胁）

PHR V **,buzz a'bout/a'round** to move around quickly, especially because you are very busy （忙得）团团转： *I've been buzzing around town all day sorting out my trip.* 我一整天都在城里转来转去，安排旅行的事情。 **,buzz 'off** (*informal*) used to tell sb rudely to go away 走开： *Just buzz off and let me get on with my work.* 走开，我得继续干活了。

■ ***noun* 1** [C, usually sing.] (*also* **buzz·ing** [U, sing.]) a continuous sound like the one that a BEE, a BUZZER or other electronic device makes 嗡嗡声；蜂鸣声： *the buzz of bees* 蜜蜂的嗡嗡声 ◇ *The buzz of the Entryphone interrupted our conversation.* 大门口对话机的蜂响声打断了我们的谈话。 ◇ *hums and buzzes from the amplifier* 扬声器发出的嗡嗡声 **2** [sing.] the sound of people talking, especially in an excited way 唧唧喳喳的谈话声： *The buzz of conversation suddenly stopped when she came into the room.* 她一踏进屋子里，热烈的谈话便戛然而止。 **3** [sing.] (*informal*) a strong feeling of pleasure, excitement or achievement （愉快、兴奋或成就的）强烈情感： *a buzz of excitement/expectation* 十分兴奋 / 期待 ◇ *She gets a buzz out of her work.* 她从工作中得到了很大乐趣。 ◇ *Flying gives me a real buzz.* 飞行真让我兴奋。 ◇ *You can sense the creative buzz in the city.* 在城市里可以感觉到创造的热情。 **4 the buzz** [sing.] (*informal*) news that people tell each other that may or may not be true 传闻；谣传 SYN **rumour**

IDM **give sb a 'buzz** (*informal*) to telephone sb 给某人打电话： *I'll give you a buzz on Monday, OK?* 我星期一给你打电话行吗？

buz·zard /ˈbʌzəd; *NAmE* -zərd/ *noun* **1** (*BrE*) a large European BIRD OF PREY (= a bird that kills other creatures for food) of the HAWK family 鵟（欧洲猛禽） **2** (*NAmE*) a large American bird like a VULTURE that eats the flesh of animals that are already dead 红头美洲鹫（食腐鸟类）

ˈbuzz cut *noun* a style of cutting the hair in which all the hair is cut very short, close to the skin of the head 寸头发型（头发理得很短，贴近头皮）

buzz·er /ˈbʌzə(r)/ *noun* an electrical device that produces a BUZZING sound as a signal 蜂鸣器

IDM at the ˈbuzzer (*NAmE*) at the end of a game or period of play 比赛结束时；游戏结束时：*He missed a three-point attempt at the buzzer.* 终场哨响时，他投三分球未中。

ˈbuzz group *noun* one of the small groups of people that a large group can be divided into in order to discuss and give their opinions about a particular subject. The information obtained is used by people doing MARKET RESEARCH. 蜂议小组，大家说小组（由大团体划分而成，组员讨论某一问题并各抒己见，意见用于市场研究）

ˈbuzz saw *noun* (*NAmE*) = CIRCULAR SAW

buzz·word /ˈbʌzwɜːd; *NAmE* -wɜːrd/ *noun* a word or phrase, especially one connected with a particular subject, that has become fashionable and popular and is used a lot in newspapers, etc.（报刊等的）时髦术语，流行行话

b/w *abbr.* (in writing 书写形式) black and white 黑白

bwana /ˈbwɑːnə/ *noun* a word used in parts of E Africa to address a man who has authority over you, for example your employer（东非部分地区用以称呼上司）主人，老板

by /baɪ/ *prep., adv.*

■ ***prep.*** **1** near sb/sth; at the side of sb/sth; beside sb/sth 靠近；在…旁边：*a house by the river* 河边的一所房子 ◇ *The telephone is by the window.* 电话在窗户旁边。◇ *Come and sit by me.* 过来挨着我坐。**2** used, usually after a passive verb, to show who or what does, creates or causes sth（常置于表示被动的动词后，表示施事者）：*He was knocked down by a bus.* 他被公共汽车撞倒了。◇ *a play by Ibsen* 易卜生写的剧本 ◇ *Who's that book by?* 谁是那本书的作者？◇ *I was frightened by the noise.* 我被那响声吓坏了。**3** used for showing how or in what way sth is done（表示方式）：*The house is heated by gas.* 这房子是煤气供暖的。◇ *May I pay by credit card?* 我能用信用卡付款吗？◇ *I will contact you by letter.* 我会给你写信联系的。◇ *to travel* ***by boat/bus/car/plane*** 乘船 / 公共汽车 / 轿车 / 飞机 ◇ *to travel* ***by air/land/sea*** 坐飞机；经陆路 / 海路 ◇ *Switch it on by pressing this button.* 按下这个开关启动它。**4** used before particular nouns without *the*, to say that sth happens as a result of sth（置于不带 the 的名词前，表示原因）由于：*They met by chance.* 他们不期而遇。◇ *I did it by mistake.* 我误做了这事。◇ *The coroner's verdict was 'death by misadventure'.* 验尸官判定是"意外致死"。**5** not later than the time mentioned; before 不迟于；在…之前：*Can you finish the work by five o'clock?* 你五点钟前能完成工作吗？◇ *I'll have it done by tomorrow.* 我明天之前让人把它弄好。◇ *By this time next week we'll be in New York.* 下星期的这个时候我们将在纽约。◇ *He ought to have arrived* ***by now/by this time***. 他现在应该已经到了。◇ ***By the time*** *(****that****) this letter reaches you I will have left the country.* 你收到这封信时，我已离开这个国家了。**6** past sb/sth 经过：*He walked by me without speaking.* 他一言不发地从我身边走过。**7** during sth; in a particular situation 在…期间；处于某种状况：*to travel* ***by day/night*** 白天 / 夜间旅行 ◇ *We had to work by candlelight.* 我们不得不借助烛光工作。**8** used to show the degree or amount of sth（表示程度、数量）：*The bullet missed him by two inches.* 子弹只差两英寸就击中他了。◇ *House prices went up by 10%.* 房价上涨了 10%。◇ *It would be better by far* (= much better) *to…* 那比…好得多。**9** from what sth shows or says; according to sth 从…看；依；按照：*By my watch it is two o'clock.* 我的表是两点钟。◇ *I could tell by the look on her face that something terrible had happened.* 从她的脸色我可以看出，发生了可怕的事情。◇ *By law, you are a child until you are 18.* 按照法律规定，18 岁之前是未成年人。**10** used to show the part of sb/sth that sb touches, holds, etc.（表示触及或抓住的人或物的部分）：*I took him by the hand.* 我拉着他的手。◇ *She seized her by the hair.* 她揪住她的头发。◇ *Pick it up by the handle!* 抓着手柄把它提起来！**11** used with *the* to show the period or quantity used for buying, selling or measuring sth（与 the 连用，表示时间或量度单位）：*We rented the car by the day.* 我们按日租用汽车。◇ *They're paid by the hour.* 他们的报酬是按小时计算的。◇ *We only sell it by the metre.* 我们只按米出售。**12** used to state the rate at which sth happens（表示速率）：*They're improving day by day.* 他们在一天天地改进。◇ *We'll do it bit by bit.* 我们会一点一点地做。◇ *It was getting worse by the minute* (= very fast). 情况急速恶化。◇ *The children came in two by two* (= in groups of two). 孩子们一对一对地走了进来。**13** used to show the measurements of sth（表示尺寸时用）：*The room measures fifteen feet by twenty feet.* 房间 15 英尺宽 20 英尺长。**14** used when multiplying or dividing（用于乘除运算）：*6 multiplied by 2 equals 12.* * 6 乘以 2 等于 12。◇ *6 divided by 2 equals 3.* * 6 除以 2 等于 3。**15** used for giving more information about where sb comes from, what sb does, etc.（补充有关出生地、职业等的信息）：*He's German by birth.* 他是德国血统的。◇ *They're both doctors by profession.* 他们两人的职业都是医生。**16** used when swearing to mean 'in the name of'（起誓时用）以…的名义：*I swear by Almighty God…* 我以全能上帝之名发誓…

IDM by the ˈby/ˈbye = BY THE WAY

■ ***adv.*** **1** past 经过：*Just drive by. Don't stop.* 直接开过去。别停车。◇ *He hurried by without speaking to me.* 他没和我说话就匆匆过去了。◇ *Excuse me, I can't get by.* 劳驾，请让开点路。◇ *Time goes by so quickly.* 时光飞逝。**2** used to say that sth is saved so that it can be used in the future（表示保留或保存时用）：*I've put some money by for college fees.* 我已经存了些钱作大学学费。**3** in order to visit sb for a short time 短暂拜访：*I'll come by this evening and pick up the books.* 我今晚过来取书。

IDM by and ˈby (*old-fashioned*) before long; soon 不久；很快：*By and by she met an old man with a beard.* 她不久就碰到了一个大胡子老头。**by and ˈlarge** used when you are saying something that is generally, but not completely, true 大体上；总的来说：*By and large, I enjoyed my time at school.* 总的说来，我在学校的日子很开心。⊃ LANGUAGE BANK AT GENERALLY

by- (*also* **bye-**) /baɪ/ *prefix* (in nouns 构成名词) **1** less important 次要的：*a by-product* 副产品 **2** near 附近：*a bystander* 旁观者

by·catch /ˈbaɪkætʃ/ *noun* [U] fish that are caught by ships by accident when other types of fish are being caught 误捕的鱼（捕捞其他种类的鱼时意外捕获）：*Thousands of small fish are thrown back into the sea as bycatch.* 成千上万误捕的鱼扔回大海中去了。

bye /baɪ/ *exclamation, noun*

■ ***exclamation*** (*also* **ˌbye-ˈbye**, **ˈbye-bye**) (*informal*) goodbye 再见；再会：*Bye! See you next week.* 再见！下星期再会。◇ *She waved bye-bye and got into the car.* 她挥手道别后就钻进了汽车。◇ *Bye for now Dad!* 再见了老爸！

■ ***noun*** (*sport* 体育) a situation in which a player or team does not have an opponent in one part of the competition and continues to the next part as if they had won 轮空（参赛者无对手而自动进入下一轮比赛）**IDM** SEE WAY *n.*

ˈbye-byes *noun*

IDM go (to) ˈbye-byes (*BrE, informal*) used by small children or to small children, to mean 'go to sleep'（儿童用语）去睡觉

ˈbye-law *noun* = BY-LAW

ˈby-election *noun* (*BrE*) an election of a new Member of Parliament to replace sb who has died or left parliament（议员等的）补缺选举，补选 ⊃ COMPARE GENERAL ELECTION

B

by·gone /ˈbaɪɡɒn; *NAmE* -ɡɔːn/ *adj.* [only before noun] happening or existing a long time ago 很久以前的；以往的：*a bygone age/era* 一个过去的时代 / 历史时期

by·gones /ˈbaɪɡɒnz; *NAmE* -ɡɔːnz/ *noun* [pl.]
IDM **let ˌbygones be ˈbygones** to decide to forget about disagreements that happened in the past 过去的事就让它过去吧

ˈby-law (*also* **ˈbye-law**) *noun* **1** (*BrE*) a law that is made by a local authority and that applies only to that area 地方法规 **2** (*NAmE*) a law or rule of a club or company （俱乐部或公司的）规章制度

by·line /ˈbaɪlaɪn/ *noun* a line at the beginning or end of a piece of writing in a newspaper or magazine that gives the writer's name （报刊文章的）署名行

by·name /ˈbaɪneɪm/ *noun* a name given to sb who has the same first name as sb else, so that it is clear who is being referred to （为区分同名者而起的）别名

BYO /ˌbiː waɪ ˈəʊ; *NAmE* ˈoʊ/ (*also* **BYOB** /biː ˌwaɪ əʊ ˈbiː; *NAmE* oʊ/) *abbr.* (used in invitations to parties, notices in restaurants, etc.) bring your own (bottle/beer) 自带酒水（全写为 bring your own (bottle / beer)，用于聚会请柬、餐厅告示等）

by·pass /ˈbaɪpɑːs; *NAmE* -pæs/ *noun, verb*
■ ***noun*** **1** (*especially BrE*) a road that passes around a town or city rather than through the centre （绕过城市的）旁路，旁道 ➲ WORDFINDER NOTE AT ROAD **2** a medical operation on the heart in which blood is directed along a different route so that it does not flow through a part that is damaged or blocked; the new route that the blood takes （给心脏接旁通管的）转流术，搭桥术；旁通管：*heart bypass surgery* 心脏搭桥手术 ◇ *a triple bypass operation* 接三通管的手术
■ ***verb*** **1 ~ sth** to go around or avoid a place 绕过；避开：*A new road now bypasses the town.* 一条新路绕城镇而过。**2 ~ sth** to ignore a rule, an official system or sb in authority, especially in order to get sth done quickly 不顾（规章制度）；不请示

ˈby-product *noun* **1** a substance that is produced during the process of making or destroying sth else 副产品：*When burnt, plastic produces dangerous by-products.* 塑料燃烧时产生出危险的副产品。 **2** a thing that happens, often unexpectedly, as the result of sth else 意外结果；副作用：*One of the by-products of unemployment is an increase in crime.* 失业带来的一大恶果是犯罪率上升。

byre /ˈbaɪə(r)/ *noun* (*old-fashioned, BrE*) a farm building in which cows are kept 牛棚 SYN **cowshed**

by·road /ˈbaɪrəʊd; *NAmE* -roʊd/ *noun* a minor road 小路；支路

by·stand·er /ˈbaɪstændə(r)/ *noun* a person who sees sth that is happening but is not involved 旁观者 SYN **onlooker**：***innocent bystanders*** *at the scene of the accident* 事故现场的无辜旁观者 ➲ SYNONYMS AT WITNESS

byte /baɪt/ *noun* a unit of information stored in a computer, equal to 8 BITS. A computer's memory is measured in bytes. 字节；位组；位元组

byway /ˈbaɪweɪ/ *noun* **1** [C] a small road that is not used very much 偏僻小路 **2 byways** [pl.] the less important areas of a subject （学科的）次要领域，冷僻部分

by·word /ˈbaɪwɜːd; *NAmE* -wɜːrd/ *noun* [usually sing.] **1 a ~ for sth** a person or thing that is a well-known or typical example of a particular quality （某种品质或特征的）代表人，代表事物，典范：*The name Chanel became a byword for elegance.* 香奈儿这个名字成了优雅的代名词。 **2** (*especially NAmE*) a word or phrase that is well known or often used 谚语；俗语

By·zan·tine /baɪˈzæntaɪn; bɪ-; -tiːn; *NAmE* ˈbɪzəntiːn/ *adj.* [usually before noun] **1** connected with Byzantium or the Eastern Roman Empire 拜占庭帝国的；东罗马帝国的 **2** used to describe ARCHITECTURE of the 5th to the 15th centuries in the Byzantine Empire, especially churches with high central DOMES and MOSAICS 拜占庭建筑风格的（尤指有高穹顶和马赛克装饰的教堂） **3** (*also* **byzantine**) (*formal*) (of an idea, a system, etc. 思想、制度等) complicated, secret and difficult to change 复杂神秘而死板的：*an organization of byzantine complexity* 拜占庭式复杂诡秘死板的机构

Cc

C

C /siː/ *noun, abbr., symbol*
■ ***noun*** (*also* **c**) [C, U] (*pl.* **Cs, C's, c's** /siːz/) **1** the third letter of the English alphabet 英语字母表的第 3 个字母：*'Cat' begins with (a) C/'C'.* * cat 一词以字母 c 开头。**2** **C** (*music* 音) the first note in the SCALE of C MAJOR * C 音（C 大调的第 1 音或音符）➲ SEE ALSO MIDDLE C **3** **C** the third highest mark/grade that a student can get for a piece of work（学业成绩）第三等，中：*She got (a) C/'C' in/for Physics.* 她物理成绩得中。
■ ***abbr.*** **1** **C.** CAPE 地角；岬角：*C. Horn* (= for example, on a map) 合恩角（例如地图标示）**2** CELSIUS, CENTIGRADE 摄氏度：*Water freezes at 0°C.* 水在零摄氏度时结冰。**3** (*also* ©) (*NAmE also* **C.**) COPYRIGHT 版权；著作权：*© Oxford University Press 2015* 版权所有，牛津大学出版社 2015 ➲ SEE ALSO C OF E, C & W
■ ***symbol*** **1** (*also* **c**) the number 100 in ROMAN NUMERALS（罗马数字）100 **2** the symbol for the chemical element CARBON（化学元素）碳

c /siː/ (*BrE*) (*also* **c.** *NAmE, BrE*) *abbr.* **1** (in writing 书写形式) CENT(S) 分（币）**2** (*also* **C**) (in writing 书写形式) century 世纪：*in the 19th c* 在 19 世纪◇(*NAmE*) *a C19th church* 一座 19 世纪的教堂 ➲ SEE ALSO CENT. **3** (*also* **ca**) (especially before dates) about; approximately (from Latin *circa*)（尤用于日期前）大约，约（源自拉丁语 circa）：*c1890* 约在 1890 年 **4** (*NAmE*) (in cooking) cup（用于烹饪）杯：*add 2c. flour* 加入两杯面粉

cab /kæb/ *noun* **1** a taxi 出租车；计程车；的士 ➲ VISUAL VOCAB PAGE V63 **2** the place where the driver sits in a bus, train or lorry/truck（公共汽车、火车、卡车的）驾驶室 ➲ VISUAL VOCAB PAGE V62

cabal /kəˈbæl; *NAmE also* -ˈbɑːl/ *noun* (*formal, usually disapproving*) a small group of people who are involved in secret plans to get political power 政治阴谋小集团

Ca·bala = KABBALAH

caba·ret /ˈkæbəreɪ; *NAmE* ˌkæbəˈreɪ/ *noun* **1** [C, U] entertainment with singing and dancing that is performed in restaurants or clubs in the evenings 卡巴莱（餐馆或夜总会于晚间提供的歌舞表演）：***a cabaret act/singer/band*** 卡巴莱表演 / 歌手 / 乐队 **2** [C] a restaurant or club where cabaret entertainment is performed（有歌舞表演的）卡巴莱餐馆，夜总会

cab·bage /ˈkæbɪdʒ/ *noun* **1** [U, C] a round vegetable with large green, purplish-red or white leaves that can be eaten raw or cooked 甘蓝；卷心菜；洋白菜：*Do you like cabbage?* 你喜欢卷心菜吗？◇ *two cabbages* 两棵洋白菜 ◇ ***white/red cabbage*** 白色的 / 红色的洋白菜 ➲ SEE ALSO CHINESE CABBAGE, PAK CHOI ➲ VISUAL VOCAB PAGE V33 **2** [C] (*BrE*) = VEGETABLE (2)

cab·bal·is·tic /ˌkæbəˈlɪstɪk/ *adj.* relating to secret or MYSTICAL beliefs 神秘信仰的；神秘论的

cabby (*also* **cab·bie**) /ˈkæbi/ *noun* (*pl.* **-ies**) (*informal*) a person who drives a taxi 出租车司机；计程车司机

caber /ˈkeɪbə(r)/ *noun* a long heavy wooden pole that is thrown into the air as a test of strength in the traditional Scottish sport of **tossing the caber**（在苏格兰传统的投掷比赛运动中使用的）长而重的木杆，长木柱

cabin /ˈkæbɪn/ *noun* **1** a small room on a ship in which you live or sleep（轮船上生活或睡觉的）隔间 **2** one of the areas for passengers to sit in a plane（飞机的）座舱 ➲ VISUAL VOCAB PAGE V57 **3** a small house or shelter, usually made of wood（通常为木制的）小屋，小棚屋：*a log cabin* 原木小屋 ➲ VISUAL VOCAB PAGE V15

ˈcabin boy *noun* a boy or young man who works as a servant on a ship（船上的）男服务员

ˈcabin crew *noun* [C+sing./pl. v.] the people whose job is to take care of passengers on a plane（飞机上的）全体乘务员 ➲ WORDFINDER NOTE AT PLANE

ˈcabin cruiser *noun* = CRUISER (2)

cab·inet 🔑 /ˈkæbɪnət/ *noun* **1** 🔑 (*usually* **the Cabinet**) [C+sing./pl. v.] a group of chosen members of a government, which is responsible for advising and deciding on government policy 内阁：*a cabinet meeting* 内阁会议 ◇ (*BrE*) *a cabinet minister* 内阁大臣 ◇ (*BrE*) *the shadow Cabinet* (= the most important members of the opposition party) 影子内阁（反对党中最重要的成员）➲ WORDFINDER NOTE AT GOVERNMENT **2** 🔑 [C] a piece of furniture with doors, drawers and/or shelves, that is used for storing or showing things 储藏柜；陈列柜：*kitchen cabinets* 橱柜 ◇ *a medicine cabinet* 药柜 ◇ *The china was displayed in a glass cabinet.* 瓷器陈列在玻璃柜里。➲ SEE ALSO FILING CABINET ➲ VISUAL VOCAB PAGE V25

cab·inet·maker /ˈkæbɪnətmeɪkə(r)/ *noun* a person who makes fine wooden furniture, especially as a job（尤指专业的）家具木工，细木工

the ˈCabinet Office *noun* [sing.] (in Britain) a government department that is responsible for the work of the Cabinet and the CIVIL SERVICE 内阁办公室（英国政府部门，负责内阁和行政部门的工作）

cab·in·et·ry /ˈkæbɪnətri/ *noun* [U] (*NAmE*) cabinets (= cupboards, especially fitted in a kitchen) 储藏柜；（尤指）橱柜

cable 🔑 /ˈkeɪbl/ *noun, verb*
■ ***noun*** **1** 🔑 [U, C] thick strong metal rope used on ships, for supporting bridges, etc.（系船用的）缆绳；（支撑桥梁等用的）钢索 ➲ PICTURE AT CORD **2** 🔑 [C, U] a set of wires, covered in plastic or rubber, that carries electricity, telephone signals, etc. 电缆；线缆：***overhead/underground cables*** 高架 / 地下电缆 ◇ *a 10 000 volt cable* * 1 万伏特高压电缆 ◇ *fibre-optic cable* 光缆 **3** [U] = CABLE TELEVISION：*We can receive up to 500 cable channels.* 我们可以接收多达 500 个有线电视频道。**4** [C] (*old-fashioned*) a message sent by electrical signals and printed out 电报
■ ***verb*** [T, I] ~ (**sb**) (*old-fashioned*) to send sb a CABLE *n.* (4)（给某人）发电报

ˈcable car *noun* **1** a vehicle that hangs from and is pulled by a moving cable and that carries passengers up and down a mountain（悬空的）缆车，索车 **2** (*especially NAmE*) a vehicle that runs on tracks and is pulled by a moving cable 有轨缆车 ➲ VISUAL VOCAB PAGE V63

ˌcable ˈtelevision (*also* **cable**, **ˌcable TˈV**) *noun* [U] a system of broadcasting television programmes along wires rather than by radio waves 有线电视

cab·ling /ˈkeɪblɪŋ/ *noun* [U] all the cables that are required for particular equipment or a particular system 成缆；（统称）缆索

ca·boo·dle /kəˈbuːdl/ *noun*
IDM **the whole (kit and) caˈboodle** (*informal*) everything 全部；全体：*I had new clothes, a new hairstyle—the whole caboodle.* 我身着新衣服，头理新发型，上下一身新。

ca·boose /kəˈbuːs/ *noun* (*NAmE*) the part at the back of a train where the person who is in charge of the train rides 守车（列车末尾供列车职工使用的车厢）

cab·ri·olet /ˈkæbriəʊleɪ; *NAmE* -oʊleɪ/ *noun* a car with a roof that can be folded down or removed（车顶可折叠或拆除的）敞篷车 **SYN** **convertible** ➲ COMPARE SOFT-TOP

ca·cao /kəˈkaʊ/ *noun* [U] a tropical tree with seeds that are used to make chocolate and COCOA; the seeds from this tree 可可（种子用以制作巧克力和可可粉）；可可豆

cache /kæʃ/ *noun, verb*
■ ***noun*** **1** a hidden store of things such as weapons 隐藏物（如武器）；（秘密）贮存物：*an arms cache* 隐藏的武器 **2** (*computing* 计) a part of a computer's memory that stores copies of data that is often needed while a program is running. This data can be accessed very quickly.

高速缓冲存储器；高速缓存

■ *verb* **1** ~ **sth** to store things in a secret place, especially weapons 匿藏，隐藏（尤指武器） **2** ~ **sth** (*computing* 计) to store data in a cache 把（数据）存入高速缓冲存储器；高速缓存： *This page is cached.* 这一页存入高速缓冲存储器了。

cachet /ˈkæʃeɪ; *NAmE* kæˈʃeɪ/ *noun* [U, sing.] (*formal*) if sth has **cachet**, it has a special quality that people admire and approve of 威信；声望 **SYN** **prestige**

cack /kæk/ *noun* [U] (*BrE, slang*) solid waste matter that is passed from the body through the BOWELS 屎

cack-handed /ˌkæk ˈhændɪd/ *adj.* (*BrE, informal, disapproving*) a **cack-handed** person often drops or breaks things or does things badly 笨手笨脚的；笨拙的 **SYN** **clumsy**

cackle /ˈkækl/ *verb, noun*

■ *verb* **1** [I] (of a chicken 鸡) to make a loud unpleasant noise 咯咯叫 **2** [I, T] (+ **speech**) to laugh in a loud unpleasant way 嘎嘎地笑： *They all cackled with delight.* 他们都高兴得嘎嘎地笑。

■ *noun* **1** the loud noise that a chicken makes（鸡的）咯咯叫声 **2** a loud unpleasant laugh（难听的）大笑声；嘎嘎的笑声

cac·oph·ony /kəˈkɒfəni; *NAmE* -ˈkɑːf-/ *noun* [U, sing.] (*formal*) a mixture of loud unpleasant sounds 刺耳的嘈杂声 ▶ **cac·oph·on·ous** /-nəs/ *adj.*

cac·tus /ˈkæktəs/ *noun* (*pl.* **cac·tuses** or **cacti** /ˈkæktaɪ/) a plant that grows in hot dry regions, especially one with thick STEMS covered in SPINES but without leaves. There are many different types of cactus. 仙人掌科植物；仙人掌 ➲ VISUAL VOCAB PAGE V11

CAD /kæd; ˌsiː eɪ ˈdiː/ *noun* [U] the abbreviation for 'computer-aided design' (the use of computers to design machines, buildings, vehicles, etc.) 计算机辅助设计，电脑辅助设计（全写为 computer-aided design）

cad /kæd/ *noun* (*old-fashioned*) a man who behaves in a dishonest or unfair way 卑鄙的人；粗鄙的人；无赖

ca·da·ver /kəˈdævə(r)/ *noun* (*specialist*) a dead human body 死尸；尸体 **SYN** **corpse**

ca·da·ver·ous /kəˈdævərəs/ *adj.* (*literary*) (of a person 人) extremely pale, thin and looking ill/sick 憔悴的；形容枯槁的

cad·die (*also* **caddy**) /ˈkædi/ *noun, verb*

■ *noun* (*pl.* **-ies**) (in GOLF 高尔夫球) a person who helps a player by carrying his or her CLUBS and equipment during a game 球童（比赛时替运动员背球棒、拿器具等）

■ *verb* (**cad·dies, caddy·ing, cad·died, cad·died**) [I] to act as a caddie in the game of GOLF （为高尔夫球手）当球童

cad·dis /ˈkædɪs/ (*also* **ˈcaddis fly**) *noun* a small insect. The young forms, called **caddis worms**, are often used for catching fish. 石蛾（幼虫常用作鱼饵）

caddy /ˈkædi/ *noun* (*pl.* **-ies**) **1** (*especially BrE*) = TEA CADDY **2** (*NAmE*) a small bag for storing or carrying small objects （装小件物品的）小包： *a sewing/make-up caddy* 针线包；化妆包 **3** = CADDIE

ca·dence /ˈkeɪdns/ *noun* **1** (*formal*) the rise and fall of the voice in speaking （说话时语调的）抑扬顿挫，起落： *He delivered his words in slow, measured cadences.* 他讲话缓慢而抑扬顿挫、把握有度。 **2** the end of a musical phrase （乐段或乐句的）收束，终止

ca·denza /kəˈdenzə/ *noun* **1** (*music* 音, *from Italian*) a short passage, usually near the end of a piece of CLASSICAL music, which is played or sung by the SOLOIST alone, and intended to show the performer's skill 华彩段，华彩乐段（通常在古典乐曲结尾，以突显独唱或独奏演员的技巧） **2** (*SAfrE*) if sb has a **cadenza**, they react suddenly and angrily to sth, especially in a way that seems unreasonable or humorous（尤指无端的或滑稽的）暴怒，大发雷霆

cadet /kəˈdet/ *noun* a young person who is training to become an officer in the police or armed forces 警官（或军官）学员；警官（或军官）候补生

cadge /kædʒ/ *verb* [T, I] ~ (**sth**) (**from/off sb**) (*BrE, informal*) to ask sb for food, money, etc. especially because you cannot or do not want to pay for sth yourself 乞讨；乞得；索取： *I managed to cadge some money off my dad.* 我设法从我父亲那里要了一些钱。 ▶ **cadger** *noun*

Cad·il·lac™ /ˈkædɪlæk/ *noun* **1** a large and expensive US make of car 凯迪拉克轿车（美国豪华轿车） **2 the ~ of sth** (*NAmE*) something that is thought of as an example of the highest quality of a type of thing 典范；极品： *This is the Cadillac of watches.* 这款手表堪称极品。

cad·mium /ˈkædmiəm/ *noun* [U] (*symb.* **Cd**) a chemical element. Cadmium is a soft poisonous bluish-white metal that is used in batteries and nuclear REACTORS. 镉

cadre /ˈkɑːdə(r); *NAmE* ˈkædri/ *noun* (*formal*) **1** [C+sing./pl. v.] a small group of people who are specially chosen and trained for a particular purpose 骨干（队伍） **2** [C] a member of this kind of group 干部

CAE /ˌsiː eɪ ˈiː/ *noun* [U] the abbreviation for 'Certificate in Advanced English' (a British test now called 'Cambridge English: Advanced' that measures a person's ability to speak and write English as a foreign language at an advanced level) 高级英语证书考试，剑桥英语第四级认证（全写为 Certificate in Advanced English，现称 Cambridge English: Advanced，英国考试，检测英语作为外语者的高级口语和写作能力）

cae·cum (*BrE*) (*NAmE* **cecum**) /ˈsiːkəm/ *noun* (*pl.* **cae·ca, ceca** /ˈsiːkə/) a small bag which is part of the INTESTINE, between the small and the large intestine 盲肠

cae·sar·ean /sɪˈzeəriən; *NAmE* -ˈzer-/ (*also* **cae·sar·ian, caeˌsarean ˈsection, caeˌsarian ˈsection**) (*US also* **ce·sar·ean, ce·sar·ian, ˈC-section**) *noun* [C, U] a medical operation in which an opening is cut in a woman's body in order to take out a baby 剖宫产，剖腹产（手术）： *an emergency caesarean* 紧急剖宫产手术 ◇ *The baby was born by caesarean section.* 那婴儿是剖腹产生下来的。 ◇ *She had to have a caesarean.* 她不得不接受剖宫产手术。 ➲ WORDFINDER NOTE AT BIRTH

Caesar salad /ˌsiːzə ˈsæləd; *NAmE* ˌsiːzər/ *noun* [U, C] a salad of LETTUCE and CROUTONS served with a mixture of oil, lemon juice, egg, etc. 凯撒色拉，凯撒沙拉（用生菜和油炸小面包块等制成）

cae·sium (*BrE*) (*NAmE* **ces·ium**) /ˈsiːziəm/ *noun* [U] (*symb.* **Cs**) a chemical element. Caesium is a soft silver-white metal that reacts strongly in water, used in PHOTO-ELECTRIC CELLS. 铯

caes·ura /sɪˈzjʊərə; *NAmE* sɪˈzjʊrə/ *noun* (*specialist*) a pause near the middle of a line of poetry 音顿（诗行中间的停顿） ➲ COMPARE ENJAMBEMENT

cafe (*also* **café**) /ˈkæfeɪ; *NAmE* kæˈfeɪ/ *noun* **1** a place where you can buy drinks and simple meals. Alcohol is not usually served in British or American cafes. 咖啡馆，小餐馆（供应饮料和便餐，在英美国家通常不供应酒类） ➲ COMPARE RESTAURANT ➲ VISUAL VOCAB PAGE V3 **2** (*SAfrE*) a small shop/store that sells sweets, newspapers, food, etc. and usually stays open later than other shops/stores 便利商店（出售糖果、报纸、食物等，通常比其他商店晚一些关门）

cafe·teria /ˌkæfəˈtɪəriə; *NAmE* -ˈtɪr-/ *noun* a restaurant where you choose and pay for your meal at a counter and carry it to a table. Cafeterias are often found in factories, colleges, hospitals, etc. 自助餐厅；自助食堂

cafe·tière /ˌkæfəˈtjeə(r); *NAmE* -ˈtjer/ (*BrE*) (*NAmE* ˌ**French ˈpress**) *noun* a special glass container for making coffee with a metal FILTER that you push down 法式咖啡壶（有活动金属过滤网） ➲ VISUAL VOCAB PAGE V26

caff /kæf/ *noun* (*BrE, informal*) a CAFE serving simple, basic food（供应便餐的）小餐馆：*a transport caff* 公路边小餐馆

caf·fein·ated /ˈkæfmeɪtɪd/ *adj.* (of coffee or tea 咖啡或茶) containing caffeine 含有咖啡因的 ➲ COMPARE DECAFFEINATED

caf·feine /ˈkæfiːn/ *noun* [U] a drug found in coffee and tea that makes you feel more active 咖啡因；咖啡碱 ➲ COLLOCATIONS AT DIET ➲ SEE ALSO DECAFFEINATED

caffè latte /ˌkæfeɪ ˈlɑːteɪ/ (*also* **latte**) *noun* (*from Italian*) a drink made by adding a small amount of strong coffee to a glass or cup of FROTHY steamed milk 热奶沫咖啡；拿铁咖啡

caf·tan *noun* = KAFTAN

cage /keɪdʒ/ *noun, verb*

■ ***noun*** a structure made of metal bars or wire in which animals or birds are kept 笼子：*a birdcage* 鸟笼 ➲ SEE ALSO RIBCAGE **IDM** SEE RATTLE *v.*

■ ***verb*** [usually passive] ~ **sth** (**up**) to put or keep an animal in a cage 把（动物）关在笼中：*The dogs are caged (up) at night.* 晚上狗被关进笼里。 ▶ **caged** *adj.*：*He paced the room like a* ***caged animal.*** 他像笼中的动物一样在房间里踱来踱去。

cagey /ˈkeɪdʒi/ *adj.* (**cagi·er, cagi·est**) ~ (**about sth**) (*informal*) not wanting to give sb information 守口如瓶的；讳莫如深的 **SYN** **evasive, secretive**：*Tony is very cagey about his family.* 托尼对自己家的事讳莫如深。 ▶ **cagi·ly** *adv.*

ca·goule (*also* **ka·goul**) /kəˈɡuːl/ *noun* (*BrE*) a long light jacket with a HOOD, worn to give protection from wind and rain 连帽式轻便长风雨衣

ca·hoots /kəˈhuːts/ *noun*

IDM **be in cahoots** (**with sb**) (*informal*) to be planning or doing sth dishonest with sb else 与…结伙；共谋；勾结（…做坏事）

cai·man (*also* **cay·man**) /ˈkeɪmən/ *noun* (*pl.* **-mans**) a N and S American REPTILE similar to an ALLIGATOR 凯门鳄

cairn /keən; *NAmE* kern/ *noun* a pile of stones which mark a special place such as the top of a mountain or a place where sb is buried 堆石标（以石堆标示山顶或某人埋葬的地点等）

ca·jole /kəˈdʒəʊl; *NAmE* kəˈdʒoʊl/ *verb* [T, I] to make sb do sth by talking to them and being very nice to them 劝诱；哄骗；诱骗 **SYN** **coax**：~ **sb** (**into sth/into doing sth**) *He cajoled me into agreeing to do the work.* 他诱骗我同意干那件活儿。 ◇ ~ **sth out of sb** *I managed to cajole his address out of them.* 我设法从他们那里套出了他的地址。 ◇ (**+ speech**) *'Please say yes,' she cajoled.* "就同意了吧。" 她哄骗道。

Cajun /ˈkeɪdʒn/ *noun, adj.*

■ ***noun*** **1** [C] a person of French origin from Louisiana who speaks an old form of French, also called Cajun 卡津人（法裔路易斯安那州人，讲旧式法语） **2** [U] a type of music originally played by Cajuns, that is a mixture of BLUES and FOLK MUSIC 卡津音乐（一种法裔路易斯安那州人的音乐，布鲁斯歌曲混合民乐）

■ ***adj.*** connected with the Cajuns, their language, music or spicy cooking 卡津人（或语言、音乐、多香料烹饪）的：*Cajun chicken/cuisine* 卡津香味鸡 / 烹饪

cake 🔑 /keɪk/ *noun, verb*

■ ***noun*** **1** 🔑 [C, U] a sweet food made from a mixture of flour, eggs, butter, sugar, etc. that is baked in an oven. Cakes are made in various shapes and sizes and are often decorated, for example with cream or ICING. 糕饼；蛋糕：*a* ***piece/slice of cake*** 一块 / 一片蛋糕 ◇ *to* ***make/bake a cake*** 做蛋糕 ◇ *a chocolate cake* 巧克力蛋糕 ◇ *a birthday cake* 生日蛋糕 ◇ (*BrE*) *a cake tin* (= for cooking a cake in) 蛋糕烤盘 ◇ (*NAmE*) *a cake pan* 蛋糕烤盘 ➲ SEE ALSO ANGEL FOOD CAKE, CHRISTMAS CAKE, FRUIT CAKE, SPONGE CAKE, WEDDING CAKE **2** [C] a food mixture that is cooked in a round flat shape 饼状食物；饼：*potato cakes* 土豆饼 ➲ SEE ALSO FISHCAKE

IDM **have your cake and ˈeat it** (*BrE*) (*also* **have your cake and eat it too** *NAmE, BrE*) to have the advantages of sth without its disadvantages; to have both things that are available 得其利而无其弊；两者兼得 **a slice/share of the ˈcake** (*BrE*) (*NAmE* **a piece/slice/share of the ˈpie**) a share of the available money or benefits that you believe you have a right to 应分得的一份钱财（或好处） **take the ˈcake** (*especially NAmE*) (*BrE also* **take the ˈbiscuit**) (*informal*) to be the most surprising, annoying, etc. thing that has happened or that sb has done 空前惊人；极其讨厌 ➲ MORE AT HOT *adj.*, ICING, PIECE *n.*

■ ***verb*** **1** [T, usually passive] ~ **sth** (**in/with sth**) to cover sth with a thick layer of sth soft that becomes hard when it dries （用厚厚一层干后即变硬的软东西）覆盖：*Her shoes were* ***caked with mud.*** 她的鞋上粘着污泥。 **2** [I] if a substance **cakes**, it becomes hard when it dries （干后）结成硬块；胶凝 ▶ **caked** *adj.*：*caked blood* 凝结了的血

cake·walk /ˈkeɪkwɔːk/ *noun* [sing.] (*informal*) something that is extremely easy to do 易如反掌的事

CAL /kæl/ *abbr.* computer assisted learning 计算机辅助学习；电脑辅助学习 ➲ COMPARE CALL

cala·bash /ˈkæləbæʃ/ *noun* **1** a container made from the hard covering of a fruit or vegetable; the fruit or vegetable from which a calabash is made 葫芦瓢；葫芦果制的容器；葫芦果 ➲ SEE ALSO GOURD **2** (*also* **ˈcalabash tree**) a tropical tree that produces a large round fruit with very hard skin, also called calabash 葫芦瓢树；蒲瓜树

cala·brese /ˈkæləbriːs; ˌkæləˈbriːs/ *noun* [U] a type of BROCCOLI (= a vegetable with a thick green STEM and green or purple flower heads) 青花菜

cala·mine /ˈkæləmaɪn/ (*also* **ˈcalamine lotion**) *noun* [U] a pink liquid that you put on burnt or sore skin to make it less painful 炉甘石洗剂（治疗皮肤灼伤或疼痛的一种粉红色水剂）

ca·lami·tous /kəˈlæmɪtəs/ *adj.* (*formal*) causing great damage to people's lives, property, etc. （对人命、财产等）引起灾难的，灾难性的 **SYN** **disastrous**

ca·lam·ity /kəˈlæməti/ *noun* [C, U] (*pl.* **-ies**) an event that causes great damage to people's lives, property, etc. 灾难；灾祸 **SYN** **disaster**

cal·cify /ˈkælsɪfaɪ/ *verb* (**cal·ci·fies, cal·ci·fy·ing, cal·ci·fied, cal·ci·fied**) [I, T] ~ (**sth**) (*specialist*) to become hard or make sth hard by adding CALCIUM salts （使）钙化，骨化 ▶ **cal·ci·fi·ca·tion** /ˌkælsɪfɪˈkeɪʃn/ *noun* [U]

cal·cite /ˈkælsaɪt/ *noun* [U] (*chemistry* 化) a white or clear mineral consisting of CALCIUM CARBONATE. It forms a major part of rocks such as LIMESTONE, MARBLE and CHALK. 方解石

cal·cium /ˈkælsiəm/ *noun* [U] (*symb.* **Ca**) a chemical element. Calcium is a soft silver-white metal that is found in bones, teeth and CHALK. 钙

ˌcalcium ˈcarbonate *noun* [U] (*symb.* **$CaCO_3$**) (*chemistry* 化) a white solid substance that exists naturally as CHALK, LIMESTONE and MARBLE 碳酸钙

cal·cul·able /ˈkælkjələbl/ *adj.* that can be calculated 可计算的；可估计的：*a calculable risk* 可预计的风险 ➲ COMPARE INCALCULABLE

cal·cu·late 🔑 /ˈkælkjuleɪt/ *verb* **1** 🔑 to use numbers to find out a total number, amount, distance, etc. 计算；核算 **SYN** **work sth↔out**：~ **sth** *Use the formula to calculate the volume of the container.* 用公式计算容器的容积。 ◇ *Benefit is calculated on the basis of average weekly earnings.* 补助金按平均周收入计算。 ◇ ~ **how much, what, etc.** *You'll need to calculate how much time the assignment will take.* 你需要算一算要花多少时间才能完成分配的任务。 ◇ **it is calculated that…** *It has been calculated that at least 47 000 jobs were lost last year.* 据估算，去年至少有 47 000 个工作岗位消失。 **2** 🔑 to guess sth or form an opinion by using all the information available 预测；推测 **SYN** **estimate**：~ **that …** *Conservationists calculate* *that hundreds of species could be lost in this area.* 自然资源保护主义者预测，数以百计的物种可能会从这个地区消失。◇ **~ how much, what, etc.** *It is impossible to calculate what influence he had on her life.* 无法估计他对她的生活产生过多大影响。

cal·cu·lated /ˈkælkjuleɪtɪd/ *adj.* [usually before noun] carefully planned to get what you want 精心策划的；蓄意的：*a calculated insult* 蓄意的侮辱 ◇ *He took* ***a calculated risk*** (= a risk that you decide is worth taking even though you know it might have bad results). 他甘冒风险。

IDM **be calculated to do sth** to be intended to do sth; to be likely to do sth 打算做；故意做；可能做：*Her latest play is calculated to shock.* 她最新推出的剧本故意要耸人听闻。◇ *This sort of life is not calculated to appeal to a young man of 20.* 这种生活对于一个 20 岁的年轻小伙子不大可能有吸引力。

cal·cu·lat·ing /ˈkælkjuleɪtɪŋ/ *adj.* (*disapproving*) good at planning things so that you have an advantage, without caring about other people 精明的；精于算计的：*a cold and calculating killer* 一个工于心计的冷酷杀手 ◇ *I never realized you could be so calculating.* 我真没有想到你会这样有心计。

cal·cu·la·tion /ˌkælkjuˈleɪʃn/ *noun* **1** [C, U] the act or process of using numbers to find out an amount 计算：*Cathy did a rough calculation.* 凯茜作了一个粗略的计算。◇ *By my calculation(s), we made a profit of £20 000 last year.* 我算了一下，我们去年赢利 2 万英镑。◇ *Our guess was confirmed by calculation.* 我们的猜测通过计算得到证实。➲ COLLOCATIONS AT SCIENTIFIC **2** [C, U] the process of using your judgement to decide what the results would be of doing sth 估计；预测；推测 **3** [U] (*disapproving*) careful planning for yourself without caring about other people 算计；自私的打算：*an act of cold calculation* 冷酷无情的算计

cal·cu·la·tor /ˈkælkjuleɪtə(r)/ *noun* a small electronic device or piece of software for calculating with numbers 计算器（指电子设备或软件）：*a pocket calculator* 袖珍计算器 ➲ VISUAL VOCAB PAGE V71

cal·cu·lus /ˈkælkjələs/ *noun* [U] the type of mathematics that deals with rates of change, for example in the slope of a curve or the speed of a falling object 微积分（学）➲ WORDFINDER NOTE AT MATHS

cal·dera /kɒlˈdeərə; -ˈdɪərə; *NAmE* kælˈderə; -ˈdɪrə; kɔːl-/ *noun* (*specialist*) a very large hole in the top of a VOLCANO, usually caused by an ERUPTION 破火山口（巨大碗口形火山凹地）

cal·dron (*US*) = CAULDRON

Cale·do·nian /ˌkælɪˈdəʊniən; *NAmE* -ˈdoʊ-/ *adj.* connected with Scotland 苏格兰的

cal·en·dar /ˈkælɪndə(r)/ *noun* **1** a page or series of pages showing the days, weeks and months of a particular year, especially one that you hang on a wall 日历；挂历：*a calendar for 2010* * 2010 年日历 ➲ VISUAL VOCAB PAGE V71 ➲ SEE ALSO ADVENT CALENDAR **2** (*NAmE*) a record of what you have to do each day; the book or piece of software in which you write this down 日程表；记事本（指纸质本或软件）**3** [usually sing.] a list of important events or dates of a particular type during the year（一年之中的）重大事件（或重要日期）一览表：*This is one of the biggest weeks in the racing calendar.* 这是全年赛马日程表中最重要的几个星期之一。**4** a system by which time is divided into fixed periods, showing the beginning and end of a year 历法：*the Islamic calendar* 伊斯兰教历

ˌcalendar ˈmonth *noun* (*specialist*) **1** one of the twelve months of the year 日历月（一年十二个月中的一个月）➲ COMPARE LUNAR MONTH **2** a period of time from a particular date in one month to the same date in the next one 一整月的时间（即从某月某日到下月同一日的期间）

ˌcalendar ˈyear *noun* (*specialist*) the period of time from 1 January to 31 December in the same year 历年（公历 1 月 1 日至 12 月 31 日）

calf /kɑːf; *NAmE* kæf/ *noun* (*pl.* **calves** /kɑːvz; *NAmE* kævz/) **1** [C] the back part of the leg between the ankle and the knee 腓肠；小腿肚：*I've torn a calf muscle.* 我拉伤了小腿肌肉。➲ VISUAL VOCAB PAGE V64 **2** [C] a young cow 小牛；牛犊 **3** [C] a young animal of some other type such as a young ELEPHANT or WHALE（象、鲸等的）崽，幼兽 **4** [U] = CALFSKIN ➲ MORE LIKE THIS 20, page R27

IDM **in/with ˈcalf** (of a cow 母牛) pregnant 怀崽的

calf·skin /ˈkɑːfskɪn; *NAmE* ˈkæf-/ (*also* **calf**) *noun* [U] soft thin leather made from the skin of calves, used especially for making shoes and clothing 小牛皮，小牛皮革（尤用于制作皮鞋和皮衣）

cali·brate /ˈkælɪbreɪt/ *verb* **~ sth** (*specialist*) to mark units of measurement on an instrument such as a THERMOMETER so that it can be used for measuring sth accurately 定标，校准，校正（刻度，以使测量准确）

cali·bra·tion /ˌkælɪˈbreɪʃn/ *noun* (*specialist*) **1** [U] the act of calibrating 定标；校准；校正：*a calibration error* 校准误差 **2** [C] the units of measurement marked on a THERMOMETER or other instrument（温度计或其他仪表上的）刻度

cali·bre (*especially US* **cali·ber**) /ˈkælɪbə(r)/ *noun* **1** [U] the quality of sth, especially a person's ability 质量；（尤指人的）能力 SYN **standard**：*He was impressed by the* ***high calibre of*** *applicants for the job.* 求职人员出色的能力给他留下了深刻印象。◇ *The firm needs more people of your calibre.* 公司需要更多像你这样有才干的人。**2** [C] the width of the inside of a tube or gun; the width of a bullet（管子、枪炮的）口径，内径；（子弹的）直径，弹径

cal·ico /ˈkælɪkəʊ; *NAmE* -koʊ/ *noun* [U] **1** (*especially BrE*) a type of heavy cotton cloth that is usually plain white（纯白）厚棉布 **2** (*especially NAmE*) a type of rough cotton cloth that has a pattern printed on it 印花粗棉布

ˈcalico cat *noun* (*NAmE*) = TORTOISESHELL (2)

cali·for·nium /ˌkælɪˈfɔːniəm; *NAmE* -ˈfɔːrn-/ *noun* [U] (*symb.* **Cf**) a chemical element. Californium is a RADIOACTIVE metal produced artificially with CURIUM or AMERICIUM. 锎（人工合成放射性化学元素）

cali·per (*especially NAmE*) = CALLIPER

ca·liph /ˈkeɪlɪf/ *noun* a title used by Muslim rulers, especially in the past 哈里发（尤为旧时穆斯林领袖的称号）

ca·liph·ate /ˈkælɪfeɪt; ˈkeɪl-; *NAmE* ˈkeɪl-/ *noun* **1** the position of a caliph 哈里发的职位 **2** an area of land that is ruled over by a caliph 哈里发的辖地

cal·is·then·ics *noun* (*NAmE*) = CALLISTHENICS

CALL /kɔːl/ *abbr.* computer assisted language learning 计算机辅助语言学习；电脑辅助语言学习 ➲ COMPARE CAL

call /kɔːl/ *verb, noun*

■ *verb*

• **GIVE NAME** 命名 **1** [T] to give sb/sth a particular name; to use a particular name or title when you are talking to sb 给…命名；称呼；把…叫作：**~ sb/sth + noun** *They decided to call the baby Mark.* 他们决定给婴儿取名马克。◇ *His name's Hiroshi but everyone calls him Hiro.* 他名叫广志，但人人都称他广。◇ *What do they call that new fabric?* 他们把那种新织品叫作什么？◇ **~ sb** *They called their first daughter after her grandmother.* 他们给大女儿取了祖母的名字。◇ *We call each other by our first names here.* 我们这儿彼此直呼其名。➲ SEE ALSO CALLED

• **DESCRIBE** 看作 **2** [T] to describe sb/sth in a particular way; to consider sb/sth to be sth 认为…是；把…看作：**~ sb/sth + noun** *I wouldn't call German an easy language.* 我并不认为德语是一门容易学的语言。◇ *Are you calling me a liar?* 你是说我撒谎？◇ *He was in the front room, or the lounge or whatever you want to call it.* 他当时在客厅，

或者说是在起居室，随便你管它叫什么。 ◇ *I make it ten pounds forty-three you owe me. Let's call it ten pounds.* 我算下来你欠我十英镑四十三便士。就算作十英镑吧。 ◇ **~ sb/sth + adj.** *Would you call it blue or green?* 你认为它是蓝色还是绿色？ ➲ SYNONYMS AT REGARD **3** [T] **~ yourself + noun** to claim that you are a particular type of person, especially when other people question whether this is true 把自己称为；自诩： *Call yourself a friend? So why won't you help me, then?* 你说你够朋友？够朋友怎么不肯帮我？ ◇ *She's no right to call herself a feminist.* 她无权以女权主义者自居。

• **SHOUT** 喊叫 **4** [I, T] to shout or say sth loudly to attract sb's attention 大声呼叫，大声说（以吸引注意力）： *I thought I heard somebody calling.* 我仿佛听见有人在呼喊。 ◇ **~ (out) to sb (for sth)** *She called out to her father for help.* 她向父亲大声呼救。 ◇ **~ (sth) out** *He called out a warning from the kitchen.* 他在厨房里大声发出警告。 ◇ **~ sth** *Did somebody call my name?* 有人叫我的名字吗？ ◇ **+ speech** *'See you later!' she called.* "再见！" 她叫道。 **5** [T, I] **~ (sb)** to ask sb to come by shouting or speaking loudly 召唤；呼唤： *Will you call the kids in for lunch?* 把孩子们叫进来吃午饭好吗？ ◇ *Did you call?* 你叫我？

• **TELEPHONE** 电话 **6** [T] to ask sb/sth to come quickly to a particular place by telephoning 打电话叫： **~ sb/sth** *to call the fire department/the police/a doctor/an ambulance* 打电话叫消防队 / 警察 / 医生 / 救护车 ◇ *The doctor has been called to an urgent case.* 医生接到电话去看急症。 ◇ *I'll call a taxi for you.* 我来打电话给你叫辆出租车。 ◇ **~ sb sth** *I'll call you a taxi.* 我来打电话给你叫辆出租车。 **7** [I, T] to telephone sb （给…）打电话： *I'll call again later.* 我过会儿再打电话来。 ◇ **~ sb/sth** *I called the office to tell them I'd be late.* 我给办公室打电话说我可能晚到一会儿。 ◇ *My brother called me from Spain last night.* 我弟弟昨晚从西班牙给我打电话来了。 ➲ NOTE AT PHONE

• **ORDER SB TO COME** 召见 **8** [T, usually passive] **+ adv./prep.** (*formal*) to order sb to come to a place 命令，召（至某处）： *Several candidates were called for a second interview.* 几个候选人被通知去参加第二次面试。 ◇ *The ambassador was called back to London by the prime minister.* 大使被首相召回伦敦。 ◇ *He felt called to the priesthood* (= had a strong feeling that he must become a priest). 他感受到要成为司铎的召唤。

• **VISIT** 拜访 **9** [I] (*especially BrE*) to make a short visit to a person or place （短暂地）访问： *I'll call round and see you on my way home.* 我想在回家的路上去看看你。 ◇ **~ on sb** *Let's call on John.* 咱们去看看约翰吧。 ◇ **~ to do sth** *He was out when I called to see him.* 我去拜访时，他不在家。

• **MEETING/STRIKE, ETC.** 集会、罢工等 **10** [T] **~ sth** to order sth to happen; to announce that sth will happen 下令举行；宣布进行： *to call a meeting/an election/a strike* 召集会议；宣布举行选举；号召罢工

• **OF BIRD/ANIMAL** 禽；兽 **11** [I] to make the cry that is typical for it 啼；鸣叫

• **IN GAMES** 比赛 **12** [T, I] **~ (sth)** to say which side of a coin you think will face upwards after it is thrown 抛硬币说正反面： *to call heads/tails* 要硬币的正面 / 反面

IDM **call sb's 'bluff** to tell sb to do what they are threatening to do, because you believe that they will not be cruel or brave enough to do it 要求…摊牌，要求…兑现其恫吓（因相信对方不至于或不敢这样做） **call sth into 'play** (*formal*) to make use of sth 利用；使用： *Chess is a game that calls into play all your powers of concentration.* 国际象棋是一项需要全神贯注的活动。 **call sth into 'question** to doubt sth or make others doubt sth 怀疑；引起怀疑 **SYN** **question**： *His honesty has never been called into question.* 他的诚实从未受到过怀疑。 **call it a 'day** (*informal*) to decide or agree to stop doing sth 结束一天的工作；到此为止；停止： *After forty years in politics I think it's time for me to call it a day* (= to retire). 从政四十年，我想现在也该退休了。 **call it 'quits** (*informal*) **1** to agree to end a contest, disagreement, etc. because both sides seem equal （因势均力敌）同意停止比赛（或争论等） **2** to decide to stop doing sth 决定停止 **call sb 'names** to use insulting words about sb 辱骂；谩骂 **call the 'shots/'tune** (*informal*) to be the person who controls a situation 控制；操纵 **call a spade a 'spade** to say exactly what you think without trying to hide your opinion 是啥说啥；直言不讳 **call 'time (on sth)** (*BrE*) to say or decide that it is time for sth to finish 宣布结束；决定结束 **call sb to ac'count (for/over sth)** to make sb explain a mistake, etc. because they are responsible for it 责成…作出解释；责问 **call sb/sth to 'order** to ask people in a meeting to be quiet so that the meeting can start or continue 要求安静下来（以便开始或继续会议）；要求遵守会议秩序 ➲ MORE AT CARPET *n.*, MIND *n.*, PAY *v.*, POT *n.*, WHAT

PHR V **'call at...** (*BrE*) (of a train, etc. 火车等) to stop at a place for a short time 停靠；（短时间）停留： *This train calls at Didcot and Reading.* 这趟列车在迪德科特和雷丁停车。 **,call sb a'way** to ask sb to stop what they are doing and to go somewhere else 叫走；把…叫到别处去： *She was called away from the meeting to take an urgent phone call.* 她被叫出会场去接一个紧急电话。 **,call 'back** | **,call sb 'back** to telephone sb again or to telephone sb who telephoned you earlier 再打电话；回电话： *She said she'd call back.* 她说她会再打电话来。 ◇ *I'm waiting for someone to call me back with a price.* 我在等人回电话报价。 **'call for sb** (*especially BrE*) to collect sb in order to go somewhere （去）接： *I'll call for you at 7 o'clock.* 我 7 点钟来接你。 **'call for sth 1** to need sth 需要： *The situation calls for prompt action.* 目前的形势需要立即采取行动。 ◇ *'I've been promoted.' 'This calls for a celebration!'* "我升职了。" "那得庆祝一下！" ➲ SEE ALSO UNCALLED FOR **2** to publicly ask for sth to happen （公开）要求： *They called for the immediate release of the hostages.* 他们要求立即释放人质。 ◇ *The opposition have called for him to resign.* 反对派已要求他辞职。 **,call sth↔'forth** (*formal*) to produce a particular reaction 引起；使产生： *His speech called forth an angry response.* 他的发言引起了一阵愤怒。 **,call 'in** to telephone a place, especially the place where you work 打电话来（工作单位等）： *Several people have called in sick today.* 今天有几个人打电话请病假。 **,call sb↔'in** to ask for the services of sb 召来，叫来（服务）： *to call in a doctor/the police* 请医生 / 叫警察来 **,call sth↔'in** to order or ask for the return of sth 下令收回；要求退回： *Cars with serious faults have been called in by the manufacturers.* 有严重缺陷的汽车已被制造商召回。 **,call sb/sth ↔'off** to order a dog or a person to stop attacking,

▼SYNONYMS 同义词辨析

call

cry out • exclaim • blurt • burst out

These words all mean to shout or say sth loudly or suddenly. 以上各词均含突然大声喊叫、说话之义。

call to shout or say sth loudly to attract sb's attention 指大声呼叫或说话以吸引注意： *I thought I heard someone calling.* 我仿佛听见有人在呼喊。

cry out (sth) to shout sth loudly, especially when you need help or are in trouble 尤指需要帮助或陷入困境时大声呼喊： *She cried out for help.* 她大声呼救。 ◇ *I cried out his name.* 我大声呼唤他的名字。

exclaim to say sth suddenly and loudly, especially because of a strong emotion 尤指因强烈的情感而突然大声说话： *'It isn't fair!' he exclaimed angrily.* "这不公平！" 他气愤地喊道。

blurt to say sth suddenly and without thinking carefully enough 指脱口而出： *He **blurted out** the answer without thinking.* 他不假思索脱口说出了答案。

burst out to say sth suddenly and loudly, especially with a lot of emotion 尤指突然激动地大声喊叫： *'He's a bully!' the little boy burst out.* "他欺负人！" 小男孩突然大叫。

PATTERNS

- to call/cry out/exclaim/blurt out (sth) **to** sb
- to call/cry out **for** sth
- to cry out/exclaim **in**/**with** sth
- to call/cry out/exclaim/blurt out/burst out **suddenly**
- to call/cry out/exclaim/burst out **loudly**

searching, etc. 把（人）叫走（不再搜查等）；把（狗）叫开（不让它咬人等） **,call sth↔'off** 🔑 to cancel sth; to decide that sth will not happen 取消；停止进行：*to call off a deal/trip/strike* 取消交易 / 旅行 / 罢工 ◇ *They have called off their engagement* (= decided not to get married). 他们已经解除婚约。◇ *The game was called off because of bad weather.* 比赛因天气恶劣被取消。 **'call on/upon sb** (*formal*) **1** to formally invite or ask sb to speak, etc. 正式邀请，要求（某人讲话等）；恭请：*I now call upon the chairman to address the meeting.* 现在请主席向大会致辞。 **2** to ask or demand that sb do sth 请求，要求，要（某人做某事）：*I feel called upon* (= feel that I ought) *to warn you that…* 我觉得我应该警告你… **,call sb 'out 1** to ask sb to come, especially to an emergency 要求某人来，召唤出动（尤指处理紧急情况）：*to call out an engineer/a plumber/the troops* 召来工程师 / 管道工；出动军队 **2** to order or advise workers to stop work as a protest 下令罢工；通知罢工 ➲ RELATED NOUN CALL-OUT **,call sb↔'up 1** 🔑 (*especially NAmE*) to make a telephone call to sb（给某人）打电话 **2** to make sb do their training in the army, etc. or fight in a war 征召（服役）；征召入伍 SYN **conscript, draft 3** to give sb the opportunity to play in a sports team, especially for their country 选入，征调（运动员为国参赛） ➲ RELATED NOUN CALL-UP **,call sth↔'up 1** to bring sth back to your mind 使回忆起；使想起 SYN **recall**: *The smell of the sea called up memories of her childhood.* 大海的气息勾起了她对童年的回忆。 **2** to use sth that is stored or kept available 调用贮存；调出备用：*I called his address up on the computer.* 我在计算机上调出了他的地址。◇ *She called up her last reserves of strength.* 她使尽了最后一点力气。

■ ***noun***

• **ON TELEPHONE** 电话 **1** 🔑 [C] (*also* **'phone call**) the act of speaking to sb on the telephone 打电话；通话：*to **get/have/receive a call** from sb* 接到某人的电话 ◇ *to give sb/to **make a call*** 给某人打电话；打个电话 ◇ *Were there any calls for me while I was out?* 我不在时有电话找我吗？◇ *I'll **take*** (= answer) ***the call** upstairs.* 我要上楼接电话。◇ *I left a message but he didn't **return my call**.* 我留了口信，但他没有回电话。◇ *a **local call*** 本地电话 ➲ NOTE AT PHONE ➲ SEE ALSO COLD-CALLING, WAKE-UP CALL

WORDFINDER 联想词：area code, dial, engaged, hold, line, message, **phone**, ring, voicemail

• **LOUD SOUND** 响亮的声音 **2** 🔑 [C] a loud sound made by a bird or an animal, or by a person to attract attention（禽、兽的）叫声；（唤起注意的）喊声：*the distinctive call of the cuckoo* 布谷鸟独特的叫声 ◇ *a call for help* 呼救声

• **VISIT** 拜访 **3** [C] a short visit to sb's house 短暂拜访：*The doctor has five calls to make this morning.* 医生今天上午要出诊五次。◇ (*old-fashioned*) ***to pay a call** on an old friend* 拜访一位老朋友

• **REQUEST/DEMAND** 请求；要求 **4** [C] ~ (**for sth**) a request, an order or a demand for sb to do sth or to go somewhere 要求；请求；呼吁：*calls for the minister to resign* 要部长辞职的要求 ◇ *calls for national unity* 国家统一的呼声 ◇ *This is the last call for passengers travelling on British Airways flight 199 to Rome.* 乘坐英国航空公司 199 次班机飞往罗马的乘客，这是最后一次通知登机。◇ (*formal*) ***a call to arms*** (= a strong request to fight in the army, etc.) 战斗号召 ➲ SEE ALSO CURTAIN CALL **5** [U] **no ~ for sth | no ~ (for sb) to do sth** no demand for sth; no reason for sb's behaviour 没有需要；没有理由（做…）：*There isn't a lot of call for small specialist shops nowadays.* 如今对小型专卖店已没有多大需求了。 **6** [C] **~ on sb/sth** a demand or pressure placed on sb/sth（对某人或某事物的）需求，压力：*She is a busy woman with many calls on her time.* 她是个大忙人，有很多事等着她去办。

• **OF A PLACE** 地方 **7** [sing.] ~ (**of sth**) (*literary*) a strong feeling of attraction that a particular place has for you（某地的）吸引力，诱惑力：*the call of the sea/your homeland* 大海的 / 家乡的魅力

• **TO A PARTICULAR JOB** 职业 **8** [sing.] ~ (**to do sth**) a strong feeling that you want to do sth, especially a particular job 召唤；呼唤；使命感

• **DECISION** 决定 **9** [C] (*informal*) a decision 决定：*It's your call!* 那是你的决定！◇ *a **good/bad** call* 正确的 / 不恰当的决定 ◇ *That's a tough call.* 那是个艰难的决定。

• **IN TENNIS** 网球 **10** [C] a decision made by the UMPIRE（裁判员的）判决：*There was a disputed call in the second set.* 第二盘比赛有一个有争议的判决。

• **IN CARD GAMES** 纸牌游戏 **11** [C] a player's BID[1] or turn to BID[1] 叫牌；吊牌

IDM **the call of 'nature** (*humorous*) the need to go to the toilet 生理需要（指上厕所） **have first 'call (on sb/sth)** to be the most important person or thing competing for sb's time, money, etc. and to be dealt with or paid for before other people or things 优先占用（时间、金钱等）；优先得到照顾（或支付）：*The children always have first call on her time.* 她的时间总是先花在孩子们身上。 **(be) on 'call** (of a doctor, police officer, etc. 医生、警察等) available for work if necessary, especially in an emergency（尤指紧急情况下）随叫随到：*I'll be on call the night of the party.* 在聚会的晚上我将随时听凭召唤。 ➲ SEE ALSO ON-CALL ➲ MORE AT BECK, CLOSE[2] *adj.*

calla lily /ˈkæləlɪli/ *noun* (*pl.* **-ies**) (*especially NAmE*) = ARUM LILY

call·back /ˈkɔːlbæk/ *noun* **1** [C] a telephone call which you make to sb who has just called you 回拨的电话；打回的电话 **2 Callback™** [U, C] = RINGBACK **3** [U, C] (*computing* 计) a process by which the user of a computer or telephone system proves their identity by contacting a computer, which then contacts them 回叫（指计算机或电话系统用户通过连接某台计算机证实自己的身份，然后该系统对之进行回调） **4** [C] (*especially NAmE*) an occasion when you are asked to return somewhere, for example for a second interview when you are trying to get a job（对求职者等的）召回

'call box *noun* **1** (*BrE*) = PHONE BOX **2** (*NAmE*) a small box beside a road, with a telephone in it, to call for help after an accident, etc.（路边供求救等用的）电话亭

'call centre (*BrE*) (*US* **'call center**) *noun* an office in which a large number of people work using telephones, for example arranging insurance for people, or taking customers' orders and answering questions 电话服务中心（安排保险、接受订单、解答问题等）

called 🔑 /kɔːld/ *adj.* [not before noun] having a particular name 叫作；称作：*What's their son called?* 他们的儿子叫什么名字？◇ *I don't know anyone called Scott.* 我不认识叫斯科特的人。◇ *I've forgotten what the firm he works for is called.* 我已经忘记他工作的公司名称。◇ *What's it called again? Yeah, that's right. A router.* 再说一遍它叫什么？对，没错，路由器。 ➲ SEE ALSO SO-CALLED

call·er /ˈkɔːlə(r)/ *noun* **1** a person who is making a telephone call 打电话者：*The caller hung up.* 打电话的人挂断了电话。◇ *an anonymous caller* 打匿名电话的人 **2** a person who goes to a house or a building 访问者；来访者 **3** a person who shouts out the steps for people performing a SQUARE DANCE or COUNTRY DANCE（方形舞或土风舞中）喊出舞步的指挥

'caller ID *noun* [U] a system that uses a device on your telephone to identify and display the telephone number of the person who is calling you（电话的）来电显示系统

'call girl *noun* a PROSTITUTE who makes her arrangements by telephone（电话）应召女郎

cal·lig·raphy /kəˈlɪɡrəfi/ *noun* [U] beautiful HANDWRITING that you do with a special pen or brush; the art of producing this 书法；书法艺术 ▸ **cal·lig·raph·er** *noun*

'call-in (*NAmE*) (*BrE* **'phone-in**) *noun* a radio or television programme in which people can telephone and make comments or ask questions about a particular subject（广播或电视的）热线直播节目，听众来电直播节目

call·ing /ˈkɔːlɪŋ/ *noun* **1** a strong desire or feeling of duty to do a particular job, especially one in which you help other people 使命感；（尤指想帮助他人的）强烈愿望，责任感 SYN **vocation**: *He realized that his calling was to preach the gospel.* 他体悟到宣讲福音是他的使命。 **2** (*formal*) a profession or career 职业；事业

ˈ**calling bell** *noun* (*IndE*) = DOORBELL

ˈ**calling card** *noun* (*NAmE*) **1** (*BrE* ˈ**visiting card**) (*also* **card** *BrE, NAmE*) (especially in the past) a small card with your name on it which you leave with sb after, or instead of, a formal visit（尤指旧时访客留下或其他人用以表示到访的）名片，拜帖 **2** (*figurative*) a sign, such as an action or a piece of work, that identifies sb or shows what they can do 名片式行为（或作品等）；能力标识 **3** = PHONECARD

cal·li·per *noun* (*BrE*) (*also* **cali·per** *NAmE, BrE*) /ˈkælɪpə(r)/ **1 callipers** [pl.] an instrument with two long thin parts joined at one end, used for measuring the DIAMETER of tubes and round objects (= the distance across them) 卡钳，测径器，两脚规，卡尺（用于测量管子、圆形物体的直径）：*a pair of callipers* 一把测径规 **2** (*BrE*) (*NAmE* **brace**) [C, usually pl.] a metal support for weak or injured legs 双脚规形夹（支撑无力或受伤的腿的金属支架）

cal·lis·then·ics (*BrE*) (*NAmE* **cal·is·then·ics**) /ˌkælɪsˈθenɪks/ *noun* [U+sing./pl. v.] physical exercises intended to develop a strong and attractive body 健美操；健身操

ˈ**call letters** *noun* [pl.] (*NAmE*) the letters that are used to identify a radio or television station（电台、电视台的）代号字母，呼号：*the call letters WNBC* 台号字母 WNBC

cal·lous /ˈkæləs/ *adj.* not caring about other people's feelings or suffering 冷酷无情的；无同情心的；冷漠的 **SYN cruel, unfeeling**：*a* ***callous killer/attitude/act*** 冷血杀手；漠不关心的态度；冷酷的行为 ◇ *a* ***callous disregard*** *for the feelings of others* 对他人感情的漠视 ▶ **cal·lous·ly** *adv.* **cal·lous·ness** *noun* [U]

cal·loused (*also* **cal·lused**) /ˈkæləst/ *adj.* (of the skin 皮肤) made rough and hard, usually by hard work 粗糙的；粗硬的；起老茧的：*calloused hands* 有老茧的双手

ˈ**call-out** *noun* an occasion when sb is called to do repairs, rescue sb, etc. 应召出勤；上门服务：*a call-out charge* 上门服务费 ◇ *ambulance call-outs* 救护车出车

cal·low /ˈkæləʊ; *NAmE* -loʊ/ *adj.* (*formal, disapproving*) young and without experience 幼稚无经验的；未谙世事的 **SYN inexperienced**：*a callow youth* 乳臭未干的年轻人

ˈ**call sign** *noun* the letters and numbers used in radio communication to identify the person who is sending a message（无线电通信的）呼叫信号，呼号

ˈ**call-up** *noun* (*BrE*) **1** [U, C, usually sing.] an order to join the armed forces（服兵役的）征召令，征集令 **SYN conscription, draft**：*to receive your* ***call-up papers*** 收到征召入伍的通知 **2** [C] the opportunity to play in a sports team, especially for your country（尤指国家队运动员的）选调，征调：*His recent form has earned him a call-up to the England squad.* 他最近的表现使他得以入选英格兰代表队。

cal·lus /ˈkæləs/ *noun* an area of thick hard skin on a hand or foot, usually caused by rubbing 胼胝，老茧（手、足上的硬皮）

cal·lused = CALLOUSED

ˈ**call waiting** *noun* [U] a telephone service that tells you if sb is trying to call you when you are using the telephone 来电等待服务，插拨服务（通话时提醒用户有人正在打进电话）

calm /kɑːm/ *adj., verb, noun*

■ *adj.* (**calm·er, calm·est**) **1** not excited, nervous or upset 镇静的；沉着的：*It is important to* ***keep calm*** *in an emergency.* 情况紧急的时候，保持镇静是重要的。◇ *Try to* ***remain calm.*** 尽量保持冷静。◇ *Her voice was surprisingly calm.* 她的声音出人意料地平静。◇ *The city is calm again* (= free from trouble and fighting) *after yesterday's riots.* 昨天的骚乱过后，城里又恢复了平静。**2** (of the sea 海洋) without large waves 风平浪静的 **3** (of the weather 天气) without wind 无风的：*a calm, cloudless day* 晴朗无风的一天 ➲ WORDFINDER NOTE AT WIND[1] ➲ MORE LIKE THIS 20, page R27 ▶ **calm·ly** *adv.*：*'I'll call the doctor,' he said calmly.* "我去请医生。"他镇定地说。 **calm·ness** *noun* [U]

■ *verb* ~ **sb/sth** to make sb/sth become quiet and more relaxed, especially after strong emotion or excitement 使平静；使镇静：*Have some tea; it'll calm your nerves.* 喝点茶吧，这会使你紧张的神经松弛下来。◇ *His presence had* ***a calming influence.*** 有他在场对大家的情绪起到了稳定作用。➲ SEE ALSO TRAFFIC CALMING

PHR V ˌ**calm** ˈ**down** | ˌ**calm sb/sth**↔ˈ**down** to become or make sb become calm（使）平静，镇静，安静：*Look, calm down! We'll find her.* 喂，镇静一点！我们会找到她的。◇ *We waited inside until things calmed down.* 我们待在室内，直到一切都恢复了平静。◇ *He took a few deep breaths to calm himself down.* 他深深地吸了几口气，使自己平静下来。

■ *noun* [C, U] **1** a quiet and peaceful time or situation 平静的时期；宁静的状态：*the calm of a summer evening* 夏日夜晚的宁静 ◇ *The police* ***appealed for calm.*** 警察要求大家保持安静。**2** a time when there is no wind 无风：*They landed in a flat calm.* 他们降落时一丝风也没有。**3** a quiet and relaxed manner 泰然自若：*Her previous calm gave way to terror.* 她先前的泰然自若已变为惊恐。

IDM the calm before the storm a calm time immediately before an expected period of violent activity or argument 暴风雨（或大动荡、激烈辩论）前的平静

▼ **WHICH WORD?** 词语辨析

calm / calmness

- The noun **calm** is usually used to talk about a peaceful time or situation. 名词 calm 通常指平静的时期或形势：*There was a short period of uneasy calm after the riot.* 动乱之后是令人不安的短暂平静。 It can also be used to describe a person's manner. 该词亦可指人的态度：*She spoke with icy calm.* 她说话时一副冷漠、若无其事的样子。 **Calmness** is usually used to talk about a person. * calmness 通常用以形容人镇定、镇静：*We admired his calmness under pressure.* 我们佩服他在压力下的镇静。

Calor gas™ /ˈkælə gæs; *NAmE* ˈkælər/ (*BrE*) (*US* ˈ**cooking gas**) *noun* [U] a type of gas stored as a liquid under pressure in metal containers and used for heating and cooking in places where there is no gas supply 罐装液化气（用于取暖和做饭）

cal·orie /ˈkæləri/ *noun* **1** a unit for measuring how much energy food will produce 大卡，千卡（测量食物含多少热量的单位）：*No sugar for me, thanks—I'm* ***counting my calories.*** 我不要糖，谢谢。我在控制摄取的热量。◇ *a* ***low-calorie drink/diet*** 低热量的饮料 / 饮食 ➲ WORDFINDER NOTE AT EAT ➲ COLLOCATIONS AT DIET **2** (*specialist*) a unit for measuring a quantity of heat; the amount of heat needed to raise the temperature of a gram of water by one degree Celsius 卡，卡路里（热量单位，或 1 克水升高 1 摄氏度时所需要的热量）

cal·or·if·ic /ˌkæləˈrɪfɪk/ *adj.* [usually before noun] **1** (*specialist*) relating to the amount of energy contained in food or fuel（热）卡的；产生热量的：*the calorific value of food* (= the quantity of heat or energy produced by a particular amount of food) 食物的热值（即某一数量的食物所产生的热量或能量） **2** (of food and drink 饮食) containing a lot of calories and likely to make you fat 高卡（路里）的；高热量的：*calorific chocolate cake* 高热量巧克力蛋糕

cal·or·im·eter /ˌkæləˈrɪmɪtə(r)/ *noun* (*specialist*) a device which measures the amount of heat in a chemical reaction 热量计；量热计

calque /kælk/ (*also* ˈ**loan translation**) *noun* (*linguistics* 语言) a word or expression in a language that is a translation of a word or expression in another language 仿造词，借译词语（外国词语的直译词）：*'Traffic calming' is a calque of the German 'Verkehrsberuhigung'.* * traffic calming 是由德语 Verkehrsberuhigung 直译过来的。

cal·umny /ˈkæləmni/ *noun* (*pl.* **-ies**) (*formal*) **1** [C] a false statement about a person that is made to damage their reputation 诬蔑，诽谤（的言论） **2** [U] the act of making such a statement 诬蔑，诽谤（的行为） **SYN** **slander**

Cal·va·dos /ˈkælvədɒs; *NAmE* ˌkælvəˈdoʊs/ *noun* [U, C] a French strong alcoholic drink made by DISTILLING apple juice （法国）苹果白兰地

C

calve /kɑːv; *NAmE* kæv/ *verb* [I] (of a cow 母牛) to give birth to a CALF 生小牛；产犊

calves PL. OF CALF

Cal·vin·ist /ˈkælvɪnɪst/ (*also* **Cal·vin·is·tic**) *adj.* **1** connected with a Church that follows the teachings of the French Protestant, John Calvin 加尔文宗的，加尔文派的（与信奉法国新教教徒约翰·加尔文教义的教派有关的） **2** having very strict moral attitudes 严守道德的 ▶ **Cal·vin·ism** *noun* [U] **Cal·vin·ist** *noun*

ca·lypso /kəˈlɪpsəʊ; *NAmE* -soʊ/ *noun* [C, U] (*pl.* **-os**) a Caribbean song about a subject of current interest; this type of music 卡利普索民歌（以时事为主题，流行于加勒比海地区）；卡利普索音乐

calyx /ˈkeɪlɪks/ *noun* (*pl.* **ca·lyxes** or **ca·ly·ces** /ˈkeɪlɪsiːz/) (*specialist*) the ring of small green leaves (called SEPALS) that protect a flower before it opens 花萼

CAM /kæm/ *abbr.* computer aided manufacturing 计算机辅助制造；电脑辅助制造

cam /kæm/ *noun* a part on a wheel that sticks out and changes the CIRCULAR movement of the wheel into up-and-down or backwards-and-forwards movement 凸轮（把圆周运动转变为上下或前后运动的机械部件）

cama·rad·erie /ˌkæməˈrɑːdəri; *NAmE* ˌkɑːməˈrɑːdəri/ *noun* [U] a feeling of friendship and trust among people who work or spend a lot of time together 同事情谊；友情

cam·ber /ˈkæmbə(r)/ *noun* a slight downward curve from the middle of a road to each side 预拱度（路面中间微拱的曲面）

cam·bric /ˈkæmbrɪk/ *noun* [U] a type of thin white cloth made from cotton or LINEN 细棉布；细亚麻布

cam·cord·er /ˈkæmkɔːdə(r); *NAmE* -kɔːrd-/ *noun* a video camera that records pictures and sound and that can be carried around （便携式）摄像机

came PAST TENSE OF COME

camel /ˈkæml/ *noun* **1** [C] an animal with a long neck and one or two HUMPS on its back, used in desert countries for riding on or for carrying goods 骆驼 ⊃ COMPARE DROMEDARY **2** [U] = CAMEL HAIR: *a camel coat* 驼毛外衣 **IDM** SEE STRAW

ˈ**camel hair** *noun* [U] (*also* **camel**) a type of thick soft pale brown cloth made from camel's hair or a mixture of camel's hair and wool, used especially for making coats 驼毛料子，驼绒料子（尤用以制外衣）：*a camel-hair coat* 驼绒外衣

cam·el·lia /kəˈmiːliə/ *noun* a bush with shiny leaves and white, red or pink flowers that look like ROSES and are also called camellias 山茶；山茶花

Cam·em·bert /ˈkæməmbeə(r); *NAmE* -ber/ *noun* [U, C] a type of soft French cheese with a strong flavour 卡芒贝尔奶酪（法国软干酪，味浓）

cameo /ˈkæmiəʊ; *NAmE* -mioʊ/ *noun* (*pl.* **-os**) **1** a small part in a film/movie or play for a famous actor （电影、戏剧中）名演员演的配角：***a cameo role/appearance*** 客串演出 ⊃ **WORDFINDER NOTE** AT ACTOR **2** a short piece of writing that gives a good description of sb/sth 小品文 **3** a piece of jewellery that consists of a raised design, often of a head, on a background of a different colour 浮雕珠宝饰物：***a cameo brooch/ring*** 浮雕针饰 / 戒指

cam·era 🔑 /ˈkæmərə/ *noun* a piece of equipment for taking photographs, moving pictures or television pictures 照相机；（电影）摄影机；（电视）摄像机：*Just point the camera and press the button.* 只要把照相机对准，然后按动快门就可以了。◇ *Cameras started clicking as soon as she stepped out of the car.* 她一跨出汽车，照相机就开始咔嚓咔嚓地响成一片。◇ ***a TV/video camera*** 电视摄像机；摄像机 ◇ *a camera crew* 摄制组

IDM **in ˈcamera** (*law* 律) in a judge's private room, without the press or the public being present 在法官的私室里；秘密地；不公开地：*The trial was held in camera.* 审判秘密进行。 **on ˈcamera** being filmed or shown on television 在摄制中；在电视上播放：*Are you prepared to tell your story on camera?* 你愿意在电视上讲述你的经历吗？

cam·era·man /ˈkæmrəmæn/, **came·ra·woman** /ˈkæmrəwʊmən/ *noun* (*pl.* **-men** /-men/, **-women** /-wɪmɪn/) a person whose job is operating a camera for making films/movies or television programmes （电影、电视节目的）摄影师，摄像师 ⊃ NOTE AT GENDER ⊃ **MORE LIKE THIS** 25, page R28 ⊃ **WORDFINDER NOTE** AT FILM

camera obscura /ˌkæmərə əbˈskjʊərə; *NAmE* -ˈskjʊrə/ *noun* an early form of camera consisting of a dark box with a tiny hole or LENS in the front and a small screen inside, on which the image appears 暗箱（早期的照相机）

ˈ**camera operator** *noun* (*also* ˈ**camera person** *pl.* ˈ**camera people**) a person whose job is operating a camera for making films/movies or television programmes （电影、电视节目的）摄影师，摄像师

cam·era·work /ˈkæmrəwɜːk; *NAmE* -wɜːrk/ *noun* [U] the style in which sb takes photographs or uses a film/movie camera 拍摄风格

cami·sole /ˈkæmɪsəʊl; *NAmE* -soʊl/ *noun* a short piece of women's underwear that is worn on the top half of the body and is held up with narrow strips of material over the shoulders （背心式）女内衣

camo·mile (*especially BrE*) (*also* **chamo·mile** *especially in NAmE*) /ˈkæməmaɪl/ *noun* [U] a plant with a sweet smell and small white and yellow flowers. Its dried leaves and flowers are used to make tea, medicine, etc. 果香菊，春黄菊，甘菊（花及叶可制茶、药等）：*camomile tea* 甘菊花茶

cam·ou·flage /ˈkæməflɑːʒ/ *noun, verb*

■ ***noun*** **1** [U] a way of hiding soldiers and military equipment, using paint, leaves or nets, so that they look like part of their surroundings（军事上的）伪装；迷彩：*a camouflage jacket* (= covered with green and brown marks and worn by soldiers) 迷彩夹克衫 ◇ *troops dressed in camouflage* 穿迷彩服的军队 **2** [U, sing.] the way in which an animal's colour or shape matches its surroundings and makes it difficult to see（动物的）保护色，拟态 **3** [U, sing.] behaviour that is deliberately meant to hide the truth 隐瞒：*Her angry words were camouflage for the way she felt.* 她以气愤的言辞掩盖自己的真实感情。

■ ***verb*** **~ sth (with sth)** to hide sb/sth by making them or it look like the things around, or like sth else 伪装；掩饰：*The soldiers camouflaged themselves with leaves.* 士兵用树叶来伪装自己。◇ *Her size was camouflaged by the long loose dress she wore.* 她穿的那件宽松长裙遮掩了她的身材。 ⊃ **SYNONYMS** AT HIDE

camp 🔑 /kæmp/ *noun, verb, adj.*

■ ***noun***

• **IN TENTS** 帐篷 **1** 🔑 [C, U] a place where people live temporarily in tents or temporary buildings 营地：*Let's return to camp.* 咱们回营地吧。◇ *to **pitch/make camp*** (= put up tents) 扎营；搭帐篷 ◇ *to break camp* (= to take down tents) 拔营 ⊃ SEE ALSO HOLIDAY CAMP

• **HOLIDAY/VACATION** 度假 **2** 🔑 [C, U] a place where young people go on holiday/vacation and take part in various activities or a particular activity 度假营：*a tennis camp* 网球度假营 ◇ *He spent two weeks at camp this summer.* 他今年夏天在度假营玩了两个星期。◇ *summer camp* 夏令营 ⊃ SEE ALSO FAT CAMP

• **PRISON, ETC.** 拘留营等 **3** 🔑 [C] (used in compounds 用于构成复合词) a place where people are kept in temporary buildings or tents, especially by a government and often for long periods （尤指政府让人长时间住宿的）营房，营

帐：*a refugee camp* 难民营 ◇ *a camp guard* 拘留营看守 ➲ SEE ALSO CONCENTRATION CAMP, PRISON CAMP, TRANSIT CAMP

- ARMY 军队 **4** [C, U] a place where soldiers live while they are training or fighting 兵营：*an army camp* 军营
- GROUP OF PEOPLE 群体 **5** [C] a group of people who have the same ideas about sth and oppose people with other ideas 阵营（指观点相同且与持不同观点者对立的集团）：*the socialist camp* 社会主义阵营 ◇ *We were in opposing camps.* 我们属于彼此对立的阵营。**6** [C] one of the sides in a competition and the people connected with it 阵营（比赛的一方及其支持者）：*There was an air of confidence in the England camp.* 英格兰队阵营信心十足。

IDM SEE FOOT *n.*

■ *verb*

- LIVE IN TENT 住帐篷 **1** [I] to put up a tent and live in it for a short time 宿营；露营：*I camped overnight in a field.* 我在田野里露营过夜。**2** [I] **go camping** to stay in a tent, especially while you are on holiday/vacation（尤指在假日）野营：*They go camping in France every year.* 他们每年去法国野营度假。➲ WORDFINDER NOTE AT HOLIDAY
- STAY FOR SHORT TIME 短暂停留 **3** [I] ~ (**out**) to live in sb's house for a short time, especially when you do not have a bed there 借住；借宿；暂住：*I'm camping out at a friend's apartment at the moment.* 我目前暂时寄宿在朋友的住处。**4** [I] (of a character in a video game) to stay in one place in order to keep attacking enemies and gain an advantage（电子游戏中的角色）蹲点（躲在一处伺机攻击）

PHR V ˌ**camp ˈout** to live outside for a short time 露宿：*Dozens of reporters camped out on her doorstep.* 许多记者在她家门口安营扎寨。ˌ**camp it ˈup** (*informal*) to behave in a very exaggerated manner, especially to attract attention to yourself or to make people laugh 装腔作势，装模作样（尤指想引人注意或令人发笑）

■ *adj.* **1** (of a man or his manner 男人或其举止) deliberately behaving in a way that some people think is typical of a HOMOSEXUAL 故意带女子气的，女性化的（被某些人认为是典型同性恋的特征） SYN **effeminate** **2** exaggerated in style, especially in a deliberately amusing way 夸张的，滑稽可笑的（尤指故意逗笑）；做作的：*The movie is a camp celebration of the fashion industry.* 这部电影夸张地颂扬时装行业。

cam·paign /kæmˈpeɪn/ *noun, verb*

■ *noun* **1** ~ (**against/for sth**) a series of planned activities that are intended to achieve a particular social, commercial or political aim 运动（为社会、商业或政治目的而进行的一系列有计划的活动）：*to* ***conduct a campaign*** 领导一场运动 ◇ *a campaign against ageism in the workplace* 反对在工作场所实行年龄歧视的运动 ◇ *the campaign for parliamentary reform* 要求议会进行改革的运动 ◇ *an anti-smoking campaign* 反对吸烟的运动 ◇ *Today police* ***launched*** (= began) ***a campaign*** *to reduce road accidents.* 警方今天发起了一场减少道路交通事故的运动。◇ *an advertising campaign* 一场广告宣传运动 ◇ *an election campaign* 竞选运动 ◇ *the President's* ***campaign team/manager*** 总统的竞选班子 / 主管 ➲ COLLOCATIONS AT VOTE **2** a series of attacks and battles that are intended to achieve a particular military aim during a war 战役 ➲ WORDFINDER NOTE AT ATTACK ➲ MORE LIKE THIS 20, page R27

■ *verb* [I, T] to take part in or lead a campaign, for example to achieve political change or in order to win an election 参加运动，领导运动（如为实现政治变革或赢得竞选）：*The party* ***campaigned vigorously*** *in the north of the country.* 该党在本国北部展开了强有力的竞选运动。◇ ~ **for/against sb/sth** *We have campaigned against whaling for the last 15 years.* 我们过去 15 年一直参加反对捕鲸的

▼ SYNONYMS 同义词辨析

campaign

battle • struggle • drive • war • fight

These are all words for an effort made to achieve or prevent sth. 以上各词均指为达到某目的或为阻止某事而作出的努力。

campaign a series of planned activities that are intended to achieve a particular social, commercial or political aim 指为社会、商业或政治目的而进行的一系列有计划的活动或运动：*the campaign for parliamentary reform* 要求议会改革的运动 ◇ *an advertising campaign* 广告宣传活动

battle a competition or an argument between people or groups of people trying to win power or control 指个人或集体为赢得权力或控制权而进行的较量、争论或斗争：*She finally won the legal battle for compensation.* 她终于赢得了这场要求赔偿的法律斗争。◇ *the endless battle between man and nature* 人与大自然永无休止的斗争

struggle a competition or an argument between people or groups of people trying to win power or control 指个人或集体为赢得权力或控制权而进行的较量、争论或斗争：*the struggle for independence* 为独立的斗争 ◇ *the struggle between good and evil* 正邪之争

BATTLE OR STRUGGLE? 用 battle 还是 struggle?

A **struggle** is always about things that seem absolutely necessary, such as life and death or freedom. A **battle** can also be about things that are not absolutely necessary, just desirable, or about the pleasure of winning. * struggle 总是用于似乎绝对必要的斗争，如关乎生死、自由等。battle 还可用于并非绝对必要的斗争，如仅仅是想得到或者为了获得胜利的满足感：*the battle/struggle between good and evil* 正邪之争 ◇ ~~*a legal struggle for compensation*~~ ◇ ~~*a struggle of wills/wits*~~

drive an organized effort by a group of people to achieve sth 指团体为达到目的而作出的有组织的努力：*the drive for greater efficiency* 为提高效率而作出的努力 ◇ *a drive to reduce energy consumption* 为减少能源消耗而发起的运动

CAMPAIGN OR DRIVE? 用 campaign 还是 drive?

A **campaign** is usually aimed at getting other people to do sth; a **drive** may be an attempt by people to get themselves to do sth. * campaign 通常指发动别人参加的运动；drive 可指让自己作出努力：*From today, we're going on an* ***economy drive*** (= we must spend less). 从今天起，我们要展开厉行节约运动。A **campaign** may be larger, more formal and more organized than a **drive**. * campaign 所指的运动可能比 drive 更大规模、更正式和更有组织。

war [sing.] an effort over a long period of time to get rid of or stop sth bad 指为消灭或阻止有害事物而进行的长期斗争：*the war against crime* 反犯罪活动的斗争

fight [sing.] the work of trying to stop or prevent sth bad or achieve sth good; an act of competing, especially in a sport 指为制止或防止坏事物或为达到好目的而进行的斗争，或指竞赛，尤指体育竞赛：*Workers won their fight to stop compulsory redundancies.* 工人赢得了阻止强制裁员的斗争。

WAR OR FIGHT? 用 war 还是 fight?

A **war** is about stopping things, like drugs and crime, that everyone agrees are bad. A **fight** can be about achieving justice for yourself. * war 用于制止人人摒弃的事物（如毒品和犯罪）而进行的斗争；fight 可用于为自己伸张正义而进行的斗争。

PATTERNS

- a campaign/battle/struggle/drive/war/fight **against** sth
- a campaign/battle/struggle/drive/fight **for** sth
- a **one-man/one-woman/personal** campaign/battle/struggle/war
- a **bitter** campaign/battle/struggle/drive/war/fight
- to **launch/embark on** a campaign/battle/drive
- to **lead/continue** the campaign/battle/struggle/drive/fight
- to **win/lose** a battle/struggle/war/fight

运动。◇ ~ **to do sth** *They are campaigning to save the area from building development.* 他们正开展一场反对在这个地区进行房地产开发的运动。▶ **cam·paign·ing** *noun* [U]

cam·paign·er /kæmˈpeɪnə(r)/ *noun* a person who leads or takes part in a campaign, especially one for political or social change （尤指政治或社会变革的）运动领导者，运动参加者：*a leading human rights campaigner* 人权运动的主要领导人 ◇ *a campaigner on environmental issues* 环保问题的活动家 ◇ *a campaigner for women priests* 主张女性也可担任司祭的倡导者 ◇ *an* ***old/veteran/seasoned campaigner*** (= a person with a lot of experience of a particular activity) 老练 / 资深 / 经验丰富的活动家 ◇ *(especially NAmE) Obama campaigners* (= people working for Obama in a campaign) 奥巴马竞选班子

cam·pa·nile /ˌkæmpəˈniːli/ *noun* a tower that contains a bell, especially one that is not part of another building （尤指独立的）钟楼

cam·pan·ology /ˌkæmpəˈnɒlədʒi; *NAmE* -ˈnɑːl-/ *noun* [U] *(formal)* the study of bells and the art of ringing bells 钟学；鸣钟术 ▶ **cam·pan·olo·gist** /-ədʒɪst/ *noun* ➲ SEE ALSO BELL-RINGER

ˈcamp bed *(BrE)* *(NAmE* **cot***)* *noun* a light narrow bed that you can fold up and carry easily 折叠床；行军床 ➲ VISUAL VOCAB PAGE V24

camp·er /ˈkæmpə(r)/ *noun* **1** a person who spends a holiday/vacation living in a tent or at a holiday camp 野营者；露营者；度假营营员 **2** *(also* **ˈcamper van***)* *(both BrE)* *(NAmE* **RV**, **recreˌational ˈvehicle***)* *(also* **motor·home** *NAmE, BrE)* a large vehicle designed for people to live and sleep in when they are travelling 野营车（供旅行时居住）➲ VISUAL VOCAB PAGE V63 **3** *(NAmE)* *(BrE* **cara·van***)* a road vehicle without an engine that is pulled by a car, designed for people to live and sleep in, especially when they are on holiday/vacation 旅行拖车，宿营拖车（无发动机，由其他车拖动，多供度假时住宿用）➲ VISUAL VOCAB PAGE V63 IDM SEE HAPPY

camp·fire /ˈkæmpfaɪə(r)/ *noun* an outdoor fire made by people who are sleeping outside or living in a tent 营火；篝火

ˌcamp ˈfollower *noun* **1** a person who supports a particular group or political party but is not a member of it（支持某一团体或政党但并非其正式成员的）追随者 **2** (in the past) a person who was not a soldier but followed an army from place to place to sell goods or services （旧时的）随军商贩，随军杂役

camp·ground /ˈkæmpɡraʊnd/ *(NAmE)* *(BrE* **camp·site**, **ˈcamping site***)* *noun* a place where people on holiday/vacation can put up their tents, park their CARAVAN/CAMPER, etc., often with toilets, water, etc. 野营地；度假营地

cam·phor /ˈkæmfə(r)/ *noun* [U] a white substance with a strong smell, used in medicine, for making plastics and to keep insects away from clothes 樟脑

camp·ing 🔑 /ˈkæmpɪŋ/ *noun* [U] living in a tent, etc. on holiday/vacation 野营度假：*Do you* ***go camping****?* 你去野营度假吗？◇ *a camping trip* 野营旅行

camp·site /ˈkæmpsaɪt/ *noun* **1** *(also* **ˈcamping site***)* *(both BrE)* *(NAmE* **ˈcamp·ground***)* a place where people on holiday/vacation can put up their tents, park their CARAVAN/CAMPER, etc., often with toilets, water, etc. 野营地；度假营地 **2** *(NAmE)* a place in a campground where you can put up one tent or park one CAMPER, etc. 露营帐篷位；野营车位

cam·pus /ˈkæmpəs/ *noun* the buildings of a university or college and the land around them （大学、学院的）校园，校区：*She lives* ***on campus*** (= within the main university area). 她住在大学校园内。◇ *campus life* 大学校园生活

cam·shaft /ˈkæmʃɑːft; *NAmE* -ʃæft/ *noun* a long straight piece of metal with a CAM on it joining parts of machinery, especially in a vehicle 凸轮轴

can[1] 🔑 /kən; *strong form* kæn/ *modal verb* ➲ SEE ALSO CAN[2] *(negative* **can·not** /ˈkænɒt; *NAmE* -nɑːt/, *short form* **can't** /kɑːnt; *NAmE* kænt/, *pt* **could** /kəd; *strong form* kʊd/, *negative* **could not**, *short form* **couldn't** /ˈkʊdnt/) **1** 🔑 used to say that it is possible for sb/sth to do sth, or for sth to happen （表示有能力做或能够发生）能，会：*I can run fast.* 我能跑得快。◇ *Can you call back tomorrow?* 明天你能回电话吗？◇ *He couldn't answer the question.* 他不能回答那个问题。◇ *The stadium can be emptied in four minutes.* 这个体育场能让观众四分钟全部离场。◇ *I can't promise anything, but I'll do what I can.* 我不能许诺什么，但会尽力而为。◇ *Please let us know if you cannot attend the meeting.* 你若不能参加会议，请通知我们。 **2** 🔑 used to say that sb knows how to do sth （表示知道如何做）懂得，会：*She can speak Spanish.* 她会讲西班牙语。◇ *Can he cook?* 他会做饭吗？◇ *I could drive a car before I left school.* 我在中学毕业前就会开车了。**3** 🔑 used with the verbs 'feel', 'hear', 'see', 'smell', 'taste'（与动词 feel、hear、see、smell、taste 连用）：*She could feel a lump in her breast.* 她摸到自己的乳房里有一个肿块。◇ *I can hear music.* 我听见有音乐声。 **4** 🔑 used to show that sb is allowed to do sth （表示允许）可以：*You can take the car, if you want.* 如果想用那辆车，你就尽管用吧。◇ *We can't wear jeans at work.* 我们工作时不准穿牛仔裤。**5** 🔑 *(informal)* used to ask permission to do sth （请求允许）可以：*Can I read your newspaper?* 我可以看一下你的报纸吗？◇ *Can I take you home?* 我送你回家好吗？**6** 🔑 *(informal)* used to ask sb to help you （请求帮助）能：*Can you help me with this box?* 你能帮我搬这个箱子吗？◇ *Can you feed the cat, please?* 请你喂一下猫好吗？**7** 🔑 used in the negative for saying that you are sure sth is not true（用于否定句，表示某事肯定不真实）：*That can't be Mary—she's in New York.* 那不可能是玛丽，她在纽约呢。◇ *He can't have slept through all that noise.* 他不可能在那种闹哄哄的环境里睡好觉。**8** 🔑 used to express doubt or surprise（表示疑惑或惊讶）究竟能，难道会，到底是：*What can they be doing?* 他们究竟在干些什么呢？◇ *Can he be serious?* 他难道会当真吗？◇ *Where can she have put it?* 她到底把它放哪儿了呢？**9** 🔑 used to say what sb/sth is often like（表示常有的行为和情形）有时会，时而可能：*He can be very tactless sometimes.* 他有时太莽撞。◇ *It can be quite cold here in winter.* 这里的冬天有时还真够冷的。**10** 🔑 used to make suggestions （提出建议）可以：*We can eat in a restaurant, if you like.* 如果你愿意，我们可以去餐馆吃饭。◇ *I can take the car if necessary.* 如果必要的话，我可以乘汽车去。**11** *(informal)* used to say that sb must do sth, usually when you are angry（表示对方必须做，通常指说话人在生气时）必须，得：*You can shut up or get out!* 你给我闭嘴，要不然就滚出去！➲ NOTE AT MODAL

▼ **WHICH WORD?** 词语辨析

can / may

- **Can** and **cannot** (or **can't**) are the most common words used for asking for, giving or refusing permission. * can 和 cannot（或 can't）是表示请求、给予或拒绝许可的最通用词：*Can I borrow your calculator?* 我可以借用你的计算器吗？◇ *You can come with us if you want to.* 如果你愿意可以跟我们一起来。◇ *You can't park your car there.* 你不能在那儿停车。
- **May** (negative **may not**) is used as a polite and fairly formal way to ask for or give permission. * may（否定式 may not）用以表示礼貌的正式请求或给予许可：*May I borrow your newspaper?* 把你的报纸借我看行吗？◇ *You may come if you wish.* 你想来的话可以来。It is often used in official signs and rules. 该词常用于正式标志和规定：*Visitors may use the swimming pool between 7 a.m. and 7 p.m.* 访客从早 7:00 到晚 7:00 可在游泳池游泳。◇ *Students may not use the college car park.* 学生不得在学院停车场停车。The form **mayn't** is hardly ever used in modern English. 现代英语几乎不用 mayn't。

IDM **as happy, simple, sweet, etc. as can be** as happy, etc. as possible 尽可能地…；要多…有多… **can't be doing with sb/sth/sb doing sth** (*informal*) used to say that you do not like sth and are unwilling to accept it（表示因不喜欢而不愿接受）无法接受…： *I can't be doing with people who complain all the time.* 我无法忍受那些整天发牢骚的人。 **no can 'do** (*informal*) used to say that you are not able or willing to do sth 干不了；不行；不成： *Sorry, no can do. I just don't have the time.* 对不起，不行。我就是没有时间。

can² /kæn/ *noun, verb* ➲ SEE ALSO CAN¹

■ ***noun*** **1** [C] (*BrE also* **tin**) [C] a metal container in which food and drink is sold（盛食品或饮料的）金属罐： *a can of beans* 豆罐头 ◇ *a beer can* 啤酒罐 ➲ VISUAL VOCAB PAGE V36 **HELP** In *NAmE* **can** is the usual word used for both food and drink. In *BrE* **can** is always used for drink, but **tin** or **can** can be used for food and other substances such as paint or varnish. 美式英语中，can 一词通常用于食品和饮料。英式英语中，can 一词总是用于饮料，但 tin 或 can 可用于食品和其他材料，如油漆、清漆等。 **2** [C] the amount contained in a can 一罐（的量）： *We drank a can of Coke each.* 我们每人喝了一罐可乐。 **3** [C] a metal or plastic container for holding or carrying liquids（装运液体用的）金属容器，塑料容器： *an oil can* 油罐 ◇ *a watering can* 洒水壶 **4** [C] a metal container in which liquids are kept under pressure and let out in a fine spray when you press a button on the lid 喷雾罐： *a can of hairspray* 一罐喷发定型剂 ➲ VISUAL VOCAB PAGE V36 **5 the can** [sing.] (*NAmE, slang*) prison 班房；监狱；牢房

▼ GRAMMAR POINT 语法说明

can / could / be able to / manage

- **Can** is used to say that somebody knows how to do something. * can 表示懂得做： *Can you play the piano?* 你会弹钢琴吗？ It is also used with verbs of seeing, noticing, etc. 该词亦与表示看见、注意到等的动词连用： *I can hear someone calling.* 我听见有人在呼叫。 and with passive infinitives. 并与不定式的被动形式连用： *The podcast can be downloaded here.* 播客可在此下载。
- **Can** or **be able to** are used to say that something is possible or that somebody has the opportunity to do something. * can 或 be able to 表示某事情有可能或某人有机会做某事： *Can you/are you able to come on Saturday?* 你星期六能来吗？
- You use **be able to** to form the future and perfect tenses and the infinitive. 用 be able to 构成将来时、完成时和动词不定式： *You'll be able to get a taxi outside the station.* 在车站外可搭乘出租车。◇ *I haven't been able to get much work done today.* 我今天未能干多少工作。◇ *She'd love to be able to play the piano.* 她很希望能弹钢琴。
- **Could** is used to talk about what someone was generally able to do in the past. * could 表示过去通常能做： *Our daughter could walk when she was nine months old.* 我们的女儿九个月大就会走路了。
- You use **was/were able to** or **manage** (but not **could**) when you are saying that something was possible on a particular occasion in the past. 关于在过去特定情况下可能的事用 was/were able to 或 manage，但不用 could： *I was able to/managed to find some useful books in the library.* 我总算在图书馆找到了一些有用的书。◇ ~~*I could find some useful books in the library.*~~ In negative sentences, **could not** can also be used. 否定句也可用 could not： *We weren't able to/didn't manage to/couldn't get there in time.* 我们未能及时赶到那儿。 **Could** is also used with this meaning with verbs of seeing, noticing, understanding, etc. 亦可用 could 加表示看见、注意到、明白等的动词表示此义： *I could see there was something wrong.* 我发觉出事了。
- **Could have** is used when you are saying that it was possible for somebody to do something in the past but they did not try. 表示过去有可能做某事但没有做，用 could have： *I could have won the game but decided to let her win.* 我本可以赢得那场比赛，但还是决定让她赢了。

6 the can [sing.] (*NAmE, slang*) the toilet 茅房；厕所

IDM **a can of 'worms** (*informal*) if you open up **a can of worms**, you start doing sth that will cause a lot of problems and be very difficult 棘手的问题；难题；麻烦事 **be in the 'can** (*informal*) (especially of filmed or recorded material 尤指影片、录像资料) to be completed and ready for use 已拍摄好；录制完毕 ➲ MORE AT CARRY

■ ***verb*** (**-nn-**) **1 ~ sth** (*especially NAmE*) to preserve food by putting it in a can 把（食品）装罐保存 **2 ~ sb** (*NAmE, informal*) to dismiss sb from their job 解雇；让…卷铺盖走人；炒…的鱿鱼 **SYN** **fire, sack**

'Canada Day *noun* (in Canada) a national holiday held on 1 July to celebrate the original joining together of PROVINCES to form Canada in 1867 加拿大国庆节（7 月 1 日，纪念 1867 年加拿大的成立）

ˌCanada 'goose *noun* a common N American GOOSE with a black head and neck 加拿大黑雁

Can·adian /kəˈneɪdiən/ *adj., noun*

■ ***adj.*** from or connected with Canada 加拿大的

■ ***noun*** a person from Canada 加拿大人

canal /kəˈnæl/ *noun* **1** a long straight passage dug in the ground and filled with water for boats and ships to travel along; a smaller passage used for carrying water to fields, crops, etc. 运河；灌溉渠： *the Panama/Suez Canal* 巴拿马 / 苏伊士运河 ◇ *an irrigation canal* 一条灌溉渠 **2** a tube inside the body through which liquid, food or air can pass 管；导管；食道；气管 ➲ SEE ALSO ALIMENTARY CANAL

ca'nal boat *noun* a long narrow boat used on canals 运河船（船体狭长） ➲ VISUAL VOCAB PAGE V59

can·al·ize (*BrE also* **-ise**) /ˈkænəlaɪz/ *verb* **1 ~ sth** (*specialist*) to make a river wider, deeper or straighter; to make a river into a canal 把（河道）加宽，加深，变直；把（河流）改建成运河 **2 ~ sth** (*formal*) to control an emotion, activity, etc. so that it is aimed at a particular purpose 把（情绪、行为等）引向某一渠道 **SYN** **channel** ▸ **can·al·iza·tion, -isa·tion** /ˌkænəlaɪˈzeɪʃn; *NAmE* -ləˈz-/ *noun* [U]

can·apé /ˈkænəpeɪ; *NAmE* ˌkænəˈpeɪ/ *noun* [usually pl.] a small biscuit or piece of bread with cheese, meat, fish, etc. on it, usually served with drinks at a party 小饼干，面包片，开胃饼（上面附有奶酪、肉、鱼等，通常在聚会上与饮料一起提供）

can·ard /kæˈnɑːd; ˈkænɑːd; *NAmE* kəˈnɑːrd; ˈkænɑːrd/ *noun* (*formal*) a false report or piece of news 虚假的报道；假新闻

can·ary /kəˈneəri; *NAmE* -ˈneri/ *noun* (*pl.* **-ies**) a small yellow bird with a beautiful song, often kept in a CAGE as a pet 金丝雀 **IDM** SEE CAT

can·asta /kəˈnæstə/ *noun* [U] a card game played with two packs of cards, in which players try to collect sets of cards 卡纳斯塔纸牌戏（用两副纸牌，参与者尽量组成牌组）

can·can /ˈkænkæn/ *noun* (*often* **the cancan**) [sing.] a fast dance in which a line of women kick their legs high in the air 康康舞，坎坎舞（女子排成一排，高高踢腿）

can·cel /ˈkænsl/ *verb* (**-ll-**, *US* **-l-**) **1** [T] **~ sth** to decide that sth that has been arranged will not now take place 取消；撤销；终止： *All flights have been cancelled because of bad weather.* 因天气恶劣，所有航班均已取消。◇ *Don't forget to cancel the newspaper* (= arrange for it not to be delivered) *before going away.* 外出前，别忘了通知人停送报纸。 ➲ COMPARE POSTPONE **2** [T, I] **~ (sth)** to say that you no longer want to continue with an agreement, especially one that has been legally arranged 撤销，取消，废除（具有法律效力的协议）： *to cancel a policy/subscription* 取消保单；停止订阅 ◇ *Is it too late to cancel my order?* 我现在取消订单是不是太晚了？ ◇ *The US has agreed to cancel debts* (= say that they no longer need to be paid) *totalling $10 million.* 美国已同意免除总

额为 1 000 万美元的债务。◇ *No charge will be made if you cancel within 10 days.* 如果在 10 天以内取消，不收费用。 **3** [T] **~ sth** to mark a ticket or stamp so that it cannot be used again 盖销，注销（票或邮票） ➲ MORE LIKE THIS 36, page R29

PHR V ˌ**cancel ˈout** | ˌ**cancel sth↔ˈout** if two or more things **cancel out** or one **cancels out** the other, they are equally important but have an opposite effect on a situation so that the situation does not change 抵消；对消： *Recent losses have cancelled out any profits made at the start of the year.* 最近的亏损抵消了年初的盈利。◇ *The advantages and disadvantages would appear to **cancel each other out**.* 看来是利弊参半。

can·cel·la·tion (US **can·cel·ation**) /ˌkænsəˈleɪʃn/ *noun* **1** [U, C] a decision to stop sth that has already been arranged from happening; a statement that sth will not happen 取消；撤销： *We need at least 24 hours' notice of cancellation.* 如欲取消，请至少提前 24 小时告知。◇ *a cancellation fee* 注销费 ◇ *Heavy seas can cause cancellation of ferry services.* 海上起大风浪会导致渡轮航班取消。◇ *Cancellations must be made in writing.* 撤销必须有书面通知。 **2** [C] something that has been cancelled 被取消了的事物： *Are there any cancellations for this evening's performance?* (= tickets that have been returned) 今晚的演出有退票吗？ **3** [U] the fact of making sth no longer valid 作废；废除；取消；中止： *the cancellation of the contract* 合同的取消

Can·cer /ˈkænsə(r)/ *noun* **1** [U] the fourth sign of the ZODIAC, the CRAB 黄道第四宫；巨蟹宫；巨蟹（星）座 **2** [sing.] a person born when the sun is in this sign, that is between 22 June and 22 July, approximately 属巨蟹座的人（约出生于 6 月 22 日至 7 月 22 日） ▸ **Can·cer·ian** /kænˈsɪəriən; NAmE -ˈsɪr-/ *noun, adj.*

can·cer 🔑 /ˈkænsə(r)/ *noun* **1** 🔑 [U, C] a serious disease in which GROWTHS of cells, also called cancers, form in the body and kill normal body cells. The disease often causes death. 癌；癌症： *lung/breast cancer* 肺癌；乳腺癌 ◇ *cancer of the bowel/stomach* 肠癌；胃癌 ◇ *Most skin cancers are completely curable.* 大多数的皮肤癌是可以完全治愈的。◇ *The cancer has spread to his stomach.* 癌已扩散到他的胃部。◇ *cancer patients* 癌症病人 ◇ *cancer research* 癌症研究 ➲ COLLOCATIONS AT ILL **2** [C] (*literary*) an evil or dangerous thing that spreads quickly （迅速蔓延的）邪恶；（社会）毒瘤： *Violence is a cancer in our society.* 暴力行为是我们社会的毒瘤。 ▸ **can·cer·ous** /ˈkænsərəs/ *adj.* : *to become cancerous* 发生癌变 ◇ ***cancerous cells/growths/tumours*** 癌细胞；癌性肿物；癌肿瘤

can·dela /kænˈdelə; -ˈdiːlə; ˈkændɪlə/ *noun* (*physics* 物) (*abbr.* **cd**) a unit for measuring the amount of light that shines in a particular direction 坎，坎德拉（光强度单位）

can·de·la·bra /ˌkændəˈlɑːbrə/ (*also less frequent* **can·de·la·brum** /ˌkændəˈlɑːbrəm/) *noun* (*pl.* **can·de·la·bra**, **can·de·la·bras**, *US also* **can·de·la·brums**) an object with several branches for holding CANDLES or lights 枝状大烛台（或灯台）

can·did /ˈkændɪd/ *adj.* **1** saying what you think openly and honestly; not hiding your thoughts 坦率的；坦诚的；直言不讳的： *a candid statement/interview* 坦率的陈述 / 会谈 ➲ SEE ALSO CANDOUR **2** a **candid** photograph is one that is taken without the person in it knowing that they are being photographed （照片）偷拍的 ▸ **can·did·ly** /ˈkændɪdli/ *adv.*

can·dida /ˈkændɪdə/ *noun* [U] (*medical* 医) the FUNGUS that can cause an infection of THRUSH 念珠菌（可导致感染鹅口疮）

can·di·dacy /ˈkændɪdəsi/ *noun* [C, U] (*pl.* **-ies**) (*also* **can·di·da·ture** *especially in BrE*) the fact of being a candidate in an election 候选人的资格（或身份）： *to **announce/declare/withdraw your candidacy** for the post* 宣布 / 宣告 / 撤销你的职位候选人资格

can·di·date 🔑 /ˈkændɪdət; -deɪt/ *noun* **1** 🔑 **~ (for sth)** a person who is trying to be elected or is applying for a job （竞选或求职的）候选人，申请人： *one of the leading candidates for the presidency* 总统职位的主要候选人之一 ◇ *a presidential candidate* 总统候选人 ◇ (*BrE*) *He stood as a candidate in the local elections.* 他作为候选人参加地方选举。◇ *There were a large number of candidates for the job.* 有许多求职者申请这份工作。 ➲ WORDFINDER NOTE AT APPLY, DEMOCRACY ➲ COLLOCATIONS AT VOTE **2** 🔑 (*BrE*) a person taking an exam 投考者；应试者；参加考试的人： *a candidate for the degree of MPhil* 攻读哲学硕士学位者 ➲ WORDFINDER NOTE AT EXAM **3 ~ (for sth)** a person or group that is considered suitable for sth or that is likely to get sth or to be sth 被认定适合者；被认定有某种结局者： *Our team is a **prime candidate for** relegation this year.* 今年我们队最有可能降级。◇ *Your father is an obvious candidate for a heart attack.* 你父亲显然是容易患心脏病的人。

can·di·da·ture /ˈkændɪdətʃə(r)/ *noun* (*especially BrE*) = CANDIDACY

can·did·ly *adv.* ➲ CANDID

can·died /ˈkændid/ *adj.* [only before noun] (of fruit or other food 水果或其他食物) preserved by boiling in sugar; cooked in sugar 蜜饯的；糖煮的；糖制的： *candied fruit* 果脯

can·dle /ˈkændl/ *noun* a round stick of WAX with a piece of string (called a WICK) through the middle which is lit to give light as it burns 蜡烛

IDM **cannot hold a candle to sb/sth** is not as good as sb or sth else 不如…好；比不上…；无法与…媲美： *His singing can't hold a candle to Bocelli's.* 他的演唱无法与波切利媲美。 ➲ MORE AT BURN *v.*, WORTH *adj.*

candle·light /ˈkændllaɪt/ *noun* [U] the light that a candle produces 烛光： *to read by candlelight* 在烛光下阅读

candle·lit /ˈkændllɪt/ *adj.* [only before noun] lit by candles 烛光照亮的： *a romantic candlelit dinner* 浪漫的烛光晚餐

candle·stick /ˈkændlstɪk/ *noun* an object for holding a candle 蜡烛台（或架） ➲ VISUAL VOCAB PAGE V23

candle·wick /ˈkændlwɪk/ *noun* [U] a type of soft cotton cloth with a raised pattern of threads, used especially for making BEDSPREADS 烛芯纱（有凸起花纹，尤用于制作床罩）

ˌ**can-ˈdo** *adj.* [only before noun] (*informal*) willing to try new things and expecting that they will be successful 勇于尝试的；积极的： ***a can-do attitude/spirit*** 乐观态度 / 精神

cand·our (*especially US* **can·dor**) /ˈkændə(r)/ *noun* [U] the quality of saying what you think openly and honestly 真诚；诚恳；坦率 SYN **frankness**: *'I don't trust him,' he said in a rare moment of candour.* "我信不过他。"他以难得的坦率说道。 ➲ SEE ALSO CANDID (1)

C & W *abbr.* COUNTRY AND WESTERN （美国的）乡村与西部音乐

candy 🔑 /ˈkændi/ *noun* [U, C] (*pl.* **-ies**) (*NAmE*) sweet food made of sugar and/or chocolate, eaten between meals; a piece of this 糖果；巧克力；一块糖（或巧克力） SYN **sweet**: *a box of candy* 一盒糖果 ◇ *a candy store* 糖果店 ◇ *a candy bar* 一条巧克力 ◇ *Who wants the last piece of candy?* 谁想要这最后一块糖？ ➲ SEE ALSO ARM CANDY, EYE CANDY

IDM **be like taking ˌcandy from a ˈbaby** (*informal*) used to emphasize how easy it is to do sth 像从娃娃手里抢糖吃；手到擒来；轻而易举

ˈ**candy apple** (*NAmE*) (*BrE* ˈ**toffee apple**) *noun* an apple covered with a thin layer of hard toffee and fixed on a stick 苹果糖，太妃苹果（外涂奶油乳脂，用扦子插起）

candy·floss /ˈkændiflɒs; NAmE -flɔːs; -flɑːs/ (*BrE*) (*NAmE* ˌ**cotton ˈcandy**) *noun* [U] a type of sweet/candy in the form of a mass of sticky threads made from melted sugar and served on a stick, especially at FAIRGROUNDS （尤指游乐场出售的）棉花糖

candy·man /ˈkændimæn/ *noun* (*pl.* **-men**) /-men/ (*US, slang*) a person who sells illegal drugs 毒品贩子

ˈcandy-striped *adj.* (of cloth or clothes 布料或衣服) with a pattern of stripes in white and another colour, especially pink 有两色条纹图案的（通常为粉白相间）

cane /keɪn/ *noun, verb*

■ ***noun*** **1** [C] the hard hollow STEM of some plants, for example BAMBOO or sugar（某些植物，如竹或甘蔗的）茎 ➲ VISUAL VOCAB PAGE V20 **2** [U] these STEMS used as a material for making furniture, etc.（用于制作家具等的）竹竿，藤条：*a cane chair* 藤椅 **3** [C] a piece of cane or a thin stick, used as a support for plants （用于支撑植物的）藤条，细竿 **4** [C] a piece of cane or a thin stick, used to help sb to walk 竹杖；藤杖；手杖 ➲ SEE ALSO WALKING STICK **5** [C] a piece of cane or a thin stick, used in the past in some schools for beating children as a punishment （旧时学校用于惩罚学童的）竹杖，藤条：*to get the cane* (= be punished with a cane) 受藤条鞭罚

■ ***verb*** **~ sb** to hit a child with a cane as a punishment 用藤条鞭打，用藤杖打，鞭笞（作为惩罚） ▶ **can·ing** *noun* [U, C]: *the abolition of caning in schools* 学校中鞭笞体罚的废除

ˈcane rat *noun* a type of large RODENT found in wild areas of Africa, which can be used for food 蔗鼠（分布于非洲荒野，其肉可食） ➲ SEE ALSO CUTTING GRASS

ˈcane sugar *noun* [U] sugar obtained from the juice of SUGAR CANE 蔗糖

ca·nine /ˈkeɪnaɪn/ *adj., noun*

■ ***adj.*** connected with dogs 犬的；似犬的

■ ***noun*** **1** (*also* **ˈcanine tooth**) one of the four pointed teeth in the front of a human's or animal's mouth （人或动物的）犬齿 ➲ COMPARE INCISOR, MOLAR **2** (*formal*) a dog 犬

can·is·ter /ˈkænɪstə(r)/ *noun* **1** a container with a lid for holding tea, coffee, etc.（装茶叶、咖啡等有盖的）小罐 **2** a strong metal container containing gas or a chemical substance, especially one that bursts when it is fired from a gun or thrown 霰弹筒：*tear-gas canisters* 催泪弹 **3** a flat round metal container used for storing film （用以放置胶片的）扁平圆金属盒：*a film canister* 胶片盒

can·ker /ˈkæŋkə(r)/ *noun* **1** [U] a disease that destroys the wood of plants and trees （植物和树木的）溃疡病，枝枯病 **2** [U] a disease that causes sore areas in the ears of animals, especially dogs and cats （尤指猫狗耳部的）溃疡，痈，疮 **3** [C] (*literary*) an evil or dangerous influence that spreads and affects people's behaviour（蔓延并影响人的行为的）邪恶，祸害，祸患，腐败

ˈcanker sore (*NAmE*) (*BrE* **ˈmouth ulcer**) *noun* a small sore area in the mouth 口腔溃疡

can·na·bis /ˈkænəbɪs/ *noun* [U] a drug made from the dried leaves and flowers or RESIN of the HEMP plant, which is smoked or eaten and which gives the user a feeling of being relaxed. Use of the drug is illegal in many countries. 大麻制品

canned /kænd/ *adj.* **1** (*BrE also* **tinned**) (of food 食品) preserved in a can 罐装的；听装的：*canned food/soup* 罐装食品 / 汤羹 **2** **~ laughter/music** the sound of people laughing or music that has been previously recorded and used in television and radio programmes （电视和电台节目中）预先录制的笑声（或音乐）

can·nel·loni /ˌkænəˈləʊni; *NAmE* -ˈloʊni/ *noun* [U] (*from Italian*) large tubes of PASTA that are served filled with meat, vegetables or cheese 加乃隆（宽管状意大利面，内填肉馅、蔬菜或奶酪等食用）

can·nery /ˈkænəri/ *noun* (*pl.* **-ies**) a factory where food is put into cans 罐头食品厂

can·ni·bal /ˈkænɪbl/ *noun* **1** a person who eats human flesh 食人肉者：*a tribe of cannibals* 食人部落 **2** an animal that eats the flesh of other animals of the same kind 同类相食的动物 ▶ **can·ni·bal·ism** /ˈkænɪbəlɪzəm/ *noun* [U]: *to practise cannibalism* 噬食同类 **can·ni·bal·is·tic** /ˌkænɪbəˈlɪstɪk/ *adj.*

can·ni·bal·ize (*BrE also* **-ise**) /ˈkænɪbəlaɪz/ *verb* **1** **~ sth** to take the parts of a machine, vehicle, etc. and use them to repair or build another 拆用（旧零件修理或装配另一部机器或车） **2** **~ sth** (*business* 商) (of a company 公司) to reduce the sales of one of its products by introducing a similar new product （公司的新产品）竞食，冲击（另一种类似产品的销售） ▶ **can·ni·bal·iza·tion, -isa·tion** /ˌkænɪbəlaɪˈzeɪʃn; *NAmE* -ləˈz-/ *noun* [U]

can·non /ˈkænən/ *noun, verb*

■ ***noun*** (*pl.* **can·non** or **can·nons**) **1** an old type of large heavy gun, usually on wheels, that fires solid metal or stone balls （通常装有轮子并发射铁弹或石弹的旧式）大炮 ➲ SEE ALSO LOOSE CANNON, WATER CANNON **2** an automatic gun that is fired from an aircraft （飞机上的）自动机关炮

■ ***verb*** [I] **+ adv./prep.** to hit sb/sth with a lot of force while you are moving 猛撞；碰撞：*He ran around the corner, cannoning into a group of kids.* 他跑过拐角时与一群小孩相撞。

can·non·ade /ˌkænəˈneɪd/ *noun* a continuous firing of large guns 连续炮轰

can·non·ball /ˈkænənbɔːl/ *noun* a large metal or stone ball that is fired from a CANNON（用旧式大炮发射的）铁弹，石弹

ˈcannon fodder *noun* [U] soldiers who are thought of not as people whose lives are important, but as material to be used up in war 炮灰

can·not 🔑 /ˈkænɒt; *NAmE* -nɑːt/ = CAN NOT: *I cannot believe the price of the tickets!* 我简直无法相信竟有这样的票价！

can·nula /ˈkænjʊlə/ *noun* (*pl.* **can·nulae** /-liː/ or **can·nulas**) (*medical* 医) a thin tube that is put into a VEIN or other part of the body, for example to give sb medicine （输药等的）插管，套管

canny /ˈkæni/ *adj.* intelligent, careful and showing good judgement, especially in business or politics（尤指在商业或政治方面）精明谨慎的，老谋深算的：*a canny politician* 老谋深算的政治家 ◇ *a canny move* 一步妙棋 ▶ **can·nily** /ˈkænɪli/ *adv.*

canoe /kəˈnuː/ *noun, verb*

■ ***noun*** a light narrow boat which you move along in the water with a PADDLE 划艇；独木舟；小划子 ➲ VISUAL VOCAB PAGE V60 ➲ SEE ALSO KAYAK

■ ***verb*** (**ca·noe·ing, ca·noed, ca·noed**) [I] (*often* **go canoeing**) to travel in a canoe 划（或乘）划艇

ca·noe·ing /kəˈnuːɪŋ/ *noun* [U] the sport of travelling in or racing a CANOE 划艇运动（或比赛）；皮划艇运动（或比赛）：*to go canoeing* 去划划艇

ca·noe·ist /kəˈnuːɪst/ *noun* a person travelling in a canoe 划划艇的人

can·ola™ /kəˈnəʊlə; *NAmE* -ˈnoʊ-/ *noun* [U] a type of cooking oil made from a variety of RAPESEED that was developed in Canada and is grown widely in N America. The plant is also referred to as **canola**. 芥花油

canon /ˈkænən/ *noun* **1** a Christian priest with special duties in a CATHEDRAL 座堂区府 **2** (*formal*) a generally accepted rule, standard or principle by which sth is judged 原则；准则；标准 **3** a list of the books or other works that are generally accepted as the genuine work of a particular writer or as being important（某作家的）真作，精品：*the Shakespeare canon* 莎士比亚的精品 ◇ *'Wuthering Heights' is a central book in the canon of English literature.* 《呼啸山庄》是英国文学经典中非常重要的一部作品。 **4** a piece of music in which singers or instruments take it in turns to repeat the MELODY (= tune) 两重轮唱（或演奏）；卡农曲

ca·non·ic·al /kəˈnɒnɪkl; *NAmE* -ˈnɑːn-/ (*also* **ca·non·ic**) *adj.* **1** included in a list of holy books that are accepted as genuine; connected with works of literature that are highly respected 被收入真经篇目的；经典的 **2** according to the law of the Christian Church 按照基督教教会法规的 **3** (*specialist*) in the simplest accepted form in mathematics（数学表达式）最简洁的

ca'nonical form *noun* (*linguistics* 语言) the most basic form of a GRAMMATICAL structure or expression, for example the infinitive in the case of a verb（语法结构或表达的）标准形式，最基本形式（如动词的不定式）

can·on·ize (*BrE also* **-ise**) /'kænənaɪz/ *verb* [usually passive] **~ sb** (of the POPE 教宗) to state officially that sb is now a SAINT 正式宣布（某人）为圣徒；宣圣；列入圣品 ➲ COMPARE BEATIFY ▶ **can·on·iza·tion, -isa·tion** /ˌkænənaɪ'zeɪʃn; *NAmE* -nə'z-/ *noun* [C, U]

ˌcanon 'law *noun* [U] the law of the Christian church 基督教教会法规

ca·noo·dle /kə'nuːdl/ *verb* [I] (*old-fashioned, informal*) (of two people 两人) to kiss and touch each other in a sexual way 亲吻爱抚

'can opener (*especially NAmE*) (*BrE also* **'tin opener**) *noun* a kitchen UTENSIL (= a tool) for opening cans of food 开罐器；罐头刀；罐头起子 ➲ VISUAL VOCAB PAGE V27

can·opy /'kænəpi/ *noun* (*pl.* **-ies**) **1** a cover that is fixed or hangs above a bed, seat, etc. as a shelter or decoration（床、座位等上面的）罩篷，遮篷，罩盖 ➲ VISUAL VOCAB PAGE V24 ➲ PICTURE AT PUSHCHAIR **2** a layer of sth that spreads over an area like a roof, especially branches of trees in a forest 顶篷；天篷；（尤指森林里的）林冠，林冠层：*The canopy of a rainforest is about 10 metres thick.* 热带雨林的林冠约有 10 米厚。 **3** (*especially NAmE*) a roof that is supported on posts and is sometimes also attached at one side to a building（有时与建筑的一侧相连的）天篷，遮篷：*a new steel entrance canopy for the building* 大楼入口处新建的钢质遮篷 ◇ *a fabric canopy to provide shade in the backyard* 后院遮阳用的织物天篷 **4** a cover for the COCKPIT of an aircraft（飞机的）座舱盖

canst /kænst/ *verb* **thou canst** (*old use*) used to mean 'you can', when talking to one person（对某人说话时表示 you can）

cant /kænt/ *noun, verb*

■ ***noun*** [U] statements, especially about moral or religious issues, that are not sincere and that you cannot trust（尤指有关道德或宗教问题的）伪善言辞，虚假的话，空话 **SYN** **hypocrisy**

■ ***verb*** [I, T] **~ (sth)** (*formal*) to be or put sth in a sloping position（使）倾斜

can't /kɑːnt; *NAmE* kænt/ *short form* cannot

Cantab /'kæntæb/ *abbr.* (used after degree titles) of Cambridge University（用于学位名称后）剑桥大学的：*James Cox MA (Cantab)* 文科硕士詹姆斯·考克斯（剑桥大学）

Can·ta·bri·gian /ˌkæntə'brɪdʒiən/ *adj.* (*formal* or *humorous*) relating to Cambridge in England, or to Cambridge University（英格兰）剑桥的；剑桥大学的

can·ta·loupe /'kæntəluːp/ *noun* a MELON (= a type of fruit) with a green skin and orange flesh 甜瓜；哈密瓜

can·tan·ker·ous /kæn'tæŋkərəs/ *adj.* bad-tempered and always complaining 脾气坏且抱怨不休的：*a cantankerous old man* 爱抱怨的倔老头

can·tata /kæn'tɑːtə/ *noun* a short musical work, often on a religious subject, sung by SOLO singers, often with a CHOIR and ORCHESTRA 康塔塔（常为宗教题材的短小音乐作品，由独唱演员演唱，常有合唱和管弦乐队伴奏）➲ COMPARE MOTET, ORATORIO

can·teen /kæn'tiːn/ *noun* **1** (*especially BrE*) a place where food and drink are served in a factory, a school, etc. 食堂；餐厅 **2** a small container used by soldiers, travellers, etc. for carrying water or other liquid（士兵、旅游者等用的）水壶 **3 ~ of cutlery** (*BrE*) a box containing a set of knives, forks and spoons（装有一套刀、叉和勺的）餐具盒

can'teen culture *noun* [U] (*BrE, disapproving*) a set of old-fashioned and unfair attitudes that are said to exist among police officers（警队内部的）陈旧不公正风气

can·ter /'kæntə(r)/ *noun, verb*

■ ***noun*** [usually sing.] a movement of a horse at a speed that is fairly fast but not very fast; a ride on a horse moving at this speed（马的）慢跑；骑马慢跑：*She set off at a canter.* 她骑着马慢跑出发。

■ ***verb*** [I, T] **~ (sth)** (of a horse or rider 马或骑手) to move or make a horse move at a canter 慢跑；使马慢跑：*We cantered along the beach.* 我们骑着马沿海滩慢跑。➲ COMPARE GALLOP *v.*, TROT *v.* (1)

can·ticle /'kæntɪkl/ *noun* a religious song with words taken from the Bible 圣歌，颂歌，赞美诗（歌词取自《圣经》）

can·ti·lever /'kæntɪliːvə(r)/ *noun* a long piece of metal or wood that sticks out from a wall to support the end of a bridge or other structure（桥梁或其他构架的）悬臂，悬桁，伸臂：*a cantilever bridge* 悬臂桥 ➲ VISUAL VOCAB PAGE V14

canto /'kæntəʊ; *NAmE* -toʊ/ *noun* (*pl.* **-os**) one of the sections of a long poem（长诗的）篇，章

can·ton /'kæntɒn; *NAmE* -tən; -tɑːn/ *noun* one of the official regions which some countries, such as Switzerland, are divided into（瑞士等国的）行政区，州

Can·ton·ese /ˌkæntə'niːz/ *noun, adj.*

■ ***noun* 1** (*also* **Yue**) [U] a form of Chinese spoken mainly in southern China, including Hong Kong 粤语；广东话 **2** [C] (*pl.* **Can·ton·ese**) a person whose first language is Cantonese 第一语言为粤语的人；广东人

■ ***adj.*** of or relating to people who speak Cantonese, or their language or culture 说粤语的人的；粤语的；广东人（或文化）的：*Cantonese cooking* 粤菜

can·ton·ment /kæn'tɒnmənt; -'tuːn-; *NAmE* kæn'tɑːn-/ *noun* a military camp, especially a permanent British military camp in India in the past 军队驻地；军队营房；（尤指旧时英军驻印度的）永久性兵站

Can·to·pop /'kæntəʊpɒp; *NAmE* 'kæntoʊpɑːp/ *noun* [U] (*SEAsianE*) a type of pop music that combines Cantonese words and Western pop music 粤语流行音乐（粤语填词，西方流行乐为曲）

can·tor /'kæntɔː(r)/ *noun* the person who leads the singing in a SYNAGOGUE or in a church CHOIR（犹太教会堂和教堂唱诗班的）领唱

Ca·nuck /kə'nʌk/ *noun* (*NAmE, informal*) a person from Canada, especially sb whose first language is French. In the US this term is sometimes offensive.（尤指第一语言为法语的）加拿大人（此称呼在美国有时含冒犯意）

Ca·nute /kə'njuːt; *NAmE* -'nuːt/ *noun* used to describe a person who tries to stop sth from happening but will never succeed 克努特式的人；妄想阻挡某事的人：*His efforts to stem the tide of violent crime have been as effective as Canute's.* 他遏制暴力犯罪增长的努力一直是螳臂挡车。 **ORIGIN** From the story of a Danish king of England who was said to have stood in front of the sea and shown people that he was not able to order the water that was moving in towards the land to turn back. The story is often changed to suggest that Canute really thought that he could turn back the sea. 源自英格兰一个丹麦裔国王的故事，据说他临海而立，向民众显示他没有能力命令冲向陆地的海水回头；这个故事常被改编，表示克努特实际上以为他能够令海水回头。

can·vas /'kænvəs/ *noun* **1** [U] a strong heavy rough material used for making tents, sails, etc. and by artists for painting on 帆布 ➲ COLLOCATIONS AT ART **2** [C] a piece of canvas used for painting on; a painting done on a piece of canvas, using oil paints（帆布）画布；油画：*a sale of the artist's early canvases* 那位画家早期油画的拍卖 ➲ WORDFINDER NOTE AT PAINTING ➲ VISUAL VOCAB

PAGE V45

IDM **under 'canvas** in a tent 在帐篷里

can·vass /'kænvəs/ *verb* **1** [I, T] to ask sb to support a particular person, political party, etc., especially by going around an area and talking to people 游说；拉选票：**~ (for sth)** *He spent the whole month canvassing for votes.* 他花了整整一个月四处游说拉选票。◇ **~ sb (for sth)** *Party workers are busy canvassing local residents.* 党务工作者正忙于游说当地居民。**2** [T] to ask people about sth in order to find out what they think about it 调查（民意）；征求（意见）：**~ sth** *He has been canvassing opinion on the issue.* 他一直在征求对这个问题的意见。◇ **~ sb** *People are being canvassed for their views on the proposed new road.* 正在就计划修建的新道路征求人们的意见。**3** [T] **~ support** to try and get support from a group of people 努力争取支持 **SYN** **drum sth↔up** **4** [T] **~ sth** to discuss an idea thoroughly 详细（或彻底）讨论：*The proposal is currently being canvassed.* 目前人们正在详细讨论这个提案。▶ **can·vass** *noun*：*to carry out a canvass* 拉选票 **can·vass·er** *noun*

can·yon /'kænjən/ *noun* a deep valley with steep sides of rock（周围有悬崖峭壁的）峡谷 **SYN** **gorge** ➲ VISUAL VOCAB PAGE V5

can·yon·ing /'kænjənɪŋ/ *noun* [U] a sport in which you jump into a mountain stream and allow yourself to be carried down at high speed 溪降运动

CAP /ˌsiː eɪ 'piː/ *abbr.* Common Agricultural Policy (of the European Union)（欧盟的）共同农业政策

cap 🔑 /kæp/ *noun, verb*

■ *noun*

• **HAT** 帽子 **1** 🔑 a type of soft flat hat with a PEAK (= a hard curved part sticking out in front). Caps are worn especially by men and boys, often as part of a uniform.（尤指男用有帽舌的）便帽，制服帽：*a school cap* 学生帽 ➲ SEE ALSO BASEBALL CAP, CLOTH CAP, MOB CAP ➲ VISUAL VOCAB PAGE V70 **2** 🔑 (usually in compounds 通常构成复合词) a soft hat that fits closely and is worn for a particular purpose 软帽：*a shower cap* 浴帽 **3** a soft hat with a square flat top worn by some university teachers and students at special ceremonies（大学师生在特别场合戴的）方帽 ➲ COMPARE MORTAR BOARD

• **IN SPORT** 体育运动 **4** (*BrE*) a cap given to sb who is chosen to play for a school, country, etc.; a player chosen to play for their country, etc.（校队、国家队等的）队员帽；（被选入国家队等的）运动员：*He won his first cap* (= was first chosen to play) *for England against France.* 他首次入选英格兰队与法国队比赛。◇ *There are three new caps in the side.* 这一方有三名新队员。

• **ON PEN/BOTTLE** 钢笔；瓶子 **5** a cover or top for a pen, bottle, etc.（钢笔、瓶子等的）帽，盖：*a lens cap* 镜头盖 ➲ VISUAL VOCAB PAGE V36 ➲ SEE ALSO FILLER CAP, HUBCAP ➲ SYNONYMS AT LID

• **LIMIT ON MONEY** 资金限额 **6** an upper limit on an amount of money that can be spent or borrowed by a particular institution or in a particular situation（可用或可借资金的）最高限额：*The government has placed a cap on local council spending.* 政府给地方议会的经费支出规定了最高限额。

• **IN TOY GUNS** 玩具枪 **7** a small paper container with EXPLOSIVE powder inside it, used especially in toy guns（尤用于玩具枪的）火药帽，火药纸

• **FOR WOMAN** 妇女 **8** (*BrE*) = DIAPHRAGM (2) ➲ SEE ALSO ICE CAP, THINKING CAP

IDM **go cap in 'hand (to sb)** (*US also* **go hat in 'hand**) to ask sb for sth, especially money, in a very polite way that makes you seem less important 谦卑地要，恭敬地讨（尤指钱） **if the cap fits (, wear it)** (*BrE*) (*NAmE* **if the shoe fits (, wear it)**) (*informal*) if you feel that a remark applies to you, you should accept it and take it as a warning or criticism 有则改之：*I didn't actually say that you were lazy, but if the cap fits…* 我并没有真的说你懒，但有则改之… ➲ MORE AT FEATHER *n.*

■ *verb* (-pp-)

• **COVER TOP** 覆盖顶部 **1** [usually passive] **~ sth (with sth)** to cover the top or end of sth with sth 用…覆盖顶部（或端部）：*mountains capped with snow* 积雪皑皑的山峰 ◇ *snow-capped mountains* 顶端积雪的群山

• **LIMIT MONEY** 限定金额 **2** [often passive] **~ sth** (*especially BrE*) to limit the amount of money that can be charged for sth or spent on sth 限额收取（或支出）：*a capped mortgage* 限额按揭

• **BEAT** 超越 **3** **~ sth** (*especially BrE*) to say or do sth that is funnier, more impressive, etc. than sth that has been said or done before 胜过；超过；比…更…：*What an amazing story. Can anyone cap that?* 这真是个精彩的故事！还有人能讲得更精彩吗？

• **TOOTH** 牙齿 **4** [usually passive] **~ sth** to put an artificial covering on a tooth to make it look more attractive 包（牙） **SYN** **crown**：*He's had his front teeth capped.* 他包了门牙。

• **IN SPORT** 体育运动 **5** [usually passive] **~ sb** (*BrE*) to choose sb to play in their country's national team for a particular sport 选入（某项体育运动的国家队）：*He has been capped more than 30 times for Wales.* 他已 30 多次入选威尔士队参加比赛。

IDM **to cap/top it 'all** (*informal*) used to introduce the final piece of information that is worse than the other bad things that you have just mentioned 最糟糕的是；最倒霉的是

cap·abil·ity **AW** /ˌkeɪpə'bɪləti/ *noun* [C, U] (*pl.* **-ies**) **1** **~ (to do sth/of doing sth)** the ability or qualities necessary to do sth 能力；才能：*Animals in the zoo have lost the capability to catch/of catching food for themselves.* 动物园的动物已经丧失自己捕食的能力。◇ ***beyond/within the capabilities*** *of current technology* 超出了当前技术能力的范围；在当前技术能力的范围以内 ◇ *Age affects the range of a person's capabilities.* 年龄影响着一个人能力的大小。**2** the power or weapons that a country has for war or for military action（国家的）军事力量，军事武器：*Britain's **nuclear/military capability*** 英国的核力量 / 军事力量

cap·able 🔑 **AW** /'keɪpəbl/ *adj.* **1** 🔑 having the ability or qualities necessary for doing sth 有能力；有才能：**~ of sth** *You are capable of better work than this.* 你有能力做得比这更好。◇ **~ of doing sth** *He's quite capable of lying to get out of trouble.* 他颇有能耐靠撒谎渡过难关。◇ *I'm perfectly capable of doing it myself, thank you.* 谢谢，我完全有能力自己做这项工作。**2** 🔑 having the ability to do things well 能力强的；足以胜任的 **SYN** **skilled, competent**：*She's a very capable teacher.* 她是一位能力很强的教师。◇ *I'll leave the organization in your capable hands.* 我要把组织工作交给你这位能手。**OPP** **incapable** ▶ **cap·ably** *adv.*

cap·acious /kə'peɪʃəs/ *adj.* (*formal*) having a lot of space to put things in 容量大的；容积大的；宽敞的 **SYN** **roomy**：*capacious pockets* 能装许多东西的大口袋

cap·aci·tance /kə'pæsɪtəns/ *noun* [U] (*physics* 物) **1** the ability of a system to store an electrical charge 电容，电容量（系统贮存电荷的能力） **2** a comparison between change in electrical charge and change in electrical POTENTIAL 电容率（电荷和电位变化之比值）

cap·aci·tor /kə'pæsɪtə(r)/ *noun* (*physics* 物) a device used to store an electrical charge 电容器

cap·acity 🔑 **AW** /kə'pæsəti/ *noun* (*pl.* **-ies**)

• **OF CONTAINER** 容器 **1** 🔑 [U, C, usually sing.] the number of things or people that a container or space can hold 容量；容积；容纳能力：*The theatre has a seating capacity of 2 000.* 那座剧院能容纳 2 000 名观众。◇ *a fuel tank with a capacity of 50 litres* 可装 50 升油的油箱 ◇ *The hall was filled **to capacity*** (= was completely full). 大厅内座无虚席。◇ *They played to a **capacity crowd*** (= one that filled all the space or seats). 他们给人山人海的观众表演。

• **ABILITY** 能力 **2** 🔑 [C, usually sing., U] the ability to understand or to do sth 领悟（或理解、办事）能力：*intellectual capacity* 智能 ◇ **~ for sth** *She has an enormous capacity for hard work.* 她特别能吃苦耐劳。◇ **~ for doing sth** *Limited resources are restricting our capacity for developing new products.* 有限的资源正制约着我们开发新产品的能力。◇ **~ to do sth** *your capacity to enjoy life* 你那享受生活乐趣的

C

能力

• **ROLE** 职责 **3** [C, usually sing.] the official position or function that sb has 职位；职责 **SYN** **role**: *acting **in her capacity as** manager* 以她作为经理的身份行事 ◇ *We are simply involved in an **advisory capacity** on the project.* 我们只不过是以顾问身份参与这个项目。

• **OF FACTORY/MACHINE** 工厂；机器 **4** [sing., U] the quantity that a factory, machine, etc. can produce 生产量；生产能力：*The factory is working at full capacity.* 这家工厂在开足马力生产。 ➲ WORDFINDER NOTE AT FACTORY, INDUSTRY

• **OF ENGINE** 发动机 **5** [C, U] the size or power of a piece of equipment, especially the engine of a vehicle（尤指车辆发动机的）容积，功率：*an engine with a capacity of 1 600 cc* 一台功率为 1.6 升的发动机

ca·pari·soned /kəˈpærɪsnd/ *adj.* in the past a **caparisoned** horse or other animal was one covered with a decorated cloth （马等）披挂装饰的；披挂马衣的

cape /keɪp/ *noun* **1** a loose outer piece of clothing that has no sleeves, fastens at the neck and hangs from the shoulders, like a CLOAK but shorter 披肩；披风；短斗篷：*a bullfighter's cape* 斗牛士的披风 **2** (*abbr.* **C.**) (often in place names 常用于地名) a piece of high land that sticks out into the sea 地角；岬角：*Cape Horn* 合恩角

caped /keɪpt/ *adj.* wearing a cape 披披肩的；披斗篷的

caper /ˈkeɪpə(r)/ *noun, verb*

■***noun*** **1** [usually pl.] the small green flower BUD of a Mediterranean bush, preserved in VINEGAR and used to flavour dishes and sauces 刺山柑花蕾（产于地中海，腌泡于醋中用作调味料） **2** (*informal*) an activity, especially one that is illegal or dangerous 活动；（尤指）不法活动，危险活动：*A call to the police should put an end to their little caper.* 给警察打个电话应该就能制止他们的胡闹。 **3** an amusing film/movie that contains a lot of action 惊险喜剧片：*a British spy caper* 英国间谍喜剧片 **4** a short jumping or dancing movement 跳跃；雀跃；蹦蹦跳跳：*He **cut a** little celebratory **caper*** (= jumped or danced a few steps) *in the middle of the road.* 他高兴得在路中央又蹦又跳的。

■***verb*** [I] (+ **adv./prep.**) (*formal*) to run or jump around in a happy and excited way 雀跃；欢跃

cap·er·cail·lie /ˌkæpəˈkeɪli; *NAmE* ˌkæpər-/ *noun* a large GROUSE (= a type of large bird) similar to a TURKEY, the male of which spreads out his tail feathers to attract females 松鸡

ca·pil·lary /kəˈpɪləri; *NAmE* ˈkæpəleri/ *noun* (*pl.* **-ies**) (*anatomy* 解) any of the smallest tubes in the body that carry blood 毛细血管 ➲ VISUAL VOCAB PAGE V64

caˈpillary action *noun* [U] (*specialist*) the force that makes a liquid move up a narrow tube 毛细作用；毛细引力（或吸力）

cap·ital /ˈkæpɪtl/ *noun, adj.*

■***noun***

• **CITY** 城市 **1** (*also* ˌ**capital ˈcity**) [C] the most important town or city of a country, usually where the central government operates from 首都；国都：*Cairo is the capital of Egypt.* 开罗是埃及的首都。 ◇ (*figurative*) *Paris, the fashion capital of the world* 巴黎，世界时装之都

• **MONEY** 金钱 **2** [sing.] a large amount of money that is invested or is used to start a business 资本；资金；启动资金：*to set up a business with a **starting capital** of £100 000* 以 10 万英镑为启动资金创办一个企业 **3** [U] wealth or property that is owned by a business or a person 财富；财产：*capital assets* 资本资产 ◇ *capital expenditure* (= money that an organization spends on buildings, equipment, etc.) 资本性支出 **4** [U] (*specialist*) people who use their money to start businesses, considered as a group 资方：*capital and labour* 资方与劳方 ➲ WORDFINDER NOTE AT INVEST, MONEY

• **LETTER** 字母 **5** (*also* ˌ**capital ˈletter**) [C] a letter of the form and size that is used at the beginning of a sentence or a name (= A,B,C rather than a,b,c) 大写字母：*Use **block capitals*** (= separate capital letters). 使用大写字母。◇ *Please write **in capitals/in capital letters**.* 请用大写字母书写。

• **ARCHITECTURE** 建筑 **6** the top part of a column 柱顶；柱头 ➲ VISUAL VOCAB PAGE V14

IDM **make capital (out) of sth** to use a situation for your own advantage 从…中捞取好处；利用…谋求私利：*The opposition parties are making political capital out of the government's problems.* 各反对党都在利用政府面临的问题捞取政治资本。

■***adj.***

• **PUNISHMENT** 惩罚 **1** [only before noun] involving punishment by death 死刑的：*a capital offence* 死罪

• **LETTER** 字母 **2** [only before noun] (of letters of the alphabet 字母表字母) having the form and size used at the beginning of a sentence or a name 大写的：*English is written with a capital 'E'.* * English 一词中字母 E 大写。 ➲ COMPARE LOWER CASE

• **EXCELLENT** 优秀 **3** (*old-fashioned*) excellent 顶好的；极好的

IDM **with a capital A, B, etc.** used to emphasize that a word has a stronger meaning than usual in a particular situation（强调有特别含义的字眼）真正地，名副其实地，不折不扣地：*He was romantic with a capital R.* 他纯属浪漫派。

ˌ**capital ˈgains** *noun* [pl.] profits that you make from selling sth, especially property （尤指出售固定资产所得的）资本收益：*to pay **capital gains tax*** 缴纳资本收益税

ˈ**capital goods** *noun* [pl.] (*business* 商) goods such as factory machines that are used for producing other goods 资本货物（如工厂用于生产其他货物的机器） ➲ COMPARE CONSUMER GOODS

ˌ**capital-inˈtensive** *adj.* (of a business, an industry, etc. 企业、行业等) needing large amounts of money in order to operate well 资本密集的 ➲ COMPARE LABOUR-INTENSIVE

cap·it·al·ism /ˈkæpɪtəlɪzəm/ *noun* [U] an economic system in which a country's businesses and industry are controlled and run for profit by private owners rather than by the government 资本主义 ➲ COMPARE SOCIALISM ➲ WORDFINDER NOTE AT SYSTEM

cap·it·al·ist /ˈkæpɪtəlɪst/ *noun, adj.*

■***noun*** **1** a person who supports capitalism 资本主义者 **2** a person who owns or controls a lot of wealth and uses it to produce more wealth 资本家

■***adj.*** (*also less frequent* **cap·it·al·is·tic** /ˌkæpɪtəˈlɪstɪk/) based on the principles of capitalism 资本主义的：*a **capitalist** society/system/economy* 资本主义社会 / 体制 / 经济

cap·it·al·ize (*BrE also* **-ise**) /ˈkæpɪtəlaɪz/ *verb* **1** ~ **sth** to write or print a letter of the alphabet as a capital; to begin a word with a capital letter 用大写字母书写（或印刷）；把…首字母大写 **2** ~ **sth** (*business* 商) to sell possessions in order to change them into money 变卖资产；变现 **3** [usually passive] ~ **sth** (*business* 商) to provide a company etc. with the money it needs to function 为…提供运营资本（或资金） ▸ **cap·it·al·iza·tion**, **-isa·tion** /ˌkæpɪtəlaɪˈzeɪʃn; *NAmE* -ləˈz-/ *noun* [U, sing.]

PHR V ˈ**capitalize on/upon sth** to gain a further advantage for yourself from a situation 充分利用；从…中获得更多的好处 **SYN** **take advantage of**: *The team failed to capitalize on their early lead.* 这个队未能充分利用开场时领先的优势。

ˌ**capital ˈletter** *noun* = CAPITAL (5)

ˌ**capital ˈpunishment** *noun* [U] punishment by death 死刑；极刑

ˌ**capital ˈsum** *noun* a single payment of money that is made to sb, for example by an insurance company 整笔应付款额（如由保险公司支付的赔偿金）

capi·ta·tion /ˌkæpɪˈteɪʃn/ *noun* [C, U] (*specialist*) a tax or payment of an equal amount for each person; the system of payments of this kind 人头税；按人摊派的费用；按人付费制度：*a capitation fee for each pupil* 按每个小学生的收费

cap·itol /ˈkæpɪtl/ *noun* **1** (*usually* **the Capitol**) [sing.] the building in Washington DC where the US Congress (= the national parliament) meets to work on new laws （美国）国会大厦 **2** [usually sing.] a building in each US state where politicians meet to work on new laws （美国）州议会大厦： *the California state capitol* 加利福尼亚州议会大厦

ˌCapitol ˈHill (*also informal* **the Hill**) *noun* [sing.] used to refer to the US Capitol and the activities that take place there 国会山（指美国国会）

ca·pitu·late /kəˈpɪtʃuleɪt/ *verb* **1** [I] ~ (**to sb/sth**) to agree to do sth that you have been refusing to do for a long time 屈服；屈从 **SYN give in** (**to sb/sth**), **yield**： *They were finally forced to capitulate to the terrorists' demands.* 他们最后被迫屈从恐怖分子的要求。 **2** [I] ~ (**to sb/sth**) to stop resisting an enemy and accept that you are defeated 投降 **SYN surrender**： *The town capitulated after a three-week siege.* 这座城镇被围困三个星期后投降了。▸ **ca·pitu·la·tion** /kəˌpɪtʃuˈleɪʃn/ *noun* [C, U]

Cap·let™ /ˈkæplət/ *noun* a long narrow tablet of medicine, with rounded ends, that you swallow 囊片；胶囊

capo·eira /ˌkæpʊˈeɪrə/ *noun* [U] a Brazilian system of movements which is similar to dance and MARTIAL ARTS 卡波埃拉（一种巴西运动，类似于舞蹈和武术）

capon /ˈkeɪpɒn; ˈkeɪpən; *NAmE* -pɑːn/ *noun* a male chicken that has been CASTRATED (= had part of its sex organs removed) and made fat for eating 阉鸡（育肥以供食用）

cap·pella ➲ A CAPPELLA

cap·puc·cino /ˌkæpuˈtʃiːnəʊ; *NAmE* -noʊ/ *noun* (*pl.* **-os**) **1** [U] a type of coffee made with hot FROTHY milk and sometimes with chocolate powder on the top 卡布奇诺咖啡（加热奶，有时上面撒有巧克力粉） **2** [C] a cup of cappuccino 一杯卡布奇诺咖啡

ca·price /kəˈpriːs/ *noun* (*formal*) **1** [C] a sudden change in attitude or behaviour for no obvious reason （态度或行为的）无缘无故突变，反复无常；任性 **SYN whim** **2** [U] the tendency to change your mind suddenly or behave unexpectedly 反复无常；善变

ca·pri·cious /kəˈprɪʃəs/ *adj.* (*formal*) **1** showing sudden changes in attitude or behaviour （态度或行为）反复无常的；任性的 **SYN unpredictable** **2** changing suddenly and quickly 变化无常的；变幻莫测的；多变的 **SYN changeable**： *a capricious climate* 变化无常的气候 ▸ **ca·pri·cious·ly** *adv.* **ca·pri·cious·ness** *noun* [U]

Cap·ri·corn /ˈkæprɪkɔːn; *NAmE* -kɔːrn/ *noun* **1** [U] the 10th sign of the ZODIAC, the Goat 黄道第十宫；摩羯宫；摩羯（星）座 **2** [C] a person born when the sun is in this sign, that is between 21 December and 20 January, approximately 属摩羯座的人（约出生于 12 月 21 日至 1 月 20 日）

ca·pri pants /kəˈpriː pænts/ (*also* **ca·pris**) *noun* [pl.] a type of trousers/pants for women ending between the knee and the foot 卡普里裤，七分裤（长及小腿的女裤）

caps /kæps/ *noun* [pl.] (*specialist*) capital letters 大写字母： *a title printed in bold caps* 以粗体大写字母印刷的标题

cap·sicum /ˈkæpsɪkəm/ *noun* (*specialist*) a type of plant which has hollow fruits. Some types of these are eaten as vegetables, either raw or cooked, for example SWEET PEPPERS or CHILLIES. 辣椒

cap·size /kæpˈsaɪz; *NAmE* ˈkæpsaɪz/ *verb* [I, T] ~ (**sth**) if a boat **capsizes** or sth **capsizes** it, it turns over in the water （船）翻，倾覆

cap·stan /ˈkæpstən/ *noun* a thick CYLINDER that winds up a rope, used for lifting heavy objects such as an ANCHOR on a ship 起锚机；绞盘

cap·stone /ˈkæpstəʊn; *NAmE* -stoʊn/ *noun* **1** a stone placed at the top of a building or wall 拱顶石；压顶石 **2** (*especially NAmE*) the best and final thing that sb achieves, thought of as making their career or life complete （使事业等臻于圆满的）顶点

cap·sule /ˈkæpsjuːl; *NAmE* ˈkæpsl; ˈkæpsuːl/ *noun* **1** a small container which has a measured amount of a medicine inside and which dissolves when you swallow it （装药物的）胶囊 ➲ WORDFINDER NOTE AT MEDICINE **2** a small plastic container with a substance or liquid inside （装物或装液体的）小塑料容器 **3** the part of a SPACECRAFT in which people travel and that often separates from the main ROCKET 太空舱；航天舱 **4** (*specialist*) a shell or container for seeds or eggs in some plants and animals （植物的）蒴果，荚膜；（动物的）囊，被膜 ➲ SEE ALSO TIME CAPSULE

Capt. *abbr.* captain 船长；机长；上尉；上校；队长

cap·tain /ˈkæptɪn/ *noun, verb*

■ ***noun*** **1** the person in charge of a ship or commercial aircraft 船长；机长： *Captain Cook* 库克船长 ◇ *The captain gave the order to abandon ship.* 船长下令弃船。 **2** an officer of fairly high rank in the navy, the army and the US AIR FORCE （海军）上校；（陆军或美国空军的）上尉： *Captain Lance Price* 兰斯・普赖斯上尉 ➲ SEE ALSO GROUP CAPTAIN ➲ WORDFINDER NOTE AT NAVY **3** the leader of a group of people, especially a sports team 首领；领导者；（尤指运动队的）队长： *She was captain of the hockey team at school.* 她过去是学校曲棍球队的队长。 **4** an officer of high rank in a US police or fire department （美国警察局的）副巡长；（美国消防署的）中队长

■ ***verb*** ~ **sth** to be a captain of a sports team or a ship 担任…的队长（或船长）

cap·tain·cy /ˈkæptənsi/ *noun* [C, usually sing., U] (*pl.* **-ies**) the position of captain of a team; the period during which sb is captain 队长职位（或任期）

ˌcaptain of ˈindustry *noun* (*pl.* **captains of industry**) used in newspapers, etc. to describe a person who manages a large business company （报章等用语）业界巨头

cap·tcha (*also* **CAPTCHA**) /ˈkæptʃə/ *noun* [C, U] a computer program that is designed to distinguish between human users and machines, often showing letters or numbers with their shape changed slightly 人机验证，验证码（一种区分计算机和人类用户的计算机程序）： *The captcha can only be solved by humans.* 只有人类能识别验证码。 **ORIGIN** An acronym from Completely Automated Public Turing test to tell Computers and Humans Apart. * captcha 是 Completely Automated Public Turing test to tell Computers and Humans Apart（全自动区分计算机和人类的公开图灵测试）的首字母缩略词。

cap·tion /ˈkæpʃn/ *noun, verb*

■ ***noun*** words that are printed underneath a picture, CARTOON, etc. that explain or describe it （图片、漫画等的）说明文字 ➲ SEE ALSO CLOSED-CAPTIONED

■ ***verb*** [usually passive] ~ **sth** to write a caption for a picture, photograph, etc. 给（图片、照片等）加说明文字

cap·tiv·ate /ˈkæptɪveɪt/ *verb* [often passive] ~ **sb** to keep sb's attention by being interesting, attractive, etc. 迷住；使着迷 **SYN enchant**： *The children were captivated by her stories.* 孩子们被她的故事迷住了。

cap·tiv·at·ing /ˈkæptɪveɪtɪŋ/ *adj.* taking all your attention; very attractive and interesting 迷人的；有魅力的；有吸引力的 **SYN enchanting**： *He found her captivating.* 他发觉她很迷人。

cap·tive /ˈkæptɪv/ *adj., noun*

■ ***adj.*** **1** kept as a prisoner or in a confined space; unable to escape 被监禁的；被关起来的；被困住的： *captive animals* 关在笼子里的动物 ◇ *They were* ***taken captive*** *by masked gunmen.* 他们被蒙面的持枪歹徒劫持了。◇ *captive breeding* (= the breeding of wild animals in zoos, etc.) 野生动物的圈养 **2** [only before noun] not free to leave a particular place or to choose what you want to do 人身自由受限制的；受控制的；无权选择的： *A salesman loves to have a* ***captive audience*** (= listening because they have no choice). 推销员喜欢不得不听的听众。

■ *noun* a person who is kept as a prisoner, especially in a war 囚徒；俘虏；战俘

cap·tiv·ity /kæp'tɪvəti/ *noun* [U] the state of being kept as a prisoner or in a confined space 监禁；关押；困住：*He was held **in captivity** for three years.* 他被监禁了三年。◇ *The bird had escaped from captivity.* 那只鸟已经逃离樊笼。

cap·tor /'kæptə(r)/ *noun* (*formal*) a person who captures a person or an animal and keeps them as a prisoner 捕获…者；捕捉者；劫持者

cap·ture /'kæptʃə(r)/ *verb, noun*

■ *verb*

• CATCH 抓住 **1** to catch a person or an animal and keep them as a prisoner or in a confined space 俘虏；俘获；捕获：**~ sb** *Allied troops captured over 300 enemy soldiers.* 盟军俘虏了 300 多名敌方士兵。◇ **~ sth** *The animals are captured in nets and sold to local zoos.* 那些动物用网捕获后被卖到当地的动物园。

• TAKE CONTROL 控制 **2** **~ sth** to take control of a place, building, etc. using force 用武力夺取；攻取；攻占：*The city was captured in 1941.* 这座城市于 1941 年被攻占。**3** **~ sth** to succeed in getting control of sth that other people are also trying to control 夺得；赢得；争得：*The company has captured 90% of the market.* 这家公司已取得九成的市场份额。

• MAKE SB INTERESTED 使感兴趣 **4** **~ sb's attention/imagination/interest** to make sb interested in sth 引起（注意、想象、兴趣）：*They use puppets to capture the imagination of younger audiences.* 他们用木偶来启发小观众的想象力。

• FEELING/ATMOSPHERE 感觉；气氛 **5** **~ sth** to succeed in accurately expressing a feeling, an atmosphere, etc. in a picture, piece of writing, film/movie, etc.（用图画、文章、电影等准确地）表达，刻画，描述 SYN **catch**：*The article captured the mood of the nation.* 这篇文章把国民的情绪把握得很准。

• FILM/RECORD/PAINT 电影；唱片；绘画 **6** [often passive] **~ sb/sth on film/tape/canvas, etc.** to film/record/paint, etc. sb/sth 拍摄；录制；绘制：*The attack was captured on film by security cameras.* 袭击事件已被保安摄像机拍摄下来。

• SB'S HEART 某人的心 **7** **~ sb's heart** to make sb love you 使…爱上（或倾心于）

• COMPUTING 计算机技术 **8** **~ sth** to put sth into a computer in a form it can use 把…输入计算机；采集

■ *noun* [U] the act of capturing sb/sth or of being captured（被）捕获；（被）俘获：*the capture of enemy territory* 占领敌方领土 ◇ *He evaded capture for three days.* 他逃避缉捕已经三天了。◇ *data capture* 数据采集

capy·bara /ˌkæpɪ'bɑːrə; *NAmE* ˌkæpə'berə/ *noun* (*pl.* **capy·bara** or **capy·baras**) an animal like a very large RABBIT with thick legs and small ears, which lives near water in S and Central America 水豚（生活于南美和中美洲水滨，腿粗耳小，形似大兔子）

car /kɑː(r)/ *noun* **1** (*also formal* **'motor car** *especially in BrE*) (*also NAmE, formal* **auto·mo·bile**) a road vehicle with an engine and four wheels that can carry a small number of passengers 小汽车；轿车：*Paula got into the car and drove off.* 葆拉钻进汽车后驾车而去。◇ *'How did you come?' 'By car.'* "你怎么来的？""开车来的。"◇ *Are you going **in the car**?* 你要开车去吗？◇ ***a car driver/manufacturer/dealer*** 汽车司机 / 制造商 / 经销商 ◇ ***a car accident/crash*** 汽车事故；撞车 ◇ *Where can I park the car?* 我可以在哪里停车呀？⊃ COLLOCATIONS AT DRIVING ⊃ VISUAL VOCAB PAGE V56 ⊃ SEE ALSO COMPANY CAR

> **WORDFINDER** 联想词：accelerate, brake, commute, **driving**, licence, motorist, **road**, road tax, **traffic**

2 (*also* **rail·car** *both NAmE*) a separate section of a train 火车车厢：*Several cars went off the rails.* 有几节火车车厢出轨了。⊃ VISUAL VOCAB PAGE V63 **3** (in compounds 构成复合词) a coach/car on a train of a particular type（某种类型的）火车车厢：***a sleeping/dining car*** 卧铺车厢；餐车

ca·rafe /kə'ræf/ *noun* a glass container with a wide neck in which wine or water is served at meals; the amount contained in a carafe（餐桌上盛酒或水的）喇叭口玻璃瓶，饮料瓶；一瓶（的量）⊃ VISUAL VOCAB PAGE V23

cara·mel /'kærəmel/ *noun* **1** [U, C] a type of hard sticky sweet/candy made from butter, sugar and milk; a small piece of this 黄油奶糖 **2** [U] burnt sugar used for adding colour and flavour to food 焦糖（用于食品着色和调味）⊃ SEE ALSO CRÈME CARAMEL **3** [U] a light brown colour 焦糖色；浅褐色

cara·mel·ize (*BrE also* **-ise**) /'kærəməlaɪz/ *verb* **1** [I] (of sugar 糖) to turn into caramel 变成焦糖 **2** [T] **~ sth** to cook sth, especially fruit, with sugar so that it is covered with caramel（尤指把水果）炒上一层焦糖

cara·pace /'kærəpeɪs/ *noun* (*specialist*) the hard shell on the back of some animals such as CRABS, that protects them（某些动物，如蟹的）头胸甲

carat /'kærət/ *noun* (*abbr.* **ct**) **1** a unit for measuring the weight of diamonds and other PRECIOUS STONES, equal to 200 milligrams 克拉（钻石或其他宝石的重量单位，等于 200 毫克）**2** (*especially BrE*) (*NAmE usually* **karat**) a unit for measuring how pure gold is. The purest gold is 24 carats. 开（黄金成色单位，纯金为 24 开）：*an 18-carat gold ring* * 18 开的金戒指

cara·van /'kærəvæn/ *noun* **1** (*BrE*) (*NAmE* **camp·er**) a road vehicle without an engine that is pulled by a car, designed for people to live and sleep in, especially when they are on holiday/vacation 旅行拖车，宿营拖车（无发动机，由其他车拖动，多供度假时住宿用）：*a caravan site/park* 旅行拖车停车场 ⊃ VISUAL VOCAB PAGE V63 **2** (*BrE*) a covered vehicle that is pulled by a horse and used for living in（供居住用的）有篷马车，大篷车：*a Gypsy caravan* 吉卜赛人的大篷车 **3** a group of people with vehicles or animals who are travelling together, especially across the desert（尤指穿越沙漠的）旅行队，车队

cara·van·ning /'kærəvænɪŋ/ *noun* [U] (*BrE*) the activity of spending a holiday/vacation in a caravan 乘旅行拖车度假

cara·van·serai /ˌkærə'vænsəraɪ; -ri/ (*especially US* **cara·van·sary** /ˌkærə'vænsəri/ *pl.* **-ies**) *noun* **1** in the past, a place where travellers could stay in desert areas of Asia and N Africa（旧时亚洲和北非沙漠地区的）商队客店 **2** (*formal*) a group of people travelling together 旅行队

cara·way /'kærəweɪ/ *noun* [U] the dried seeds of a plant of the PARSLEY family, used to give flavour to food 葛缕子干籽（用于食物调味）：*caraway seeds* 葛缕子籽

carb /kɑːb; *NAmE* kɑːrb/ *noun* (*informal*) = CARBOHYDRATE

car·bine /'kɑːbaɪn; *NAmE* 'kɑːrb-/ *noun* a short light RIFLE 卡宾枪

carbo·hy·drate /ˌkɑːbəʊ'haɪdreɪt; *NAmE* ˌkɑːrboʊ-/ *noun* **1** (*also informal* **carb**) [C, U] a substance such as sugar or STARCH that consists of CARBON, HYDROGEN and OXYGEN. Carbohydrates in food provide the body with energy and heat. 碳水化合物；糖类 **2** **carbohydrates** (*also informal* **carbs**) [pl.] foods such as bread, potatoes and rice that contain a lot of carbohydrate 含碳水化合物的食物；淀粉质食物

car·bol·ic /kɑː'bɒlɪk; *NAmE* kɑːr'bɑːlɪk/ (*also* **car,bolic 'acid**) *noun* [U] a chemical that kills bacteria, used as an ANTISEPTIC and as a DISINFECTANT (= to prevent infection from spreading) 石炭酸，苯酚（用作消毒剂）：*carbolic soap* 石炭酸皂

'car bomb *noun* a bomb hidden inside or under a car 汽车炸弹

car·bon /'kɑːbən; *NAmE* 'kɑːrb-/ *noun* **1** [U] (*symb.* **C**) a chemical element. Carbon is found in all living things, existing in a pure state as diamond and GRAPHITE. 碳：*carbon fibre* 碳纤维 **2** [U] used when referring to the gas CARBON DIOXIDE in terms of the effect it has on the earth's climate in causing GLOBAL WARMING 碳（指导致全球变暖的二氧化碳气体）: *carbon emissions/levels/taxes* 碳排放；碳水平；碳税 ◇ (*BrE*) *How do we move to a low carbon economy?* 我们如何转向低碳经济？ **3** [C] = CARBON COPY **4** [C] a piece of CARBON PAPER 复写纸

car·bon·ate /ˈkɑːbəneɪt; *NAmE* ˈkɑːrbənət/ *noun* (*chemistry* 化) a salt that contains CARBON and OXYGEN together with another chemical 碳酸盐

car·bon·ated /ˈkɑːbəneɪtɪd; *NAmE* ˈkɑːrb-/ *adj.* (*specialist*) (of a drink 饮料) containing small bubbles of CARBON DIOXIDE 含二氧化碳的；起泡的 SYN **fizzy**

ˌcarbon ˌcapture and ˈstorage (*also* **ˌcarbon ˌcapture and sequeˈstration**) *noun* [U] the process of collecting CARBON DIOXIDE produced by burning coal, oil, etc. and other industrial processes, and storing it so that it does not affect the atmosphere 碳收集与储存，碳捕获与封存（将煤、石油等燃烧及其他工业过程所产生的二氧化碳收集并储存） ➲ SEE ALSO CARBON SEQUESTRATION

ˌcarbon ˈcopy (*also* **car·bon**) *noun* **1** a copy of a document, letter, etc. made with CARBON PAPER（文件、信等的）复写本 ➲ SEE ALSO CC *abbr.* **2** a person or thing that is very similar to sb/sth else 极相像的人；极类似的事物: *She is a carbon copy of her sister.* 她跟她姐姐长得一模一样。

ˈcarbon credit *noun* **1** a key element in the system of national and international CARBON TRADING. A country or organization has the right to produce a particular amount of CARBON DIOXIDE and other gases that cause GLOBAL WARMING, which is expressed in terms of **carbon credits**, which may be traded between countries or organizations. 碳信用（指有权拥有且可交易的温室气体排放量）: *The sale of carbon credits can finance renewable energy projects.* 碳信用额的销售可为可再生能源项目提供资金。 **2** a CARBON OFFSET, which a person or company may choose to buy as a way of reducing the level of CARBON DIOXIDE for which they are responsible 碳补偿信用额（购入后用以抵消自身碳排放量）: *Wind energy companies sell carbon credits to consumers.* 风能公司向消费者出售碳补偿信用额。

ˈcarbon cycle *noun* [C, U] the processes by which carbon is changed from one form to another within the environment, for example in plants and when wood or oil is burned 碳循环（指碳在自然环境中的形式变化过程）

ˌcarbon ˈdating (*also formal* **ˌradiocarbon ˈdating**) *noun* [U] a method of calculating the age of very old objects by measuring the amounts of different forms of carbon in them 碳定年法（根据测定古物不同形态的碳含量以计算年代）

ˌcarbon ˈdebt *noun* the difference between the effects of the CARBON FOOTPRINT of a country, group, person, etc. and anything that has been agreed or done to reduce these effects 碳债务，碳债（碳足迹效应与已承诺或已实施的碳减排之间的差额）: *A massive carbon debt will be created when the forests are harvested.* 采伐森林将产生巨额碳债务。

ˌcarbon diˈoxide *noun* [U] (*symb.* CO_2) a gas breathed out by people and animals from the lungs or produced by burning CARBON 二氧化碳

ˌcarbon ˈfootprint *noun* a measure of the amount of carbon dioxide that is produced by the daily activities of a person or company 碳足迹（日常活动所产生的碳排放量的量度方式）: *Flying is the biggest contribution to my carbon footprint.* 乘坐飞机在我的碳足迹中占有的比例最大。 ➲ COLLOCATIONS AT ENVIRONMENT

car·bon·ic acid /kɑːˌbɒnɪk ˈæsɪd; *NAmE* kɑːrˌbɑːnɪk-/ *noun* [U] (*chemistry* 化) a very weak acid that is formed when carbon dioxide is dissolved in water 碳酸

car·bon·ifer·ous /ˌkɑːbəˈnɪfərəs; *NAmE* ˌkɑːrb-/ *adj.* (*geology* 地) **1** producing or containing coal 产煤的；含煤（或碳）的 **2 Carboniferous** of the period in the earth's history when layers of coal were formed underground 石炭纪的

car·bon·ize (*BrE also* **-ise**) /ˈkɑːbənaɪz; *NAmE* ˈkɑːrb-/ *verb* **1** [I, T] ~ (**sth**) to become CARBON, or to make sth become carbon （使）碳化；（使）焦化 **2** [T] ~ **sth** to cover sth with CARBON 给…涂碳 ▸ **car·bon·iza·tion, -isa·tion** /ˌkɑːbənaɪˈzeɪʃn; *NAmE* ˌkɑːrbənəˈz-/ *noun* [U]

ˌcarbon monˈoxide /ˌkɑːbən mənˈɒksaɪd; *NAmE* ˌkɑːrbən mənˈɑːksaɪd/ *noun* [U] (*symb.* **CO**) a poisonous gas formed when CARBON burns partly but not completely. It is produced when petrol/gas is burnt in car engines. 一氧化碳

ˌcarbon ˈneutral *adj.* in which the amount of CARBON DIOXIDE produced has been reduced to nothing or is balanced by actions that protect the environment 碳平衡的（指碳排放量减低为零，或通过环保措施抵消排放） SYN **zero-carbon**: *All of these fuels are renewable and carbon neutral.* 所有这些燃料都可再生并达至碳中和。

ˌcarbon ˈoffset *noun* [C, U] a way for a company or person to reduce the level of CARBON DIOXIDE for which they are responsible by paying money to a company that works to reduce the total amount produced in the world, for example by planting trees 碳补偿，碳抵消（出钱给从事全球减少碳排放的公司，以降低自身碳排放水平）: *carbon offset initiatives for air travellers* 供航空旅客采用的碳补偿倡议 ➲ COMPARE CARBON CREDIT

ˈcarbon paper *noun* [U] thin paper with a dark substance on one side, that is used between two sheets of paper for making copies of written or typed documents 复写纸

ˌcarbon ˌsequeˈstration *noun* [U] the process of storing CARBON DIOXIDE that has been collected and removed from the atmosphere, in solid or liquid form 碳固存，碳封存，碳截存（把从大气中收集并清除的二氧化碳以固态或液态形式封存） ➲ SEE ALSO CARBON CAPTURE AND STORAGE

ˈcarbon trading (*also* **eˈmissions trading**) *noun* [U] a system that gives countries and organizations the right to produce a particular amount of CARBON DIOXIDE and other gases that cause GLOBAL WARMING, and allows them to sell this right 碳排放权交易；碳交易

ˌcar ˈboot sale *noun* (*BrE*) an outdoor sale where people sell things that they no longer want, using tables or the backs of their cars to put the goods on（于户外摆放在桌子上或车尾行李厢里的）旧货销售，旧货市场

Car·bor·un·dum™ /ˌkɑːbəˈrʌndəm; *NAmE* ˌkɑːrb-/ *noun* [U] (*chemistry* 化) a very hard black solid substance, used as an ABRASIVE 金刚砂，碳化硅（用作研磨材料）

car·boy /ˈkɑːbɔɪ; *NAmE* ˈkɑːrbɔɪ/ *noun* a large round bottle, usually protected by an outer frame of wood and used for storing and transporting dangerous liquids 大瓶，大罐（通常有木架保护，用于贮藏和运输危险液体）

ˈcar bra *noun* = BRA (2)

car·bun·cle /ˈkɑːbʌŋkl; *NAmE* ˈkɑːrb-/ *noun* **1** a large painful swelling under the skin 痈 **2** a bright red JEWEL, usually cut into a round shape 红榴石；红宝石；红玉

car·bur·et·tor (*BrE*) (*NAmE* **car·bur·etor**) /ˌkɑːbəˈretə(r); *NAmE* ˈkɑːrbəreɪtər/ *noun* the part of an engine, for example in a car, where petrol/gas and air are mixed together 汽化器，化油器（汽车发动机部件）

car·cass (*BrE also*, *less frequent* **car·case**) /ˈkɑːkəs; *NAmE* ˈkɑːrkəs/ *noun* the dead body of an animal, especially of a large one or of one that is ready for cutting up as meat 动物尸体；（尤指供食用的）畜体

car·cino·gen /kɑːˈsɪnədʒən; *NAmE* kɑːrˈs-/ *noun* a substance that can cause cancer 致癌物

car·cino·gen·ic /ˌkɑːsɪnəˈdʒenɪk; *NAmE* ˌkɑːrs-/ *adj.* likely to cause cancer 致癌的

car·cin·oma /ˌkɑːsɪˈnəʊmə; *NAmE* ˌkɑːrsɪˈnoʊmə/ *noun* (*medical* 医) a cancer that affects the top layer of the skin or the LINING of the body's internal organs 癌（影响上皮组织或腹腔器官内膜的恶性肿瘤）

ˈcar crash *noun* **1** an accident in which a car hits sth, for example another vehicle, usually causing damage and often killing or injuring the passengers 撞车事故；车祸 **2** (*informal*) a very unsuccessful event or situation that people often find interesting 糗事；尴尬局面；糟糕境地：*Her life is turning into a car crash.* 她的生活变得糗事连连。◇ *The whole industry is a car crash—even major investment won't save it now.* 整个行业一塌糊涂，现在连大笔投资也无法挽救它。◇ *car-crash television* 哗众取宠的电视节目 ➲ COMPARE TRAIN WRECK (2)

C

card /kɑːd; *NAmE* kɑːrd/ *noun, verb*

■ ***noun***

• **PAPER** 纸 **1** [U] (*BrE*) thick stiff paper 卡片纸；厚纸片；薄纸板：*a piece of card* 一张卡片纸 ◇ *The model of the building was made of card.* 建筑物的模型是用厚纸片制作的。

• **WITH INFORMATION** 资料 **2** [C] a small piece of stiff paper or plastic with information on it, especially information about sb's identity（尤指显示个人资料的）卡片：*a membership card* 会员卡 ◇ *an appointment card* 预约卡 ➲ SEE ALSO GREEN CARD, IDENTITY CARD, LOYALTY CARD, RED CARD, REPORT CARD at REPORT *n.* (5), YELLOW CARD **3** [C] = BUSINESS CARD: *Here's my card if you need to contact me again.* 如果你需要再和我联系，这是我的名片。**4** [C] = VISITING CARD

• **FOR MONEY** 代替货币 **5** [C] a small piece of plastic, especially one given by a bank or shop/store, used for buying things or obtaining money 信用卡；现金卡；储值卡：*I put the meal on* (= paid for it using) *my card.* 我用信用卡支付餐费。➲ SEE ALSO CASH CARD, CHARGE CARD, CHIP CARD, CREDIT CARD, DEBIT CARD, PHONECARD, SIM CARD, SMART CARD, SWIPE CARD

• **WITH A MESSAGE** 信息 **6** [C] a piece of stiff paper that is folded in the middle and has a picture on the front of it, used for sending sb a message with your good wishes, an invitation, etc. 贺卡；慰问卡；请柬：*a **birthday/get-well/good luck card*** 生日贺卡；祝愿康复卡；幸运贺卡 ➲ SEE ALSO CHRISTMAS CARD, GREETINGS CARD **7** [C] = POSTCARD: *Did you get my card from Italy?* 你收到我从意大利寄出的明信片了吗？

• **IN GAMES** 游戏 **8** [C] = PLAYING CARD: (*BrE*) *a pack of cards* 一副纸牌 ◇ (*NAmE*) *a deck of cards* 一副纸牌 ➲ VISUAL VOCAB PAGE V41 ➲ SEE ALSO TRUMP CARD, WILD CARD

> **WORDFINDER** 联想词：ace, cut, deal, **gambling**, hand, jack, shuffle, suit, trump

9 **cards** [pl.] a game or games in which PLAYING CARDS are used 纸牌游戏：*Who wants to play cards?* 谁想玩牌？◇ *I've never been very good at cards.* 我打牌的技术向来不高。◇ *Let's have a game of cards.* 咱们来玩纸牌吧。◇ *She won £20 at cards.* 她打牌赢了 20 英镑。

• **COMPUTING** 计算机技术 **10** [C] a small device containing an electronic CIRCUIT that is part of a computer or added to it, enabling it to perform particular functions 电路板卡；插件：*a printed circuit card* 印刷电路卡 ◇ *a **graphics/network/sound card*** 图形卡；网卡；声卡 ➲ SEE ALSO EXPANSION CARD

• **PERSON** 人 **11** [C] (*old-fashioned, informal*) an unusual or amusing person 怪人；引人发笑的人；活宝

• **HORSE RACES** 赛马 **12** [C] a list of all the races at a particular RACE MEETING (= a series of horse races)（赛马大会的）赛事一览表

• **FOR WOOL/COTTON** 毛；棉 **13** [C] (*specialist*) a machine or tool used for cleaning and COMBING wool or cotton before it is spun 梳理机；梳理工具

IDM **sb's best/strongest/winning ˈcard** something that gives sb an advantage over other people in a particular situation 某人的王牌；最强有力的一招；制胜的绝招 **get your ˈcards** (*BrE, informal*) to be told to leave a job 被解雇；被炒鱿鱼 **give sb their ˈcards** (*BrE, informal*) to make sb leave their job 解雇；开除；炒…的鱿鱼 **have a card up your ˈsleeve** to have an idea, a plan, etc. that will give you an advantage in a particular situation and that you keep secret until it is needed 有锦囊妙计；留有一招 **hold all the ˈcards** (*informal*) to be able to control a particular situation because you have an advantage over other people 能控制局势；应付自如；占上风 **hold/keep/play your cards close to your ˈchest** to keep your ideas, plans, etc. secret 守口如瓶；秘而不宣 **lay/put your cards on the ˈtable** to tell sb honestly what your plans, ideas, etc. are 摊牌；（把计划或想法等）和盘托出 **on the ˈcards** (*BrE*) (*NAmE* **in the ˈcards**) (*informal*) likely to happen 可能发生的；可能的：*The merger has been on the cards for some time now.* 合并的事情已经酝酿了一段时间。**play the ... card** to mention a particular subject, idea or quality in order to gain an advantage 打…牌；出…招：*He accused his opponent of playing the immigration card during the campaign.* 他指责对手在竞选活动中打移民牌。➲ SEE ALSO RACE CARD **play your ˈcards right** to deal successfully with a particular situation so that you achieve some advantage or sth that you want 办事精明；做事有盘算；处理得当 ➲ MORE AT TIP *v.*, STACKED

■ ***verb*** **1** ~ **sth** (*specialist*) to clean wool using a wire instrument（用钢丝刷）梳理 **2** ~ **sb** (*NAmE, informal*) to ask a person to show their identity card as a means of checking how old they are, for example if they want to buy alcohol 要求出示身份证（以确认年龄，如购酒时）

car·da·mom /ˈkɑːdəməm; *NAmE* ˈkɑːrd-/ *noun* [U] the dried seeds of a SE Asian plant, used in cooking as a spice 豆蔻干籽（用作调味料）➲ VISUAL VOCAB PAGE V35

card·board /ˈkɑːdbɔːd; *NAmE* ˈkɑːrdbɔːrd/ *noun, adj.*

■ ***noun*** [U] stiff material like very thick paper, often used for making boxes 硬纸板，卡纸板（常用于制造盒子）：*a cardboard box* 纸板盒 ◇ *a piece of cardboard* 一张硬纸板

■ ***adj.*** [only before noun] not seeming real or genuine 不真实的；虚假的：*a novel with superficial cardboard characters* 人物不真实而又缺乏深度的小说

ˌcardboard ˈcity *noun* (*BrE*) an area of a city where people who have nowhere to live sleep outside, protected only by cardboard boxes（城市中无家可归者聚集过夜的）纸箱街区

ˈcard-carrying *adj.* [only before noun] known to be an official and usually active member of a political organization（政治组织）正式成员的：*a card-carrying member of the Conservative Party* 保守党正式党员

ˈcard catalog (*NAmE*) (*BrE* **ˈcard index**, **index**) *noun* a box of cards with information on them, arranged in alphabetical order 卡片目录（或索引）➲ VISUAL VOCAB PAGE V71

ˈcard game *noun* a game in which playing cards are used 纸牌游戏

card·hold·er /ˈkɑːdhəʊldə(r); *NAmE* ˈkɑːrdhoʊl-/ *noun* a person who has a credit card from a bank, etc. 持有信用卡的人；持卡人

car·diac /ˈkɑːdiæk; *NAmE* ˈkɑːrd-/ *adj.* [only before noun] (*medical* 医) connected with the heart or heart disease 心脏的；心脏病的：***cardiac disease/failure/surgery*** 心脏病；心力衰竭；心脏手术 ◇ *to suffer **cardiac arrest*** (= an occasion when a person's heart stops temporarily or permanently) 心脏停搏

car·di·gan /ˈkɑːdɪɡən; *NAmE* ˈkɑːrd-/ (*NAmE also* **ˌcardigan ˈsweater**) *noun* a knitted jacket made of wool, usually with no COLLAR and fastened with buttons at the front（无领）开襟毛衣 ➲ VISUAL VOCAB PAGE V68

car·din·al /ˈkɑːdɪnl; *NAmE* ˈkɑːrd-/ *noun, adj.*

■ ***noun*** **1** a priest of the highest rank in the Roman Catholic Church. Cardinals elect and advise the POPE. 枢机；枢机主教：*Cardinal Newman* 纽曼枢机主教 **2** (*also* **ˌcardinal ˈnumber**) a number, such as 1, 2 and 3 (or one, two and three), used to show quantity rather than order 基数；纯数 ➲ COMPARE ORDINAL **3** a N American bird. The male cardinal is bright red. 红衣凤头鸟（见于北美，雄鸟为鲜红色）

■ ***adj.*** [only before noun] (*formal*) most important; having other things based on it 最重要的；基本的：*Respect for* *life is a cardinal principle of English law.* 尊重生命是英国法律最重要的原则。

ˌcardinal ˈpoints *noun* [pl.] (*specialist*) the four main points (North, South, East and West) of the COMPASS 基本方位，方位基点（罗盘上的北、南、东、西）

ˌcardinal ˈsin *noun* **1** (*sometimes humorous*) an action that is a serious mistake or that other people disapprove of 严重过失；过错：*He committed the cardinal sin of criticizing his teammates.* 他犯了指责队友的大错。 **2** a serious SIN in the Christian Church（基督教中严重的）罪，罪孽

ˈcard index (*also* **index**) (*both BrE*) (*NAmE* **ˈcard catalog**) *noun* a box of cards with information on them, arranged in alphabetical order 卡片目录（或索引） ➲ VISUAL VOCAB PAGE V71

cardio /ˈkɑːdiəʊ; *NAmE* ˈkɑːrdioʊ/ *noun* [U] (*informal*) exercises to make your heart work harder, that you do to keep yourself fit 健心运动：*Cardio is the answer if you want to lose weight.* 想减肥就得做健心运动。◇ *cardio exercise/workouts* 健心体操 / 锻炼 ➲ SEE ALSO CARDIOVASCULAR

cardio- /ˈkɑːdiəʊ; *NAmE* ˈkɑːrdioʊ/ *combining form* (in nouns, adjectives and adverbs 构成名词、形容词和副词) connected with the heart 心脏的：*cardiogram* 心电图

car·di·olo·gist /ˌkɑːdiˈɒlədʒɪst; *NAmE* ˌkɑːrdiˈɑːl-/ *noun* a doctor who studies and treats heart diseases 心脏病医生；心脏病学家 ➲ WORDFINDER NOTE AT SPECIALIST ▶ **car·di·ology** /-dʒi/ *noun* [U]

car·dio·vas·cu·lar /ˌkɑːdiəʊˈvæskjələ(r); *NAmE* ˌkɑːrdioʊ-/ *adj.* (*medical* 医) connected with the heart and the BLOOD VESSELS (= the tubes that carry blood around the body) 心血管的

card·phone /ˈkɑːdfəʊn; *NAmE* ˈkɑːrdfoʊn/ *noun* (*BrE*) a public telephone in which you use a plastic card (= a PHONECARD) instead of money 磁卡电话

ˈcard reader *noun* **1** an electronic device that reads data stored on a credit card, MEMBERSHIP card, etc.（读取信用卡、会员卡等数据的）读卡机，读卡器：*a credit card reader* 信用卡读卡器 **2** an electronic device, that you can attach to or that is part of a computer, printer, etc., which reads or transfers data from a memory device（计算机、打印机等的）卡片读入机，读卡器

ˈcard sharp *noun* a person who cheats in games of cards in order to make money（玩纸牌时）作弊赢钱的人，耍老千的人

ˈcard swipe *noun* an electronic device through which you pass a credit card, etc. in order to record the information on it, open a door, etc. 读卡机；磁卡识别机

ˈcard table *noun* a small table for playing card games on, especially one that you can fold（折叠式）牌桌

> **WORD FAMILY**
> **care** *noun, verb*
> **careful** *adj.* (≠ careless)
> **carefully** *adv.* (≠ carelessly)
> **caring** *adj.* (≠ uncaring)

care /keə(r); *NAmE* ker/ *noun, verb*

■ ***noun*** **1** [U] the process of caring for sb/sth and providing what they need for their health or protection 照料；照顾；照看；护理：*medical/patient care* 医疗保健；病人护理 ◇ *How much do men share housework and the care of the children?* 男人分担多少做家务和照看小孩的工作？ ◇ *the provision of care for the elderly* 对老人的赡养 ◇ ***skin/hair care** products* 护肤品；护发品 ➲ SEE ALSO COMMUNITY CARE, DAY CARE, EASY-CARE, HEALTH CARE, INTENSIVE CARE **2** [U] attention or thought that you give to sth that you are doing so that you will do it well and avoid mistakes or damage 小心；谨慎：*She chose her words **with care**.* 她措辞谨慎。◇ *Great care is needed when choosing a used car.* 选购旧车时要特别小心。◇ *Fragile—handle with care* (= written on a container holding sth which is easily broken or damaged) 易碎物品，小心轻放 **3** [C, usually pl., U] (*formal*) a feeling of worry or anxiety; something that causes problems or anxiety 忧虑；焦虑；引起烦恼的事；令人焦虑的事：*I felt free from the cares of the day as soon as I left the building.* 我一离开那栋大楼便觉得轻松自在，不再为那天的事烦心了。◇ *Sam looked as if he **didn't have a care in the world**.* 萨姆看上去好像什么事都不操心似的。

IDM **ˈcare of sb** (*NAmE also* **in ˈcare of sb**) (*abbr.* **c/o**) used when writing to sb at another person's address（以别人的地址给某人写信时用）由某人转交：*Write to him care of his lawyer.* 写给他的信由他的律师转交。 **in ˈcare** (*BrE*) (of children 儿童) living in an institution run by the local authority rather than with their parents 由福利院收养：*The two girls were **taken into care** after their parents were killed.* 两个女孩在父母遇害后由福利院收养。 **in the care of sb/in sb's care** being cared for by sb 由…照管：*The child was left in the care of friends.* 小孩留给朋友照管。 **take ˈcare** (*informal*) used when saying goodbye（告别用语）走好，保重：*Bye! Take care!* 再见！多保重！ **take care (that…/to do sth)** to be careful 小心；当心：*Take care (that) you don't drink too much!* 当心别喝得太多！◇ *Care should be taken to close the lid securely.* 盖子应小心扣紧。 **take care of sb/sth/yourself** **1** to care for sb/sth/yourself; to be careful about sth 照顾；照料；爱护；小心：*Who's taking care of the children while you're away?* 你外出时谁来照料孩子？◇ *She takes great care of her clothes.* 她非常爱惜自己的衣服。◇ *He's old enough to take care of himself.* 他已经不小了，能照顾自己了。 **2** to be responsible for or to deal with a situation or task 负责；处理：*Don't worry about the travel arrangements. They're all being taken care of.* 别担心旅行安排，一切都会有人照管的。◇ *Celia takes care of the marketing side of things.* 西莉亚负责产品营销方面的事宜。 **under the care of sb** receiving medical care from sb 接受某人的治疗：*He's under the care of Dr Parks.* 他在接受帕克斯医生的治疗。

> **▼SYNONYMS** 同义词辨析
>
> **care**
>
> **caution • prudence**
>
> These are all words for attention or thought that you give to sth in order to avoid mistakes or accidents. 以上各词均指小心、谨慎。
>
> **care** attention or thought that you give to sth that you are doing so that you will do it well and avoid mistakes or damage 指小心、谨慎以做好某事，同时避免出现错误或损失：*She chose her words with care.* 她措辞谨慎。
>
> **caution** care that you take in order to avoid danger or mistakes; not taking any risks 指小心、谨慎，以免发生危险或错误：*The utmost caution must be exercised when handling explosives.* 处理爆炸品一定要慎之又慎。
>
> **prudence** (*rather formal*) being sensible and careful when you make judgements and decisions; avoiding unnecessary risks 指判断和决策时谨慎、慎重，处事时避免不必要的风险：*As a matter of prudence, keep a record of all your financial transactions.* 为慎重起见，请记下你所有的财务往来。 **NOTE** **Prudence** is used particularly in financial contexts. * prudence 尤用于金融、财务语境。
>
> **PATTERNS**
> - to do sth **with** care/caution/prudence
> - **great/extreme** care/caution/prudence
> - to **use/exercise** care/caution/prudence
> - to **proceed with** care/caution

■ ***verb*** (not used in the progressive tenses 不用于进行时) **1** [I, T] to feel that sth is important and worth worrying about 关注；在意；担忧：***I don't care*** (= I will not be upset) *if I never see him again!* 即使我永远再也见不到他，我也不在乎！◇ *He threatened to fire me, **as if I cared!*** 他威胁要解雇我，好像我多在乎似的！◇ **~ about sth** *She cares deeply about environmental issues.* 她对环境问题深感担忧。◇ **~ what/whether, etc.** *I don't care what he thinks.* 我才不管他怎么想呢。◇ **~ that…** *She doesn't seem to care* that he's been married four times before. 她似乎不介意他以前结过四次婚。 **2** ⚷ [I] ~ (**about sb**) to like or love sb and worry about what happens to them 关心；关怀： *He genuinely cares about his employees.* 他真诚地关心他的雇员。 **3** [T] ~ **to do sth** to make the effort to do sth 努力做： *I've done this job more times than I care to remember.* 这事我都记不清做了多少遍了。

IDM **couldn't care 'less** (*informal*) used to say, often rudely, that you do not think that sb/sth is important or worth worrying about （常用于无礼地表示）不在乎，不在意： *Quite honestly, I couldn't care less what they do.* 说实在的，我才不在乎他们做什么。 **for all you, I, they, etc. care** (*informal*) used to say that a person is not worried about or interested in what happens to sb/sth 漠不关心；无动于衷；全然不在乎： *I could be dead for all he cares!* 我是死是活，他才不关心呢！ **who 'cares? | what do I, you, etc. care?** (*informal*) used to say, often rudely, that you do not think that sth is important or interesting （常用于无礼地表示）管它呢，谁管呢： *Who cares what she thinks?* 谁管她怎么想呢！ **Would you care for sth? | Would you care to do sth?** (*formal*) used to ask sb politely if they would like sth or would like to do sth, or if they would be willing to do sth （礼貌问语）您想要，您喜欢，您愿意： *Would you care for another drink?* 您再来一杯好吗？ ◇ *If you'd care to follow me, I'll show you where his office is.* 如果您愿意跟我走，我会把您领到他的办公室去。 ➲ NOTE AT WANT ➲ MORE AT DAMN *n.*, FIG, HOOT *n.*, TUPPENCE

PHR V **'care for sb 1** ⚷ to look after sb who is sick, very old, very young, etc. 照顾，照料（病、老、幼者等） **SYN** **take care of**: *She moved back home to care for her elderly parents.* 她搬回家住，好照料年迈的双亲。 ➲ SEE ALSO UNCARED FOR **2** to love or like sb very much 深深地爱；非常喜欢： *He cared for her more than she realized.* 她不知道他是多么在乎她。 ➲ SYNONYMS AT LOVE **not 'care for sb/sth** (*formal*) to not like sb/sth 不喜欢： *He didn't much care for her friends.* 他不太喜欢她的朋友。

▼ **WHICH WORD?** 词语辨析

take care of / look after / care for

- You can **take care of** or, especially in *BrE*, **look after** someone who is very young, very old, or sick, or something that needs keeping in good condition. 照看小孩、老人、病人或物品可用 take care of，英式英语尤用 look after： *We've asked my mother to take care of/look after the kids while we're away.* 我们已请我母亲在我们外出时照看孩子。 ◇ *You can borrow my camera if you promise to take care of/look after it.* 只要你答应把我的照相机保管好就可以借去用。
- In more formal language you can also **care for** someone. 在较正式用语中，照看或照顾某人亦可用 care for： *She does some voluntary work, caring for the elderly.* 她干一些照顾老人的义务工作。 But **care for** is more commonly used to mean 'like'. 但 care for 较常用于表示喜欢： *I don't really care for spicy food.* 我其实不喜欢吃辛辣食物。

'care assistant *noun* (*BrE*) = CARE WORKER

ca·reen /kəˈriːn/ *verb* [I] + **adv./prep.** (*especially NAmE*) (of a person or vehicle 人或车辆) to move forward very quickly especially in a way that is dangerous or uncontrolled （尤指危险或失控地）猛冲，疾驶 **SYN** **hurtle**

ca·reer ⚷ /kəˈrɪə(r); *NAmE* kəˈrɪr/ *noun, verb*

■ ***noun* 1** ⚷ the series of jobs that a person has in a particular area of work, usually involving more responsibility as time passes 生涯；职业： *a career in politics* 从政生涯 ◇ *a teaching career* 教学生涯 ◇ *What made you decide on a career as a vet?* 是什么驱使你选择兽医这种职业的？ ◇ *She has been concentrating on her career.* 她一直专心致志于她的本职工作。 ◇ *a change of career* 改换职业 ◇ *That will be a good career move* (= something that will help your career). 那将是事业发展上明智的一步。 ◇ *a career soldier/diplomat* (= a professional one) 职业军人；外交人员 ◇ (*BrE*) *a careers adviser/officer* (= a person whose job is to give people advice and information about jobs) 职业顾问；就业指导员 ➲ SYNONYMS AT WORK ➲ COLLOCATIONS AT JOB **2** ⚷ the period of time that you spend in your life working or doing a particular thing 经历；事业： *She started her career as an English teacher.* 她以当英语教师开始了她的职业生涯。 ◇ *He is playing the best tennis of his career.* 他正处于他网球事业的巅峰时期。 ◇ *My school career was not very impressive.* 我的学业成绩并不很出色。

■ ***verb*** [I] + **adv./prep.** (of a person or vehicle 人或车辆) to move forward very quickly, especially in an uncontrolled way （尤指失控地）猛冲，疾驰，飞奔 **SYN** **hurtle**: *The vehicle careered across the road and hit a cyclist.* 那辆车横冲过马路，撞上了一个骑自行车的人。

ca'reer break *noun* a period of time when you do not do your usual job, for example because you have children to care for 离职期（如因照料小孩之需）

ca·reer·ist /kəˈrɪərɪst; *NAmE* -ˈrɪr-/ *noun* (*often disapproving*) a person whose career is more important to them than anything else 视事业重于一切的人；事业狂 ▸ **ca·reer·ism** *noun* [U]

ca'reer woman *noun* a woman whose career is more important to her than getting married and having children 职业妇女，职业女性（视事业比结婚生孩子更重要的女人）

care·free /ˈkeəfriː; *NAmE* ˈkerf-/ *adj.* having no worries or responsibilities 无忧无虑的；无牵挂的；无责任的： *He looked happy and carefree.* 他看起来轻松愉快。 ◇ *a carefree attitude/life* 轻松自在的态度；无忧无虑的生活

care·ful ⚷ /ˈkeəfl; *NAmE* ˈkerfl/ *adj.* **1** ⚷ [not before noun] giving attention or thought to what you are doing so that you avoid hurting yourself, damaging sth or doing sth wrong 小心；注意；谨慎： *Be careful!* 小心！ ◇ ~ **to do sth** *He was careful to keep out of sight.* 他小心翼翼地躲开别人的视线。 ◇ ~ **not to do sth** *Be careful not to wake the baby.* 注意别吵醒了宝宝。 ◇ ~ **when/what/how, etc.** *You must be careful when handling chemicals.* 搬运化学品必须小心谨慎。 ◇ ~ **of/about/with sth** *Be careful of the traffic.* 注意交通安全。 ◇ *Please be careful with my glasses* (= Don't break them). 请当心别打碎我的眼镜。 ◇ ~ (**that**) … *Be careful you don't bump your head.* 留神别撞了你的头。 ➲ EXPRESS YOURSELF AT WARN **2** ⚷ giving a lot of attention to details 细致的；精心的；慎重的： *a careful piece of work* 精雕细琢的作品 ◇ *a careful examination of the facts* 对事实的仔细调查 ◇ *After careful consideration we have decided to offer you the job.* 经过慎重考虑后，我们决定给你这份工作。 **OPP** **careless** ▸ **care·ful·ly** ⚷ /ˈkeəfəli; *NAmE* ˈker-/ *adv.*： *Please listen carefully.* 请仔细地听。 ◇ *She put the glass down carefully.* 她小心翼翼地放下玻璃杯。 ◇ *Drive carefully.* 小心开车。 **OPP** **carelessly** **care·ful·ness** *noun* [U]

IDM **you can't be too 'careful** used to warn sb that they should take care to avoid danger or problems 无论怎样小心也不会过分；越小心越好： *Don't stay out in the sun for too long—you can't be too careful.* 别在太阳底下待得太久，你得尽量小心。 **careful with money** not spending money on unimportant things 花钱精打细算；不乱花钱

care·giver /ˈkeəgɪvə(r); *NAmE* ˈkerg-/ (*NAmE*) (*BrE* **carer**) *noun* a person who takes care of a sick or old person at home 照料家居老弱病患者的人；家庭护理员

'care home *noun* (*BrE*) a place where people live and are cared for when they cannot live at home or look after themselves 护理院；照护所： *a care home for the elderly* 养老院 ➲ WORDFINDER NOTE AT OLD

'care label *noun* a label attached to the inside of a piece of clothing, giving instructions about how it should be washed and ironed （衣服的）熨洗须知标签

care·less ⚷ /ˈkeələs; *NAmE* ˈkerləs/ *adj.* **1** ⚷ not giving enough attention and thought to what you are doing, so that you make mistakes 不小心的；不仔细的；粗心的： *It was careless of me to leave the door open.* 怪我粗心忘了关

门。◇ *Don't be so* **careless** *about/with spelling.* 别那么粗心大意地犯拼写错误。◇ *a* **careless** *worker/driver* 粗心大意的工人 / 司机 OPP **careful 2** 🔑 resulting from a lack of attention and thought 粗心造成的；疏忽引起的： *a* **careless** *mistake/error* 疏忽造成的错误 / 差错 **3** ~ **of sth** (*formal*) not at all worried about sth 不担忧的；无忧无虑的： *He seemed careless of his own safety.* 他仿佛把自己的安危置之度外。**4** not showing interest or effort 淡漠的；不关心的；漫不经心的 SYN **casual**: *She gave a careless shrug.* 她漠然地耸了耸肩。◇ *a* **careless** *laugh/smile* 淡然的一笑 ▶ **care·less·ly** 🔑 *adv.*： *Someone had carelessly left a window open.* 有人粗心大意忘了关一扇窗。◇ *She threw her coat carelessly onto the chair.* 她把外套随手扔在了椅子上。◇ *'I don't mind,' he said carelessly.* "我无所谓。" 他满不在乎地说。 **care·less·ness** *noun* [U]： *a moment of carelessness* 一时的疏忽大意

care·line /ˈkeəlaɪn; *NAmE* ˈkerl-/ *noun* a telephone service that you can call to get advice or information on a company's products（公司的）产品咨询热线，服务热线，客服热线： *Call our customer careline for advice.* 请拨打我们的客户服务热线咨询。

carer /ˈkeərə(r); *NAmE* ˈker-/ (*BrE*) (*NAmE* **care·giver**) *noun* a person who takes care of a sick or old person at home 照料家居老弱病患者的人；家庭护理员

ca·ress /kəˈres/ *verb, noun*
- *verb* ~ **sb/sth** to touch sb/sth gently, especially in a sexual way or in a way that shows affection 抚摩；爱抚： *His fingers caressed the back of her neck.* 他的手指抚摩着她的后颈。
- *noun* a gentle touch or kiss to show you love sb 抚摩；爱抚；亲吻

caret /ˈkærət/ *noun* a mark (^) placed below a line of printed or written text to show that words or letters should be added at that place in the text 脱字号；补注号

care·taker /ˈkeəteɪkə(r); *NAmE* ˈkert-/ *noun, adj.*
- *noun* **1** (*BrE*) (*NAmE, ScotE* **jani·tor**) (*NAmE also* **cus·to·dian**) a person whose job is to take care of a building such as a school or a block of flats or an apartment building（建筑物的）管理员，看管人，看门人 **2** (*especially NAmE*) a person who takes care of a house or land while the owner is away（主人外出时房地产的）看管人，代管人 **3** (*especially NAmE*) a person such as a teacher, parent, nurse, etc., who takes care of other people 照看人；监护人；护理人员
- *adj.* [only before noun] in charge for a short time, until a new leader or government is chosen 临时代理的；暂时主管的： *a* **caretaker** *manager/government* 代经理；看守政府

ˈcare worker (*also* **ˈcare assistant**) (*both BrE*) *noun* a person whose job is to help and take care of people who are mentally ill, sick or disabled, especially those who live in special homes or hospitals（精神病人、残疾人，尤指住院治疗者的）护理员

care·worn /ˈkeəwɔːn; *NAmE* ˈkerwɔːrn/ *adj.* looking tired because you have a lot of worries 忧虑憔悴的

cargo /ˈkɑːɡəʊ; *NAmE* ˈkɑːrɡoʊ/ *noun* [C, U] (*pl.* **-oes**, *NAmE also* **-os**) the goods carried in a ship or plane（船或飞机装载的）货物： *The tanker began to spill its cargo of oil.* 油轮已开始漏油。◇ *a cargo ship* 货船

ˈcargo pants (*also* **car·goes**) (*BrE also* **com·bats**, **ˈcombat trousers**) *noun* [pl.] loose trousers that have pockets in various places, for example on the side of the leg above the knee 工装裤（多口袋，宽松） ➲ VISUAL VOCAB PAGE V68

Carib·bean /ˌkærɪˈbiːən; kəˈrɪbiən/ *noun, adj.*
- *noun* **the Caribbean** the region consisting of the Caribbean Sea and its islands, including the West Indies, and the coasts which surround it 加勒比海地区（指加勒比海及其岛屿，包括西印度群岛及其周围海岸）
- *adj.* connected with the Caribbean 加勒比海地区的；加勒比海诸岛的

cari·bou /ˈkærɪbuː/ *noun* (*pl.* **cari·bou**) a N American REINDEER 北美驯鹿

cari·ca·ture /ˈkærɪkətʃʊə(r); *NAmE* -tʃər; -tʃʊr/ *noun, verb*
- *noun* **1** [C] a funny drawing or picture of sb that exaggerates some of their features 人物漫画 **2** [C] a description of a person or thing that makes them seem ridiculous by exaggerating some of their characteristics 夸张的描述： *He had unfairly presented a caricature of my views.* 他歪曲了我的观点。**3** [U] the art of drawing or writing caricatures 漫画艺术；漫画手法 ➲ WORDFINDER NOTE AT COMEDY ▶ **cari·ca·tur·ist** *noun*
- *verb* [often passive] ~ **sb/sth** (**as sth**) to produce a caricature of sb; to describe or present sb as a type of person you would laugh at or not respect 把…画成漫画；滑稽地描述： *She was unfairly caricatured as a dumb blonde.* 她被不公正地丑化成了一个傻头傻脑的金发女郎。

car·ies /ˈkeəriːz; *NAmE* ˈker-/ *noun* [U] (*medical* 医) decay in teeth or bones 龋齿；骨疡；骨疽： *dental caries* 龋

car·il·lon /kəˈrɪljən; *NAmE* ˈkærəlɑːn/ *noun* **1** a set of bells on which tunes can be played, sometimes using a keyboard 组钟；大钟琴 **2** a tune played on bells 组钟乐曲；钟乐

car·ing /ˈkeərɪŋ; *NAmE* ˈker-/ *adj.* [usually before noun] kind, helpful and showing that you care about other people 乐于助人的；关心他人的；体贴人的： *He's a very caring person.* 他是个非常体贴别人的人。◇ *Children need a caring environment.* 儿童需要一个充满关怀的环境。◇ *a* **caring** *profession* (= a job that involves looking after or helping other people) 护理职业

car·jack·ing /ˈkɑːdʒækɪŋ; *NAmE* ˈkɑːrdʒ-/ *noun* [U, C] the crime of forcing the driver of a car to take you somewhere or give you their car, using threats and violence 劫持汽车（罪）；劫车（罪） ➲ COMPARE HIJACKING at HIJACK ▶ **car·jack** *verb* ~ **sth** **car·jack·er** *noun*

car·load /ˈkɑːləʊd; *NAmE* ˈkɑːrloʊd/ *noun* the number of people or amount of things that a car is carrying or is able to carry 汽车荷载量

car·mine /ˈkɑːmaɪn; *NAmE* ˈkɑːrm-/ *adj.* (*formal*) dark red in colour 深红色的；暗红色的 ▶ **car·mine** *noun* [U]

carn·age /ˈkɑːnɪdʒ; *NAmE* ˈkɑːrn-/ *noun* [U] the violent killing of a large number of people 大屠杀 SYN **slaughter**: *a scene of carnage* 大屠杀的场面

car·nal /ˈkɑːnl; *NAmE* ˈkɑːrnl/ *adj.* [usually before noun] (*formal* or *law* 律) connected with the body or with sex 肉体的；肉欲的；性欲的： *carnal desires/appetites* 肉欲 ▶ **car·nal·ly** /ˈkɑːnəli; *NAmE* ˈkɑːrn-/ *adv.*

ˌcarnal ˈknowledge *noun* [U] (*old-fashioned* or *law* 律) = SEXUAL INTERCOURSE

car·na·tion /kɑːˈneɪʃn; *NAmE* kɑːrˈn-/ *noun* a white, pink, red or yellow flower, often worn as a decoration on formal occasions（丁）香石竹；康乃馨： *He was wearing a carnation in his buttonhole.* 他在扣眼里插了一朵康乃馨。➲ VISUAL VOCAB PAGE V11

car·ne·lian /kɑːˈniːliən; *NAmE* kɑːrˈn-/ (*also* **cor·nel·ian**) *noun* [C, U] a red, brown or white stone, used in jewellery 光玉髓（宝石）

car·ni·val /ˈkɑːnɪvl; *NAmE* ˈkɑːrn-/ *noun* **1** [C, U] a public festival, usually one that happens at a regular time each year, that involves music and dancing in the streets, for which people wear brightly coloured clothes 狂欢节；嘉年华： *There is a local carnival every year.* 当地每年都举行狂欢节。◇ *the carnival in Rio* 里约热内卢的狂欢节 ◇ *a carnival atmosphere* 狂欢节的气氛 **2** [C] (*NAmE*) = FAIR (1) **3** (*NAmE*) (*BrE* **fete**, **fair**) [C] an outdoor entertainment at which people can play games to win prizes, buy food and drink, etc., usually arranged to make money for a special purpose 露天游乐会；义卖游乐会 **4** [sing.] ~ **of sth** (*formal*) an exciting or brightly coloured mixture of things 激动人心的事物组合；五彩缤纷的事物组合： *this summer's carnival of sport* 今年夏季的体育盛会

car·ni·vore /ˈkɑːnɪvɔː(r); *NAmE* ˈkɑːrn-/ *noun* any animal that eats meat 食肉动物 ➲ COMPARE HERBIVORE, INSECTIVORE, OMNIVORE ▸ **car·ni·vor·ous** /kɑːˈnɪvərəs; *NAmE* kɑːrˈn-/ *adj.*: *a carnivorous diet* 多肉的饮食 ➲ COMPARE OMNIVOROUS

carob /ˈkærəb/ (*also* ˈ**carob tree**) *noun* a southern European tree with dark brown fruit that can be made into a powder that tastes like chocolate 角豆树（产于南欧，果实可制粉，味道似巧克力）

carol /ˈkærəl/ *noun, verb*
■ *noun* (*also* ˈ**Christmas carol**) a Christian religious song sung at Christmas 圣诞颂歌
■ *verb* (**-ll-**, *US* **-l-**) [I, T] ~ (**sth**) | + **speech** to sing sth in a cheerful way 欢乐地唱

ˈ**carol singing** *noun* [U] the singing of Christmas carols especially in a church or outdoors, often to collect money for charity 圣诞报佳音（尤指在教堂或户外唱圣诞颂歌）▸ ˈ**carol singer** *noun*

carom /ˈkærəm/ *verb* [I] (*especially NAmE*) to hit a surface and come off it fast at a different angle 撞击后弹开

car·ot·ene /ˈkærətiːn/ *noun* [U] a red or orange substance found in carrots and other plants 胡萝卜素 ➲ SEE ALSO BETA-CAROTENE

ca·rotid ar·tery /kəˈrɒtɪd ɑːtəri; *NAmE* -ˈrɑːt- ɑːrt-/ *noun* (*anatomy* 解) either of the two large ARTERIES in the neck that carry blood to the head 颈动脉

ca·rouse /kəˈraʊz/ *verb* [I] (*literary*) to spend time drinking alcohol, laughing and enjoying yourself in a noisy way with other people 痛饮狂欢；狂饮作乐

car·ou·sel /ˌkærəˈsel/ *noun* **1** (*especially NAmE*) = MERRY-GO-ROUND (1) ➲ PICTURE AT ROUNDABOUT **2** a moving belt from which you collect your bags at an airport （机场的）行李传送带

carp /kɑːp; *NAmE* kɑːrp/ *noun, verb*
■ *noun* [C, U] (*pl.* **carp**) a large FRESHWATER fish that is used for food 鲤鱼
■ *verb* [I] ~ (**at sb**) (**about sb/sth**) to keep complaining about sb/sth in an annoying way 不停地抱怨；唠叨

car·pal /ˈkɑːpl; *NAmE* ˈkɑːrpl/ *noun* (*anatomy* 解) any of the eight small bones that form the wrist 腕骨

carpal ˈ**tunnel syndrome** *noun* [U] (*medical* 医) a painful condition of the hand and fingers caused by pressure on a nerve because of repeated movements over a long period 腕管综合征（手腕长期受力压迫神经引起手和手指疼痛）

ˈ**car park** *noun* (*BrE*) an area or a building where people can leave their cars 停车场；停车房 ➲ SEE ALSO GARAGE *n.* (1), MULTI-STOREY CAR PARK ➲ COMPARE PARKING LOT

carpe diem /ˌkɑːpeɪ ˈdiːem; ˈdaɪem; *NAmE* ˌkɑːrpeɪ/ *exclamation* (*from Latin*) an expression used when you want to say that sb should not wait, but should take an opportunity as soon as it appears 抓住机遇；把握时机

car·pel /ˈkɑːpl; *NAmE* ˈkɑːrpl/ *noun* (*biology* 生) the part of a plant in which seeds are produced 心皮（植物长出子实的部分）➲ VISUAL VOCAB PAGE V11

car·pen·ter /ˈkɑːpəntə(r); *NAmE* ˈkɑːrp-/ *noun* a person whose job is making and repairing wooden objects and structures 木工；木匠 ➲ COMPARE JOINER

car·pen·try /ˈkɑːpəntri; *NAmE* ˈkɑːrp-/ *noun* [U] **1** the work of a carpenter 木工；木工工艺；木匠活 **2** things made by a carpenter 木工制品；木器；木作

car·pet 🔑 /ˈkɑːpɪt; *NAmE* ˈkɑːrpɪt/ *noun, verb*
■ *noun* **1** 🔑 [U] a thick WOVEN material made of wool, etc. for covering floors or stairs 地毯：*a roll of carpet* 一卷地毯 **2** 🔑 [C] a piece of carpet used as a floor covering, especially when shaped to fit a room（尤指铺满房间的一块）地毯：*to lay a carpet* 铺地毯 ◇ *a bedroom carpet* 卧室地毯 ◇ (*BrE*) *We have* **fitted carpets** (= carpets from wall to wall) *in our house.* 我们家的地上都铺了地毯。➲ VISUAL VOCAB PAGE V24 ➲ SEE ALSO CARPETING (1), RED CARPET, RUG (1) **3** [C] ~ (**of sth**) (*literary*) a thick layer of sth on the ground 覆盖地面的一层厚东西：*a carpet of snow* 一层厚厚的雪

IDM **(be/get called) on the** ˈ**carpet** (*informal, especially NAmE*) called to see sb in authority because you have done sth wrong（因做错事）被上司叫去训斥：*I got called on the carpet for being late.* 我因为迟到被叫去训了一顿。➲ MORE AT SWEEP *v.*

■ *verb* [usually passive] **1** ~ **sth** to cover the floor of a room with a carpet 用地毯铺（房间）的地板：*The hall was carpeted in blue.* 大厅铺上了蓝色的地毯。**2** ~ **sth** (**with/in sth**) (*literary*) to cover sth with a thick layer of sth 把…厚厚地覆盖；厚厚地铺上：*The forest floor was carpeted with wild flowers.* 森林的地面上长满了野花。**3** ~ **sb** (*informal, especially BrE*) to speak angrily to sb because they have done sth wrong 训斥；斥责 SYN **reprimand**

ˈ**carpet bag** *noun* a bag used in the past for carrying your things when travelling （旧时的）毛毡旅行包

car·pet·bag·ger /ˈkɑːpɪtbæɡə(r); *NAmE* ˈkɑːrp-/ *noun* **1** (*disapproving*) a politician who tries to be elected in an area where he or she is not known and is therefore not welcome（在知名度不高的地区参加竞选因而不受当地欢迎的）外来政客 **2** a person from the northern states of the US who went to the South after the Civil War in order to make money or get political power（美国内战后去南方）投机钻营的北方人

ˈ**carpet-bomb** *verb* **1** ~ **sth** to drop a large number of bombs onto every part of an area 对（某地）实行地毯式轰炸 **2** ~ **sb** (*business* 商) to send an advertisement to a very large number of people, especially by email（尤指通过电子邮件）广泛散发广告 ▸ ˈ**carpet-bombing** *noun* [U]

car·pet·ing /ˈkɑːpɪtɪŋ; *NAmE* ˈkɑːrp-/ *noun* **1** [U] carpets in general or the material used for carpets （统称）地毯；地毯织料：*new offices with wall-to-wall carpeting* 房内铺满地毯的新办公室 ◇ (*NAmE*) *We need new carpeting* (= a new carpet) *in the living room.* 我们的起居室里需要铺新地毯了。**2** [C] (*BrE, informal*) an act of speaking angrily to sb because they have done sth wrong 训斥；斥责

ˈ**carpet slipper** *noun* [usually pl.] (*old-fashioned, BrE*) a type of SLIPPER (= a shoe that you wear in the house), with the upper part made of cloth （布面）室内拖鞋；软拖鞋

ˈ**carpet sweeper** *noun* a simple machine for cleaning carpets, with a long handle and brushes that go around 地毯清扫器

ˈ**car pool** *noun* **1** a group of car owners who take turns to drive everyone in the group to work, so that only one car is used at a time 合伙用车的一伙人（一群各自都有汽车的人每次轮流开一辆车送大家上班）**2** (*BrE*) (*also* ˈ**motor pool** *US, BrE*) a group of cars owned by a company or an organization, that its staff can use （公司或机构的）公用车队

car·pool /ˈkɑːpuːl; *NAmE* ˈkɑːr-/ *verb* [I] if a group of people **carpool**, they travel to work together in one car and divide the cost between them 合伙用车；拼车

car·port /ˈkɑːpɔːt; *NAmE* ˈkɑːrpɔːrt/ *noun* a shelter for a car, usually built beside a house and consisting of a roof supported by posts （沿房搭建的）汽车棚

car·rel /ˈkærəl/ *noun* a small area with a desk, separated from other desks by a dividing wall or screen, where one person can work in a library（图书馆内备有书桌供单人用的）研习间

car·riage /ˈkærɪdʒ/ *noun* **1** (*also* **coach**) (*both BrE*) (*NAmE* **car**) [C] a separate section of a train for carrying passengers（火车的）客车厢：*a railway carriage* 铁路客车厢 ➲ WORDFINDER NOTE AT TRAIN ➲ VISUAL VOCAB PAGE V63 **2** [C] a road vehicle, usually with four wheels, that is pulled by one or more horses and was used in the past to carry people（旧时载客的）四轮马车：*a horse-drawn carriage* 四轮马车 **3** (*BrE*) (*also* **hand·ling** *NAmE, BrE*) [U] (*formal*) the act or cost of transporting goods from one place to another 运输；运费：*£16.95 including VAT and carriage* * 16.95 英镑，包含增值税和运费 **4** [C] a moving part of a machine that supports or moves another part, for example on a TYPEWRITER（打字机等机器上的）滑动托架：*a carriage return* (= the act of starting a new line when typing) 回车 **5** [sing.] (*old-fashioned*) the way in which sb holds and moves their head and body 仪态；举止 SYN **bearing** ➲ SEE ALSO BABY CARRIAGE, UNDERCARRIAGE

'carriage clock *noun* a small clock inside a case with a handle on top 带提手的钟

'carriage house (*US*) (*BrE* **'mews house**) *noun* a house in a row of houses converted from stables (= buildings used to keep horses in) 马厩改建的房屋

car·riage·way /'kærɪdʒweɪ/ *noun* (*BrE*) **1** one of the two sides of a MOTORWAY or other large road, used by traffic moving in the same direction （高速公路等的）单方向路：*the eastbound carriageway of the M50* * 50 号高速公路的东向路 ➲ SEE ALSO DUAL CARRIAGEWAY **2** the part of a road intended for vehicles, not people walking, etc. 车行道；行车道 ➲ WORDFINDER NOTE AT ROAD

car·rier /'kæriə(r)/ *noun* **1** a company that carries goods or passengers from one place to another, especially by air （尤指经营空运的）运输公司 **2** a military vehicle or ship that carries soldiers or equipment from one place to another 军用运输车；运输舰；航空母舰：*an armoured personnel carrier* 装甲运兵车 ➲ SEE ALSO AIRCRAFT CARRIER, PEOPLE CARRIER **3** a person or an animal that passes a disease to other people or animals but does not suffer from it 带菌者，病原携带者（自身不受感染而传播疾病的人或动物） **4** a metal frame that is fixed to a bicycle and used for carrying bags （自行车的）载物架 **5** a person or thing that carries sth 搬运人；运送人；运输工具：*Aquarius, the Water Carrier* 宝瓶座 ◇ *a baby carrier* (= for carrying a baby on your back or in front of you) （用于前胸或后背的）婴儿背带 **6** (*BrE*) = CARRIER BAG **7** a company that provides a telephone or Internet service 电话公司；互联网公司；通信公司：*a telecoms carrier* 通信公司

'carrier bag (*also* **car·rier**) (*both BrE*) (*NAmE* **'shopping bag**) *noun* a paper or plastic bag for carrying shopping （纸或塑料的）购物袋，手提袋 ➲ VISUAL VOCAB PAGE V36

'carrier pigeon *noun* a PIGEON (= a type of bird) that has been trained to carry messages 信鸽

car·rion /'kæriən/ *noun* [U] the decaying flesh of dead animals （死动物的）腐肉：*crows feeding on carrion* 以腐肉为食的乌鸦 ➲ VISUAL VOCAB PAGE V12

'carrion crow *noun* a type of medium-sized CROW 小嘴乌鸦

car·rot 🔑 /'kærət/ *noun* **1** 🔑 [U, C] a long pointed orange root vegetable 胡萝卜：*grated carrot* 擦成丝的胡萝卜 ◇ *a pound of carrots* 一磅胡萝卜 ➲ VISUAL VOCAB PAGE V34 **2** [C] a reward promised to sb in order to persuade them to do sth （为说服人做事所许诺的）酬报，好处 SYN **incentive**：*They are holding out a carrot of $120 million in economic aid.* 他们许诺给予 1.2 亿美元的经济援助。

IDM **the carrot and (the) stick (approach)** if you use the **carrot and stick approach**, you persuade sb to try harder by offering them a reward if they do, or a punishment if they do not 胡萝卜加大棒；威逼利诱

car·roty /'kærəti/ *adj.* (*sometimes disapproving*) (of hair 头发) orange in colour 胡萝卜色的；橘红色的

carry 🔑 /'kæri/ *verb* (**car·ries**, **carry·ing**, **car·ried**, **car·ried**)

• **TAKE WITH YOU** 带走 **1** 🔑 [T] **~ sb/sth** to support the weight of sb/sth and take them or it from place to place; to take sb/sth from one place to another 拿；提；搬；扛；背；抱；运送：*He was carrying a suitcase.* 他提着一个手提箱。◇ *She carried her baby in her arms.* 她怀里抱着她的婴儿。◇ *The injured were carried away on stretchers.* 伤员用担架抬走了。◇ *a train carrying commuters to work* 运送上班乘客的市郊往返列车 **2** 🔑 [T] **~ sth** to have sth with you and take it wherever you go 携带；佩带：*Police in many countries carry guns.* 许多国家的警察都带枪。◇ *I never carry much money on me.* 我身上从不多带钱。

• **OF PIPES/WIRES** 管道；线路 **3** 🔑 [T] **~ sth** to contain and direct the flow of water, electricity, etc. 输送，传输，传送（水、电等）：*a pipeline carrying oil* 输油管道 ◇ *The veins carry blood to the heart.* 静脉把血液输送到心脏。

• **DISEASE** 疾病 **4** [T] **~ sth** if a person, an insect, etc. **carries** a disease, they are infected with it and might spread it to others although they might not become sick themselves 传播；传染：*Ticks can carry a nasty disease which affects humans.* 蜱可传播危害人类的严重疾病。

• **REMEMBER** 记忆 **5** [T] **~ sth in your head/mind** to be able to remember sth 能记住；能回想起

• **SUPPORT WEIGHT** 承重 **6** [T] **~ sth** to support the weight of sth 支撑；承载：*A road bridge has to carry a lot of traffic.* 公路桥必须承载很多来往车辆。

• **RESPONSIBILITY** 责任 **7** [T] **~ sth** to accept responsibility for sth; to suffer the results of sth 承担（责任）；承受（结果）：*He is carrying the department* (= it is only working because of his efforts). 他支撑着这个部门的工作。◇ *Their group was targeted to* **carry the burden** *of job losses.* 他们那个小组被选中成为裁员的目标。

• **HAVE AS QUALITY/FEATURE** 具有品质 / 特点 **8** [T] **~ sth** to have sth as a quality or feature 具有（某品质或特点）：*Her speech carried the ring of authority.* 她的讲话带着权威的口吻。◇ *My views don't* **carry much weight** *with* (= have much influence on) *the boss.* 我的意见对老板起不了多少作用。◇ *Each bike carries a ten-year guarantee.* 每辆自行车保修十年。 **9** [T] **~ sth** to have sth as a result 带有，带来（某种结果或后果）：*Crimes of violence carry heavy penalties.* 暴力犯罪要受到严惩。◇ *Being a combat sport, karate* **carries with it** *the risk of injury.* 作为一项格斗运动，空手道有受伤的风险。

• **OF THROW/KICK** 扔；踢 **10** [I] **+ noun + adv./prep.** if sth that is thrown, kicked, etc. **carries** a particular distance, it travels that distance before stopping 扔（或踢等）到…距离：*The fullback's kick carried 50 metres into the crowd.* 后卫一脚把球踢出 50 米远，落入人群中。

• **OF SOUND** 声音 **11** [I] **(+ adv./prep.)** if a sound **carries**, it can be heard a long distance away 传得很远

• **TAKE TO PLACE/POSITION** 带到…地方 / 位置 **12** [T] **~ sth/sb to/into sth** to take sth/sb to a particular point or in a particular direction 使向…前进；把…推进到：*The war was carried into enemy territory.* 战争已推进到敌方境内。◇ *Her abilities carried her to the top of her profession.* 她的才能使她在本行业中出类拔萃。

• **APPROVAL/SUPPORT** 赞成；支持 **13** [T, usually passive] **~ sth** to approve of sth by more people voting for it than against it（以票数多出）通过：*The resolution was carried by 340 votes to 210.* 这项决议以 340 票对 210 票获得通过。 **14** [T] to win the support or sympathy of sb; to persuade people to accept your argument 赢得…支持（或同情）；劝说…接受论点：**~ sb** *His moving speech was enough to carry the audience.* 他感人的演讲足以赢得听众的支持。◇ **~ sth** *She nodded in agreement, and he saw he had carried his point.* 她同意地点点头，他明白他的话已收到效果。

• **HAVE LABEL** 有标签 **15** [T] **~ sth** to have a particular label or piece of information attached 贴有（标签）；附有（信息）：*Cigarettes carry a health warning.* 香烟上标注着有害健康的警告。

• **NEWS STORY** 新闻报道 **16** [T] **~ sth** if a newspaper or broadcast **carries** a particular story, it publishes or broadcasts it 刊登；登载；播出；报道

• **ITEM IN STORE** 商店商品 **17** [T] **~ sth** if a shop/store **carries** a particular item, it has it for sale 销售；出售：*We* **carry a range** *of educational software.* 我们出售各种教育软件。

• **BABY** 婴儿 **18** [T] **be carrying sb** to be pregnant with sb 怀孕；怀胎：*She was carrying twins.* 她怀上了双胞胎。

• **YOURSELF** 自己 **19** [T] **~ yourself + adv./prep.** to hold or move your head or body in a particular way 保持姿态；做姿势：*to carry yourself well* 姿势正确

• **ADDING NUMBERS** 加法 **20** [T] **~ sth** to add a number to the next column on the left when adding up numbers, for example when the numbers add up to more than ten 进位

IDM **be/get carried aˈway** to get very excited or lose control of your feelings 变得很激动；失去自制力： *I got carried away and started shouting at the television.* 我激动得不能自持，冲着电视机大叫起来。 **carry all/everything beˈfore you** to be completely successful 全胜；大获成功 **carry the ˈball** (*US, informal*) to take responsibility for getting sth done 承担责任： *My co-worker was sick, so I had to carry the ball.* 我的搭档病了，所以我得负起全责。 **carry the ˈcan (for sb/sth)** (*BrE, informal*) to accept the blame for sth, especially when it is not your fault 承受责难；（尤指）代人受过，背黑锅 **carry a torch for sb** to be in love with sb, especially sb who does not love you in return 爱上（尤指单相思）；痴恋 ➲ MORE AT DAY, FAR *adv.*, FAST *adv.*, FETCH

PHR V **ˌcarry sb ˈback (to sth)** to make sb remember a time in the past 使回想起；使回忆： *The smell of the sea carried her back to her childhood.* 大海的气息勾起了她童年的回忆。 **ˌcarry sth↔ˈforward** (*also* **ˌcarry sth↔ˈover**) to move a total amount from one column or page to the next 把总金额转入次栏（或次页）；过账；结转 **ˌcarry sth↔ˈoff 1** to win sth 赢得；获得： *He carried off most of the prizes.* 他赢得了大多数的奖项。 **2** to succeed in doing sth that most people would find difficult 成功地对付，不费劲地处理（大多数人认为难以应付的事）： *She's had her hair cut really short, but she can carry it off.* 她把头发剪得非常短，但她还是驾驭得了这种发型。 **ˌcarry ˈon 1** 🔑 (*especially BrE*) to continue moving 继续移动： *Carry on until you get to the junction, then turn left.* 继续往前走到交叉路口，然后向左转。 **2** (*informal*) to argue or complain noisily 争吵；吵闹；吵闹地抱怨： *He was shouting and carrying on.* 他在大吵大闹。 ➲ RELATED NOUN CARRY-ON **ˌcarry ˈon (with sth)** | **ˌcarry sth↔ˈon** 🔑 to continue doing sth 继续做；坚持干： *Carry on with your work while I'm away.* 我不在时你要接着干。 ◇ *After he left I just tried to carry on as normal* (= do the things I usually do). 他离开后，我就像往常一样继续努力干。 ◇ *Carry on the good work!* 干得不错，继续努力吧！ ◇ **carry on doing sth** *He carried on peeling the potatoes.* 他不停地削土豆皮。 **ˌcarry ˈon (with sb)** (*old-fashioned*) to have a sexual relationship with sb when you should not （与…）有不正当的男女关系： *His wife found out he'd been carrying on with another woman.* 他的妻子发现他和另一个女人勾勾搭搭。 **ˌcarry sth↔ˈout 1** 🔑 to do sth that you have said you will do or have been asked to do 履行；实施；执行；落实： *to carry out a promise/a threat/a plan/an order* 把承诺/威胁/计划/命令付诸行动 **2** 🔑 to do and complete a task 完成（任务）： *to carry out an inquiry/an investigation/a survey* 进行查询/调查/考察 ◇ *Extensive tests have been carried out on the patient.* 已对患者进行了全面检查。 **ˌcarry ˈover** to continue to exist in a different situation （在不同情况下）继续存在，保持下去： *Attitudes learned at home carry over into the playground.* 家里养成的作风会表现在游戏场上。 **ˌcarry sth↔ˈover 1** to keep sth from one situation and use it or deal with it in a different situation 运用；应用 **2** to delay sth until a later time 延迟；延期： *The match had to be carried over until Sunday.* 比赛不得不推迟到星期天。 **3** = CARRY STH↔FORWARD **ˌcarry sb ˈthrough** | **ˌcarry sb ˈthrough sth** to help sb to survive a difficult period 帮助…渡过难关： *His determination carried him through the ordeal.* 他靠坚强的信心渡过了难关。 **ˌcarry sth ˈthrough** to complete sth successfully 成功完成；顺利实现： *It's a difficult job but she's the person to carry it through.* 这是一项艰巨的工作，但她这个人是能够顺利完成的。 **ˌcarry ˈthrough (on/with sth)** (*NAmE*) to do what you have said you will do 履行（承诺）： *He has proved he can carry through on his promises.* 他已证明他能履行自己的诺言。

carry·cot /ˈkærikɒt; *NAmE* -kɑːt/ *noun* (*BrE*) a small bed for a baby, with handles at the sides so you can carry it 手提式婴儿床 ➲ PICTURE AT PUSHCHAIR

ˈcarry-on *noun* **1** [usually sing.] (*BrE, informal*) a display of excitement, anger or silly behaviour over sth unimportant （对小事的）大惊小怪，歇斯底里发作，愚蠢的举动： *What a carry-on!* 真是大惊小怪！ **2** (*NAmE*) a small bag or case that you carry onto a plane with you （可随身携带上飞机的）小包，小行李箱： *Only one carry-on is allowed.* 随身只能携带一个小包。 ◇ *carry-on baggage* 随身携带的行李

ˈcarry-out *noun* (*US, ScotE*) = TAKEAWAY : *Let's get a carry-out.* 咱们叫份儿外卖吧。 ◇ *carry-out coffees* 外卖咖啡

ˈcarry-over *noun* **1** [usually sing.] something that remains or results from a situation in the past 保存的事物；遗留下的东西；影响；结果： *His neatness is a carry-over from his army days.* 他爱整洁的习惯是他当兵时养成的。 **2** an amount of money that has not been used and so can be used later 结转下期的款项： *The £20 million included a £7 million carry-over from last year's underspend.* 这笔 2 000 万英镑的款项包括了去年结转的 700 万英镑。

ˈcar seat *noun* **1** (*also* **ˈchild seat**) a special safety seat for a child, that can be fitted into a car （可安装在汽车上的）儿童安全座椅 **2** a seat in a car 汽车座位

car·sick /ˈkɑːsɪk; *NAmE* ˈkɑːrsɪk/ *adj.* [not usually before noun] feeling ill/sick because you are travelling in a car 晕车： *Do you get carsick?* 你晕车吗？ ▶ **car·sick·ness** *noun* [U]

cart /kɑːt; *NAmE* kɑːrt/ *noun, verb*

■ ***noun* 1** a vehicle with two or four wheels that is pulled by a horse and used for carrying loads （两轮或四轮）运货马车： *a horse and cart* 一套马车 **2** (*also* **hand·cart**) a light vehicle with wheels that you pull or push by hand 手推车；手拉车 **3** (*NAmE*) (*BrE* **trol·ley**) a small vehicle with wheels that can be pushed or pulled along and is used for carrying things 手推车；手拉车： *a baggage cart* 行李车 ◇ *a serving cart* 上菜手推车 **4** (*especially NAmE*) = SHOPPING CART : *Add to cart.* 加入购物车。 **5** (*NAmE*) (*BrE* **buggy**) a small car, often without a roof or doors, used for a particular purpose （常指无顶无门的）专用小汽车： *a golf cart* 高尔夫球具车

IDM **put the ˌcart before the ˈhorse** to put or do things in the wrong order 本末倒置；因果倒置

■ ***verb* 1 ~ sth (+ adv./prep.)** to carry sth in a cart or other vehicle 用马车运送；用车装运： *The rubbish is then carted away for recycling.* 垃圾接着被运去作回收处理。 **2 ~ sth + adv./prep.** (*informal*) to carry sth that is large, heavy or awkward in your hands 用手提（笨重物品）： *We had to cart our luggage up six flights of stairs.* 我们得把行李提着上六段楼梯。 **3 ~ sb + adv./prep.** (*informal*) to take sb somewhere, especially with difficulty 强行带走；抓走： *The demonstrators were carted off to the local police station.* 示威游行者被强行带到当地的警察局。

carte blanche /ˌkɑːt ˈblɑ̃ʃ; *NAmE* ˌkɑːrt/ *noun* [U] (*from French*) **~ (to do sth)** the complete freedom or authority to do whatever you like 自由行使权；全权

car·tel /kɑːˈtel; *NAmE* kɑːrˈtel/ *noun* [C+sing./pl. v.] a group of separate companies that agree to increase profits by fixing prices and not competing with each other 卡特尔，企业联盟（通过统一价格、防止竞争来增加共同利润）

Car·te·sian /kɑːˈtiːziən; -ʒən; *NAmE* kɑːrˈt-/ *adj.* connected with the French PHILOSOPHER Descartes and his ideas about philosophy and mathematics （法国哲学家和数学家）笛卡尔的；笛卡尔主义的

cart·horse /ˈkɑːthɔːs; *NAmE* ˈkɑːrthɔːrs/ *noun* a large strong horse used especially in the past for heavy work on farms （尤指旧时在农场干重活的）强壮高大的马

car·til·age /ˈkɑːtɪlɪdʒ; *NAmE* ˈkɑːrt-/ *noun* [U, C] the strong white TISSUE that is important in support and especially in joints to prevent the bones rubbing against each other 软骨 ➲ VISUAL VOCAB PAGE V64

car·ti·la·gin·ous /ˌkɑːtɪˈlædʒɪnəs; *NAmE* ˌkɑːrt-/ *adj.* (*anatomy* 解) made of cartilage 软骨的；软骨构成的

cart·load /ˈkɑːtləʊd; *NAmE* ˈkɑːrtloʊd/ *noun* **1** the amount of sth that fills a CART 一大车的装载量 **2** [usually pl.] (*informal*) a large amount of sth 大量；大批

car·tog·raph·er /kɑːˈtɒɡrəfə(r); *NAmE* kɑːrˈtɑːɡ-/ *noun* a person who draws or makes maps 制图员；地图绘制员

car·tog·raphy /kɑːˈtɒɡrəfi; *NAmE* kɑːrˈtɑːɡ-/ *noun* [U] the art or process of drawing or making maps 制图学；地图绘制 ▸ **carto·graph·ic** /ˌkɑːtəˈɡræfɪk; *NAmE* ˌkɑːrt-/ *adj.*

car·ton /ˈkɑːtn; *NAmE* ˈkɑːrtn/ *noun* **1** a light cardboard or plastic box or pot for holding goods, especially food or liquid; the contents of a carton（尤指装食品或液体的）硬纸盒，塑料盒，塑料罐；硬纸盒（或塑料盒）所装物品：*a milk carton/a carton of milk* 牛奶盒；一盒牛奶 ➲ VISUAL VOCAB PAGE V36 **2** (*NAmE*) a large container in which goods are packed in smaller containers（内装小盒的）大包装盒：*a carton of cigarettes* 一条香烟

car·toon /kɑːˈtuːn; *NAmE* kɑːrˈt-/ *noun* **1** an amusing drawing in a newspaper or magazine, especially one about politics or events in the news（报刊中尤与政治或时事有关的）漫画，讽刺画 ➲ EXPRESS YOURSELF AT DESCRIBE **2** = COMIC STRIP **3** (*also* ˌ**animated carˈtoon**) a film/movie made by photographing a series of gradually changing drawings or models, so that they look as if they are moving 动画片；卡通片：*a Walt Disney cartoon* 迪士尼动画片 ◇ *a cartoon character* 动画片人物 **4** (*specialist*) a drawing made by an artist as a preparation for a painting 草图；底图

car·toon·ist /kɑːˈtuːnɪst; *NAmE* kɑːrˈt-/ *noun* a person who draws cartoons 漫画家；动画片画家

car·touche /kɑːˈtuːʃ; *NAmE* kɑːr-/ *noun* an OBLONG or OVAL shape which contains a set of ancient Egyptian HIEROGLYPHS, often representing the name and title of a king or queen（常印有古埃及国王或王后名号的）象形文字长方形（或椭圆）图框

cart·ridge /ˈkɑːtrɪdʒ; *NAmE* ˈkɑːrt-/ *noun* **1** (*NAmE also* **shell**) a tube or case containing EXPLOSIVE and a bullet or SHOT, for shooting from a gun 枪弹；子弹 **2** a case containing sth that is used in a machine, for example film for a camera, ink for a printer, etc. Cartridges are put into the machine and can be removed and replaced when they are finished or empty. 胶片盒；暗盒；墨盒 **3** a thin tube containing ink which you put inside a pen（钢笔的）笔芯，墨水囊

ˈ**cartridge paper** *noun* [U] (*BrE*) thick strong paper for drawing on 绘画纸；图画纸

ˈ**cart track** *noun* (*BrE*) a rough track that is not suitable for ordinary cars, etc.（崎岖不平的）马车道，大车道

cart·wheel /ˈkɑːtwiːl; *NAmE* ˈkɑːrt-/ *noun* **1** a fast physical movement in which you turn in a circle sideways by putting your hands on the ground and bringing your legs, one at a time, over your head 侧手翻；侧身筋斗：*to do/turn cartwheels* 做侧手翻 **2** the wheel of a CART（马车或手推车）车轮 ▸ **cart·wheel** *verb* [I]

carve /kɑːv; *NAmE* kɑːrv/ *verb* **1** [T, I] to make objects, patterns, etc. by cutting away material from wood or stone 雕刻：**~ sth** *a carved doorway* 雕花的门道 ◇ **~ sth from/out of sth** *The statue was carved out of a single piece of stone.* 这座雕像是用整块石料雕成的。◇ **~ sth into/in sth** *The wood had been carved into the shape of a flower.* 木头雕成了花朵状。◇ **~ in sth** *She carves in both stone and wood.* 她既做石雕也做木雕。 ➲ COLLOCATIONS AT ART **2** [T] **~ sth (on sth)** to write sth on a surface by cutting into it 刻：*They carved their initials on the desk.* 他们把自己姓名的首字母刻在书桌上。 **3** [T, I] to cut a large piece of cooked meat into smaller pieces for eating 把（熟肉）切成块：**~ (sth) | ~ (sb) sth** *Who's going to carve the turkey?* 谁来把火鸡切成小块？ **4** [T, no passive] to work hard in order to have a successful career, reputation, etc. 艰苦创业；奋斗取得（事业、名声等）：**~ sth (out)** *He succeeded in carving out a career in the media.* 他在传媒界闯出了一片天地。◇ **~ sth (out) for yourself** *She has carved a place for herself in the fashion world.* 她已在时装界谋得一席之地。 IDM SEE STONE *n.*

PHR V ˌ**carve sth↔ˈup** (*disapproving*) to divide a company, an area of land, etc. into smaller parts in order to share it between people 划分；瓜分

car·very /ˈkɑːvəri; *NAmE* ˈkɑːrv-/ *noun* (*pl.* **-ies**) (*BrE*) a restaurant that serves ROAST meat 烤肉餐馆

ˈ**carve-up** *noun* [sing.] (*BrE, informal, disapproving*) the dividing of sth such as a company or a country into separate parts 划分；瓜分

carv·ing /ˈkɑːvɪŋ; *NAmE* ˈkɑːrvɪŋ/ *noun* **1** [C, U] an object or a pattern made by cutting away material from wood or stone 雕刻品；雕刻图案；雕像 **2** [U] the art of making objects in this way 雕刻术 ➲ VISUAL VOCAB PAGE V45

ˈ**carving knife** *noun* a large sharp knife for cutting cooked meat 切（熟）肉刀 ➲ VISUAL VOCAB PAGE V27

ˈ**car wash** *noun* a place with special equipment, where you can pay to have your car washed 洗车处；洗车场

cary·atid /ˌkæriˈætɪd/ *noun* (*architecture* 建) a statue of a female figure used as a supporting PILLAR in a building 女像柱

Casa·nova /ˌkæsəˈnəʊvə; ˌkæzə-; *NAmE* -ˈnoʊvə/ *noun* a man who has sex with a lot of women 浪荡公子；风流浪子 ➲ MORE LIKE THIS 17, page R27 ORIGIN From Giovanni Jacopo Casanova, an Italian man in the 18th century who was famous for having sex with many women. 源自卡萨诺瓦（Giovanni Jacopo Casanova)。这名 18 世纪的意大利人以放荡不羁的生活而闻名。

cas·bah = KASBAH

cas·cade /kæˈskeɪd/ *noun, verb*

■ *noun* **1** a small WATERFALL, especially one of several falling down a steep slope with rocks 小瀑布（尤指一连串瀑布中的一支） **2** a large amount of water falling or pouring down 倾泻；流注：*a cascade of rainwater* 如注的雨水 **3** (*formal*) a large amount of sth hanging down 大簇的下垂物：*Her hair tumbled in a cascade down her back.* 她的长发瀑布般地倾泻在后背上。 **4** (*formal*) a large number of things falling or coming quickly at the same time 倾泻（或涌出）的东西：*He crashed to the ground in a cascade of oil cans.* 他随着一连串的油桶跌落坠地。

■ *verb* **1** [I] + **adv./prep.** to flow downwards in large amounts 倾泻；流注：*Water cascaded down the mountainside.* 水从山腰倾泻而下。 **2** [I] + **adv./prep.** (*formal*) to fall or hang in large amounts 大量落下；大量垂悬：*Blonde hair cascaded over her shoulders.* 她的金发像瀑布似的披落在肩头。

case 🔑 /keɪs/ *noun, verb*

■ *noun*

• **SITUATION** 情况 **1** 🔑 [C] a particular situation or a situation of a particular type 具体情况；事例；实例：*In some cases people have had to wait several weeks for an appointment.* 在某些情况下，人们必须等上好几周才能得到约见。◇ *The company only dismisses its employees in cases of gross misconduct.* 这家公司只有在雇员严重渎职时才予以解聘。◇ *It's a* **classic case** (= a very typical case) *of bad planning.* 这是计划不当的一个典型事例。 ➲ SEE ALSO WORST-CASE ➲ SYNONYMS AT EXAMPLE, SITUATION **2** 🔑 **the case** [sing.] **~ (that...)** the true situation 实情；事实：*If that is the case* (= if the situation described is true), *we need more staff.* 如果真是那样，那我们就需要更多的员工了。◇ *It is simply not the case that prison conditions are improving.* 监狱条件得到改善的情况绝非事实。 **3** 🔑 [C, usually sing.] a situation that relates to a particular person or thing 特殊情况：*In your case, we are prepared to be lenient.* 根据你的情况，我们可以从宽处理。◇ *I cannot make an exception in your case* (= for you and not for others). 我不能对你破例。◇ *Every application will be decided* **on a case-by-case basis** (= each one will be considered separately). 各项申请将根据各自情况逐一审定。 ➲ SYNONYMS AT EXAMPLE

• **POLICE INVESTIGATION** 警方调查 **4** 🔑 [C] a matter that is being officially investigated, especially by the police（尤指警方）侦查的案情，调查的案件：*a murder case* 谋杀案 ◇ *a case of theft* 盗窃案 ➲ COLLOCATIONS AT CRIME

• **IN COURT** 法院 **5** 🔑 [C] a question to be decided in court 待裁决的案件：*The case will be heard next week.* 此案下周审理。◇ *a court case* 诉讼案件 ◇ *to win/lose a case* 胜诉；败诉 ➲ SEE ALSO TEST CASE

• **ARGUMENTS** 论据 **6** [C, usually sing.] ~ (**for/against sth**) a set of facts or arguments that support one side in a trial, a discussion, etc. （在审判、讨论等中支持一方的）论据，理由，辩词：*the **case for the defence/prosecution*** 有利于被告 / 原告的论据 ◇ *Our lawyer didn't think we **had a case*** (= had enough good arguments to win in a court of law). 我们的律师认为我们论据不足，无法赢得官司。◇ *the **case for/against** private education* 赞成 / 反对实行私立学校教育的理由 ◇ *The report **makes out a strong case*** (= gives good arguments) *for spending more money on hospitals.* 报告充分阐明了增加医院经费的理由。◇ *You will each be given the chance to **state your case**.* 你们每人都有机会陈述理由。

• **CONTAINER** 容器 **7** [C] (often in compounds 常构成复合词) a container or covering used to protect or store things; a container with its contents or the amount that it contains 容器；箱；盒；套；罩；容器及内装物；（容器的）容量：*a pencil case* 铅笔盒 ◇ *a jewellery case* 首饰盒 ◇ *a packing case* (= a large wooden box for packing things in) 包装箱 ◇ *The museum was full of stuffed animals in glass cases.* 博物馆摆满了放在玻璃柜里的动物标本。◇ *a case* (= 12 bottles) *of champagne* 一箱（12 瓶）香槟酒 ➲ PICTURE AT CLOCK ➲ SEE ALSO VANITY CASE **8** [C] = SUITCASE：*Let me carry your case for you.* 我来帮你提箱子吧。

• **OF DISEASE** 疾病 **9** [C] the fact of sb having a disease or an injury; a person suffering from a disease or an injury 病例；病案；病人；伤员：*a severe case of typhoid* 伤寒重病例 ◇ *The most serious cases were treated at the scene of the accident.* 受伤最严重的人在事故现场就得到了救治。

• **PERSON** 人 **10** [C] a person who needs, or is thought to need, special treatment or attention （需特别对待或注意的）人：*He's a hopeless case.* 他是无可救药了。

• **GRAMMAR** 语法 **11** [C, U] the form of a noun, an adjective or a pronoun in some languages, that shows its relationship to another word 格（某些语言中表示名词、形容词或代词与另一词关系的形式）：*the **nominative/accusative/genitive case*** 主格；宾格；所有格 ◇ *Latin nouns have case, number and gender.* 拉丁语名词有格、数和性。 ➲ WORDFINDER NOTE AT GRAMMAR

IDM **as the ˌcase may ˈbe** used to say that one of two or more possibilities is true, but which one is true depends on the circumstances 根据具体情况；视情况而定：*There may be an announcement about this tomorrow—or not, as the case may be.* 这件事明天可能有个声明，也可能没有，那要看情况了。 **be on sb's ˈcase** (*informal*) to criticize sb all the time 不停地指责某人：*She's always on my case about cleaning my room.* 她老是对我的房间需要打扫的事指责个没完。 **be on the ˈcase** to be dealing with a particular matter, especially a criminal investigation 处理事件（尤指刑事侦查）：*We have two agents on the case.* 我们有两名探员在侦查此案。 **get off my ˈcase** (*informal*) used to tell sb to stop criticizing you 别再批评我 **a case in ˈpoint** a clear example of the problem, situation, etc. that is being discussed 明证；恰当的例证 ➲ LANGUAGE BANK AT E.G. **in ˈany case** whatever happens or may have happened 无论如何；不管怎样：*There's no point complaining now—we're leaving tomorrow in any case.* 现在抱怨毫无意义，不管怎样我们明天都要离开。 **(just) in case (...)** because of the possibility of sth happening 以防；以防万一：*You'd better take the keys in case I'm out.* 你最好带上钥匙以防我不在家。◇ *You probably won't need to call—but take my number, just in case.* 你很可能无需打电话，不过还是记下我的电话号码吧，以防万一。◇ *In case* (= if it is true that) *you're wondering why Jo's here—let me explain...* 我来解释一下吧，免得你奇怪乔为什么在这儿。 **in case of sth** (often on official notices 常用于正式通知) if sth happens 如果；假使：*In case of fire, ring the alarm bell.* 如遇火警，即按警铃。 **in ˈthat case** if that happens or has happened; if that is the situation 既然那样；假使那样的话：*'I've made up my mind.' 'In that case, there's no point discussing it.'* "我已经拿定主意了。" "既然如此，讨论这件事就毫无意义了。" ➲ MORE AT DOG *n.*, REST *v.*

■***verb***

IDM **case the joint** (*informal*) to look carefully around a building so that you can plan how to steal things from it at a later time （为日后行窃）踩点，踩道，探路

case·book /ˈkeɪsbʊk/ *noun* a written record kept by doctors, lawyers, etc. of cases they have dealt with （医生、律师等保存的）书面记录，病历，案卷

cased /keɪst/ *adj.* ~ **in sth** completely covered with a particular material 用…完全覆盖的：*The towers are made of steel cased in granite.* 这些塔楼是钢结构，花岗岩贴面。 ➲ SEE ALSO CASING

ˌcase ˈhistory *noun* a record of a person's background, past illnesses, etc. that a doctor or SOCIAL WORKER studies （医生用的）病历；（社会工作者用的）个案史

ˈcase law *noun* [U] (*law* 律) law based on decisions made by judges in earlier cases 判例法，案例法（以已往的判例为依据的法律） ➲ COMPARE COMMON LAW, STATUTE LAW ➲ SEE ALSO TEST CASE

case·load /ˈkeɪsləʊd; *NAmE* -loʊd/ *noun* all the people that a doctor, SOCIAL WORKER, etc. is responsible for at one time（医生、社会工作者等负责的）个案总量，总人数，工作量：*a heavy caseload* (= a large number of people) 繁重的工作量

case·ment /ˈkeɪsmənt/ (*also* **ˌcasement ˈwindow**) *noun* a window that opens on HINGES like a door 平开窗；竖铰链窗；门式窗 ➲ VISUAL VOCAB PAGE V18

ˌcase-ˈsensitive *adj.* (*computing* 计) a program which is **case-sensitive** recognizes the difference between capital letters and small letters （程序）能识别大小写字母的，区分大小写的

ˈcase study *noun* a detailed account of the development of a person, a group of people or a situation over a period of time 个案研究；专题研究；案例研究

case·work /ˈkeɪswɜːk; *NAmE* -wɜːrk/ *noun* [U] social work (= work done to help people in the community with special needs) involving the study of a particular person's family and background 社会工作（指帮助社区特殊困难者）

case·work·er /ˈkeɪswɜːkə(r); *NAmE* -wɜːrk-/ *noun* (*especially NAmE*) a SOCIAL WORKER who helps a particular person or family in the community with special needs 社会工作者（帮助社区特殊困难者）

cash /kæʃ/ *noun, verb*

■***noun*** [U] **1** money in the form of coins or notes/bills 现金：*How much cash do you have on you?* 你身上带着多少现金？◇ *Payments can be made by card or **in cash**.* 用卡或现金付款均可。◇ *Customers are offered a 10% discount if they **pay cash**.* 顾客若付现金，可获九折优惠。◇ *The thieves stole £500 **in cash**.* 小偷盗走 500 英镑现金。 ➲ COLLOCATIONS AT FINANCE ➲ PICTURE AT MONEY ➲ SEE ALSO HARD CASH, PETTY CASH ➲ SYNONYMS AT MONEY **2** (*informal*) money in any form（任何形式的）金钱，资金：*The museum needs to find ways of raising cash.* 博物馆需要找到募集资金的途径。◇ *I'm short of cash right now.* 我眼下正缺钱。◇ *I'm constantly **strapped for cash*** (= without enough money). 我总是缺钱。

IDM **cash ˈdown** (*BrE*) (*also* **ˌcash up ˈfront** *NAmE, BrE*) with immediate payment of cash 即付现款；即期付款：*to pay for sth cash down* 用现款支付 **ˌcash in ˈhand** (*BrE, informal*) if you pay for goods and services **cash in hand**, you pay in cash, especially so that the person being paid can avoid paying tax on the amount 现金支付（尤指受款人可避税） **ˌcash on deˈlivery** (*abbr.* **COD**) a system of paying for goods when they are delivered 货到付款；交货付现

■***verb*** ~ **a cheque/check** to exchange a cheque/check for the amount of money that it is worth 兑现支票

IDM **cash in your ˈchips** (*informal*) to die 死

PHR V **ˌcash ˈin (on sth)** (*disapproving*) to gain an advantage for yourself from a situation, especially in a way that other people think is wrong or immoral 从中牟利；捞到好处：*The film studio is being accused of cashing in on the singer's death.* 那家电影制片厂被指责利用这位歌手的死来赚钱。 **ˌcash sth↔ˈin** to exchange sth, such as an insurance policy, for money before the date on which it would normally end 把（保险单等）提前兑成现金 ˌ**cash ˈup** (*BrE*) (*NAmE* ˌ**cash ˈout**) to add up the amount of money that has been received in a shop/store, club, etc., especially at the end of the day（商店、俱乐部等在每天营业结束时）结算当日进款

ˌ**cash and ˈcarry** *noun* [C, U] a large WHOLESALE shop/store that sells goods in large quantities at low prices to customers from other businesses who pay in cash and take the goods away themselves; the system of buying and selling goods in this way 现款自运批发商店；付现自运批发

cash·back (*BrE*) (*US* **cash-back**) /ˈkæʃbæk/ *noun* **1** [U] if you ask for **cashback** when you are paying for goods in a shop/store with a DEBIT CARD (= a plastic card that takes money directly from your bank account), you get a sum of money in cash, that is added to your bill 现金提取（指借记卡持有者可在商店刷卡付账时提取小额现金，此现金附加在购物账单上） **2** [U, C] a sum of money that is offered to people who buy particular products or services（购买某些特定商品或支付某些特定服务费时的）现金返还，现金折扣： *There's £200 cashback on this computer if you buy before January 31.* 在 1 月 31 日前购买这台电脑可获得 200 英镑的现金返还。

ˈ**cash bar** *noun* a bar at a wedding, party, etc., at which the guests have to pay for their own drinks rather than getting them free（婚礼、聚会等场合的）售饮料柜台

ˈ**cash box** *noun* a box with a lock for keeping money in, usually made of metal 钱箱；银箱

ˈ**cash card** *noun* (*BrE*) (*US* **ATˈM card**) a plastic card used to get money from a CASH MACHINE (= a machine in or outside a bank) 现金卡；自动取款卡 ➲ COMPARE CREDIT CARD, DEBIT CARD

ˈ**cash cow** *noun* (*business* 商) the part of a business that always makes a profit and that provides money for the rest of the business 金牛，摇钱树，赢利部门（一企业中始终赢利并给其他部门提供资金的部门）

ˈ**cash crop** *noun* a crop grown for selling, rather than for use by the person who grows it 商品作物；经济作物 ➲ COMPARE SUBSISTENCE

ˈ**cash desk** *noun* (*BrE*) the place in a shop/store where you pay for goods that you have bought 收款处；收银台

ˈ**cash dispenser** *noun* (*BrE*) = CASH MACHINE

ˌ**cashed ˈup** *adj.* (*informal, especially AustralE*) very rich 有大把钱的；富得流油的： *Mark was cashed up that night, so he got the drinks.* 马克那天晚上有一大笔钱，所以酒都归他买了。◇ *support from cashed-up investors* 腰缠万贯的投资者的资助

cashew /ˈkæʃuː; kæˈʃuː/ (*also* ˈ**cashew nut**) *noun* the small curved nut of the tropical American **cashew tree**, used in cooking and often eaten salted with alcoholic drinks 腰果（产于美洲热带，用于烹饪，常盐渍后佐酒） ➲ VISUAL VOCAB PAGE V35

ˈ**cash flow** *noun* [C, U] the movement of money into and out of a business as goods are bought and sold 现金流（量）；资金流（量）： *a healthy cash flow* (= having enough money to make payments when necessary) 良好的资金周转状况 ◇ *cash-flow problems* 资金周转问题

cash·ier /kæˈʃɪə(r); *NAmE* -ˈʃɪr/ *noun, verb*

■ *noun* a person whose job is to receive and pay out money in a bank, shop/store, hotel, etc. 出纳员

■ *verb* [usually passive] **~ sb** to make sb leave the army, navy, etc. because they have done sth wrong 开除…的军籍

cash·less /ˈkæʃləs/ *adj.* done or working without using cash 不用现金的： *We are moving towards the cashless society.* 我们正在向不用现钞的社会发展。

ˈ**cash machine** (*BrE also* ˈ**cash dispenser**, **cash·point™** /ˈkæʃpɔɪnt/) (*also* **ATM** *NAmE, BrE*) (*also* **ABM** *CanE*) *noun* a machine in or outside a bank, etc., from which you can get money from your bank account using a special plastic card 自动取款机 ➲ COLLOCATIONS AT FINANCE

cash·mere /ˈkæʃmɪə(r); ˌkæʃˈm-; *NAmE* ˈkæʒmɪr; ˈkæʃ-/ *noun* [U] fine soft wool made from the long hair of a type of GOAT, used especially for making expensive clothes（山羊绒）开司米；山羊绒；克什米尔羊毛

ˈ**cash register** (*BrE also* **till**) (*NAmE also* **regis·ter**) *noun* a machine used in shops/stores, restaurants, etc. that has a drawer for keeping money in, and that shows and records the amount of money received for each thing that is sold 现金收入记录机；现金出纳机

ˈ**cash-starved** *adj.* [only before noun] without enough money, usually because another organization, such as the government, has failed to provide it 资金不足的（尤指政府等提供的资金不到位）： *cash-starved public services* 资金匮乏的公共事业

ˈ**cash-strapped** *adj.* [only before noun] without enough money资金短缺的： ***cash-strapped governments/shoppers*** 缺资金的政府；缺钱的购物者

cas·ing /ˈkeɪsɪŋ/ *noun* [C, U] a covering that protects sth 箱；盒；套；罩

ca·sino /kəˈsiːnəʊ; *NAmE* -noʊ/ *noun* (*pl.* **-os**) a public building or room where people play gambling games for money 赌场 ➲ WORDFINDER NOTE AT GAMBLING

cask /kɑːsk; *NAmE* kæsk/ *noun* a small wooden BARREL used for storing liquids, especially alcoholic drinks; the amount contained in a cask 小木桶；酒桶；一桶（的量）： *a wine cask/a cask of wine* 酒桶；一桶酒

cas·ket /ˈkɑːskɪt; *NAmE* ˈkæs-/ *noun* **1** a small decorated box for holding jewellery or other valuable things, especially in the past（尤指旧时放珠宝等贵重物品的）精致小盒，装饰精美的小箱 **2** (*NAmE*) (*also* **coffin** *especially in BrE*) a box in which a dead body is buried or CREMATED 棺材；棺椁；棺木

Cas·san·dra /kəˈsændrə/ *noun* a person who predicts that sth bad will happen, especially a person who is not believed（尤指无人相信的）凶事预言者 ➲ MORE LIKE THIS 17, page R27 **ORIGIN** From the name of a princess in ancient Greek stories to whom Apollo gave the ability to predict the future. After she tricked him, he stopped people believing her. 源自古希腊神话中一位公主的名字。阿波罗神给她预言能力，她欺骗阿波罗后，阿波罗使人不相信她的预言。

cas·sava /kəˈsɑːvə/ (*also* **man·ioc**) *noun* [U] **1** a tropical plant with many branches and long roots that you can eat 木薯（热带植物，多枝长根，可食用） **2** the roots of this plant, which can be boiled, fried, ROASTED or made into flour 木薯块根（可制成木薯粉）

cas·ser·ole /ˈkæsərəʊl; *NAmE* -roʊl/ *noun* **1** [C, U] a hot dish made with meat, vegetables, etc. that are cooked slowly in liquid in an oven 炖烧菜，炖锅菜（有肉、蔬菜等）： *a chicken casserole* 炖鸡 ◇ *Is there any casserole left?* 还剩有炖锅菜吗？ **2** [C] (*also* ˈ**casserole dish**) a container with a lid used for cooking meat, etc. in liquid in an oven 炖锅；砂锅 ➲ VISUAL VOCAB PAGE V28 ▶ **cas·ser·ole** *verb* **~ sth**

cas·sette /kəˈset/ *noun* **1** a small flat plastic case containing tape for playing or recording music or sound 磁带盒；盒式磁带；卡式磁带： *a **cassette recorder/player*** 盒式磁带录音机 / 放音机 ◇ *available **on cassette*** 已录制成磁带 ◇ *a video cassette* (= for recording sound and pictures) 盒式录像带 **2** a plastic case containing film that can be put into a camera 胶片盒；暗盒

cas·sock /ˈkæsək/ *noun* a long piece of clothing, usually black or red, worn by some Christian priests and other people with special duties in a church（基督教会教士等穿的黑或红色的）长袍

cas·sou·let /ˈkæsʊleɪ/ *noun* [U] (*from French*) a dish consisting of meat and BEANS cooked slowly in liquid 法式锅菜（有鲜肉和白扁豆）

cas·so·wary /ˈkæsəwəri; -weəri; *NAmE* -weri/ *noun* (*pl.* **-ies**) a very large bird related to the EMU, that does not fly. It is found mainly in New Guinea. 鹤鸵（主要生长于新几内亚）

C

cast /kɑːst; *NAmE* kæst/ *verb, noun*

■ *verb* (**cast, cast**)

• **A LOOK/GLANCE/SMILE** 瞧；瞥；笑 **1** [T] ~ (**sb**) **sth** to look, smile, etc. in a particular direction 向…投以（视线、笑容等）： *She cast a welcoming smile in his direction.* 她向他微笑以示欢迎。

• **LIGHT/A SHADOW** 光；影子 **2** [T] ~ **sth** (**over sth**) to make light, a shadow, etc. appear in a particular place 投射（光、影子等）： *The setting sun cast an orange glow over the mountains.* 橘红色的夕阳辉映着群山。◇ (*figurative*) *The sad news cast a shadow over the proceedings* (= made people feel unhappy). 这个坏消息给事件的进程蒙上了一层阴影。

• **DOUBT** 怀疑 **3** [T] ~ **doubt/aspersions** (**on/upon sth**) to say, do or suggest sth that makes people doubt sth or think that sb is less honest, good, etc. 使人怀疑；造谣中伤： *This latest evidence casts serious doubt on his version of events.* 最新的证据使人们十分怀疑他对事件的说法。

• **FISHING LINE** 钓鱼线 **4** [I, T] ~ (**sth**) to throw one end of a FISHING LINE into a river, etc. 投（钓线）；抛（钓钩）

• **THROW** 投；掷 **5** [T] ~ **sb/sth** (*literary*) to throw sb/sth somewhere, especially using force 扔；掷；抛： *The priceless treasures had been cast into the Nile.* 价值连城的珍宝被扔进了尼罗河。◇ *They cast anchor at nightfall.* 他们傍晚抛锚停泊。

• **SKIN** 皮 **6** [T] ~ **sth** when a snake **casts** its skin, the skin comes off as part of a natural process （蛇）蜕（皮） SYN **shed**

• **SHOE** 蹄铁 **7** [T] ~ **sth** if a horse **casts** a shoe, the shoe comes off by accident （马）踢落（蹄铁）

• **ACTORS** 演员 **8** [T] to choose actors to play the different parts in a film/movie, play, etc.; to choose an actor to play a particular role 分配角色；选派角色： ~ **sth** *The play is being cast in both the US and Britain.* 目前正在英美两国挑选这部戏剧的演员。◇ ~ **sb** (**as sb**) *He has cast her as an ambitious lawyer in his latest movie.* 他选定她在他最近的一部影片里扮演一名雄心勃勃的律师。

• **DESCRIBE** 描写 **9** [T] to describe or present sb/yourself in a particular way 把某人描写成；把某人表现为： ~ **sb/yourself** (**as sth**) *He cast himself as the innocent victim of a hate campaign.* 他把自己说成是无辜的受害者，声誉受到刻意诋毁。◇ ~ **sb/yourself** (**in sth**) *The press were quick to cast her in the role of the 'other woman'.* 新闻界很快把她描述成"第三者"的角色。

• **VOTE** 表决 **10** [T] ~ **a/your vote/ballot** (**for sb/sth**) to vote for sb/sth 投票

• **SHAPE METAL** 模铸金属 **11** [T] ~ **sth** (**in sth**) to shape hot liquid metal, etc. by pouring it into a hollow container (called a MOULD) 浇铸；铸造： *a statue cast in bronze* 青铜铸像 ◇ (*figurative*) *an artist **cast in the mould of*** (= very similar to) *Miró* 风格酷似米罗的一名艺术家

IDM **cast your mind back** (**to sth**) to make yourself think about sth that happened in the past 回顾；回想： *I want you to cast your minds back to the first time you met.* 我要你们回忆初次见面的情景。 **cast your net wide** to consider a lot of different people, activities, possibilities, etc. when you are looking for sth 撒开大网（搜寻时考虑面要宽） **cast a 'spell** (**on sb/sth**) to use words that are thought to be magic and have the power to change or influence sb/sth （对…）施魔法，念咒语 ➲ MORE AT ADRIFT, CAUTION *n.*, DIE *n.*, EYE *n.*, LIGHT *n.*, LOT *n.*

PHR V ˌ**cast aˈbout/aˈround for sth** to try hard to think of or find sth, especially when this is difficult 苦苦思索；四处寻找： *She cast around desperately for a safe topic of conversation.* 她绞尽脑汁寻找稳妥的话题。 ˌ**cast sb/sth↔aˈside** (*formal*) to get rid of sb/sth because you no longer want or need them 抛弃；丢弃 SYN **discard** **be** ˌ**cast aˈway** to be left somewhere after a SHIPWRECK （船遇难后幸存者）流落某处 ➲ RELATED NOUN CASTAWAY **be** ˌ**cast ˈdown** (**by sth**) (*literary*) to be sad or unhappy about sth （因某事）沮丧，不愉快 ➲ SEE ALSO DOWNCAST ˌ**cast ˈoff** | ˌ**cast sth↔ˈoff** **1** to undo the ropes that are holding a boat in a fixed position, in order to sail away 解缆；解（船）；解缆出航 **2** (in knitting 编织) to remove STITCHES from the needles in a way that forms an edge that will not come undone 收针 ˌ**cast sth↔ˈoff** (*formal*) to get rid of sth because you no longer want or need it 抛弃；丢弃： *The town is still trying to cast off its dull image.* 该镇仍在努力摆脱自己沉闷无趣的形象。 ˌ**cast ˈon** | ˌ**cast sth↔ˈon** (in knitting 编织) to put the first row of STITCHES on a needle 起针；放针 ˌ**cast sb/sth↔ˈout** (*literary*) to get rid of sb/sth, especially by using force 驱逐；赶走： *He claimed to have the power to cast out demons.* 他宣称有驱魔的神力。 ➲ RELATED NOUN OUTCAST

■ *noun*

• **ACTORS** 演员 **1** [C+sing./pl. v.] all the people who act in a play or film/movie （一出戏剧或一部电影的）全体演员： *The whole cast performs/perform brilliantly.* 全体演员都表现出色。◇ *members of the cast* 剧组成员 ◇ *an **all-star cast*** (= including many well-known actors) 明星云集的演员阵容 ◇ *the **supporting cast*** (= not the main actors, but the others) 配角演员 ◇ *a cast list* 演员表 ➲ WORDFINDER NOTE AT ACTOR, PLAY

• **IN SHAPING METAL** 模铸金属 **2** [C] an object that is made by pouring hot liquid metal, etc. into a MOULD (= a specially shaped container) 铸件；铸造品 **3** [C] a shaped container used to make an object 模子；铸模 SYN **mould**

• **APPEARANCE** 外表 **4** [sing.] (*formal*) the way that a person or thing is or appears 特性；特征；外表；外貌： *He has an unusual **cast of mind**.* 他的思想与众不同。◇ *I disliked the arrogant cast to her mouth.* 我不喜欢她傲慢的口吻。

• **THROW** 投 **5** [C] an act of throwing sth, especially a fishing line 投，掷，抛（钓线）

• **ON ARM/LEG** 手臂；腿 **6** [C] = PLASTER CAST (1)： *Her **leg's in a cast**.* 她的一条腿打上了石膏。 ➲ SEE ALSO OPENCAST

cas·ta·nets /ˌkæstəˈnets/ *noun* [pl.] a musical instrument that consists of two small round pieces of wood that you hold in the hand and hit together with the fingers to make a noise. Castanets are used especially by Spanish dancers. 响板（西班牙人跳舞时常用的伴奏乐器） ➲ VISUAL VOCAB PAGE V37

cast·away /ˈkɑːstəweɪ; *NAmE* ˈkæst-/ *noun* a person whose ship has sunk (= who has been SHIPWRECKED) and who has had to swim to a lonely place, usually an island （沉船后）游泳逃生到孤岛等荒僻处的人

caste /kɑːst; *NAmE* kæst/ *noun* **1** [C] any of the four main divisions of Hindu society, originally those made according to functions in society （印度教的四大）种姓： *the caste system* 种姓制度 ◇ *high-caste Brahmins* 高级种姓婆罗门 **2** [C] a social class, especially one whose members do not allow others to join it （尤指禁止其他等级成员进入的）社会阶层，社会等级： *the ruling caste* 统治阶层 **3** [U] the system of dividing society into classes based on differences in family origin, rank or wealth 社会等级制度

cas·tel·lated /ˈkæstəleɪtɪd/ *adj.* (*architecture* 建) built in the style of a castle with BATTLEMENTS 像城堡的；有城垛的；有雉堞的

cas·tel·la·tions /ˌkæstəˈleɪʃnz/ *noun* [pl.] the top edge of a castle wall, that has regular spaces along it 城堡雉堞

cas·ter (*NAmE*) = CASTOR

ˌ**caster ˈsugar** (*also* ˌ**castor ˈsugar**) *noun* [U] (*BrE*) white sugar in the form of very fine grains, used in cooking 幼砂糖

cas·ti·gate /ˈkæstɪɡeɪt/ *verb* ~ **sb/sth/yourself** (**for sth**) (*formal*) to criticize sb/sth/yourself severely 严厉批评；申斥： *He castigated himself for being so stupid.* 他责怪自己太笨。 ▶ **cas·ti·ga·tion** /ˌkæstɪˈɡeɪʃn/ *noun* [U]

cast·ing /ˈkɑːstɪŋ; *NAmE* ˈkæst-/ *noun* **1** [U] the process of choosing actors for a play or film/movie 角色分配；演员挑选 **2** [C] an object made by pouring hot liquid metal, etc. into a MOULD (= a specially shaped container) 铸件；铸造品

ˌ**casting couch** *noun* used to refer to a process in which actors are chosen for a film/movie, etc. if they have sex with the person in charge of choosing the actors 床第选角（为争演角色与负责选派角色者发生性关系）

ˌ**casting 'vote** *noun* [usually sing.] the vote given by the person in charge of an official meeting to decide an issue when votes on each side are equal（会议主席在赞成票和反对票票数相等时所投的）决定票

ˌ**cast 'iron** *noun* [U] a hard type of iron that does not bend easily and is shaped by pouring the hot liquid metal into a MOULD (= a specially shaped container) 铸铁

ˌ**cast-'iron** *adj.* **1** made of cast iron 铸铁制的： *a cast-iron bridge* 铸铁桥 **2** (*BrE*) very strong or certain; that cannot be broken or fail 有力的；确实的；坚定不移的： *a* ***cast-iron guarantee/promise*** 永不反悔的保证；铁誓 ◇ *a* ***cast-iron excuse/alibi*** 有说服力的辩解；不在犯罪现场的确凿证据 ➲ COMPARE IRONCLAD

cas·tle 🔑 /ˈkɑːsl; *NAmE* ˈkæsl/ *noun* **1** a large strong building with thick high walls and towers, built in the past by kings or queens, or other important people, to defend themselves against attack 城堡；堡垒 ➲ VISUAL VOCAB PAGE V15 ➲ SEE ALSO SANDCASTLE **2** (*also* **rook**) (in CHESS 国际象棋) any of the four pieces placed in the corner squares of the board at the start of the game, usually made to look like a castle 车 ➲ VISUAL VOCAB PAGE V42

IDM **(build) castles in the 'air** (to have) plans or dreams that are not likely to happen or come true（建）空中楼阁；幻想；空想 ➲ MORE AT MAN *n.*

ˈ**cast-off** (*especially BrE*) (*also* **'hand-me-down** *especially in NAmE*) *noun* [usually pl.] a piece of clothing that the original owner no longer wants to wear 被抛弃的衣物 ▶ **'cast-off** (*also* **'hand-me-down**) *adj.* : *a cast-off overcoat* 被丢弃的大衣

cas·tor (*BrE*) (*NAmE* **cas·ter**) /ˈkɑːstə(r); *NAmE* ˈkæs-/ *noun* one of the small wheels fixed to the bottom of a piece of furniture so that it can be moved easily（家具底部的）小脚轮，万向轮 ➲ VISUAL VOCAB PAGE V71

ˌ**castor 'oil** *noun* [U] a thick yellow oil obtained from a tropical plant and used in the past as a type of medicine, usually as a LAXATIVE 蓖麻油

ˌ**castor 'sugar** *noun* [U] = CASTER SUGAR

cas·trate /kæˈstreɪt; *NAmE* ˈkæstreɪt/ *verb* ~ **sth/sb** to remove the TESTICLES of a male animal or person 割除（男子或雄性动物）的睾丸；阉割 ▶ **cas·tra·tion** /kæˈstreɪʃn/ *noun* [U, C]

cas·ual /ˈkæʒuəl/ *adj.*, *noun*

■ *adj.*

• **WITHOUT CARE/ATTENTION** 不介意；不注意 **1** [usually before noun] not showing much care or thought; seeming not to be worried; not wanting to show that sth is important to you 不经意的；无忧无虑的；漫不经心的；不在乎的： *a casual manner* 漫不经心的样子 ◇ *It was just a casual remark—I wasn't really serious.* 我只是随便说说，并不当真。◇ *He tried to sound casual, but I knew he was worried.* 他讲话时试图显得不在乎，但我知道他心里着急。 ◇ *They have a casual attitude towards safety* (= they don't care enough). 他们对安全问题采取无所谓的态度。 **2** [usually before noun] without paying attention to detail 马虎的；疏忽的： *a casual glance* 随便扫一眼 ◇ *It's obvious even to the casual observer.* 即便再马虎的人也能一眼看明白是怎么回事。

• **NOT FORMAL** 非正式 **3** not formal 非正式的；随便的： *casual clothes* (= comfortable clothes that you choose to wear in your free time) 便装 ◇ *family parties and other casual occasions* 家庭聚会和其他非正式场合

• **WORK** 工作 **4** [usually before noun] not permanent; not done, or doing sth regularly 临时的；不定期的： ***casual workers/labour*** 临时工 ◇ *Students sometimes do casual work in the tourist trade.* 学生有时做些旅游方面的零工。◇ *They are employed* ***on a casual basis*** (= they do not have a permanent job with the company). 他们被雇为临时工。

• **RELATIONSHIP** 关系 **5** [usually before noun] without deep affection 感情不深的；疏远的： *a casual acquaintance* 泛泛之交 ◇ *a casual friendship* 一般的友谊 ◇ *to have casual sex* (= to have sex without having a steady relationship with that partner) 做露水鸳鸯

• **BY CHANCE** 偶然 **6** [only before noun] happening by chance; doing sth by chance 偶然的；碰巧的： *a* ***casual encounter/meeting*** 不期而遇；邂逅 ◇ *a casual passer-by* 碰巧过路的人 ◇ *The exhibition is interesting to both the enthusiast and the casual visitor.* 热心的爱好者和碰巧来参观的人都认为这个展览有意思。◇ *The disease is not spread by casual contact.* 此病不会通过偶然接触传染。

▶ **cas·ual·ly** *adv.* : *'What did he say about me?' she asked as casually as she could.* "他说了我什么？" 她尽量装着不在意地问。◇ *They chatted casually on the phone.* 他们在电话上闲聊。◇ *dressed casually in jeans and T-shirt* 随便穿着牛仔裤和 T 恤衫 **cas·ual·ness** *noun* [U]: *He was sure that the casualness of the gesture was deliberate.* 他确信那似乎漫不经心的姿态是有意装出来的。

■ *noun*

• **CLOTHES** 服装 **1 casuals** (*BrE*) [pl.] informal clothes or shoes 便装；便鞋： *dressed in casuals* 穿着便装

• **WORKER** 工人 **2** [C] a casual worker (= one who does not work permanently for a company) 临时工

casu·al·iza·tion /ˌkæʒuəlaɪˈzeɪʃn; *NAmE* -ləˈz-/ *noun* [U] the practice of employing temporary staff for short periods instead of permanent staff, in order to save costs 雇用临时工制（以节省开支）

casu·alty /ˈkæʒuəlti/ *noun* (*pl.* **-ies**) **1** [C] a person who is killed or injured in war or in an accident （战争或事故的）伤员，亡者，遇难者： *road casualties* 交通事故伤亡人员 ◇ *Both sides had suffered* ***heavy casualties*** (= many people had been killed). 双方都伤亡惨重。 ➲ WORDFINDER NOTE AT CONFLICT ➲ COLLOCATIONS AT WAR **2** [C] a person that suffers or a thing that is destroyed when sth else takes place 受害者；毁坏物；损坏物 SYN **victim**: *She became a casualty of the reduction in part-time work* (= she lost her job). 她成了裁减兼职工作的受害人。◇ *Small shops have been a casualty of the recession.* 小商店在经济萧条中深受其害。 **3** [U] (*also* **'casualty department**, ˌ**accident and e'mergency**) (*all BrE*) (*NAmE* **e'mergency room**) the part of a hospital where people who need urgent treatment are taken 急诊室： *The victims were rushed to casualty.* 受伤者被迅速送往急救室。 ➲ WORDFINDER NOTE AT ACCIDENT

casu·is·try /ˈkæʒuɪstri/ *noun* [U] (*formal, disapproving*) a way of solving moral or legal problems by using clever arguments that may be false 诡辩（指用似是而非的论点解决伦理或法律问题）

casus belli /ˌkeɪsəs ˈbelaɪ; ˌkɑːsʊs ˈbeliː/ *noun* (*pl.* **casus belli**) (*formal*) an act or situation that is used to justify a war 交战理由；开战借口

cat 🔑 /kæt/ *noun* **1** a small animal with soft fur that people often keep as a pet. Cats catch and kill birds and mice. 猫： *cat food* 猫粮 ➲ SEE ALSO KITTEN, TOMCAT **2** a wild animal of the cat family 猫科动物： *the big cats* (= LIONS, TIGERS, etc.) 大型猫科动物（狮、虎等） ➲ SEE ALSO FAT CAT, WILDCAT *n.*

IDM **be the cat's 'whiskers/py'jamas** (*informal*) to be the best thing, person, idea, etc. 最棒的东西（或人、主意等）： *He thinks he's the cat's whiskers* (= he has a high opinion of himself). 他自以为了不起。 **let the 'cat out of the bag** to tell a secret carelessly or by mistake （无意中）泄露秘密： *I wanted it to be a surprise, but my sister let the cat out of the bag.* 我想给大家来个惊喜，可我妹妹却先说漏了嘴。 **like a ˌcat on hot 'bricks** (*BrE*) *NAmE* **like a ˌcat on a hot tin 'roof** very nervous 局促不安；如坐针毡；像热锅上的蚂蚁： *She was like a cat on hot bricks before her driving test.* 她考驾驶执照前十分紧张不安。 **like a cat that's got the 'cream** (*BrE*) (*US* **like the cat that got/ate/swallowed the can'ary**) very pleased with yourself 扬扬得意；踌躇满志 SYN **smug look like sth the 'cat brought/dragged in** (*informal*) (of a person 人) to look dirty and untidy 穿着邋遢；衣衫褴褛；不修边幅 **not have/stand a cat in 'hell's chance (of doing sth)** to have no chance at all 毫无机会 **play (a game of) ,cat and 'mouse with sb | play a ,cat-and-'mouse game with sb** to play a cruel game with sb in your power by changing your behaviour very often, so that they become nervous and do not know what to expect 和某人玩起猫捉老鼠的游戏；要弄 **put/set the cat among the 'pigeons** (*BrE*) to say or do sth that is likely to cause trouble 引起麻烦；招惹是非 **when the cat's a'way the mice will 'play** (*saying*) people enjoy themselves more and behave with greater freedom when the person in charge of them is not there 猫儿不在，老鼠玩得自在（指管事的不在，下面的玩个痛快） ➲ MORE AT CURIOSITY, HERD *v.*, RAIN *v.*, ROOM *n.*, WAY *n.*

ca·tab·ol·ism (*also* **ka·tab·ol·ism**) /kəˈtæbəlɪzəm/ *noun* [U] (*biology* 生) the process by which chemical structures are broken down and energy is released 分解代谢

cata·clysm /ˈkætəklɪzəm/ *noun* (*formal*) a sudden disaster or a violent event that causes change, for example a flood or a war （突然降临的）大灾难，大灾变，大动乱 ▸ **cata·clys·mic** /ˌkætəˈklɪzmɪk/ *adj.* [usually before noun]

cata·combs /ˈkætəkuːmz; *NAmE* -koʊmz/ *noun* [pl.] a series of underground tunnels used for burying dead people, especially in ancient times （尤指古代纵横交错的）地下墓穴

cata·falque /ˈkætəfælk/ *noun* a decorated platform on which the dead body of a famous person is placed before a funeral 灵柩台

Cata·lan /ˈkætəlæn/ *noun, adj.*
■ ***noun* 1** [U] a language spoken in Catalonia, Andorra, the Balearic Islands and parts of southern France 加泰罗尼亚语（通行于西班牙加泰罗尼亚、安道尔、巴利阿里群岛和法国南部一些地区） **2** [C] a person who was born in or who lives in Catalonia 加泰罗尼亚人
■ ***adj.*** connected with Catalonia, its people, its language, or its culture 加泰罗尼亚的；加泰罗尼亚人（或语言、文化）的

cata·lepsy /ˈkætəlepsi/ *noun* [U] (*medical* 医) a condition in which sb's body becomes stiff and they temporarily become unconscious 僵住；僵住症；强直性昏厥；倔强症 ▸ **cata·lep·tic** /ˌkætəˈleptɪk/ *adj.* [only before noun]

cata·logue (*NAmE also* **cata·log**) /ˈkætəlɒɡ; *NAmE* -lɔːɡ; -lɑːɡ/ *noun, verb*
■ ***noun* 1** a complete list of items, for example of things that people can look at or buy 目录；目录簿：*a mail-order catalogue* (= a book showing goods for sale to be sent to people's homes) 邮购商品目录 ◇ *to consult the library catalogue* 查看图书馆目录 ◇ *An illustrated catalogue accompanies the exhibition.* 展览会有插图目录。◇ *an online catalogue* 联机目录 **2** a long series of things that happen (usually bad things) 一连串（糟糕）事：*a catalogue of disasters/errors/misfortunes* 接二连三的灾难 / 错误 / 不幸
■ ***verb* 1 ~ sth** to arrange a list of things in order in a catalogue; to record sth in a catalogue 列入目录；编入目录 **2 ~ sth** to give a list of things connected with a particular person, event, etc. 记载，登记（某人、某事等的详情）：*Interviews with the refugees catalogue a history of discrimination and violence.* 对难民的采访记录下了一部歧视和暴力的历史。

cata·lyse (*BrE*) (*NAmE* **cata·lyze**) /ˈkætəlaɪz/ *verb* **~ sth** (*chemistry* 化) to make a chemical reaction happen faster 催化

cata·lyst /ˈkætəlɪst/ *noun* **1** (*chemistry* 化) a substance that makes a chemical reaction happen faster without being changed itself 催化剂 ➲ WORDFINDER NOTE AT CHEMISTRY **2 ~ (for sth)** a person or thing that causes a change 促使变化的人；引发变化的因素：*I see my role as being a catalyst for change.* 我认为我的角色是促成变革。

cata·lyt·ic con·vert·er /ˌkætəˌlɪtɪk kənˈvɜːtə(r); *NAmE* -ˈvɜːrt-/ *noun* a device used in the EXHAUST system of vehicles to reduce the damage caused to the environment 催化转化器，催化式排气净化器（用以净化机动车废气）

cata·ma·ran /ˌkætəməˈræn/ *noun* a fast sailing boat with two HULLS 双体船 ➲ VISUAL VOCAB PAGE V59 ➲ COMPARE TRIMARAN

cata·mite /ˈkætəmaɪt/ *noun* (*old use*) a boy kept as a SLAVE for a man to have sex with 娈童；当性奴的男童

catapult (*BrE*) / **slingshot** (*NAmE*) 弹弓

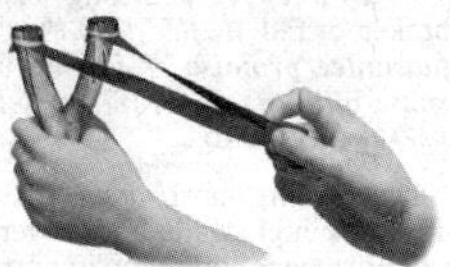

cata·pult /ˈkætəpʌlt/ *noun, verb*
■ ***noun* 1** (*BrE*) (*NAmE* **sling·shot**) a stick shaped like a Y with a rubber band attached to it, used by children for shooting stones 弹弓 **2** a weapon used in the past to throw heavy stones （旧时的）石弩，弩炮 **3** a machine used for sending planes up into the air from a ship 弹射器（用以从舰船上弹射飞机升空）
■ ***verb*** [T, I] to throw sb/sth or be thrown suddenly and violently through the air （被）猛掷，猛扔：**~ (sb/sth) + adv./prep.** *She was catapulted out of the car as it hit the wall.* 汽车撞墙时，她被甩出车外。◇ (*figurative*) *The movie catapulted him to international stardom.* 这部电影使他一跃成为国际明星。

cat·ar·act /ˈkætərækt/ *noun* **1** a medical condition that affects the LENS of the eye and causes a gradual loss of sight 白内障 **2** (*literary*) a large steep WATERFALL 大瀑布

ca·tarrh /kəˈtɑː(r)/ *noun* [U] thick liquid (called PHLEGM) that you have in your nose and throat because, for example, you have a cold 卡他；黏膜炎

ca·tas·trophe /kəˈtæstrəfi/ *noun* **1** a sudden event that causes many people to suffer 灾难；灾祸；横祸 **SYN** **disaster**: *Early warnings of rising water levels prevented another major catastrophe.* 提前发出的洪水水位上涨警报防止了又一次的重大灾害。 **2** an event that causes one person or a group of people personal suffering, or that makes difficulties 不幸事件；困难：*The attempt to expand the business was a catastrophe for the firm.* 扩展业务的尝试使这家公司陷入困境。◇ *We've had a few catastrophes with the food for the party.* 我们为聚会准备食物时遇到了一些困难。 ▸ **cata·stroph·ic** /ˌkætəˈstrɒfɪk; *NAmE* -ˈstrɑː-/ *adj.* **SYN** **disastrous**: *catastrophic effects/losses/results* 灾难性的影响 / 损失 / 结果 ◇ (*US*) *a catastrophic illness* (= one that costs a very large amount to treat) 要花费巨资治疗的疾病 **cata·stroph·ic·al·ly** /-kli/ *adv.*

cata·to·nia /ˌkætəˈtəʊniə; *NAmE* -ˈtoʊ-/ *noun* [U] (*medical* 医) a condition resulting from a mental illness, especially SCHIZOPHRENIA, in which a person does not move for long periods 畸张症；紧张症

cata·ton·ic /ˌkætəˈtɒnɪk; *NAmE* -ˈtɑːnɪk/ *adj.* (*medical* 医) not able to move or show any reaction to things because of illness, shock, etc. 紧张型的；紧张性的

cat·bird seat /ˈkætbɜːd siːt; *NAmE* -bɜːrd/ *noun*
IDM **be in the 'catbird seat** (*NAmE*) to have an advantage over other people or be in control of a situation 处于有利地位；控制着局势

'cat burglar *noun* a thief who climbs up the outside of a building in order to enter it and steal sth 翻墙入室的窃贼；飞贼

cat·call /ˈkætkɔːl/ *noun* [usually pl.] a noise or shout expressing anger at or disapproval of sb who is speaking or performing in public （表示愤怒或反对的）嘘声，不满之声

catch /kætʃ/ *verb, noun*

■ ***verb*** (**caught**, **caught** /kɔːt/)

• **HOLD** 接住 **1** [T, I] ~ (**sth**) to stop and hold a moving object, especially in your hands 接住；截住；拦住： *She managed to catch the keys as they fell.* 她接住了落下的钥匙。◇ *'Throw me over that towel, will you?' 'OK. Catch!'* "请你把毛巾扔过来好吗？" "好，接住！" ◇ *The dog caught the stick in its mouth.* 狗衔住了木棍。 **2** [T] ~ **sth** to hold a liquid when it falls 接（落下的液体）： *The roof was leaking and I had to use a bucket to catch the drips.* 屋顶漏雨，我不得不用桶来接。 **3** [T] ~ **sb/sth** (+ **adv./prep.**) to take hold of sb/sth 抓住；握住： *He* ***caught hold of*** *her arm as she tried to push past him.* 她试图从他身边挤过去时，他一把抓住了她的手臂。

• **CAPTURE** 捉住 **4** [T] ~ **sb/sth** to capture a person or an animal that tries or would try to escape 逮住；捕捉；捕获： *The murderer was never caught.* 这个杀人犯一直未抓到。◇ *Our cat is hopeless at catching mice.* 我们的猫绝对捉不到老鼠。◇ *How many fish did you catch?* 你捕到几条鱼？

• **SB DOING STH** 某人正做某事 **5** [T] to find or discover sb doing sth, especially sth wrong 当场发现（或发觉）： ~ **sb doing sth** *I caught her smoking in the bathroom.* 我撞见她在盥洗室里抽烟。◇ ***You wouldn't catch me*** *working* (= I would never work) *on a Sunday!* 你绝对不会看到我在星期日工作！ ◇ ~ **yourself doing sth** *She caught herself wondering whether she had made a mistake.* 她发觉自己在怀疑是否犯了错误。◇ ~ **sb + adv./prep.** *He was caught with bomb-making equipment in his home.* 他被发现家里藏有制造炸弹的设备。◇ *Mark walked in and* ***caught them at it*** (= in the act of doing sth wrong). 马克走了进去，当场发现他们正在干坏事。◇ *thieves* ***caught in the act*** 偷窃时被当场抓住的窃贼 ◇ *You've caught me at a bad time* (= at a time when I am busy). 你现在来找我可不是时候。

• **BUS/TRAIN/PLANE** 公共汽车；火车；飞机 **6** [T] ~ **sth** to be in time for a bus, train, plane, etc. and get on it 赶上（公共汽车、火车、飞机等）： *We caught the 12.15 from Oxford.* 我们赶上了 12:15 从牛津发出的火车。◇ *I must go—I have a train to catch.* 我得走了，我要赶火车。

• **BE IN TIME** 及时 **7** [T] ~ **sb/sth** to be in time to do sth, talk to sb, etc. 及时做（或谈等）： *I caught him just as he was leaving the building.* 他正要离开大楼时，我追上了他。◇ *I was hoping to catch you at home* (= to telephone you at home when you were there). 我本希望赶上你在家的时候给你打电话。◇ *The illness can be treated provided it's caught* (= discovered) *early enough.* 此病若及早发现是可医治的。◇ (*BrE*) *to* ***catch the post*** (= post letters before the box is emptied) （寄信）赶上邮局的收信时刻 ◇ (*BrE, informal*) *Bye for now!* ***I'll catch you later*** (= speak to you again later). 再见！下次再谈。

• **SEE/HEAR** 看见；听到 **8** [T] ~ **sth** (*informal, especially NAmE*) to see or hear sth; to attend sth 看见；听到；出席；参加： *Let's eat now and maybe we could catch a movie later.* 咱们现在就吃吧，也许还能赶上一场电影。➲ SYNONYMS AT SEE

• **HAPPEN UNEXPECTEDLY** 意外地发生 **9** [T] ~ **sb** to happen unexpectedly and put sb in a difficult situation 使突然遭受： *His arrival* ***caught*** *me* ***by surprise***. 他的到来让我感到意外。◇ *She* ***got caught in*** *a thunderstorm.* 她遇上了雷雨。

• **ILLNESS** 疾病 **10** [T] to get an illness 得病；染疾： ~ **sth** *to catch measles* 染上麻疹 ◇ ~ **sth from sb** *I think I must have caught this cold from you.* 我的感冒想必是你传染的。

• **BECOME STUCK** 被缠住 **11** [I, T] to become stuck in or on sth; to make sth become stuck （被）钩住，夹住，绊住： ~ (**in/on sth**) *Her dress caught on a nail.* 她的连衣裙被钉子钩住了。◇ ~ **sth** (**in/on sth**) *He caught his thumb in the door.* 他的拇指被门夹住了。

• **HIT** 打 **12** [T] to hit sb/sth 击中；打： ~ **sb/sth + adv./prep.** *The stone caught him on the side of the head.* 他头的侧面被石头击中。◇ ~ **sb sth + adv./prep.** *She caught him a blow on the chin.* 她一拳打在他下巴上。

• **NOTICE** 注意到 **13** [T] ~ **sth** to notice sth only for a moment 察觉；瞥见： *She* ***caught sight*** *of a car in the distance.* 她瞥见远处有一辆车。◇ *He* ***caught a glimpse*** *of himself in the mirror.* 他看了一眼镜子中的自己。◇ *I caught a look of surprise on her face.* 我发现她面露惊奇。◇ *He caught* ***a whiff*** *of her perfume.* 他闻到一股她身上的香水味。

• **HEAR/UNDERSTAND** 听见；理解 **14** [T] ~ **sth** to hear or understand sth 听清楚；领会： *Sorry, I didn't quite catch what you said.* 对不起，我没听清楚你的话。

• **INTEREST** 兴趣 **15** [T] ~ **sb's interest, imagination, attention, etc.** if sth **catches** your interest, etc., you notice it and feel interested in it 引起，激发（兴趣、想象、注意等）

• **SHOW ACCURATELY** 逼真地显示 **16** [T] ~ **sth** to show or describe sth accurately 逼真再现；准确描绘 SYN **capture**: *The artist has caught her smile perfectly.* 艺术家完美地捕捉到她的微笑。

• **LIGHT** 光 **17** [T] ~ **sth** if sth **catches** the light or the light **catches** it, the light shines on it and makes it shine too （光）照射；受到（光的）照射： *The knife gleamed as it* ***caught the light***. 刀在光照下闪闪发亮。

• **THE SUN** 太阳 **18** [T] ~ **the sun** (*informal*) if you **catch the sun**, you become red or brown because of spending time in the sun 晒黑；晒红；晒成棕色

• **BURN** 燃烧 **19** [T, I] ~ (**fire**) to begin to burn 烧着；着（火）： *The wooden rafters caught fire.* 木椽子着火了。◇ *These logs are wet: they won't catch.* 这些木柴是湿的，烧不着。

• **IN CRICKET** 板球 **20** [T] ~ **sb** to make a player unable to continue BATTING by catching the ball they have hit before it touches the ground （在球落地前）接住球

IDM **catch your 'breath 1** to stop breathing for a moment because of fear, shock, etc. （由于恐惧、震惊等）屏息，屏气 **2** to breathe normally again after running or doing some tiring exercise （跑或激烈运动后）喘口气 **catch your 'death (of 'cold)** (*old-fashioned, informal*) to catch a very bad cold 患重感冒 **catch sb's 'eye** to attract sb's attention 引起某人注意；惹人注目： *Can you catch the waiter's eye?* 你能引起服务员的注意吗？ **'catch it** (*BrE*) (*NAmE* **catch 'hell**, **'get it**) (*informal*) to be punished or spoken to angrily about sth 受罚；受斥责： *If your dad finds out you'll really catch it!* 要是你老爸知道了，你非挨骂不可！ **catch sb 'napping** to get an advantage over sb by doing sth when they are not expecting it and not ready for it 使人措手不及；乘其不备 **catch sb on the 'hop** (*informal*) to surprise sb by doing sth when they are not expecting it and not ready for it 使某人措手不及 **catch sb red-'handed** to catch sb in the act of doing sth wrong or committing a crime 当场抓住；现场捕获 **catch sb with their 'pants down** (*BrE also* **catch sb with their 'trousers down**) (*informal*) to arrive or do sth when sb is not expecting it and not ready, especially when they are in an embarrassing situation 使突陷窘境；乘人措手不及；出其不意；冷不防 ➲ MORE AT BALANCE *n.*, CLEFT *adj.*, EARLY *adj.*, FANCY *n.*, RAW *n.*, ROCK *n.*, SHORT *adv.*

PHR V **'catch at sth** = CLUTCH/CATCH AT STH/SB **,catch 'on** to become popular or fashionable 受欢迎；流行起来；变得时髦： *He invented a new game, but it never really caught on.* 他发明了一种新的游戏，但从未真正流行起来。 **,catch 'on (to sth)** (*informal*) to understand sth 理解： *He is very quick to catch on to things.* 他领悟能力很强。 **,catch sb 'out 1** to surprise sb and put them in a difficult position 使突陷困境： *Many investors were caught out by the fall in share prices.* 许多投资者由于股价下跌而突然陷入困境。 **2** to show that sb does not know much or is doing sth wrong 抓住某人的短处；指出无知；指出过失： *They tried to catch her out with a difficult question.* 他们试图用一道难题去难倒她。 **,catch 'up on sth 1** to spend extra time doing sth because you have not done it earlier 补做（未做的事）；赶做；补上： *I have a lot of work to catch up on.* 我有许多工作要补做。 **2** (*also* **,catch 'up**) to find out about things that have happened 了解（已发生的事情）： *We spent the evening catching up* (*on each other's news*). 我们那一晚上都一直在彼此通报情况。 **be/get ,caught 'up in sth** to become involved in sth, especially when you do not want to be 被卷入；陷入： *Innocent passers-by got caught up in the riots.* 无辜的过路人被卷入了那场暴乱。 **,catch 'up (with sb)** (*BrE also* **,catch sb 'up**) **1** to reach sb who is ahead by going faster 赶上，追上（某人）： *Go on ahead. I'll catch up with you.* 你先走，我随后赶上你。◇ *I'll catch you up.* 我会追上你的。 **2** to reach the same level or standard as sb who was better or more advanced 赶上，达到（某水平）： *After missing a term through illness he had to work hard to catch up with the others.* 他因病休学一学期，不得不努力学习，好赶上别的同学。 ˌ**catch ˈup with sb 1** to finally start to cause problems for sb after they have managed to avoid this for some time 产生（曾设法避免的）问题： *She was terrified that one day her past problems would catch up with her.* 她十分害怕过去的问题总有一天又会来困扰她。 **2** if the police or authorities **catch up with** sb, they find and punish them after some time 终于查到某人头上： *The law caught up with him years later when he had moved to Spain.* 多年后，他已移居西班牙，最终还是受到法律的制裁。

■ *noun*

• **OF BALL** 球 **1** [C] an act of catching sth, for example a ball 接（球等）： *to make a catch* 接球

• **AMOUNT CAUGHT** 捕获量 **2** [C] the total amount of things that are caught 总捕获量： *a huge catch of fish* 捕获大量的鱼

• **FASTENING** 固着装置 **3** [C] a device used for fastening sth 扣拴物；扣件： *a catch on the door* 门闩 ◇ *safety catches for the windows* 安全窗钩

• **DIFFICULTY** 困难 **4** [C, usually sing.] (*informal*) a hidden difficulty or disadvantage 隐藏的困难；暗藏的不利因素： *All that money for two hours' work—what's the catch?* 干了两小时的活就给那么多钱，这里面有什么鬼？

• **CHILD'S GAME** 儿童游戏 **5** [U] a child's game in which two people throw a ball to each other （儿童）传接球游戏

• **PERSON** 人 **6** [sing.] (*old-fashioned*) a person that other people see as a good person to marry, employ, etc. 理想的对象；意中人；雇用的好对象；看中的人

IDM **(a) catch-22 | a catch-22 situation** (*informal*) a difficult situation from which there is no escape because you need to do one thing before doing a second, but you need to do the second thing before you can do the first 进退维谷的局面： *I can't get a job because I haven't got anywhere to live but I can't afford a place to live until I get a job—it's a catch-22 situation.* 我没有住所就找不到工作，但是没有工作就没钱租房子，这真是左右为难。

ˈ**catch-all** *noun* **1** (*especially NAmE*) a thing for holding many small objects 装杂物的容器；放杂物的东西 **2** a group or description that includes different things and that does not state clearly what is included or not 笼统的一类（或描述） ▸ ˈ**catch-all** *adj.* [only before noun]: *a catch-all phrase/term* 含义甚广的短语 / 术语

catch·er /ˈkætʃə(r)/ *noun* **1** (in BASEBALL 棒球) the player who stands behind the BATTER and catches the ball if he or she does not hit it 接手 ➲ VISUAL VOCAB PAGE V47 **2** (usually in compounds 通常构成复合词) a person or thing that catches sth 捕捉者；捕捉器： *a rat catcher* 捕鼠器

catch·ing /ˈkætʃɪŋ/ *adj.* [not before noun] **1** (of a disease 疾病) easily caught by one person from another 有传染性 **SYN** **infectious** **2** (of an emotion or a mood 情感或情绪) passing quickly from one person to another 有感染力 **SYN** **infectious**: *Try to be as enthusiastic as possible (enthusiasm is catching)!* 尽量表现出热情（热情具有感染力）！

catch·line /ˈkætʃlaɪn/ *noun* **1** (*specialist*) a short line of text which can be easily noticed, for example at the top of a page （页面顶端等处）引人注目的语句，醒目的字行 **2** a phrase used in an advertisement 广告语

catch·ment area /ˈkætʃmənt eəriə; *NAmE* eriə/ *noun* **1** the area from which a school takes its students, a hospital its patients, etc. （学校的）招生地区；（医院等的）服务地区 **2** (*also* **catch·ment**) (*specialist*) the area from which rain flows into a particular river or lake 汇水区；汇水面积

catch·penny /ˈkætʃpeni/ *adj.* (*old-fashioned*) (of a product or service 产品或服务) produced or provided just to make money, without being of good quality（劣质）只求赚钱的

catch·phrase /ˈkætʃfreɪz/ *noun* a popular phrase that is connected with the politician or entertainer who used it and made it famous 名言；流行语；时兴的话

ˈ**catch-up** *noun* **1** [U] the act of trying to reach the same level or standard as sb who is ahead of you（向别人水平的）追赶： *It was a month of catch-up for them.* 他们那个月急起直追。 **2** [C, sing.] an occasion when two or more people meet to discuss what has happened since the last time they met 谈论近况： *We must get together for a catch-up.* 我们得聚在一起说说各自的近况。◇ *I have a catch-up meeting with my manager at two.* 我和我的经纪人约好两点钟见面聊聊近况。 **3** [U] a service that allows you to watch television programmes on a computer or a special television after the time when they were originally broadcast 电视节目回放服务（通过电脑等收看）： *catch-up TV* 电视回放

IDM **play ˈcatch-up** to try to equal sb that you are competing against in a sport or game（在体育运动或比赛中）拼命赶超： *After our bad start to the season we were always playing catch-up.* 我们在赛季初表现不佳，之后一直在努力追赶。

catch·word /ˈkætʃwɜːd; *NAmE* -wɜːrd/ *noun* a word or phrase that is used to express a particular idea, typically in order to get people's attention 口号；关键词： *In education, 'quality' is the catchword.* 教育的关键词是"质量"。

catchy /ˈkætʃi/ *adj.* (*informal*) (**catch·ier**, **catchi·est**) (of music or the words of an advertisement 音乐或广告词) pleasing and easily remembered 悦耳易记的： *a catchy tune/slogan* 容易上口的乐曲 / 口号

ˈ**cat door** (*NAmE*) (*BrE* ˈ**cat flap**) *noun* a hole cut in the bottom of the door to a house, covered by a piece of plastic that swings, so a pet cat can go in and out （门下供家猫进出的）活动板猫洞

cat·ech·ism /ˈkætəkɪzəm/ *noun* [usually sing.] a set of questions and answers that are used for teaching people about the beliefs of the Christian religion（基督教的）教理问答

cat·egor·ic·al /ˌkætəˈɡɒrɪkl; *NAmE* -ˈɡɔːr-/ *adj.* [usually before noun] (*formal*) expressed clearly and in a way that shows that you are very sure about what you are saying 明确的；绝对的： *to make a categorical statement* 发表明确声明 ◇ *to give a categorical assurance* 提供绝对保证 ▸ **cat·egor·ic·al·ly** /-kli/ *adv.*: *He categorically rejected our offer.* 他断然拒绝我们的提议。

cat·egor·ize **AW** (*BrE also* **-ise**) /ˈkætəɡəraɪz/ *verb* to put people or things into groups according to what type they are 将…分类；把…加以归类 **SYN** **classify**: **~ sb/sth** *Participants were categorized according to age.* 参加者按年龄分组。◇ **~ sb/sth as sth** *His latest work cannot be categorized as either a novel or an autobiography.* 他最近的作品既不属于小说也不属于自传。 ▸ **cat·egor·iza·tion, -isa·tion** **AW** /ˌkætəɡəraɪˈzeɪʃn; *NAmE* -rəˈz-/ *noun* [U, C]

cat·egory **AW** /ˈkætəɡəri; *NAmE* -ɡɔːri/ *noun* (*pl.* **-ies**) a group of people or things with particular features in common（人或事物的）类别，种类 **SYN** **class**: *Students over 25 fall into a different **category**.* * 25 岁以上的学生属另一类。◇ *The results can be divided into three **main categories**.* 结果可分为三大类。

cater /ˈkeɪtə(r)/ *verb* [I, T] to provide food and drinks for a social event（为社交活动）提供饮食，承办餐宴： (*BrE*) **~ for sb/sth** *Most of our work now involves catering for weddings.* 我们现在的工作多半是承办婚宴。◇ (*NAmE*) **~ sth** *Who will be catering the wedding?* 谁来承办婚宴？

PHRV ˈ**cater for sb/sth** to provide the things that a particular person or situation needs or wants 满足需要；适合： *The class caters for all ability ranges.* 这个班对各种不同水平的人都适合。 ˈ**cater to sb/sth** to provide the things that a particular type of person wants, especially things that you do not approve of 满足需要；迎合： *They only publish novels which cater to the mass market.* 他们只出版迎合大众市场的小说。

cater·er /ˈkeɪtərə(r)/ *noun* a person or company whose job is to provide food and drinks at a business meeting or for a special occasion such as a wedding（商务会议或婚礼等的）酒席承办商，饮食服务公司

cater·ing /ˈkeɪtərɪŋ/ *noun* [U] the work of providing food and drinks for meetings or social events（会议或社交活动的）饮食服务，餐宴承办： *Who did the catering for your son's wedding?* 你儿子的婚宴是由谁承办的？

cat·er·pil·lar /ˈkætəpɪlə(r); *NAmE* -tərp-/ *noun* a small creature like a WORM with legs, that develops into a BUTTERFLY or MOTH (= flying insects with large, sometimes brightly coloured, wings). Caterpillars eat the leaves of plants. 蠋，毛虫（蝴蝶或蛾的幼虫） ➲ VISUAL VOCAB PAGE V13

ˈ**Caterpillar track™** (*especially BrE*) *noun* a metal belt fastened around the wheels of a heavy vehicle, used for travelling over rough or soft ground 卡特彼勒履带（重型车辆使用）

cat·er·waul /ˈkætəwɔːl; *NAmE* ˈkætər-/ *verb* [I] to make the loud unpleasant noise that is typical of a cat（猫）号叫

cat·fight /ˈkætfaɪt/ *noun* (*informal*) a fight between women 猫斗（指女人之间的打斗）

cat·fish /ˈkætfɪʃ/ *noun, verb*

■ *noun* (*pl.* **cat·fish**) **1** a large fish with long stiff hairs, like a cat's WHISKERS, around its mouth. There are several types of catfish, most of which are FRESHWATER fish. 鲇鱼（多为淡水鱼） **2** (*slang*) a person who pretends to be sb else, usually sb who does not really exist, on a SOCIAL NETWORKING website in order to deceive other people（在社交网站上）用虚拟身份行骗者

■ *verb* [I, T] to pretend to be sb else on a SOCIAL NETWORKING website in order to deceive other people（在社交网站上）用虚拟身份行骗

ˈ**cat flap** (*BrE*) (*NAmE* ˈ**cat door**) *noun* a hole cut in the bottom of the door to a house, covered by a piece of plastic that swings, so a pet cat can go in and out（门上供家猫进出的）活动板猫洞

cat·gut /ˈkætɡʌt/ (*also* **gut**) *noun* [U] thin strong string made from animals' INTESTINES and used in making musical instruments 肠线（用于制乐器的弦）

cath·ar·sis /kəˈθɑːsɪs; *NAmE* -ˈθɑːrs-/ *noun* [U, C] (*pl.* **cath·arses** /-siːz/) (*specialist*) the process of releasing strong feelings, for example through plays or other artistic activities, as a way of providing relief from anger, suffering, etc. 宣泄，净化（如通过戏剧或其他艺术活动） ▶ **cath·ar·tic** /kəˈθɑːtɪk; *NAmE* -ˈθɑːrt-/ *adj.*： *It was a cathartic experience.* 那是一次情感宣泄的体验。

cath·edral /kəˈθiːdrəl/ *noun* the main church of a district, under the care of a BISHOP (= a priest of high rank) 主教座堂；教区总教堂： *St Paul's Cathedral* 圣保罗大教堂 ◇ (*BrE*) *a cathedral city* 有主教座堂的城市

Cath·er·ine wheel /ˈkæθrɪn wiːl/ (*especially BrE*) (*NAmE usually* **pin·wheel**) *noun* a round flat FIREWORK that spins around when lit 凯瑟琳车轮式焰火；转轮烟火

cath·eter /ˈkæθɪtə(r)/ *noun* a thin tube that is put into the body in order to remove liquid such as URINE 导管（如导尿管）

cath·ode /ˈkæθəʊd; *NAmE* -oʊd/ *noun* (*specialist*) the ELECTRODE in an electrical device where REDUCTION occurs; the negative electrode in an ELECTROLYTIC cell and the positive electrode in a battery 阴极；（电解池的）负极；（原电池的）正极 ➲ COMPARE ANODE

ˌ**cathode ˈray tube** *noun* a VACUUM tube which was used in the past inside a television or computer screen, etc. from which a stream of ELECTRONS produced images on the screen 阴极射线管

Cath·olic /ˈkæθlɪk/ *noun* = ROMAN CATHOLIC： *They're Catholics.* 他们是天主教徒。 ▶ **Cath·oli·cism** /kəˈθɒləsɪzəm; *NAmE* -ˈθɑːlə-/ *noun* [U] = ROMAN CATHOLICISM

cath·olic /ˈkæθlɪk/ *adj.* **1 Catholic** = ROMAN CATHOLIC： *Are they Catholic or Protestant?* 他们是天主教徒还是新教徒？ ◇ *a Catholic church* 天主教教堂 **2** (*often* **Catholic**) (*specialist*) connected with all Christians or the whole Christian Church 全体基督教徒的；基督教会的 **3** (*formal*) including many or most things 包罗万象的；广泛的： *to have catholic tastes* (= to like many different things) 爱好广泛的

cat·ion /ˈkætaɪən/ *noun* (*chemistry* 化, *physics* 物) an ION with a positive electrical CHARGE 正离子；阳离子 ➲ COMPARE ANION

cat·kin /ˈkætkɪn/ *noun* a long thin hanging bunch, or short standing group, of soft flowers on the branches of trees such as the WILLOW 柔荑花序 ➲ VISUAL VOCAB PAGE V10

cat·mint /ˈkætmɪnt/ (*also* **cat·nip** /ˈkætnɪp/) *noun* [U] a plant that has white flowers with purple spots, leaves covered with small hairs and a smell that is attractive to cats 假荆芥；猫薄荷

cat·nap /ˈkætnæp/ *noun* a short sleep 小睡；打盹儿；瞌睡 ▶ **cat·nap** *verb* (**-pp-**) [I]

cat-o'-nine-tails /ˌkæt ə ˈnaɪn teɪlz/ *noun* [sing.] a WHIP made of nine strings with knots in them, that was used to punish prisoners in the past 九尾鞭（用九条带结的细绳编成，旧时鞭打囚犯用）

CAT scan /ˈkæt skæn/ (*also* ˌ**CˈT scan**) *noun* a medical examination that uses a computer to produce an image of the inside of sb's body from X-RAY or ULTRASOUND pictures 计算机层析成像扫描

cat's cradle 翻线戏

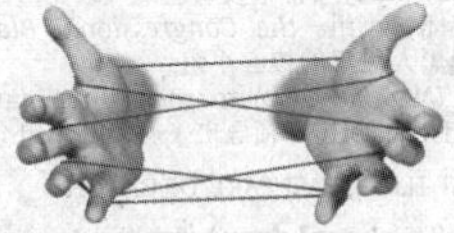

ˌ**cat's ˈcradle** *noun* **1** [U] a game in which you wrap string around the fingers of both hands to make different patterns 翻线戏，翻绳儿，挑绷子（游戏） **2** [C] a pattern made with string in a game of cat's cradle 翻线戏花样

Cats·eye™ /ˈkætsaɪ/ *noun* (*BrE*) one of a line of small objects that are fixed into a road and that reflect a car's lights in order to guide traffic at night 猫眼（固定安装在道路上的夜间反光路标）

cat·suit /ˈkætsuːt; *BrE also* -sjuːt/ *noun* a piece of women's clothing that fits closely and covers the body and legs 女式紧身连衣裤

cat·tery /ˈkætəri/ *noun* (*pl.* **-ies**) a place where people can pay to leave their cats to be cared for while they are away 猫代养所

cat·tle /ˈkætl/ *noun* [pl.] cows and BULLS that are kept as farm animals for their milk or meat 牛： *a herd of cattle* 一群牛 ◇ *twenty head of cattle* (= twenty cows) 二十头牛 ◇ *dairy/beef cattle* 乳牛；菜牛 ➲ COLLOCATIONS AT FARMING ➲ VISUAL VOCAB PAGE V7

ˈ**cattle class** *noun* [U] (*humorous*) the way of travelling on a plane, a train, etc. that costs the least and is the least comfortable 经济舱；牛栏位： *We were in cattle class on the plane so we were very cramped.* 我们坐在飞机的经济舱，局促得很。

cat·tle duff·ing /ˈkætl dʌfɪŋ/ *noun* (*AustralE*) the stealing of cows 偷牛；盗牛

ˈcattle grid (*BrE*) (*NAmE* **ˈcattle guard**) *noun* metal bars that are placed over a hole that has been made in the road. Cars can pass over the metal bars but animals such as sheep and cows cannot. 拦畜沟栅（铺在公路坑上的金属架，车辆可通过，但牛羊过不去）

C

catty /ˈkæti/ *adj.* (*informal*) (**cat·tier**, **cat·ti·est**) (of a woman 女人) saying unkind things about other people 散布流言蜚语的；刁钻刻薄的；搬弄是非的 SYN **bitchy, spiteful**: *a catty comment* 尖酸刻薄的话 ▶ **cat·ti·ness** *noun* [U]

ˌcatty-ˈcorner(ed) (*also* **ˌkitty-ˈcorner(ed)**) *adj., adv.* (*NAmE, informal*) opposite and at a DIAGONAL angle from sth/sb 成对角线（的）；斜对面（的）：*a restaurant catty-corner from the theater* 斜对着剧院的餐馆 ◇ *Motorcyclists cut catty-cornered across his yard.* 骑摩托车的人斜穿过他的院子。

cat·walk /ˈkætwɔːk/ *noun* **1** (*NAmE also* **run·way**) the long stage that models walk on during a fashion show（时装表演时供模特儿用的）狭长表演台，T 型台 ⊃ COLLOCATIONS AT FASHION **2** a narrow platform for people to walk on, for example along the outside of a building or a bridge（楼房旁、桥面等处的）狭窄人行通道

Cau·ca·sian /kɔːˈkeɪziən; kɔːˈkeɪʒn/ *noun* a member of any of the races of people who have pale skin 白种人；高加索人 ▶ **Cau·ca·sian** *adj.*

cau·cus /ˈkɔːkəs/ *noun, verb*

■ *noun* (*especially NAmE*) **1** a meeting of the members or leaders of a political party to choose candidates or to decide policy; the members or leaders of a political party as a group（由领导人或一般成员参加的为挑选候选人或制定政策的）政党会议；（政党的）全体成员，领导班子 ⊃ WORDFINDER NOTE AT CONGRESS **2** a group of people with similar interests, often within a larger organization or political party（常指较大组织或政党内部志趣相投的）派别，小集团，小组：*the Congressional Black Caucus* 美国国会提倡黑人民权的核心小组

■ *verb* [I, T] (*NAmE*) ~ (**sb**) to meet in a caucus or other group to discuss sth 开领导班子会；开小组会议

caught PAST TENSE, PAST PART. OF CATCH

caul·dron (*US also* **cal·dron**) /ˈkɔːldrən/ *noun* a large deep pot for boiling liquids or cooking food over a fire 大锅：*a witch's cauldron* 女巫的大锅 ◇ (*figurative*) *The stadium was a seething cauldron of emotion.* 体育场内群情沸腾。

cauli·flower /ˈkɒliflaʊə(r); *NAmE* ˈkɔːli-; ˈkɑːli-/ *noun* [U, C] a vegetable with green leaves around a large hard white head of flowers 花椰菜；菜花：*Do you like cauliflower?* 你喜欢菜花吗？◇ *two cauliflowers* 两个花椰菜 ⊃ VISUAL VOCAB PAGE V33

ˌcauliflower ˈcheese (*BrE*) (*NAmE* **ˌcauliflower with ˈcheese**) *noun* [U] a hot dish of cauliflower cooked and served in a cheese sauce 奶酪菜花

ˌcauliflower ˈear *noun* an ear that is permanently swollen because it has been hit many times（因多次遭殴打而永久肿胀的）菜花状耳

caulk /kɔːk/ *verb* ~ **sth** to fill the holes or cracks in sth, especially a ship, with a substance that keeps out water 补（船）的漏洞；填（船）缝

causal /ˈkɔːzl/ *adj.* **1** (*formal*) connected with the relationship between two things, where one causes the other to happen 因果关系的；前因后果的；原因的：*the causal relationship between poverty and disease* 贫穷与疾病的因果关系 **2** ~ **conjunction/connective** (*grammar* 语法) a word such as *because* that introduces a statement about the cause of sth 表示因果关系的（连接词，如 because）▶ **caus·al·ly** /-əli/ *adv.*：*Are the two factors causally connected?* 这两个因素有因果关系吗？

caus·al·ity /kɔːˈzæləti/ (*also* **caus·ation**) *noun* [U] (*formal*) the relationship between sth that happens and the reason for it happening; the principle that nothing can happen without a cause 因果关系；因果律（或性）

caus·ation /kɔːˈzeɪʃn/ *noun* [U] (*formal*) **1** the process of one event causing or producing another event 诱因；起因；原因 **2** = CAUSALITY

causa·tive /ˈkɔːzətɪv/ *adj.* **1** (*formal*) acting as the cause of sth 成为原因的；起因的：*Smoking is a causative factor in several major diseases.* 抽烟是引起几种主要疾病的病因。**2** (*grammar* 语法) a **causative verb** expresses a cause, for example *blacken* which means 'to cause to become black' 使役的（动词，如 blacken）⊃ COMPARE ERGATIVE, INCHOATIVE

cause /kɔːz/ *noun, verb*

■ *noun* **1** [C] the person or thing that makes sth happen 原因；起因：*Unemployment is a major cause of poverty.* 失业是贫困的主要原因。◇ *There was discussion about the fire and its likely cause.* 对那场火灾及其可能的起因进行了讨论。◇ *Drinking and driving is one of the most common causes of traffic accidents.* 酒后驾车是导致交通事故最常见的原因之一。**2** [U] ~ (**for sth**) a reason for having particular feelings or behaving in a particular way 理由；动机；缘故：*There is no* ***cause for concern.*** 没有理由担忧。◇ *The food was excellent—I had no* ***cause for complaint.*** 饭菜好极了，我没理由抱怨。◇ ***with/without good cause*** (= with/without a good reason) 理由充分；无缘无故 **3** [C] an organization or idea that people support or fight for（支持或为之奋斗的）事业，目标，思想：*Animal welfare campaigners raised £70 000 for their cause last year.* 动物保护主义者去年为保护动物募集了 7 万英镑。◇ ***a good cause*** (= an organization that does good work, such as a charity) 崇高的事业 ◇ *fighting for the Republican cause* 为共和党的事业而奋斗 ⊃ SEE ALSO LOST CAUSE **4** [C] (*law* 律) a case that goes to court 诉讼案

IDM **be for/in a good ˈcause** worth doing, because it is helping other people 做好事；行善 ⊃ MORE AT COMMON *adj.*

■ *verb* to make sth happen, especially sth bad or unpleasant 使发生；造成；引起；导致：~ **sth** *Do they know what caused the fire?* 他们知道引起这场火灾的原因吗？◇ *Are you* ***causing trouble*** *again?* 你又在惹麻烦吗？◇ *deaths caused by dangerous driving* 危险驾驶造成的死亡 ◇ ~ **sth for sb** *The bad weather is causing problems for many farmers.* 恶劣的天气正给许多农民造成困难。◇ ~ **sb sth** *The project is still causing him a lot of problems.* 这项工程现在仍然给他带来许多的麻烦。◇ ~ **sth to do sth** *The poor harvest caused prices to rise sharply.* 收成不好导致物价急剧上涨。

▼ LANGUAGE BANK 用语库

cause

X causes Y * X 导致 Y

- *Childhood obesity can* ***cause/lead to*** *long-term health problems.* 儿童肥胖可能导致长期的健康问题。
- *Changes in lifestyle and diet over the last twenty years have* ***caused/led to/resulted in*** *a sharp increase in childhood obesity.* 过去二十年生活方式及饮食的变化导致肥胖儿童数量急剧上升。
- *Several factors, including changes in diet and lifestyle,* ***have contributed to*** *the increase in childhood obesity.* 包括饮食及生活方式变化在内的多个因素促使肥胖儿童数量增加。
- *Research suggests that fast food and soft drinks directly* ***contribute to*** *childhood obesity.* 研究表明快餐和软饮料会直接导致儿童肥胖。
- *Genetics, lifestyle and diet* ***are*** *all important* ***factors*** *in cases of childhood obesity.* 基因、生活方式和饮食都是造成儿童肥胖的重要因素。
- *Even small changes in lifestyle and diet can* ***bring about*** *significant weight loss.* 甚至生活方式及饮食的细微变化都可能带来明显的体重下降。

⊃ LANGUAGE BANK AT CONSEQUENTLY, THEREFORE

'cause *conj.* = COS[1]

cause célèbre /ˌkɔːz seˈlebrə/ *noun* (*from French*) (*pl.* **causes célèbres** /ˌkɔːz seˈlebrə/) an issue that attracts a lot of attention and is supported by a lot of people 广受关注的有争议问题

cause·way /ˈkɔːzweɪ/ *noun* a raised road or path across water or wet ground （穿越水面或湿地的）堤道

caus·tic /ˈkɔːstɪk/ *adj.* **1** (of a chemical substance 化学物质) able to destroy or dissolve other substances 腐蚀性的；苛性的 SYN **corrosive** **2** critical in a bitter or SARCASTIC way 尖酸刻薄的；挖苦的；讥讽的 SYN **scathing**: *caustic comments/wit* 刻薄话；长于讽刺 ▸ **caus·tic·al·ly** /-kli/ *adv.*

ˌ**caustic ˈsoda** *noun* [U] a chemical used in making paper and soap 苛性钠；烧碱；氢氧化钠

caut·er·ize (*BrE also* **-ise**) /ˈkɔːtəraɪz/ *verb* **~ sth** (*medical* 医) to burn a wound, using a chemical or heat, in order to stop the loss of blood or to prevent infection 烧灼，烙（用化学药剂或高温烧灼伤口以止血或消毒）

cau·tion /ˈkɔːʃn/ *noun, verb*

▪*noun* **1** [U] care that you take in order to avoid danger or mistakes; not taking any risks 谨慎；小心；慎重：*extreme/great caution* 特别谨慎；小心翼翼 ◇ *Statistics should be treated* ***with caution***. 对待统计数字要小心。➲ SYNONYMS AT CARE **2** [C] (*BrE*) a warning that is given by the police to sb who has committed a crime that is not too serious （警察向犯轻罪的人发出的）警告：*As a first offender, she got off with a caution.* 她由于是初犯，被从轻发落，只受到了警告。 **3** [U, C] (*formal*) a warning or a piece of advice about a possible danger or risk （对危险或风险的）警告，告诫：*a* ***word/note of caution*** 一句警告 ◇ *Some cautions must be mentioned—for example good tools are essential to do the job well.* 有些忠告一定得说，如：工欲善其事，必先利其器。

IDM **throw/cast caution to the ˈwind(s)** to stop caring about how dangerous sth might be; to start taking risks 不顾危险；鲁莽行事；冒险

▪*verb* **1** [I, T] to warn sb about the possible dangers or problems of sth 警告；告诫；提醒：**~ against sth** *I would caution against getting too involved.* 我要提出警告，别介入太深。◇ **~ sb against/about sth** *Sam cautioned him against making a hasty decision.* 萨姆告诫他不要草率作出决定。◇ **~ (sb) that...** *The government cautioned that pay increases could lead to job losses.* 政府警告说增加工资会导致失业。◇ **~ sb to do sth** *Employees were cautioned to be careful about what they said to people outside the company.* 员工受到告诫，对公司外的人说话要小心谨慎。◇ **~ (sb) + speech** *'I'd take care if I were you,' she cautioned (him).* "我要是你，我会当心的。" 她提醒（他）道。**2** [T] **~ sb** (*BrE, law* 律) to warn sb officially that anything they say may be used as evidence against them in court 警告，提醒（某人说的任何话都可能在法庭上被当作对其不利的证据）：*Suspects must be cautioned before any questions are asked.* 嫌疑犯在回答问题前必须得到提醒。**3** [T, usually passive] (*BrE, law* 律) **~ sb (for sth)** to warn sb officially that they will be punished if they do sth wrong or illegal again 警告（某人不得再做错事或非法的事）：*She wasn't sent to the juvenile court; instead she was cautioned.* 她未被送上少年法庭，而是受到了警告。

cau·tion·ary /ˈkɔːʃənəri; *NAmE* -neri/ *adj.* giving advice or a warning 劝告的；告诫的；警告的：*a* ***cautionary tale*** *about the problems of buying a computer* 有关购买计算机时可能遇到种种问题的告诫 ◇ *In her conclusion, the author sounds a* ***cautionary note***. 作者在结尾时敲响了警钟。

cau·tious /ˈkɔːʃəs/ *adj.* being careful about what you say or do, especially to avoid danger or mistakes; not taking any risks 小心的；谨慎的：*The government has been cautious in its response to the report.* 政府对此报道反应谨慎。◇ *They've taken a very* ***cautious approach***. 他们采取了十分谨慎的态度。◇ *They expressed cautious optimism about a solution to the crisis.* 他们对解决危机持谨慎的乐观态度。 ◇ **~ about sb/sth | ~ about doing sth** *He was very cautious about committing himself to anything.* 他谨小慎微，从不轻易作出承诺。▸ **cau·tious·ly** *adv.*: *She looked cautiously around and then walked away from the house.* 她先小心地环顾了一下四周，然后才离开了房子。◇ *I'm cautiously optimistic.* 我持谨慎的乐观态度。 **cau·tious·ness** *noun* [U]

▼**WHICH WORD?** 词语辨析

cautious / careful

- A **cautious** person is nervous that something may be dangerous or unwise, so they only do it very slowly or after a lot of thought. (opposite = **rash**) * cautious 指人因担心某事危险或不明智而缓慢行事或小心谨慎。（反义词为 rash）
- A **careful** person is not nervous but does take extra care to make sure that everything is correct or nothing goes wrong. (opposite = **careless**) * careful 指人并非担心害怕，但为确保万无一失而做事小心仔细。（反义词为 careless）
- Notice also 还要注意：

  Be careful/Take care *when you drive on icy roads.* 在冰霜覆盖的道路上驾驶时要小心。

  Caution/Warning*—thin ice.* 小心 / 警告 —— 冰薄勿踏。

cava /ˈkɑːvə/ *noun* [U, C] a type of SPARKLING white wine (= with bubbles) from Spain 卡瓦酒（西班牙发泡白葡萄酒）

cav·al·cade /ˌkævlˈkeɪd/ *noun* a line of people on horses or in vehicles forming part of a ceremony （参加典礼的）骑马队列，车队

Cava·lier /ˌkævəˈlɪə(r); *NAmE* -ˈlɪr/ *noun* a supporter of the King in the English Civil War (1642–49) 骑士（英格兰内战中支持国王者） ➲ COMPARE ROUNDHEAD

cava·lier /ˌkævəˈlɪə(r); *NAmE* -ˈlɪr/ *adj.* [usually before noun] not caring enough about sth important or about the feelings of other people 漫不经心的；不在乎的：*The government takes a* ***cavalier attitude*** *to the problems of prison overcrowding.* 政府对监狱拥挤不堪的问题不闻不问。 ▸ **cava·lier·ly** *adv.*

cav·alry /ˈkævlri/ *noun* (*usually* **the cavalry**) [sing.+sing./pl. v.] (in the past) the part of the army that fought on horses; the part of the modern army that uses ARMOURED vehicles （旧时的）骑兵；装甲兵

cave /keɪv/ *noun, verb*

▪*noun* a large hole in the side of a hill or under the ground 山洞；洞穴：*the mouth* (= the entrance) *of the cave* 洞口 ◇ *a* ***cave-dweller*** (= a person who lives in a cave) 穴居人 ➲ VISUAL VOCAB PAGE V5

▪*verb*

PHR V ˌ**cave ˈin (on sb/sth)** (of a roof, wall, etc. 房顶、墙等) to fall down and towards the centre 塌落；塌陷；坍塌：*The ceiling suddenly caved in on top of them.* 他们头顶的天花板突然塌落。 ➲ RELATED NOUN CAVE-IN ˌ**cave ˈin (to sth)** to finally do what sb wants after you have been strongly opposing them 让步；屈服；屈从：*The President is unlikely to cave in to demands for a public inquiry.* 总统未必会同意进行公开调查。 ➲ SEE ALSO CAVING

cav·eat /ˈkæviæt/ *noun* (*formal, from Latin*) a warning that particular things need to be considered before sth can be done 警告；告诫

cav·eat emp·tor /ˌkæviæt ˈemptɔː(r)/ *noun* (*from Latin*) the principle that a person who buys sth is responsible for finding any faults in the thing they buy 买主购物自行小心（买主购物时有责任检查所购货物是否有问题）

ˈ**cave-in** *noun* the fact of sth suddenly collapsing （突然的）塌陷，坍塌，倒塌

cave·man /ˈkeɪvmæn/ *noun* (*pl.* **-men** /-men/) **1** a person who lived in a CAVE thousands of years ago （数千年前的）穴居人 **2** (*informal*) a man who behaves in an aggressive way 野蛮的人；粗野的人

ˈcave painting *noun* a PREHISTORIC painting on the walls of a CAVE, often showing animals and hunting scenes （史前期画有动物和狩猎场面的）洞穴壁画

C

caver /ˈkeɪvə(r)/ (*also* **pot·holer** *BrE*) (*NAmE* **spe·lunk·er**) *noun* a person who goes into CAVES under the ground as a sport or hobby 探察洞穴者（以此为体育运动或业余爱好） ➲ COMPARE SPELEOLOGIST

cav·ern /ˈkævən; *NAmE* -vərn/ *noun* a CAVE, especially a large one 大洞穴；大山洞

cav·ern·ous /ˈkævənəs; *NAmE* -vərn-/ *adj.* (*formal*) (of a room or space 房间或空间) very large and often empty and/or dark; like a CAVE 大而空的；又黑又深的；像洞穴的

cav·iar (*also* **cavi·are**) /ˈkæviɑː(r)/ *noun* [U] the eggs of some types of fish, especially the STURGEON, that are preserved using salt and eaten as a very special and expensive type of food （尤指用鲟鱼子腌制的）鱼子酱

cavil /ˈkævl/ *verb* (**-ll-**, *especially US* **-l-**) [I] ~ (**at sth**) (*formal*) to make unnecessary complaints about sth 无端抱怨；挑剔；吹毛求疵 **SYN** **quibble**

cav·ing /ˈkeɪvɪŋ/ (*BrE also* **pot·hol·ing**) (*NAmE* **spe·lunk·ing**) *noun* [U] the sport or activity of going into CAVES under the ground 洞穴探察：*He had always wanted to go caving.* 他过去一直想探索洞穴。 ➲ VISUAL VOCAB PAGE V44

cav·ity /ˈkævəti/ *noun* (*pl.* **-ies**) (*formal* or *specialist*) **1** a hole or empty space inside sth solid 洞；孔；窟窿；腔：*the abdominal cavity* 腹腔 **2** a hole in a tooth （龋齿的）窝洞，洞 ➲ WORDFINDER NOTE AT DENTIST

ˌcavity ˈwall *noun* a wall consisting of two walls with a space between them, designed to prevent heat from escaping （有保暖作用的）空心墙，夹壁墙：*cavity wall insulation* 空心墙隔热

ca·vort /kəˈvɔːt; *NAmE* kəˈvɔːrt/ *verb* [I] + **adv./prep.** to jump or move around in a noisy, excited and often sexual way 欢跃；欢蹦乱跳；嬉戏；放荡地玩乐：*The photos showed her cavorting on the beach with her new lover.* 这些照片展现了她和新欢在海滩上放荡嬉戏的情景。

caw /kɔː/ *noun* the loud, unpleasant sound that is made by birds such as CROWS and ROOKS 鸦叫声；聒耳的叫声 ▸ **caw** *verb* [I] ➲ MORE LIKE THIS 4, page R25

cay·enne /keɪˈen/ (*also* **ˌcayenne ˈpepper**) *noun* [U] a type of red pepper used in cooking to give a hot flavour to food 红辣椒

cay·man = CAIMAN

CB /ˌsiː ˈbiː/ *noun* [U] the abbreviation for 'Citizens' Band' (a range of waves on a radio on which people can talk to each other over short distances, especially when driving) 民用波段，民用电台频带（全写为 Citizens' Band，在短距离内，尤指驾车时可通话的无线电波段）：*A truck driver used his CB radio to call for help.* 卡车司机用民用波段无线电呼救。

CBE /ˌsiː biː ˈiː/ *noun* the abbreviation for 'Commander (of the Order) of the British Empire' (an award given in Britain to some people for a special achievement) 英帝国高级勋位获得者，英帝国司令勋衔获得者（全写为 Commander (of the Order) of the British Empire，英国授予有特殊功绩的人的奖励）：*He was made a CBE in 2012.* 他在 2012 年获颁英帝国高级勋位。◇ *Shami Chakrabarti CBE* 英帝国高级勋爵沙米·查克拉巴提

CBI /ˌsiː biː ˈaɪ/ *abbr.* Confederation of British Industry (an important organization to which businesses and industries belong) 英国产业联合会

CBS /ˌsiː biː ˈes/ *abbr.* Columbia Broadcasting System (an American recording and broadcasting company that produces records, television programmes, etc.) （美国）哥伦比亚广播公司

CBSA /ˌsiː biː es ˈeɪ/ *abbr.* Canadian Border Services Agency (the department of the Canadian government that deals with people coming into the country and with taxes on goods that are bought and sold) 加拿大边境服务局（负责出入境和海关检查）

CBT /ˌsiː biː ˈtiː/ (*also* **ˌcognitive beˈhavioural therapy** /ˌkɒɡnətɪv bɪˌheɪvjərəl ˈθerəpi; *NAmE* ˌkɑːɡ-/, **ˌcognitive ˈtherapy** /ˌkɒɡnətɪv ˈθerəpi; *NAmE* ˌkɑːɡ-/) *noun* [U] a type of PSYCHOTHERAPY in which you are encouraged to change the way you think about yourself and the world 认知行为疗法，认识疗法（全写为 cognitive behavioural therapy，一种心理疗法，鼓励人改变认知自我和世界的方式）

cc /ˌsiː ˈsiː/ *abbr.*, *verb*

■ ***abbr.*** **1** carbon copy (to) (used on business letters and emails to show that a copy is being sent to another person) 副本，抄送（用于商务书信和电子邮件，表示副本同时发送给另一人）：*to Luke Peters, cc Janet Gold* 寄卢克·彼得斯，抄送珍妮特·戈尔德 **2** cubic centimetre(s) 立方厘米；毫升；西西：*an 850cc engine* * 850 毫升发动机

■ ***verb*** (**cc's, cc'ing, cc'ed, cc'ed** /ˌsiː ˈsiːd/) **~ sth** (**to sb**) | **~ sb sth** (*informal*) to send sb a copy of a letter or email message that you are sending to sb else 抄送（将信函或电邮同时发送给收信人以外的人）：*Her message was sent to the company president and cc'ed to us.* 她的邮件发给了公司总裁，同时抄送我们了。

CCTV /ˌsiː siː tiː ˈviː/ *abbr.* CLOSED-CIRCUIT TELEVISION 闭路电视

CCU /ˌsiː siː ˈjuː/ *noun* **1** the abbreviation for 'critical care unit' (= part of a hospital that provides intensive care) 危重症监护病房，加护病房（全写为 critical care unit） **2** the abbreviation for 'coronary care unit' or 'cardiac care unit' (= part of a hospital that provides care for people with heart conditions) 冠心病监护治疗病房，心脏病加护病房（全写为 coronary care unit 或 cardiac care unit）

CD 🔑 /ˌsiː ˈdiː/ (*also* **disc**) *noun* the abbreviation for 'compact disc' (a small disc on which sound or information is recorded. CDs are played on a special machine called a **CD player**.) 光盘，激光唱片，光碟（全写为 compact disc）：*His albums are available on CD and online.* 他的专辑可以购买 CD 或在线获得。 ➲ COLLOCATIONS AT MUSIC

ˌCˈD burner (*also* **ˌCˈD writer**) *noun* a piece of software or equipment used for copying sound or information from a computer onto a CD 光盘刻录机；光盘刻录软件

CD-I (*US* **CDI™**) /ˌsiː diː ˈaɪ/ *noun* **1** [U] the abbreviation for 'compact disc interactive' (a MULTIMEDIA system which uses CDs that can react to instructions given by the user) 光碟交互播放系统（全写为 compact disc interactive，一种受使用者指令控制的多媒体光盘系统） **2** [C] the type of CD that this type of system uses 交互式光碟

CD-R™ /ˌsiː diː ˈɑː(r)/ *noun* [C, U] the abbreviation for 'compact disc recordable' (a CD on which information, sound and pictures can be recorded once only) 可录光碟（可作一次性刻录，全写为 compact disc recordable）

Cdr (*also* **Cdr.** *especially in US*) *abbr.* (in writing 书写形式) COMMANDER 海军中校；高级警官：*Cdr (John) Stone* （约翰·）斯通警官

Cdre *abbr.* (in writing 书写形式) = COMMODORE

CD-ROM /ˌsiː diː ˈrɒm; *NAmE* ˈrɑːm/ *noun* [C, U] the abbreviation for 'compact disc read-only memory' (a CD on which large amounts of information, sound and pictures can be stored, for use on a computer) 只读光盘存储器，只读光碟（全写为 compact disc read-only memory）：*The software package contains 5 CD-ROMs.* 这个软件包由 5 张只读光盘组成。◇ *The encyclopedia is available on CD-ROM.* 百科全书有光盘版。◇ *a CD-ROM drive* (= in a computer) 只读光盘驱动器 ➲ VISUAL VOCAB PAGE V73 ➲ COMPARE ROM

CD-RW /ˌsiː diː ɑː ˈdʌbljuː; *NAmE* ɑːr/ *noun* [C, U] the abbreviation for 'compact disc rewritable' (a CD on which information, sound and pictures can be recorded and removed more than once) 可重写光碟（全写为 compact disc rewritable）

CDT /ˌsiː diː ˈtiː/ *abbr.* CENTRAL DAYLIGHT TIME 中部夏令时

ˌCˈD writer *noun* = CD BURNER

CE /ˌsiː ˈiː/ *abbr.* **1** (in Britain) Church of England 英国国教会；英格兰圣公会 **2** (*also* **C.E.** *especially in NAmE*) Common Era (the period since the birth of Christ when the Christian CALENDAR starts counting years). CE can be used to give dates in the same way as AD. 基督纪元，公元（表示日期时用法同 AD） ➲ COMPARE AD, BC, BCE

cease 🔑 AW /siːs/ *verb* [I, T] (*formal*) to stop happening or existing; to stop sth from happening or existing （使）停止，终止，结束：*Welfare payments cease as soon as an individual starts a job.* 一旦就业，即停发福利救济。◇ **~ to do sth** *You never cease to amaze me!* 你总能让我感到惊奇！◇ **~ sth** *They voted to cease strike action immediately.* 他们投票决定立即停止罢工。◇ *He ordered his men to cease fire* (= stop shooting). 他命令手下停止射击。◇ **~ doing sth** *The company ceased trading in June.* 这家公司已于六月停业。 ➲ SEE ALSO CESSATION IDM SEE WONDER *n.*

cease·fire /ˈsiːsfaɪə(r)/ *noun* a time when enemies agree to stop fighting, usually while a way is found to end the fighting permanently （通常指永久性的）停火，停战 SYN **truce**：*a call for an immediate ceasefire* 要求立即停火的呼吁 ◇ *Observers have reported serious violations of the ceasefire.* 观察员报告说停火协议遭到严重破坏。 ➲ WORDFINDER NOTE AT PEACE ➲ COLLOCATIONS AT WAR

cease·less AW /ˈsiːsləs/ *adj.* (*formal*) not stopping; seeming to have no end 不停的；（好像）无休止的，不断的 SYN **constant, interminable** ▶ **cease·less·ly** *adv.*

cecum (*NAmE*) (*BrE* **cae·cum**) /ˈsiːkəm/ *noun* (*pl.* **ceca** /ˈsiːkə/) a small bag which is part of the INTESTINE, between the small and the large intestine 盲肠

cedar /ˈsiːdə(r)/ *noun* **1** (*also* **ˈcedar tree**) [C] a tall EVERGREEN tree with wide spreading branches 雪松 **2** (*also* **cedar·wood**) [U] the hard red wood of the cedar tree, which has a sweet smell 雪松木

cede /siːd/ *verb* **~ sth (to sb)** (*formal*) to give sb control of sth or give them power, a right, etc., especially unwillingly 割让；让给；转让：*Alsace-Lorraine was ceded to Germany by France in 1871.* 法国于 1871 年将阿尔萨斯－洛林割让给德国。 ➲ SEE ALSO CESSION

ce·dilla /sɪˈdɪlə/ *noun* the mark placed under the letter *c* in French, Portuguese, etc. to show that it is pronounced like an *s* rather than a *k*, as in *français*; a similar mark under *s* in Turkish and some other languages 下加符，下加变音符（法语、葡萄牙语等 c 字母下面加的符号，表示发音像 s 而不像 k，如 français；土耳其语和其他一些语言中 s 字母下有类似的符号）

CEFR /ˌsiː iː ef ˈɑː(r)/ *abbr.* Common European Framework of Reference for languages (a description of the language abilities of students at different levels of learning, that can be used to help different countries to compare standards and create teaching programmes) 欧洲共同语言参考标准（全写为 Common European Framework of Reference for languages，对学生的语言能力水平作分级描述，有助于各国对比标准和制订教学方案）：*The course is suitable for students at CEFR level B1.* 本课程适合欧洲共同语言参考标准 B1 级的学生。

cei·lidh /ˈkeɪli/ *noun* a social occasion with music and dancing, especially in Scotland and Ireland （苏格兰、爱尔兰有音乐舞蹈的）同乐会，社交集会

ceil·ing 🔑 /ˈsiːlɪŋ/ *noun* **1** 🔑 the top inside surface of a room 天花板；顶棚：*She lay on her back staring up at the ceiling.* 她仰卧着凝视天花板。◇ *a large room with a high ceiling* 屋顶很高的大房间 **2** the highest limit or amount of sth 最高限度；上限；最大限量：*price ceilings* 最高限价 ➲ COMPARE FLOOR *n.* (7) **3** (*specialist*) the greatest height at which a particular aircraft is able to fly 升限；最高飞行限度 ➲ SEE ALSO GLASS CEILING IDM SEE HIT *v.*

ˈceiling rose (*also* **rose**) *noun* (*specialist*) a round object that is fixed to the ceiling of a room for the wires of an electric light to go through （天花板或顶棚的）灯线盒

celeb /səˈleb/ *noun* (*informal*) = CELEBRITY (1)

cele·brant /ˈselɪbrənt/ *noun* **1** a priest who leads a church service, especially the COMMUNION (1) service; a person who attends a service 主持宗教仪式（尤指圣餐）的神父；参加教堂仪式的人 **2** (*NAmE*) a person who is celebrating sth, for example at a party 参加聚会（或庆典）的人

cele·brate 🔑 /ˈselɪbreɪt/ *verb* **1** 🔑 [I, T] to show that a day or an event is important by doing sth special on it 庆祝；庆贺：*Jake's passed his exams. We're going out to celebrate.* 杰克已通过考试，我们要外出庆祝一下。◇ **~ sth** *We celebrated our 25th wedding anniversary in Florence.* 我们在佛罗伦萨庆祝结婚 25 周年。◇ *How do people celebrate New Year in your country?* 你们国家的人怎样庆贺新年？

> **WORDFINDER** 联想词：anniversary, birthday, commemorate, festivity, jubilee, occasion, parade, party, reception

2 [T] **~ sth** to perform a religious ceremony, especially the Christian COMMUNION (1) service 主持宗教仪式（尤指圣餐） **3** [T] **~ sb/sth** (*formal*) to praise sb/sth 赞美；颂扬；歌颂：*a movie celebrating the life and work of Nelson Mandela* 颂扬纳尔逊•曼德拉生平事迹的影片

cele·brated /ˈselɪbreɪtɪd/ *adj.* famous for having good qualities 著名的；闻名的；驰名的：*a celebrated painter* 著名的画家

cele·bra·tion 🔑 /ˌselɪˈbreɪʃn/ *noun* **1** 🔑 [C] a special event that people organize in order to celebrate sth 庆典；庆祝活动：*birthday/wedding celebrations* 生日 / 结婚庆典 **2** 🔑 [U, C] the act of celebrating sth 庆祝；颂扬：*Her triumph was a* ***cause for celebration***. 她的胜利是庆祝的理由。◇ *a party* ***in celebration of*** *their fiftieth wedding anniversary* 庆祝他们金婚纪念的聚会 ◇ *The service was a celebration of his life* (= praised what he had done in his life). 举行的宗教礼仪颂扬了他的一生。

cele·bra·tory /ˌseləˈbreɪtəri; *NAmE* ˈseləbrətɔːri/ *adj.* celebrating sth or marking a special occasion 庆祝的；庆典的：*a* ***celebratory drink/dinner*** 喜庆酒 / 宴会

ce·leb·rity /səˈlebrəti/ *noun* (*pl.* **-ies**) **1** (*also informal* **celeb**, *informal* **sleb**) [C] a famous person 名人；名流：*TV celebrities* 电视名人 **2** [U] the state of being famous 名望；名誉；著名 SYN **fame**：*Does he find his new celebrity intruding on his private life?* 他是否感觉到他最近的成名侵扰了他的私生活？

cel·eri·ac /səˈleriæk/ *noun* [U] a large white root vegetable which is a type of CELERY and which is eaten raw or cooked 块根芹；根芹菜

cel·ery /ˈseləri/ *noun* [U] a vegetable with long crisp light green STEMS that are often eaten raw 芹菜：(*BrE*) *a stick of celery* 一根芹菜 ◇ (*NAmE*) *a stalk of celery* 一根芹菜 ➲ VISUAL VOCAB PAGE V33

cel·esta /səˈlestə/ (*also* **ce·leste** /səˈlest/) *noun* a small musical instrument with a keyboard, that produces a sound like bells 钢片琴

ce·les·tial /səˈlestiəl; *NAmE* -tʃl/ *adj.* [usually before noun] (*formal* or *literary*) of the sky or of heaven 天空的；天上的：***celestial bodies*** (= the sun, moon, stars, etc.) 天体 ◇ *celestial light/music* 天体光；仙乐 ➲ COMPARE TERRESTRIAL (2)

ce·liac dis·ease (*NAmE*) (*BrE* **coel·iac disease**) /ˈsiːliæk dɪziːz/ *noun* a disease in which sb cannot DIGEST food (= break it down in their body) because their body is very sensitive to GLUTEN (= a PROTEIN that is found in WHEAT) 乳糜泻（因麸胶过敏引起的消化不良）

celi·bate /ˈselɪbət/ *adj., noun*

■ *adj.* **1** not married and not having sex, especially for religious reasons （尤指因宗教原因）独身的，不结婚的，没有性生活的： *celibate priests* 独身的教士 **2** not having sex 无性生活的；禁欲的： *I've been celibate for the past six months.* 我已禁欲六个月。 ▸ **celi·bacy** /ˈselɪbəsi/ *noun* [U]: *a vow of celibacy* 独身誓言

■ *noun* (*formal*) a person who has chosen not to marry; a person who never has sex 独身主义者；禁欲者；从不过性生活的人

cell /sel/ *noun* **1** a room for one or more prisoners in a prison or police station 单间牢房；牢房 ➲ SEE ALSO PADDED CELL ➲ WORDFINDER NOTE AT PRISON **2** a small room without much furniture in which a MONK or NUN lives （修道士或修女住的）小房间 **3** the smallest unit of living matter that can exist on its own. All plants and animals are made up of cells. 细胞： *blood cells* 血细胞 ◇ *the nucleus of a cell* 细胞核 ➲ SEE ALSO STEM CELL ➲ WORDFINDER NOTE AT BIOLOGY **4** each of the small sections that together form a larger structure, for example a HONEYCOMB （大结构中的）小隔室（如蜂房巢室） **5** a device for producing an electric current, for example by the action of chemicals or light 电池： *a photoelectric cell* 光电池 **6** a small group of people who work as part of a larger political organization, especially secretly（尤指秘密的）政治小组，基层组织： *a terrorist cell* 恐怖分子小组 **7** one of the small squares in a SPREADSHEET computer program in which you enter a single piece of data（计算机电子表格的）单元格 **8** (*informal, especially NAmE*) = CELL PHONE

cel·lar /ˈselə(r)/ *noun* **1** an underground room often used for storing things 地窖；地下室： *a coal cellar* 贮煤地窖 **2** = WINE CELLAR ➲ SEE ALSO SALT CELLAR

cell·ist /ˈtʃelɪst/ *noun* a person who plays the CELLO 大提琴手；大提琴演奏者

cell·mate /ˈselmeɪt/ *noun* a prisoner with whom another prisoner shares a cell 同牢难友

cello /ˈtʃeləʊ; *NAmE* -loʊ/ (*also formal* **vio·lon·cello**) *noun* (*pl.* **-os**) a musical instrument with strings, shaped like a large VIOLIN. The player sits down and holds the cello between his or her knees. 大提琴 ➲ VISUAL VOCAB PAGE V38

Cel·lo·phane™ /ˈseləfeɪn/ *noun* [U] a thin transparent plastic material used for wrapping things 赛璐玢（用于包装的玻璃纸）

ˈcell phone /ˈselfəʊn; *NAmE* ˈselfoʊn/ (*also* ˌ**cellular ˈphone**, *informal* **cell**) (*especially NAmE*) (*BrE usually* ˌ**mobile ˈphone**, **mo·bile**) *noun* a telephone that does not have wires and works by radio, that you can carry with you and use anywhere 移动电话；手机： *cell phone users* 移动电话用户 ◇ *I talked to her on my cell phone.* 我用手机跟她通话。 ◇ *The use of cellular phones is not permitted on most aircraft.* 大多数飞机上禁止使用手机。 ➲ COLLOCATIONS AT PHONE

cel·lu·lar /ˈseljələ(r)/ *adj.* **1** connected with or consisting of the cells of plants or animals 细胞的；由细胞组成的： *cellular structure/processes* 细胞结构／变化过程 **2** connected with a telephone system that works by radio instead of wires（无线电话）蜂窝状的： *a cellular network* 蜂窝式网络系统 ◇ *cellular radio* 蜂窝式无线传输系统 **3** (*BrE*) (of cloth 布料) loosely WOVEN for extra warmth 网状的；网眼的： *cellular blankets* 网眼毯

cel·lu·lite /ˈseljulaɪt/ *noun* [U] a type of fat that some people get below their skin, which stops the surface of the skin looking smooth 皮下脂肪团

cel·lu·loid /ˈseljulɔɪd/ *noun* [U] **1** a thin transparent plastic material made in sheets, used in the past for cinema film （旧时摄影用的）胶片，赛璐珞片 **2** (*old-fashioned*) used as a way of referring to films/movies 电影

cel·lu·lose /ˈseljuləʊs; *NAmE* -loʊs/ *noun* [U] **1** a natural substance that forms the cell walls of all plants and trees and is used in making plastics, paper, etc. 纤维素 **2** any COMPOUND of cellulose used in making paint, LACQUER, etc.（用于制作涂料、漆等的）纤维素化合物

Cel·sius /ˈselsiəs/ (*also* **centi·grade**) *adj.* (*abbr.* **C**) of or using a scale of temperature in which water freezes at 0° and boils at 100° 摄氏的： *It will be a mild night, around nine degrees Celsius.* 晚间天气温和，温度约九摄氏度。 ◇ *the Celsius Scale* 摄氏温标 ▸ **Cel·sius** *noun* [U]: *temperatures in Celsius and Fahrenheit* 摄氏和华氏温度

Celt /kelt/ *noun* **1** a member of a race of people from western Europe who settled in ancient Britain before the Romans came 凯尔特人（在罗马人之前定居不列颠的西欧人） **2** a person whose ANCESTORS were Celts, especially one from Ireland, Wales, Scotland, Cornwall or Brittany （尤指来自爱尔兰、威尔士、苏格兰、康沃尔或布列塔尼的）凯尔特人后裔

Cel·tic /ˈkeltɪk/ *adj.* connected with the Celts or their language 凯尔特人的；凯尔特语的： *Celtic history* 凯尔特人的历史

ˌ**Celtic ˈcross** *noun* a cross with the vertical part longer than the horizontal part and a circle round the centre 凯尔特十字（垂直线比水平线长，中间有圆环）

the ˌ**Celtic ˈfringe** *noun* [sing.] (*BrE*) the people in Ireland and western parts of Britain whose ANCESTORS were CELTS, often used to refer to Ireland, Scotland and Wales 凯尔特外缘（祖先为凯尔特人的爱尔兰和不列颠西部的人，常用以指爱尔兰、苏格兰和威尔士）

ce·ment /sɪˈment/ *noun, verb*

■ *noun* [U] **1** a grey powder made by burning CLAY and LIME that sets hard when it is mixed with water. Cement is used in building to stick bricks together and to make very hard surfaces. 水泥 ➲ WORDFINDER NOTE AT CONSTRUCTION **2** the hard substance that is formed when cement becomes dry and hard （干燥后硬化的）水泥： *a floor of cement* 水泥地板 ◇ *a cement floor* 水泥地板 ➲ SEE ALSO CONCRETE *n.*, MORTAR *n.* (1) **3** a soft substance that becomes hard when dry and is used for sticking things together or filling in holes 胶合剂；胶接剂；黏固剂： *dental cement* (= for filling holes in teeth) 补牙用的黏固剂 **4** (*formal*) something that unites people in a common interest （共同利益联合起来的）纽带，凝聚力： *values which are the cement of society* 使社会具有凝聚力的价值观念

■ *verb* **1** [often passive] **~ A and B (together)** to join two things together using cement, glue, etc.（用水泥、胶等）黏结，胶合 **2 ~ sth** to make a relationship, an agreement, etc. stronger 加强，巩固（关系、协定等） SYN **strengthen**: *The President's visit was intended to cement the alliance between the two countries.* 总统的访问是为了加强两国的联盟。

cemen·ta·tion /ˌsiːmenˈteɪʃn/ *noun* [U] **1** (*chemistry* 化) the process of changing a metal by heating it together with a powder （金属的）渗镀 **2** (*geology* 地) the process of grains of sand, etc. sticking together to form SEDIMENTARY rocks （沙土等的）胶结，胶结作用

ceˈment mixer (*also* ˈ**concrete mixer**) *noun* a machine with a drum that holds sand, water and cement and turns to mix them together 混凝土搅拌机；搅拌车 ➲ VISUAL VOCAB PAGE V63

cem·et·ery /ˈsemətri; *NAmE* -teri/ *noun* (*pl.* **-ies**) an area of land used for burying dead people, especially one that is not beside a church（尤指不靠近教堂的）墓地，坟地，公墓 ➲ COMPARE CHURCHYARD, GRAVEYARD (1) ➲ WORDFINDER NOTE AT DIE

ceno·taph /ˈsenətɑːf; *NAmE* -tæf/ *noun* a MONUMENT built in memory of soldiers killed in war who are buried somewhere else （为葬于他处的阵亡士兵建立的）纪念碑

cen·ser /ˈsensə(r)/ *noun* a container for holding and burning INCENSE (= a substance that produces a pleasant smell), used especially during religious ceremonies （尤用于宗教仪式等的）香炉

cen·sor /'sensə(r)/ *noun, verb*

■ ***noun*** a person whose job is to examine books, films/movies, etc. and remove parts which are considered to be offensive, immoral or a political threat（书籍、电影等的）审查员，审查官

■ ***verb*** **~ sth** to remove the parts of a book, film/movie, etc. that are considered to be offensive, immoral or a political threat 删剪（书籍、电影等中被认为犯忌、违反道德或政治上危险的内容）：*The news reports had been* ***heavily censored.*** 这些新闻报道已被大幅删剪。

cen·sori·ous /sen'sɔːriəs/ *adj.* (*formal*) tending to criticize people or things a lot 爱挑剔的；吹毛求疵的 **SYN critical**

cen·sor·ship /'sensəʃɪp; *NAmE* -sərʃ-/ *noun* [U] the act or policy of CENSORING books, etc. 审查；检查；审查制度：*press censorship* 新闻审查制度 ◇ *The decree imposed strict censorship of the media.* 这个法令强制实行严格的媒体审查制度。 ⊃WORDFINDER NOTE AT JOURNALIST

cen·sure /'senʃə(r)/ *noun, verb*

■ ***noun*** [U] (*formal*) strong criticism 严厉的批评；斥责；谴责：*a vote of censure on the government's foreign policy* 投票表决谴责政府的外交政策

■ ***verb*** **~ sb (for sth)** (*formal*) to criticize sb severely, and often publicly, because of sth they have done（公开地）严厉斥责，谴责 **SYN rebuke**: *He was censured for leaking information to the press.* 他因泄露消息给新闻界而受到谴责。

cen·sus /'sensəs/ *noun* (*pl.* **cen·suses**) the process of officially counting sth, especially a country's population, and recording various facts（官方的）统计；人口普查；人口调查

cent 🔑 /sent/ *noun* (*abbr.* **c**, **ct**) a coin and unit of money worth 1% of the main unit of money in many countries, for example of the US dollar or of the euro 分（辅币单位，相当于许多国家主币面值的 1%，如美元或欧元的 1%）；分币 ⊃SEE ALSO PER CENT *n.*, RED CENT

IDM **put in your two 'cents' worth** (*NAmE*) (*BrE* **put in your two 'pennyworth**, **put in your two 'penn'orth**) (*informal*) to give your opinion about sth, even if other people do not want to hear it 发表意见（即使别人不想听）

cent. *abbr.* century 世纪：*in the 20th cent.* 在 20 世纪

cen·taur /'sentɔː(r)/ *noun* (in ancient Greek stories) a creature with a man's head, arms and upper body on a horse's body and legs（古希腊神话中的）半人半马怪

cen·ten·ar·ian /ˌsentɪ'neəriən; *NAmE* -'ner-/ *noun* a person who is 100 years old or more 人瑞；百岁人瑞

cen·ten·ary /sen'tiːnəri; *NAmE* -'tenəri/ (*pl.* **-ies**) (*especially BrE*) (*NAmE usually* **cen·ten·nial**) *noun* the 100th anniversary of an event * 100 周年纪念：*The club will celebrate its centenary next year.* 俱乐部明年要庆祝成立一百周年。◇ *the centenary year* 一百周年纪念年 ⊃SEE ALSO BICENTENARY, TERCENTENARY

cen·ten·nial /sen'teniəl/ (*especially NAmE*) (*BrE usually* **cen·ten·ary**) *noun* the 100th anniversary of an event * 100 周年纪念：*The year 1889 was the centennial of the inauguration of George Washington.* * 1889 年是乔治·华盛顿就职一百周年纪念。 ⊃SEE ALSO BICENTENNIAL

cen·ter (*US*) = CENTRE

cen·ter·board, **cen·tered**, **cen·ter·fold**, **cen·ter·piece** (*US*) = CENTREBOARD, CENTRED, CENTREFOLD, CENTREPIECE

centi- /'sentɪ/ *combining form* (in nouns 构成名词) **1** hundred 一百：*centipede* 蜈蚣 **2** (often used in units of measurement 常用于计量单位) one hundredth 百分之一：*centimetre* 厘米

centi·grade /'sentɪgreɪd/ *adj.* = CELSIUS：*a temperature of 40 degrees centigrade* * 40 摄氏度的温度 ▶ **centi·grade** *noun* [U]: *temperatures in centigrade and Fahrenheit* 摄氏和华氏温度

centi·gram (*also* **centi·gramme**) /'sentɪgræm/ *noun* a unit for measuring weight. There are 100 centigrams in a gram. 厘克

centi·litre (*especially US* **centi·liter**) /'sentɪliːtə(r)/ *noun* (*abbr.* **cl**) a unit for measuring liquids. There are 100 centilitres in a litre. 厘升

centi·metre 🔑 (*especially US* **centi·meter**) /'sentɪmiːtə(r)/ *noun* (*abbr.* **cm**) a unit for measuring length. There are 100 centimetres in a metre. 厘米

centi·pede /'sentɪpiːd/ *noun* a small creature like an insect, with a long thin body and many legs 蜈蚣

cen·tral 🔑 /'sentrəl/ *adj.* **1** 🔑 most important 最重要的；首要的；主要的：*The central issue is that of widespread racism.* 最重要的问题是种族主义到处泛滥。◇ *She has been a central figure in the campaign.* 她一直是这场运动的主要人物。◇ *Prevention also plays a central role in traditional medicine.* 预防在传统医学中也起着主导作用。◇ *Reducing inflation is* ***central to*** (= is an important part of) *the government's economic policy.* 减少通货膨胀是政府经济政策重要的组成部分。 ⊃SYNONYMS AT MAIN **2** 🔑 having power or control over other parts 起支配作用的；有控制力的：*the central committee* (= of a political party)（政党的）中央委员会 ◇ *The organization has a central office in York.* 该组织在约克设有总部。 **3** 🔑 in the centre of an area or object 在中心的；中央的：*central London* 伦敦中心区 ◇ *Central America/Europe/Asia* 中美洲；中欧；中亚 ◇ *the central area of the brain* 大脑中枢 **4** 🔑 easily reached from many areas 容易到达的；交通方便的；四通八达的：*The flat is very central—just five minutes from Princes Street.* 这座公寓位于市中心，离王子街只需要五分钟。◇ *a central location* 中心位置 **5** (*phonetics* 语音) (of a vowel 元音) produced with the centre of the tongue in a higher position than the front or the back, for example /ɜː/ in *bird* 中央的（发音时舌高点在口腔中间位置） ⊃COMPARE BACK *adj.* (4), FRONT *adj.* (2) ▶ **cen·tral·ity** /sen'trælәti/ *noun* [U] (*formal*): *the centrality of the family as a social institution* 家庭作为一种社会机构的重要性 **cen·tral·ly** /'sentrəli/ *adv.*: *The hotel is centrally located for all major attractions.* 这家旅馆位于中心地带，前往所有主要景点都很方便。◇ *a centrally planned economy* 中央计划经济 ◇ *Is the house centrally heated* (= does it have central heating)? 这房子有中央供暖吗？

ˌCentral A'merica *noun* [U] the part of N America that consists of Guatemala, Belize, Honduras, El Salvador, Nicaragua, Costa Rica and Panama 中美洲（包括危地马拉、伯利兹、洪都拉斯、萨尔瓦多、尼加拉瓜、哥斯达黎加以及巴拿马） ▶ **ˌCentral A'merican** *adj., noun*

ˌcentral 'bank *noun* a national bank that does business with the government and other banks, and issues the country's coins and paper money 中央银行

ˌcentral 'casting *noun* [U] a company or a department that supplies actors, usually for small, STEREOTYPICAL film roles 角色分派中心（通常分派模式化次要电影角色的公司或部门）：(*figurative*) *He looked like an absent-minded professor straight out of central casting.* 他看起来就像径直从角色分派中心走出来的心不在焉的教授。

ˌCentral 'Daylight Time *noun* [U] (*abbr.* **CDT**) the time used in summer in the central US and Canada, which is five hours behind UTC 中部夏令时（美国中部和加拿大中部的夏令时，比协调世界时晚五小时）

ˌCentral Euroˌpean 'Summer Time *noun* [U] (*abbr.* **CEST**) the time used in summer in central and part of western Europe, which is two hours ahead of UTC 欧洲中部夏令时间，中欧夏令时（用于中欧及部分西欧地区，比协调世界时早两个小时）

ˌCentral Euro'pean Time *noun* [U] (*abbr.* **CET**) the time used in winter in central and part of western Europe, which is one hour ahead of UTC 欧洲中部时间（欧洲中部和西欧部分地区的冬季时间，比协调世界时早一小时）

C

ˌ**central ˈgovernment** *noun* [U, C] the government of a whole country, rather than LOCAL GOVERNMENT which is concerned with smaller areas 中央政府

ˌ**central ˈheating** *noun* [U] a system for heating a building from one source which then sends the hot water or hot air around the building through pipes 集中供热；中央供暖（系统）➲ COLLOCATIONS AT DECORATE

ˌ**Central Inˈtelligence Agency** *noun* [sing.] = CIA

cen·tral·ism /ˈsentrəlɪzəm/ *noun* [U] a way of organizing sth, such as government or education, that involves one central group of people controlling the whole system 中央集权制（或主义）；集中制 ▸ **cen·tral·ist** *adj.*: *centralist control of schools* 学校的集中控制

cen·tral·ize (*BrE also* **-ise**) /ˈsentrəlaɪz/ *verb* **~ sth** to give the control of a country or an organization to a group of people in one particular place 集权控制；实行集中：*a highly centralized system of government* 高度中央集权的政府体制 ▸ **cen·tral·iza·tion, -isa·tion** /ˌsentrəlaɪˈzeɪʃn; *NAmE* -ləˈz-/ *noun* [U]: *the centralization of political power* 政治权力的集中

ˌ**central ˈlocking** *noun* [U] a system for locking a car in which all the doors can be locked or opened at the same time（汽车的）中央门锁系统，中央控制门锁

ˌ**central ˈnervous system** *noun* (*anatomy* 解) the part of the system of nerves in the body that consists of the brain and the SPINAL CORD 中枢神经系统 ➲ SEE ALSO NERVOUS SYSTEM

ˌ**central ˈprocessing unit** *noun* (*computing* 计) (*abbr.* **CPU**) the part of a computer that controls all the other parts of the system 中央处理器；中央处理机

ˌ**central reserˈvation** (*BrE*) (*NAmE* **me·dian**, **ˈmedian strip**) *noun* a narrow strip of land that separates the two sides of a major road such as a MOTORWAY or INTERSTATE（高速公路、州际公路等的）中央隔离带

ˌ**Central ˈStandard Time** *noun* [U] (*abbr.* **CST**) the time used in winter in the central US and Canada, which is six hours behind UTC 中部标准时间（美国中部和加拿大中部的冬季时间，比协调世界时晚六小时）

ˈ**Central time** *noun* [U] the time at the line of LONGITUDE 90°W, which is the standard time in the central US and Canada 中部时间（指西经 90 度的时间，是美国中部和加拿大的标准时间）

centre 🔑 (*especially US* **cen·ter**) /ˈsentə(r)/ *noun, verb*

■ *noun*

• **MIDDLE** 中间 **1** 🔑 [C] the middle point or part of sth 中心点；中心；正中；中央：*the centre of a circle* 圆心 ◇ *a long table in the centre of the room* 房间中央的长桌 ◇ *chocolates with soft centres* 软心巧克力糖 ➲ PICTURE AT CIRCLE

• **TOWN/CITY** 城镇；城市 **2** 🔑 [C] (*especially BrE*) (*NAmE usually* **down·town** [usually sing.]) the main part of a town or city where there are a lot of shops/stores and offices （市镇的）中心区：*in the* **town/city centre** 在镇 / 市中心区 ◇ *the centre of town* 市中心 ◇ *a town-centre car park* 市中心停车场 **3** 🔑 [C] a place or an area where a lot of people live; a place where a lot of business or cultural activity takes place 人口集中的地区；商业中心区；文化中心区：*major urban/industrial centres* 主要城市 / 工业中心 ◇ *a centre of population* 人口密集区 ◇ *Small towns in South India serve as economic and cultural centres for the surrounding villages.* 印度南部的小城镇是周围村庄的经济文化中心。

• **BUILDING** 建筑物 **4** 🔑 [C] a building or place used for a particular purpose or activity 中心；活动中心：*a* **shopping/sports/leisure/community centre** 购物 / 运动 / 休闲 / 社区中心 ◇ *the Centre for Policy Studies* 政策研究中心

• **OF EXCELLENCE** 优秀 **5** [C] **~ of excellence** a place where a particular kind of work is done extremely well 居领先地位的中心；（某领域中成绩突出的）中心

• **OF ATTENTION** 注意 **6** [C, usually sing.] the point towards which people direct their attention 中心；聚集点：*Children like to be the* **centre of attention**. 小孩子喜欢受到大家的关注。◇ *The prime minister is* **at the centre of** *a political row over leaked Cabinet documents.* 首相成了内阁文件泄密而引起的一场政治风波的中心人物。

• **-CENTRED** 以…为中心 **7** (in adjectives 构成形容词) having the thing mentioned as the most important feature or centre of attention 有…最重要特征的；有…中心的；以…为中心的：*a child-centred approach to teaching* 以儿童为中心的教学法 ➲ SEE ALSO SELF-CENTRED

• **IN POLITICS** 政治 **8** (*usually* **the centre**) [sing.] a MODERATE (= middle) political position or party, between the extremes of LEFT-WING and RIGHT-WING parties 中间派；中间党：*a party of the centre* 中间党派

• **IN SPORT** 体育运动 **9** [C] (in some team sports 用于某些团体运动) a player or position in the middle of the pitch/ field, court, etc. 中锋；中锋位置 IDM SEE FRONT *n.*, LEFT *adj.*

■ *verb* **~ sth** to move sth so that it is in the centre of sth else 把…放在中央：*Carefully centre the photograph on the page and stick it in place.* 把照片小心地放在页面中央并粘贴好。

PHR V ˈ**centre around/on/round/upon sb/sth** | ˈ**centre sth around/on/round/upon sb/sth** to be or make sb/sth become the person or thing around which most activity, etc. takes place 把…当作中心；（使）成为中心：*State occasions always centred around the king.* 国家庆典总是以国王为中心。◇ *Discussions were centred on developments in Eastern Europe.* 讨论围绕着东欧的发展这一中心议题进行。ˈ**centre sth in...** [usually passive] to make somewhere the place where an activity or event takes place 使活动等集中于…：*Most of the fighting was centred in the north of the capital.* 战斗大多集中在首都北部。

ˌ**centre ˈback** (*especially US* ˌ**center ˈback**) (*also* ˌ**centre ˈhalf**, *especially US* ˌ**center ˈhalf**) *noun* (in football (SOCCER) and some other sports 足球及其他一些体育运动) a player or position in the middle of the back line of players 中后卫；中后卫位置

centre·board (*especially US* **cen·ter·board**) /ˈsentəbɔːd; *NAmE* ˈsentərbɔːrd/ *noun* a board that can be passed through a hole in the bottom of a sailing boat to keep it steady when sailing（帆船的）稳向板龙骨

cen·tred (*especially US* **cen·tered**) /ˈsentəd; *NAmE* -ərd/ *adj.* (*especially NAmE*) calm, sensible and emotionally in control 冷静的；理智的：*My family helps to keep me centred.* 家人帮助我保持冷静。➲ SEE ALSO CENTRE *n.* (7)

centre·fold (*especially US* **cen·ter·fold**) /ˈsentəfəʊld; *NAmE* -tərfoʊld/ *noun* **1** a large picture, often of a young woman with few or no clothes on, folded to form the middle pages of a magazine（杂志内常刊登性感女郎照片的）中间插页 **2** a person whose picture is the centrefold of a magazine 中间插页人物

ˌ**centre ˈforward** (*especially US* ˌ**center ˈforward**) *noun* (in football (SOCCER) and some other sports 足球及其他一些体育运动) a player or position in the middle of the front line of players 中锋；中锋位置

ˌ**centre ˈhalf** (*especially US* ˌ**center ˈhalf**) *noun* = CENTRE BACK

ˌ**centre-ˈleft** (*especially US* ˌ**center-ˈleft**) (*BrE also* ˌ**left-of-ˈcentre**, *US also* ˌ**left-of-ˈcenter**) *adj.* (*politics* 政) supporting both CAPITALISM and gradual social change 中左的（指支持资本主义和渐进式社会改革的）：*a centre-left coalition government* 中间靠左的联合政府 ▸ ˌ**centre-ˈleft** (*especially US* ˌ**center-ˈleft**) *noun* [sing.]: *Most of the centre-left will give their support.* 大多数中左派将给予支持。

ˌ**centre of ˈgravity** (*especially US* ˌ**center of ˈgravity**) *noun* (*pl.* **centres/centers of gravity**) the point in an object at which its weight is considered to act（物体的）重心

centre·piece (*especially US* **cen·ter·piece**) /ˈsentəpiːs; *NAmE* -tərp-/ *noun* **1** [sing.] the most important item 最重要的项目（或物品）：*This treaty is the centrepiece of the government's foreign policy.* 这个条约是政府外交政策最重要的一环。**2** a decoration for the centre of a table 桌子中央的装饰品

ˌcentre-ˈright (*especially US* **ˌcenter-ˈright**) (*also* **ˌright-of-ˈcentre**, *especially US* **ˌright-of-ˈcenter**) *adj.* (*politics* 政) supporting CAPITALISM and accepting some social change 中右的（指支持资本主义并接受某些社会改革的）：*Europe's centre-right parties* 欧洲的中右党派 ▶ **ˌcentre-ˈright** (*especially US* **ˌcenter-ˈright**) *noun* [sing.]: *a politician of the centre-right* 中右派从政者

ˌcentre ˈspread (*especially US* **ˌcenter ˈspread**) *noun* the two facing middle pages of a newspaper or magazine （报纸或杂志的）中间跨页

ˌcentre ˈstage (*especially US* **ˌcenter ˈstage**) *noun* [U] an important position where sb/sth can easily get people's attention 重要位置；中心；核心：*Education is **taking centre stage** in the government's plans.* 教育正在成为政府计划的核心。◇ *This region continues to **occupy centre stage** in world affairs.* 这个地区继续在国际舞台上占主导地位。▶ **ˌcentre ˈstage** (*especially US* **ˌcenter ˈstage**) *adv.*：*The minister said, 'We are putting full employment centre stage.'* 部长说："我们正在把充分就业放到首要位置。"

-centric /ˈsentrɪk/ *suffix* **1** having a particular centre 以…为中心；有…中心：*geocentric* 以地球为中心的 **2** (*often disapproving*) based on a particular way of thinking 基于…思路；以…想法为出发点：*Eurocentric* 欧洲中心主义的 ◇ *ethnocentric* 种族中心主义的

cen·tri·fu·gal /ˌsentrɪˈfjuːgl; senˈtrɪfjəgl/ *adj.* (*specialist*) moving or tending to move away from a centre 离心的

ˌcentriˌfugal ˈforce (*also* **cenˈtrifugal force**) *noun* (*physics* 物) a force that appears to cause an object travelling around a centre to fly away from the centre and off its CIRCULAR path 离心力

cen·tri·fuge /ˈsentrɪfjuːdʒ/ *noun* a machine with a part that spins around to separate substances, for example liquids from solids, by forcing the heavier substance to the outer edge 离心机；离心分离机；离心过滤机

cen·tri·pet·al /senˈtrɪpɪtl; ˌsentrɪˈpiːtl/ *adj.* (*specialist*) moving or tending to move towards a centre 向心的

cen·trist /ˈsentrɪst/ *noun* a person with political views that are not extreme （政治上的）中间派，温和派 SYN **moderate** ▶ **cen·trist** *adj.*

cen·tur·ion /senˈtjʊəriən; *NAmE* -ˈtʃʊr-/ *noun* (in ancient Rome) an army officer who commanded 100 soldiers 百夫长（古罗马军队中管理 100 名士兵的军官）

cen·tury 🔑 /ˈsentʃəri/ *noun* (*pl.* **-ies**) **1** 🔑 a period of 100 years * 100 年；百年 **2** 🔑 (*abbr.* **c**, **cent.**) any of the periods of 100 years before or after the birth of Christ 世纪：*the 20th century* (= AD 1901–2000 or 1900–1999) * 20 世纪 ◇ *eighteenth-century writers* * 18 世纪的作家 **3** (in CRICKET 板球) a score of 100 RUNS by one player （一个运动员所得的）100 分 IDM SEE TURN *n.*

CEO /ˌsiː iː ˈəʊ; *NAmE* ˈoʊ/ *abbr.* chief executive officer (the person with the highest rank in a business company) 总裁；首席执行官 ➲ WORDFINDER NOTE AT BUSINESSMAN

cep /sep/ *noun* a type of MUSHROOM which many people consider to be one of the best to eat 牛肝菌（一种可食用的蘑菇）

ceph·al·ic /sɪˈfælɪk; *BrE also* keˈfælɪk/ *adj.* (*anatomy* 解) in or related to the head 头的；（头）颅的

ceph·alo·pod /ˈsefələpɒd; *NAmE* -pɑːd/ *noun* (*biology* 生) a type of MOLLUSC with a combined head and body and large eyes. Cephalopods have arms and/or TENTACLES (= long thin parts like arms), which may have SUCKERS (= round parts that suck) on them. OCTOPUS and SQUID are cephalopods. 头足类，头足纲动物（如章鱼和乌贼）➲ VISUAL VOCAB PAGE V13

cer·am·ic /səˈræmɪk/ *noun* **1** [C, usually pl.] a pot or other object made of CLAY that has been made permanently hard by heat 陶瓷制品；陶瓷器：*an exhibition of ceramics by Picasso* 毕加索陶瓷作品展 **2** **ceramics** [U] the art of making and decorating ceramics 制陶艺术；陶瓷装潢艺术 ▶ **cer·am·ic** *adj.*：*ceramic tiles* 瓷砖

cer·eal /ˈsɪəriəl; *NAmE* ˈsɪr-/ *noun* **1** [C] one of various types of grass that produce grains that can be eaten or are used to make flour or bread. WHEAT, BARLEY and RYE are all cereals. 谷类植物：*cereal crops* 谷类作物 ➲ WORDFINDER NOTE AT CROP ➲ VISUAL VOCAB PAGE V35 **2** [U] the grain produced by cereal crops 谷物 **3** [C, U] food made from the grain of cereals, often eaten for breakfast with milk （常加牛奶作早餐用的）谷类食物：*breakfast cereals* 谷类早餐食物 ◇ *a bowl of cereal* 一碗麦片粥

ce·re·bel·lum /ˌserəˈbeləm/ *noun* (*pl.* **ce·re·bel·lums** or **cere·bella** /-ˈbelə/) (*anatomy* 解) the part of the brain at the back of the head that controls the activity of the muscles 小脑

cere·bral /ˈserəbrəl; *NAmE* səˈriːbrəl/ *adj.* **1** relating to the brain 大脑的；脑的：*a cerebral haemorrhage* 脑出血 **2** (*formal*) relating to the mind rather than the feelings 理智的；智力的 SYN **intellectual**：*His poetry is very cerebral.* 他的诗富有理性。

ˌcerebral ˈpalsy *noun* [U] a medical condition usually caused by brain damage before or at birth that causes the loss of control of movement in the arms and legs 大脑性瘫痪

cere·brum /səˈriːbrəm; ˈserəbrəm/ *noun* (*pl.* **ce·re·bra** /-brə/) (*anatomy* 解) the front part of the brain, responsible for thoughts, emotions and personality 脑；大脑

cere·mo·nial /ˌserɪˈməʊniəl; *NAmE* -ˈmoʊ-/ *adj.*, *noun*

■ ***adj.*** relating to or used in a ceremony 礼仪的；礼节的；用于礼仪的：*ceremonial occasions* 礼仪场合 ◇ *a ceremonial sword* 礼仪佩剑 ▶ **cere·mo·ni·al·ly** /-niəli/ *adv.*

■ ***noun*** [U, C] the system of rules and traditions that states how things should be done at a ceremony or formal occasion 礼仪；礼节：*The visit was conducted with all due ceremonial.* 访问按照一切应有的礼仪进行。

cere·mo·ni·ous /ˌserəˈməʊniəs; *NAmE* -ˈmoʊ-/ *adj.* (*formal*) behaving or performed in an extremely formal way 讲究礼仪的 OPP **unceremonious** ▶ **cere·mo·ni·ous·ly** *adv.*

cere·mony 🔑 /ˈserəməni; *NAmE* -moʊni/ *noun* (*pl.* **-ies**) **1** 🔑 [C] a public or religious occasion that includes a series of formal or traditional actions 典礼；仪式：*an awards/opening ceremony* 颁奖 / 开幕仪式 ◇ *a wedding/marriage ceremony* 婚礼 ➲ WORDFINDER NOTE AT WEDDING ➲ COLLOCATIONS AT MARRIAGE **2** [U] formal behaviour; traditional actions and words used on particular formal occasions 礼节；礼仪；礼貌

IDM **stand on ˈceremony** to behave formally 讲究客套；拘于礼节：*Please don't stand on ceremony* (= Please be natural and relaxed) *with me.* 请别跟我讲客套。**without ˈceremony** in a very rough or informal way 粗鲁无礼；不拘礼节；随便：*He found himself pushed without ceremony out of the house and the door slammed in his face.* 他被毫不客气地推出屋子，门砰的一声当着他的面关上了。➲ SEE ALSO MASTER OF CEREMONIES

cer·ise /səˈriːz; səˈriːs/ *adj.* pinkish-red in colour 鲜红色的；樱桃色的 ▶ **cer·ise** *noun* [U]

cer·ium /ˈsɪəriəm; *NAmE* ˈsɪr-/ *noun* [U] (*symb.* **Ce**) a chemical element. Cerium is a silver-white metal used in the production of glass and CERAMICS. 铈

cert /sɜːt; *NAmE* sɜːrt/ *noun* (*BrE, informal*) a thing that is sure to happen or be successful 必然发生的事；确定无疑的事；有把握成功的事 SYN **certainty**：*That horse is a **dead cert for*** (= is sure to win) *the next race.* 那匹马下一场比赛准赢。

cert. *abbr.* **1** CERTIFICATE 证明；证明书 **2** CERTIFY （书面）证明，证实

cer·tain 🔑 /ˈsɜːtn; *NAmE* ˈsɜːrtn/ *adj.*, *pron.*

■ ***adj.*** **1** 🔑 that you can rely on to happen or to be true 确实；确定；肯定：*The climbers face certain death if the rescue today is unsuccessful.* 救援行动如果今天不能成功，登山队员必死无疑。◇ **~ (that)...** *It is certain that they will* *agree.* 他们一定会同意。◇ **~ to do sth** *She looks certain to win an Oscar.* 看来奥斯卡金像奖非她莫属。◇ *They are certain to agree.* 他们一定会同意。◇ **~ of sth/of doing sth** *If you want to be certain of getting a ticket, book now.* 要想有把握买到票，现在就得预订。 ➲ SYNONYMS AT SURE **2** firmly believing sth; having no doubts 确信；确定；无疑：**~ (that)**… *She wasn't certain (that) he had seen her.* 她不敢肯定他见过她。◇ **~ of/about sth** *Are you absolutely certain about this?* 你对这事绝对确信无疑吗？◇ **~ who/where, etc.…** *I'm not certain who was there.* 我无法确定谁当时在场。◇ ***To my certain knowledge** he was somewhere else at the time* (= I am sure about it). 我敢肯定他当时不在现场。 **3** used to mention a particular thing, person or group without giving any more details about it or them（不提及细节时用）某事，某人，某种：*For certain personal reasons I shall not be able to attend.* 由于某种个人原因，我将不能出席。◇ *Certain people might disagree with this.* 某些人对这事可能不会赞同。◇ *They refused to release their hostages unless certain conditions were met.* 除非某些条件得到满足，否则他们不会释放人质。 **4** (*formal*) used with a person's name to show that the speaker does not know the person（与人名连用，表示说话者不识其人）某某，某位，一位叫…的：*It was a certain Dr Davis who performed the operation.* 是一位叫戴维斯的医生做的手术。 **5** slight; noticeable, but difficult to describe 轻微的；微小的；显而易见却难以描述的：*That's true, **to a certain extent**.* 在一定程度上的确如此。◇ *I felt there was a certain coldness in her manner.* 我觉得她的态度有点冷淡。

IDM **for ˈcertain** without doubt 肯定；确定；无疑：*I can't say for certain when we'll arrive.* 我说不准我们什么时候能到。 **make certain (that…)** to find out whether sth is definitely true 弄确实；弄清楚；弄明白：*I think there's a bus at 8 but you'd better call to make certain.* 好像 8 点有一班公共汽车，不过你最好打电话弄清楚。 **make certain of sth/of doing sth** to do sth in order to be sure that sth else will happen 确保（做某事）：*You'll have to leave soon to make certain of getting there on time.* 你得快点出发，好确保准时到达那里。 **of a certain ˈage** if you talk about a person being **of a certain age**, you mean that they are no longer young but not yet old 不算年轻的；年纪不轻的；中年的：*The show appeals to an audience of a certain age.* 这个节目中年观众感兴趣。

▼ **SYNONYMS 同义词辨析**

certain

bound • sure • definite • guaranteed

These are all words describing sth that will definitely happen or is definitely true. 以上各词均指某事肯定、必定会发生或属实。

certain that you can rely on to happen or be true 指确实、确定、肯定（会发生或是事实）：*It's certain that they will agree.* 他们肯定会同意。◇ *They are certain to agree.* 他们肯定会同意。

bound [not before noun] certain to happen, or to do or be sth 指肯定会、一定会 NOTE **Bound** is only used in the phrase *bound to do/be, etc.* * bound 只用于 bound to do/be 等短语中：*There are bound to be changes when the new system is introduced.* 新系统引进后肯定会有变化。◇ *You've done so much work—you're bound to pass the exam.* 你下了这么大功夫，一定能通过考试。

sure certain to happen or be true; that can be trusted or relied on 指必定、无疑（会发生或是事实）或不容置疑、确切、可靠：*She's sure to be picked for the team.* 她肯定会入选该队。◇ *It's sure to rain.* 一准会下雨。

definite (*rather informal*) certain to happen; that is not going to change 指必将发生、不会改变：*Is it definite that he's leaving?* 他肯定要离开吗？

guaranteed certain to have a particular result 指肯定会、必定会（有特定结果）：*That kind of behaviour is guaranteed to make him angry.* 那样的行为肯定会让他生气。

PATTERNS
- certain/sure **of** sth
- certain/bound/sure/guaranteed **to do sth**
- certain/definite **that…**
- **I couldn't say for** certain/sure/definite.

▼ **EXPRESS YOURSELF 情景表达**

Expressing certainty or uncertainty 表示确定或不确定

When you are stating what has happened or is going to happen, you can say how certain or uncertain you are about what you are saying. 陈述已经或将要发生之事时对自己所言表示确定或不确定：

- ***I'm sure/100% certain/absolutely positive*** *I left my keys on the table.* 我肯定我把钥匙落在桌子上了。
- ***There's no doubt in my mind that*** *this is the best option.* 我心里确信无疑，这是最佳选择。
- ***Without a doubt,/No question,*** *this is where it was.* 毫无疑问，它原来就在这里。
- ***I'm not (at all) sure*** *what time they arrive,* ***to be honest.*** 老实说，我（一点也）拿不准他们什么时候到。
- ***I rather doubt*** *they'll call back.* (*BrE*) 我有点儿怀疑他们是否会回电话。

■ ***pron.*** **certain of…** (*formal*) used for talking about some members of a group of people or things without giving their names（不提及人或事物的名称时用）某些：*Certain of those present were unwilling to discuss the matter further.* 某些在场的人不愿意进一步讨论这个问题。

cer·tain·ly /ˈsɜːtnli; *NAmE* ˈsɜːrtnli/ *adv.* **1** without doubt 无疑；确定；肯定 SYN **definitely**：*Without treatment, she will almost certainly die.* 要是不治疗，她十有八九会死。◇ *Certainly, the early years are crucial to a child's development.* 毫无疑问，幼年对儿童的发展至关重要。◇ *I'm certainly never going there again.* 我肯定不会再去那里了。 ➲ NOTE AT SURELY ➲ LANGUAGE BANK AT NEVERTHELESS **2** (used in answer to questions 用于回答问题) of course 当然；行：*'May I see your passport, Mr Scott?' 'Certainly.'* "斯科特先生，请出示您的护照好吗？""当然可以。"◇ *'Do you think all this money will change your life?' 'Certainly not.'* "你认为这些钱会改变你的生活吗？""当然不会。"

cer·tainty /ˈsɜːtnti; *NAmE* ˈsɜːrtnti/ *noun* (*pl.* **-ies**) **1** [C] a thing that is certain 确实的事；必然的事：*political/moral certainties* 政治上/道德上确定无疑的事◇ *Her return to the team now seems a certainty.* 她的归队现在似乎已成定局。 **2** [U] the state of being certain 确信；确实；确定性：*There is no certainty that the president's removal would end the civil war.* 总统下台是否会结束内战现在还很难说。◇ *I can't say **with** any **certainty** where I'll be next week.* 我根本说不准我下周会在什么地方。

cer·ti·fi·able /ˈsɜːtɪfaɪəbl; *NAmE* ˈsɜːrt-/ *adj.* **1** a person who is **certifiable** can or should be officially stated to be INSANE 可证明患有精神病的；应被证明为精神病患者的：(*informal*) *He's certifiable* (= he's crazy). 他脑子有问题。 **2** (*especially NAmE*) good enough to be officially accepted or recommended 可接纳的；可推荐的 ► **cer·ti·fi·ably** *adv.*：*certifiably insane* 确认患有精神病的

cer·tifi·cate *noun, verb*

■ ***noun*** /səˈtɪfɪkət; *NAmE* sərˈt-/ (*abbr.* **cert.**) **1** an official document that may be used to prove that the facts it states are true 证明；证明书：*a **birth/marriage/death certificate*** 出生/结婚/死亡证明 **2** an official document proving that you have completed a course of study or passed an exam; a qualification obtained after a course of study or an exam 文凭；结业证书；合格证书：*a Postgraduate Certificate in Education* (= a British qualification for teachers) 教育学研究生证书（英国教师资格证书） ➲ WORDFINDER NOTE AT DOCUMENT, TRAINING

■ ***verb*** /səˈtɪfɪkeɪt; *NAmE* sərˈt-/ **~ sb (to do sth)** (*BrE*) to give sb an official document proving that they have successfully completed a training course, especially for a particular profession 发给结业证书；（尤指）发给职业培训证书

cer·tifi·cated /sə'tɪfɪkeɪtɪd; *NAmE* sər't-/ *adj.* having the certificate which shows that the necessary training for a particular job has been done 持有职业培训证书的；有执业资格的

cer·ti·fi·ca·tion /ˌsɜːtɪfɪ'keɪʃn; *NAmE* ˌsɜːrt-/ *noun* [U] (*specialist*) **1** the act of CERTIFYING sth 证明；鉴定：*the medical certification of the cause of death* 为死因出具医学鉴定书 **2** the process of giving certificates for a course of education 出具课程结业证书：*the certification of the exam modules* 出具考试课程结业证书

ˌcertified 'cheque (*BrE*) (*NAmE* **ˌcertified 'check**) *noun* a cheque that a bank guarantees 保付支票；保兑支票

ˌcertified 'mail (*NAmE*) (*BrE* **reˌcorded de'livery**) *noun* [U] a method of sending a letter or package in which the person sending it gets an official note to say it has been posted and the person receiving it must sign a form when it is delivered 挂号邮寄（寄件人会收到发件通知，收件人需签收）➲ COMPARE REGISTERED MAIL

ˌcertified ˌpublic ac'countant (*NAmE*) (*BrE* **ˌchartered ac'countant**) *noun* a fully trained and qualified ACCOUNTANT 注册会计师；特许会计师

cer·tify /'sɜːtɪfaɪ; *NAmE* 'sɜːrt-/ *verb* (**cer·ti·fies**, **cer·ti·fy·ing**, **cer·ti·fied**, **cer·ti·fied**) **1** (*formal*) to state officially, especially in writing, that sth is true （尤指书面）证明，证实：**~ (that)...** *He handed her a piece of paper certifying (that) she was in good health.* 他递给她一份证明其健康状况良好的文件。◇ *This* (= this document) *is to certify that...* 兹证明…◇ **~ sb/sth + adj.** *He was certified dead on arrival.* 他送达时被证实已死亡。◇ **~ sb/sth (as) sth** *The accounts were certified (as) correct by the finance department.* 账目经财务部门证实无误。◇ **~ sb/sth to be/do sth** *The plants must be certified to be virus free.* 这些植物必须具备无病毒证明。 **2** [usually passive] **~ sb (as sth)** to give sb an official document proving that they are qualified to work in a particular profession 颁发（或授予）专业合格证书 **3** [usually passive] **~ sb (+ adj.)** (*law* 律) to officially state that sb is mentally ill, so that they can be given medical treatment 证明（某人）患有精神病：*Patients must be certified before they can be admitted to the hospital.* 该医院只接纳经证明患有精神病的人。

cer·ti·tude /'sɜːtɪtjuːd; *NAmE* 'sɜːrtɪtuːd/ *noun* [U, C] (*formal*) a feeling of being certain; a thing about which you are certain 确信；确定；确实的事：*'You will like Rome,' he said, with absolute certitude.* "你会喜欢罗马的。"他深信不疑地说道。◇ *the collapse of moral certitudes* 道德信念的崩溃

cer·ul·ean /sɪ'ruːliən/ *adj.* (*literary*) deep blue in colour 深蓝色的；蔚蓝色的

ceru·men /sɪ'ruːmən/ *noun* [U] (*specialist*) a substance like WAX which is produced in the ear 耵聍；耳垢 SYN **earwax**

cer·vical /'sɜːvɪkl; sə'vaɪkl; *NAmE* 'sɜːrvɪkl/ *adj.* [only before noun] (*anatomy* 解) **1** connected with the cervix 宫颈的：*cervical cancer* 宫颈癌 **2** connected with the neck 颈的：*the cervical spine* 颈椎

ˌcervical 'smear *noun* (*BrE*) = SMEAR TEST

cer·vix /'sɜːvɪks; *NAmE* 'sɜːrv-/ *noun* (*pl.* **cer·vi·ces** /-vɪsiːz/ or **cer·vi·xes** /-vɪksɪz/) (*anatomy* 解) the narrow passage at the opening of a woman's WOMB 子宫颈

ce·sar·ean, **ce·sar·ian** (*US*) = CAESAREAN

ces·ium (*NAmE*) (*BrE* **cae·sium**) /'siːziəm/ *noun* [U] (*symb.* **Cs**) a chemical element. Cesium is a soft silver-white metal that reacts strongly in water, used in PHOTOELECTRIC CELLS. 铯

ces·sa·tion /se'seɪʃn/ *noun* [U, C] (*formal*) the stopping of sth; a pause in sth 停止；终止；中断；暂停：*Mexico called for an immediate cessation of hostilities.* 墨西哥要求立即停止敌对行动。

ces·sion /'seʃn/ *noun* [U, C] (*formal*) the act of giving up land or rights, especially to another country after a war（尤指战争结束后领土的）割让；（权利的）放弃 ➲ SEE ALSO CEDE

cess·pit /'sespɪt/ (*also* **cess·pool** /'sespuːl/) *noun* **1** a covered hole or container in the ground for collecting waste from a building, especially from the toilets（覆盖的）粪池，污水坑，垃圾坑 **2** a place where dishonest or immoral people gather 藏污纳垢的场所：*a cesspit of corruption* 堕落腐化的渊薮

CET /ˌsiː iː 'tiː/ *abbr.* CENTRAL EUROPEAN TIME 欧洲中部时间

cet·acean /sɪ'teɪʃn/ *adj., noun* (*biology* 生)
■ ***adj.*** (*also* **cet·aceous** /sɪ'teɪʃəs/) connected with the group of creatures that includes WHALES and DOLPHINS 鲸目动物的；鲸类的
■ ***noun*** a WHALE, DOLPHIN, or other sea creature that belongs to the same group 鲸类 ➲ **VISUAL VOCAB** PAGE V12

cf. *abbr.* (in writing 书写形式) compare 比较

CFC /ˌsiː ef 'siː/ *noun* [C, U] the abbreviation for 'chlorofluorocarbon', a type of gas used especially in AEROSOLS (= types of container that release liquid in the form of a spray). CFCs are harmful to the earth's OZONE LAYER. 氯氟碳化物；氯氟烃（全写为 chlorofluorocarbon，尤用于喷雾剂，对臭氧层有害）

CFL /ˌsiː ef 'el/ *abbr.* Canadian Football League (the organization of professional football teams in Canada) 加拿大（职业）橄榄球联合会；加拿大橄榄球联盟

CGI /ˌsiː dʒiː 'aɪ/ *abbr.* computer-generated imagery 计算机生成影像：*The movie 'Dinosaur' combines CGI animation with live-action location shots.* 《恐龙》这部电影结合了计算机成像动画和实地拍摄的画面。

chaat /tʃɑːt/ *noun* [U] a S Asian dish consisting of fruit or vegetables with spices 南亚香料炒水果（或蔬菜）

cha·cha /'tʃɑːtʃɑː/ *noun* (*IndE*) **1** an uncle 叔叔；舅舅；伯父；姑丈；姨丈 **2** a male cousin of your parents 表（或堂）叔；表（或堂）伯；表（或堂）舅 **3** a male friend of your family （一家人的）男性朋友

cha-cha /'tʃɑː tʃɑː/ (*also* **'cha-cha-cha**) *noun* a S American dance with small fast steps 恰恰舞（南美洲小快步舞）：*to dance/do the cha-cha* 跳恰恰舞

cha-ching /tʃə'tʃɪŋ/ *exclamation* (*NAmE, informal*) = KA-CHING

chad /tʃæd/ *noun* the small piece that is removed when a hole is made in a piece of card, etc.（在卡片等上打孔时打出的）孔屑

cha·dor /'tʃɑːdɔː(r)/ *noun* a large piece of cloth that covers a woman's head and upper body so that only the face can be seen, worn by some Muslim women 卡多尔（穆斯林妇女使用的一种盖头，遮盖头部和上身，只露出脸）

chafe /tʃeɪf/ *verb* **1** [I, T] if skin **chafes**, or if sth **chafes** it, it becomes sore because the thing is rubbing against it 擦痛；擦得红肿：*Her wrists chafed where the rope had been.* 她的手腕上给绳子勒过的地方都磨红了。◇ **~ sth** *The collar was far too tight and chafed her neck.* 衣领特别紧，把她脖子擦痛了。 **2** [I] **~ (at/under sth)** (*formal*) to feel annoyed and impatient about sth, especially because it limits what you can do（尤指因受限制而）恼怒，烦恼，焦躁：*He soon chafed at the restrictions of his situation.* 他很快便因为处处受到限制而感到恼火。

chaff /tʃɑːf; *NAmE* tʃæf/ *noun, verb*
■ ***noun*** [U] **1** the outer covering of the seeds of grain such as WHEAT, which is separated from the grain before it is eaten 谷壳；糠 **2** STRAW (= dried STEMS of WHEAT) and HAY (= dried grass) cut up as food for cows（作为牛饲料的）麦秸，干草 IDM SEE WHEAT
■ ***verb*** **~ sb** (*old-fashioned* or *formal*) to make jokes about

sb in a friendly way（友善地）开玩笑，取笑，打趣 SYN **tease**

chaf·finch /ˈtʃæfɪntʃ/ *noun* a small European bird of the FINCH family 苍头燕雀（见于欧洲）

C

ˈ**chafing dish** *noun* a metal pan used for keeping food warm at the table 暖锅；布菲炉

chag·rin /ˈʃæɡrɪn; *NAmE* ʃəˈɡrɪn/ *noun* [U] (*formal*) a feeling of being disappointed or annoyed 失望；恼怒；烦恼；懊恼 ▶ **chag·rined** *adj.*

chai /tʃaɪ/ *noun* [U] a type of Indian tea, made especially by boiling tea leaves with milk, sugar and spices 印度奶茶

chain /tʃeɪn/ *noun, verb*

■ *noun*

• **METAL RINGS** 金属链 **1** [C, U] a series of connected metal rings, used for pulling or fastening things; a length of chain used for a particular purpose 链子；链条；锁链：*a short length of chain* 一截短链条 ◇ *She wore a heavy gold chain around her neck.* 她戴着一条粗实的金项链。◇ *The mayor wore his chain of office.* 市长佩戴着标志他职务的链徽。◇ *a bicycle chain* 自行车链条 ◇ *The prisoners were kept* ***in chains*** (= with chains around their arms and legs, to prevent them from escaping). 囚犯戴着镣铐。➲ PICTURE AT ROPE ➲ VISUAL VOCAB PAGES V55, V70

• **CONNECTED THINGS** 相关连的事 **2** [C] a series of connected things or people 一系列，一连串（人或事）：*to set in motion a* ***chain of events*** 触发一连串的事件 ◇ ***a chain of command*** (= a system in an organization by which instructions are passed from one person to another) 指挥系统 ◇ ***mountain/island chains*** 山脉；岛群 ◇ *Volunteers formed a* ***human chain*** *to rescue precious items from the burning house.* 志愿者排成一条长龙，从着火的房子里手传手把贵重物品抢救出来。➲ SEE ALSO FOOD CHAIN

• **OF SHOPS/HOTELS** 商店；旅馆 **3** [C] a group of shops/stores or hotels owned by the same company 连锁商店（或旅馆）：*a chain of supermarkets/a supermarket chain* 连锁超市

• **RESTRICTION** 限制 **4** [C, usually pl.] (*formal* or *literary*) a thing that restricts sb's freedom or ability to do sth 约束；束缚：*the chains of fear/misery* 恐惧的桎梏；苦难的枷锁

• **IN HOUSE BUYING** 购房 **5** [C, usually sing.] (*BrE*) a situation in which a number of people selling and buying houses must each complete the sale of their house before buying from the next person 连环式（指一群房主先售后购的置业方式） IDM SEE BALL *n.*, LINK *n.*, WEAK

■ *verb* [often passive] to fasten sth with a chain; to fasten sb/sth to another person or thing with a chain, so that they do not escape or get stolen 用锁链拴住（或束缚、固定）：~ **sb/sth** *The doors were always locked and chained.* 那些门总是上着锁链。◇ ~ **sb/sth up** *The dog was chained up for the night.* 夜间那条狗用链子拴起来。◇ ~ **sb/sth to sb/sth** *She chained her bicycle to the gate.* 她用链子把自行车锁在大门上。◇ (*figurative*) *I've been chained to my desk all week* (= because there was so much work). 我整个星期都在伏案工作，脱不开身。

ˈ**chain gang** *noun* a group of prisoners chained together and forced to work 一群被链子拴在一起服劳役的囚犯

ˈ**chain letter** *noun* a letter sent to several people asking them to make copies of the letter and send them on to more people 连锁信（收信人复印多份寄出）

ˌ**chain-ˌlink ˈfence** *noun* a fence made of wire in a diamond pattern 钢丝网眼栅栏

ˈ**chain mail** (*also* **mail**) *noun* [U] ARMOUR (= covering to protect the body when fighting) made of small metal rings linked together 锁子甲（护身铠甲）

ˌ**chain reˈaction** *noun* **1** (*chemistry* 化, *physics* 物) a chemical or nuclear change that forms products which themselves cause more changes and new products 链（式）反应 **2** a series of events, each of which causes the next（事情的）连锁反应：*It set off a chain reaction in the international money markets.* 这一事件在国际货币市场上引起了连锁反应。

chain·saw /ˈtʃeɪnsɔː/ *noun* a tool made of a chain with sharp teeth set in it, that is driven by a motor and used for cutting wood 链锯

ˈ**chain-smoke** *verb* [I, T] ~ (**sth**) to smoke cigarettes continuously, lighting the next one from the one you have just smoked 一支接一支地吸（烟） ▶ ˈ**chain-smoker** *noun*

ˈ**chain store** (*BrE also* **mul·tiple**, ˌ**multiple ˈstore**) *noun* a shop/store that is one of a series of similar shops/stores owned by the same company 连锁商店

chair /tʃeə(r); *NAmE* tʃer/ *noun, verb*

■ *noun* **1** [C] a piece of furniture for one person to sit on, with a back, a seat and four legs 椅子：*a table and chairs* 一套桌椅 ◇ *Sit on your chair!* 坐在你的椅子上！◇ *an old man asleep in a chair* (= an ARMCHAIR) 在扶手椅里睡着了的老人 ➲ VISUAL VOCAB PAGE V22,V23 ➲ SEE ALSO ARMCHAIR *n.*, DECKCHAIR, EASY CHAIR, HIGH CHAIR, MUSICAL CHAIRS, ROCKING CHAIR, WHEELCHAIR **2 the chair** [sing.] the position of being in charge of a meeting or committee; the person who holds this position（主持会议或委员会的）主席席位；委员长职位；（会议或委员会的）主席；委员长：*She takes the chair in all our meetings.* 她主持我们所有的会议。◇ *Who is in the chair today?* 今天谁主持？◇ *He was elected chair of the city council.* 他当选为市议会主席。➲ WORDFINDER NOTE AT CLUB, DEBATE, MEETING ➲ MORE LIKE THIS 25, page R28 **3** [C] the position of being in charge of a department in a university（大学的）系主任：*He holds the chair of philosophy at Oxford.* 他是牛津大学哲学系的系主任。 **4 the chair** [sing.] (*US, informal*) = ELECTRIC CHAIR

■ *verb* ~ **sth** to act as the chairman or chairwoman of a meeting, discussion, etc. 担任（会议、讨论等的）主席；主持（会议、讨论等）：*Who's chairing the meeting?* 谁主持这次会议？

chair·lift /ˈtʃeəlɪft; *NAmE* ˈtʃer-/ *noun* a series of chairs hanging from a moving cable, for carrying people up and down a mountain 缆椅

chair·man /ˈtʃeəmən; *NAmE* ˈtʃer-/ *noun* (*pl.* **-men** /-mən/) **1** the person in charge of a meeting, who tells people when they can speak, etc.（会议的）主席，主持人 **2** the person in charge of a committee, a company, etc.（委员会的）委员长，主席；（公司等的）董事长：*the chairman of the board of governors* (= of a school) 校董会主席 ◇ *The chairman of the company presented the annual report.* 公司董事长提交了年度报告。➲ WORDFINDER NOTE AT BUSINESSMAN ➲ NOTE AT GENDER ➲ MORE LIKE THIS 25, page R28

chair·man·ship /ˈtʃeəmənʃɪp; *NAmE* ˈtʃer-/ *noun* **1** [C] the position of a chairman or chairwoman（男或女）主席职位：*the chairmanship of the committee* 委员会的主席职位 **2** [U] the state of being a chairman or chairwoman（男或女）主席的任职：*under her skilful chairmanship* 在她这位主席的英明领导下

chair·per·son /ˈtʃeəpɜːsn; *NAmE* ˈtʃerpɜːrsn/ *noun* (*pl.* **-per·sons**) a chairman or chairwoman（男或女）主席，主持人，委员长，董事长 ➲ SEE ALSO CHAIR *n.* (2) ➲ MORE LIKE THIS 25, page R28

chair·woman /ˈtʃeəwʊmən; *NAmE* ˈtʃer-/ *noun* (*pl.* **-women** /-wɪmɪn/) a woman in charge of a meeting, a committee or an organization（会议、委员会或机构的）女主席，女主持人，女委员长，女董事长 ➲ NOTE AT GENDER ➲ MORE LIKE THIS 25, page R28

chaise /ʃeɪz/ *noun* a CARRIAGE pulled by a horse or horses, used in the past（旧时的）马车

chaise longue /ˌʃeɪz ˈlɒŋ; *NAmE* ˈlɔːŋ/ *noun* (*pl.* **chaises longues** /ˌʃeɪz ˈlɒŋ; *NAmE* ˈlɔːŋ/) (*from French*) **1** a long low seat with a back and one arm, on which the person sitting can stretch out their legs 躺椅 **2** (*NAmE*) (*also informal* **chaise lounge**) a long chair with a back that can be vertical for sitting or flat for lying on outdoors

活动睡椅（可在户外竖起当座椅或平放当躺椅） ➲ VISUAL VOCAB PAGE V22

chakra /ˈtʃʌkrə/ *noun* (in YOGA 瑜伽) each of the main centres of spiritual power in the human body 轮（人体精神集中点之一）

cha·let /ˈʃæleɪ; *NAmE* ʃæˈleɪ/ *noun* **1** a wooden house with a roof that slopes steeply down over the sides, usually built in mountain areas, especially in Switzerland（尤指瑞士山区的）小木屋 **2** (*BrE*) a small house or HUT, especially one used by people on holiday/vacation at the sea（尤指海边度假用的）小屋，棚屋

chal·ice /ˈtʃælɪs/ *noun* a large cup for holding wine, especially one from which wine is drunk in the Christian COMMUNION (1) service 大酒杯；（尤指基督教的）圣爵 IDM SEE POISON *v.*

chalk /tʃɔːk/ *noun, verb*

■ ***noun*** **1** [U] a type of soft white stone 白垩: *the chalk cliffs of southern England* 英格兰南部的白垩质峭壁 **2** [U, C] a substance similar to chalk made into white or coloured sticks for writing or drawing（白色或彩色的）粉笔: *a **piece/stick of chalk*** 一支粉笔 ◇ *drawing diagrams with chalk on the blackboard* 用粉笔在黑板上画图表 ◇ *a box of coloured chalks* 一盒彩色粉笔

IDM **ˌchalk and ˈcheese** (*BrE*) if two people or things are like **chalk and cheese** or as different as **chalk and cheese**, they are completely different from each other 截然不同；天渊之别 ➲ MORE LIKE THIS 13, page R26 ➲ MORE AT LONG *adj.*

■ ***verb*** **~ sth (up) (on sth)** to write or draw sth with chalk 用粉笔写（或画）: *She chalked (up) the day's menu on the board.* 她把当天的菜单用粉笔写在黑板上。

PHR V **ˌchalk ˈup sth** (*informal*) to achieve or record a success, points in a game, etc. 获得，取得（成功）；记下，记录（成就、比赛得分等）: *The team chalked up their tenth win this season.* 这支队本赛季已赢了十场比赛。 **ˌchalk sth ˈup to sth** (*NAmE, informal*) to consider that sth is caused by sth 把某事归因于: *We can chalk that win up to a lot of luck.* 我们可以把那次胜利归因于好运十足。IDM SEE EXPERIENCE *n.*

chalk·board /ˈtʃɔːkbɔːd; *NAmE* -bɔːrd/ *noun* (*especially NAmE*) = BLACKBOARD

chalky /ˈtʃɔːki/ *adj.* containing chalk or like chalk 含（或似）白垩的；含（或似）粉笔的

chal·lan /ˈtʃʌlən/ *noun, verb* (*IndE*)

■ ***noun*** **1** a document in which an official claim is made by the police that sb has committed a crime or a traffic offence（警方的）指控书，交通违章通知书: *The police filed a challan against the four accused in the case.* 警方呈交了对本案四名被告的起诉状。 ◇ *He was issued a challan for the traffic offence and agreed to pay a fine.* 他因交通违章收到罚单，并同意支付罚款。 **2** an official form or document relating to a payment, such as a receipt or an INVOICE 收据；发票: *You need to show a copy of the fee payment challan before you can take the exam.* 须出示缴费收据的副本才能参加考试。

■ ***verb*** **~ sb** (of the police) to accuse sb formally of an illegal act, especially a traffic offence（警方）指控…违法（尤指交通违章）: *The traffic policeman challaned him for not wearing a helmet.* 交警指控他未戴头盔违章。

chal·lenge 🔑 AW /ˈtʃælɪndʒ/ *noun, verb*

■ ***noun*** **1** 🔑 a new or difficult task that tests sb's ability and skill 挑战；艰巨任务: *an **exciting/interesting challenge*** 刺激的 / 富趣味的挑战 ◇ *The role will be the biggest challenge of his acting career.* 扮演这个角色将是他演艺生涯中最大的挑战。 ◇ *to **face a challenge*** (= to have to deal with one) 面临挑战 ◇ *Destruction of the environment is one of the most **serious challenges** we face.* 环境的破坏是我们所面临的最严峻的挑战之一。 ◇ *Schools must **meet the challenge** of new technology* (= deal with it successfully). 学校必须迎接新技术的挑战。 ➲ WORDFINDER NOTE AT ADVENTURE **2** 🔑 an invitation or a suggestion to sb that they should enter a competition, fight, etc. 挑战书；（比赛、打斗等的）邀请，提议: *to **accept/take up a challenge*** 接受挑战 ◇ *to **mount a challenge*** 发起挑战 **3** 🔑 **~ (to sth)** a statement or an action that shows that sb refuses to accept sth and questions whether it is right, legal, etc. 质询；质疑；提出异议: *It was a direct challenge to the president's authority.* 这是对主席权威的直接质疑。 ◇ *Their legal challenge was unsuccessful.* 他们提出的法律质疑未能成功。

■ ***verb*** **1** 🔑 **~ sth** to question whether a statement or an action is right, legal, etc.; to refuse to accept sth 对…怀疑（或质疑）；拒绝接受 SYN **dispute**: *The story was completely untrue and was successfully challenged in court.* 此案情纯属捏造，已在法庭上被揭穿。 ◇ *She does not like anyone challenging her authority.* 她不喜欢任何人挑战她的权威。 ◇ *This discovery challenges traditional beliefs.* 这项发现是对传统信念的冲击。 ➲ LANGUAGE BANK AT ARGUE **2** 🔑 to invite sb to enter a competition, fight, etc.; to suggest strongly that sb should do sth (especially when you think that they might be unwilling to do it) 向（某人）挑战；（尤指在对方不情愿时）强烈建议（某人做某事）: **~ sb (to sth)** *Mike challenged me to a game of chess.* 迈克硬逼着要和我下一盘棋。 ◇ **~ sb to do sth** *The opposition leader challenged the prime minister to call an election.* 反对党领袖要求首相宣布进行大选。 **3** 🔑 **~ sb** to test sb's ability and skills, especially in an interesting way 考查，考验（能力和技巧）: *The job doesn't really challenge her.* 这项工作不能真正考验出她的能力。 **4** **~ sb** to order sb to stop and say who they are or what they are doing 盘问；查问: *We were challenged by police at the border.* 我们在边境受到警察盘问。

chal·lenged /ˈtʃælɪndʒd/ *adj.* (used with an adverb 与副词连用) a way of referring to sb who has a DISABILITY of some sort 伤残的；有残疾的: *a competition for physically challenged athletes* 残疾运动员的比赛 ◇ (*humorous*) *I'm financially challenged at the moment* (= I have no money). 我眼下身无分文。 HELP **Challenged** was intended to be a polite way of referring to sb with a DISABILITY but it soon came to be used in a humorous way and is now no longer considered very polite. * challenged 原为指称残疾人的委婉说法，但很快成为幽默用法，现已不再被视为很礼貌。

chal·len·ger AW /ˈtʃælɪndʒə(r)/ *noun* a person who competes with sb else in sport or in politics for an important position that the other person already holds（体育运动或政治的）挑战者: *the official challenger for the world championship title* 世界冠军头衔的正式挑战者

chal·len·ging AW /ˈtʃælɪndʒɪŋ/ *adj.* **1** difficult in an interesting way that tests your ability 挑战性的；考验能力的: *challenging work/questions/problems* 具有挑战性的工作 / 提问 / 问题 ◇ *a challenging and rewarding career as a teacher* 富有挑战性且有意义的教师职业 ➲ SYNONYMS AT DIFFICULT **2** done in a way that invites people to disagree or argue with you, or shows that you disagree with them 挑起争论的；不赞同的: *She gave him a challenging look. 'Are you really sure?' she demanded.* 她用挑衅的眼光看了他一眼。"你敢肯定吗？"她问道。

cham·ber 🔑 /ˈtʃeɪmbə(r)/ *noun* **1** 🔑 [C] a hall in a public building that is used for formal meetings 会议厅: *The members left the council chamber.* 议员离开了会议厅。 ◇ *the **Senate/House chamber*** 参议院 / 众议院会议厅 ➲ SEE ALSO CHAMBER OF COMMERCE **2** (*also* **Chamber**) [C+sing./pl. v.] one of the parts of a parliament（议会的）议院: *the **Lower/Upper Chamber*** (= in Britain, the House of Commons/House of Lords) 下议院；上议院 ◇ *the Chamber of Deputies in the Italian parliament* 意大利国会的众议院 ◇ *Under Senate rules, the chamber must vote on the bill by this Friday.* 根据规定，参议院必须在本星期五以前投票表决此项议案。 ➲ WORDFINDER NOTE AT PARLIAMENT **3** 🔑 [C] (in compounds 构成复合词) a room used for the particular purpose that is mentioned（作特定用途的）房间，室: *a burial chamber* 墓室 ◇ *Divers transfer from the water to a decompression chamber.* 潜水员从水里转入减压舱。 ➲ SEE ALSO GAS CHAMBER **4** [C] a space in the body, in a plant or in a machine, which is separated from the rest（人体、植物或机器内的）腔，室: *the chambers of the heart* 心腔 ◇ *the rocket's combustion chamber* 火箭燃

C

烧室 ◇ *the chamber of a gun* (= the part that holds the bullets) 枪膛 **5** [C] a space under the ground which is almost completely closed on all sides 洞穴：*They found themselves in a vast underground chamber.* 他们发现身处一个地下大洞穴。 **6** [C] (*old use*) a bedroom or private room 卧室；寝室；私人房间

C

cham·ber·lain /ˈtʃeɪmbəlɪn; *NAmE* -bərlɪn/ *noun* an official who managed the home and servants of a king, queen or important family in the past（国王或女王的）内侍；（旧时贵族的）管家

cham·ber·maid /ˈtʃeɪmbəmeɪd; *NAmE* -bərm-/ *noun* a woman whose job is to clean bedrooms, usually in a hotel（通常指旅馆内）打扫房间的女工

ˈchamber music *noun* [U] CLASSICAL music written for a small group of instruments 室内乐（为小型乐队谱写的古典乐曲）

ˌChamber of ˈCommerce *noun* a group of local business people who work together to help business and trade in a particular town 商会

ˌchamber of ˈhorrors *noun* [sing.] a part of a museum displaying objects used to kill people in a cruel and painful way or scenes showing how they died （博物馆中的）恐怖物像陈列室

ˈchamber orchestra *noun* a small group of musicians who play CLASSICAL music together 室内乐队（演奏古典乐曲的小型乐队）

ˈchamber pot (*also slang, offensive* **piss·pot**) *noun* a round container that people in the past had in the bedroom and used for URINATING in at night （旧时的）夜壶，尿壶 ➲ COMPARE POTTY *n.*

cha·meleon /kəˈmiːliən/ *noun* **1** a small LIZARD (= a type of REPTILE) that can change colour according to its surroundings 避役；变色蜥蜴；变色龙 **2** (*often disapproving*) a person who changes their behaviour or opinions according to the situation 见风使舵的人；善变的人

cham·fer /ˈtʃæmfə(r)/ *noun* (*specialist*) a cut made along an edge or on a corner so that it slopes rather than being at 90° 斜切面；削角

cham·ois *noun* (*pl.* **cham·ois**) **1** /ˈʃæmwɑː; *NAmE* ˈʃæmi/ [C] an animal like a small DEER, that lives in the mountains of Europe and Asia （欧亚山区的）岩羚羊 **2** /ˈʃæmi/ (*also* **sham·my**) (*BrE also* **ˌchamois ˈleather**, **ˌshammy ˈleather**) [U, C] a type of soft leather, made from the skin of GOATS, sheep, etc.; a piece of this, used especially for cleaning windows （由山羊、绵羊等的皮制成的）麂皮；（尤指）擦窗用的软皮革；擦拭用的软皮 **3** /ˈʃæmi/ [U] (*NAmE*) a type of soft thick cotton cloth, used especially for making shirts （尤指制衬衣用的）厚软棉织物

chamo·mile (*especially NAmE*) (*also* **camo·mile** *especially in BrE*) /ˈkæməmaɪl/ *noun* [U] a plant with a sweet smell and small white and yellow flowers. Its dried leaves and flowers are used to make tea, medicine, etc. 苹果菊，春黄菊，甘菊（花及叶可制茶、药等）：*chamomile tea* 苹果菊茶

champ /tʃæmp/ *verb, noun*

▪ ***verb*** [I, T] ~ (sth) (especially of horses 尤指马) to bite or eat sth noisily 大声地咬（或咀嚼）

IDM **ˌchamping at the ˈbit** (*informal*) impatient to do or start doing sth 迫不及待；急不可耐

▪ ***noun*** an informal way of referring to a champion, often used in newspapers （常用于报章，champion 的非正式写法）冠军：*Scottish champs celebrate victory!* 苏格兰的冠军庆祝胜利！

cham·pagne /ʃæmˈpeɪn/ *noun* [U, C] a French SPARKLING white wine (= one with bubbles) that is drunk on special occasions 香槟酒：*a glass of champagne* 一杯香槟酒

ˌchampagne ˈsocialist *noun* (*BrE, disapproving*) a person who has SOCIALIST ideas but is rich or has social advantages 香槟酒社会主义者（有社会主义思想但富有或享有社会特权）

cham·pers /ˈʃæmpəz; *NAmE* -pərz/ *noun* [U] (*BrE, informal*) = CHAMPAGNE

cham·pion /ˈtʃæmpiən/ *noun, verb*

▪ ***noun*** **1** a person, team, etc. that has won a competition, especially in a sport 冠军；第一名；优胜者：*the world basketball champions* 世界篮球冠军 ◇ *a* ***champion jockey/boxer/swimmer*** 获得冠军的赛马骑师 / 拳击手 / 游泳运动员 ◇ *the reigning champion* (= the person who is champion now) 本届冠军 ➲ WORDFINDER NOTE AT SPORT **2** ~ (**of sth**) a person who fights for, or speaks in support of, a group of people or a belief 斗争者；捍卫者；声援者；拥护者：*She was a champion of the poor all her life.* 她终身都是穷苦人的卫士。

▪ ***verb*** ~ **sth** to fight for or speak in support of a group of people or a belief 为…而斗争；捍卫；声援：*He has always championed the cause of gay rights.* 他一直在为争取同性恋者的权利而斗争。

cham·pion·ship /ˈtʃæmpiənʃɪp/ *noun* **1** (*also* **cham·pion·ships** [pl.]) a competition to find the best player or team in a particular sport 锦标赛：*the National Basketball Association Championship* * NBA 总决赛 ◇ *He won a silver medal at the European Championships.* 他获得了欧洲锦标赛的银牌。 **2** the position of being a champion 冠军地位：*They've held the championship for the past two years.* 他们在过去的两年里一直保持着冠军地位。 **3 the Championship** the football (SOCCER) league in England and Wales that has the second best teams in it, after the PREMIERSHIP (2)（英格兰和威尔士的）足球冠军联赛（仅次于足球超级联赛）

chance 🔑 /tʃɑːns; *NAmE* tʃæns/ *noun, verb, adj.*

▪ ***noun*** **1** 🔑 [C, U] a possibility of sth happening, especially sth that you want （尤指希望发生的事的）可能性：**~ of doing sth** *Is there any chance of getting tickets for tonight?* 有可能弄到今晚的票吗？ ◇ *She has only* ***a slim chance*** *of passing the exam.* 她通过考试的希望很渺茫。 ◇ **~ that…** *There's a* ***slight chance*** *that he'll be back in time.* 他及时赶回来的可能性不大。 ◇ *There is* ***no chance*** *that he will change his mind.* 他不可能改变主意。 ◇ **~ of sth happening** *What chance is there of anybody being found alive?* 找到生还者的希望有多大？ ◇ **~ of sth** *Nowadays a premature baby* ***has a very good chance*** *of survival.* 如今早产儿存活的希望非常大。 ◇ *The operation has a* ***fifty-fifty chance*** *of success.* 这次手术成功和失败的可能性各占一半。 ◇ *an* ***outside chance*** (= a very small one) 非常小的可能性 ◇ *The chances are a million to one against being struck by lightning.* 遭雷击的可能性是微乎其微的。 **2** 🔑 [C] a suitable time or situation when you have the opportunity to do sth 机会；机遇；时机：*It was the chance she had been waiting for.* 那正是她一直等待的机会。 ◇ *Jeff deceived me once already—I won't give him* ***a second chance.*** 杰夫已骗过我一次，我不会再给他机会。 ◇ *This is your* ***big chance*** (= opportunity for success). 这是你成功的大好机会。 ◇ **~ of sth** *We won't* ***get another chance*** *of a holiday this year.* 我们今年不会再有机会度假了。 ◇ **~ to do sth** *Please* ***give me a chance*** *to explain.* 请给我一个解释的机会。 ◇ *Tonight is your* ***last chance*** *to catch the play at your local theatre.* 今晚是你在本地剧院看这出戏的最后一次机会。 ◇ **~ for sb to do sth** *There will be a chance for parents to look around the school.* 家长将有机会参观学校。 **3** 🔑 [C] an unpleasant or dangerous possibility 风险；冒险：*When installing electrical equipment don't* ***take any chances.*** *A mistake could kill.* 安装电器设备时千万不要冒险，一个失误就可能要人命。 **4** 🔑 [U] the way that some things happen without any cause that you can see or understand 偶然；碰巧；意外：*I met her* ***by chance*** (= without planning to) *at the airport.* 我碰巧在机场遇见她。 ◇ *Chess is not a* ***game of chance.*** 国际象棋不是靠运气取胜的。 ◇ *It was* ***pure chance*** *that we were both there.* 我们俩当时都在场纯属巧合。 ◇ *We'll plan everything very carefully and* ***leave nothing to chance.*** 我们将非常周密地筹划一切，决不留任何纰漏。 ➲ SYNONYMS AT LUCK

IDM **as ˌchance would ˈhave it** happening in a way that

was lucky, although it was not planned 凑巧；碰巧：*As chance would have it, John was going to London too, so I went with him.* 赶巧约翰也去伦敦，所以我跟他一块儿去了。 **be ˌin with a ˈchance (of doing sth)** (*BrE, informal*) to have the possibility of succeeding or achieving sth 有可能成功；有机会获得：*'Do you think we'll win?' 'I think we're in with a chance.'* "你认为我们会获胜吗？" "我觉得有可能。" ◊ *He's in with a good chance of passing the exam.* 他大有可能考试合格。 **by ˈany chance** used especially in questions, to ask whether sth is true, possible, etc.（尤用于问句，询问是否真实、可能等）或许，可能：*Are you in love with him, by any chance?* 或许你爱上他了？ **the chances ˈare (that)...** (*informal*) it is likely that... 可能…：*The chances are you won't have to pay.* 你可能不用付钱。 **ˈchance would be a fine thing** (*BrE, informal*) people say **chance would be a fine thing** to show that they would like to do or have the thing that sb has mentioned, but that they do not think that it is very likely 苦于没有机会 **give sb/sth half a ˈchance** to give sb/sth some opportunity to do sth 给…一些机会：*That dog will give you a nasty bite, given half a chance.* 只要一有机会，那条狗就会狠咬你一口。 **ˈno chance** (*informal*) there is no possibility 不可能：*'Do you think he'll do it?' 'No chance.'* "你认为他会做这事吗？" "不可能。" **on the ˈoff chance (that)** because of the possibility of sth happening, although it is unlikely 抱（一线）希望；碰碰运气：*I didn't think you'd be at home but I just called by on the off chance.* 我想你不会在家，只是碰碰运气顺路来看一下。 **stand a ˈchance (of doing sth)** to have the possibility of succeeding or achieving sth 有可能成功；有机会获得：*The driver didn't stand a chance of stopping in time.* 司机根本不可能及时刹车。 **take a ˈchance (on sth)** to decide to do sth, knowing that it might be the wrong choice 冒险：*We took a chance on the weather and planned to have the party outside.* 我们怀着天气可能会好的侥幸心理筹划到户外聚会。 **take your ˈchances** to take a risk or to use the opportunities that you have and hope that things will happen in the way that you want 碰运气：*He took his chances and jumped into the water.* 他冒险跳进水里。 ➲ MORE AT CAT, DOG *n.*, EVEN *adj.*, EYE *n.*, FAT *adj.*, FIGHT *v.*, SNOWBALL *n.*, SPORTING

■ ***verb*** **1** [T] (*informal*) to risk sth, although you know the result may not be successful 冒险；拿…去冒风险：**~ sth** *She was **chancing her luck** driving without a licence.* 她无照驾车，完全是在冒险。 ◊ *'Take an umbrella.' 'No, I'll **chance it** (= take the risk that it may rain).'* "带上伞吧。" "不带了，我就冒冒险吧。" ◊ **~ doing sth** *I stayed hidden; I couldn't chance coming out.* 我躲了起来，不能冒险出去。 **2** *linking verb* (*formal*) to happen or to do sth by chance 偶然发生；碰巧：**~ to do sth** *If I do chance to find out where she is, I'll inform you immediately.* 要是我真的碰巧发现她的行踪，会立即通知你的。 ◊ *They chanced to be staying at the same hotel.* 他们碰巧住在同一家旅馆。 ◊ **it chanced (that)...** *It chanced (that) they were staying at the same hotel.* 碰巧他们住在同一家旅馆。

IDM **ˌchance your ˈarm** (*BrE, informal*) to take a risk although you will probably fail 冒险一试；碰碰运气

PHR V **ˈchance on/upon sb/sth** (*formal*) to find or meet sb/sth unexpectedly or by chance 偶然发现；碰巧遇到：*One day he chanced upon Emma's diary and began reading it.* 有一天他偶然发现了埃玛的日记，便开始读了起来。

■ ***adj.*** [only before noun] not planned 意外的；偶然的；碰巧的 SYN **unplanned**：*a chance meeting/encounter* 邂逅

chan·cel /ˈtʃɑːnsl; *NAmE* ˈtʃænsl/ *noun* the part of a church near the ALTAR, where the priests and the CHOIR (= singers) sit during services（教堂的）圣坛

chan·cel·lery /ˈtʃɑːnsələri; *NAmE* ˈtʃæn-/ *noun* (*pl.* **-ies**) **1** [C, usually sing.] the place where a chancellor has his or her office 大臣（或大法官等）的官署 **2** [sing.+sing./pl. v.] the staff in the department of a chancellor 大臣（或大法官等）官署的全体工作人员

chan·cel·lor /ˈtʃɑːnsələ(r); *NAmE* ˈtʃæns-/ (*also* **Chancel·lor**) *noun* (often used in a title 常用于头衔) **1** the head of government in Germany or Austria（德国或奥地利的）总理：*Chancellor Merkel* 默克尔总理 **2** (*BrE*) = CHANCELLOR OF THE EXCHEQUER: *MPs waited for the chancellor's announcement.* 议员们等待着财政大臣发布公告。 **3** the official head of a university in Britain. Chancellor is an HONORARY title.（英国大学的）名誉校长 ➲ COMPARE VICE CHANCELLOR **4** the head of some American universities（某些美国大学的）校长 **5** used in the titles of some senior state officials in Britain（用于英国某些高级政府官员的头衔）：*the Lord Chancellor* (= a senior law official) 大法官

ˌChancellor of the Exˈchequer *noun* (in Britain) the government minister who is responsible for financial affairs（英国）财政大臣

chan·cer /ˈtʃɑːnsə(r); *NAmE* ˈtʃænsər/ *noun* (*BrE, informal*) a person who is always looking for opportunities to gain an advantage, even when they do not deserve to do so 投机者；钻空子的人

chan·cery /ˈtʃɑːnsəri; *NAmE* ˈtʃæns-/ *noun* [sing.] **1 Chancery** (*law* 律) a division of the High Court in Britain（英国）高等法院的大法官法庭 **2** (*especially BrE*) an office where public records are kept 公共档案馆；公共档案室 **3** (*also* **ˈchancery court**) a court in the US that decides legal cases based on the principle of EQUITY（美国）衡平法院 **4** the offices where the official representative of a country works, in another country 大使馆（或领事馆）办公处

chancy /ˈtʃɑːnsi; *NAmE* ˈtʃænsi/ *adj.* (*informal*) involving risks and UNCERTAINTY 有风险的；不确定的 SYN **risky**

chan·de·lier /ˌʃændəˈlɪə(r); *NAmE* -ˈlɪr/ *noun* a large round frame with branches that hold lights or CANDLES. Chandeliers are decorated with many small pieces of glass and hang from the ceiling. 枝形吊灯

chand·ler /ˈtʃɑːndlə(r); *NAmE* ˈtʃænd-/ (*also* **ˈship's chandler**) *noun* a person or shop/store that sells equipment for ships 船用杂货商（或杂货店）

change /tʃeɪndʒ/ *verb, noun*

■ ***verb***

• **BECOME/MAKE DIFFERENT**（使）变化 **1** [I] to become different 改变；变化：*Rick hasn't changed. He looks exactly the same as he did at school.* 里克一点儿没变，他和上学时一模一样。 ◊ *changing attitudes towards education* 不断变化的对教育的看法 ◊ *Her life changed completely when she won the lottery.* 买彩票中奖后她的生活完全变了。 **2** [T] **~ sb/sth** to make sb/sth different 使不同：*Fame hasn't really changed him.* 名声并没有使他有丝毫改变。 ◊ *Computers have changed the way people work.* 计算机已改变了人的工作方式。 **3** [I, T] to pass or make sb/sth pass from one state or form into another（使）变换，改换，变成：*Wait for the traffic lights to change.* 等待交通灯变换颜色。 ◊ **~ (from A) to/into B** *The lights changed from red to green.* 交通灯已由红变绿。 ◊ *Caterpillars change into butterflies.* 毛虫变成蝴蝶。 ◊ **~ sb/sth (from A) to/into B** *With a wave of her magic wand, she changed the frog into a handsome prince.* 她魔杖一挥，把青蛙变成了英俊的王子。 **4** [T] **~ sth** to stop having one state, position or direction and start having another 转换；变更：*Leaves change colour in autumn.* 树叶在秋天改变颜色。 ◊ *The wind has changed direction.* 风向已经变了。 ◊ *Our ship changed course.* 我们的船改变了航向。

• **REPLACE** 代替 **5** [T] to replace one thing, person, service, etc. with sth new or different 替代；替换；更换：**~ sb/sth** *I want to change my doctor.* 我想另找一位医生看病。 ◊ *That back tyre needs changing.* 那个后轮胎需要更换。 ◊ **~ sb/sth (for sb/sth)** *We change our car every two years.* 我们的车每两年更换一次。 ◊ *We changed the car for a bigger one.* 我们换了一辆较大的车。 ◊ **~ sth (to sth)** *Marie changed her name when she got married.* 玛丽婚后改了姓。 ◊ *She changed her name to his.* 她改用了他的姓氏。

• **EXCHANGE** 交换 **6** [T] (used with a plural object 与复数宾语连用) to exchange positions, places, etc. with sb else, so that you have what they have, and they have what you have 互换；交换：**~ sth** *At half-time the teams change ends.* 球队在半场时交换场地。 ◊ *Can we change*

C

seats? 咱们可以交换一下座位吗？ ◇ **~ sth with sb** *Can I change seats with you?* 我可以和您换一下座位吗？

• **CLOTHES** 衣物 **7** [I, T] to put on different or clean clothes 换衣服；更衣：*I went into the bedroom to change.* 我走进卧室更衣。◇ **~ into sth** *She changed into her swimsuit.* 她换上了游泳衣。◇ **~ out of sth** *You need to change out of those wet things.* 你该把那些湿衣服换掉。◇ **~ sth** (*especially NAmE*) *I didn't have time to **change clothes** before the party.* 我没时间在聚会前更换衣服。 ◇ (*especially BrE*) *I didn't have time to **get changed** before the party* (= to put different clothes on). 我没时间在聚会前更换衣服。

• **BABY** 婴儿 **8** [T] **~ sb/sth** to put clean clothes or a clean NAPPY/DIAPER on a baby 更换（衣服或尿布）：*She can't even change a nappy.* 她连换尿布都不会。◇ *The baby needs changing.* 该给婴儿换尿布了。 ◇ *There are baby changing facilities in all our stores.* 我们所有的商店都有供顾客给婴儿换尿布的地方。

• **BED** 床 **9** [T] **~ sth** to put clean sheets, etc. on a bed 换（床单等）：*to change the sheets* 换床单 ◇ *Could you help me change the bed?* 你帮我换一下床单好吗？

• **MONEY** 钱 **10** [T] to exchange money into the money of another country 把（货币）兑换（成另一种货币）：**~ sth** *Where can I change my traveller's cheques?* 哪里可以兑换旅行支票？ ◇ **~ sth into sth** *to change dollars into yen* 把美元兑换成日元 **11** [T] to exchange money for the same amount in different coins or notes 换零钱：**~ sth** *Can you change a £20 note?* 你能把一张 20 英镑的钞票换成零钱吗？ ◇ **~ sth for/into sth** *to change a dollar bill for four quarters* 把一元美钞换为四个二十五分币

• **GOODS** 货品 **12** [T] **~ sth (for sth)** (*BrE*) to exchange sth that you have bought for sth else, especially because there is sth wrong with it; to give a customer a new item because there is sth wrong with the one they have bought 退换；掉换：*This shirt I bought's too small—I'll have to change it for a bigger one.* 我买的这件衬衫太小，得换件大一点的。 ◇ *Of course we'll change it for a larger size, Madam.* 夫人，我们当然会给您掉换件大号的。

• **BUS/TRAIN/PLANE** 公共汽车；火车；飞机 **13** [I, T] to go from one bus, train, etc. to another in order to continue a journey 换乘；转乘：*Where do I have to change?* 我该在哪儿换车？ ◇ *Change at Reading (for London).* 在雷丁换车（去伦敦）。 ◇ **~ sth** *I stopped in Moscow only to change planes.* 我为了转机才在莫斯科停留。 ➲ SEE ALSO UNCHANGING

IDM **change 'hands** to pass to a different owner 换主人；易主；转手：*The house has changed hands several times.* 这房子已几易其主。 **change horses in mid'stream** to change to a different or new activity while you are in the middle of sth else; to change from supporting one person or thing to another 中流换马；中途变卦；转而支持另外的人（或事） **change your/sb's 'mind** to change a decision or an opinion 改变决定（或看法、主意）：*Nothing will make me change my mind.* 什么都不能让我改变主意。 **change your 'tune** (*informal*) to express a different opinion or behave in a different way when your situation changes 改变口风；转变态度；变卦：*Wait until it happens to him—he'll soon change his tune.* 等着瞧吧，到他遇上这事时，他很快就会改变看法了。 **change your 'ways** to start to live or behave in a different way from before 开始过另一种生活；换个活法 ➲ MORE AT CHOP *v.*, LEOPARD, PLACE *n.*

PHR V **,change sth↔a'round/'round** to move things or people into different positions 改变…的位置：*You've changed all the furniture around.* 你改变了所有家具的位置。 **,change 'back (into sb/sth)** to return to a previous situation, form, etc. 恢复原状；还原；复原 **,change 'back (into sth)** to take off your clothes and put on what you were wearing earlier 换回（原来穿的衣服）：*She changed back into her work clothes.* 她又换上了工作服。**,change sth 'back (into sth)** to exchange an amount of money into the CURRENCY that it was in before 把（钱）换回（原货币）：*You can change back unused dollars into pounds at the bank.* 你可以到银行把没有用掉的美元兑换回英镑。 **,change 'down** (*BrE*) to start using a lower gear when you are driving a car, etc. （开车等）换低一挡，换成低速挡，降挡：*Change down into second.* 把车降到第二挡。 **,change 'over (from sth) (to sth)** to change from one system or position to another 改变系统（或位置）：*The farm has changed over to organic methods.* 农场已改用有机耕作方法。 ➲ RELATED NOUN CHANGEOVER **,change 'up** (*BrE*) to start using a higher gear when driving a car, etc. （开车等）换高一挡，换成高速挡，加挡：*Change up into fifth.* 把车加到第五挡。

■ ***noun***

• **DIFFERENCE** 差别 **1** [C, U] **~ (in/to sth)** the act or result of sth becoming different 改变；变化；变更；变革：*a change in the weather* 天气的变化 ◇ *important changes to the tax system* 税收制度的重大变革 ◇ *There was **no change** in the patient's condition overnight.* 病人整夜病情稳定。◇ *She is someone who hates change.* 她是十分讨厌变革的那种人。 ◇ *social/political/economic change* 社会 / 政治 / 经济变革

• **STH NEW AND INTERESTING** 新奇有趣的事 **2** **a change** [sing.] **~ (from sth)** the fact of a situation, a place or an experience being different from what is usual and therefore likely to be interesting, enjoyable, etc.（会令人感兴趣或可喜的）变化，变更：*Finishing early was **a welcome change**.* 能早日结束是个可喜的变化。 ◇ *Let's stay in tonight **for a change**.* 咱们今晚换换口味，就待在家里吧。 ◇ *Can you just listen **for a change**?* 你就当一回听众，好吗？ ◇ *It **makes a change** to read some good news for once.* 破例读到点好消息，真让人高兴。

• **REPLACING STH** 代替 **3** [C] **~ (of sth) | ~ (from sth to sth)** the process of replacing sth with sth new or different; a thing that is used to replace sth 替代；更换；替代物：*a change of address* 地址的变更 ◇ *a change of government* 政府的更迭 ◇ *a change from agriculture to industry* 从农业向工业转换 ◇ *There will be a crew change when we land at Dubai.* 我们在迪拜着陆后将更换机组人员。 ◇ (*BrE*) *Let's get away for the weekend. **A change of scene*** (= time in a different place) *will do you good.* 咱们出去度周末吧，换换环境会对你有好处的。

• **OF CLOTHES** 衣物 **4** **~ of clothes, etc.** [C] an extra set of clothes, etc. 额外一套衣物（等）：*She packed a change of clothes for the weekend.* 她已收拾好度周末的一套换洗衣物。 ◇ *I keep a change of shoes in the car.* 我在车里放有一双供替换的鞋。

• **MONEY** 钱 **5** [U] the money that you get back when you have paid for sth giving more money than the amount it costs 找给的零钱；找头：*Don't forget your change!* 别忘了找给你的零钱！ ◇ *That's 40p change.* 这是找给您的 40 便士。 ◇ *The ticket machine gives change.* 自动售票机可以找零。 **6** [U] coins rather than paper money 辅币；硬币；分币：*Do you have any change for the parking meter?* 你有投进停车计时器的硬币吗？ ◇ *a dollar **in change*** (= coins that together are worth one dollar) 总值一美元钱的硬币 ◇ *I didn't have any **small change*** (= coins of low value) *to leave as a tip.* 我没有零钱留下来付小费。 ◇ *He puts his **loose change** in a money box for the children.* 他把身上的零钱放进了给孩子的钱箱。 ◇ *Could you give me **change for** a ten pound note* (= coins or notes that are worth this amount)? 你能换给我十英镑的零钱吗？ ➲ SYNONYMS AT MONEY

• **OF BUS/TRAIN/PLANE** 公共汽车；火车；飞机 **7** [C] an occasion when you go from one bus, train or plane to another during a journey 换车；转车；换机：*The journey involved three changes.* 这趟旅行中转乘过三次。

• **IN A WOMAN'S LIFE** 女性生命 **8** **the change** [sing.] (*informal*) = MENOPAUSE

IDM **a change for the 'better/'worse** a person, thing, situation, etc. that is better/worse than the previous or present one 变好（或坏） **a ,change of 'heart** if you have **a change of heart**, your attitude towards sth changes, usually making you feel more friendly, helpful, etc. 改变态度，改变看法（通常指变得更友好、有益等） **a ,change of 'mind** an act of changing what you think about a situation, etc. 改变看法；改变主意 **get no change out of sb** (*BrE, informal*) to get no help or information from sb （从某人处）得不到帮助，打听不到消息 ➲ MORE AT RING² *v.*, WIND¹ *n.*

change·able /ˈtʃeɪndʒəbl/ *adj.* likely to change; often changing 可能变化的；易变的；常变的 SYN **unpredictable**: *The weather is very changeable at this time of year.*

年年在这个时候天气都变化无常。 ➲ COMPARE UNCHANGEABLE ▸ **change·abil·ity** /ˌtʃeɪndʒəˈbɪləti/ *noun* [U]

changed /tʃeɪndʒd/ *adj.* [only before noun] (of people or situations 人或情况) very different from what they were before 与以前截然不同的；变化大的；已变的： *She's a **changed woman** since she got that job.* 她自从得到了那份工作，变得判若两人。 ◇ *This will not be possible in the changed economic climate.* 这在经济气候已经改变的条件下是不可能的。 **OPP** **unchanged**

change·less /ˈtʃeɪndʒləs/ *adj.* (*formal*) never changing 永远不变的；永恒的

change·ling /ˈtʃeɪndʒlɪŋ/ *noun* (*literary*) a child who is believed to have been secretly left in exchange for another, especially (in stories) by FAIRIES （尤指童话中被仙女）偷换后留下的孩童

the ˌchange of ˈlife *noun* [sing.] (*informal*) = MENOPAUSE

change·over /ˈtʃeɪndʒəʊvə(r); *NAmE* -oʊv-/ *noun* a change from one system, or method of working to another （系统或工作方法的）改变，转变，更换 **SYN** **switch**： *the changeover from a manual to a computerized system* 由手工操作向计算机化系统的转换 ◇ *a changeover period* 转变时期

ˈchange purse *noun* (*NAmE*) a small bag made of leather, plastic, etc. for carrying coins （装硬币的）零钱包 ➲ **VISUAL VOCAB PAGE V69** ➲ COMPARE PURSE *n.* (1)

chan·ger /ˈtʃeɪndʒə(r)/ *noun* (often in compounds 常构成复合词) **1** a piece of equipment that holds several discs, etc. and is able to switch between them （光盘等的）换片装置；光盘转换器； 光碟更换器： *The car comes with white leather seats and a 6-CD changer.* 这辆车配置了白色皮座椅和一台 6 碟光盘换片装置。 **2** a person or thing that changes sth, usually in order to improve it 改变者；改进者： *The whole experience was a life changer for me.* 这整个经历改变了我的一生。

ˈchanging room *noun* (*especially BrE*) a room for changing clothes in, especially before playing sports （尤指做运动前使用的）更衣室 ➲ COMPARE LOCKER ROOM ➲ SEE ALSO FITTING ROOM ➲ **MORE LIKE THIS** 9, page R26

chan·nel 🔑 **AW** /ˈtʃænl/ *noun, verb*

■ ***noun***

• **ON TELEVISION/RADIO** 电视；无线电 **1** 🔑 [C] a television station 电视台： *What's on Channel 4 tonight?* 第 4 台今晚有什么节目？ ◇ *a **movie/sports channel*** 电影台；体育台 ◇ *to **change/switch channels*** 换频道 ➲ **COLLOCATIONS** AT TELEVISION **2** 🔑 [C] a band of radio waves used for broadcasting television or radio programmes 频道；波段： ***terrestrial/satellite channels*** 地面 / 卫星频道

• **FOR COMMUNICATING** 交流 **3** 🔑 [C] (*also* **channels** [pl.]) a method or system that people use to get information, to communicate, or to send sth somewhere 途径；渠道；系统： *Complaints must be made **through the proper channels**.* 投诉必须通过正当途径进行。 ◇ *The newsletter is a useful **channel of communication** between teacher and students.* 简讯是有助于师生沟通的渠道。 ◇ *The company has worldwide distribution channels.* 这家公司拥有遍布全世界的销售网络。

• **FOR IDEAS/FEELINGS** 思想感情 **4** [C] a way of expressing ideas and feelings （表达的）方式，方法，手段： *The campaign provided a channel for protest against the war.* 这场运动是反对战争的一种方式。 ◇ *Music is a great channel for releasing your emotions.* 音乐是宣泄情感的好方法。

• **WATER** 水 **5** [C] a passage that water can flow along, especially in the ground, on the bottom of a river, etc. 水渠；沟渠；河槽： *drainage channels in the rice fields* 稻田的排水沟 **6** [C] a deep passage of water in a river or near the coast that can be used as route for ships 水道；航道 **7** [C] a passage of water that connects two areas of water, especially two seas 海峡： *the Bristol Channel* 布里斯托尔海峡 **8 the Channel** [sing.] the area of sea between England and France, also known as **the English Channel** 英吉利海峡： *the Channel Tunnel* 英吉利海峡隧道 ◇ *cross-Channel ferries* 横渡英吉利海峡的渡船 ◇ *news from across the Channel* (= from France) 来自英吉利海峡对岸（指法国）的消息

■ ***verb*** (**-ll-**, *especially US* **-l-**)

• **IDEAS/FEELINGS** 思想感情 **1 ~ sth** (**into sth**) to direct money, feelings, ideas, etc. towards a particular thing or purpose 为…引资；引导；贯注： *He channels his aggression into sport.* 他把他的好斗劲头倾注于体育比赛之中。

• **MONEY/HELP** 金钱；帮助 **2 ~ sth** (**through sth**) to send money, help, etc. using a particular route （利用某途径）输送资金，提供帮助： *Money for the project will be channelled through local government.* 这个项目的资金将由地方政府提供。

• **WATER/LIGHT** 水；光 **3 ~ sth** to carry or send water, light, etc. through a passage （经过通道）输送，传送： *A sensor channels the light signal along an optical fibre.* 传感器沿光导纤维输送光信号。

• **SPIRIT/CHARACTER** 灵魂；角色 **4 ~ sb** to act as a MEDIUM (5) (= a person who claims to be able to communicate with the spirits of dead people) for sb 充当…的灵媒： *He believed that he could channel an ancestor from two hundred years ago.* 他相信自己能充当两百年前一位祖先的灵媒。 **5 ~ sb** to behave in the manner of sb else, as though that person has given you the idea or desire to act in that way 像…附体一样： *When he sang, he would channel Nat King Cole.* 他演唱时犹如纳京高附体。 ➲ **MORE LIKE THIS** 36, page R29

ˈchannel-hop *verb* (**-pp-**) (*also* **ˈchannel-surf**) [I] to repeatedly switch from one television channel to another 不断地转换电视频道

the ˈChannel Islands *noun* [pl.] a group of islands near the north-western coast of France that belong to Britain but have their own parliaments and laws 海峡群岛（位于法国西北海岸附近，隶属英国，但有自己的议会和法律）

chant /tʃɑːnt; *NAmE* tʃænt/ *noun, verb*

■ ***noun*** **1** [C] words or phrases that a group of people shout or sing again and again 反复呼喊的话语；重复唱的歌词： *The crowd broke into chants of 'Out! Out!'* 人群爆发出一阵阵"下台！下台！"的呼喊声。 ◇ *football chants* 此起彼伏的足球助威声 **2** [C, U] a religious song or prayer or a way of singing, using only a few notes that are repeated many times （音调简单重复的）圣歌，祷文，吟唱： *a Buddhist chant* 佛教唱诵 ➲ SEE ALSO GREGORIAN CHANT

■ ***verb*** **1** [I, T] to sing or shout the same words or phrases many times 反复唱；反复呼喊： *A group of protesters, chanting and carrying placards, waited outside.* 一群抗议者等候在外面，举着标语牌不停地喊着口号。 ◇ **~ sth** *The crowd chanted their hero's name.* 人群不断地呼唤着自己英雄的名字。 ◇ *'Resign! Resign!' they chanted.* "辞职！辞职！"他们反复喊叫着。 **2** [I, T] **~** (**sth**) to sing or say a religious song or prayer using only a few notes that are repeated many times 唱圣歌；吟咏祷文 ▸ **chant·ing** *noun* [U]: *The chanting rose in volume.* 圣歌的声音渐渐响亮起来。

chant·er /ˈtʃɑːntə(r); *NAmE* ˈtʃæntər/ *noun* (*music* 音) the part of a set of BAGPIPES that is like a pipe with finger holes, on which the music is played （风笛的）曲调管

chan·ter·elle /ˈʃɑːntərel; ʃɑːntəˈrel/ *noun* a yellowish MUSHROOM that grows in woods and has a hollow part in the centre 鸡油菌（食用蘑菇）

chant·euse /ʃɑːnˈtɜːz/ *noun* (*from French*) a female singer of popular songs, especially in a NIGHTCLUB （尤指夜总会的）流行歌曲女歌手

chan·try /ˈtʃɑːntri; *NAmE* ˈtʃæntri/ *noun* (*pl.* **-ies**) (*also* **ˌchantry ˈchapel**) a small church or part of a church paid for by sb, so that priests could say prayers for them there after their death （由某人捐款建造并为之做追思弥撒用的）附属礼拜堂，祈唱堂

chanty *noun* (*pl.* **-ies**) (*also* **chantey**) (*both US*) /ˈʃænti/ (*BrE, CanE* **shanty**, **ˈsea shanty**) a song that sailors traditionally used to sing while pulling ropes, etc. 水手号子（旧时水手边拉绳索等边唱的歌）

Cha·nuk·kah, **Cha·nu·kah** = HANUKKAH

C

chaos /ˈkeɪɒs; NAmE ˈkeɪɑːs/ *noun* [U] a state of complete confusion and lack of order 混乱；杂乱；紊乱：*economic/political/domestic chaos* 经济 / 政治 / 国内的混乱 ◇ *Heavy snow has caused* ***total chaos*** *on the roads.* 大雪导致道路上交通一片混乱。◇ *The house was* ***in chaos*** *after the party.* 聚会后，房子里一片狼藉。

ˈ**chaos theory** *noun* [U] (*mathematics* 数) the study of a group of connected things that are very sensitive so that small changes in conditions affect them very much 混沌理论

cha·ot·ic /keɪˈɒtɪk; NAmE -ˈɑːtɪk/ *adj.* in a state of complete confusion and lack of order 混乱的；杂乱的；紊乱的：*The traffic in the city is chaotic in the rush hour.* 在上下班高峰时间，城市的交通混乱不堪。▶ **cha·ot·ic·al·ly** /keɪˈɒtɪkli; NAmE -ˈɑːtɪk-/ *adv.*

chap /tʃæp/ *noun* (*BrE, informal, becoming old-fashioned*) used to talk about a man in a friendly way（对男子的友好称呼）家伙，伙计：*He isn't such a bad chap really.* 他这个家伙并不真的这么坏。

chap. *abbr.* (in writing 书写形式) chapter 章；篇；回

chap·ar·ral /ˌʃæpəˈræl/ *noun* [U] (*NAmE*) an area of dry land that is covered with small bushes 查帕拉尔群落

cha·patti (*also* **cha·pati**) /tʃəˈpæti; -ˈpɑːti/ *noun* a type of flat round S Asian bread（南亚）薄饼

chapel /ˈtʃæpl/ *noun* **1** [C] a small building or room used for Christian worship in a school, prison, large private house, etc.（学校、监狱、私人宅院等基督教徒礼拜用的）小教堂：*a college chapel* 学院的小教堂 **2** [C] a separate part of a church or CATHEDRAL, with its own ALTAR, used for some services and private prayer（教堂内的）分堂，小教堂 **3** [C, U] the word for a church used in some Christian DENOMINATIONS, for example by Nonconformists in Britain（基督教某些教派如英国的非圣公会新教教徒做礼拜的）教堂：*a Methodist chapel* 循道宗教堂 ◇ *a Mormon chapel* 摩门教教堂 ◇ *She always went to chapel on Sundays.* 她总是在星期天去教堂做礼拜。 **4** [C] a small building or room used for funeral services, especially at a CEMETERY or CREMATORIUM（尤指墓地或火葬场的）殡仪馆，殡仪室 **5** [C+sing./pl. v.] (*BrE*) a branch of a trade/labor union in a newspaper office or printing house; the members of the branch（报馆或印刷所的）工会分会，工会分会会员

ˌ**chapel of ˈrest** *noun* (*BrE*) a room at an UNDERTAKER'S where dead bodies are kept before the funeral（殡仪馆的）停尸间，停尸室

chap·er·one (*also* **chap·eron**) /ˈʃæpərəʊn; NAmE -oʊn/ *noun, verb*

▪ ***noun*** **1** (in the past) an older woman who, on social occasions, took care of a young woman who was not married（旧时未婚少女社交时的）年长女伴 **2** a person who takes care of children in public, especially when they are working, for example as actors（尤指儿童表演时的）在场监护人 **3** (*NAmE*) a person, such as a parent or a teacher, who goes with a group of young people on a trip or to a dance to encourage good behaviour（未成年人集体旅行的）保护人，监护人；（未成年人舞会上的）行为引导人

▪ ***verb*** ~ **sb** to act as a chaperone for sb, especially a woman 当女子陪伴人；做引导人

chap·kan /ˈtʃæpkən/ *noun* a long coat worn by men, especially in northern India and Pakistan 查普坎（尤指印度北方和巴基斯坦等地男子穿的长外套）

chap·lain /ˈtʃæplɪn/ *noun* a priest or other Christian minister who is responsible for the religious needs of people in a prison, hospital, etc. or in the armed forces（监狱、医院、军队等的）教士，牧师，神父；特遣牧师 ➲ COMPARE PADRE, PRIEST (1)

chap·lain·cy /ˈtʃæplɪnsi/ *noun* (*pl.* **-ies**) the position or work of a chaplain; the place where a chaplain works 特遣牧师的职位（或职责）；特遣牧师工作的地方

chap·let /ˈtʃæplət/ *noun* a circle of leaves, flowers or JEWELS worn on the head（用叶、花或珠宝做成的）花冠

chap·pal /ˈtʃæpəl/ *noun* (*IndE*) a type of light comfortable open shoe that usually has a piece of leather that goes between the big toe and the toe next to it, or leather bands that go over the foot 人字拖；皮凉鞋

chapped /tʃæpt/ *adj.* (of the skin or lips 皮肤或唇) rough, dry and sore, especially because of wind or cold weather（尤指因风吹或天冷而）皲裂的，开裂的

cha·prasi /tʃʌˈprɑːsiː/ *noun* (*IndE*) an office worker of low rank who does small tasks, such as delivering messages 办公室勤杂员

chaps /tʃæps/ *noun* [pl.] leather coverings worn as protection over trousers/pants by COWBOYS, etc. when riding a horse（牛仔等骑马时穿的）皮护腿套裤，皮套裤：*a pair of chaps* 一条皮套裤

chap·ter 🔑 AW /ˈtʃæptə(r)/ *noun* **1** 🔑 (*abbr.* **chap.**) [C] a separate section of a book, usually with a number or title（书的）章，篇，回：*I've just finished Chapter 3.* 我刚完成第 3 章。◇ *in the* ***previous/next/last chapter*** 在前 / 下 / 最后一章 ◇ *Have you read the chapter on the legal system?* 你读过论述法律制度的那一章吗？ **2** [C] a period of time in a person's life or in history（人生或历史的）时期，时代，篇章：*a difficult chapter in our country's history* 我们国家历史上的一段困难时期 **3** [C+sing./pl. v.] all the priests of a CATHEDRAL or members of a religious community 主教座堂全体教士；宗教团体的全体成员：*a meeting of the dean and chapter* 座堂主任牧师和全体教士的会议 **4** [C] (*especially NAmE*) a local branch of a society, club, etc.（社团、俱乐部等的）地方分会：*the local chapter of the Rotary club* 扶轮社的地方分会

IDM ˌ**chapter and ˈverse** the exact details of sth, especially the exact place where particular information may be found 准确细节；（尤指信息的）确切出处：*I can't give chapter and verse, but that's the rough outline of our legal position.* 我无法提供准确细节，但那是我们所处法律地位的大致情况。 **a ˌchapter of ˈaccidents** (*BrE*) a series of unfortunate events 接二连三的不幸事故；接踵而来的灾祸；祸不单行

ˌ**Chapter ˈ11** *noun* [U] (*law* 律) in the US, a section of the law dealing with BANKRUPTCY (= being unable to pay debts), that allows companies to stop paying their debts in the normal way while they try to find a solution to their financial problems 美国破产法第十一章，破产保护（允许公司在解决财务问题期间停止偿还债务）：*The company has* ***filed for Chapter 11*** *bankruptcy protection.* 公司已经按破产法第十一章的规定申请破产保护。➲ COMPARE ADMINISTRATION (6)

ˌ**Chapter ˈ7** *noun* [U] (*law* 律) in the US, a section of the law dealing with BANKRUPTCY (= being unable to pay debts), that allows a court to take property belonging to a company or person which is then sold to pay their debts 美国破产法第七章，破产清算（允许法院清算变卖财产以偿还债务）➲ COMPARE LIQUIDATION (1)

ˈ**chapter house** *noun* a building where all the priests of a CATHEDRAL or members of a religious community meet 座堂会议厅；宗教团体会议厅

char /tʃɑː(r)/ *verb, noun*

▪ ***verb*** (**-rr-**) **1** [I, T] ~ (**sth**) to become black by burning; to make sth black by burning it（使）烧黑，烧焦 ➲ SEE ALSO CHARRED ➲ SYNONYMS AT BURN **2** [I] (*old-fashioned, BrE*) to work as a cleaner in a house 当家庭清洁工

▪ ***noun*** (*old-fashioned, BrE*) **1** [C] = CHARWOMAN **2** [U] (*informal*) tea 茶：*a cup of char* 一杯茶

chara·banc /ˈʃærəbæŋ/ *noun* (*old-fashioned, BrE*) an early type of bus, used in the past especially for pleasure trips（尤指用于游览的老式）旅游车，游览车

char·ac·ter 🔑 /ˈkærəktə(r)/ *noun*

• **QUALITIES/FEATURES** 品质；特点 **1** 🔑 [C, usually sing.] all the qualities and features that make a person, groups of people, and places different from others （人、集体的）品质，性格；（地方的）特点，特性：*to have a **strong/weak character*** 个性强 / 不强 ◇ ***character traits/defects*** 性格特点 / 弱点 ◇ *The book gives a fascinating insight into Mrs Obama's character.* 这部书对奥巴马夫人的性格作了生动的剖析。◇ *Generosity is part of the American character.* 慷慨是美国人性格的一部分。◇ *The character of the neighbourhood hasn't changed at all.* 这片街区的风貌依旧。 **2** 🔑 [C, usually sing., U] the way that sth is, or a particular quality or feature that a thing, an event or a place has （事物、事件或地方的）特点，特征，特色 SYN **nature**: *the delicate character of the light in the evening* 夜间灯火所具有的那种柔和的特点 ◇ *buildings that are very simple **in character*** 造型很简洁的建筑物 **3** 🔑 [U] (*approving*) strong personal qualities such as the ability to deal with difficult or dangerous situations 勇气；毅力：*Everyone admires her strength of character and determination.* 每一个人都钦佩她坚强的性格和决心。◇ *He showed great character returning to the sport after his accident.* 他在出了事故后仍能重返体坛表现出他顽强的毅力。◇ *Adventure camps are considered to be **character-building*** (= meant to improve sb's strong qualities). 冒险野营生活被认为能磨炼意志。 **4** 🔑 [U] (*usually approving*) the interesting or unusual quality that a place or a person has （地方或人的）与众不同之处，特色：*The modern hotels here have no real character.* 此处的现代化旅馆毫无特色可言。◇ *a face with a lot of character* 与众不同的面孔

• **STRANGE/INTERESTING PERSON** 古怪的 / 有趣的人 **5** [C] (*informal*) (used with an adjective 与形容词连用) a person, particularly an unpleasant or strange one（令人讨厌的或古怪的）人：*There were some really strange characters hanging around the bar.* 有些不三不四的人在酒吧周围游荡。 **6** [C] (*informal*) an interesting or unusual person（有趣的或不同寻常的）人：*She's a character!* 她真是个有趣的人！

• **REPUTATION** 名誉 **7** [C, U] (*formal*) the opinion that people have of you, particularly of whether you can be trusted or relied on 名誉；声望；名气：*She was a victim of **character assassination*** (= an unfair attack on the good opinion people had of her). 她是诽谤行为的受害者。◇ ***a slur/attack on his character*** 对他名誉的诋毁 / 攻击 ◇ *My teacher agreed to be a **character witness** for me in court.* 我的老师同意出庭做我的品德信誉见证人。◇ ***a character reference*** (= a letter that a person who knows you well writes to an employer to tell them about your good qualities) 品德证明书

• **IN BOOK/PLAY/MOVIE** 书；戏剧；电影 **8** 🔑 [C] a person or an animal in a book, play or film/movie（书籍、戏剧或电影中的）人物，角色：*a **major/minor character** in the book* 书中的主要 / 次要人物 ◇ *cartoon characters* 动画片中的角色 ➲ WORDFINDER NOTE AT BOOK ➲ COLLOCATIONS AT LITERATURE

WORDFINDER 联想词：anti-hero, baddy, goody, hero, love interest, narrator, protagonist, trait, villain

• **SYMBOL/LETTER** 符号；字母 **9** [C] a letter, sign, mark or symbol used in writing, in printing or on computers（书写、印刷或计算机上的）文字，字母，符号：*Chinese characters* 汉字 ◇ *a line 30 characters long* 长达 30 字符的一行 ◇ *The URL contained non-standard characters like question marks.* * URL 地址包含问号等非标准字符。➲ PICTURE AT IDEOGRAM

IDM **ˌin ˈcharacter | ˌout of ˈcharacter** typical/not typical of a person's character 符合（或不符合）某人的性格：*Her behaviour last night was completely out of character.* 她昨晚的举止与她的性格截然不符。 **ˌin ˈcharacter (with sth)** in the same style as sth（与…）风格相同：*The new wing of the museum was not really in character with the rest of the building.* 博物馆新建的配楼与大楼其他部分的风格有些不一样。

ˈcharacter actor *noun* an actor who always takes the parts of interesting or unusual people 性格演员

char·ac·ter·ful /ˈkærəktəfl; *NAmE* -tərfl/ *adj.* very interesting and unusual 很有趣且富有特色的

char·ac·ter·is·tic 🔑 /ˌkærəktəˈrɪstɪk/ *adj., noun*

■ ***adj.*** 🔑 ~ (**of sth/sb**) very typical of sth or of sb's character 典型的；独特的；特有的：*She spoke with characteristic enthusiasm.* 她说话带着特有的热情。 OPP **uncharacteristic** ▸ **char·ac·ter·is·tic·al·ly** *adv.*: *Characteristically, Helen paid for everyone.* 一如既往，海伦为每一个人付了费。

■ ***noun*** 🔑 ~ (**of sth/sb**) a typical feature or quality that sth/sb has 特征；特点；品质：*The need to communicate is a key characteristic of human society.* 需要交流是人类社会最重要的一个特征。◇ *The two groups of children have quite different characteristics.* 这两组儿童具有截然不同的特点。◇ *Personal characteristics, such as age and sex are taken into account.* 个人的特征，如年龄和性别等，都要考虑进去。◇ *genetic characteristics* 遗传特征

char·ac·ter·iza·tion (*BrE also* **-isa·tion**) /ˌkærəktəraɪˈzeɪʃn; *NAmE* -rəˈz-/ *noun* [U, C] **1** the way that a writer makes characters in a book or play seem real（对书或戏剧中人物的）刻画，描绘，塑造 **2** (*formal*) the way in which sb/sth is described or defined 描述方法；界定方法 SYN **portrayal**: *This is an unfair characterization of the Prime Minister.* 这是对首相不公正的描述。

char·ac·ter·ize (*BrE also* **-ise**) /ˈkærəktəraɪz/ *verb* (*formal*) **1** ~ **sb/sth** to be typical of a person, place or thing 是…的特征；以…为典型：*the rolling hills that characterize this part of England* 成为英格兰这一地区特征的绵延起伏的丘陵地 **2** ~ **sb/sth** [often passive] to give sb/sth its typical or most noticeable qualities or features 使…具有特点（或最引人注目的特征）：*The city is characterized by tall modern buildings in steel and glass.* 这座城市的特点是钢铁和玻璃建造的现代化高楼大厦林立。 **3** ~ **sb/sth (as sth)** to describe or show the qualities of sb/sth in a particular way 描述，刻画，表现（…的特征、特点）：*activities that are characterized as 'male' or 'female' work* 被描述为"男性"或"女性"工作的各种活动

char·ac·ter·less /ˈkærəktələs; *NAmE* -tərləs/ *adj.* having no interesting qualities 无特征的；无个性的；平凡的

ˈcharacter recognition *noun* [U] the ability of a computer to read numbers or letters that are printed or written by hand 字符识别（计算机读取印刷或手写数字或字母的能力）➲ SEE ALSO OPTICAL CHARACTER RECOGNITION

cha·rade /ʃəˈrɑːd; *NAmE* ʃəˈreɪd/ *noun* **1** [C] a situation in which people pretend that sth is true when it clearly is not 明显的伪装；做戏；装模作样 SYN **pretence**: *Their whole marriage had been a charade—they had never loved each other.* 他们的整个婚姻都是在做戏，他们从未相爱过。 **2 charades** [U] a game in which one player acts out the syllables of a word or title and the other players try to guess what it is 打哑谜猜字游戏：*Let's play charades.* 咱们来玩打哑谜猜字游戏吧。

char·broil /ˈtʃɑːbrɔɪl; *NAmE* ˈtʃɑːr-/ *verb* ~ **sth** to cook meat or other food over CHARCOAL 炭烤，炭炙（肉等食物）

char·coal /ˈtʃɑːkəʊl; *NAmE* ˈtʃɑːrkoʊl/ *noun* [U] **1** a black substance made by burning wood slowly in an oven with little air. Charcoal is used as a fuel or for drawing. 炭，木炭（可作燃料或供作画）：*charcoal-grilled steaks* 用木炭烤制的牛排 ◇ *a charcoal drawing* 炭笔画 **2** (*also* **ˌcharcoal ˈgrey**) a very dark grey colour 深灰色 ➲ MORE LIKE THIS 15, page R26

chard /tʃɑːd; *NAmE* tʃɑːrd/ (*also* **ˌSwiss ˈchard**) *noun* [U] a vegetable with large green leaves and thick white, yellow or red STEMS 莙荙菜；厚皮菜

charge 🔑 /tʃɑːdʒ; *NAmE* tʃɑːrdʒ/ *noun, verb*

■ ***noun***

• **MONEY** 钱 **1** 🔑 [C, U] ~ (**for sth**) the amount of money that sb asks for goods and services（商品和服务所需的）要价，收费：*We have to make a small charge for refreshments.* 我们得收取少量茶点费。◇ *admission charges* 入场费 ◇ *Delivery is free of charge.* 免费送货。➲ SYNONYMS AT RATE **2** [C, U] (*NAmE, informal*) = ACCOUNT (3), CHARGE

ACCOUNT, CREDIT ACCOUNT: *Would you like to put that on your charge?* 你愿意把这笔费用记在你的账上吗? ◇ *'Are you paying cash?' 'No, it'll be a charge.'* "你用现金支付吗?" "不，记账吧。"

• **OF CRIME/STH WRONG** 罪行; 过失 **3** [C, U] an official claim made by the police that sb has committed a crime 指控; 控告: *criminal charges* 刑事指控 ◇ *a murder/an assault charge* 谋杀罪的 / 侵犯人身罪的指控 ◇ *He will be sent back to England* ***to face a charge of*** (= to be on trial for) *armed robbery.* 他将被遣返回英国面临持械抢劫罪的指控。◇ *They decided to* ***drop the charges*** *against the newspaper and settle out of court.* 他们已决定撤销对那家报纸的指控，在庭外和解。◇ *After being questioned by the police, she was released* ***without charge.*** 她被警察传讯后无罪释放。➲ COLLOCATIONS AT JUSTICE **4** [C] a statement accusing sb of doing sth wrong or bad 指责; 谴责 SYN **allegation**: *She rejected the charge that the story was untrue.* 她否认了说她编造事实的指责。◇ *Be careful you don't* ***leave yourself open to charges*** *of political bias.* 你要小心别留下把柄，让人家指责你带有政治偏见。

• **RESPONSIBILITY** 职责 **5** [U] a position of having control over sb/sth; responsibility for sb/sth 主管; 掌管; 照管; 职责; 责任: *She has charge of the day-to-day running of the business.* 她负责掌管日常业务。◇ *They left the au pair* ***in charge of*** *the children for a week.* 他们把孩子留给做换工的照料一周。◇ *He* ***took charge of*** *the farm after his father's death.* 他在父亲去世后掌管了农场。◇ *I'm leaving the school in your charge.* 我这就把学校交给你掌管。**6** [C] (*formal* or *humorous*) a person that you have responsibility for and care for 被照管的人; 受照料者

• **ELECTRICITY** 电 **7** [C, U] the amount of electricity that is put into a battery or carried by a substance (电池的) 充电量; (带电物质的) 电荷: *a* ***positive/negative charge*** 正电荷; 负电荷 ➲ WORDFINDER NOTE AT ELECTRICITY **8** the act of putting electricity into a battery or the time when this happens (电池) 充电; 充电时间: *He put his phone* ***on charge.*** 他给他的手机充电。

• **RUSH/ATTACK** 猛冲; 攻击 **9** [C] a sudden rush or violent attack, for example by soldiers, wild animals or players in some sports 突然猛冲; 猛攻; 冲锋: *He led the charge down the field.* 他带头沿着球场冲杀过去。

• **EXPLOSIVE** 炸药 **10** [C] the amount of EXPLOSIVE needed to fire a gun or make an explosion (射击或爆炸需要的) 炸药量 ➲ SEE ALSO DEPTH CHARGE

• **STRONG FEELING** 强烈感情 **11** [sing.] the power to cause strong feelings 感染力; 震撼力: *the emotional charge of the piano piece* 那首钢琴曲扣人心弦的感染力

• **TASK** 任务 **12** [sing.] (*formal*) a task or duty 任务; 责任: *His charge was to obtain specific information.* 他的任务是收集具体的信息。

IDM **bring/press/prefer 'charges against sb** (*law* 律) to accuse sb formally of a crime so that there can be a trial in court 起诉; 控告 **get a 'charge out of sth** (*NAmE*) to get a strong feeling of excitement or pleasure from sth 从…中得到快感 (或快乐、乐趣)

■ *verb*

• **MONEY** 钱 **1** [T, I] to ask an amount of money for goods or a service 收费; 要价: **~ sth for sth** *What did they charge for the repairs?* 他们收了多少修理费? ◇ *The restaurant charged £20 for dinner.* 这家餐馆收了 20 英镑的餐费。◇ **~ sb for sth** *We won't charge you for delivery.* 我们送货不收费。◇ **~ sth at sth** *Calls are charged at 36p per minute.* 电话费按每分钟 36 便士收取。◇ **~ sb sth (for sth)** *He only charged me half price.* 他只收我半价。◇ **~ for sth** *Do you think museums should charge for admission?* 你认为博物馆应该收入场费吗? ◇ **~ (sb) to do sth** *The bank doesn't charge to stop a payment.* 银行不收取停止付款的手续费。**2** [T] to record the cost of sth as an amount that sb has to pay 把…记在账上; 在某人账上记入: **~ sth to sth** *They charge the calls to their credit-card account.* 他们用信用卡账户支付电话费。◇ (*NAmE*) **~ sth** *Don't worry. I'll* ***charge it*** (= pay by credit card). 别担心，我会用信用卡付款的。

• **WITH CRIME/STH WRONG** 犯罪; 过失 **3** [T] to accuse sb formally of a crime so that there can be a trial in court 控告; 起诉: **~ sb** *Several people were arrested but nobody was charged.* 有数人被捕，但均未受到起诉。◇ **~ sb with sth/with doing sth** *He was charged with murder.* 他被指控犯有谋杀罪。➲ WORDFINDER NOTE AT POLICE **4** [T] **~ sb (with sth/with doing sth)** (*formal*) to accuse sb publicly of doing sth wrong or bad 指责; 谴责: *Opposition MPs charged the minister with neglecting her duty.* 反对党议员指责这名女部长玩忽职守。

• **RUSH/ATTACK** 猛冲; 攻击 **5** [I, T] to rush forward and attack sb/sth 猛冲; 猛攻; 冲锋: *The bull put its head down and charged.* 公牛低下头猛冲过来。◇ **~ (at) sb/sth** *We charged at the enemy.* 我们向敌人发起冲锋。**6** [I] + **adv./prep.** to rush in a particular direction 向…方向冲去: *The children charged down the stairs.* 孩子们冲下了楼梯。◇ *He came charging into my room and demanded to know what was going on.* 他冲进我的房间，要求知道发生了什么事。

• **WITH ELECTRICITY** 电 **7** [T] to pass electricity through sth so that it is stored there 充电: **~ sth** *I need to charge my phone.* 我需要给我的手机充电。◇ **~ sth up** *The shaver can be charged up and used when travelling.* 这种电动剃须刀可充电供旅行使用。

• **WITH RESPONSIBILITY/TASK** 职责; 任务 **8** [T] (usually passive 通常用于被动语态) (*formal*) to give sb a responsibility or task 赋予…职责 (或任务); 使…承担责任 (或任务): **~ sb with sth** *The committee has been charged with the development of sport in the region.* 委员会已被赋予在该地区发展体育运动的职责。◇ **~ sb with doing sth** *The governing body is charged with managing the school within its budget.* 学校管理部门负有在预算范围内管理好学校的职责。

• **WITH STRONG FEELING** 强烈感情 **9** [T] (usually passive 通常用于被动语态) **~ sth (with sth)** (*literary*) to fill sb with an emotion 使充满 (…情绪): *The room was charged with hatred.* 这个房间里充满了敌意。

• **GLASS** 玻璃杯 **10** [T] **~ sth** (*BrE, formal*) to fill a glass 注满 (玻璃杯): *Please charge your glasses and drink a toast to the bride and groom!* 请各位斟满酒杯向新娘、新郎敬酒!

• **GUN** 枪 **11** [T] **~ sth** (*old use*) to load a gun 装 (弹药)

charge·able /ˈtʃɑːdʒəbl; *NAmE* ˈtʃɑːrdʒ-/ *adj.* **~ (to sb/sth)** **1** (of a sum of money 一笔钱) that must be paid by sb 应支付的; 应偿付的: *Any expenses you may incur will be chargeable to the company.* 你的所有开销均由本公司支付。 **2** (of income or other money that you earn 正常收入或其他所得) that you must pay tax on 应征税的: ***chargeable earnings/income*** 应征税的工资 / 收入

ˈcharge account *noun* (*NAmE*) = ACCOUNT (3)

ˈcharge capping *noun* [U] (*BrE*) the act of setting a limit on the amount of money that the local government of an area can charge people in order to pay for public services (地方政府为公共服务向公众收取的) 收费限额

ˈcharge card *noun* a small plastic card provided by a shop/store which you use to buy goods there, paying for them later (购物的) 赊购卡，记账卡 ➲ SEE ALSO CREDIT CARD

charged /tʃɑːdʒd; *NAmE* tʃɑːrdʒd/ *adj.* **~ (with sth)** full of or causing strong feelings or opinions 充满 (某种情绪或想法) 的; 紧张的: *a highly charged atmosphere* 一触即发的紧张气氛 ◇ *a politically charged issue* 极具政治敏感性的问题 ◇ *The dialogue is charged with menace.* 对话充满威胁。

chargé d'af·faires /ˌʃɑːʒeɪ dæˈfeə(r); *NAmE* ˌʃɑːrʒeɪ dæˈfer/ *noun* (*pl.* **chargés d'af·faires** /ˌʃɑːʒeɪ dæˈfeə(r); *NAmE* ˌʃɑːrʒeɪ dæˈfer/) (*from French*) **1** an official who takes the place of an AMBASSADOR in a foreign country when he or she is away 临时代办 (大使不在时代行其职责) **2** an official below the rank of AMBASSADOR who acts as the senior representative of his or her country in a foreign country where there is no AMBASSADOR 代办 (出使没有派驻大使的国家，其级别低于大使的外交代表)

charge·hand /ˈtʃɑːdʒhænd; *NAmE* ˈtʃɑːrdʒ-/ *noun* (*BrE*) a worker in charge of others on a particular job, but below the rank of a FOREMAN 副领班; 副组长

'charge nurse *noun* (*BrE*) a nurse, especially a man, who is in charge of a hospital WARD 主管护士，护士长（多为男性）

char·ger /'tʃɑːdʒə(r); *NAmE* 'tʃɑːrdʒ-/ *noun* **1** a piece of equipment for loading a battery with electricity 充电器：*a phone charger* 手机充电器 **2** (*old use*) a horse that a soldier rode in battle in the past （旧时的）军马，战马

'charge sheet *noun* a record kept in a police station of the names of people that the police have stated to be guilty of a crime (= that they have charged) （警察局的）被起诉者名录

charge·sheet /'tʃɑːdʒʃiːt; *NAmE* 'tʃɑːrdʒ-/ *verb* [T] ~ **sb** (**for sth**) (*IndE*) to accuse sb formally of committing an offence and to ask for an official reply or defence （因某事）起诉，控告（某人）

char·grill /'tʃɑːgrɪl; *NAmE* 'tʃɑːr-/ *verb* ~ **sth** [usually passive] to cook meat, fish or vegetables over a very high heat so that the outside is slightly burnt 高温烤炙，高温烧烤（至表皮焦黄）

char·iot /'tʃæriət/ *noun* an open vehicle with two wheels, pulled by horses, used in ancient times in battle and for racing （古代用于战斗或比赛的）双轮敞篷马车

char·iot·eer /ˌtʃæriə'tɪə(r); *NAmE* -'tɪr/ *noun* the driver of a chariot 驾双轮马车的人

cha·risma /kə'rɪzmə/ *noun* [U] the powerful personal quality that some people have to attract and impress other people 超凡的个人魅力；感召力；号召力：*The President has great personal charisma.* 总统具有超凡的个人魅力。◇ *a lack of charisma* 缺乏个人魅力

cha·ris·mat·ic /ˌkærɪz'mætɪk/ *adj.*, *noun*
■ *adj.* **1** having charisma 有超凡魅力的；有号召力（或感召力）的：*a charismatic leader* 魅力超凡的领袖 **2** (of a Christian religious group 基督教宗教团体) believing in special gifts from God; worshipping in a very enthusiastic way 灵恩派的；灵恩运动的 ▶ **cha·ris·mat·ic·al·ly** /-kli/ *adv.*
■ *noun* (*often* **Charismatic**) a charismatic Christian 有特恩的基督徒

char·it·able /'tʃærətəbl/ *adj.* **1** connected with a charity or charities 慈善团体的；慈善事业的：***a charitable institution/foundation/trust*** 慈善机构 / 基金会 / 基金机构 ◇ ***a charitable donation/gift*** 慈善捐赠 / 赠品 ◇ (*BrE*) *to have* ***charitable status*** (= to be an official charity) 是认可的慈善机构 **2** helping people who are poor or in need 慈善的；行善的；布施的：*His later years were devoted largely to* ***charitable work.*** 他晚年主要致力于慈善工作。 **3** kind in your attitude to other people, especially when you are judging them 仁爱的；宽厚的；宽容的：*Let's be charitable and assume she just made a mistake.* 咱们宽容些吧，就当她只是犯了个错误。 **OPP** **uncharitable** ▶ **char·it·ably** /-bli/ *adv.*：*Try to think about him a little more charitably.* 看待他这个人尽量大度一点吧。

char·ity 🔑 /'tʃærəti/ *noun* (*pl.* **-ies**) **1** 🔑 [C] an organization for helping people in need 慈善机构（或组织）：*Many charities sent money to help the victims of the famine.* 许多慈善机构捐款赈济饥民。◇ *The concert will raise money for local charities.* 这场音乐会将为当地慈善机构募捐。➲ WORDFINDER NOTE AT POOR **2** 🔑 [U] the aim of giving money, food, help, etc. to people who are in need 慈善；赈济；施舍：*Most of the runners in the London Marathon are* ***raising money for charity.*** 大多数人参加伦敦马拉松赛跑是为慈善事业募集资金。◇ *Do you give much to charity?* 慈善捐助你捐得多吗？◇ *a charity concert* (= organized to get money for charity) 慈善音乐会 ◇ *to* ***live on/off charity*** (= to live on money which other people give you because you are poor) 靠赈济生活

> **WORDFINDER** 联想词：appeal, benefit, collection, donation, fundraiser, handout, telethon, volunteer, welfare

3 [U] (*formal*) kindness and sympathy towards other people, especially when you are judging them 仁爱；宽容；宽厚：*Her article showed no charity towards her former friends.* 她的文章对她以前的朋友毫不宽容。

IDM **charity begins at 'home** (*saying*) you should help and care for your own family, etc. before you start helping other people 博爱始于自家

'charity shop (*BrE*) (*NAmE* **'thrift shop/store**) *noun* a shop/store that sells clothes and other goods given by people to raise money for a charity 慈善商店（通过出售捐赠的衣物等募集慈善资金）

char·lady /'tʃɑːleɪdi; *NAmE* 'tʃɑːr-/ *noun* (*pl.* **-ies**) (*old-fashioned, BrE*) = CHARWOMAN

char·la·tan /'ʃɑːlətən; *NAmE* 'ʃɑːrl-/ *noun* a person who claims to have knowledge or skills that they do not really have 假充内行的人；骗子

charles·ton /'tʃɑːlstən; *NAmE* 'tʃɑːrl-/ *noun* (*usually* **the charleston**) [sing.] a fast dance that was popular in the 1920s 查尔斯顿舞（流行于 20 世纪 20 年代的快步舞）

char·ley horse /'tʃɑːli hɔːs; *NAmE* 'tʃɑːrli hɔːrs/ *noun* [usually sing.] (*NAmE, informal*) = CRAMP (1)：*Ow! I just got a charley horse in my leg.* 哎唷！我的腿抽筋了。

char·lie /'tʃɑːli; *NAmE* 'tʃɑːrli/ *noun* (*old-fashioned, BrE, informal*) a silly person 蠢人；傻瓜；笨蛋：*You must have felt a proper charlie!* 你一定觉得自己是个十足的笨蛋！

charm /tʃɑːm; *NAmE* tʃɑːrm/ *noun, verb*
■ *noun* **1** [U] the power of pleasing or attracting people 魅力；魔力；吸引力：*a man of great charm* 富有魅力的男人 ◇ *The hotel is full of charm and character.* 这家旅馆风格独特，极具吸引力。 **2** [C] a feature or quality that is pleasing or attractive 迷人的特征；吸引人的特性；妩媚：*her physical charms* (= her beauty) 她那妩媚的外貌 **3** [C] a small object worn on a chain or BRACELET, that is believed to bring good luck （链子或手镯上的）吉祥小饰物：*a lucky charm* 吉祥饰物 ◇ *a charm bracelet* 吊饰手镯 ➲ WORDFINDER NOTE AT LUCK ➲ VISUAL VOCAB PAGE V70 **4** [C] an act or words believed to have magic power 魔法；咒语；符咒 **SYN** **spell**
IDM **ˌwork like a 'charm** to be immediately and completely successful 立见功效；效验如神 ➲ MORE AT THIRD ORDINAL NUMBER
■ *verb* **1** [T, I] ~ (**sb**) to please or attract sb in order to make them like you or do what you want 吸引；迷住：*He was charmed by her beauty and wit.* 他被她的才貌迷住了。◇ *Her words had lost their power to charm.* 她的话再也没有吸引力了。 **2** [T] ~ **sb/sth** to control or protect sb/sth using magic, or as if using magic （以魔法或似用魔法）控制，保护：*He has led* ***a charmed life*** (= he has been lucky even in dangerous or difficult situations). 他的日子过得如有神佑（即使遇到艰险都能逢凶化吉）。
PHR V **ˌcharm sth 'out of sb** to obtain sth such as information, money, etc. from sb by using charm 利用魅力从…获取

ˌcharmed 'circle *noun* [sing.] a group of people who have special influence 有特别影响力的一群人

charm·er /'tʃɑːmə(r); *NAmE* 'tʃɑːrm-/ *noun* a person who acts in a way that makes them attractive to other people, sometimes using this to influence others 使人着迷的人；有吸引力的人；施展魅力的人 ➲ SEE ALSO SNAKE CHARMER

charm·ing /'tʃɑːmɪŋ; *NAmE* 'tʃɑːrmɪŋ/ *adj.* **1** very pleasant or attractive 令人着迷的；迷人的；吸引人的：*The cottage is tiny, but it's charming.* 这间村舍虽小，却十分迷人。◇ *She's a charming person.* 她是个有魅力的人。 **2** (*ironic, informal*) used to show that you have a low opinion of sb's behaviour （表示对某人的行为评价不高）真是太好了：*They left me to tidy it all up myself. Charming, wasn't it?* 他们留下我一个人来收拾这一切。真是照顾我哟，不是吗？ ▶ **charm·ing·ly** *adv.*

charm·less /'tʃɑːmləs; *NAmE* 'tʃɑːrm-/ *adj.* (*formal*) not at all pleasant or interesting 无魅力的；无吸引力的；无趣的：*a charmless industrial town* 一座毫无吸引力的工业城镇

ˈcharm offensive *noun* a situation in which a person, for example a politician, is especially friendly and pleasant in order to get other people to like them and to support their opinions 魅力攻势（如政客为拉拢民众所采取的）

ˈcharm school *noun* (*old-fashioned* or *humorous*) a school where young people are taught to behave in a polite way （青少年）礼仪学校

char·nel house /ˈtʃɑːnl haʊs; *NAmE* ˈtʃɑːrnl/ *noun* a place used in the past for keeping dead human bodies or bones （旧时）存放尸骨的地方

char·poy /ˈtʃɑːpɔɪ; *NAmE* ˈtʃɑːrpɔɪ/ *noun* (*IndE*) a light wooden or metal frame, usually with many ropes stretched and tied across it, that you can sleep on 轻便床（木架或金属架，床面通常由绳索编成）

charred /tʃɑːd; *NAmE* tʃɑːrd/ *adj.* [usually before noun] burnt and black 烧焦的；烧黑的：*the charred remains of a burnt-out car* 被烧焦的轿车残骸

charts 图表

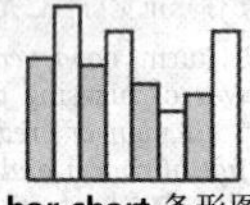

bar chart 条形图

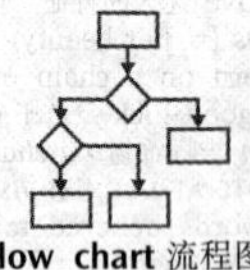

flow chart 流程图

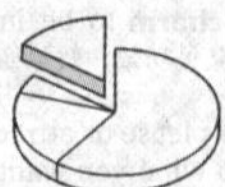

pie chart 饼分图

chart 🔑 AW /tʃɑːt; *NAmE* tʃɑːrt/ *noun, verb*

■ *noun* **1** 🔑 [C] a page or sheet of information in the form of diagrams, lists of figures, etc. 图表：*a weather chart* 天气图 ◇ *a sales chart* (= showing the level of a company's sales) 销售图表 ➲ LANGUAGE BANK AT ILLUSTRATE ➲ SEE ALSO BAR CHART, FLOW CHART, PIE CHART **2** [C] a detailed map of the sea 海图：*a naval chart* 海军航图 **3 the charts** [pl.] (*especially BrE*) a list, produced each week, of the songs or albums that have sold the most copies or been DOWNLOADED or listened to via STREAMING (2) the most frequently （歌曲或唱片每周销售、下载或流播数量）排行榜：*The album went straight into the charts at number 1.* 这张专辑一进入流行唱片排行榜便占首位。◇ *to top the charts* (= to be the song or album that has sold more copies than all the others) 位居排行榜之首

IDM ˌ**off the ˈcharts** (*informal, especially NAmE*) extremely high in level 高得离谱；高极了：*World demand for the product is off the charts.* 此产品的世界需求量高极了。

■ *verb* **1** 🔑 **~ sth** to record or follow the progress or development of sb/sth 记录，跟踪（进展或发展）：*The exhibition **charts the history of** the palace.* 展览记载了这座王宫的历史。 **2 ~ sth** to plan a course of action 计划行动步骤；制订计划：*She had carefully charted her route to the top of her profession.* 她周密地制订了达到她职业巅峰的行动计划。 **3 ~ sth** to make a map of an area 绘制区域地图 SYN **map**：*Cook charted the coast of New Zealand in 1768.* 库克于 1768 年绘制了新西兰的海岸图。

char·ter /ˈtʃɑːtə(r); *NAmE* ˈtʃɑːrt-/ *noun, verb*

■ *noun* **1** [C] a written statement describing the rights that a particular group of people should have （说明某部分民众应有权利的）宪章：*the European Social Charter of workers' rights* 欧洲工人权利社会宪章 **2** [C] a written statement of the principles and aims of an organization （表明某一组织之宗旨和原则的）宪章，章程 SYN **constitution**：*the United Nations Charter* 联合国宪章 **3** [C] an official document stating that a ruler or government allows a new organization, town or university to be established and gives it particular rights （统治者或政府准许成立新的组织、城镇、大学等并授予某些权利的）特许状，许可证，凭照：*The Royal College received its charter as a university in 1967.* 皇家学院于 1967 年获得升格为大学的特许状。 **4** [sing.] **~ (for sth)** (*BrE*) a law or policy that seems likely to help people do sth bad （法律或政策的）不完善，漏洞，缺陷：*The new law will be a charter for unscrupulous financial advisers.* 新的法律会使不诚实的金融顾问有机可乘。◇ *a blackmailer's charter* 敲诈者可钻的法律空子 **5** [U] the hiring of a plane, boat, etc. （飞机、船等的）租赁：*a yacht available for charter* 可供租赁的游艇

■ *verb* **1 ~ sth** to hire/rent a plane, boat, etc. for your own use 包租（飞机、船等）：*a chartered plane* 包机 ➲ WORDFINDER NOTE AT PLANE **2 ~ sth** to state officially that a new organization, town or university has been established and has special rights 特许设立；给予…特权；发给许可证（或凭照）

char·tered /ˈtʃɑːtəd; *NAmE* ˈtʃɑːrtərd/ *adj.* [only before noun] **1** (*BrE*) qualified according to the rules of a professional organization that has a royal charter （持有皇家特许状的专业组织认定为）合格的，特许的：***a chartered accountant/surveyor/engineer*** 特许会计师 / 测量师 / 工程师 **2** (of an aircraft, a ship or a boat 飞机或船) hired for a particular purpose 包租的；租赁的：*a chartered plane* 包机

ˌ**chartered acˈcountant** (*BrE*) (*US* ˌ**certified public acˈcountant**) *noun* a fully trained and qualified ACCOUNTANT 特许会计师；注册会计师

ˈ**charter flight** *noun* a flight in an aircraft in which all the seats are paid for by a travel company and then sold to their customers 包机；包机航班 ➲ COMPARE SCHEDULED FLIGHT

ˌ**charter ˈmember** (*NAmE*) (*BrE* ˌ**founder ˈmember**) *noun* one of the first members of a society, an organization, etc., especially one who helped start it （社团、组织等的）创始人，发起人，创建人

char·treuse /ʃɑːˈtrɜːz; *NAmE* ʃɑːrˈtruːz/ *noun* **1** [U, C] a green or yellow LIQUEUR (= a strong sweet alcoholic drink) 察吐士酒，荨麻酒（一种烈性甜酒，呈绿色或黄色） **2** [U] a pale yellow or pale green colour 浅黄色；浅绿色

ˈ**chart-topping** *adj.* [only before noun] (of a singer, an ALBUM (2), etc. 歌手、音乐专辑等) having reached the highest position in the music CHARTS 位居流行音乐排行榜榜首的：*his latest chart-topping hit* 他大受欢迎、占据排行榜首位的新作 ▸ ˈ**chart-topper** *noun*

char·woman /ˈtʃɑːwʊmən; *NAmE* ˈtʃɑːr-/ *noun* (*pl.* **-women** /-wɪmɪn/) (*also* **char**, **char·lady**) (*all BrE, old-fashioned*) a woman whose job is to clean a house, an office building, etc. 女清洁工

chary /ˈtʃeəri; *NAmE* ˈtʃeri/ *adj.* **~ of sth/of doing sth** not willing to risk doing sth; fearing possible problems if you do sth 不愿冒风险的；小心谨慎的；谨小慎微的 SYN **wary**

chase 🔑 /tʃeɪs/ *verb, noun*

■ *verb*

• **RUN/DRIVE AFTER** 追赶；追逐 **1** 🔑 [T, I] to run, drive, etc. after sb/sth in order to catch them 追赶；追逐；追捕：**~ sb/sth** *My dog likes chasing rabbits.* 我的狗喜欢追捕兔子。◇ *The kids **chased each other** around the kitchen table.* 孩子们围着厨房的桌子相互追逐嬉戏。◇ **~ after sb/sth** *He chased after the burglar but couldn't catch him.* 他追赶那个盗贼却没有抓住他。➲ WORDFINDER NOTE AT HUNT

• **MONEY/WORK/SUCCESS** 钱；工作；成功 **2** [T] **~ sth** to try to obtain or achieve sth, for example money, work or success 努力获得；争取得到：*Too many people are chasing* *too few jobs nowadays.* 如今有太多的人在角逐寥寥无几的工作职位。◇ *The team is chasing its first win in five games.* 这支队伍正全力争取五场比赛的首场胜利。

- **MAN/WOMAN** 男女 **3** [I, T] (*informal*) to try to persuade sb to have a sexual relationship with you 追求；求爱： **~ after sb** *Kevin's been chasing after Joan for months.* 凯文几个月来一直在追求琼。◇ **~ sb** *Girls are always chasing him.* 姑娘们总是在追求他。
- **REMIND SB** 提醒 **4** [T] **~ sb** (*informal*) to persuade sb to do sth that they should have done already 催促： *I need to chase him about organizing the meeting.* 我得催他有关筹办会议的事。
- **RUSH** 急奔 **5** [I] **+ adv./prep.** (*informal*) to rush or hurry somewhere 急奔；急赶；匆忙地走： *I've been **chasing around** town all morning looking for a present for Sharon.* 为了送给莎伦一件礼物，我一上午都在满城奔走寻觅。
- **METAL** 金属 **6** [T] **~ sth** (*specialist*) to cut patterns or designs on metal 镂刻；雕刻： *chased silver* 雕花银器

IDM **chase your (own) 'tail** (*informal*) to be very busy but in fact achieve very little 瞎忙活；徒劳无功

PHR V **,chase sb/sth↔a'way, 'off, 'out, etc.** to force sb/sth to run away 驱逐；赶走 **,chase sb↔'up** to contact sb in order to remind them to do sth that they should have done already 催促： *We need to chase up all members who have not yet paid.* 我们得催促所有未付费的成员交费。 **,chase sth↔'up** (*BrE*) (*NAmE* **,chase sth↔'down**) to find sth that is needed; to deal with sth that has been forgotten 找寻（所需的东西）；催办： *My job was to chase up late replies.* 我的工作是催促迟迟未答复者。

■ ***noun***

- **RUNNING/DRIVING AFTER** 追赶；追逐 **1** [C] (often used with *the* 常与 the 连用) an act of running or driving after sb/sth in order to catch them 追赶；追捕；追逐： *The thieves were caught by police after a short chase.* 经过短暂追捕，小偷被警察擒获。◇ *a high-speed car chase* 一场汽车的高速角逐 ◇ *We lost him in the narrow streets and had to **give up the chase*** (= stop chasing him). 我们在狭窄的街道上被他甩掉，不得不放弃对他的追捕。◇ *to **take up the chase*** (= start chasing sb) 开始追捕行动
- **FOR SUCCESS/MONEY/WORK** 成功；钱；工作 **2** [sing.] a process of trying hard to get sth 努力获得；争取： *Three teams are involved in the chase for the championship.* 有三支队伍角逐冠军的宝座。
- **IN SPORT** 体育运动 **3** **the chase** [sing.] hunting animals as a sport 打猎 **4** [C] = STEEPLECHASE ➲ SEE ALSO WILD GOOSE CHASE

IDM **cut to the 'chase** (*informal*) to stop wasting time and start talking about the most important thing 不绕圈子直截了当地说；开门见山： *Right, let's cut to the chase. How much is it going to cost?* 对啦，咱们开门见山吧。这要多少钱？ **give 'chase** to run after sb/sth in order to catch them 追逐；追赶；追捕： *We gave chase along the footpath.* 我们开始沿小路追赶。

chaser /'tʃeɪsə(r)/ *noun* **1** a drink that you have after another of a different kind, for example a stronger alcoholic drink after a weak one 续酒，追饮酒（饮淡酒后喝的烈性酒或饮烈性酒后喝的淡酒）： *a beer with a whisky chaser* 喝啤酒后接着喝威士忌酒 **2** a horse for STEEPLECHASE racing (= in which horses must jump over a series of fences) （参加障碍赛的）马

Chas·id·ism /'xæsɪdɪzəm/ *noun* [U] = HASIDISM

chasm /'kæzəm/ *noun* **1** [C] (*literary*) a deep crack or opening in the ground （地上的）深裂口，裂隙，深坑 **2** [sing.] **~ (between A and B)** (*formal*) a very big difference between two people or groups, for example because they have different attitudes （两个人或团体之间的）巨大分歧，显著差别 **SYN** **gulf**

chas·sis /'ʃæsi/ *noun* (*pl.* **chas·sis** /-siz/) the frame that a vehicle is built on （车辆的）底盘，底座，底架

chaste /tʃeɪst/ *adj.* **1** (*old-fashioned*) not having sex with anyone; only having sex with the person that you are married to 贞洁的；忠贞的： *to remain chaste* 保持贞洁 **2** (*formal*) not expressing sexual feelings 不含有性意味的；纯洁的： *a **chaste kiss** on the cheek* 在面颊上纯洁的一吻 **3** (*formal*) simple and plain in style; not decorated （风格）简朴的，朴实的；不修饰的： *the cool, chaste interior of the hall* 清爽朴实的大厅内部 ▶ **chaste·ly** *adv.* : *He kissed her chastely on the cheek.* 他在她的脸上留下了纯洁的一吻。

chas·ten /'tʃeɪsn/ *verb* [often passive] **~ sb** (*formal*) to make sb feel sorry for sth they have done 使内疚；使懊悔： *He felt **suitably chastened** and apologized.* 他恰当地感到内疚并表示歉意。◇ *She gave them a chastening lecture.* 她给他们做了一次令他们深感汗颜的演讲。◇ *It was a **chastening experience**.* 那是一次让人接受磨炼的经历。

chas·tise /tʃæ'staɪz/ *verb* **1 ~ sb (for sth/for doing sth)** (*formal*) to criticize sb for doing sth wrong 批评；指责；责备： *He chastised the team for their lack of commitment.* 他指责队伍未竭尽全力。 **2 ~ sb** (*old-fashioned*) to punish sb physically 体罚 **SYN** **beat** ▶ **chas·tise·ment** /tʃæ'staɪzmənt; 'tʃæstɪzmənt/ *noun* [U]

chas·tity /'tʃæstəti/ *noun* [U] the state of not having sex with anyone or only having sex with the person you are married to; being CHASTE （性方面的）忠贞；贞洁；贞操： *vows of chastity* (= those taken by some priests) （神父的）忠贞誓言

'chastity belt *noun* a device worn by some women in the past to prevent them from being able to have sex （旧时防止妇女私通的）贞操带

chat /tʃæt/ *verb, noun*

■ ***verb*** (-tt-) **1** [I] to talk in a friendly informal way to sb 闲聊；闲谈；聊天： **~ (to/with sb)** *My kids spend hours chatting on the phone to their friends.* 我的几个孩子在电话上和朋友聊天一聊就是几个小时。◇ **~ away (to/with sb)** *Within minutes of being introduced they were chatting away like old friends.* 他们经人介绍认识才几分钟，便一见如故地聊个没完。◇ **~ about sth/sb** *What were you chatting about?* 你们聊了些什么？ **2** [I] **~ (away) (to/with sb) | ~ (about sth/sb)** to exchange messages with other people on the Internet, especially in a CHAT ROOM （尤指在网上聊天室的）闲聊，聊天，交谈： *He's been on the computer all morning, chatting with his friends.* 他整个上午都在上网和朋友聊天。 ➲ WORDFINDER NOTE AT WEB ➲ MORE LIKE THIS 36, page R29

PHR V **,chat sb↔'up** (*BrE, informal*) to talk in a friendly way to sb you are sexually attracted to （受异性吸引而）亲昵地攀谈，与某人搭讪： *She went straight over and tried to chat him up.* 她径直走了过去试图同他搭讪。

■ ***noun*** **1** [C] a friendly informal conversation 闲聊；闲谈；聊天： *I just called in for a chat.* 我只是来聊聊天。◇ *I had a long chat with her.* 我和她闲聊了很久。 ➲ SYNONYMS AT DISCUSSION **2** [U] talking, especially informal conversation （尤指非正式的）谈话，讲话： *That's enough chat from me—on with the music!* 我不再多讲了，继续欣赏音乐吧！ ➲ SYNONYMS AT DISCUSSION **3** [U, C] communication between people on the Internet 网上聊天： *chat software* 聊天软件 ◇ *Internet chat services* 互联网聊天服务 ◇ *Fans are invited to an online chat.* 爱好者获邀参与网上聊天。

cha·teau (*also* **châ·teau**) /'ʃætəʊ; *NAmE* ʃæ'toʊ/ *noun* (*pl.* **cha·teaux**, **châ·teaux** or **cha·teaus**, **châ·teaus** /-təʊz; *NAmE* -toʊz/) (*from French*) a castle or large country house in France （法国的）城堡，乡间别墅

chat·line /'tʃætlaɪn/ *noun* **1** a telephone service which allows a number of people who call in separately to have a conversation, especially for fun （消遣性的）热线电话交谈服务 **2** a telephone service which people can call to talk to sb about sex in order to feel sexually excited 热线电话色情交谈服务

'chat room *noun* an area on the Internet where people can communicate with each other, usually about one particular topic （互联网上的）聊天室 ➲ COLLOCATIONS AT EMAIL

'chat show (*BrE*) (*also* **'talk show** *NAmE, BrE*) *noun* a television or radio programme in which famous people are asked questions and talk in an informal way about their work and opinions on various topics （电视或电台的）访谈节目：*a chat-show host* 访谈节目主持人 ➲ WORDFINDER NOTE AT PROGRAMME

C

chat·tel /ˈtʃætl/ *noun* [C, U] (*law* 律 or *old-fashioned*) something that belongs to you （个人的）财产，动产 ➲ SEE ALSO GOODS AND CHATTELS

chat·ter /ˈtʃætə(r)/ *verb, noun*
■ ***verb*** **1** [I] ~ **(away/on)** **(to sb)** **(about sth)** to talk quickly and continuously, especially about things that are not important 喋喋不休；唠叨；饶舌：*They chattered away happily for a while.* 他们高兴地闲扯了一会儿。◇ *The children chattered to each other excitedly about the next day's events.* 孩子们很兴奋，没完没了地谈论着第二天的活动。 **2** [I] (of teeth 牙齿) to knock together continuously because you are cold or frightened （因冷或害怕）打颤 **3** [I] (of birds or MONKEYS 禽或猴) to make a series of short high sounds 鸣叫；啼啭；啁啾；唧唧叫；吱吱叫
IDM **the ˈchattering classes** (*BrE, usually disapproving*) the people in society who like to give their opinions on political or social issues 喜欢（对政治或社会问题）发表意见的人
■ ***noun*** [U] **1** continuous rapid talk about things that are not important 唠叨的话；喋喋不休：*Jane's constant chatter was beginning to annoy him.* 简无休止的唠叨开始使他心烦。◇ *idle chatter* 无聊的唠叨 **2** a series of quick short high sounds that some animals make 鸣叫声；啼啭声；吱吱叫声：*the chatter of monkeys* 猴子的吱吱叫声 **3** a series of short sounds made by things knocking together 碰击声；咯咯声；打颤声：*the chatter of teeth* 牙齿打颤的咯咯声

chat·ter·box /ˈtʃætəbɒks; *NAmE* ˈtʃætərbɑːks/ *noun* (*informal*) a person who talks a lot, especially a child 话多的人，话匣子（尤指小孩）

chatty /ˈtʃæti/ *adj.* (**chat·tier**, **chat·ti·est**) (*informal*) **1** talking a lot in a friendly way 爱说话的；爱闲聊的；健谈的：*You're very chatty today, Alice.* 艾丽斯，你今天很健谈。 **2** having a friendly informal style 闲聊式的：*a chatty letter* 一封聊天式的信

ˈchat-up *noun* [C, U] (*BrE, informal*) an occasion when a person is talking to sb in a way that shows they are interested in them sexually 亲昵攀谈；搭讪：*Is that your best **chat-up line**?* 那是你最拿手的调情话吗？

chauf·feur /ˈʃəʊfə(r); *NAmE* ʃoʊˈfɜːr/ *noun, verb*
■ ***noun*** a person whose job is to drive a car, especially for sb rich or important （尤指富人或要人的）司机
■ ***verb*** **~ sb** to drive sb in a car, usually as your job 为某人开车；当司机：*He was chauffeured to all his meetings.* 他由司机开车送去参加所有的会议。◇ *a chauffeured limousine* 有专职司机驾驶的豪华轿车

chau·vin·ism /ˈʃəʊvɪnɪzəm; *NAmE* ˈʃoʊ-/ *noun* [U] (*disapproving*) **1** an aggressive and unreasonable belief that your own country is better than all others 沙文主义 **2** = MALE CHAUVINISM

chau·vin·ist /ˈʃəʊvɪnɪst; *NAmE* ˈʃoʊ-/ *noun* **1** = MALE CHAUVINIST **2** a person who has an aggressive and unreasonable belief that their own country is better than all others 沙文主义者 ▸ **chau·vin·is·tic** /ˌʃəʊvɪˈnɪstɪk; *NAmE* ˌʃoʊ-/ (*also less frequent* **chau·vin·ist**) *adj.* **chau·vin·is·tic·al·ly** /-kli/ *adv.*

chav /tʃæv/ *noun* (*BrE, slang*) a young person, often without a high level of education, who typically behaves in a loud and annoying way and wears designer clothes 低俗的年轻人（一般受教育程度低、举止放浪、穿名牌服装）

ChB /ˌsiː eɪtʃ ˈbiː/ *abbr.* (*BrE*) Bachelor of Surgery 外科医学士

cheap 🔑 /tʃiːp/ *adj., adv.*
■ ***adj.*** (**cheap·er**, **cheap·est**)
• LOW PRICE 低价 **1** 🔑 costing little money or less money than you expected 花钱少的；便宜的；廉价的 SYN **inexpensive**：*cheap fares* 便宜的票价 ◇ *Personal computers are cheap and getting cheaper.* 个人电脑现在价格便宜，以后还会越来越便宜。◇ *Cycling is a cheap way to get around.* 骑自行车是一种省钱的出行方式。◇ *The printer isn't exactly cheap at £200.* 价格为 200 英镑的打印机并不是很便宜。◇ *immigrant workers, used as a source of **cheap labour*** (= workers who are paid very little, especially unfairly) 作为廉价劳动力来源的移民工人 ➲ SEE ALSO DIRT CHEAP OPP **expensive** **2** 🔑 charging low prices 收费低廉的：*a cheap restaurant/hotel* 收费低廉的餐馆 / 旅馆 ◇ (*BrE*) *We found a **cheap and cheerful** cafe* (= one that is simple and charges low prices but is pleasant). 我们找到了一家价格低廉环境宜人的咖啡馆。 OPP **expensive**
• POOR QUALITY 劣质 **3** 🔑 (*disapproving*) low in price and quality 价低质劣的：*cheap perfume/jewellery/shoes* 低价劣质香水 / 珠宝 / 鞋 ◇ (*BrE*) *a **cheap and nasty** bottle of wine* 一瓶便宜的劣质葡萄酒
• UNKIND 不友好 **4** unpleasant or unkind and rather obvious 令人讨厌的；明显不友好的；不和善的：*I was tired of his cheap jokes at my expense.* 我讨厌他拿我开低级庸俗的玩笑。
• LOW STATUS 地位低下 **5** (*disapproving*) having a low status and therefore not deserving respect 卑微的；卑贱的；可鄙的：*He's just a cheap crook.* 他简直是个卑鄙的骗子。◇ *His treatment of her made her **feel cheap*** (= ashamed, because she had lost her respect for herself). 他那样对待她使她感到很丢脸。
• NOT GENEROUS 不大方 **6** (*NAmE*) (*BrE* **mean**) (*informal, disapproving*) not liking to spend money 小气的；抠门儿的：*Don't be so cheap!* 别这么小气！
▸ **cheap·ness** *noun* [U]
IDM **cheap at the ˈprice** (*also* **cheap at ˈtwice the price**) (*BrE also* **cheap at ˈhalf the price**) so good or useful that the cost does not seem too much 价钱虽高但还合算 **on the ˈcheap** spending less money than you usually need to spend to do sth 低廉地；廉价地：*a guide to decorating your house on the cheap* 房屋廉价装潢指南 ➲ MORE AT LIFE
■ ***adv.*** (*comparative* **cheap·er**, *no superlative*) (*informal*) for a

▼ SYNONYMS 同义词辨析

cheap

competitive • budget • affordable • reasonable • inexpensive

These words all describe a product or service that costs little money or less money than you expected. 以上各词均指产品或服务花钱少或低于预期。

cheap costing little money or less money than you expected; charging low prices 指花钱少、便宜、收费低廉
NOTE **Cheap** can also be used in a disapproving way to suggest that sth is poor quality as well as low in price.
* cheap 亦可作贬义，指价低质劣：*a bottle of cheap perfume* 一瓶低价劣质香水

competitive (of prices, goods or services) as cheap as or cheaper than those offered by other companies; able to offer goods or services at competitive prices 指价格、产品或服务收费方面具有竞争力

budget [only before noun] (used especially in advertising) cheap because it offers only a basic level of service（尤用于广告）指仅提供基本服务因而价格低廉

affordable cheap enough for most people to afford 指多数人买得起或负担得来的

reasonable (of prices) not too expensive 指价格不太高、公道的

inexpensive (*rather formal*) cheap 指不昂贵
NOTE **Inexpensive** is often used to mean that sth is good value for its price. It is sometimes used instead of **cheap**, because **cheap** can suggest that sth is poor quality.
* inexpensive 常含物有所值之义，有时用以代替 cheap，因为 cheap 可有质量低劣的含义。

PATTERNS
- cheap/competitive/budget/affordable/reasonable **prices/fares/rates**
- cheap/competitive/budget/affordable/inexpensive **products/services**

low price 低价地；廉价地；便宜地：*I got this dress cheap in a sale.* 这件衣服是我在大减价时便宜买的。

IDM **be ˌgoing ˈcheap** to be offered for sale at a lower price than usual 降价出售；廉价销售 **sth does not come ˈcheap** something is expensive 昂贵；不便宜：*Violins like this don't come cheap.* 像这样的小提琴不会便宜。

cheap·en /ˈtʃiːpən/ *verb* **1 ~ sb/yourself** to make sb lose respect for himself or herself 使丧失威信；使贬低 SYN **degrade**: *She never cheapened herself by lowering her standards.* 她从不降低标准来贬低自己。 **2 ~ sth** to make sth lower in price 降低…的价格：*to cheapen the cost of raw materials* 降低原材料的成本 **3 ~ sth** to make sth appear to have less value 使贬值；贬低：*The movie was accused of cheapening human life.* 有人指责这部电影贬低了人的生命价值。

cheap·ly 🔑 /ˈtʃiːpli/ *adv.* without spending or costing much money 便宜地；廉价地；低廉地：*I'm sure I could buy this more cheaply somewhere else.* 我相信我能在别的地方更便宜地买到这种物品。◇ *a cheaply made movie* 一部低成本电影

cheapo /ˈtʃiːpəʊ; *NAmE* -poʊ/ *adj.* [only before noun] (*informal, disapproving*) cheap and often of poor quality 价廉质劣的

cheap·skate /ˈtʃiːpskeɪt/ *noun* (*informal, disapproving*) a person who does not like to spend money 小气鬼；守财奴

cheat 🔑 /tʃiːt/ *verb, noun*

■ *verb* **1** 🔑 [T] **~ sb/sth** to trick sb or make them believe sth which is not true 欺骗；蒙骗：*She is accused of attempting to cheat the taxman.* 她被指控企图蒙骗税务员。◇ *Many people* ***feel cheated*** *by the government's refusal to hold a referendum.* 由于政府拒绝举行全民投票表决，许多人都觉得上当受骗。◇ *He* ***cheated his way*** *into the job.* 他骗取了这份工作。 **2** 🔑 [I] **~ (at sth)** to act in a dishonest way in order to gain an advantage, especially in a game, a competition, an exam, etc.（尤指在游戏、比赛、考试等中）作弊，舞弊：*He cheats at cards.* 他玩牌爱作弊。◇ *You're not allowed to look at the answers—****that's cheating****.* 你们不许看答案，那是作弊。 **3** [I] **~ (on sb)** (of sb who is married or who has a regular sexual partner 已婚或有固定性伴侣的人) to have a secret sexual relationship with sb else 与他人有秘密性关系；对某人不忠（或不贞）

IDM **cheat ˈdeath** (often used in newspapers 常用于报章) to survive in a situation where you could have died 死里逃生；幸免于难

PHR V **ˈcheat sb of sth | ˌcheat sb ˈout of sth** 🔑 to prevent sb from having sth, especially in a way that is not honest or fair（尤指用不诚实或不正当的手段）阻止某人得到某物：*They cheated him out of his share of the profits.* 他们施展伎俩，不让他获得他的那份利润。

■ *noun* (*especially BrE*) **1** 🔑 (*also* **cheat·er** *especially in NAmE*) [C] a person who cheats, especially in a game（尤指游戏中的）作弊者，骗子：*You little cheat!* 你这小滑头！ **2** [sing.] something that seems unfair or dishonest, for example a way of doing sth with less effort than it usually needs 欺骗手段；欺诈行为：*It's really a cheat, but you can use ready-made pastry if you want.* 这样做其实是骗人，但如果你愿意的话，可以用现成的油酥面团。 **3** [C] (*computing* 计) a program you can use to move immediately to the next stage of a computer game without needing to play the game（电脑游戏的）秘技，欺骗程序，作弊软件：*There's a cheat you can use to get to the next level.* 有种秘技，你可以用来到达下一关。

ˈcheat sheet *noun* (*informal*) a set of notes to help you remember important information, especially one taken secretly into an exam room 备忘纸条；（尤指考试用的）作弊纸条，夹带

check 🔑 /tʃek/ *verb, noun, exclamation*

■ *verb*

• **EXAMINE** 检查 **1** 🔑 [T] **~ sth (for sth)** to examine sth to see if it is correct, safe or acceptable 检查；审查；核查；检验：*Check the container for cracks or leaks.* 检验容器是否有裂缝或者漏洞。◇ *She gave me the minutes of the meeting to read and check.* 她把会议记录交给我审阅。◇ *Check*

▼ **SYNONYMS 同义词辨析**

cheat

fool • deceive • betray • take in • trick • con

These words all mean to make sb believe sth that is not true, especially in order to get what you want. 以上各词均含使人误信之义，尤指有目的地这样做。

cheat to make sb believe sth that is not true, in order to get money or sth else from them 指为得到钱财或其他东西而欺骗、欺诈：*She is accused of attempting to cheat the taxman.* 她被指控企图蒙骗税务员。◇ *He cheated his way into the job.* 他骗取了这份工作。 NOTE **Cheat** also means to act in a dishonest way in order to gain an advantage, especially in a game, competition or exam. * cheat 亦指在游戏、竞赛或考试中作弊、舞弊：*You're not allowed to look at the answers—****that's cheating****.* 你们不许看答案，那是作弊。

fool to make sb believe sth that is not true, especially in order to laugh at them or to get what you want 指蒙骗、愚弄：*Just don't be fooled into investing any money with them.* 别上当受骗，同他们一起搞什么投资。

deceive to make sb believe sth that is not true, especially sb who trusts you, in order to get what you want 尤指利用别人的信任欺骗、蒙骗、诓骗：*She deceived him into handing over all his savings.* 她把他所有的积蓄都骗走了。

betray to hurt sb who trusts you, especially by deceiving them or not being loyal to them 指辜负别人的信任、出卖：*She felt betrayed when she found out the truth about him.* 她发现他的真实情况时，感到受了欺骗。

take sb in [often passive] to deceive sb, usually in order to get what you want 指为个人目的而欺骗、蒙骗：*I was taken in by her story.* 我被她的花言巧语蒙骗了。

trick to deceive sb, especially in a clever way, in order to get what you want 尤指以巧妙的方式欺骗、欺诈

con (*informal*) to deceive sb, especially in order to get money from them or get them to do sth for you 尤指为获取钱财或使人为自己做事而欺骗、哄骗、诈骗：*They had been conned out of £100 000.* 他们被骗走了 10 万英镑。

WHICH WORD? 词语辨析

Many of these words involve making sb believe sth that is not true, but some of them are more disapproving than others. **Deceive** is probably the worst because people typically deceive friends, relations and others who know and trust them. People may *feel cheated/betrayed* by sb in authority who they trusted to look after their interests. If sb **takes you in**, they may do it by acting a part and using words and charm effectively. If sb **cheats/fools/tricks/cons** you, they may get sth from you and make you feel stupid. However, sb might **fool** you just as a joke; and to **trick** sb is sometimes seen as a clever thing to do, if the person being tricked is seen as a bad person who deserves it. 以上各词多含使人将假话信以为真之义，但其中有些词贬义较另一些词强。deceive 大概贬义最强，主要指欺骗朋友、亲戚和其他认识和信任自己的人。相信掌权者能够顾全自己利益却遭欺骗可用 feel cheated/betrayed。通过装腔作势或花言巧语等骗人用 take sb in。哄骗、愚弄他人用 cheat/fool/trick/con。只为开玩笑可用 fool。如果被戏弄者是应该受到惩罚的坏人，可用 trick，表示计谋巧妙。

PATTERNS

- to cheat/fool/trick/con sb **out of** sth
- to cheat/fool/deceive/betray/trick/con sb **into doing sth**
- to **feel** cheated/fooled/deceived/betrayed/tricked/conned
- to fool/deceive **yourself**
- to cheat/trick/con **your way** into sth

the oil and water before setting off. 出发前应查看一下油和水。◇ *Check your work before handing it in.* 交作业前先检查一遍。

C

- **MAKE SURE** 确定 **2** 🔑 [I, T] to find out if sth/sb is present, correct or true or if sth is how you think it is 查明；查看；核实；弄确实：*'Is Mary in the office?' 'Just a moment. I'll go and check.'* "玛丽在办公室吗？" "请稍等，我去看看。" ◇ **~ sth** *Hang on—I just need to check my email.* 稍等，我得查看一下我的电邮。◇ **~ (that)...** *Go and check (that) I've locked the windows.* 去查看一下我是不是把窗户锁上了。◇ **~ (with sb) (what/whether, etc....)** *You'd better check with Jane what time she's expecting us tonight.* 你最好向简核实一下她今晚见我们的时间。➲ SEE ALSO CROSS-CHECK, DOUBLE-CHECK
- **CONTROL** 控制 **3** [T] **~ sth** to control sth; to stop sth from increasing or getting worse 控制；抑制；阻止：*The government is determined to check the growth of public spending.* 政府决心要控制公共开支的增长。 **4** [T] to stop yourself from saying or doing sth or from showing a particular emotion 克制，抑制（做某事或表露感情）：**~ sth** *to check your anger/laughter/tears* 忍住怒火 / 笑 / 眼泪 ◇ **~ yourself** *She wanted to tell him the whole truth but she checked herself—it wasn't the right moment.* 她本想告诉他全部真相，但是又忍住了——还不是时候。
- **COATS/BAGS/CASES** 外套；包；箱子 **5** [T] **~ sth** (*NAmE*) to leave coats, bags, etc. in an official place (called a CHECKROOM) while you are visiting a club, restaurant, etc. 存放；寄放：*Do you want to check your coats?* 你们要寄放外套吗？ **6** [T] **~ sth** (*NAmE*) to leave bags or cases with an official so that they can be put on a plane or train 托运（行李）
- **MAKE MARK** 标上符号 **7** [T] **~ sth** (*NAmE*) (*BrE* **tick**) to put a mark (✓) next to an item on a list, an answer, etc. 标记号；打上钩；打对号：*Check the box next to the right answer.* 在正确答案旁边的方框中打钩。

PHR V ˌ**check ˈin (at...)** 🔑 to go to a desk in a hotel, an airport, etc. and tell an official there that you have arrived（在旅馆、机场等）登记，报到：*Please check in at least an hour before departure.* 请至少在飞机起飞前一小时办理登机手续。◇ *We've checked in at the hotel.* 我们已经在旅馆登记入住。➲ RELATED NOUN CHECK-IN ˌ**check sth↔ˈin** 🔑 to leave bags or cases with an official to be put on a plane or train 托运（行李）：*We checked in our luggage and went through to the departure lounge.* 我们托运行李后直接进入候机室。➲ RELATED NOUN CHECK-IN ˈ**check into...** 🔑 to arrive at a hotel or private hospital to begin your stay there 登记入住（旅馆或私立医院）：*He checked into a top London clinic yesterday for an operation on his knee.* 他昨天住进了伦敦一家最高级的诊所，准备做膝部手术。ˌ**check sb/sth↔ˈoff** (*NAmE*) (*BrE* ˌ**tick sb/sth ˈoff**) to put a mark (✓) beside a name or an item on a list to show that sth has been dealt with 给…画上钩；给…打核对号：*Check the names off as the guests arrive.* 客人到来时在其姓名旁打钩。ˈ**check on sb/sth** 🔑 to make sure that there is nothing wrong with sb/sth 核实，检查（是否一切正常）：*I'll just go and check on the children.* 我正要去看看孩子们。ˌ**check ˈout** to be found to be true or acceptable after being examined（经检查）得到证实，获得证明：*The local police found her story didn't check out.* 当地警方证实她的说法不成立。ˌ**check ˈout (of...)** 🔑 to pay your bill and leave a hotel, etc. 结账离开（旅馆等）：*Guests should check out of their rooms by noon.* 客人务请在中午以前办理退房手续。➲ RELATED NOUN CHECKOUT (2) ˌ**check sb/sth↔ˈout** **1** to find out if sth is correct, or if sb is acceptable 调查；查证；核实：*The police are checking out his alibi.* 警察在查证他不在案发现场的证据。◇ *We'll have to check him out before we employ him.* 我们得先调查一下才雇用他。 **2** (*informal*) to look at or examine a person or thing that seems interesting or attractive 察看，观察（有趣或有吸引力的人或事物）：*Check out the prices at our new store!* 看一看我们新商店的价格吧！◇ *Hey, check out that car!* 嘿，看看那辆车！ ˌ**check sth↔ˈout** to borrow sth from an official place, for example a book from a library（从图书馆等）借出：*The book has been checked out in your name.* 这本书已用你的名字从图书馆借出。 ˌ**check ˈover/ˈthrough↔sth** 🔑 to examine sth carefully to make sure that it is correct or acceptable 仔细检查；核对；核查：*Check over your work for mistakes.* 仔细检查你的作业以防有错。ˌ**check ˈup on sb** 🔑 to make sure that sb is doing what they should be doing 监督；督促：*My parents are always checking up on me.* 我父母总是督促我。ˌ**check ˈup on sth** to find out if sth is true or correct 查证；核实：*I need to check up on a few things before I can decide.* 我得核实几件事情才能作决定。

■ ***noun***

- **EXAMINATION** 检查 **1** 🔑 [C] **~ (for/on sth)** an act of making sure that sth is safe, correct or in good condition by examining it 检查，查看（是否安全、正确、状况良好）：*Could you give the tyres a check?* 你能检查一下轮胎吗？◇ *a health check* 体格检查 ◇ *The drugs were found in their car during a routine check by police.* 警方在例行检查时在他们的车里搜出了毒品。◇ *a check for spelling mistakes* 拼写错误检查 ◇ *I'll just have a quick check to see if the letter's arrived yet.* 我要快速查看一下，看看那封信是否已经寄到。◇ *It is vital to* ***keep a check on*** *your speed* (= look at it regularly in order to control it). 经常检查并控制你的车速

▼ **SYNONYMS** 同义词辨析

check

examine • inspect • go over sth

These words all mean to look closely to make sure that everything is correct, in good condition, or acceptable. 以上各词均含仔细检查、审查之义。

check to look at sth closely to make sure that everything is correct, in good condition, safe or satisfactory 指检查、审查、核查，以确保完好、正常和安全：*Check your work before handing it in.* 交作业前先检查一遍。

examine to look at sb/sth closely to see if there is anything wrong or to find the cause of a problem 指仔细检查或检验人或事物，以确认有无问题或找出问题所在：*The goods were examined for damage on arrival.* 货物到达时已检查是否有破损。

inspect to look at sb/sth closely to make sure that everything is satisfactory; to officially visit a school, factory, etc. in order to check that rules are being obeyed and that standards are acceptable 指检查、查看、审视，以确保一切妥当；视察（学校、工厂等）：*Make sure you inspect the goods before signing for them.* 要确保在签收货物之前进行检验。◇ *The Tourist Board inspects all recommended hotels at least once a year.* 旅游局至少每年视察一次所有举荐的旅馆。

CHECK, EXAMINE OR INSPECT? 用 check、examine 还是 inspect?

All these words can be used when you are looking for possible problems, but only **check** is used for mistakes. 以上各词均可用于检查可能出现的问题，但检查错误只用 check：~~Examine/Inspect your work before handing it in.~~ Only **examine** is used when looking for the cause of a problem. 查找问题的原因只用 examine：~~The doctor checked/inspected her but could find nothing wrong.~~ **Examine** is used more often about a professional person. * examine 较常用于专业人员所做的检查：*The surveyor examined the walls for signs of damp.* 房屋鉴定人检查了墙壁，看是否有水渍。 **Inspect** is used more often about an official. * inspect 较常用于官方检查：*Public health officials were called in to inspect the restaurant.* 公共卫生官员被召来视察了这家餐馆。

go over sth to check sth carefully for mistakes, damage or anything dangerous 指仔细检查是否有错误、损坏或危险：*Go over your work for spelling mistakes before you hand it in.* 交作业前仔细检查一下拼写错误。

PATTERNS

- to check/examine/inspect/go over (sth) **for** sth
- to check/examine/inspect/go over sth **to see if/whether...**
- to check/examine/inspect/go over sth **carefully/thoroughly**

是至关重要的。➲ SEE ALSO REALITY CHECK
- **INVESTIGATION** 调查 **2** [C] ~ (**on sb/sth**) an investigation to find out more information about sth 调查；审查：*The police **ran a check** on the registration number of the car.* 警方对那辆车的牌照号码进行了调查。◇ *Was any check made on Mr Morris when he applied for the post?* 莫里斯先生申请这个职位时对他进行调查了吗？
- **CONTROL** 控制 **3** [C] ~ (**on/to sth**) (*formal*) something that delays the progress of sth else or stops it from getting worse 阻碍进程的事物；阻止恶化的事物：*A cold spring will provide a natural check on the number of insects.* 寒冷的春季会自然控制昆虫的数量。 **4 checks** [pl.] (*formal*) rules that are designed to control the amount of power, especially political power, that one person or group has（对政治等权力的）规定，条令，约束 ➲ SEE ALSO CHECKS AND BALANCES
- **PATTERN** 图案 **5** [C, U] a pattern of squares, usually of two colours（通常指双色的）方格图案，方格，格子：*Do you prefer checks or stripes?* 你喜欢方格还是条纹？◇ *a check shirt/suit* 格子衬衫 / 西服 ◇ *a yellow and red check skirt* 红黄色相间的方格裙子 ➲ SEE ALSO CHECKED ➲ **WORDFINDER NOTE** AT PATTERN
- **MONEY** 钱 **6** [C] (*US*) = CHEQUE **7** [C] (*NAmE*) = BILL (2)：*Can I have the check, please?* 请给我结账。➲ **SYNONYMS** AT BILL
- **FOR COATS/BAGS** 外套；包 **8** [C] (*NAmE*) **coat ~** a place in a club, restaurant, etc. where you can leave your coat or bag（俱乐部、餐馆等外套、包的）寄存处，存放处 **9** [C] (*NAmE*) a ticket that you get when you leave your coat, bag, etc. in, for example, a restaurant or theatre（餐馆或剧院等的）存物牌，存放证
- **IN GAME** 竞技活动 **10** [U] (in CHESS 国际象棋) a position in which a player's king (= the most important piece) can be directly attacked by the other player's pieces 被将军的局面：*There, you're in check.* 瞧，将你一军。➲ SEE ALSO CHECKMATE
- **MARK** 符号 **11** (*also* ˈ**check mark**) (*both NAmE*) (*BrE* **tick**) [C] a mark (✓) put beside a sum or an item on a list, usually to show that it has been checked or done or is correct 核对号；对号；钩号 ➲ COMPARE CROSS *n.* (1), X *symbol* (4)

IDM ▸ **hold/keep sth in ˈcheck** to keep sth under control so that it does not spread or get worse 控制；制止 ➲ MORE AT RAIN CHECK

■ ***exclamation*** used to show that you agree with sb or that sth on a list has been dealt with 行；已经办好：*'Do you have your tickets?' 'Check.' 'Passport?' 'Check.'* "你有票吗？" "有。" "护照呢？" "有。"

check·book *noun* (*US*) = CHEQUEBOOK

check·box /ˈtʃekbɒks; *NAmE* -bɑːks/ (*BrE also* **tick·box**) *noun* a small square on a computer screen that you click on with the mouse to choose whether a particular function is switched on or off（计算机屏幕上的）复选框

checked /tʃekt/ *adj.* having a pattern of squares, usually of two colours 有方格图案的（常为双色）：*checked material* 印有方格图案的布料 ➲ SEE ALSO CHECK *v.*

check·er /ˈtʃekə(r)/ *noun* ➲ SEE ALSO CHECKERS **1** (*especially US*) a person who works at the CHECKOUT in a supermarket（超市的）收款员，收银员 **2** (in compounds 构成复合词) a computer program that you use to check sth, for example the spelling and grammar of sth you have written（计算机的）检查程序：*a **spelling/grammar/virus checker*** 拼写 / 语法 / 病毒检查程序 **3** a person who checks things 检验员；审核员：*a quality control checker* 质量控制检验员

check·er·board /ˈtʃekəbɔːd; *NAmE* ˈtʃekərbɔːrd/ (*NAmE*) (*BrE* **draught·board**) *noun* a board with black and white squares, used for playing DRAUGHTS/CHECKERS 国际跳棋棋盘；西洋跳棋棋盘

check·ered *adj.* (*especially NAmE*) = CHEQUERED

check·ers /ˈtʃekəz; *NAmE* -ərz/ (*NAmE*) (*BrE* **draughts**) *noun* [U] a game for two players using 24 round pieces on a board marked with black and white squares 国际跳棋；西洋跳棋

ˈ**check-in** *noun* **1** [C, U] the place where you go to at an airport to leave your suitcases, etc. and show your ticket（机场的）登机手续办理处 **2** [U] the act of confirming your intention to take a particular flight and your personal details either at an airport or using a computer（在机场或电脑上）办理登机手续：*Do you know your check-in time?* 你知道办理登机手续的时间吗？◇ (*BrE*) *the check-in desk* 办理登机手续的服务台 ◇ (*NAmE*) *the check-in counter* 办理登机手续的服务台 ➲ **WORDFINDER NOTE** AT AIRPORT

ˈ**checking account** (*US*) (*BrE* ˈ**current account**) (*CanE* ˈ**chequing account**) *noun* a type of bank account that you can take money out of at any time, and that provides you with a CHEQUEBOOK and CASH CARD 活期存款账户；往来账户 ➲ COMPARE DEPOSIT ACCOUNT

check·list /ˈtʃeklɪst/ *noun* a list of the things that you must remember to do, to take with you or to find out（记事）清单，一览表

check·mate /ˌtʃekˈmeɪt; ˈtʃekmeɪt/ (*also* **mate**) *noun* [U] **1** (in CHESS 国际象棋) a position in which one player cannot prevent his or her king (= the most important piece) being captured and therefore loses the game 将死；输棋 ➲ SEE ALSO CHECK *n.* (10) ➲ COMPARE STALEMATE (2) **2** a situation in which sb has been completely defeated 败局；败北；彻底战败 ▸ **check·mate** (*also* **mate**) *verb*: **~ sb/sth** *His king had been checkmated.* 他的王棋已被将死。◇ *She hoped the plan would checkmate her opponents.* 她希望这一计划能彻底战胜对手。

check·out /ˈtʃekaʊt/ *noun* **1** [C] the place where you pay for the things that you are buying in a supermarket（超市的）付款台，付款处：***a checkout assistant/operator*** 付款台助手 / 收银员 **2** [U] the time when you leave a hotel at the end of your stay（在旅馆）结账离开的时间：*At checkout, your bill will be printed for you.* 结账时，旅馆会把你的账单打印给你。 **3** [U] part of the process of online shopping in which the customer enters delivery information and pays for the item（网购）结算（输入送货信息并付款）：*Proceed to checkout.* 去结算。

check·point /ˈtʃekpɔɪnt/ *noun* a place, especially on a border between two countries, where people have to stop so their vehicles and documents can be checked（边防）检查站；边防关卡

check·room /ˈtʃekruːm; -rʊm/ *noun* (*NAmE*) = CLOAKROOM (1)

ˌ**checks and ˈbalances** *noun* [pl.] **1** influences in an organization or political system which help to keep it fair and stop a small group from keeping all the power 制约与平衡（为保持机构或政体内的公正并防止权力集中于小团体） **2** (in the US) the principle of government by which the President, Congress and the Supreme Court each have some control over the others 三权分立（美国政府中总统、国会以及最高法院之间相互制约的政体原则）➲ COMPARE SEPARATION OF POWERS ➲ **WORDFINDER NOTE** AT GOVERNMENT

check·sum /ˈtʃeksʌm/ *noun* (*computing* 计) the total of the numbers in a piece of digital data, used to check that the data is correct 检查和（用以校验数据项的和）

ˈ**check-up** *noun* an examination of sth, especially a medical one to make sure that you are healthy 检查；（尤指）体格检查：*to **go for/to have a check-up*** 去做体检 ◇ *a **medical/dental/routine/thorough check-up*** 体格 / 牙科 / 常规 / 全面检查 ➲ **WORDFINDER NOTE** AT DENTIST

Ched·dar /ˈtʃedə(r)/ (*also* ˌ**Cheddar** ˈ**cheese**) (*both BrE*) (*NAmE* **cheddar**, ˌ**cheddar** ˈ**cheese**) *noun* [U] a type of hard yellow cheese 切达干酪（一种黄色硬奶酪）

cheek /tʃiːk/ *noun, verb*

■ ***noun*** **1** [C] either side of the face below the eyes 面颊；脸颊：***chubby/rosy/pink cheeks*** 丰满的 / 红润的 / 粉红的脸颊 ◇ *He kissed her on both cheeks.* 他亲吻了她的双

颊。◇ *Couples were dancing* ***cheek to cheek.*** 成双成对的舞伴在跳贴面舞。➲ COLLOCATIONS AT PHYSICAL ➲ VISUAL VOCAB PAGE V64 **2 -cheeked** (in adjectives 构成形容词) having the type of cheeks mentioned 有…面颊的；面颊…的：***chubby-cheeked/rosy-cheeked/hollow-cheeked*** 双颊丰满 / 红润 / 瘦削 ➲ MORE LIKE THIS 8, page R25 **3** [C] (*informal*) either of the BUTTOCKS 半边屁股 **4** [U, sing.] (*BrE*) talk or behaviour that people think is annoying, rude or lacking in respect 令人讨厌（或粗鲁、无礼）的话（或行为）SYN **nerve**: *What a cheek!* 真不要脸！◇ *He* ***had the cheek*** *to ask his ex-girlfriend to babysit for them.* 他竟厚着脸皮要他以前的女朋友为他们临时照看小孩。◇ *I think they've* ***got a cheek*** *making you pay to park the car.* 我想不到他们居然有脸要你付停车费。

IDM **ˌcheek by ˈjowl** (**with sb/sth**) very close to sb/sth（和…）紧靠着，紧挨着 **turn the other ˈcheek** to make a deliberate decision to remain calm and not to act in an aggressive way when sb has hurt you or made you angry（受到伤害或被激怒时）甘心容忍，不予回击 ➲ MORE AT ROSE *n.*, TONGUE *n.*

▪ ***verb*** **~ sb** (*BrE, informal*) to speak to sb in a rude way that shows a lack of respect 对…粗鲁无礼地说

cheek·bone /ˈtʃiːkbəʊn; *NAmE* -boʊn/ *noun* the bone below the eye 颧骨 ➲ VISUAL VOCAB PAGE V64

cheeky /ˈtʃiːki/ *adj.* (**cheek·ier, cheeki·est**) (*informal*) rude in an amusing or an annoying way 厚脸皮的；鲁莽的；放肆的：*You cheeky monkey!* 你这厚脸皮的猴崽子！◇ *a cheeky grin* 厚颜无耻的龇牙一笑 ◇ *You're getting far too cheeky!* 你太放肆了！➲ SYNONYMS AT RUDE ▶ **cheek·ily** *adv.* **cheeki·ness** *noun* [U]

cheep /tʃiːp/ *verb* [I] (of young birds 雏鸟) to make short high sounds 唧唧叫；吱吱叫 ▶ **cheep** *noun*

cheer /tʃɪə(r); *NAmE* tʃɪr/ *noun, verb*

▪ ***noun*** ➲ SEE ALSO CHEERS **1** [C] a shout of joy, support or praise 欢呼声；喝彩声：*A great cheer went up from the crowd.* 观众爆发出一阵热烈的欢呼声。◇ *cheers of encouragement* 鼓励的喝彩声 ◇ ***Three cheers for the winners!*** (= used when you are asking a group of people to cheer three times, in order to CONGRATULATE sb, etc.) 为优胜者欢呼三次吧！OPP **boo** **2** [C] (*NAmE*) a special song or poem used by CHEERLEADERS（拉拉队的）加油歌，加油诗 **3** [U] (*formal* or *literary*) an atmosphere of happiness 欢乐（或幸福）的气氛

▪ ***verb*** **1** [I, T] to shout loudly, to show support or praise for sb, or to give them encouragement 欢呼；喝彩；加油：*We all cheered as the team came on to the field.* 球队入场时我们都为之欢呼。◇ *Cheering crowds greeted their arrival.* 欢呼的人群欢迎他们的到来。◇ **~ sb** *The crowd cheered the President as he drove slowly by.* 当总统的车缓缓经过时，群众向他欢呼致意。➲ SYNONYMS AT SHOUT OPP **boo** **2** [T] **~ sb** [usually passive] to give hope, comfort or encouragement to sb 鼓励；鼓舞：*She was cheered by the news from home.* 来自家里的消息使她受到鼓舞。▶ **cheer·ing** *noun* [U]: *He came on stage amid clapping and cheering.* 他在掌声和欢呼声中走上舞台。**cheer·ing** *adj.*: *The results of the test were very cheering.* 化验结果令人欢欣鼓舞。

PHR V **ˌcheer sb↔ˈon** to give shouts of encouragement to sb in a race, competition, etc.（赛跑、比赛等中）以喝彩声鼓励，为（某人）加油 **ˌcheer ˈup | ˌcheer sb/sth↔ˈup** to become more cheerful; to make sb/sth more cheerful（使）变得更高兴，振奋起来：*Oh, come on—cheer up!* 噢，得了，高兴起来吧！◇ *Give Mary a call; she needs cheering up.* 给玛丽打个电话，她需要人安慰。◇ *Bright curtains can cheer up a dull room.* 色彩鲜艳的窗帘可以让单调的房间变得亮丽起来。

cheer·ful 🔑 /ˈtʃɪəfl; *NAmE* ˈtʃɪrfl/ *adj.* **1** 🔑 happy, and showing it by the way that you behave 快乐的；高兴的；兴高采烈的：*You're not your usual cheerful self today.* 你今天不像往常那么快快乐乐的。◇ *a cheerful, hard-working employee* 快快乐乐勤奋工作的雇员 ◇ *a cheerful smile/voice* 欢快的微笑 / 说话声 **2** 🔑 giving you a feeling of happiness 令人愉快的：*a bright, cheerful restaurant* 明亮宜人的餐馆 ◇ *walls painted in cheerful* (= light and bright) *colours* 用亮丽色彩涂饰的墙壁 ◇ *a chatty, cheerful letter* 一封令人愉快的拉家常的信 ▶ **cheer·ful·ly** 🔑 /-fəli/ *adv.*: *to laugh/nod/whistle cheerfully* 欢快地笑 / 点头 / 吹口哨 ◇ *I could cheerfully have killed him when he said that* (= I would have liked to). 他说那话时我真想把他宰了。◇ *She cheerfully admitted that she had no experience at all* (= she wasn't afraid to do so). 她坦然承认她毫无经验。**cheer·ful·ness** *noun* [U]

cheerio /ˌtʃɪəriˈəʊ; *NAmE* ˌtʃɪriˈoʊ/ *exclamation* (*BrE, informal*) goodbye 再见：*Cheerio! I'll see you later.* 再见！回头见。

cheer·lead·er /ˈtʃɪəliːdə(r); *NAmE* ˈtʃɪrl-/ *noun* **1** (especially in the US) one of the members of a group of young people (usually women) wearing special uniforms, who encourage the crowd to CHEER for their team at a sports event 拉拉队队员（尤见于美国，通常为女性）**2** a person who supports a particular politician, idea, or way of doing sth（某一政治家、某种观点或做法等的）支持者，摇旗呐喊者 ▶ **cheer·leading** /ˈtʃɪəliːdɪŋ; *NAmE* ˈtʃɪrliːdɪŋ/ *noun* [U]: *a* ***cheerleading squad/team*** 拉拉队 ◇ *the President's continued cheerleading for the 'strong dollar'* 总统为"强势美元"不断摇旗呐喊

cheer·less /ˈtʃɪələs; *NAmE* ˈtʃɪrl-/ *adj.* (*formal*) (of a place, etc. 地方等) without warmth or colour so it makes you feel depressed 阴冷的；阴暗的；阴郁的 SYN **gloomy**: *a dark and cheerless room* 黑暗阴森的房间

cheers /tʃɪəz; *NAmE* tʃɪrz/ *exclamation* **1** a word that people say to each other as they lift up their glasses to drink（用于祝酒）干杯 **2** (*BrE, informal*) thank you 谢谢：*'Have another biscuit.' 'Cheers.'* "再来一块饼干。""谢谢。" **3** (*BrE, informal*) goodbye 再见：*Cheers then. See you later.* 告辞了。再见。

cheery /ˈtʃɪəri; *NAmE* ˈtʃɪri/ *adj.* (**cheer·ier, cheeri·est**) (*informal*) (of a person or their behaviour 人或行为) happy and cheerful 高兴的；兴高采烈的：*a* ***cheery remark/smile/wave*** 开心的话 / 微笑 / 挥手 ◇ *He left with a cheery 'See you again soon'.* 他高兴地说了声"希望早日再见到你"就离开了。▶ **cheer·ily** *adv.*

cheese 🔑 /tʃiːz/ *noun* **1** 🔑 [U, C] a type of food made from milk that can be either soft or hard and is usually white or yellow in colour; a particular type of this food 干酪；奶酪：*Cheddar cheese* 切达干酪 ◇ *goat's cheese* (= made from the milk of a GOAT) 山羊奶酪（由山羊奶制成）◇ *a cheese* ***sandwich/salad*** 奶酪三明治 / 色拉 ◇ *a* ***chunk/piece/slice of cheese*** 一厚块 / 块 / 薄片奶酪 ◇ *a selection of French cheeses* 精选的法国奶酪 ◇ *a cheese knife* (= a knife with a special curved blade with two points on the end, used for cutting and picking up pieces of cheese) 干酪刀 ➲ VISUAL VOCAB PAGE V23 ➲ SEE ALSO AMERICAN CHEESE, BLUE CHEESE, CAULIFLOWER CHEESE, COTTAGE CHEESE, CREAM CHEESE, MACARONI CHEESE **2** **cheese!** what you ask sb to say before you take their photograph "茄子"（要求照相的人说的口形词）

IDM SEE BIG *adj.*, CHALK *n.*, HARD *adj.*

cheese·board /ˈtʃiːzbɔːd; *NAmE* -bɔːrd/ *noun* **1** a board that is used to cut cheese on 干酪切板 ➲ VISUAL VOCAB PAGE V23 **2** a variety of cheeses that are served at the end of a meal（一餐饭结束前上的）干酪拼盘 ➲ VISUAL VOCAB PAGE V23

cheese·bur·ger /ˈtʃiːzbɜːgə(r); *NAmE* -bɜːrg-/ *noun* a HAMBURGER with a slice of cheese on top of the meat 干酪汉堡包

cheese·cake /ˈtʃiːzkeɪk/ *noun* [C, U] a cold DESSERT (= a sweet dish) made from a soft mixture of CREAM CHEESE, sugar, eggs, etc. on a base of cake or crushed biscuits/cookies, sometimes with fruit on top 奶酪蛋糕（冷甜食）：*a strawberry cheesecake* 草莓奶酪蛋糕 ◇ *Is there any cheesecake left?* 还有奶酪蛋糕吗？

cheese·cloth /ˈtʃiːzklɒθ; *NAmE* -klɔːθ/ *noun* [U] a type of loose cotton cloth used especially for making shirts（尤指制衬衣用的）薄纱棉布

ˌ**cheesed ˈoff** *adj.* [not before noun] ~ (**with/about sb/sth**) (*BrE, informal*) annoyed or bored 厌烦；厌倦；烦恼

ˈ**cheese-paring** *adj.* (*disapproving*) not liking to spend money 吝啬的；吝惜金钱的 SYN **mean** ▶ ˈ**cheese-paring** *noun* [U]

ˌ**cheese ˈstraw** *noun* a stick of PASTRY with cheese in it, eaten as a SNACK 干酪酥条；乳酪酥条

cheesy /ˈtʃiːzi/ *adj.* (**chees·ier, cheesi·est**) **1** (*informal*) not very good or original, and without style, in a way that is embarrassing but amusing 拙劣可笑的；令人尴尬发笑的：*a cheesy horror movie* 拙劣可笑的恐怖片 **2** (*informal*) too emotional or romantic, in a way that is embarrassing 过于多愁善感的：*a cheesy love song* 伤感的情歌 **3** (of a smile 笑容) done in an exaggerated and probably not sincere way 刻意的；做作的：*She had a* ***cheesy grin*** *on her face.* 她勉强虚伪地龇牙笑了一笑。 **4** smelling or tasting of cheese 干酪气味的；干酪味道的

chee·tah /ˈtʃiːtə/ *noun* a wild animal of the cat family, with black spots, that runs very fast 猎豹

chef /ʃef/ *noun* a professional cook, especially the most senior cook in a restaurant, hotel, etc. 厨师；（尤指餐馆、旅馆等的）主厨，厨师长

chef-d'oeuvre /ˌʃeɪ ˈdɜːvrə; *NAmE also* ˈduːvrə/ *noun* (*pl.* **chefs-d'oeuvre** /ˌʃeɪ ˈdɜːvrə; *NAmE also* ˈduːvrə/) (*from French, formal*) a very good piece of work, especially the best work by a particular artist, writer, etc. （尤指某一艺术家、作家等的）杰作，代表作 SYN **masterpiece**

ˌ**chef's ˈsalad** (*also* ˌ**chef ˈsalad**) *noun* (*NAmE*) a large salad consisting of LETTUCE, tomato and other vegetables with slices of cheese and meat such as chicken or HAM on top 主厨色拉，主厨沙拉（用莴苣、番茄等蔬菜制成，上面配有干酪片和鸡肉、火腿等肉片）

ˌ**Chelsea ˈtractor** *noun* (*BrE, informal, disapproving*) a large vehicle such as an SUV that is designed to be used in the country but is used in towns and cities instead of a normal car 切尔西拖拉机（指在城镇中使用的越野车之类的大车）：*the environmental cost of driving a Chelsea tractor* 驾驶切尔西拖拉机所产生的环境污染成本

chem·ical 🔑 AW /ˈkemɪkl/ *adj., noun*

■ *adj.* **1** 🔑 connected with chemistry 与化学有关的；化学的：*a chemical element* 化学元素 ◇ *the chemical industry* 化学工业 **2** 🔑 produced by or using processes which involve changes to atoms or MOLECULES 用化学方法制造的；化学作用的：***chemical reactions/processes*** 化学反应 / 过程 ▶ **chem·ic·al·ly** AW /-kli/ *adv.*：*The raw sewage is chemically treated.* 未经处理的污水要进行化学处理。

■ *noun* 🔑 a substance obtained by or used in a chemical process 化学制品；化学品

ˌ**chemical engiˈneering** *noun* [U] the study of the design and use of machines in industrial chemical processes 化学工程 ▶ ˌ**chemical engiˈneer** *noun*

ˌ**chemical ˈwarfare** *noun* [U] the use of poisonous gases and chemicals as weapons in a war 化学战

ˌ**chemical ˈweapon** *noun* a weapon that uses poisonous gases and chemicals to kill and injure people 化学武器 ➲ COMPARE BIOLOGICAL WEAPON

che·mise /ʃəˈmiːz/ *noun* a piece of women's underwear or a NIGHTDRESS 女式内衣；女式睡衣

chem·ist 🔑 /ˈkemɪst/ *noun* **1** (*also* **disˈpensing chem·ist**) (*both BrE*) (*NAmE* **drug·gist**) a person whose job is to prepare and sell medicines, and who works in a shop 药剂师；药商 ➲ COMPARE PHARMACIST (1) **2** 🔑 **chemist's** (*pl.* **chem·ists**) (*BrE*) a shop/store that sells medicines and usually also soap, make-up, etc. 药房，药店（通常也出售肥皂、化妆品等）：*You can obtain the product from all good chemists.* 你可从各大药房买到这种产品。 ◇ *Take this prescription to the chemist's.* 带着这张药方到药房去。 ◇ *I'll get it at the chemist's.* 我要去药房买。 ◇ *a chemist's/chemist shop* 药房 ➲ SEE ALSO DRUGSTORE ➲ COMPARE PHARMACY (1) ➲ MORE LIKE THIS 34, page R29 **3** 🔑 a scientist who studies chemistry 化学家：*a research chemist* 从事研究工作的化学家

chem·is·try 🔑 /ˈkemɪstri/ *noun* [U] **1** 🔑 the scientific study of the structure of substances, how they react when combined or in contact with one another, and how they behave under different conditions 化学：*a degree in chemistry* 化学学位 ◇ *the university's chemistry department* 那所大学的化学系 ◇ ***inorganic/organic chemistry*** 无机 / 有机化学 ➲ SEE ALSO BIOCHEMISTRY

WORDFINDER 联想词：acid, catalyst, compound, formula, molecule, pH, react, solution, valency

2 (*specialist*) the chemical structure and behaviour of a particular substance 物质的化学组成（或性质）：*the chemistry of copper* 铜的化学性质 ◇ *The patient's blood chemistry was monitored regularly.* 那名患者的血液化学成分受到了定时的监测。 **3** the relationship between two people, usually a strong sexual attraction （常指有强烈性吸引力的）两人间的关系：*sexual chemistry* 相互吸引的两性关系 ◇ *The chemistry just wasn't right.* 他俩就是擦不出火花。

chemo /ˈkiːməʊ; *NAmE* -moʊ/ *noun* [U] (*informal*) = CHEMOTHERAPY

chemo·recep·tor /ˈkiːməʊrɪseptə(r); *NAmE* ˈkiːmoʊ-/ *noun* (*biology* 生) a cell or sense organ that is sensitive to chemical STIMULI, making a response possible 化学感受器（对化学刺激敏感的细胞或感觉器官）

chemo·ther·apy /ˌkiːməʊˈθerəpi; *NAmE* -moʊ-/ (*also informal* **chemo**) *noun* [U] the treatment of disease, especially cancer, with the use of chemical substances （尤指对癌的）化学治疗，化学疗法，化疗 ➲ COMPARE RADIATION (3), RADIOTHERAPY ➲ WORDFINDER NOTE AT CURE

che·nille /ʃəˈniːl/ *noun* [U] a type of thick, soft thread; cloth made from this 绳绒线；雪尼尔花线；绳绒织物：*a chenille sweater* 雪尼尔线套头衫

cheong·sam /tʃɒŋˈsæm; *NAmE* ˈtʃɑːŋsæm/ *noun* (*from Chinese*) a straight, tightly fitting silk dress with a high neck and short sleeves and an opening at the bottom on each side, worn by women from China and Indonesia 旗袍

cheque 🔑 (*BrE*) (*US* **check**) /tʃek/ *noun* a printed form that you can write on and sign as a way of paying for sth instead of using money 支票：*a cheque for £50* 一张 50 英镑的支票 ◇ *to write a cheque* 开支票 ◇ *to make a cheque out to sb* 给某人开出一张支票 ◇ *to pay by cheque* 用支票支付 ◇ *to cash a cheque* (= to get or give money for a cheque) 兑现支票 ➲ COLLOCATIONS AT FINANCE ➲ PICTURE AT MONEY ➲ SEE ALSO BLANK CHEQUE, TRAVELLER'S CHEQUE

cheque·book (*BrE*) (*US* **check·book**) /ˈtʃekbʊk/ *noun* a book of printed cheques 支票簿 ➲ PICTURE AT MONEY

ˌ**chequebook ˈjournalism** *noun* [U] (*BrE, disapproving*) the practice of journalists paying people large amounts of money to give them personal or private information for a newspaper story 支票簿新闻（指记者用重金购买的独家新闻）

che·quered (*BrE*) (*also* **check·ered** *NAmE, BrE*) /ˈtʃekəd; *NAmE* -kərd/ *adj.* **1** ~ **past/history/career** a person's past, etc. that contains both successful and not successful periods 成功与失败并存的（过去、历史、事业） **2** having a pattern of squares of different colours 有不同颜色方格图案的

the ˌ**chequered ˈflag** (*BrE*) (*also* **the check·ered flag** *NAmE, BrE*) *noun* a flag with black and white squares that is waved when a driver has finished a motor race （赛车到达终点时挥动的）黑白方格旗

ˈ**chequing account** *noun* (*CanE*) = CURRENT ACCOUNT

C

cher·ish /ˈtʃerɪʃ/ *verb* (*formal*) **1 ~ sb/sth** to love sb/sth very much and want to protect them or it 珍爱；钟爱；爱护：*Children need to be cherished.* 儿童需要无微不至的呵护。◇ *her most* ***cherished*** *possession* 她最珍爱的物品 **2 ~ sth** to keep an idea, a hope or a pleasant feeling in your mind for a long time 抱有（信念、希望）；怀有（好感）；怀念：*Cherish the memory of those days in Paris.* 怀念在巴黎的岁月。

Chero·kee /ˈtʃerəkiː/ *noun* (*pl.* **Chero·kee** or **Chero·kees**) a member of a Native American people, many of whom now live in the US states of Oklahoma and North Carolina 切罗基人（美洲土著，很多现居于美国俄克拉何马州和北卡罗来纳州）

che·root /ʃəˈruːt/ *noun* a type of CIGAR with two open ends （两端开口的）雪茄烟

cherry /ˈtʃeri/ *noun, adj.*

■ ***noun*** (*pl.* **-ies**) **1** [C] a small soft round fruit with shiny red or black skin and a large seed inside 樱桃 ➲ VISUAL VOCAB PAGE V32 **2** (*also* ˈ**cherry tree**) [C] a tree on which cherries grow, or a similar tree, grown for its flowers 樱桃树；樱花树：*cherry blossom* 樱花 ◇ *a winter-flowering cherry* 冬季开花的樱桃树 **3** (*also* **cherry·wood** /ˈtʃeriwʊd/) [U] the wood of the cherry tree 樱桃木 **4** (*also* ˌ**cherry ˈred**) [U] a bright red colour 樱桃色；鲜红色 ➲ MORE LIKE THIS 15, page R26 IDM SEE BITE *n.*

■ ***adj.*** (*also* ˌ**cherry ˈred**) bright red in colour 樱桃色的；鲜红色的：*cherry lips* 樱唇

ˈ**cherry-pick** *verb* [T, I] ~ (**sb/sth**) to choose the best people or things from a group and leave those which are not so good 筛选；精选

ˈ**cherry picker** *noun* **1** a type of tall CRANE which lifts people up so that they can work in very high places 樱桃夹式升降台；车载升降台 **2** a person who picks CHERRIES 摘樱桃的人

ˈ**cherry tomato** *noun* a type of very small tomato 樱桃番茄

cherub /ˈtʃerəb/ *noun* **1** (*pl.* **cher·ubs** or **cher·ubim** /-bɪm/) (in art 艺术) a type of ANGEL, shown as a small fat, usually male, child with wings 小天使（常被绘为有翅膀的胖男孩） ➲ COMPARE SERAPH **2** (*pl.* **cher·ubs**) (*informal*) a pretty child; a child who behaves well 可爱的小孩；乖小孩 ▸ **cher·ub·ic** /tʃəˈruːbɪk/ *adj.* (*formal*)：*a cherubic face* (= looking round and innocent, like a small child's) 胖乎乎、天真无邪的娃娃脸

cher·vil /ˈtʃɜːvɪl; *NAmE* ˈtʃɜːrvɪl/ *noun* [U] a plant with leaves that are used in cooking as a HERB 峨参（叶用作调料）

chess /tʃes/ *noun* [U] a game for two people played on a board marked with black and white squares on which each playing piece (representing a king, queen, castle, etc.) is moved according to special rules. The aim is to put the other player's king in a position from which it cannot escape (= to CHECKMATE it). 国际象棋：*Alex plays chess as a hobby.* 亚历克斯把下棋作为业余爱好。➲ VISUAL VOCAB PAGE V42

chess·board /ˈtʃesbɔːd; *NAmE* -bɔːrd/ *noun* a board with 64 black and white squares that chess is played on 国际象棋棋盘 ➲ VISUAL VOCAB PAGE V42

chess·man /ˈtʃesmæn/ *noun* (*pl.* **-men** /-men/) any of the 32 pieces used in the game of chess 国际象棋棋子

chest 🔑 /tʃest/ *noun* **1** 🔑 the top part of the front of the body, between the neck and the stomach 胸部；胸膛：*The bullet hit him in the chest.* 子弹击中了他的胸部。◇ *She gasped for breath, her chest heaving.* 她喘着气，胸部不停地起伏。◇ *a chest infection* 胸部感染 ◇ *chest pains* 胸部疼痛 ◇ *a hairy chest* 毛茸茸的胸部 ➲ COLLOCATIONS AT PHYSICAL ➲ VISUAL VOCAB PAGE V64 **2 -chested** (in adjectives 构成形容词) having the type of chest mentioned 有…胸的；胸部…的：*flat-chested* 胸部扁平的 ◇ *broad-chested* 胸部宽阔的 ➲ MORE LIKE THIS 8, page R25 **3** a large strong box, usually made of wood, used for storing things in and/or moving them from one place to another （常为木制的）大箱子：*a medicine chest* 药箱 ◇ *a treasure chest* 财宝箱 ➲ SEE ALSO HOPE CHEST, TEA CHEST, WAR CHEST

IDM ˌ**get sth off your ˈchest** to talk about sth that has been worrying you for a long time so that you feel less anxious 倾吐心里的烦恼；吐出心事；一吐为快 ➲ MORE AT CARD *n.*

ches·ter·field /ˈtʃestəfiːld; *NAmE* ˈtʃestərf-/ *noun* **1** a type of SOFA that has arms and a back that are all the same height 切斯特菲尔德长沙发（扶手和靠背同高） **2** (*CanE*) any type of SOFA 长沙发

chest·nut /ˈtʃesnʌt/ *noun, adj.*

■ ***noun*** **1** (*also* ˈ**chestnut tree**) [C] a large tree with spreading branches, that produces smooth brown nuts inside cases which are covered with SPIKES. There are several types of chestnut tree. 栗树 ➲ SEE ALSO HORSE CHESTNUT (1) **2** [C] a smooth brown nut of a chestnut tree, some types of which can be eaten 栗子；板栗：*roast chestnuts* 炒板栗 ➲ VISUAL VOCAB PAGE V35 ➲ SEE ALSO WATER CHESTNUT ➲ COMPARE CONKER (1) **3** [U] a deep reddish-brown colour 栗色；深红棕色 **4** [C] a horse of a reddish-brown colour 栗色马；红棕马 **5 old chestnut** [C] (*informal*) an old joke or story that has been told so many times that it is no longer amusing or interesting 陈腐的笑话；老掉牙的故事

■ ***adj.*** reddish-brown in colour 栗色的；红棕色的

ˌ**chest of ˈdrawers** *noun* (*pl.* **chests of drawers**) (*NAmE also* **bur·eau**, **dresser**) a piece of furniture with drawers for keeping clothes in 五斗橱；（有抽屉的）衣橱 ➲ VISUAL VOCAB PAGE V24

chesty /ˈtʃesti/ *adj.* (*informal, especially BrE*) suffering from or showing signs of chest disease 患胸部疾病的；有胸部疾病征兆的

chev·ron /ˈʃevrən/ *noun* **1** a line or pattern in the shape of a V * V 形线条；V 形图案 **2** a piece of cloth in the shape of a V which soldiers and police officers wear on their uniforms to show their rank（军人、警察制服上表示军衔或警衔的）V 形标志

chew 🔑 /tʃuː/ *verb, noun*

■ ***verb*** **1** 🔑 [I, T] to bite food into small pieces in your mouth with your teeth to make it easier to swallow 咀嚼；嚼碎：**~ (at/on/through sth)** *After the operation you may find it difficult to chew and swallow.* 手术后你咀嚼和吞咽可能会感到困难。◇ **~ sth (up)** *teeth designed for chewing meat* 用于咀嚼肉食的牙齿 ◇ *He is always chewing gum.* 他总是在嚼口香糖。 **2** [I, T] to bite sth continuously, for example because you are nervous or to taste it （因为紧张等）咬住，不停地啃；（为尝味道）不停地咀嚼：**~ on sth** *Rosa chewed on her lip and stared at the floor.* 罗莎咬着嘴唇，眼睛盯着地板。◇ *The dog was chewing on a bone.* 那只狗在一个劲儿地啃骨头。◇ **~ sth** *to chew your nails* 啃指甲

IDM ˌ**chew the ˈfat** (*informal*) to have a long friendly talk with sb about sth （长时间）闲聊，闲扯 ➲ MORE AT BITE *v.*

PHR V ˌ**chew sb ˈout** (*NAmE, informal*) to tell sb angrily that you do not approve of their actions 气愤地骂（某人）：*He got chewed out by the boss for lying.* 他因说谎遭到老板的痛骂。 ˌ**chew sth↔ˈover** to think about or discuss sth slowly and carefully 仔细考虑；深思熟虑；详细讨论

■ ***noun*** **1** an act of chewing sth 咀嚼 **2** a type of sweet/candy that you chew 口香糖 **3** a piece of TOBACCO that you chew 供嚼用的烟草

ˈ**chewing gum** (*also* **gum**) *noun* [U] a sweet/candy that you chew but do not swallow 口香糖 ➲ MORE LIKE THIS 28, page R28

ˈ**chewing-stick** *noun* a stick made from the STEM or root of particular plants that you chew at one end and then use to clean your teeth (used in some parts of Africa and Asia) 咀嚼洁齿棒（用于非洲和亚洲的一些地区，取材于植物根茎）

chewy /ˈtʃuːi/ *adj.* (**chew·ier**, **chewi·est**) (of food 食物) needing to be chewed a lot before it can be swallowed 需要多嚼的；不易嚼烂的；耐嚼的 ➲ WORDFINDER NOTE AT CRISP

Chey·enne /ʃaɪˈen/ *noun* (*pl.* **Chey·enne** or **Chey·ennes**) a member of a Native American people, many of whom now live in the US states of Oklahoma and Montana 夏延人（美洲土著，很多现居于美国俄克拉何马州和蒙大拿州）

chez /ʃeɪ/ *prep.* (*from French*) at the home of 在…家：*I spent a pleasant evening chez the Stewarts.* 我在斯图尔特家度过了一个愉快的夜晚。

chi /kaɪ/ *noun* the 22nd letter of the Greek alphabet (Χ, χ) 希腊字母表的第 22 个字母

chiaro·scuro /kiˌɑːrəˈskʊərəʊ; *NAmE* -ˈskʊroʊ/ *noun* [U] (*art* 美术) the way light and shade are shown; the contrast between light and shade 明暗对比法；明暗对比

chi·as·mus /kaɪˈæzməs; *NAmE* kɪˈæz-/ *noun* [U, C] (*pl.* **chi·as·mi** /kaɪˈæzmi; kɪˈæz-/) (*specialist*) a technique used in writing or in speeches, in which words, ideas, etc. are repeated in reverse order 回环，交错配列（对词、思想等的倒序重复排列）

chic /ʃiːk/ *adj.* very fashionable and elegant 时髦的；优雅的；雅致的 **SYN** **stylish**：*She is always so chic, so elegant.* 她总是那么时髦，那么优雅。◇ *a chic new restaurant* 雅致的新餐馆 ▸ **chic** *noun* [U]：*a perfectly dressed woman with an air of chic that was unmistakably French* 一位衣着讲究、明显地流露出法国式优雅姿态的女士

chi·ca /ˈtʃiːkə/ *noun* (*US, from Spanish, informal*) a girl or young woman 小妞；姑娘

Chi·cana /tʃɪˈkɑːnə; *BrE also* ʃɪ-; -ˈkeɪnə/ *noun* (*especially US, from Spanish*) a girl or woman living in the US whose family came from Mexico 女奇卡诺人（墨西哥裔美国女孩或妇女）➲ COMPARE CHICANO, HISPANIC *n.*, LATINO

chi·cane /ʃɪˈkeɪn/ *noun* (*BrE*) a sharp double bend, either on a track where cars race, or on an ordinary road to stop vehicles from going too fast （赛车或一般车道上防止车速过快的）双急转弯

chi·can·ery /ʃɪˈkeɪnəri/ *noun* [U] (*formal*) the use of complicated plans and clever talk in order to trick people 欺诈；诈骗；欺骗

Chi·cano /tʃɪˈkɑːnəʊ; *NAmE* -noʊ; *BrE also* ʃɪ-; -ˈkeɪn-/ *noun* (*pl.* **-os**) (*especially US, from Spanish*) a person living in the US whose family came from Mexico 奇卡诺人（墨西哥裔美国人）➲ COMPARE CHICANA, HISPANIC *n.*, LATINO

chi·chi /ˈʃiːʃiː/ *adj.* used to describe a style of decoration that contains too many details and lacks taste （装饰）华丽而俗气的，繁琐俗气的

chick /tʃɪk/ *noun* **1** a baby bird, especially a baby chicken 雏鸟；（尤指）雏鸡，小鸡 **2** (*old-fashioned, sometimes offensive*) a way of referring to a young woman 少女；少妇；小妞儿

chicka·dee /ˈtʃɪkədiː; ˌtʃɪkəˈdiː/ *noun* a small N American bird of the TIT family. There are many types of chickadee. 北美山雀

chick·en /ˈtʃɪkɪn/ *noun, verb, adj.*

■ ***noun*** **1** [C] a large bird that is often kept for its eggs or meat 鸡：*They keep chickens in the back yard.* 他们在后院养鸡。◇ *free-range chickens* 自由放养的鸡 ➲ COMPARE COCK *n.* (1), HEN ➲ VISUAL VOCAB PAGE V12 **2** [U] meat from a chicken 鸡肉：***fried/roast chicken*** 炸鸡；烧鸡 ◇ ***chicken stock/soup*** 原汁鸡汤；鸡汤 ◇ ***chicken breasts/livers/thighs*** 鸡胸脯肉；鸡肝；鸡大腿 ◇ *chicken and chips* 炸鸡块配炸薯条 ➲ SEE ALSO SPRING CHICKEN

IDM **a ˌchicken-and-ˈegg situation, problem, etc.** a situation in which it is difficult to tell which one of two things was the cause of the other 鸡与蛋孰先难定的情况；因果难定的问题 **play ˈchicken** to play a game in which people do sth dangerous for as long as they can to show how brave they are. The person who stops first has lost the game. 比试胆量 ➲ MORE AT COUNT *v.*, HEADLESS, HOME *adv.*

■ ***verb***

PHR V **ˌchicken ˈout (of sth/of doing sth)** (*informal*) to decide not to do sth because you are afraid 因害怕而放弃；临阵退缩；胆怯

■ ***adj.*** [not before noun] (*informal*) not brave; afraid to do sth 胆怯；懦弱；怯懦 **SYN** **cowardly**

ˈchicken feed *noun* [U] (*informal*) an amount of money that is not large enough to be important 一笔微不足道的钱；一小笔钱

ˈchicken flu *noun* [U] = BIRD FLU

chick·en·pox /ˈtʃɪkɪnpɒks; *NAmE* -pɑːks/ *noun* [U] a disease, especially of children, that causes a slight fever and many spots on the skin 水痘：***to catch/get/have chickenpox*** 染上 / 患上 / 得了水痘

ˈchicken run *noun* an area surrounded by a fence in which chickens are kept 养鸡场

chick·en·shit /ˈtʃɪkɪnʃɪt/ *noun, adj.*

■ ***noun*** [U] (*NAmE, slang*) nonsense 废话；瞎说；胡说八道

■ ***adj.*** (*NAmE, slang*) (of a person 人) not brave 胆怯的；懦弱的；怯懦的 **SYN** **cowardly**

ˈchicken wire *noun* [U] thin wire made into sheets like nets with a pattern of shapes with six sides 六角形网眼铁丝网

ˈchick flick *noun* (*informal*) a film/movie that is intended especially for women 女性电影（旨在迎合女性口味的电影）

ˈchick lit *noun* [U] (*informal*) novels that are intended especially for women, often with a young, single woman as the main character 小妞文学（旨在迎合女性口味、主角常为单身少女的小说）

chick·pea /ˈtʃɪk piː/ *noun* (*especially BrE*) (*NAmE usually* **gar·banzo**, **garˈbanzo bean**) a hard round seed, like a light brown PEA, that is cooked and eaten as a vegetable 鹰嘴豆（浅棕色的硬圆豆，可烹食）➲ VISUAL VOCAB PAGE V34

ˈchickpea flour *noun* = GRAM FLOUR

chick·weed /ˈtʃɪkwiːd/ *noun* [U] a small plant with white flowers that often grows as a WEED over a wide area 繁缕（杂草，花白色）

chi·co /ˈtʃiːkəʊ; *NAmE* -koʊ/ *noun* (*pl.* **-os**) (*US, from Spanish, informal*) a boy or young man 小家伙；小伙子

chic·ory /ˈtʃɪkəri/ *noun* [U] **1** (*BrE*) (*NAmE* **en·dive**) [C, U] a small pale green plant with bitter leaves that are eaten raw or cooked as a vegetable. The root can be dried and used with or instead of coffee. 菊苣（根干燥后可与咖啡同饮或作其替代品） **2** (*NAmE*) (*BrE* **en·dive**) (*NAmE also* **ˌcurly ˈendive**, **fri·sée**) a plant with green curly leaves that are eaten raw as a vegetable （卷叶）欧洲菊苣

chide /tʃaɪd/ *verb* (*formal*) to criticize or blame sb because they have done sth wrong 批评；指责；责备 **SYN** **rebuke**：**~ sb/yourself (for sth/for doing sth)** *She chided herself for being so impatient with the children.* 她责怪自己对孩子不够耐心。◇ **~ (sb) + speech** *'Isn't that a bit selfish?' he chided.* "那不有点自私吗？" 他责备道。

chief /tʃiːf/ *adj., noun*

■ ***adj.*** **1** [only before noun] most important 最重要的；首要的；主要的：*the chief cause/problem/reason* 主要原因 / 问题 / 理由 ◇ *one of the President's chief rivals* 总统的主要政敌之一 ➲ SYNONYMS AT MAIN ➲ MORE LIKE THIS 32, page R28 **2** (*often* **Chief**) [only before noun] highest in rank 最高级别的；为首的；首席的：*the Chief Education Officer* 首席教育官 ◇ *the chief financial officer of the company* 公司的首席财务官 ◇ *Detective Chief Inspector Williams* 总督察威廉斯 **3** **-in-ˈchief** (in nouns 构成名词) of the highest rank 最高级别的；为首的：*commander-in-chief* 总司令 ➲ SEE ALSO CHIEFLY

■ ***noun*** **1** a person with a high rank or the highest rank

C

in a company or an organization（公司或机构的）首领，头目，最高领导人：*army/industry/police chiefs* 部队首长；行业巨擘；警察局长 **2** (often as a title 常用作头衔) a leader or ruler of a people or community 首领；酋长；族长：*Chief Buthelezi* 布特莱齐酋长 ◇ *Chief Crazy Horse* "疯马"酋长

IDM **too many ˌchiefs and not enough ˈIndians** (*BrE, informal*) used to describe a situation in which there are too many people telling other people what to do, and not enough people to do the work 将多兵少；官多兵少

ˌchief ˈconstable *noun* (in Britain) a senior police officer who is in charge of the police force in a particular area（英国）地区警察局长：*Chief Constable Brian Turner* 地区警察局长布赖恩·特纳

ˌchief eˈxecutive *noun* **1** the person with the highest rank in a company or an organization（公司或机构的）总经理，总裁 **2 Chief Executive** the President of the US 美国总统

ˌchief eˈxecutive officer *noun* (*abbr.* **CEO**) the person in a company who has the most power and authority 总裁；首席执行官

ˌchief inˈspector *noun* (in Britain) a police officer above the rank of an INSPECTOR（英国警察的）总巡官，总督察

ˌchief ˈjustice (*also* **Chief Justice**) *noun* the most important judge in a court, especially the US Supreme Court 首席法官；（尤指）美国最高法院首席法官

chief·ly /ˈtʃiːfli/ *adv.* not completely, but as a most important part 主要地；首要地 **SYN** **primarily, mainly**: *We are chiefly concerned with improving educational standards.* 我们主要关心的是提高教育水平。◇ *He's travelled widely, chiefly in Africa and Asia.* 他游历了许多地方，主要在非洲和亚洲。

ˌchief of ˈstaff *noun* (*pl.* **chiefs of staff**) an officer of very high rank, responsible for advising the person who commands each of the armed forces 参谋长；参谋总长 ➲ SEE ALSO JOINT CHIEFS OF STAFF

ˌchief opeˈrations officer (*also* **ˌchief ˈoperating officer**) *noun* = COO

ˌchief superinˈtendent *noun* (in Britain) a police officer above the rank of SUPERINTENDENT（英国警察的）总警司，警务长

chief·tain /ˈtʃiːftən/ *noun* the leader of a people or a CLAN in Scotland 首领；酋长；（苏格兰的）族长

chif·fon /ˈʃɪfɒn; *NAmE* ʃɪˈfɑːn/ *noun* [U] a type of fine transparent cloth made from silk or NYLON, used especially for making clothes 雪纺绸，薄绸，尼龙绸（尤用于制衣）

chig·ger (*also* **jig·ger**) *noun* /ˈtʃɪɡə(r); ˈdʒɪɡə(r); *NAmE* ˈtʃɪɡər/ a small FLEA that lives in tropical regions and lays eggs under a person's or an animal's skin, causing painful areas on the skin 恙螨

chi·gnon /ˈʃiːnjɒn; *NAmE* -jɑːn/ *noun* (*from French*) a style for women's hair in which the hair is pulled back and twisted into a smooth knot at the back（女人的）发髻 ➲ VISUAL VOCAB PAGE V65

chi·hua·hua /tʃɪˈwɑːwə; *NAmE* -ˈwɑːwɑː/ *noun* a very small dog with smooth hair 吉娃娃狗（体型小，毛平滑）

chi·kun·gun·ya /ˌtʃɪkənˈɡʌnjə/ *noun* [U] a disease similar to DENGUE caused by a virus, found in E Africa and parts of Asia and carried by MOSQUITOES 奇昆古尼亚热（东非和亚洲部分地区的一种类似登革热的病毒性传染病，由蚊子传播）

chil·blain /ˈtʃɪlbleɪn/ *noun* [usually pl.] a painful red swelling on the hands or feet that is caused by cold or bad CIRCULATION of the blood 冻疮

child 🔑 /tʃaɪld/ *noun* (*pl.* **chil·dren** /ˈtʃɪldrən/) **1** 🔑 a young human who is not yet an adult 儿童；小孩：*a child of three/a three-year-old child* 三岁小孩 ◇ *men, women and children* 男人、女人及儿童 ◇ *an unborn child* 胎儿 ◇ *not suitable for young children* 不适于幼儿 ◇ *I lived in London as a child.* 我小时候住在伦敦。◇ *a child star* 童星 ➲ WORDFINDER NOTE AT BABY, FAMILY, PREGNANT ➲ SEE ALSO BRAINCHILD, LATCHKEY CHILD, POSTER CHILD, SCHOOLCHILD **2** 🔑 a son or daughter of any age 儿子；女儿：*They have three grown-up children.* 他们有三个成年的孩子。◇ *a support group for adult children of alcoholics* 帮助酗酒者成年子女的小组 ◇ *They can't* ***have children.*** 他们不能生孩子。➲ SEE ALSO GODCHILD, GRANDCHILD, LOVE CHILD, ONLY CHILD, STEPCHILD ➲ COMPARE KID *n.* (1) **3** a person who is strongly influenced by the ideas and attitudes of a particular time or person 深受…影响的人：*a child of the 90s* 属于 20 世纪 90 年代的人 **4** (*disapproving*) an adult who behaves like a child and is not MATURE or responsible 孩子气的人；幼稚的人；不负责任的人

IDM **be with ˈchild** (*old-fashioned*) to be pregnant 怀孕；有喜 **be ˈchild's play** (*informal*) to be very easy to do, so not even a child would find it difficult 极容易做；轻而易举

▼ **COLLOCATIONS 词语搭配**

Children 孩子

Having a baby/child 怀孕

- **want** a baby/a child/kids 想要孩子
- **start** a family 生孩子
- **conceive/be expecting/be going to have** a baby/child 怀孕
- **miss** your period 月经未按期来
- **become/get/be/find out that you are** pregnant 怀孕了；发现怀孕了
- **have** a baby/a child/kids/a son/a daughter/twins/a family 有一个宝宝 / 一个孩子 / 孩子 / 一个儿子 / 一个女儿 / 一对双胞胎 / 孩子
- **have** a normal/a difficult/an unwanted pregnancy; an easy/a difficult/a home birth 正常 / 历经艰难 / 意外怀孕；顺产；难产；在家中分娩
- **be in/go into/induce** labour/(*especially US*) labor 分娩；催产
- **have/suffer/cause** a miscarriage 流产；引起流产
- **give birth to** a child/baby/daughter/son/twins 生了一个孩子 / 一个宝宝 / 一个女儿 / 一个儿子 / 一对双胞胎

Parenting 养育；抚养；教养

- **bring up**/ (*especially NAmE*) **raise** a child/family 抚养孩子
- **care for**/ (*especially BrE*) **look after** a baby/child/kid 照顾小孩
- **change** (*BrE*) a nappy/(*NAmE*) a diaper/a baby 换尿布；给婴儿换尿布
- **feed/breastfeed/bottle-feed** a baby 喂孩子；给孩子哺乳；用奶瓶喂养孩子
- **be entitled to/go on** maternity/paternity leave 有权利休 / 正在休产假 / 陪产假
- **go back/return to work** after maternity leave 产假后回到工作岗位
- **need/find/get** a babysitter/good quality affordable childcare 需要 / 找到一个临时保姆 / 负担得起的高质量儿童保育
- **balance/combine work and** childcare/child-rearing/family life 平衡 / 兼顾工作与照顾小孩 / 抚养小孩 / 家庭生活
- **educate/teach/home-school** a child/kid 教育孩子；给孩子家庭教育
- **punish/discipline/spoil** a child/kid 惩罚 / 管教 / 娇惯孩子
- **adopt** a baby/child/kid 收养小孩
- **offer a baby for/put a baby up for** adoption 把小孩给人收养
- (*especially BrE*) **foster** a child/kid 代养小孩
- **be placed with/be raised by** foster parents 被交给寄养父母；由寄养父母抚养

ˈchild abuse *noun* [U] the crime of harming a child in a physical, sexual or emotional way 摧残儿童；虐待儿童：*victims of child abuse* 受虐待的儿童

child·bear·ing /ˈtʃaɪldbeərɪŋ; *NAmE* -ber-/ *noun* [U] the process of giving birth to children 分娩；生孩子：*women of childbearing age* 育龄妇女

ˌchild ˈbenefit *noun* [U] (in Britain) money that the government regularly pays to parents of children up to a particular age 儿童补助金（由英国政府定期发给儿童的父母，直至儿童长到某一年龄为止）

child·birth /ˈtʃaɪldbɜːθ; *NAmE* -bɜːrθ/ *noun* [U] the process of giving birth to a baby 分娩；生孩子：*pregnancy and childbirth* 怀孕及分娩 ◇ *His wife died **in childbirth**.* 他妻子生孩子的时候死了。

child·care /ˈtʃaɪldkeə(r); *NAmE* -ker/ *noun* [U] the care of children, especially while parents are at work （尤指父母上班时的）儿童保育，儿童照管：*childcare facilities for working parents* 为职业父母提供的照管儿童的设施 ➲ COLLOCATIONS AT CHILD

child·hood /ˈtʃaɪldhʊd/ *noun* [U, C] the period of sb's life when they are a child 童年；幼年；孩童时期：*childhood, adolescence and adulthood* 童年、青少年及成年 ◇ *in early childhood* 在婴幼儿时期 ◇ ***childhood memories/experiences*** 童年的回忆 / 经历 ◇ *She had a happy childhood.* 她有一个幸福的童年。◇ *childhood cancer* 儿童癌症 ➲ COLLOCATIONS AT AGE

IDM **a/sb's second ˈchildhood** a time in the life of an adult person when they behave like a child again 老小孩时期；行为像小孩的晚年时期

child·ish /ˈtʃaɪldɪʃ/ *adj.* **1** connected with or typical of a child 孩子的；孩子气的；稚嫩的：*childish handwriting* 稚嫩的笔迹 **2** (*disapproving*) (of an adult 成人) behaving in a stupid or silly way 幼稚的；天真的 SYN **immature**: *Don't be so childish!* 别那么幼稚！ OPP **mature** ➲ COMPARE CHILDLIKE ▶ **child·ish·ly** *adv.*：*to behave childishly* 举止幼稚 **child·ish·ness** *noun* [U]

child·less /ˈtʃaɪldləs/ *adj.* having no children 无子女的；无后代的：*a **childless couple/marriage*** 无子女的夫妇 / 婚姻生活

child·like /ˈtʃaɪldlaɪk/ *adj.* (*usually approving*) having the qualities that children usually have, especially INNOCENCE 孩子般的；童稚的；单纯的；（尤指）天真无邪的：***childlike enthusiasm/simplicity/delight*** 孩子般的热情 / 淳朴 / 兴高采烈 ➲ COMPARE CHILDISH

child·mind·er /ˈtʃaɪldmaɪndə(r)/ *noun* (*BrE*) a person who is paid to care for children while their parents are at work. A childminder usually does this in his or her own home. （通常指在自己家中）受雇照看孩子者 ➲ SEE ALSO BABYSITTER

child·proof /ˈtʃaɪldpruːf/ *adj.* designed so that young children cannot open, use, or damage it 防孩童开启（或使用、损坏）的；对孩童安全的：*childproof containers for medicines* 防孩童开启的药瓶

ˈchild restraint *noun* a belt, or small seat with a belt, that is used in a car to control and protect a child （汽车的）儿童安全带，儿童安全座椅

ˈchild seat *noun* = CAR SEAT (1)

chili /ˈtʃɪli/ (*NAmE*) **1** [C] = CHILLI **2** [U] = CHILLI CON CARNE

chill /tʃɪl/ *noun, verb, adj.*

■ ***noun*** **1** [sing.] a feeling of being cold 寒冷；寒意；凉意：*There's a chill in the air this morning.* 今天早晨寒气袭人。◇ *A small fire was burning to **take the chill off** the room.* 房间里生着小火炉驱寒。 **2** [C] an illness caused by being cold and wet, causing fever and SHIVERING (= shaking of the body) 着凉；受寒 **3** [sing.] a feeling of fear 害怕的感觉：*a chill of fear/apprehension* 一阵害怕 / 恐惧 ◇ *His words **sent a chill down her spine**.* 他的话让她觉得毛骨悚然。

■ ***verb*** **1** [T, usually passive] ~ **sb** to make sb very cold 使很冷；使冰冷：*They were chilled by the icy wind.* 凛冽的寒风吹得他们遍体冰凉。◇ *Let's go home, I'm **chilled to the bone*** (= very cold). 咱们回家吧，我感到寒气刺骨。 **2** [I, T] when food or a drink **chills** or when sb **chills** it, it is made very cold but it does not freeze （使）冷却；（被）冷藏：*Let the pudding chill for an hour until set.* 把布丁冷却一小时直至凝固成形。◇ ~ **sth** *This wine is best served chilled.* 这种葡萄酒冰镇后饮用最佳。◇ *chilled foods* (= for example in a supermarket) 冷藏食物 **3** [T] ~ **sb/sth** (*literary*) to frighten sb 使恐惧；恐吓；吓唬：*His words chilled her.* 他的话使她不寒而栗。◇ *What he saw **chilled his blood/chilled him to the bone**.* 他看到的情景使他毛骨悚然。 **4** [I] (*informal*) = CHILL OUT：*We went home and chilled in front of the TV.* 我们回家坐在电视机前放松了一下。◇ *Just chill, Mum, everything's going to be OK.* 妈妈，放松些，一切都会没事的。

PHR V **ˌchill ˈout** (*informal*) to spend time relaxing; to relax and stop feeling angry or nervous about sth 放松；冷静；镇静：*They sometimes meet up to chill out and watch a movie.* 他们有时聚在一起，看场电影放松一下。◇ *Sit down and chill out!* 坐下来冷静一下！

■ ***adj.*** (*formal*) (especially of weather and the wind 尤指天气和风) cold, in an unpleasant way 寒冷的；冷飕飕的；阴冷的：*the chill grey dawn* 寒冷阴沉的拂晓 ◇ *a chill wind* 寒风

chill·ax /tʃɪˈlæks/ *verb* [I] (*slang*) to relax and stop feeling angry or nervous about sth 冷静；放松：*Chillax, dude—I'm on your team.* 别紧张，哥们儿，我和你一伙的。➲ MORE LIKE THIS 1, page R25

ˌchilled-ˈout (*also* **chilled**) *adj.* (*informal*) very relaxed 十分放松的；休闲舒适的：*a chilled-out atmosphere* 轻松的气氛 ◇ *He felt totally chilled.* 他感觉完全放松了下来。

ˈchill factor *noun* the extent to which the wind makes the air feel colder; a number which represents this 风寒效应；风寒指数

chilli (*BrE*) (*NAmE* **chili**) /ˈtʃɪli/ *noun* (*pl.* **chil·lies**, *NAmE* **chilies**) **1** (*also* **ˈchilli pepper**, *NAmE also* **ˈchili pepper**) [C, U] the small green or red fruit of a type of pepper plant that is used in cooking to give a hot taste to food, often dried or made into powder, also called chilli or chilli powder 辣椒（辣椒粉亦称 chilli 或 chilli powder）➲ VISUAL VOCAB PAGE V33 **2** [U] = CHILLI CON CARNE

chilli con carne /ˌtʃɪli kɒn ˈkɑːni; *NAmE* kɑːn ˈkɑːrni/ (*especially BrE*) (*BrE also* **chilli**) (*NAmE also* **chili**) *noun* [U] a hot spicy Mexican dish made with meat, BEANS and chillies 辣味肉豆（墨西哥菜肴）

chill·ing /ˈtʃɪlɪŋ/ *adj.* frightening, usually because it is connected with sth violent or cruel （常与残暴有关）令人恐惧的，令人害怕的：*a chilling story* 令人毛骨悚然的故事 ◇ *The film evokes chilling reminders of the war.* 这部电影使人回忆起战争的可怕场景。

chill·out /ˈtʃɪlaʊt/ *noun* [U] a style of electronic music that is not fast or lively and is intended to make you relaxed and calm 舒放音乐（节奏平缓、让人放松的电子音乐）

ˈchill pill /ˈtʃɪl pɪl/ *noun* (*informal*) if you say that sb should take a chill pill, you mean that they need to be calmer or to relax 冷静药丸（用于习语 take a chill pill，意为冷静或放松一下）：*He's always so stressed out—he really needs to take a chill pill!* 他总是那么紧张，他的确需要放松一下！

chilly /ˈtʃɪli/ *adj.* (**chill·ier**, **chilli·est**) **1** (especially of the weather or a place, but also of people 尤指天气或地方，亦指人) too cold to be comfortable 寒冷的；阴冷的：*It's chilly today.* 今天很寒冷。◇ *I was feeling chilly.* 我感到冷得难受。➲ SYNONYMS AT COLD **2** not friendly 不友好的；冷淡的；冷漠的：*The visitors got a chilly reception.* 客人遭到了冷遇。 ▶ **chil·li·ness** *noun* [U]

chime /tʃaɪm/ *verb, noun*

■ ***verb*** [I, T] (of a bell or a clock 铃或时钟) to ring; to show the time by making a ringing sound 鸣响；敲响；报时：*I heard the clock chime.* 我听见钟响报时。◇ *Eight o'clock* *had already chimed.* 已敲过八点钟了。◊ ~ **sth** *The clock chimed midday.* 时钟响过正午十二点。

PHR V **ˌchime ˈin (with sth)** to join or interrupt a conversation 插嘴；打断谈话：*He kept chiming in with his own opinions.* 他不断插话发表自己的意见。◊ + **speech** *'And me!' she chimed in.* "还有我！" 她插嘴道。 **chime (in) with sth** (of plans, ideas, etc. 计划、主意等) to agree with sth; to be similar to sth 与…相一致（或相似）：*His opinions chimed in with the mood of the nation.* 他的主张与国民的心态相吻合。

■ ***noun*** a ringing sound, especially one that is made by a bell 响亮清晰的声音；（尤指）铃声，钟声：*door chimes* 门铃声 ➲ SEE ALSO WIND CHIMES

chi·mera (*also* **chi·maera**) /kaɪˈmɪərə; *NAmE* -ˈmɪrə/ *noun* **1** (in ancient Greek stories) a creature with a LION's head, a GOAT's body and a snake's tail, that can breathe out fire 喀迈拉（古希腊神话中狮头、羊身、蛇尾的吐火怪物） **2** (*formal*) an impossible idea or hope 妄想；幻想；空想 **3** (*biology* 生) an ORGANISM (= a living thing) that contains a mixture of GENETICALLY different TISSUES 嵌合体（含有两种以上基因型组织的有机体）

chim·ney /ˈtʃɪmni/ *noun* **1** a structure through which smoke or steam is carried up away from a fire, etc. and through the roof of a building; the part of this that is above the roof 烟囱；烟道；（屋顶上的）烟囱管：*He threw a bit of paper onto the fire and it flew up the chimney.* 他把一小片纸扔进火里，纸飘进了烟道。◊ *the factory chimneys of an industrial landscape* 工厂烟囱林立的工业区景观 ➲ VISUAL VOCAB PAGE V18 **2** (*specialist*) a narrow opening in an area of rock that a person can climb up （岩石间可供攀登的）狭孔，狭缝

ˈchimney breast *noun* (*BrE*) the wall around the bottom part of a chimney, above a FIREPLACE 壁炉腔

ˈchimney piece *noun* (*BrE*) a brick or stone structure that is built over a FIREPLACE 壁炉台

ˈchimney pot *noun* (*BrE*) a short wide pipe that is placed on top of a chimney 烟囱管帽 ➲ VISUAL VOCAB PAGE V18

ˈchimney stack *noun* (*BrE*) **1** the part of the chimney that is above the roof of a building （屋顶上的）烟囱体 **2** (*NAmE* **smoke·stack**) a very tall chimney, especially one in a factory （尤指工厂的）高烟囱

ˈchimney sweep (*also* **sweep**) *noun* a person whose job is to clean the inside of chimneys 烟囱清扫工

chim·pan·zee /ˌtʃɪmpænˈziː/ (*also informal* **chimp**) *noun* a small intelligent African APE (= an animal like a large MONKEY without a tail) 黑猩猩 ➲ VISUAL VOCAB PAGE V12

chin 🔑 /tʃɪn/ *noun* the part of the face below the mouth and above the neck 颏；下巴 ➲ COLLOCATIONS AT PHYSICAL ➲ VISUAL VOCAB PAGE V64 ➲ SEE ALSO DOUBLE CHIN

IDM **(keep your) ˈchin up** (*informal*) used to tell sb to try to stay cheerful even though they are in a difficult or unpleasant situation 振作起来；不气馁；不灰心：*Chin up! Only two exams left.* 别泄气！只剩下两门考试了。 **take sth on the ˈchin** (*informal*) **1** to accept a difficult or unpleasant situation without complaining, trying to make excuses, etc. （无怨无悔地）承受某事 **2** (*NAmE*) to be damaged or badly affected by something 受损；受到严重影响 ➲ MORE AT CHUCK *v.*

china /ˈtʃaɪnə/ *noun* [U] **1** white CLAY which is baked and used for making delicate cups, plates, etc. 瓷；瓷料：*a china vase* 瓷花瓶 ➲ SEE ALSO BONE CHINA **2** cups, plates, etc. that are made of china 瓷制品；瓷器：*She got out the best china.* 她制作最好的瓷器。 IDM SEE BULL

ˌchina-ˈblue *adj.* pale greyish-blue in colour 瓷蓝的；浅灰蓝的 ▸ **ˌchina ˈblue** *noun* [U] ➲ MORE LIKE THIS 15, page R26

ˌchina ˈclay *noun* [U] = KAOLIN

China·town /ˈtʃaɪnətaʊn/ *noun* [U, C] the area of a city where many people of Chinese origin live and there are Chinese shops/stores and restaurants 唐人街；中国城

chin·chilla /tʃɪnˈtʃɪlə/ *noun* **1** [C] an animal like a RABBIT with soft silver-grey fur. Chinchillas are often kept on farms for their fur. 毛丝鼠（似兔，皮毛银灰色，常养殖以获取毛皮） **2** [U] the skin and fur of the chinchilla, used for making expensive coats, etc. 毛丝鼠毛皮（用以制作名贵大衣等）

Chi·nese /ˌtʃaɪˈniːz/ *adj.*, *noun*

■ ***adj.*** from or connected with China 中国的

■ ***noun*** (*pl.* **Chi·nese**) **1** [C] a person from China, or whose family was originally from China 中国人；华裔；华人 **2** [U] the language of China 中国话；汉语；中文

ˌChinese ˈcabbage *noun* [U] (*BrE also* **ˌChinese ˈleaves** [pl.], **ˌChinese ˈleaf** [U]) a type of vegetable that is eaten cooked or in salads. There are two types of Chinese cabbage, one with long light-green leaves and thick white STEMS which is similar to LETTUCE and one with darker green leaves and thicker white STEMS. The first type is usually called 'Chinese leaves' in British English and the second type is called 'pak choi' (*BrE*) or 'bok choy' (*NAmE*). 白菜；大白菜

ˌChinese ˈchequers (*BrE*) (*NAmE* **ˌChinese ˈcheckers**) *noun* [U] a game for two to six players who try to move the playing pieces from one corner to the opposite corner of the board, which is shaped like a star （弹子）跳棋 ➲ VISUAL VOCAB PAGE V42

ˌChinese ˈlantern *noun* **1** a lamp that is inside a paper case, with a handle to carry it 灯笼 **2** a plant with white flowers and round orange fruits inside a material like paper 酸浆

ˌChinese ˈwhispers *noun* [U] (*BrE*) the situation when information is passed from one person to another and gets slightly changed each time 口传失真（消息从一个人向另一个人传播时每次都发生一些变化）

Ching·lish /ˈtʃɪŋglɪʃ/ *noun* [U] (*informal*) language which is a mixture of ENGLISH and CHINESE, especially a type of English that includes many Chinese words and/or follows Chinese grammar rules 中式英语

Chink /tʃɪŋk/ *noun* (*taboo, slang*) a very offensive word for a Chinese person （对中国人的蔑称）中国佬

chink /tʃɪŋk/ *noun, verb*

■ ***noun*** **1** a narrow opening in sth, especially one that lets light through （尤指光线可进入的）裂口，缝隙，裂缝：*a chink in the curtains* 窗帘上的缝隙 **2** ~ **of light** a small area of light shining through a narrow opening 一缕，一束，一线（从缝隙间射入的光） **3** [usually sing.] the light ringing sound that is made when glass objects or coins touch （玻璃物品或硬币的）轻微碰撞声，叮当声：*the chink of glasses* 玻璃杯相碰的叮当声

IDM **a chink in sb's ˈarmour** a weak point in sb's argument, character, etc., that can be used in an attack （论点、性格等易受攻击的）弱点，缺陷，薄弱环节

■ ***verb*** [I, T] when glasses, coins or other glass or metal objects **chink** or when you **chink** them, they make a light ringing sound （使）叮当响 SYN **clink**：*the sound of bottles chinking* 瓶子叮当的碰撞声 ◊ ~ **sth** *We chinked glasses and drank to each other's health.* 我们互相碰杯，祝对方身体健康。

chin·less /ˈtʃɪnləs/ *adj.* (of a man 男子) having a very small chin (often thought of as a sign of a weak character) 下巴短小的（常被认为性格软弱）

IDM **a chinless ˈwonder** (*BrE, humorous, disapproving*) a young, upper-class man who is weak and stupid 上流脓包；上流青年懦夫

chi·nois·erie /ʃɪnˈwɑːzəri/ *noun* [U] (*art* 美术) the use of Chinese images, designs and techniques in Western art, furniture and ARCHITECTURE 中国式风格，中国艺术风格（见于西方艺术、家具、建筑）

chi·nook /tʃɪˈnuːk; ʃɪ-/ *noun* **1** (*also* **chiˌnook ˈwind**) a warm dry wind that blows down the east side of the Rocky Mountains at the end of winter 奇努克风（冬末从落基山脉东侧吹下来的干燥暖风） **2** (*also* **chi,nook 'salmon**) a large N Pacific SALMON which is eaten as food 奇努克鲑，王鲑，大鳞大麻哈鱼，大鳞鲑鱼（产于北太平洋的食用鱼）

chinos /'tʃiːnəʊz; *NAmE* -noʊz/ *noun* [pl.] informal trousers/pants made from strong cotton 斜纹布裤：*a pair of chinos* 一条斜纹布裤

chintz /tʃɪnts/ *noun* [U, C] a type of shiny cotton cloth with a printed design, especially of flowers, used for making curtains, covering furniture, etc. 轧光印花棉布（用于制作窗帘、家具套等）

chintzy /'tʃɪntsi/ *adj.* **1** covered in or decorated with chintz 用轧光印花棉布覆盖（或装饰）的 **2** (*NAmE, informal*) cheap and not attractive 便宜而俗气的；廉价的 **3** (*NAmE, humorous*) not willing to spend money 吝啬的；小气的 SYN **cheap, stingy**

'chin-up *noun* (*especially NAmE*) = PULL-UP

chin·wag /'tʃɪnwæg/ *noun* [sing.] (*BrE, informal*) a friendly, informal conversation with sb that you know well（与熟人的）闲谈，闲聊 SYN **chat**

chips (*BrE*) (*also* **French fries** *NAmE, BrE*)
炸薯条

crisps (*BrE*) / **chips** (*NAmE*)
炸薯片

chip /tʃɪp/ *noun, verb*

■ ***noun*** **1** the place from which a small piece of wood, glass, etc. has broken from an object（木头、玻璃等的）缺口，缺损处：*This mug has a chip in it.* 这缸子有个豁口。 ➲ PICTURE AT BROKEN **2** a small piece of wood, glass, etc. that has broken or been broken off an object（木头、玻璃等破损后留下的）碎屑，碎片，碎渣：*chips of wood* 碎木屑 ◇ *chocolate chip cookies* (= biscuits containing small pieces of chocolate) 碎粒巧克力饼干 **3** (*BrE*) (*also* **,French 'fry, fry** *NAmE, BrE*) [usually pl.] a long thin piece of potato fried in oil or fat 油炸土豆条；炸薯条：*All main courses are served with chips or baked potato.* 所有的主菜都配有炸土豆条或烤土豆。 ➲ SEE ALSO FISH AND CHIPS **4** (*also* **po'tato chip**) (*both NAmE*) (*BrE* **crisp, po,tato 'crisp**) a thin round slice of potato that is fried until hard then dried and eaten cold. Chips are sold in bags and have many different flavours. 油炸土豆片；炸薯片 **5** = TORTILLA CHIP **6** = MICROCHIP：*chip technology* 芯片科技 ➲ SEE ALSO V-CHIP **7** a small flat piece of plastic used to represent a particular amount of money in some types of gambling（作赌注用的）筹码：(*figurative*) *The release of prisoners was used as a bargaining chip.* 释放战俘被用作讨价还价的筹码。 ➲ WORDFINDER NOTE AT GAMBLING **8** (*also* **'chip shot**) (in GOLF, football (SOCCER), etc. 高尔夫球、足球等) an act of hitting or kicking a ball high in the air so that it lands within a short distance（高尔夫球）近穴击球，切削击球；（足球）撮球 ➲ SEE ALSO BLUE-CHIP

IDM **a ,chip off the old 'block** (*informal*) a person who is very similar to their mother or father in the way that they look or behave （相貌或性格）酷似父亲或母亲的人 **have a 'chip on your shoulder (about sth)** (*informal*) to be sensitive about sth that happened in the past and become easily offended if it is mentioned because you think that you were treated unfairly （因受过委屈而变得）敏感，好生气 **have had your 'chips** (*BrE, informal*) to be in a situation in which you are certain to be defeated or killed 注定要失败（或完蛋） **when the chips are 'down** (*informal*) used to refer to a difficult situation in which you are forced to decide what is important to you 在危急关头；在关键时刻：*I'm not sure what I'll do when the chips are down.* 我拿不准到了关键时刻我会干出些什么事来。 ➲ MORE AT CASH *v.*

■ ***verb*** (**-pp-**) **1** [T, I] ~ (**sth**) to damage sth by breaking a small piece off it; to become damaged in this way 打破；弄缺；被损坏：*a badly chipped saucer* 破损厉害的碟子 ◇ *She chipped one of her front teeth.* 她锛了一颗门牙。 ◇ *These plates chip easily.* 这些盘子容易破损。 ➲ PICTURE AT BROKEN **2** [T] ~ **sth + adv./prep.** to cut or break small pieces off sth with a tool 切下，削下，凿下（碎片、屑片）：*Chip away the damaged area.* 把损坏的部分凿掉。 ◇ *The fossils had been chipped out of the rock.* 那些化石已从岩石上被凿了下来。 **3** [T, I] ~ (**sth**) (especially in GOLF and football (SOCCER) 尤指高尔夫球和足球) to hit or kick the ball so that it goes high in the air and then lands within a short distance 撮高（球）；近穴击（球） **4** [T] ~ **potatoes** (*BrE*) to cut potatoes into long thin pieces and fry them in deep oil 将（土豆）切条油炸 **5** [T] ~ **sth** to put a MICROCHIP under the skin of a dog or other animal so that it can be identified if it is lost or stolen （为辨认而在狗或其他动物的皮下）植入微芯片

PHR V **,chip a'way at sth** to keep breaking small pieces off sth 不停地削（或凿）：*He was chipping away at the stone.* 他不停地凿那块石头。 ◇ (*figurative*) *They chipped away at the power of the government* (= gradually made it weaker). 他们不断削弱政府的权力。 **,chip 'in (with sth)** (*informal*) **1** to join in or interrupt a conversation; to add sth to a conversation or discussion 插话；插嘴；（对谈话或讨论）作补充：*Pete and Anne chipped in with suggestions.* 皮特和安妮插话提出了建议。 ◇ **+ speech** *'That's different,' she chipped in.* "那可不一样。" 她插嘴说道。 **2** (*also* **,chip 'in sth**) to give some money so that a group of people can buy sth together 凑份子 SYN **contribute**：*If everyone chips in we'll be able to buy her a really nice present.* 如果大家都凑钱，我们就能给她买件很好的礼物。 ◇ *We each chipped in (with) £5.* 我们每人凑了 5 英镑。 **,chip 'off | ,chip sth↔'off** to damage sth by breaking a small piece off it; to be damaged in this way（小块地）损坏，毁坏，剥落，被损坏，被毁坏：*He chipped off a piece of his tooth.* 他锛缺了一点牙齿。 ◇ *The paint had chipped off.* 油漆已经剥落。

,chip and 'PIN (*also* **chip and pin**) *noun* [U] a system of paying for sth with a credit card or DEBIT CARD in which the card has information stored on it in the form of a MICROCHIP and you prove your identity by typing a number (your PIN) rather than by signing your name 芯片卡付款系统，智能卡付款系统（信用卡或借记卡上带有存储信息的微型芯片，付款时输入密码即可）：*Chip and PIN is designed to combat credit card fraud.* 智能卡系统是专为防止信用卡诈骗设计的。

chip·board /'tʃɪpbɔːd; *NAmE* -bɔːrd/ *noun* [U] a type of board that is used for building, made of small pieces of wood that are pressed together and stuck with glue 刨花板；碎木胶合板

'chip card *noun* a plastic card on which information is stored in the form of a MICROCHIP 芯片卡；智能卡：*Chip cards will be the money of the future.* 智能卡将是未来的货币。

chip·munk /'tʃɪpmʌŋk/ *noun* a small N American animal of the SQUIRREL family, with light and dark marks on its back 花鼠，金花鼠，花栗鼠（栖于北美，属松鼠科）

chipo·lata /ˌtʃɪpəˈlɑːtə/ *noun* (*especially BrE*) a small thin SAUSAGE 契普拉塔小香肠

chip·per /ˈtʃɪpə(r)/ *adj., noun*
■ ***adj.*** (*informal*) cheerful and lively 生气勃勃的
■ ***noun*** **1** a machine which cuts wood into very small pieces 木材削片机 **2** a device which cuts potatoes into chips/fries 土豆条机；薯条机 **3** (*ScotE, IrishE, informal*) a chip shop 薯条店

chip·pings /ˈtʃɪpɪŋz/ *noun* [pl.] (*BrE*) small pieces of stone or wood 碎石；木屑

chippy /ˈtʃɪpi/ *noun, adj.*
■ ***noun*** (*also* **chip·pie**) (*pl.* **-ies**) (*BrE, informal*) **1** = CHIP SHOP **2** = CARPENTER
■ ***adj.*** (*informal*) (of a person 人) getting annoyed or offended easily 易怒的；易生气的

ˈchip shop (*also informal* **chip·py**, **chip·pie**) *noun* (in Britain) a shop that cooks and sells fish and chips and other fried food for people to take home and eat（在英国以炸鱼薯条为主的）油炸食品外卖店

ˈchip shot *noun* = CHIP (8)

chiro·mancy /ˈkaɪrəʊmænsi; *NAmE* ˈkaɪroʊ-/ *noun* [U] the practice of telling what will happen in the future by looking at the lines on sb's PALMS 手相术 **SYN** **palmistry** ▸ **chiro·man·cer** /ˈkaɪrəʊmænsə(r); *NAmE* ˈkaɪroʊ-/ *noun*

chir·opo·dist /kɪˈrɒpədɪst; *NAmE* kɪˈrɑːp-/ (*especially BrE*) (*NAmE usually* **po·dia·trist**) *noun* a person whose job is the care and treatment of people's feet 足病诊疗师；足部护理师

chir·opody /kɪˈrɒpədi; *NAmE* kɪˈrɑːp-/ (*especially BrE*) (*NAmE usually* **po·dia·try**) *noun* [U] the work of a chiropodist 足病治疗

chiro·prac·tic /ˌkaɪərəʊˈpræktɪk; *NAmE* -roʊ-/ *noun* [U] the medical profession which involves treating some diseases and physical problems by pressing and moving the bones in a person's SPINE or joints; the work of a chiropractor 捏积（疗法）；脊柱推拿（疗法）

chiro·prac·tor /ˈkaɪərəʊpræktə(r); *NAmE* -roʊ-/ *noun* a person whose job involves treating some diseases and physical problems by pressing and moving the bones in a person's SPINE or joints 捏积医师；推拿师 ➲ COMPARE OSTEOPATH ➲ **WORDFINDER NOTE AT TREATMENT**

chirp /tʃɜːp; *NAmE* tʃɜːrp/ (*also* **chir·rup**) *verb* **1** [I] (of small birds and some insects 小鸟或某些昆虫) to make short high sounds 吱喳叫；唧唧叫；发啁啾声 **2** [I, T] to speak in a lively and cheerful way 轻松愉快地讲（话）；喊喊喳喳地说 ▸ **chirp** (*also* **chir·rup**) *noun*

chirpy /ˈtʃɜːpi; *NAmE* ˈtʃɜːrpi/ *adj.* (*informal*) lively and cheerful; in a good mood 活泼快活的；轻松愉快的；心情好的 ▸ **chirp·ily** *adv.* **chirpi·ness** *noun* [U]

chir·rup /ˈtʃɪrəp/ *verb, noun* = CHIRP

chisel /ˈtʃɪzl/ *noun, verb*
■ ***noun*** a tool with a sharp flat edge at the end, used for shaping wood, stone or metal 凿子；錾子 ➲ **VISUAL VOCAB** PAGES V21, V45
■ ***verb*** (**-ll-**, *especially US* **-l-**) [T, I] ~ (**sth**) (+ **adv./prep.**) to cut or shape wood or stone with a chisel（用凿子）凿，刻，雕：*A name was chiselled into the stone.* 石头上刻着一个名字。◇ *She was chiselling some marble.* 她在雕刻大理石。▸ **chisel·ler** (*especially US* **chisel·er**) /ˈtʃɪzlə(r)/ *noun*

chis·elled (*BrE*) (*especially US* **chis·eled**) /ˈtʃɪzld/ *adj.* (of a person's face 人的脸部) having clear strong features 轮廓鲜明的

chi-square test /ˌkaɪ ˈskweə test; *NAmE* ˈskwer/ *noun* (*statistics* 统计) a calculation that is used to test how well a set of data fits the results that were expected according to a theory * χ^2 检验；卡方检验

chit /tʃɪt/ *noun* **1** a short written note, signed by sb, showing an amount of money that is owed, or giving sb permission to do sth 欠账字据；欠条；（允许某人去做某事的）便条 **2** (*old-fashioned, disapproving*) a young woman or girl, especially one who is thought to have no respect for older people（尤指对老人无礼的）毛丫头；不知礼的年轻女子

ˈchit-chat *noun* [U] (*informal*) conversation about things that are not important 闲聊；聊天；闲谈 **SYN** **chat** ➲ MORE LIKE THIS 11, page R26

chit·ter·lings /ˈtʃɪtəlɪŋz; *NAmE* ˈtʃɪtər-/ *noun* [pl.] pig's INTESTINES, eaten as food（食用）猪小肠

chiv·al·rous /ˈʃɪvəlrəs/ *adj.* (of men 男人) polite, kind and behaving with honour, especially towards women（尤指对女人）彬彬有礼的，殷勤的，体贴的 **SYN** **gallant** ▸ **chiv·al·rous·ly** *adv.*

chiv·alry /ˈʃɪvəlri/ *noun* [U] **1** polite and kind behaviour that shows a sense of honour, especially by men towards women（尤指男人对女人的）彬彬有礼，殷勤，体贴 **2** (in the Middle Ages) the religious and moral system of behaviour which the perfect KNIGHT was expected to follow（中世纪的）骑士制度

chives /tʃaɪvz/ *noun* [pl.] the long thin leaves of a plant with purple flowers. Chives taste like onions and are used to give flavour to food. 北葱，细香葱（长细叶，开紫色花，味似洋葱）➲ **VISUAL VOCAB** PAGE V35 ▸ **chive** *adj.* [only before noun]: *a chive and garlic dressing* 细香葱蒜泥调料

chivvy /ˈtʃɪvi/ *verb* (**chiv·vies**, **chivvy·ing**, **chiv·vied**, **chiv·vied**) ~ **sb** (**into sth/along**) | ~ **sb to do sth** to try and make sb hurry or do sth quickly, especially when they do not want to do it 强求；催促：*He chivvied them into the car.* 他催促他们上车。

chla·mydia /kləˈmɪdiə/ *noun* [U] (*medical* 医) a disease caused by bacteria, which is caught by having sex with an infected person 衣原体病（通过与病患者性交传染）

chlor·ide /ˈklɔːraɪd/ *noun* [U, C] (*chemistry* 化) a COMPOUND of CHLORINE and another chemical element 氯化物 ➲ SEE ALSO SODIUM CHLORIDE

chlor·in·ate /ˈklɔːrɪneɪt/ *verb* ~ **sth** to put chlorine in sth, especially water 氯化 ▸ **chlor·in·ation** /ˌklɔːrɪˈneɪʃn/ *noun* [U]: *a chlorination plant* 氯气消毒装置

chlor·ine /ˈklɔːriːn/ *noun* [U] (*symb.* **Cl**) a chemical element. Chlorine is a poisonous greenish gas with a strong smell. It is often used in swimming pools to keep the water clean. 氯；氯气

chloro·fluoro·car·bon /ˌklɔːrəʊˈfluərəʊkɑːbən; *NAmE* ˌklɔːroʊˈflɔroʊkɑːrbən/ *noun* (*chemistry* 化) a CFC; a COMPOUND containing CARBON, FLUORINE and CHLORINE that is harmful to the OZONE LAYER 氯氟碳化物，氯氟烃（对臭氧层有害）

chloro·form /ˈklɒrəfɔːm; *NAmE* ˈklɔːrəfɔːrm/ *noun* [U] (*symb.* **$CHCl_3$**) a clear liquid used in the past in medicine, etc. to make people unconscious, for example before an operation 氯仿，三氯甲烷（旧时医用麻醉剂）

chloro·phyll /ˈklɒrəfɪl; *NAmE* ˈklɔːr-/ *noun* [U] the green substance in plants that absorbs light from the sun to help them grow 叶绿素 ➲ SEE ALSO PHOTOSYNTHESIS

chloro·plast /ˈklɒrəplɑːst; *NAmE* ˈklɔːrəplæst/ *noun* (*biology* 生) the structure in plant cells that contains CHLOROPHYLL and in which PHOTOSYNTHESIS takes place 叶绿体

choc /tʃɒk; *NAmE* tʃɑːk/ *noun* (*BrE, informal*) a chocolate 巧克力；朱古力：*a box of chocs* 一盒巧克力

choca·hol·ic = CHOCOHOLIC

choccy /ˈtʃɒki; *NAmE* ˈtʃɑːki/ *noun* (*pl.* **-ies**) [U, C] (*BrE, informal*) chocolate; a sweet/candy made of chocolate 巧克力；巧克力糖果：*a box of choccies* 一盒巧克力糖果

ˈchoc ice *noun* (*BrE*) a small block of ice cream covered with chocolate 巧克力脆皮冰淇淋；紫雪糕

chock-a-block /ˌtʃɒk ə ˈblɒk; *NAmE* ˌtʃɑːk ə ˈblɑːk/ (*also* **chocka** /ˈtʃɒkə; *NAmE* ˈtʃɑːkə/) *adj.* [not before noun] ~ (**with sth/sb**) (*informal*) very full of things or people pressed close together 充满；挤满；塞满：*The shelves were chock-a-block with ornaments.* 架子上堆满了装饰品。◇ *It was chock-a-block in town today* (= full of people). 今天城里人多得不得了。

chock-full /ˌtʃɒk ˈfʊl; *NAmE* ˌtʃɑːk/ *adj.* [not before noun] ~ (**of sth/sb**) (*informal*) completely full 塞满；挤满；充满

choco·hol·ic (*also* **choca·hol·ic**) /ˌtʃɒkəˈhɒlɪk; *NAmE* ˌtʃɑːkəˈhɑːlɪk; -ˈhɔːlɪk/ *noun* (*informal*) a person who likes chocolate very much and eats a lot of it 嗜食巧克力的人

choc·olate /ˈtʃɒklət; *NAmE* ˈtʃɑːk-; ˈtʃɔːk-/ *noun* **1** [U] a hard brown sweet food made from COCOA BEANS, used in cooking to add flavour to cakes, etc. or eaten as a sweet/candy 巧克力；朱古力：*a* ***bar/piece of chocolate*** 一条 / 一块巧克力 ◇ *a chocolate cake* 巧克力蛋糕 ◇ *a chocolate factory* 巧克力制造厂 ➲ SEE ALSO MILK CHOCOLATE, PLAIN CHOCOLATE **2** [C] a sweet/candy that is made of or covered with chocolate 巧克力糖；夹心巧克力糖：*a box of chocolates* 一盒巧克力糖 **3** [U, C] (*BrE*) = HOT CHOCOLATE：*a mug of drinking chocolate* 一杯巧克力饮料 ➲ COMPARE COCOA **4** [U] a dark brown colour 深褐色；巧克力色

ˈ**chocolate-box** *adj.* [only before noun] (*BrE*) (especially of places 尤指地方) very pretty, but in a way that does not seem real 如糖罐上描绘的；华丽但不真实的；花里胡哨的：*a chocolate-box village* 装饰得花里胡哨的村庄

choice /tʃɔɪs/ *noun, adj.*

■ ***noun*** **1** [C] ~ (**between A and B**) an act of choosing between two or more possibilities; something that you can choose 选择；挑选；抉择：*women forced to make a choice between family and career* 被迫在家庭和事业之间作出抉择的妇女 ◇ *We are faced with a difficult choice.* 我们面临着困难的抉择。◇ *We aim to help students make more informed career choices.* 我们旨在帮助学生作出更有依据的职业抉择。◇ *There is a wide range of choices open to you.* 你有很多选择。➲ SYNONYMS AT OPTION ➲ EXPRESS YOURSELF AT WHY **2** [U, sing.] the right to choose or the possibility of choosing 选择权；选择的可能性：*If I had the choice, I would stop working tomorrow.* 如果让我选择，我明天就停止工作。◇ *He* ***had no choice*** *but to leave* (= this was the only thing he could do). 除了离去，他别无选择。◇ *She's going to do it. She doesn't have* ***much choice****, really, does she?* 她就要做那件事了。她真的没有多少选择的余地了，不是吗？◇ *This government is committed to extending parental choice in education.* 本届政府承诺扩大父母在教育方面的选择权。**3** [C] a person or thing that is chosen 入选者；被选中的东西：*She's the obvious choice for the job.* 她是这个职位当然的人选。◇ *Hawaii remains a popular choice for winter vacation travel.* 夏威夷一直是深受人们青睐的冬季假日旅游胜地。◇ *This colour wasn't my first choice.* 这种颜色并非我的首选。◇ *She wouldn't be my choice as manager.* 我不会选她做经理。**4** [sing., U] the number or range of different things from which to choose 供选择的品种；可选的范围：*The menu has a good choice of desserts.* 菜单上有多种甜食可供选择。◇ *There wasn't* ***much choice*** *of colour.* 可供选择的颜色不多。➲ SEE ALSO HOBSON'S CHOICE, MULTIPLE-CHOICE

IDM **by ˈchoice** because you have chosen 出于自己的选择：*I wouldn't go there by choice.* 让我选择，我不会去那里。**of ˈchoice (for sb/sth)** (used after a noun 用于名词后) that is chosen by a particular group of people or for a particular purpose 精选的；特选的：*It's the software of choice for business use.* 这是商务专用软件。**of your ˈchoice** that you choose yourself 自己选择（或选定）的：*First prize will be a meal for two at the restaurant of your choice.* 头等奖是一顿双人餐，餐馆任选。➲ MORE AT PAY *v.*, SPOILT

■ ***adj.*** (**choicer**, **choicest**) [only before noun] **1** (especially of food 尤指食物) of very good quality 优质的；上等的；优选的 **2** (*NAmE*) (of meat 肉) of very good, but not the highest, quality（质量）中上等的 **3** ~ **words/phrases** (*humorous*) rude or offensive language（言语）粗鲁的，无礼的：*She summed up the situation in a few choice phrases.* 她用粗鲁的两三句话总结了情况。◇ *He used some pretty choice language.* 他出言不逊。

> ▼ **SYNONYMS 同义词辨析**
>
> **choice**
>
> **favourite • preference • selection • pick**
>
> These are all words for a person or thing that is chosen, or that is liked more than others. 以上各词均指选中或特别喜爱的人或事物。
>
> **choice** a person or thing that is chosen 指入选者、选中的东西：*She's the obvious choice for the job.* 她是这个职位当然的人选。
>
> **favourite/favorite** a person or thing that you like more than the others of the same type 指同类人或事物中最喜欢的一个：*Which one's your favourite?* 你最喜欢哪一个？
>
> **preference** a thing that is liked better or best 指偏爱的或最喜爱的事物：*Tastes and preferences vary from individual to individual.* 人的爱好和选择各不相同。
>
> **FAVOURITE OR PREFERENCE? 用favourite还是preference?**
>
> Your **favourites** are the things you like best, and that you have, do, listen to, etc. often; your **preferences** are the things that you would rather have or do if you can choose. * favourite 指最喜欢因而常有、常做或常听等的事物；preference 指在可以选择的情况下会较喜欢有或做的事物。
>
> **selection** a number of people or things that have been chosen from a larger group 指从大群中选出来的一组人或物：*A selection of reader's comments are published below.* 下面选登了部分读者评论。
>
> **pick** (*rather informal*) a person or thing that is chosen 指入选者、选中的东西：*She was his pick for best actress.* 她是他认为最好的女演员。
>
> **PATTERNS**
>
> - sb's choice/favourite/pick **for** sth
> - sb's choice/selection/pick **as** sth
> - an **obvious** choice/favourite/selection
> - a(n) **excellent**/**good**/**popular**/**fine** choice/selection

choir /ˈkwaɪə(r)/ *noun* **1** [C+sing./pl. v.] a group of people who sing together, for example in church services or public performances（教堂的）唱诗班；（公开演出的）合唱团，歌唱队：*She sings in the school choir.* 她是校合唱队的成员。➲ COLLOCATIONS AT MUSIC **2** [C] the part of a church where the choir sits during services（教堂）唱经楼，唱诗席

choir·boy /ˈkwaɪəbɔɪ; *NAmE* ˈkwaɪərbɔɪ/, **choir·girl** /ˈkwaɪəɡɜːl; *NAmE* ˈkwaɪərɡɜːrl/ *noun* a boy or girl who sings in the choir of a church 唱诗班的男童（或女童）➲ SEE ALSO CHORISTER

choir·mas·ter /ˈkwaɪəmɑːstə(r); *NAmE* ˈkwaɪərmæstər/ *noun* a person who trains a CHOIR to sing 唱诗班指挥；合唱团指挥

choke /tʃəʊk; *NAmE* tʃoʊk/ *verb, noun*

■ ***verb*** **1** [I, T] to be unable to breathe because the passage to your lungs is blocked or you cannot get enough air; to make sb unable to breathe（使）窒息，哽噎：*She almost* ***choked to death*** *in the thick fumes.* 她几乎被浓烟呛死。◇ ~ **on sth** *He was choking on a piece of toast.* 他被一块烤面包噎得喘不过气来。◇ ~ **sb** *Very small toys can choke a baby.* 很小的玩具可使婴儿窒息。**2** [T] ~ **sb** to make sb stop breathing by squeezing their throat（掐住喉咙）使停止呼吸，使窒息 SYN **strangle**：*He may have been choked or poisoned.* 他可能是被掐死或毒死的。**3** [I, T] to be unable to speak normally especially because of strong emotion; to make sb feel too emotional to speak normally（尤指感情激动而）说不出话来；使哽咽：~ (**with sth**) *His voice was choking with rage.* 他气得声音哽咽。◇

~ sth *Despair choked her words.* 她绝望得说不出话来。◇ *'I can't bear it,' he said in a choked voice.* "我实在忍不下去了。"他声音哽咽地说道。➲ SEE ALSO CHOKED **4** [T] to block or fill a passage, space, etc. so that movement is difficult 阻塞，塞满，堵塞（通道、空间等）：**~ sth (with sth)** *The pond was choked with rotten leaves.* 池塘被腐烂的叶子塞满了。◇ **~ sth up (with sth)** *The roads are choked up with traffic.* 几条马路都在塞车。 **5** [I] (*NAmE, informal*) to fail at sth, for example because you are nervous（因紧张等而）失败，失灵，失去作用

PHR V ˌ**choke sth↔ˈback** to try hard to prevent your feelings from showing 强忍住；抑制；克制：*to choke back* ***tears/anger/sobs*** 强忍住眼泪 / 愤怒 / 哭泣 ˌ**choke sth↔ˈdown** to swallow sth with difficulty 硬咽；硬吞 ˌ**choke sth↔ˈoff 1** to prevent or limit sth 阻止；制止；限制：*High prices have choked off demand.* 高昂的价格制约了需求。 **2** to interrupt sth; to stop sth 打断；停止；终止：*Her screams were suddenly choked off.* 她的尖叫声戛然而止。 ˌ**choke ˈout | choke out sth** to say sth with great difficulty because you feel a strong emotion （因感情激动而）哽咽着说，哽咽地说出某事：*He choked out a reply.* 他哽咽着回答。◇ **+ speech** *'I hate you!' she choked out.* "我恨你！"她哽咽着说道。 ˌ**choke ˈup** (*NAmE*) to find it difficult to speak, because of the strong emotion that you are feeling （因感情激动而）哽咽：*She choked up when she began to talk about her mother.* 她开始谈起母亲时，便哽咽着说不出话来。

■ *noun* **1** a device that controls the amount of air flowing into the engine of a vehicle （车辆发动机的）进气门 **2** an act or the sound of choking 窒息；哽噎；哽噎声；呛住的声音

choked /tʃəʊkt; *NAmE* tʃoʊkt/ *adj.* [not before noun] **~ up (about sth) | ~ (about sth)** (*informal*) upset or angry about sth, so that you find it difficult to speak 心烦意乱，愤怒，生气（而难以说出话来）

choker /ˈtʃəʊkə(r); *NAmE* ˈtʃoʊ-/ *noun* a piece of jewellery or narrow band of cloth worn closely around the neck 贴颈项链；项圈

chola /ˈtʃəʊlə; *NAmE* ˈtʃoʊlə/ *noun* (*from Spanish*) a woman from Latin America who has both Spanish and Native American ANCESTORS 拉美混血女子（西班牙人与美洲土著的混血女性后裔）➲ COMPARE CHOLO

chol·era /ˈkɒlərə; *NAmE* ˈkɑːl-/ *noun* [U] a disease caught from infected water that causes severe DIARRHOEA and VOMITING and often causes death 霍乱

chol·er·ic /ˈkɒlərɪk; *NAmE* ˈkɑːl-/ *adj.* (*formal*) easily made angry 易怒的；暴躁的；动辄发怒的 **SYN** **bad-tempered**

chol·es·terol /kəˈlestərɒl; *NAmE* -rɔːl/ *noun* [U] a substance found in blood, fat and most TISSUES of the body. Too much cholesterol can cause heart disease. 胆固醇 ➲ COLLOCATIONS AT DIET

cholo /ˈtʃəʊləʊ; *NAmE* ˈtʃoʊloʊ/ *noun* (*pl.* **-os**) a person from Latin America who has both Spanish and Native American ANCESTORS 拉美混血儿（西班牙人与美洲土著的混血后裔）➲ COMPARE CHOLA

chomp /tʃɒmp; *NAmE* tʃɑːmp; tʃɔːmp/ *verb* [I, T] to eat or bite food noisily 大声地吃（或咬、咀嚼食物） **SYN** **munch**：**~ (away) (on/through sth)** *She was chomping away on a bagel.* 她在嘎嘣嘎嘣地啃着一个硬面包圈。◇ **~ sth** *He* ***chomped his way*** *through two hot dogs.* 他呼哧呼哧地吃掉了两个热狗。

choo-choo /ˈtʃuː tʃuː/ *noun* (*pl.* **choo-choos**) a child's word for a train （儿语）火车

chook /tʃʊk/ *noun* (*AustralE, NZE, informal*) **1** a chicken 鸡 **2** an offensive word for an older woman （含冒犯意）老太婆

choose 🔑 /tʃuːz/ *verb* (**chose** /tʃəʊz; *NAmE* tʃoʊz/, **chosen** /ˈtʃəʊzn; *NAmE* ˈtʃoʊzn/) **1** 🔑 [I, T] to decide which thing or person you want out of the ones that are available 选择；挑选；选取：*You choose, I can't decide.* 你来选吧，我拿不定主意。◇ *There are plenty of restaurants to choose from.* 有许多餐馆可供选择。◇ **~ between A and/or B** *She had to choose between staying in the UK or going home.* 她不得不在留在英国和回国之间作出选择。◇ **~ sth** *Sarah chose her words carefully.* 萨拉措辞谨慎。◇ *This site has been chosen for the new school.* 这块场地已被选作新学校的校址。◇ **~ A from B** *We have to choose a new manager from a shortlist of five candidates.* 我们得从最终人选名单上的五位候选人中选出一个新经理。◇ **~ sb/sth as/for sth** *He chose banking as a career.* 他选择了从事银行业。◇ *We chose Phil McSweeney as/for chairperson.* 我们选菲尔・麦克斯威尼当主席。◇ **~ whether, what, etc....** *You'll have to choose whether to buy it or not.* 买还是不买，你得作出选择。◇ **~ to do sth** *We chose to go by train.* 我们选择乘火车去。◇ **~ sb to be/do sth** *We chose Phil McSweeney to be chairperson.* 我们选菲尔・麦克斯威尼当主席。➲ MORE LIKE THIS 26, page R28 **2** 🔑 [I, T] to prefer or decide to do sth 宁愿；情愿；决定：*Employees can retire at 60 if they choose.* 如果雇员愿意的话，可在 60 岁退休。◇ **~ to do sth** *Many people choose not to marry.* 许多人情愿不结婚。➲ SEE ALSO CHOICE

IDM **there is nothing/not much/little to choose between A and B** there is very little difference between two or more things or people 不相上下；难分高低；相差无几 ➲ MORE AT PICK *v.*

▼ SYNONYMS 同义词辨析

choose

select • pick • decide • opt • go for

These words all mean to decide which thing or person you want out of the ones that are available. 以上各词均含选择、挑选人或物之义。

choose to decide which thing or person you want out of the ones that are available 指选择、选取人或物：*You choose—I can't decide.* 你来选吧，我拿不定主意。

select [often passive] to choose sb/sth, usually carefully, from a group of people or things 指仔细选择、挑选：*He was selected for the team.* 他已入选进队了。◇ *a randomly selected sample of 23 schools* 随机抽选的 23 所学校

pick (*rather informal*) to choose sb/sth from a group of people or things 指选择、挑选：*She picked the best cake for herself.* 她为自己挑了一块最好的蛋糕。

CHOOSE, SELECT OR PICK? 用 choose、select 还是 pick?

Choose is the most general of these words and the only one that can be used without an object. When you **select** sth, you choose it carefully, unless you actually say that it is *selected randomly/at random*. **Pick** is a more informal word and often a less careful action, used especially when the choice being made is not very important. * choose 在以上各词中含义最广，也是唯一可以不带宾语的词。select 表示仔细挑选，除非表明 select randomly/at random（随机选取）。pick 较非正式，常指随意挑选，尤用于所作选择不甚重要的事情。

decide to choose between two or more possibilities 指在两个或更多可能的情况中作出抉择、决定、选择：*We're still trying to* ***decide on*** *a venue.* 我们仍在设法选定一个活动地点。

opt to choose to take or not to take a particular course of action 指选择是否采取某种行动：*After graduating she opted for a career in music.* 毕业后她选择了从事音乐工作。◇ *After a lot of thought, I* ***opted against*** *buying a motorbike.* 经过反复考虑，我决定不买摩托车。

go for sth (*rather informal*) to choose sth 指选择某物：*I think I'll go for the fruit salad.* 我想要水果色拉。

PATTERNS

- to choose/select/pick/decide **between** A and/or B
- to choose/select/pick A **from** B
- to opt/go **for** sb/sth
- to choose/decide/opt **to do sth**
- to choose/select/pick sb/sth **carefully/at random**
- **randomly** chosen/selected/picked

chooser /ˈtʃuːzə(r)/ *noun* IDM SEE BEGGAR *n.*

choosy /ˈtʃuːzi/ *adj.* (**choos·ier**, **choosi·est**) (*informal*) careful in choosing; difficult to please 精挑细选的；爱挑剔的；难以取悦的 SYN **fussy**, **picky**: *I'm very choosy about my clothes.* 我对自己的衣着很讲究。

chop /tʃɒp; *NAmE* tʃɑːp/ *verb, noun*

■ *verb* (-pp-) **1** to cut sth into pieces with a sharp tool such as a knife 切碎；剁碎；砍；劈：**~ sth** *He was chopping logs for firewood.* 他在把原木劈成柴火。◇ *Add the finely chopped onions.* 加入切碎的洋葱。◇ **~ sth (up) (into sth)** *Chop the carrots up into small pieces.* 把胡萝卜切成小块。◇ (*figurative*) *The country was chopped up into small administrative areas.* 这个国家被划分为若干小的行政区。➲ COLLOCATIONS AT COOKING ➲ VISUAL VOCAB PAGE V30 **2** [usually passive] **~ sth (from sth) (to sth)** (*informal*) to reduce sth by a large amount; to stop sth（大幅度地）削减，降低；取消；终止 SYN **cut**: *The share price was chopped from 50 pence to 20 pence.* 股价由每股 50 便士猛降至 20 便士。**3** **~ sb/sth** to hit sb/sth with a short downward stroke or blow 向下猛击

IDM ˌ**chop and ˈchange** (*BrE, informal*) to keep changing your mind or what you are doing 变化无常；反复变换 ➲ MORE LIKE THIS 13, page R26

PHR V ˈ**chop (away) at sth** to aim blows at sth with a heavy sharp tool such as an AXE 对准…砍去（或猛击） ˌ**chop sth↔ˈdown** to make sth, such as a tree, fall by cutting it at the base with a sharp tool 砍伐，伐倒（如树木） ˌ**chop sth↔ˈoff (sth)** to remove sth by cutting it with a sharp tool 砍掉；砍下；砍断：*He chopped a branch off the tree.* 他从那棵树上砍下一根树枝。◇ (*informal*) *Anne Boleyn had her head chopped off.* 安妮•博林被斩首。

■ *noun* **1** [C] a thick slice of meat with a bone attached to it, especially from a pig or sheep 猪（或羊等）排：*a* ***pork/lamb chop*** 猪排；羊排 **2** [C] an act of cutting sth with a quick downward movement using an AXE or a knife 砍；劈；剁 **3** [C] an act of hitting sb/sth with the side of your hand in a quick downward movement 掌劈：*a karate chop* 空手道中的掌劈 **4** **chops** [pl.] (*informal*) the part of a person's or an animal's face around the mouth（人或动物的）嘴周围的地方：*The dog sat licking its chops.* 那只狗坐着在舔嘴。**5** **chops** [pl.] the technical skill of an actor or a JAZZ or rock musician（演员、爵士乐手或摇滚乐手的）技艺：*He has the acting chops to carry a major film.* 他的演技足以撑起一部大片。

IDM **get/be given the ˈchop** (*BrE, informal*) **1** (of a person 人) to be dismissed from a job 被解雇；被撤职：*The whole department has been given the chop.* 整个部门的员工都已被解雇。**2** (of a plan, project, etc. 计划、工程等) to be stopped or ended 被取消；被终止：*Three more schemes have got the chop.* 又有三个方案被砍掉了。**be for the ˈchop** (*BrE, informal*) **1** (of a person 人) to be likely to be dismissed from a job 可能遭裁员：*Who's next for the chop?* 下一个轮到谁被裁员？**2** (of a plan, project, etc. 计划、工程等) to be likely to be stopped or ended 可能被取消（或终止）**not much ˈchop** (*AustralE, NZE, informal*) not very good or useful 不算好的；不太有用的

ˌ**chop-ˈchop** *exclamation* (*informal*) hurry up! 快，赶快：*Chop-chop! We haven't got all day!* 快！快！我们的时间不多！ORIGIN From pidgin English based on a Chinese word for 'quick'. 源自汉语"快"字的洋泾浜英语。

chop·per /ˈtʃɒpə(r); *NAmE* ˈtʃɑːp-/ *noun* **1** [C] (*informal*) = HELICOPTER **2** [C] a large heavy knife or small AXE 大砍刀；小斧头 **3** [C] (*NAmE*) a type of motorcycle with a very long piece of metal connecting the front wheel to the HANDLEBARS（特制的）前轮伸出式摩托车 **4** **choppers** [pl.] (*informal*) teeth 牙齿

ˈ**chopping board** (*BrE*) (*NAmE* ˈ**chopping block**, ˈ**cutting board**) *noun* a board made of wood or plastic used for cutting meat or vegetables on 砧板；切菜板 ➲ VISUAL VOCAB PAGE V27

choppy /ˈtʃɒpi; *NAmE* ˈtʃɑːpi/ *adj.* (**chop·pier**, **chop·pi·est**) **1** (of the sea, etc. 海洋等) with a lot of small waves; not calm 波浪起伏的；不平静的：*choppy waters* 波浪起伏的水面 **2** (*NAmE, disapproving*) (of a style of writing 文体) containing a lot of short sentences and changing topics too often 不连贯的；支离破碎的

chop·stick /ˈtʃɒpstɪk; *NAmE* ˈtʃɑːp-/ *noun* [usually pl.] either of a pair of thin sticks that are used for eating with, especially in some Asian countries 筷子 ➲ VISUAL VOCAB PAGE V23 ➲ PICTURE AT STICK

chop suey /ˌtʃɒp ˈsuːi; *NAmE* ˌtʃɑːp/ *noun* [U] a Chinese-style dish of small pieces of meat fried with vegetables and served with rice 炒杂烩（中式菜，碎肉和蔬菜一起炒后配米饭吃）

choral /ˈkɔːrəl/ *adj.* connected with, written for or sung by a CHOIR (= a group of singers) 唱诗班的；为唱诗班谱写的；由唱诗班演唱的；合唱的：*choral music* 合唱音乐

chor·ale /kɒˈrɑːl; *NAmE* kəˈræl; -ˈrɑːl/ *noun* **1** a piece of church music sung by a group of singers 众赞歌 **2** (*especially NAmE*) a group of singers; a CHOIR 合唱队；唱诗班

chord /kɔːd; *NAmE* kɔːrd/ *noun* **1** (*music* 音) two or more notes played together 和弦；和音 **2** (*mathematics* 数) a straight line that joins two points on a curve 弦 ➲ PICTURE AT CIRCLE ➲ SEE ALSO VOCAL CORDS

IDM **strike/touch a ˈchord (with sb)** to say or do sth that makes people feel sympathy or enthusiasm 引起同情（或共鸣）：*The speaker had obviously struck a chord with his audience.* 讲演者显然已引起了听众的共鸣。

chore /tʃɔː(r)/ *noun* **1** a task that you do regularly 日常事务；例行工作：*doing the* ***household/domestic chores*** 干家务杂活 **2** an unpleasant or boring task 令人厌烦的任务；乏味无聊的工作：*Shopping's a real chore for me.* 对我来说，购物真是件苦差事。

cho·rea /kəˈriə/ *noun* [U] (*medical* 医) a condition in which parts of the body make quick sudden movements that cannot be controlled 舞蹈症（身体部位不自主地抽动）

choreo·graph /ˈkɒriəgrɑːf; -græf; *NAmE* ˈkɔːriəgræf/ *verb* **~ sth** to design and arrange the steps and movements for dancers in a BALLET or a show（为芭蕾舞或表演）设计舞蹈动作，编舞：(*figurative*) *There was some carefully choreographed flag-waving as the President drove by.* 总统的车经过时，人们按精心编排的动作挥舞着旗帜。➲ WORDFINDER NOTE AT DANCE

chore·og·raphy /ˌkɒriˈɒgrəfi; *NAmE* ˌkɔːriˈɑːg-/ *noun* [U] the art of designing and arranging the steps and movements in dances, especially in BALLET; the steps and movements in a particular ballet or show（尤指芭蕾舞的）编舞艺术，舞蹈设计 ▸ **chore·og·raph·er** /ˌkɒriˈɒgrəfə(r); *NAmE* ˌkɔːriˈɑːg-/ *noun* **choreo·graph·ic** /ˌkɒriəˈgræfɪk; *NAmE* ˌkɔːriəˈg-/ *adj.*

chor·ic /ˈkɔːrɪk; *BrE also* ˈkɒrɪk/ *adj.* (*specialist*) relating to or performed by a CHORUS (6) in a play, etc.（古希腊戏剧）歌队表演的

chor·is·ter /ˈkɒrɪstə(r); *NAmE* ˈkɔːr-; ˈkɑːr-/ *noun* a person who sings in the CHOIR of a church 唱诗班成员

chor·izo /tʃəˈriːzəʊ; *NAmE* -zoʊ/ *noun* [U, C] (*pl.* **-os**) (*from Spanish*) a spicy Spanish or Latin American SAUSAGE 西班牙（或拉美）辣味香肠

chor·tle /ˈtʃɔːtl; *NAmE* ˈtʃɔːrtl/ *verb* [I, T] to laugh loudly with pleasure or because you are amused 开怀大笑；高兴得咯咯笑；哈哈大笑：*Gill chortled with delight.* 吉尔高兴得哈哈大笑。▸ **chor·tle** *noun*

chorus /ˈkɔːrəs/ *noun, verb*

■ *noun* **1** [C] part of a song that is sung after each VERSE 副歌 SYN **refrain**: *Everyone joined in the chorus.* 唱到副歌时，大家都加入进来。**2** [C] a piece of music, usually part of a larger work, that is written for a CHOIR (= a group of singers) 合唱曲：*the Hallelujah Chorus*《哈利路亚合唱曲》**3** [C+sing./pl. v.] (often in names 常用于名称) a large group of singers 合唱团；歌咏队 SYN **choir**: *the Bath Festival Chorus* 巴斯音乐节大合唱团 **4** [C+sing./pl. v.] a group of performers who sing and dance in a musical show 歌舞队：*the chorus line* (= a line of singers and dancers performing together) 排成一排同台表演的歌舞演员 ➲ WORDFINDER NOTE AT OPERA **5** **a ~ of sth** [sing.] the sound of a lot of people expressing approval or disapproval at the same time 齐声，异口同声（表示同意或不同意）：***a chorus of praise/complaint*** 一片赞扬声 / 抱怨声 ◇ *a chorus of voices calling for her resignation* 异口同声要求她辞职 ➲ SEE ALSO DAWN CHORUS **6** [sing.+sing./pl. v.] (in ancient Greek drama 古希腊戏剧) a group of performers who comment together on the events of the play 歌队，合唱队（对剧情加以评论） **7** [sing.] (especially in 16th century drama 尤指在 16 世纪的戏剧中) an actor who speaks the opening and closing words of the play（开场白和收场白的）朗诵演员

IDM **in chorus** all together 一起；一齐；同时 SYN **in unison**: *'Thank you,' they said in chorus.* "谢谢。" 他们齐声说道。

■ ***verb*** **~ sth** to sing or say sth all together 合唱；齐声说；异口同声地说：*'Hello, Paul,' they chorused.* "你好，保罗。" 他们齐声问候道。

'chorus girl *noun* a girl or young woman who is a member of the chorus in a musical show, etc. 合唱团女性成员

chose PAST TENSE OF CHOOSE

chosen PAST PART. OF CHOOSE

chough /tʃʌf/ *noun* a bird of the CROW family, with blue-black feathers and red legs 山鸦

choux pastry /ˌʃuː ˈpeɪstri/ *noun* [U] a type of very light PASTRY made with eggs, used to make ECLAIRS and PROFITEROLES 泡芙面团

chow /tʃaʊ/ *noun* **1** [U] (*slang*) food 吃的东西 **2** (*also* **'chow chow**) [C] a dog with long thick hair, a curled tail and a blue-black tongue, originally from China 松狮狗（原产中国，毛厚长，尾卷曲，舌蓝黑色）

chow·der /ˈtʃaʊdə(r)/ *noun* [U] a thick soup made with fish and vegetables 杂烩羹（用鱼加蔬菜烹制）：*clam chowder* 蛤肉菜汤 ➲ SEE ALSO BISQUE

chowk /tʃaʊk/ *noun* (*IndE*) an open area with a market at a place where two roads meet in a city （城市交叉路口处的）集市广场：*Chandni Chowk* 昌德尼集市

chow mein /ˌtʃaʊ ˈmeɪn/ *noun* [U] a Chinese-style dish of fried NOODLES served with small pieces of meat and vegetables（中式）炒面：*chicken chow mein* 鸡肉炒面

Chrimbo (*also* **Crimbo**) /ˈkrɪmbəʊ; *NAmE* -boʊ/ *noun* [U] (*BrE, informal*) Christmas 圣诞节

Chris·sake /ˈkraɪseɪk/ (*also* **Chris·sakes** /-seɪks/) *noun* [U] (*taboo, informal*)

IDM **for 'Chrissake** a swear word that many people find offensive, used to show that you are angry, annoyed or surprised（很多人认为含冒犯意，表示生气、恼火或吃惊）天哪，上帝：*For Chrissake, listen!* 天哪，听！

Christ /kraɪst/ (*also* **Jesus**, **ˌJesus 'Christ**) *noun, exclamation*

■ ***noun*** the man that Christians believe is the son of God and on whose teachings the Christian religion is based 基督；耶稣基督

■ ***exclamation*** (*taboo, informal*) a swear word that many people find offensive, used to show that you are angry, annoyed or surprised （很多人认为含冒犯意，表示生气、恼火或吃惊）天哪：*Christ! Look at the time—I'm late!* 天哪！看看时间，我迟到了！

chris·ten /ˈkrɪsn/ *verb* **1** to give a name to a baby at his or her baptism to welcome him or her into the Christian Church （施洗时）为…命名；给…施洗：**~ sb + noun** *The child was christened Mary.* 这孩子受洗时取名玛丽。◇ **~ sb** *Did you have your children christened?* 你的孩子都受洗了吗？**2** **~ sb/sth (+ noun)** to give a name to sb/sth 给…取名（或命名）：*This area has been christened 'Britain's last wilderness'.* 这个地区被命名为"英国最后的荒野"。◇ *They christened the boat 'Oceania'.* 他们把这条船命名为"大洋洲号"。**3** **~ sth** (*informal*) to use sth for the first time 首次使用

Chris·ten·dom /ˈkrɪsndəm/ *noun* [U] (*old-fashioned*) all the Christian people and countries of the world（全世界的）基督教徒，信奉基督教的国家

chris·ten·ing /ˈkrɪsnɪŋ/ *noun* a Christian ceremony in which a baby is officially named and welcomed into the Christian Church （基督教的）洗礼 ➲ COMPARE BAPTISM

Chris·tian /ˈkrɪstʃən/ *adj., noun*

■ ***adj.*** **1** based on or believing the teachings of Jesus Christ 基督教的；信奉基督教的：***the Christian Church/faith/religion*** 基督教会；基督教的信仰；基督教 ◇ *She had a Christian upbringing.* 她从小接受基督教教育。◇ *a Christian country* 信奉基督教的国家 **2** connected with Christians 基督教徒的：*the Christian sector of the city* 城市的基督教徒区 **3** (*also* **christian**) showing the qualities that are thought of as typical of a Christian; good and kind 有基督教徒品行的；慈善的；仁慈的；友爱的

■ ***noun*** a person who believes in the teachings of Jesus Christ or has been BAPTIZED in a Christian church 基督徒；基督教徒：*Only 10% of the population are now practising Christians.* 现在仅有 10% 的人口是积极参与宗教活动的基督徒。

the 'Christian era *noun* [sing.] the period of time that begins with the birth of Christ 基督纪元；公元

Chris·tian·ity /ˌkrɪstiˈænəti/ *noun* [U] the religion that is based on the teachings of Jesus Christ and the belief that he was the son of God 基督教

'Christian name *noun* (in Western countries) a name given to sb when they are born or when they are CHRISTENED; a personal name, not a family name （西方人的）圣名，教名，洗礼名：*We're all on Christian-name terms here.* 我们这里所有的人都用教名相互称呼。➲ COMPARE FIRST NAME

ˌChristian 'Science *noun* [U] the beliefs of a religious group called **the Church of Christ, Scientist**, which include the belief that the physical world is not real and that you can cure illness only by prayer 基督教科学（基督教科学派的信仰，认为客观世界是不真实的，只有通过祈祷才能治愈疾病） ▶ **ˌChristian 'Scientist** *noun*

Christ·mas /ˈkrɪsməs/ *noun* [U, C] **1** (*also* **ˌChristmas 'Day**) 25 December, the day when Christians celebrate the birth of Christ 圣诞节（12 月 25 日）：***Christmas dinner/presents*** 圣诞大餐 / 礼物 ➲ SEE ALSO BOXING DAY **2** (*also* **Christ·mas·time**) the period that includes Christmas Day and the days close to it 圣诞节期间：***the Christmas holidays/vacation*** 圣诞节假期 ◇ *Are you spending Christmas with your family?* 你和家人共度圣诞节假日吗？◇ *Happy Christmas!* 圣诞快乐！◇ *Merry Christmas and a Happy New Year!* 圣诞快乐并恭贺新禧！➲ SEE ALSO WHITE CHRISTMAS

'Christmas box *noun* (*BrE, old-fashioned*) a small gift, usually of money, given at Christmas to sb who provides a service during the year, for example a POSTMAN （给邮差等服务人员的）圣诞节礼品，圣诞礼金

'Christmas cake *noun* [C, U] a fruit cake covered with MARZIPAN and ICING, traditionally eaten in Britain and some other countries at Christmas （英国和其他一些国家传统的）圣诞蛋糕（上面覆有杏仁蛋白糊和糖霜）

'Christmas card *noun* a card with a picture on it that you send to friends and relatives at Christmas with your good wishes 圣诞贺卡

'Christmas carol *noun* = CAROL

ˌChristmas 'cracker *noun* = CRACKER (2)

ˌChristmas 'Eve *noun* [U, C] the day before Christmas Day, 24 December; the evening of this day 圣诞节前一天（12 月 24 日）；圣诞夜，平安夜（12 月 24 日晚）

ˌChristmas 'pudding *noun* [C, U] a hot PUDDING (= a sweet dish) like a dark fruit cake, traditionally eaten in Britain at Christmas （英国传统的）圣诞布丁

ˌChristmas ˈstocking (*also* **stock·ing**) *noun* a long sock which children leave out when they go to bed on Christmas Eve so that it can be filled with presents 圣诞袜（圣诞夜小孩睡前留在外边供装圣诞礼物的长袜）

Christ·massy /ˈkrɪsməsi/ *adj.* (*informal*) typical of Christmas 具有圣诞节特征的： *We put up the decorations and the tree and started to feel Christmassy at last.* 我们布置好了装饰品和圣诞树，终于有了圣诞节的气氛。

Christ·mas·time /ˈkrɪsməstaɪm/ *noun* [U, C] = CHRISTMAS (2)

ˈChristmas tree *noun* an EVERGREEN tree, or an artificial tree that looks similar, that people cover with decorations and coloured lights and have in their homes or outside at Christmas 圣诞树

chroma /ˈkrəʊmə; *NAmE* ˈkroʊmə/ *noun* [U] (*specialist*) the degree to which a colour is pure or strong, or the fact that it is pure or strong 色度；彩度；色品饱和度

chro·mat·ic /krəˈmætɪk/ *adj.* (*music* 音) of the **chromatic scale**, a series of musical notes that rise and fall in SEMITONES/HALF STEP 半音（阶）的 ➲ COMPARE DIATONIC

chro·ma·tog·raphy /ˌkrəʊməˈtɒɡrəfi; *NAmE* ˌkroʊməˈtɑːɡ-/ *noun* [U] (*chemistry* 化) the separation of a mixture by passing it through a material through which some parts of the mixture travel further than others 层析，层谱法（利用混合物各部分在介质中的通透距离差异而将其分离的方法） ▸ **chro·ma·to·graph·ic** /krəʊˌmætəˈɡræfɪk; *NAmE* ˌkroʊ-/ *adj.*

chrome /krəʊm; *NAmE* kroʊm/ *noun* [U] a hard shiny metal used especially as a covering which protects another metal; chromium or an ALLOY of chromium and other metals 铬；铬合金

ˌchrome ˈsteel (*also* **ˌchromium ˈsteel**) *noun* [U] a hard steel containing CHROMIUM that is used for making tools 铬钢（用以制作工具）

chro·mium /ˈkrəʊmiəm; *NAmE* ˈkroʊ-/ *noun* [U] (*symb.* **Cr**) a chemical element. Chromium is a hard grey metal that shines brightly when polished and is often used to cover other metals in order to prevent them from RUSTING. 铬： *chromium-plated steel* 镀铬的钢

ˌchromium ˈsteel *noun* [U] = CHROME STEEL

chromo·some /ˈkrəʊməsəʊm; *NAmE* ˈkroʊməsoʊm/ *noun* (*biology* 生) one of the very small structures like threads in the NUCLEI (= central parts) of animal and plant cells, that carry the GENES 染色体 ➲ SEE ALSO SEX CHROMOSOME, X CHROMOSOME, Y CHROMOSOME ➲ WORDFINDER NOTE AT BIOLOGY ▸ **chromo·somal** /ˌkrəʊməˈsəʊməl; *NAmE* ˌkroʊməˈsoʊməl/ *adj.* : *chromosomal abnormalities* 染色体畸变

chron·ic /ˈkrɒnɪk; *NAmE* ˈkrɑːn-/ *adj.* **1** (especially of a disease 尤指疾病) lasting for a long time; difficult to cure or get rid of 长期的；慢性的；难以治愈（或根除）的： *chronic bronchitis/arthritis/asthma* 慢性支气管炎 / 关节炎 / 哮喘 ◇ *the country's chronic unemployment problem* 该国长期存在的失业问题 ◇ *a chronic shortage of housing in rural areas* 农村地区住房的长期匮乏 OPP **acute 2** having had a disease for a long time 长期患病的： *a chronic alcoholic/depressive* 慢性酒精中毒者；长期抑郁症患者 **3** (*BrE, informal*) very bad 糟透的；拙劣的： *The film was just chronic.* 这部电影简直糟透了。 ▸ **chron·ic·al·ly** /ˈkrɒnɪkli; *NAmE* ˈkrɑːn-/ *adv.* : *a hospital for the chronically ill* 慢性病医院

ˌchronic faˈtigue syndrome (*BrE also* **ME**, **my·al·gic en·ceph·alo·my·eli·tis**) *noun* [U] an illness that makes people feel extremely weak and tired and that can last a long time 肌痛性脑脊髓炎；慢性疲劳综合征

chron·icle /ˈkrɒnɪkl; *NAmE* ˈkrɑːn-/ *noun, verb*
■ *noun* a written record of events in the order in which they happened 编年史；历史： *the Anglo-Saxon Chronicle* 《盎格鲁 - 撒克逊人编年史》 ◇ *Her latest novel is a chronicle of life in a Devon village.* 她的最近一部小说是德文郡一个小村庄的生活纪事。
■ *verb* ~ **sth** (*formal*) to record events in the order in which they happened 把…载入编年史；按事件顺序记载： *Her achievements are chronicled in a new biography out this week.* 她的成就已载入本周出版的一本新传记中。 ▸ **chron·ic·ler** /ˈkrɒnɪklə(r); *NAmE* ˈkrɑːn-/ *noun*

chrono- /ˈkrɒnəʊ; *NAmE* ˈkrɑːnoʊ/ *combining form* (in nouns, adjectives and adverbs 构成名词、形容词和副词) connected with time 与时间有关的： *chronological* 按发生时间顺序排列的

chrono·graph /ˈkrɒnəɡrɑːf; *NAmE* ˈkrɑːnəɡræf/ *noun* **1** a device for recording time extremely accurately 计时仪 **2** a STOPWATCH 秒表；跑表

chrono·logic·al /ˌkrɒnəˈlɒdʒɪkl; *NAmE* ˌkrɑːnəˈlɑːdʒ-/ *adj.* **1** (of a number of events 许多事件) arranged in the order in which they happened 按发生时间顺序排列的： *The facts should be presented* ***in chronological order***. 这些事实应按时间先后顺序陈述。 **2** ~ **age** (*formal*) the number of years a person has lived as opposed to their level of physical, mental or emotional development 实际年龄（相对于身体、智力或情感方面的发展而言） ➲ COMPARE MENTAL AGE ▸ **chrono·logic·al·ly** /-kli/ *adv.*

chron·ology /krəˈnɒlədʒi; *NAmE* -ˈnɑːl-/ *noun* (*pl.* **-ies**) [U, C] the order in which a series of events happened; a list of these events in order 按事件发生的年代排列的顺序；年表： *Historians seem to have confused the chronology of these events.* 历史学家好像把这些事件发生的年代顺序搅混了。 ◇ *a chronology of Mozart's life* 莫扎特生平年表

chron·om·eter /krəˈnɒmɪtə(r); *NAmE* -ˈnɑːm-/ *noun* a very accurate clock, especially one used at sea 天文钟（尤用于航海）

chrys·alis /ˈkrɪsəlɪs/ *noun* (*also* **chrys·alid**) the form of an insect, especially a BUTTERFLY or MOTH, while it is changing into an adult inside a hard case, also called a chrysalis （尤指蝴蝶或蛾的）蛹，蛹壳 ➲ VISUAL VOCAB PAGE V13 ➲ COMPARE PUPA

chrys·an·the·mum /krɪˈsænθəməm; -ˈzæn-/ *noun* a large, brightly coloured garden flower that is shaped like a ball and is made up of many long narrow PETALS 菊花 ➲ VISUAL VOCAB PAGE V11

chub /tʃʌb/ *noun* (*pl.* **chub**) a FRESHWATER fish with a thick body 查布鱼；圆鳍雅罗鱼；白鲑

chubby /ˈtʃʌbi/ *adj.* (**chub·bier**, **chub·bi·est**) slightly fat in a way that people usually find attractive 胖乎乎的；圆胖的： ***chubby cheeks/fingers/hands*** 胖乎乎的脸颊 / 手指 / 手 ▸ **chub·bi·ness** *noun* [U]

chuck /tʃʌk/ *verb, noun*
■ *verb* **1** (*informal, especially BrE*) to throw sth carelessly or without much thought（随便或贸然地）扔，抛： ~ **sth** (+ **adv./prep.**) *He chucked the paper in a drawer.* 他把那篇文章顺手丢进了抽屉。 ◇ ~ **sb sth** *Chuck me the newspaper, would you?* 请你把报纸扔给我好吗？ ➲ SYNONYMS AT THROW **2** (*informal*) to give up or stop doing sth 放弃；停止；终止： ~ **sth** *You haven't chucked your job!* 你还没有辞掉你的工作！ ◇ ~ **sth in/up** *I'm going to* ***chuck it all in*** (= give up my job) *and go abroad.* 我要离职出国。 **3** ~ **sb** (*BrE, informal*) to leave your boyfriend or girlfriend and stop having a relationship with him or her 与…终止（或断绝）恋爱关系： *Has he chucked her?* 他把她甩了吗？ **4** ~ **sth** (*informal*) to throw sth away 扔掉；丢弃；抛弃： *That's no good—just chuck it.* 那东西毫无用处，扔掉吧。
IDM **chuck sb under the chin** (*old-fashioned*) to touch sb gently under the chin in a friendly way 轻抚某人的下巴 **it's ˈchucking it down** (*BrE, informal*) it's raining heavily 下着倾盆大雨；大雨滂沱
PHR V **ˌchuck sth↔aˈway** | **ˌchuck sth↔ˈout** (*informal*) to throw sth away 扔掉；丢弃；抛弃： *Those old clothes can be chucked out.* 那些旧衣服可以扔掉了。 **ˌchuck sb ˈoff (sth)** | **ˌchuck sb ˈout (of sth)** (*informal*) to force sb to leave a place or a job 撵走；解雇： *They got chucked off the bus.* 他们被赶下了公共汽车。 ◇ *You can't just chuck*

C

him out. 你不能只把他解雇了事。

■**noun 1** [C] a part of a tool such as a DRILL that can be adjusted to hold sth tightly（固定钻头等用的）夹盘，卡盘，夹头 ➲ VISUAL VOCAB PAGE V21 **2** [sing.] (*NEngE, informal*) a friendly way of addressing sb（熟人之间友好的称呼）小亲亲：*What's up with you, chuck?* 你怎么了，亲爱的？ **3** (*also* ˌ**chuck** ˈ**steak**) [U] meat from the shoulder of a cow 牛肩胛肉

ˌ**chucker** ˈ**out** *noun* (*BrE, informal*) a person employed to make people leave a social event if they have not been invited or if they cause trouble（在社交场合撵走无关人员或闹事者的）护卫，护场员

chuckle /ˈtʃʌkl/ *verb* [I] ~ (**at/about sth**) to laugh quietly 低声轻笑；轻声地笑：*She chuckled at the memory.* 想起这件事她就暗自发笑。▸ **chuckle** *noun*：*She gave a chuckle of delight.* 她高兴得轻声笑了出来。

chuffed /tʃʌft/ *adj.* [not before noun] ~ (**about sth**) (*BrE, informal*) very pleased 很愉快；很高兴；很满意

chuff·ing /ˈtʃʌfɪŋ/ *adj.* (*NEngE, slang*) a mild swear word that some people use when they are annoyed, to avoid saying 'fucking' 昏了头的，不像话的（用以替代 fucking）：*The whole chuffing world's gone mad.* 全世界的人都他妈的疯了。

chug /tʃʌg/ *verb, noun*

■**verb** (**-gg-**) **1** [I] (+ **adv./prep.**) to move making the sound of an engine running slowly（发动机缓慢运转时）发出突突声：*The boat chugged down the river.* 小船突突地沿江而下。 **2** [T] ~ **sth** (*NAmE, slang*) to drink all of sth quickly without stopping 一饮而尽；一口气喝完

■**noun** the sound made by a chugging engine（发动机的）突突声

chug·ger /ˈtʃʌgə(r)/ *noun* a person who approaches people in the street, asking them to give money to a particular charity 街头慈善募捐者 ➲ MORE LIKE THIS 1, page R25 ORIGIN From **charity** and **mugger**. 源自 charity 和 mugger。

chukka /ˈtʃʌkə/ *noun* one of the periods of 7½ minutes into which a game of POLO is divided（马球比赛的）一局（7 分半钟）

chum /tʃʌm/ *noun* (*old-fashioned, informal*) a friend 朋友；友人；伙伴：*an old school chum* 老校友

chummy /ˈtʃʌmi/ *adj.* (*old-fashioned, informal*) very friendly 非常友好的；亲切的 ▸ **chum·mi·ness** *noun* [U]

chump /tʃʌmp/ *noun* (*old-fashioned, informal*) a stupid person 笨蛋；傻瓜；蠢货：*Don't be such a chump!* 别这么蠢！

chun·der /ˈtʃʌndə(r)/ *verb* [I] (*BrE, informal*) to VOMIT 呕吐；呕出 ▸ **chun·der** *noun* [U]

chunk /tʃʌŋk/ *noun* **1** a thick solid piece that has been cut or broken off sth 厚块；厚片；大块：*a chunk of cheese/masonry* 一块厚厚的奶酪 / 砖石 **2** (*informal*) a fairly large amount of sth 相当大的量：*I've already written a fair chunk of the article.* 我已写出文章相当大的部分。 **3** (*linguistics* 语言) a phrase or group of words which can be learnt as a unit by sb who is learning a language. Examples of chunks are 'Can I have the bill, please?' and 'Pleased to meet you'. 语块（话语组成部分） IDM SEE BLOW *v.*

chunk·ing /ˈtʃʌŋkɪŋ/ *noun* [U] (*linguistics* 语言) the use of chunks in language 组块；断句；分拆；划分话语成分

chunky /ˈtʃʌŋki/ *adj.* (**chunki·er**, **chunki·est**) **1** thick and heavy 粗重的；厚实的；结实的：*a chunky gold bracelet* 沉甸甸的金手镯 ◇ (*BrE*) *a chunky sweater* 厚实的套头毛衣 **2** having a short strong body 敦实的；矮胖的：*a squat chunky man* 矮胖敦实的男人 **3** (of food 食品) containing thick pieces（含有）厚片的，大块的：*chunky marmalade* 含果肉的果酱

chun·ter /ˈtʃʌntə(r)/ *verb* [I] ~ (**on**) (**about sth**) (*BrE, informal*) to talk or complain about sth in a way that other people think is boring or annoying 咕哝；抱怨 SYN **witter**

church 🔑 /tʃɜːtʃ; *NAmE* tʃɜːrtʃ/ *noun* **1** 🔑[C] a building where Christians go to worship（基督教的）教堂，礼拜堂：*a church tower* 教堂塔楼 ◇ *The procession moved into the church.* 人们排着队走进教堂。◇ *church services* 教堂礼拜仪式 **2** 🔑[U] a service or services in a church 礼拜；礼拜仪式：*How often do you **go to church**?* 你多久去教堂做一次礼拜？ ◇ (*BrE*) *They're **at church*** (= attending a church service). 他们在做礼拜。 ◇ (*NAmE*) *They're **in church**.* 他们在做礼拜。◇ *Church is at 9 o'clock.* 礼拜仪式 9 点钟开始。 ➲ COLLOCATIONS AT RELIGION ➲ NOTE AT SCHOOL **3** 🔑 **Church** [C] a particular group of Christians 基督教教派：*the Anglican Church* 圣公会 ◇ *the Catholic Church* 天主教会 ◇ *the Free Churches* 自由教会 ➲ SEE ALSO DENOMINATION (1) **4** 🔑 (**the**) **Church** [sing.] the ministers of the Christian religion; the institution of the Christian religion 基督教牧师；基督教机构：*The Church has a duty to condemn violence.* 基督教会有义务谴责暴力。 ◇ *the conflict between Church and State* 教会与政府的冲突 ◇ *to go into the Church* (= to become a Christian minister) 成为基督教牧师 IDM SEE BROAD *adj.*

church·goer /ˈtʃɜːtʃgəʊə(r); *NAmE* ˈtʃɜːrtʃgoʊər/ *noun* a person who goes to church services regularly 按时去教堂做礼拜的人 ▸ **church·going** *noun* [U]

church·man /ˈtʃɜːtʃmən; *NAmE* ˈtʃɜːrtʃ-/ *noun* (*pl.* **-men** /-mən/) a member of the Christian CLERGY or of a church（基督教）圣职人员，神职人员 ➲ COMPARE CHURCHWOMAN, CLERGYMAN, CLERGYWOMAN

the ˌ**Church of** ˈ**England** *noun* (*abbr.* **CE**, **C of E**) [sing.] the official Church in England, whose leader is the Queen or King 英国国教会；英格兰圣公会

the ˌ**Church of** ˈ**Scotland** *noun* [sing.] the official (Presbyterian) Church in Scotland 苏格兰长老会

church·war·den /ˌtʃɜːtʃˈwɔːdn; *NAmE* ˌtʃɜːrtʃˈwɔːrdn/ *noun* (in the Anglican Church 圣公会的) a person who is chosen by the members of a church to take care of church property and money 堂会理事（管理教会财务）

church·woman /ˈtʃɜːtʃwʊmən; *NAmE* ˈtʃɜːrtʃ-/ *noun* (*pl.* **church·women** /-wɪmɪn/) a female member of a Christian church（基督教）女信徒，女教友，女教徒 ➲ COMPARE CHURCHMAN, CLERGYWOMAN

churchy /ˈtʃɜːtʃi; *NAmE* ˈtʃɜːr-/ *adj.* (**church·ier**, **churchi·est**) (*disapproving*) (of a person 人) religious in a way that involves going to church, PRAYING, etc. a lot, but often not accepting other people's views 表现得热衷教会活动的；恪守教会仪式的

church·yard /ˈtʃɜːtʃjɑːd; *NAmE* ˈtʃɜːrtʃjɑːrd/ *noun* an area of land around a church, often used for burying people in 教堂庭院（常用作墓地） ➲ COMPARE CEMETERY, GRAVEYARD (1)

churi·dar /ˈtʃʊrɪdɑː(r)/ *noun* tight trousers worn with a KAMEEZ or KURTA （配克米兹或库尔塔长袖上衣穿的）紧身长裤

churl /tʃɜːl; *NAmE* tʃɜːrl/ *noun* (*old-fashioned*) a rude unpleasant person 粗鲁无礼的人；粗野的人

churl·ish /ˈtʃɜːlɪʃ; *NAmE* ˈtʃɜːrlɪʃ/ *adj.* (*formal*) rude or bad-tempered 粗鲁无礼的；粗野的；脾气坏的：*It would be churlish to refuse such a generous offer.* 拒绝这样一个慷慨的提议未免失礼。 ▸ **churl·ish·ly** *adv.* **churl·ish·ness** *noun* [U]

churn /tʃɜːn; *NAmE* tʃɜːrn/ *verb, noun*

■**verb 1** [I, T] if water, mud, etc. **churns**, or if sth **churns it** (**up**), it moves or is moved around violently 剧烈搅动；（使）猛烈翻腾：~ (**up**) *The water churned beneath the huge ship.* 水在巨轮下面剧烈翻滚。◇ ~ **sth** (**up**) *Vast crowds had churned the field into a sea of mud.* 大批大批的人把场地踩得一片泥泞。 **2** [I, T] ~ (**sth**) if your stomach **churns** or if sth **churns** your stomach, you feel a strong, unpleasant feeling of worry, disgust or fear 反胃，恶心（忧虑、厌恶或恐惧的强烈感觉）：*My stomach churned as* *the names were read out.* 名单一宣布，我就觉得胃里翻腾得难受。 **3** [I, T] ~ (**sb**) (**up**) to feel or to make sb feel upset or emotionally confused （使）感到不安，心烦意乱： *Conflicting emotions churned inside him.* 相互矛盾的情绪使他感到心烦意乱。 **4** [T] ~ **sth** to turn and stir milk in a special container in order to make butter 用搅乳器搅（乳，以制作黄油）

PHR V ˌ**churn sth**↔ˈ**out** (*informal, often disapproving*) to produce sth quickly and in large amounts （粗制滥造地）大量生产，大量炮制

■ ***noun*** **1** a machine in which milk or cream is shaken to make butter （制作黄油的）搅乳器 **2** (*BrE*) a large metal container in which milk was carried from a farm in the past （旧时）盛奶大罐，奶桶

ˈ**churn rate** *noun* (*business* 商) the number of people who stop using a product and change to another or who leave the company they work for and go to another 客户流失率；员工流失率

chute /ʃuːt/ *noun* **1** a tube or passage down which people or things can slide（人或物可顺势滑下的）斜槽，溜道： *a* ***water chute*** (= at a swimming pool) 滑水槽 ◇ *a* ***laundry/rubbish/garbage chute*** (= from the upper floors of a high building) 洗衣滑槽；垃圾道（高层建筑上面各层用的） **2** (*informal*) = PARACHUTE

ˌ**Chutes and ˈLadders™** *noun* [U] (*US*) a children's game played on a special board with pictures of chutes and ladders on it. Players move their pieces up the ladders to go forward and down the chutes to go back. 滑道梯子棋（儿童游戏，棋盘上有滑道和梯子的图案，棋子遇梯子往前走，遇滑道则往回走） ➲ SEE ALSO SNAKES AND LADDERS

chut·ney /ˈtʃʌtni/ *noun* [U] a cold thick sauce made from fruit, sugar, spices and VINEGAR, eaten with cold meat, cheese, etc. 酸辣酱

chutz·pah /ˈxʊtspə; ˈhʊ-/ *noun* [U] (*often approving*) behaviour, or a person's attitude, that is rude or shocking but so confident that people may feel forced to admire it 无所顾忌；敢作敢为 SYN **nerve**

Ci *abbr.* CURIE 居里（放射性活度单位）

CIA /ˌsiː aɪ ˈeɪ/ *abbr.* Central Intelligence Agency (a department of the US government which collects information about other countries, often secretly) （美国）中央情报局

cia·batta /tʃəˈbætə; -ˈbɑːtə/ *noun* [U, C] (*from Italian*) a type of Italian bread made in a long flat shape; a SANDWICH made with this type of bread 拖鞋面包（一种意大利扁平长面包）；拖鞋三明治

ciao /tʃaʊ/ *exclamation* (*from Italian, informal*) goodbye 再见

ci·cada /sɪˈkɑːdə; *NAmE* sɪˈkeɪdə/ *noun* a large insect with transparent wings, common in hot countries. The male makes a continuous high sound after dark by making two MEMBRANES (= pieces of thin skin) on its body VIBRATE (= move very fast). 蝉；知了

CID /ˌsiː aɪ ˈdiː/ *abbr.* Criminal Investigation Department (the department of the British police force that is responsible for solving crimes) （英国警察）刑事调查部

-cide *combining form* (in nouns 构成名词) **1** the act of killing 杀死；毁灭： *suicide* 自杀 ◇ *genocide* 种族灭绝 **2** a person or thing that kills 杀手；杀灭剂： *insecticide* 杀虫剂 ▸ **-cidal** (in adjectives 构成形容词)： *homicidal* 有杀人倾向的

cider /ˈsaɪdə(r)/ *noun* **1** (*BrE*) (*NAmE* ˈ**hard cider**) [U, C] an alcoholic drink made from the juice of apples 苹果酒： ***dry/sweet cider*** 干 / 甜苹果酒 ◇ *cider apples* 酿造果酒的苹果 ◇ *a cider press* (= for squeezing the juice from apples) 苹果榨汁器 **2** (*NAmE*) [U, C] a drink made from the juice of apples that does not contain alcohol 苹果汁 **3** [C] a glass of cider 一杯苹果酒（或苹果汁） ➲ COMPARE PERRY

cigar /sɪˈɡɑː(r)/ *noun* a roll of dried TOBACCO leaves that people smoke, like a cigarette but bigger and without paper around it 雪茄烟： *cigar smoke* 雪茄烟雾 IDM SEE CLOSE² *adj.*

cig·ar·ette 🔑 /ˌsɪɡəˈret; *NAmE* ˈsɪɡəret/ *noun* a thin tube of paper filled with TOBACCO, for smoking 香烟；纸烟；卷烟： *a* ***packet/pack of cigarettes*** 一包香烟 ◇ *to light a cigarette* 点燃一支香烟

cigaˈrette end (*BrE*) (*also* **cigaˈrette butt** *NAmE, BrE*) *noun* the part of a cigarette that is left when sb has finished smoking it 香烟头；烟蒂

cigaˈrette holder *noun* a narrow tube for holding a cigarette in while you are smoking 香烟烟嘴

cigaˈrette lighter *noun* = LIGHTER (1)

cigaˈrette paper *noun* a thin piece of paper in which people roll TOBACCO to make their own cigarettes 卷烟纸

cig·ar·illo /ˌsɪɡəˈrɪləʊ; *NAmE* -loʊ/ *noun* (*pl.* **-os**) a small CIGAR 小雪茄

ciggy /ˈsɪɡi/ *noun* (*pl.* **-ies**) (*informal*) a cigarette 香烟

ci·lan·tro /sɪˈlæntrəʊ; *NAmE* -troʊ/ *noun* [U] (*NAmE*) the leaves of the CORIANDER plant, used in cooking as a HERB 芫荽叶，香菜叶（用于调味） ➲ VISUAL VOCAB PAGE V35

cil·iary muscle /ˈsɪliəri mʌsl/ *noun* (*anatomy* 解) a muscle in the eye that controls how much the LENS curves 睫状肌（控制眼睛晶状体弯曲度） ➲ VISUAL VOCAB PAGE V64

C.-in-C. /ˌsiː ɪn ˈsiː/ *abbr.* COMMANDER-IN-CHIEF 总司令；最高统帅

cinch /sɪntʃ/ *noun, verb*

■ ***noun*** [sing.] (*informal*) **1** something that is very easy 很容易的事；小菜 SYN **doddle**： *The first question is a cinch.* 第一个问题是小菜一碟。 **2** (*especially NAmE*) a thing that is certain to happen; a person who is certain to do sth 必然发生的事；必做某事的人： *He's a cinch to win the race.* 这场比赛他必赢无疑。

■ ***verb*** **1** ~ **sth** (*especially NAmE*) to fasten sth tightly around your waist; to be fastened around sb's waist 在腰间系住 **2** ~ **sth** (*NAmE*) to fasten a GIRTH around a horse （给马）系上肚带 **3** ~ **sth** (*NAmE, informal*) to make sth certain 弄确实；弄清楚；确保

cin·der /ˈsɪndə(r)/ *noun* [usually pl.] a small piece of ASH or partly burnt coal, wood, etc. that is no longer burning but may still be hot 灰烬；余烬： *a cinder track* (= a track for runners made with finely crushed cinders) 用细煤渣铺成的跑道 IDM SEE BURN *v.*

ˈ**cinder block** (*NAmE*) (*BrE* ˈ**breeze block**) *noun* a light building block, made of sand, coal ASHES and CEMENT 煤渣砌块，焦渣砖（用沙、煤渣和水泥制成）

Cin·der·ella /ˌsɪndəˈrelə/ *noun* [usually sing.] a person or thing that has been ignored and deserves to receive more attention 灰姑娘；未得到应有注意的人（或事物）： *For years radio has been the Cinderella of the media world.* 多年来电台广播在传媒界中一直不受重视。 ➲ MORE LIKE THIS 16, page R27 ORIGIN From the European fairy tale about a beautiful girl, **Cinderella**, who was treated in a cruel way by her two ugly sisters. She had to do all the work and received no reward or thanks until she met and married Prince Charming. 源自欧洲童话，美丽的灰姑娘（Cinderella）受两个丑陋的姐姐虐待，被迫干所有的活儿，毫无回报，直至后来遇上了白马王子并与之缔结良缘。

cine /ˈsɪni/ *adj.* [only before noun] (*BrE*) connected with films/movies and the film/movie industry 电影的；电影业的： *a* ***cine camera/film/photographer*** 电影摄影机 / 胶片 / 摄影师

cine·aste (*also* **cine·ast**) /ˈsɪniæst/ *noun* (*from French*) a person who knows a lot about films/movies and is very enthusiastic about them 电影爱好者；影迷

cin·ema 🔑 /ˈsɪnəmə/ *noun* **1** 🔑 (*especially BrE*) (*NAmE usually* ˈ**movie theater, theater**) [C] a building in which films/movies are shown 电影院： *the local cinema* 当地的电影院 ➲ VISUAL VOCAB PAGE V3 **2** **the cinema** [sing.] (*BrE*) (*NAmE* **the movies**) when you go to **the cinema** or to **the movies**, you go to a cinema/movie theater to see a film/movie （去电影院）看电影： *I used to go to the cinema every week.* 我过去每周都去看电影。 **3** [U, sing.] (*especially BrE*) (*NAmE usually* **the movies**) films/movies as an art or an industry 电影艺术；电影制片业： *one of the great successes of British cinema* 英国电影艺术的巨大成就之一 ➲ WORDFINDER NOTE AT FILM

'cinema-goer *noun* (*BrE*) = FILM-GOER

cine·mat·ic /ˌsɪnəˈmætɪk/ *adj.* (*specialist*) connected with films/movies and how they are made 电影的；电影制作的： ***cinematic effects/techniques*** 电影制作效果 / 技术

cine·ma·tog·raphy /ˌsɪnəməˈtɒɡrəfi; *NAmE* -ˈtɑːɡ-/ *noun* [U] (*specialist*) the art or process of making films/movies, especially the photography and CAMERAWORK 电影摄制艺术；电影摄制方法 ▸ **cine·ma·tog·raph·er** /ˌsɪnəməˈtɒɡrəfə(r); *NAmE* -ˈtɑːɡ-/ *noun* **cine·ma·tog·raph·ic** /ˌsɪnəmətəˈɡræfɪk/ *adj.*

cine·phile /ˈsɪnifaɪl/ *noun* a person who is very interested in films/movies 电影爱好者；影迷

cinna·bar /ˈsɪnəbɑː(r)/ *noun* [U] **1** a bright red mineral that is sometimes used to give colour to things 辰砂，朱砂（可用作颜料） **2** the bright red colour of cinnabar 朱红色

cin·na·mon /ˈsɪnəmən/ *noun* [U] the inner BARK of a SE Asian tree, used in cooking as a spice, especially to give flavour to sweet foods 肉桂皮，桂皮香料（东南亚一种树的内层树皮，尤用于甜食调味） ➲ VISUAL VOCAB PAGE V35

ci·pher (*also* **cy·pher**) /ˈsaɪfə(r)/ *noun* **1** [U, C] a secret way of writing, especially one in which a set of letters or symbols is used to represent others 密码；暗号 SYN **code**: *a message in cipher* 密码信 ➲ SEE ALSO DECIPHER **2** [C] (*formal, disapproving*) a person or thing of no importance 无足轻重的人；无关紧要的东西 **3** (*BrE*) the first letters of sb's name combined in a design and used to mark things （姓名首字母的）拼合字，花押

circa /ˈsɜːkə; *NAmE* ˈsɜːrkə/ *prep.* (*from Latin*) (*abbr.* **c**) (used with dates 与日期连用) about 大约： *born circa 150 BC* 生于约公元前 150 年

cir·ca·dian /sɜːˈkeɪdiən; *NAmE* sɜːrˈk-/ *adj.* [only before noun] (*specialist*) connected with the changes in the bodies of people or animals over each period of 24 hours（每 24 小时人或动物体内变化）昼夜节律的，生理节奏的

cir·cle /ˈsɜːkl; *NAmE* ˈsɜːrkl/ *noun, verb*

■ *noun* **1** a completely round flat shape 圆；圆形： *Cut out two circles of paper.* 剪出两个圆形纸片。 ➲ PICTURE AT CONIC SECTION ➲ SEE ALSO SEMICIRCLE **2** the line that forms the edge of a circle 圆周；圆圈： *Draw a circle.* 画一个圆圈。 ◇ *She walked the horse round **in a circle**.* 她牵着马遛圈子。 ➲ SEE ALSO ANTARCTIC CIRCLE, ARCTIC CIRCLE, TURNING CIRCLE **3** a thing or a group of people or things shaped like a circle 圆形物；环状物；圈；环： *a circle of trees/chairs* 一圈树 / 椅子 ◇ *The children stood in a circle.* 孩子们站成一圈。 ➲ SEE ALSO CORN CIRCLE, CROP CIRCLE **4** (*also* **bal·cony**) an upper floor of a theatre or cinema/movie theater where the seats are arranged in curved rows （剧院或电影院的）弧形楼座： *We had seats in the circle.* 我们坐的是楼座座位。 ➲ SEE ALSO DRESS CIRCLE ➲ WORDFINDER NOTE AT THEATRE **5** a group of people who are connected because they have the same interests, jobs, etc.（相同兴趣、职业等的人形成的）圈子，阶层，界： *the family circle* 家庭圈子 ◇ *She's well known in theatrical circles.* 她在戏剧界赫赫有名。 ◇ *a large **circle of friends*** 一大群朋友 ➲ SEE ALSO CHARMED CIRCLE, INNER CIRCLE, VICIOUS CIRCLE

IDM **come, turn, etc. full 'circle** to return to the situation in which you started, after a series of events or experiences（事情或经历）兜了一圈回到原处 **go round in 'circles** to work hard at sth or discuss sth without

▼ COLLOCATIONS 词语搭配

Cinema / the movies 电影

Watching 观看

- **go to/take sb to** (**see**) a film/movie 去 / 带某人去看电影
- **go to/sit in** (*BrE*) the cinema/(*NAmE*) the (movie) theater 去 / 在看电影
- **rent** a film/movie/DVD 租借影片 / DVD 光碟
- **download/stream** a film/movie 下载 / 用串流传输方式播放电影
- **burn/copy/rip** a DVD 刻录 / 复制 / 转压一张 DVD 碟片
- **see/watch** a film/movie/DVD/preview/trailer 观看电影 / DVD 碟片 / 预映 / 预告片

Showing 放映；播放

- **show/screen** a film/movie 放映电影
- **promote/distribute/review** a film/movie 宣传 / 发行 / 评论电影
- (*BrE*) **be on at** the cinema 在电影院上映
- **be released on/come out on/be out on** DVD 发行 DVD
- **captivate/delight/grip/thrill** the audience 使观众着迷 / 高兴 / 感兴趣 / 激动
- **do well/badly** at the box office 票房好 / 不好
- **get a lot of/live up to the** hype 受到大肆炒作；与天花乱坠的广告宣传相符

Film-making 电影制作

- **write/co-write** a film/movie/script/screenplay 写 / 合写一部电影剧本
- **direct/produce/make/shoot/edit** a film/movie/sequel 导演 / 制作 / 拍摄 / 编辑电影 / 续集
- **make** a romantic comedy/a thriller/an action movie 拍摄一部浪漫喜剧 / 惊悚片 / 动作片
- **do/work on** a sequel/remake 拍摄续集；重拍
- **film/shoot** the opening scene/an action sequence/footage (of sth) 拍摄（…的）开场戏 / 一套动作 / 连续镜头
- **compose/create/do/write** the soundtrack 制作电影声带
- **cut/edit** (**out**) a scene/sequence 剪辑掉一个镜头 / 一组镜头

Acting 表演

- **have/get/do** an audition 试演
- **get/have/play** a leading/starring/supporting role 得以饰演 / 饰演主角 / 配角
- **play** a character/James Bond/the bad guy 饰演一个人物 / 詹姆斯·邦德 / 反面角色
- **act in/appear in/star in** a film/movie/remake 出演 / 主演一部影片 / 翻拍电影
- **do/perform/attempt** a stunt 做 / 尝试特技表演
- **work in/make it big in** Hollywood 在好莱坞工作 / 取得成功
- **forge/carve/make/pursue** a career in Hollywood 在好莱坞闯出 / 追求一番事业

Describing films 描述电影

- the camera **pulls back/pans over sth/zooms in** (**on sth**) 摄影机拉回 / 追拍 / 推近…
- the camera **focuses on sth/lingers on sth** 摄影机聚焦于 / 长时间拍摄某物
- **shoot sb/show sb** in extreme close-up 用特写镜头拍摄 / 表现某人
- **use** odd/unusual camera angles 采用奇特的 / 不同寻常的摄影机角度
- **be filmed/shot** on location/in a studio 在外景地 / 摄影棚拍摄
- **be set/take place** in London/in the '60s 以伦敦 / 60 年代为背景
- **have** a happy ending/plot twist 有美满的结局 / 出人意料的情节转折

circles 圆

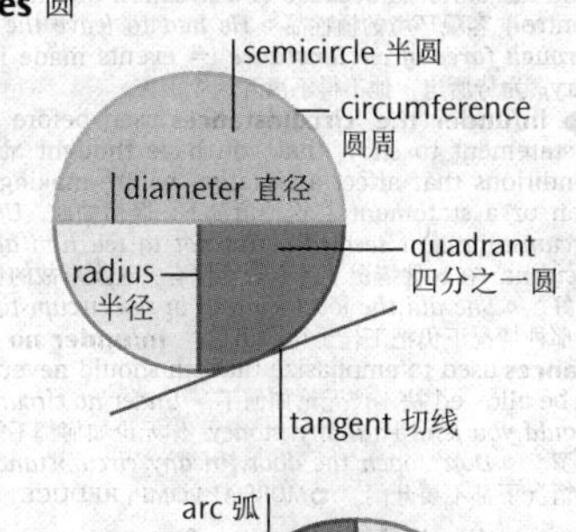

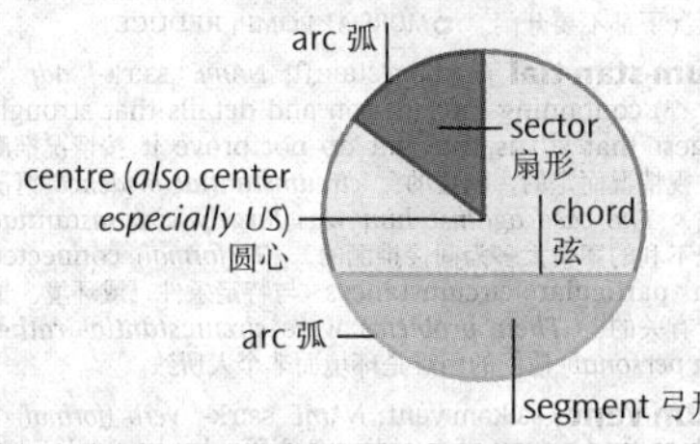

making any progress 在原地绕圈子；总是回到同一个问题 **run round in 'circles** (*informal*) to be busy doing sth without achieving anything important or making progress 徒劳无功；瞎忙；空忙

■ ***verb*** **1** [I, T] to move in a circle, especially in the air （尤指在空中）盘旋，环行，转圈： **~ (around) (above/over sb/sth)** *Seagulls circled around above his head.* 海鸥在他的头顶上盘旋。◇ **~ sth** *The plane circled the airport to burn up excess fuel.* 飞机在机场上空盘旋以耗掉多余的燃料。 **2** [T] **~ sth** to draw a circle around sth 围绕…画圈；圈出；圈起： *Spelling mistakes are circled in red ink.* 拼写错误都用红笔圈了出来。

IDM **circle the 'wagons** (*NAmE*) to join together with people who have the same ideas and beliefs as you, and avoid contact with those who do not, who may threaten or attack you （联合理念相同者）结成统一战线： *When your way of life is threatened, you have to circle the wagons and defend yourself.* 当你的生活方式受到威胁时，你必须与他人结盟保护自己。 ORIGIN From the practice of arranging a WAGON TRAIN in a circle to defend against attack. 源自将马拉篷车队围成一圈以抵御进攻的做法。

cir·clet /'sɜːklət; *NAmE* 'sɜːrk-/ *noun* a round band made of PRECIOUS METAL, flowers, etc., worn around the head for decoration 圆箍饰环，环形饰物（用贵重金属、花等制作，戴在头上）

cir·cuit /'sɜːkɪt; *NAmE* 'sɜːrkɪt/ *noun* **1** a line, route or journey around a place 环行；环行路线： *The race ended with eight laps of a city centre circuit.* 比赛以环绕城中心跑八圈结束。◇ *The earth takes a year to make a circuit of* (= go around) *the sun.* 地球绕太阳运行一周需要一年的时间。 **2** the complete path of wires and equipment along which an electric current flows 电路；线路： *an electrical circuit* 电路 ◇ *a circuit diagram* (= one showing all the connections in the different parts of the circuit) 电路图 ➲ SEE ALSO INTEGRATED CIRCUIT, PRINTED CIRCUIT, SHORT CIRCUIT **3** (in sport 体育运动) a series of games or matches in which the same players regularly take part 巡回赛： *the women's tennis circuit* 女子网球巡回赛 **4** a track for cars or motorcycles to race around 赛车道 **5** a series of places or events of a particular kind at which the same people appear or take part 巡回；巡游： *the lecture/cabaret circuit* 巡回讲学；卡巴莱歌舞巡回表演 ➲ SEE ALSO CLOSED-CIRCUIT TELEVISION **6** a regular journey made by a judge to hear court cases in each of the courts of law in a particular area （法官的）巡回审判： *a circuit court/judge* 巡回法院 / 法官 ➲ MORE LIKE THIS 20, page R27

'circuit board *noun* a board that holds electrical circuits inside a piece of electrical equipment 电路板；线路板

'circuit breaker *noun* a device that can automatically stop an electric current if it becomes dangerous （自动断电的）断路器

cir·cu·it·ous /sə'kjuːɪtəs; *NAmE* sər'k-/ *adj.* (*formal*) (of a route or journey 路线或旅程) long and not direct 迂回的；绕道的；曲折的 SYN **roundabout** ▸ **cir·cu·it·ous·ly** *adv.*

cir·cuit·ry /'sɜːkɪtri; *NAmE* 'sɜːrk-/ *noun* [U] a system of electrical CIRCUITS or the equipment that forms this 电路系统；电路；电路装置

'circuit training *noun* [U] a type of training in sport in which different exercises are each done for a short time 循环训练（轮番做不同的体育运动，每种只做很短时间）

cir·cu·lar /'sɜːkjələ(r); *NAmE* 'sɜːrk-/ *adj., noun*

■ ***adj.*** **1** shaped like a circle; round 圆形的；环形的；圆的： *a circular building* 圆形建筑物 **2** moving around in a circle 环行的；绕圈的： *a circular tour of the city* 环城游览 **3** (of an argument or a theory 论点或理论) using an idea or a statement to prove sth which is then used to prove the idea or statement at the beginning 循环论证的（以一种观点证明另一观点，接着再用后一种观点反过来去证明前一观点） **4** (of a letter 信函) sent to a large number of people 大量送发的；传阅的 ▸ **cir·cu·lar·ity** /ˌsɜːkjə'lærəti; *NAmE* ˌsɜːrk-/ *noun* [U]: *There is a dangerous circularity about this argument.* 这个论点存在着危险的循环论证。

■ ***noun*** a printed letter, notice or advertisement that is sent to a large number of people at the same time （同时送达很多人的）印刷信函（或通知、广告）

ˌcircular 'saw (*NAmE also* **'buzz saw**) *noun* a SAW in the form of a metal disc that turns quickly, driven by a motor, and is used for cutting wood, etc. 圆锯

cir·cu·late /'sɜːkjəleɪt; *NAmE* 'sɜːrk-/ *verb* **1** [I, T] when a liquid, gas or air **circulates** or **is circulated**, it moves continuously around a place or system （液体或气体）环流，循环： *The condition prevents the blood from circulating freely.* 这种病会阻碍血液的畅通循环。◇ **~ sth** *Cooled air is circulated throughout the building.* 冷气在整座大楼循环。 **2** [I, T] **~ (sth)** if a story, an idea, information, etc. **circulates** or if you **circulate** it, it spreads or it is passed from one person to another 传播；流传；散布： *Rumours began to circulate about his financial problems.* 有关他财务问题的谣言开始流传开来。 **3** [T] **~ sth (to sb)** to send goods or information to all the people in a group 传送；传递；传阅： *The document will be circulated to all members.* 这份文件将在所有成员间传阅。 **4** [I] to move around a group, especially at a party, talking to different people （尤指在聚会上）往来应酬，周旋

cir·cu·la·tion /ˌsɜːkjə'leɪʃn; *NAmE* ˌsɜːrk-/ *noun* **1** [U] the movement of blood around the body 血液循环： *Regular exercise will improve blood circulation.* 经常锻炼会促进血液循环。◇ *to have* ***good/bad circulation*** 血液循环良好 / 不畅 **2** [U] the passing or spreading of sth from one person or place to another 传递；流传；流通： *the* ***circulation of money/information/ideas*** 货币的流通；消息的传播；观念的流行 ◇ *A number of forged tickets are* ***in circulation.*** 有一些假入场券在流通。◇ *The coins were* ***taken out of circulation.*** 这种硬币已停止流通。◇ *Copies of the magazine were* ***withdrawn from circulation.*** 这期杂志有不少已从市场上收回。 **3** [U] the fact that sb takes part in social activities at a particular time （某段时间的）社交活动，交际： *Anne has been ill but now she's* ***back in circulation.*** 安妮一直生病，但现在又回来参加社交活动了。◇ ***I was out of circulation*** *for months after the baby was born.* 孩子出生后我有几个月都没有参加社交活动。 **4** [C, usually sing.] the usual number of copies of a newspaper or magazine that are sold each day, week, etc. （报刊）发行量，销售量： *a daily circulation of more than one million* 日发行量超过一百万份 **5** [U, C] the movement of sth (for example air, water, gas, etc.) around an area or inside a system or machine（气、水等的）环流，循环

cir·cu·la·tory /ˌsɜːkjəˈleɪtəri; *NAmE* ˈsɜːrkjələtɔːri/ *adj.* relating to the circulation of the blood 血液循环的

C

cir·cum·cise /ˈsɜːkəmsaɪz; *NAmE* ˈsɜːrk-/ *verb* **1 ~ sb** to remove the FORESKIN of a boy or man for religious or medical reasons（因宗教或医学原因）对（男子）行割礼，环切（男子）的包皮 **2 ~ sb** to cut off part of the sex organs of a girl or woman 切除（女子）的阴蒂

cir·cum·ci·sion /ˌsɜːkəmˈsɪʒn; *NAmE* ˌsɜːrk-/ *noun* [U, C] the act of circumcising sb; the religious ceremony when sb, especially a baby, is circumcised 包皮环切术；阴蒂切除术；（宗教仪式尤指为男婴施行的）切礼

cir·cum·fer·ence /səˈkʌmfərəns; *NAmE* sərˈk-/ *noun* [C, U] a line that goes around a circle or any other curved shape; the length of this line 圆周；圆周长：*the circumference of the earth* 地球的周长 ◇ *The earth is almost 25 000 miles **in circumference**.* 地球的周长大约为 25 000 英里。➲ PICTURE AT CIRCLE ➲ COMPARE PERIMETER

cir·cum·flex /ˈsɜːkəmfleks; *NAmE* ˈsɜːrk-/ (*also* **ˌcircum·flex ˈaccent**) *noun* the mark placed over a vowel in some languages to show how it should be pronounced, as over the *o* in *rôle* 音调符号（标在元音字母上表发音，如 rôle 一词中 o 字母上的符号）➲ COMPARE ACUTE ACCENT, GRAVE², TILDE, UMLAUT

cir·cum·lo·cu·tion /ˌsɜːkəmləˈkjuːʃn; *NAmE* ˌsɜːrk-/ *noun* [U, C] (*formal*) using more words than are necessary, instead of speaking or writing in a clear, direct way 迂回曲折的说法

cir·cum·navi·gate /ˌsɜːkəmˈnævɪɡeɪt; *NAmE* ˌsɜːrk-/ *verb* **~ sth** (*formal*) to sail all the way around sth, especially all the way around the world 环绕…航行；（尤指）环绕地球航行 ▸ **cir·cum·navi·ga·tion** /ˌsɜːkəmˌnævɪˈɡeɪʃn; *NAmE* ˌsɜːrk-/ *noun* [U]

cir·cum·scribe /ˈsɜːkəmskraɪb; *NAmE* ˈsɜːrk-/ *verb* **1** [often passive] **~ sth** (*formal*) to limit sb/sth's freedom, rights, power, etc. 限制，约束（自由、权利、权力等）SYN **restrict**: *The power of the monarchy was circumscribed by the new law.* 君主统治的权力受到了新法律的制约。**2 ~ sth** (*specialist*) to draw a circle around another shape 画…的外接圆 ▸ **cir·cum·scrip·tion** /ˌsɜːkəmˈskrɪpʃn; *NAmE* ˌsɜːrk-/ *noun* [U]

cir·cum·spect /ˈsɜːkəmspekt; *NAmE* ˈsɜːrk-/ *adj.* (*formal*) thinking very carefully about sth before doing it, because there may be risks involved 小心谨慎的；考虑周密的；慎重的 SYN **cautious** ▸ **cir·cum·spec·tion** /ˌsɜːkəmˈspekʃn; *NAmE* ˌsɜːrk-/ *noun* [U] **cir·cum·spect·ly** *adv.*

cir·cum·stance 🔑 AW /ˈsɜːkəmstəns; -stɑːns; -stæns; *NAmE* ˈsɜːrkəmstæns/ *noun* **1** 🔑 [C, usually pl.] the conditions and facts that are connected with and affect a situation, an event or an action 条件；环境；状况：*The company reserves the right to cancel this agreement in certain circumstances.* 本公司保留在一定条件下取消这项协议的权利。◇ *changing social and political circumstances* 正在变化的社会和政治环境 ◇ *I know I can trust her in any circumstance.* 我知道我在任何情况下都能信任她。◇ *Police said there were no **suspicious circumstances** surrounding the boy's death.* 警方说关于男孩死亡一事没有发现可疑的情况。◇ *The ship sank in mysterious circumstances.* 那艘船神秘地沉没了。◇ *She never discovered the true circumstances of her birth.* 她从未弄清她身世的真相。➲ SYNONYMS AT SITUATION **2** 🔑 **circumstances** [pl.] the conditions of a person's life, especially the money they have 境况；境遇；（尤指）经济状况：*Grants are awarded according to your **financial circumstances**.* 补助金根据经济状况发给。◇ ***family/domestic/personal circumstances*** 家庭 / 个人经济状况 **3** [U] (*formal*) situations and events that affect and influence your life and that are not in your control 命运；客观环境：*a **victim of circumstance*** (= a person who has suffered because of a situation that they cannot control) 客观环境的牺牲品 ◇ *He had to leave the country through **force of circumstance*** (= events made it necessary). 为势所迫，他不得不离开这个国家。

IDM **in/under the ˈcircumstances** used before or after a statement to show that you have thought about the conditions that affect a situation before making a decision or a statement 在这种情况下；既然如此：*Under the circumstances, it seemed better not to tell him about the accident.* 在这种情况下，不告诉他有关这次事故的情况似乎更好。◇ *She did the job very well in the circumstances.* 她在那种情况下仍把工作干得很出色。 **in/under no circumstances** used to emphasize that sth should never happen or be allowed 决不；无论如何不：*Under no circumstances should you lend Paul any money.* 你无论如何都不能借钱给保罗。◇ *Don't open the door, in any circumstances.* 在任何情况下都不要开门。➲ MORE AT POMP, REDUCE

cir·cum·stan·tial /ˌsɜːkəmˈstænʃl; *NAmE* ˌsɜːrk-/ *adj.* **1** (*law* 律) containing information and details that strongly suggest that sth is true but do not prove it 按情况推测的；视情况而定的；间接的：*circumstantial evidence* 情况证据 ◇ *The case against him was largely circumstantial.* 对他不利的案情大多为间接推测的。 **2** (*formal*) connected with particular circumstances 与特定条件（或环境、情况）有关的：*Their problems were circumstantial rather than personal.* 他们的困难是环境而非个人所致。

cir·cum·vent /ˌsɜːkəmˈvent; *NAmE* ˌsɜːrk-/ *verb* (*formal*) **1 ~ sth** to find a way of avoiding a difficulty or a rule 设法回避；规避：*They found a way of circumventing the law.* 他们找到了规避法律的途径。 **2 ~ sth** to go or travel around sth that is blocking your way 绕过；绕行；绕道旅行 ▸ **cir·cum·ven·tion** /ˌsɜːkəmˈvenʃn; *NAmE* ˌsɜːrk-/ *noun* [U]

cir·cus /ˈsɜːkəs; *NAmE* ˈsɜːrkəs/ *noun* **1** [C] a group of entertainers, sometimes with trained animals, who perform skilful or amusing acts in a show that travels around to different places 马戏团 **2 the circus** [sing.] a show performed by circus entertainers, usually in a large tent called the BIG TOP 马戏表演（常在大帐篷里进行）：*We took the children to the circus.* 我们带孩子去看了马戏表演。**3** [sing.] (*informal, disapproving*) a group of people or an event that attracts a lot of attention 引人注意的人（或事）；热闹场面：*A media circus surrounded the royal couple wherever they went.* 无论王室夫妇走到何处，他们的身后都会跟着一大群媒体记者。◇ *the American electoral circus* 美国大选的热闹场面 **4** [C] (*BrE*) (used in some place names) a round open area in a town where several streets meet（用于一些地名）圆形广场，圆环（广场），环形交叉路口：*Piccadilly Circus* 皮卡迪利广场 **5** [C] (in ancient Rome 古罗马) a place like a big round outdoor theatre for public games, races, etc. 露天圆形竞技场

cirque /sɜːk; *NAmE* sɜːrk/ *noun* (*geology* 地) = CORRIE

cir·rho·sis /səˈrəʊsɪs; *NAmE* -ˈroʊ-/ *noun* [U] a serious disease of the LIVER, caused especially by drinking too much alcohol 肝硬化；肝硬变

cir·rus /ˈsɪrəs/ *noun* [U] (*specialist*) a type of light cloud that forms high in the sky 卷云

CIS /ˌsiː aɪ ˈes/ *abbr.* Commonwealth of Independent States (a group of independent countries that were part of the Soviet Union until 1991) 独立国家联合体，独联体（由 1991 年之前原属苏联的主权国家组成）

cissy (*BrE*) = SISSY

cis·tern /ˈsɪstən; *NAmE* -tərn/ *noun* a container in which water is stored in a building, especially one in the roof or connected to a toilet（尤指屋顶上的）蓄水箱，贮水箱；（抽水马桶的）水箱 ➲ VISUAL VOCAB PAGE V25

cita·del /ˈsɪtədəl; -del/ *noun* (in the past) a castle on high ground in or near a city where people could go when the city was being attacked（旧时的）城堡，要塞，堡垒：(*figurative*) *citadels of private economic power* 私人经济力量的堡垒

cit·ation AW /saɪˈteɪʃn/ *noun* (*formal*) **1** [C] words or lines taken from a book or a speech 引语；引文；引述 SYN

quotation 2 [C] an official statement about sth special that sb has done, especially about acts of courage in a war 表彰；表扬；（尤指对战争中英勇表现的）嘉奖令：*a citation for bravery* 因勇敢而受到的嘉奖 **3** [U] an act of citing or being cited （被）引用，引证：*Space does not permit the citation of the examples.* 篇幅有限，示例从略。**4** [C] (*NAmE*) = SUMMONS (1): *The judge issued a contempt citation against the woman for violating a previous court order.* 法官对上一次拒不遵守庭谕的那名妇女发出了藐视法庭的传讯。

cite AW /saɪt/ *verb* (*formal*) **1 ~ sth (as sth)** to mention sth as a reason or an example, or in order to support what you are saying 提及（原因）；举出（示例）；列举：*He cited his heavy workload as the reason for his breakdown.* 他提到巨大的工作负荷是导致他精神崩溃的原因。➲ SYNONYMS AT MENTION **2 ~ sth** to speak or write the exact words from a book, an author, etc. 引用；引述；援引 SYN **quote 3 ~ sb (for sth)** (*law* 律) to order sb to appear in court; to name sb officially in a legal case 传唤；传讯：*She was cited in the divorce proceedings.* 她在离婚诉讼中被传唤。**4 ~ sb (for sth)** to mention sb officially or publicly because they deserve special praise 嘉奖；表彰；表扬：*He was cited for bravery.* 他因表现勇敢而得到嘉奖。

citi·fied /ˈsɪtɪfaɪd/ *adj.* (*usually disapproving*) characteristic of a city 有城市特征的；城市气的：*his citified surroundings* 他那充满市井气息的环境

citi·zen 🔑 /ˈsɪtɪzn/ *noun* **1** a person who has the legal right to belong to a particular country 公民：*She's Italian by birth but is now an Australian citizen.* 她生于意大利，但现在是澳大利亚公民。◇ *British citizens living in other parts of the European Union* 居住在欧盟其他地区的英国公民 **2** a person who lives in a particular place 居民；市民：*the citizens of Budapest* 布达佩斯市民 ◇ *When you're old, people treat you like a **second-class citizen**.* 当你年迈时，人们会把你当成二等公民对待。➲ SEE ALSO SENIOR CITIZEN ➲ COMPARE SUBJECT *n.* (6)

ˌcitizen ˈjournalism *noun* [U] reports and pictures of events recorded by ordinary people and shown on the Internet 公民新闻；网民新闻：*citizen journalism websites* 公民新闻网站 ▶ **ˌcitizen ˈjournalist** *noun*

citi·zen·ry /ˈsɪtɪzənri/ *noun* [sing.+sing./pl. v.] (*formal*) (less *formal* in *NAmE* 在美式英语中正式程度较低) all the citizens of a particular town, country, etc. 全体市民（或公民）

ˌcitizen's arˈrest *noun* an arrest made by a member of the public, not by the police 公民扭送

ˈCitizens' Band *noun* [U] = CB

citi·zen·ship /ˈsɪtɪzənʃɪp/ *noun* [U] **1** the legal right to belong to a particular country 公民身份；公民资格：*French citizenship* 法国国籍 ◇ *You can apply for citizenship after five years' residency.* 居住满五年可申请公民身份。➲ COLLOCATIONS AT RACE **2** the state of being a citizen and accepting the responsibilities of it 公民义务：*an education that prepares young people for citizenship* 培养年轻人履行公民义务的教育

cit·ric /ˈsɪtrɪk/ *adj.* relating to fruit such as lemons, oranges and LIMES 柠檬的；酸橙的；柑橘类水果的：*a citric flavour* 柠檬味

cit·ric acid /ˌsɪtrɪk ˈæsɪd/ *noun* [U] a weak acid found in the juice of lemons and other sour fruits 柠檬酸

cit·ron /ˈsɪtrən/ *noun* [C, U] a yellow fruit like a large lemon 枸橼；香橼

cit·ron·ella /ˌsɪtrəˈnelə/ *noun* [U] a type of grass from which an oil used in PERFUMES and soap is obtained 香茅（香茅油用于香水和肥皂）

cit·rus /ˈsɪtrəs/ *noun* [U] fruit belonging to the group of fruit that includes oranges, lemons, LIMES and GRAPEFRUIT 柑橘类果实：***citrus fruit/trees/growers*** 柑橘果实 / 果树 / 种植者 ◇ *fabric in bright citrus shades* (= orange, yellow or green) 色调鲜艳的橙黄色布料 ➲ VISUAL VOCAB PAGE V33

city 🔑 /ˈsɪti/ *noun* (*pl.* **-ies**) **1** [C] a large and important town 都市；城市：*the city centre* 市中心 ◇ *one of the world's most beautiful cities* 世界上最优美的城市之一 ◇ *a major city* 大城市 ◇ *the country's **capital city*** 这个国家的首都 ◇ *Mexico City* 墨西哥城 ➲ VISUAL VOCAB PAGE V3 ➲ SEE ALSO INNER CITY

WORDFINDER 联想词：amenity, ghetto, high-rise, metropolitan, population, slum, suburb, **town**, urban

2 [C] (*BrE*) a town that has been given special rights by a king or queen, usually one that has a CATHEDRAL （由国王或女王授予特权，通常有大教堂的）特许市：*the city of York* 约克特许市 **3** [C] (*NAmE*) a town that has been given special rights by the state government （由政府授予特权的）特权市 **4** [sing.+sing./pl. v.] all the people who live in a city 全市居民：*The city turned out to welcome the victorious team home.* 全市居民倾城而出欢迎凯旋的队伍。**5 the City** [sing.] (*BrE*) Britain's financial and business centre, in the oldest part of London 伦敦商业区，伦敦城（伦敦最古老的金融商务中心）：*a City stockbroker* 伦敦商业区的证券经纪人 ◇ *What is the City's reaction to the cut in interest rates?* 伦敦金融界对削减利率的反应如何？ **6** [U] (*informal*) used after other nouns to say that a place is full of a particular thing （用于其他名词之后）充满…的地方：*It's not exactly fun city here is it?* 这里并不是好玩的地方，对吧？ IDM SEE FREEDOM

the ˌCity and ˈGuilds Institute *noun* [sing.] (in Britain) an organization that gives qualifications in technical subjects and practical skills 英国伦敦城市行业协会（颁发职业技能证书的机构）

ˈcity desk *noun* **1** (*BrE*) the department of a newspaper that deals with financial news （报社的）财经新闻部 **2** (*NAmE*) the department of a newspaper that deals with local news （报社的）地方新闻部

ˈcity editor *noun* **1** (*BrE*) a journalist who is responsible for financial news in a newspaper or magazine （报刊的）财经新闻编辑 **2** (*NAmE*) a journalist who is responsible for local news in a newspaper or magazine （报刊的）地方新闻编辑

ˌcity ˈfather *noun* [usually pl.] a person with experience of governing a city 城市元老（有城市管理经验者）

ˌcity ˈgent *noun* (*BrE, informal*) a business person, especially a man who works in the financial area of London （尤指在伦敦金融区工作的）商人

ˌcity ˈhall *noun* [C, U] (*NAmE*) the local government of a city and the offices it uses 市政府；市政厅

city·scape /ˈsɪtiskeɪp/ *noun* the appearance of a city or urban area, especially in a picture; a picture of a city （尤指图画中的）城市景象，城市风光；城市风光画（或照片）

ˌcity ˈslicker *noun* (*informal, often disapproving*) a person who behaves in a way that is typical of people who live in big cities 油头滑脑的城里人；城里老油子；城里滑头

ˌcity ˈstate *noun* (especially in the past) an independent state consisting of a city and the area around it (for example, Athens in ancient times) （尤指旧时的）城邦（如古代雅典）

civet /ˈsɪvɪt/ *noun* **1** [C] a wild animal like a cat, that lives in central Africa and Asia 灵猫，麝猫（分布于中非和亚洲） **2** [U] a substance with a strong smell, obtained from a civet, and used in making PERFUME 麝猫香，灵猫香（用于制作香水）

civic /ˈsɪvɪk/ *adj.* [usually before noun] **1** officially connected with a town or city 市政的；城市的；城镇的：***civic buildings/leaders*** 市政建筑物 / 领导人 **2** connected with the people who live in a town or city 市民的；城镇居民的：*a sense of **civic pride*** (= pride that people feel for their town or city) 作为某市市民的自豪感 ◇ ***civic duties/responsibilities*** 市民的义务 / 职责

ˌcivic ˈcentre *noun* **1** (*BrE*) the area where the public buildings are, in a town 市中心 **2 civic center** (*NAmE*) a large building where public entertainments and meetings are held 市政大厦；市政中心： *Atlanta Civic Center* 亚特兰大市政大厦

ˌcivic ˈholiday *noun* (*CanE*) a holiday that is taken on the first Monday in August in all of Canada apart from Quebec, Alberta and Prince Edward Island 市政日（八月的第一个星期一，除魁北克、艾伯塔和爱德华王子岛省之外加拿大各地的假日）

civ·ics /ˈsɪvɪks/ *noun* [U] (*especially NAmE*) the school subject which studies the way government works and deals with the rights and duties that you have as a citizen and a member of a particular society 公民学；市政学 ➲ MORE LIKE THIS 29, page R28

civil 🔑 AW /ˈsɪvl/ *adj.* **1** 🔑 [only before noun] connected with the people who live in a country 国民的；平民的： *civil unrest* (= that is caused by groups of people within a country) 民众的骚乱 ➲ SEE ALSO CIVIL WAR **2** 🔑 [only before noun] connected with the state rather than with religion or with the armed forces 国家的，政府的（非宗教或军事的）： *a civil marriage ceremony* 非宗教仪式的结婚典礼 **3** [only before noun] involving personal legal matters and not criminal law 民事的（非刑事的）： *a civil court* 民事法庭 ➲ COMPARE CRIMINAL *adj.* (2) ➲ SEE ALSO CIVIL LAW **4** polite in a formal way but possibly not friendly 有礼貌的；客气的 OPP **uncivil** ▶ **civ·il·ly** /ˈsɪvəli/ *adv.*： *She greeted him civilly but with no sign of affection.* 她礼貌地向他打招呼，但没有一丝爱意。

ˌcivil deˈfence (*especially US* **ˌcivil deˈfense**) *noun* [U] the organization and training of ordinary people to protect themselves from attack during a war or, in the US, from natural disasters such as HURRICANES 民防

ˌcivil disoˈbedience *noun* [U] refusal by a large group of people to obey particular laws or pay taxes, usually as a form of peaceful political protest 非暴力反抗；温和抵抗；不合作主义 ➲ WORDFINDER NOTE AT PROTEST

ˌcivil engiˈneering *noun* [U] the design, building and repair of roads, bridges, CANALS, etc.; the study of this as a subject 土木工程；土木工程学 ▶ **ˌcivil engiˈneer** *noun*

ci·vil·ian /səˈvɪliən/ *noun* a person who is not a member of the armed forces or the police 平民；老百姓；庶民 ➲ COLLOCATIONS AT WAR ▶ **ci·vil·ian** *adj.* [usually before noun]： *He left the army and returned to civilian life.* 他从军队退了役，重新过上平民百姓的生活。 ➲ COMPARE MILITARY *n.*

ci·vil·ity /səˈvɪləti/ *noun* (*formal*) **1** [U] polite behaviour 彬彬有礼的行为；礼貌；客气： *Staff members are trained to treat customers with civility at all times.* 员工经过培训，要做到任何时候都以礼待客。 **2 civilities** [pl.] remarks that are said only in order to be polite 客套话；客气话

civ·il·iza·tion (*BrE also* **-isa·tion**) /ˌsɪvəlaɪˈzeɪʃn; *NAmE* -ləˈz-/ *noun* **1** [U] a state of human society that is very developed and organized 文明： *the technology of modern civilization* 现代文明的技术 ◇ *The Victorians regarded the railways as bringing progress and civilization.* 维多利亚时代的人认为铁路带来了进步和文明。 **2** [U, C] a society, its culture and its way of life during a particular period of time or in a particular part of the world（特定时期或地区的）社会文明： *the civilizations of ancient Greece and Rome* 古希腊和古罗马的社会文明 ◇ *diseases that are common in Western civilization* 西方文明社会的常见病 **3** [U] all the people in the world and the societies they live in, considered as a whole 文明世界；文明社会： *Environmental damage threatens the whole of civilization.* 环境的破坏威胁着整个文明世界。 **4** [U] (*often humorous*) a place that offers you the comfortable way of life of a modern society 人类文明的生活： *It's good to be back in civilization after two weeks in a tent!* 在帐篷里住了两个星期后又回到人类文明的生活可真好呀！

civ·il·ize (*BrE also* **-ise**) /ˈsɪvəlaɪz/ *verb* **~ sb/sth** to educate and improve a person or a society; to make sb's behaviour or manners better 教化；开化；使文明；使有教养： *The girls in a class tend to have a civilizing influence on the boys.* 班上的女生往往能让男生文雅起来。

civ·il·ized (*BrE also* **-ised**) /ˈsɪvəlaɪzd/ *adj.* **1** well organized socially with a very developed culture and way of life 文明的；开化的： *the civilized world* 文明世界 ◇ *rising crime in our so-called civilized societies* 在我们所谓文明社会中日益增多的犯罪行为 ◇ *civilized peoples* 文明的民族 **2** having laws and customs that are fair and morally acceptable 有法制伦理的；有道德的： *No civilized country should allow such terrible injustices.* 凡有法制伦理的国家都不该允许这种可怕的不公正行为。 **3** having or showing polite and reasonable behaviour 有礼貌的；有教养的；举止得体的： *We couldn't even have a civilized conversation any more.* 我们之间甚至连礼貌的寒暄都没有了。 **4** typical of a comfortable and pleasant way of life（生活）惬意的，愉快舒适的： *Breakfast on the terrace—how civilized!* 在阳台上用早餐，真是惬意无比！ OPP **uncivilized**

ˌcivil ˈlaw *noun* [U] law that deals with the rights of private citizens rather than with crime 民法

ˌcivil ˈliberty *noun* [C, usually pl., U] the right of people to be free to say or do what they want while respecting others and staying within the law 公民自由

the ˈCivil List *noun* [sing.] before 2013, a sum of money given to the British royal family each year by Parliament（2013 年前英国议会每年提供的）王室年俸 ➲ SEE ALSO THE SOVEREIGN GRANT

ˌcivil ˈmarriage *noun* a marriage with no religious ceremony 公证结婚，世俗结婚（不采用宗教仪式）

ˌcivil ˈpartnership *noun* (in some countries) a legal relationship between two people of the same sex, with the same legal status as marriage （某些国家）合法伴侣关系（同性伴侣享有与婚姻同等的法律地位） ▶ **ˌcivil ˈpartner** *noun*

ˌcivil ˈrights *noun* [pl.] the rights that every person in a society has, for example to be treated equally, to be able to vote, work, etc. whatever their sex, race or religion 公民权： *the civil rights leader Martin Luther King* 民权领袖马丁·路德·金 ➲ WORDFINDER NOTE AT SOCIETY

the ˌcivil ˈrights movement *noun* [sing.] (in the US) the campaign in the 1950s and 1960s to change the laws so that African Americans have the same rights as others （美国）民权运动（20 世纪 50 年代和 60 年代非裔美国人争取平等权利的运动） ➲ COLLOCATIONS AT RACE

ˌcivil ˈservant *noun* a person who works in the civil service（政府的）公务员，文职人员

the ˌcivil ˈservice *noun* [sing.] the government departments in a country and the people who work for them, except the armed forces, judges and elected politicians（政府的）文职部门，行政部门；（统称）政府工作人员，公务员

ˌcivil ˈwar *noun* **1** [C, U] a war between groups of people in the same country 内战： *the Spanish Civil War* 西班牙内战 ◇ *30 years of bitter civil war* * 30 年惨烈的内战 ➲ COLLOCATIONS AT WAR **2 the Civil War** the war fought in the US between the northern and the southern states in the years 1861 to 1865 美国内战，美国南北战争（1861–1865 年）

civ·vies /ˈsɪviz/ *noun* [pl.] (*slang*) (used by people in the armed forces) ordinary clothes, not military uniform（军人穿的）便服

Civvy Street /ˈsɪvi striːt/ *noun* [U] (*old-fashioned, BrE, slang*) ordinary life outside the armed forces （非军队的）平民生活，老百姓生活

CJD /ˌsiː dʒeɪ ˈdiː/ *abbr.* CREUTZFELDT-JAKOB DISEASE 克罗伊茨费尔特－雅各布病；克－雅脑病

cl *abbr.* (*pl.* **cl** or **cls**) CENTILITRE 厘升： *75cl* * 75 厘升

C

clack /klæk/ *verb* [I] if two hard objects **clack**, they make a short loud sound when they hit each other 发出啪嗒声；噼啪作响；使咔哒地响：*Her heels clacked on the marble floor.* 她的鞋后跟在大理石地面上发出咔哒咔哒的响声。▶ **clack** *noun* [sing.]: *the clack of high heels on the floor* 高跟鞋在地板上发出的咔咔声 ◇ *the clack of her knitting needles* 她的织针发出的啪嗒啪嗒声

clad /klæd/ *adj.* (*usually formal*) **1** ~ (**in sth**) (often used after an adverb or in compounds 常用于副词后或构成复合词) wearing a particular type of clothing 穿…衣服的 **SYN** **dressed**: *She was clad in blue velvet.* 她身着蓝色的天鹅绒服装。◇ ***warmly/scantily clad*** 衣着暖和 / 暴露 ◇ *leather-clad motorcyclists* 穿皮外套的摩托车手 **2 -clad** (in compounds 构成复合词) covered in a particular thing …覆盖的：*snow-clad hills* 白雪覆盖的山峦

clad·ding /ˈklædɪŋ/ *noun* [U] a covering of a hard material, used as protection 镀层；保护层

claim 🔑 /kleɪm/ *verb, noun*

■ *verb*

• **SAY STH IS TRUE** 表示真实性 **1** 🔑 [T] to say that sth is true although it has not been proved and other people may not believe it 宣称；声称；断言：~ (**that**)… *He claims (that) he was not given a fair hearing.* 他声称他未得到公正的申诉机会。◇ ~ (**sb/sth**) **to be/do sth** *I don't claim to be an expert.* 我不敢自称为专家。◇ ~ **sth** *Scientists are claiming a major breakthrough in the fight against cancer.* 科学家宣称治疗癌症已有重大的突破。◇ **it is claimed that…** *It was claimed that some doctors were working 80 hours a week.* 据说有些医生每周工作 80 小时。➲ LANGUAGE BANK AT ARGUE

• **DEMAND LEGAL RIGHT** 要求合法权利 **2** 🔑 [T] ~ **sth** to demand or ask for sth because you believe it is your legal right to own or to have it 要求（拥有）；索取；认领：*A lot of lost property is never claimed.* 许多失物从未被认领。◇ *He claimed political asylum.* 他要求政治避难。

• **MONEY** 金钱 **3** 🔑 [T, I] to ask for money from the government or a company because you have a right to it 索要；索取：~ **sth** *He's not entitled to claim unemployment benefit.* 他无权要求领取失业救济金。◇ ~ **sth from sth** *She claimed damages from the company for the injury she had suffered.* 她因受伤向公司要求获得损害赔偿金。◇ *You could have claimed the cost of the hotel room from your insurance.* 你本可以从你的保险中索取旅馆住房费。◇ ~ (**on sth**) (**for sth**) *You can claim on your insurance for that coat you left on the train.* 你可按你的保险索赔你遗忘在火车上的大衣。

• **ATTENTION/THOUGHT** 注意；思考 **4** [T] ~ **sth** to get or take sb's attention 引起注意：*A most unwelcome event claimed his attention.* 一件非常讨厌的事情需要他去考虑。

• **GAIN/WIN** 获得；赢得 **5** [T] ~ **sth** to gain, win or achieve sth 获得；赢得；取得：*She has finally claimed a place on the team.* 她终于成了那支队伍的队员。

• **CAUSE DEATH** 导致死亡 **6** [T] ~ **sth** (of a disaster, an accident, etc. 灾难、事故等) to cause sb's death 夺走，夺去（生命）：*The car crash claimed three lives.* 那次撞车事故导致三人死亡。

PHR V ˌ**claim sth↔ˈback** to ask or demand to have sth returned because you have a right to it 索回；要回：*You can claim back the tax on your purchases.* 你可以要求退回购物时缴纳的税款。

■ *noun*

• **SAYING STH IS TRUE** 表示真实 **1** 🔑 [C] ~ (**that**…) a statement that sth is true although it has not been proved and other people may not agree with or believe it 声称；宣称；断言：*The singer has denied the magazine's claim that she is leaving the band.* 这名歌手已否认那家杂志有关她要离开乐队的说法。

• **LEGAL RIGHT** 合法权利 **2** 🔑 [C, U] ~ (**on/to sth**) a right that sb believes they have to sth, especially property, land, etc. （尤指对财产、土地等要求拥有的）所有权：*They had no claim on the land.* 他们无权索要那块土地。◇ *She has more claim to the book's success than anybody* (= she deserves to be praised for it). 她为这本书的成功立了头功。

• **FOR MONEY** 钱款 **3** 🔑 [C] ~ (**for sth**) a request for a sum of money that you believe you have a right to, especially from a company, the government, etc. （尤指向公司、政府等）索款，索赔：*You can **make a claim** on your insurance policy.* 你可按保险单索赔。◇ *to **put in a claim** for an allowance* 提出领取津贴的要求 ◇ *a claim for £2 000* 要求 2 000 英镑的索赔 ◇ *Make sure your claims for expenses are submitted by the end of the month.* 你的费用一定要在月底以前办理报销。◇ *a three per cent **pay claim*** 提高工资 3% 的要求 ◇ *Complete a **claim form*** (= an official document which you must use in order to request money from an organization). 填写索赔表格。

IDM ˌ**claim to ˈfame** (*often humorous*) one thing that makes a person or place important or interesting 一举出名的事；成名的一件事：*His main claim to fame is that he went to school with the Prime Minister.* 他出名主要是因为他曾经是首相的中学同学。 **have a claim on sb** to have the right to demand time, attention, etc. from sb 对某人有…的要求权 **lay claim to sth** to state that you have a right to own sth 声称对…的拥有权；提出对…的所有权 **make no claim** used when you are saying that you cannot do sth （表示不能做某事）自认为不：*I make no claim to understand modern art.* 我自认为不懂现代艺术。➲ MORE AT STAKE *v.*

▼ **SYNONYMS** 同义词辨析

claim

allegation • assertion

These are all words for a statement that sth is true, although it has not been proved. 以上各词均表示未经证实的说法。

claim a statement that sth is true, although it has not been proved 指声称、宣称、断言

allegation (*rather formal*) a public statement that is made without giving proof, accusing sb of doing sth that is wrong or illegal 指无证据的说法、指控

assertion (*rather formal*) a statement of sth that you strongly believe to be true, although it has not been proved 指明确肯定、断言

CLAIM OR ASSERTION? 用 claim 还是 assertion?

When the point in doubt is a matter of opinion, not fact, use **assertion**. 表示坚持观点而非断言属实，用 assertion: ~~She made sweeping claims about the role of women in society.~~ When you are talking about a matter of fact you can use either word; an **assertion** may be slightly stronger than a **claim** and it is a more formal word. 表示断言属实，两词可以通用。assertion 比 claim 语气稍强，且更正式。

PATTERNS

- a(n) claim/allegation/assertion **that**…
- a(n) claim/allegation/assertion **about**/**of** sth
- **false**/**unfounded**/**conflicting** claims/allegations/assertions
- to **make**/**deny** a(n) claim/allegation/assertion
- to **withdraw** a(n) claim/allegation

claim·ant /ˈkleɪmənt/ *noun* **1** a person who claims sth because they believe they have a right to it 要求者；索要者 **2** a person who is receiving money from the state because they are unemployed, etc. （因失业等）领取救济金者

clair·voy·ance /kleəˈvɔɪəns; *NAmE* klerˈv-/ *noun* [U] the power that some people claim to have to be able to see future events or to communicate with people who are dead or far away 预知能力；通灵能力；遥感能力 ▶ **clair·voy·ant** /kleəˈvɔɪənt; *NAmE* klerˈv-/ *noun*：*to consult a clairvoyant* 咨询先知 **clair·voy·ant** *adj.*

clam /klæm/ *noun, verb*

■ *noun* a SHELLFISH that can be eaten. It has a shell in two parts that can open and close. 蛤；蛤蜊；蚌：*clam chowder/soup* 蛤蜊杂烩汤；蛤蜊汤 ➲ PICTURE AT

SHELLFISH

■ *verb* (-mm-)

PHR V ˌ**clam ˈup (on sb)** (*informal*) to refuse to speak, especially when sb asks you about sth（尤指被询问时）拒绝说话，拒不开口，闭口不言

clam·bake /ˈklæmbeɪk/ *noun* (*NAmE*) an outdoor party, especially for eating clams and other SEAFOOD 野餐会；（尤指）烤蛤及海鲜野餐会

clam·ber /ˈklæmbə(r)/ *verb* [I] + **adv./prep.** to climb or move with difficulty or a lot of effort, using your hands and feet（吃力地）攀登，攀爬 SYN **scramble**: *The children clambered up the steep bank.* 孩子们攀登上了陡峭的河岸。

clammy /ˈklæmi/ *adj.* (**clam·mier**, **clam·mi·est**) damp in an unpleasant way 黏糊糊的；湿漉漉的：*His skin felt cold and clammy.* 他的皮肤摸上去冷冰冰湿乎乎的。◇ *clammy hands* 又湿又黏的双手

clam·our (*especially US* **clamor**) /ˈklæmə(r)/ *verb, noun*

■ *verb* **1** [I, T] (*formal*) to demand sth loudly 大声（或吵闹）地要求：~ **(for sth)** *People began to clamour for his resignation.* 人们开始大声疾呼要求他辞职。◇ ~ **to do sth** *Everyone was clamouring to know how much they would get.* 大家都吵闹着想知道他们能得到多少。◇ + **speech** *'Play with us!' the children clamoured.* "跟我们一起玩吧！" 孩子们吵吵嚷嚷地要求道。 **2** [I] (of many people 许多人) to shout loudly, especially in a confused way（尤指乱哄哄地）大声地喊叫，呼叫

■ *noun* [sing., U] (*formal*) **1** a loud noise especially one that is made by a lot of people or animals 喧闹声；嘈杂声；吵闹：*the clamour of the market* 市场上鼎沸的人声 **2** ~ **(for sth)** a demand for sth made by a lot of people 民众的要求：*The clamour for her resignation grew louder.* 民众要求她辞职的呼声越来越高。▶ **clam·or·ous** /ˈklæmərəs/ *adj.*

clamp /klæmp/ *verb, noun*

■ *verb* **1** [T] to hold sth tightly, or fasten two things together, with a clamp（用夹具）夹紧，夹住，固定：~ **A to B** *Clamp one end of the plank to the edge of the table.* 把厚木板的一端用夹具固定在桌子的边上。◇ ~ **A and B (together)** *Clamp the two halves together until the glue dries.* 用夹具把两半物品夹紧，待胶干后再松开。**2** [T, I] to hold or fasten sth very tightly so that it does not move; to be held tightly 紧紧抓住；紧夹住；被抓住；被夹紧：~ **sth + adv./prep.** *He had a cigar clamped between his teeth.* 他嘴里叼着一根雪茄。◇ *She clamped a pair of headphones over her ears.* 她把一副耳机戴在两边耳朵上。◇ + **adv./prep.** *Her lips clamped tightly together.* 她的双唇紧闭。◇ ~ **(sth) + adj.** *He clamped his mouth shut.* 他紧闭着嘴。**3** [T, often passive] ~ **sth/sb** (*BrE*) to fix a clamp *n.* (2) to a car's wheel so that the car cannot be driven away 用夹锁锁住（车轮）➲ WORDFINDER NOTE AT TRAFFIC

PHR V ˌ**clamp ˈdown (on sb/sth)** to take strict action in order to prevent sth, especially crime 严厉打击（犯罪等）：*a campaign by police to clamp down on street crime* 警方严厉打击街头犯罪的运动 ➲ RELATED NOUN CLAMPDOWN ˈ**clamp sth on sb** (*especially NAmE*) to force sb to accept sth such as a restriction or law 强制…接受（限制或法律等）：*The army* ***clamped a curfew on*** *the city.* 军队对这座城市实行了宵禁。

■ *noun* **1** a tool for holding things tightly together, usually by means of a screw 夹具；夹子；夹钳 ➲ VISUAL VOCAB PAGE V72 **2** (*also* ˈ**wheel clamp**) (*both BrE*) (*US* ˌ**Denver** ˈ**boot**, **boot**) a device that is attached to the wheel of a car that has been parked illegally, so that it cannot be driven away 车轮夹锁（用于锁住违章停放的车辆）

clamp·down /ˈklæmpdaʊn/ *noun* [usually sing.] sudden action that is taken in order to stop an illegal activity 严禁，制止，取缔（非法活动）：*a clampdown on drinking and driving* 严禁酒后驾车

clam·shell /ˈklæmʃel/ *adj.* [only before noun] having a lid or other part that opens and shuts like the shell of a CLAM 蛤壳式的；掀盖式的：*a* ***clamshell phone*** 翻盖式手机 ▶ **clam·shell** *noun*

clan /klæn/ *noun* [C+sing./pl. v.] **1** a group of families who are related to each other, especially in Scotland（尤指苏格兰的）宗族，氏族，家族：*the Macleod clan* 麦克劳德氏族 ◇ *clan warfare* 宗族冲突 **2** (*informal, sometimes humorous*) a very large family, or a group of people who are connected because of a particular thing 庞大的家族；宗派；帮派；小集团：*one of a growing clan of stars who have left Hollywood* 脱离了好莱坞的那帮人数日益增多的明星中的一员

clan·des·tine /klænˈdestɪn; ˈklændəstaɪn/ *adj.* (*formal*) done secretly or kept secret 暗中从事的；保密的；秘密的：*a* ***clandestine meeting/relationship*** 秘密会议 / 关系

clang /klæŋ/ *verb* [I, T] to make a loud ringing sound like that of metal being hit; to cause sth to make this sound（使）叮当作响，铿锵作响 SYN **clank**: *Bells were clanging in the tower.* 塔楼上的钟当当地敲响了。◇ + **adj.** *The gates clanged shut.* 大门咣的一声合上了。◇ ~ **sth + adv./prep.** *The trams clanged their way along the streets.* 有轨电车哐啷哐啷沿街驶过。◇ *He clanged a spoon against a glass.* 他用勺子叮叮当当地敲玻璃杯。 ▶ **clang** (*also* **clang·ing**) *noun* [usually sing.]

clang·er /ˈklæŋə(r)/ *noun* (*BrE, informal*) an obvious and embarrassing mistake 明显且令人难堪的错误：*Mentioning her ex-husband was a bit of a clanger.* 提及她的前夫是有点令人难堪的失言。◇ *He was always* ***dropping clangers*** (= making embarrassing mistakes or remarks). 他总是出岔子，令人十分尴尬。

clang·our (*especially US* **clangor**) /ˈklæŋgə(r)/ *noun* (*formal*) a continuous loud crashing or ringing sound（持续的）铿锵声，叮当声 ▶ **clang·or·ous** /ˈklæŋgərəs/ *adj.*

clank /klæŋk/ *verb* [I, T] to make a loud sound like pieces of metal hitting each other; to cause sth to make this sound（使）发出叮当声，发出当啷声：*clanking chains* 叮当作响的镣铐 ◇ + **adj.** *I heard a door clank shut.* 我听见门咣的一声关上了。◇ ~ **sth** *The guard clanked his heavy ring of keys.* 看守把他的那串沉甸甸的钥匙弄得叮当响。▶ **clank** (*also* **clank·ing**) *noun* [usually sing.]

clan·nish /ˈklænɪʃ/ *adj.* (*often disapproving*) (of members of a group 集团成员) not showing interest in people who are not in the group 小集团的；宗派的；排他的

clans·man /ˈklænzmən/ *noun* (*pl.* **-men** /-mən/) a member of a CLAN 氏族（或宗族）成员；宗派（或小集团）的成员

clap /klæp/ *verb, noun*

■ *verb* (-pp-) **1** [I, T] to hit your open hands together several times to show that you approve of or have enjoyed sth 鼓掌，拍手（表示赞许或欣赏）：*The audience cheered and clapped.* 观众又是喝彩又是鼓掌。◇ ~ **sb/sth** *Everyone clapped us when we went up to get our prize.* 我们上前领奖时，大家都为我们鼓掌。 **2** [I, T] to hit your open hands together 拍手；击掌：*Everyone clapped in time to the music.* 大家合着音乐的节奏拍手。◇ ~ **your hands** *She clapped her hands in delight.* 她高兴地拍起手来。◇ *He clapped his hands for silence.* 他拍手要大家安静下来。 **3** [T] ~ **sb on the back/shoulder** to lightly hit sb with your open hand, usually in a friendly way（常指友好地）轻拍某人的背（或肩） **4** [T] ~ **sth/sb + adv./prep.** to put sth/sb somewhere quickly and suddenly 急速放置：*'Oh dear!' she cried,* ***clapping a hand*** *over her mouth.* "哎呀！" 她叫道，急急用手捂住了嘴。◇ *to* ***clap sb in irons/jail/prison*** 迅速把某人关进监狱 ▶ **clap·ping** *noun* [U]: *I could hear the sound of clapping from the other room.* 我听得见另一个房间里传来的鼓掌声。IDM SEE EYE *n.*

■ *noun* **1** [sing.] an act of clapping the hands; the sound this makes 鼓掌；拍手；掌声；拍手声：*Give him a clap!* (= to praise sb at the end of a performance) 为他鼓掌吧！ **2** [C] a sudden loud noise 砰然巨响；霹雳声：*a clap of thunder* 一声霹雳 **3** (*also* **the clap**) [U] (*informal*) a disease of the sexual organs, caught by having sex with an infected person 淋病 SYN **gonorrhoea**

clap·board /ˈklæpbɔːd; *NAmE* ˈklæbərd/ *noun* [U] (*especially NAmE*) = WEATHERBOARD

C

Clap·ham omni·bus /ˌklæpəm ˈɒmnɪbəs; *NAmE* ˈɑːmnɪbəs/ *noun*
IDM the man on the ˌClapham ˈomnibus (*BrE, informal, old-fashioned*) an ordinary person who is typical of many others 普通人；正常人： *Can you persuade the man on the Clapham omnibus that it is useful?* 你能让普通人相信这个有用吗？

ˌclapped ˈout *adj.* (*BrE, informal*) (of a car or machine 汽车或机器) old and in bad condition 破旧的；残破的；破烂的： *The van's totally clapped out.* 那辆货车已破得不成样子。◇ *a clapped-out old Mini* 又旧又破的迷你牌汽车

clap·per /ˈklæpə(r)/ *noun* the piece of metal inside a bell that hits the sides and makes the bell ring 钟锤；钟舌；铃舌
IDM like the ˈclappers (*BrE, informal*) extremely fast 特别快；飞快；疾速： *to* ***run/ride/drive like the clappers*** 飞快地奔跑；骑马飞奔；驾车疾驰

clap·per·board /ˈklæpəbɔːd; *NAmE* ˈklæpərbɔːrd/ *noun* a device that is used when making films/movies. It consists of two connected boards that are hit together at the start of a scene, and its purpose is to help to match the pictures with the sound. （拍摄电影用的）场记板，拍板

clap·trap /ˈklæptræp/ *noun* [U] (*informal*) stupid talk that has no value 无聊的蠢话；废话

claque /klæk/ *noun* a group of people who are paid to clap or BOO a performer or public speaker 受雇喝（倒）彩的一伙人；职业观众

claret /ˈklærət/ *noun* **1** [U, C] a dry red wine, especially from the Bordeaux area of France. There are several types of claret. （尤指产于法国波尔多地区的）干红葡萄酒 **2** [U] a dark red colour 深红色；暗红色

clar·ify AW /ˈklærəfaɪ/ *verb* (**clari·fies, clari·fy·ing, clari·fied, clari·fied**) **1** (*formal*) to make sth clearer or easier to understand 使更清晰易懂；阐明；澄清： **~ sth** ***to clarify a situation/problem/issue*** 澄清情况 / 问题 ◇ *I hope this* ***clarifies my position.*** 我希望这能阐明我的立场。◇ **~ what/how, etc.…** *She asked him to clarify what he meant.* 她要他说清楚他是什么意思。➲ LANGUAGE BANK AT DEFINE **2 ~ sth** to make sth, especially butter, pure by heating it （尤指通过加热使黄油）纯净，净化： *clarified butter* 已净化的黄油 ▶ **clari·fi·ca·tion AW** /ˌklærəfɪˈkeɪʃn/ *noun* [U, C]: *I am* ***seeking clarification of*** *the regulations.* 我正在努力弄清楚这些规则。

clari·net /ˌklærəˈnet/ *noun* a musical instrument of the WOODWIND group. It is shaped like a pipe and has a REED and a MOUTHPIECE at the top that you blow into. 单簧管；黑管 ➲ VISUAL VOCAB PAGE V38

cla·ri·net·tist (*NAmE* **cla·ri·net·ist**) /ˌklærəˈnetɪst/ *noun* a person who plays the clarinet 单簧管（或黑管）演奏者

clar·ion call /ˈklæriən kɔːl/ *noun* [sing.] (*formal*) a clear message or request for people to do sth 口号；号召；召唤

clar·ity AW /ˈklærəti/ *noun* [U] **1** the quality of being expressed clearly 清晰；清楚；明确： *a lack of clarity in the law* 法律上不明确 **2** the ability to think about or understand sth clearly 清晰的思维（或理解）能力： ***clarity of thought/purpose/vision*** 思路清楚；目的明确；视野清晰 **3** if a picture, substance or sound has **clarity**, you can see or hear it very clearly, or see through it easily （画面、物质或声音的）清晰，清楚，清澈： *the clarity of sound on a CD* 激光唱片的清晰音质

clash /klæʃ/ *noun, verb*
■ ***noun***
• **FIGHT** 打斗 **1 ~ (with sb) | ~ (between A and B)** a short fight between two groups of people （两群人之间的）打斗，打架，冲突： *Clashes broke out between police and demonstrators.* 警方与示威者发生了冲突。➲ SYNONYMS AT FIGHT
• **ARGUMENT** 争论 **2 ~ (with sb) (over sth) | ~ (between A and B) (over sth)** an argument between two people or groups of people who have different beliefs and ideas 争论；辩论；争执 **SYN conflict**： *a head-on clash between the two leaders over education policy* 两位领导人就教育政策进行的针锋相对的争论
• **DIFFERENCE** 差异 **3** the difference that exists between two things that are opposed to each other 差别；差异；分歧 **SYN conflict**： ***a clash of interests/opinions/cultures*** 利益冲突；意见分歧；文化差异 ◇ ***a personality clash*** *with the boss* 与老板的个性不合
• **OF TWO EVENTS** 两件事 **4** a situation in which two events happen at the same time so that you cannot go to or see them both （时间上的）冲突，矛盾： *a clash in the timetable/schedule* 时间安排有冲突
• **OF COLOURS** 颜色 **5** the situation when two colours, designs, etc. look ugly when they are put together 不协调；不和谐；搭配不当
• **LOUD NOISE** 大声 **6** a loud noise made by two metal objects being hit together （金属的）撞击声： ***a clash of cymbals/swords*** 铙钹的敲击声；剑的撞击声
• **IN SPORT** 体育运动 **7** (used in newspapers, about sports 用于报章中有关体育运动的报道) an occasion when two teams or players compete against each other 交锋；交战；比赛： *Bayern's clash with Roma in the Champions League* 拜仁队在欧洲冠军联赛中与罗马队的交锋
■ ***verb***
• **FIGHT/COMPETE** 打斗；比赛 **1** [I] **~ (with sb)** to come together and fight or compete in a contest 打斗；冲突；比赛： *The two sets of supporters clashed outside the stadium.* 双方的支持者在体育场外打了起来。◇ *The two teams clash in tomorrow's final.* 这两支队将在明天的决赛中厮杀。
• **ARGUE** 争论 **2** [I] **~ (with sb) (over/on sth)** to argue or disagree seriously with sb about sth, and to show this in public （公开地）争论，辩论，争辩： *The leaders and members clashed on the issue.* 领袖和下属的成员在这个问题上产生了分歧。◇ *The leaders clashed with party members on the issue.* 政党领袖与该党党员在这个问题上产生了分歧。
• **BE DIFFERENT** 差异 **3** [I] **~ (with sth)** (of beliefs, ideas or personalities 信念、思想或个性) to be very different and opposed to each other 迥然不同；不相容；抵触： *His left-wing views clashed with his father's politics.* 他的左翼观点与他父亲的政见分歧很大。◇ *His views and his father's clashed.* 他的观点与他父亲的观点相抵触。◇ *They have clashing personalities.* 他们的个性迥然相异。
• **OF TWO EVENTS** 两件事 **4** [I] **~ (with sth)** (of events 活动) to happen at the same time so that you cannot go to or see them both （时间上）相冲突，相矛盾： *Unfortunately your party clashes with a wedding I'm going to.* 不巧得很，你的聚会和我要参加的婚礼在时间上有冲突。◇ *There are two good movies on TV tonight, but they clash.* 今晚电视有两部好电影，但播出时间有冲突。
• **OF COLOURS** 颜色 **5** [I] **~ (with sth)** (of colours, patterns or styles 颜色、图案或风格) to look ugly when put together 不协调；不和谐；搭配不当： *The wallpaper clashes with the carpet.* 墙纸与地毯的色彩不协调。◇ *The wallpaper and the carpet clash.* 墙纸和地毯的色彩不相配。
• **MAKE LOUD NOISE** 发出大声 **6** [I, T] to hit together and make a loud ringing noise; to make two metal objects do this （使）撞击出巨大的响声；（使）当啷作响： **~ (together)** *The long blades clashed together.* 长刀相击铿然作响。◇ **~ sth (together)** *She clashed the cymbals.* 她当啷一声敲响铙钹。

clasp /klɑːsp; *NAmE* klæsp/ *verb, noun*
■ ***verb*** **1 ~ sth** to hold sth tightly in your hand 握紧；攥紧；抓紧： *He leaned forward, his* ***hands clasped*** *tightly together.* 他俯身向前，双手十字交错地紧握着。◇ *They clasped hands* (= held each other's hands). 他们相互紧握着对方的手。◇ *I stood there, clasping the door handle.* 我站在那里，紧攥着门把手。➲ SYNONYMS AT HOLD **2 ~ sb/sth** to hold sb/sth tightly with your arms around them 抱紧；紧紧拥抱： *She clasped the children in her arms.* 她把孩子紧紧地搂在怀里。◇ *He* ***clasped*** *her* ***to him.*** 他紧紧地拥抱着她。 **3 ~ sth (+ adv./prep.)** to fasten sth with a clasp 扣紧；扣住；扣牢： *She clasped the bracelet around her wrist.* 她把手镯戴上手腕扣牢。

■ *noun* **1** [C] a device that fastens sth, such as a bag or the ends of a belt or a piece of jewellery （包、皮带或首饰的）搭扣，扣环： *the clasp of a necklace/handbag* 项链扣环；手提包扣 ➲ VISUAL VOCAB PAGE V70 **2** [sing.] a tight hold with your hand or in your arms 紧握；紧攥；紧抱： *He took her hand in his firm warm clasp.* 他用温暖的手紧紧握住她的手。

C

class /klɑːs; *NAmE* klæs/ *noun, verb, adj.*

■ *noun*

• IN EDUCATION 教育 **1** [C+sing./pl. v.] a group of students who are taught together 班；班级： *We were in the same class at school.* 我们在上学时同过班。◇ *She is the youngest in her class.* 她在班里年龄最小。◇ *He came* **top of the class**. 他在全班名列前茅。◇ *The whole class was/were told to stay behind after school.* 全班被告知放学后留下。**2** [C, U] an occasion when a group of students meet to be taught 课；上课 SYN **lesson**: *I was late for a class.* 我上课迟到了。◇ *See me after class.* 下课后来见我。◇ *She works hard* **in class** (= during the class). 她在课堂上学习用功。◇ *I have a history class at 9 o'clock.* 我 9 点钟有历史课。➲ COLLOCATIONS AT EDUCATION **3** [C] (*also* **classes** [pl.]) a series of classes on a particular subject（某科目的）系列课程 SYN **course**: *I've been* **taking classes** *in pottery.* 我一直在上陶器制作技术课。◇ *Are you still doing your French evening class?* 你还在夜校学习法语吗？ **4** [C+sing./pl. v.] (*especially NAmE*) a group of students who finish their studies at school, college or university in a particular year 同届毕业生： *the class of 2008* * 2008 届毕业生

• IN SOCIETY 社会 **5** [C+sing./pl. v.] one of the groups of people in a society that are thought of as being at the same social or economic level 阶级；阶层： *the working/middle/upper class* 工人 / 中产 / 上层阶级 ◇ *The party tries to appeal to all classes of society.* 这个政党尽力吸引社会各阶层人士。◇ *the professional classes* 专业阶层 **6** [U] the way that people are divided into different social and economic groups 社会等级： *differences of class, race or gender* 社会等级、种族或性别差异 ◇ *the class system* 社会等级制度 ◇ *a society in which class is more important than ability* 一个社会等级比能力更为重要的社会 ➲ WORDFINDER NOTE AT SOCIETY

• GROUP OF PEOPLE/ANIMALS 人 / 动物群体 **7** [C] a group of people, animals or things that have similar characteristics or qualities 种类；类别；等级： *It was good accommodation for a hotel of this class.* 就这种档次的旅馆来说，住宿条件算是不错了。◇ *different classes of drugs* 不同种类的毒品 ◇ *Dickens was* **in a different class** *from* (= was much better than) *most of his contemporaries.* 与大多数的同辈相比，狄更斯要出色得多。◇ *As a jazz singer she's* **in a class of her own** (= better than most others). 作为爵士乐歌手，她比大多数同行都要出色。➲ SEE ALSO FIRST-CLASS, HIGH-CLASS, LOW-CLASS, SECOND-CLASS

• SKILL/STYLE 技巧；风格 **8** [U] an elegant quality or a high level of skill that is impressive 优雅；典雅；高超： *She* **has class** *all right—she looks like a model.* 她的确风姿婀雅，看上去像模特儿一样。◇ *There's a real touch of class about this team.* 这支队确实技艺超群。

• IN TRAIN/PLANE 火车；飞机 **9** [C] (especially in compounds 尤用于构成复合词) each of several different levels of comfort that are available to travellers in a plane, etc. 等级；舱位等级： *He always travels business class.* 他总是坐公务舱旅行。◇ *The first-class compartment is situated at the front of the train.* 头等车厢位于火车的前部。➲ SEE ALSO BUSINESS CLASS, ECONOMY CLASS SYNDROME, FIRST CLASS *n.*, SECOND-CLASS, THIRD-CLASS, TOURIST CLASS

• OF UNIVERSITY DEGREE 大学学位 **10** [C] (especially in compounds 尤用于构成复合词) one of the levels of achievement in a British university degree exam（英国学位考试的）等级： *a* ***first-/second-/third-class*** *degree* 一级优等 / 二级优等 / 第三等学位

• BIOLOGY 生物学 **11** [C] a group into which animals, plants, etc. that have similar characteristics are divided, below a PHYLUM（动植物等分类的）纲 ➲ COMPARE FAMILY *n.* (5), GENUS, SPECIES ➲ WORDFINDER NOTE AT BREED

IDM SEE CHATTER *v.*

■ *verb* [often passive] **~ sb/sth** (**as sth**) to think or decide that sb/sth is a particular type of person or thing 把…看作（或分类、归类） SYN **classify**: *Immigrant workers were classed as aliens.* 移民来的工人被归入侨民类。

■ *adj.* [only before noun] (*informal*) very good 很好的；优秀的；出色的： *a* ***class player/performer*** 优秀的选手 / 表演者 ◇ *She's a real* ***class act.*** 她真是魅力非凡。

ˌclass ˈaction *noun* (*NAmE*) a type of LAWSUIT that is started by a group of people who have the same problem 集体诉讼

ˈclass-conscious *adj.* very aware of belonging to a particular social class and of the differences between social classes 有阶级意识的；有社会阶层意识的 ▸ **ˈclass-conscious·ness** *noun* [U]

clas·sic AW /ˈklæsɪk/ *adj., noun*

■ *adj.* [usually before noun] **1** accepted or deserving to be accepted as one of the best or most important of its kind 最优秀的；第一流的： *a classic novel/study/goal* 最佳小说 / 研究 / 进球 ➲ WORDFINDER NOTE AT WRITE **2** (*also* **clas·sic·al**) with all the features you would expect to find; very typical 有代表性的；典型的： ***a classic example*** *of poor communication* 缺乏有效沟通的典型实例 ◇ *She displayed the classic symptoms of depression.* 她显现出了抑郁症的典型症状。◇ *I made the classic mistake of clapping in a pause in the music!* 我犯了一个常见错误，在乐曲演奏暂停的间歇鼓起掌来。**3** elegant, but simple and traditional in style or design; not affected by changes in fashion（风格或设计）典雅的，古朴的；传统的： *a classic grey suit* 一套典雅的灰色服装 ◇ *classic design* 古朴典雅的设计 ◇ ***classic cars*** (= cars which are no longer made, but which are still popular) 古典雅致的老式车 **4** (*informal*) people say **That's classic!** when they find sth very amusing, when they think sb has been very stupid or when sth annoying, but not surprising, happens 惹笑的；愚蠢（或令人讨厌）而又不足为奇的： *She's not going to help? Oh, that's classic!* 她不来帮忙？哦，那不足为奇！

■ *noun* **1** [C] a book, film/movie or song which is well known and considered to be of very high quality, setting standards for other books, etc.（书、电影或歌曲的）经典作品，名著，杰作： *English classics such as 'Alice in Wonderland'* 英语经典作品如《艾丽丝漫游奇境记》◇ *The novel may become a modern classic.* 这部小说可能会成为

▼ WHICH WORD? 词语辨析

classic / classical

These adjectives are frequently used with the following nouns. 以上形容词常与下列名词连用：

classic ~	classical ~
example	music
case	ballet
novel	architecture
work	scholar
car	period

• **Classic** describes something that is accepted as being of very high quality and one of the best of its kind. * classic 指经典的、优秀的、一流的： *a classic movie/work* 经典影片 / 作品 It is also used to describe a typical example of something 该词亦可表示典型的： *a classic example/mistake* 典型的例子 / 错误 or something elegant but simple and traditional. 或表示古典的、典雅的： *classic design* 典雅的设计

• **Classical** describes a form of traditional Western music and other things that are traditional in style. * classical 表示西方古典音乐及其他传统的事物： *a classical composer* 古典派作曲家 ◇ *a classical theory* 古典学说 It is also used to talk about things that are connected with the culture of Ancient Greece and Rome. 该词亦可修饰与古希腊和古罗马文化有关的事物： *a classical scholar* 古典学者 ◇ *classical mythology* 古典神话

现代名著。**2** [C] a thing that is an excellent example of its kind 优秀的典范：*That match was a classic.* 那场比赛堪称经典。**3 Classics** [U] the study of ancient Greek and Roman culture, especially their languages and literature 古希腊与古罗马的文化研究（尤指对其语言与文学的研究）：*a degree in Classics* 古希腊与古罗马文化研究的学位

clas·sic·al AW /ˈklæsɪkl/ *adj.* [usually before noun] **1** widely accepted and used for a long time; traditional in style or idea 古典的；经典的；传统的：*the classical economics of Smith and Ricardo* 斯密与李嘉图的古典经济学 ◊ *the classical theory of unemployment* 传统的失业理论 ◊ *classical and modern ballet* 古典与现代芭蕾舞 **2** connected with or influenced by the culture of ancient Greece and Rome 和古希腊与古罗马文化相关的；受古希腊与古罗马文化影响的：*classical studies* 古希腊与古罗马的文化研究 ◊ *a classical scholar* (= an expert in Latin and Greek) 研究拉丁文与希腊文的学者 **3** (of music 音乐) written in a Western musical tradition, usually using an established form (for example a SYMPHONY) and not played on electronic instruments. Classical music is generally considered to be serious and to have a lasting value. 古典的：*He plays classical music, as well as pop and jazz.* 他演奏流行音乐和爵士乐，同时也演奏古典音乐。◊ *a **classical composer/violinist*** 古典音乐作曲家 / 小提琴手 ➲ COLLOCATIONS AT MUSIC **4** = CLASSIC (2)：*These are classical examples of food allergy.* 这些是食物过敏的典型病例。**5** (of a language 语言) ancient in its form and no longer used in a spoken form 古文的；文言的：*classical Arabic* 古阿拉伯语 **6** simple and attractive 简洁优美的；朴实美观的：*the classical elegance of the design* 设计简洁典雅 ▶ **clas·sic·al·ly** /-kli/ *adv.*：*Her face is classically beautiful.* 她的长相具有古典美。◊ *a **classically trained** singer* 受过古典派训练的歌手

clas·si·cism /ˈklæsɪsɪzəm/ *noun* [U] **1** a style of art and literature that is simple and elegant and is based on the styles of ancient Greece and Rome. Classicism was popular in Europe in the 18th century. 古典主义（基于古希腊与古罗马风格，18 世纪盛行于欧洲） **2** a style or form that has simple, natural qualities and pleasing combinations of parts 古典风格

clas·si·cist /ˈklæsɪsɪst/ *noun* **1** a person who studies ancient Greek or Latin 古希腊文化研究者；拉丁文化研究者；古典学者 **2** a person who follows classicism in art or literature（艺术或文学上的）古典主义者

clas·si·fi·able /ˈklæsɪfaɪəbl/ *adj.* that you can or should CLASSIFY 可分类（或级别）的；应分类（或级别）的：*The information was not easily classifiable.* 此信息不易分类。◊ *top-secret or classifiable information* 绝密或机密信息

clas·si·fi·ca·tion /ˌklæsɪfɪˈkeɪʃn/ *noun* **1** [U] the act or process of putting people or things into a group or class (= of CLASSIFYING them) 分类；归类；分级：*a style of music that defies classification* (= is like no other) 独特的音乐风格 **2** [C] a group, class, division, etc. into which sb or sth is put 类别；等级；门类 **3** [U] (*biology* 生) the act of putting animals, plants, etc. into groups, classes or divisions according to their characteristics（动植物等的）分类 ➲ WORDFINDER NOTE AT BREED **4** [C] (*specialist*) a system of arranging books, tapes, magazines, etc. in a library into groups according to their subject（图书馆的书、磁带、杂志等的）分类系统，编目

clas·si·fied /ˈklæsɪfaɪd/ *adj.* [usually before noun] **1** (of information 信息) officially secret and available only to particular people 机密的；保密的：***classified information/documents/material*** 机密信息 / 文件 / 材料 OPP **unclassified** **2** with information arranged in groups according to subjects 分类的；归类的：*a classified catalogue* 分类目录 **3 classifieds** *noun* [pl.] = CLASSIFIED ADVERTISEMENTS

ˌclassified adˈvertisements (*also* ˌ**classified ˈads**, ˈ**classifieds**) (*BrE also* ˈ**small ads**) (*NAmE also* ˈ**want ads**) *noun* [pl.] the section in a newspaper with small advertisements arranged in groups according to their subject, that are placed by people or small companies who want to buy or sell sth, find or offer a job, etc.（报章上的）分类广告

clas·si·fier /ˈklæsɪfaɪə(r)/ *noun* (*grammar* 语法) an AFFIX or word which shows that a word belongs to a group of words with similar meanings. For example the prefix 'un' is a classifier that shows the word is negative. 分类成分，分类词（能显示同义所属关系，如前缀 un 是表示反义的分类成分）

clas·sify /ˈklæsɪfaɪ/ *verb* (**clas·si·fies**, **clas·si·fy·ing**, **clas·si·fied**, **clas·si·fied**) **1 ~ sth** to arrange sth in groups according to features that they have in common 分类；归类：*The books in the library **are classified according to** subject.* 图书馆的书按学科分类。◊ *Patients **are classified into** three categories.* 病人被归为三种类型。**2 ~ sb/sth as sth** to decide which type or group sb/sth belongs to 划分；界定：*Only eleven of these accidents were classified as major.* 这些事故中只有十一例被判定为重大事故。

class·less /ˈklɑːsləs; *NAmE* ˈklæs-/ *adj.* **1** (*approving*) with no divisions into social classes 无阶级的：*Will Britain ever become a classless society?* 英国会有可能成为无阶级的社会吗？**2** not clearly belonging to a particular social class 不明显属于社会某阶级（或阶层）的：*a classless accent* 不带社会阶层特征的口音 ▶ **class·less·ness** *noun* [U]

class·mate /ˈklɑːsmeɪt; *NAmE* ˈklæs-/ *noun* a person who is or was in the same class as you at school or college 同班同学

class·room /ˈklɑːsruːm; -rʊm; *NAmE* ˈklæs-/ *noun* a room where a class of children or students is taught 教室；课堂：*classroom activities* 课堂活动 ◊ *the use of computers in the classroom* 在课堂使用计算机 ➲ VISUAL VOCAB PAGE V72

ˌclass ˈstruggle (*also* ˌ**class ˈwar**) *noun* [U, sing.] (*politics* 政) opposition between the different social classes in society, especially that described in Marxist theory（尤指马克思主义理论描述的）阶级斗争

classy /ˈklɑːsi; *NAmE* ˈklæsi/ *adj.* (**classi·er**, **classi·est**) (*informal*) of high quality; expensive and/or fashionable 上等的；豪华的；时髦的：*a classy player* 优秀选手 ◊ *a classy hotel/restaurant* 豪华的旅馆 / 餐馆

clat·ter /ˈklætə(r)/ *verb* **1** [I] if hard objects **clatter**, they knock together and make a loud noise（硬物相碰）发出响亮的撞击声：*He dropped the knife and it clattered on the stone floor.* 他一失手，刀子当啷一声掉到石头地面上。◊ *Her cup clattered in the saucer.* 她的杯子把茶碟碰得叮当响。**2** [I] + **adv./prep.** to move making a loud noise like hard objects knocking together 移动发出（像硬物碰撞）的响声：*The cart clattered over the cobbles.* 马车哐当哐当地行驶在卵石路上。◊ *She heard him clattering around downstairs.* 她听到他在楼下咔哒咔哒地走来走去。▶ **clat·ter** (*also* **clat·ter·ing**) *noun* [sing.]：*the clatter of horses' hoofs* 嗒嗒的马蹄声

clause AW /klɔːz/ *noun* **1** (*grammar* 语法) a group of words that includes a subject and a verb, and forms a sentence or part of a sentence 从句；子句；分句：*In the sentence 'They often go to Italy because they love the food', 'They often go to Italy' is the main clause and 'because they love the food' is a subordinate clause.* 在 They often go to Italy because they love the food 这个句子里，They often go to Italy 是主句，because they love the food 是从句。**2** an item in a legal document that says that a particular thing must or must not be done（法律文件的）条款 ➲ WORDFINDER NOTE AT DOCUMENT

claus·tro·pho·bia /ˌklɔːstrəˈfəʊbiə; *NAmE* -ˈfoʊ-/ *noun* [U] an extreme fear of being in a small confined place; the unpleasant feeling that a person gets in a situation which restricts them 幽闭恐怖（症）；因受限制而产生的不适感：*to suffer from claustrophobia* 患幽闭恐怖症 ◊ *She felt she had to escape from the claustrophobia of family life.* 她感到她得摆脱家庭生活的那种幽闭感觉了。➲ COMPARE AGORAPHOBIA

claus·tro·pho·bic /ˌklɔːstrəˈfəʊbɪk; *NAmE* -ˈfoʊ-/ *adj.* giving you claustrophobia; suffering from claustrophobia

引起幽闭恐怖的；患幽闭恐怖症的： *the claustrophobic atmosphere of the room* 房间里的幽闭恐怖气氛 ◇ *to feel claustrophobic* 感到幽闭恐怖 ▶ **claus·tro·pho·bic** *noun*

C

clave /kleɪv; 'klɑːveɪ/ *noun* **1** one of a pair of wooden sticks that are hit together to make a sound 响棒（打击乐器，成双） **2** a rhythm that forms the basis of Latin music 响棒节奏（拉丁音乐的一个基本节奏）

clavi·chord /'klævɪkɔːd; *NAmE* -kɔːrd/ *noun* an early type of musical instrument, like a piano with a very soft tone 击弦键琴

clav·icle /'klævɪkl/ *noun* (*anatomy* 解) the COLLARBONE 锁骨 ➲ VISUAL VOCAB PAGE V64

claw /klɔː/ *noun, verb*

■ ***noun*** **1** one of the sharp curved nails on the end of an animal's or a bird's foot （动物或禽类的）爪，脚爪，脚趾 ➲ VISUAL VOCAB PAGE V12 **2** a long, sharp curved part of the body of some types of SHELLFISH, used for catching and holding things （水生有壳动物的）螯，钳： *the claws of a crab* 螃蟹的螯 ➲ PICTURE AT SHELLFISH ➲ VISUAL VOCAB PAGE V13 **3** part of a tool or machine, like a claw, used for holding, pulling or lifting things 爪形夹具；（机械的）爪 ➲ VISUAL VOCAB PAGE V21 ➲ SEE ALSO CLAW HAMMER

IDM **get your claws into sb** **1** (*disapproving*) if a woman **gets her claws** into a man, she tries hard to make him marry her or to have a relationship with her （女人）死死缠住（男人） **2** to criticize sb severely 严厉批评： *Wait until the media gets its claws into her.* 等着媒体来严厉批驳她吧。 ➲ MORE AT RED *adj.*

■ ***verb*** [I, T] to scratch or tear sb/sth with claws or with your nails （用爪子或手指甲）抓，撕，挠： **~ at sb/sth** *The cat was clawing at the leg of the chair.* 那只猫在抓挠椅子腿。 ◇ **~ sb/sth** *She had clawed Stephen across the face.* 她抓过斯蒂芬的脸。 ◇ (*figurative*) *His hands clawed the air.* 他的双手在空中乱抓。

IDM **claw your way back, into sth, out of sth, to sth, etc.** to gradually achieve sth or move somewhere by using a lot of determination and effort 努力逐步获得；艰难地移动： *She clawed her way to the top of her profession.* 她努力不懈，终于爬到了职业的顶峰。 ◇ *Slowly, he clawed his way out from under the collapsed building.* 他艰难地从倒塌的大楼废墟底下慢慢爬了出来。

PHR V ˌ**claw sth**↔'**back** **1** to get sth back that you have lost, usually by using a lot of effort 设法捞回；费力地挽回 **2** (of a government 政府) to get back money that has been paid to people, usually by taxing them （常通过税收手段）收回（已支付给民众的钱款） ➲ RELATED NOUN CLAWBACK

claw·back /'klɔːbæk/ *noun* (*BrE, business* 商) the act of getting money back from people it has been paid to; the money that is paid back 收回（款）；追回（款）

ˈ**claw hammer** *noun* a hammer with one split, curved side that is used for pulling out nails 鱼尾锤；拔钉锤；羊角榔头

clay /kleɪ/ *noun* [U] a type of heavy, sticky earth that becomes hard when it is baked and is used to make things such as pots and bricks 黏土；陶土 ➲ SYNONYMS AT SOIL IDM SEE FOOT *n.*

ˈ**clay court** *noun* a TENNIS COURT that has a surface made of clay 红土网球场；沙地网球场

clayey /'kleɪi/ *adj.* containing clay; like clay 含黏土的；黏土质的；似黏土的： *clayey soil* 黏性土壤

clay·more /'kleɪmɔː(r)/ *noun* a large SWORD with a broad blade with two sharp edges that was used in Scotland in the past （旧时苏格兰的）双刃大刀

ˌ**clay 'pigeon shooting** (*BrE*) (*NAmE* **'skeet shooting**) *noun* a sport in which a disc of baked clay (called a **clay pigeon**) is thrown into the air for people to shoot at 泥鸽飞靶射击运动

clean 🔑 /kliːn/ *adj., verb, adv., noun*

■ ***adj.*** (**clean·er, clean·est**)

• **NOT DIRTY** 清洁 **1** 🔑 not dirty 洁净的；干净的： *Are your hands clean?* 你的手干净吗？ ◇ *to **wipe sth clean*** 把某物擦干净 ◇ *The hotel was **spotlessly*** (= extremely) ***clean**.* 这家旅馆干净得一尘不染。 ◇ (*BrE*) *It is your responsibility to **keep** the room **clean and tidy**.* 保持房间整洁是你的职责。 ◇ (*NAmE*) ***Keep** your room **neat and clean**.* 保持房间整洁。 ◇ *I can't find a clean shirt* (= one I haven't worn since it was washed). 我找不到一件干净的衬衫。 **2** 🔑 having a clean appearance and clean surroundings 爱干净的；爱整洁的： *Cats are very clean animals.* 猫是很爱干净的动物。

• **NOT HARMFUL** 无害 **3** 🔑 free from harmful or unpleasant substances 无有害物的；无污染的： *clean drinking water* 洁净的饮用水 ◇ *clean air* 清洁的空气 ◇ *cleaner cars* (= not producing so many harmful substances) 环保型汽车

• **PAPER** 纸 **4** 🔑 [usually before noun] with nothing written on it 空白的；未写过字的： *a clean sheet of paper* 一张空白纸

• **NOT OFFENSIVE** 文明 **5** 🔑 not offensive or referring to sex; not doing anything that is considered immoral or bad 文明的；无色情的；正派的： *The entertainment was **good clean fun** for the whole family.* 这种娱乐文明有趣，对全家老少都适合。 ◇ *Keep the jokes clean please!* 开玩笑请文明点！ ◇ *The sport has a very clean image.* 这项运动享有很文明的声誉。

• **NOT ILLEGAL** 合法 **6** 🔑 not showing or having any record of doing sth that is against the law 无犯罪记录的；守法的；清白的： *a **clean driving licence/driver's license*** 无违章记录的驾驶执照 ◇ *a clean police record* 无犯罪记录 **7** (*informal*) not owning or carrying anything illegal such as drugs or weapons 没有私藏（或携带）违禁品（如毒品、武器等）的： *The police searched her but she was clean.* 警察搜了她的身，但未发现她携带任何违禁品。

• **FAIR** 公正 **8** played or done in a fair way and within the rules 公平的；守规则的；不违例的： *It was a tough but clean game.* 这是一场打得艰苦但却是规规矩矩的比赛。

• **SMOOTH/SIMPLE** 平整；简洁 **9** having a smooth edge, surface or shape; simple and regular 边缘平整的；表面平滑的；简洁规则的： *A sharp knife makes a clean cut.* 快刀切得整齐。 ◇ *a modern design with clean lines and a bright appearance* 线条流畅、外观明快的现代设计

• **ACCURATE** 准确 **10** done in a skilful and accurate way 动作熟练而准确的；干净利落的： *The plane made a clean take-off.* 飞机起飞得干净利落。

• **TASTE/SMELL** 味道；气味 **11** tasting, smelling or looking pleasant and fresh 清醇的；清新的： *The wine has a clean taste and a lovely golden colour.* 这葡萄酒味道清醇，色泽金黄。 ➲ COMPARE UNCLEAN

IDM **as clean as a 'whistle** (*informal*) very clean 干干净净 ➲ MORE LIKE THIS 14, page R26 **a clean bill of 'health** a report that says sb is healthy or that sth is in good condition 健康证明；合格证明 **a clean 'break** **1** a complete separation from a person, an organization, a way of life, etc. （与人、组织、生活方式等的）彻底决裂： *She wanted to make a clean break with the past.* 她想与过去完全断绝。 **2** a break in a bone in one place 一处骨折 **a clean 'sheet/'slate** a record of your work or behaviour that does not show any mistakes or bad things that you have done 无过错记录；清白的历史： *No government operates with a completely clean sheet.* 没有任何政府执政一点也不失误。 ◇ *They kept a clean sheet in the match* (= no goals were scored against them). 他们在比赛中未失一球。 **make a clean 'breast of sth** to tell the truth about sth so that you no longer feel guilty 彻底坦白；如实供认；把…和盘托出 **make a clean sweep (of sth)** **1** to remove all the people or things from an organization that are thought to be unnecessary or need changing 全部撤换；彻底清除 **2** to win all the prizes or parts of a game or competition; to win an election completely （比赛或竞赛中）大获全胜，包揽（所有奖项）；获得选举全胜： *China made a clean sweep of the medals in the gymnastics events.* 中国队在体操比赛中包揽了所有的奖牌。 ◇ *The opinion poll suggests a clean sweep for the Democrats.* 民意测验表明民主党有可能大获全胜。 ➲ MORE AT NOSE *n.*, WIPE *v.*

■ ***verb*** **1** 🔑 [T, I] **~ (sth)** to make sth free from dirt or dust by washing or rubbing it 除去…的灰尘；使…干净；打扫： *to clean the windows/bath/floor* 擦窗户／浴缸／地板 ◇ *to clean a wound* 洗净伤口 ◇ *Have you **cleaned your teeth**?* 你

刷牙了吗？ ◇ *The villa is cleaned twice a week.* 这栋别墅一周打扫两次。 ◇ *I spent all day cooking and cleaning.* 我一整天都忙着做饭和打扫卫生。 ➲ SEE ALSO DRY-CLEAN, SPRING-CLEAN **2** [I] to become clean 变干净: *This oven cleans easily* (= is easy to clean). 这烤箱容易擦洗。 **3** [T] ~ **sth** = DRY-CLEAN : *This coat is filthy. I'll **have it cleaned**.* 这件大衣脏了，我得送去干洗。 **4** [T] ~ **sth** to remove the inside parts of a fish, chicken, etc. before you cook it （烹调前给鱼、鸡等）清除内脏

IDM **clean 'house** (*NAmE*) **1** to remove people or things that are not necessary or wanted 清除不必要的人（或事物）；裁减: *The new manager said he wanted to clean house.* 新上任的经理说他要裁员。 **2** to make your house clean 打扫房屋 **clean up your 'act** (*informal*) to start behaving in a moral or responsible way 改邪归正；重新做人: *He cleaned up his act and came off drugs.* 他已改邪归正戒掉了毒品。

PHR V **,clean sth↔'down** to clean sth thoroughly 彻底打扫；使…彻底干净: *All the equipment should be cleaned down regularly.* 所有设备都应该定期彻底打扫。 **'clean sth off/from sth** | **,clean sth↔'off** to remove sth from sth by brushing, rubbing, etc. 把…刷（或擦）掉: *I cleaned the mud off my shoes.* 我刷掉了鞋子上的泥土。 **,clean sth ↔'out** to clean the inside of sth thoroughly 把（某物）内部彻底打扫干净: *I must clean the fish tank out.* 我必须把养鱼缸彻底清洗干净。 **,clean sb 'out** (*informal*) to use all of sb's money 耗尽（某人的）钱；用光（某人的）钱: *Paying for all those drinks has cleaned me out.* 购买那些饮料把我的钱花得一干二净。 **,clean sb/sth 'out** (*informal*) to steal everything from a person or place 洗劫: *The burglars totally cleaned her out.* 窃贼把她洗劫一空。 **,clean 'up** (*informal*) to win or make a lot of money 赢钱；赚大钱；发财: *This film should clean up at the box offices.* 这部电影在票房收入上应该能赚大钱。 **,clean (yourself) 'up** 🔑 (*informal*) to make yourself clean, usually by washing 把（身体）洗干净: *I need to change and clean up.* 我需要换洗一下。 ◇ *Go and clean yourself up.* 去梳洗干净吧。 ◇ *You'd better **get cleaned up**.* 你最好去梳洗一下。 ➲ RELATED NOUN CLEAN-UP **,clean 'up** | **,clean sth↔'up** to remove dirt, etc. from somewhere 打扫（或清除）干净: *He always expected other people to **clean up after** him* (= when he had made the place dirty or untidy). 他总是指望别人来打扫他弄脏了的地方。 ◇ *Who's going to clean up this mess?* 这么又脏又乱的，谁来清理？ ◇ *to clean up beaches after an oil spillage* 清理石油泄漏后被污染的海滩 ➲ RELATED NOUN CLEAN-UP **,clean sth↔'up** to remove crime and immoral behaviour from a place or an activity 清除（某地或某活动中的）犯罪及不道德行为；清理；整顿: *The new mayor is determined to clean up the city.* 新上任的市长决心要整治好这座城市。 ◇ *Soccer needs to **clean up its image**.* 足球界的形象需要改善。 ➲ RELATED NOUN CLEAN-UP

■ *adv.* (*informal*) used to emphasize that an action takes place completely （行动）彻底地，完全地: *The thief got clean away.* 那小偷已逃之夭夭。 ◇ *I clean forgot about calling him.* 我把给他打电话的事忘得一干二净。

IDM **come clean (with sb) (about sth)** to admit and explain sth that you have kept as a secret 全盘招供；和盘托出: *Isn't it time the government came clean about their plans for education?* 这难道不是政府彻底说明教育计划的时候了吗？

■ *noun* [sing.] the act or process of cleaning sth 打扫；清扫: *The house needed a good clean.* 这房子需要彻底打扫。

> **▼SYNONYMS 同义词辨析**
>
> **clean**
>
> **wash • rinse • cleanse • dry-clean**
>
> These words all mean to remove dirt from sth, especially by using water and/or soap. 以上各词均含打扫、洗净之义，尤指用水、肥皂等。
>
> **clean** to remove dirt or dust from sth, especially by using water or chemicals 指除去灰尘、打扫，尤指用水或化学品洗净、擦净 : *The villa is cleaned twice a week.* 这栋别墅一周打扫两次。 ◇ *Have you cleaned your teeth?* 你刷牙了吗？ ◇ *This coat is filthy. I'll have it cleaned* (= dry-cleaned). 这件大衣脏了，我得送去干洗。
>
> **wash** to remove dirt from sth using water and usually soap 指洗、洗涤 : *He quickly washed his hands and face.* 他很快把手和脸洗了。 ◇ *These jeans need washing.* 这条牛仔裤该洗了。
>
> **rinse** to remove dirt, etc. from sth using clean water only, not soap; to remove the soap from sth with clean water after washing it 指用清水冲洗、清洗、冲掉皂液 : *Make sure you rinse all the soap out.* 一定要把皂液冲洗干净。
>
> **cleanse** to clean your skin or a wound 指清洁（皮肤）、清洗（伤口）
>
> **dry-clean** to clean clothes using chemicals instead of water 指干洗
>
> **PATTERNS**
>
> - to clean/wash/rinse/cleanse sth **in/with** sth
> - to clean/wash/rinse sth **from** sth
> - to clean/wash/cleanse a **wound**
> - to clean/wash the **car/floor**
> - to wash/rinse your **hair**
> - to **have sth** cleaned/washed/dry-cleaned

,clean and 'jerk *noun* an exercise in WEIGHTLIFTING in which a bar with weights is lifted to the shoulder, and then raised above the head （举重）挺举

,clean-'cut *adj.* (especially of a young man 尤指年轻男子) looking neat and clean and therefore socially acceptable 外表整洁的: *Simon's clean-cut good looks* 西蒙整洁英俊的外表

clean·er /'kliːnə(r)/ *noun* **1** a person whose job is to clean other people's houses or offices, etc. 清洁工: *an office cleaner* 办公室清洁工 **2** a machine or substance that is used for cleaning 吸尘器；清洁剂；去污剂: *a vacuum cleaner* 真空吸尘器 ◇ *a bottle of kitchen cleaner* 一瓶厨房清洁剂 **3 cleaner's** (*pl.* **cleaners**) (*also* **,dry-'cleaner's**) a shop/store where clothes, curtains, etc. are cleaned, especially with chemicals 干洗店: *Can you pick up my suit from the cleaner's?* 你能帮我从干洗店取回我的套装吗？

IDM **take sb to the 'cleaners** (*informal*) **1** to steal all of sb's money, etc., or to get it using a trick 将某人洗劫一空；偷光（或骗尽）某人的钱财 **2** to defeat sb completely 彻底打败某人: *Our team got taken to the cleaners.* 我们队被打得一败涂地。

clean·ing /'kliːnɪŋ/ *noun* [U] the work of making the inside of a house, etc. clean 打扫；扫除；清洁: *They pay someone to **do the cleaning**.* 他们花钱雇人打扫。 ➲ VISUAL VOCAB PAGE V21

'cleaning lady (*also* **'cleaning woman**) *noun* a woman whose job is to clean the rooms and furniture in an office, a house, etc. （办公室、房屋等的）清洁女工

,clean-'limbed *adj.* (of a person 人) thin and with a good shape 体形修长优美的；苗条的: *a clean-limbed model* 身材苗条的模特儿

clean·li·ness /'klenlinəs/ *noun* [U] the state of being clean or the habit of keeping things clean 清洁；干净；爱干净的习惯: *Some people are obsessive about cleanliness.* 有些人有洁癖。

,clean-'living *adj.* (of a person 人) living a healthy life, by not drinking alcohol, not having sex with a lot of different people, etc. 生活健康正派的

clean·ly /'kliːnli/ *adv.* **1** easily and smoothly in one movement 干净利落地；利索地: *The boat moved cleanly through the water.* 小船在水面上轻快地行进。 **2** in a clean way 清洁地；干净地: *fuel that burns cleanly* 环保型的燃料

cleanse /klenz/ *verb* **1** [T, I] ~ **(sth)** to clean your skin or a wound 清洁（皮肤）；清洗（伤口）: *a cleansing cream* 洁肤霜 ➲ SYNONYMS AT CLEAN **2** [T] ~ **sb (of/from sth)**

(*literary*) to take away sb's guilty feelings or SIN 使免除（罪过）；使净化 ➲ SEE ALSO ETHNIC CLEANSING

cleans·er /ˈklenzə(r)/ *noun* **1** a liquid or cream for cleaning your face, especially for removing make-up（尤指用于清除脸上化妆的）洁肤液，洁肤霜 ➲ WORDFINDER NOTE AT MAKE-UP **2** a substance that contains chemicals and is used for cleaning things 清洁剂

ˌclean-ˈshaven *adj.* a man who is **clean-shaven** does not have a beard or MOUSTACHE (= hair that has been allowed to grow on the face) 胡子刮净的；刮过脸的

ˈclean-up *noun* [usually sing.] the process of removing dirt, pollution, or things that are considered bad or immoral from a place 清扫；清除（污染物）；清理；整顿：*the clean-up of the river* 河流清理 ◇ *a clean-up campaign* 整顿运动

clear 🔑 /klɪə(r); *NAmE* klɪr/ *adj.*, *verb*, *adv.*, *noun*

> **WORD FAMILY**
> **clear** *adj.* (≠ unclear)
> **clearly** *adv.*
> **clarity** *noun*
> **clarify** *verb*

■ ***adj.*** (**clear·er**, **clear·est**)

• **WITHOUT CONFUSION/DOUBT** 清晰；无疑问 **1** 🔑 easy to understand and not causing any confusion 清晰易懂的；明白清楚的；不含混的：*She gave me clear and precise directions.* 她给了我清晰而准确的指示。◇ *Are these instructions clear enough?* 这些说明够清楚了吗？◇ *You'll do as you're told, is that clear?* 叫你做什么你就去做什么，明白吗？◇ *This behaviour must stop—do I* ***make myself clear*** (= express myself clearly so there is no doubt about what I mean)? 这种行为必须停止。我讲清楚了吧？◇ *I hope I* ***made it clear*** *to him that he was no longer welcome here.* 我希望我已经给他讲清楚他在这里不再受欢迎。**2** 🔑 obvious and leaving no doubt at all 明显的；显然的；明确的：*This is a clear case of fraud.* 这无疑是一桩诈骗案。◇ *She won the election by a clear majority.* 她以明显的多数赢得选举。◇ *His height gives him a clear advantage.* 他的身高使他具有明显的优势。◇ **~ (to sb) (that)...** ***It was*** *quite* ***clear*** *to me* ***that*** *she was lying.* 我十分清楚她在撒谎。◇ **~ what, how, whether, etc....** *It is not clear what they want us to do.* 我们不清楚他们要我们做什么。➲ LANGUAGE BANK AT EVIDENCE, IMPERSONAL **3** 🔑 having or feeling no doubt or confusion 无疑的；清楚的；明白的：**~ about/on sth** *Are you clear about the arrangements for tomorrow?* 你清楚明天的安排吗？◇ *My memory is not clear on that point.* 那一点我记不清了。◇ **~ what, how, whether, etc....** *I'm still not clear what the job involves.* 我仍然不明白这项工作包括哪些内容。◇ *We need a* ***clear understanding*** *of the problems involved.* 我们需要了解清楚所涉及的各种问题。➲ SYNONYMS AT SURE ➲ EXPRESS YOURSELF AT EXPLAIN

• **MIND** 头脑 **4** 🔑 thinking in a sensible and logical way, especially in a difficult situation（尤指在困境中）思维敏锐而有逻辑的，头脑清醒的：*a clear thinker* 思维清晰的人 ◇ *You'll need to* ***keep a clear head*** *for your interview.* 你面试时要保持清醒的头脑。

• **EASY TO SEE/HEAR** 容易看见/听到 **5** 🔑 easy to see or hear 容易看见的；听得清的：*The photo wasn't very clear.* 这张照片不太清晰。◇ *The voice on the phone was clear and strong.* 电话上的声音清晰洪亮。◇ *She was in Australia but I could hear her voice* ***as clear as a bell.*** 她虽然在澳大利亚，但我却能非常清楚地听到她的声音。

• **TRANSPARENT** 透明 **6** 🔑 that you can see through 透明的；清澈的：*The water was so clear we could see the bottom of the lake.* 湖水清澈见底。◇ *clear glass* 透明的玻璃 ◇ *a clear colourless liquid* 透明的无色液体

• **SKY/WEATHER** 天空；天气 **7** 🔑 without cloud or MIST 无云（或雾）的；晴朗的：*a clear blue sky* 晴朗的碧空 ◇ *On a clear day you can see France.* 天气晴朗时你可以看见法国。

• **SKIN** 皮肤 **8** without spots or marks 无斑（或疤痕）的：*clear skin* 没有丝毫斑点的皮肤 ◇ *a clear complexion* 无瑕的面庞

• **EYES** 眼睛 **9** bright and lively 明亮有神的

• **NOT BLOCKED** 无阻碍 **10 ~ (of sth)** free from things that are blocking the way or covering the surface of sth 畅通无阻的；无障碍的；（表面）收拾干净的：*The road was clear and I ran over.* 路上没有东西挡着，我就跑了过来。◇ *All exits must be kept clear of baggage.* 所有出口必须保持通畅，不得堆放行李。◇ *You won't get a clear view of the stage from here.* 从这里看舞台，你的视野会受到遮挡。◇ *I always leave a clear desk at the end of the day.* 每天工作结束时，我总是把桌面收拾干净。

• **CONSCIENCE** 良心 **11** if you have a **clear** CONSCIENCE or your CONSCIENCE is **clear**, you do not feel guilty 无罪的；清白的；问心无愧的

• **FREE FROM STH BAD** 与坏事不沾边 **12 ~ of sth** free from sth that is unpleasant 摆脱掉（不愉快事物）的：*They were still not clear of all suspicion.* 他们仍未解除所有的嫌疑。◇ *We are finally clear of debt.* 我们终于偿清了债务。

• **NOT TOUCHING/NEAR** 不接触；不靠近 **13** [not before noun] **~ (of sb/sth)** not touching sth; a distance away from sth 不接触；远离：*The plane climbed until it was clear of the clouds.* 飞机爬升直至穿出了云层。◇ *Make sure you park your car clear of the entrance.* 切莫把车停在入口处。

• **PERIOD OF TIME** 一段时间 **14** [only before noun] whole or complete 全部的；整体的；完整的：*Allow three clear days*

> ▼ **SYNONYMS 同义词辨析**
>
> **clear**
>
> **obvious • apparent • evident • plain**
>
> These words all describe sth that is easy to see or understand and leaves no doubts or confusion. 以上各词均形容事物显而易见、明白易懂、清楚、明确。
>
> **clear** easy to see or understand and leaving no doubts 指显而易见的、明白易懂的、清楚的、明确的：*It was quite clear to me that she was lying.* 我十分清楚她在撒谎。
>
> **obvious** easy to see or understand 指明显的、显然的、易理解的：*It's obvious from what he said that something is wrong.* 根据他所说的，显然是出问题了。
>
> **apparent** [not usually before noun] (*rather formal*) easy to see or understand 指显而易见、明白易懂、显然：*It was apparent from her face that she was really upset.* 从面容上一眼就可以看出她确实心绪烦乱。
>
> **evident** (*rather formal*) easy to see or understand 指清楚的、明白的、显然的：*The orchestra played with evident enjoyment.* 管弦乐队演奏得兴致勃勃。
>
> **plain** easy to see or understand 指清楚的、明显的、浅白的：*He* ***made it*** *very* ***plain*** *that he wanted us to leave.* 他明确表示要我们离开。
>
> **WHICH WORD? 词语辨析**
>
> These words all have almost exactly the same meaning. There are slight differences in register and patterns of use. If you *make sth clear/plain*, you do so deliberately because you want people to understand sth; if you *make sth obvious*, you usually do it without meaning to. 以上各词意思几乎相同，只是在语体风格和句型使用上稍有区别。make sth clear/plain 表示刻意为使别人明白；make sth obvious 通常并非刻意：~~*I hope I make myself obvious.*~~ ◇ ~~*Try not to make it so clear/plain.*~~ In the expressions *clear majority*, *for obvious reasons*, *for no apparent reason* and *plain to see*, none of the other words can be used instead. You can have *a clear/an obvious/a plain case of sth* but not ~~*an evident case of sth*~~. 在 clear majority（明显多数）、for obvious reasons（因为显而易见的原因）、for no apparent reason（没有明显的原因）和 plain to see（显而易见）中，表示"明显"的词不能替换。可以用 clear/obvious/plain case of sth（明显的情况），但不能用 an evident case of sth。
>
> **PATTERNS**
>
> • clear/obvious/apparent/evident/plain **to** sb/sth
> • clear/obvious/apparent/evident/plain **that/what/who/how/where/why...**
> • to **seem/become/make sth** clear/obvious/apparent/evident/plain
> • **perfectly/quite/very** clear/obvious/apparent/evident/plain

for the letter to arrive. 信要整整三天才能寄到。

- **SUM OF MONEY** 款项 **15** [only before noun] remaining when taxes, costs, etc. have been taken away（扣除税项、成本等后）净的，纯的 **SYN net**: *They had made a clear profit of £2 000.* 他们已赚得 2 000 英镑的净利。
- **PHONETICS** 语音学 **16** (of a speech sound 语音) produced with the central part of the tongue close to the top of the mouth. In many accents of English, clear /l/ is used before a vowel, as in *leave*. 清晰的 **OPP dark**

IDM be clear 'sailing (*US*) = BE PLAIN SAILING **(as) clear as 'day** easy to see or understand 显而易见；容易理解 **(as) clear as 'mud** (*informal, humorous*) not clear at all; not easy to understand 一点不清楚；难懂：*Oh well, that's all as clear as mud, then.* 哎呀，那么一来这真是成了一本糊涂账了。➲ MORE AT FIELD *n.*, HEAD *n.*, LOUD *adv.*

■ ***verb***

- **REMOVE STH/SB** 移动某物；使某人离去 **1** 🔑 [T] to remove sth that is not wanted or needed from a place 移走，搬走，清除（不需要的东西）：**~ sth** *I had cleared my desk before I left.* 离开前我清理干净了办公桌。◊ *It was several hours before the road was cleared after the accident.* 事故过去几小时后这条道路才被疏通。◊ *It's your turn to* ***clear the table*** (= to take away the dirty plates, etc. after a meal). 该轮到你收拾餐桌了。◊ *She* ***cleared a space*** *on the sofa for him to sit down.* 她在沙发上清出一个空位让他坐下。◊ **~ A (of B)** *I cleared my desk of papers.* 我清理好了写字台上的文件。◊ *The streets had been cleared of snow.* 街道上的积雪已被清除干净。◊ **~ B (from/off A)** *Clear all those papers off the desk.* 把桌子上所有那些文件都拿走。◊ *The remains of the snow had been cleared from the streets.* 街道上的残雪已被清扫干净。➲ SEE ALSO CLEAR AWAY **2** 🔑 [T] **~ sth** to make people leave a place 使人离开：*After the bomb warning, police cleared the streets.* 接到有炸弹的警告后，警察疏散了街上的行人。
- **NOT BE BLOCKED** 不受阻碍 **3** 🔑 [I] to move freely again; to no longer be blocked 恢复畅通；不再受阻：*The traffic took a long time to clear after the accident.* 事故后很久交通才恢复畅通。◊ *The boy's lungs cleared and he began to breathe more easily.* 男孩的肺部恢复通畅后，呼吸开始比较轻松。
- **OF LIQUID** 液体 **4** 🔑 [I] when a liquid **clears**, it becomes transparent and you can see through it 变透明；变清澈：*The muddy water slowly cleared.* 浑浊的水慢慢变得清澈起来。
- **OF SMOKE, ETC.** 烟等 **5** 🔑 [I] **~ (away)** when smoke, FOG, etc. **clears**, it disappears so that it is easier to see things（烟、雾等）消散，散去，消失：*The mist will clear by mid-morning.* 雾将在上午十时左右消散。
- **OF SKY/WEATHER** 天空；天气 **6** [I] when the sky or the weather **clears**, it becomes brighter and free of cloud or rain 变明朗；转晴；放晴：*The sky cleared after the storm.* 暴风雨过后，天转晴了。◊ *The rain is clearing slowly.* 雨渐渐停下来。
- **YOUR HEAD/MIND** 头脑；思路 **7** [I, T] if your head or mind **clears**, or you **clear** it, you become free of thoughts that worry or confuse you or the effects of alcohol, a blow, etc. and you are able to think clearly（使）变清醒，变清晰：*As her mind cleared, she remembered what had happened.* 头脑清醒之后，她想起了所发生的一切。◊ **~ sth** *I went for a walk to clear my head.* 我去散一会儿步，好清醒清醒头脑。
- **OF FACE/EXPRESSION** 脸色；表情 **8** [I] if your face or expression **clears**, you stop looking angry or worried 变平静；变开朗
- **PROVE SB INNOCENT** 证明无罪 **9** [T] **~ sb (of sth)** to prove that sb is innocent 证明无罪（或无辜）：*She was cleared of all charges against her.* 对她的所有指控均已撤销。◊ *Throughout his years in prison, he fought to* ***clear his name***. 在整个服刑期间，他奋力证明自己名誉的清白。
- **GIVE OFFICIAL PERMISSION** 批准 **10** [T] to give or get official approval for sth to be done 批准；准许；得到许可：**~ sth** *His appointment had been cleared by the board.* 他的任命已由董事会批准。◊ **~ sth with sb/sth** *I'll have to* ***clear it with*** *the manager.* 这事我须要获得经理的准许。**11** [T] **~ sth** to give official permission for a person, a ship, a plane or goods to leave or enter a place 批准（人、船只、飞机或货物）离境（或入境）；使通过（海关）：*The plane had been cleared for take-off.* 飞机已获准起飞。◊ *to clear goods through customs* 给货物结关 **12** [T] **~ sb** to decide officially, after finding out information about sb, that they can be given special work or allowed to see secret papers （经审查后）正式批准（某人）做机密工作（或阅读机密文件）：*She hasn't been cleared by security.* 她未获保安部门批准做机要工作。
- **MONEY** 款项 **13** [I, T] **~ (sth)** if a payment that is made into your bank account **clears**, or a bank **clears** it, the money is available for you to use （付款）到账；（银行）将（付款）划入账户：*Cheques usually take three working days to clear.* 兑现支票通常需要三个工作日。 **14** [T] **~ sth** to gain or earn a sum of money as profit 获利；净赚：*She cleared £1 000 on the deal.* 她在那笔交易中净赚 1 000 英镑。 **15** [T] **~ sth** if you **clear** a debt or a loan, you pay all the money back 偿清，还清（债务或贷款）
- **GET OVER/PAST** 越过；通过 **16** [T] **~ sth** to jump over or get past sth without touching it （无接触地）跃过，越过，通过：*The horse cleared the fence easily.* 那匹马轻松地跃过了栅栏。◊ *The car only just cleared* (= avoided hitting) *the gatepost.* 那辆汽车通过时险些撞上门柱。
- **IN SPORT** 体育运动 **17** [T, I] **~ (sth)** (in football (SOCCER) and some other sports 足球及其他一些体育运动) if you **clear** a ball, or a ball **clears**, it is kicked or hit away from the area near your own goal 将（球）击离己方球门区；（球）滚离己方球门区

IDM clear the 'air to improve a difficult or TENSE situation by talking about worries, doubts, etc. （通过倾诉）改变困境，缓解紧张状态，改善气氛 **clear the 'decks** (*informal*) to prepare for an activity, event, etc. by removing anything that is not essential to it 清除障碍准备行动 **clear your 'throat** to cough so that you can speak clearly 清喉咙；清嗓子 **clear the way (for sth/for sth to happen)** to remove things that are stopping the progress or movement of sth （为…）清除障碍，扫清道路：*The ruling could clear the way for extradition proceedings.* 这项裁决也许能为引渡程序铺平道路。➲ MORE AT COAST *n.*, COBWEB

PHR V ,clear a'way | ,clear sth↔a'way to remove sth because it is not wanted or needed, or in order to leave a clear space 把…清除掉（以留出空间）：*He cleared away and made coffee.* 他把东西收拾好以后煮了咖啡。◊ *It's time your toys were cleared away.* 现在该收走你的玩具了。**,clear 'off** (*informal*) to go or run away 离开；逃离；逃跑：*He cleared off when he heard the police siren.* 他听到警笛便逃之夭夭。◊ *You've no right to be here. Clear off!* 你无权在这里，走开！ **,clear 'out (of...)** (*informal*) to leave a place quickly 迅速离开：*He cleared out with all the money and left her with the kids.* 他卷款而逃，把孩子丢给她。 **,clear 'out | ,clear sth↔'out** 🔑 to make sth empty and clean by removing things or throwing things away 把…清空；清理；丢掉：*to clear out a drawer/room* 把抽屉 / 房间腾空 ◊ *We cleared out all our old clothes.* 我们扔掉了所有的旧衣服。◊ *I found the letters when I was clearing out after my father died.* 我在父亲去世后清理遗物时发现了这些信件。➲ RELATED NOUN CLEAR-OUT **,clear 'up 1** 🔑 (of the weather 天气) to become fine or bright 转晴；放晴；变晴朗：*I hope it clears up this afternoon.* 我希望今天下午天气放晴。 **2** (of an illness, infection, etc. 疾病、感染等) to disappear 痊愈；治愈；消失：*Has your rash cleared up yet?* 你的皮疹消失了吗？ **,clear 'up | ,clear sth↔'up** 🔑 to make sth clean and neat 使整洁；清理：*It's time to clear up.* 该打扫了。◊ *I'm fed up with* ***clearing up after you!*** 你弄脏了的地方总是要我来打扫，我受够了！◊ *Clear up your own mess!* 看你把这里弄得又脏又乱的，你自己来收拾吧！ **,clear sth↔'up** 🔑 to solve or explain sth 解决；解答；解释：*to clear up a* ***mystery/difficulty/misunderstanding*** 揭开谜团；解决困难；消除误会

■ ***adv.***

- **NOT NEAR/TOUCHING** 不靠近；不触及 **1** 🔑 **~ (of sth)** away from sth; not near or touching sth 离开；不靠近；不接触：*Stand clear of the train doors.* 不要靠近列车门站立。◊ *He injured his arm as he jumped clear of the car.* 他跳离汽车时手臂受了伤。◊ *By lap two Walker was two metres clear of the rest of the runners.* 跑第二圈时，沃克已领先了

其他赛跑者两米。

• ALL THE WAY 一直 **2** (*especially NAmE*) all the way to sth that is far away 一直（到远处）: *She could see clear down the highway into the town.* 她顺着公路一直望去，能看到远处的那座城镇。

IDM **keep/stay/steer clear (of sb/sth)** to avoid a person or thing because it may cause problems 避开；回避；躲避 ➲MORE AT WAY *n.*

■*noun*

IDM **in the 'clear** (*informal*) no longer in danger or thought to be guilty of sth 不再有危险；不再被认为有罪: *It seems that the original suspect is in the clear.* 好像原先的嫌疑犯已被认定无罪。

clear·ance /ˈklɪərəns; *NAmE* ˈklɪr-/ *noun* **1** [C, U] the removal of things that are not wanted 清除；排除；清理: *forest clearances* 伐空的林地 ◇ *slum clearance* (= the removal of houses that are in very bad condition in an area of a town) 拆除贫民窟 ◇ *a clearance sale* (= in a shop/store, when goods are sold cheaply to get rid of them quickly) 清仓大甩卖 **2** [U, C] the amount of space or distance that is needed between two objects so that they do not touch each other 净空；间距；间隙: *There is not much clearance for vehicles passing under this bridge.* 车辆在这座桥下通过时没有多少余隙。◇ *a clearance of one metre* 一米的间距 **3** [U, C] official permission that is given to sb before they can work somewhere, have particular information, or do sth they want to do（录用或准许接触机密以前的）审查许可，审核批准: *I'm waiting for clearance from headquarters.* 我在等待总部的录用审查许可。◇ *All employees at the submarine base require security clearance.* 所有潜水艇基地的雇员必须得到安全部门的审查许可方可录用。 **4** [U] official permission for a person or vehicle to enter or leave an airport or a country（人、交通工具进出机场或出入境的）许可，准许: *The pilot was waiting for clearance for take-off.* 飞行员在等待起飞的许可。 **5** [U, C] the process of a payment into a bank account being confirmed by the bank, so the money is available for you to use（付款的）到账 **6** [C] a **clearance** in football (SOCCER) and some other sports is when a player kicks or hits the ball away from the goal of his or her own team（足球及其他一些体育运动中的）解围

ˌ**clear-ˈcut** *adj.* definite and easy to see or identify 明确的；明显的；易辨认的: *There is no clear-cut answer to this question.* 这个问题没有确切的答案。

ˌ**clear-ˈheaded** *adj.* able to think in a clear and sensible way, especially in a difficult situation（尤指在困境中）头脑清醒的，明白事理的

clear·ing /ˈklɪərɪŋ; *NAmE* ˈklɪrɪŋ/ *noun* **1** [C] an open space in a forest where there are no trees 林中空地 SYN **glade** ➲VISUAL VOCAB PAGE V5 **2** [U] (in Britain) the system used by universities to find students for the places on their courses that have not been filled shortly before the beginning of the academic year（英国大学的）补录（学年开始前补招学生填补空缺名额）: *She got into university through clearing.* 她通过补录上了大学。◇ *You can apply for a place through the clearing system.* 你可以通过补录系统申请一个名额。◇ *The university has a limited number of clearing places this year.* 今年这所大学的补录名额有限。

ˈ**clearing bank** *noun* (in Britain) a bank that uses a clearing house when dealing with other banks（英国）清算银行，票据交换银行

ˈ**clearing house** *noun* **1** a central office that banks use in order to pay each other money and exchange cheques, etc.（银行）票据交换所，清算中心，结算所 **2** an organization that collects and exchanges information on behalf of people or other organizations 信息交换机构；信息交流所

clear·ly 🔑 /ˈklɪəli; *NAmE* ˈklɪrli/ *adv.* **1** 🔑 in a way that is easy to see or hear 清楚地；清晰地: *Please speak clearly after the tone.* 请听到信号后清楚地讲话。 **2** 🔑 in a way that is sensible and easy to understand 明白地；易懂地: *She explained everything very clearly.* 她把一切都解释得很明白。 **3** 🔑 used to emphasize that what you are saying is obvious and true 明显地；显然地 SYN **obviously**: *Clearly, this will cost a lot more than we realized.* 显而易见，这将比我们以前了解到的花费要多得多。

clear·ness /ˈklɪənəs; *NAmE* ˈklɪrnəs/ *noun* [U] (much less frequent than *clarity* 远不及 clarity 一词用得频繁) the state of being clear 清楚；清晰；明确

ˈ**clear-out** *noun* [usually sing.] (*informal, especially BrE*) a process of getting rid of things or people that you no longer want 清理；清除: *have a clear-out* 清理一下

ˌ**clear-ˈsighted** *adj.* understanding or thinking clearly; able to make good decisions and judgements 明白的；头脑清楚的；有眼光的

ˈ**clear-up** *noun* (*BrE*) the process of removing rubbish and tidying things 打扫清理: *a massive clear-up operation* 大扫除活动

clear·way /ˈklɪəweɪ; *NAmE* ˈklɪrweɪ/ *noun* (in Britain) a road on which vehicles must not stop（英国）禁停公路

cleat /kliːt/ *noun* **1** [C] a small wooden or metal bar fastened to sth, on which ropes may be fastened by winding（可绕绳索的）小木桩，金属桩 **2** [C] a piece of rubber on the bottom of a shoe, etc. to stop it from slipping（鞋底等的）防滑钉 **3 cleats** [pl.] (*NAmE*) shoes with cleats, often worn for playing sports 防滑（运动）鞋 ➲COMPARE FOOTBALL BOOT, SPIKE *n.* (2), STUD (3)

cleav·age /ˈkliːvɪdʒ/ *noun* **1** [C, U] the space between a woman's breasts that can be seen above a dress that does not completely cover them（妇女穿低胸服时露出的）乳沟 **2** [C] (*formal*) a difference or division between people or groups（个人或集团之间的）差异，差别，分歧

cleave /kliːv/ *verb* (**cleaved**, **cleaved**) HELP Less commonly, **cleft** /kleft/ and **clove** /kləʊv; *NAmE* kloʊv/ are used for the past tense, and **cleft** and **cloven** /ˈkləʊvn; *NAmE* ˈkloʊvn/ for the past participle. 过去式 cleft 或 clove 以及过去分词 cleft 或 cloven 比较不常用。 **1** [T] **~ sth** (*old-fashioned* or *literary*) to split or cut sth in two using sth sharp and heavy 劈开；砍开；剁开: *She cleaved his skull (in two) with an axe.* 她用斧头把他的颅骨劈成两半。◇ (*figurative*) *His skin was cleft with deep lines.* 他的皮肤布满深深的皱纹。 **2** [I, T] (*old-fashioned* or *literary*) to move quickly through sth 迅速穿过；迅速穿越: **~ through sth** *a ship cleaving through the water* 破浪前进的船 ◇ **~ sth** *The huge boat cleaved the darkness.* 那艘巨轮在黑暗中破浪前行。 **3** [I] **~ to sth/sb** (*literary*) to stick close to sth/sb 紧贴；紧挨: *Her tongue clove to the roof of her mouth.* 她的舌头紧紧地贴着上腭。 **4** (**cleaved**, **cleaved**) [I] **~ to sth** (*formal*) to continue to believe in or be loyal to sth 坚信；信守；忠于: *to cleave to a belief/idea* 坚守信仰 / 信念 IDM ➲SEE CLEFT *adj.*

cleav·er /ˈkliːvə(r)/ *noun* a heavy knife with a broad blade, used for cutting large pieces of meat 砍肉刀；剁肉刀 ➲VISUAL VOCAB PAGE V27

clef /klef/ *noun* (*music* 音) a symbol at the beginning of a line of printed music (called a STAVE or STAFF) that shows the PITCH of the notes on it 谱号: *the treble/bass clef* 高音 / 低音谱号 ➲PICTURE AT MUSIC

cleft /kleft/ *noun, adj.* ➲SEE ALSO CLEAVE

■*noun* a natural opening or crack, for example in the ground or in rock, or in a person's chin（自然的）裂口，裂缝: *a cleft in the rocks* 岩石的裂缝

■*adj.*

IDM **be (caught) in a cleft 'stick** to be in a difficult situation when any action you take will have bad results 进退维谷；陷入困境

ˌ**cleft ˈlip** *noun* a condition in which sb is born with their upper lip split 唇裂；兔唇

ˌ**cleft ˈpalate** *noun* a condition in which sb is born with the roof of their mouth split, making them unable to speak clearly 腭裂

ˌ**cleft ˈsentence** *noun* (*grammar* 语法) a sentence that begins with 'it' or 'that' and has a following clause, for example, 'it is you that I love', or 'that is my mother you're insulting' 分裂句（以 it 或 that 开始，后接从句）

cle·ma·tis /'klemətɪs; klə'meɪtɪs/ *noun* [C, U] a climbing plant with large white, purple or pink flowers 铁线莲，转子莲（开白、紫或粉红色花的攀缘植物）

clem·ency /'klemənsi/ *noun* [U] (*formal*) kindness shown to sb when they are being punished; willingness not to punish sb so severely （对受惩罚的人表现出的）仁慈，慈悲；宽恕；宽容 **SYN** **mercy**: *a plea for clemency* 乞求开恩

clem·ent /'klemənt/ *adj.* (*formal*) **1** (especially of weather 尤指天气) mild and pleasant 温和的；温暖的 **OPP** **in·clement** **2** showing kindness and MERCY to sb who is being punished （对受惩罚的人）仁慈的，宽恕的，宽容的

clem·en·tine /'kleməntiːn/ *noun* a fruit like a small orange 小柑橘

clench /klentʃ/ *verb* **1** [T, I] ~ (**sth**) when you **clench** your hands, teeth, etc., or when they **clench**, you press or squeeze them together tightly, usually showing that you are angry, determined or upset （通常表示愤怒、决心或不安时）捏紧，攥紧（拳头等），咬紧（牙齿等）: *He* ***clenched his fists*** *in anger.* 他愤怒地攥紧了拳头。◇ *Through* ***clenched teeth*** *she told him to leave.* 她咬牙切齿地叫他离开。◇ *His fists clenched slowly until his knuckles were white.* 他的拳头慢慢地捏紧，直捏得指关节都发白了。**2** [T] ~ **sth** (**in/between sth**) to hold sth tightly and firmly 握紧；抓牢；攥住: *Her pen was clenched between her teeth.* 她咬着笔。

clere·story /'klɪəstɔːri; *NAmE* 'klɪrs-/ *noun* (*pl.* **-ies**) (*architecture* 建) the upper part of a wall in a large church, with a row of windows in it, above the level of the lower roofs（大教堂中在高于周围屋顶的墙壁上开的）侧天窗，高侧窗

clergy /'klɜːdʒi; *NAmE* 'klɜːrdʒi/ (*often* **the clergy**) *noun* [pl.] the priests or ministers of a religion, especially of the Christian Church（统称）圣职人员，神职人员: *All the local clergy were asked to attend the ceremony.* 所有当地的圣职人员都获邀参加这个仪式。◇ *The new proposals affect both clergy and laity.* 新的提案使神职人员与平信徒都会受到影响。➲ COLLOCATIONS AT RELIGION ➲ COMPARE LAITY

cler·gy·man /'klɜːdʒimən; *NAmE* 'klɜːrdʒ-/ *noun* (*pl.* **-men** /-mən/) a male priest or minister in the Christian Church （男）圣职人员，神职人员 ➲ COMPARE CHURCHMAN, PRIEST

cler·gy·wo·man /'klɜːdʒiwʊmən; *NAmE* 'klɜːrdʒ-/ *noun* (*pl.* **-women** /-wɪmɪn/) a female priest or minister in the Christian Church （女）圣职人员，神职人员 ➲ COMPARE CHURCHMAN

cler·ic /'klerɪk/ *noun* **1** (*old-fashioned* or *formal*) a member of the clergy 圣职人员；神职人员 **2** a religious leader in any religion 宗教领袖；宗教领导人: *Muslim clerics* 穆斯林教职人员

cler·ic·al /'klerɪkl/ *adj.* **1** connected with office work 办公室工作的: ***clerical workers/staff/assistants*** 办公室工作人员；全体办事员；文书助理 ◇ *a clerical error* (= one made in copying or calculating sth) 笔误（誊写或计算中的错误） **2** connected with the CLERGY (= priests) 圣职人员的；神职人员的: *a* ***clerical collar*** (= one that fastens at the back, worn by some priests) 圣职人员白领

clerk 🔑 /klɑːk; *NAmE* klɜːrk/ *noun, verb*

■ ***noun*** **1** 🔑 a person whose job is to keep the records or accounts in an office, shop/store etc. 职员；簿记员；文书: *an office clerk* 办公室职员 ➲ SEE ALSO FILING CLERK **2** 🔑 an official in charge of the records of a council, court, etc. （议会、法院等的）书记员: *the Town Clerk* 市政府书记员 ◇ *the Clerk of the Court* 法院书记员 ➲ SEE ALSO CLERK OF WORKS, COUNTY CLERK, PARISH CLERK **3** 🔑 (*NAmE*) = SALES CLERK: *The clerk at the counter gave me too little change.* 柜台的售货员给我少找了零钱。 **4** (*also* **'desk clerk**) (*both NAmE*) a person whose job is dealing with people arriving at or leaving a hotel 旅馆服务台接待员 **SYN** **receptionist**

■ ***verb*** [I] (*NAmE*) to work as a clerk 当职员（或文书、书记员）: *a clerking job* 职员工作

ˌclerk of 'works *noun* (*BrE*) a person whose job is to be in charge of repairs to buildings or of building works, for an organization or institution 物业维修（或建筑工程）管理人员

clever 🔑 /'klevə(r)/ *adj.* (**clever·er**, **clever·est**) **HELP** You can also use **more clever** and **most clever**. 亦可用 more clever 和 most clever。 **1** 🔑 (*especially BrE*) quick at learning and understanding things 聪明的；聪颖的 **SYN** **intelligent**: *a clever child* 聪明伶俐的孩子 ◇ *Clever girl!* 多么聪慧的女孩！◇ *How clever of you to work it out!* 你解决了这个问题真是太聪明了！◇ ***He's too clever by half, if you ask me*** (= it annoys me or makes me suspicious). 恕我直言，他未免聪明过头了。➲ SYNONYMS AT INTELLIGENT **2** 🔑 ~ (**at sth**) (*especially BrE*) skilful 熟练的；灵巧的: *She's clever at getting what she wants.* 她想把什么东西弄到手的时候总是很精的。◇ *He's clever with his hands.* 他的手很灵巧。**3** 🔑 showing intelligence or skill, for example in the design of an object, in an idea or sb's actions 精巧的；精明的: *a clever little gadget* 精巧的小器具 ◇ *What a clever idea!* 多么精明的主意！◇ *That wasn't very clever* (= what you just did wasn't sensible), *was it?* 那样做不太明智，不是吗？ **4** (*BrE, informal, disapproving*) quick with words in a way that annoys people or does not show respect 油腔滑调的: *Don't you get clever with me!* 别跟我油嘴滑舌的！▸ **clev·er·ly** *adv.* **clev·er·ness** *noun* [U] **IDM** SEE BOX *v.*

'clever Dick (*also* **'clever clogs**) *noun* (*both BrE, informal, disapproving*) a person who thinks they are always right or that they know everything 自以为总是对（或无所不知）的人；自以为是的人

cli·ché (*also* **cliche**) /'kliːʃeɪ; *NAmE* kliː'ʃeɪ/ *noun* (*disapproving*) **1** [C] a phrase or an idea that has been used so often that it no longer has much meaning and is not interesting 陈词滥调；陈腐的套语: *She trotted out the old cliché that 'a trouble shared is a trouble halved.'* 她又重复了"与人说愁愁减半"的陈词滥调。 **2** [U] the use of clichés in writing or speaking 使用陈词滥调 ▸ **cli·chéd** *adj.*: *a clichéd view of upper-class life* 对上层社会的生活所持的陈腐看法

click 🔑 /klɪk/ *verb, noun*

■ ***verb*** **1** 🔑 [I, T] to make or cause sth to make a short sharp sound （使）发出咔哒声，咔哒（或咔嚓）响: (**+ adv./prep.**) *The cameras clicked away.* 照相机咔嚓咔嚓地不停拍照。◇ *The bolt clicked into place.* 门闩咔哒一声插上了。◇ **+ adj.** *The door* ***clicked shut.*** 门咔哒一声关上了。◇ **~ sth** *He* ***clicked his fingers*** *at the waiter.* 他冲服务员打了个响指。◇ *Polly* ***clicked her tongue*** *in annoyance.* 波利气得舌头发出啧啧声。 ➲ MORE LIKE THIS 3, page R25 **2** 🔑 [T, I] to choose a particular function or item on a computer screen, etc., by pressing one of the buttons on a mouse or TOUCHPAD （用鼠标或在触摸板上）点击，单击: **~ sth** *Click the OK button to start.* 单击 OK 按钮启动。◇ **~** (**on sth**) *I clicked on the link to the next page of the website.* 我单击链接好翻到网站的下一页。 ◇ *To run a window, just double-click on the icon.* 要运行视窗，只需双击图标即可。 ➲ SEE ALSO DOUBLE-CLICK ➲ WORDFINDER NOTE AT KEYBOARD **3** [I] (*informal*) to suddenly become clear or understood 被突然明白；豁然开朗: *Suddenly it* ***clicked****—we'd been talking about different people.* 我们突然领悟到原来我们谈论的不是同一个人。◇ *It all* ***clicked into place.*** 一切都豁然开朗。 **4** [I] (*informal*) to become friends with sb at once; to become popular with sb （与某人）即刻成为朋友；受（某人）的欢迎: *We met at a party and clicked immediately.* 我们在聚会上相识，一见如故。 ◇ **~ with sb** *He's never really clicked with his students.* 他从未真正受到过他的学生的欢迎。 **5** [I] (*informal*) to work well together 配合默契；运作协调: *The team don't seem to have clicked yet.* 这支队伍好像还没能配合默契。

PHR V **ˌclick 'through** (**to sth**) to visit a website by clicking on an electronic link or advertisement on

another web page 点击，点进，点通（链接网站）
■ *noun* **1** a short sharp sound 短而尖的声音；咔哒（或咔嚓）声： *The door closed with a click.* 门咔哒一声关上了。 **2** the act of pressing the button on a computer mouse or TOUCHPAD （对计算机鼠标或触摸板的）点击，单击 **3** (*phonetics* 语音) a speech sound made by pressing the tongue against the top of the mouth or the part of the mouth behind the upper front teeth, then releasing it quickly, causing air to be sucked in. Clicks are found especially in southern African languages.（尤见于非洲南部某些语言的）吸气音： *click languages* 有吸气音的语言 **4** = KLICK

click·able /ˈklɪkəbl/ *adj.* (*computing* 计) if text or an image is **clickable**, you can click on it with the mouse or TOUCHPAD in order to make sth happen （文本或图像）可点击的

click·jack·ing /ˈklɪkdʒækɪŋ/ *noun* [U] (*informal*) the practice of adding hidden HYPERLINKS to documents on the Internet, causing users to make purchases, perform actions on SOCIAL NETWORKING sites, etc. without their knowledge 点击劫持，点阅绑架（把隐藏的超级链接添加于互联网文件，导致用户在不知情的情况下购买商品或介入社交网站操作等）： *a clickjacking attack* 点击劫持攻击

click·stream /ˈklɪkstriːm/ *noun* a record of all the websites a person visits when spending time on the Internet 点击流路径（个人浏览网站的记录）

ˈclick-through /ˈklɪk θruː/ *noun* **1** the action of following a link on a web page to another website, especially a commercial one （尤指对商业网站链接的）点击进入，点阅： *The number of click-throughs to the site has increased in recent weeks.* 该网站的点进量在最近几周有所增加。◇ *Unfortunately, the advert is still achieving a low click-through rate.* 可惜的是，这则广告的点击率仍然很低。 **2** a link on a web page to another website, especially a commercial one（网页上指向另一个网站，尤其是商业网站的）链接： *The click-throughs on the site to other companies aren't always very useful.* 这家网站连到其他公司的链接并不总是很有用。

cli·ent /ˈklaɪənt/ *noun* **1** a person who uses the services or advice of a professional person or organization 委托人；当事人；客户： *a lawyer with many famous clients* 接受许多名人委托的律师 ◇ *to act on behalf of a client* 代表当事人 ◇ *Social workers must always consider the best interests of their clients.* 社会工作者必须时刻考虑其当事人的最佳利益。 **2** (*computing* 计) a computer that is linked to a SERVER （连接在服务器上的）客户机

cli·en·tele /ˌkliːənˈtel; *NAmE* ˌklaɪənˈtel/ *noun* [sing.+sing./pl. v.] all the customers or clients of a shop/store, restaurant, organization, etc.（统称）顾客，主顾，客户： *an international clientele* 国际客户网

ˌclient-ˈserver *adj.* [only before noun] (*computing* 计) (of a computer system 计算机系统) in which a central SERVER provides data to a number of computers connected together in a network 客户服务器的 ➲ SEE ALSO PEER-TO-PEER

ˌclient ˈstate *noun* a country which depends on a larger and more powerful country for support and protection （依赖强国的）附庸国

cliff /klɪf/ *noun* a high area of rock with a very steep side, often at the edge of the sea or ocean （常指海洋边的）悬崖，峭壁： *the cliff edge/top* 悬崖边缘 / 顶端 ◇ *the chalk cliffs of southern England* 英格兰南部的白垩质峭壁 ◇ *a castle perched high on the cliffs above the river* 高高耸立在临河峭壁上的城堡 ➲ WORDFINDER NOTE AT COAST ➲ VISUAL VOCAB PAGE V5

cliff·hang·er /ˈklɪfhæŋə(r)/ *noun* a situation in a story, film/movie, competition, etc. that is very exciting because you cannot guess what will happen next, or you do not find out immediately what happens next （故事、电影、竞赛等扣人心弦的）悬念： *The first part of the serial ended with a real cliffhanger.* 这部连续剧的第一集以扣人心弦的悬念告终。 ▸ **cliff·hang·ing** *adj.*

cliff·top /ˈklɪftɒp; *NAmE* -tɑːp/ *noun* the area of land at the top of a cliff 悬崖顶 ➲ VISUAL VOCAB PAGE V5

cli·mac·tic /klaɪˈmæktɪk/ *adj.* (*formal*) (of an event or a point in time 事情或时刻) very exciting, most important 非常激动人心的；高潮的；最重要的

cli·mate /ˈklaɪmət/ *noun* **1** [C, U] the regular pattern of weather conditions of a particular place 气候： *a mild/temperate/warm/wet climate* 温和的 / 暖和的 / 温暖的 / 潮湿的气候 ◇ *the harsh climate of the Arctic regions* 北极地区的恶劣气候 ➲ WORDFINDER NOTE AT EARTH

> **WORDFINDER** 联想词： arid, continental climate, equatorial, frigid, harsh, humidity, rainfall, tropical, zone

2 [C] an area with particular weather conditions 气候区： *They wanted to move to a warmer climate.* 他们想迁移到气候较温暖的地区。 **3** [C] a general attitude or feeling; an atmosphere or a situation which exists in a particular place 倾向；思潮；风气；环境气氛： *the present political climate* 当前的政治气候 ◇ *the current* ***climate of opinion*** (= what people generally are thinking about a particular issue) 目前的舆论倾向 ◇ ***a climate of suspicion/violence*** 怀疑 / 暴力的风气 ◇ *We need to create a climate in which business can prosper.* 我们需要创造一个有利于商业繁荣的环境。

ˈclimate change *noun* [U] changes in the earth's weather, including changes in temperature, wind patterns and RAINFALL, especially the increase in the temperature of the earth's atmosphere that is caused by the increase of particular gases, especially CARBON DIOXIDE 气候变化： *the threat of global climate change* 全球气候变化的威胁 ➲ COLLOCATIONS AT ENVIRONMENT ➲ COMPARE GLOBAL WARMING

cli·mat·ic /klaɪˈmætɪk/ *adj.* [only before noun] connected with the climate of a particular area 与某一地区气候有关的： ***climatic changes/conditions*** 气候变化 / 条件 ▸ **cli·mat·ic·al·ly** /-kli/ *adv.*

cli·mat·ology /ˌklaɪməˈtɒlədʒi; *NAmE* -ˈtɑːl-/ *noun* [U] the scientific study of climate 气候学 ▸ **cli·ma·to·logic·al** /ˌklaɪmətəˈlɒdʒɪkl; *NAmE* -ˈlɑːdʒ-/ *adj.* **cli·mat·olo·gist** /ˌklaɪməˈtɒlədʒɪst; *NAmE* -ˈtɑːl-/ *noun*

cli·max /ˈklaɪmæks/ *noun, verb*
■ *noun* **1** the most exciting or important event or point in time（重要事情或时刻的）高潮，极点，顶点： ***to come to/reach a climax*** 达到极点 ◇ *the climax of his political career* 他政治生涯的巅峰 **2** the most exciting part of a play, piece of music, etc. that usually happens near the end（戏剧、音乐等通常接近结束时出现的）高潮 **3** the highest point of sexual pleasure 性高潮 SYN **orgasm** ➲ COMPARE ANTICLIMAX
■ *verb* **1** [I, T] to come to or form the best, most exciting, or most important point in sth 达成（或形成）极点（或顶点、高潮）： **~ with/in sth** *The festival will climax on Sunday with a gala concert.* 星期天的音乐盛会将把这次会演推向高潮。◇ **~ sth** (*especially NAmE*) *The sensational verdict climaxed a six-month trial.* 那项引起轰动的裁决使长达六个月的审判达到了高潮。 **2** [I] to have an ORGASM 达到性高潮

climb /klaɪm/ *verb, noun*
■ *verb*
• **GO UP** 上去 **1** [T, I] **~ (up) (sth)** to go up sth towards the top 攀登；爬： *to climb a mountain/hill/tree/wall* 爬山；爬树；爬墙 ◇ *She climbed up the stairs.* 她爬上了楼梯。◇ *The car slowly climbed the hill.* 汽车缓慢地爬上了山坡。◇ *As they climbed higher, the air became cooler.* 他们攀登得越高，空气就越凉。
• **GO THROUGH/DOWN/OVER** 通过；下去；越过 **2** [I] **+ adv./prep.** to move somewhere, especially with difficulty or effort （尤指吃力地向某处）爬： *I climbed through the window.* 我从窗口爬过去。◇ *Sue climbed into bed.* 休吃力地爬上床。◇ *Can you climb down?* 你能爬下去吗？◇ *The boys climbed over the wall.* 那些男孩翻过了那堵墙。

• MOUNTAIN/ROCK, ETC. 山、岩石等 **3** **go climbing** to go up mountains or climb rocks as a hobby or sport 登山，攀岩（作为业余爱好或运动）: *He likes to go climbing most weekends.* 在多数周末他都喜欢去登山。
• AIRCRAFT/SUN, ETC. 飞机、太阳等 **4** [I] to go higher in the sky 爬升；上升: *The plane climbed to 33 000 feet.* 飞机爬升到 33 000 英尺。
• SLOPE UP 倾斜着上升 **5** [I] to slope upwards 倾斜上升: *From here the path climbs steeply to the summit.* 这条小路从这里突然变陡，直上山顶。
• OF PLANTS 植物 **6** [I] to grow up a wall or frame（沿墙或架子）攀缘生长: *a climbing rose* 攀缘生长的玫瑰
• INCREASE 增加 **7** [I] (of temperature, a country's money, etc. 温度、国家的货币等) to increase in value or amount 上升；增值；升值: *The dollar has been climbing all week.* 整个星期美元一直在升值。◇ *The paper's circulation continues to climb.* 这份报纸的发行量持续增长。
• IMPROVE POSITION/STATUS 提高身份 / 地位 **8** [I] ~ **(to sth)** to move to a higher position or social rank by your own effort （靠自己的努力）晋升，提高社会地位: *In a few years he had climbed to the top of his profession.* 他在几年内攀上了职业的巅峰。◇ *The team has now climbed to fourth in the league.* 这支队现已上升到联赛的第四名。
IDM SEE BANDWAGON ➲ MORE LIKE THIS 20, page R27
PHR V ˌ**climb ˈdown (over sth)** to admit that you have made a mistake or that you were wrong 承认做错事；认错 ➲ RELATED NOUN CLIMBDOWN
■ *noun*
• MOUNTAIN/STEPS 山；台阶 **1** an act of climbing up a mountain, rock or large number of steps; a period of time spent climbing 攀登；攀缘；爬阶梯；攀登用的时间: *an exhausting climb* 令人精疲力竭的攀登 ◇ *It's an hour's climb to the summit.* 爬到顶峰需要一小时。 **2** a mountain or rock which people climb up for sport（登山或攀岩运动的）山，岩: *Titan's Wall is the mountain's hardest rock climb.* "巨人墙"是这座山最难攀登的一段山岩。
• INCREASE 增加 **3** [usually sing.] an increase in value or amount 增值；升值；增加: *the dollar's climb against the euro* 美元对欧元的升值
• TO A HIGHER POSITION OR STATUS 提高身份 / 地位 **4** [usually sing.] progress to a higher status, standard or position （地位、标准、身份的）跃升，提高，晋升: *a rapid climb to stardom* 一跃而成为明星 ◇ *the long slow climb out of the recession* 经济衰退期后长时间的缓慢复苏

climb·down /ˈklaɪmdaʊn/ *noun* (*BrE*) an act of admitting that you were wrong, or of changing your position in an argument 认错；（争论中）改变立场，让步: *The Chancellor was forced into a humiliating climbdown on his economic policies.* 财政大臣被迫狼狈地承认他的经济政策存在失误。

climb·er /ˈklaɪmə(r)/ *noun* **1** a person who climbs (especially mountains) or an animal that climbs 攀登者；登山者；攀爬的动物: *climbers and hill walkers* 登山者和山地徒步旅行者 ◇ *Monkeys are efficient climbers.* 猴子的攀缘能力很强。 **2** a climbing plant 攀缘植物 ➲ VISUAL VOCAB PAGE V20 ➲ SEE ALSO SOCIAL CLIMBER

climb·ing /ˈklaɪmɪŋ/ *noun* [U] the sport or activity of climbing rocks or mountains 登山运动；攀岩活动: *to go climbing* 去登山 ◇ *a climbing accident* 登山事故

ˈ**climbing frame** (*BrE*) (*NAmE* ˈ**jungle gym**) *noun* a structure made of metal bars joined together for children to climb and play on 攀爬架（儿童游乐设施）➲ PICTURE AT FRAME ➲ VISUAL VOCAB PAGE V41

ˈ**climbing wall** *noun* a wall with parts to hold onto, usually inside a building, for people to practise climbing on （室内供练习用的）攀登墙，攀岩墙

clime /klaɪm/ *noun* [usually pl.] (*literary* or *humorous*) a country with a particular kind of climate （具有某种气候的）地区，地带；气候带: *I'm heading for sunnier climes next month.* 我下个月要去阳光比较明媚的地区。

clinch /klɪntʃ/ *verb, noun*
■ *verb* (*informal*) **1** ~ **sth** to succeed in achieving or winning sth 成功取得；赢得: ***to clinch an argument/a deal/a victory*** 赢得辩论；成交；赢得胜利 **2** ~ **sth** to provide the answer to sth; to settle sth that was not certain 提供解决办法；解决；确定: *'I'll pay your airfare.' 'Okay, that clinches it—I'll come with you.'* "我会帮你付飞机票。""好，就这么说定，我跟你一起去。"◇ *a clinching argument* 让人折服的论证
■ *noun* **1** (*informal*) a position in which two lovers hold each other tightly （恋人相互的）搂抱，拥抱 SYN **embrace** **2** a position in a fight in which two opponents hold each other tightly（格斗中双方的）互相扭抱

clinch·er /ˈklɪntʃə(r)/ *noun* [usually sing.] (*informal*) a fact, a remark or an event that settles an argument, a decision or a competition 起决定性作用的事实（或话语、事情）

cline /klaɪn/ *noun* a series of similar items in which each is almost the same as the ones next to it, but the last is very different from the first 渐变群，梯度变异（群体中相邻的两个成员相差无几，但第一个和最后一个之间差异极明显）SYN **continuum**

cling /klɪŋ/ *verb* (**clung, clung** /klʌŋ/) **1** [I] to hold on tightly to sb/sth 抓紧；紧握；紧抱: ~ **to sb/sth** *survivors clinging to a raft* 紧紧抓住救生筏的幸存者 ◇ ~ **on to sb/sth** *She clung on to her baby.* 她紧紧抱住她的婴儿。◇ ~ **on** *Cling on tight!* 紧紧抓住！◇ ~ **together** *They clung together, shivering with cold.* 他们紧紧地抱在一起，冷得直发抖。➲ SYNONYMS AT HOLD **2** [I] to stick to sth 粘住；附着: *a dress that clings* (= fits closely and shows the shape of your body) 紧身连衣裙 ◇ ~ **to sth** *The wet shirt clung to his chest.* 湿衬衫紧贴在他的胸部。◇ *The smell of smoke still clung to her clothes.* 烟味仍附着在她的衣服上不散。 **3** [I] ~ **(to sb)** (*usually disapproving*) to stay close to sb, especially because you need them emotionally（尤指情感上）依恋，依附: *After her mother's death, Sara clung to her aunt more than ever.* 萨拉在母亲去世后比以往任何时候都更依附于她的姨妈。
PHR V ˈ**cling to sth** | ˌ**cling ˈon to sth** to be unwilling to get rid of sth, or stop doing sth 不愿放弃；坚持: *Throughout the trial she had clung to the belief that he was innocent.* 在整个审判中，她都坚信他是清白的。◇ *He had one last hope to cling on to.* 他还抱着最后的一线希望。◇ *She managed to cling on to life for another couple of years.* 她顽强地又活了几年。

ˈ**cling film** (*BrE*) (*NAmE* ˈ**plastic wrap**, **Saˈran Wrap™**) *noun* [U] a thin transparent plastic material that sticks to a surface and to itself, used especially for wrapping food （尤指包装食物的）透明薄膜，塑料保鲜膜

cling·ing /ˈklɪŋɪŋ/ (*also* **clingy** /ˈklɪŋi/) *adj.* **1** (of clothes or material 衣服或衣料) sticking to the body and showing its shape 紧身的；贴身的 **2** (*usually disapproving*) needing another person too much （对别人）依赖性强的，离不开的: *a clinging child* 缠人的孩子

clin·ic /ˈklɪnɪk/ *noun* **1** a building or part of a hospital where people can go for special medical treatment or advice 诊所；（医院的）门诊部: *the local family planning clinic* 当地的计划生育诊所 **2** (*especially BrE*) a period of time during which doctors give special medical treatment or advice 门诊时间；会诊时间: *The antenatal clinic is on Wednesdays.* 产前检查时间为星期三。 **3** (*especially BrE*) a private hospital or one that treats health problems of a particular kind 私人诊所；专科医院: *He is being treated at the London clinic.* 他正在伦敦一家私人诊所接受治疗。◇ *a rehabilitation clinic for alcoholics* 戒酒康复专科诊所 **4** (*NAmE*) a building shared by a group of doctors who work together 门诊治疗部；医疗中心 **5** an occasion in a hospital when medical students learn by watching a specialist examine and treat patients 临床实习；临床教学 **6** an occasion at which a professional person, especially a SPORTSMAN or SPORTSWOMAN gives advice and training （尤指运动员举办的）讲习班，培训班，研习班: *a coaching clinic for young tennis players* 为年轻网球运动员举办的培训班

clin·ic·al /ˈklɪnɪkl/ *adj.* **1** [only before noun] relating to the examination and treatment of patients and their illnesses 临床的；临床诊断的: *clinical research* (= done on patients, not just considering theory) 临床研究 ◇ *clinical* *training* (= the part of a doctor's training done in a hospital) 临床培训 ◇ *clinical trials of a drug* 药物的临床试验 **2** (*disapproving*) cold and calm and without feeling or sympathy 冷淡的；无动于衷的；无同情心的：*He watched her suffering with clinical detachment.* 他无动于衷地看着她受苦。 **3** (*disapproving*) (of a room, building, etc. 房间、建筑物等) very plain; without decoration 简陋的；无装饰的 ▸ **clin·ic·al·ly** /-kli/ *adv.*：*clinically dead* (= judged to be dead from the condition of the body) 临床死亡的（从身体的状况判断为死亡的）◇ *clinically depressed* 临床诊断为抑郁症的

clin·ician /klɪˈnɪʃn/ *noun* a doctor, PSYCHOLOGIST, etc. who has direct contact with patients 临床医师

clink /klɪŋk/ *verb, noun*

■ ***verb*** [I, T] to make or cause sth to make a sharp ringing sound, like that of glasses being hit against each other （使）发出叮当声，叮当作响 SYN **chink**: *clinking coins* 叮当响的硬币 ◇ **~ sth** *They clinked glasses and drank to each other's health.* 他们碰杯互祝身体健康。

■ ***noun*** [sing.] **1** (*also* **clink·ing**) a sharp ringing sound like the sound made by glasses being hit against each other 叮当声 **2** (*old-fashioned, slang*) prison 班房；牢房

clink·er /ˈklɪŋkə(r)/ *noun* **1** [U, C] the hard rough substance left after coal has burnt at a high temperature; a piece of this substance 煤渣；炉渣；煤渣块 **2** [sing.] (*NAmE*) a wrong musical note 错误的音符：*The singer hit a clinker.* 那名歌手唱错了一个音符。

clip /klɪp/ *noun, verb*

■ ***noun*** **1** [C] (often in compounds 常构成复合词) a small metal or plastic object used for holding things together or in place（金属或塑料的）夹子，回形针：*a hair clip* 发夹 ◇ *toe clips on a bicycle* 自行车上的踏脚夹套 ➲ VISUAL VOCAB PAGE V71 ➲ SEE ALSO BICYCLE CLIP, BULLDOG CLIP™, PAPER CLIP **2** [C] a piece of jewellery that fastens to your clothes 首饰别针：*a diamond clip* 钻石别针 **3** [sing.] the act of cutting sth to make it shorter 剪短；修剪：*He gave the hedge a clip.* 他把树篱修剪了一下。**4** [C] a short part of a film/movie that is shown separately 电影片段：*Here is a clip from her latest movie.* 这是她最新电影的片段。**5** [C] (*BrE, informal*) a quick hit with your hand （用手）猛击，抽打：*She gave him **a clip round the ear** for being cheeky.* 她因他放肆给了他一记耳光。**6** [C] a set of bullets in a metal container that is placed in or attached to a gun for firing 子弹夹；弹匣

IDM **at a fast, good, steady, etc. ˈclip** (*especially NAmE*) quickly 迅速；很快地

■ ***verb*** (**-pp-**) **1** [T, I] to fasten sth to sth else with a clip; to be fastened with a clip 夹住；别住；被夹住：**~ sth + adv./prep.** *He **clipped** the microphone (**on**) **to** his collar.* 他把麦克风别在衣领上。◇ ***Clip** the pages **together**.* 把这些散页夹在一起。◇ **+ adv./prep.** *Do those earrings clip on?* 那些耳环是夹戴的吗？ **2** [T] to cut sth with scissors or SHEARS, in order to make it shorter or neater; to remove sth from somewhere by cutting it off 剪（掉）；修剪：**~ sth** *to clip a hedge* 修剪树篱 ◇ **~ sth from sth/off (sth)** *He clipped off a length of wire.* 他剪掉了一段金属线。**3** [T] to hit the edge or side of sth 碰撞（某物的边缘或侧面）：**~ sth** *The car clipped the kerb as it turned.* 汽车转弯时撞上了马路牙子。◇ **~ sth + adv./prep.** *She clipped the ball into the net.* 她把球斜推入网。 **4** [T] **~ sth (out of/from sth)** to cut sth out of sth else using scissors 从…剪下：*to clip a coupon (out of the paper)* （从报纸上）剪下赠券

IDM **clip sb's ˈwings** to restrict a person's freedom or power 限制某人的自由（或权力）

PHR V **ˌclip sth ˈoff sth** (*informal*) to reduce the time that it takes to do sth by a particular length of time 缩短，削减（做某事的时间）：*She clipped two seconds off her previous best time.* 她把自己之前的最佳纪录缩短了两秒。

ˈclip art *noun* [U] (*computing* 计) pictures and symbols that are stored in computer programs or on websites for computer users to copy and add to their own documents 剪贴画（计算机程序或网站中供用户复制自用的图像和符号）

clip·board /ˈklɪpbɔːd; *NAmE* -bɔːrd/ *noun* **1** a small board with a clip at the top for holding papers, used by sb who wants to write while standing or moving around 写字夹板；带夹写字板 ➲ VISUAL VOCAB PAGE V71 **2** (*computing* 计) a place in a computer's memory where information from a computer file is stored for a time until it is added to another file（临时存储信息的）剪贴板

clip-clop /ˈklɪp klɒp; *NAmE* klɑːp/ *noun* a sound like the sound of a horse's HOOFS on a hard surface （像马蹄踏在硬路面上发出的）嗒嗒声，嘚嘚声 ➲ MORE LIKE THIS 3, page R25

ˈclip joint *noun* (*informal, disapproving*) a NIGHTCLUB which charges prices that are too high （收费偏高的）宰客夜总会

ˈclip-on *adj.* [only before noun] fastened to sth with a CLIP 用夹子夹住的；用别针别牢的：*clip-on earrings* 夹式耳环 ➲ VISUAL VOCAB PAGE V70

clipped /klɪpt/ *adj.* (of a person's way of speaking 说话方式) clear and fast but not very friendly 清脆快速但不太友好的：*his clipped military tones* 他那短促的军人语调

clip·per /ˈklɪpə(r)/ *noun* **1 clippers** [pl.] a tool for cutting small pieces off things 剪具：*a pair of clippers* 一把剪子 ➲ SEE ALSO NAIL CLIPPERS **2** a fast sailing ship, used in the past （旧时的）快速帆船

clip·ping /ˈklɪpɪŋ/ *noun* **1** [usually pl.] a piece cut off sth 剪下物：***hedge/nail clippings*** 剪下的树篱 / 指甲 **2** (*especially NAmE*) (*also* **ˈpress clipping** *BrE, NAmE*) (*BrE also* **cut·ting**, **ˈpress cutting**) an article or a story that you cut from a newspaper or magazine and keep 剪报；杂志剪辑资料

clique /kliːk/ *noun* [C+sing./pl. v.] (*often disapproving*) a small group of people who spend their time together and do not allow others to join them 派系；私党；小集团；小圈子

cliquey /ˈkliːki/ (*also* **cliqu·ish** /ˈkliːkɪʃ/) *adj.* (*disapproving*) tending to form a clique; controlled by cliques 有派系倾向的；有结成小集团倾向的；派系控制的：*He found the school very cliquey and elitist.* 他发现这所学校很排外并以精英自居。

clit·oris /ˈklɪtərɪs/ *noun* the small sensitive organ just above the opening of a woman's VAGINA which becomes larger when she is sexually excited 阴蒂；阴核 ▸ **clit·or·al** /ˈklɪtərəl/ *adj.* [only before noun]

Cllr *abbr.* (*BrE*) (used before names in writing) COUNCILLOR （书写形式，用于姓名前）市议员，政务委员会委员：*Cllr Michael Booth* 市议员迈克尔•布思

cloak /kləʊk; *NAmE* kloʊk/ *noun, verb*

■ ***noun*** **1** [C] a type of coat that has no sleeves, fastens at the neck and hangs loosely from the shoulders, worn especially in the past （尤指旧时的）披风，斗篷 **2** [sing.] (*literary*) a thing that hides or covers sb/sth 遮盖物：*They left under the cloak of darkness.* 他们在黑暗的掩护下离开了。

■ ***verb*** **~ sth (in sth)** [often passive] (*literary*) to cover or hide sth 遮盖；掩盖：*The hills were cloaked in thick mist.* 大雾笼罩着群山。 ◇ *The meeting was **cloaked in** mystery.* 会议笼罩着神秘的气氛。 ▸ **cloaked** *adj.*：*a tall cloaked figure* (= a person wearing a cloak) 一个穿着披风、身材很高的人

ˌcloak-and-ˈdagger *adj.* [only before noun] **cloak-and-dagger** activities are secret and mysterious, sometimes in a way that people think is unnecessary or ridiculous 秘密的，神秘兮兮的（有时被认为不必要或荒谬）

cloak·room /ˈkləʊkruːm; -rʊm; *NAmE* ˈkloʊk-/ *noun* **1** (*especially BrE*) (*NAmE usually* **check·room**, **ˈcoat check**, **coat·room**) a room in a public building where people can leave coats, bags, etc. for a time 衣帽间；衣帽寄放处 **2** (*BrE*) a room that contains a toilet or toilets 厕所；卫生间；洗手间 ➲ NOTE AT TOILET

clob·ber /ˈklɒbə(r); *NAmE* ˈklɑːb-/ *verb, noun*
■ ***verb*** (*informal*) **1 ~ sb** to hit sb very hard 狠击；狠揍；猛打 **2** [often passive] **~ sb/sth** to affect sb badly or to punish them, especially by making them lose money 极大地打击；惩罚；使受到（严重经济损失）：*The paper got clobbered with libel damages of half a million pounds.* 该报被罚以五十万英镑的诽谤损害赔偿金。 **3** [usually passive] **~ sb/sth** to defeat sb completely 彻底战胜（或击败）：*We got clobbered in the game on Saturday.* 我们在星期六的比赛中一败涂地。
■ ***noun*** [U] (*BrE, informal*) a person's clothes or equipment 衣服；随身物品 SYN **stuff**

cloche /klɒʃ; *NAmE* kloʊʃ/ *noun* **1** (*also* ˌ**cloche** ˈ**hat**) a woman's hat, shaped like a bell, and fitting close to the head, worn especially in the 1920s（尤指 20 世纪 20 年代的）钟形女帽 **2** a glass or plastic cover placed over young plants to protect them from cold weather（保护植物幼苗不受冻的）玻璃罩，塑料罩 ➲ VISUAL VOCAB PAGE V20

clocks and watches 钟表

clock /klɒk; *NAmE* klɑːk/ *noun, verb*
■ ***noun*** **1** [C] an instrument for measuring and showing time, in a room, on the wall of a building or on a computer screen (not worn or carried like a watch) 时钟；钟：*It was ten past six by the kitchen clock.* 厨房的钟六点十分了。◇ *The* ***clock struck*** *twelve/midnight.* 时钟已敲响十二点 / 午夜十二点。◇ *The* ***clock is fast/slow.*** 这钟走得快了 / 慢了。◇ *The clock has stopped.* 钟停了。◇ *the* ***clock face*** (= the front part of a clock with the numbers on) 钟面 ◇ *The* ***hands of the clock*** *crept slowly around.* 钟的时针在缓慢地走着。◇ *Ellen heard the loud* ***ticking of the clock*** *in the hall.* 埃伦听见大厅的钟滴答滴答地大声走着。➲ SEE ALSO ALARM CLOCK, BIOLOGICAL CLOCK, BODY CLOCK, CARRIAGE CLOCK, CUCKOO CLOCK, GRANDFATHER CLOCK, O'CLOCK, TIME CLOCK **2 the clock** [sing.] (*informal*) = MILOMETER：*a used car with 20 000 miles on the clock* 一辆计程器上累计行程为 2 万英里的旧汽车

IDM **against the** ˈ**clock** if you do sth **against the clock**, you do it fast in order to finish before a particular time 抢时间；争分夺秒 **around/round the** ˈ**clock** all day and all night without stopping 日夜不停；夜以继日 **put the clocks forward/back** (*BrE*) (*NAmE* **set/move the clocks ahead/back**) to change the time shown by clocks, usually by one hour, when the time changes officially, for example at the beginning and end of summer（夏时制开始和结束时）把时钟拨快 / 拨回（一般为一个小时） **put/turn the** ˈ**clock back 1** to return to a situation that existed in the past; to remember a past age 倒退；复旧；怀旧：*I wish we could turn the clock back two years and give the marriage another chance.* 我但愿时光能倒退两年，再给我们的婚姻一次机会。 **2** (*disapproving*) to return to old-fashioned methods or ideas 开倒车：*The new censorship law will turn the clock back 50 years.* 新的审查制度将使社会倒退回 50 年前的状态。 **run down/out the** ˈ**clock** (*US*) if a sports team tries to **run down/out the clock** at the end of a game, it stops trying to score and just tries to keep hold of the ball to stop the other team from scoring 消耗掉剩余的比赛时间（比赛接近结束时，球队不想进球而只设法控制住球，以阻止对方进球得分） ➲ COMPARE TIME-WASTING (2) **the clocks go forward/back** the time changes officially, for example at the beginning and end of summer（夏时制）时钟被拨快 / 拨回 ➲ MORE AT BEAT *v.*, RACE *n.*, STOP *v.*, WATCH *v.*
■ ***verb*** **1 ~ sth** to reach a particular time or speed 达到（某时间或速度）：*He clocked 10.09 seconds in the 100 metres final.* 他 100 米决赛跑出了 10.09 秒的速度。 **2** to measure the speed at which sb/sth is travelling 测…的速度：**~ sb doing sth** *The police clocked her doing over 100 miles an hour.* 警察测出她的车速每小时超过 100 英里。◇ **~ sb/sth (at sth)** *Wind gusts at 80 m.p.h. were clocked at Rapid City.* 据测拉皮德城的狂风速度为每小时 80 英里。 **3 ~ sb | ~ that... | ~ what/where, etc....** (*BrE, informal*) to notice or recognize sb 注意到；认出：*I clocked her in the driving mirror.* 我从汽车后视镜里注意到她。 **4 ~ sth** (*BrE, informal*) to illegally reduce the number of miles shown on a vehicle's MILOMETER (= instrument that measures the number of miles it has travelled) in order to make the vehicle appear to have travelled fewer miles than it really has 非法减少（车辆）计程器上的里程数；回拨（车辆）里程表作弊

PHR V ˌ**clock** ˈ**in/**ˈ**on** (*BrE*) (*NAmE* ˌ**punch** ˈ**in**) to record the time at which you arrive at work, especially by putting a card into a machine（尤指用机器）记录上班时间，上班打卡 ˌ**clock** ˈ**out/**ˈ**off** (*BrE*) (*NAmE* ˌ**punch** ˈ**out**) to record the time at which you leave work, especially by putting a card into a machine（尤指用机器）记录下班时间，下班打卡 ˌ**clock** ˈ**up sth** to reach a particular amount or number 达到（某一数量或数目）：*On the trip we clocked up over 1 800 miles.* 这次旅行我们的行程超过了 1 800 英里。◇ *He has clocked up more than 25 years on the committee.* 他担任委员会的委员已超过 25 年。

clock·er /ˈklɒkə(r); *NAmE* ˈklɑːk-/ *noun* (*informal*) **1** (*BrE*) a person who illegally changes a car's MILOMETER so that the car seems to have travelled fewer miles than it really has 倒拨里程表的人；里程表作弊者 **2** (*NAmE*) a person who sells illegal drugs, especially COCAINE or CRACK（可卡因等的）毒品贩子

ˌ**clock** ˈ**radio** *noun* a clock combined with a radio that can be set to come on at a particular time in order to wake sb up 收音机闹钟 ➲ VISUAL VOCAB PAGE V24

ˈ**clock speed** *noun* [U] (*computing* 计) the speed at which a computer operates 时钟频率（计算机的运行速率）：*This machine has a clock speed of 2.6GHz.* 这台机器的时钟频率为 2.6 千兆赫。

ˈ**clock tower** *noun* a tall tower, usually part of another building, with a clock at the top 钟楼 ➲ VISUAL VOCAB PAGE V3

ˈ**clock-watcher** *noun* (*disapproving*) a worker who is always checking the time to make sure that they do not work longer than they need to 老是看时间等下班的人

clock·wise /ˈklɒkwaɪz; *NAmE* ˈklɑːk-/ *adv., adj.* moving around in the same direction as the hands of a clock 顺时针方向（的）：*Turn the key clockwise.* 把钥匙按顺时针方向扭动。◇ *a clockwise direction* 顺时针方向 OPP **anti-clockwise, counterclockwise**

clock·work /ˈklɒkwɜːk; *NAmE* ˈklɑːkwɜːrk/ *noun* [U] machinery with wheels and SPRINGS 齿轮发条装置：*clockwork toys* (= toys that you wind up with a key) 有齿轮发条装置的玩具

IDM **go/run like** ˈ**clockwork** to happen according to plan; to happen without difficulties or problems 按计划进行；进展顺利 ➲ MORE AT REGULAR *adj.*

clod /klɒd; *NAmE* klɑːd/ *noun* **1** [usually pl.] a lump of earth or CLAY 泥块；土块 **2** (*informal*) a stupid person 笨蛋；蠢人；傻瓜

clod·hop·per /ˈklɒdhɒpə(r); *NAmE* ˈklɑːdhɑːp-/ *noun* (*informal*) **1** [usually pl.] a large heavy shoe 笨重的大鞋子 **2** (*disapproving*) an awkward or CLUMSY person 笨拙的人；笨蛋

clog /klɒg; *NAmE* klɑːg; klɔːg/ *verb, noun*

■ ***verb*** (**-gg-**) [T, often passive, I] to block sth or to become blocked（使）阻塞，堵塞：**~ sth (up) (with sth)** *The narrow streets were clogged with traffic.* 狭窄的街道上交通堵塞。◇ *Tears clogged her throat.* 她哽咽了。◇ **~ (up) (with sth)** *Within a few years the pipes began to clog up.* 没有几年管子就开始堵塞了。

■ ***noun*** a shoe that is completely made of wood or one that has a thick wooden SOLE and a leather top 木底鞋；木鞋；木屐 ➲ VISUAL VOCAB PAGE V69 **IDM** SEE POP *v.*

ˈclog dance *noun* a dance that is performed by people wearing clogs 木底鞋舞

clois·ter /ˈklɔɪstə(r)/ *noun* **1** [C, usually pl.] a covered passage with ARCHES around a square garden, usually forming part of a CATHEDRAL, CONVENT or MONASTERY（常为教堂、修院或寺院的）回廊；修院（或圣堂）禁地 ➲ VISUAL VOCAB PAGE V14 **2** [sing.] life in a CONVENT or MONASTERY 修院（或寺院）的生活

clois·tered /ˈklɔɪstəd; *NAmE* -tərd/ *adj.* (*formal*) protected from the problems and dangers of normal life 隐居的；躲开尘世纷争的：*a cloistered life* 隐居的生活 ◇ *the cloistered world of the university* 与世隔绝的大学

clone /kləʊn; *NAmE* kloʊn/ *noun, verb*

■ ***noun*** **1** (*biology* 生) a plant or an animal that is produced naturally or artificially from the cells of another plant or animal and is therefore exactly the same as it 克隆动物（或植物）；无性繁殖动物（或植物）；复制动物（或植物）**2** (*sometimes disapproving*) a person or thing that seems to be an exact copy of another 好像一模一样的人；复制品；仿造品；翻版

■ ***verb*** **1 ~ sth** to produce an exact copy of an animal or a plant from its cells 以无性繁殖技术复制；克隆：*A team from the UK were the first to successfully clone an animal.* 英国的一个小组率先克隆动物成功。◇ *Dolly, the cloned sheep* 复制羊多利 **2 ~ sth** to illegally make an electronic copy of stored information from a person's credit card or mobile/cell phone so that you can make payments or phone calls but the owner of the card or phone receives the bill 非法复制，克隆（复制他人信用卡或手机的存储信息，从而使卡主或机主付费）

clonk /klɒŋk; *NAmE* klɑːŋk/ *noun* (*informal*) a short loud sound of heavy things hitting each other（重物的）碰击声，哐当声 ▸ **clonk** *verb* [I, T] **~ (sth)**

close¹ 🔑 /kləʊz; *NAmE* kloʊz/ *verb, noun* ➲ SEE ALSO CLOSE²

■ ***verb***

• **WINDOW/DOOR, ETC.** 窗、门等 **1** 🔑 [T, I] **~ (sth)** to put sth into a position so that it covers an opening; to get into this position 关；关闭；闭上 **SYN** **shut**: *Would anyone mind if I closed the window?* 我关上窗户会有人介意吗？◇ *She closed the gate behind her.* 她关上了身后的大门。◇ *It's dark now—let's close the curtains.* 天黑了，咱们拉上窗帘吧。◇ *I closed my eyes against the bright light.* 我闭上眼睛以防强光的照射。◇ *The doors open and close automatically.* 这些门自动开关。**OPP** **open**

• **BOOK/UMBRELLA, ETC.** 书、伞等 **2** 🔑 [T] **~ sth (up)** to move the parts of sth together so that it is no longer open 合上；合拢 **SYN** **shut**: *to close a book/an umbrella* 合上书；收起伞 **OPP** **open**

• **SHOP/STORE/BUSINESS, ETC.** 店铺、商店、公司等 **3** 🔑 [T, often passive, I] to make the work of a shop/store, etc. stop for a period of time; to not be open for people to use（使）关门，关闭（一段时间）；不开放：**~ sth (for sth)** *The museum has been closed for renovation.* 博物馆已闭馆整修。◇ **~ sth (to sb/sth)** *The road was closed to traffic for two days.* 这条路封闭了两天。◇ **~ (for sth)** *What time does the bank close?* 那家银行什么时候关门？◇ *We close for lunch between twelve and two.* 十二点至两点是我们的午餐歇业时间。**OPP** **open** **4** 🔑 [T, I] **~ (sth)** (*also* **ˌclose ˈdown, ˌclose sth↔ˈdown**) if a company, shop/store, etc. **closes**, or if you **close** it, it stops operating as a business 停业；关闭；歇业；倒闭：*The club was closed by the police.* 那家夜总会被警察查封了。◇ *The hospital closed at the end of last year.* 这所医院去年年底关闭。◇ *The play closed after just three nights.* 这部剧仅上演了三个晚上就停演了。**OPP** **open**

• **END** 结束 **5** 🔑 [T, I] to end or make sth end（使）结束，终止：*The meeting will close at 10.00 p.m.* 会议将在晚上10点结束。◇ *The offer closes at the end of the week.* 优惠将在本周末截止。◇ **~ sth** *to close a meeting/debate* 结束会议/辩论 ◇ *to close a case/an investigation* 结案；结束调查 ◇ *to close an account* (= to stop keeping money in a bank account) 注销账户 ◇ *The subject is now closed* (= we will not discuss it again). 这个话题的讨论现在已告结束。**OPP** **open** ➲ EXPRESS YOURSELF AT FINISH

• **FINANCE** 金融 **6** [I] **~ (at sth)** to be worth a particular amount at the end of the day's business 收盘：*Shares in the company closed at 265p.* 这家公司的股票收盘价为265便士。◇ *closing prices* 收盘价

• **DISTANCE/DIFFERENCE** 距离；差别 **7** [T, I] **~ (sth)** to make the distance or difference between two people or things smaller; to become smaller or narrower（使）缩小，接近；变小；变窄：*These measures are aimed at* ***closing the gap*** *between rich and poor.* 这些措施旨在缩小贫富差距。◇ *The gap between the two top teams is closing all the time.* 两支顶尖球队的差距一直在缩小。

• **HOLD FIRMLY** 牢牢抓住 **8** [T, I] **~ (sth) about/around/over sb/sth** to hold sth/sb firmly 把…牢牢抱住（或抓住、握住）：*She closed her hand over his.* 她牢牢抓住他的手不放。◇ *Her hand closed over his.* 她牢牢抓住他的手不放。

IDM **close the book on sth** to stop doing sth because you no longer believe you will be successful or will find a solution（因相信不会成功或没有结论而）放弃：*The police have closed the book on the case* (= they have stopped trying to solve it). 警方已经放弃侦破此案。**close its doors** (of a business, etc. 企业等) to stop trading 停业；歇业；关闭：*The factory closed its doors for the last time*

▼ **WHICH WORD?** 词语辨析

close / shut

You can **close** and **shut** doors, windows, your eyes, mouth, etc. 关门、关窗、闭眼、闭嘴等用 close 或 shut 均可。

- **Shut** can suggest more noise and is often found in phrases such as *slammed shut, banged shut, snapped shut.* * shut 可含发出较大声音之义，常见于 slammed shut、banged shut、snapped shut（砰的一声关上）等短语中。
- **Shut** is also usually used for containers such as boxes, suitcases, etc. 关上盒子、手提箱等亦常用 shut。
- To talk about the time when shops, offices, etc. are not open, use **close** or **shut**. 商店、办事处等停业或不办公用 close 或 shut 均可：*What time do the banks close/shut?* 银行什么时候关门？◇ *A strike has shut the factory.* 罢工使工厂停业。You can also use **closed** or **shut** (*NAmE* usually **closed**). 亦可用 closed 或 shut（美式英语常用 closed）表示：*The store is closed/shut today.* 这家商店今天不营业。Especially in *NAmE*, **shut** can sound less polite. 尤其在美式英语中，shut 听起来欠礼貌。
- **Closed** is used in front of a noun, but **shut** is not. * closed 可用于名词前，shut 则不能：*a closed window* 关着的窗户
- We usually use **closed** about roads, airports, etc. 道路封闭、机场关闭等常用 closed：*The road is closed because of the snow.* 这条路因下雪而封闭。
- **Close** is also used in formal English to talk about ending a meeting or conversation. * close 亦用于正式英语中，表示结束会议或谈话。

C

in 2009. 这家工厂最后于 2009 年关闭。 **close your 'mind to sth** to refuse to think about sth as a possibility 对…拒不考虑（或置之不理、置若罔闻） **close 'ranks 1** if a group of people **close ranks**, they work closely together to defend themselves, especially when they are being criticized （尤指受到批评时）抱团，携手合作：*It's not unusual for the police to close ranks when one of their officers is being investigated.* 在一位警员受到调查时，警察抱团的事并不罕见。 **2** if soldiers **close ranks**, they move closer together in order to defend themselves （士兵）成密集队形，相互靠拢 ➲MORE AT DOOR, EAR, EYE *n.*

PHR V **,close 'down** (*BrE*) when a radio or television station **closes down**, it stops broadcasting at the end of the day（电台或电视台在一天的播送后）结束播放，停止播音 ➲RELATED NOUN CLOSE-DOWN **,close 'down | ,close sth↔'down** = CLOSE¹ (4)：*All the steelworks around here were closed down in the 1980s.* 这一带的所有钢铁厂都在 20 世纪 80 年代关闭了。 ➲RELATED NOUN CLOSE-DOWN OPP **open up** **,close 'in 1** when the days **close in**, they become gradually shorter during the autumn/fall （秋季白天）逐渐变短 **2** if the weather **closes in**, it gets worse （天气）变坏 **3** when the night **closes in**, it gets darker（夜色）加浓；（夜幕）降临：*They huddled around the fire as the night closed in.* 夜幕降临的时候，他们聚拢在炉火旁。 **,close 'in (on sb/sth)** to move nearer to sb/sth, especially in order to attack them （尤指为了进攻）逼近，靠近：*The lions closed in on their prey.* 狮子逼近它们的猎物。 **,close sth↔'off** to separate sth from other parts so that people cannot use it 隔离；封锁：*The entrance to the train station was closed off following the explosion.* 爆炸发生后随即封锁了火车站入口。 **,close sth ↔'out** (*NAmE*) **1** to finish or settle sth 结束；了结：*The band closes the album out with an instrumental track.* 乐队在这张专辑的最后以一首器乐曲收尾。 ◇ *A rock concert closed out the festivities.* 一场摇滚音乐会为庆典活动画下句点。 **2** to sell goods very cheaply in order to get rid of them quickly 削价销售；清仓处理；大甩卖 ➲ RELATED NOUN CLOSEOUT **,close 'over sb/sth** to surround and cover sb/sth 笼罩；遮盖；淹没：*The water closed over his head.* 水没过他的头顶。 **,close 'up 1** when a wound **closes up**, it heals （伤口）愈合 **2** to hide your thoughts or emotions 避而不谈（思想感情）：*She closed up when I asked about her family.* 我问起她的家人时她避而不谈。 **,close 'up | ,close sth↔'up 1** to shut and lock sth such as a shop/store or a building, especially for a short period of time （尤指临时）关门停业，锁上门：*Why don't we close up and go out for lunch?* 我们何不关上门出去吃顿午饭？ ◇ *Can the last one out close up the office?* 最后离开的人把办公室锁上好吗？ OPP **open up 2** to come closer together; to bring people or things closer together （使）靠拢，靠紧：*Traffic was heavy and cars were closing up behind each other.* 交通拥挤不堪，汽车一辆紧挨一辆地前行。 **3** to become narrower and less open 变狭窄：*Every time he tried to speak, his throat closed up with fear.* 每当他试图讲话时，他都害怕得喉咙发紧说不出话来。 OPP **open up**

■***noun*** [sing.] (*formal*) the end of a period of time or an activity （一段时间或活动的）结束，终结，终了：*at the close of the 17th century* 在 17 世纪末 ◇ *His life was* ***drawing to a close****.* 他的生命正走向终点。 ◇ *Can we* ***bring*** *this meeting* ***to a close****?* 我们可以结束会议了吗？

close² 🔑 /kləʊs; *NAmE* kloʊs/ *adj., adv., noun* ➲SEE ALSO CLOSE¹

■***adj.*** (**closer, clos·est**)

• **NEAR** 接近 **1** 🔑[not usually before noun] ~ (**to sb/sth**) | ~ (**together**) near in space or time（在空间、时间上）接近：*Our new house is close to the school.* 我们的新房子离学校很近。 ◇ *I had no idea the beach was so close.* 我不知道海滩会这么近。 ◇ *The two buildings are* ***close together****.* 两座建筑物相距很近。 ◇ *This is the closest we can get to the beach by car.* 开车去海滩到了这儿就再也不能往前走了。 ◇ *We all have to work* ***in close proximity*** (= near each other). 我们都不得不紧挨在一起工作。 ◇ *The President was shot* ***at close range*** (= from a short distance away). 总统遭到了近距离的枪击。 ◇ *The children are close to each other in age.* 这些儿童彼此的年龄很接近。 ◇ *Their birthdays are very* ***close together****.* 他们的生日挨得很近。 ➲NOTE AT NEAR

• **ALMOST/LIKELY** 几乎；可能 **2** 🔑[not before noun] ~ **to sth** | ~ **to doing sth** almost in a particular state; likely to do sth soon 几乎（处于某种状态）；可能（快要做某事）：*He was close to tears.* 他几乎掉眼泪了。 ◇ *The new library is close to completion.* 新图书馆快要竣工了。 ◇ *She knew she was close to death.* 她知道自己将不久于人世。 ◇ *We are close to signing the agreement.* 我们可能很快要签订协议。

• **RELATIONSHIP** 关系 **3** 🔑 ~ (**to sb**) knowing sb very well and liking them very much 亲密的；密切的：*Jo is a very* ***close friend****.* 乔是一个很亲密的朋友。 ◇ *She is very close to her father.* 她和父亲的关系很亲密。 ◇ *She and her father are very close.* 她和父亲的关系很亲密。 ◇ *We're a very close family.* 我们全家彼此亲密无间。 **4** 🔑 near in family relationship（家庭关系）亲近的：*close relatives, such as your mother and father, and brothers and sisters* 近亲，如父母和兄弟姊妹 OPP **distant** **5** 🔑very involved in the work or activities of sb else, usually seeing and talking to them regularly（与某人的工作或活动）紧密相关的，密切的：*He is one of the prime minister's closest advisers.* 他是首相最亲信的顾问之一。 ◇ *The college has close links with many other institutions.* 这所学院与其他许多的机构有着紧密的联系。 ◇ *She has kept in* ***close contact*** *with the victims' families.* 她与受害者的家人一直保持着密切的联系。 ◇ *We keep in* ***close touch*** *with the police.* 我们与警方保持着密切联系。

• **CAREFUL** 仔细 **6** 🔑[only before noun] careful and thorough 细致的；严密的；周密的：*Take a* ***close look*** *at this photograph.* 仔细看看这张照片。 ◇ ***On closer examination*** *the painting proved to be a fake.* 经过更加仔细的查看，那幅画被证实是件赝品。 ◇ *Pay* ***close attention*** *to what I am telling you.* 要认真听我给你讲的话。

• **SIMILAR** 相似 **7** 🔑 ~ (**to sth**) very similar to sth else or to an amount 酷似的；几乎相等的：*There's a close resemblance* (= they look very similar). 彼此间有酷似之处。 ◇ *His feeling for her was close to hatred.* 他对她的感情近乎仇恨。 ◇ *The total was close to 20% of the workforce.* 总数接近劳动力的 20%。 ◇ *We tried to match the colours, but this is the closest we could get.* 我们尽量使颜色搭配协调，但最好也只能做到这样了。

• **COMPETITION/ELECTION, ETC.** 竞争、选举等 **8** 🔑 won by only a small amount or distance 实力相差无几的；仅以些微之差获胜的：*a* ***close contest/match/election*** 双方实力很接近的竞赛 / 比赛；胜负双方差距很小的选举 ◇ *It was a very* ***close finish****.* 比赛结果的胜负双方差距极小。 ◇ *I think it's going to be close.* 我认为这将是一场势均力敌的角逐。 ◇ *Our team came a* ***close second*** (= nearly won). 我们队以微弱差距屈居第二。 ◇ *The game was closer than the score suggests.* 双方实力比得分所显示的要更接近。 ◇ *The result is going to be* ***too close to call*** (= either side may win). 双方实力非常接近，因此结果无法预料。

• **ALMOST BAD RESULT** 近乎于不好的结果 **9** used to describe sth, usually a dangerous or unpleasant situation, that nearly happens（通常指危险或不愉快的情况几乎发生）差一点儿，险些：*Phew! That was close—that car nearly hit us.* 啊！好险！那辆车差点儿撞上我们。 ◇ *We caught the bus in the end but it was close* (= we nearly missed it). 虽然我们最后总算赶上了那趟公共汽车，但也是够悬的。

• **WITHOUT SPACE** 无空间 **10** with little or no space in between 空隙极小的；无空隙的；密集的；紧凑的：*over 1 000 pages of close print* * 1 000 多页字体密集的印刷品 ◇ *The soldiers advanced in close formation.* 士兵排着密集的队形前进。

• **CUT SHORT** 剪短 **11** cut very short, near to the skin 剪到齐根的；剪得很短的：*a* ***close haircut/shave*** 剪到齐根的头发；刮剃干净

• **GUARDED** 戒备 **12** [only before noun] carefully guarded 严加戒备的；守卫严密的：*The donor's identity is a close secret.* 捐赠人的身份是保密的。 ◇ *She was kept under close arrest.* 她被严密监禁。

• **WEATHER/ROOM** 天气；房间 **13** warm in an uncomfortable way because there does not seem to be enough fresh air 闷热的；不通风的 SYN **stuffy**

• **PRIVATE** 私人 **14** [not before noun] ~ (**about sth**) not willing to give personal information about yourself （对自己的个人信息）守口如瓶：*He was close about his past.* 他对他

的过去守口如瓶。

- **MEAN** 吝啬 **15** [not before noun] (*BrE*) not liking to spend money 吝啬；小气：*She's always been very close with her money.* 她用钱总是很吝啬。
- **PHONETICS** 语音学 **16** (*also* **high**) (of a vowel 元音) produced with the mouth in a relatively closed position 闭塞音的，闭的（发音时口形相对闭合的）➲ COMPARE OPEN *adj.* (19)

▸ **close·ly** adv. : *I sat and watched everyone very closely* (= carefully). 我坐着仔细观察每一个人。◇ *He walked into the room, closely followed by the rest of the family.* 他走进房间，后面紧跟着他的家人。◇ *a closely contested election* 实力相差无几的竞选 ◇ *She closely resembled her mother at the same age.* 她与她母亲在相同的年龄时长相酷似。◇ *The two events are closely connected.* 两起事件之间有密切的联系。 **close·ness** noun [U]

IDM **at/from ˌclose ˈquarters** very near 很近；非常靠近：*fighting at close quarters* 近距离作战 **close, but no ciˈgar** (*informal, especially NAmE*) used to tell sb that their attempt or guess was almost but not quite successful 很接近，但还是输了；猜得差不多，但不完全对 **a ˌclose ˈcall/ˈshave** (*informal*) a situation in which you only just manage to avoid an accident, etc. 侥幸避免事故；侥幸脱险；幸免于难 **a close ˈthing** a situation in which success or failure is equally possible 成败机会各半：*We got him out in the end, but it was a close thing.* 我们最后总算把他救了出来，可那是真险啊。 **close to ˈhome** if a remark or topic of discussion is **close to home**, it is accurate or connected with you in a way that makes you uncomfortable or embarrassed （话语或讨论的话题）因点中要害而使人局促不安（或尴尬）：*Her remarks about me were embarrassingly close to home.* 她说我的那些话使我尴尬不已。 **keep a close ˈeye/ˈwatch on sb/sth** to watch sb/sth carefully 密切注视；严密监视：*Over the next few months we will keep a close eye on sales.* 在今后的几个月里我们将密切关注销售情况。➲ MORE AT HAND *n.*, HEART

■ *adv.* (**closer, clos·est**) near; not far away 接近；靠近；紧挨着；不远地：*They sat close together.* 他们紧挨着坐在一起。◇ *Don't come too close!* 别靠得太近！◇ *She held Tom close and pressed her cheek to his.* 她紧紧地抱着汤姆，并把脸紧贴在他的脸上。◇ *I couldn't get close enough to see.* 我无法靠得很近去看清楚。◇ *A second police car followed close behind.* 第二辆警车紧紧跟在后面。

IDM **close at ˈhand** near; in a place where sb/sth can be reached easily 在附近；在触手可及的地方：*There are good cafes and a restaurant close at hand.* 附近有几家挺不错的咖啡馆和一家餐馆。 **close ˈby (sb/sth)** at a short distance (from sb/sth) （离…）不远；在不远处；在近旁：*Our friends live close by.* 我们的朋友住得不远。◇ *The route passes close by the town.* 这条路离那座城镇不远。 **close on | close to** almost; nearly 几乎；接近；差不多：*She is close on sixty.* 她快满六十岁了。◇ *It is close on midnight.* 时近午夜。◇ *a profit close to £200 million* 接近 2 亿英镑的利润 **a close-run ˈthing** a situation in which sb only just wins or loses, for example in a competition or an election （比赛或选举等中的）险胜，差距很小的败北 **close ˈto | close ˈup** in a position very near to sth 在很近处；很近地：*The picture looks very different when you see it close to.* 这幅画贴近看时就很不一样。 **close up to sb/sth** very near in space to sb/sth （在空间上）离…很近：*She snuggled close up to him.* 她紧紧地依偎着他。 **come close (to sth/to doing sth)** to almost reach or do sth 几乎达到；差不多：*He'd come close to death.* 他曾与死神擦肩而过。◇ *We didn't win but we came close.* 我们输了，但离赢只差了那么一小点儿。 **run sb/sth ˈclose** (*BrE*) to be nearly as good, fast, successful, etc. as sb/sth else 与…不相上下；可与…媲美：*Germany ran Argentina very close in the final.* 在决赛中，德国队发挥得几乎和阿根廷队一样出色。➲ MORE AT CARD *n.*, MARK *n.*, SAIL *v.*

■ *noun* **1** (*BrE*) (especially in street names 尤用于街道名称) a street that is closed at one end 一端不通的街道；死胡同；死巷道：*Brookside Close* 布鲁克赛德巷 **2** the grounds and buildings that surround and belong to a CATHEDRAL 大教堂所属的周围场地及建筑物

close-cropped /ˌkləʊs ˈkrɒpt; *NAmE* ˌkloʊs ˈkrɑːpt/ *adj.* (of hair, grass, etc. 头发、草等) cut very short 剪得很短的

closed /kləʊzd; *NAmE* kloʊzd/ *adj.* **1** shut 关闭；封闭：*Keep the door closed.* 让门关着吧。 **2** [not before noun] shut, especially of a shop/store or public building that is not open for a period of time 关闭；（尤指一段时间）停止营业，不开放：*The museum is closed on Mondays.* 博物馆每逢星期一闭馆。◇ *This road is closed to traffic.* 这条道路暂停通行。 **3** not willing to accept outside influences or new ideas 封闭的；闭关自守的；不愿接受新思想的：*a closed society* 闭关自守的社会 ◇ *He has a closed mind.* 他思想僵化守旧。 **4** [usually before noun] limited to a particular group of people; not open to everyone 只限于某些人的；仅为少数人的；不向公众开放的：*a closed membership* 只限于少数人的成员资格 OPP **open** ➲ NOTE AT CLOSE[1]

IDM **behind closed ˈdoors** without the public being allowed to attend or know what is happening; in private 与外界隔绝；秘密地；暗地里 **a closed ˈbook (to sb)** a subject or person that you know nothing about 对之一窍不通的事物；不了解的人

ˌclosed-ˈcaptioned *adj.* (*NAmE*) (of a TV programme 电视节目) having CAPTIONS that can only be read if you have a special machine (= a DECODER) 闭路字幕的（用解码器才能阅读）

ˌclosed-ˌcircuit ˈtelevision *noun* [U] (*abbr.* **CCTV**) a television system that works within a limited area, for example a public building, to protect it from crime 闭路电视

close-down /ˈkləʊz daʊn; *NAmE* ˈkloʊz/ *noun* [U, sing.] the stopping of work, especially permanently, in an office, a factory, etc. （尤指永久的）停工，停业；倒闭

ˈclosed season *noun* [sing.] = CLOSE SEASON (1)

ˌclosed ˈshop *noun* a factory, business, etc. in which employees must all be members of a particular trade/labor union 只雇用某工会会员的工厂（或企业等）➲ WORDFINDER NOTE AT UNION

ˈclosed syllable *noun* (*phonetics* 语音) a syllable which ends with a consonant, for example *sit* 闭音节（以辅音结束的音节，如 sit）

close-fitting /ˌkləʊs ˈfɪtɪŋ; *NAmE* ˌkloʊs/ *adj.* (of clothes 衣服) fitting tightly, showing the shape of the body 紧身的

close harmony /ˌkləʊs ˈhɑːməni; *NAmE* ˌkloʊs ˈhɑːrməni/ *noun* [U] (*music* 音) a style of singing in HARMONY in which the different notes are close together 密集和声（声部紧靠在一起）

close-knit /ˌkləʊs ˈnɪt; *NAmE* ˌkloʊs/ (*also less frequent* **ˌclosely-ˈknit**) *adj.* (of a group of people 一群人) having strong relationships with each other and taking a close, friendly interest in each other's activities and problems 紧密结合在一起的；志同道合的；意气相投的：*the close-knit community of a small village* 小村庄里抱团的村民

close-mouthed /ˌkləʊs ˈmaʊðd; *NAmE* ˌkloʊs/ *adj.* [not usually before noun] not willing to say much about sth because you want to keep a secret 守口如瓶；口紧；缄口不言

close-out /ˈkləʊzaʊt; *NAmE* ˈkloʊz-/ *noun* (*NAmE*) an occasion when goods are sold cheaply in order to get rid of them quickly 削价销售；清仓处理；大甩卖

close-range /ˌkləʊs ˈreɪndʒ; *NAmE* ˌkloʊs/ *adj.* [only before noun] at or from a short distance 近距离的：*The close-range shot was blocked by the goalkeeper.* 那次近距离的射门被守门员截住了。

close-run /ˌkləʊs ˈrʌn; *NAmE* ˌkloʊs/ *adj.* [usually before noun] (of a race or competition 比赛或竞争) won by a very small amount or distance 险胜的：*The election was a close-run thing.* 这次选举是一次险胜。

close season /ˈkləʊz siːzn; *NAmE* ˈkloʊz/ *noun* [sing.] (*BrE*) **1** (*also* **ˈclosed season** *NAmE, BrE*) the time of year when it is illegal to kill particular kinds of animal, bird and fish because they are breeding 禁猎期；禁渔期 OPP **open**

season 2 (*NAmE* ˈ**off season**) (in sport 体育运动) the time during the summer when teams do not play important games （夏季的）休赛期

close-set /ˌkləʊs ˈset; *NAmE* ˌkloʊs/ *adj.* very close together 紧靠在一起的；很近的：*close-set eyes* 长得距离很近的眼睛

closet /ˈklɒzɪt; *NAmE* ˈklɑːzət/ *noun, adj., verb*
■ ***noun*** (*especially NAmE*) a small room or a space in a wall with a door that reaches the floor, used for storing things 贮藏室；壁橱：*a walk-in closet* 步入式衣帽间 ➲ VISUAL VOCAB PAGE V24 ➲ COMPARE CUPBOARD (2), WARDROBE (1) ➲ SEE ALSO WATER CLOSET
IDM **come out of the ˈcloset** to admit sth openly that you kept secret before, especially because of shame or embarrassment 公开承认秘密（尤指因耻辱或尴尬而一直保守着的秘密）；"出柜"：*Homosexuals in public life are now coming out of the closet.* 公众人物中的同性恋者如今逐渐公开自己的性取向。➲ SEE ALSO COME OUT (10) at COME *v.* ➲ MORE AT SKELETON
■ ***adj.*** [only before noun] used to describe people who want to keep some fact about themselves secret 隐藏（身份等）的；不公开（个人信息）的：*closet gays* 不公开表明的同性恋者 ◇ *I suspect he's a closet fascist.* 我怀疑他是秘密的法西斯分子。
■ ***verb*** **~ sb/yourself + adv./prep.** to put sb in a room away from other people, especially so that they can talk privately with sb, or so that they can be alone 把…关在房间里（尤指为了私下会谈或避免他人打扰）：*He was closeted with the President for much of the day.* 他与总统闭门进行了几乎一整天的密谈。◇ *She had closeted herself away in her room.* 她把自己关在房间里不见任何人。

close-up /ˈkləʊs ʌp; *NAmE* ˈkloʊs/ *noun* [C, U] a photograph, or picture in a film/movie, taken very close to sb/sth so that it shows a lot of detail （照片、电影的）特写，特写镜头：*a close-up of a human eye* 人眼睛的特写镜头 ◇ *It was strange to see her own face* ***in close-up*** *on the screen.* 在屏幕上看见她自己的脸部特写使她感到奇怪。◇ *close-up pictures of the planet* 这颗行星的特写照片

clos·ing /ˈkləʊzɪŋ; *NAmE* ˈkloʊzɪŋ/ *adj., noun*
■ ***adj.*** [only before noun] coming at the end of a speech, a period of time or an activity （讲话、时段或活动）接近尾声的，结尾的，结束的：*his closing remarks* 他的结束语 ◇ *the closing stages of the game* 比赛的结束阶段 OPP **opening**
■ ***noun*** [U] the act of shutting sth such as a factory, hospital, school, etc. permanently （永久的）停业，关闭；倒闭：*the closing of the local school* 当地学校的关闭 OPP **opening**

ˈ**closing date** *noun* the last date by which sth must be done, such as applying for a job or entering a competition 截止日期 ➲ WORDFINDER NOTE AT COMPETITION

ˈ**closing time** *noun* [C, U] the time when a pub, shop/store, bar, etc. ends business for the day and people have to leave （酒馆、商店等的）打烊时间

clos·ure /ˈkləʊʒə(r); *NAmE* ˈkloʊ-/ *noun* **1** [C, U] the situation when a factory, school, hospital, etc. shuts permanently （永久的）停业，关闭；倒闭：*factory closures* 工厂倒闭 ◇ *The hospital has been threatened with closure.* 这家医院面临着关闭的威胁。**2** [C, U] the temporary closing of a road or bridge （路或桥的）暂时封闭 **3** [U] the feeling that a difficult or an unpleasant experience has come to an end or been dealt with in an acceptable way （因困境结束或事情得到妥善处理等的）宽慰；如释重负：*The conviction of their son's murderer helped to give them a sense of closure.* 谋杀儿子的凶手被判罪，让他们得到了一些安慰。

clot /klɒt; *NAmE* klɑːt/ *noun, verb*
■ ***noun*** **1** = BLOOD CLOT：*They removed a clot from his brain.* 他们从他的大脑里取出了一个血块。**2** (*old-fashioned, BrE, informal*) a stupid person 蠢人；笨蛋；傻瓜
■ ***verb*** (**-tt-**) [I, T] **~ (sth)** when blood or cream **clots** or when sth **clots** it, it forms thick lumps or clots （使血或乳脂）凝结成块：*a drug that stops blood from clotting during operations* 手术时防止血液凝结成块的药物 ◇ *the blood clotting agent, Factor 8* 凝血因子 VIII ➲ MORE LIKE THIS 36, page R29

cloth /klɒθ; *NAmE* klɔːθ/ *noun* (*pl.* **cloths** /klɒθs; *NAmE* klɔːðz/) **1** [U] material made by WEAVING or knitting cotton, wool, silk, etc. 织物；布料：***woollen/cotton cloth*** 毛料；棉布料 ◇ *bandages made from strips of cloth* 用布条做的绷带 ◇ *the* ***cloth industry/trade*** 纺织业；布业贸易 ◇ *a cloth bag* 布袋 ➲ SYNONYMS AT FABRIC **2** [C] (often in compounds 常构成复合词) a piece of cloth, often used for a special purpose, especially cleaning things or covering a table （一块）布；（尤指一块）抹布，桌布：*Wipe the surface with a damp cloth.* 用湿布擦拭表面。➲ SEE ALSO DISHCLOTH, DROP CLOTH, FLOORCLOTH, TABLECLOTH **3 the cloth** [sing.] (*literary*) used to refer to Christian priests as a group （统称）牧师，神父：*a man of the cloth* 一位牧师 IDM SEE COAT *n.*

ˌ**cloth ˈcap** (*also* ˌ**flat ˈcap**) (*both BrE*) *noun* a soft cap, normally made of wool, traditionally a symbol of working men 布帽，羊毛软帽（传统上为劳工的象征）：*The party has shed its cloth cap image* (= it is not just a working-class party any more). 这个政党已经摆脱纯工人阶级的形象。➲ VISUAL VOCAB PAGE V70

clothe /kləʊð; *NAmE* kloʊð/ *verb* **1 ~ sb/yourself/sth (in sth)** (*formal*) to dress sb/yourself 给…穿衣：*They clothe their children in the latest fashions.* 他们给他们的孩子穿最时髦的服装。◇ (*figurative*) *Climbing plants clothed the courtyard walls.* 攀缘植物给院墙披上了外衣。**2 ~ sb** to provide clothes for sb to wear 为（某人）提供衣服：*the costs of feeding and clothing a family* 一家人的衣食费用

ˈ**cloth-eared** *adj.* (*BrE, informal, disapproving*) (of a person 人) unable to hear or understand things clearly 耳背的；呆头呆脑的

clothed /kləʊðd; *NAmE* kloʊðd/ *adj.* [not usually before noun] **~ (in sth)** dressed in a particular way 衣着…；穿…衣服：*a man clothed in black* 黑衣男子 ◇ *She jumped* ***fully clothed*** *into the water.* 她没有脱衣服就跳进了水里。◇ (*figurative*) *The valley was clothed in trees and shrubs.* 树林和灌木丛覆盖着山谷。

clothes /kləʊðz; kləʊz; *NAmE* kloʊðz; kloʊz/ *noun* [pl.] the things that you wear, such as trousers/pants, dresses and jackets 衣服；服装：*I bought some new clothes for the trip.* 我为这次旅行买了一些新衣服。◇ *to* ***put on/take off your clothes*** 穿上 / 脱下衣服 ◇ *Bring* ***a change of clothes*** *with you.* 你要带上一套换洗衣服。◇ *She has no* ***clothes sense*** (= she does not know what clothes look attractive). 她不懂穿着打扮。➲ COLLOCATIONS AT FASHION ➲ VISUAL VOCAB PAGES V66-68 IDM SEE EMPEROR ➲ SYNONYMS ON NEXT PAGE

ˈ**clothes hanger** *noun* = HANGER

ˈ**clothes horse** *noun* **1** (*BrE*) a wooden or plastic folding frame that you put clothes on to dry after you have washed them 晾衣架；晒衣架 **2** (*disapproving*) a person, especially a woman, who is too interested in fashionable clothes 讲究衣着的人，追求时装的人（尤指女性）

ˈ**clothes line** (*BrE*) (*also* **line** *NAmE, BrE*) (*BrE also* ˈ**washing line**) *noun* a piece of thin rope or wire, attached to posts, that you hang clothes on to dry outside after you have washed them 晒衣绳

ˈ**clothes peg** (*BrE*) (*NAmE* ˈ**clothes·pin**) *noun* = PEG (3) ➲ PICTURE AT PEG

clo·thier /ˈkləʊðiə(r); *NAmE* ˈkloʊ-/ *noun* (*formal*) a person or company that makes or sells clothes or cloth 服装制造（或销售）商；衣料商

cloth·ing /ˈkləʊðɪŋ; *NAmE* ˈkloʊðɪŋ/ *noun* [U] clothes, especially a particular type of clothes 衣服；（尤指某种）服装：*protective clothing* 防护服 ◇ *the high cost of food and clothing* 衣食的昂贵费用 ◇ *an* ***item/article of clothing*** 一件衣服 ➲ SYNONYMS AT CLOTHES IDM SEE WOLF *n.*

▼ SYNONYMS 同义词辨析

clothes

clothing • garment • dress • wear • gear

These are all words for the things that you wear, such as shirts, jackets, dresses and trousers/pants. 以上各词均指衣服、服装。

clothes [pl.] the things that you wear, such as shirts, jackets, dresses and trousers/pants 指衣服、服装

clothing [U] (*rather formal*) clothes, especially a particular type of clothes 指衣服，尤指某种类型的服装：*warm clothing* 保暖服

CLOTHES OR CLOTHING? 用 clothes 还是 clothing?

Clothing is more formal than **clothes** and is used especially to mean 'a particular type of clothes'. There is no singular form of **clothes** or **clothing**: *a piece/an item/an article of clothing* is used to talk about one thing that you wear such as a dress or shirt. * clothing 较 clothes 更正式，尤用以指某种类型的服装。clothes 或 clothing 无单数形式，指一件衣服用 a piece/an item/an article of clothing。

garment (*formal*) a piece of clothing 指一件衣服：*He was wearing a strange shapeless garment.* 他穿着一件不成形的奇怪衣服。NOTE **Garment** should only be used in formal or literary contexts; in everyday contexts use *a piece of clothing*. * garment 只用于正式场合或文学语境，在日常生活中，一件衣服用 a piece of clothing。

dress [U] clothes, especially when worn in a particular style or for a particular occasion 指着装、衣着，尤指某种样式或某种场合穿的衣服：*We were allowed to wear casual dress on Fridays.* 我们在星期五可以穿便服。

wear [U] (usually in compounds) clothes for a particular purpose or occasion, especially when it is being sold in shops/stores （通常构成复合词）指为特定用途或场合穿的衣服，尤指商店中售卖的衣服：*the children's wear department* 童装部

gear [U] (*informal*) clothes 指衣服、服装：*Her friends were all wearing the latest gear* (= fashionable clothes). 她的朋友都穿着最新款的衣服。

PATTERNS

- **casual** clothes/clothing/dress/wear/gear
- **evening/formal** clothes/dress/wear
- **designer/sports** clothes/clothing/garments/wear/gear
- **children's/men's/women's** clothes/clothing/garments/wear
- to **have on/be in/wear** ...clothes/garments/dress/gear

ˌ**clotted** ˈ**cream** *noun* [U] a very thick type of cream made by slowly heating milk, made and eaten especially in Britain （尤指在英国用文火加热牛奶制作的）凝脂奶油：*scones and jam with clotted cream* 夹有凝脂奶油和果酱的烤饼

ˈ**clotting factor** *noun* [C, U] (*biology* 生) any of the substances in the blood which help it to CLOT (= become thick and form lumps) 凝血因子 ➲ MORE LIKE THIS 9, page R26

cloud /klaʊd/ *noun, verb*

■ *noun* **1** [C, U] a grey or white mass made of very small drops of water, that floats in the sky 云；云朵：*The sun went behind a cloud.* 太阳躲到了一朵云的后面。◇ *The plane was flying in cloud most of the way.* 飞机一路大多在云层里飞行。➲ COLLOCATIONS AT WEATHER ➲ SEE ALSO STORM CLOUD, THUNDERCLOUD **2** [C] a large mass of sth in the air, for example dust or smoke, or a number of insects flying all together 一团，一大片（尘雾、烟雾或一群飞行的昆虫等）**3** [C] something that makes you feel sad or anxious 阴影；忧郁；焦虑；令人忧虑的事：*Her father's illness* ***cast a cloud over*** *her wedding day.* 她父亲的病给她的结婚喜庆日蒙上了一层阴影。◇ *The only dark* ***cloud on the horizon*** *was that they might have to move house.* 唯一的忧虑是他们可能得搬家。◇ *He still has* ***a cloud*** *of suspicion* ***hanging over him.*** 大家仍然在怀疑他。**4 the cloud** [sing.] a network of SERVERS (= computers that control or supply information to other computers) on which data and software can be stored or managed and to which users have access over the Internet 云（可存储或管理数据和软件的服务器网络，用户通过互联网访问）：*Key company documents are now stored in the cloud, so you no longer need to save them to your computer's hard drive.* 公司最重要的文档现在存储在云端，因此不必再将它们保存到计算机硬盘。

IDM **every cloud has a silver 'lining** (*saying*) every sad or difficult situation has a positive side 黑暗中总有一线光明；朵朵乌云衬银边，处处黑暗透光明 **on cloud 'nine** (*old-fashioned, informal*) extremely happy 极其快乐；乐不可支 **under a 'cloud** if sb is **under a cloud**, other people think that they have done sth wrong and are suspicious of them 有嫌疑；被怀疑 ➲ MORE AT HEAD *n.*

■ *verb* **1** [T] ~ **sth** if sth **clouds** your judgement, memory, etc., it makes it difficult for you to understand or remember sth clearly 使难以理解；使记不清楚；使模糊：*Doubts were beginning to cloud my mind.* 诸多疑问开始使我的思路变模糊了。◇ *His judgement was clouded by jealousy.* 妒忌心干扰了他的判断力。**2** [I, T] (*formal*) (of sb's face 脸色) to show sadness, fear, anger, etc.; to make sb look sad, afraid, angry, etc. 显得阴沉（或恐惧、愤怒等）；看起来忧愁（或害怕、愤怒等）：~ (**over**) *Her face clouded over with anger.* 她满面怒容。◇ ~ **sth** *Suspicion clouded his face.* 他狐疑满面。**3** [T] ~ **the issue** to make sth you are discussing or considering less clear, especially by introducing subjects that are not connected with it （尤指用无关的话题来）混淆，搅混（问题）**4** [I] ~ (**over**) (of the sky 天空) to fill with clouds 布满云：*It was beginning to cloud over.* 天空开始阴云密布。**5** [T] ~ **sth** to make sth less pleasant or enjoyable 使减少乐趣；使不快：*His last years were clouded by financial worries.* 由于经济窘困，他的晚年生活过得闷闷不乐。**6** [I, T] if glass, water, etc. **clouds**, or if sth **clouds** it, it becomes less transparent （使）不透明；（使）模糊：~ (**with sth**) *Her eyes clouded with tears.* 泪水模糊了她的眼睛。◇ ~ **sth** *Steam had clouded the mirror.* 水蒸气使镜子变得模糊不清。

cloud·burst /ˈklaʊdbɜːst; *NAmE* -bɜːrst/ *noun* a sudden very heavy fall of rain （骤然降下的）大暴雨，倾盆大雨

ˈ**cloud computing** *noun* [U] a way of using computers in which data and software are stored or managed on a network of SERVERS (= computers that control or supply information to other computers), to which users have access over the Internet 云计算；云端运算

ˌ**cloud** ˈ**cuckoo land** (*BrE*) (*NAmE* ˈ**la-la land**) *noun* [U] (*informal, disapproving*) if you say that sb is living **in cloud cuckoo land**, you mean that they do not understand what a situation is really like, but think it is much better than it is 幻想世界；脱离现实的幻境

ˈ**cloud forest** *noun* [C, U] a forest in tropical or SUBTROPICAL parts of the world that usually has thick cloud at the level of the tops of the trees （热带或亚热带的）云雾林 ➲ COMPARE RAINFOREST

cloud·less /ˈklaʊdləs/ *adj.* clear; with no clouds 晴朗的；无云的：*a cloudless sky* 晴朗的天空

cloudy /ˈklaʊdi/ *adj.* (**cloud·ier, cloudi·est**) **1** (of the sky or the weather 天空或天气) covered with clouds; with a lot of clouds 被云遮住的；阴云密布的；阴天的；多云的：*a grey, cloudy day* 灰暗多云的一天 OPP **clear 2** (of liquids 液体) not clear or transparent 不清澈的；不透明的；浑浊的 ▶ **cloudi·ness** *noun* [U]

clout /klaʊt/ *noun, verb*

■ *noun* **1** [U] power and influence 影响力；势力：***political/financial clout*** 政治 / 经济势力 ◇ *I knew his opinion carried a lot of clout with them.* 我知道他的观点对他们很有影响力。**2** [C, usually sing.] (*informal*) a blow with the hand or a hard object （用手或硬物的）击，打

■ ***verb*** **~ sb** (*informal*) to hit sb hard, especially with your hand（尤指用手）猛击，重打

clove /kləʊv; *NAmE* kloʊv/ *noun* **1** [C, U] the dried flower of a tropical tree, used in cooking as a spice, especially to give flavour to sweet foods. Cloves look like small nails. 丁香（热带树木的干花，形似小钉子，用于烹饪调味，尤用作甜食的香料）➲ VISUAL VOCAB PAGE V35 **2** [C] **a garlic ~ | a ~ of garlic** one of the small separate sections of a BULB (= the round underground part) of GARLIC 蒜瓣 ➲ VISUAL VOCAB PAGE V33 ➲ SEE ALSO CLEAVE

ˌcloven ˈhoof *noun* the foot of an animal such as a cow, a sheep, or a GOAT, that is divided into two parts （牛、羊等的）偶蹄，分趾蹄

clo·ver /ˈkləʊvə(r); *NAmE* ˈkloʊ-/ *noun* [U] a small wild plant that usually has three leaves on each STEM and purple, pink or white flowers that are shaped like balls 三叶草；车轴草： *a four-leaf clover* (= one with four leaves instead of three, thought to bring good luck) 四叶车轴草（一般为三叶，故被认为可带来好运）

IDM **be/live in clover** (*informal*) to have enough money to be able to live a very comfortable life 过舒适优裕的生活

clover·leaf /ˈkləʊvəliːf; *NAmE* ˈkloʊvər-/ *noun* (*NAmE*) a place where a number of main roads meet at different levels, with curved sections that form the pattern of a four-leaf clover 四叶苜蓿叶形立交路口

clown /klaʊn/ *noun, verb*

■ ***noun*** **1** an entertainer who wears funny clothes and a large red nose and does silly things to make people laugh 丑角；小丑： (*figurative*) *Robert was always the class clown* (= he did silly things to make the other students laugh). 那时候罗伯特总是班里的活宝。 **2** (*disapproving*) a person that you disapprove of because they act in a stupid way 蠢货；笨蛋： *What do those clowns in the government think they are doing?* 政府里的那些蠢货自以为他们在做什么呢？

■ ***verb*** [I] ~ (**around**) (*often disapproving*) to behave in a silly way, especially in order to make other people laugh （尤指为逗人笑而故意）做出蠢相

clown·fish /ˈklaʊnfɪʃ/ *noun* a type of brightly coloured SALTWATER fish that lives with SEA ANEMONES and is protected from their stings 小丑鱼；海葵鱼

clown·ish /ˈklaʊnɪʃ/ *adj.* like a clown; silly 小丑似的；滑稽的；愚蠢的；傻的

cloy /klɔɪ/ [I] (of sth pleasant or sweet 美好的事物或香甜的东西) to start to become slightly disgusting or annoying, because there is too much of it （因过量而）让人腻烦： *After a while, the rich sauce begins to cloy.* 过了一会儿，浓味沙司开始显得油腻了。

cloy·ing /ˈklɔɪɪŋ/ *adj.* (*formal*) **1** (of food, a smell, etc. 食物、气味等) so sweet that it is unpleasant 甜得发腻的；使人腻烦的 **2** using emotion in a very obvious way, so that the result is unpleasant （感情过于外露而）令人腻烦的： *the cloying sentimentality of her novels* 她的小说中令人厌烦的感伤情调 ▸ **cloy·ing·ly** *adv.*

cloze test /ˈkləʊz test; *NAmE* ˈkloʊz/ *noun* a type of test in which you have to put suitable words in spaces in a text where words have been left out 填空测验

club /klʌb/ *noun, verb*

■ ***noun***

• **FOR ACTIVITY/SPORT** 活动；体育运动 **1** [C+sing./pl. v.] (especially in compounds 尤用于构成复合词) a group of people who meet together regularly, for a particular activity, sport, etc. 俱乐部；社团；会： *a **golf/tennis, etc. club*** 高尔夫球、网球等俱乐部 ◇ *a **chess/film/movie, etc. club*** 国际象棋、电影等俱乐部 ◇ *to **join/belong to a club*** 加入俱乐部；是某俱乐部成员 ◇ *The club has/have voted to admit new members.* 俱乐部通过投票同意接纳新成员。➲ SEE ALSO FAN CLUB, YOUTH CLUB

WORDFINDER 联想词： AGM, the chair, hobby, member, newsletter, secretary, society, subscription, treasurer

2 [C] the building or rooms that a particular club uses （俱乐部使用的）建筑设施，活动室： *We had lunch at the golf club.* 我们在高尔夫球俱乐部吃了午饭。◇ *the club bar* 俱乐部酒吧 ➲ SEE ALSO COUNTRY CLUB, HEALTH CLUB **3** [C+sing./pl. v.] (*BrE*) a professional sports organization that includes the players, managers, owners and members 职业运动俱乐部： *Manchester United Football Club* 曼联职业足球俱乐部

• **MUSIC/DANCING** 音乐；舞蹈 **4** [C] a place where people, especially young people, go and listen to music, dance, etc. （尤指年轻人听音乐、跳舞等的）俱乐部，夜总会： *a jazz club* 爵士乐夜总会 ◇ *the club scene in Newcastle* 纽卡斯尔的夜总会场景 ➲ SEE ALSO CLUBBING, NIGHTCLUB, STRIP CLUB

• **SOCIAL** 社交 **5** [C+sing./pl. v.] (especially in Britain) an organization and a place where people can meet together socially or stay（尤指英国）俱乐部： *He's a member of several London clubs.* 他是伦敦几个俱乐部的会员。

• **SELLING BOOKS/CDS** 销售书 / 激光唱片 **6** [C] an organization that sells books, CDs, etc. cheaply to its members （以优惠价出售图书、激光唱片等给成员的）读者俱乐部，听众俱乐部，…会： *a music club* 音乐听众俱乐部 ➲ SEE ALSO BOOK CLUB

• **WEAPON** 武器 **7** [C] a heavy stick with one end thicker than the other, that is used as a weapon 击棍（一头粗一头细）➲ SEE ALSO BILLY CLUB

• **IN GOLF** 高尔夫球 **8** [C] = GOLF CLUB (1)

• **IN CARD GAMES** 纸牌游戏 **9 clubs** [pl., U] one of the four sets of cards (called SUITS) in a PACK/DECK of cards. The clubs have a black design shaped like three black leaves on a short STEM. 梅花： *the five/queen/ace of clubs* 梅花五 / Q / A ➲ VISUAL VOCAB PAGE V42 **10** [C] one card from the SUIT called clubs 梅花牌： *I played a club.* 我出梅花。

IDM **be in the club** (*BrE, informal*) to be pregnant 怀孕；肚子大了 ➲ MORE AT JOIN *v.*

■ ***verb*** (**-bb-**) **1** [T] **~ sb/sth** to hit a person or an animal with a heavy stick or similar object 用棍棒（或类似棍棒之物）打： *The victim was **clubbed to death** with a baseball bat.* 受害者被人用棒球球棒殴打致死。 **2** [I] **go clubbing** (*informal*) to spend time dancing and drinking in NIGHTCLUBS 泡夜总会 ➲ MORE LIKE THIS 36, page R29

PHR V **ˌclub toˈgether** (*BrE*) if two or more people **club together**, they each give an amount of money and the total is used to pay for sth 凑份子；分担费用： *We clubbed together to buy them a new television.* 我们凑钱给他们买了一台新电视机。

club·bing /ˈklʌbɪŋ/ *noun* [U] the activity of going to NIGHTCLUBS regularly 泡夜总会： *They **go clubbing** most weekends.* 他们大多数周末都去泡夜总会。 ▸ **club·ber** *noun* ： *The venue was packed with 3 000 clubbers.* 会场被 3 000 名俱乐部会员挤得满满的。

ˈclub car *noun* (*NAmE*) a coach/car on a train with comfortable chairs and tables, where you can buy sth to eat or drink （火车的）休闲车厢（设有舒适桌椅，并出售食品饮料）

ˈclub class *noun* [U] (*BrE*) = BUSINESS CLASS

ˌclub ˈfoot *noun* [C, U] a foot that has been DEFORMED (= badly shaped) since birth （先天性的）畸形足 ▸ **ˌclub-ˈfooted** *adj.*

club·house /ˈklʌbhaʊs/ *noun* the building used by a club, especially a sports club （尤指体育）俱乐部会所

club·land /ˈklʌblænd/ *noun* [U] (*BrE*) popular NIGHTCLUBS in general and the people who go to them; an area of a town where there are a lot of NIGHTCLUBS 受欢迎的夜总会及其顾客；夜总会区： *modern clubland* 现代夜总会区 ◇ *London's clubland* 伦敦的夜总会区

ˌclub ˈsandwich *noun* a SANDWICH consisting of three slices of bread with two layers of food between them 总会三明治（三片面包，两层夹馅）

cluck /klʌk/ *verb, noun*

■ ***verb*** **1** [I] when a chicken **clucks**, it makes a series of short low sounds （鸡）咯咯地叫，发出咯咯声 **2** [I] to make a short low sound with your tongue to show that

C

you feel sorry for sb or that you disapprove of sth（表示遗憾或不赞成）发出啧啧声：*The teacher clucked sympathetically at the child's story.* 对那小孩讲述的遭遇，老师啧啧地表示同情。

■ ***noun*** the low, short sounds that a chicken makes（鸡的）咯咯声：(*figurative*) *a* ***cluck of impatience/annoyance*** 不耐烦 / 气恼的啧啧声

clucky /ˈklʌki/ *adj.* (*AustralE, NZE, informal*) **1** (of a HEN) sitting or ready to sit on eggs（母鸡）孵蛋的，准备孵蛋的 **SYN** **broody** **2** (of a woman) wanting to have a baby（女人）想生孩子的 **SYN** **broody**

clue /kluː/ *noun, verb*

■ ***noun*** **1** ~ (**to sth**) an object, a piece of evidence or some information that helps the police solve a crime（帮助警方破案的）线索，迹象：*The police think the videotape may hold some vital clues to the identity of the killer.* 警方认为那盘录像带可能录有能确认凶手身份的一些重要线索。 **2** ~ (**to sth**) a fact or a piece of evidence that helps you discover the answer to a problem（问题答案的）线索，提示：*Diet may hold the clue to the causes of migraine.* 饮食习惯有可能揭示偏头痛的原因。 **3** some words or a piece of information that helps you find the answers to a CROSSWORD, a game or a question（纵横填字谜、游戏或问题的）提示词语，解答提示：*'You'll never guess who I saw today!' 'Give me a clue.'* "你绝对猜不着我今天见到谁了！""给我提示一下吧。"

IDM **not have a ˈclue** (*informal*) **1** to know nothing about sth or about how to do sth 一无所知；不知怎么做：*I don't have a clue where she lives.* 我完全不知道她住在哪里。 **2** (*disapproving*) to be very stupid 很愚蠢；很笨拙：*Don't ask him to do it—he doesn't have a clue!* 这事别叫他做，他笨极了。

■ ***verb***

PHR V **ˌclue sb ˈin (on sth)** (*informal*) to give sb the most recent information about sth 给（某人）提供最新信息：*He's just clued me in on the latest developments.* 他刚给我提供了最新的进展情况。

ˌclued-ˈup (*BrE*) (*NAmE* **ˌclued-ˈin**) *adj.* ~ (**on sth**) (*informal*) knowing a lot about sth; having a lot of information about sth（对某事）很熟悉，所知甚多

clue·less /ˈkluːləs/ *adj.* (*informal, disapproving*) very stupid; not able to understand or to do sth 很愚蠢的；（对某事）不懂的，无能的：*He's completely clueless about computers.* 他对计算机一窍不通。

clump /klʌmp/ *noun, verb*

■ ***noun*** **1** a small group of things or people very close together, especially trees or plants; a bunch of sth such as grass or hair（尤指树或植物的）丛，簇，束，串；（人的）群，组；（草的）堆；（毛发的）绺：*a* ***clump of trees/bushes*** 树丛；灌木丛 **2** the sound made by sb putting their feet down very heavily 沉重的脚步声

■ ***verb*** **1** [I] **+ adv./prep.** (*especially BrE*) to put your feet down noisily and heavily as you walk 以沉重的脚步行走：*The children clumped down the stairs.* 孩子们脚步嗵嗵地走下了楼梯。 **2** [I, T] ~ (**together**) | ~ **A and B** (**together**) to come together or be brought together to form a tight group 聚集；被聚集成群：*Galaxies tend to clump together in clusters.* 星系往往聚集形成星团。

clumpy /ˈklʌmpi/ *adj.* (of shoes and boots 鞋和靴) big, thick and heavy 大而厚重的

clumsy /ˈklʌmzi/ *adj.* (**clum·sier, clum·si·est**) **1** (of people and animals 人和动物) moving or doing things in a very awkward way 笨拙的；不灵巧的：*I spilt your coffee. Sorry—that was clumsy of me.* 我弄洒了你的咖啡。对不起，我真是笨手笨脚的。◇ *His clumsy fingers couldn't untie the knot.* 他的手很笨拙，无法解开这个结。 **2** (of actions and statements 行动和陈述) done without skill or in a way that offends people 无技巧的；冒犯人的；不得体的：*She made* ***a clumsy attempt*** *to apologize.* 她本想道歉，但措辞生硬。 **3** (of objects 物体) difficult to move or use easily; not well designed 难以移动的；难用的；设计欠佳的 **4** (of processes 程序) awkward; too complicated to understand or use easily 难处理的；复杂难懂的；使用不便的：*The complaints procedure is clumsy and time-consuming.* 申诉程序复杂耗时。 ▶ **clum·si·ly** /-ɪli/ *adv.* **clum·si·ness** *noun* [U]

clung PAST TENSE, PAST PART. OF CLING

clunk /klʌŋk/ *noun* a dull sound made by two heavy objects hitting each other（重物的）碰撞声，哐啷声 ▶ **clunk** *verb* [I]

clunk·er /ˈklʌŋkə(r)/ *noun* (*NAmE, informal*) **1** an old car in bad condition 破旧不堪的汽车 **2** a serious mistake 严重的错误；大错

clunky /ˈklʌŋki/ *adj.* (*informal*) heavy and awkward 笨重的：*clunky leather shoes* 笨重的皮鞋 ◇ (*figurative*) *The movie is ruined by wooden acting and clunky dialogue.* 这部电影被木讷的表演和笨拙的对白给毁了。

clus·ter /ˈklʌstə(r)/ *noun, verb*

■ ***noun*** **1** a group of things of the same type that grow or appear close together（同类物丛生或聚集的）簇，团，束，串：*a cluster of stars* 星团 ◇ *The plant bears its flowers in clusters.* 这种植物开花成簇。◇ *a leukaemia cluster* (= an area where there are more cases of the disease than you would expect) 白血病高发区 **2** a group of people, animals or things close together（人或动物的）群，团，组；（物品的）堆，批：*a cluster of spectators* 一群观众 ◇ *a little cluster of houses* 挤在一起的几栋房屋 **3** (*phonetics* 语音) a group of consonants which come together in a word or phrase, for example /str/ at the beginning of *string* 辅音丛；辅音连缀：*a consonant cluster* 辅音丛 ➲ WORDFINDER NOTE AT PRONUNCIATION

■ ***verb*** [I] to come together in a small group or groups 群聚；聚集：**~ together** *The children clustered together in the corner of the room.* 孩子们聚集在房间的角落里。◇ **~ around/round sb/sth** *The doctors* ***clustered*** *anxiously* ***around*** *his bed.* 医生焦急地围在他的床边。

ˈcluster bomb *noun* a type of bomb that throws out smaller bombs when it explodes 集束炸弹；子母弹

clutch /klʌtʃ/ *verb, noun*

■ ***verb*** **1** [T, I] to hold sb/sth tightly 紧握；抱紧；抓紧 **SYN** **grip**：**~ sth (+ adv./prep.)** *He clutched the child to him.* 他紧紧地抱住小孩。◇ *She stood there, the flowers still clutched in her hand.* 她站在那里，手里仍然紧握着花束。◇ **+ adv./prep.** *I clutched on to the chair for support.* 我紧紧抓住椅子撑着身体。➲ SYNONYMS AT HOLD **2** [T, I] to take hold of sth suddenly, because you are afraid or in pain（因害怕或痛苦）突然抓住：**~ sth** *He gasped and clutched his stomach.* 他喘着气突然按住自己的胃部。◇ **~ at sb/sth** (*figurative*) *Fear clutched at her heart.* 她突然感到一阵恐惧袭上心头。**IDM** SEE STRAW ➲ SYNONYMS AT HOLD

PHR V **ˈclutch/ˈcatch at sth/sb** to try to quickly get hold of sth/sb 试图一把抓住 **SYN** **grab**

■ ***noun*** **1** [C] the PEDAL in a car or other vehicle that you press with your foot so that you can change gear（汽车等换挡用的）离合器踏板：*Put your foot on the clutch.* 把你的脚放在离合器踏板上。➲ COLLOCATIONS AT DRIVING ➲ VISUAL VOCAB PAGE V56 **2** [C] a device in a machine that connects and DISCONNECTS working parts, especially the engine and the gears（尤指发动机和排挡的）离合器：*The car needs a new clutch.* 这辆车需要换一个新的离合器了。 **3** **a ~ of sth** [sing.] a group of people, animals or things 一群（人或动物）；一批（物品）：*He's won a whole clutch of awards.* 他获了一大堆奖。 **4** **clutches** [pl.] (*informal*) power or control 势力范围；控制；掌管：*He managed to escape* ***from*** *their* ***clutches***. 他设法摆脱了他们的控制。◇ *Now that she had him* ***in her clutches***, *she wasn't going to let go.* 她既然已经把他控制在自己手里，就不打算让他脱身。 **5** [C, usually sing.] a tight hold on sb/sth 攫住；紧紧抓住 **SYN** **grip**：(*figurative*) *She felt the sudden clutch of fear.* 她突然感到一阵恐惧。 **6** [C] a group of eggs that a bird lays at one time; the young birds that come out of a group of eggs at the same time（一次下的）一窝蛋；（同时孵出的）一窝小鸟 **7** [C] (*especially NAmE*) = CLUTCH BAG

ˈclutch bag (*NAmE also* **clutch**) *noun* a small, flat bag that women carry in their hands, especially on formal occasions （尤指出席正式场合时用的）女式小手提包 ➲ VISUAL VOCAB PAGE V69

clut·ter /ˈklʌtə(r)/ *verb, noun*

■ ***verb*** **~ sth (up) (with sth/sb)** to fill a place with too many things, so that it is untidy 凌乱地塞满；乱堆放：*Don't clutter the page with too many diagrams.* 别用太多的图表来堆砌版面。◇ *I don't want all these files cluttering up my desk.* 我不想看到这么多文档乱堆在我的桌子上。◇ *(figurative) Try not to clutter your head with trivia.* 尽量别满脑子都想些鸡毛蒜皮的事。

■ ***noun*** [U, sing.] *(disapproving)* a lot of things in an untidy state, especially things that are not necessary or are not being used; a state of confusion 杂乱的东西（尤指不需要的或无用的）；杂乱 **SYN** **mess**：*There's always so much clutter on your desk!* 你桌子上总有那么多乱七八糟的东西！◇ *There was a clutter of bottles and tubes on the shelf.* 架子上胡乱堆满了瓶子和管子。

clut·tered /ˈklʌtəd; *NAmE* -tərd/ *adj.* **~ (up) (with sb/sth)** covered with, or full of, a lot of things or people, in a way that is untidy 杂乱的；凌乱的；挤满的：*a **cluttered room/desk*** 乱七八糟的房间 / 桌面 ◇ *(figurative) a cluttered mind* 杂乱无序的思路 **OPP** **uncluttered**

cm *abbr.* (*pl.* **cm** or **cms**) CENTIMETRE 厘米

CMS /ˌsiː em ˈes/ *noun* the abbreviation for 'content management system' (a piece of software that is used to organize, manage or change the content of a website) 网站内容管理系统（全写为 content management system）：*The CMS enables employees to add and edit web pages without the support of a web developer.* 网站内容管理系统使得员工无需网站开发人员支援就能够在网页上进行添加和编辑操作。

CND /ˌsiː en ˈdiː/ *abbr.* Campaign for Nuclear Disarmament (a British organization whose aim is to persuade countries to get rid of their nuclear weapons) 核裁军运动（英国反核运动组织）

CNN /ˌsiː en ˈen/ *abbr.* Cable News Network (an American broadcasting company that sends television news programmes all over the world) 有线电视新闻网（美国广播公司，向全世界播送新闻节目）

CO /ˌsiː ˈəʊ; *NAmE* ˈoʊ/ *abbr.* Commanding Officer (an officer who commands a group of soldiers, sailors, etc.) 指挥官；指挥长

Co. /kəʊ; *NAmE* koʊ/ *abbr.* **1** (*business* 商) company 公司；商号；商行：*Pitt, Briggs & Co.* 皮特 – 布里格斯公司 **2** (in writing 书写形式) county 郡；县 **3 and co.** *(informal)* and other members of a group of people 及其他成员；及其一伙：*Were Jane and co. at the party?* 简那几个人都参加聚会了吗？

co- /kəʊ; *NAmE* koʊ/ *prefix* (used in adjectives, adverbs, nouns and verbs 构成形容词、副词、名词和动词) together with 和…一起；共同；联合：*co-produced* 合作生产的 ◇ *cooperatively* 合作地 ◇ *co-author* 合著者 ◇ *coexist* 共存 ➲ MORE LIKE THIS 6, page R25

c/o /ˌsiː ˈəʊ; *NAmE* ˈoʊ/ *abbr.* (used on letters to a person staying at sb else's house) care of（用于投递给寄居人的信件上）由…转交：*Mr P Brown, c/o Ms M Jones* * M. 琼斯女士转交 P. 布朗先生

coach 🔑 /kəʊtʃ; *NAmE* koʊtʃ/ *noun, verb*

■ ***noun*** **1** 🔑 [C] a person who trains a person or team in sport（体育运动的）教练：*a **basketball/football/tennis, etc. coach*** 篮球、足球、网球等教练 ◇ *Italy's national coach* 意大利国家队教练 **2** [C] *(BrE)* a person who gives private lessons to sb, often to prepare them for an exam 私人教师；（多指）考前辅导教师：*a maths coach* 数学应试辅导教师 **3** [C] = LIFE COACH **4** 🔑 [C] a comfortable bus for carrying passengers over long distances 长途汽车；长途客车：*They went to Italy on a **coach tour**.* 他们乘长途客车去意大利旅游。◇ *Travel is **by coach** overnight to Berlin.* 旅程为乘一夜长途汽车去柏林。◇ *a **coach station*** (= where coaches start and end their journey) 长途汽车总站 ◇ *a **coach party*** (= a group of people travelling together on a coach) 乘坐长途客车的旅游团 ➲ VISUAL VOCAB PAGE V62 **5** 🔑 [C] *(BrE)* = CARRIAGE (1)：*a railway coach* 火车车厢 **6** [C] a large closed vehicle with four wheels, pulled by horses, used in the past for carrying passengers（旧时载客的）四轮大马车 ➲ SEE ALSO STAGECOACH **7** [U] *(NAmE)* the cheapest seats in a plane（客机的）经济舱：*to fly coach* 坐飞机经济舱 ◇ ***coach fares/passengers/seats*** 飞机经济舱票价 / 乘客 / 座位 **IDM** SEE DRIVE *v.*

■ ***verb*** **1** to train sb to play a sport, to do a job better, or to improve a skill（对体育运动、工作或技能进行）训练，培训，指导：**~ sb (in/for sth)** *Her father coached her for the Olympics.* 她的父亲训练她备战奥林匹克运动会。◇ **~ sb (to do sth)** *She has coached hundreds of young singers.* 她培养了许许多多的青年歌手。◇ **~ sth** *He coaches basketball and soccer.* 他执教篮球和足球。**2 ~ sb (in/for sth)** *(especially BrE)* to give a student extra teaching in a particular subject especially so that they will pass an exam 辅导（尤指为让学员通过考试）**3 ~ sb (in/on sth) | ~ sb (to do sth)** to give sb special instructions for what they should do or say in a particular situation 指示；特殊指导；专门传授：*They believed the witnesses had been coached on what to say.* 他们认为证人所作的证词是别人教他们那样说的。

ˈcoach house *noun* a building where CARRIAGES pulled by horses are or were kept 马车房

coach·ing /ˈkəʊtʃɪŋ; *NAmE* ˈkoʊtʃ-/ *noun* [U] **1** the process of training sb to play a sport, to do a job better or to improve a skill（体育运动、工作或技能的）训练，培训，指导：*a coaching session* 集训期 **2** *(especially BrE)* the process of giving a student extra teaching in a particular subject（某科目上的）辅导 ➲ WORDFINDER NOTE AT TRAINING

ˈcoaching inn *noun* in the past, an INN along a route used by horses, at which horses could be changed 驿马旅馆，驿站（旧时可换驿马的旅馆）

coach·load /ˈkəʊtʃləʊd; *NAmE* ˈkoʊtʃloʊd/ *noun* *(BrE)* a group of people travelling together in a coach（乘同一长途客车旅游的）团体旅客：*Tourists were arriving **by the coachload**.* 整团整团的游客乘着长途客车到达。

coach·man /ˈkəʊtʃmən; *NAmE* ˈkoʊtʃ-/ *noun* (*pl.* **-men** /-mən/) (in the past) a man who drove a COACH pulled by horses （旧时）马车夫

coach·work /ˈkəʊtʃwɜːk; *NAmE* ˈkoʊtʃwɜːrk/ *noun* [U] *(BrE)* the metal outer part of a road or railway/railroad vehicle 汽车（或火车）车身

co·agu·late /kəʊˈæɡjuleɪt; *NAmE* koʊ-/ *verb* [I, T] **~ (sth)** if a liquid **coagulates** or sth **coagulates** it, it becomes thick and partly solid 凝固；使凝结 **SYN** **congeal**：*Blood began to coagulate around the edges of the wound.* 血液开始在伤口的边缘凝固。 ▸ **co·agu·la·tion** /kəʊˌæɡjuˈleɪʃn; *NAmE* koʊ-/ *noun* [U]

coal 🔑 /kəʊl; *NAmE* koʊl/ *noun* **1** 🔑 [U] a hard black mineral that is found below the ground and burnt to produce heat 煤：*I put more coal on the fire.* 我往火里加了些煤。◇ *a lump of coal* 一块煤 ◇ *a coal fire* 煤火 ◇ *a coal mine* 煤矿 ◇ *the coal industry* 煤炭工业 **2** [C] a piece of coal, especially one that is burning （尤指燃烧着的）煤块：*A hot coal fell out of the fire and burnt the carpet.* 一块燃烧着的煤块从火炉里掉出来把地毯烧了。

IDM **carry, take, etc. coals to ˈNewcastle** *(BrE)* to take goods to a place where there are already plenty of them; to supply sth where it is not needed 多此一举 **ORIGIN** Newcastle-upon-Tyne, in the north of England, was once an important coal-mining centre. 英格兰北部泰恩河畔纽卡斯尔曾是重要的煤矿开采中心。 ➲ MORE AT HAUL *v.*, RAKE *v.*

ˌcoal-ˈblack *adj.* very dark in colour 乌黑的；漆黑的：*coal-black eyes* 乌黑的眼睛 ➲ MORE LIKE THIS 15, page R26

co·alesce /ˌkəʊəˈles; *NAmE* ˌkoʊə-/ *verb* [I] **~ (into/with sth)** *(formal)* to come together to form one larger group, substance, etc. 合并；联合；结合 **SYN** **amalgamate**：*The puddles had coalesced into a small stream.* 地面上水洼子里的水汇流成了一条小溪。 ▸ **co·ales·cence** /ˌkəʊəˈlesns; *NAmE* ˌkoʊə-/ *noun* [U]

coal·face /ˈkəʊlfeɪs; *NAmE* ˈkoʊl-/ (*also* **face**) *noun* the place deep inside a mine where the coal is cut out of the rock（煤矿井里的）回采工作面，采煤工作面

IDM **at the ˈcoalface** (*BrE*) where the real work is done, not just where people talk about it 在工作现场；在工作第一线：*Many of the best ideas come from doctors at the coalface.* 许多最好的意见都来自临床医师。

coal·field /ˈkəʊlfiːld; *NAmE* ˈkoʊl-/ *noun* a large area where there is a lot of coal under the ground 煤田

ˌcoal-ˈfired *adj.* using coal as fuel 用煤作燃料的；烧煤的：*a coal-fired power station* 一座燃煤火力发电站

ˈcoal gas *noun* [U] a mixture of gases produced from coal, that can be used for electricity and heating 煤气

coal·house /ˈkəʊlhaʊs; *NAmE* ˈkoʊl-/ *noun* a small building for storing coal, especially in sb's garden in the past（尤指旧时家中花园的）煤库，煤屋

co·ali·tion /ˌkəʊəˈlɪʃn; *NAmE* ˌkoʊə-/ *noun* **1** [C+sing./pl. v.] a government formed by two or more political parties working together（两党或多党）联合政府：*to form a coalition* 组成联合政府 ◇ *a two-party coalition* 两党联合的政府 ◇ *a coalition government* 联合政府 ➲ WORDFINDER NOTE AT PARLIAMENT **2** [C+sing./pl. v.] a group formed by people from several different groups, especially political ones, agreeing to work together for a particular purpose（尤指多个政治团体的）联合体，联盟：*a coalition of environmental and consumer groups* 环境保护和消费者团体的联盟 **3** [U] the act of two or more groups joining together 联合；结合；联盟：*They didn't rule out coalition with the Social Democrats.* 他们不排除与社会民主党人结盟的可能性。

coal·man /ˈkəʊlmən; *NAmE* ˈkoʊl-/ *noun* (*pl.* **-men** /-mən/) a man whose job is to deliver coal to people's houses 送煤工

ˈcoal mine (*also* **pit**) *noun* a place underground where coal is dug 煤矿

ˈcoal miner *noun* a person whose job is digging coal in a coal mine 煤矿工人

ˈcoal scuttle (*also* **scuttle**) *noun* a container with a handle, used for carrying coal and usually kept beside the FIREPLACE（通常置于壁炉边的）煤斗，煤筐，煤桶

ˈcoal tar *noun* [U] a thick black sticky substance produced when gas is made from coal（制作煤气时产生的）煤焦油，煤沥青

coarse /kɔːs; *NAmE* kɔːrs/ *adj.* (**coars·er**, **coars·est**) **1** (of skin or cloth 皮肤或布料) rough 粗糙的；粗织的：*coarse hands/linen* 粗糙的手；粗亚麻布 OPP **smooth**, **soft** **2** consisting of relatively large pieces 粗的；大颗粒的：*coarse sand/salt/hair* 粗沙；粗盐；粗糙的毛发 OPP **fine** **3** rude and offensive, especially about sex 粗鲁无礼的，粗俗的（尤指涉及性的）SYN **vulgar**：*coarse manners/laughter* 粗俗的举止 / 笑声 ▸ **coarse·ly** *adv.*：*coarsely chopped onions* (= cut into large pieces) 剁成大块的洋葱 ◇ *He laughed coarsely at her.* 他粗鲁无礼地嘲笑她。**coarse·ness** *noun* [U]

ˌcoarse ˈfish *noun* (*pl.* **coarse fish**) (*BrE*) any fish, except SALMON and TROUT, that lives in rivers and lakes rather than in the sea 粗鱼，杂鱼（指肉质粗糙的淡水鱼，不包括鲑和鳟鱼）

ˌcoarse ˈfishing *noun* [U] (*BrE*) the sport of catching coarse fish 捕捉杂鱼运动：*to go coarse fishing* 去捕捉杂鱼

coars·en /ˈkɔːsn; *NAmE* ˈkɔːrsn/ *verb* **1** [I, T] to become or make sth become thicker and/or rougher（使）变厚，变粗糙：*Her hair gradually coarsened as she grew older.* 随着年龄的增长，她的头发逐渐变粗糙了。◇ **~ sth** *His features had been coarsened by the weather.* 气候使他的容貌变得粗糙。**2** [T, I] **~ (sb)** to become or make sb become less polite and often offensive in the way they behave（使）变得粗鲁无礼：*The six long years in prison had coarsened him.* 六年漫长的监狱生活使他变得粗鲁无礼。

coast /kəʊst; *NAmE* koʊst/ *noun, verb*

■ ***noun*** [C, U] the land beside or near to the sea or ocean 海岸；海滨：*a town on the south coast of England* 英格兰南海岸的一座城镇 ◇ *islands off the west coast of Ireland* 爱尔兰西海岸的岛屿 ◇ *a trip to the coast* 海滨旅游 ◇ *We walked along the coast for five miles.* 我们沿着海岸步行了五英里。◇ *the Welsh coast* 威尔士海岸 ◇ *a pretty stretch of coast* 一段美丽的海岸线 ◇ *the coast road* 滨海道路 ➲ WORDFINDER NOTE AT SEA ➲ VISUAL VOCAB PAGE V5

WORDFINDER 联想词：beach, cliff, dune, headland, inlet, promontory, **sea**, shore, tide

IDM **the ˌcoast is ˈclear** (*informal*) there is no danger of being seen or caught 没有被发现（或抓住）的危险：*As soon as the coast was clear he climbed in through the*

▼ **SYNONYMS** 同义词辨析

coast

beach • seaside • coastline • sand • seashore

These are all words for the land beside or near to the sea, a river or a lake. 以上各词均指海滨、河岸或湖畔。

coast the land beside or near to the sea or ocean 指海岸、海滨：*a town on the south coast of England* 英格兰南海岸的一座城镇 ◇ *The coast road is closed due to bad weather.* 由于天气恶劣，滨海公路暂时封闭。NOTE It is nearly always **the coast**, except when it is uncountable. 除用作不可数名词外，coast 几乎总是与 the 连用：*That's a pretty stretch of coast.* 那是一段美丽的海岸线。

beach an area of sand, or small stones, beside the sea or a lake 指有沙石的海滩、海滨或湖滨：*She took the kids to the beach for the day.* 她带了孩子去海滩玩一天。◇ *sandy beaches* 沙滩

seaside (*especially BrE*) an area that is by the sea, especially one where people go for a day or a holiday 尤指人们游玩、度假的海边、海滨：*a trip to the seaside* 去海滨旅行 NOTE It is always **the seaside**, except when it is used before a noun. 除用于名词前外，seaside 总是与 the 连用：*a seaside resort* 海滨胜地 **The seaside** is British English; in American English **seaside** is only used before a noun. * the seaside 为英式英语，在美式英语中，seaside 只用于名词前。

coastline the land along a coast, especially when you are thinking of its shape or appearance 指沿海地带，尤其是海岸线、海岸地形或轮廓：*California's rugged coastline* 加利福尼亚州崎岖的海岸线

sand a large area of sand on a beach 指沙滩：*We went for a walk along the sand.* 我们去沙滩上散了散步。◇ *a resort with miles of golden sands* 有着绵延数英里金色沙滩的度假胜地

the seashore the land along the edge of the sea or ocean, usually where there is sand and rocks 通常指有沙石的海岸、海滨：*He liked to look for shells on the seashore.* 他喜欢在海滨捡贝壳。

BEACH OR SEASHORE? 用 beach 还是 seashore?

Beach is usually used to talk about a sandy area next to the sea where people lie in the sun or play, for example when they are on holiday/vacation. **Seashore** is used more to talk about the area by the sea in terms of things such as waves, sea shells, rocks, etc., especially where people walk for pleasure. * beach 通常指海边的沙滩，人们度假时可以躺着沐浴阳光或玩乐；seashore 多指有海浪、贝壳、岩石等的海岸，尤指人们散步消遣的海滨。

PATTERNS

- **along** the coast/beach/coastline/seashore
- **on** the coast/beach/coastline/sands/seashore
- **at** the coast/beach/seaside/seashore
- **by** the coast/seaside/seashore
- a(n) **rocky/unspoiled** coast/beach/coastline
- **to go to** the coast/beach/seaside/seashore

window. 等到四下无人，他便从窗户爬了进去。

■ ***verb*** **1** [I] (**+ adv./prep.**) (of a car or a bicycle 汽车或自行车) to move, especially down a hill, without using any power（尤指不用动力向山坡下）滑行，惯性滑行：*The car coasted along until it stopped.* 汽车随惯性而下直至滑行停止。◇ *She took her feet off the pedals and coasted downhill.* 她把脚从自行车的踏板上抬开，沿山坡滑行而下。**2** [I] (**+ adv./prep.**) (of a vehicle 交通工具) to move quickly and smoothly, without using much power（不用多少动力）快速平稳地移动：*The plane coasted down the runway.* 飞机顺着跑道平稳滑行。**3** [I] ~ (**through/to sth**) to be successful at sth without having to try hard 不费力地取得成功：*He coasted through his final exams.* 他毫不费劲地通过了期终考试。**4** [I] ~ (**along**) (*disapproving*) to put very little effort into sth（做事）不出力：*You're just coasting—it's time to work hard now.* 你根本是在应付，现在该努力干了。**5** [I] (of a ship 船) to stay close to land while sailing around the coast 沿海岸航行

coast·al /ˈkəʊstl; *NAmE* ˈkoʊstl/ *adj.* [usually before noun] of or near a coast 沿海的；靠近海岸的：***coastal waters/resorts/scenery*** 沿海水域；海滨胜地 / 风景 ◇ *a* ***coastal path*** (= one that follows the line of the coast) 滨海小道 ➲ VISUAL VOCAB PAGE V5 ➲ COMPARE INLAND *adj.*

coast·eer·ing /ˌkəʊstˈɪərɪŋ; *NAmE* ˌkoʊstˈɪrɪŋ/ *noun* [U] the sport of following a route around a coast by climbing, jumping off CLIFFS and swimming 海岸攀岩（沿着海岸路线攀爬、跳下悬崖和游泳的运动）

coast·er /ˈkəʊstə(r); *NAmE* ˈkoʊst-/ *noun* **1** a small flat object which you put under a glass to protect the top of a table 玻璃杯垫 ➲ VISUAL VOCAB PAGE V22 **2** a ship that sails from port to port along a coast 航行于沿海港口间的轮船 ➲ SEE ALSO ROLLER COASTER

coast·guard /ˈkəʊstɡɑːd; *NAmE* ˈkoʊstɡɑːrd/ *noun* **1** (*usually* **the coastguard**) [sing.] an official organization (in the US a branch of the armed forces) whose job is to watch the sea near a coast in order to help ships and people in trouble, and to stop people from breaking the law 海岸警卫队（在美国隶属于军队）：*The coastguard was alerted.* 海岸警卫队已接到报警。◇ *They radioed Dover Coastguard.* 他们用无线电和多佛海岸警卫队联络。◇ *a coastguard station* 海岸警卫队驻地 **2** [C] (*especially BrE*) (*US usually* **coast·guards·man** /ˈkəʊstɡɑːdzmən; *NAmE* ˈkoʊstɡɑːrdz-/ *pl.* **-men** /-mən/) a member of this organization 海岸警卫队队员

coast·line /ˈkəʊstlaɪn; *NAmE* ˈkoʊst-/ *noun* the land along a coast, especially when you are thinking of its shape or appearance 海岸线；海岸地形（或轮廓）；沿海地带：*a* ***rugged/rocky/beautiful coastline*** 崎岖的 / 多岩石的 / 美丽的海岸线 ◇ *to protect the coastline from oil spillage* 保护海岸线不受石油泄漏的污染 ➲ SYNONYMS AT COAST

coat 🔑 /kəʊt; *NAmE* koʊt/ *noun, verb*

■ ***noun*** **1** 🔑 a piece of outdoor clothing that is worn over other clothes to keep warm or dry. Coats have sleeves and may be long or short. 外套；外衣；大衣：*a fur/leather coat* 毛皮 / 皮大衣 ◇ *a long winter coat* 冬天穿的长大衣 ◇ *to* ***put on/take off your coat*** 穿上 / 脱下外套 ➲ VISUAL VOCAB PAGE V66 ➲ SEE ALSO DUFFEL COAT, GREATCOAT, HOUSECOAT, OVERCOAT, PETTICOAT, RAINCOAT, TRENCH COAT **2** (*NAmE*) (*old-fashioned in BrE* 英式英语中为老式用法) a jacket that is worn as part of a suit（套装的）上装，上衣 ➲ SEE ALSO FROCK COAT, MORNING COAT, TAILCOAT, WAISTCOAT **3** 🔑 the fur, hair or wool that covers an animal's body 动物皮毛：*a dog with a* ***smooth/shaggy coat*** 皮毛光滑的 / 蓬乱的狗 ➲ VISUAL VOCAB PAGE V12 **4** 🔑 a layer of paint or some other substance that covers a surface 涂料层；覆盖层：*to give the walls a second coat of paint* 给墙刷上第二层涂料 ➲ SEE ALSO TOPCOAT, UNDERCOAT

IDM **ˌcut your ˈcoat acˌcording to your ˈcloth** (*saying*) to do only what you have enough money to do and no more 量入为出

■ ***verb*** [often passive] ~ **sth** (**with/in sth**) to cover sth with a layer of a substance 给…涂上一层；用…覆盖：*cookies thickly coated with chocolate* 外面涂有厚厚一层巧克力的曲奇 ◇ *A film of dust coated the table.* 桌上覆盖着一层灰尘。➲ SEE ALSO SUGAR-COATED

ˈ**coat check** *noun* (*NAmE*) = CLOAKROOM (1)

ˈ**coat hanger** *noun* = HANGER

coati /kəʊˈɑːti; *NAmE* koʊ-/ (*also* **co·ati·mundi** /kəʊˌɑːtiˈmʌndi; *NAmE* koʊ-/) *noun* a small animal with a long nose and a long tail with lines across it, which lives mainly in Central and S America 南美浣熊（主要生活于中美和南美）

coat·ing /ˈkəʊtɪŋ; *NAmE* ˈkoʊt-/ *noun* a thin layer of a substance covering a surface（薄的）覆盖层，涂层：*a thin coating of chocolate* 薄薄一层巧克力 ◇ *a disk with a magnetic coating* 磁盘

ˌ**coat of ˈarms** *noun* (*pl.* **coats of arms**) (*also* **arms**) a design or a SHIELD that is a special symbol of a family, city or other organization 盾形纹章；盾徽：*the royal coat of arms* 皇家盾徽

coat·room /ˈkəʊtruːm; -rʊm; *NAmE* ˈkoʊt-/ *noun* (*NAmE*) = CLOAKROOM (1)

ˈ**coat stand** *noun* a stand with hooks for hanging coats and hats on 衣帽架

ˈ**coat-tails** *noun* [pl.]

IDM **on sb's coat-tails** using the success and influence of another person to help yourself become successful 利用他人的成就和声望（帮助自己成功）：*She got where she is today on her brother's coat-tails.* 她倚仗她哥哥的声望爬上了今天的位置。

ˌ**co-ˈauthor** *noun* a person who writes a book or an article with sb else（书或文章的）合著者 ▶ ˌ**co-ˈauthor** *verb* ~ **sth** ˌ**co-ˈauthor·ship** *noun* [U]

coax /kəʊks; *NAmE* koʊks/ *verb* to persuade sb to do sth by talking to them in a kind and gentle way 哄劝；劝诱 SYN **cajole**：~ **sb/sth** (**into doing sth**) *She coaxed the horse into coming a little closer.* 她哄着那匹马让它再靠近了一点。◇ ~ **sb/sth** (**into/out of sth**) *He was coaxed out of retirement to help the failing company.* 他退休之后又被力劝出山帮助濒临破产的公司。◇ ~ **sb/sth** (**+ adv./prep.**) *She had to coax the car along.* 她得耐着性子发动汽车往前开。◇ ~ (**sb/sth**) **+ speech** *'Nearly there,' she coaxed.* "快要到啦。"她哄着说。

PHR V **coax sth out of/from sb** to gently persuade sb to do sth or give you sth 哄劝；哄诱得到：*The director coaxed a brilliant performance out of the cast.* 经过导演悉心劝说，全体演员完成了一场精彩的表演。

coax·ing /ˈkəʊksɪŋ; *NAmE* ˈkoʊ-/ *noun* [U] gentle attempts to persuade sb to do sth or to get a machine to start 试图劝诱；耐心地发动（机器）：*No amount of coaxing will make me change my mind.* 任你费尽口舌也不会说服我改变主意。▶ **coax·ing** *adj.* **coax·ing·ly** *adv.*

COB /ˌsiː əʊ ˈbiː; *NAmE* oʊ/ *abbr.* close of business (the time when business ends for the day) 营业时间结束，下班（全写为 close of business）：*We need to come to a decision by COB tomorrow.* 我们得在明天下班前做出决定。

cob /kɒb; *NAmE* kɑːb/ *noun* **1** = CORNCOB：*corn on the cob* 玉米棒子 **2** a strong horse with short legs 短腿壮马 **3** (*BrE*) a round LOAF of bread 圆面包：*a crusty cob* 脆皮圆面包

co·balt /ˈkəʊbɔːlt; *NAmE* ˈkoʊ-/ *noun* [U] **1** (*symb.* **Co**) a chemical element. Cobalt is a hard silver-white metal, often mixed with other metals and used to give a deep blue-green colour to glass. 钴 **2** (*also* ˌ**cobalt ˈblue**) a deep blue-green colour 深蓝色；钴蓝 ➲ MORE LIKE THIS 15, page R26

cob·ber /ˈkɒbə(r); *NAmE* ˈkɑːb-/ *noun* (*AustralE, NZE, informal*) (used especially by a man addressing another man 尤用作男子间的称呼) a friend 伙计；老兄；兄弟

C

cob·ble /ˈkɒbl; NAmE ˈkɑːbl/ *verb* ~ **sth** (*old-fashioned*) to make or repair shoes 制（鞋）；修补（鞋）
PHR V ˌ**cobble sth↔toˈgether** to produce sth quickly and without great care or effort, so that it can be used but is not perfect 草率匆忙地制作；胡乱拼凑；粗制滥造：*The essay was cobbled together from some old notes.* 这篇文章是用以前的一些笔记胡乱拼凑而成的。

cob·bled /ˈkɒbld; NAmE ˈkɑːbld/ *adj.* (of streets and roads 街道和道路) having a surface that is made of COBBLES 铺有鹅卵石的

cob·bler /ˈkɒblə(r); NAmE ˈkɑːb-/ *noun* **1** [C] a type of fruit or meat PIE with a thick cake or PASTRY layer on top 厚皮水果馅饼（或肉饼）：*peach cobbler* 桃子馅饼 **2** [C] a person who repairs shoes 修鞋匠 ⊃COMPARE SHOEMAKER **3** [U] **cobblers** (*BrE, informal*) nonsense 胡说；废话：*He said it was all a load of cobblers.* 他说那完全是一派胡言。

cob·bles /ˈkɒblz; NAmE ˈkɑːblz/ (*also* **cobble·stones**) *noun* [pl.] small stones used to make the surfaces of roads, especially in the past （尤指旧时铺路面用的）小石头，鹅卵石

cobble·stones /ˈkɒblstəʊnz; NAmE ˈkɑːblstoʊnz/ *noun* [pl.] = COBBLES ▶ **cobble·stone** *adj.* [only before noun]

COBOL /ˈkəʊbɒl; NAmE ˈkoʊbɔːl/ *noun* [U] an early computer language used in business programs * COBOL 语言（早期的一种商用计算机程序语言）

cobra /ˈkəʊbrə; NAmE ˈkoʊ-/ *noun* a poisonous snake that can spread the skin at the back of its neck to make itself look bigger. Cobras live in Asia and Africa. 眼镜蛇（毒蛇，分布于亚洲和非洲） ⊃VISUAL VOCAB PAGE V13

cob·web /ˈkɒbweb; NAmE ˈkɑːb-/ *noun* a fine net of threads made by a spider to catch insects; a single thread of this net (usually used when it is old and covered with dirt) 蜘蛛网，蜘蛛丝（常指落满灰尘的旧蛛网）：*Thick cobwebs hung in the dusty corners.* 积有灰尘的角落挂着厚厚的蜘蛛网。◇ *He brushed a cobweb out of his hair.* 他拂去了头发上的蜘蛛丝。 ⊃SEE ALSO SPIDER'S WEB, WEB (1) ▶ **cob·webbed** /ˈkɒbwebd; NAmE ˈkɑːb-/ *adj.*：*cobwebbed corners* 布满蜘蛛网的角落
IDM **blow/clear the ˈcobwebs away** to help sb start sth in a fresh, lively state of mind 使头脑清醒；使振作精神：*A brisk walk should blow the cobwebs away.* 轻快的散步可以使人头脑清醒。

coca /ˈkəʊkə; NAmE ˈkoʊ-/ *noun* [U] a tropical bush whose leaves are used to make the drug COCAINE 古柯（热带灌木，叶子用于制作可卡因）

Coca-Cola™ /ˌkəʊkə ˈkəʊlə; NAmE ˌkoʊkə ˈkoʊlə/ (*also informal* **Coke™**) *noun* **1** [U, C] a popular type of COLA drink 可口可乐（饮料） **2** [C] a glass, bottle or can of Coca-Cola 一杯（或一瓶、一罐）可口可乐

co·caine /kəʊˈkeɪn; NAmE koʊˈkeɪn/ (*also informal* **coke**) *noun* [U] a powerful drug that some people take illegally for pleasure and can become ADDICTED to. Doctors sometimes use it as an ANAESTHETIC. 可卡因；古柯碱

coc·cyx /ˈkɒksɪks; NAmE ˈkɑːk-/ *noun* (*pl.* **coc·cyxes** or **coc·cy·ges** /ˈkɒksɪdʒiːz; NAmE ˈkɑːk-/) (*anatomy* 解) the small bone at the bottom of the SPINE 尾骨 SYN **tailbone** ⊃VISUAL VOCAB PAGE V64

coch·in·eal /ˌkɒtʃɪˈniːl; NAmE ˈkɑːtʃəniːl/ *noun* [U] a bright red substance used to give colour to food 胭脂虫红颜料（用于食物）

coch·lea /ˈkɒkliə; NAmE ˈkoʊk-; ˈkɑːk-/ *noun* (*pl.* **coch·leae** /-klii/) (*anatomy* 解) a small curved tube inside the ear, which contains a small part that sends nerve signals to the brain when sounds cause it to VIBRATE 耳蜗

cock /kɒk; NAmE kɑːk/ *noun, verb*
■*noun* **1** (*BrE*) (*also* **roost·er** *NAmE, BrE*) [C] an adult male chicken 公鸡；雄鸡：*The cock crowed.* 公鸡啼叫。 ⊃COMPARE HEN (1) **2** [C] (especially in compounds 尤用于构成复合词) a male of any other bird 雄禽：*a cock pheasant* 雄雉 ⊃SEE ALSO PEACOCK **3** [C] (*taboo, slang*) a PENIS 鸡巴 **4** [C] = STOPCOCK ⊃SEE ALSO BALLCOCK **5** [sing.] (*old-fashioned, BrE, slang*) used as a friendly form of address between men（男子间友好的称呼）老兄，家伙，伙计 ⊃SEE ALSO HALF-COCK
■*verb* **1** ~ **sth** to raise a part of your body so that it is vertical or at an angle 立起，竖起，翘起（身体部位）：*The dog cocked its leg by every tree on our route* (= in order to URINATE). 这狗在我们一路上走过每棵树时都抬起一条腿（撒尿）。◇ *He cocked an inquisitive eyebrow at her.* 他扬眉向她投以询问的目光。◇ *She cocked her head to one side and looked at me.* 她抬起头侧向一边看着我。◇ *The dog stood listening, its ears cocked.* 那狗站着，竖起耳朵听动静。 **2** ~ **a gun/pistol/rifle** to raise the HAMMER on a gun so that it is ready to fire 扣（或扳）上扳机准备射击
IDM **cock an ear/eye at sth/sb** to look at or listen to sth/sb carefully and with a lot of attention 侧耳倾听；凝神细看 **cock a snook at sb/sth** (*BrE*) to say or do sth that clearly shows you do not respect sb/sth （说话或做事）明显地表示蔑视；轻蔑；不屑一顾：*to cock a snook at authority* 蔑视权威
PHR V ˌ**cock sth↔ˈup** (*BrE, slang*) to ruin sth by doing it badly, or by making a careless or stupid mistake 把…搞糟（或弄得一塌糊涂） SYN **bungle**：*I really cocked that exam up!* 我那次考试考砸了！◇ *She cocked up all the arrangements for the party.* 她把聚会的安排搞得一塌糊涂。 ⊃RELATED NOUN COCK-UP

cock·ade /kɒˈkeɪd; NAmE kɑː-/ *noun* a decorated BADGE or an arrangement of RIBBONS, feathers, etc. that is worn in a hat to show military rank, membership of a political party, etc. 帽章，帽花结（显示军衔、政党身份等）

cock-a-doodle-doo /ˌkɒk ə ˌduːdl ˈduː; NAmE ˌkɑːk/ *noun* the word for the sound that a COCK/ROOSTER makes （公鸡的啼声）喔喔喔

ˌ**cock-a-ˈhoop** *adj.* [not usually before noun] ~ (**about/at/over sth**) (*informal*) very pleased and excited, especially about achieving sth 得意扬扬

cock-a-leekie /ˌkɒk ə ˈliːki; NAmE ˌkɑːk/ (*also* ˌ**cock-a-leekie ˈsoup**) *noun* [U] a type of Scottish soup, made with chicken and LEEKS (= long vegetables that taste like onions)（苏格兰）鸡肉韭菜汤

cock·ama·mie (*also* **cock·ama·my**) /ˈkɒkəmeɪmi; NAmE ˈkɑːk-/ *adj.* (*NAmE, informal*) (of an idea, a story, etc. 主意、故事等) silly; not to be believed 荒诞可笑的；不可信的

ˌ**cock and ˈbull story** *noun* a story that is unlikely to be true but is used as an explanation or excuse 荒唐的解释；荒诞的借口

cocka·tiel /ˌkɒkəˈtiːl; NAmE ˌkɑːk-/ *noun* an Australian PARROT with a grey body and a yellow and orange face 鸡尾鹦鹉，玄凤（产于澳大利亚，毛灰色，面部黄色带橙斑）

cocka·too /ˌkɒkəˈtuː; NAmE ˈkɑːkətuː/ *noun* (*pl.* **-oos**) an Australian bird of the PARROT family, with a large row of feathers (called a CREST) standing up on its head 凤头鹦鹉，葵花鹦鹉（见于澳大利亚）

cock·cha·fer /ˈkɒktʃeɪfə(r); NAmE ˈkɑːk-/ (*also* ˈ**May bug**) *noun* a large brown insect that flies and makes a loud noise in early evening in summer 鳃角金龟；五月甲虫；大栗鳃角金龟

cock·crow /ˈkɒkkrəʊ; NAmE ˈkɑːkkroʊ/ *noun* [U] (*literary*) the time of the day when it is becoming light 黎明；拂晓 SYN **dawn**

ˌ**cocked ˈhat** *noun* IDM SEE KNOCK *v.*

cock·er /ˈkɒkə(r); NAmE ˈkɑːk-/ (*also* ˌ**cocker ˈspaniel**) *noun* a small SPANIEL (= type of dog) with soft hair 可卡犬（小型软毛猎犬）

cock·erel /ˈkɒkərəl; NAmE ˈkɑːk-/ *noun* a young male chicken 小公鸡

cock·eyed /ˈkɒkaɪd; *NAmE* ˈkɑːk-/ *adj.* (*informal*) **1** not level or straight 倾斜的；歪斜的 SYN **crooked**: *Doesn't that picture look cockeyed to you?* 你不觉得那张画挂歪了吗？ **2** not practical; not likely to succeed 不切实际的；不大可能成功的： *a cockeyed scheme to make people use less water* 让大众少用水的不切实际的计划

cock·fight /ˈkɒkfaɪt; *NAmE* ˈkɑːk-/ *noun* a fight between two adult male chickens, watched as a sport and illegal in many countries 斗鸡 ▶ **cock·fight·ing** *noun* [U]

cockle /ˈkɒkl; *NAmE* ˈkɑːkl/ *noun* a small SHELLFISH that can be eaten 鸟蛤（可食用的有壳小水生动物） IDM ➲ SEE WARM *v.*

cockle·shell /ˈkɒklʃel; *NAmE* ˈkɑːkl-/ *noun* **1** the shell of a cockle 鸟蛤壳 **2** a small light boat 轻舟；小舟

cock·ney /ˈkɒkni; *NAmE* ˈkɑːkni/ *noun* **1** [C] a person from the East End of London 伦敦东区的人 **2** [U] the way of speaking that is typical of cockneys 伦敦东区的口音（或土腔）： *a cockney accent* 伦敦东区口音

cock·pit /ˈkɒkpɪt; *NAmE* ˈkɑːk-/ *noun* the area in a plane, boat or racing car where the pilot or driver sits （飞机、船或赛车的）驾驶舱，驾驶座 ➲ VISUAL VOCAB PAGES V61, V57

cock·roach /ˈkɒkrəʊtʃ; *NAmE* ˈkɑːkroʊtʃ/ (*also NAmE, informal* **roach**) *noun* a large brown insect with wings, that lives in houses, especially where there is dirt 蟑螂

cock·sucker /ˈkɒksʌkə(r); *NAmE* ˈkɑːk-/ *noun* (*taboo, slang*) an offensive word used to insult sb, usually a man 狗杂种，浑蛋（通常指男人）

cock·sure /ˌkɒkˈʃʊə(r); ˌkɒkˈʃɔː(r); *NAmE* ˌkɑːkˈʃʊr/ *adj.* (*old-fashioned, informal*) confident in a way that is annoying to other people and that they might find offensive 过分自信的；自高自大的；自以为是的

cock·tail /ˈkɒkteɪl; *NAmE* ˈkɑːk-/ *noun* **1** [C] a drink usually made from a mixture of one or more SPIRITS (= strong alcoholic drinks) and fruit juice. It can also be made without alcohol. 鸡尾酒： *a* ***cocktail bar/cabinet/lounge*** 鸡尾酒酒吧 / 陈列柜 / 酒吧间 **2** [C, U] a dish of small pieces of food, usually served cold 凉菜；冷盘： *a prawn/shrimp cocktail* 大虾 / 小虾冷盘 ◇ *fruit cocktail* 什锦水果丁 **3** [C] a mixture of different substances, usually ones that do not mix together well 混合物（通常由不太相融的物质掺和而成）： *a lethal cocktail of drugs* 致命的混合药物 ➲ SEE ALSO MOLOTOV COCKTAIL

ˈcocktail dress *noun* a dress that is suitable for formal social occasions （正式社交场合穿的）短裙

ˈcocktail party *noun* a formal social occasion, usually in the early evening, when people drink COCKTAILS or other alcoholic drinks 鸡尾酒会

ˈcocktail stick *noun* (*BrE*) a small, sharp piece of wood on which small pieces of food are placed, for guests to eat at parties （聚会用的）取食签

ˈcock-teaser (*also* **ˈcock-tease**, **ˈprick-teaser**, **ˈprick-tease**) *noun* (*taboo, slang*) an offensive word used to describe a woman who makes a man think she will have sex with him when she will not 煽情骚货（含冒犯意，指激起男人性欲而不与之性交的女人）

ˈcock-up *noun* (*BrE, informal*) a mistake that spoils people's arrangements; sth that has been spoilt because it was badly organized （打乱了原先所作安排的）差错；（因组织不当而造成的）混乱，一团糟： *There's been a bit of a cock-up over the travel arrangements.* 旅行安排出了点儿岔子。

cocky /ˈkɒki; *NAmE* ˈkɑːki/ *adj.* (**cock·ier**, **cocki·est**) (*informal*) too confident about yourself in a way that annoys other people 过分自信的；自以为是的 ▶ **cocki·ness** *noun* [U]

cocoa /ˈkəʊkəʊ; *NAmE* ˈkoʊkoʊ/ *noun* **1** [U, C] dark brown powder made from the crushed seeds (called **cocoa beans**) of a tropical tree 可可粉 **2** [U, C] a hot drink made by mixing cocoa powder with milk and/or water and usually sugar 热可可（饮料）： *a mug of cocoa* 一大杯热可可饮料 **3** [C] a cup of cocoa 一杯热可可饮料 ➲ COMPARE CHOCOLATE (3), DRINKING CHOCOLATE

ˈcocoa butter *noun* [U] fat that is obtained from cocoa BEANS and is used in making chocolate and COSMETICS 可可油，可可脂（用于制作巧克力和化妆品）

co·co·nut /ˈkəʊkənʌt; *NAmE* ˈkoʊ-/ *noun* **1** [C] the large nut of a tropical tree called a **coconut palm**. It grows inside a hard shell and contains a soft white substance that can be eaten and juice that can be drunk. 椰子 ➲ VISUAL VOCAB PAGE V33 **2** [U] the soft white substance inside a coconut, used in cooking （用于烹调的）椰子肉，椰蓉： *desiccated coconut* 椰子干 ◇ *coconut biscuits/cookies* 椰蓉饼干 ◇ *coconut oil* 椰子油

ˈcoconut butter *noun* [U] a solid substance inside coconuts that is used to make soap, CANDLES, etc. 椰子油（用以制作肥皂、蜡烛等）

ˌcoconut ˈmatting *noun* [U] (*BrE*) a material used to cover floors that is made from the hair inside the outer shell of coconuts （制地垫的）椰衣

ˈcoconut shy *noun* (*pl.* **coconut shies**) (*BrE*) an outdoor entertainment in which people try to knock coconuts off stands by throwing balls at them 打椰子游戏（掷球把椰子从支架上击落）

co·coon /kəˈkuːn/ *noun, verb*

■ ***noun*** **1** a covering of silk threads that some insects make to protect themselves before they become adults 茧 **2** a soft covering that wraps all around a person or thing and forms a protection 保护膜；防护层；软罩： (*figurative*) *the cocoon of a caring family* 家庭中相互关爱所形成的保护

■ ***verb*** [usually passive] **~ sb/sth (in sth)** to protect sb/sth by surrounding them or it completely with sth 把…包围起来保护；（用…）完全保护起来： *We were warm and safe, cocooned in our sleeping bags.* 我们在睡袋里睡觉，暖和又安全。

co·coon·ing /kəˈkuːnɪŋ/ *noun* [U] the habit of spending more of your free time at home and less time going out and doing things with other people 蚕茧式生活，宅在家（指业余时间大多待在家里而很少外出交往）

coco·yam /ˈkəʊkəʊjæm; *NAmE* ˈkoʊkoʊ-/ *noun* [C, U] (*WAfrE*) a plant whose roots can be cooked and eaten or made into flour 芋头： *roasted cocoyam* 烤芋头 ➲ SEE ALSO FUFU

COD /ˌsiː əʊ ˈdiː; *NAmE* oʊ/ *abbr.* cash on delivery or (in American English) collect on delivery (payment for goods will be made when the goods are delivered) 货到付款；交货付现

cod /kɒd; *NAmE* kɑːd/ *noun, adj.*

■ ***noun*** [C, U] (*pl.* **cod**) (*also* **cod·fish**) a large sea fish with white flesh that is used for food 鳕鱼： *fishing for cod* 捕鳕鱼 ◇ *cod fillets* 鳕鱼鱼片

■ ***adj.*** [only before noun] (*BrE, informal*) not genuine or real 假的；伪的；不真实的： *a cod American accent* 假装的美国口音 ◇ *cod psychology* 伪心理学

coda /ˈkəʊdə; *NAmE* ˈkoʊdə/ *noun* the final passage of a piece of music （乐曲的）后奏，尾声；结尾乐段： (*figurative*) *The final two months were a miserable coda to the President's first period in office.* 总统首届任期的最后两个月非常糟糕。

cod·dle /ˈkɒdl; *NAmE* ˈkɑːdl/ *verb* **1 ~ sb** (*often disapproving*) to treat sb with too much care and attention 娇惯；娇养；溺爱 ➲ COMPARE MOLLYCODDLE **2 ~ sth** to cook eggs in water slightly below boiling point （在略低于沸点的水里）煮（蛋）

code 🔑 AW /kəʊd; *NAmE* koʊd/ *noun, verb*

■ ***noun*** **1** 🔑 [C, U] (often in compounds 常构成复合词) a system of words, letters, numbers or symbols that represent a message or record information secretly or in a shorter form 密码；暗码；电码；代码： *to* ***break/crack a code*** (= to understand and read the message) 破译密码 ◇ *It's written* ***in code.*** 那是用密码写的。 ◇ *Tap your code* *number into the machine.* 把你的密码数字输入机器。◇ *In the event of the machine not operating correctly, an* ***error code*** *will appear.* 如果机器运转不正常，就会出现错误代码。 ➲ SEE ALSO AREA CODE, BARCODE, MORSE CODE, POSTCODE, SORT CODE, ZIP CODE **2** [C] = DIALLING CODE： *There are three codes for London.* 伦敦有三个电话区号。 **3** [U] (*computing* 计) a system of computer programming instructions （代）码 ➲ SEE ALSO MACHINE CODE, SOURCE CODE ➲ **WORDFINDER NOTE** AT PROGRAM **4** [C] a set of moral principles or rules of behaviour that are generally accepted by society or a social group 道德准则；行为规范： *a strict code of conduct* 严格的行为准则 **5** [C] a system of laws or written rules that state how people in an institution or a country should behave 法典；法规： *the penal code* 刑法典 ➲ SEE ALSO DRESS CODE, HIGHWAY CODE

■ *verb* **1** [T] ~ **sth** to write or print words, letters, numbers, etc. on sth so that you know what it is, what group it belongs to, etc. 为…编码： *Each order is coded separately.* 每份订单都单独编号。 **2** [T] ~ **sth** to put a message into code so that it can only be understood by a few people 把…译成密码 **3** [T, I] ~ (**sth**) (*computing* 计) to write a computer program by putting one system of numbers, words and symbols into another system 编程序；编码 ➲ COMPARE ENCODE (2)

coded /ˈkəʊdɪd; *NAmE* ˈkoʊ-/ *adj.* **1** [only before noun] a **coded** message or **coded** information is written or sent using a special system of words, letters, numbers, etc. that can only be understood by a few other people or by a computer 密码的；暗码的；编码的： *a coded warning of a bomb at the airport* 告知机场有炸弹的密码警报 **2** expressed in an indirect way 间接表达的： *There was coded criticism of the government from some party members.* 一些党员对政府进行了间接的批评。

co·deine /ˈkəʊdiːn; *NAmE* ˈkoʊ-/ *noun* [U] a drug used to reduce pain 可待因（用于减轻疼痛）

ˈcode name *noun* a name used for a person or thing in order to keep the real name secret 代号 ▶ **ˈcode-named** *adj.* [not before noun]： *a drug investigation, code-named Snoopy* 代号为史努比的一次毒品调查行动

ˌcode of ˈpractice *noun* (*pl.* **codes of practice**) a set of standards that members of a particular profession agree to follow in their work 行业规则；职业准则

co·depend·ency /ˌkəʊdɪˈpendənsi; *NAmE* ˌkoʊ-/ *noun* [U] (*psychology* 心) a situation in which two people have a close relationship in which they rely too much on each other emotionally, especially when one person is caring for the other one（两人在感情等方面的）互为依赖 ▶ **co·depend·ent** *adj., noun*

CODESA /kəʊˈdesə; *NAmE* koʊ-/ *abbr.* Convention for a Democratic South Africa (in the past, the group of politicians who discussed how South Africa would become a DEMOCRACY) 民主南非大会（讨论南非如何成为民主国家）

ˈcode-sharing *noun* [U] (*specialist*) an agreement between two or more AIRLINES to carry each other's passengers and use their own set of letters and numbers for flights provided by another airline 代码共享协议（航空公司之间可相互运送乘客并互用航班号）

ˈcode switching *noun* [U] (*linguistics* 语言) the practice of changing between languages when you are speaking 语码切换（说话中不同语言间的变换）

codex /ˈkəʊdeks; *NAmE* ˈkoʊ-/ *noun* (*pl.* **co·di·ces** /ˈkəʊdɪsiːz; ˈkɒd-; *NAmE* ˈkoʊ-; ˈkɑːd-/ or **codexes**) **1** an ancient text in the form of a book 古书手抄本 **2** an official list of medicines or chemicals 药典

cod·fish /ˈkɒdfɪʃ; *NAmE* ˈkɑːd-/ (*pl.* **cod·fish**) = COD

cod·ger /ˈkɒdʒə(r); *NAmE* ˈkɑːdʒ-/ *noun* (*informal*) **old ~** an informal way of referring to an old man that shows that you do not respect him 老家伙；老头儿

co·di·cil /ˈkəʊdɪsɪl; *NAmE* ˈkɑːdəsl/ *noun* (*law* 律) an instruction that is added later to a WILL, usually to change a part of it 遗嘱修改附录

co·dify /ˈkəʊdɪfaɪ; *NAmE* ˈkɑːd-/ *verb* (**co·di·fies, co·di·fy·ing, co·di·fied, co·di·fied**) ~ **sth** (*specialist*) to arrange laws, rules, etc. into a system 把…编成法典 ▶ **co·difi·ca·tion** /ˌkəʊdɪfɪˈkeɪʃn; *NAmE* ˌkɑːd-/ *noun* [U]

ˌcod liver ˈoil *noun* [U] a thick yellow oil from the LIVER of COD (= a type of fish), containing a lot of VITAMINS A and D and often given as a medicine 鱼肝油

cod·piece /ˈkɒdpiːs; *NAmE* ˈkɑːd-/ *noun* a piece of cloth, especially a decorative one, attached to a man's lower clothing and covering his GENITALS, worn in Europe in the 15th and 16th centuries 遮阴布（15、16 世纪欧洲男子加贴在紧身裤中，常带装饰）

cods·wal·lop /ˈkɒdzwɒləp; *NAmE* ˈkɑːdzwɑːləp/ *noun* [U] (*old-fashioned, BrE, informal*) nonsense 废话；胡言乱语： *I've never heard such a load of old codswallop in my life.* 我这辈子还从没有听到过这么一大堆胡说八道。

coed /ˌkəʊˈed; *NAmE* ˌkoʊ-/ *noun* (*old-fashioned, NAmE*) a female student at a co-educational school or college（男女同校的）女生

ˌco-eduˈcational (*also informal* **coed**) *adj.* (of a school or an EDUCATIONAL system 学校或教育体制) where girls and boys are taught together 男女同校的 ▶ **ˌco-eduˈcation** *noun* [U]

co·ef·fi·cient /ˌkəʊɪˈfɪʃnt; *NAmE* ˌkoʊ-/ *noun* **1** (*mathematics* 数) a number which is placed before another quantity and which multiplies it, for example 3 in the quantity 3x 系数 **2** (*physics* 物) a number that measures a particular property (= characteristic) of a substance（测定物质某种特性的）系数： *the coefficient of friction* 摩擦系数

coela·canth /ˈsiːləkænθ/ *noun* a large fish found mainly in the seas near Madagascar. It was thought to be EXTINCT until one was discovered in 1938. 腔棘鱼，矛尾鱼（产于马达加斯加附近海域，1938 年发现之前被认为已灭绝）

coel·iac disease (*BrE*) (*NAmE* **celiac disease**) /ˈsiːliæk dɪziːz/ *noun* [U] a disease in which sb cannot DIGEST food (= break it down in their body) because their body is very sensitive to GLUTEN (= a substance that is found in flour, especially WHEAT flour) 乳糜泻（因麸质过敏引起的消化不良）

co·erce /kəʊˈɜːs; *NAmE* koʊˈɜːrs/ *verb* ~ **sb** (**into sth/into doing sth**) | ~ **sb** (**to do sth**) (*formal*) to force sb to do sth by using threats 强迫；胁迫；迫使： *They were coerced into negotiating a settlement.* 他们被迫商讨协定。

co·er·cion /kəʊˈɜːʃn; *NAmE* koʊˈɜːrʒn/ *noun* [U] (*formal*) the action of making sb do sth that they do not want to do, using force or threatening to use force 强迫；胁迫： *He claimed he had only acted under coercion.* 他声称他只是受了胁迫才采取行动。

co·er·cive /kəʊˈɜːsɪv; *NAmE* koʊˈɜːrsɪv/ *adj.* (*formal*) using force or the threat of force 用武力的；强制的；胁迫的： ***coercive measures/powers*** 强制的措施 / 力量

co·eval /kəʊˈiːvl; *NAmE* koʊ-/ *adj.* (*formal*) ~ (**with sth**) (of two or more things 两个或以上的事物) having the same age or date of origin（与…）同龄，同时代，同时期出现： *The industry is coeval with the construction of the first railways.* 这一产业和初期铁路的建造相伴而生。

co·ex·ist /ˌkəʊɪɡˈzɪst; *NAmE* ˌkoʊ-/ *verb* [I] ~ (**with sb/sth**) (*formal*) to exist together in the same place or at the same time, especially in a peaceful way 共存；（尤指）和平共处： *The illness frequently coexists with other chronic diseases.* 这种病往往与其他慢性病同时存在。◇ *English speakers now coexist peacefully with their Spanish-speaking neighbours.* 讲英语的人现在与他们讲西班牙语的邻居和睦相处。◇ *Different traditions coexist successfully side by side.* 不同的传统和谐地共存着。

co·ex·ist·ence /ˌkəʊɪɡˈzɪstəns; *NAmE* ˌkoʊ-/ *noun* [U] the state of being together in the same place at the same time 共处；共存： *to live in **uneasy/peaceful coexistence** within one nation* 在一个国家内难以 / 和平共存

C of E /ˌsiː əv ˈiː/ *abbr.* Church of England 英国国教会；英格兰圣公会 ➲ SEE ALSO CE

cof·fee /ˈkɒfi; *NAmE* ˈkɔː-; ˈkɑː-/ *noun* **1** [U, C] the ROASTED seeds (called **coffee beans**) of a tropical bush; a powder made from them（烘烤过的）咖啡豆；咖啡粉： ***decaffeinated/instant coffee*** 不含咖啡因的 / 速溶咖啡 ◇ ***ground/real coffee*** 现磨现煮的咖啡 ◇ *a jar of coffee* 一罐咖啡 ◇ *a blend of Brazilian and Colombian coffees* 巴西和哥伦比亚的混合咖啡 ◇ *coffee ice cream* 咖啡冰淇淋 **2** [U, C] a hot drink made from coffee powder and boiling water. It may be drunk with milk and/or sugar added. 咖啡（热饮料）： ***black/white coffee*** (= without/with milk) 不加奶的 / 加奶的咖啡 ◇ *Tea or coffee?* 要茶还是要咖啡？ ◇ *I'll just make the coffee.* 我就来煮咖啡。 ◇ *Let's talk over coffee* (= while drinking coffee). 咱们边喝咖啡边聊吧。 **3** [C] a cup of coffee 一杯咖啡： *Two strong black coffees, please.* 请来两杯不加奶的浓咖啡。 **4** [U] the colour of coffee mixed with milk; light brown 咖啡色；浅褐色；浅棕色 IDM SEE WAKE *v.*

ˈ**coffee bar** *noun* **1** (*BrE*) (*also* ˈ**coffee shop** *NAmE, BrE*) a place, sometimes in a store, train station, etc., where you can buy coffee, tea, other drinks without alcohol and sometimes simple meals 小咖啡厅（有时设在商店、火车站等内；供应咖啡、茶、其他无酒精饮料及便餐） **2** (*NAmE*) a small restaurant that sells special sorts of coffee and cakes 小咖啡馆（专卖咖啡和糕点）

ˈ**coffee break** *noun* a short period of rest when you stop working and drink coffee 工间喝咖啡休息时间： *to have a coffee break* 工间喝咖啡休息

ˈ**coffee cake** *noun* (*NAmE*) a small cake with melted sugar on top that people eat with coffee 咖啡糕（配咖啡的糕点，表面淋上糖浆）

ˈ**coffee house** *noun* **1** a restaurant serving coffee, etc., especially one of a type popular in Britain in the 18th century or one in a city in Central Europe（尤指流行于英国 18 世纪或中欧城市里的）咖啡馆： *the coffee houses of Vienna* 维也纳的咖啡馆 **2** (*NAmE*) a restaurant serving coffee, etc. where people go to listen to music, poetry, etc.（可听音乐、诗歌等的）咖啡馆

ˈ**coffee machine** *noun* **1** = COFFEE MAKER **2** a machine that you put coins in to get a cup of coffee 投币咖啡机

ˈ**coffee maker** (*also* ˈ**coffee machine**) *noun* a small machine for making cups of coffee 煮咖啡机 ➲ VISUAL VOCAB PAGE V26

ˈ**coffee morning** *noun* (*BrE*) a social event held in the morning, often at a person's house, where money is usually given to help a charity 咖啡早茶会（通常在某人家里为慈善募款而举行）

ˈ**coffee shop** *noun* a small restaurant, often in a store, hotel, etc., where coffee, tea, other drinks without alcohol and simple food are served 小咖啡厅（常设在商店、旅馆等内，供应咖啡、茶、其他无酒精饮料及小吃）

ˈ**coffee table** *noun* a small low table for putting magazines, cups, etc. on, usually in front of a SOFA 咖啡桌；茶几 ➲ VISUAL VOCAB PAGE V22

ˈ**coffee-table book** *noun* a large expensive book containing many pictures or photographs, that is designed for people to look through rather than to read carefully 咖啡桌图书（多供浏览，开本大，插图丰富，较昂贵）

cof·fer /ˈkɒfə(r); *NAmE* ˈkɔːf-; ˈkɑːf-/ *noun* **1** [C] a large strong box, used in the past for storing money or valuable objects（旧时的）保险柜，贵重物品箱 **2** (*also* **coffers**) [pl.] a way of referring to the money that a government, an organization, etc. has available to spend（政府、机构等的）金库，资金： *The nation's coffers are empty.* 国库空虚。

cof·fin /ˈkɒfɪn; *NAmE* ˈkɔːfɪn; ˈkɑːfɪn/ (*especially BrE*) (*NAmE usually* **cas·ket**) *noun* a box in which a dead body is buried or CREMATED 棺材；棺椁；棺木 ➲ WORDFINDER NOTE AT DIE IDM SEE NAIL *n.*

cog /kɒɡ; *NAmE* kɑːɡ/ *noun* **1** one of a series of teeth on the edge of a wheel that fit between the teeth on the next wheel and cause it to move（齿轮的）轮齿，嵌齿 ➲ PICTURE AT COGWHEEL **2** = COGWHEEL

IDM **a cog in the maˈchine/ˈwheel** (*informal*) a person who is a small part of a large organization（大机构中的）小职员，小成员

co·gent /ˈkəʊdʒənt; *NAmE* ˈkoʊ-/ *adj.* (*formal*) strongly and clearly expressed in a way that influences what people believe 有说服力的；令人信服的 SYN **convincing**: *She put forward some cogent reasons for abandoning the plan.* 她为放弃这个计划提出了一些具有说服力的理由。 ▶ **co·gency** /ˈkəʊdʒənsi; *NAmE* ˈkoʊ-/ *noun* [U] **co·gent·ly** *adv.*

cogi·tate /ˈkɒdʒɪteɪt; *NAmE* ˈkɑːdʒ-/ *verb* [I] ~ (**about/on sth**) (*formal*) to think carefully about sth 仔细思考；慎重考虑；深思熟虑 ▶ **cogi·ta·tion** /ˌkɒdʒɪˈteɪʃn; *NAmE* ˌkɑːdʒ-/ *noun* [U, C]

co·gnac /ˈkɒnjæk; *NAmE* ˈkoʊn-/ *noun* **1** [U, C] a type of fine BRANDY made in western France 科尼亚克白兰地酒，干邑（产于法国西部） **2** [C] a glass of cognac 一杯科尼亚克白兰地酒

cog·nate /ˈkɒɡneɪt; *NAmE* ˈkɑːɡ-/ *adj., noun*

■ ***adj.*** **1** (*linguistics* 语言) having the same origin as another word or language（词或语言）同源的，同族的，同语系的： *'Haus' in German is cognate with 'house' in English.* 德语中的 Haus 一词与英语中的 house 同源。 ◇ *German and Dutch are cognate languages.* 德语和荷兰语是同源语言。 **2** (*formal*) related in some way and therefore similar 相关的；类似的： *a cognate development* 相关的发展

■ ***noun*** (*linguistics* 语言) a word that has the same origin as another 同源词： *'Haus' and 'house' are cognates.* * Haus 和 house 是同源词。

cog·ni·tion /kɒɡˈnɪʃn; *NAmE* kɑːɡ-/ *noun* [U] (*psychology* 心) the process by which knowledge and understanding is developed in the mind 认知；感知；认识

cog·ni·tive /ˈkɒɡnətɪv; *NAmE* ˈkɑːɡ-/ *adj.* [usually before noun] connected with mental processes of understanding 认知的；感知的；认识的： *a child's cognitive development* 儿童的认知发展 ◇ *cognitive psychology* 认知心理学

ˌ**cognitive beˌhavioural ˈtherapy** (*US* ˌ**cognitive beˌhavioral ˈtherapy**) (*also* ˌ**cognitive ˈtherapy**) *noun* [U] = CBT

cog·ni·zance (*BrE also* **-i·sance**) /ˈkɒɡnɪzəns; *NAmE* ˈkɑːɡ-/ *noun* [U] (*formal*) knowledge or understanding of sth 认识；获知；领悟 ▶ **cog·ni·zant**, **-i·sant** *adj.* [not before noun]: *cognizant of the importance of the case* 认识到这个论据的重要性

IDM **take cognizance of sth** (*law* 律) to understand or consider sth; to take notice of sth 获知；察知；考虑到；注意到

co·gnos·centi /ˌkɒnjəˈʃenti; *NAmE* ˌkɑːn-/ *noun* [pl.] **the cognoscenti** (*from Italian, formal*) people with a lot of knowledge about a particular subject 专家；行家

cog·wheel /ˈkɒɡwiːl; *NAmE* ˈkɑːɡ-/ (*also* **cog**) *noun* a wheel with a series of teeth on the edge that fit between the teeth on the next wheel and cause it to move 齿轮 ➲ PICTURE ON NEXT PAGE

co·habit /kəʊˈhæbɪt; *NAmE* koʊ-/ *verb* [I] ~ (**with sb**) (*formal*) (usually of a man and a woman 通常指男女) to live together and have a sexual relationship without being married（无婚姻关系）同居 ▶ **co·hab·it·ation** /ˌkəʊˌhæbɪˈteɪʃn; *NAmE* ˌkoʊ-/ *noun* [U]

co·here /kəʊˈhɪə(r); *NAmE* koʊˈhɪr/ *verb* (*formal*) **1** [I] ~ (**with sth**) (of different ideas, arguments, sentences, etc. 不同的看法、论点、句子等) to have a clear logical

cogwheel 齿轮

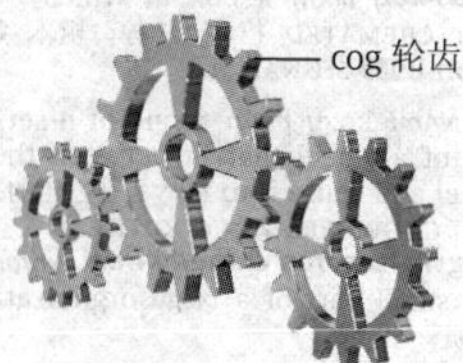

connection so that together they make a whole 连贯；一致：*This view does not cohere with their other beliefs.* 这个观点与他们的其他看法不一致。**2** [I] (of people 人) to work closely together 齐心协力；团结一致：*It can be difficult to get a group of people to cohere.* 要使一群人做到彼此一条心有时候很困难。

co·her·ence AW /kəʊˈhɪərəns; *NAmE* koʊˈhɪr-/ *noun* [U] (*formal*) the situation in which all the parts of sth fit together well 连贯性；条理性：*The points you make are fine, but the whole essay lacks coherence.* 你提出的论点很好，但整篇文章缺乏呼应连贯。OPP **incoherence**

co·her·ent AW /kəʊˈhɪərənt; *NAmE* koʊˈhɪr-/ *adj.* **1** (of ideas, thoughts, arguments, etc. 看法、思想、论点等) logical and well organized; easy to understand and clear 合乎逻辑的；有条理的；清楚易懂的：*a **coherent narrative/account/explanation*** 条理清楚的叙述 / 描述 / 阐述 ◇ *a coherent policy for the transport system* 运输系统方面的一个前后一致的政策 **2** (of a person 人) able to talk and express yourself clearly 有表达能力的；能表述清楚的：*She only became coherent again two hours after the attack.* 她发病两小时之后才恢复了清楚说话的能力。OPP **incoherent** ▸ **co·her·ent·ly** AW *adv.*

co·he·sion /kəʊˈhiːʒn; *NAmE* koʊ-/ *noun* [U] **1** (*formal*) the act or state of keeping together 黏合；结合；凝聚性 SYN **unity**: *the cohesion of the nuclear family* 核心家庭的内聚性 ◇ ***social/political/economic cohesion*** 社会 / 政治 / 经济凝聚性 **2** (*physics* 物, *chemistry* 化) the force causing MOLECULES of the same substance to stick together 内聚力；黏聚力

co·he·sive /kəʊˈhiːsɪv; *NAmE* koʊ-/ *adj.* (*formal*) **1** forming a united whole 结成一个整体的：*a cohesive group* 一个紧密团结的群体 **2** causing people or things to become united 使结合的；使凝结的；使内聚的：*the cohesive power of shared suffering* 共患难的内聚力 ◇ *well-structured sentences illustrating the use of cohesive markers such as 'nevertheless' and 'however'* 能够表明像 nevertheless 和 however 这类连词用法的结构严谨的句子 ▸ **co·he·sive·ness** *noun* [U]

co·hort /ˈkəʊhɔːt; *NAmE* ˈkoʊhɔːrt/ *noun* [C+sing./pl. v.] **1** (*specialist*) a group of people who share a common feature or aspect of behaviour（有共同特点或举止类同的）一群人，一批人：*the 1999 birth cohort* (= all those born in 1999) * 1999 年出生的同龄人口 **2** (*disapproving*) a member of a group of people who support another person 同伙；支持者：*Robinson and his cohorts were soon ejected from the hall.* 鲁滨逊及其同伙很快被赶出了大厅。

coif·fure /kwɑːˈfjʊə(r); *NAmE* -ˈfjʊr/ *noun* (*from French, formal* or *humorous*) the way in which a person's hair is arranged 发式；发型 SYN **hairstyle**

coil /kɔɪl/ *verb, noun*

▪ ***verb*** [I, T] to wind into a series of circles; to make sth do this（使）缠绕，盘绕：**~ up** *The snake coiled up, ready to strike.* 那条蛇盘绕起来准备攻击。◇ **~ round, around, etc. sth** *Mist coiled around the tops of the hills.* 薄雾盘绕着山巅。◇ **~ sth (+ adv./prep.)** *to coil a rope into a loop* 把绳索盘绕成圈 ◇ *Her hair was coiled on top of her head.* 她把头发盘在头顶上。◇ *a coiled spring* 螺旋状弹簧 ➲ PICTURE AT KNOT

▪ ***noun*** **1** a series of circles formed by winding up a length of rope, wire, etc.（绳索、金属线等的）圈，卷，盘：*a coil of wire* 一圈金属线 **2** one circle of rope, wire, etc. in a series 一圈（绳索、金属线等）：*Shake the rope and let the coils unwind.* 抖动绳索把绳圈展开。◇ *a snake's coils* 蛇的盘圈 **3** a length of wire, wound into circles, that can carry electricity 线圈；绕组 **4** = IUD

coin /kɔɪn/ *noun, verb*

▪ ***noun*** **1** [C] a small flat piece of metal used as money（一枚）硬币；金属货币：*a euro coin* 欧元硬币 ➲ PICTURE AT MONEY **2** [U] money made of metal（统称）硬币：*notes and coin* 纸币和硬币 IDM ▸ SEE SIDE *n.*, TWO

▪ ***verb*** **1 ~ sth** to invent a new word or phrase that other people then begin to use 创造（新词语）：*The term 'cardboard city' was coined to describe communities of homeless people living in cardboard boxes.* 人们创造了 cardboard city 一词，用来指居住在纸板棚里的无家可归者所聚集的地区。**2 ~ sth** to make coins out of metal 铸（币）；造（硬币）

IDM **be ˈcoining it (in) | be ˌcoining ˈmoney** (*BrE, informal*) to earn a lot of money quickly or easily 暴富；赚大钱；发大财 SYN **rake in** **to coin a ˈphrase 1** used to introduce a well-known expression that you have changed slightly in order to be funny（引出为逗趣而稍加改动的名言）**2** used to show that you are aware that you are using an expression that is not new 套用一句老话；用老话来说：*Oh well, no news is good news, to coin a phrase.* 噢，常言道，没有消息就是好消息。

coin·age /ˈkɔɪnɪdʒ/ *noun* **1** [U] the coins used in a particular place or at a particular time; coins of a particular type（统称某地或某时期的）金属货币；（某种）硬币：*Roman coinage* 古罗马时期的硬币 ◇ ***gold/silver/bronze coinage*** 金币；银币；铜币 **2** [U] the system of money used in a particular country（国家的）货币制度：*decimal coinage* 十进位货币制 **3** [C, U] a word or phrase that has been invented recently; the process of inventing a word or phrase 新创的词语；新词语的创造：*new coinages* 新创的词语

ˈcoin box *noun* (*BrE, old-fashioned*) a public telephone that you put coins in to operate 投币式公用电话

co·in·cide AW /ˌkəʊɪnˈsaɪd; *NAmE* ˌkoʊ-/ *verb* **1** [I] (of two or more events 两件或更多的事情) to take place at the same time 同时发生：*It's a pity our trips to New York don't coincide.* 真遗憾我们的纽约之行不在同一时间。◇ **~ with sth** *The strike was timed to coincide with the party conference.* 那次罢工选择在召开政党大会的同一时间举行。**2** [I] (*formal*) (of ideas, opinions, etc. 想法、意见等) to be the same or very similar 相同；相符；极为类似：*The interests of employers and employees do not always coincide.* 雇主和雇员的利益并不总是一致的。◇ **~ with sth** *Her story coincided exactly with her brother's.* 她和她弟弟所讲的完全一致。**3** [I] (*formal*) (of objects or places 物品或地方) to meet; to share the same space 相接；相交；位置重合；重叠：*At this point the two paths coincide briefly.* 两条小路在这个地方有一小段合了在一起。◇ **~ with sth** *The present position of the house coincides with that of an earlier dwelling.* 这栋房子现在的位置恰与原住宅的位置一致。

co·in·ci·dence AW /kəʊˈɪnsɪdəns; *NAmE* koʊ-/ *noun* **1** [C, U] the fact of two things happening at the same time by chance, in a surprising way（令人吃惊的）巧合，巧事：***a strange/an extraordinary/a remarkable coincidence*** 奇怪的 / 不寻常的 / 惊人的巧合 ◇ ***What a coincidence!*** *I wasn't expecting to see you here.* 真巧！我没料到会在这里见到你。◇ *It's **not a coincidence that** none of the directors are women* (= it did not happen by chance). 没有一位董事是女性，这并非偶然。◇ ***By** (**sheer**) **coincidence,** I met the person we'd been discussing the next day.* 真是巧了，我在第二天就遇见了我们一直在谈论的那个人。➲ SYNONYMS AT LUCK ➲ WORDFINDER NOTE AT LUCK **2** [sing.] (*formal*) the fact of things being present at the same time 同时存在；并存：*the coincidence of inflation and unemployment* 通货膨胀与失业的并存 **3** [sing.] (*formal*) the fact of two or more opinions, etc. being the same（意见等的）相同，相符，一致：*a coincidence of interests between the two partners* 两个合伙人之间利益的一致

co·in·ci·dent AW /kəʊˈɪnsɪdənt; NAmE koʊ-/ *adj.* ~ (**with sth**) (*formal*) happening in the same place or at the same time 在同一地方发生的；同时发生的

co·in·ci·dent·al AW /kəʊˌɪnsɪˈdentl; NAmE koʊ-/ *adj.* [not usually before noun] happening by chance; not planned 巧合；碰巧；非计划之中：*I suppose your presence here today is not **entirely coincidental**.* 我认为你今天来这里不完全是碰巧。◇ *It's **purely coincidental that** we both chose to call our daughters Emma.* 我们俩都给自己的女儿取名叫埃玛，这完全是巧合。▶ **co·in·ci·den·tal·ly** /-təli/ *adv.*：*Coincidentally, they had both studied in Paris.* 碰巧的是，他们俩都在巴黎学习过。

coir /ˈkɔɪə(r)/ *noun* [U] rough material made from the shells of COCONUTS, used for making ropes, for covering floors, etc. 椰子壳粗纤维（用于制作绳索、地板垫等）

co·itus /ˈkɔɪtəs; ˈkəʊɪtəs; NAmE ˈkoʊ-/ *noun* [U] (*medical* 医 or *formal*) = SEXUAL INTERCOURSE

coitus interruptus /ˌkɔɪtəs ɪntəˈrʌptəs; ˌkəʊɪtəs; NAmE ˌkoʊ-/ *noun* [U] an act of SEXUAL INTERCOURSE in which the man removes his PENIS from the woman's body before he EJACULATES, in order to prevent the woman from becoming pregnant （为防止受孕而在射精前抽出阴茎的）不完全性交

Coke™ /kəʊk; NAmE koʊk/ *noun* [C, U] (*informal*) = COCA-COLA™：*Can I have a Diet Coke?* 给我来一罐健怡可口可乐好吗？

coke /kəʊk; NAmE koʊk/ *noun* [U] **1** (*informal*) = COCAINE **2** a black substance that is produced from coal and burnt to provide heat 焦炭

Col. *abbr.* (in writing 书写形式) COLONEL 上校：*Col. Stewart* 斯图尔特上校

col /kɒl; NAmE kɑːl/ *noun* (*specialist*) a low point between two higher points in a mountain range （山脉中两个山峰之间的）山口 SYN **pass**

col. *abbr.* (in writing 书写形式) COLUMN 栏

cola /ˈkəʊlə; NAmE ˈkoʊlə/ *noun* **1** [U, C] a sweet brown, FIZZY drink (= with bubbles) that does not contain alcohol. Its flavour comes from the seeds of a W African tree (the **cola tree**) and other substances. 可乐饮料 **2** [C] a glass, can or bottle of cola 一杯（或一罐、一瓶）可乐 ➲ SEE ALSO COCA-COLA™, COKE™

col·an·der /ˈkʌləndə(r); NAmE ˈkɑːl-/ *noun* a metal or plastic bowl with a lot of small holes in it, used for DRAINING water from vegetables, etc. after washing or cooking 滤器；滤锅 ➲ VISUAL VOCAB PAGE V27

ˈcola nut (*also* **ˈkola nut**) *noun* the seed of the cola tree, that can be chewed or made into a drink 可乐果（可咀嚼或制作饮料）

cold 🔑 /kəʊld; NAmE koʊld/ *adj., noun, adv.*

■ *adj.* (**cold·er, cold·est**)

• LOW TEMPERATURE 低温 **1** 🔑 having a lower than usual temperature; having a temperature lower than the human body 寒冷的；冷的：*I'm cold. Turn the heating up.* 我觉得冷，把暖气温度调高一点。◇ *to **feel/look cold*** 感觉/看起来冷 ◇ *cold hands and feet* 冷手凉脚 ◇ *a cold room/house* 寒冷的房间/屋子 ◇ *hot and cold water in every room* 每个房间都供给的冷热水 ◇ *Isn't it cold today?* 今天真冷，是不是？◇ *It's **freezing cold**.* 天气寒冷彻骨。◇ *to **get/turn colder*** 变得更冷 ◇ ***bitterly cold** weather* 严寒的天气 ◇ *the coldest May on record* 有记载以来最冷的五月 ◇ (*BrE*) *The water has gone cold.* 水已变凉。

• FOOD/DRINK 食物；饮料 **2** 🔑 not heated; cooled after being cooked 未热过的；已凉的；冷却的：*a cold drink* 冷饮 ◇ *Hot and cold food is available in the cafeteria.* 自助餐厅有冷热食物供应。◇ *cold chicken for lunch* 午餐的鸡肉冷盘

• UNFRIENDLY 不友好 **3** 🔑 (of a person 人) without emotion; unfriendly 冷漠的；不友好的：*to give sb a **cold look/stare/welcome*** 冷冷地看某人一眼/瞪着某人/迎接某人 ◇ *Her manner was **cold and distant**.* 她的态度冷漠而疏远。◇ *He was staring at her with **cold eyes**.* 他用冷漠的眼光盯着她。

• LIGHT/COLOURS 光线；颜色 **4** 🔑 seeming to lack warmth, in an unpleasant way 冷的；冷色的；寒色的：*clear cold light* 清寒的光 ◇ *cold grey skies* 冷灰色的天空

• ROUTE 路径 **5** not easy to find 不易发现的：*The police followed the robbers to the airport but then the **trail went cold**.* 警察追踪抢劫犯到了机场，但是后来却失去了他们的踪迹。

• IN GAMES 游戏 **6** used in children's games to say that the person playing is not close to finding a person or thing, or to guessing the correct answer （儿童游戏中）离目标远的，未猜中的

• UNCONSCIOUS 失去知觉 **7 out ~** [not before noun] (*informal*) unconscious 失去知觉：*He was knocked out cold in the second round.* 他在第二轮中被击倒，失去了知觉。

• FACTS 事实 **8 the ~ facts/truth** facts with nothing added to make them more interesting or pleasant 真实的；客观的 ➲ SEE ALSO COLDLY, COLDNESS

IDM **a cold ˈfish** a person who seems unfriendly and without strong emotions 冷漠无情的人 **get/have cold ˈfeet** (*informal*) to suddenly become nervous about doing sth that you had planned to do 临阵胆怯；畏缩：*He was going to ask her but he got cold feet and said nothing.* 他本来是想问她的，可事到临头他却胆怯得什么也没有说。 **give sb the cold ˈshoulder** (*informal*) to treat sb in an unfriendly way 冷漠对待；使受到冷遇 ➲ SEE ALSO COLD-SHOULDER **in cold ˈblood** acting in a way that is

▼ **SYNONYMS** 同义词辨析

cold

cool • freezing • chilly • lukewarm • tepid

These words all describe sb/sth that has a low temperature. 以上各词均表示温度低。

cold having a temperature that is lower than usual or lower than the human body; (of food or drink) not heated; cooled after being cooked 指寒冷的、冷的，（食物、饮料）凉的、冷的：*I'm cold. Turn the heating up.* 我觉得冷，把暖气温度调高一点。◇ *Outside it was bitterly cold.* 外面非常寒冷。◇ *a cold wind* 寒风 ◇ *hot and cold water* 热水和凉水 ◇ *It's cold chicken for lunch.* 午餐有鸡肉冷盘。

cool (*often approving*) fairly cold, especially in a pleasant way 指凉爽的、凉快的：*a long cool drink* 一大口冷饮 ◇ *We found a cool place to sit.* 我们找了一个凉快的地方坐下来。

freezing extremely cold; having a temperature below 0° Celsius 指极冷的、冰冻的、冰点以下的：*It's absolutely freezing outside.* 外面冷得不得了。◇ *I'm freezing!* 我要冻僵了！

chilly (*rather informal*) too cold to be comfortable 指寒冷的、阴冷的：*Bring a coat. It might turn chilly later.* 带件大衣，过一会儿天气可能会变冷。

lukewarm (*often disapproving*) slightly warm, sometimes in an unpleasant way 指微温的、不冷不热的、温吞的：*Her coffee was now lukewarm.* 她的咖啡变得微温。

tepid (*often disapproving*) slightly warm, sometimes in an unpleasant way 指微温的、不冷不热的、温吞的：*a jug of tepid water* 一壶温水

LUKEWARM OR TEPID? 用 lukewarm 还是 tepid?

There is really no difference in meaning or use between these words. 以上两词在含义和用法上无实际区别。

PATTERNS

- to **feel**/**get** cold/cool/chilly
- cold/cool/freezing/chilly **air**/**weather**
- a cold/cool/freezing/chilly **wind**
- cold/cool/freezing/lukewarm/tepid **water**
- a cold/cool/lukewarm/tepid **shower**/**bath**
- cold/lukewarm/tepid **tea**/**coffee**/**food**
- a cold/cool **drink**
- **It's** cold/chilly/freezing outside.

C

deliberately cruel; with no pity 残忍地；蓄意地；冷酷地；无情地：*to kill sb in cold blood* 残忍地杀害某人 **in the cold light of day** when you have had time to think calmly about sth; in the morning when things are clearer 有时间冷静考虑时；在头脑更清醒些的第二天早晨：*These things always look different in the cold light of day.* 这些事情在冷静地考虑后总会显得不同。 **leave sb 'cold** to fail to affect or interest sb 未打动某人；无法引起某人的兴趣：*Most modern art leaves me cold.* 大多数的现代艺术引不起我的兴趣。 **pour/throw cold 'water on sth** to give reasons for not being in favour of sth; to criticize sth 泼冷水；批评；责备 ➲ MORE AT BLOOD *n.*, BLOW *v.*, HOT *adj.*

■ *noun*

• **LOW TEMPERATURE** 低温 **1** [U] a lack of heat or warmth; a low temperature, especially in the atmosphere 冷；寒冷；（尤指）低气温：*He shivered with cold.* 他冻得发抖。◇ *Don't stand outside **in the cold**.* 别站在外面冻着。◇ *She doesn't seem to **feel the cold**.* 她好像不觉得冷。◇ *You'll **catch your death of cold*** (= used to warn sb they could become ill if they do not keep warm in cold weather). 你会冻出病的。

• **ILLNESS** 疾病 **2** [C] (*also less frequent* **the ˌcommon 'cold**) a common illness that affects the nose and/or throat, making you cough, SNEEZE, etc. 感冒；伤风；着凉：*I've got a cold.* 我感冒了。◇ *a **bad/heavy/slight cold*** 严重 / 重 / 轻微感冒 ◇ *to **catch a cold*** 患感冒 ➲ COLLOCATIONS AT ILL

IDM **come in from the 'cold** to become accepted or included in a group, etc. after a period of being outside it 不再受冷落（或排斥） **leave sb ˌout in the 'cold** to not include sb in a group or an activity 冷落；排斥 ➲ MORE AT CATCH *v.*

■ *adv.* **1** (*NAmE*) suddenly and completely 突然彻底：*His final request stopped her cold.* 他最后的请求突然阻止了她。**2** without preparing 毫无准备地：*I can't just walk in there cold and give a speech.* 我不能什么准备都没有，进去就发表演讲。

ˌcold-'blooded *adj.* **1** (of people and their actions 人及其行为) showing no feelings or pity for other people 冷酷的；无情的；残酷的：*a cold-blooded killer* 冷酷无情的杀手 **2** (*biology* 生) (of animals, for example fish or snakes 动物，如鱼或蛇) having a body temperature that depends on the temperature of the surrounding air or water 冷血的 ➲ COMPARE WARM-BLOODED ▶ **ˌcold-'blooded·ly** *adv.*

ˌcold-'calling *noun* [U] the practice of telephoning sb that you do not know, in order to sell them sth 推销商品的电话 ➲ WORDFINDER NOTE AT ADVERTISE ▶ **ˌcold 'call** *noun*

ˌcold 'cash (*NAmE*) (*BrE* **ˌhard 'cash**) *noun* [U] money, especially in the form of coins and notes, that you can spend 现金（尤指硬币和纸币）

ˌcold 'comfort *noun* [U] the fact that sth that would normally be good does not make you happy because the whole situation is bad 于事无补的安慰；不起作用的慰藉：*A small drop in the inflation rate was cold comfort for the millions without a job.* 对数百万失业者来说，通货膨胀率的微降是不起什么作用的安慰。

'cold cream *noun* [U] a thick white cream that people use for cleaning their face or making their skin soft 洁面乳；润肤膏

'cold cuts *noun* [pl.] (*especially NAmE*) slices of cooked meat that are served cold 冷盘肉片

'cold frame (*also* **frame**) *noun* a small wooden or metal frame covered with glass that you grow seeds or small plants in to protect them from cold weather 冷床，阳畦（保护育种或幼苗抗寒的床框） ➲ PICTURE AT FRAME ➲ VISUAL VOCAB PAGE V20

ˌcold 'fusion *noun* [U] (*physics* 物) NUCLEAR FUSION that takes place at or near room temperature 冷核聚变

ˌcold-'hearted *adj.* not showing any love or sympathy for other people; unkind 冷酷无情的；无同情心的；不仁慈的 ➲ COMPARE WARM-HEARTED

coldie /ˈkəʊldi; *NAmE* ˈkoʊl-/ *noun* (*AustralE, informal*) a cold can or bottle of beer 一罐（或一瓶）冰镇啤酒

cold·ly /ˈkəʊldli; *NAmE* ˈkoʊld-/ *adv.* without any emotion or warm feelings; in an unfriendly way 冷淡地；冷漠地；不友好地

cold·ness /ˈkəʊldnəs; *NAmE* ˈkoʊld-/ *noun* [U] **1** the lack of warm feelings; unfriendly behaviour 冷淡；冷漠；不友好的举止：*She was hurt by the coldness in his voice.* 他说话的冷漠语气让她很伤心。 **2** the state of being cold 冷；寒冷：*the icy coldness of the water* 冰冷彻骨的水 OPP **warmth**

ˌcold-'shoulder *verb* ~ **sb** to treat sb in an unfriendly way 冷待；冷落；慢待 ➲ SEE ALSO GIVE SB THE COLD SHOULDER at COLD *adj.*

'cold snap *noun* (*informal*) a sudden short period of very cold weather （短时间的）骤冷期

'cold sore (*NAmE also* **'fever blister**) *noun* a small painful spot on the lips or inside the mouth that is caused by a virus 唇疱疹

'cold spell *noun* a period when the weather is colder than usual 寒冷期

ˌcold 'storage *noun* [U] a place where food, etc. can be kept fresh or frozen until it is needed; the storing of sth in such a place 冷藏库；冷藏：(*figurative*) *I've had to **put my plans into cold storage*** (= I've decided not to carry them out immediately but to keep them for later). 我不得不把我的计划暂时搁置起来。

'cold store *noun* a room where food, etc. can be kept at a low temperature in order to keep it in good condition 冷藏室；冷藏库

ˌcold 'sweat *noun* [usually sing.] a state when you have sweat on your face or body but still feel cold, usually because you are very frightened or anxious（通常因恐惧或焦急而出的）冷汗：*to break out into a cold sweat* 出了一身冷汗 ◇ *I woke up in a cold sweat about the interview.* 梦中的面试情景吓得我在一身冷汗中惊醒。

ˌcold 'turkey *noun* [U] the unpleasant state that drug ADDICTS experience when they suddenly stop taking a drug; a way of treating drug ADDICTS that makes them experience this state （吸毒成瘾者）突然戒毒时的痛苦；（治疗吸毒成瘾者的）突然戒毒方法 ▶ **ˌcold 'turkey** *adv.*：*I quit smoking cold turkey.* 我用突然戒烟法戒了烟。

ˌcold 'war *noun* [sing., U] (*often* **Cold War**) a very unfriendly relationship between two countries who are not actually fighting each other, usually used about the situation between the US and the Soviet Union after the Second World War 冷战（通常指第二次世界大战后美国与苏联之间的对峙局面）

cole·slaw /ˈkəʊlslɔː; *NAmE* ˈkoʊl-/ *noun* [U] pieces of raw CABBAGE, carrot, onion, etc., mixed with MAYONNAISE and eaten with meat or salads 凉拌菜丝（用生圆白菜、胡萝卜、洋葱等切丝与蛋黄酱搅拌而成）

coley /ˈkəʊli; *NAmE* ˈkoʊli/ *noun* [C, U] (*pl.* **coley** or **coleys**) a N Atlantic fish that is used for food 绿青鳕（产于北大西洋）

colic /ˈkɒlɪk; *NAmE* ˈkɑːlɪk/ *noun* [U] severe pain in the stomach and BOWELS, suffered especially by babies （尤指婴儿的）急性腹痛，腹绞痛 ▶ **col·icky** *adj.*

col·itis /kəˈlaɪtɪs/ *noun* [U] (*medical* 医) a disease that causes pain and swelling in the COLON (= part of the BOWELS) 结肠炎

col·lab·or·ate /kəˈlæbəreɪt/ *verb* **1** [I] to work together with sb in order to produce or achieve sth 合作；协作：*Researchers around the world are collaborating to develop a new vaccine.* 世界各地的研究人员正在合作培育一种新的疫苗。◇ ~ **(with sb) (on sth)** *We have collaborated on many projects over the years.* 这些年来我们合作搞了许多项目。◇ ~ **(with sb) (in sth/in doing sth)** *She agreed to collaborate with him in writing her biography.* 她同意与他合作撰写她

的传记。 **2** [I] ~ (**with sb**) (*disapproving*) to help the enemy who has taken control of your country during a war 通敌；勾结敌人

col·lab·or·ation /kəˌlæbəˈreɪʃn/ *noun* **1** [U, C] the act of working with another person or group of people to create or produce sth 合作；协作：*It was a collaboration that produced extremely useful results.* 这是一次带来极其有益的成果的合作。◇ ~ (**with sb**) (**on sth**) *She wrote the book* ***in collaboration*** *with one of her students.* 她和她的一个学生合写了这本书。◇ *The government worked in close collaboration with teachers on the new curriculum.* 政府和教师就新的课程进行了紧密协作。◇ ~ (**between A and B**) *collaboration between the teachers and the government* 教师和政府间的合作 **2** [C] a piece of work produced by two or more people or groups of people working together 合作成果（或作品） **3** [U] (*disapproving*) the act of helping the enemy during a war when they have taken control of your country 通敌；勾结敌人

col·lab·ora·tive /kəˈlæbərətɪv; *NAmE* -reɪtɪv/ *adj.* [only before noun] (*formal*) involving, or done by, several people or groups of people working together 合作的；协作的；协力的：***collaborative projects/studies/research*** 合作项目 / 研究 ◇ *a* ***collaborative effort/venture*** 共同的努力；合作企业 ▸ **col·lab·ora·tive·ly** *adv.*

col·lab·or·ator /kəˈlæbəreɪtə(r)/ *noun* **1** a person who works with another person to create or produce sth such as a book 合作者；协作者；合著者 **2** (*disapproving*) a person who helps the enemy in a war, when they have taken control of the person's country 通敌者

col·lage /ˈkɒlɑːʒ; *NAmE* kəˈlɑːʒ/ *noun* **1** [U, C] the art of making a picture by sticking pieces of coloured paper, cloth, or photographs onto a surface; a picture that you make by doing this 拼贴艺术；拼贴画 **2** [C] a collection of things, which may be similar or different 收集品；收藏品：*an interesting collage of 1960s songs* 有趣的 20 世纪 60 年代歌曲的收藏集

col·lagen /ˈkɒlədʒən; *NAmE* ˈkɑːl-/ *noun* [U] a PROTEIN found in skin and bone, sometimes INJECTED into the body, especially the face, to improve its appearance 胶原蛋白，胶原（存在于皮肤和骨骼中的蛋白质，可通过注射来美容等）：*collagen injections* 胶原蛋白注射

col·lapse AW /kəˈlæps/ *verb, noun*

■ ***verb***

• **OF BUILDING** 建筑物 **1** [I] to fall down or fall in suddenly, often after breaking apart（突然）倒塌，坍塌 SYN **give way**：*The roof collapsed under the weight of snow.* 房顶在雪的重压下突然坍塌下来。

• **OF SICK PERSON** 病人 **2** [I] to fall down (and usually become unconscious), especially because you are very ill/sick（尤指因病重而）倒下，昏倒，晕倒：*He collapsed in the street and died two hours later.* 他昏倒在街上，两小时后死了。

• **RELAX** 放松 **3** [I] (*informal*) to sit or lie down and relax, especially after working hard（尤指工作劳累后）坐下，躺下放松：*When I get home I like to collapse on the sofa and listen to music.* 回到家时，我喜欢倒在沙发上听音乐。

• **FAIL** 失败 **4** [I] to fail suddenly or completely 突然失败；崩溃；瓦解 SYN **break down**：*Talks between management and unions have collapsed.* 资方与工会的谈判已告破裂。◇ *All opposition to the plan has collapsed.* 所有反对此计划的力量均已消除。

• **OF PRICES/CURRENCIES** 价格；货币 **5** [I] to decrease suddenly in amount or value（突然）降价，贬值；暴跌：*Share prices collapsed after news of poor trading figures.* 在交易数额不佳的消息公布后，股票价格暴跌。

• **FOLD** 折叠 **6** [I, T] ~ (**sth**) to fold sth into a shape that uses less space; to be able to be folded in this way 折叠；套缩；可折叠（或套缩） SYN **fold**：*The table collapses for easy storage.* 这桌子可折叠起来方便存放。

• **MEDICAL** 医学 **7** [I, T] ~ (**sth**) if a lung or BLOOD VESSEL **collapses** or **is collapsed**, it falls in and becomes flat and empty（肺或血管）萎陷

▸ **col·lapsed** AW *adj.*：*collapsed buildings* 坍塌的建筑物 ◇ *a collapsed investment bank* 破产的投资银行 ◇ *a collapsed lung* 萎陷的肺

■ ***noun***

• **FAILURE** 失败 **1** [C, usually sing., U] a sudden failure of sth, such as an institution, a business or a course of action（机构、生意、行动等的）突然失败，倒闭，崩溃：*the collapse of law and order in the area* 该地区治安的瘫痪 ◇ *The peace talks were* ***on the verge of collapse.*** 和平谈判濒于破裂。

• **OF BUILDING** 建筑物 **2** [U] the action of a building suddenly falling（突然的）倒塌，塌陷，垮掉：*The walls were strengthened to protect them from collapse.* 围墙已加固以防倒塌。

• **ILLNESS** 疾病 **3** [U, C, usually sing.] a medical condition when a person suddenly becomes very ill/sick, or when sb falls because they are ill/sick or weak 病倒；（因病或体弱的）昏倒，晕倒：*a state of* ***mental/nervous collapse*** 精神 / 神经的崩溃状态 ◇ *She was taken to hospital after her collapse at work.* 她在工作时晕倒后被送进了医院。

• **OF PRICES/CURRENCIES** 价格；货币 **4** [C, usually sing.] a sudden fall in value 突然降价；突然贬值；暴跌：*the collapse of share prices/the dollar/the market* 股票价格 / 美元 / 市场价格暴跌

col·laps·ible AW /kəˈlæpsəbl/ *adj.* that can be folded flat or made into a smaller shape that uses less space 可折叠的；可套缩的：*a* ***collapsible chair/boat/bicycle*** 折叠式椅子 / 小船 / 自行车

col·lar /ˈkɒlə(r); *NAmE* ˈkɑːl-/ *noun, verb*

■ ***noun*** **1** the part around the neck of a shirt, jacket or coat that usually folds down 衣领；领子：*a coat with a fur collar* 毛皮领大衣 ◇ *I turned up my collar against the wind* (= to keep warm). 我把衣领竖起来挡风。◇ *He always wears* ***a collar and tie*** *for work.* 他上班总是系着领带。 ➲ VISUAL VOCAB PAGE V66 ➲ SEE ALSO BLUE-COLLAR, DOG COLLAR, WHITE-COLLAR, WING COLLAR **2** a band of leather or plastic put around the neck of an animal, especially a dog（动物，尤指狗的）颈圈：*a* ***collar and lead/leash*** 颈圈和系带 **3** (*specialist*) a band made of a strong material that is put round sth, such as a pipe or a piece of machinery, to make it stronger or to join two parts together（管子或机器部件的）圈，箍 IDM SEE HOT *adj.*

■ ***verb*** (*informal*) **1** ~ **sb** to capture sb and hold them tightly so that they cannot escape from you 抓住；捉住；揪住；逮住：*Police collared the culprit as he was leaving the premises.* 罪犯正离开现场时，警察逮住了他。 **2** ~ **sb** to stop sb in order to talk to them 拦住（某人以与其）谈话：*I was collared in the street by a woman doing a survey.* 我在大街上给一个做民意调查的女人拦住问话。

col·lar·bone /ˈkɒləbəʊn; *NAmE* ˈkɑːlərboʊn/ *noun* either of the two bones that go from the base of the neck to the shoulders 锁骨 SYN **clavicle** ➲ VISUAL VOCAB PAGE V64

col·lard greens /ˈkɒlɑːd ɡriːnz; *NAmE* ˈkɑːlərd/ (*also* **collards**) *noun* [pl.] (*NAmE*) = KALE

col·lar·less /ˈkɒlələs; *NAmE* ˈkɑːlərləs/ *adj.* with no collar 无领的：*a collarless shirt* 无领衬衫

col·late /kəˈleɪt/ *verb* **1** ~ **sth** to collect information together from different sources in order to examine and compare it 核对，校勘，对照（不同来源的信息）：*to* ***collate data/information/figures*** 核对资料 / 信息 / 数据 **2** ~ **sth** to collect pieces of paper or the pages of a book, etc. and arrange them in the correct order 整理（文件或书等） ▸ **col·la·tion** /kəˈleɪʃn/ *noun* [U]：*the collation of information* 信息的整理

col·lat·eral /kəˈlætərəl/ *noun, adj.*

■ ***noun*** [U] (*finance* 财) property or sth valuable that you promise to give to sb if you cannot pay back money that you borrow 抵押物；担保品

■ ***adj.*** (*formal*) connected with sth else, but in addition to it and less important 附属的；附加的；附带的：*collateral benefits* 附加津贴 ◇ *The government denied that there had been any* ***collateral damage*** (= injury to ordinary people or buildings) *during the bombing raid.* 政府否认空袭期间有任何附带性的破坏（即对平民或建筑物的损害）。

C

col·league 🔑 AW /ˈkɒliːɡ; *NAmE* ˈkɑːliːɡ/ *noun* a person that you work with, especially in a profession or a business 同事；同僚；同人：*a colleague of mine from the office* 我办公室的一位同事 ◊ *We were friends and colleagues for more than 20 years.* * 20 多年来我们既是朋友又是同事。◊ *the Prime Minister and his Cabinet colleagues* 首相及其内阁同僚

col·lect 🔑 /kəˈlekt/ *verb, adj., adv.*

▪ *verb*

• BRING TOGETHER 汇集 **1** 🔑 [T] to bring things together from different people or places 收集；采集 SYN **gather**: **~ sth** *to* ***collect data/evidence/information*** 收集资料/证据/信息 ◊ *We're collecting signatures for a petition.* 我们在为请愿书收集签名。◊ **~ sth from sb/sth** *Samples were collected from over 200 patients.* 已从 200 多名病人取样。

• AS HOBBY 业余爱好 **2** 🔑 [T] **~ sth** to buy or find things of a particular type and keep them as a hobby 收藏；搜集；收集：*to* ***collect stamps/postcards, etc.*** 集邮、收藏明信片等 ➲ SEE ALSO STAMP COLLECTING ➲ **VISUAL VOCAB** PAGE V45

▼ SYNONYMS 同义词辨析

collect

gather • accumulate • amass

These words all mean to get more of sth over a period of time, or to increase in quantity over a period of time. 以上各词均含收集、聚积、积累之义。

collect to bring things or information together from different people or places; to gradually increase in amount in a place 指收集、采集、聚积、积累：*We've been collecting data from various sources.* 我们一直从各种渠道收集资料。◊ *Dirt had collected in the corners of the room.* 房间的角落里积满了灰尘。NOTE People sometimes **collect** things of a particular type as a hobby. 作为爱好收藏物品用 collect：*to collect stamps* 集邮

gather to bring things together that have been spread around; to collect information from different sources 指收拢、归拢（分散的东西），搜集、收集（情报）：*I waited while he* ***gathered up*** *his papers.* 他整理文件时我就在一旁等待。◊ *Detectives have spent months gathering evidence.* 侦探花了数月时间搜集证据。

COLLECT OR GATHER? 用 collect 还是 gather?

Both **collect** and **gather** can be used in the same way to talk about bringing together data, information or evidence. When talking about things, **gather** is used with words like *things, belongings* or *papers* when the things are spread around within a short distance. **Collect** is used for getting examples of sth from different people or places that are physically separated. * collect 和 gather 均可指收集资料、情报或证据。将分散在附近的东西、财物或文件收拢用 gather；从不同的人或分散的地方收集样品用 collect。

accumulate (*rather formal*) to gradually get more and more of sth over a period of time; to gradually increase in number or quantity over a period of time 指积累、聚积，（数量）逐渐增加：*I seem to have accumulated a lot of books.* 我好像已经积存了很多书。◊ *Debts began to accumulate.* 债务开始增加。

amass (*rather formal*) to collect sth in large quantities, especially money, debts or information 指大量积累、积聚（尤指金钱、债务或情报）：*He amassed a fortune from silver mining.* 他靠开采银矿积累了一笔财富。

PATTERNS

- to collect/gather/accumulate/amass **data**/**evidence**/**information**
- to accumulate/amass **a fortune**/**debts**
- **dirt**/**dust**/**debris** collects/accumulates
- to **gradually**/**slowly** collect/gather/accumulate (sth)

• OF PEOPLE 人 **3** [I] to come together in one place to form a larger group 聚集；集合；汇集 SYN **gather**: *A crowd began to collect in front of the embassy.* 人群开始聚集在大使馆的前面。

• INCREASE IN AMOUNT 数量增加 **4** 🔑 [I, T] to gradually increase in amount in a place; to gradually obtain more and more of sth in a place 聚积；积聚；积累 SYN **accumulate**: *Dirt had collected in the corners of the room.* 房间的角落里积满了灰尘。◊ **~ sth** *We seem to have collected an enormous number of boxes* (= without intending to). 我们似乎无意中积存了大量的盒子。◊ *That guitar's been sitting* ***collecting dust*** (= not being used) *for years now.* 那把吉他至今已尘封多年。

• TAKE AWAY 取走 **5** 🔑 [T] to go somewhere in order to take sb/sth away 领取；收走；接走：**~ sth (from…)** *What day do they collect the rubbish/garbage?* 他们哪天收运垃圾？◊ *The package is waiting to be collected.* 这包裹在等人领取。◊ (*BrE*) **~ sb (from…)** *She's gone to collect her son from school.* 她到学校接她儿子去了。

• MONEY 金钱 **6** 🔑 [I, T] to ask people to give you money for a particular purpose 募捐；募集：**~ (for sth)** *We're collecting for local charities.* 我们正在为当地慈善机构募捐。◊ **~ sth (for sth)** *We collected over £300 for the appeal.* 我们为此吁请募集了 300 多英镑。 **7** [T] **~ sth** to obtain the money, etc. that sb owes, for example by going to their house to get it 收（欠款）；（上门）收（账）：*to* ***collect rent/debts/tax*** 收租金；讨债；征税

• RECEIVE/WIN 收到；赢得 **8** [T, I] **~ (sth)** to receive sth; to win sth 收到；赢得；获得：*She collected £25 000 in compensation.* 她得到了 25 000 英镑赔偿金。◊ *to collect a prize/a medal* 获奖；赢得奖牌

IDM **collect yourself/your thoughts** **1** to try to control your emotions and become calm （尽力）镇定下来，敛神专注：*I'm fine—I just need a minute to collect myself.* 我没事，只是需要稍稍镇定一下。 **2** to prepare yourself mentally for sth 做好精神准备：*She paused to collect her thoughts before entering the interview room.* 她停下来定了定神，才走进面试室。

PHR V **colˌlect sth↔up** to bring together things that are no longer being used 把某物收起搁置：*Would somebody collect up all the dirty glasses?* 谁来把这些脏玻璃杯收拾一下好吗？

▪ *adj.* (*NAmE*) (of a telephone call 电话) paid for by the person who receives the call 由受话人付费的：*to make a collect call* 打对方付费电话 ➲ SEE ALSO REVERSE *v.* (7)

▸ **col·lect** *adv.*：*to call sb collect* 给某人打由受话人付费的电话

col·lect·able (*also* **col·lect·ible**) /kəˈlektəbl/ *adj.* worth collecting because it is beautiful or may become valuable 值得收藏（或收集、采集）的 ▸ **col·lect·able** (*also* **col·lect·ible**) *noun* [usually pl.]

col·lect·ed /kəˈlektɪd/ *adj.* **1** [not before noun] very calm and in control of yourself 镇静；冷静；泰然：*She always stays* ***cool, calm and collected*** *in a crisis.* 她在危急关头总是很冷静镇定，处之泰然。 **2** **~ works, papers, poems, etc.** all the books, etc. written by one author, published in one book or in a set 收成全集的

col·lec·tion 🔑 /kəˈlekʃn/ *noun*

• GROUP OF OBJECTS/PEOPLE 一批物品；一群人 **1** 🔑 [C] a group of objects, often of the same sort, that have been collected （常指同类的）收集物，收藏品：*a* ***stamp/coin, etc. collection*** 邮票、硬币等收藏品 ◊ *The painting comes from his private collection.* 这幅画来自他的私人收藏。 **2** [C] a group of objects or people 一批物品；一群人：*There was a collection of books and shoes on the floor.* 地板上有成堆的书和鞋。◊ *There is always a strange collection of runners in the London Marathon.* 每次总会有一批稀奇古怪的选手参加伦敦马拉松比赛。

• TAKING AWAY/BRINGING TOGETHER 取走；聚集 **3** 🔑 [C, U] an act of taking sth away from a place; an act of bringing things together into one place 取走；拿走；聚集；聚积：***refuse/garbage collection*** 废物/垃圾的收运 ◊ *The last collection from this postbox is at 5.15.* 这邮筒最后一次收信的时间是 5:15。◊ *Your suit will be ready for collection on Tuesday.* 你的套装可在星期二领取。◊ *The first stage in research is data collection.* 研究工作的第一步是收集资料。

➲ COMPARE PICKUP *n.* (4)

• **POEMS/STORIES/MUSIC** 诗歌；故事；音乐 **4** [C] a group of poems, stories or pieces of music published together as one book, disc, etc. 作品集：*a collection of stories by women writers* 女作家小说集

• **MONEY** 金钱 **5** [C] an act of collecting money to help a charity or during a church service; the money collected（为慈善机构或做礼拜时的）募捐，募集；募集的钱：*a house-to-house collection for Cancer Research* 为资助癌症研究挨门逐户进行的募捐 ◇ *The total collection last week amounted to £250.* 上周的募捐总额达 250 英镑。➲ WORDFINDER NOTE AT CHARITY

• **NEW CLOTHES** 新衣服 **6** [C] a range of new clothes or items for the home that are designed, made and offered for sale, often for a particular season（常为季节性推出的）系列时装（或家用品）：*Armani's stunning new autumn collection* 款式新颖靓丽的阿玛尼秋装系列 ➲ COLLOCATIONS AT FASHION

col·lect·ive /kəˈlektɪv/ *adj., noun*

■ ***adj.*** [usually before noun] **1** done or shared by all members of a group of people; involving a whole group or society 集体的；共有的；共同的：***collective leadership/decision-making/responsibility*** 集体领导 / 决策；共同责任 ◇ *collective memory* (= things that a group of people or a community know or remember, that are often passed from parents to children) 集体记忆 **2** used to refer to all members of a group 全体成员的；总体的：*The collective name for mast, boom and sails on a boat is the 'rig'.* 船的桅杆、帆桁和帆总称为"索具"。▸ **col·lect·ive·ly** *adv.*：*the collectively agreed rate* 共同商定的费率 ◇ *We have had a successful year, both collectively and individually.* 我们这一年干得不错，无论是整体还是个人都取得了成功。◇ *rain, snow and hail, collectively known as 'precipitation'* (= as a group) 总称为"降水"的雨、雪和冰雹

■ ***noun*** a group of people who own a business or a farm and run it together; the business that they run 企业集团；合作农场；集体企业：*an independent collective making films for television* 为电视制作影片的独立集体企业

col,lective 'bargaining *noun* [U] discussions between a trade/labor union and an employer about the pay and working conditions of the union members（劳资双方就工资和工作条件进行的）集体谈判 ➲ WORDFINDER NOTE AT UNION

col,lective 'farm *noun* a large farm, or a group of farms, owned by the government and run by a group of people 集体农场

col,lective 'noun *noun* (*grammar* 语法) a singular noun, such as *committee* or *team*, that refers to a group of people, animals or things and, in British English, can be used with either a singular or a plural verb. In American English it must be used with a singular verb. 集合名词（如 committee 或 team，在英式英语中既可用单数也可用复数动词；在美式英语中必须用单数动词）

col,lective un'conscious *noun* [sing.] (*psychology* 心) the part of the unconscious mind that is thought to be shared with other humans because it is passed from generation to generation 集体无意识（普遍存在于人类，成因是遗传）

col·lect·iv·ism /kəˈlektɪvɪzəm/ *noun* [U] the political system in which all farms, businesses and industries are owned by the government or by all the people 集体主义；（一切农场、工商企业都归政府或全民所有的）公有制 ▸ **col·lect·iv·ist** *adj.*

col·lect·iv·ize (*BrE also* **-ise**) /kəˈlektɪvaɪz/ *verb* [often passive] **~ sth** to join several private farms, industries, etc. together so that they are controlled by the community or by the government 使公有化，使集体化（将若干私营农场、工业企业等合并，使之归集体或政府所有）▸ **col·lect·iv·iza·tion, -isa·tion** /kə,lektɪvaɪˈzeɪʃn; *NAmE* -vəˈz-/ *noun* [U]

col·lect·or /kəˈlektə(r)/ *noun* **1** (especially in compounds 尤用于构成复合词) a person who collects things, either as a hobby or as a job 收集者；收藏家：*a stamp collector* 集邮者 ◇ ***ticket/tax/debt collectors*** 收票员；收税员；讨债人 **2** the chief officer of a district in some S Asian countries（南亚某些国家的）地方行政长官

col·lect·or·ate /kəˈlektərət/ *noun* **1** (in some S Asian countries) the area under the authority of a collector（一些南亚国家的）地方行政长官辖区，行政区 **2** the office in which a collector is based 地方行政长官办公室

col'lector's item *noun* a thing that is valued because it is very old or rare, or because it has some special interest 收藏家的珍藏；珍藏品；珍品

col·leen /ˈkɒliːn; *NAmE* kɑːˈl-/ *noun* **1** (*IrishE*) a girl or young woman 女孩；少妇 **2** (*old-fashioned* or *humorous*) a girl or young woman from Ireland 爱尔兰女孩；爱尔兰少妇

col·lege 🔑 /ˈkɒlɪdʒ; *NAmE* ˈkɑːl-/ *noun* **1** 🔑 [C, U] (often in names 常用于名称) (in Britain) a place where students go to study or to receive training after they have left school（英国）学院，职业学校，技术学校：*a college of further education* (= providing education and training for people over 16) 进修学院 ◇ *a secretarial college* 文秘职业学校 ◇ *the Royal College of Art* 皇家艺术学院 ◇ *a* ***college course/library/student*** 学院的课程 / 图书馆 / 学生 ◇ *She's at college.* 她在学院读书。➲ SEE ALSO COMMUNITY COLLEGE (1), SIXTH-FORM COLLEGE ➲ WORDFINDER NOTE AT TRAINING **2** 🔑 [C, U] (often in names 常用于名称) (in the US) a university where students can study for a degree after they have left school（美国）大学：*Carleton College* 卡尔顿大学 ◇ *a* ***college campus/student*** 大学校园 / 学生 ◇ *a private college* 私立大学 ◇ *He got interested in politics when he was* ***in college***. 他在上大学时开始对政治感兴趣。◇ *She's away* ***at college*** *in California.* 她去加利福尼亚州上大学了。◇ *He's hoping to* ***go to college*** *next year.* 他希望明年上大学。➲ COLLOCATIONS AT EDUCATION ➲ SEE ALSO COMMUNITY COLLEGE (2) **3** [C, U] (*CanE*) a place where you can study for higher or more specialist qualifications after you finish high school 高等专科学校；高等职业学院 **4** [C, U] one of the separate institutions that some British universities, such as Oxford and Cambridge, are divided into（英国大学如牛津和剑桥中独立的）学院：*King's College, Cambridge* 剑桥大学的国王学院 ◇ *a tour of Oxford colleges* 参观牛津大学的各学院 ◇ *Most students live in college.* 大多数学生住在学院里。**5** (in the US) one of the main divisions of some large universities（美国一些规模

▼ **BRITISH/AMERICAN** 英式 / 美式英语

college / university

- In both *BrE* and *NAmE* a **college** is a place where you can go to study after you leave secondary school. In Britain you can go to a **college** to study or to receive training in a particular skill. In the US you can study for your first degree at a **college**. A **university** offers more advanced degrees in addition to first degrees. 在英式英语和美式英语中，college 均指中学毕业后的学习场所。在英国，college 提供高等或专职教育。在美国，college 开设初级学位课程。university 除开设初级学位课程外还有更高学位的课程。
- In *NAmE* **college** is often used to mean a **university**, especially when talking about people who are studying for their first degree. **The** is not used when you are talking about someone studying there. 在美式英语中，college 常指大学 (university)，尤用来谈论攻读学士学位。表示上大学不用定冠词 the：*My son has gone away to college.* 我儿子上大学去了。◇ *'Where did you go to college?' 'Ohio State University.'* "你在什么地方上的大学？""俄亥俄州立大学。"
- In *BrE* you can say 英式英语可以说：*My daughter is at university.* 我女儿在上大学。In *NAmE* you cannot use **university** or **college** in this way. You use it with **a** or **the** to mean a particular university or college. 在美式英语中，university 和 college 不能这样用，表示上某所大学，应在 university 或 college 之前加 a 或 the：*I didn't want to go to a large university.* 我当时不想去大的综合性大学读书。

C

大的大学的）学院：*The history department is part of the College of Arts and Sciences.* 历史系是文理学院的一部分。**6** [C+sing./pl. v.] the teachers and/or students of a college（学院的）师生，教师，学生 **7** [C] (especially in names, in Britain and some other countries 在英国和其他一些国家尤用于名称) a SECONDARY SCHOOL, especially one where you must pay（尤指必须交费的）中学，公学：*Eton College* 伊顿公学 **8** [C] (usually in names 通常用于名称) an organized group of professional people with special interests, duties or powers 学会；协会；社团：*the Royal College of Physicians* 皇家医师协会 ◇ *the American College of Cardiology* 美国心脏病研究学会 ➲ SEE ALSO ELECTORAL COLLEGE

col·le·gi·ate /kəˈliːdʒiət/ *adj.* **1** relating to a college or its students 大学的；学院的；大学生的：*collegiate life* 大学生活 **2** (*BrE*) divided into a number of colleges 分为学院的：*a collegiate university* 设有若干学院的大学

col͵legiate ˈinstitute *noun* (in some parts of Canada) a public high school（加拿大某些地区的）公立高中

col·lide /kəˈlaɪd/ *verb* **1** [I] if two people, vehicles, etc. **collide**, they crash into each other; if a person, vehicle, etc. **collides** with another, or with sth that is not moving, they crash into it 碰撞；相撞：*The car and the van collided head-on in thick fog.* 那辆小轿车和货车在浓雾中迎面相撞。◇ **~ with sth/sb** *The car collided head-on with the van.* 那辆小轿车与货车迎面相撞。◇ *As he fell, his head collided with the table.* 他跌倒时头部撞上了桌子。➲ SYNONYMS AT CRASH **2** [I] **~ (with sb) (over sth)** (*formal*) (of people, their opinions, etc. 人、意见等) to disagree strongly 严重不一致；冲突；抵触：*They regularly collide over policy decisions.* 他们经常在政策决策上发生冲突。➲ SEE ALSO COLLISION

col·lider /kəˈlaɪdə(r)/ *noun* (*physics* 物) a machine for making two streams of PARTICLES move at high speed and crash into each other 对撞机（使两束高速运动的粒子相互冲撞）

col·lie /ˈkɒli; *NAmE* ˈkɑːli/ *noun* a dog of which there are several types. Those with long pointed noses and long thick hair are popular as pets. Smaller collies with shorter hair are often trained to help control sheep on a farm. 科利牧羊狗

col·lier /ˈkɒliə(r); *NAmE* ˈkɑːl-/ *noun* **1** (*old-fashioned, especially BrE*) = COAL MINER **2** a ship that carries coal 运煤船

col·liery /ˈkɒliəri; *NAmE* ˈkɑːl-/ *noun* (*pl.* **-ies**) a coal mine with its buildings and equipment 煤矿（包括建筑物和设备在内）

col·li·gate /ˈkɒlɪgeɪt; *NAmE* ˈkɑːl-/ *verb* [I, T] **~ (with sth) | ~ sth (with sth) 1** (*formal*) if two ideas, facts, etc. **colligate**, or **are colligated**, they are linked together by a single explanation or theory（使）发生紧密联系 **2** (*linguistics* 语言) if two words **colligate**, or **are colligated**, they occur together and are linked by grammar（使）结成类联结

col·li·sion /kəˈlɪʒn/ *noun* [C, U] **~ (with sb/sth) | ~ (between/of A and B) 1** an accident in which two vehicles or people crash into each other 碰撞（或相撞）事故：*a collision between two trains* 两列火车相撞事故 ◇ *Stewart was injured in a collision with another player.* 斯图尔特与另一选手相撞受了伤。◇ *a head-on collision* (= between two vehicles that are moving towards each other)（车辆的）迎头相撞 ◇ *a mid-air collision* (= between two aircraft while they are flying)（两架飞机的）空中相撞 ◇ *His car was* ***in collision with*** *a motorbike.* 他的车和一辆摩托车撞上了。**2** (*formal*) a strong disagreement between two people or between opposing ideas, opinions, etc.; the meeting of two things that are very different（两人之间或对立意见、看法等之间的）冲突，抵触：*a collision between two opposing points of view* 两种对立观点的冲突 ◇ *In his work we see the collision of two different traditions.* 在他的作品中我们看到两种不同传统的碰撞。

IDM **be on a colˈlision course (with sb/sth) 1** to be in a situation which is almost certain to cause a disagreement or argument 几乎发生冲突（或争端、纠纷）：*I was on a collision course with my boss over the sales figures.* 我和我的老板在销售数字问题上差点发生争执。**2** to be moving in a direction in which it is likely that you will crash into sb/sth 朝着可能会碰撞的方向移动；有可能相撞的趋势：*A giant iceberg was on a collision course with the ship.* 巨大的冰山朝着可能与船相撞的方向漂移。

col·lo·cate /ˈkɒləkeɪt; *NAmE* ˈkɑːl-/ *verb* [I] (*linguistics* 语言) **~ (with sth)** (of words 词语) to be often used together in a language 搭配；连用：*'Bitter' collocates with 'tears' but 'sour' does not.* * bitter 可与 tears 搭配，而 sour 则不可。◇ *'Bitter' and 'tears' collocate.* * bitter 和 tears 可搭配使用。 ▸ **col·lo·cate** /ˈkɒləkət; *NAmE* ˈkɑːl-/ *noun*: *'Bitter' and 'tears' are collocates.* * bitter 和 tears 可搭配使用。

col·lo·ca·tion /͵kɒləˈkeɪʃn; *NAmE* ͵kɑːl-/ *noun* (*linguistics* 语言) **1** [C] a combination of words in a language, that happens very often and more frequently than would happen by chance 词组；组合：*'Resounding success' and 'crying shame' are English collocations.* * resounding success 和 crying shame 是英语里的两个搭配词组。**2** [U] the fact of two or more words often being used together, in a way that happens more frequently than would happen by chance（词语的）搭配，连用：*Advanced students need to be aware of the importance of collocation.* 层次较高的学生需要意识到词语搭配的重要性。

col·lo·quial /kəˈləʊkwiəl; *NAmE* -ˈloʊ-/ *adj.* (of words and language 词语和语言) used in conversation but not in formal speech or writing 会话的；口语的 SYN **informal** ▸ **col·lo·qui·al·ly** /-kwiəli/ *adv.*

col·lo·qui·al·ism /kəˈləʊkwiəlɪzəm; *NAmE* -ˈloʊ-/ *noun* a word or phrase that is used in conversation but not in formal speech or writing 口语；口语体；俗语

col·lo·quium /kəˈləʊkwiəm; *NAmE* -ˈloʊ-/ *noun* (*pl.* **col·lo·quia** /kəˈləʊkwiə; *NAmE* -ˈloʊ-/) a formal academic SEMINAR or conference 学术研讨会；学术会议

col·lo·quy /ˈkɒləkwi; *NAmE* ˈkɑːl-/ *noun* (*pl.* **-ies**) (*formal*) a conversation 谈话；会谈

col·lude /kəˈluːd/ *verb* [I] (*formal, disapproving*) to work together secretly or illegally in order to trick other people 密谋；勾结；串通：**~ (with sb) (in sth/in doing sth)** *Several people had colluded in the murder.* 这起谋杀案是几个人串通策划的。◇ **~ (with sb) (to do sth)** *They colluded with terrorists to overthrow the government.* 他们与恐怖分子密谋推翻政府。

col·lu·sion /kəˈluːʒn/ *noun* [U] (*formal, disapproving*) secret agreement especially in order to do sth dishonest or to trick people 密谋；勾结；串通：*The police were corrupt and were operating* ***in collusion with*** *the drug dealers.* 警察腐败，与毒品贩子内外勾结。◇ *There was collusion between the two witnesses* (= they gave the same false evidence). 两个证人串通作伪证。 ▸ **col·lu·sive** /kəˈluːsɪv/ *adj.*

colly·wob·bles /ˈkɒliwɒblz; *NAmE* ˈkɑːliwɑː-/ *noun* [pl.] (*old-fashioned, BrE, informal*) **1** a nervous feeling of fear and worry 紧张；担心 **2** a pain in the stomach 肚子痛

colo·bus /ˈkɒləbəs; *NAmE* ˈkɑːl-/ (*also* **ˈcolobus monkey**) *noun* a small African MONKEY with a long tail, that eats leaves（非洲）疣猴

co·logne /kəˈləʊn; *NAmE* kəˈloʊn/ (*also* **eau de cologne**) *noun* [U] a type of light PERFUME 科隆香水；古龙香水

colon /ˈkəʊlən; *NAmE* ˈkoʊ-/ *noun* **1** the mark (:) used to introduce a list, a summary, an explanation, etc. or before reporting what sb has said 冒号 ➲ COMPARE SEMICOLON **2** (*anatomy* 解) the main part of the large INTESTINE (= part of the BOWELS) 结肠 ➲ VISUAL VOCAB PAGE V64

col·onel /ˈkɜːnl; *NAmE* ˈkɜːrnl/ *noun* (*abbr.* **Col.**) an officer of high rank in the army, the MARINES, or the US AIR FORCE（陆军、海军陆战队或美国空军）上校：*Colonel Jim Edge* 吉姆•埃奇上校

ˌColonel ˈBlimp *noun* = BLIMP (2)

co·lo·nial /kəˈləʊniəl; *NAmE* -ˈloʊ-/ *adj.*, *noun*

■ ***adj.*** **1** connected with or belonging to a country that controls another country 殖民的；殖民国家的：*a colonial power* 殖民强国 ◇ *Tunisia achieved independence from French colonial rule in 1956.* 突尼斯于 1956 年从法国的殖民统治下获得独立。◇ *Western colonial attitudes* 西方的殖民主义态度 ➲ SEE ALSO COLONY (1) **2** (*often* **Colonial**) typical of or connected with the US at the time when it was still a British COLONY （美国）具有英属殖民地时期特色的，英属殖民地时期的：*life in colonial times* 英属殖民地时期的美国生活

■ ***noun*** a person who lives in a COLONY and who comes from the country that controls it 生活在殖民地的宗主国居民：*British colonials in India* 生活在印度这块殖民地上的英国人

co·lo·ni·al·ism /kəˈləʊniəlɪzəm; *NAmE* -ˈloʊ-/ *noun* [U] the practice by which a powerful country controls another country or other countries 殖民主义：*European colonialism* 欧洲殖民主义 ▸ **co·lo·ni·al·ist** *adj.*, *noun*：*colonialist laws* 殖民主义的法律

co·lo·nic /kəˈlɒnɪk; *NAmE* -ˈlɑːn-/ *adj.* (*anatomy* 解) connected with the COLON (= part of the BOWELS) 结肠的：***colonic irrigation*** (= the process of washing out the COLON with water) 灌肠

col·on·ist /ˈkɒlənɪst; *NAmE* ˈkɑːl-/ *noun* a person who settles in an area that has become a COLONY 殖民地定居者

col·on·ize (*BrE also* **-ise**) /ˈkɒlənaɪz; *NAmE* ˈkɑː-/ *verb* **1 ~ sth** to take control of an area or a country that is not your own, especially using force, and send people from your own country to live there 在（某国家或地区）建立殖民地；移民于殖民地：*The area was colonized by the Vikings.* 这一地区曾为维京人的殖民地。➲ WORDFINDER NOTE AT EXPLORE **2 ~ sth** (*biology* 生) (of animals or plants 动物或植物) to live or grow in large numbers in a particular area（在某一地区）聚居，大批生长：*The slopes are colonized by flowering plants.* 坡地上长满了开花植物。◇ *Bats had colonized the ruins.* 蝙蝠聚居在这片废墟上。 ▸ **col·on·iza·tion**, **-isa·tion** /ˌkɒlənaɪˈzeɪʃn; *NAmE* ˌkɑːlənəˈz-/ *noun* [U]：*the colonization of the 'New World'* "新大陆"的殖民 ◇ *plant colonization* 植物的拓植 **col·on·izer**, **-iser** *noun*

col·on·nade /ˌkɒləˈneɪd; *NAmE* ˌkɑːl-/ *noun* a row of stone columns with equal spaces between them, usually supporting a roof 列柱；柱廊 ➲ VISUAL VOCAB PAGE V14 ▸ **col·on·naded** /ˌkɒləˈneɪdɪd; *NAmE* ˌkɑːl-/ *adj.*

col·ony /ˈkɒləni; *NAmE* ˈkɑːl-/ *noun* (*pl.* **-ies**) **1** [C] a country or an area that is governed by people from another, more powerful, country 殖民地：*former British colonies* 前英国殖民地 **2** [sing.+sing./pl. v.] a group of people who go to live permanently in a colony 殖民地定居者群体 **3** [C+sing./pl. v.] a group of people from the same place or with the same work or interests who live in a particular city or country or who live together （来自同一地方，职业或兴趣相同的）聚居人群：*the American colony in Paris* 聚居巴黎的美国侨民 ◇ *an artists' colony* 聚居的艺术家 **4** [C] (*IndE*) a small town set up by an employer or an organization for its workers（雇主或机构设立的）职工城，职工居住区 **5** [C+sing./pl. v.] (*biology* 生) a group of plants or animals that live together or grow in the same place （同地生长的植物或动物）群体，集落，群：*a colony of ants* 蚁群 ◇ *a bird colony* 鸟群

color (*especially US*) = COLOUR **HELP** You will find most words formed with **color** at the spelling **colour**. 大多数由 color 构成的词都可在拼写为 colour 的词条下找到。

col·or·ant (*especially US*) = COLOURANT

col·or·ation (*BrE also* **col·our·ation**) /ˌkʌləˈreɪʃn/ *noun* [U] (*specialist*) the natural colours and patterns on a plant or an animal （植物或动物的）自然色彩，自然花纹

col·ora·tura /ˌkɒlərəˈtʊərə; *NAmE* ˌkʌlərəˈtʊrə/ *noun* [U] (*music* 音, *from Italian*) complicated passages for a singer, for example in OPERA 花腔：*a coloratura soprano* (= one who often sings coloratura passages) 花腔女高音歌手 ➲ WORDFINDER NOTE AT OPERA

ˈcolor bar (*especially US*) = COLOUR BAR

ˈcolor-blind (*especially US*) = COLOUR-BLIND

ˈcolor code (*especially US*) = COLOUR CODE

col·ored (*especially US*) = COLOURED

color·fast (*especially US*) = COLOUR FAST

col·or·ful (*especially US*) = COLOURFUL

ˈcolor guard *noun* (*US*) a small group of people who carry official flags in a ceremony 掌旗仪仗队

col·or·ing (*especially US*) = COLOURING

col·or·ist, **col·or·istic** (*especially US*) = COLOURIST, COLOURISTIC

col·or·ize (*BrE also* **col·our·ize**) /ˈkʌləraɪz/ *verb* **~ sth** (*specialist*) to add colour to a black and white film/movie, using a computer process （借助计算机）给（黑白影片）着色

col·or·less (*especially US*) = COLOURLESS

ˈcolor line (*also* **ˈcolor bar**) (*both US*) (*BrE* **ˈcolour bar**) *noun* [usually sing.] a social system which does not allow black people the same rights as white people 肤色障碍；种族歧视；种族障碍

ˈcolor scheme (*especially US*) = COLOUR SCHEME

ˈcolor separation (*especially US*) = COLOUR SEPARATION

col·os·sal /kəˈlɒsl; *NAmE* kəˈlɑːsl/ *adj.* extremely large 巨大的；庞大的：*a colossal statue* 巨大的雕像 ◇ *The singer earns a colossal amount of money.* 那歌手现在可赚大钱了。

col·os·sus /kəˈlɒsəs; *NAmE* -ˈlɑːs-/ *noun* **1** [sing.] (*formal*) a person or thing that is extremely important or large in size 巨人；巨物 **2** [C] (*pl.* **co·lossi** /kəˈlɒsaɪ; *NAmE* -ˈlɑːs-/) an extremely large statue 巨型雕像

col·os·tomy /kəˈlɒstəmi; *NAmE* kəˈlɑːs-/ *noun* (*pl.* **-ies**) (*medical* 医) an operation in which part of a person's COLON (= the lower part of the BOWELS) is removed and an opening is made in the ABDOMEN through which the person can get rid of waste matter from the body 结肠造口术

col·os·trum /kəˈlɒstrəm; *NAmE* -ˈlɑːs-/ *noun* [U] the substance produced in the breasts of a new mother, which has a lot of ANTIBODIES which help her baby to resist disease 初乳（含丰富的抗体，有助于婴儿免疫）

col·our 🔑 (*especially US* **color**) /ˈkʌlə(r)/ *noun*, *verb*

■ ***noun***

• **RED, GREEN, ETC.** 颜色 **1** 🔑 [C, U] the appearance that things have that results from the way in which they reflect light. Red, orange and green are colours. 颜色；色彩：*What's your favourite colour?* 你最喜欢的颜色是什么？ ◇ ***bright/dark/light colours*** 鲜艳的 / 深 / 浅颜色 ◇ *available in 12 different colours* 有 12 种不同的颜色可供挑选 ◇ *the colour of the sky* 天空的颜色 ◇ *Her hair is a reddish-brown colour.* 她的头发是棕红色的。◇ *Foods which go through a factory process lose much of their colour, flavour and texture.* 经过工厂加工的食品会在色泽、味道和口感方面大受损失。◇ *The garden was a mass of colour.* 花园里五彩缤纷。 **2** 🔑 [U] (usually before another noun 通常用于另一名词前) the use of all the colours, not only black and white 彩色：*a colour TV* 彩色电视机 ◇ ***colour photography/printing*** 彩色摄影 / 印刷 ◇ *a full-colour brochure* 彩色小册子 ◇ *Do you dream* ***in colour?*** 你的梦是彩色的吗？

• **OF SKIN** 皮肤 **3** 🔑 [U, C] the colour of a person's skin, when it shows the race they belong to （人种的）肤色：*discrimination on the grounds of race, colour or religion* 以种族、肤色或宗教信仰为理由的歧视 ◇ (*especially NAmE*) ***a person/man/woman of colour*** (= who is not white)

有色人种的人 / 男子 / 女子
• **OF FACE** 面孔 **4** [U] a red or pink colour in sb's face, especially when it shows that they look healthy or that they are embarrassed（尤指脸色的）红润，粉红；（尴尬时的）脸红：*The fresh air brought colour to their cheeks.* 新鲜空气使他们的脸颊红润。◇ *Colour flooded her face when she thought of what had happened.* 她想起发生的事情，脸涨得通红。◇ *His face was drained of colour* (= he looked pale and ill). 他脸上毫无血色。
• **SUBSTANCE** 物质 **5** [C, U] a substance that is used to give colour to sth 颜料；染料：*a semi-permanent hair colour that lasts six to eight washes* 经得起洗涤六至八次的半永久性染发剂 ➲ SEE ALSO WATERCOLOUR
• **INTERESTING DETAILS** 有趣的细节 **6** [U] interesting and exciting details or qualities 趣味；乐趣：*The old town is full of colour and attractions.* 这座古城姿彩纷呈，引人入胜。◇ *Her acting added warmth and colour to the production.* 她的表演给这出戏增添了生气和趣味。◇ *to add/give/lend colour to sth* (= make it brighter, more interesting, etc.) 给某物增色 ➲ SEE ALSO LOCAL COLOUR
• **OF TEAM/COUNTRY, ETC.** 队、国家等 **7 colours** [pl.] the particular colours that are used on clothes, flags, etc. to represent a team, school, political party or country（用于服装、旗帜等代表团队、学校、政党或国家的）色彩：*Red and white are the team colours.* 红白两色是这支队的队服色。◇ *Spain's national colours* 西班牙国旗的颜色 ◇ (*figurative*) *There are people of different political colours on the committee.* 委员会由来自不同政党的成员组成。**8 colours** [pl.] (*especially BrE*) a flag, BADGE, etc. that represents a team, country, ship, etc.（代表团队、国家、船等的）旗帜，徽章：*Most buildings had a flagpole with the national colours flying.* 大多数的建筑物都有悬挂着国旗的旗杆。◇ *sailing under the French colours* 挂法国国旗航行

▼ **SYNONYMS** 同义词辨析

colour

shade • hue • tint • tinge

These words all describe the appearance of things, resulting from the way in which they reflect light. 以上各词均表示颜色、色彩。

colour/color the appearance that things have, resulting from the way in which they reflect light. Red, green and blue are colours. 指颜色、色彩（如红色、绿色、蓝色）：*What's your favourite colour?* 你最喜欢的颜色是什么？◇ *bright/dark/light colours* 鲜艳的 / 深 / 浅颜色

shade a particular form of a colour, especially when describing how light or dark it is. Sky blue is a shade of blue. 指色彩的浓淡深浅、色度（如天蓝是蓝色的一种）

hue (*literary* or *technical*) a colour or a particular shade of a colour 指颜色、色度、色调：*His face took on an unhealthy, whitish hue.* 他的脸上透出一丝病态的苍白。

tint a shade or small amount of a particular colour; a faint colour covering a surface 指色调、淡色彩、一层淡色：*leaves with red and gold autumn tints* 金秋时节略呈红黄色的树叶

tinge a small amount of a colour 指微量、少许颜色：*There was a pink tinge to the sky.* 天空略带一点淡淡的粉红色。

TINT OR TINGE? 用 tint 还是 tinge?

You can say 可以说：*a reddish tint/tinge* or 或：*a tinge of red* 略带一点淡红色 but not 但不说：~~*a tint of red*~~
Tint is often used in the plural, but **tinge** is almost always singular. * tint 常用作复数，但 tinge 几乎总是作单数。

PATTERNS
• a **warm/rich** colour/shade/hue/tint
• a **bright/vivid/vibrant/dark/deep** colour/shade/hue
• a **pale/pastel/soft/subtle/delicate** colour/shade/hue
• a **light/strong/neutral/natural** colour/shade

IDM **see the colour of sb's 'money** (*informal*) to make sure that sb has enough money to pay for sth 确定某人有支付能力 ➲ MORE AT FLYING *adj.*, LEND, NAIL *v.*, TRUE *adj.* ➲ SEE ALSO OFF COLOUR
■ *verb*
• **PUT COLOUR ON STH** 着色 **1** [I, T] to put colour on sth using paint, coloured pencils, etc.（用颜料、彩色笔等）为…着色：*The children love to draw and colour.* 儿童喜欢画画和涂颜色。◇ *a colouring book* (= with pictures that you can add colour to) 涂色画册 ◇ **~ sth** *How long have you been colouring* (= DYEING) *your hair?* 你染发有多长时间了？◇ **~ sth + adj.** *He drew a monster and coloured it green.* 他画了一个怪物，把它涂成绿色。
• **OF FACE** 面孔 **2** [I] **~ (at sth)** (of a person or their face 人或其面孔) to become red with embarrassment（因尴尬而）脸红 **SYN** **blush**：*She coloured at his remarks.* 她听到他的话脸红了。
• **AFFECT** 影响 **3** [T] **~ sth** to affect sth, especially in a negative way（尤指负面地）影响：*This incident coloured her whole life.* 这事件影响了她的一生。◇ *Don't let your judgement be coloured by personal feelings.* 不要让你的判断受到个人感情的影响。

PHR V **,colour sth↔'in** to put colour inside a particular area, shape, etc. using coloured pencils, CRAYONS, etc.（用彩色笔、蜡笔等）给…涂色，给…着色：*I'll draw a tree and you can colour it in.* 我来画一棵树，你给它涂上颜色。

col·our·ant (*especially US* **col·or·ant**) /ˈkʌlərənt/ *noun* a substance that is used to put colour in sth, especially a person's hair 着色剂；染色剂（尤指染发剂）

col·our·ation (*BrE*) = COLORATION

'colour bar (*especially US* **'color bar, color line**) *noun* [usually sing.] a social system which does not allow black people the same rights as white people 肤色障碍；种族歧视；种族障碍

'colour-blind (*especially US* **'color-blind**) *adj.* **1** unable to see the difference between some colours, especially red and green 色盲的 **2** treating people with different coloured skin in exactly the same way（对待不同肤色的人）一视同仁的，无种族歧视的 ▸ **'colour-blindness** (*especially US* **'color-blindness**) *noun* [U]

'colour code (*especially US* **'color code**) *noun* a system of marking things with different colours so that you can easily identify them 色标（法），色码（法）（用不同颜色表示识别标记）▸ **'colour-coded** (*especially US* **'color-coded**) *adj.*：*The files have labels that are colour-coded according to subject.* 这些档案按主题内容贴有色标。

col·oured 🔑 (*especially US* **col·ored**) /ˈkʌləd; *NAmE* -ərd/ *adj.*, *noun*
■ *adj.* **1** 🔑 (often in compounds 常构成复合词) having a particular colour or different colours 有…色的；色彩…的：*brightly coloured balloons* 色彩鲜艳的气球 ◇ *coloured lights* 彩灯 ◇ *She was wearing a cream-coloured suit.* 她穿着一身米色套装。**2** (*old-fashioned* or *offensive*) (of a person 人) from a race that does not have white skin 有色人种的 **3 Coloured** (in South Africa) having parents who are of different races（南非）混血种的
■ *noun* **1** (*old-fashioned* or *offensive*) a person who does not have white skin 有色人种的人 **2 Coloured** (in South Africa) a person whose parents are of different races（南非）混血种的人

'colour fast (*especially US* **'color·fast**) *adj.* cloth that is **colour fast** will not lose colour when it is washed（织物）不退色的，不变色的，不掉色的

col·our·ful (*especially US* **col·or·ful**) /ˈkʌləfl; *NAmE* -ərfl/ *adj.* **1** full of bright colours or having a lot of different colours 颜色鲜艳的；五彩缤纷的：*colourful shop windows* 五彩缤纷的商店橱窗 ◇ *The male birds are more colourful than the females.* 这种鸟雄性比雌性更加色彩艳丽。**2** interesting or exciting; full of variety, sometimes in a way that is slightly shocking 有趣的；令人激动的；丰富多彩的（有时达到了有些令人震惊的程度）：***a colourful history/past/career*** 丰富多彩的历史 / 过去 / 经历 ◇ *one of the book's most colourful characters* 这部书中最有趣的人物

之一 ▸ **col·our·ful·ly** (*especially US* **col·or·ful·ly**) *adv.*: *The street was colourfully decorated with flags and bunting.* 街道用彩旗和彩带装点得绚丽多彩。◇ *The tragic tale is told well and colourfully.* 这个悲惨的故事讲得生动而扣人心弦。

col·our·ing (*especially US* **col·or·ing**) /ˈkʌlərɪŋ/ *noun* **1** [U, C] a substance that is used to give a particular colour to food（食物的）着色剂，色素： *red **food colouring*** 红色食物着色剂 **2** [U] the colour of a person's skin, eyes and hair（皮肤、眼睛和头发的）颜色： *Blue suited her fair colouring.* 蓝色适合于她白皙的肤色。 **3** [U] the colours that exist in sth, especially a plant or an animal（尤指动植物的）天然色，色彩： *insects with vivid yellow and black colouring* 躯体带有鲜黄色和黑色的昆虫

col·our·ist (*especially US* **col·or·ist**) /ˈkʌlərɪst/ *noun* a person who uses colour, especially an artist or a hairdresser 用色彩者；（尤指）画家，着色师，染发师

col·our·istic (*also* **col·or·istic**) /ˌkʌləˈrɪstɪk/ *adj.* (*specialist*) showing or relating to a special use of colour 着色的；用色的： *colouristic effects* 着色效果

col·our·ize (*BrE*) = COLORIZE

col·our·less (*especially US* **col·or·less**) /ˈkʌlələs; *NAmE* -lərl-/ *adj.* **1** without colour or very pale 无色的；苍白的： *a colourless liquid like water* 像水一样无色的液体 ◇ *colourless lips* 苍白的嘴唇 **2** not interesting 无趣的；枯燥的 SYN **dull**： *a colourless personality* 乏味的个性

ˈ**colour scheme** (*especially US* ˈ**color scheme**) *noun* the way in which colours are arranged, especially in the furniture and decoration of a room（尤指房间家具和装饰的）色彩设计，色彩搭配

ˈ**colour separation** (*especially US* ˈ**color separation**) *noun* (*specialist*) **1** [C] one of four images of sth made using only the colours CYAN, MAGENTA, yellow or black. The four images containing these colours are then used together to print an image in full colour. 分色制版图片（用青、洋红、黄、黑制成的四张制版用单色图片之一） **2** [U] the process that is used to do this 分色制版

ˈ**colour supplement** *noun* (*BrE*) a magazine printed in colour and forming an extra part of a newspaper, particularly on Saturdays or Sundays（尤指星期六或星期日报纸的）彩色增刊

col·our·way (*especially US* **col·or·way**) /ˈkʌləweɪ; *NAmE* -lərw-/ *noun* a colour or combination of colours which a piece of clothing, etc. is available in（衣料等可供挑选的）色彩设计，颜色搭配，配色： *The designs are available in two colourways: red/grey or blue/grey.* 这些式样有两组配色：红灰色或蓝灰色。

colt /kəʊlt; *NAmE* koʊlt/ *noun* **1** a young male horse up to the age of four or five（四或五岁以下的）雄马驹 ➲ COMPARE FILLY, STALLION **2** (*BrE*) a member of a sports team consisting of young players（年轻运动队的）队员 **3 Colt™** a type of small gun 科耳特左轮手枪

colt·ish /ˈkəʊltɪʃ; *NAmE* ˈkoʊlt-/ *adj.* (of a person 人) moving with a lot of energy but in an awkward way 活跃但笨拙的

col·um·bine /ˈkɒləmbaɪn; *NAmE* ˈkɑːl-/ *noun* **1** [C, U] a garden plant with delicate leaves and pointed blue flowers that hang down 耧斗菜 **2 Col·um·bine** [sing.] a female character in traditional Italian theatre 科隆比纳（意大利传统戏剧中的女角）

Col·um·bus Day /kəˈlʌmbəs deɪ/ *noun* [U, C] a national holiday in the US on the second Monday in October when people celebrate the arrival of Christopher Columbus in America in 1492 哥伦布纪念日（美国节日，在十月第二个星期一，纪念哥伦布 1492 年到达美洲大陆）

col·umn 🔑 /ˈkɒləm; *NAmE* ˈkɑːləm/ *noun* **1** 🔑 a tall, solid, vertical post, usually round and made of stone, which supports or decorates a building or stands alone as a MONUMENT 柱；（通常为）圆形石柱；纪念柱： *The temple is supported by marble columns.* 这座庙宇由大理石柱支撑。◇ *Nelson's Column in London* 伦敦的纳尔逊纪念碑 ➲ VISUAL VOCAB PAGE V14 **2** 🔑 a thing shaped like a column 圆柱状物；柱形物： *a column of smoke* (= smoke rising straight up) 烟柱 ➲ SEE ALSO SPINAL COLUMN, STEERING COLUMN **3** 🔑 (*abbr.* **col.**) one of the vertical sections into which the printed page of a book, newspaper, etc. is divided（书、报纸等印刷页上的）栏： *a column of text* 一栏正文 ◇ *a dictionary with two columns per page* 每页有两栏正文的字典 ◇ *Put a mark in the appropriate column.* 在适当的栏里标上记号。 ◇ *Their divorce filled a lot of **column inches** in the national papers* (= got a lot of attention). 他们的离婚引起了多家全国性报纸的关注。 **4** 🔑 a part of a newspaper or magazine which appears regularly and deals with a particular subject or is written by a particular writer（报刊的）专栏，栏目： *the gossip/financial column* 漫谈 / 财经专栏 ◇ *I always read her column in the local paper.* 我一直读她在当地报纸上的专栏文章。 ➲ SEE ALSO AGONY COLUMN, PERSONAL COLUMN **5** 🔑 a series of numbers or words arranged one under the other down a page 纵行（数字或字）： *to add up a column of figures* 把纵行数字相加 **6** a long, moving line of people or vehicles（人或车辆排成行移动的）长列，纵队： *a long column of troops and tanks* 部队和坦克的长列纵队 ➲ SEE ALSO FIFTH COLUMN ➲ **MORE LIKE THIS** 20, page R27

col·um·nist /ˈkɒləmnɪst; *NAmE* ˈkɑːl-/ *noun* a journalist who writes regular articles for a newspaper or magazine 专栏作家 ➲ **WORDFINDER NOTE** AT NEWSPAPER

coma /ˈkəʊmə; *NAmE* ˈkoʊmə/ *noun* a deep unconscious state, usually lasting a long time and caused by serious illness or injury 昏迷： *to **go into/be in a coma*** 陷入 / 处于昏迷状态

Com·an·che /kəˈmæntʃi/ *noun* (*pl.* **Com·an·che** or **Com·an·ches**) a member of a Native American people, many of whom live in the US state of Oklahoma 科曼切人（美洲土著，很多居于美国俄克拉何马州）

co·ma·tose /ˈkəʊmətəʊs; *NAmE* ˈkoʊmətoʊs/ *adj.* **1** (*medical* 医) deeply unconscious; in a coma 不省人事的；昏迷的 **2** (*humorous*) extremely tired and lacking in energy; sleeping deeply 困乏的；无精打采的；酣睡的

comb /kəʊm; *NAmE* koʊm/ *noun, verb*

■***noun*** **1** [C] a flat piece of plastic or metal with a row of thin teeth along one side, used for making your hair neat; a smaller version of this worn by women in their hair to hold it in place or as a decoration 梳子；篦子；压发梳 ➲ **VISUAL VOCAB** PAGE V25 **2** [C, usually sing.] the act of using a comb on your hair 梳理（头发）： *Your hair needs a good comb.* 你的头发得好好梳理一下。 **3** [C, U] = HONEYCOMB **4** [C] the soft, red piece of flesh on the head of a male chicken（公鸡的）鸡冠 IDM ➤ SEE FINE-TOOTH COMB

■***verb*** **1** [T] ~ **sth** to pull a comb through your hair in order to make it neat 梳，梳理（头发）： *Don't forget to comb your hair!* 别忘了梳一下头发！ ◇ *Her hair was neatly combed back.* 她的头发整齐地梳到后面。 **2** [T, I] to search sth carefully in order to find sb/sth 仔细搜索；搜寻 SYN **scour**： ~ **sth** *I combed the shops looking for something to wear.* 我跑遍商店寻找可穿的东西。 ◇ ~ **sth for sb/sth** *The police combed the area for clues.* 警察彻底搜索了那个地区以寻找线索。 ◇ ~ **through sth** (**for sb/sth**) *They combed through the files for evidence of fraud.* 他们查遍档案搜寻欺诈的证据。 **3** [T] ~ **sth** (*specialist*) to make wool, cotton, etc. clean and straight using a special comb so that it can be used to make cloth 梳理（羊毛、棉花等）

PHR V ˌ**comb sth**↔ˈ**out** to pull a comb through hair in order to make it neat or to remove knots from it 梳整；梳去（发结）

com·bat /ˈkɒmbæt; *NAmE* ˈkɑːm-/ *noun, verb*

■***noun*** [U, C] fighting or a fight, especially during a time of war 搏斗；打仗；战斗： *He was killed **in combat**.* 他在战斗中阵亡。 ◇ ***armed/unarmed combat*** (= with/without weapons) 武装 / 非武装对抗 ◇ *combat troops* 作战部队 ◇ *combat boots* 军靴 ➲ SEE ALSO SINGLE COMBAT

■***verb*** (**-t-** or **-tt-**) **1** ~ **sth** to stop sth unpleasant or harmful from happening or from getting worse 防止；减轻： *measures to **combat** crime/inflation/unemployment/*

disease 防止犯罪 / 通货膨胀 / 失业 / 疾病的措施 **2** **~ sb** (*formal*) to fight against an enemy 战斗；与…搏斗

com·bat·ant /ˈkɒmbətənt; *NAmE* ˈkɑːm-/ *noun* a person or group involved in fighting in a war or battle 参战者；战斗人员；战士 ➲ COMPARE NON-COMBATANT

ˈcombat fatigue (*also* **ˈbattle fatigue**) *noun* [U] mental problems caused by being in a war for a long period of time 战斗疲劳

ˈcombat fatigues (*also* **ˈbattle fatigues**) *noun* [pl.] clothes that soldiers wear for fighting that are covered in brown and green marks to make them difficult to see （士兵穿的）战斗服，迷彩服

com·bat·ive /ˈkɒmbətɪv; *NAmE* kəmˈbætɪv/ *adj.* ready and willing to fight or argue 好战的；好斗的；好争论的：*in a* ***combative mood/spirit*** 斗志昂扬；锐气旺盛

com·bats /ˈkɒmbæts; *NAmE* ˈkɑːm-/ (*also* **ˈcombat trousers**) *noun* [pl.] (*BrE*) = CARGO PANTS

combi = KOMBI

com·bin·ation 🔑 /ˌkɒmbɪˈneɪʃn; *NAmE* ˌkɑːm-/ *noun* **1** 🔑 [C] two or more things joined or mixed together to form a single unit 结合体；联合体；混合体：*His treatment was a combination of surgery, radiation and drugs.* 对他的治疗是把手术、放射和药物结合起来。◇ *What an unusual combination of flavours!* 多么与众不同的混合风味啊！◇ *Technology and good management. That's a* ***winning combination*** (= one that will certainly be successful). 技术加良好的管理，这是取胜的组合。**2** 🔑 [U] the act of joining or mixing together two or more things to form a single unit 结合；联合；混合：*The firm is working on a new product* ***in combination with*** *several overseas partners.* 这家公司与几家海外合伙人在联合开发新产品。◇ *These paints can be used individually or* ***in combination.*** 这些涂料可单独或混合使用。**3** [C] a series of numbers or letters used to open a combination lock（用于开密码锁的）数码组合，字码组合：*I can't remember the combination.* 我不记得密码锁的密码了。**4 combinations** (*BrE*) [pl.] a piece of underwear covering the body and legs, worn in the past（旧时的）连裤内衣

combiˈnation lock *noun* a type of lock which can only be opened by using a particular series of numbers or letters 密码锁；暗码锁；转字锁

com·bine 🔑 *verb, noun*

■ *verb* /kəmˈbaɪn/ **1** 🔑 [I, T] to come together to form a single thing or group; to join two or more things or groups together to form a single one （使）结合，组合，联合，混合：*Hydrogen and oxygen combine to form water.* 氢与氧化合成水。◇ **~ with sth** *Hydrogen combines with oxygen to form water.* 氢与氧化合成水。◇ **~ to do sth** *Several factors had combined to ruin our plans.* 几种因素加在一起毁了我们的计划。◇ **~ sth** *Combine all the ingredients in a bowl.* 把所有的配料放在碗里拌匀。◇ **~ sth with sth** *Combine the eggs with a little flour.* 把鸡蛋和少量的面粉搅匀。◇ **~ A and B (together)** *Combine the eggs and the flour.* 把鸡蛋和面粉搅匀。◇ *The German team scored a* ***combined total*** *of 652 points.* 德国队综合得分为 652 分。**2** 🔑 [T] to have two or more different features or characteristics; to put two or more different things, features or qualities together 兼有；兼备；使融合（或并存）：**~ sth** *We are still looking for someone who combines all the necessary qualities.* 我们仍在寻觅兼具所有必要才能的人选。◇ **~ A and/with B** *The hotel combines comfort with convenience.* 这家旅馆既舒适又方便。◇ *This model combines a printer and scanner.* 这种型号兼备打印机和扫描仪的功能。◇ *They have successfully combined the old with the new in this room.* 他们在这个房间里成功地把古老和现代的风格融为一体。◇ *a kitchen and dining room combined* 厨房兼饭厅 **3** 🔑 [T] **~ A and/with B** to do two or more things at the same time 同时做（两件或以上的事）；兼做；兼办：*The trip will combine business with pleasure.* 此次旅行将把公干和游玩结合起来。◇ *She has successfully combined a career and bringing up a family.* 她成功地兼顾了事业和抚养子女。**4** [I, T] to come together in order to work or act together; to put two things or groups together so that they work or act together 合并；协力：*They combined against a common enemy.* 他们联手对付共同的敌人。◇ **~ sth (with sth)** *the combined effects of the two drugs* 两种药物的复合疗效 ◇ *You should try to combine exercise with a healthy diet.* 你应该试着把锻炼和健康饮食结合起来。◇ *It took the* ***combined efforts*** *of both the press and the public to bring about a change in the law.* 这项法律的变更来自媒体和公众的通力合作。**IDM** SEE FORCE *n.*

■ *noun* /ˈkɒmbaɪn; *NAmE* ˈkɑːm-/ **1** (*BrE also* **ˌcombine ˈharvester**) a large farm machine which cuts a crop and separates the grains from the rest of the plant 联合收割机 **2** a group of people or organizations acting together in business 集团；联合企业

comˈbining form *noun* (*grammar* 语法) a form of a word that can combine with another word or another combining form to make a new word, for example *techno-* and *-phobe* in *technophobe* 构词成分，组合形式（能与另一词或另一构词成分构成新词，如 technophobe 一词中的 techno- 和 -phobe）

combo /ˈkɒmbəʊ; *NAmE* ˈkɑːmboʊ/ *noun* (*pl.* **-os**) (*informal*) **1** a small band that plays JAZZ or dance music 小型爵士乐队；小型伴舞乐队 **2** (*especially NAmE*) a number of different things combined together, especially different types of food 混合物；（尤指食物的）杂烩，组合餐：*I'll have the steak and chicken combo platter.* 我要牛排和鸡组合餐。

com·bust /kəmˈbʌst/ *verb* [I, T] **~ (sth)** to start to burn; to start to burn sth 开始燃烧；开始烧

com·bust·ible /kəmˈbʌstəbl/ *adj.* able to begin burning easily 易燃的；可燃的 **SYN** **flammable**：***combustible material/gases*** 易燃材料 / 气体

com·bus·tion /kəmˈbʌstʃən/ *noun* [U] **1** the process of burning 燃烧 **2** (*specialist*) a chemical process in which substances combine with the OXYGEN in the air to produce heat and light （快速）氧化

comˈbustion chamber *noun* a space in which combustion takes place, for example in an engine （发动机等的）燃烧室

come 🔑 /kʌm/ *verb, prep., exclamation, noun*

■ *verb* (**came** /keɪm/, **come**)

• **TO A PLACE** 地方 **1** 🔑 [I] to move to or towards a person or place 来：**(+ adv./prep.)** *He came into the room and shut the door.* 他进了房间，把门关上。◇ *She comes to work by bus.* 她乘公共汽车来上班。◇ *My son is coming home soon.* 我儿子很快就要回家了。◇ *Come here!* 到这儿来！◇ *Come and see us soon!* 快点来看我们吧！◇ ***Here comes Jo!*** (= Jo is coming) 乔来啦！◇ *There's a storm coming.* 暴风雨就要来了。◇ **~ to do sth** *They're coming to stay for a week.* 他们要来待上一星期。**HELP** In spoken English **come** can be used with **and** plus another verb, instead of with **to** and the infinitive, to show purpose or to tell sb what to do. 在口语中表示目的或告诉某人如何做时，come 可与 and 加另一动词使用，而不用 to 和动词不定式：*When did she last come and see you?* 她上一次来看你是什么时候？◇ *Come and have your dinner.* 过来吃饭。The **and** is sometimes left out, especially in *NAmE*. * and 有时被省掉，尤其在美式英语中：***Come have*** *your dinner.* 过来吃饭。**2** 🔑 [I] **~ (to…)** to arrive at or reach a place 来到；到达，抵达（某地）：*They continued until they came to a river.* 他们继续往前一直来到河边。◇ *What time did you come* (= to my house)? 你什么时候到（我家）的？◇ *Spring came late this year.* 今年春天来得晚。◇ *Your breakfast is coming soon.* 你的早餐很快就到。◇ *Have any letters come for me?* 有给我的来信吗？◇ *Help came at last.* 救援终于到了。◇ *The CD comes* ***complete*** *with all the words of the songs.* 这张光盘配有歌曲的全部歌词。◇ *The time has come* (= now is the moment) *to act.* 采取行动的时机到了。**3** 🔑 [I] to arrive somewhere in order to do sth or get sth 来做；来取；来拿：**~ for sth** *I've come for my book.* 我来拿我的书。◇ **~ about sth** *I've come about my book.* 我来拿我的书。◇ **~ to do sth** *I've come to get my book.* 我来拿我的书。◇ **~ doing sth** *He came looking for me.* 他来找我。**4** 🔑 [I] to move or

C

travel, especially with sb else, to a particular place or in order to be present at an event 来（尤指相聚、往某地或出席活动）: *I've only come for an hour.* 我来了才一个小时。◇ *Thanks for coming* (= to my house, party, etc.). 谢谢光临。◇ **~ (to sth) (with sb)** *Are you coming to the club with us tonight?* 你今晚和我们一起去俱乐部吗？◇ **~ doing sth** *Why don't you come skating tonight?* 今晚来溜冰好吗？

• **RUNNING/HURRYING ETC.** 奔跑、匆忙等 **5** [I] **~ doing sth** (+ **adv.prep.**) to move in a particular way or while doing sth else （以某种方式）来；边…边来: *The children came running into the room.* 孩子们跑着进了房间。

• **TRAVEL** 行进 **6** [I] + **noun** to travel a particular distance 行进（某段距离）: *We've come 50 miles this morning.* 我们今天上午走了 50 英里。◇ (*figurative*) *The company has* **come a long way** (= made lot of progress) *in the last 5 years.* 公司在过去的 5 年里取得了巨大进步。

• **HAPPEN** 发生 **7** [I] to happen 发生: *The agreement came after several hours of negotiations.* 协议经过几小时的谈判后才达成。◇ *The rains came too late to do any good.* 雨季来得太晚，什么用也没有。◇ **~ as sth** *Her death came as a terrible shock to us.* 她的死使我们极为震惊。◇ *His resignation came as no surprise.* 他的辞职毫不令人惊讶。 **8** [T] **~ to do sth** used in questions to talk about how or why sth happened （用于疑问句，表示怎么或为什么）: *How did he come to break his leg?* 他怎么把腿弄断的？◇ *How do you come to be so late?* 你怎么这么晚？

• **TO A POSITION/STATE** 位置；状态 **9** [I] + **adv./prep.** (not used in the progressive tenses 不用于进行时) to have a particular position 位于，处于（某位置）: *That comes a long way down my list of priorities.* 在我的优先事项中，那事远没那么紧要。◇ *His family comes first* (= is the most important thing in his life). 他把家庭放在首位。◇ *She came second* (= received the second highest score) *in the exam.* 她这次考试名列第二。 **10** [I] **~ to/into sth** used in many expressions to show that sth has reached a particular state （用于许多词组）达到，进入（某种状态）: *At last winter* **came to an end**. 冬天终于结束了。◇ *He* **came to power** *in 2006.* 他于 2006 年上台执政。◇ *When will they* **come to a decision**? 他们何时会作出决定？◇ *The trees are coming into leaf.* 树开始长叶子了。 **11** [I] (not used in the progressive tenses 不用于进行时) (of goods, products, etc. 货品、产品等) to be available or to exist in a particular way 可提供；有（货）: **~ in sth** *This dress comes in black and red.* 这款连衣裙有黑、红两种颜色。◇ **+ adj.** (*informal*) *New cars don't* **come cheap** (= they are expensive). 新汽车没有便宜的。 **12** [I, T] to become 成为；变成；变得: **+ adj.** *The buttons had come undone.* 纽扣都松开了。◇ *The handle came loose.* 这把手松了。◇ *Everything will* **come right** *in the end.* 一切到最后都会好起来的。◇ **~ to do sth** *This design came to be known as the Oriental style.* 这种设计后来被称为东方风格。 **13** [T] **~ to do sth** to reach a point where you realize, understand or believe sth 达到（认识、理解或相信的程度）: *In time she came to love him.* 她终于爱上了他。◇ *She had come to see the problem in a new light.* 她开始从新的角度来看待这个问题。◇ *I've come to expect this kind of behaviour from him.* 对于他的这种举止我渐渐不感到意外了。

• **SEX** 性 **14** [I] (*informal*) to have an ORGASM 达到性高潮

IDM **HELP** Most idioms containing **come** are at the entries for the nouns or adjectives in the idioms, for example **come a cropper** is at **cropper**. 大多数含 come 的习语，都可在该等习语中的名词或形容词相关词条找到，如 come a cropper 在词条 cropper 下。 **be as ˌclever, ˌstupid, etc. as they ˈcome** (*informal*) to be very clever, stupid, etc. 非常聪明（或愚蠢等） **ˌcome aˈgain?** (*informal*) used to ask sb to repeat sth （要求重复）再说一遍，你说什么来着: *'She's an entomologist.' 'Come again?' 'An entomologist—she studies insects.'* "她是昆虫学家。" "请再说一遍？" "昆虫学家，她是研究昆虫的。" **ˌcome and ˈgo 1** to arrive and leave; to move freely 来去；来往；自由走动: *They had a party next door—we heard people coming and going all night.* 他们在隔壁聚会，我们整夜都听见人来人往的声音。 **2** to be present for a short time and then go away 时来时去；忽隐忽现: *The pain in my leg comes and goes.* 我的腿时而疼时而不疼。 **come ˈeasily, ˈnaturally, etc. to sb** (of an activity, a skill, etc. 活动、技能等) to be easy, natural, etc. for sb to do （对某人而言）轻而易举（或生来就会等）: *Acting comes naturally to her.* 她天生就会表演。 **ˌcome over (all) ˈfaint, ˈdizzy, ˈgiddy, etc.** (*old-fashioned, BrE, informal*) to suddenly feel ill/sick or faint 突然感到昏眩（或眩晕、头晕等） **come the...** (*informal*) to play the part of a particular type of person; to behave in a particular way 扮演（某类人）；以（某种方式）行事: *Don't come the innocent with me.* 别跟我扮无辜。 **come to ˈnothing | not ˈcome to anything** to be unsuccessful; to have no successful result 不成功；失败；毫无成果: *How sad that all his hard work should come to nothing.* 他的所有辛勤劳动竟全部付诸东流，太让人伤心了。◇ *Her plans didn't come to anything.* 她的计划全落空了。 **come to ˈthat | if it comes to ˈthat** (*informal, especially BrE*) used to introduce sth extra that is connected with what has just been said （引出与刚提及的事物相关的事）说起…来，既然如此，假如那样的话: *I don't really trust him—nor his wife, come to that.* 我不太信任他。说起信任，我也不信任他的妻子。 **ˌcome what ˈmay** despite any problems or difficulties you may have 不管出现什么问题；无论有什么困难；不管怎样: *He promised to support her come what may.* 他答应不管出现什么问题都支持她。 **how come (...)?** (*informal*) used to say you do not understand how sth can happen and would like an explanation （用以表示不理解情况是如何发生的，希望得到解释）怎么回事，怎么发生的，怎样解释: *'I think you owe me some money.' 'How come?'* "你好像欠我钱。" "怎么会呢？" ◇ *If she spent five years in Paris, how come her French is so bad?* 既然她在巴黎待了五年，她的法语怎么还会这样糟糕？ **not ˈcome to much** to not be important or successful 不重要；无关紧要；不成功 **to ˈcome** (used after a noun 用于名词后) in the future 将来；未来的: *They may well regret the decision* **in years to come**. 他们过几年之后很可能会为这个决定而后悔。◇ *This will be a problem* **for some time to come** (= for a period of time in the future). 这将是未来一段时期里的一个问题。 **when it comes to sth/to doing sth** when it is a question of sth 当涉及某事（或做某事）时: *When it comes to getting things done, he's useless.* 一涉及做事，他便不中用了。 **where sb is ˈcoming from** (*informal*) somebody's ideas, beliefs, personality, etc. that makes them say what they have said （决定某人言论的）某人的全部背景: *I see where you're coming from* (= I understand what you mean). 我明白你究竟是什么意思。

PHR V **ˌcome aˈbout (that...)** to happen 发生: *Can you tell me how the accident came about?* 你能告诉我事故是怎样发生的吗？

ˌcome aˈcross (*also* **ˌcome ˈover**) **1** to be understood 被理解；被弄懂: *He spoke for a long time but his meaning didn't really come across.* 他讲了很久，但并没有人真正理解他的意思。 **2** to make a particular impression 给人以…印象；使产生…印象: *She comes across well in interviews.* 她在面试中常给人留下很好的印象。◇ *He came over as a sympathetic person.* 他给人的印象是一个富有同情心的人。 **ˈcome across sb/sth** [no passive] to meet or find sb/sth by chance （偶然）遇见，碰见，发现: *I came across children sleeping under bridges.* 我偶然发现睡在桥下的孩子。◇ *She came across some old photographs in a drawer.* 她在抽屉里偶然发现了一些旧照片。 **ˌcome aˈcross (with sth)** [no passive] to provide or supply sth when you need it （需要时）提供，供给，给予: *I hoped she'd come across with some more information.* 我希望她能再提供更多的信息。

ˌcome ˈafter sb [no passive] to chase or follow sb 追赶；追逐；追随

ˌcome aˈlong 1 to arrive; to appear 到达；抵达；出现: *When the right opportunity comes along, she'll take it.* 适当的机会来临时，她会抓住的。 **2** to go somewhere with sb 跟随；跟着来: *I'm glad you came along.* 有你跟我一起来，我很高兴。 **3** (*informal*) to improve or develop in the way that you want 进步；进展 **SYN** **progress**: *Your French has come along a lot recently.* 你的法语最近进步很大。 **4** used in orders to tell sb to hurry, or to try harder （用于命令）赶快，加把劲: *Come along! We're late.* 快点！我们迟到了。◇ *Come along! It's easy!* 再加把劲！这很

C

容易！

ˌcome aˈpart to break into pieces 破碎；破裂：*The book just came apart in my hands.* 这本书就在我手中散开了。◇ (*figurative*) *My whole life had **come apart at the seams**.* 我的整个生活都崩溃了。

ˌcome aˈround/ˈround 1 (*also* ˌcome ˈto) to become conscious again 恢复知觉；苏醒：*Your mother hasn't yet come round from the anaesthetic.* 你的母亲麻醉后还没有苏醒过来。 2 (of a date or a regular event 日期或有规律的事) to happen again 再度发生；再次出现：*My birthday seems to come around quicker every year.* 我的生日似乎一年比一年来得快。 ˌcome aˈround/ˈround (to…) to come to a place, especially sb's house, to visit for a short time 短暂访问（尤指某人的家）：*Do come around and see us some time.* 务必抽空来看看我们。 ˌcome aˈround/ˈround (to sth) to change your mood or your opinion 改变心态；改变观点：*He'll never come round to our way of thinking.* 他绝不会改变观点与我们的思路一致。

ˈcome at sb [no passive] to move towards sb as though you are going to attack them 扑向（某人）：*She came at me with a knife.* 她拿着刀子向我扑过来。◇ (*figurative*) *The noise came at us from all sides.* 噪音从四面八方向我们袭来。 ˈcome at sth to think about a problem, question, etc. in a particular way （用某方法）考虑，思考 SYN approach：*We're getting nowhere—let's come at it from another angle.* 我们这样会毫无进展，还是换个角度考虑一下吧。

ˌcome aˈway (from sth) to become separated from sth 分离；脱离：*The plaster had started to come away from the wall.* 灰泥已开始从墙上剥落。 ˌcome aˈway with sth [no passive] to leave a place with a particular feeling or impression （带着某种感觉或印象）离开：*We came away with the impression that all was not well with their marriage.* 我们离开时有一种印象：他们的婚姻并不十分美满。

ˌcome ˈback 1 to return 回来；返回：*You came back* (= came home) *very late last night.* 你昨晚回来得很晚。◇ *The colour was coming back to her cheeks.* 她的双颊又泛起了红晕。◇ (*figurative*) *United came back from being two goals down to win 3–2.* 联队在先失两球的情况下将比分扳回，最终以 3:2 取胜。 ➲ SYNONYMS AT RETURN 2 to become popular or successful again 再度流行；再次成功：*Long hair for men seems to be coming back in.* 男子留长发好像又在流行了。 ➲ RELATED NOUN COMEBACK (2)

ˌcome ˈback (at sb) (with sth) to reply to sb angrily or with force 强有力地（或愤怒地）答复；反驳：*She came back at the speaker with some sharp questions.* 她用一些尖锐的提问来反驳讲话人。 ➲ RELATED NOUN COMEBACK (3)

ˌcome ˈback (to sb) to return to sb's memory 恢复记忆；回想起：*It's all coming back to me now.* 现在我全都回想起来了。◇ *Once you've been in France a few days, your French will soon come back.* 只要在法国待上几天，你的法语就会很快恢复起来。 ˌcome ˈback to sth [no passive] to return to a subject, an idea, etc. 回到（主题、想法等）上来：*Let's come back to the point at issue.* 咱们还是回到问题的焦点吧。◇ *It all comes back to a question of money.* 一切又回到钱的问题上来了。

ˈcome before sb/sth [no passive] (*formal*) to be presented to sb/sth for discussion or a decision 被提交给…讨论（或作决定）：*The case comes before the court next week.* 这案件在下周庭审。

ˌcome beˈtween sb and sb [no passive] to damage a relationship between two people 损害…之间的关系；离间：*I'd hate anything to come between us.* 我不喜欢任何有损我们之间关系的事情。

ˌcome ˈby (sth) (*NAmE*) to make a short visit to a place, in order to see sb （为看望某人）作短暂拜访：*She came by the house.* 她来家里看了一下。 ˈcome by sth 1 to manage to get sth 设法得到（或获得）：*Jobs are hard to come by these days.* 如今找工作很难。 2 to receive sth 收到；得到：*How did you come by that scratch on your cheek?* 你脸颊上的抓伤是怎么来的？

ˌcome ˈdown 1 to break and fall to the ground 崩塌；坍塌：*The ceiling came down with a terrific crash.* 随着一声可怕的巨响，天花板塌了下来。 2 (of rain, snow, etc. 雨、雪等) to fall 落下；降落：*The rain came down in torrents.* 大雨滂沱。 3 (of an aircraft 飞机) to land or fall from the sky 着陆；降落；从空中坠落：*We were forced to come down in a field.* 我们被迫降落在田野里。 4 if a price, a temperature, a rate, etc. **comes down**, it gets lower （价格、温度、比率等）下降，降低：*The price of gas is coming down.* 煤气价格在下跌。◇ *Gas is coming down in price.* 煤气价格在下跌。 5 to decide and say publicly that you support or oppose sb 决定并宣布（支持或反对）：*The committee came down in support of his application.* 委员会决定并宣布支持他的申请。 6 to reach as far down as a particular point 下垂，向下延伸（到某一点）：*Her hair comes down to her waist.* 她的头发垂至腰部。 ˌcome ˈdown (from…) (*BrE, formal*) to leave a university, especially Oxford or Cambridge, at the end of a term or after finishing your studies （尤指在牛津或剑桥期末或学业结束后）离开大学，大学毕业 OPP come up (to…) ˌcome ˈdown (from…) (to…) to come from one place to another, usually from the north of a country to the south, or from a larger place to a smaller one 从…到…（通常指从一国的北部到南部，或从大地方到小地方） ˌcome ˈdown on sb [no passive] (*informal*) to criticize sb severely or punish sb 斥责；训斥；惩罚：*Don't come down too hard on her.* 不要太严厉地责备她。◇ *The courts are coming down heavily on young offenders.* 法庭对年轻罪犯实行严惩。 ˌcome ˈdown (to sb) to have come from a long time in the past （从很久以前）流传下来：*The name has come down from the last century.* 这名称是从上个世纪流传下来的。 ˌcome ˈdown to sth [no passive] to be able to be explained by a single important point 可归结为；可归纳为：*What **it comes down to** is either I get more money or I leave.* 归结起来就是：不给我加薪，我就辞职。 ˌcome ˈdown with sth [no passive] to get an illness that is not very serious 患，得，染上（小病）：*I think I'm coming down with flu.* 我想我得了流感。

ˌcome ˈforward to offer your help, services, etc. 主动提供（帮助或服务等）：*Several people came forward with information.* 有几个人自动站出来提供了信息。◇ *Police have asked witnesses of the accident to come forward.* 警方呼吁事故的目击者出来提供线索。

ˈcome from… (not used in the progressive tenses 不用于进行时) to have as your place of birth or the place where you live 出生于；来自：*She comes from London.* 她是伦敦人。◇ *Where do you come from?* 你是什么地方的人？ ˈcome from sth 1 to start in a particular place or be produced from a particular thing 始于；产自；来自：*Much of our butter comes from New Zealand.* 我们的黄油大多产自新西兰。◇ *This wool comes from goats, not sheep.* 这种羊毛是山羊毛，不是绵羊毛。◇ *This poem comes from his new book.* 这首诗出自他的新书。◇ *Where does her attitude come from?* 她的态度因何而起？◇ *Where's that smell coming from?* 那种气味是哪里来的？◇ *He comes from a family of actors.* 他出身于演员世家。◇ *'She doesn't try hard enough.' 'That's rich, **coming from you*** (= you do not try hard either).' "她没有竭尽全力。" "你自己也没尽力，还说别人。" 2 = COME OF/FROM STH

ˌcome ˈin 1 when the TIDE **comes in**, it moves towards the land （潮水）上涨；涨潮 OPP go out 2 to finish a race in a particular position （赛跑比赛中）取得（某名次）：*My horse came in last.* 我的马跑了最后一名。 3 to become fashionable 变时髦；时兴；流行：*Long hair for men came in in the sixties.* 男子留长发在 60 年代流行开来。 OPP go out 4 to become available 可提供；可利用：*We're still waiting for copies of the book to come in.* 我们仍然在等这本书进货。 5 to have a part in sth 在…中起作用；参与：*I understand the plan perfectly, but I can't see where I come in.* 我完全了解这项计划，可是不明白我能起什么作用。 6 to arrive somewhere; to be received 到达；被收到：*The train is coming in now.* 火车现正进站。◇ *News is coming in of a serious plane crash in France.* 刚收到的消息说法国发生了一起严重的飞机坠毁事故。◇ *She has over a thousand pounds a month coming in from her investments.* 她每月从自己的投资中得到超过一千英镑的收入。 7 to take part in a discussion 参加讨论：*Would you like to come in at this point, Susan?* 苏珊，你愿意在此刻发表意见吗？ 8 (of a law or rule 法律或规则) to be introduced; to begin to be used 被推行；开始被采用 ˌcome ˈin for sth [no passive] to receive sth, especially sth unpleasant 遭到；受到：*The government's economic policies have come in for a lot of criticism.* 政府的经济政策遭到了很多批评。 **ˌcome ˈin (on sth)** to become involved in sth 卷入；陷入：*If you want to come in on the deal, you need to decide now.* 如果你要做这笔交易，你得现在作出决定。

ˌcome ˈinto sth [no passive] **1** to be left money by sb who has died 继承，得到（遗产）：*She came into a fortune when her uncle died.* 她在叔叔去世后继承了一大笔财产。 **2** to be important in a particular situation （在某种情形下）是重要的：*I've worked very hard to pass this exam—luck doesn't come into it.* 我为通过这次考试下了很大的苦功，运气不是主要的。

ˈcome of/from sth to be the result of sth 是…的结果：*I made a few enquiries, but nothing **came of it** in the end.* 我做过一些查询，但到头来却毫无结果。 ◇ **come of/from doing sth** *That comes of eating too much!* 那是吃得太多的结果！

ˌcome ˈoff 1 🔑 to be able to be removed 能被去掉（或除去）：*Does this hood come off?* 这风帽能卸下来吗？ ◇ *That mark won't come off.* 那污点去不掉。 **2** (*informal*) to take place; to happen 举行；发生：*Did the trip to Rome ever come off?* 去罗马的事最后成了吗？ **3** (*informal*) (of a plan, etc. 计划等) to be successful; to have the intended effect or result 成功；达到预期效果（或结果）：*They had wanted it to be a surprise but the plan didn't come off.* 他们本想一鸣惊人，然而计划却流产了。 **4 come off well, badly, etc.** (*informal*) to be successful/not successful in a fight, contest, etc. （搏斗、比赛等）成功，不成功：*I thought they came off very well in the debate.* 我认为他们在辩论中表现非常出色。 **ˌcome ˈoff (sth) 1** to fall from sth 从…掉下（或落下）：*to come off your bicycle/horse* 从自行车 / 马上跌下 **2** 🔑 to become separated from sth 与…分离（或分开）：*When I tried to lift the jug, the handle came off in my hand.* 我刚想提起水壶，壶把子就掉在我的手中了。◇ *A button had come off my coat.* 我的外套掉了一颗纽扣。 **ˌcome ˈoff it** (*informal*) used to disagree with sb rudely （粗鲁地表示不同意）别胡扯，别胡说，住口：*Come off it! We don't have a chance.* 别胡扯了！我们没机会。 **ˌcome ˈoff sth** [no passive] to stop taking medicine, a drug, alcohol, etc. 停止（服药、吸毒、饮酒等）：*I've tried to get him to come off the tranquillizers.* 我试图说服他停止服用镇静剂。

ˌcome ˈon 1 (of an actor 演员) to walk onto the stage 登台；出场；上场 **2** (of a player 运动员) to join a team during a game （比赛中）上场：*Owen came on for Brown ten minutes before the end of the game.* 终场前十分钟，欧文上场替换了布朗。 **3** 🔑 (*informal*) to improve or develop in the way you want 改进；改善；发展；完善：*The project is coming on fine.* 这项工程进展顺利。 **4** 🔑 used in orders to tell sb to hurry or to try harder （用于命令）赶快，加把劲：*Come on! We don't have much time.* 快点！我们时间不多了。◇ *Come on! Try once more.* 加把劲！再试一次。 **5** 🔑 used to show that you know what sb has said is not correct （表示知道某人所说的话不正确）得了吧：*Oh, come on—you know that isn't true!* 咳，得了吧，你知道那不是真的！ **6** (usually used in the progressive tenses 通常用于进行时) (of an illness or a mood 疾病或心情) to begin 开始：*I can feel a cold coming on.* 我觉得要感冒了。◇ *I think there's rain coming on.* 我看要下雨了。◇ **come on to do sth** *It came on to rain.* 天下起雨来了。 **7** (of a TV programme, etc. 电视节目等) to start 开始：*What time does the news come on?* 新闻报道什么时候开始？ **8** 🔑 to begin to operate 开始运转（或运行）：*Set the oven to come on at six.* 把烤箱设定在六点钟开始烘烤。◇ *When does the heating come on?* 什么时间来暖气？ **ˈcome on/upon sb/sth** [no passive] (*formal*) to meet or find sb/sth by chance 偶然遇见；偶然发现 **ˌcome ˈon to sb** (*informal*) to behave in a way that shows sb that you want to have a sexual relationship with them 勾引，勾搭（想与其发生性关系） ➲ RELATED NOUN COME-ON

ˌcome ˈon to sth [no passive] to start talking about a subject 开始讨论（某一主题）：*I'd like to come on to that question later.* 我想稍后再讨论那个问题。

ˌcome ˈout 1 🔑 when the sun, moon or stars **come out**, they appear （太阳、月亮或星星）出现，露出：*The rain stopped and the sun came out.* 雨停后太阳出来了。 **2** (of flowers 花朵) to open 盛开；开花：*The daffodils came out early this year.* 水仙花今年开得早。 **3** 🔑 to be produced or published 出版；发行；发表：*When is her new novel coming out?* 她的新小说何时出版？ **4** 🔑 (of news, the truth, etc. 消息、真相等) to become known 被获知；为人所知：*The full story came out at the trial.* 案情始末在审判时真相大白。◇ **it comes out that…** *It came out that he'd been telling lies.* 后来才知道他一直在说谎。 **5** if a photograph **comes out**, it is a clear picture when it is developed and printed （照片）冲洗（或洗印）清楚：*Some of the photos from our trip didn't come out.* 我们旅行的一些照片冲洗的效果不好。 **6** to be shown clearly 显示；显出：*Her best qualities come out in a crisis.* 她的优秀品质在危难之际显示了出来。 **7** when words **come out**, they are spoken 说出；讲出：*I tried to say 'I love you,' but the words wouldn't come out.* 我想说"我爱你"，但这话怎么也说不出口。 **8** to say publicly whether you agree or disagree with sth 公开表明（同意或不同意）：*He came out against the plan.* 他公开表示反对这个计划。◇ *In her speech, the senator came out in favour of a change in the law.* 这位参议员在她的讲话中公开赞成修改法律。 **9** (*BrE*) to stop work and go on strike 罢工 **10** to no longer hide the fact that you are HOMOSEXUAL 不再隐瞒自己是同性恋者的事实；公开表明自己是同性恋者；"出柜" **11** (of a young UPPER-CLASS girl, especially in the past 尤指旧时上层社会的少女) to be formally introduced into society （经正式介绍）初入社交界 **ˌcome ˈout (of sth)** 🔑 **1** (of an object 物体) to be removed from a place where it is fixed （从固定处）除掉，去掉：*This nail won't come out.* 这颗钉子拔不出来。 **2** 🔑 (of dirt, a mark, etc. 污垢、污迹等) to be removed from sth by washing or cleaning 洗掉；清除：*These ink stains won't come out of my dress.* 我衣服上的这些墨水斑点洗不掉。◇ *Will the colour come out* (= become faint or disappear) *if I wash it?* 我若用水洗，它会掉色吗？ **ˌcome ˈout at sth** [no passive] to add up to a particular cost or sum 总共；共计：*The total bill comes out at £500.* 账单金额总计为 500 英镑。 **ˌcome ˈout in sth** [no passive] (of a person 人) to become covered in spots, etc. on the skin （皮肤上）布满（斑点等）：*Hot weather makes her come out in a rash.* 炎热的天气使她起了皮疹。 **ˌcome ˈout of yourself** to relax and become more confident and friendly with other people 精神放松、更加自信和友好地与他人交往：*It was when she started drama classes that she really came out of herself.* 她是在开始学习戏剧课程时才真正不再害羞。 **ˌcome ˈout of sth** [no passive] to develop from sth 由…产生（或形成）：*The book came out of his experiences in India.* 这本书取材于他在印度的经历。◇ *Rock music came out of the blues.* 摇滚乐起源于布鲁斯音乐。 **ˌcome ˈout with sth** [no passive] to say sth, especially sth surprising or rude 说出（尤指令人吃惊或粗鲁的话）：*He came out with a stream of abuse.* 他讲了一连串的脏话。◇ *She sometimes comes out with the most extraordinary remarks.* 她有时说起话来语惊四座。

ˌcome ˈover 1 (*BrE, informal*) to suddenly feel sth 突然感到：**+ adj.** *to come over funny/dizzy/faint* 突然感到可笑 / 眩晕 / 昏眩 ◇ *I come over all shy whenever I see her.* 我每次看到她时都会突然感到很害羞。 **2** = COME ACROSS：*He came over well in the interview.* 他在面试中给人留下了很好的印象。 **ˌcome ˈover (to…)** to come to a place, especially sb's house, to visit for a short time （尤指到某人家中）短暂造访 **ˌcome ˈover (to…) (from…)** to travel from one place to another, usually over a long distance （通常远距离地）从…到，从…来：*Why don't you come over to England in the summer?* 你为何不在夏天来英格兰呢？ ◇ *Her grandparents came over from Ireland during the famine.* 她的祖父母是在饥荒时期从爱尔兰迁移过来的。

ˌcome ˈover (to sth) to change from one side, opinion, etc. to another 改变立场（或看法等） **ˌcome ˈover sb** [no passive] to affect sb 影响某人：*A fit of dizziness came over her.* 她感到一阵头晕目眩。◇ ***I can't think what came over me*** (= I do not know what caused me to behave in that way). 我不知道我是怎么了。

ˌcome ˈround | **ˌcome ˈround (to sth)** (*BrE*) = COME AROUND/ROUND

ˌcome ˈthrough (of news or a message 消息或信息) to

arrive by telephone, radio, etc. or through an official organization （用电话、无线电等或由官方机构）传来： *A message is just coming through.* 刚有消息传来。 ˌ**come ˈthrough (sth)** to get better after a serious illness or to avoid serious injury （重病后）康复；避免受严重伤害 SYN **survive**: *With such a weak heart she was lucky to come through the operation.* 她的心脏很弱，手术后能活下来真是幸运。 ˌ**come ˈthrough (with sth)** to successfully do or complete sth that you have promised to do （成功地）履行诺言，实现诺言： *We were worried she wouldn't be able to handle it, but she came through in the end.* 我们担心她没有能力处理那件事，然而她最终说到做到了。 ◇ *The bank finally came through with the money.* 这家银行终于兑现了那笔钱。

ˌ**come ˈto** = COME AROUND/ROUND ˌ**come to your'self** (*old-fashioned*) to return to your normal state 恢复常态 ˈ**come to sb** [no passive] (of an idea 主意) to enter your mind 被想出： *The idea came to me in the bath.* 我泡澡时想出了这个主意。 ◇ **come to sb that…** *It suddenly came to her that she had been wrong all along.* 她突然意识到她一开始就错了。 ˈ**come to sth** [no passive] **1** to add up to sth 合计；共计；总共： *The bill came to $30.* 账单金额总计为 30 美元。 ◇ *I never expected those few items to come to so much.* 我根本没想到就那么几件东西合计起来竟要花这么多钱。 **2** to reach a particular situation, especially a bad one 达到（某状况，尤指坏的局面）： *The doctors will operate if necessary—but it may not come to that.* 必要时医生会施行手术，但也许还不至于此。 ◇ *Who'd have thought things would come to this* (= become so bad)? 谁会想到事情竟会变成这个样子？

ˌ**come toˈgether** if two or more different people or things **come together**, they form a united group 合成一体；结合；联合： *Three colleges have come together to create a new university.* 三所学院合并成了一所新的大学。 ◇ *Bits and pieces of things he'd read and heard were coming together, and he began to understand.* 他把读到和听到的零碎片段综合起来，便逐渐明白了。

ˈ**come under sth** [no passive] **1** to be included in a particular group 归入；归类： *What heading does this come under?* 这该归入哪一个主题？ **2** to be a person that others are attacking or criticizing 成为（攻击或批评的）目标： *The head teacher came under a lot of criticism from the parents.* 校长受到了家长的很多批评。 **3** to be controlled or influenced by sth 被…控制；受…影响： *All her students came under her spell.* 她所有的学生都被她迷住了。

ˌ**come ˈup 1** (of plants 植物) to appear above the soil 长出地面；破土而出： *The daffodils are just beginning to come up.* 那些水仙花刚开始破土发芽。 **2** (of the sun 太阳) to rise 升起： *We watched the sun come up.* 我们观看了日出。 **3** to happen 发生： *I'm afraid something urgent has come up.* 恐怕有紧急事情发生。 ◇ *We'll let you know if any vacancies come up.* 一有空缺，我们就会通知你。 **4** to be mentioned or discussed 被提及；被讨论： *The subject came up in conversation.* 谈话中提到了这个话题。 ◇ *The question is bound to come up at the meeting.* 会上一定会讨论这个问题。 **5** (of an event or a time 事情或时间) to be going to happen very soon 即将发生（或出现、到来）： *Her birthday is coming up soon.* 她的生日就快到了。 **6** to be dealt with by a court （由法院）审理： *Her divorce case comes up next month.* 她的离婚案在下月审理。 **7** if your number, name, ticket, etc. **comes up** in a betting game, it is chosen and you win sth （在博彩游戏中指号码、名字、奖券等）被抽中，中奖 **8** (*informal*) (usually used in the progressive tenses 通常用于进行时) to arrive; to be ready soon 来到；马上备妥： *'Is lunch ready?' 'Coming up!'* "午餐准备好了吗？" "马上就好！" ˌ**come ˈup (to…)** (*BrE, formal*) to arrive at a university, especially Oxford or Cambridge, at the beginning of a term or in order to begin your studies （尤指在牛津或剑桥学期开学时）到校上学 OPP **come down (from…)** ˌ**come ˈup (to…) (from…)** to come from one place to another, especially from the south of a country to the north or from a smaller place to a larger one （从…）上到…（通常指从一国的南部到北部，或从小地方到大地方）： *Why don't you come up to Scotland for a few days?* 你为何不上苏格兰来住几天？ ˌ**come ˈup (to sb)** to move towards sb, in order to talk to them （为攀谈而）走到跟前，走近： *He came up to me and asked me the way to the station.* 他走到我跟前打听去车站的路。 ˌ**come ˈup against sb/sth** [no passive] to be faced with or opposed by sb/sth 面对；遭到…的反对： *We expect to come up against a lot of opposition to the plan.* 我们预料这个计划会遭到很多人的反对。 ˌ**come ˈup for sth** [no passive] **1** to be considered for a job, an important position, etc. 被考虑为…的候选人： *She comes up for re-election next year.* 她明年将再度参加竞选。 **2** to be reaching the time when sth must be done 接近（期限）： *His contract is coming up for renewal.* 他的合同快到续订期了。 ˌ**come ˈup to sth** [no passive] **1** to reach as far as a particular point 达到（某点）： *The water came up to my neck.* 水淹到了我的脖子。 **2** to reach an acceptable level or standard 达到（认可的水平或标准）： *His performance didn't really come up to his usual high standard.* 他的表现没有真正达到他往常的高水平。 ◇ *Their trip to France didn't come up to expectations.* 他们的法国之行未尽如人意。 ˌ**come ˈup with sth** [no passive] to find or produce an answer, a sum of money, etc. 找到（答案）；拿出（一笔钱等）： *She came up with a new idea for increasing sales.* 她想出了增加销售量的新主意。 ◇ *How soon can you come up with the money?* 你什么时候能拿出这笔钱？

ˈ**come upon sb/sth** = COME ON/UPON SB/STH

■ ***prep.*** (*old-fashioned, informal*) when the time mentioned comes （提及的时间）到来： *They would have been married forty years come this June.* 到今年六月他们结婚就有四十年了。

■ ***exclamation*** (*old-fashioned*) used when encouraging sb to be sensible or reasonable, or when showing slight disapproval （鼓励某人要有理智或通情达理，或表示不太赞同）嗨，得啦，好啦： *Oh come now, things aren't as bad as all that.* 哦，好啦，情况并不是那么糟。 ◇ *Come, come, Miss Jones, you know perfectly well what I mean.* 得啦，得啦，琼斯小姐，你完全知道我的意思。

■ ***noun*** [U] (*slang*) SEMEN 精液；精子

come·back /ˈkʌmbæk/ *noun* **1** [usually sing.] if a person in public life makes a **comeback**, they start doing sth again which they had stopped doing, or they become popular again 复出；重返；再度受欢迎： *an ageing pop star trying to stage a comeback* 试图重返歌坛的已经上了年纪的流行音乐歌星 **2** if a thing makes a **comeback**, it becomes popular and fashionable or successful again 再度流行并变得时髦；再度获得成功 **3** (*informal*) a quick reply to a critical remark （对批评迅速作出的）反驳，回应 SYN **retort 4** a way of holding sb responsible for sth wrong which has been done to you 可因自身受到伤害而追究某人的责任： *You agreed to the contract, so now you have no comeback.* 你同意了这份合同，所以现在你不能追究他人的责任了。

com·edian /kəˈmiːdiən/ *noun* an entertainer who makes people laugh by telling jokes or funny stories （讲笑话或趣事的）滑稽演员

com·edi·enne /kəˌmiːdiˈen/ *noun* (*old-fashioned*) a female entertainer who makes people laugh by telling jokes or funny stories 女滑稽演员；女喜剧演员

come·down /ˈkʌmdaʊn/ *noun* [usually sing.] (*informal*) a situation in which a person is not as important as before, or does not get as much respect from other people 失势；落泊；潦倒

com·edy /ˈkɒmədi; *NAmE* ˈkɑːm-/ *noun* (*pl.* **-ies**) **1** [C, U] a play or film/movie that is intended to be funny, usually with a happy ending; plays and films/movies of this type 喜剧；喜剧片： *a romantic comedy* 浪漫喜剧： *slapstick comedy* 打闹剧 ⇨ COMPARE TRAGEDY ⇨ SEE ALSO BLACK *adj.* (9), SITUATION COMEDY

WORDFINDER 联想词： caricature, funny, joke, parody, pun, sketch, slapstick, spoof, take-off

2 [U] an amusing aspect of sth 滑稽；幽默；诙谐 SYN **humour**: *He didn't appreciate the comedy of the situation.* 他未领略到这种局面的滑稽可笑之处。

ˌ**comedy of ˈmanners** *noun* an amusing play, film/movie, or book that shows the silly behaviour of a particular group of people 风俗喜剧，风尚喜剧（讽刺某群体行为的戏剧、电影或书籍）

ˌ**come-ˈhither** *adj.* [only before noun] (of sb's expression 表情) appearing to be trying to attract sb sexually 勾引的；调情的： *a come-hither look* 挑逗的眼神

come·ly /ˈkʌmli/ *adj.* (*literary*) (especially of a woman 尤指女子) pleasant to look at 标致的；秀丽的 SYN **attractive**

ˈ**come-on** *noun* [usually sing.] (*informal*) an object or action which is intended to attract sb or to persuade them to do sth 引诱；诱惑；劝诱： *She was definitely giving him the come-on* (= trying to attract him sexually). 她肯定是在勾引他。

comer /ˈkʌmə(r)/ *noun* **1 all comers** [pl.] anyone who is interested in, or comes forward for, sth, especially a competition（尤指对比赛）感兴趣的人，到场者，参加者： *The event is open to all comers.* 所有人均可参加这项比赛。 **2** (with adjectives 与形容词连用) a person who arrives somewhere 到达者 ➲ SEE ALSO LATECOMER, NEWCOMER **3** (*NAmE, informal*) a person who is likely to be successful 可能成功者

com·est·ible /kəˈmestɪbl/ *adj., noun* (*formal*)
■ ***adj.*** that can be eaten 可食用的 SYN **edible**
■ ***noun*** [usually pl.] an item of food 食物

comet /ˈkɒmɪt; *NAmE* ˈkɑːmət/ *noun* a mass of ice and dust that moves around the sun and looks like a bright star with a tail 彗星；扫帚星 ➲ WORDFINDER NOTE AT UNIVERSE

come·up·pance /kʌmˈʌpəns/ *noun* [sing.] (*informal*) a punishment for sth bad that you have done, that other people feel you really deserve 报应；应得的惩罚： *I was glad to see that the bad guy **got his comeuppance** at the end of the movie.* 我很高兴看到那个坏蛋在电影的结尾受到了应有的惩罚。

com·fit /ˈkʌmfɪt/ *noun* (*old-fashioned*) a sweet/candy consisting of a nut, seed or fruit covered with sugar 果仁糖果；蜜饯

com·fort 🔑 /ˈkʌmfət; *NAmE* -fərt/ *noun, verb*

> **WORD FAMILY**
> **comfort** *noun, verb*
> **comfortable** *adj.*
> (≠ uncomfortable)
> **comfortably** *adv.*
> (≠ uncomfortably)
> **comforting** *adj.*

■ ***noun*** **1** 🔑 [U] the state of being physically relaxed and free from pain; the state of having a pleasant life, with everything that you need 舒服；安逸；舒适： *These tennis shoes are designed **for comfort** and performance.* 这些网球鞋的设计以舒适为本，打起球来发挥更出色。 ◇ *You can now watch the latest movies **in the comfort of** your own home.* 你现在可以在自己家舒舒服服地看最新电影。 ◇ *The hotel offers a high standard of comfort and service.* 这家旅馆提供高标准的舒适享受和优质服务。 ◇ *They had enough money to live **in comfort** in their old age.* 他们有足够的钱舒舒服服地安度晚年。 **2** 🔑 [U] a feeling of not suffering or worrying so much; a feeling of being less unhappy 安慰；慰藉；宽慰 SYN **consolation**： *to **take/draw comfort** from sb's words* 从某人的话中得到安慰 ◇ *I tried to offer a few **words of comfort**.* 我试图说上几句安慰的话。 ◇ *The sound of gunfire **was too close for comfort**.* 炮火声太近，让人恐慌不安。 ◇ *If **it's any comfort to** you, I'm in the same situation.* 就当是一句安慰的话，我的情况也跟你一样。 ◇ *His words were of **little comfort** in the circumstances.* 在这种情况下，他的话起不了什么安慰作用。 ◇ ***comfort food*** (= food that makes you feel better) 安慰性食品 **3** 🔑 [sing.] a person or thing that helps you when you are suffering, worried or unhappy 令人感到安慰的人（或事物）： *The children have **been a great comfort to** me through all of this.* 在我经历这一切的日子里，孩子们一直是我的莫大安慰。 ◇ *It's a comfort to know that she is safe.* 知道她安然无恙是令人宽慰的事。 ➲ SEE ALSO COLD COMFORT **4** 🔑 [C, usually pl.] a thing that makes your life easier or more comfortable 舒适的设施（或条件）： *The hotel has all modern comforts/every modern comfort.* 这家旅馆拥有各种现代化的舒适设施。 ◇ *material comforts* (= money and possessions) 物质上的舒适条件（钱财） ➲ SEE ALSO CREATURE COMFORTS

■ ***verb*** to make sb who is worried or unhappy feel better by being kind and sympathetic towards them 安慰；抚慰；宽慰： **~ sb** *The victim's widow was today being comforted by family and friends.* 受害人的遗孀今天正受到亲属和朋友的安慰。 ◇ *She comforted herself with the thought that it would soon be spring.* 她想到春天很快就要来临，以此来宽慰自己。 ◇ **it comforts sb to do sth** *It comforted her to feel his arms around her.* 感受到他的拥抱使她得到安慰。

com·fort·able 🔑 /ˈkʌmftəbl; *BrE also* -fət-; *NAmE also* -fərt-/ *adj.*
• **CLOTHES/FURNITURE** 衣服；家具 **1** 🔑 (of clothes, furniture, etc. 衣服、家具等) making you feel physically relaxed; pleasant to wear, sit on, etc. 使人舒服的；舒适的： *It's such a comfortable bed.* 这床真舒服。 ◇ *These new shoes are not very comfortable.* 这双新鞋穿起来不太舒服。 ◇ *a warm comfortable house* 温暖舒适的房子 OPP **uncomfortable**
• **PHYSICALLY RELAXED** 轻松 **2** 🔑 feeling physically relaxed in a pleasant way; warm enough, without pain, etc. 愉快放松的；舒服的；安逸的： *Are you comfortable?* 你感觉舒服吗？ ◇ *She shifted into a more comfortable position on the chair.* 她在椅子上换了个更舒适的姿势。 ◇ *Please **make yourself comfortable** while I get some coffee.* 我去冲咖啡，您别拘束。 ◇ *The patient is comfortable* (= not in pain) *after his operation.* 病人手术后感觉良好。 OPP **uncomfortable**
• **CONFIDENT** 有信心 **3** 🔑 confident and not worried or afraid 自信而无忧虑的；自在的： *He's more comfortable with computers than with people.* 比起与人相处，他和电脑打交道更能应付自如。 OPP **uncomfortable**
• **HAVING MONEY** 有钱 **4** 🔑 having enough money to buy what you want without worrying about the cost 富裕的；宽裕的： *They're not millionaires, but they're certainly very comfortable.* 他们不是百万富翁，但也很富裕。 ➲ SYNONYMS AT RICH
• **VICTORY** 胜利 **5** quite large; allowing you to win easily 相当大的；轻松取胜的： *The party won with a comfortable majority.* 该政党以明显的多数票获胜。 ◇ *a comfortable 2–0 win* 以 2:0 轻取

com·fort·ably 🔑 /ˈkʌmftəbli; *BrE also* -fət-; *NAmE also* -fərt-/ *adv.* **1** 🔑 in a comfortable way 舒服地；舒适地；安逸地： *All the rooms were comfortably furnished.* 所有的房间都配置了舒适的家具。 ◇ *If you're all sitting comfortably, then I'll begin.* 要是你们都坐好了，那么我就开始。 **2** with no problem 没问题；容易地 SYN **easily**： *He can comfortably afford the extra expense.* 他支付这些额外的费用毫无问题。 ◇ *They are comfortably ahead in the opinion polls.* 他们在民意测验中遥遥领先。

IDM ˌ**comfortably ˈoff** having enough money to buy what you want without worrying too much about the cost 生活富裕；丰衣足食

ˈ**comfort blanket** *noun* (*BrE*) = SECURITY BLANKET (1)： *You can't use food as a comfort blanket.* 你不能拿食物当安慰。

ˈ**comfort eating** *noun* [U] the act of eating sth to make yourself feel happier rather than because you are hungry 安慰性进食： *Years of depression caused him to turn to comfort eating.* 多年的抑郁导致他靠吃东西寻求安慰。

com·fort·er /ˈkʌmfətə(r); *NAmE* -fərt-/ *noun* **1** a person or thing that makes you feel calmer or less worried 令人感到安慰（或慰藉）的人（或事物） **2** (*NAmE*) a type of thick cover for a bed 加衬芯床罩 ➲ COMPARE QUILT

com·fort·ing /ˈkʌmfətɪŋ; *NAmE* -fərt-/ *adj.* making you feel calmer and less worried or unhappy 令人安慰的： *her comforting words* 她说的那些令人安慰的话 ◇ *It's comforting to know that you'll be there.* 知道你要去那里令人感到欣慰。 ▸ **com·fort·ing·ly** *adv.*

com·fort·less /ˈkʌmfətləs; *NAmE* -fərt-/ *adj.* (*formal*) without anything to make a place more comfortable 没有舒适设施的

ˈcomfort zone *noun* **1** (*sometimes disapproving*) a place or situation in which you feel safe or comfortable, especially when you choose to stay in this situation instead of trying to work harder or achieve more 舒适区，放松区，安乐窝（尤指自我放松、不追求更高成就的状态）：*Stepping outside your comfort zone and trying new things can be a great experience.* 走出你的安乐窝去尝试一下新事物会是个很棒的经历。◇ *We cannot afford to have anyone operating in a comfort zone.* 我们可用不起工作中贪图安逸不求上进的人。 **2** (*approving*) (especially in sport 尤用于体育运动) a state in which you feel confident and are performing at your best 最佳状态：*I knew if I could find my comfort zone I would be difficult to beat.* 我知道如果我能达到自己的最佳状态就难以被打败。

com·frey /ˈkʌmfri/ *noun* [U, C] a plant with large leaves covered with small hairs and small bell-shaped flowers 聚合草（长细茸大叶，开铃状小花）

comfy /ˈkʌmfi/ *adj.* (**com·fier**, **com·fi·est**) (*informal*) comfortable 舒服的；舒适的：*a comfy armchair/bed* 舒适的扶手椅 / 床 HELP **More comfy** is also common as a comparative. 比较级 more comfy 也常用。

comic /ˈkɒmɪk; *NAmE* ˈkɑːmɪk/ *adj., noun*

■ ***adj.*** **1** amusing and making you laugh 滑稽的；使人发笑的：*a comic monologue/story* 滑稽的长篇独白 / 故事 ◇ *The play is both comic and tragic.* 这部剧既滑稽又悲惨。◇ *She can always be relied on to provide* ***comic relief*** (= sth to make you laugh) *at a boring party.* 在沉闷的聚会上，她总是能搞些笑料调剂气氛。 ➲ SYNONYMS AT FUNNY **2** [only before noun] connected with comedy (= entertainment that is funny and that makes people laugh) 喜剧的：*a comic opera* 滑稽歌剧 ◇ *a comic actor* 喜剧演员 ➲ WORDFINDER NOTE AT STORY

■ ***noun*** **1** an entertainer who makes people laugh by telling jokes or funny stories 喜剧演员 SYN **comedian** **2** (*NAmE also* **ˈcomic book**) a magazine, especially for children, that tells stories through pictures （尤指儿童看的）连环画杂志 **3 the comics** [pl.] (*NAmE*) the section of a newspaper that contains COMIC STRIPS （报章上的）连环漫画栏

com·ic·al /ˈkɒmɪkl; *NAmE* ˈkɑːm-/ *adj.* funny or amusing, especially because it is strange or ridiculous 滑稽可笑的；奇特有趣的 ▶ **com·ic·al·ly** /-kli/ *adv.*

ˈcomic strip (*also* **car·toon**) (*BrE also* **ˌstrip carˈtoon**) (*NAmE also* **strip**) *noun* a series of drawings inside boxes that tell a story and are often printed in newspapers （常登载于报纸上的）连环漫画

com·ing /ˈkʌmɪŋ/ *noun, adj.*

■ ***noun*** [sing.] **the ~ of sth** the time when sth new begins （新事物的）到来，来临：*With the coming of modern technology, many jobs were lost.* 随着现代技术的到来，许多工作岗位不复存在。

IDM **ˌcomings and ˈgoings** (*informal*) the movement of people arriving at and leaving a particular place 来来往往：*It's hard to keep track of the children's comings and goings.* 这些孩子来来往往，很难跟得上他们的行踪。

■ ***adj.*** [only before noun] happening soon; next 即将发生的；下一个的：*in the coming months* 在随后的几个月里 ◇ *This coming Sunday is her birthday.* 下个星期天是她的生日。

ˌcoming of ˈage *noun* [sing.] the time when a person reaches the age at which they have an adult's legal rights and responsibilities 成年；成人年龄

comma /ˈkɒmə; *NAmE* ˈkɑːmə/ *noun* the mark (,) used to separate the items in a list or to show where there is a slight pause in a sentence 逗号 ➲ SEE ALSO INVERTED COMMAS

com·mand /kəˈmɑːnd; *NAmE* kəˈmænd/ *noun, verb*

■ ***noun***

• **ORDER** 命令 **1** [C] an order given to a person or an animal（给人或动物的）命令：*Begin when I give the command.* 我发出命令时开始。◇ *You must obey the captain's commands.* 你必须服从船长的命令。 ➲ WORDFINDER NOTE AT ARMY, NAVY

• **FOR COMPUTER** 计算机 **2** [C] an instruction given to a computer 指令；命令

WORDFINDER 联想词：connect, desktop, drag, enter, insert, refresh, scroll, select, toggle

• **CONTROL** 控制 **3** [U] control and authority over a situation or a group of people 控制；管辖；指挥：*He has 1 200 men under his command.* 他掌管着 1 200 人。◇ *He* ***has command of*** *1 200 men.* 有 1 200 人由他管辖。◇ *The police arrived and* ***took command of*** *the situation.* 警察到达后就控制了局势。◇ *For the first time in years, she felt* ***in command of*** *her life.* 多少年来第一次，她觉得生活掌握在自己的手里。◇ *He looked relaxed and totally* ***in command of himself***. 他看起来很轻松，有绝对的自信完全能控制住自己。◇ *Who is* ***in command*** *here?* 这里谁负责？ ➲ SEE ALSO SECOND IN COMMAND

• **IN ARMY** 军队 **4 Command** [C] a part of an army, AIR FORCE, etc. that is organized and controlled separately; a group of officers who give orders （陆军、空军等的）兵团，军区，指挥部，司令部：*Bomber Command* 轰炸机组的指挥部

• **KNOWLEDGE** 知识 **5** [U, sing.] **~ (of sth)** your knowledge of sth; your ability to do or use sth, especially a language 知识；（尤指对语言的）掌握，运用能力：*Applicants will be expected to have (a) good command of English.* 申请人必须精通英语。

IDM **at your comˈmand** if you have a skill or an amount of sth **at your command**, you are able to use it well and completely 可自由使用；可支配 **be at sb's comˈmand** (*formal*) to be ready to obey sb 听候某人的吩咐；服从某人的支配：*I'm at your command—what would you like me to do?* 我听从您的吩咐，您要我做什么？ ➲ MORE AT WISH *n.*

■ ***verb***

• **ORDER** 命令 **1** [T] (of sb in a position of authority 掌权者) to tell sb to do sth 命令 SYN **order**: **~ sb to do sth** *He commanded his men to retreat.* 他命令手下撤退。◇ **~ sth** *She commanded the release of the prisoners.* 她下令释放囚犯。◇ **+ speech** *'Come here!' he commanded (them).* "过来！"他命令（他们）道。◇ **~ that…** (*formal*) *The commission intervened and commanded that work on the building cease.* 委员会进行了干预，下令那栋大楼必须停建。◇ (*BrE also*) *The commission commanded that work on the building should cease.* 委员会下令那栋大楼必须停建。

• **IN ARMY** 军队 **2** [T, I] **~ (sb/sth)** to be in charge of a group of people in the army, navy, etc. 指挥，统率（陆军、海军等）：*The troops were commanded by General Haig.* 部队由黑格将军统率。

• **DESERVE AND GET** 应得 **3** [T, no passive] (not used in the progressive tenses 不用于进行时) **~ sth** to deserve and get sth because of the special qualities you have 应得；博得；值得：*to command sympathy/support* 值得同情 / 支持 ◇ *She was able to command the respect of the class.* 她赢得了全班的尊敬。◇ *The headlines commanded her attention.* 那些标题引起了她的注意。◇ *As a top lawyer, he can expect to command a six-figure salary.* 作为首屈一指的律师，他可望拿到六位数的薪资。

• **VIEW** 视野 **4** [T, no passive] (not used in the progressive tenses 不用于进行时) **~ sth** (*formal*) to be in a position from where you can see or control sth 居高临下地掌控；俯瞰：*The hotel commands a fine view of the valley.* 从这家旅馆俯瞰下面的峡谷一览无余。

• **CONTROL** 控制 **5** [T, no passive] (not used in the progressive tenses 不用于进行时) **~ sth** (*formal*) to have control of sth; to have sth available for use 控制；拥有…可供使用；掌管：*The party was no longer able to command a majority in Parliament.* 该党已不能在国会中再占有多数。◇ *the power and finances commanded by the police* 警方掌握的权力和资金

com·mand·ant /ˈkɒməndænt; *NAmE* ˈkɑːm-/ *noun* the officer in charge of a particular military group or institution 司令；指挥官

comˌmand eˈconomy *noun* = PLANNED ECONOMY

com·man·deer /ˌkɒmənˈdɪə(r); *NAmE* ˌkɑːmənˈdɪr/ *verb* **~ sth** to take control of a building, a vehicle, etc. for military purposes during a war, or by force for your own use （战争期间为军事目的而）强征，征用；强占 SYN **requisition**

com·mand·er /kəˈmɑːndə(r); *NAmE* -ˈmæn-/ *noun* **1** a person who is in charge of sth, especially an officer in charge of a particular group of soldiers or a military operation 负责人；（尤指）司令官，指挥官：*military/allied/field/flight commanders* 军事 / 盟军 / 战地 / 飞行指挥官 ◇ *the commander of the expedition* 探险队队长 **2** (*abbr.* **Cdr**) an officer of fairly high rank in the British or American navy（英国或美国）海军中校 **3** (*abbr.* **Cdr**) (in Britain) a London police officer of high rank（英国）伦敦高级警官

comˌmander-in-ˈchief (*abbr.* **C.-in-C.**) *noun* (*pl.* **commanders-in-chief**) the officer who commands all the armed forces of a country or all its forces in a particular area 总司令；最高统帅

com·mand·ing /kəˈmɑːndɪŋ; *NAmE* -ˈmæn-/ *adj.* **1** [only before noun] in a position of authority that allows you to give formal orders 指挥的；统帅的：*Who is your commanding officer?* 谁是你们的指挥官？ **2** [usually before noun] if you are in a **commanding position** or have a **commanding lead**, you are likely to win a race or competition （速度竞赛或比赛）居领先位置的，遥遥领先的 **3** [usually before noun] powerful and making people admire and obey you 权威的；威严的：*a* ***commanding figure/presence/voice*** 威严的人物 / 气派 / 说话声 **4** [only before noun] if a building is in a **commanding position** or has a **commanding view**, you can see the area around very well from it 居高临下的；视野宽阔的：*The castle occupies a commanding position on a hill.* 城堡占据着山上居高临下的位置。

com·mand·ment /kəˈmɑːndmənt; *NAmE* -ˈmæn-/ *noun* a law given by God, especially any of **the Ten Commandments** given to the Jews in the Bible 诫条（尤指《圣经》中上帝给犹太人的十诫之一） ➲ COLLOCATIONS AT RELIGION

comˈmand module *noun* the part of a SPACECRAFT that remains after the rest has separated from it, where the controls and the people that operate them are located（航天器中载人和控制仪器的）指挥舱，指令舱

com·mando /kəˈmɑːndəʊ; *NAmE* kəˈmændoʊ/ *noun* (*pl.* **-os**) a soldier or a group of soldiers who are trained to make quick attacks in enemy areas 突击手；突击队；突击队员

IDM **go comˈmando** (*informal, humorous*) to not wear underwear under your clothes 不穿内衣；空身穿外衣

comˌmand perˈformance *noun* [usually sing.] a special performance, for example at a theatre, that is given for a head of state（为国家元首举行的）专场演出，御前演出

com·media dell'arte /kɒˌmeɪdɪə del ˈɑːteɪ; *NAmE* kəˌmeɪdɪə del ˈɑːrteɪ/ *noun* [U] (*from Italian*) traditional Italian theatre in which the same characters appeared in different plays 即兴喜剧，假面喜剧（意大利的一种传统戏剧，相同的角色出现在不同的戏剧中）

com·mem·or·ate /kəˈmeməreɪt/ *verb* **~ sth/sb** to remind people of an important person or event from the past with a special action or object; to exist to remind people of a person or an event from the past （用…）纪念；作为…的纪念：*A series of movies will be shown to commemorate the 30th anniversary of his death.* 为纪念他逝世 30 周年，有一系列的电影将要上映。◇ *A plaque commemorates the battle.* 设了一块匾额来纪念那次战役。 ➲ WORDFINDER NOTE AT CELEBRATE

com·mem·or·ation /kəˌmeməˈreɪʃn/ *noun* [U, C] an action, or a ceremony, etc. that makes people remember and show respect for an important person or event in the past 纪念；纪念仪式：*a commemoration service* 纪念仪式 ◇ *a statue* ***in commemoration of*** *a national hero* 纪念民族英雄的雕像

com·mem·ora·tive /kəˈmemərətɪv; *NAmE* -əreɪt-/ *adj.* intended to help people remember and respect an important person or event in the past 纪念的：*commemorative stamps* 纪念邮票

com·mence AW /kəˈmens/ *verb* [I, T] (*formal*) to begin to happen; to begin sth 开始发生；开始；着手：*The meeting is scheduled to commence at noon.* 会议定于午间召开。◇ *I will be on leave during the week commencing 15 February.* 我将从 2 月 15 日开始一周的休假。◇ **~ with sth** *The day commenced with a welcome from the principal.* 那天由校长致欢迎词开始。 ◇ **~ sth** *She commenced her medical career in 1956.* 她于 1956 年开始行医。◇ **~ doing sth** *We commence building next week.* 我们下周破土动工。◇ **~ to do sth** *Operators commenced to build pipelines in 1862.* 运营商于 1862 年开始兴建管道。 ➲ SYNONYMS AT START

com·mence·ment AW /kəˈmensmənt/ *noun* [U, C, usually sing.] **1** (*formal*) beginning 开始；开端：*the commencement of the financial year* 财政年度的开始 **2** (*NAmE*) a ceremony at which students receive their academic degrees or DIPLOMAS 学位授予典礼；毕业典礼 SYN **graduation**

com·mend /kəˈmend/ *verb* **1 ~ sb (for sth/for doing sth) | ~ sb (on sth/on doing sth)** to praise sb/sth, especially publicly （尤指公开地）赞扬，称赞，表扬：*She was commended on her handling of the situation.* 她因妥善处理了那个局面而受到表扬。◇ *His designs were* ***highly commended*** *by the judges* (= they did not get a prize but they were especially praised). 他的设计受到了评委的高度赞扬。 **2 ~ sb/sth (to sb)** (*formal*) to recommend sb/sth to sb 推荐；举荐：*She is an excellent worker and I commend her to you without reservation.* 她工作出色，我毫无保留地把她推荐给你。◇ *The movie* ***has little to commend it*** (= it has few good qualities). 这部电影乏善可陈。 **3 ~ itself to sb** (*formal*) if sth **commends** itself to sb, they approve of it 受到赞同；得到认可：*His outspoken behaviour did not commend itself to his colleagues.* 他直言不讳的行为不受他同事的欢迎。 **4 ~ sb/sth to sb** (*formal*) to give sb/sth to sb in order to be taken care of 把…托付给（或委托于）：*We commend her soul to God.* 我们把她的灵魂托付给上帝。

com·mend·able /kəˈmendəbl/ *adj.* (*formal*) deserving praise and approval 值得赞扬（或嘉许）的：*commendable honesty* 值得称赞的诚实 ▸ **com·mend·ably** /-əbli/ *adv.*

com·men·da·tion /ˌkɒmenˈdeɪʃn; *NAmE* ˌkɑːm-/ *noun* **1** [U] (*formal*) praise; approval 赞扬；称赞；赞成；嘉许 **2** [C] **~ (for sth)** an award or official statement giving public praise for sb/sth 奖品；奖励；表扬：*a commendation for bravery* 因勇敢而受到的嘉奖

com·men·sal /kəˈmensl/ *adj.* (*biology* 生) living on another animal or plant and getting food from the situation, but doing no harm 共生的；共栖的：*commensal organisms* 共栖体 ▸ **com·men·sal·ism** /kəˈmenslɪzəm/ *noun* [U]

com·men·sur·ate /kəˈmenʃərət/ *adj.* **~ (with sth)** (*formal*) matching sth in size, importance, quality, etc. （在大小、重要性、质量等方面）相称的，相当的：*Salary will be commensurate with experience.* 薪金将会与资历相称。 OPP **incommensurate** ▸ **com·men·sur·ate·ly** *adv.*

com·ment 🔑 AW /ˈkɒment; *NAmE* ˈkɑːm-/ *noun, verb*

■ ***noun*** **1** 🔑 [C, U] **~ (about/on sth)** something that you say or write which gives an opinion on or explains sb/sth 议论；评论；解释：*Have you any comment to make about the cause of the disaster?* 你对发生灾难的原因有何评论？◇ *She* ***made*** *helpful* ***comments*** *on my work.* 她对我的工作提出了有益的意见。◇ *The director was not available for comment.* 经理抽不出时间来发表评论。 ◇ *He handed me the document without comment.* 他未作任何解释就把文件交给了我。◇ (*especially BrE*) *What she said was* ***fair comment*** (= a reasonable criticism). 她所讲的是合乎情理的批评。➲

SYNONYMS AT STATEMENT **2** [sing., U] criticism that shows the faults of sth 批评；指责： *The results are a clear comment on government education policy.* 这些结果是对政府教育政策明显的批评。◇ *There was a lot of comment about his behaviour.* 对他的行为举止有很多的议论。

IDM **ˌno ˈcomment** (said in reply to a question, usually from a journalist 通常用于回答记者的问题) I have nothing to say about that 无可奉告： *'Will you resign, sir?' 'No comment!'* "先生，你会辞职吗？""无可奉告！"

■ ***verb*** [I, T] ~ (**on/upon sth**) to express an opinion about sth 表达意见： *I don't feel I can comment on their decision.* 我觉得我无法对他们的决定作出评论。◇ *He refused to comment until after the trial.* 他拒绝在审判前作任何评论。◇ ~ **that…** *A spokesperson commented that levels of carbon dioxide were very high.* 发言人称二氧化碳的含量很高。◇ + **speech** *'Not his best performance,' she commented to the woman sitting next to her.* "这不是他的最佳表现。"她对坐在她旁边的女士议论道。

▼ SYNONYMS 同义词辨析

comment

note • remark • observe

These words all mean to say or write a fact or opinion. 以上各词均指口头或书面说明事实或发表意见。

comment to express an opinion or give facts about sth 指发表意见或说明事实： *He refused to comment until after the trial.* 他拒绝在审判前作任何评论。

note (*rather formal*) to mention sth because it is important or interesting 指特别提到或指出： *He noted in passing that the company's record on safety issues was not good.* 他顺便提到该公司在安全方面的记录不好。

remark to say or write what you have noticed about a situation 指说起、谈论、评论： *Critics remarked that the play was not original.* 评论家指出这部戏剧缺乏创意。

observe (*formal*) to say or write what you have noticed about a situation 指说起、谈论、评论： *She observed that it was getting late.* 她说天色晚了。

COMMENT, REMARK OR OBSERVE? 用 comment、remark 还是 observe?

If you **comment on** sth you say sth about it; if you **remark on** sth or **observe** sth, you say sth about it that you have noticed: there is often not much difference between the three. However, while you can *refuse to comment* (without *on*), you cannot 'refuse to remark' or 'refuse to observe' (without *on*). * comment on 表示谈论某事，remark on 或 observe 表示谈论或评论注意到的事物。以上三词通常无大的区别，但拒绝评论可说 refuse to comment（不带 on），不能说 refuse to remark 或 refuse to observe（不带 on）： ~~*He refused to remark/observe until after the trial.*~~

PATTERNS

- to comment/note/remark/observe **that…**
- to comment on/note/remark/observe **how…**
- to comment/remark **on** sth
- to comment/remark/observe **to** sb
- **'It's long,'** he commented/noted/remarked/observed.

com·men·tary AW /ˈkɒməntri; *NAmE* ˈkɑːmənteri/ *noun* (*pl.* **-ies**) ~ (**on sth**) **1** [C, U] a spoken description of an event that is given while it is happening, especially on the radio or television（尤指电台或电视台所作的）实况报道，现场解说： *a sports commentary* 体育实况报道 ◇ *Our reporters will give* ***a running commentary*** (= a continuous one) *on the election results as they are announced.* 我们的记者将对选举的公布结果作实况追踪报道。◇ *He kept up* ***a running commentary*** *on everyone who came in or went out.* 他不断地对上下场的每一名队员进行解说。**2** [C] a written explanation or discussion of sth such as a book or a play 注释；解释；评注；评论： *a critical commentary on the final speech of the play* 对这剧本结尾的台词所作的批判性评论 **3** [C, U] a criticism or discussion of sth 批评；议论： *The petty quarrels were a sad commentary on the state of the government.* 这些鸡毛蒜皮的争吵说明了政府的状况很糟糕。◇ *political commentary* 政治评论

com·men·tate /ˈkɒmənteɪt; *NAmE* ˈkɑːm-/ *verb* [I] ~ (**on sth**) to give a spoken description of an event as it happens, especially on television or radio（尤指在电视台或电台上）作实况报道，作现场解说： *Who will be commentating on the game?* 谁来对这场比赛作现场解说？

com·men·ta·tor AW /ˈkɒmənteɪtə(r); *NAmE* ˈkɑːm-/ *noun* ~ (**on sth**) **1** a person who is an expert on a particular subject and talks or writes about it on television or radio, or in a newspaper（电视台、电台或报章的）评论员： *a political commentator* 政治评论员 **2** a person who describes an event while it is happening, especially on television or radio（尤指电视台或电台的）现场解说员，实况播音员： *a* ***television/sports commentator*** 电视台/体育运动实况解说员

com·merce /ˈkɒmɜːs; *NAmE* ˈkɑːmɜːrs/ *noun* [U] trade, especially between countries; the buying and selling of goods and services（尤指国际间的）贸易；商业；商务： *leaders of industry and commerce* 工商界领导人 ➲ WORDFINDER NOTE AT TRADE ➲ SEE ALSO CHAMBER OF COMMERCE

com·mer·cial /kəˈmɜːʃl; *NAmE* kəˈmɜːrʃl/ *adj., noun*

■ ***adj.*** **1** [usually before noun] connected with the buying and selling of goods and services 贸易的；商业的： *the commercial heart of the city* 城市的商业中心 ◇ *a commercial vehicle* (= one that is used for carrying goods or passengers who pay) 商用车辆 ➲ SYNONYMS AT ECONOMIC **2** [only before noun] making or intended to make a profit 赢利的；以获利为目的的： *The movie was not a commercial success* (= did not make money). 这部电影票房收入不佳。◇ *commercial baby foods* 市面上的婴儿食品 ◇ *the first commercial flights across the Atlantic* 头几次横跨大西洋的商业飞行 ➲ SYNONYMS AT SUCCESSFUL **3** (*disapproving*) more concerned with profit and being popular than with quality 偏重利润和声望的；商业化的： *Their more recent music is far too commercial.* 他们最近的音乐过分商业化了。**4** (of television or radio 电视或电台) paid for by the money charged for broadcasting advertisements 由广告收入支付的；商业性的： *a commercial radio station/TV channel* 商业电台/电视频道 ▸ **com·mer·cial·ly** /-ʃəli/ *adv.* : *commercially produced/grown/developed* 商业化生产的/种植的/开发的 ◇ *The product is not yet commercially available.* 这种产品还没有上市。◇ *His invention was not commercially successful.* 他的发明从赢利角度看并不成功。

■ ***noun*** an advertisement on the radio or on television（电台或电视播放的）广告 ➲ SYNONYMS AT ADVERTISEMENT ➲ COLLOCATIONS AT TELEVISION

com·mer·cial·ism /kəˈmɜːʃəlɪzəm; *NAmE* -ˈmɜːrʃl-/ *noun* [U] (*disapproving*) the fact of being more interested in making money than in the value or quality of things 商业主义；赢利主义

com·mer·cial·ize (*BrE also* **-ise**) /kəˈmɜːʃəlaɪz; *NAmE* -ˈmɜːrʃl-/ *verb* [often passive] ~ **sth** to use sth to try to make a profit, especially in a way that other people do not approve of（尤指不择手段地）利用…牟利；商业化： *Their music has become very commercialized in recent years.* 他们的音乐近几年非常商业化了。▸ **com·mer·cial·iza·tion, -isa·tion** /kəˌmɜːʃəlaɪˈzeɪʃn; *NAmE* -ˌmɜːrʃələˈz-/ *noun* [U]

comˌmercial ˈtraveller *noun* (*old-fashioned, BrE*) = SALES REPRESENTATIVE

com·mie /ˈkɒmi; *NAmE* ˈkɑːmi/ *noun* (*especially NAmE*) an insulting way of referring to sb that you think has ideas similar to those of COMMUNISTS or SOCIALISTS, or who is a member of a COMMUNIST or SOCIALIST party（侮辱性用语）有共产思想的人，共党分子

com·min·gle /kəˈmɪŋgl/ *verb* [I, T] (*formal* or *specialist*) to mix two or more things together or to be mixed, when it is impossible for the things to be separated afterwards 混合；掺和：~ (**with sth**) *The fluid must be prevented from commingling with other fluids.* 一定要避免将这种液体与其他液体混合。◇ ~ **sth** (**with sth**) (*finance* 财) *Campaign funds must not be commingled with other money.* 竞选经费切忌与其他款项合并。

com·mis·er·ate /kəˈmɪzəreɪt/ *verb* [I, T] ~ (**with sb**) (**on/about/for/over sth**) | + **speech** to show sb sympathy when they are upset or disappointed about sth 同情；怜悯：*She commiserated with the losers on their defeat.* 她对失败的一方表示同情。

com·mis·er·ation /kəˌmɪzəˈreɪʃn/ *noun* [U, C] (*formal*) an expression of sympathy for sb who has had sth unpleasant happen to them, especially not winning a competition（尤指对某人未赢得比赛而表示的）同情：*I offered him my commiseration.* 我对他表示同情。◇ *Commiserations to the losing team!* 落败的队伍太可惜了！

com·mis·sar /ˌkɒmɪˈsɑː(r); *NAmE* ˌkɑːm-/ *noun* an officer of the Communist Party, especially in the past in the Soviet Union（尤指旧时苏联的）政治委员，政委

com·mis·sar·iat /ˌkɒmɪˈseəriət; *NAmE* ˌkɑːmɪˈser-/ *noun* **1** a department of the army that is responsible for food supplies 军需处 **2** a government department in the Soviet Union before 1946（1946 年以前苏联的）人民委员部

com·mis·sary /ˈkɒmɪsəri; *NAmE* ˈkɑːmɪseri/ *noun* (*pl.* **-ies**) (*NAmE*) **1** a shop/store that sells food, etc. in a military base, a prison, etc.（军事基地、监狱等处出售食品等的）杂货商店 **2** a restaurant for people working in a large organization, especially a film studio（大型机构，尤指电影制片厂的）员工餐厅

com·mis·sion 🔑 AW /kəˈmɪʃn/ *noun, verb*

■ ***noun***

• **OFFICIAL GROUP** 官方团体 **1** 🔑 (*often* **Commission**) [C] an official group of people who have been given responsibility to control sth, or to find out about sth, usually for the government（通常为政府管控或调查某事的）委员会：*the European Commission* 欧洲委员会 ◇ (*BrE*) *The government has set up a* ***commission of inquiry*** *into the disturbances at the prison.* 政府成立了一个委员会来调查监狱骚乱事件。◇ *a commission on human rights* 人权委员会

• **MONEY** 金钱 **2** 🔑 [U, C] an amount of money that is paid to sb for selling goods and which increases with the amount of goods that are sold 佣金；回扣：*You get a 10% commission on everything you sell.* 你可从你售出的每件商品中获得 10% 的佣金。◇ *He earned £2 000 in commission last month.* 他上个月挣了 2 000 英镑的佣金。◇ *In this job you work* ***on commission*** (= are paid according to the amount you sell). 你做这份工作按销售额提成。➲ WORDFINDER NOTE AT PAY **3** 🔑 [U] an amount of money that is charged by a bank, etc. for providing a particular service（银行等的）手续费：*1% commission is charged for cashing traveller's cheques.* 兑现旅行支票收取 1% 的手续费。

• **FOR ART/MUSIC, ETC.** 艺术、音乐等 **4** 🔑 [C] a formal request to sb to design or make a piece of work such as a building or a painting（请某人作建筑设计或作一幅画等的）正式委托

• **IN ARMED FORCES** 军队 **5** [C] an officer's position in the armed forces 军官职务

• **OF CRIME** 犯罪 **6** [U] (*formal*) the act of doing sth wrong or illegal 做错事；犯罪：*the commission of a crime* 犯罪

IDM **in/out of comˈmission** available/not available to be used 可 / 不可使用：*Several of the airline's planes are temporarily out of commission and undergoing safety checks.* 这家航空公司有几架飞机暂时不能使用，正在接受安全检查。

■ ***verb***

• **PIECE OF ART/MUSIC, ETC.** 艺术、音乐等作品 **1** 🔑 to officially ask sb to write, make or create sth or to do a task for you 正式委托（谱写、制作、创作或完成）：~ **sb to do sth** *She has been commissioned to write a new national anthem.* 她已受委托谱写新国歌。◇ ~ **sth** *Publishers have commissioned a French translation of the book.* 出版商已委托人把这本书译成法语。

• **IN ARMED FORCES** 军队 **2** [usually passive] to choose sb as an officer in one of the armed forces 任命…为军官：~ **sb** *She was commissioned in 2014.* 她于 2014 年被任命为军官。◇ ~ **sb** (**as**) **sth** *He has just been commissioned (as a) pilot officer.* 他刚被任命为空军少尉。

com·mis·sion·aire /kəˌmɪʃəˈneə(r); *NAmE* -ˈner/ *noun* (*BrE, becoming old-fashioned*) a person in uniform whose job is to stand at the entrance to a hotel, etc. and open the door for visitors, find them taxis, etc.（在旅馆等门口为来宾开门、叫出租车等的）穿制服的看门人，门童 ➲ SEE ALSO DOORMAN

comˌmissioned ˈofficer *noun* an officer in the armed forces who has a higher rank, such as a captain or a GENERAL 军官（如上尉或将军）➲ COMPARE NON-COMMISSIONED OFFICER

com·mis·sion·er AW /kəˈmɪʃənə(r)/ *noun* **1** (*usually* **Commissioner**) a member of a COMMISSION (= an official group of people who are responsible for controlling sth or finding out about sth)（委员会的）委员，专员，特派员：*the Church Commissioners* (= the group of people responsible for controlling the financial affairs of the Church of England) 英格兰国教会财政管理委员会委员 ◇ *European Commissioners* 欧洲委员会委员 **2** (*also* **poˈlice commissioner** *especially in NAmE*) the head of a particular police force in some countries 警察局长；警长 **3** the head of a government department in some countries（政府部门的）首长，长官：*the* ***agriculture/health, etc. commissioner*** 农业、卫生等厅长 ◇ *Commissioner Rhodes was unavailable for comment.* 罗兹局长无暇评论。➲ SEE ALSO HIGH COMMISSIONER **4** (in the US) an official chosen by a sports association to control it（美国体育协会的）总干事，主管人：*the baseball commissioner* 棒球协会总干事

comˌmissioner for ˈoaths *noun* (*BrE*) a lawyer who has official authority to be present when sb makes a formal promise that a written statement that they will use as evidence in court is true 监誓官（得到正式任命在法庭上主持宣誓的律师）

the Comˌmission on Civil ˈRights *noun* [sing.] (in the US) a government organization that works for equal rights for all Americans 民权委员会（美国政府机构，宗旨是争取全体美国人的平等权利）

com·mit 🔑 AW /kəˈmɪt/ *verb* (**-tt-**)

• **CRIME** 犯罪 **1** 🔑 [T] ~ **a crime, etc.** to do sth wrong or illegal 做出（错事）；犯（罪）：*to* ***commit murder/adultery*** 犯凶杀罪 / 通奸罪 ◇ *Most crimes are committed by young men.* 多数罪行都是年轻人犯下的。◇ *appalling crimes committed against innocent children* 对无辜儿童犯下的骇人听闻的罪行

• **SUICIDE** 自杀 **2** 🔑 [T] ~ **suicide** to kill yourself deliberately 自杀

• **PROMISE/SAY DEFINITELY** 承诺；肯定地说 **3** 🔑 [T, often passive] to promise sincerely that you will definitely do sth, keep to an agreement or arrangement, etc. 承诺，保证（做某事、遵守协议或遵从安排等）：~ **sb/yourself** (**to sth/to doing sth**) *The President is committed to reforming health care.* 总统承诺要改革卫生保健制度。◇ *Borrowers should think carefully before committing themselves to taking out a loan.* 借款人应当慎重考虑之后再行借贷。◇ ~ **sb/yourself to do sth** *Both sides committed themselves to settle the dispute peacefully.* 双方承诺和平解决争端。**4** [T] ~ **yourself** (**to sth**) to give an opinion or make a decision openly so that it is then difficult to change it（公开地）表达意见，作出决定（以致日后难以更改）：*You don't have to commit yourself now, just think about it.* 你不必现在表态，只需考虑一下这件事。➲ SEE ALSO NON-COMMITTAL

• **BE LOYAL** 忠诚 **5** [I] ~ (**to sb/sth**) to be completely loyal to one person, organization, etc. or give all your time and effort to your work, an activity, etc. 忠于（某个人、机构等）；全心全意投入（工作、活动等）：*Why are so many men scared to commit?* (= say they will be loyal to one person) 为什么有这么多的男人害怕许诺忠诚于人？ ➲ SEE ALSO COMMITTED

• **MONEY/TIME** 金钱；时间 **6** [T] **~ sth** to spend money or time on sth/sb 花（钱或时间）：*The council has committed large amounts of money to housing projects.* 市政会在住宅项目上投入了大量资金。

• **TO HOSPITAL/PRISON** 医院；监狱 **7** [T, often passive] **~ sb to sth** to order sb to be sent to a hospital, prison, etc. （下令）把（某人）送进（医院或监狱等）：*She was committed to a psychiatric hospital.* 她被送进了精神病院。

• **SB FOR TRIAL** 某人受审 **8** [T] **~ sb** to send sb for trial in court 把（某人）送交法庭受审

• **STH TO MEMORY** 记住 **9** [T] **~ sth to memory** to learn sth well enough to remember it exactly 把…学好记牢：*She committed the instructions to memory.* 她把指令记得很牢。

• **STH TO PAPER/WRITING** 用纸记下；书写 **10** [T] **~ sth to paper/writing** to write sth down 把…记（或写）下来 ➲ MORE LIKE THIS 36, page R29

com·mit·ment AW /kəˈmɪtmənt/ *noun* **1** [C, U] a promise to do sth or to behave in a particular way; a promise to support sb/sth; the fact of committing yourself 承诺；许诺；允诺承担；保证：**~ (to sb/sth)** *She doesn't want to* **make a** *big emotional* **commitment** *to Steve at the moment.* 她不想在此刻对史蒂夫在感情上作出重大的承诺。◇ *the government's commitment to public services* 政府对公共服务作出的承诺 ◇ **~ to do/doing sth** *The company's commitment to providing quality at a reasonable price has been vital to its success.* 这家公司保证供货质优价廉的承诺对它的成功起了决定性的作用。**2** [U] **~ (to sb/sth)** the willingness to work hard and give your energy and time to a job or an activity （对工作或活动的）献身，奉献，投入：*A career as an actor requires one hundred per cent commitment.* 干演员这一行需要百分之百的投入。 **3** [C] a thing that you have promised or agreed to do, or that you have to do 已承诺（或同意）的事；不得不做的事：*He's busy for the next month with filming commitments.* 他正忙于准备已经承诺下个月接拍的电影工作。◇ *Women very often have to juggle work with their family commitments.* 妇女经常要工作和家庭两头忙。**4** [U, C] **~ (of sth) (to sth)** agreeing to use money, time or people in order to achieve sth 花费，使用（资金、时间、人力）：*the commitment of resources to education* 对教育的资源投入 ◇ *Achieving success at this level requires a commitment of time and energy.* 取得这种水平的成就需要花费时间和精力。

com·mit·tal /kəˈmɪtl/ *noun* [U] (*specialist*) the official process of sending sb to prison or to a mental hospital 收监；拘押；送入（精神病院）：*He was released on bail pending committal proceedings.* 他交保获释正在候审。

com·mit·ted AW /kəˈmɪtɪd/ *adj.* (*approving*) willing to work hard and give your time and energy to sth; believing strongly in sth 尽心尽力的；坚信的；坚定的：*a committed member of the team* 忠于职守的队员 ◇ *They are committed socialists.* 他们是坚定的社会主义者。OPP **uncommitted**

com·mit·tee /kəˈmɪti/ *noun* [C+sing./pl. v.] a group of people who are chosen, usually by a larger group, to make decisions or to deal with a particular subject 委员会：*She's on the management committee.* 她任管理委员会委员。◇ *The committee has/have decided to close the restaurant.* 委员会已决定关闭这家餐馆。◇ *a committee member/a member of the committee* 委员会的委员 ◇ *a committee meeting* 委员会的会议 ➲ WORDFINDER NOTE AT MEETING

com·mode /kəˈməʊd; NAmE kəˈmoʊd/ *noun* **1** a piece of furniture that looks like a chair but has a toilet under the seat 座椅式便桶 **2** a piece of furniture, especially an old or ANTIQUE one, with drawers for storing things in （尤指旧式或古董）有抽屉的柜橱，五斗橱

com·modi·ous /kəˈməʊdiəs; NAmE -ˈmoʊ-/ *adj.* (*formal*) having a lot of space 宽敞的

com·mod·ity AW /kəˈmɒdəti; NAmE -ˈmɑːd-/ *noun* (*pl.* **-ies**) **1** (*economics* 经) a product or a raw material that can be bought and sold 商品：*rice, flour and other basic commodities* 稻米、面粉和其他基本商品 ◇ *a drop in commodity prices* 商品价格的下跌 ◇ *Crude oil is the world's most important commodity.* 原油是世界上最重要的商品。➲ SYNONYMS AT PRODUCT **2** (*formal*) a thing that is useful or has a useful quality 有用的东西；有使用价值的事物：*Water is a precious commodity that is often taken for granted in the West.* 水很宝贵，但在西方国家人们往往意识不到这一点。

com·mo·dore /ˈkɒmədɔː(r); NAmE ˈkɑːm-/ *noun* (*abbr.* **Cdre**) an officer of high rank in the navy 海军准将：*Commodore John Barry* 约翰•巴里海军准将

com·mon /ˈkɒmən; NAmE ˈkɑːmən/ *adj.*, *noun*

■ ***adj.*** (**com·mon·er**, **com·mon·est**) HELP **More common** and **most common** are more frequent. * more common 和 most common 更为常见。 **1** happening often; existing in large numbers or in many places 常见的；通常的；普遍的：*Jackson is a common English name.* 杰克逊是常见的英语人名。◇ *Breast cancer is the most common form of cancer among women in this country.* 乳腺癌是这个国家妇女中最常见的一种癌症。◇ *Some birds which were once a* **common sight** *are now becoming rare.* 有些曾经随处可见的鸟类现在日益稀少。◇ *a common spelling mistake* 常犯的拼写错误 OPP **uncommon** **2** [usually before noun] **~ (to sb/sth)** shared by or belonging to two or more people or by the people in a group 共有的；共享的；共同的：*They share a common interest in photography.* 他们在摄影方面兴趣相投。◇ *basic features which are common to all human languages* 所有人类语言共有的基本特征 ◇ *We are working together for a common purpose.* 我们在为一个共同的目标一起工作。◇ *common ownership of the land* 土地的共同所有权 ◇ *This decision was taken for the* **common good** (= the advantage of everyone). 作出这个决定是为了共同的利益。◇ *It is, by* **common consent**, *Scotland's prettiest coast* (= everyone agrees that it is). 这是苏格兰公认的最美丽的海岸。 **3** [only before noun] ordinary; not unusual or special 普通的；平常的；寻常的；平凡的：*the common garden frog* 园地里常见的青蛙 ◇ *Shakespeare's work was popular among* **the common people** *in his day.* 莎士比亚的作品在他那个年代很受平民百姓的欢迎。◇ *In most people's eyes she was nothing more than a* **common criminal**. 在多数人的眼里她只不过是个普通的罪犯。◇ *You'd think he'd have the* **common courtesy** *to apologize* (= this would be the polite behaviour that people would expect). 你还以为他会懂得起码的礼貌去道个歉呢。◇ *It's only* **common decency** *to let her know what's happening* (= people would expect it). 出于礼貌，该让她知道正在发生的事。 **4** (*BrE, disapproving*) typical of sb from a low social class and not having good manners 粗俗的；庸俗的：*She thought he was very common and uneducated.* 她认为他很粗俗且无教养。

IDM **ˌcommon or ˈgarden** (*BrE*) (*NAmE* **ˈgarden-variety**) (*informal*) ordinary; with no special features 普通的；平常的；一般的 **the ˌcommon ˈtouch** the ability of a powerful or famous person to talk to and understand ordinary people （有权势者或名人的）平易近人的品质，亲民作风 **make common ˈcause with sb** (*formal*) to be united with sb about sth that you both agree on, believe in or wish to achieve 与某人联合起来，与某人合作（以达到共同的目的） ➲ MORE AT KNOWLEDGE

■ ***noun*** **1** [C] an area of open land in a town or village that anyone may use 公共用地；公地：*We went for a walk on the common.* 我们在公地上散步。◇ *Wimbledon Common* 温布尔登公地 **2 commons** [sing.] (*US*) a large room where students can eat in a school, college, etc. （学校、大学等的）学生公共食堂：*The commons is next to the gym.* 学生公共食堂在体育馆的旁边。➲ SEE ALSO COMMONS

IDM **have sth in common (with sb)** (of people 人) to have the same interests, ideas, etc. as sb else （兴趣、想法等方面）相同：*Tim and I have nothing in common./I have nothing in common with Tim.* 我和蒂姆毫无共同之处。 **have sth in common (with sth)** (of things, places, etc. 东西、地方等) to have the same features, characteristics, etc. 有相同的特征（或特点等）：*The two cultures have a lot in common.* 这两种文化具有许多相同之处。 **in**

common (*specialist*) by everyone in a group 共有；公有：*They hold the property as tenants in common.* 作为共同租赁人，他们共同占用这份房地产。 **in common with sb/sth** (*formal*) in the same way as sb/sth 与…相同：*Britain, in common with many other industrialized countries, has experienced major changes over the last 100 years.* 与许多其他工业化国家一样，英国在过去 100 年里经历了重大的变化。

the ˌcommon ˈcold *noun* [sing.] = COLD (2)

ˌcommon deˈnominator *noun* **1** (*mathematics* 数) a number that can be divided exactly by all the numbers below the line in a set of FRACTIONS 公分母 ➲ COMPARE DENOMINATOR **2** an idea, attitude or experience that is shared by all the members of a group（想法、态度或经验的）共同点 ➲ SEE ALSO LOWEST COMMON DENOMINATOR

com·mon·er /ˈkɒmənə(r); *NAmE* ˈkɑːm-/ *noun* a person who does not come from a royal or NOBLE family 平民 ➲ COMPARE ARISTOCRAT

ˌCommon ˈEra *noun* [sing.] (*abbr.* **CE**) the period since the birth of Christ when the Christian CALENDAR starts counting years 公元：*1890 CE* 公元 1890 年

ˌcommon ˈground *noun* [U] opinions, interests and aims that you share with sb, although you may not agree with them about other things（观点、利益和目标的）共同基础，共同点，一致点：*Despite our disagreements, we have been able to find some common ground.* 尽管我们存在分歧，但仍能找到一些共同点。

com·mon·hold /ˈkɒmənhəʊld; *NAmE* ˈkɑːmənhoʊld/ *noun* [U] (*BrE, law* 律) a system in which each person owns their flat/apartment in a building but the building and shared areas are owned by everyone together 公寓楼共有制度（住户共同拥有楼房及公用区域）

ˈcommon land *noun* [U] (*BrE*) land that belongs to or may be used by the local community 公共用地；公地

ˌcommon ˈlaw *noun* [U] (in some countries) the part of the law that has been developed from customs and from decisions made by judges, not created by Parliament（某些国家）普通法，习惯法，判例法 ➲ COMPARE CASE LAW, STATUTE LAW

ˌcommon-law ˈhusband, ˌcommon-law ˈwife *noun* a person that a woman or man has lived with for a long time and who is recognized (in some countries though not the UK) as a husband or wife, without a formal marriage ceremony（未举行结婚仪式的）事实婚姻的男方，事实婚姻的女方

com·mon·ly 🔑 /ˈkɒmənli; *NAmE* ˈkɑːm-/ *adv.* usually; very often; by most people 通常；常常；大多数人地：*Christopher is commonly known as Kit.* 克里斯托弗通常被称为基特。◇ *commonly held opinions* 多数人持有的观点 ◇ *This is one of the most commonly used methods.* 这是最常采用的方法之一。

ˌcommon ˈmarket *noun* **1** [C, usually sing.] a group of countries that have agreed on low taxes on goods traded between countries in the group, and higher fixed taxes on goods imported from countries outside the group 共同市场（成员国之间实行低关税贸易，对从成员国之外的国家进口的商品规定较高关税） **2 the Common Market** [sing.] a former name of the European Union 欧洲共同市场（欧洲联盟旧称）

ˌcommon ˈnoun *noun* (*grammar* 语法) a word such as *table, cat* or *sea*, that refers to an object or a thing but is not the name of a particular person, place or thing 普通名词（如 table、cat 或 sea） ➲ COMPARE ABSTRACT NOUN, PROPER NOUN

com·mon·place /ˈkɒmənpleɪs; *NAmE* ˈkɑːm-/ *adj., noun*

▪ ***adj.*** done very often, or existing in many places, and therefore not unusual 平凡的；普通的；普遍的：*Computers are now commonplace in primary classrooms.* 计算机如今在小学教室里很普遍。

▪ ***noun*** (*formal*) **1** [usually sing.] an event, etc. that happens very often and is not unusual 常见的事；平常的事 **2** a remark, etc. that is not new or interesting 平淡无奇的言语等；老生常谈

ˈcommonplace book *noun* (especially in the past) a book into which you copy parts of other books, poems, etc. and add your own comments（尤指旧时的）摘录本，摘记簿

ˌcommon ˈrat *noun* = BROWN RAT

ˈcommon room *noun* (*especially BrE*) a room used by the teachers or students of a school, college, etc. when they are not teaching or studying（学校、学院等的）公共休息室

the Com·mons /ˈkɒmənz; *NAmE* ˈkɑːm-/ *noun* [pl.] = HOUSE OF COMMONS ➲ COMPARE THE LORDS

ˌcommon ˈsense *noun* [U] the ability to think about things in a practical way and make sensible decisions 常识：*For goodness' sake, just use your common sense!* 我的老天，你也凭常识想想！◇ *a common-sense approach to a problem* 按常理解决问题的方法

com·mon·wealth /ˈkɒmənwelθ; *NAmE* ˈkɑːm-/ *noun* [sing.] **1 the Commonwealth** an organization consisting of the United Kingdom and other countries, including most of the countries that used to be part of the British Empire 英联邦（由英国和其他大多数曾经隶属于大英帝国的国家组成）：*a member of the Commonwealth* 英联邦成员国 ◇ *Commonwealth countries* 英联邦国家 **2** (*usually* **the Commonwealth**) used in the official names of, and to refer to, some states of the US (Kentucky, Massachusetts, Pennsylvania and Virginia)（用于美国肯塔基、马萨诸塞、宾夕法尼亚和弗吉尼亚四州的正式名称中）州：*the Commonwealth of Virginia* 弗吉尼亚州 ◇ *The city and the Commonwealth have lost a great leader.* 这座城市和这个州失去了一位伟大的领袖。 **3** (*NAmE*) an independent country that is strongly connected to the US（与美国联系紧密的）自治政区：*Puerto Rico remains a US commonwealth, not a state.* 波多黎各至今仍然是美国的一个自治政区，而不是一个州。 **4** (*usually* **Commonwealth**) used in the names of some groups of countries or states that have chosen to be politically linked with each other（用于某些政治上相互有联系的国家集团的名称）联合体：*the Commonwealth of Independent States* (*CIS*) 独立国家联合体（独联体）

com·mo·tion /kəˈməʊʃn; *NAmE* -ˈmoʊ-/ *noun* [C, usually sing., U] sudden noisy confusion or excitement（突然发生的）喧闹，骚乱，骚动：*I heard a commotion and went to see what was happening.* 我听到一阵喧闹，便去看看发生了什么事情。◇ *The crowd waiting outside was causing a commotion.* 在外面等待的人群眼看就要发生骚乱。

com·mu·nal /kəˈmjuːnl; *BrE also* ˈkɒmjənl/ *adj.* **1** shared by, or for the use of, a number of people, especially people who live together（尤指居住在一起的人）共享的，共有的，共用的 SYN **shared**：***a communal kitchen/garden, etc.*** 共用的厨房、花园等 ◇ *As a student he tried communal living for a few years.* 当学生时他尝试过几年集体生活。 **2** involving different groups of people in a community（集体中）不同群体的，各团体的：*communal violence between religious groups* 不同教派之间的暴力冲突 ▶ **com·mu·nal·ly** *adv.*：*The property was owned communally.* 这财产属集体所有。

com·mu·nal·ism /kəˈmjuːnəlɪzəm; ˈkɒmjənəl-; *NAmE* ˈkɑːm-/ *noun* [U] **1** the fact of living together and sharing possessions and responsibilities 公社生活 **2** (*IndE*) a strong sense of belonging to a particular, especially religious, community, which can lead to extreme behaviour or violence towards others 集团主义（可能排外）

com·mune *noun, verb*

▪ ***noun*** /ˈkɒmjuːn; *NAmE* ˈkɑːm-/ [C+sing./pl. v.] **1** a group of people who live together and share responsibilities, possessions, etc.（共同生活、分担责任、共享财产等的）群体，公社：*a 1970s hippy commune* * 20 世纪 70 年代的嬉皮士群体 **2** the smallest division of local government in

France and some other countries （法国及其他一些国家的）最小的行政区
■ **verb** /kə'mjuːn/
PHR V **com'mune with sb/sth** (*formal*) to share your emotions and feelings with sb/sth without speaking 与…默默分享情感（或沟通、交融）： *He spent much of this time* ***communing with nature.*** 他这个时期的许多时间都沉浸在大自然中。

C

com·mu·nic·able AW /kə'mjuːnɪkəbl/ *adj.* (*formal*) that sb can pass on to other people or communicate to sb else 可传染的；可传达的： *communicable diseases* 传染性疾病

com·mu·ni·cant /kə'mjuːnɪkənt/ *noun* a person who receives COMMUNION in a Christian church service 领受圣餐（或圣体）者

com·mu·ni·cate AW /kə'mjuːnɪkeɪt/ *verb*
• EXCHANGE INFORMATION 交流信息 **1** [I, T] to exchange information, news, ideas, etc. with sb （与某人）交流（信息或消息、意见等）；沟通： *We only communicate by email.* 我们只是互通电邮。◇ *They communicated in sign language.* 他们用手语沟通。◇ **~ with sb/sth** *Dolphins use sound to communicate with each other.* 海豚用声音相互沟通。◇ **~ sth (to sb)** *to communicate information/a message to sb* 把情报 / 信息传递给某人 ➲ SYNONYMS AT TALK
• SHARE IDEAS/FEELINGS 分享想法 / 感情 **2** [I, T] to make your ideas, feelings, thoughts, etc. known to other people so that they understand them 传达，传递（想法、感情、思想等）： *Candidates must be able to communicate effectively.* 候选人必须善于有效地表达自己。◇ **~ sth (to sb)** *He was eager to communicate his ideas to the group.* 他急于把他的想法传达给小组。◇ *Her nervousness was communicating itself to the children.* 她紧张不安的情绪传递给了孩子们。◇ **~ how/what, etc.…** *They failed to communicate what was happening and why.* 他们没说清楚当时发生了什么以及起因是什么。 **3** [I] **~ (with sb)** to have a good relationship because you are able to understand and talk about your own and other people's thoughts, feelings, etc. 沟通： *The novel is about a family who can't communicate with each other.* 这部小说写的是一个成员间彼此无法沟通的家庭。
• DISEASE 疾病 **4** [T, usually passive] **~ sth** to pass a disease from one person, animal, etc. to another 传染；传播： *The disease is communicated through dirty drinking water.* 这种疾病通过不干净的饮用水传播。
• OF TWO ROOMS 两个房间 **5** [I] if two rooms **communicate**, they are next to each other and you can get from one to the other 相通；相连： *a* ***communicating door*** (= one that connects two rooms) 连通门

com·mu·ni·ca·tion AW /kəˌmjuːnɪ'keɪʃn/ *noun* **1** [U] the activity or process of expressing ideas and feelings or of giving people information 表达；交流；交际；传递： *Speech is the fastest method of communication between people.* 说话是人与人之间最快捷的沟通方法。◇ *All channels of communication need to be kept open.* 所有沟通渠道都要保持畅通。 ◇ *Doctors do not always have good* ***communication skills.*** 医生不一定都具备良好的交际能力。◇ *non-verbal communication* 非言语交际 ◇ *We are in regular communication by email.* 我们定期通过电子邮件联系。 **2** [U] (*also* **communications** [pl.]) methods of sending information, especially telephones, radio, computers, etc. or roads and railways 通信；交通联系： ***communication systems/links/technology*** 通信系统 / 线路 / 技术 ◇ *The new airport will improve communications between the islands.* 新机场将改善岛屿间的交通联系。 ◇ *Snow has prevented communication with the outside world for three days.* 大雪使得与外界的通信联系中断了三天。 **3** [C] (*formal*) a message, letter or telephone call 信息；书信；电话： *a communication from the leader of the party* 来自政党领袖的信息

com·mu·ni·ca·tive AW /kə'mjuːnɪkətɪv; *NAmE* -keɪtɪv/ *adj.* **1** willing to talk and give information to other people 乐意沟通的： *I don't find him very communicative.* 我发觉他不太爱说话。 OPP **uncommunicative** **2** connected with the ability to communicate in a language, especially a foreign language 语言交际能力的（尤指用外语）： *communicative skills* 语言交际能力

the com'municative approach *noun* [sing.] (*also* **comˌmunicative 'language teaching** [U]) a method of teaching a foreign language which stresses the importance of learning to communicate information and ideas in the language 交际法（外语教学中强调语言交际作用）

comˌmunicative 'competence *noun* [U] (*linguistics* 语言) a person's ability to communicate information and ideas in a foreign language （外语）交际能力

com·mu·ni·ca·tor /kə'mjuːnɪkeɪtə(r)/ *noun* a person who communicates sth to others 沟通的人；交流者： *an effective/skilled/successful communicator* 有效的 / 熟练的 / 成功的交际者 ◇ *a poor communicator* 不善于交流的人 ➲ SYNONYMS AT SPEAKER

com·mu·nion /kə'mjuːniən/ *noun* **1** (*also* **Com·mu·nion**, **ˌHoly Com'munion**) [U] a ceremony in the Christian Church during which people eat bread and drink wine in memory of the last meal that Christ had with his DISCIPLES（基督教教会的）圣餐仪式，领受圣体： *to go to Communion* (= attend church for this celebration) 去参加圣餐仪式 ◇ *to* ***take/receive communion*** (= receive the bread and wine) 领受圣餐 ➲ SEE ALSO EUCHARIST, MASS (1) **2** [U] **~ (with sb/sth)** (*formal*) the state of sharing or exchanging thoughts and feelings; the feeling of being part of sth （思想感情的）交流，交融： *poets living in communion with nature* 与大自然情感交融的诗人 **3** [C] (*specialist*) a group of people with the same religious beliefs 教派；教会；宗教团体： *the Anglican communion* 圣公会

com·mu·ni·qué /kə'mjuːnɪkeɪ; *NAmE* kəˌmjuːnə'keɪ/ *noun* an official statement or report, especially to newspapers （尤指对报界发布的）公报

com·mun·ism /'kɒmjunɪzəm; *NAmE* 'kɑːm-/ *noun* [U] **1** a political movement that believes in an economic system in which the state controls the means of producing everything on behalf of the people. It aims to create a society in which everyone is treated equally. 共产主义 **2** **Communism** the system of government by a ruling Communist Party, such as in the former Soviet Union 共产主义制度 ➲ COMPARE CAPITALISM ➲ WORDFINDER NOTE AT SYSTEM

com·mun·ist /'kɒmjənɪst; *NAmE* 'kɑːm-/ *noun* **1** a person who believes in or supports communism 共产主义者；共产主义的支持者 **2** **Communist** a member of a Communist Party 共产党党员 ▸ **com·mun·ist** (*also* **Communist**) *adj.*: *communist ideology* 共产主义的思想体系 ◇ *a Communist country/government/leader* 共产主义的国家 / 政府 / 领袖

the 'Communist Party *noun* a political party that supports COMMUNISM or rules in a COMMUNIST country 共产党

com·mu·nity AW /kə'mjuːnəti/ *noun* (*pl.* **-ies**) **1** [sing.] all the people who live in a particular area, country, etc. when talked about as a group 社区；社会： *The* ***local community*** *was shocked by the murders.* 当地社会对这些谋杀案感到震惊。◇ *health workers based in the community* (= working with people in a local area) 以社区为基地的保健工作人员 ◇ ***the international community*** (= the countries of the world as a group) 国际社会 ◇ *good community relations with the police* 社区与警方之间的良好关系 ◇ (*NAmE*) ***community parks/libraries*** (= paid for by the local town/city) 社区公园 / 图书馆 **2** [C+sing./pl. v.] a group of people who share the same religion, race, job, etc. 团体；社团；界： *the Polish community in London* 在伦敦的波兰侨民团体 ◇ *ethnic communities* 种族团体 ◇ *the farming community* 农业界 **3** [U] the feeling of sharing things and belonging to a group in the place where you live 共享；共有： *There is a strong sense of community in this town.* 这个镇上有一种强烈的社区意识。◇ *community spirit* 团体精神 ➲ COLLOCATIONS AT TOWN **4** [C] (*biology* 生)

a group of plants and animals growing or living in the same place or environment （动植物的）群落

com,munity 'care (*also* **,care in the com'munity**) *noun* [U] (*BrE*) medical and other care for people who need help over a long period, which allows them to live at home rather than in a hospital 社区护理服务（让长期需要帮助者在家中接受医疗等）

com'munity centre (*BrE*) (*NAmE* **com'munity center**) *noun* a place where people from the same area can meet for social events or sports or to take classes 社区活动中心

com'munity college *noun* **1** (*also* **com'munity school**) (in Britain) a SECONDARY SCHOOL that is open to adults from the local community as well as to its own students 社区中学（在英国除接收本校学生外亦向当地社区成人开放） **2** (in the US) a college that is mainly for students from the local community and that offers programmes that are two years long, including programmes in practical skills 社区学院（美国为社区成员提供两年制课程，包括职业技术训练）

com,munity 'language learning *noun* [U] a method of teaching a foreign language that uses small groups and other ways of reducing students' anxiety （外语的）群体语言学习法

com,munity 'order *noun* (*BrE, law* 律) (in the UK) a decision, made in court, to give a punishment that involves helping people in the community, having treatment for an addiction, etc. instead of going to prison （英国）社区服务令（须完成法院规定的社区服务工作或接受戒瘾治疗等，无须入狱）： *He was sentenced to a community order that involved psychological counselling.* 他被判社区服务，需要接受心理辅导。

com,munity 'property *noun* [U] (*NAmE, law* 律) property that is considered to belong equally to a married couple （夫妻的）共同财产，共有财产

com,munity 'sentence *noun* (*BrE, law* 律) (in the UK) a punishment, given by a court, that involves helping people in the community, having treatment for an addiction, etc. instead of going to prison （英国）社区刑罚，社区服务刑（须完成法院规定的社区服务工作或接受戒瘾治疗等，无须入狱）： *She was given a two-year community sentence for the assault on her neighbour.* 她因袭击邻居被判处两年社区刑。

com,munity 'service *noun* [U] work helping people in the local community that sb does without being paid, either because they want to, or because they have been ordered to by a court as a punishment 社区服务（自愿或因受法庭惩罚的无偿劳动）

com·mut·able /kə'mju:təbl/ *adj.* **1** (of a place or a distance 地方或距离) close enough or short enough to make travelling to work every day a possibility 上下班方便的；（离工作地点）近的 **2** (*law* 律) a **commutable** punishment can be made less severe （刑罚）可减轻的 **3** (*formal*) able to be changed 可改变的；可变换的

com·mu·ta·tion /,kɒmju'teɪʃn; *NAmE* ,kɑ:m-/ *noun* [C, U] **1** (*law* 律) the act of making a punishment less severe 减刑： *a commutation of the death sentence to life imprisonment* 由死刑减为终身监禁 **2** (*finance* 财) the act of replacing one method of payment with another; a payment that is replaced with another 代偿；折合偿付；代偿金

com·mu·ta·tive /kə'mju:tətɪv/ *adj.* (*mathematics* 数) (of a calculation 计算) giving the same result whatever the order in which the quantities are shown 交换的（排列次序不影响结果）

com·mu·ta·tor /'kɒmjuteɪtə(r); *NAmE* 'kɑ:m-/ *noun* (*physics* 物) **1** a device that connects a motor to the electricity supply （马达）转换开关，转换器 **2** a device for changing the direction in which electricity flows （电流）换向器

com·mute /kə'mju:t/ *verb, noun*

■ ***verb*** **1** [I, T] to travel regularly by bus, train, car, etc. between your place of work and your home （乘公共汽车、火车、汽车等）上下班往返，经常往返（于两地）： **~ (from A) (to B)** *She commutes from Oxford to London every day.* 她每天上下班往返于牛津与伦敦之间。◇ **~ between A and B** *He spent that year commuting between New York and Chicago.* 那年他穿梭来往于纽约与芝加哥之间。◇ *I live **within commuting distance of** Dublin.* 我住在离都柏林上下班可乘公交车往返的地方。◇ **~ sth** *People are prepared to commute long distances if they are desperate for work.* 亟需得到工作的人会愿意长途乘车往返上下班。 ➲ WORDFINDER NOTE AT CAR, JOURNEY **2** [T] **~ sth (to sth)** (*law* 律) to replace one punishment with another that is less severe 减刑 **3** [T] **~ sth (for/into sth)** (*finance* 财) to exchange one form of payment, for sth else 代偿

■ ***noun*** the journey that a person makes when they commute to work 上下班路程： *a two-hour commute into downtown Washington* 去华盛顿中心区两小时的上下班路程 ◇ *I have only a short commute to work.* 我上班的路程很短。

com·muter /kə'mju:tə(r)/ *noun* a person who travels into a city to work each day, usually from quite far away （远距离）上下班往返的人： (*BrE*) *the **commuter belt*** (= the area around a city where people live and from which they travel to work in the city) 上班族居住地带

comp /kɒmp; *NAmE* kɑ:mp/ *noun* (*informal*) **1** [C] (*BrE*) = COMPREHENSIVE： *Her children go to the local comp.* 她的孩子们上当地的综合中学。 **2** [C] (*BrE*) = COMPETITION **3** [C] (*NAmE*) a COMPLIMENTARY ticket, meal, etc. (= one that you do not have to pay for) 赠品（如入场券、膳食等） **4** [U] (*NAmE*) = COMPENSATION： ***comp time*** (= time off work given for working extra hours) （加班后的）补休时间

com·pact *adj., noun, verb*

■ ***adj.*** /kəm'pækt; 'kɒmpækt; *NAmE* 'kɑ:m-/ **1** smaller than is usual for things of the same kind 小型的；袖珍的： *a compact camera* 袖珍照相机 **2** using or filling only a small amount of space 紧凑的；体积小的： *The kitchen was compact but well equipped.* 这间厨房虽然空间小但设备齐全。 **3** closely and firmly packed together 紧密的；坚实的： *a compact mass of earth* 一堆压得很结实的泥土 **4** (of a person or an animal 人或动物) small and strong 矮小而健壮的： *He had a compact and muscular body.* 他个子矮小，身体健壮。 ▶ **com·pact·ly** *adv.* **com·pact·ness** *noun* [U]

■ ***noun*** /'kɒmpækt; *NAmE* 'kɑ:m-/ **1** (*NAmE*) a small car 小汽车 ➲ COMPARE SUBCOMPACT **2** a small flat box with a mirror, containing powder that women use on their faces 带镜小粉盒 ➲ VISUAL VOCAB PAGE V65 **3** (*formal*) a formal agreement between two or more people or countries 协定；协议；契约；合约

■ ***verb*** /kəm'pækt/ [usually passive] **~ sth** to press sth together firmly 把…紧压在一起（或压实）： *a layer of compacted snow* 压紧的一层雪

,compact 'disc *noun* = CD

com·padre /kɒm'pɑ:dreɪ; *NAmE* kəm-/ *noun* (*NAmE, informal, from Spanish*) a friend or sb with whom you spend a lot of time 朋友；同伴

com·pan·ion /kəm'pæniən/ *noun* **1** a person or an animal that travels with you or spends a lot of time with you 旅伴；伴侣；陪伴： *travelling companions* 旅伴 ◇ (*figurative*) *Fear was the hostages' constant companion.* 人质一直都感到恐惧不安。 ➲ WORDFINDER NOTE AT FRIEND **2** a person who has similar tastes, interests, etc. to your own and whose company you enjoy （爱好、志趣等相投的）伙伴，同伴： *She was a charming dinner companion.* 与她同桌进餐使人感到十分高兴。◇ *His younger brother is not much of a companion for him.* 他的弟弟和他志趣不太相投。◇ *They're drinking companions* (= they go out drinking together). 他们是酒友。 **3** a person who shares in your work, pleasures, sadness, etc. 同甘共苦的伙伴： *We became companions in misfortune.* 我们成了患难之交。 **4** a person, usually a woman, employed to live with and help sb, especially sb old or ill/sick 陪护（通常受雇照料老人或病人） **5** one of a pair of things that go together or can be used together 成对的物品之一；一副物品中的一个： *A companion volume is soon to be published.* 这卷书的姊妹篇即将问世。 **6** used in book titles to describe a book giving useful facts and information on a particular subject （用于书名）指南，手册： *A Companion to French Literature* 《法国文学指南》 ➲ SEE ALSO BOON COMPANION

com·pan·ion·able /kəm'pæniənəbl/ *adj.* friendly 朋友般的；友好的；友善的 ▸ **com·pan·ion·ably** /-əbli/ *adv.*

com·pan·ion·ship /kəm'pæniənʃɪp/ *noun* [U] the pleasant feeling that you have when you have a friendly relationship with sb and are not alone 友情；交谊；友谊： *They meet at the club for companionship and advice.* 他们在俱乐部相会是为了联谊和寻求建议。 ◇ *She had only her cat for companionship.* 她只有猫儿做伴。

com·pan·ion·way /kəm'pæniənweɪ/ *noun* (*specialist*) a set of stairs on a ship （船上的）升降口扶梯

com·pany 🔑 /'kʌmpəni/ *noun* (*pl.* **-ies**)

• **BUSINESS** 商业 **1** 🔑 [C+sing./pl. v.] (*abbr.* **Co.**) (often in names 常用于名称) a business organization that makes money by producing or selling goods or services 公司；商号；商行： *the largest computer company in the world* 全球最大的计算机公司 ◇ *the National Bus Company* 全国公共汽车公司 ◇ *She joined the company in 2009.* 她于 2009 年加入这家公司。 ◇ *Company profits were 5% lower than last year.* 公司的利润比去年降低了 5%。 ➲ COLLOCATIONS AT BUSINESS

WORDFINDER 联想词： agent, **business**, competitor, customer, director, **employ**, franchise, manager, shareholder

• **THEATRE/DANCE** 戏剧；舞蹈 **2** 🔑 (often in names 常用于名称) [C+sing./pl. v.] a group of people who work or perform together 剧团；演出团： *a* ***theatre/dance, etc. company*** 剧团、舞蹈团等 ◇ *the Royal Shakespeare Company* 皇家莎士比亚戏剧团

• **BEING WITH SB** 与某人在一起 **3** 🔑 [U] the fact of being with sb else and not alone 陪伴；做伴： *I enjoy Jo's company* (= I enjoy being with her). 我喜欢和乔在一起。 ◇ *She enjoys her own company* (= being by herself) *when she is travelling.* 她喜爱独自旅行。 ◇ *The children are very* ***good company*** (= pleasant to be with) *at this age.* 和这个年龄的孩子在一起很开心。 ◇ *a pleasant evening in the company of friends* 与朋友一起度过的愉快夜晚 ◇ *He's coming with me* ***for company***. 他要陪伴我一起来。

• **GUESTS** 宾客 **4** [U] (*formal*) guests in your house 宾客；来宾： *I didn't realize you* ***had company***. 我不知道你有客人。

• **GROUP OF PEOPLE** 一群人 **5** [U] (*formal*) a group of people together 在一起的一群人： *She told the assembled company what had happened.* 她把发生的事告诉了聚会的人。 ◇ *It is bad manners to whisper* ***in company*** (= in a group of people). 在众人面前窃窃私语是不礼貌的行为。

• **SOLDIERS** 士兵 **6** [C+sing./pl. v.] a group of soldiers that is part of a BATTALION 连队

IDM **the 'company sb keeps** the people that sb spends time with 某人所交往的人；伙伴；与之为伍的人： *Judging by the company he kept, Mark must have been a wealthy man.* 根据马克所交往的人来判断，他一定是位富翁。 **get into/keep bad 'company** to be friends with people that others disapprove of 与坏人交往 **in company with sb/sth** (*formal*) together with or at the same time as sb/sth 与…一起；与…同时： *She arrived in company with the ship's captain.* 她与船长一起到达。 ◇ *The US dollar went through a difficult time, in company with the oil market.* 美元与石油市场同时经历了艰难时期。 **in good 'company** if you say that sb is **in good company**, you mean that they should not worry about a mistake, etc. because sb else, especially sb more important, has done the same thing 无伤大雅（表示不必为错误等担忧，因为他人，尤其是更重要的人也犯过同样的错误） **keep sb 'company** to stay with sb so that they are not alone 做伴；陪伴： *I'll keep you company while you're waiting.* 你等待时我会陪伴你。 **two's 'company (, three's a 'crowd)** (*saying*) used to suggest that it is better to be in a group of only two people than have a third person with you as well 两人成伴（三人太多） ➲ MORE AT PART *v.*, PRESENT *adj.*

company 'car *noun* a car which is provided by the company that you work for （为工作人员提供的）公司车

com·par·able /'kɒmpərəbl; *NAmE* 'kɑːm-/ *adj.* ~ **(to/with sb/sth)** similar to sb/sth else and able to be compared 类似的；可比较的： *A comparable house in the south of the city would cost twice as much.* 一栋类似的房子位于城南就要贵一倍。 ◇ *The situation in the US is not directly comparable to that in the UK.* 美国的情况与英国的不能直接相比。 ◇ *Inflation is now at a rate comparable with that in other European countries.* 现在通货膨胀率已经和欧洲其他国家的差不多了。 ▸ **com·par·abil·ity** /ˌkɒmpərə'bɪləti; *NAmE* ˌkɑːm-/ *noun* [U]: *Each group will have the same set of questions, in order to ensure comparability.* 为确保可比性，每一组将得到一套同样的问题。

com·para·tive /kəm'pærətɪv/ *adj.*, *noun*

▪ ***adj.*** **1** connected with studying things to find out how similar or different they are 比较的；相比的： *a comparative study of the educational systems of two countries* 两国教育制度的比较研究 ◇ *comparative linguistics* 比较语言学 **2** measured or judged by how similar or different it is to sth else 比较而言的；相对的 **SYN** **relative**: *Then he was living in comparative comfort* (= compared with others or with his own life at a previous time). 他那时生活比较舒适。 ◇ *The company is a comparative newcomer to the software market* (= other companies have been in business much longer). 就软件市场来说，这家公司相对而言就是新手了。 **3** (*grammar* 语法) relating to adjectives or adverbs that express more in amount, degree or quality, for example *better, worse, slower* and *more difficult* （形容词或副词）比较级的（如 better、worse、slower 和 more difficult） ➲ COMPARE SUPERLATIVE *adj.*

▪ ***noun*** (*grammar* 语法) the form of an adjective or adverb that expresses more in amount, degree or quality （形容词或副词的）比较级形式： *'Better' is the comparative of 'good' and 'more difficult' is the comparative of 'difficult'.* * better 是 good 的比较级； more difficult 是 difficult 的比较级。 ➲ COMPARE SUPERLATIVE *n.*

com·para·tive·ly /kəm'pærətɪvli/ *adv.* as compared to sth/sb else 比较上；相对地 **SYN** **relatively**: *The unit is comparatively easy to install and cheap to operate.* 这种设备比较容易安装而且用起来便宜。 ◇ *He died comparatively young* (= at a younger age than most people die). 他死时年纪并不大。 ◇ *comparatively few/low/rare/recent* 比较少 / 低 / 罕见；时间上相对较近的

com·pare 🔑 /kəm'peə(r); *NAmE* -'per/ *verb*, *noun*

▪ ***verb*** **1** 🔑 (*abbr.* **cf.**, **cp.**) [T] to examine people or things to see how they are similar and how they are different 比较；对比： **~ A and B** *It is interesting to compare their situation and ours.* 把他们的状况与我们的相比很有意思。 ◇ *We compared the two reports carefully.* 我们仔细地比较了两个报告。 ◇ **~ A with/to B** *We carefully compared the first report with the second.* 我们仔细比较了第一份报告和第二份报告。 ◇ *My own problems seem insignificant* ***compared with*** *other people's.* 与别人的问题相比，我自己的问题算不得什么。 ◇ *I've had some difficulties, but they were* ***nothing compared to*** *yours* (= they were not nearly as bad as yours). 我遇到了一些困难，但与你的困难比起来就算不上什么了。 ◇ *Standards in health care have improved enormously compared to 40 years ago.* 与 40 年前相比，卫生保健的水平得到了极大提高。 ➲ LANGUAGE BANK AT CONTRAST, ILLUSTRATE **2** 🔑 [I] **~ with/to sb/sth** to be similar to sb/sth else, either better or worse 与…类似（或相似）： *This school compares with the best in the country* (= it is as good as them). 这所学校可与全国最好的学校媲美。 ◇ *This house doesn't compare with our previous one* (= it is not as good). 这房子比不上我们以前的。 ◇ *Their prices* ***compare favourably*** *to those of their competitors.* 他们的价格比竞争者的要优惠。 **3** 🔑 [T] **~ A to B** to show or state that sb/sth is similar to sb/sth else 表明…与…相似；将…比作： *The critics compared his work to that of Martin Amis.* 评论家把他的作品和马丁•埃米斯的相提并论。

IDM **compare 'notes (with sb)** if two or more people **compare notes**, they each say what they think about the same event, situation, etc. （与…）交换看法（或意见等）
you can't compare ˌapples and 'oranges (*NAmE*) it is impossible to say that one thing is better than another if the two are completely different（因两样事物完全不同）不具可比性，不能相提并论：*They are both great but you can't compare apples and oranges.* 他们两个都很不错，但是不可相提并论。

▪*noun*

IDM **beyond/without com'pare** (*literary*) better than anything else of the same kind 无与伦比；举世无双

com·pari·son /kəmˈpærɪsn/ *noun* **1** [U] ~ (**with sb/sth**) the process of comparing two or more people or things 比较：*Comparison with other oil-producing countries is extremely interesting.* 与其他石油生产国作一比较是很有意思的。◇ *I enclose the two plans* ***for comparison.*** 兹附上两份计划以供比较。◇ *The education system* ***bears/stands no comparison with*** (= is not as good as) *that in many Asian countries.* 这种教育制度比不上许多亚洲国家的教育制度。 **2** [C] an occasion when two or more people or things are compared 对比；相比：**~ of A and B** *a comparison of the rail systems in Britain and France* 英国和法国铁路系统的比较 ◇ **~ of A with B** *a comparison of men's salaries with those of women* 男女薪酬的比较 ◇ **~ between A and B** *comparisons between Britain and the rest of Europe* 英国与欧洲其他国家之间的各种比较 ◇ **~ of A to B** *a comparison of the brain to a computer* (= showing what is similar) 将大脑比作计算机 ◇ **~ (with sth)** *It is difficult to* ***make a comparison*** *with her previous book—they are completely different.* 这很难与她以前的书相比，两者是截然不同的。◇ *You can* ***draw comparisons*** *with the situation in Ireland* (= say how the two situations are similar). 这种情形可与爱尔兰的相比。 ➲ LANGUAGE BANK AT SIMILARLY

IDM **by comparison** used especially at the beginning of a sentence when the next thing that is mentioned is compared with sth in the previous sentence（尤用于句首）比较起来，较之：*By comparison, expenditure on education increased last year.* 相比之下，去年教育经费增加了。 **by/in comparison (with sb/sth)** when compared with sb/sth （与…）相比较：*The second half of the game was dull by comparison with the first.* 与上半场相比，比赛的下半场有些沉闷。◇ *The tallest buildings in London are small in comparison with New York's skyscrapers.* 伦敦最高的建筑物与纽约的摩天大厦一比就相形见绌。 **there's no com'parison** used to emphasize the difference between two people or things that are being compared（强调比较之下的差别）无法相比，根本不能相提并论：*In terms of price there's no comparison* (= one thing is much more expensive than the other). 在价格方面无法相比。 ➲ MORE AT PALE *v.*

com·part·ment /kəmˈpɑːtmənt; *NAmE* -ˈpɑːrt-/ *noun* **1** one of the separate sections which a coach/car on a train is divided into（铁路客车车厢分隔成的）隔间 **2** one of the separate sections that sth such as a piece of furniture or equipment has for keeping things in（家具或设备等的）分隔间，隔层：*The desk has a secret compartment.* 这书桌有一个秘密暗格。◇ *There is a handy storage compartment beneath the oven.* 在烤箱的下面有一个便利的橱柜。 ➲ SEE ALSO GLOVE COMPARTMENT

com·part·men·tal·ize (*BrE also* **-ise**) /ˌkɒmpɑːtˈmentəlaɪz; *NAmE* kəmˌpɑːrt-/ *verb* **~ sth (into sth)** to divide sth into separate sections, especially so that one thing does not affect the other 分隔；隔开；划分：*Life today is rigidly compartmentalized into work and leisure.* 当今的生活被严格划分为工作和休闲两部分。

com·pass /ˈkʌmpəs/ *noun* **1** (*also* **magˌnetic 'compass**) [C] an instrument for finding direction, with a needle that always points to the north 罗盘；罗经；指南针；罗盘仪：*a map and compass* 地图和指南针 ◇ *the* ***points of the compass*** (= N, S, E, W, etc.) 罗经方位点（东、南、西、北等） ➲ WORDFINDER NOTE AT MAP ➲ VISUAL VOCAB PAGE V44 **2** [C] (*also* **compasses** [pl.]) an instrument with two long thin parts joined together at the top, used for drawing circles and measuring distances on a map 圆规；两脚规：*a pair of compasses* 一副圆规 **3** [sing.] (*formal*) a range or an extent, especially of what can be achieved in a particular situation 范围；范畴；界限：*the compass of a singer's voice* (= the range from the lowest to the highest note that he or she can sing) 歌手的音域

com·pas·sion /kəmˈpæʃn/ *noun* [U] ~ (**for sb**) a strong feeling of sympathy for people who are suffering and a desire to help them 同情；怜悯：*to feel/show compassion* 感到/表示同情

com·pas·sion·ate /kəmˈpæʃənət/ *adj.* feeling or showing sympathy for people who are suffering 有同情心的；表示怜悯的：*He was allowed to go home on compassionate grounds* (= because he was suffering). 他因为得到同情而获准回家。 ▸ **com·pas·sion·ate·ly** *adv.*

comˌpassionate 'leave *noun* [U] time that you are allowed to be away from work because sb in your family is ill/sick or has died 恩恤休假；恩假（因家人生病或去世而准许的休假）

com·pati·bil·ity AW /kəmˌpætəˈbɪləti/ *noun* [U] ~ (**with sb/sth**) | ~ (**between A and B**) **1** the ability of people or things to live or exist together without problems 和睦相处；并存；相容 **2** the ability of machines, especially computers, and computer programs to be used together（尤指计算机及程序的）兼容性，相容性

com·pat·ible AW /kəmˈpætəbl/ *adj.* **1** ~ (**with sth**) (of machines, especially computers, or software 机器，尤指计算机，或软件) able to be used together 兼容的；可共用的：*The new system will be compatible with existing equipment.* 新的系统将与现有的设备相互兼容。 **2** ~ (**with sth**) (of ideas, methods or things 想法、方法或事物) able to exist or be used together without causing problems 可共存的；可共用的；兼容的：*Are measures to protect the environment compatible with economic growth?* 保护环境的措施与经济的增长协调吗？ ◇ *compatible blood groups* 相容的血型 **3** ~ (**with sb**) if two people are **compatible**, they can have a good relationship because they have similar ideas, interests, etc.（因思想、志趣等相投而）关系好的，和睦相处的 OPP **incompatible** ▸ **com·pat·ibly** /-əbli/ *adv.*

com·pat·riot /kəmˈpætriət; *NAmE* -ˈpeɪt-/ *noun* a person who was born in, or is a citizen of, the same country as sb else 同胞；同国人 SYN **countryman**：*He played against one of his compatriots in the semi-final.* 他在半决赛中与他的一位同胞选手对垒。

com·pel /kəmˈpel/ *verb* (**-ll-**) (*formal*) **1** to force sb to do sth; to make sth necessary 强迫；迫使；使必须：**~ sb to do sth** *The law can compel fathers to make regular payments for their children.* 这项法律可强制父亲定期支付子女的费用。◇ ***I feel compelled to*** *write and tell you how much I enjoyed your book.* 我觉得必须写信告诉你我是多么欣赏你的书。◇ **~ sth** *Last year ill health compelled his retirement.* 去年他因身体不好被迫退休了。 **2** ~ **sth** (not used in

compasses 指南针；圆规

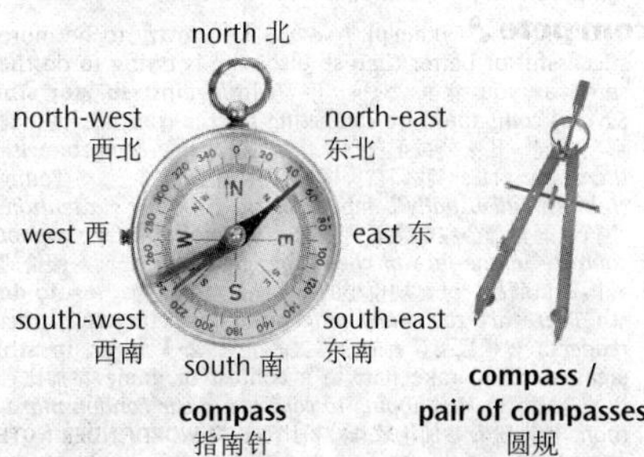

compass 指南针

compass / pair of compasses 圆规

the progressive tenses 不用于进行时) to cause a particular reaction 引起反应: *He spoke with an authority that compelled the attention of the whole crowd.* 他用权威的口气讲话，引起了整个人群的注意。➲ SEE ALSO COMPULSION

C

com·pel·ling /kəm'pelɪŋ/ *adj.* **1** that makes you pay attention to it because it is so interesting and exciting 引人入胜的；扣人心弦的：*Her latest book makes compelling reading.* 她新出的书读起来扣人心弦。➲ SYNONYMS AT INTERESTING **2** so strong that you must do sth about it 非常强烈的；不可抗拒的：*a* ***compelling need/desire*** 非常强烈的需要 / 欲望 **3** that makes you think it is true 令人信服的：*There is no compelling reason to believe him.* 没有令人信服的理由让人相信他。◇ *compelling evidence* 有说服力的证据 ▸ **com·pel·ling·ly** *adv.*：*compellingly attractive* 具有无法抗拒的魅力

com·pen·dious /kəm'pendiəs/ *adj.* (*formal*) containing all the necessary facts about sth 简明扼要的；概括的：*a compendious description* 简要说明

com·pen·dium /kəm'pendiəm/ *noun* (*pl.* **com·pen·dia** /-diə/ or **com·pen·diums**) a collection of facts, drawings and photographs on a particular subject, especially in a book（尤指书中某题材事实、图画及照片的）汇编，概要

com·pen·sate AW /'kɒmpenseɪt; *NAmE* 'kɑːm-/ *verb* **1** [I] ~ (**for sth**) to provide sth good to balance or reduce the bad effects of damage, loss, etc. 补偿；弥补 SYN **make up for**: *Nothing can compensate for the loss of a loved one.* 失去心爱的人是无法补偿的。**2** [T] ~ **sb** (**for sth**) to pay sb money because they have suffered some damage, loss, injury, etc. 给（某人）赔偿（或赔款）：*Her lawyers say she should be compensated for the suffering she had been caused.* 她的律师说她应该为所遭受的痛苦得到赔偿。▸ **com·pen·sa·tory** AW /ˌkɒmpen'seɪtəri; *NAmE* kəm'pensətɔːri/ *adj.*: *He received a compensatory payment of $20 000.* 他获得了 2 万美元的赔偿金。

com·pen·sa·tion AW /ˌkɒmpen'seɪʃn; *NAmE* ˌkɑːm-/ *noun* **1** [U, C] ~ (**for sth**) something, especially money, that sb gives you because they have hurt you, or damaged sth that you own; the act of giving this to sb 补偿（或赔偿）物；（尤指）赔偿金，补偿金；赔偿：*to* ***claim/award/receive compensation*** 要求 / 判给 / 得到赔偿金 ◇ *to pay compensation for injuries at work* 支付工伤赔偿金 ◇ *to receive £10 000* ***in compensation*** 得到赔偿金 1 万英镑 **2** [C, usually pl.] ~ (**for sth**) things that make a bad situation better 使坏的情况变好的事物；（对不利局面的）补偿：*I wish I were young again, but getting older has its compensations.* 我要是能再次年轻就好了，但上了年纪也有上了年纪的好处。

com·père /'kɒmpeə(r); *NAmE* 'kɑːmper/ *noun, verb*

■ ***noun*** (*BrE*) a person who introduces the people who perform in a television programme, a show in a theatre, etc.（电视节目等的）主持人；（剧院等的）报幕员 SYN **emcee**: *to act as (a) compère* 当节目主持人

■ ***verb*** [T, I] ~ (**sth**) (*BrE*) to act as a compère for a show 做（演出）主持人；做报幕员

com·pete 🔑 /kəm'piːt/ *verb* **1** 🔑 [I] to try to be more successful or better than sb else who is trying to do the same as you 竞争；对抗：~ (**with/against sb**) (**for sth**) *Several companies are competing for the contract.* 为得到那项合同，几家公司正在竞争。◇ *We can't compete with them on price.* 我们在价格上无法与他们竞争。◇ *Young children will usually compete for their mother's attention.* 小孩子通常都会在母亲面前争宠。◇ *Small traders cannot compete in the face of cheap foreign imports.* 面对廉价的外国进口商品，经营规模小的商人无法与之抗衡。◇ **~ to do sth** *There are too many magazines competing to attract readers.* 竞相吸引读者的杂志太多了。**2** 🔑 [I] ~ (**in sth**) (**against sb**) to take part in a contest or game 参加比赛（或竞赛）：*He's hoping to compete in the London marathon.* 他期盼着参加伦敦马拉松比赛。➲ WORDFINDER NOTE AT SPORT

com·pe·tence /'kɒmpɪtəns; *NAmE* 'kɑːm-/ *noun* **1** (*also less frequent* **com·pe·ten·cy**) [U, C] ~ (**in sth**) | ~ (**in doing sth**) the ability to do sth well 能力；胜任：*to gain a high level of competence in English* 获得高水平的英语能力 ◇ *professional/technical competence* 专业 / 技术能力 OPP **incompetence 2** [U] (*law* 律) the power that a court, an organization or a person has to deal with sth（法庭、机构或人的）权限，管辖权：*The judge has to act within the competence of the court.* 法官必须在法庭的权限范围内行使权力。◇ *outside sb's area of competence* 超出某人的权限范围 **3** [C] (*also less frequent* **com·pe·ten·cy**) (*specialist*) a skill that you need in a particular job or for a particular task 技能；本领：*The syllabus lists the knowledge and competences required at this level.* 教学大纲列出了这一级水平要求掌握的知识和技能。

com·pe·tency /'kɒmpɪtənsi; *NAmE* 'kɑːm-/ *noun* (*pl.* **-ies**) = COMPETENCE

com·pe·tent /'kɒmpɪtənt; *NAmE* 'kɑːm-/ *adj.* ~ (**to do sth**) **1** having enough skill or knowledge to do sth well or to the necessary standard 足以胜任的；有能力的；称职的：*Make sure the firm is competent to carry out the work.* 要确保这家公司有能力完成这项工作。◇ *He's very competent in his work.* 他工作十分称职。OPP **incompetent 2** of a good standard but not very good 合格的；不错的；尚好的 **3** having the power to decide sth 有决定权的：*The case was referred to a competent authority.* 事情已交给有关当局处理。▸ **com·pe·tent·ly** *adv.*：*to perform competently* 出色地完成

com·pe·ti·tion 🔑 /ˌkɒmpə'tɪʃn; *NAmE* ˌkɑːm-/ *noun* **1** 🔑 [U] ~ (**between/with sb**) (**for sth**) a situation in which people or organizations compete with each other for sth that not everyone can have 竞争；角逐：*There is now intense competition between schools to attract students.* 现在学校之间为了招揽学生展开了激烈竞争。◇ *We are* ***in competition with*** *four other companies for the contract.* 我们在与其他四家公司竞争这项合同。◇ *We won the contract in the face of* ***stiff competition***. 面对激烈的竞争，我们赢得了这项合同。**2** 🔑 [C] an event in which people compete with each other to find out who is the best at sth 比赛；竞赛：*a* ***music/photo, etc. competition*** 音乐、摄影等比赛 ◇ *to* ***enter/win/lose a competition*** 参加 / 赢得 / 输掉比赛

> WORDFINDER 联想词：closing date, disqualify, judge, prize, round, runner-up, submit, tiebreaker, winner

3 the competition [sing.+sing./pl. v.] the people who are competing against sb 竞争者；对手：*We'll be able to assess the competition at the conference.* 我们可以在会上对竞争对手进行估量。

com·peti·tive 🔑 /kəm'petətɪv/ *adj.* **1** 🔑 used to describe a situation in which people or organizations compete against each other 竞争的：***competitive games/sports*** 竞技性的比赛 / 体育运动 ◇ *Graduates have to fight for jobs in a* ***highly competitive*** *market.* 毕业生不得不在竞争激烈的市场上奋力争取工作。**2** 🔑 ~ (**with sb/sth**) as good as or better than others（与…）一样好的；（比…）更好的；有竞争力的：*a shop selling clothes at competitive prices* (= as low as any other shop) 在服装价格上有竞争力的商店 ◇ *We need to work harder to remain competitive with other companies.* 我们需要更加努力工作以便在与其他公司的竞争中不落下风。◇ *to gain a* ***competitive advantage*** *over rival companies* 占有超越对手公司的竞争优势 ➲ SYNONYMS AT CHEAP **3** 🔑 (of a person 人) trying very hard to be better than others 努力竞争的；一心求胜的：*You have to be highly competitive to do well in sport these days.* 如今你必须有强烈的竞争意识才能在体育运动中取得好成绩。OPP **uncompetitive** ▸ **com·peti·tive·ly** *adv.*：*competitively priced goods* 价格上具有竞争力的商品 **com·peti·tive·ness** *noun* [U]：*the competitiveness of British industry* 英国工业的竞争力

com·peti·tor /kəm'petɪtə(r)/ *noun* **1** a person or an organization that competes against others, especially in business（尤指商业方面的）竞争者，对手：***our main/major competitor*** 我们主要的竞争对手 ➲ WORDFINDER NOTE AT COMPANY **2** a person who takes part in a competition 参赛者；竞赛者：*Over 200 competitors entered the race.* * 200 多名选手参加了赛跑。

com·pil·ation AW /ˌkɒmpɪˈleɪʃn; *NAmE* ˌkɑːm-/ *noun* **1** [C] a collection of items, especially pieces of music or writing, taken from different places and put together 收集；选编；选辑：*Her latest album is a compilation of all her best singles.* 她的最新专辑收录了她所有的最佳单曲。◇ *a compilation album* 一张选辑 **2** [U] the process of compiling sth 编纂；编著；编写：*the compilation of a dictionary* 词典的编纂

com·pile AW /kəmˈpaɪl/ *verb* **1 ~ sth** to produce a book, list, report, etc. by bringing together different items, articles, songs, etc. 编写（书、列表、报告等）；编纂：*We are trying to compile a list of suitable people for the job.* 我们在努力编制一份适合做这项工作的人员的名单。◇ *The album was compiled from live recordings from last year's tour.* 这张专辑由去年巡回演出的实况录音汇编而成。**2 ~ sth** (*computing* 计) to translate instructions from one computer language into another so that a particular computer can understand them 编译

com·piler /kəmˈpaɪlə(r)/ *noun* **1** a person who compiles sth 编纂者；汇编者；编著者 **2** (*computing* 计) a program that translates instructions from one computer language into another for a computer to understand 编译程序；编译器

com·pla·cency /kəmˈpleɪsnsi/ *noun* [U] (*usually disapproving*) a feeling of satisfaction with yourself or with a situation, so that you do not think any change is necessary; the state of being complacent 自满；自得；自鸣得意：*Despite signs of an improvement in the economy, there is no room for complacency.* 尽管在经济方面有改善的迹象，但仍不容自满。

com·pla·cent /kəmˈpleɪsnt/ *adj.* ~ (**about sb/sth**) (*usually disapproving*) too satisfied with yourself or with a situation, so that you do not feel that any change is necessary; showing or feeling complacency 自满的；自鸣得意的；表现出自满的：*a dangerously complacent attitude to the increase in unemployment* 对失业增加抱满不在乎的危险态度 ◇ *We must not become complacent about progress.* 我们决不能因进步变得自满。▸ **com·pla·cent·ly** *adv.*

com·plain 🔑 /kəmˈpleɪn/ *verb* [I, T] to say that you are annoyed, unhappy or not satisfied about sb/sth 抱怨；埋怨；投诉；发牢骚：**~ (to sb) (about/of sth)** *I'm going to complain to the manager about this.* 我要就这件事向经理投诉。◇ *The defendant complained of intimidation during the investigation.* 被告申诉在调查期间受到了恐吓。◇ *She never complains, but she's obviously exhausted.* 她虽然从不抱怨，但显然已疲惫不堪。◇ (*informal*) *'How are you?' 'Oh, I can't complain* (= I'm all right).*'* "你好吗？" "啊，没的抱怨的。" ◇ **~ (that)**... *He **complained bitterly** that he had been unfairly treated.* 他愤懑地诉说他所受到的不公平待遇。◇ **+ speech** *'It's not fair,' she complained.* "这不公平。" 她抱怨道。

PHR V **com'plain of sth** to say that you feel ill/sick or are suffering from a pain 诉说（病情或痛苦）：*She left early, complaining of a headache.* 她说自己头疼，很早就离开了。

com·plain·ant /kəmˈpleɪnənt/ *noun* (*law* 律) = PLAINTIFF

com·plaint 🔑 /kəmˈpleɪnt/ *noun* **1** 🔑 [C] a reason for not being satisfied; a statement that sb makes saying that they are not satisfied 不满的原因；抱怨；埋怨；投诉；控告：**~ (about sb/sth)** *The most common complaint is about poor service.* 最常见的投诉与服务差有关。◇ *We received a number of complaints from customers about the lack of parking facilities.* 我们收到了来自顾客的许多投诉，抱怨缺乏停车设施。◇ *I'd like to **make a complaint** about the noise.* 我要就噪音问题提出投诉。◇ **~ (against sb/sth)** *I believe you have a complaint against one of our nurses.* 我认为你对我们的一位护士有怨言。◇ **~ (that...)** *a **complaint that** he had been unfairly treated* 对他受到了不公正待遇的投诉 ◇ *a **formal complaint*** 正式控告 ◇ (*formal*) *to **file/lodge*** (= make) ***a complaint*** 提出控告 **2** 🔑 [U] the act of complaining 抱怨；埋怨；投诉：*I can see **no grounds for complaint**.* 我找不到抱怨的理由。◇ *a letter of complaint* 投诉信 **3** [C] an illness, especially one that is not serious, and often one that affects a particular part of the body （尤指不严重、常影响身体某部位的）疾病：*a skin complaint* 皮肤病

▼ **SYNONYMS 同义词辨析**

complain

protest • object • grumble • moan • whine

These words all mean to say that you are annoyed, unhappy or not satisfied about sb/sth. 以上各词均含对人或事物感到恼怒、不高兴或不满之义。

complain to say that you are annoyed, unhappy or not satisfied about sb/sth 指抱怨、埋怨、投诉、发牢骚：*I'm going to complain to the manager about this.* 我要就这件事向经理投诉。

protest to say or do sth to show that you disagree with or disapprove of sth, especially publicly; to give sth as a reason for protesting 指公开反对、抗议或申辩：*Students took to the streets to **protest against** the decision.* 学生走上街头抗议这项决定。

object to say that you disagree with or disapprove of sth; to give sth as a reason for objecting 指不同意、不赞成、反对或抗辩：*If nobody objects, we'll postpone the meeting till next week.* 如果没有人反对，我们就把会议推迟到下周。◇ *He objected that the police had arrested him without sufficient evidence.* 他抗辩说警察没有充分证据就逮捕了他。

grumble (*rather informal, disapproving*) to complain about sb/sth in a bad-tempered way 指咕哝、嘟囔、发牢骚：*They kept grumbling that they were cold.* 他们不停地嘟囔着说冷。

moan (*BrE, rather informal, disapproving*) to complain about sb/sth in an annoying way 指抱怨、埋怨：*What are you moaning on about now?* 你在抱怨什么呢？

whine (*rather informal, disapproving*) to complain in an annoying, crying voice 指哭哭啼啼或哭嚷着诉说：*Stop whining!* 别哭哭啼啼的！◇ *'I want to go home,' whined Toby.* "我要回家。" 托比哼哼唧唧地说。NOTE **Whine** is often used to talk about the way that young children complain. * whine 通常用于小孩子抱怨。

PATTERNS

- to complain/protest/grumble/moan/whine **about** sth
- to complain/protest/grumble/moan **at** sth
- to complain/protest/object/grumble/moan/whine **to** sb
- to complain/protest/object/grumble/moan/whine **that...**

▼ **EXPRESS YOURSELF 情景表达**

Making a complaint 提出投诉

You can express your dissatisfaction when something you buy is of poor quality or the standard of service you receive is not good enough in various ways. 对所购劣质商品或得到的低标准服务表达不满可以用多种方式：

- *I'm afraid I'm not satisfied with this.* 恐怕我对此不太满意。
- ***I'm sorry. This isn't acceptable/good enough.*** *We've been waiting half an hour.* 对不起，这是不可接受的。我们已经等半个小时了。
- ***I'd like to make a complaint.*** *The radio I bought doesn't work.* 我要投诉。我买的收音机有故障。
- ***Excuse me—this isn't what I asked for.*** *I'm having/I ordered the soup, not the salad.* 对不起，这不是我点的。我要的是汤，不是色拉。
- ***I'd like to speak to the manager. I've got a complaint*** *about something I bought.* 我要找经理。我对我买的东西不满意。

C

com·plai·sant /kəmˈpleɪzənt/ *adj.* (*old-fashioned*) ready to accept other people's actions and opinions and to do what other people want 顺从的；殷勤的 ▸ **com·plai·sance** /kəmˈpleɪzəns/ *noun* [U]

com·plect·ed /kəmˈplektɪd/ *adj.* (*NAmE, informal*) (used with adjectives 与形容词连用) with skin and a COMPLEXION of the type mentioned 肤色…的: ***fair/dark complected*** 肤色白皙 / 黝黑

com·ple·ment AW *verb, noun*

■*verb* /ˈkɒmplɪment; *NAmE* ˈkɑːm-/ ~ **sth** to add to sth in a way that improves it or makes it more attractive 补充；补足；使完美；使更具吸引力: *The excellent menu is complemented by a good wine list.* 佳肴佐以美酒，堪称完美无缺。◇ *The team needs players who* ***complement each other.*** 球队需要能够相互取长补短的队员。 ➲ NOTE AT COMPLIMENT

■*noun* /ˈkɒmplɪmənt; *NAmE* ˈkɑːm-/ **1** ~ (**to sth**) a thing that adds new qualities to sth in a way that improves it or makes it more attractive 补充物；补足物 **2** the complete number or quantity needed or allowed 足数；足额: *We've taken our full complement of trainees this year.* 我们今年接收的实习生已满员。 **3** (*grammar* 语法) a word or phrase, especially an adjective or a noun, that is used after linking verbs such as *be* and *become*, and describes the subject of the verb. In some descriptions of grammar it is used to refer to any word or phrase which is GOVERNED by a verb and usually comes after the verb in a sentence. 补足语；补语: *In the sentences 'I'm angry' and 'He became a politician', 'angry' and 'politician' are complements.* 在句子 I'm angry 和 He became a politician 中，angry 和 politician 为补语。

com·ple·men·tary AW /ˌkɒmplɪˈmentri; *NAmE* ˌkɑːm-/ *adj.* ~ (**to sth**) two people or things that are **complementary** are different but together form a useful or attractive combination of skills, qualities or physical features 互补的；补充的；相互补足的: *The school's approach must be complementary to that of the parents.* 学校与家长的教育方法必须相辅相成。 ➲NOTE AT COMPLIMENT

ˌcomplementary ˈangle *noun* (*geometry* 几何) either of two angles which together make 90° 余角 ➲ COMPARE SUPPLEMENTARY ANGLE

ˌcomplementary ˈcolour (*especially US* **ˌcomplementary ˈcolor**) *noun* (*specialist*) **1** a colour that, when mixed with another colour, gives black or white 互补色，补色（与另外一种颜色混合成为黑色或白色的颜色） **2** a colour that gives the greatest contrast when combined with a particular colour 对比色（与某特定颜色形成最大色差的颜色）: *The designer has chosen the complementary colours blue and orange.* 设计师选取了蓝和橙黄两种对比色。

ˌcomplementary ˈmedicine *noun* [U] medical treatment that is not part of the usual scientific treatment used in Western countries, for example ACUPUNCTURE 辅助性医疗（不属于西方国家通常采用的科学疗法，如针灸） ➲**WORDFINDER NOTE AT TREATMENT**

com·ple·men·ta·tion /ˌkɒmplɪmenˈteɪʃn; *NAmE* ˌkɑːm-/ *noun* [U] **1** the fact of complementing sth 补充 **2** (*grammar* 语法) the complements of a verb in a clause （动词的）补足语，补语

com·ple·men·tizer (*BrE also* **-iser**) /ˈkɒmplɪməntaɪzə(r); *NAmE* ˈkɑːm-/ *noun* (*grammar* 语法) a word or part of a word that shows a clause is being used as a complement 补语化成分

com·plete 🔑 /kəmˈpliːt/ *adj., verb*

■*adj.* **1** 🔑 [usually before noun] used when you are emphasizing sth, to mean 'to the greatest degree possible' (用以强调) 完全的，彻底的 SYN **total**: *We were in complete agreement.* 我们意见完全一致。◇ *a complete change* 彻底的变化 ◇ *in complete silence* 万籁俱寂 ◇ *a complete stranger* 素不相识的人 ◇ *It came as a complete surprise.* 这事来得十分意外。◇ *I felt a complete idiot.* 我觉得自己是个十足的笨蛋。 **2** 🔑 including all the parts, etc. that are necessary; whole 全部的；完整的；整个的: *I've collected the complete set.* 我收集了全套。◇ *a complete guide to events in Oxford* 牛津活动盛事完全手册 ◇ *the* ***complete works*** *of Tolstoy* 托尔泰全集 ◇ *You will receive payment for each complete day that you work.* 你将按你每一整天的工作领取报酬。 OPP **incomplete** **3** ~ **with sth** [not before noun] including sth as an extra part or feature 包括，含有（额外部分或特征）: *The furniture comes complete with tools and instructions for assembly.* 这件家具备有组装工具和说明书。◇ *The book, complete with CD, costs £35.* 此书包括光盘，售价 35 英镑。 **4** 🔑 [not before noun] finished 完成；结束: *Work on the office building will be complete at the end of the year.* 办公大楼工程将于年底竣工。 OPP **incomplete** ▸ **com·plete·ness** *noun* [U]: *the accuracy and completeness of the information* 信息的准确完整性 ◇ *For the sake of completeness, all names are given in full.* 为完整起见，所有名称均用全名。

■*verb* **1** 🔑 [often passive] ~ **sth** to finish making or doing sth 完成；结束: *She's just completed a master's degree in Law.* 她刚读完法律硕士学位。◇ *The project should be completed within a year.* 这项工程必须在一年之内完成。 **2** 🔑 ~ **sth** to write all the information you are asked for on a form 填写（表格） SYN **fill in/out**: *2 000 shoppers completed our questionnaire.* * 2 000 名顾客填写了我们的调查表。 **3** 🔑 ~ **sth** to make sth whole or perfect 使完整；使完美: *I only need one more card to complete the set.* 我只差一张卡片就配齐全套了。

com·plete·ly 🔑 /kəmˈpliːtli/ *adv.* (used to emphasize the following word or phrase 用于强调紧跟其后的词或短语) in every way possible 彻底地；完全地；完整地 SYN **totally**: *completely different* 截然不同 ◇ *completely and utterly broke* 彻底破产 ◇ *I've completely forgotten her name.* 我完全把她的名字给忘了。 ◇ *The explosion completely destroyed the building.* 爆炸完全毁掉了那栋大楼。

com·ple·tion /kəmˈpliːʃn/ *noun* **1** [U] the act or process of finishing sth; the state of being finished and complete 完成；结束: *the completion of the new hospital building* 新医院大楼的竣工 ◇ *Satisfactory completion of the course does not ensure you a job.* 圆满完成课程并不能保证你能得到工作。◇ *The project is* ***due for completion*** *in the spring.* 这项工程预定在明年春季竣工。◇ *The road is* ***nearing completion*** (= it is nearly finished). 这条道路快要完工了。◇ *the date of completion/the completion date* 竣工日期 **2** [U, C] (*BrE*) the formal act of completing the sale of property, for example the sale of a house （房地产等的）完成交易，完成交割

com·plex 🔑 AW *adj., noun*

■*adj.* /ˈkɒmpleks; *NAmE* kəmˈpleks; ˈkɑːm-/ **1** 🔑 made of many different things or parts that are connected; difficult to understand 复杂的；难懂的；费解的 SYN **complicated**: *complex machinery* 结构复杂的机器 ◇ *the complex structure of the human brain* 错综复杂的人脑构造 ◇ *a complex argument/problem/subject* 复杂难懂的论证 / 问题 / 科目 **2** (*grammar* 语法) (of a word or sentence 单词或句子) containing one main part (= the ROOT of a word or MAIN CLAUSE of a sentence) and one or more other parts (called AFFIXES or SUBORDINATE CLAUSES) 复合的（指词根加有词缀或主句含有从句） ➲COMPARE COMPOUND *adj.*

■*noun* /ˈkɒmpleks; *NAmE* ˈkɑːm-/ **1** a group of buildings of a similar type together in one place （类型相似的）建筑群: *a sports complex* 综合体育场 ◇ *an industrial complex* (= a site with many factories) 工业建筑群 ➲**SYNONYMS** AT BUILDING **2** a group of things that are connected 相关联的一组事物: *This is just one of a whole complex of issues.* 这仅仅是所有相关的问题之一。 **3** (especially in compounds 尤用于构成复合词) a mental state that is not normal 不正常的精神状态；情结: *to suffer from a guilt complex* 蒙受负罪感之苦 ➲ SEE ALSO INFERIORITY COMPLEX, OEDIPUS COMPLEX, PERSECUTION COMPLEX **4** if sb has a **complex** about sth, they are worried about it in way that is not normal （对某事）不正常的忧虑

com·plex·ion /kəmˈplekʃn/ *noun* **1** the natural colour and condition of the skin on a person's face 面色；肤色；气色: *a pale/bad complexion* 苍白的 / 病态的脸色 ➲ **COLLOCATIONS** AT PHYSICAL **2** [usually sing.] the general character of sth （事物的）性质，特性： *a move which changed the political complexion of the country* 改变国家政局的举措

IDM **put a new/different com'plexion on sth** to change the way that a situation appears 使形势改观

com·plex·ity AW /kəm'pleksəti/ *noun* **1** [U] the state of being formed of many parts; the state of being difficult to understand 复杂性；难懂： *the increasing complexity of modern telecommunication systems* 日益复杂的现代电信系统 ◇ *I was astonished by the size and complexity of the problem.* 这个问题的复杂性和涉及面之广使我感到惊讶。 **2 complexities** [pl.] the features of a problem or situation that are difficult to understand 难题；难以理解的局势： *the complexities of the system* 这一系统的复杂之处

ˌcomplex 'number *noun* (*mathematics* 数) a number containing both a REAL NUMBER and an IMAGINARY NUMBER 复数

com·pli·ance /kəm'plaɪəns/ *noun* [U] ~ (**with sth**) the practice of obeying rules or requests made by people in authority 服从；顺从；遵从： *procedures that must be followed to ensure full compliance with the law* 为确保严格遵守法律所必须遵行的程序 ◇ *Safety measures were carried out* ***in compliance with*** *paragraph 6 of the building regulations.* 遵照建筑规程的第 6 条实施了安全措施。 OPP **non-compliance** ➲ SEE ALSO COMPLY

com·pli·ant /kəm'plaɪənt/ *adj.* **1** (*usually disapproving*) too willing to agree with other people or to obey rules 顺从的；百依百顺的；俯首帖耳的： *By then, Henry seemed less compliant with his wife's wishes than he had six months before.* 与六个月以前相比，亨利当时对他妻子的意愿似乎已不那么百依百顺了。 ◇ *We should not be producing compliant students who do not dare to criticize.* 我们不应当把学生培养成不敢批评的唯唯诺诺的人。 **2** in agreement with a set of rules （与一系列规则）符合的，一致的： *This site is HTML compliant.* 这个网站支持 HTML 语言。 ➲ SEE ALSO COMPLY

com·pli·cate 🔑 /'kɒmplɪkeɪt; *NAmE* 'kɑːm-/ *verb* ~ **sth** to make sth more difficult to do, understand or deal with 使复杂化： *I do not wish to complicate the task more than is necessary.* 我不想使这项任务不必要地复杂化。 ◇ ***To complicate matters*** *further, there will be no transport available till 8 o'clock.* 使事情更难办的是 8 点钟之前不会有交通工具。 ◇ *The issue* ***is complicated by the fact that*** *a vital document is missing.* 一份重要文件的丢失使这个问题复杂化了。

com·pli·cated 🔑 /'kɒmplɪkeɪtɪd; *NAmE* 'kɑːm-/ *adj.* made of many different things or parts that are connected; difficult to understand 复杂的；难懂的 SYN **complex**： *a complicated system* 复杂的系统 ◇ *The instructions look very complicated.* 这说明书看起来很难懂。 ◇ *It's all very complicated—but I'll try and explain.* 尽管这一切都很难理解，但我会尽力解释。

com·pli·ca·tion /ˌkɒmplɪ'keɪʃn; *NAmE* ˌkɑːm-/ *noun* **1** [C, U] a thing that makes a situation more complicated or difficult 使更复杂化（或更困难）的事物： *The bad weather added a further complication to our journey.* 恶劣的天气给我们的旅行增加了更多的困难。 **2** [C, usually pl.] (*medical* 医) a new problem or illness that makes treatment of a previous one more complicated or difficult 并发症： *She developed complications after the surgery.* 她手术后出现了并发症。

com·pli·cit /kəm'plɪsɪt/ *adj.* ~ (**in/with sb/sth**) involved with other people in sth wrong or illegal （与某人在某事上）同谋的，串通的： *Several officers were complicit in the cover-up.* 几名军官串通一气隐瞒真相。

com·pli·city /kəm'plɪsəti/ *noun* [U] ~ (**in sth**) (*formal*) the act of taking part with another person in a crime 同谋；共犯；勾结 SYN **collusion**： *to be guilty of complicity in the murder* 犯凶杀同谋罪 ◇ *evident complicity between the two brothers* 两兄弟间明显的串通一气

com·pli·ment *noun, verb*

■ *noun* /'kɒmplɪmənt; *NAmE* 'kɑːm-/ **1** [C] a remark that expresses praise or admiration of sb 赞扬；称赞： ***to pay sb a compliment*** (= to praise them for sth) 对某人表示赞扬 ◇ *'You understand the problem because you're so much older.'* ***'I'll take that as a compliment!'*** "您是能理解这个问题的，因为您年纪大那么多。" "就当你这是夸奖吧！" ◇ *It's* ***a great compliment*** *to be asked to do the job.* 获聘请做这项工作是一项极大的荣誉。 ◇ ***to return the compliment*** (= to treat sb in the same way as they have treated you) 照样回敬 **2 compliments** [pl.] (*formal*) polite words or good wishes, especially when used to express praise and admiration 致意；问候；祝贺： *My compliments to the chef!* 请向厨师代为致意！ ◇ (*BrE*) *Compliments of the season!* (= for Christmas or the New Year) 谨致节日的祝贺！（圣诞节或新年时的贺辞） ◇ *Please accept these flowers* ***with the compliments of*** (= as a gift from) *the manager.* 请接受经理送的鲜花。 IDM SEE BACKHANDED

■ *verb* /'kɒmplɪment; *NAmE* 'kɑːm-/ ~ **sb** (**on sth**) to tell sb that you like or admire sth they have done, their appearance, etc. 赞美；称赞；钦佩： *She complimented him on his excellent German.* 她夸奖他德语棒极了。

com·pli·men·tary /ˌkɒmplɪ'mentri; *NAmE* ˌkɑːm-/ *adj.* **1** given free 免费的；赠送的： *complimentary tickets for the show* 演出赠券 **2** ~ (**about sth**) expressing admiration, praise, etc. 表示钦佩的；赞美的： *a complimentary remark* 赞美的言辞 ◇ *She was extremely complimentary about his work.* 她对他的工作给予了高度评价。 OPP **uncomplimentary** ➲ NOTE AT COMPLIMENT

'compliments slip *noun* (*BrE*) a small piece of paper printed with the name of a company, that is sent out together with information, goods, etc. （附在信息、货物等上印有公司名称的）赠礼便条，礼帖

com·ply /kəm'plaɪ/ *verb* (**com·plies, com·ply·ing, com·plied, com·plied**) [I] ~ (**with sth**) to obey a rule, an order, etc. 遵从；服从；顺从： *They refused to comply with the UN resolution.* 他们拒绝遵守联合国的决议。 ➲ SEE ALSO COMPLIANCE

compo /'kɒmpəʊ; *NAmE* 'kɑːmpoʊ/ *noun* [U] (*AustralE, NZE, informal*) money that is paid to a worker if he/she gets injured at work 工伤赔偿费 SYN **compensation**

com·pon·ent AW /kəm'pəʊnənt; *NAmE* -'poʊ-/ *noun* one of several parts of which sth is made 组成部分；成分；部件： *the components of a machine* 机器部件 ◇ *the car component industry* 汽车零部件制造业 ◇ ***Key components*** *of the government's plan are…* 政府计划的主要组成部分是… ◇ *Trust is a* ***vital component*** *in any relationship.* 在任何关系中，信任都是一个至关重要的因素。 ► **com·pon·ent** *adj.* [only before noun]： *Break the problem down into its* ***component parts.*** 把这个问题分解成若干组成部分。

▼ WHICH WORD? 词语辨析

compliment / complement

- These words have similar spellings but completely different meanings. If you **compliment** someone, you say something very nice to them. 这两个词拼写相似，但意义完全不同。compliment 指赞美、称赞： *She complimented me on my English.* 她夸奖我的英语好。 If one thing **complements** another, the two things work or look better because they are together. * complement 表示相辅相成、相配合： *The different flavours complement each other perfectly.* 不同的味道搭配在一起，可口极了。
- The adjectives are also often confused. 这两个词的形容词形式亦常混淆。 **Complimentary**： *She made some very complimentary remarks about my English.* 她对我的英语赞赏有加。 It can also mean 'free'. 该词亦含免费赠送之义： *There was a complimentary basket of fruit in our room.* 我们房间里有一篮免费赠送的水果。 **Complementary**： *The team members have different but complementary skills.* 队员技术不同但能互补。

com·pon·en·tial an·aly·sis /ˌkɒmpəˈnenʃl əˈnæləsɪs; NAmE ˌkɑːm-/ *noun* [U] (*linguistics* 语言) the study of meaning by analysing the different parts of words（语义的）成分分析

C

com·port /kəmˈpɔːt; NAmE -ˈpɔːrt/ *verb* **~ yourself + adv./prep.** (*formal*) to behave in a particular way 行为表现；举止：*She always comports herself with great dignity.* 她的举止总是很端庄。

com·port·ment /kəmˈpɔːtmənt; NAmE -ˈpɔːrt-/ *noun* [U] (*formal*) the way in which sb/sth behaves 行为；举止；表现：*She won admiration for her comportment during the trial.* 她在选拔赛中的表现得到了赞赏。

com·pose /kəmˈpəʊz; NAmE -ˈpoʊz/ *verb* **1** [T] (not used in the progressive tenses 不用于进行时) **~ sth** (*formal*) to combine together to form a whole 组成，构成（一个整体）**SYN** **make sth↔up**: *Ten men compose the committee.* 委员会由十人组成。➲ SEE ALSO COMPOSED (1) **2** [T, I] **~ (sth)** to write music 作曲；创作（音乐）：*Mozart composed his last opera shortly before he died.* 莫扎特在创作出他最后一部歌剧后不久便去世了。 **3** [T] **~ a letter/speech/poem** to write a letter, etc. usually with a lot of care and thought 撰写（信函、讲稿、诗歌等）：*She composed a letter of protest.* 她写了一封抗议信。➲ WORDFINDER NOTE AT MESSAGE **4** [T, no passive] (*formal*) to manage to control your feelings or expression 使镇静；使平静：**~ yourself** *Emma frowned, making an effort to compose herself.* 埃玛皱起了眉头，努力使自己镇定下来。◇ **~ sth** *I was so confused that I could hardly compose my thoughts.* 我心烦意乱难以镇定思绪。➲ SEE ALSO COMPOSURE

com·posed /kəmˈpəʊzd; NAmE -ˈpoʊzd/ *adj.* **1 be composed of sth** (*formal*) to be made or formed from several parts, things or people 由…组成（或构成）的：*The committee is composed mainly of lawyers.* 委员会主要由律师组成。➲ SYNONYMS AT CONSIST **2** [not usually before noun] calm and in control of your feelings 镇静；镇定；平静：*She seemed outwardly composed.* 她表面上好像很镇静。

com·poser /kəmˈpəʊzə(r); NAmE -ˈpoʊz-/ *noun* a person who writes music, especially CLASSICAL music（尤指古典音乐的）创作者；作曲者；作曲家

com·pos·ite /ˈkɒmpəzɪt; NAmE kəmˈpɑːzət/ *adj., noun*

■ ***adj.*** [only before noun] made of different parts or materials 合成的；混成的；复合的：*a composite picture* (= one made from several pictures) 合成照片

■ ***noun*** **1** something made by putting together different parts or materials 合成物；混合物；复合材料：*The document was a composite of information from various sources.* 这份文件是不同来源信息的综合。 **2** (*also* **comˈposite sketch**) (*both US*) (*BrE* **Iden·ti·kit™**) a set of drawings of different features that can be put together to form the face of a person, especially sb wanted by the police, using descriptions given by people who saw the person; a picture made in this way 容貌拼图（根据目击者描述拼制出人的面部画像，尤用于警方要捉拿的人）

com·pos·ition /ˌkɒmpəˈzɪʃn; NAmE ˌkɑːm-/ *noun* **1** [U] the different parts which sth is made of; the way in which the different parts are organized 成分；构成；组合方式：*the chemical composition of the soil* 土壤的化学成分 ◇ *the composition of the board of directors* 董事会的组成 ➲ SYNONYMS AT STRUCTURE **2** [C] (*formal*) a piece of music or art, or a poem（音乐、艺术、诗歌的）作品：*one of Beethoven's finest compositions* 贝多芬最优美的音乐作品之一 **3** [U] the act of COMPOSING sth 作曲；创作：*pieces performed in the order of their composition* 按作曲顺序表演的作品 **4** [U] the art of writing music 作曲艺术：*to study composition* 学习作曲艺术 **5** [C] a short text that is written as a school exercise; a short essay 作文；小论文 **6** [U] (*art* 美术) the arrangement of people or objects in a painting or photograph（绘画、摄影的）构图

com·posi·tor /kəmˈpɒzɪtə(r); NAmE -ˈpɑːz-/ *noun* a person who arranges text on a page before printing 排版人员

com·pos men·tis /ˌkɒmpəs ˈmentɪs; NAmE ˌkɑːm-/ *adj.* [not before noun] (*from Latin, formal* or *humorous*) having full control of your mind 能完全控制神志；心智健全 **OPP** **non compos mentis**

com·post /ˈkɒmpɒst; NAmE ˈkɑːmpoʊst/ *noun, verb*

■ ***noun*** [U, C] a mixture of decayed plants, food, etc. that can be added to soil to help plants grow 混合肥料；堆肥：*potting compost* (= a mixture of soil and compost that you can buy to grow new plants in) 盆栽混合肥料 ➲ VISUAL VOCAB PAGE V9

■ ***verb*** **1 ~ sth** to make sth into compost 把…制成堆肥 **2 ~ sth** to put compost on or in sth 施堆肥于

ˈcompost bin *noun* a container in the garden where leaves, plants, etc. are put to make compost（花园里的）堆肥桶；落叶垃圾桶 ➲ VISUAL VOCAB PAGE V20

ˈcompost heap (*especially BrE*) (*NAmE usually* **ˈcompost pile**) *noun* a place in the garden where leaves, plants, etc. are piled, to make compost（花园里的）堆肥处；园中落叶堆

com·pos·ure /kəmˈpəʊʒə(r); NAmE -ˈpoʊ-/ *noun* [U] the state of being calm and in control of your feelings or behaviour 沉着；镇静；镇定：***to keep/lose/recover/regain your composure*** 保持 / 失去 / 恢复镇静

com·pote /ˈkɒmpɒt; NAmE ˈkɑːmpoʊt/ *noun* [C, U] a cold DESSERT (= a sweet dish) made of fruit that has been cooked slowly with sugar（加糖慢火煮过后冷却的）糖渍水果，蜜饯

com·pound **AW** *noun, adj., verb*

■ ***noun*** /ˈkɒmpaʊnd; NAmE ˈkɑːm-/ **1** a thing consisting of two or more separate things combined together 复合物；混合物 **2** (*chemistry* 化) a substance formed by a chemical reaction of two or more elements in fixed amounts relative to each other 化合物：*Common salt is a compound of sodium and chlorine.* 普通食盐是钠和氯的化合物。➲ COMPARE ELEMENT, MIXTURE ➲ WORDFINDER NOTE AT CHEMISTRY **3** (*grammar* 语法) a noun, an adjective or a verb made of two or more words or parts of words, written as one or more words, or joined by a hyphen. *Travel agent*, *dark-haired* and *bathroom* are all compounds. 复合词 **4** an area surrounded by a fence or wall in which a factory or other group of buildings stands 有围栏（或围墙）的场地（内有工厂或其他建筑群）：*a prison compound* 监狱场地

■ ***adj.*** /ˈkɒmpaʊnd; NAmE ˈkɑːm-/ [only before noun] (*specialist*) formed of two or more parts 复合的：*a compound adjective, such as fair-skinned* 复合形容词，如 fair-skinned ◇ *A compound sentence contains two or more clauses.* 复合句包含两个或多个从句。

■ ***verb*** /kəmˈpaʊnd/ **1** [often passive] **~ sth** to make sth bad become even worse by causing further damage or problems 使加重；使恶化：*The problems were compounded by severe food shortages.* 严重的食物短缺使问题进一步恶化。 **2 be compounded of/from sth** (*formal*) to be formed from sth 由…构成（或形成）：*The DNA molecule is compounded from many smaller molecules.* 脱氧核糖核酸分子是由许多更小的分子组成的。 **3** [often passive] **~ sth (with sth)** (*formal* or *specialist*) to mix sth together 混合；掺和；拌和：*liquid soaps compounded with disinfectant* 用消毒剂混合制成的皂液 **4 ~ sth** (*finance* 财) to pay or charge interest on an amount of money that includes any interest already earned or charged 支付，收取（复利）

ˌcompound ˈeye *noun* (*biology* 生) an eye like that of most insects, made up of several parts that work separately 复眼

ˌcompound ˈfracture *noun* an injury in which a bone in the body is broken and part of the bone comes through the skin 开放性骨折 ➲ COMPARE SIMPLE FRACTURE

ˌcompound ˈinterest *noun* [U] interest that is paid both on the original amount of money saved and on the interest that has been added to it 复利 ➲ COMPARE SIMPLE INTEREST

com·pre·hend /ˌkɒmprɪˈhend; *NAmE* ˌkɑːm-/ *verb* [I, T] (often used in negative sentences 常用于否定句) (*formal*) to understand sth fully 理解；领悟；懂：*He stood staring at the dead body, unable to comprehend.* 他站在那里，盯着那具尸体，弄不明白是怎么回事。◇ **~ sth** *The infinite distances of space are too great for the human mind to comprehend.* 太空的广阔无垠是人类无法理解的。◇ **~ how/why, etc....** *She could not comprehend how someone would risk people's lives in that way.* 她不明白怎么会有人竟拿人们的生命那样去冒险。◇ **~ that...** *He simply could not comprehend that she could be guilty.* 他就是搞不懂她怎么会有罪。➲ SYNONYMS AT UNDERSTAND

com·pre·hen·sible /ˌkɒmprɪˈhensəbl; *NAmE* ˌkɑːm-/ *adj.* ~ (**to sb**) (*formal*) that can be understood by sb 可理解的；能懂的：*easily/readily comprehensible to the average reader* 一般读者容易懂的 OPP **incomprehensible** ▶ **com·pre·hen·sib·il·ity** /ˌkɒmprɪˌhensəˈbɪləti; *NAmE* ˌkɑːm-/ *noun* [U]

com·pre·hen·sion /ˌkɒmprɪˈhenʃn; *NAmE* ˌkɑːm-/ *noun* **1** [U] the ability to understand 理解力；领悟能力：*speech and comprehension* 说话能力和理解力 ◇ *His behaviour was completely* ***beyond comprehension*** (= impossible to understand). 他的举止完全令人费解。◇ *She had no comprehension of what was involved.* 她不明白所涉及的事情。**2** [U, C] an exercise that trains students to understand a language（语言学习中的）理解练习（或训练）：*listening comprehension* 听力练习 ◇ *a reading comprehension* 阅读理解练习

com·pre·hen·sive AW /ˌkɒmprɪˈhensɪv; *NAmE* ˌkɑːm-/ *adj., noun*

■ ***adj.*** **1** including all, or almost all, the items, details, facts, information, etc., that may be concerned 全部的；所有的；（几乎）无所不包的；详尽的 SYN **complete, full**：*a comprehensive list of addresses* 详尽的地址目录 ◇ *a comprehensive study* 全面的研究 ◇ *comprehensive insurance* (= covering all risks) 综合保险 **2** (*BrE*) (of education 教育) designed for students of all abilities in the same school 综合性的（接收各种资质的学生）▶ **com·pre·hen·sive·ness** *noun* [U]

■ ***noun*** (*also* **compreˈhensive school**) (*also informal* **comp**) (in Britain) a SECONDARY SCHOOL for young people of all levels of ability（英国为各种资质的学生设立的）综合中学

com·pre·hen·sive·ly AW /ˌkɒmprɪˈhensɪvli; *NAmE* ˌkɑːm-/ *adv.* completely; thoroughly 完全地；彻底地：*They were comprehensively beaten in the final.* 他们在决赛中一败涂地。

com·press *verb, noun*

■ ***verb*** /kəmˈpres/ **1** [T, I] to press or squeeze sth together or into a smaller space; to be pressed or squeezed in this way （被）压紧，压缩：**~ sth** (**into sth**) *compressed air/gas* 压缩空气 / 气体 ◇ **~** (**into sth**) *Her lips compressed into a thin line.* 她的双唇抿成了一道缝。**2** [T] **~ sth** (**into sth**) to reduce sth and fit it into a smaller space or amount of time 精简；浓缩；压缩 SYN **condense**：*The main arguments were compressed into one chapter.* 主要的论证被压缩为一个章节。**3** [T] **~ sth** (*computing* 计) to make computer files, etc. smaller so that they use less space on a disk, etc. 压缩（文件等）OPP **decompress** ▶ **com·pres·sion** /kəmˈpreʃn/ *noun* [U]：*the compression of air* 空气的压缩 ◇ *data compression* 数据压缩

■ ***noun*** /ˈkɒmpres; *NAmE* ˈkɑːm-/ a cloth that is pressed onto a part of the body to stop the loss of blood, reduce pain, etc.（止血、减痛等的）敷布，压布

com·pres·sor /kəmˈpresə(r)/ *noun* a machine that compresses air or other gases 压气机；压缩机

com·prise AW /kəmˈpraɪz/ *verb* (not used in the progressive tenses 不用于进行时) (*formal*) **1** (*also* **be comprised of**) **~ sth** to have sb/sth as parts or members 包括；包含；由…组成 SYN **consist of**：*The collection comprises 327 paintings.* 那一组收藏有 327 幅画。◇ *The committee is comprised of representatives from both the public and private sectors.* 委员会由政府和私人部门的双方代表组成。**2 ~ sth** to be the parts or members that form sth 是（某事物的）组成部分；组成；构成 SYN **make up**：*Older people comprise a large proportion of those living in poverty.* 在那些生活贫困的人中，老年人占有很大的比例。➲ SYNONYMS AT CONSIST ➲ LANGUAGE BANK AT PROPORTION

com·prom·ise /ˈkɒmprəmaɪz; *NAmE* ˈkɑːm-/ *noun, verb*

■ ***noun*** **1** [C] an agreement made between two people or groups in which each side gives up some of the things they want so that both sides are happy at the end 妥协；折中；互让；和解：*After lengthy talks the two sides finally* ***reached a compromise.*** 双方经过长期的商谈终于达成了妥协。◇ *In any relationship, you have to* ***make compromises.*** 在任何关系当中，人们都得作出让步。◇ ***a compromise solution/agreement/candidate*** 折中的解决方案 / 协议 / 候选人 **2** [C] **~** (**between A and B**) a solution to a problem in which two or more things cannot exist together as they are, in which each thing is reduced or changed slightly so that they can exist together 妥协（或折中）方案：*This model represents the best compromise between price and quality.* 这种型号是平衡了价格和质量的最佳折中方案。**3** [U] the act of reaching a compromise 达成妥协（或和解）：*Compromise is an inevitable part of life.* 妥协是生活不可避免的一部分。◇ *There is no prospect of compromise in sight.* 目前还没有和解的希望。

■ ***verb*** **1** [I] to give up some of your demands after a disagreement with sb, in order to reach an agreement（为达成协议而）妥协，折中，让步：*Neither side is prepared to compromise.* 双方都不愿意妥协。◇ **~** (**with sb**) (**on sth**) *After much argument, the judges finally compromised on* (= agreed to give the prize to) *the 18-year old pianist.* 经过激烈争论，评委终于同意那个 18 岁的钢琴演奏者获奖。◇ *They were unwilling to compromise with the terrorists.* 他们不愿与恐怖分子妥协。**2** [T, I] to do sth that is against your principles or does not reach standards that you have set 违背（原则）；达不到（标准）：**~ sth** *I refuse to compromise my principles.* 我拒绝在原则问题上妥协。◇ **~** (**on sth**) *We are not prepared to compromise on safety standards.* 我们不愿在安全标准问题上放松。**3** [T] **~ sb/sth/yourself** to bring sb/sth/yourself into danger or under suspicion, especially by acting in a way that is not very sensible（尤指因行为不很明智）使陷入危险，使受到怀疑：*She had already compromised herself by accepting his invitation.* 她接受了他的邀请，这件事已经使她的声誉受到了损害。◇ *Defeat at this stage would* ***compromise their chances*** (= reduce their chances) *of reaching the finals of the competition.* 在这个阶段的失败会减少他们进入决赛的机会。

com·prom·is·ing /ˈkɒmprəmaɪzɪŋ; *NAmE* ˈkɑːm-/ *adj.* if sth is **compromising**, it shows or tells people sth that you want to keep secret, because it is wrong or embarrassing 有失体面的；不宜泄露的：*compromising photos* 不宜公开的照片 ◇ *They were discovered together in a* ***compromising situation.*** 他们被人发现在一起，场面有伤风化。

comp·trol·ler /kənˈtrəʊlə(r); *NAmE* -ˈtroʊ-/ *noun* = CONTROLLER (3)

com·pul·sion /kəmˈpʌlʃn/ *noun* **1** [U, C] (*formal*) strong pressure that makes sb do sth that they do not want to do 强迫；强制：**~** (**to do sth**) *You are under no compulsion to pay immediately.* 没有人强迫你立刻付款。◇ **~** (**on sb**) **to do sth** *There are no compulsions on students to attend classes.* 没有强求学生上课。**2** [C] **~** (**to do sth**) a strong desire to do sth, especially sth that is wrong, silly or dangerous（尤指做不正确、愚蠢或危险事的）强烈欲望，冲动 SYN **urge**：*He felt a great compulsion to tell her everything.* 他感到一阵强烈的冲动，想要把一切都告诉她。➲ SEE ALSO COMPEL

com·pul·sive /kəmˈpʌlsɪv/ *adj.* **1** (of behaviour 行为) that is difficult to stop or control 难以制止的；难控制的：***compulsive eating/spending/gambling*** 强迫性进食 / 消费；上瘾的赌博 **2** (of people 人) not being able to control their behaviour 无法控制行为的；禁不住的：***a compulsive drinker/gambler/liar*** 酗酒成性的酒徒；嗜赌成癖的赌徒；说谎成性的人 **3** that makes you pay attention to it because it is so interesting and exciting 引人入胜的：*The programme made compulsive viewing.* 这节目引人入胜，

收看起来欲罢不能。▶ **com·pul·sive·ly** *adv.*： *She watched him compulsively.* 她情不自禁地注视着他。◇ *a compulsively readable book* 引人入胜、非读不可的书

com·pul·sory /kəmˈpʌlsəri/ *adj.* that must be done because of a law or a rule（因法律或规则而）必须做的，强制的，强迫的 SYN **mandatory**： ***It is compulsory for** all motorcyclists to wear helmets.* 所有骑摩托车的人都必须戴头盔，这是强制性的。◇ *English is a **compulsory subject** at this level.* 英语在这一级别是必修科目。◇ ***compulsory education/schooling*** 义务教育 ◇ *compulsory redundancies* 强制裁员 OPP **voluntary** ▶ **com·pul·sor·ily** /kəmˈpʌlsərəli/ *adv.*： *Over 600 workers were made compulsorily redundant.* * 600 多名工人遭到强制性裁员。

com,pulsory 'purchase *noun* [U, C] (*BrE*) an occasion when sb is officially ordered to sell land or property to the government or other authority（政府等对土地或财产的）强制征购，强制性购买： *a compulsory purchase order* 强制征购令

com·punc·tion /kəmˈpʌŋkʃn/ *noun* [U] (also [C] in *NAmE* 美式英语亦作可数名词) ~ (**about doing sth**) (*formal*) a guilty feeling about doing sth 内疚；愧疚： *She felt no compunction about leaving her job.* 她对自己的辞职一点儿也不感到懊悔。◇ *He had lied to her without compunction.* 他向她撒了谎却毫无愧疚。◇ (*NAmE*) *She has no compunctions about rejecting the plan.* 她对拒绝那个计划丝毫也不后悔。

com·pu·ta·tion AW /ˌkɒmpjuˈteɪʃn; *NAmE* ˌkɑːm-/ *noun* [C, U] (*formal*) an act or the process of calculating sth 计算；计算过程： *All the statistical computations were performed by the new software system.* 所有的统计计算均由新的软件系统完成。◇ *an error in the computation* 计算错误

com·pu·ta·tion·al AW /ˌkɒmpjuˈteɪʃənl; *NAmE* ˌkɑːm-/ *adj.* [usually before noun] using or connected with computers 使用计算机的；与计算机有关的： *computational methods* 用计算机做的方法 ◇ *a computational approach* 通过计算机进行

compu,tational lin'guistics *noun* [U] the study of language and speech using computers 计算语言学（用计算机进行语言分析）

com·pute AW /kəmˈpjuːt/ *verb* ~ **sth** (*formal*) to calculate sth 计算；估算： *The losses were computed at £5 million.* 损失估算为 500 万英镑。▶ **com·put·able** AW *adj.*

com·puter 🔑 AW /kəmˈpjuːtə(r)/ *noun* an electronic machine that can store, organize and find information, do calculations and control other machines 计算机；电脑： *a personal computer* 个人电脑 ◇ *Our sales information is processed by computer.* 我们的销售信息是用计算机处理的。◇ *a computer program* 计算机程序 ◇ ***computer software/hardware/graphics*** 计算机软件 / 硬件 / 制图 ◇ *a computer error* 计算机错误 ◇ *computer-aided design* 计算机辅助设计 ➲ VISUAL VOCAB PAGE V73 ➲ SEE ALSO DESKTOP COMPUTER, MICROCOMPUTER, PERSONAL COMPUTER, SUPERCOMPUTER

> **WORDFINDER 联想词**： display, drive, **keyboard**, memory, platform, **program**, reboot, router, screen

com'puter game *noun* a game played on a computer 电脑游戏

com·pu·ter·ize (*BrE also* **-ise**) /kəmˈpjuːtəraɪz/ *verb* **1** ~ **sth** to provide a computer or computers to do the work of sth 用计算机做；使计算机化；使电脑化： *The factory has been fully computerized.* 这家工厂已完全计算机化了。**2** ~ **sth** to store information on a computer 用计算机存储，用电脑存储（信息）： *computerized databases* 计算机化数据库 ◇ *The firm has computerized its records.* 那家公司已把记录存入计算机。▶ **com·pu·ter·iza·tion, -isa·tion** /kəmˌpjuːtəraɪˈzeɪʃn; *NAmE* -rəˈz-/ *noun* [U]

com,puter-'literate (*also* **com·puter·ate** /kəmˈpjuːtərət/) *adj.* able to use computers well 能熟练使用计算机的；会用电脑的 ▶ **com,puter 'literacy** *noun* [U]

com,puter 'science *noun* [U] the study of computers and how they can be used 计算机科学；电脑科学： *a degree in computer science* 计算机科学学位 ▶ **com,puter 'scientist** *noun*

com·put·ing AW /kəmˈpjuːtɪŋ/ *noun* [U] the fact of using computers 计算；计算机技术；信息处理技术： *to work in computing* 从事信息处理 ◇ *to study computing* 从事数据处理研究 ◇ ***educational/network/scientific computing*** 教育 / 网络 / 科学信息处理技术 ◇ ***computing power/services/skills/systems*** 数据处理能力 / 服务 / 技术 / 系统 ➲ VISUAL VOCAB PAGES V73-74

com·rade /ˈkɒmreɪd; *NAmE* ˈkɑːmræd/ *noun* **1** a person who is a member of the same COMMUNIST or SOCIALIST political party as the person speaking（共产党或社会主义政党的）同志 **2** (*also* **,comrade-in-'arms**) (*old-fashioned*) a friend or other person that you work with, especially as soldiers during a war 朋友；同事；（尤指战争期间的）战友： *They were old army comrades.* 他们是部队的老战友。➲ WORDFINDER NOTE AT FRIEND ▶ **com·rade·ly** /ˈkɒmreɪdli; *NAmE* ˈkɑːmrædli/ *adj.* **com·rade·ship** /ˈkɒmreɪdʃɪp; *NAmE* ˈkɑːmræd-/ *noun* [U] (*formal*)： *There was a sense of comradeship between them.* 他们之间存在着一种同志情谊。

Con. *abbr.* (in British politics) CONSERVATIVE *n.* (1)（英国政治）保守党党员，保守党支持者

con /kɒn; *NAmE* kɑːn/ *noun, verb*

■ ***noun*** (*informal*) **1** [sing.] (*also BrE, formal* **'confidence trick**) (*also NAmE, formal* **'confidence game**) a trick; an act of cheating sb 诡计；骗局；欺骗： *The so-called bargain was just a big con!* 这种所谓的减价优惠只不过是个大骗局！◇ (*BrE*) *a con trick* 骗人的花招 ◇ (*NAmE*) *a con game* 骗局 ◇ *He's a real **con artist*** (= a person who regularly cheats others). 他真是个行骗老手。➲ SEE ALSO CONMAN, MOD CONS **2** [C] = CONVICT IDM SEE PRO *n.*

■ ***verb*** (**-nn-**) (*informal*) to trick sb, especially in order to get money from them or persuade them to do sth for you（尤指为钱财或使人为自己做某事而）欺骗，哄骗，诈骗： ~ **sb** (**into doing sth**) *I was conned into buying a useless car.* 我上当受骗买了辆不能用的汽车。◇ ~ **sb** (**out of sth**) *They had been conned out of £100 000.* 他们被骗走了 10 万英镑。◇ ~ **your way into sth** *He conned his way into the job using false references.* 他用假的推荐信骗取了那份工作。➲ SYNONYMS AT CHEAT

con·ation /kəˈneɪʃn/ *noun* [U] (*philosophy* 哲, *psychology* 心) a mental process that makes you want to do sth or decide to do sth 意动；意图 ▶ **cona·tive** /ˈkɒnətɪv; *NAmE* ˈkɑːn-/ *adj.*

con·cat·en·ation /kənˌkætəˈneɪʃn/ *noun* (*formal*) a series of things or events that are linked together 一系列相关联的事物（或事件）： *a strange **concatenation of events*** 一连串奇怪的事

con·cave /kɒnˈkeɪv; *NAmE* kɑːnˈk-; ˈkɑːn-/ *adj.* (of an outline or a surface 轮廓或表面) curving in 凹的；凹面的： *a **concave lens/mirror*** 凹透镜；凹镜 OPP **convex**

con·cav·ity /ˌkɒnˈkævəti; *NAmE* ˌkɑːn-/ *noun* (*pl.* **-ies**) (*specialist*) **1** [U] the quality of being concave (= curving in) 凹；凹陷 **2** [C] a shape or place that curves in 凹形；凹状；凹陷处

con·ceal /kənˈsiːl/ *verb* (*formal*) to hide sb/sth 隐藏；隐瞒；掩盖： ~ **sb/sth** *The paintings were concealed beneath a thick layer of plaster.* 那些画被隐藏在厚厚的灰泥层下面。◇ *Tim could barely conceal his disappointment.* 蒂姆几乎掩饰不住自己的失望。◇ *She sat down to **conceal the fact that** she was trembling.* 她坐下来以不让人看出她在发抖。◇ ~ **sb/sth from sb/sth** *For a long time his death was concealed from her.* 他的死瞒了很长时间都没告诉她。➲ SYNONYMS AT HIDE ➲ SEE ALSO ILL-CONCEALED

con·ceal·er /kənˈsiːlə(r)/ *noun* [U, C] a skin-coloured cream or powder used to cover spots or marks on the skin or dark circles under the eyes 遮瑕膏；遮瑕粉 ➲ VISUAL VOCAB PAGE V65

con·ceal·ment /kənˈsiːlmənt/ *noun* [U] (*formal*) the act of hiding sth; the state of being hidden 隐藏；隐瞒；掩盖：

the concealment of crime 对罪行的隐瞒 ◇ *Many animals rely on concealment for protection.* 许多动物靠藏匿自己来自保。

con·cede /kən'siːd/ *verb* **1** [T] to admit that sth is true, logical, etc. 承认（某事属实、合乎逻辑等）：**+ speech** *'Not bad,' she conceded grudgingly.* "不错。" 她勉强承认道。◇ **~ (that)**… *He was forced to concede (that) there might be difficulties.* 他被迫承认可能会有困难。◇ **~ sth** *I had to concede the logic of this.* 我得承认这件事情有它的逻辑。◇ **~ sth to sb** *He reluctantly **conceded the point** to me.* 他不情愿地向我承认了这一点。◇ **~ sb sth** *He reluctantly conceded me the point.* 他不情愿地向我承认了这一点。◇ **it is conceded that…** ***It must be conceded that** different judges have different approaches to these cases.* 必须承认不同的法官会采用不同的方法来判定这些案件。➲ SYNONYMS AT ADMIT **2** [T] to give sth away, especially unwillingly; to allow sb to have sth （尤指勉强地）让与，让步；允许：**~ sth (to sb)** *The President was obliged to concede power to the army.* 总统被迫把权力让给军队。◇ *England conceded a goal immediately after half-time.* 英格兰队在下半场一开始就被攻入一球。◇ **~ sb sth** *Women were only conceded full voting rights in the 1950s.* 妇女在 20 世纪 50 年代才被容许完全享有选举权。**3** [I, T] **~ (defeat)** to admit that you have lost a game, an election, etc. 承认（比赛、选举等失败）：*After losing this decisive battle, the general was forced to concede.* 输掉了这场决定性的战役后，那位将军不得不承认失败。◇ *Injury forced Hicks to concede defeat.* 受伤后，希克斯被迫认输。➲ SEE ALSO CONCESSION

▼ **EXPRESS YOURSELF 情景表达**

Conceding a point 承认对方有理

When you want to show that the other person has convinced you with their argument, at least partially, you can concede. 表示信服他人的论点，或至少在某程度上接受对方的意见，可以用不同的方式：

- ***Yes, I suppose you're right.*** (*especially BrE*) 是的，我想你是对的。
- ***Yes, I guess you're right.*** (*especially NAmE*) 是的，我想你是对的。
- ***Yes, I see what you mean.*** 是的，我明白你的意思。
- ***OK, I take/see your point about the expense, but I still think it's worth it.*** 好吧，我理解你对这笔支出的看法，但我还是认为这是值得的。
- ***Well, I guess you've got a point there.*** 嗯，我想你说的有道理。
- ***OK, that's a good point.*** 嗯，这话说得很对。
- ***No, possibly/I guess not.*** 不，应该不行 / 我想不行。
- ***I suppose not.*** (*BrE*) 我想不行。
- ***Well/Yes/OK, I hadn't really appreciated/understood that before.*** 好吧，我以前真的不了解那一点。
- ***Well, I can't/won't argue with that.*** 好吧，我不得不承认那一点。
- ***That's true. We'll need to take that into consideration.*** 确实如此。我们需要考虑这一点。

con·ceit /kən'siːt/ *noun* **1** [U] (*disapproving*) too much pride in yourself and what you do 自负；骄傲自大 **2** [C] (*formal*) an artistic effect or device, especially one that is very clever or tries to be very clever but does not succeed 别出心裁但不实用的效果；巧妙但不实用的东西：*The ill-advised conceit of the guardian angel dooms the film from the start.* 对守护天使的蹩脚设计弄巧成拙，从一开始就注定这部电影要失败。**3** [C] (*specialist*) a clever expression in writing or speech that involves a comparison between two things 巧妙的言辞；别出心裁的比喻 **SYN** **metaphor**：*The idea of the wind singing is a romantic conceit.* 风儿在唱歌这一巧妙的比喻很有浪漫色彩。

con·ceit·ed /kən'siːtɪd/ *adj.* (*disapproving*) having too much pride in yourself and what you do 自负的；骄傲自大的：*a very conceited person* 极其自命不凡的人 ◇ *It's very conceited of you to assume that your work is always the best.* 你认为你的工作总是最好的，真是太自大了。▶ **con·ceit·ed·ly** *adv.*

con·ceiv·able **AW** /kən'siːvəbl/ *adj.* that you can imagine or believe 可想象的；可信的 **SYN** **possible**：*It is conceivable that I'll see her tomorrow.* 我可能明天会见到她。◇ *a beautiful city with buildings of every conceivable age and style* 拥有各个时代和各种风格建筑物的美丽城市 **OPP** **inconceivable** ▶ **con·ceiv·ably** **AW** /-əbli/ *adv.*：*The disease could conceivably be transferred to humans.* 这种疾病可能会传染给人类。

C

con·ceive **AW** /kən'siːv/ *verb* **1** [T] (*formal*) to form an idea, a plan, etc. in your mind; to imagine sth 想出（主意、计划等）；想象；构想；设想：**~ sth** *He conceived the idea of transforming the old power station into an arts centre.* 他想出了把旧发电站改造为艺术中心的主意。◇ **~ of sth (as sth)** *God is often conceived of as male.* 上帝常常被想象为男性。◇ **~ (that)**… *I cannot conceive (= I do not believe) (that) he would wish to harm us.* 我无法想象他会存心伤害我们。◇ **~ what/how, etc.…** *I cannot conceive what it must be like.* 我想象不出它会是什么样子。**2** [I, T] when a woman **conceives** or **conceives a child**, she becomes pregnant 怀孕；怀胎：*She is unable to conceive.* 她不能怀孕。◇ **~ sb** *Their first child was conceived on their wedding night.* 他们的第一个小孩是在新婚之夜怀上的。➲ SEE ALSO CONCEPTION

> **WORD FAMILY**
> **conceive** *verb*
> **conceivable** *adj.*
> (≠ inconceivable)
> **conceivably** *adv.*
> **concept** *noun*
> **conception** *noun*
> **conceptual** *adj.*

con·cen·trate 🔑 **AW** /'kɒnsntreɪt; *NAmE* 'kɑːn-/ *verb*, *noun*

■ ***verb*** **1** 🔑 [I, T] to give all your attention to sth and not think about anything else 集中（注意力）；聚精会神：**~ (on sth/on doing sth)** *I can't concentrate with all that noise going on.* 吵闹声不绝于耳，我无法集中精神。◇ **~ sth** *Nothing **concentrates the mind** better than the knowledge that you could die tomorrow* (= it makes you think very clearly). 没有什么比知道自己明天就可能会死去更能让人定下心来去思考种种问题的了。◇ **~ sth (on sth/on doing sth)** *I decided to **concentrate all my efforts** on finding somewhere to live.* 我决定全力以赴找个住的地方。**2** [T] **~ sth + adv./prep.** to bring sth together in one place 使…集中（或集合、聚集）：*Power is largely concentrated in the hands of a small elite.* 权力主要集中在少数精英人物的手里。◇ *We need to concentrate resources on the most run-down areas.* 我们需要把资源集中用于最衰败的地区。◇ *Fighting was concentrated around the towns to the north.* 战斗集中在北方诸城镇的周围进行。**3** [T] **~ sth** (*specialist*) to increase the strength of a substance by reducing its volume, for example by boiling it （使）浓缩 **SYN** **reduce**

PHR V **'concentrate on sth** 🔑 to spend more time doing one particular thing than others 集中时间做某事：*In this lecture I shall concentrate on the early years of Charles's reign.* 这一节课我将着重讲查理王朝的早期统治时期。

■ ***noun*** [C, U] a substance that is made stronger because water or other substances have been removed 浓缩物：*mineral concentrates found at the bottom of rivers* 在河底发现的精矿 ◇ *jams made with fruit juice concentrate* 用浓缩果汁做的果酱

con·cen·trated **AW** /'kɒnsntreɪtɪd; *NAmE* 'kɑːn-/ *adj.* **1** showing determination to do sth 决心要做的；全力以赴的：*He made a concentrated effort to finish the work on time.* 他全力以赴以按时完成这项工作。**2** (of a substance 物质) made stronger because water or other substances have been removed 浓缩的：*concentrated orange juice* 浓缩橙汁 ◇ *a concentrated solution of salt in water* 浓缩盐水溶液 **3** if sth exists or happens in a **concentrated** way, there is a lot of it in one place or at one time 密集的；集中的：*concentrated gunfire* 密集的炮火

con·cen·tra·tion 🔑 **AW** /ˌkɒnsn'treɪʃn; *NAmE* ˌkɑːn-/ *noun* **1** 🔑 [U] the ability to direct all your effort and attention on one thing, without thinking of other things 专心；专注：*This book requires a great deal of concentration.*

这本书需要全神贯注才能读懂。◇ *Tiredness affects your powers of concentration.* 疲劳影响注意力的集中。**2** [U] ~ (**on sth**) the process of people directing effort and attention on a particular thing 关注；重视：*a need for greater concentration on environmental issues* 更加关注环境问题的必要性 **3** [C] ~ (**of sth**) a lot of sth in one place 集中；聚集：*a concentration of industry in the north of the country* 该国北部的工业集中地 **4** [C, U] the amount of a substance in a liquid or in another substance 浓度；含量：*glucose concentrations in the blood* 血液中的葡萄糖含量

concen'tration camp *noun* a type of prison, often consisting of a number of buildings inside a fence, where political prisoners, etc. are kept in extremely bad conditions 集中营：*a Nazi concentration camp* 纳粹集中营

concentric circles 同心圆

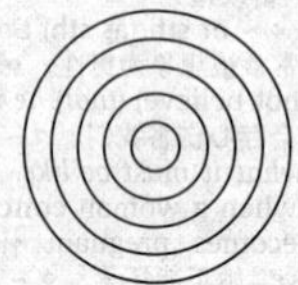

con·cen·tric /kən'sentrɪk/ *adj.* (*geometry* 几何) (of circles 圆) having the same centre 同心的：*concentric rings* 同心环

con·cept 🔑 AW /'kɒnsept; *NAmE* 'kɑːn-/ *noun* an idea or a principle that is connected with sth ABSTRACT 概念；观念：~ (**of sth**) *the concept of social class* 社会等级的概念 ◇ *concepts such as 'civilization' and 'government'* 诸如"文明"和"政府"的概念 ◇ *He can't grasp the basic concepts of mathematics.* 他无法掌握数学的基本概念。◇ ~ (**that…**) *the concept that everyone should have equality of opportunity* 人人应当机会均等的观念

'concept album *noun* a collection of pieces of popular music, all having the same theme and recorded on one ALBUM (2) （流行音乐）概念专辑，主题唱片（所有曲目为同一主题）

con·cep·tion AW /kən'sepʃn/ *noun* **1** [U] the process of forming an idea or a plan 构思；构想；设想：*The plan was brilliant in its conception but failed because of lack of money.* 尽管这计划构想绝妙，但终因资金不足而告流产。**2** [C, U] ~ (**of sth**) | ~ (**that…**) an understanding or a belief of what sth is or what sth should be 理解（认为某事怎样或应该怎样）：*Marx's conception of social justice* 马克思对社会公平概念的理解 ◇ *He has* ***no conception of*** *how difficult life is if you're unemployed.* 他不懂得失业后生活会是怎样的艰难。**3** [U, C] the process of an egg being FERTILIZED inside a woman's body so that she becomes pregnant 怀孕；受孕：*the moment of conception* 受孕的一刻 ➲ WORDFINDER NOTE AT PREGNANT ➲ SEE ALSO CONCEIVE

con·cep·tual AW /kən'septʃuəl/ *adj.* (*formal*) related to or based on ideas 概念（上）的；观念（上）的：*a conceptual framework within which children's needs are assessed* 对儿童需求进行评估的概念框架 ◇ *a conceptual model* 概念模式 ▶ **con·cep·tu·al·ly** AW /kən'septʃuəli/ *adv.*：*conceptually similar/distinct* 概念上相似 / 不同

con,ceptual 'art *noun* [U] art in which the idea which the work of art represents is considered to be the most important thing about it 概念艺术，观念艺术（将艺术品的思想作为精髓）

con·cep·tual·ism /kən'septʃuəlɪzəm/ *noun* [U] (*philosophy* 哲) the theory that general ideas such as 'beauty' and 'red' exist only as ideas in the mind 概念论（认为"美"、"红"等笼统概念只存在于头脑中）▶ **con·cep·tual·ist** /kən'septʃuəlɪst/ *noun*

con·cep·tu·al·ize AW (*BrE also* **-ise**) /kən'septʃuəlaɪz/ *verb* ~ **sth** (**as sth**) (*formal*) to form an idea of sth in your mind 构思；使形成观念；将…概念化（为…）

con·cern 🔑 /kən'sɜːn; *NAmE* -'sɜːrn/ *verb, noun*

■ *verb*

• **AFFECT/INVOLVE** 影响；涉及 **1** 🔑 [often passive] ~ **sb/sth** to affect sb/sth; to involve sb/sth 影响；涉及；牵涉：*Don't interfere in what doesn't concern you.* 不要管与自己无关的事。◇ *The loss was a tragedy for* ***all concerned*** (= all those affected by it). 这损失对有关各方来说都是极大的不幸。◇ *Where our children's education is concerned, no compromise is acceptable.* 在事关我们的孩子的教育问题上，那是毫无妥协余地的。◇ *The individuals concerned have some explaining to do.* 涉及的每个人都要作出解释。◇ ***To whom it may concern…*** (= used for example, at the beginning of a public notice or of a job reference about sb's character and ability) 敬启者…（如用于公告或求职推荐信的开头）◇ *Everyone who* ***was*** *directly* ***concerned in*** (= had some responsibility for) *the incident has now resigned.* 所有与该事件有直接牵连的人现在均已辞职。

• **BE ABOUT** 关于 **2** 🔑 ~ **sth** (*also* **be concerned with sth**) to be about sth 与…有关；涉及：*The story concerns the prince's efforts to rescue Pamina.* 这故事讲的是王子奋力解救帕米娜。◇ *The book is primarily concerned with Soviet-American relations during the Cold War.* 这部书主要讲的是冷战时期的苏美关系。◇ *This chapter concerns itself with the historical background.* 本章旨在讲述历史背景。◇ *One major difference between these computers* ***concerns the way*** *in which they store information.* 这些计算机彼此之间的一个主要差异涉及其存储信息的方式。

• **WORRY SB** 使某人担心 **3** 🔑 to worry sb 让（某人）担忧：~ **sb** *What concerns me is our lack of preparation for the change.* 让我担心的是我们对事态的变化缺乏准备。◇ ~ **sb that…** *It concerns me that you no longer seem to care.* 你似乎不再在乎，这令我担忧。➲ SEE ALSO CONCERNED

• **TAKE AN INTEREST** 感兴趣 **4** ~ **yourself with/about sth** to take an interest in sth （对…）感兴趣：*He didn't concern himself with the details.* 他对细节不感兴趣。

• **CONSIDER IMPORTANT** 认为重要 **5 be concerned to do sth** (*formal*) to think it is important to do sth 认为（做某事）重要：*She was concerned to write about situations that everybody could identify with.* 她认为应该写大家都能产生共鸣的情境。IDM SEE FAR *adv.*

■ *noun*

• **WORRY** 担忧 **1** 🔑 [U, C] a feeling of worry, especially one that is shared by many people （尤指许多人共同的）担心，忧虑：~ (**about sth/sb**) *There is growing concern about violence on television.* 人们对电视上充斥暴力内容的忧虑日益加重。◇ *In the meeting, voters raised concerns about health care.* 选民在会上提出了对卫生保健状况的担忧。◇ ~ (**for sth/sb**) *She hasn't been seen for four days and there is concern for her safety.* 她已四天不见踪影，大家对她的安全很担心。◇ ~ (**over sth/sb**) *The report expressed concern over continuing high unemployment.* 报告表达了对失业率居高不下的忧虑。◇ ~ (**that…**) *There is widespread concern that new houses will be built on protected land.* 人们普遍对在保护区建新的房屋感到忧虑。◇ *Stress at work is* ***a matter of concern to*** *staff and management.* 工作压力是一件让员工和管理人员都关切的事。◇ *The President's health was giving serious* ***cause for concern.*** 总统的健康正引起公众的严重关切。➲ COMPARE UNCONCERN

• **DESIRE TO PROTECT** 保护的愿望 **2** 🔑 [U] a desire to protect and help sb/sth 关爱；关心：*parents' concern for their children* 父母对子女的关爱

• **STH IMPORTANT** 重要的事 **3** 🔑 [C] something that is important to a person, an organization, etc. （对人、组织等）重要的事情：*What are your main concerns as a writer?* 作为一名作家，你主要关注的是哪些问题？◇ *The government's primary concern is to reduce crime.* 政府的头等大事是减少犯罪。

• **RESPONSIBILITY** 责任 **4** [C, usually sing.] (*formal*) something that is your responsibility or that you have a right to know about （某人）负责的事，有权知道的事：*This matter is their concern.* 这件事由他们负责。◇ *How much money I make is none of your concern.* 我赚多少钱没有必要告诉你。

• **COMPANY** 公司 **5** [C] a company or business 公司；商行；

企业 SYN firm: *a major publishing concern* 一家大出版公司 IDM SEE GOING *adj.*

con·cerned /kən'sɜːnd; *NAmE* -'sɜːrnd/ *adj.* **1** worried and feeling concern about sth 担心的；忧虑的：*Concerned parents held a meeting.* 忧心忡忡的家长们开了一次会。◇ **~ about/for sth** *The President is deeply concerned about this issue.* 总统对这个问题深感担忧。◇ **~ for sth** *He didn't seem in the least concerned for her safety.* 对她的安全他似乎一点都不担心。◇ **~ (that)...** *She was concerned that she might miss the turning and get lost.* 她担心自己会错过转弯的地方而迷路。 ➲ SYNONYMS AT WORRIED **2** **~ (about/with sth)** interested in sth 感兴趣的；关切的；关注的：*They were more concerned with how the other women had dressed than with what the speaker was saying.* 他们对其他女人的衣着打扮比对演讲者的讲话更加感兴趣。 OPP **unconcerned** IDM SEE FAR *adv.*

con·cern·ing /kən'sɜːnɪŋ; *NAmE* -'sɜːrn-/ *prep.* (*formal*) about sth; involving sb/sth 关于；涉及：*He asked several questions concerning the future of the company.* 他问了几个有关公司前途的问题。◇ *All cases concerning children are dealt with in a special children's court.* 所有涉及儿童的案件均由儿童特别法庭审理。

con·cert /'kɒnsət; *NAmE* 'kɑːnsərt/ *noun* a public performance of music 音乐会；演奏会：*a concert of music by Bach* 巴赫作品音乐会 ◇ *a **classical/rock/pop concert*** 古典 / 摇滚 / 流行音乐会 ◇ *They're **in concert** at Wembley Arena.* 他们在温布利体育馆举行音乐会。◇ *a **concert hall/pianist*** 音乐厅；在音乐会上演奏的钢琴家 ➲ COLLOCATIONS AT MUSIC

> **WORDFINDER** 联想词：audience, auditorium, interval, microphone, perform, programme, soloist, support, venue

IDM **in concert with sb/sth** (*formal*) working together with sb/sth 与…合作（或同心协力）

con·cer·tante /ˌkɒntʃə'tænteɪ; -ti; *NAmE* ˌkɑːn-/ *adj.* [only before noun] (*music* 音, *from Italian*) related to a piece of music which contains an important part for a SOLO singer or player and which is similar to a CONCERTO in character 具有协奏曲性质的

'concert band *noun* a large group of people who play wind instruments together, and who perform in a concert hall 管乐团 ➲ COMPARE MILITARY BAND

con·cert·ed /kən'sɜːtɪd; *NAmE* -'sɜːrt-/ *adj.* [only before noun] done in a planned and determined way, especially by more than one person, government, country, etc. 努力的；共同筹划决定的；同心协力的：*a **concerted approach/attack/campaign*** 商定的方法；联合攻击；协同运动 ◇ *She has begun to **make a concerted effort to** find a job.* 她开始尽全力寻找工作。

con·cert·goer /'kɒnsətgəʊə(r); *NAmE* 'kɑːnsərtgoʊər/ *noun* a person who regularly goes to concerts, especially of CLASSICAL music 常去听音乐会的人（尤指古典音乐会）

ˌconcert 'grand *noun* a piano of the largest size, used especially for concerts 大型三角钢琴；音乐会大钢琴

con·cer·tina /ˌkɒnsə'tiːnə; *NAmE* ˌkɑːnsər't-/ *noun, verb*

■ ***noun*** a musical instrument like a small ACCORDION, that you hold in both hands. You press the ends together and pull them apart to produce sounds. 六角手风琴 ➲ PICTURE AT ACCORDION

■ ***verb*** (**con·cer·tina·ing**, **con·cer·tinaed**, **con·cer·tinaed**) [I] (*BrE*) to fold up like a concertina （像六角手风琴一样）折起，折叠：*The truck crashed into the tree and concertinaed.* 货车撞在树上撞扁了。

con·cert·mas·ter /'kɒnsətmɑːstə(r); *NAmE* 'kɑːnsərtmæs-/ (*especially NAmE*) (*BrE also* **lead·er**) *noun* the most important VIOLIN player in an ORCHESTRA （管弦乐队的）首席小提琴手

con·certo /kən'tʃɜːtəʊ; *NAmE* -'tʃɜːrtoʊ/ *noun* (*pl.* **-os**) a piece of music for one or more SOLO instruments playing with an ORCHESTRA 协奏曲：*a piano concerto* 钢琴协奏曲 ◇ *a concerto for flute and harp* 长笛与竖琴协奏曲

con·ces·sion /kən'seʃn/ *noun* **1** [C, U] something that you allow or do, or allow sb to have, in order to end an argument or to make a situation less difficult 让步；妥协：*The firm will be forced to **make concessions** if it wants to avoid a strike.* 要想避免罢工，公司将不得不作出一些让步。◇ *to win a concession from sb* 取得某人的让步 ◇ ***a major/an important concession*** 重大的让步 ◇ *She **made no concession** to his age; she expected him to work as hard as she did.* 她丝毫也不体谅他的年龄，要求他干得像她一样卖力。 ➲ SEE ALSO CONCEDE **2** [U] the act of giving sth or allowing sth; the act of CONCEDING 承认；给予；许可；让步：*the concession of university status to some colleges* 对某些学院升为大学的许可 ◇ (*especially NAmE*) *McCain's concession speech* (= when he admitted that he had lost the election) 麦凯恩承认竞选失败的讲话 **3** [C, usually pl.] (*BrE*) a reduction in an amount of money that has to be paid; a ticket that is sold at a reduced price to a particular group of people 减价；（对某类人的）减价票：*tax concessions* 税收减免 ◇ *Tickets are £3; there is a £1 concession for students.* 票价为 3 英镑，学生票减免 1 英镑。◇ *Adults £2.50, concessions £2, family £5.* 成人、优惠、家庭票价分别为 2.50 英镑、2 英镑、5 英镑。 **4** [C] a right or an advantage that is given to a group of people, an organization, etc., especially by a government or an employer （尤指由政府或雇主给予的）特许权，优惠：*The Bolivian government has granted logging concessions covering 22 million hectares.* 玻利维亚政府批准了在 2 200 万公顷土地上的伐木特许权。 **5** [C] the right to sell sth in a particular place; the place where you sell it, sometimes an area which is part of a larger building or store （在某地的）特许经营权；（有时为大型建筑物或商场中的）销售场地，摊位：*the burger concessions at the stadium* 体育场内的汉堡包小吃摊

con·ces·sion·aire /kənˌseʃə'neə(r); *NAmE* -'ner/ *noun* (*especially BrE*) a person or a business that has been given a concession to sell sth （销售）特许权获得者；特许经销商

con·ces·sion·ary /kən'seʃənəri; *NAmE* -neri/ *adj.* [usually before noun] (*BrE*) costing less money for people in particular situations; given as a CONCESSION (3) （在某种情况下）花费少的；优惠的；减价的：***concessionary rates/fares/travel*** 优惠费率 / 票价 / 旅行

con·ces·sive /kən'sesɪv/ *adj.* (*grammar* 语法) (of a preposition or conjunction 介词或连词) used at the beginning of a clause to say that the action of the main clause is in fact true or possible, despite the situation. 'Despite' and 'although' are concessive words. 表示让步的

conch /kɒntʃ; *NAmE* kɑːntʃ/ *noun* the shell of a sea creature which is also called a conch 海螺壳；海螺

con·chie (*also* **con·chy**) /'kɒntʃi; *NAmE* 'kɑːn-/ *noun* (*pl.* **-ies**) (*BrE, informal, old-fashioned*) a CONSCIENTIOUS OBJECTOR 出于道义原因而拒服兵役者

con·cierge /'kɒnsieəʒ; *NAmE* kɔːn'sjerʒ; kɑːn'sjerʒ/ *noun* (*from French*) **1** a person, especially in France, who takes care of a building containing flats/apartments and checks people entering and leaving the building （尤指法国公寓等处的）看门人，司阍 **2** (*especially NAmE*) a person in a hotel whose job is to help guests by giving them information, arranging theatre tickets, etc. （旅馆中负责提供信息、订票等的）服务台职员

con·cili·ate /kən'sɪlieɪt/ *verb* **~ sb** (*formal*) to make sb less angry or more friendly, especially by being kind and pleasant or by giving them sth （尤指通过和蔼友善或送给某物来）平息…的怒火，抚慰，安抚 SYN **pacify** ▶ **con·cili·ation** /kənˌsɪli'eɪʃn/ *noun* [U]: *A conciliation service helps to settle disputes between employers and workers.* 调解机构帮助解决劳资纠纷。

con·cili·ator /kən'sɪlieɪtə(r)/ *noun* a person or an organization that tries to make angry people calm so that they can discuss or solve their problems successfully 调解者；抚慰者；调解机构

con·cili·atory /kənˈsɪliətəri; *NAmE* -tɔːri/ *adj.* having the intention or effect of making angry people calm 调解的；抚慰的；意在和解的；和解的：*a* ***conciliatory approach/attitude/gesture/move*** 调解的方法；和解的态度 / 姿态 / 行动

C

con·cise /kənˈsaɪs/ *adj.* **1** giving only the information that is necessary and important, using few words 简明的；简练的；简洁的：*a concise summary* 简明扼要的总结 ◇ *clear concise instructions* 言简意赅的说明 **2** [only before noun] (of a book 书) shorter than the original book, on which it was based 简略的；简缩的；简明的：*a concise dictionary* 简明词典 ▸ **con·cise·ly** *adv.* **con·cise·ness** (*also less frequent* **con·ci·sion** /kənˈsɪʒn/) *noun* [U]

con·clave /ˈkɒŋkleɪv; *NAmE* ˈkɑːŋ-/ *noun* (*formal*) a meeting to discuss sth in private; the people at this meeting 秘密会议；秘密会议与会者

con·clude 🔑 **AW** /kənˈkluːd/ *verb* **1** 🔑 [T] (not used in the progressive tenses 不用于进行时) to decide or believe sth as a result of what you have heard or seen 断定；推断出；得出结论：**~ sth (from sth)** *What do you conclude from that?* 你从中得出了什么结论？◇ **~ (that)...** *The report concluded (that) the cheapest option was to close the laboratory.* 这份报告认为最省钱的做法是关闭实验室。◇ **~ from sth that...** *He concluded from their remarks that they were not in favour of the plan.* 他从他们的话语中推断出他们不赞同此项计划。◇ **it is concluded that...** *It was concluded that the level of change necessary would be low.* 结论是需要作出的变更程度很低。◇ **+ speech** *'So it should be safe to continue,' he concluded.* "那么继续下去应该是安全的。"他推断说。➲ LANGUAGE BANK AT CONCLUSION **2** 🔑 [I, T] (*formal*) to come to an end; to bring sth to an end（使）结束，终止：*Let me make just a few concluding remarks.* 我来讲几句话作为结束语。◇ **~ with sth** *The programme concluded with Stravinsky's 'Rite of Spring'.* 演出节目以斯特拉文斯基的《春之祭》结束。◇ **~ by doing sth** *He concluded by wishing everyone a safe trip home.* 他讲话结束时祝愿大家回家一路平安。◇ **~ sth (with sth)** *The commission concluded its investigation last month.* 委员会在上个月终止了调查。◇ **+ speech** *'Anyway, she should be back soon,' he concluded.* "反正她快回来了。"他最后说道。 **3** [T] **~ sth (with sb)** (*formal*) to arrange and settle an agreement with sb formally and finally 达成，订立，缔结（协定）：*They concluded a treaty with Turkey.* 他们同土耳其缔结了一项条约。◇ *A trade agreement was concluded between the two countries.* 两国之间签署了贸易协定。

con·clu·sion 🔑 **AW** /kənˈkluːʒn/ *noun* **1** 🔑 [C] something that you decide when you have thought about all the information connected with the situation 结论；推论：*I've* ***come to the conclusion*** *that he's not the right person for the job.* 我断定他不适合做这项工作。◇ *It took the jury some time to* ***reach the conclusion*** *that she was guilty.* 陪审团花了很长时间才得出结论认为她有罪。◇ *New evidence might* ***lead to the conclusion*** *that we are wrong.* 根据新的证据可能会推断出我们是错的。◇ *We can safely* ***draw some conclusions*** *from our discussion.* 从讨论中我们可以有把握地得出一些结论。➲ COLLOCATIONS AT SCIENTIFIC **2** 🔑 [C, usually sing.] the end of sth such as a speech or a piece of writing 结束；结果；结尾；结局：*The conclusion of the book was disappointing.* 这部书的结尾令人失望。◇ ***In conclusion*** (= finally), *I would like to thank...* 最后，我想感谢…◇ *If we took this argument to its* ***logical conclusion...*** 假如我们把这个论点归结到合乎其逻辑的结论… **3** [U] the formal and final arrangement of sth official 签订；达成；缔结 **SYN** **completion**：*the successful conclusion of a trade treaty* 贸易条约的成功签署 ➲ EXPRESS YOURSELF AT FINISH

IDM **jump/leap to conˈclusions | jump/leap to the conˈclusion that...** to make a decision about sb/sth too quickly, before you know or have thought about all the facts 匆忙下结论；贸然断定：*There I go again—jumping to conclusions.* 我又犯老毛病了——匆忙草率地下结论。➲ MORE AT FOREGONE

con·clu·sive **AW** /kənˈkluːsɪv/ *adj.* proving sth, and allowing no doubt or confusion 结论性的；不容置疑的；确凿的：***conclusive evidence/proof/results*** 确凿的证据；不容置疑的结果 **OPP** **inconclusive** ▸ **con·clu·sive·ly** **AW** *adv.*：*to prove sth conclusively* 确凿地证明某事

con·coct /kənˈkɒkt; *NAmE* -ˈkɑːkt/ *verb* **1 ~ sth** to make sth, especially food or drink, by mixing different things 调制，调合，配制（尤指食物或饮料）：*The soup was concocted from up to a dozen different kinds of fish.* 这种汤是用多达十几种不同的鱼熬制而成的。 **2 ~ sth** to invent a story, an excuse, etc. 虚构，杜撰，编造（故事、借口等）**SYN** **cook up, make up**：*She concocted some elaborate story to explain her absence.* 她精心编造了解释她缺席的一些谎言。

con·coc·tion /kənˈkɒkʃn; *NAmE* -ˈkɑːkʃn/ *noun* a strange or unusual mixture of things, especially drinks or medicines（古怪或少见的）混合物，调合物，调配品（尤指饮料或药物）：*a concoction of cream and rum* 奶油和朗姆酒调制的怪味饮料

con·comi·tant /kənˈkɒmɪtənt; *NAmE* -ˈkɑːm-/ *adj., noun*

■ ***adj.*** (*formal*) happening at the same time as sth else, especially because one thing is related to or causes the other（尤指相关联的或有因果关系的事）同时发生的，伴随的，相伴的

■ ***noun*** (*formal*) a thing that happens at the same time as sth else 同时发生的事；伴随（或相伴）的事物

con·cord /ˈkɒŋkɔːd; *NAmE* ˈkɑːŋkɔːrd/ *noun* [U] **1 ~ (with sb)** (*formal*) peace and agreement 和谐；和睦；协调 **SYN** **harmony**：*living in concord with neighbouring states* 与邻国和睦相处 **OPP** **discord** **2** [U] **~ (with sth)** (*grammar* 语法) (of words in a phrase 短语中的单词) the fact of having the same NUMBER, GENDER or PERSON（数、性或人称的）一致 **SYN** **agreement**

▼ LANGUAGE BANK 用语库

conclusion

Summing up an argument 总结论点

- ***In conclusion****, the study has provided useful insights into the issues relating to people's perception of crime.* 综上所述，本研究为人们对犯罪活动的认识问题提供了有益的见解。
- *Based on this study,* ***it can be concluded that*** *the introduction of new street lighting did not reduce reported crime.* 基于这项研究可以得出这样的结论：增加街道照明设备并没有使犯罪案件报案数量减少。
- ***To sum up****, no evidence can be found to support the view that improved street lighting reduces reported crime.* 总而言之，没有证据表明街道照明的改进能使犯罪案件报案数量减少。
- *The available evidence clearly* ***leads to the conclusion that*** *the media do have an influence on the public perception of crime.* 现有证据显然可以得出这一结论：公众对犯罪活动的认识确实受到媒体的影响。
- ***The main conclusion to be drawn from*** *this study is that public perception of crime is significantly influenced by crime news reporting.* 本研究可以得出的一个主要结论是：公众对犯罪活动的认识受到犯罪新闻报道的很大影响。
- ***This study has shown that*** *people's fear of crime is out of all proportion to crime itself.* 本研究表明，人们对犯罪活动的恐惧与犯罪活动本身并不相称。
- *Fear of crime is out of all proportion to the actual level of crime, and the reasons for this* ***can be summarized as follows****. First...* 对犯罪活动的恐惧与实际犯罪水平并不相称，其原因可归结为以下几点。第一，…
- ***Overall/In general****, women are more likely than men to feel insecure walking alone after dark.* 一般情况下，天黑后独自行走，女人比男人更容易感到不安全。

➲ LANGUAGE BANK AT EMPHASIS, FIRST, GENERALLY

con·cord·ance /kən'kɔːdəns; *NAmE* -'kɔːrd-/ *noun* **1** [C] an alphabetical list of the words used in a book, etc. showing where and how often they are used（书籍等中按字母顺序排列的）词语索引：*a Bible concordance*《圣经》用语索引 **2** [C] a list produced by a computer that shows all the examples of an individual word in a book, etc.（计算机显示的）语汇索引 **3** [U] (*specialist*) the state of being similar to sth or CONSISTENT with it 相似；一致；协调：*There is reasonable concordance between the two sets of results.* 两组结果之间有着合理的一致。

con·cordat /kən'kɔːdæt; *NAmE* -'kɔːrd-; *BrE also* kɒn-/ *noun* an agreement, especially between the Roman Catholic Church and the state（尤指罗马教廷与各国政府订立的）政教协定，政教条约

con·course /'kɒŋkɔːs; *NAmE* 'kɑːŋkɔːrs/ *noun* a large, open part of a public building, especially an airport or a train station（尤指机场或火车站的）大厅，广场：*the station concourse* 车站大厅

con·crete 🔑 /'kɒŋkriːt; *NAmE* 'kɑːŋ-/ *adj., noun, verb*
■ ***adj.*** **1** 🔑 made of concrete 混凝土制的：*a concrete floor* 混凝土地面 **2** 🔑 based on facts, not on ideas or guesses 确实的，具体的（而非想象或猜测的）：***concrete evidence/proposals/proof*** 确凿的证据；具体的建议；确实的证明 ◇ *'It's only a suspicion,' she said, 'nothing concrete.'*"那只是怀疑，"她说，"没有任何确实的依据。"◇ *It is easier to think* ***in concrete terms*** *rather than in the abstract.* 结合具体的事物来思考要比抽象思考容易些。➲ COMPARE ABSTRACT *adj.* (1) **3** a **concrete** object is one that you can see and feel 有形的；实在的 ▸ **con·crete·ly** *adv.*
■ ***noun*** 🔑 [U] building material that is made by mixing together CEMENT, sand, small stones and water 混凝土：*a slab of concrete* 混凝土板
■ ***verb*** **~ sth** (**over**) to cover sth with concrete 用混凝土覆盖：*The garden had been concreted over.* 花园里铺设了混凝土。

ˌconcrete 'jungle *noun* [usually sing.] a way of describing a city or an area that is unpleasant because it has many large modern buildings and no trees or parks 混凝土丛林（指高楼林立、无树木无公园因而单调沉闷的现代化城市或地区）

'concrete mixer *noun* = CEMENT MIXER

ˌconcrete 'poetry *noun* [U] poetry in which the meaning or effect is communicated partly by using patterns of words or letters that are visible on the page 实体诗歌（部分借助于字词或字母组合的视象方法表达）

con·cu·bine /'kɒŋkjubaɪn; *NAmE* 'kɑːŋ-/ *noun* (especially in some societies in the past) a woman who lives with a man, often in addition to his wife or wives, but who is less important than they are（尤指旧时某些社会里的）妾，姨太太，小老婆

con·cu·pis·cence /kən'kjuːpɪsns/ *noun* [U] (*formal, often disapproving*) strong sexual desire 强烈的性欲；淫欲 SYN **lust**

con·cur /kən'kɜː(r)/ *verb* (**-rr-**) [I, T] **~ (with sb) (in sth)** | **~ (with sth)** | **~ (that…)** | **(+ speech)** (*formal*) to agree 同意；赞同：*Historians have concurred with each other in this view.* 历史学家在这个观点上已取得一致意见。◇ *The coroner concurred with this assessment.* 验尸官同意这个鉴定。

con·cur·rence /kən'kʌrəns; *NAmE* -'kɜːr-/ *noun* (*formal*) **1** [U, sing.] agreement 同意；一致：*The doctor may seek the concurrence of a relative before carrying out the procedure.* 医生可能会征得亲属的同意后再施行此项手术。 **2** [sing.] an example of two or more things happening at the same time 同时发生；同时出现：*an unfortunate concurrence of events* 几件事情不幸同时发生

con·cur·rent AW /kən'kʌrənt; *NAmE* -'kɜːr-/ *adj.* **~ (with sth)** existing or happening at the same time 并存的；同时发生的：*He was imprisoned for two concurrent terms of 30 months and 18 months.* 他被判处 30 个月和 18 个月的监禁，合并执行。▸ **con·cur·rent·ly** AW *adv.*：*The prison sentences will run concurrently.* 所判的几个刑期合并执行。

con·cuss /kən'kʌs/ *verb* **~ sb** to hit sb on the head, making them become unconscious or confused for a short time 使脑部受到震荡 ▸ **con·cussed** *adj.*：*She was concussed after the fall.* 她跌倒造成了脑震荡。

con·cus·sion /kən'kʌʃn/ *noun* [U] (This word is only [C] in *NAmE*. 在美式英语中只作可数名词) a temporary loss of CONSCIOUSNESS caused by a blow to the head; the effects of a severe blow to the head such as confusion and temporary loss of physical and mental abilities 脑震荡：(*BrE*) *He was taken to hospital with concussion.* 他因脑震荡被送进医院。◇ (*NAmE*) *He was taken to the hospital with a concussion.* 他因脑震荡被送进医院。

con·demn /kən'dem/ *verb*
• **EXPRESS DISAPPROVAL** 表示反对 **1** **~ sb/sth (for/as sth)** to express very strong disapproval of sb/sth, usually for moral reasons（通常因道义上的原因而）谴责，指责：*The government issued a statement condemning the killings.* 政府发表声明谴责这些凶杀事件。◇ *The editor of the newspaper was condemned as lacking integrity.* 这家报纸的主编被指责为缺乏操守。
• **SB TO PUNISHMENT** 处以刑罚 **2** [usually passive] to say what sb's punishment will be 宣判；判处（某人某种刑罚） SYN **sentence**：**~ sb (to sth)** *He was condemned to death for murder and later hanged.* 他因谋杀罪被判处死刑后被绞死了。◇ **~ sb to do sth** *She was condemned to hang for killing her husband.* 她因杀害亲夫被处以绞刑。
• **SB TO DIFFICULT SITUATION** 把某人置于困境 **3** [usually passive] **~ sb to sth** to force sb to accept a difficult or unpleasant situation 迫使…接受困境（或不愉快的状况） SYN **doom**：*He was condemned to a life of hardship.* 他不得不过苦日子。◇ *They were condemned to spend every holiday on a rainy campsite.* 他们得在阴雨连绵的野营地度过每一个假日，徒叹奈何。
• **STH DANGEROUS** 危险的事物 **4** [usually passive] **~ sth (as sth)** to say officially that sth is not safe enough to be used 宣告使用…不安全：*a condemned building* 一座已宣告不能居住的危楼 ◇ *The meat was condemned as unfit to eat.* 这种肉被宣告不宜食用。
• **SHOW GUILT** 表明有罪 **5** **~ sb** to show or suggest that sb is guilty of sth 证明（或表明）有罪：*She is condemned out of her own mouth* (= her own words show that she is guilty). 她自己说的话显示她有罪责。➲ **MORE LIKE THIS** 20, page R27

con·dem·na·tion /ˌkɒndem'neɪʃn; *NAmE* ˌkɑːn-/ *noun* [U, C] **~ (of sb/sth)** an expression of very strong disapproval 谴责；指责：*There was widespread condemnation of the invasion.* 那次侵略遭到了人们普遍的谴责。

conˌdemned 'cell *noun* (*BrE*) a prison cell where a person who is going to be punished by death is kept 死囚牢房

con·den·sa·tion /ˌkɒnden'seɪʃn; *NAmE* ˌkɑːn-/ *noun* **1** [U] drops of water that form on a cold surface when warm water VAPOUR becomes cool 凝结的水珠 **2** [U] the process of a gas changing to a liquid （气体）冷凝，凝结 **3** [C, usually sing., U] (*formal*) the process of making a book, etc. shorter by taking out anything that is not necessary（书等的）简缩

con·dense /kən'dens/ *verb* **1** [I, T] to change from a gas into a liquid; to make a gas change into a liquid （由气体）冷凝；（使气体）凝结：**~ (into sth)** *Steam condenses into water when it cools.* 蒸汽冷却时凝结为水。◇ **~ sth (into sth)** *The steam was condensed rapidly by injecting cold water into the cylinder.* 由于汽缸中注入了冷水，蒸汽迅速凝结了。➲ **WORDFINDER NOTE AT** LIQUID **2** [I, T] **~ (sth)** if a liquid **condenses** or you **condense** it, it becomes thicker and stronger because it has lost some of its water （使）浓缩，变浓，变稠 SYN **reduce**：*Condense the soup by boiling it for several minutes.* 煮几分钟把汤熬浓。 **3** [T] **~ sth (into sth)** to put sth such as a piece of writing into fewer words; to put a lot of information into a small space 简缩；压缩（文字、信息等）：*The article was condensed into just two pages.* 这篇文章被简

缩成仅两页。◇ *The author has condensed a great deal of material into just 100 pages.* 作者在短短 100 页中浓缩了大量信息。

con͵densed 'milk *noun* [U] a type of thick sweet milk that is sold in cans 炼乳

con·dens·er /kən'densə(r)/ *noun* **1** a device that cools gas in order to change it into a liquid 冷凝器 **2** a device that receives or stores electricity, especially in a car engine（尤指汽车发动机内的）电容器

con·des·cend /ˌkɒndɪ'send; *NAmE* ˌkɑːn-/ *verb* **1** [T] **~ to do sth** (*often disapproving*) to do sth that you think it is below your social or professional position to do 屈尊；俯就 SYN **deign**: *We had to wait almost an hour before he condescended to see us.* 我们等了几乎一小时他才屈尊大驾来见我们。 **2** [I] **~ to sb** to behave towards sb as though you are more important and more intelligent than they are（对某人）表现出优越感: *When giving a talk, be careful not to condescend to your audience.* 发表讲话时，注意别对听众表现出高人一等的样子。 ▶ **con·des·cen·sion** /ˌkɒndɪ'senʃn; *NAmE* ˌkɑːn-/ *noun* [U]: *Her smile was a mixture of pity and condescension.* 她的微笑中夹杂着怜悯与傲慢。

con·des·cend·ing /ˌkɒndɪ'sendɪŋ; *NAmE* ˌkɑːn-/ *adj.* behaving as though you are more important and more intelligent than other people 表现出优越感的；居高临下的: *He has a condescending attitude towards women.* 他对女性总是居高临下。 ▶ **con·des·cend·ing·ly** *adv.*

con·dign /kən'daɪn/ *adj.* (*formal*) (of a punishment 惩罚) appropriate to the crime 适当的；应得的

con·di·ment /'kɒndɪmənt; *NAmE* 'kɑːn-/ *noun* [usually pl.] **1** a substance such as salt or pepper that is used to give flavour to food 调味料；作料 **2** (*especially NAmE*) a sauce, etc. that is used to give flavour to food, or that is eaten with food 调味汁（或酱等）；酱料

con·di·tion 🔑 /kən'dɪʃn/ *noun, verb*

■ ***noun***

• **STATE OF STH** 事物的状态 **1** 🔑 [U, sing.] the state that sth is in 状态；状况: *to be **in bad/good/excellent condition*** 处于糟糕的 / 良好的 / 极佳的状态 ◇ *a used car in perfect condition* 车况完好的旧车

• **MEDICAL** 医学上 **2** 🔑 [U, sing.] the state of sb's health or how fit they are 健康状况: *He is overweight and **out of condition*** (= not physically fit). 他体重超重，健康状况不佳。◇ *You are **in no condition*** (= too ill/sick, etc.) *to go anywhere.* 你的身体太差，哪儿都不宜去。◇ *The motorcyclist was in a **critical condition** in hospital last night.* 那位摩托车手昨晚在医院生命垂危。 **3** 🔑 [C] an illness or a medical problem that you have for a long time because it is not possible to cure it（因不可能治愈而长期患有的）疾病: *a medical condition* 疾病◇ *He suffers from a serious **heart condition**.* 他患有严重的心脏病。 ➲ WORDFINDER NOTE AT HEALTH ➲ SYNONYMS AT DISEASE

> **WORDFINDER** 联想词: anorexia, autism, bipolar disorder, dementia, depression, **mentally**, paranoia, psychosis, schizophrenia

• **CIRCUMSTANCES** 环境 **4** 🔑 **conditions** [pl.] the circumstances or situation in which people live, work or do things（居住、工作或做事情的）环境，境况，条件: ***living/housing/working conditions*** 生活 / 住房 / 工作条件 ◇ *changing economic conditions* 不断变化的经济状况 ◇ *neglected children living **under** the most appalling **conditions*** 生活在最恶劣环境下的无人关注的儿童 ◇ *a strike to improve **pay and conditions*** 要求提高工资和改善工作条件的罢工 ➲ SYNONYMS AT SITUATION **5** 🔑 **conditions** [pl.] the physical situation that affects how sth happens（影响某事发生的）物质环境，状态，条件: *The plants grow best in cool, damp conditions.* 这种植物最适合在阴凉、潮湿的环境下生长。 ◇ ***freezing/icy/humid, etc. conditions*** 冰冻、结冰、潮湿等的气候条件◇ *Conditions are ideal* (= the weather is very good) *for sailing today.* 今天是乘帆船航海的理想天气。◇ *treacherous **driving conditions*** 危险的行车环境

• **RULE** 规则 **6** 🔑 [C] a rule or decision that you must agree to, sometimes forming part of a contract or an official agreement 条件；条款；要件: *the **terms and conditions** of employment* 雇用的条款◇ *The offer is **subject to** certain **conditions**.* 此项优惠受制于某些条件。 ◇ *They agreed to lend us the car **on condition that*** (= only if) *we returned it before the weekend.* 他们同意借车给我们，条件是周末以前归还。 ◇ *They will give us the money **on one condition** —that we pay it back within six months.* 他们给我们提供资金有一个条件，即我们在六个月以内偿还。 ◇ (*especially NAmE*) *They agreed **under the condition that** the matter be dealt with promptly.* 他们同意了，前提是要迅速处理这件事。◇ *Congress can **impose strict conditions** on the bank.* 国会可能会迫使这家银行接受苛刻的条件。◇ *They have agreed to the ceasefire provided their **conditions are met**.* 他们已经同意停火，只要他们提出的条件得到满足。

• **NECESSARY SITUATION** 必要的条件 **7** 🔑 [C] a situation that must exist in order for sth else to happen（先决）条件；前提: *a necessary condition for economic growth* 经济增长的必要条件◇ *A good training programme is one of the conditions for successful industry.* 良好的培训计划是企业成功的先决条件。

• **STATE OF GROUP** 群体状况 **8** [sing.] (*formal*) the state of a particular group of people because of their situation in life, their problems, etc.（某群体的）生存状态，处境: *He spoke angrily about the condition of the urban poor.* 他愤怒地谈论城市贫民的处境。◇ *Work is basic to **the human condition*** (= the fact of being alive). 劳动是人类生存的基本条件。

IDM **on 'no condition** (*US also* **under 'no condition**) (*formal*) not in any situation; never 无论如何都不；决不: *You must on no condition tell them what happened.* 你决不能告诉他们所发生的事。 ➲ MORE AT MINT *n.*

> ▼ **WHICH WORD?** 词语辨析
>
> **condition / state**
>
> The following adjectives are frequently used with these nouns. 下列形容词常与这两个名词连用:
>
> | ~ condition | ~ state |
> |---|---|
> | good | present |
> | excellent | current |
> | physical | mental |
> | poor | solid |
> | human | no |
> | perfect | emotional |
> | no | physical |
> | better | natural |
>
> • **State** is a more general word than **condition** and is used for the condition that something is in at a particular time. It can be used without an adjective. * state 较 condition 通用，指特定时间的状况，可不加形容词: *the present state of medical knowledge* 目前医学知识的状况◇ *We're worried about his mental state.* 我们担心他的精神状况。◇ *What a state this room is in* (= very bad). 这房间真糟糕。
>
> • **Condition** is used with an adjective and refers especially to the appearance, quality or working order of somebody or something. * condition 与形容词连用，尤指人或事物的外观、品质或工作状况: *The car is in excellent condition.* 这辆汽车的车况好极了。

■ ***verb*** **1** [usually passive] to train sb/sth to behave in a particular way or to become used to a particular situation 训练；使习惯于；使适应: **~ sb/sth (to sth)** *the difference between inborn and **conditioned reflexes*** (= reactions that are learned/not natural) 先天反应与条件反射的差异 ◇ *Patients can become conditioned to particular forms of treatment.* 病人会习惯某些治疗方式。◇ **~ sb/sth to do sth**

The rats had been conditioned to ring a bell when they wanted food. 这些老鼠已经过训练，想吃食物时就会按铃。 **2** ~ **sb/sth** to have an important effect on sb/sth; to influence the way that sth happens 对…具有重要影响；影响（某事发生的方式）：*Gender roles are often conditioned by cultural factors.* 文化因素常常对性别的角色有着重要的影响。 **3** ~ **sth** to keep sth such as your hair or skin healthy 保持（头发或皮肤等的）健康；养护：*a shampoo that cleans and conditions hair* 可清洁并养护头发的洗发剂 ◇ *a polish for conditioning leather* 皮革护理油

con·di·tion·al /kən'dɪʃənl/ *adj., noun*

■ ***adj.*** **1** ~ (**on/upon sth**) depending on sth 附带条件的；依…而定的：***conditional approval/acceptance*** 有条件的批准 / 接受 ◇ *Payment is conditional upon delivery of the goods* (= if the goods are not delivered, the money will not be paid). 货到方付款。◇ *He was found guilty and given a* ***conditional discharge*** (= allowed to go free on particular conditions). 他被判定有罪并被判处有条件的释放。◇ *a conditional offer* (= that depends on particular conditions being met) 有条件的要约 OPP **unconditional** **2** [only before noun] (*grammar* 语法) expressing sth that must happen or be true if another thing is to happen or be true 条件的：*a* ***conditional sentence/clause*** 条件句 / 从句 ▶ **con·di·tion·al·ly** /-ʃənəli/ *adv.*: *The offer was made conditionally.* 这个报价附有条件。

■ ***noun*** (*grammar* 语法) **1** [C] a sentence or clause that begins with *if* or *unless* and expresses a condition 条件句，条件从句（由 if 或 unless 引导的） **2 the conditional** [sing.] the form of a verb that expresses a conditional action, for example *should* in *If I should die...* 动词的条件式（如 should 用在 If I should die...）：*the* ***present/past/perfect conditional*** 现在 / 过去 / 完成条件式 ◇ *the* ***first/second/third conditional*** 第一 / 第二 / 第三条件式

con·di·tion·er /kən'dɪʃənə(r)/ *noun* [C, U] **1** a liquid that makes hair soft and shiny after washing 护发剂；护发素：*shampoo and conditioner* 洗发剂与护发素 **2** a liquid, used after washing clothes, that makes them softer（洗衣后用的）柔顺剂：*fabric conditioner* 织物柔顺剂

con·di·tion·ing /kən'dɪʃənɪŋ/ *noun* [U] the training or experience that an animal or a person has that makes them behave in a particular way in a particular situation 训练；熏陶；条件作用：*Is personality the result of conditioning from parents and society, or are we born with it?* 个性是受父母和社会熏陶的结果，还是我们生而有之？ ➲ SEE ALSO AIR CONDITIONING

condo /'kɒndəʊ; *NAmE* 'kɑːndoʊ/ *noun* (*pl.* **-os**) (*NAmE, informal*) = CONDOMINIUM

con·dol·ence /kən'dəʊləns; *NAmE* -'doʊ-/ *noun* [C, usually pl., U] sympathy that you feel for sb when a person in their family or that they know well has died; an expression of this sympathy 吊唁；慰唁：***to give/offer/express your condolences*** 表示慰唁 ◇ *Our condolences go to his wife and family.* 向他的妻子和家人谨致吊慰之意。◇ *a letter of condolence* 吊唁信

con·dom /'kɒndɒm; *NAmE* 'kɑːndəm/ *noun* **1** (*BrE also* **sheath**) (*also NAmE, formal* or *specialist* **prophy·lac·tic**) a thin rubber covering that a man wears over his PENIS during sex to stop a woman from becoming pregnant or to protect against disease（男用）避孕套，保险套，安全套，阴茎套 **2 female condom** a thin rubber device that a woman wears inside her VAGINA during sex to prevent herself from becoming pregnant（女用）避孕套

con·do·min·ium /ˌkɒndə'mɪniəm; *NAmE* ˌkɑːn-/ (*also informal* **condo**) *noun* (*especially NAmE*) an apartment building or group of houses in which each flat/apartment/house is owned by the person living in it but the shared areas are owned by everyone together; a flat/apartment/house in such a building or group of houses 公寓（套房私有，其他地方属业主共有）；公寓的套房；公寓的单元

con·done /kən'dəʊn; *NAmE* -'doʊn/ *verb* ~ **sth** | ~ (**sb**) **doing sth** to accept behaviour that is morally wrong or to treat it as if it were not serious 容忍；纵容：*Terrorism can never be condoned.* 决不能容忍恐怖主义。

con·dor /'kɒndɔː(r); *NAmE* 'kɑːn-/ *noun* a large bird of the VULTURE family, that lives mainly in S America 神鹰，大秃鹰（主要栖居在南美洲）

con·du·cive /kən'djuːsɪv; *NAmE* -'duːs-/ *adj.* ~ **to sth** making it easy, possible or likely for sth to happen 有助于…的发生：*Chairs in rows are not as conducive to discussion as chairs arranged in a circle.* 椅子成排摆放不如成圈摆放便于讨论。

con·duct 🔑 AW *verb, noun*

■ ***verb*** /kən'dʌkt/ **1** 🔑 [T] ~ **sth** (*formal*) to organize and/or do a particular activity 组织；安排；实施；执行：*to* ***conduct an experiment/an inquiry/a survey*** 进行实验 / 询问 / 调查 ◇ *The negotiations have been conducted in a positive manner.* 已积极进行过谈判。 **2** 🔑 [T, I] ~ (**sth**) to direct a group of people who are singing or playing music 指挥（歌唱或音乐演奏）：*a concert by the London Philharmonic Orchestra, conducted by Marin Alsop* 由马林•阿尔索普指挥、伦敦爱乐乐团演奏的音乐会 **3** [T] ~ **sb/sth** + **adv./prep.** (*formal*) to lead or guide sb through or around a place 带领；引导；为（某人）导游：*a* ***conducted tour*** *of Athens* (= one with a guide, giving information about it) 有导游陪同的雅典之行 ◇ *The guide conducted us around the ruins of the ancient city.* 导游带领我们游览了古城遗迹。 **4** [T] ~ **yourself** + **adv./prep.** (*formal*) to behave in a particular way 举止；表现：*He conducted himself far better than expected.* 他表现得比预料的要好得多。**5** [T] ~ **sth** (*specialist*) (of a substance 物质) to allow heat or electricity to pass along or through it 传导（热或电等能量）：*Copper conducts electricity well.* 铜的导电性能好。
➲ WORDFINDER NOTE AT ELECTRICITY

■ ***noun*** /'kɒndʌkt; *NAmE* 'kɑːn-/ [U] (*formal*) **1** 🔑 a person's behaviour in a particular place or in a particular situation（人在某地或某种情况下的）行为，举止：*The sport has a strict code of conduct.* 这种体育运动有严格的行为规范。 **2** ~ **of sth** the way in which a business or an activity is organized and managed 经营方式；管理方法；实施办法：*There was growing criticism of the government's conduct of the war.* 政府对战争的指挥方式受到越来越多的指责。 ➲ SEE ALSO SAFE CONDUCT

con·duct·ance /kən'dʌktəns/ *noun* [U] (*physics* 物) the degree to which an object allows electricity or heat to pass through it 电导（率）；（热）传导性

con·duc·tion /kən'dʌkʃn/ *noun* [U] (*physics* 物) the process by which heat or electricity passes through a material（热或电等能量的）传导

con·duct·ive /kən'dʌktɪv/ *adj.* (*physics* 物) able to CONDUCT electricity, heat, etc. 导电（或热等）的；能传导（电、热等）的 ▶ **con·duct·iv·ity** /ˌkɒndʌk'tɪvəti; *NAmE* ˌkɑːn-/ *noun* [U]

conˌductive eduˈcation *noun* [U] a treatment for people with CEREBRAL PALSY that was developed in Hungary and that involves special physical exercises and learning methods 引导式教育（治疗脑瘫的方法，在匈牙利开发，包括特定的动作训练和学习方法）

con·duct·or /kən'dʌktə(r)/ *noun* **1** a person who stands in front of an ORCHESTRA, a group of singers etc., and directs their performance, especially sb who does this as a profession（管弦乐队、合唱队等的）指挥；职业指挥 **2** (*BrE also* **guard**) a person who is in charge of a train and travels with it, but does not drive it 列车长 **3** (*BrE*) a person whose job is to collect money from passengers on a bus or train or check their tickets（公共汽车）售票员；（火车）检票员：*a bus conductor* 公共汽车售票员 **4** (*physics* 物) a substance that allows electricity or heat to pass along it or through it 导体（导电或导热等的物质）：*Wood is a poor conductor.* 木头是不良导体。 ➲ SEE ALSO LIGHTNING CONDUCTOR

con·duc·tress /kən'dʌktrəs/ *noun* (*BrE, old-fashioned*) a woman who collects money from passengers on a bus or checks their tickets（公共汽车的）女售票员

C

con·duit /ˈkɒndjuɪt; *NAmE* ˈkɑːnduɪt/ *noun* **1** (*specialist*) a pipe, channel or tube which liquid, gas or electrical wire can pass through（液体、气体或电线的）管道，导管 **2** (*formal*) a person, an organization or a country that is used to pass things or information to other people or places 中转人；中转机构；中转国：*The organization had acted as a conduit for money from the arms industry.* 那家机构充当了从军工业向他处中转资金的渠道。

cone /kəʊn; *NAmE* koʊn/ *noun, verb*

■ ***noun*** **1** a solid or hollow object with a round flat base and sides that slope up to a point（实心或空心的）圆锥体 ➲ PICTURE AT SOLID ➲ SEE ALSO CONIC *n.*, CONICAL **2** a solid or hollow object that is shaped like a cone（实心或空心的）圆锥形物：*a paper cone full of popcorn* 装满爆玉米花的锥形纸筒 ◇ *the cone of a volcano* 火山锥 ➲ SEE ALSO NOSE CONE **3** (*also* **ˈtraffic cone**) a plastic object shaped like a cone and often red and white, or yellow, in colour, used on roads to show where vehicles are not allowed to go, for example while repairs are being done 锥形交通标，锥形桶，路锥（常为红白色或红黄色的塑料锥形物，表示在维修道路等时禁止车辆通行）➲ **WORDFINDER NOTE** AT TRAFFIC **4** (*also old-fashioned* **cornet**) a piece of thin crisp biscuit shaped like a cone, which you can put ice cream in to eat it（盛冰淇淋的）锥形蛋卷筒 **5** the hard dry fruit of a PINE or FIR tree（松树或冷杉的）球果：*a pine cone* 松树球果 ➲ **VISUAL VOCAB PAGE V10** ➲ SEE ALSO FIR CONE

■ ***verb***

PHR V ˌ**cone sth↔ˈoff** to close a road or part of a road by putting a line of cones across it 用锥形交通标关闭（道路或道路的一部分）

con·fab /ˈkɒnfæb; *NAmE* ˈkɑːn-/ *noun* (*informal*) **1** an informal private discussion or conversation 私人谈话；闲谈 **2** (*NAmE*) a meeting or conference of the members of a profession or group（行业或团体）会议：*the annual movie confab in Cannes* 在戛纳举行的电影年会

con·fabu·la·tion /kənˌfæbjəˈleɪʃn/ *noun* [C, U] (*formal*) **1** a story that sb has invented in their mind; the act of inventing a story in your mind 虚构的故事；虚构 **2** a conversation; the activity of having a conversation 谈话；闲谈

con·fec·tion /kənˈfekʃn/ *noun* **1** (*formal*) a cake or other sweet food that looks very attractive（精美诱人的）甜点，甜食 **2** a thing such as a building or piece of clothing, that is made in a skilful or complicated way 精工制作的物品（如建筑物或衣物）

con·fec·tion·er /kənˈfekʃənə(r)/ *noun* a person or a business that makes or sells cakes and sweets/candy（制作或销售糕饼和糖果的）甜食商，甜食业

conˈfectioner's sugar (*also* **ˈpowdered sugar**) (*both US*) (*BrE* **ˈicing sugar**) *noun* [U] fine white powder made from sugar, that is mixed with water to make icing （制糖霜用的）糖粉

con·fec·tion·ery /kənˈfekʃənəri; *NAmE* -ʃəneri/ *noun* [U] sweets/candy, chocolate, etc. 甜食（糖果、巧克力等）

con·fed·er·acy /kənˈfedərəsi/ *noun* **1** [C] a union of states, groups of people or political parties with the same aim 联盟；同盟；联邦 **2** **the Confederacy** [sing.] = CONFEDERATE STATES

con·fed·er·ate /kənˈfedərət/ *noun, adj.*

■ ***noun*** **1** a person who helps sb, especially to do sth illegal or secret 同谋；同伙；从犯；共犯 **SYN** **accomplice** **2** **Confederate** a person who supported the Confederate States in the American Civil War（美国内战期间）南部邦联的支持者

■ ***adj.*** **1** belonging to a confederacy 联盟的；同盟的；联邦的 **2** **Confederate** connected with the Confederate States（美国内战期间）南部邦联的：*the Confederate flag* 南部邦联旗

the Conˌfederate ˈStates *noun* [pl.] (*also* **the Confederacy**) the eleven southern states of the US which left the United States in 1860–1, starting the American Civil War（美国）南部邦联（1860 – 1861 年脱离合众国从而引发南北战争的美国南部 11 州）

con·fed·er·ation /kənˌfedəˈreɪʃn/ *noun* **1** an organization consisting of countries, businesses, etc. that have joined together in order to help each other 联盟；联合体：*the Confederation of British Industry* 英国工业联合会 **2** **Confederation** (in Canada) the joining together of PROVINCES and TERRITORIES forming Canada, which began 1 July, 1867 加拿大联邦（从 1867 年 7 月 1 日起由若干省和地区组成加拿大）

con·fer **AW** /kənˈfɜː(r)/ *verb* (**-rr-**) (*formal*) **1** [I] ~ (**with sb**) (**on/about sth**) to discuss sth with sb, in order to exchange opinions or get advice 商讨；协商；交换意见：*He wanted to confer with his colleagues before reaching a decision.* 他想与他的同事先商议一下再作出决定。 **2** [T] ~ **sth** (**on/upon sb**) to give sb an award, a university degree or a particular honour or right 授予，颁发（奖项、学位、荣誉或权利）：*An honorary degree was conferred on him by Oxford University in 2009.* 牛津大学于 2009 年授予他荣誉学位。 ➲ **MORE LIKE THIS** 36, page R29

con·fer·ence 🔑 **AW** /ˈkɒnfərəns; *NAmE* ˈkɑːn-/ *noun* **1** 🔑 a large official meeting, usually lasting for a few days, at which people with the same work or interests come together to discuss their views（通常持续几天的大型正式）会议，研讨会：*The hotel is used for exhibitions, conferences and social events.* 这家旅馆用于举行展览、大型会议和社交活动。 ◇ *a* ***conference room/centre/hall*** 会议室；会议中心；会议厅 ◇ *She is attending a three-day conference on AIDS education.* 她正在出席一个为期三天的有关艾滋病教育的会议。 ◇ *The conference will be held in Glasgow.* 会议将在格拉斯哥举行。 ◇ *delegates to the Labour Party's annual conference* 参加工党年会的代表

> **WORDFINDER** 联想词：delegate, exhibition, name tag, plenary, register, speaker, talk, venue, workshop

2 🔑 a meeting at which people have formal discussions（正式）讨论会，商讨会：*Ministers from all four countries involved will meet at the* ***conference table*** *this week.* 有关四国将各派部长于本周开会协商。 ◇ *He was* ***in conference*** *with his lawyers all day.* 他与他的律师们商讨了一整天。 ➲ SEE ALSO PRESS CONFERENCE **3** (*especially NAmE*) a group of sports teams that play against each other in a league 体育协会（或联合会）：*Southeast Conference football champions* 东南部联盟的橄榄球联赛

ˈconference call *noun* a telephone call in which three or more people take part 电话会议

con·fer·en·cing /ˈkɒnfərənsɪŋ; *NAmE* ˈkɑːn-/ *noun* the activity of organizing or taking part in meetings, especially when people are in different places and use telephones, computers, or video to communicate 召集（或参加）会议（尤指电话、网络或视频会议）：*video conferencing* 召开视频会议

con·fer·ment /kənˈfɜːmənt; *NAmE* -ˈfɜːrm-/ *noun* [U, C] (*formal*) the action of giving sb an award, a university degree or a particular honour or right（奖项、学位、荣誉或权利的）授予，颁发

con·fess /kənˈfes/ *verb* **1** [I, T] to admit, especially formally or to the police, that you have done sth wrong or illegal 供认，坦白，承认（错误或罪行）：*After hours of questioning, the suspect confessed.* 经过数小时的审问后，嫌疑犯终于招供。 ◇ ~ **to sth/to doing sth** *She confessed to the murder.* 她供认犯了谋杀罪。 ◇ ~ (**that**)... *He confessed that he had stolen the money.* 他承认他偷了那笔钱。 ◇ ~ **sth** *We persuaded her to confess her crime.* 我们说服她坦白她的罪行。 **2** [I, T] to admit sth that you feel ashamed or embarrassed about 承认（自己感到羞愧或尴尬的事）：~ **sth** *She was reluctant to confess her ignorance.* 她不愿承认她的无知。 ◇ ~ **to sth/to doing sth** *I must confess to knowing nothing about computers.* 我得承认对电脑一窍不通。 ◇ ~ (**that**)... *I confess (that) I know nothing about computers.* 我承认我对电脑一窍不通。 ◇ **+ speech** *'I know nothing about them,' he confessed.* "我对他们一无所知。"他承认道。 ◇ ~ **yourself + adj.** (*formal*) *I confess myself bewildered by their explanation.* 我承认他们的解释使我感

到困惑。➲ SEE ALSO SELF-CONFESSED ➲ SYNONYMS AT ADMIT **3** [I, T] ~ (**sth**) (**to sb**) (especially in the Roman Catholic Church 尤指天主教) to tell God or a priest about the bad things you have done so that you can say that you are sorry and be forgiven 忏悔；悔过；告罪；告解 **4** [T] ~ **sb** (of a priest 神父) to hear sb confess their SINS (= the bad things they have done) 聆听（某人的）忏悔（或告罪、告解）

con·fes·sion /kənˈfeʃn/ *noun* **1** [C, U] a statement that a person makes, admitting that they are guilty of a crime; the act of making such a statement 供词；供状；认罪；供认；坦白：*After hours of questioning by police, she made a full confession.* 经过警察数小时的审问，她供认了全部罪行。**2** [C, U] a statement admitting sth that you are ashamed or embarrassed about; the act of making such a statement（对使自己羞愧或尴尬的事的）表白，承认 SYN **admission**: *I've a confession to make—I lied about my age.* 我有错要承认，我谎报了年龄。**3** [U, C] (especially in the Roman Catholic Church 尤指天主教) a private statement to a priest about the bad things that you have done（向神父作的）告罪，告解：*to go to confession* 去告解 ◇ *to hear sb's confession* 听某人告解 **4** [C] (*formal*) a statement of your religious beliefs, principles, etc.（宗教的）信仰表白：*a confession of faith* 宗教信仰表白

con·fes·sion·al /kənˈfeʃənl/ *noun* a private place in a church where a priest listens to people making confessions（教堂内的）告解室，告解亭，忏悔室

con·fes·sor /kənˈfesə(r)/ *noun* a Roman Catholic priest who listens to sb's CONFESSION (3) 听告解神父

con·fetti /kənˈfeti/ *noun* [U] small pieces of coloured paper that people often throw at weddings over people who have just been married, or (in the US) at other special events （在婚礼或美国其他特殊活动中撒的）五彩纸屑

con·fi·dant (*feminine* **con·fi·dante**) /ˈkɒnfɪdænt; ˌkɒnfɪˈdɑːnt; *NAmE* ˈkɑːnfɪdænt/ *noun* a person that you trust and who you talk to about private or secret things（可吐露秘密的）知己，密友：*a* ***close/trusted confidant*** *of the President* 总统的密友 / 亲信

con·fide /kənˈfaɪd/ *verb* to tell sb secrets and personal information that you do not want other people to know （向某人）吐露（秘密、隐私等）：**~ sth** (**to sb**) *She confided all her secrets to her best friend.* 她向她最要好的朋友倾吐了自己所有的秘密。◇ ~ (**to sb**) **that**… *He confided to me that he had applied for another job.* 他向我透露他已申请另一份工作。◇ + **speech** *'It was a lie,' he confided.* "这是谎言。"他透露说。

PHR V **conˈfide in sb** to tell sb secrets and personal information because you feel you can trust them 向（认为可信赖的人）透露秘密（或隐私）：*It is important to have someone you can confide in.* 有一位心腹知己很重要。

con·fi·dence 🔑 /ˈkɒnfɪdəns; *NAmE* ˈkɑːn-/ *noun*

• **BELIEF IN OTHERS** 对他人的信心 **1** 🔑 [U] ~ (**in sb/sth**) the feeling that you can trust, believe in and be sure about the abilities or good qualities of sb/sth 信心；信任；信赖：*The players all* ***have confidence in*** *their manager.* 队员都信赖他们的教练。◇ *A fall in unemployment will help to restore consumer confidence.* 失业人数的下降会有助于恢复消费者的信心。◇ *a lack of confidence in the government* 对政府缺乏信任 ◇ *The new contracts have undermined the confidence of employees.* 新的合同动摇了雇员们的信心。◇ *She has every confidence in her students' abilities.* 她完全相信她学生的能力。➲ SEE ALSO VOTE OF CONFIDENCE, VOTE OF NO CONFIDENCE

• **BELIEF IN YOURSELF** 对自己的信心 **2** 🔑 [U] a belief in your own ability to do things and be successful 自信心；把握：*He answered the questions* ***with confidence.*** 他自信地回答了那些问题。◇ *People often* ***lose confidence*** *when they are criticized.* 人受到批评时经常会失去信心。◇ *He* ***gained confidence*** *when he went to college.* 他上大学后增强了自信。◇ *She suffers from a* ***lack of confidence.*** 她深受缺乏自信心之苦。◇ *While girls* ***lack confidence,*** *boys often overestimate their abilities.* 女孩通常缺乏自信，而男孩则往往会高估自己的能力。◇ *I didn't have any confidence in myself at school.* 我在学校时对自己毫无信心。

• **FEELING CERTAIN** 感到有把握 **3** 🔑 [U] the feeling that you are certain about sth 把握；肯定：*They could not say* ***with confidence*** *that he would be able to walk again after the accident.* 他们不能肯定他经过那场事故后还能行走。◇ *He expressed his* ***confidence that*** *they would win.* 他表示了自己的信心：他们必定取胜。

• **TRUST** 信任 **4** [U] a feeling of trust that sb will keep information private （对某人会保守秘密的）信任，信赖：*Eva told me about their relationship* ***in confidence.*** 伊娃对我透露了他们俩的关系这个秘密。◇ *This is in the* ***strictest confidence.*** 这事切勿外传。◇ *It took a long time to gain her confidence* (= make her feel she could trust me). 我花了很长的时间才赢得她的信任。

• **A SECRET** 秘密 **5** [C] (*formal*) a secret that you tell sb（向某人透露的）秘密，机密：*The girls exchanged confidences.* 女孩子们相互吐露自己的心事。◇ *I could never forgive Mike for betraying a confidence.* 迈克泄露了秘密，我绝不会原谅他。

IDM **be in sb's confidence** to be trusted with sb's secrets 受某人信任；是某人的心腹：*He is said to be very much in the President's confidence.* 据说他深受总统的信任。**take sb into your confidence** to tell sb secrets and personal information about yourself 向某人吐露内心秘密（或隐私）：*She took me into her confidence and told me about the problems she was facing.* 她把我当成知己，把她面临的种种难题都向我和盘托出。

ˈconfidence trick (*BrE*) (*NAmE* **ˈconfidence game**) *noun* (*formal*) = CON

ˈconfidence trickster *noun* (*BrE, formal*) a person who tricks others into giving him or her money, etc. 行骗者；骗子

con·fi·dent 🔑 /ˈkɒnfɪdənt; *NAmE* ˈkɑːn-/ *adj.* **1** 🔑 feeling sure about your own ability to do things and be successful 自信的；有自信心的：*She was in a relaxed, confident mood.* 她的心态从容而自信。◇ *The teacher wants the children to feel confident about asking questions when they don't understand.* 教师要孩子们遇到不懂的就大胆提问。➲ SEE ALSO SELF-CONFIDENT **2** 🔑 feeling certain that sth will happen in the way that you want or expect 肯定的；确信的；有把握的：**~ of sth/doing sth** *The team feels confident of winning.* 这个队觉得有把握取胜。◇ **~ that**… *I'm confident that you will get the job.* 我肯定你能得到那份工作。➲ SYNONYMS AT SURE ► **con·fi·dent·ly** 🔑 *adv.*

con·fi·den·tial /ˌkɒnfɪˈdenʃl; *NAmE* ˌkɑːn-/ *adj.* **1** meant to be kept secret and not told to or shared with other people 机密的；保密的；秘密的：***confidential information/documents*** 机密情报 / 文件 ◇ *Your medical records are* ***strictly confidential*** (= completely secret). 你的病历是绝对保密的。**2** (of a way of speaking 说话的方式) showing that what you are saying is private or secret 隐秘的；秘密的：*He spoke in a confidential tone, his voice low.* 他低声用隐秘的语气说话。**3** [only before noun] trusted with private or secret information 受信任的；委以机密的：*a confidential secretary* 机要秘书 ► **con·fi·den·tial·ly** *adv.*: *She told me confidentially that she is going to retire early.* 她私下告诉我她要提早退休。

con·fi·den·tial·ity /ˌkɒnfɪˌdenʃiˈæləti; *NAmE* ˌkɑːn-/ *noun* [U] a situation in which you expect sb to keep information secret 保密；机密：*They signed a confidentiality agreement.* 他们签署了一份保守机密的协议。◇ *All letters will be treated with complete confidentiality.* 所有信件将按绝密处置。

con·fid·ing /kənˈfaɪdɪŋ/ *adj.* [usually before noun] showing trust; showing that you want to tell sb a secret 信任的；推心置腹的：*a confiding relationship* 可以推心置腹的关系 ► **con·fid·ing·ly** *adv.*

con·fig·ur·ation /kənˌfɪɡəˈreɪʃn; *NAmE* -ˌfɪɡjəˈr-/ *noun* **1** (*formal* or *specialist*) an arrangement of the parts of sth or a group of things; the form or shape that this arrangement produces 布局；结构；构造；格局；形状 **2** (*computing* 计) the equipment and programs that form a computer system and the way that these are set up to run（计算机的）配置

con·fig·ure /kənˈfɪɡə(r); *NAmE* -ˈfɪɡjər/ *verb* [usually passive] ~ sth (*specialist*) to arrange sth in a particular way, especially computer equipment; to make equipment or software work in the way that the user prefers （按特定方式）安置；（尤指对计算机设备进行）配置；对（设备或软件进行）设定 ➲ WORDFINDER NOTE AT SOFTWARE

con·fine 🔑 AW /kənˈfaɪn/ *verb* **1** 🔑 **~ sb/sth to sth** [often passive] to keep sb/sth inside the limits of a particular activity, subject, area, etc. 限制；限定 SYN **restrict**: *The work will not be confined to the Glasgow area.* 此项工作不会局限于格拉斯哥地区。◇ *I will **confine myself** to looking at the period from 1900 to 1916.* 我将把自己考察的范围限定在 1900 年至 1916 年这段时间以内。 **2** 🔑 **~ sb/sth** (in sth) [usually passive] to keep a person or an animal in a small or closed space 监禁；禁闭: *Keep the dog confined in a suitable travelling cage.* 把狗关进适于旅行的笼子里。◇ *Here the river is confined in a narrow channel.* 这条河在这里流入狭窄的河槽。◇ *The soldiers concerned were **confined to barracks*** (= had to stay in the BARRACKS, as a punishment). 有关的士兵已受到禁闭在营房的处分。 **3** **be confined to bed, a wheelchair, etc.** to have to stay in bed, in a WHEELCHAIR, etc. 使离不开（或受困于床、轮椅等）: *She was confined to bed with the flu.* 她因患流感卧病在床。◇ *He was confined to a wheelchair after the accident.* 经过那场事故后他就离不开轮椅了。

con·fined 🔑 AW /kənˈfaɪnd/ *adj.* [usually before noun] (of a space or an area 空间或场地) small and surrounded by walls or sides 狭窄而围起来的: *It is cruel to keep animals in confined spaces.* 把动物关在狭小的空间里是残忍的。

con·fine·ment /kənˈfaɪnmənt/ *noun* **1** [U] the state of being forced to stay in a closed space, prison, etc., the act of putting sb there 禁闭；监禁；关押: *her confinement to a wheelchair* 半步离不开轮椅对她的束缚 ◇ *years of confinement as a political prisoner* 作为政治犯被监禁的岁月 ➲ SEE ALSO SOLITARY CONFINEMENT **2** [U, C] (*formal* or *old-fashioned*) the time when a woman gives birth to a baby 分娩；产期: *the expected date of confinement* 预产期 ◇ *a **hospital/home confinement*** 在医院 / 家中分娩

con·fines /ˈkɒnfaɪnz; *NAmE* ˈkɑːn-/ *noun* [pl.] (*formal*) limits or borders 范围；界限；边界: *It is beyond the confines of human knowledge.* 这超出了人类的知识范围。◇ *the confines of family life* 家庭生活的范围

con·firm 🔑 AW /kənˈfɜːm; *NAmE* -ˈfɜːrm/ *verb* **1** 🔑 to state or show that sth is definitely true or correct, especially by providing evidence（尤指提供证据来）证实，证明，确认: **~ sth** *Rumours of job losses were later confirmed.* 裁员的传言后来得到了证实。◇ *His guilty expression confirmed my suspicions.* 他内疚的表情证实了我的猜疑。◇ *Please write to confirm your reservation* (= say that it is definite). 预订后请来函确认。◇ **~ (that)…** *Has everyone confirmed (that) they're coming?* 他们是不是每个人都确定了一定会来？◇ **~ what/when, etc.…** *Can you confirm what happened?* 你能证实一下发生了什么事吗？◇ **it is confirmed that…** *It has been confirmed that the meeting will take place next week.* 已经确定会议将于下个星期举行。 **2** 🔑 **~ sth | ~ sb (in sth)** to make sb feel or believe sth even more strongly 使感觉更强烈；使确信: *The walk in the mountains confirmed his fear of heights.* 在山里步行使他更加确信自己有恐高症。 **3** 🔑 to make a position, an agreement, etc. more definite or official; to establish sb/sth firmly 批准（职位、协议等）；确认；认可: **~ sth** *After a six-month probationary period, her position was confirmed.* 经过六个月的试用期后，她获准正式担任该职。◇ **~ sb as sth** *He was confirmed as captain for the rest of the season.* 他被正式任命在这个赛季剩下的时间内担任队长。◇ **~ sb in sth** *I'm very happy to confirm you in your post.* 我很高兴确认你担任此职位。 **4** [usually passive] **~ sb** to make sb a full member of the Christian Church（给某人）施放坚振，施坚信礼: *She was baptized when she was a month old and confirmed when she was thirteen.* 她出生一个月时受洗礼，十三岁时受坚信礼。

con·firm·ation AW /ˌkɒnfəˈmeɪʃn; *NAmE* ˌkɑːnfərˈm-/ *noun* [U, C] **1** a statement, letter, etc. that shows that sth is true, correct or definite 证实；确认书；证明书: *I'm still waiting for confirmation of the test results.* 我仍在等待考试结果的通知书。 **2** a ceremony at which a person becomes a full member of the Christian Church 坚振；坚振礼；坚信礼 **3** a Jewish ceremony similar to a BAR MITZVAH or BAT MITZVAH but usually for young people over the age of 16 坚振礼（通常为 16 岁以上犹太年轻人举行的仪式）

con·firmed /kənˈfɜːmd; *NAmE* -ˈfɜːrmd/ *adj.* [only before noun] having a particular habit or way of life and not likely to change 成习惯的；根深蒂固的: ***a confirmed bachelor*** (= a man who is not likely to get married, often used in newspapers to refer to a HOMOSEXUAL man) 抱定独身主义的男子（报章常用以指同性恋者）

con·fis·cate /ˈkɒnfɪskeɪt; *NAmE* ˈkɑːn-/ *verb* **~ sth** to officially take sth away from sb, especially as a punishment（尤指作为惩罚）没收，把…充公: *Their land was confiscated after the war.* 他们的土地在战后被没收。◇ *The teacher threatened to confiscate their phones if they kept using them in class.* 老师警告说，如果他们上课时继续使用手机就予以没收。 ▶ **con·fis·ca·tion** /ˌkɒnfɪˈskeɪʃn; *NAmE* ˌkɑːnfɪˈskeɪʃn/ *noun* [U, C]

con·flag·ra·tion /ˌkɒnfləˈɡreɪʃn; *NAmE* ˌkɑːn-/ *noun* (*formal*) a very large fire that destroys a lot of land or buildings 大火灾；大火

con·flate /kənˈfleɪt/ *verb* **~ A and/with B** (*formal*) to put two or more things together to make one new thing 合并；合成；混合 ▶ **con·fla·tion** /kənˈfleɪʃn/ *noun* [U, C]

con·flict 🔑 AW *noun, verb*

■ ***noun*** /ˈkɒnflɪkt; *NAmE* ˈkɑːn-/ [C, U] **~ (between A and B) | ~ (over sth)** **1** 🔑 a situation in which people, groups or countries are involved in a serious disagreement or argument 冲突；争执；争论: *a conflict between two cultures* 两种文化的冲突 ◇ *The violence was the result of political and ethnic conflicts.* 那次暴动是政治与种族冲突的结果。◇ *She found herself **in conflict with** her parents over her future career.* 她发现自己在将来择业的问题上与父母存在着分歧。◇ *John often **comes into conflict** with his boss.* 约翰经常和他的老板发生争执。◇ *The government has done nothing to **resolve the conflict** over nurses' pay.* 政府未采取任何措施来解决护士工资问题引发的冲突。 **2** 🔑 a violent situation or period of fighting between two countries（军事）冲突；战斗: ***armed/military conflict*** 武装 / 军事冲突 ➲ COLLOCATIONS AT WAR

> **WORDFINDER** 联想词: aggression, arms, **army**, attack, casualty, defend, hostile, territory, **war**

3 🔑 a situation in which there are opposing ideas, opinions, feelings or wishes; a situation in which it is difficult to choose 抵触；矛盾；不一致: *The story tells of a classic conflict between love and duty.* 这故事讲的是典型的爱情与责任之间的矛盾。◇ *Her diary was a record of her inner conflict.* 她的日记记录了她内心的矛盾。◇ *Many of these ideas appear to be **in conflict with** each other.* 这些观念中有许多看上去似乎相互矛盾。

IDM **conflict of ˈinterest(s)** a situation in which sb has two jobs, aims, roles, etc. and cannot treat both of them equally and fairly at the same time 利益（或利害）冲突: *There was a conflict of interest between his business dealings and his political activities.* 他的商务交往与政治活动之间出现利益冲突。

■ ***verb*** 🔑 /kənˈflɪkt/ [I] **~ (with sth)** if two ideas, beliefs, stories, etc. **conflict**, it is not possible for them to exist together or for them both to be true（两种思想、信仰、说法等）冲突，抵触 SYN **clash**: ***conflicting emotions/interests/loyalties*** 相互矛盾的感情 / 利益 / 忠诚 ◇ *These results conflict with earlier findings.* 这些结果与早期的发现相矛盾。◇ *Reports conflicted on how much of the aid was reaching the famine victims.* 对于究竟有多少援助到了饥民手里，相关报告的说法彼此矛盾。

'conflict diamond (*also* **'blood diamond**) *noun* a diamond that has not been shaped by cutting and that is sold illegally to provide money for an armed conflict 冲突钻石，血钻（未经打磨，用于非法交易，为武装冲突提供资金）：*The organization is trying to combat trade in conflict diamonds in the war zone.* 该组织正全力打击交战区的血钻石交易。

con·flict·ed /kən'flɪktɪd/ *adj.* (*especially NAmE*) confused about what to do or choose because you have strong but opposing feelings 因心理冲突而不知所措的

con·flu·ence /'kɒnfluəns; *NAmE* 'kɑːn-/ *noun* [usually sing.] **1** (*specialist*) the place where two rivers flow together and become one （河流的）汇合处，汇流处，交汇处 **2** (*formal*) the fact of two or more things becoming one （事物的）汇合，汇聚，汇集：*a confluence of social factors* 多种社会因素的汇集

con·form AW /kən'fɔːm; *NAmE* -'fɔːrm/ *verb* **1** [I] to behave and think in the same way as most other people in a group or society 顺从，顺应（大多数人或社会）；随潮流：*There is considerable pressure on teenagers to conform.* 青少年被大力要求守规矩。◇ **~ to sth** *He refused to conform to the local customs.* 他拒绝遵从当地的风俗习惯。➲ WORDFINDER NOTE AT BEHAVIOUR, SOCIETY **2** [I] **~ to/with sth** to obey a rule, law, etc. 遵守，遵从，服从（规则、法律等）SYN **comply**：*The building does not conform with safety regulations.* 这座建筑物不符合安全条例。 **3** [I] **~ to sth** to agree with or match sth 相一致；相符合；相吻合：*It did not conform to the usual stereotype of an industrial city.* 这和工业城市那种千篇一律的格局不一样。

con·form·able AW /kən'fɔːməbl; *NAmE* -'fɔːrm-/ *adj.* **~ to/with sth** (*formal*) similar in form or nature to sth; in agreement with sth （与…）相似的，相配的 SYN **consistent**：*What happens in cases where common law is not conformable to the constitution?* 普通法与宪法相抵牾时该怎么办？ ▸ **con·form·abil·ity** AW /kənˌfɔːmə'bɪləti; *NAmE* -ˌfɔːrmə'bɪləti/ *noun* [U]

con·form·ance AW /kən'fɔːməns; *NAmE* -'fɔːrm-/ *noun* [U] **~ (to/with sth)** (*formal*) the fact of following the rules or standards of sth 遵从；恪守 SYN **conformity**：*You need to ensure conformance to strict quality guidelines.* 你得保证遵守严格的质量基准。

con·form·ation AW /ˌkɒnfɔː'meɪʃn; *NAmE* ˌkɑːnfɔːr'm-/ *noun* [U, C] (*formal*) the way in which sth is formed; the structure of sth, especially an animal 构造；结构；形态；（尤指动物的）身体构造

con·form·ist AW /kən'fɔːmɪst; *NAmE* -'fɔːrm-/ *noun* (*often disapproving*) a person who behaves and thinks in the same way as most other people and who does not want to be different 顺从者；随波逐流者；循规蹈矩的人 ▸ **con·form·ist** *adj.* ➲ SEE ALSO NONCONFORMIST

con·form·ity AW /kən'fɔːməti; *NAmE* -'fɔːrm-/ *noun* [U] **~ (to/with sth)** (*formal*) behaviour or actions that follow the accepted rules of society （对社会规则的）遵从，遵守
IDM **in con'formity with sth** following the rules of sth; conforming to sth 遵循（规则）；与…相符合（或一致）：*regulations that are in conformity with European law* 符合欧洲法律的条例

con·found /kən'faʊnd/ *verb* (*formal*) **1 ~ sb** to confuse and surprise sb 使困惑惊讶；使惊疑 SYN **baffle**：*The sudden rise in share prices has confounded economists.* 股价的突然上涨使经济学家大惑不解。 **2 ~ sb/sth** to prove sb/sth wrong 证明…有错：*to confound expectations* 证明期望有误 ◇ *She confounded her critics and proved she could do the job.* 她驳倒了批评者的看法，证明自己能够胜任那项工作。 **3 ~ sb** (*old-fashioned*) to defeat an enemy 击败，战胜（敌人）
IDM **con'found it/you!** (*old-fashioned*) used to show that you are angry about sth/with sb （表示愤怒）真讨厌，去你的

con·found·ed /kən'faʊndɪd/ *adj.* [only before noun] (*old-fashioned*) used when describing sth to show that you are annoyed （表示某事令人厌烦）讨厌的，该死的

con·fra·ter·nity /ˌkɒnfrə'tɜːnɪti; *NAmE* ˌkɑːnfrə'tɜːr-/ *noun* (*pl.* **-ies**) (*formal*) a group of people who join together especially for a religious purpose or to help other people （尤指宗教、慈善事业的）团体，协会

con·front 🔑 /kən'frʌnt/ *verb* **1** 🔑 **~ sb/sth** (of problems or a difficult situation 问题或困境) to appear and need to be dealt with by sb 使…无法回避；降临于：*the economic problems confronting the country* 这个国家所面临的经济问题 ◇ *The government found itself confronted by massive opposition.* 政府发现自己遭到了强烈的反对。 **2** 🔑 **~ sth** to deal with a problem or difficult situation 处理，解决（问题或困境）SYN **face up to**：*She knew that she had to confront her fears.* 她心里明白自己必须克服恐惧心理。 **3** 🔑 **~ sb** to face sb so that they cannot avoid seeing and hearing you, especially in an unfriendly or dangerous situation 面对；对抗；与（某人）对峙：*This was the first time he had confronted an armed robber.* 这是他第一次面对一个武装劫匪。 **4** 🔑 **~ sb with sb/sth** to make sb face or deal with an unpleasant or difficult person or situation 使面对，使面临，使对付（令人不快或难处的人、场合）：*He confronted her with a choice between her career or their relationship.* 他要她在事业和他们两人关系之间作出抉择。 **5 be confronted with sth** to have sth in front of you that you have to deal with or react to 面对（某事物）：*Most people when confronted with a horse will pat it.* 大多数人遇见马时都会轻轻地拍拍它。

con·fron·ta·tion /ˌkɒnfrʌn'teɪʃn; *NAmE* ˌkɑːnfrən-/ *noun* [U, C] **~ (with sb) | ~ (between A and B)** a situation in which there is an angry disagreement between people or groups who have different opinions 对抗；对峙；冲突：*She wanted to avoid another confrontation with her father.* 她想避免和父亲再次发生冲突。◇ *confrontation between employers and unions* 资方与工会之间的对峙

con·fron·ta·tion·al /ˌkɒnfrʌn'teɪʃnl; *NAmE* ˌkɑːnfrən-/ *adj.* tending to deal with people in an aggressive way that is likely to cause arguments, rather than discussing things with them 对抗性的；挑起冲突的

Con·fu·cian /kən'fjuːʃən/ *adj.* [usually before noun] based on or believing the teachings of the Chinese PHILOSOPHER Confucius 儒家的；儒学的；孔子学说的 ▸ **Con·fu·cian** *noun* **Con·fu·cian·ism** *noun* [U]

con·fus·able /kən'fjuːzəbl/ *adj.* if two things are **confusable**, it is easy to confuse them 易混淆的：*'Historic' and 'historical' are easily confusable.* * historic 和 historical 容易搞混。◇ *The various types of owl are easily confusable with one another.* 各种猫头鹰之间很容易弄混。▸ **con·fus·able** *noun*：*confusables such as 'principle' and 'principal'* * principle 和 principal 之类容易混淆的词

con·fuse 🔑 /kən'fjuːz/ *verb* **1** 🔑 **~ sb** to make sb unable to think clearly or understand sth 使糊涂；使迷惑：*They confused me with conflicting accounts of what happened.* 他们对发生的事所作的陈述自相矛盾，使我迷惑不解。 **2** 🔑 **~ A and/with B** to think wrongly that sb/sth is sb/sth else （将…）混淆，混同 SYN **mix up**：*People often confuse me and my twin sister.* 人们常常把我和我的孪生妹妹搞错。◇ *Be careful not to confuse quantity with quality.* 注意不要把数量与质量混淆了。 **3** 🔑 **~ sth** to make a subject more difficult to understand 使更难于理解：*His comments only served to confuse the issue further.* 他的评论只是把问题弄得更加复杂。

con·fused 🔑 /kən'fjuːzd/ *adj.* **1** 🔑 unable to think clearly or to understand what is happening or what sb is saying 糊涂的；迷惑的：*People are confused about all the different labels on food these days.* 人们如今被那些五花八门的食物标签搞得稀里糊涂。◇ *He was depressed and in a confused state of mind.* 他意志消沉，脑子里乱成一团。◇ *I'm confused—say all that again.* 我被搞糊涂了，把那件事从头到尾再说一遍吧。 **2** 🔑 not clear or easy to understand 不清楚的；混乱的；难懂的：*The children gave a confused account of what had happened.* 孩子们把发生的事叙述得颠三倒四。▸ **con·fused·ly** /-ədli/ *adv.*

C

con·fus·ing /kən'fjuːzɪŋ/ *adj.* difficult to understand; not clear 难以理解的；不清楚的：*The instructions on the box are very confusing.* 盒子上的使用说明令人费解。◇ *a very confusing experience* 让人莫名其妙的经历 ▶ **con·fus·ing·ly** *adv.*

con·fu·sion /kən'fjuːʒn/ *noun* **1** [U, C] ~ (**about/over sth**) | ~ (**as to sth**) a state of not being certain about what is happening, what you should do, what sth means, etc. 不确定；困惑：*There is some confusion about what the correct procedure should be.* 对于应该采取什么正确步骤，还是有些不明确。◇ *a confusion as to what to do next* 不清楚下一步该怎么办 **2** [U, C] ~ (**between A and B**) the fact of making a mistake about who sb is or what sth is 混淆；混同：*To avoid confusion, please write the children's names clearly on all their school clothes.* 为避免搞错，请在孩子所有的校服上写清楚他们各自的姓名。◇ *confusion between letters of the alphabet like 'o' or 'a'* 像 o 或 a 这类字母之间的易于混淆 **3** [U] a feeling of embarrassment when you do not understand sth and are not sure what to do in a situation 困窘；尴尬；局促不安：*He looked at me* ***in confusion*** *and did not answer the question.* 他困窘地看着我，没有回答问题。 **4** [U] a confused situation in which people do not know what action to take （让人不知所措的）混乱局面，乱成一团：*Fighting had broken out and all was chaos and confusion.* 战斗爆发了，一切都陷入了混乱不堪的状态。◇ *Her unexpected arrival threw us into total confusion.* 她的突然到来使得我们不知所措，乱成一团。

con·fute /kən'fjuːt/ *verb* ~ **sb/sth** (*formal*) to prove a person or an argument to be wrong 驳倒；驳斥

conga /'kɒŋɡə; *NAmE* 'kɑːŋɡə/ *noun* **1** a fast dance in which the dancers follow a leader in a long winding line, with each person holding on to the person in front; a piece of music for this dance 康茄舞；康茄舞乐曲 **2** (*also* '**conga drum**) a tall narrow drum that you play with your hands 康茄鼓（用手击打的狭长鼓） ➲ VISUAL VOCAB PAGE V37

con·geal /kən'dʒiːl/ *verb* [I] (of blood, fat, etc. 血液、脂肪等) to become thick or solid 变稠；凝结：*congealed blood* 凝固了的血 ◇ *The cold remains of supper had congealed on the plate.* 晚餐剩下的冷饭菜已经凝结在盘子上了。◇ (*figurative*) *The bitterness and tears had congealed into hatred.* 愤懑与眼泪凝结成了仇恨。

con·gen·ial /kən'dʒiːniəl/ *adj.* (*formal*) **1** (of a person 人) pleasant to spend time with because their interests and character are similar to your own 意气相投的；志趣相投的；合得来的：*a congenial colleague* 意气相投的同事 **2** ~ (**to sb**) (of a place, job, etc. 地方、工作等) pleasant because it suits your character 相宜的；合意的；适宜的：*a congenial working environment* 宜人的工作环境 **3** ~ (**to sth**) (*formal*) suitable for sth 适合的；适当的：*a situation that was congenial to the expression of nationalist opinions* 适于表达民族主义者意见的场合

con·geni·tal /kən'dʒenɪtl/ *adj.* **1** (of a disease or medical condition 疾病或健康问题) existing since or before birth 先天的；天生的：*congenital abnormalities* 先天畸形 **2** [only before noun] existing as part of a person's character and not likely to change 生性的；生就的：*a congenital inability to tell the truth* 生就不会说实话 **3** [only before noun] (of a person 人) born with a particular illness 生来有病的：(*figurative*) *a congenital liar* (= one who will not change) 生性好说谎的人 ▶ **con·geni·tal·ly** /-təli/ *adv.*

con·ger /'kɒŋɡə(r); *NAmE* 'kɑːŋ-/ (*also* ˌ**conger 'eel**) *noun* a large EEL (= a long thin fish) that lives in the sea 康吉鳗（海产鳗类）

con·gest·ed /kən'dʒestɪd/ *adj.* **1** ~ (**with sth**) crowded; full of traffic 拥挤的；挤满的；（交通）堵塞的：*congested city streets* 交通拥塞的城市街道 ◇ *Many of Europe's airports are heavily congested.* 欧洲许多机场都十分拥挤。 **2** (*medical* 医) (of a part of the body 身体部位) blocked with blood or MUCUS 充血的；黏液阻塞的

con·ges·tion /kən'dʒestʃən/ *noun* [U] **1** the state of being crowded and full of traffic （交通）拥塞；塞车：*traffic congestion and pollution* 交通拥塞和污染 ➲ COLLOCATIONS AT TOWN **2** (*medical* 医) the state of part of the body being blocked with blood or MUCUS 充血；淤血；黏液阻塞：*congestion of the lungs* 肺淤血 ◇ *medicine to relieve nasal congestion* 治疗鼻塞的药

con'gestion charge *noun* (*BrE*) an amount of money that people have to pay for driving their cars into the centre of some cities as a way of stopping the city centre from becoming too full of traffic 交通拥塞费，进城费（为缓解市中心塞车状况而收取） ▶ **con'gestion charging** *noun* [U]

con·glom·er·ate /kən'glɒmərət; *NAmE* -'glɑːm-/ *noun* **1** [C] (*business* 商) a large company formed by joining together different firms 联合大公司；企业集团：*a media conglomerate* 大众传媒联合体 **2** [sing.] (*formal*) a number of things or parts that are put together to form a whole 合成物；组合物；聚合物 **3** [U] (*geology* 地) a type of rock made of small stones held together by dried CLAY 砾岩

con·glom·er·ation /kənˌglɒmə'reɪʃn; *NAmE* -ˌglɑːm-/ *noun* **1** [C, usually sing.] **a** ~ (**of sth**) (*formal*) a mixture of different things that are found all together 混合物；聚集物：*a conglomeration of buildings of different sizes and styles* 大小和风格各异的建筑楼群 **2** [U] the process of forming a conglomerate or the state of being a conglomerate 聚集过程；聚集状态

con·grats /kən'græts/ *noun* [pl.] (*informal*) = CONGRATULATIONS

con·gratu·late /kən'grætʃuleɪt/ *verb* **1** ~ **sb** (**on sth**) to tell sb that you are pleased about their success or achievements 向（某人）道贺；祝贺：*I congratulated them all on their results.* 我为他们取得的成就向他们所有人表示祝贺。◇ *The authors are to be congratulated on producing such a clear and authoritative work.* 向创作出这样一部具有权威性又清晰易懂的作品的作者们祝贺。 **2** ~ **yourself** (**on sth**) to feel pleased and proud because you have achieved sth or been successful at sth（为成就或成功）感到自豪，引以为豪：*You can congratulate yourself on having done an excellent job.* 你应该为你出色的工作感到自豪。

▼ **EXPRESS YOURSELF 情景表达**

Congratulating somebody on an achievement or a family event 表示祝贺

When someone tells you some good news about their family, or what they have done, you can congratulate them. 得知某人家有喜事或取得成就时向其表示祝贺可以用多种方式：

- ***Congratulations on*** *your engagement! I hope you'll be very happy.* 恭喜你们订婚！祝你们幸福美满。
- ***Well done*** *for passing your driving test.* (*BrE*) 你通过了驾驶执照考试，很不错！
- ***Good job*** *on passing your exams.* (*NAmE*) 你考试及格了，真棒！
- *I hear you did very well in your exams/you've got a new job/you've had a baby—**congratulations!*** (*BrE*) 听说你考得非常好 / 找到了新工作 / 喜得贵子 —— 恭喜恭喜！
- *Jo tells me you're getting married—**congratulations!*** 乔告诉我你要结婚了，恭喜！

Responses 回应：

- ***Thank you very much.*** 多谢。
- ***Oh, thanks!*** 哦，谢谢！

con·gratu·la·tion /kənˌgrætʃu'leɪʃn/ *noun* **1** **congratulations** [pl.] a message congratulating sb (= saying that you are happy about their good luck or success) 祝贺；恭贺；贺辞：*to **offer/send your congratulations to sb*** 向某人致以祝贺 **2** **Congratulations!** used when you want to congratulate sb （用以向人祝贺）祝

贺，恭喜：*'We're getting married!' 'Congratulations!'* "我们要结婚了！""恭喜恭喜！"◇ *Congratulations on your exam results!* 祝贺你考出了好成绩！ **3** [U] the act of congratulating sb 祝贺：*a letter of congratulation* 贺信

con·gratu·la·tory /kənˌɡrætʃuˈleɪtəri; *NAmE* kənˈɡrætʃələtɔːri/ *adj.* expressing congratulations 祝贺的；恭贺的：*a congratulatory message* 贺辞

con·gre·gate /ˈkɒŋɡrɪɡeɪt; *NAmE* ˈkɑːŋ-/ *verb* [I] to come together in a group 群集；聚集；集合：*Young people often congregate in the main square in the evenings.* 年轻人傍晚时经常聚集在大广场上。

con·gre·ga·tion /ˌkɒŋɡrɪˈɡeɪʃn; *NAmE* ˌkɑːŋ-/ *noun* [C+sing./pl. v.] **1** a group of people who are gathered together in a church to worship God, not including the priest and CHOIR （教堂的）会众：*The congregation stood to sing the hymn.* 会众站起来唱圣歌。➲ COLLOCATIONS AT RELIGION **2** a group of people who regularly attend a particular place of worship （定期去特定地方做礼拜的）会众 ▸ **con·gre·ga·tion·al** /-ʃənl/ *adj.*

Con·gre·ga·tion·al·ism /ˌkɒŋɡrɪˈɡeɪʃnəlɪzəm; *NAmE* ˌkɑːŋ-/ *noun* [U] a type of Christianity in which the congregation of each church is responsible for its own affairs 公理制，公理主义（主张各地方教会独立行事） ▸ **Con·gre·ga·tion·al** *adj.* **Con·gre·ga·tion·al·ist** *noun*

con·gress /ˈkɒŋɡres; *NAmE* ˈkɑːŋɡrəs/ *noun* **1** [C] a large formal meeting or series of meetings where representatives from different groups discuss ideas, make decisions, etc. 代表大会：*an international congress of trades unions* 工会国际代表大会 **2** [C+sing./pl. v.] **Congress** (in the US and some other countries) the name of the group of people who are elected to make laws, in the US consisting of the Senate and the HOUSE OF REPRESENTATIVES （美国及其他一些国家的）国会，议会：*Congress will vote on the proposals tomorrow.* 国会明天将对提案进行投票表决。➲ COLLOCATIONS AT POLITICS

> **WORDFINDER** 联想词：caucus, electoral college, House of Representatives, nomination, president, primary, running mate, senate, swing state

3 [C+sing./pl. v.] used in the names of political parties in some countries（用于某些国家的政党名称）国民大会：*the African National Congress* 非洲人国民大会

con·gres·sion·al /kənˈɡreʃənl/ *adj.* [only before noun] related to or belonging to a congress or the Congress in the US 立法机构的；代表大会的；（美国）国会的：*a congressional committee/bill* 代表委员会；国会议案 ◇ *the midterm Congressional elections* 国会的中期选举

con·gress·man /ˈkɒŋɡresmən; *NAmE* ˈkɑːŋɡrəs-/, **con·gress·woman** /ˈkɒŋɡreswʊmən; *NAmE* ˈkɑːŋɡrəs-/ *noun* (*often* **Congressman, Congresswoman**) (*pl.* **-men** /-mən/, **-women** /-wɪmɪn/) (*also* **con·gress·person, Con·gress·person** /-pɜːsn; *NAmE* -pɜːrsn/) a member of Congress in the US, especially the House of Representatives （尤指美国众议院的）国会议员；众议员 ➲ MORE LIKE THIS 25, page R28

con·gru·ent /ˈkɒŋɡruənt; *NAmE* ˈkɑːŋ-/ *adj.* **1** (*geometry* 几何) having the same size and shape 全等的；叠合的：*congruent triangles* 全等三角形 **2** ~ (**with sth**) (*formal*) suitable for sth; appropriate in a particular situation 适合的；适当的；恰当的；相称的 ▸ **con·gru·ence** /ˈkɒŋɡruəns; *NAmE* ˈkɑːŋ-/ *noun* [U]

conic /ˈkɒnɪk; *NAmE* ˈkɑːnɪk/ *adj., noun* (*geometry* 几何)
■ *adj.* of or related to a CONE 圆锥（体）的
■ *noun* = CONIC SECTION

con·ic·al /ˈkɒnɪkl; *NAmE* ˈkɑːn-/ *adj.* shaped like a CONE 锥形的；圆锥形的；圆锥的

ˌconic ˈsection (*also* **conic**) *noun* (*geometry* 几何) a shape formed when a flat surface meets a CONE with a round base 圆锥曲线；二次曲线

con·ifer /ˈkɒnɪfə(r); ˈkəʊn-; *NAmE* ˈkɑːn-; ˈkoʊn-/ *noun* any tree that produces hard dry fruit called CONES. Most conifers are EVERGREEN (= have leaves that stay on the tree all year). 针叶树 ➲ VISUAL VOCAB PAGE V5 ▸ **con·ifer·ous** /kəˈnɪfərəs/ *adj.*: *coniferous trees/forests* 针叶树；针叶林

con·jec·ture /kənˈdʒektʃə(r)/ *noun, verb*
■ *noun* (*formal*) **1** [C] an opinion or idea that is not based on definite knowledge and is formed by guessing 猜测；推测 SYN **guess**: *The truth of his conjecture was confirmed by the newspaper report.* 新闻报道证明了他的推测果然不假。 **2** [U] the forming of an opinion or idea that is not based on definite knowledge 揣测；臆测：*What was going through the killer's mind is a matter for conjecture.* 凶手当时心里是怎样想的，这个问题只能由人们去推测了。 ➲ SEE ALSO GUESSWORK ▸ **con·jec·tural** /kənˈdʒektʃərəl/ *adj.*
■ *verb* [I, T] (*formal*) to form an opinion about sth even though you do not have much information on it 猜测；推测 SYN **guess**: ~ (**about sth**) *We can only conjecture about what was in the killer's mind.* 我们只能猜测当时凶手心里想的是什么。◇ ~ **what/how, etc.…** *We can only conjecture what was in the killer's mind.* 我们只能猜测当时凶手心里想的是什么。◇ ~ **that…** *He conjectured that the population might double in ten years.* 他推测人口在十年后可能会增加一倍。◇ ~ **sth** *She conjectured the existence of a completely new species.* 她推测有一个全新物种存在。◇ ~ **sth to do sth** *The remains are conjectured to be thousands of years old.* 据推测，这些古迹有几千年的历史。

con·join /kənˈdʒɔɪn/ *verb* [I, T] ~ (**sth**) (*formal*) to join together; to join two or more things together 结合；连接；把…结成一体

conˌjoined ˈtwin *noun* (*specialist*) (*also* **ˌSiamese ˈtwin**) one of two people who are born with their bodies joined together in some way, sometimes sharing the same organs 联体儿

con·joint /kənˈdʒɔɪnt/ *adj.* [usually before noun] (*formal*) combining all or both the people or things involved 联合的；共同的；协同的 ▸ **con·joint·ly** *adv.*

con·ju·gal /ˈkɒndʒəɡl; *NAmE* ˈkɑːn-/ *adj.* [only before noun] (*formal*) connected with marriage and the sexual relationship between a husband and wife 婚姻的；夫妻间的：*conjugal love* 夫妻间的恩爱

ˌconjugal ˈrights *noun* [pl.] the rights that a husband and wife each has in a marriage, especially the right to have sex with their partner 婚姻权利；配偶权利

con·ju·gate /ˈkɒndʒəɡeɪt; *NAmE* ˈkɑːn-/ *verb* (*grammar* 语法) **1** [T] ~ **sth** to give the different forms of a verb, as they vary according to NUMBER, PERSON, tense, etc. （根据数、人称、时态等）列举动词的变化形式 **2** [I] (of a verb 动词) to have different forms, showing NUMBER, PERSON,

conic sections 圆锥曲线

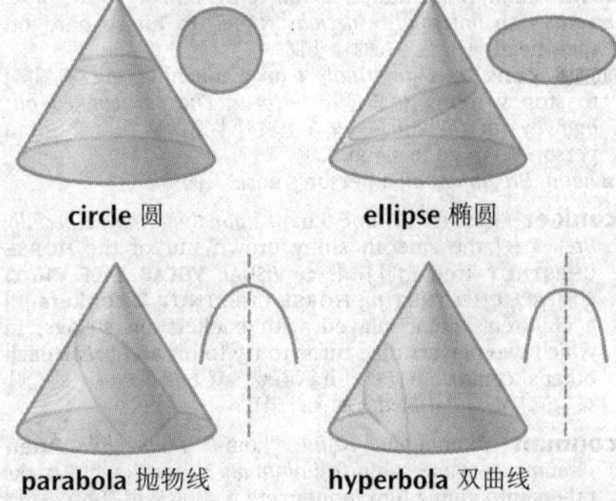

tense, etc. （表示数、人称、时态等）有词形变化形式：*How does this verb conjugate?* 这个动词有哪些词形变化？ ➲ COMPARE DECLINE *v.* (3) ➲ **WORDFINDER NOTE** AT GRAMMAR

C

con·ju·ga·tion /ˌkɒndʒuˈɡeɪʃn; *NAmE* ˌkɑːndʒə-/ *noun* (*grammar* 语法) **1** [C, U] the way in which a verb conjugates 动词的变化形式：*a verb with an irregular conjugation* 不规则动词 **2** [C] a group of verbs that conjugate in the same way 词形变化相同的一类动词：*Latin verbs of the second conjugation* 属于第二种词形变化的拉丁语动词

con·junc·tion /kənˈdʒʌŋkʃn/ *noun* **1** [C] (*grammar* 语法) a word that joins words, phrases or sentences, for example 'and', 'but', 'or' 连词，连接词（如 and、but、or） **2** [C] (*formal*) a combination of events, etc., that causes a particular result（引起某种结果的事物等的）结合，同时发生：*The conjunction of low inflation and low unemployment came as a very pleasant surprise.* 低通货膨胀与低失业的同时出现是一大惊喜。 **3** [C, U] (*astronomy* 天) the fact of stars, planets, etc. passing close together as seen from the earth （恒星、行星等的）合

IDM **in conˈjunction with** (*formal*) together with 与…一起：*The police are working in conjunction with tax officers on the investigation.* 警方正和税务官员协同进行调查。◇ *The system is designed to be used in conjunction with a word processing program.* 本系统是为与文字处理程序配合使用而设计的。

con·junc·tiv·itis /kənˌdʒʌŋktɪˈvaɪtɪs/ *noun* [U] an infectious eye disease that causes pain and swelling in part of the eye 结膜炎

con·jure /ˈkʌndʒə(r)/ *verb* [I, T] to do clever tricks such as making things seem to appear or disappear as if by magic 变魔术；变戏法；使…变戏法般地出现（或消失）：*Her grandfather taught her to conjure.* 她的祖父教她变魔术。◇ **~ sth + adv./prep.** *He could conjure coins from behind people's ears.* 他可以从人们的耳朵后面变出硬币来。

IDM SEE NAME *n.*

PHR V ˌ**conjure sth↔ˈup 1** to make sth appear as a picture in your mind 使…呈现于脑际；使想起 SYN **evoke**：*That smell always conjures up memories of holidays in France.* 那种气味总是勾起对法国度假那段日子的回忆。 **2** to make sb/sth appear by using special magic words 用咒语使…出现 **conjure sth from/out of sth** to create sth or make sth appear in a surprising or unexpected way 令人惊讶地创造出；使意外地出现：*He conjured a delicious meal out of a few leftovers.* 他居然用几样吃剩的东西做出了可口的一餐。

con·jur·ing /ˈkʌndʒərɪŋ/ *noun* [U] entertainment in the form of magic tricks, especially ones which seem to make things appear or disappear 变魔术；变戏法：*a conjuring trick* 魔术

con·juror (*also* **con·jurer**) /ˈkʌndʒərə(r)/ *noun* a person who performs conjuring tricks 魔术师；变戏法的人

conk /kɒŋk; *NAmE* kɑːŋk; kɔːŋk/ *verb, noun*

■ *verb* **~ sb** (*informal, especially NAmE*) to hit sb hard on their head 重击（某人的）头部

PHR V ˌ**conk ˈout** (*informal*) **1** (of a machine, etc. 机器等) to stop working 停止运转；失灵：*The car conked out halfway up the hill.* 汽车在上坡时半途抛锚了。 **2** (of a person 人) to go to sleep 入睡；睡着

■ *noun* (*BrE, informal*) a person's nose 人的鼻子

conk·er /ˈkɒŋkə(r); *NAmE* ˈkɑːŋ-/ *noun* (*informal, especially BrE*) **1** [C] the smooth shiny brown nut of the HORSE CHESTNUT tree 七叶树果 ➲ **VISUAL VOCAB** PAGE V10 ➲ COMPARE CHESTNUT *n.*, HORSE CHESTNUT **2 conkers** [U] a children's game played with conkers on strings, in which two players take turns to try to hit and break each other's conker 康克戏（儿童游戏，双方用系在绳上的七叶果轮流互击，以击破对方的七叶果）

conman /ˈkɒnmæn; *NAmE* ˈkɑːn-/ *noun* (*pl.* **-men** /ˈkɒnmen; *NAmE* ˈkɑːn-/) (*informal*) a man who tricks others into giving him money, etc. （诈取钱财等的）骗子

con·nect 🔑 /kəˈnekt/ *verb*

• **JOIN** 连接 **1** 🔑 [T, I] **~ (A to/with/and B)** to join together two or more things; to be joined together （使）连接；联结：*The towns are connected by train and bus services.* 这些城镇由火车和公共汽车连接起来。◇ *The canal was built to connect Sheffield with the Humber estuary.* 修建这条运河是为了将设菲尔德和亨伯河河口连接起来。◇ *a connecting door* (= one that connects two rooms) 连通两间房的门 ◇ *The rooms on this floor connect.* 这层楼的房间是相通的。

• **ELECTRICITY/GAS/WATER** 电；煤气；水 **2** 🔑 [T] **~ sth (to sth)** to join sth to the main supply of electricity, gas, water, etc. or to another piece of equipment 使…连接；接通：*First connect the printer to the computer.* 首先把打印机与计算机接通。◇ *We're waiting for the telephone to be connected.* 我们等待着接通电话。 OPP **disconnect** ➲ **WORDFINDER NOTE** AT ELECTRICITY

• **INTERNET** 互联网 **3** 🔑 [I, T] **~ (sb) (to sth)** to join a computer or a mobile device to the Internet or to a computer network（使计算机或移动设备）连接（到互联网或计算机网络）：*Click 'Continue' to connect to the Internet.* 点击 Continue 连接到互联网。 OPP **disconnect** ➲ **WORDFINDER NOTE** AT COMMAND

• **LINK** 联系 **4** 🔑 [T] **~ sb/sth (with sb/sth)** to notice or make a link between people, things, events, etc. 注意到…有关联；把…联系起来 SYN **associate**：*There was nothing to connect him with the crime.* 他与那起犯罪毫无关联。◇ *I was surprised to hear them mentioned together: I had never connected them before.* 听到有人把他们牵扯在一起让我很吃惊；我以前从未把他们联起来想过。

• **OF TRAIN/BUS/PLANE** 火车；公共汽车；飞机 **5** [I] **~ (with sth)** to arrive just before another one leaves so that passengers can change from one to the other 衔接；联运：*His flight to Amsterdam connects with an afternoon flight to New York.* 他飞往阿姆斯特丹的班机与下午飞往纽约的一趟航班相衔接。◇ *There's a connecting flight at noon.* 中午有一趟相衔接的航班。

• **TELEPHONE LINES** 电话线 **6** [T] **~ sb** to join telephone lines so that people can speak to each other 为（某人）接通电话；连接 SYN **put through**：*Hold on please, I'm trying to connect you.* 请别挂电话，我在尽力给您接通。 OPP **disconnect**

• **FORM RELATIONSHIP** 建立关系 **7** [I] **~ (with sb)** to form a good relationship with sb so that you like and understand each other （与某人）建立良好关系，沟通：*They met a couple of times but they didn't really connect.* 尽管他们见了几次面，但仍未真正建立起良好的关系。

• **HIT** 击 **8** [I] **~ (with sb/sth)** (*informal, especially NAmE*) to hit sb/sth 打（某人）；击中（某物）：*The blow connected and she felt a surge of pain.* 她遭到沉重的一击，感到一阵疼痛。

PHR V **conˌnect sth↔ˈup (to sth) | conˌnect ˈup (to sth)** to join sth to a supply of electricity, gas, etc. or to another piece of equipment; to be joined in this way 将…（与电源、煤气、设备等）连接起来，接通：*She connected up the two computers.* 她把两台计算机连接起来。 OPP **disconnect**

con·nect·ed 🔑 /kəˈnektɪd/ *adj.* **~ (with sb/sth)** (of two or more things or people) having a link between them （两个或以上的事物或人）有联系的，相关的：*market prices and other connected matters* 市场价格及其他相关事宜 ◇ *They are connected by marriage.* 他们是姻亲。◇ *jobs connected with the environment* 与环境有关的工作 ◇ *The two issues are* **closely connected**. 这两个问题紧密相关。 OPP **unconnected** ➲ SEE ALSO WELL CONNECTED

con·nect·ed·ness /kəˈnektɪdnəs/ *noun* [U] **~ (to/with sb/sth)** a feeling that you have a link with sb/sth or are part of a group 相关感；归属感：*the benefits of helping students feel a sense of connectedness to their school* 帮助学生感到自己是学校一分子的益处

con·nec·tion 🔑 (*BrE also*, *old-fashioned* **con·nex·ion**) /kəˈnekʃn/ *noun*

• **LINK** 联系 **1** 🔑 [C] something that connects two facts, ideas, etc.（两种事实、想法等的）联系，关联 SYN **link**：**~ (between A and B)** *Scientists have established a connection between cholesterol levels and heart disease.* 科学家已证实胆固醇含量与心脏病之间有关联。◇ **~ (with sth)** *a*

direct/close/strong connection** with sth* 与某事有直接的/密切的/牢固的联系 ◇ *How did you **make the connection (= realize that there was a connection between two facts that did not seem to be related)*?* 你怎么看出来有这种关系的？

• **BEING CONNECTED** 连接 **2** [U, C] ~ (**to sth**) the act of connecting or the state of being connected 联结；接通；连接：*Connection to the gas supply was delayed for three days.* 接通煤气延迟了三天。◇ *I'm having problems with my Internet connection.* 我的互联网连接有问题。

• **IN ELECTRICAL SYSTEM** 电力系统 **3** [C] a point, especially in an electrical system, where two parts connect 连接点；（尤指电力系统的）接头：*A faulty connection caused the machine to stop.* 线路接错导致机器停止运转。

• **TRAIN/BUS/PLANE** 火车；公共汽车；飞机 **4** [C] a train, bus or plane at a station or an airport that a passenger can take soon after getting off another in order to continue their journey 转车；转机；联运：*We arrived in good time for the connection to Paris.* 我们到达后有充分的时间接上去巴黎的联运。➲ WORDFINDER NOTE AT TRAIN **5** [C, usually pl.] a means of travelling to another place 旅行交通工具：*There are good bus and train connections between the resort and major cities.* 在度假胜地与主要城市之间有着便利的公共汽车和火车运输。

• **PERSON/ORGANIZATION** 人；机构 **6** [C, usually pl.] a person or an organization that you know and that can help or advise you in your social or professional life 有社交或业务关系的人（或机构）SYN **contact**：*One of my business connections gave them my name.* 我生意上的一个关系户向他们提供了我的名字。

• **DISTANT RELATIVES** 远亲 **7 connections** [pl.] people who are your relatives, but not members of your close family 亲戚；旁系亲属：*She is British but also has German connections.* 她是英国人，但也有德国亲戚。

IDM **in connection with sb/sth** for reasons connected with sb/sth 与…有关（或相关）：*A man has been arrested in connection with the murder of the teenager.* 一名男子因与该谋杀少年案有关而被捕。◇ *I am writing to you in connection with your recent job application.* 我写此信与你最近求职一事有关。**in this/that connection** (*formal*) for reasons connected with sth recently mentioned 由于这（或那）事；为此

con·nect·ive /kəˈnektɪv/ *adj., noun*

▪ ***adj.*** (*medical* 医) that connects things 连接的；结缔的：*connective tissue* 结缔组织

▪ ***noun*** (*grammar* 语法) a word that connects two parts of a sentence 连接词；关联词：*Don't overuse a causal connective like 'because'.* 不要过多地使用像 because 这样表示原因的连接词。

con·nec·tiv·ity /ˌkɒnekˈtɪvəti; *NAmE* ˌkɑːn-/ *noun* [U] (*specialist*) the state of being connected or the degree to which two things are connected 连通性；连接（度）；联结（度）：*ISDN connectivity allows computers to communicate over a network.* 综合业务数字网连接实现了计算机网络通信。

con·nec·tor /kəˈnektə(r)/ *noun* a thing that links two or more things together 连接物；连接器；连线：*a cable connector* 电缆连接器

con·ning tower /ˈkɒnɪŋ taʊə(r); *NAmE* ˈkɑːnɪŋ/ *noun* a raised structure on a SUBMARINE containing the PERISCOPE （潜水艇的）指挥塔

con·nip·tion /kəˈnɪpʃn/ (*also* **conˈniption fit**) *noun* (*old-fashioned, NAmE*) a sudden attack of anger or fear 突发的怒火；一阵惊恐：*He had a conniption when he heard the news.* 他听到消息后大发雷霆。

con·niv·ance /kəˈnaɪvəns/ *noun* [U] (*disapproving*) help in doing sth wrong; the failure to stop sth wrong from happening 共谋；纵容；默许：*The crime was committed with the connivance of a police officer.* 这项罪行是在警察的纵容下发生的。

con·nive /kəˈnaɪv/ *verb* (*formal, disapproving*) **1** [I] ~ **at/in sth** to seem to allow sth wrong to happen 纵容；默许；放任：*She knew that if she said nothing she would be conniving in an injustice.* 她知道她如果什么也不说就是在纵容不公正的行为。**2** [I] ~ (**with sb**) (**to do sth**) to work together with sb to do sth wrong or illegal 共谋；狼狈为奸；同流合污 SYN **conspire**：*The government was accused of having connived with the security forces to permit murder.* 政府被指控与安全部队狼狈为奸放任谋杀。

con·niv·ing /kəˈnaɪvɪŋ/ *adj.* (*disapproving*) behaving in a way that secretly hurts others or deliberately fails to prevent others from being hurt 暗算他人的；故意纵容的

con·nois·seur /ˌkɒnəˈsɜː(r); *NAmE* ˌkɑːnəˈsɜːr; -ˈsʊr/ *noun* an expert on matters involving the judgement of beauty, quality or skill in art, food or music 鉴赏家；鉴定家；行家：*a connoisseur of Italian painting* 意大利绘画鉴赏家 ◇ *a wine connoisseur* 葡萄酒鉴定家

con·no·ta·tion /ˌkɒnəˈteɪʃn; *NAmE* ˌkɑːn-/ *noun* an idea suggested by a word in addition to its main meaning 含义；隐含意义：*The word 'professional' has connotations of skill and excellence.* * professional 这个词隐含着技艺和专长的意思。◇ *negative connotations* 贬义 ➲ COMPARE DENOTATION ➲ WORDFINDER NOTE AT WORD

con·note /kəˈnəʊt; *NAmE* kəˈnoʊt/ *verb* ~ **sth** (*formal*) (of a word 词) to suggest a feeling, an idea, etc. as well as the main meaning 意味着；暗示；隐含 ➲ COMPARE DENOTE

con·nub·ial /kəˈnjuːbiəl; *NAmE* -ˈnuː-/ *adj.* (*literary*) related to marriage, or the relationship between husband and wife 婚姻的；夫妻（关系）的

con·quer /ˈkɒŋkə(r); *NAmE* ˈkɑːŋ-/ *verb* **1** ~ **sb/sth** to take control of a country or city and its people by force 占领；攻克；征服：*The Normans conquered England in 1066.* 诺曼人于 1066 年征服了英格兰。◇ ***conquered peoples/races/territories*** 被征服的民族/种族；被占领的领土 **2** ~ **sb** to defeat sb, especially in a competition, race, etc. （尤指比赛、赛跑等中）击败，战胜：*The world champion conquered yet another challenger last night.* 昨晚这位世界冠军又战胜了一名挑战者。**3** ~ **sth** to succeed in dealing with or controlling sth （成功地）对付，克服，控制：*The only way to conquer a fear is to face it.* 克服恐惧的唯一方法是正视恐惧。◇ *Mont Blanc was conquered* (= successfully climbed) *in 1786.* 勃朗峰于 1786 年被征服。**4** ~ **sth** to become very popular or successful in a place 在（某地）很受欢迎；在（某地）成功：*The band is now setting out to conquer the world.* 这支乐队现在要出发去征服世界。

con·queror /ˈkɒŋkərə(r); *NAmE* ˈkɑːŋ-/ *noun* a person who conquers 征服者；占领者；胜利者：*William the Conqueror* (= King William I of England) 征服者威廉（英国国王威廉一世）

con·quest /ˈkɒŋkwest; *NAmE* ˈkɑːŋ-/ *noun* **1** [C, U] the act of taking control of a country, city, etc. by force 征服；占领：*the Norman Conquest* (= of England in 1066) 诺曼征服（即 1066 年诺曼人征服英格兰）**2** [C] an area of land taken by force 占领（或征服）的地区：*the Spanish conquests in South America* 西班牙人在南美洲的占领地 **3** [C] (*usually humorous*) a person that sb has persuaded to love them or to have sex with them （爱情或性方面）被俘虏的人：*I'm just one of his many conquests.* 我仅仅是他的众多俘虏之一。**4** [U] the act of gaining control over sth that is difficult or dangerous （对困难、危险等的）控制：*the conquest of inflation* 对通货膨胀的控制

con·quis·ta·dor /kɒnˈkwɪstədɔː(r); -ˈkɪst-; *NAmE* kɑːn-/ *noun* (*pl.* **con·quis·ta·dores** /kɒnˌkwɪstəˈdɔːreɪz; -ˌkɪstə-; *NAmE* kɑːn-/ or **con·quis·ta·dors**) (*from Spanish*) one of the Spanish people who took control of Mexico and Peru by force in the 16th century （16 世纪侵占墨西哥和秘鲁的）西班牙征服者

con·san·guin·ity /ˌkɒnsæŋˈgwɪnəti; *NAmE* ˌkɑːn-/ *noun* [U] (*formal*) relationship by birth in the same family 同宗；血缘；血亲关系

con·science /ˈkɒnʃəns; *NAmE* ˈkɑːn-/ *noun* **1** [C, U] the part of your mind that tells you whether your actions are right or wrong 良心；良知：*to have a **clear/guilty conscience*** (= to feel that you have done right/wrong) 问心

无愧 / 有愧 ◇ *This is a **matter of** individual **conscience*** (= everyone must make their own judgement about it). 这关系到个人的良知。◇ *He won't let it trouble his conscience.* 他不会让这件事搞得自己良心不安的。➲ SEE ALSO SOCIAL CONSCIENCE **2** [U, C] a guilty feeling about sth you have done or failed to do 内疚；愧疚：*She was seized by a sudden pang of conscience.* 她突然感到一阵内疚。◇ *I have a terrible conscience about it.* 我对此事深感愧疚。**3** [U] the fact of behaving in a way that you feel is right even though this may cause problems 凭良心：*freedom of conscience* (= the freedom to do what you believe to be right) 凭良心行事的自由 ◇ *Emilia is the voice of conscience in the play.* 埃米莉亚在这出戏中是良知的代言人。➲ SEE ALSO PRISONER OF CONSCIENCE

IDM **in (all/good) conscience** (*formal*) believing your actions to be fair （认为行为）公正地，公平地，凭良心 SYN **honestly**: *We cannot in all conscience refuse to help.* 凭良心我们不能拒绝去帮助别人。 **on your 'conscience** making you feel guilty for doing or failing to do sth 使人内疚；良心不安：*I'll write and apologize. I've had it on my conscience for weeks.* 我要写信赔礼道歉。几个星期以来我都为此而良心不安。➲ MORE AT PRICK *v.*

'conscience-stricken *adj.* feeling guilty about sth you have done or failed to do 内疚的；不安的；受良心责备的

con·scien·tious /ˌkɒnʃiˈenʃəs; *NAmE* ˌkɑːn-/ *adj.* taking care to do things carefully and correctly 勤勉认真的；一丝不苟的：*a conscientious student/teacher/worker* 勤勉认真的学生；一丝不苟的老师；认真负责的工人 ▶ **con·scien·tious·ly** *adv.*: *She performed all her duties conscientiously.* 她认真负责地履行自己的所有职责。**con·scien·tious·ness** *noun* [U]

ˌconscientious ob'jector *noun* a person who refuses to serve in the armed forces for moral reasons 出于道义原因而拒服兵役者 ➲ COMPARE DRAFT DODGER, PACIFIST

con·scien·tize (*BrE also* **-ise**) /ˈkɒnʃəntaɪz; *NAmE* ˈkɑːn-/ *verb* **~ sb/yourself** (*SAfrE*) to make sb/yourself aware of important social or political issues 使意识到（重大社会或政治问题）；使觉悟：*People need to be conscientized about their rights.* 需要让人们明白自己的权利。

con·scious /ˈkɒnʃəs; *NAmE* ˈkɑːn-/ *adj.* **1** [not before noun] aware of sth; noticing sth 意识到；注意到：**~ of sth** *She's very conscious of the problems involved.* 她完全意识到了所涉及的问题。◇ **~ of doing sth** *He became acutely conscious of having failed his parents.* 他深深感到自己辜负了父母的期望。◇ **~ that…** *I was vaguely conscious that I was being watched.* 我隐隐约约地觉察到有人在监视我。 OPP **unconscious** ➲ SEE ALSO CLASS-CONSCIOUS, SELF-CONSCIOUS **2** able to use your senses and mental powers to understand what is happening 神志清醒的；有知觉的；有意识的：*A patient who is not fully conscious should never be left alone.* 神志并非完全清醒的病人必须时刻有人照料。 OPP **unconscious** **3** (of actions, feelings, etc. 行为、感情等) deliberate or controlled 慎重的；有意的；刻意的：*to make a **conscious decision*** 作出慎重的决定 ◇ *I made a **conscious effort** to get there on time.* 我刻意约束自己准时到达那里。◇ *a conscious act of cruelty* 蓄意的残暴行径 OPP **unconscious** ➲ COMPARE SUBCONSCIOUS *adj.* **4** being particularly interested in sth 特别感兴趣的；关注的：*environmentally conscious* 有环保意识的 ◇ *They have become increasingly health-conscious.* 他们的健康意识越来越强。▶ **con·scious·ly** *adv.*: *Consciously or unconsciously, you made a choice.* 不管是有意还是无意，你已作出了选择。

con·scious·ness /ˈkɒnʃəsnəs; *NAmE* ˈkɑːn-/ *noun* [U] **1** the state of being able to use your senses and mental powers to understand what is happening 清醒状态；知觉：*I can't remember any more—I must have **lost consciousness**.* 我什么都想不起来了，我当时一定是失去了知觉。◇ *She did not **regain consciousness** and died the next day.* 她再也没有苏醒过来，第二天便去世了。 **2** the state of being aware of sth 觉察；感觉；意识 SYN **awareness**: *his consciousness of the challenge facing him* 他对所面临的挑战的清醒意识 ◇ ***class-consciousness*** (= consciousness of different classes in society) 阶级意识 **3** the ideas and opinions of a person or group 观念；看法：*her newly developed political consciousness* 她最近形成的政治观念 ➲ SEE ALSO STREAM OF CONSCIOUSNESS

'consciousness-raising *noun* [U] the process of making people aware of important social and political issues （社会或政治）觉悟提高，意识加强

con·script *verb, noun*

■ ***verb*** /kənˈskrɪpt/ (*especially BrE*) (*NAmE usually* **draft**) [usually passive] **~ sb (into sth)** to make sb join the armed forces 征募；征召 SYN **call up**: *He was conscripted into the army in 1939.* 他于 1939 年应征入伍。

■ ***noun*** /ˈkɒnskrɪpt; *NAmE* ˈkɑːn-/ (*especially BrE*) (*US usually* **draft·ee**) a person who has been conscripted to join the armed forces 应征入伍者：*young army conscripts* 年轻的应征士兵 ◇ ***conscript soldiers/armies*** 应征入伍的士兵；由应征入伍者组成的部队 ➲ COMPARE VOLUNTEER *n.* (3)

con·scrip·tion /kənˈskrɪpʃn/ *noun* [U] (*especially BrE*) (*US usually* **the draft**) the practice of ordering people by law to serve in the armed forces 征募；征兵 SYN **call-up**

con·se·crate /ˈkɒnsɪkreɪt; *NAmE* ˈkɑːn-/ *verb* **1 ~ sth** to state officially in a religious ceremony that sth is holy and can be used for religious purposes 祝圣；圣化；奉献：*The church was consecrated in 1853.* 这座教堂于 1853 年祝圣。◇ *consecrated ground* 经祝圣的地方 **2 ~ sth** (in Christian belief 基督教信仰) to make bread and wine into the body and blood of Christ 祝圣饼酒；成圣体 **3 ~ sb (as) (sth)** to state officially in a religious ceremony that sb is now a priest, etc. 祝圣神职人员：*He was consecrated (as) bishop last year.* 他于去年被祝圣为主教。 **4 ~ sth/sb/yourself to sth** (*formal*) to give sth/sb/yourself to a special purpose, especially a religious one （尤指为宗教而）奉献，献身 ▶ **con·se·cra·tion** /ˌkɒnsɪˈkreɪʃn; *NAmE* ˌkɑːn-/ *noun* [C, U]: *the consecration of a church/bishop* 教堂 / 主教祝圣礼

con·secu·tive /kənˈsekjətɪv/ *adj.* [usually before noun] following one after another in a series, without interruption 连续不断的：*She was absent for nine consecutive days.* 她一连缺席了九天。◇ *He is beginning his fourth consecutive term of office.* 他开始了第四届任期。▶ **con·secu·tive·ly** *adv.*

con·sen·su·al /kənˈsenʃuəl/ *adj.* (*formal*) **1** which people in general agree with 一致同意的：*a consensual approach* 一致赞成的方法 **2** (of an activity 活动) which the people taking part have agreed to （参与者）同意的，赞同的：*consensual sex* 两厢情愿的性行为

con·sen·sus AW /kənˈsensəs/ *noun* [sing., U] an opinion that all members of a group agree with 一致的意见；共识：**~ (about/on sth)** *She is skilled at achieving consensus on sensitive issues.* 她擅长就敏感问题进行斡旋，从而达成共识。◇ *There is a growing **consensus of opinion** on this issue.* 对这个问题的看法日趋一致。◇ *an attempt to **reach a consensus*** 达成共识的尝试 ◇ **~ (among sb) (about/on sth)** *There is a general consensus among teachers about the need for greater security in schools.* 教师们对必须加强学校的安全工作有普遍的共识。◇ **~ (that…)** *There seems to be a consensus that the plan should be rejected.* 看来人们一致同意放弃这一计划。

con·sent AW /kənˈsent/ *noun, verb*

■ ***noun*** **1** [U] **~ (to sth)** permission to do sth, especially given by sb in authority 同意；准许；允许：*Children under 16 cannot **give consent** to medical treatment.* * 16 岁以下的儿童不得自行同意接受治疗。◇ *The written consent of a parent is required.* 要求有家长的书面同意。◇ *to **refuse/withhold** your **consent*** 拒不同意 ◇ *He is charged with taking a car **without** the owner's **consent**.* 他因未征得车主的同意自行开走车而受到指控。 ➲ SEE ALSO AGE OF CONSENT **2** [U] agreement about sth 同意；赞同：*She was chosen as leader **by common consent*** (= everyone agreed to the choice). 大家一致同意选她为领导人。◇ ***By mutual consent** they didn't go out* (= they both agreed not to). 他俩一致同意不出门了。 **3** [C] an official document giving permission for sth 正式批准文件；批文

■ ***verb*** [I] (*rather formal*) to agree to sth or give your permission for sth 同意；准许；允许：*When she told them what she intended they readily consented.* 她告诉他们她的打算时，他们欣然同意。◇ **~ to sth** *He reluctantly consented to his daughter's marriage.* 他勉强同意了女儿的婚事。◇ **~ to do sth** *She finally consented to answer our questions.* 她最终同意回答我们的问题。➲ SYNONYMS AT AGREE ➲ MORE LIKE THIS 26, page R28

con,senting 'adult *noun* a person who is considered old enough, by law, to decide whether they should agree to have sex; a person who has agreed to have sex 到达法定性成熟年龄的已成年人；同意发生性行为的已成年人

con·se·quence 🔑 AW /ˈkɒnsɪkwəns; *NAmE* ˈkɑːnsəkwens/ *noun* **1** 🔑 [C] **~ (of sth) (for sb/sth)** a result of sth that has happened 结果；后果：*This decision could have **serious consequences** for the industry.* 这项决定可能对该行业造成严重后果。◇ *Two hundred people lost their jobs **as a direct consequence** of the merger.* 合并一事直接导致二百人失去了工作。◇ *He drove too fast with tragic consequences.* 他开车太快，结果酿成惨剧。◇ *to **suffer/face/take the consequences** of your actions* 自食其果；面对 / 承担自己行为的后果 ➲ SYNONYMS AT RESULT ➲ LANGUAGE BANK AT CONSEQUENTLY **2** [U] (*formal*) importance 重要性：*Don't worry. It's **of no consequence**.* 别担心，这无关紧要。

IDM **in consequence (of sth)** (*formal*) as a result of sth 由于；作为…的结果：*The child was born deformed in consequence of an injury to the mother.* 由于母亲受过伤，这小孩生下来是畸形的。

con·se·quent AW /ˈkɒnsɪkwənt; *NAmE* ˈkɑːnsəkwənt/ *adj.* (*formal*) happening as a result of sth 随之发生的；作为结果的 SYN **resultant**：*the lowering of taxes and the consequent increase in spending* 税收降低与随之引起的消费增长 ◇ **~ on/upon sth** *the responsibilities consequent upon the arrival of a new child* 新生儿出世后随之而来的职责

con·se·quen·tial /ˌkɒnsɪˈkwenʃl; *NAmE* ˌkɑːnsəˈk-/ *adj.* (*formal*) **1** happening as a result or an effect of sth 随之而来的；相应发生的；作为结果的 SYN **resultant**：*retirement and the consequential reduction in income* 退休与随之而来的收入减少 **2** important; that will have important results 重要的；将产生重大结果的：*The report discusses a number of consequential matters that are yet to be decided.* 这份报告讨论了许多有待决定的重大问题。OPP **inconsequential** ▶ **con·se·quen·tial·ly** /-ʃəli/ *adv.*

con·se·quent·ly AW /ˈkɒnsɪkwəntli; *NAmE* ˈkɑːnsəkwentli/ *adv.* as a result; therefore 因此；所以：*This poses a threat to agriculture and the food chain, and consequently to human health.* 这会对农业和食物链造成威胁，因而危及人的健康。

con·ser·vancy /kənˈsɜːvənsi; *NAmE* -ˈsɜːrv-/ *noun* **1 Conservancy** [sing.+sing./pl. v.] a group of officials who control the use of a port, a river, an area of land, etc. （港口、河流、地区等的）管理机构：*the Thames Conservancy* 泰晤士河管理委员会 ◇ *Texas Nature Conservancy* 得克萨斯州自然资源管理委员会 **2** [U] (*formal*) the protection of the natural environment （对自然环境的）保护 SYN **conservation**：*nature conservancy* 自然环境的保护

con·ser·va·tion /ˌkɒnsəˈveɪʃn; *NAmE* ˌkɑːnsərˈv-/ *noun* [U] **1** the protection of the natural environment （对自然环境的）保护 SYN **conservancy**：*to be interested in wildlife conservation* 对野生动物保护感兴趣 ➲ WORDFINDER NOTE AT GREEN **2** the official protection of buildings that have historical or artistic importance（官方对历史或艺术建筑的）保护；文物保护 **3** the act of preventing sth from being lost, wasted, damaged or destroyed 防止流失（或浪费、损害、毁坏）；保持；保护：*to encourage the **conservation of water/fuel*** 鼓励节约用水 / 燃料 ◇ *energy conservation* 能源的节约 ➲ SEE ALSO CONSERVE *v.*

conser'vation area *noun* (in the UK) an area where the natural environment or the buildings are protected by law from being damaged or changed （英国自然环境或建筑物的）保护区

con·ser·va·tion·ist /ˌkɒnsəˈveɪʃənɪst; *NAmE* ˌkɑːnsərˈv-/ *noun* a person who takes an active part in the protection of the environment 自然环境保护主义者：*a meeting of local conservationists* 当地自然环境保护主义者的会议

con·ser·va·tism /kənˈsɜːvətɪzəm; *NAmE* -ˈsɜːrv-/ *noun* [U] **1** the tendency to resist great or sudden change 保守；守旧：*the innate conservatism of older people* 老年人固有的保守性 **2** (*also* **Conservatism**) the political belief that society should change as little as possible 保守主义：*an examination of the political theories of conservatism and liberalism* 对保守主义和自由主义政治理论的审视 **3** (*usually* **Conservatism**) the principles of the Conservative Party in British politics （英国）保守党的原则

con·ser·va·tive 🔑 /kənˈsɜːvətɪv; *NAmE* -ˈsɜːrvə-/ *adj., noun*

■ ***adj.*** **1** 🔑 opposed to great or sudden social change; showing that you prefer traditional styles and values 保守的；守旧的：*the conservative views of his parents* 他父母的保守观念 ◇ *Her style of dress was never conservative.* 她的服装式样一点儿也不保守。 **2** (*usually* **Conservative**) connected with the British Conservative Party（英国）保守党的：*Conservative members/supporters* 保守党的党员 / 支持者 **3** 🔑 (of an estimate 估计) lower than what is probably the real amount or number 低于实际数量的；保守的：***At a conservative estimate**, he'll be earning £50 000.* 按照保守的估计，他会赚到 5 万英镑。▶ **con·ser·va·tive·ly** *adv.*

■ ***noun*** **1** (*usually* **Conservative**) (*abbr.* **Con.**) a member or supporter of the British Conservative Party（英国）保守党党员，保守党支持者 **2** a conservative person 保守者；因循守旧者

the Con'servative Party *noun* [sing.+sing./pl. v.] one of the main British political parties, on the political right, which especially believes in FREE ENTERPRISE and that industry should be privately owned 保守党（英国主要政党之一，尤其信奉自由企业制度及产业私有化）

con·ser·va·toire /kənˈsɜːvətwɑː(r); *NAmE* -ˈsɜːrv-/ (*BrE*) (*NAmE* **con·ser·va·tory**) *noun* a school or college at which people are trained in music and theatre 音乐（或戏剧）专科学校（或学院）

con·ser·va·tor /kənˈsɜːvətə(r); *NAmE* -ˈsɜːrv-/ *noun* a person who is responsible for repairing and preserving

▼ **LANGUAGE BANK 用语库**

consequently

Describing the effect of something 描述某事的影响

- ***One consequence of** changes in diet over recent years has been a dramatic increase in cases of childhood obesity.* 近年来饮食变化带来的一个结果是儿童肥胖人数急剧上升。
- *Many parents today do not have time to cook healthy meals for their children. **Consequently/As a consequence**, many children grow up eating too much junk food.* 现在许多家长没有时间给孩子做健康的饭菜，结果造成许多孩子在成长过程中吃过多的垃圾食品。
- *Many children spend their free time watching TV instead of playing outside. **As a result**, more and more of them are becoming overweight.* 许多孩子把他们的闲暇时间都花在看电视上，而不是进行户外活动，从而导致越来越多的孩子变得肥胖。
- *Last year junk food was banned in schools. **The effect of this has been to** create a black market in the playground, with pupils bringing sweets from home to sell to other pupils.* 去年学校禁售垃圾食品，结果是学校操场上出现了垃圾食品的黑市交易，有的学生把从家里带来的甜食卖给其他学生。

➲ NOTE AT EFFECT
➲ LANGUAGE BANK AT CAUSE, THEREFORE

works of art, buildings and other things of cultural interest 文物修复员；文物保护员

con·ser·va·tory /kənˈsɜːvətri; *NAmE* -ˈsɜːrvətɔːri/ *noun* (*pl.* **-ies**) **1** a room with glass walls and a glass roof that is built on the side of a house. Conservatories are used for sitting in to enjoy the sun, and to protect plants from cold weather. （靠房屋一侧用玻璃建造的）温室，暖房 ➲ VISUAL VOCAB PAGE V20 **2** (*NAmE*) (*BrE* **con·ser·va·toire**) a school or college at which people are trained in music and theatre 音乐（或戏剧）专科学校（或学院）

C

con·serve *verb, noun*

■ ***verb*** /kənˈsɜːv; *NAmE* -ˈsɜːrv/ **1 ~ sth** to use as little of sth as possible so that it lasts a long time 节省；节约：*Help to conserve energy by insulating your home.* 对房屋做隔热处理来帮助节约能源。**2 ~ sth** to protect sth and prevent it from being changed or destroyed 保护；保存；保藏：*new laws to conserve wildlife in the area* 保护该地区野生动物的新法令 ➲ SEE ALSO CONSERVATION

■ ***noun*** /ˈkɒnsɜːv; *NAmE* ˈkɑːnsɜːrv/ [C, U] jam containing large or whole pieces of fruit（含有大块或整块水果的）果酱，蜜饯

con·sider 🔑 /kənˈsɪdə(r)/ *verb* **1** 🔑 [I, T] to think about sth carefully, especially in order to make a decision （尤指为作出决定而）仔细考虑，细想：*I'd like some time to consider.* 我希望有些时间考虑一下。◇ **~ sth** *She considered her options.* 她仔细考虑了自己的各种选择。◇ *a **carefully considered** response* 经过仔细考虑的回复 ◇ *The company is being actively considered as a potential partner* (= it is thought possible that it could become one). 这家公司正在被积极考虑为可能的合作伙伴。◇ **~ doing sth** *We're considering buying a new car.* 我们在考虑买一辆新车。◇ **~ how/what, etc.…** *We need to consider how the law might be reformed.* 我们得斟酌法律应如何修订。◇ *He was considering what to do next.* 他在考虑下一步怎么办。➲ LANGUAGE BANK AT ABOUT ➲ MORE LIKE THIS 27, page R28 **2** 🔑 [T] to think of sb/sth in a particular way 认为；以为；觉得：**~ sb/sth + noun | ~ sb/sth (to be) sth | ~ sb/sth (as) sth** *He considers himself an expert on the subject.* 他认为自己是这门学科的专家。◇ *This award is considered (to be) a great honour.* 这项奖被视为极大的荣誉。◇ *These workers are considered (as) a high-risk group.* 这些工人被视为高风险人群。◇ **~ sb/sth + adj. | ~ sb/sth (to be) sth** ***Consider yourself lucky*** *you weren't fired.* 你没被解雇，算是万幸。◇ *Who do you consider (to be) responsible for the accident?* 你认为谁对这起事故负有责任？◇ **~ sb/sth to do sth** *He's generally considered to have the finest tenor voice in the country.* 普遍认为他是全国最佳男高音歌手。◇ **~ (that)…** *She considers that it is too early to form a definite conclusion.* 她认为现在下确切的结论还为时过早。◇ **it is considered that…** *It is considered that the proposed development would create much-needed jobs.* 人们认为所提出的发展计划将创造急需的就业机会。 ➲ SYNONYMS AT REGARD **3** 🔑 [T] **~ sb/sth** to think about sth, especially the feelings of other people, and be influenced by it when making a decision, etc. 体谅；考虑到；顾及：*You should consider other people before you act.* 你在行动之前应当考虑到别人。 **4** [T] **~ sb/sth** (*formal*) to look carefully at sb/sth 端详；注视：*He stood there, considering the painting.* 他站在那里，凝视着那幅画。

IDM **all things conˈsidered** thinking carefully about all the facts, especially the problems or difficulties, of a situation 从各方面看来；考虑到所有情况；总而言之：*She's had a lot of problems since her husband died but she seems quite cheerful, all things considered.* 自从丈夫死后，她面临很多困难，但总的来说她看上去情绪还是挺乐观的。 **your conˌsidered oˈpinion** your opinion that is the result of careful thought 成熟的意见；经过深思熟虑的意见

con·sid·er·able 🔑 AW /kənˈsɪdərəbl/ *adj.* (*rather formal*) great in amount, size, importance, etc. 相当多（或大、重要等）的 SYN **significant**：*The project wasted a considerable amount of time and money.* 那项工程耗费了相当多的时间和资金。◇ *Damage to the building was considerable.* 对这栋建筑物的损坏相当严重。

con·sid·er·ably 🔑 AW /kənˈsɪdərəbli/ *adv.* (*formal*) much; a lot 非常；很；相当多地 SYN **significantly**：*The need for sleep varies considerably from person to person.* 不同的人对睡眠的需要差异相当大。

con·sid·er·ate /kənˈsɪdərət/ *adj.* always thinking of other people's wishes and feelings; careful not to hurt or upset others 考虑周到的；为（他人）着想的；体谅的；体贴的 SYN **thoughtful**：*She is always polite and considerate towards her employees.* 她对待雇员总是客客气气，关心体谅。◇ *It was very considerate of him to wait.* 他一直在等候着，真是体贴。 OPP **inconsiderate** ▸ **con·sid·er·ate·ly** *adv.*

con·sid·er·ation 🔑 /kənˌsɪdəˈreɪʃn/ *noun* **1** 🔑 [U, C] (*formal*) the act of thinking carefully about sth 仔细考虑；深思；斟酌：*Careful consideration should be given to issues of health and safety.* 健康与安全的问题应该认真予以考虑。◇ *The proposals are currently **under consideration*** (= being discussed). 那些提案目前正在审议中。◇ *After a few moments' consideration, he began to speak.* 他想了片刻后开始讲话。◇ *a consideration of the legal issues involved* 对有关法律问题的考虑 **2** 🔑 [C] something that must be thought about when you are planning or deciding sth （作计划或决定时）必须考虑的事（或因素、原因）：***economic/commercial/environmental/practical considerations*** 需要考虑的经济 / 商业 / 环境 / 实际因素 ◇ *Time is another important consideration.* 时间是另一个需要考虑的重要因素。 **3** 🔑 [U] **~ (for sb/sth)** the quality of being sensitive towards others and thinking about their wishes and feelings （对他人的）考虑周到，体谅，顾及：*They showed no consideration whatsoever for my feelings.* 他们根本不体谅我的感受。◇ *Journalists stayed away from the funeral **out of consideration for** the bereaved family.* 出于对亡人家属的考虑，新闻记者没有到葬礼现场。 **4** [C] (*formal*) a reward or payment for a service 报酬；酬金；支付款

IDM **in consideration of sth** (*formal*) as payment for sth 作为…的报酬（或酬劳）：*a small sum in consideration of your services* 对你服务的微薄酬金 **take sth into consideration** 🔑 to think about and include a particular thing or fact when you are forming an opinion or making a decision 考虑到；顾及：*The candidates' experience and qualifications will be taken into consideration when the decision is made.* 作决定时要考虑候选人的经验和资格。◇ *Taking everything into consideration, the event was a great success.* 总的说来，这项活动取得了极大的成功。 ➲ MORE AT MATURE *adj.*

con·sider·ing /kənˈsɪdərɪŋ/ *prep., conj., adv.* used to show that you are thinking about a particular fact, and are influenced by it, when you make a statement about sth 考虑到；就…而言；鉴于：*She's very active, considering her age.* 就她的年龄来说，她是十分活跃的。◇ *Considering he's only just started, he knows quite a lot about it.* 鉴于他才刚刚开始，他懂得的已经不少了。◇ (*informal*) *You've done very well, considering* (= in the difficult circumstances). 考虑到处境的艰难，你已经做得相当不错了。

con·sign /kənˈsaɪn/ *verb* (*formal*) **1 ~ sb/sth to sth** to put sb/sth somewhere in order to get rid of them/it （为摆脱而）把…置于，把…交付给：*I consigned her letter to the wastebasket.* 我把她的信丢进了废纸篓。◇ *What I didn't want was to see my mother consigned to an old people's home.* 我所不愿意的是看到我母亲被送进养老院。 **2 ~ sb/sth to sth** to put sb/sth in an unpleasant situation 把…置于（令人不快的境地）；打发；发落：*The decision to close the factory has **consigned** 6 000 people **to the scrap-heap**.* 关闭那家工厂的决定使 6 000 人遭到了遗弃。◇ *A car accident consigned him to a wheelchair for the rest of his life.* 一次车祸使他落得在轮椅上度过余生。 **3 ~ sth to sb** to give or send sth to sb 交给；交付；寄送

con·sign·ment /kənˈsaɪnmənt/ *noun* **1** [C] a quantity of goods that are sent or delivered somewhere 装运的货物；运送物：*a consignment of medicines* 运送的一批药物 **2** [U] the act of sending or delivering sb/sth 发送；投递；递送

conˈsignment shop (*also* **conˈsignment store**) *noun* (*NAmE*) a shop/store where people take their old clothes, etc. to be sold to sb else. The consignment shop keeps part of the money after an item is sold and gives the other part to the person who brought it in. 委托商行；寄售店

con·sist AW /kən'sɪst/ *verb* (not used in the progressive tenses 不用于进行时)

PHR V **con'sist in sth** (*formal*) to have sth as the main or only part or feature 存在于；在于： *The beauty of the city consists in its magnificent buildings.* 这座城市的美就在于它那些宏伟的建筑。◇ **consist in doing sth** *True education does not consist in simply being taught facts.* 真正的教育并不在于仅仅讲授事实。 **con'sist of sb/sth** to be formed from the people or things mentioned 由…组成（或构成）： *The committee consists of ten members.* 委员会由十人组成。◇ *Their diet consisted largely of vegetables.* 他们的日常饮食以蔬菜为主。◇ **consist of doing sth** *Most of the fieldwork consisted of making tape recordings.* 现场工作多半为进行磁带录音。

▼ **SYNONYMS 同义词辨析**

consist of sb/sth

comprise • make up sth • constitute • be composed of sb/sth

These words all mean to be formed from the things or people mentioned, or to be the parts that form sth. 以上各词均表示由某些人或事物组成、构成某事物。

consist of sb/sth to be formed from the people, things or activities mentioned 指由人、事物或活动组成、构成： *Their diet consists largely of vegetables.* 他们的日常饮食以蔬菜为主。

comprise (*rather formal*) to be formed from the things or people mentioned 指由…组成、构成： *The collection comprises 327 paintings.* 这组收藏有 327 幅画。 NOTE **Comprise** can also be used to refer to the parts or members of sth. * comprise 亦可指组成、构成： *Older people comprise a large proportion of those living in poverty.* 在那些生活贫困的人中，老年人占很大的比例。 However, this is less frequent. 不过这种用法不常见。

make up sth (*rather informal*) to be the parts or people that form sth 指组成、构成： *Women make up 56% of the student numbers.* 女生占学生人数的 56%。

constitute (*formal*) to be the parts or people that form sth 指组成、构成： *People under the age of 40 constitute the majority of the labour force.* * 40 岁以下的人占劳动力的大多数。

be composed of sb/sth (*rather formal*) to be formed from the things or people mentioned 指由…组成、构成： *Around 15% of our diet is composed of protein.* 我们的饮食中大约 15% 是蛋白质。

WHICH WORD? 词语辨析

Consist of sb/sth is the most general of these words and the only one that can be used for activities with the *-ing* form of a verb. * consist of 是这组词中最通用、也是唯一可与动词 -ing 形式连用、表示包含…活动的词： *My work at that time just consisted of typing letters.* 我那时的工作就是打印信件。 The other main difference is between those verbs that take the whole as the subject and the parts as the object 另一主要区别在于有些词是将整体作为主语，部分作为宾语： *The group consists of/comprises/is made up of/is composed of ten people.* 这个小组由十个人组成。 and those that take the parts as the subject and the whole as the object. 另一些词则是将部分作为主语，整体作为宾语： *Ten people make up/constitute/comprise the group.* 这个小组由十个人组成。 It is not correct to use 'comprises of' or 'is composed by/from'. 用 comprise of 或 is composed by/from 均不正确。

con·sist·ency AW /kən'sɪstənsi/ *noun* (*pl.* **-ies**) **1** [U] (*approving*) the quality of always behaving in the same way or of having the same opinions, standard, etc.; the quality of being consistent 一致性；连贯性： *She has played with great consistency all season.* 她整个赛季表现相当稳定。◇ *We need to ensure the consistency of service to our customers.* 我们对客户要确保服务的连贯性。 OPP **inconsistency** **2** [C, U] the **consistency** of a mixture or a liquid substance is how thick, smooth, etc. it is 黏稠度；密实度；平滑度；坚实度： *Beat the ingredients together to a creamy consistency.* 把配料搅拌成乳脂状。◇ *The cement should have the consistency of wet sand.* 水泥的稠度应如湿沙。

con·sist·ent AW /kən'sɪstənt/ *adj.* **1** (*approving*) always behaving in the same way, or having the same opinions, standards, etc. 一致的；始终如一的： *She's not very consistent in the way she treats her children.* 她对待孩子反复无常。◇ *He has been Milan's most consistent* (= most consistently good) *player this season.* 他是米兰队这个赛季状态最稳定的队员。◇ *We must be consistent in applying the rules.* 我们在实施这些规则时必须保持一贯性。◇ *a consistent approach to the problem* 解决问题的一贯方法 **2** happening in the same way and continuing for a period of time 连续的；持续的： *the party's consistent failure to come up with any new policies* 这个政党长时间提不出任何新政策 ◇ *a pattern of consistent growth in the economy* 经济持续增长的模式 **3 ~ with sth** in agreement with sth; not CONTRADICTING sth 与…一致的；相符的；符合的；不矛盾的： *The results are entirely consistent with our earlier research.* 这些结果与我们早些时候的研究完全吻合。◇ *injuries consistent with a fall from an upper storey* (= similar to those such a fall would have caused) 和从楼上摔下来的情形相符合的伤处 **4** (of an argument or a set of ideas 论点或一系列的观点) having different parts that all agree with each other 相互连贯的： *a well-thought-out and consistent argument* 经过深思熟虑的、相互连贯的论点 OPP **inconsistent** ▸ **con·sist·ent·ly** AW *adv.*： *Her work has been of a consistently high standard.* 她的工作一直是高水准的。◇ *We have argued consistently for a change in the law.* 我们一直力主更改法律。

con·sola·tion /ˌkɒnsə'leɪʃn; *NAmE* ˌkɑːn-/ *noun* [U, C] a thing or person that makes you feel better when you are unhappy or disappointed 使感到安慰的人（或物）；安慰；慰藉 SYN **comfort**： *a few words of consolation* 几句安慰的话 ◇ *If it's any consolation, she didn't get the job, either.* 不知道这算不算得上安慰，她也没有得到那份工作。◇ *The children were a great consolation to him when his wife died.* 他妻子去世后，几个孩子就是他极大的安慰。

conso'lation prize *noun* a small prize given to sb who has not won a competition 安慰奖；鼓励奖

con·sola·tory /kən'sɒlətəri; *NAmE* kən'soʊlətɔːri; -'sɑːlə-/ *adj.* (*formal*) intended to make sb who is unhappy or disappointed feel better 安慰的；慰藉的

con·sole¹ /kən'səʊl; *NAmE* -'soʊl/ *verb* to give comfort or sympathy to sb who is unhappy or disappointed 安慰；抚慰；慰藉 SYN **comfort**： **~ sb/yourself** *Nothing could console him when his wife died.* 他妻子去世后，什么事情也不能使他感到宽慰。◇ *She put a consoling arm around his shoulders.* 她搂住他肩膀以示安慰。 ◇ **~ sb/yourself with sth** *Console yourself with the thought that you did your best.* 你可以安慰自己的是你已经尽了最大的努力。◇ **~ sb/yourself that...** *I didn't like lying but I consoled myself that it was for a good cause.* 我不愿意撒谎，但我安慰自己那是出于好意。 ◇ **~ sb + speech** *'Never mind,' Anne consoled her.* "没关系。"安妮安慰她说。

con·sole² /'kɒnsəʊl; *NAmE* 'kɑːnsoʊl/ *noun* **1** a flat surface which contains all the controls and switches for a machine, a piece of electronic equipment, etc. （机器、电子设备等的）控制台，操纵台，仪表板 **2** (*also* **'games console**) a small electronic device for playing video games 游戏机

con·soli·date /kən'sɒlɪdeɪt; *NAmE* -'sɑːl-/ *verb* **1** [T, I] **~ (sth)** to make a position of power or success stronger so that it is more likely to continue 使加强；使巩固： *With this new movie he has* **consolidated** *his* **position** *as the country's leading director.* 他新执导的影片巩固了他作为全

C

国最佳导演的地位。◇ *Italy consolidated their lead with a second goal.* 意大利队的第二个进球巩固了其领先的地位。**2** [T, I] ~ (**sth**) (*specialist*) to join things together into one; to be joined into one（使）结成一体，合并：*All the debts have been consolidated.* 所有债项均已合并。◇ *consolidated accounts* 合并账目 ◇ *The two companies consolidated for greater efficiency.* 为提高效率，这两家公司已合并。▶ **con·soli·da·tion** /kənˌsɒlɪˈdeɪʃn; *NAmE* -ˌsɑːl-/ *noun* [U]: *the consolidation of power* 权力的巩固 ◇ *the consolidation of Japan's banking industry* 日本银行业的合并

con·sommé /kənˈsɒmeɪ; *NAmE* ˌkɑːnsəˈmeɪ/ *noun* [U] a clear soup made with the juices from meat 清炖肉汤

con·son·ance /ˈkɒnsənəns; *NAmE* ˈkɑːn-/ *noun* **1** [U] ~ (**with sth**) (*formal*) agreement 一致；协调：*a policy that is popular because of its consonance with traditional party doctrine* 因与传统的政党宗旨一致而受欢迎的政策 **2** [U, C] (*music* 音) a combination of musical notes that sound pleasing together 协和音程 OPP **dissonance**

con·son·ant /ˈkɒnsənənt; *NAmE* ˈkɑːn-/ *noun, adj.*
■ *noun* **1** (*phonetics* 语音) a speech sound made by completely or partly stopping the flow of air being breathed out through the mouth 辅音 **2** a letter of the alphabet that represents a consonant sound, for example 'b', 'c', 'd', 'f', etc. 辅音字母（如 b、c、d、f 等）➲ COMPARE VOWEL ➲ WORDFINDER NOTE AT PRONUNCIATION
■ *adj.* ~ **with sth** (*formal*) agreeing with or being the same as sth else（与…）一致的，符合的，相同的，和谐的

con·son·ant·al /ˌkɒnsəˈnæntl; *NAmE* ˌkɑːn-/ *adj.* (*phonetics* 语音) relating to or consisting of a consonant or consonants 辅音的；辅音组成的 ➲ COMPARE VOCALIC

con·sort *noun, verb*
■ *noun* /ˈkɒnsɔːt; *NAmE* ˈkɑːnsɔːrt/ **1** the husband or wife of a ruler（统治者的）配偶：*the Prince Consort* (= the queen's husband) 女王的丈夫 **2** a group of old-fashioned musical instruments, or a group of musicians who play music from several centuries ago 一组（古乐器）；（演奏几世纪前音乐的）一组乐师
■ *verb* /kənˈsɔːt; *NAmE* kənˈsɔːrt/ [I] ~ **with sb** (*formal*) to spend time with sb that other people do not approve of 厮混；鬼混：*He is known to have consorted with prostitutes.* 众所周知他曾与妓女厮混在一起。

con·sor·tium /kənˈsɔːtiəm; *NAmE* -ˈsɔːrt-/ *noun* (*pl.* **con·sor·tiums** or **con·sor·tia** /-tiə; *BrE also* -ˈsɔːʃə; *NAmE also* -ˈsɔːrʃə/) a group of people, countries, companies, etc. who are working together on a particular project（合作进行某项工程的）财团，银团，联营企业：*the Anglo-French consortium that built the Channel Tunnel* 修建英吉利海峡隧道的英法财团

con·spicu·ous /kənˈspɪkjuəs/ *adj.* easy to see or notice; likely to attract attention 易见的；明显的；惹人注意的：*Mary's red hair always made her conspicuous at school.* 玛丽的红头发在学校里总是很惹眼。◇ *I felt very conspicuous in my new car.* 坐在我的新车里，我感到十分惹人注目。◇ *The advertisements were all posted in a conspicuous place.* 广告都贴在了显眼的地方。◇ *The event was a conspicuous success* (= a very great one). 这项活动至为成功。OPP **inconspicuous** ▶ **con·spicu·ous·ly** *adv.*：*Women were conspicuously absent from* (= there were surprisingly few women on) *the planning committee.* 引人注意的是，规划委员会里没有一位女性委员。**con·spicu·ous·ness** *noun* [U]
IDM **conˌspicuous by your ˈabsence** not present in a situation or place, when it is obvious that you should be there（本应在场）因缺席而招人注意：*When it came to cleaning up afterwards, Anne was conspicuous by her absence.* 后来到打扫时，本应在场的安妮却因为不在而引起了注意。

conˌspicuous conˈsumption *noun* [U] the buying of expensive goods in order to impress people and show them how rich you are 夸耀性消费；炫耀性购买

con·spir·acy /kənˈspɪrəsi/ *noun* [C, U] (*pl.* **-ies**) a secret plan by a group of people to do sth harmful or illegal 密谋策划；阴谋：~ (**to do sth**) *a conspiracy to overthrow the government* 颠覆政府的阴谋 ◇ ~ (**against sb/sth**) *conspiracies against the president* 反对总统的阴谋诡计 ◇ ~ (**to sth**) *They were charged with conspiracy to murder.* 他们被指控秘密策划谋杀。◇ *a* ***conspiracy of silence*** (= an agreement not to talk publicly about sth which should be made public) 保持缄默的密约（对该公开的事情不公开谈论的约定）◇ *a* ***conspiracy theory*** (= the belief that a secret conspiracy is responsible for a particular event) 阴谋论（认为某事件背后有阴谋）

con·spir·ator /kənˈspɪrətə(r)/ *noun* a person who is involved in a conspiracy 共谋者；搞阴谋的人

con·spira·tor·ial /kənˌspɪrəˈtɔːriəl/ *adj.* **1** connected with, or like, a conspiracy 阴谋的；密谋的；似阴谋的 **2** (of a person's behaviour 个人的举止) suggesting that a secret is being shared 会意的；心照不宣的：*'I know you understand,' he said and gave a conspiratorial wink.* "我知道你明白。"他说道，会意地眨一眨眼。▶ **con·spira·tori·al·ly** *adv.*

con·spire /kənˈspaɪə(r)/ *verb* (*formal*) **1** [I] to secretly plan with other people to do sth illegal or harmful 密谋；图谋；阴谋：~ (**with sb**) (**against sb**) *They were accused of conspiring against the king.* 他们被指控密谋反对国王。◇ ~ (**together**) (**to do sth**) *They deny conspiring together to smuggle drugs.* 他们否认共谋走私毒品。◇ ~ (**with sb**) (**to do sth**) *She admitted conspiring with her lover to murder her husband.* 她承认与情夫密谋杀害亲夫。**2** [I] (of events 事件) to seem to work together to make sth bad happen 似乎共同导致（不良后果）：~ **against sb/sth** *Circumstances had conspired against them.* 各种情况都凑在一起和他们作对。◇ ~ **to do sth** *Everything conspired to make her life a misery.* 她事事不顺，生活悲惨。

con·stable /ˈkʌnstəbl; *NAmE* ˈkɑːn-/ *noun* **1** (*BrE*) (used especially when talking to a police officer of the lowest rank 尤与最低级别的警察谈话时用) = POLICE CONSTABLE：*Have you finished your report, Constable?* 警察，你的报告完成了吗？➲ SEE ALSO CHIEF CONSTABLE **2** (in the US 美国) a peace officer with some of the powers of a police officer, typically in a small town（通常指小城镇的）警员，治安官

con·stabu·lary /kənˈstæbjələri; *NAmE* -leri/ *noun* [C +sing./pl. v.] (*pl.* **-ies**) (in Britain) the police force of a particular area or town（英国某地区或城镇的）警察部队

con·stancy AW /ˈkɒnstənsi; *NAmE* ˈkɑːn-/ *noun* [U] (*formal*) **1** the quality of staying the same and not changing 稳定性；持久不变；始终如一 **2** (*approving*) the quality of being faithful 忠诚；忠实；忠贞 SYN **fidelity**：*He admired her courage and constancy.* 他钦佩她的勇气和忠贞。

con·stant 🔑 AW /ˈkɒnstənt; *NAmE* ˈkɑːn-/ *adj., noun*
■ *adj.* **1** 🔑 [usually before noun] happening all the time or repeatedly 连续发生的；不断的；重复的：*constant interruptions* 无休止的干扰 ◇ *a constant stream of visitors all day* 整天络绎不绝的游客 ◇ *Babies need constant attention.* 婴儿一刻也离不开人。◇ *This entrance is in constant use.* 此入口经常使用。**2** 🔑 that does not change 不变的；固定的；恒定的 SYN **fixed**：*travelling at a constant speed of 50 m.p.h.* 以每小时 50 英里的速度匀速行驶
■ *noun* (*specialist*) a number or quantity that does not vary 常数；常量 OPP **variable**

con·stant·ly 🔑 AW /ˈkɒnstəntli; *NAmE* ˈkɑːn-/ *adv.* all the time; repeatedly 始终；一直；重复不断地：*Fashion is constantly changing.* 时尚总是日新月异。◇ *Heat the sauce, stirring constantly.* 加热调味汁并不停地搅动。

con·sta·tive /ˈkɒnstətɪv; kənˈsteɪtɪv; *NAmE* ˈkɑːn-/ *adj.* (*grammar* 语法) stating that sth is real or true 描述的，述愿的（陈述真实的事物）➲ SEE ALSO PERFORMATIVE

con·stel·la·tion /ˌkɒnstəˈleɪʃn; *NAmE* ˌkɑːn-/ *noun* **1** a group of stars that forms a shape in the sky and has a name 星座 ➲ WORDFINDER NOTE AT UNIVERSE **2** (*formal*) a group of related ideas, things or people 一系列（相关的想法、事物）；一群（相关的人）：*a constellation of Hollywood talent* 一群好莱坞天才

con·ster·na·tion /ˌkɒnstəˈneɪʃn; *NAmE* ˌkɑːnstərˈn-/ *noun* [U] (*formal*) a worried, sad feeling after you have received an unpleasant surprise 惊愕；惊恐 **SYN dismay**: *The announcement of her retirement caused consternation among tennis fans.* 她宣布挂拍告退的消息引起了网球迷的震惊。

con·sti·pated /ˈkɒnstɪpeɪtɪd; *NAmE* ˈkɑːn-/ *adj.* unable to get rid of waste material from the BOWELS easily 便秘的

con·sti·pa·tion /ˌkɒnstɪˈpeɪʃn; *NAmE* ˌkɑːn-/ *noun* [U] the condition of being unable to get rid of waste material from the BOWELS easily (= being constipated) 便秘

con·stitu·ency AW /kənˈstɪtjuənsi; *NAmE* -tʃu-/ (*pl.* **-ies**) *noun* **1** (*especially BrE*) [C] a district that elects its own representative to parliament （选举议会议员的）选区：*Unemployment is high in her constituency.* 她的选区的失业人数居高不下。◊ *He owns a house in his Darlington constituency.* 他在自己的选区达灵顿拥有一座房子。➲ WORDFINDER NOTE AT DEMOCRACY **2** [C+sing./pl. v.] the people who live in and vote in a particular district 选区的选民：*constituency opinion* 选区选民的意见 **3** [C+sing./pl. v.] a particular group of people in society who are likely to support a person, an idea or a product （统称）支持者

con·stitu·ent AW /kənˈstɪtjuənt; *NAmE* -tʃu-/ *noun, adj.*

■ ***noun*** **1** a person who lives, and can vote in a constituency （选区的）选民，选举人：*She has the full support of her constituents.* 她得到本区选民的全力支持。 **2** one of the parts of sth that combine to form the whole 成分；构成要素

■ ***adj.*** [only before noun] (*formal*) forming or helping to make a whole 组成的；构成的：*to break something up into its* ***constituent parts/elements*** 把某物分离为各个组成部分 / 要素

conˌstituent asˈsembly *noun* [C+sing./pl. v.] a group of elected representatives with the power to make or change a country's CONSTITUTION 立宪会议（有权制定或修改国家宪法）

con·sti·tute AW /ˈkɒnstɪtjuːt; *NAmE* ˈkɑːnstətuːt/ *verb* (*formal*) **1** *linking verb* **+ noun** (not used in the progressive tenses 不用于进行时) to be considered to be sth （被认为或看作）是；被算作：*Does such an activity constitute a criminal offence?* 难道这样的活动也算刑事犯罪吗？◊ *The increase in racial tension constitutes a threat to our society.* 种族间紧张状态的升级是对我们社会的一种威胁。 **2** *linking verb* **+ noun** (not used in the progressive tenses 不用于进行时) to be the parts that together form sth 组成；构成 **SYN make up**: *Female workers constitute the majority of the labour force.* 女性雇员占劳动力的多数。➲ SYNONYMS AT CONSIST **3** [T, usually passive] **~ sth** to form a group legally or officially （合法或正式地）成立，设立 **SYN establish, set up**: *The committee was constituted in 1974 by an Act of Parliament.* 该委员会是根据议会法于 1974 年设立的。

con·sti·tu·tion AW /ˌkɒnstɪˈtjuːʃn; *NAmE* ˌkɑːnstəˈtuːʃn/ *noun* **1** [C] the system of laws and basic principles that a state, a country or an organization is governed by 宪法；章程：*your right to vote under the constitution* 根据宪法所拥有的选举权 ◊ *According to the constitution...* 依照宪法…… ◊ *to propose a new amendment to the Constitution* 提出一项新的宪法修正案 ◊ *the South African Constitution* 南非宪法 ➲ WORDFINDER NOTE AT GOVERNMENT **2** [C] the condition of a person's body and how healthy it is 身体素质；体质；体格：*to have a* ***healthy/strong/weak constitution*** 体质健康 / 强壮 / 虚弱 **3** [U, C] (*formal*) the way sth is formed or organized 构成；构造 **SYN structure**: *the genetic constitution of cells* 细胞的基因构造 **4** [U] (*formal*) the act of forming sth 组成；形成 **SYN establishment**: *He recommended the constitution of a review committee.* 他建议设立审查委员会。

con·sti·tu·tion·al AW /ˌkɒnstɪˈtjuːʃənl; *NAmE* ˌkɑːnstəˈtuː-/ *adj., noun*

■ ***adj.*** **1** [only before noun] connected with the constitution of a country or an organization 宪法的；章程的：***constitutional government/reform*** 立宪政体；宪法的修改 ◊ *a constitutional amendment* 宪法修正案 **2** allowed or limited by the constitution of a country or an organization 宪法准许的；受宪法限制的；受章程限制的：*They can't pass this law. It's not constitutional.* 他们无法通过这项法律，它不符合宪法。◊ ***constitutional rights*** 宪法规定的权利 ◊ *a* ***constitutional monarchy*** (= a country with a king or queen whose power is controlled by a set of laws and basic principles) 君主立宪国家 **OPP unconstitutional** **3** [usually before noun] related to the body's ability to stay healthy, be strong and fight illness 身体素质的；体质的；体格的：*constitutional remedies* 体质顺势疗法 ▸ **con·sti·tu·tion·al·ly** AW /-ʃənəli/ *adv.*: *constitutionally guaranteed rights* 受到宪法保障的权利 ◊ *He was much weakened constitutionally by the disease.* 那场病使得他体质大大减弱。

■ ***noun*** (*old-fashioned* or *humorous*) a short walk that people take because it is good for their health 保健散步

Consˌtitutional ˈCourt *noun* [sing.] in South Africa, the highest court dealing with cases related to the constitution 宪法法院（南非处理与宪法相关案件的最高法院）

con·sti·tu·tion·al·ism /ˌkɒnstɪˈtjuːʃənəlɪzəm; *NAmE* ˌkɑːnstəˈtuː-/ *noun* [U] a belief in constitutional government 立宪主义

con·sti·tu·tion·al·ity /ˌkɒnstɪˌtjuːʃəˈnæləti; *NAmE* ˌkɑːnstəˌtuː-/ *noun* [U] (*specialist*) the fact that sth is acceptable according to a CONSTITUTION 符合宪法：*They questioned the constitutionality of the law.* 他们质疑这项法律是否符合宪法。

con·sti·tu·tive AW /kənˈstɪtjutɪv; ˈkɒnstɪt-; *NAmE* ˈkɑːnstɪtuːtɪv/ *adj.* (*formal*) **~ (of sth)** forming a part, often an essential part, of sth 组成部分的；本质的；基本的：*Memory is constitutive of identity.* 记忆是身份的一个重要构成部分。

con·strain AW /kənˈstreɪn/ *verb* (*formal*) **1** [usually passive] **~ sb to do sth** to force sb to do sth or behave in a particular way 强迫；强制；迫使：*The evidence was so compelling that he* ***felt constrained to*** *accept it.* 证据是那样的令人折服，他觉得不得不接受。 **2** [often passive] to restrict or limit sb/sth 限制；限定；约束：**~ sth** *Research has been constrained by a lack of funds.* 研究工作因经费不足而受限制。◊ **~ sb (from doing sth)** *She felt constrained from continuing by the threat of losing her job.* 由于受到失去工作的威胁，她感到很难再坚持下去。➲ SEE ALSO UNCONSTRAINED

con·strained /kənˈstreɪnd/ *adj.* (*formal*) not natural; forced or too controlled 不自然的；强迫的；过于受约束的：*constrained emotions* 受压抑的情感

con·straint AW /kənˈstreɪnt/ *noun* **1** [C] a thing that limits or restricts sth, or your freedom to do sth 限制；限定；约束 **SYN restriction**: ***constraints of time/money/space*** 时间 / 资金 / 空间的限制 ◊ ***financial/economic/legal/political constraints*** 财政 / 经济 / 法律 / 政治约束 ◊ **~ on sth** *This decision will impose serious constraints on all schools.* 这项决定将使所有的学校受到各种严格的限制。➲ SYNONYMS AT LIMIT **2** [U] strict control over the way that you behave or are allowed to behave 约束；严管：*At last we could relax and talk without constraint.* 我们终于可以放松下来，无拘无束地谈话了。

con·strict /kənˈstrɪkt/ *verb* **1** [I, T] to become tighter or narrower; to make sth tighter or narrower （使）紧缩，缩窄：*Her* ***throat constricted*** *and she swallowed hard.* 她喉咙发紧，使劲地咽了一下唾沫。◊ **~ sth** *a drug that constricts the blood vessels* 收缩血管的药 **2 ~ sb** to limit or restrict what sb is able to do 限制；限定；抑制；约束：*Film-makers of the time were constricted by the censors.* 那时的电影制作人受到了审查官的限制。◊ *constricting rules and regulations* 具有约束性的规章制度 ▸ **con·strict·ed** *adj.*: *Her throat felt dry and constricted.* 她感到喉咙发干发紧。◊ *a constricted vision of the world* 受到局限的对世界的认识 **con·stric·tion** /kənˈstrɪkʃn/ *noun* [U, C]: *a feeling of constriction in the chest* 胸部的压迫感 ◊ *political constrictions* 政治上的约束

C

con·struct 🔑 AW *verb, noun*

■ *verb* /kən'strʌkt/ **1** 🔑 [often passive] to build or make sth such as a road, building or machine 建筑；修建；建造：**~ sth** *When was the bridge constructed?* 那座桥是何时修建的？ ◇ **~ sth from/out of/of sth** *They constructed a shelter out of fallen branches.* 他们用落下的枯树枝搭了个窝棚。 ➲ SYNONYMS AT BUILD **2** 🔑 **~ sth** to form sth by putting different things together 组成；创建 SYN **put together**: *You must learn how to construct a logical argument.* 你必须学会怎样确立合乎逻辑的论点。 ◇ *to construct a theory* 创立一种理论 ◇ *a well-constructed novel* 构思巧妙的小说 **3** **~ sth** (*geometry* 几何) to draw a line or shape according to the rules of mathematics （按照数学规则）编制，绘制：*to construct a triangle* 画一个三角形

■ *noun* /'kɒnstrʌkt; *NAmE* 'kɑːn-/ (*formal*) **1** an idea or a belief that is based on various pieces of evidence which are not always true （根据不总是真实的各种证据得出的）构想，观念，概念：*a contrast between lived reality and the construct held in the mind* 现实生活与头脑所持概念之间的明显差别 **2** (*linguistics* 语言) a group of words that form a phrase （短语的）结构成分，结构体 **3** a thing that is built or made 建造物；构筑物；制成物

con·struc·tion 🔑 AW /kən'strʌkʃn/ *noun*

• **OF ROADS/BUILDINGS** 道路；建筑物 **1** 🔑 [U] the process or method of building or making sth, especially roads, buildings, bridges, etc. 建筑；建造；施工：*the construction industry* 建筑业 ◇ *road construction* 道路的施工 ◇ *Work has begun on the construction of the new airport.* 新机场的修建已经开工。 ◇ *Our new offices are still* ***under construction*** (= being built). 我们的新办公楼尚在修建中。 ◇ *the construction of a new database* 新数据库的建立

WORDFINDER 联想词：cement, foundation, girder, joist, masonry, plaster, rubble, scaffolding, site

2 🔑 [U] the way that sth has been built or made 建造（或构造）的方式：*strong in construction* 结构坚固 ◇ *ships of steel construction* 钢结构船 ➲ SYNONYMS AT STRUCTURE

• **BUILDING/STRUCTURE** 建筑；结构 **3** [C] (*formal*) a thing that has been built or made 建造物；构筑物；制成物：*The summer house was a simple wooden construction.* 那座避暑别墅是简单的木结构建筑。

• **GRAMMAR** 语法 **4** [C] the way in which words are used together and arranged to form a sentence, phrase, etc. （句子、短语等的）结构：*grammatical constructions* 语法结构

• **OF THEORY, ETC.** 理论等 **5** [U, C] the creating of sth from ideas, opinions and knowledge （理念、观点和知识的）创造，创立，建立：*the construction of a new theory* 新理论的创立

• **MEANING** 含义 **6** [C] (*formal*) the way in which words, actions, statements, etc. are understood by sb（对词语、行为、陈述等的）解释，说明，理解 SYN **interpretation**: *What construction do you put on this letter* (= what do you think it means)? 你对这封信如何理解？

con·struc·tion·al /kən'strʌkʃənl/ *adj.* connected with the making or building of things 建造的；构造的；建筑的

con'struction paper *noun* [U] (*NAmE*) thick coloured paper that people cut out to make designs, models, etc. （做设计、模型等的）彩色美术纸

con'struction site *noun* (*especially NAmE*) = BUILDING SITE

con·struct·ive AW /kən'strʌktɪv/ *adj.* having a useful and helpful effect rather than being negative or with no purpose 建设性的；有助益的；积极的：***constructive criticism/suggestions/advice*** 建设性的批评 / 提议 / 忠告 ◇ *His work involved helping hyperactive children to use their energy in a constructive way.* 他的工作包括帮助患有多动症的儿童建设性地利用他们的精力。 ◇ *The government is encouraging all parties to play a constructive role in the reform process.* 政府鼓励所有的政党在改革过程中发挥建设性的作用。 ➲ COMPARE DESTRUCTIVE ▸ **con·struct·ive·ly** *adv.*

con,structive dis'missal *noun* [U] (*BrE, law* 律) a situation in which you are forced to leave your job because it is changed in a way that makes it impossible for you to continue doing it 推定解雇，变工解雇（指通过改变工作条件而迫使雇员自动离职）

con·struct·or /kən'strʌktə(r)/ *noun* a person or company that builds things, especially cars or aircraft （尤指汽车或飞机的）建造者，制造者，建造商

con·strue /kən'struː/ *verb* [usually passive] (*formal*) to understand the meaning of a word, a sentence or an action in a particular way 理解；领会 SYN **interpret**: **~ sth** *He considered how the remark was to be construed.* 他考虑这话该如何理解。 ◇ **~ sth as sth** *Her words could hardly be construed as an apology.* 她的话怎么想都不像是道歉。

con·sul /'kɒnsl; *NAmE* 'kɑːnsl/ *noun* a government official who is the representative of his or her country in a foreign city 领事：*the British consul in Miami* 英国驻迈阿密领事 ➲ COMPARE AMBASSADOR ▸ **con·su·lar** /'kɒnsjələ(r); *NAmE* 'kɑːnsəl-/ *adj.*：*consular officials* 领事

con·sul·ate /'kɒnsjələt; *NAmE* 'kɑːnsəl-/ *noun* the building where a consul works 领事馆 ➲ COMPARE EMBASSY (2)

con·sult 🔑 AW /kən'sʌlt/ *verb* **1** 🔑 [T, I] to go to sb for information or advice 咨询；请教：**~ sb** *If the pain continues, consult your doctor.* 如果疼痛持续不消退，要请医生诊治。 ◇ **~ sb about sth** *Have you consulted your lawyer about this?* 你就此事咨询过你的律师吗？ ◇ *a consulting engineer* (= one who has expert knowledge and gives advice) 顾问工程师 ◇ (*NAmE*) **~ with sb** (**about/on sth**) *Consult with your physician about possible treatments.* 向你的医生咨询可行的治疗方案。 **2** 🔑 [T, I] to discuss sth with sb to get their permission for sth, or to help you make a decision （与某人）商议，商量（以得到许可或帮助决策）：**~ sb** *You shouldn't have done it without consulting me.* 你不该不和我商量就做了这件事。 ◇ **~ sb about/on sth** *I expect to be consulted about major issues.* 我认为重大问题必须找我商量。 ◇ **~ with sb** (**about/on sth**) *I need to consult with my colleagues on the proposals.* 我需要和我的同事商讨这些建议。 ➲ SYNONYMS AT TALK **3** 🔑 [T] **~ sth** to look in or at sth to get information 查阅；查询；参看 SYN **refer to**: *He consulted the manual.* 他查阅了使用说明书。

con·sult·ancy AW /kən'sʌltənsi/ *noun* (*pl.* **-ies**) **1** [C] a company that gives expert advice on a particular subject to other companies or organizations 咨询公司：*a* ***management/design/computer, etc. consultancy*** 管理 / 设计 / 计算机等咨询公司 **2** [U] expert advice that a company or person is paid to provide on a particular subject 专家咨询：*consultancy fees* 咨询费

con·sult·ant AW /kən'sʌltənt/ *noun* **1** a person who knows a lot about a particular subject and is employed to give advice about it to other people 顾问：*a firm of management consultants* 管理咨询公司 ◇ **~ on sth** *the President's consultant on economic affairs* 总统的经济事务顾问 ➲ WORDFINDER NOTE AT BUSINESSMAN **2** (*BrE*) a hospital doctor of the highest rank who is a specialist in a particular area of medicine 高级顾问医师；会诊医师：*a consultant in obstetrics* 产科顾问医师 ◇ *a consultant surgeon* 外科顾问医师 ➲ COMPARE REGISTRAR (3) ➲ WORDFINDER NOTE AT HOSPITAL

con·sult·ation AW /,kɒnsl'teɪʃn; *NAmE* ,kɑːn-/ *noun* **1** [U] the act of discussing sth with sb or with a group of people before making a decision about it 咨询；商讨；磋商：*a* ***consultation document/paper/period/process*** 咨询文件 / 论文 / 期 / 过程 ◇ *acting* ***in consultation with*** *all the departments involved* 和所有有关部门磋商后行事 ◇ *The decision was taken after close consultation with local residents.* 这项决定是在与当地居民仔细磋商后作出的。 ➲ SYNONYMS AT DISCUSSION **2** [C] a formal meeting to discuss sth 商讨会；协商会：*extensive consultations between the two countries* 两国之间的广泛磋商 ➲ SYNONYMS AT DISCUSSION **3** [C] a meeting with an expert, especially a doctor, to get advice or treatment （向专家请教的）咨询会；（尤指）就诊 ➲ SYNONYMS AT INTERVIEW **4** [U] the act of looking for information in a book, etc. 查找；查

阅；查看：*There is a large collection of texts available for consultation on-screen.* 有大量的文本可通过电脑查阅。

con·sulta·tive AW /kənˈsʌltətɪv/ *adj.* giving advice or making suggestions 咨询的；顾问的 SYN **advisory**：*a* ***consultative committee/body/document*** 咨询委员会／机构／文件

conˈsulting room *noun* a room where a doctor talks to and examines patients 诊疗室

con·sum·able /kənˈsjuːməbl; *NAmE* -ˈsuːm-/ *adj., noun* (*business* 商)

■ ***adj.*** intended to be bought, used and then replaced 可消耗的；会用尽的：*consumable electronic goods* 电子消费品

■ ***noun*** **con·sum·ables** [pl.] goods that are intended to be used fairly quickly and then replaced 消耗品：*computer consumables such as CD-Rs and printer cartridges* 可录光盘、打印机墨盒之类的电脑耗材

con·sume AW /kənˈsjuːm; *NAmE* -ˈsuːm/ *verb* (*formal*) **1 ~ sth** to use sth, especially fuel, energy or time 消耗，耗费（尤指燃料、能量或时间）：*The electricity industry consumes large amounts of fossil fuels.* 电力工业消耗大量的化石燃料。 **2 ~ sth** to eat or drink sth 吃；喝；饮：*Before he died he had consumed a large quantity of alcohol.* 他死亡前喝了大量的酒。**3 ~ sb (with sth)** [usually passive] to fill sb with a strong feeling 使充满（强烈的感情）：*Carolyn was consumed with guilt.* 卡罗琳深感内疚。◇ *Rage consumed him.* 他无比愤怒。 **4 ~ sth** (of fire 火) to completely destroy sth 烧毁；毁灭：*The hotel was quickly consumed by fire.* 那座旅馆很快被大火吞噬。 ➲ SEE ALSO ALL-CONSUMING, CONSUMING, CONSUMPTION, TIME-CONSUMING

con·sumer 🔑 AW /kənˈsjuːmə(r); *NAmE* -ˈsuː-/ *noun* a person who buys goods or uses services 消费者；顾客；用户：***consumer demand/choice/rights*** 消费者的需求／选择／权利 ◇ *Health-conscious consumers want more information about the food they buy.* 注重身体健康的消费者想得到更多有关他们所购买的食物的信息。 ◇ *a* ***consumer society*** (= one where buying and selling is considered to be very important) 消费社会 ◇ *Tax cuts will boost* ***consumer confidence*** *after the recession.* 减税将增强消费者在经济衰退后的信心。 ➲ COMPARE PRODUCER (1)

conˌsumer ˈdurables (*BrE*) (*NAmE* **ˈdurable goods**) *noun* [pl.] (*business* 商) goods which are expected to last for a long time after they have been bought, such as cars, televisions, etc. 耐用消费品（如汽车、电视机等）

conˈsumer goods *noun* [pl.] goods such as food, clothing, etc. bought by individual customers 消费品 ➲ COMPARE CAPITAL GOODS

con·sumer·ism /kənˈsjuːmərɪzəm; *NAmE* -ˈsuː-/ *noun* [U] (*sometimes disapproving*) the buying and using of goods and services; the belief that it is good for a society or an individual person to buy and use a large quantity of goods and services 消费；消费主义（认为高消费对社会和个人有利） ▸ **con·sumer·ist** *adj.*：*consumerist values* 消费主义的价值观

conˌsumer ˈprice index (*BrE also* **conˌsumer ˈprices index**) *noun* [sing.] (*abbr.* **CPI**) a list of the prices of some ordinary goods and services which shows how much these prices change each month 居民消费价格指数；消费价格指数 ➲ SEE ALSO RETAIL PRICE INDEX

con·sum·ing /kənˈsjuːmɪŋ; *NAmE* -ˈsuː-/ *adj.* [only before noun] (of a feeling, an interest, etc. 感情、兴趣等) so strong or important that it takes up all your time and energy 强烈的；重要的；令人着迷的：*Basketball is his* ***consuming passion.*** 篮球令他着迷。 ➲ SEE ALSO ALL-CONSUMING, TIME-CONSUMING

con·sum·mate¹ /kənˈsʌmət; ˈkɒnsəmət; *NAmE* ˈkɑːn-/ *adj.* [usually before noun] (*formal*) extremely skilled; perfect 技艺高超的；完美的：*She was a consummate performer.* 她是个技艺非凡的表演者。◇ *He played the shot with consummate skill.* 他以高超的技巧投球进篮。◇ (*disapproving*) *a consummate liar* 撒谎高手 ▸ **con·sum·mate·ly** *adv.*

con·sum·mate² /ˈkɒnsəmeɪt; *NAmE* ˈkɑːn-/ *verb* (*formal*) **1 ~ sth** to make a marriage or a relationship complete by having sex（初次）行房；通过性交使（婚姻或两人的关系）圆满：*The marriage lasted only a week and was never consummated.* 那段婚姻仅维持了一星期，期间从未行房。 **2 ~ sth** to make sth complete or perfect 使完整；使完美

con·sum·ma·tion /ˌkɒnsəˈmeɪʃn; *NAmE* ˌkɑːn-/ *noun* [C, U] **1** the act of making a marriage or relationship complete by having sex （初次）行房；通过性交使婚姻或两人关系圆满 **2** the fact of making sth complete or perfect 完成；使完美：*The paintings are the consummation of his life's work.* 这些画是他毕生努力的完美结晶。

con·sump·tion AW /kənˈsʌmpʃn/ *noun* [U] **1** the act of using energy, food or materials; the amount used （能量、食物或材料的）消耗，消耗量：*the production of fuel for* ***domestic consumption*** (= to be used in the country where it is produced) 供国内消耗的燃料生产 ◇ *Gas and oil consumption always increases in cold weather.* 燃气和燃油的消耗量在天冷时总会增加。 ◇ *The meat was declared unfit for* ***human consumption.*** 这种肉被宣布不适于人食用。◇ *He was advised to reduce his alcohol consumption.* 他被劝告减少饮酒。 ◇ *Her speech to party members was not intended for* ***public consumption*** (= to be heard by the public). 她对党员发表的讲话并不打算公诸大众。 ➲ SEE ALSO CONSUME **2** the act of buying and using products 消费：*Consumption rather than saving has become the central feature of contemporary societies.* 现代社会的主要特征是消费而不是储蓄。 ➲ SEE ALSO CONSPICUOUS CONSUMPTION, CONSUME **3** (*old-fashioned*) a serious infectious disease of the lungs 肺病；肺痨；肺结核 SYN **tuberculosis**

con·sump·tive /kənˈsʌmptɪv/ *noun* (*old-fashioned*) a person who suffers from consumption (= a disease of the lungs) 肺痨（或肺结核）患者 ▸ **con·sump·tive** *adj.*

cont. (*also* **contd**) *abbr.* continued 继续的；连续的：*cont. on p74* 下接第 74 页

con·tact 🔑 AW /ˈkɒntækt; *NAmE* ˈkɑːn-/ *noun, verb*

■ ***noun***

• **ACT OF COMMUNICATING** 联系 **1** 🔑 [U] **~ (with sb) | ~ (between A and B)** the act of communicating with sb, especially regularly （尤指经常的）联系，联络：*I don't have much contact with my uncle.* 我和叔父甚少联系。◇ *There is little contact between the two organizations.* 这两个机构相互之间没有什么联系。◇ *Have you kept* ***in contact with*** *any of your friends from college* (= do you still see them or speak or write to them)? 你和你大学里的朋友还保持联系吗？ ◇ *She's* ***lost contact with*** (= no longer sees or writes to) *her son.* 她和儿子失去了联系。 ◇ *I finally* ***made contact with*** (= succeeded in speaking to or meeting) *her in Paris.* 我最终在巴黎与她取得了联系。 ◇ *The organization* ***put me in contact with*** *other people in a similar position* (= gave me their addresses or telephone numbers). 这家机构为我提供了其他和我情况相似的人的联系方法。 ◇ *two people avoiding* ***eye contact*** (= avoiding looking directly at each other) 避免目光相遇的两个人 ◇ *Here's my* ***contact number*** (= temporary telephone number) *while I'm away.* 这是我外出时的联系电话。 ◇ *I'll give you my* ***contact details*** (= telephone number, email address, etc.). 我会给你我的具体联系方式。

• **TOUCHING SB/STH** 接触 **2** 🔑 [U] the state of touching sth 触摸；接触：*His fingers were briefly* ***in contact with*** *the ball.* 他的手指稍稍地碰了一下球。 ◇ *This substance should not* ***come into contact with*** *food.* 这种物质切莫与食物接触。 ◇ *a fear of physical contact* 对身体接触的恐惧感 ◇ *This pesticide kills insects* ***on contact*** (= as soon as it touches them). 这种杀虫剂昆虫一触即死。

• **MEETING SB/STH** 遇到某人／事物 **3** 🔑 [U] the state of meeting sb or having to deal with sth 遇见（某人）；碰上（要处理的事）：*In her job she often* ***comes into contact with*** (= meets) *lawyers.* 她在工作中常与律师接触。 ◇ *Children should be* ***brought into contact with*** *poetry at an* early age. 儿童应该在幼年就接触诗歌。

• RELATIONSHIP 关系 4 [C, usually pl.] an occasion on which you meet or communicate with sb; a relationship with sb 会见；交往；人际关系： *We have good contacts with the local community.* 我们与当地社区关系甚好。 ◇ *The company has maintained trade contacts with India.* 这家公司和印度一直保持着贸易往来。

• PERSON 人 5 [C] a person that you know, especially sb who can be helpful to you in your work 熟人；（尤指）社会关系： ***social/personal contacts*** 社会上的 / 私下的熟人 ◇ *I've made some useful contacts in journalism.* 我在新闻界结交了一些有用的人。

• ELECTRICAL 电 6 [C] an electrical connection （电流的）接触，接通；接触器： *The switches close the contacts and complete the circuit.* 这些开关可接通形成闭合电路。

• FOR EYES 眼睛 7 **contacts** [pl.] (*informal*) = CONTACT LENS

• MEDICAL 医学 8 [C] a person who may be infectious because he or she has recently been near to sb with a CONTAGIOUS disease（与传染病患者的）接触者 IDM SEE POINT *n.*

■ ***verb*** ~ **sb** to communicate with sb, for example by telephone or letter 联系，联络（如用电话或信件）： *I've been trying to contact you all day.* 我一整天都在设法与你联系。

▶ **con·tact·able** AW *adj.*: *I'll be contactable on this number:...* 这个号码可以联系到我：…

'contact lens (*also informal* **con·tact, lens**) *noun* [usually pl.] a small round piece of thin plastic that you put on your eye to help you see better 隐形眼镜片： *to wear **contact lenses*** 戴隐形眼镜

con·tact·less /'kɒntæktləs; *NAmE* 'kɑːn-/ *adj.* relating to the technology that allows a SMART CARD (= a small plastic card used to store information electronically), mobile/cell phone, etc. to contact an electronic device that it is not connected to, usually in order to make a payment 无触点感应的；非接触式（技术）的： *contactless cards* 非接触式卡 ◇ *a contactless payment* 一笔非接触式支付款项

'contact sport *noun* a sport in which players have physical contact with each other 接触式运动（运动员之间有身体接触） OPP **non-contact sport**

con·ta·gion /kən'teɪdʒən/ *noun* **1** [U] the spreading of a disease by people touching each other 接触传染： *There is no risk of contagion.* 没有接触传染的风险。 **2** [C] (*old use*) a disease that can be spread by people touching each other 接触性传染病 **3** [C] (*formal*) something bad that spreads quickly by being passed from person to person（不良事物的快速）传播，蔓延，扩散 ➲ COMPARE INFECTION (1)

con·ta·gious /kən'teɪdʒəs/ *adj.* **1** a **contagious** disease spreads by people touching each other （疾病）接触传染的： *Scarlet fever is highly contagious.* 猩红热的接触传染性很强。 ◇ (*figurative*) *His enthusiasm was contagious* (= spread quickly to other people). 他的热情富有感染力。 ◇ *a contagious laugh* 有感染力的笑声 **2** [not usually before noun] if a person is **contagious**, they have a disease that can be spread to other people by touch 患接触性传染病 ➲ COMPARE INFECTIOUS ▶ **con·ta·gious·ly** *adv.*

con·tain /kən'teɪn/ *verb* (not used in the progressive tenses 不用于进行时) **1** ~ **sth** if sth **contains** sth else, it has that thing inside it or as part of it 包含；含有；容纳： *This drink doesn't contain any alcohol.* 这种饮料不含任何酒精。 ◇ *Her statement contained one or two inaccuracies.* 她的陈述有一两处不准确。 ◇ *a brown envelope containing dollar bills* 装有钞票的棕色信封 ◇ *The bottle contains* (= can hold) *two litres.* 此瓶容量为两升。 **2** to keep your feelings under control 控制，克制，抑制（感情） SYN **restrain**: ~ **sth** *She was unable to contain her excitement.* 她无法抑制内心的激动。 ◇ ~ **yourself** *I was so furious I just couldn't **contain myself*** (= I had to express my feelings). 我气愤极了，简直无法克制自己。 **3** ~ **sth** to prevent sth harmful from spreading or getting worse 防止…蔓延（或恶化）： *to contain an epidemic* 防止流行病的蔓延 ◇ *Government forces have failed to contain the rebellion.* 政府军未能遏止叛乱。

con·tain·er /kən'teɪnə(r)/ *noun* **1** a box, bottle, etc. in which sth can be stored or transported 容器： *Food will last longer if kept in an airtight container.* 如果贮藏在密封的容器里，食物能保存比较久的时间。 **2** a large metal or wooden box of a standard size in which goods are packed so that they can easily be lifted onto a ship, train, etc. to be transported 集装箱；货柜： *a container ship* (= one designed to transport such containers) 集装箱船 ➲ VISUAL VOCAB PAGE V59

con·tain·er·ized (*also* **-ised**) /kən'teɪnəraɪzd/ *adj.* packed and transported in CONTAINERS 封装运输的；集装箱装运的；货柜装运的： *containerized cargo* 集装箱载运的货物 ▶ **con·tain·er·iza·tion, -isa·tion** /kən,teɪnəraɪ'zeɪʃn; *NAmE* -rə'z-/ *noun* [U]

con·tain·ment /kən'teɪnmənt/ *noun* [U] (*formal*) **1** the act of keeping sth under control so that it cannot spread in a harmful way 控制；抑制： *the containment of the epidemic* 对流行病的控制 **2** the act of keeping another country's power within limits so that it does not become too powerful （对另一个国家力量的）遏制： *a policy of containment* 遏制政策

con·tam·in·ant /kən'tæmɪnənt/ *noun* (*specialist*) a substance that makes sth IMPURE 致污物；污染物： *Filters do not remove all contaminants from water.* 过滤器无法过滤掉水中的所有污染物。

con·tam·in·ate /kən'tæmɪneɪt/ *verb* **1** ~ **sth** (**with sth**) to make a substance or place dirty or no longer pure by adding a substance that is dangerous or carries disease 污染；弄脏 SYN **adulterate**: *The drinking water has become contaminated with lead.* 饮用水被铅污染了。 ◇ ***contaminated blood/food/soil*** 受到污染的血液 / 食物 / 土壤 **2** ~ **sth** (*formal*) to influence people's ideas or attitudes in a bad way 玷污，毒害，腐蚀（人的思想或品德）： *They were accused of contaminating the minds of our young people.* 他们被指控毒害我们青少年的心灵。 ➲ SEE ALSO UNCONTAMINATED ▶ **con·tam·in·ation** /kən,tæmɪ'neɪʃn/ *noun* [U]: *radioactive contamination* 放射性污染 ➲ SEE ALSO CROSS-CONTAMINATION

contd *abbr.* = CONT.

con·tem·plate /'kɒntəmpleɪt; *NAmE* 'kɑːn-/ *verb* **1** [T] to think about whether you should do sth, or how you should do sth 考虑；思量；思忖 SYN **consider, think about/of**: ~ **sth** *You're too young to be contemplating retirement.* 你考虑退休还太年轻。 ◇ ~ **doing sth** *I have never contemplated living abroad.* 我从未考虑过去国外居住。 ◇ ~ **how/what, etc....** *He continued while she contemplated how to answer.* 她还在考虑如何回答时，他就继续往下说了。 **2** [T] to think carefully about and accept the possibility of sth happening 考虑接受（发生某事的可能性）： ~ **sth** *The thought of war is too awful to contemplate.* 战争太可怕了，真不敢去想。 ◇ ~ **how/what, etc....** *I can't contemplate what it would be like to be alone.* 我不能想象独自一人会是个什么样子。 ◇ ~ **that...** *She contemplated that things might get even worse.* 她想到事情可能会变得更糟。 **3** [T, I] ~ (**sth**) (*formal*) to think deeply about sth for a long time 深思熟虑；沉思；苦思冥想： *to contemplate your future* 仔细盘算未来 ◇ *She lay in bed, contemplating.* 她躺在床上冥思苦想。 **4** [T] ~ **sb/sth** (*formal*) to look at sb/sth in a careful way for a long time 端详；审视 SYN **stare at**: *She contemplated him in silence.* 她默默地注视着他。

con·tem·pla·tion /,kɒntəm'pleɪʃn; *NAmE* ,kɑːn-/ *noun* [U] (*formal*) **1** the act of thinking deeply about sth 深思；沉思： *He sat there deep in contemplation.* 他坐在那里沉思着。 ◇ *a few moments of quiet contemplation* 默默沉思的片刻 ◇ *a life of prayer and contemplation* 祈祷与冥思的生活 **2** the act of looking at sth in a calm and careful way 凝视；默默注视： *She turned from her contemplation of the photograph.* 她从凝视着的那张照片上移开目光。

IDM **in contem'plation** (*formal*) being considered 考虑中： *By 1613 even more desperate measures were in* *contemplation.* 到 1613 年，甚至考虑要采取更为孤注一掷的措施。

con·tem·pla·tive /kən'templətɪv/ *adj.* (*formal*) **1** thinking quietly and seriously about sth 沉思默想的；深思熟虑的： *She was in contemplative mood.* 她陷入沉思之中。 **2** spending time thinking deeply about religious matters （对宗教问题）冥想的，敛心默祷的： *the contemplative life* (= life in a religious community) 宗教上的默观生活

con·tem·por·an·eous /kənˌtempə'reɪniəs/ *adj.* ~ (**with** sb/sth) (*formal*) happening or existing at the same time 同时发生（或存在）的；同时期的；同时代的 **SYN contemporary**: *How do we know that the signature is contemporaneous with the document?* 我们怎样才能知道这个签字和文件是同一个时间的呢？ ◇ ***contemporaneous events/accounts*** 同一时期的事情 / 记述 ▶ **con·tem·por·an·eous·ly** *adv.*

con·tem·por·ary 🔑 AW /kən'temprəri; *NAmE* -pəreri/ *adj.*, *noun*

■*adj.* **1** 🔑 ~ (**with** sb/sth) belonging to the same time 属同时期的；同一时代的： *We have no contemporary account of the battle* (= written near the time that it happened). 我们没有当时人们对这一战役的记载。 ◇ *He was contemporary with the dramatist Congreve.* 他与剧作家康格里夫属于同一时代。 **2** 🔑 belonging to the present time 当代的；现代的 **SYN modern**: *life in contemporary Britain* 当代英国的生活 ◇ ***contemporary fiction/music/dance*** 当代小说 / 音乐 / 舞蹈

■*noun* (*pl.* **-ies**) a person who lives or lived at the same time as sb else, especially sb who is about the same age 同代人；同辈人；同龄人： *She and I were contemporaries at college.* 她和我在大学是同学。 ◇ *He was a contemporary of Freud and may have known him.* 他是弗洛伊德的同代人，可能认识弗洛伊德。

con·tempt /kən'tempt/ *noun* [U, sing.] **1** the feeling that sb/sth is without value and deserves no respect at all 蔑视；轻蔑；鄙视： *She looked at him **with contempt**.* 她轻蔑地看着他。 ◇ *I shall treat that suggestion with the contempt it deserves.* 我对那项建议当然会不屑一顾。 ◇ *His treatment of his children is **beneath contempt*** (= so unacceptable that it is not even worth feeling contempt for). 他对待自己子女的那种行径为人所不齿。 ◇ *Politicians seem to be generally **held in contempt** by ordinary people.* 一般百姓似乎普遍看不起从政者。 ◇ ~ **for sb/sth** *They had shown a contempt for the values she thought important.* 他们对她所认为重要的价值表示蔑视。 **2** ~ **for sth** a lack of worry or fear about rules, danger, etc. （对规则、危险等的）藐视，不顾： *The firefighters showed a contempt for their own safety.* 那些消防队员已把他们自己的安全置之度外。 ◇ *His remarks betray a staggering contempt for the truth* (= are completely false). 他的话表明他完全无视事情的真相。 **3** = CONTEMPT OF COURT： *He could be jailed for two years for contempt.* 他由于藐视法庭可能被监禁两年。 ◇ *She was held **in contempt** for refusing to testify.* 她因拒绝作证而被判藐视法庭罪。 **IDM** SEE FAMILIARITY

con·tempt·ible /kən'temptəbl/ *adj.* (*formal*) not deserving any respect at all 可轻蔑的；可鄙的；卑劣的 **SYN despicable**: *contemptible behaviour* 卑劣的行为

conˌtempt of 'court (*also* **con·tempt**) *noun* [U] the crime of refusing to obey an order made by a court; not showing respect for a court or judge 藐视法庭（罪）： *Any person who disregards this order will be in contempt of court.* 凡漠视本法令者将被判藐视法庭罪。

con·temp·tu·ous /kən'temptʃuəs/ *adj.* feeling or showing that you have no respect for sb/sth 蔑视的；鄙视的；表示轻蔑的 **SYN scornful**: *She gave him a contemptuous look.* 她鄙夷地看了他一眼。 ◇ ~ **of sb/sth** *He was contemptuous of everything I did.* 他对我所做的一切都不屑一顾。 ▶ **con·temp·tu·ous·ly** *adv.*： *to laugh contemptuously* 轻蔑地大笑

con·tend /kən'tend/ *verb* **1** [T] ~ **that...** (*formal*) to say that sth is true, especially in an argument （尤指在争论中）声称，主张，认为 **SYN maintain**: *I would contend that the minister's thinking is flawed on this point.* 我倒认为部长的想法在这一点上有漏洞。 **2** [I] ~ (**for sth**) to compete against sb in order to gain sth 竞争；争夺： *Three armed groups were contending for power.* 三个武装集团在争夺权力。

PHR V con'tend with sth/sb to have to deal with a problem or with a difficult situation or person （不得不）应付，处理，对付： *Nurses often have to contend with violent or drunken patients.* 护士经常不得不应付粗暴的或喝醉酒的病人。

con·tend·er /kən'tendə(r)/ *noun* a person who takes part in a competition or tries to win sth 竞争者；角逐者；争夺者： *a contender for a gold medal in the Olympics* 奥运金牌的争夺者 ◇ *a **leading/serious/strong contender** for the party leadership* 该党领导权最重要的 / 强劲的 / 有实力的角逐者

con·tent¹ 🔑 /'kɒntent; *NAmE* 'kɑːn-/ *noun* ➲ SEE ALSO CONTENT² **1** 🔑 **contents** [pl.] the things that are contained in sth 所容纳之物；所含之物；内容： *He tipped the contents of the bag onto the table.* 他把提包里的东西倒在桌子上。 ◇ *Fire has caused severe damage to the contents of the building.* 大火导致那栋大楼里的东西严重损毁。 ◇ *She hadn't read the letter and so was unaware of its contents.* 她没有看过那封信，所以对其内容一无所知。 **2** 🔑 **contents** [pl.] the different sections that are contained in a book （书的）目录，目次： *a table of contents* (= the list at the front of a book) 目录 ◇ *a contents page* 目录页 **3** 🔑 [sing.] the subject matter of a book, speech, programme, etc. （书、讲话、节目等的）主题，主要内容： *Your tone of voice is as important as the content of what you have to say.* 你的讲话声调和你要讲的内容同样重要。 ◇ *The content of the course depends on what the students would like to study.* 课程的内容取决于学生愿意学什么。 ◇ *Her poetry has a good deal of political content.* 她的诗歌包含大量的政治内容。 **4** 🔑 [sing.] (following a noun 用于名词后) the amount of a substance that is contained in sth else 含量；容量： *food with a high fat content* 脂肪含量高的食物 ◇ *the alcohol content of a drink* 饮料的酒精含量 **5** [U] (*computing* 计) the information or other material contained on a website or other digital media （网站或其他数字媒介上的）内容： *online content providers* 网络内容提供商

con·tent² /kən'tent/ *adj.*, *verb*, *noun* ➲ SEE ALSO CONTENT¹

■*adj.* [not before noun] **1** ~ (**with sth**) happy and satisfied with what you have 满意；满足： *Not content with stealing my boyfriend* (= not thinking that this was enough), *she has turned all my friends against me.* 她偷走了我的男朋友还不满足，又挑起我所有的朋友和我作对。 ◇ *He seemed more content, less bitter.* 他看起来比较满意，不那么愤愤不平。 ◇ *He had to be content with third place.* 他只好屈居第三名。 ➲ SYNONYMS AT HAPPY **2** ~ **to do sth** willing to do sth 愿意： *I was content to wait.* 我愿意等候。 ➲ COMPARE CONTENTED

■*verb* **1** ~ **yourself with sth** to accept and be satisfied with sth and not try to have or do sth better 满足；满意；知足： *Martina contented herself with a bowl of soup.* 马丁娜喝了一碗汤就心满意足了。 **2** ~ **sb** (*formal*) to make sb feel happy or satisfied 使满意；使满足： *My apology seemed to content him.* 我的道歉好像使他感到满意。

■*noun* = CONTENTMENT **IDM** SEE HEART

con·tent·ed /kən'tentɪd/ *adj.* [usually before noun] showing or feeling happiness or satisfaction, especially because your life is good （尤指因生活好而）满意的，惬意的，满足的： *a contented smile* 惬意的微笑 ◇ *He was a contented man.* 他是个心满意足的人。 ➲ COMPARE CONTENT² *adj.* **OPP discontented** ➲ SYNONYMS AT HAPPY ▶ **con·tent·ed·ly** *adv.*： *She smiled contentedly.* 她心满意足地笑了。

'content farm *noun* (*also* **'content mill**) a website that includes a large quantity of material, which may be of low quality or taken from other sources, but which enables the site to appear high on the list of results given by a SEARCH ENGINE 内容农场，文字工厂（资料繁杂的网站，其内容或许低质或许东拼西凑，但在搜索引擎的结果列表上排位靠前）

con·ten·tion /kənˈtenʃn/ *noun* (*formal*) **1** [U] angry disagreement between people 争吵；争执；争论 SYN **dispute**: *One area of contention is the availability of nursery care.* 争论的一个方面是提供幼儿照顾的问题。◇ *a point of contention* 争论点 **2** [C] ~ (**that...**) a belief or an opinion that you express, especially in an argument （尤指争论时的）看法，观点：*It is our client's contention that the fire was an accident.* 我们当事人的看法是这场火灾属于意外事故。◇ *I would reject that contention.* 我不会同意那种观点。

IDM **in conˈtention** (**for sth**) with a chance of winning sth 有机会赢得：*Only three teams are now in contention for the title.* 现在只有三个队有机会夺冠。**out of conˈtention** (**for sth**) without a chance of winning sth 没有机会赢得 ➲ MORE AT BONE *n.*

con·ten·tious /kənˈtenʃəs/ *adj.* (*formal*) **1** likely to cause disagreement between people 可能引起争论的：*a contentious issue/topic/subject* 有争议的问题 / 话题 / 主题 ◇ *Both views are highly contentious.* 两种观点都很有争议。OPP **uncontentious** **2** liking to argue; involving a lot of arguing 爱争论的；充满争吵的：*a contentious meeting* 争论不休的会议

con·tent·ment /kənˈtentmənt/ (*also less frequent* **content**) *noun* [U] a feeling of happiness or satisfaction 满意；满足：*He has found contentment at last.* 他最终得到了满足。◇ *a sigh of contentment* 满足地舒一口气 ➲ COMPARE DISCONTENT ➲ SYNONYMS AT SATISFACTION

ˈcontent mill *noun* = CONTENT FARM

ˈcontent provider *noun* an organization that supplies information that can be used on a website （互联网）内容提供者，内容供应商

ˈcontent word *noun* (*linguistics* 语言) a noun, a verb, an adjective or an adverb whose main function is to express meaning 实义词；实词 ➲ COMPARE FUNCTION WORD

con·test 🔑 *noun, verb*

■ *noun* /ˈkɒntest; *NAmE* ˈkɑːn-/ **1** 🔑 a competition in which people try to win sth 比赛；竞赛：*a singing contest* 歌咏比赛 ◇ *a talent contest* 新秀大奖赛 ◇ *to* ***enter/win/lose a contest*** 参加 / 赢得竞赛；竞赛失败 ➲ SEE ALSO BEAUTY CONTEST **2** 🔑 ~ (**for sth**) a struggle to gain control or power （控制权或权力的）争夺，竞争：*a contest for the leadership of the party* 争夺政党的领导权 ➲ WORDFINDER NOTE AT DEMOCRACY

IDM **be ˌno ˈcontest** used to say that one side in a competition is so much stronger or better than the other that it is sure to win easily （表示竞争中的一方过于强大或出色）完全不是对手，毫无竞争可言

■ *verb* /kənˈtest/ **1** ~ **sth** to take part in a competition, election, etc. and try to win it 争取赢得（比赛、选举等）：*Three candidates contested the leadership.* 有三位候选人角逐领导权。◇ *a* ***hotly/fiercely/keenly contested*** *game* (= one in which the players try very hard to win and the scores are close) 竞争十分激烈的比赛 **2** ~ **sth** to formally oppose a decision or statement because you think it is wrong 争辩；就…提出异议：*to contest a will* (= try to show that it was not correctly made in law) 对遗嘱提出质疑 ◇ *The divorce was not contested.* 这桩离婚案没有人提出异议。

con·test·ant /kənˈtestənt/ *noun* a person who takes part in a contest 比赛者；竞争者：*Please welcome our next contestant.* 请欢迎我们的下一位竞赛选手。

con·text 🔑 AW /ˈkɒntekst; *NAmE* ˈkɑːn-/ *noun* [C, U] **1** 🔑 the situation in which sth happens and that helps you to understand it （事情发生的）背景，环境，来龙去脉：*This speech needs to be* ***set in the context of*** *Britain in the 1960s.* 这篇演说需要放到 20 世纪 60 年代的英国这一背景之下来看待。◇ *His decision can only be understood* ***in context.*** 只有了解来龙去脉才能明白他的决定。**2** 🔑 the words that come just before and after a word, phrase or statement and help you to understand its meaning 上下文；语境：*You should be able to guess the meaning of the word from the context.* 你应该能从上下文猜出这个词的含义。◇ *This quotation has been taken* ***out of context*** (= repeated without referring to the rest of the text). 这条引文断章取义。

con·text·ual AW /kənˈtekstʃuəl/ *adj.* (*formal*) connected with a particular context 上下文的；与上下文有关的；与语境相关的：*contextual information* 与上下文有关的信息 ◇ *contextual clues to the meaning* 上下文提供的理解其含义的线索 ▶ **con·text·ual·ly** /kənˈtekstʃuəli/ *adv.*

con·text·ual·ize AW (*BrE also* **-ise**) /kənˈtekstʃuəlaɪz/ *verb* ~ **sth** (*formal*) to consider sth in relation to the situation in which it happens or exists 将…置于背景中考虑；将…置于上下文中理解 ▶ **con·text·ual·iza·tion**, **-isa·tion** /kənˌtekstʃuəlaɪˈzeɪʃn; *NAmE* -ləˈz-/ *noun* [U]

con·tigu·ous /kənˈtɪɡjuəs/ *adj.* (*formal* or *specialist*) touching or next to sth 相接的；相邻的：*The countries are contiguous.* 这些国家互相接壤。◇ ~ **with/to sth** *The bruising was not contiguous to the wound.* 这青肿块不在伤口边上。▶ **con·tigu·ity** /ˌkɒntɪˈɡjuːəti; *NAmE* ˌkɑːn-/ *noun* [U]

con·tin·ence /ˈkɒntɪnəns; *NAmE* ˈkɑːn-/ *noun* [U] **1** (*formal*) the control of your feelings, especially your desire to have sex （感情的）节制，自制；（尤指）性欲的节制 **2** the ability to control the BLADDER and BOWELS （大小便的）自控能力，节制力 OPP **incontinence** ▶ **con·tin·ent** /ˈkɒntɪnənt; *NAmE* ˈkɑːn-/ *adj.* OPP **incontinent**

con·tin·ent 🔑 /ˈkɒntɪnənt; *NAmE* ˈkɑːn-/ *noun* **1** 🔑 [C] one of the large land masses of the earth such as Europe, Asia or Africa 大陆；陆地；洲：*the continent of Africa* 非洲大陆 ◇ *the African continent* 非洲大陆 **2 the Continent** [sing.] (*BrE*) the main part of the continent of Europe, not including Britain or Ireland 欧洲大陆（不包括英国和爱尔兰）：*We're going to spend a weekend on the Continent.* 我们要去欧洲大陆度周末。

con·tin·en·tal /ˌkɒntɪˈnentl; *NAmE* ˌkɑːn-/ *adj., noun*

■ *adj.* **1** (*also* **Continental**) [only before noun] (*BrE*) of or in the continent of Europe, not including Britain and Ireland 欧洲大陆的（不包括英国和爱尔兰）：*a popular continental holiday resort* 受欢迎的欧洲大陆度假胜地 ◇ *Britain's continental neighbours* 英国的欧洲大陆邻国 **2** (*BrE*) following the customs of countries in western and southern Europe 随（西、南欧国家）大陆风俗的：*a continental lifestyle* 西、南欧大陆的生活方式 ◇ *The shutters and the balconies make the street look almost continental.* 活动护窗和阳台使这条街看起来颇具欧洲大陆风格。**3** [only before noun] connected with the main part of the N American continent 北美大陆的：*Prices are often higher in Hawaii than in the continental United States.* 夏威夷的物价常常比美国大陆高。**4** forming part of, or typical of, any of the seven main land masses of the earth 大洲的；大陆的：*continental Antarctica/Asia/Europe* 南极洲 / 亚洲 / 欧洲大陆 ◇ *to study continental geography* 研究大陆地理学

■ *noun* (*BrE, old-fashioned, often disapproving*) a person who lives in the continent of Europe （欧洲）大陆人：*The continentals have never understood our preference for warm beer.* 欧洲大陆人根本不理解我们为什么喜欢喝温啤酒。

ˌcontinental ˈbreakfast *noun* a light breakfast, usually consisting of coffee and bread rolls with butter and jam 欧陆式早餐，简易早餐（通常包括咖啡和黄油果酱圆面包）➲ COMPARE ENGLISH BREAKFAST

ˌcontinental ˈclimate *noun* a fairly dry pattern of weather with very hot summers and very cold winters, that is typical of the central regions of the US, Canada and Russia, for example 大陆（性）气候 ➲ WORDFINDER NOTE AT CLIMATE

ˌcontinental ˈdrift *noun* [U] (*geology* 地) the slow movement of the continents towards and away from each other during the history of the earth 大陆漂移 ➲ SEE ALSO PLATE TECTONICS

ˌcontinental ˈshelf *noun* [usually sing.] (*geology* 地) the area of land on the edge of a continent that slopes into the ocean 大陆架

C

ˌ**continental ˈslope** *noun* [sing.] (*geology* 地) the steep surface that goes down from the outer edge of the continental shelf to the ocean floor 大陆坡

con·tin·gency /kənˈtɪndʒənsi/ *noun* (*pl.* **-ies**) an event that may or may not happen 可能发生的事；偶发（或不测、意外）事件 **SYN** **possibility**: *We must consider all possible contingencies.* 我们必须考虑一切可能发生的事。◇ *to make **contingency plans*** (= plans for what to do if a particular event happens or does not happen) 拟订应变计划 ◇ *a **contingency fund*** (= to pay for sth that might happen in the future) 意外开支准备金

conˈtingency fee *noun* (in the US) an amount of money that is paid to a lawyer only if the person he or she is advising wins in court（美国）成功酬金（胜诉才付给律师）

con·tin·gent /kənˈtɪndʒənt/ *noun, adj.*

■ ***noun*** [C+sing./pl. v.] **1** a group of people at a meeting or an event who have sth in common, especially the place they come from, that is not shared by other people at the event（志趣相投、尤指来自同一地方的）一组与会者，代表团：*The largest contingent was from the United States.* 最大的会议代表团来自美国。◇ *A strong contingent of local residents were there to block the proposal.* 由当地居民组成的强大的代表团在那里阻止通过这项提案。**2** a group of soldiers that are part of a larger force（军队的）分遣队，小分队：*the French contingent in the UN peacekeeping force* 联合国维和部队的法国分队

■ ***adj.*** **1** ~ (**on/upon sth**) (*formal*) depending on sth that may or may not happen 依情况而定的：*All payments are contingent upon satisfactory completion dates.* 所有的付款须视是否如期完成。**2** ~ **worker/work/job** (*business* 商) a person, or work done by a person, who does not have a permanent contract with a company 临时工；临时工作：*the spread of contingent work throughout the economy* 临时工作在整个经济领域的扩展 ▶ **con·tin·gent·ly** *adv.*

con·tin·ual /kənˈtɪnjuəl/ *adj.* [only before noun] **1** repeated many times in a way that is annoying（令人厌烦地）多次重复的，频繁的：***continual complaints/interruptions*** 反复的抱怨 / 打搅 **2** continuing without interruption 接连不断的；连续的；频频的 **SYN** **continuous**: *He was in a continual process of rewriting his material.* 他一直在不断地改写他的材料。◇ *We lived in continual fear of being discovered.* 我们长期生活在害怕被发现的恐惧中。◇ *Her daughter was a continual source of delight to her.* 她的女儿是她无限快乐的源泉。➲ NOTE AT CONTINUOUS ▶ **con·tinu·al·ly** /-juəli/ *adv.*：*They argue continually about money.* 他们没完没了地为钱争吵。◇ *the need to adapt to new and continually changing circumstances* 需要适应又新又不断变化的情况 ◇ *New products are continually being developed.* 新产品正源源不断地开发出来。

con·tinu·ance /kənˈtɪnjuəns/ *noun* **1** [U] (*formal*) the state of continuing to exist or function 继续；持续：*We can no longer support the President's continuance in office.* 我们不能再支持总统继续任职。**2** [C] (*NAmE, law* 律) a decision that a court case should be heard later 延期审理：*The judge refused his motion for a continuance.* 法官拒绝他要求延期审理的动议。

con·tinu·ant /kənˈtɪnjuənt/ *noun* (*phonetics* 语音) a consonant that is pronounced with the breath passing through the throat, so that the sound can be continued. /f/, /l/ and /m/ are examples of continuants. 延续音 ▶ **con·tinu·ant** *adj.* [only before noun]: *continuant consonants* 延续辅音

con·tinu·ation /kənˌtɪnjuˈeɪʃn/ *noun* **1** [U, sing.] an act or the state of continuing 继续；连续；持续：*They are anxious to ensure the continuation of the economic reform programme.* 他们渴望确保经济改革计划持续下去。◇ ~ **in sth** *This year saw a continuation in the upward trend in sales.* 今年销售呈持续增长的趋势。**2** [C] something that continues or follows sth else 延续部分；续篇：*Her new book is a continuation of her autobiography.* 她的新书是她自传的续篇。**3** [C] something that is joined on to sth else and forms a part of it 附加物；延续物：*There are plans to build a continuation of the bypass next year.* 已有计划明年修建这条支路的延长线。

con·tinue 🔑 /kənˈtɪnjuː/ *verb* **1** 🔑 [I, T] to keep existing or happening without stopping 持续；继续存在；不断发生：*The exhibition continues until 25 July.* 展览举行至 7 月 25 日为止。◇ *The trial is expected to continue for three months.* 预计审判要持续三个月。◇ ~ **to do sth** *The rain continued to fall all afternoon.* 这场雨整整一下午都下个不停。◇ ~ **doing sth** *The rain continued falling all afternoon.* 这场雨整整一下午都下个不停。**2** 🔑 [I, T] to keep doing sth without stopping 继续做；不停地干：~ **doing sth** *She wanted to continue working until she was 60.* 她想要继续工作到 60 岁。◇ ~ **to do sth** *He continued to ignore everything I was saying.* 他仍对我所说的一切置若罔闻。◇ ~ (**with sth**) *Are you going to continue with the project?* 你要继续做这个项目吗？◇ ~ **sth** *The board of inquiry is continuing its investigations.* 调查委员会在继续做调查。**3** 🔑 [I] (+ **adv./prep.**) to go or move further in the same direction（朝相同方向）走，移动；延伸：*The path continued over rough, rocky ground.* 这条小路穿过了崎岖不平的石头地。◇ *He continued on his way.* 他继续走他的路。**4** 🔑 [I] ~ (**as sth**) to remain in a particular job or condition 留任；维持原状：*I want you to continue as project manager.* 我要你留任项目经理。◇ *She will continue in her present job until a replacement can be found.* 在找到替换人员以前，她将继续做她目前的工作。**5** 🔑 [I, T] to start or start sth again after stopping for a time（停顿后）继续，再开始 **SYN** **resume**: *The story continues in our next issue.* 这篇故事我们将在下一期里继续刊载。◇ ~ **sth** *The story will be continued in our next issue.* 这篇故事我们将在下一期里继续刊载。**6** 🔑 [I, T] to start speaking again after stopping（停顿后）继续说，接着说：*Please continue—I didn't mean to interrupt.* 请继续往下说，我并非有意打断你的话。◇ + **speech** *'In fact,' he continued, 'I'd like to congratulate you.'*“其实，”他接着说，“我想向你表示祝贺。”

con·tinued /kənˈtɪnjuːd/ (*also* **con·tinu·ing** /kənˈtɪnjuɪŋ/) *adj.* [only before noun] existing in the same state without change or interruption 继续不变的；连续不断的：*We are grateful for your **continued/continuing support**.* 我们对你们始终不渝的支持不胜感激。◇ *continued interest* 持久的兴趣 ◇ *continuing involvement* 不断的参与

conˌtinuing eduˈcation *noun* [U] = ADULT EDUCATION

con·tinu·ity /ˌkɒntɪˈnjuːəti; *NAmE* ˌkɑːntəˈnuː-/ *noun* (*pl.* **-ies**) **1** [U] the fact of not stopping or not changing 连续性；持续性：*to **ensure/provide/maintain continuity** of fuel supplies* 确保 / 提供 / 保持燃料供给的连续性 **OPP** **discontinuity** **2** [U, C] a logical connection between the parts of sth, or between two things（逻辑上的）连接，联结：*The novel fails to achieve narrative continuity.* 这部小说叙述不连贯。◇ *There are obvious continuities between diet and health.* 日常饮食与健康之间有着明显的逻辑关联。**OPP** **discontinuity** **3** [U] (*specialist*) the organization of a film/movie or television programme, especially making sure that people's clothes, objects, etc. are the same from one scene to the next（电影或电视节目场景中服装、物体等的）一致性，衔接

con·tinuo /kənˈtɪnjuəʊ; *NAmE* -juoʊ/ *noun* [U] (*music* 音, *from Italian*) a musical part played to accompany another instrument, in which a line of low notes is shown with figures to represent the higher notes to be played above them 数字低音；通奏低音：*a trio for two violins and continuo* 两小提琴与通奏低音的三声中部

con·tinu·ous 🔑 /kənˈtɪnjuəs/ *adj.* **1** 🔑 happening or existing for a period of time without interruption 不断的；持续的；连续的：*She was in continuous employment until the age of sixty-five.* 她一直工作到 65 岁。◇ *The rain has been continuous since this morning.* 从早上到现在这雨就没停过。**2** 🔑 spreading in a line or over an area without any spaces 延伸的；遍布的：*a continuous line of traffic* 络绎不绝的车辆 **3** 🔑 (*informal*) repeated many times 反复的；频繁的 **SYN** **continual**: *For four days the town suffered continuous attacks.* 那座城镇连续四天遭到了袭击。**HELP** **Continual** is much more frequent in this meaning.

此义更多用 continual。**4** (*grammar* 语法) = PROGRESSIVE (3)：*the continuous tenses* 进行时态 ▶ **con·tin·u·ous·ly** *adv.*: *He has lived and worked in France almost continuously since 1990.* 自从 1990 年以来，他差不多一直在法国居住和工作。

C

▼ WHICH WORD? 词语辨析

continuous / continual

These adjectives are frequently used with the following nouns. 这两个形容词常与下列名词连用：

continuous ~	continual ~
process	change
employment	problems
flow	updating
line	questions
speech	pain
supply	fear

- **Continuous** describes something that continues without stopping. * continuous 指持续的、不间断的。
- **Continual** usually describes an action that is repeated again and again. * continual 通常指一再重复。
- The difference between these two words is now disappearing. In particular, **continual** can also mean the same as **continuous** and is used especially about undesirable things. 上述两词的差异正逐渐消失，特别是 continual 亦含有与 continuous 相同的意义，尤指不希望发生的事： *Life was a continual struggle for them.* 生活对他们来说就是不断的挣扎。 However, **continuous** is much more frequent in this sense. 不过，用 continuous 表达此义常见得多。

con,tinuous as'sessment *noun* [U] (*BrE*) a system of giving a student a final mark/grade based on work done during a course of study rather than on one exam 连续性评定（学生的最后成绩不是根据一次考试而是根据课程作业）

con·tinuum /kən'tɪnjuəm/ *noun* (*pl.* **con·tinua** /-juə/) a series of similar items in which each is almost the same as the ones next to it but the last is very different from the first （相邻两者相似但起首与末尾截然不同的）连续体 SYN **cline**: *It is impossible to say at what point along the continuum a dialect becomes a separate language.* 要说出同一语言的方言差异到什么程度才成为另一种语言是不可能的。

con·tort /kən'tɔːt; *NAmE* -'tɔːrt/ *verb* [I, T] to become twisted or make sth twisted out of its natural or normal shape （使）扭曲，走样： *His face contorted with anger.* 他脸都气歪了。◇ **~ sth** *Her mouth was contorted in a snarl.* 她龇牙咧嘴地怒吼着。 ▶ **con·tort·ed** *adj.*: *contorted limbs/bodies* 扭曲的四肢 / 躯体 ◇ (*figurative*) *It was a contorted version of the truth.* 这是对事实的歪曲。

con·tor·tion /kən'tɔːʃn; *NAmE* -'tɔːrʃn/ *noun* **1** [U] the state of the face or body being twisted out of its natural shape （脸部或躯体的）扭曲，变形，走样： *Their bodies had suffered contortion as a result of malnutrition.* 由于营养不良他们的躯体都变了形。 **2** [C] a movement which twists the body out of its natural shape 扭曲的动作（或姿势）： *His facial contortions amused the audience of schoolchildren.* 他扮鬼脸逗得小学生观众都笑起来了。◇ (*figurative*) *We had to go through all the usual contortions* (= a difficult series of actions) *to get a ticket.* 我们照例得费尽心机才能弄到一张票。

con·tor·tion·ist /kən'tɔːʃənɪst; *NAmE* -'tɔːrʃ-/ *noun* a performer who does contortions of their body to entertain others 柔体杂技演员

con·tour /'kɒntʊə(r); *NAmE* 'kɑːntʊr/ *noun* **1** the outer edges of sth; the outline of its shape or form 外形；轮廓： *The road follows the natural contours of the coastline.* 这条路沿着海岸线的自然轮廓延伸。◇ *She traced the contours of his face with her finger.* 她用一根手指拂过他脸部的轮廓。 **2** (*also* **'contour line**) a line on a map that joins points that are the same height above sea level （地图上连接相同海拔各点的）等高线： *a contour map* (= a map that includes these lines) 等高线地图

con·toured /'kɒntʊəd; *NAmE* 'kɑːntʊrd/ *adj.* **1** with a specially designed outline that makes sth attractive or comfortable 外形设计独特的： *It is smoothly contoured to look like a racing car.* 这辆车外形设计流畅，看起来像赛车。 **2** having or showing contours 标示等高线的： *contoured hills/maps* 标有等高线的山峦 / 地图

contra- /'kɒntrə; *NAmE* 'kɑːntrə/ *combining form* **1** (in nouns, verbs and adjectives 构成名词、动词和形容词) against; opposite 反对；相反： *contraflow* 一侧双向行驶 ◇ *contradict* 反驳 **2** (in nouns 构成名词) (*music* 音) having a PITCH an OCTAVE below 声音低八度的： *a contrabassoon* 低音大管

con·tra·band /'kɒntrəbænd; *NAmE* 'kɑːn-/ *noun* [U] goods that are illegally taken into or out of a country （非法带入或带出国境的）禁运品，走私货： *contraband goods* 违禁货物 ◇ *to smuggle contraband* 走私违禁品

con·tra·cep·tion /ˌkɒntrə'sepʃn; *NAmE* ˌkɑːn-/ *noun* [U] the practice of preventing a woman from becoming pregnant; the methods of doing this 避孕（法）；节育（法） SYN **birth control**: *to give advice about contraception* 就避孕方法提供咨询

con·tra·cep·tive /ˌkɒntrə'septɪv; *NAmE* ˌkɑːn-/ *noun* a drug, device or practice used to prevent a woman from becoming pregnant 避孕药；避孕用具；避孕措施： *oral contraceptives* 口服避孕药 ▶ **con·tra·cep·tive** *adj.* [only before noun]: *a contraceptive pill* 避孕药丸 ◇ *contraceptive advice/precautions/methods* 避孕咨询 / 措施 / 方法

con·tract AW *noun, verb*

■ ***noun*** /'kɒntrækt; *NAmE* 'kɑːn-/ **1** an official written agreement 合同；合约；契约： *a contract of employment* 雇佣合同 ◇ *a research contract* 从事研究的合同 ◇ **~ with sb** *to* **enter into/make/sign a contract** *with the supplier* 与供应商签订合同 ◇ **~ between A and B** *These clauses form part of the contract between buyer and seller.* 这些条款构成买卖双方所签合同的一部分。 ◇ **~ for sth** *a contract for the supply of vehicles* 提供车辆的合约 ◇ **~ to do sth** *to* **win/be awarded a contract** *to build a new school* 获得承建一所新学校的合同 ◇ *a* **contract worker** (= one employed on a contract for a fixed period of time) 合同工 ◇ *I was* **on a** *three-year* **contract** *that expired last week.* 我签订的三年期合同已于上周期满。 ◇ **Under the terms of the contract** *the job should have been finished yesterday.* 根据合同的条款，这项工作本应于昨天完成。 ◇ *She is* **under contract to** (= has a contract to work for) *a major American computer firm.* 她已签约为一家大型美国计算机公司工作。 ◇ *The offer has been accepted,* **subject to contract** (= the agreement is not official until the contract is signed). 此报价已获接受，尚须以签约为准。 ◇ *They were sued for* **breach of contract** (= not keeping to a contract). 他们被指控违约。 ⇨ WORDFINDER NOTE AT DEAL, EMPLOY **2 ~ (on sb)** (*informal*) an agreement to kill sb for money （雇用杀人的）协议，合同： *to take out a contract on sb* 雇凶手杀害某人

■ ***verb*** /kən'trækt/ **1** [I, T] to become less or smaller; to make sth become less or smaller （使）收缩，缩小： *Glass contracts as it cools.* 玻璃遇冷收缩。 ◇ *a contracting market* 萎缩的市场 ◇ *The heart muscles contract to expel the blood.* 心脏肌肉收缩以挤压出血液。 ◇ **~ sth** *The exercise consists of stretching and contracting the leg muscles.* 此项训练包括伸展和收缩腿部肌肉。 ◇ **~ sth to sth** *'I will' and 'I shall' are usually contracted* (= made shorter) *to 'I'll'.* * I will 和 I shall 通常缩写成 I'll。 OPP **expand 2** [T] **~ sth** (*formal* or *medical* 医) to get an illness 感染（疾病）；得（病）： *to contract AIDS/a virus/a disease* 感染艾滋病 / 病毒 / 疾病 **3** [T] to make a legal agreement with sb for them to work for you or provide you with a service 与…

订立合同（或契约）：**~ sb to do sth** *The player is contracted to play until August.* 这位选手签约参加比赛到八月份。◇ **~ sb** (**to sth**) *Several computer engineers have been contracted to the finance department.* 有几位计算机工程师与财务部门签订了合同。 **4** [I] **~ to do sth** to make a legal agreement to work for sb or provide them with a service 订立…的合同（或契约）：*She has contracted to work 20 hours a week.* 她已签订每周工作 20 小时的合同。 **5** [T] **~ a marriage/an alliance** (**with sb**) (*formal*) to formally agree to marry sb/form an ALLIANCE with sb （与…）订立（婚约）；（与…）缔结（同盟） ➲ MORE LIKE THIS 21, page R27

PHR V **con,tract 'in** (**to sth**) (*BrE*) to formally agree that you will take part in sth 订约参与 **con,tract 'out** (**of sth**) (*BrE*) to formally agree that you will not take part in sth 订约不参与；退出（或不参加）…合约：*Many employees contracted out of the pension plan.* 许多雇员退出了养老金计划的合约。 **con,tract sth ↔ 'out** (**to sb**) to arrange for work to be done by another company rather than your own 订约把…承包出去

,contract 'bridge *noun* [U] the standard form of the card game BRIDGE, in which points are given only for sets of cards that are BID[1] and won 定约桥牌（桥牌的标准形式，只能按叫到的定约取得成局奖分）

con·tract·ile /kən'træktaɪl/ *adj.* (*biology* 生) (of living TISSUE, organs, etc. 活组织、器官等) able to contract or, of an opening or tube, become narrower 可收缩的；（开口或管）可变窄的

con·trac·tion /kən'trækʃn/ *noun* **1** [U] the process of becoming smaller 收缩；缩小：*the expansion and contraction of the metal* 金属的膨胀与收缩 ◇ *The sudden contraction of the markets left them with a lot of unwanted stock.* 股票市场骤然收缩，让他们剩下了许多无人要的股票。 **OPP** **expansion** **2** [C, U] a sudden and painful contracting of muscles, especially of the muscles around a woman's WOMB, that happens when she is giving birth to a child （肌肉的）收缩，挛缩；（尤指分娩时的）子宫收缩：*The contractions started coming every five minutes.* 子宫开始每隔五分钟收缩一次。 ➲ WORDFINDER NOTE AT BIRTH **3** [C] (*linguistics* 语言) a short form of a word 词的缩约形式：*'He's' may be a contraction of 'he is' or 'he has'.* * he's 可以是 he is 或 he has 的缩写形式。

con·tract·or **AW** /kən'træktə(r)/ *noun* a person or company that has a contract to do work or provide goods or services for another company 承包人；承包商；承包公司：*a* ***building/haulage, etc. contractor*** 建筑、货运等承包商 ◇ *to employ an outside contractor* 雇用外来承包商

con·tract·ual /kən'træktʃuəl/ *adj.* connected with the conditions of a legal written agreement; agreed in a contract 合同的；契约的；按合同（或契约）规定的 ▸ **con·trac·tu·al·ly** /kən'træktʃuəli/ *adv.*

con·tra·dict **AW** /,kɒntrə'dɪkt; *NAmE* ,kɑːn-/ *verb* **1** to say that sth that sb else has said is wrong, and that the opposite is true 反驳；驳斥；批驳：**~ sth** *All evening her husband contradicted everything she said.* 整个晚上她说什么丈夫都反驳。◇ **~ sb/yourself** *You've just* ***contradicted yourself*** (= said the opposite of what you said before). 你恰好与你刚才说的自相矛盾。◇ **~ (sb) + speech** *'No, it's not,' she contradicted (him).* "不，不是的。" 她反驳（他）说。 **2 ~ sth | ~ each other** (of statements or pieces of evidence 陈述或证据) to be so different from each other that one of them must be wrong 相抵触；相矛盾；相反：*The two stories contradict each other.* 这两种说法相互抵触。 ➲ LANGUAGE BANK AT EVIDENCE

con·tra·dic·tion **AW** /,kɒntrə'dɪkʃn; *NAmE* ,kɑːn-/ *noun* **1** [C, U] **~ (between A and B)** a lack of agreement between facts, opinions, actions, etc. （事实、看法、行动等的）不一致，矛盾，对立：*There is a contradiction between the two sets of figures.* 这两组数据相互矛盾。 ◇ *His public speeches are* ***in direct contradiction to*** *his personal lifestyle.* 他的公开言论与他本人的生活方式恰恰相反。 ◇ *How can we resolve this apparent contradiction?* 我们怎样才能解决这个明显的矛盾呢？ **2** [U, C] the act of saying that sth that sb else has said is wrong or not true; an example of this 反驳；驳斥：*I think I can say,* ***without fear of contradiction****, that…* 就算有人反驳，我也敢说… ◇ *Now you say you both left at ten—that's a contradiction of your last statement.* 你现在说你们俩是十点钟离开的，这可和你上次的说法不一致。

IDM **a ,contradiction in 'terms** a statement containing two words that contradict each other's meaning 自相矛盾的说法：*A 'nomad settlement' is a contradiction in terms.* "游牧者的定居"是用词上的自相矛盾。

con·tra·dict·ory **AW** /,kɒntrə'dɪktəri; *NAmE* ,kɑːn-/ *adj.* containing or showing a contradiction 相互矛盾的；对立的；不一致的 **SYN** **conflicting**：*We are faced with two apparently contradictory statements.* 我们面前这两种说法显然是矛盾的。 ◇ *The advice I received was often contradictory.* 我所得到的建议常常是相互矛盾的。

con·tra·dis·tinc·tion /,kɒntrədɪ'stɪŋkʃn; *NAmE* ,kɑːn-/ *noun*

IDM **in contradistinction to sth/sb** (*formal*) in contrast with sth/sb 与…相对比（或截然不同）

con·tra·flow /'kɒntrəfləʊ; *NAmE* 'kɑːntrəfloʊ/ *noun* (*BrE*) a system that is used when one half of a large road is closed for repairs, and the traffic going in both directions has to use the other half （道路一侧关闭维修时实行的）一侧双向行驶：*A contraflow system is in operation on this section of the motorway.* 这段高速公路的一侧正在实行双向行驶。 ➲ WORDFINDER NOTE AT TRAFFIC

con·tra·indi·cate /,kɒntrə'ɪndɪkeɪt; *NAmE* ,kɑːn-/ *verb* **~ sth** (*medical* 医) if a drug or treatment is **contraindicated**, there is a medical reason why it should not be used in a particular situation 禁忌使用（某种药物或疗法）：*This drug is contraindicated in patients with asthma.* 这种药哮喘病人禁用。

con·tra·indi·ca·tion /,kɒntrə,ɪndɪ'keɪʃn; *NAmE* ,kɑːn-/ *noun* (*medical* 医) a possible reason for not giving sb a particular drug or medical treatment （对某种药物或疗法的）禁忌

con·tralto /kən'træltəʊ; *NAmE* -toʊ/ *noun* (*pl.* **-os**) = ALTO

con·trap·tion /kən'træpʃn/ *noun* a machine or piece of equipment that looks strange 奇异的机械；奇特的装置：*She showed us a strange contraption that looked like a satellite dish.* 她给我们看了一个奇怪的玩意儿，样子像碟形卫星信号接收器。

con·tra·pun·tal /,kɒntrə'pʌntl; *NAmE* ,kɑːn-/ *adj.* (*music* 音) having two or more tunes played together to form a whole 对位的 ➲ SEE ALSO COUNTERPOINT *n.* (1)

con·trari·wise /kən'treəriwaɪz; *NAmE* -'trer-/ *adv.* (*formal*) **1** used at the beginning of a sentence or clause to introduce a contrast （用于句首或从句的开头以引出对比）相反，在另一方面 **2** in the opposite way 以相反的方式：*It worked contrariwise—first you dialled the number, then you put the money in.* 这部电话的操作方式相反，要先拨号码，然后投入钱币。

con·trary[1] **AW** /'kɒntrəri; *NAmE* 'kɑːntreri/ *adj.*, *noun* ➲ SEE ALSO CONTRARY[2]

■ ***adj.*** **1 ~ to sth** different from sth; against sth 与之相异的；相对立的；相反的：***Contrary to popular belief,*** *many cats dislike milk.* 与普遍的看法相反，许多猫不喜欢牛奶。◇ *The government has decided that the publication of the report would be 'contrary to the public interest'.* 政府认为发表这份报告将会"违背公众的利益"。 **2** [only before noun] completely different in nature or direction （在性质或方向上）截然不同的，完全相反的 **SYN** **opposite**：***contrary advice/opinions/arguments*** 完全相反的建议 / 观点 / 论点 ◇ *The contrary view is that prison provides an excellent education—in crime.* 截然不同的看法是监狱可以提供极好的教育 —— 在犯罪方面。

■ ***noun*** **the contrary** [sing.] the opposite fact, event or situation 相反的事实（或事情、情况）：*In the end the contrary was proved true: he was innocent and she was guilty.* 最后证明事实正好相反：他是无辜的，而她则有罪。

IDM **on the 'contrary** used to introduce a statement that says the opposite of the last one 与此相反；恰恰相反：*'It* *must have been terrible.' 'On the contrary, I enjoyed every minute.'* "那一定是很糟糕。" "恰恰相反，我非常喜欢。" ˌ**quite the ˈcontrary** used to emphasize that the opposite of what has been said is true 恰恰相反；正相反：*I don't find him funny at all. Quite the contrary.* 正相反，我觉得他一点儿也不可笑。 **to the ˈcontrary** showing or proving the opposite 相反的；相反地：*Show me some evidence to the contrary* (= proving that sth is not true). 给我看看有什么相反的证据吧。◇ *I will expect to see you on Sunday unless I hear anything to the contrary* (= that you are not coming). 我星期天等你，除非你说不来了。

con·trary² AW /kənˈtreəri; *NAmE* -ˈtreri/ *adj.* (*formal, disapproving*) (usually of children 通常指小孩) behaving badly; choosing to do or say the opposite of what is expected 乖戾的；好与人作对的；逆反的；犟的：*She was such a contrary child—it was impossible to please her.* 这孩子老跟人作对，没法让她高兴。➲ SEE ALSO CONTRARY¹ ▶ **con·trar·ily** AW *adv.* **con·trari·ness** *noun* [U]

con·trast 🔑 AW *noun, verb*

■ ***noun*** /ˈkɒntrɑːst; *NAmE* ˈkɑːntræst/ **1** 🔑 [C, U] a difference between two or more people or things that you can see clearly when they are compared or put close together; the fact of comparing two or more things in order to show the differences between them 明显的差异；对比；对照：~ (**between A and B**) *There is an obvious contrast between the cultures of East and West.* 东西方文化之间有明显的差异。◇ ~ (**to sb/sth**) *The company lost $7 million this quarter* ***in contrast to*** *a profit of $6.2 million a year earlier.* 这家公司本季度亏损了 700 万美元，与去年同期 620 万美元的盈利形成了对照。◇ *The situation when we arrived was in* ***marked contrast*** *to the news reports.* 我们到达时的局势与新闻报道的截然不同。◇ *The poverty of her childhood* ***stands in total contrast to*** *her life in Hollywood.* 她孩提时的贫困处境与她在好莱坞的生活有着天壤之别。◇ ~ (**with sb/sth**) *to show a* ***sharp/stark/striking contrast*** *with sth* 与某事物形成鲜明 / 明显 / 显著的对比 ◇ ~ (**in sth**) *A wool jacket complements the silk trousers and provides an interesting contrast in texture.* 毛料上衣配真丝长裤，质地上的差异非常有趣。◇ *When you look at their new system, ours seems very old-fashioned* ***by contrast***. 看一看他们的新系统，就显得我们的系统陈旧过时了。◇ ~ (**of sth**) *Careful contrast of the two plans shows some important differences.* 把两个计划仔细地加以对比就可看出一些重要的差异。**2** [C, usually sing.] ~ (**to sb/sth**) a person or thing that is clearly different from sb/sth else 明显不同的人（或事物）：*The work you did today is quite a contrast to* (= very much better/worse than) *what you did last week.* 你今天的表现与上周截然不同。**3** [U] differences in colour or in light and dark, used in photographs and paintings to create a special effect（摄影或绘画中的）颜色反差，明暗对比：*The artist's use of contrast is masterly.* 这位艺术家娴熟地运用了明暗对比。**4** [U] the amount of difference between light and dark in a photograph or the picture on a television screen（照片或电视图像的）明暗对比度，反差：*Use this button to adjust the contrast.* 用此按钮调节图像明暗的对比度。

■ ***verb*** /kənˈtrɑːst; *NAmE* -ˈtræst/ **1** 🔑 [T] ~ (**A and/with B**) to compare two things in order to show the differences between them 对比；对照：*It is interesting to contrast the British legal system with the American one.* 把英国的法制与美国的加以对比很有意思。◇ *The poem contrasts youth and age.* 这首诗对比了青年与老年。**2** 🔑 [I] ~ (**with sth**) to show a clear difference when close together or when compared（靠近或作比较时）显出明显的差异，形成对比：*Her actions* ***contrasted sharply*** *with her promises.* 她的行为与她的诺言相差甚远。◇ *Her actions and her promises contrasted sharply.* 她的行为与她的诺言相差甚远。

> ▼ **LANGUAGE BANK** 用语库
>
> **contrast**
>
> Highlighting differences 突出差异 / 不同
>
> - *This survey* ***highlights a number of differences in*** *the way that teenage boys and girls in the UK spend their free time.* 这项民意测验凸显出英国十几岁的男孩和女孩在打发闲暇时间上的诸多不同。
> - ***One of the main differences between*** *the girls* ***and*** *the boys who took part in the research was the way in which they use the Internet.* 参与了这项研究的女生和男生之间的主要差异之一在于他们使用互联网的方式。
> - ***Unlike*** *the girls, who use the Internet mainly to keep in touch with friends, the boys questioned in this survey tend to use the Internet for playing computer games.* 女生使用互联网主要是和朋友联系，这一点和男生不同，参与调查的男生往往是使用互联网来玩电脑游戏。
> - *The girls* ***differ from*** *the boys* ***in that*** *they tend to spend more time keeping in touch with friends on the telephone or on social networking websites.* 与男生不同的是，女生往往花更多的时间通过电话或社交网站与朋友保持联系。
> - ***Compared to*** *the boys, the girls spend much more time chatting to friends on the telephone.* 与男生相比，女生花在与朋友电话聊天上的时间要多得多。
> - *On average the girls spend four hours a week chatting to friends on the phone.* ***In contrast***, *very few of the boys spend more than five minutes a day talking to their friends in this way.* 女生平均每周花四个小时与朋友电话聊天。相比之下，很少有男生每天以这种方式与朋友聊天五分钟以上。
> - *The boys prefer competitive sports and computer games,* ***whereas/while*** *the girls seem to enjoy more cooperative activities, such as shopping with friends.* 男生更喜欢竞技性体育运动和电脑游戏，而女生似乎更喜欢合作性活动，比如与朋友一起购物。
> - *When the girls go shopping, they mainly buy clothes and cosmetics. The boys,* ***on the other hand***, *tend to purchase computer games or gadgets.* 女生购物时主要买衣服和化妆品，而男生往往会买电脑游戏或小器具。
>
> ➲ LANGUAGE BANK AT GENERALLY, ILLUSTRATE, PROPORTION, SIMILARLY, SURPRISING

con·trast·ing 🔑 AW /kənˈtrɑːstɪŋ; *NAmE* -ˈtræs-/ *adj.* [usually before noun] very different in style, colour or attitude（在式样、颜色或态度上）极不相同的，差异大的：*bright, contrasting colours* 鲜艳斑斓的色彩 ◇ *The book explores contrasting views of the poet's early work.* 此书探讨了人们对这位诗人早期作品截然不同的观点。

con·trast·ive AW /kənˈtrɑːstɪv; *NAmE* -ˈtræs-/ *adj.* (*linguistics* 语言) showing the differences between languages 作对比研究的：*a contrastive analysis of British and Australian English* 对英式英语和澳大利亚英语的对比分析

con·tra·vene /ˌkɒntrəˈviːn; *NAmE* ˌkɑːn-/ *verb* ~ **sth** (*formal*) to do sth that is not allowed by a law or rule 违犯，违反（法律或规则） SYN **infringe**：*The company was found guilty of contravening safety regulations.* 那家公司被判违反了安全条例。 ▶ **con·tra·ven·tion** /ˌkɒntrəˈvenʃn; *NAmE* ˌkɑːn-/ *noun* [U, C] SYN **infringement**：*These actions are* ***in contravention of*** *European law.* 这些行动违反了欧洲的法律。

con·tre·temps /ˈkɒntrətɒ̃; *NAmE* ˈkɑːntrətɑ̃ː; ˈkɔ̃ːntrətɑ̃ː/ *noun* (*pl.* **con·tre·temps**) (*from French, formal* or *humorous*) an unfortunate event or embarrassing disagreement with another person 不幸事情；令人难堪的龃龉

con·trib·ute 🔑 AW /kənˈtrɪbjuːt; *BrE also* ˈkɒntrɪbjuːt/ *verb* **1** 🔑 [T, I] to give sth, especially money or goods, to help sb/sth 捐献，捐赠（尤指金钱或物品）；捐助：~ **sth** (**to/towards sth**) *We contributed £5 000 to the earthquake fund.* 我们向地震基金捐赠了 5 000 英镑。◇ ~ (**to/towards sth**) *Would you like to contribute to our collection?* 你愿意给我们的募捐捐款吗？◇ *Do you wish to contribute?* 你想捐助吗？**2** 🔑 [I] ~ (**to sth**) to be one of the causes of sth 是…的原因之一：*Medical negligence was said to have contributed to her death.* 据说医务人员的玩忽职守是她死亡的原因之一。◇ *Human error may have been a* ***contributing factor***. 人为过错可能是一个起作用的因素。 ➲ LANGUAGE BANK AT CAUSE **3** 🔑 [I, T] to increase, improve or add to sth 增加；增进；添加（到某物）：~ **to sth** *Immigrants have contributed to British culture in many ways.* 移民在许多方面都对英国文化有所贡献。◇ ~ **sth to sth** *This book* *contributes little to our understanding of the subject.* 此书对我们了解这门学科助益甚少。 **4** [T, I] to write things for a newspaper, magazine, or a radio or television programme; to speak during a meeting or conversation, especially to give your opinion（为报纸、杂志、电台或电视节目）撰稿；（在会议或会谈期间）讲话，（尤指）发表意见： **~ sth (to sth)** *She contributed a number of articles to the magazine.* 她给这家杂志撰写了一些稿件。◇ **~ (to sth)** *He contributes regularly to the magazine 'New Scientist'.* 他定期给《新科学家》杂志撰稿。◇ *We hope everyone will contribute to the discussion.* 我们希望大家都能参与讨论。

con·tri·bu·tion AW /ˌkɒntrɪˈbjuːʃn; NAmE ˌkɑːn-/ *noun* **1** [C] a sum of money that is given to a person or an organization in order to help pay for sth 捐款；捐资 SYN **donation**： **~ (to sth)** *to **make a contribution** to charity* 给慈善事业捐款 ◇ *a substantial contribution* 一笔数额相当大的捐款 ◇ *All contributions will be gratefully received.* 我们对所有捐资表示感谢。◇ **~ (toward(s) sth/doing sth)** *valuable contributions towards the upkeep of the cathedral* 对维修大教堂很重要的捐资 **2** [C] **~ (to sth)** a sum of money that you pay regularly to your employer or the government in order to pay for benefits such as health insurance, a pension, etc.（给雇主或政府用作医疗保险、养老金等津贴的）定期缴款： *monthly contributions to the pension scheme* 养老金计划的每月分摊款额 ➲ SYNONYMS AT PAYMENT **3** [C, usually sing.] an action or a service that helps to cause or increase sth 贡献；促成作用： **~ (to sth)** *He **made a** very positive **contribution** to the success of the project.* 他对项目的成功作出了非常积极的贡献。◇ *the car's contribution to the greenhouse effect* 汽车对加剧温室效应所起的作用 ◇ **~ (toward(s) sth/doing sth)** *These measures would make a valuable contribution towards reducing industrial accidents.* 这些措施将会对减少工业事故起重要的作用。 **4** [C] **~ (to sth)** an item that forms part of a book, magazine, broadcast, discussion, etc.（书、杂志、广播、讨论等部分内容的）一则，一条，稿件： *an important contribution to the debate* 这次辩论一项重要的内容 ◇ *All contributions for the May issue must be received by Friday.* 所有要在五月这一期发表的稿件必须在星期五以前寄到。 **5** [U] **~ (to sth)** the act of giving sth, especially money, to help a person or an organization 捐赠；捐助；（尤指）捐款： *We rely entirely on voluntary contribution.* 我们全靠自愿捐赠。

con·tribu·tor AW /kənˈtrɪbjətə(r)/ *noun* **1 ~ (to sth)** a person who writes articles for a magazine or a book, or who talks on a radio or television programme or at a meeting（杂志或书的）撰稿人，投稿人；（电台、电视节目中的）嘉宾；（会议的）发言人 **2 ~ (to sth)** a person or thing that provides money to help pay for sth, or support sth 捐款者；捐赠者；作出贡献者： *Older people are important contributors to the economy.* 老一辈人为发展经济作出了重要贡献。 **3 ~ (to sth)** something that helps to cause sth 促成物： *Sulphur dioxide is a pollutant and a major contributor to acid rain.* 二氧化硫是一种污染物，并且是形成酸雨的主要因素。

con·tribu·tory /kənˈtrɪbjətəri; NAmE -tɔːri/ *adj.* [usually before noun] **1** helping to cause sth 促成的；促进的；起作用的： *Alcohol is a **contributory factor** in 10% of all road accidents.* 所有交通事故中有 10% 是酒后驾车造成的。 **2** involving payments from the people who will benefit 需要受益人付钱的： *a **contributory** pension **scheme/plan*** (= paid for by both employers and employees) 由雇主与雇员共同出资的养老金计划 OPP **non-contributory**

con·trite /kənˈtraɪt; BrE also ˈkɒntraɪt/ *adj.* (*formal*) very sorry for sth bad that you have done 深感懊悔的；痛悔的 ▶ **con·trite·ly** *adv.* **con·tri·tion** /kənˈtrɪʃn/ *noun* [U]: *a look of contrition* 追悔莫及的神色

con·triv·ance /kənˈtraɪvəns/ *noun* (*formal*) **1** [C, U] (*usually disapproving*) something that sb has done or written that does not seem natural; the fact of seeming artificial 非自然之物；人工产物；矫揉造作： *The film is spoilt by unrealistic contrivances of plot.* 这部电影被不实际的牵强情节给毁了。◇ *The story is told with a complete absence of contrivance.* 这故事讲得毫不矫揉造作。 **2** [C] a clever or complicated device or tool made for a particular purpose 精巧（或复杂）的装置；专用工具 **3** [C, U] a clever plan or trick; the act of using a clever plan or trick 计谋；圈套；采用计谋（或圈套）： *an ingenious contrivance to get her to sign the document without reading it* 使她未经过目就签署文件的妙计

con·trive /kənˈtraɪv/ *verb* (*formal*) **1 ~ to do sth** to manage to do sth despite difficulties（不顾困难而）设法做到： *She contrived to spend a couple of hours with him every Sunday evening.* 每周星期日晚上她都设法与他待上几个小时。 **2 ~ sth** to succeed in making sth happen despite difficulties（克服困难）促成某事： *I decided to contrive a meeting between the two of them.* 我决定设法让他们双方见上一面。 **3 ~ sth** to think of or make sth, for example a plan or a machine, in a clever way 巧妙地策划；精巧地制造（如机器）： *They contrived a plan to defraud the company.* 他们精心策划要欺诈那家公司。

con·trived /kənˈtraɪvd/ *adj.* (*disapproving*) planned in advance and not natural or genuine; written or arranged in a way that is not natural or realistic 预谋的；不自然的；人为的；做作的： *a contrived situation* 人为的状况 ◇ *The book's happy ending seemed contrived.* 这部书大团圆的结局读来让人感到不真实。

con·trol /kənˈtrəʊl; NAmE kənˈtroʊl/ *noun, verb*

■ ***noun***

• **POWER** 权力 **1** [U] **~ (of/over sb/sth)** the power to make decisions about how a country, an area, an organization, etc. is run（对国家、地区、机构等的）管理权，控制权，支配权： *The party is expecting to **gain control of** the council in the next election.* 该党期待着在下次选举中获得对地方议会的控制权。◇ *The Democrats will probably **lose control of** Congress.* 民主党很可能失去对国会的控制。◇ *A military junta **took control of the country**.* 政变上台的军政府接管了这个国家。◇ *The city is **in the control of** enemy forces.* 那座城市现处于敌军的控制之下。◇ *The city is **under enemy control**.* 那座城市现处于敌人的控制之下。 **2** [U] **~ (of/over sb/sth)** the ability to make sb/sth do what you want 控制（或操纵）能力： *The teacher **had no control** over the children.* 那位老师管不住学生。◇ *She struggled to **keep control of** her voice.* 她竭力控制住自己的声音。◇ *She **lost control** of her car on the ice.* 她在冰上开车失去了控制。◇ *He got so angry he **lost control*** (= shouted and said or did things he would not normally do). 他气得失去了自制。◇ *Owing to **circumstances beyond our control**, the flight to Rome has been cancelled.* 由于出现了我们无法控制的情况，飞往罗马的航班已被取消。◇ *The coach made the team work hard on ball control* (= in a ball game). 教练让全队努力练习控球。 ➲ SEE ALSO SELF-CONTROL

• **LIMITING/MANAGING** 限制；管理 **3** [U, C] **~ (of/on sth)** (often in compounds 常构成复合词) the act of restricting, limiting or managing sth; a method of doing this 限制；限定；约束；管理；管制： *traffic control* 交通管制 ◇ *talks on arms control* 军备控制谈判 ◇ *government controls on trade and industry* 政府对工商业的管理 ◇ *A new advance has been made in the control of malaria.* 在控制疟疾方面已取得新的进展。◇ *Price controls on food were ended.* 对食物价格的控制已告结束。◇ *a pest control officer* 虫害防治员 ➲ SEE ALSO BIRTH CONTROL, QUALITY CONTROL ➲ SYNONYMS AT LIMIT

• **IN MACHINE** 机器 **4** [C, usually pl.] the switches and buttons, etc. that you use to operate a machine or a vehicle（机器或车辆的）操纵装置，开关，按钮： *the controls of an aircraft* 飞机的操纵装置 ◇ *the control panel* 控制面板 ◇ *the volume control of a CD player* 激光唱片机的音量调节器 ◇ *The co-pilot was **at the controls** when the plane landed.* 副驾驶员操纵着飞机着陆。 ➲ SEE ALSO REMOTE CONTROL

• **IN EXPERIMENT** 实验 **5** [C] (*specialist*) a person, thing or group used as a standard of comparison for checking the results of a scientific experiment; an experiment whose result is known, used for checking working methods 对照标准；（检验工作方法的）参照实验： *One group was treated with the new drug, and the **control group** was given a sugar pill.* 一组采用新药治疗，而对照检验组服用的

C

则是糖丸。

• **PLACE** 地点 **6** [sing.] a place where orders are given or where checks are made; the people who work in this place 指挥（或检查、控制）站；指挥（或检查、控制）人员： *air traffic control* 空中交通管制中心 ◇ *We went through passport control and into the departure lounge.* 我们通过护照检查站进入了候机大厅。 ◇ *This is Mission Control calling the space shuttle Discovery.* 地面指挥中心现在呼叫航天飞机"发现号"。

• **ON COMPUTER** 计算机 **7** [U] (*also* **con'trol key** [sing.]) (on a computer keyboard) a key that you press when you want to perform a particular operation （键盘上的）控制键 ⮊ **WORDFINDER NOTE** AT KEYBOARD

IDM **be in control (of sth)** **1** to direct or manage an organization, an area or a situation 掌管，管理，控制，操纵（某机构、地区或局势）： *He's reached retiring age, but he's still firmly in control.* 他虽然已到退休年龄，但仍大权在握。 ◇ *There has been some violence after the match, but the police are now in control of the situation.* 比赛后发生了一些暴力事件，但是现在警方已控制了局势。 **2** to be able to organize your life well and keep calm 处之泰然；安之若素： *In spite of all her family problems, she's really in control.* 她虽然家庭问题重重，却能完全处之泰然。 **be/get/run/etc. out of con'trol** to be or become impossible to manage or to control 无法管理；失去控制： *The children are completely out of control since their father left.* 这些孩子自他们的父亲离开后就无法无天了。 ◇ *A truck ran out of control on the hill.* 一辆卡车在山上失去了控制。 **be under con'trol** to be being dealt with successfully 被控制住；处于控制之下： *Don't worry—everything's under control!* 别担心，一切都控制住了！ **bring/get/keep sth under con'trol** to succeed in dealing with sth so that it does not cause any damage or hurt anyone 控制得住，抑制得住（从而不造成损害）： *It took two hours to bring the fire under control.* 花了两个小时才控制住火势。 ◇ *Please keep your dog under control!* 请管好你的狗！

■ *verb* **(-ll-)**

• **HAVE POWER** 拥有权力 **1** **~ sb/sth** to have power over a person, company, country, etc. so that you are able to decide what they must do or how it is run 指挥；控制；掌管；支配： *By the age of 21 he controlled the company.* 他 21 岁就掌管了公司。 ◇ *The whole territory is now controlled by the army.* 现在全境都在军队的控制之下。 ◇ *Can't you control your children?* 你就不能管管你这些孩子？

• **LIMIT/MANAGE** 限制；管理 **2** to limit sth or make it happen in a particular way 限制；限定： **~ sth** *government attempts to control immigration* 政府试图限制移民的措施 ◇ *Many biological processes are controlled by hormones.* 许多生物变化过程都是由激素控制的。 ◇ **~ what/how, etc....** *Parents should control what their kids watch on television.* 父母应该限定孩子看什么样的电视节目。 **3** **~ sth** to stop sth from spreading or getting worse 阻止蔓延（或恶化）： *Firefighters are still trying to control the blaze.* 消防队员仍在尽力控制火势的蔓延。 ◇ *She was given drugs to control the pain.* 给她服用了镇痛药。

• **MACHINE** 机器 **4** **~ sth** to make sth, such as a machine or system, work in the way that you want it to 操纵，控制（机器或系统等）： *This knob controls the volume.* 此旋钮调节音量。 ◇ *The traffic lights are controlled by a central computer.* 交通信号灯由中心计算机控制。

• **STAY CALM** 保持镇静 **5** to manage to make yourself remain calm, even though you are upset or angry 抑制；克制： **~ yourself** *I was so furious I couldn't control myself and I hit him.* 我气得无法自制，就打了他。 ◇ **~ sth** *He was finding it difficult to control his feelings.* 他觉得很难克制住自己的感情。 ⮊ **MORE LIKE THIS** 36, page R29

con'trol freak *noun* (*informal, disapproving*) a person who always wants to be in control of their own and others' lives, and to organize how things are done 好多管事的人；爱指挥别人的人

con·trol·lable /kən'trəʊləbl; *NAmE* -'troʊ-/ *adj.* that can be controlled 可控制（或管理、操纵、支配）的

con·trolled /kən'trəʊld; *NAmE* -'troʊld/ *adj.* **1** done or arranged in a very careful way 十分小心完成的；精心安排的： *a controlled explosion* 控制爆破 ◇ *a controlled environment* 受到控制的生态环境 **2** limited, or managed by law or by rules （受法律或规则）限制的，控制的，管制的： *controlled airspace* 管制空域 **3** **-controlled** (in compounds 构成复合词) managed by a particular group, or in a particular way （受某团体或用某种方式）管理的，控制的，操纵的： *a British-controlled company* 英资公司 ◇ *computer-controlled systems* 用计算机控制的系统 **4** remaining calm and not getting angry or upset 保持冷静的；克制的： *She remained quiet and controlled.* 她沉默不语保持克制。 ⮊ COMPARE UNCONTROLLED

con,trolled e'conomy *noun* (*economics* 经) a type of economic system in which a government controls its country's industries and decides what goods should be produced and in what amounts 管制经济（由政府控制国家工业并决定产品的种类与数量）

con,trolled 'substance *noun* (*specialist*) an illegal drug 受管制药品；毒品： *to be arrested for possession of a controlled substance* 因藏有毒品而被捕

con·trol·ler /kən'trəʊlə(r); *NAmE* -'troʊ-/ *noun* **1** a person who manages or directs sth, especially a large organization or part of an organization （尤指大型机构或部门的）管理者，控制者，指挥者 ⮊ SEE ALSO AIR TRAFFIC CONTROLLER **2** (*specialist*) a device that controls or REGULATES a machine or part of a machine （机器或部件的）控制器，调节器： *a temperature controller* 温控器 **3** (*also* **comp·trol·ler**) a person who is in charge of the financial accounts of a business company （公司的）财务总管

con,trolling 'interest *noun* [usually sing.] the fact of owning enough shares in a company to be able to make decisions about what the company should do 控制股权

con'trol tower *noun* a building at an airport from which the movements of aircraft are controlled （机场的）指挥塔台，控制塔，指挥调度台

con·tro·ver·sial **AW** /ˌkɒntrə'vɜːʃl; *NAmE* ˌkɑːntrə'vɜːrʃl/ *adj.* causing a lot of angry public discussion and disagreement 引起争论的；有争议的： *a* ***highly controversial*** *topic* 颇有争议的话题 ◇ *a controversial plan to build a new road* 有争议的修建新道路计划 ◇ *Winston Churchill and Richard Nixon were both controversial figures.* 温斯顿·丘吉尔和理查德·尼克松都是有争议的人物。 **OPP** **non-controversial, uncontroversial** ▸ **con·tro·ver·sial·ly** **AW** *adv.*

con·tro·versy **AW** /'kɒntrəvɜːsi; *NAmE* 'kɑːntrəvɜːrsi; *BrE also* kən'trɒvəsi/ *noun* [U, C] (*pl.* **-ies**) **~ (over/about/surrounding sb/sth)** public discussion and argument about sth that many people strongly disagree about, disapprove of, or are shocked by （公开的）争论，争议，论战： *to* ***arouse/cause controversy*** 引起争论 ◇ *a bitter controversy* ***over/about*** *the site of the new airport* 有关新机场选址的激烈争论 ◇ *the controversy surrounding his latest movie* 围绕他最近一部电影的争论 ◇ *The President resigned amid considerable controversy.* 总统在激烈的争议中辞职了。

con·tro·vert /ˌkɒntrə'vɜːt; *NAmE* 'kɑːntrəvɜːrt/ *verb* **~ sth** (*formal*) to say or prove that sth is not true 驳斥；反驳 **SYN** **refute** ⮊ SEE ALSO INCONTROVERTIBLE

con·tu·ma·cious /ˌkɒntju'meɪʃəs; *NAmE* ˌkɑːntu-/ *adj.* (*old use* or *law* 律) lacking respect for authority 藐视权威的；违抗的；不服从的

con·tu·sion /kən'tjuːʒn; *NAmE* -'tuː-/ *noun* [C, U] (*medical* 医) an injury to part of the body that does not break the skin 挫伤 **SYN** **bruise**

con·un·drum /kə'nʌndrəm/ *noun* **1** a confusing problem or question that is very difficult to solve 令人迷惑的难题；复杂难解的问题 **2** a question, usually involving a trick with words, that you ask for fun 谜语 **SYN** **riddle**

con·ur·ba·tion /ˌkɒnɜː'beɪʃn; *NAmE* ˌkɑːnɜːr'b-/ *noun* (*formal*) a large area where towns have grown and joined together, often around a city （有卫星城镇的）大都市，集合城市

con·va·lesce /ˌkɒnvəˈles; *NAmE* ˌkɑːn-/ *verb* [I] (*formal*) to spend time getting your health and strength back after an illness 逐步康复；（身体）恢复 SYN **recuperate**: *She is convalescing at home after her operation.* 手术后她正在家休养康复。

con·va·les·cence /ˌkɒnvəˈlesns; *NAmE* ˌkɑːn-/ *noun* [sing., U] a period of time when you get well again after an illness or a medical operation; the process of getting well 康复期；恢复期；康复：*You need four to six weeks' convalescence.* 你需要四至六个星期的康复期。

con·va·les·cent /ˌkɒnvəˈlesnt; *NAmE* ˌkɑːn-/ *adj.* connected with convalescence; in the process of convalescence 康复期的；正在康复的；渐愈的：*a convalescent home* (= a type of hospital where people go to get well after an illness) 康复医院 ◇ *a convalescent child* 逐渐康复的小孩 ▶ **con·va·les·cent** *noun* : *I treated him as a convalescent, not as a sick man.* 我把他当作正在康复的人，而不是病人。

con·vec·tion /kənˈvekʃn/ *noun* [U] (*specialist*) the process in which heat moves through a gas or a liquid as the hotter part rises and the cooler, heavier part sinks（热通过气体或液体的）运流，对流

con·vect·or /kənˈvektə(r)/ (*also* **conˈvector heater**) *noun* a device for heating the air in a room using convection 对流加热器；换流器

con·vene AW /kənˈviːn/ *verb* (*formal*) **1** [T] ~ **sth** to arrange for people to come together for a formal meeting 召集，召开（正式会议）：*to convene a meeting* 召开会议 ◇ *A Board of Inquiry was convened immediately after the accident.* 事故后立即成立了调查委员会。 **2** [I] to come together for a formal meeting （为正式会议而）聚集，集合：*The committee will convene at 11.30 next Thursday.* 委员会将在下星期四上午 11:30 开会。 ⮕ WORDFINDER NOTE AT MEETING

con·vener (*also* **con·venor**) /kənˈviːnə(r)/ *noun* **1** a person who arranges meetings of groups or committees 会议召集人 **2** (*BrE*) a senior official of a trade/labor union at a factory or other place of work（工厂或基层单位的）资深工会领导人

con·veni·ence /kənˈviːniəns/ *noun* **1** [U] the quality of being useful, easy or suitable for sb 方便；适宜；便利：*We have provided seats **for the convenience** of our customers.* 为方便顾客我们备有座位。 ◇ ***For** (**the sake of**) **convenience**, the two groups have been treated as one in this report.* 为方便起见，这两个组在本报告中被视为一组。 ◇ *In this resort you can enjoy all the **comfort and convenience** of modern tourism.* 在这个度假胜地你可享受所有现代旅游的舒适与便利。 ⮕ COMPARE INCONVENIENCE *n.* ⮕ SEE ALSO FLAG OF CONVENIENCE, MARRIAGE OF CONVENIENCE **2** [C] something that is useful and can make things easier or quicker to do, or more comfortable 便利的事物（或设施）；方便的用具：*It was a great convenience to have the school so near.* 学校这么近真是太方便了。 ◇ *The house had all the modern conveniences* (= central heating, etc.) *that were unusual at that time.* 这座房子拥有在当时并不常见的所有现代化设施。 ⮕ SEE ALSO PUBLIC CONVENIENCE

IDM **at sb's conˈvenience** (*formal*) at a time or a place which is suitable for sb 在（某人）方便时；在（某人）适宜的地点：*Can you telephone me at your convenience to arrange a meeting?* 你能不能在你方便时给我来个电话，安排见一次面？ ⮕ MORE AT EARLY *adj.*

conˈvenience food *noun* [C, U] food that you buy frozen or in a box or can, that you can prepare and cook very quickly and easily 方便食品；便利食品

conˈvenience store *noun* (*especially NAmE*) a shop/store that sells food, newspapers, etc. and often stays open 24 hours a day 便利店（常为 24 小时营业）

con·veni·ent /kənˈviːniənt/ *adj.* **1** ~ (**for sb/sth**) useful, easy or quick to do; not causing problems 实用的；便利的；方便的；省事的：*It is very convenient to pay by credit card.* 用信用卡付款非常方便。 ◇ *You'll find these meals quick and convenient to prepare.* 你会发现准备这样的饭既快又省事。 ◇ *Fruit is a convenient source of vitamins and energy.* 水果是维生素和能量的便利来源。 ◇ *A bicycle is often more convenient than a car in towns.* 在城镇骑自行车常常比开车更方便。 ◇ *I can't see him now—it isn't convenient.* 我现在不便见他。 ◇ *I'll call back at a more convenient time.* 在比较方便的时候我会回电话的。 ◇ (*disapproving*) *He used his wife's birthday as a convenient excuse for not going to the meeting.* 他说要给妻子过生日，利用这个借口，就不去参加会议了。 **2** near to a particular place; easy to get to 附近的；近便的；容易到达的：(*BrE*) ~ (**for sth**) *The house is very convenient for several schools.* 这座房子离几所学校很近。 ◇ (*NAmE*) ~ (**to sth**) *The hotel is convenient to downtown.* 这家旅馆离市中心很近。 OPP **inconvenient** ▶ **con·veni·ent·ly** *adv.* : *The report can be conveniently divided into three main sections.* 这份报告不用费事就可划分为三个主要部分。 ◇ *The hotel is conveniently situated close to the beach.* 那家旅馆坐落在海滩附近，非常方便。 ◇ *She conveniently forgot to mention that her husband would be at the party, too* (= because it suited her not to say). 她没有提她丈夫也要参加聚会，她觉得还是不提为好。

con·venor = CONVENER

con·vent /ˈkɒnvənt; *NAmE* ˈkɑːnvent; -vənt/ *noun* **1** a building in which NUNS (= members of a female religious community) live together 女隐修院；女修道院 ⮕ COLLOCATIONS AT RELIGION **2** (*also* ˈ**convent school**) a school run by NUNS 女修会开办的学校

con·ven·tion AW /kənˈvenʃn/ *noun* **1** [C, U] the way in which sth is done that most people in a society expect and consider to be polite or the right way to do it 习俗；常规；惯例：*social conventions* 社会习俗 ◇ ***By convention** the deputy leader was always a woman.* 按惯例，这一领导职务的副职总是由女性担任。 ◇ *She is a young woman who enjoys flouting conventions.* 她是一位喜欢无视传统习俗的年轻女子。 ⮕ WORDFINDER NOTE AT SOCIETY **2** [C] a large meeting of the members of a profession, a political party, etc. （从业者、政党成员等的）大会，集会 SYN **conference**: *to hold a convention* 召开大会 ◇ *the Democratic Party Convention* (= to elect a candidate for president) 民主党代表大会（选出总统候选人） **3** [C] an official agreement between countries or leaders （国家或首脑间的）公约，协定，协议：*the Geneva convention* 日内瓦公约 ◇ *the United Nations convention on the rights of the child* 联合国儿童权利公约 **4** [C, U] a traditional method or style in literature, art or the theatre （文学、艺术或戏剧的）传统手法，传统风格：*the conventions of Greek tragedy* 希腊悲剧的传统手法

con·ven·tion·al AW /kənˈvenʃənl/ *adj.* **1** (*often disapproving*) tending to follow what is done or considered acceptable by society in general; normal and ordinary, and perhaps not very interesting 依照惯例的；遵循习俗的；墨守成规的；普通平凡的：***conventional behaviour/morality*** 循规蹈矩的行为；传统的道德规范 ◇ *She's very conventional in her views.* 她的观点很守旧。 OPP **unconventional** **2** [usually before noun] following what is traditional or the way sth has been done for a long time 传统的；习惯的：***conventional methods/approaches*** 传统方法 ◇ ***conventional medicine*** 传统医学 ◇ *It's not a hotel, in the conventional sense, but rather a whole village turned into a hotel.* 这不是一家传统意义上的旅馆，而是整个村庄变身而成的度假村。 ◇ *You can use a microwave or cook it in a conventional oven.* 你可以用微波炉或传统烤箱烹制。 OPP **unconventional** **3** [usually before noun] (especially of weapons 尤指武器) not nuclear 非核的；常规的：***conventional forces/weapons*** 常规部队 / 武器 ◇ *a conventional power station* (= using oil or coal as fuel, rather than nuclear power) 常规电站 ▶ **con·ven·tion·al·ity** /kənˌvenʃəˈnæləti/ *noun* [U] **con·ven·tion·al·ly** AW /-ʃənəli/ *adv.* : *conventionally dressed* 衣着传统的 ◇ *conventionally grown food* (= grown according to conventional methods) 用传统方法种植的粮食 IDM SEE WISDOM

con·ven·tion·eer /kən,venʃə'nɪə(r); *NAmE* -'nɪr/ *noun* (*NAmE*) a person who is attending a convention 与会者；大会代表

con·verge /kən'vɜːdʒ; *NAmE* -'vɜːrdʒ/ *verb* **1** [I] ~ (**on...**) (of people or vehicles 人或车辆) to move towards a place from different directions and meet 汇集；聚集；集中：*Thousands of supporters converged on London for the rally.* 成千上万的支持者从四面八方汇聚伦敦参加集会。**2** [I] (of two or more lines, paths, etc. 多条线、小路等) to move towards each other and meet at a point（向某一点）相交，会合：*There was a signpost where the two paths converged.* 两条小路的相交处有一路标。**3** [I] if ideas, policies, aims, etc. **converge**, they become very similar or the same（思想、政策、目标等）十分相似，相同 OPP **diverge** ▶ **con·ver·gent** /-dʒənt/ *adj.*：*convergent lines/opinions* 相交的线条；趋于一致的意见 **con·ver·gence** *noun* [U]

con·ver·sant /kən'vɜːsnt; *NAmE* -'vɜːrs-/ *adj.* ~ **with sth** (*formal*) knowing about sth; familiar with sth 通晓的；熟悉的：*You need to become fully conversant with the company's procedures.* 你得对公司的程序了如指掌。

con·ver·sa·tion 🔑 /,kɒnvə'seɪʃn; *NAmE* ,kɑːnvər's-/ *noun* [C, U] ~ (**with sb**) (**about sth**) an informal talk involving a small group of people or only two; the activity of talking in this way（非正式）交谈，谈话：*a telephone conversation* 电话交谈 ◇ *I had a long conversation with her the other day.* 前几天我与她作了一次长谈。◇ *The main* ***topic of conversation*** *was the likely outcome of the election.* 谈话的主题是选举可能的结果。◇ *Don was* ***deep in conversation*** *with the girl on his right.* 唐与他右边的女孩在专心交谈。◇ (*BrE*) *to* ***get into conversation*** *with sb* 开始与某人攀谈 ◇ (*NAmE*) *to* ***get into a conversation*** *with sb* 开始与某人攀谈 ◇ *The conversation turned to gardening.* 话题转到了园艺上。◇ *I tried to* ***make conversation*** (= to speak in order to appear polite). 我设法找些话题。

➲ SYNONYMS AT DISCUSSION ➲ EXPRESS YOURSELF AT OPEN

con·ver·sa·tion·al /,kɒnvə'seɪʃənl; *NAmE* ,kɑːnvər's-/ *adj.* **1** not formal; as used in conversation 非正式的；用于交谈的；口语的 SYN **colloquial**：*a casual and conversational tone* 不拘礼节的谈话语气 ◇ *I learnt conversational Spanish at evening classes.* 我在夜校学过西班牙语会话。**2** [only before noun] connected with conversation 交谈的；谈话的；会话的：*Men have a more direct conversational style.* 男人交谈比较直截了当。▶ **con·ver·sa·tion·al·ly** *adv.*：*'Have you been here long?' he asked conversationally.* "你来这里很久了吗？" 他攀谈着问道。

con·ver·sa·tion·al·ist /,kɒnvə'seɪʃənəlɪst; *NAmE* ,kɑːnvər's-/ *noun* a person who is good at talking to others, especially in an informal way 健谈的人；能聊的人

conver'sation piece *noun* **1** an object that is talked about a lot because it is unusual（因不寻常而成为）话题；谈资 **2** (*art* 美术) a type of painting in which a group of people are shown in the countryside or in a home 人物风俗画；乡村（或室内）风情画

conver'sation stopper *noun* (*informal*) an unexpected or shocking remark, which people do not know how to reply to 噎人的话；令人瞠目结舌的话

con·verse[1] /kən'vɜːs; *NAmE* -'vɜːrs/ *verb* [I] ~ (**with sb**) (*formal*) to have a conversation with sb 交谈；谈话

➲ MORE LIKE THIS 21, page R27

con·verse[2] AW /'kɒnvɜːs; *NAmE* 'kɑːnvɜːrs/ *noun* **the converse** [sing.] (*formal*) the opposite or reverse of a fact or statement 相反的事物；（事实或陈述的）反面：*Building new roads increases traffic and the converse is equally true: reducing the number and size of roads means less traffic.* 修筑新的道路会增加交通流量，反过来也是同样的道理：减少道路的数量和规模就意味着减少交通流量。

➲ MORE LIKE THIS 21, page R27 ▶ **con·verse** *adj.*：*the converse effect* 相反的效果

con·verse·ly AW /'kɒnvɜːsli; *NAmE* 'kɑːnvɜːrs-/ *adv.* (*formal*) in a way that is the opposite or reverse of sth 相反地；反过来：*You can add the fluid to the powder, or, conversely, the powder to the fluid.* 可把液体加入粉末，或者相反，把粉末加入液体。

con·ver·sion AW /kən'vɜːʃn; *NAmE* -'vɜːrʒn; -ʃn/ *noun* **1** [U, C] ~ (**from sth**) (**into/to sth**) the act or process of changing sth from one form, use or system to another 转变；转换；转化：*the conversion of farm buildings into family homes* 农场建筑物改建为家庭住宅 ◇ *No conversion from analogue to digital data is needed.* 没有必要把模拟转换为数字数据。◇ *a metric conversion table* (= showing how to change METRIC amounts into or out of another system) 公制换算表 ◇ *a firm which specializes in house conversions* (= turning large houses into several smaller flats/apartments) 专营房屋改建的公司 **2** [U, C] ~ (**from sth**) (**to sth**) the process or experience of changing your religion or beliefs（宗教或信仰的）改变；皈依；归附：*the conversion of the Anglo-Saxons by Christian missionaries* 基督教传教士使盎格鲁 — 撒克逊人的信仰改变 ◇ *his conversion from Judaism to Christianity* 他由犹太教改信基督教 **3** [C] (in RUGBY and AMERICAN FOOTBALL 橄榄球和美式足球) a way of scoring extra points after scoring a TRY or a TOUCHDOWN（持球过对方球门线触地或达阵后的）附加得分 **4** [C] **barn/loft** ~ a building or room that has been changed so that it can be used for a different purpose, especially for living in（尤指为居住而）改建的房屋

con'version van (*also* **'van conversion**) *noun* (*US*) a vehicle in which the back part behind the driver has been arranged as a living space 改装旅行车

con·vert 🔑 AW *verb, noun*

■ *verb* /kən'vɜːt; *NAmE* -'vɜːrt/ **1** 🔑 [T, I] to change or make sth change from one form, purpose, system, etc. to another（使）转变，转换，转化：~ **sth** (**into sth**) *The hotel is going to be converted into a nursing home.* 那家旅馆将被改建成私人疗养院。◇ *What rate will I get if I convert my dollars into euros?* 如果我把美元兑换成欧元，汇率是多少？◇ ~ (**from sth**) (**into/to sth**) *We've converted from oil to gas central heating.* 我们已经把中央供热系统由燃油改成了燃气。**2** 🔑 [I] ~ **into/to sth** to be able to be changed from one form, purpose, or system to another 可转变为；可变换成：*a sofa that converts into a bed* 可改作床用的沙发 **3** 🔑 [I, T] to change or make sb change their religion or beliefs（使）改变（宗教或信仰）；（使）皈依，归附：~ (**from sth**) (**to sth**) *He converted from Christianity to Islam.* 他由基督教改信伊斯兰教。◇ ~ **sb** (**from sth**) (**to sth**) *She was soon converted to the socialist cause.* 她不久便转而献身于社会主义事业了。**4** [I, T] to change an opinion, a habit, etc. 改变（观点、习惯等）：~ (**from sth**) **to sth** *I've converted to organic food.* 我改吃有机食物了。◇ ~ **sb** (**from sth**) (**to sth**) *I didn't use to like opera but my husband has converted me.* 我过去不喜欢歌剧，但我丈夫改变了我。**5** [T] ~ **sth** (in RUGBY and AMERICAN FOOTBALL 橄榄球和美式足球) to score extra points after a TRY or a TOUCHDOWN（在持球过对方球门线触地或达阵后）获得附加分 IDM SEE PREACH

■ *noun* /'kɒnvɜːt; *NAmE* 'kɑːnvɜːrt/ ~ (**from sth**) (**to sth**) a person who has changed their religion, beliefs or opinions 改变宗教（或信仰、观点）的人；皈依者：*a convert to Islam* 改信伊斯兰教的人 ◇ *converts from other faiths* 来自其他宗教信仰的皈依者 ◇ *a* ***convert to the cause*** 一个转而支持这项事业的人

con·vert·er (*also* **con·ver·tor**) /kən'vɜːtə(r); *NAmE* -'vɜːrt-/ *noun* **1** a person or thing that converts sth 使发生转化的人（或物）；转换器：*a catalytic converter* 催化转换器 **2** (*physics* 物) a device for converting ALTERNATING CURRENT into DIRECT CURRENT or the other way around 变流器 **3** (*physics* 物) a device for converting a radio signal from one FREQUENCY to another（改变无线电信号的）变频器

con·vert·ible AW /kən'vɜːtəbl; *NAmE* -'vɜːrt-/ *adj., noun*

■ *adj.* that can be changed to a different form or use 可改变的；可转换的；可兑换的：*a convertible sofa* (= one that can be used as a bed) 可当作床用的沙发 ◇ *convertible currencies* (= ones that can be exchanged for those of other

countries) 可兑换的货币 ◇ **~ into/to sth** *The bonds are convertible into ordinary shares.* 债券可兑换为普通股。 ▶ **con·vert·ibil·ity** /kənˌvɜːtəˈbɪləti; *NAmE* -ˌvɜːrt-/ *noun* [U]
■ *noun* a car with a roof that can be folded down or taken off 活动顶篷式汽车 ➲ VISUAL VOCAB PAGE V56

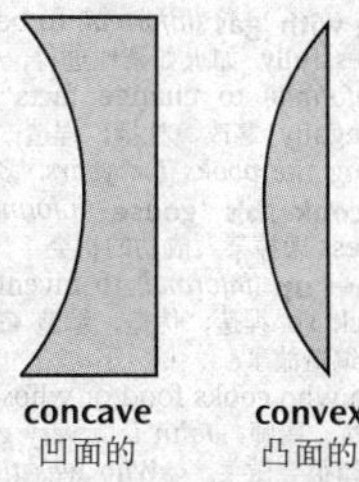

con·vex /ˈkɒnveks; *NAmE* ˈkɑːn-/ *adj.* (of an outline or a surface 外形或表面) curving out 凸出的；凸面的： *a convex lens/mirror* 凸透镜；凸镜 OPP **concave** ▶ **con·vex·ity** /kɒnˈveksəti; *NAmE* kɑːnˈv-/ *noun* [U]

con·vey /kənˈveɪ/ *verb* **1** to make ideas, feelings, etc. known to sb 表达，传递（思想、感情等） SYN **communicate**： **~ sth** *Colours like red convey a sense of energy and strength.* 红色之类的颜色可给人以充满活力与力量的感觉。 ◇ **~ sth to sb** (*formal*) *Please convey my apologies to your wife.* 请向你的妻子转达我的歉意。 ◇ **~ how, what, etc....** *He tried desperately to convey how urgent the situation was.* 他不顾一切地试图说明情况是多么紧急。 ◇ **~ that...** *She did not wish to convey that they were all at fault.* 她不愿表示出他们人人都有错。 **2 ~ sb/sth (from...) (to...)** (*formal*) to take, carry or transport sb/sth from one place to another 传送；运送；输送： *Pipes convey hot water from the boiler to the radiators.* 管道把热水从锅炉输送到暖气片。

con·vey·ance /kənˈveɪəns/ *noun* **1** [U] (*formal*) the process of taking sb/sth from one place to another 传送；运送；输送： *the conveyance of goods by rail* 由火车运输货物 **2** [C] (*formal*) a vehicle 运载（或交通）工具；车辆： *horse-drawn conveyances* 马车 **3** [C] (*law* 律) a legal document that moves property from one owner to another 财产转让证书

con·vey·an·cer /kənˈveɪənsə(r)/ *noun* a lawyer who is an expert in conveyancing 财产转让业务人

con·vey·an·cing /kənˈveɪənsɪŋ/ *noun* [U] (*law* 律) the branch of law concerned with moving property from one owner to another 财产转让（事务）

con·vey·or /kənˈveɪə(r)/ *noun* **1** = CONVEYOR BELT **2** (*also* **con·vey·er**) (*formal*) a person or thing that carries sth or makes sth known 运送者；传送者；传播者；传达者

con'veyor belt (*also* **con·vey·or**) *noun* a continuous moving band used for transporting goods from one part of a building to another, for example products in a factory or suitcases in an airport 传送带，输送带（如输送工厂的产品或机场的行李）

con·vict *verb, noun*
■ *verb* /kənˈvɪkt/ [often passive] **~ sb (of sth)** to decide and state officially in court that sb is guilty of a crime 定罪；宣判…有罪： *a convicted murderer* 已定罪的谋杀犯 ◇ *He was convicted of fraud.* 他被判犯有诈骗罪。 OPP **acquit** ➲ COLLOCATIONS AT JUSTICE
■ *noun* /ˈkɒnvɪkt; *NAmE* ˈkɑːn-/ (*also informal* **con**) a person who has been found guilty of a crime and sent to prison 已决犯；服刑囚犯： *an escaped convict* 越狱犯 ➲ MORE LIKE THIS 21, page R27

con·vic·tion /kənˈvɪkʃn/ *noun* **1** [C, U] **~ (for sth)** the act of finding sb guilty of a crime in court; the fact of having been found guilty 判罪；定罪；证明有罪： *She has six previous convictions for theft.* 她有六次盗窃前科。 ◇ *He plans to appeal against his conviction.* 他不服判决，准备上诉。 ◇ *an offence which carries, on conviction, a sentence of not more than five years' imprisonment* 定罪后可判处五年或五年以下监禁的罪行 OPP **acquittal** ➲ COLLOCATIONS AT JUSTICE **2** [C, U] **~ (that...)** a strong opinion or belief 坚定的看法（或信念）： *strong* ***political/moral convictions*** 坚定不移的政治 / 道德信念 ◇ *She was motivated by deep religious conviction.* 她的行动是出于虔诚的宗教信仰。 ◇ *a conviction that all would be well in the end* 最终一切都会好起来的坚定信念 **3** [U] the feeling or appearance of believing sth strongly and of being sure about it 深信；坚信；坚定；肯定： *'Not true!' she said with conviction.* “不真实！” 她肯定地说道。 ◇ *He said he agreed but his voice lacked conviction.* 他说他赞同，但语气不坚定。 ◇ *The leader's speech in defence of the policy didn't* ***carry much conviction.*** 那位领导人为政策辩护的讲话不是很有说服力。
IDM SEE COURAGE

con·vince 🔑 AW /kənˈvɪns/ *verb* **1** 🔑 to make sb/yourself believe that sth is true 使确信；使相信；使信服： **~ sb/yourself (of sth)** *You'll need to convince them of your enthusiasm for the job.* 你要使他们相信你对这份工作的热忱。 ◇ **~ sb/yourself (that)...** *I'd convinced myself (that) I was right.* 我确信自己是正确的。 **2** 🔑 **~ sb to do sth** to persuade sb to do sth 说服，劝说（某人做某事）： *I've been trying to convince him to see a doctor.* 我一直劝他去看病。 ➲ NOTE AT PERSUADE

con·vinced AW /kənˈvɪnst/ *adj.* **1** [not before noun] completely sure about sth 坚信；深信；确信： *Sam nodded but he didn't look convinced.* 萨姆点了点头，可他看起来并没有信服。 ◇ **~ of sth** *I am convinced of her innocence.* 我坚信她是清白无辜的。 ◇ **~ that...** *I am convinced that she is innocent.* 我坚信她是清白无辜的。 OPP **unconvinced** ➲ SYNONYMS AT SURE **2** [only before noun] believing strongly in a particular religion or set of political ideas 坚信不移的；有坚定宗教信仰（或政治信念）的： *a convinced Christian* 虔诚的基督徒

con·vin·cing AW /kənˈvɪnsɪŋ/ *adj.* that makes sb believe that sth is true 令人信服的；有说服力的： *a* ***convincing argument/explanation/case*** 有说服力的论点 / 解释 / 事例 ◇ *She sounded very convincing to me* (= I believed what she said). 我觉得她的话很有说服力。 ◇ *a* ***convincing victory/win*** (= an easy one) 令人折服的胜利 OPP **unconvincing** ▶ **con·vin·cing·ly** AW *adv.* : *Her case was convincingly argued.* 她的辩词很有说服力。 ◇ *They won convincingly.* 他们赢得令人信服。

con·viv·ial /kənˈvɪviəl/ *adj.* cheerful and friendly in atmosphere or character （气氛或性格）欢快友好的 SYN **sociable**： *a convivial evening/atmosphere* 欢乐的夜晚 / 气氛 ◇ *convivial company* 快乐的伙伴 ▶ **con·vivi·al·ity** /kənˌvɪviˈæləti/ *noun* [U]

con·vo·ca·tion /ˌkɒnvəˈkeɪʃn; *NAmE* ˌkɑːn-/ *noun* (*formal*) **1** [C] a large formal meeting, especially of Church officials or members of a university （尤指教会或大学的）大型正式会议 **2** [U] the act of calling together a convocation 召集会议 **3** [C] (*NAmE*) a ceremony held in a university or college when students receive their degrees （大学的）学位授予典礼，毕业典礼

con·voke /kənˈvəʊk; *NAmE* -ˈvoʊk/ *verb* **~ sb/sth** (*formal*) to gather together a group of people for a formal meeting 召集，召开（会议） SYN **convene**

con·vo·luted /ˈkɒnvəluːtɪd; *NAmE* ˈkɑːn-/ *adj.* **1** extremely complicated and difficult to follow 错综复杂的；晦涩难懂的： *a* ***convoluted argument/explanation*** 晦涩费解的论证 / 阐述 ◇ *a book with a convoluted plot* 情节错综复杂的书 **2** (*formal*) having many twists or curves 盘绕的；弯曲的： *a convoluted coastline* 蜿蜒的海岸线

con·vo·lu·tion /ˌkɒnvəˈluːʃn; *NAmE* ˌkɑːn-/ *noun* [usually pl.] (*formal*) **1** a thing that is very complicated and difficult to follow 错综复杂的东西；晦涩费解的事： *the bizarre convolutions of the story* 那故事错综复杂的离奇情节 **2** a twist or curve, especially one of many （尤指其中之一的）盘绕，弯曲： *the convolutions of the brain* 脑回

con·vol·vu·lus /kən'vɒlvjələs; *NAmE* -'vɑːlv-/ *noun* [C, U] a wild plant with TRIANGULAR leaves and flowers that are shaped like TRUMPETS. It climbs up walls, fences, etc. and twists itself around other plants. 旋花属植物

C

con·voy /'kɒnvɔɪ; *NAmE* 'kɑːn-/ *noun* a group of vehicles or ships travelling together, especially when soldiers or other vehicles travel with them for protection（尤指有士兵护送的）车队，船队： *a* ***convoy of trucks/lorries/freighters*** 被护送的卡车 / 货船队 ◇ *A United Nations* ***aid convoy*** *loaded with food and medicine finally got through to the besieged town.* 一支联合国援助车队载着食物和药物终于抵达了被围困的城镇。

IDM **in 'convoy** (of travelling vehicles 行驶中的车辆) as a group; together 结队；组队： *We drove in convoy because I didn't know the route.* 因为我不熟悉路线，所以我们结队行驶。

con·vulse /kən'vʌls/ *verb* **1** [T, I] ~ **(sb)** **(with sth)** (*rather formal*) to cause a sudden shaking movement in sb's body; to make this movement 使痉挛（或抽筋）；（身体）震动（或抖动）： *A violent shiver convulsed him.* 剧烈的颤抖使他抽搐不已。◇ *His whole body convulsed.* 他全身痉挛。 **2** [T] **be convulsed with laughter, anger, etc.** to be laughing so much, so angry, etc. that you cannot control your movements （因笑、生气等）全身抖动

con·vul·sion /kən'vʌlʃn/ *noun* [usually pl.] (*rather formal*) **1** a sudden shaking movement of the body that cannot be controlled 痉挛；抽搐 SYN **fit**: *The child went into convulsions.* 那孩子全身抽搐起来。 **2** a sudden important change that happens to a country or an organization 动乱；骚动 SYN **upheaval**

con·vul·sive /kən'vʌlsɪv/ *adj.* (of movements or actions 动作或行动) sudden and impossible to control 突然而无法控制的；痉挛的；抽搐的： *a* ***convulsive movement/attack/fit*** 痉挛的动作 / 发作 ◇ *Her breath came in convulsive gasps.* 她突然喘不过气来。 ▶ **con·vul·sive·ly** *adv.*： *weeping convulsively* 抽泣

COO /ˌsiː əʊ 'əʊ; *NAmE* oʊ 'oʊ/ *abbr.* Chief Operations Officer or Chief Operating Officer (the person who manages the day-to-day activities or work of a company or other institution) 首席运营官，营运长（全写为 Chief Operations Officer 或 Chief Operating Officer）

coo /kuː/ *verb, exclamation*

■ *verb* (**coo·ing, cooed, cooed**) **1** [I] when a DOVE¹ (1) or a PIGEON **coos**, it makes a soft low sound （鸽子）咕咕叫 ➲ MORE LIKE THIS 4, page R25 **2** [I, T] (+ **speech**) to say sth in a soft quiet voice, especially to sb you love （尤指对所爱的人）轻柔低语，柔情地说 IDM SEE BILL *v.* ▶ **coo** *noun*

■ *exclamation* (*BrE, old-fashioned, informal*) used to show that you are surprised （表示惊讶）唔，嗬： *Coo, look at him!* 唔，看看他！ ➲ MORE LIKE THIS 2, page R25

ˌco-oc'cur *verb* [I] to occur together or at the same time 同现；共现： *The words 'heavy' and 'rain' co-occur frequently.* * heavy 和 rain 两词经常同时出现。 ▶ **co-oc'currence** *noun* [U]

cooee /'kuːiː/ *exclamation* (*old-fashioned, BrE, informal*) used as a way of attracting sb's attention （用以引起注意）喂，嗨

IDM **within 'cooee (of)** (*AustralE, NZE*) not far (from) （离…）不远；（在…）附近： *There's loads of cheap accommodation within cooee of the airport.* 机场附近有很多便宜住处。

cook 🔑 /kʊk/ *verb, noun*

■ *verb* **1** 🔑 [I, T] to prepare food by heating it, for example by boiling, baking or frying it 烹饪；烹调： *Where did you learn to cook?* 你在哪里学的烹调？ ◇ ~ **sth** *What's the best way to cook trout?* 鳟鱼怎么做最好吃？ ◇ *Who's going to cook supper?* 谁来做晚饭？ ◇ *He cooked lunch for me.* 他给我做了午餐。 ◇ ~ **sb sth** *He cooked me lunch.* 他给我做了午餐。 ➲ COLLOCATIONS AT COOKING ➲ VISUAL VOCAB PAGES V28-31 **2** 🔑 [I] (of food 食物) to be prepared by boiling, baking, frying, etc 煮（或烘烤、煎炸等）： *While the pasta is cooking, prepare the sauce.* 煮意大利面的时候，准备酱汁。 **3** [I] **be cooking** (*informal*) to be planned secretly 密谋；秘密策划： *Everyone is being very secretive—there's something cooking.* 人人都神秘兮兮的，准是在搞什么鬼把戏。

IDM **be cooking with 'gas** (*informal*) to be doing sth very well and successfully 如火如荼地进行；做得起劲 **ˌcook the 'books** (*informal*) to change facts or figures dishonestly or illegally 篡改；杜撰；捏造： *His accountant had been cooking the books for years.* 多年来他的会计师一直在做假账。 **cook sb's 'goose** (*informal*) to ruin sb's chances of success 毁掉某人成功的机会

PHR V **ˌcook sth↔'up** (*informal*) to invent sth, especially in order to trick sb 捏造；伪造；编造 SYN **concoct**: *to cook up a story* 编造故事

■ *noun* 🔑 a person who cooks food or whose job is cooking 做饭的人；炊事员；厨师： *John is a very good cook* (= he cooks well). 约翰很会做菜。 ◇ *Who was the cook* (= who cooked the food)? 谁做的饭菜？ ◇ *She was employed as a cook in a hotel.* 她受雇在一家旅馆做厨师。 ➲ COMPARE CHEF

IDM **too many cooks spoil the 'broth** (*saying*) if too many people are involved in doing sth, it will not be done well 厨师多了烧坏汤；人多手杂反坏事；人多添乱

cook·book /'kʊkbʊk/ (*BrE also* **'cookery book**) *noun* a book that gives instructions on cooking and how to cook individual dishes 烹饪书；烹饪菜谱；食谱

'cook-chill *adj.* [only before noun] (*BrE*) food prepared by the **cook-chill** method is cooked, kept at a low temperature and then heated again （食品）做熟后冷藏备用的

cook·er 🔑 /'kʊkə(r)/ (*BrE*) (*NAmE* **range**) (*also* **stove** *NAmE, BrE*) *noun* a large piece of equipment for cooking food, containing an oven and gas or electric rings on top （带烤箱、燃气炉或电炉的）厨灶，炉具： *a gas cooker* 燃气厨灶 ◇ *an electric cooker* 电灶 ➲ SEE ALSO PRESSURE COOKER

cook·ery /'kʊkəri/ *noun* [U] (*especially BrE*) the art or activity of preparing and cooking food 烹饪术；烹饪；烹调： *a cookery course* 烹饪课程 ◇ *Italian cookery* 意大利烹饪

'cookery book *noun* (*BrE*) = COOKBOOK

cook·house /'kʊkhaʊs/ *noun* an outdoor kitchen, for example in a military camp （如军营中的）户外厨房，露天厨房

cookie 🔑 /'kʊki/ *noun* (*pl.* **-ies**) **1** 🔑 (*especially NAmE*) a small flat sweet cake for one person, usually baked until crisp 曲奇饼： *chocolate chip cookies* 巧克力碎片曲奇 ◇ *a cookie jar* 饼干罐 ➲ COMPARE BISCUIT (1), CRACKER (1) ➲ SEE ALSO FORTUNE COOKIE **2** **smart/tough ~** (*NAmE, informal*) a smart/tough person 精明强干的人；坚强的人 **3** (*computing* 计) a computer file with information in it that is sent to the central SERVER each time a particular person uses a NETWORK or the Internet 小甜饼（用户使用网络或互联网时发给中央服务器信息的信息记录）： *Learn about our cookie policy.* 了解我们的浏览记录 (cookie) 政策。 ➲ WORDFINDER NOTE AT WEBSITE ➲ COLLOCATIONS AT EMAIL IDM SEE WAY *n.*

'cookie cutter *noun, adj.*

■ *noun* (*NAmE*) an object used for cutting biscuits in a particular shape 饼干成型切割刀

■ *adj.* **'cookie-cutter** [only before noun] (*NAmE, disapproving*) having no special characteristics; not original in any way 千篇一律的；俗套的： *Handmade goods appeal to those who are tired of cookie-cutter products.* 手工制品受到那些已厌倦划一产品的人的欢迎。

'cookie jar *noun* (*NAmE*) a container for biscuits 饼干罐

IDM **get caught/found with your hand in the 'cookie jar** (*informal*) to be discovered when doing sth that is illegal or dishonest 当场就擒；当场被发现

'cookie sheet (*NAmE*) (*BrE* **'baking sheet, 'baking tray**) *noun* a small sheet of metal used for baking food on （小片）烘烤板（或盘）

cook·ing /ˈkʊkɪŋ/ *noun, adj.*
■*noun* [U] **1** the process of preparing food 烹饪；烹调：*My husband does all the cooking.* 我丈夫把做饭全包了下来。◇ *a book on Indian cooking* 一本关于印度烹饪的书 ➲ VISUAL VOCAB PAGES V28-31 **2** food that has been prepared in a particular way（用某种方法烹制的）食物，饭菜：*The restaurant offers traditional home cooking* (= food similar to that cooked at home). 这家餐馆供应传统的家常菜。◇ *They serve good French cooking.* 他们供应美味的法国菜。
■*adj.* suitable for cooking rather than eating raw or drinking 适于烹饪的（不宜于生吃或直接饮用的）：*cooking sherry* 烹饪用的雪利酒

ˈcooking apple *noun* any type of apple that is suitable for cooking, rather than eating raw 烹调用的苹果 ➲ COMPARE EATING APPLE

ˈcooking gas (*US*) (*BrE* **Calor gas™**) *noun* [U] a type of gas stored as a liquid under pressure in metal containers and used for heating and cooking in places where there is no gas supply 灌装液化气（用于取暖和做饭）

cook·out /ˈkʊkaʊt/ *noun* (*NAmE, informal*) a meal or party when food is cooked over an open fire outdoors, for example at a beach 露天烧烤餐；野外烧烤宴会 ➲ COMPARE BARBECUE *n.*

cook·shop /ˈkʊkʃɒp; *NAmE* -ʃɑːp/ *noun* (*BrE*) a shop/store where equipment for cooking with is sold 炊具店；厨具店

cook·ware /ˈkʊkweə(r); *NAmE* -wer/ *noun* [U] pots and containers used in cooking 炊具；烹饪用具 ➲ WORDFINDER NOTE AT STORE

cool /kuːl/ *adj., verb, noun*
■*adj.* (**cool·er, cool·est**)
• FAIRLY COLD 凉爽 **1** fairly cold; not hot or warm 凉的；凉爽的；凉快的：*a cool breeze/drink/climate* 凉爽的微风；清凉的饮料；凉快的气候 ◇ *Cooler weather is forecast for the weekend.* 预报本周末天气较凉。◇ *Let's sit in the shade and keep cool.* 咱们坐在背阴处乘凉吧。◇ *Store lemons in a cool dry place.* 把柠檬贮存在干燥凉爽的地方。➲ SYNONYMS AT COLD
• COLOURS 颜色 **2** making you feel pleasantly cool 使人感到凉爽的；冷色的：*a room painted in cool greens and blues* 涂成令人感到凉爽的绿色和蓝色的房间
• CALM 冷静 **3** calm; not excited, angry or emotional 冷静的；镇静的；平静的：*Keep cool!* 保持冷静！◇ *She tried to remain **cool, calm and collected*** (= calm). 她试图保持冷静、沉着、镇定。◇ *He has a **cool head*** (= he stays calm in an emergency). 他头脑冷静。
• NOT FRIENDLY/ENTHUSIASTIC 不友好/热情 **4** not friendly, interested or enthusiastic 不友好的；冷淡的；冷漠的：*She was decidedly cool about the proposal.* 她对这个提议显然十分冷淡。◇ *They gave the Prime Minister **a cool reception**.* 他们对首相态度冷淡。
• APPROVING 赞许 **5** (*informal*) used to show that you admire or approve of sth because it is fashionable, attractive and often different（因时髦、漂亮且与众不同而）令人钦佩的，绝妙的，酷的：*You look pretty cool with that new haircut.* 你新剪的发型真酷。◇ *It's a cool movie.* 那部电影真棒。➲ SYNONYMS AT GREAT **6** (*informal*) people say **Cool!** or **That's cool** to show that they approve of

▼COLLOCATIONS 词语搭配

Cooking 烹饪；烹调

Preparing 准备
- **prepare** a dish/a meal/a menu/dinner/the fish 准备一道菜/一顿饭/一份菜单/正餐/鱼
- **weigh out** 100g/4oz of sugar/the ingredients 称出 100 克/4 盎司的糖/食材
- **wash/rinse** the lettuce/spinach/watercress 洗生菜/菠菜/西洋菜
- **chop/slice/dice** the carrots/onions/potatoes 把胡萝卜/洋葱/土豆切碎/切成片/切成丁
- **peel** the carrots/onion/potatoes/garlic/orange 给胡萝卜/洋葱/土豆/大蒜/橘子去皮
- **grate** a carrot/the cheese/some nutmeg 将胡萝卜/干酪/一些肉豆蔻磨碎
- **remove/discard** the bones/seeds/skin 去骨；去籽；去皮
- **blend/combine/mix** (**together**) the flour and water/all the ingredients 把面粉和水/所有的食材和在一起
- **beat/whisk** the cream/eggs/egg whites 搅打奶油/鸡蛋/鸡蛋清
- **knead/shape/roll** (**out**) the dough 揉捏/定型/擀平面团

Cooking 烹饪
- **heat** the oil in a frying pan 在平底煎锅里将油烧热
- **preheat/heat** the oven/(*BrE*) the grill/(*NAmE*) the broiler 将烤箱/烤架预热/加热
- **bring to** (*BrE*) the boil/(*NAmE*) a boil 使沸腾
- **stir** constantly/gently with a wooden spoon 用木勺子不停地/轻轻地搅拌
- **reduce** the heat 把温度调低
- **simmer** gently for 20 minutes/until reduced by half 用文火炖 20 分钟/炖到量减少一半
- **melt** the butter/chocolate/cheese/sugar 使黄油/巧克力/奶酪/糖融化
- **brown** the meat for 8–20 minutes 把肉加热 8 至 20 分钟使之成棕色
- **drain** the pasta/the water from the pot/in a colander 把意大利面滤干；把水从锅里滤出来/滤到滤器里
- **mash** the potatoes/banana/avocado 把土豆/香蕉/油梨捣碎

Ways of cooking 烹饪方式
- **cook** food/fish/meat/rice/pasta/a Persian dish 烹饪食物/鱼/肉/米饭/意大利面食/波斯菜
- **bake** (a loaf of) bread/a cake/(*especially NAmE*) cookies/(*BrE*) biscuits/a pie/potatoes/fish/scones/muffins 烤（一条）面包/一个蛋糕/曲奇饼/小甜饼/馅饼/土豆/鱼/司康饼/小松糕
- **boil** cabbage/potatoes/an egg/water 煮洋白菜/土豆/鸡蛋；烧开水
- **fry/deep-fry/stir-fry** the chicken/vegetables 煎/油炸/炒鸡肉/蔬菜
- **grill** meat/steak/chicken/sausages/a hot dog 烧烤肉/牛排/鸡肉/香肠/热狗
- **roast** potatoes/peppers/meat/chicken/lamb 烘烤土豆/甜椒/肉/鸡肉/羊羔肉
- **sauté** garlic/mushrooms/onions/potatoes/vegetables 炒大蒜/蘑菇/洋葱/土豆/蔬菜
- **steam** rice/vegetables/spinach/asparagus/dumplings 蒸米饭/蔬菜/菠菜/芦笋/饺子
- **toast** bread/nuts 烤面包/坚果
- **microwave** food/popcorn/(*BrE*) a ready meal 用微波炉烹调（或加热）食物/爆米花/预制餐

Serving 上菜
- **serve** in a glass/on a bed of rice/with potatoes 盛在玻璃杯里上；上盖饭；和土豆一起上
- **arrange** the slices on a plate/in a layer 把切片在盘子里摆好/铺成一层
- **carve** the meat/lamb/chicken/turkey 把肉/羊羔肉/鸡肉/火鸡肉切成块
- **dress/toss** a salad 给色拉加调味酱；拌色拉
- **dress with/drizzle with** olive oil/vinaigrette 浇上橄榄油/色拉调味汁
- **top with** a slice of lemon/a scoop of ice cream/whipped cream/syrup 上面放一片柠檬/一勺冰淇淋/搅打好的奶油/糖浆
- **garnish with** a sprig of parsley/fresh basil leaves/lemon wedges/a slice of lime/a twist of orange 用一小枝欧芹/新鲜的罗勒叶/柠檬角/一片酸橙/一卷橘子皮做饰菜
- **sprinkle with** salt/sugar/herbs/parsley/freshly ground black pepper 撒上盐/糖/香草/欧芹/刚磨碎的黑胡椒

C

sth or agree to a suggestion（表示满意或赞同）妙极的，酷的：*'We're meeting Jake for lunch and we can go on the yacht in the afternoon.' 'Cool!'* "我们和杰克一起吃午饭，下午乘游艇玩去。""棒极了！" ◇ *'Can you come at 10.30 tomorrow?' 'That's cool.'* "你明天10:30能来吗？""没问题。" ◇ *I was surprised that she got the job, but **I'm cool with it*** (= it's not a problem for me). 我没想到她会得到这份工作，不过对我来说无所谓。

• CONFIDENT 自信 **7** (*informal*) calm and confident in a way that lacks respect for other people, but makes people admire you as well as disapprove 孤傲冷漠的；满不在乎的：*She just took his keys and walked out with them, cool as you please.* 她拿了他的钥匙就跟他们走了，你看多有个性。

• MONEY 金钱 **8** [only before noun] (*informal*) used about a sum of money to emphasize how large it is（强调金额之大）整整的，足足的：*The car cost a cool thirty thousand.* 那辆车花了整整三万。➲ SEE ALSO COOLLY, COOLNESS

IDM (as) ˌ**cool as a ˈcucumber** very calm and controlled, especially in a difficult situation（尤指在困难情况下）非常冷静，泰然自若 **play it ˈcool** (*informal*) to deal with a situation in a calm way and not show what you are really feeling 沉着应付；冷静处理；不动声色 ➲ MORE AT LONG *adj.*

■ *verb*

• BECOME COLDER 变凉 **1** [I, T] to become or to make sb/sth become cool or cooler（使）变凉，冷却：*Glass contracts as it cools.* 玻璃遇冷收缩。◇ **~ sth** *The cylinder is cooled by a jet of water.* 这种气缸是用喷水冷却的。

• BECOME CALMER 变得冷静 **2** [I] to become calmer, less excited or less enthusiastic 冷静下来；镇静下来；冷淡下来：*I think we should wait until tempers have cooled.* 我认为我们应该等到怒火平息下来再说。◇ *Relations between them have definitely cooled* (= they are not as friendly with each other as they were). 他们之间的关系已明显地冷下来。

IDM ˈ**cool it!** (*informal*) used to tell sb to be calmer and less excited or angry（用于劝说）冷静下来，沉住气，别激动，息怒 ˌ**cool your ˈheels** (*informal*) to have to wait for sb/sth 不得不等待；久等

PHR V ˌ**cool ˈdown/ˈoff** **1** to become cool or cooler 变凉；冷却下来：*We cooled off with a swim in the lake.* 在湖里游泳后我们感到凉快了。 **2** to become calm, less excited or less enthusiastic 镇静下来；变冷淡；不再那么激动：*I think you should wait until she's cooled down a little.* 我觉得你应该等她镇静一点再说。 ˌ**cool sb↔down/ˈoff** **1** to make sb feel cooler 使感到凉快（或凉爽）：*Drink plenty of cold water to cool yourself down.* 多喝点凉水，让自己凉快凉快。 **2** to make sb calm, less excited or less enthusiastic 使冷静；使平静；使冷淡：*A few hours in a police cell should cool him off.* 在警察局班房里关上几个小时就会使他平静下来。ˌ**cool sth↔down/ˈoff** to make sth cool or cooler 使（某物）变凉；使冷却下来 ˌ**cool ˈout** (*informal*) to relax and become calm after a period of activity or stress 放松下来；镇静下来 SYN **chill out**：*It's a wonderful place to cool out with a glass of beer.* 这儿真是个不错的地方，可以喝杯啤酒放松一下。◇ *It sounds like he needs some time to cool out.* 听起来，他还需要一段时间镇静下来。

■ *noun* **the cool** [sing.] cool air or a cool place 凉气；凉快的地方：*the cool of the evening* 夜晚的凉爽

IDM **keep your cool** (*informal*) to remain calm in a difficult situation（在困难的情况下）保持冷静，沉着 **lose your cool** (*informal*) to become angry or excited 火冒三丈；失去冷静

coola·bah *noun* = COOLIBAH

cool·ant /ˈkuːlənt/ *noun* [C, U] a liquid that is used for cooling an engine, a nuclear REACTOR, etc. 冷却剂，冷却介质（用于发动机、核反应堆等）

ˈ**cool bag** (*also* ˈ**cool box**) *noun* (*BrE*) a bag or box which keeps food or drinks cold and which can be used for a PICNIC 冰袋，冰盒（用于保存野餐食物或饮料）➲ SEE ALSO COOLER

cool·drink /ˈkuːldrɪŋk/ *noun* (*SAfrE*) = SOFT DRINK

cool·er /ˈkuːlə(r)/ *noun* **1** [C] a container or machine which cools things, especially drinks, or keeps them cold 冷却器；冷藏器：*the office water cooler* 办公室的饮水冷却器 ◇ (*especially NAmE*) *They took a cooler full of drinks to the beach.* 他们把冷藏器装满饮料带到了海滩。➲ VISUAL VOCAB PAGE V71 **2** [C] (*NAmE*) a drink with ice and usually wine in it（通常有冰和酒的）清凉饮料：*a wine cooler* 含酒的清凉饮料

ˌ**cool-ˈheaded** *adj.* calm; not showing excitement or nerves 头脑冷静的；沉着的：*a cool-headed assessment of the situation* 对局势头脑冷静的估计

coo·li·bah (*also* **coola·bah**) /ˈkuːlɪbɑː/ *noun* an Australian tree that produces a strong hard wood 蓝叶桉

coolie /ˈkuːli/ *noun* (*old-fashioned, taboo*) an offensive word for a worker in Eastern countries with no special skills or training 苦力（含冒犯意，指东方国家里没有专门技能或未受过训练的工人）

ˈ**cooling centre** (*US* ˈ**cooling center**) *noun* (in the US) an AIR-CONDITIONED public place where people can go to cool down, get a drink, etc. when the weather is very hot 避暑中心（美国在天气酷热时开放的有空调的公共场所）

ˌ**cooling-ˈoff period** *noun* **1** a period of time during which two sides in a disagreement try to reach an agreement before taking further action, for example by going on strike（争执双方试图达成协议的）冷却期，冷静期 **2** a period of time after sb has agreed to buy sth, such as an insurance plan, during which they can change their mind（在同意购买某物如保险计划后可改变主意的）可变更期，等待期

ˈ**cooling tower** *noun* a large high round building used in industry for cooling water before it is used again 冷却塔

cool·ly /ˈkuːlli/ *adv.* **1** in a way that is not friendly or enthusiastic 冷漠地；冷淡地：*'We're just good friends,' she said coolly.* "我们仅仅是好朋友而已。"她冷冷地说道。◇ *He received my suggestion coolly.* 他对我的建议反应冷淡。 **2** in a calm way 冷静地；沉着地

cool·ness /ˈkuːlnəs/ *noun* [U] the quality of being cool 凉；凉爽；凉快；冷静；冷漠：*the delicious coolness of the water* 清凉爽口的水 ◇ *I admire her coolness under pressure.* 我佩服她在压力下能保持冷静。◇ *I noticed a certain coolness* (= lack of friendly feeling) *between them.* 我觉察到他们之间有些冷淡。

coon /kuːn/ *noun* (*taboo, slang*) a very offensive word for a black person（冒犯语，指黑人）黑鬼

ˈ**co-op** *noun* (*informal*) a COOPERATIVE shop/store, society or business 合作商店；合作社；合作性商业机构：*a housing co-op* 住房合作社

coop /kuːp/ *noun, verb*

■ *noun* a CAGE for chickens, etc.（关鸡等的）笼子 IDM SEE FLY *v.*

■ *verb*

PHR V ˌ**coop sb/sth ˈup** [usually passive] to keep a person or an animal inside a building or in a small space 把…关（或禁锢）起来；拘禁

coop·er /ˈkuːpə(r)/ *noun* a person who makes BARRELS 制桶工人；箍桶匠

co·oper·ate AW (*BrE also* **co-operate**) /kəʊˈɒpəreɪt; *NAmE* koʊˈɑːp-/ *verb* **1** [I] **~ (with sb) (in/on sth)** to work together with sb else in order to achieve sth 合作；协作：*The two groups agreed to cooperate with each other.* 这两个组同意相互协作。◇ *They had cooperated closely in the planning of the project.* 他们曾密切合作，共同规划这一项目。 **2** [I] **~ (with sb) (in/on sth)** to be helpful by doing what sb asks you to do 协助；配合：*Their captors told them they would be killed unless they cooperated.* 抓住他们的人说如果他们不配合就杀掉他们。

co·oper·ation AW (*BrE also* **co-operation**) /kəʊˌɒpəˈreɪʃn; *NAmE* koʊˌɑːp-/ *noun* [U] **1** the fact of doing sth together or of working together towards a shared aim 合作；协

作： ~ (**with sb**) (**in doing sth**) *a report produced by the government in cooperation with the chemical industry* 政府与化工行业合作提出的一份报告 ◇ ~ (**between A and B**) *We would like to see closer cooperation between parents and schools.* 我们希望家长和学校有更加紧密的合作。 **2** ~ (**in doing sth**) willingness to be helpful and do as you are asked 协助；配合： *We would be grateful for your cooperation in clearing the hall as quickly as possible.* 你们若大力协助尽快把大厅腾空，我们将不胜感激。

co·opera·tive AW (*BrE also* **co-operative**) /kəʊˈɒpərətɪv; *NAmE* koʊˈɑːp-/ *adj., noun*

■ ***adj.*** **1** [usually before noun] involving doing sth together or working together with others towards a shared aim 合作的；协作的；同心协力的： *Cooperative activity is essential to effective community work.* 要把社区工作做好，协作活动是必不可少的。 **2** helpful by doing what you are asked to do 协助的；配合的： *Employees will generally be more cooperative if their views are taken seriously.* 如果雇员的意见得到认真对待，他们一般都会更加配合。 OPP **uncooperative** **3** [usually before noun] (*business* 商) owned and run by the people involved, with the profits shared by them 共同拥有共同经营利益共享的；合作的： *a cooperative farm* 合作农场 ▶ **co·opera·tive·ly** AW (*BrE also* **co-operatively**) *adv.*

■ ***noun*** a cooperative business or other organization 合作企业；合作社组织： *agricultural cooperatives in India* 印度的农业合作社 ◇ *The factory is now a workers' cooperative.* 这家工厂现为工人合作企业。

ˌco-ˈopt *verb* **1** ~ **sb** (**onto/into sth**) to make sb a member of a group, committee, etc. by the agreement of all the other members （经所有成员同意）增选（某人）为委员： *She was co-opted onto the board.* 她获增选为董事会成员。 **2** ~ **sb** (**onto/into sth**) to include sb in sth, often when they do not want to be part of it 拉拢；笼络

co·ord·in·ate AW (*BrE also* **co-ordinate**) *verb, noun*

■ ***verb*** /kəʊˈɔːdɪneɪt; *NAmE* koʊˈɔːrd-/ **1** ~ **sth** to organize the different parts of an activity and the people involved in it so that it works well 使协调；使相配合： *They appointed a new manager to coordinate the work of the team.* 为协调这个队的工作，他们任用了一位新经理。 ◇ *We need to develop a coordinated approach to the problem.* 我们需要制订一个协调一致的方式来解决这个问题。 **2** [T] ~ **sth** to make the different parts of your body work well together 使（身体各部位）动作协调；协同动作 ➲ SEE ALSO UNCOORDINATED **3** [I, T] ~ (**sth**) (**with sth**) (*rather formal*) if you **coordinate** clothes, furniture, etc. or if they **coordinate**, they look nice together （使衣服、家具等）搭配，协调： *This shade coordinates with a wide range of other colours.* 这种深浅的颜色可与很多颜色搭配。 ▶ **co·ord·in·ator** (*BrE also* **co-ordinator**) *noun* : *The campaign needs an effective coordinator.* 这场运动需要一个能干的协调人。

■ ***noun*** /kəʊˈɔːdɪnət; *NAmE* koʊˈɔːrd-/ **1** [C] either of two numbers or letters used to fix the position of a point on a map or GRAPH 坐标： *the x, y coordinates of any point on a line* 一条线上任意一点的 x、y 坐标 **2** **coordinates** [pl.] (used in shops/stores etc. 商店等用) pieces of clothing that can be worn together because, for example, the colours look good together（颜色协调的）配套服装，套装

coordinate clause /kəʊˌɔːdɪnət ˈklɔːz; *NAmE* koʊˌɔːrd-/ *noun* (*grammar* 语法) each of two or more parts of a sentence, often joined by *and, or, but*, etc., that make separate statements that each have an equal importance 并列分句，并列子句（常由 and、or、but 等连接） ➲ COMPARE SUBORDINATE CLAUSE

Coˌordinated Uniˌversal ˈTime *noun* [U] = UTC

coˌordinating conˈjunction *noun* (*grammar* 语法) a word such as *or, and* or *but*, that connects clauses or sentences of equal importance 并列连词 ➲ COMPARE SUBORDINATING CONJUNCTION

co·ord·in·ation AW (*BrE also* **co-ordination**) /kəʊˌɔːdɪˈneɪʃn; *NAmE* koʊˌɔːrd-/ *noun* [U] **1** the act of making parts of sth, groups of people, etc. work together in an efficient and organized way 协作；协调；配合： *a need for greater coordination between departments* 各部门间加强配合的必要 ◇ *a lack of coordination in conservation policy* 环保政策的不协调 ◇ *a pamphlet produced by the government* ***in coordination with*** (= working together with) *the Sports Council* 政府与体育委员会合作发行的小册子 ◇ *advice on colour coordination* (= choosing colours that look nice together, for example in clothes or furniture) 对颜色搭配的建议 **2** the ability to control your movements well 协调动作的能力： *You need good hand-eye coordination to play ball games.* 玩球类游戏，手和眼的动作要协调好。

coot /kuːt/ *noun* **1** a black bird with a white FOREHEAD and beak that lives on or near water 白骨顶，蹼鸡（黑色水鸟，额和喙为白色） **2** **old** ~ (*NAmE, informal*) a stupid person 笨蛋；傻瓜 IDM SEE BALD

cop /kɒp; *NAmE* kɑːp/ *noun, verb*

■ ***noun*** (*informal*) a police officer 警察： *Somebody call the cops!* 去个人报警啊！ ◇ *children playing* ***cops and robbers*** 在玩警察抓小偷的孩子们 ◇ *a TV cop show* 电视警察节目

IDM **not much ˈcop** (*BrE, slang*) not very good 不太好；不怎么样： *He's not much cop as a singer.* 他的歌唱得不怎么样。 ➲ MORE AT FAIR *adj.*

■ ***verb*** (-pp-) (*informal*) **1** ~ **sth** to receive or suffer sth unpleasant 遭受；忍受： *He copped all the hassle after the accident.* 他在事故发生后各种的麻烦都受了。 **2** ~ **sth** to notice sth 注意到： *Cop a load of this!* (= Listen to this) 听听这一大套！

IDM **cop hold of sth** (*BrE, informal*) to take hold of sth 抓住，握住（某物） **cop a ˈplea** (*NAmE, informal*) to admit in court to being guilty of a small crime in the hope of receiving less severe punishment for a more serious crime 避重就轻地认罪（以求轻判） ➲ COMPARE PLEA BARGAINING **ˈcop it** (*BrE, slang*) **1** to be punished 被罚；受罚 **2** to be killed 被杀

PHR V **ˌcop ˈoff** (**with sb**) (*BrE, slang*) to start a sexual or romantic experience with sb （与某人）开始发生性关系，调情： *Who did he cop off with at the party?* 他在聚会上与谁调情？ **ˌcop ˈout** (**of sth**) (*informal*) to avoid or stop doing sth that you should do because you are afraid, lazy, etc. （因害怕、懒惰等而）逃避，回避： *You're not going to cop out at the last minute, are you?* 你不是打算临阵脱逃吧？ ➲ RELATED NOUN COP-OUT

cope /kəʊp; *NAmE* koʊp/ *verb, noun*

■ ***verb*** [I] to deal successfully with sth difficult （成功地）对付，处理 SYN **manage**: *I got to the stage where I wasn't coping any more.* 到了这个阶段，我已经无法应付了。 ◇ ~ **with sth** *He wasn't able to cope with the stresses and strains of the job.* 对付这项工作的紧张与压力，他无能为力。 ◇ *Desert plants are adapted to cope with extreme heat.* 沙漠植物适于耐酷热。

■ ***noun*** a long loose piece of clothing worn by priests on special occasions （圣职人员在特定礼仪中穿的）斗篷式祭衣，大圆衣

copier /ˈkɒpiə(r); *NAmE* ˈkɑːp-/ *noun* (*especially NAmE*) = PHOTOCOPIER

ˈco-pilot *noun* a second pilot who helps the main pilot in an aircraft （飞机的）副驾驶员

cop·ing /ˈkəʊpɪŋ; *NAmE* ˈkoʊpɪŋ/ *noun* (*architecture* 建) the top row of bricks or stones, usually sloping, on a wall 压顶板

co·pi·ous /ˈkəʊpiəs; *NAmE* ˈkoʊ-/ *adj.* in large amounts 大量的；充裕的；丰富的 SYN **abundant**: *copious* (= large) *amounts of water* 大量的水 ◇ *I took copious notes.* 我做了详尽的笔记。 ◇ *She supports her theory with copious evidence.* 她以大量的论据来支持自己的理论。 ▶ **co·pi·ous·ly** *adv.* : *bleeding copiously* 大量出血

ˈcop-out *noun* (*informal, disapproving*) a way of avoiding doing sth that you should do, or an excuse for not doing it 逃避（或躲避）的方法；（不做某事的）借口： *Not turning up was just a cop-out.* 不露面只不过是在逃避而已。

cop·per /ˈkɒpə(r); *NAmE* ˈkɑːp-/ *noun* **1** [U] (*symb.* **Cu**) a chemical element. Copper is a soft reddish-brown metal used for making electric wires, pipes and coins. 铜: *a copper mine* 铜矿 ◇ *copper pipes* 铜管 ◇ *copper-coloured hair* 红棕色的头发 **2 coppers** [pl.] (*BrE*) brown coins that do not have much value 铜币: *I only paid a few coppers for it.* 我只花了几个铜板买下这东西。 **3** [C] (*BrE, informal*) a police officer 警察

ˌcopper ˈbeech *noun* a tall type of BEECH tree with smooth BARK and reddish-brown leaves 紫叶山毛榉

ˌcopper-ˈbottomed *adj.* (*BrE*) that you can trust or rely on completely 完全可靠的；稳妥的： *a copper-bottomed guarantee* 完全可信的保证

cop·per·head /ˈkɒpəhed; *NAmE* ˈkɑːpər-/ *noun* one of several types of poisonous snake that are a brownish colour 铜头蛇

cop·per·plate /ˈkɒpəpleɪt; *NAmE* ˈkɑːpər-/ *noun* [U] a neat old-fashioned way of writing with sloping letters joined together 铜版体（老式书写体，笔画工整倾斜、相互连接）；工整的手写体

cop·pery /ˈkɒpəri; *NAmE* ˈkɑːp-/ *adj.* similar to or having the colour of COPPER 似铜的；紫铜色的： *coppery hair* 红棕色的头发

cop·pice /ˈkɒpɪs; *NAmE* ˈkɑːp-/ *verb, noun*
■ *verb* [T, I] ~ (**sth**) (*specialist*) to cut back young trees in order to make them grow faster 修剪（小树）以助长
■ *noun* = COPSE

copra /ˈkɒprə; *NAmE* ˈkɑːprə/ *noun* [U] the dried white flesh of COCONUTS 椰仁干

copse /kɒps; *NAmE* kɑːps/ (*also* **cop·pice**) *noun* a small area of trees or bushes growing together 萌生林 ➲ VISUAL VOCAB PAGE V3

ˈcop shop *noun* (*informal*) a police station 警察局；局子

cop·ter /ˈkɒptə(r); *NAmE* ˈkɑːp-/ *noun* (*informal*) = HELICOPTER

cop·ula /ˈkɒpjələ; *NAmE* ˈkɑːp-/ *noun* (*grammar* 语法) = LINKING VERB

copu·late /ˈkɒpjuleɪt; *NAmE* ˈkɑːp-/ *verb* [I] ~ (**with sb/sth**) (*specialist*) to have sex 性交；交媾；交配；交尾 ► **copu·la·tion** /ˌkɒpjuˈleɪʃn; *NAmE* ˌkɑːp-/ *noun* [U]

copy /ˈkɒpi; *NAmE* ˈkɑːpi/ *noun, verb*
■ *noun* (*pl.* **-ies**) **1** [C] ~ (**of sth**) a thing that is made to be the same as sth else, especially a document or a work of art （尤指文件或艺术品的）复印件，副本，复制品： *I will send you a copy of the report.* 我会把这个报告的复印本寄给你。 ◇ *The thieves replaced the original painting with a copy.* 盗贼们用摹本换走了原画。 ◇ *You should* **make a copy** *of the disk as a backup.* 你应该将磁盘复制一个备份。 ➲ SEE ALSO HARD COPY **2** [C] a single example of a book, newspaper, etc. of which many have been made （书、报纸等的）一本，一册，一份： *a copy of 'The Times'* 一份《泰晤士报》 ◇ *The book sold 20 000 copies within two weeks.* 这本书在两周内销售了 2 万册。 ➲ SEE ALSO BACK COPY **3** [U] written material that is to be printed in a newspaper, magazine, etc.; news or information that can be used in a newspaper article or advertisement （报刊等的）稿件；（可用于报纸文章或广告的）消息，信息： *The subeditors prepare the reporters' copy for the paper and write the headlines.* 助理编辑处理记者为报纸写的稿件并加标题。 ◇ *This will make great copy for the advertisement.* 这可当作这则广告的绝妙广告词。 **4** [C] = PHOTOCOPY: *Could I have ten copies of this page, please?* 请把这一页给我复印十份好吗？ **5** [C] (*IndE*) a book used by students for writing exercises, etc. in 作业本；练习本
■ *verb* (**cop·ies, copy·ing, cop·ied, cop·ied**) **1** [T] ~ **sth** to make sth that is exactly like sth else 复制；复印；仿造；临摹： *They copied the designs from those on Greek vases.* 他们临摹希腊花瓶上的图案。 ◇ *Everything in the computer's memory can be copied onto DVDs.* 计算机内存里的所有资料都可以复制到 DVD 光盘上。 ➲ WORDFINDER NOTE AT FILE **2** [T] to write sth exactly as it is written somewhere else 抄写；誊写： ~ **sth** (**from sth**) (**into/onto sth**) *She copied the phone number into her address book.* 她把那个电话号码抄写在自己的通讯录上。 ◇ ~ **sth** (**down/out**) *I copied out several poems.* 我抄录了几首诗歌。 **3** [T] ~ **sb/sth** to behave or do sth in the same way as sb else 模仿；效法；仿效 SYN **imitate**: *She copies everything her sister does.* 她一切都效仿她的姐姐。 ◇ *Their tactics have been copied by other terrorist organizations.* 他们的手段已被其他恐怖组织效仿。 **4** [I] ~ (**from/off sb**) to cheat in an exam, school work, etc. by writing what sb else has written and pretending it is your own work 作弊；抄袭 **5** [T] ~ **sth** (*especially NAmE*) = PHOTOCOPY

PHR V **ˌcopy sb ˈin** (**on sth**) to send sb a copy of a letter, an email message, etc. that you are sending to sb else 把（信件、电邮等）抄送某人；给某人寄…的副本： *Can you copy me in on your report?* 你的报告给我抄送一份好吗？

copy·book /ˈkɒpibʊk; *NAmE* ˈkɑːp-/ *noun, adj.*
■ *noun* a book, used in the past by children in school, containing examples of writing which school students had to copy （旧时有书法范例的）习字帖，练字本 IDM SEE BLOT *v.*
■ *adj.* [only before noun] (*BrE*) done exactly how it should be done （做得）精确的，准确的： *It was a copybook operation by the police.* 警方的这一行动非常出色。

copy·cat /ˈkɒpikæt; *NAmE* ˈkɑːp-/ *noun, adj.*
■ *noun* (*informal, disapproving*) used especially by children about and to a person who copies what sb else does because they have no ideas of their own （尤为儿童用语，指无主见的）模仿者，抄袭者，好跟人学的人
■ *adj.* [only before noun] (of crimes 罪行) similar to and seen as copying an earlier well-known crime 模仿犯罪的

ˈcopy editor *noun* a person whose job is to correct and prepare a text for printing 文字编辑 ► **ˈcopy-edit** *verb* [T, I]

copy·ist /ˈkɒpiɪst; *NAmE* ˈkɑːp-/ *noun* a person who makes copies of written documents or works of art 缮写员；誊写员；抄写员；临摹者

copy·right /ˈkɒpiraɪt; *NAmE* ˈkɑːp-/ *noun, adj., verb*
■ *noun* [U, C] ~ (**in/on sth**) if a person or an organization holds the **copyright** on a piece of writing, music, etc., they are the only people who have the legal right to publish, broadcast, perform it, etc., and other people must ask their permission to use it or any part of it 版权；著作权： *Who owns the copyright on this song?* 谁拥有这首歌曲的版权？ ◇ *Copyright expires seventy years after the death of the author.* 版权在作者去世七十年后期满无效。 ◇ *They were sued for* **breach/infringement** *of copyright.* 他们被指控侵犯版权。
■ *adj.* (*abbr.* **C**) protected by copyright; not allowed to be copied without permission 受版权保护的；未经准许不得复制的： *copyright material* 版权资料
■ *verb* ~ **sth** to get the copyright for sth 获得…的版权

ˈcopyright library *noun* in the UK and Ireland, a library that must receive a copy of every book that is published in the country 版本图书馆（在英国和爱尔兰，国内出版的每一种图书都必须收藏一册）

ˈcopy typist *noun* (*BrE*) a person whose job is to type things that they copy from written documents （文件的）副本打字员

copy·writer /ˈkɒpiraɪtə(r); *NAmE* ˈkɑːp-/ *noun* a person whose job is to write the words for advertising material 广告文字撰写人（或撰稿人）

co·quet·ry /ˈkɒkɪtri; *NAmE* ˈkoʊk-/ *noun* [U] (*literary*) behaviour that is typical of a coquette 卖弄风情；卖俏；媚态

co·quette /kɒˈket; *NAmE* koʊˈket/ *noun* (*literary, often disapproving*) a woman who behaves in a way that is intended to attract men 卖弄风情的女人 SYN **flirt** ► **co·quet·tish** /kɒˈketɪʃ; *NAmE* koʊˈk-/ *adj.*: *a coquettish smile* 卖弄风骚的微笑 **co·quet·tish·ly** *adv.*

cor /kɔː(r)/ (*also* ˌ**cor** ˈ**bli·mey**) *exclamation* (*BrE*, *old-fashioned*, *informal*) used when you are surprised, pleased or impressed by sth（惊讶、欣喜或感动时说）啊呀，天哪：*Cor! Look at that!* 啊呀！看看那个！

cor·acle /ˈkɒrəkl; *NAmE* ˈkɔːr-; ˈkɑːr-/ *noun* a small round boat with a wooden frame, used in Wales and Ireland 科拉科尔小艇（威尔士和爱尔兰用的木结构圆形小船）

coral /ˈkɒrəl; *NAmE* ˈkɔːrəl; ˈkɑːrəl/ *noun*, *adj.*
■ ***noun*** **1** [U] a hard substance that is red, pink or white in colour, and that forms on the bottom of the sea from the bones of very small creatures. Coral is often used in jewellery. 珊瑚：***coral reefs/islands*** 珊瑚礁；珊瑚岛 ◇ *a coral necklace* 珊瑚项链 **2** [C] a creature that produces coral 珊瑚虫
■ ***adj.*** pink or red in colour, like coral 珊瑚色的；红色的；粉红的：*coral lipstick* 珊瑚色的唇膏

cor ang·lais /ˌkɔːr ˈɒŋgleɪ; *NAmE* ɔːŋˈgleɪ/ *noun* (*pl.* **cors anglais** /ˌkɔːr ˈɒŋgleɪ; *NAmE* ɔːŋˈgleɪ/) (*especially BrE*) (*also* ˌ**English** ˈ**horn** *especially in NAmE*) a musical instrument of the WOODWIND group, like an OBOE but larger and playing lower notes 英国管；次中音双簧管

cor·bel /ˈkɔːbl; *NAmE* ˈkɔːrbl/ *noun* (*architecture* 建) a piece of stone or wood that sticks out from a wall to support sth, for example an ARCH（墙壁上的）托臂，梁托

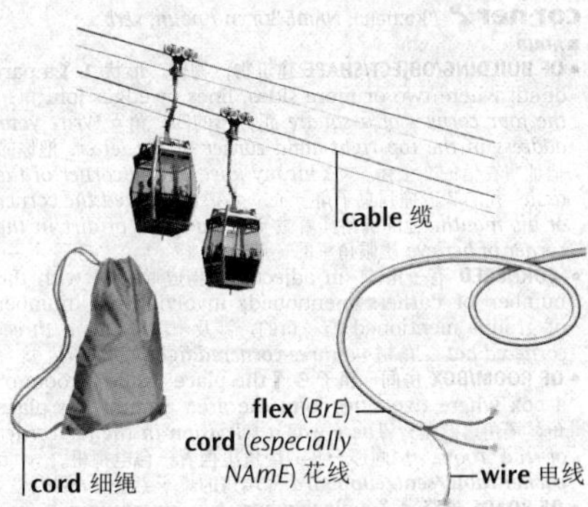

cord /kɔːd; *NAmE* kɔːrd/ *noun* **1** [U, C] strong thick string or thin rope; a piece of this（结实的）粗线，细绳；一根粗线（或细绳）：***a piece/length of cord*** 一根 / 一段粗线 ◇ *picture cord* (= used for hanging pictures) 画的挂绳 ◇ *a silk bag tied with a gold cord* 用金线捆扎的丝绸包 **2** (*especially NAmE*) (*BrE also* **flex**) [C, U] a piece of wire that is covered with plastic, used for carrying electricity to a piece of equipment 软线；花线；皮线：*an electrical cord* 电线 ◇ *telephone cord* 电话线 ➲ SEE ALSO CORDLESS **3** [U] = CORDUROY：*a cord jacket* 灯芯绒夹克 **4** **cords** (*also old-fashioned* **cor·du·roys**) [pl.] trousers/pants made of CORDUROY 灯芯绒裤子：*a pair of cords* 一条灯芯绒裤子 ➲ SEE ALSO SPINAL CORD, UMBILICAL CORD, VOCAL CORDS

cord·ed /ˈkɔːdɪd; *NAmE* ˈkɔːrd-/ *adj.* **1** (of cloth 布料) having raised lines 有凸纹的；有棱的 SYN **ribbed** **2** (of a muscle 肌肉) TENSE and standing out so that it looks like a piece of cord 绷紧鼓起的 **3** that has a cord attached 系（或附）有绳（或线）的：*a corded phone* 有线电话 OPP **cordless**

cor·dial /ˈkɔːdiəl; *NAmE* ˈkɔːrdʒəl/ *adj.*, *noun*
■ ***adj.*** (*formal*) pleasant and friendly 热情友好的；和蔼可亲的：*a* ***cordial atmosphere/meeting/relationship*** 亲切友好的气氛 / 会议 / 关系 ▶ **cor·di·al·ity** /ˌkɔːdiˈæləti; *NAmE* ˌkɔːrdʒiˈæ-/ *noun* [U]：*I was greeted with a show of cordiality.* 我受到了热情友好的接待。
■ ***noun*** **1** (*BrE*) [U, C] a sweet drink that does not contain alcohol, made from fruit juice. It is drunk with water added.（不含酒精、加水饮用的）甜果汁饮料：*blackcurrant cordial* 黑醋栗果汁饮料 **2** [U, C] (*NAmE*) = LIQUEUR **3** [C] a glass of cordial 一杯甜果汁饮料

cor·di·al·ly /ˈkɔːdiəli; *NAmE* ˈkɔːrdʒəli/ *adv.* (*formal*) **1** in a pleasant and friendly manner 热情友好地；和蔼可亲地：*You are cordially invited to a celebration for Mr Michael Brown on his retirement.* 热诚邀请您参加为迈克尔·布朗先生退休举行的庆祝会。**2** (used with verbs showing dislike 与动词连用表示厌恶) very much 非常；十分；很：*They cordially detest each other.* 他们彼此仇视。

cord·ite /ˈkɔːdaɪt; *NAmE* ˈkɔːrd-/ *noun* [U] an EXPLOSIVE used in bullets, bombs, etc. 无烟线状火药

cord·less /ˈkɔːdləs; *NAmE* ˈkɔːrd-/ *adj.* (of a telephone or an electrical tool 电话或电动工具) not connected to its power supply by wires 不用电线与电源相连的；无电线的；无塞绳式的：*a* ***cordless phone/drill*** 无绳电话；无塞绳式电钻 OPP **corded**

cor·don /ˈkɔːdn; *NAmE* ˈkɔːrdn/ *noun*, *verb*
■ ***noun*** a line or ring of police officers, soldiers, etc. guarding sth or stopping people from entering or leaving a place（由警察、士兵等组成的）警戒线，封锁线：*Demonstrators broke through the police cordon.* 示威者冲破了警方的警戒线。➲ WORDFINDER NOTE AT POLICE
■ ***verb***
PHR V ˌ**cordon sth**↔ˈ**off** to stop people from getting into an area by surrounding it with police, soldiers, etc.（由警察、士兵等）包围，警戒，封锁：*Police cordoned off the area until the bomb was made safe.* 警方封锁了这个地区直到炸弹被安全拆除为止。

cor·don bleu /ˌkɔːdɒ̃ ˈblɜː; *NAmE* ˌkɔːrdɔ̃ː/ *adj.* [usually before noun] (*from French*) of the highest standard of skill in cooking 烹饪手艺高超的：*a cordon bleu chef* 烹饪大师 ◇ *cordon bleu cuisine* 名厨师烹制的菜肴

cor·du·roy /ˈkɔːdərɔɪ; *NAmE* ˈkɔːrd-/ *noun* **1** (*also* **cord**) [U] a type of strong soft cotton cloth with a pattern of raised parallel lines on it, used for making clothes 灯芯绒：*a corduroy jacket* 灯芯绒夹克 **2** **cor·du·roys** [pl.] (*old-fashioned*) = CORDS

core 🔑 AW /kɔː(r)/ *noun*, *adj.*, *verb*
■ ***noun*** **1** 🔑 the hard central part of a fruit such as an apple, that contains the seeds（水果的）果心，核儿 ➲ VISUAL VOCAB PAGE V32 **2** 🔑 the central part of an object（物体的）中心部分：*the earth's core* 地核 ◇ *the core of a nuclear reactor* 核反应堆的活性区 **3** 🔑 the most important or central part of sth 最重要的部分；核心；要点；精髓：*the core of the argument* 争论的核心 ◇ *Concern for the environment is* ***at the core*** *of our policies.* 对环境的关注是我们政策的核心。**4** a small group of people who take part in a particular activity（参加某项活动的）一小群人：*He gathered a small core of advisers around him.* 他的周围聚集了一帮谋士。➲ SEE ALSO HARD CORE
IDM **to the ˈcore** so that the whole of a thing or a person is affected 直至核心；十足；透顶：*She was shaken to the core by the news.* 这消息使她大为震惊。◇ *He's a politician to the core* (= in all his attitudes and actions). 他是个十足的政客。
■ ***adj.*** **1** most important; main or essential 最重要的；主要的；基本的：*core subjects* (= subjects that all the students have to study) *such as English and mathematics* 诸如英语和数学等核心科目 ◇ *the core curriculum* 核心课程 ◇ *We need to concentrate on our* ***core business***. 我们需要集中在核心业务上。◇ *The use of new technology is core to our strategy.* 运用新技术是我们策略的关键。**2** **~ beliefs, values, principles, etc.** the most important or central beliefs, etc. of a person or group 核心（信念、价值、原则等）：*The party is losing touch with its core values.* 这个党正在逐渐偏离其核心价值观。**3** used to describe the most important members of a group 核心成员的；骨干的：*The team is built around a core group of players.* 这个队是以几名骨干队员为核心构建的。
■ ***verb*** **~ sth** to take out the core of a fruit 去掉（水果）的果心；去（水果）的核儿

C

C

co·referen·tial /ˌkəʊrefəˈrenʃl; *NAmE* ˌkoʊ-/ *adj.* (*linguistics* 语言) if two words or expressions are **coreferential**, they refer to the same thing. For example, in the sentence 'I had a camera but I lost it', 'a camera' and 'it' are coreferential. 同指的（两个词或短语所指称的对象相同）

ˌco-reˈspondent *noun* (*law* 律) a person who is said to have committed ADULTERY with the husband or wife of sb who is trying to get divorced（通奸引起的离婚诉讼中的）共同被告

corgi /ˈkɔːgi; *NAmE* ˈkɔːrgi/ *noun* (*pl.* **corgis**) a small dog with short legs and a pointed nose 柯吉犬（短腿尖鼻）

cori·an·der /ˌkɒriˈændə(r); *NAmE* ˌkɔːr-/ *noun* [U] a plant whose leaves are used in cooking as a HERB and whose seeds are used in cooking as a spice 芫荽；香菜 ➲ COMPARE CILANTRO ➲ **VISUAL VOCAB** PAGE V35

Cor·inth·ian /kəˈrɪnθiən/ *adj.* [usually before noun] (*architecture* 建) used to describe a style of ARCHITECTURE in ancient Greece that has thin columns with decorations of leaves at the top 科林斯式的（古希腊建筑风格，采用顶部雕刻叶饰的细圆柱）：***Corinthian columns/capitals*** 科林斯式柱 / 柱头

cork /kɔːk; *NAmE* kɔːrk/ *noun, verb*

■ ***noun*** **1** [U] a light, soft material that is the thick BARK of a type of Mediterranean OAK tree 木栓，软木（一种地中海橡树皮）：*a cork mat* 软木垫 ◇ *cork tiles* 软木薄砌块 **2** [C] a small round object made of cork or plastic, that is used for closing bottles, especially wine bottles（尤指酒瓶的）软木塞，塑料塞 ➲ **VISUAL VOCAB** PAGE V36 ➲ **SYNONYMS** AT LID

■ ***verb*** **~ sth** to close a bottle with a cork 用软木塞封（瓶）**OPP** **uncork**

cork·age /ˈkɔːkɪdʒ; *NAmE* ˈkɔːrk-/ *noun* [U] the money that a restaurant charges if you want to drink wine there that you have bought somewhere else（餐馆对顾客自备酒水所收取的）开瓶费

corked /kɔːkt; *NAmE* kɔːrkt/ *adj.* (of wine 酒) with a bad taste because the cork has decayed （因软木塞腐朽而）味道不佳的，带瓶塞异味的

cork·er /ˈkɔːkə(r); *NAmE* ˈkɔːrk-/ *noun* [usually sing.] (*old-fashioned, BrE, informal*) a person or thing that is extremely good, beautiful or amusing 杰出（或非凡）的人；绝色佳丽；趣味无穷的事物

cork·screw /ˈkɔːkskruː; *NAmE* ˈkɔːrk-/ *noun, verb*

■ ***noun*** a tool for pulling CORKS from bottles. Most corkscrews have a handle and a long twisted piece of metal for pushing into the cork. 瓶塞钻；螺旋开瓶起子 ➲ **VISUAL VOCAB** PAGE V27

■ ***verb*** [I] (+ **adv./prep**) to move in a particular direction while turning in circles （顺某方向）做螺旋式转动

corm /kɔːm; *NAmE* kɔːrm/ *noun* the small round underground part of some plants, from which the new plant grows every year （植物的）球茎

cor·mor·ant /ˈkɔːmərənt; *NAmE* ˈkɔːrm-/ *noun* a large black bird with a long neck that lives near the sea or other areas of water 鸬鹚

corn /kɔːn; *NAmE* kɔːrn/ *noun* **1** (*BrE*) [U] any plant that is grown for its grain, such as WHEAT; the grain of these plants （小麦等）谷物；谷粒：*a field of corn* 一片庄稼 ◇ ***ears/sheaves of corn*** 谷穗；一捆捆的谷物 ➲ **COLLOCATIONS** AT FARMING **2** (*NAmE*) (*BrE* **maize**) [U] a tall plant grown for its large yellow grains that are used for making flour or eaten as a vegetable; the grains of this plant 玉蜀黍；玉米 ➲ **VISUAL VOCAB** PAGE V35 ➲ SEE ALSO CORNCOB, CORN ON THE COB **3** (*NAmE*) (*BrE* **sweet·corn**) [U] the yellow seeds of a type of corn (MAIZE) plant, also called corn, which grow on thick STEMS and are cooked and eaten as a vegetable 玉米 ➲ **VISUAL VOCAB** PAGE V33 **4** [C] a small area of hard skin on the foot, especially the toe, that is sometimes painful（尤指脚趾上的）钉胼，鸡眼

ˌcorn ˈbeef *noun* [U] = CORNED BEEF

the ˈCorn Belt *noun* the US states of the Midwest where CORN (MAIZE) is an important crop 玉米带（美国中西部盛产玉米的几个州）

corn·bread /ˈkɔːnbred; *NAmE* ˈkɔːrn-/ *noun* [U] (*NAmE*) a kind of flat bread made with CORN (MAIZE) flour 玉米面包；玉米粉糕

ˈcorn chip *noun* (*NAmE*) a thin, crisp piece of food made from crushed CORN (MAIZE) that has been fried 炸玉米片

ˈcorn circle *noun* = CROP CIRCLE

corn·cob /ˈkɔːnkɒb; *NAmE* ˈkɔːrnkɑːb/ (*especially BrE*) (*also* **cob** *NAmE, BrE*) *noun* the long hard part of the MAIZE (CORN) plant that the rows of yellow grains grow on 玉米芯；玉米穗轴

cor·nea /ˈkɔːniə; *NAmE* ˈkɔːrniə/ *noun* (*anatomy* 解) the transparent layer which covers and protects the outer part of the eye 角膜 ➲ **VISUAL VOCAB** PAGE V64 ▶ **cor·neal** /ˈkɔːniəl; *NAmE* ˈkɔːrn-/ *adj.* [only before noun]: *a corneal transplant* 角膜移植

corned beef /ˌkɔːnd ˈbiːf; *NAmE* ˌkɔːrnd/ (*also* **ˌcorn ˈbeef**) *noun* [U] beef that has been cooked and preserved using salt, often sold in cans （常为罐装的）咸牛肉

cor·ne·lian /kɔːˈniːliən; *NAmE* kɔːrˈn-/ *noun* = CARNELIAN

cor·ner 🔑 /ˈkɔːnə(r); *NAmE* ˈkɔːrn-/ *noun, verb*

■ ***noun***

• **OF BUILDING/OBJECT/SHAPE** 建筑物；物体；形状 **1** 🔑 a part of sth where two or more sides, lines or edges join 角：*the four corners of a square* 正方形的四个角 ◇ *Write your address in the top right-hand corner of the letter.* 把你的地址写在信的右上角。◇ *I hit my knee on the corner of the table.* 我的膝盖撞到桌子角上了。◇ *A smile lifted the corner of his mouth.* 他的嘴角挂着微笑。◇ *a speck of dirt in the corner of her eye* 她眼角里的一点灰尘

• **-CORNERED** 有…角 **2** (in adjectives 构成形容词) with the number of corners mentioned; involving the number of groups mentioned 有…角的；涉及…群体的：*a three-cornered hat* 三角帽 ◇ *a three-cornered fight* 三方争斗

• **OF ROOM/BOX** 房间；箱子 **3** 🔑 the place inside a room or a box where two sides join; the area around this place 角；墙角；壁角：*There was a television in the far corner of the room.* 房间那一头的墙角里摆着一台电视机。◇ *a **corner table/seat/cupboard*** 靠墙角的桌子 / 座位 / 橱柜

• **OF ROADS** 道路 **4** 🔑 a place where two streets join 街角；拐角：*There was a group of youths standing on the **street corner**.* 有一群年轻人站在街角。◇ *Turn right at the corner of Sunset and Crescent Heights Boulevards.* 在夕阳街和新月山庄大街路口向右转。◇ *There's a hotel **on/at the corner** of my street.* 我住的那条街拐角上有一家旅馆。◇ *The wind hit him as he **turned the corner**.* 他一拐过街角，狂风就向他袭来。 **5** 🔑 a sharp bend in a road （道路的）急转弯：*The car was taking the corners too fast.* 那车急转弯时开得太快。

• **AREA/REGION** 地区；区域 **6** a region or an area of a place (sometimes used for one that is far away or difficult to reach) （有时指偏僻或难以到达的）区域，地区：*She lives in a quiet corner of rural Yorkshire.* 她居住在约克郡乡间一个僻静的地方。◇ *Students come here **from the four corners** of the world.* 学生从世界各地来到这里。◇ *He knew every corner of the old town.* 他熟悉这座古镇的每个角落。

• **DIFFICULT SITUATION** 困境 **7** [usually sing.] a difficult situation 困境；窘境：*to **back/drive/force sb into a corner*** 把某人逼入困境 ◇ *They had got her in a corner, and there wasn't much she could do about it.* 他们把她逼得走投无路，而且她也没有什么办法脱身。◇ *He was used to talking his way out of **tight corners**.* 他惯于凭借口才摆脱困境。

• **IN SPORT** 体育运动 **8** (in sports such as football (SOCCER) and HOCKEY 足球、曲棍球等) a free kick or hit that you take from the corner of your opponent's end of the field 角球：*to take a corner* 开角球 ◇ *The referee awarded a corner.* 裁判员判给了一次角球。 ➲ SEE ALSO CORNER KICK **9** (in BOXING and WRESTLING 拳击运动和摔跤) any of the four corners of a RING[1]; the supporters who help in the corner 场角；（场角处的）辅助人员

IDM **(just) around/round the ˈcorner** very near 很近；在

附近：*Her house is just around the corner.* 她的房子就在附近。◇ (*figurative*) *There were good times around the corner* (= they would soon come). 好时光很快就会来临。 **cut 'corners** (*disapproving*) to do sth in the easiest, cheapest or quickest way, often by ignoring rules or leaving sth out（常不按规则或省略地）用最简捷经济的方式做事，图省事；（做事）走捷径 **cut the 'corner** (*also* **cut off the 'corner** *especially in BrE*) to go across the corner of an area and not around the sides of it, because it is quicker 走捷径；抄近道 **see sth out of the corner of your 'eye** to see sth by accident or not very clearly because you see it from the side of your eye and are not looking straight at it 偶然瞟见；睨视：*Out of the corner of her eye, she saw him coming closer.* 她用眼一瞟，见他正向她走过来。 **turn the 'corner** to pass a very important point in an illness or a difficult situation and begin to improve（患病时期）转危为安，脱离危险，好转；渡过难关；脱离困境 ➲ MORE AT FIGHT *v.*, TIGHT *adj.*

■ ***verb***

• **TRAP SB** 使落入圈套 **1** [T, often passive] **~ sb/sth** to get a person or an animal into a place or situation from which they cannot escape 使（人或动物）走投无路；逼…入绝境：*The man was finally cornered by police in a garage.* 那人最终被警方逼到了车库里。◇ *If cornered, the snake will defend itself.* 蛇在被逼得走投无路时会自卫。 **2** [T] **~ sb** to go towards sb in a determined way, because you want to speak to them 硬要走近想与（某人）说话：*I found myself cornered by her on the stairs.* 我发觉她在楼梯上迎面过来非要与我说话。

• **THE MARKET** 市场 **3** [T] **~ the market (in sth)** to get control of the trade in a particular type of goods 垄断（某种货品的交易）：*They've cornered the market in silver.* 他们垄断了白银市场。

• **OF VEHICLE/DRIVER** 车辆；司机 **4** [I] to go around a corner 转弯；拐弯：*The car has excellent cornering* (= it is easy to steer around corners). 这汽车的转弯性能极佳。

cor·ner·back /ˈkɔːnəbæk; *NAmE* ˈkɔːrnər-/ *noun* (in AMERICAN FOOTBALL 美式足球) a defending player whose position is outside and behind the LINEBACKERS（列阵于线卫后侧的）角卫

'corner kick (*also* **cor·ner**) *noun* (in football (SOCCER) 足球) a free kick that you take from the corner of your opponent's end of the field 角球；踢角球

'corner shop *noun* (*BrE*) a small shop that sells food, newspapers, cigarettes, etc., especially one near people's houses（尤指住宅区附近的）小商店，街头小店

cor·ner·stone /ˈkɔːnəstəʊn; *NAmE* ˈkɔːrnərstoʊn/ *noun* **1** (*especially NAmE*) a stone at the corner of the base of a building, often laid in a special ceremony 基石；奠基石 **2** the most important part of sth that the rest depends on 最重要部分；基础；柱石：*This study is the cornerstone of the whole research programme.* 此项研究是整个研究计划的基础。

cor·net /ˈkɔːnɪt; *NAmE* ˈkɔːrnɪt/ *noun* **1** a BRASS musical instrument like a small TRUMPET 短号 **2** (*BrE, old-fashioned*) = CONE (4)：*an ice-cream cornet* 蛋卷冰淇淋

cor·netto /kɔːˈnetəʊ; *NAmE* kɔːrˈnetoʊ/ *noun* (*pl.* **cor·netti** /-ti/) (*from Italian*) an early musical instrument consisting of a curved tube with holes in that you cover with your fingers while blowing into the end 木管号，科尔内管（早期乐器）

'corn exchange *noun* (*BrE*) a building where grain used to be bought and sold（旧时）谷物市场

corn·field /ˈkɔːnfiːld; *NAmE* ˈkɔːrn-/ *noun* a field in which CORN is grown 小麦田；玉米田

corn·flakes /ˈkɔːnfleɪks; *NAmE* ˈkɔːrn-/ *noun* [pl.] small crisp yellow pieces of crushed MAIZE (CORN), usually eaten with milk and sugar for breakfast 脆玉米片（通常加牛奶和糖作早餐）

corn·flour /ˈkɔːnflaʊə(r); *NAmE* ˈkɔːrn-/ (*BrE*) (*NAmE* **corn·starch**) *noun* [U] fine white flour made from MAIZE (CORN), used especially for making sauces thicker（精制）玉米粉；（尤指）玉米淀粉

corn·flower /ˈkɔːnflaʊə(r); *NAmE* ˈkɔːrn-/ *noun* a small wild plant with blue flowers 矢车菊

cor·nice /ˈkɔːnɪs; *NAmE* ˈkɔːrnɪs/ *noun* (*architecture* 建) a decorative border around the top of the walls in a room or on the outside walls of a building 檐口；楣；檐板；飞檐

Corn·ish /ˈkɔːnɪʃ; *NAmE* ˈkɔːrnɪʃ/ *noun, adj.*

■ ***noun*** [U] the Celtic language that was spoken in Cornwall in England. Nobody now uses Cornish as a first language. 康沃尔语（从前通行于英格兰康沃尔地区）

■ ***adj.*** connected with Cornwall, or its people, language or culture 康沃尔的；康沃尔人（或语言、文化）的

ˌCornish 'Cream *noun* [U] CLOTTED CREAM (= a very thick type of cream) from Cornwall 康沃尔浓缩奶油

Corn·ish pasty /ˌkɔːnɪʃ ˈpæsti; *NAmE* ˌkɔːrnɪʃ/ *noun* (*BrE*) a small PIE in the shape of a half circle, containing meat and vegetables 康沃尔菜肉馅饼

corn·meal /ˈkɔːnmiːl; *NAmE* ˈkɔːrn-/ *noun* [U] flour made from CORN (MAIZE) 玉米面

ˌcorn on the 'cob *noun* [U] MAIZE (CORN) that is cooked with all the grains still attached to the inner part and eaten as a vegetable 玉米棒子 ➲ VISUAL VOCAB PAGE V33

'corn pone (*also* **pone**) (*both US*) *noun* [U] a type of bread made from CORN (MAIZE) and water 玉米面包；玉米饼

corn·rows /ˈkɔːnrəʊz; *NAmE* ˈkɔːrnroʊz/ *noun* [pl.] a HAIRSTYLE worn especially by black women, in which the hair is put into lines of PLAITS along the head（尤指黑人妇女梳的）玉米垄发式 ➲ VISUAL VOCAB PAGE V65

corn·starch /ˈkɔːnstɑːtʃ; *NAmE* ˈkɔːrnstɑːrtʃ/ (*NAmE*) (*BrE* **corn·flour**) *noun* [U] fine white flour made from CORN (MAIZE), used especially for making sauces thicker（精制）玉米粉；（尤指）玉米淀粉

ˌcorn 'syrup *noun* [U] a thick sweet liquid made from CORN (MAIZE) and used in cooking 玉米糖浆

cor·nu·co·pia /ˌkɔːnjuˈkəʊpiə; *NAmE* ˌkɔːrnjuˈkoʊpiə/ *noun* **1** (*also* **ˌhorn of 'plenty**) a decorative object shaped like an animal's horn, shown in art as full of fruit and flowers 丰饶角，丰饶角饰（艺术作品中装满水果和鲜花、形似动物角的装饰物） **2** (*formal*) something that is or contains a large supply of good things 丰盛；丰富；丰饶：*The book is a cornucopia of good ideas.* 这部书里有无数好主意。

corny /ˈkɔːni; *NAmE* ˈkɔːrni/ *adj.* (**corn·ier**, **corni·est**) (*informal*) not original; used too often to be interesting or to sound sincere 陈旧的；过时的；陈词滥调的；老生常谈的：*a corny joke/song* 老掉牙的笑话/歌曲 ◇ *I know it sounds corny, but it really was love at first sight!* 我知道这听起来像陈词滥调，然而的确是一见钟情啊！

cor·olla /kəˈrɒlə; *NAmE* -ˈrɑːlə; -ˈroʊlə/ *noun* (*biology* 生) the ring of PETALS around the central part of a flower 花冠

cor·ol·lary /kəˈrɒləri; *NAmE* ˈkɔːrəleri; ˈkɑːr-/ *noun* (*pl.* **-ies**) **~ (of/to sth)** (*formal* or *specialist*) a situation, an argument or a fact that is the natural and direct result of another one 必然的结果（或结论）

cor·ona /kəˈrəʊnə; *NAmE* -ˈroʊ-/ *noun* (*pl.* **co·ro·nae** /-niː/) (*astronomy* 天) (*also informal* **halo**) a ring of light seen around the sun or moon, especially during an ECLIPSE 华；（尤指在日食或月食期间的）日冕，日华，月华

cor·on·ary /ˈkɒrənri; *NAmE* ˈkɔːrəneri; ˈkɑːrəneri/ *adj.* (*medical* 医) connected with the heart, particularly the ARTERIES that take blood to the heart 冠状动脉的：*coronary (heart) disease* 冠状动脉（心脏）病 ◇ *a coronary patient* (= sb suffering from coronary disease) 冠状动脉疾病患者

ˌcoronary 'artery *noun* (*anatomy* 解) either of the two ARTERIES that supply blood to the heart 冠状动脉

ˌ**coronary thromˈbosis** (*also informal* **cor·on·ary**) *noun* [C, U] (*medical* 医) a blocking of the flow of blood by a blood CLOT in an ARTERY supplying blood to the heart 冠状动脉血栓形成 ➲ COMPARE HEART ATTACK

C

cor·on·ation /ˌkɒrəˈneɪʃn; *NAmE* ˌkɔːr-; ˌkɑːr-/ *noun* a ceremony at which a crown is formally placed on the head of a new king or queen 加冕；加冕典礼

cor·on·er /ˈkɒrənə(r); *NAmE* ˈkɔːr-; ˈkɑːr-/ *noun* an official whose job is to discover the cause of any sudden, violent or suspicious death by holding an INQUEST 验尸官

cor·onet /ˈkɒrənet; *NAmE* ˌkɔːrəˈnet; ˌkɑːr-/ *noun* **1** a small crown worn on formal occasions by princes, princesses, lords, etc. （王子、公主、贵族等戴的）冠冕 **2** a round decoration for the head, especially one made of flowers （尤指用花制作的）冠状头饰；花冠

Corp. *abbr.* CORPORATION （大）公司

cor·pora PL. OF CORPUS

cor·poral /ˈkɔːpərəl; *NAmE* ˈkɔːrp-/ *noun* (*abbr.* **Cpl**) a member of one of the lower ranks in the army, the MARINES or the British AIR FORCE （陆军、海军陆战队或英国空军的）下士：*Corporal Smith* 史密斯下士

ˌ**corporal ˈpunishment** *noun* [U] the physical punishment of people, especially by hitting them 体罚；肉刑

cor·por·ate AW /ˈkɔːpərət; *NAmE* ˈkɔːrp-/ *adj.* [only before noun] **1** connected with a corporation 公司的：***corporate finance/planning/strategy*** 公司的财务 / 计划 / 策略 ◇ ***corporate identity*** (= the image of a company, that all its members share) 公司形象 ◇ ***corporate hospitality*** (= when companies entertain customers to help develop good business relationships) 公司对顾客的热情招待 **2** (*specialist*) forming a CORPORATION 组成公司（或团体）的；法人的：*The BBC is a **corporate body**.* 英国广播公司为法人团体。◇ *The law applies to both individuals and corporate bodies.* 本法律既适用于个人也适用于法人团体。**3** involving or shared by all the members of a group 社团的；全体的；共同的：*corporate responsibility* 共同的责任

ˌ**corporate ˈraider** *noun* (*business* 商) a person or company that regularly buys large numbers of shares in other companies against their wishes, either to control the company or to sell the shares again for a large profit 公司掠夺者（经常强行大量购买其他公司股份的个人或公司，以对其加以控制或高价出售股份而获利）

cor·por·ation AW /ˌkɔːpəˈreɪʃn; *NAmE* ˌkɔːrp-/ *noun* **1** (*abbr.* **Corp.**) a large business company （大）公司：*multinational corporations* 跨国公司 ◇ *the Chrysler corporation* 克莱斯勒公司 **2** an organization or a group of organizations that is recognized by law as a single unit 法人；法人团体：*urban development corporations* 城市开发集团公司 **3** (*BrE*) a group of people elected to govern a large town or city and provide public services 市政委员会

ˌ**corpoˈration tax** *noun* [U] (*BrE*) a tax that companies pay on their profits 公司税

cor·por·at·ism /ˈkɔːpərətɪzəm; *NAmE* ˈkɔːrp-/ *noun* [U] the control of a country, etc. by large groups, especially businesses 社团主义（以产业社团等作为政治代表机关支配人民的活动）

cor·por·at·or /ˈkɔːpəreɪtə(r); *NAmE* ˈkɔːrp-/ *noun* (*IndE*) an elected member of the government of a town or city 市政当局成员

cor·por·eal /kɔːˈpɔːriəl; *NAmE* kɔːrˈp-/ *adj.* (*formal*) **1** that can be touched; physical rather than spiritual 物质的；有形的；实体的：*his corporeal presence* 他的大驾亲临 **2** of or for the body 身体的；肉体的；身体所需的：*corporeal needs* 身体的需要

corps /kɔː(r)/ *noun* (*pl.* **corps** /kɔːz; *NAmE* kɔːrz/) [C+sing./pl. v.] **1** a large unit of an army, consisting of two or more DIVISIONS （由两个或以上师组成的）军，兵团：*the commander of the third army corps* 陆军第三军团的指挥官 **2** one of the groups of an army with a special responsibility （陆军）特种部队：*the Royal Army Medical Corps* 英国皇家陆军医疗队 **3** a group of people involved in a particular job or activity （从事某工作或活动的）一群人，一组人：*a corps of trained and experienced doctors* 一队训练有素并富有经验的医生 ➲ SEE ALSO DIPLOMATIC CORPS, PRESS CORPS

corps de bal·let /ˌkɔː də ˈbæleɪ; *NAmE* ˌkɔːr də bæˈleɪ/ *noun* [C+sing./pl. v.] (*from French*) dancers in a BALLET company who dance together as a group （芭蕾舞团的）群舞演员

corpse /kɔːps; *NAmE* kɔːrps/ *noun*

■ ***noun*** a dead body, especially of a human 尸体；（尤指人的）死尸，尸首

cor·pu·lent /ˈkɔːpjələnt; *NAmE* ˈkɔːrp-/ *adj.* (*formal*) (of a person 人) fat. People say ‘corpulent’ to avoid saying ‘fat’. 发福的，富态的（委婉说法，与 fat 同义） ▶ **cor·pu·lence** *noun* [U]

cor·pus /ˈkɔːpəs; *NAmE* ˈkɔːrpəs/ *noun* (*pl.* **cor·pora** /ˈkɔːpərə; *NAmE* ˈkɔːrpərə/ or **cor·puses** /-sɪz/) (*specialist*) a collection of written or spoken texts （书面或口语的）文集，文献，汇编；语料库：*a corpus of 100 million words of spoken English* 含有 1 亿单词的英语口语语料库 ◇ *the whole corpus of Renaissance poetry* 文艺复兴时期诗歌的总汇 ➲ SEE ALSO HABEAS CORPUS

cor·puscle /ˈkɔːpʌsl; *NAmE* ˈkɔːrp-/ *noun* (*anatomy* 解) any of the red or white cells found in blood （红或白）血球，血细胞：***red/white corpuscles*** 红血球；白血球

cor·ral /kəˈrɑːl; *NAmE* -ˈræl/ *noun, verb*

■ ***noun*** (in N America) a fenced area for horses, cows, etc. on a farm or RANCH （北美农牧场的）畜栏，围栏：*They drove the ponies into a corral.* 他们把矮种马赶进了畜栏。

■ ***verb*** (**-ll-**, *US also* **-l-**) **1 ~ sth** to force horses or cows into a corral 把（马或牛）赶入围栏（或关进畜栏） **2 ~ sb** to gather a group of people together and keep them in a particular place 把（一群人）集中起来关在一起

cor·rect /kəˈrekt/ *adj., verb*

■ ***adj.* 1** accurate or true, without any mistakes 准确无误的；精确的；正确的 SYN **right**：*Do you have the correct time?* 你的表走得准吗？ ◇ *the correct answer* 正确答案 ◇ *Please check that these details are correct.* 请检查这些细节是否准确无误。◇ *‘Are you in charge here?’ ‘That's correct.’* “你是这里的负责人吗？”“是的。”◇ *Am I correct in saying that you know a lot about wine?* 你对酒了解颇深，我说得对吧？ OPP **incorrect** ➲ SYNONYMS AT TRUE **2** right and suitable, so that sth is done as it should be done 恰当

▼ **EXPRESS YOURSELF** 情景表达

Correcting yourself 纠正自己的话

When you say something that was not quite what you intended, you can correct yourself in various ways. 说话词不达意时可以用多种方式加以修正：

- *I'll be there at five fifteen, **I mean** five fifty—ten to six.* 我会在 5 点 15 分到那儿，不，应该是 5 点 50 分，差 10 分钟 6 点。
- *It'll be Tuesday—**sorry, I meant to say** Thursday.* 那就是星期二。不对，我想说的是星期四。
- ***Sorry, what I mean is,** we need two handouts per person.* 抱歉，我的意思是我们每个人需要两份讲义。
- *We can meet in the conference centre—**or rather** in front of the centre.* 我们可以在会议中心，确切地讲是在会议中心前面会合。
- *The painter—**or should I say**, the sculptor—was born in Padua.* 这名画家，应该说是雕塑家，生于帕多瓦。
- *It's one t and double s—**no, sorry,** one s and double t.* 是一个 t 和两个 s。不，搞错了，应该是一个 s 和两个 t。
- *It's on the fifth floor—**no, actually,** it's the fourth.* 是在六楼，不，实际上是在五楼。
- *Can I get two lattes and an espresso—**no, scratch that,** three lattes.* (*NAmE, informal*) 请给我来两杯拿铁和一杯浓缩咖啡。不，不要那个，要三杯拿铁。

的；合适的：*Do you know the correct way to shut the machine down?* 你知道这台机器该怎么关吗？◇ *I think you've made the correct decision.* 我认为你的决定是正确的。➲ SYNONYMS AT RIGHT **3** taking care to speak or behave in a way that follows the accepted standards or rules（举止言谈）符合公认准则的，得体的：*a correct young lady* 举止得体的年轻女士 ◇ *He is always very correct in his speech.* 他说话总是很有分寸。OPP **incorrect** ➲ SEE ALSO POLITICALLY CORRECT ▶ **cor·rect·ly** adv.：*Have you spelled it correctly?* 你把它拼写对了吗？◇ *They reasoned, correctly, that she was away for the weekend.* 他们的推断没错，她出去度周末了。◇ *He was looking correctly grave.* 他表情严肃得体。**cor·rect·ness** noun [U]：*The correctness of this decision may be doubted.* 此项决定是否正确值得怀疑。➲ SEE ALSO POLITICAL CORRECTNESS IDM SEE PRESENT *adj.*

■ *verb* **1** ~ **sth** to make sth right or accurate, for example by changing it or removing mistakes 改正；纠正；修正：*Read through your work and correct any mistakes that you find.* 从头至尾看一遍你们的作业，发现的错误都要改正过来。◇ *Their eyesight can be corrected in just a few minutes by the use of a laser.* 他们的视力用激光只要几分钟就可矫正。◇ *They issued a statement correcting the one they had made earlier.* 他们发表了一份声明，更正早先声明中的错误。**2** ~ **sth** (of a teacher 教师) to mark the mistakes in a piece of work (and sometimes give a mark/grade to the work) 批改；改：*I spent all evening correcting essays.* 我整个晚上都在批改论文。**3** to tell sb that they have made a mistake 指出错误：~ **sb** *Correct me if I'm wrong, but isn't this last year's brochure?* 这不是去年的小册子吗？若是我说错了就请指出。◇ *Yes, you're right—I stand corrected* (= I accept that I made a mistake). 是的，你说得对。承蒙指正。◇ ~ **(sb)** + **speech** *'It's Yates, not Wates,' she corrected him.* "那是 Yates 而不是 Wates。" 她纠正他道。

cor·rec·tion /kəˈrekʃn/ noun, exclamation

■ *noun* **1** [C] a change that makes sth more accurate than it was before 改正；纠正；修正：*I've made a few small corrections to your report.* 我对你的报告作了几处小的修改。◇ *The paper had to publish a correction to the story.* 这家报纸不得不对这则新闻报道发一个更正。**2** [U] the act or process of correcting sth 改正的行动（或过程）：*There are some programming errors that need correction.* 有一些程序错误需要改正。**3** [U] (*old-fashioned*) punishment 惩罚；处罚；惩治：*the correction of young offenders* 对失足青少年的管教

■ *exclamation* (*informal*) used when you want to correct sth that you have just said（想纠正刚说过的话时用）改正，更正：*I don't know. Correction—I do know, but I'm not going to tell you.* 我不知道。不，我知道不假，但不打算告诉你。

cor·rec·tion·al /kəˈrekʃənl/ *adj.* [only before noun] (*especially NAmE*) concerned with improving the behaviour of criminals, usually by punishing them 改造的：*a correctional center/institution/facility* (= a prison) 监狱

corˈrection fluid noun [U] a white liquid that you use to cover mistakes that you make when you are writing or typing, and that you can write on top of 涂改液；修正液 ➲ VISUAL VOCAB PAGE V71 ➲ SEE ALSO TIPP-EX™, WITEOUT™

cor·rect·ive /kəˈrektɪv/ *adj., noun*

■ *adj.* (*formal*) designed to make sth right that was wrong before 改正的；纠正的；矫正的：*We need to take corrective action to halt this country's decline.* 我们得采取纠偏行动来阻止这个国家的衰落。◇ *corrective measures* 纠偏措施 ◇ *corrective surgery/glasses* 矫正外科 / 眼镜

■ *noun* ~ **(to sth)** (*formal*) something that helps to give a more accurate or fairer view of sb/sth 起纠正作用的东西；修改；纠正：*I should like to add a corrective to what I have written previously.* 我想对我先前写的内容进行补充修改。

cor·rel·ate /ˈkɒrəleɪt; NAmE ˈkɔːr-; ˈkɑːr-/ verb (*formal*) **1** [I] if two or more facts, figures, etc. **correlate** or if a fact, figure, etc. **correlates** with another, the facts are closely connected and affect or depend on each other 相互关联影响；相互依赖：*The figures do not seem to correlate.* 这些数字似乎毫不相干。◇ ~ **with sth** *A high-fat diet correlates with a greater risk of heart disease.* 高脂肪饮食与增加心脏病发作的风险密切相关。**2** [T] ~ **sth** to show that there is a close connection between two or more facts, figures, etc. 显示（两个或多个事实或数字等）的紧密联系：*Researchers are trying to correlate the two sets of figures.* 研究人员正试图展示这两组数字的相关性。▶ **cor·rel·ate** noun

cor·rel·ation /ˌkɒrəˈleɪʃn; NAmE ˌkɔːr-/ noun [C, U] a connection between two things in which one thing changes as the other does 相互关系；相关；关联：~ **(between A and B)** *There is a direct correlation between exposure to sun and skin cancer.* 暴露在太阳下与皮肤癌直接相关。◇ ~ **(of A with B)** *the correlation of social power with wealth* 社会权力与财富的相关性

cor·rela·tive /kəˈrelətɪv/ noun (*formal*) a fact or an idea that is closely related to or depends on another fact or idea 紧密相关；相互关联 ▶ **cor·rela·tive** *adj.*

cor·res·pond AW /ˌkɒrəˈspɒnd; NAmE ˌkɔːrəˈspɑːnd; ˌkɑː-/ *verb* **1** [I] to be the same as or match sth 相一致；符合 SYN **agree, tally**：*Your account and hers do not correspond.* 你说的情况与她说的不相符。◇ ~ **with sth** *Your account of events does not correspond with hers.* 你对事情的陈述与她说的不相符。◇ ~ **to sth** *The written record of the conversation doesn't correspond to* (= is different from) *what was actually said.* 那次谈话的文字记录与原话不符。**2** [I] ~ **(to sth)** to be similar to or the same as sth else 类似于；相当于：*The British job of Lecturer corresponds roughly to the US Associate Professor.* 英国的讲师职位大致相当于美国的副教授。**3** [I] ~ **(with sb)** (*formal*) to write letters to sb and receive letters from them 通信

cor·res·pond·ence AW /ˌkɒrəˈspɒndəns; NAmE ˌkɔːrəˈspɑːn-; ˌkɑː-/ noun (*formal*) **1** [U] ~ **(with sb)** the letters a person sends and receives 来往信件；往来书信：***personal/private correspondence*** 私人来往信件 ◇ *The editor welcomes correspondence from readers on any subject.* 编辑欢迎读者有关任何问题的来信。◇ *the **correspondence column/page*** (= in a newspaper) 读者来信专栏 / 版面 ◇ *Jane Austen's correspondence with her sister* 简·奥斯汀与她姐姐的往来信件 **2** [U, C] ~ **(with sb)** the activity of writing letters 通信；通信联系：*I refused to enter into any correspondence* (= to exchange letters) *with him about it.* 我拒绝就此问题与他通信联系。◇ *We have been **in correspondence** for months.* 我们通信几个月了。◇ *We kept up a correspondence for many years.* 我们保持了很多年的通信联系。**3** [C, U] ~ **(between A and B)** a connection between two things; the fact of two things being similar 相关；相似：*There is a close correspondence between the two extracts.* 这两段摘录如出一辙。

corre'spondence course noun a course of study that you do at home, using books and exercises sent to you by post/mail or by email 函授课程

cor·res·pond·ent /ˌkɒrəˈspɒndənt; NAmE ˌkɔːrəˈspɑːn-; ˌkɑː-/ noun **1** a person who reports news from a particular country or on a particular subject for a newspaper or a television or radio station 记者；通讯员：*the BBC's political correspondent* 英国广播公司的政治新闻记者 ◇ *a **foreign/war/sports, etc. correspondent*** 驻外、战地、体育等记者 ◇ *our Delhi correspondent* 我们驻德里的通讯员 ➲ WORDFINDER NOTE AT JOURNALIST **2** (used with an adjective 与形容词连用) a person who writes letters to another person 通信者：*She's a poor correspondent* (= she does not write regularly). 她是个懒于写信的人。

cor·res·pond·ing AW /ˌkɒrəˈspɒndɪŋ; NAmE ˌkɔːrəˈspɑːn-; ˌkɑː-/ *adj.* matching or connected with sth that you have just mentioned 符合的；相应的；相关的 SYN **equivalent**：*A change in the money supply brings a corresponding change in expenditure.* 货币供应量的改变随即引起支出的相应改变。◇ *Profits have risen by 15 per cent compared with the corresponding period last year.* 与去年同期相比利润增长了 15%。◇ *The Redskins lost to the Cowboys in the corresponding game last year.* 在去年那场两队的交锋中，

红皮队输给了牛仔队。◇ **~ to sth** *Give each picture a number corresponding to its position on the page.* 按所在页面位置给每一幅画编上相对应的号码。▶ **cor·res·pond·ing·ly** AW *adv.*: *a period of high demand and correspondingly high prices* 需求大、价格相应较高的时期

corres'ponding angles (*also* **'F angles**) *noun* [pl.] (*geometry* 几何) equal angles formed on the same side of a line that crosses two parallel lines 同位角；对应角 ➲ PICTURE AT ANGLE ➲ COMPARE ALTERNATE ANGLES

cor·ri·dor /ˈkɒrɪdɔː(r); *NAmE* ˈkɔːr-; ˈkɑːr-/ *noun* **1** (*NAmE also* **hall·way**) a long narrow passage in a building, with doors that open into rooms on either side（建筑物内的）走廊，过道，通道：*His room is along the corridor.* 他的房间就在走廊边。➲ VISUAL VOCAB PAGE V72 **2** a passage on a train（火车上的）走道，过道，通道 **3** a long narrow strip of land belonging to one country that passes through the land of another country; a part of the sky over a country that planes, for example from another country, can fly through 走廊（一国领土通过他国境内的狭长地带）；空中走廊（一国领空中允许他国飞机经过的区域）➲ SEE ALSO AIR CORRIDOR **4** a long narrow strip of land that follows the course of an important road or river（沿着重要道路或河道的）狭长地带：*the electronics industry in the M4 corridor* * 4 号高速公路沿线一带的电子工业区

IDM **the corridors of 'power** (*sometimes humorous*) the higher levels of government, where important decisions are made 权力走廊（高层政治决策机构）

cor·rie /ˈkɒri; *NAmE* ˈkɔːri; ˈkɑːri/ (*also* **cirque**, **cwm**) *noun* (*geology* 地) a round hollow area in the side of a mountain 山侧圆形凹地

cor·rob·or·ate /kəˈrɒbəreɪt; *NAmE* -ˈrɑːb-/ *verb* [T, I, often passive] **~ (sth)** (*formal*) to provide evidence or information that supports a statement, theory, etc. 证实，确证（陈述、理论等）SYN **confirm**: *The evidence was corroborated by two independent witnesses.* 此证据被两名独立证人证实。◇ *corroborating evidence* 证实的证据 ▶ **cor·rob·or·ation** /kəˌrɒbəˈreɪʃn; *NAmE* -ˌrɑːbə-/ *noun* [U]

cor·rob·ora·tive /kəˈrɒbərətɪv; *NAmE* kəˈrɑːbəreɪtɪv/ *adj.* (*formal*) [usually before noun] giving support to a statement or theory（对陈述或理论）提供支持的；使确凿的：*Is there any* ***corroborative evidence*** *for this theory?* 是否有进一步说明问题的论据来支持这个理论？

cor·rode /kəˈrəʊd; *NAmE* kəˈroʊd/ *verb* [T, I] **~ (sth)** to destroy sth slowly, especially by chemical action; to be destroyed in this way 腐蚀；侵蚀：*Acid corrodes metal.* 酸腐蚀金属。◇ (*figurative*) *Corruption corrodes public confidence in a political system.* 腐败可削弱公众对政治制度的信心。◇ *The copper pipework has corroded in places.* 铜管有几处受到了腐蚀。▶ **cor·ro·sion** /kəˈrəʊʒn; *NAmE* -ˈroʊ-/ *noun* [U]: *Look for signs of corrosion.* 寻找腐蚀的痕迹。◇ *Clean off any corrosion before applying the paint.* 先把锈迹清除干净再涂油漆。➲ VISUAL VOCAB PAGE V7

cor·ro·sive /kəˈrəʊsɪv; *NAmE* -ˈroʊ-/ *adj.* **1** tending to destroy sth slowly by chemical action 腐蚀性的；侵蚀性的：*the corrosive effects of salt water* 盐水的腐蚀作用 ◇ *corrosive acid* 具有腐蚀作用的酸 **2** (*formal*) tending to damage sth gradually 损害性的；逐渐起破坏作用的：*Unemployment is having a corrosive effect on our economy.* 失业对我国的经济起着破坏作用。

cor·ru·gated /ˈkɒrəgeɪtɪd; *NAmE* ˈkɔːr-; ˈkɑːr-/ *adj.* shaped into a series of regular folds that look like waves 起皱的；波纹形的：*a* ***corrugated iron*** *roof* 波纹铁屋顶 ◇ *corrugated cardboard* 瓦楞纸板

cor·rupt /kəˈrʌpt/ *adj.*, *verb*

■ ***adj.*** **1** (of people 人) willing to use their power to do dishonest or illegal things in return for money or to get an advantage 贪污的；受贿的；腐败的；营私舞弊的：*a corrupt regime* 贪污腐败的政权 ◇ *corrupt officials accepting bribes* 接受贿赂的贪官污吏 **2** (of behaviour 行为) dishonest or immoral 不诚实的；不道德的：*corrupt practices* 徇私舞弊 ◇ *The whole system is inefficient and corrupt.* 整个体系都效率低下并且腐败堕落。**3** (*computing* 计) containing changes or faults, and no longer in the original state 已变换的；有缺陷的；有错误的：*corrupt software* 已受损的软件 ◇ *The file on the disk seems to be corrupt.* 这张磁盘上的文件好像有错误。▶ **cor·rupt·ly** *adv.*

■ ***verb*** **1** [T] **~ sb** to have a bad effect on sb and make them behave in an immoral or dishonest way 使腐化；使堕落：*He was corrupted by power and ambition.* 权力与野心使他腐化堕落。◇ *the corrupting effects of great wealth* 巨大财富的腐蚀作用 **2** [T, often passive] **~ sth** to change the original form of sth, so that it is damaged or spoiled in some way 破坏；损坏：*a corrupted form of Buddhism* 一种蜕变了的佛教 **3** [T, I] **~ (sth)** (*computing* 计) to cause mistakes to appear in a computer file, etc. with the result that the information in it is no longer correct 引起（计算机文件等的）错误；破坏：*The program has somehow corrupted the system files.* 这程序莫名其妙地导致系统文件出错了。◇ *corrupted data* 被破坏数据 ◇ *The disk will corrupt if it is overloaded.* 磁盘如果过载，数据就会出错。

cor·rupt·ible /kəˈrʌptəbl/ *adj.* that can be corrupted 易腐蚀的；易腐败的；可收买的 OPP **incorruptible**

cor·rup·tion /kəˈrʌpʃn/ *noun* **1** [U] dishonest or illegal behaviour, especially of people in authority 腐败；贪污；贿赂；受贿：*allegations of* ***bribery and corruption*** 对贿赂与贪污的指控 ◇ *The new district attorney has promised to fight police corruption.* 新上任的地方检察官承诺要打击警察腐败。➲ COLLOCATIONS AT CRIME **2** [U] the act or effect of making sb change from moral to immoral standards of behaviour 堕落；腐蚀：*He claimed that sex and violence on TV led to the corruption of young people.* 他断言电视中所宣扬的色情与暴力诱使青少年堕落。**3** [C, usually sing.] the form of a word or phrase that has become changed from its original form in some way（单词或短语的）变体：*The word 'holiday' is a corruption of 'holy day'.* 单词 holiday 是 holy day 的变体。

cor·sage /kɔːˈsɑːʒ; *NAmE* kɔːrˈsɑːʒ/ *noun* a small bunch of flowers that is worn on a woman's dress, for example at a wedding（婚礼等女服上佩戴的）小花束

cor·set /ˈkɔːsɪt; *NAmE* ˈkɔːrsɪt/ *noun* a piece of women's underwear, fitting the body tightly, worn especially in the past to make the waist look smaller（尤指旧时妇女束腰的）紧身内衣

cor·tège (*also* **cor·tege** *especially in US*) /kɔːˈteʒ; -ˈteɪʒ; *NAmE* kɔːrˈteʒ/ *noun* a line of cars or people moving along slowly at a funeral 送葬车队（或行列、队伍）SYN **funeral procession**

cor·tex /ˈkɔːteks; *NAmE* ˈkɔːrt-/ *noun* (*pl.* **cor·ti·ces** /ˈkɔːtɪsiːz; *NAmE* ˈkɔːrt-/) (*anatomy* 解) the outer layer of an organ in the body, especially the brain 皮层；皮质；（尤指）大脑皮层：*the* ***cerebral/renal cortex*** (= around the brain/KIDNEY) 大脑 / 肾皮质 ▶ **cor·tic·al** /ˈkɔːtɪkl; *NAmE* ˈkɔːrt-/ *adj.*

cor·ti·sone /ˈkɔːtɪzəʊn; -səʊn; *NAmE* ˈkɔːrtəsoʊn; -zoʊn/ *noun* [U] (*medical* 医) a HORMONE used in the treatment of diseases such as ARTHRITIS, to reduce swelling 可的松（用于治疗关节炎等缓解肿胀的激素）

cor·us·cate /ˈkɒrəskeɪt; *NAmE* ˈkɔːr-; ˈkɑːr-/ *verb* (*literary*) **1** [I] (of light 光) to flash 闪耀；闪烁 **2** [I] (of a person 人) to be full of life, enthusiasm or humour 充满活力；朝气蓬勃；幽默风趣 ▶ **cor·us·cat·ing** *adj.*: *coruscating wit* 敏

corrugated 波纹形的

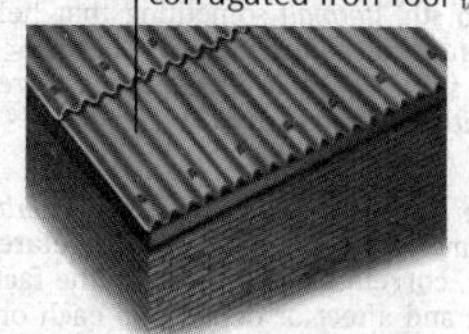

捷的才思 **cor·us·cat·ing·ly** *adv.*: *coruscatingly brilliant* 熠熠生辉

cor·vette /kɔːˈvet; *NAmE* kɔːrˈvet/ *noun* a small fast ship used in war to protect other ships from attack 小型护卫舰

cos[1] (*also* **'cos**, **'cause**, **coz**) /kəz; *BrE also* kɒz/ *conj.* (*BrE, informal*) because 因为： *I can't see her at all, cos it's too dark.* 天太黑，我根本看不见她。

cos[2] *abbr.* (in writing 书写形式) COSINE 余弦

COSATU /kəʊˈsɑːtuː; *NAmE* koʊ-/ *abbr.* the Congress of South African Trade Unions (= a political organization in South Africa that represents many unions) 南非工会大会；南非总工会

cosh /kɒʃ; *NAmE* kɑːʃ/ *noun, verb*

■ ***noun*** (*especially BrE*) a short thick heavy stick, for example a piece of metal or solid rubber, that is used as a weapon （用作武器的）金属短棍，实心橡胶棒

IDM **under the 'cosh** (*BrE, informal*) experiencing a lot of pressure 压力沉重： *Our side was under the cosh for most of the second half.* 我方在下半场的大部分时间里经受着很大的压力。

■ ***verb* ~ sb** (*especially BrE*) to hit sb hard with a cosh or sth similar 用短棒打；用短棒之类的东西打

ˌco-'signatory *noun* one of two or more people who sign a formal document （正式文件的）联署人： *co-signatories of/to the treaty* 条约的联署人

co·sine /ˈkəʊsaɪn; *NAmE* ˈkoʊ-/ *noun* (*abbr.* **cos**) (*mathematics* 数) the RATIO of the length of the side next to an ACUTE ANGLE in a RIGHT-ANGLED triangle to the length of the longest side (= the HYPOTENUSE) 余弦 ➲ COMPARE SINE, TANGENT (2)

cos lettuce /ˌkɒs ˈletɪs; ˌkɒz; *NAmE* ˌkɑːs; ˌkɔːs/ (*BrE*) (*NAmE* **ro·maine**) *noun* [C, U] a type of LETTUCE with long crisp leaves 长叶莴苣

cos·met·ic /kɒzˈmetɪk; *NAmE* kɑːz-/ *noun, adj.*

■ ***noun*** [usually pl.] a substance that you put on your face or body to make it more attractive 化妆品；美容品： *the cosmetics industry* 化妆品行业 ◇ *a cosmetic company* 化妆品公司 ◇ *cosmetic products* 化妆产品 ➲ COLLOCATIONS AT FASHION

■ ***adj.*** **1** improving only the outside appearance of sth and not its basic character 装门面的；表面的： *These reforms are not merely cosmetic.* 这些改革不仅仅是装点门面的。◇ *She dismissed the plan as a cosmetic exercise to win votes.* 她认为这项计划是为了赢得选票所做的表面文章。 **2** connected with medical treatment that is intended to improve a person's appearance 整容的： *cosmetic surgery* 整容外科 ◇ *cosmetic dental work* 牙齿整形 ► **cos·met·ic·al·ly** /-kli/ *adv.*

cos·mic /ˈkɒzmɪk; *NAmE* ˈkɑːz-/ *adj.* [usually before noun] **1** connected with the whole universe 宇宙的： *Do you believe in a cosmic plan?* 你相信冥冥中的安排吗？ ➲ WORDFINDER NOTE AT UNIVERSE **2** very great and important 巨大且重要的： *This was disaster on a cosmic scale.* 这是塌天大祸。

ˌcosmic 'dust *noun* [U] (*astronomy* 天) very small pieces of matter floating in space 宇宙尘

ˌcosmic 'rays *noun* [pl.] RAYS that reach the earth from outer space 宇宙线

cos·mol·ogy /kɒzˈmɒlədʒi; *NAmE* kɑːzˈmɑːl-/ *noun* [U] the scientific study of the universe and its origin and development 宇宙学 ► **cosmo·logic·al** /ˌkɒzməˈlɒdʒɪkl; *NAmE* ˌkɑːzməˈlɑːdʒ-/ *adj.* **cos·molo·gist** /kɒzˈmɒlədʒɪst; *NAmE* kɑːzˈmɑːl-/ *noun*

cosmo·naut /ˈkɒzmənɔːt; *NAmE* ˈkɑːz-/ *noun* an ASTRONAUT from the former Soviet Union （苏联的）宇航员，航天员，太空人

cosmo·pol·itan /ˌkɒzməˈpɒlɪtən; *NAmE* ˌkɑːzməˈpɑːl-/ *adj., noun*

■ ***adj.*** (*approving*) **1** containing people of different types or from different countries, and influenced by their culture 世界性的；全球各国的；有各国人的；受各国文化影响的： *a cosmopolitan city/resort* 国际性的都市 / 度假胜地 ◇ *The club has a cosmopolitan atmosphere.* 这个俱乐部具有世界文化的气氛。 **2** having or showing a wide experience of people and things from many different countries 接触过许多国家的人（或事物）的；见过世面的；见识广的： *people with a truly cosmopolitan outlook* 真正具有世界眼光的人 ◇ *cosmopolitan young people* 见多识广的年轻人

■ ***noun*** a person who has experience of many different parts of the world 周游世界的人： *She's a real cosmopolitan.* 她是个真正的四海为家的人。

cos·mos /ˈkɒzmɒs; *NAmE* ˈkɑːzmoʊs; -məs/ **the cosmos** *noun* [sing.] the universe, especially when it is thought of as an ordered system （尤指被视为有序体系时的）宇宙： *the structure of the cosmos* 宇宙的结构 ◇ *our place in the cosmos* 我们在宇宙中的位置

cos·set /ˈkɒsɪt; *NAmE* ˈkɑːs-/ *verb* **~ sb** (*often disapproving*) to treat sb with a lot of care and give them a lot of attention, sometimes too much 宠爱；溺爱；娇惯 **SYN** **pamper**

cost /kɒst; *NAmE* kɔːst/ *noun, verb*

■ ***noun*** **1** [C, U] the amount of money that you need in order to buy, make or do sth 费用；花费；价钱： *the **high/low cost** of housing* 住宅的高昂 / 低廉费用 ◇ *A new computer system has been installed **at a cost of** £80 000.* 新的计算机系统已安装，费用为 8 万英镑。 ◇ *The plan had to be abandoned on grounds of cost.* 由于经费的原因此项计划被迫放弃。 ◇ *We did not even make enough money to **cover the cost** of the food.* 我们挣的钱甚至无法糊口。 ◇ *Consumers will have to **bear the full cost** of these pay increases.* 消费者将不得不承担增加工资所需的全部费用。 ◇ *The total cost to you* (= the amount you have to pay) *is £3 000.* 你总共要支付 3 000 英镑。 ➲ SYNONYMS AT PRICE **2** **costs** [pl.] the total amount of money that needs to be spent by a business 成本： *The use of cheap labour helped to keep costs down.* 使用廉价劳动力有助于降低成本。 ◇ *to **cut/reduce costs*** 降低成本 ◇ ***running/operating/labour costs*** 营运 / 经营 / 人工成本 ◇ *We have had to raise our prices because of rising costs.* 因为成本不断上涨，我们不得不提高价格。 ➲ COLLOCATIONS AT BUSINESS **3** [U, sing.] the effort, loss or damage that is involved in order to do or achieve sth （为做某事涉及的）努力，代价，损失： *the terrible cost of the war in death and suffering* 这场战争造成的死亡与苦难的惨重代价 ◇ *the environmental cost of nuclear power* 核动力对环境的破坏 ◇ *She saved him from the fire but **at the cost of** her own life* (= she died). 她从火中把他救了出来，却牺牲了自己的生命。 ◇ *He worked non-stop for three months, **at** considerable **cost** to his health.* 他连续不断地工作了三个月，大大损害了自己的身体健康。 ◇ *I felt a need to please people, whatever **the cost in** time and energy.* 我感到一定要使人们满意，耗费多少时间和精力都在所不惜。 **4** **costs** (*NAmE also* **'court costs**) [pl.] the sum of money that sb is ordered to pay for lawyers, etc. in a legal case 诉讼费用： *He was ordered to pay £2 000 costs.* 他被责令缴纳 2 000 英镑诉讼费。

IDM **at 'all cost/costs** whatever is needed to achieve sth 不惜任何代价： *You must stop the press from finding out at all costs.* 你必须不惜一切代价阻止媒体查明真相。 **at 'any cost** under any circumstances 在任何情况下；无论如何： *He is determined to win at any cost.* 他决心无论如何要争取胜利。 **at 'cost** for only the amount of money that is needed to make or get sth, without any profit being added on 按成本；按成本价格： *goods sold at cost* 按成本价销售的商品 **know/learn/find sth to your 'cost** to know sth because of sth unpleasant that has happened to you 付出过代价（或吃了苦头）才知道： *He's a ruthless businessman, as I know to my cost.* 我吃了苦头后才知道他是个无情的商人。 ➲ MORE AT COUNT *v.*

■ ***verb*** (**cost, cost**) **HELP** In sense 4 **costed** is used for the past tense and past participle. 作第 4 义时过去式和过去分词用 costed。 **1** if sth **costs** a particular amount of money, you need to pay that amount in order to buy, make or do it 需付费；价钱为： **~ sth** *How much did it cost?* 这东西要多少钱？ ◇ *I didn't get it because it cost too much.* 因

为那东西太昂贵我没买。 ◇ *Tickets cost ten dollars each.* 每张票价为十美元。 ◇ *Calls to the helpline cost 38p per minute.* 打服务热线每分钟为 38 便士。 ◇ *Don't use too much of it—it **cost a lot of money**.* 这东西很贵，不要用得太多。 ◇ *All these reforms will **cost money*** (= be expensive). 所有这些改革都要花很多钱。 ◇ *Good food need not **cost a fortune*** (= cost a lot of money). 好食物不一定要花很多的钱。 ◇ **~ sb sth** *The meal cost us about £40.* 这顿饭花了我们约 40 英镑。 ◇ *This is costing the taxpayer £10 billion a year.* 这要花费纳税人每年 100 亿英镑。 ◇ **~ sth to do sth** *The hospital will cost an estimated £2 billion to build.* 修建这座医院估计要耗费 20 亿英镑。 ◇ *It costs a fortune to fly first class.* 乘坐飞机头等舱要花一大笔钱。 **2** to cause the loss of sth 使丧失；使损失： **~ sb sth** *That one mistake almost cost him his life.* 那一个差错几乎使他丧命。 ◇ *A late penalty cost United the game* (= meant that they did not win the game). 临近终场点球得分使得联队输掉那场比赛。 ◇ **~ sth** *The closure of the factory is likely to cost 1 000 jobs.* 那家工厂一关闭，很可能 1 000 个工作岗位就没有了。 **3 ~ sb sth** to involve you in making an effort or doing sth unpleasant 使付出努力；使做不愉快的事： *The accident cost me a visit to the doctor.* 那事故害得我去看了一趟医生。 ◇ *Financial worries cost her many sleepless nights.* 她为钱发愁，许多夜晚无法入睡。 ➲ MORE LIKE THIS 33, page R28 **4** (**costed, costed**) [usually passive] to estimate how much money will be needed for sth or the price that should be charged for sth 估算成本；估价： **~ sth** *The project needs to be costed in detail.* 这项工程需要作详细的成本估算。 ◇ *Their accountants have costed the project at $8.1 million.* 他们的会计师估算此项工程成本为 810 万美元。 ◇ **~ sth out** *Have you costed out these proposals yet?* 你估算过这些提案所涉及的费用吗？ ➲ SEE ALSO COSTING

▼ **SYNONYMS 同义词辨析**

costs

spending • expenditure • expenses • overheads • outlay

These are all words for money spent by a government, an organization or a person. 以上各词均指政府、机构或个人的开支、支出、花费。

costs the total amount of money that needs to be spent by a business 指成本： *labour/production costs* 人工 / 生产成本 ◇ *rising costs* 正在上涨的成本

spending the amount of money that is spent, especially by a government or an organization 尤指政府或机构的开支、支出、花销： *public spending* 公共开支 ◇ *More spending on health was promised.* 已承诺增加医疗开支。

expenditure (*rather formal*) an amount of money spent by a government, an organization or a person 指政府、机构或个人的开支、支出、花费： *expenditure on education* 教育支出

expenses money that has to be spent by a person or an organization; money that you spend while you are working which your employer will pay back to you later 指个人或机构必需的开支、花费或报销的费用： *legal expenses* 律师费 ◇ *travel expenses* 差旅费

overhead(s) the regular costs of running a business or an organization, such as rent, electricity and wages 指经费、运营费用、经常性开支： *High overheads mean small profit margins.* 经费开销大意味着利润低。

outlay the money that you have to spend in order to start a new business or project, or in order to save yourself money or time later 指启动新业务或项目所必要的开支、费用或为了节省后期投入而使用的经费： *The best equipment is costly but is well worth the outlay.* 最好的设备花费大，但这种开支很值得。

PATTERNS

- spending/expenditure/outlay **on** sth
- **high/low** costs/spending/expenditure/expenses/overheads
- **total** costs/spending/expenditure/expenses/overheads/outlay
- **capital** costs/spending/expenditure/expenses/outlay
- **household** costs/spending/expenditure/expenses
- **government/public/education/health** costs/spending/expenditure
- to **increase/reduce** costs/spending/expenditure/expenses/overheads/the outlay

IDM **cost sb 'dear** to make sb suffer a lot 使饱尝苦头；使付出沉重的代价： *That one mistake has cost him dear over the years.* 那一个差错使他多年来付出了沉重的代价。 **it will 'cost you** (*informal*) used to say that sth will be expensive 贵得很；要花很多钱： *There is a deluxe model available, but it'll cost you.* 有豪华型的，但贵得很。 ➲ MORE AT ARM *n.*

'cost accounting *noun* [U] (*business* 商) the process of recording and analysing the costs involved in running a business 成本会计

cos·tal /'kɒstl; *NAmE* 'kɑːstl/ *adj.* (*anatomy* 解) connected with the RIBS 肋骨的；肋部的

'co-star *noun, verb*

■ ***noun*** one of two or more famous actors who appear together in a film/movie or play （电影或戏剧中的）联袂主演明星

■ ***verb*** (**-rr-**) **1** [I] **~ (with sb)** to appear as one of the main actors with sb in a play or film/movie （在电影或戏剧中）与其他明星联合主演： *a new movie in which Russell Crowe co-stars with Cate Blanchett* 由罗素·克劳和凯特·布兰切特联袂主演的一部新电影 **2** [T] **~ sb** (of a film/movie or play 电影或戏剧) to have two or more famous actors acting in it （由明星演员）联袂主演，合演： *a new movie co-starring Russell Crowe and Cate Blanchett* 由罗素·克劳和凯特·布兰切特联袂主演的一部新电影

'cost-benefit *noun* [U] (*economics* 经) the relationship between the cost of doing sth and the value of the benefit that results from it 成本效益： *cost-benefit analysis* 成本效益分析

'cost-cutting *noun* [U] the reduction of the amount of money spent on sth, especially because of financial difficulty （尤指因财政困难的）成本削减： *Deliveries of mail could be delayed because of cost-cutting.* 由于削减成本，邮件的递送可能会延迟。 ◇ *a **cost-cutting exercise/measure/programme*** 成本削减的实施 / 措施 / 计划

,cost-ef'fective *adj.* giving the best possible profit or benefits in comparison with the money that is spent 有最佳利润的；有成本效益的；划算的 ► **,cost-ef'fect·ive·ness** *noun* [U]

cos·ter·mon·ger /'kɒstəmʌŋɡə(r); *NAmE* 'kɑːstərm-/ *noun* (*BrE*) (in the past) a person who sold fruit and vegetables in the street （旧时的）水果蔬菜小贩

cost·ing /'kɒstɪŋ; *NAmE* 'kɔːst-/ *noun* an estimate of how much money will be needed for sth 成本估算： *Here is a detailed costing of our proposals.* 这是我们的方案的详细成本估算。 ◇ *You'd better do some costings.* 你最好作一些成本估算。

cost·ly /'kɒstli; *NAmE* 'kɔːst-/ *adj.* (**cost·lier, cost·li·est**) HELP It is also very common to use **more costly** and **most costly**. 亦可用 more costly 和 most costly。 **1** costing a lot of money, especially more than you want to pay 花钱多的；昂贵的；价钱高的 SYN **expensive**: *Buying new furniture may prove too costly.* 购买新家具可能会花钱太多。 ➲ SYNONYMS AT EXPENSIVE **2** causing problems or the loss of sth 引起困难的；造成损失的 SYN **expensive**: *a costly mistake/failure* 造成重大损失的错误 / 失败 ◇ *Mining can be costly in terms of lives* (= too many people can die). 采矿有时会造成重大的生命损失。 ► **cost·li·ness** *noun* [U]

the ,cost of 'living *noun* [sing.] the amount of money that people need to pay for food, clothing and somewhere to live 生活费用： *a steady rise in the cost of living* 生活费用的持续上升 ◇ *Despite the high cost of living, London is a great place to live.* 尽管生活费用昂贵，伦敦依然是一个居住的好地方。

,cost 'price *noun* [U] the cost of producing sth or the price at which it is sold without profit 成本价： *Copies of* *the CD can be purchased at cost price.* 这光盘可按成本价购买。 ➲ COMPARE SELLING PRICE

cos·tume /ˈkɒstjuːm; *NAmE* ˈkɑːstuːm/ *noun* **1** [C, U] the clothes worn by people from a particular place or during a particular historical period（某地或某历史时期的）服装，装束 ➲ SEE ALSO NATIONAL COSTUME **2** [C, U] the clothes worn by actors in a play or film/movie, or worn by sb to make them look like sb/sth else 戏装；装扮用服装：*The actors were still in costume and make-up.* 这些演员仍是戏装打扮。◇ *She has four costume changes during the play.* 她在这出戏里要换四次服装。◇ *He went to the party in a giant chicken costume.* 他打扮成一只大鸡去参加聚会。◇ *a costume designer* 戏装设计师 ➲ WORDFINDER NOTE AT STAGE **3** [C] (*BrE, informal*) = SWIMMING COSTUME

cos·tumed /ˈkɒstjuːmd; *NAmE* ˈkɑːstuːmd/ *adj.* [usually before noun] wearing a costume 着戏装的

ˈcostume drama *noun* [C, U] a play or film/movie set in the past 古装戏；古装电影

ˈcostume jewellery *noun* [U] large heavy jewellery that can look expensive but is made with cheap materials（廉价）人造珠宝饰物

ˈcostume party *noun* (*NAmE*) a party where all the guests wear special clothes, in order to look like a different person, an animal, etc. 化装舞会

cos·tu·mier /kɒsˈtjuːmiə(r); *NAmE* kɑːsˈtuːmieɪ/ (*BrE*) (*NAmE* **ˈcos·tu·mer**) *noun* a person or company that makes COSTUMES or has COSTUMES to hire, especially for the theatre（尤指戏剧演出的）戏装制作人，服装公司，戏装出租商：*a firm of theatrical costumiers* 戏剧服装出租公司

cosy (*BrE*) (*NAmE* **cozy**) /ˈkəʊzi; *NAmE* ˈkoʊzi/ *adj., verb*

■ ***adj.*** (**cosi·er, cosi·est, cozi·er, cozi·est**) **1** warm, comfortable and safe, especially because of being small or confined（尤指因地方小或封闭而）温暖舒适的 SYN snug：*a cosy little room* 温暖舒适的小房间 ◇ *a cosy feeling* 惬意的感觉 ◇ *I felt warm and cosy sitting by the fire.* 坐在炉火旁，我感到又暖和又舒服。 **2** friendly and private 亲密无间的；密切的：*a cosy chat with a friend* 与朋友亲切的闲聊 **3** (*often disapproving*) easy and convenient, but not always honest or right 轻易得到的，轻松的（但不一定是诚实或正当的）：*The firm has a cosy relationship with the Ministry of Defence.* 这家公司与国防部关系密切。◇ *The danger is that things get too cosy.* 危险在于一切都来得太容易。 ▸ **cosi·ly** (*BrE*) (*NAmE* **cozi·ly**) *adv.*: *sitting cosily by the fire* 暖融融地坐在炉火旁 **cosi·ness** (*BrE*) (*NAmE* **cozi·ness**) *noun* [U]: *the warmth and cosiness of the kitchen* 厨房的温暖与舒适

■ ***verb*** (**cosies, cosy·ing, cosied, cosied**)

PHR V **ˌcosy ˈup to sb** (*BrE*) (*NAmE* **ˌcozy ˈup to sb**) (*informal*) to act in a friendly way towards sb, especially sb who will be useful to you 献殷勤；取悦

cot /kɒt; *NAmE* kɑːt/ *noun* **1** (*BrE*) (*NAmE* **crib**) a small bed with high sides for a baby or young child（有围栏的）幼儿床：*a travel cot* (= one that can be moved around easily, used when travelling) 旅行幼儿床 ➲ VISUAL VOCAB PAGE V24 ➲ SEE ALSO CARRYCOT **2** (*NAmE*) (*BrE* **ˈcamp bed**) a light narrow bed that you can fold up and carry easily 折叠床；行军床 ➲ VISUAL VOCAB PAGE V24

ˈcot death (*BrE*) (*NAmE* **ˈcrib death**) *noun* [U, C] the sudden death while sleeping of a baby that appears to be healthy 婴儿猝死

co·terie /ˈkəʊtəri; *NAmE* ˈkoʊ-/ *noun* [C+sing./pl. v.] (*formal, often disapproving*) a small group of people who have the same interests and do things together but do not like to include others（志趣相同、合伙做事而排外的）小圈子，小集团

co·ter·min·ous /kəʊˈtɜːmɪnəs; *NAmE* koʊˈtɜːrm-/ *adj.* [not usually before noun] (*formal*) **1 ~ (with sth)** (of countries or areas 国家或地区) sharing a border 享有共同边界；毗连；接壤 **2 ~ (with sth)** (of things or ideas 事物或看法) having so much in common that they are almost the same as each other 几乎一致；差不多相同

cot·tage /ˈkɒtɪdʒ; *NAmE* ˈkɑːt-/ *noun* a small house, especially in the country 小屋；（尤指）村舍，小别墅：*a charming country cottage with roses around the door* 门口周围开着玫瑰花的迷人的乡村小屋 ◇ (*BrE*) *a holiday cottage* 度假小别墅 ➲ VISUAL VOCAB PAGE V16

ˌcottage ˈcheese *noun* [U] soft white cheese with small lumps in it 农家干酪（含小块的白色软干酪）

ˌcottage ˈhospital *noun* (*BrE*) a small hospital in a country area 乡村小医院；乡间诊疗所

ˌcottage ˈindustry *noun* a small business in which the work is done by people in their homes 家庭手工业：*Weaving and knitting are traditional cottage industries.* 编织和针织是传统的家庭手工业。

ˌcottage ˈloaf *noun* (*BrE*) a LOAF of bread consisting of a large round piece with a smaller round piece on top 农家面包（用大、小两个圆面包叠在一起）

ˌcottage ˈpie *noun* [C, U] = SHEPHERD'S PIE

cot·tager /ˈkɒtɪdʒə(r); *NAmE* ˈkɑːt-/ *noun* (*BrE*) (especially in the past) a person who lives in a small house or cottage in the country（尤指旧时的）住农舍者，村民

cot·ta·ging /ˈkɒtɪdʒɪŋ; *NAmE* ˈkɑːt-/ *noun* [U] (*BrE, slang*) the practice of HOMOSEXUAL men looking for sexual partners in a public toilet/bathroom（男性同性恋者）在公共卫生间寻找性伴侣

cot·ton /ˈkɒtn; *NAmE* ˈkɑːtn/ *noun, verb*

■ ***noun*** [U] **1** a plant grown in warm countries for the soft white hairs around its seeds that are used to make cloth and thread 棉，棉花（植株）：*cotton fields/plants* 棉田；棉株 ◇ *bales of cotton* 大包的棉花 **2** the cloth made from the cotton plant 棉织物；棉布：*The sheets are 100% pure cotton.* 这些被单是 100% 的纯棉。◇ *a cotton shirt/skirt* 棉布衬衫 / 裙子 ◇ *printed cotton cloth* 印花棉布 ◇ *the cotton industry* 棉纺织业 ◇ *a cotton mill* 棉纺厂 **3** (*especially BrE*) thread that is used for sewing 棉线；棉纱：*sewing cotton* 缝纫用棉线 ◇ *a cotton reel* 棉线轴 ➲ VISUAL VOCAB PAGE V45 **4** (*NAmE*) (*US also* **abˌsorbent ˈcotton**) (*BrE* **ˌcotton ˈwool**) a soft mass of white material that is used for cleaning the skin or a wound 药棉；脱脂棉：*Use a cotton ball to apply the lotion.* 用棉球涂护肤液。

■ ***verb***

PHR V **ˌcotton ˈon (to sth)** (*informal*) to begin to understand or realize sth without being told 明白；领悟；意识到：*I suddenly cottoned on to what he was doing.* 我突然明白了他在做什么。 **ˈcotton (up) to sb/sth** (*NAmE, informal*) to make an attempt to be friendly to sb 向…讨好；巴结；与…套近乎

the ˈCotton Belt *noun* the states in the southern US where cotton was the main crop 棉花带（美国南部盛产棉花的几个州）

ˌcotton ˈbud (*BrE*) (*also* **ˈQ-tip™** *NAmE, BrE*) *noun* a small stick with COTTON WOOL at each end, used for cleaning inside the ears, etc.（用于清洁耳朵内部等的）棉签

ˌcotton ˈcandy (*NAmE*) (*BrE* **candy·floss**) *noun* [U] a type of sweet/candy in the form of a mass of sticky threads made from melted sugar and served on a stick, especially at FAIRGROUNDS（尤指游乐场出售的）棉花糖

ˈcotton gin (*also* **gin**) *noun* a machine for separating the seeds of a cotton plant from the cotton 轧棉机；轧花机

cotton·mouth /ˈkɒtnmaʊθ; *NAmE* ˈkɑːtn-/ (*also* **ˌcotton-mouth ˈmoccasin, ˌwater ˈmoccasin**) *noun* a poisonous snake which lives near water in the US 棉口蛇，水蝮蛇（毒蛇，生活于美国水滨）

cot·ton·wood /ˈkɒtnwʊd; *NAmE* ˈkɑːtn-/ (*also* **ˈcotton-wood tree**) *noun* a type of N American POPLAR tree, with seeds that are covered in hairs that look like white cotton 棉白杨，三角叶杨（产于北美）

C

ˌcotton ˈwool (*BrE*) (*US* **(abˌsorbent) ˈcotton**) *noun* [U] a soft mass of white material that is used for cleaning the skin or a wound 药棉；脱脂棉：*cotton wool balls* 药用棉球

couch /kaʊtʃ/ *noun, verb*

■ ***noun*** **1** a long comfortable seat for two or more people to sit on 长沙发；长榻 **SYN** **settee, sofa** ➲ VISUAL VOCAB PAGE V22 **2** a long piece of furniture like a bed, especially in a doctor's office（尤指诊室内的）诊察台：*on the psychiatrist's couch* 在精神病医生的诊察台上

■ ***verb*** [usually passive] **~ sth (in sth)** (*formal*) to say or write words in a particular style or manner（用某种文体或方式）表达，措辞：*The letter was deliberately **couched in** very vague **terms**.* 这封信故意写得含糊其词。

couch·ette /kuːˈʃet/ *noun* a narrow bed on a train, that folds down from the wall（列车上的）折叠式卧铺

ˈcouch potato *noun* (*informal, disapproving*) a person who spends a lot of time sitting and watching television 老泡在电视机前的人

cou·gar /ˈkuːɡə(r)/ *noun* (*especially NAmE*) **1** = PUMA **2** an older woman who seeks a sexual relationship with a much younger man "狼虎女"（追求比自己年轻得多的男子并想与之发生性关系的老女人）

cough 🔑 /kɒf; *NAmE* kɔːf/ *verb, noun*

■ ***verb*** **1** 🔑 [I] to force out air suddenly and noisily through your throat, for example when you have a cold 咳嗽：*I couldn't stop coughing.* 我咳嗽不止。◇ *to **cough nervously/politely/discreetly*** 紧张地 / 斯文地 / 小心翼翼地咳嗽 **2** [T] **~ sth (up)** to force sth out of your throat or lungs by coughing（从喉咙或肺中）咳出：*Sometimes she coughed (up) blood.* 她有时咯血。**3** [I] (of an engine 发动机) to make a sudden unpleasant noise 突然发出刺耳的声音

PHR V **ˌcough ˈup** | **ˌcough sth↔ˈup** (*informal*) to give sth, especially money, unwillingly 勉强给（尤指钱）：*Steve finally coughed up the money he owed us.* 史蒂夫最终勉强归还了他欠我们的钱。

■ ***noun*** **1** 🔑 an act or a sound of coughing 咳嗽；咳嗽声：*She gave a little cough to attract my attention.* 她轻轻地咳了一声以引起我的注意。**2** 🔑 an illness or infection that makes you cough often 咳嗽病：*to have a **dry/persistent/hacking cough*** 干咳；顽固的咳嗽；频繁地干咳 ◇ *My cold's better, but I can't seem to shake off this cough.* 我感冒好些了，但这咳嗽好像老也不好。➲ SEE ALSO WHOOPING COUGH

cough·ing 🔑 /ˈkɒfɪŋ; *NAmE* ˈkɔːfɪŋ/ *noun* [U] the action of coughing 咳嗽：*Another fit of coughing seized him.* 他那咳嗽又一次发作了。

ˈcough mixture (*BrE*) (*also* **ˈcough syrup**, **ˈcough medicine** *BrE, NAmE*) *noun* [U] liquid medicine that you take for a cough 止咳药水；止咳合剂

could 🔑 /kəd; *strong form* kʊd/ *modal verb* (*negative* **could not**, *short form* **couldn't** /ˈkʊdnt/) **1** 🔑 used as the past tense of 'can'（用于 can 的过去式）：*She said that she couldn't come.* 她说她来不了。◇ *I couldn't hear what they were saying.* 我听不见他们在说些什么。◇ *Sorry, I couldn't get any more.* 对不起，我无法弄到更多了。➲ NOTE AT CAN[1] **2** 🔑 used to ask if you can do sth（询问是否可做某事）能，可以：*Could I use your phone, please?* 请让我用一下你的电话可以吗？◇ *Could we stop by next week?* 我们下周能过来一下吗？**3** 🔑 used to politely ask sb to do sth for you（礼貌地请求别人做事）能，可以：*Could you babysit for us on Friday?* 你星期五帮我们看一下孩子好吗？**4** 🔑 used to show that sth is or might be possible（表示可能性）可能：*I could do it now, if you like.* 如果你愿意的话，我现在就可以做这事。◇ *Don't worry—they could have just forgotten to call.* 别担心，他们可能只是忘了打电话。◇ *You couldn't have left it on the bus, could you?* 你不可能把它落在公共汽车上了吧？◇ *'Have some more cake.' 'Oh, I couldn't, thank you* (= I'm too full).' "再来点蛋糕吧。" "谢谢你，我吃不下了。" **5** 🔑 used to suggest sth（用于建议）可以：*We could write a letter to the director.* 我们不妨给主管写封信。◇ *You could always try his home number.* 你总可以试着给他在家里打电话呀。**6** 🔑 used to show that you are annoyed that sb did not do sth（对某人未做某事表示恼怒）本来可以：*They could have let me know they were going to be late!* 他们要晚来，也该早告诉我一声呀！**7** (*informal*) used to emphasize how strongly you want to express your feelings（强调感觉）真想：*I'm so fed up I could scream!* 我烦透了，非大喊大叫不可！➲ NOTE AT MODAL

IDM **could do with sth** (*informal*) used to say that you need or would like to have sth（表示需要或希望有）想要：*I could do with a drink!* 我真想喝一杯！◇ *Her hair could have done with a wash.* 她的头发该洗一洗了。

cou·lis /ˈkuːli; *NAmE* kuːˈliː/ *noun* (*pl.* **cou·lis**) (*from French*) a thin fruit sauce 稀果酱

cou·lomb /ˈkuːlɒm; *NAmE* -lɑːm; -loːm/ *noun* (*abbr.* **C**) (*physics* 物) a unit for measuring electric charge 库，库仑（电量单位）

coun·cil 🔑 /ˈkaʊnsl/ *noun* [C+sing./pl. v.] (*often* **the Council**) **1** 🔑 a group of people who are elected to govern an area such as a city or county（市、郡等的）政务委员会，地方议会：*a **city/county/borough/district council*** 市 / 郡 / 自治市 / 区政务委员会 ◇ *She's on the local council.* 她是地方议会的议员。◇ ***a council member/meeting*** 政务委员会委员 / 会议 **2** 🔑 (*BrE*) the organization that provides services in a city or county, for example education, houses, libraries, etc. 市政（或地方管理）服务机构：***council workers/services*** 市政工作人员 / 部门 **3** a group of people chosen to give advice, make rules, do research, provide money, etc.（顾问、立法、研究、基金等）委员会：*the Medical Research Council* 医学研究会 ◇ *In Britain, the Arts Council gives grants to theatres.* 英国的艺术委员会向剧院提供资金。**4** (*formal*) (especially in the past) a formal meeting to discuss what action to take in a particular situation（尤指旧时讨论采取什么行动的）协商会议：*The King held a council at Nottingham from 14 to 19 October 1330.* 国王于 1330 年 10 月 14 日至 19 日在诺丁汉召集协商会议。➲ SEE ALSO PRIVY COUNCIL

ˈcouncil chamber *noun* (*BrE*) a large room in which a council meets 会议厅；会议室；议事室

ˈcouncil estate *noun* (*BrE*) a large group of houses built by a local council 地方当局所属地产；地方政府建的住宅群

ˈcouncil house, **ˈcouncil flat** *noun* (*BrE*) a house or flat rented from the local council 地方政府出租的住房（或公寓）

coun·cil·lor (*NAmE also* **coun·cil·or**) /ˈkaʊnsələ(r)/ *noun* (*abbr.* **Cllr**) a member of a council 市议员；政务委员会委员：*Councillor Ann Jones* 安·琼斯委员 ◇ *Talk to your local councillor about the problem.* 关于这个问题可与你那里的政务委员谈一谈。➲ SEE ALSO COUNCILMAN, COUNCILWOMAN

coun·cil·man /ˈkaʊnslmən/ *noun* (*pl.* **-men** /-mən/) (*US*) = COUNCILLOR

ˌcouncil of ˈwar *noun* (*pl.* **councils of war**) (*BrE*) a meeting to discuss how to deal with an urgent and difficult situation（为处理紧急和困难局势而召开的）紧急会议

ˈcouncil tax *noun* (*often* **the council tax**) [sing., U] (in Britain) a tax charged by local councils, based on the value of a person's home（英国根据个人住房的价值而收取的）市政税

coun·cil·woman /ˈkaʊnslwʊmən/ *noun* (*pl.* **-women** /-wɪmɪn/) (*US*) = COUNCILLOR

coun·sel /ˈkaʊnsl/ *noun, verb*

■ ***noun*** [U, C] **1** (*formal*) advice, especially given by older people or experts; a piece of advice（尤指年长者或专家的）劝告，忠告，建议：*Listen to the counsel of your elders.* 要听从长辈的忠告。◇ *In the end, wiser counsels prevailed.* 高明的建议最终占了上风。**2** (*law* 律) a lawyer or group of lawyers representing sb in court 法律顾问；律师：*to be represented by counsel* 由律师代表 ◇ *the counsel* *for the defence/prosecution* 被告 / 原告的律师 ◊ ***defence/prosecuting counsel*** 被告 / 原告的律师 ◊ *The court then heard counsel for the dead woman's father.* 法庭接着听取了女死者的父亲所请律师的陈述。 ➲ **WORDFINDER NOTE** AT TRIAL ➲ **COLLOCATIONS** AT JUSTICE ➲ SEE ALSO QUEEN'S COUNSEL ➲ NOTE AT LAWYER

IDM **a counsel of des'pair** (*formal*) advice not to try to do sth because it is too difficult 知难而退的建议 **a counsel of per'fection** (*formal*) advice that is good but that is difficult or impossible to follow 听上去完美却难以实行的建议 **keep your own 'counsel** (*formal*) to keep your opinions, plans, etc. secret 将自己意见（或计划等）保密；不暴露自己的意图

■ ***verb*** (**-ll-**, *especially US* **-l-**) **1 ~ sb** to listen to and give support or professional advice to sb who needs help 提供专业咨询：*Therapists were brought in to counsel the bereaved.* 请了治疗专家来给死者的亲属做心理辅导。 **2** (*formal*) to advise sb to do sth 建议，劝告（做某事）：**~ sth** *Most experts counsel caution in such cases.* 大多数专家建议在这样的情况下要谨慎从事。 ◊ **~ sb to do sth** *He counselled them to give up the plan.* 他建议他们放弃此项计划。 ➲ **MORE LIKE THIS** 36, page R29

coun·sel·ling (*especially US* **coun·sel·ing**) /ˈkaʊnsəlɪŋ/ *noun* [U] professional advice about a problem 咨询；辅导：*marriage guidance counselling* 婚姻指导咨询 ◊ *a student counselling service* 学生辅导服务

coun·sel·lor (*especially US* **coun·sel·or**) /ˈkaʊnsələ(r)/ *noun* **1** a person who has been trained to advise people with problems, especially personal problems（尤指针对私人问题的）顾问；辅导顾问：*a marriage guidance counsellor* 婚姻指导顾问 **2** (*NAmE, IrishE*) a lawyer 律师 **3** (*NAmE*) a person who is in charge of young people at a summer camp 夏令营负责人

count 🔑 /kaʊnt/ *verb, noun*

■ ***verb***

• **SAY NUMBERS** 数数 **1** 🔑 [I] to say numbers in the correct order（按顺序）数数：*Billy can't count yet.* 比利还不会数数。 ◊ **~ to/up to sth** *She can count up to 10 in Italian.* 她可以用意大利语数到 10。 ◊ **~ (from sth) to/up to sth** *to count from 1 to 10* 从 1 数到 10

• **FIND TOTAL** 得到总数 **2** 🔑 [T, I] to calculate the total number of people, things, etc. in a particular group 计算（或清点）总数：**~ sth (up)** *The diet is based on counting calories.* 这个饮食安排以热量统计为根据。 ◊ **~ (up) how many…** *She began to count up how many guests they had to invite.* 她开始计算他们得邀请多少位客人。 ◊ **~ from…** *There are 12 weeks to go, counting from today.* 从今天算起还有 12 个星期。

• **INCLUDE** 包括 **3** 🔑 [T] **~ sb/sth** to include sb/sth when you calculate a total 把…算入；包括：*We have invited 50 people, not counting the children.* 不算小孩，我们邀请了 50 人。

• **MATTER** 有重要性 **4** 🔑 [I] (not used in the progressive tenses 不用于进行时) to be important 重要 **SYN** **matter**: *Every point in this game counts.* 这场比赛每一分都很重要。 ◊ ***It's the thought that counts*** (= used about a small but kind action or gift). 贵在心意。 ◊ **~ for sth** *The fact that she had apologized counted for nothing with him.* 她已道歉，但他认为这没有用。

• **ACCEPT OFFICIALLY** 正式接纳 **5** 🔑 [I, T] to be officially accepted; to accept sth officially（被）正式接纳，正式认可：*Don't go over that line or your throw won't count.* 别越过那条线，否则你的投掷就会被判无效。 ◊ **~ sth** *Applications received after 1 July will not be counted.* * 7 月 1 日以后收到的申请书将不予受理。

• **CONSIDER** 认为 **6** [I, T] to consider sb/sth in a particular way; to be considered in a particular way 认为；看作；算作；被视为：**~ (sb/sth) as sb/sth** *For tax purposes that money counts/is counted as income.* 那笔钱算作收入，需要纳税。 ◊ **~ sb/sth/yourself + adv./prep.** *I count him among my closest friends.* 我把他看作我最亲密的朋友之一。 ◊ **~ sb/sth/yourself + adj.** *I count myself lucky to have known him.* 和他相识，我觉得很幸运。 ◊ **~ sb/sth/yourself + noun** *She counts herself one of the lucky ones.* 她认为自己是一个幸运儿。

IDM **be able to count sb/sth on (the fingers of) one 'hand** used to say that the total number of sb/sth is very small 屈指可数；寥寥无几 **…and 'counting** used to say that a total is continuing to increase（总数）仍在继续增加：*The movie's ticket sales add up to $39 million, and counting.* 这部电影的票房共 3 900 万美元，还在继续上升。 **count your 'blessings** to be grateful for the good things in your life 知足 **don't count your 'chickens (before they are 'hatched)** (*saying*) you should not be too confident that sth will be successful, because sth may still go wrong 不要蛋未孵化先数小鸡；别过早打如意算盘 **count the cost (of sth)** to feel the bad effects of a mistake, an accident, etc. 感受（错误、事故等造成的）不利后果：*The town is now counting the cost of its failure to provide adequate flood protection.* 这个镇未采取充分的防洪措施，现在尝到苦头了。 **count 'sheep** to imagine that sheep are jumping over a fence and to count them, as a way of getting to sleep 数（假想中跳过栅栏的）羊以求入睡 **stand up and be 'counted** to say publicly that you support sb or you agree with sth 公开表示支持（或赞同） **who's 'counting?** (*informal*) used to say that you do not care how many times sth happens（表示不管发生多少次）谁在乎呢，管它呢：*I've seen the film five times, but who's counting?* 这部电影我看了五遍，管它呢。

PHR V **ˌcount a'gainst sb | ˌcount sth a'gainst sb** to be considered or to consider sth to be a disadvantage in sb（被）认为对某人不利：*For that job her lack of experience may count against her.* 她缺乏经验可能对她申请那份工作不利。 **ˌcount 'down (to sth)** to think about a future event with pleasure or excitement and count the minutes, days, etc. until it happens 倒计时：*She's already counting down to the big day.* 她已经在为这一重大日子倒计时了。 ➲ RELATED NOUN COUNTDOWN **ˌcount sb 'in** to include sb in an activity 把某人算入；包括：*I hear you're organizing a trip to the game next week? Count me in!* 我听说你们将在下周组织旅行去看比赛？把我也算上！ **'count on sb/sth** 🔑 to trust sb to do sth or to be sure that sth will happen 依赖，依靠，指望（某人做某事）；确信（某事会发生） **SYN** **bank on**: *'I'm sure he'll help.' 'Don't count on it.'* "我肯定他会帮忙的。" "那可靠不住。" ◊ **count on sb/sth to do sth** *I'm counting on you to help me.* 我就靠你帮我啦。 ◊ **count on sb/sth doing sth** *Few people can count on having a job for life.* 很少人会指望一辈子都干一个工作。 ◊ *We can't count on this warm weather lasting.* 我们不能指望这暖和的天气会持久。 ➲ **SYNONYMS** AT TRUST **ˌcount sb/sth↔'out** to count things one after the other as you put them somewhere（放置东西时）逐一地数出：*She counted out $70 in $10 bills.* 她数出了 70 美元，都是 10 美元一张的。 **ˌcount sb 'out** to not include sb in an activity 不把某人算入；不包括：*If you're going out tonight you'll have to count me out.* 假如你们今晚要出去，就别把我算在内。 **ˌcount to'wards/to'ward sth** to be included as part of sth that you hope to achieve in the future 被包括在内（成为将来所得的一部分）：*Students gain college credits which count towards their degree.* 学生获得的学分将计入其学位积分。

■ ***noun***

• **TOTAL** 总数 **1** [usually sing.] an act of counting to find the total number of sth; the total number that you find 数出总数；总数：*The bus driver did a quick count of the empty seats.* 公共汽车司机很快地数了数空位。 ◊ *If the election result is close, there will be a second count.* 如果选举结果很接近，将进行第二次计票。 ◊ *The body count* (= the total number of people who have died) *stands at 24.* 死亡人数总计为 24 人。 ➲ SEE ALSO HEADCOUNT

• **SAYING NUMBERS** 数数 **2** [usually sing.] an act of saying numbers in order beginning with 1（按顺序的）数数，点数：*Raise your leg and hold for a count of ten.* 抬起一条腿，保持这一姿势，直至数到十。 ◊ *He was knocked to the ground and stayed down for a count of eight* (= in boxing). 他被击倒在地，躺在地上直至数到八（拳击用语）。

• **MEASUREMENT** 度量 **3** [usually sing.] (*specialist*) a measurement of the amount of sth contained in a particular substance or area（某物质在某物或面积中）量的计数：*a raised white blood cell count* 升高了的白血球数 ➲ SEE ALSO BLOOD COUNT, POLLEN COUNT

• **CRIME** 罪行 **4** (*law* 律) a crime that sb is accused of committing （被指控的）罪状，事项：*They were found guilty on all counts.* 他们被判各项罪名成立。◇ *She appeared in court on three counts of fraud.* 她因三项诈骗罪而出庭受审。

- **IN DISCUSSION/ARGUMENT** 讨论；争论 **5** [usually pl.] a point made during a discussion or an argument （讨论或争论的）论点，观点，问题，事项：*I disagree with you on both counts.* 我对你的两个观点均不敢苟同。
- **RANK/TITLE** 等级；头衔 **6** (in some European countries) a NOBLEMAN of high rank, similar to an EARL in Britain 伯爵（欧洲一些国家相当于英国 earl 的贵族封号）：*Count Tolstoy* 托尔斯泰伯爵 ➲ SEE ALSO COUNTESS

IDM **at the last 'count** according to the latest information about the numbers of sth 根据有关…数字的最新消息：*She'd applied for 30 jobs at the last count.* 根据有关的最新消息她申请过 30 个职位。 **keep (a) count (of sth)** to remember or keep a record of numbers or amounts of sth over a period of time （在一段时期内）记得数目，数得清，记录：*Keep a count of your calorie intake for one week.* 把你一星期的卡路里摄入量记录下来。 **lose count (of sth)** to forget the total of sth before you have finished counting it 数不清：*I lost count and had to start again.* 我数着数着忘了，不得不从头开始数。◇ *She had lost count of the number of times she'd told him to be careful* (= she could not remember because there were so many). 她不知多少次告诉过他要小心。 **ˌout for the 'count** (*BrE*) (*NAmE* **ˌdown for the 'count**) **1** (of a BOXER 拳击手) unable to get up again within ten seconds after being knocked down （被击倒后的十秒钟以内）无法再站立起来 **2** in a deep sleep 熟睡；酣睡

count·able /ˈkaʊntəbl/ *adj.* (*grammar* 语法) a noun that is **countable** can be used in the plural or with *a* or *an*, for example *table*, *cat* and *idea* （名词）可数的 **OPP** **uncountable**

count·down /ˈkaʊntdaʊn/ *noun* ~ (**to sth**) **1** [sing., U] the action of counting seconds backwards to zero, for example before a SPACECRAFT is launched 倒数读秒，倒计时（如发射宇宙飞船时） ➲ WORDFINDER NOTE AT SPACE **2** [sing.] the period of time just before sth important happens 大事临近的时期：*the countdown to the wedding* 婚礼的临近

coun·ten·ance /ˈkaʊntənəns/ *noun, verb*

- *noun* (*formal* or *literary*) a person's face or their expression 面容；脸色；面部表情
- *verb* ~ **sth** | ~ (**sb**) **doing sth** (*formal*) to support sth or agree to sth happening 支持；赞成；同意 **SYN** **consent to**：*The committee refused to countenance his proposals.* 委员会拒不同意他的方案。

coun·ter /ˈkaʊntə(r)/ *noun, verb, adv.*

- *noun* **1** a long flat surface over which goods are sold or business is done in a shop/store, bank, etc. （商店、银行等的）柜台：*I asked the woman* ***behind the counter*** *if they had any postcards.* 我问柜台后面的女售货员是否有明信片。 ➲ WORDFINDER NOTE AT SHOP **2** (*also* **counter·top**) (*both NAmE*) (*BrE* **work·top**, **'work surface**) a flat surface in a kitchen for preparing food on （厨房的）操作台 ➲ VISUAL VOCAB PAGE V26 **3** a small disc used for playing or scoring in some board games （某些棋盘游戏的）筹码，棋子 ➲ VISUAL VOCAB PAGE V42 ➲ SEE ALSO BARGAINING COUNTER at BARGAINING CHIP **4** (especially in compounds 尤用于构成复合词) an electronic device for counting sth （电子）计数器，计算器：*The needle on the rev counter soared.* 转速计的指针猛升。 ➲ VISUAL VOCAB PAGE V56 ➲ SEE ALSO GEIGER COUNTER ➲ COMPARE BEAN COUNTER **5** [usually sing.] ~ (**to sb/sth**) (*formal*) a response to sb/sth that opposes their ideas, position, etc. （对意见、态度等的）反对，反驳：*The employers' association was seen as a counter to union power.* 雇主协会被看作是工会权力的对头。

IDM **over the 'counter** goods, especially medicines, for sale **over the counter** can be bought without a PRESCRIPTION (= written permission from a doctor to buy a medicine) or special licence （尤指购药）不凭处方：*These tablets are available over the counter.* 这些药片不用处方就可买到。 ➲ SEE ALSO OVER-THE-COUNTER **under the 'counter** goods that are bought or sold **under the counter** are sold secretly and sometimes illegally （商品销售）秘密地，暗地里，非法地

- *verb* **1** [T, I] to reply to sb by trying to prove that what they said is not true 反驳；驳斥：~ **sb/sth** *Such arguments are not easily countered.* 这种论点不易反驳。◇ ~ **that…** *I tried to argue but he countered that the plans were not yet finished.* 我试图争辩，但他却申辩说各项计划尚未完成。◇ ~ (**sb**) + **speech** *'But I was standing right here!' he countered.* "但我那时就站在这儿！"他反驳道。◇ ~ (**sb/sth**) **with sth** *Butler has countered with a lawsuit against the firm.* 巴特勒反诉了这家公司。 **2** [T] ~ **sth** to do sth to reduce or prevent the bad effects of sth 抵制；抵消 **SYN** **counteract**：*Businesses would like to see new laws to counter late payments of debts.* 商界希望见到对付债务逾期不还的新法律出台。
- *adv.* ~ **to sth** in the opposite direction to sth; in opposition to sth 逆向地；相反地；反对地：*The government's plans* ***run counter*** *to agreed European policy on this issue.* 政府的计划违反了有关这个问题已协商好的欧盟政策。

counter- /ˈkaʊntə(r)/ *combining form* (in nouns, verbs, adjectives and adverbs 构成名词、动词、形容词和副词) **1** against; opposite 逆；反对；相反；对立：*counterterrorism* 反恐怖主义 ◇ *counter-argument* 相对立的论点 **2** CORRESPONDING 相应；对应：*counterpart* 对方职位相当的人

coun·ter·act /ˌkaʊntərˈækt/ *verb* ~ **sth** to do sth to reduce or prevent the bad or harmful effects of sth 抵制；抵消；抵抗 **SYN** **counter**：*These exercises aim to counteract the effects of stress and tension.* 这些训练动作旨在缓解压力与紧张。

ˈcounter-attack *noun, verb*

- *noun* an attack made in response to the attack of an enemy or opponent in war, sport or an argument （战争、体育运动或争论中的）反攻，反击
- *verb* [I, T] ~ (**sb**) to make an attack in response to the attack of an enemy or opponent in war, sport or an argument （在战争、体育运动或争论中）反攻，反击 **SYN** **retaliate**

coun·ter·bal·ance *verb, noun*

- *verb* /ˌkaʊntəˈbæləns; *NAmE* ˌkaʊntərˈb-/ ~ **sth** (*formal*) to have an equal but opposite effect to sth else 抗衡；抵消；对…起平衡作用 **SYN** **offset**：*Parents' natural desire to protect their children should be counterbalanced by the child's need for independence.* 父母保护孩子的本能愿望应当与孩子独立的需要相平衡。
- *noun* /ˈkaʊntəbæləns; *NAmE* ˈkaʊntərb-/ (*also* **coun·ter·weight**) [usually sing.] ~ (**to sth**) a thing that has an equal but opposite effect to sth else and can be used to limit the bad effects of sth 平衡抵消物；平衡重（或块、锤）：*The accused's right to silence was a vital counterbalance to the powers of the police.* 被告人的沉默权对警方的权力是一种至关重要的抗衡。

coun·ter·blast /ˈkaʊntəblɑːst; *NAmE* ˈkaʊntərblæst/ *noun* ~ (**to sth**) a very strong spoken or written reply to sth that has been said or written （对言论或文章的）强硬驳斥

coun·ter·claim /ˈkaʊntəkleɪm; *NAmE* -tərk-/ *noun* a claim made in reply to another claim and different from it 反要求；反索赔；反诉

coun·ter·clock·wise /ˌkaʊntəˈklɒkwaɪz; *NAmE* -tərˈklɑːk-/ (*NAmE*) (*BrE* **anti·clock·wise**) *adv., adj.* in the opposite direction to the movement of the hands of a clock 逆时针方向（的） **OPP** **clockwise**

coun·ter·cul·ture /ˈkaʊntəkʌltʃə(r); *NAmE* -tərk-/ *noun* [C, U] a way of life and set of ideas that are opposed to those accepted by most of society; a group of people who share such a way of life and such ideas 反主流文化；反正统文化；反主流文化的群体

ˌcounter-ˈespionage *noun* [U] secret action taken by a country to prevent an enemy country from finding out its secrets 反间谍活动

coun·ter·fac·tual /ˌkaʊntəˈfæktʃuəl; *NAmE* -tər-/ *adj.* (*formal*) connected with what did not happen or what is not the case 反事实的；虚拟的： *counterfactual questions such as 'What if the President had not been assassinated?'* "假如总统没有遇刺会怎么样？"之类的反事实问题 ◇ *an interesting exercise in counterfactual history* 假设历史并非如此的一个有趣活动 ▶ **coun·ter·fac·tual** *noun* : *'What if' questions involving counterfactuals are familiar in historical speculations.* "若非如此，将会怎样？"这样的反事实假设在历史思考中很常见。

coun·ter·feit /ˈkaʊntəfɪt; *NAmE* -tərf-/ *adj., verb*
■ *adj.* (*formal*) (of money and goods for sale 钱币及商品) made to look exactly like sth in order to trick people into thinking that they are getting the real thing 伪造的；仿造的；假冒的 SYN **fake**: *counterfeit watches* 冒牌手表 ◇ *Are you aware these notes are counterfeit?* 你觉察到这些钞票是伪造的吗？ OPP **genuine** ▶ **coun·ter·feit** *noun* ➲ COMPARE FORGERY
■ *verb* **~ sth** (*formal*) to make an exact copy of sth in order to trick people into thinking that it is the real thing 伪造；仿造；制假 ➲ COMPARE FORGE *v.* (2) ▶ **coun·ter·feit·ing** *noun* [U]

coun·ter·feit·er /ˈkaʊntəfɪtə(r); *NAmE* -tərf-/ *noun* a person who counterfeits money or goods 伪造者；仿造者；制假者 ➲ COMPARE FORGER

coun·ter·foil /ˈkaʊntəfɔɪl; *NAmE* -tərfɔɪl/ *noun* (*BrE*) the part of a cheque, ticket, etc. that you keep when you give the other part to sb else （支票、票据等的）存根，票根 SYN **stub**

ˌcounter-inˈsurgency *noun* [U] action taken against a group of people who are trying to take control of a country by force 反叛乱；反暴动

ˌcounter-inˈtelligence *noun* [U] secret action taken by a country to prevent an enemy country from finding out its secrets, for example by giving them false information; the department of a government, etc. that is responsible for this 反情报秘密行动；反情报政府部门

ˌcounter-inˈtuitive *adj.* the opposite of what you would expect or what seems to be obvious 反直觉的；与正常预期相反的： *These results seem counter-intuitive.* 这些结果似乎与预料的相反。 ▶ **ˌcounter-inˈtuitive·ly** *adv.*

coun·ter·mand /ˌkaʊntəˈmɑːnd; *NAmE* ˈkaʊntərmænd/ *verb* **~ sth** (*formal*) to cancel an order that has been given, especially by giving a different order 取消，撤销（尤指代以不同的新命令或订单）

coun·ter·meas·ure /ˈkaʊntəmeʒə(r); *NAmE* -tərm-/ *noun* a course of action taken to protect against sth that is considered bad or dangerous 对策；对抗手段；反措施

coun·ter·of·fen·sive /ˈkaʊntərəfensɪv/ *noun* an attack made in order to defend against enemy attacks 反攻；反击

coun·ter·pane /ˈkaʊntəpeɪn; *NAmE* -tərp-/ *noun* (*old-fashioned, BrE*) = BEDSPREAD

coun·ter·part /ˈkaʊntəpɑːt; *NAmE* -tərpɑːrt/ *noun* a person or thing that has the same position or function as sb/sth else in a different place or situation 职位（或作用）相当的人；对应的事物： *The Foreign Minister held talks with his Chinese counterpart.* 外交部长与中国的同级官员举行了会谈。 ◇ *The women's shoe, like its male counterpart, is specifically designed for the serious tennis player.* 像同类的男款鞋一样，这款女鞋是专为认真从事网球运动的人设计的。 ➲ COMPARE YOUR OPPOSITE NUMBER at OPPOSITE *adj.*

coun·ter·point /ˈkaʊntəpɔɪnt; *NAmE* -tərp-/ *noun, verb*
■ *noun* **1** [U] (*music* 音) the combination of two or more tunes played together to form a single piece of music 对位法，对位（各声部互相结合） SYN **polyphony**: *The two melodies are played in counterpoint.* 用对位法来演奏这两首曲调。 ➲ SEE ALSO CONTRAPUNTAL **2** [C] **~ (to sth)** (*music* 音) a tune played in combination with another one 复调 **3** [U, C] (*formal*) a pleasing or interesting contrast 惬意（或有趣）的对比： *This work is in austere counterpoint to that of Gaudi.* 这件作品的质朴风格与高迪的形成了有趣的对比。
■ *verb* **~ sth (with/against sth)** (*formal*) to contrast sth with sth else; to form a contrast with sth 用…作对比；与…形成对比

coun·ter·pro·duct·ive /ˌkaʊntəprəˈdʌktɪv; *NAmE* -tərp-/ *adj.* having the opposite effect to the one which was intended 产生相反效果；事与愿违；适得其反： *counter-productive behaviour/policies/effects* 适得其反的行为 / 政策 / 效果 ➲ COMPARE PRODUCTIVE

ˌcounter-ˌrevoˈlution *noun* [C, U] opposition to or violent action against a government that came to power as a result of a revolution, in order to destroy and replace it 反革命；反革命活动

ˌcounter-ˌrevoˈlutionary *noun* a person involved in a counter-revolution 反革命分子 ▶ **ˌcounter-ˌrevoˈlu·tion·ary** *adj.*

coun·ter·sign /ˈkaʊntəsaɪn; *NAmE* -tərs-/ *verb* **~ sth** (*specialist*) to sign a document that has already been signed by another person, especially in order to show that it is valid 联署，副署，会签（文件）

coun·ter·tenor /ˈkaʊntətenə(r); ˌkaʊntəˈtenə(r); *NAmE* ˈkaʊntər-/ *noun* a man who is trained to sing with a very high voice; a male ALTO 高男高音；假声男高音 ➲ COMPARE ALTO *n.*

counter·terror·ism /ˌkaʊntəˈterərɪzəm; *NAmE* ˌkaʊntər-/ *noun* [U] action taken to prevent the activities of political groups who use violence to try to achieve their aims 反恐怖主义 ▶ **counter·terror·ist** /ˌkaʊntəˈterərɪst; *NAmE* ˌkaʊntər-/ *adj.*

coun·ter·top /ˈkaʊntətɒp; *NAmE* ˈkaʊntərtɑːp/ *noun* (*NAmE*) = COUNTER (2)

coun·ter·vail·ing /ˈkaʊntəveɪlɪŋ; *NAmE* -tərv-/ *adj.* [only before noun] (*formal*) having an equal but opposite effect 抗衡的；抵消的

coun·ter·weight /ˈkaʊntəweɪt; *NAmE* -tərw-/ *noun* [usually sing.] = COUNTERBALANCE

count·ess /ˈkaʊntəs; -es/ *noun* **1** a woman who has the rank of a COUNT or an EARL 女伯爵 **2** the wife of a COUNT or an EARL 伯爵夫人： *the Earl and Countess of Rosebery* 罗斯伯里伯爵及夫人

count·less /ˈkaʊntləs/ *adj.* [usually before noun] very many; too many to be counted or mentioned 无数的；数不胜数的；数不尽的： *I've warned her countless times.* 我警告过她无数次了。 ◇ *The new treatment could save Emma's life and the lives of countless others.* 新的疗法可拯救埃玛的生命以及无数其他人的生命。 ➲ COMPARE UNCOUNTABLE

ˈcount noun *noun* (*grammar* 语法) a countable noun 具数名词；可数名词 OPP **uncount noun**

coun·tri·fied /ˈkʌntrifaɪd/ *adj.* (*often disapproving*) like the countryside or the people who live there 像乡下的；像乡下人的；乡土气的；土里土气的

coun·try /ˈkʌntri/ *noun* (*pl.* **-ies**) **1** [C] an area of land that has or used to have its own government and laws 国；国家： *European countries* 欧洲国家 ◇ *leading industrial countries* 最重要的工业国家 ◇ *She didn't know what life in a* ***foreign country*** *would be like.* 她不知道外国的生活会是什么样。 ◇ *It's good to meet people from* ***different parts of the country.*** 结识来自这个国家不同地区的人是有益的。 **2** [U] (often following an adjective 常置于形容词后) an area of land, especially with particular physical features, suitable for a particular purpose or connected with a particular person or people （尤指具有某种自然特征、适于某目的或与某种人有关的）地区，区域： ***open/wooded, etc. country*** 空旷、树木繁茂等的地区 ◇ *superb* ***walking country*** 极佳的徒步旅行区域 ◇ *Explore Thomas Hardy country.* 踏访托马斯·哈代小说描写的地区。 ➲ SEE ALSO BACKCOUNTRY **3** **the country** [sing.] the people of a country; the nation as a whole 全国人民；国民；全民： *They have the support of most of the country.* 他们有大多数国民的支持。 ◇ *The rich benefited from the* *reforms, not the **country** as a whole.* 富人而不是全体国民得益于这些改革。 ➲ SEE ALSO MOTHER COUNTRY, OLD COUNTRY, UP-COUNTRY **4** **the country** [sing.] any area outside towns and cities, with fields, woods, farms, etc. 乡下；乡村： *to live **in the country*** 住在乡下 ◇ *We spent a pleasant day in the country.* 我们在乡下度过了愉快的一

▼ SYNONYMS 同义词辨析

country

landscape • countryside • terrain • land • scenery

These are all words for areas away from towns and cities, with fields, woods and farms. 以上各词均指远离城镇，有田野、树林和农场的地区。

country (often **the country**) an area that is away from towns and cities, especially one with particular natural features（常作 the country）尤指具有自然特征的乡下、乡村： *She lives in the country.* 她住在乡下。◇ *an area of wooded country* 树木覆盖的乡村地区

landscape everything that you can see when you look across a large area of land, especially in the country 尤指乡村的风景或景色： *This pattern of woods and fields is typical of the English landscape.* 这种林地与田野的格局是典型的英格兰乡村景色。

countryside land outside towns and cities, with fields, woods and farms 指乡村、农村 NOTE **Countryside** is usually used when you are talking about the beauty or peacefulness of a country area. * countryside 通常用于强调乡村地区的美丽或宁静： *a little village in the French countryside* 法国乡间的小村庄

terrain (*formal*) land 指地带、土地 NOTE **Terrain** is used when you are describing the natural features of an area, for example if it is rough, flat, etc. * terrain 用于描述某地区的地形或地势： *The truck bumped its way over the rough terrain.* 卡车在崎岖不平的地面上颠簸行进。

land (usually **the land**) the countryside; the way people live in the country as opposed to in towns and cities（通常作 the land）指与城镇相对的农村、农村生活方式： *Many younger people are leaving the land to find work in the cities.* 许多较年轻的人陆续离开农村到城市去找工作。

scenery the natural features of an area, such as mountains, valleys, rivers and forests, especially when these are attractive to look at 指自然风景、景色、风光： *We stopped on the mountain pass to admire the scenery.* 我们在山口停下来欣赏风景。

PATTERNS

- **mountainous/mountain/wild/rugged** country/landscape/countryside/terrain/scenery
- **beautiful/glorious/dramatic** country/landscape/countryside/scenery
- **open** country/landscape/countryside/terrain/land
- **rolling** country/landscape/countryside
- to **protect** the landscape/countryside/land

▼ WHICH WORD? 词语辨析

country / state

- **Country** is the most usual, neutral word for a geographical area that has or used to have its own government. * country 是指国家的最普通的中性词。
- **State** emphasizes the political organization of an area under an independent government. Especially in *BrE*, it can also mean the government. * state 侧重指独立政府统治下的政权机构，尤其在英式英语中，该词亦可指政府： *the member states of the EU* 欧盟成员国 ◇ *The state provides free education.* 政府提供免费教育。
  In *NAmE* **the state** usually refers to one of the 50 states of the US, not to the government of the country as a whole. 在美式英语中，the state 通常指美国 50 个州中的一个州，而非指作为一个整体的国家政府。

天。◇ *a country lane* 乡间小路 ➲ COLLOCATIONS AT TOWN **5** [U] = COUNTRY AND WESTERN： *pop, folk and country* 流行、民间和乡村音乐

IDM **across 'country** directly across fields, etc.; not by a main road（直接）穿越田野；不走大路： *riding across country* 骑马穿过田野 ➲ SEE ALSO CROSS-COUNTRY **go to the 'country** (*BrE*) (of a government 政府) to hold an election to choose a new parliament 举行大选（以组成新的议会） ➲ MORE AT FREE *adj.*

,country and 'western (*abbr.* **C & W**) (*also* **'country music, country**) *noun* [U] a type of music in the style of the traditional music of the southern and western US（美国的）乡村与西部音乐： *a country and western singer* 乡村与西部音乐歌手

,country 'bumpkin (*also* **bump·kin**) *noun* (*disapproving*) a person from the countryside who seems stupid 乡巴佬；土包子

'country club *noun* a club in the country, or on the edge of a town, where people can play sports and go to social events（体育运动和社交的）乡村俱乐部

,country 'cousin *noun* a person from the country who does not know much about life in the city, and who dresses or behaves in a way that shows this 乡下人

,country 'dance *noun* (*BrE*) a type of traditional dance, especially one in which couples dance in long lines or circles 乡村舞，土风舞（尤为长排对舞或圆圈舞） ▶ **,country 'dancing** *noun* [U]

,country 'house *noun* (*BrE*) a large house in the country, especially one that belongs or used to belong to a rich important family（尤指有地位富人家庭的）乡间宅第，别墅

coun·try·made /'kʌntrimeɪd/ *adj.* (*IndE*) not made by a professional person 非专业制作的；土造的： *a country-made pistol* 土制手枪

coun·try·man /'kʌntrimən/ *noun* (*pl.* **-men** /-mən/) **1** a person born in or living in the same country as sb else 同国人；同胞；同乡 SYN **compatriot**： *The champion looks set to play his **fellow countryman** in the final.* 看来这位冠军在决赛中会遇上他的同胞。 **2** a man living or born in the country, not in the town 乡下人；农村人

,country 'mile *noun* (*becoming old-fashioned, especially BrE*) a long distance 远程；长距离；长途： *He won the race by a country mile.* 他遥遥领先赢了比赛。

'country music *noun* [U] = COUNTRY AND WESTERN

,country 'seat *noun* (*BrE*) = SEAT (7)

coun·try·side /'kʌntrisaɪd/ *noun* [U] land outside towns and cities, with fields, woods, etc. 乡村；农村： *The surrounding countryside is windswept and rocky.* 这周围的乡村风多石头多。 ◇ *magnificent views over open countryside* 开阔乡村的壮丽景色 ◇ *Everyone should enjoy the right of access to the countryside.* 人人都应享有进入乡村的权利。 ➲ SYNONYMS AT COUNTRY ➲ COLLOCATIONS AT TOWN ➲ VISUAL VOCAB PAGE V3

coun·try·wide /,kʌntri'waɪd/ *adj.* over the whole of a country 遍及全国的；全国性的 SYN **nationwide**： *a countrywide mail-order service* 全国性的邮购服务 ▶ **coun·try·wide** *adv.*： *The film will be released in London in March and countrywide in May.* 这部电影将于三月在伦敦发行，五月在全国发行。

coun·try·woman /'kʌntriwʊmən/ *noun* (*pl.* **-women** /-wɪmɪn/) **1** a woman living or born in the country, not the town 农村女人；乡下女人 **2** a woman born or living in the same country as sb else 女同胞

county /'kaʊnti/ *noun, adj.*

- ***noun*** (*pl.* **-ies**) (*abbr.* **Co.**) an area of Britain, Ireland or the US that has its own government（英国、爱尔兰的）郡；（美国的）县： *the southern counties* 南部各郡 ◇ *county boundaries* 郡分界线 ◇ *Orange County* 奥兰治县 ➲ SEE ALSO HOME COUNTIES
- ***adj.*** (*BrE, usually disapproving*) typical of English upper-class people 典型英格兰上流社会人物的；世家子弟的

ˌ**county ˈclerk** *noun* (in the US) an elected county official who is responsible for elections and who keeps records of who owns buildings in the county, etc.（美国负责选举及房产登记等的）县政官员

ˌ**county ˈcouncil** *noun* [C+sing./pl. v.] (in Britain) a group of people elected to the local government of a county（英国的）郡政务委员会，郡议会：*a member of Lancashire County Council* 兰开夏郡政务委员会委员 ▶ ˌ**county ˈcouncillor** *noun*

ˌ**county ˈcourt** *noun* a local court. In Britain county courts only deal with private disagreements but in the US they also deal with criminal cases. 郡法院（在英国受理私人纠纷）；县法院（在美国受理私人纠纷和刑事案件）➲ COMPARE CROWN COURT

ˌ**county ˈtown** (*BrE*) (*NAmE* ˌ**county ˈseat**) *noun* the main town of a county, where its government is 郡（或县）首府；郡（或县）城

coun·ty·wide /ˌkaʊntiˈwaɪd/ *adj.* over the whole of a county 遍及全郡（或县）的；全郡（或县）的 ▶ **coun·ty·wide** *adv.*

coup /kuː/ *noun* (*pl.* **coups** /kuːz/) **1** (*also* **coup d'état**) a sudden change of government that is illegal and often violent 政变：*He seized power in a military coup in 2008.* 他在 2008 年的军事政变中夺取了政权。◇ *to **stage/mount a coup*** 发动政变 ◇ *an attempted coup* 政变未遂 ◇ ***a failed/an abortive coup*** 失败的 / 流产的政变 ◇ *She lost her position in a boardroom coup* (= a sudden change of power among senior managers in a company). 她在董事会的人事突变中失去了职位。 **2** the fact of achieving sth that was difficult to do 努力办到难办的事：*Getting this contract has been quite a coup for us.* 把这份合同争取到手让我们费了很大力气。

coup de grâce /ˌkuː də ˈɡrɑːs/ *noun* [sing.] (*from French, formal*) **1** an action or event that finally ends sth that has been getting weaker or worse 最后的一击：*My disastrous exam results dealt the coup de grâce to my university career.* 我考试考得一塌糊涂，这就断送了我的大学生涯。 **2** a hit or shot that finally kills a person or an animal, especially to put an end to their suffering（尤指解除痛苦的）致命的一击 SYN **death blow**

coup d'état /ˌkuː deɪˈtɑː/ *noun* (*pl.* **coups d'état** /ˌkuː deɪˈtɑː/) = COUP (1)

coup de théâtre /ˌkuː də teɪˈɑːtrə/ *noun* (*pl.* **coups de théâtre** /ˌkuː də teɪˈɑːtrə/) (*from French*) **1** something very dramatic and surprising that happens, especially in a play（尤指戏剧中）剧情的突变 **2** a play, show, etc. which is very successful 非常成功的戏剧（或演出等）

coupé /ˈkuːpeɪ; *NAmE* kuːˈpeɪ/ (*NAmE also* **coupe** /kuːp/) *noun* a car with two doors and usually a sloping back（通常斜背的）双门小汽车

couple 🔑 AW /ˈkʌpl/ *noun, verb*

■ ***noun*** HELP In *BrE* a plural verb is usually used in all 3 senses. 在英式英语中 3 义均常用复数动词。 **1** 🔑 [sing.+sing./pl. v.] ~ (**of sth**) two people or things 两人；两件事物：*I saw a couple of men get out.* 我看见有两个男人出去了。 **2** 🔑 [sing.+sing./pl. v.] ~ (**of sth**) a small number of people or things 几个人；几件事物 SYN **a few**：*a couple of minutes* 几分钟 ◇ *We went there a couple of years ago.* 我们几年前去过那里。◇ *I've seen her a couple of times before.* 我以前见过她几次。◇ *I'll be with you in a minute. There are a couple of things I have to do first.* 我一会儿就到你那里去。我有几件事情得先处理一下。◇ *There are a couple more files to read first.* 还有几份档案要先看一看。◇ *We can do it in the **next couple of** weeks.* 我们可在今后几个星期里完成这件事。◇ *The **last couple of** years have been difficult.* 最近的几年一直是困难重重。 **3** 🔑 [C+sing./pl. v.] two people who are seen together, especially if they are married or in a romantic or sexual relationship（人）一对；（尤指）夫妻，情侣：*married couples* 几对夫妇 ◇ *a young/an elderly couple* 年轻 / 老年夫妇 ◇ *Several couples were on the dance floor.* 有几对情侣在跳舞。◇ *The couple was/were married in 2006.* 这对夫妇于 2006 年结婚。➲ COLLOCATIONS AT MARRIAGE IDM SEE SHAKE *n.* ▶ **a couple** 🔑 *pron.*：*Do you need any more glasses? I've got a couple I can lend you.* 你还需要玻璃杯吗？我有几个可以借给你。**couple** *det.* (*NAmE, informal*)：*It's only a couple blocks away.* 那地方离这里只有几个街区。

■ ***verb*** **1** [T, usually passive] to join together two parts of sth, for example two vehicles or pieces of equipment（把车辆或设备等）连接，结合：**~ A and B together** *The two train cars had been coupled together.* 两节火车车厢已经挂上钩了。◇ **~ A (to B)** *CDTV uses a CD-ROM system that is coupled to a powerful computer.* 动态视频系统使用的是与大功率计算机相连的只读光盘系统。 **2** [I] (*formal*) (of two people or animals 两人或两动物) to have sex 性交；交配
PHR V ˈ**couple sb/sth with sb/sth** [usually passive] to link one thing, situation, etc. to another 把…与…连接起来：*Overproduction, coupled with falling sales, has led to huge losses for the company.* 生产过剩加上销售下降使这家公司遭受巨大损失。

coup·let /ˈkʌplət/ *noun* two lines of poetry of equal length one after the other 对句（相连的两行长度相等的诗句）；对联：*a poem written in rhyming couplets* 用押韵对句写成的诗 ➲ SEE ALSO HEROIC COUPLET ➲ WORDFINDER NOTE AT POETRY

coup·ling AW /ˈkʌplɪŋ/ *noun* **1** [usually sing.] an action of joining or combining two things 连接；结合；联结：*a coupling of Mozart's Prague Symphony and Schubert's Unfinished Symphony* (= for example, on the same CD) 编排在一起的莫扎特的《布拉格交响曲》与舒伯特的《未完成交响曲》（如在同一张光盘上） **2** (*formal*) an act of having sex 性交：*illicit couplings* 不正当的性交 **3** (*specialist*) a thing that joins together two parts of sth, two vehicles or two pieces of equipment 联轴器；（连接车辆的）车钩

cou·pon /ˈkuːpɒn; *NAmE* -pɑːn; ˈkjuː-/ *noun* **1** a small piece of printed paper that you can exchange for sth or that gives you the right to buy sth at a cheaper price than normal 配给券；（购物）票证，优惠券：*money-off coupons* 优惠券 ◇ *clothing coupons* 服装票 ◇ *an international reply coupon* 国际通用预付回信邮资券 **2** a printed form, often cut out from a newspaper, that is used to enter a competition, order goods, etc.（常为剪自报章的）参赛表，订货单：*Fill in and return the attached coupon.* 填写所附上的参赛表并寄回。

cour·age 🔑 /ˈkʌrɪdʒ; *NAmE* ˈkɜːr-/ *noun* [U] the ability to do sth dangerous, or to face pain or opposition, without showing fear 勇气；勇敢；无畏；胆量 SYN **bravery**：*He showed great courage and determination.* 他表现得十分勇敢和果断。◇ *I haven't yet **plucked up the courage** to ask her.* 我还鼓不起勇气去问她。◇ ***moral/physical courage*** 道德勇气；胆识 ◇ *courage in the face of danger* 面对危险时的胆量 ➲ SEE ALSO DUTCH COURAGE
IDM **have/lack the courage of your conˈvictions** to be/not be brave enough to do what you feel to be right 有 / 没有勇气做自己认为正确的事 **take courage** (**from sth**) to begin to feel happier and more confident because of sth（因某事而）鼓起勇气 **take your ˌcourage in both ˈhands** to make yourself do sth that you are afraid of 鼓起勇气（做自己害怕做的事）；敢作敢为：*Taking her courage in both hands, she opened the door and walked in.* 她壮着胆打开门，走了进去。➲ MORE AT SCREW *v.*

cour·age·ous /kəˈreɪdʒəs/ *adj.* showing courage 勇敢的；无畏的 SYN **brave**：*a very courageous decision* 十分勇敢的决定 ◇ *I hope people will be courageous enough to speak out against this injustice.* 我希望人们能敢于大胆说出来，反对这种不公。OPP **cowardly** ▶ **cour·age·ous·ly** *adv.*

cour·gette /kʊəˈʒet; kɔːˈʒet; *NAmE* kʊrˈʒet/ (*BrE*) (*NAmE* **zuc·chini**) *noun* a long vegetable with dark green skin and white flesh（深绿皮）密生西葫芦，小胡瓜 ➲ VISUAL VOCAB PAGE V34

cour·ier /ˈkʊriə(r)/ *noun* **1** a person or company whose job is to take packages or important papers somewhere

（递送包裹或重要文件的）信使，通讯员，专递公司：*We sent the documents by courier.* 我们派了信使送交这些文件。 **2** (*BrE*) a person who is employed by a travel company to give advice and help to a group of tourists on holiday（旅游公司的）导游 ▶ **cour·ier** *verb*: **~ sth** *Courier that letter—it needs to get there today* (= send it by courier). 那封信必须今天到达，用专递寄吧。

course /kɔːs; *NAmE* kɔːrs/ *noun, verb*

■ ***noun***

• **EDUCATION** 教育 **1** [C] **~ (in/on sth)** a series of lessons or lectures on a particular subject（有关某学科的系列）课程，讲座：*a **French/chemistry, etc. course*** 法语、化学等课程 ◇ *to **take/do a course** in art and design* 攻读美术与设计课程 ◇ *to **go on a** management training **course*** 去参加管理培训讲座 ◇ *The college **runs** specialist language **courses**.* 这所学院开设有专门语言课程。 ➲ WORDFINDER NOTE AT STUDY, TRAINING ➲ COLLOCATIONS AT EDUCATION ➲ SEE ALSO CORRESPONDENCE COURSE, CRASH *adj.*, FOUNDATION COURSE, INDUCTION COURSE, REFRESHER COURSE, SANDWICH COURSE **2** [C] (*especially BrE*) a period of study at a college or university that leads to an exam or a qualification（大学中要进行考试或取得资格的）课程：*a degree course* 学位课程 ◇ *a two-year postgraduate course leading to a master's degree* 两年制硕士研究生课程 ➲ COMPARE PROGRAMME *n.* (5)

• **DIRECTION** 方向 **3** [U, C, usually sing.] a direction or route followed by a ship or an aircraft（船或飞机的）航向，航线：*The plane was **on/off course*** (= going/not going in the right direction). 飞机航向正确 / 偏离。◇ *He radioed the pilot to **change course**.* 他用无线电通知飞行员改变航向。◇ *They **set a course** for the islands.* 他们确定了去群岛的航线。**4** [C, usually sing.] the general direction in which sb's ideas or actions are moving 方针；行动方向：*The president appears likely to **change course** on some key issues.* 总统看起来可能要在某些重要问题上改变方针。◇ *Politicians are often obliged to steer a course between incompatible interests.* 政治家常常被迫在互不相容的利益集团之间开辟航道。

• **ACTION** 行动 **5** (*also* ˌ**course of** ˈ**action**) [C] a way of acting in or dealing with a particular situation 行动方式；处理方法：*There are various courses open to us.* 我们有多种处理方法可采取。 ◇ *What course of action would you recommend?* 你想推荐什么办法呢？ ◇ *The wisest course would be to say nothing.* 最明智的对策是缄口不语。

• **DEVELOPMENT** 发展 **6** [sing.] **~ of sth** the way sth develops or should develop 进展；进程：*an event that changed the **course of history*** 改变了历史进程的事件 ◇ *The unexpected **course of events** aroused considerable alarm.* 意外的事态发展引起了相当大的恐慌。

• **PART OF MEAL** 菜肴 **7** [C] any of the separate parts of a meal 一道菜：*a four-course dinner* 有四道菜的正餐 ◇ *The main course was roast duck.* 主菜是烤鸭。 ➲ WORDFINDER NOTE AT RESTAURANT ➲ COLLOCATIONS AT RESTAURANT

• **FOR GOLF** 高尔夫球 **8** [C] = GOLF COURSE：*He set a new course record.* 他创下了高尔夫球的新纪录。

• **FOR RACES** 比赛 **9** [C] an area of land or water where races are held 比赛场地；跑道；赛船水道；泳道：*She was overtaken on the last stretch of the course.* 她在最后一个直道上被超过。 ➲ SEE ALSO ASSAULT COURSE, RACECOURSE

• **OF RIVER** 江河 **10** [C, usually sing.] the direction a river moves in 江河流向：*The path follows the course of the river.* 小路沿河道延伸。➲ WORDFINDER NOTE AT RIVER

• **MEDICAL TREATMENT** 医疗 **11** [C] **~ (of sth)** a series of medical treatments, pills, etc.（医疗、服药等的）疗程：*to prescribe a course of antibiotics* 开一个疗程抗生素的处方

• **IN WALL** 墙壁 **12** [C] a continuous layer of bricks, stone, etc. in a wall（砖、石等墙的）层：*A new damp-proof course could cost £1 000 or more.* 新的防潮层可花掉 1 000 英镑以上。

IDM **in course of sth** (*formal*) going through a particular process 在…的过程中：*The new textbook is in course of preparation.* 新的教科书正在准备之中。 **in/over the course of...** (used with expressions for periods of time 与表示时间段的词组连用) during 在…期间；在…的时候：*He's seen many changes in the course of his long life.* 他在漫长的一生中目睹了许许多多的变化。◇ *The company faces major challenges over the course of the next few years.* 这家公司今后几年将面临重大的挑战。 **in the course of ˈtime** when enough time has passed 总有一天；最后；终于 **SYN** **eventually**：*It is possible that in the course of time a cure for cancer will be found.* 治疗癌症的方法终有一天能找到。 **in the ordinary, normal, etc. course of events, things, etc.** as things usually happen 按通常情况；在一般情况下；通常 **SYN** **normally**：*In the normal course of things we would not treat her disappearance as suspicious.* 在一般情况下，她不露面，我们也不会觉得有什么可疑之处。**of course 1** (*also* **course**) (*informal*) used to emphasize that what you are saying is true or correct（强调所说的话属实或正确）当然：*'Don't you like my*

▼ **BRITISH/AMERICAN 英式 / 美式英语**

course / program

• In *BrE* **course** is used for a series of lessons or lectures on a particular subject. 在英式英语中，course 指某学科的系列课程或讲座：*a physics course* 物理课程 ◇ *a course of ten lectures* 有十次讲座的课程 In *NAmE* you would say 美式英语说：*a physics course/program* 物理课程 ◇ *a program of ten lectures* 有十次讲座的课程

• In *NAmE* a **course** is usually an individual unit that forms part of a longer period of study. 在美式英语中，course 通常指较长学习阶段中的一个独立单元：*I have to take a physics course/class.* 我得参加一个物理课程。 This is called a **module** in Britain, especially in a college or university. 在英国，尤其是高等院校，这种独立单元叫 module。

• In *BrE* **course** can also mean a period of study at a college or university. 英式英语的 course 亦可指高等教育的一个阶段：*a two-year college course* 两年的大学课程 In *NAmE* you would say 美式英语说：*a two-year college program* 两年的大学课程

▼ **MORE ABOUT ... 补充说明**

of course

• **Of course** is often used to show that what you are saying is not surprising or is generally known or accepted. For this reason, and because it can be difficult to get the right intonation, you may not sound polite if you use **of course** or **of course not** when you answer a request for information or permission. It can be safer to use a different word or phrase. * of course 常用以表示所说的事不足为奇或理所当然。与此同时，由于可能不容易掌握恰当的语调，用 of course 或 of course not 回答询问或请求时可能显得不礼貌。因此，用其他词语或短语可能更稳妥。

• *'Is this the right room for the English class?' 'Yes, it is.'* “这是上英语课的教室吗？”“是的。”◇ ~~*'Of course.'*~~ or ~~*'Of course it is.'*~~

• *'Can I borrow your dictionary?' 'Certainly.'* (*formal*) “我可以借用一下你的词典吗？”“当然可以。”（正式）◇ *'Sure.'* (*informal*) “当然可以。”（非正式）

• *'Do you mind if I borrow your dictionary?' 'Not at all.'* “我借用一下你的词典行吗？”“没问题。”◇ *'Go ahead.'* (*informal*) “拿吧。”（非正式）

• If you say **of course**/**of course not** it may sound as though you think the answer to the question is obvious and that the person should not ask. In the same way, **of course** should not be used as a reply to a statement of fact or when someone expresses an opinion. 如果用 of course/of course not 回答，听起来就好像是说答案太明显，用不着问。同样，of course 不宜用于回应别人对事实的陈述或意见的表达：*'It's a lovely day.' 'It certainly is.'*/*'Yes it is.'* “天气真好。”“确实真好。”/“是的，真好。”◇ ~~*'Of course it is.'*~~ ◇ *'I think you'll enjoy that play.' 'I'm sure I will.'*/*'Yes, it sounds really good.'* “我想你会喜欢那出戏的。”“我肯定会的。”/“是的，这戏看来真棒。”◇ ~~*'Of course.'*~~

mother?' 'Of course I do!' "难道你不喜欢我母亲？" "当然喜欢！" ◇ *'Will you be there?' 'Course I will.'* "你会去那里吗？" "当然会。" **2** (*also* **course**) (*informal*) used as a polite way of giving sb permission to do sth（允许某人做某事的客气说法）当然：*'Can I come, too?' 'Course you can.'* "我也可以来吗？" "当然可以。" ◇ *'Can I have one of those pens?' 'Of course—help yourself.'* "我能在那些笔中拿一支吗？" "当然，自己拿吧。" **3** (*informal*) used as a polite way of agreeing with what sb has just said（礼貌地同意某人刚说的话）当然：*'I did all I could to help.' 'Of course,' he murmured gently.* "我尽全力帮忙了。" "当然。" 他轻声低语道。 **4** used to show that what you are saying is not surprising or is generally known or accepted（表示所说的事不令人惊讶或具有普遍性）当然，自然：*Ben, of course, was the last to arrive.* 本当然是最后一个到的。◇ *Of course, there are other ways of doing this.* 当然还有别的方法做这件事。 ➲ LANGUAGE BANK AT NEVERTHELESS **of 'course not** (*also* **'course not**) used to emphasize the fact that you are saying 'no'（强调不同意）当然不：*'Are you going?' 'Of course not.'* "你要去吗？" "当然不去。" ◇ *'Do you mind?' 'No, of course not.'* "你介意吗？" "不，当然不介意。" **on 'course for sth/to do sth** likely to achieve or do sth because you have already started to do it（因为已开始做而）很可能做成（或做）：*The American economy is on course for higher inflation than Britain by the end of the year.* 美国经济很可能在今年年底前出现比英国高的通货膨胀。 **run/take its 'course** to develop in the usual way and come to the usual end 任其发展；听其自然：*When her tears had run their course, she felt calmer and more in control.* 等她哭够了，她就比较镇静，比较克制了。◇ *With minor ailments the best thing is often to let nature take its course.* 对于小病，往往最好是听其自然。 ➲ MORE AT COLLISION, DUE *adj.*, HORSE *n.*, MATTER *n.*, MIDDLE *adj.*, PAR, PERVERT *v.*, STAY *v.*

■ *verb* [I] + **adv./prep.** (*literary*) (of liquid 液体) to move or flow quickly 快速地流动；奔流

course·book /ˈkɔːsbʊk; *NAmE* ˈkɔːrs-/ *noun* (*BrE*) a book for studying from, used regularly in class 教科书；课本

ˌcourse of 'action *noun* (*pl.* **courses of action**) = COURSE (5)

course·ware /ˈkɔːsweə(r); *NAmE* ˈkɔːrswer/ *noun* [U] (*computing* 计) computer programs that are designed to be used to teach a subject 课件；教学软件

course·work /ˈkɔːswɜːk; *NAmE* ˈkɔːrswɜːrk/ *noun* [U] work that students do during a course of study, not in exams, that is included in their final mark/grade（计入最终成绩的）课程作业：*Coursework accounts for 40% of the final marks.* 课程作业占最后总成绩的 40%。

cours·ing /ˈkɔːsɪŋ; *NAmE* ˈkɔːr-/ *noun* [U] the sport of hunting animals with dogs, using sight rather than smell 追踪狩猎（凭借猎狗的视力而不是嗅觉追捕猎物）：*hare coursing* 追踪野兔

court /kɔːt; *NAmE* kɔːrt/ *noun, verb*

■ ***noun***

• **LAW** 法律 **1** [C, U] the place where legal trials take place and where crimes, etc. are judged 法院；法庭；审判庭：*the* ***civil/criminal courts*** 民事 / 刑事法庭 ◇ *Her lawyer made a statement outside the court.* 她的律师在法庭外面发表了一份声明。◇ *She will appear* ***in court*** *tomorrow.* 她明天出庭。◇ *They* ***took*** *their landlord* ***to court*** *for breaking the contract.* 因为房东毁约，他们把他告上了法庭。◇ *The case took five years to* ***come to court*** (= to be heard by the court). 那案件历时五年才被法庭受理。◇ *There wasn't enough evidence to* ***bring the case to court*** (= start a trial). 没有足够的证据可把此案提交法庭。◇ *He won the* ***court case*** *and was awarded damages.* 他胜诉得到了赔偿金。◇ *She can't pay her tax and is facing* ***court action***. 她缴不起税，将面临法庭诉讼。◇ *The case was* ***settled out of court*** (= a decision was reached without a trial). 这案件已庭外和解。 ➲ SEE ALSO COURTHOUSE (1), COURTROOM ➲ WORDFINDER NOTE AT LAW ➲ COLLOCATIONS AT JUSTICE ➲ NOTE AT SCHOOL **2** **the court** [sing.] the people in a court, especially those who make the decisions, such as the judge and JURY 全体出庭人员；（尤指）全体审判人员：*Please tell the court what happened.* 请向法庭陈述事情的经过。 ➲ SEE ALSO CONTEMPT OF COURT, COUNTY COURT, CROWN COURT, HIGH COURT, JUVENILE COURT, SUPREME COURT

• **FOR SPORT** 体育运动 **3** [C] a place where games such as TENNIS are played（网球等的）球场：*a* ***tennis/squash/badminton court*** 网球场；壁球场；羽毛球场 ◇ *He won after only 52 minutes* ***on court***. 他上场仅 52 分钟就赢得了胜利。 ➲ VISUAL VOCAB PAGES V47, V48 ➲ SEE ALSO CLAY COURT, GRASS COURT

• **KINGS/QUEENS** 国王；女王 **4** [C, U] the official place where kings and queens live 王宫；宫殿；宫廷：*the court of Queen Victoria* 维多利亚女王的宫廷 **5** **the court** [sing.] the king or queen, their family, and the people who work for them and/or give advice to them 王室人员；王宫人员

• **BUILDINGS** 建筑物 **6** [C] = COURTYARD **7** (*abbr.* **Ct**) [C] used in the names of blocks of flats or apartment buildings, or of some short streets; (in Britain) used in the name of some large houses（用于套房、公寓或某些短街区的名称）公寓大楼，短街；（英国用于某些大型宅第的名称）宅第，邸宅 **8** [C] a large open section of a building, often with a glass roof 建筑物的开阔部分（常有玻璃房顶）；大厅；馆：*the food court at the shopping mall* 大型购物中心的食品区

IDM **hold 'court (with sb)** to entertain people by telling them interesting or funny things（讲趣闻或笑话）使人快乐，逗人乐 **rule/throw sth out of 'court** to say that sth is completely wrong or not worth considering, especially in a trial（尤指在法庭上）指明完全错误，不予考虑，不予受理：*The charges were thrown out of court.* 这些指控未予受理。◇ *Well that's my theory ruled out of court.* 唉，那就是我遭到摒弃的意见。 ➲ MORE AT BALL *n.*, LAUGH *v.*, PAY *v.*

▼ **WHICH WORD?** 词语辨析

court / law court / court of law

• All these words can be used to refer to a place where legal trials take place. **Court** and (*formal*) **court of law** usually refer to the actual room where cases are judged. **Courtroom** is also used for this. **Law court** (*BrE*) is more often used to refer to the building. 以上各词均可指法庭或法院。court 和 court of law（正式说法）通常指法庭、审判室，courtroom 亦用于此义。law court（英式英语）多指法院这座建筑物：*The prison is opposite the law court.* 监狱在法院对面。**Courthouse** is used for this in *NAmE*. 美式英语用 courthouse 表达此义。

■ ***verb***

• **TRY TO PLEASE** 试图取悦 **1** [T] **~ sb** to try to please sb in order to get sth you want, especially the support of a person, an organization, etc.（为有所求，尤指为寻求支持而）试图取悦，讨好，争取 SYN **cultivate**：*Both candidates have spent the last month courting the media.* 两位候选人在过去的一个月里都在取悦媒体。

• **TRY TO GET** 试图得到 **2** [T] **~ sth** (*formal*) to try to obtain sth 试图获得；博取：*He has never courted popularity.* 他从不追求名望。

• **INVITE STH BAD** 招致灾祸 **3** [T] **~ sth** (*formal*) to do sth that might result in sth unpleasant happening 招致，酿成，导致（不愉快的事）：*to* ***court danger/death/disaster*** 招致危险 / 死亡 / 灾难 ◇ *As a politician he has often courted controversy.* 作为政治人物，他常常招致争议。

• **HAVE RELATIONSHIP** 建立感情 **4** [T] **~ sb** (*old-fashioned*) if a man **courts** a woman, he spends time with her and tries to make her love him, so that they can get married（向女子）求爱，求婚 **5** **be courting** [I] (*old-fashioned*) (of a man and a woman 男女) to have a romantic relationship before getting married 恋爱：*At that time they had been courting for several years.* 当时他们已经谈了好几年的恋爱了。 ➲ SEE ALSO COURTSHIP (1)

• **ANIMALS** 动物 **6** **~ sth** (of a male bird or other animal) to try to attract a mate（雄鸟或其他雄性动物）求偶

ˈcourt card (*BrE*) (*also* **ˈface card** *NAmE, BrE*) *noun* a PLAYING CARD with a picture of a king, queen or JACK on it 人头牌，花牌（纸牌的 K、Q 或 J） ➲ VISUAL VOCAB PAGE V42

C

ˈcourt costs *noun* [pl.] (*NAmE*) = COSTS

cour·te·ous /ˈkɜːtiəs; *NAmE* ˈkɜːrt-/ *adj.* polite, especially in a way that shows respect 有礼貌的；客气的；（尤指）恭敬的，谦恭的：*a courteous young man* 彬彬有礼的年轻人 ◇ *The hotel staff are friendly and courteous.* 旅馆服务人员友好而有礼貌。 **OPP** **discourteous** ▶ **cour·te·ous·ly** *adv.*

cour·tesan /ˌkɔːtɪˈzæn; *NAmE* ˈkɔːrtɪzn/ *noun* (in the past) a PROSTITUTE, especially one with rich customers（旧时尤指伺候富豪的）高级妓女

cour·tesy /ˈkɜːtəsi; *NAmE* ˈkɜːrt-/ *noun, adj.*

■ ***noun*** (*pl.* **-ies**) **1** [U] polite behaviour that shows respect for other people 礼貌；谦恭；彬彬有礼 **SYN** **politeness**：*I was treated with the utmost courtesy by the staff.* 我受到了工作人员极有礼貌的接待。 ◇ *It's only* ***common courtesy*** *to tell the neighbours that we'll be having a party* (= the sort of behaviour that people would expect). 告诉邻居我们要举行聚会，这是起码的礼貌。 **2** [C, usually pl.] (*formal*) a polite thing that you say or do when you meet people in formal situations（正式场合见面时的）客气话，礼貌：*an exchange of courtesies before the meeting* 会议开始前互致问候

IDM **courtesy of sb/sth 1** (*also* **by courtesy of sb/sth**) with the official permission of sb/sth and as a favour 承蒙…的允许（或好意）：*The pictures have been reproduced by courtesy of the British Museum.* 承蒙大英博物馆惠允，复制了这些画。 **2** given as a prize or provided free by a person or an organization 蒙…提供；赞助；赠送：*Win a weekend in Rome, courtesy of Fiat.* 赢了就可以获得菲亚特公司提供的到罗马度周末的机会。 **3** as the result of a particular thing or situation 作为…的结果：*Viewers can see the stadium from the air, courtesy of a camera fastened to the plane.* 由于飞机上安装有摄像机，电视观众可从空中鸟瞰体育场。 **do sb the courtesy of doing sth** to be polite by doing the thing that is mentioned（做提及的事）对某人表示礼貌：*Please do me the courtesy of listening to what I'm saying.* 请耐心听一听我的话。 **have the courtesy to do sth** to know when you should do sth in order to be polite 知道何时该做…（以示礼貌）：*You think he'd at least have the courtesy to call to say he'd be late.* 谁都会觉得他至少应该懂得打个电话说一声他要晚来。

■ ***adj.*** [only before noun] (of a bus, car, etc. 公共汽车、小轿车等) provided free, at no cost to the person using it 免费乘坐（或使用）的：*A* ***courtesy bus*** *operates between the hotel and the town centre.* 有免费接送的公共汽车往返于旅馆和市中心之间。 ◇ *The dealer will provide you with a* ***courtesy car*** *while your vehicle is being repaired.* 车辆维修期间，经销商会提供免费使用的汽车。

ˈcourtesy call *noun* **1** (*also* **ˈcourtesy visit**) a formal or official visit, usually by one important person to another, just to be polite, not to discuss important business（正式或官方的）礼节性拜访 **2** a telephone call from a company to one of its customers, for example to see if they are satisfied with the company's service 礼节性征询电话（如公司征询顾客对服务是否满意）

ˈcourtesy light *noun* a small light inside a car which is automatically switched on when sb opens the door（汽车内的）门控照明灯

ˈcourtesy title *noun* a title that sb is allowed to use but which has no legal status（无法律实效的）尊称

court·house /ˈkɔːthaʊs; *NAmE* ˈkɔːrt-/ *noun* **1** (*especially NAmE*) a building containing courts of law 法院大楼 ➲ NOTE AT COURT **2** (in the US) a building containing the offices of a county government（美国）县政府大楼

court·ier /ˈkɔːtiə(r); *NAmE* ˈkɔːrt-/ *noun* (especially in the past) a person who is part of the COURT of a king or queen（尤指旧时的）侍臣，侍从，廷臣

court·ly /ˈkɔːtli; *NAmE* ˈkɔːrt-/ *adj.* (*formal* or *literary*) extremely polite and full of respect, especially in an old-fashioned way（尤指老式）极其恭敬有礼的，温文尔雅的

ˌcourtly ˈlove *noun* [U] a tradition in literature, especially in Medieval times, involving the faithful love of a KNIGHT for his married LADY, with whom he can never have a relationship 典雅爱情（尤指中世纪的一种文学传统，指骑士对贵妇人的忠贞但无结果的爱情）

ˌcourt ˈmartial *noun* [C, U] (*pl.* **courts martial**) a military court that deals with members of the armed forces who break military law; a trial at such a court 军事法庭；军事法庭的审判；军法审判：*He was convicted at a court martial.* 他在军事法庭上被判有罪。 ◇ *All the men now face court martial.* 现在所有这些军人都面临军事法庭的审判。

ˌcourt-ˈmartial *verb* (**-ll-**, *US* **-l-**) [often passive] **~ sb** to hold a trial of sb in a military court（在军事法庭上）举行审判；以军法审判：*He was court-martialled for desertion.* 他因擅离职守受到了军法审判。

ˌcourt of apˈpeal *noun* **1** (*pl.* **courts of appeal**) a court that people can go to in order to try and change decisions that have been made by a lower court 上诉法院 ➲ SEE ALSO APPELLATE COURT **2** **ˌCourt of Apˈpeal** [sing.] (*BrE*) the highest court in Britain (apart from the Supreme Court), that can change decisions made by a lower court（英国）上诉法院（仅次于最高法院的司法机构） **3** **ˌCourt of Apˈpeals** [C] (*US*) one of the courts in the US that can change decisions made by a lower court（美国）上诉法院

ˌcourt of ˈclaims *noun* (*pl.* **courts of claims**) (*US*) a court in the US that hears claims made against the government（美国）求偿法院（负责审理对政府的申诉案件）

ˌcourt of inˈquiry (*also* **ˌcourt of enˈquiry**) *noun* (*pl.* **courts of inquiry/enquiry**) (*BrE*) a special official group of people that investigates a particular problem 调查庭

ˌcourt of ˈlaw *noun* (*pl.* **courts of law**) (*formal*) (*also* **law court**) a room or building where legal cases are judged 法庭；法院 ➲ NOTE AT COURT

ˌCourt of ˈSession *noun* in Scotland, the highest court that deals with CIVIL cases (= not criminal cases)（苏格兰）最高民事法院

ˌcourt ˈorder *noun* a decision that is made in court about what must happen in a particular situation 法庭命令（或指令、庭谕）

court·room /ˈkɔːtruːm; -rʊm; *NAmE* ˈkɔːrt-/ *noun* a room in which trials or other legal cases are held 法庭；审判室 ➲ NOTE AT COURT

court·ship /ˈkɔːtʃɪp; *NAmE* ˈkɔːrt-/ *noun* **1** [C, U] (*old-fashioned*) the time when two people have a romantic relationship before they get married; the process of developing this relationship 求爱期；求爱；追求：*They married after a short courtship.* 他们恋爱不久便结婚了。 ◇ *Mr Elton's courtship of Harriet* 埃尔顿先生对哈丽雅特的追求 **2** [U] the special way animals behave in order to attract a mate for producing young animals（动物的）求偶：*courtship displays* 求偶的炫耀行为 **3** [U] **~ (of sb/sth)** (*formal*) the process or act of attracting a business partner, etc. 招商：*the company's courtship by the government* 政府向公司献殷勤

ˈcourt shoe (*BrE*) (*NAmE* **pump**) *noun* a woman's formal shoe that is plain and does not cover the top part of the foot 船鞋，半高跟鞋（正式场合穿的素色女鞋） ➲ VISUAL VOCAB PAGE V69

ˌcourt ˈtennis (*NAmE*) (*BrE* **ˈreal tennis**) (*AustralE* **ˈroyal tennis**) *noun* [U] an old form of tennis played inside a building with a hard ball 庭院网球（使用硬球的旧式室内网球运动）

court·yard /ˈkɔːtjɑːd; *NAmE* ˈkɔːrtjɑːrd/ (*also* **court**) *noun* an open space that is partly or completely surrounded by buildings and is usually part of a castle, a large house, etc.（通常为城堡、大宅第等的）庭院，院子，天井：*the central/inner courtyard* 中心／内庭院

cous·cous /ˈkʊskʊs; ˈkuːskuːs/ *noun* [U] a type of N African food made from crushed WHEAT; a dish of meat and/or vegetables with couscous（北非的）蒸粗麦粉食物

cousin /ˈkʌzn/ *noun* **1** (*also* ˌ**first ˈcousin**) a child of your aunt or uncle 同辈表亲（或堂亲）；堂兄（或弟、姊、妹）；表兄（或弟、姊、妹）：*She's my cousin.* 她是我的表妹。◇ *We're cousins.* 我们是表亲。➲ SEE ALSO COUNTRY COUSIN, SECOND COUSIN **2** a person who is in your wider family but who is not closely related to you 远房亲戚；远亲：*He's a distant cousin of mine.* 他是我远房的一个表亲。 **3** [usually pl.] a way of describing people from another country who are similar in some way to people in your own country 兄弟的…国人民（对与本民族有某些类似的另一国家人民的说法）：*our American cousins* 我们兄弟的美国人民 **4** [usually pl.] a way of describing things that are similar or related in some way 同族；同类：*Asian elephants are smaller than their African cousins.* 亚洲象比它们的非洲同类小些。

ˈcousin brother *noun* (*IndE, informal*) a male cousin of your own generation 堂（或表）兄；堂（或表）弟

ˈcousin sister *noun* (*IndE, informal*) a female cousin of your own generation 堂（或表）姐；堂（或表）妹

cou·ture /kuˈtjʊə(r); *NAmE* -ˈtʊr/ *noun* [U] (*from French*) the design and production of expensive and fashionable clothes; these clothes 时装设计制作；时装：*a couture evening dress* 昂贵时髦的晚礼服 ➲ SEE ALSO HAUTE COUTURE

cou·tur·ier /kuˈtjʊəriеɪ; *NAmE* -ˈtʊr-/ *noun* (*from French*) a person who designs, makes and sells expensive, fashionable clothes, especially for women（尤指）女装设计师；时装裁缝；女装商人 SYN **fashion designer**

co·va·lent /ˌkəʊˈveɪlənt; *NAmE* ˌkoʊ-/ *adj.* (*chemistry* 化) (of a chemical BOND 化学键) sharing a pair of ELECTRONS 共价的 ➲ COMPARE IONIC

cove /kəʊv; *NAmE* koʊv/ *noun* **1** a small bay (= an area of sea that is partly surrounded by land) 小海湾：*a secluded cove* 僻静的小海湾 ➲ VISUAL VOCAB PAGE V5 **2** (*old-fashioned, BrE, informal*) a man 家伙；汉子；小子

coven /ˈkʌvn/ *noun* a group or meeting of WITCHES 女巫团；女巫的聚会

cov·en·ant /ˈkʌvənənt/ *noun* a promise to sb, or a legal agreement, especially one to pay a regular amount of money to sb/sth 承诺；合同；协约；（尤指定期付款的）契约：*God's covenant with Abraham* 上帝与亚伯拉罕的立约 ◇ *a covenant to a charity* 向慈善机构定期捐款的契约 ▸ **cov·en·ant** *verb*：**~ sth (to sb/sth)** *All profits are covenanted to medical charities.* 已立约把所有收益捐给医疗慈善机构。

Cov·en·try /ˈkɒvəntri; *NAmE* ˈkɑːv-/ *noun*

IDM **send sb to ˈCoventry** (*BrE*) to refuse to speak to sb, as a way of punishing them for sth that they have done 拒绝与某人交谈（作为惩罚）

cover /ˈkʌvə(r)/ *verb, noun*

■ *verb*

• **HIDE/PROTECT** 隐藏；保护 **1** [T] **~ sth (with sth)** to place sth over or in front of sth in order to hide or protect it 掩蔽；遮盖：*Cover the chicken loosely with foil.* 用锡箔把鸡肉松松地盖起来。◇ *She covered her face with her hands.* 她双手掩面。◇ (*figurative*) *He laughed to cover (= hide) his nervousness.* 他哈哈大笑以掩饰他紧张的心情。➲ SYNONYMS AT HIDE

• **SPREAD OVER SURFACE** 覆盖 **2** [T] **~ sth** to lie or spread over the surface of sth 盖；覆盖：*Snow covered the ground.* 大雪覆盖了大地。◇ *Much of the country is covered by forest.* 森林覆盖着这个国家的大片土地。**3** [T] to put or spread a layer of liquid, dust, etc. on sb/sth 撒上，洒上，溅上（一层液体、尘土等）：**~ sb/sth in sth** *The players were soon covered in mud.* 那些运动员很快就浑身溅满了泥。◇ **~ sb/sth with sth** *The wind blew in from the desert and covered everything with sand.* 风从沙漠那边吹来，把一切都蒙上了一层沙子。

• **INCLUDE** 包括 **4** [T] **~ sth** to include sth; to deal with sth 包括；包含；涉及；处理：*The survey covers all aspects of the business.* 调查包括这家企业的各个方面。◇ *The lectures* ***covered a lot of ground*** (= a lot of material, subjects, etc.). 这些讲座涉及的内容极为广泛丰富。◇ *the sales team covering the northern part of the country* (= selling to people in that area) 负责这个国家北部地区的销售队伍 ◇ *Do the rules cover* (= do they apply to) *a case like this?* 这些规则适用于这样的情况吗？

• **MONEY** 款项 **5** [T] **~ sth** to be or provide enough money for sth 足以支付；够付：*$100 should cover your expenses.* *100 美元该足够支付你的费用了。◇ *Your parents will have to cover your tuition fees.* 你的父母得支付你的学费。◇ *The show barely* ***covered its costs.*** 这场演出勉强够本。

• **DISTANCE/AREA** 距离；面积 **6** [T] **~ sth** to travel the distance mentioned 行走（一段路程）：*By sunset we had covered thirty miles.* 到日落时我们已走了三十英里。◇ *They walked for a long time and* ***covered a good deal of ground.*** 他们步行了很长时间，走了一大段路。**7** [T] **~ sth** to spread over the area mentioned 占（一片面积）：*The reserve covers an area of some 1 140 square kilometres.* 保护区占地面积大约 1 140 平方公里。

• **REPORT NEWS** 报道新闻 **8** [T] **~ sth** to report on an event for television, a newspaper, etc.; to show an event on television 报道；电视报道：*She's covering the party's annual conference.* 她正在报道这个政党的年会新闻。◇ *The BBC will cover all the major games of the tournament.* 英国广播公司将报道这次锦标赛的所有重要赛事。

• **FOR SB** 代替某人 **9** [I] **~ for sb** to do sb's work or duties while they are away 代替，顶替，替补（某人工作或履行职责）：*I'm covering for Jane while she's on leave.* 简休假时我来顶替她工作。 **10** [I] **~ for sb** to invent a lie or an excuse that will stop sb from getting into trouble（为免他人陷入麻烦而用谎话或借口）遮掩，掩盖，敷衍：*I have to go out for a minute—will you cover for me if anyone asks where I am?* 我得出去一会儿，假如有人问起我在哪里，你能为我搪塞一下吗？

• **WITH INSURANCE** 保险 **11** [T] to protect sb against loss, injury, etc. by insurance 给…保险：**~ sb/sth (against/for sth)** *Are you fully covered for fire and theft?* 你是否买了足够的火险和盗窃险？◇ **~ sb/sth to do sth** *Does this policy cover my husband to drive?* 这份保险单是否保我丈夫的驾车险？

• **AGAINST BLAME** 防遭指责 **12** [T] **~ yourself (against sth)** to take action in order to protect yourself against being blamed for sth 采取预防行动（以使自己免遭责备）：*One reason doctors take temperatures is to cover themselves against negligence claims.* 医生测量体温的一个原因是免得因玩忽职守而遭索赔。

• **WITH GUN** 用枪 **13** [T] **~ sb** to protect sb by threatening to shoot at anyone who tries to attack them 掩护：*Cover me while I move forward.* 掩护我前进。 **14** [T] **~ sb/sth** to aim a gun at a place or person so that nobody can escape or shoot 用枪瞄准（以致无人可逃跑或开枪）：*The police covered the exits to the building.* 警方用枪封锁了那栋大楼的出口。◇ *Don't move—we've* ***got you covered!*** 不许动！我们的枪口正对着你们！

• **SONG** 歌曲 **15** [T] **~ sth** to record a new version of a song that was originally recorded by another band or singer 翻唱（原来由另一乐队或歌手演唱的歌曲）：*They've covered an old Rolling Stones number.* 他们翻唱了滚石乐队的一首老歌。

IDM **cover all the ˈbases** to consider and deal with all the things that could happen or could be needed when you are arranging sth 考虑周全；面面俱到 **cover your ˈback** (*informal*) (*NAmE also* **cover your ˈass** *taboo, slang*) to realize that you may be blamed or criticized for sth later and take action to avoid this 粉饰污点；防止可预见的指责：*Get everything in writing in order to cover your back.* 一切都要立字为据，以绝后患。 **cover your ˈtracks** to try and hide what you have done, because you do not want other people to find out about it 掩盖自己的行径：*He had attempted to cover his tracks by making her death appear like suicide.* 他使她的死亡看起来像是自杀，企图以此掩盖自己的罪行。➲ MORE AT MULTITUDE

PHR V ˌ**cover sth↔ˈin** to put a covering or roof over

an open space（给露天场地）装顶盖，加顶 **ˌcover sth↔ˈover** to cover sth completely so that it cannot be seen（完全）盖住，遮住 SYN **conceal**: *The Roman remains are now covered over by office buildings.* 这些罗马时代的遗址现已被栋栋办公大楼完全遮住。 **ˌcover ˈup | ˌcover yourself ˈup** to put on more clothes 加（或多）穿衣服；穿暖和 **ˌcover sth↔ˈup** 🔑 **1** to cover sth completely so that it cannot be seen（完全）盖住，遮住：*He covered up the body with a sheet.* 他用一条布单把尸体盖上了。 **2** 🔑 (*disapproving*) to try to stop people from knowing the truth about a mistake, a crime, etc. 掩盖（错误、罪行等的）真相 ➲ RELATED NOUN COVER-UP

■ ***noun***

• **PROTECTION/SHELTER** 保护；遮蔽物 **1** 🔑 [C] a thing that is put over or on another thing, usually to protect it or to decorate it 覆盖物；掩蔽物；套子；罩子：*a cushion cover* 靠垫套 ◇ *a plastic waterproof cover for the stroller* 手推童车的塑料防水篷 ➲ VISUAL VOCAB PAGE V72 ➲ SEE ALSO DUST COVER, LOOSE COVER **2** [U] a place that provides shelter from bad weather or protection from an attack 躲避处；避难所；庇护所：*Everyone ran* ***for cover*** *when it started to rain.* 雨下起来时，大家都跑着找地方避雨。◇ *The climbers* ***took cover*** *from the storm in a cave.* 登山者在山洞里躲避暴风雨。◇ *After the explosion the street was full of people* ***running for cover***. 爆炸发生以后，满街的人都奔跑着找躲避处。

• **OF BOOK** 书 **3** 🔑 [C] the outside of a book or a magazine（书刊的）封面，封皮：*the* ***front/back cover*** 封面；封底 ◇ *Her face was* ***on the cover*** (= the front cover) *of every magazine.* 各种杂志的封面都有她的头像。 ◇ *He always reads the paper* ***from cover to cover*** (= everything in it). 他总是把报纸从头到尾全看一遍。

• **INSURANCE** 保险 **4** (*BrE*) (*NAmE* **cov·er·age**) [U] **~ (against sth)** protection that an insurance company provides by promising to pay you money if a particular event happens（保险公司的）保险：*accident cover* 事故保险 ◇ *cover against accidental damage* 意外损害保险 ➲ WORDFINDER NOTE AT INSURANCE

• **WITH WEAPONS** 武器 **5** [U] support and protection that is provided when sb is attacking or in danger of being attacked 掩护；防护：*The ships needed air cover* (= protection by military planes) *once they reached enemy waters.* 一到达敌方的水域，船只就需要空中掩护。

• **TREES/PLANTS** 树木；植物 **6** [U] trees and plants that grow on an area of land（生长在一个地区的）植被：*The total forest cover of the earth is decreasing.* 地球上森林覆盖的总面积正在减少。

• **CLOUD/SNOW** 云；雪 **7** [U] the fact of the sky being covered with cloud or the ground with snow（云层的）遮盖；（雪的）覆盖：*Fog and low cloud cover are expected this afternoon.* 预计今天下午有雾和低空云层。 ◇ *In this area there is snow cover for six months of the year.* 这个地区一年中有六个月被积雪覆盖。

• **ON BED** 床上 **8 the covers** [pl.] the sheets, BLANKETS, etc. on a bed 床单；床罩；毯子；被子：*She threw back the covers and leapt out of bed.* 她掀开被子跳下床来。

• **SONG** 歌曲 **9** [C] = COVER VERSION

• **HIDING STH** 隐藏 **10** [C, usually sing.] **~ (for sth)** activities or behaviour that seem honest or true but that hide sb's real identity or feelings, or that hide sth illegal（对身份、感情或违法事情的）掩盖，掩饰：*His work as a civil servant was a cover for his activities as a spy.* 他以公务员的工作来掩护他搞间谍活动。◇ *Her over-confident attitude was a cover for her nervousness.* 她以过分自信的态度来掩饰她紧张的心情。 ◇ *It would only take one phone call to* ***blow their cover*** (= make known their true identities and what they were really doing). 只要拨打一个电话就可揭穿他们的伪装。

• **FOR SB'S WORK** 代替某人工作 **11** [U] the fact of sb doing another person's job when they are away or when there are not enough staff 代替工作；代劳；替补：*It's the manager's job to organize cover for staff who are absent.* 安排他人顶替缺席的员工是经理的工作。◇ *Ambulance drivers provided only emergency cover during the dispute.* 纠纷期间救护车司机只提供急救替班。

IDM **break ˈcover** to leave a place that you have been hiding in, usually at a high speed 匆匆离开隐蔽处；冲出躲藏处 **under ˈcover 1** pretending to be sb else in order to do sth secretly（为秘密活动）伪装着，装扮着，冒名顶替：*a police officer working under cover* 做隐蔽工作的警察 **2** under a structure that gives protection from the weather 在…下（避风雨） **under (the) cover of sth** hidden or protected by sth 在…的掩护（或保护）下：*Later, under cover of darkness, they crept into the house.* 后来他们在夜幕的掩护下溜进了房子。 **under separate ˈcover** (*business* 商) in a separate envelope 另函：*The information you requested is being forwarded to you under separate cover.* 现另函寄上所要资料。 ➲ MORE AT JUDGE *v.*

cov·er·age /ˈkʌvərɪdʒ/ *noun* **1** [U] the reporting of news and sport in newspapers and on the radio and television 新闻报道：***media/newspaper/press coverage*** 媒体 / 报纸 / 报刊的报道 ◇ *tonight's* ***live coverage*** *of the hockey game* 今晚曲棍球比赛的现场直播 ➲ WORDFINDER NOTE AT JOURNALIST **2** [U] the range or quality of information that is included in a book or course of study, on television, etc.（书、课程学习、电视等的）信息范围，信息质量：*magazines with extensive coverage of diet and health topics* 包含大量饮食与健康话题的杂志 ◇ *The volume offers an incomplete coverage of the history of philosophy.* 这本书所涵盖的哲学史并不完整。 **3** [U, C, usually sing.] the amount of sth that sth provides; the extent to which sth covers an area or a group of people 提供的数量；覆盖范围：*Immunization coverage against fatal diseases has increased to 99% in some countries.* 在一些国家致命疾病免疫注射的覆盖面已达到 99%。 ◇ *The service has a coverage of 90% of the UK population.* 该服务覆盖了英国 90% 的人口。 **4** (*NAmE*) (*BrE* **cover**) [U] protection that an insurance company provides by promising to pay you money if a particular event happens（保险公司的）保险：*insurance coverage* 保险范围 ◇ *Medicaid health coverage for low-income families* 对低收入家庭的医疗保险

cov·er·alls /ˈkʌvərɔːlz/ (*NAmE*) (*BrE* **overalls**) *noun* [pl.] a loose piece of clothing like a shirt and trousers/pants in one piece, made of heavy cloth and usually worn over other clothing by workers doing dirty work 工装连衣裤；工装服 ➲ PICTURE AT OVERALL

ˈcover charge *noun* [usually sing.] an amount of money that you pay in some restaurants or clubs in addition to the cost of the food and drink（餐馆或俱乐部中饮食之外的）服务费

covered 🔑 /ˈkʌvəd; *NAmE* -vərd/ *adj.* **1** 🔑 [not before noun] **~ in/with sth** having a layer or amount of sth on it 盖着一层；盖满：*His face was covered in blood.* 他满脸是血。◇ *The walls were covered with pictures.* 这些墙上挂满了画。 **2** 🔑 having a roof over it 有顶的：*a covered area of the stadium with seats* 体育场有顶的座席区域

ˌcovered ˈwagon *noun* a large wooden vehicle with a curved roof made of cloth, that is pulled by horses, used especially in the past in N America by people travelling across the land to the west（尤指旧时用于横跨北美大陆到西部的）大篷马车

ˈcover girl *noun* a young woman whose photograph is on the front of a magazine（杂志的）封面女郎

cov·er·ing 🔑 /ˈkʌvərɪŋ/ *noun* **1** 🔑 a layer of sth that covers sth else（一层）覆盖层，遮盖物：*a thick covering of snow on the ground* 地上厚厚的一层积雪 **2** 🔑 a layer of material such as carpet or WALLPAPER, used to cover, decorate and protect floors, walls, etc. 装饰（或保护）性覆盖物：***floor/wall coverings*** 地板 / 墙壁覆盖物 **3** 🔑 a piece of material that covers sth 覆盖某物的一块（或一片）材料：*He pulled the plastic covering off the dead body.* 他拉掉了盖在尸体上的塑料布。

ˌcovering ˈletter (*BrE*) (*NAmE* **ˈcover letter**) *noun* a letter containing extra information that you send with sth 附信（与某物一起寄出）

cov·er·let /ˈkʌvələt; *NAmE* -vərl-/ *noun* (*old-fashioned*) a type of BEDSPREAD to cover a bed 床罩

ˈcover story *noun* **1** the main story in a magazine, that goes with the picture shown on the front cover 封面故事（杂志中与封面图片有关的内容） **2** a story that is invented in order to hide sth, especially a person's identity or their reasons for doing sth（尤指掩饰身份或做某事原因的）托辞，借口

cov·ert *adj., noun*
■ ***adj.*** /ˈkʌvət; ˈkəʊvɜːt; *NAmE* ˈkoʊvɜːrt/ (*formal*) secret or hidden, making it difficult to notice 秘密的；隐蔽的；暗中的： ***covert operations/surveillance*** 暗中活动 / 监视 ◇ *He stole a covert glance at her across the table.* 他隔着桌子偷偷地瞥了她一眼。➲ COMPARE OVERT ▶ **cov·ert·ly** *adv.* : *She watched him covertly in the mirror.* 她从镜子里偷偷地望着他。
■ ***noun*** /ˈkʌvət; *NAmE* -vərt/ an area of thick low bushes and trees where animals can hide（动物可藏身的）矮树丛，灌木林

ˈcover-up *noun* [usually sing.] action that is taken to hide a mistake or an illegal activity from the public （对过失或不法活动的）掩盖，掩饰: *Government sources denied there had been a deliberate cover-up.* 政府方面否认了有故意掩饰的行为。

ˈcover version (*also* **cover**) *noun* a new recording of an old song by a different band or singer（由不同乐队演奏或不同歌手演唱的）翻唱版本

covet /ˈkʌvət/ *verb* ~ **sth** (*formal*) to want sth very much, especially sth that belongs to sb else 渴望；贪求（尤指别人的东西）；觊觎: *He had long coveted the chance to work with a famous musician.* 他一直渴望有机会与著名音乐家合作。◇ *They are this year's winners of the coveted trophy* (= that everyone would like to win). 他们获得了本年度人人觊觎的大奖。

cov·et·ous /ˈkʌvətəs/ *adj.* (*formal*) having a strong desire for the things that other people have 贪求的；垂涎的 ▶ **cov·et·ous·ness** *noun* [U]

cow 🔑 /kaʊ/ *noun, verb*
■ ***noun*** **1** 🔑 a large animal kept on farms to produce milk or beef 母牛；奶牛；菜牛；肉牛: *cow's milk* 牛奶 ◇ *a herd of dairy cows* (= cows kept for their milk) 一群奶牛 ➲ COMPARE BULL (1), CALF (2), HEIFER ➲ SEE ALSO CATTLE **2** the female of the ELEPHANT, WHALE and some other large animals 雌象；雌鲸；大型雌性动物 ➲ COMPARE BULL (2) **3** (*slang, disapproving*) an offensive word for a woman 婆娘；娘儿们: *You stupid cow!* 你这蠢婆娘！ **4** (*AustralE, NZE*) an unpleasant person, thing or situation 讨厌的人（或事物、情况） ➲ SEE ALSO CASH COW, SACRED COW
IDM ▶ **have a ˈcow** (*NAmE, informal*) to become very angry or anxious about sth 暴跳如雷；焦虑不安: *Don't have a cow—it's no big deal.* 别发火，没什么大不了。 **till the ˈcows come home** (*informal*) for a very long time; for ever 很长时间；永远
■ ***verb*** [usually passive] ~ **sb** to frighten sb in order to make them obey you 恐吓；吓唬；威胁；胁迫 SYN **intimidate**: *She was easily cowed by people in authority.* 她很容易被有权势的人吓住。

cow·ard /ˈkaʊəd; *NAmE* -ərd/ *noun* (*disapproving*) a person who is not brave or who does not have the courage to do things that other people do not think are especially difficult 胆小鬼；懦夫；胆怯者: *You coward! What are you afraid of?* 你这胆小鬼！你怕什么呢？ ◇ *I'm a real coward when it comes to going to the dentist.* 我一去看牙医就胆战心惊。 ▶ **cow·ard·ly** *adj.* : *a cowardly attack on a defenceless man* 欺负一个没有自卫能力的人的不光彩行为

cow·ard·ice /ˈkaʊədɪs; *NAmE* -ərd-/ *noun* [U] fear or lack of courage 惧怕；胆小；懦弱 OPP **bravery, courage**

cow·bell /ˈkaʊbel/ *noun* a bell that is put around a cow's neck so that the cow can easily be found 牛颈铃

cow·boy /ˈkaʊbɔɪ/ *noun* **1** (*NAmE also* **cow·poke** *old-fashioned* or *humorous*) a man who rides a horse and whose job is to take care of CATTLE in the western parts of the US（美国西部的）牛仔，骑马牧人: *cowboy boots* 牛仔靴 ➲ VISUAL VOCAB PAGE V69 **2** a man like this as a character in a film/movie about the American West（美国西部影片中的）牛仔: *children playing a game of cowboys and Indians* 玩美国西部牛仔与印第安人游戏的孩子们 **3** (*BrE, informal, disapproving*) a dishonest person in business, especially sb who produces work of bad quality or charges too high a price（尤指产品质量差或索价太高的）奸商

ˈcowboy hat *noun* a hat with a wide BRIM, worn by American cowboys （美国牛仔戴的）牛仔帽 ➲ VISUAL VOCAB PAGE V70

cow·catch·er /ˈkaʊkætʃə(r)/ *noun* (*NAmE*) a pointed metal structure at the front of a train that is used for pushing things off the track （火车机车前的）排障器

ˈcow chip *noun* (*US*) a very hard COWPAT 硬牛粪团

cowed /kaʊd/ *adj.* made to feel afraid and that you are not as good as sb else 使感到胆怯的；自惭形秽的 ➲ SEE ALSO COW *v.*

cower /ˈkaʊə(r)/ *verb* [I] to bend low and/or move backwards because you are frightened （因恐惧而）蜷缩，畏缩，退缩: *A gun went off and people cowered behind walls and under tables.* 一声枪响，人们缩到墙后或桌子底下躲起来。

cow·girl /ˈkaʊɡɜːl; *NAmE* -ɡɜːrl/ *noun* a female COWBOY in the American West （美国西部的）女牛仔，女牧工

cow·hand /ˈkaʊhænd/ *noun* a person whose job is taking care of cows 牧牛工；放牛人

cow·hide /ˈkaʊhaɪd/ *noun* [U] strong leather made from the skin of a cow （母）牛皮革

cowl /kaʊl/ *noun* **1** a large loose covering for the head, worn especially by MONKS （尤指修道士戴的）大兜帽，大风帽 **2** a cover for a CHIMNEY, etc., usually made of metal. Cowls often turn with the wind and are designed to improve the flow of air or smoke. 烟囱罩，通风帽（常可随风转动以利通风或排烟）

cow·lick /ˈkaʊlɪk/ *noun* a piece of hair that grows in a different direction from the rest of your hair and is difficult to make lie flat 翘起的一绺头发

cowl·ing /ˈkaʊlɪŋ/ *noun* (*specialist*) a metal cover for an engine, especially on an aircraft 整流罩；（尤指）飞机引擎罩 ➲ VISUAL VOCAB PAGE V57

ˈcowl neck *noun* a COLLAR on a woman's sweater that hangs in several folds （女性套衫的）重褶领

ˈco-worker *noun* a person that sb works with, doing the same kind of job 共同工作者；合作者；同事；同僚 SYN **colleague**

ˈcow parsley *noun* [U] a European wild plant with a lot of very small white flowers that look like LACE 峨参，饰带花（原产欧洲，开小白花）

cow·pat /ˈkaʊpæt/ (*BrE*) *noun* a round flat piece of solid waste from a cow 牛粪团

cow·pea /ˈkaʊpiː/ *noun* a type of BEAN that is white with a black spot and is grown for food 豇豆，黑眼豆（供食用）: *Cowpeas are an important crop in many African countries.* 黑眼豆是很多非洲国家的重要作物。

cow·poke /ˈkaʊpəʊk; *NAmE* -poʊk/ *noun* (*NAmE, old-fashioned* or *humorous*) = COWBOY

cow·rie /ˈkaʊri/ *noun* a small shiny shell that was used as money in the past in parts of Africa and Asia 宝贝贝壳（旧时亚非部分地区用作货币的小贝壳）

cow·shed /ˈkaʊʃed/ *noun* a farm building in which cows are kept 牛棚；牛舍

cow·slip /ˈkaʊslɪp/ *noun* a small wild plant with yellow flowers with a sweet smell 樱草；欧洲樱草；黄花九轮草；野生报春花

cox /kɒks; *NAmE* kɑːks/ *noun, verb*
■ ***noun*** (*also* **cox·swain**) the person who controls the

direction of a ROWING BOAT while other people are ROWING（划艇的）舵手
■ *verb* [T, I] ~ (sth) to control the direction of a ROWING BOAT while other people are ROWING; to act as a cox（为划艇）掌舵；当（划艇的）舵手

cox·swain /ˈkɒksn; *NAmE* ˈkɑːksn/ *noun* **1** the person who is in charge of a LIFEBOAT and who controls its direction（救生艇的）艇长，舵手 **2** = COX

coy /kɔɪ/ *adj.* **1** shy or pretending to be shy and innocent, especially about love or sex, and sometimes in order to make people more interested in you（尤指对爱情或性爱）羞羞答答的，假装害羞无知的，故作忸怩的：*She gave me a coy smile.* 她羞答答地对我笑了笑。 **2** ~ (about sth) not willing to give information about sth, or answer questions that tell people too much about you 不愿提供信息的；不肯作答的；含糊其词的 SYN **reticent**: *She was a little coy about how much her dress cost.* 她对她那条连衣裙花了多少钱有点吞吞吐吐。 ▸ **coyly** *adv.* **coy·ness** *noun* [U]

coy·ote /kaɪˈəʊti; *NAmE* -ˈoʊti; *BrE also* kɔɪ-; *NAmE also* ˈkaɪoʊt/ (*also* **ˈprairie wolf**) *noun* a N American wild animal of the dog family 丛林狼，草原狼（犬科动物，分布于北美）

coy·pu /ˈkɔɪpuː/ *noun* (*pl.* **coy·pus** or **coy·pu**) a large S American animal, like a BEAVER, that lives near water 河狸鼠（南美洲动物）

coz *conj.* = COS[1]

cozy (*NAmE*) (*BrE* **cosy**) /ˈkəʊzi; *NAmE* ˈkoʊzi/ *adj.*, *verb*
■ *adj.* (**cozi·er**, **cozi·est**, **cosi·er**, **cosi·est**) **1** warm, comfortable and safe, especially because of being small or confined（尤指因地方小或封闭而）温暖舒适的 SYN **snug**: *a cozy little room* 温暖舒适的小房间 ◇ *a cozy feeling* 惬意的感觉 ◇ *I felt warm and cozy sitting by the fire.* 坐在炉火旁，我感到又暖和又舒服。 **2** friendly and private 亲密无间的；密切的：*a cozy chat with a friend* 与朋友亲切的闲聊 **3** (*often disapproving*) easy and convenient, but not always honest or right 轻易得到的，轻松的（但不一定是诚实或正当的）：*The firm has a cozy relationship with the Department of Defense.* 这家公司与国防部关系密切。 ◇ *The danger is that things get too cozy.* 危险在于一切都来得太容易。 ▸ **cozi·ly** (*NAmE*) (*BrE* **cosi·ly**) *adv.*: *sitting cozily by the fire* 暖融融地坐在炉火旁 **cozi·ness** (*NAmE*) (*BrE* **cosi·ness**) *noun* [U]: *the warmth and coziness of the kitchen* 厨房的温暖与舒适
■ *verb* (**cozies**, **cozy·ing**, **cozied**, **cozied**)
PHR V ˌ**cozy ˈup to sb** (*NAmE*) (*BrE* ˌ**cosy ˈup to sb**) (*informal*) to act in a friendly way towards sb, especially sb who will be useful to you 献殷勤；取悦

cp. *abbr.* (in writing 书写形式) compare 比较

CPE /ˌsiː piː ˈiː/ *noun* [U] the abbreviation for 'Certificate of Proficiency in English' (a British test, now called 'Cambridge English: Proficiency' that measures a person's ability to speak and write English at a very advanced level) 熟练英语证书考试，剑桥英语第五级认证（全写为 Certificate of Proficiency in English，现称 Cambridge English: Proficiency，英国考试，检测英语作为外语者的高级口语和写作能力）

CPI /ˌsiː piː ˈaɪ/ *abbr.* CONSUMER PRICE INDEX 居民消费价格指数；消费价格指数

Cpl (*BrE*) (*NAmE* **Cpl.**) *abbr.* (in writing 书写形式) CORPORAL 下士

CPR /ˌsiː piː ˈɑː(r)/ *noun* [U] the abbreviation for 'cardiopulmonary resuscitation' (breathing air into the mouth of an unconscious person and pressing on their chest to keep them alive by sending air around their body) 心肺复苏（全写为 cardiopulmonary resuscitation，包括进行人工呼吸和体外心脏按压）

CPU /ˌsiː piː ˈjuː/ *abbr.* (*computing* 计) central processing unit (the part of a computer that controls all the other parts of the system) 中央处理器

CRA /ˌsiː ɑːr ˈeɪ/ *abbr.* Canada Revenue Agency (the department of the Canadian government that deals with personal income tax) 加拿大税务局

crab /kræb/ *noun* **1** [C] a sea creature with a hard shell, eight legs and two PINCERS (= curved and pointed arms for catching and holding things). Crabs move sideways on land. 蟹；螃蟹 ⊃ VISUAL VOCAB PAGE V13 ⊃ SEE ALSO HERMIT CRAB **2** [U] meat from a crab, used for food 蟹肉：*dressed crab* 经加工的螃蟹 **3** **crabs** (*informal*) the condition caused by having LICE (called **crab lice**) in the hair around the GENITALS 阴虱病

ˈ**crab apple** *noun* a tree that produces fruit like small hard sour apples, also called crab apples 酸苹果树；花红树；沙果树

crabbed /ˈkræbɪd; kræbd/ *adj.* **1** (*literary*) (of sb's writing 笔迹) small and difficult to read 小而难辨认的 **2** (*old-fashioned*) = CRABBY

crabby /ˈkræbi/ *adj.* (*informal*) (of people 人) bad-tempered and unpleasant 脾气乖戾的；易怒的

crab·grass /ˈkræbɡrɑːs; *NAmE* -ɡræs/ *noun* [U] (*especially NAmE*) a type of grass that grows where it is not wanted, spreads quickly and is hard to get rid of 马唐，指草（多为杂草，难以根除）

ˈ**crab stick** *noun* a small pink stick made from pressed pieces of fish that have been flavoured to taste like CRAB 蟹肉棒，蟹肉条（用鱼肉糜加香料制成）

crab·wise /ˈkræbwaɪz/ *adv.* (of a movement 移动) in a sideways direction, like a CRAB 向一边地；横向似螃蟹地

crack 🔑 /kræk/ *verb*, *noun*, *adj.*
■ *verb*
• **BREAK** 破裂 **1** 🔑 [I, T] to break without dividing into separate parts; to break sth in this way 破裂；裂开；断裂：*The ice cracked as I stepped onto it.* 我一踩冰就裂了。 ◇ ~ **sth** *He has cracked a bone in his arm.* 他的手臂有一处骨裂。 ◇ *Her lips were dry and cracked.* 她的嘴唇干裂了。 **2** 🔑 [I, T] to break open or into pieces; to break sth in this way 砸开；破开；砸碎；打碎：**+ adv./prep.** *A chunk of the cliff had cracked off in a storm.* 悬崖上的一块石头在暴风雨中崩塌下来。 ◇ (*figurative*) *His face cracked into a smile.* 他脸上绽放了微笑。 ◇ ~ **sth** *to crack a nut* 把坚果砸开 ◇ ~ **sth + adv./prep.** *She cracked an egg into the pan.* 她往锅里打了一个鸡蛋。
• **HIT** 击中 **3** [T] ~ **sth/sb (on/against sth)** to hit sth/sb with a short hard blow 重击；猛击：*I cracked my head on the low ceiling.* 我的头撞上了低矮的天花板。 ◇ *He cracked me on the head with a ruler.* 他用尺子猛击我的头部。
• **MAKE SOUND** 发出声音 **4** [I, T] to make a sharp sound; to make sth do this（使）发出爆裂声，噼啪作响：*A shot cracked across the ridge.* 一颗炮弹飞过山脊爆炸了。 ◇ [no passive] ~ **sth** *He* **cracked his whip** *and galloped away.* 他抽响鞭子，策马飞奔而去。
• **OF VOICE** 嗓音 **5** [I] if your voice **cracks**, it changes in depth, volume, etc. suddenly and in a way that you cannot control（突然）变嘶哑，变沙哑：*In a voice cracking with emotion, he told us of his son's death.* 他悲恸失声地告诉我们他儿子去世的消息。
• **UNDER PRESSURE** 在压力下 **6** [I] to no longer be able to function normally because of pressure（因压力而）吃不消，崩溃，瓦解：*Things are terrible at work and people are cracking under the strain.* 工作情况很糟糕，人们因过度紧张越来越吃不消了。 ◇ *They questioned him for days before he cracked.* 他们审讯他多日后他就垮掉了。 ◇ *The old institutions are cracking.* 旧的制度正在瓦解。
• **FIND SOLUTION** 找到解决方法 **7** [T] ~ **sth** to find the solution to a problem, etc.; to find the way to do sth difficult 找到解决（难题等的）方法：*to crack the enemy's code* 破译敌人的密码 ◇ (*informal*) *After a year in this job I think* **I've got it cracked!** 干了一年后，我觉得我已知道怎样做这项工作了！
• **STOP SB/STH** 阻止 **8** [T] ~ **sth** to find a way of stopping or defeating a criminal or an enemy 阻止，打击，击败，

战胜（罪犯或敌人）：*Police have cracked a major drugs ring.* 警方破获了一个重大的贩毒集团。

• OPEN BOTTLE 开瓶 **9** [T] ~ **(open) a bottle** (*informal*) to open a bottle, especially of wine, and drink it 开瓶；（尤指）开瓶饮酒

• A JOKE 玩笑 **10** [T] ~ **a joke** (*informal*) to tell a joke 说（笑话）；开（玩笑）

IDM **get 'cracking** (*informal*) to begin immediately and work quickly 立即大干起来 SYN **get going**: *There's a lot to be done, so let's get cracking.* 要做的工作很多，咱们马上就干吧。 **not all, everything, etc. sb's cracked 'up to be** (*informal*) not as good as people say 不像人们说的那么好：*He's not nearly such a good writer as he's cracked up to be.* 他远不是人们所说的那种优秀作家。 **crack the 'whip** to use your authority or power to make sb work very hard, usually by treating them in a strict way 压迫；役使 ➲ MORE AT NUT *n.*, SLEDGEHAMMER

PHR V **,crack 'down (on sb/sth)** to try harder to prevent an illegal activity and deal more severely with those who are caught doing it 竭力取缔；严厉打击；镇压：*Police are cracking down on drug dealers.* 警方正在严厉打击毒品贩子。 ➲ RELATED NOUN CRACKDOWN **,crack 'on (with sth)** (*BrE, informal*) to work hard at sth so that you finish it quickly; to pass or continue quickly （为尽快完成而）努力干；（急速）经过，穿过；快速继续下去：*If we crack on with the painting we should finish it today.* 只要我们拼命干，今天应该就能刷完漆。◇ *Time was cracking on and we were nowhere near finished.* 时间飞逝，可我们却远远没有完成。 **,crack 'up** (*informal*) **1** to become ill, either physically or mentally, because of pressure （因压力造成身体或精神）垮掉，崩溃：*You'll crack up if you carry on working like this.* 你再这样干下去，身体会垮掉的。 **2** to start laughing a lot 开始大笑起来：*He walked in and everyone just cracked up.* 他一进来，人人都捧腹大笑起来。 **,crack sb 'up** (*informal*) to make sb laugh a lot 使大笑起来：*Gill's so funny, she just cracks me up.* 吉尔滑稽极了，逗得我哈哈大笑。

■ *noun*

• BREAK 裂缝 **1** [C] ~ **(in sth)** a line on the surface of sth where it has broken but not split into separate parts 裂纹；裂缝：*This cup has a crack in it.* 这杯子有一道裂痕。◇ *Cracks began to appear in the walls.* 墙壁开始出现裂缝了。◇ (*figurative*) *The cracks* (= faults) *in the government's economic policy are already beginning to show.* 政府经济政策中的失误已开始显露出来。 ➲ PICTURE AT BROKEN

• NARROW OPENING 缝隙 **2** [C] a narrow space or opening 缝隙；狭缝；窄缝：*She peeped through the crack in the curtains.* 她透过窗帘的缝隙窥视。◇ *The door opened a crack* (= a small amount). 那门开了一条缝。

• SOUND 声响 **3** [C] a sudden loud noise （突然的）爆裂声，噼啪声：*a crack of thunder* 一声霹雳 ◇ *the sharp crack of a rifle shot* 尖厉的步枪声

• HIT 击中 **4** [C] ~ **(on sth)** a sharp blow that can be heard （可听到响声的）重击，猛击：*She fell over and got a nasty crack on the head.* 她跌倒了，脑袋重重地磕了一下。

• ATTEMPT 尝试 **5** [C] ~ **(at sth)** | ~ **(at doing sth)** (*informal*) an occasion when you try to do sth 尝试；试做 SYN **attempt**: *She hopes to have another crack at the world record this year.* 她希望今年再一次冲击世界纪录。

• DRUG 毒品 **6** (*also* **,crack co'caine**) [U] a powerful, illegal drug that is a form of COCAINE 强效可卡因：*a crack addict* 吸强效可卡因成瘾的人

• JOKE 玩笑 **7** [C] (*informal*) a joke, especially a critical one （尤指挖苦人的）玩笑，俏皮话：*He made a very unfair crack about her looks.* 他开玩笑地损了一下她的长相，言语很是刻薄。

• CONVERSATION 交谈 **8** (*also* **craic**) [U, sing.] (*IrishE, informal*) a good time; friendly, enjoyable talk 好时光；友好愉快的交谈：*Where's the crack tonight?* 今晚去哪里逍遥？◇ *He's a person who enjoys a drink and a bit of crack.* 他是个喜欢喝两杯又爱聊天的人。

IDM **at the crack of 'dawn** (*informal*) very early in the morning 黎明；破晓；清晨 ➲ MORE AT FAIR *adj.*

■ *adj.* [only before noun] expert and highly trained; excellent at sth 训练有素的；技艺高超的；优秀的；一流的：*crack troops* 精锐部队 ◇ *He's a crack shot* (= accurate and skilled at shooting). 他是个神枪手。

crack·brained /'krækbreɪnd/ *adj.* (*informal*) crazy and unlikely to succeed 疯狂而难以成功的：*a crackbrained idea* 异想天开的想法

crack·down /'krækdaʊn/ *noun* ~ **(on sb/sth)** severe action taken to restrict the activities of criminals or of people opposed to the government or sb in authority 严厉的打击；镇压：*a military crackdown on student protesters* 对抗议的学生实行的军事镇压 ◇ *a crackdown on crime* 对犯罪的严厉打击

cracked /krækt/ *adj.* **1** damaged with lines in its surface but not completely broken 破裂的；有裂纹的：*a cracked mirror/mug* 有裂纹的镜子／杯子 ◇ *He suffered cracked ribs and bruising.* 他断了肋骨还有挫伤。◇ *She passed her tongue over her cracked lips and tried to speak.* 她用舌头舔了一下干裂的嘴唇，试图要说话。 ➲ PICTURE AT BROKEN **2** (of sb's voice 嗓音) sounding rough with sudden changes in how loud or high it is, because the person is upset （因心烦意乱而突然）粗声的，沙哑的：*'I'm just fine,' she said in a cracked voice.* "我真的挺好。"她声音沙哑地说道。 **3** [not before noun] (*informal*) crazy 疯狂；发疯：*I think he must be cracked, don't you?* 我认为他一定是疯了，你说是不是？

Christmas cracker 彩包爆竹

crack·er /'krækə(r)/ *noun* **1** a thin dry biscuit that is often salty and usually eaten with cheese 薄脆饼干（多为咸味，常与干酪一起食用） ➲ SEE ALSO CREAM CRACKER, GRAHAM CRACKER **2** (*also* **,Christmas 'cracker**) a tube of coloured paper that makes a loud EXPLOSIVE sound when it is pulled open by two people. Crackers usually contain a paper hat, a small present and a joke, and are used in Britain at Christmas parties and meals. 彩包爆竹，彩色拉炮（在英国用于圣诞聚会和聚餐，通常装有纸帽、小礼品及笑话纸条）：*Who wants to pull this cracker with me?* 谁来跟我拉响这个彩炮？ ➲ SEE ALSO FIRECRACKER **3** (*BrE, informal*) something that you think is very good, funny, etc. （认为）十分愉快的事，滑稽可笑的事：*It was a cracker of a goal.* 这球进得真精彩。◇ *I've got a joke for you. It's a real cracker!* 我给你讲个笑话。好笑死了！ **4** (*NAmE, slang*) an offensive word for a poor white person with little education from the southern US （对几乎未受过教育的美国南方贫苦白人的轻蔑语）车把式 **5** (*informal*) a person who illegally finds a way of looking at or stealing information on sb else's computer system 破密高手（非法浏览或窃取他人的计算机系统上的信息） **6** (*old-fashioned, BrE, informal*) an attractive woman 有魅力的女人；迷人的女子

crack·er·jack /'krækədʒæk; *NAmE* -kərdʒæk/ *noun* (*NAmE, informal*) an excellent person or thing 出色的人；优质的东西 ▶ **crack·er·jack** *adj.*

crack·ers /'krækəz; *NAmE* -kərz/ *adj.* [not before noun] (*BrE, informal*) crazy 疯狂；发狂：*That noise is driving me crackers.* 那噪声闹得我简直要疯了。

crack·head /'krækhed/ *noun* (*slang*) a person who uses the illegal drug CRACK 强效可卡因瘾君子

'crack house *noun* a place where people sell CRACK (= a type of illegal drug) 强效可卡因毒品站

crack·ing /'krækɪŋ/ *noun, adj.*

■ *noun* [U] **1** lines on a surface where it is damaged or beginning to break 裂纹；裂缝；裂痕：*All planes are being inspected for possible cracking and corrosion.* 所有的飞机都在接受检查，看是否有裂纹和腐蚀现象。 **2** the sound of sth cracking 爆裂声；噼啪声：*the cracking of* thunder/twigs 霹雳声；细枝发出的噼啪声

■**adj.** [usually before noun] (*BrE, informal*) excellent 优秀的；出色的；极好的；顶呱呱的：*That was a cracking goal.* 这球进得真精彩。◇ *She's in cracking form at the moment.* 她这会儿状态好极了。◇ *We set off **at a cracking pace*** (= very quickly). 我们迅速地出发了。▶ **crack·ing** *adv.*：*a cracking good* (= extremely good) *dinner* 一顿佳肴美餐

crackle /ˈkrækl/ *verb, noun*

■**verb** [I] to make short sharp sounds like sth that is burning in a fire（像东西在火里燃烧一样）发爆裂声，噼啪作响：*A log fire crackled in the hearth.* 炉中的木柴烧得噼啪作响。◇ *The radio crackled into life.* 收音机嘎嘎地响了起来。◇ (*figurative*) *The atmosphere crackled with tension.* 气氛顿时紧张了起来。

■**noun** [U, C] a series of short sharp sounds（一连串的）噼啪声；噼里啪啦的响声：*the distant crackle of machine-gun fire* 远处机枪扫射的噼啪声 ▶ **crack·ly** /ˈkrækli/ *adj.*：*She picked up the phone and heard a crackly voice saying: 'Sue here.'* 她拿起电话，听到一个刺耳的声音在说："我是休。"

crack·ling /ˈkræklɪŋ/ *noun* **1** [U, sing.] a series of sharp sounds（一连串的）爆裂声，噼啪声：*He could hear the crackling of burning trees.* 他可以听见树木燃烧发出的噼啪声。**2** [U] (*BrE*) (*US* **crack·lings** [pl.]) the hard skin of PORK (= meat from a pig) that has been cooked in the oven（烤猪肉的）脆皮

crack·pot /ˈkrækpɒt; *NAmE* -pɑːt/ *noun* (*informal*) a person with strange or crazy ideas 有古怪想法的人；怪人 ▶ **crack·pot** *adj.* [only before noun]：***crackpot ideas/theories*** 离奇古怪的想法 / 理论

-cracy *combining form* (in nouns 构成名词) the government or rule of …的政府；…的统治：*democracy* 民主政体 ◇ *bureaucracy* 官僚体制

cra·dle /ˈkreɪdl/ *noun, verb*

■**noun** **1** a small bed for a baby which can be pushed gently from side to side 摇篮：*She rocked the baby to sleep in its cradle.* 她摇动摇篮哄婴儿入睡。➲ VISUAL VOCAB PAGE V24 **2** [usually sing.] **~ of sth** the place where sth important began 策源地；发源地；发祥地：*Greece, the cradle of Western civilization* 希腊，西方文明的摇篮 **3** (*BrE*) a small platform that can be moved up and down the outside of a high building, used by people cleaning windows, etc.（高楼外供清洁窗户等用的）吊架，托架，吊篮 **4** the part of a telephone on which the RECEIVER rests（电话机的）听筒架，叉托支架

IDM **from the ˌcradle to the ˈgrave** a way of referring to the whole of a person's life, from birth until death 一生；一世；从生到死 ➲ MORE AT ROB

■**verb** **~ sb/sth** to hold sb/sth gently in your arms or hands 轻轻抱着：*The old man cradled the tiny baby in his arms.* 老汉把幼小的婴儿轻轻抱在怀里。

ˈcradle cap *noun* [U] a skin condition that causes dry rough yellow areas on top of a baby's head 乳痂

ˈcradle-snatcher (*BrE*) (*NAmE* **ˈcradle-robber**) *noun* (*disapproving*) a person who has a sexual relationship with a much younger person 与比自己年轻得多的人发生性关系者 ▶ **ˈcradle-snatch** (*BrE*) (*NAmE* **ˈcradle-rob**) *verb* [I]

craft 🔑 /krɑːft; *NAmE* kræft/ *noun, verb*

■**noun** **1** 🔑 [C, U] an activity involving a special skill at making things with your hands 手艺；工艺：*traditional crafts like basket-weaving* 像编篮子之类的传统工艺 ◇ *a **craft fair/workshop*** 手工艺品交易会 / 制作坊 ◇ *Craft, Design and Technology* (= a subject in some British schools) 工艺、设计与技术（英国某些学校中的科目）➲ SEE ALSO ARTS AND CRAFTS **2** 🔑 [sing.] all the skills needed for a particular activity 技巧；技能；技艺：*chefs who learned their craft in top hotels* 在高级酒店学过烹调技艺的厨师 ◇ *the writer's craft* 写作技巧 **3** [U] (*formal, disapproving*) skill in making people believe what you want them to believe 诡计；手腕；骗术：*He knew how to win by craft and diplomacy what he could not gain by force.* 他擅长于通过计谋和外交手腕赢得他用武力无法得到的东西。**4** [C] (*pl.* **craft**) (*formal*) a boat or ship 小船；船：*Hundreds of small craft bobbed around the liner as it steamed into the harbour.* 班轮驶进港口时，周围的许多小船颠簸起来。◇ *a **landing/pleasure craft*** 登陆艇；游艇 **5** [C] (*pl.* **craft**) an aircraft or SPACECRAFT 飞行器；飞机；航天器；宇宙飞船；航天飞机

■**verb** [usually passive] **~ sth** to make sth using special skills, especially with your hands（尤指用手工）精心制作 SYN **fashion**：*All the furniture is crafted from natural materials.* 所有的家具均采用天然材料精心制作而成。◇ *a carefully crafted speech* 精心准备的讲话 ➲ SEE ALSO HAND-CRAFTED

ˈcraft knife *noun* (*BrE*) a very sharp knife used for cutting paper or thin pieces of wood 裁纸刀；削木刀

crafts·man /ˈkrɑːftsmən; *NAmE* ˈkræf-/ (*also* **crafts·person**) *noun* (*pl.* **-men** /-mən/) a skilled person, especially one who makes beautiful things by hand 工匠；手艺人；工艺师：*rugs handmade by local craftsmen* 由当地工艺师手工制作的小地毯 ◇ *It is clearly the work of a master craftsman.* 很明显这是工艺大师的作品。➲ SEE ALSO CRAFTSWOMAN

crafts·man·ship /ˈkrɑːftsmənʃɪp; *NAmE* ˈkræf-/ *noun* [U] **1** the level of skill shown by sb in making sth beautiful with their hands 手艺；技艺：*The whole house is a monument to her craftsmanship.* 那整座房子是她技艺的一座丰碑。**2** the quality of design and work shown by sth that has been made by hand 精工细作：*the superb craftsmanship of the carvings* 这些雕刻品的一流工艺

crafts·person /ˈkrɑːftspɜːsn; *NAmE* ˈkræftspɜːrsn/ *noun* (*pl.* **-people** /-piːpl/) = CRAFTSMAN

crafts·woman /ˈkrɑːftswʊmən; *NAmE* ˈkræf-/ *noun* (*pl.* **-women** /-wɪmɪn/) a skilled woman, especially one who makes beautiful things by hand 女工匠；女手艺人；女巧匠；女工艺师 ➲ NOTE AT GENDER

craft·work /ˈkrɑːftwɜːk; *NAmE* ˈkræftwɜːrk/ *noun* [U] work done by a CRAFTSMAN 工艺品

crafty /ˈkrɑːfti; *NAmE* ˈkræfti/ *adj.* (**craft·ier**, **crafti·est**) (*usually disapproving*) clever at getting what you want, especially by indirect or dishonest methods 巧妙的；（尤指）狡诈的，诡计多端的 SYN **cunning, wily**：*He's a crafty old devil.* 他是个奸诈狡猾的老家伙。◇ *one of the party's craftiest political strategists* 这个政党最精明的政治战略家之一 ▶ **craft·ily** *adv.* **crafti·ness** *noun* [U]

crag /kræg/ *noun* a high steep rough mass of rock 悬崖；峭壁；绝壁：*a castle set on a crag above the village* 位于村子上方悬崖上的城堡

craggy /ˈkrægi/ *adj.* **1** having many crags 多峭壁的；峻峭的：*a craggy coastline* 陡峭的海岸 **2** (*usually approving*) (of a man's face 男人的脸) having strong features and deep lines 轮廓分明有皱纹的

craic *noun* = CRACK (8)

cram /kræm/ *verb* (**-mm-**) **1** [T, I] to push or force sb/sth into a small space; to move into a small space with the result that it is full 把…塞进；挤满；塞满：**~ sb/sth into/onto sth** *He crammed eight people into his car.* 他往他的车里硬塞进八个人。◇ **~ sth in** *I could never cram in all that she does in a day.* 我可做不了她在一天之内所做的事情。◇ **~ sth + adv./prep.** *I managed to cram down a few mouthfuls of food.* 我好歹狼吞虎咽地吃了几口东西。◇ **~ sth** *Supporters crammed the streets.* 街上挤满了支持者。◇ **~ sth full** *I bought a large basket and crammed it full of presents.* 我买了个大篮子，然后把它装满礼物。◇ **~ into/onto sth** *We all managed to cram into his car.* 我们大家好歹都挤进了他的车。**2** [I] **~ (for sth)** (*NAmE, informal* or *rather old-fashioned, BrE*) to learn a lot of things in a short time, in preparation for an exam（为应考）临时死记硬背 SYN **swot**：*He's been cramming for his exams all week.* 他整个星期都一直在拼命准备应考。

crammed /kræmd/ *adj.* **1 ~ (with sb/sth)** full of things or people 塞满的；挤满的 SYN **packed**：*All the shelves were crammed with books.* 所有的架子上都堆满了书。◇ *The room was **crammed full** of people.* 房间里挤满了人。◇ *The article was **crammed full** of ideas.* 这篇文章包含着许多想

法。 **2** [not before noun] if people are **crammed** into a place, there is not much room for them in it 拥挤不堪 SYN **packed**: *We were crammed four to an office.* 我们四个人挤在一间办公室里。

cram·mer /ˈkræmə(r)/ *noun* (*BrE*) a school or book that prepares people quickly for exams（应付考试的）强化训练补习学校；（为应付考试而编写的）强化训练用书

cramp /kræmp/ *noun, verb*

■ ***noun*** **1** [U, C] (*NAmE also* ˈ**charley horse**) a sudden pain that you get when the muscles in a particular part of your body contract, usually caused by cold or too much exercise 痛性痉挛；抽筋：(*BrE*) *to get cramp in your leg* 腿部抽筋 ◇ (*NAmE*) *to get a cramp in your leg* 腿部抽筋 ➲ SEE ALSO WRITER'S CRAMP **2** **cramps** [pl.] severe pain in the stomach（腹部）绞痛

■ ***verb*** **~ sth** to prevent the development or progress of sb/sth 阻碍，阻止（发展或进步）SYN **restrict**: *Tighter trade restrictions might cramp economic growth.* 较严格的贸易限制会妨碍经济的增长。

IDM **cramp sb's ˈstyle** (*informal*) to stop sb from behaving in the way they want to 束缚…的手脚；使不能放开手脚（或施展才能）

cramped /kræmpt/ *adj.* **1** a **cramped** room, etc. does not have enough space for the people in it 狭窄的；狭小的：*working in cramped conditions* 在拥挤的环境里工作 **2** (of people 人) not having room to move freely 拥挤的；缺少自由活动空间的 **3** (of sb's writing 字迹) with small letters close together and therefore difficult to read 密小难认的；密密麻麻的

cram·pon /ˈkræmpɒn; *NAmE* -pɑːn/ *noun* [usually pl.] a metal plate with pointed pieces of metal underneath, worn on sb's shoes when they are walking or climbing on ice and snow 带钉铁鞋底（用以在冰雪上行走或攀登）

cran·berry /ˈkrænbəri; *NAmE* -beri/ *noun* (*pl.* **-ies**) a small sour red BERRY that grows on a small bush and is used in cooking 越橘，小红莓（用于烹饪）：*cranberry sauce* 越橘调味汁

crane /kreɪn/ *noun, verb*

■ ***noun*** **1** a tall machine with a long arm, used to lift and move building materials and other heavy objects 起重机；吊车 ➲ VISUAL VOCAB PAGE V3 **2** a large bird with long legs and a long neck 鹤 ➲ SEE ALSO BLUE CRANE

■ ***verb*** [I, T] to lean or stretch over sth in order to see sth better; to stretch your neck（为看得更清楚而）探着身子；伸长（脖子）：**(+ adv./prep.)** *People were craning out of the windows and waving.* 人们把头探出窗外挥手致意。◇ **~ sth** *She **craned her neck** to get a better view of the stage.* 她伸长了脖子看舞台，好看清楚些。

ˈcrane fly (*also informal* ˌ**daddy-ˈlong-legs**) *noun* a flying insect with very long legs 大蚊（腿长）

cra·nium /ˈkreɪniəm/ *noun* (*pl.* **cra·ni·ums** or **cra·nia** /ˈkreɪniə/) (*anatomy* 解) the bone structure that forms the head and surrounds and protects the brain 颅；颅骨；头盖骨 SYN **skull** ➲ VISUAL VOCAB PAGE V64 ▶ **cra·nial** /ˈkreɪniəl/ *adj.* [only before noun]: *cranial nerves/injuries* 颅神经 / 外伤

crank /kræŋk/ *noun, verb*

■ ***noun*** **1** (*disapproving*) a person with ideas that other people find strange（想法）古怪的人 SYN **eccentric**: *Vegetarians are no longer dismissed as cranks.* 素食者不再被视为有怪癖的人。**2** (*NAmE*) a person who easily gets angry or annoyed 脾气坏的人；容易恼怒的人 **3** a bar and handle in the shape of an L that you pull or turn to produce movement in a machine, etc.（L 字形）曲柄，曲轴 ➲ VISUAL VOCAB PAGE V55

■ ***verb*** **~ sth (up)** to make sth turn or move by using a crank 用曲柄转动（或启动）：*to crank an engine* 用曲柄发动引擎 ◇ (*figurative*) *He has a limited time to crank the reforms into action.* 他启动各项改革的时间很有限。

PHR V ˌ**crank sth↔ˈout** (*informal*) to produce a lot of sth quickly, especially things of low quality 快速地大量制造；（尤指）粗制滥造 SYN **turn out** ˌ**crank sth↔ˈup** (*informal*) **1** to make a machine, etc. work or work at a higher level 使机器运转；使…提高效率 **2** to make music, etc. louder（把音乐等的音量）开大，调高 SYN **turn sth↔up**: *Crank up the volume!* 把音量放大些！

crank·shaft /ˈkræŋkʃɑːft; *NAmE* -ʃæft/ *noun* (*specialist*) a long piece of metal in a vehicle that connects the engine to the wheels and helps turn the engine's power into movement 曲轴；曲柄轴

cranky /ˈkræŋki/ *adj.* (*informal*) **1** (*BrE*) strange 古怪的；怪异的 SYN **eccentric**: ***cranky ideas/schemes*** 离奇古怪的想法 / 计划 **2** (*especially NAmE*) bad-tempered 脾气坏的：*The kids were getting tired and a little cranky.* 孩子们越来越累，脾气也有些变坏了。

cranny /ˈkræni/ *noun* (*pl.* **-ies**) a very small hole or opening, especially in a wall（尤指墙上的）小孔，缝隙，裂缝 IDM SEE NOOK

crap /kræp/ *noun, adj., verb*

■ ***noun*** (*taboo, slang*) **1** [U] nonsense 废话；胡说；胡扯：*He's so full of crap.* 他净胡说八道。◇ *Let's **cut the crap** and get down to business.* 咱们别说废话了，开始干正事吧。◇ (*BrE*) *You're talking a **load of crap**!* 你这是一派胡言！◇ (*NAmE*) *What a **bunch of crap**!* 真是废话连篇！**2** [U] something of bad quality 质量差的东西；蹩脚货：*This work is complete crap.* 这件作品蹩脚透顶。◇ (*BrE*) *Her latest film is a **load of crap**.* 她最近的一部电影很糟糕。◇ (*NAmE*) *Her latest movie is a **bunch of crap**.* 她最近的一部电影很糟糕。HELP More acceptable words are **rubbish**, **garbage**, **trash** or **junk**. 更常用的词有 rubbish、garbage、trash 或 junk。**3** [U] criticism or unfair treatment 批评；非难；不公正的待遇：*I'm not going to take this crap any more.* 我再也不受这种委屈了。**4** [U] solid waste matter from the BOWELS 屎 SYN **excrement** **5** [sing.] an act of emptying solid waste matter from the BOWELS 拉屎：*to have a crap* 拉屎 IDM SEE BUG *v.*

■ ***adj.*** (*BrE, taboo, slang*) bad; of very bad quality 坏的；糟糕的；劣质的：*a crap band* 很差劲的乐队 ◇ *The concert was crap.* 那场音乐会演得很差。▶ **crap** *adv.*: *The team played crap yesterday.* 这个队昨天的表现很差劲。

■ ***verb*** **(-pp-)** [I] (*taboo, slang*) to empty solid waste from the BOWELS 拉屎 SYN **defecate** HELP A more polite way of expressing this is 'to go to the toilet/lavatory' (*BrE*), 'to go to the bathroom' (*NAmE*), or 'to go'. A more formal expression is 'to empty the bowels'. 比较有礼貌的表达方式为 to go to the toilet / lavatory（英式英语）、to go to the bathroom（美式英语）或 to go。比较正式的表达方式为 to empty the bowels。

crappy /ˈkræpi/ *adj.* (**crap·pier**, **crap·pi·est**) [usually before noun] (*slang*) of very bad quality 劣质的；蹩脚的：*a crappy novel* 粗制滥造的小说

craps /kræps/ *noun* [U] (*NAmE*) a gambling game played with two DICE 双骰子赌博戏：*to shoot craps* (= play this game) 掷双骰子赌博 ▶ **crap** *adj.* [only before noun]: *a crap game* 掷双骰子的赌博

crap·shoot /ˈkræpʃuːt/ *noun* (*NAmE*) **1** a game of CRAPS 双骰子赌博戏 **2** (*informal*) a situation whose success or result is based on luck rather than on effort or careful organization 碰运气的事

crash 🔑 /kræʃ/ *noun, verb, adj.*

■ ***noun***

• **VEHICLE ACCIDENT** 交通事故 **1** 🔑 (*NAmE also* **wreck**) an accident in which a vehicle hits sth, for example another vehicle, usually causing damage and often injuring or killing the passengers 撞车；碰撞；相撞：*A girl was killed yesterday in a crash involving a stolen car.* 昨天有个女孩在一桩涉及被盗汽车的撞车事故中丧生。◇ *a car/plane crash* 汽车撞车事故；飞机失事 ➲ COLLOCATIONS AT DRIVING

• **LOUD NOISE** 巨响 **2** 🔑 [usually sing.] a sudden loud noise made, for example, by sth falling or breaking（倒下、破碎等突然的）碰撞声，破裂声，碎裂声：*The tree fell with a great crash.* 那棵树哗啦一声倒了。◇ *The first distant crash of thunder shook the air.* 远处的第一声霹雳震撼了天空。

• **IN FINANCE/BUSINESS** 金融；商业 **3** 🔑 a sudden serious fall in the price or value of sth; the occasion when a business,

etc. fails 暴跌；倒闭；破产；失败 SYN **collapse**: *the 1987 stock market crash* * 1987 年的股票市场暴跌
• COMPUTING 计算机技术 **4** a sudden failure of a machine or system, especially of a computer or computer system（机器或系统，尤指计算机或计算机系统的）崩溃
■ *verb*
• **OF VEHICLE** 交通工具 **1** [I, T] if a vehicle **crashes** or the driver **crashes** it, it hits an object or another vehicle, causing damage 碰撞；撞击：*I was terrified that the plane would crash.* 飞机可能会失事，我吓坏了。◇ *We're going to crash, aren't we?* 我们要坠毁了，是不是？◇ **~ into sth** *A truck went out of control and crashed into the back of a bus.* 货车失控撞上了一辆公共汽车的尾部。◇ **~ sth (into sth)** *He crashed his car into a wall.* 他的汽车撞到了墙上。
• **HIT HARD/LOUD NOISE** 猛撞；巨响 **2** [I, T] to hit sth hard while moving, causing noise and/or damage; to make sth hit sb/sth in this way（使）猛撞，碰撞：**+ adv./prep.** *A brick crashed through the window.* 砖块哗啦一声砸入了窗户。◇ *With a sweep of his hand he sent the glasses crashing to the floor.* 他一挥手把眼镜摔到地上摔碎了。◇ **+ adj.** *The door crashed open.* 那门砰的一声给砸开了。◇ **~ sth + adj.** *She stormed out of the room and crashed the door shut behind her.* 她愤怒地冲出房间并随手把门砰的一声关上。**3** [I] to make a loud noise 使发出巨响：*Thunder crashed overhead.* 头顶上雷声隆隆。
• **IN FINANCE/BUSINESS** 金融；商业 **4** [I] (of prices, a business, shares, etc. 价格、公司、股票等) to lose value or fail suddenly and quickly（突然）贬值，倒闭，失败；暴跌：*Share prices crashed to an all-time low yesterday.* 昨天股票价格暴跌到了历史最低。◇ *The company crashed with debts of £50 million.* 那家公司由于负债 5 000 万英镑而告破产。
• **COMPUTING** 计算机技术 **5** [I, T] **~ (sth)** if a computer **crashes** or you **crash** a computer, it stops working suddenly 崩溃：*Files can be lost if the system suddenly crashes.* 要是计算机系统突然崩溃，文件就可能丢失。
• **PARTY** 聚会 **6** [T] **~ sth** (*informal*) = GATECRASH
• **IN SPORT** 体育运动 **7** [I] **(+ adv./prep)** (*especially BrE*) to lose very badly in a sports game（比赛中）溃败，惨败：*The team crashed to their worst defeat this season.* 那支队遭受了本赛季最严重的一次惨败。
• **SLEEP** 睡觉 **8** [I] **~ (out)** (*informal*) to fall asleep; to sleep somewhere you do not usually sleep 入睡；（在不常睡觉的地方）睡觉：*I was so tired I crashed out on the sofa.* 我累极了，在沙发上就睡着了。◇ *I've come to crash on your floor for a couple of nights.* 我来你家打几个晚上的地铺。
• **MEDICAL** 医学 **9** [I] if sb **crashes**, their heart stops beating 心脏停止跳动

IDM **a crashing 'bore** (*old-fashioned, BrE*) a very boring person 讨厌透顶的人

PHR V **,crash 'out (of sth)** (*BrE, sport* 体育) to lose a game with the result that you have to stop playing in a competition 被淘汰：*They crashed out of the World Cup after a 2–1 defeat to Brazil.* 他们以 1:2 输给巴西队之后在世界杯赛中被淘汰出局。

■ *adj.* [only before noun] involving hard work or a lot of effort over a short period of time in order to achieve quick results 应急的；速成的：*a crash course in computer programming* 计算机编程速成课程 ◇ *a crash diet* 快速减肥规定饮食

> ▼ **SYNONYMS 同义词辨析**
>
> **crash**
>
> **slam • collide • smash • wreck**
>
> These are all words that can be used when sth, especially a vehicle, hits sth else very hard and is damaged or destroyed. 以上各词均含碰撞、撞击之义，尤指撞车。
>
> **crash** (*rather informal*) to hit an object or another vehicle, causing damage; to make a vehicle do this 指（使）物体或交通工具碰撞或撞击：*I was terrified that the plane would crash.* 我很害怕飞机会失事。
>
> **slam (sth) into/against sb/sth** to crash into sth with a lot of force; to make sth do this 指（使）重重地撞上：*The car skidded and slammed into a tree.* 汽车打滑，砰的一声撞到树上。
>
> **collide** (*rather formal*) (of two vehicles or people) to crash into each other; (of a vehicle or person) to crash into sb/sth else 指交通工具或人碰撞、相撞或撞上：*The car and the van collided head-on in thick fog.* 那辆小轿车和货车在浓雾中迎面相撞。
>
> **smash** (*rather informal*) to crash into sth with a lot of force; to make sth do this; to crash a car 指（使）猛烈撞击、猛烈碰撞或撞车：*Ram-raiders smashed a stolen car through the shop window.* 飙车抢劫者驾着偷来的汽车撞破商店橱窗。
>
> **CRASH, SLAM OR SMASH?** 用 crash、slam 还是 smash?
>
> **Crash** is used especially to talk about vehicles and can be used without a preposition. * crash 尤指交通工具碰撞，可不与介词连用：*We're going to crash, aren't we?* 我们要坠毁了，是不是？ In this meaning **slam** and **smash** always take a preposition. * slam 和 smash 表示此义时总是与介词连用：~~*We're going to slam/smash, aren't we?*~~ They are used for a much wider range of things than just vehicles. **Crash** can also be used for other things, if used with a preposition. 两词均可用于除交通工具外的范围更广的事物。crash 与介词连用也可用于其他事物：*He crashed down the telephone receiver.* 他砰的一声将电话听筒摔下来。
>
> **wreck** to crash a vehicle and damage it so badly that it is not worth repairing 指使交通工具彻底毁坏
>
> **PATTERNS**
> • **two vehicles** crash/collide
> • **two vehicles** crash/slam/smash **into each other**
> • to crash/smash/wreck **a car**

'crash barrier (*BrE*) (*NAmE* **'guard rail**) *noun* a strong low fence or wall at the side of a road or between the two halves of a major road such as a MOTORWAY or INTERSTATE（高速公路或州际公路上的）防撞护栏，防撞墙

'crash helmet *noun* a hat made of very strong material and worn when riding a motorcycle to protect the head（骑摩托车的）防护头盔，安全帽 ➲ VISUAL VOCAB PAGE V70

'crash-land *verb* [I, T] **~ (sth)** if a plane **crash-lands** or a pilot **crash-lands** it, the pilot lands it roughly in an emergency, usually because it is damaged and cannot land normally 迫降；强行着陆 ▶ **,crash 'landing** *noun*：*to make a crash landing* 实施迫降

'crash team *noun* (*BrE*) a team of people in a hospital who are ready to make patients start breathing or become conscious again after they have almost died（医院里救治濒死病人的）急救小组，抢救小组

'crash-test *verb* **~ sth** to deliberately crash a new vehicle under controlled conditions in order to test how it reacts or to improve its safety 撞击试验（检验新车反应或改进安全性能） ▶ **'crash test** *noun*

,crash-test 'dummy *noun* a model of a person used in crash tests to see what would happen to a driver or passenger in a real crash 撞击试验假人（当作驾驶者或乘客）

crass /kræs/ *adj.* very stupid and showing no sympathy or understanding 愚蠢而无同情心的 SYN **insensitive**: *the crass questions all disabled people get asked* 所有残疾人都会碰到的愚蠢而缺乏同情心的提问 ◇ *an act of crass* (= great) *stupidity* 愚不可及的行为 ▶ **crass·ly** *adv.* **crass·ness** *noun* [U]

-crat *combining form* (in nouns 构成名词) a member or supporter of a particular type of government or system（某政体或体制的）成员，支持者：*democrat* 民主主义者 ◇ *bureaucrat* 官僚主义者 ▶ **-cratic** (in adjectives 构成形容词)：*aristocratic* 贵族的

crate /kreɪt/ *noun, verb*
■ *noun* **1** a large wooden container for transporting goods

大木箱，板条箱（运货用）：*a crate of bananas* 一箱香蕉 **2** a container made of plastic or metal divided into small sections, for transporting or storing bottles 塑料分格箱，金属分格箱（运送或存放瓶子用）：*a beer crate* 啤酒箱 **3** the amount of sth contained in a crate 一箱（的量）：*They drank two crates of beer.* 他们喝了两箱啤酒。

■ ***verb*** **~ sth (up)** to pack sth in a crate 把…装入大木箱（或板条箱、分格箱）

cra·ter /ˈkreɪtə(r)/ *noun* **1** a large hole in the top of a VOLCANO 火山口 **2** a large hole in the ground caused by the explosion of a bomb or by sth large hitting it（由炸弹爆炸或巨物撞击形成的）坑：*a meteorite crater* 陨石坑

cra·vat /krəˈvæt/ (*NAmE also* **ascot**) *noun* a short wide strip of silk, etc. worn by men around the neck, folded inside the COLLAR of a shirt（男用）阔领带

crave /kreɪv/ *verb* **1** [T, I] **~ (for) sth | ~ to do sth** to have a very strong desire for sth 渴望；热望 **SYN long for**：*She has always craved excitement.* 她总盼望得到刺激。 **2** [T] **~ sth** (*BrE, old use*) to ask for sth seriously 恳求；请求：*I must crave your pardon.* 我必须恳求您原谅。

cra·ven /ˈkreɪvn/ *adj.* (*formal, disapproving*) lacking courage 胆小的；胆怯的；怯懦的 **SYN cowardly OPP brave** ▶ **craven·ly** *adv.*

crav·ing /ˈkreɪvɪŋ/ *noun* a strong desire for sth 强烈的愿望；渴望；热望：**~ (for sth)** *a craving for chocolate* 非常想吃巧克力 ◇ **~ (to do sth)** *a desperate craving to be loved* 对被爱的极度渴望

craw /krɔː/ *noun* the part of a bird's throat where food is kept（禽的）嗉囊，嗉子 **IDM** ➔ SEE STICK *v.*

craw·fish /ˈkrɔːfɪʃ/ *noun* (*especially NAmE*) = CRAYFISH

crawl /krɔːl/ *verb, noun*

■ ***verb*** **1** [I] **(+ adv./prep.)** to move forward on your hands and knees, with your body close to the ground 爬；爬行；匍匐行进：*Our baby is just starting to crawl.* 我们的宝宝刚开始会爬。◇ *A man was crawling away from the burning wreckage.* 一个男人正爬离燃烧着的残骸。 **2** [I] **(+ adv./prep.)** when an insect **crawls**, it moves forward on its legs（昆虫）爬行：*There's a spider crawling up your leg.* 有只蜘蛛正顺着你的腿往上爬。 **3** [I] **(+ adv./ prep.)** to move forward very slowly 缓慢行进：*The traffic was crawling along.* 来往车辆缓缓而行。◇ *The weeks crawled by.* 几个星期慢慢地过去了。 **4** [I] **~ (to sb)** (*informal, disapproving*) to be too friendly or helpful to sb in authority, in a way that is not sincere, especially in order to get an advantage from them 卑躬屈膝；谄媚；巴结；拍马屁：*She's always crawling to the boss.* 她对老板总是谄媚奉承。

IDM ➔ SEE SKIN *n.*, WOODWORK

PHR V **be ˈcrawling with sth** (*informal*) to be full of or completely covered with people, insects or animals, in a way that is unpleasant 挤满；爬满：*The place was crawling with journalists.* 这地方挤满了记者。◇ *Her hair was crawling with lice.* 她的头发上爬满了虱子。

■ ***noun*** **1** [sing.] a very slow speed 缓慢的速度：*The traffic slowed to a crawl.* 来往的车辆放缓速度慢慢前行。➔ SEE ALSO PUB CRAWL **2** (*often* **the crawl**) [sing., U] a fast swimming stroke that you do lying on your front moving one arm over your head, and then the other, while kicking with your feet 爬泳；自由泳：*a swimmer doing the crawl* 游自由泳的运动员 ➔ VISUAL VOCAB PAGE V48

crawl·er /ˈkrɔːlə(r)/ *noun* (*informal*) **1** (*BrE, disapproving*) a person who tries to get sb's favour by praising them, doing what will please them, etc. 奴颜婢膝的人；马屁精 **2** a thing or person that crawls, such as a vehicle, an insect or a baby 爬行物（如车辆、昆虫等）；爬行的人（如婴儿等）➔ SEE ALSO KERB-CRAWLER at KERB-CRAWLING

cray·fish /ˈkreɪfɪʃ/ (*especially BrE*) (*also* **craw·fish** *NAmE, BrE*) *noun* [C, U] (*pl.* **cray·fish, craw·fish**) an animal like a small LOBSTER, that lives in rivers and lakes and can be eaten, or one like a large lobster, that lives in the sea and can be eaten 淡水螯虾；刺龙虾

crayon /ˈkreɪən/ *noun* a coloured pencil or stick of soft coloured CHALK or WAX, used for drawing 彩色铅笔（或粉笔、蜡笔） ▶ **crayon** *verb* [I, T] **~ (sth)**

craze /kreɪz/ *noun* **~ (for sth)** an enthusiastic interest in sth that is shared by many people but that usually does not last very long; a thing that people have a craze for（通常为一时的）狂热，疯狂；风行一时的东西 **SYN fad**：*the latest fitness craze to sweep the country* 最近风靡全国的健身热

crazed /kreɪzd/ *adj.* **~ (with sth)** (*formal*) full of strong feelings and lacking control 疯狂的；发狂的：***crazed with fear/grief/jealousy*** 害怕 / 伤心 / 嫉妒得发疯 ◇ *a crazed killer roaming the streets* 在街上游荡的丧心病狂的杀手

crazy 🔑 /ˈkreɪzi/ *adj., noun*

■ ***adj.*** (**cra·zier, crazi·est**) (*informal*) **1** 🔑 not sensible; stupid 不理智的；疯狂的；愚蠢的；傻的：*Are you crazy? We could get killed doing that.* 你疯了？我们那样做会丧命的。◇ *She must be crazy to lend him money.* 她把钱借给他，一定是疯了。◇ *He drove like an idiot, passing in the craziest places.* 他像白痴一样净把车往最不可思议的地方开。◇ *What a crazy idea!* 这个想法真荒唐！◇ *I know it sounds crazy but it just might work.* 我知道这听起来很疯狂，但也许行得通。 **2** 🔑 very angry 非常气愤：*That noise* ***is driving me crazy.*** 那噪声吵得我快发疯了。◇ *Marie says* ***he went crazy,*** *and smashed the room up.* 玛丽说他气得发疯，把房间里的东西都砸碎了。 **3** 🔑 **~ (about sth)** (often in compounds 常构成复合词) very enthusiastic or excited about sth 热衷的；狂热的：*Rick is crazy about football.* 里克对足球着了迷。◇ *He's football-crazy.* 他是个足球迷。◇ *I'm not crazy about Chinese food* (= I don't like it very much). 我并不十分热衷于中餐。◇ *The crowd* ***went crazy*** *when the band came on stage.* 乐队出场时，观众欣喜若狂。◇ *You're so beautiful you're* ***driving me crazy.*** 你真美，弄得我神魂颠倒了。 **4** 🔑 **~ about sb** liking sb very much; in love with sb 迷恋的；爱上的：*I've been crazy about him since the first time I saw him.* 我从第一次见到他就爱上他了。 **5** 🔑 mentally ill; INSANE 患精神病的；精神失常（或错乱）的：*She's crazy—she ought to be locked up.* 她疯了，应该把她关起来。➔ SYNONYMS AT MAD ▶ **crazi·ly** *adv.* **cra·zi·ness** *noun* [U]

IDM **like ˈcrazy/ˈmad** (*informal*) very fast, hard, much, etc. 非常快地；拼命地；疯狂地：*We worked like crazy to get it done on time.* 我们拼命地干，好按时完成这项工作。

■ ***noun*** (*pl.* **-ies**) (*informal, especially NAmE*) a crazy person 疯子

ˈcrazy golf *noun* [U] (*BrE*) = MINIGOLF

ˌcrazy ˈpaving *noun* [U] (*BrE*) pieces of stone of different shapes and sizes, fitted together on the ground to make a path or PATIO（用不规则形状的石块拼成的）错铺地面

ˌcrazy ˈquilt *noun* (*NAmE*) a type of QUILT in which small pieces of cloth of different shape, colour, design and size are sewn together 百衲被 ➔ COMPARE PATCHWORK (1)

creak /kriːk/ *verb, noun*

■ ***verb*** [I] to make the sound that a door sometimes makes when you open it or that a wooden floor sometimes makes when you step on it 嘎吱作响（开门或踩上木地板等时发出的声音）：*She heard a floorboard creak upstairs.* 她听见楼上的地板发出嘎吱嘎吱的响声。◇ *a creaking* ***bed/gate/stair*** 嘎吱作响的床 / 大门 / 楼梯 ◇ *The table creaked and groaned under the weight.* 那张桌子在重压下嘎吱嘎吱作响。◇ **+ adj.** *The door creaked open.* 门嘎吱一声开了。

IDM **ˌcreak under the ˈstrain** if a system or service **creaks under the strain**, it cannot deal effectively with all the things it is expected to do or provide 因负担过重而效率低下；由于压力过大而运转不灵

■ ***noun*** [C] (*also* **creak·ing** [U, C]) a sound, for example that sometimes made by a door when it opens or shuts, or by a wooden floor when you step on it 嘎吱声：*the creak/creaking of the door* 门的嘎吱声 ◇ *Distant creaks and groans echoed eerily along the dark corridors.* 远处嘎吱嘎吱的声音回响在漆黑的走廊里，怪可怕的。

C

creaky /ˈkriːki/ *adj.* **1** making creaks 嘎吱作响的：*a creaky old chair* 嘎吱作响的旧椅子 **2** old and not in good condition 老朽的；破旧的；摇摇欲坠的：*the country's creaky legal machinery* 这个国家摇摇欲坠的司法机构

cream /kriːm/ *noun, adj., verb*

■ *noun* **1** [U] the thick pale yellowish-white FATTY liquid that rises to the top of milk, used in cooking or as a type of sauce to put on fruit, etc. 奶油；乳脂：*strawberries and cream* 加奶油的草莓 ◇ *Would you like milk or cream in your coffee?* 你的咖啡里要牛奶还是奶油？◇ ***fresh/whipped cream*** 新鲜的 / 搅打过的奶油 ◇ (*BrE*) *cream cakes* (= containing cream) 奶油蛋糕 ◇ (*BrE*) ***double/single cream*** (= thick/thin cream) 浓奶油；稀奶油 ➲ SEE ALSO CLOTTED CREAM, ICE CREAM, SALAD CREAM, SOUR CREAM, WHIPPING CREAM **2** [C] (in compounds 构成复合词) a sweet/candy that has a soft substance like cream inside 奶油夹心糖：*a **chocolate/peppermint cream*** 巧克力 / 薄荷奶油夹心糖 **3** [U, C] a soft substance or thick liquid used on your skin to protect it or make it feel soft; a similar substance used for cleaning things 护肤霜；洁净剂；清洗液：*hand/moisturizing cream* 护手霜；润肤霜 ◇ *antiseptic cream* 抗菌药膏 ◇ *a cream cleaner* 乳液清洁剂 ➲ SEE ALSO COLD CREAM, FACE CREAM, SHAVING CREAM **4** [U] a pale yellowish-white colour 奶油色；淡黄色；米色 **5 the ~ of sth** the best people or things in a particular group 精英；精华；精髓：*the cream of New York society* 纽约社会的精英 ◇ ***the cream of the crop*** *of this season's movies* 本季电影的最佳影片 IDM SEE CAT

■ *adj.* pale yellowish-white in colour 奶油色的；淡黄色的；米色的：*a cream linen suit* 米色的亚麻布套装

■ *verb* **1 ~ sth (together)** to mix things together into a soft smooth mixture 把…搅成糊状（或奶油状）混合物：*Cream the butter and sugar together.* 把黄油和糖搅成糊状。**2 ~ sb** (*NAmE, informal*) to completely defeat sb 彻底打败；狠揍：*We got creamed in the first round.* 我们在第一轮就被彻底打败了。

PHR V **ˌcream sb/sth↔ˈoff** to take sth away, usually the best people or things or an amount of money, in order to get an advantage for yourself 提取（精华）；选取（最好的人或物）；取走（某数额的金钱）：*The best students were creamed off by the grammar schools.* 最好的学生都已被文法学校录取。

ˌcream ˈcheese *noun* [U, C] soft white cheese containing a lot of cream 奶油干酪

ˌcream ˈcracker *noun* (*BrE*) a dry biscuit, often eaten with cheese 奶油饼干（常与奶酪一起食用）

cream·er /ˈkriːmə(r)/ *noun* **1** [U] a liquid or powder that you can put in coffee, etc. instead of cream or milk（替代奶油或牛奶的可放入咖啡等中的）拌末，植脂末，咖啡伴侣：*non-dairy creamer* 不含奶的植脂末 **2** [C] (*NAmE*) a small container for holding and pouring cream 小奶油壶；小奶油罐；小奶油瓶

cream·ery /ˈkriːməri/ *noun* (*pl.* **-ies**) a place where milk and cream are made into butter and cheese 乳品厂

ˌcream ˈpuff *noun* (*NAmE*) **1** = PROFITEROLE **2** (*slang, disapproving*) a person who is not strong or brave 弱者；懦夫 SYN **wimp**

ˌcream ˈsoda *noun* [U, C] (*especially NAmE*) a FIZZY drink (= one with bubbles) that tastes of VANILLA 奶油苏打水

ˌcream ˈtea *noun* (*BrE*) a special meal eaten in the afternoon, consisting of tea with SCONES, jam and thick cream（下午进食的）奶油茶点

creamy /ˈkriːmi/ *adj.* (**cream·ier, creami·est**) **1** thick and smooth like cream; containing a lot of cream 像奶油的；光滑细腻的；含乳脂的：*a **creamy sauce/soup*** 奶油调味汁 / 汤羹 ➲ WORDFINDER NOTE AT CRISP **2** pale yellowish-white in colour 奶油色的；淡黄色的；米色的：*creamy skin* 淡黄色的皮肤

crease /kriːs/ *noun, verb*

■ *noun* **1** an untidy line that is made in cloth or paper when it is pressed or crushed 褶痕；皱痕：*She smoothed the creases out of her skirt.* 她把裙子上的皱褶弄平。◇ *a shirt made of crease-resistant material* 用防皱布料制作的衬衫 **2** a neat line that you make in sth, for example when you fold it 褶缝；褶线：*trousers with a sharp crease in the legs* 裤线笔挺的裤子 ➲ VISUAL VOCAB PAGE V66 **3** a line in the skin, especially on the face（皮肤上，尤指脸上的）皱纹：*creases around the eyes* 眼睛周围的皱纹 **4** (in CRICKET 板球) a white line on the ground near each WICKET that marks the position of the BOWLER and the BATSMAN（投手和击球员的）位置线，区域线；投球线；击球线

■ *verb* **1** [T, I] **~ (sth)** to make lines on cloth or paper by folding or crushing it; to develop lines in this way 弄皱；压褶；（使）起褶子：*Pack your suit carefully so that you don't crease it.* 把你的西装小心装好以免弄皱。**2** [T, I] **~ (sth)** to make lines in the skin; to develop lines in the skin（皮肤）皱起；（使）起皱纹：*A frown creased her forehead.* 她一皱眉，额头显出了皱纹。◇ *Her face creased into a smile.* 她的脸上露出了微笑。▶ **creased** *adj.*：*I can't wear this blouse. It's creased.* 我不能穿这件衬衫，它皱了。

PHR V **ˌcrease ˈup | ˌcrease sb ˈup** (*BrE, informal*) to start laughing or make sb start laughing（使）大笑起来 SYN **crack up, crack sb up**：*Ed creased up laughing.* 埃德哈哈大笑起来。◇ *Her jokes really creased me up.* 她的笑话真让我笑死了。

cre·ate AW /kriˈeɪt/ *verb* **1 ~ sth** to make sth happen or exist 创造；创作；创建：*Scientists disagree about how the universe was created.* 科学家对宇宙是怎样形成的有分歧。◇ *The main purpose of industry is to create wealth.* 工业的主要宗旨是创造财富。◇ *The government plans to create more jobs for young people.* 政府计划为年轻人创造更多的就业机会。◇ *Create a new directory and put all your files into it.* 创建一个新的目录，然后把你所有的文件都放进去。◇ *Try this new dish, created by our head chef.* 品尝一下这道新菜吧，是我们厨师长首创的。➲ SYNONYMS AT MAKE **2 ~ sth** to produce a particular feeling or impression 造成，引起，产生（感觉或印象）：*The company is trying to create a young energetic image.* 这家公司正试图塑造一个充满活力的年轻形象。◇ *The announcement only succeeded in creating confusion.* 那通告反而引起了混乱。◇ *They've painted it red to create a feeling of warmth.* 他们把它刷成红色以营造一种温暖的感觉。 **3** to give sb a particular rank or title 授予；册封：**~ sth** *The government has created eight new peers.* 政府新封了八个贵族。◇ **~ sth + noun** *He was created a baronet in 1715.* 他于 1715 年被封为准男爵。

cre·ation AW /kriˈeɪʃn/ *noun* **1** [U] the act or process of making sth that is new, or of causing sth to exist that did not exist before 创造；创建：*the process of database creation* 数据库的创建过程 ◇ *wealth creation* 财富的创造 ◇ *He had been with the company since its creation in 1989.* 他从 1989 年公司成立以来就一直在那里工作。 ➲ SEE ALSO JOB CREATION **2** [C] (*often humorous*) a thing that sb has made, especially sth that shows ability or imagination 作品；创作：*a literary creation* 文学作品 ◇ *The cake was a delicious creation of sponge, cream and fruit.* 这蛋糕是用松糕、奶油和水果制作的，又好吃，又好看。**3** (*usually* **the Creation**) [sing.] the making of the world, especially by God as described in the Bible（尤指《圣经》所述由上帝）创造天地 **4** (*often* **Creation**) [U] the world and all the living things in it 世界；天地万物

cre·ation·ism /kriˈeɪʃnɪzəm/ *noun* [U] the belief that the universe was made by God exactly as described in the Bible 创造论（认为万物皆按《圣经》所述由上帝创造）▶ **cre·ation·ist** *adj., noun*

creˈation science *noun* [U] science that tries to find proof that God created the world 创造科学（旨在找到上帝创造世界的证据）

cre·ative AW /kriˈeɪtɪv/ *adj., noun*

■ *adj.* **1** [only before noun] involving the use of skill and the imagination to produce sth new or a work of art 创造（性）的；创作的：*a course on **creative writing*** (= writing stories, plays and poems) 文学创作课程 ◇ *the creative and performing arts* 创作与表演艺术 ◇ ***creative thinking*** (= thinking about problems in a new way or thinking of new ideas) 创造性思维 ◇ *the company's creative team* 公司的创新组 ◇ *the creative process* 创作的过程 **2** having the skill and ability to produce sth new, especially a work of art; showing this ability 有创造力的；（尤指艺术作品）创作的；表现创造力的：*She's very creative—she writes poetry and paints.* 她极富创造力，既赋诗又作画。◇ *Do you have any ideas? You're the creative one.* 你有何高见？你是有创见的人。▸ **cre·ative·ly** AW *adv.* **cre·ativ·ity** AW *noun* [U]: *Creativity and originality are more important than technical skill.* 创造力和原创性比专门技术更为重要。

■ *noun* **1** [C] a person who is creative 富于创造力的人；搞创作的人：*The exhibition features the paintings of local creatives.* 这个展览会展出的是当地画家的作品。 **2** [U] creative ideas or material 创意；创作素材：*We need to produce better creative if we want to attract big clients.* 要吸引大客户，我们就得拿出更好的创意。

cre,ative ac'counting *noun* [U] (*disapproving*) a way of doing or presenting the accounts of a business that might not show what the true situation really is 创造性做账（指用取巧的方法入账）

cre·ator AW /kri'eɪtə(r)/ *noun* **1** [C] a person who has made or invented a particular thing 创造者；创作者；发明者：*Walt Disney, the creator of Mickey Mouse* 沃尔特•迪士尼 —— 米老鼠的创作者 **2 the Creator** [sing.] God 造物主；上帝；天主

crea·ture /'kriːtʃə(r)/ *noun* **1** a living thing, real or imaginary, that can move around, such as an animal 生物；动物：*The dormouse is a shy, nocturnal creature.* 睡鼠是一种在夜间活动的胆小动物。◇ *respect for all* ***living creatures*** 对所有生物的尊重 ◇ *strange creatures from outer space* 来自外太空的怪物 **2** (especially following an adjective 尤置于形容词后) a person, considered in a particular way（具有某种特征的）人：*You pathetic creature!* 你这可怜的家伙！◇ *She was an exotic creature with long red hair and brilliant green eyes.* 她有着红色长发、明亮碧眼，是个少见的异域美人。◇ *He always goes to bed at ten—he's* ***a creature of habit*** (= he likes to do the same things at the same time every day). 他总在十点钟上床睡觉，是个严守生活习惯的人。

IDM **a/the creature of sb | sb's creature** (*formal, disapproving*) a person or thing that depends completely on sb else and is controlled by them 傀儡

,creature 'comforts *noun* [pl.] all the things that make life, or a particular place, comfortable, such as good food, comfortable furniture or modern equipment 使人舒适的所有东西（如食物、家具或现代化设备）；物质享受

crèche (*also* **creche**) /kreʃ/ *noun* **1** (*BrE*) a place where babies and small children are taken care of while their parents are working, studying, shopping, etc. 日托托儿所 ➲ COMPARE DAY NURSERY **2** (*NAmE*) (*BrE* **crib**) a model of the scene of Jesus Christ's birth, placed in churches and homes at Christmas 圣诞马槽（表现耶稣诞生的情景）

cred /kred/ *noun* [U] = STREET CRED

cre·dence /'kriːdns/ *noun* [U] (*formal*) **1** a quality that an idea or a story has that makes you believe it is true 可信性；真实性：*Historical evidence* ***lends credence to*** *his theory.* 史学根据使他的理论更为可信。**2** belief in sth as true 信任；信念：*They could* ***give*** *no* ***credence*** *to the findings of the survey.* 他们不相信这次调查的结果。◇ *Alternative medicine has been* ***gaining credence*** (= becoming more widely accepted) *recently.* 近来替代疗法越来越得到大众的认可。

cre·den·tial /krə'denʃl/ *verb* ~ **sb** (*NAmE*) to provide sb with credentials 提供证明书（或证件）

cre·den·tials /krə'denʃlz/ *noun* [pl.] **1** ~ (**as/for sth**) the qualities, training or experience that make you suitable to do sth 资格；资历：*He has all the credentials for the job.* 他做这项工作完全够格。◇ *She will first have to establish her leadership credentials.* 她得首先证明她有担任领导的资格。 **2** documents such as letters that prove that you are who you claim to be, and can therefore be trusted 资格证书；证明书；证件

cred·ibil·ity /,kredə'bɪləti/ *noun* [U] the quality that sb/sth has that makes people believe or trust them 可信性；可靠性：*to* ***gain/lack/lose credibility*** 获取 / 缺乏 / 失去信任 ◇ *The prosecution did its best to* ***undermine the credibility*** *of the witness.* 控方竭力削弱证人的可信性。◇ *Newspapers were talking of a* ***credibility gap*** *between what he said and what he did.* 各家报纸都在议论他言行不一。➲ SEE ALSO STREET CRED

cred·ible /'kredəbl/ *adj.* **1** that can be believed or trusted 可信的；可靠的 SYN **convincing**: *a* ***credible explanation/witness*** 可信的解释 / 证人 ◇ *It is just not credible that she would cheat.* 她会行骗简直难以置信。 **2** that can be accepted, because it seems possible that it could be successful（因看似可能成功而）可接受的 SYN **viable**: *Community service is seen as the only credible alternative to imprisonment.* 除监禁外，社区劳动被看作是唯一可接受的选择。 ▸ **cred·ibly** /-əbli/ *adv.*: *We can credibly describe the band's latest album as their best yet.* 我们完全可以说，这支乐队的最新专辑是他们迄今的最佳作品。

credit AW /'kredɪt/ *noun, verb*

■ *noun*

• **BUY NOW–PAY LATER** 赊购 **1** [U] an arrangement that you make, with a shop/store for example, to pay later for sth you buy 赊购；赊欠：*to* ***get/refuse credit*** 允许 / 拒绝赊购 ◇ *We bought the dishwasher* ***on credit***. 我们赊购了一台洗碗机。◇ *to offer* ***interest-free credit*** (= allow sb to pay later, without any extra charge) 提供免息赊购 ◇ *a* ***credit agreement*** 信贷协定 ◇ ***credit facilities/terms*** 信贷业务；赊欠期 ◇ *Your* ***credit limit*** *is now £2 000.* 你的信用额度现在为 2 000 英镑。◇ *He's a bad* ***credit risk*** (= he is unlikely to pay the money later). 他有欠账不还的危险。➲ COMPARE HIRE PURCHASE

• **MONEY BORROWED** 借款 **2** [U, C] money that you borrow from a bank; a loan（从银行借的）借款；贷款：*The bank refused further credit to the company.* 银行拒绝再给那家公司提供贷款。 ➲ **WORDFINDER NOTE AT** BANK, LOAN ➲ **COLLOCATIONS AT** FINANCE **3** [U] the status of being trusted to pay back money to sb who lends it to you（偿还欠款的）信誉，信用：*Her credit isn't good anywhere now.* 她借钱不还，弄得声名狼藉。

• **MONEY IN BANK** 银行存款 **4** [U] if you or your bank account are **in credit**, there is money in the account 结余 **5** [C, U] a sum of money paid into a bank account; a record of the payment （付入银行账户的）存款金额，贷记：*a credit of £50* * 50 英镑的贷记 ◇ *You'll be paid by direct credit into your bank account.* 给你的付款将直接存入你的银行账户。 OPP **debit**

• **MONEY BACK** 返回的钱 **6** [C, U] (*specialist*) a payment that sb has a right to for a particular reason 有权索要的款项：*a tax credit* 课税扣除

• **PRAISE** 赞扬 **7** [U] ~ (**for sth**) praise or approval because you are responsible for sth good that has happened 赞扬；称赞；认可：*He's a player who rarely seems to get the credit he deserves.* 他这个选手好像很少得到应得的赞扬。◇ *I can't take all the credit for the show's success—it was a team effort.* 演出成功不能都算成我一个人的功劳，这是集体努力的结果。◇ *We did all the work and she gets all the credit!* 工作都是我们干的，而功劳却都归了她！◇ *Credit will be given in the exam for good spelling and grammar.* 考试中拼写和语法出色者将受到表扬。◇ *At least give him credit for trying* (= praise him because he tried, even if he did not succeed). 至少该表扬他尝试过。 ➲ COMPARE BLAME *n.*, DISCREDIT *n.* **8** [sing.] ~ **to sb/sth** a person or thing whose qualities or achievements are praised and who therefore earns respect for sb/sth else 为…赢得荣誉的人（或事物）：*She is a credit to the school.* 她为学校赢得了荣誉。

• **ON MOVIE/TV PROGRAMME** 电影；电视节目 **9** [C, usually pl.] the act of mentioning sb who worked on a project such as a film/movie or a television programme（电影或电视节目演职人员的）片头字幕，片尾字幕：*She was given a programme credit for her work on the costumes for the play.* 她为这出戏准备服装，被列入剧目制作人员名单。

◇ *The credits* (= the list of all the people involved) *seemed to last almost as long as the film!* 演职人员字幕持续的时间几乎与这部电影一样长!

• UNIT OF STUDY 学习单元 **10** [C] a unit of study at a college or university (in the US, also at a school); the fact of having successfully completed a unit of study（大学，以及美国中小学的）学习单元，学分: *My math class is worth three credits.* 我的数学课为三个学分。

IDM **do sb credit | do credit to sb/sth** if sth **does credit** to a person or an organization, they deserve to be praised for it 使值得赞扬（或表扬）: *Your honesty does you great credit.* 你的诚实值得大大表扬。 **have sth to your credit** to have achieved sth 完成; 取得: *He's only 30, and he already has four novels to his credit.* 他年仅 30，却已著有四部小说。 **on the 'credit side** used to introduce the good points about sb/sth, especially after the bad points have been mentioned（尤用于提及缺点之后）就优点方面而言 **to sb's credit** making sb deserve praise or respect 使值得赞扬; 使受尊重: *To his credit, Jack never told anyone exactly what had happened.* 杰克对发生的事守口如瓶，值得赞扬。

■ *verb*

• PUT MONEY IN BANK 往银行存钱 **1** to add an amount of money to sb's bank account（给银行账户）存入金额; 把…记入贷方; 贷记（银行账户）: **~ A (with B)** *Your account has been credited with $50 000.* 已把 5 万美元存入你的账户。◇ **~ B (to A)** *$50 000 has been credited to your account.* 已把 5 万美元存入你的账户。OPP **debit**

• WITH ACHIEVEMENT 成就 **2** [usually passive] to believe or say that sb is responsible for doing sth, especially sth good 认为是…的功劳; 把…归于: **~ sb** *All the contributors are credited on the title page.* 所有撰稿人的姓名均刊登在扉页上。◇ **~ A with B** *The company is credited with inventing the industrial robot.* 发明工业机器人是那家公司的功劳。◇ **~ B to A** *The invention of the industrial robot is credited to the company.* 工业机器人的发明应归功于那家公司。

• WITH QUALITY 品质 **3 ~ A with B** to believe that sb/sth has a particular good quality or feature 认为…有（良好的品质或特点）: *I credited you with a little more sense.* 我认为你更有见识。**4** [usually passive] **~ sb/sth as sth** to believe that sb/sth is of a particular type or quality 认为…属（某种类或性质）: *The cheetah is generally credited as the world's fastest animal.* 普遍认为猎豹是世界上跑得最快的动物。

• BELIEVE 相信 **5 ~ sth | ~ what, how, etc.... | ~ that...** (*BrE*) (used mainly in questions and negative sentences 主要用于疑问句和否定句) to believe sth, especially sth surprising or unexpected 相信（尤指令人惊奇或意外的事物）: *He's been promoted—would you credit it?* 他被擢升了，你相信吗?

cred·it·able /ˈkredɪtəbl/ *adj.* (*formal*) **1** of a quite good standard and deserving praise or approval 值得赞扬的; 应当认可的 SYN **praiseworthy**: *It was a very creditable result for the team.* 对这支队来说，这比赛结果是十分值得称道的。**2** morally good 道德上好的; 高尚的 SYN **admirable**: *There was nothing very creditable in what he did.* 他这事做得可实在不怎么样。▶ **cred·it·ably** /ˈkredɪtəbli/ *adv.*

ˈcredit account *noun* (*BrE*) = ACCOUNT (3)

ˈcredit card *noun* a small plastic card that you can use to buy goods and services and pay for them later 信用卡: *All major credit cards are accepted at our hotels.* 我们的旅馆接受所有主要的信用卡。➲ PICTURE AT MONEY ➲ SEE ALSO CHARGE CARD, DEBIT CARD, STORE CARD

ˈcredit crunch *noun* [usually sing.] (*economics* 经) an economic condition in which it suddenly becomes difficult and expensive to borrow money 信贷紧缩

ˈcredit note *noun* (*BrE*) a letter that a shop/store gives you when you have returned sth and that allows you to have goods of the same value in exchange 贷项凭单（退货时发给的凭证，可换取等值的商品）

cred·it·or AW /ˈkredɪtə(r)/ *noun* a person, company, etc. that sb owes money to 债权人; 债主; 贷方 ➲ COMPARE DEBTOR

ˈcredit rating *noun* a judgement made by a bank, etc. about how likely sb is to pay back money that they borrow, and how safe it is to lend money to them（银行等作出的）信用等级评定

ˈcredit transfer *noun* (*BrE*) the process of sending money from one person's bank account to another's 银行转账

ˈcredit union *noun* an organization that lends money to its members at low rates of interest 互助储金会，信用合作社（向会员提供低息贷款）

credit·worthy /ˈkredɪtwɜːði; *NAmE* -wɜːrði/ *adj.* able to be trusted to pay back money that is owed; safe to lend money to 可信赖偿还欠款的; 信誉好的; 信用可靠的; 借贷安全的 ▶ **credit·worthi·ness** *noun* [U]

credo /ˈkriːdəʊ; ˈkreɪdəʊ; *NAmE* -doʊ/ *noun* (*pl.* **-os**) (*formal*) a set of beliefs 信条 SYN **creed**

cre·du·lity /krɪˈdjuːləti; *NAmE* -ˈduː-/ *noun* [U] (*formal*) the ability or willingness to believe that sth is real or true 轻信: *The plot of the novel stretches credulity to the limit* (= it is almost impossible to believe). 这部小说的情节牵强得几乎令人无法相信。

credu·lous /ˈkredjələs; *NAmE* -dʒə-/ *adj.* (*formal*) too ready to believe things and therefore easy to trick 轻信的; 易受骗的 SYN **gullible** ➲ COMPARE INCREDULOUS

Cree /kriː/ *noun* (*pl.* **Cree** or **Crees**) a member of a Native American people, many of whom live in central Canada 克里人（美洲土著，很多居于加拿大中部）

creed /kriːd/ *noun* **1** [C] a set of principles or religious beliefs 信念; 原则; 纲领; 宗教信仰: *people of all races, colours and creeds* 各种种族、肤色和宗教信仰的人 ◇ *discrimination on the basis of race, colour or creed* 基于种族、肤色或宗教信仰的歧视 ◇ *What is his political creed?* 他的政治信仰是什么? **2 the Creed** [sing.] a statement of Christian belief that is spoken as part of some church services（基督教）信经

Creek /kriːk/ *noun* (*pl.* **Creek** or **Creeks**) a member of a Native American people, many of whom now live in the US state of Oklahoma 克里克人（美洲土著，很多现居于美国俄克拉何马州）

creek /kriːk/ *noun* **1** (*BrE*) a narrow area of water where the sea flows into the land 小海湾; 小港湾 SYN **inlet 2** (*NAmE, AustralE, NZE*) a small river or stream 小河; 小溪

IDM **up the 'creek (without a 'paddle)** (*informal*) in a difficult or bad situation 处于困境（或窘境）: *I was really up the creek without my car.* 离了我那辆汽车真是不方便。

creel /kriːl/ *noun* a BASKET for holding fish that have just been caught（钓鱼用的）鱼篓

creep /kriːp/ *verb, noun*

■ *verb* (**crept, crept** /krept/) HELP In the phrasal verb **creep sb out, creeped** is used for the past simple and past participle. 在短语动词 creep sb out 中，creep 的过去式和过去分词均为 creeped。**1** [I] (**+ adv./prep.**) (of people or animals 人或动物) to move slowly, quietly and carefully, because you do not want to be seen or heard 悄悄地缓慢行进; 蹑手蹑脚地移动: *I crept up the stairs, trying not to wake my parents.* 为了尽量不吵醒父母，我蹑手蹑脚地上了楼。**2** [I] (**+ adv./prep.**) (*NAmE*) to move with your body close to the ground; to move slowly on your hands and knees 匍匐行进; 爬行 SYN **crawl 3** [I] (**+ adv./prep.**) to move or develop very slowly 非常缓慢地行进; 不知不觉产生; 渐渐出现: *Her arms crept around his neck.* 她的双臂慢慢地搂住了他的脖子。◇ *A slight feeling of suspicion crept over me.* 我渐渐地产生了一丝疑虑。**4** [I] (**+ adv./prep.**) (of plants 植物) to grow along the ground or up walls using long STEMS or roots 蔓生; 蔓延 ➲ SEE ALSO CREEPER **5** [I] **~ (to sb)** (*BrE, informal, disapproving*) to be too friendly or helpful to sb in authority in a way that is not sincere, especially in order to get an advantage from them 谄媚; 巴结; 拍马屁 IDM SEE FLESH *n.*

PHR V ˌ**creep ˈin/ˈinto sth** to begin to happen or affect sth 开始发生（或影响）：*As she became more tired, errors began to creep into her work.* 由于越来越疲劳，她的工作开始出现差错。ˌ**creep sb ˈout** (**creeped, creeped**) (*NAmE, informal*) to make sb feel afraid, uncomfortable or disgusted 使人感到害怕（或不舒服、恶心）：*He said the empty streets creeped him out.* 他说空旷的街道令他毛骨悚然。ˌ**creep ˈup** to gradually increase in amount, price, etc. （数量、价格等）逐渐增长：*House prices are creeping up again.* 住房价格又在渐渐上涨。ˌ**creep ˈup on sb 1** to move slowly nearer to sb, usually from behind, without being seen or heard （通常从后面）缓慢地悄悄靠近：*Don't creep up on me like that!* 别那样蹑手蹑脚地靠近我！ **2** to begin to affect sb, especially before they realize it （尤指不知不觉地）开始影响（某人）：*Tiredness can easily creep up on you while you're driving.* 开车时会很容易不知不觉就累了。

■ ***noun* 1** [C] (*informal*) a person that you dislike very much and find very unpleasant 讨厌鬼：*He's a nasty little creep!* 他这小子真让人讨厌！ **2** [C] (*BrE, informal*) a person who is not sincere but tries to win your approval by being nice to you 讨好卖乖的人；谄媚奉承的人；马屁精 **3** [U] (in compounds 构成复合词) (*often disapproving*) the development of a project beyond the goal that was originally agreed （对既定目标的）偏离：*The World Bank has been accused of **mission creep** when seeking to address these concerns.* 世界银行被指控在寻求处理这些重大事务时偏离使命。◇ *The inclusion of health data on identity cards was condemned as **function creep**.* 在身份证中包含健康资料被谴责为超出功能范围。

IDM **give sb the ˈcreeps** (*informal*) to make sb feel nervous and slightly frightened, especially because sb/sth is unpleasant or strange 吓人；使惊慌；使心里发毛

creep·er /ˈkriːpə(r)/ *noun* a plant that grows along the ground, up walls, etc., often winding itself around other plants 蔓生植物；攀缘植物 ➲SEE ALSO VIRGINIA CREEPER

creep·ing /ˈkriːpɪŋ/ *adj.* [only before noun] (of sth bad 坏事) happening or moving gradually and not easily noticed （不知不觉地）逐渐发生的，缓慢行进的：*creeping inflation* 慢慢加剧的通货膨胀

creepy /ˈkriːpi/ *adj.* (**creep·ier, creepi·est**) (*informal*) **1** causing an unpleasant feeling of fear or slight horror 令人毛骨悚然的；令人不寒而栗的 **SYN** **scary**：*a creepy ghost story* 令人毛骨悚然的鬼故事 ◇ *It's kind of creepy down in the cellar!* 地窖里真有点令人不寒而栗！ **2** strange in a way that makes you feel nervous 怪异的，离奇的（使人感到紧张） **SYN** **spooky**：*What a creepy coincidence.* 多么离奇的巧合。

creepy-crawly /ˌkriːpi ˈkrɔːli/ *noun* (*pl.* **-ies**) (*informal*) an insect, a WORM, etc. when you think of it as unpleasant （使人厌恶的）爬虫，蠕虫

cre·mains /krɪˈmeɪnz/ *noun* [pl.] (*NAmE*) the powder that is left after a dead person's body has been CREMATED (= burned) 骨灰 **SYN** **ashes**

cre·mate /krəˈmeɪt/ *verb* [often passive] **~ sb/sth** to burn a dead body, especially as part of a funeral ceremony 焚烧，火化（尸体）；（尤指）火葬

cre·ma·tion /krəˈmeɪʃn/ *noun* **1** [U] the act of cremating sb 火化 **2** [C] a funeral at which the dead person is cremated 火葬；火化仪式 ➲WORDFINDER NOTE AT DIE

crema·tor·ium /ˌkreməˈtɔːriəm/ *noun* (*pl.* **crema·toria** /-ˈtɔːriə/ or **crema·tor·iums**) (*NAmE also* **crema·tory** /ˈkriːmətɔːri; ˈkrem-/ *pl.* **-ies**) a building in which the bodies of dead people are burned 火葬场

crème brûlée /ˌkrem bruːˈleɪ/ *noun* [C, U] (*pl.* **crèmes brûlées** /ˌkrem bruːˈleɪ/) (*from French*) a cold DESSERT (= a sweet dish) made from cream, with burnt sugar on top 焦糖奶油（冷甜点）

crème caramel /ˌkrem ˈkærəmel/ *noun* [C, U] (*pl.* **crèmes caramel** /ˌkrem ˈkærəmel/, **crème caramels** /ˌkrem ˈkærəmelz/) (*BrE, from French*) (*NAmE* **flan**) a cold DESSERT (= a sweet dish) made from milk, eggs and sugar 焦糖蛋奶（冷甜点）

crème de la crème /ˌkrem də lɑː ˈkrem/ *noun* [sing.] (*from French, formal* or *humorous*) the best people or things of their kind 精英；精华；精髓：*This school takes only the crème de la crème.* 这所学校只招收高材生。

crème de menthe /ˌkrem də ˈmɒnθ; *NAmE* ˈmenθ/ *noun* [U, C] (*pl.* **crèmes de menthe** /ˌkrem də ˈmɒnθ; *NAmE* ˈmenθ/) (*from French*) a strong sweet alcoholic drink made with MINT 薄荷烈性甜酒

crème fraiche /ˌkrem ˈfreʃ/ *noun* [U] (*from French*) thick cream with a slightly sour taste 鲜浓奶油，生奶油（略带酸味）

cren·el·lated (*US also* **cren·el·ated**) /ˈkrenəleɪtɪd/ *adj.* (*specialist*) (of a tower, castle, etc. 塔楼、城堡等) having BATTLEMENTS 有雉堞的

Cre·ole /ˈkriːəʊl; *NAmE* -oʊl/ (*also* **creole**) *noun* **1** [C] a person of mixed European and African race, especially one who lives in the West Indies 克里奥尔人（尤指居住在西印度群岛的欧洲人和非洲人的混血儿） **2** [C] a person whose ANCESTORS were among the first Europeans who settled in the West Indies or S America, or one of the French or Spanish people who settled in the southern states of the US 克里奥尔人（指首批定居在西印度群岛或南美的欧洲人的后裔，或定居在美国南部诸州的法国人和西班牙人的后裔）：*Creole cookery* 克里奥尔式烹饪方法 **3** [U, C] a language formed when a mixture of a European language with a local language (especially an African language spoken by SLAVES in the West Indies) is spoken as a first language 克里奥尔语（欧洲语言和当地语言的混合语，尤指与西印度群岛奴隶讲的非洲语言的混合语） ➲COMPARE PIDGIN

cre·ol·ize (*BrE also* **-ise**) /ˈkriːəlaɪz; *BrE also* ˈkrɪə-/ *verb* **~ sth** (*linguistics* 语言) to change a language by combining it with a language from another place 使（语言）克里奥尔语化；使混合化：*Creolized forms of Latin were spoken in various parts of Europe.* 当时欧洲各地区都讲克里奥尔语形式的拉丁语。▶ **cre·ol·iza·tion, -isa·tion** /ˌkriːəlaɪˈzeɪʃn; *NAmE* -ləˈz-; *BrE also* ˈkrɪəlaɪzeɪʃn/ *noun* [U, C]

creo·sote /ˈkriːəsəʊt; *NAmE* -soʊt/ *noun, verb*

■ ***noun*** [U] a thick brown liquid that is made from COAL TAR, used to preserve wood 杂酚油，木馏油（用于木材防腐）

■ ***verb* ~ sth** to paint or preserve sth with creosote 用杂酚油涂抹（或防腐）

crêpe (*also* **crepe**) /kreɪp/ *noun* **1** [U] a type of light thin cloth, made especially from cotton or silk, with a surface that is covered in lines and folds （尤指用棉和丝织的）绉；绉纱；绉布：*a black crêpe dress* 黑色绉绸连衣裙 ◇ *a crêpe bandage* 弹力绷带 **2** [U] a type of strong rubber with a rough surface, used for making the SOLES of shoes 绉胶（制鞋底用）：*crêpe-soled shoes* 绉胶底鞋 **3** /krep/ [C] a thin PANCAKE 薄煎饼

ˈ**crêpe paper** *noun* [U] a type of thin brightly coloured paper that stretches and has a surface covered in lines and folds, used especially for making decorations （尤用于装饰的）彩色皱纹纸

crept PAST TENSE, PAST PART. OF CREEP

cre·pus·cul·ar /krɪˈpʌskjələ(r)/ *adj.* (*literary*) related to the period of the evening when the sun has just gone down but there is still some light in the sky 黄昏的

cres·cendo /krəˈʃendəʊ; *NAmE* -doʊ/ *noun* (*pl.* **-os**) [C, U] **1** (*music* 音, *from Italian*) a gradual increase in how loudly a piece of music is played or sung （音乐的）渐强 **OPP** **diminuendo 2** a gradual increase in noise; the loudest point of a period of continuous noise 逐渐增强的喧闹声；持续噪声的最高点 **SYN** **swell**：*Voices rose in a crescendo and drowned him out.* 人们讲话的声音越来越大，盖过了他的声音。◇ (*figurative*) *The advertising campaign reached a crescendo just before Christmas.* 圣诞节前夕，广告攻势达到了高潮。

cres·cent /ˈkresnt; *BrE also* ˈkreznt/ *noun* **1** [C] a curved shape that is wide in the middle and pointed at each end 新月形；月牙形：*a crescent moon* 新月 **2** [C] (often used in street names 常用于街道名称) a curved street with a row of houses on it 新月形街区（一排房屋）：*I live at 7 Park Crescent.* 我住在帕克新月街 7 号。 **3 the Crescent** [sing.] the curved shape that is used as a symbol of Islam 新月（伊斯兰教的象征）➲ SEE ALSO RED CRESCENT

cress /kres/ *noun* [U] a small plant with thin STEMS and very small leaves, often eaten in salads and SANDWICHES 水芥（常放在色拉和三明治中食用） ➲ SEE ALSO WATERCRESS

crest /krest/ *noun, verb*
■ *noun* **1** [usually sing.] ~ (**of sth**) the top part of a hill or wave 山顶；顶峰；波峰；浪尖：*surfers riding the crest of the wave* 正在浪峰上冲浪的运动员 ➲ VISUAL VOCAB PAGE V5 **2** a design used as the symbol of a particular family, organization, etc., especially one that has a long history（尤指象征历史悠久的家族、机构等的）饰章，纹章：*the university crest* 大学的徽章 **3** a group of feathers that stand up on top of a bird's head 鸟冠；羽冠 ➲ VISUAL VOCAB PAGE V12
IDM **the crest of a/the ˈwave** a situation in which sb is very successful, happy, etc. 顶峰时期；极其成功；春风得意 ➲ MORE AT RIDE *v.*
■ *verb* **1** [T] ~ **sth** (*formal*) to reach the top of a hill, mountain or wave 到达山顶（或浪峰）：*He slowed the pace as they crested the ridge.* 当他们到达山脊时，他放慢了步伐。 **2** [I] (*NAmE*) (of a flood, wave, etc. 洪水、波浪等) to reach its highest level before it falls again 到达洪峰；达到顶点：(*figurative*) *The level of debt crested at a massive $290 billion in 2009.* * 2009 年的巨额债务高达 2 900 亿美元。

crest·ed /ˈkrestɪd/ *adj.* **1** marked with a crest 有饰章的：*crested notepaper* 有饰章的信笺 **2** used especially in names of birds or animals which have a crest（尤用于鸟兽名称）有鸟冠的，有羽冠的：*crested newts* 冠欧螈

crest·fall·en /ˈkrestfɔːlən/ *adj.* sad and disappointed because you have failed and you did not expect to 垂头丧气的；灰心失望的；沮丧的

Cret·aceous /krɪˈteɪʃəs/ *adj.* (*geology* 地) of the PERIOD between around 146 and 65 million years ago, when dinosaurs lived (until they died out); of the rocks formed during this time 白垩纪的 ▸ **the Cret·aceous** *noun* [sing.]

cre·tin /ˈkretɪn; *NAmE* ˈkriːtn/ *noun* (*informal, offensive*) a very stupid person 笨蛋；傻瓜；白痴：*Why did you do that, you cretin?* 你为什么这样做，你这个傻瓜？ ▸ **cret·in·ous** /ˈkretɪnəs; *NAmE* ˈkriːtnəs/ *adj.*

Creutzfeldt-Jakob disease /ˌkrɔɪtsfelt ˈjækɒb dɪziːz; *NAmE* ˈjækɔːb/ *noun* [U] (*abbr.* **CJD**) a brain disease that causes gradual loss of control of the mind and body and, finally, death. It is believed to be caused by PRIONS and is linked to BSE in cows. 克罗伊茨费尔特－雅各布病，克－雅脑病（俗称疯牛病，被认为由朊病毒引起并与牛海绵状脑病有关的致命脑病）

cre·vasse /krəˈvæs/ *noun* a deep open crack, especially in ice, for example in a GLACIER （尤指冰川等的）裂缝，裂隙，冰隙

crev·ice /ˈkrevɪs/ *noun* a narrow crack in a rock or wall （岩石或墙壁的）裂缝，裂隙，裂口

crew /kruː/ *noun, verb*
■ *noun* **1** [C+sing./pl. v.] all the people working on a ship, plane, etc.（轮船、飞机等上面的）全体工作人员：*None of the passengers and crew were injured.* 没有一个乘客和机组人员受伤。◇ *crew members* 全体机组人员 ➲ SEE ALSO AIRCREW, CABIN CREW, FLIGHT CREW **2** [C+sing./pl. v.] all the people working on a ship, plane etc. except the officers who are in charge（轮船、飞机等上面不包括高级职员的）全体船员，全体乘务员：*the officers and crew* 负责人员和全体乘务员 **3** [C+sing./pl. v.] a group of people with special skills working together 技术人员团队；专业团队：*a film/camera crew* 电影摄制组；摄制组 ◇ *an ambulance crew* 救护车急救组 ➲ SEE ALSO GROUND CREW **4** [sing.] (*usually disapproving*) a group of people 一群（或一帮、一伙）人：*The people she invited were a pretty **motley crew*** (= a strange mix of types of people). 她邀请的人相当杂。 **5** [C+sing./pl. v.] a team of people who ROW[1] boats in races（赛艇的）划船队员，划船队：*a member of the Cambridge crew* 剑桥大学划船队的队员 **6** [U] (*NAmE*) the sport of ROWING with other people in a boat 赛艇运动：*I'm thinking of going out for crew this semester* (= joining the ROWING team). 这学期我打算参加赛艇队。
■ *verb* [T, I] to be part of a crew, especially on a ship 当（尤指船上的）工作人员：~ (**sth**) *Normally the boat is crewed by five people.* 通常这条船配有五名船员。◇ ~ (**for sb**) *I crewed for him on his yacht last summer.* 去年夏天我在他的游艇上当船员。

ˈcrew cut *noun* a HAIRSTYLE for men in which the hair is cut very short 平头（男式发型）➲ VISUAL VOCAB PAGE V65 ▸ **ˈcrew-cut** *adj.*：*crew-cut teenagers* 留平头的青少年

crew·man /ˈkruːmən/ *noun* (*pl.* **-men** /-mən/) a member of a CREW, usually a man 船员，乘务员（通常为男性）

ˌcrew ˈneck *noun* a round neck on a sweater, etc.（套头毛衣等的）圆领，水手领 ➲ VISUAL VOCAB PAGE V68

crib /krɪb/ *noun, verb*
■ *noun* **1** (*NAmE*) (*BrE* **cot**) a small bed with high sides for a baby or young child（有围栏的）幼儿床 ➲ VISUAL VOCAB PAGE V24 **2** a long open box that horses and cows can eat from（马、牛的）饲料槽 SYN **manger 3** (*BrE*) (*NAmE* **crèche**) a model of the scene of Jesus Christ's birth, placed in churches and homes at Christmas 圣诞马槽（表现耶稣诞生的情景）**4** (*informal*) written information such as answers to questions, often used dishonestly by students in tests（考试作弊用的）夹带：*a crib sheet* 夹带的答案纸 **5** = CRIBBAGE **6** (*NAmE, informal*) the house, flat/apartment, etc. where sb lives 住所；公寓；居所
■ *verb* **1** (**-bb-**) [I, T] ~ (**sth**) (**from sb**) (*old-fashioned*) to dishonestly copy work from another student or from a book（学生在考试或做作业时）抄袭，剽窃 **2** [I] ~ (**about sth**) (*BrE, old-fashioned* or *IndE*) to complain about sb/sth in a bad-tempered way 抱怨；发牢骚

crib·bage /ˈkrɪbɪdʒ/ (*also* **crib**) *noun* [U] a card game in which players score points by collecting different combinations of cards. The score is kept by putting small PEGS in holes in a board. 克里比奇牌戏（用小木钉插在有孔的木板上记分）

ˈcrib death (*NAmE*) (*BrE* **ˈcot death**) *noun* [U, C] the sudden death while sleeping of a baby that appears to be healthy 婴儿猝死

crick /krɪk/ (*NAmE also* **kink**) *noun* [usually sing.] a sudden painful stiff feeling in the muscles of your neck or back（颈或背部的）痛性痉挛 ▸ **crick** *verb*：~ **sth** *I suffered a cricked neck during a game of tennis.* 我在一次网球比赛时脖子扭了。

crick·et /ˈkrɪkɪt/ *noun* **1** [U] a game played on grass by two teams of 11 players. Players score points (called RUNS) by hitting the ball with a wooden BAT and running between two sets of vertical wooden sticks, called STUMPS. 板球（运动）：*a **cricket match/team/club/ball*** 板球比赛 / 运动队 / 俱乐部；板球 ➲ VISUAL VOCAB PAGE V47 **2** [C] a small brown jumping insect that makes a loud high sound by rubbing its wings together 蟋蟀；蛐蛐：*the chirping of crickets* 蟋蟀的唧唧叫声
IDM **not ˈcricket** (*old-fashioned, BrE, informal*) unfair; not HONOURABLE 不公正；不光明正大；不光彩；见不得人

crick·et·er /ˈkrɪkɪtə(r)/ *noun* a cricket player 板球运动员

cricket·ing /ˈkrɪkɪtɪŋ/ *adj.* [only before noun] playing cricket; connected with cricket 打板球的；与板球有关的：*cricketing nations* 打板球的国家 ◇ *a cricketing jersey* 板球运动衫

cri de cœur /ˌkriː də ˈkɜː(r)/ *noun* (*pl.* **cris de cœur** /ˌkriː də ˈkɜː(r)/) (*from French*) an act of asking for sth, or protesting, in a way that shows you care deeply about sth 发自内心的要求（或抗议）；恳求；激烈抗议

C

cried PAST TENSE, PAST PART. OF CRY

crier /ˈkraɪə(r)/ *noun* = TOWN CRIER

cri·key /ˈkraɪki/ *exclamation* (*BrE, old-fashioned, informal*) used to show that sb is surprised or annoyed（惊讶或恼怒时说）哎呀，哎哟，唷：*Crikey, is that the time?* 哎呀，都这会儿啦？

Crimbo = CHRIMBO

crime /kraɪm/ *noun* **1** [U] activities that involve breaking the law 犯罪活动；不法行为：*an increase in violent crime* 暴力犯罪活动的增加 ◇ *the fight against crime* 与犯罪活动的斗争 ◇ *Stores spend more and more on* ***crime prevention*** *every year.* 商店每年在防止犯罪方面的花费越来越多。◇ ***petty/serious crime*** 轻微的 / 严重的犯罪 ◇ *the connection between drugs and* ***organized crime*** 毒品与有组织犯罪之间的联系 ◇ *He* ***turned to crime*** *when he dropped out of school.* 他辍学后走上犯罪道路。◇ *The* ***crime rate*** *is rising.* 犯罪率正在上升。◇ ***crime fiction/novels*** (= stories about crime) 犯罪小说 ◇ ***crime figures/statistics*** 犯罪数字 / 统计数字 ◇ *She's a* ***crime writer*** (= she writes stories about crime). 她是犯罪小说作家。➲ WORDFINDER NOTE AT LAW ➲ COLLOCATIONS AT JUSTICE **2** [C] ~ (**against sb**) an illegal act or activity that can be punished by law 罪；罪行：*to* ***commit a crime*** (= do sth illegal) 犯罪 ◇ *The massacre was a* ***crime against humanity.*** 这场大屠杀是一桩反人类的罪行。➲ SEE ALSO WAR CRIME **3 a crime** [sing.] (*informal*) an act that you think is immoral or is a big mistake 不道德的行为；罪过：*It's a crime to waste so much money.* 挥霍这么多钱是一种罪过。

ˈcrime wave *noun* [sing.] a situation in which there is a sudden increase in the number of crimes that are committed 犯罪高潮

crim·inal /ˈkrɪmɪnl/ *adj., noun*

■ ***adj.* 1** [usually before noun] (*rather formal* or *law* 律) connected with or involving crime 犯罪的；犯法的；涉及犯罪的：***criminal offences/behaviour*** 刑事犯罪；犯罪行为 ◇ ***criminal damage*** (= the crime of damaging sb's property deliberately) 刑事损害 ◇ ***criminal negligence*** (= the illegal act of sb failing to do sth that they should do, with the result that sb else is harmed) 过失犯罪 **2** [only before noun] connected to the laws that deal with crime 刑法的；刑事的：*criminal law* 刑法 ◇ *the criminal justice system* 刑事审判制度 ◇ *a criminal lawyer* 刑事诉讼律师 ◇ *to bring criminal charges against sb* 对某人提起刑事诉讼 ➲ COMPARE CIVIL (3) **3** morally wrong 道德上错误的；不道德的：*This is a criminal waste of resources.* 这是一种浪费资源的可耻行为。

■ ***noun*** a person who commits a crime 罪犯：*Society does not know how to deal with* ***hardened criminals*** (= people who regularly commit crimes and are not sorry for what they do). 社会不知道怎样处置惯犯。◇ (*especially NAmE*) *a* ***career criminal*** 职业罪犯 ➲ COLLOCATIONS AT CRIME

crim·in·al·ity /ˌkrɪmɪˈnæləti/ *noun* [U] the fact of people being involved in crime; criminal acts 犯罪；有罪；犯罪行为

crim·in·al·ize (*BrE also* **-ise**) /ˈkrɪmɪnəlaɪz/ *verb* **1 ~ sth** to make sth illegal by passing a new law（通过新的法律）使不合法，使非法：*The use of opium was not criminalized until fairly recently.* 直到最近抽鸦片才被判定为非法。**2 ~ sb** to make sb a criminal by making their activities illegal 使成为罪犯 ▶ **crim·in·al·iza·tion, -isa·tion** /ˌkrɪmɪnəlaɪˈzeɪʃn; *NAmE* -ləˈz-/ *noun* [U]

crim·in·al·ly /ˈkrɪmɪnəli/ *adv.* according to the laws that deal with crime 刑法上；刑事上；在犯罪方面：*criminally insane* 精神不正常而犯罪的

ˌcriminal ˈrecord *noun* = RECORD (6)

▼ **COLLOCATIONS 词语搭配**

Crime 犯罪

Committing a crime 犯罪

- **commit** a crime/a murder/a violent assault/a brutal killing/an armed robbery/fraud 犯罪 / 谋杀罪 / 暴力侵犯他人身体罪 / 残杀罪 / 持械抢劫罪 / 诈骗罪
- **be involved in** terrorism/a suspected arson attack/people smuggling/human trafficking 参与恐怖主义活动；涉嫌纵火袭击；参与人口走私 / 人口贩卖
- **engage/participate in** criminal activity/illegal practices/acts of mindless vandalism 参与犯罪活动 / 非法活动 / 愚昧的故意毁坏他人财产的行为
- **steal** sb's wallet/purse/(*BrE*) mobile phone/(*NAmE*) cell phone 偷某人的钱包 / 手机
- **rob** a bank/a person/a tourist 抢劫银行 / 他人 / 游客
- **break into**/(*BrE*) **burgle**/(*NAmE*) **burglarize** a house/a home/an apartment 入室盗窃
- **hijack** a plane/ship/bus 劫持飞机 / 轮船 / 公共汽车
- **smuggle** drugs/weapons/arms/immigrants 走私毒品 / 武器 / 军火；偷运移民
- **launder** drug money (through sth) （通过…）洗毒资
- **forge** documents/certificates/passports 伪造文件 / 证件 / 护照
- **take/accept/pay sb/offer (sb)** a bribe 索取 / 收受贿赂；向（某人）行贿
- **run** a phishing/an email/an Internet scam 进行网络钓鱼 / 电子邮件 / 互联网诈骗

Fighting crime 打击犯罪

- **combat/fight** crime/terrorism/corruption/drug trafficking 打击犯罪 / 恐怖主义 / 腐败 / 贩毒
- **prevent/stop** credit-card fraud/child abuse/software piracy 防止 / 阻止信用卡诈骗 / 虐待儿童 / 软件盗版
- **deter/stop** criminals/burglars/thieves/shoplifters/vandals 威慑 / 阻止犯罪分子 / 入室盗窃者 / 小偷 / 商店扒手 / 故意破坏公物者
- **reduce/tackle/crack down on** knife/gun/violent/street crime/(*especially BrE*) antisocial behaviour 减少 / 处理 / 严厉打击持刀 / 持枪 / 暴力 / 街头犯罪 / 反社会行为
- **foil** a bank raid/a terrorist plot 挫败一起银行抢劫案 / 一次恐怖分子的阴谋
- **help/support/protect** the victims of crime 帮助 / 支持 / 保护犯罪活动的受害者

Investigating crime 调查犯罪活动

- **report** a crime/a theft/a rape/an attack/(*especially BrE*) an incident to the police 向警方举报不法行为 / 偷窃案 / 强奸案 / 袭击事件 / 暴力事件
- **witness** the crime/attack/murder/incident 目击犯罪 / 袭击 / 谋杀 / 暴力事件
- **investigate** a murder/(*especially NAmE*) a homicide/a burglary/a robbery/the alleged incident 调查谋杀案 / 蓄意杀人案 / 入室盗窃案 / 抢劫案 / 涉嫌的暴力事件
- **conduct/launch/pursue** an investigation (into…)/(*especially BrE*) a police/murder inquiry 进行 / 开始 / 继续（对…的）调查 / 警方调查 / 谋杀案调查
- **investigate/reopen** a criminal/murder case 调查 / 重新审理犯罪 / 谋杀案件
- **examine/investigate/find fingerprints at** the crime scene/the scene of crime 仔细检查 / 调查 / 查找犯罪现场的指纹
- **collect/gather** forensic evidence 收集法医证据
- **uncover** new evidence/a fraud/a scam/a plot/a conspiracy/political corruption/a cache of weapons 发现新证据 / 诈骗 / 欺诈 / 密谋 / 阴谋 / 政治腐败 / 私藏武器
- **describe/identify** a suspect/the culprit/the perpetrator/the assailant/the attacker 描述 / 指认嫌疑犯 / 罪犯 / 作恶者 / 攻击者 / 袭击者
- **question/interrogate** a suspect/witness 询问嫌疑人 / 目击证人
- **solve/crack** the case 破案

➲ COLLOCATIONS AT JUSTICE

C

crim·in·ology /ˌkrɪmɪˈnɒlədʒi; NAmE -ˈnɑːl-/ *noun* [U] the scientific study of crime and criminals 犯罪学 ▶ **crim·ino·logic·al** /ˌkrɪmɪnəˈlɒdʒɪkl; NAmE -ˈlɑːdʒ-/ *adj.* **crim·in·olo·gist** /-dʒɪst/ *noun*

crimp /krɪmp/ *verb, noun*
■ *verb* **1** ~ **sth** to make curls in sb's hair by pressing it with a heated tool 烫发；使（头发）拳曲；使（头发）成波形 **2** ~ **sth** to press cloth or paper into small folds 把（织物或纸）压出皱纹；使起皱 **3** ~ **sth** (*NAmE, informal*) to restrict the growth or development of sth 阻止，妨碍（某事物的发展）
■ *noun*
IDM **put a ˈcrimp in/on sth** (*NAmE, informal*) to have a bad or negative effect on sth 对…造成阻碍；对…有负面影响；损害

crim·son /ˈkrɪmzn/ *adj.* dark red in colour 深红色的；暗红色的：*She went crimson* (= her face became very red because she was embarrassed). 她的脸羞得通红。▶ **crim·son** *noun* [U]

cringe /krɪndʒ/ *verb* **1** [I] to move back and/or away from sb because you are afraid 畏缩；怯退 SYN **cower**：*a child cringing in terror* 吓得直退缩的小孩 **2** [I] to feel very embarrassed and uncomfortable about sth 感到尴尬不安；觉得难为情：*I cringe when I think of the poems I wrote then.* 每当我想起我那时写的诗歌就感到很难堪。

cringe·worthy /ˈkrɪndʒwɜːði; NAmE -wɜːrði/ (*also* **ˈcringe-making**) *adj.* (*both BrE, informal*) making you feel embarrassed or uncomfortable 令人感到尴尬（或不舒服）的：*It was a cringeworthy performance from start to finish.* 演出从头到尾叫人不舒服。

crin·kle /ˈkrɪŋkl/ *verb, noun*
■ *verb* [I, T] to become covered with or to form a lot of thin folds or lines, especially in skin, cloth or paper（尤指皮肤、布料或纸张）变皱，起皱纹：*He smiled, his eyes crinkling.* 他眯着眼睛笑了。◇ *Her face crinkled up in a smile.* 她笑得满脸都是皱纹。◇ ~ **sth** *The binding had faded and the pages were crinkled.* 书的封皮已经退色，纸张也皱巴巴的。
■ *noun* a very thin fold or line made on paper, cloth or skin 褶痕；皱纹

crin·kly /ˈkrɪŋkli/ *adj.* **1** having a lot of thin folds or lines 多褶皱的；多皱纹的：*crinkly silver foil* 布满褶皱的银箔 **2** (of hair 头发) having a lot of small curls or waves 多鬈发的；多波浪的

crin·ol·ine /ˈkrɪnəlɪn/ *noun* a frame that was worn under a skirt by some women in the past in order to give the skirt a very round full shape（旧时的）裙衬，裙撑，裙架

cripes /kraɪps/ *exclamation* (*BrE, old-fashioned, informal*) used to show that sb is surprised or annoyed（表示惊讶或恼怒）天哪，啊呀

crip·ple /ˈkrɪpl/ *verb, noun*
■ *verb* **1** [usually passive] ~ **sb** to damage sb's body so that they are no longer able to walk or move normally 使残废；使跛；使成瘸子 SYN **disable**：*He was crippled by polio as a child.* 他幼年患过小儿麻痹症，结果腿就瘸了。◇ *to be crippled with arthritis* 因患关节炎而腿瘸 **2** [usually passive] ~ **sb/sth** to seriously damage or harm sb/sth 严重毁坏（或损害）：*The pilot tried to land his crippled plane.* 飞行员试图驾驶损坏严重的飞机着陆。▶ **crip·pling** *adj.*：*a crippling disease* 严重损害健康的疾病 ◇ *crippling debts* 导致经济瘫痪的债务
■ *noun* (*old-fashioned* or *offensive*) a person who is unable to walk or move normally because of a disease or injury 伤残人；残疾人；跛子；瘸子：(*figurative*) *He's an emotional cripple* (= he cannot express his feelings). 他是个感情有缺陷的人。HELP People now use **disabled person** instead of 'cripple'. 人们现在说 disabled person，而不说 cripple。

cri·sis 🔑 /ˈkraɪsɪs/ *noun* [C, U] (*pl.* **cri·ses** /-siːz/) **1** 🔑 a time of great danger, difficulty or confusion when problems must be solved or important decisions must be made 危机；危急关头：*a* ***political/financial crisis*** 政治/金融危机 ◇ *the government's latest* ***economic crisis*** 政府最近的经济危机 ◇ *The business is still* ***in crisis*** *but it has survived the worst of the recession.* 这家公司虽然仍处于危机之中，但已经挺过了经济衰退最严重的日子。◇ *The Labour Party was facing an* ***identity crisis.*** 工党当时正面临着身份危机。◇ *an expert in* ***crisis management*** 危机处理专家 ◇ *We provide help to families in crisis situations.* 我们向处于困境的家庭提供帮助。◇ *In times of crisis I know which friends I can turn to.* 在危难关头我知道能投靠哪些朋友。◇ *The party was suffering a* ***crisis of confidence*** *among its supporters* (= they did not trust it any longer). 当时这个政党在其支持者中正遭受信任危机。➲ SEE ALSO MIDLIFE CRISIS **2** 🔑 a time when a problem, a bad situation or an illness is at its worst point 危难时刻；病危期：*Their marriage has reached crisis point.* 他们的婚姻已到了岌岌可危的地步。◇ *The fever has passed its crisis.* 发烧已过危险期。➲ SEE ALSO CRITICAL (3)

crisp 🔑 /krɪsp/ *adj., noun, verb*
■ *adj.* (**crisp·er, crisp·est**) (*usually approving*) **1** 🔑 (of food 食物) (*also* **crispy**) pleasantly hard and dry 脆的；酥脆的：*Bake until the pastry is golden and crisp.* 把油酥面团烤至金黄酥脆。

WORDFINDER 联想词： chewy, creamy, crunchy, greasy, juicy, mushy, rubbery, tender, tough

2 🔑 (of fruit and vegetables 水果和蔬菜) (*also* **crispy**) firm and fresh 鲜脆的；脆嫩的：*a* ***crisp apple/lettuce*** 新鲜脆生的苹果 / 生菜 **3** (of paper or cloth 纸张或布料) fresh and clean; new and slightly stiff without any folds in it 洁净的；挺括的：*a crisp new $5 bill* 一张崭新挺括的 5 美元钞票 ◇ *a crisp white shirt* 洁净挺括的白衬衫 **4** (of the air or the weather 空气或天气) pleasantly dry and cold 凉爽的；清新的；干燥寒冷让人舒畅的：*a crisp winter morning* 冬天一个干冷的早晨 ◇ *The air was crisp and clear and the sky was blue.* 空气清新，天空碧蓝。 **5** (of snow, leaves, etc. 雪、树叶等) firm or dry and making a pleasant noise when crushed（踩踏时发出）脆响的：*deep, crisp snow* 踩上去咯吱作响的厚积雪 **6** (of sounds, images, etc. 声音、图像等) pleasantly clear and sharp 清脆悦耳的；清晰分明的：*The recording sounds very crisp, considering its age.* 考虑到这录音已年代久远，听起来声音还是挺清楚的。**7** (*sometimes disapproving*) (of a person's way of speaking 说话的方式) quick and confident in a way that suggests that the person is busy or is not being friendly 简短干脆的（表明某人忙或不友好）：*Her answer was crisp, and she gave no details.* 她的回答简短而干脆，没有提供细节。▶ **crisp·ly** *adv.*：*crisply fried potatoes* 脆炸土豆片 ◇ *'Take a seat,' she said crisply.* "坐下。"她干脆地说。 **crisp·ness** *noun* [U]：*The salad had lost its crispness.* 这色拉已经不脆了。
■ *noun* **1** (*also* **poˌtato ˈcrisp**) (*both BrE*) (*NAmE* **chip, poˈtato chip**) a thin round slice of potato that is fried until hard then dried and eaten cold. Crisps are sold in bags and have many different flavours. 油炸土豆片，炸薯片（有多种风味，袋装）➲ PICTURE AT CHIP **2** (*NAmE*) (*BrE* **crum·ble**) [U, C] a DESSERT (= a sweet dish) made from fruit that is covered with a rough mixture of flour, butter and sugar, cooked in the oven and usually served hot 水果酥，酥脆水果甜点（通常烤熟趁热吃）：*apple crisp* 苹果酥 IDM SEE BURN *v.*
■ *verb* [I, T] ~ (**sth**) to become or make sth crisp （使）变脆

crisp·bread /ˈkrɪspbred/ *noun* [C, U] a thin crisp biscuit made of WHEAT or RYE, often eaten with cheese or instead of bread 薄脆麦饼干（用小麦或黑麦制成，常与奶酪同吃，或替代面包）

crispy /ˈkrɪspi/ *adj.* (*approving*) = CRISP：*crispy batter* 炸土豆片用的面糊

criss-cross /ˈkrɪs krɒs; NAmE krɔːs/ *adj., verb*
■ *adj.* [usually before noun] with many straight lines that cross each other 十字交叉的；纵横交错的：*a criss-cross pattern* 十字形图案 ▶ **criss-cross** *noun* [sing.]：*a criss-cross of streets* 纵横交错的街道
■ *verb* [T, I] ~ (**sth**) | ~ **sth** (**with sth**) to make a pattern on sth with many straight lines that cross each other 构成十字形（或交叉）图案：*The city is criss-crossed with canals.* 这座城市里运河纵横交错。➲ MORE LIKE THIS 11, page R26

cri·ter·ion 🔑 AW /kraɪˈtɪəriən; *NAmE* -ˈtɪr-/ *noun* (*pl.* **cri·teria** /-riə/) a standard or principle by which sth is judged, or with the help of which a decision is made（评判或作决定的）标准，准则，原则：*The main criterion is value for money.* 主要的标准是要划算。◇ *What criteria are used for assessing a student's ability?* 用什么标准来评定一个学生的能力？ ⊃ MORE LIKE THIS 30, page R28

crit·ic /ˈkrɪtɪk/ *noun* **1** a person who expresses opinions about the good and bad qualities of books, music, etc. 批评家；评论家；评论员：*a **music/theatre/literary, etc. critic*** 音乐、戏剧、文学等评论家 ◇ *The critics loved the movie.* 评论家喜爱这部电影。 ⊃ WORDFINDER NOTE AT WRITE **2** a person who expresses disapproval of sb/sth and talks about their bad qualities, especially publicly 批评者；挑剔的人：*She is one of the ruling party's most outspoken critics.* 她是最直言不讳地批评执政党的人之一。◇ *a critic of private health care* 对私营医疗保健服务持批评态度的人

crit·ic·al 🔑 /ˈkrɪtɪkl/ *adj.*

- **EXPRESSING DISAPPROVAL** 表示不赞成 **1** 🔑 expressing disapproval of sb/sth and saying what you think is bad about them 批评的；批判性的；挑剔的：***a critical comment/report*** 批判性的评论 / 报道 ◇ *The supervisor is always very critical.* 主管总是很挑剔。◇ **~ of sb/sth** *Tom's parents were highly critical of the school.* 汤姆的父母对学校提出了强烈的批评。
- **IMPORTANT** 重要 **2** 🔑 extremely important because a future situation will be affected by it 极重要的；关键的；至关紧要的 SYN **crucial**：*a critical factor in the election campaign* 竞选活动的关键因素 ◇ *Reducing levels of carbon dioxide in the atmosphere is **of critical importance**.* 减少大气层中的二氧化碳含量极其重要。◇ *Your decision is **critical to** our future.* 你的决定对我们的将来至关重要。 ⊃ SYNONYMS AT ESSENTIAL
- **SERIOUS/DANGEROUS** 严重；危险 **3** 🔑 serious, uncertain and possibly dangerous 安危攸关的；危急的：*The first 24 hours after the operation are the most critical.* 病人手术后头 24 小时是最危险的。◇ *a critical moment in our country's history* 我国历史上的一个危急关头 ◇ *One of the victims of the fire remains **in a critical condition**.* 大火的一位受害者依然病情危急。 ⊃ SEE ALSO CRISIS
- **MAKING CAREFUL JUDGEMENTS** 审慎判断 **4** 🔑 involving making fair, careful judgements about the good and bad qualities of sb/sth 有判断力的；判断公正（或审慎）的：*Students are encouraged to develop critical thinking instead of accepting opinions without questioning them.* 鼓励学生培养批判性思维，而非不加质疑地接受观点。
- **OF ART/MUSIC/BOOKS, ETC.** 艺术、音乐、书等 **5** [only before noun] according to the judgement of critics of art, music, literature, etc. 根据（艺术、音乐、文学等）评论家的：*the film director's greatest critical success* 那位电影导演从评论界获得的最大成功 ◇ *In her day she never received the **critical acclaim*** (= praise from the critics) *she deserved.* 她在世时从未从评论家处获得她应得的赞扬。

▶ **crit·ic·al·ly** /-ɪkli/ *adv.*：*She spoke critically of her father.* 她谈到父亲时颇有微词。◇ *He is **critically ill** in intensive care.* 他病得很重，正处于特护之中。◇ *I looked at myself critically in the mirror.* 我对着镜子，挑剔地打量着自己。

ˌcritical ˈmass *noun* [U, sing.] **1** (*physics* 物) the smallest amount of a substance that is needed for a nuclear CHAIN REACTION to take place（核链式反应的）临界质量 **2** the minimum amount of resources, number of customers, etc. needed to start or support a project or an activity, or the minimum size that a project or activity needs to be in order to be successful（启动或支持项目或活动所需的）最小资源量，最低人数；（项目或活动成功所需的）最小规模：*The company needs one million customers to reach critical mass and start making a profit.* 公司需要 100 万客户才能达到临界规模并开始赢利。◇ *TV via Internet could only be developed once a critical mass of households had broadband access.* 在足够多的家庭拥有宽带接入时，网络电视才能开发。

ˌcritical ˈpath *noun* [sing.] (*specialist*) the order of work that should be followed to complete a project as fast and as cheaply as possible（又快又省完成项目必须遵循的）关键路径

ˌcritical ˈtheory *noun* [U] a way of thinking about and examining culture and literature by considering the social, historical and IDEOLOGICAL forces that affect it and make it the way it is 批判理论，批评理论（从社会、历史及意识形态所产生的影响出发，思考和探讨文化和文学）

ˌcritical ˈthinking *noun* [U] the process of analysing information in an objective way, in order to make a judgement about it 批判性思维；批判性思考：***Critical thinking skills*** *enable students to evaluate information.* 批判性思维能力使学生能够对信息作出评估。

criti·cism 🔑 /ˈkrɪtɪsɪzəm/ *noun* **1** 🔑 [U, C] the act of expressing disapproval of sb/sth and opinions about their faults or bad qualities; a statement showing disapproval 批评；批判；责备；指责：*The plan has attracted criticism from consumer groups.* 这项计划引起了各消费者组织的指责。◇ *People in public life must always be **open to criticism*** (= willing to accept being criticized). 公众人物必须随时准备接受批评。◇ *Ben is very sensitive, he just can't **take criticism**.* 本很敏感，就是接受不了批评。◇ *to offer sb **constructive criticism*** (= that is meant to be helpful) 给某人提出建设性的批评意见 ◇ *I didn't mean it as a criticism.* 我没有要责备的意思。◇ ***criticisms levelled at*** (= aimed at) *journalists* 针对记者的批评 ◇ **~ of sb/sth** *There was **widespread criticism** of the government's handling of the disaster.* 政府对灾难的处理方式遭到了普遍的批评。◇ **~ that…** *My only criticism of the house is that it is on a main road.* 我对这座房子唯一的不满是它处于一条大路上。 OPP **praise** **2** 🔑 [U] the work or activity of making fair, careful judgements about the good and bad qualities of sb/sth, especially books, music, etc.（尤指对书、音乐等的）评论文章，评论：*literary criticism* 文学批评

criti·cize 🔑 (*BrE also* **-ise**) /ˈkrɪtɪsaɪz/ *verb* **1** 🔑 [I, T] to say that you disapprove of sb/sth; to say what you do not like or think is wrong about sb/sth 批评；批判；挑剔；指责：*All you ever do is criticize!* 你就只知道批评！◇ **~ sb/sth** *The decision was criticized by environmental groups.* 这个决定受到了环保团体的批评。◇ **~ sb/sth for sth** *The government has been criticized for not taking the problem seriously.* 政府因没有认真对待这个问题而受到指责。 OPP **praise** **2** 🔑 [T] **~ sth** to judge the good and bad qualities of sth 评论；评价：*We were taught how to criticize poems.* 我们学习了怎样评论诗歌。

cri·tique /krɪˈtiːk/ *noun, verb*

- ***noun*** a piece of written criticism of a set of ideas, a work of art, etc. 评论；评论文章：*a feminist critique of Freud's theories* 从女权主义的角度对弗洛伊德理论所作的批评
- ***verb*** **~ sth** to write or give your opinion of, or reaction to, a set of ideas, a work of art, etc. 写评论；对…发表评论；评判：*Her job involves critiquing designs by fashion students.* 她的工作包括评判时装专业学生的设计。

crit·ter /ˈkrɪtə(r)/ *noun* (*NAmE, informal*) a living creature 生物：*wild critters* 野生的生物

croak /krəʊk; *NAmE* kroʊk/ *verb, noun*

- ***verb*** **1** [I] to make a rough low sound, like the sound a FROG makes 发出（像青蛙的）低沉沙哑声；呱呱地叫 **2** [I, T] to speak or say sth with a rough low voice 用低沉而沙哑的声音说话：*I had a sore throat and could only croak.* 我喉咙痛，只能哑着嗓子说话。◇ **~ sth** *He managed to croak a greeting.* 他勉强用沙哑的嗓音打招呼。◇ **+ speech** *'I'm fine,' she croaked.* "我没事。" 她哑着嗓子说。**3** [I] (*slang*) to die 死；咽气
- ***noun*** a rough low sound made in the throat, like the sound made by a FROG（像青蛙发出的）低沉沙哑的声音，呱呱的叫声

croaky /ˈkrəʊki; *NAmE* ˈkroʊ-/ *adj.* (*informal*) (of sb's voice 嗓音) deep and rough, especially because of a sore throat（尤指因嗓子疼痛而）低沉沙哑的

croc /krɒk; *NAmE* krɑːk/ *noun* (*informal*) = CROCODILE

cro·chet /ˈkrəʊʃeɪ; *NAmE* kroʊˈʃeɪ/ *noun, verb*
■ ***noun*** [U] a way of making clothes, etc. from wool or cotton using a special thick needle with a hook at the end to make a pattern of connected threads 钩针编织 ➲ VISUAL VOCAB PAGE V45
■ ***verb*** (**cro·chet·ing**, **cro·cheted**) [T, I] ~ (**sth**) to make sth using crochet 用钩针编织：*a crocheted shawl* 钩针编织的披肩

crock /krɒk; *NAmE* krɑːk/ *noun* **1** **crocks** [pl.] (*old-fashioned*) cups, plates, dishes, etc. 陶器；瓦器 **2** [C] (*old use*) a large pot made of baked CLAY 瓦罐；坛子 **3** [C] (*BrE, informal*) an old person 老家伙；老朽的人 **4** [C] (*BrE, informal*) an old car in bad condition 破旧的汽车
IDM **a ˌcrock of ˈshit** (*taboo, slang, especially NAmE*) something that is not true 屁话；胡说八道 ➲ MORE AT GOLD *n.*

crocked /krɒkt; *NAmE* krɑːkt/ *adj.* [not before noun] (*NAmE, slang*) drunk 喝醉了；醉醺醺

crock·ery /ˈkrɒkəri; *NAmE* ˈkrɑːk-/ *noun* [U] **1** (*especially BrE*) plates, cups, dishes, etc. 陶器；瓦器 **2** (*NAmE*) dishes, etc. that you use in the oven（烤箱用的）碟，盘，杯，碗

croco·dile /ˈkrɒkədaɪl; *NAmE* ˈkrɑːk-/ (*also informal* **croc**) *noun* **1** [C] a large REPTILE with a long tail, hard skin and very big JAWS. Crocodiles live in rivers and lakes in hot countries. 鳄鱼 **2** [U] crocodile skin made into leather（做成皮革的）鳄鱼皮：*crocodile shoes* 鳄鱼皮皮鞋 **3** [C] (*BrE*) a long line of people, especially children, walking in pairs 成对纵列行进的人（尤指儿童）
IDM **ˈcrocodile tears** if sb SHEDS (= cries) **crocodile tears**, they pretend to be sad about sth, but they are not really sad at all 鳄鱼的眼泪；假慈悲

ˈcrocodile clip (*especially BrE*) (*also* **ˈalligator clip** *especially NAmE*) *noun* an object with sharp teeth used for holding things together, that is held closed by a spring and that you squeeze to open 鳄鱼嘴夹：*Use the crocodile clips to attach the cables to the battery.* 用鳄鱼嘴夹把电缆接到蓄电池上。

cro·cus /ˈkrəʊkəs; *NAmE* ˈkroʊ-/ *noun* a small yellow, purple or white flower that appears in early spring 番红花

croft /krɒft; *NAmE* krɔːft/ *noun* (*BrE*) a small farm or the house on it, especially in Scotland （尤指苏格兰的）小农场，小农场上的住宅

croft·er /ˈkrɒftə(r); *NAmE* ˈkrɔːft-/ *noun* (*BrE*) a person who rents or owns a small family farm, especially in Scotland（尤指苏格兰的）家庭小农场的佃户，家庭小农场主

Crohn's disease /ˈkrəʊnz dɪziːz; *NAmE* ˈkroʊnz/ *noun* [U] a disease affecting the lower INTESTINES, in which they develop many sore areas. The disease lasts for many years and is difficult to cure. 克罗恩病，局限性肠炎，节段性肠炎（引起大肠直肠多部位长年疼痛）

crois·sant /ˈkrwæsɒ̃; *NAmE* krwɑːˈsɑ̃ː; krəˈsɑːnt/ *noun* (*from French*) a small sweet roll with a curved shape, eaten especially at breakfast 羊角面包；新月形面包；牛角面包

crone /krəʊn; *NAmE* kroʊn/ *noun* (*literary*) an ugly old woman 丑陋的老太婆

crony /ˈkrəʊni; *NAmE* ˈkroʊni/ *noun* [usually pl.] (*pl.* **-ies**) (*often disapproving*) a person that sb spends a lot of time with 好友；密友：*He was playing cards with his cronies.* 他当时正与他那些狐朋狗友玩牌。

cro·ny·ism /ˈkrəʊniɪzəm; *NAmE* ˈkroʊ-/ *noun* [U] (*disapproving*) the situation in which people in power give jobs to their friends 任人唯亲；任用亲信

crook /krʊk/ *noun, verb, adj.*
■ ***noun*** **1** (*informal*) a dishonest person 骗子 SYN **criminal**: *That salesman is a real crook.* 那推销员真是个骗子。**2** ~ **of your arm/elbow** the place where your arm bends at the elbow 臂弯；肘弯 **3** a long stick with a hook at one end, used especially in the past by SHEPHERDS for catching sheep（尤指旧时牧羊人捕羊用的）曲柄杖 IDM SEE HOOK *n.*
■ ***verb*** ~ **sth** to bend your finger or arm 使（手指或手臂）弯曲
■ ***adj.*** [not usually before noun] (*AustralE, NZE, informal*) ill/sick 生病；有病；不舒服

crooked /ˈkrʊkɪd/ *adj.* **1** not in a straight line; bent or twisted 不直的；弯曲的；扭曲的：*a crooked nose/smile* 鹰钩鼻；不自然的微笑 ◇ *a village of crooked streets* 街道弯弯曲曲的村庄 ◇ *Your glasses are on crooked.* 你的眼镜歪了。OPP **straight** **2** dishonest 不诚实的；欺诈的：*a crooked businessman/deal* 奸商；不正当的交易 **3** ~ (**on sb**) (*AustralE, informal*) annoyed 生（某人的）气：*It's not you I'm* ***crooked on***, *it's him.* 我不是生你的气，是生他的气。➲ MORE LIKE THIS 22, page R27 ▸ **crook·ed·ly** *adv.*

croon /kruːn/ *verb* [T, I] ~ (**sth**) to sing sth quietly and gently 低声哼唱：*She gently crooned a lullaby.* 她轻声哼唱了一支摇篮曲。

croon·er /ˈkruːnə(r)/ *noun* (*old-fashioned*) a male singer who sings slow romantic songs（慢唱浪漫歌曲的）男歌手

crop 🔑 /krɒp; *NAmE* krɑːp/ *noun, verb*
■ ***noun***
• **PLANTS FOR FOOD** 庄稼 **1** 🔑 [C] a plant that is grown in large quantities, especially as food 庄稼；作物：*Sugar is an important crop on the island.* 糖料作物是这个岛上的一种重要作物。◇ ***crop rotation/production/yield*** 农作物轮作 / 生产 / 产量 ◇ *The crops are regularly sprayed with pesticides.* 农作物定期喷洒杀虫剂。➲ WORDFINDER NOTE AT FARM ➲ COLLOCATIONS AT FARMING ➲ VISUAL VOCAB PAGE V3 ➲ SEE ALSO CASH CROP

> **WORDFINDER** 联想词： blight, cereal, genetically modified, grain, harvest, monoculture, organic, staple, yield

2 🔑 [C] the amount of grain, fruit, etc. that is grown in one season（谷物、水果等一季的）收成，产量 SYN **harvest**: *a fall in this year's coffee crop* 今年咖啡产量的下降 ◇ *We are looking forward to a* ***bumper crop*** (= a very large one). 我们期盼着大丰收。
• **GROUP OF PEOPLE** 一群人 **3** [sing.] **a ~ of sth** a group of people who do sth at the same time; a number of things that happen at the same time（同时做某事的）一群人，一批人；（同时发生的）一些事情：*the current crop of trainees* 现在的这批实习生 ◇ *She is really* ***the cream of the crop*** (= the best in her group). 她的确是那批人中的精英。◇ ***a crop of disasters/injuries*** 一连串的灾难 / 伤害
• **WHIP** 鞭子 **4** [C] a short WHIP used by horse riders（骑手的）短马鞭：*a riding crop* 骑马用的短马鞭
• **HAIR** 头发 **5** [C] a very short HAIRSTYLE 短发 **6** [sing.] **a ~ of dark, fair, etc. hair/curls** hair that is short and thick 短而密的头发：*He had a thick crop of black curly hair.* 他有一头浓黑鬈曲的短发。
• **OF BIRD** 鸟 **7** (*specialist*) a part of a bird's throat shaped like a bag where food is stored before it passes into the stomach 嗉囊
■ ***verb*** (**-pp-**)
• **HAIR** 头发 **1** [T] ~ **sth** (+ **adj.**) to cut sb's hair very short 剪短：*closely cropped hair* 剪得很短的头发
• **PHOTOGRAPH** 照片 **2** [T] ~ **sth** (*specialist*) to cut off part of a photograph or picture 剪裁，裁切（照片或图画）
• **OF ANIMALS** 动物 **3** [T] ~ **sth** to bite off and eat the tops of plants, especially grass 啃吃（青草或其他植物上面的部分）
• **PLANTS** 植物 **4** [I] (of plants 植物) to produce a crop 有收成：*The potatoes cropped well this year.* 今年马铃薯丰收。**5** [T] ~ **sth** to use land to grow crops 种地；种庄稼：*The river valley is intensively cropped.* 河谷里种满了庄稼。
PHR V **ˌcrop ˈup** to appear or happen, especially when it is not expected（尤指意外地）出现，发生 SYN **come up**: *His name just cropped up in conversation.* 交谈时无意中就提到了他的名字。◇ *I'll be late—something's cropped up at home.* 我要晚一点来，家里突然出了点事。

ˈcrop circle (*also* **ˈcorn circle**) *noun* a round area in a field of crops that has suddenly become flat. Some people say that crop circles were made by creatures from outer space. 麦田圈（庄稼地里突然变平的一块圆形地，传说是外星生物所为）

'crop dusting *noun* [U] the practice of spraying crops with chemicals such as PESTICIDES from a plane 作物喷洒（用飞机给农作物喷洒农药等）

crop·per /ˈkrɒpə(r); *NAmE* ˈkrɑːp-/ *noun*
IDM **come a 'cropper** (*BrE, informal*) **1** (of a person 人) to fall over 跌倒；摔倒；栽跟头 **2** to have a failure or near disaster 失败；惨败：*We nearly came a cropper in the second half of the game.* 在比赛的下半场我们差一点就输掉了。

'crop top *noun* a woman's informal piece of clothing for the upper body, cut short so that the stomach can be seen（女式）露腹短上衣，露脐装

cro·quet /ˈkrəʊkeɪ; *NAmE* kroʊˈkeɪ/ *noun* [U] a game played on grass in which players use wooden hammers (called MALLETS) to knock wooden balls through a series of HOOPS (= curved wires) 槌球（在草地上进行，以木槌击木球穿过一连串的铁圈）

cro·quette /krəʊˈket; *NAmE* kroʊ-/ *noun* a small amount of MASHED potato, fish, etc., shaped into a ball or tube, covered with BREADCRUMBS and fried（用土豆泥、鱼馅等裹以面包屑做成的）炸丸子，炸条块

crore /krɔː(r)/ *number* (*plural verb* 复数动词) (*pl.* **crore** or **crores**) (*IndE*) ten million; one hundred LAKH 一千万

cro·sier (*also* **croz·ier**) /ˈkrəʊziə(r); *NAmE* ˈkroʊʒər/ *noun* a long stick, usually curved at one end, carried by a BISHOP (= a Christian priest of high rank) at religious ceremonies（主教的）牧杖，权杖

cross /krɒs; *NAmE* krɔːs/ *noun, verb, adj.*
■ *noun*
• **MARK ON PAPER** 纸上符号 **1** [C] a mark or an object formed by two lines crossing each other (× or +); the mark (×) is often used on paper to show sth 叉字形记号；十字形记号：*I've put a cross on the map to show where the hotel is.* 我已在地图上打叉标出了旅馆的位置。◇ *Put a tick if the answer is correct and a cross if it's wrong.* 答案正确打钩，错误打叉。◇ *Sign your name on the form where I've put a cross.* 在表格上我打叉的地方签上你的名字。◇ *Those who could not write signed with a cross.* 不会写字的人画十字代替签名。➲ SEE ALSO NOUGHTS AND CROSSES ➲ COMPARE TICK *n.* (1)
• **FOR PUNISHMENT** 惩罚 **2** [C] a long vertical piece of wood with a shorter piece across it near the top. In the past people were hung on crosses and left to die as a punishment.（旧时用以处死人的）十字架
• **CHRISTIAN SYMBOL** 基督教标记 **3 the Cross** [sing.] the cross that Jesus Christ died on, used as a symbol of Christianity（耶稣钉死在上面的）十字架 **4** [C] an object, a design, a piece of jewellery, etc. in the shape of a cross, used as a symbol of Christianity 十字架物品（或设计、首饰等）：*She wore a small gold cross on a chain around her neck.* 她脖子上戴了一条项链，上面挂着个金的小十字架。
• **MEDAL** 勋章 **5** (*usually* **Cross**) [C] a small decoration in the shape of a cross that is given to sb as an honour for doing sth very brave（表彰英勇行为的）十字勋章
• **MIXTURE** 混合物 **6** [C, usually sing.] ~ (**between A and B**) a mixture of two different things, breeds of animal, etc. 混合物；（动物等的）杂种，杂交品种：*The play was a cross between a farce and a tragedy.* 这出戏把闹剧和悲剧交织为一体。◇ *A mule is a cross between a horse and a donkey.* 骡是马和驴杂交的产物。➲ SEE ALSO HYBRID
• **IN SPORT** 体育运动 **7** [C] (in football (SOCCER) or HOCKEY 足球或曲棍球) a kick or hit of the ball across the field rather than up or down it 横传 ➲ SEE ALSO RED CROSS
IDM **have a (heavy) 'cross to bear** to have a difficult problem that makes you worried or unhappy but that you have to deal with 有本难念的经；有苦难要忍受：*We all have our crosses to bear.* 家家有本难念的经。
■ *verb*
• **GO/PUT ACROSS** 穿越；使交叉 **1** [I, T] to go across; to pass or stretch from one side to the other 穿越；越过；横过；渡过：~ (**over**) *I waved and she crossed over* (= crossed the road towards me). 我挥了挥手，她便横穿马路朝我走来。◇ ~ (**over**) (**from…**) (**to/into…**) *We crossed from Dover to Calais.* 我们从多佛尔横渡到加来。◇ ~ **sth** *to cross a/the road* 横穿道路 ◇ *to cross the sea/mountains* 越过大海；翻越高山 ◇ *to cross France by train* 乘火车穿越法国 ◇ *The bridge crosses the River Dee.* 这座桥横跨迪河。◇ *A look of annoyance* ***crossed her face.*** 恼怒的神色从她脸上掠过。◇ *They crossed the finishing line together* (= in a race). 他们同时越过终点线。◇ ~ **over sth** *He crossed over the road and joined me.* 他穿过马路和我会合。 **2** [I] to pass across each other 交叉；相交：*The roads cross just outside the town.* 这些道路正好在城外交叉。◇ *The straps cross over at the back and are tied at the waist.* 带子在背后交叉，然后系在腰部。◇ *Our letters must have crossed in the mail* (= each was sent before the other was received). 我们的信一定是在路上相互错过了。◇ *We seem to have a* ***crossed line*** (= a telephone call that interrupts another call because of a wrong connection). 我们的电话好像串线了。 **3** [T] ~ **sth** to put or place sth across or over sth else 使交叉；使交叠：*to* ***cross your arms/legs*** (= place one arm or leg over the other) 交叉两臂 / 双腿 ◇ *She sat with her legs crossed.* 她跷着二郎腿坐着。◇ *a flag with a design of two crossed keys* 有两把钥匙交叉图案的旗帜
• **OPPOSE** 反对 **4** [T] ~ **sb** to oppose sb or speak against them or their plans or wishes 反对，反驳，否定（某人或计划、意愿）：*She's really nice until you cross her.* 她待人确实很好，除非你跟她作对。◇ (*literary*) *He had been* ***crossed in love*** (= the person he loved was not faithful to him). 他所爱的人背叛了他。
• **MIX ANIMALS/PLANTS** 杂交 **5** [T] ~ **A with B** | ~ **A and B** to make two different types of animal breed together; to mix two types of plant to form a new one 使杂交；使异种交配：*A mule is the product of a horse crossed with a donkey.* 骡是马和驴杂交的产物。◇ (*figurative*) *He behaved like an army officer crossed with a professor.* 他的举止既像军官又像教授。
• **IN SPORT** 体育运动 **6** [I] (in football (SOCCER) or HOCKEY 足球或曲棍球) to kick or pass a ball sideways across the field 横传
• **DRAW LINE** 画线 **7** [T] ~ **sth** to draw a line across sth 画横线于：*to cross your t's* (= the letters in writing) 写 t 上面的一横 ◇ (*BrE*) *to cross a cheque* (= to draw two lines across it so that it can only be paid through a bank account) 在支票上画线（使支票只能经银行账户兑现）
• **MAKE CHRISTIAN SYMBOL** 做基督教的标记 **8** [T] ~ **yourself** to make the sign of the cross (= the Christian symbol) on your chest（在胸口上）画十字圣号
IDM **cross your 'fingers** to hope that your plans will be successful (sometimes putting one finger across another as a sign of hoping for good luck) 祈求成功（有时使手指交叉为祈求好运的手势）：*I'm crossing my fingers that my proposal will be accepted.* 但愿我的建议能被采纳。◇ *Keep your fingers crossed!* 祈求好运吧！ **cross my 'heart (and hope to die)** (*informal*) used to emphasize that you are telling the truth or will do what you promise 我发誓（否则不得好死）：*I saw him do it—cross my heart.* 我看见是他干的，我可以发誓。 **cross your 'mind** (of thoughts, etc. 想法等) to come into your mind 掠过心头；出现在脑海 **SYN** **occur to sb**: *It never crossed my mind that she might lose* (= I was sure that she would win). 我从来没想过她会失败。 **ˌcross sb's ˌpalm with 'silver** to give sb money so that they will do you a favour, especially tell your FORTUNE 为得到好处而给某人钱；（尤指）付钱请人算命 **ˌcross sb's 'path | people's ˌpaths 'cross** if sb crosses sb's path or their paths cross, they meet by chance 偶然相遇；不期而遇；邂逅：*I hope I never cross her path again.* 但愿我永远不再碰见她。◇ *Our paths were to cross again many years later.* 许多年以后我们又不期而遇了。 **cross 'swords (with sb)** to fight or argue with sb（与某人）交锋，争论 **cross that bridge when you 'come to it** to worry about a problem when it actually happens and not before 临机应变（不用事前操心）➲ MORE AT DOT *v.*, WIRE *n.*
PHR V **ˌcross sb/sth↔'off | ˌcross sb/sth 'off sth** to draw a line through a person's name or an item on a list

because they/it is no longer required or involved（从名单或清单上）画掉，删掉：*We can cross his name off; he's not coming.* 他不来了，我们可以把他的名字画掉了。

ˌ**cross sth**↔ˈ**out/ˈthrough** to draw a line through a word, usually because it is wrong 画掉，删掉（错字）

ˌ**cross ˈover (to/into sth)** to move or change from one type of culture, music, political party, etc. to another（从某种文化、音乐、政党等）转变，变换：*a cult movie that has crossed over to mass appeal* 由部分人推崇转变为大众喜爱的电影 ➲ RELATED NOUN CROSSOVER

■ **adj.** (**cross·er, cross·est**) ~ (**with sb**) (*especially BrE*) annoyed or quite angry 恼怒的；十分愤怒的；生气的：*I was cross with him for being late.* 我因他迟到而十分生气。◇ *Please don't* **get cross**. *Let me explain.* 请别发火，让我来解释一下。➲ SYNONYMS AT ANGRY ▶ **cross·ly** *adv.*：*'Well what did you expect?' she said crossly.* "咳，你还想怎么着？"她气愤地说。

cross- /krɒs; *NAmE* krɔːs/ *combining form* (in nouns, verbs, adjectives and adverbs 构成名词、动词、形容词和副词) involving movement or action from one thing to another or between two things 从一事物到另一事物的运动（或动作）；两事物间的运动（或动作）；横过；穿越：*cross-Channel ferries* 横渡英吉利海峡的渡船 ◇ *cross-fertilize* 异花授粉 ◇ *crossfire* 交叉火力

cross·bar /ˈkrɒsbɑː(r); *NAmE* ˈkrɔːs-/ *noun* **1** the bar joining the two vertical posts of a goal（足球球门的）横梁 ➲ VISUAL VOCAB PAGE V48 **2** the bar between the seat and the HANDLEBARS of a man's bicycle（自行车的）横梁 ➲ VISUAL VOCAB PAGE V55

ˈ**cross-bencher** *noun* (*BrE*) a member of the British House of Lords who does not belong to a particular political party（英国上议院的）无党派议员，中立议员 ▶ ˈ**cross benches** *noun* [pl.]: *members who sit on the cross benches* 坐在中立议员席的议员

cross·bones /ˈkrɒsbəʊnz; *NAmE* ˈkrɔːsboʊnz/ *noun* [pl.] ➲ SKULL AND CROSSBONES

ˈ**cross-border** *adj.* [only before noun] involving activity across a border between two countries 跨越国境的：*a cross-border raid by guerrillas* 游击队越过国境的袭击 ➲ WORDFINDER NOTE AT ALLY

cross·bow /ˈkrɒsbəʊ; *NAmE* ˈkrɔːsboʊ/ *noun* a weapon which consists of a BOW² *n.* (1) that is fixed onto a larger piece of wood, and that shoots short heavy arrows (called BOLTS) 弩；弩弓；十字弓 ➲ PICTURE AT BOLT

ˈ**cross-breed** *verb, noun*

■ **verb** [T, I] ~ (**sth**) to make an animal or a plant breed with a different breed; to breed with an animal or a plant of a different breed 使杂交；杂交繁育：*cross-bred sheep* 杂交羊 ▶ ˌ**cross-ˈbreeding** *noun* [U]

■ **noun** an animal or a plant that is a result of cross-breeding 杂交品种（动物或植物）➲ COMPARE HYBRID (1)

ˌ**cross-ˈcheck** *verb* to make sure that information, figures, etc. are correct by using a different method or system to check them（用不同的方法或系统）核查，核对；交叉检查：~ **sth** *Cross-check your answers with a calculator.* 用计算器核对一下你的答案。◇ ~ **sth against sth** *Baggage should be cross-checked against the names of individual passengers.* 必须再把行李与各位旅客的姓名核对一遍。▶ ˈ**cross-check** *noun*

ˌ**cross-contam·iˈn·ation** *noun* [U] the process by which harmful bacteria spread from one substance to another（病菌的）交叉污染

ˌ**cross-ˈcountry** *adj., adv., noun*

■ **adj.** [usually before noun], **adv.** **1** across fields or open country rather than on roads or a track 越野（的）：*cross-country running* 越野赛跑 ◇ *We rode cross-country.* 我们驾车越野前行。**2** from one part of a country to the other, especially not using main roads or routes（尤指通过越野）横越全国（的）：*cross-country train journeys* 穿越全国的火车旅行 **3** involving two or more countries 跨国的；多国的：*The report contains the findings of a cross-country comparison of crime statistics.* 这份报告包含犯罪数据跨国比较的调查结果。

■ **noun** **1** **the cross-country** [sing.] a cross-country running or SKIING race 越野赛跑；越野滑雪比赛 **2** [U] the sport of running or SKIING across country 越野赛跑运动；越野滑雪运动 ➲ COMPARE DOWNHILL *n.*

ˌ**cross-country ˈskiing** *noun* [U] the sport of SKIING across the countryside, rather than down mountains 越野滑雪（与高山滑雪相对）➲ VISUAL VOCAB PAGE V52

ˌ**cross-ˈcultural** *adj.* involving or containing ideas from two or more different countries or cultures 跨文化的；涉及多种文化的

ˈ**cross-current** *noun* **1** a current of water in a river or in the sea that flows across the main current（穿过河流或海域主流的）交叉水流 **2** [usually pl.] (*formal*) a set of beliefs or ideas that are different from others, especially from those that most people hold 岔流思想（尤指与多数人不同的信仰、观点或看法）

ˌ**cross-curˈricu·lar** *adj.* (*BrE*) affecting or connected with different parts of the school CURRICULUM 跨课程的；与多种课程有关的

ˌ**cross-ˈdressing** *noun* [U] the practice of wearing clothes usually worn by a person of the opposite sex, especially for sexual pleasure（尤指为得到性快感而）穿异性服装 SYN transvestism ▶ ˌ**cross-ˈdresser** *noun*

ˌ**cross-eˈxamine** *verb* ~ **sb** to question sb carefully and in a lot of detail about answers that they have already given, especially in court（尤指在法庭上对证词细节的）盘问，反诘：*The witness was cross-examined for over two hours.* 那位证人被盘问了两个多小时。➲ COLLOCATIONS AT JUSTICE ▶ ˌ**cross-eˌxamiˈn·ation** *noun* [U, C]: *He broke down* **under cross-examination** (= while he was being cross-examined) *and admitted his part in the assault.* 他经不起严密的诘问，招认了他曾参与那次殴打。

ˌ**cross-ˈeyed** *adj.* having one or both eyes looking towards the nose 内斜视的；对眼的；斗鸡眼的

ˌ**cross-ˈfertil·ize** (*BrE also* **-ise**) *verb* **1** ~ **sth** (*biology* 生) to FERTILIZE a plant using POLLEN from a different plant of the same SPECIES 异花授粉 **2** ~ **sth** to help sth develop in a useful or positive way by mixing ideas from a different area 吸收其他领域的思想以促发展：*The study of psychology has recently been widely cross-fertilized by new discoveries in genetics.* 心理学研究最近从遗传学的新发现中受益匪浅。▶ ˌ**cross-ˌfertil·iˈza·tion, -iˈsa·tion** *noun* [U, sing.]

cross·fire /ˈkrɒsfaɪə(r); *NAmE* ˈkrɔːs-/ *noun* [U] the firing of guns from two or more directions at the same time, so that the bullets cross 交叉火力：*The doctor was killed in crossfire as he went to help the wounded.* 那位医生去救助伤员时在交叉火力中丧生。◇ (*figurative*) *When two industrial giants clash, small companies can get* **caught in the crossfire** (= become involved and suffer as a result). 两工业巨头交火时，小公司难免遭殃。

ˈ**cross-hatch** *verb* ~ **sth** (*specialist*) to mark or colour sth with two sets of parallel lines crossing each other 用交叉的平行线画出（或着色）；交叉排线 ▶ ˈ**cross-hatching** *noun* [U]

ˈ**cross head** *noun* a screw with a cross shape in the top 十字头螺钉

ˈ**cross-infection** *noun* [U] (*medical* 医) an occasion when sb passes an infection to sb who has a different infection 交叉感染

cross·ing /ˈkrɒsɪŋ; *NAmE* ˈkrɔːs-/ *noun* **1** a place where you can safely cross a road, a river, etc., or from one country to another（通过道路、河流等的）安全通行处；人行横道；渡口；（从一国到另一国的）过境处：*The child was killed when a car failed to stop at the crossing.* 汽车在人行横道线未能停车，结果把小孩撞死了。◇ *The next crossing point is a long way downstream.* 下一个渡口在下游方向很远的地方。◇ *He was arrested by guards at the border crossing.* 他在边境过境处被卫兵逮捕。➲ SEE ALSO LEVEL CROSSING, PEDESTRIAN CROSSING, PELICAN

CROSSING, ZEBRA CROSSING **2** a place where two lines, two roads or two tracks cross（线的）交叉点；（道路的）十字路口；（轨道的）交叉道口 SYN **intersection** **3** a journey across a sea or a wide river（海洋或宽阔江河的）横渡：*a three-hour ferry crossing* 三小时的轮渡 ◇ *a rough crossing from Dover to Calais* 从多佛尔到加来波涛汹涌的横渡 ◇ *the first Atlantic crossing* 首次横渡大西洋 **4** an act of going from one side to another 穿越；横越：*attempted crossings of the border* 穿越边境未遂

cross-legged /ˌkrɒs ˈlegd; ˈlegɪd; *NAmE* ˌkrɔːs/ *adv.* sitting on the floor with your legs pulled up in front of you and with one leg or foot over the other 盘腿 ▸ **cross-legged** *adj.*：*the cross-legged figure of the Hindu god* 盘腿打坐的印度教神像

cross·over /ˈkrɒsəʊvə(r); *NAmE* ˈkrɔːsoʊ-/ *noun* the process or result of changing from one area of activity or style of doing sth to another（活动范围或风格的）改变，转型，变化：*The album was an exciting jazz-pop crossover.* 这张唱片中收集了爵士乐与流行音乐两种风格相结合的精彩作品。

cross·piece /ˈkrɒspiːs; *NAmE* ˈkrɔːs-/ *noun* (*specialist*) a piece of a structure or a tool that lies or is fixed across another piece 横档；横杆

ˌcross-ˈplatform *adj.* (of a computer program or an electronic device 计算机程序或电子仪器) that can be used with different types of computers or programs 交叉平台的，跨平台的（能兼容不同类型的计算机或程序）

ˌcross-ˈpollin·ate *verb* **~ sth** (*biology* 生) to move POLLEN from a flower or plant onto another flower or plant so that it produces seeds 使异花传粉；为（植物）异花授粉 ▸ **ˌcross-polliˈn·ation** *noun* [U]

ˌcross ˈpost *noun* (*also* **cross-post**) a message, an image, an article, etc. that has been put at two or more online locations 跨页贴出的信息（或图像、文章等）；跨版多贴文：*I ran a cross post from the site.* 我从该网站转发了一篇文章。◇ *One of your cross-posts sparked a debate.* 你转发的一个帖子引发了论战。

ˌcross-ˈpost *verb* [T, I] to put a message, an image, an article, etc. at two or more online locations 跨页发表；跨页张贴；交叉发布；跨版多贴：*You can cross-post items from/to your own blog.* 你可以跨页张贴自己博客里的内容 / 把内容转贴到自己的博客。

ˌcross-proˈmotion *noun* [C, U] (*business* 商) a set of advertisements or other activities that are designed to help a company sell two different products, or to help two companies sell their products or services together 交叉推销（同时推销一个公司的两种商品或两个公司的产品或服务）

ˌcross ˈpurposes *noun* [pl.] if two people are **at cross purposes**, they do not understand each other because they are talking about or aiming at different things, without realizing it（由于谈论或针对不同事情而未意识到的）相互不理解，相互误解：*I think we're talking at cross purposes; that's not what I meant at all.* 我想我们是说到两下里去了，我根本不是那个意思。

ˌcross-ˈquestion *verb* **~ sb** to question sb thoroughly and often in a way that seems aggressive 盘问；追问

ˌcross-reˈfer *verb* (**-rr-**) [T, I] **~ (sth) to sth** to refer to another text or part of a text, especially to give more information about sth 给…注相互参照项；将…指向参照项；交互参照：*The entry for 'polygraph' is cross-referred to the entry for 'lie detector'.* 词条 polygraph 注有指向词条 lie detector 的参照项。

ˌcross ˈreference *noun* **~ (to sth)** a note that tells a reader to look in another part of a book or file for further information（指向…的）参见项；交互参照

cross·roads /ˈkrɒsrəʊdz; *NAmE* ˈkrɔːsroʊdz/ *noun* (*pl.* **cross·roads**) a place where two roads meet and cross each other 十字路口：*At the next crossroads, turn right.* 在下一个十字路口向右拐。◇ (*figurative*) *He has reached a career crossroads* (= he must decide which way to go next in his career). 他的事业发展到了一个十字路口。➲ SEE ALSO INTERSECTION (1), JUNCTION (1)
IDM **at a/the ˈcrossroads** at an important point in sb's life or development（人生或发展）处于关键时刻，在紧要关头

ˈcross section *noun* **1** [C, U] what you see when you cut through the middle of sth so that you can see the different layers it is made of; a drawing of this view 横截面（图）；剖面（图）；断面（图）：*a diagram representing a cross section of the human eye* 表现人眼的剖面图 ◇ *the human eye* **in cross section** 人眼的剖面图 **2** [C, usually sing.] a group of people or things that are typical of a larger group 典型的一群人（或事物）：*a representative cross section of society* 一群具有代表性的社会典型人物

ˌcross-ˈselling *noun* [U] (*business* 商) the activity of selling a different extra product to a customer who is already buying a product from a company 交叉销售（向现有顾客推销另一产品）

ˈcross street *noun* (*NAmE*) a street that crosses another street 交叉的街；十字街

cross·talk /ˈkrɒstɔːk; *NAmE* ˈkrɔːs-/ *noun* [U] (*specialist*) a situation in which a communications system is picking up the wrong signals（通信系统的）串扰，串音

cross·town /ˌkrɒsˈtaʊn; *NAmE* ˌkrɔːs-/ *adj.* (*NAmE*) going from one side of a town or city to the other 穿过市镇的：*a crosstown bus* 穿越市区的公共汽车

ˈcross-trainer *noun* **1** a piece of exercise equipment that you use standing up, with parts that you push up and down with your feet and parts that you hold onto and push with your arms 多功能健身器 **2** a type of sports shoe that can be worn for more than one kind of sport 多功能运动鞋

ˈcross-training *noun* [U] the activity of training in sports other than your main sport in order to make yourself fitter and able to do your main sport better 交叉训练（同时参加多项运动训练提高身体素质，进而提高自己在主项上的竞技水平）

cross·walk /ˈkrɒswɔːk; *NAmE* ˈkrɔːs-/ (*NAmE*) (*BrE* **peˌdestrian ˈcrossing**) *noun* a part of a road where vehicles must stop to allow people to cross 人行横道；行人穿越道 ➲ VISUAL VOCAB PAGE V3 ➲ SEE ALSO ZEBRA CROSSING

cross·wind /ˈkrɒswɪnd; *NAmE* ˈkrɔːs-/ *noun* a wind that is blowing across the direction that you are moving in 侧风

cross·wise /ˈkrɒswaɪz; *NAmE* ˈkrɔːs-/ *adv.* **1** across, especially from one corner to the opposite one 横过地；贯穿地；（尤指）对角横穿地，斜穿地：*Cut the fabric crosswise.* 把那块布对角剪开。**2** in the form of a cross 成十字地；交叉地

cross·word /ˈkrɒswɜːd; *NAmE* ˈkrɔːswɜːrd/ (*also* **ˈcrossword puzzle**) *noun* a game in which you have to fit words across and downwards into spaces with numbers in a square diagram. You find the words by solving CLUES. 纵横字谜；纵横填字游戏：*to* **do a/the crossword** 做纵横填字游戏 ◇ *I've finished the crossword apart from 3 across and 10 down.* 这份纵横字谜除横 3 竖 10 以外我都填完了。➲ VISUAL VOCAB PAGE V43

crotch /krɒtʃ; *NAmE* krɑːtʃ/ (*also* **crutch**) *noun* **1** the part of the body where the legs join at the top, including the area around the GENITALS（人体的）胯部，两腿分叉处 **2** the part of a pair of trousers/pants, etc. that covers the crotch 裤裆：*There's a hole in the crotch.* 裤裆上有个洞。

crot·chet /ˈkrɒtʃɪt; *NAmE* ˈkrɑːtʃ-/ (*BrE*) (*NAmE* **ˈquarter note**) *noun* (*music* 音) a note that lasts half as long as a MINIM/HALF NOTE 四分音符 ➲ PICTURE AT MUSIC

crot·chety /ˈkrɒtʃəti; *NAmE* ˈkrɑːtʃ-/ *adj.* (*informal*) bad-tempered; easily made angry 脾气坏的；易怒的；动辄生气的：*He was tired and crotchety.* 他累了，动不动就发火。

C

crotch·less /ˈkrɒtʃləs; *NAmE* ˈkrɑːtʃ-/ *adj.* (of underwear 内衣) having a hole at the CROTCH 开裆的；无裆的

crouch /kraʊtʃ/ *verb, noun*
■ *verb* [I] (+ **adv./prep.**) to put your body close to the ground by bending your legs under you 蹲；蹲下；蹲伏 SYN **squat**: *He crouched down beside her.* 他在她的旁边蹲了下来。◇ *Doyle crouched behind a hedge.* 多伊尔蹲在篱笆后面。 ▶ **crouched** *adj.*: *She sat crouched in a corner.* 她蹲坐在一个角落里。
PHR V **ˈcrouch over sb/sth** to bend over sb/sth so that you are very close to them or it 俯身接近: *He crouched over the papers on his desk.* 他俯身看他桌上的文件。
■ *noun* [sing.] a crouching position 蹲着的姿势: *She dropped to a crouch.* 她俯身蹲了下来。

croup /kruːp/ *noun* [U] a disease of children that makes them cough a lot and have difficulty breathing 哮吼（儿童疾病，咳得厉害，呼吸困难）

croup·ier /ˈkruːpieɪ; *NAmE also* -piər/ *noun* a person whose job is to be in charge of a gambling table and collect and pay out money, give out cards, etc.（负责收付钱、发牌等的）赌台管理员，赌台主持人 ➲ WORDFINDER NOTE AT GAMBLING

crou·ton /ˈkruːtɒn; *NAmE* -tɑːn/ *noun* a small piece of cold crisp fried bread served in soup or as part of a salad（放在汤或色拉里的）油炸面包丁

Crow /krəʊ; *NAmE* kroʊ/ *noun* (*pl.* **Crow** or **Crows**) a member of a Native American people, many of whom live in the US state of Montana 克劳人（美洲土著，很多居于美国蒙大拿州）

crow /krəʊ; *NAmE* kroʊ/ *noun, verb*
■ *noun* **1** a large bird, completely or mostly black, with a rough unpleasant cry 乌鸦 **2** a sound like that of a COCK/ROOSTER crowing（像雄鸡的）啼叫声，喔喔叫声: *She gave a little crow of triumph.* 她轻轻地发出了胜利的欢呼声。
IDM **as the ˈcrow flies** in a straight line 成直线地；笔直地: *The villages are no more than a mile apart as the crow flies.* 这些村庄直线距离相隔不超过一英里。➲ MORE AT EAT, STONE *v.*
■ *verb* **1** [I] (of a COCK/ROOSTER 雄鸡) to make repeated loud high sounds, especially early in the morning（尤指在清晨）啼叫，打鸣 **2** [I, T] (*disapproving*) to talk too proudly about sth you have achieved, especially when sb else has been unsuccessful（尤指在其他人不成功时）扬扬自得地夸口，自鸣得意 SYN **boast, gloat**: ~ (**about/over sth**) *He won't stop crowing about his victory.* 他滔滔不绝地夸耀自己的胜利。◇ + **speech** *'I've won, I've won!' she crowed.* "我赢了，我赢了！" 她得意忘形地叫道。◇ ~ **that…** *He crowed that they had sold out in one day.* 他扬扬得意地炫耀他们一天内就全部售完了。**3** [I] (*BrE*) (of a baby 婴儿) to make happy sounds 欢叫

crow·bar /ˈkrəʊbɑː(r); *NAmE* ˈkroʊ-/ *noun* a straight iron bar, usually with a curved end, used for forcing open boxes and moving heavy objects 铁撬棍

crowd 🔑 /kraʊd/ *noun, verb*
■ *noun* **1** 🔑 [C+sing./pl. v.] a large number of people gathered together in a public place, for example in the streets or at a sports game 人群；观众: *He pushed his way through the crowd.* 他在人群中往前挤。◇ *A small crowd had gathered outside the church.* 一小群人聚集在教堂的外面。◇ *Police had to break up the crowd.* 警方不得不驱散人群。◇ *Crowds of people poured into the street.* 人们成群结队涌上街头。◇ *I want to get there early to avoid the crowds.* 我想早点儿赶到那里，免得拥挤。◇ *The match attracted a capacity crowd of 80 000.* 这场比赛爆满，吸引了 8 万名观众。◇ *The crowd cheered the winning hit.* 观众为那决胜的一击而欢呼。◇ *crowd control* 人群控制 ◇ *crowd trouble* 群众闹事 ◇ *A whole crowd of us (= a lot of us) are going to the ball.* 我们一大帮人要去参加舞会。◇ *He left the hotel surrounded by crowds of journalists.* 他在大群记者的包围下离开了酒店。 **2** [C+sing./pl. v.] (*informal, often disapproving*) a particular group of people 一伙人；一帮人: *Bob introduced her to some of the usual crowd* (= people who often meet each other). 鲍勃把她介绍给常见面的几个朋友。◇ *the bright young theatrical crowd* 这帮年轻聪明的戏剧演员 **3 the crowd** [sing.] (*sometimes disapproving*) ordinary people, not special or unusual in any way 群众；民众；老百姓；凡夫俗子: *We all like to think we **stand out from the crowd*** (= are different from and better than other people). 我们都喜欢认为自己胜人一筹。◇ *He prefers to be **one of the crowd**.* 他宁愿做个凡夫俗子。◇ *She's quite happy to **follow the crowd**.* 她就愿意随大溜。
■ *verb* **1** ~ **sth** to fill a place so there is little room to move 挤满；塞满；使…拥挤: *Thousands of people crowded the narrow streets.* 成千上万的人把狭窄的街道挤得水泄不通。 **2** ~ **sth** to fill your mind so that you can think of nothing else 涌上（心头）；涌入（脑海）: *Memories crowded his mind.* 往事涌上他的心头。 **3** ~ **sb** (*informal*) to stand very close to sb so that they feel uncomfortable or nervous 挤，靠近，挤在一旁（以致使人不舒服或紧张）
PHR V **ˌcrowd aˈround/ˈround (sb/sth)** to gather in large numbers around sb/sth 聚集在…周围；聚拢: *We all crowded around the stove to keep warm.* 我们都挤在炉边取暖。◇ *Photographers were crowding around outside.* 摄影师聚集在外面。 **ˌcrowd ˈin (on sb) | ˌcrowd ˈinto sth** (of thoughts, questions, etc. 想法、问题等) to fill your mind so that you can think of nothing else 涌上（心头）；涌入（脑海）: *Too many uncomfortable thoughts were crowding in on her.* 她心乱如麻。◇ *Memories came crowding into her mind.* 往事一齐涌上她的心头。 **ˌcrowd ˈinto/ˈonto sth | ˌcrowd ˈin** to move in large numbers into a small space 大批涌入（狭小的空间）: *We all crowded into her office to sing 'Happy Birthday'.* 我们全都涌进她的办公室，唱"祝你生日快乐"。 **ˌcrowd sb/sth ˈinto/ˈonto sth | ˌcrowd sb/sth ˈin** to put many people or things into a small space 把…装满（或塞满）: *Guests were crowded into the few remaining rooms.* 客人都给塞进了剩下的几个房间。 **ˌcrowd sb/sth ˈout** to fill a place so that other people or things are kept out 把（其他人或物）排挤在外

crowd·ed 🔑 /ˈkraʊdɪd/ *adj.* ~ (**with sth**) **1** 🔑 having a lot of people or too many people 人（太）多的；拥挤的: *crowded streets* 拥挤的街道 ◇ *a crowded bar* 挤满人的酒吧 ◇ *In the spring the place is crowded with skiers.* 春季这地方满是滑雪的人。◇ *London was very crowded.* 伦敦拥挤不堪。➲ COMPARE UNCROWDED **2** 🔑 full of sth 充满的；挤满的: *a room crowded with books* 堆满书籍的房间 ◇ *We have a very crowded schedule.* 我们的日程排得满满的。

crowd·fund·ing /ˈkraʊdfʌndɪŋ/ *noun* [U] the practice of funding a project or an activity by raising many small amounts of money from a large number of people, usually using the Internet 众筹，大众集资（向大众募集小额资金，通常利用互联网进行）: *They raised the money for the film through crowdfunding.* 他们通过众筹为影片筹措资金。

ˈcrowd-pleaser *noun* (*informal*) a person or performance that always pleases an audience 取悦观众的人（或表演）

ˈcrowd-puller *noun* (*informal*) a person or thing that always attracts a large audience 吸引大量观众的人（或事物）

crowd·sour·cing /ˈkraʊdsɔːsɪŋ; *NAmE* -sɔːrsɪŋ/ *noun* [U] the activity of getting information or help for a project or a task from a large number of people, typically using the Internet 众包，众源（向大众寻求信息或帮助，尤利用互联网进行）: *The newspaper uses crowdsourcing to gather information for its website.* 这家报纸采用众包模式为其网站收集信息。 ▶ **crowd·source** *verb* ~ **sth**

crown 🔑 /kraʊn/ *noun, verb*
■ *noun*
• **OF KING/QUEEN** 国王；女王 **1** 🔑 [C] an object in the shape of a circle, usually made of gold and PRECIOUS STONES, that a king or queen wears on his or her head on official occasions 王冠；皇冠；冕 **2 the Crown** [sing.] the government of a country, thought of as being represented by a king or queen 王国政府；王国: *land owned by the Crown*

王国的土地 ◇ *a Minister of the Crown* 王国的大臣 ◇ *Who's appearing for the Crown* (= bringing a criminal charge against sb on behalf of the state) *in this case?* 谁将在此案中代表王国政府出庭？ **3 the crown** [sing.] the position or power of a king or queen 王位；王权：*She refused the crown* (= refused to become queen). 她拒绝接受王位。◇ *his claim to the French crown* 他声称有继任法国王位的权利

• **OF FLOWERS/LEAVES** 花；树叶 **4** [C] a circle of flowers, leaves, etc. that is worn on sb's head, sometimes as a sign of victory 花冠（戴在头上，有时象征胜利）

• **IN SPORTS COMPETITION** 体育竞赛 **5** [C, usually sing.] (*informal*) the position of winning a sports competition 冠军宝座；桂冠：*She is determined to retain her Wimbledon crown.* 她决心卫冕她的温布尔登网球赛的冠军宝座。

• **OF HEAD/HAT** 头；帽 **6** (*usually* **the crown**) [sing.] the top part of the head or a hat 头顶；帽顶 ➲ VISUAL VOCAB PAGES V64, V70

• **HIGHEST PART** 顶部 **7** (*usually* **the crown**) [sing.] the highest part of sth（某物的）顶部，顶端：*the crown of a hill* 山顶

• **ON TOOTH** 牙齿 **8** [C] an artificial cover for a damaged tooth（受损牙齿的）人造冠 ➲ WORDFINDER NOTE AT DENTIST

• **SHAPE** 形状 **9** [C] anything in the shape of a crown, especially as a decoration or a BADGE 王冠状物（尤指饰物或徽章）

• **MONEY** 货币 **10** [C] a unit of money in several European countries 克朗（欧洲一些国家的货币单位）：*Czech crowns* 捷克克朗 **11** [C] an old British coin worth five SHILLINGS (= now 25p) * 5 先令的英国旧币（等于现在的 25 便士）

IDM SEE JEWEL

■ ***verb***

• **KING/QUEEN** 国王；女王 **1** to put a crown on the head of a new king or queen as a sign of royal power 为…加冕：**~ sb** *Queen Elizabeth was crowned in 1953.* 伊丽莎白女王于 1953 年加冕。◇ **~ sb + noun** *The prince was soon to be crowned King of England.* 王子不久就要被立为英格兰国王了。

• **COVER TOP** 覆盖顶部 **2** [usually passive] **~ sth (with sth)** to form or cover the top of sth 形成…顶部；给…加顶：*His head was crowned with a mop of brown curls.* 他长了一头蓬乱的棕色鬈发。

• **MAKE COMPLETE** 使完成 **3** [often passive] **~ sth (with sth)** to make sth complete or perfect, especially by adding an achievement, a success, etc.（尤指通过增添成就、成功等）使圆满，使完美：*The award of the Nobel Prize has crowned a glorious career in physics.* 荣获诺贝尔奖使其物理学研究的辉煌事业达到了顶点。◇ *Their efforts were finally crowned with success.* 他们的努力终于取得圆满成功。

• **HIT ON HEAD** 击打头部 **4 ~ sb** (*old-fashioned, informal*) to hit sb on the head 敲（某人）的脑壳

• **TOOTH** 牙齿 **5 ~ sth** to put an artificial cover on a tooth（在牙齿上）镶人造冠 SYN **cap**：*I've had one of my teeth crowned.* 我的一颗牙齿镶了假齿冠。

IDM **to crown it 'all** (*BrE, informal*) used to say that sth is the final and worst event in a series of unpleasant or annoying events（在一系列不愉快或讨厌的事件中）最糟糕的是：*It was cold and raining, and, to crown it all, we had to walk home.* 天气寒冷又下着雨，最糟的是我们得走着回家。

ˌCrown 'Colony *noun* a COLONY ruled directly by the British government 英国政府直辖殖民地

ˌCrown 'Court *noun* (in England and Wales 英格兰和威尔士) a court which deals with criminal cases, with a judge and JURY 刑事法院（有法官和陪审团）➲ COMPARE COUNTY COURT

crown·ing /ˈkraʊnɪŋ/ *adj.* [only before noun] making sth perfect or complete 使完美的；使圆满的：*The cathedral is the* ***crowning glory*** *of the city.* 大教堂是这座城市至高无上的骄傲。◇ *His 'Beethoven' sculpture is seen as the crowning achievement of his career.* 人们认为他制作的贝多芬雕像是他在事业上取得的最高成就。

ˌcrown 'jewels *noun* [pl.] the crown and other objects worn or carried by a king or queen on formal occasions 御宝（国王或女王在正式场合佩戴的饰物）

ˌcrown 'prince *noun* (in some countries) a prince who will become king when the present king or queen dies（某些国家的）王储，皇太子

ˌcrown prinˈcess *noun* **1** the wife of a crown prince 王储妃；皇太子妃 **2** (in some countries) a princess who will become queen when the present king or queen dies（某些国家的）女王储

ˌCrown 'prosecutor *noun* in England and Wales, a lawyer who works for the state（英格兰和威尔士的）皇家检察官

ˈcrow's feet *noun* [pl.] lines in the skin around the outer corner of a person's eye（眼角的）鱼尾纹

ˈcrow's nest *noun* a platform at the top of a ship's MAST (= the post that supports the sails) from which sb can see a long way and watch for land, danger, etc. 桅杆瞭望台

croz·ier = CROSIER

cru·cial 🔑 AW /ˈkruːʃl/ *adj.* extremely important, because it will affect other things 至关重要的；关键性的 SYN **critical**, **essential**：*a* ***crucial factor/issue/decision*** 关键性的因素 / 问题 / 决定 ◇ *topics of crucial importance* 至关重要的课题 ◇ *The next few weeks are going to be crucial.* 今后几个星期是关键。◇ **~ to/for sth** *Winning this contract is crucial to the success of the company.* 赢得这份合同对这家公司的成败至关重要。◇ **~ that...** ***It is crucial that*** *we get this right.* 我们把这个问题弄明白是极其重要的。◇ *Parents* ***play a crucial role*** *in preparing their child for school.* 父母对孩子做好上学的准备起着至关重要的作用。◇ *He wasn't there* ***at the crucial moment*** (= when he was needed most). 紧要关头他却不在那里。➲ SYNONYMS AT ESSENTIAL ➲ LANGUAGE BANK AT EMPHASIS, VITAL ▶ **cru·cial·ly** AW /-ʃəli/ *adv.*：*crucially important* 极其重要

cru·cible /ˈkruːsɪbl/ *noun* **1** a pot in which substances are heated to high temperatures, metals are melted, etc. 坩埚；熔炉 ➲ VISUAL VOCAB PAGE V72 **2** (*formal* or *literary*) a place or situation in which people or ideas are tested severely, often creating sth new or exciting in the process 熔炉；严峻的考验；磨炼

cru·ci·fix /ˈkruːsəfɪks/ *noun* a model of a cross with a figure of Jesus Christ on it, as a symbol of the Christian religion（十字架）苦像；耶稣受难像

cru·ci·fix·ion /ˌkruːsəˈfɪkʃn/ *noun* (*sometimes* **Crucifixion**) **1** [C, U] the act of killing sb by fastening them to a cross 钉死在十字架上：*the Crucifixion* (= of Jesus) 耶稣被钉在十字架上 **2** [C] a painting or other work of art representing the crucifixion of Jesus Christ 十字架苦像（耶稣受难的画像或艺术品）

cru·ci·form /ˈkruːsɪfɔːm; NAmE -fɔːrm/ *adj.* (*specialist*) (especially of buildings 尤指建筑物) in the shape of a cross 十字形的

cru·cify /ˈkruːsɪfaɪ/ *verb* (**cru·ci·fies**, **cru·ci·fy·ing**, **cru·ci·fied**, **cru·ci·fied**) **1 ~ sb** to kill sb as a punishment by fastening them to a wooden cross 把（某人）钉（或捆）在木十字架上处死 **2 ~ sb** (*informal*) to criticize or punish sb very severely 严厉批评；严惩；折磨：*The prime minister was crucified in the press for his handling of the affair.* 首相因处理此事的方式而受到新闻界的严厉抨击。

crud /krʌd/ *noun* [U] (*informal*) any dirty or unpleasant substance 脏东西；污垢；渣滓

cruddy /ˈkrʌdi/ *adj.* (**crud·dier**, **crud·di·est**) (*informal, especially NAmE*) bad, dirty or of low quality 糟糕的；邋遢的；蹩脚的：*We got really cruddy service in that restaurant last time.* 我们上次在那家餐馆得到的服务实在差极了。

crude /kruːd/ *adj., noun*

■ ***adj.*** (**cruder**, **cru·dest**) **1** simple and not very accurate but giving a general idea of sth 粗略的；简略的；大概的：***In crude terms****, the causes of mental illness seem to be of three main kinds.* 简略地说，导致精神病的原因看起

来主要有三种。 **2** (of objects or works of art 物体或艺术品) simply made, not showing much skill or attention to detail 粗糙的；粗制的：*a crude drawing of a face* 脸部的略图 **3** (of people or the way they behave 人或行为方式) offensive or rude, especially about sex 冒犯的，粗俗的，粗鲁的（尤其有关性的） **SYN** **vulgar**: *crude jokes/language* 粗俗的笑话 / 语言 **4** [usually before noun] (of oil and other natural substances 油和其他自然物质) in its natural state, before it has been treated with chemicals 天然的；自然的：*crude oil/metal* 原油；未经提炼的金属 ▶ **crude·ly** *adv.*: *a crudely drawn ship* 粗略勾画出来的船 ◇ *To put it crudely, the poor are going without food so that the rich can drive cars.* 简而言之，穷人无饭吃，富人才有车开。**crude·ness** *noun* [U]

■ ***noun*** (*also* ˌ**crude ˈoil**) [U] oil in its natural state, before it has been treated with chemicals 原油；石油：*50 000 barrels of crude* * 5 万桶石油

cru·di·tés /ˈkruːdɪteɪ; *NAmE* ˌkruːdɪˈteɪ/ *noun* [pl.] (*from French*) pieces of raw vegetables that are eaten at the beginning of a meal （用餐开始时食用的）生菜色拉

cru·dity /ˈkruːdəti/ *noun* [U, C] (*pl.* **-ies**) the fact of being CRUDE; an example of sth CRUDE 粗糙，简陋，粗俗，粗鲁（的事例）：*Despite the crudity of their methods and equipment, the experiment was a considerable success.* 尽管他们的方法和设备较为粗陋，那次实验却相当成功。◇ *the novel's structural crudities* 那部小说粗糙的结构 ◇ *The crudity of her language shocked him.* 她粗鄙的语言使他感到震惊。

cruel /ˈkruːəl/ *adj.* (**cruel·ler**, **cruel·lest**) **1** ~ (**to sb/sth**) having a desire to cause pain and suffering 残酷的；冷酷的；残忍的；残暴的：*a cruel dictator* 残暴的独裁者 ◇ *I can't stand people who are cruel to animals.* 我无法容忍虐待动物的人。◇ *Her eyes were cruel and hard.* 她目光冷酷逼人。◇ *Sometimes you have to* ***be cruel to be kind*** (= make sb suffer because it will be good for them later). 有时候为了某人好你就得对他狠。 **OPP** **kind** **2** causing pain or suffering 引起痛苦的：*a* ***cruel punishment/joke*** 残酷的惩罚；挖苦人的笑话 ◇ *Her father's death was a* ***cruel blow.*** 父亲去世对她是一大打击。▶ **cruel·ly** /ˈkruːəli/ *adv.*: *The dog had been cruelly treated.* 那条狗受过虐待。◇ *I was cruelly deceived.* 我被骗得惨透了。

cruelty /ˈkruːəlti/ *noun* (*pl.* **-ies**) **1** [U] ~ (**to sb/sth**) behaviour that causes pain or suffering to others, especially deliberately （尤指蓄意的）残酷，残忍，残暴：*cruelty to animals* 对动物的虐待 ◇ *The deliberate cruelty of his words cut her like a knife.* 他故意说的那些残酷无情的话对她像刀割一样。 **OPP** **kindness** **2** [C, usually pl.] a cruel action 残暴的行为 **3** [C, U] something that happens that seems unfair 不公；不平：*the cruelties of life* 生活中的种种不公

cruet /ˈkruːɪt/ *noun* a small container, or set of containers, for salt, pepper, oil, etc. for use on the table at meals （餐桌上的）调味瓶，一组调味瓶

cruise /kruːz/ *noun, verb*

■ ***noun*** a journey by sea, visiting different places, especially as a holiday/vacation 乘船游览；航行：*I'd love to go on a round-the-world cruise.* 我很想乘船周游世界。◇ *a luxury cruise ship* 豪华游轮 ➲ WORDFINDER NOTE AT HOLIDAY ➲ COLLOCATIONS AT TRAVEL

■ ***verb*** **1** [I, T] to travel in a ship or boat visiting different places, especially as a holiday/vacation 乘船游览：(+ **adv./prep.**) *They cruised down the Nile.* 他们沿尼罗河而下乘船游览。◇ ~ **sth** *We spent two weeks cruising the Bahamas.* 我们花了两个星期乘船游览巴哈马群岛。 **2** [I] (+ **adv./prep.**) (of a car, plane, etc. 汽车、飞机等) to travel at a steady speed 以平稳的速度行驶：*a light aircraft cruising at 4 000 feet* 一架在 4 000 英尺高度巡航的轻型飞机 ◇ *a cruising speed of 50 miles an hour* 每小时 50 英里平稳行驶的速度 **3** [I, T] (of a car, etc. or its driver 汽车等或驾驶员) to drive along slowly, especially when you are looking at or for sth （尤指查看或寻找时）慢速行驶，巡行：+ **adv./prep.** *She cruised around the block looking for a parking space.* 她绕着那个街区慢慢行驶，想找个停车位。◇ ~ **sth** *Taxis cruised the streets, looking for fares.* 出租汽车在街上缓慢行驶招揽顾客。 **4** [I] + **adv./prep.** to win or achieve sth easily 轻而易举赢得（或获得）；轻取：*The home team cruised to victory.* 主队轻松取胜。 **5** [I, T] ~ (**sth**) (*slang*) to go around in public places looking for a sexual partner （在公共场所）寻觅性伙伴，猎艳

ˈ**cruise control** *noun* [U] a device in a vehicle that allows it to stay at the speed that the driver has chosen 定速巡航装置（让车辆以选定速度行驶）

ˌ**cruise ˈmissile** *noun* a large weapon with a WARHEAD that flies close to the ground and is guided by its own computer to an exact place 巡航导弹

cruiser /ˈkruːzə(r)/ *noun* **1** a large fast ship used in war 巡洋舰 **2** (*also* ˈ**cabin cruiser**) a boat with a motor and room for people to sleep, used for pleasure trips （可住宿的）舱式游艇 ➲ VISUAL VOCAB PAGE V59 **3** (*NAmE*) a police car 巡逻警车

crumb /krʌm/ *noun* **1** a very small piece of food, especially of bread or cake, that has fallen off a larger piece 食物碎屑；（尤指）面包屑，糕饼屑：*She stood up and brushed the crumbs from her sweater.* 她站起身掸掉了毛衣上的面包屑。 **2** a small piece or amount 一点；少许；少量：*a few crumbs of useful information* 点滴有用的消息 ◇ *The government's only* ***crumb of comfort*** *is that their opponents are as confused as they are.* 政府唯一聊以自慰的是反对派与他们一样困惑不解。➲ MORE LIKE THIS 20, page R27

crum·ble /ˈkrʌmbl/ *verb, noun*

■ ***verb*** **1** [I, T] to break or break sth into very small pieces （使）破碎，成碎屑：*Rice flour makes the cake less likely to crumble.* 这种糕饼用米粉做不那么容易碎。◇ ~ **sth** *Crumble the cheese over the salad.* 把干酪弄成碎屑洒在色拉上。 **2** [I] if a building or piece of land **is crumbling**, parts of it are breaking off 坍塌；损坏；崩裂：*buildings crumbling into dust* 渐渐坍塌的建筑物 ◇ *crumbling stonework* 不断破裂的石制建筑 ◇ *The cliff is gradually crumbling away.* 峭壁正在逐渐崩坍。 **3** [I] to begin to fail or get weaker or to come to an end （开始渐渐）衰退，衰弱；崩溃；瓦解；消亡：*a crumbling business/relationship* 逐渐衰败的企业；日益恶化的关系 ◇ ~ **away** *All his hopes began to crumble away.* 他所有的希望开始化为泡影。◇ ~ **into/to sth** *The empire finally crumbled into dust.* 这个帝国最终崩溃了。 **IDM** SEE WAY *n.*

■ ***noun*** (*BrE*) (*NAmE* **crisp**) [U, C] a DESSERT (= a sweet dish) made from fruit that is covered with a rough mixture of flour, butter and sugar, cooked in the oven and usually served hot 酥皮水果甜点：*apple crumble and custard* 酥皮苹果甜点心加蛋奶沙司

crum·bly /ˈkrʌmbli/ *adj.* that easily breaks into very small pieces 易碎的；脆的：*crumbly soil/cheese* 易碎的土壤 / 干酪

crumbs /krʌmz/ *exclamation* (*old-fashioned, BrE, informal*) used to show that you are surprised （惊讶时说）哎呀，哎哟，天哪：*Oh crumbs! Is that the time?* 啊，天哪！都这会儿啦？

crummy /ˈkrʌmi/ *adj.* (*informal*) of very bad quality 劣质的；低劣的；糟糕的：*Most of his songs are pretty crummy.* 他的歌曲大多糟糕透顶。

crum·pet /ˈkrʌmpɪt/ *noun* (*BrE*) **1** [C] a small flat round cake with small holes in the top, eaten hot with butter （上层有孔，涂上黄油趁热吃的）小圆烤饼 **2** [U] (*slang*) an offensive way of referring to people who are sexually attractive, usually women （对性感的人的蔑称，通常指女人）

crum·ple /ˈkrʌmpl/ *verb* **1** [T, I] ~ (**sth**) (**up**) (**into sth**) to crush sth into folds; to become crushed into folds 压皱；（使）变皱，起皱：*She crumpled the letter up into a ball and threw it on the fire.* 她把那封信揉成一团扔进了火里。◇ *This material crumples very easily.* 这种布料很容易起皱。 ➲ PICTURE AT SQUEEZE **2** [I] ~ (**up**) if your face **crumples**, you look sad and disappointed, as if you might cry （脸）沮丧地皱起，哭丧着 **3** [I] ~ (**up**) to fall down in an uncontrolled way because you are injured, unconscious, drunk, etc.（因受伤、失去知觉、喝醉而）瘫倒 SYN **collapse**: *He crumpled up in agony.* 他极度痛苦地瘫倒在地。▶ **crump·led** *adj.*: ***crumpled clothes/papers*** 皱巴巴的衣服 / 纸张 ◇ *A crumpled figure lay motionless in the doorway.* 门口躺着一个人，蜷缩成一团，一动不动。

ˈcrumple zone *noun* the part of a car that is designed to crumple easily if there is an accident, to protect the people in the car（汽车的）防撞缓冲区

crunch /krʌntʃ/ *noun, verb, adj.*

■ ***noun*** **1** [C, usually sing.] a noise like the sound of sth firm being crushed 压碎声；碎裂声: *the crunch of feet on snow* 脚踩着雪发出的嘎吱嘎吱声 ◇ *The car drew up with a crunch of gravel.* 那辆汽车在沙砾路上嘎吱一声停了下来。**2 the crunch** [sing.] (*informal*) an important and often unpleasant situation or piece of information 紧要关头；困境；症结；令人不快的重要消息: ***The crunch came*** *when she returned from America.* 她从美国回来以后，危机就出现了。◇ *He always says he'll help but* ***when it comes to the crunch*** (= when it is time for action) *he does nothing.* 他口口声声说一定帮忙，然而到关键时候却不行动。◇ *The crunch is that we can't afford to go abroad this year.* 症结在于我们今年负担不起出国的费用。**3** [C, usually sing.] a situation in which there is suddenly not enough of sth, especially money（突发的）不足，短缺；（尤指）缺钱: *the* ***budget/energy/housing crunch*** 预算 / 能源 / 住房短缺 **4** [C] = SIT-UP

■ ***verb*** **1** [T, I] ~ (**on**) **sth** to crush sth noisily between your teeth when you are eating 嘎吱嘎吱地嚼: *She crunched her apple noisily.* 她吃苹果发出嘎嚓嘎嚓的声音。**2** [I, T] ~ (**sth**) to make or cause sth to make a noise like sth hard being crushed（使）发出碎裂声 SYN **scrunch**: *The snow crunched under our feet.* 积雪在我们脚下嘎吱作响。**3** [I] + **adv./prep.** to move over a surface, making a loud crushing noise（在路上）行进发出响声: *I crunched across the gravel to the front door.* 我嘎吱嘎吱走过石子路来到前门。**4** [T] ~ **sth** (*computing* 计) to deal with large amounts of data very quickly（快速大量地）处理信息；数字捣弄 ➲ SEE ALSO NUMBER CRUNCHING

PHR V ˌ**crunch sth**↔ˈ**up** to crush sth completely 彻底压碎（或碾碎）: *He crunched up the empty pack and threw it out of the window.* 他把小空纸包揉成一团丢出了窗外。

■ ***adj.*** [only before noun] (*informal*) a **crunch** meeting, sports game, etc. is very important and may be the last chance to succeed（会议、体育竞赛等）至关重要的，最后一线胜机的: *Sunday's crunch game with Leeds* 星期天与利兹队决一雌雄的比赛

crunchy /ˈkrʌntʃi/ *adj.* (**crunch·ier, crunchi·est**) (*approving*) (especially of food 尤指食物) firm and crisp and making a sharp sound when you bite or crush it 脆的；爽脆的；脆口的: *a crunchy salad* 脆口的色拉 ➲ WORDFINDER NOTE AT CRISP

crunk /krʌŋk/ *noun* [U] a type of music, similar to RAP *n.* (2) or HIP HOP (1), that contains phrases that are repeated many times and has a strong BASS[1] *n.* (1) beat 旷克，旷克乐（与说唱音乐或嘻哈音乐类似，包含重复多次的乐句和强烈的低音节奏）

cru·sade /kruːˈseɪd/ *noun, verb*

■ ***noun*** **1** ~ (**for/against sth**) | ~ (**to do sth**) a long and determined effort to achieve sth that you believe to be right or to stop sth that you believe to be wrong（长期坚定不移的）斗争，运动 SYN **campaign**: *to lead a crusade against crime* 领导打击犯罪活动的运动 ◇ *a moral crusade* 提倡道德的运动 **2** (*sometimes* **Crusade**) any of the wars fought in Palestine by European Christian countries against the Muslims in the Middle Ages（中世纪的）十字军东征

■ ***verb*** [I] to make a long and determined effort to achieve sth that you believe to be right or to stop sth you believe to be wrong 长期坚定不移地奋斗 SYN **campaign**

cru·sader /kruːˈseɪdə(r)/ *noun* a person who takes part in a crusade 十字军战士；（某）运动的参加者: *moral crusaders* 提倡道德运动的志士

crush 🔑 /krʌʃ/ *verb, noun*

■ ***verb*** **1** 🔑 [T] ~ **sb/sth** to press or squeeze sth so hard that it is damaged or injured, or loses its shape 压坏；压伤；挤压变形: *The car was completely crushed under the truck.* 小轿车被卡车压得完全变形了。◇ *They crush the olives with a heavy wooden press.* 他们用沉重的木制压榨机把橄榄压碎。◇ *Several people were* ***crushed to death*** *in the accident.* 好几个人在事故中被压死了。**2** 🔑 [T] ~ **sb/sth + adv./prep.** to push or press sb/sth into a small space 把…挤入，将…塞进（狭小的空间内）: *Over twenty prisoners were crushed into a small dark cell.* 二十多名囚犯被塞在一间黑暗狭小的牢房里。**3** 🔑 [T] ~ **sth** to break sth into small pieces or into a powder by pressing hard 压碎；捣碎；碾成粉末: *Add two cloves of crushed garlic.* 加入两瓣捣碎的蒜。➲ PICTURE AT SQUEEZE **4** [T, I] ~ (**sth**) to become or make sth full of folds or lines（使）变皱，起皱 **5** [T] ~ **sb** to use violent methods to defeat people who are opposing you 镇压；（用暴力）制伏 SYN **put down, quash**: *The army was sent in to crush the rebellion.* 军队被派去平息叛乱。**6** ~ **sb** to destroy sb's confidence or happiness 破坏，毁坏（某人的信心或幸福）: *She felt completely crushed by the teacher's criticism.* 老师的批评使她觉得自己一无是处。

■ ***noun*** **1** [C, usually sing.] a crowd of people pressed close together in a small space（狭小空间中）拥挤的人群: *a big crush in the theatre bar* 剧院酒吧里拥挤不堪的人群 ◇ *I couldn't find a way through the crush.* 人太挤，我挤不过去。**2** [C] ~ (**on sb**) a strong feeling of love, that usually does not last very long, that a young person has for sb older（通常指年轻人对年长者的短暂的）热恋，迷恋: *a schoolgirl crush* 女学生的迷恋 ◇ *I had a huge crush on her.* 我对她爱慕至极。**3** [U, C] a drink made from fruit juice 果汁饮料

ˈcrush barrier *noun* (*BrE*) a temporary metal fence used for keeping back a crowd 防挤栏杆，临时栅栏（用以阻挡人群）

crush·er /ˈkrʌʃə(r)/ *noun* (often in compounds 常构成复合词) a machine or tool for crushing sth 压碎机；压榨机；破碎机: *a garlic crusher* 压蒜器 ➲ VISUAL VOCAB PAGE V27

crush·ing /ˈkrʌʃɪŋ/ *adj.* [usually before noun] used to emphasize how bad or severe sth is（强调糟糕或严重的程度）惨重的，毁坏性的: *a* ***crushing defeat*** *in the election* 在选举中的惨败 ◇ *The shipyard has been dealt another* ***crushing blow*** *with the failure to win this contract.* 由于未能赢得这份合同，造船厂又遭到了一次惨重的打击。▶ **crush·ing·ly** *adv.*

crust /krʌst/ *noun* **1** [C, U] the hard outer surface of bread 面包皮: *sandwiches with the crusts cut off* 切掉面包皮的三明治 **2** [C, usually sing.] a layer of PASTRY, especially on top of a PIE 糕饼（尤指馅饼）酥皮: *Bake until the crust is golden.* 把糕饼烤至外皮呈金黄色。**3** [C, U] a hard layer or surface, especially above or around sth soft or liquid（尤指软物或液体上面、周围的）硬层，硬表面: *a thin crust of ice* 一层薄冰 ◇ *the earth's crust* 地壳 ➲ SEE ALSO UPPER CRUST IDM ➤ SEE EARN

crust·acean /krʌˈsteɪʃn/ *noun* (*specialist*) any creature with a soft body that is divided into sections, and a hard outer shell. Most crustaceans live in water. CRABS, LOBSTERS and SHRIMPS are all crustaceans. 甲壳动物（如螃蟹、龙虾和小虾）➲ VISUAL VOCAB PAGE V13 ➲ COMPARE SHELLFISH

crust·ed /ˈkrʌstɪd/ *adj.* [not usually before noun] ~ (**with sth**) having a hard layer or covering of sth 有硬皮；有外壳

crusty /ˈkrʌsti/ *adj., noun*

■ ***adj.*** (**crust·ier, crusti·est**) **1** (of food 食物) having a hard outer layer 有硬皮的；有外壳的: *fresh crusty bread* 新鲜的脆皮面包 **2** (*informal*) (especially of older people 尤指老年人) bad-tempered; easily irritated 脾气坏的；易发怒的: *a crusty old man* 脾气暴躁的老人

■ ***noun*** (*also* **crustie**) (*pl.* **-ies**) (*BrE, informal*) a person who usually has no permanent home, has a dirty or untidy appearance, and rejects the way that most people live in Western society（抗拒西方传统的）邋遢流浪汉；居无定所抗拒传统的人

crutch /krʌtʃ/ *noun* **1** one of two long sticks that you put under your arms to help you walk after you have injured your leg or foot（腿或脚受伤者用的）腋杖：*After the accident I spent six months* ***on crutches.*** 事故后我用了六个月的腋杖。 **2** (*usually disapproving*) a person or thing that gives you help or support but often makes you depend on them too much 依靠；依赖 **3** = CROTCH

crux /krʌks/ *noun* [sing.] **the ~** (**of sth**) the most important or difficult part of a problem or an issue（难题或问题的）关键，最难点，症结 **SYN** **nub**：*Now we come to the* ***crux of the matter.*** 现在我们来谈问题的症结。

cry /kraɪ/ *verb, noun*

■ ***verb*** (**cries, cry·ing, cried, cried**) **1** [I, T] to produce tears from your eyes because you are unhappy or hurt 哭；哭泣：*It's all right. Don't cry.* 不要紧，别哭了。◇ *I just couldn't stop crying.* 我哭得停不下来。◇ **~ for sb/sth** *The baby was crying for* (= because it wanted) *its mother.* 婴儿哭着要妈妈。◇ **~ about/over sth** *There's nothing to cry about.* 没有什么值得哭的。◇ **~ with sth** *He felt like crying with rage.* 他气得想哭。◇ **+ speech** *'Waaa!' she cried.* "哇！" 她哭出声来。◇ *I found him* ***crying his eyes out*** (= crying very much). 我看他哭得很伤心。◇ *That night she* ***cried herself to sleep.*** 那天晚上她哭着哭着就睡着了。 **2** [I, T] to shout loudly 喊叫；呼喊；呼叫：**~ for sth** *She ran to the window and cried for help.* 她跑到窗口呼喊救命。◇ **+ speech** *'You're safe!' Tom cried in delight.* "你安全啦！" 汤姆高兴地大声说道。 ➲ SYNONYMS AT SHOUT **3** [I] (of a bird or an animal 鸟或动物) to make a loud unpleasant noise 发出刺耳的叫声；嗥叫；吠：*Seagulls followed the boat, crying loudly.* 海鸥追随着那条船，高声鸣叫着。

IDM **ˌcry ˈfoul** (*informal*) to complain that sb else has done sth wrong or unfair 抱怨；埋怨 **cry over spilt ˈmilk** (*BrE*) (*US* **cry over spilled ˈmilk**) to waste time worrying about sth that has happened that you cannot do anything about 枉为无可挽回的事忧伤；作于事无补的担忧：*As the saying goes—* ***it's no use crying over spilt milk.*** 常言道：覆水难收，后悔也于事无补。 **cry ˈwolf** to call for help when you do not need it, with the result that when you do need it people do not believe you 喊"狼来了"；谎报险情；发假警报 **for ˌcrying out ˈloud** (*informal*) used to show you are angry or surprised（表示愤怒或惊讶）哎呀，我的天哪，真是岂有此理：*For crying out loud! Why did you have to do that?* 真是岂有此理！你为什么非得干那种事？ ➲ MORE AT LAUGH *v.*, SHOULDER *n.*

▼ VOCABULARY BUILDING 词汇扩充

Cry 表示哭、流泪的词

To **cry** is the most general word for producing tears when you are unhappy or hurt, or when you are extremely happy. * cry 泛指因悲伤、痛苦或喜悦而流泪。

- To **sob** means to cry noisily, taking sudden, sharp breaths. * sob 指啜泣、抽噎。
- To **wail** means to cry in a loud high voice. * wail 指嚎啕大哭。
- To **whimper** means to cry making low, weak noises. * whimper 指低声啜泣、呜咽。
- To **weep** (*literary* or *formal*) means to cry quietly for a long time. * weep （文学或正式用语）指饮泣。

All these verbs can be used like 'say'. 以上动词均与 say 用法相同：*'I don't want you to go,' she cried/wailed/sobbed.* "我不想你走。"她哭 / 号哭 / 抽噎着说。

- To **be in tears** means to be crying. * be in tears 指流泪。
- To **burst into tears** means to suddenly begin to cry. * burst into tears 指突然哭起来。
- To **cry your eyes out** means to cry a lot or for a long time, because you are very sad. * cry one's eyes out 指痛哭不止。

PHR V **ˌcry ˈoff** (*BrE, informal*) to say that you cannot do sth that you promised to do 撤回前言；取消诺言；打退堂鼓：*She said she was coming to the party, but cried off at the last moment.* 她说过她要来参加聚会，可到最后一刻又变卦了。 **ˌcry ˈout** to make a loud sound without words because you are hurt, afraid, surprised, etc.（因伤痛、害怕、惊讶等）大叫，叫喊：*She tried to stop herself from crying out.* 她试图控制住自己不叫出声来。◇ *to* ***cry out in fear/alarm/pain*** 害怕 / 惊慌 / 疼痛得大叫起来 **ˌcry ˈout/ˌcry ˈout sth** to shout sth loudly 大声呼喊：*She cried out for help.* 她大声呼救。◇ *She cried out his name.* 她大声呼唤着他的名字。◇ **+ speech** *'Help!' he cried out.* "救命啊！" 他大声呼叫着。 ➲ SYNONYMS AT CALL **ˌcry ˈout for sth** (usually used in the progressive tenses 通常用于进行时) to need sth very much 迫切需要：*The company is crying out for fresh new talent.* 公司急需具有最新理念的人才。

■ ***noun*** (*pl.* **cries**) **1** [C] a loud sound without words that expresses a strong feeling（表达强烈感情的）叫喊，叫声：*to* ***give a cry of anguish/despair/relief/surprise/terror, etc.*** 发出痛苦、绝望、如释重负、惊讶、恐怖等的叫声 **2** [C] a loud shout 大喊；大叫；呼喊：*With a cry of 'Stop thief!' he ran after the boy.* 他一边喊"抓贼啊！"一边追赶那男孩。◇ *Her answer was greeted with cries of outrage.* 她的回答引起了一片愤怒的吼叫。 **3** [C] the sound made by a bird or an animal（鸟的）鸣叫，啼叫；（动物的）嗥叫，吠：*the cry of gulls circling overhead* 海鸥在头顶上盘旋着发出的鸣叫 **4** [sing.] an action or a period of crying 哭；一阵哭泣：*I felt a lot better after a good long cry.* 我痛痛快快哭了一场，好受多了。 **5** [C] **~ (for sth)** an urgent demand or request for sth 迫切需要；恳求：*Her suicide attempt was really* ***a cry for help.*** 她企图自杀实际上表明她迫切需要帮助。 **6** [C] (especially in compounds 尤用于构成复合词) a word or phrase that expresses a group's beliefs and calls people to action 口号：*a battle cry* 战斗口号

IDM **in full ˈcry** talking or shouting loudly and in an enthusiastic way 激情呐喊；大声疾呼：*The Leeds supporters were in full cry.* 利兹队的球迷在激动地呐喊。 ➲ MORE AT FAR *adj.*, HUE

cry·baby /ˈkraɪbeɪbi/ *noun* (*pl.* **-ies**) (*informal, disapproving*) a person, especially a child, who cries too often or without good reason 爱哭的人，动不动就哭的人（尤指小孩）：*Don't be such a crybaby.* 别动不动就哭鼻子。

cry·ing /ˈkraɪɪŋ/ *adj., noun*

■ ***adj.*** [only before noun]

IDM **be a crying ˈshame** (*informal*) used to emphasize that you think sth is extremely bad or shocking（用于强调）极其糟糕，令人震惊：*It's a crying shame to waste all that food.* 那么些食物都浪费了，真是太不像话了。 **a crying ˈneed (for sth)** a great and urgent need for sth 迫切的需要

■ ***noun*** [U] the sound or act of crying 哭泣声；哭泣：*the crying of terrified children* 小孩受了惊吓的哭声

cryo·gen·ic /ˌkraɪəˈdʒenɪk/ *adj.* (*physics* 物) involving the use of very low temperatures 低温的；深冷的：*a cryogenic storage system* 低温冷藏系统

cryo·gen·ics /ˌkraɪəˈdʒenɪks/ *noun* [U] (*physics* 物) the scientific study of the production and effects of very low temperatures 低温学 ➲ COMPARE CRYONICS

cry·on·ics /kraɪˈɒnɪks; *NAmE* -ˈɑːn-/ *noun* [U] (*medical* 医) the process of freezing a body at the moment of its death with the hope that it will be brought back to life at some future time 人体冷冻法（把人体在死亡时冷冻起来以期在将来起死回生） ➲ COMPARE CRYOGENICS

crypt /krɪpt/ *noun* a room under the floor of a church, used especially in the past as a place for burying people（尤指旧时做墓穴用的）教堂地下室

cryp·tic /ˈkrɪptɪk/ *adj.* with a meaning that is hidden or not easily understood 含义隐晦的；晦涩难懂的 **SYN** **mysterious**：*a* ***cryptic message/remark/smile*** 令人困惑的信息 / 话语 / 微笑 ◇ *a cryptic crossword clue* 扑朔迷离的纵横字谜线索 ▸ **cryp·tic·al·ly** /-kli/ *adv.*：*'Yes and no,' she replied cryptically.* "又是又不是。" 她回答得很隐晦。

crypto- /ˈkrɪptəʊ; *NAmE* -toʊ/ *combining form* (in nouns 构成名词) secret 秘密的；保密的；隐蔽的： *a crypto-communist* 地下共产党员

crypt·og·raphy /krɪpˈtɒɡrəfi; *NAmE* -ˈtɑːɡ-/ *noun* [U] the art of writing or solving codes 密码学

crypto·spor·id·ium /ˌkrɪptəʊspəˈrɪdiəm; *NAmE* ˌkrɪptoʊ-/ *noun* a PARASITE found in water that causes infections inside the body 隐孢子虫（水中寄生虫，可引致体内受感染）

crys·tal /ˈkrɪstl/ *noun* **1** [C] a small piece of a substance with many even sides, that is formed naturally when the substance becomes solid 结晶；晶体： ***ice/salt crystals*** 冰 / 盐的结晶体 **2** [U, C] a clear mineral, such as QUARTZ, used in making jewellery and decorative objects 水晶（如石英，用于制作珠宝饰物）： *a pair of crystal earrings* 一对水晶耳环 **3** [U] glass of very high quality 水晶玻璃： *a* ***crystal chandelier/vase*** 水晶玻璃枝形吊灯 / 花瓶 **4** [C] (*NAmE*) a piece of glass or plastic that covers the face of a watch 石英玻璃表护面；塑料表护面；表蒙子 ➲ SEE ALSO LIQUID CRYSTAL DISPLAY **5** = METH

ˌcrystal ˈball *noun* a clear glass ball used by people who claim they can predict what will happen in the future by looking into it （占卜用的）水晶球： *Without a crystal ball, it's impossible to say where we'll be next year.* 没有水晶球预卜未来，我们说不准明年处境会如何。

ˌcrystal ˈclear *adj.* **1** (of glass, water, etc. 玻璃、水等) completely clear and bright 清澈透明的；晶莹的 **2** very easy to understand; completely obvious 浅显易懂的；显而易见的： *I want to make my meaning crystal clear.* 我想把我的意思解释得清清楚楚。

crys·tal·line /ˈkrɪstəlaɪn/ *adj.* **1** (*specialist*) made of or similar to CRYSTALS 结晶的；水晶制的；晶状的： ***crystalline structure/rocks*** 晶体结构；结晶岩 **2** (*formal*) very clear 清澈的；透明的；晶莹的 SYN **transparent**: *water of crystalline purity* 清澈纯净的水

crys·tal·lize (*BrE also* **-ise**) /ˈkrɪstəlaɪz/ *verb* **1** [I, T] (of thoughts, plans, beliefs, etc. 想法、计划、信仰等) to become clear and fixed; to make thoughts, beliefs, etc. clear and fixed 变明确；使（想法、信仰等）明确： *Our ideas began to crystallize into a definite plan.* 我们的想法开始形成了一个明确的计划。◇ **~ sth** *The final chapter crystallizes all the main issues.* 最后一章澄清了所有的主要问题。 **2** [I, T] **~ (sth)** (*specialist*) to form or make sth form into CRYSTALS （使）形成晶体，结晶： *The salt crystallizes as the water evaporates.* 盐在水分蒸发时结晶。 ▶ **crys·tal·liza·tion, -isa·tion** /ˌkrɪstəlaɪˈzeɪʃn; *NAmE* -ləˈz-/ *noun* [U, sing.]

crys·tal·lized (*BrE also* **-ised**) /ˈkrɪstəlaɪzd/ *adj.* (especially of fruit 尤指水果) preserved in and covered with sugar 蜜饯的；用糖渍的

crystal·log·raphy /ˌkrɪstəˈlɒɡrəfi; *NAmE* -ˈlɑːɡ-/ *noun* [U] the branch of science that deals with CRYSTALS 晶体学；结晶学 ▶ **crystal·log·raph·er** /ˌkrɪstəˈlɒɡrəfə(r); *NAmE* -ˈlɑːɡ-/ *noun*

crystal meth *noun* = METH

ˈcrystal set (*also* **ˌcrystal ˈradio**) *noun* a simple early radio which was listened to wearing HEADPHONES（早期用耳机的）晶体检波收音机，矿石收音机

the CSA /ˌsiː es ˈeɪ/ *abbr.* the Child Support Agency (a government organization in Britain that decides how much money a parent who does not live with a child must contribute to support the child. It was replaced by the Child Maintenance Service in 2017.) 儿童支持局，子女抚养代理局（英国政府机构，负责规定与子女分开居住的家长应支付的抚养费数额，该机构于 2017 年被"儿童抚养服务局"所取代）

ˈC-section *noun* (*NAmE*) = CAESAREAN

CS gas /ˌsiː es ˈɡæs/ *noun* [U] a gas that stings the eyes, producing tears and making it difficult to breathe. CS gas is sometimes used to control crowds. 催泪性毒气（或瓦斯） ➲SEE ALSO TEAR GAS

CST /ˌsiː es ˈtiː/ *abbr.* CENTRAL STANDARD TIME 中部标准时间

Ct (*also* **Ct.** *especially in NAmE*) *abbr.* (used in written addresses) COURT *n.* (7)（用于书写地址）公寓楼，宅第： *30 Willow Ct* 威洛公寓楼 30 号

ct (*also* **ct.** *especially in NAmE*) *abbr.* **1** (in writing 书写形式) CARAT 开；克拉： *an 18ct gold ring* 一枚 18 开的金戒指 **2** (in writing 书写形式) CENT(S) 分（币）： *50 cts* * 50 分

CTC /ˌsiː tiː ˈsiː/ *abbr.* (in the UK) City Technology College (a school in a town or city that teaches technology, science and mathematics to young people between the ages of 11 and 18) 城市技术学院（全写为 City Technology College，在英国向 11 至 18 岁的青少年教授科技和数学）

CT scan /ˌsiː ˈtiː skæn/ *noun* = CAT SCAN

cu. *abbr.* (in writing 书写形式) CUBIC 立方的： *a volume of 2 cu. m* (= 2 cubic metres) * 2 立方米的体积

cub /kʌb/ *noun* **1** [C] a young BEAR, LION, FOX, etc.（熊、狮、狐狸等的）幼兽，崽： *a lioness guarding her cubs* 守护幼崽的母狮 **2 the Cubs** (*BrE*) (*US* **the ˈCub Scouts**) [pl.] a branch of the SCOUT ASSOCIATION for boys between the ages of eight and ten or eleven 幼童军（八至十或十一岁的男孩组成的童子军的一部分）： *to join the Cubs* 参加幼童军 **3 Cub** (*also* **ˈCub Scout**) [C] a member of the Cubs 幼童军成员 ➲COMPARE BROWNIE (2), (3)

Cuban /ˈkjuːbən/ *adj., noun*
■***adj.*** from or connected with Cuba 古巴的
■***noun*** a person from Cuba 古巴人

cub·by·hole /ˈkʌbihəʊl; *NAmE* -hoʊl/ *noun* **1** a small room or a small space 小房间；斗室；狭小的空间： *My office is a cubbyhole in the basement.* 我的办公室是地下室的一间小屋。 **2** (*SAfrE*) a small space or shelf facing the front seats of a car where you can keep papers, maps, etc.（汽车前排座前放纸或地图等的）格架 ➲ COMPARE GLOVE COMPARTMENT

cube /kjuːb/ *noun, verb*
■***noun*** **1** a solid or hollow figure with six equal square sides 立方体；立方形 ➲ PICTURE AT SOLID **2** a piece of sth, especially food, with six sides 立方形的东西（尤指食物）： *Cut the meat into cubes.* 把肉切成丁儿。 ➲ SEE ALSO ICE CUBE, STOCK CUBE, SUGAR CUBE **3** (*mathematics* 数) the number that you get when you multiply a number by itself twice 立方；三次幂： *The cube of 5 (5^3) is 125 (5×5×5).* * 5 的立方（5^3）是 125。
■***verb*** **1** [usually passive] **~ sth** (*mathematics* 数) to multiply a number by itself twice 求…的立方： *10 cubed is 1 000.* * 10 的立方是 1 000。 **2 ~ sth** to cut food into cubes 把（食物）切成小方块 SYN **dice**

ˌcube ˈroot *noun* (*mathematics* 数) a number which, when multiplied by itself twice, produces a particular number 立方根： *The cube root of 64 ($\sqrt[3]{64}$) is 4.* * 64 的立方根是 4。 ➲COMPARE SQUARE ROOT

cubic /ˈkjuːbɪk/ *adj.* **1** (*abbr.* **cu.**) [only before noun] used to show that a measurement is the volume of sth, that is the height multiplied by the length and the width 立方的： ***cubic centimetres/inches/metres*** 立方厘米 / 英寸 / 米 **2** measured or expressed in cubic units 用立方单位度量（或表示）的： *the cubic capacity of a car's engine* 汽车发动机汽缸的容量 **3** having the shape of a cube 立方形的： *a cubic figure* 立方形

cu·bicle /ˈkjuːbɪkl/ *noun* a small room that is made by separating off part of a larger room（大房间分隔出的）小房间，隔间： *a shower cubicle* 淋浴小单间 ◇ (*BrE*) *a changing cubicle* (= for example at a public swimming pool) 更衣室隔间 ◇ (*especially NAmE*) *an office cubicle* 办公室的隔间

cu·bism /ˈkjuːbɪzəm/ (*also* **Cubism**) *noun* [U] a style and movement in early 20th century art in which objects and people are represented as GEOMETRIC shapes, often shown from many different angles at the same time (20

世纪初艺术的）立体主义，立体派 ▶ **cu·bist** (*also* **Cubist**) *noun*: *The exhibition includes works by the Cubists.* 这个展览包括立体派的作品。 **cu·bist** (*also* **Cubist**) *adj.* [usually before noun]: *cubist paintings* 立体派的绘画

C

cubit /ˈkjuːbɪt/ *noun* an ancient measurement of length, about 45 cm or the length from the elbow to the end of the fingers 肘尺，腕尺（古代长度单位，约 45 厘米，或自肘至指尖的长度）

cu·boid /ˈkjuːbɔɪd/ *noun, adj.*
■ *noun* (*geometry* 几何) a solid object which has six sides at RIGHT ANGLES to each other 长方体；矩形体
■ *adj.* shaped approximately like a CUBE 近似立方形的

ˌcub reˈporter *noun* a young newspaper REPORTER without much experience 缺少经验的年轻记者；初出茅庐的记者

cuck·old /ˈkʌkəʊld; *NAmE* -oʊld/ *noun, verb*
■ *noun* (*old use, disapproving*) a man whose wife has sex with another man 妻子有外遇的人；戴绿帽子的人
■ *verb* (*old use*) **1** **~ sb** (of a man 男人) to make another man a cuckold by having sex with his wife 给（另一男人）戴绿帽子；与（某人）的妻子通奸 **2** **~ sb** (of a woman 女人) to make her husband a cuckold by having sex with another man 使（丈夫）戴绿帽子；使（丈夫）当王八

cuckoo /ˈkʊkuː/ *noun, adj.*
■ *noun* (*pl.* **-oos**) a bird with a call that sounds like its name. Cuckoos leave their eggs in the nests of other birds. 杜鹃（鸟）；布谷鸟 ➲ SEE ALSO CLOUD CUCKOO LAND
■ *adj.* [not before noun] (*old-fashioned, informal*) crazy 疯狂；狂热

ˈcuckoo clock *noun* a clock that has a small toy bird inside that comes out every hour and marks the hours with a sound like that of a cuckoo 布谷鸟自鸣钟（钟内有小玩具鸟每个整点出现，报时声似布谷鸟叫声）

cu·cum·ber /ˈkjuːkʌmbə(r)/ *noun* [C, U] a long vegetable with dark green skin and light green flesh, that is usually eaten raw 黄瓜 ➲ VISUAL VOCAB PAGE V34 ➲ SEE ALSO SEA CUCUMBER IDM SEE COOL *adj.*

cud /kʌd/ *noun* [U] the food that cows and similar animals bring back from the stomach into the mouth to chew again （牛等动物）反刍的食物，倒嚼的食物：*cows chewing the cud* 在咀嚼反刍食物的牛

cud·dle /ˈkʌdl/ *verb, noun*
■ *verb* [I, T] to hold sb/sth close in your arms to show love or affection 拥抱；搂抱 SYN **hug**: *A couple of teenagers were kissing and cuddling on the doorstep.* 一对年轻人在门阶上亲吻拥抱。◇ **~ sth (+ adj.)** *The little boy cuddled the teddy bear close.* 小男孩紧紧地搂着玩具熊。
PHR V **ˌcuddle ˈup (to/against sb/sth)** | **ˌcuddle ˈup (together)** to sit or lie very close to sb/sth 紧靠…而坐（或躺）；依偎：*She cuddled up against him.* 她依偎着他。◇ *We cuddled up together under the blanket.* 我们盖着毯子依偎在一起。
■ *noun* [usually sing.] the action of holding sb close in your arms to show love or affection 拥抱；搂抱 SYN **hug**: *to give sb a cuddle* 拥抱某人

cud·dly /ˈkʌdli/ *adj.* (*informal*) (**cud·dlier**, **cud·dli·est**) **1** (*approving*) if a person is **cuddly**, they make you want to cuddle them 令人想拥抱的 **2** [only before noun] (of a child's toy 儿童玩具) soft and designed to be cuddled 柔软而令人想搂抱的：*a cuddly rabbit* 逗人爱抚的玩具兔

cudgel /ˈkʌdʒl/ *noun, verb*
■ *noun* a short thick stick that is used as a weapon（用作武器的）短棒，粗短棍
IDM **take up (the) cudgels on behalf of sb/sth** (*old-fashioned*) to defend or support sb/sth strongly 坚决保卫；毅然支持
■ *verb* (*BrE*) (**-ll-**, *especially US* **-l-**) **~ sb** to hit sb with a cudgel 用短棒打
IDM **cudgel your ˈbrains** (*old-fashioned, BrE*) to think very hard 冥思苦想；绞尽脑汁

cue /kjuː/ *noun, verb*
■ *noun* **1** an action or event that is a signal for sb to do sth 暗示；提示；信号：**~ (for sth)** *Jon's arrival was a cue for more champagne.* 乔恩一来就意味着要喝更多的香槟酒了。◇ **~ (to do sth)** *I think that's my cue to explain why I'm here.* 我想这就是要我解释一下我为什么到这里来。**2** a few words or an action in a play that is a signal for another actor to do sth（戏剧的）提示，暗示，尾白：*She stood in the wings and waited for her cue to go on.* 她站在舞台侧面等待着出场的提示。➲ WORDFINDER NOTE AT PERFORMANCE **3** a long wooden stick with a leather tip, used for hitting the ball in the games of BILLIARDS, POOL and SNOOKER（台球等的）球杆，弹子棒 ➲ VISUAL VOCAB PAGE V44
IDM **(right) on cue** at exactly the moment you expect or that is appropriate 恰好在这时；就在这时候：*'Where is that boy?' As if on cue, Simon appeared in the doorway.* "那男孩在哪里？" 西蒙像是接到了信号一样刚好出现在门口。**take your ˈcue from sb/sth** to copy what sb else does as an example of how to behave or what to do 模仿…的样子做；学…的样：*Investors are taking their cue from the big banks and selling dollars.* 投资者效法大银行卖出美元。
■ *verb* (**cue·ing**, **cued**, **cued**) **~ sb** to give sb a signal so they know when to start doing sth 给（某人）暗示（或提示）：*Can you cue me when you want me to begin speaking?* 你要我开始讲话时能给我暗示一下吗？

ˈcue ball *noun* the ball that is hit with the cue in games such as BILLIARDS and SNOOKER（台球和斯诺克等的）白球，母球 ➲ VISUAL VOCAB PAGE V44

ˈcue card *noun* a large card held up behind a television camera so that it can be read by actors or television PRESENTERS but cannot be seen on television 提词板，提示板（给电视演员或节目主持人看）➲ COMPARE AUTOCUE™

cuff /kʌf/ *noun, verb*
■ *noun* **1** [C] the end of a coat or shirt sleeve at the wrist 袖口：*a collar and cuffs of white lace* 带白色蕾丝花边的衣领和袖口 ➲ VISUAL VOCAB PAGE V68 **2** **cuffs** [pl.] (*informal*) = HANDCUFFS **3** (*NAmE*) (*BrE* **ˈturn-up**) [C] the bottom of the leg of a pair of trousers/pants that has been folded over on the outside（裤脚的）外翻边，外卷边 **4** [C] a light hit with an open hand 用掌轻拍：*to give sb a friendly cuff* 友好地轻轻拍某人一下
IDM **ˌoff the ˈcuff** (of speaking, remarks, etc. 讲话、话语等) without previous thought or preparation 未经思考（或准备）；即兴：*I'm just speaking off the cuff here—I haven't seen the results yet.* 我只是在这里即兴说说而已，我还没看到结果呢。◇ *an off-the-cuff remark* 即席发言
■ *verb* **~ sb** to hit sb quickly and lightly with your hand, especially in a way that is not serious 用手轻快地拍（某人）：*She cuffed him lightly around his head.* 她轻轻地在他头上拍了几下。

cuff·link /ˈkʌflɪŋk/ *noun* [usually pl.] one of a pair of small decorative objects used for fastening shirt cuffs together（衬衫的）袖口链扣，袖扣：*a pair of gold cufflinks* 一对袖口金链扣 ➲ VISUAL VOCAB PAGE V70

cuis·ine /kwɪˈziːn/ *noun* [U, C] (*from French*) **1** a style of cooking 烹饪；风味：*Italian cuisine* 意大利式烹饪 **2** the food served in a restaurant (usually an expensive one)（通常指昂贵的餐馆中的）饭菜，菜肴：*The hotel restaurant is noted for its excellent cuisine.* 这家旅馆的餐厅以美味佳肴闻名遐迩。➲ SEE ALSO HAUTE CUISINE, NOUVELLE CUISINE ➲ WORDFINDER NOTE AT RESTAURANT

cul-de-sac /ˈkʌl də sæk/ *noun* (*pl.* **cul-de-sacs** or **culs-de-sac**) (*from French*) a street that is closed at one end 死胡同；死巷

cu·lin·ary /ˈkʌlɪnəri; *NAmE* -neri/ *adj.* [only before noun] (*formal*) connected with cooking or food 烹饪的；食物的：*culinary skills* 烹饪技能 ◇ *Savour the culinary delights of Mexico.* 品尝墨西哥的美味。

cull /kʌl/ *verb, noun*
■ *verb* **~ sth** to kill a particular number of animals of a

group in order to prevent the group from getting too large 部分捕杀，选择性宰杀（为防止动物种群量过多而杀掉其中一定数量）

PHR V **'cull sth from sth** to choose or collect sth from a source or several different sources 选出；挑出；采集：*an exhibition of paintings culled from regional art galleries* 从各地区画廊中精选出来的绘画作品展

■ ***noun*** the act of killing some animals (usually the weakest ones) of a group in order to prevent the group from getting too large（为防止动物种群量过多而通常对最弱者的）选择性宰杀：*the annual seal cull* 每年对海豹的选择性宰杀

cul·min·ate /'kʌlmɪneɪt/ *verb* [I] ~ (**in/with sth**) (*formal*) to end with a particular result, or at a particular point （以某种结果）告终；（在某一点）结束：*a gun battle which culminated in the death of two police officers* 一场造成两名警察死亡的枪战 ◇ *Months of hard work culminated in success.* 几个月的艰辛工作终于取得了成功。 ◇ *Their summer tour will culminate at a spectacular concert in London.* 在伦敦举行的一场精彩的音乐会将为他们的夏季巡回演出画上句号。

cul·min·ation /ˌkʌlmɪ'neɪʃn/ *noun* [sing.] (*formal*) the highest point or end of sth, usually happening after a long time 顶点；巅峰；高潮；终点：*The reforms marked the successful culmination of a long campaign.* 这些改革标志着一场长期运动的胜利结束。

cu·lottes /kjuː'lɒts; *NAmE* kuː'lɑːts/ *noun* [pl.] women's wide short trousers/pants that are made to look like a skirt 裙裤：*a pair of culottes* 一条裙裤

culp·able /'kʌlpəbl/ *adj.* (*formal*) responsible and deserving blame for having done sth wrong 应受责备的；难辞其咎的 ▶ **culp·abil·ity** /ˌkʌlpə'bɪləti/ *noun* [U] **culp·ably** /'kʌlpəbli/ *adv.*

ˌculpable 'homicide *noun* [U] (*law* 律) in some countries, the crime of killing sb illegally but not deliberately（一些国家的）应受惩罚的杀人罪 ➲ COMPARE JUSTIFIABLE HOMICIDE

cul·prit /'kʌlprɪt/ *noun* **1** a person who has done sth wrong or against the law 犯错的人；罪犯：*The police quickly identified the real culprits.* 警方很快查出了真正的罪犯。 **2** a person or thing responsible for causing a problem 肇事者；引起问题的事物：*The main culprit in the current crisis seems to be modern farming techniques.* 当前这场危机的罪魁祸首好像是现代农业技术。

cult /kʌlt/ *noun, adj.*

■ ***noun*** **1** [usually sing.] ~ (**of sth**) a way of life, an attitude, an idea, etc. that has become very popular（对生活方式、态度、观念等的）狂热，时尚，崇拜：*the cult of physical fitness* 健身热 ◇ *An extraordinary* ***personality cult*** *had been created around the leader.* 在这位领导人的周围兴起了一场异乎寻常的个人崇拜。 **2** a small group of people who have extreme religious beliefs and who are not part of any established religion（有极端宗教信仰的）异教团体：*Their son ran away from home and joined a cult.* 他们的儿子离家出走，加入了一个异教团体。 **3** (*formal*) a system of religious beliefs and practices 宗教信仰；宗教习俗：*the Chinese cult of ancestor worship* 中国人供奉祖先的习俗

■ ***adj.*** [only before noun] very popular with a particular group of people; treating sb/sth as a cult figure, etc. 受特定群体欢迎的；作为偶像崇拜的：*a* ***cult movie/book*** 风靡一时的电影／书 ◇ *The singer has become a* ***cult figure*** *in America.* 那位歌手在美国已成为人们狂热崇拜的偶像。 ◇ *The cartoon has achieved* ***cult status.*** 这部动画片达到了风靡一时的地步。 ◇ *The TV series has a* ***cult following*** *among young people.* 那部电视连续剧在年轻人中拥有一批狂热的追随者。

cul·tiv·able /'kʌltɪvəbl/ *adj.* (of land 土地) that can be used to grow crops 可耕作的；可耕种的

cul·ti·var /'kʌltɪvɑː(r)/ *noun* (*specialist*) a type of plant that has been deliberately developed to have particular features 栽培种；栽培品种

cul·ti·vate /'kʌltɪveɪt/ *verb* (*formal*) **1** ~ **sth** to prepare and use land for growing plants or crops 耕；耕作：*The land around here has never been cultivated.* 这一带的土地从未开垦过。 ➲ WORDFINDER NOTE AT FARM **2** ~ **sth** to grow plants or crops 种植；栽培；培育 SYN **grow**: *The people cultivate mainly rice and beans.* 这里的人们主要种植水稻和豆类。 **3** ~ **sb/sth** (*sometimes disapproving*) to try to get sb's friendship or support 建立（友谊）；结交（朋友）；获得（支持）：*He purposely tried to cultivate good relations with the press.* 他特意设法与新闻界搞好关系。 ◇ *It helps if you go out of your way to cultivate the local people.* 主动结交当地人大有好处。 **4** ~ **sth** to develop an attitude, a way of talking or behaving, etc. 逐渐形成（某种态度、谈话或举止方式等）：*She cultivated an air of sophistication.* 她养成了一派精明练达的气度。

cul·ti·vated /'kʌltɪveɪtɪd/ *adj.* **1** (of people 人) having a high level of education and showing good manners 有教养的；有修养的；举止文雅的 SYN **cultured** **2** (of land 土地) used to grow crops 用于耕作的：*cultivated fields* 耕地 **3** (of plants that are also wild 野生植物) grown on a farm, etc. in order to be sold （为出售而）栽培的，培植的：*cultivated mushrooms* 培植的蘑菇 OPP **wild**

cul·ti·va·tion /ˌkʌltɪ'veɪʃn/ *noun* [U] **1** the preparation and use of land for growing plants or crops 耕种；种植；栽培：*fertile land that is* ***under cultivation*** (= being CULTIVATED) 肥沃的耕地 ◇ ***rice/wheat, etc. cultivation*** 水稻、小麦等的种植 ➲ SEE ALSO SHIFTING CULTIVATION **2** the deliberate development of a particular relationship, quality or skill （关系的）培植；（品质或技巧的）培养：*the cultivation of a good relationship with local firms* 发展与当地公司的良好关系

cul·ti·va·tor /'kʌltɪveɪtə(r)/ *noun* **1** a person who CULTIVATES (= grows crops on) the land 耕种者；种植者；栽培者 **2** a machine for breaking up soil and destroying WEEDS (= plants growing where they are not wanted) 中耕机；松土除草机

cul·tural 🔑 AW /'kʌltʃərəl/ *adj.* [usually before noun] **1** 🔑 connected with the culture of a particular society or group, its customs, beliefs, etc. 与文化有关的；文化的：*cultural differences between the two communities* 这两个群体之间的文化差异 ◇ *economic, social and cultural factors* 经济、社会和文化因素 **2** 🔑 connected with art, literature, music, etc. 与艺术、文学、音乐等有关的：*a cultural event* 文化活动 ◇ *Europe's cultural heritage* 欧洲的文化遗产 ◇ *The orchestra is very important for the cultural life of the city.* 管弦乐队对这座城市的文化生活而言非常重要。 ▶ **cul·tur·al·ly** AW /-rəli/ *adv.*

cul·ture 🔑 AW /'kʌltʃə(r)/ *noun, verb*

■ ***noun***

• **WAY OF LIFE** 生活方式 **1** 🔑 [U] the customs and beliefs, art, way of life and social organization of a particular country or group 文化，文明（指国家或群体的风俗、信仰、艺术、生活方式及社会组织）：***European/Islamic/African/American, etc. culture*** 欧洲、伊斯兰、非洲、美国等文化 ◇ *working-class culture* 工人阶级的文化 **2** 🔑 [C] a country, group, etc. with its own beliefs, etc. 文化（指拥有特定信仰等的国家、群体等）：*The children are taught to respect different cultures.* 孩子们受到教导要尊重不同的文化。 ◇ *the effect of technology on traditional cultures* 技术对各种传统文化的影响 ➲ WORDFINDER NOTE AT SOCIETY

• **ART/MUSIC/LITERATURE** 艺术；音乐；文学 **3** 🔑 [U] art, music, literature, etc., thought of as a group 文化（艺术、音乐、文学等的统称）：*Venice is a beautiful city full of culture and history.* 威尼斯是一座具有深厚文化和历史底蕴的美丽城市。 ◇ ***popular culture*** (= that is enjoyed by a lot of people) 大众文化 ◇ *the Minister for Culture* 文化部长

• **BELIEFS/ATTITUDES** 看法；态度 **4** 🔑 [C, U] the beliefs and attitudes about sth that people in a particular group or organization share 文化（某群体或组织的一致看法和态度）：*The political cultures of the United States and Europe are very different.* 美国的政治观和欧洲的大不相同。 ◇ *A culture of failure exists in some schools.* 在某些学校中存在着失败文化。 ◇ *company culture* 企业文化 ◇ *We are living in a consumer culture.* 我们生活在一种消费文化

之中。

- **GROWING/BREEDING** 种植；养殖 **5** [U] (*specialist*) the growing of plants or breeding of particular animals in order to get a particular substance or crop from them 种植；栽培；养殖；培育：*the culture of silkworms* (= for silk) 桑蚕养殖
- **CELLS/BACTERIA** 细胞；细菌 **6** [C] (*biology* 生, *medical* 医) a group of cells or bacteria, especially one taken from a person or an animal and grown for medical or scientific study, or to produce food; the process of obtaining and growing these cells 培养物；培养细胞；培养细菌；（为医疗、科研或食品生产而作的细胞或细菌的）培养：*a culture of cells from the tumour* 肿瘤细胞的培养 ◇ *Yogurt is made from active cultures.* 酸奶是由活性培养菌制成的。◇ *to do/take a throat culture* 采集喉部培养细胞

■ ***verb*** **~ sth** (*biology* 生, *medical* 医) to grow a group of cells or bacteria for medical or scientific study 培养（细胞或细菌）

cul·tured AW /ˈkʌltʃəd; *NAmE* -tʃərd/ *adj.* **1** (of people 人) well educated and able to understand and enjoy art, literature, etc. 有教养的；有修养的；文雅的 SYN **cultivated** OPP **uncultured** **2** (of cells or bacteria 细胞或细菌) grown for medical or scientific study（为医学或科学研究）培养的 **3** (of PEARLS 珍珠) grown artificially 人工养殖的

ˈ**culture shock** *noun* [C, U] a feeling of confusion and anxiety that sb may feel when they live in or visit another country 文化冲击，文化休克（指在异国生活或访问时的一种困惑不安的感觉）

ˈ**culture vulture** *noun* (*humorous*) a person who is very interested in serious art, music, literature, etc. 文化狂热分子

cul·vert /ˈkʌlvət; *NAmE* -vərt/ *noun* a tunnel that carries a river or a pipe for water under a road 涵（洞）；（道路下面的）排水管

cum /kʌm/ *prep.* (used for linking two nouns 用于连接两个名词) and; as well as 和；与；及：*a bedroom-cum-study* 卧室兼书房

cum·ber·some /ˈkʌmbəsəm; *NAmE* -bərs-/ *adj.* **1** large and heavy; difficult to carry 大而笨重的；难以携带的 SYN **bulky**：*cumbersome machinery* 笨重的机器 **2** slow and complicated 缓慢复杂的：*cumbersome legal procedures* 繁琐的法律程序 **3** (of words or phrases 单词或短语) long or complicated 冗长的；累赘的；复杂的：*The organization changed its cumbersome title to something easier to remember.* 这家机构把它那复杂累赘的名称改得简单好记一些了。

cumin /ˈkjuːmɪn; ˈkʌm-/ *noun* [U] the dried seeds of the cumin plant, used in cooking as a spice 莳萝籽；土茴香籽：*cumin seeds* 土茴香籽 ➲ VISUAL VOCAB PAGE V35

cum laude /ˌkʊm ˈlɔːdi; ˈlaʊdeɪ/ *adv., adj.* (*from Latin*) (in the US) at the third of the three highest levels of achievement that students can reach when they finish their studies at college 以优等成绩（美国大学毕业的成绩等级，为三等优异成绩的第三等）：*He graduated cum laude.* 他以优等成绩毕业。➲ COMPARE MAGNA CUM LAUDE, SUMMA CUM LAUDE

cum·mer·bund /ˈkʌməbʌnd; *NAmE* -mərb-/ *noun* a wide band of silk, etc. worn around the waist, especially under a DINNER JACKET（尤指男式晚礼服的）宽腰带

cu·mu·la·tive /ˈkjuːmjələtɪv; *NAmE* -leɪtɪv/ *adj.* **1** having a result that increases in strength or importance each time more of sth is added（在力量或重要性方面）聚积的，积累的，渐增的：*the* ***cumulative effect*** *of human activity on the world environment* 人类活动对世界生态环境日积月累的影响 **2** including all the amounts that have been added previously 累计的；累积的：*the monthly sales figures and the cumulative total for the past six months* 每月的销售数字和过去六个月的累计总数 ▶ **cu·mu·la·tive·ly** *adv.*

cu·mu·lo·nim·bus /ˌkjuːmələʊˈnɪmbəs; *NAmE* -loʊ-/ *noun* [U] (*specialist*) a high mass of thick cloud with a flat base, often seen during THUNDERSTORMS 积雨云（常伴有雷阵雨）

cu·mu·lus /ˈkjuːmjələs/ *noun* [U] (*specialist*) a type of thick white cloud 积云

cu·nei·form /ˈkjuːnɪfɔːm; *NAmE* -fɔːrm/ *noun* [U] an ancient system of writing used in Persia and Assyria（古代波斯和亚述的）楔形文字

cun·ni·lin·gus /ˌkʌnɪˈlɪŋgəs/ *noun* [U] the act of touching a woman's sex organs with the mouth and tongue in order to give sexual pleasure 舔阴（用口和舌接触女性生殖器）

cun·ning /ˈkʌnɪŋ/ *adj., noun*

■ ***adj.*** **1** (*disapproving*) able to get what you want in a clever way, especially by tricking or cheating sb 狡猾的；奸诈的；诡诈的 SYN **crafty, wily**：*a cunning liar* 花言巧语的骗子 ◇ *He was as cunning as a fox.* 他像狐狸一样狡猾。**2** clever and skilful 灵巧的；精巧的；巧妙的 SYN **ingenious**：*It was a cunning piece of detective work.* 那是一篇构思巧妙的侦探作品。▶ **cun·ning·ly** *adv.*：*The microphone was cunningly concealed in the bookcase.* 话筒被巧妙地隐藏在书柜里。

■ ***noun*** [U] the ability to achieve sth by tricking or cheating other people in a clever way 狡猾；诡诈；狡黠 SYN **craftiness**：*It took energy and cunning just to survive.* 既要花力气又要有心计才能维持生存。◇ *She used low cunning* (= dishonest behaviour) *to get what she wanted.* 她用了卑鄙的欺诈手段来获取她想得到的东西。

cunt /kʌnt/ *noun* (*taboo, slang*) **1** a woman's VAGINA and outer sexual organs 屄；女性阴部 **2** a very offensive word used to insult sb and to show anger or dislike（用于辱骂）讨厌鬼，龟孙子，王八蛋：*You stupid cunt!* 你这傻屄！

cup 🔑 /kʌp/ *noun, verb*

■ ***noun*** **1** 🔑 [C] a small container shaped like a bowl, usually with a handle, used for drinking tea, coffee, etc. 杯子：*a teacup* 茶杯 ◇ *a coffee cup* 咖啡杯 ◇ *a cup and saucer* 一套杯碟 ◇ *a paper cup* 纸杯 ➲ VISUAL VOCAB PAGE V23 **2** 🔑 [C] the contents of a cup 一杯（的量）：*She drank the whole cup.* 她把那一杯全喝下去了。◇ *Would you like a cup of tea?* 你想喝杯茶吗？ **3** 🔑 [C] a unit for measuring quantity used in cooking in the US; a metal or plastic container used to measure this quantity 杯（美国用作烹饪的计量单位）；量杯（金属或塑料量器）：*two cups of flour and half a cup of butter* 两杯面粉加上半杯黄油 **4** 🔑 [C] a thing shaped like a cup 杯状物：*an egg cup* 蛋杯 **5** 🔑 [C] a gold or silver cup on a STEM, often with two handles, that is given as a prize in a competition 奖杯；优胜杯：*She's won several cups for skating.* 她已多次荣获滑冰比赛的奖杯。◇ *He lifted the cup for the fifth time this year* (= it was the fifth time he had won). 他今年第五次举起了奖杯。➲ PICTURE AT MEDAL **6** 🔑 [sing.] (*usually* **Cup**) a sports competition in which a cup is given as a prize 杯赛：*the World Cup* 世界杯赛 **7** [C] one of the two parts of a BRA that cover the breast（胸罩的）罩杯：*a C cup* 罩杯尺寸为C的胸罩 **8** [C, U] a drink made from wine mixed with, for example, fruit juice（由葡萄酒与果汁等调制的）混合饮料 **9** [C] (*NAmE*) (in GOLF 高尔夫球) a hollow in the ground that you must get the ball into 球洞 **10** [C] (*NAmE*) a piece of plastic that a man wears over his sex organs to protect them while he is playing a sport（体育运动时保护男子生殖器的）护裆；裆部护具

IDM **in your ˈcups** (*old-fashioned*) having drunk too much alcohol 喝醉：*He gets very maudlin when he's in his cups.* 他酒醉就顾影自怜。 **not sb's cup of ˈtea** (*informal*) not what sb likes or is interested in 非某人所好；不合某人心意：*An evening at the opera isn't everyone's cup of tea.* 并不是所有人都喜欢晚上去听歌剧。◇ *He's nice enough but not really my cup of tea.* 他这人挺不错，但不是我特喜欢的那种人。➲ MORE AT SLIP *n.*

■ ***verb*** (**-pp-**) **1** **~ your hand(s)** (**around/over sth**) to make your hands into the shape of a bowl 使（手）窝成杯状：*She held the bird gently in cupped hands.* 她双手轻轻地捧着那只小鸟。**2** **~ sth** (**in your hands**) to hold sth, making your hands into a round shape 使（双手）成圆状托起：*He cupped her face in his hands and kissed her.* 他用双手捧着她的脸吻她。

cup·board /ˈkʌbəd; *NAmE* -bərd/ *noun* **1** a piece of furniture with doors and shelves used for storing dishes, food, clothes, etc. 橱柜；食物柜；衣柜：*kitchen cupboards* 厨房用的橱柜 **2** (*BrE*) (*NAmE* **closet**) a space in a wall with a door that reaches the ground, used for storing things 壁橱：*built-in cupboards* 壁橱 SEE ALSO AIRING CUPBOARD, BROOM CUPBOARD

IDM **the ˌcupboard is ˈbare** (*BrE*) used to say that there is no money for sth 食橱是空的（指没钱购买）：*They are seeking more funds but the cupboard is bare.* 他们正在寻求更多的资金，然而根本找不到。ORIGIN This expression refers to a children's nursery rhyme about Old Mother Hubbard, who had nothing in her cupboard to feed her dog. 源自一首关于老妈哈伯德的儿歌。她的食橱里没有喂狗的东西。**ˈcupboard love** (*BrE*) affection that sb, especially a child, shows towards sb else in order to get sth（尤指小孩）有所企图的亲热 MORE AT SKELETON

cup·cake /ˈkʌpkeɪk/ (*especially NAmE*) (*BrE also* **ˈfairy cake**) *noun* a small cake, baked in a paper container shaped like a cup and often with ICING on top（常撒有糖霜的）纸杯蛋糕

ˈcup final (*also* **Cup Final**) *noun* (*BrE*) (especially in football (SOCCER) 尤指足球) the last match in a series of matches in a competition that gives a cup as a prize to the winners 优胜杯决赛；锦标赛决赛：*cup final tickets* 优胜杯决赛票 ◊ *the FA Cup Final* 足协杯赛决赛

cup·ful /ˈkʌpfʊl/ *noun* the amount that a cup will hold 一杯（的量）；满杯：*3 cupfuls of water* * 3 满杯水 SEE ALSO CUP *n.* (2)

Cupid /ˈkjuːpɪd/ *noun* **1** the Roman god of love who is shown as a beautiful baby boy with wings, carrying a BOW² *n.* (1) and arrow（罗马爱神）丘比特 **2** **cupid** [C] a picture or statue of a baby boy who looks like Cupid 似罗马爱神丘比特的画像（或雕塑）

IDM **play ˈCupid** to try to start a romantic relationship between two people 扮演丘比特角色；牵线撮合

cu·pid·ity /kjuːˈpɪdəti/ *noun* [U] (*formal*) a strong desire for more wealth, possessions, power, etc. than a person needs 贪心；贪婪 SYN **greed**

cu·pola /ˈkjuːpələ/ *noun* a round part on top of a building (like a small DOME) 小穹顶 VISUAL VOCAB PAGE V14

cuppa /ˈkʌpə/ *noun* (*BrE, informal*) a cup of tea 一杯茶：*Do you fancy a cuppa?* 你想来一杯茶吗？

cup·ping /ˈkʌpɪŋ/ *noun* [U] a way of treating pain by putting special cups on the skin and heating them so that the flow of blood to the skin increases 拔火罐；杯吸法

ˈcup tie *noun* (*BrE*) (especially in football (SOCCER) 尤指足球) a match between two teams in a competition that gives a cup as a prize to the winner 优胜杯赛比赛

cur /kɜː(r)/ *noun* (*old-fashioned, disapproving*) an aggressive dog, especially a MONGREL 恶狗；（尤指）杂种狗

cur·able /ˈkjʊərəbl; *NAmE* ˈkjʊr-/ *adj.* (of an illness 疾病) that can be cured 可医治的；可治愈的：*Most skin cancers are curable if treated early.* 如果及早治疗，多数的皮肤癌是可治好的。OPP **incurable**

cura·çao /ˌkjʊərəˈsəʊ; -ˈseɪəʊ; *NAmE* ˌkjuːrəˈsoʊ; -ˈsaʊ/ *noun* [U, C] a strong alcoholic drink made from the skin of bitter oranges 库拉索酒（橙皮烈酒）

cur·acy /ˈkjʊərəsi; *NAmE* ˈkjʊr-/ *noun* (*pl.* **-ies**) the position of a curate¹; the time that sb is a curate¹ 助理牧师的职位；助理牧师的任期

cur·ate¹ /ˈkjʊərət; *NAmE* ˈkjʊrət/ *noun* SEE ALSO CURATE² (in the Anglican Church 圣公会) an assistant to a VICAR (= a priest, who is in charge of the church or churches in a particular area)（某教区的）助理牧师

IDM **the/a ˌcurate's ˈegg** (*BrE*) something that has some good parts and some bad ones 好坏兼有之物；瑕瑜互见之物

cur·ate² /kjʊəˈreɪt; *NAmE* kjʊˈr-/ *verb* **1 ~ sth** to select, organize and look after the objects or works of art in a museum or an ART GALLERY, etc. 管理（博物馆或美术馆的藏品）；策展 **2 ~ sth** (especially on the Internet) to collect, select and present information or items such as pictures, video, music, etc. for people to use or enjoy, using your professional or expert knowledge（尤在互联网上）精选并分享，策展（信息、图片、视频、音乐等）：*A UK rock band are curating the BBC's digital music station for a week.* 一支英国摇滚乐队在英国广播公司的数字音乐台进行为期一周的内容策展。

cura·tive /ˈkjʊərətɪv; *NAmE* ˈkjʊr-/ *adj.* (*formal*) able to cure illness 能治病的；有疗效的 SYN **healing**：*the curative properties of herbs* 药草治病的功效 COMPARE PREVENTIVE

cur·ator /kjʊəˈreɪtə(r); *NAmE* kjʊˈr-/ *noun* a person whose job is to be in charge of the objects or works of art in a museum or an ART GALLERY, etc.（博物馆或美术馆等的）馆长，负责人，策展人

curb /kɜːb; *NAmE* kɜːrb/ *verb, noun*

■ *verb* **~ sth** to control or limit sth, especially sth bad 控制，抑制，限定，约束（尤指不好的事物）SYN **check**：*He needs to learn to curb his temper.* 他得学着控制自己的脾气。◊ *A range of policies have been introduced aimed at curbing inflation.* 为了抑制通货膨胀实施了一系列的政策。

■ *noun* **1** **~ (on sth)** something that controls and puts limits on sth 起控制（或限制）作用的事物：*curbs on government spending* 对政府开支的限制措施 **2** (*NAmE*) (*BrE* **kerb**) the edge of the raised path at the side of a road, usually made of long pieces of stone（由条石砌成的）路缘，道牙，马路牙子：*The bus mounted the curb* (= went onto the SIDEWALK/PAVEMENT) *and hit a tree.* 那辆公交车开上路缘撞到了一棵树上。VISUAL VOCAB PAGE V3

curb·side (*NAmE*) (*BrE* **kerb·side**) /ˈkɜːbsaɪd; *NAmE* ˈkɜːrb-/ *noun* [U] the side of the street or path near the CURB/KERB 人行道靠近路缘的部分

curb·stone (*NAmE*) (*BrE* **kerb·stone**) /ˈkɜːbstəʊn; *NAmE* ˈkɜːrbstoʊn/ *noun* a block of stone or concrete in a CURB/KERB 路缘石

curd /kɜːd; *NAmE* kɜːrd/ *noun* [U] (*also* **curds** [pl.]) a thick soft substance that is formed when milk turns sour 凝乳（牛奶变酸后形成的稠而软的物质）

ˈcurd cheese *noun* [U, C] (*BrE*) a type of soft cheese 凝乳（软）干酪 COMPARE QUARK (2)

cur·dle /ˈkɜːdl; *NAmE* ˈkɜːrdl/ *verb* **1** [I, T] **~ (sth)** when a liquid, especially milk, **curdles** or sth **curdles** it, it separates into solid and liquid parts（使）凝结，结成酸乳 **2** [I, T] **~ (sth)** if sth **curdles** your blood or makes your blood **curdle**, it makes you extremely frightened or shocked 吓得血液凝固；使心惊胆战 SEE ALSO BLOOD-CURDLING

cure /kjʊə(r); *NAmE* kjʊr/ *verb, noun*

■ *verb* **1** **~ sb (of sth)** to make a person or an animal healthy again after an illness 治愈，治好（病人或动物）：*Will you be able to cure him, Doctor?* 医生，你能把他治好吗？ WORDFINDER NOTE AT DOCTOR COLLOCATIONS AT ILL

> **WORDFINDER** 联想词：chemotherapy, **disease**, **drug**, injection, medication, osteopathy, palliative, physiotherapy, radiotherapy

2 **~ sth** to make an illness go away 治好（疾病）：*TB is a serious illness, but it can be cured.* 肺结核虽然是一种严重的疾病，但可治愈。 **3 ~ sth** to deal with a problem successfully 解决，了结（问题）：*I finally managed to cure the rattling noise in my car.* 我最终设法解决了我汽车发出的格格响声。 **4 ~ sb of sth** to stop sb from behaving in a particular way, especially a way that is bad or annoying 矫正，改正（某人的不良行为） **5 ~ sth** to treat food or TOBACCO with smoke, salt or heat, etc. in order to preserve it（用熏、腌、加热等方法）加工贮藏（食物或烟草）IDM SEE KILL v.

■ *noun* **1** ~ (**for sth**) a medicine or medical treatment that cures an illness 药；药物；疗法：*the search for a cure for cancer* 对癌症治愈方法的研究 ◇ *There is no known cure but the illness can be treated.* 这种病尚没有确切的治愈方法，但可以医治。 **2** the act of curing sb of an illness or the process of being cured 治疗；疗程：*Doctors cannot effect a cure if the disease has spread too far.* 假如这种疾病已扩散得厉害，医生也无计可施。 ◇ *The cure took six weeks.* 此疗程花了六个星期。 **3** ~ (**for sth**) something that will solve a problem, improve a bad situation, etc.（解决问题、改善糟糕情况等的）措施，对策：*a cure for poverty* 解决贫穷问题的措施 IDM SEE PREVENTION

ˈcure-all *noun* something that people believe can cure any problem or any disease 万灵药；灵丹妙药 SYN **panacea**

cur·few /ˈkɜːfjuː; *NAmE* ˈkɜːrf-/ *noun* [C, U] **1** a law which says that people must not go outside after a particular time at night until the morning; the time after which nobody must go outside 宵禁令；宵禁时间：*The army imposed a dusk-to-dawn curfew.* 军队强制实行黄昏至黎明的宵禁。 ◇ *You must get home before curfew.* 你必须在实行宵禁之前回到家中。 ➲ COLLOCATIONS AT WAR **2** (*NAmE*) a time when children must be home in the evening 儿童晚间必须在家的时间：*I have a 10 o'clock curfew.* 我得遵守晚上 10 点之前回家的规定。

curie /ˈkjʊəri; *NAmE* ˈkjʊri/ *noun* (*abbr.* **Ci**) (*physics* 物) a unit for measuring RADIOACTIVITY 居里（放射性活度单位）

curio /ˈkjʊəriəʊ; *NAmE* ˈkjʊrioʊ/ *noun* (*pl.* **-os**) a small object that is rare or unusual, often sth that people collect（常指收藏的）小件稀有物

curi·os·ity /ˌkjʊəriˈɒsəti; *NAmE* ˌkjʊriˈɑːs-/ *noun* (*pl.* **-ies**) **1** [U, sing.] ~ (**about sth**) | ~ (**to do sth**) a strong desire to know about sth 好奇心；求知欲：*Children show curiosity about everything.* 儿童对一切事物都显露出好奇心。 ◇ *a certain curiosity to see what would happen next* 有点想知道接下来会发生什么的好奇心 ◇ *The letter wasn't addressed to me but I opened it* ***out of curiosity***. 那封信不是写给我的，然而我却出于好奇把它拆开了。 ◇ *His answer did not* ***satisfy my curiosity*** *at all.* 他的答复丝毫没有满足我的好奇心。 ◇ *Sophie's* ***curiosity was aroused*** *by the mysterious phone call.* 那个神秘的电话引起了索菲的好奇心。 ◇ *intellectual curiosity* 求知欲 ◇ *'Why do you ask?' 'Oh, just* ***idle curiosity*** (= no particular reason).' "你为什么要问？" "哦，只是好奇而已。" **2** [C] an unusual and interesting thing 罕见而有趣之物；奇物；珍品：*The museum is full of historical curiosities.* 这座博物馆有许多珍奇历史文物。

IDM **curiosity killed the ˈcat** (*saying*) used to tell sb not to ask questions or try to find out about things that do not concern them 好奇害死猫（让人别提问或打听与己无关的事情）

curi·ous /ˈkjʊəriəs; *NAmE* ˈkjʊr-/ *adj.* **1** ~ (**about sth**) | ~ (**to do sth**) having a strong desire to know about sth 求知欲强的；好奇的 SYN **inquisitive**：*They were very curious about the people who lived upstairs.* 他们对住在楼上的人感到很好奇。 ◇ *I was curious to find out what she had said.* 我真想弄清楚她说了些什么。 ◇ *Everyone was* ***curious as to*** *why Mark was leaving.* 马克为什么要离去，大家都感到好奇。 ◇ *He is such a curious boy, always asking questions.* 他这个孩子求知欲很强，总是爱提问。 **2** ~ (**that…**) strange and unusual 稀奇古怪；奇特；不寻常：*There was a curious mixture of people in the audience.* 观众中有各色人等，显得很怪。 ◇ *It was a curious feeling, as though we were floating on air.* 那是一种奇特的感觉，我们仿佛在空中飘浮。 ◇ ***It was curious that*** *she didn't tell anyone.* 她没有告诉任何人，这很反常。 ▸ **curi·ous·ly** *adv.*: *'Are you really an artist?' Sara asked curiously.* "你真是画家吗？" 萨拉好奇地问道。 ◇ *His clothes were curiously old-fashioned.* 他的衣服式样陈旧古怪。 ◇ *Curiously enough, a year later exactly the same thing happened again.* 说来也怪，一模一样的事情在一年以后又发生了。

cur·ium /ˈkjʊəriəm; *NAmE* ˈkjʊr-/ *noun* [U] (*symb.* **Cm**) a chemical element. Curium is a RADIOACTIVE metal produced artificially from PLUTONIUM. 锔（放射性化学元素）

curl /kɜːl; *NAmE* kɜːrl/ *verb, noun*

■ *verb* **1** [I, T] ~ (**sth**) to form or make sth form into a curl or curls 卷；（使）拳曲，鬈曲：*His hair curls naturally.* 他的头发天生鬈曲。 **2** [I, T] to form or make sth form into a curved shape（使）成拳曲状；蜷缩：(**+ adv./prep.**) *The cat curled* ***into a ball*** *and went to sleep.* 那只猫蜷缩成一团睡着了。 ◇ **~ sth** (**+ adv./prep.**) *She curled her legs up under her.* 她盘腿坐着。 **3** [I, T] to move while forming into a twisted or curved shape; to make sth do this（使）呈螺旋（或卷曲）状移动；（使）旋绕；缭绕：(**+ adv./prep.**) *The smoke curled steadily upwards.* 烟袅袅上升。 ◇ **~ sth** (**+ adv./prep.**) *He turned and curled the ball around the goalkeeper.* 他转身把球一盘，绕过了守门员。 **4** [T, I] ~ (**sth**) if you **curl** your lip or your lip **curls**, you move your lip upwards and sideways to show that you think sb/sth is stupid or that you are better than they are 噘起（嘴唇）；撇（嘴）IDM SEE TOE *n.*

PHR V **ˌcurl ˈup | be ˌcurled ˈup** to lie or sit with your back curved and your arms and legs bent close to your body 蜷曲着躺（或坐）：*She curled up and closed her eyes.* 她蜷成一团，闭上了眼睛。 ➲ PICTURE AT CURVED **ˌcurl ˈup | ˌcurl sb ˈup** (*BrE, informal*) to become or make sb become very embarrassed（使）感到十分尴尬 **ˌcurl ˈup | ˌcurl sth↔ˈup** to form or make sth form into a tightly curled shape（使）形成紧紧的卷曲状：*The paper started to shrivel and curl up in the heat.* 那张纸在高温下开始起皱卷曲。

■ *noun* **1** [C] a small bunch of hair that forms a curved or round shape（一绺）鬈发：*Her hair was a mass of curls.* 她满头鬈发。 ◇ *The baby had dark eyes and dark curls.* 那婴孩长着深色的眼睛和深色的鬈发。 **2** [C, U] the tendency of hair to form curls（头发）拳曲：*His hair had a natural curl.* 他的头发是自然鬈。 **3** [C] a thing that forms a curved or round shape 卷状物；螺旋状物：*a curl of smoke* 一缕青烟 ◇ *Decorate the cake with curls of chocolate.* 用圈状巧克力来装饰这个蛋糕。 ◇ *a contemptuous curl of the lip* (= an expression showing disapproval) 轻蔑地撇一撇嘴

curl·er /ˈkɜːlə(r); *NAmE* ˈkɜːrl-/ *noun* [usually pl.] a small plastic or metal tube which you can wrap wet hair around in order to make it curl 卷发夹 SYN **roller**

cur·lew /ˈkɜːljuː; *NAmE* ˈkɜːrl-/ *noun* a bird with a long thin beak that curves downwards, that lives near water 杓鹬

cur·li·cue /ˈkɜːlɪkjuː; *NAmE* ˈkɜːrl-/ *noun* (*specialist*) a decorative curl or twist in writing or in a design（书法、图案等的）花饰旋曲

curl·ing /ˈkɜːlɪŋ; *NAmE* ˈkɜːrlɪŋ/ *noun* [U] a game played on ice, in which players slide heavy flat stones towards a mark 冰壶，冰上溜石（将重石片滑向一目标）

ˈcurling tongs *noun* (*also* **tongs**) [pl.] (*both BrE*) (*NAmE* **ˈcurling iron** [C]) a tool that is heated and used for curling hair 烫发钳；卷发钳

curly /ˈkɜːli; *NAmE* ˈkɜːrli/ *adj.* (**curl·ier**, **curli·est**) having a lot of curls or a curved shape 有鬈发（或毛）的；拳曲状的：*short curly hair* 短鬈发 ◇ *a dog with a curly tail* 卷尾巴的狗 ➲ PICTURE AT CURVED ➲ VISUAL VOCAB PAGE V65 OPP **straight**

ˌcurly ˈendive *noun* [C, U] = CHICORY (2)

cur·mudg·eon /kɜːˈmʌdʒən; *NAmE* kɜːrˈm-/ *noun* (*old-fashioned*) a bad-tempered person, often an old one 脾气坏的人（常指老年人）▸ **cur·mudg·eon·ly** *adj.*

cur·rant /ˈkʌrənt; *NAmE* ˈkɜːr-/ *noun* **1** a small dried GRAPE, used in cakes, etc. 小葡萄干（用于糕饼等）：*a currant bun* 葡萄干小圆面包 **2** (usually in compounds 通常构成复合词) a small black, red or white BERRY that grows in bunches on bushes 穗醋栗；醋栗；茶藨子：*blackcurrants* 黑茶藨子 ◇ *currant bushes* 醋栗灌木丛

cur·rency AW /ˈkʌrənsi; *NAmE* ˈkɜːr-/ *noun* (*pl.* -ies) **1** [C, U] the system of money that a country uses 通货；货币：*trading in foreign currencies* 买卖外汇 ◇ *a single European currency* 统一的欧洲货币 ◇ *You'll need some cash in* ***local currency*** *but you can also use your credit card.* 你将需要一些当地的货币现金，但也可使用信用卡。➲ SEE ALSO HARD CURRENCY **2** [U] the fact that sth is used or accepted by a lot of people 通用；流行；流传：*The term 'post-industrial' now has* ***wide currency.*** "后工业化"这个术语现已广为使用。◇ *The qualification has* ***gained currency*** *all over the world.* 这种资格在全世界都得到了普遍认可。

cur·rent 🔑 /ˈkʌrənt; *NAmE* ˈkɜːr-/ *adj., noun*

■ ***adj.*** **1** 🔑 [only before noun] happening now; of the present time 现时发生的；当前的；现在的：*current prices* 时价 ◇ *a budget for the current year* 今年的预算 ◇ *your current employer* 你现在的雇主 ➲ NOTE AT ACTUAL **2** 🔑 being used by or accepted by most people 通用的；流通的；流行的：*words that are no longer current* 已不再通用的词

■ ***noun*** **1** 🔑 the movement of water in the sea or a river; the movement of air in a particular direction（海洋或江河的）水流，潮流；气流：*He swam to the shore against a* ***strong current.*** 他逆着急流游向岸边。◇ *Birds use warm air currents to help their flight.* 鸟利用暖气流助飞。➲ WORDFINDER NOTE AT RIVER **2** 🔑 the flow of electricity through a wire, etc. 电流：*a 15 amp electrical current* * 15 安培的电流 ➲ SEE ALSO AC, DC **3** the fact of particular ideas, opinions or feelings being present in a group of people 思潮；潮流；趋向：*Ministers are worried by this current of anti-government feeling.* 部长们对这股反政府情绪感到担忧。

ˈ**current account** (*BrE*) (*US* ˈ**checking account**, *CanE* ˈ**chequing account**) *noun* a type of bank account that you can take money out of at any time, and that provides you with a CHEQUEBOOK and CASH CARD 活期存款账户；往来账户 ➲ COMPARE DEPOSIT ACCOUNT

ˌ**current afˈfairs** *noun* [pl.] events of political or social importance that are happening now 时事

cur·rent·ly 🔑 /ˈkʌrəntli; *NAmE* ˈkɜːr-/ *adv.* at the present time 现时；目前；当前；时下：*The hourly charge is currently £35.* 现在每小时收费是 35 英镑。◇ *Currently, over 500 students are enrolled on the course.* 目前有 500 多名学生注册学习这门课程。◇ *All the options are* ***currently available.*** 所有的方案现在均可选择。◇ *This matter is currently being discussed.* 这个问题现正在讨论之中。

cur·ricu·lar /kəˈrɪkjələ(r)/ *adj.* connected with the curriculum of a school, etc. 课程的 ➲ SEE ALSO EXTRA-CURRICULAR

cur·ricu·lum /kəˈrɪkjələm/ *noun* (*pl.* **cur·ric·ula** /-lə/ or **cur·ricu·lums**) the subjects that are included in a course of study or taught in a school, college, etc.（学校等的）全部课程：*the school curriculum* 学校课程 ◇ (*BrE*) *Spanish is on the curriculum.* 西班牙语已纳入课程内容。◇ (*NAmE*) *Spanish is in the curriculum.* 西班牙语已纳入课程内容。➲ COLLOCATIONS AT EDUCATION ➲ COMPARE SYLLABUS

cur·ricu·lum vitae /kəˌrɪkjələm ˈviːtaɪ/ (*abbr.* **CV**) *noun* **1** (*BrE*) (*NAmE* **ré·sumé**) a written record of your education and the jobs you have done, that you send when you are applying for a job（求职用的）履历，简历：*Applications with a full curriculum vitae and two references should reach the Principal by June 12th.* 申请书连同完整的个人简历和两封推荐信必须在 6 月 12 日以前送达校长处。**2** (*also* **vita**) (*US*) a record of a university/college teacher's education and where they have worked, also including a list of books and articles that they have published and courses that they have taught, used when they are applying for a job（大学教师求职用的）工作履历

cur·ried /ˈkʌrid; *NAmE* ˈkɜːr-/ *adj.* [only before noun] cooked with hot spices 用咖喱烹调的：***curried chicken/beef/eggs, etc.*** 咖喱鸡肉、牛肉、鸡蛋等

curry /ˈkʌri; *NAmE* ˈkɜːri/ *noun, verb*

■ ***noun*** [C, U] a S Asian dish of meat, vegetables, etc. cooked with hot spices, often served with rice 咖喱菜：*a chicken curry* 一道咖喱鸡肉 ◇ *Would you like some more curry?* 你想再来一点咖喱菜吗？

■ ***verb*** (**cur·ries**, **curry·ing**, **cur·ried**, **cur·ried**) **~ sth** to make curry out of meat or vegetables 以（肉或蔬菜）烹制咖喱菜

IDM **curry ˈfavour (with sb)** (*disapproving*) to try to get sb to like or support you by praising or helping them a lot 讨好；奉承；拍马屁

ˈ**curry leaf** *noun* [C, U] a type of SHRUB (= a large plant) or small tree grown in India and Sri Lanka; the leaf of this tree, widely used as a spice in Indian cooking 咖喱树（生长在印度和斯里兰卡的一种灌木或小乔木）；咖喱叶（咖喱树的叶子，在印度烹饪中广泛地用作香料）

ˈ**curry powder** *noun* [U] a powder made from a mixture of spices, used to give a hot flavour to food, especially curry 混合辣味调料粉；（尤指）咖喱粉

curse /kɜːs; *NAmE* kɜːrs/ *noun, verb*

■ ***noun*** **1** [C] a rude or offensive word or phrase that some people use when they are very angry 咒骂语；骂人话 SYN **oath, swear word**：*He muttered a curse at the other driver.* 他低声咒骂对方司机。**2** [C] a word or phrase that has a magic power to make sth bad happen 咒；咒语：*The family thought that they were* ***under a curse.*** 这家人认为他们受人诅咒而遭了殃。➲ COMPARE HEX **3** [C] something that causes harm or evil 祸根；祸端；祸水：*the curse of drug addiction* 吸毒成瘾的祸害 ◇ *Noise is a curse of modern city life.* 噪音是现代城市生活的一大祸根。**4 the curse** [sing.] (*old-fashioned, informal*) = MENSTRUATION

■ ***verb*** **1** [I] to swear 诅咒：*He hit his head as he stood up and cursed loudly.* 他站起来时撞了头，便破口大骂。**2** [T] to say rude things to sb or think rude things about sb/sth 咒骂；诅咒；在心里诅咒：**~ sb/sth/yourself** *She cursed her bad luck.* 她骂自己运气不好。◇ **~ sb/sth/yourself for sth** *He cursed himself for his stupidity.* 他咒骂自己愚蠢。**3** [T] **~ sb/sth** to use a magic word or phrase against sb in order to harm them 念咒语诅咒：*Legend has it that the whole village had been cursed by a witch.* 传说整座村庄遭到了巫婆的诅咒。➲ COMPARE HEX

PHR V **be ˈcursed with sth** to continuously suffer from or be affected by sth bad 不断因…而遭殃；为…所苦；受…之害：*She seems cursed with bad luck.* 她好像运气不好连连遭殃。

cursed *adj.* **1** /kɜːst; *NAmE* kɜːrst/ having a curse *n.* (2) on it; suffering from a curse *n.* (2) 带有符咒的；遭受诅咒之苦的：*The necklace was cursed.* 这条项链上附有会给人带来灾难的符咒。◇ *The whole family seemed cursed.* 全家人仿佛都受到诅咒遭了殃。**2** /ˈkɜːsɪd; *NAmE* ˈkɜːrsɪd/ [only before noun] (*old-fashioned*) unpleasant; annoying 使人不愉快的；可恨的；讨厌的

cur·sive /ˈkɜːsɪv; *NAmE* ˈkɜːrs-/ *adj.* (*specialist*) (of HANDWRITING 笔迹) with the letters joined together 连笔的；草书的；草写体的

cur·sor /ˈkɜːsə(r); *NAmE* ˈkɜːrs-/ *noun* a small mark on a computer screen that can be moved and that shows the position on the screen where, for example, text will be added（计算机屏幕上的）光标，游标 ➲ WORDFINDER NOTE AT KEYBOARD ➲ VISUAL VOCAB PAGE V74

curs·ory /ˈkɜːsəri; *NAmE* ˈkɜːrs-/ *adj.* (*often disapproving*) done quickly and without giving enough attention to details 粗略的；仓促的 SYN **brief, perfunctory**：***a cursory glance/examination/inspection*** 匆匆的一瞥；粗略的审查 / 检查 ▶ **cur·sor·ily** /ˈkɜːsərəli; *NAmE* ˈkɜːrs-/ *adv.*

curt /kɜːt; *NAmE* kɜːrt/ *adj.* (of a person's manner or behaviour 人的举止或行为) appearing rude because very few words are used, or because sth is done in a very quick way 简短而失礼的；唐突无礼的 SYN **abrupt, brusque**：*a curt reply* 唐突无礼的答复 ◇ *a curt nod* 草草的点头 ◇ *His tone was curt and unfriendly.* 他说话的语调粗暴无礼。▶ **curt·ly** *adv.* **curt·ness** *noun* [U]

cur·tail /kɜːˈteɪl; *NAmE* kɜːrˈt-/ *verb* **~ sth** (*formal*) to limit sth or make it last for a shorter time 限制；缩短；减缩：*Spending on books has been severely curtailed.* 购书开支已

被大大削减。◇ *The lecture was curtailed by the fire alarm going off.* 那次讲座被突然鸣响的火警中断了。 ▸ **cur·tail·ment** *noun* [U]: *the curtailment of civil liberties* 对公民自由的限制

C

cur·tain /ˈkɜːtn; *NAmE* ˈkɜːrtn/ *noun, verb*

▪***noun*** **1** [C] a piece of cloth that is hung to cover a window 窗帘: *to **draw/pull/close the curtains*** (= to pull them across the window so they cover it) 把窗帘拉上 ◇ ***to draw/draw back/pull back the curtains*** (= to open them, so that the window is no longer covered) 把窗帘拉开 ◇ *It was ten in the morning but the curtains were still drawn* (= closed). 已是早上十点钟了，可窗帘还拉着。◇ *a pair of curtains* 一对窗帘 ➲ SEE ALSO DRAPE *n.* ➲ **VISUAL VOCAB** PAGE V22 **2** [C] (*NAmE*) (*BrE* ˌ**net ˈcurtain**) a very thin piece of cloth that you hang at a window, which allows light to enter but stops people outside from being able to see inside 网眼帘子 **3** [C] a piece of cloth that is hung up as a screen in a room or around a bed, for example 帘；幔；（遮隔房间的）帷幔；床帷: *a shower curtain* 淋浴帘 ➲ SEE ALSO IRON CURTAIN **4** [sing.] a piece of thick, heavy cloth that hangs in front of the stage in the theatre（舞台上的）幕，幕布，帷幕: *The audience was waiting for the curtain to rise* (= for the play to begin). 观众在等待开幕。◇ *There was tremendous applause when the curtain came down* (= the play ended). 幕落时响起了经久不息的掌声。◇ *We left just before the **final curtain**.* 我们刚好在演出结束前离开。◇ (*figurative*) *The curtain has fallen on her long and distinguished career* (= her career has ended). 她那漫长而成就卓著的职业生涯已告结束。◇ (*figurative*) *It's time to face the **final curtain*** (= the end; death). 人生的戏该落幕了。➲**WORDFINDER NOTE AT STAGE** **5** [C, usually sing.] a thing that covers, hides or protects sth 覆盖物；隐蔽物；防护物: ***a curtain of rain/smoke*** 雨幕；烟幕 ◇ *She pushed back the curtain of brown hair from her eyes.* 她把棕色的头发从眼前拢到脑后。

IDM **be ˈcurtains (for sb)** (*informal*) to be a situation without hope or that you cannot escape from 绝望的处境；无法摆脱的困境；完蛋: *When I saw he had a gun, I thought it was curtains for me.* 我一见他有枪，就想这下子我算是完了。 **bring down the ˈcurtain on sth | bring the ˈcurtain down on sth** to finish or mark the end of sth 结束；标志着…的终结: *His sudden decision to retire brought down the curtain on a distinguished career.* 他突然决定退休，结束了他成就斐然的职业生涯。

▪***verb*** **~ sth** to provide curtains for a window or a room 给（窗户或房间）装上帘子

PHR V ˌ**curtain sth↔ˈoff** to separate an area of a room with a curtain or curtains 用帘子隔开

ˈ**curtain call** *noun* the time in the theatre when the actors come to the front of the stage at the end of a play to receive the APPLAUSE of the audience（演员的）谢幕

ˈ**curtain-raiser** *noun* **1 ~ (to sth)** a small event that prepares for a more important one（重大事件的）前奏，序曲 **2 ~ (to sth)** a short performance before the main performance in a theatre, etc.（剧院等主要剧目演出前的）序幕，开场小戏

curtsy (*also* **curt·sey**) /ˈkɜːtsi; *NAmE* ˈkɜːrtsi/ *noun* (*pl.* **-ies** or **-eys**) a formal sign made by a woman in a dance or to say hello or goodbye to an important person, by bending her knees with one foot in front of the other（女子行的）屈膝礼 ▸ **curtsy** *verb* (**curt·sies, curt·sy·ing, curt·sied, curt·sied**) (*also* **curt·sey**) [I]: **~ (to sb)** *She curtsied to the Queen.* 她向女王行了屈膝礼。

curv·aceous /kɜːˈveɪʃəs; *NAmE* kɜːrˈv-/ *adj.* (*informal*) used in newspapers, etc. to describe a woman whose body has attractive curves（报章等描述女子）有曲线美的，体形优美的

curv·ature /ˈkɜːvətʃə(r); *NAmE* ˈkɜːrv-/ *noun* [U, C] (*specialist*) the state of being curved; the amount that sth is curved 曲率；弯曲；曲度: *the curvature of the earth* 地球的曲度 ◇ *curvature of the spine* 脊柱弯曲

curve /kɜːv; *NAmE* kɜːrv/ *noun, verb*

▪***noun*** **1** a line or surface that bends gradually; a smooth bend 曲线；弧线；曲面；弯曲: *the delicate curve of her ear* 她耳朵的优美曲线 ◇ *a pattern of straight lines and curves* 直线与曲线交织的图案 ◇ (*especially NAmE*) *a curve in the road* 道路上的拐弯处 ◇ (*especially NAmE*) *The driver lost control on a curve and the vehicle hit a tree.* 司机在拐弯处失控，车撞到了一棵树上。◇ *to plot a curve on a graph* 在图上绘出一条曲线 ◇ (*specialist*) *the unemployment-income curve* (= a line on a GRAPH showing the relationship between the number of unemployed people and national income) 失业与国民收入曲线 ➲ SEE ALSO LEARNING CURVE **2** (*also* ˈ**curve ball**) (*NAmE*) (in BASEBALL 棒球) a ball that moves in a curve when it is thrown to the BATTER（投向击球员的）曲线球: (*figurative*) *One of the journalists **threw** the senator **a curve*** (= surprised him by asking a difficult question). 一名记者向那位参议员提出了一个出乎意料的难题。

IDM **ahead of/behind the ˈcurve** (*especially NAmE, business* 商) in advance of or behind a particular trend 引领 / 落后于潮流: *Our expert advice will help you stay ahead of the curve.* 我们的专业建议将有助于你保持引领潮流。◇ *We've fallen behind the curve when it comes to developing new digital products.* 就开发新的数字产品而论，我们已经落后了。

▪***verb*** [I, T] **~ (sth) (+ adv./prep.)** to move or make sth move in the shape of a curve; to be in the shape of a curve（使）沿曲线移动；呈曲线形: *The road curved around the bay.* 那条路沿海湾呈曲线伸展。◇ *The ball curved through the air.* 球在空中沿曲线移动。◇ *His lips curved in a smile.* 他咧嘴笑了。◇ *A smile curved his lips.* 他咧嘴笑了。

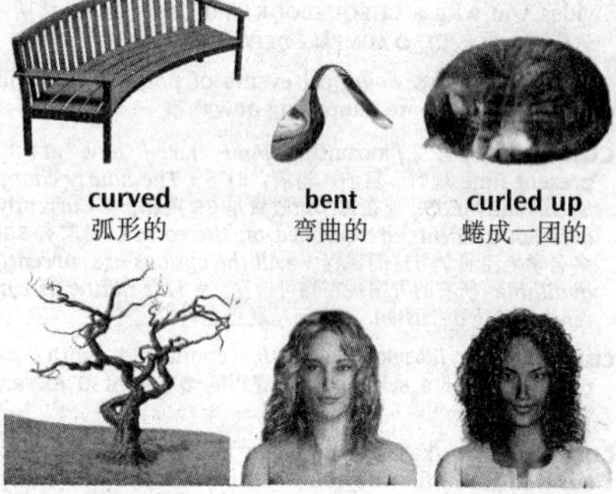

curved 弧形的 | **bent** 弯曲的 | **curled up** 蜷成一团的

twisted 扭曲的 | **wavy** 波状的 | **curly** 鬈曲的

curved /kɜːvd; *NAmE* kɜːrvd/ *adj.* having a round shape 呈弯曲状的；弧形的: *a curved path/roof/blade* 蜿蜒的小路；拱顶；弧形刀片

curvi·lin·ear /ˌkɜːvɪˈlɪniə(r); *NAmE* ˌkɜːrv-/ *adj.* (*formal*) consisting of a curved line or lines 曲线的；由曲线组成的

curvy /ˈkɜːvi; *NAmE* ˈkɜːrvi/ *adj.* (*informal*) having curves 有曲线的；弯曲的: *a curvy body* 富有曲线美的身段 ◇ *curvy lines* 弯弯曲曲的线条

cush·ion /ˈkʊʃn/ *noun, verb*

▪***noun*** **1** (*NAmE also* **pil·low**) a cloth bag filled with soft material or feathers that is used, for example, to make a seat more comfortable 软垫；坐垫；靠垫: *matching curtains and cushions* 颜色协调的窗帘与靠垫 ◇ *a floor cushion* (= a large cushion that you put on the floor to sit on) 地板坐垫 ◇ *a pile of scatter cushions* (= small cushions, often in bright colours, that you put on chairs, etc.) 一堆小靠垫 ◇ (*figurative*) *a cushion of moss on a rock* 岩石上的一层苔藓 ➲ **VISUAL VOCAB** PAGE V22 **2** a layer of sth between two surfaces that keeps them apart（隔离两个表

面的）垫：*A hovercraft rides on a cushion of air.* 气垫船悬浮在气垫上行驶。**3** [usually sing.] **~ (against sth)** something that protects you against sth unpleasant that might happen 起保护（或缓冲）作用的事物：*His savings were a comfortable cushion against financial problems.* 他的积蓄好比一个舒适的垫子，可以缓解财务问题。◇ *The team built up a safe cushion of two goals in the first half.* 球队上半场射进两球，吃了颗定心丸。**4** (in the game of BILLIARDS, etc. 台球等运动) the soft inside edge along each side of the table, that the balls BOUNCE off（台球桌内侧边缘的）弹性衬里 ➲ VISUAL VOCAB PAGE V44

■ ***verb*** **1 ~ sth** to make the effect of a fall or hit less severe（跌倒或碰撞时）起缓冲作用，缓和冲击：*My fall was cushioned by the deep snow.* 积雪很厚，我跌得不重。**2 ~ sb/sth (against/from sth)** to protect sb/sth from being hurt or damaged or from the unpleasant effects of sth 缓和打击：*The south of the country has been cushioned from the worst effects of the recession.* 国家南部保护得好，没有受到经济衰退造成的最恶劣影响。◇ *He broke the news of my brother's death to me, making no effort to* ***cushion the blow*** (= make the news less shocking). 他把我弟弟死亡的消息直接告诉了我，没有试图减轻此事对我的打击。 **3** [usually passive] **~ sth** to make sth soft with a cushion（用垫子）使柔和，使松软

cushy /ˈkʊʃi/ *adj.* (**cush·ier**, **cushi·est**) (*informal, often disapproving*) very easy and pleasant; needing little or no effort 轻松愉快的；安逸的；不费劲的：*a cushy job* 不费心劳神的工作

IDM **a cushy ˈnumber** (*BrE*) an easy job; a pleasant situation that other people would like 轻松的工作；美差；令人羡慕的轻松状态

cusp /kʌsp/ *noun* **1** (*specialist*) a pointed end where two curves meet（两曲线相交的）尖点，会切点，交点：*the cusp of a leaf* 叶尖 **2** the time when one sign of the ZODIAC ends and the next begins（黄道十二宫的）两宫会切的时辰：*I was born* ***on the cusp*** *between Virgo and Libra.* 我生于室女宫和天秤宫会切的时辰。◇ (*figurative*) *He was on the cusp between small acting roles and moderate fame.* 他这个配角演员现在已是小荷初露尖尖角。

cuss /kʌs/ *verb, noun*

■ ***verb*** [I, T] **~ (sb/sth)** (*old-fashioned, informal*) to swear at sb 诅咒；咒骂：*My dad used to come home drunk, shouting and cussing.* 我爹以前常常喝醉了回家，又是喊又是骂。

■ ***noun*** (*old-fashioned, informal*) **1** used with a negative adjective to describe a person（与贬义形容词一起用于描述人）家伙：*He's an awkward cuss.* 他是个笨家伙。 **2** = CURSE (1)：*cuss words* 骂人话

cussed /ˈkʌsɪd/ *adj.* (*old-fashioned, informal*) (of people 人) not willing to be helpful 不愿帮助的 SYN **stubborn** ▶ **cuss·ed·ly** *adv.* **cuss·ed·ness** *noun* [U]

cus·tard /ˈkʌstəd; *NAmE* -tərd/ *noun* **1** [U] (*especially BrE*) (*NAmE usually* ˌ**custard ˈsauce**) a sweet yellow sauce made from milk, sugar, eggs and flour, usually served hot with cooked fruit, PUDDINGS, etc. 蛋奶沙司（通常与熟水果、布丁等一同食用）：*apple pie and custard* 苹果馅饼加蛋奶沙司 **2** [C, U] a mixture of eggs, milk and sugar baked until it is firm （烤制的）蛋奶糕，蛋挞

ˌ**custard ˈpie** *noun* a flat PIE filled with sth soft and wet that looks like custard, that performers throw at each other to make people laugh（表演者互相投掷逗乐用的）蛋奶馅饼

cus·to·dial /kʌˈstəʊdiəl; *NAmE* -ˈstoʊ-/ *adj.* [usually before noun] (*law* 律) **1** involving sending sb to prison 监禁的；拘留的：*The judge gave him a* ***custodial sentence*** (= sent him to prison). 法官判处他监禁。 **2** connected with the right or duty of taking care of sb; having CUSTODY 监护权的；监管职责的；有监护权的：*The mother is usually the custodial parent after a divorce.* 离婚后母亲通常拥有孩子的监护权。 OPP **non-custodial**

cus·to·dian /kʌˈstəʊdiən; *NAmE* -ˈstoʊ-/ *noun* **1** a person who takes responsibility for taking care of or protecting sth 监护人；看守人；保管人：*the museum's custodians* 博物馆的管理员 ◇ *a self-appointed custodian of public morals* 自封的公共道德的卫道士 **2** (*NAmE*) (*BrE* **care·taker**) (*NAmE also*, *ScotE* **jani·tor**) a person whose job is to take care of a building such as a school or a block of flats or an apartment building（建筑物的）管理员，看管人，看门人

cus·tody /ˈkʌstədi/ *noun* [U] **1** the legal right or duty to take care of or keep sb/sth; the act of taking care of sth/sb 监护权；保管权；监护；保管：*Who will* ***have custody*** *of the children?* 谁来负责监护这些孩子？ ◇ *The divorce court awarded custody to the child's mother.* 离婚法庭把监护权判给了孩子的母亲。◇ *The parents were locked in a bitter battle for custody.* 双亲陷入了一场对孩子监护权的激烈争夺之中。 ◇ *The bank provides* ***safe custody*** *for valuables.* 这家银行提供对贵重物品的安全保管服务。◇ *The castle is now* ***in the custody of*** *the state.* 现在那座城堡由国家照管。 ➲ COLLOCATIONS AT MARRIAGE **2** the state of being in prison, especially while waiting for trial（尤指在候审时的）拘留，拘押，羁押： *After the riot, 32 people were taken into* ***police custody***. 那场暴乱后，有 32 人被警方拘留。 ◇ (*BrE*) *He was* ***remanded in custody***, *charged with the murder of a policeman.* 他被控谋杀一名警察，正在羁押候审。 ➲ SEE ALSO YOUTH CUSTODY

cus·tom 🔑 /ˈkʌstəm/ *noun, adj.*

■ ***noun*** ➲ SEE ALSO CUSTOMS **1** 🔑 [C, U] **~ (of doing sth)** an accepted way of behaving or of doing things in a society or a community 风俗；习俗：*an* ***old/ancient custom*** 旧的 / 古老的习俗 ◇ *the custom of giving presents at Christmas* 在圣诞节赠送礼物的习俗 ◇ *It's a* ***local custom***. 这是当地的风俗习惯。 ◇ ***It is the custom*** *in that country for women to marry young.* 女子早婚是那个国家的风俗。 ➲ WORDFINDER NOTE AT SOCIETY **2** [sing.] (*formal* or *literary*) the way a person always behaves（个人的）习惯，习性，惯常行为 SYN **habit, practice**： *It was her custom to rise early.* 早起是她的习惯。 ◇ *As was his custom, he knocked three times.* 一如既往，他敲了三下。**3** [U] (*BrE, formal*) (*also* **business** *NAmE, BrE*) the fact of a person or people buying goods or services at a shop/store or business（顾客对商店的）惠顾，光顾： *Thank you for your custom. Please call again.* 谢谢您的惠顾，请下次再来。◇ *We've lost a lot of custom since prices went up.* 自从价格上涨以来我们失去了很多生意。

■ ***adj.*** [only before noun] (*especially NAmE*) = CUSTOM-BUILT, CUSTOM-MADE: *a custom motorcycle* 定制的摩托车

cus·tom·ary /ˈkʌstəməri; *NAmE* -meri/ *adj.* **1** if sth is **customary**, it is what people usually do in a particular place or situation 习俗的；习惯的 SYN **usual**: *Is it customary to tip hairdressers in this country?* 这个国家兴不兴给理发师小费？ **2** typical of a particular person（某人）特有的，独特的，典型的 SYN **habitual**: *She arranged everything with her customary efficiency.* 她以她特有的高效率把一切都已安排妥当。 ▶ **cus·tom·ar·ily** /ˈkʌstəmərəli; *NAmE* ˌkʌstəˈmerəli/ *adv.*

ˌ**custom-ˈbuilt** (*also* **cus·tom** *especially in NAmE*) *adj.* designed and built for a particular person（为某人）设计建造的，定做的

cus·tom·er 🔑 /ˈkʌstəmə(r)/ *noun* **1** 🔑 a person or an organization that buys sth from a shop/store or business 顾客；主顾；客户： *one of the shop's* ***best/biggest customers*** 此商店最佳 / 最大的客户之一 ◇ *They know me—I'm a* ***regular customer***. 我是老主顾，他们都认识我。 ◇ *the* ***customer service*** *department* 客户服务部 ◇ *The firm has excellent customer relations.* 此公司与客户关系极好。 ➲ WORDFINDER NOTE AT COMPANY ➲ COLLOCATIONS AT SHOPPING **2** (*old-fashioned, informal*) used after an adjective to describe a particular type of person（用于形容词之后描述某类型的人）家伙：*an awkward customer* 难对付的家伙

ˈ**customer base** *noun* [usually sing.] (*business* 商) all the people who buy or use a particular product or service（统称某种产品或服务的）客户：*We need to appeal to a wider customer base.* 我们需要吸引更广泛的客户。

ˈ**customer-facing** *adj.* [only before noun] (*business* 商) dealing directly with customers or used by customers 面

向客户的：*customer-facing operations such as call centres* 呼叫中心之类的客户服务 ◇ *customer-facing software applications* 面向客户的软件应用程序

C

cus·tom·ize (*BrE also* **-ise**) /ˈkʌstəmaɪz/ *verb* **~ sth** to make or change sth to suit the needs of the owner 定制，定做，改制（以满足顾主的需要）：*You can customize the software in several ways.* 你可用几种方法按需要编制这个软件。 ▶ **cus·tom·ized**, **-ised** *adj.*：*a customized car* 按需要定制的汽车

ˌcustom-ˈmade (*also* **cus·tom** *especially in NAmE*) *adj.* designed and made for a particular person（为某人）设计定做的，定制的 ➲ SEE ALSO BESPOKE (1)

cus·toms 🔑 /ˈkʌstəmz/ *noun* [pl.] **1** 🔑 (*usually* **Customs**) (*BrE also* **ˌRevenue and ˈCustoms**) the government department that collects taxes on goods bought and sold and on goods brought into the country, and that checks what is brought in（政府部门）海关：*French Customs have arrested two men.* 法国海关逮捕了两名男子。◇ *a customs officer* 海关官员 **HELP** *NAmE* uses a singular verb with **customs** in this meaning. 美式英语 customs 作此义时使用单数动词。**2** 🔑 the place at a port or an airport where your bags are checked as you come into a country（港口或机场的）海关：*to go through customs and passport control* 通过海关和交验护照 **3** 🔑 the taxes that must be paid to the government when goods are brought in from other countries 关税；进口税：*to pay customs on sth* 为某物缴纳关税 ◇ ***customs duty/duties*** 进口税 ➲ SYNONYMS AT TAX ➲ COMPARE EXCISE[1]

ˈcustoms union *noun* a group of states that agree to have the same taxes on imported goods 关税同盟（缔约国按统一关税进口商品）

cut 🔑 /kʌt/ *verb, noun*

■ *verb* (**cut·ting**, **cut**, **cut**)

• **WOUND/HOLE** 伤口；破口 **1** 🔑 [T, I] to make an opening or a wound in sth, especially with a sharp tool such as a knife or scissors 切；割；割破；划破：**~ sth** *She cut her finger on a piece of glass.* 一块玻璃把她的手指头划破了。◇ **~ yourself** *He cut himself* (= his face) *shaving.* 他刮胡子把脸刮破了。◇ **~ sth + adj.** *She had fallen and* ***cut*** *her head* ***open***. 她摔了一跤，把头磕破了。◇ **~ through sth** *You need a powerful saw to cut through metal.* 切割金属需要用功率大的锯。◇ (*figurative*) *The canoe cut through the water.* 独木舟划破水面前行。

• **REMOVE WITH KNIFE** 用刀切下 **2** 🔑 [T] to remove sth or a part of sth, using a knife, etc.（用刀等从某物上）切下，割下：**~ sth** (**from sth**) *He cut four thick slices from the loaf.* 他从一条面包上切下四厚片。◇ *a bunch of cut flowers* 一束剪下的花朵 ◇ **~ sb sth** *I cut them all a piece of birthday cake.* 我给他们每个人都切了一块生日蛋糕。◇ **~ sth for sb** *I cut a piece of birthday cake for them all.* 我给他们每个人都切了一块生日蛋糕。**3** [T] **~ sth** (**in sth**) to make or form sth by removing material with a knife, etc. 切成；割成；剪成；削成；凿成：*The climbers cut steps in the ice.* 攀登者在冰上凿出踩脚处。◇ *Workmen* ***cut a hole*** *in the pipe.* 工人在管子上切了一个口。

• **DIVIDE** 分开 **4** 🔑 [T] to divide sth into two or more pieces with a knife, etc.（用刀等将某物）切成，割成：**~ sth** *Don't cut the string, untie the knots.* 不要剪断绳子，把结解开。◇ **~ sth in/into sth** *He cut the loaf into thick slices.* 他把那条面包切成了厚片。◇ *The bus was cut in two by the train.* 那辆公共汽车被火车撞成两截。◇ *Now cut the tomatoes in half.* 把西红柿都切成两半。

• **HAIR/NAILS/GRASS, ETC.** 头发、指甲、草等 **5** 🔑 [T] to make sth shorter by cutting 剪短；修剪：**~ sth** ***to cut your hair/nails*** 理发；剪指甲 ◇ ***to cut the grass/lawn/hedge*** 修剪草 / 草坪 / 树篱 ◇ **~ sth + adj.** ***He's had his hair cut*** *really short.* 他头发理得真短。

• **RELEASE** 释放 **6** [T] to allow sb to escape from somewhere by cutting the rope, object, etc. that is holding them（割断绳子、某物等）让（某人）逃跑，释放：**~ sb** (**from sth**) *The injured driver had to be cut from the wreckage.* 受伤的司机不得不等到把汽车残骸拆开才逃出来。◇ **~ sb + adj.** *Two survivors were* ***cut free*** *after being trapped for twenty minutes.* 两名幸存者受困二十分钟后才被解救出来。

• **CLOTHING** 服装 **7** [T, usually passive] **~ sth + adj.** to design and make a piece of clothing in a particular way 剪裁：*The swimsuit was cut high in the leg.* 这件游泳衣的腿部开口很高。

• **ABLE TO CUT/BE CUT** 可切割；可被切割 **8** 🔑 [I] to be capable of cutting 可用于切割；能切割：*This knife won't cut.* 这把刀不快。**9** [I] to be capable of being cut 可被切割：*Sandstone cuts easily.* 沙岩容易切割。

• **REDUCE** 减少 **10** 🔑 [T] to reduce sth by removing a part of it 削减；缩减；裁减：**~ sth** ***to cut prices/taxes/spending/production*** 削价；减税；缩减开支；降低产量 ◇ *Buyers will bargain hard to* ***cut the cost of*** *the house they want.* 买主会竭力讨价还价以压低他们想买的房子的价格。◇ **~ sth by…** *His salary has been cut by ten per cent.* 他的薪金减少了百分之十。◇ **~ sth** (**from…**) (**to…**) *Could you cut your essay from 5 000 to 3 000 words?* 请把你的文章从 5 000 字删减到 3 000 字好吗？

• **REMOVE** 删除 **11** 🔑 [T] **~ sth** (**from sth**) to remove sth from sth 删剪；删节：*This scene was cut from the final version*

▼ **SYNONYMS** 同义词辨析

cut

slash • cut sth back • scale sth back • rationalize • downsize

These words all mean to reduce the amount or size of sth, especially of an amount of money or a business.
以上各词均含减少、缩小之义，尤指削减经费、缩减生意。

cut to reduce sth, especially an amount of money that is demanded, spent, earned, etc. or the size of a business 指削减、缩减、裁减（尤指经费、开支、收入或生意规模）：*The President has promised to cut taxes significantly.* 总统承诺大幅度减税。◇ *Buyers will bargain hard to cut the cost of the house they want.* 买主会竭力讨价还价以压低他们想买的房子的价格。◇ *His salary has been cut by ten per cent.* 他的薪金减少了百分之十。◇ *Could you cut your essay from 5 000 to 3 000 words?* 请把你的文章从 5 000 字删减至 3 000 字好吗？

slash [often passive] (*rather informal*) (often used in newspapers) to reduce sth by a large amount（常用于报章）指大幅度削减、大大降低：*The workforce has been slashed by half.* 职工人数裁减了一半。

cut sth back/cut back on sth to reduce sth, especially an amount of money or business 指削减、缩减、裁减（尤指经费或生意）：*We had to cut back production.* 我们只得减产了。

scale sth back (*especially NAmE* or *business*) to reduce sth, especially an amount of money or business 指削减、缩减、裁减（尤指经费或生意）：*The IMF has scaled back its growth forecasts for the next decade.* 国际货币基金组织已经调低对未来十年的增长预测。

rationalize (*BrE, business*) to make changes to a business or system, in order to make it more efficient, especially by spending less money 指对企业或制度进行合理化改革、使合理化、使有经济效益

downsize (*business*) to make a company or an organization smaller by reducing the number of jobs in it, in order to reduce costs 指公司或机构精简人员以降低成本 **NOTE** **Downsize** is often used by people who want to avoid saying more obvious words like 'dismiss' or 'make redundant' because they sound too negative. 人们通常使用 downsize 以避免使用 dismiss 或 make redundant 等词义直白的词，因为这些词听起来过于负面。

PATTERNS

• to cut/slash/cut back on/scale back/rationalize **spending/production**
• to cut/slash/cut back on **jobs**
• to cut/slash/downsize **the workforce**
• to cut/slash/rationalize **the cost** of sth
• to cut/slash **prices/taxes/the budget**
• to cut sth/slash sth/cut sth back **drastically**

of the movie. 这场戏在电影的最终版本中被删剪了。

- COMPUTING 计算机技术 **12** [I, T] ~ (sth) to DELETE (= remove) part of a text on a computer screen in order to place it somewhere else 剪切：*You can **cut and paste** between different programs.* 可在不同的程序之间进行剪切和粘贴。
- STOP 停止 **13** [T] ~ sth (*informal*) used to tell sb to stop doing sth（让人停止做某事）：*Cut the chatter and get on with your work!* 别闲聊了，继续干活吧！
- END 结束 **14** [T] ~ sth to completely end a relationship or all communication with sb 断绝（关系）；终止（沟通） SYN **sever**: *She has cut all ties with her family.* 她已经和家人完全断绝关系。
- IN MOVIE/TV 电影；电视 **15** [T] ~ sth to prepare a film/movie or tape by removing parts of it or putting them in a different order 剪辑；剪接 SYN **edit** ➲ SEE ALSO DIRECTOR'S CUT **16** [I] (usually used in orders 通常用于指令) to stop filming or recording 停止拍片（或录音、录像）：*The director shouted 'Cut!'* "停！"导演大声喊道。 **17** [I] ~ (from sth) to sth (in films/movies, radio or television 电影、无线电广播或电视) to move quickly from one scene to another 切换画面；转换：*The scene cuts from the bedroom to the street.* 镜头从卧室转换到街道。
- MISS CLASS 旷课 **18** [T] ~ sth (*informal, especially NAmE*) to stay away from a class that you should go to 旷（课）；缺（课）；逃学：*He's always **cutting class**.* 他总是旷课。
- UPSET 使不安 **19** [T] ~ sb to hurt sb emotionally（从感情上）伤害：*His cruel remarks cut her deeply.* 他那些无情的话深深地刺痛了她的心。
- IN CARD GAMES 纸牌游戏 **20** [I, T] ~ (sth) to divide a PACK/DECK of PLAYING CARDS by lifting a section from the top, in order to reveal a card to decide who is to play first, etc. 切牌，抽牌（为决定谁先出牌等）：*Let's cut for dealer.* 咱们切牌决定由谁发牌吧。 ➲ WORDFINDER NOTE AT CARD
- GEOMETRY 几何学 **21** [T] ~ sth (of a line 一条线) to cross another line（与另一条线）相交：*The line cuts the circle at two points.* 那条线与圆相交于两点。
- A TOOTH 牙齿 **22** [T] ~ a tooth to have a new tooth beginning to appear through the GUM 开始长（新牙）：*When did she cut her first tooth?* 她什么时候长出了第一颗牙？
- A DISC, ETC. 激光唱片等 **23** [T] ~ a disc, etc. to make a recording of music on a record, CD, etc. 灌制（唱片）；制作（激光唱片等）：*The Beatles cut their first disc in 1962.* 披头士乐队于 1962 年灌制了他们的第一张唱片。
- DRUG 毒品 **24** [T] ~ sth (with sth) to mix an illegal drug such as HEROIN with another substance 把（海洛因等）与另一种物质掺和

IDM HELP Most idioms containing **cut** are at the entries for the nouns and adjectives in the idioms, for example **cut your losses** is at **loss**. 大多数含 cut 的习语，都可在该等习语中的名词及形容词相关词条找到，如 cut your losses 在词条 loss 下。 **cut and 'run** (*informal*) to make a quick or sudden escape 急忙逃走；撒腿就跑 **(not) 'cut it** (*informal*) to (not) be as good as is expected or needed（不）如预想的一般好；（不）像所需要的那么好：*He won't cut it as a professional singer.* 他的歌艺未达到专业歌手水平。

PHR V **,cut a'cross sth 1** to affect or be true for different groups that usually remain separate 影响，符合，适用于（分离的不同群体）：*Opinion on this issue cuts across traditional political boundaries.* 人们对这个问题的看法超越了传统的政治界限。 **2** (*also* **,cut 'through sth**) to go across sth in order to make your route shorter 抄近路穿过；走近路：*I usually cut across the park on my way home.* 我回家常抄近路，打公园里头走。

,cut sth↔a'way (from sth) to remove sth from sth by cutting 切除；割掉；砍掉；剪去：*They cut away all the dead branches from the tree.* 他们把这棵树上的枯枝全都砍掉了。

,cut sth↔back 1 ⚷ (*also* **,cut 'back (on sth)**) to reduce sth 减少；削减；缩减：*If we don't sell more we'll have to cut back production.* 我们若不能多销，就必须减产。◇ *to cut back on spending* 削减开支 ➲ RELATED NOUN CUTBACK **2** to make a bush, etc. smaller by cutting branches off 剪枝；修剪 SYN **prune**: *to cut back a rose bush* 给玫瑰丛剪枝

,cut sb↔down (*formal*) to kill sb 杀死（某人）：*He was cut down by an assassin's bullet.* 他被刺客的子弹击中身亡。 **,cut sth↔'down** ⚷ to make sth fall down by cutting it at the base（自根基部分）砍倒：*to cut down a tree* 齐根砍倒一棵树 **,cut sth↔'down (to…) | ,cut 'down (on sth)** ⚷ to reduce the size, amount or number of sth 削减，缩小（尺寸、数量或数目）：*We need to cut the article down to 1 000 words.* 我们得把这篇文章压缩到 1 000 字。◇ *The doctor told him to cut down on his drinking.* 医生劝他少喝酒。◇ *I won't have a cigarette, thanks—I'm trying to cut down* (= smoke fewer). 谢谢，我不抽。我现在尽量少抽烟。

,cut 'in 1 if a motor or an engine **cuts in**, it starts working（马达或发动机）发动：*Emergency generators cut in.* 应急发电机启动了。 **2** (*NAmE*) (*BrE* **,push 'in**) to go in front of other people who are waiting 加塞儿；插队 **,cut 'in (on sb/sth) 1** to interrupt sb when they are speaking 打断（谈话）；插嘴 SYN **butt in (on sb/sth)**: *She kept cutting in on our conversation.* 我们谈话时她老是插嘴。◇ + speech *'Forget it!' she cut in.* "算了吧！"她插嘴道。 **2** (of a vehicle or its driver 车辆或驾驶者) to move suddenly in front of another vehicle, leaving little space between the two vehicles 超车抢道 **,cut sb 'in (on sth)** (*informal*) to give sb a share of the profit in a business or an activity 让（某人）分享利润

,cut sb↔off 1 [often passive] to interrupt sb who is speaking on the telephone by breaking the connection 中断（电话通话）：*We were cut off in the middle of our conversation.* 我们电话打到一半就断线了。 **2** to refuse to let sb receive any of your property after you die 剥夺继承权 SYN **disinherit**: *He **cut** his son **off without a penny**.* 他完全剥夺了儿子的继承权。 **,cut sb/sth↔'off 1** to interrupt sb and stop them from speaking 打断（某人并阻止其讲话）：*My explanation was cut off by loud protests.* 我的解释被强烈的抗议声打断了。 **2** ⚷ [often passive] to stop the supply of sth to sb 停止，中断（供给）：*Our water supply has been cut off.* 我们断水了。◇ *They were cut off for not paying their phone bill.* 他们未付电话费，被停机了。 **,cut sth↔off 1** ⚷ (*also* **,cut sth 'off sth**) to remove sth from sth larger by cutting 切掉；割掉；砍掉；剪掉：*He had his finger cut off in an accident at work.* 他在一次工伤中被切断了手指。◇ (*figurative*) *The winner cut ten seconds off* (= ran the distance ten seconds faster than) *the world record.* 获胜者比世界纪录快了十秒。 ➲ SEE ALSO CUT-OFF **2** ⚷ to block or get in the way of sth 阻碍；阻挡；堵塞：*They cut off the enemy's retreat.* 他们切断了敌人的退路。◇ *The new factory cuts off our view of the hills.* 新建的工厂挡住了我们观山景的视线。 **,cut sb/sth 'off (from sb/sth)** ⚷ [often passive] to prevent sb/sth from leaving or reaching a place or communicating with people outside a place 切断…的去路（或来路）；使…与外界隔绝：*The army was cut off from its base.* 那支部队与基地失去了联络。◇ *She feels very cut off living in the country.* 她住在乡间感到很闭塞。◇ *He **cut himself off** from all human contact.* 他断绝了与所有人的联系。

,cut 'out if a motor or an engine **cuts out**, it suddenly stops working（马达或发动机）突然熄火，停止运转 ➲ RELATED NOUN CUT-OUT **,cut sb↔'out (of sth)** to not allow sb to be involved in sth 不让某人参与；把某人排除在…之外：*Don't cut your parents out of your lives.* 别把父母排除在你的生活之外。◇ *Furious, his mother cut him out of her will* (= refused to let him receive any of her property after she died). 他母亲一怒之下，在遗嘱中没有给他任何遗产。 **,cut sth↔'out 1** ⚷ to make sth by cutting 裁剪：*She cut the dress out of some old material.* 她用一些旧布料裁剪出了那件连衣裙。◇ (*figurative*) *He's cut out a niche for himself* (= found a suitable job) *in journalism.* 他在新闻界找到了一份适合自己的工作。 ➲ RELATED NOUN CUT-OUT **2** ⚷ to leave sth out of a piece of writing, etc. 删除；删去 SYN **omit**: *I would cut out the bit about working as a waitress.* 我想删掉做女服务员的那段经历。 **3** (*informal*) used to tell sb to stop doing or saying sth annoying（让人停止做或说恼人的事）住口，打住：*I'm sick of you two arguing—just **cut it out**!* 你们俩吵来吵去让我烦死了，住口吧！ **4** to block sth, especially light 阻挡（尤指光线）：*Tall trees cut out the sunlight.* 高高的树木遮住了阳光。 **,cut sth↔'out (of sth)** ⚷ **1** ⚷ to remove sth

C

from sth larger by cutting, usually with scissors（通常用剪刀）剪下：*I cut this article out of the newspaper.* 我从报纸上剪下了这篇文章。**2** to stop doing, using or eating sth 停止做（或使用、食用）：*I've been advised to cut sugar out of my diet.* 有人劝我饮食要忌糖。**be ˌcut ˈout for sth | be ˌcut ˈout to be sth** (*informal*) to have the qualities and abilities needed for sth 具有所需素质及才能；是…的材料：*He's not cut out for teaching.* 他不适于做教学工作。◇ *He's not cut out to be a teacher.* 他不是当教师的材料。

ˌcut ˈthrough sth 1 = CUT ACROSS STH (2) **2** (*also* **ˌcut sth ˈthrough sth**) to make a path or passage through sth by cutting 开辟（出路或通道）：*They used a machete to cut through the bush.* 他们用大砍刀在灌木林中劈出了一条路。◇ *The prisoners* ***cut their way through*** *the barbed wire.* 囚犯们切断铁丝网开出一条路逃之夭夭。

ˌcut ˈup (*NAmE, informal*) to behave in a noisy and silly way 胡闹；吵吵嚷嚷地出洋相 **ˌcut sb↔ˈup** (*informal*) **1** to injure sb badly by cutting or hitting them （严重地）割伤，打伤：*He was very badly cut up in the fight.* 他在这场斗殴中伤得很重。**2** [usually passive] to upset sb emotionally 使伤心；使悲伤；使难受：*She was pretty cut up about them leaving.* 他们这一走使她伤心极了。**ˌcut sb/sth↔ˈup** (*BrE*) to suddenly drive in front of another vehicle in a dangerous way（危险地）突然超车 **ˌcut sth↔ˈup** 🔑 to divide sth into small pieces with a knife, etc. 切碎；剁碎：*He cut up the meat on his plate.* 他在盘子上把肉切成小块。

■***noun***

• **WOUND** 伤口 **1** 🔑 a wound caused by sth sharp 伤口；划口：*cuts and bruises on the face* 脸上的伤口和淤伤 ◇ *Blood poured from the deep cut on his arm.* 鲜血从他手臂上深深的伤口中涌出。

• **HOLE** 开口 **2** 🔑 a hole or an opening in sth, made with sth sharp （锋利物留下的）开口，破口：*Using sharp scissors, make a small cut in the material.* 用锋利的剪刀在这块布料上剪一个小口。

• **REDUCTION** 削减 **3** 🔑 ~ (**in sth**) a reduction in amount, size, supply, etc.（数量、尺寸、供应等的）削减，减少，缩减：***price/tax/job cuts*** 减价；减税；裁员 ◇ *They had to take a 20% cut in pay.* 他们不得不接受减薪 20%。◇ *They announced cuts in public spending.* 他们宣布缩减公共开支。➲SEE ALSO POWER CUT, SHORTCUT

• **OF HAIR** 头发 **4** 🔑 [usually sing.] an act of cutting sb's hair; the style in which it is cut 理发；发型：*Your hair could do with a cut* (= it is too long). 你该理发了。◇ *a cut and blow-dry* 理发带吹干 ➲SEE ALSO BUZZ CUT

• **OF CLOTHING** 服装 **5** [usually sing.] the shape and style that a piece of clothing has because of the way the cloth is cut（剪裁的）款式，式样：*the elegant cut of her dress* 她的连衣裙的典雅款式

• **SHARE OF MONEY** 钱的份额 **6** a share in sth, especially money（尤指钱的）份，份额：*They were rewarded with a cut of 5% from the profits.* 他们得到了占利润 5% 份额的酬报。

• **OF MOVIE/PLAY, ETC.** 电影、戏剧等 **7** ~ (**in sth**) an act of removing part of a film/movie, play, piece of writing, etc. 删剪；删节：*The director objected to the cuts ordered by the censor.* 导演反对按审查员的指令作删剪。◇ *She made some cuts before handing over the finished novel.* 她交定稿之前对小说作了一些删节。

• **MEAT** 肉 **8** a piece of meat cut from an animal（从动物躯体上）割下的一块肉：*a lean cut of pork* 一块瘦猪肉 ◇ *cheap cuts of stewing lamb* 廉价的炖羊肉块 ➲ SEE ALSO COLD CUTS

IDM **a cut above sb/sth** better than sb/sth 优于；比…高一等；胜…一筹：*His latest novel is* ***a cut above the rest.*** 他最近出版的小说比其他的小说都好。 **the cut and ˈthrust (of sth)** (*BrE*) the lively or aggressive way that sth is done 激烈交锋：*the cut and thrust of political debate* 政治辩论中的唇枪舌剑 **make the ˈcut 1** to reach or maintain the required standard 达标；保持水准：*I had to explain to the applicants why they didn't make the cut.* 我不得不向那些申请人解释他们为什么不符合资格。**2** (in golf) to achieve a good enough score to be able to take part in the next stage of a competition（高尔夫球）晋级：*Woods needed a 69 to make the cut.* 伍兹需要打出 69 杆才能晋级。**3** (of a film/movie, play, piece of writing, etc. 电影、戏剧、文章等) to be included after parts have been removed 经删剪后收录：*When a book is made into a movie not every scene will make the cut.* 一本书改编成电影时，并不是每个片段都会保留。

ˌcut and ˈdried *adj.* [not usually before noun] decided in a way that cannot be changed or argued about 已成定局；不容更改：*The inquiry is by no means cut and dried.* 调查之事远未盖棺定论。

cu·ta·ne·ous /kjuˈteɪniəs/ *adj.* (*anatomy* 解) connected with the skin 皮肤（上）的

cut·away /ˈkʌtəweɪ/ *adj.*, *noun*

■***adj.*** [only before noun] (of a model or diagram 模型或图表) with some outside parts left out, in order to show what the inside looks like 局部剖视的：*a cutaway picture of the inside of a nuclear reactor* 核反应堆内部的局部剖视图

■***noun*** **1** (*especially NAmE*) ~ (**to sb/sth**) (on television, in a film/movie, etc. 电视、电影等中) a picture that shows sth different from the main thing that is being shown 切出镜头：*There was a cutaway to Jackson's guest at the side of the stage.* 镜头切换到了舞台一侧杰克逊的嘉宾。**2** a model or diagram with some outside parts left out, in order to show what the inside looks like 局部剖视模型；局部剖视图

cut·back /ˈkʌtbæk/ *noun* [usually pl.] ~ (**in sth**) a reduction in sth 削减；缩减；减少：*cutbacks in public spending* 公共开支的削减 ◇ *staff cutbacks* 裁员

ˌcut-ˈdown *adj.* [only before noun] reduced in length, size or range 缩减的；缩小的：*a cut-down version of the program* 这个程序的简化版

cute /kjuːt/ *adj.* (**cuter**, **cutest**) **1** pretty and attractive 可爱的；漂亮迷人的：*a cute little baby* 逗人喜爱的小宝宝 ◇ (*BrE*) *an unbearably cute picture of two kittens* (= it seems SENTIMENTAL) 让人爱得不得了的两只小猫的图片 **2** (*informal, especially NAmE*) sexually attractive 有性吸引力的；性感的：*Check out those cute guys over there!* 瞧那边那些性感的家伙！**3** (*informal, especially NAmE*) clever, sometimes in an annoying way because a person is trying to get an advantage for himself or herself 精明的，机灵的（有时使人厌烦）：*She had a really cute idea.* 她有一个精明绝顶的主意。◇ *Don't get cute with me!* 别跟我耍滑头！ ▶ **cute·ly** *adv.*: *to smile cutely* 可爱地一笑 **cute·ness** *noun* [U]

cutesy /ˈkjuːtsi/ *adj.* (*informal*) too pretty or attractive in a way that is annoying or not realistic 矫揉造作的；忸怩作态的

ˌcut ˈglass *noun* [U] glass with patterns cut in it 雕花玻璃；刻花玻璃：*a cut-glass vase* 雕花玻璃花瓶

cut·icle /ˈkjuːtɪkl/ *noun* an area of hard skin at the base of the nails on the fingers and toes（手指甲或脚指甲根部的）甲小皮 ➲VISUAL VOCAB PAGE V64

cutie /ˈkjuːti/ *noun* (*informal*) a person who is attractive or kind 俏人儿；大好人：*He's a real cutie.* 他这个人真有魅力。

cut·lass /ˈkʌtləs/ *noun* a short SWORD with a curved blade that was used as a weapon by sailors and PIRATES in the past（旧时水手和海盗用的）短剑，短弯刀

cut·lery /ˈkʌtləri/ *noun* [U] **1** (*especially BrE*) (*NAmE usually* **flat·ware**, **sil·ver·ware**) knives, forks and spoons, used for eating and serving food 餐具（刀、叉和匙）➲VISUAL VOCAB PAGE V23 **2** (*NAmE*) knives, etc. that are sharp 刀具

cut·let /ˈkʌtlət/ *noun* **1** a thick slice of meat, especially LAMB or PORK (= meat from a pig), that is cooked and served with the bone still attached 厚肉片；（尤指羊或猪）肉排 **2** (in compounds 构成复合词) finely chopped pieces of meat, fish, vegetables, etc. that are pressed together into a flat piece, covered with BREADCRUMBS and cooked（肉、鱼肉、蔬菜等剁碎后外裹面包屑做成的）炸饼：*nut cutlets* 果仁炸饼

ˈcut-off *noun, adj.*

■ ***noun*** **1** a point or limit when you stop sth 截止点；界限：*Is there a cut-off point between childhood and adulthood?* 童年与成年之间有分界线吗？ **2** the act of stopping the supply of something 停止供应：*The government announced a cut-off in overseas aid.* 政府宣布停止对外援助。**3 cut-offs** [pl.] trousers/pants that have been made shorter by cutting off part of the legs 剪短的裤子：*wearing frayed cut-offs* 身着毛边的剪短的裤子

■ ***adj.*** [only before noun] (of trousers/pants 裤子) made shorter by cutting off part of the legs 裤腿剪短的：*cut-off jeans* 裤腿剪短的牛仔裤

ˈcut-out *noun* **1** a shape cut out of paper, wood, etc.（从纸、木等）剪下的图样：*a cardboard cut-out* 从硬纸板剪下的图形 **2** a piece of safety equipment that stops an electric current from flowing through sth（电流的）断路器，保险装置：*A cut-out stops the kettle boiling dry.* 断流装置避免水壶干烧。

ˌcut-ˈprice *adj.* [only before noun] (*especially BrE*) (*NAmE usually* **ˌcut-ˈrate**) **1** sold at a reduced price 减价出售的；削价的：***cut-price goods/fares*** 减价商品 / 票 **2** selling goods at a reduced price 出售减价商品的：***a cut-price store/supermarket*** 折价商品店 / 超市

cut·ter /ˈkʌtə(r)/ *noun* **1** (usually in compounds 通常构成复合词) a person or thing that cuts 切割工；剪裁工；切割工具；剪裁工具：*a pastry cutter* 油酥饼切刀 **2 cutters** [pl.] (usually in compounds 通常构成复合词) a tool for cutting 切割工具：*a pair of wire cutters* 一把钢丝钳 **3** a small fast ship 小快艇 **4** a ship's boat, used for travelling between the ship and land （行驶于大船与岸边之间的）小艇，接应船

ˈcut-throat *adj.* [usually before noun] (of an activity 活动) in which people compete with each other in aggressive and unfair ways 竞争激烈的；残酷无情的；不公的：*the cut-throat world of politics* 斗得你死我活的政界

ˌcut-throat ˈrazor *noun* a RAZOR (= a tool used for shaving) with a long sharp blade 折叠式剃须刀 ➲ COMPARE SAFETY RAZOR

cut·ting /ˈkʌtɪŋ/ *noun, adj.*

■ ***noun*** **1** (*also* **ˈpress cutting**) (*both BrE*) (*also* **clip·ping**, **ˈpress clipping** *NAmE, BrE*) an article or a story that you cut from a newspaper or magazine and keep 剪报；杂志剪辑资料：***newspaper/press cuttings*** 剪报 **2** a piece cut off a plant that will be used to grow a new plant 插枝，插条（从植物上截取的一段供扦插的枝条）**3** (*BrE*) a narrow open passage that is dug through high ground for a road, railway/railroad or CANAL（为修道路、铁路或运河从高地开凿出来的）路堑，河道

■ ***adj.*** [usually before noun] **1** unkind and likely to hurt sb's feelings 尖刻的；刻薄的；挖苦人的 SYN **biting**：*a cutting remark* 尖酸刻薄的言辞 **2** (of winds 风) cold in a sharp and unpleasant way 凛冽的；刺骨的 SYN **biting**

ˈcutting board (*NAmE*) (*BrE* **ˈchop·ping board**) *noun* a board made of wood or plastic used for cutting meat or vegetables on 砧板；切菜板

ˌcutting ˈedge *noun* [sing.] **1 the ~ (of sth)** the newest, most advanced stage in the development of sth（处于某事物发展的）尖端，最前沿，领先阶段：*working **at the cutting edge** of computer technology* 在计算机技术的最前沿工作 ➲ COMPARE BLEEDING EDGE **2** an aspect of sth that gives it an advantage 有利方面；优势：*We're relying on him to give the team a cutting edge.* 我们指望他给这个队带来优势。▸ **ˌcutting-ˈedge** *adj.*：*cutting-edge technology/research/science/design* 尖端技术；前沿研究 / 科学；新锐设计

ˈcutting grass *noun* = GRASSCUTTER

ˈcutting room *noun* a room in which the different parts of a film/movie are cut and put into order（影片的）剪辑室，剪接室 ➲ MORE LIKE THIS 9, page R26

cuttle·fish /ˈkʌtlfɪʃ/ *noun* (*pl.* **cuttle·fish**) a sea creature with eight arms, two TENTACLES (= long thin parts like arms) and a wide flat shell inside its body, that produces a black substance like ink when it is attacked 乌贼；墨鱼；墨斗鱼

cutup /ˈkʌtʌp/ *noun* (*NAmE, informal*) a person who behaves in a silly way in order to attract attention and make people laugh（引人注意和逗笑的）活宝，出尽洋相的人

CV /ˌsiː ˈviː/ (*BrE*) (*NAmE* **résumé**) *noun* the abbreviation for 'curriculum vitae' (a written record of your education and the jobs you have done, that you send when you are applying for a job) 履历，简历（全写为 curriculum vitae）：*Send a full CV with your job application.* 随求职申请书寄上详尽的个人履历。➲ WORDFINDER NOTE AT APPLY ➲ COLLOCATIONS AT JOB

cwm /kʊm/ *noun* (*geology* 地) = CORRIE

ˈC-word *noun* (*informal, sometimes offensive*) used to replace a word beginning with C that you do not want to say, for example the offensive swear word 'cunt', or 'cancer' * C 开头的词（用以替代不想说出口的以 C 开头的冒犯性脏话等，如 cunt、cancer）：*An employee who uses the C-word to a colleague will be suspended.* 雇员对同事说 C 开头的词将被停职。◇ *I hate it when people refer to cancer as the C-word.* 我不喜欢有人把癌症说成是 C 开头的词。➲ COMPARE F-WORD

cwt *abbr.* (*pl.* **cwt**) (in writing 书写形式) HUNDREDWEIGHT 英担

cwtch /kʊtʃ/ *verb* [I, T] **~ (sb)** (*WelshE*) to be held close in sb's arms in a loving way; to hold sb in this way（被）紧紧拥抱：*Cwtch up to your mam!* 去拥抱你妈妈！▸ **cwtch** *noun*

-cy, **-acy** *suffix* (in nouns 构成名词) **1** the state or quality of 具有…的状态（或性质）：*infancy* 幼年 ◇ *accuracy* 精确性 **2** the status or position of 具有…的地位（或职位）：*chaplaincy* 特遣牧师的职位

cyan /ˈsaɪən/ *noun* [U] (*specialist*) a greenish-blue colour, used in printing 蓝绿色，青色（用于印刷）

cy·an·ide /ˈsaɪənaɪd/ *noun* [U] a highly poisonous chemical 氰化物（剧毒化学品）

cyber- /ˈsaɪbə(r)/ *combining form* (in nouns and adjectives 构成名词和形容词) connected with electronic communication networks, especially the Internet 计算机的，电脑的，网络的（尤指互联网）：*cybernetics* 控制论 ◇ *cybercafe* 网吧

cyber·attack /ˈsaɪbərətæk/ *noun* the act of trying to damage or destroy a computer network, computer system or website by secretly changing information on it without permission 网络攻击：*Fourteen people were arrested for launching a cyberattack on the company's website.* 十四人因对公司网站发动网络攻击而被捕。➲ COMPARE CYBERTHREAT

cyber·bully /ˈsaɪbəbʊli; *NAmE* ˈsaɪbər-/ *noun* (*pl.* **-ies**) a person who uses messages on SOCIAL NETWORKING sites, emails, TEXT MESSAGES, etc. to frighten or upset sb 网络欺凌者（利用社交网站信息、电子邮件、手机短信等恐吓或骚扰他人）

cyber·bully·ing /ˈsaɪbəbʊliɪŋ; *NAmE* ˈsaɪbər-/ *noun* [U] the activity of using messages on SOCIAL NETWORKING sites, emails, TEXT MESSAGES, etc. to frighten or upset sb 网络欺凌：*The school provides guidance for parents on how to deal with issues such as cyberbullying.* 学校为家长如何应对网络欺凌等问题提供指导。

cyber·cafe /ˈsaɪbəkæfeɪ; *NAmE* ˈsaɪbər-/ *noun* a CAFE with computers on which customers can use the Internet, send emails, etc. 网吧

cyber·crime /ˈsaɪbəkraɪm; *NAmE* ˈsaɪbər-/ *noun* [U, C] crime that is committed using the Internet, for example by stealing sb's personal or bank details or infecting their computer with a virus 网络犯罪

C

cyber·naut /ˈsaɪbənɔːt; *NAmE* ˈsaɪbərnɔːt/ *noun* (*computing* 计) **1** a person who wears special devices in order to experience VIRTUAL REALITY 虚拟现实体验者；虚拟实境体验者 **2** a person who uses the Internet 网络用户；网民

cy·ber·net·ics /ˌsaɪbəˈnetɪks; *NAmE* -bərˈn-/ *noun* [U] the scientific study of communication and control, especially concerned with comparing human and animal brains with machines and electronic devices 控制论（对信息传递和控制的科学研究，尤涉及人和动物大脑与机器和电子装置的比较） ➲ MORE LIKE THIS 29, page R28 ▶ **cy·ber·net·ic** *adj.*

cyber·punk /ˈsaɪbəpʌŋk; *NAmE* -bərp-/ *noun* [U] stories set in an imaginary future world controlled by technology and computers 电脑科幻小说（以受技术与电脑控制的虚构未来世界为背景）

cyber·sex /ˈsaɪbəseks; *NAmE* ˈsaɪbər-/ *noun* [U] communication between people using the Internet which makes them sexually excited 网络性爱，网交（借由互联网上的沟通获得性快感）

cyber·space /ˈsaɪbəspeɪs; *NAmE* -bərs-/ *noun* [U] the imaginary place where electronic messages, etc. exist while they are being sent between computers 网络空间

cyber·squat·ting /ˈsaɪbəskwɒtɪŋ; *NAmE* ˈsaɪbərskwɑːtɪŋ/ *noun* [U] the illegal activity of buying and officially recording an address on the Internet that is the name of an existing company or a well-known person, with the intention of selling it to the owner in order to make money 域名抢注（抢先注册已有的公司名或名人的域名以便能出售赚钱） ▶ **cyber·squat·ter** *noun*

cyber·threat /ˈsaɪbəθret; *NAmE* ˈsaɪbər-/ *noun* the possibility that sb will try to damage or destroy a computer network, computer system or website by secretly changing information on it without permission 网络威胁：*The company isn't doing enough to secure its systems against cyberthreats.* 公司在保护其系统免遭网络威胁方面做得还不够。 ➲ COMPARE CYBERATTACK

cy·borg /ˈsaɪbɔːg; *NAmE* -bɔːrg/ *noun* (in SCIENCE FICTION stories 科幻故事) a creature that is part human, part machine 半人半机器的生物

cyc·la·men /ˈsɪkləmən; *NAmE* ˈsaɪk-/ *noun* (*pl.* **cyc·la·men** or **cyc·la·mens**) a plant with pink, purple or white flowers that grow on long STEMS pointing downwards, often grown indoors 仙客来（常在室内种植，花朵下垂，呈粉红色、紫色或白色）

cycle 🔑 AW /ˈsaɪkl/ *noun*, *verb*
■ *noun* **1** 🔑 a bicycle or motorcycle 自行车；摩托车：*We went for a cycle ride on Sunday.* 我们星期天骑自行车去兜风了。◇ *a* ***cycle route/track*** 自行车车道 / 赛道 ➲ VISUAL VOCAB PAGE V55 ➲ SEE ALSO BIKE *n.* **2** 🔑 the fact of a series of events being repeated many times, always in the same order 循环：*the cycle of the seasons* 四季的循环 ➲ SEE ALSO LIFE CYCLE **3** a complete set or series, for example of movements in a machine 整套，整个系列（如机器的运转）：*eight cycles per second* 每秒转动八次 ◇ *the rinse cycle* (= in a washing machine)（洗衣机的）漂洗运转过程
■ *verb* 🔑 [I] (+adv./prep.) (*especially BrE*) to ride a bicycle; to travel by bicycle 骑自行车；骑自行车旅行：*I usually cycle home through the park.* 我通常骑自行车穿过公园回家。➲ COMPARE BICYCLE *v.*, BIKE *v.*

ˈcycle lane (*BrE*) (*NAmE* **ˈbicycle lane**, *informal* **ˈbike lane**) *noun* a part of a road that only bicycles are allowed to use 自行车道 ➲ VISUAL VOCAB PAGE V3

ˈcycle rickshaw (*also* **ˈcycle-rickshaw**) *noun* a vehicle like a bicycle with three wheels, with a covered seat for passengers behind the driver, used especially in some Asian countries 人力三轮车（尤见于一些亚洲国家）

cyc·lic AW /ˈsaɪklɪk; ˈsɪk-/ (*also* **cyc·lic·al** /ˈsaɪklɪkl; ˈsɪk-/) *adj.* [usually before noun] repeated many times and always happening in the same order 循环的；周期的：*the cyclic processes of nature* 自然界的循环过程 ◇ *Economic activity often follows a cyclical pattern.* 经济活动常常遵循周期性模式。 ▶ **cyc·lic·al·ly** *adv.*：*events that occur cyclically* 周期性出现的事情

cyc·ling 🔑 /ˈsaɪklɪŋ/ *noun* [U] the sport or activity of riding a bicycle 骑自行车运动（或活动）：*to go cycling* 去骑自行车 ◇ *Cycling is Europe's second most popular sport.* 骑自行车是欧洲第二流行的体育运动。◇ *cycling shorts* 自行车运动短裤 ➲ VISUAL VOCAB PAGE V52

WORDFINDER 联想词： back-pedal, dismount, handlebar, pedal, ride, saddle, speed, tandem, velodrome

cyc·list /ˈsaɪklɪst/ *noun* a person who rides a bicycle 骑自行车的人 ➲ COMPARE BICYCLIST

cyclo-cross /ˈsaɪkləʊ krɒs; *NAmE* ˈsaɪkloʊ krɔːs/ *noun* [U] the sport of racing bicycles over rough ground, which in places is too difficult to ride on so you have to carry your bicycle and run 自行车越野赛（遇到特别崎岖的路面时需携车跑步）

cyc·lone /ˈsaɪkləʊn; *NAmE* -kloʊn/ *noun* a violent tropical storm in which strong winds move in a circle 气旋；旋风 ➲ COMPARE HURRICANE, TYPHOON ➲ WORDFINDER NOTE AT DISASTER ▶ **cyc·lon·ic** /saɪˈklɒnɪk; *NAmE* -ˈklɑːn-/ *adj.*

Cy·clops /ˈsaɪklɒps; *NAmE* -klɑːps/ *noun* (in ancient Greek stories) a giant with only one eye in the middle of his face（古希腊神话中的）库克罗普斯，独眼巨人

cyclo·tron /ˈsaɪklətrɒn; *NAmE* ˈsaɪklətrɑːn/ *noun* (*physics* 物) a machine which makes atoms or ELECTRONS move more quickly, using electrical and MAGNETIC FIELDS 回旋加速器

cyg·net /ˈsɪgnət/ *noun* a young SWAN (= a large white bird with a long neck that lives on or near water) 幼天鹅

cy·lin·der /ˈsɪlɪndə(r)/ *noun* **1** a solid or hollow figure with round ends and long straight sides 圆柱；圆柱体；圆筒 ➲ PICTURE AT SOLID **2** an object shaped like a cylinder, especially one used as a container（尤指用作容器的）圆筒状物：*a* ***gas/oxygen cylinder*** 气罐；氧气瓶 ➲ VISUAL VOCAB PAGE V72 **3** the hollow tube in an engine, shaped like a cylinder, inside which the PISTON moves（发动机的）气缸：*a six-cylinder engine* 六缸发动机
IDM **working/firing on all ˈcylinders** (*informal*) using all your energy to do sth; working as well as possible 竭尽全力；尽力干好；开足马力

cy·lin·dric·al /səˈlɪndrɪkl/ *adj.* shaped like a cylinder 圆柱形的；圆筒状的：*huge cylindrical gas tanks* 巨大的圆柱形贮气罐

cym·bal /ˈsɪmbl/ *noun* a musical instrument in the form of a round metal plate. It is hit with a stick, or two cymbals are hit against each other. 钹，铙钹（打击乐器）：*a* ***clash/crash of cymbals*** 铙钹的敲击声 ➲ VISUAL VOCAB PAGE V37

Cymru /ˈkʌmri/ *noun* the name for 'Wales' in the Welsh language（威尔士语）威尔士 ➲ SEE ALSO PLAID CYMRU

cynic /ˈsɪnɪk/ *noun* **1** a person who believes that people only do things to help themselves, rather than for good or sincere reasons 认为人皆自私的人；愤世嫉俗者 **2** a person who does not believe that sth good will happen or that sth is important 悲观者；怀疑者：*Cynics will say that there is not the slightest chance of success.* 悲观的人会说根本不可能取得成功。 ▶ **cyni·cism** /ˈsɪnɪsɪzəm/ *noun* [U]：*In a world full of cynicism she was the one person I felt I could trust.* 在这个人人都互相猜忌的世界里，只有她一个我认为是可以信赖的。

cyn·ic·al /ˈsɪnɪkl/ *adj.* **1** believing that people only do things to help themselves rather than for good or honest reasons 认为人皆自私的；愤世嫉俗的：*Do you have to be so cynical about everything?* 你非得怀疑一切吗？◇ *a cynical view/smile* 愤世嫉俗的观点；讥笑 **2** not believing that sth good will happen or that sth is important 悲观的；怀疑的：*I'm a bit cynical about the benefits of the plan.* 我对这项计划的成效有点儿怀疑。**3** not caring that sth might hurt other people, if there is some advantage for you 只顾自己不顾他人的；见利忘义的： *a cynical disregard for the safety of others* 只顾自己不顾他人安危 ◇ *a deliberate and cynical foul* 存心恶意犯规 ▶ **cyn·ic·al·ly** /-kli/ *adv.*

cyn·o·sure /ˈsɪnəzjʊə(r); ˈsɪnəʃʊə(r); ˈsaɪn-; *NAmE* ˈsaɪnəʃʊr; ˈsɪn-/ *noun* [sing.] (*formal*) a person or thing that is the centre of attention 引人注目的人（或事物）；注意的中心： *Ruth was the cynosure of all eyes.* 鲁思吸引了所有的目光。

cy·pher = CIPHER

cy·press /ˈsaɪprəs/ *noun* a tall straight EVERGREEN tree 柏树

Cy·ril·lic /səˈrɪlɪk/ *adj.* the Cyrillic alphabet is used to write Russian, Bulgarian, Serbian, Ukrainian and some other Slavic languages 西里尔字母的（用于俄语、保加利亚语、塞尔维亚语、乌克兰语及其他一些斯拉夫语族语言） ▶ **Cy·ril·lic** *noun* [U]

cyst /sɪst/ *noun* a GROWTH containing liquid that forms in or on a person's or an animal's body and may need to be removed 囊肿；囊；包囊

cys·tic fi·bro·sis /ˌsɪstɪk faɪˈbrəʊsɪs; *NAmE* -ˈbroʊ-/ *noun* [U] a serious medical condition that some people are born with, in which GLANDS in the lungs and other organs do not work correctly. It often leads to infections and can result in early death. 囊性纤维化

cyst·itis /sɪˈstaɪtɪs/ *noun* [U] an infection of the BLADDER, especially in women, that causes frequent, painful URINATION 膀胱炎

cy·tol·o·gy /saɪˈtɒlədʒi; *NAmE* -ˈtɑːl-/ *noun* [U] the scientific study of the structure and function of cells from living things 细胞学

cyto·megalo·virus /ˌsaɪtəʊˈmegələʊvaɪrəs; *NAmE* ˌsaɪtəʊˈmegəloʊ-/ *noun* (*medical* 医) a virus that usually causes mild infections, but that can be serious for people with AIDS or for new babies 巨细胞病毒（对艾滋病人或新生儿有危险）

cy·to·plasm /ˈsaɪtəʊplæzəm; *NAmE* -toʊ-/ *noun* [U] (*biology* 生) all the living material in a cell, not including the NUCLEUS 细胞质；胞质；胞浆 ▶ **cy·to·plas·mic** /ˌsaɪtəʊˈplæzmɪk; *NAmE* -toʊ-/ *adj.* ➲COMPARE PROTOPLASM

czar, **czar·ina**, **czar·ism**, **czar·ist** = TSAR, TSARINA, TSARISM, TSARIST

C

Dd

D /diː/ *noun, abbr., symbol*
■ ***noun*** (*also* **d**) [C, U] (*pl.* **Ds**, **D's**, **d's** /diːz/) **1** the fourth letter of the English alphabet 英语字母表的第 4 个字母：*'Dog' begins with (a) D/'D'.* * dog 一词以字母 d 开头。 **2 D** (*music* 音) the second note in the SCALE of C MAJOR * D 音（C 大调的第 2 音或音符） **3 D** the fourth highest mark/grade that a student can get for a piece of work, showing that it is not very good （学业成绩）第四等，差：*He got (a) D/'D' in/for Geography.* 他的地理成绩得 D。➲ SEE ALSO D-DAY
■ ***abbr.*** (*also* **D.** *especially in NAmE*) (in politics in the US 美国政治) DEMOCRAT; DEMOCRATIC 民主党人；民主党的
■ ***symbol*** the number 500 in ROMAN NUMERALS （罗马数字） 500

d. *abbr.* **1** (in writing 书写形式) died 去世；逝世：*Emily Clifton, d. 1865* 埃米莉·克利夫顿，卒于 1865 年 **2 d** (in the system of money used in the past in Britain) a PENNY （英国旧币制中的）便士

-d *suffix* ➲ -ED

DA (*BrE*) (*US* **D.A.**) /ˌdiː ˈeɪ/ *noun* = DISTRICT ATTORNEY

dab /dæb/ *verb, noun*
■ ***verb*** (**-bb-**) **1** to touch sth lightly, usually several times 轻触，轻拍，轻拭，轻揩（几下）：**~ sth** *She dabbed her eyes and blew her nose.* 她轻轻擦了几下眼睛，擤了擤鼻涕。◇ **~ at sth** *He dabbed at the cut with his handkerchief.* 他用手帕轻轻按了按伤口。 **2 ~ sth + adv./prep.** to put sth on a surface with quick light movements 轻搽；轻涂；轻敷：*She dabbed a little perfume behind her ears.* 她朝耳后搽了点香水。
■ ***noun*** **1** a small amount of a liquid, cream or powder that is put on a surface in a quick gentle movement 少量，一点点（轻敷于表面的液体、乳霜或化妆用粉）：*She put a dab of perfume behind her ears.* 她朝耳后搽了点香水。 **2** an act of gently touching or pressing sth without rubbing 轻触，轻按（但不揉擦）：*He gave the cut a quick dab with a towel.* 他麻利地用毛巾按了按伤口。 **3** a small flat fish 黄盖鲽（小比目鱼） **4** (*WelshE*) a person or thing 人；东西：*He's in hospital again. **Poor dab**.* 他又住医院了，怪可怜的。

dab·ble /ˈdæbl/ *verb* **1** [I] **~ (in/with sth)** to take part in a sport, an activity, etc. but not very seriously 涉猎；涉足；浅尝：*He dabbles in local politics.* 他开始涉足地方政坛。 **2** [T] **~ sth (in sth)** to move your hands, feet, etc. around in water 玩水；嬉水：*She dabbled her toes in the stream.* 她把脚趾浸在小河里嬉水。

ˌdab ˈhand *noun* (*BrE, informal*) a person who is very good at doing sth or using sth 能手；高手：*He's a dab hand at cooking spaghetti.* 他是煮意大利面条的高手。◇ *She's a dab hand with a paintbrush.* 她是绘画能手。

dacha /ˈdætʃə/ *noun* a Russian country house （俄国的）乡间宅第，别墅

dachs·hund /ˈdæksnd; *NAmE* ˈdɑːkshʊnd/ (*also BrE, informal* **ˈsausage dog**) *noun* a small dog with a long body, long ears and very short legs 猎獾狗，腊肠狗（身长、腿短、耳朵大）

da·coit /dəˈkɔɪt/ *noun* (*IndE*) a member of a group of armed thieves 武装匪徒；强盗

dac·tyl /ˈdæktɪl/ *noun* (*specialist*) a unit of sound in poetry consisting of one strong or long syllable followed by two weak or short syllables （诗歌的）扬抑抑格，长短短格

dad 🔑 /dæd/ *noun* (*informal*) (often used as a name 常用作称呼) father 爸爸；爹爹：*That's my dad over there.* 那边那位是我爸爸。◇ *Do you live with your mum or your dad?* 你和妈妈还是和爸爸住在一起？◇ *Is it OK if I borrow the car, Dad?* 爸爸，借用一下汽车好吗？

Dada /ˈdɑːdɑː/ *noun* [U] an early 20th century movement in art, literature, music and film which made fun of social and artistic conventions 达达主义（20 世纪早期兴起的文艺运动，以嘲讽社会和艺术传统为特征） ▶ **Dada·ism** /ˈdɑːdɑːɪzəm/ *noun* [U] **Dada·ist** /ˈdɑːdɑːɪst/ *noun*

dada /ˈdɑːdɑː/ *noun* (*IndE*) **1** an older brother or male cousin 哥哥；表兄；堂兄 **2** used after the first name of an older man as a polite way of addressing him 伯伯，叔叔（敬称，用于年长男性的名字后） **3** the father of your father 祖父；爷爷 **4** a leader of a GANG *n.* (1) （犯罪团伙的）头目，老大

daddy /ˈdædi/ *noun* (*pl.* **-ies**) used especially by and to young children, and often as a name, to mean 'father' （尤作儿语）爸爸：*What does your daddy look like?* 你爸爸长得什么样？◇ *Daddy, where are you?* 爸爸，你在哪儿？◇ *Come to Daddy.* 到爸爸这儿来。

ˌdaddy-ˈlong-legs *noun* (*pl.* **daddy-long-legs**) (*informal*) **1** = CRANE FLY **2** (*NAmE*) a small creature like a spider with very long legs 长脚爷叔；盲蛛

dado /ˈdeɪdəʊ; *NAmE* -doʊ/ *noun* (*pl.* **-os**, *NAmE* **-oes**) the lower part of the wall of a room when it is a different colour or material from the top part 墙裙；护壁板

ˈdado rail *noun* a raised line around the wall of a room, that separates the dado from the upper part of the wall （墙裙顶端的）护壁条

dae·mon /ˈdiːmən/ *noun* a creature in stories from ancient Greece that is half man and half god （古希腊神话中的）半神半人的精灵

daf·fo·dil /ˈdæfədɪl/ *noun* a tall yellow spring flower shaped like a TRUMPET. It is a national symbol of Wales. 黄水仙（威尔士的民族象征） ➲ VISUAL VOCAB PAGE V11

daffy /ˈdæfi/ *adj.* (**daf·fier**, **daf·fi·est**) (*informal*) silly 傻的；愚蠢的

daft /dɑːft; *NAmE* dæft/ *adj.* (**daft·er**, **daft·est**) (*informal*) silly, often in a way that is amusing 笨的；傻的；愚蠢可笑的：*Don't be so daft!* 别那么犯傻了！◇ *She's not as daft as she looks.* 她并不像看上去那么傻。◇ *What a daft thing to say!* 这样说真是太愚蠢了！ ▶ **daft·ness** *noun* [U]
IDM **ˌdaft as a ˈbrush** (*BrE, informal*) very silly 傻得很；愚蠢透顶

dag /dæg/ *noun* (*informal*) **1** (*AustralE, NZE*) a person who is strange or different in an amusing way 怪人；滑稽的人 **2** (*AustralE*) a person who is not fashionable 不入时的人；土包子 **3** (*AustralE, NZE*) a dirty piece of wool that hangs down from a sheep's bottom （羊屁股下面的）脏毛；羊股沟毛

dagaa /dəˈgɑː/ *noun* [C, U] (*pl.* **dagaa**) (*EAfrE*) small fish that are dried to preserve them, and often fried and then cooked with tomatoes and milk to make a STEW 小鱼干（常炸过后与番茄和牛奶同煮，做成炖菜）

dagga /ˈdæxə/ *noun* [U] (*SAfrE*) = MARIJUANA：*She was arrested for smoking dagga.* 她吸大麻被捕。

dag·ger /ˈdægə(r)/ *noun* a short pointed knife that is used as a weapon 匕首；短剑 ➲ PICTURE AT SWORD ➲ SEE ALSO CLOAK-AND-DAGGER
IDM **at daggers ˈdrawn** (*BrE*) if two people are **at daggers drawn**, they are very angry with each other 剑拔弩张；势不两立 **look ˈdaggers at sb** to look at sb in a very angry way 对某人怒目而视

daggy /ˈdægi/ *adj.* (*AustralE, informal*) **1** not fashionable 不时髦的；过时的；土气的：*a daggy restaurant* 土里土气的餐馆 **2** untidy or dirty 凌乱的；肮脏的

dago /ˈdeɪgəʊ; *NAmE* -goʊ/ *noun* (*pl.* **-os** or **-oes**) (*taboo, slang*) a very offensive word for a person from Italy, Spain or Portugal 拉丁佬（对意大利人、西班牙人或葡萄牙人的蔑称）

da·guerre·otype (*also* **da·guerro·type**) /dəˈgerətaɪp/ *noun* a photograph taken using an early process that used a silver plate and MERCURY gas （早期的）达盖尔银版照片

dah·lia /ˈdeɪliə; *NAmE* ˈdæliə/ *noun* a large brightly coloured garden flower, often shaped like a ball 大丽花属

dai·kon /ˈdaɪkɒn; *NAmE* -kɑːn/ *noun* [U, C] = MOOLI

the Dáil /dɔɪl/ *noun* [sing.+sing./pl. v.] one of the parts of the parliament of the Republic of Ireland, whose members are elected by the people （爱尔兰共和国的）众议院

daily /ˈdeɪli/ *adj., adv., noun*

■*adj.* [only before noun] **1** happening, done or produced every day 每日的；日常的：*a daily routine/visit/newspaper* 日常事务；每日一次的访问；日报 ◇ *events affecting the **daily lives** of millions of people* 影响数百万人日常生活的事件 ◇ *Invoices are signed **on a daily basis**.* 发票按日签发。 **2** connected with one day's work 每个工作日的；按日的：*They charge a daily rate.* 他们按日收费。

IDM **your daily ˈbread** the basic things that you need to live, especially food 生计；（尤指）每日的食物

■*adv.* every day 每日；每天：*The machines are inspected twice daily.* 机器每日检查两次。

■*noun* (*pl.* **-ies**) **1** a newspaper published every day except Sunday （除星期日外每日发行的）日报：*The story was in all the dailies.* 这则新闻刊登在所有日报上。 **2** (*also* ˌ**daily ˈhelp**) (*old-fashioned, BrE*) a person employed to come to sb's house each day to clean it and do other jobs （不寄宿的）仆人

dainty /ˈdeɪnti/ *adj.* (**dain·tier**, **dain·ti·est**) **1** (of people and things 人和物) small and delicate in a way that people find attractive 娇小的；娇美的；精致的；小巧的 SYN **delicate**: *dainty feet* 娇小可爱的脚 ◇ *a dainty porcelain cup* 小巧玲珑的瓷杯 **2** (of movements 举止) careful, often in a way that suggests good manners 文雅的；优雅的；高雅的 SYN **delicate**: *She took a dainty little bite of the apple.* 她文雅地咬了一小口苹果。 ▸ **dain·tily** *adv.*: *She blew her nose as daintily as possible.* 她尽量文雅地擤了擤鼻涕。 **dain·ti·ness** *noun* [U]

dai·quiri /ˈdaɪkɪri; ˈdæk-/ *noun* an alcoholic drink made from RUM mixed with fruit juice, sugar, etc. 代基里酒（由朗姆酒与果汁、糖等掺和而成）

dairy /ˈdeəri; *NAmE* ˈderi/ *noun, adj.*

■*noun* (*pl.* **-ies**) **1** [C] a place on a farm where milk is kept and where butter and cheese are made 牛奶场；乳品场 ➲ WORDFINDER NOTE AT FARM **2** [C] a company that sells milk, eggs, cheese and other milk products 乳品公司；乳品店 **3** [C] (*NZE*) a small local shop （当地的）小商店，小铺：*I went to buy a paper at the corner dairy.* 我到街角的小店去买了份报纸。 **4** [U] milk, eggs, cheese and other milk products 乳制品：*The doctor told me to eat less red meat and dairy.* 医生告诫我要少吃红肉和乳制品。

■*adj.* [only before noun] **1** made from milk 牛奶的；奶制的；乳品的：***dairy products/produce*** 乳制品 **2** connected with the production of milk rather than meat 乳品业的；生产乳品的：*the dairy industry* 乳品业 ◇ ***dairy cattle/farmers*** 乳牛；乳牛场工人 ◇ *a **dairy cow/farm*** 乳牛；乳牛场

dairy·maid /ˈdeərimeɪd; *NAmE* ˈderi-/ *noun* (*old-fashioned*) a woman who works in a dairy *n.* (1) 挤奶女工；乳牛场女工

dairy·man /ˈdeərimən; *NAmE* ˈderi-/ *noun* (*pl.* **-men** /-mən/) **1** a man who works in a dairy *n.* (1) 挤奶工人；乳牛场工人 **2** a man who owns or manages a dairy *n.* (2) and sells the products 乳牛场主；乳品商

dais /ˈdeɪɪs/ *noun* a stage, especially at one end of a room, on which people stand to make speeches to an audience （尤指房间一端的）讲台，高台

daisy /ˈdeɪzi/ *noun* (*pl.* **-ies**) a small wild flower with white PETALS around a yellow centre; a taller plant with similar but larger flowers 雏菊（花）；（类似雏菊，但花稍大的）菊科植物 IDM SEE PUSH *v.* ➲ SEE ALSO MICHAELMAS DAISY ➲ VISUAL VOCAB PAGE V11

ˈ**daisy chain** *noun* a string of daisies tied together to wear around the neck, etc. 雏菊花环

ˈ**daisy cutter** *noun* **1** (in CRICKET or BASEBALL 板球或棒球) a ball hit or thrown to roll or BOUNCE low along the ground 擦地球；地滚球；滚地球 **2** a very powerful bomb dropped from an aircraft that explodes close to the ground and causes a lot of destruction over a large area 摘菊使者（杀伤范围大的空投炸弹）；滚地球炸弹

ˈ**daisy wheel** *noun* a small disc, used in some printers and TYPEWRITERS, with metal letters around the edge which print onto paper （打印机或打字机的）菊瓣字轮：*a daisy wheel printer* 菊瓣字轮打印机

daks /dæks/ *noun* [pl.] (*AustralE, NZE, informal*) an informal word used to mean trousers 裤子

dal (*also* **dhal**) /dɑːl/ *noun* [U] a S Asian dish made from LENTILS or other PULSES (= seeds from certain plants) 豆泥糊（用扁豆或其他豆子做的印度菜肴）

dala-dala /ˈdælə dælə/ *noun* (in Tanzania) a privately owned road vehicle with seats for about twelve people, that carries passengers and has a driver that you pay to take you somewhere, usually along a fixed route with other stops for people to get on and off 达拉达拉小巴士（坦桑尼亚的一种私营公交车）

dale /deɪl/ *noun* (*literary* or *dialect*) a valley, especially in northern England （尤指英格兰北部的）山谷，峪：*the Yorkshire Dales* 约克郡山谷

Dalit /ˈdʌlɪt/ *noun* (in the traditional Indian CASTE system) a member of the caste that is considered the lowest and that has the fewest advantages 达利特人，贱民（传统印度种姓制度中地位最低、最弱势的人）：*the Dalits' struggle for social and economic rights* 贱民争取社会和经济权利的斗争

dal·li·ance /ˈdæliəns/ *noun* [U, C] (*old-fashioned* or *humorous*) **1** the behaviour of sb who is dallying with sb/sth 嬉戏；戏弄：*It turned out to be his last dalliance with the education system.* 这一次竟成了他对教育体制最后的嘲弄。 **2** a sexual relationship that is not serious 调情；调戏

dally /ˈdæli/ *verb* (**dal·lies**, **dally·ing**, **dal·lied**, **dal·lied**) [I] (*old-fashioned*) to do sth too slowly; to take too much time making a decision 蹉跎（时光）；延误；拖拉

PHR V ˈ**dally with sb/sth** (*old-fashioned*) to treat sb/sth in a way that is not serious enough 轻率地对待；玩弄；戏弄 ➲ SEE ALSO DILLY-DALLY

Dal·ma·tian /dælˈmeɪʃn/ *noun* a large dog that has short white hair with black spots 达尔马提亚狗（带黑色斑点的白色短毛大狗）

dam /dæm/ *noun, verb*

■*noun* **1** a barrier that is built across a river in order to stop the water from flowing, used especially to make a RESERVOIR (= a lake for storing water) or to produce electricity 水坝；拦河坝 ➲ WORDFINDER NOTE AT RIVER **2** (*specialist*) the mother of some animals, especially horses 母兽；（尤指）母马，骒马 ➲ COMPARE SIRE *n.* (1) **3** = DENTAL DAM

■*verb* (**-mm-**) ~ **sth** (**up**) to build a dam across a river, especially in order to make an artificial lake for use as a water supply, etc. （在河上）筑坝

dam·age /ˈdæmɪdʒ/ *noun, verb*

■*noun* **1** [U] ~ (**to sth**) physical harm caused to sth which makes it less attractive, useful or valuable （有形的）损坏，破坏，损失：***serious/severe/extensive/permanent/minor damage*** 重大的 / 严重的 / 大范围的 / 永久性的 / 轻微的损坏 ◇ ***brain/liver etc. damage*** 脑、肝等损伤 ◇ ***fire/smoke/bomb/storm damage*** 火灾损失；烟雾熏坏；炸弹毁坏；暴风雨破坏 ◇ *The earthquake caused damage to property estimated at $6 million.* 地震造成大约 600 万美元的财产损失。◇ *The storm didn't **do** much **damage**.* 暴风雨并未造成严重损失。◇ *Let's take a look at the damage.* 让我们看看损失情况吧。◇ *I insist on paying for the damage.* 我

▼ SYNONYMS 同义词辨析

damage

hurt • harm • impair

These words all mean to have a bad effect on sb/sth. 以上各词均含伤害、损害之义。

damage to cause physical harm to sth, making it less attractive, useful or valuable; to have a bad effect on sb/sth's life, health, happiness or chances of success 指毁坏、破坏、伤害、损害： *The fire badly damaged the town hall.* 火灾使市政厅遭到严重破坏。◇ *emotionally damaged children* 感情上受伤害的孩子

hurt (*rather informal*) to have a bad effect on sb/sth's life, health, happiness or chances of success 指伤害、损害： *Hard work never hurt anyone.* 努力工作绝无害处。

harm to have a bad effect on sb/sth's life, health, happiness or chances of success 指伤害、损害： *Pollution can harm marine life.* 污染会危及海洋生物。

DAMAGE, HURT OR HARM? 用 damage、hurt 还是 harm?

Hurt is slightly less formal than **damage** or **harm**, especially when it is used in negative statements. 与 damage 或 harm 相比，hurt 稍非正式，用于否定句时尤其如此： *It won't hurt him to have to wait a bit.* 等上一会儿对他无妨。◇ ~~*It won't damage/harm him to have to wait a bit.*~~ **Harm** is also often used to talk about ways in which things in the natural world such as *wildlife* and the *environment* are affected by human activity. * harm 亦常用来表示自然界中的事物（如野生生物和环境）受到人类活动的影响。

impair (*rather formal*) to damage sb's health, abilities or chances 指损害、削弱（健康、能力或机会）： *Even one drink can impair driving performance.* 即使一杯酒也可能影响驾驶操作。

PATTERNS

- to damage/hurt/harm/impair sb's **chances**
- to damage/hurt/harm sb's **interests/reputation**
- to damage/harm/impair sb's **health**
- to **seriously/greatly** damage/hurt/harm/impair sb/sth
- to **badly/severely** damage/hurt/impair sb/sth

坚持要赔偿损失。◇ *Make sure you insure your camera against loss or damage.* 一定要给你的照相机投保，以防丢失或损坏。 **2** 🔑 [U] ~ (**to sb/sth**) harmful effects on sb/sth 损害；伤害： *emotional damage resulting from divorce* 离婚引起的感情伤害 ◇ *damage to a person's reputation* 对个人名誉的损害 ◇ *This could cause serious damage to the country's economy.* 这可能对国家的经济造成严重破坏。◇ *I'm going—I've done enough damage here already.* 我要走了，我在这里造成的损害已经够大了。 **3 damages** [pl.] an amount of money that a court decides should be paid to sb by the person, company, etc. that has caused them harm or injury （法院判定的）损害赔偿金： *He was ordered to pay damages totalling £30 000.* 他被责令支付总额为 3 万英镑的损害赔偿金。◇ *They intend to sue for damages.* 他们打算起诉，要求赔偿损失。◇ *Ann was awarded £6 000 (in) damages.* 安被判予 6 000 英镑的损害赔偿金。

IDM **what's the 'damage?** (*informal*) a way of asking how much sth costs 要花多少钱

■ *verb* 🔑 ~ **sth/sb** to harm or spoil sth/sb 损害；伤害；毁坏；破坏： *The fire badly damaged the town hall.* 火灾使市政厅遭到严重破坏。◇ *Several vehicles were damaged in the crash.* 好几辆汽车在撞车事故中损坏了。◇ *Smoking seriously damages your health.* 吸烟严重损害人体健康。◇ *The allegations are likely to damage his political career.* 这些指控有可能对他的政治生涯造成伤害。◇ *emotionally damaged children* 感情上受伤害的孩子 ➲ COLLOCATIONS AT INJURY

ˌdamage limiˈtation (*also* **ˌdamage conˈtrol** *especially in NAmE*) *noun* [U] the process of trying to limit the amount of damage that is caused by sth 损害控制

dam·aging /ˈdæmɪdʒɪŋ/ *adj.* causing damage; having a bad effect on sb/sth 造成破坏的；有害的；损害的： ***damaging consequences/effects*** 破坏性的后果 / 影响 ◇ **~ to sb/sth** *Lead is potentially damaging to children's health.* 铅对儿童的健康具有潜在损害。

Da·mas·cus /dəˈmæskəs/ *noun*

IDM **the road to Daˈmascus** an experience that results in a great change in a person's attitudes or beliefs 通往大马士革之路；（观点或信仰的）翻然转变： *Spending a night in jail was his road to Damascus.* 在监狱里度过的一夜彻底改变了他的人生观。 ORIGIN From the story in the Bible in which St Paul hears the voice of God on the road to Damascus and becomes a Christian. 源自《圣经》故事，圣保罗在前往大马士革的路上听到了上帝的召唤，于是皈依基督。

dam·ask /ˈdæməsk/ *noun* [U] a type of thick cloth, usually made from silk or LINEN, with a pattern that is visible on both sides 花缎；锦缎： *a damask tablecloth* 织花桌布

dame /deɪm/ *noun* **1 Dame** (in Britain) a title given to a woman as a special honour because of the work she has done 女爵士（英国授予有贡献的女性的荣誉称号）： *Dame Maggie Smith* 玛吉・史密斯女爵士 **2** (*old-fashioned, NAmE, informal*) a woman 女人 **3** = PANTOMIME DAME

damn /dæm/ *exclamation, adj., verb, adv., noun*

■ ***exclamation*** (*also old-fashioned* **dam·mit** /ˈdæmɪt/, **ˈdamn it**) (*informal*) a swear word that people use to show that they are annoyed, disappointed, etc. （表示厌烦、失望等）该死，他妈的，讨厌： *Oh damn! I forgot he was coming.* 真该死！我把他要来这事儿给忘了。 ➲ MORE LIKE THIS 20, page R27

■ ***adj.*** (*also* **damned**) [only before noun] (*informal*) **1** a swear word that people use to show that they are annoyed with sb/sth （表示厌烦）可恶的，讨厌的，该死的： *Where's that damn book!* 那该死的书在哪儿呢！◇ *The damned thing won't start!* 这混账东西就是发动不起来！◇ *It's none of your damn business!* 关你屁事！◇ *He's a damn nuisance!* 他真是个该死的讨厌鬼！ **2** a swear word that people use to emphasize what they are saying （加强语气）十足的，完全的： *What a damn shame!* 真是太遗憾了！ IDM SEE THING

■ ***verb*** **1 ~ sb/sth** (*informal*) used when swearing at sb/sth to show that you are angry （表示愤怒）该死，混账： *Damn you! I'm not going to let you bully me.* 你这个浑蛋！甭想欺负我。◇ *Damn this machine! Why won't it work?* 这该死的机器！怎么就是发动不起来？ **2 ~ sb** (of God 上帝) to decide that sb must suffer in hell 令（某人）下地狱 **3 ~ sb/sth** to criticize sb/sth very strongly 强烈指责；谴责；狠狠批评： *The film was damned by the critics for its mindless violence.* 这部影片因无谓的暴力受到评论家的强烈谴责。

IDM **damn the consequences, expense, etc.** (*informal*) used to say that you are going to do sth even though you know it may be expensive, have bad results, etc. 置后果（或费用等）于不顾： *Let's celebrate and damn the expense!* 管它花多少钱，咱们先庆祝一番再说！ **damn sb/sth with faint ˈpraise** to praise sb/sth only a little, in order to show that you do not really like them/it 用冷漠的赞扬贬低；寓贬于褒；名褒实贬 **I'll be damned!** (*old-fashioned, informal*) used to show that you are very surprised about sth （表示惊奇）真没想到，真叫我吃惊 **I'm damned if...** (*informal*) used to show that you refuse to do sth or do not know sth 我决不…；我绝对不…： *I'm damned if I'll apologize!* 我决不道歉！◇ *I'm damned if I know who he is.* 我根本不认识他。 ➲ MORE AT NEAR *adv.*

■ ***adv.*** (*also* **damned**) (*informal*) **1** a swear word that people use to show that they are annoyed with sb/sth （表示厌烦）该死，讨厌，十足，完全： *Don't be so damn silly!* 别那么傻了！◇ *What a damn stupid question!* 这问题问得真是愚蠢透顶！◇ *You* ***know damn well*** (= you know very well) *what I mean!* 我的意思你再清楚不过了！◇ *I'll damn well leave tonight* (= I am determined to). 我今晚一定得离开。 **2** a swear word that people use to emphasize what they are saying （加强语气）非常，十分，极： *damn good* 好得不得了 ◇ *We got out pretty damned fast!* 我们一溜烟似的走了！◇ *I'm damn sure she had no idea.* 我敢肯定她不知道。

IDM **damn ˈall** (*BrE*) nothing 毫无；丝毫不；完全没有： *I*

know damn all about computers. 我对计算机一窍不通。

■ ***noun***

IDM **not care/give a 'damn (about sb/sth)** (*informal*) to not care at all about sb/sth （对…）毫不在乎

dam·nable /'dæmnəbl/ *adj.* (*old-fashioned*) bad or annoying 糟糕的；讨厌的 ▶ **dam·nably** /'dæmnəbli/ *adv.*

dam·na·tion /dæm'neɪʃn/ *noun* [U] the state of being in hell; the act of sending sb to hell 天谴；罚入地狱：*eternal damnation* 永罚

damned /dæmd/ *adj., adv., noun*

■ ***adj., adv.*** = DAMN

■ ***noun*** **the damned** [pl.] people who are forced to live in hell after they die 下地狱的灵魂

damned·est /'dæmdɪst/ *noun, adj.* (*informal*)

IDM **the damnedest…** (*especially NAmE*) the most surprising… 最令人惊奇（的）；最奇妙（的）：*It's the damnedest thing I ever saw.* 这是我见过的最奇妙的玩意。 **do/try your 'damnedest (to do sth)** to try as hard as you can (to do sth) 全力以赴；尽力而为；竭尽全力：*She did her damnedest to get it done on time.* 她竭尽全力按时把它完成了。

damn·ing /'dæmɪŋ/ *adj.* critical of sb/sth; suggesting that sb is guilty 谴责的；诅咒的；可以定罪的：***damning criticism/evidence*** 谴责性的批评；足以定罪的证据 ◇ *a* ***damning conclusion/report*** 可以定罪的结论 / 报告 ◇ *Her report is expected to deliver a damning indictment of education standards.* 人们预料她的报告会对教育水平予以强烈谴责。

Damo·cles /'dæməkli:z/ *noun* IDM SEE SWORD

damp 🔑 /dæmp/ *adj., noun, verb*

■ ***adj.*** 🔑 (**damp·er, damp·est**) slightly wet, often in a way that is unpleasant 潮湿的；微湿的；湿气重的：*The cottage was cold and damp.* 这小屋又冷又湿。◇ *It feels damp in here.* 这地方使人感到潮乎乎的。◇ *damp clothes* 潮湿的衣服 ◇ *Wipe the surface with a damp cloth.* 用湿布擦表面。 ➲ SYNONYMS AT WET ▶ **damp·ly** *adv.*：*The blouse clung damply to her skin.* 衬衫湿漉漉地贴在她身上。

IDM **a damp 'squib** (*BrE, informal*) an event that is disappointing because it is not as exciting or impressive as expected 哑炮；令人失望的事；令人扫兴的事

■ ***noun*** [U] (*BrE*) the state of being damp; areas on a wall, etc. that are damp 潮湿；潮气；湿气；湿块：*The old house smells of damp.* 这老房子散发出一股潮气。◇ *Those marks above the window look like damp to me.* 窗子上面的那些印迹看上去像是水渍。

■ ***verb*** **~ sth** = DAMPEN：*She damped a towel and wrapped it round his leg.* 她弄湿毛巾，把它裹在他的腿上。

PHR V **,damp sth↔'down 1** to make a fire burn more slowly or stop burning 使（火）减弱；灭火 **2** to make an emotion or a feeling less strong 抑制，控制（情绪、感情等）

'damp course (*also* **'damp-proof course**) *noun* (*both BrE*) a layer of material near the bottom of a wall that is used to stop damp rising from the ground （墙脚的）防潮层

damp·en /'dæmpən/ *verb* **1** (*also less frequent* **damp**) **~ sth** to make sth slightly wet 弄湿；使潮湿：*Perspiration dampened her face and neck.* 她的脸和脖子都汗津津的。◇ *He dampened his hair to make it lie flat.* 他把头发弄湿，梳得平平的。 **2 ~ sth** to make sth such as a feeling or a reaction less strong 抑制，控制，减弱（感情、反应等）：*None of the setbacks could* ***dampen his enthusiasm*** *for the project.* 任何挫折都不能减弱他对这个项目的热情。 ◇ *She wasn't going to let anything* ***dampen her spirits*** *today.* 她不想让任何事情来影响她今天的兴致。

damp·er /'dæmpə(r)/ *noun* **1** a piece of metal that can be moved to allow more or less air into a fire so that the fire burns more or less strongly （调节空气流量，控制炉火燃烧的）风门，气闸，挡板 **2** a device in a piano that is used to reduce the level of the sound produced （钢琴的）制音器，减音器

IDM **put a 'damper on sth** (*BrE also* **put a 'dampener on sth**) (*informal*) to make sth less enjoyable, successful, etc. 抑制；使扫兴；使沮丧

damp·ness /'dæmpnəs/ *noun* [U] the fact or state of being damp 潮湿：*To avoid dampness, air the room regularly.* 为避免潮湿，房间要经常通风。

'damp-proof course *noun* = DAMP COURSE

dam·sel /'dæmzl/ *noun* (*old use*) a young woman who is not married 少女；姑娘；闺女

IDM **a ,damsel in di'stress** (*humorous*) a woman who needs help 落难女子；需要帮助的女子

dam·sel·fly /'dæmzlflaɪ/ *noun* (*pl.* **-ies**) an insect with a long thin body and two pairs of wings 豆娘

dam·son /'dæmzn/ *noun* a small purple fruit, like a PLUM 西洋李子（果实呈紫色，类似李子）：*a damson tree* 西洋李子树

dan /dæn/ *noun* **1** one of the levels in KARATE or JUDO （空手道或柔道的）段 **2** a person who has reached a particular level in KARATE or JUDO （空手道或柔道的）入段选手

dance 🔑 /dɑ:ns; *NAmE* dæns/ *noun, verb*

■ ***noun*** **1** 🔑 [C] a series of movements and steps that are usually performed to music; a particular example of these movements and steps 舞蹈；舞步：*a* ***dance class/routine*** 舞蹈课；一套舞蹈动作 ◇ *Find a partner and practise these new* ***dance steps.*** 找个舞伴来练习这些新舞步。◇ *Do you know any other Latin American dances?* 你会跳其他拉美舞蹈吗？ ◇ *The next dance will be a waltz.* 接下来是华尔兹舞。

> **WORDFINDER** 联想词：ballet, ballroom, band, choreograph, floor, folk dance, **music**, partner, step

2 🔑 [U] the art of dancing, especially for entertainment 舞蹈（艺术）：*an evening of drama, music and dance* 戏剧、音乐和舞蹈晚会 ◇ ***modern/classical dance*** 现代 / 古典舞蹈 ◇ *a* ***dance company/troupe*** 舞蹈团；舞蹈队 **3** 🔑 [C] an act of dancing 跳舞：*Let's have a dance.* 咱们跳个舞吧。 ◇ *He did a little dance of triumph.* 他兴高采烈地跳了几步舞。 **4** 🔑 [C] a social event at which people dance 舞会：*We hold a dance every year to raise money for charity.* 我们每年举行一场舞会，为慈善事业募捐。 **5** 🔑 [C] a piece of music for dancing to 舞曲：*The band finished with a few slow dances.* 乐队最后演奏了几首节奏缓慢的舞曲。 IDM SEE LEAD[1] *v.*, SONG

■ ***verb*** **1** 🔑 [I] to move your body to the sound and rhythm of music 跳舞：*Do you want to dance?* 你想跳舞吗？ ◇ *He asked me to dance.* 他邀请我跳舞。 ◇ *They stayed up all night singing and dancing.* 他们唱啊，跳啊，一宿没睡。◇ *They danced to the music of a string quartet.* 他们随着弦乐四重奏乐曲跳舞。◇ *Ruth danced all evening with Richard.* 整个晚上鲁思都和理查德跳舞。◇ *Ruth and Richard danced together all evening.* 鲁思和理查德整晚都在一起跳舞。 **2** 🔑 [T] **~ sth** to do a particular type of dance 跳…舞：*to dance the tango* 跳探戈舞 ◇ *to dance a waltz* 跳华尔兹舞 **3** [I] to move in a lively way 跳跃；雀跃；轻快地移动：*The children danced around her.* 孩子们在她周围蹦蹦跳跳。◇ *The sun shone on the sea and the waves danced and sparkled.* 太阳照在海面上，碧浪翻滚，波光粼粼。 ◇ *The words danced before her tired eyes.* 这些字在她疲乏的眼前晃动。

IDM **,dance at'tendance on sb** (*BrE, formal*) to be with sb and do things to help and please them 讨好；奉承；迎合 **,dance the 'night away** to dance for the whole evening or night 整夜（或通宵达旦）跳舞 **dance to sb's 'tune** to do whatever sb tells you to 听从某人的指挥；唯命是从；言听计从

'dance band *noun* a group of musicians who play music at dances 伴舞乐队

'dance floor *noun* an area where people can dance in a hotel, club, etc. （旅馆、俱乐部等供客人跳舞的）舞场，舞池

'dance hall *noun* a large public room where people pay to go and dance (more common in the past than now) 舞厅（营业性的，此义稍旧） ➲ COMPARE BALLROOM

dan·cer /ˈdɑːnsə(r); *NAmE* ˈdæn-/ *noun* a person who dances or whose job is dancing 跳舞者；舞蹈演员：*She's a fantastic dancer.* 她的舞跳得非常好。◇ *He's a dancer with the Royal Ballet.* 他是皇家芭蕾舞团的舞蹈演员。

dan·cing /ˈdɑːnsɪŋ; *NAmE* ˈdæn-/ *noun* [U] moving your body to music 跳舞；舞蹈：*dancing classes* 舞蹈课 ◇ *There was music and dancing till two in the morning.* 音乐和舞蹈一直持续到凌晨两点。➲ SEE ALSO COUNTRY DANCING at COUNTRY DANCE, LAP DANCING, POLE DANCING, TABLE DANCING

D

dan·delion /ˈdændɪlaɪən/ *noun* a small wild plant with a bright yellow flower that becomes a soft white ball of seeds called a **dandelion clock** 蒲公英 ➲ VISUAL VOCAB PAGE V11

dan·di·fied /ˈdændɪfaɪd/ *adj.* (*old-fashioned, disapproving*) (of a man 男子) caring a lot about his clothes and appearance 讲究衣着和外表的；好打扮的；油头粉面的

dan·dle /ˈdændl/ *verb* **~ sb** (*old-fashioned*) to play with a baby or young child by moving them up and down on your knee 摇逗（放在膝上的孩子）

dan·druff /ˈdændrʌf/ *noun* [U] very small pieces of dead skin, seen as a white dust in a person's hair 头皮屑

dandy /ˈdændi/ *noun, adj.*

■ ***noun*** (*pl.* **-ies**) (*old-fashioned*) a man who cares a lot about his clothes and appearance 讲究衣着和外表的男人；好打扮的男人

■ ***adj.*** (*old-fashioned, especially NAmE*) very good 非常好的；极佳的

dang /dæŋ/ *adj., adv., exclamation* (*NAmE, informal*) a mild swear word, used instead of DAMN 倒霉，该死（婉辞，与 damn 同义）：*It's just dang stupid!* 简直太愚蠢了！

dan·ger /ˈdeɪndʒə(r)/ *noun* **1** [U] **~ (of sth)** the possibility of sth happening that will injure, harm or kill sb, or damage or destroy sth 危险；风险：*Danger! Keep Out!* 危险！请勿入内！◇ *Children's lives are **in danger** every time they cross this road.* 孩子们每次过这条马路都面临着生命危险。◇ *Doctors said she is now **out of danger*** (= not likely to die). 医生说她已脱离危险。**2** [C, U] the possibility of sth bad or unpleasant happening （坏事或不快之事发生的）可能性，危险：*There is no danger of a bush fire now.* 目前没有山林大火之虞。◇ **~ of sth** *The building is **in danger of** collapsing.* 这栋建筑有垮塌的危险。◇ *How many factory workers are **in danger of** losing their jobs?* 有多少产业工人可能失业？◇ *'Nicky won't find out, will she?' 'Oh, no, there's no danger of that.'* "尼基不会察觉吧，会吗？" "不会，绝对不会的。" ◇ **~ that…** *There is a danger that the political disorder of the past will return.* 昔日的政治动乱可能会重演。**3** [C] **~ (to sb/sth)** a person or thing that may cause damage, or harm sb 危险的人；危险因素；危害；威胁：*Smoking is a serious danger to health.* 吸烟严重危害健康。◇ *Police said the man was a danger to the public.* 警方说这个男人对公众是个危险。◇ *the hidden dangers in your home* 家里潜在的危险因素 ➲ SEE ALSO ENDANGER

IDM **be on/off the 'danger list** (*BrE*) to be so ill/sick that you may die; to no longer be very ill/sick 病危；病入膏肓；病势危急（或好转）；（病人）转危为安

'danger money (*BrE*) (*US* **'hazard pay**, **'danger pay**) *noun* [U] extra pay for doing work that is dangerous 危险工作津贴

dan·ger·ous /ˈdeɪndʒərəs/ *adj.* likely to injure or harm sb, or to damage or destroy sth 有危险的；引起危险的；不安全的：*a dangerous road/illness/sport* 危险的道路/疾病/运动 ◇ *dangerous levels of carbon monoxide* 达到危险程度的一氧化碳含量 ◇ *The prisoners who escaped are violent and dangerous.* 这些逃犯残暴而危险。◇ *The situation is **highly dangerous**.* 形势十分危急。◇ (*BrE*) *a conviction for dangerous driving* 判危险驾驶罪 ◇ **~ for sb** *The traffic here is very dangerous for children.* 这里的交通对孩子很危险。◇ **~ for sb to do sth** *It would be dangerous for you to stay here.* 你待在这儿不安全。▶ **dan·ger·ous·ly** *adv.*：*She was standing dangerously close to the fire.* 她站得离火太近，有危险。◇ *His father is dangerously ill* (= so ill that he might die). 他父亲病危。◇ *Mel enjoys living dangerously* (= doing things that involve risk or danger). 梅尔喜欢冒险活动。

IDM **dangerous 'ground** a situation or subject that is likely to make sb angry, or that involves risk 令人气愤的场合（或话题）；危险处境：*We'd be **on dangerous ground** if we asked about race or religion.* 我们要是问到种族或宗教问题，就很可能会冒犯人。

dan·gle /ˈdæŋgl/ *verb* **1** [I] **(+adv./prep.)** to hang or swing freely 悬垂；悬挂；悬荡；悬摆：*Gold charms dangled from her bracelet.* 她的手链上挂着许多金饰物。◇ *A single light bulb dangled from the ceiling.* 天花板上孤零零地悬吊着一只灯泡。◇ *He sat on the edge with his legs dangling over the side.* 他耷拉着双腿坐在边缘上。**2** [T] **~ sth** to hold sth so that it hangs or swings freely 提着（某物，任其自然下垂或摆动）；来回摆动着：*She dangled her car keys nervously as she spoke.* 她说话时紧张地晃动着她那串汽车钥匙。▶ **dan·gly** /ˈdæŋgli/ *adj.*：*a pair of dangly earrings* 一对耳坠 ➲ VISUAL VOCAB PAGE V70

IDM **keep/leave sb 'dangling** (*informal*) to keep sb in an uncertain state by not telling them sth that they want to know（不对人言明而）使心里没底，使无把握，使拿不准：*She kept him dangling for a week before making her decision.* 她让他忐忑不安了一个星期才作出决定。

PHR V **,dangle sth be'fore/in 'front of sb** to offer sb sth good in order to persuade them to do sth 诱惑；吊胃口

,dan·gling par'ti·ciple *noun* (*grammar* 语法) a participle that relates to a noun that is not mentioned 垂悬分词（相关的名词没有出现的分词）HELP 'Dangling participles' are not considered correct. In the sentence 'While walking home, my phone rang', 'walking' is a dangling participle. A correct form of the sentence would be 'While I was walking home, my phone rang'. "垂悬分词"被认为是不正确的。在 While walking home, my phone rang 中，walking 是垂悬分词。正确句式应是 While I was walking home, my phone rang。

Dan·ish /ˈdeɪnɪʃ/ *adj., noun*

■ ***adj.*** from or connected with Denmark 丹麦的

■ ***noun*** **1** [U] the language of Denmark 丹麦语 **2** [C] = DANISH PASTRY

,Danish 'pastry (*especially BrE*) (*also* **Dan·ish** *NAmE, BrE*) *noun* a sweet cake made of light PASTRY, often containing apple, nuts, etc. and/or covered with ICING 丹麦酥皮甜饼

dank /dæŋk/ *adj.* (especially of a place 尤指地方) damp, cold and unpleasant 阴冷潮湿的；阴湿的：*a dark dank cave* 阴暗潮湿的洞穴 ▶ **dank·ness** *noun* [U]

dap·per /ˈdæpə(r)/ *adj.* (of a man 男人) small with a neat appearance and nice clothes 矮小利落的；衣冠楚楚的

dap·pled /ˈdæpld/ *adj.* marked with spots of a different colour; with areas of light and shade 有斑点的；花斑的；光影斑驳的：*the cool dappled light under the trees* 树下凉爽斑驳的光

dap·ple grey (*BrE*) (*NAmE* **dapple gray**) /ˌdæpl ˈgreɪ/ *adj.* (of a horse 马) grey or white with darker round marks 灰色（或白色）带深色斑点的；菊花青色的 ▶ **dap·ple grey** *noun*

Darby and Joan /ˌdɑːbi ən ˈdʒəʊn; *NAmE* ˌdɑːrbi ən ˈdʒoʊn/ *noun* [pl.] (*BrE*) a way of referring to an old couple who are happily married 幸福的老夫妻

dare /deə(r); *NAmE* der/ *verb, noun*

■ ***verb*** **1** (not usually used in the progressive tenses 通常不用于进行时) to be brave enough to do sth 敢于；胆敢：*She said it as loudly as she dared.* 她壮着胆子大声说了出来。◇ **~ (to) do sth** *He didn't dare (to) say what he thought.* 他不敢说出他的想法。◇ *They daren't ask for any more money.* 他们不敢再要钱了。◇ (*literary*) *She dared not breathe a word of it to anybody.* 她对任何人都只字不敢提及此事。◇ *There was something, **dare I say it**, a little* unusual about him. 要我说啊，他这人有那么一点怪。 2 [T] to persuade sb to do sth dangerous, difficult or embarrassing so that they can show that they are not afraid 激（某人做某事）；问（某人）有没有胆量（做某事）: ~ **sb** *Go on! Take it! I dare you.* 来呀！接受吧！我谅你也不敢。◇ **~ sb to do sth** *Some of the older boys had dared him to do it.* 几个大男孩激他，问他敢不敢干这事。 ➲ NOTE AT MODAL

IDM **don't you dare!** (*informal*) used to tell sb strongly not to do sth （让人绝不要做某事）你敢，谅你不敢: *'I'll tell her about it.' 'Don't you dare!'* "我要把这事告诉她。" "你敢！" ◇ *Don't you dare say anything to anybody.* 谅你不敢对任何人提起这事儿。 **how 'dare you, etc.** used to show that you are angry about sth that sb has done （表示气愤）你竟然，你竟敢: *How dare you talk to me like that?* 你竟敢这样对我说话？ ◇ *How dare she imply that I was lying?* 她竟敢暗示我在撒谎？ **I dare say** (*also* **I daresay** *especially in BrE*) used when you are saying that sth is probable 我想；很可能；大概: *I dare say you know about it already.* 你大概已经知道了。

▼GRAMMAR POINT 语法说明

dare

- **Dare** (sense 1) usually forms negatives and questions like an ordinary verb and is followed by an infinitive with *to*. It is most common in the negative. * dare（第 1 义）通常与一般动词一样构成否定式和疑问式，后接带 to 的动词不定式，最常用于否定句中： *I didn't dare to ask.* 我不敢问。◇ *He won't dare to break his promise.* 他不敢食言。◇ *You told him? How did you dare?* 你告诉他了？你竟敢？ ◇ *I hardly dared to hope she'd remember me.* 我几乎不敢指望她会记得我。 In positive sentences a phrase like **not be afraid** is often used instead. 在肯定句中常用 not be afraid 代替： *She wasn't afraid* (= she dared) *to tell him the truth.* 她敢对他讲实话。
- It can also be used like a modal verb especially in present tense negative forms in *BrE*, and is followed by an infinitive without *to*. * dare 亦可以情态动词方式使用，尤其在英式英语中的现在时否定式，后接不带 to 的动词不定式： *I daren't tell her the truth.* 我不敢对她讲实话。
- In spoken English, the forms of the ordinary verb are often used with an infinitive without *to*. 在英语口语中，此普通动词的各种形式常与不带 to 的不定式连用： *Don't you dare tell her what I said!* 谅你不敢告诉她我说的话！◇ *I didn't dare look at him.* 我不敢看他。

■***noun*** [usually sing.] something dangerous, difficult or embarrassing that you try to persuade sb to do, to see if they will do it 激将；挑战: (*BrE*) *He climbed onto the roof* ***for a dare.*** 他受到激将才爬上房顶。◇ (*NAmE*) *She learned to fly* ***on a dare.*** 她在激将下学会了驾驶飞机。

dare·devil /ˈdeədevl; *NAmE* ˈderd-/ *noun* a person who enjoys doing dangerous things, in a way that other people may think is stupid 鲁莽大胆的人；蛮干的人；冒失鬼: *a reckless daredevil* 轻举妄动的冒失鬼 ▶ **dare·devil** *adj.* [only before noun]: *Don't try any daredevil stunts.* 别去做那些玩儿命的惊险动作。

dar·ing /ˈdeərɪŋ; *NAmE* ˈder-/ *adj., noun*

■***adj.*** brave; willing to do dangerous or unusual things; involving danger or taking risks 勇敢的；敢于冒险的: *a daring walk in space* 勇敢的太空漫步 ◇ *There are plenty of activities at the resort for the less daring.* 度假胜地有许多活动是供不太敢于冒险的人玩的。◇ *The gallery was known for putting on daring exhibitions.* 该画廊以其举办的大胆画展而享有盛名。◇ *a daring strapless dress in black silk* 大胆袒露的黑绸无吊带连衣裙 ▶ **dar·ing·ly** *adv.*

■***noun*** [U] courage and the willingness to take risks 大胆；勇敢；胆量: *the skill and daring of the mountain climbers* 登山者的技能和胆量

dark 🔑 /dɑːk; *NAmE* dɑːrk/ *adj., noun*

■***adj.*** (**dark·er**, **dark·est**)

- WITH LITTLE LIGHT 光线暗淡 **1** 🔑 with no or very little light, especially because it is night 黑暗的；昏暗的；阴暗的: *a dark room/street/forest* 黑暗的房间；昏暗的街道；黑黝黝的森林 ◇ *What time does it* ***get dark*** *in summer?* 夏天什么时候天黑？◇ *It was dark outside and I couldn't see much.* 外面很黑，我看不清。 OPP **light**
- COLOURS 颜色 **2** 🔑 not light; closer in shade to black than to white 深色的；暗色的: ***dark blue/green/red, etc.*** 深蓝色、墨绿色、深红色等 ◇ *Darker colours are more practical and don't show stains.* 深色不显脏，更实用。 OPP **light, pale** **3** 🔑 having a colour that is close to black 近乎黑色的: *a dark suit* 深色的西服 ◇ *dark-coloured wood* 深色木材 ◇ *The dark clouds in the sky meant that a storm was coming.* 天空中的乌云预示暴风雨即将来临。
- HAIR/SKIN/EYES 头发；皮肤；眼睛 **4** 🔑 brown or black in colour 褐色的；黝黑的；乌黑的: *Sue has long dark hair.* 休留着长长的黑发。◇ *Even if you have dark skin, you still need protection from the sun.* 即使你皮肤黝黑，仍需要防晒。 **5** 🔑 (of a person 人) having dark hair, eyes, etc. 有深色头发（或眼睛等）的: *a dark handsome stranger* 一位黑头发的英俊陌生人 OPP **fair** ➲ WORDFINDER NOTE AT BLONDE
- MYSTERIOUS 神秘 **6** 🔑 mysterious; hidden and not known about 神秘的；隐秘的；隐藏的: *There are no dark secrets in our family.* 我们家没有隐秘。
- EVIL 邪恶 **7** evil or frightening 邪恶的；阴险的；凶恶的: *There was a darker side to his nature.* 他本性中有阴险的一面。◇ *the dark forces of the imagination* 幻想中的邪恶势力
- WITHOUT HOPE 无希望 **8** unpleasant and without any hope that sth good will happen 忧郁的；不快的；无望的: *the darkest days of Fascism* 法西斯统治下最黑暗的日子 ◇ *The film is a dark vision of the future.* 这部影片预示着黯淡无光的未来。
- PHONETICS 语音学 **9** (of a speech sound 语音) produced with the back part of the tongue close to the back of the mouth. In many accents of English, dark /l/ is used after a vowel, as in *ball*. 模糊的 OPP **clear**

IDM **a dark 'horse 1** (*BrE*) a person who does not tell other people much about their life, and who surprises other people by having interesting qualities 深藏不露的人 **2** a person taking part in a race, etc. who surprises everyone by winning 出人意料的获胜者；黑马 **keep sth 'dark** (*BrE, informal*) to keep sth secret and not tell people about it 对…保密；隐瞒；隐藏

■***noun***

- NO LIGHT 无光 **1** 🔑 **the dark** [sing.] the lack of light in a place, especially because it is night 黑暗；暗处: *All the lights went out and we were left* ***in the dark.*** 灯全熄了，我们周围一片黑暗。◇ *Are the children afraid of the dark?* 孩子们怕黑吗？◇ *animals that can see in the dark* 在黑暗中能看见东西的动物
- COLOUR 颜色 **2** 🔑 [U] an amount of sth that is dark in colour 暗色；阴影: *patterns of light and dark* 明暗相间的图案

IDM **after/before dark** after/before the sun goes down and it is night 天黑后 / 前；黄昏后 / 前: *Try to get home before dark.* 尽量在天黑前回家。◇ *Don't go out alone after dark.* 天黑后不要单独外出。 **in the 'dark (about sth)** knowing nothing about sth （对某事）全然不知: *Workers were kept in the dark about the plans to sell the company.* 工人全然不知出售公司的计划。◇ *She arrived at the meeting as much in the dark as everyone else.* 她到会时与其他人一样毫不知情。 **a shot/stab in the 'dark** a guess; sth you do without knowing what the result will be 瞎猜；盲动；盲干: *The figure he came up with was really just a shot in the dark.* 他得出的数字实际上只是瞎猜而已。 ➲ MORE AT LEAP *n.*

the 'dark ages *noun* [pl.] **1 the Dark Ages** the period of European history between the end of the Roman Empire and the 10th century AD 黑暗时代（欧洲历史上从罗马帝国衰亡至公元 10 世纪的时期） **2** (*often humorous*) a period of history or a time when sth was not developed or modern 不发达的历史时期: *Back in the dark ages of computing, in about 1980, they started a software*

D

company. 早在计算机尚未普及的时代，约 1980 年，他们就创办了软件公司。

ˌdark ˈchocolate (*BrE also* **ˌplain ˈchocolate**) *noun* [U] dark brown chocolate with a slightly bitter taste, made without milk being added 黑巧克力；纯巧克力 ➲ COMPARE MILK CHOCOLATE

D

dark·en /ˈdɑːkən; *NAmE* ˈdɑːrk-/ *verb* **1** [I, T] to become dark; to make sth dark（使）变暗，变黑：*The sky began to darken as the storm approached.* 暴风雨来临时天空变得黑沉沉的。◇ **~ sth** *We walked quickly through the darkened streets.* 我们快步穿过黑魆魆的街道。◇ *a darkened room* 变暗了的房间 **2** [I, T] to become unhappy or angry; to make sb unhappy or angry（使）忧郁，生气，不快：*Her mood darkened at the news.* 听到这消息，她的心情暗淡起来。◇ *Luke's face darkened* (= he looked angry). 卢克沉下脸来。◇ **~ sth** *It was a tragedy that darkened his later life.* 这场悲剧给他后来的岁月蒙上了阴影。

IDM **never darken my ˈdoor again** (*old-fashioned, humorous*) used to tell sb never to come to your home again 再不要跨进我的门槛；再不许踏进我的家门

ˌdark ˈglasses *noun* [pl.] glasses that have dark-coloured LENSES 墨镜 ➲ SEE ALSO SUNGLASSES

darkie /ˈdɑːki; *NAmE* ˈdɑːrki/ *noun* (*taboo, old-fashioned*) a very offensive word for a black person（蔑称）黑人，黑鬼

dark·ling /ˈdɑːklɪŋ; *NAmE* ˈdɑːrk-/ *adj.* (*literary*) becoming dark or connected with the dark 渐暗的；昏暗的；黑暗的：*the darkling sky* 渐暗的天空

dark·ly /ˈdɑːkli; *NAmE* ˈdɑːrk-/ *adv.* **1** in a threatening or unpleasant way 威胁地；险恶地；负面地：*He hinted darkly that all was not well.* 他悲观地暗示并非一切都顺利。 **2** showing a dark colour 漆黑地；乌黑地：*Her eyes burned darkly.* 她的眼里满是怒火。

ˌdark ˈmatter *noun* [U] (*astronomy* 天) according to some theories, material that exists in space but does not reflect any light 暗物质（根据一些理论，指太空中不反射光的物质）

dark·ness /ˈdɑːknəs; *NAmE* ˈdɑːrk-/ *noun* [U] **1** the state of being dark, without any light 黑暗；阴暗；漆黑：*After a few minutes our eyes got used to the darkness.* 几分钟后我们的眼睛就适应了黑暗。◇ *The house was plunged into* ***total darkness*** *when the electricity was cut off.* 停电后，整座房子陷入一片黑暗。◇ *The sun went down and* ***darkness fell*** (= it became night). 夕阳西下，夜幕降临。◇ *There is an extra hour of darkness on winter mornings.* 冬天的早晨天亮晚一个小时。◇ *Parking is not allowed during the* ***hours of darkness.*** 夜间禁止停放车辆。◇ *Her face was* ***in darkness.*** 她的脸处于暗处。◇ *They managed to escape* ***under cover of darkness.*** 他们设法在夜色掩护下逃跑了。 **2** the quality or state of being dark in colour 墨色；暗色；深色：*It depends on the darkness of your skin.* 这取决于你肤色的深浅。 **3** (*literary*) evil 邪恶；罪恶：*the forces of darkness* 邪恶势力

dark·room /ˈdɑːkruːm; -rʊm; *NAmE* ˈdɑːrk-/ *noun* a room that can be made completely dark, where you can take film out of a camera and develop photographs（冲洗胶片的）暗室

ˌdark ˈstar *noun* (*astronomy* 天) an object in space similar to a star, that produces no light or very little light 不发光天体（太空中类似星体但不发光的物体）

dar·ling /ˈdɑːlɪŋ; *NAmE* ˈdɑːrlɪŋ/ *noun, adj.*

■ ***noun*** **1** (*informal*) a way of addressing sb that you love 亲爱的；宝贝：*What's the matter, darling?* 怎么啦，亲爱的？ **2** a person who is very friendly and kind 亲切友好的人：*You are a darling, Hugo.* 雨果，你真好。 **3 the ~ of sb/sth** a person who is especially liked and very popular 备受宠爱的人；宠儿：*She is the darling of the newspapers and can do no wrong.* 她是新闻界的大红人，不可能做错事的。

■ ***adj.*** [only before noun] (*informal*) much loved; very attractive, special, etc. 备受喜爱的；可爱的；迷人的：*My darling daughter.* 我的宝贝女儿。◇ *'Darling Henry,' the letter began.* "亲爱的亨利"，信的开头这样写道。

darm·stadt·ium /ˈdɑːmʃtætiəm; *NAmE* ˈdɑːrm-/ *noun* [U] (*symb.* **Ds**) a chemical element. Darmstadtium is a RADIOACTIVE element that is produced artificially. 鐽（人造放射性化学元素）

darn /dɑːn; *NAmE* dɑːrn/ *verb, noun, adj., adv.*

■ ***verb*** [T, I] **~ (sth)** to repair a hole in a piece of clothing by sewing STITCHES across the hole 织补；缝补：*to darn socks* 补袜子

IDM **ˈdarn it!** (*informal, especially NAmE*) used as a mild swear word to show that you are angry or annoyed about sth, to avoid saying 'damn' 见鬼，真气人，真糟糕（婉辞，与 damn 同义）：*Darn it! I've lost my keys!* 真见鬼，我的钥匙丢了！ **I'll be ˈdarned!** (*informal, especially NAmE*) used to show that you are surprised about sth（表示吃惊）真没想到，真叫我吃惊

■ ***noun*** a place on a piece of clothing that has been repaired by darning 织补处

■ ***adj.*** (*also* **darned**) (*informal*) used as a mild swear word, to emphasize sth（加强语气）该死的，讨厌的：*Why don't you switch the darn thing off and listen to me!* 把那讨厌的东西关掉，专心听我讲话好不好！

■ ***adv.*** (*also* **darned**) (*informal*) used as a mild swear word, instead of saying DAMN, to mean 'extremely' or 'very' 极其，非常（婉辞，与 damn 同义）：*You had a darn good try.* 你这一试再好不过了。◇ *It's darn cold tonight.* 今天晚上冷得要命。

darned /dɑːnd; *NAmE* dɑːrnd/ *adj., adv.* = DARN：*That's a darned good idea!* 这真是绝妙的好主意！ ▸ **darned·est** *adj.*

dart /dɑːt; *NAmE* dɑːrt/ *noun, verb*

■ ***noun*** **1** [C] a small pointed object, sometimes with feathers to help it fly, that is shot as a weapon or thrown in the game of darts 镖；飞镖：*a poisoned dart* 有毒的飞镖 ➲ VISUAL VOCAB PAGE V44 **2 darts** [U] a game in which darts are thrown at a round board marked with numbers for scoring. Darts is often played in British pubs. 掷镖游戏（常见于英国酒吧里）：*a darts match* 掷镖赛 ➲ VISUAL VOCAB PAGE V44 **3** [sing.] a sudden quick movement 猛冲；突进；飞奔 SYN **dash**：*She* ***made a dart for*** *the door.* 她朝门口冲去。 **4** [sing.] (*literary*) a sudden feeling of a strong emotion 突发的强烈情感：*Nina felt a sudden dart of panic.* 尼娜突然感到一阵恐慌。 **5** [C] a pointed fold that is sewn in a piece of clothing to make it fit better 省缝，缝褶（为使衣服更合身而在衣料上缝进去的部分）

■ ***verb*** **1** [I] **+ adv./prep.** to move suddenly and quickly in a particular direction 猛冲；突进；飞奔：*A dog darted across the road in front of me.* 一条狗突然在我面前窜过马路。◇ *Her eyes darted around the room, looking for Greg.* 她迅速环视了一下房间，寻找格雷格。 **2** [T] to look at sb suddenly and quickly（朝某人猛然）看，瞥：**~ a glance/look (at sb)** *He darted an impatient look at Vicky.* 他不耐烦地朝维基瞥了一眼。◇ **~ sb a glance/look** *He darted Vicky an impatient look.* 他不耐烦地瞥了维基一眼。

dart·board /ˈdɑːtbɔːd; *NAmE* ˈdɑːrtbɔːrd/ *noun* a round board used in the game of darts（掷镖游戏的）镖靶 ➲ VISUAL VOCAB PAGE V44

Dar·win·ism /ˈdɑːwɪnɪzəm; *NAmE* ˈdɑːr-/ *noun* [U] (*biology* 生) the theory that living things EVOLVE by NATURAL SELECTION, developed by Charles Darwin in the 19th century 达尔文主义，达尔文学说（查尔斯·达尔文于 19 世纪创立的学说，认为生物通过自然选择而进化） ▸ **Dar·win·ian** /dɑːˈwɪniən; *NAmE* dɑːr-/ *adj.*：*Darwinian ideas* 达尔文思想

dash /dæʃ/ *noun, verb*

■ ***noun***

• **STH DONE QUICKLY** 匆忙做完的事 **1** [sing.] **a ~ (for sth)** an act of going somewhere suddenly and/or quickly 猛冲；突进；急奔：*When the doors opened, there was a* ***mad dash*** *for seats.* 门一开，人们便疯狂地朝座位奔去。◇ *a 60-mile dash to safety* 急奔 60 英里到达安全的地方 ◇ *He jumped off the bus and* ***made a dash for*** *the nearest bar.*

他跳下公共汽车，直奔近处的酒吧。◇ *We waited for the police to leave then* ***made a dash for it*** (= left quickly in order to escape). 我们等警察离开后便迅速逃走。 **2** [sing.] an act of doing sth quickly because you do not have enough time 匆忙；匆促；仓促： *a last-minute dash to buy presents* 利用最后一点时间匆忙买礼物

• **SMALL AMOUNT** 少量 **3** [C, usually sing.] ~ **(of sth)** a small amount of sth that is added to sth else 少量，少许（添加物）： *Add a dash of lemon juice.* 加少量柠檬汁。◇ *The rug adds a dash of colour to the room.* 小地毯为房间增添了点色彩。➲ COMPARE SPLASH *n.* (4)

• **SYMBOL** 符号 **4** [C] the mark (—) used to separate parts of a sentence, often instead of a colon or in pairs instead of brackets/parentheses 破折号 ➲ COMPARE HYPHEN

• **RACE** 赛跑 **5** [C, usually sing.] *(especially NAmE)* a race in which the people taking part run very fast over a short distance 短跑 **SYN** **sprint**: *the 100-meter dash* 百米赛跑

• **WAY OF BEHAVING** 行为举止 **6** [U] *(old-fashioned, approving)* a way of behaving that combines style, enthusiasm and confidence 气魄；活力；冲劲；锐气

• **PART OF CAR** 汽车部件 **7** [C] *(informal)* = DASHBOARD (1) ➲ SEE ALSO PEBBLE-DASH

IDM **cut a 'dash** *(BrE)* to look attractive in a particular set of clothes, especially in a way that makes other people notice you （穿上某套衣服后）风度翩翩，引人注目： *He cut quite a dash in his uniform.* 他穿着这身制服显得特帅。

■ ***verb***

• **GO QUICKLY** 急冲 **1** [I] to go somewhere very quickly 急奔；急驰；猛冲 **SYN** **rush**: *I must dash* (= leave quickly), *I'm late.* 我得赶紧走，来不及了。 ◇ **+ adv./prep.** *She dashed off to keep an appointment.* 她急匆匆地赶去赴约。 ◇ *He dashed along the platform and jumped on the train.* 他沿站台猛跑，纵身跳上火车。

• **THROW/BEAT** 投掷；击打 **2** [T, I] to throw sth or make sth fall violently onto a hard surface; to beat against a surface 猛掷；猛击；猛撞： **~ sth + adv./prep.** *The boat was dashed repeatedly against the rocks.* 小船一次又一次撞在岩石上。 ◇ **+ adv./prep.** *The waves were dashing against the harbour wall.* 海浪撞击着港湾的坝堤。

IDM **dash sb's 'hopes** to destroy sb's hopes by making what they were hoping for impossible 使某人的希望化为泡影（或破灭） **dash (it)! | dash it all!** *(old-fashioned, BrE)* used to show that you are annoyed about sth （表示厌烦）真见鬼，真糟糕，真混账

PHRV **,dash sth↔'off** to write or draw sth very quickly 仓促写出；草草画成： *I dashed off a note to my brother.* 我急急忙忙给我弟弟写了个字条。

dash·board /'dæʃbɔːd; *NAmE* -bɔːrd/ *noun* **1** *(also* **fa·scia***)* *(also informal* **dash** *especially in NAmE)* the part of a car in front of the driver that has instruments and controls in it （汽车上的）仪表板 ➲ VISUAL VOCAB PAGE V56 **2** a diagram that shows important information, typically one that gives an outline of a business（主要业务数据的）动态监控面板： *an executive dashboard showing key performance indicators* 显示关键运营指标的监控管理面板 **3** a page on a website where you can access information about its various functions（网站的）主控面板（从中可以了解网站的不同功能）

dash·ed /dæʃt/ *adj.* [only before noun] *(BrE, old-fashioned, informal)* used as a mild swear word by some people to emphasize sth or to show they are annoyed （表示强调或不耐烦）该死的，讨厌的

dash·iki /'dɑːʃɪki/ *noun* a loose shirt or longer piece of clothing worn by men in W Africa, often made from cloth with brightly coloured patterns 达西基（西非男子穿的花哨而宽松的衬衫或套衫）

dash·ing /'dæʃɪŋ/ *adj.* *(old-fashioned)* **1** (usually of a man 通常指男人) attractive, confident and elegant 风度翩翩的；自信的；潇洒的： *a dashing young officer* 风度翩翩的年轻军官 ◇ *his dashing good looks* 他英俊潇洒的容貌 **2** (of a thing 物品) attractive and fashionable 时髦的；流行的： *his dashing red waistcoat* 他时髦的红背心

das·tard·ly /'dæstədli; *NAmE* -tərd-/ *adj.* *(old-fashioned)* evil and cruel 邪恶残忍的： *My first part was Captain O'Hagarty, a dastardly villain in a children's play.* 我演的第一个角色是奥哈格蒂船长，一部儿童剧中的恶棍。

data 🔑 **AW** /'deɪtə; *BrE also* 'dɑːtə; *NAmE also* 'dætə/ *noun* (used as a plural noun in technical English, when the singular is *datum* 在科技英语中用作复数名词，其单数形式是 datum) **1** 🔑 [U, pl.] facts or information, especially when examined and used to find out things or to make decisions 数据；资料；材料： *This data was collected from 69 countries.* 这资料是从 69 个国家收集来的。◇ *the analysis/interpretation of the data* 数据分析 / 解读 ◇ *raw data* (= that has not been analysed) 原始资料 ◇ *demographical/historical/personal data* 人口统计资料；史料；个人资料 ◇ *(specialist) These data show that most cancers are detected as a result of clinical follow-up.* 这些数据表明多数癌症是由临床随访查出的。➲ COLLOCATIONS AT SCIENTIFIC **2** 🔑 [U] information that is stored by a computer （存储在计算机中的）数据资料： *data retrieval* (= ways of storing or finding information on a computer) 数据检索 ➲ WORDFINDER NOTE AT FILE, PROGRAM ➲ MORE LIKE THIS 30, page R28

data·bank /'deɪtəbæŋk; *NAmE also* 'dætə-/ *noun* a large amount of data on a particular subject that is stored in a computer （存储在计算机中某一题材的）数据库

data·base /'deɪtəbeɪs; *NAmE also* 'dætə-/ *noun* an organized set of data that is stored in a computer and can be looked at and used in various ways （存储在计算机中的）数据库

,database 'management system *noun* *(abbr.* **DBMS***)* *(computing* 计*)* a system for organizing and managing a large amount of data 数据库管理系统

dat·able /'deɪtəbl/ *adj.* that can be dated to a particular time 可测定日期的；可确定年代的： *pottery that is datable to the second century* 可确定产于二世纪的陶器

'data capture *noun* [U] the action or process of collecting data, especially using computers 数据采集（尤指利用计算机）

'data mining *noun* [U] *(computing* 计*)* looking at large amounts of information that has been collected on a computer and using it to provide new information 数据挖掘

,data 'processing *noun* [U] *(computing* 计*)* a series of actions that a computer performs on data to produce an output 数据处理

'data projector *(also* **projector***)* *noun* a piece of equipment that takes data and images from a computer and shows them on a wall or large screen 数码放映机；数码投影仪 ➲ COMPARE OVERHEAD PROJECTOR, PROJECTOR, SLIDE PROJECTOR ➲ VISUAL VOCAB PAGE V71

,data pro'tection *noun* [U] legal restrictions that keep information stored on computers private and that control who can read it or use it 数据保护

'data set *noun* *(computing* 计*)* a collection of data which is treated as a single unit by a computer 数据集

'data warehouse *noun* a large amount of data which comes from different parts of a business and which is stored together 数据仓库（汇集企业各部门信息的大量数据）

date 🔑 /deɪt/ *noun, verb*

■ ***noun***

• **PARTICULAR DAY** 日期 **1** 🔑 [C] a particular day of the month, sometimes in a particular year, given in numbers and words 日期；日子： *'What's the date today?' 'The 10th.'* "今天几号？" "10 号。"◇ *Write* ***today's date*** *at the top of the page.* 在页面顶端写上今天的日期。◇ *We need to* ***fix a date*** *for the next meeting.* 我们得为下次会议定个日期。◇ *They haven't* ***set a date*** *for the wedding yet.* 他们尚未确定举行婚礼的日期。◇ *I can't come on that date.* 那个日子我来不了。◇ *Please give your name, address and* ***date of birth***. 请报姓名、地址和出生日期。 ◇ *(especially NAmE) name, address and* ***birth date*** 姓名、地址和出生日期 ◇ *There's no date on this letter.* 这封信未注明日期。➲ SEE

ALSO BEST-BEFORE DATE, CLOSING DATE, SELL-BY DATE
• PAST TIME/FUTURE 过去；将来 **2** [sing., U] a time in the past or future that is not a particular day 年代；时期；时候：*The details can be added* **at a later date.** 细节可过些时候再补充进去。◇ *The work will be carried out* **at a future date.** 这项工作将来再做。◇ *a building of late Roman date* 罗马时代后期的建筑
• ARRANGEMENT TO MEET 约见 **3** [C] an arrangement to meet sb at a particular time 会晤时间；约见时间：*Call me next week and we'll try and* **make a date.** 下周打电话给我，我们争取定个见面时间。◇ *Next Friday? Fine—it's a date!* 下星期五？好，就约在那天吧！
• ROMANTIC MEETING 异性约会 **4** [C] a meeting that you have arranged with a boyfriend or girlfriend or with sb who might become a boyfriend or girlfriend 约会；幽会：*I've got a date with Lucy tomorrow night.* 明天晚上我与露西有个约会。◇ *Paul's not coming. He's got a* **hot date** (= an exciting one). 保罗不来了。他有一个朝思夜盼的幽会。 ➲COLLOCATIONS AT MARRIAGE ➲SEE ALSO BLIND DATE, DOUBLE DATE **5** [C] (*especially NAmE*) a boyfriend or girlfriend with whom you have arranged a date 约会对象：*My date is meeting me at seven.* 我的对象七点钟与我见面。 ➲WORDFINDER NOTE AT LOVE
• FRUIT 果实 **6** [C] a sweet sticky brown fruit that grows on a tree called a **date palm**, common in N Africa and W Asia （北非和西亚常见的海枣树的）海枣，椰枣
IDM **to 'date** until now 迄今为止；到目前为止；直到现在：*To date, we have received over 200 replies.* 到目前为止，我们已收到 200 多封回信。◇ *The exhibition contains some of his best work to date.* 这个展览有他迄今为止一些最好的作品。 ➲SEE ALSO OUT OF DATE, UP TO DATE
■*verb*
• WRITE DATE 写日期 **1** [T] **~ sth** to write or print the date on sth 注明日期；写上日期：*Thank you for your letter dated 24th March.* 你 3 月 24 日来函收悉，谢谢。
• FIND AGE 确定年代 **2** [T] **~ sth (at/to sth)** to say when sth old existed or was made 确定年代：*The skeleton has been dated at about 2000 BC.* 这骨架的年代为公元前 2000 年左右。
• OF CLOTHES/WORDS 衣服；词语 **3** [I] to become old-fashioned 过时；不流行：*She designs classic clothes which do not date.* 她设计的服装式样古朴，不会过时。
• PERSON 人 **4** [T] **~ sb** if sth **dates** you, it shows that you are fairly old or older than the people you are with 使显老；使显得年龄大：*I was at the Woodstock festival—that dates me, doesn't it?* 我参加了伍德斯托克摇滚音乐节，那说明我老了，是不是？
• HAVE RELATIONSHIP 有恋爱关系 **5** [T, I] **~ (sb)** (*especially NAmE*) to have a romantic relationship with sb 与（某人）谈恋爱：*She's been dating Ron for several months.* 她与罗恩谈恋爱已有数月。
PHR V **,date 'back (to...)** | **'date from...** to have existed since a particular time in the past or for the length of time mentioned 追溯到；始于；自…至今：*The college dates back to medieval times.* 这所学院创办于中世纪。◇ *The custom dates back hundreds of years.* 这一习俗可以追溯到几百年前。◇ *a law dating from the 17th century* 自 17 世纪起沿用至今的一条法律

date·book /'deɪtbʊk/ (*NAmE*) (*BrE* **diary**) *noun* a book with spaces for each day of the year in which you can write down things you have to do in the future （工作日程）记事簿

dated /'deɪtɪd/ *adj.* old-fashioned; belonging to a time in the past 过时的；陈旧的：*These ideas seem a bit dated now.* 这些想法现在似乎有些过时了。 ➲COMPARE UNDATED

'Date Line *noun* = INTERNATIONAL DATE LINE

'date rape *noun* [U] the crime of RAPING sb, committed by a person he or she has gone out with on a DATE (4) 约会强奸（罪）

'dat·ing agency (*also* **'dat·ing service**) *noun* a business or an organization that arranges meetings between single people who want to begin a romantic relationship 婚姻介绍所：*He met his wife through a* **computer dating agency.** 他是通过电脑红娘认识他妻子的。

dat·ive /'deɪtɪv/ *noun* (*grammar* 语法) (in some languages 用于某些语言) the form of a noun, a pronoun or an adjective when it is the INDIRECT OBJECT of a verb or is connected with the INDIRECT OBJECT 与格（名词、代词或形容词用作间接宾语或与间接宾语相关时的一种形式）：*In the sentence, 'I sent her a postcard', the word 'her' is* **in the dative.** 在 I sent her a postcard 一句中，her 一词处于与格。 ➲COMPARE ABLATIVE, ACCUSATIVE, GENITIVE, LOCATIVE, NOMINATIVE, VOCATIVE ▶ **dat·ive** *adj.*: *the dative case* 与格

datum /'deɪtəm/ *noun* (*pl.* **data**) (*specialist*) a fact or piece of information 数据；资料 ➲SEE ALSO DATA ➲MORE LIKE THIS 30, page R28

daub /dɔːb/ *verb, noun*
■*verb* **~ A on, etc. B | ~ B with A | ~ sth + adv./prep.** to spread a substance such as paint, mud, etc. thickly and/or carelessly onto sth （用颜料、油漆、灰泥等）涂抹，乱涂，乱画：*The walls of the building were daubed with red paint.* 这栋建筑的墙上随意涂了一层红色涂料。
■*noun* **1** [U] a mixture of CLAY, etc. that was used in the past for making walls （旧时抹墙用的）粗灰泥：*walls made of* **wattle and daub** 用枝条和灰泥做成的墙 **2** [C] a small amount of a substance such as paint that has been spread carelessly （乱涂乱画的）少量颜料，涂料：*a daub of lipstick* 薄薄一层唇膏 **3** [C] a badly painted picture 拙劣的画

daugh·ter /'dɔːtə(r)/ *noun* **1** a person's female child 女儿：*We have two sons and a daughter.* 我们有两儿一女。◇ *They have three grown-up daughters.* 他们有三个成年的女儿。◇ *She's the daughter of an Oxford professor.* 她是牛津大学一位教授的女儿。 ➲COLLOCATIONS AT CHILD ➲SEE ALSO GOD-DAUGHTER, GRANDDAUGHTER, STEP-DAUGHTER **2** (*literary*) a woman who belongs to a particular place or country, etc. （某地、某国等的）妇女：*one of the town's most famous daughters* 这座城镇最著名的女性之一

'daughter-in-law *noun* (*pl.* **daughters-in-law**) the wife of your son 儿媳妇 ➲COMPARE SON-IN-LAW

daunt /dɔːnt/ *verb* [usually passive] **~ sb** to make sb feel nervous and less confident about doing sth 使胆怯；使气馁；使失去信心 SYN **intimidate**: *She was a brave woman but she felt daunted by the task ahead.* 她是一个勇敢的女人，但对面前的任务却感到信心不足。 ▶ **daunt·ing** *adj.* SYN **intimidating**: *She has the* **daunting** *task of cooking for 20 people every day.* 她每天得做 20 个人的饭，这是一项可怕的任务。◇ *Starting a new job can be a* **daunting prospect.** 开始一项新工作有时会让人望而却步。 **daunt·ing·ly** *adv.*
IDM **nothing 'daunted** (*BrE, formal*) confident about sth difficult you have to do 无所畏惧；毫不气馁：*Nothing daunted, the people set about rebuilding their homes.* 人们毫不气馁，又开始重建家园。

daunt·less /'dɔːntləs/ *adj.* (*literary*) not easily frightened or stopped from doing sth difficult 无所畏惧的；吓不倒的；勇敢的 SYN **resolute**

dau·phin /'dəʊfæ̃; -fæn; *NAmE* 'doʊ-/ *noun* (*old use*) the oldest son of the king of France （法国）王长子

David and Goliath /ˌdeɪvɪd ənd ɡə'laɪəθ/ *adj.* used to describe a situation in which a small or weak person or organization tries to defeat another much larger or stronger opponent 强弱悬殊；以弱战强：*The match looks like being a David and Goliath contest.* 比赛看上去像是一场力量悬殊的较量。 ORIGIN From the Bible story in which Goliath, a giant, is killed by the boy David with a stone. 源自《圣经》故事，巨人歌利亚被男孩大卫以石击杀。

daw·dle /'dɔːdl/ *verb* [I] to take a long time to do sth or go somewhere 拖延；磨蹭；游荡：*Stop dawdling! We're going to be late!* 别磨蹭了，咱们快迟到了！◇ **+ adv./prep.** *They dawdled along by the river, laughing and talking.* 他们沿河边闲逛，一路谈笑风生。

dawn /dɔːn/ *noun, verb*

■ ***noun*** **1** [U, C] the time of day when light first appears 黎明；拂晓；破晓 SYN **daybreak, sunrise**: *They start work* ***at dawn***. 天一亮他们就开始干活了。◇ *It's almost dawn.* 天快亮了。◇ *We arrived in Sydney as* ***dawn broke*** (= as the first light could be seen). 黎明时分我们到达了悉尼。◇ *I woke up just before dawn.* 我正好在拂晓前醒来。◇ *summer's early dawns* 夏日早到的黎明 ◇ *He works* ***from dawn till dusk*** (= from morning till night). 他从早到晚地工作。➲ COMPARE DUSK **2** [sing.] **~ (of sth)** the beginning or first signs of sth 开端；曙光；萌芽: *the* ***dawn of civilization/time/history*** 文明/时代/历史的开端 ◇ *Peace marked a new dawn in the country's history.* 和平使这个国家的历史翻开了新的一页。IDM SEE BREAK *n.*, CRACK *n.*

■ ***verb*** **1** [I] (of a day or a period of time 一天或一个时期) to begin 开始: *The following morning dawned bright and warm.* 第二天一大早阳光和煦。◇ *A new technological age had dawned.* 新技术时代已经开始。 **2** [I] to become obvious or easy to understand 变得明朗；开始清楚: *Slowly the awful truth dawned.* 可怕的事实慢慢地清晰起来。IDM SEE LIGHT *n.*

PHR V **'dawn on sb** [no passive] if sth **dawns on you**, you begin to realize it for the first time 使开始明白；使渐渐领悟；使开始理解: **it dawns on sb that…** *Suddenly it dawned on me that they couldn't possibly have met before.* 我突然明白他们以前不可能见过面。

the ˌdawn 'chorus *noun* [sing.] the sound of birds singing very early in the morning 破晓时的鸟鸣声

day /deɪ/ *noun* **1** [C] a period of 24 hours 一天；一日: *I saw Tom three days ago.* 我三天前见过汤姆。◇ *'What day is it today?' 'Monday.'* "今天星期几？" "星期一。" ◇ *We're going away* ***in a few days/in a few days' time***. 我们过几天就要离开了。◇ *They left* ***the day before yesterday*** (= two days ago). 他们前天就走了。◇ *We're meeting* ***the day after tomorrow*** (= in two days). 我们后天要见面。◇ *New Year's Day* 元旦 ◇ *Take the medicine three times* ***a day***. 每日服药三次。◇ *We can't go there today. You can go* ***another day***. 我们今天不能去那儿。你可以改天去。➲ SEE ALSO FIELD DAY, OFF DAY, RED-LETTER DAY, SPORTS DAY **2** [U] the time between when it becomes light in the morning and when it becomes dark in the evening 白昼；白天: *The sun was shining* ***all day***. 白天一直阳光明媚。◇ *I could sit and watch the river* ***all day long***. 我可以整天坐在这里看那条河。◇ *He works at night and sleeps* ***during the day***. 他晚上干活，白天睡觉。◇ *Nocturnal animals sleep* ***by day*** *and hunt by night.* 夜行动物白天睡觉晚上猎食。 **3** [C, usually sing.] the hours of the day when you are awake, working, etc. 工作日；一天的活动时间: *a seven-hour* ***working day*** 七小时工作日 ◇ *It's been* ***a long day*** (= I've been very busy). 忙了一整天了。◇ *Did you have a good day?* 你这一天过得顺利吗？◇ *She didn't do a* ***full day's work***. 她并没干一整天的工作。◇ *I took a half day off yesterday.* 昨天我休假半天。◇ (*NAmE*) *Have a nice day!* 祝你度过愉快的一天！➲ SEE ALSO WORKDAY **4** [C, usually pl.] a particular period of time or history 时期；时代: *in Queen Victoria's day* 在维多利亚女王时代 ◇ *the* ***early days*** *of computers* 计算机早期阶段 ◇ *Most women stayed at home* ***in those days***. 在那个时代大多数妇女都待在家里。◇ (*informal*) *in the* ***old days*** (= in the past) 早先 ➲ SEE ALSO GLORY DAYS, HEYDAY, NOWADAYS, PRESENT DAY HELP There are many other compounds ending in **day**. You will find them at their place in the alphabet. 以 day 结尾的复合词还有很多，可在各字母中的适当位置查到。

IDM **all in a day's 'work** part of your normal working life and not unusual 日常工作的一部分；习以为常；不足为奇 **any day (now)** (*informal*) very soon 很快: *The letter should arrive any day now.* 信该很快就到了。 **carry/win the 'day** (*formal*) to be successful against sb/sth 得胜；占上风；取得成功: *Despite strong opposition, the ruling party carried the day.* 尽管遭到强烈反对，执政党还是获胜了。 **day after 'day** each day repeatedly (used especially when sth is boring or annoying) 日复一日，一天又一天（尤指枯燥无味、令人厌烦）: *She hates doing the same work day after day.* 她讨厌日复一日做同样的工作。 **day by 'day** all the time; a little at a time and gradually 一天天；逐日: *Day by day his condition improved.* 他的健康状况一天天好转。 **day 'in, day 'out** every day for a long period of time 日复一日，天天（指不间断） **a day of 'reckoning** the time when sb will have to deal with the result of sth that they have done wrong, or be punished for sth bad that they have done 遭报应的日子；受到惩罚的日子 **sb's/sth's days are 'numbered** a person or thing will not continue to live, exist or be successful for much longer （指人）死期不远了，得意的日子屈指可数了；（指物）用不了多久了，寿命不长了: *His days as leader of the party are numbered.* 他作为党的领袖的日子已屈指可数了。 **from day 'one** (*informal*) from the beginning 从一开始；从第一天: *It's never worked from day one.* 这从一开始就行不通。 **from day to 'day 1** with no thoughts or plans for the future 过一天算一天: *They live from day to day, looking after their sick daughter.* 他们过一天算一天，日复一日地照顾着生病的女儿。 **2** if a situation changes **from day to day**, it changes often 天天，一天又一天（指经常变化）: *A baby's need for food can vary from day to day.* 婴儿对食物的需要天天都在变化。 **from ˌone day to the 'next** if a situation changes **from one day to the next**, it is uncertain and not likely to stay the same each day 一天又一天（表示不知未来如何）: *I never know what to expect from one day to the next.* 一天又一天我从不知道会发生什么。 **have had your 'day** to no longer be successful, powerful, etc. 得意之时已过；风光不再；日渐衰败: *She's had her day as a supermodel.* 她作为超级模特儿的辉煌日子已一去不复返。 **have seen/known better 'days** (*humorous*) to be in poor condition 穷困潦倒；昔盛今衰；曾辉煌过: *Our car has seen better days!* 我们的汽车曾辉煌一时！ **if he's, she's, etc. a 'day** (*informal*) (used when talking about sb's age) at least （谈论某人年龄）至少: *He must be 70 if he's a day!* 他至少 70 岁了！ **in sb's 'day 1** during the part of sb's life when they were most successful, famous, etc. （某人的）昔日盛时，鼎盛时期: *She was a great dancer in her day.* 她曾是红极一时的舞蹈家。 **2** when sb was young 年轻时；当年: *In my day, there were plenty of jobs when you left school.* 我年轻时，毕业后就业机会很多。 **in 'this day and age** now, in the modern world 当代；当今；在今天这个时代 **it's not sb's 'day** (*informal*) used when several unfortunate or unpleasant things happen on the same day 祸不单行；特别倒霉的一天: *My car broke down and then I locked myself out—it's just not my day!* 我的汽车抛锚了，我又把钥匙锁到车里，真是祸不单行！ **make sb's 'day** to make sb feel very happy on a particular day 使某人一天非常快活: *The phone call from Mike really made my day.* 迈克打来电话，真让我高兴了一整天。 **make a day of it** (*informal*) to make a particular enjoyable activity last for a whole day instead of only part of it 痛痛快快玩一整天 **not have all 'day** to not have much time 时间不多了: *Come on! We don't have all day!* 快一点！我们的时间不多了！ **of sb's 'day** during a particular period of time when sb lived 某人生活的时代: *the best player of his day* 他那个时代最优秀的运动员 ◇ *Bessie Smith was the Madonna of her day.* 贝西•史密斯是她那个时代的麦当娜。 **of the 'day** that is served on a particular day in a restaurant（餐馆）当日特别供应: *soup of the day* 当日供应的汤 **oh my 'days** used to emphasize what you are saying when you are surprised, shocked or annoyed （吃惊或恼火时加强语气）我的天啊: *Oh my days! Is that true?* 我的天啊！那是真的吗？ **'one day** at some time in the future, or on a particular day in the past 有朝一日；（过去）某一天: *One day, I want to leave the city and move to the country.* 有朝一日，我要离开城市搬到乡下去。◇ *One day, he walked out of the house with a small bag and never came back.* 一天，他带了个小提包走出家门，再也没有回来。 **'one of these days** before a long time has passed 不久；日内: *One of these days you'll come back and ask me to forgive you.* 你很快就会回来请求我原谅的。 **one of those 'days** (*informal*) a day when there are a lot of mistakes and a lot of things go wrong 诸事不顺的日子；倒霉的日子: *It's been one of those days!* 这一天真倒霉！ **'some day** at an unknown time in the future 将来有一天；总有一天: *Some day I'll be famous.* 总有一天我会成名的。 **take it/things one ˌday at a 'time** (*informal*) to not think about what will happen in the future 得过

且过；做一天和尚撞一天钟；过一天算一天：*I don't know if he'll get better. We're just taking it one day at a time.* 我不知道他还能不能好转，我们只有过一天算一天。 **'that'll be the day** (*informal, ironic*) used when you are saying that sth is very unlikely to happen 那样的事永远不可能；哪有那样的事：*Paul? Apologize? That'll be the day!* 保罗？道歉？那真是太阳从西边出来了！ **'these days** (*informal*) used to talk about the present, especially when you are comparing it with the past（尤用于拿现在和过去比较）如今，而今：*These days kids grow up so quickly.* 如今孩子们成长得真快。 **'those were the days** (*informal*) used to suggest that a time in the past was happier or better than now（指过去）那才是好时光，那才是好年头 **to the 'day** exactly 恰好；刚好；一天不差：*It's been three years to the day since we met.* 我们整整三年没见面了。 **to this 'day** even now, when a lot of time has passed 直到如今；甚至现在：*To this day, I still don't understand why he did it.* 我直到今天仍然不明白他当时为什么那样做。 ➲ MORE AT BACK *adv.*, BORN *v.*, BREAK *n.*, CALL *v.*, CLEAR *adj.*, COLD *adj.*, DEED, DOG *n.*, EARLY *adj.*, END *n.*, END *v.*, EVIL *adj.*, FORTH, GIVE *v.*, LATE *adv.*, LIVE[1], LIVELONG, NICE, NIGHT, NINE, OLD, ORDER *n.*, OTHER, PASS *v.*, PLAIN *adj.*, RAINY, ROME, SALAD, SAVE *v.*, TIME *n.*

'day boy *noun* (*BrE*) a boy DAY PUPIL （寄宿学校的）走读男生

day·break /ˈdeɪbreɪk/ *noun* [U] the time of day when light first appears 黎明；拂晓；破晓；天亮 **SYN** **dawn**：*We left before daybreak.* 我们是在黎明前离开的。

'day care *noun* [U] care for small children, or for old or sick people, away from home, during the day 日托；日间护理：*Day care is provided by the company she works for.* 她工作的那家公司有日托。

'day care center (*NAmE*) (*BrE* **'day nursery, nursery**) *noun* a place where small children are cared for while their parents are at work 日间托儿所 ➲ COMPARE NURSERY SCHOOL

'day centre (*BrE*) (*especially US* **'day center**) *noun* a place that provides care for old or sick people during the day （老人或病人）日间护理站，日间照顾中心

day·dream /ˈdeɪdriːm/ *noun* pleasant thoughts that make you forget about the present 白日梦；幻想；空想：*She stared out of the window, lost in a daydream.* 她凝视窗外，沉浸在幻想之中。 ▶ **day·dream** *verb* [I]: ~ (**about sb/sth**) *I would spend hours daydreaming about a house of my own.* 我常常一连几个小时幻想有一所自己的房子。

'day girl *noun* (*BrE*) a girl DAY PUPIL （寄宿学校的）走读女生

Day-Glo™ /ˈdeɪ gləʊ; *NAmE* gloʊ/ *adj.* having a very bright orange, yellow, green or pink colour 日辉牌荧光色的：*Day-Glo cycling shorts* 荧光色骑行短裤

'day job *noun* [sing.] the paid work that sb normally does 日常的有薪工作；（白天的）正职

IDM **don't give up the 'day job** (*informal, humorous*) used to tell sb that they should continue doing what they are used to, rather than trying sth new which they are likely to fail at 别放弃白天的正职（别放弃老本行去尝试没有把握的新事物）：*So you want to be a writer? Well my advice is, don't give up the day job.* 这么说你想成为一个作家了？得了，我劝你不要放弃老本行。

day·light /ˈdeɪlaɪt/ *noun* [U] the light that comes from the sun during the day 日光：*They emerged from the church into the bright daylight.* 他们走出教堂来到明亮的日光下。◇ *The street looks very different* **in daylight**. 大街在白天看来大不一样。◇ *They left* **before daylight** (= before the sun had risen). 他们天亮前就走了。➲ WORDFINDER NOTE AT SUN

IDM **,daylight 'robbery** (*informal*) the fact of sb charging too much money for sth 漫天要价；敲竹杠：*You wouldn't believe some of the prices they charge; it's daylight robbery.* 他们的要价有一些你都不会相信，简直就是在光天化日之下抢劫呀！➲ MORE AT BROAD *adj.*

day·lights /ˈdeɪlaɪts/ *noun* [pl.]

IDM **beat/knock the (living) 'daylights out of sb** (*informal*) to hit sb very hard several times and hurt them very much 狠揍某人 **frighten/scare the (living) 'daylights out of sb** (*informal*) to frighten sb very much 吓得某人六神无主（或魂飞魄散）

,daylight 'saving time (*abbr.* **DST**) (*also* **'daylight time**) (*both NAmE*) (*BrE* **'summer time**) *noun* [U] the period during which in some countries the clocks are put forward one hour, so that it is light for an extra hour in the evening 夏令时（有些国家实行夏时制，将时钟拨快一小时，以节约照明能源）

day·long /ˈdeɪlɒŋ; *NAmE* -lɔːŋ/ *adj.* [only before noun] (*especially NAmE*) lasting for a whole day 全天的；整天的；终日的：*a daylong meeting* 一整天的会议

'day nursery (*also* **nursery**) (*both BrE*) (*NAmE* **'day care center**) *noun* a place where small children are cared for while their parents are at work 日间托儿所 ➲ COMPARE CRÈCHE (1), NURSERY SCHOOL

,day 'off *noun* (*pl.* **days off**) a day on which you do not have to work 休假日；休息日：*Most weeks, Sunday is my only day off.* 我多半只有星期天才休息。◇ *Why not take a few days off?* 为什么不休息几天呢？

the ,Day of 'Judgement *noun* [sing.] = JUDGEMENT DAY

,day 'out *noun* (*pl.* **days out**) a trip or visit somewhere for a day 一日游：*We had a day out in the country.* 我们在乡下玩了一天。➲ SYNONYMS AT TRIP

'day pupil (*BrE*) (*also* **'day student** *NAmE, BrE*) *noun* a school student who goes to a BOARDING SCHOOL but lives at home （寄宿学校的）走读生

,day re'lease *noun* (*BrE*) [U] a system of allowing employees days off work for education （职工）脱产学习，脱产进修制度，进修休假制度：*time off for study on day release* 请假脱产学习的时间 ◇ *a day release course* 脱产进修课程

,day re'turn *noun* (*BrE*) a ticket at a reduced price for a journey to a place and back again on the same day （打了折的）当日往返车票

'day room *noun* a room in a hospital or other institution where people can sit, relax, watch television, etc. during the day （医院或其他机构的）日间娱乐室，日间休息室

'day school *noun* **1** (*old-fashioned*) a private school with students who live at home and only go to school during the day 私立走读学校；私立日校 ➲ COMPARE BOARDING SCHOOL **2** (*BrE*) a course of education lasting one day, at which a particular topic is discussed 为期一天的专题讲座：*a day school at Leeds University on women in Victorian times* 利兹大学为期一天的关于维多利亚时代妇女的专题讲座

'day student (*especially NAmE*) (*BrE also* **'day pupil**) *noun* a school student who goes to a BOARDING SCHOOL but lives at home （寄宿学校的）走读生

day·time /ˈdeɪtaɪm/ *noun* [U] the period during the day between the time when it gets light and the time when it gets dark 白天；白昼；日间：*You don't often see this bird* **in (the) daytime**. 这种鸟白天不常见。◇ *The park is open* **during (the) daytime**. 这个公园日间开放。◇ *Daytime temperatures never fell below 30°C.* 日间温度从未低于 30 摄氏度。◇ *Please give your name and daytime phone number.* 请提供姓名和日间联络电话。

,day-to-'day *adj.* [only before noun] **1** planning for only one day at a time 按日计划的；逐日的；每天的：*I have organized the cleaning* **on a day-to-day basis**, *until our usual cleaner returns.* 我已逐日安排好清洁工作，直到我们的清洁工回来为止。 **2** involving the usual events or tasks of each day 日常工作的；例行的：*She has been looking after the* **day-to-day running** *of the school.* 她一直在负责学校的日常管理工作。

'day trading *noun* [U] (*finance* 财) buying and selling shares very quickly on the same day using the Internet in order to make a profit from small price changes 当日交易（用互联网即日频繁买卖股票，从微小差价中获利） ▶ **'day trader** *noun*

'day trip *noun* a trip or visit completed in one day 一日游： *a day trip to France* 法国一日游 ▶ **'day tripper** *noun* (*BrE*)

day·wear /'deɪweə(r); *NAmE* -wer/ *noun* [U] clothes for wearing every day, for example for working or shopping, not for special occasions 便服；日常衣服

daze /deɪz/ *noun*

IDM **in a daze** in a confused state 迷茫；茫然；恍惚： *I've been in a complete daze since hearing the news.* 自从听到那消息，我一直茫然不知所措。

dazed /deɪzd/ *adj.* unable to think clearly, especially because of a shock or because you have been hit on the head （由于震惊或头部受到撞击）神志不清的，茫然的： *Survivors waited for the rescue boats, dazed and frightened.* 生还者不知所措，心有余悸，等待着救援船只。◇ *Jimmy was still dazed by the blow to his head.* 吉米由于头部被击，仍然神志不清。

daz·zle /'dæzl/ *verb, noun*

■ *verb* [often passive] **1** [T, I] ~ (**sb**) if a strong light **dazzles** you, it is so bright that you cannot see for a short time （强光等）使目眩，使眼花 SYN **blind**: *He was momentarily dazzled by the strong sunlight.* 强烈的阳光使他一时睁不开眼。 **2** [T] ~ **sb** to impress sb a lot with your beauty, skill, etc.（美貌、技能等）使倾倒，使赞叹不已，使眼花缭乱： *He was dazzled by the warmth of her smile.* 她那温柔的微笑使他神魂颠倒。 ▶ **daz·zling** *adj.* SYN **brilliant**: *a dazzling display of oriental dance* 令人陶醉的东方舞蹈表演 **daz·zlingly** *adv.*： *She was dazzlingly beautiful.* 她美得让人倾倒。

■ *noun* [U, sing.] **1** the quality that bright light has that stops you from seeing clearly 耀眼眩目；令人眼花缭乱 **2** a thing or quality that impresses you but may prevent you from understanding or thinking clearly 令人眼花缭乱的东西（或特性）

d.b.a. /ˌdiː biː 'eɪ/ *abbr.* (*US*) doing business as 以…公司名义营业： *Philip Smith, d.b.a. Phil's Signs* 用菲尔标志公司名义经营的菲利普•史密斯

DBIS /ˌdiː biː aɪ 'es/ *abbr.* (in Britain) Department for Business, Innovation and Skills （英国）商业、创新与技能部

DBMS /ˌdiː biː em 'es/ *abbr.* DATABASE MANAGEMENT SYSTEM 数据库管理系统

DBS /ˌdiː biː 'es/ *abbr.* (in the UK) Disclosure and Barring Service (formerly called the Criminal Records Bureau), a government body that checks to see whether people have committed crimes which make them unsuitable for certain jobs, e.g. working with children, or to adopt children （英国）犯罪记录披露与禁止从业局（全写为 Disclosure and Barring Service，旧称 the Criminal Records Bureau，核查某人有无犯罪记录，从而判断其是否适合做与儿童接触的工作或收养孩子等）： *a DBS check* 犯罪记录核查

DC /ˌdiː 'siː/ *abbr.* **1** DIRECT CURRENT 直流；直流电流 ➲ COMPARE ALTERNATING CURRENT **2** District of Columbia in the US 美国哥伦比亚特区： *Washington, DC* 华盛顿（哥伦比亚特区）

DCMS /ˌdiː siː em 'es/ *abbr.* (in Britain) Department for Culture, Media and Sport （英国）文化、媒体和体育部

DD /ˌdiː 'diː/ *abbr.* (*informal*) (especially in TEXT MESSAGES, emails, etc.) darling daughter 宝贝女儿（全写为 darling daughter，尤用于短信、电邮等）： *My DD is nearly a year old now.* 我的宝贝女儿快一岁了。

'D-Day *noun* [U] a date on which sth important is expected to happen 重大事情预定发生日；计划行动开始日 ORIGIN From the name given to 6 June 1944, the day on which the British, US and other armies landed on the beaches of northern France in the Second World War. 源自 1944 年 6 月 6 日第二次世界大战时，英美及其他国家的军队这天在法国北部海滩登陆的行动。

DDT /ˌdiː diː 'tiː/ *noun* [U] a chemical used, especially in the past, for killing insects that harm crops 滴滴涕（旧时尤用作农业杀虫剂）

de- /diː/ *prefix* (in verbs and related nouns, adjectives and adverbs 构成动词及相关的名词、形容词和副词) **1** the opposite of …的反义： *decentralization* 权力分散 **2** removing sth 除掉；去掉；取消： *to defrost the refrigerator* (= remove layers of ice from it) 给冰箱除霜 ➲ MORE LIKE THIS 6, page R25

dea·con /'diːkən/ *noun* **1** (in the Roman Catholic, Anglican and Orthodox Churches) a religious leader just below the rank of a priest （天主教、圣公会和东正教会的）执事，会吏 **2** (in some Nonconformist Churches) a person who is not a member of the CLERGY, but who helps a minister with church business affairs （某些不信奉英国国教的教会中协助管理教会事务的）助祭

dea·con·ess /ˌdiːkə'nes; *NAmE* 'diːkənəs/ *noun* (in some Christian Churches) a woman who has duties that are similar to those of a deacon （某些基督教会中的）女执事，女会吏，女助祭

de·activ·ate /ˌdiː'æktɪveɪt/ *verb* ~ **sth** to make sth such as a device or chemical process stop working 使（仪器等）停止工作；使失活；使（化学过程）灭活化（或减活化、钝化）： *Do you know how to deactivate the alarm?* 你知道如何让闹钟不响吗？

dead 🔑 /ded/ *adj., noun, adv.*

■ *adj.*

• **NOT ALIVE** 不活 **1** 🔑 no longer alive 死的；失去生命的；枯萎的： *My mother's dead; she died in 1987.* 我母亲不在了，她是 1987 年去世的。◇ *a dead person/animal* 死人；死去的动物 ◇ *dead leaves/wood/skin* 枯叶；枯木；死皮 ◇ *He was shot dead by a gunman outside his home.* 他在家门外被持枪歹徒开枪打死。◇ *Catherine's* ***dead body*** *lay peacefully on the bed.* 凯瑟琳的尸体安详地躺在床上。◇ *He* ***dropped dead*** (= died suddenly) *last week.* 他上星期突然就死了。◇ *The poor child looks* ***more dead than alive***. 这孩子看上去半死不活的，真可怜。◇ (*figurative*) *In ten years he'll be* ***dead and buried*** *as a politician.* 他作为从政者十年后就不会有人记得了。

• **IDEA/BELIEF/PLAN** 想法；信念；计划 **2** 🔑 [not before noun] no longer believed in or aimed for 不再有人相信（或争取）： *Many believe the peace plan is dead.* 许多人认为和平计划已成泡影。◇ *Unfortunately racism is not yet dead.* 不幸的是种族歧视仍未消亡。◇ *Though the idea may be dead, it is far from being buried* (= people still talk about it, even though there is nothing new to say). 尽管这种思想可能已无人相信，但还远没被人遗忘。

• **NOT USED** 不用 **3** 🔑 belonging to the past; no longer practised or fashionable 过时的；已废弃的；不流行的： *Is the Western a dead art form?* 西部电影这种艺术形式过时了吗？◇ *a dead language* (= one that is no longer spoken, for example Latin) 死语言（不再通用，如拉丁语）

• **FINISHED** 用完 **4** (*informal*) finished; not able to be used any more 用完了的；不能再用的： *dead matches* 划过的火柴 ◇ *There were two dead bottles of wine on the table.* 桌子上有两个空酒瓶。

• **MACHINE** 机器 **5** 🔑 (of machines or equipment 机器或设备) not working because of a lack of power （因为缺电）不运行的，不转动的： *a dead battery* 用完的电池 ◇ *Suddenly the phone* ***went dead***. 电话突然没声音了。

• **PLACE** 地方 **6** (*informal, disapproving*) very quiet, without activity or interest 死气沉沉的；无活力的；无趣的： *There were no theatres, no cinemas, no coffee bars. It was dead as anything.* 那时既无剧院，又无电影院，也无咖啡馆，死气沉沉。

• **BUSINESS** 商业 **7** (*informal, disapproving*) without activity; with nobody buying or selling anything 停滞的；萧条的： *'The market is absolutely dead this morning,' said one foreign exchange trader.* "今天早上市场萧条极了。" 一个外汇交易员说道。◇ *Winter is traditionally the dead season* for the housing market. 冬天历来是住房市场的萧条期。

• TIRED 疲劳 **8** [not usually before noun] (*informal*) extremely tired; not well 筋疲力尽；身体不好：***half dead*** *with cold and hunger* 饥寒交迫，筋疲力尽 ◇ *She felt* ***dead on her feet*** *and didn't have the energy to question them further.* 她觉得累死了，没有力气继续审问他们了。

• WITHOUT FEELING 无感觉 **9** [not before noun] (of a part of the body 身体部位) unable to feel because of cold, etc. （由于冷等）失去知觉，麻木 SYN **numb**: *My left arm had gone dead.* 我的左胳臂已经麻木了。 **10 ~ to sth** unable to feel or understand emotions 无动于衷；麻木不仁；无感觉 SYN **insensitive**: *He was dead to all feelings of pity.* 他毫无同情心。 **11** (especially of sb's voice, eyes or face 尤指嗓音、眼神或脸色) showing no emotion 无表情的；冷漠的；漠不关心的 SYN **expressionless**: *She said, 'I'm sorry, too,' in a quiet, dead voice.* 她平静而冷漠地说："我也很抱歉。" ◇ *His usually dead grey eyes were sparkling.* 他那平日冷漠的灰眼睛突然亮了起来。

• COMPLETE/EXACT 完全；精确 **12** [only before noun] complete or exact 完全的；精确的；全然的：*a* ***dead silence/calm*** 死寂；完全静止 ◇ *the* ***dead centre*** *of the target* 靶子正中心 ◇ *The car gave a sudden jerk and came to a* ***dead stop.*** 汽车猛然一颠，猝然停下。◇ (*BrE*) *This horse is a* ***dead cert*** *for* (= will certainly win) *the race tomorrow.* 这匹马明天比赛一定能赢。◇ *She crumpled to the floor* ***in a dead faint*** (= completely unconscious). 她倒在地上全然不省人事。

• NEVER ALIVE 无生命 **13** never having been alive 无生命的；非生物的：*dead matter* (= for example rock) 无生命物质（如岩石）◇ *a dead planet* (= one with no life on it) 无生命存在的行星

• IN SPORT 体育运动 **14** outside the playing area 是死球；出界

IDM **be dead and 'gone** (*informal*) to be dead 死了；不存在了：*You'll be sorry you said that when I'm dead and gone.* 我死后你会为你说的话感到后悔的。 **be a dead 'ringer for sb** (*informal*) to look very like sb 酷似，极像（某人）；（和某人）一模一样：*She's a dead ringer for a girl I used to know.* 她酷似我以前认识的一个女孩。 **(as) ˌdead as a/the 'dodo** (*BrE, informal*) completely dead; no longer interesting or valid 完全过时；不再引人注目；失效 ➲ MORE LIKE THIS 14, page R26 **(as) ˌdead as a 'doornail** (*informal*) completely dead 完全死了的；死僵了的 **a ˌdead 'duck** (*informal*) a plan, an event, etc. that has failed or is certain to fail and that is therefore not worth discussing 已失败（或注定要失败、毫无讨论价值）的计划（或事情等） **the dead hand of sth** an influence that controls or restricts sth（控制或阻碍事物发展的）影响：*We need to free business from the dead hand of bureaucracy.* 我们必须摆脱官僚主义对工作的严重影响。 **ˌdead in the 'water** a person or plan that is **dead in the water** has failed and has little hope of succeeding in the future （人或计划）失败，无成功希望：*His leadership campaign is dead in the water.* 他参加领导层竞选无望成功。 **dead 'meat** (*informal*) in serious trouble 处境艰难；倒大霉：*If anyone finds out, you're dead meat.* 如果有人发现，你可要倒大霉了。 **ˌdead on ar'rival** (*abbr.* **DOA**) **1** (of an accident victim or other patient) already dead when arriving at hospital（事故受害者或病人）到达医院时已经死亡：*She was pronounced dead on arrival.* 她在送达医院时即被宣布死亡。 **2** (*NAmE, informal*) very unlikely to be successful; not working when it is delivered 已不可能成功；到货即损；到达时已无用：*The bill was dead on arrival in the Senate.* 这项法案在参议院就不可能通过。 ◇ *The software was DOA.* 这软件送达时已经损坏。 **ˌdead to the 'world** fast asleep 熟睡；沉睡；酣睡 **over ˌmy dead 'body** (*informal*) used to show you are strongly opposed to sth（表示强烈反对）除非我死了，我死也不：*She moves into our home over my dead body.* 除非我死了，否则她别想搬进我们家。 **sb wouldn't be seen/caught 'dead...** (*informal*) used to say that you would not like to wear particular clothes, or to be in a particular situation （表示不愿穿戴某衣物或处于某种环境）死也不愿意：*She wouldn't be seen dead in a hat.* 她最讨厌戴帽子。◇ *He wouldn't be caught dead going to a club with his mother.* 他死也不愿意跟母亲一起去俱乐部。 ➲ MORE AT FLOG, KNOCK *v.*

■ ***noun*** **the dead 1** [pl.] people who have died 死人；死者：*The dead and wounded in that one attack amounted to 6 000.* 仅那一次进攻就死伤达 6 000 人。 **2** [sing.] the state of being dead 死：*Christians believe that God raised Jesus from the dead.* 基督徒相信上帝使耶稣复活。◇ (*figurative*) *In nine years he has brought his party back from the dead almost to the brink of power.* 九年来他使该党起死回生，甚至差点成为执政党。 ➲ MORE LIKE THIS 24, page R28

IDM **in the ˌdead of 'night** (*BrE also* **at ˌdead of 'night**) in the quietest part of the night 深夜；在夜晚万籁俱寂时：*I crept out of bed in the dead of night and sneaked downstairs.* 深夜我悄悄地从床上爬起来，蹑手蹑脚地下了楼。 **in the ˌdead of 'winter** in the coldest part of winter 在隆冬；在严冬

■ ***adv.*** (*informal*)

• COMPLETELY 完全 **1** completely; exactly 完全地；全然地；确实地：*You're dead right!* 你完全正确！◇ (*BrE*) *a dead straight road* 笔直的道路 ◇ (*BrE*) *The train was dead on time.* 火车正点出发。◇ *He's dead against the idea.* 他坚决反对这个想法。◇ *The sight made him* ***stop dead in his tracks*** (= stop suddenly). 一看这情景，他惊呆了。◇ *She's* ***dead set on*** *getting* (= determined to get) *this new job.* 她打定主意要得到这个新工作。

• VERY 非常 **2** (*BrE, informal*) very; extremely 非常；绝对；极度：*The instructions are dead easy to follow.* 这些指令很容易执行。◇ *You were dead lucky to get that job.* 你得到那份工作，真是太幸运了。◇ *I was dead scared.* 我怕得要死。

IDM **cut sb 'dead** (*BrE*) to pretend not to have seen sb; to refuse to say hello to sb 假装没看见，不理睬（某人）：*She saw me, recognized me and cut me dead.* 她看见了我，也认出了我，却不理睬我。 ➲ MORE AT RIGHT *n.*

ˌdead 'beat (*also* **beat**) *adj.* [not before noun] (*informal*) very tired 筋疲力尽；疲惫不堪：*You look dead beat.* 你好像累得够呛。

dead·beat /ˈdedbiːt/ *noun* (*informal*) **1** (*especially NAmE*) a lazy person; a person with no job and no money, who is not part of normal society 懒人；二流子；身无分文的无业者 **2** (*NAmE*) a person or company that tries to avoid paying their debts 赖账者；赖债者；不讲信用的公司 **3** (*also* **ˌdeadbeat 'dad**) (*NAmE*) a father who does not live with his children and does not pay their mother any money to take care of them（不与子女同住，也不支付抚养费的）无良父亲，失职父亲

dead·bolt /ˈdedbəʊlt; *NAmE* -boʊlt/ (*especially NAmE*) (*BrE also* **dead·lock**) *noun* a type of lock on a door that needs a key to open or close it 需用钥匙开关的门锁

dead·en /ˈdedn/ *verb* **~ sth** to make sth such as a sound, a feeling, etc. less strong 使（声音、感觉等）减弱；使缓和；使迟钝 SYN **dull**: *He was given drugs to deaden the pain.* 给了他止痛药。 ▸ **dead·en·ing** *adj.* [only before noun]: *the deadening effect of alcohol on your reactions* 酒精对反应的抑制作用

ˌdead 'end *noun* **1** a road, passage, etc. that is closed at one end 一头封死的道路（或通道等）：*The first street we tried turned out to be a dead end.* 我们想走的头一条路结果是条死胡同。 **2** a point at which you can make no further progress in what you are doing 绝境；僵局：*We had come to a dead end in our research.* 我们的研究工作已陷入绝境。◇ *He's in a* ***dead-end job*** *in the local factory* (= one with low wages and no hope of promotion). 他在当地工厂的工作是没有前途的。◇ *These negotiations are a* ***dead-end street*** (= they have reached a point where no further progress is possible). 谈判陷入僵局。

dead·head /ˈdedhed/ *verb* **~ sth** to remove dead flowers from a plant 摘掉（植物）的枯花

ˌdead 'heat *noun* **1** (*especially BrE*) a result in a race when two of those taking part finish at exactly the same time（速度比赛中两个参赛者）同时到达终点，成绩并列 **2** (*NAmE*) a situation during a race or competition, etc. when two or more people are at the same level 势均力敌；不分胜负；不相上下：*The two candidates are* ***in a dead heat*** *in the polls.* 两名候选人在民意测验中势均力敌。

ˌ**dead ˈletter** *noun* **1** [usually sing.] a law or an agreement that still exists but that is ignored 无人遵守的法律；形同虚设的协定；空文 **2** (*especially NAmE*) a letter that cannot be delivered to an address or to the person who sent it 死信；无法投递（或退回）的邮件

dead·line /ˈdedlaɪn/ *noun* ~ (**for sth**) a point in time by which sth must be done 最后期限；截止日期：*I prefer to* ***work to a deadline****.* 我喜欢按规定的期限完成工作。◇ *The deadline for applications is 30 April.* 交申请书的截止日期是 4 月 30 日。◇ *the January 15 deadline set by the United Nations* 联合国规定的 1 月 15 日最后期限

dead·lock /ˈdedlɒk; *NAmE* -lɑːk/ *noun* **1** [sing., U] a complete failure to reach agreement or settle an argument 僵持；僵局；相持不下 SYN **stalemate**：*European agriculture ministers failed to* ***break the deadlock*** *over farm subsidies.* 欧洲各国农业部长在农业补贴问题上未能打破僵局。◇ (*BrE*) *The strike appeared to have reached deadlock.* 罢工好像已陷入僵局。◇ (*NAmE, BrE*) *The strike has reached a deadlock.* 罢工已陷入僵局。 **2** (*BrE*) (*also* **dead·bolt** *NAmE, BrE*) [C] a type of lock on a door that needs a key to open or close it 需用钥匙开关的门锁 ▸ **dead·locked** *adj.* [not before noun]：*Despite months of discussion the negotiations remained deadlocked.* 尽管已讨论数月，谈判仍僵持不下。

ˌ**dead ˈloss** *noun* [usually sing.] (*BrE, informal*) a person or thing that is not helpful or useful 无用的人（或物）；废物：*He may be a very talented designer, but as a manager he's a dead loss.* 他可能是一个很有天赋的设计师，但作为经理他却很无能。

dead·ly /ˈdedli/ *adj., adv.*

■ *adj.* (**dead·lier**, **dead·li·est**) HELP **More deadly** and **deadliest** are the usual forms. You can also use **most deadly**. 常用 more deadly 和 deadliest，亦可用 most deadly。 **1** causing or likely to cause death（可能）致命的，致死的 SYN **lethal**：*a* ***deadly weapon/disease*** 致命的武器 / 疾病 ◇ ***deadly poison*** 剧毒 ◇ *The cobra is one of the world's deadliest snakes.* 眼镜蛇是世界上最致命的蛇类之一。◇ *The terrorists have chosen to play a deadly game with the civilian population.* 恐怖分子决意要同平民百姓玩死亡游戏。 **2** [only before noun] extreme; complete 极度的；十足的；彻底的：*I'm* ***in deadly earnest****.* 我是非常认真的。◇ *We sat* ***in deadly silence****.* 我们默不作声地坐着。◇ *They are* ***deadly enemies*** (= are full of hatred for each other). 他们是不共戴天的仇敌。 **3** extremely effective, so that no defence is possible 非常有效的；无法防御的：*His aim is deadly* (= so accurate that he can kill easily). 他弹无虚发。◇ *It was the deadly striker's 11th goal of the season.* 这是杀手前锋本赛季的第 11 个进球。 **4** (*informal*) very boring 枯燥的；令人厌烦的：*The lecture was absolutely deadly.* 这讲座简直无聊透了。

■ *adv.* **1** (*informal*) extremely 极其；非常：***deadly serious/dull*** 极其严肃认真 / 乏味 **2** = DEATHLY：***deadly pale/cold*** 死一般地苍白；冷得要死

dead·ly night·shade /ˌdedli ˈnaɪtʃeɪd/ (*also* **bella·donna**) *noun* [U] a very poisonous plant with purple flowers and black BERRIES 颠茄（有毒，开紫花，结黑色浆果）

ˌ**deadly ˈsin** *noun* one of the seven actions for which you can go to hell, in Christian tradition 七罪宗之一，大罪（基督教指罪恶的根源）：*Greed is one of the seven deadly sins.* 贪婪是七罪宗之一。

dead·pan /ˈdedpæn/ *adj.* without any expression or emotion; often pretending to be serious when you are joking 面无表情的；不带感情色彩的；冷面幽默的：*deadpan humour* 冷面幽默

ˌ**dead ˈweight** *noun* [usually sing.] **1** a thing that is very heavy and difficult to lift or move （难以搬动的）重物 **2** a person or thing that makes it difficult for sth to succeed or change 重负；累赘

ˌ**dead ˈwood** *noun* [U] people or things that have become useless or unnecessary in an organization 冗员；废物

ˈ**dead zone** *noun* **1** a place or a period of time in which nothing happens 空白地带，空白期（没有事情发生）：*The town is a cultural dead zone.* 这个镇子是个文化荒原。 **2** an area which separates two places, groups of people, etc. 隔离带：*The UN is trying to maintain a dead zone between the warring groups.* 联合国正试图在交战方之间保留隔离带。 **3** a place where a mobile/cell phone does not work because no signal can be received 盲区，静区（无手机信号） **4** (*biology* 生) an area of water in which animals cannot live because there is not enough OXYGEN 死水区（因缺氧而使动物无法生存）

deaf 🔑 /def/ *adj.* (**deaf·er**, **deaf·est**) **1** 🔑 unable to hear anything or unable to hear very well 聋的：*to* ***become/go deaf*** 变聋 ◇ *She was born deaf.* 她天生耳聋。➲ SEE ALSO STONE DEAF, TONE-DEAF **2 the deaf** *noun* [pl.] people who cannot hear 耳聋的人；聋子：*television subtitles for the deaf and hard of hearing* 为耳聋和耳背者做的电视字幕 ➲ MORE LIKE THIS 24, page R28 **3** [not before noun] ~ **to sth** not willing to listen or pay attention to sth 不愿听；不去注意：*He was deaf to my requests for help.* 他对我的求助充耳不闻。▸ **deaf·ness** *noun* [U]

IDM (**as**) ˌ**deaf as a ˈpost** (*informal*) very deaf 全聋；聋得什么也听不见 ➲ MORE LIKE THIS 14, page R26 **fall on deaf ˈears** to be ignored or not noticed by other people 不被理睬；不被注意；被置若罔闻：*Her advice fell on deaf ears.* 她的忠告没有受到重视。 **turn a deaf ˈear** (**to sb/sth**) to ignore or refuse to listen to sb/sth （对…）置之不理，充耳不闻：*He turned a deaf ear to the rumours.* 他对这些谣言置若罔闻。

deaf·en /ˈdefn/ *verb* [usually passive] **1** ~ **sb** to make sb unable to hear the sounds around them because there is too much noise 使震得耳朵发聋：*The noise of the siren was deafening her.* 汽笛声震得她耳朵都快聋了。 **2** ~ **sb** to make sb deaf 使聋；使听不见

deaf·en·ing /ˈdefnɪŋ/ *adj.* very loud 震耳欲聋的；极喧闹的：*deafening applause* 掌声如雷 ◇ *The noise of the machine was deafening.* 机器的轰鸣声震耳欲聋。◇ *The government's response to the report has been a* ***deafening silence*** (= it was very noticeable that nothing was said or done). 政府对此报道显然置之不理。▸ **deaf·en·ing·ly** *adv.*

ˌ**deaf ˈmute** *noun* (*sometimes offensive*) a person who is unable to hear or speak 聋哑人

deal 🔑 /diːl/ *verb, noun*

■ *verb* (**dealt**, **dealt** /delt/)

• **CARDS** 纸牌游戏 **1** [I, T] to give cards to each player in a game of cards 发牌：*Whose turn is it to deal?* 该谁发牌了？◇ ~ (**sth**) (**out**) (**to sb**) *Start by dealing out ten cards to each player.* 首先给每家发十张牌。◇ ~ **sb sth** *He dealt me two aces.* 他给我发了两张 A 牌。➲ WORDFINDER NOTE AT CARD

• **DRUGS** 毒品 **2** [I, T] ~ (**sth**) to buy and sell illegal drugs 非法买卖毒品；贩毒：*You can often see people dealing openly on the streets.* 经常可以看到一些人在大街上公然买卖毒品。➲ WORDFINDER NOTE AT DRUG

IDM **deal sb/sth a ˈblow | deal a ˈblow to sb/sth** (*formal*) **1** to be very shocking or harmful to sb/sth 令…震惊；给…以打击；使…受到伤害：*Her sudden death dealt a blow to the whole country.* 她突然逝世，举国上下为之震惊。 **2** to hit sb/sth 给…一击；打击 **deal with it** used to tell sb that they cannot change a situation so they must accept it （用以告诉某人无法改变现状）接受现实吧：*That's the way it is, so deal with it!* 就是这个样子，接受现实吧！➲ MORE AT WHEEL *v.*

PHR V ˈ**deal in sth** **1** 🔑 to buy and sell a particular product 经营，买卖（某一产品） SYN **trade in**：*The company deals in computer software.* 这个公司经营计算机软件。 **2** to accept sth as a basis for your decisions, attitudes or actions 作为依据加以接受：*We don't deal in rumours or guesswork.* 我们不听信谣言，也不胡乱猜测。 ˌ**deal sb ˈin** (*informal, especially NAmE*) to include sb in an activity 将某人算在里边；让某人参与：*That sounds great. Deal me in!* 这听起来太棒了。算我一个！ ˌ**deal sth↔ˈout** **1** to share sth out among a group of people 分发；分配

SYN distribute: *The profits were dealt out among the investors.* 利润分给了投资者。 **2** to say what punishment sb should have 给予（判决、处罚）: *Many judges deal out harsher sentences to men than to women.* 许多法官对男性比对女性的判决更严厉。 **'deal with sb** 🔑 to take appropriate action in a particular situation or according to who you are talking to, managing, etc. 对付；应付；对待 SYN **handle**: *She is used to dealing with all kinds of people in her job.* 她已习惯于和工作中遇到的各种各样的人打交道。 **'deal with sb/sth** 🔑 to do business with a person, a company or an organization 与…做生意 **'deal with sth 1** 🔑 to solve a problem, perform a task, etc. 解决；处理；应付: *to deal with enquiries/issues/complaints* 处理各种询问 / 问题 / 投诉 ◇ *Have you dealt with these letters yet?* 这些信件你处理了吗？ ◇ *He's good at dealing with pressure.* 他善于应付压力。 **2** 🔑 to be about sth 涉及；论及；关于: *Her poems often deal with the subject of death.* 她的诗经常涉及死亡这一主题。 ➲ LANGUAGE BANK AT ABOUT

■ *noun*

• A LOT 很多 **1** 🔑 [sing.] **a good/great ~** much; a lot 大量；很多: *They spent a great deal of money.* 他们花了大量的钱。 ◇ *It took a great deal of time.* 这费了很多时间。 ◇ *I'm feeling a good deal better.* 我感觉好多了。 ◇ *We see them a great deal* (= often). 我们经常见到他们。

• BUSINESS AGREEMENT 商业协议 **2** 🔑 [C] an agreement, especially in business, on particular conditions for buying or doing sth 协议；（尤指）交易: *to **make/sign/conclude/close a deal** (with sb)* （与某人）达成一笔交易 ◇ (*informal*) *Did you **cut a deal*** (= make one)? 你们交易做成了吗？ ◇ ***We did a deal** with the management on overtime.* 我们与资方在加班问题上达成了一项协议。 ◇ *They were hoping for a better pay deal.* 他们希望达成一项提高工资的协议。 ◇ ***A deal was struck** after lengthy negotiations.* 经过漫长的谈判终于达成了协议。 ◇ ***The deal fell through*** (= no agreement was reached). 交易没有谈成。 ◇ *I got a **good deal** on the car* (= bought it cheaply). 我这辆小汽车买得很便宜。 ◇ ***It's a deal!*** (= I agree to your terms) 就这么办吧！ ◇ *Listen. **This is the deal*** (= this is what we have agreed and are going to do). 听着，下面是我们达成的协议。 ➲ COLLOCATIONS AT BUSINESS ➲ SEE ALSO PACKAGE *n.* (3)

WORDFINDER 联想词: acquisition, bid, broker, contract, merger, negotiation, offer, proposal, takeover

• TREATMENT 待遇 **3** [C, usually sing.] the way that sb/sth is treated 待遇: *If elected, the party has promised a **new deal*** (= better and fairer treatment) *for teachers.* 该党承诺如果当选将给教师更好的待遇。 ◇ *They knew they'd been given a **raw/rough deal*** (= been treated unfairly). 他们知道自己受到了不公正待遇。 ◇ *We tried to ensure that everyone got a **fair deal**.* 我们尽力保证每个人都受到公平待遇。 ◇ *It was a **square deal** for everyone.* 这对任何人来说都是公平合理的。

• IN CARD GAMES 纸牌游戏 **4** [C, usually sing.] the action of giving out cards to the players 发牌: *It's your deal.* 该你发牌了。

• WOOD 木材 **5** [U] (*especially BrE*) the soft pale wood of FIR or PINE trees, especially when it is cut into boards for making things 冷杉木；松木板: *a deal table* 松木桌子

IDM **what's the 'deal?** (*informal*) what is happening in the present situation? 出了什么事；怎么啦: *What's the deal? Do you want to go out or not?* 怎么啦？你想不想出去？ ➲ MORE AT BIG *adj.*, DONE *adj.*, STRIKE *v.*

'deal-breaker *noun* something that causes sb to reject a deal in politics or business 砸买卖的事: *The candidate's support for the war is the deal-breaker* (= people will not vote for the candidate because of it). 候选人因为支持这场战争而失去了选民。

deal·er /ˈdiːlə(r)/ *noun* **1** a person whose business is buying and selling a particular product 交易商；贸易商: *an art/antique dealer* 艺术品经销商；古董商 ◇ **~ in sth** *He's a dealer in second-hand cars.* 他经销二手汽车。 ➲ SEE ALSO WHEELER-DEALER **2** a person who sells illegal drugs 贩毒者，毒品贩子 **3** the person who gives out the cards in a card game （纸牌游戏的）发牌者

deal·er·ship /ˈdiːləʃɪp; *NAmE* -lərʃ-/ *noun* a business that buys and sells products, especially cars, for a particular company; the position of being a dealer who can buy and sell sth 专项商品（尤指汽车）经销店；专项商品经销: *a Ford dealership* 福特汽车经销店

deal·ing /ˈdiːlɪŋ/ *noun* **1 dealings** [pl.] business activities; the relations that you have with sb in business （商业）活动，往来: *Have you **had** any previous **dealings with** this company?* 你曾与这家公司有过业务往来吗？ ◇ *I knew nothing of his business dealings.* 我对他生意上的事一概不知道。 ◇ *She has always been very polite in her dealings with me.* 她在与我交往的过程中总是彬彬有礼。 **2** [U] a way of doing business with sb 经营作风；经营方式: *a reputation for **fair/honest dealing*** 公平交易 / 诚信经营的美名 **3** [U, C] buying and selling 买卖；交易: *drug dealing* 毒品交易 ◇ *dealings in shares* 股票交易

dealt PAST TENSE, PAST PART. OF DEAL

dean /diːn/ *noun* **1** (in the Anglican Church 圣公会) a priest of high rank who is in charge of the other priests in a CATHEDRAL 座堂主任牧师 **2** (*also* ˌ**rural 'dean**) (*BrE*) a priest who is in charge of the priests of several churches in an area （乡间主管若干教堂牧师的）主任牧师 **3** a person in a university who is in charge of a department of studies （大学的）学院院长，系主任 **4** (in a college or university, especially at Oxford or Cambridge) a person who is responsible for the discipline of students （大学，尤指牛津、剑桥大学的）学监 **5** (*NAmE*) = DOYEN

dean·ery /ˈdiːnəri/ *noun* (*pl.* **-ies**) **1** a group of PARISHES controlled by a dean (2) 总铎区；（统辖若干教区的）主任牧师管辖区 **2** the office or house of a dean (1), (2) 主任牧师办公室（或住所）

ˌ**dean's 'list** *noun* (in the US) a list that is published every year of the best students in a college or university （美国大学的）年度优秀学生名单

dear 🔑 /dɪə(r); *NAmE* dɪr/ *adj., exclamation, noun, adv.*

■ *adj.* (**dear·er, dear·est**) **1** 🔑 loved by or important to sb 亲爱的；宝贵的；珍视的: *He's one of my dearest friends.* 他是我最亲密的朋友之一。 ◇ **~ to sb** *Her daughter is very dear to her.* 她的女儿是她心爱的宝贝。 **2** 🔑 **Dear** used at the beginning of a letter before the name or title of the person that you are writing to （用于信函抬头的名字或头衔前）亲爱的: *Dear Sir or Madam* 亲爱的先生 / 女士 ◇ *Dear Mrs Jones* 亲爱的琼斯太太 **3** [not usually before noun] (*BrE*) expensive; costing a lot of money 昂贵；价格高: *Everything's so dear now, isn't it?* 现在什么东西都那么贵，是不是？ OPP **cheap**

IDM **dear old/little...** used to describe sb in a way that shows affection （表示亲昵喜爱）亲爱的: *Dear old Sue! I knew she'd help.* 亲爱的休啊！我知道她会帮忙的。 ◇ *Their baby's a dear little thing.* 他们的宝宝真是个小乖乖。 **hold sb/sth 'dear** (*formal*) to care very much for sb/sth; to value sb/sth highly 非常关心；十分看重；极为珍视: *He had destroyed everything we held dear.* 他把我们珍视的一切都给毁了。 ➲ MORE AT HEART, LIFE, NEAR *adj.*

■ *exclamation* used in expressions that show that you are surprised, upset, annoyed or worried （惊奇、不安、烦恼、担忧等时说）啊，哎呀，糟糕，天哪: ***Oh dear!** I think I've lost my purse!* 糟糕，我可能把钱包给丢了！ ◇ ***Oh dear!** What a shame.* 天哪，太可惜啦！ ◇ ***Dear me!** What a mess!* 哎呀，真是一团糟！ ◇ ***Dear oh dear!** What are you going to do now?* 哎呀呀，你现在怎么办呢？

■ *noun* **1** (*informal*) a kind person 仁慈的人；可爱的人: *Isn't he a dear?* 他不是很可爱吗？ ◇ ***Be a dear and** fetch me my coat.* 劳驾把外套给我拿来。 **2** used when speaking to sb you love （称呼所爱的人）亲爱的: *Would you like a drink, dear?* 喝点什么吗，亲爱的？ ◇ *Come here, my dear.* 上这儿来，亲爱的。 **3** used when speaking to sb in a friendly way, for example by an older person to a young person or a child （对较年轻的人或孩子说话时用）亲爱的，乖乖: *What's your name, dear?* 你叫什么名字，亲爱的？ ➲ COMPARE DUCK *n.* (4)

▪***adv.*** (*BrE*) at a high price 高价地；昂贵地：*to buy cheap and sell dear* 贱买贵卖 IDM ➤ SEE COST *v.*

dear·est /ˈdɪərɪst; *NAmE* ˈdɪr-/ *adj., noun*
▪***adj.*** (*old-fashioned*) **1** used when writing to sb you love（给所爱的人写信时用）最亲爱的：*'Dearest Nina', the letter began.* "最亲爱的尼娜"，信的开端这样写道。**2** [usually before noun] that you feel deeply 深切的；由衷的：*It was her* ***dearest wish*** *to have a family.* 有一个家是她由衷的希望。
▪***noun*** (*old-fashioned*) used when speaking to sb you love（称呼所爱的人）亲爱的：*Come (my) dearest, let's go home.* 好啦，亲爱的，咱们回家吧。IDM ➤ SEE NEAR *adj.*

dearie /ˈdɪəri; *NAmE* ˈdɪri/ *noun* (*old-fashioned, BrE, informal*) used to address sb in a friendly way（表示友好的称呼）亲爱的，乖乖：*Sit down, dearie.* 坐下，亲爱的。

dear·ly /ˈdɪəli; *NAmE* ˈdɪrli/ *adv.* **1** very much 非常；很：*She loves him dearly.* 她深深地爱着他。◇ *I would* ***dearly like/love*** *to know what he was thinking.* 我很想知道他在想什么。◇ ***dearly beloved*** (= used by a minister at a Christian church service to address people) 最亲爱的教友们（神职人员对参礼信众的称呼）**2** in a way that causes a lot of suffering or damage, or that costs a lot of money 代价极大地；高价地；昂贵地：*Success has* ***cost him dearly.*** 他为成功付出了高昂的代价。◇ *She* ***paid dearly*** *for her mistake.* 她因犯错误而付出了巨大的代价。

dearth /dɜːθ; *NAmE* dɜːrθ/ *noun* [sing.] ~ (**of sth**) a lack of sth; the fact of there not being enough of sth 缺乏；不足 SYN **scarcity**：*There was a dearth of reliable information on the subject.* 关于这个课题缺乏可靠资料。

death 🔑 /deθ/ *noun* **1** 🔑[C] the fact of sb dying or being killed 死；死亡：*a* ***sudden/violent/peaceful, etc. death*** 猝死、横死、安详的死等 ◇ *the anniversary of his wife's death* 他妻子的忌日 ◇ *an increase in deaths from cancer* 癌症死亡人数的增加 ◇ *He died a slow and painful death.* 他缓慢而痛苦地死去。**2** 🔑[U] the end of life; the state of being dead 生命的终止；死亡状态：*Two children were burnt* ***to death*** *in the fire* (= they died as a result of the fire). 两个孩子被大火烧死。◇ *He's drinking himself* ***to death*** (= so that it will kill him). 他这样喝酒非醉死不可。◇ *Police are trying to establish the* ***cause of death.*** 警方在设法确定死因。◇ *Do you believe in* ***life after death?*** 你相信来世吗？◇ *a* ***death camp*** (= a place where prisoners are killed, usually in a war) 死亡集中营（常指战争中杀害俘虏的地方）◇ *He was* ***sentenced to death*** (= to be EXECUTED). 他被判处死刑。**3** 🔑[U] ~ **of sth** the permanent end or destruction of sth 永久的灭亡；毁灭；破灭：*the death of all my plans* 我所有计划的破灭 ◇ *the death of fascism* 法西斯主义的灭亡 **4** (*also* **Death**) [U] (*literary*) the power that destroys life, imagined as human in form 死神：*Death is often shown in paintings as a human skeleton.* 死神在绘画作品中常以骷髅形式出现。➲ SEE ALSO SUDDEN DEATH
IDM ➤ **at death's ˈdoor** (*often humorous*) so ill/sick that you may die（因病重）生命危在旦夕；病危 **be the ˈdeath of sb** (*informal*) to worry or upset sb very much 让某人担心得要命；使某人深感不安：*Those kids will be the death of me.* 为那些孩子操心会把我累死。 **ˌdo sth to ˈdeath** to do or perform sth so often that people become tired of seeing or hearing it 做烦了；看腻了；听厌了：*That joke's been done to death.* 那个笑话都听腻了。 **frighten/scare sb to ˈdeath** to frighten sb very much 把某人吓得要命 **look/feel like death warmed ˈup** (*BrE*) (*NAmE* **like death warmed ˈover**) (*informal*) to look or feel very ill/sick or tired 看起来病得厉害（或疲惫不堪）；感到很不舒服（或累得要命） **put sb to death** to kill sb as a punishment 处死；处决 SYN **execute**：*The prisoner will be put to death at dawn.* 囚犯将在黎明时被处死。 **to death** extremely; very much 极度；非常：*to be bored to death* 腻烦得要命 ◇ *I'm* ***sick to death*** *of your endless criticism.* 你这无休止的指责真让我烦死了。 **to the death** until sb is dead 至死；到底；永远：*a fight to the death* 战斗到底 ➲ MORE AT CATCH *v.*, CHEAT *v.*, DICE *v.*, DIE *v.*, FATE, FIGHT *v.*, FLOG, GRIM, KISS *n.*, LIFE, MATTER *n.*

death·bed /ˈdeθbed/ *noun* [usually sing.] the bed in which sb is dying or dies 临终床：*a* ***deathbed confession/conversion*** 临终告解 / 皈依 ◇ *He told me the truth* ***on his deathbed*** (= as he lay dying). 他临终时向我吐露了实情。◇ *She* ***was on her deathbed*** (= going to die very soon). 她已生命垂危。◇ (*humorous*) *You'd have to be practically on your deathbed before the doctor would come and see you!* 你非病到就要一命呜呼的时候医生才会来看你！

ˈdeath blow *noun* an event that destroys or puts an end to sth 导致毁灭的事情；致命的一击：*They thought the arrival of television would* ***deal a death blow*** *to mass cinema audiences.* 他们认为电视的问世将使观众涌向影院的现象不复存在。

ˈdeath certificate *noun* an official document, signed by a doctor, that states the cause and time of sb's death 死亡证书

ˈdeath duty *noun* [usually pl.] (*old-fashioned, BrE*) = INHERITANCE TAX

ˈdeath knell (*also* **knell**) *noun* [sing.] an event that means that the end or destruction of sth will come soon 丧钟；死亡的征兆；预示毁灭的事件

death·less /ˈdeθləs/ *adj.* never dying or forgotten 不死的；不朽的；永恒的 SYN **immortal**：(*ironic*) *written in his usual deathless prose* (= very bad) 用他那万世不变的笔调写成

death·ly /ˈdeθli/ (*also less frequent* **dead·ly**) *adv.* like a dead person; suggesting death 死一般地；让人想到死亡：*Her face was deathly pale.* 她的脸色死一般苍白。◇ *The house was deathly still.* 房子一片死寂。▶ **death·ly** *adj.*：*A* ***deathly hush*** *fell over the room as he walked in.* 他进去时，房间里变得死一般的寂静。

ˈdeath mask *noun* a model of the face of a person who has just died, made by pressing a soft substance over their face and removing it when it becomes hard（用柔软物质压在死人脸上，变硬后取出制成的）死人面部模型

the ˈdeath penalty *noun* [sing.] the punishment of being killed that is used in some countries for very serious crimes 死刑；极刑：*the* ***abolition/return of the death penalty*** 死刑的废除 / 恢复 ◇ *The two men are* ***facing the death penalty.*** 这二人面临死刑。➲ COLLOCATIONS AT JUSTICE

ˈdeath rate *noun* **1** the number of deaths every year for every 1 000 people in the population of a place 死亡率（某地每年每 1 000 人的死亡人数）：*a* ***high/low death rate*** 高 / 低死亡率 **2** the number of deaths every year from a particular disease or in a particular group （某种疾病或某个群体的）死亡率：*Death rates from heart disease have risen considerably in recent years.* 近年来心脏病的死亡率大大上升了。

ˈdeath rattle *noun* [sing.] a sound sometimes heard in the throat of a dying person 临终喉鸣

ˌdeath ˈrow *noun* [U] the cells in a prison for prisoners who are waiting to be killed as punishment for a serious crime 死囚牢房；死囚区：*prisoners* ***on death row*** 死囚区的犯人 ➲ WORDFINDER NOTE AT PRISON ➲ COLLOCATIONS AT JUSTICE

ˈdeath sentence *noun* the legal punishment of being killed for a serious crime 死刑：***to be given/to receive the death sentence*** *for murder* 因谋杀罪被判死刑

ˈdeath's head *noun* a human SKULL (= the bone structure of the head) used as a symbol of death 骷髅头（象征死亡）

ˈdeath squad *noun* a group of people who are ordered by a government to kill other people, especially the government's political opponents（受命于政府谋杀政敌等的）处决小队，暗杀小组

ˈdeath throes *noun* [pl.] **1** the final stages of sth just before it comes to an end 临终；末日；最后阶段：*The regime is now in its death throes.* 这一政权大势已去。**2** violent pains and movements at the moment of death 临终的剧痛；死前的挣扎

'death toll *noun* the number of people killed in an accident, a war, a disaster, etc.（事故、战争、灾难等的）死亡人数

death·trap /ˈdeθtræp/ *noun* (*informal*) a building, vehicle, etc. that is dangerous and could cause sb's death 死亡陷阱（潜藏祸患的建筑物、车辆等）: *The cars blocking the exits could turn this place into a deathtrap.* 堵住出口的汽车可能使这地方成为死亡陷阱。

D

'death warrant *noun* an official document stating that sb should receive the punishment of being killed for a crime that they have committed 死刑执行令: *The President* ***signed the death warrant.*** 总统签署了死刑执行令。◇ *If you pay the ransom, you may be signing your son's death warrant.* 如果你付赎金，可能就要了你儿子的命。◇ (*figurative*) *By withdrawing the funding, the government signed the project's death warrant.* 政府撤回资金，也就是对这项工程判了死刑。

ˌdeath-watch ˈbeetle *noun* a small insect that eats into old wood, making sounds like a watch TICKING 红毛窃蠹（专蛀旧木，发出类似表的嘀嗒声的小甲虫）

'death wish *noun* [sing.] a desire to die, often that sb is not aware of（常指无意识的）死亡愿望

deb /deb/ *noun* (*informal*) = DEBUTANTE

de·bacle /deɪˈbɑːkl; dɪˈb-/ *noun* an event or a situation that is a complete failure and causes embarrassment 大败；崩溃；垮台；灾祸

debar /dɪˈbɑː(r)/ *verb* (**-rr-**) [usually passive] **~ sb (from sth/ from doing sth)** (*formal*) to officially prevent sb from doing sth, joining sth, etc. 阻止，禁止（某人做某事、加入某团体等）: *He was debarred from holding public office.* 他被禁止担任公职。

de·base /dɪˈbeɪs/ *verb* **~ sb/sth** to make sb/sth less valuable or respected 降低…的价值；败坏…的名誉 **SYN** **devalue**: *Sport is being debased by commercial sponsorship.* 体育运动因受商业赞助而降低了声誉。▶ **de·base·ment** *noun* [U]

de·bat·able **AW** /dɪˈbeɪtəbl/ *adj.* not certain because people can have different ideas and opinions about the thing being discussed 可争辩的；有争议的 **SYN** **arguable, questionable**: *a debatable point* 有争议的观点 ◇ ***It is highly debatable whether*** *conditions have improved for low-income families.* 低收入家庭的生活状况是否已得到改善是一个颇有争议的问题。

de·bate 🔑 **AW** /dɪˈbeɪt/ *noun, verb*

■ *noun* [C, U] **~ (on/about/over sth)** **1** 🔑 a formal discussion of an issue at a public meeting or in a parliament. In a debate two or more speakers express opposing views and then there is often a vote on the issue.（在公共集会上或议会里就某问题进行的、常以表决结束的）辩论: *a debate on abortion* 关于堕胎的辩论 ◇ *The minister opened the debate* (= was the first to speak). 部长在辩论时率先发言。◇ *The motion* ***under debate*** (= being discussed) *was put to a vote.* 辩论中的动议已付诸表决。◇ *After a long debate, Congress approved the proposal.* 经过长时间辩论，国会通过了这项提议。➲ SYNONYMS AT DISCUSSION ➲ COLLOCATIONS AT POLITICS

> **WORDFINDER** 联想词: argument, ayes, chair, the floor, motion, propose, second[1], **speak**, vote

2 🔑 an argument or a discussion expressing different opinions（各自发表不同意见的）争论，辩论，讨论: *a* ***heated/wide-ranging/lively debate*** 激烈的／广泛的／热烈的争论 ◇ *the current debate about tax* 目前关于税收的讨论 ◇ *There had been much debate on the issue of childcare.* 人们对儿童照管问题议论纷纷。◇ *Whether he deserves what has happened to him is* ***open to debate/a matter for debate*** (= cannot be certain or decided yet). 他是否罪有应得还有待于讨论。◇ *The theatre's future is a subject of considerable debate.* 剧院的前途是一个颇有争议的问题。

■ *verb* **1** 🔑 [T, I] to discuss sth, especially formally, before making a decision or finding a solution（尤指正式）讨论，辩论 **SYN** **discuss**: **~ (sth)** *Politicians will be debating the bill later this week.* 政界将在本周晚些时候讨论这个议案。◇ *The question of the origin of the universe is still* ***hotly debated*** (= strongly argued about) *by scientists.* 关于宇宙起源问题，科学家仍在激烈辩论。◇ **~ whether, what, etc....** *The committee will debate whether to lower the age of club membership to 16.* 委员会将讨论是否将参加俱乐部的年龄限制放宽到 16 岁。➲ SYNONYMS AT TALK **2** [I, T] to think carefully about sth before making a decision 仔细考虑；思考；盘算: **~ (with yourself)** *She debated with herself for a while, and then picked up the phone.* 她仔细琢磨了一会儿，然后拿起了电话。◇ **~ whether, what, etc....** *We're debating whether or not to go skiing this winter.* 我们盘算着今年冬天是否去滑雪。◇ **~ doing sth** *For a moment he debated going after her.* 他仔细思考了片刻要不要去追求她。▶ **de·bat·ing** *noun* [U]: *a debating society at a school* 学校的辩论社团

de·bater /dɪˈbeɪtə(r)/ *noun* a person who is involved in a debate 参加讨论者；争论者

de·bauched /dɪˈbɔːtʃt/ *adj.* a **debauched** person is immoral in their sexual behaviour, drinks a lot of alcohol, takes drugs, etc. 道德败坏的；淫荡的；沉湎酒色的；嗜毒的 **SYN** **depraved, dissolute**

de·bauch·ery /dɪˈbɔːtʃəri/ *noun* [U] immoral behaviour involving sex, alcohol or drugs 道德败坏；淫荡；沉湎酒色（或毒品）

de·ben·ture /dɪˈbentʃə(r)/ *noun* (*finance* 财) an official document that is given by a company, showing it has borrowed money from a person and stating the interest payments that it will make to them（公司）债券

de·bili·tate /dɪˈbɪlɪteɪt/ *verb* (*formal*) **1** **~ sb/sth** to make sb's body or mind weaker 使身心衰弱；使衰竭；使虚弱: *a debilitating disease* 使人虚弱的疾病 **2** **~ sth** to make a country, an organization, etc. weaker 削弱（国家、机构等）的力量；使软弱无力: *Prolonged strike action debilitated the industry.* 长时间的罢工削弱了这个行业的活力。

de·bil·ity /dɪˈbɪləti/ *noun* [U, C] (*pl.* **-ies**) (*formal*) physical weakness, especially as a result of illness（尤指疾病引起的）体弱，虚弱，衰弱

debit /ˈdebɪt/ *noun, verb*

■ *noun* **1** a written note in a bank account or other financial record of a sum of money owed or spent 借记；借方；收方: *on the debit side of an account* 账户的借方 ◇ (*figurative*) *On the debit side* (= a negative result will be that) *the new shopping centre will increase traffic problems.* 负面影响是新购物中心会使交通问题加剧。 **2** a sum of money taken from a bank account 借项 **OPP** **credit** ➲ SEE ALSO DIRECT DEBIT ➲ WORDFINDER NOTE AT BANK

■ *verb* **~ sth** when a bank **debits** an account, it takes money from it 记入（账户）的借方；借记: *The money will be debited from your account each month.* 这笔钱将逐月记入你账户的借方。 **OPP** **credit** ➲ COLLOCATIONS AT FINANCE

'debit card *noun* a plastic card that can be used to take money directly from your bank account when you pay for sth 借记卡；借方卡 ➲ COMPARE CREDIT CARD

de·bon·air /ˌdebəˈneə(r); *NAmE* -ˈner/ *adj.* (*old-fashioned*) (usually of men 通常指男人) fashionable and confident 温雅自信的；潇洒的

de·brief /ˌdiːˈbriːf/ *verb* **~ sb (on sth)** to ask sb questions officially, in order to get information about the task that they have just completed 正式询问，盘问（某人执行任务的情况）: *He was taken to a US airbase to be debriefed on the mission.* 他被带到美国空军基地汇报执行任务情况。➲ COMPARE BRIEF *v.* (1) ▶ **de·brief·ing** *noun* [U, C]: *a debriefing session* 执行任务情况汇报会

deb·ris /ˈdebriː; ˈdeɪ-; *NAmE* dəˈbriː/ *noun* [U] **1** pieces of wood, metal, brick, etc. that are left after sth has been destroyed 残骸；碎片；破片: *Emergency teams are still clearing the debris from the plane crash.* 各抢救小组仍在清理失事飞机的残骸。 **2** (*formal*) rubbish/garbage or pieces of material that are left somewhere and are not wanted 垃圾；残渣；废弃物：*Clear away leaves and other garden debris from the pond.* 把池塘里的树叶和其他庭园垃圾清除干净。

debt /det/ *noun* **1** [C] a sum of money that sb owes 借款；欠款；债务：*I need to **pay off** all my **debts** before I leave the country.* 我得在离开该国前偿清所有债务。◇ *an outstanding debt of £300* 有待偿还的 300 英镑债务 ◇ *He had **run up** credit card **debts** of thousands of dollars.* 他积欠了数千美元的信用卡借款。 ➲ WORDFINDER NOTE AT LOAN ➲ COLLOCATIONS AT FINANCE **2** [U] the situation of owing money, especially when you cannot pay 负债情况：*He died heavily **in debt**.* 他死时负债累累。◇ *The club is £4 million **in debt**.* 这家俱乐部负债 400 万英镑。◇ *We were poor but we never **got into debt**.* 我们穷是穷，但从不负债。◇ *It's hard to stay **out of debt** when you are a student.* 当学生很难不负债。◇ *a country's foreign debt burden* 国家的外债负担 ➲ SEE ALSO BAD DEBT **3** [C, usually sing.] the fact that you should feel grateful to sb because they have helped you or been kind to you 人情债；情义；恩情：*to **owe a debt of gratitude to sb*** 欠某人的情 ◇ *I would like to acknowledge my debt to my teachers.* 我想向我的老师表达我的感激之情。

IDM **be in sb's 'debt** (*formal*) to feel grateful to sb for their help, kindness, etc. 欠某人的人情债；受某人的恩惠；感激某人

debt·or /ˈdetə(r)/ *noun* a person, a country or an organization that owes money 债务人；借方 OPP **creditor**

debug /ˌdiːˈbʌɡ/ *verb* (**-gg-**) ~ **sth** (*computing* 计) to look for and remove the faults in a computer program 排错；调试；除错

de·bug·ger /ˌdiːˈbʌɡə(r)/ *noun* a computer program that helps to find and correct mistakes in other programs 调试程序，排错程序（可帮助找出并修正其他程序中的错误）

de·bunk /ˌdiːˈbʌŋk/ *verb* ~ **sth** to show that an idea, a belief, etc. is false; to show that sth is not as good as people think it is 批判；驳斥；揭穿…的真相：*His theories have been debunked by recent research.* 最近的研究证明了他的理论不成立。

debut (*also* **début**) /ˈdeɪbjuː; ˈdebjuː; *NAmE* deɪˈbjuː/ *noun, verb*

■ ***noun*** the first public appearance of a performer or sports player （演员、运动员的）首次亮相；初次登台（或上场）：*He will **make his debut** for the first team this week.* 本周他将在第一支出场的队伍中首次亮相。◇ *the band's debut album* 这个乐队首次推出的专辑

■ ***verb*** **1** [I] (of a performer or show) to make a first public appearance （演员）首次亮相，初次登台；（表演）首次上演：*The ballet will debut next month in New York.* 这出芭蕾舞剧将于下月在纽约首演。 **2** [T] ~ **sth** (*especially NAmE, business* 商) to present a new product or advertising campaign to the market 推出，首发（新产品、广告宣传）：*They will debut the products at the trade show.* 他们将在商品展销会上推出新产品。

debu·tante /ˈdebjutɑːnt/ (*also informal* **deb**) *noun* a young, rich or UPPER-CLASS woman who is going to fashionable social events for the first time 首次进入上流社交场合的富家年轻女子

deca- /ˈdekə/ *combining form* (in nouns 构成名词) ten; having ten 十；有十的：*decathlon* 十项全能运动 ➲ COMPARE DECI-

dec·ade AW /ˈdekeɪd; dɪˈkeɪd/ *noun* a period of ten years, especially a continuous period, such as 1910–1919 or 2000–2009 十年，十年期（尤指一个年代）

deca·dence /ˈdekədəns/ *noun* [U] (*disapproving*) behaviour, attitudes, etc. which show a fall in standards, especially moral ones, and an interest in pleasure and enjoyment rather than more serious things 堕落；颓废；贪图享乐：*the decadence of modern Western society* 现代西方社会的颓废现象

deca·dent /ˈdekədənt/ *adj.* (*disapproving*) having or showing low standards, especially moral ones, and an interest only in pleasure and enjoyment rather than serious things 堕落的；颓废的；贪图享乐的：*the decadent rich* 贪图享乐的富豪 ◇ *a **decadent lifestyle/society*** 堕落的生活方式；腐朽的社会

De·caf™ (*also* **de·caff**) (*both BrE*) (*NAmE* **decaf**) /ˈdiːkæf/ *noun* [U, C] (*informal*) decaffeinated coffee 低咖（脱咖啡因咖啡）：(*BrE*) *Regular coffee or Decaf?* 你要普通咖啡还是低咖？◇ *I'll have a decaff, please.* 请给我来一杯低咖。

de·caf·fein·ated /ˌdiːˈkæfɪneɪtɪd/ *adj.* (of coffee or tea 咖啡或茶) with most or all of the CAFFEINE removed （全）脱咖啡因的 ▶ **de·caf·fein·ated** *noun* [U, C]

decal /ˈdiːkæl/ *noun* (*NAmE*) = TRANSFER (5)

deca·litre (*US* **deca·liter**, **deka·liter**) /ˈdekəliːtə(r)/ *noun* a unit for measuring volume, equal to 10 litres 十升

deca·metre (*US* **deca·meter**, **deka·meter**) /ˈdekəmiːtə(r)/ *noun* a unit for measuring length, equal to 10 metres 十米

de·camp /dɪˈkæmp/ *verb* [I] ~ (**from…**) (**to…**) to leave a place suddenly, often secretly 逃亡；潜逃

de·cant /dɪˈkænt/ *verb* ~ **sth** (**into sth**) to pour liquid, especially wine, from one container into another （把液体，尤指酒）倒入，注入

de·cant·er /dɪˈkæntə(r)/ *noun* a glass bottle, often decorated, that wine and other alcoholic drinks are poured into from an ordinary bottle before serving 雕花玻璃酒瓶

de·capi·tate /dɪˈkæpɪteɪt/ *verb* ~ **sb/sth** to cut off sb's head 杀头；斩首 SYN **behead**：*His decapitated body was found floating in a canal.* 人们发现他被斩首的尸体漂浮在一条水渠里。 ▶ **de·capi·ta·tion** /dɪˌkæpɪˈteɪʃn/ *noun* [U, C]

de·car·bon·ize (*BrE also* **-ise**) /ˌdiːˈkɑːbənaɪz; *NAmE* -ˈkɑːr-/ *verb* ~ **sth** to replace FOSSIL FUELS with a fuel that is less harmful to the environment （使用低碳环保能源取代化石燃料）降低…的碳排放，使环保：*If we decarbonize electricity then through electric cars we can decarbonize transport.* 假如我们能使用环保的方式发电，然后通过使用电动车，就可以使交通出行变得环保。 ▶ **de·car·bon·iz·ation**, **-is·ation** /diːˌkɑːbənaɪˈzeɪʃn; *NAmE* -ˌkɑːrbənə-/ *noun* [U]

deca·syl·lable /ˈdekəsɪləbl/ *noun* (*specialist*) a line of poetry with ten syllables 十音节诗行 ▶ **deca·syl·lab·ic** /ˌdekəsɪˈlæbɪk/ *adj.*：*a decasyllabic line* 十音节诗行

dec·ath·lete /dɪˈkæθliːt/ *noun* a person who competes in a decathlon 十项全能运动员

dec·ath·lon /dɪˈkæθlən/ *noun* a sporting event in which people compete in ten different sports 十项全能运动 ➲ COMPARE BIATHLON, HEPTATHLON, PENTATHLON, TRIATHLON

decay /dɪˈkeɪ/ *noun, verb*

■ ***noun*** [U] **1** the process or result of being destroyed by natural causes or by not being cared for (= of decaying) 腐烂；腐朽：*tooth decay* 蛀牙 ◇ *The landlord had let the building **fall into decay**.* 房东任由房子变得破烂不堪。◇ *The smell of death and decay hung over the town.* 城镇上空弥漫着死亡和腐烂的气味。 **2** the gradual destruction of a society, an institution, a system, etc. （社会、机构、制度等的）衰败，衰退，衰落：***economic/moral/urban decay*** 经济衰退；道德败坏；城市衰落 ◇ *the decay of the old industries* 旧工业的衰败

■ ***verb*** **1** [I, T] ~ (**sth**) to be destroyed gradually by natural processes; to destroy sth in this way （使）腐烂，腐朽 SYN **rot**：*decaying leaves/teeth/food* 烂叶；蛀齿；腐烂食物 **2** [I] if a building or an area **decays**, its condition slowly becomes worse （建筑、地方等）破败，衰落，衰败：*decaying inner city areas* 衰败中的内城区 **3** [I] to become less powerful and lose influence over people, society, etc. （力量、影响等）衰弱，衰退，衰减：*decaying standards of morality* 日趋低下的道德标准

de·cease /dɪˈsiːs/ *noun* [U] (*law* 律 or *formal*) the death of a person 死亡；亡故

de·ceased /dɪˈsiːst/ *adj.* (*law* 律 or *formal*) **1** dead 死去了的；已死的；亡故的：*her deceased parents* 她已故的双亲 **2 the deceased** *noun* (*pl.* **the deceased**) a person who has died, especially recently 死者；已故者

de·ceit /dɪˈsiːt/ *noun* [U, C] dishonest behaviour that is intended to make sb believe sth that is not true; an example of this behaviour 欺骗，欺诈（行为）；诡计 **SYN deception**: *He was accused of lies and deceit.* 他被指控撒谎和欺诈。◇ *Everyone was involved in this web of deceit.* 所有人都牵涉到这起诈骗勾当之中了。◇ *Their marriage was an illusion and a deceit.* 他们的婚姻是虚假的、不真实的。

de·ceit·ful /dɪˈsiːtfl/ *adj.* (*formal*) behaving in a dishonest way by telling lies and making people believe things that are not true 不诚实的；骗人的 **SYN dishonest** ▸ **de·ceit·ful·ly** /-fəli/ *adv.* **de·ceit·ful·ness** *noun* [U]

de·ceive /dɪˈsiːv/ *verb* **1** [T] to make sb believe sth that is not true 欺骗；蒙骗；诓骗：**~ sb** *Her husband had been deceiving her for years.* 她丈夫多年来一直在欺骗她。◇ **~ sb into doing sth** *She deceived him into handing over all his savings.* 她把他所有的积蓄都骗了出来。➲ SYNONYMS AT CHEAT **2** [T] **~ yourself (that…)** to refuse to admit to yourself that sth unpleasant is true 欺骗（自己）：*You're deceiving yourself if you think he'll change his mind.* 如果你认为他会改变主意，那你是在欺骗自己。 **3** [T, I] **~ (sb)** to make sb have a wrong idea about sb/sth 使人误信；误导 **SYN mislead**: *Unless my eyes deceive me, that's his wife.* 如果我没有看错的话，那是他的妻子。➲ SEE ALSO DECEPTIVE ▸ **de·ceiver** *noun* **IDM** SEE FLATTER

> **WORD FAMILY**
> deceive *verb*
> deceit *noun*
> deceitful *adj.*
> deception *noun*
> deceptive *adj.*

de·cel·er·ate /ˌdiːˈseləreɪt/ *verb* (*formal*) **1** [I, T] **~ (sth)** to reduce the speed at which a vehicle is travelling （使）减速行驶；降低运行速度 **2** [I, T] **~ (sth)** to become or make sth become slower （使）减缓，变慢 **SYN slow down**: *Economic growth decelerated sharply in June.* 六月份经济增长大幅度减缓。 **OPP accelerate** ▸ **de·cel·er·ation** /ˌdiːseləˈreɪʃn/ *noun* [U]

De·cem·ber /dɪˈsembə(r)/ *noun* [U, C] (*abbr.* **Dec.**) the 12th and last month of the year 十二月 **HELP** To see how **December** is used, look at the examples at **April**. * December 的用法见词条 April 下的示例。

de·cency /ˈdiːsnsi/ *noun* **1** [U] honest, polite behaviour that follows accepted moral standards and shows respect for others 正派；得体；彬彬有礼：*Her behaviour showed a total lack of* ***common decency.*** 她的举止显示她连起码的礼节都不懂。◇ *Have you no* ***sense of decency?*** 你礼貌都不懂吗？◇ *He might* ***have had the decency to*** *apologize.* 他其实应该道个歉的。 **2 the decencies** [pl.] (*formal*) standards of behaviour in society that people think are acceptable 礼仪；行为准则：*the basic decencies of civilized society* 文明社会的基本行为准则

de·cent /ˈdiːsnt/ *adj.* **1** of a good enough standard or quality 像样的；相当不错的；尚好的：(*informal*) *a decent meal/job/place to live* 相当不错的饭菜 / 工作 / 住所 ◇ *I need a decent night's sleep.* 我需要好好地睡上一夜。 **2** (of people or behaviour 人或行为举止) honest and fair; treating people with respect 正派的；公平的；合乎礼节的：*ordinary, decent, hard-working people* 勤劳、正派的普通人 ◇ *Everyone said he was a decent sort of guy.* 人人都说他是个品行端正的小伙子。 **3** acceptable to people in a particular situation 得体的；合宜的；适当的：*a decent burial* 体面的葬礼 ◇ *That dress isn't decent.* 那件连衣裙不够雅观。◇ *She ought to have waited for a decent interval before getting married again.* 她再次嫁人也应该适当等上一段时间。 **4** (*informal*) wearing enough clothes to allow sb to see you 穿好了衣服的；适宜于见人的：*I can't go to the door—I'm not decent.* 我不能去开门，我还没穿好衣服。➲ COMPARE INDECENT ▸ **de·cent·ly** *adv.*
IDM **to do the decent ˈthing** to do what people or society expect, especially in a difficult situation （尤指在困境中）做人心所向的事，做体面事：*He did the decent thing and resigned.* 他做得很体面，辞职了。

de·cen·tral·ize (*BrE also* **-ise**) /ˌdiːˈsentrəlaɪz/ *verb* [T, I] **~ (sth)** to give some of the power of a central government, organization, etc. to smaller parts or organizations around the country 分散，下放（权力）；将…的权力下放：*decentralized authority/administration* 下放了的权力 / 行政权 **OPP centralize** ▸ **de·cen·tral·iza·tion, -isa·tion** /ˌdiːˌsentrəlaɪˈzeɪʃn; *NAmE* -ləˈz-/ *noun* [U, sing.]

de·cep·tion /dɪˈsepʃn/ *noun* **1** [U] the act of deliberately making sb believe sth that is not true (= of DECEIVING them) 欺骗；蒙骗；诓骗 **SYN deceit**: *a drama full of lies and deception* 充满谎言和欺骗的一出戏 ◇ *He was accused of obtaining property by deception.* 他被指控骗取钱财。 **2** [C] a trick intended to make sb believe sth that is not true 诡计；骗术；骗局 **SYN deceit**: *The whole episode had been a cruel deception.* 这起事件从头到尾就是一个残酷的骗局。

de·cep·tive /dɪˈseptɪv/ *adj.* likely to make you believe sth that is not true 欺骗性的；误导的；骗人的 **SYN misleading**: *a deceptive advertisement* 虚假广告 ◇ *Appearances can often be deceptive* (= things are not always what they seem to be). 外表常常靠不住。◇ *the deceptive simplicity of her writing style* (= it seems simple but is not really) 她那看似简单实则不然的写作风格 ▸ **de·cep·tive·ly** *adv.*: *a deceptively simple idea* 貌似简单的想法

deci- /ˈdesɪ/ *combining form* (in nouns; often used in units of measurement 构成名词，常用于计量单位) one tenth 十分之一：*decilitre* 分升 ➲ COMPARE DECA-

deci·bel /ˈdesɪbel/ *noun* a unit for measuring how loud a sound is 分贝（声音强度的单位）

de·cide /dɪˈsaɪd/ *verb* **1** [I, T] to think carefully about the different possibilities that are available and choose one of them 对…作出抉择；决定；选定：*It's up to you to decide.* 这事由你来决定吧。◇ **~ between A and B** *It was difficult to decide between the two candidates.* 很难在这两个候选人之间决定取舍。◇ **~ against sth** *They decided against taking legal action.* 他们决定不提起诉讼。◇ **~ what, whether, etc.…** *I can't decide what to wear.* 我拿不定主意穿什么。◇ **~ (that)…** *She decided (that) she wanted to live in France.* 她决定要住在法国。◇ **~ to do sth** *We've decided not to go away after all.* 我们到底还是决定不离开。◇ **~ sth** *We might be hiring more people but nothing has been decided yet.* 我们或许会再多雇些人，不过现在什么都还没定下来。◇ **it is decided (that)…** *It was decided (that) the school should purchase new software.* 已经决定学校要购买新软件。➲ MORE LIKE THIS 26, page R28 **2** [T, I] (*law* 律) to make an official or legal judgement 裁决；判决：**~ sth** *The case will be decided by a jury.* 这案件将由陪审团裁决。◇ **~ for/in favour of sb | ~ in sb's favour** *The Appeal Court decided in their favour.* 上诉法院作出了有利于他们的裁定。◇ **~ against sb** *It is always possible that the judge may decide against you.* 法官判你败诉总是有可能的。 **3** [T, I] to affect the result of sth 影响（或决定）…的结果：**~ (sth)** *A mixture of skill and good luck decided the outcome of the game.* 技术和运气结合在一起决定了比赛的结果。◇ **~ if, whether, etc.…** *A number of factors decide whether a movie will be successful or not.* 一部电影成功与否是由许多因素决定的。 **4** [T] to be the reason why sb does sth 成为（某人）做某事的原因：*For most customers, price is* ***the deciding factor.*** 对大多数顾客来说，价格是决定性因素。◇ **~ sb (to do sth)** *They offered me free accommodation for a year, and that decided me.* 他们愿意免费为我提供一年的住宿，这就使我下定了决心。

> **WORD FAMILY**
> decide *verb*
> decision *noun* (≠ indecision)
> decisive *adj.* (≠ indecisive)
> undecided *adj.*

PHR V **deˈcide on/upon sth** to choose sth from a number of possibilities 决定；选定：*We're still trying to decide on a venue.* 我们仍然在设法选定一个会场。

de·cided /dɪˈsaɪdɪd/ *adj.* **1** [only before noun] obvious and definite 明显的；明白无误的；确实无疑的：*His height was a decided advantage in the job.* 干这项工作，他的身高是明显优势。**2** (*especially BrE*) having very strong opinions 坚定的；坚决的：*She was a very decided young woman, eager to do some good in the world.* 她是一个非常坚定的年轻女子，渴望在世上做点有益的事。◇ *The child is very decided about what she wants and doesn't want.* 这孩子对她想要和不想要的东西非常有主见。➲ COMPARE UNDECIDED

de·cided·ly /dɪˈsaɪdɪdli/ *adv.* **1** (used with an adjective or adverb 与形容词或副词连用) definitely and in an obvious way 确实；肯定；显然：*Amy was looking decidedly worried.* 埃米看上去显然是忧心忡忡。**2** in a way that shows that you are sure and determined about sth 果断地；坚决地；坚定地：*'I won't go,' she said decidedly.* "我不去。"她果断地说。

de·cider /dɪˈsaɪdə(r)/ *noun* [usually sing.] the game, race, etc. that will decide who the winner is in a competition 决胜局；决赛

de·cidu·ous /dɪˈsɪdʒuəs; -dju-/ *adj.* (of a tree, bush etc. 树、灌木等) that loses its leaves every year 落叶的 ➲ COMPARE EVERGREEN ➲ VISUAL VOCAB PAGE V10

decile /ˈdesaɪl; *NAmE also* ˈdesl/ *noun* (*statistics* 统计) one of ten equal groups into which a collection of things or people can be divided according to the DISTRIBUTION of a particular VARIABLE 十分位数：*families in the top decile of income* (= the 10% of families with the highest income) 收入排在前十分位的家庭

deci·litre (*especially US* **deci·liter**) /ˈdesɪliːtə(r)/ *noun* a unit for measuring liquids. There are 10 decilitres in a litre. 分升；十分之一升

deci·mal /ˈdesɪml/ *adj., noun*

■ ***adj.*** based on or counted in tens or tenths 十进位的；小数的：*the decimal system* 十进制

■ ***noun*** (*also* ˌ**decimal ˈfraction**) a FRACTION (= a number less than one) that is shown as a dot or point followed by the number of tenths, HUNDREDTHS, etc. 小数：*The decimal 0.61 stands for 61 hundredths.* 小数 0.61 代表 61%。➲ COMPARE VULGAR FRACTION

deci·mal·ize (*BrE also* **-ise**) /ˈdesɪməlaɪz/ *verb* **1** ~ **sth** to change a system of coins or weights and measurements to a decimal system 把（币制或度量衡）改为十进制 **2** ~ **sth** to express an amount using the decimal system instead of the system it is already expressed in 把（数量）化为小数：*The question asks you to decimalize the fraction ⅞.* 这道题要求你将分数 ⅞ 化为小数。▸ **deci·mal·iza·tion**, **-isa·tion** /ˌdesɪməlaɪˈzeɪʃn; *NAmE* -ləˈz-/ *noun* [U]

ˌ**decimal ˈplace** *noun* the position of a number after a decimal point 小数位：*The figure is* ***accurate to two decimal places.*** 这个数精确到小数点后两位。

ˌ**decimal ˈpoint** *noun* a dot or point used to separate the whole number from the tenths, HUNDREDTHS, etc. of a decimal, for example in 0.61 小数点

deci·mate /ˈdesɪmeɪt/ *verb* **1** [usually passive] ~ **sth** to kill large numbers of animals, plants or people in a particular area 大量毁灭，大批杀死（某地区的动物、植物或人）：*The rabbit population was decimated by the disease.* 这种疾病使大批兔子死亡。**2** ~ **sth** (*informal*) to severely damage sth or make sth weaker 严重破坏；大大削弱：*Cheap imports decimated the British cycle industry.* 廉价进口产品严重削弱了英国的自行车工业。▸ **deci·ma·tion** /ˌdesɪˈmeɪʃn/ *noun* [U]

deci·metre (*especially US* **deci·meter**) /ˈdesɪmiːtə(r)/ *noun* a unit for measuring length. There are 10 decimetres in a metre. 分米；十分之一米

de·cipher /dɪˈsaɪfə(r)/ *verb* ~ **sth** to succeed in finding the meaning of sth that is difficult to read or understand 破译，辨认（难认、难解的东西）：*to decipher a code* 破译密码 ◇ *Can anyone decipher his handwriting?* 有谁能辨认他的字迹？➲ SEE ALSO INDECIPHERABLE

de·ci·sion 🔑 /dɪˈsɪʒn/ *noun* **1** [C] ~ (**on/about sth**) | ~ (**to do sth**) a choice or judgement that you make after thinking and talking about what is the best thing to do （作出的）决定，抉择：*to* ***make a decision*** (= to decide) 作出决定 ◇ (*BrE*) *to* ***take a decision*** (= to decide) 作出决定 ◇ *We need a decision on this by next week.* 我们得在下周前就这一问题作出决定。◇ *Who* ***took the decision*** *to go ahead with the project?* 是谁决定开始这项工程的？◇ *He is really bad at* ***making decisions.*** 他的确不善于决策。◇ *We finally* ***reached a decision*** (= decided after some difficulty). 我们终于作出了抉择。◇ *We must* ***come to a decision*** *about what to do next by tomorrow.* 我们必须最晚明天就下一步做什么作出决定。◇ *a big* (= an important) *decision* 一项重大的抉择 ◇ *The final decision is yours.* 最终的决定权属于你。◇ *It's a difficult decision for any doctor.* 这对任何医生来说都是一个困难的决定。◇ *The editor's decision is final.* 编辑定了就不再改了。◇ *Mary is the decision-maker in the house.* 家里的事玛丽说了算。**2** (*also* **de·cisive·ness**) [U] the ability to decide sth clearly and quickly 决断（力）；果断：*This is not a job for someone who lacks decision.* 不果断的人不适宜做这工作。OPP **indecision** **3** [U] the process of deciding sth 作决定；决策：*The moment of decision had arrived.* 决策的时刻已经到了。

deˈcision-making *noun* [U] the process of deciding about sth important, especially in a group of people or in an organization 决策 ▸ **deˈcision-maker** *noun*

de·cisive /dɪˈsaɪsɪv/ *adj.* **1** very important for the final result of a particular situation 决定性的；关键的：*a* ***decisive factor/victory/battle*** 决定性的因素 / 胜利 / 战役 ◇ *She has* ***played a decisive role*** *in the peace negotiations.* 她在和谈中起了关键作用。◇ *a* ***decisive step*** (= an important action that will change a situation) *towards a cleaner environment* 朝着更清洁的环境迈出的关键一步 ➲ SYNONYMS AT ESSENTIAL **2** able to decide sth quickly and with confidence 坚决的；果断的；决断的：*decisive management* 果断的管理层 ◇ *The government must take* ***decisive action*** *on gun control.* 政府必须在枪支管制方面采取果断措施。OPP **indecisive** ▸ **de·cisive·ly** *adv.*

de·cisive·ness /dɪˈsaɪsɪvnəs/ *noun* [U] = DECISION (2)

deck /dek/ *noun, verb*

■ ***noun*** **1** the top outside floor of a ship or boat 甲板；舱面：*I was the only person* ***on deck*** *at that time of night.* 夜里当时只有我一个人在甲板上。◇ *As the storm began, everyone disappeared* ***below deck(s).*** 暴风雨来临时，所有的人都躲到甲板下面去了。**2** one of the floors of a ship or a bus （船或公共汽车的）一层，层面：*the* ***upper/lower/main deck*** *of a ship* 船的上层 / 下层 / 主甲板 ◇ *We sat on the top deck of the bus.* 我们坐在公共汽车的上层。◇ *My cabin is on deck C.* 我的舱位在 C 层甲板。➲ SEE ALSO DOUBLE-DECKER (1), FLIGHT DECK, SINGLE-DECKER **3** (*also* ˌ**deck of ˈcards**) (*both especially NAmE*) (*especially BrE* **pack**) a complete set of 52 PLAYING CARDS 一副（为 52 张）➲ VISUAL VOCAB PAGE V41 **4** a wooden floor that is built outside the back of a house where you can sit and relax （屋后供休憩的）木制平台 ➲ VISUAL VOCAB PAGE V20 **5** a part of a SOUND SYSTEM that records and/or plays sounds on a disc or tape （唱机的）转盘装置；（音响系统的）走带机构，录音座：*a cassette/tape deck* 磁带转动机械装置 IDM SEE CLEAR *v.*, HAND *n.*, HIT *v.*

■ ***verb*** **1** [often passive] ~ **sb/sth** (**out**) (**in/with sth**) to decorate sb/sth with sth 装饰；布置；打扮：*The room was decked out in flowers and balloons.* 房间里装点着鲜花和气球。**2** ~ **sb** (*informal*) to hit sb very hard so that they fall to the ground 用力击倒；打倒在地；揍趴下

deck·chair /ˈdektʃeə(r); *NAmE* -tʃer/ *noun* a folding chair with a seat made from a long strip of material on a wooden or metal frame, used for example on a beach （沙滩等处用的）帆布折叠椅 ➲ VISUAL VOCAB PAGE V20

deck·hand /ˈdekhænd/ *noun* a worker on a ship who does work that is not skilled 舱面水手；普通水手

deck·ing /ˈdekɪŋ/ *noun* [U] wood used to build a floor (called a DECK) in the garden/yard next to or near a house （房屋外的）平台木板

ˈ**deck shoe** *noun* a flat shoe made of strong cloth or soft leather, with a soft SOLE which does not slip 平底帆布鞋，平底软皮鞋（鞋底防滑）

D

de·claim /dɪˈkleɪm/ *verb* [T, I] **~ (against) sth | ~ that... | + speech** (*formal*) to say sth loudly; to speak loudly and with force about sth you feel strongly about, especially in public （尤指在公众前）慷慨激昂地宣讲，慷慨陈词：*She declaimed the famous opening speech of the play.* 她慷慨激昂地朗诵了这出戏中著名的开场白。◇ *He declaimed against the evils of alcohol.* 他慷慨陈词，猛烈抨击酗酒的罪恶。

dec·lam·ation /ˌdekləˈmeɪʃn/ *noun* (*formal*) **1** [U] the act of speaking or of expressing sth to an audience in a formal way 朗诵；雄辩 **2** [C] a speech or piece of writing that strongly expresses feelings and opinions 慷慨激昂的演说（词）

de·clama·tory /dɪˈklæmətəri; *NAmE* -tɔːri/ *adj.* (*formal*) expressing feelings or opinions in a strong way in a speech or a piece of writing 慷慨陈词的；雄辩演说的

dec·lar·ation /ˌdekləˈreɪʃn/ *noun* **1** [C, U] an official or formal statement, especially about the plans of a government or an organization; the act of making such a statement 公告；宣告；宣言：*to **issue/sign a declaration*** 发布 / 签署公告 ◇ *the declaration of war* 宣战 ◇ *the Declaration of Independence* (= of the United States) （美国）独立宣言 **2** [C] a written or spoken statement, especially about what people feel or believe 声明（书）；宣布；表白；宣称：*a **declaration of love/faith/guilt*** 表白爱情；表达信念；宣判有罪 ➲ SYNONYMS AT STATEMENT **3** [C] an official written statement giving information 申报（单）：*a declaration of income* 收益申报表 ◇ *customs declarations* (= giving details of goods that have been brought into a country) 报关单（带入境内物品的详细清单）

de·clara·tive /dɪˈklærətɪv/ *adj.* (*grammar* 语法) (of a sentence 句子) in the form of a simple statement 陈述的

de·clare 🔑 /dɪˈkleə(r); *NAmE* dɪˈkler/ *verb* **1** 🔑 [T] to say sth officially or publicly 公布；宣布；宣告：**~ sth** *The government has declared a state of emergency.* 政府已宣布进入紧急状态。◇ *Germany **declared war on** France on 1 August 1914.* 德国在 1914 年 8 月 1 日向法国宣战。◇ *The government has **declared war on** (= officially stated its intention to stop) illiteracy.* 政府已宣布要扫除文盲。◇ **~ that...** *The court declared that strike action was illegal.* 法庭宣判罢工为非法。◇ **~ sth + noun** *The area has been declared a national park.* 这地区已宣布为国家公园。◇ **~ sth to be sth** *The painting was declared to be a forgery.* 这幅画被判定为赝品。◇ **~ sth + adj.** *The contract was declared void.* 这份合同被宣布无效。◇ *I declare this bridge open.* 我宣布这座大桥正式启用。 **2** 🔑 [T] to state sth firmly and clearly 表明；宣称；断言：**+ speech** *'I'll do it!' Tom declared.* "让我来！"汤姆果断地说。◇ **~ that...** *He declared that he was in love with her.* 他声称他已爱上她。◇ **~ sth** *Few people dared to declare their opposition to the regime.* 很少有人敢宣称他们反对这个政权。◇ **~ yourself + adj./noun** *She declared herself extremely hurt by his lack of support.* 她说自己非常伤心，因为没有得到他的支持。 **3** 🔑 [T] **~ sth** to tell the tax authorities how much money you have earned 申报（收益）：*All income must be declared.* 所有收益必须申报。 **4** 🔑 [T] **~ sth** to tell customs officers (= at the border of a country) that you are carrying goods on which you should pay tax 申报（应纳税物品）：*Do you have anything to declare?* 你有什么要申报的吗？ **5** [I] (in CRICKET 板球) to decide to end your INNINGS (= the period during which your team is BATTING) before all your players have BATTED （在击球员还未全部出局时）宣布结束赛局，宣布停止击球

PHR V **deˌclare aˈgainst sb/sth** (*formal*) to say publicly that you do not support sb/sth 声明反对；表示不赞成 **deˈclare for sb/sth** (*formal*) to say publicly that you support sb/sth 声明支持；表示赞成

▼ **SYNONYMS** 同义词辨析

declare

state • indicate • announce

These words all mean to say sth, usually firmly and clearly and often in public. 以上各词均含表明、宣称、宣布之义。

declare (*rather formal*) to say sth officially or publicly; to state sth firmly and clearly 指公布、宣布、表明、宣称：*to declare war* 宣战 ◇ *The painting was declared to be a forgery.* 这幅画被判定为赝品。

state (*rather formal*) to formally write or say sth, especially in a careful and clear way 指陈述、说明、声明：*He has already stated his intention to run for election.* 他已声明打算参加竞选。

indicate (*rather formal*) to state sth, sometimes in a way that is slightly indirect 指表明、暗示：*During our meeting, he indicated his willingness to cooperate.* 在我们会晤期间，他提及了合作的意愿。

announce to tell people officially about a decision or plans; to give information about sth in a public place, especially through a loudspeaker; to say sth in a loud and/or serious way 指宣布、宣告、（通过广播）通知：*They haven't formally announced their engagement yet.* 他们还没有正式宣布订婚。◇ *Has our flight been announced yet?* 广播通知了我们的航班没有？

DECLARE OR ANNOUNCE? 用 declare 还是 announce?

Declare is used more often for giving judgements; **announce** is used more often for giving facts. * declare 较常用于表明意见、看法；announce 较常用于说明事实：~~The painting was announced to be a forgery.~~ ◇ ~~They haven't formally declared their engagement yet.~~

PATTERNS

- to declare/state/indicate/announce **that...**
- to declare/state sb/sth **to be** sth
- to declare/state/indicate/announce **your intention** to do sth
- to declare/state/announce sth **formally/publicly/officially**
- to declare/state/announce sth **firmly/confidently**

de·clared /dɪˈkleəd; *NAmE* -ˈklerd/ *adj.* [only before noun] stated in an open way so that people know about it 公开宣布（或声明、表态）的 **SYN** **professed**: *the government's declared intention to reduce crime* 政府公开宣布的减少犯罪的计划

de·clas·sify /ˌdiːˈklæsɪfaɪ/ *verb* (**de·clas·si·fies, de·clas·si·fy·ing, de·clas·si·fied, de·clas·si·fied**) **~ sth** to state officially that secret government information is no longer secret 将（政府机密文件）解密：*declassified **information/documents*** 已解密的情报 / 文件 **OPP** **classify** ▸ **de·clas·si·fi·ca·tion** /ˌdiːˌklæsɪfɪˈkeɪʃn/ *noun* [U]

de·clen·sion /dɪˈklenʃn/ *noun* (*grammar* 语法) **1** [C] a set of nouns, adjectives or pronouns that change in the same way to show CASE, number and GENDER （名词、形容词或代词显示性、数、格的）变格 **2** [U] the way in which some sets of nouns, adjectives and pronouns change their form or endings to show CASE, number or GENDER （名词、形容词和代词显示性、数、格的）词形变化

de·cline 🔑 **AW** /dɪˈklaɪn/ *noun, verb*

■ ***noun*** 🔑 [C, usually sing., U] **~ (in sth) | ~ (of sth)** a continuous decrease in the number, value, quality, etc. of sth （数量、价值、质量等的）减少，下降，衰落，衰退：*a **rapid/sharp/gradual decline*** 迅速 / 急剧 / 逐渐下降 ◇ ***urban/economic decline*** 城市衰落；经济衰退 ◇ *The company reported a small decline in its profits.* 公司报告其

利润略有减少。◇ *An increase in cars has resulted in the decline of public transport.* 小汽车的增加导致了公共交通的减少。◇ *The town* ***fell into*** *(**a**)* ***decline*** (= started to be less busy, important, etc.) *after the mine closed.* 这个镇在矿井关闭后开始衰落。◇ *Industry in Britain has been* ***in decline*** *since the 1970s.* 英国工业自 20 世纪 70 年代以来一直在走下坡路。 ➲WORDFINDER NOTE AT TREND

■*verb* **1** [I] (*rather formal*) to become smaller, fewer, weaker, etc. 减少；下降；衰弱；衰退： *Support for the party continues to decline.* 对该党的支持继续下降。◇ *The number of tourists to the resort declined by 10% last year.* 去年到这个胜地旅游的人数减少了 10%。◇ *Her health was declining rapidly.* 她的健康状况迅速恶化。 **2** [I, T] (*formal*) to refuse politely to accept or to do sth 谢绝；婉言拒绝 SYN **refuse**[1]: *I offered to give them a lift but they declined.* 我主动提议开车送他们，但他们婉言谢绝了。◇ **~ sth** *to* ***decline an offer/invitation*** 谢绝对方的主动帮助 / 邀请 ◇ **~ to do sth** *Their spokesman declined to comment on the allegations.* 他们的发言人拒绝对这些指控加以评论。 **3** [I, T] **~ (sth)** (*grammar* 语法) if a noun, an adjective or a pronoun **declines**, it has different forms according to whether it is the subject or the object of a verb, whether it is in the singular or plural, etc. When you **decline** a noun, etc., you list these forms. （根据名词、形容词或代词在句中的作用）变格，使发生词形变化 ➲ COMPARE CONJUGATE

IDM **sb's declining 'years** (*literary*) the last years of sb's life 暮年；晚年

de·clut·ter (*also* **de-clutter**) /diːˈklʌtə(r)/ *verb* [I, T] to remove things that you do not use so that you have more space and can easily find things when you need them 清除，清理（无用杂物）： *Moving is a good opportunity to declutter.* 搬家是清理无用杂物的好时机。◇ **~ sth** *a 7-step plan to help you declutter your home* 帮你把家清理干净的 7 步骤计划

de·code /ˌdiːˈkəʊd; *NAmE* -ˈkoʊd/ *verb* **1 ~ sth** to find the meaning of sth, especially sth that has been written in code 解（码）；破译（尤指密码） SYN **decipher 2 ~ sth** to receive an electronic signal and change it into pictures that can be shown on a television screen 译解（电子信号）： *decoding equipment* 电子信号译码设备 **3 ~ sth** (*linguistics* 语言) to understand the meaning of sth in a foreign language 译解，理解（外文） ➲COMPARE ENCODE

de·coder /ˌdiːˈkəʊdə(r); *NAmE* -ˈkoʊ-/ *noun* a device that changes an electronic signal into a form that people can understand, such as sound and pictures （电子信号）解码器，译码器： *a* ***satellite/video decoder*** 卫星 / 视频解码器

dé·col·le·tage /ˌdeɪkɒlˈtɑːʒ; *NAmE* -kɑːləˈt-/ (*also* **dé·col·leté** /deɪˈkɒlteɪ; *NAmE* ˌdeɪkɑːlˈteɪ/) *noun* (*from French*) the top edge of a woman's dress, etc. that is designed to be very low in order to show her shoulders and the top part of her breasts （女装的）低胸露肩领 ▸ **dé·col·leté** *adj.*

de·col·on·iza·tion (*BrE also* **-isa·tion**) /diːˌkɒlənaɪˈzeɪʃn; *NAmE* -ˌkɑːlənəˈz-/ *noun* [U] the process of a COLONY or COLONIES becoming independent 非殖民（地）化；殖民地独立

de·com·mis·sion /ˌdiːkəˈmɪʃn/ *verb* **~ sth** to officially stop using weapons, a nuclear power station, etc. 正式停止使用（武器、核电站等）

de·com·pose /ˌdiːkəmˈpəʊz; *NAmE* -ˈpoʊz/ *verb* **1** [I, T] to be destroyed gradually by natural chemical processes 腐烂 SYN **decay, rot**: *a decomposing corpse* 正在腐烂的尸体 ◇ *As the waste materials decompose, they produce methane gas.* 废物腐烂时会产生沼气。◇ **~ sth** *a decomposed body* 已经腐烂了的尸体 **2** [T, I] **~ (sth) (into sth)** (*specialist*) to divide sth into smaller parts; to divide into smaller parts （使）分解 ▸ **de·com·pos·ition** /ˌdiːkɒmpəˈzɪʃn; *NAmE* -kɑːm-/ *noun* [U]: *the decomposition of organic waste* 有机垃圾的分解

de·com·press /ˌdiːkəmˈpres/ *verb* **1** [I, T] **~ (sth)** to have the air pressure in sth reduced to a normal level or to reduce it to its normal level （使）减压；（给）卸压 **2** [T] **~ sth** (*computing* 计) to return files, etc. to their original size after they have been COMPRESSED 解压缩（将压缩文件等恢复到原大小） OPP **compress**

de·com·pres·sion /ˌdiːkəmˈpreʃn/ *noun* [U] **1** a reduction in air pressure; the act of reducing the pressure of the air 减压；卸压： *a* ***decompression chamber*** (= a piece of equipment that DIVERS sit in so that they can return slowly to normal air pressure after being deep in the sea) 减压舱（潜水员深海作业后坐在其中恢复到正常气压）◇ ***decompression sickness*** (= severe pain and difficulty in breathing experienced by DIVERS who come back to the surface of deep water too quickly) 减压病（潜水员从深水迅速回到水面后感到的剧痛和呼吸困难） ➲SEE ALSO BEND *n.* (2) **2** (*specialist*) the act or process of allowing sth that has been compressed (= made smaller) to fill the space that it originally took up 解压缩（将压缩的东西恢复到原状）

de·com·pres·sor /ˌdiːkəmˈpresə(r)/ *noun* (*BrE*) **1** (*specialist*) a device for reducing pressure in a vehicle's engine （机动车发动机的）减压装置，减压器 **2** (*computing* 计) a computer program which returns files, etc. to their original size after they have been COMPRESSED 解压缩程序

de·con·gest·ant /ˌdiːkənˈdʒestənt/ *noun* a medicine that helps sb with a cold to breathe more easily 减充血药： *a nasal decongestant* 鼻塞通药

de·con·se·crate /ˌdiːˈkɒnsɪkreɪt; *NAmE* -ˈkɑːn-/ *verb* **~ sth** (*religion* 宗) to stop using sth, especially a building, for a religious purpose 停止把（建筑物等）用于宗教目的；把…改作俗用： *a deconsecrated church* 改作俗用的教堂 ▸ **de·con·se·cra·tion** /ˌdiːˌkɒnsɪˈkreɪʃn; *NAmE* -ˌkɑːn-/ *noun* [U]

de·con·struct /ˌdiːkənˈstrʌkt/ *verb* **1 ~ sth** (*specialist*) (in literature and philosophy 文学和哲学) to analyse a text in order to show that there is no fixed meaning within the text but that the meaning is created each time in the act of reading 解构（文本没有固定意义，只有在阅读中才获得意义） **2 ~ sth (into sth)** to separate sth into the parts from which it is made up and put them together again in a different way 拆分后重组： *Picasso deconstructed his subjects into cubes and colours.* 毕加索将他的表现对象拆解重组为一个个小方块和不同的颜色。◇ *deconstructed lasagne* 散煮千层面

de·con·struc·tion /ˌdiːkənˈstrʌkʃn/ *noun* [U] (*specialist*) (in literature and philosophy 文学和哲学) a theory that states that it is impossible for a text to have one fixed meaning, and emphasizes the role of the reader in the production of meaning 解构理论（文本不可能只有一个固定含义，强调读者在意义发生过程中的作用） ➲ COMPARE STRUCTURALISM ▸ **de·con·struc·tion·ist** *noun, adj.*： *a deconstructionist critic/approach* 解构主义评论家 / 方法

de·con·tam·in·ate /ˌdiːkənˈtæmɪneɪt/ *verb* **~ sth** to remove harmful substances from a place or thing 清除有害物质；排除…的污染： *the process of decontaminating areas exposed to radioactivity* 清除受放射污染地区有害物质的过程 ▸ **de·con·tam·in·ation** /ˌdiːkənˌtæmɪˈneɪʃn/ *noun* [U]

de·con·trol /ˌdiːkənˈtrəʊl; *NAmE* -ˈtroʊl/ *verb* (**-ll-**) **~ sth** (*formal, especially NAmE*) if a government **decontrols** sth, it removes legal controls from it 解除对…的控制；撤销对…的管制 SYN **deregulate** ▸ **de·con·trol** *noun* [U]

decor /ˈdeɪkɔː(r); *NAmE* deɪˈkɔːr/ *noun* [U, C, usually sing.] the style in which the inside of a building is decorated （建筑内部的）装饰布局，装饰风格： *interior decor* 室内装饰风格 ◇ *the restaurant's elegant new decor* 餐馆内部雅致的新装潢

dec·or·ate /ˈdekəreɪt/ *verb* **1** [T] **~ sth (with sth)** to make sth look more attractive by putting things on it 装饰；装潢： *They decorated the room with flowers and balloons.* 他们用花和气球装饰了房间。◇ *The cake was decorated to look like a car.* 这蛋糕装饰得像一辆汽车。 **2** [I, T] (*especially BrE*) to put paint, WALLPAPER, etc. on the walls and ceilings of a room or house 粉刷；油漆；糊墙纸： *I hate decorating.* 我讨厌粉刷墙壁。◇ *He has his* *own painting and decorating business.* 他经营自己的油漆和粉刷墙壁生意。◇ **~ sth** *We need to decorate the sitting room.* 我们需要将客厅粉刷一下。◇ *The sitting room needs decorating.* 客厅需要粉刷。 **3** [T] **~ sth** to be placed on sth in order to make it look more attractive 点缀；装点 **SYN adorn**: *Photographs of actors decorated the walls of the restaurant.* 演员的照片装点着餐馆的墙壁。 **4** [T, usually passive] **~ sb (for sth)** to give sb a MEDAL as a sign of respect for sth they have done 授给（某人）勋章（或奖章）

dec·or·ation /ˌdekəˈreɪʃn/ *noun* **1** [C, usually pl.] a thing that makes sth look more attractive on special occasions 装饰品：*Christmas decorations* 圣诞节装饰品 ◇ *a table decoration* 餐桌装饰物 **2** [U, C] a pattern, etc. that is added to sth and that stops it from being plain 装饰图案：*the elaborate decoration on the carved wooden door* 木雕门上精美的装饰图案 **3** [U] the style in which sth is decorated 装饰风格：*a Chinese theme in the interior decoration* 室内装饰的中国主题 **4** [U] (*BrE*) the act or process of decorating sth such as the inside of a house by painting it, etc.（房屋内部等的）装饰，装潢 **5** [C] a MEDAL that is given to sb as an honour 勋章；奖章

dec·ora·tive /ˈdekərətɪv; *NAmE* ˈdekəreɪtɪv/ *adj.* (of an object or a building 物体或建筑) decorated in a way that makes it attractive; intended to look attractive or pretty 装饰性的；作装饰用的：*The mirror is functional yet decorative.* 这镜子能照人，但也有装饰作用。◇ *purely decorative arches* 纯属装饰性的拱门

ˌdecorative ˈarts *noun* [pl.] artistic activities which produce objects which are useful and beautiful at the same time 装饰艺术

dec·or·ator /ˈdekəreɪtə(r)/ *noun* a person whose job is painting and decorating houses （房屋的）油漆匠，裱糊匠

dec·or·ous /ˈdekərəs/ *adj.* (*formal*) polite and appropriate in a particular social situation; not shocking 礼貌得体的；端庄稳重的 **SYN proper**: *a decorous kiss* 礼貌得体的一吻 ▶ **dec·or·ous·ly** *adv.*

de·corum /dɪˈkɔːrəm/ *noun* [U] (*formal*) polite behaviour that is appropriate in a social situation 礼貌得体；端庄稳重 **SYN propriety**

dé·coup·age (*especially NAmE* **de·coup·age**) *noun* [U] (*art* 美术) /ˌdeɪkuˈpɑːʒ/ the art of decorating furniture or other objects by cutting out pictures or designs on paper and sticking them onto the surface 剪纸装饰艺术

de·couple /diːˈkʌpl/ *verb* **~ sth (from sth)** (*formal*) to end the connection or relationship between two things （使两事物）分离，隔断

decoy /ˈdiːkɔɪ/ *noun* [C] **1** an animal or a bird, or a model of one, that attracts other animals or birds, especially so that they can be shot by people who are hunting them （诱捕鸟兽的）动物，假兽，假鸟 **2** a thing or a person that is used to trick sb into doing what you want them to do, going where you want them to go, etc. 诱饵；诱惑物；用作诱饵的人 ▶ **decoy** *verb* **~ sth**

de·crease *verb, noun*

■ *verb* /dɪˈkriːs/ [I, T] (*rather formal*) to become or make sth become smaller in size, number, etc. （使大小、数量等）减少，减小，降低： **~ (from sth) (to sth)** *The number of new students decreased from 210 to 160 this year.* 今年新生人数从 210 减少到 160。◇ *a decreasing population* 逐渐减少的人口 ◇ **~ by sth** *The price of wheat has decreased by 5%.* 小麦价格降低了 5%。◇ **~ in sth** *This species of bird is decreasing in numbers every year.* 这种鸟的数量在逐年减少。◇ **~ sth** *People should decrease the amount of fat they eat.* 人们应减少脂肪的摄入量。 **OPP increase**

■ *noun* /ˈdiːkriːs/ [C, U] the process of reducing sth or the amount that sth is reduced by 减少；降低；减少量 **SYN reduction**: **~ (in sth)** *There has been some decrease in military spending this year.* 今年的军费开支有所减少。◇ **~ (of sth)** *a decrease of nearly 6% in the number of visitors to the museum* 参观博物馆人数下降将近 6% **OPP increase** ⊃ MORE LIKE THIS 21, page R27

de·cree /dɪˈkriː/ *noun, verb*

■ *noun* **1** [C, U] an official order from a ruler or a government that becomes the law 法令；政令：*to issue/sign a decree* 颁布 / 签署法令 ◇ *a leader who rules by decree* (= not in a DEMOCRATIC way) 专制统治者 **2** [C] a decision that is made in court （法院的）裁定，判决

▼ **COLLOCATIONS** 词语搭配

Decorating and home improvement 装饰和改善房屋

Houses 房屋

- **refurbish/renovate/**(*BrE*) **do up** a building/a house 整修 / 翻新 / 修缮楼房 / 房屋
- **convert** a building/house/room into homes/offices/(*especially NAmE*) apartments/(*BrE*) flats 把楼房 / 房子 / 房间 / 改建成住房 / 办公室 / 公寓
- **extend/enlarge** a house/building/room/kitchen 扩建 / 扩大房屋 / 楼房 / 房间 / 厨房
- **build** (*BrE*) an extension (to the back/rear of a house)/(*NAmE*) an addition (on/to sth)/(*BrE*) a conservatory （在房子后面）扩建；（在某处）增建；建造暖房
- **knock down/demolish** a house/home/building/wall 推倒 / 拆除房子 / 住房 / 楼房 / 墙壁
- **knock out/through** the wall separating two rooms 将两个房间的隔墙打通

Decoration 装饰

- **furnish/paint/**(*especially BrE*) **decorate** a home/a house/an apartment/a flat/a room 布置 / 油漆 / 装饰住房 / 房子 / 公寓 / 房间
- **be decorated** in bright colours/(*especially US*) colors/in a traditional style/with flowers/with paintings 用明亮的色彩 / 传统风格 / 花朵 / 绘画装饰
- **paint/plaster** the walls/ceiling 给墙壁 / 天花板上刷油漆 / 抹灰
- **hang/put up/strip off/remove** the wallpaper 贴 / 去除墙纸
- **install/replace/remove** the bathroom fixtures/(*BrE*) fittings 安装 / 更换 / 拆除浴室的固定装置 / 附加设备
- **build/put up** shelves 搭架子
- **lay** wooden flooring/timber decking/floor tiles/a carpet/a patio 铺设木地板 / 平台木板 / 地砖 / 地毯 / 露台
- **put up/hang/take down** a picture/painting/poster/curtain 挂上 / 取下图画 / 绘画 / 海报 / 帘子

DIY/home improvement 自己动手；房屋改造

- **do** (*BrE*) DIY/carpentry/the plumbing/the wiring 自己动手做；做木匠活；铺设管道；铺设线路
- **make** home improvements 改造房屋
- **add/install** central heating/underfloor heating/insulation 添加 / 安装中央供暖系统 / 地暖系统 / 隔热材料
- **fit/install** double-glazing/a smoke alarm 安装双层玻璃 / 烟雾报警器
- **insulate** your house/your home/the walls/the pipes/the tanks/(*especially BrE*) the loft 在房子 / 住房 / 墙壁 / 管道 / 热水箱 / 阁楼里加隔热装置
- **fix/repair** a roof/a leak/a pipe/the plumbing/a leaking (*especially BrE*) tap/(*NAmE usually*) faucet 维修房顶 / 裂缝 / 管子 / 管道系统 / 漏水的水龙头
- **block/clog (up)/unblock/unclog** a pipe/sink 堵住 / 疏通管道 / 洗涤池
- **make/drill/fill** a hole 开 / 钻 / 填一个洞
- **hammer (in)/pull out/remove** a nail 锤进 / 拔出钉子
- **tighten/untighten/loosen/remove** a screw 拧紧 / 拧松 / 拧开螺丝钉
- **saw/cut/treat/stain/varnish/paint** wood 锯 / 切割 / 加工木料；给木料上色 / 上清漆 / 上油漆

■ *verb* (**de·cree·ing**, **de·creed**, **de·creed**) [T, I] to decide, judge or order sth officially 裁定；判决；颁布：~ (**sth**) *The government decreed a state of emergency.* 政府下令进入紧急状态。◇ ~ **what, how, etc....** *We cannot decree what the committee should do.* 我们不能决定委员会应该做什么。◇ **it is decreed that...** *It was decreed that the following day would be a holiday.* 法令宣布第二天为休假日。

de,cree 'absolute *noun* [sing.] (*BrE, law* 律) an order from a court that finally ends a marriage, making the two people divorced（法院对离婚诉讼的）绝对判决，最终判决：*The period between the decree nisi and the decree absolute was six weeks.* 离婚初期判决和最终判决之间的期限当时为六个星期。

decree nisi /dɪˌkriː ˈnaɪsaɪ/ *noun* [sing.] (*BrE, law* 律) an order from a court that a marriage will end after a fixed amount of time unless there is a good reason why it should not（法院对离婚诉讼的）非绝对判决，初期判决

de·crepit /dɪˈkrepɪt/ *adj.* (of a thing or person 物或人) very old and not in good condition or health 衰老的；老朽的；破旧的

de·crepi·tude /dɪˈkrepɪtjuːd; *NAmE* -tuːd/ *noun* [U] (*formal*) the state of being old and in poor condition or health 衰老；老朽；破旧

de·crim·in·al·ize (*BrE also* **-ise**) /diːˈkrɪmɪnəlaɪz/ *verb* ~ **sth** to change the law so that sth is no longer illegal（改变法律以）使合法化：*There are moves to decriminalize some soft drugs.* 已采取步骤使某些软毒品合法化。**OPP** **criminalize** ▸ **de·crim·in·al·iza·tion**, **-isa·tion** /diːˌkrɪmɪnəlaɪˈzeɪʃn; *NAmE* -ləˈz-/ *noun* [U]

decry /dɪˈkraɪ/ *verb* (**de·cries**, **de·cry·ing**, **de·cried**, **de·cried**) ~ **sb/sth** (**as sth**) (*formal*) to strongly criticize sb/sth, especially publicly（公开）谴责；（强烈）批评 **SYN** **condemn**：*The measures were decried as useless.* 这些措施受到指责，说是不起作用。

de·crypt /diːˈkrɪpt/ *verb* ~ **sth** (*computing* 计) to change information that is in code into ordinary language so that it can be understood by anyone 脱密；给…解密 **OPP** **encrypt** ▸ **de·cryp·tion** /diːˈkrɪpʃn/ *noun* [U] **OPP** **encryption**

dedi·cate /ˈdedɪkeɪt/ *verb* **1** to give a lot of your time and effort to a particular activity or purpose because you think it is important 把…奉献给 **SYN** **devote**：~ **yourself/sth to sth** *She dedicates herself to her work.* 她献身于自己的工作。◇ ~ **yourself/sth to doing sth** *He dedicated his life to helping the poor.* 他毕生致力于帮助穷人。**2** ~ **sth to sb** to say at the beginning of a book, a piece of music or a performance that you are doing it for sb, as a way of thanking them or showing respect（在书、音乐或演出的前部）题献词：*This book is dedicated to my parents.* 谨以此书献给我的父母。**3** to hold an official ceremony to say that a building or an object has a special purpose or is special to the memory of a particular person 为…举行奉献典礼；为（建筑物等）举行落成典礼：~ **sth** *The chapel was dedicated in 1880.* 这座小教堂于 1880 年举行献堂典礼。◇ ~ **sth to sb/sth** *A memorial stone was dedicated to those who were killed in the war.* 为阵亡将士纪念碑举行了落成典礼。

dedi·cated /ˈdedɪkeɪtɪd/ *adj.* **1** working hard at sth because it is very important to you 献身的；专心致志的；一心一意的 **SYN** **committed**：*a dedicated teacher* 富有献身精神的教师 ◇ ~ **to sth** *She is dedicated to her job.* 她对工作专心致志。**2** [only before noun] designed to do only one particular type of work; used for one particular purpose only 专用的；专门用途的：*Software is exported through a dedicated satellite link.* 软件通过专用卫星链路出口。➲ MORE LIKE THIS 32, page R28

dedi·ca·tion /ˌdedɪˈkeɪʃn/ *noun* **1** [U] ~ (**to sth**) (*approving*) the hard work and effort that sb puts into an activity or a purpose because they think it is important 献身；奉献 **SYN** **commitment**：*hard work and dedication* 勤奋和奉献 **2** [C] a ceremony that is held to show that a building or an object has a special purpose or is special to the memory of a particular person（建筑物等的）落成典礼 **3** [C] the words that are used at the beginning of a book, piece of music, a performance, etc. to offer it to sb as a sign of thanks or respect 题献（作者在书、音乐作品、演出等开始前表示将其献给某人的一段话）

de·duce **AW** /dɪˈdjuːs; *NAmE* dɪˈduːs/ *verb* (*formal*) to form an opinion about sth based on the information or evidence that is available 推论；推断；演绎 **SYN** **infer**：~ **sth** (**from sth**) *We can deduce a lot from what people choose to buy.* 从人们选购的东西可以作出多方面的推断。◇ ~ (**from sth**) **that, what, how, etc....** *Can we deduce from your silence that you do not approve?* 你保持沉默，我们是否可以据此而推断出你不赞成？➲ SEE ALSO DEDUCTION ▸ **de·du·cible** /dɪˈdjuːsəbl; *NAmE* -ˈduːs-/ *adj.*

de·duct /dɪˈdʌkt/ *verb* [often passive] to take away money, points, etc. from a total amount（从总量中）扣除，减去 **SYN** **subtract**：~ **sth** *Ten points will be deducted for a wrong answer.* 答错一题扣十分。◇ ~ **sth from sth** *The cost of your uniform will be deducted from your wages.* 制服费将从你的工资中扣除。

de·duct·ible /dɪˈdʌktəbl/ *adj.*, *noun*

■ *adj.* that can be taken away from an amount of money you earn, from tax, etc. 可扣除的；可减免的：*These costs are deductible from profits.* 这些费用可从利润中扣除。◇ *tax-deductible expenses* (= that you do not have to pay tax on) 可减免税款的开支

■ *noun* (*NAmE*) (*BrE* **ex·cess**) the part of an insurance claim that a person has to pay while the insurance company pays the rest 免赔额；自负额：*a policy with a very high deductible* 免赔额极高的保单

de·duc·tion **AW** /dɪˈdʌkʃn/ *noun* **1** [U, C] the process of using information you have in order to understand a particular situation or to find the answer to a problem 演绎；推论；推理：*He arrived at the solution by a simple process of deduction.* 他通过一番简单的推理得出了解决问题的方法。◇ *If my deductions are correct, I can tell you who the killer was.* 如果我的推论正确的话，我可以告诉你谁是凶手。➲ COMPARE INDUCTION (3) ➲ SEE ALSO DEDUCE **2** [U, C] the process of taking an amount of sth, especially money, away from a total; the amount that is taken away 扣除（额）；减去（数）：*deductions from your pay for tax, etc.* 从工资中扣除税金等的数额 ◇ *tax deductions* 减税额 ➲ WORDFINDER NOTE AT PAY

de·duct·ive /dɪˈdʌktɪv/ *adj.* [usually before noun] using knowledge about things that are generally true in order to think about and understand particular situations or problems 演绎的；推论的；推理的：***deductive logic/reasoning*** 演绎逻辑 / 推理 ➲ COMPARE INDUCTIVE (1)

deed /diːd/ *noun* **1** (*formal, literary*) a thing that sb does that is usually very good or very bad 行为；行动 **SYN** **act**：***a brave/a charitable/an evil/a good deed*** 勇敢的行为；善举；恶行；善行 ◇ *a tale of heroic deeds* 英雄事迹的故事 **2** (often plural in BrE 在英式英语中常用复数) a legal document that you sign, especially one that proves that you own a house or a building（尤指房产）契约，证书：*the deeds of the house* 房契 ➲ WORDFINDER NOTE AT DOCUMENT, HOME ➲ COLLOCATIONS AT HOUSE ➲ SEE ALSO TITLE DEED

IDM **your good deed for the 'day** a helpful, kind thing that you do（所做的）好事，善事

,deed of 'covenant *noun* (*BrE*) an agreement to pay a regular amount of money to sb/sth, especially a charity, that means that they also receive the tax that would have to be paid on this money 付款契据（承诺定期捐款的契约，受款人可兼获为此款所应缴的税额）：*Signing a deed of covenant makes £1 worth £1.20.* 签署一张付款契据就使 1 英镑价值变为 1.2 英镑。

'deed poll *noun* [U, sing.] (*BrE*) a legal document signed by only one person, especially in order to change their name 单务契约，单边契据（由一方签立，尤为更改姓名）：*Smith changed his name **by deed poll** to Jervis-Smith.* 史密斯通过单边契据将自己的名字更改为杰维斯－史密斯。

dee·jay /ˈdiːdʒeɪ/ *noun, verb*
■*noun* (*informal*) = DISC JOCKEY
■*verb* [I] to perform as a DISC JOCKEY, especially in a club（尤指在俱乐部）当唱片节目主持人

deem /diːm/ *verb* **~ sth + noun/adj. | ~ sth to be sth | ~ (that)...** (*formal*) (not usually used in the progressive tenses 通常不用于进行时) to have a particular opinion about sth 认为；视为；相信 **SYN consider**: *The evening was deemed a great success.* 大家认为这次晚会非常成功。◇ *She* ***deemed it*** *prudent not to say anything.* 她认为什么都不说是明智的。◇ *They would take any action* ***deemed necessary.*** 他们会采取认为必要的任何行动。

deep /diːp/ *adj., adv., noun*

WORD FAMILY
deep *adj., adv.*
deeply *adv.*
deepen *verb*
depth *noun*

■*adj.* (**deep·er, deep·est**)
• **TOP TO BOTTOM** 由顶向底 **1** having a large distance from the top or surface to the bottom 深的；厚的：*a deep hole/well/river* 很深的洞 / 井 / 河 ◇ *deep water/snow* 深水；厚雪 **OPP shallow**
• **FRONT TO BACK** 由前向后 **2** having a large distance from the front edge to the furthest point inside 纵深的；宽的：*a deep cut/wound* 很深的划口 / 伤口 ◇ *a deep space* 深邃的空间 **OPP shallow**
• **MEASUREMENT** 量度 **3** used to describe or ask about the depth of sth 有…深的：*The water is only a few inches deep.* 这水只有几英寸深。◇ *How deep is the wound?* 伤口有多深？
• **-DEEP** 有…深 **4** (in adjectives 构成形容词) as far up or down as the point mentioned 远至…的；有…深的：*The water was only waist-deep so I walked ashore.* 水只有齐腰深，所以我涉水上了岸。 **5** (in adjectives 构成形容词) in the number of rows mentioned, one behind the other 成…排的；有…层的：*They were standing three-deep at the bar.* 他们在吧台前站成三排。
• **BREATH/SIGH** 呼吸；叹息 **6** [usually before noun] taking in or giving out a lot of air 深（呼吸）的：*She took a deep breath.* 她深深地吸了一口气。◇ *He gave a deep sigh.* 他深深地叹了一口气。
• **SOUNDS** 声音 **7** low 深沉的；低沉的：*I heard his deep warm voice filling the room.* 我听到他低沉暖人的话语在整个房间里回荡。◇ *a* ***deep roar/groan*** 低沉的轰鸣声 / 呻吟声
• **COLOURS** 颜色 **8** strong and dark 深的：*a rich deep red* 浓重的深红色 **OPP pale**
• **SLEEP** 睡眠 **9** a person in a **deep** sleep is difficult to wake 酣睡的；沉睡的：*to be in a* ***deep sleep/trance/coma*** 酣睡；昏睡；昏迷 **OPP light**
• **SERIOUS** 严重 **10** extreme or serious 极度的；严重的：*He's* ***in deep trouble.*** 他陷入极度困境之中。◇ *a deep economic recession* 严重的经济衰退 ◇ *The affair had exposed deep divisions within the party.* 这件事暴露出党内的严重分歧。◇ *a place of great power and of deep significance* 具有重大影响力和深远意义的地方
• **EMOTIONS** 情感 **11** strongly felt 强烈的；深切的；衷心的 **SYN sincere**: *deep respect* 深深的敬意 ◇ *a deep sense of loss* 强烈的失落感
• **KNOWLEDGE** 知识 **12** showing great knowledge or understanding 渊博的；深刻的：*a deep understanding* 深刻的理解
• **DIFFICULT TO UNDERSTAND** 难以理解 **13** difficult to understand 深奥的；难懂的；难解的 **SYN profound**: *This discussion's getting too deep for me.* 这讨论越来越深奥，使我难以理解。◇ *He pondered, as if over some deep philosophical point.* 他沉思着，仿佛在思索某个深奥的哲学问题。
• **INVOLVED** 深陷 **14 ~ in sth** fully involved in an activity or a state 专心；全神贯注；深陷：*to be* ***deep in thought/conversation*** 陷入深思；专心谈话 ◇ *He is often so deep in his books that he forgets to eat.* 他常常专心于读书以致忘了吃饭。◇ *The firm ended up* ***deep in debt.*** 这家公司最后债台高筑。
• **PERSON** 人 **15** if a person is **deep**, they hide their real feelings and opinions 深沉的；摸不透的；城府深的：*She's always been a deep one, trusting no one.* 她这个人一直城府很深，对谁也不相信。
• **IN SPORT** 体育运动 **16** to or from a position far down or across the field 远端的：*a deep ball from Brown* 布朗踢到球场远端的一脚球 ➲SEE ALSO DEPTH

IDM **go off the ˈdeep end** (*informal*) to suddenly become very angry or emotional（突然）火冒三丈，大发脾气，非常激动 **in deep ˈwater(s)** (*informal*) in trouble or difficulty 在困境中；在危难中 **jump/be thrown in at the ˈdeep end** (*informal*) to start or be made to start a new and difficult activity that you are not prepared for （使）陷入未曾料到的艰难处境，一筹莫展：*Junior hospital doctors are thrown in at the deep end in their first jobs.* 医院的初级医生开始工作时会遇上未曾料到的困难。➲MORE AT DEVIL, SHIT *n.*

■*adv.* (**deep·er, deep·est**) **~ (below, into, under, etc.)** a long way below the surface of sth or a long way inside or into sth 深深地；在深处；至深处：*Dig deeper!* 再挖深点！◇ *The miners were trapped deep underground.* 矿工被困在地下深处。◇ *whales that feed deep beneath the waves* 在大海深处进食的鲸鱼 ◇ *He gazed deep into her eyes.* 他深深凝视着她的眼睛。◇ *They sat and talked* ***deep into the night*** (= until very late). 他们坐着谈话，一直谈到深夜。◇ *deep in the forest* 在森林深处 ◇ *He stood with his hands deep in his pockets.* 他双手深插在衣袋里站着。

IDM **deep ˈdown 1** if you know sth **deep down**, you know your true feelings about sth, although you may not admit them to yourself 在内心深处；在心底：*Deep down I still loved him.* 我在内心深处仍然爱着他。 **2** if sth is true **deep down**, it is really like that, although it may not be obvious to people 本质上；实际上；事实上：*He seems confident but deep down he's quite insecure.* 他好像很有信心，实际上却没什么把握。 **go/run ˈdeep** (of emotions, beliefs, etc. 情感、信仰等) to be felt in a strong way, especially for a long time 强烈；深厚；深入内心：*Dignity and pride run deep in this community.* 尊严和骄傲已深深扎根于这个群体之中。➲MORE AT DIG *v.*, STILL *adj.*

▼WHICH WORD? 词语辨析

deep / deeply

• The adverbs **deep** and **deeply** can both mean 'a long way down or into something'. **Deep** can only mean this and is more common than **deeply** in this sense. It is usually followed by a word like *into* or *below*. 副词 deep 和 deeply 均含由上到下或从外到里距离大的意思。deep 只含此义，而且用于此义时较 deeply 常用，其后通常接 into 或 below：*We decided to go deeper into the jungle.* 我们决定继续深入丛林。
• **Deeply** usually means 'very much'. * deeply 常含非常之义：*deeply in love* 深爱 ◇ *deeply shocked* 大为震惊
You can use **deep down** (but not **deeply**) to talk about a person's real nature. 表示人的本性、心地可用 deep down（但不能用 deeply）：*She can seem stern, but deep down she's a very kind person.* 她可能看上去严厉，其实心地非常善良。◇ ~~*She can seem stern, but deeply she's a very kind person.*~~

■*noun* **1 the deep** [sing.] (*literary*) the sea 海；海洋 **2 the deep** [sing.], **the deeps** [pl.] a deep part of sth; the deepest part of sth 深处；最深处：*in the deep of night/winter* (= in the middle of the night/of winter) 在深夜 / 隆冬 ◇ *the deeps of Loch Ness* 尼斯湖的深处 ◇ (*figurative*) *the deeps of sorrow* 悲伤的深渊

Dee·pa·vali *noun* /ˌdiːpəˈvɑːliː/ = DIWALI

ˌdeep-ˈdyed *adj.* (*NAmE*) having a particular characteristic or opinion very strongly 特性明显的；立场鲜明的；十足的：*a deep-dyed socialist* 立场鲜明的社会主义者

deep·en /ˈdiːpən/ *verb* **1** [I, T] **~ (sth) (into sth)** if an emotion or a feeling **deepens**, or if sth **deepens** it, it becomes stronger（使情感、感觉等）加强，变强烈：*Their friendship soon deepened into love.* 他们的友谊很快发展成为爱情。 **2** [I, T] **~ (sth)** to become worse; to make sth worse（使）变糟，恶化，严重：*Warships were sent in as the crisis deepened.* 危机加重时军舰便奉命来到现场。◇ *a deepening economic recession* 越来越严重的经济衰退 **3** [I, T] to become deeper; to make sth deeper（使）变深；加深：*The water deepened gradually.* 水渐渐变深了。◇ *His frown deepened.* 他的眉头皱得更紧了。◇ **~ sth** *There were plans to deepen a stretch of the river.* 曾经有过加深一段河道的计划。 **4** [T] **~ sth** to improve your knowledge or understanding of sth 增长（知识）；加深（理解）：*an opportunity for students to deepen their understanding of different cultures* 学生加深理解不同文化的机会 **5** [I, T] **~ (sth)** if colour or light **deepens** or if sth **deepens** it, it becomes darker（使色泽、光线等）变浓；（使）变昏暗：*deepening shadows* 越来越暗的阴影 **6** [I, T] **~ (sth) (to sth)** if a sound or voice **deepens** or if you **deepen** it, it becomes lower or you make it lower（使声音）变低沉：*His voice deepened to a growl.* 他的声音变成了低沉的怒吼。 **7** [I] if your breathing **deepens**, you breathe more deeply than usual 深（呼吸）；喘（大气）

ˌdeep ˈfreeze (*BrE*) (*US* **Deep·freeze™**, **ˌdeep ˈfreezer**) *noun* = FREEZER

ˌdeep-ˈfrozen *adj.* preserved at an extremely low temperature 深冻冷藏的

ˌdeep-ˈfry *verb* [usually passive] **~ sth** to cook food in oil that covers it completely 油炸：*deep-fried chicken pieces* 油炸鸡块

deep·ly 🔑 /ˈdiːpli/ *adv.* **1** 🔑 very; very much 很；非常；极其：*She is deeply religious.* 她非常虔诚。◇ *They were deeply disturbed by the accident.* 这个事故使他们深感不安。◇ *Opinion is **deeply divided** on this issue.* 对这个问题的意见分歧很大。◇ ***deeply rooted** customs/ideas* 根深蒂固的习俗 / 思想 ◇ ***deeply held** beliefs/convictions/views* (= that sb feels very strongly) 坚定不移的信仰 / 信念 / 观点 **2** 🔑 used with some verbs to show that sth is done in a very complete way（与某些动词连用）深刻地，强烈地，深沉地：*to **breathe/sigh/exhale deeply*** (= using all of the air in your lungs) 深呼吸；深深地叹息；长长地呼气 ◇ ***sleep deeply*** (= in a way that makes it difficult for you to wake up) 酣睡 ◇ *to **think deeply*** (= about all the aspects of sth) 沉思 **3** 🔑 to a depth that is quite a long way from the surface of sth 至深处：*to drill deeply into the wood*（钻头）往木头深处钻 ➲ NOTE AT DEEP

ˌdeep-ˈrooted, **ˌdeep-ˈseated** *adj.* [usually before noun] (of feelings and beliefs 感情和信仰) very fixed and strong; difficult to change or to destroy 根深蒂固的；强烈的；坚定的：*a deep-rooted desire* 强烈的愿望 ◇ *The country's political divisions are deep-seated.* 这个国家的政治分歧根深蒂固。

ˈdeep-sea (*also less frequent* **ˈdeep-water**) *adj.* [only before noun] of or in the deeper parts of the sea 深海的：*a deep-sea diver* 深海潜水员 ◇ ***deep-sea fishing/diving*** 深海捕鱼 / 潜水

ˌdeep-ˈset *adj.* (*formal*) eyes that are **deep-set** seem to be quite far back in a person's face（眼睛）深陷的

ˌdeep-ˈsix *verb* [usually passive] **~ sth** (*NAmE, informal*) to decide not to do or use sth that you had planned to do or use 放弃；抛弃；丢弃：*Plans to build a new mall were deep-sixed after protests from local residents.* 修建新购物中心的计划由于当地居民反对而终止。

the ˌDeep ˈSouth *noun* [sing.] the southern states of the US, especially Georgia, Alabama, Mississippi, Louisiana and South Carolina 美国南部诸州（尤指佐治亚、亚拉巴马、密西西比、路易斯安那和南卡罗来纳州）

ˈdeep structure (*also* **ˈD-structure**) *noun* (*grammar* 语法) the basic relationships between the different parts of a sentence, which show how we think when we are using language 深层结构 ➲ COMPARE SURFACE STRUCTURE

ˌdeep vein thromˈbosis *noun* [U, C] (*abbr.* **DVT**) (*medical* 医) a serious condition caused by a blood CLOT (= a thick mass of blood) forming in a VEIN 深静脉血栓形成：*Passengers on long-haul flights are being warned about the risks of deep vein thrombosis.* 长途航班上的乘客须注意可能出现深静脉血栓。

ˈdeep-water *adj.* = DEEP-SEA

deer /dɪə(r); *NAmE* dɪr/ *noun* (*pl.* **deer**) an animal with long legs, that eats grass, leaves, etc. and can run fast. Most male deer have ANTLERS (= horns shaped like branches). There are many types of deer. 鹿：*a herd of deer* 一群鹿 ◇ *a deer park* 鹿苑 ➲ SEE ALSO FALLOW DEER, RED DEER, REINDEER, ROE DEER, DOE, FAWN *n.* (1), STAG

deer·stalk·er /ˈdɪəstɔːkə(r); *NAmE* ˈdɪrs-/ *noun* a cap with two PEAKS, one in front and one behind, and two pieces of cloth which are usually tied together on top but can be folded down to cover the ears 猎鹿帽（前后各有一帽舌，两块护耳可系于帽顶）

def /def/ *adj.* (*slang*) excellent 极好的；很棒的：*a def band* 出色的乐队

de·face /dɪˈfeɪs/ *verb* **~ sth** to damage the appearance of sth especially by drawing or writing on it 损伤…的外貌（尤指乱涂、乱写） ▶ **de·face·ment** *noun* [U]

de facto /ˌdeɪ ˈfæktəʊ; *NAmE* -toʊ/ *adj.* [usually before noun] (*from Latin, formal*) existing as a fact although it may not be legally accepted as existing 实际上存在的（不一定合法）：*The general took de facto control of the country.* 这位将军实际上控制了整个国家。 ▶ **de facto** *adv.*：*He continued to rule the country de facto.* 实际上，他继续统治着这个国家。 ➲ COMPARE DE JURE

defae·cate, **defae·ca·tion** (*BrE*) = DEFECATE, DEFECATION

def·am·ation /ˌdefəˈmeɪʃn/ *noun* [U, C] (*formal*) the act of damaging sb's reputation by saying or writing bad or false things about them 诬蔑；诽谤；中伤：*The company sued for defamation.* 这家公司因受到诽谤而提起诉讼。

de·fama·tory /dɪˈfæmətri; *NAmE* -tɔːri/ *adj.* (*formal*) (of speech or writing 说话或文章) intended to harm sb by saying or writing bad or false things about them 诬蔑的；诽谤的；中伤的

de·fame /dɪˈfeɪm/ *verb* **~ sb/sth** (*formal*) to harm sb by saying or writing bad or false things about them 诬蔑；诽谤；中伤

de·fault /dɪˈfɔːlt; ˈdiːfɔːlt/ *noun, verb*

■ ***noun*** **1** [U, C] failure to do sth that must be done by law, especially paying a debt 违约（尤指未偿付债务）：*The company is in default on the loan.* 这家公司拖欠借款。◇ *Mortgage defaults have risen in the last year.* 按揭借款违约在近一年里呈上升趋势。 **2** [U, C, usually sing.] (*computing* 计) what happens or appears if you do not make any other choice or change 默认；系统设定值；缺省值；预置值：*The default option is to save your work every five minutes.* 默认设置为每五分钟存盘一次。◇ *What is your default browser?* 你的默认浏览器是什么？

IDM **by deˈfault** **1** a game or competition can be won **by default** if there are no other people, teams, etc. taking part（比赛）因其他参赛者不到场，由于对手缺席（而胜出） **2** if sth happens **by default**, it happens because you have not made any other decision or choices which would make things happen in a different way 由于没有特别作出决定（或选择） **in deˈfault of sth** (*formal*) because of a lack of sth 由于缺乏…；因为没有…：*They accepted what he had said **in default of** any evidence to disprove it.* 由于缺乏相反的证据，他们相信了他的话。

■ ***verb*** **1** [I] **~ (on sth)** to fail to do sth that you legally have to do, especially by not paying a debt 违约，不履行义务（尤指不偿还债务）：*to default on a loan/debt* 拖欠借款 / 债务 ◇ *defaulting borrowers/tenants* 不偿还债务的借款人；拖欠租金的承租人 **2** [I] **~ (to sth)** (*computing* 计) to happen when you do not make any other choice or change 默认；预设；预置 ▶ **de·fault·er** *noun*：*mortgage defaulters* 抵押贷款违约者

de·feat 🔑 /dɪˈfiːt/ *verb, noun*

■ ***verb*** **1** 🔑 **~ sb/sth** to win against sb in a war, competition, sports game, etc. 击败；战胜 **SYN** **beat**：*He*

D

defeated the champion in three sets. 他三盘击败了冠军。◇ a defeated army 败军 **2** ~ **sth** to stop sth from being successful 使失败；阻挠；挫败：*The motion was defeated by 19 votes.* 这项动议以差额 19 票被否决。◇ *Staying late at the office to discuss shorter working hours rather **defeats the object of the exercise!*** 迟迟待在办公室讨论缩短工作时间恰恰是在阻挠这一目标的实现！ **3** ~ **sb** (*formal*) if sth **defeats** you, you cannot understand it 使困惑；难住：*The instruction manual completely defeated me.* 这操作指南把我完全弄糊涂了。

■ ***noun*** **1** [U, C] failure to win or to be successful 失败；战败；挫败：*The party faces defeat in the election.* 这个党面临选举失败。◇ *a **narrow/heavy defeat*** 惜败；惨败 ◇ *The world champion has only had two defeats in 20 fights.* 这个世界冠军在 20 场比赛中只败过两场。◇ *They finally had to **admit defeat*** (= stop trying to be successful). 他们最后只得认输。 **2** [C, usually sing.] the act of winning a victory over sb/sth 击败；战胜：*the defeat of fascism* 战胜法西斯主义

de·feat·ist /dɪˈfiːtɪst/ *adj.* expecting not to succeed, and showing it in a particular situation 失败主义（者）的：*a **defeatist attitude/view*** 失败主义的态度 / 观点 ▶ **de·feat·ist** *noun*：*He is a pessimist and a defeatist.* 他是悲观主义者，也是失败主义者。 **de·feat·ism** *noun* [U]

de·fe·cate (*BrE also* **defae·cate**) /ˈdefəkeɪt; ˈdiː-/ *verb* [I] (*formal*) to get rid of solid waste from your body through your BOWELS 排便 ▶ **de·fe·ca·tion** (*BrE also* **defae·ca·tion**) /ˌdefəˈkeɪʃn; ˌdiː-/ *noun* [U]

de·fect *noun, verb*

■ ***noun*** /ˈdiːfekt; dɪˈfekt/ a fault in sth or in the way it has been made which means that it is not perfect 缺点；缺陷；毛病：*a speech defect* 言语缺陷 ◇ *a defect in the glass* 玻璃杯的缺陷

■ ***verb*** /dɪˈfekt/ [I] ~ (**from sth**) (**to sth**) to leave a political party, country, etc. to join another that is considered to be an enemy 背叛；叛变；投敌 ▶ **de·fec·tion** /dɪˈfekʃn/ *noun* [U, C]：~ (**from sth**) (**to sth**) *There have been several defections from the ruling party.* 执政党已有好几位党员倒戈。 **de·fect·or** *noun*

de·fect·ive /dɪˈfektɪv/ *adj.* having a fault or faults; not perfect or complete 有缺点的；有缺陷的；有毛病的 SYN **faulty**：*defective goods* 有缺陷的商品 ◇ *Her hearing was found to be slightly defective.* 经检查，她的听力有点缺陷。 ▶ **de·fect·ive·ly** *adv.* **de·fect·ive·ness** *noun* [U]

de·fence (*especially US* **de·fense**) /dɪˈfens/ *noun*

• **PROTECTION AGAINST ATTACK** 防御 **1** [U] the act of protecting sb/sth from attack, criticism, etc. 防御；保护；保卫：*soldiers who died **in defence of** their country* 为保卫祖国而献身的战士 ◇ *When her brother was criticized she **leapt to his defence**.* 她的哥哥受到批评时，她马上跳出来卫护。◇ *What points can be raised in defence of this argument?* 有什么论点能提出来为这个说法辩护呢？◇ *I have to say **in her defence** that she knew nothing about it beforehand.* 我得为她说句话，她事先并不知道此事。 ➲ SEE ALSO SELF-DEFENCE **2** [C, U] ~ (**against sth**) something that provides protection against attack from enemies, the weather, illness, etc. 防御物；防务；防御能力：*The town walls were built as a defence against enemy attacks.* 城墙是为防御敌人袭击而修建的。◇ *The harbour's sea defences are in poor condition.* 港口的海防工事状况很差。◇ *The body has natural **defence mechanisms** to protect it from disease.* 人体对疾病具有先天性防御机制。 ◇ *Humour is a more effective defence than violence.* 幽默是比暴力更有效的防御武器。 **3** [U] the organization of the people and systems that are used by a government to protect a country from attack 国防机构；国防体系：(*BrE*) *the Ministry of Defence* 国防部 ◇ (*NAmE*) *the Department of Defense* 国防部 ◇ *Further cuts in defence spending are being considered.* 目前正在考虑进一步削减国防开支。

• **SUPPORT** 支持 **4** [C] something that is said or written in order to support sth 辩解；辩白：*a defence of Marxism* 为马克思主义辩解

• **LAW** 法律 **5** [C] what is said in court to prove that a person did not commit a crime; the act of presenting this argument in court 辩护；辩词；答辩：*Her defence was that she was somewhere completely different at the time of the crime.* 她的辩词是案发时她根本就不在现场。◇ *He wanted to conduct his own defence.* 他想自己为自己辩护。 **6 the defence** [sing.+sing./pl. v.] the lawyer or lawyers whose job is to prove in court that a person did not commit a crime 辩护律师 ➲ COMPARE PROSECUTION (2)

• **IN SPORT** 体育运动 **7** [sing., U] the players who must prevent the other team from scoring; the position of these players on the sports field 防守队员；防守；后卫：*Welford cut through the defence to score the winning goal.* 韦尔福特突破防守射进了制胜的一球。◇ (*BrE*) *She plays **in defence**.* 她打防守。◇ (*NAmE*) *He plays **on defense**.* 他打防守。 ➲ COMPARE ATTACK *n.* (8), OFFENSE (2) **8** [C] a contest, game, etc. in which the previous winner or winners compete in order to try to win again 卫冕赛：*Barcelona's defence of the Champions League title* 欧洲冠军联赛巴塞罗那队的冠军卫冕赛

de·fence·less (*especially US* **de·fense·less**) /dɪˈfensləs/ *adj.* weak; not able to protect yourself; having no protection 软弱的；不能自卫的；无防御的：*defenceless children* 没有自卫能力的儿童 ◇ *The village is defenceless against attack.* 这个村庄毫无防御能力。 ▶ **de·fence·less·ness** (*especially US* **de·fense·less·ness**) *noun* [U]

de·fend /dɪˈfend/ *verb*

• **PROTECT AGAINST ATTACK** 防御 **1** [T, I] to protect sb/sth from attack 防御；保护；保卫：~ **sb/yourself/sth** *Troops have been sent to defend the borders.* 已派出部队去守卫边疆。◇ ~ **sb/yourself/sth from/against sb/sth** *All our officers are trained to defend themselves against knife attacks.* 我们所有的警察都接受过自卫训练，能够对付持刀袭击。◇ ~ **against sb/sth** *It is impossible to defend against an all-out attack.* 防御全面进攻是不可能的。 ➲ **WORDFINDER NOTE** AT ARMY, CONFLICT

• **SUPPORT** 支持 **2** [T] to say or write sth in support of sb/sth that has been criticized 辩解；辩白：~ **sth** *How can you defend such behaviour?* 你怎能为这种行为辩解呢？◇ ~ **sb/yourself/sth from/against sb/sth** *Politicians are skilled at defending themselves against their critics.* 从政者都善于为自己辩解，反驳别人的批评。

• **IN SPORT** 体育运动 **3** [I, T] ~ (**sth**) (in sports 体育运动) to protect your own goal to stop your opponents from scoring 防守 OPP **attack**

• **IN COMPETITIONS** 竞赛 **4** [T] ~ **sth** to take part in a competition that you won the last time and try to win it again 参加比赛（或选举）保住（头衔、席位等）：*He is **defending champion**.* 他在参加卫冕赛。◇ *She will be **defending her title** at next month's championships.* 她将在下月的锦标赛上争取蝉联冠军。◇ (*politics* 政) *He intends to defend his seat in the next election.* 他想在下届选举中寻求连任。

• **LAW** 法律 **5** [T, I] ~ (**sb/yourself**) to act as a lawyer for sb who has been charged with a crime （为…）辩护；当辩护律师：*He has employed one of the UK's top lawyers to defend him.* 他请了英国一位顶尖律师为他辩护。 ➲ COMPARE PROSECUTE (2)

de·fend·ant /dɪˈfendənt/ *noun* the person in a trial who is accused of committing a crime, or who is being sued by another person 被告人；被告 ➲ **WORDFINDER NOTE** AT TRIAL ➲ **COLLOCATIONS** AT JUSTICE ➲ COMPARE ACCUSED, PLAINTIFF

de·fend·er /dɪˈfendə(r)/ *noun* **1** a player who must stop the other team from scoring in games such as football (SOCCER), HOCKEY, etc. 防守队员；后卫 **2** a person who defends and believes in protecting sth 守卫者；保护人；防御者：*a passionate defender of human rights* 热诚的人权卫士

de·fense, **de·fense·less**, **de·fense·less·ness** (*especially US*) = DEFENCE, DEFENCELESS, DEFENCELESSNESS

de·fens·ible /dɪˈfensəbl/ *adj.* **1** able to be supported by reasons or arguments that show that it is right or should be allowed 可辩解的；合乎情理的；有正当理由的：*Is abortion morally defensible?* 堕胎从道德上讲合乎

情理吗? OPP indefensible 2 (of a place 地方) able to be defended from an attack 可防御的；可守护的

de·fen·sive /dɪˈfensɪv/ *adj., noun*

■ ***adj.*** **1** protecting sb/sth against attack 防御的；保护的；保卫的：*a defensive measure* 防御措施 ◇ *Troops took up a defensive position around the town.* 部队在全城采取了守势。 ➲ COMPARE OFFENSIVE *adj.* (3) **2** behaving in a way that shows that you feel that people are criticizing you 戒备的；怀有戒心的；自卫的：*Don't ask him about his plans—he just gets defensive.* 别问他有什么计划，他老存有戒心。 **3** (*sport* 体育) connected with trying to prevent the other team or player from scoring points or goals 防守的：*defensive play* 防守型打法 ➲ COMPARE OFFENSIVE *adj.* (4) ▸ **de·fen·sive·ly** *adv.* **de·fen·sive·ness** *noun* [U]

■ ***noun***

IDM **on/onto the deˈfensive** acting in a way that shows that you expect to be attacked or criticized; having to defend yourself 处于防御姿态；处于戒备状态；采取守势：*Their questions about the money put her on the defensive.* 他们问到钱的问题时，她就警觉起来。 ◇ *Warnings of an enemy attack forced the troops onto the defensive.* 敌军显示出进攻的迹象，部队不得不进入戒备状态。

deˌfensive ˈmedicine *noun* [U] (*especially NAmE*) medical treatment that involves more tests, operations, etc. than a person really needs because a doctor is worried that a claim or complaint may be made against them in court if they make a mistake in the treatment they give 防御性医疗，自卫性医疗（医生担心因误诊被起诉而让病人做过多的化验、手术等）

defer /dɪˈfɜː(r)/ *verb* (**-rr-**) ~ (**doing**) **sth** (*formal*) to delay sth until a later time 推迟；延缓；展期 SYN **put off**：*The department deferred the decision for six months.* 这个部门推迟了六个月才作决定。 ◇ *She had applied for deferred admission to college.* 她已申请延期入学。 ▸ **de·fer·ment**, **de·fer·ral** /dɪˈfɜːrəl/ *noun* [U, C]

PHR V **deˈfer to sb/sth** (*formal*) to agree to accept what sb has decided or what they think about sb/sth because you respect him or her 遵从；听从；顺从：*We will defer to whatever the committee decides.* 我们遵从委员会的任何决定。

def·er·ence /ˈdefərəns/ *noun* [U] behaviour that shows that you respect sb/sth 尊重；遵从；听从：*The women wore veils **in deference to** the customs of the country.* 这些妇女戴着面纱是遵从这个国家的习俗。 ◇ *The flags were lowered **out of deference to** the bereaved family.* 降旗是出于对死者家属的尊重。 ▸ **def·er·en·tial** /ˌdefəˈrenʃl/ *adj.* **def·er·en·tial·ly** /-ʃəli/ *adv.*

de·fi·ance /dɪˈfaɪəns/ *noun* [U] open refusal to obey sb/sth 违抗；反抗；拒绝服从：*a look/an act/a gesture of defiance* 反抗的神色 / 行动 / 表示 ◇ *Nuclear testing was resumed **in defiance of** an international ban.* 尽管国际上明令禁止，核试验又在进行了。

deˈfiance campaign *noun* (in South Africa in the past, especially in the period after 1952) a series of activities in which black people refused to obey laws that were not fair 抗法运动（尤指 1952 年之后，南非黑人拒绝遵守不公平的法律规定）

de·fi·ant /dɪˈfaɪənt/ *adj.* openly refusing to obey sb/sth, sometimes in an aggressive way 公然违抗的；反抗的；挑衅的：*a defiant teenager* 一个反叛的少年 ◇ *The terrorists sent a defiant message to the government.* 恐怖分子向政府发出了挑战书。 ▸ **de·fi·ant·ly** *adv.*

de·fib·ril·la·tion /ˌdiːfɪbrɪˈleɪʃn/ *noun* [U] (*medical* 医) the use of a controlled electric shock from a defibrillator to return the heart to its natural rhythm 心脏除颤（用电击）

de·fib·ril·la·tor /diːˈfɪbrɪleɪtə(r)/ *noun* (*medical* 医) a piece of equipment used to control the movements of the heart muscles by giving the heart a controlled electric shock 除颤器（通过电击心脏控制心肌运动）

de·fi·ciency /dɪˈfɪʃnsi/ *noun* (*pl.* **-ies**) (*formal*) **1** [U, C] ~ (**in/of sth**) the state of not having, or not having enough of, sth that is essential 缺乏；缺少；不足 SYN **shortage**：*Vitamin deficiency in the diet can cause illness.* 饮食中缺乏维生素会导致疾病。 ◇ *a deficiency of Vitamin B* 缺乏维生素 B **2** [C] ~ (**in/of sth**) a fault or a weakness in sth/sb that makes it or them less successful 缺点；缺陷：*deficiencies in the computer system* 计算机系统的种种缺陷

de·fi·cient /dɪˈfɪʃnt/ *adj.* (*formal*) **1** ~ (**in sth**) not having enough of sth, especially sth that is essential 缺乏的；缺少的；不足的：*a diet that is deficient in vitamin A* 缺乏维生素 A 的饮食 **2** not good enough 有缺点的；有缺陷的：*Deaf people are sometimes treated as being mentally deficient.* 耳聋的人有时被看作智力不健全。

def·icit /ˈdefɪsɪt/ *noun* **1** (*economics* 经) the amount by which money spent or owed is greater than money earned in a particular period of time 赤字；逆差；亏损：*a **budget/trade deficit*** 预算赤字；贸易逆差 ◇ *The trade balance has been **in deficit** for the past five years.* 过去五年来贸易状况一直是逆差。 ➲ COLLOCATIONS AT INTERNATIONAL ➲ COMPARE SURPLUS *n.* (2) **2** (*formal*) the amount by which sth, especially an amount of money, is too small or smaller than sth else 不足额；缺款额；缺少：*There's a deficit of $3 million in the total needed to complete the project.* 完成这项工程所需资金还缺少 300 万美元。 ◇ *The team has to come back from a 2–0 deficit in the first half.* 这支队得扳回上半场 0:2 的落后局面。

de·fied PAST TENSE, PAST PART. OF DEFY

de·file¹ /dɪˈfaɪl/ *verb* ~ **sth** (*formal* or *literary*) to make sth dirty or no longer pure, especially sth that people consider important or holy 弄脏；玷污；糟蹋；亵渎：*Many victims of burglary feel their homes have been defiled.* 许多家门被撬的人都感到自己的家被玷污了。 ◇ *The altar had been defiled by vandals.* 圣坛受到破坏公物者的肆意践踏。 ▸ **de·file·ment** *noun* [U, C]

de·file² /dɪˈfaɪl; ˈdiːfaɪl/ *noun* (*formal*) a narrow way through mountains 山中狭径

de·fine 🔑 AW /dɪˈfaɪn/ *verb* **1** 🔑 to say or explain what the meaning of a word or phrase is 解释（词语的含义）；给…下定义：**~ sth** *The term 'mental illness' is difficult to define.* "精神病"这个词很难下定义。 ◇ **~ sth as sth** *Life imprisonment is defined as 60 years under state law.* 按照州法律终身监禁定义为 60 年。 ➲ LANGUAGE BANK ON NEXT PAGE **2** 🔑 to describe or show sth accurately 阐明；明确；界定：**~ sth** *We need to define the task ahead very clearly.* 我们需要明确今后的任务。 ◇ *The difficulty of a problem was **defined in terms of** how long it took to complete.* 问题的难易度是以解决这个问题所花时间的长短而定的。 ◇ **~ what, how, etc.…** *It is difficult to define what makes him so popular.* 很难解释清楚什么原因使他如此走红。 **3** **~ sth** to show clearly a line, shape or edge 画出…的线条；描出…的外形；确定…的界线；界定：*The mountain was **sharply defined** against the sky.* 那座山在天空的衬托下显得轮廓分明。 ▸ **de·fin·able** AW *adj.*

deˌfined ˈbenefit *noun* a fixed amount of money that will be paid by a PENSION PLAN, especially when this amount is based on your salary at the end of your working life and the number of years you worked （养老金计划的）固定收益

deˌfined contriˈbution *noun* fixed payments that are made to a PENSION PLAN, where the amount that will be paid out can change （养老金计划的）固定缴款

de·fin·ing /dɪˈfaɪnɪŋ/ *adj.* = RESTRICTIVE (2)

deˈfining vocabulary *noun* a set of carefully chosen words used to write the explanations in some dictionaries （词典的）释义词汇

def·in·ite 🔑 AW /ˈdefɪnət/ *adj., noun*

■ ***adj.*** **1** 🔑 ~ (**that…**) sure or certain; unlikely to change 肯定的；确定的；不会改变的：*Can you give me a definite answer by tomorrow?* 你最晚明天能给我一个确定的答复吗？ ◇ *Is it definite that he's leaving?* 他肯定要离开吗？ ◇ *I've heard rumours, but nothing definite.* 我听到一些流言，但都不确定。 ◇ *a definite offer of a job* 明确给予一份

D

▼ LANGUAGE BANK 用语库

define

Defining terms 为术语下定义

- ***It is important to clarify what is meant by** climate change.* 说清楚"气候变化"的含义很重要。
- *Climate change **can / may be defined as** 'the long-term fluctuations in temperature, precipitation, wind and other aspects of the earth's climate'.* 气候变化可以被定义为"地球气候在温度、降水量、风力及其他方面的长期波动"。
- ***A generally accepted definition of** global warming **is** the gradual increase in the overall temperature of the earth's atmosphere due to the greenhouse effect.* 对于全球变暖，普遍接受的一种定义是：由于受到温室效应的影响，地球大气层总体温度逐渐上升。
- *The greenhouse effect **is defined** by the author **as** the process by which heat from the sun is trapped in the earth's atmosphere, causing the temperature of the earth to rise.* 作者将温室效应定义为：地球大气层锁住来自太阳的热量，导致地球温度上升的过程。
- *The author **uses the term** climate change **to refer to** any significant change in measures of climate lasting for an extended period.* 作者使用"气候变化"这个术语来指代任何持续较长时间的气候的显著变化。
- ***The term** 'carbon footprint' **refers to** the amount of carbon dioxide released into the atmosphere as a result of the activities of an individual or organization.* "碳足迹"这个术语指的是由于个人或组织的活动排放到大气层中的二氧化碳的量。
- *Scientists suggest that increased carbon dioxide in the atmosphere will result in an increase in global temperatures, and **the term** 'global warming' **is used** to describe this phenomenon.* 科学家认为大气层中二氧化碳的增加会导致全球气温上升，"全球变暖"这个术语就是用来描述这种现象的。

➲ LANGUAGE BANK AT FIRST

工作 ◇ *I'm not sure—I can find out **for definite** if you like.* 我没把握，如果你愿意，我可以去核实。 ◇ *That's definite then, is it?* 那么，那是确切的了，是吗？ ◇ *They have very definite ideas on how to bring up children.* 关于如何培养孩子，他们有非常明确的想法。 ➲ SYNONYMS AT CERTAIN **2** 🔑 easily or clearly seen or understood; obvious 清楚的；明显的 SYN **clear**: *The look on her face was a definite sign that something was wrong.* 一看她的神色就知道出事了。 ◇ *There was a definite feeling that things were getting worse.* 人们明显感到事情越来越糟。 **3** [not before noun] **~ (about something) | ~ (that...)** (of a person 人) sure that sth is true or that sth is going to happen and stating it to other people 肯定；有把握：*I'm definite about this.* 我对这事毫无疑问。

■ ***noun*** [sing.] (*informal*) sth that you are certain about or that you know will happen; sb who is sure to do sth 肯定的事（或人）：*'We're moving our office to Glasgow.' 'That's a definite, is it?'* "我们的办事处要搬到格拉斯哥去。""这事儿定了，是吗？" ◇ *'Is Sarah coming to the party?' 'Yes, she's a definite.'* "萨拉要来参加聚会吗？""是的，她肯定来。"

ˌdefinite ˈarticle *noun* (*grammar* 语法) the word *the* in English, or a similar word in another language 定冠词（如英语中的 the） ➲ COMPARE INDEFINITE ARTICLE

def·in·ite·ly 🔑 AW /ˈdefɪnətli/ *adv.* **1** 🔑 (*informal*) a way of emphasizing that sth is true and that there is no doubt about it 肯定；没问题；当然；确实：*I definitely remember sending the letter.* 我记得这封信肯定发出去了。 ◇ *'Was it what you expected?' 'Yes, definitely.'* "那是你所期待的吗？""当然是。" ◇ *'Do you plan to have children?' 'Definitely not!'* "你们打算要孩子吗？""绝对没这个打算！" ◇ *Some old people want help; others most definitely do not.* 有些老人想要得到帮助，有些却根本不需要。 **2** 🔑 in a way that is certain or that shows that you are certain 确切地；明确地；清楚地：*The date of the move has not been definitely decided yet* (= it may change). 搬迁日期还未完全确定下来。 ◇ *Please say definitely whether you will be coming or not.* 请说清楚，你来还是不来。

def·in·ition 🔑 AW /ˌdefɪˈnɪʃn/ *noun* **1** 🔑 [C, U] an explanation of the meaning of a word or phrase, especially in a dictionary; the act of stating the meanings of words and phrases （尤指词典里的词或短语的）释义；解释：*clear simple definitions* 简单明了的释义 ◇ *Neighbours **by definition** live close by* (= this is what being a neighbour means). 顾名思义，"邻居"就要住在邻近的地方。 ➲ LANGUAGE BANK AT DEFINE ➲ WORDFINDER NOTE AT DICTIONARY, WORD **2** 🔑 [C] what an idea, etc. means 定义：*What's your definition of happiness?* 你对幸福的定义是什么？ **3** [U] the quality of being clear and easy to see 清晰度：*The definition of the digital TV pictures is excellent.* 数字电视图像的清晰度很高。

de·fini·tive AW /dɪˈfɪnətɪv/ *adj.* **1** final; not able to be changed 最后的；决定性的；不可更改的：*a **definitive agreement/answer/statement*** 最后的协议 / 答复 / 声明 ◇ *The **definitive version** of the text is ready to be published.* 文本的正稿已备妥，可以发表了。 **2** [usually before noun] considered to be the best of its kind and almost impossible to improve 最佳的；最完整可靠的：*the definitive biography of Einstein* 最完整可靠的爱因斯坦传记 ▶ **de·fini·tive·ly** *adv.*

de·flate *verb* **1** /dɪˈfleɪt; ˌdiː-/ [T, I] **~ (sth)** to let air or gas out of a tyre, BALLOON, etc.; to become smaller because of air or gas coming out 放掉（轮胎、气球等的）气；（使）瘪下来 **2** /dɪˈfleɪt/ [T, often passive] **~ sb/sth** to make sb feel less confident; to make sb/sth feel or seem less important 使泄气；挫败…的锐气：*All the criticism had left her feeling totally deflated.* 所有这些批评使她彻底失去了信心。 **3** /ˌdiː-/ [T] **~ sth** (*economics* 经) to reduce the amount of money being used in a country so that prices fall or stay steady 紧缩（通货） ➲ COMPARE INFLATE, REFLATE

de·fla·tion /ˌdiːˈfleɪʃn/ *noun* [U] **1** (*economics* 经) a reduction in the amount of money in a country's economy so that prices fall or remain the same 通货紧缩 ➲ COLLOCATIONS AT ECONOMY **2** the action of air being removed from sth 放气；抽气；泄气 OPP **inflation** ▶ **de·fla·tion·ary** /ˌdiːˈfleɪʃənri; *NAmE* -neri/ *adj.*：*deflationary policies* 通货紧缩政策

de·flect /dɪˈflekt/ *verb* **1** [I, T] to change direction or make sth change direction, especially after hitting sth （尤指击中某物后）偏斜，转向，使偏斜，使转向：*The ball deflected off Reid's body into the goal.* 球打在里德身上反弹进球门。 ◇ **~ sth** *He raised his arm to try to deflect the blow.* 他举起手臂试图挡开这一击。 **2** [T] **~ sth** to succeed in preventing sth from being directed towards you 转移；引开 SYN **divert**: *All attempts to **deflect attention** from his private life have failed.* 本想转移人们对他私生活的注意，但一切努力都失败了。 ◇ *She sought to **deflect criticism** by blaming her family.* 她责怪她的家人，企图以此转移对她的批评。 **3** [T] **~ sb (from sth)** to prevent sb from doing sth that they are determined to do 阻止（某人做已决定做的事）：*The government will not be deflected from its commitments.* 政府决不会因任何阻碍而放弃承诺。

de·flec·tion /dɪˈflekʃn/ *noun* [U, C, usually sing.] a sudden change in the direction that sth is moving in, usually after it has hit sth; the act of causing sth to change direction （常指击中某物后）突然转向，偏斜，偏离：*the angle of deflection* 偏斜度 ◇ *the deflection of the missile away from its target* 导弹偏离目标 ◇ *The goal was scored with a deflection off the goalkeeper.* 这个入球是球打在守门员身上反弹入网的。

de·flower /ˌdiːˈflaʊə(r)/ *verb* **~ sb** (*old-fashioned, literary*) to have sex with a woman who has not had sex before 奸污（处女）；夺去（女子）的贞操

de·fog /ˌdiːˈfɒɡ; *NAmE* -ˈfɔːɡ; -ˈfɑːɡ/ *verb* (**-gg-**) [T, I] **~ (sth)** (*NAmE*) (*BrE* **de·mist**) to remove the CONDENSATION from a car's windows so that you can see clearly 除去（汽车玻璃上的）雾水

de·fo·liant /ˌdiːˈfəʊliənt; *NAmE* -ˈfoʊ-/ *noun* [C, U] a chemical that removes the leaves from plants, sometimes used as a weapon in war 落叶剂（有时用作军事武器）

de·foli·ate /ˌdiːˈfəʊlieɪt; *NAmE* -ˈfoʊ-/ *verb* ~ **sth** (*specialist*) to destroy the leaves of trees or plants, especially with chemicals（尤指用化学物质）除去…的叶 ▶ **de·foli·ation** /ˌdiːˌfəʊliˈeɪʃn; *NAmE* -ˌfoʊ-/ *noun* [U]

de·for·est /ˌdiːˈfɒrɪst; *NAmE* -ˈfɔːr-; -ˈfɑːr-/ *verb* [usually passive] ~ **sth** to cut down and destroy all the trees in a place 砍掉（某地）的树林；毁掉（某地）的森林：*Two thirds of the region has been deforested in the past decade.* 在过去十年里这个地区的森林有三分之二被毁掉。

de·for·est·ation /ˌdiːˌfɒrɪˈsteɪʃn; *NAmE* -ˌfɔːr-; -ˌfɑːr-/ *noun* [U] the act of cutting down or burning the trees in an area 毁林；滥伐森林；烧林 ➲ COLLOCATIONS AT ENVIRONMENT ➲ VISUAL VOCAB PAGE V6 ➲ COMPARE AFFORESTATION, REFORESTATION

de·form /dɪˈfɔːm; *NAmE* -ˈfɔːrm/ *verb* ~ **sth** to change or spoil the usual or natural shape of sth 改变…的外形；损毁…的形状；使成畸形：*The disease had deformed his spine.* 疾病导致他脊柱变形。

de·form·ation /ˌdiːfɔːˈmeɪʃn; *NAmE* -fɔːrˈm-/ *noun* **1** [U] the process or result of changing and spoiling the normal shape of sth 损形；变形；畸形 **2** [C] a change in the normal shape of sth as a result of injury or illness 破相；变丑；残废：*a deformation of the spine* 脊柱的畸变

de·formed /dɪˈfɔːmd; *NAmE* -ˈfɔːrmd/ *adj.* (of a person or a part of the body 人或身体部位) having a shape that is not normal because it has grown wrongly 畸形的；变形的：*She was born with deformed hands.* 她的双手天生畸形。

de·form·ity /dɪˈfɔːməti; *NAmE* -ˈfɔːrm-/ *noun* (*pl.* **-ies**) [C, U] a condition in which a part of the body is not the normal shape because of injury, illness or because it has grown wrongly（身体的）畸形 SYN **malformation**：*Drugs taken during pregnancy may cause physical deformity in babies.* 妊娠期服用的药物可能引起婴儿身体畸形。

DEFRA /ˈdefrə/ *abbr.* (in Britain) Department for Environment, Food and Rural Affairs（英国）环境、食品和乡村事务部

de·frag·ment /ˌdiːfræɡˈment/ (*also informal* **de·frag** /ˌdiːˈfræɡ/) *verb* ~ **sth** (*computing* 计) to organize the files on a computer so that information relating to each file is stored in the same area, so the computer works faster 整理（计算机磁盘）碎片

de·fraud /dɪˈfrɔːd/ *verb* [I, T] to get money illegally from a person or an organization by tricking them 骗取，诈取（…的钱财）：*All three men were charged with conspiracy to defraud.* 三人均被控密谋诈骗。◇ ~ **sb (of sth)** *They were accused of defrauding the company of $14 000.* 他们被控诈骗该公司 14 000 美元。

de·fray /dɪˈfreɪ/ *verb* ~ **costs/expenses** (*formal*) to give sb back the money that they have spent on sth 支付，付给（已开支的款项）

de·friend /ˌdiːˈfrend/ *verb* = UNFRIEND

de·frock /ˌdiːˈfrɒk; *NAmE* -ˈfrɑːk/ *verb* [usually passive] ~ **sb** to officially remove a priest from his or her job, because he or she has done sth wrong 免去（行为不端的牧师）的圣职：*a defrocked priest* 被免职的祭司

de·frost /ˌdiːˈfrɒst; *NAmE* -ˈfrɔːst/ *verb* **1** [I, T] to become or make sth warmer, especially food, so that it is no longer frozen 解冻，使解冻（尤指食物）：*It will take about four hours to defrost.* 解冻要花四小时左右。◇ ~ **sth** *Make sure you defrost the chicken completely before cooking.* 一定要让冻鸡化透后再烹调。➲ COMPARE DE-ICE, MELT (1), THAW *v.* (3), UNFREEZE (1) **2** [T, I] ~ **(sth)** when you **defrost** a fridge/refrigerator or FREEZER, or when it **defrosts**, you remove the ice from it 给（冰箱或冷冻柜）除霜；除霜 **3** [T] ~ **sth** (*NAmE*) to remove ice from the surface of a car's windows 除去（汽车玻璃上的）冰霜 ▶ **de·frost·er** *noun*

deft /deft/ *adj.* **1** (of a person's movements 人的动作) skilful and quick 熟练的；灵巧的；机敏的：***deft hands/fingers/footwork*** 灵活的手 / 手指 / 步法 ◇ *He finished off the painting with a few deft strokes of the brush.* 他用画笔熟练地勾上几笔，这幅画就完成了。 **2** skilful 熟练的；有技巧的：*her deft command of the language* 她对这种语言的充分掌握 ▶ **deft·ly** *adv.*：*I threw her a towel which she deftly caught.* 我扔给她一块毛巾，她敏捷地接住了。◇ *They deftly avoided answering my questions.* 他们机智地避开了我的问题。 **deft·ness** *noun* [U]

de·funct /dɪˈfʌŋkt/ *adj.* (*formal*) no longer existing, operating or being used 已灭绝的；不再起作用的；不再使用的

de·fuse /ˌdiːˈfjuːz/ *verb* **1** ~ **sth** to stop a possibly dangerous or difficult situation from developing, especially by making people less angry or nervous 缓和；平息：*Local police are trying to defuse racial tension in the community.* 当地的警察竭力缓和这个社区种族间的紧张关系。 **2** ~ **sth** to remove the FUSE from a bomb so that it cannot explode 拆除（炸弹）的引信

defy /dɪˈfaɪ/ *verb* (**de·fies**, **defy·ing**, **de·fied**, **de·fied**) **1** ~ **sb/sth** to refuse to obey or show respect for sb in authority, a law, a rule, etc. 违抗；反抗；蔑视：*I wouldn't have dared to defy my teachers.* 我可不敢不听老师的话。◇ *Hundreds of people today defied the ban on political gatherings.* 今天有数百人违抗禁止政治集会的规定。 **2** ~ **belief, explanation, description, etc.** to be impossible or almost impossible to believe, explain, describe, etc. 不可能，无法（相信、解释、描绘等）：*a political move that defies explanation* 无法解释的政治举动 ◇ *The beauty of the scene defies description.* 景色之美简直难以描绘。 **3** ~ **sth** to successfully resist sth to a very unusual degree 经受住；顶住；抗住：*The baby boy* ***defied all the odds and survived*** (= stayed alive when it seemed certain that he would die). 这名男婴九死一生活了下来。

> **WORD FAMILY**
> **defy** *verb*
> **defiance** *noun*
> **defiant** *adj.*

IDM **I defy you/anyone to do sth** used to say that sb should try to do sth, as a way of emphasizing that you think it is impossible to do it 激，挑动（某人尽力做你认为不可能的事）：*I defy anyone not to cry at the end of the film.* 我倒要看看有谁在电影结尾时不哭。

deg. *abbr.* DEGREE(S) 度，度数（温度单位）：*26 deg. C* * 26 摄氏度

de·gen·er·ate *verb, adj., noun*

■ ***verb*** /dɪˈdʒenəreɪt/ [I] to become worse, for example by becoming lower in quality or weaker 恶化；蜕变；衰退 SYN **deteriorate**：*Her health degenerated quickly.* 她的健康状况迅速恶化。◇ ~ **into sth** *The march degenerated into a riot.* 示威游行变成了暴乱。

■ ***adj.*** /dɪˈdʒenərət/ **1** having moral standards that have fallen to a level that is very low and unacceptable to most people 堕落的；颓废的：*a degenerate popular culture* 颓废的大众文化 **2** (*specialist*) having returned to a simple structure; lacking sth that is usually present 退化的；简并的 ▶ **de·gen·er·acy** /dɪˈdʒenərəsi/ *noun* [U]

■ ***noun*** /dɪˈdʒenərət/ a person whose behaviour shows moral standards that have fallen to a very low level 堕落的人

de·gen·er·ation /dɪˌdʒenəˈreɪʃn/ *noun* [U] the process of becoming worse or less acceptable in quality or condition 蜕化；衰退；堕落：*social/moral degeneration* 社会倒退；道德沦丧 ◇ *Intensive farming in the area has caused severe degeneration of the land.* 这个地区的集约化农业使得土壤严重贫瘠化。

de·gen·era·tive /dɪˈdʒenərətɪv/ *adj.* (*specialist*) (of an illness 疾病) getting or likely to get worse as time passes（随着时间的推移）变性的，退行性的：*degenerative diseases such as arthritis* 诸如关节炎之类的变性病

de·grad·able /dɪˈɡreɪdəbl/ *adj.* (*especially NAmE, specialist*) that can be changed to a simpler form 可降级的；可降低的；可降解的 ➲ SEE ALSO BIODEGRADABLE

deg·rad·ation /ˌdeɡrəˈdeɪʃn/ *noun* [U] **1** a situation in which sb has lost all SELF-RESPECT and the respect of other people 堕落；落魄，潦倒（的境况）：*the degradation of being sent to prison* 被关进监狱的落魄境况 **2** (*specialist*) the process of sth being damaged or made worse 毁坏，恶化（过程）：*environmental degradation* 环境恶化

D

de·grade /dɪˈɡreɪd/ *verb* **1** [T] **~ sb** to show or treat sb in a way that makes them seem not worth any respect or not worth taking seriously 降低…身份；侮辱…的人格；使受屈辱：*This poster is offensive and degrades women.* 这张海报冒失无礼，有辱女性尊严。 **2** [I, T] **~ (sth)** (*specialist*) to change or make sth change to a simpler chemical form （使）退化，降解；分解 **3** [T] **~ sth** (*specialist*) to make sth become worse, especially in quality 降低，削弱（尤指质量）

de·grad·ing /dɪˈɡreɪdɪŋ/ *adj.* treating sb as if they have no value, so that they lose their SELF-RESPECT and the respect of other people 有辱人格的；降低身份的；贬低的：*the inhuman and degrading treatment of prisoners* 犯人所受的不人道和侮辱性待遇

de·grease /ˌdiːˈɡriːs/ *verb* **~ sth** to remove GREASE or oil from sth 除去…的脂肪（或油污）

de·gree 🔑 /dɪˈɡriː/ *noun* **1** 🔑 [C] a unit for measuring angles 度，度数（角的量度单位）：*an angle of ninety degrees (90°)* * 90 度角 **2** 🔑 [C] (*abbr.* **deg.**) a unit for measuring temperature 度，度数（温度单位）：*Water freezes at 32 degrees Fahrenheit (32°F) or zero/nought degrees Celsius (0°C).* 水在 32 华氏度或零摄氏度结冰。 **3** 🔑 [C, U] the amount or level of sth 程度：*Her job demands a high degree of skill.* 她的工作要求有高超的技能。◇ *I agree with you **to a certain degree**.* 我在某种程度上同意你的观点。◇ *To what degree can parents be held responsible for a child's behaviour?* 父母应在多大程度上对孩子的行为负责呢？◇ *Most pop music is influenced, to a greater or lesser degree, by the blues.* 多数流行音乐都不同程度地受到布鲁斯音乐的影响。 **4** 🔑 [C] the qualification obtained by students who successfully complete a university or college course （大学）学位：*My brother has a master's degree from Harvard.* 我哥哥有哈佛大学的硕士学位。◇ *She has a degree in Biochemistry from Queen's University.* 她有女王大学的生物化学学位。◇ *a four-year degree course* 四年的学位课程 ➲ WORDFINDER NOTE AT UNIVERSITY ➲ COLLOCATIONS AT EDUCATION **5** [C] (*BrE*) a university or college course, normally lasting three years or more （大学通常三年或以上的）学位课程：*I'm hoping to do a chemistry degree.* 我希望攻读化学学位课程。 **6** [C] a level in a scale of how serious sth is 严重程度（或级别）：*murder in the first degree* (= of the most serious kind) 一级谋杀（最严重）◇ *first-degree murder* 一级谋杀 ◇ *third-degree* (= very serious) *burns* 三度烧伤（非常严重）

IDM **by deˈgrees** slowly and gradually 逐渐地；渐渐地：*By degrees their friendship grew into love.* 他们的友谊逐渐发展成为爱情。 ➲ MORE AT NTH

de·hu·man·ize (*BrE also* **-ise**) /ˌdiːˈhjuːmənaɪz/ *verb* **~ sb** to make sb lose their human qualities such as kindness, pity, etc. 使丧失人性；使无人性：*the dehumanizing effects of poverty and squalor* 贫穷和肮脏的环境造成丧失人性的结果 ▶ **de·hu·man·iza·tion, -isa·tion** /diːˌhjuːmənaɪˈzeɪʃn; *NAmE* -nəˈz-/ *noun* [U]

de·hu·midi·fier /ˌdiːhjuːˈmɪdɪfaɪə(r)/ *noun* an electrical machine for removing water from the air 抽湿机；除湿器；干燥机 ➲ SEE ALSO HUMIDIFIER

de·hy·drate /diːˈhaɪdreɪt; ˌdiːhaɪˈdreɪt/ *verb* **1** [T, usually passive] **~ sth** to remove the water from sth, especially food, in order to preserve it 使（食物）脱水 **2** [I, T] to lose too much water from your body; to make a person's body lose too much water （身体）失水，脱水；使（身体）脱水：*Runners can dehydrate very quickly in this heat.* 天这样热，赛跑运动员很快会脱水。◇ **~ sb** *the dehydrating effects of alcohol* 酒精引起的脱水 ▶ **de·hy·dra·tion** /ˌdiːhaɪˈdreɪʃn/ *noun* [U]：*to suffer from dehydration* 受脱水之苦 **de·hy·drated** /ˌdiːhaɪˈdreɪtɪd/ *adj.*：*Drink lots of water to avoid becoming dehydrated.* 要大量饮水，以免脱水。

de-ice /ˌdiː ˈaɪs/ *verb* **~ sth** to remove the ice from sth 除去…上的冰 ➲ COMPARE DEFROST, MELT (1), THAW *v.* (3), UNFREEZE (1)

de-icer /ˌdiː ˈaɪsə(r)/ *noun* [C, U] a substance that is put on a surface to remove ice or to stop it from forming 除冰剂

deic·tic /ˈdaɪktɪk; ˈdeɪktɪk/ *adj.* (*linguistics* 语言) relating to a word or an expression whose meaning depends on who says it, where they are, who they are talking to, etc., for example 'you', 'me', 'here', 'next week' （词语或表达方式）指示的（如 you、me、here、next week 等）

deify /ˈdeɪɪfaɪ; ˈdiːɪfaɪ/ *verb* (**dei·fies, dei·fy·ing, dei·fied, dei·fied**) **~ sb** (*formal*) to treat or worship sb as a god 把（某人）奉若神明；把（某人）尊为神；崇拜 ▶ **dei·fi·ca·tion** /ˌdeɪɪfɪˈkeɪʃn; ˌdiːɪfɪˈkeɪʃn/ *noun* [U]：*the deification of medieval kings* 对中世纪国王的神化

deign /deɪn/ *verb* **~ to do sth** (*disapproving*) to do sth in a way that shows you think you are too important to do it 屈尊，俯就，降低身份（做某事） SYN **condescend**：*She just grunted, not deigning to look up from the page.* 她只咕哝了一声，继续看书，不屑抬起头来看一眼。

deism /ˈdeɪɪzəm; ˈdiːɪz-/ *noun* [U] belief in God, especially a God that created the universe but does not take part in it 自然神论，理神论（认为上帝创造世界后让其自然运行） ▶ **deist** /ˈdeɪɪst; ˈdiːɪst/ *noun* **de·is·tic** /deɪˈɪstɪk; diːˈɪ-/ *adj.*

deity /ˈdeɪəti; ˈdiːəti/ *noun* (*pl.* **-ies**) **1** [C] a god or GODDESS 神；女神：*Greek/Roman/Hindu deities* 希腊 / 罗马 / 印度教诸神 **2 the Deity** [sing.] (*formal*) God 上帝；天主

deixis /ˈdeɪksɪs; ˈdaɪksɪs/ *noun* [U] (*linguistics* 语言) the function or use of DEICTIC words or expressions (= ones whose meaning depends on where, when or by whom they are used) 指示功能；指示词的使用

déjà vu /ˌdeɪʒɑː ˈvuː/ *noun* [U] (*from French*) the feeling that you have previously experienced sth which is happening to you now 似曾经历过的感觉：*I had a strong sense of déjà vu as I entered the room.* 进这房间时我有一种似曾来过的强烈感觉。

de·ject·ed /dɪˈdʒektɪd/ *adj.* unhappy and disappointed 沮丧的；情绪低落的；垂头丧气的 SYN **despondent**：*She looked so dejected when she lost the game.* 她输掉比赛时情绪显得非常低落。 ▶ **de·ject·ed·ly** *adv.*

de·jec·tion /dɪˈdʒekʃn/ *noun* [U] a feeling of unhappiness and disappointment 沮丧；情绪低落；垂头丧气

de jure /ˌdeɪ ˈdʒʊəri; *NAmE* ˈdʒʊri/ *adj., adv.* (*from Latin, law* 律) according to the law 根据法律；在法律上：*He held power de jure and de facto* (= both according to the law and in reality). 他无论在法律上还是实际上都大权在握。 ➲ COMPARE DE FACTO

deka·liter /ˈdekəliːtə(r)/ *noun* (*US*) = DECALITRE

deka·meter /ˈdekəmiːtə(r)/ *noun* (*US*) = DECAMETRE

dekko /ˈdekəʊ; *NAmE* -koʊ/ *noun*

IDM **have a dekko (at sth)** (*old-fashioned, BrE, slang*) to look (at sth) 看，望（某物）；（对…）看一眼 ORIGIN From the Hindi word for 'look!', used by the British army in India in the past. 源自印地语表示"看！"的词，过去由驻印度英军使用。

delay 🔑 /dɪˈleɪ/ *noun, verb*

■ ***noun*** **1** 🔑 [C] a period of time when sb/sth has to wait because of a problem that makes sth slow or late 延迟（或耽搁、拖延）的时间：*Commuters will face long delays on the roads today.* 路远乘车上下班的人今天要在路上耽误很多时间了。◇ *We apologize for the delay in answering your letter.* 来信收悉，迟复为歉。◇ *a delay of two hours/a two-hour delay* 两小时的延误 ➲ COLLOCATIONS AT TRAVEL

2 [C, U] a situation in which sth does not happen when it should; the act of delaying 延期；耽搁；延误：*There's no time for delay.* 没有时间了，不能拖延了。◇ *Report it to the police* ***without delay*** (= immediately). 赶快将此事报告警方。

■ ***verb*** 1 [I, T] to not do sth until a later time or to make sth happen at a later time 延迟；延期；推迟 SYN **defer**: *Don't delay—call us today!* 别拖延，今天就给我们打电话！◇ **~ sth** *The judge will delay his verdict until he receives medical reports on the offender.* 法官将推迟判决，直到收到有关违法者的医疗报告。◇ *She's suffering a* ***delayed reaction*** (= a reaction that did not happen immediately) *to the shock.* 她正在承受着冲击所带来的滞后反应。◇ **~ doing sth** *He delayed telling her the news, waiting for the right moment.* 他没有马上把消息告诉她，等有了适当的时机再说。 ➲ MORE LIKE THIS 27, page R28 2 [T] **~ sb** to make sb late or force them to do sth more slowly 使迟到；使耽搁；使拖延 SYN **hold up**: *Thousands of commuters were delayed for over an hour.* 数千名乘车上下班的人被耽搁了一个多小时。◇ *The government is accused of using* ***delaying tactics*** (= deliberately doing sth to delay a process, decision, etc.). 政府被指责故意采取拖延战术。

de·lect·able /dɪˈlektəbl/ *adj.* 1 (of food and drink 食物或饮料) extremely pleasant to taste, smell or look at 美味可口的；香甜的；宜人的 SYN **delicious**: *the delectable smell of freshly baked bread* 新烤面包的香味 2 (*humorous*) (of a person 人) very attractive 妩媚动人的；有迷惑力的；有吸引力的：*his delectable body* 他健美的身体

de·lect·ation /ˌdiːlekˈteɪʃn/ *noun* [U] (*formal* or *humorous*) enjoyment or entertainment 享受；愉快；娱乐 SYN **delight**

dele·gate *noun, verb*

■ ***noun*** /ˈdelɪɡət/ 1 a person who is chosen or elected to represent the views of a group of people and vote and make decisions for them 代表；会议代表：*Congress delegates rejected the proposals.* 国会代表拒绝了这些提议。 2 a person who attends a conference 参会人员；会议出席者：*The conference was attended by delegates from 56 countries.* 此次会议有来自 56 个国家的代表出席。 ➲ WORDFINDER NOTE AT CONFERENCE

■ ***verb*** /ˈdelɪɡeɪt/ 1 [I, T] to give part of your work, power or authority to sb in a lower position than you 授（权）；把（工作、权力等）委托（给下级）：*Some managers find it difficult to delegate.* 有些经理认为难以做到下放权力。◇ **~ (sth) (to sb)** *The job had to be delegated to an assistant.* 这工作得交给助手负责。 2 [T] **~ sb to do sth** [usually passive] to choose sb to do sth 选派（某人做某事）：*I've been delegated to organize the Christmas party.* 我被选派来组织圣诞聚会。 ➲ MORE LIKE THIS 21, page R27

dele·ga·tion /ˌdelɪˈɡeɪʃn/ *noun* 1 [C+sing./pl. v.] a group of people who represent the views of an organization, a country, etc. 代表团：*the Dutch delegation to the United Nations* 出席联合国会议的荷兰代表团 ◇ *a delegation of teachers* 教师代表团 ➲ COLLOCATIONS AT INTERNATIONAL 2 [U] the process of giving sb work or responsibilities that would usually be yours 委托；委派：*delegation of authority/decision-making* 授予权力 / 决策权

de·lete /dɪˈliːt/ *verb* **~ sth (from sth)** to remove sth that has been written or printed, or that has been stored on a computer 删去；删除：*Your name has been deleted from the list.* 你的名字已从名单上删掉。◇ *This command deletes files from the directory.* 这一指令把文档从目录中删除。◇ (*BrE*) *Mr/Mrs/Ms* (***delete as appropriate***) 先生 / 太太 / 女士（删去不适用者） ➲ WORDFINDER NOTE AT FILE ➲ COLLOCATIONS AT EMAIL ▶ **de·le·tion** /dɪˈliːʃn/ *noun* [U, C]: *He made several deletions to the manuscript.* 他在原稿上删去了好几处。

dele·teri·ous /ˌdeləˈtɪəriəs; *NAmE* -ˈtɪr-/ *adj.* (*formal*) harmful and damaging 有害的；造成伤害的；损害的

deli /ˈdeli/ *noun* = DELICATESSEN

de·lib·er·ate *adj., verb*

■ ***adj.*** /dɪˈlɪbərət/ 1 done on purpose rather than by accident 故意的；蓄意的；存心的 SYN **intentional, planned**: *a deliberate act of vandalism* 故意毁坏公物的行为 ◇ *The speech was a deliberate attempt to embarrass the government.* 这一发言蓄意使政府难堪。 OPP **unintentional** 2 (of a movement or an action 动作或行为) done slowly and carefully 不慌不忙的；小心翼翼的；从容不迫的：*She spoke in a slow and deliberate way.* 她说话慢条斯理不慌不忙。

■ ***verb*** /dɪˈlɪbəreɪt/ [I, T] (*formal*) to think very carefully about sth, usually before making a decision 仔细考虑；深思熟虑；反复思考：*The jury deliberated for five days before finding him guilty.* 陪审团认真讨论了五天才裁定他有罪。◇ **~ (on) whether, what, etc.…** *They deliberated (on) whether to continue with the talks.* 他们仔细考虑了是否继续谈判的问题。

de·lib·er·ate·ly /dɪˈlɪbərətli/ *adv.* 1 done in a way that was planned, not by chance 故意；蓄意；存心 SYN **intentionally, on purpose**: *She's been deliberately ignoring him all day.* 她故意整天都不理他。 2 slowly and carefully 不慌不忙地；小心翼翼地；从容不迫地：*He packed up his possessions slowly and deliberately.* 他慢慢地、小心翼翼地收拾好自己的物品。

de·lib·er·ation /dɪˌlɪbəˈreɪʃn/ *noun* (*formal*) 1 [U, C, usually pl.] the process of carefully considering or discussing sth 细想；考虑；商议；审议：*After ten hours of deliberation, the jury returned a verdict of 'not guilty'.* 经过十小时的商议，陪审团宣告了"无罪"的裁决。◇ *The deliberations of the committee are completely confidential.* 委员会的审议过程是绝对保密的。 2 [U] the quality of being slow and careful in what you say or do（说话或办事）从容，审慎：*She signed her name with great deliberation.* 她非常审慎地签上了自己的名字。

deli·cacy /ˈdelɪkəsi/ *noun* (*pl.* **-ies**) 1 [U] the quality of being, or appearing to be, easy to damage or break 脆弱；娇嫩：*the delicacy of the fabric* 织物的精细脆弱 2 [U] the quality of being done carefully and gently 仔细；温柔：*the delicacy of his touch* 他那温柔的抚摸 3 [U] very careful behaviour in a difficult situation so that nobody is offended 周到；体贴 SYN **tact**: *She handled the situation with great sensitivity and delicacy.* 她慎重而周到地处理了这个情况。 4 [U] the fact that a situation is difficult and sb may be easily offended 棘手；微妙：*I need to talk to you about a matter of some delicacy.* 我需要与你谈个有点棘手的问题。 5 [C] a type of food considered to be very special in a particular place 精美的食物；佳肴 SYN **speciality**: *local delicacies* 当地的美味佳肴

deli·cate /ˈdelɪkət/ *adj.* 1 easily damaged or broken 易损的；易碎的；脆弱的 SYN **fragile**: *delicate china teacups* 易碎的瓷茶杯 ◇ *The eye is one of the most delicate organs of the body.* 眼睛是人体最娇弱的器官之一。◇ *the delicate ecological balance of the rainforest* 热带雨林极易被破坏的生态平衡 ◇ *Babies have very delicate skin.* 婴儿的皮肤非常娇嫩。◇ *a cool wash cycle for delicate fabrics* 精细织物冷洗程序 2 (of a person 人) not strong and easily becoming ill/sick 虚弱的；纤弱的：***a delicate child/constitution*** 纤弱的孩子 / 体质 3 small and having a beautiful shape or appearance 纤细的；微小的；精美的；小巧玲珑的：*his delicate hands* 他纤细的手 4 made or formed in a very careful and detailed way 精致的；精细的；精密的：*the delicate mechanisms of a clock* 钟的精密机件 5 showing or needing skilful, careful or sensitive treatment 熟练的；需要技巧的；需要小心处理的；微妙的：*I admired your delicate handling of the situation.* 我佩服你应付这种局面的娴熟技巧。◇ *a delicate problem* 微妙的问题 ◇ *The delicate surgical operation took five hours.* 这精细的外科手术花了五个小时。 6 (of colours, flavours and smells 颜色、味道、气味) light and pleasant; not strong 柔和的；清淡可口的；清香的 SYN **subtle**: ***a delicate fragrance/flavour*** 清新的芳香；鲜美的味道 ◇ *a river scene painted in delicate watercolours* 用柔和的水彩画的河景 ▶ **deli·cate·ly** *adv.*: *He stepped delicately over the broken glass.* 他小心翼翼地跨过碎玻璃。◇ *delicately balanced flavours* 精心调配的味道

D

deli·ca·tes·sen /ˌdelɪkəˈtesn/ (*also* **deli**) *noun* a shop/store or part of one that sells cooked meats and cheeses, and special or unusual foods that come from other countries（出售熟肉、干酪和进口风味食品的）熟食店，熟食柜台

D

de·li·cious /dɪˈlɪʃəs/ *adj.* **1** having a very pleasant taste or smell 美味的；可口的；芬芳的：*Who cooked this? It's delicious.* 谁做的？味道好极了。 **2** (*literary*) extremely pleasant or enjoyable 令人愉快的；令人开心的；宜人的：*the delicious coolness of the breeze* 微风送爽 ▶ **de·li·cious·ly** *adv.*：*deliciously creamy soup* 可口的奶油汤

de·light /dɪˈlaɪt/ *noun, verb*

■ ***noun*** **1** [U] a feeling of great pleasure 高兴；愉快；快乐 SYN **joy**：*a feeling of sheer/pure delight* 十分高兴的心情 ◊ *The children squealed* ***with delight*** *when they saw the puppy.* 孩子们看到小狗时高兴得大声尖叫。 ◊ *She won the game easily,* ***to the delight of*** *all her fans.* 这场比赛她赢得很轻松，令所有的崇拜者大为高兴。 ◊ *He* ***takes*** *(****great****)* ***delight in*** (= enjoys) *proving others wrong.* 他以证实别人出错为（一大）快事。 ➲ SYNONYMS AT PLEASURE **2** [C] something that gives you great pleasure 令人高兴的事；乐事；乐趣 SYN **joy**：*This guitar is a delight to play.* 这吉他弹起来很惬意。 ◊ *the delights of living in the country* 生活在乡村的乐趣

■ ***verb*** ~ **sb** to give sb a lot of pleasure and enjoyment 使高兴；使愉快；使快乐：*This news will delight his fans all over the world.* 这消息将使全世界崇拜他的人都感到高兴。

PHR V **deˈlight in sth/doing sth** [no passive] to enjoy doing sth very much, especially sth that makes other people feel embarrassed, uncomfortable, etc. 以…为乐（尤指做使别人感到尴尬、不舒服的事）

de·light·ed /dɪˈlaɪtɪd/ *adj.* very pleased 高兴的；愉快的；快乐的：*a delighted smile* 愉快的微笑 ◊ ~ **to do sth** *I'd be absolutely delighted to come.* 我非常乐意前来。 ◊ ~ **that…** *I was delighted that you could stay.* 你能留下来我很高兴。 ◊ ~ **by/at sth** *She was delighted by/at the news of the wedding.* 听到婚礼的消息她很高兴。 ◊ ~ **with sth** *I was delighted with my presents.* 我对我收到的礼物很满意。 ➲ SYNONYMS AT GLAD ▶ **de·light·ed·ly** *adv.*

de·light·ful /dɪˈlaɪtfl/ *adj.* very pleasant 使人快乐的；令人愉快的；宜人的 SYN **charming**：*a delightful book/restaurant/town* 令人愉快的书；舒适的餐馆；宜人的城镇 ◊ *a delightful child* 讨人喜欢的孩子 ➲ SYNONYMS AT WONDERFUL ▶ **de·light·ful·ly** /dɪˈlaɪtfəli/ *adv.*

de·limit /diˈlɪmɪt/ *verb* ~ **sth** (*formal*) to decide what the limits of sth are 定…的界限；限定；界定

de·lin·eate /dɪˈlɪnieɪt/ *verb* ~ **sth** (*formal*) to describe, draw or explain sth in detail（详细地）描述，描画，解释：*Our objectives need to be precisely delineated.* 我们的目标需详细解释清楚。 ◊ *The ship's route is clearly delineated on the map.* 这条船的航线清楚地标在地图上。 ▶ **de·lin·ea·tion** /dɪˌlɪniˈeɪʃn/ *noun* [U, C]

de·lin·quency /dɪˈlɪŋkwənsi/ *noun* [U, C] (*pl.* **-ies**) bad or criminal behaviour, usually of young people（常指青年人的）犯罪，违法行为：*an increase in juvenile delinquency* 青少年犯罪的增加

de·lin·quent /dɪˈlɪŋkwənt/ *adj.* **1** (especially of young people or their behaviour 尤指青年人或其行为) showing a tendency to commit crimes 有违法倾向的：*delinquent teenagers* 不良青少年 **2** (*NAmE, finance* 财) having failed to pay money that is owed 拖欠债务的；欠债未还的：*a delinquent borrower* 欠债未还的借款人 **3** (*NAmE, finance* 财) (of a sum of money 款项) not having been paid in time 到期未付的：*a delinquent loan* 逾期未还的贷款 ▶ **de·lin·quent** *noun* ➲ SEE ALSO JUVENILE DELINQUENT

deli·quesce /ˌdelɪˈkwes/ *verb* (*formal*) **1** [I] to become liquid as a result of decaying（因腐烂而）融解 **2** [I] (*chemistry* 化) to become liquid as a result of absorbing water from the air 潮解 ▶ **deli·ques·cence** /ˌdelɪˈkwesns/ *noun* [U]

de·li·ri·ous /dɪˈlɪriəs; *BrE also* -ˈlɪəriəs/ *adj.* **1** in an excited state and not able to think or speak clearly, usually because of fever 极度亢奋的，精神错乱的，语无伦次的（常由发烧引起）：*He became delirious and couldn't recognize people.* 他已精神错乱，谁都不认得了。 **2** extremely excited and happy 极度兴奋的；特别愉快的：*The crowds were delirious with joy.* 人群欣喜若狂。 ▶ **de·li·ri·ous·ly** *adv.*

de·lir·ium /dɪˈlɪriəm; *BrE also* -ˈlɪəriəm/ *noun* [U] a mental state where sb becomes delirious, usually because of illness 谵妄，神志失常，说胡话（常由疾病引起）：*fits of delirium* 一阵阵胡言乱语

de·lir·ium tre·mens /dɪˌlɪriəm ˈtriːmenz; *BrE also* -ˌlɪəriəm/ *noun* [U] (*medical* 医) = DTs

de·liver /dɪˈlɪvə(r)/ *verb*

• **TAKE GOODS/LETTERS** 送货/信 **1** [T, I] to take goods, letters, etc. to the person or people they have been sent to; to take sb somewhere 递送；传送；交付；运载：~ **sth** *Do you have your milk delivered?* 你的牛奶是让别人送吗？ ◊ ~ **(sth) to sb/sth** *Leaflets have been delivered to every household.* 传单已发送到每家每户。 ◊ ~ **(to sb/sth)** *We promise to deliver within 48 hours.* 我们承诺在 48 小时内送到。

• **GIVE SPEECH** 发表演说 **2** [T] ~ **sth** to give a speech, talk, etc. or other official statement 发表；宣布；发布：*She is due to deliver a lecture on genetic engineering.* 根据安排她要作一个关于遗传工程的讲座。 ◊ *He delivered his lines confidently.* 他信心十足地说了他的台词。 ◊ *The jury finally delivered its verdict.* 陪审团终于宣布了裁决。

• **KEEP PROMISE** 履行诺言 **3** [I, T] to do what you promised to do or what you are expected to do; to produce or provide what people expect you to 履行诺言；不负所望；兑现：*He has promised to finish the job by June and I am sure he will deliver.* 他答应在六月底完成这项工作，我相信他会履行诺言。 ◊ ~ **on sth** *She always delivers on her promises.* 她总是信守诺言。 ◊ ~ **sth** *If you can't deliver improved sales figures, you're fired.* 如果你不能按照要求提高销售额，就会被解雇。 ◊ *The team delivered a stunning victory last night.* 昨晚这个队不负众望，大获全胜。

• **GIVE TO SB'S CONTROL** 交某人控制 **4** [T] ~ **sb/sth (up/over) (to sb)** (*formal*) to give sb/sth to sb else so that they are under this person's control 交出；交付；移交：*They delivered their prisoner over to the invading army.* 他们把俘虏交给了侵略军。

• **BABY** 婴儿 **5** [T] ~ **a baby** to help a woman to give birth to a baby 助产；接生：*The baby was delivered by Caesarean section.* 这个婴儿是剖腹产下的。 **6** [T] **be delivered of a baby** (*formal*) to give birth to a baby 分娩；生孩子：*She was delivered of a healthy boy.* 她生下一个健康的男孩儿。 ➲ WORDFINDER NOTE AT BIRTH

• **THROW** 投掷 **7** [T] ~ **sth** to throw or aim sth 投掷；把…瞄准；用…对准：*He* ***delivered the blow*** (= hit sb hard) *with all his force.* 他打这一下使出了全身的力气。

• **RESCUE** 解救 **8** [T] ~ **sb (from sth)** (*old use*) to rescue sb from sth bad 解救；拯救；使摆脱 SYN **save** IDM SEE GOODS, SIGN *v.*

de·liver·able /dɪˈlɪvərəbl/ *noun* [usually pl.] a product that a company promises to have ready for a customer 应交付的产品：*computer software deliverables* 应交付的计算机软件

de·liv·er·ance /dɪˈlɪvərəns/ *noun* [U] ~ **(from sth)** (*formal*) the state of being rescued from danger, evil or pain 解救；拯救；解脱

de·liv·ery /dɪˈlɪvəri/ *noun* (*pl.* **-ies**) **1** [U, C] the act of taking goods, letters, etc. to the people they have been sent to 传送；递送；交付：*a delivery van* 厢式送货车 ◊ *Please pay for goods* ***on delivery*** (= when you receive them). 请货到付款。 ◊ *Allow 28 days* ***for delivery.*** 请留出 28 天送货时间。 ◊ *Is there a* ***postal/mail delivery*** *on Saturdays?* 星期六送邮件吗？ ◊ (*formal*) *When can you* ***take delivery of*** (= be available to receive) *the car?* 你何时能提取那辆汽车？ ◊ (*figurative*) *the delivery of public services* 提供公共事业服务 **2** [C, U] the process of giving birth to a baby 分娩：*an* ***easy/difficult delivery*** 顺产；难产 ◊ *a* ***delivery room/ward*** (= in a hospital, etc.) 产房；产科病

房 **3** [sing.] the way in which sb speaks, sings a song, etc. in public 演讲方式；表演风格：*The beautiful poetry was ruined by her poor delivery.* 这优美的诗被她拙劣的朗诵给糟蹋了。 **4** [C] a ball that is thrown, especially in CRICKET or BASEBALL 投球（尤指板球或棒球）：*a fast delivery* 一个快投球 IDM SEE CASH *n.*

dell /del/ *noun* (*literary*) a small valley with trees growing in or around it （里面或周围有树的）小山谷

de·louse /ˌdiːˈlaʊs/ *verb* **~ sb/sth** to remove LICE (= small insects) from sb's hair or from an animal's coat 除去（头发或动物皮毛上的）虱子

Del·phic /ˈdelfɪk/ *adj.* **1** relating to the ancient Greek ORACLE at Delphi (= the place where people went to ask the gods for advice or information about the future) 德尔斐神谕的 **2** (*often* **delphic**) (*formal*) with a meaning that is deliberately hidden or difficult to understand 隐晦的；难以理解的：*a delphic utterance* 令人费解的话

del·phin·ium /delˈfɪniəm/ *noun* a tall garden plant with blue or white flowers growing up its STEM 翠雀，飞燕草属（高株园艺植物，开蓝花或白花）

delta /ˈdeltə/ *noun* **1** the fourth letter of the Greek alphabet (Δ, δ) 希腊字母表的第 4 个字母 **2** an area of land, shaped like a triangle, where a river has split into several smaller rivers before entering the sea 三角洲：*the Nile Delta* 尼罗河三角洲

del·toids /ˈdeltɔɪdz/ (*also informal* **delts** /delts/) *noun* [pl.] (*anatomy* 解) the thick triangle-shaped muscles that cover the shoulder joints 三角肌（覆盖于肩关节）

de·lude /dɪˈluːd/ *verb* to make sb believe sth that is not true 欺骗；哄骗 SYN **deceive**: **~ sb** *You poor deluded creature.* 你这上了当的可怜虫。◇ **~ yourself** *He's deluding himself if he thinks it's going to be easy.* 他要是以为那事很容易，那就是自己欺骗自己。◇ **~ sb/yourself into doing sth** *Don't be deluded into thinking that we are out of danger yet.* 不要误以为我们已脱离危险。◇ **~ yourself that...** *She had been deluding herself that he loved her.* 她一直欺骗自己说他爱着她。 ➲ SEE ALSO DELUSION

del·uge /ˈdeljuːdʒ/ *noun, verb*

■ ***noun*** [usually sing.] **1** a sudden very heavy fall of rain 暴雨；大雨；洪水 SYN **flood** **2** a large number of things that happen or arrive at the same time 涌现的事物；蜂拥而至的事物：*a **deluge of calls/complaints/letters*** 接连不断的电话；没完没了的投诉；纷至沓来的信件

■ ***verb*** **1 ~ sb/sth (with sth)** [usually passive] to send or give sb/sth a large number of things at the same time 使涌来；使充满 SYN **flood, inundate**: *We have been deluged with applications for the job.* 申请这个工作的求职信使我们应接不暇。 **2** [often passive] **~ sth** (*formal*) to flood a place with water 泛滥；淹没：*The campsite was deluged by a flash flood.* 露营地被突发的洪水淹没。

de·lu·sion /dɪˈluːʒn/ *noun* **1** [C] a false belief or opinion about yourself or your situation 错觉；谬见；妄想：*the delusions of the mentally ill* 精神病患者的妄想 ◇ *Don't go getting **delusions of grandeur*** (= a belief that you are more important than you actually are). 不要变得妄自尊大。 **2** [U] the act of believing or making yourself believe sth that is not true 自欺 ➲ SEE ALSO DELUDE

de·lu·sive /dɪˈluːsɪv/ (*also* **de·lu·sory** /dɪˈluːsəri; -zəri/) *adj.* (*formal*) not real or true 不真实的；虚假的 SYN **deceptive**

de·luxe /ˌdəˈlʌks; -ˈlʊks/ *adj.* [usually before noun] of a higher quality and more expensive than usual 高级的；豪华的 SYN **luxury**: *a deluxe hotel* 豪华酒店

delve /delv/ *verb* [I] **+ adv./prep.** to search for sth inside a bag, container, etc. （在手提包、容器等中）翻找 SYN **dig**: *She delved in her handbag for a pen.* 她在手提包里翻找钢笔。

PHR V **ˌdelve ˈinto sth** to try hard to find out more information about sth 探索；探究；查考：*She had started to delve into her father's distant past.* 她开始探究她父亲久已逝去的岁月。

Dem. *abbr.* (in politics in the US) DEMOCRAT; DEMOCRATIC （美国政治）民主党人，民主党的

dema·gogue /ˈdeməɡɒɡ; *NAmE* -ɡɑːɡ/ *noun* (*disapproving*) a political leader who tries to win support by using arguments based on emotion rather than reason 蛊惑民心的政客 ▸ **dema·gog·ic** /ˌdeməˈɡɒɡɪk; *NAmE* -ˈɡɑːɡ-/ *adj.* **dema·gogy** /ˈdeməɡɒɡi; *NAmE* -ɡɑːɡi/ *noun* [U]

de·mand /dɪˈmɑːnd; *NAmE* dɪˈmænd/ *noun, verb*

■ ***noun*** **1** [C] **~ (for sth/that...)** a very firm request for sth; sth that sb needs （坚决的）要求；所需之物：*a demand for higher pay* 增加工资的要求 ◇ *demands that the law on gun ownership should be changed* 要求修改枪械持有法的呼声 ◇ *firms attempting to **meet/satisfy** their customers' **demands*** (= to give them what they are asking for) 尽力满足客户要求的商行 **2** **demands** [pl.] **~ (of sth)** | **~ (on sb)** things that sb/sth makes you do, especially things that are difficult, make you tired, worried, etc. （尤指困难、使人劳累、令人担忧等的）要求：*the demands of children/work* 孩子烦人的事；工作中累人的事 ◇ *Flying **makes** enormous **demands** on pilots.* 驾驶飞机对飞行员要求很高。 **3** [U, C] **~ (for sth/sb)** the desire or need of customers for goods or services which they want to buy or use （顾客的）需求，需要：*to meet the demand for a product* 满足对某产品的需求 ◇ *There's an increased demand for organic produce these days.* 目前对有机农产品有更大的需求。◇ *Demand is exceeding supply.* 供不应求。 ➲ COLLOCATIONS AT ECONOMY

IDM **by popular deˈmand** because a lot of people have asked for sth 由于许多人的要求；由于普遍要求：*By popular demand, the play will run for another week.* 应广大观众要求，这出戏将加演一周。 **in deˈmand** wanted by a lot of people 需求大：*Good secretaries are always in*

▼ **SYNONYMS 同义词辨析**

demand

require • expect • insist • ask

These words all mean to say that sb should do or have sth. 以上各词均含要求之义。

demand to ask for sth very firmly; to say very firmly that sb should have or do sth 指强烈要求、坚决要求：*She demanded an immediate explanation.* 她强烈要求立即作出解释。

require [often passive] (*rather formal*) to make sb do or have sth, especially because it is necessary according to a law or set of rules or standards 指要求做（某事）、达到（某水平），尤指根据法规或规定：*All candidates will be required to take a short test.* 所有候选人都要做一个小测验。

expect to demand that sb should do, have or be sth, especially because it is their duty or responsibility 指要求、认为应得、指望，尤因义务或责任：*I expect to be paid promptly for the work.* 我要求即时付工钱。

insist to demand that sth happens or that sb agrees to do sth 指坚决要求、坚持：*I didn't want to go but he insisted.* 我并不想去，但他硬要我去。◇ *We **insist on** the highest standards at all times.* 我们始终坚持最高标准。

ask to expect or demand sth 指期望、要求：*You're asking too much of him.* 你对他要求过分了。

DEMAND, EXPECT OR ASK? 用 demand、expect 还是 ask?

Ask is not as strong as **demand** or **expect**, both of which can be more like a command. * ask 不如 demand 和 expect 语气强烈，demand 和 expect 更像命令。

PATTERNS

- to demand/require/expect/ask sth **of/from** sb
- to demand/require/expect/insist/ask **that...**
- to require/expect/ask sb **to do sth**
- to demand/require/expect/ask **a lot/too much/a great deal**
- to **be too much to** expect/ask

demand. 优秀的秘书总是很抢手。 **on de'mand** done or happening whenever sb asks 一经要求： *Feed the baby on demand.* 宝宝需要时再喂食。◇ *on-demand printing of books* 书籍按需印刷 ➲ SEE ALSO SUPPLY AND DEMAND

■ *verb* **1** to ask for sth very firmly 强烈要求： **~ sth** *She demanded an immediate explanation.* 她强烈要求立即作出解释。◇ **~ that…** *The UN has demanded that all troops be withdrawn.* 联合国已要求撤出所有部队。◇ (*BrE also*) *They are demanding that all troops should be withdrawn.* 他们强烈要求所有部队撤离。◇ **~ to do sth** *I demand to see the manager.* 我坚决要求见经理。◇ **+ speech** *'Who the hell are you?' he demanded angrily.* "你到底是谁？"他气势汹汹地查问道。 ➲ SYNONYMS AT ASK **2** **~ sth** to need sth in order to be done successfully 需要： *This sport demands both speed and strength.* 这项运动既需要速度也需要体力。

de'mand draft *noun* (*IndE*) a printed form on which your bank account details are written, that you can order from a bank in order to pay for sth. The money is taken from your account when you order it and the person you want to pay must then take the draft to a bank to receive the money. 即期汇票；见票即付汇票

de·mand·ing /dɪ'mɑːndɪŋ; *NAmE* -'mæn-/ *adj.* **1** (of a piece of work 工作) needing a lot of skill, patience, effort, etc. 要求高的；需要高技能（或耐性等）的；费力的： *The work is physically demanding.* 这工作需要有很好的体力。 ➲ SYNONYMS AT DIFFICULT **2** (of a person 人) expecting a lot of work or attention from others; not easily satisfied 要求极严的；苛求的；难满足的： *a demanding boss/child* 苛刻的老板；难满足的孩子 OPP **undemanding**

de·mar·cate /'diːmɑːkeɪt; *NAmE* -mɑːrk-/ *verb* **~ sth** (*formal*) to mark or establish the limits of sth 标出…的界线；给…划界： *Plots of land have been demarcated by barbed wire.* 一块块土地都用带刺的铁丝网圈了起来。

de·mar·ca·tion /ˌdiːmɑː'keɪʃn; *NAmE* -mɑːr'k-/ *noun* [U, C] a border or line that separates two things, such as types of work, groups of people or areas of land （工种、人群、土地等的）划分，区分，界线： *It was hard to draw clear lines of demarcation between work and leisure.* 在工作和闲暇之间很难划出明确的界限。◇ *social demarcations* 社会阶层的划分

de·mean /dɪ'miːn/ *verb* **1** **~ yourself** to do sth that makes people have less respect for you 降低身份；失去尊重： *I wouldn't demean myself by asking for charity.* 我决不低三下四地乞求施舍。 **2** **~ sb/sth** to make people have less respect for sb/sth 贬低；贬损；使失尊严 SYN **degrade**: *Such images demean women.* 这些形象有损妇女尊严。

de·mean·ing /dɪ'miːnɪŋ/ *adj.* putting sb in a position that does not give them the respect that they should have 降低身份的；失去尊严的 SYN **humiliating**: *He found it demeaning to work for his former employee.* 他觉得为自己以前的雇员工作有失体面。

de·mean·our (*especially US* **de·meanor**) /dɪ'miːnə(r)/ *noun* [U] (*formal*) the way that sb looks or behaves 外表；风度；行为；举止: *He maintained a professional demeanour throughout.* 他始终保持着专业人士的风度。

de·men·ted /dɪ'mentɪd/ *adj.* **1** (*especially BrE*) behaving in a crazy way because you are extremely upset or worried 极度焦躁不安的；忧虑失常的；发狂的： *I've been nearly demented with worry about you.* 我一直为你担心，都快发疯了。 **2** (*old-fashioned* or *medical* 医) having a mental illness 痴呆的；发狂的 ▸ **de·men·ted·ly** *adv.*

de·men·tia /dɪ'menʃə/ *noun* [U] (*medical* 医) a serious mental DISORDER caused by brain disease or injury, that affects the ability to think, remember and behave normally 痴呆 ➲ SEE ALSO SENILE DEMENTIA ➲ WORDFINDER NOTE AT CONDITION, OLD

dem·er·ara sugar /ˌdeməreərə 'ʃʊgə(r); *NAmE* -rerə/ *noun* [U] (*BrE*) a type of rough brown sugar 德梅拉拉蔗糖

de·merge /ˌdiː'mɜːdʒ; *NAmE* -'mɜːrdʒ/ *verb* [T, I] **~ (sth)** (*BrE, business* 商) to separate a company into smaller companies, usually into the companies that had previously been joined together; to be split in this way 将（合并公司）分拆；（公司）分拆

de·mer·ger /ˌdiː'mɜːdʒə(r); *NAmE* -'mɜːrdʒ-/ *noun* [C, U] (*BrE, business* 商) the act of separating a company from a larger company, especially when they had previously been joined together （尤指合并公司的）分拆

de·merit /diː'merɪt/ *noun* (*formal*) **1** [usually pl.] a fault in sth or a disadvantage of sth 过失；缺点；短处： *the merits and demerits of the scheme* 这个方案的优缺点 **2** (*NAmE*) a mark on sb's school record showing that they have done sth wrong （学校给学生记的）过失分： *You'll get three demerits if you're caught smoking on school grounds.* 在校内抽烟一经发现将被记过失分三分。

de·mesne /də'meɪn/ *noun* **1** (in the past) land attached to a MANOR (= large house) that was kept by the owners for their own use （旧时）领主自留地产 **2** (*old use*) a region or large area of land 地区；地域

demi- /'demi/ *prefix* (in nouns 构成名词) half; partly 半；部分： *demigod* 半神半人 ➲ MORE LIKE THIS 6, page R25

demi·god /'demigɒd; *NAmE* -gɑːd/ *noun* **1** a minor god, or a BEING that is partly a god and partly human 次神；半神半人 **2** a ruler or other person who is treated like a god 尊为神明的统治者；被神化的人物

demi·john /'demidʒɒn; *NAmE* -dʒɑːn/ *noun* a very large bottle with a narrow opening at the top, for holding and transporting water, wine, etc. 小口大肚瓶；细颈大瓶

de·mili·tar·ize (*BrE also* **-ise**) /ˌdiː'mɪlɪtəraɪz/ *verb* [usually passive] **~ sth** to remove military forces from an area 从…撤军；使非军事化： *a* ***demilitarized zone*** 非军事区 OPP **militarize** ▸ **de·mili·tar·iza·tion**, **-isa·tion** /ˌdiːˌmɪlɪtəraɪ'zeɪʃn; *NAmE* -rə'z-/ *noun* [U]

demi-monde /ˌdemi 'mɒnd; *NAmE* 'mɑːnd/ *noun* [sing.] (*from French*) people whose behaviour or beliefs prevent them from being fully accepted as part of the main group in society 不完全被社会接受的人；行为（或信仰）不受社会尊重的人

de·mise /dɪ'maɪz/ *noun* [sing.] **1** the end or failure of an institution, an idea, a company, etc. 终止；失败；倒闭 **2** (*formal* or *humorous*) death 死亡；逝世；一命呜呼： *his* ***imminent/sudden/sad demise*** 他死到临头；他的猝死；他悲惨的死亡

de·mist /ˌdiː'mɪst/ (*BrE*) (*NAmE* **de·fog**) *verb* **~ sth** to remove the CONDENSATION from a car's windows so that you can see clearly 除去（汽车玻璃上的）雾水

de·mist·er /ˌdiː'mɪstə(r)/ *noun* a device, spray, etc. that removes CONDENSATION, especially from the windows of a car （尤指汽车挡风玻璃的）除雾器，除雾剂

demi·urge /'demiɜːdʒ; *NAmE* -ɜːrdʒ/ *noun* (*literary*) **1** a BEING that is responsible for creating the world 巨匠造物主（创世者） **2** a BEING that controls the part of the world which is not spiritual 巨匠造物主（物质世界的控制者）

demo /'deməʊ; *NAmE* -moʊ/ *noun, verb*

■ ***noun*** (*pl.* **-os**) (*informal*) **1** (*especially BrE*) = DEMONSTRATION (1): *They all went on the demo.* 他们都参加了示威游行。 **2** = DEMONSTRATION (2): ***I'll give you a demo.*** 我来给你作个示范。 ➲ WORDFINDER NOTE AT SOFTWARE **3** a record or tape with an example of sb's music on it 试样唱片；录音样带： *a demo tape* 一盘录音样带

■ ***verb*** **~ sth** to use sth, especially a piece of software, to show sb or to see for yourself how it works 试用（尤指软件）；演示；示范： *He demoed the new program he had just created.* 他演示了他刚编写的新程序。◇ *Can I demo the software before I buy it?* 在购买此软件之前，我能先试用一下吗？

demo- *prefix* (in nouns, adjectives and adverbs 构成名词、形容词和副词) connected with people or population 与人（或人口）有关的： *democracy* 民主 ◇ *democratic* 民主的

demob /ˌdiːˈmɒb; *NAmE* -ˈmɑːb/ *verb* (**-bb-**) [usually passive] **~ sb** (*BrE, informal*) = DEMOBILIZE : *He was demobbed in 1946.* 他于 1946 年复员。 ▶ **demob** *noun* [U] (*BrE*)

de·mo·bil·ize (*BrE also* **-ise**) /dɪˈməʊbəlaɪz; *NAmE* diːˈmoʊ-/ (*also BrE, informal* **demob**) *verb* **~ sb** to release sb from military service, especially at the end of a war （尤指战后）使退伍，使复员 ➲ COMPARE MOBILIZE ▶ **de·mo·bil·iza·tion, -isa·tion** /dɪˌməʊbəlaɪˈzeɪʃn; *NAmE* -ˌmoʊbələˈz-/ *noun* [U]

de·moc·racy /dɪˈmɒkrəsi; *NAmE* -ˈmɑːk-/ *noun* (*pl.* **-ies**) **1** [U] a system of government in which all the people of a country can vote to elect their representatives 民主；民主政体；民主制度：*parliamentary democracy* 议会民主 ◇ *the principles of democracy* 民主原则 **2** [C] a country which has this system of government 民主国家：*Western democracies* 西方民主国家 ◇ *I thought we were supposed to be living in a democracy.* 我还以为我们应该是生活在一个民主国家里。 **3** [U] fair and equal treatment of everyone in an organization, etc., and their right to take part in making decisions 民主精神；民主权利；民主：*the fight for justice and democracy* 为正义和民主的斗争 ➲ WORDFINDER NOTE AT SYSTEM

WORDFINDER 联想词：candidate, constituency, contest, election, majority, manifesto, poll, referendum, swing vote

demo·crat /ˈdeməkræt/ *noun* **1** a person who believes in or supports democracy 民主主义者 **2 Democrat** (*abbr.* **D, Dem.**) a member or supporter of the Democratic Party of the US（美国）民主党党员，民主党人，民主党支持者 ➲ COMPARE REPUBLICAN *n.* (2)

demo·crat·ic /ˌdeməˈkrætɪk/ *adj.* **1** (of a country, state, system, etc. 国家、政府、制度等) controlled by representatives who are elected by the people of a country; connected with this system 民主的；民主政体的；民主制度的：*a democratic country* 民主国家 ◇ *a democratic system* 民主制度 ◇ *democratic government* 民主政府 **2** based on the principle that all members have an equal right to be involved in running an organization, etc. 民主权利的：*democratic participation* 民主参与 ◇ *a democratic decision* 民主决策 **3** based on the principle that all members of society are equal rather than divided by money or social class 有民主精神的；平等的：*a democratic society* 民主社会 ◇ *democratic reforms* 民主改革 **4 Democratic** (*abbr.* **Dem., D**) connected with the Democratic Party in the US（美国）民主党的：*the Democratic senator from Oregon*（美国）俄勒冈州的民主党参议员 ▶ **demo·crat·ic·al·ly** /-kli/ *adv.*：*a democratically elected government* 民主选举的政府 ◇ *democratically controlled* 民主监管的 ◇ *The decision was taken democratically.* 这是通过民主讨论作出的决策。

the Demo'cratic Party *noun* [sing.] one of the two main political parties in the US, usually considered to be in favour of social reform 民主党（美国两大主要政党之一，通常被认为主张社会改革）➲ COMPARE REPUBLICAN PARTY

dem·oc·ra·tize (*BrE also* **-ise**) /dɪˈmɒkrətaɪz; *NAmE* -ˈmɑːk-/ *verb* **~ sth** (*formal*) to make a country or an institution more democratic 使民主化 ▶ **dem·oc·ra·tiza·tion, -isa·tion** /dɪˌmɒkrətaɪˈzeɪʃn; *NAmE* -ˌmɑːkrətəˈz-/ *noun* [U]

demo·graph·ic /ˌdeməˈɡræfɪk/ *noun, adj.*

■ *noun* **1 demographics** [pl.] (*statistics* 统计) data relating to the population and different groups within it 人口统计数据：*the demographics of radio listeners* 电台听众统计数据 **2** [C] (*business* 商) a group of customers who are of a similar age, the same sex, etc. 同类客户群体：*The products are designed to appeal to a young demographic.* 这些产品是为吸引年轻一代客户而设计的。 ◇ *the 18–30 demographic* * 18 至 30 岁的客户群

■ *adj.* relating to the population and different groups within it 人口的；人口学的：***demographic changes/trends/factors*** 人口结构变化 / 发展趋势 / 统计要素 ▶ **demo·graph·ic·al·ly** *adv.*

dem·og·raphy /dɪˈmɒɡrəfi; *NAmE* -ˈmɑːɡ-/ *noun* [U] the changing number of births, deaths, diseases, etc. in a community over a period of time; the scientific study of these changes 人口统计；人口统计学；人口学：*the social demography of Africa* 非洲社会人口统计 ▶ **dem·og·raph·er** /dɪˈmɒɡrəfə(r); *NAmE* -ˈmɑːɡ-/ *noun*

de·mol·ish /dɪˈmɒlɪʃ; *NAmE* -ˈmɑːl-/ *verb* **1 ~ sth** to pull or knock down a building 拆毁，拆除（建筑物）：*The factory is due to be demolished next year.* 这个工厂定于明年拆除。 **2 ~ sth** to destroy sth accidentally （意外）毁坏，破坏：*The car had skidded across the road and demolished part of the wall.* 汽车打滑冲过马路，把部分墙撞塌了。 **3 ~ sth** to show that an idea or theory is completely wrong 推翻，驳倒（观点或理论）：*A recent book has demolished this theory.* 最近出版的一本书推翻了这种理论。 **4 ~ sb/sth** to defeat sb easily and completely 轻易而彻底地打败：*They demolished New Zealand 44–6 in the final.* 他们在决赛中以 44:6 大败新西兰队。 **5 ~ sth** (*BrE, informal*) to eat sth very quickly 狼吞虎咽地吃；贪婪地吃：*The children demolished their burgers and chips.* 孩子们狼吞虎咽地吃了汉堡包和炸土豆条。 ▶ **demo·li·tion** /ˌdeməˈlɪʃn/ *noun* [U, C]：*The whole row of houses is scheduled for demolition.* 整排房子均列入拆除计划。 ◇ *His speech did a very effective* ***demolition job*** *on the government's proposals.* 他的发言非常成功地驳倒了政府的提案。

ˌdemolition 'derby (*NAmE*) (*BrE* **'stock-car racing**) *noun* [C] a type of race in which the competing cars are allowed to hit each other 撞车大赛（参赛车辆可以相互碰撞）

demon /ˈdiːmən/ *noun* **1** an evil spirit 恶魔；魔鬼：*demons torturing the sinners in Hell* 地狱里折磨罪人的魔鬼 **2** (*informal*) a person who does sth very well or with a lot of energy 技艺出众的人；精力充沛的人：*He skis like a demon.* 他滑雪技艺超群。 **3** something that causes a person to worry and makes them unhappy （使人担忧和不快的）邪恶事物：*the demons of jealousy* 恶魔一样的嫉妒心

IDM **the demon 'drink** (*BrE, humorous*) alcoholic drink 含酒精饮料

de·mon·ic /diˈmɒnɪk; *NAmE* -ˈmɑːn-/ *adj.* connected with, or like, a demon 恶魔的；魔鬼似的；恶魔般的：*demonic forces* 邪恶势力 ◇ *a demonic appearance* 魔鬼般的外表

de·mon·ize (*BrE also* **-ise**) /ˈdiːmənaɪz/ *verb* **~ sb/sth** to describe sb/sth in a way that is intended to make other people think of them or it as evil or dangerous 把…描绘成魔鬼（或危险人物等）；将…妖魔化：*He was demonized by the right-wing press.* 他被右翼报章描写成了魔鬼。 ▶ **de·mon·iza·tion, -isa·tion** /ˌdiːmənaɪˈzeɪʃn; *NAmE* -nəˈz-/ *noun* [U]

dem·on·strable AW /dɪˈmɒnstrəbl; *NAmE* -ˈmɑːn-; *BrE also* ˈdemənstrəbl/ *adj.* (*formal*) that can be shown or proved 明显的；可表明的；可论证的；可证明的：*a demonstrable need* 明显的需要 ▶ **dem·on·strably** AW /-bli/ *adv.*：*demonstrably unfair* 显然不公平

dem·on·strate AW /ˈdemənstreɪt/ *verb* **1** [T] to show sth clearly by giving proof or evidence 证明；证实；论证；说明：**~ that...** *These results demonstrate convincingly that our campaign is working.* 这些结果有力地证明，我们的运动已见成效。 ◇ **~ sth (to sb)** *Let me demonstrate to you some of the difficulties we are facing.* 我来向你说明一下我们面临的一些困难。 ◇ **~ how, what, etc....** *His sudden departure had demonstrated how unreliable he was.* 他突然离去，这说明他是多么不可靠。 ◇ **~ sb/sth to be sth** *The theories were demonstrated to be false.* 这些理论已被证明是错误的。 ◇ **it is demonstrated that...** *It has been demonstrated that this drug is effective.* 这药已证实是有效的。 ➲ LANGUAGE BANK AT EVIDENCE **2** [T] **~ sth** to show by your actions that you have a particular quality, feeling or opinion 表达；表露；表现；显露 SYN **display**: *You need to demonstrate more self-control.* 你得表现出更强的自制力。 ◇ *We want to demonstrate our commitment to human rights.* 我们想展示我们对人权的热情投入。 **3**

[T] to show and explain how sth works or how to do sth 示范；演示： ~ **sth** (**to sb**) *Her job involves demonstrating new educational software.* 她的工作包括演示新的教学软件。 ◇ ~ (**to sb**) **how, what, etc.…** *Let me demonstrate to you how it works.* 让我来为你演示一下它是怎么运行的。 **4** [I] to take part in a public meeting or march, usually as a protest or to show support for sth 游行示威 SYN **protest**: ~ (**against sth**) *students demonstrating against the war* 参加反战示威游行的学生 ◇ ~ (**in favour/support of sth**) *They are demonstrating in favour of free higher education.* 他们参加示威游行，要求实行免费高等教育。 ➲ WORDFINDER NOTE AT PROTEST

D

de·mon·stra·tion AW /ˌdemənˈstreɪʃn/ *noun* **1** (*also informal* **demo** *especially in BrE*) [C] ~ (**against sb/sth**) a public meeting or march at which people show that they are protesting against or supporting sb/sth 游行示威： *to **take part in/go on a demonstration*** 参加 / 进行示威游行 ◇ *to **hold/stage a demonstration*** 举行示威游行 ◇ ***mass demonstrations** in support of the exiled leader* 支持流亡领导人的群众集会 ◇ *anti-government demonstrations* 反政府示威游行 ◇ *a **peaceful/violent demonstration*** 和平 / 暴力示威 ➲ COMPARE MARCH *n.* (1) **2** (*also informal* **demo**) [C, U] an act of showing or explaining how sth works or is done 示范；示范表演；演示： *We were given a brief demonstration of the computer's functions.* 我们看了这种计算机各种功能的简短演示。 ◇ *a practical demonstration* 实际操作示范 ◇ *We provide demonstration of videoconferencing over the Internet.* 我们提供网络视频会议的演示。 **3** [C, U] an act of giving proof or evidence for sth 证明；证实；论证；说明： *a demonstration of the connection between the two sets of figures* 论证这两组数字间的联系 ◇ *a demonstration of how something that seems simple can turn out to be very complicated* 说明看似简单的东西实际上可能非常复杂 **4** [C] an act of showing a feeling or an opinion 表达；表露；表现；显露： *a public demonstration of affection* 公开表露爱慕之情 ◇ *a demonstration of support for the reforms* 表示对改革的支持

de·mon·stra·tive AW /dɪˈmɒnstrətɪv; *NAmE* -ˈmɑːn-/ *adj., noun*

■ ***adj.*** **1** showing feelings openly, especially feelings of affection 公开表露感情（尤指爱慕之情）的；感情外露的： *Some people are more demonstrative than others.* 有些人更容易流露感情。 ◇ *a demonstrative greeting* 热情的问候 **2** (*grammar* 语法) used to identify the person or thing that is being referred to 指示的： *'This' and 'that' are demonstrative pronouns.* * this 和 that 是指示代词。 ▶ **de·mon·stra·tive·ly** AW *adv.*

■ ***noun*** (*grammar* 语法) a demonstrative pronoun or determiner 指示代词；限定词

dem·on·stra·tor AW /ˈdemənstreɪtə(r)/ *noun* **1** a person who takes part in a public meeting or march in order to protest against sb/sth or to show support for sb/sth （集会或游行的）示威者 **2** a person whose job is to show or explain how sth works or is done 示范者；演示者

de·mor·al·ize (*BrE also* **-ise**) /dɪˈmɒrəlaɪz; *NAmE* -ˈmɔːr-/ *verb* [usually passive] ~ **sb** to make sb lose confidence or hope 使泄气；使意志消沉；使士气低落 SYN **dishearten**: *Constant criticism is enough to demoralize anybody.* 频繁的批评足以使任何人意志消沉。 ▶ **de·mor·al·ized**, **-ised** *adj.* : *The workers here seem very demoralized.* 这里的工人显得十分沮丧。 **de·mor·al·iz·ing**, **-is·ing** *adj.* : *the demoralizing effects of unemployment* 失业造成的使人沮丧的后果 **de·mor·al·iza·tion**, **-isa·tion** /dɪˌmɒrəlaɪˈzeɪʃn; *NAmE* -ˌmɔːrələˈz-/ *noun* [U]

de·mote /ˌdiːˈməʊt; *NAmE* -ˈmoʊt/ *verb* [often passive] ~ **sb** (**from sth**) (**to sth**) to move sb to a lower position or rank, often as a punishment 使降级，使降职，使降低地位（常作为惩罚） OPP **promote** ▶ **de·mo·tion** /ˌdiːˈməʊʃn; *NAmE* -ˈmoʊ-/ *noun* [C, U]

dem·ot·ic /dɪˈmɒtɪk; *NAmE* -ˈmɑːt-/ *adj.* (*formal*) used by or typical of ordinary people 民众的；通俗的；大众化的

de·mo·tiv·ate /ˌdiːˈməʊtɪveɪt; *NAmE* -ˈmoʊ-/ *verb* ~ **sb** to make sb feel that it is not worth making an effort 使失去动力；使变得消极： *Failure can demotivate students.* 失败会挫伤学生的积极性。 ▶ **de·mo·tiv·at·ing** *adj.* **de·mo·tiv·ated** *adj.* **de·mo·tiv·ation** /ˌdiːməʊtɪˈveɪʃn; *NAmE* -moʊ-/ *noun* [U]

demur /dɪˈmɜː(r)/ *verb, noun*

■ ***verb*** (**-rr-**) [I] (+ **speech**) (*formal*) to say that you do not agree with sth or that you refuse to do sth 表示反对；提出异议；拒绝： *At first she demurred, but then finally agreed.* 她一开始表示反对，但最终还是同意了。

■ ***noun***

IDM **without deˈmur** (*formal*) without objecting or hesitating 毫无异议；毫不犹豫： *They accepted without demur.* 他们接受了，没有提出异议。

de·mure /dɪˈmjʊə(r); *NAmE* dɪˈmjʊr/ *adj.* **1** (of a woman or a girl 女子) behaving in a way that does not attract attention to herself or her body; quiet and serious 娴静的；端庄的 SYN **modest**: *a demure young lady* 娴静的年轻女士 **2** suggesting that a woman or girl is demure （女子的举止或衣服等）显得庄重的 SYN **modest**: *a demure smile* 矜持的微笑 ◇ *a demure navy blouse with a white collar* 严肃庄重的白领海军军服上衣 ▶ **de·mure·ly** *adv.*

de·mys·tify /ˌdiːˈmɪstɪfaɪ/ *verb* (**de·mys·ti·fies**, **de·mys·ti·fy·ing**, **de·mys·ti·fied**, **de·mys·ti·fied**) ~ **sth** to make sth easier to understand and less complicated by explaining it in a clear and simple way 使明白易懂；深入浅出地解释 ▶ **de·mys·ti·fi·ca·tion** /ˌdiːˌmɪstɪfɪˈkeɪʃn/ *noun* [U]

den /den/ *noun* **1** the hidden home of some types of wild animal 兽穴；兽窝： *a **bear's/lion's den*** 熊的 / 狮子的洞穴 **2** (*disapproving*) a place where people meet in secret, especially for some illegal or immoral activity 窝点，窝子（尤指非法或邪恶活动秘密聚会处）： *a den of thieves* 贼窝 ◇ *a **drinking/gambling den*** 酗酒窝点；赌窟 ◇ *He thought of New York as **a den of iniquity**.* 他把纽约视为罪恶的渊薮。 **3** (*NAmE*) a room in a house where people go to relax, watch television, etc. 休息室 **4** (*old-fashioned, BrE, informal*) a room in a house where a person can work or study without being disturbed 书斋；书房： *He would often retire to his den.* 他往往是回自己的书房去。 **5** a secret place, often made roughly with walls and a roof, where children play （儿童的）隐蔽玩耍处： *They made themselves a den in the woods.* 他们在树林里为自己搭了个窝，在里面玩。 IDM SEE BEARD *v.*, LION

de·nation·al·ize (*BrE also* **-ise**) /ˌdiːˈnæʃnəlaɪz/ *verb* ~ **sth** to sell a company or an industry so that it is no longer owned by the government 使私有化；使非国有化 SYN **privatize** OPP **nationalize** ▶ **de·nation·al·iza·tion**, **-isa·tion** /ˌdiːˌnæʃnəlaɪˈzeɪʃn; *NAmE* -ləˈz-/ *noun* [U]

den·drite /ˈdendraɪt/ (*also* **den·dron** /ˈdendrɒn; *NAmE* -drɑːn/) *noun* (*biology* 生) a short branch at the end of a nerve cell, which receives signals from other cells 树突（位于神经元末端的树枝状突起，接收其他神经元传来的信号） ➲ COMPARE AXON ▶ **den·drit·ic** /ˌdenˈdrɪtɪk/ *adj.* : *dendritic cells* 树突细胞

den·gue /ˈdeŋɡi/ (*also* **ˈden·gue fever**, **ˈbreak·bone fever**) *noun* [U] a disease caused by a virus carried by MOSQUITOES, that is found in tropical areas and causes fever and severe pain in the joints 登革热（由蚊子传播的热带疾病，症状为发烧和关节剧痛）

deni·able AW /dɪˈnaɪəbl/ *adj.* that can be denied 可否认的；可拒绝的 OPP **undeniable**

de·nial AW /dɪˈnaɪəl/ *noun* **1** [C] ~ (**of sth/that…**) a statement that says sth is not true or does not exist 否认；否定： *the prisoner's repeated denials of the charges against him* 囚犯再三否认对他的指控 ◇ *The terrorists issued a denial of responsibility for the attack.* 恐怖分子发表声明，否认对这次袭击负责。 ◇ *an official denial that there would be an election before the end of the year* 对年底前将进行选举的正式否认 **2** [C, U] (a) ~ **of sth** a refusal to allow sb to have sth they have a right to expect 拒绝给予，剥夺（应有的权利）： *the denial of basic human rights* 剥夺基本人权 **3** [U] (*psychology* 心) a refusal to accept that sth unpleasant or painful is true 拒绝接受，拒不承认（令人

不快、痛苦的事）：*The patient is still **in denial**.* 病人仍然拒不接受事实。

den·ier /ˈdeniə(r)/ *noun* (*especially BrE*) a unit for measuring how fine threads of NYLON, silk, etc. are 旦，旦尼尔（测量尼龙线、丝线等的纤度单位）：*15 denier tights* * 15 旦的连裤袜

deni·grate /ˈdenɪɡreɪt/ *verb* **~ sb/sth** (*formal*) to criticize sb/sth unfairly; to say sb/sth does not have any value or is not important 诋毁；诽谤；贬低 SYN **belittle**: *I didn't intend to denigrate her achievements.* 我不是想贬低她的成绩。 ▶ **deni·gra·tion** /ˌdenɪˈɡreɪʃn/ *noun* [U]

denim /ˈdenɪm/ *noun* **1** [U] a type of strong cotton cloth that is usually blue and is used for making clothes, especially jeans 蓝粗棉布；劳动布；牛仔布：*a denim jacket* 牛仔布夹克衫 ➲ VISUAL VOCAB PAGE V66 ORIGIN From the French *serge de Nîmes*, meaning 'serge (= a type of cloth) from the town of Nîmes'. 源自法语 serge de Nîmes，意为尼姆城产的哔叽。 **2 denims** [pl.] (*old-fashioned*) trousers/pants made of denim 牛仔裤 SYN **jeans**

deni·zen /ˈdenɪzn/ *noun* (*formal* or *humorous*) a person, an animal or a plant that lives, grows or is often found in a particular place（某地区的）居民，常客，动物，植物 SYN **inhabitant**: *polar bears, denizens of the frozen north* 北极熊，在冰天雪地的北方生活的动物 ◇ *the denizens of the local pub* 当地酒吧的常客

de·nom·in·ate /dɪˈnɒmɪneɪt; *NAmE* -ˈnɑːm-/ *verb* **1 ~ sth (in sth)** to express an amount of money using a particular unit 以（某种货币）为单位：*The loan was denominated in US dollars.* 这笔贷款是以美元计算的。 **2 ~ sb (as) sth** (*formal*) to give sth a particular name or description 将…命名为；称…为：*These payments are denominated as 'fees' rather than 'salary'.* 这几笔付款称为"费用"而不是"工资"。

de·nom·in·ation /dɪˌnɒmɪˈneɪʃn; *NAmE* -ˌnɑːm-/ *noun* (*formal*) **1** a branch of the Christian Church（基督教）教派，宗派：*Christians of all denominations attended the conference.* 基督教所有教派的人都出席了这次会议。 **2** a unit of value, especially of money（尤指钱的）面额，面值：*coins and banknotes of various denominations* 各种面额的硬币和纸币

de·nom·in·ation·al /dɪˌnɒmɪˈneɪʃənl; *NAmE* -ˌnɑːm-/ *adj.* belonging to a particular branch of the Christian Church（基督教）教派的，宗派的

de·nom·in·ator /dɪˈnɒmɪneɪtə(r); *NAmE* -ˈnɑːm-/ *noun* (*mathematics* 数) the number below the line in a FRACTION showing how many parts the whole is divided into, for example 4 in ¾ 分母 ➲ COMPARE NUMERATOR, COMMON DENOMINATOR (1)

de·nota·tion AW /ˌdiːnəʊˈteɪʃn; *NAmE* -noʊ-/ *noun* (*specialist*) the act of naming sth with a word; the actual object or idea to which the word refers 指称；指称之物；指称意义；外延 ➲ COMPARE CONNOTATION ▶ **de·nota·tion·al** /ˌdiːnəʊˈteɪʃnl; *NAmE* -noʊ-/ *adj.*

de·note AW /dɪˈnəʊt; *NAmE* dɪˈnoʊt/ *verb* (*formal*) **1 ~ sth | ~ that...** to be a sign of sth 标志；预示；象征 SYN **indicate**: *A very high temperature often denotes a serious illness.* 高烧常常表示病得很重。 **2 ~ sth | ~ what, when, etc....** to mean sth 表示；意指 SYN **represent**: *In this example 'X' denotes the time taken and 'Y' denotes the distance covered.* 在这个例子中，X 表示所用的时间，Y 表示所行的距离。◇ *The red triangle denotes danger.* 红色三角形表示危险。◇ *Here 'family' denotes mother, father and children.* 此处的 family 指母亲、父亲和孩子。 ➲ COMPARE CONNOTE

de·noue·ment (*also* **dé·noue·ment**) /ˌdeɪˈnuːmɒ̃; *NAmE* ˌdeɪnuːˈmɑ̃ː/ *noun* (*from French*) the end of a play, book, etc., in which everything is explained or settled; the end result of a situation（戏剧、小说等的）结局，收场；（事情的）结果 ➲ WORDFINDER NOTE AT DRAMA

de·nounce /dɪˈnaʊns/ *verb* **1** to strongly criticize sb/sth that you think is wrong, illegal, etc. 谴责；指责；斥责：**~ sb/sth** *She publicly denounced the government's handling of the crisis.* 她公开谴责政府处理这场危机的方式。◇ **~ sb/sth as sth** *The project was denounced as a scandalous waste of public money.* 这项工程被斥责为可耻的公款挥霍。 **2** to tell the police, the authorities, etc. about sb's illegal political activities 告发（某人从事非法政治活动）：**~ sb as sth** *They were denounced as spies.* 他们被揭发是间谍。◇ **~ sb (to sb)** *Many people denounced their neighbours to the secret police.* 许多人向秘密警察告发自己的邻居。 ➲ SEE ALSO DENUNCIATION

dense /dens/ *adj.* (**dens·er**, **dens·est**) **1** containing a lot of people, things, plants, etc. with little space between them 密集的；稠密的：*a **dense crowd/forest*** 密集的人群；密林 ◇ *areas of dense population* 人口密集地区 **2** difficult to see through 浓密的；浓重的 SYN **thick**: *dense **fog/smoke/fumes*** 浓雾；浓烟；浓烈的气体 **3** (*informal*) stupid 愚笨的；迟钝的；笨拙的：*How can you be so dense?* 你怎么会这么笨？ **4** difficult to understand because it contains a lot of information（信息量大得）难理解的，难懂的：*a dense piece of writing* 难懂的文章 **5** (*specialist*) heavy in relation to its size 密度大的；密实的：*Less dense substances move upwards to form a crust.* 密度小的物质向上浮动并形成一硬层。 ▶ **dense·ly** *adv.*：*a **densely populated** area* 人口密集地区 ◇ ***densely covered/packed*** 盖得 / 塞得严实的

dens·ity /ˈdensəti/ *noun* (*pl.* **-ies**) **1** [U] the quality of being dense; the degree to which sth is dense 密集；稠密；密度；浓度：*population density* 人口密度 ◇ *low density forest* 低密度森林 **2** [C, U] (*physics* 物) the thickness of a solid, liquid or gas measured by its mass per unit of volume 密度（固体、液体或气体单位体积的质量）：*the density of a gas* 一种气体的密度 **3** [U] (*computing* 计) the amount of space available on a disk for recording data 密度（磁盘存储数据的可用空间）

dent /dent/ *verb, noun*

■ ***verb*** **1 ~ sth** to make a hollow place in a hard surface, usually by hitting it 使凹陷；使产生凹痕：*The back of the car was badly dented in the collision.* 汽车尾部被撞后严重凹陷。 **2 ~ sth** to damage sb's confidence, reputation, etc. 损害，伤害，挫伤（信心、名誉等）：*It seemed that nothing could dent his confidence.* 似乎任何事情都不会使他的信心受挫。

■ ***noun*** a hollow place in a hard surface, usually caused by sth hitting it 凹痕；凹坑；凹部：*a large dent in the car door* 车门上一大块凹陷

IDM **make, etc. a ˈdent in sth** to reduce the amount of sth, especially money 减少，削减（尤指资金）：*The lawyer's fees will make a dent in our finances.* 律师费将耗去我们一部分资金。

dent·al /ˈdentl/ *adj.* [only before noun] **1** connected with teeth 牙齿的；牙科的：***dental disease/care/treatment/health*** 牙齿疾病 / 护理 / 治疗 / 健康 ◇ *a dental appointment* 牙科预约 ◇ *dental records* 牙科病历 ◇ (*BrE*) *a dental surgery* (= where a dentist sees patients) 牙科诊所 **2** (*phonetics* 语音) (of a consonant 辅音) produced with the tongue against the upper front teeth, for example /θ/ and /ð/ in *thin* and *this* 齿音的

ˈdental dam (*also* **dam**) *noun* **1** a small rubber sheet used by dentists to keep a tooth separate from the other teeth 橡皮障（牙医用的牙齿阻隔膜） **2** a small rubber sheet used to protect the mouth during sex（性交时用的）口腔保护膜；口交保险膜

ˈdental floss (*also* **floss**) *noun* [U] a type of thread that is used for cleaning between the teeth 洁牙线；牙线

ˈdental hygienist *noun* (*especially NAmE*) = HYGIENIST

ˈdental surgeon *noun* (*formal*) = DENTIST (1)

den·tine /ˈdentiːn/ (*NAmE also* **den·tin** /ˈdentɪn/) *noun* [U] (*biology* 生) the hard substance that forms the main part of a tooth under the ENAMEL 牙质；牙本质；齿质

den·tist 🔑 /ˈdentɪst/ *noun* **1** (*also formal* **ˈdental surgeon**) a person whose job is to take care of people's teeth 牙科医生 **2 dentist's** (*pl.* **dentists**) a place where a dentist sees patients 牙科诊所：*an appointment at the dentist's* 牙科诊所的门诊预约 ➲ **MORE LIKE THIS** 34, page R29

WORDFINDER 联想词：anaesthetic, cavity, check-up, crown, dentures, drill, extract, filling, hygienist

D

den·tis·try /ˈdentɪstri/ *noun* [U] **1** the medical study of the teeth and mouth 牙科学 **2** the work of a dentist 牙科医术；牙医的工作：*preventive dentistry* 预防牙科

den·ti·tion /denˈtɪʃn/ *noun* [U, C] (*specialist*) the arrangement or condition of a person's or an animal's teeth 齿列，齿系（人或动物的牙列或牙齿状况）

den·tures /ˈdentʃəz; *NAmE* -tʃərz/ *noun* [pl.] artificial teeth on a thin piece of plastic (= a PLATE), worn by sb who no longer has all their own teeth 义齿；假牙 ➲ WORDFINDER NOTE AT DENTIST ▸ **den·ture** *adj.*：*denture adhesive* 义齿黏附剂 ➲ COMPARE FALSE TEETH, PLATE *n.* (14)

de·nude /dɪˈnjuːd; *NAmE* dɪˈnuːd/ *verb* [usually passive] **~ sth (of sth)** (*formal*) to remove the covering, features, etc. from sth, so that it is exposed 剥光；使裸露；使光秃：*hillsides denuded of trees* 光秃秃没有树的山坡

de·nun·ci·ation /dɪˌnʌnsiˈeɪʃn/ *noun* [C, U] **~ (of sb/sth)** (*formal*) an act of criticizing sb/sth strongly in public（公开）谴责，斥责，指责：*an angry denunciation of the government's policies* 愤怒谴责政府的政策 ◇ *All parties joined in bitter denunciation of the terrorists.* 所有党派同仇敌忾地痛斥恐怖分子。➲ SEE ALSO DENOUNCE

Den·ver boot /ˈdenvə buːt; *NAmE* -vər/ (*also* **boot**) (*both US*) (*BrE* **clamp**, **ˈwheel clamp**) *noun* a device that is attached to the wheel of a car that has been parked illegally, so that it cannot be driven away 车轮夹锁（用于锁住违章停放的车辆）

deny 🔑 AW /dɪˈnaɪ/ *verb* (**de·nies**, **deny·ing**, **de·nied**, **de·nied**) **1** 🔑 to say that sth is not true 否认；否定：**~ sth** *to deny a claim/a charge/an accusation* 否认某种说法 / 指控 / 指责 ◇ *The spokesman refused either to confirm or deny the reports.* 发言人对那些报道不置可否。◇ **~ (that)...** *She denied (that) there had been any cover-up.* 她否认有任何隐瞒。◇ ***There's no denying** (the fact) **that** quicker action could have saved them.* 无可否认，如果行动快一点，本来是救得了他们的。◇ **it is denied that...** ***It can't be denied that** we need to devote more resources to this problem.* 无可否认，我们需要投入更多的资源来解决这个问题。◇ **~ doing sth** *He denies attempting to murder his wife.* 他否认企图谋杀妻子。➲ **MORE LIKE THIS** 27, page R28 **2** 🔑 **~ sth** to refuse to admit or accept sth 拒绝承认；拒绝接受：*She denied all knowledge of the incident.* 她矢口否认知晓此事的任何情况。◇ *The department denies responsibility for what occurred.* 这个部门拒绝为所发生的事承担责任。**3** (*formal*) to refuse to allow sb to have sth that they want or ask for 拒绝；拒绝给予：**~ sb sth** *They were denied access to the information.* 他们试图取得这个情报被拒。◇ **~ sth to sb** *Access to the information was denied to them.* 他们无法得到这个情报。**4 ~ yourself (sth)** (*formal*) to refuse to let yourself have sth that you would like to have, especially for moral or religious reasons（尤因道德或宗教原因）节制，克制，戒绝

WORD FAMILY
deny *verb*
denial *noun*
undeniable *adj.*
undeniably *adv.*

de·odor·ant /diˈəʊdərənt; *NAmE* diˈoʊ-/ *noun* [C, U] a substance that people put on their bodies to prevent or hide unpleasant smells 除臭剂，解臭剂（用于消除体臭）：(*a*) *roll-on deodorant* 走珠式除臭剂 ➲ SEE ALSO ANTIPERSPIRANT

dep. *abbr.* (in writing 书写形式) DEPART (1); DEPARTURE 离开；出发；启程 ➲ COMPARE ARR. (1)

de·part /dɪˈpɑːt; *NAmE* dɪˈpɑːrt/ *verb* (*rather formal*) **1** [I, T] to leave a place, especially to start a trip 离开；离去；起程；出发：**~ (for...) (from...)** *Flights for Rome depart from Terminal 3.* 飞往罗马的班机从 3 号航站楼出发。◇ *She waited until the last of the guests had departed.* 她一直等到最后一位客人离开。◇ **~ sth** (*NAmE*) *The train departed Amritsar at 6.15 p.m.* 火车在下午 6 点 15 分离开了阿姆利则。OPP **arrive** **2** [I, T] (*NAmE*) to leave your job 离职：*the departing president* 行将卸任的总裁 ◇ **~ sth** *He departed his job December 16.* 他于 12 月 16 日离职。➲ SEE ALSO DEPARTURE

IDM **depart this ˈlife** to die. People say 'depart this life' to avoid saying 'die'. 离开人世，去世，亡故（委婉说法，与 die 同义）

PHR V **deˈpart from sth** to behave in a way that is different from usual 违反，背离（常规）：*Departing from her usual routine, she took the bus to work.* 她一反常态乘公共汽车上班了。

de·part·ed /dɪˈpɑːtɪd; *NAmE* -ˈpɑːrt-/ *adj.* [only before noun] (*formal*) **1** dead. People say 'departed' to avoid saying 'dead'. 去世的，已故的（委婉说法，与 dead 同义）：*your dear departed brother* 你挚爱的亡兄 **2 the departed** *noun* (*pl.* **the de·part·ed**) the person who has died 去世者；亡故者

de·part·ment 🔑 /dɪˈpɑːtmənt; *NAmE* -ˈpɑːrt-/ *noun* (*abbr.* **Dept**) a section of a large organization such as a government, business, university, etc.（政府、企业等的）部门，局，科；（大学的）院，系：*the Department of Health* 卫生署 ◇ *the Treasury Department* 财政部 ◇ *a **government/university, etc. department*** 政府部门、大学学系等 ◇ *the **marketing/sales, etc. department*** 营销、销售等部门 ◇ *the children's department* (= in a large store) 儿童用品部 ◇ *the English department* 英语系 ➲ SEE ALSO POLICE DEPARTMENT, STATE DEPARTMENT

IDM **be sb's department** (*informal*) to be sth that sb is responsible for or knows a lot about 某人的职责范围（或知识范围）：*Don't ask me about it—that's her department.* 这事别问我，那是她的职责范围。

de·part·ment·al /ˌdiːpɑːtˈmentl; *NAmE* -pɑːrt-/ *adj.* [only before noun] connected with a department rather than with the whole organization 部门的；分部的：*a departmental manager* 部门经理

deˈpartment store *noun* a large shop/store that is divided into several parts, each part selling a different type of goods 百货公司；大百货商店

de·par·ture 🔑 /dɪˈpɑːtʃə(r); *NAmE* -ˈpɑːrt-/ *noun* **1** 🔑 [C, U] **~ (from...)** the act of leaving a place; an example of this 离开；起程；出发：*His sudden departure threw the office into chaos.* 他的突然离去使整个办公室陷入一片混乱。◇ *Flights should be confirmed 48 hours before departure.* 航班应在起飞前 48 小时予以确认。◇ *They had received no news of him since his departure from the island.* 自从他离开这座岛后，他们再没听过他的消息。OPP **arrival** ➲ WORDFINDER NOTE AT JOURNEY **2** 🔑 [C] a plane, train, etc. leaving a place at a particular time（在特定时间）离开的飞机（或火车等）：*arrivals and departures* 到站和离站班次 ◇ *All departures are from Manchester.* 所有离站班次都从曼彻斯特出发。◇ *the **departure lounge/time/gate*** 候机（或车）室；离站时间；登机（或上车）口 ◇ *the **departures board*** 离站时刻牌 OPP **arrival** **3** [C] **~ (from sth)** an action that is different from what is usual or expected 背离；违反；逾越：*It was a radical departure from tradition.* 这从根本上违背了传统。◇ *Their latest single represents **a new departure** for the band.* 他们最新推出的单曲唱片体现了这支乐队的新尝试。IDM SEE POINT *n.*

de·pend 🔑 /dɪˈpend/ *verb*

IDM **deˈpending on** 🔑 according to 视乎；决定于：*Starting salary varies from £26 000 to £30 500, depending on experience.* 起薪为 26 000 至 30 500 英镑不等，依个人经验而定。◇ *He either resigned or was sacked, depending on who you talk to.* 他或是辞职了，或是被辞退了，这要看你跟谁讲了。**that deˈpends | it (all) deˈpends** 🔑 used to say that you are not certain about sth because other things have to be considered 那得看情况：*'Is he coming?' 'That depends. He may not have the time.'* "他来吗？" "那要看情况。他不一定有时间。" ◇ *I don't know if we can* *help—it all depends.* 我不知道我们能不能帮上忙，一切都得看情况而定。◇ *I might not go. It depends how tired I am.* 我不一定去。这要看我累不累。◇ *'Your job sounds fun.' 'It depends what you mean by 'fun'.'* "你的工作听起来很有乐趣。" "这就要看你说的'乐趣'是什么意思了。" ◇ *I shouldn't be too late. But it depends if the traffic's bad.* 我应该不会太迟。不过这取决于交通是否拥挤了。

PHR V **de'pend on/upon sb/sth** **1** to rely on sb/sth and be able to trust them 依靠；信赖：*He was the sort of person you could depend on.* 他这个人你是可以信赖的。◇ **depend on/upon sb/sth to do sth** *He knew he could depend upon her to deal with the situation.* 他知道可以依靠她来应付这种局面。➲ SYNONYMS AT TRUST **2** to be sure or expect that sth will happen 确信；相信；指望 SYN **count on sb/sth**：*Depend upon it* (= you can be sure) *we won't give up.* 请相信，我们决不会放弃。◇ **depend on/upon sb/sth doing sth** *Can we depend on you coming in on Sunday?* 我们能指望你星期天来参加吗？◇ (*formal*) *You can depend on his coming in on Sunday.* 你放心，他星期天一定来参加。◇ **depend on/upon sb/sth to do sth** (*ironic*) *You can depend on her to be* (= she always is) *late.* 她保准迟到。 **de'pend on/upon sb/sth (for sth)** (not usually used in the progressive tenses 通常不用于进行时) to need money, help, etc. from sb/sth else for a particular purpose 需要，依靠（提供资金、帮助等）：*The community depends on the shipping industry for its survival.* 这个社区靠航运业维持生活。◇ *I don't want to depend too much on my parents.* 我不想过度依靠父母。 **de'pend on/upon sth** (not used in the progressive tenses 不用于进行时) to be affected or decided by sth 受…的影响；由…决定；取决于：*Does the quality of teaching depend on class size?* 教学质量取决于每个班的人数吗？◇ *It would depend on the circumstances.* 这要视情况而定。◇ **depend on/upon how, what, etc....** *Whether we need more food depends on how many people turn up.* 我们是否需要更多的食物，这要视到场人数而定。

▼ GRAMMAR POINT 语法说明

depend on

- In informal English, it is quite common to say **depend** rather than **depend on** before words like *what, how* or *whether.* 在非正式英语中，在 what、how 或 whether 等词前常用 depend 而非 depend on：*It depends what you mean by 'hostile'.* 那得看你所说的 hostile 的含义。 In formal written English, **depend** should always be followed by *on* or *upon.* 在正式的书面英语中，depend 后总是跟 on 或 upon：*It depends on how you define the term 'hostile'.* 那得看你怎么定义 hostile 这个词。 *Upon* is more formal and less frequent than *on.* * upon 较正式，不如 on 常用。

de·pend·able /dɪˈpendəbl/ *adj.* that can be relied on to do what you want or need 可信赖的；可靠的 SYN reliable ▶ **de·pend·abil·ity** /dɪˌpendəˈbɪləti/ *noun* [U]

de·pend·ant /dɪˈpendənt/ (*BrE, CanE*) (*also* **de·pend·ent** *NAmE, BrE*) *noun* a person, especially a child, who depends on another person for a home, food, money, etc. 受扶养者（尤指孩子）；靠他人生活者

de·pend·ence /dɪˈpendəns/ *noun* [U] **1** ~ **(on/upon sb/sth)** the state of needing the help and support of sb/sth in order to survive or be successful（生存或成功必需的）依靠，依赖，依存：*his dependence on his parents* 他对父母的依赖 ◇ *Our relationship was based on mutual dependence.* 我们的关系建立在相互依存的基础上。◇ *the dependence of Europe on imported foods* 欧洲对进口食品的依赖 ◇ *financial/economic dependence* 财政/经济依赖 OPP **independence** **2** (*also* **de·pend·ency**) the state of being ADDICTED to sth (= unable to stop taking or using it) 瘾：*drug/alcohol dependence* 毒瘾；酒瘾 ➲ WORDFINDER NOTE AT DRUG **3** ~ **of A and B** (*specialist*) the fact of one thing being affected by another 相关（性）；相依（性）：*the close dependence of soil and landforms* 土壤和地貌的密切相关

de·pend·ency /dɪˈpendənsi/ *noun* (*pl.* **-ies**) **1** [U] ~ **(on/upon sb/sth)** the state of relying on sb/sth for sth, especially when this is not normal or necessary（尤指不正常或不必要的）依靠，依赖：*financial dependency* 财政上的依赖 ◇ *Their aim is to reduce people's dependency on the welfare state.* 他们旨在减少人们对福利制度的依赖。◇ *the **dependency culture*** (= a way of life in which people depend too much on money from the government) 依赖文化（过分依赖政府资助）➲ COMPARE CODEPENDENCY **2** [C] a country, an area, etc. that is controlled by another country 附属国；附属地 **3** = DEPENDENCE (2)

de·pend·ent /dɪˈpendənt/ *adj., noun*

■ *adj.* **1** needing sb/sth in order to survive or be successful 依靠的；依赖的：*a woman with several dependent children* 一个女人带着几个未自立的孩子 ◇ ~ **on/upon sb/sth** *You can't be dependent on your parents all your life.* 你不可能一辈子靠父母生活。◇ ~ **on/upon sb/sth for sth** *The festival is heavily dependent on sponsorship for its success.* 这次节日庆祝活动成功与否，在很大程度上就看赞助了。 **2** ~ **on/upon sth** ADDICTED to sth (= unable to stop taking or using it) 有瘾的：*to be dependent on drugs* 有毒瘾 **3** ~ **on/upon sth** (*formal*) affected or decided by sth 受…的影响；取决于：*A child's development is dependent on many factors.* 孩子的成长受多种因素影响。◇ *The price is dependent on how many extras you choose.* 价格取决于你挑选额外收费项目的多少。

■ *noun* (*especially NAmE*) = DEPENDANT

deˌpendent ˈclause *noun* (*grammar* 语法) = SUBORDINATE CLAUSE

deˌpendent ˈvariable *noun* (*mathematics* 数) a VARIABLE whose value depends on another variable 因变量；因变数

de·per·son·al·ize (*BrE also* **-ise**) /diːˈpɜːsənəlaɪz; *NAmE* -ˈpɜːrs-/ *verb* ~ **sth** [often passive] to make sth less personal so that it does not seem as if humans with feelings and personality are involved 使非个性化；使不掺杂个人感情

de·pict /dɪˈpɪkt/ *verb* (*rather formal*) **1** to show an image of sb/sth in a picture 描绘；描画：~ **sb/sth (as sb/sth)** *a painting depicting the Virgin and Child* 一幅描绘童贞马利亚和圣子耶稣的画 ◇ ~ **sb/sth doing sth** *The artist had depicted her lying on a bed.* 画家画了她躺在床上的画像。 **2** to describe sth in words, or give an impression of sth in words or with a picture 描写；描述；刻画：~ **sb/sth** *The novel depicts French society in the 1930s.* 这部小说描述了 20 世纪 30 年代的法国社会。◇ ~ **sb/sth as sb/sth** *The advertisements depict smoking as glamorous and attractive.* 这些广告把吸烟描绘得充满刺激和富有吸引力。 ▶ **de·pic·tion** /dɪˈpɪkʃn/ *noun* [U, C]：*They object to the movie's depiction of gay people.* 他们反对这部影片对同性恋者的刻画。

de·pila·tor /ˈdepɪleɪtə(r); *NAmE* dɪˈpɪlətɔːr/ *noun* a device which removes hair from your body by pulling it out 拔毛器；脱毛器

de·pila·tory /dɪˈpɪlətri; *NAmE* -tɔːri/ *noun* (*pl.* **-ies**) a substance used for removing body hair 脱毛剂 ▶ **de·pila·tory** *adj.* [only before noun]：*depilatory creams* 脱毛乳膏

de·plane /diːˈpleɪn/ *verb* [I] (*NAmE*) to get off a plane 下飞机 SYN **disembark**

de·plete /dɪˈpliːt/ *verb* [usually passive] ~ **sth** (*formal*) to reduce sth by a large amount so that there is not enough left 大量减少；耗尽；使枯竭：*Food supplies were severely depleted.* 食物供应已严重不足。 ▶ **de·ple·tion** /dɪˈpliːʃn/ *noun* [U]：*ozone depletion* 臭氧耗损 ◇ *the depletion of fish stocks* 鱼类存量锐减

de·plor·able /dɪˈplɔːrəbl/ *adj.* (*formal*) very bad and unacceptable, often in a way that shocks people 糟透的；令人震惊的；令人愤慨的 SYN **appalling**：*a deplorable incident* 令人愤慨的事件 ◇ *They were living in the most deplorable conditions.* 他们生活在最糟糕的环境里。◇ *The acting was deplorable.* 那演技糟透了。 ▶ **de·plor·ably**

/-əbli/ *adv.* : *They behaved deplorably.* 他们的表现糟透了。◇ ***deplorably high/low/bad*** 高 / 低 / 糟得令人吃惊

de·plore /dɪˈplɔː(r)/ *verb* **~ sth** (*formal*) to strongly disapprove of sth and criticize it, especially publicly 公开谴责；强烈反对： *Like everyone else, I deplore and condemn this killing.* 我同所有人一样强烈谴责这桩凶杀案。

D

de·ploy /dɪˈplɔɪ/ *verb* **1 ~ sb/sth** (*specialist*) to move soldiers or weapons into a position where they are ready for military action 部署，调度（军队或武器）： *2 000 troops were deployed in the area.* 那个地区部署了 2 000 人的部队。◇ *At least 5 000 missiles were deployed along the border.* 沿边境至少部署了 5 000 枚导弹。 **2 ~ sth** (*formal*) to use sth effectively 有效地利用；调动： *to deploy arguments/resources* 利用论据 / 资源 ▶ **de·ploy·ment** *noun* [U, C]

de·popu·late /ˌdiːˈpɒpjuleɪt; *NAmE* -ˈpɑːp-/ *verb* [usually passive] **~ sth** to reduce the number of people living in a place 使人口减少： *Whole stretches of land were laid waste and depopulated.* 一片片土地荒芜，人口减少。▶ **de·popu·la·tion** /ˌdiːˌpɒpjuˈleɪʃn; *NAmE* -ˌpɑːp-/ *noun* [U]

de·port /dɪˈpɔːt; *NAmE* dɪˈpɔːrt/ *verb* **~ sb** to force sb to leave a country, usually because they have broken the law or because they have no legal right to be there 把（违法者或无居留权的人）驱逐出境；递解出境 ▶ **de·port·ation** /ˌdiːpɔːˈteɪʃn; *NAmE* -pɔːrˈt-/ *noun* [C, U]: *Several of the asylum seekers now face deportation.* 寻求避难的人中有几个正面临递解出境。◇ *a deportation order* 驱逐出境令

de·port·ee /ˌdiːpɔːˈtiː; *NAmE* -pɔːr-/ *noun* a person who has been DEPORTED or is going to be deported 被驱逐出境者；被判处驱逐出境者

de·port·ment /dɪˈpɔːtmənt; *NAmE* -ˈpɔːrt-/ *noun* [U] (*formal*) **1** (*BrE*) the way in which a person stands and moves 风度；仪态： *lessons for young ladies in deportment and etiquette* 年轻女士的礼仪课 **2** (*old-fashioned, especially NAmE*) the way in which a person behaves 行为；举止

de·pose /dɪˈpəʊz; *NAmE* dɪˈpoʊz/ *verb* **~ sb** to remove sb, especially a ruler, from power 罢免；废黜： *The president was deposed in a military coup.* 总统在军事政变中被废黜。

de·posit 🔑 /dɪˈpɒzɪt; *NAmE* -ˈpɑːz-/ *noun, verb*

■***noun***

• **MONEY** 钱 **1** 🔑 [usually sing.] **a ~ (on sth)** a sum of money that is given as the first part of a larger payment 订金；订钱 **SYN** **down payment**: *They normally ask you to pay $100 (as a) deposit.* 他们通常要求付 100 美元（作为）订金。◇ (*BrE*) *We've put down a 5% deposit on the house.* 我们已支付了房款的 5% 作为订金。 ➲ SYNONYMS AT PAYMENT ➲ WORDFINDER NOTE AT LOAN ➲ COLLOCATIONS AT HOUSE **2** 🔑 [usually sing.] a sum of money that is paid by sb when they rent sth and that is returned to them if they do not lose or damage the thing they are renting 押金： *to pay a deposit* 付押金 **3** a sum of money that is paid into a bank account 存款： *Deposits can be made at any branch.* 在任何一家分行都可以存钱。 **OPP** **withdrawal** ➲ WORDFINDER NOTE AT BANK ➲ COLLOCATIONS AT FINANCE **4** (in the British political system) the amount of money that a candidate in an election to Parliament has to pay, and that is returned if he/she gets enough votes 竞选保证金（英国议员候选人预付，获得足够的票数则退还）： *All the other candidates **lost their deposits**.* 所有其余候选人都失掉了竞选保证金。

• **SUBSTANCE** 物质 **5** a layer of a substance that has formed naturally underground （地下自然形成的）沉积物，沉积层： ***mineral/gold/coal deposits*** 矿床；金矿；煤藏 **6** a layer of a substance that has been left somewhere, especially by a river, flood, etc., or is found at the bottom of a liquid （尤指河流、洪水、液体等的）沉积物，淤积物： *The rain left a deposit of mud on the windows.* 雨水在窗上留下一层泥。◇ *fatty deposits in the arteries of the heart* 心动脉中的脂肪沉积

■***verb***

• **PUT DOWN** 放下 **1 ~ sb/sth + adv./prep.** to put or lay sb/sth down in a particular place 放下；放置： *She deposited a pile of books on my desk.* 她把一摞书放在我的书桌上。◇ (*informal*) *I was whisked off in a taxi and deposited outside the hotel.* 一辆出租车匆匆把我送到旅馆外面，让我下了车。

• **LEAVE SUBSTANCE** 留存物质 **2 ~ sth** (especially of a river or a liquid 尤指河流或液体) to leave a layer of sth on the surface of sth, especially gradually and over a period of time 使沉积；使沉淀；使淤积： *Sand was deposited which hardened into sandstone.* 沙经沉积固结形成沙岩。

• **MONEY** 钱 **3** 🔑 **~ sth** to put money into a bank account 将（钱）存入银行；存储： *Millions were deposited in Swiss bank accounts.* 巨额款项存入了瑞士的银行账户。 **4** 🔑 **~ sth** to pay a sum of money as the first part of a larger payment; to pay a sum of money that you will get back if you return in good condition sth that you have rented 付（订金）；付（保证金）；付（押金）

• **PUT IN SAFE PLACE** 存放 **5 ~ sth (in sth) | ~ sth (with sb/sth)** to put sth valuable or important in a place where it will be safe 寄放，寄存（贵重物品）： *Guests may deposit their valuables in the hotel safe.* 旅客可将贵重物品寄存在旅馆的保险柜里。

deˈposit account *noun* (*BrE*) a type of account at a bank or BUILDING SOCIETY that pays interest on money that is left in it 储蓄存款账户 ➲ COMPARE CURRENT ACCOUNT

de·pos·ition /ˌdepəˈzɪʃn/ *noun* **1** [U, C] (*specialist*) the natural process of leaving a layer of a substance on rocks or soil; a substance left in this way 沉积（物）；沉淀（物）；淤积（物）： ***marine/river deposition*** 海洋 / 河流沉积物 **2** [U, C] the act of removing sb, especially a ruler, from power 罢免；废黜： *the deposition of the King* 废黜国王 **3** [C] (*law* 律) a formal statement, taken from sb and used in court 书面证词

de·pos·it·or /dɪˈpɒzɪtə(r); *NAmE* -ˈpɑːz-/ *noun* a person who puts money in a bank account 储户；存户

de·posi·tory /dɪˈpɒzɪtri; *NAmE* dɪˈpɑːzətɔːri/ *noun* (*pl.* **-ies**) a place where things can be stored 贮藏室；存放处；仓库

depot /ˈdepəʊ; *NAmE* ˈdiːpoʊ/ *noun* **1** a place where large amounts of food, goods or equipment are stored （大量物品的）贮藏处，仓库： *an arms depot* 军械库 **2** (*BrE*) a place where buses or other vehicles are kept and repaired 车库；修车厂 **3** (*NAmE*) a small station where trains or buses stop 火车小站；公共汽车小站

de·prave /dɪˈpreɪv/ *verb* **~ sb** (*formal*) to make sb morally bad 使堕落；使腐化；败坏 **SYN** **corrupt**: *In my view this book would deprave young children.* 我认为这本书会腐蚀儿童。

de·praved /dɪˈpreɪvd/ *adj.* (*formal*) morally bad 道德败坏的；堕落的；腐化的 **SYN** **wicked, evil**: *This is the work of a depraved mind.* 这是思想堕落者所为。

de·prav·ity /dɪˈprævəti/ *noun* [U] (*formal*) the state of being morally bad 堕落；腐化 **SYN** **wickedness**: *a life of depravity* 腐化的生活

dep·re·cate /ˈdeprəkeɪt/ *verb* **~ sth** (*formal*) to feel and express strong disapproval of sth 对…表示极不赞成；强烈反对 ▶ **dep·re·cat·ing** (*also less frequent* **dep·re·ca·tory** /ˌdeprəˈkeɪtəri; *NAmE* ˈdeprɪkətɔːri/) *adj.* : *a deprecating comment* 表示反对的评论 **dep·re·cat·ing·ly** *adv.*

de·pre·ci·ate /dɪˈpriːʃieɪt/ *verb* **1** [I] to become less valuable over a period of time 贬值；跌价： *New cars start to depreciate as soon as they are on the road.* 新车一上路就开始贬值。◇ *Shares continued to depreciate on the stock markets today.* 今日股市股价继续下跌。 **OPP** **appreciate** **2** [T] **~ sth** (*business* 商) to reduce the value, as stated in the company's accounts, of a particular ASSET over a particular period of time 折旧： *The bank depreciates PCs over a period of five years.* 这家银行把个人计算机的折旧年限定为五年。 **3** [T] **~ sth** (*formal*) to make sth seem unimportant or of no value 贬低；轻视： *I had no intention of depreciating your contribution.* 我并不想贬低你的贡献。 ▶ **de·pre·ci·ation** /dɪˌpriːʃiˈeɪʃn/ *noun* [U]: *currency depreciation* 货币贬值 ◇ *the depreciation of fixed assets* 固定资产折旧

dep·re·da·tion /ˌdeprəˈdeɪʃn/ *noun* [usually pl.] (*formal*) acts that cause damage to people's property, lives, etc. 掠夺；劫掠；破坏

de·press AW /dɪˈpres/ *verb* **1** to make sb sad and without enthusiasm or hope 使抑郁；使沮丧；使消沉；使失去信心：**~ sb** *Wet weather always depresses me.* 阴雨天总使我心情抑郁。◇ **it depresses sb to do sth** *It depresses me to see so many young girls smoking.* 看到这么多女孩抽烟令我感到很沮丧。 **2 ~ sth** to make trade, business, etc. less active 使萧条；使不景气：*The recession has depressed the housing market.* 经济衰退导致住房市场不景气。 **3 ~ sth** to make the value of prices or wages lower 降低（价格）；减少（工资）：*to* ***depress wages/prices*** 减少工资；降低价格 **4 ~ sth** (*formal*) to press or push sth down, especially part of a machine 按，压，推下（尤指机器部件）：*to depress the clutch pedal* (= when driving) （开车时）踩离合器踏板

de·pres·sant /dɪˈpresnt/ *noun* (*medical* 医) a drug which slows the rate of the body's functions 抑制剂 ➲ SEE ALSO ANTIDEPRESSANT

de·pressed AW /dɪˈprest/ *adj.* **1** very sad and without hope 抑郁的；沮丧的；意志消沉的：*She felt very depressed about the future.* 她感到前途无望。 **2** suffering from the medical condition of DEPRESSION 患抑郁症的 **3** (of a place or an industry 地方或行业) without enough economic activity or jobs for people 不景气的；萧条的；经济困难的：*an attempt to bring jobs to depressed areas* 给经济萧条地区创造就业机会的努力 **4** having a lower amount or level than usual 低于一般水准的；降低了的；削弱了的：*depressed prices* 降低了的价格

de·press·ing AW /dɪˈpresɪŋ/ *adj.* making you feel very sad and without enthusiasm 令人抑郁的；令人沮丧的；令人消沉的：*a* ***depressing sight/thought/experience*** 令人沮丧的景象 / 想法 / 经历 ◇ *Looking for a job these days can be very depressing.* 如今求职有时会令人非常沮丧。 ▶ **de·press·ing·ly** *adv.*：*a depressingly familiar experience* 令人感到腻烦的经历

de·pres·sion AW /dɪˈpreʃn/ *noun* **1** [U] a medical condition in which a person feels very sad and anxious and often has physical SYMPTOMS such as being unable to sleep, etc. 抑郁症；精神忧郁：*clinical depression* 临床抑郁症 ◇ *She suffered from severe depression after losing her job.* 她失业后患了严重的抑郁症。 ➲ WORDFINDER NOTE AT CONDITION ➲ SEE ALSO POSTNATAL DEPRESSION, POST-PARTUM DEPRESSION **2** [U, C] the state of feeling very sad and without hope 抑郁；沮丧；消沉：*There was a feeling of gloom and depression in the office when the news of the job cuts was announced.* 裁员消息宣布时办公室里一片忧郁和沮丧的气氛。 **3** [C, U] a period when there is little economic activity and many people are poor or without jobs 萧条期；（经济）衰退；不景气：*The country was in the grip of (an) economic depression.* 当时国家处于经济萧条期。◇ *the great Depression of the 1930s* * 20 世纪 30 年代的经济大萧条 **4** [C] (*formal*) a part of a surface that is lower than the parts around it 洼地；凹地；坑 SYN **hollow**：*Rainwater collects in shallow depressions on the ground.* 雨水积在地上的浅坑里。 **5** [C] (*specialist*) a weather condition in which the pressure of the air becomes lower, often causing rain 低气压；气压降低 ➲ COMPARE ANTICYCLONE

de·pres·sive /dɪˈpresɪv/ *adj., noun*
■ ***adj.*** connected with the medical condition of depression 患抑郁症的；抑郁的：*depressive illness* 抑郁症
■ ***noun*** a person who is suffering from the medical condition of depression 抑郁症患者 ➲ SEE ALSO MANIC-DEPRESSIVE

de·pres·sor /dɪˈpresə(r)/ *noun* = TONGUE DEPRESSOR

de·priv·ation /ˌdeprɪˈveɪʃn/ *noun* [U, C] the fact of not having sth that you need, like enough food, money or a home; the process that causes this 贫困；丧失；剥夺：*neglected children suffering from social deprivation* 遭社会遗弃无人照管的孩子 ◇ *sleep deprivation* 睡眠剥夺 ◇ *the deprivation of war* (= the suffering caused by not having enough of some things) 战时的物品匮乏

de·prive /dɪˈpraɪv/ *verb*
PHR V **deˈprive sb/sth of sth** to prevent sb from having or doing sth, especially sth important 剥夺；使丧失；使不能享有：*They were imprisoned and deprived of their basic rights.* 他们遭到监禁并被剥夺了基本权利。 ◇ *Why should you* ***deprive yourself*** *of such simple pleasures?* 你为什么连这种简单的乐事也不让自己享受一下呢？

de·prived /dɪˈpraɪvd/ *adj.* without enough food, education, and all the things that are necessary for people to live a happy and comfortable life 贫穷的；贫困的；穷苦的：*a* ***deprived childhood/background/area*** 贫穷的童年 / 出身 / 地区 ◇ ***economically/emotionally/socially deprived*** 经济困难的；感情失落的；社会遗弃的 ➲ SYNONYMS AT POOR

Dept (*also* **Dept.** *especially in NAmE*) *abbr.* (in writing 书写形式) department 部；部门；系

depth /depθ/ *noun*
• **MEASUREMENT** 量度 **1** [C, U] the distance from the top or surface to the bottom of sth 向下的距离；深（度）；纵深：*What's the depth of the water here?* 这儿的水有多深？ ◇ *Water was found* ***at a depth of*** *30 metres.* 在 30 米深处找到了水。◇ *They dug down* ***to a depth of*** *two metres.* 他们挖到两米深。◇ *Many dolphins can dive to depths of 200 metres.* 许多海豚可潜到 200 米深。 ◇ *The oil well extended several hundreds of feet* ***in depth.*** 油井向下延伸了数百英尺。◇ *the depth of a cut/wound/crack* 划口 / 伤口 / 裂口深度 **2** [C, U] the distance from the front to the back of sth 向里的距离；深（度）：*The depth of the shelves is 30 centimetres.* 书架的深度为 30 厘米。
• **OF FEELINGS** 感觉 **3** [U] the strength and power of feelings 深厚；诚挚；强烈：*the depth of her love* 她那爱情之深
• **OF KNOWLEDGE** 知识 **4** [U] (*approving*) the quality of knowing or understanding a lot of details about sth; the ability to provide and explain these details 渊博；深刻；洞察力：*a writer of great wisdom and depth* 有卓越智慧和洞察力的作家 ◇ *a job that doesn't require any great* ***depth of knowledge*** 不需要多么高深知识的工作 ◇ *His ideas lack depth.* 他的想法缺乏深度。
• **DEEPEST PART** 最深处 **5** [C, usually pl.] the deepest, most extreme or serious part of sth 最深处；深渊；极限：*the* ***depths of the ocean*** 海洋深处 ◇ *to live* ***in the depths of the country*** (= a long way from a town) 住在偏远地区 ◇ *in the* ***depths of winter*** (= when it is coldest) 在隆冬季节 ◇ *She was* ***in the depths of despair.*** 她处于绝望的深渊。◇ *He gazed into the depths of her eyes.* 他深深凝视着她的眼睛。 ◇ *Her paintings reveal* ***hidden depths*** (= unknown and interesting things about her character). 她的画表现出她内心深处的东西。
• **OF COLOUR** 颜色 **6** [U] the strength of a colour 浓度；强度：*Strong light will affect the depth of colour of your carpets and curtains.* 强烈的阳光会使你的地毯和窗帘退色。
• **PICTURE/PHOTOGRAPH** 画；照片 **7** [U] (*specialist*) the quality in a work of art or a photograph which makes it appear not to be flat 立体感 ➲ SEE ALSO DEEP *n.*
IDM **ˌin ˈdepth** in a detailed and thorough way 全面；深入；详细：*I haven't looked at the report in depth yet.* 我还没有细看这份报告。◇ *an in-depth study* 深入研究 **be out of your ˈdepth 1** (*BrE*) to be in water that is too deep to stand in with your head above water 在水深没顶（或够不着底）的地方 **2** to be unable to understand sth because it is too difficult; to be in a situation that you cannot control 非某人所能理解；为某人力所不及：*He felt totally out of his depth in his new job.* 他感到自己根本不能胜任这新工作。 ➲ MORE AT PLUMB *v.*

ˈdepth charge *noun* a bomb that is set to explode underwater, used to destroy SUBMARINES （用以摧毁潜艇的）深水炸弹

ˌdepth of ˈfield (*also* **ˌdepth of ˈfocus**) *noun* (*specialist*) the distance between the nearest and the furthest objects that a camera can produce a clear image of at the same time 景深（照相机能同时清晰拍摄的最近和最远物体之间的距离）

dep·u·ta·tion /ˌdepjuˈteɪʃn/ *noun* [C+sing./pl. v.] a small group of people who are asked or allowed to act or speak for others 代表团

de·pute /dɪˈpjuːt/ *verb* **~ sb to do sth** [often passive] (*formal*) to give sb else the authority to represent you or do sth for you 向（某人）授权；把权委托给 SYN **delegate**: *He was deputed to put our views to the committee.* 他获授权向委员会表达我们的观点。

depu·tize (*BrE also* **-ise**) /ˈdepjutaɪz/ *verb* [I] **~ (for sb)** to do sth that sb in a higher position than you would usually do 担任代表；充当代理人：*Ms Green has asked me to deputize for her at the meeting.* 格林女士请我代表她出席会议。

dep·uty /ˈdepjuti/ *noun* (*pl.* **-ies**) **1** a person who is the next most important person below a business manager, a head of a school, a political leader, etc. and who does the person's job when he or she is away 副手；副职；代理：*I'm acting as deputy till the manager returns.* 我在经理回来之前代行他的职务。◇ *the deputy head of a school* 副校长 **2** the name for a member of parliament in some countries（某些国家的）议员 **3** (in the US) a police officer who helps the SHERIFF of an area（美国协助地方治安官办案的）警官

de·racin·ate /ˌdiːˈræsmeɪt/ *verb* **~ sb** (*formal*) to force sb to leave the place or situation in which they feel comfortable 迫使（某人）离开熟悉的环境；使背井离乡 ▶ **de·racin·ated** /ˌdiːˈræsmeɪtɪd/ *adj.*

de·rail /dɪˈreɪl/ *verb* [I, T] (of a train 火车) to leave the track; to make a train do this （使）脱轨，出轨：*The train derailed and plunged into the river.* 火车脱轨栽进了河里。◇ **~ sth** (*figurative*) *This latest incident could derail the peace process.* 最近这个事件可能会扰乱和平进程。▶ **de·rail·ment** *noun* [C, U]

de·rail·leur /dɪˈreɪljə(r)/ *noun* (*specialist*) a type of gear on a bicycle that works by lifting the chain from one gear wheel to another larger or smaller one 拨链器，变速器（自行车换挡装置）

de·ranged /dɪˈreɪndʒd/ *adj.* unable to behave and think normally, especially because of mental illness 精神错乱的；精神失常的；疯狂的：*mentally deranged* 精神错乱 ◇ *a deranged attacker* 疯狂的攻击者 ▶ **de·range·ment** *noun* [U]: *He seemed to be on the verge of total derangement.* 他似乎已濒临精神崩溃的边缘。

derby /ˈdɑːbi; *NAmE* ˈdɜːrbi/ *noun* (*pl.* **-ies**) **1** (*NAmE*) = BOWLER (2) **2** (*BrE*) a sports competition between teams from the same area or town 德比，同城大战（同地区两队间的比赛）：*a **local derby** between the two North London sides* 两支北伦敦队之间的一场同城德比 ◇ *a derby match* 地区体育比赛 **3** a race or sports competition 速度比赛；体育竞赛：*a motorcycle derby* 摩托车大赛 ➲ SEE ALSO DEMOLITION DERBY **4 Derby** used in the name of several horse races which happen every year 德比马赛（特指几个一年一度的马赛）：*the Epsom Derby* 埃普瑟姆马赛 ◇ *the Kentucky Derby* 肯塔基马赛

de·regu·late AW /ˌdiːˈregjuleɪt/ *verb* [often passive] **~ sth** to free a trade, a business activity, etc. from rules and controls 撤销对（贸易、商业活动等）的管制；解除控制 SYN **decontrol**: *deregulated financial markets* 放宽了管制的金融市场 ▶ **de·regu·la·tion** AW /ˌdiːˌreɡjuˈleɪʃn/ *noun* [U] **de·regu·la·tory** /ˌdiːˈregjələtəri; *NAmE* -tɔːri/ *adj.* [only before noun]: *deregulatory reforms* 撤销管制的改革

dere·lict /ˈderəlɪkt/ *adj., noun*

■ ***adj.*** (especially of land or buildings 尤指土地或建筑物) not used or cared for and in bad condition 荒废的；被弃置的；破旧的：***derelict land/buildings/sites*** 荒废的土地；被废弃的建筑物；破旧的遗址

■ ***noun*** (*formal*) a person without a home, a job or property 无家可归者；乞丐；社会弃儿 SYN **vagrant**: *derelicts living on the streets* 流落街头的乞丐

dere·lic·tion /ˌderəˈlɪkʃn/ *noun* (*formal*) **1** [U] the state of being derelict 荒废；弃置；破旧不堪：***industrial/urban dereliction*** 工业 / 城市废墟 ◇ *a house in a state of dereliction* 破旧不堪的房屋 **2** [U, sing.] **~ of duty** (*formal* or *law* 律) the fact of deliberately not doing what you ought to do, especially when it is part of your job 玩忽职守；渎职：*The police officers were found guilty of serious **dereliction of duty**.* 这些警察被判犯有严重渎职罪。

de·ride /dɪˈraɪd/ *verb* [often passive] **~ sb/sth (as sth)** | **+ speech** (*formal*) to treat sb/sth as ridiculous and not worth considering seriously 嘲笑；愚弄；揶揄 SYN **mock**: *His views were derided as old-fashioned.* 他的观点被当作旧思想受到嘲弄。

de ri·gueur /ˌdə rɪˈgɜː(r)/ *adj.* [not before noun] (*from French*) considered necessary if you wish to be accepted socially 合乎礼节；按照习俗；按照时尚：*Evening dress is de rigueur at the casino.* 按照习俗在赌场要穿晚礼服。

de·ri·sion /dɪˈrɪʒn/ *noun* [U] a strong feeling that sb/sth is ridiculous and not worth considering seriously, shown by laughing in an unkind way or by making unkind remarks 嘲笑；取笑；奚落 SYN **scorn**: *Her speech was greeted with howls of derision.* 她的演讲受到阵阵嘲笑。◇ *He became an object of universal derision.* 他成了众人嘲弄的对象。

de·ri·sive /dɪˈraɪsɪv/ (*also less frequent* **de·ri·sory**) *adj.* unkind and showing that you think sb/sth is ridiculous 嘲笑的；嘲弄的；取笑的：*She gave a short, derisive laugh.* 她讥讽地笑了笑。▶ **de·ri·sive·ly** *adv.*

de·ri·sory /dɪˈraɪsəri/ *adj.* (*formal*) **1** too small or of too little value to be considered seriously 少得可笑的；少得可怜的；不屑一顾的 SYN **laughable**: *They offered us a derisory £50 a week.* 他们每周给我们 50 英镑，少得可怜。**2** = DERISIVE

der·iv·ation AW /ˌderɪˈveɪʃn/ *noun* [U, C] the origin or development of sth, especially a word （尤指词语的）起源，由来，派生：*a word of Greek derivation* 源自希腊语的词

de·riva·tive AW /dɪˈrɪvətɪv/ *noun, adj.*

■ ***noun*** a word or thing that has been developed or produced from another word or thing 派生词；衍生字；派生物；衍生物：*'Happiness' is a derivative of 'happy'.* * happiness 是 happy 的派生词。◇ *Crack is a highly potent and addictive derivative of cocaine.* 强效纯可卡因是一种药效极强、容易使人上瘾的可卡因制剂。

■ ***adj.*** (*usually disapproving*) copied from sth else; not having new or original ideas 模仿他人的；缺乏独创性的：*a **derivative design/style*** 沿袭前人的设计 / 样式

de·rive AW /dɪˈraɪv/ *verb*

PHR V **de'rive from sth | be de'rived from sth** to come or develop from sth 从…衍生出；起源于；来自：*The word 'politics' is derived from a Greek word meaning 'city'.* * politics 一词源自希腊语，意思是 city。 **de'rive sth from sth 1** (*formal*) to get sth from sth （从…中）得到，获得：*He derived great pleasure from painting.* 他从绘画中得到极大的乐趣。 **2** (*specialist*) to obtain a substance from sth （从…中）提取：*The new drug is derived from fish oil.* 这种新药是从鱼油中提炼出来的。

derma·titis /ˌdɜːməˈtaɪtɪs; *NAmE* ˌdɜːrm-/ *noun* [U] (*medical* 医) a skin condition in which the skin becomes red, swollen and sore 皮炎

derma·tolo·gist /ˌdɜːməˈtɒlədʒɪst; *NAmE* ˌdɜːrməˈtɑːl-/ *noun* a doctor who studies and treats skin diseases 皮肤病医生；皮肤病专家 ➲ WORDFINDER NOTE AT SPECIALIST

derma·tol·ogy /ˌdɜːməˈtɒlədʒi; *NAmE* ˌdɜːrməˈtɑːl-/ *noun* [U] the scientific study of skin diseases 皮肤病学 ▶ **derma·to·logi·cal** /ˌdɜːmətəˈlɒdʒɪkl; *NAmE* ˌdɜːrmətəˈlɑːdʒ-/ *adj.*

der·mis /ˈdɜːmɪs; *NAmE* ˈdɜːr-/ *noun* [U] (*biology* 生) the skin 真皮

dero·gate /ˈderəgeɪt/ *verb* **~ sth** (*formal*) to state that sth or sb is without worth 贬低；贬损

PHR V **'derogate from sth** to ignore a responsibility or duty 忽视责任

dero·ga·tion /ˌderəˈɡeɪʃn/ *noun* [U, C] (*formal*) **1** an occasion when a rule or law is allowed to be ignored （法规等的）部分废除 **2** words or actions which show that sb or sth is considered to have no worth 含有贬义的言辞（或行为）

de·roga·tory /dɪˈrɒɡətri; *NAmE* dɪˈrɑːɡətɔːri/ *adj.* (*formal*) showing a critical attitude towards sb 贬低的；贬义的 SYN **insulting**: *derogatory remarks/comments* 贬斥的言辞 / 评论

der·rick /ˈderɪk/ *noun* **1** a tall machine used for moving or lifting heavy weights, especially on a ship; a type of CRANE 转臂起重机；（尤指船上的）吊杆式起重机 **2** a tall structure over an OIL WELL for holding the DRILL (= the machine that makes the hole in the ground for getting the oil out) （油井的）井架，钻塔

derring-do /ˌderɪŋ ˈduː/ *noun* [U] (*old-fashioned, humorous*) brave actions, like those in adventure stories 大胆冒险行为；英勇行为

der·vish /ˈdɜːvɪʃ; *NAmE* ˈdɜːrvɪʃ/ *noun* a member of a Muslim religious group whose members make a promise to stay poor and live without comforts or pleasures. They perform a fast lively dance as part of their worship. 德尔维希教团成员（属伊斯兰教，尚苦行，狂舞为其崇拜仪式的一部分）: *He threw himself around the stage like a whirling dervish.* 他在台上转圈，如同跳旋转舞蹈的苦行僧一样。

de·sal·in·ation /ˌdiːˌsælɪˈneɪʃn/ *noun* [U] the process of removing salt from sea water （海水的）脱盐: *a desalination plant* 脱盐工厂

de·scale /ˌdiːˈskeɪl/ *verb* **~ sth** (*BrE*) to remove the SCALE (= the hard white material left on pipes, etc. by water when it is heated) from sth 除去（热水管道等的）水垢

des·cant /ˈdeskænt/ *noun* (*music* 音) a tune that is sung or played at the same time as, and usually higher than, the main tune 高于主旋律的曲调；狄斯康特

ˌdescant reˈcorder (*BrE*) (*NAmE* **soˌprano reˈcorder**) *noun* (*music* 音) the most common size of RECORDER (= a musical instrument in the shape of a pipe that you blow into), with a high range of notes 高音竖笛

des·cend /dɪˈsend/ *verb* **1** [I, T] (*formal*) to come or go down from a higher to a lower level 下来；下去；下降: *The plane began to descend.* 飞机开始降落。◇ *The results, ranked* ***in descending order*** (= from the highest to the lowest) *are as follows…* 结果按递减顺序排列如下…◇ **~ sth** *She descended the stairs slowly.* 她缓慢地走下楼梯。OPP **ascend** **2** [I] (*formal*) (of a hill, etc. 山等) to slope downwards 下斜；下倾: *At this point the path descends steeply.* 小路从这里陡然而下。OPP **ascend** **3** [I] (*literary*) (of night, DARKNESS, a mood, etc. 夜晚、黑暗、情绪等) to arrive and begin to affect sb/sth 降临；来临 SYN **fall**: *Night descends quickly in the tropics.* 热带地区天黑得快。◇ **~ on/upon sb/sth** *Calm descended on the crowd.* 人群平静下来。

PHR V **be desˈcended from sb** to be related to sb who lived a long time ago 是某人的后裔: *He claims to be descended from a Spanish prince.* 他声称是一位西班牙王子的后裔。 **desˈcend into sth** [no passive] (*formal*) to gradually get into a bad state 逐渐陷入: *The country was descending into chaos.* 这个国家陷入一片混乱。 **desˈcend on/upon sb/sth** to visit sb/sth in large numbers, sometimes unexpectedly （突然）大批来访: *Hundreds of football fans descended on the city.* 数百名足球迷蜂拥入城。 **desˈcend to sth** [no passive] to do sth that makes people stop respecting you 降低身份去做；竟做出；堕落到…地步: *They descended to the level of personal insults.* 他们竟卑鄙到进行人身侮辱的地步。

des·cend·ant /dɪˈsendənt/ *noun* **1** a person's **descendants** are their children, their children's children, and all the people who live after them who are related to them 后裔；后代；子孙: *He was an O'Conor and a* ***direct descendant*** *of the last High King of Ireland.* 他属于奥康纳家族，是爱尔兰最后一位君王的嫡系后裔。◇ *Many of them are descendants of the original settlers.* 他们中许多人都是早期移民的后裔。 **2** something that has developed from sth similar in the past （由过去类似物发展来的）派生物

des·cent /dɪˈsent/ *noun* (*formal*) **1** [C, usually sing.] an action of coming or going down 下降；下倾: *The plane began its descent to Heathrow.* 飞机开始向希思罗机场降落。◇ (*figurative*) *the country's swift descent into anarchy* 国家迅速陷入无政府状态 OPP **ascent** **2** [C] a slope going downwards 斜坡；坡道: *There is a gradual descent to the sea.* 有一片斜坡缓缓伸延到海边。OPP **ascent** **3** [U] a person's family origins 血统；祖籍；祖先；出身 SYN **ancestry**: *to be of Scottish descent* 祖籍是苏格兰 ◇ **~ from sb** *He traces his line of descent from the Stuart kings.* 他的家族可追溯到斯图亚特王朝。 ➲ WORDFINDER NOTE AT RELATION

de·scribe 🔑 /dɪˈskraɪb/ *verb* **1** 🔑 to say what sb/sth is like 描述；形容；把…称为: **~ sb/sth (to/for sb)** *Can you describe him to me?* 你能向我描述一下他的样子吗？◇ **~ sb/sth as sth** *The man was described as tall and dark, and aged about 20.* 据描述这男人高个子，深色皮肤，年龄在 20 岁左右。◇ *Jim was described by his colleagues as 'unusual'.* 吉姆被同事们称为"不寻常"的人。◇ **~ how, what, etc.…** *Describe how you did it.* 谈谈你是怎样做这事的。◇ **~ (sb/sth) doing sth** *Several people described seeing strange lights in the sky.* 好几个人都说看到天上出现了奇异光芒。 **2 ~ sth** (*formal* or *specialist*) to make a movement which has a particular shape; to form a particular shape 沿…形状移动；画出…图形；形成…形状: *The shark described a circle around the shoal of fish.* 这条鲨鱼围绕着鱼群游动。▸ **de·scrib·able** *adj.*

▼ **EXPRESS YOURSELF** 情景表达

Describing a picture 描述图片

In some exams, you have to describe what you see in a picture or photograph. Here are some useful phrases.
有些考试会要求描述图片或照片内容。下面是一些有用的短语：

- ***The picture shows*** *a family gathered around a kitchen table.* 照片中一家人围坐在餐桌旁。
- ***This is a picture/photo of*** *a busy city street.* 这张图 / 照片里是一条繁华的城市街道。
- ***In the foreground/background, we can see*** *a group of protesters.* 在前景 / 背景中，我们可以看到一群示威者。
- ***In the bottom right-hand corner/top left-hand corner, there's*** *a child sitting alone.* 在右下角 / 左上角，有一个孩子孤零零地坐在那里。
- ***On the left/On the right/In the middle,*** *someone is standing with a bottle in his hand.* 在左边 / 右边 / 中间，站着一个手里拿着瓶子的人。
- ***In the cartoon, we can see*** *two people looking at a newspaper headline.* 在漫画中，我们可以看到两个人在看报纸的大字标题。
- ***The cartoonist has drawn*** *the man* ***to represent*** *a typical businessman.* 漫画家把这个男人画成一个典型的商人。

de·scrip·tion 🔑 /dɪˈskrɪpʃn/ *noun* **1** 🔑 [C, U] **~ (of sb/sth)** a piece of writing or speech that says what sb/sth is like; the act of writing or saying in words what sb/sth is like 描写（文字）；形容；说明: *to give a* ***detailed/full description*** *of the procedure* 对程序作详细的 / 详尽的说明 ◇ *a* ***brief/general description*** *of the software* 软件的简要 / 概括性说明 ◇ *Police have issued a description of the gunman.* 警方发布通告，描述了持枪歹徒的特征。◇ *'Scared stiff' is an apt description of how I felt at that moment.* "吓得呆若木鸡"是我当时感受的贴切描述。 ◇ *a personal pain that goes* ***beyond description*** (= is too great to express in words) 难以言表的个人痛苦 ◇ *the novelist's powers of* *description* 小说家的叙述才能 **2** [C] **of some, all, every, etc.** ~ of some, etc. type 类型: *boats of every description/ all descriptions* 各种类型的船 ◇ *Their money came from trade of some description.* 他们的钱是做某种生意赚来的。◇ *medals, coins and things of that description* 纪念章、硬币以及诸如此类的东西

IDM **answer/fit a description** (**of sb/sth**) to be like a particular person or thing 与描述的…相像: *A child answering the description of the missing boy was found safe and well in London yesterday.* 昨天在伦敦发现了一个与失踪男孩情况相符的孩子，安然无恙。 ⊃ MORE AT BEGGAR *v.*

de·scrip·tive /dɪˈskrɪptɪv/ *adj.* **1** saying what sb/sth is like; describing sth 描写的；叙述的；说明的: *the descriptive passages in the novel* 小说中的描写性段落 ◇ *The term I used was meant to be purely descriptive* (= not judging). 我所用的措辞是纯叙述性的（并非作出判断）。 **2** (*linguistics* 语言) saying how language is actually used, without giving rules for how it should be used 描写性的（描述语言的实际应用而非使用规则） OPP **prescriptive**

de·scrip·tor /dɪˈskrɪptə(r)/ *noun* (*linguistics* 语言) a word or expression used to describe or identify sth 叙词

des·cry /dɪˈskraɪ/ *verb* (**des·cries, des·cry·ing, des·cried, des·cried**) ~ **sb/sth** (*literary*) to suddenly see sb/sth 突然看到；突然发现

dese·crate /ˈdesɪkreɪt/ *verb* ~ **sth** to damage a holy thing or place or treat it without respect 亵渎（圣物或圣地）: *desecrated graves* 被亵渎的坟墓 ▶ **dese·cra·tion** /ˌdesɪˈkreɪʃn/ *noun* [U]: *the desecration of a cemetery* 亵渎墓地 ◇ (*figurative*) *the desecration of the countryside by new roads* 新公路糟蹋了乡村

de·seg·re·gate /ˌdiːˈsegrɪgeɪt/ *verb* ~ **sth** to end the policy of SEGREGATION in a place in which people of different races are kept separate in public places, etc. 废除…的种族隔离 ▶ **de·seg·re·ga·tion** /ˌdiːˌsegrɪˈgeɪʃn/ *noun* [U]

de·select /ˌdiːsɪˈlekt/ *verb* **1** ~ **sb** if the local branch of a political party in Britain **deselects** the existing Member of Parliament, it does not choose him or her as a candidate at the next election （英国）取消（现任议员）的候选人资格，否决（现任议员）为下届候选人 **2** ~ **sth** (*computing* 计) to remove sth from the list of possible choices on a computer menu（从计算机选单上）撤销选定 ▶ **de·selec·tion** *noun* [U]

de·sen·si·tize (*BrE also* **-ise**) /ˌdiːˈsensətaɪz/ *verb* [usually passive] **1** ~ **sb/sth** (**to sth**) to make sb/sth less aware of sth, especially a problem or sth bad, by making them become used to it 使（尤指对不好的事）不再敏感: *People are increasingly becoming desensitized to violence on television.* 大众对电视上的暴力镜头越来越麻木了。 **2** ~ **sb/sth** (*specialist*) to treat sb/sth so that they will stop being sensitive to physical or chemical changes, or to a particular substance 使脱敏；降低敏感反应 ▶ **de·sen·si·tiza·tion, -isa·tion** /ˌdiːˌsensətaɪˈzeɪʃn; *NAmE* -təˈz-/ *noun* [U]

des·ert *noun, verb*

■ ***noun*** /ˈdezət; *NAmE* ˈdezərt/ ⊃ SEE ALSO DESERTS [C, U] a large area of land that has very little water and very few plants growing on it. Many deserts are covered by sand. 沙漠；荒漠；荒原: *the Sahara Desert* 撒哈拉大沙漠 ◇ *Somalia is mostly desert.* 索马里大部分地区都是荒漠。◇ *burning desert sands* 沙漠里灼热的沙 ◇ (*figurative*) *a cultural desert* (= a place without any culture) 文化沙漠

■ ***verb*** /dɪˈzɜːt; *NAmE* dɪˈzɜːrt/ **1** [T] ~ **sb** to leave sb without help or support 抛弃，离弃，遗弃（某人） SYN **abandon**: *She was deserted by her husband.* 她被丈夫遗弃了。 **2** [T, often passive] ~ **sth** to go away from a place and leave it empty 舍弃，离弃（某地方） SYN **abandon**: *The villages had been deserted.* 这些村庄已经荒无人烟了。◇ *The owl seems to have deserted its nest.* 这只猫头鹰似乎不要这个窝了。 **3** [I, T] ~ (**sth**) to leave the armed forces without permission 擅离（部队）；逃走；开小差: *Large numbers of soldiers deserted as defeat became inevitable.* 战败已成定局，许多士兵开小差跑了。 **4** [T] ~ **sth** (**for sth**) to stop using, buying or supporting sth 废弃，放弃，撇下不管: *Why did you desert teaching for politics?* 你为什么弃教从政呢？ **5** [T] ~ **sb** if a particular quality **deserts** you, it is not there when you need it 背离；使失望: *Her courage seemed to desert her for a moment.* 她一时间似乎失去了勇气。 ▶ **de·ser·tion** /dɪˈzɜːʃn; *NAmE* -ˈzɜːr-/ *noun* [U, C]: *She felt betrayed by her husband's desertion.* 她感到丈夫遗弃她辜负了她的心。◇ *The army was badly affected by desertions.* 开小差使部队大受影响。 IDM SEE SINK *v.*

ˈ**desert boot** *noun* a SUEDE boot that just covers the ankle 沙漠靴（齐踝深的幼山羊皮皮靴）

des·ert·ed /dɪˈzɜːtɪd; *NAmE* -ˈzɜːrt-/ *adj.* **1** (of a place 地方) with no people in it 无人居住的；空寂无人的: *deserted streets* 空无一人的街道 **2** left by a person or people who do not intend to return 被抛弃的；被遗弃的；被舍弃的 SYN **abandoned**: *a deserted village* 被舍弃的村庄 ◇ *deserted wives* 遭遗弃的妻子

de·sert·er /dɪˈzɜːtə(r); *NAmE* -ˈzɜːrt-/ *noun* a person who leaves the army, navy, etc. without permission (= DESERTS) 逃兵；开小差的人

desert·ifi·ca·tion /dɪˌzɜːtɪfɪˈkeɪʃn; *NAmE* -ˌzɜːrt-/ *noun* [U] (*specialist*) the process of becoming or making sth a desert 沙漠化

ˌ**desert ˈisland** *noun* a tropical island where no people live 热带荒岛

des·erts /dɪˈzɜːts; *NAmE* dɪˈzɜːrts/ *noun* [pl.]

IDM **sb's** (**just**) **deserts** what sb deserves, especially when it is sth bad 应得的惩罚；报应: *The family of the victim said that the killer had **got his just deserts** when he was jailed for life.* 受害者家属说杀人犯被判终身监禁是得到了他应有的惩罚。

de·serve /dɪˈzɜːv; *NAmE* dɪˈzɜːrv/ *verb* (not used in the progressive tenses 不用于进行时) if sb/sth **deserves** sth, it is right that they should have it, because of the way they have behaved or because of what they are 值得；应得；应受: ~ **sth** *You deserve a rest after all that hard work.* 辛苦劳累那么久，你该休息一下了。◇ *The report deserves careful consideration.* 这报告应该给予认真考虑。◇ *One player in particular deserves a mention.* 有一名运动员特别值得表扬。◇ *What have I done to deserve this?* 我做了什么事而要得到这种待遇呢？ ◇ ~ **to do sth** *They didn't deserve to win.* 他们不该赢。◇ *He deserves to be locked up for ever for what he did.* 他做了这样的事，应该终身监禁。◇ ~ **doing sth** *Several other points deserve mentioning.* 其他几点值得一提。

IDM **sb deˌserves a ˈmedal** (*informal*) used to say that you admire sb because they have done sth difficult or unpleasant（用以夸奖某人完成了艰巨任务）应给某人授勋 ˌ**get what you deˈserve** | **deˌserve all/everything you ˈget** (*informal*) used to say that you think sb has earned the bad things that happen to them 罪有应得 ⊃ MORE AT TURN *n.*

de·served·ly /dɪˈzɜːvɪdli; *NAmE* -ˈzɜːrv-/ *adv.* in the way that is deserved; correctly 应得地；恰如其分地；理所当然地: *The restaurant is deservedly popular.* 这餐馆为大众喜爱是理所当然的。◇ *He has just been chosen for the top job, and **deservedly so**.* 他刚被选中担任这一要职，这是理所当然的。 OPP **undeservedly**

de·serv·ing /dɪˈzɜːvɪŋ; *NAmE* -ˈzɜːrv-/ *adj.* ~ (**of sth**) (*formal*) that deserves help, praise, a reward, etc. 值得的；应得的: *to give money to a deserving cause* 把钱捐给值得赞助的事业 ◇ *This family is one of the most deserving cases.* 这是最应当得到帮助的一户人家。◇ *an issue deserving of attention* 值得注意的问题 OPP **undeserving**

dés·ha·billé /ˌdezæbiːˈjeɪ/ (*also* **dis·ha·bille** /ˌdɪsəˈbiːl; -ˈbiː/) *noun* [U] (*formal* or *humorous*) the state of wearing no clothes or very few clothes 赤身裸体；一丝不挂；衣不蔽体: *in a state of déshabillé* 一丝不挂

desi (*also* **deshi**) /ˈdeɪsi/ *adj., noun*

■ ***adj.*** **1** local or belonging to a particular place; Indian, Pakistani, Bangladeshi, or Sri Lankan 本地的；当地的；南亚的: *Many people in the city prefer desi food to the type that is sold by foreign fast food chains.* 城里很多人

喜欢本地南亚口味的食物胜过外国快餐连锁店卖的食物。◊ *a desi film* 南亚影片 ➲ COMPARE VIDESHI *adj.* **2** not mixed with other substances 纯的；纯粹的；没有杂质的：*desi ghee* 纯印度酥油 **3** (*disapproving*) typical of the country or country people; simple and basic 土里土气的；简陋的：*Modern consumers weren't attracted by the desi images of rural life shown in the adverts.* 现代消费者并未被广告中呈现的乡村土气的画面所吸引。

■ ***noun*** a person of Indian, Pakistani, Bangladeshi, or Sri Lankan birth or origin who lives abroad 南亚侨民

des·ic·cated /ˈdesɪkeɪtɪd/ *adj.* **1** (of food 食物) dried in order to preserve it 脱水的；干燥法保存的：*desiccated coconut* 椰子干 **2** (*specialist*) completely dry 干涸的；枯竭的：*treeless and desiccated soil* 无树的荒芜干旱土地

des·ic·ca·tion /ˌdesɪˈkeɪʃn/ *noun* [U] (*specialist*) the process of becoming completely dry 干涸；枯竭

de·sid·er·atum /dɪˌzɪdəˈrɑːtəm; -ˈreɪtəm/ *noun* (*pl.* **de·sid·er·ata** /-ɑːtə; -eɪtə/) (*from Latin, formal*) a thing that is wanted or needed 想望的东西；需要的东西

de·sign 🔑 AW /dɪˈzaɪn/ *noun, verb*

■ ***noun***

• **ARRANGEMENT** 布置 **1** 🔑 [U, C] the general arrangement of the different parts of sth that is made, such as a building, book, machine, etc. 设计；布局；安排：*The basic design of the car is very similar to that of earlier models.* 这种汽车的基本设计与早期的型号非常相似。◊ *special new design features* 特别的新型设计风格 ◊ *The magazine will appear in a new design from next month.* 从下月起这本杂志将以新的设计问世。

• **DRAWING/PLAN/MODEL** 图样；方案；模型 **2** 🔑 [U] the art or process of deciding how sth will look, work, etc. by drawing plans, making models, etc. 设计艺术；构思：*a course in art and design* 美术及设计课程 ◊ *a design studio* 设计室 ◊ *computer-aided design* 计算机辅助设计 ◊ *the design and development of new products* 新产品的设计和开发 ➲ SEE ALSO INTERIOR DESIGN **3** 🔑 [C] ~ (**for sth**) a drawing or plan from which sth may be made 设计图样；设计方案：*designs for aircraft* 飞机的设计图样 ◊ *new and original designs* 别具一格的新型设计方案

• **PATTERN** 图案 **4** 🔑 [C] an arrangement of lines and shapes as a decoration 装饰图案；花纹 SYN **pattern**: ***floral/abstract/geometric designs*** 花卉 / 抽象 / 几何图案 ◊ *The tiles come in a huge range of colours and designs.* 瓷砖有各种各样的颜色和图案。

• **INTENTION** 意图 **5** [U, C] a plan or an intention 打算；意图；目的：*It happened—whether **by accident or design**—that the two of them were left alone after all the others had gone.* 不知道是偶然还是有意安排，其他人走后，竟然只剩下他们两个人。◊ *It is all part of his **grand design**.* 这都是他那宏图大略的一部分。➲ MORE LIKE THIS 20, page R27

IDM **have designs on sb** (*formal* or *humorous*) to want to start a sexual relationship with sb 企图占有某人；存心与某人发生性关系；对…存心不良 **have designs on sth** (*formal*) to be planning to get sth for yourself, often in a way that other people do not approve of 企图将某物据为己有；图谋得到某物；打…的鬼主意：*Rumours spread that the Duke had designs on the crown* (= wanted to make himself king). 谣传公爵觊觎王位。

■ ***verb***

• **DRAW PLANS** 设计 **1** 🔑 to decide how sth will look, work, etc., especially by drawing plans or making models 设计；制图；构思：**~ sth** *to design a car/a dress/an office* 设计汽车 / 连衣裙 / 办公室 ◊ *a badly designed kitchen* 设计很糟糕的厨房 ◊ **~ sth for sb/sth** *They asked me to design a poster for the campaign.* 他们请我为这次运动设计一张海报。◊ **~ sb sth** *Could you design us a poster?* 你能为我们设计一张海报吗？

• **PLAN STH** 计划 **2** 🔑 **~ sth** to think of and plan a system, a way of doing sth, etc. 计划；筹划；制订：*We need to design a new syllabus for the third year.* 我们需要为三年级学生制订一个新的课程大纲。

• **FOR SPECIAL PURPOSE** 特定目的 **3** 🔑 [usually passive] to make, plan or intend sth for a particular purpose or use 制造；设计；意欲：**~ sth** (**for sth**) *The method is specifically designed for use in small groups.* 这方法是专为小组活动设计的。◊ **~ sth** (**as sth**) *This course is primarily designed as an introduction to the subject.* 这门课程开设的主要目的是教授这门学科的导论。◊ **~ sth to do sth** *The programme is designed to help people who have been out of work for a long time.* 这项计划的目的是为长期失业者提供帮助。

des·ig·nate *verb, adj.*

■ ***verb*** /ˈdezɪɡneɪt/ [often passive] (*formal*) **1** to say officially that sb/sth has a particular character or name; to describe sb/sth in a particular way 命名；指定；认定：**~ sb/sth** (**as**) **sth** *This area has been designated* (*as*) *a National Park.* 本区已定为国家公园。◊ **~ sb/sth** (**as being/having sth**) *Several pupils were designated as having moderate or severe learning difficulties.* 几名学生被认定有一定或严重学习困难。◊ *a designated nature reserve* 指定的自然保护区 ◊ *designated seats for the elderly* 老人专座 **2** to choose or name sb for a particular job or position 选定，指派，委任（某人任某职）：**~ sb/sth** *The director is allowed to designate his/her successor.* 主任获准选定自己的继任人。◊ **~ sb** (**as**) **sth** *Who has she designated* (*as*) *her deputy?* 她委任了谁为她的副手？◊ **~ sb to do sth** *the man designated to succeed the president* 被指派接替主席职务的男人 **3** **~ sth** (**by sth**) to show sth using a particular mark or sign 标明；标示；指明：*The different types are designated by the letters A, B and C.* 不同的类型分别用字母 A、B 和 C 标明。

■ ***adj.*** /ˈdezɪɡneɪt; -nət/ [after noun] (*formal*) chosen to do a job but not yet having officially started it（已受委派）尚未上任；（已当选）尚未就职：*an interview with the director designate* 与未到任主任的面谈

ˌdesignated ˈdriver *noun* (*informal*) the person who agrees to drive and not drink alcohol when people go to a party, a bar, etc. 指定驾车人（同意去聚会、酒吧等不饮酒而为他人开车）

ˌdesignated ˈhitter *noun* (in BASEBALL 棒球) a player who is named at the start of the game as the person who will hit the ball in place of the PITCHER 指定击球员（比赛开始即指定为击球手而非投球手）

des·ig·na·tion /ˌdezɪɡˈneɪʃn/ *noun* (*formal*) **1** [U] ~ (**as sth**) the action of choosing a person or thing for a particular purpose, or of giving them or it a particular status 选定；指定；委任：*The district is under consideration for designation as a conservation area.* 正在考虑将这个地区指定为保护区。 **2** [C] a name, title or description 名称；称号；称呼：*Her official designation is Financial Controller.* 她的正式职衔是财务总监。

de·sign·er AW /dɪˈzaɪnə(r)/ *noun, adj.*

■ ***noun*** a person whose job is to decide how things such as clothes, furniture, tools, etc. will look or work by making drawings, plans or patterns 设计者；构思者：***a fashion/jewellery, etc. designer*** 时装、珠宝等设计师 ◊ *an industrial designer* 工业设计师

■ ***adj.*** [only before noun] made by a famous designer; expensive and having a famous brand name 由著名设计师设计的；标有设计师姓名的；名牌的：*designer jeans* 名牌牛仔裤 ◊ *designer labels* 设计师品牌 ◊ *designer water* 名牌饮用水 ◊ *He had a trendy haircut, an earring and **designer stubble*** (= a short beard, grown for two or three days and thought to look fashionable). 他理了个时髦的发型，戴着一只耳环，还留着时髦的胡子茬儿。➲ COLLOCATIONS AT FASHION

deˌsigner ˈbaby *noun* (used especially in newspapers 尤用于报纸) a baby that is born from an EMBRYO which was selected from a number of embryos produced using IVF, for example because the parents want a baby that can provide cells to treat a brother's or sister's medical condition 定制婴儿，设计婴儿（借助体外受精技术选取胚胎而生出的婴儿，以提供细胞治疗哥哥或姐姐的病）

deˌsigner ˈdrug *noun* a drug produced artificially, usually one that is illegal 人造毒品

de·sir·able /dɪˈzaɪərəbl/ *adj.* **1** (*formal*) that you would like to have or do; worth having or doing 想望的；可取的；值得拥有的；值得做的：*She chatted for a few minutes* about the qualities she considered **desirable in** a secretary. 她用了几分钟谈了谈她认为一个秘书应有的品质。 ◇ *Such measures are desirable, if not essential.* 这些措施即使不是必要，也是可取的。◇ *The house has many desirable features.* 这栋房子有许多吸引人的特点。◇ *highly desirable* 非常可取 ◇ **~ that** (*BrE*) *It is* ***desirable that*** *interest rates should be reduced.* 利率下调是可取的。◇ (*NAmE*) *It is* ***desirable that*** *interest rates be reduced.* 利率下调是可取的。◇ **~ (for sb) (to do sth)** *It is no longer* ***desirable for*** *adult children to live with their parents.* 孩子长大成人后还与父母住在一起就不太可取了。 **OPP** **undesirable** **2** (of a person 人) causing other people to feel sexual desire 引起性欲的；性感的 ▸ **de·sir·abil·ity** /dɪˌzaɪərəˈbɪləti/ *noun* [U]: (*formal*) *No one questions the desirability of cheaper fares.* 没有人质疑票价下调是件好事。

de·sire /dɪˈzaɪə(r)/ *noun, verb*

■ ***noun*** **1** [C, U] a strong wish to have or do sth 愿望；欲望；渴望：*enough money to satisfy all your desires* 足够的钱来满足你所有的欲望 ◇ **~ for sth** *a strong desire for power* 强烈的权力欲◇ **~ to do sth** *She felt an overwhelming desire to return home.* 她感到一种难以遏制的想回家的愿望。◇ (*formal*) *I have no desire* (= I do not want) *to discuss the matter further.* 我不想再谈此事。◇ (*formal*) *He has expressed a desire to see you.* 他表示想见见你。 **2** [U, C] **~ (for sb)** a strong wish to have sex with sb 情欲；肉欲；性欲：*She felt a surge of love and desire for him.* 她对他骤生爱意，欲火攻心。 **3** [C, usually sing.] a person or thing that is wished for 想望的人；渴望的事物：*When she agreed to marry him he felt he had achieved* ***his heart's desire.*** 当她答应嫁给他时，他感到终于得到了自己的心上人。

■ ***verb*** (not used in the progressive tenses 不用于进行时) **1** (*formal*) to want sth; to wish for sth 渴望；期望；想望：**~ sth** *We all desire health and happiness.* 我们都渴望健康和幸福。◇ *The house had everything you could desire.* 这房子你要什么有什么。◇ *The medicine did not achieve* ***the desired effect.*** 这种药未达到预期效果。◇ **~ (sb/sth) to do sth** *Fewer people desire to live in the north of the country.* 想住在这个国家北方的人更少。 **2** **~ sb** to be sexually attracted to sb 被（某人）吸引；对（某人）产生性欲：*He still desired her.* 他依然渴望拥有她。

IDM **leave a lot, much, something, etc. to be deˈsired** to be bad or unacceptable 还有许多（或一些等）需要改进的地方

de·sir·ous /dɪˈzaɪərəs/ *adj.* [not before noun] **~ (of sth/of doing sth) | ~ (to do sth)** (*formal*) having a wish for sth; wanting sth 渴望；想望；希望：*At that point Franco was desirous of prolonging the war.* 那时，佛朗哥希望战争能延续下去。

de·sist /dɪˈzɪst; dɪˈsɪst/ *verb* [I] **~ (from sth/from doing sth)** (*formal*) to stop doing sth 停止；结束：*They agreed to desist from the bombing campaign.* 他们同意停止大规模轰炸。

desk /desk/ *noun* **1** a piece of furniture like a table, usually with drawers in it, that you sit at to read, write, work, etc. 书桌；写字台；办公桌：*He used to be a pilot but now he has* ***a desk job.*** 他曾是飞行员，但现在做办公室工作。 ➲ VISUAL VOCAB PAGE V71 **2** a place where you can get information or be served at an airport, a hotel, etc.（机场、旅馆等的）问讯处，服务台：*the check-in desk*（机场）登机手续办理处◇ *the reception desk* 接待处 ➲ SEE ALSO CASH DESK, FRONT DESK **3** an office at a newspaper, television company, etc. that deals with a particular subject（报社、电视台等的）办公处，部，室，组：*the sports desk* 体育部 ➲ SEE ALSO CITY DESK, NEWS DESK

ˈdesk clerk *noun* (*NAmE*) = CLERK (4)

de·skill /diːˈskɪl/ *verb* **~ sth** (*specialist*) to reduce the amount of skill that is needed to do a particular job 减低（某工作）的技术要求 ▸ **de·skill·ing** *noun* [U]

desk·mate /ˈdeskmeɪt/ *noun* (*EAfrE*) a person who sits or sat next to you in class at school（学校班上的）同桌

desk·top /ˈdesktɒp; *NAmE* -tɑːp/ *noun* **1** the top of a desk 桌面 **2** a screen on a computer which shows the ICONS of the programs that can be used 桌面（显示使用程序图标的计算机屏幕） ➲ WORDFINDER NOTE AT COMMAND ➲ VISUAL VOCAB PAGE V74 **3** = DESKTOP COMPUTER

ˌdesktop comˈputer (*also* **desk·top**) *noun* a computer with a keyboard, screen and main processing unit, that fits on a desk 台式计算机；台式电脑 ➲ COMPARE LAPTOP, NOTEBOOK (3)

ˌdesktop ˈpublishing *noun* [U] (*abbr.* **DTP**) the use of a small computer and a printer to produce a small book, a magazine or other printed material 桌面出版（用小型电脑和打印机做编辑出版）

deso·late *adj., verb*

■ ***adj.*** /ˈdesələt/ **1** (of a place 地方) empty and without people, making you feel sad or frightened 无人居住的；荒无人烟的；荒凉的：*a bleak and desolate landscape* 一片荒凉的景色 **2** very lonely and unhappy 孤独凄凉的；不幸的；忧伤的 **SYN** **forlorn**

■ ***verb*** /ˈdesəleɪt/ [usually passive] **~ sb** (*literary*) to make sb feel sad and without hope 使感到悲惨；使感到凄凉；使悲伤绝望：*She had been desolated by the death of her friend.* 朋友的去世使她感到十分悲伤。

deso·la·tion /ˌdesəˈleɪʃn/ *noun* [U] (*formal*) **1** the feeling of being very lonely and unhappy 孤寂；悲哀；忧伤 **2** the state of a place that is ruined or destroyed and offers no joy or hope to people 废墟；荒芜；荒凉：*a scene of utter desolation* 满目疮痍的景象

des·pair /dɪˈspeə(r); *NAmE* dɪˈsper/ *noun, verb*

■ ***noun*** [U] the feeling of having lost all hope 绝望：*She uttered a cry of despair.* 她发出了绝望的叫声。◇ *A deep sense of despair overwhelmed him.* 深深的绝望使他痛苦不堪。◇ *He gave up the struggle* ***in despair.*** 他绝望地放弃了斗争。◇ *One harsh word would send her into* ***the depths of despair.*** 一句严厉的话就会使她陷入极度的绝望之中。◇ *Eventually,* ***driven to despair,*** *he threw himself under a train.* 他被逼得走投无路，最后卧轨自杀了。 ➲ SEE ALSO DESPERATE

IDM **be the despair of sb** to make sb worried or unhappy, because they cannot help 令某人担心（或绝望）：*My handwriting was the despair of my teachers.* 我的字写得很差，使老师们感到十分失望。 ➲ MORE AT COUNSEL *n.*

■ ***verb*** [I] to stop having any hope that a situation will change or improve 绝望；失去希望；丧失信心：*Don't despair! We'll think of a way out of this.* 别灰心！我们会找到出路的。◇ **~ of sth/sb** *I despair of him; he can't keep a job for more than six months.* 我对他都绝望了，他做任何工作都不超过半年。◇ **~ of doing sth** *They'd almost despaired of ever having children.* 他们对生孩子几乎不抱任何希望了。

des·pair·ing /dɪˈspeərɪŋ; *NAmE* -ˈsper-/ *adj.* showing or feeling the loss of all hope 表示绝望的；感到绝望的；没有希望的：*a* ***despairing cry/look/sigh*** 绝望的呼声 / 神情 / 叹息 ◇ *With every day that passed he became ever more despairing.* 随着日子一天天过去，他越来越绝望。 ▸ **des·pair·ing·ly** *adv.*：*She looked despairingly at the mess.* 她一看这乱糟糟的样子，心就凉了。

des·patch (*BrE*) = DISPATCH

des·per·ado /ˌdespəˈrɑːdəʊ; *NAmE* -doʊ/ *noun* (*pl.* **-oes** or **-os**) (*old-fashioned*) a man who does dangerous and criminal things without caring about himself or other people 暴徒；歹徒；亡命之徒

des·per·ate /ˈdespərət/ *adj.* **1** feeling or showing that you have little hope and are ready to do anything without worrying about danger to yourself or others（因绝望而）不惜冒险的，不顾一切的，拼命的：*The prisoners grew increasingly desperate.* 犯人因绝望而越来越胆大妄为。◇ *Stores are getting desperate after two years of poor sales.* 两年来销路不畅，商店不惜冒起险来。◇ *Somewhere out there was a desperate man, cold, hungry, hunted.* 那外面有个男人又冷又饿，还有人追捕他，走投无路了。◇ *I heard sounds of a desperate struggle in the next room.* 我听到隔壁房间里有拼命挣扎的声音。 **2** [usually before noun] (of an action 行为) giving little hope of success; tried when everything else has failed 绝望的；孤注一掷的；铤而走险的： ***a desperate bid** for freedom* 孤注一掷争取自由的努力 ◇ *She clung to the edge **in a desperate attempt** to save herself.* 为了活命，她拼命抓住边缘。 ◇ *His increasing financial difficulties forced him to take **desperate measures**.* 不断增加的经济困难迫使他采取了铤而走险的办法。 ◇ *Doctors were fighting a **desperate battle** to save the little girl's life.* 医生们不惜一切地奋力抢救小女孩的生命。 **3** [not usually before noun] needing or wanting sth very much 非常需要；极想；渴望： **~ (for sth)** *He was so desperate for a job he would have done anything.* 他当时太想找份工作了，什么事都愿意干。 ◇ *(informal) I'm desperate for a cigarette.* 我很想抽支烟。 ◇ **~ (to do sth)** *I was absolutely desperate to see her.* 我极想见到她。 **4** (of a situation 情况) extremely serious or dangerous 极严重的；极危险的；很危急的： *The children are **in desperate need** of love and attention.* 这些孩子非常需要爱心和关注。 ◇ *They face a desperate shortage of clean water.* 他们面临洁净水的严重短缺。 ▶ **des·per·ate·ly** *adv.* : ***desperately ill/unhappy/lonely*** 病得厉害；极为不快；极其孤独 ◇ *He took a deep breath, desperately trying to keep calm.* 他深深地吸了口气，竭尽全力保持镇定。 ◇ *They desperately wanted a child.* 他们非常想要一个孩子。 ◇ *She looked desperately around for a weapon.* 她在四下里找，急于弄到一件武器。

des·per·ation /ˌdespəˈreɪʃn/ *noun* [U] the state of being desperate 绝望；拼命；铤而走险： ***In desperation**, she called Louise and asked for her help.* 在走投无路的情况下，她给路易丝打了个电话请她帮忙。 ◇ *There was a note of desperation in his voice.* 听他的语气他急得要命。 ◇ *an act of sheer desperation* 完全不顾一切的行为

de·spic·able /dɪˈspɪkəbl; ˈdespɪkəbl/ *adj.* *(formal)* very unpleasant or evil 令人厌恶的；可鄙的；卑鄙的： ***a despicable act/crime*** 卑鄙的行为 / 罪行 ◇ *I hate you! You're despicable.* 我恨你！你真卑鄙。

de·spise /dɪˈspaɪz/ *verb* **~ sb/sth** (not used in the progressive tenses 不用于进行时) to dislike and have no respect for sb/sth 鄙视；蔑视；看不起： *She despised gossip in any form.* 她对任何形式的流言蜚语都嗤之以鼻。 ◇ *He despised himself for being so cowardly.* 他为自己如此怯懦而自惭形秽。 ➲ SYNONYMS AT HATE

de·spite AW /dɪˈspaɪt/ *prep.* **1** used to show that sth happened or is true although sth else might have happened to prevent it 即使；尽管 SYN **in spite of**: *Her voice was shaking despite all her efforts to control it.* 尽管她竭尽全力控制自己，声音仍然在颤抖。 ◇ *Despite applying for hundreds of jobs, he is still out of work.* 尽管他申请了数百个工作，但仍然在失业中。 ◇ *She was good at physics **despite the fact that** she found it boring.* 尽管她认为物理枯燥无味，她却学得很好。 ➲ LANGUAGE BANK AT HOWEVER **2 despite yourself** used to show that sb did not intend to do the thing mentioned 尽管（自己）不愿意 SYN **in spite of**: *He had to laugh despite himself.* 他不想笑，但没法不笑。

de·spoil /dɪˈspɔɪl/ *verb* **~ sth (of sth)** *(literary)* to steal sth valuable from a place; to make a place less attractive by damaging or destroying it 抢劫；掠夺；蹂躏；破坏 SYN **plunder**

des·pond·ent /dɪˈspɒndənt; *NAmE* -ˈspɑːn-/ *adj.* **~ (about sth)** *(especially NAmE)* | **~ (over sth)** sad, without much hope 苦恼的；沮丧的；泄气的；失望的 SYN **dejected**: *She was becoming increasingly despondent about the way things were going.* 她对事情的发展越来越失望。 ▶ **des·pond·ency** /dɪˈspɒndənsi; *NAmE* -ˈspɑːn-/ *noun* [U]: *a mood of despondency* 沮丧的心情 ◇ *Life's not all gloom and despondency.* 生活并不都是悲观和失望。 **des·pond·ent·ly** *adv.*

des·pot /ˈdespɒt; *NAmE* ˈdespɑːt/ *noun* a ruler with great power, especially one who uses it in a cruel way 专制统治者；专制君主；暴君： *an enlightened despot* (= one who tries to use his/her power in a good way) 开明的专制君主 ▶ **des·pot·ic** /dɪˈspɒtɪk; *NAmE* -ˈspɑːt-/ *adj.* : ***despotic power/rule*** 至高无上的权力；专制统治

des·pot·ism /ˈdespətɪzəm/ *noun* [U] the rule of a despot 专制统治；独裁制；暴政

des res /ˌdez ˈrez/ *noun* [usually sing.] *(BrE, humorous)* an attractive house, especially a large one (from the words 'desirable residence') 理想的房子（desirable residence 的缩略形式）

des·sert /dɪˈzɜːt; *NAmE* dɪˈzɜːrt/ *noun* [U, C] sweet food eaten at the end of a meal（饭后）甜点，甜食： *What's for dessert?* 餐后甜点吃什么？ ◇ *a rich chocolate dessert* 腻人的巧克力甜点 ◇ *a dessert wine* 餐末甜酒 ◇ *(BrE) the dessert trolley* (= a table on wheels from which you choose your dessert in a restaurant)（餐厅内）送甜点的手推车 ➲ COLLOCATIONS AT RESTAURANT ➲ COMPARE AFTERS, PUDDING (1), SWEET *n.* (2)

des·sert·spoon /dɪˈzɜːtspuːn; *NAmE* -ˈzɜːrt-/ *noun* **1** a spoon of medium size 中型匙；点心匙 ➲ VISUAL VOCAB PAGE V23 **2** *(also* **des·sert·spoon·ful** /-fʊl/) the amount a dessertspoon can hold 一点心匙（的量）

de·sta·bil·ize *(BrE also* **-ise**) /ˌdiːˈsteɪbəlaɪz/ *verb* **~ sth** to make a system, country, government, etc. become less firmly established or successful 使（制度、国家、政府等）动摇；使不安定；使不稳定： *Terrorist attacks were threatening to destabilize the government.* 恐怖袭击威胁着政府的稳定。 ◇ *The news had a destabilizing effect on the stock market.* 这消息引起了股市的动荡。 ➲ COMPARE STABILIZE ▶ **de·sta·bil·iza·tion, -isa·tion** /ˌdiːˌsteɪbəlaɪˈzeɪʃn; *NAmE* -ləˈz-/ *noun* [U]

des·tin·ation /ˌdestɪˈneɪʃn/ *noun, adj.*

■ ***noun*** a place to which sb/sth is going or being sent 目的地；终点： *popular **holiday destinations** like the Bahamas* 像巴哈马那样深受大众喜爱的度假胜地 ◇ ***to arrive at/reach your destination*** 到达目的地 ◇ *Our luggage was checked all the way through to our **final destination**.* 我们的行李一直被托运到最终目的地。 ➲ WORDFINDER NOTE AT JOURNEY

■ ***adj.*** **~ hotel/store/restaurant, etc.** a hotel, store, etc. that people will make a special trip to visit 作为目的地的（旅馆、商店、饭店等）

des·tined /ˈdestɪnd/ *adj.* *(formal)* **1** having a future which has been decided or planned at an earlier time, especially by FATE 预定；注定；（尤指）命中注定： **~ for sth** *He was destined for a military career, like his father before him.* 他命中注定要步父亲的后尘，过戎马生涯。 ◇ **~ to do sth** *We seem destined never to meet.* 我们似乎是命中注定无缘相见。 **2 ~ for...** on the way to or intended for a place 开往；运往；前往 SYN **bound**: *goods destined for Poland* 运往波兰的货物

des·tiny /ˈdestəni/ *noun* *(pl.* **-ies**) **1** [C] what happens to sb or what will happen to them in the future, especially things that they cannot change or avoid 命运；天命；天数： *the destinies of nations* 国家的命运 ◇ *He wants to be in control of his own destiny.* 他想要掌握自己的命运。 **2** [U] the power believed to control events 主宰事物的力量；命运之神 SYN **fate**: *I believe there's some force guiding us—call it God, destiny or fate.* 我总认为有某种力量在指引着我们，称之为上帝也罢，天意也罢，还是命运也罢。 ➲ SYNONYMS AT LUCK

des·ti·tute /ˈdestɪtjuːt; *NAmE* -tuːt/ *adj.* **1** without money, food and the other things necessary for life 贫困的；贫穷的；赤贫的： *When he died, his family was left completely destitute.* 他死时家里一贫如洗。 **2 the destitute** *noun* [pl.] people who are destitute 穷人；贫民 ➲ MORE LIKE THIS 24, page R28 **3 ~ of sth** *(formal)* lacking sth 缺乏；没有；毫无： *They seem destitute of ordinary human feelings.* 他们似乎一点人情味都没有。 ▶ **des·ti·tu·tion** /ˌdestɪˈtjuːʃn; *NAmE* -ˈtuːʃn/ *noun* [U]: *homelessness and destitution* 无家可归且一无所有

de·stock /ˌdiːˈstɒk; *NAmE* -ˈstɑːk/ *verb* [I, T] **~ (sth)** *(BrE, business* 商) to reduce the amount of goods in a shop/store, the amount of materials kept available for making sth in a factory, etc. 减少存货；减少库存；去库存

D

de-stress /ˌdiː ˈstres/ *verb* [I, T] **~ (sb/yourself)** to relax after working hard or experiencing stress; to reduce the amount of stress that you experience 放松；舒缓压力；减少压力：*De-stress yourself with a relaxing bath.* 舒舒服服洗个澡放松一下。

des·troy /dɪˈstrɔɪ/ *verb* **1** **~ sth/sb** to damage sth so badly that it no longer exists, works, etc. 摧毁；毁灭；破坏：*The building was completely destroyed by fire.* 这栋建筑物被大火彻底焚毁了。◇ *They've destroyed all the evidence.* 他们销毁了一切证据。◇ *Heat gradually destroys vitamin C.* 加热会逐渐破坏维生素 C。◇ *You have destroyed my hopes of happiness.* 你毁掉了我得到幸福的希望。◇ *Failure was slowly destroying him* (= making him less and less confident and happy). 失败渐渐地把他毁了。 **2** **~ sth** to kill an animal deliberately, usually because it is sick or not wanted （因动物有病或不再需要而）杀死，消灭，人道毁灭：*The injured horse had to be destroyed.* 这匹马受了伤，只好把它杀了。➲ SEE ALSO SOUL-DESTROYING

WORD FAMILY
destroy *verb*
destroyer *noun*
destruction *noun*
destructive *adj.*
indestructible *adj.*

des·troy·er /dɪˈstrɔɪə(r)/ *noun* **1** a small fast ship used in war, for example to protect larger ships 驱逐舰 **2** a person or thing that destroys 破坏者；毁灭者：*Sugar is the destroyer of healthy teeth.* 糖会危害健康的牙齿。

de·struc·tion /dɪˈstrʌkʃn/ *noun* [U] the act of destroying sth; the process of being destroyed 摧毁；毁灭；破坏：*the destruction of the rainforests* 对热带雨林的破坏 ◇ *weapons of mass destruction* 大规模杀伤性武器 ◇ *a tidal wave bringing* ***death and destruction*** *in its wake* 带来死亡与破坏的海啸 ◇ *The central argument is that capitalism* ***sows the seeds of its own destruction*** (= creates the forces that destroy it). 主要论点是资本主义播下了自我毁灭的种子。

de·struc·tive /dɪˈstrʌktɪv/ *adj.* causing destruction or damage 引起破坏（或毁灭）的；破坏（或毁灭）性的：*the destructive power of modern weapons* 现代武器的毁灭性力量 ◇ *the destructive effects of anxiety* 焦虑的破坏性影响 ➲ COMPARE CONSTRUCTIVE ▸ **de·struc·tive·ly** *adv.* **de·struc·tive·ness** *noun* [U]

des·ul·tory /ˈdesəltri; *NAmE* -tɔːri/ *adj.* (*formal*) going from one thing to another, without a definite plan and without enthusiasm 漫无目的的；无条理的；随意的：*I wandered about in a desultory fashion.* 我漫无目的地四处游荡。◇ *a desultory conversation* 漫无边际的谈话 ▸ **des·ul·tor·ily** *adv.*

Det *abbr.* (*BrE*) (in writing 书写形式) DETECTIVE 侦探：*Det Insp* (= Inspector) *Cox* 考克斯探长

de·tach /dɪˈtætʃ/ *verb* **1** [T, I] to remove sth from sth larger; to become separated from sth 拆卸；（使）分开，脱离：**~ sth** *Detach the coupon and return it as soon as possible.* 将表格撕下后尽快寄回。◇ **~ sth from sth** *One of the panels had become detached from the main structure.* 一块镶板已从主体结构上脱落。◇ **~ (from sth)** *The skis should detach from the boot if you fall.* 要是你跌倒了，滑雪板就会脱离靴子。➲ COMPARE ATTACH (1) **2** [T] **~ yourself (from sb/sth)** (*formal*) to leave or separate yourself from sb/sth 挣脱；摆脱；离开：*She detached herself from his embrace.* 她挣脱了他的拥抱。◇ (*figurative*) *I tried to detach myself from the reality of these terrible events.* 我尽力使自己从这些可怕事件的现实中摆脱出来。 **3** [T] **~ sb/sth** (*specialist*) to send a group of soldiers, etc. away from the main group, especially to do special duties 派遣；分遣；分派

de·tach·able /dɪˈtætʃəbl/ *adj.* that can be taken off 可拆卸的；可分开的 SYN **removable**：*a coat with a detachable hood* 带有活风帽的外套

de·tached /dɪˈtætʃt/ *adj.* **1** (of a house 房子) not joined to another house on either side 单独的；独立的；不连接的 ➲ COMPARE SEMI-DETACHED **2** showing a lack of feeling 不带感情的；超然的；冷漠的 SYN **indifferent**：*She wanted him to stop being so cool, so detached, so cynical.* 她希望他不再那么冷酷无情，那么无动于衷，那么愤世嫉俗。 **3** (*approving*) not influenced by other people or by your own feelings 客观的；公正的；无偏见的 SYN **impartial**：*a detached observer* 客观的观察者

de·tach·ment /dɪˈtætʃmənt/ *noun* **1** [U] the state of not being involved in sth in an emotional or personal way 超然；超脱；冷漠：*He answered with an air of detachment.* 他回答时带着冷漠的神态。◇ *She felt a sense of detachment from what was going on.* 她对眼前发生的事感到很超然。OPP **involvement** **2** [U] (*approving*) the state of not being influenced by other people or by your own feelings 公正；客观；独立：*In judging these issues a degree of critical detachment is required.* 在裁决这些争议时须要有一定程度的公正判断力。 **3** [C] a group of soldiers, ships, etc. sent away from a larger group, especially to do special duties 分遣队；支队；特遣小分队：*a detachment of artillery* 炮兵支队 **4** [U] the act of detaching sth; the process of being detached from sth 拆卸；分离；分遣：*to suffer detachment of the retina* 出现视网膜脱落

de·tail /ˈdiːteɪl; *NAmE also* dɪˈteɪl/ *noun, verb*

■ ***noun***

• **FACTS/INFORMATION** 事实；信息 **1** [C] a small individual fact or item; a less important fact or item 细微之处；枝节；琐事：*an expedition planned down to the last detail* 计划详尽的探险 ◇ *He stood still, absorbing every detail of the street.* 他一动不动地站着，不放过街上的每一细微之处。◇ *Tell me the main points now; leave* ***the details*** *till later.* 现在把要点告诉我，细节留到以后再说。 **2** [U] the small facts or features of sth, when you consider them all together 详情；细节：*This issue will be discussed* ***in*** *more* ***detail*** *in the next chapter.* 这个问题将在下一章详细论述。◇ *The research has been carried out with scrupulous* ***attention to detail.*** 研究工作一丝不苟地完成了。◇ *He had* ***an eye for detail*** (= noticed and remembered small details). 他很善于发现并记住细节。◇ *The fine detail of the plan has yet to be worked out.* 这个方案的具体细节尚未制订出来。 **3** **details** [pl.] information about sth 具体情况；（关于某事物的）资料，消息：*Please supply the following details: name, age and sex.* 请提供下列资料：姓名、年龄及性别。◇ *Further details and booking forms are available on request.* 备有详细资料和订购单以供索取。◇ *They didn't give any details about the game.* 他们没有提供这场比赛的具体情况。◇ *'We had a terrible time—' 'Oh, spare me the details* (= don't tell me any more).*'* "我们倒霉透了…" "唉呀，别给我细说了。"

• **SMALL PARTS** 细部 **4** [C, U] a small part of a picture or painting; the smaller or less important parts of a picture, pattern, etc. when you consider them all together （照片、绘画等的）细部，局部，次要部分：*This is a detail from the 1844 Turner painting.* 这是透纳 1844 年画作的局部。◇ *a huge picture with a lot of detail in it* 一幅有很多细微之处的巨型画

• **SOLDIERS** 士兵 **5** [C] a group of soldiers given special duties 特遣队；小分队；支队

IDM **go into ˈdetail(s)** to explain sth fully 详细叙述；逐一说明：*I can't go into details now; it would take too long.* 我现在不能细说，太费工夫。

■ ***verb***

• **GIVE FACTS/INFORMATION** 详述 **1** **~ sth** to give a list of facts or all the available information about sth 详细列举；详细说明；详述：*The brochure details all the hotels in the area and their facilities.* 这本小册子详细介绍了当地所有旅馆及其设施。

• **ORDER SOLDIER** 派遣士兵 **2** [often passive] **~ sb (to do sth)** to give an official order to sb, especially a soldier, to do a particular task 派遣；选派；分遣：*Several of the men were detailed to form a search party.* 几个人被派组成一个搜索队。

• **CLEAN CAR** 清洗汽车 **3** **~ sth** (*NAmE*) to clean a car extremely thoroughly 彻底清洗（汽车）：*He got work for a while detailing cars.* 他干了一段时间的清洗汽车的工作。

de·tailed 🔑 /ˈdiːteɪld; *NAmE also* dɪˈteɪld/ *adj.* giving many details and a lot of information; paying great attention to details 详细的；细致的；精细的： *a **detailed description/analysis/study*** 详细的描述 / 分析 / 研究 ◇ *He gave me **detailed instructions** on how to get there.* 他详细地告诉我如何去那里。

de·tail·ing /ˈdiːteɪlɪŋ; *NAmE also* dɪˈteɪlɪŋ/ *noun* [U] small details put on a building, piece of clothing, etc., especially for decoration （建筑、服装等的）装饰细部

de·tain /dɪˈteɪn/ *verb* **1 ~ sb** to keep sb in an official place, such as a police station, a prison or a hospital, and prevent them from leaving 拘留；扣押： *One man has been detained for questioning.* 一个男人被拘留审问。 ➲ WORDFINDER NOTE AT POLICE **2 ~ sb** (*formal*) to delay sb or prevent them from going somewhere 耽搁；留住；阻留： *I'm sorry—he'll be late; he's been detained at a meeting.* 对不起，他要晚点儿到，他因会议耽搁了。 ➲ SEE ALSO DETENTION

de·tain·ee /ˌdiːteɪˈniː/ *noun* a person who is kept in prison, usually because of his or her political opinions （通常因政治主张）被拘留者，被扣押者

de·tect AW /dɪˈtekt/ *verb* **~ sth** to discover or notice sth, especially sth that is not easy to see, hear, etc. 发现；查明；侦察出： *The tests are designed to detect the disease early.* 这些检查旨在早期查出疾病。 ◇ *an instrument that can detect small amounts of radiation* 能检测微量辐射的仪器 ◇ *Do I detect a note of criticism?* 这好像带有批评的意味吧？ ➲ SYNONYMS AT NOTICE ▶ **de·tect·able** AW *adj.*： *The noise is barely detectable by the human ear.* 这种声音人的耳朵几乎是察觉不到的。 OPP **undetectable**

de·tec·tion AW /dɪˈtekʃn/ *noun* [U] the process of detecting sth; the fact of being detected 侦查；探测；察觉；发现： *crime prevention and detection* 犯罪的预防和侦查 ◇ *Last year the detection rate for car theft was just 13%.* 去年汽车盗窃案的侦破率仅为 13%。 ◇ *Many problems, however, escape detection.* 然而许多问题却未被察觉。 ◇ *Early detection of cancers is vitally important.* 癌症的早期查出是极为重要的。

de·tect·ive AW /dɪˈtektɪv/ *noun* (*abbr.* **Det**) **1** a person, especially a police officer, whose job is to examine crimes and catch criminals 侦探；警探： *Detective Inspector (Roger) Brown* （罗杰·）布朗探长 ◇ *detectives from the anti-terrorist squad* 反恐怖主义小组的侦探 ◇ *a **detective story/novel*** 侦探故事 / 小说 ➲ SEE ALSO STORE DETECTIVE ➲ WORDFINDER NOTE AT POLICE **2** a person employed by sb to find out information about sb/sth 私人侦探 ➲ SEE ALSO PRIVATE DETECTIVE

de·tect·or AW /dɪˈtektə(r)/ *noun* a piece of equipment for discovering the presence of sth, such as metal, smoke, EXPLOSIVES or changes in pressure or temperature 探测器；侦察器；检测器： *a smoke detector* 烟雾检测器

dé·tente (*also* **de·tente** *especially in NAmE*) /ˌdeɪˈtɑːnt/ *noun* [U] (*from French, formal*) an improvement in the relationship between two or more countries which have been unfriendly towards each other in the past （国际紧张关系的）缓和，改善

de·ten·tion /dɪˈtenʃn/ *noun* **1** [U] the state of being kept in a place, especially a prison, and prevented from leaving 拘留；扣押；监禁： *a sentence of 12 months' detention in a young offender institution* 在青少年教养院拘禁 12 个月的判决 ◇ *police powers of arrest and detention* 警方的逮捕和拘留权 ◇ *allegations of torture and detention without trial* 拷打和未经审判便进行关押的指控 ◇ *a detention camp* 拘留营 **2** [U, C] the punishment of being kept at school for a time after other students have gone home 放学后留校，留堂（处罚学生）： *They can't give me (a) detention for this.* 他们不能因为这事罚我课后留下来。 ➲ SEE ALSO DETAIN

deˈtention centre (*BrE*) (*NAmE* **deˈtention center**) *noun* **1** a place where young people who have committed offences are kept in detention 少年管教所 **2** a place where people are kept in detention, especially people who have entered a country illegally （尤指非法入境者的）收容所，拘留营

de·tenu (*also* **de·tenue**) /diˈtenjuː/ *noun* (*IndE*) a person who is held in prison, especially while waiting for trial 羁押候审者；囚犯

deter /dɪˈtɜː(r)/ *verb* (**-rr-**) [T, I] **~ (sb) (from sth/from doing sth)** to make sb decide not to do sth or continue doing sth, especially by making them understand the difficulties and unpleasant results of their actions 制止；阻止；威慑；使不敢： *I told him I wasn't interested, but he wasn't deterred.* 我已告诉他我不感兴趣，可他却不罢休。 ◇ *The high price of the service could deter people from seeking advice.* 这么高的服务费可能使咨询者望而却步。 ➲ SEE ALSO DETERRENT

de·ter·gent /dɪˈtɜːdʒənt; *NAmE* -ˈtɜːrdʒ-/ *noun* [U, C] a liquid or powder that helps remove dirt, for example from clothes or dishes 洗涤剂；去垢剂；洗衣粉

de·teri·or·ate /dɪˈtɪəriəreɪt; *NAmE* -ˈtɪr-/ *verb* [I] to become worse 变坏；恶化；退化： *Her health deteriorated rapidly, and she died shortly afterwards.* 她的健康状况急剧恶化，不久便去世了。 ◇ *deteriorating weather conditions* 不断恶化的天气状况 ◇ **~ into sth** *The discussion quickly deteriorated into an angry argument.* 这场讨论迅速演变成愤怒的争吵。 ▶ **de·teri·or·ation** /dɪˌtɪəriəˈreɪʃn; *NAmE* -ˌtɪr-/ *noun* [U, C]： *a serious deterioration in relations between the two countries* 两国关系的严重恶化

de·ter·min·able /dɪˈtɜːmɪnəbl; *NAmE* -ˈtɜːrm-/ *adj.* (*formal*) that can be found out or calculated 可确定的；可查明的；可计算出的： *During the third month of pregnancy the sex of the child becomes determinable.* 孩子的性别在妊娠期第三个月便可查明。

de·ter·min·ant /dɪˈtɜːmɪnənt; *NAmE* -ˈtɜːrm-/ *noun* (*formal*) a thing that decides whether or how sth happens 决定因素；决定条件

de·ter·min·ate /dɪˈtɜːmɪnət; *NAmE* -ˈtɜːrm-/ *adj.* (*formal*) fixed and definite 固定的；确定的： *a sentence with a determinate meaning* 具有确定意义的句子 OPP **indeterminate**

de·ter·min·ation 🔑 /dɪˌtɜːmɪˈneɪʃn; *NAmE* -ˌtɜːrm-/ *noun* **1** 🔑 [U] the quality that makes you continue trying to do sth even when this is difficult 决心；坚毅；坚定： ***fierce/grim/dogged determination*** 坚强的 / 不屈不挠的 / 顽强的决心 ◇ *He fought the illness with courage and determination.* 他勇敢顽强地与疾病作斗争。 ◇ *They had survived by sheer determination.* 他们全凭坚强的决心幸存下来。 ◇ **~ to do sth** *I admire her determination to get it right.* 我赞赏她非把事情办好的决心。 **2** [U] (*formal*) the process of deciding sth officially （正式）决定，确定，规定： *factors influencing the determination of future policy* 影响未来决策的各种因素 **3** [U, C] (*specialist*) the act of finding out or calculating sth 查明；测定；计算： *Both methods rely on the accurate determination of the pressure of the gas.* 两种方法都依赖于对气体压力的准确测定。

de·ter·mine 🔑 /dɪˈtɜːmɪn; *NAmE* -ˈtɜːrm-/ *verb* (*formal*) **1** 🔑 [T] to discover the facts about sth; to calculate sth exactly 查明；测定；准确算出 SYN **establish**： **~ sth** *An inquiry was set up to determine the cause of the accident.* 已展开调查以确定事故原因。 ◇ **~ what, whether, etc....** *We set out to determine exactly what happened that night.* 我们着手查明那天晚上发生的事情。 ◇ **it is determined that...** *It was determined that she had died of natural causes.* 已确认她是自然死亡。 **2** [T] **~ sth | ~ what, whether, etc....** to make sth happen in a particular way or be of a particular type 决定；形成；支配；影响： *Age and experience will be **determining factors** in our choice of candidate.* 年龄和经验是我们选择候选人的决定因素。 ◇ *Upbringing plays an important part in determining a person's character.* 后天培养对于一个人性格的形成起着重要作用。 **3** [T] to officially decide and/or arrange sth 确定；裁决；安排： **~ sth** *A date for the meeting has yet to be determined.* 会议

D

日期尚待确定。◇ ~ (that)... *The court determined (that) the defendant should pay the legal costs.* 法庭裁决由被告支付诉讼费用。 **4** [T, I] **~ to do sth | ~ (that)... | ~ on sth** to decide definitely to do sth 决定，决心（做某事）： *They determined to start early.* 他们决定早点儿出发。

de·ter·mined /dɪˈtɜːmɪnd; *NAmE* -ˈtɜːrm-/ *adj.* **1** [not before noun] **~ (to do sth)** if you are **determined** to do sth, you have made a firm decision to do it and you will not let anyone prevent you 决心；决定；决意： *I'm determined to succeed.* 我决心要获得成功。 **2** showing a person's determination to do sth 坚定的；坚决的；坚毅的： *a determined effort to stop smoking* 坚决戒烟的努力 ◇ *The proposal had been dropped in the face of determined opposition.* 这项建议因遭到坚决反对而撤销。 IDM SEE BOUND *adj.* ▸ **de·ter·mined·ly** *adv.*

de·ter·miner /dɪˈtɜːmɪnə(r); *NAmE* -ˈtɜːrm-/ *noun* (*grammar* 语法) (abbreviation *det.* in this dictionary 本词典缩略为 det.) a word such as *the*, *some*, *my*, etc. that comes before a noun to show how the noun is being used 限定词（置于名词前起限定作用，如 the、some、my 等）

de·ter·min·ism /dɪˈtɜːmɪnɪzəm; *NAmE* -ˈtɜːrm-/ *noun* [U] (*philosophy* 哲) the belief that people are not free to choose what they are like or how they behave, because these things are decided by their surroundings and other things over which they have no control 决定论（排除自由意志，认为个性或行为均由环境和自己不能控制的因素所决定） ▸ **de·ter·min·is·tic** /dɪˌtɜːmɪˈnɪstɪk; *NAmE* -ˌtɜːrm-/ *adj.*

de·ter·rent /dɪˈterənt; *NAmE* -ˈtɜːr-/ *noun* **~ (to sb/sth)** a thing that makes sb less likely to do sth (= that deters them) 威慑因素；遏制力： *Hopefully his punishment will act as a deterrent to others.* 对他的惩罚但愿能起到杀一儆百的作用。 ◇ *the country's **nuclear deterrents*** (= nuclear weapons that are intended to stop an enemy from attacking) 这个国家核武器的威慑力 ▸ **de·ter·rence** /dɪˈterəns; *NAmE* -ˈtɜːr-/ *noun* [U] (*formal*) **de·ter·rent** *adj.* : *a deterrent effect* 遏制作用

de·test /dɪˈtest/ *verb* (not used in the progressive tenses 不用于进行时) **~ sb/sth | ~ doing sth** to hate sb/sth very much 厌恶；憎恨；讨厌 SYN **loathe**: *They detested each other on sight.* 他们互相看着就不顺眼。 ⊃ SYNONYMS AT HATE ▸ **de·test·ation** /ˌdiːteˈsteɪʃn/ *noun* [U]

de·test·able /dɪˈtestəbl/ *adj.* that deserves to be hated 可憎的；可恨的；令人讨厌的： *All terrorist crime is detestable, whoever the victims.* 无论受害者是谁，一切恐怖主义罪行都是可憎的。

de·throne /ˌdiːˈθrəʊn; *NAmE* -ˈθroʊn/ *verb* **~ sb** to remove a king or queen from power; to remove sb from a position of authority or power 废黜（国王或女王）；撵下台；免（某人）的职；罢（某人）的官

det·on·ate /ˈdetəneɪt/ *verb* [I, T] **~ (sth)** to explode, or to make a bomb or other device explode （使）爆炸；引爆；起爆： *Two other bombs failed to detonate.* 另外两枚炸弹未引爆。 ⊃ SYNONYMS AT EXPLODE

det·on·ation /ˌdetəˈneɪʃn/ *noun* [C, U] an explosion; the action of making sth explode 爆炸；起爆；引爆

det·on·ator /ˈdetəneɪtə(r)/ *noun* a device for making sth, especially a bomb, explode 引爆装置；雷管；起爆管

de·tour /ˈdiːtʊə(r); *NAmE* -tʊr/ *noun, verb*

■ ***noun*** **1** a longer route that you take in order to avoid a problem or to visit a place 绕行的路；迂回路；兜圈子： *We had to make a detour around the flooded fields.* 我们只得绕道避开被洪水淹没的田野。 ◇ *It's well worth making a detour to see the village.* 绕道去参观一下这村子很是值得。 **2** (*NAmE*) (*BrE* **di·ver·sion**) a road or route that is used when the usual one is closed 临时绕行路；临时支路

■ ***verb*** [I, T] (*NAmE*) **~ (sb/sth) (to...)** to take a longer route in order to avoid a problem or to visit a place; to make sb/sth take a longer route （使）绕道，绕行： *The President detoured to Chicago for a special meeting.* 总统绕道到芝加哥参加一个特别会议。

detox /ˈdiːtɒks; *NAmE* -tɑːks/ *noun* [U] (*informal*) **1** the process of removing harmful substances from your body by only eating and drinking particular things 排毒（通过控制饮食种类将有害物质排出体外） **2** = DETOXIFICATION: *a detox clinic* 戒瘾（诊）所 ◇ *He's gone into detox.* 他进了戒毒所。

de·toxi·fi·ca·tion /diːˌtɒksɪfɪˈkeɪʃn; *NAmE* -ˌtɑːks-/ (*also informal* **detox**) *noun* [U] treatment given to people to help them stop drinking alcohol or taking drugs 戒酒；戒毒： *a detoxification unit* 戒毒所 ⊃ WORDFINDER NOTE AT DRUG

de·toxi·fy /ˌdiːˈtɒksɪfaɪ; *NAmE* -ˈtɑːks-/ *verb* (**de·toxi·fies**, **de·toxi·fy·ing**, **de·toxi·fied**, **de·toxi·fied**) **1 ~ sth** to remove harmful substances or poisons from sth 排毒；解毒；去毒；除去…的毒素 **2 ~ sb** to treat sb in order to help them stop drinking too much alcohol or taking drugs 戒酒；戒毒

de·tract /dɪˈtrækt/ *verb*

PHR V **deˈtract from sth | deˈtract sth from sth** (not used in the progressive tenses 不用于进行时) to make sth seem less good or enjoyable 减损；毁损；贬低 SYN **take away from**: *He was determined not to let anything detract from his enjoyment of the trip.* 他下决心这次旅行不让任何事情影响他的兴致。

de·tract·or /dɪˈtræktə(r)/ *noun* [usually pl.] (*especially formal*) a person who tries to make sb/sth seem less good or valuable by criticizing it 诋毁者；贬低者；恶意批评者

de·train /ˌdiːˈtreɪn/ *verb* [I, T] **~ (sb)** (*formal*) to leave a train or make sb leave a train （使）下火车

det·ri·ment /ˈdetrɪmənt/ *noun* [U, C, usually sing.] (*formal*) the act of causing harm or damage; sth that causes harm or damage 伤害；损害；造成伤害（或损害）的事物

IDM **to the detriment of sb/sth | to sb/sth's detriment** resulting in harm or damage to sb/sth （结果）不利于，有害于，有损于： *He was engrossed in his job to the detriment of his health.* 他全身心地投入工作结果损害了他的健康。 **without detriment (to sb/sth)** not resulting in harm or damage to sb/sth （结果）无害于，无损于

det·ri·ment·al /ˌdetrɪˈmentl/ *adj.* **~ (to sb/sth)** (*formal*) harmful 有害的；不利的 SYN **damaging**: *the sun's **detrimental effect** on skin* 日光对皮肤的伤害 ◇ *The policy will be detrimental to the peace process.* 这项政策将不利于和平进程。 ▸ **det·ri·men·tal·ly** /-təli/ *adv.*

de·tritus /dɪˈtraɪtəs/ *noun* [U] **1** (*specialist*) natural waste material that is left after sth has been used or broken up 碎屑；风化物；残渣；腐殖质： *organic detritus from fish and plants* 鱼和植物的有机碎屑 **2** (*formal*) any kind of rubbish/garbage that is left after an event or when sth has been used 瓦砾；碎石；垃圾；废物 SYN **debris**: *the detritus of everyday life* 日常生活垃圾

de trop /ˌdə ˈtrəʊ; *NAmE* ˈtroʊ/ *adj.* [not before noun] (*from French, formal*) not wanted, especially in a social situation with other people（尤指在社交场合）不受欢迎，不需要，多余

deuce /djuːs; *NAmE* duːs/ *noun* **1** [U, C] (in TENNIS 网球) the situation when both players have 40 as a score, after which one player must win two points one after the other in order to win the game 局末平分 **2** [C] (*NAmE*) a PLAYING CARD with two PIPS on it 二点的纸牌： *the deuce of clubs* 梅花二 **3 the deuce** [sing.] (*old-fashioned, informal*) used in questions to show that you are annoyed （用于问句中表示烦恼、厌恶）到底，究竟： *What the deuce is he doing?* 他到底在干什么？

deuced /djuːst; *NAmE also* duːst/ *adj.* [only before noun] (*old use*) used for emphasizing feelings, especially anger, disappointment or surprise （强调生气、失望、惊讶等感情）非常的，极其的： *The man's a deuced fool!* 那个男人真是个傻瓜！ ▸ **deuced** *adv.* : *It's deuced awkward.* 那事真令人难堪。

deur·me·kaar /ˌdjɜːməˈkɑː(r); *NAmE* ˌdjɜːrm-/ *adj.* (*SAfrE, informal*) in a confused state 混乱的；迷惑的

deus ex mach·ina /ˌdeɪʊs eks ˈmækɪnə/ *noun* [sing.] (*literary*) an unexpected power or event that saves a situation that seems without hope, especially in a play or novel （尤指剧本或小说中）机械降神，扭转乾坤的力量

deu·ter·ium /djuːˈtɪəriəm; *NAmE* -ˈtɪr-; duːˈt-/ *noun* [U] (*symb.* **D**) (*chemistry* 化) an ISOTOPE (= a different form) of HYDROGEN with twice the mass of the usual isotope 氘，重氢（氢的同位素）

Deutsch·mark /ˈdɔɪtʃmɑːk; *NAmE* -mɑːrk/ (*also* **mark**) *noun* (*abbr.* **DM**) the former unit of money in Germany (replaced in 2002 by the euro) 德国马克（德国货币单位，于 2002 年为欧元所取代）

de·value /ˌdiːˈvæljuː/ *verb* **1** [I, T] ~ (**sth**) (**against sth**) (*finance* 财) to reduce the value of the money of one country when it is exchanged for the money of another country 使（货币）贬值 **OPP** **revalue** **2** [T] ~ **sth** to give a lower value to sth, making it seem less important than it really is 降低…的价值；贬低：*Work in the home is often ignored and devalued.* 家务劳动常常被忽视和贬低。 ▸ **de·valu·ation** /ˌdiːˌvæljuˈeɪʃn/ *noun* [C, U]: *There has been a further small devaluation against the dollar.* 兑美元的比值继续小幅下跌。

Deva·nag·ari /ˌdeɪvəˈnɑːɡəri; ˌdev-/ *noun* [U] the alphabet used to write Sanskrit, Hindi and some other Indian languages 天城体文字，伽里字母（用于梵语、印地语及其他印度语言）

dev·as·tate /ˈdevəsteɪt/ *verb* **1** ~ **sth** to completely destroy a place or an area 彻底破坏；摧毁；毁灭：*The bomb devastated much of the old part of the city.* 这颗炸弹炸毁了旧城的一大片地方。 **2** [often passive] ~ **sb** to make sb feel very shocked and sad 使震惊；使极为忧伤；使极为悲痛

dev·as·tated /ˈdevəsteɪtɪd/ *adj.* extremely upset and shocked 极度不安的；极为震惊的：*His family is absolutely devastated.* 他的一家感到极为震惊。

dev·as·tat·ing /ˈdevəsteɪtɪŋ/ *adj.* **1** causing a lot of damage and destruction 破坏性极大的；毁灭性的 **SYN** **disastrous**：*a* ***devastating explosion/fire/cyclone*** 毁灭性的爆炸 / 火灾 / 旋风 ◇ *Oil spills are having a* ***devastating effect*** *on coral reefs in the ocean.* 石油泄漏对海洋里的珊瑚礁有着毁灭性影响。 ◇ *He received devastating injuries in the accident.* 他在这次事故中受到致命伤害。 ◇ *It will be a* ***devastating blow*** *to the local community if the factory closes.* 如果这家工厂倒闭，将给当地居民以毁灭性的打击。 **2** extremely shocking to a person 令人震惊的；骇人的：*the devastating news that her father was dead* 她父亲去世的惊人消息 **3** impressive and powerful 给人印象深刻的；令人钦佩的；强有力的：*his devastating performance in the 100 metres* 他在 100 米赛跑中的惊人表现 ◇ *Her smile was devastating.* 她的笑容令人倾倒。 ◇ *a devastating attack on the President's economic record* 针对总统的经济政绩发动的猛烈抨击 ▸ **dev·as·tat·ing·ly** *adv.*：*a devastatingly handsome man* 富有魅力的美男子

dev·as·ta·tion /ˌdevəˈsteɪʃn/ *noun* [U] great destruction or damage, especially over a wide area （尤指大面积的）毁灭，破坏，蹂躏：*The bomb caused widespread devastation.* 炸弹造成大面积破坏。

de·velop 🔑 /dɪˈveləp/ *verb*

• **GROW BIGGER/STRONGER** 发展；壮大 **1** [I, T] to gradually grow or become bigger, more advanced, stronger, etc.; to make sth do this （使）成长，发展，壮大：*The child is developing normally.* 这孩子发育正常。 ◇ ~ (**from sth**) (**into sth**) *The place has rapidly developed from a small fishing community into a thriving tourist resort.* 这地方由原来的小渔村迅速发展成一个繁荣的旅游胜地。 ◇ ~ **sth** (**from sth**) (**into sth**) *She developed the company from nothing.* 她白手起家创办了这家公司。

• **NEW IDEA/PRODUCT** 新思想 / 产品 **2** [T] ~ **sth** to think of or produce a new idea, product, etc. and make it successful 开发；研制：*The company develops and markets new software.* 这家公司开发并销售新软件。 ➲ SYNONYMS AT MAKE

• **DISEASE/PROBLEM** 疾病；问题 **3** [I, T] ~ (**sth**) to begin to have sth such as a disease or a problem; to start to affect sb/sth 患（病）；出现（问题）；（疾病）开始侵袭；（问题）开始影响：*Her son developed asthma when he was two.* 她的儿子两岁时患了哮喘。 ◇ *The car developed engine trouble and we had to stop.* 汽车发动机出了故障，我们只好停下来。

• **HAPPEN/CHANGE** 发生；变化 **4** [I] to start to happen or change, especially in a bad way （尤指开始向坏的方面）发展，变化：*A crisis was rapidly developing in the Gulf.* 海湾危机迅速加剧。 ◇ *We need more time to see how things develop before we take action.* 我们采取行动之前需要有更多时间观察情况的发展。

• **BECOME BETTER** 变得更好 **5** [T, I] ~ (**sth**) to start to have a skill, ability, quality, etc. that becomes better and stronger; to become better and stronger 加强；增强；发挥：*He's developed a real flair for management.* 他在管理方面已经变得很有一套。 ◇ *Their relationship has developed over a number of years.* 多年来他们的情谊日益深厚。

• **BUILD HOUSES** 建房 **6** [T] ~ **sth** to build new houses, factories, etc. on an area of land, especially land that was not being used effectively before 修建；开发：*The site is being developed by a French company.* 这块地正由一家法国公司开发利用。

• **IDEA/STORY** 想法；叙述 **7** [T] ~ **sth** to make an idea, a story, etc. clearer by explaining it further 详尽阐述；阐明 **SYN** **elaborate**：*She develops the theme more fully in her later books.* 她在后来写的书中更详尽地阐明了这个主题。

• **PHOTOGRAPHS** 照片 **8** [T] ~ **sth** to treat film which has been used to take photographs with chemicals so that the pictures can be seen 使（胶卷）显影；显像；冲洗（胶片）：*I had the film developed yesterday.* 我昨天把胶卷拿去冲印了。

de·veloped /dɪˈveləpt/ *adj.* **1** (of a country, society, etc. 国家、社会等) having many industries and a complicated economic system 发达的；高度发展的：*financial aid to less developed countries* 对欠发达国家的经济援助 ◇ *The average citizen in the* ***developed world*** *uses over 155kg of paper per year.* 发达国家中普通公民每年的用纸量超过 155 公斤。 ➲ COMPARE UNDERDEVELOPED **2** in an advanced state 先进的；成熟的：*children with highly developed problem-solving skills* 具有非常熟练解决问题能力的孩子 ➲ SEE ALSO WELL DEVELOPED

de·vel·op·er /dɪˈveləpə(r)/ *noun* **1** [C] a person or company that buys land or buildings in order to build new houses, shops/stores, etc., or to improve the old ones, and makes a profit from doing this （房地产）开发商，开发公司：*property developers* 房地产开发商 **2** [C] a person or a company that designs and creates new products （新产品的）开发者，研制者：*a software developer* 软件开发人员 **3** [U] a chemical substance that is used for developing photographs from a film 显影剂

de·vel·op·ing /dɪˈveləpɪŋ/ *adj.* [only before noun] (of a country, society, etc. 国家、社会等) poor, and trying to make its industry and economic system more advanced 发展中的：***developing countries/nations/economies*** 发展中国家 / 经济体 ➲ COMPARE UNDERDEVELOPED

de·vel·op·ment 🔑 /dɪˈveləpmənt/ *noun*

• **GROWTH** 发展 **1** [U] the gradual growth of sth so that it becomes more advanced, stronger, etc. 发展；发育；成长；壮大：*a baby's development in the womb* 胎儿在子宫内的发育 ◇ *the development of basic skills such as literacy and numeracy* 诸如识字与识数等基本技能的发展 ◇ *career development* 职业的发展

• **NEW PRODUCT** 新产品 **2** [U, C] the process of producing or creating sth new or more advanced; a new or advanced product 开发；研制；研制成果：*the development of vaccines against tropical diseases* 热带疾病疫苗的研制 ◇ *developments in aviation technology* 航空技术的开发成果 ◇ *This piece of equipment is an exciting new development.* 这台设备是一项振奋人心的最新研究成果。 ➲ SEE ALSO RESEARCH AND DEVELOPMENT

• NEW EVENT 新事态 **3** [C] a new event or stage that is likely to affect what happens in a continuing situation （新的）发展事态，进展情况，发展阶段：*the latest developments in the war* 战争的最新进展情况 ◇ *Are there further developments in the investigation?* 调查有新的进展吗？

• NEW BUILDINGS 新建筑 **4** [C] a piece of land with new buildings on it 新建住宅区；新开发区：*a **commercial/business/housing development*** 商业开发区；新建住宅区 ➲ SEE ALSO RIBBON DEVELOPMENT **5** [U] the process of using an area of land, especially to make a profit by building on it, etc.（尤指房地产的）开发：*He bought the land for development.* 他买了这块地准备开发。

de·vel·op·men·tal /dɪˌveləpˈmentl/ *adj.* **1** in a state of developing or being developed 发育中的；进化中的；开发中的：*The product is still at a developmental stage.* 这种产品仍处于研制阶段。 **2** connected with the development of sb/sth 发展的；成长的；进化的：*developmental psychology* 发展心理学 ▶ **de·vel·op·men·tal·ly** *adv.*

deˈvelopment area *noun* (*BrE*) an area where new industries are encouraged in order to create jobs 开发区

Devi /ˈdeɪvi/ *noun* (*IndE*) **1** [C] a female god 提毗；女神 **2** used after the first name of a Hindu woman as a polite way of addressing her 提毗（敬称，用于印度教女教徒的名字后）

de·vi·ant /ˈdiːviənt/ *adj.* different from what most people consider to be normal and acceptable 不正常的；异常的；偏离常轨的：***deviant behaviour/sexuality*** 偏常行为 / 性行为 ▶ **de·vi·ant** *noun*：*sexual deviants* 性偏离者 **de·vi·ance** /-viəns/, **de·vi·ancy** /ˈdiːviənsi/ *noun* [U]：*a study of social deviance and crime* 对社会偏常行为和犯罪行为的研究

de·vi·ate AW /ˈdiːvieɪt/ *verb* [I] ~ (**from sth**) to be different from sth; to do sth in a different way from what is usual or expected 背离；偏离；违背：*The bus had to deviate from its usual route because of a road closure.* 因为道路封闭，公共汽车只得绕道而行。 ◇ *He never deviated from his original plan.* 他从未偏离自己最初的计划。

de·vi·ation AW /ˌdiːviˈeɪʃn/ *noun* **1** [U, C] ~ (**from sth**) the act of moving away from what is normal or acceptable; a difference from what is expected or acceptable 背离；偏离；违背：*deviation from the previously accepted norms* 违背事先接受的准则 ◇ *sexual deviation* 性偏离 ◇ *a deviation from the plan* 违背计划 **2** [C] ~ (**from sth**) (*specialist*) the amount by which a single measurement is different from the average 偏差：*a compass deviation of 5°* (= from true north) 罗盘偏差 5 度（相对正北而言） ➲ SEE ALSO STANDARD DEVIATION

de·vice AW /dɪˈvaɪs/ *noun* **1** an object or a piece of equipment that has been designed to do a particular job 装置；仪器；器具；设备：*a water-saving device* 节水装置 ◇ *devices such as tablet PCs and mobile phones* 平板电脑和手机等设备 ◇ *electrical labour-saving devices around the home* 节省劳力的各种家用电器 **2** a bomb or weapon that will explode 炸弹；爆炸性武器；爆炸装置：*A powerful device exploded outside the station.* 一枚威力巨大的炸弹在车站外爆炸了。 ◇ *the world's first atomic device* 世界第一枚原子弹 **3** a method of doing sth that produces a particular result or effect 手段；策略；方法；技巧：*Sending advertising by email is very successful as a marketing device.* 作为一种营销手段，用电子邮件发送广告是非常成功的。 **4** a plan or trick that is used to get sth that sb wants 花招；计谋；诡计：*The report was a device used to hide rather than reveal problems.* 这份报告不是揭露问题而是要花招掩盖问题。

IDM **leave sb to their own deˈvices** to leave sb alone to do as they wish, and not tell them what to do 听任某人自行其是；对某人不加干涉

devil /ˈdevl/ *noun* **1 the Devil** (in the Christian, Jewish and Muslim religions 基督教、犹太教和伊斯兰教) the most powerful evil BEING 魔王；撒旦 SYN **Satan** **2** an evil spirit 魔鬼；恶魔：*They believed she was possessed by devils.* 他们认为她是魔鬼附身。 **3** (*informal*) a person who behaves badly, especially a child 淘气鬼；冒失鬼；调皮鬼：*a naughty little devil* 小淘气鬼 **4** (*informal*) used to talk about sb and to emphasize an opinion that you have of them（强调对某人的看法）人，家伙：*I miss the old devil, now that he's gone.* 老家伙这一走，我还真想他。 ◇ *She's off to Greece for a month—lucky devil!* 她休假去希腊一个月，真够幸运的！

IDM **be a ˈdevil** (*BrE*) people say **Be a devil!** to encourage sb to do sth that they are not sure about doing（用以鼓励）别怕，勇敢点：*Go on, be a devil, buy both of them.* 来，怕什么，两个都买了吧。 **better the ˌdevil you ˈknow (than the ˌdevil you ˈdon't)** (*saying*) used to say that it is easier and wiser to stay in a bad situation that you know and can deal with rather than change to a new situation which may be much worse 熟悉的魔鬼比不熟悉的魔鬼好；不要嫌熟悉的环境不好，换个不熟悉的环境可能更糟 **between the ˌdevil and the ˌdeep blue ˈsea** in a difficult situation where there are two equally unpleasant or unacceptable choices 进退维谷；左右为难 **the ˈdevil** (*old-fashioned*) very difficult or unpleasant 非常困难；令人非常不快：*These berries are the devil to pick because they're so small.* 这些浆果太小了，很难摘。 **the ˌdevil looks after his ˈown** (*saying*) bad people often seem to have good luck 坏人多好运；坏蛋自有鬼照顾；恶人自有恶人帮 **the devil makes work for idle ˈhands** (*saying*) people who do not have enough to do often start to do wrong 人闲生是非：*She blamed the crimes on the local jobless teenagers. 'The devil makes work for idle hands,' she would say.* 她认为那些违法活动是当地的无业青少年所为，总是说："人一闲，惹麻烦。" **a ˈdevil of a job/time** (*old-fashioned*) a very difficult or unpleasant job or time 费力（或令人讨厌）的事；难熬（或令人不快）的日子：*I've had a devil of a job finding you.* 我费了九牛二虎之力才找到你。 **go to the ˈdevil!** (*old-fashioned, informal*) used, in an unfriendly way, to tell sb to go away 滚开；见鬼去；去你的 **like the ˈdevil** (*old-fashioned, informal*) very hard, fast, etc. 拼命；卖力；飞快：*We ran like the devil.* 我们跑得飞快。 **speak/talk of the ˈdevil** (*informal*) people say **speak/talk of the devil** when sb they have been talking about appears unexpectedly 说到某人，某人就到：*Well, speak of the devil—here's Alice now!* 嘀，说谁谁到 —— 瞧，艾丽斯这就来啦！ **what, where, who, why, etc. the ˈdevil...** (*old-fashioned*) used in questions to show that you are annoyed or surprised（用于问句表示烦恼或吃惊）究竟…，到底…：*What the devil do you think you're doing?* 你到底知不知道自己在干什么？ ➲ MORE AT PAY *v.*, SELL *v.*

devil·ish /ˈdevəlɪʃ/ *adj.* **1** cruel or evil 残忍邪恶的；恶毒的：*a devilish conspiracy* 恶毒的阴谋活动 **2** morally bad, but in a way that people find attractive 魔鬼似的，恶魔似的（但具吸引力）：*He was handsome, with a devilish charm.* 他英俊漂亮，具有魔鬼般的迷惑力。

devil·ish·ly /ˈdevəlɪʃli/ *adv.* (*old-fashioned*) extremely; very 极其；非常：*a devilishly hot day* 酷热的一天

dev·illed (*BrE*) (*US* **dev·iled**) /ˈdevld/ *adj.* cooked in a thick liquid containing hot spices 用辣味浓汤炖的

ˌdevil-may-ˈcare *adj.* [usually before noun] cheerful and not worrying about the future 乐天的；无忧无虑的；无所顾忌的

dev·il·ment /ˈdevlmənt/ (*also* **dev·il·ry** /ˈdevlri/) *noun* [U] (*formal*) wild behaviour that causes trouble 捣乱；恶作剧 SYN **mischief**

ˌdevil's ˈadvocate *noun* a person who expresses an opinion that they do not really hold in order to encourage a discussion about a subject 故意唱反调的人；故意持不同意见的人：*Often the interviewer will need **to play devil's advocate** in order to get a discussion going.* 采访者常常需要故意唱唱反调好让访谈继续下去。

de·vi·ous /ˈdiːviəs/ *adj.* **1** behaving in a dishonest or indirect way, or tricking people, in order to get sth 不诚实的；不直率的；欺诈的 SYN **deceitful, underhand**：*a devious politician* 不诚实的政治家 ◇ *He got rich by devious means.* 他不择手段大发横财。 **2** ~ **route/path** a route or path that is not straight but has many changes in direction; not direct 迂回的（路线）；曲折的（道路）：*a devious route from the airport* 出机场的曲折路线 ▶ **de·vi·ous·ly** *adv.* **de·vi·ous·ness** *noun* [U]

de·vise /dɪˈvaɪz/ *verb* ~ sth to invent sth new or a new way of doing sth 发明；设计；想出 **SYN** **think up**: *A new system has been devised to control traffic in the city.* 控制城市交通的新系统已经设计出来。

de·voice /ˌdiːˈvɔɪs/ *verb* ~ sth (*phonetics* 语音) to make a speech sound, usually a consonant, VOICELESS 使（辅音等）清化

de·void /dɪˈvɔɪd/ *adj.* ~ **of sth** completely lacking in sth 完全没有；缺乏：*The letter was devoid of warmth and feeling.* 这封信既无热情又无感情。

de·vo·lu·tion /ˌdiːvəˈluːʃn; *NAmE* ˌdev-/ *noun* [U] the act of giving power from a central authority or government to an authority or a government in a local region （中央政府向地方政府的）权力下放，权力转移，分权

de·volve /dɪˈvɒlv; *NAmE* -ˈvɑːlv/ *verb*

PHRV **deˈvolve on/upon sb/sth** (*formal*) **1** if property, money, etc. **devolves on/upon** you, you receive it after sb else dies （财产、金钱等遗产）转给，传给，移交 **2** if a duty, responsibility, etc. **devolves on/upon** you, it is given to you by sb at a higher level of authority （职责、责任等）交由…接替，委托…承担 **deˈvolve sth to/on/upon sb** to give a duty, responsibility, power, etc. to sb who has less authority than you（将职责、责任、权力等）移交，转交，委任：*The central government devolved most tax-raising powers to the regional authorities.* 中央政府将大部分征税权移交给了地方当局。

de·volved /dɪˈvɒlvd; *NAmE* -ˈvɑːlvd/ *adj.* if power or authority is **devolved**, it has been passed to sb who has less power （职权）已移交的，下放的，委任的：*devolved responsibility* 已移交的责任 ◇ *a system of devolved government* 治理权力下放制

de·vote 🔑 **AW** /dɪˈvəʊt; *NAmE* dɪˈvoʊt/ *verb*

PHRV **deˈvote yourself to sb/sth** 🔑 to give most of your time, energy, attention, etc. to sb/sth 献身；致力；专心：*She devoted herself to her career.* 她全力倾注于自己的事业。 **deˈvote sth to sth** 🔑 to give an amount of time, attention, etc. to sth 把…用于：*I could only devote two hours a day to the work.* 我一天只能在这个工作上花两个小时。

de·voted 🔑 /dɪˈvəʊtɪd; *NAmE* -ˈvoʊt-/ *adj.* ~ (**to sb/sth**) having great love for sb/sth and being loyal to them 挚爱的；忠诚的；全心全意的：*They are devoted to their children.* 他们深爱着自己的孩子。◇ *a devoted son/friend/fan* 孝子；忠诚的朋友；狂热的崇拜者 ➲ SYNONYMS AT LOVE ▶ **de·voted·ly** *adv.*

de·votee /ˌdevəˈtiː/ *noun* **1** ~ (**of sb/sth**) a person who admires and is very enthusiastic about sb/sth（狂热的）崇拜者，爱好者：*a devotee of science fiction* 科幻小说的狂热爱好者 **2** ~ (**of sb/sth**) a very religious person who belongs to a particular group 虔诚的宗教信徒：*devotees of Krishna* （印度教）黑天的虔诚信徒

de·vo·tion **AW** /dɪˈvəʊʃn; *NAmE* -ˈvoʊ-/ *noun* **1** [U, sing.] ~ (**to sb/sth**) great love, care and support for sb/sth 挚爱；关爱；关照：*His devotion to his wife and family is touching.* 他对妻子和家人的关爱感人至深。 **2** [U, sing.] ~ (**to sb/sth**) the action of spending a lot of time or energy on sth 奉献；忠诚；专心；热心 **SYN** **dedication**: *her devotion to duty* 她对职责的忠诚 ◇ *Her devotion to the job left her with very little free time.* 她全身心投入工作，几乎没有闲暇。 **3** **devotions** [pl.] prayers and other religious practices 宗教敬拜

de·vo·tion·al /dɪˈvəʊʃənl; *NAmE* -ˈvoʊ-/ *adj.* (of music, etc. 音乐等) connected with or used in religious services 用于祈祷的；宗教仪式的

de·vour /dɪˈvaʊə(r)/ *verb* **1** ~ sth to eat all of sth quickly, especially because you are very hungry（尤指因饥饿而）狼吞虎咽地吃光 **SYN** **gobble** **2** to read or look at sth with great interest and enthusiasm 津津有味地看；如饥似渴地读：*She devoured everything she could lay her hands on: books, magazines and newspapers.* 无论是书、杂志，还是报纸，只要能弄到手，她都看得津津有味。 **3** ~ sb/sth (*formal*) to destroy sb/sth 吞没；吞噬；毁灭 **SYN** **engulf**: *Flames devoured the house.* 大火吞噬了这栋房子。

IDM **be devoured by sth** to be filled with a strong emotion that seems to control you 心中充满（强烈的情感）：*She was devoured by envy and hatred.* 她心中充满嫉妒和憎恨。

de·vout /dɪˈvaʊt/ *adj.* (of a person 人) believing strongly in a particular religion and obeying its laws and practices 笃信宗教的；虔诚的：*a devout Christian/Muslim* 虔诚的基督徒 / 穆斯林 ▶ **de·vout·ly** *adv.*: *a devoutly Catholic region* 笃信天主教的地区 ◇ *She devoutly* (= very strongly) *hoped he was telling the truth.* 她诚挚地希望他讲的是实情。

dew /djuː; *NAmE* duː/ *noun* [U] the very small drops of water that form on the ground, etc. during the night 露；露水：*The grass was wet with early morning dew.* 清晨的露水使得青草湿漉漉的。

dew·berry /ˈdjuːbəri; *NAmE* ˈduːberi; ˈdjuː-/ *noun* (*pl.* **-ies**) a small soft black or blue-black fruit like a BLACKBERRY, or the bush that it grows on 露莓（浆果）；露莓（灌木）

dew·drop /ˈdjuːdrɒp; *NAmE* ˈduːdrɑːp/ *noun* a small drop of dew or other liquid 露珠；水珠

Dewey deci·mal clas·si·fi·ca·tion /ˌdjuːi ˈdesɪml klæsɪfɪˈkeɪʃn; *NAmE also* ˌduːi/ (*also* **ˈDewey sys·tem**) *noun* [sing.] an international system for arranging books in a library 杜威十进分类法（图书馆藏书分类法）

ˈdew point *noun* [sing.] (*specialist*) the temperature at which air can hold no more water. Below this temperature the water comes out of the air in the form of drops. 露点（空气中水汽含量达到饱和的气温，低于此温度时水汽从空气中析出凝成水珠）

dewy /ˈdjuːi; *NAmE* duːi/ *adj.* wet with DEW 露水打湿的；带露水的

ˌdewy-ˈeyed *adj.* (*disapproving*) showing emotion about sth, perhaps with a few tears in the eyes 动感情的；感伤的；泪汪汪的 **SYN** **sentimental**

dex·ter·ity /dekˈsterəti/ *noun* [U] skill in using your hands or your mind （手）灵巧，熟练；（思维）敏捷，灵活：*You need manual dexterity to be good at video games.* 玩好电子游戏手要灵巧。◇ ***mental/verbal dexterity*** 智能；说话技巧

dex·ter·ous (*also* **dex·trous**) /ˈdekstrəs/ *adj.* (*formal*) skilful with your hands; skilfully done 灵巧的；熟练的；敏捷的 ▶ **dex·ter·ous·ly** (*also* **dex·trous·ly**) *adv.*

dex·trose /ˈdekstrəʊz; -əʊs; *NAmE* -oʊz; -oʊs/ *noun* [U] (*chemistry* 化) a form of GLUCOSE (= a type of natural sugar) 右旋糖（一种天然糖）

DFID /ˌdiː ef aɪ ˈdiː/ *abbr.* (in Britain) Department for International Development （英国）国际发展部

DH /ˌdiː ˈeɪtʃ/ *abbr.* (in Britain) Department of Health （英国）卫生部

dhaba /ˈdɑːbə/ *noun* (*IndE*) a small cheap restaurant where Punjabi food is served, with basic furniture and facilities, and often with an open front and tables outside （提供旁遮普食物的）塔吧，小饭馆

dhal = DAL

dhania /ˈdɑːniə/ *noun* [U] (*EAfrE, IndE, SAfrE*) the leaves or seeds of the CORIANDER plant, used to flavour food 香菜叶，香菜籽（用作调味料）

dhan·sak /ˈdʌnsɑːk; ˈdænsæk/ *noun* an Indian meat or vegetable dish cooked with LENTILS and CORIANDER 兵豆香菜炖肉，炒兵豆香菜（印度菜肴）

dharma /ˈdɑːmə; *NAmE* ˈdɑːr-/ *noun* [U] (in Indian religion 印度宗教) truth or law that affects the whole universe 法，达摩（影响整个宇宙的真理或规则）

dharna /ˈdɜːnə; -nɑː; *NAmE* ˈdɜːrn-/ *noun* (*IndE*) **1** an act of lying flat on the floor with your face down as an act of worship in a TEMPLE 达尔那（在寺庙中伏地朝拜） **2** a form of protest in which a group of people refuse to leave a factory, public place, etc. 静坐抗议

dhoti /ˈdəʊti; *NAmE* ˈdoʊti/ *noun* a long piece of cloth worn by Hindu men. It is sometimes tied round the waist, with the lower part passed between the legs and put into the cloth at the back, so that the knees are usually covered. （印度男子的）多蒂腰布

dhow /daʊ/ *noun* an Arab ship with one large sail in the shape of a triangle 阿拉伯三角帆船

dhur·rie (*also* **dur·rie**) /ˈdʌri/ *noun* a heavy cotton RUG (= small carpet) from S Asia 达里（南亚产的小块厚棉地毯）

DI /ˌdiː ˈaɪ/ *noun* the abbreviation for 'Detective Inspector' (a British police officer of middle rank) 探长（全写为 Detective Inspector，英国中级警官）：*DI Ross* 罗斯探长

di- /daɪ/ *combining form* (*chemistry* 化) (in nouns that are names of chemical COMPOUNDS 构成化合物名词) containing two atoms or groups of the type mentioned 含有两个原子的；含有两组…物质的：*carbon dioxide* 二氧化碳

dia·betes /ˌdaɪəˈbiːtiːz/ *noun* [U] a medical condition which makes the patient produce a lot of URINE and feel very thirsty. There are several types of diabetes. 糖尿病

dia·bet·ic /ˌdaɪəˈbetɪk/ *adj., noun*
■ ***adj.*** **1** having or connected with diabetes 糖尿病的；患糖尿病的：*She's diabetic.* 她患有糖尿病。◇ *a diabetic patient* 糖尿病患者 ◇ *diabetic complications* 糖尿病并发症 **2** suitable for or used by sb who has diabetes 适合糖尿病患者的；专供糖尿病患者吃的：*a diabetic diet* 适合糖尿病患者的饮食
■ ***noun*** a person who suffers from DIABETES 糖尿病患者

dia·bol·ical /ˌdaɪəˈbɒlɪkl; *NAmE* -ˈbɑːl-/ *adj.* **1** (*informal, especially BrE*) extremely bad or annoying 糟糕透顶的；烦人的；讨厌的 **SYN** **terrible**: *The traffic was diabolical.* 交通状况糟糕透了。 **2** (*also less frequent* **dia·bol·ic** /ˌdaɪəˈbɒlɪk; *NAmE* -ˈbɑːl-/) morally bad and evil; like a DEVIL 道德败坏的；邪恶的；恶魔似的 ▸ **dia·bol·ic·al·ly** /-kli/ *adv.*

dia·chron·ic /ˌdaɪəˈkrɒnɪk; *NAmE* -ˈkrɑːn-/ *adj.* (*specialist*) relating to the way sth, especially a language, has developed over time （尤指语言研究）历时的 ➲ COMPARE SYNCHRONIC

dia·crit·ic /ˌdaɪəˈkrɪtɪk/ *noun* (*linguistics* 语言) a mark such as an accent, placed over, under or through a letter in some languages, to show that the letter should be pronounced in a different way from the same letter without a mark 变音符，附加符号（置于字母上方、下方或穿过字母，表示发音不同） ▸ **dia·crit·ic·al** /-ˈkrɪtɪkl/ *adj.*: *diacritical marks* 变音符

dia·dem /ˈdaɪədem/ *noun* a crown, worn especially as a sign of royal power 王冠；冕

di·aer·esis (*BrE*) (*US* **di·er·esis**) /daɪˈerəsɪs/ (*pl.* **di·aer·eses**, **di·er·eses** /-siːz/) *noun* (*specialist*) the mark placed over a vowel to show that it is pronounced separately, as in *naïve* 分音符（标在元音上面，表示单独发音，如 naïve）

diag·nose /ˈdaɪəgnəʊz; ˌdaɪəgˈnəʊz; *NAmE* -ˈnoʊs/ *verb* [T, I] to say exactly what an illness or the cause of a problem is 诊断（疾病）；判断（问题的原因）：**~ (sth)** *The test is used to diagnose a variety of diseases.* 此项化验可用于诊断多种疾病。◇ **~ sth as sth** *The illness was diagnosed as cancer.* 此病诊断为癌症。◇ **~ sb with sth** *He has recently been diagnosed with angina.* 他最近被诊断出患有心绞痛。◇ **~ sb (as) sth** *He was diagnosed (as) a diabetic when he was 64.* 他 64 岁时被诊断患有糖尿病。◇ **~ sb + adj./noun** *He was diagnosed (a) diabetic.* 他被诊断患有糖尿病。➲ WORDFINDER NOTE AT EXAMINE ➲ COLLOCATIONS AT ILL

diag·no·sis /ˌdaɪəgˈnəʊsɪs; *NAmE* -ˈnoʊ-/ *noun* [C, U] (*pl.* **diag·noses** /-siːz/) **~ (of sth)** the act of discovering or identifying the exact cause of an illness or a problem 诊断；（问题原因的）判断：*diagnosis of lung cancer* 肺癌的诊断 ◇ *They are waiting for the doctor's diagnosis.* 他们正在等待医生的诊断结果。◇ *An accurate* ***diagnosis was made*** *after a series of tests.* 准确的诊断是在一系列的检查后作出的。

diag·nos·tic /ˌdaɪəgˈnɒstɪk; *NAmE* -ˈnɑːs-/ *adj., noun*
■ ***adj.*** [usually before noun] (*specialist*) connected with identifying sth, especially an illness 诊断的；判断的：*to carry out* ***diagnostic assessments/tests*** 进行诊断性评估 / 化验 ◇ *specific conditions which are diagnostic of AIDS* 诊断为艾滋病的具体症状
■ ***noun*** (*computing* 计) **1** (*also* ˌ**diagˈnostic program**) [C] a program used for identifying a computer fault 诊断程序（诊断计算机的错误） **2** [C] a message on a computer screen giving information about a fault 诊断提示（计算机出错误的显示） **3 diagnostics** [U] the practice or methods of diagnosis 诊断；诊断法

di·ag·onal /daɪˈægənl/ *adj., noun*
■ ***adj.*** (of a straight line 直线) at an angle; joining two opposite sides of sth at an angle 斜线的；对角线的：*diagonal stripes* 斜纹 ▸ **di·ag·onal·ly** /-nəli/ *adv.*: *Walk diagonally across the field to the far corner and then turn left.* 斜着穿过这块地到远角处，然后朝左转。
■ ***noun*** a straight line that joins two opposite sides of sth at an angle; a straight line that is at an angle 对角线；斜线

dia·gram 🔑 /ˈdaɪəgræm/ *noun* a simple drawing using lines to explain where sth is, how sth works, etc. 简图；图解；图表；示意图：*a diagram of the wiring system* 线路系统图 ◇ *The results are shown in diagram 2.* 结果显示在表 2 上。 ▸ **dia·gram·mat·ic** /ˌdaɪəgrəˈmætɪk/ *adj.* **dia·gram·mat·ic·al·ly** /-kli/ *adv.*

dial /ˈdaɪəl/ *noun, verb*
■ ***noun*** **1** the face of a clock or watch, or a similar control on a machine, piece of equipment or vehicle that shows a measurement of time, amount, speed, temperature, etc. 表盘；刻度盘；标度盘；仪表盘：*an alarm clock with a luminous dial* 夜光闹钟 ◇ *Check the tyre pressure on the dial.* 检查一下仪表盘显示的车胎压力。➲ SEE ALSO SUNDIAL **2** the round control on a radio, cooker/stove, etc. that you turn in order to adjust sth, for example to choose a particular station or to choose a particular temperature （收音机、炉、灶等的）调节盘，控制盘 **3** the round part on some older telephones, with holes for the fingers, that you move around to call a particular number （旧式电话机的）拨号盘
■ ***verb*** (**-ll-**, *NAmE* **-l-**) [T, I] **~ (sth)** to use a telephone by pushing buttons or turning the dial to call a number 拨（电话号码）：*He dialled the number and waited.* 他拨号后便等着通话。◇ *Dial 0033 for France.* 打电话到法国拨 0033。➲ WORDFINDER NOTE AT CALL ➲ COLLOCATIONS AT PHONE

dia·lect /ˈdaɪəlekt/ *noun* [C, U] the form of a language that is spoken in one area with grammar, words and pronunciation that may be different from other forms of the same language 地方话；土话；方言：*the Yorkshire dialect* 约克郡方言 ➲ COMPARE ACCENT *n.* (1), IDIOLECT ➲ WORDFINDER NOTE AT LANGUAGE ▸ **dia·lect·al** /ˌdaɪəˈlektl/ *adj.*

dia·lect·ic /ˌdaɪəˈlektɪk/ *noun* [sing.] (*also less frequent* **dia·lect·ics** [U]) **1** (*philosophy* 哲) a method of discovering the truth of ideas by discussion and logical argument and by considering ideas that are opposed to each other 辩证法 **2** (*formal*) the way in which two aspects of a situation affect each other 对立（一个情况的两个方面彼此影响） ▸ **dia·lect·ic·al** /-kl/ *adj.*

diaˌlectical maˈterialism *noun* [U] (*philosophy* 哲) the Marxist theory that all change results from opposing social forces, which come into conflict because of material needs 辩证唯物主义

dial·ler (*BrE*) (*NAmE* **dial·er**) /ˈdaɪələ(r)/ *noun* a computer program or piece of equipment which calls telephone numbers automatically 自动拨号程序；自动拨号器

ˈ**dialling code** (*also* **code**) *noun* (*BrE*) the numbers that are used for a particular town, area or country, in front of an individual telephone number（电话的）区号：*international dialling codes* 国际区号 ➲COMPARE AREA CODE

ˈ**dialling tone** (*BrE*) (*NAmE* ˈ**dial tone**) *noun* the sound that you hear when you pick up a telephone that means you can make a call（电话的）拨号音

ˈ**dialog box** (*BrE also* ˈ**dialogue box**) *noun* a box that appears on a computer screen asking the user to choose what they want to do next（计算机屏幕上的）对话窗，对话框 ➲VISUAL VOCAB PAGE V74

dia·logue (*NAmE also* **dia·log**) /ˈdaɪəlɒg; *NAmE* -lɑːg; -lɔːg/ *noun* [C, U] **1** conversations in a book, play, or film/movie（书、戏剧或电影中的）对话，对白：*The novel has long descriptions and not much dialogue.* 这部小说描述多对话少。◇ *dialogues for language learners* 供语言学习者学习的对话 ➲ SYNONYMS AT DISCUSSION ➲ WORDFINDER NOTE AT DRAMA, FILM, PLOT **2** a formal discussion between two groups or countries, especially when they are trying to solve a problem, end a disagreement, etc.（尤指集体或国家间为解决问题、结束争端等进行的）对话：*The President told waiting reporters there had been a constructive dialogue.* 总统告诉等候的记者，刚才进行了一次富有建设性的对话。➲COMPARE MONOLOGUE

ˈ**dial-up** *adj.* [only before noun] using a telephone line and a MODEM to connect your computer to the Internet 拨号上网的

dia·ly·sis /ˌdaɪˈæləsɪs/ *noun* [U] (*specialist*) a process for separating substances from a liquid, especially for taking waste substances out of the blood of people with damaged KIDNEYS 透析，渗析（尤指将废物从肾病病人的血液中分离出来）：***kidney/renal dialysis*** 肾透析 ◇ *a dialysis machine* 透析机

dia·manté /ˌdiːəˈmɒnteɪ; *NAmE* ˌdiːəmɑːnˈteɪ/ *adj.* decorated with glass that is cut to look like diamonds 镶嵌钻石状玻璃饰品的；珠光的：*diamanté earrings* 珠光耳环

dia·man·tine /ˌdaɪəˈmæntiːn/ *adj.* (*specialist*) **1** made from, or looking like, diamonds （像）钻石的 **2** very hard or strong 坚硬的；坚固的

diam·eter /daɪˈæmɪtə(r)/ *noun* **1** a straight line going from one side of a circle or any other round object to the other side, passing through the centre 直径；对径：*the diameter of a tree trunk* 树干的直径 ◇ *The dome is 42.3 metres **in diameter**.* 这个穹顶直径为 42.3 米。➲ PICTURE AT CIRCLE ➲COMPARE RADIUS (1) **2** (*specialist*) a measurement of the power of an instrument to MAGNIFY sth 放大率；放大倍数：*a lens magnifying 300 diameters* (= making sth look 300 times larger than it really is) 放大 300 倍的透镜

dia·met·ric·al /ˌdaɪəˈmetrɪkl/ *adj.* [usually before noun] **1** used to emphasize that people or things are completely different 截然相反的；完全不同的：*He's the **diametrical opposite** of his brother.* 他和他的弟弟截然不同。**2** relating to the DIAMETER of sth 直径的

dia·met·ric·al·ly /ˌdaɪəˈmetrɪkli/ *adv.* **~ opposed/opposite** completely different 完全（不同）；截然（相反）：*We hold diametrically opposed views.* 我们的观点大相径庭。

dia·mond 🔑 /ˈdaɪəmənd/ *noun* **1** 🔑 [U, C] a clear PRECIOUS STONE of pure CARBON, the hardest substance known. Diamonds are used in jewellery and also in industry, especially for cutting glass. 金刚石；钻石：*a ring with a diamond in it* 钻石戒指 ◇ *a **diamond ring/necklace*** 钻石戒指 / 项链 ◇ *She was wearing her diamonds* (= jewellery with diamonds in it). 她戴着钻石首饰。◇ *The lights shone like diamonds.* 灯光像钻石一样闪闪发亮。➲ SEE ALSO ROUGH DIAMOND **2** 🔑 [C] a shape with four straight sides of equal length and with angles that are not RIGHT ANGLES 菱形 **3 diamonds** [pl., U] one of the four SUITS (= sets) in a PACK/DECK of cards. The cards are marked with red diamond shapes.（纸牌的）方块：*the ten of diamonds* 方块十 ➲ VISUAL VOCAB PAGE V42 **4** [C] a card of this SUIT （一张）方块牌：*You must play a diamond if you have one.* 如果你有方块就必须出。**5** [C] (in BASEBALL 棒球) the space inside the lines that connect the four BASES; also used to mean the whole BASEBALL field 内场；棒球场

ˌ**diamond in the** ˈ**rough** (*NAmE*) (*BrE* ˌ**rough** ˈ**diamond**) *noun* a person who has many good qualities even though they do not seem to be very polite, educated, etc. 外粗内秀的人

ˌ**diamond** ˈ**jubilee** *noun* [usually sing.] the 60th anniversary of an important event, especially of sb becoming king/queen; a celebration of this event 钻石大庆，60 周年庆典（尤指国王或女王登基 60 周年纪念日）➲ COMPARE GOLDEN JUBILEE, SILVER JUBILEE

ˌ**diamond** ˈ**wedding** (*BrE*) (*NAmE* ˌ**diamond anni**ˈ**versary**) (*also* ˌ**diamond** ˈ**wedding anniversary** *NAmE, BrE*) *noun* the 60th anniversary of a wedding 钻石婚（结婚 60 周年纪念）➲COMPARE GOLDEN WEDDING, RUBY WEDDING, SILVER WEDDING

dia·mor·phine /ˌdaɪəˈmɔːfiːn; *NAmE* -ˈmɔːrf-/ *noun* [U] a powerful drug that is made from OPIUM and used to reduce pain 二乙酰吗啡，海洛因（用以镇痛）

di·aper /ˈdaɪəpə(r); *NAmE* ˈdaɪpər/ (*NAmE*) (*BrE* **nappy**) *noun* a piece of soft cloth or other thick material that is folded around a baby's bottom and between its legs to absorb and hold its body waste 尿布：*a diaper rash* 尿布疹

di·aph·an·ous /daɪˈæfənəs/ *adj.* (*formal*) (of cloth 布料) so light and fine that you can almost see through it 轻薄半透明的

dia·phragm /ˈdaɪəfræm/ *noun* **1** (*anatomy* 解) the layer of muscle between the lungs and the stomach, used especially to control breathing 膈；膈膜；横膈膜 **2** (*BrE also* **cap**) a rubber or plastic device that a woman places inside her VAGINA before having sex to prevent SPERM from entering the WOMB and making her pregnant 子宫帽（避孕用具）**3** any thin piece of material used to separate the parts of a machine, etc.（机器等的）隔膜，隔板 **4** (*specialist*) a thin disc used to turn electronic signals into sound and sound into electronic signals in telephones, LOUDSPEAKERS, etc.（电话机、扬声器等的）膜片，膜件，振动膜

diar·ist /ˈdaɪərɪst/ *noun* a person who writes a diary, especially one that is later published 日记作者；日志记载者：*Samuel Pepys, the famous 17th century diarist* 塞缪尔 • 佩皮斯，17 世纪著名的日记作者

diar·rhoea (*BrE*) (*NAmE* **diar·rhea**) /ˌdaɪəˈrɪə; *NAmE* -ˈriːə/ (*also informal* **the runs**) *noun* [U] an illness in which waste matter is emptied from the BOWELS much more frequently than normal, and in liquid form 腹泻：*Symptoms include diarrhoea and vomiting.* 症状有腹泻和呕吐。

diary 🔑 /ˈdaɪəri/ *noun* (*pl.* **-ies**) **1** 🔑 (*BrE*) (*NAmE* **datebook**) a book with spaces for each day of the year in which you can write down things you have to do in the future（工作日程）记事簿：*a desk diary* 台式记事簿 ◇ *I'll make a note of our next meeting in my diary.* 我将把下次会议的事记在我的记事簿上。➲ VISUAL VOCAB PAGE V71 **2** 🔑 a book in which you can write down the experiences you have each day, your private thoughts, etc. 日记；日记簿：*Do you **keep a diary*** (= write one regularly)? 你经常记日记吗？➲ SEE ALSO JOURNAL, VIDEO DIARY ➲ NOTE AT AGENDA

dias·pora /daɪˈæspərə/ *noun* [sing.] (*formal*) **1 the diaspora** the movement of the Jewish people away from their own country to live and work in other countries（犹太人的）大流散 **2** the movement of people from any

D

nation or group away from their own country （任何民族或群体的）大移居

di·atom·ic /ˌdaɪəˈtɒmɪk; NAmE -ˈtɑːmɪk/ *adj.* (*chemistry* 化) consisting of two atoms 双原子的

dia·ton·ic /ˌdaɪəˈtɒnɪk; NAmE -ˈtɑːn-/ *adj.* (*music* 音) using only the notes of the appropriate MAJOR or MINOR SCALE 自然的 ➲ COMPARE CHROMATIC

dia·tribe /ˈdaɪətraɪb/ *noun* ~ (**against sb/sth**) (*formal*) a long and angry speech or piece of writing attacking and criticizing sb/sth （无休止的）指责；（长篇）抨击，谴责：*He launched a bitter diatribe against the younger generation.* 他对年轻一代发起了猛烈的抨击。

di·aze·pam /daɪˈæzəpæm/ *noun* [U] (*medical* 医) a drug that is used to make people feel less anxious and more relaxed 安定；苯甲二氮䓬

dibs /dɪbz/

IDM **dibs on…** (*NAmE, informal*) (*BrE* **bags (I)…**) used to claim sth as yours before sb else can claim it …是我的；我要求…

dice /daɪs/ *noun, verb*

■ *noun* (*pl.* **dice**) **1** (*also* **die** *especially in NAmE*) [C] a small CUBE of wood, plastic, etc., with a different number of spots on each of its sides, used in games of chance 骰子；色子：*a pair of dice* 一对骰子 ◇ *to* ***roll/throw/shake the dice*** 滚 / 掷 / 摇骰子 **2** [U] a game played with dice 掷骰游戏；掷骰赌博：*We played dice all night.* 我们掷了一夜的骰子。➲ VISUAL VOCAB PAGE V42

IDM **no ˈdice** (*informal, especially NAmE*) used to show that you refuse to do sth, or that sth cannot be done （表示拒绝做或某事做不成）不行，不成，没门儿：*'Did you get that job?' 'No dice.'* "你得到那份工作了吗？" "不行啊。" ➲ MORE AT LOAD *v.*

■ *verb* ~ **sth** to cut meat, vegetables, etc. into small square pieces 将（肉、菜等）切成小方块；将…切成丁：*diced carrots* 胡萝卜丁 ➲ VISUAL VOCAB PAGE V30

IDM **dice with death** (*informal*) to risk your life by doing sth that you know is dangerous 冒生命危险；玩命

dicey /ˈdaɪsi/ *adj.* (*informal*) uncertain and dangerous 前途未卜的；冒险的；危险的 SYN **risky**

di·chot·omy /daɪˈkɒtəmi; NAmE -ˈkɑːt-/ *noun* [usually sing.] (*pl.* **-ies**) ~ (**between A and B**) (*formal*) the separation that exists between two groups or things that are completely opposite to and different from each other 一分为二；二分法

dick /dɪk/ *noun* (*taboo, slang*) **1** a man's PENIS 鸡巴；屌 **2** = DICKHEAD ➲ SEE ALSO CLEVER DICK

dick·ens /ˈdɪkɪnz/ *noun* **the dickens** (*old-fashioned, informal*) **1** used in questions instead of 'devil' to show that you are annoyed or surprised （用于问句代替 devil，表示烦恼或吃惊）究竟，到底：*Where the dickens did he go?* 他究竟上哪儿去了？ **2** (*NAmE*) used when you are saying how attractive, etc. sb is （某人）…极了，太…了，多么…啊：*cute as the dickens* 可爱极了

Dick·ens·ian /dɪˈkenziən/ *adj.* connected with or typical of the novels of Charles Dickens, which often describe social problems and bad social conditions 狄更斯文体的；具有狄更斯小说特点的；类似狄更斯笔下描述的：*a Dickensian slum* 类似狄更斯笔下的贫民窟

dicker /ˈdɪkə(r)/ *verb* [I] ~ (**with sb**) (**over sth**) (*especially NAmE*) to argue about or discuss sth with sb, especially in order to agree on a price 讨价还价；议价；讲价 SYN **bargain**

dick·head /ˈdɪkhed/ (*also* **dick**) *noun* (*taboo, slang*) a very rude way of referring to sb, especially a man, that you think is stupid 笨蛋，蠢货，蠢家伙（尤用于辱骂男性） SYN **idiot**

dicky /ˈdɪki/ *adj., noun*

■ *adj.* (*old-fashioned, BrE, informal*) not healthy; not working correctly 虚弱的；有病的；工作不正常的：*a dicky heart* 虚弱的心脏

■ *noun* (*also* **dickey**) (*pl.* **dickies** or **dickeys**) (*IndE*) the BOOT/TRUNK of a car （汽车后部的）行李厢

ˈdicky bird *noun* (*BrE*) (used by or when speaking to young children 儿语) a bird 鸟儿；小鸟儿

IDM **not say, hear, etc. a dicky bird** (*BrE, informal*) to say, hear, etc. nothing 什么也没说（或没听见等）：*He won't say a dicky bird, but we think he knows who did it.* 他什么都不肯说，但是我们认为他知道是谁干的。ORIGIN This idiom is from rhyming slang, in which 'dicky bird' stands for 'word'. 源自同韵俚语，其中 dicky bird（小鸟儿）代表 word。

di·coty·ledon /ˌdaɪkɒtɪˈliːdən; NAmE -kɑːt-/ (*also* **dicot** /ˈdaɪkɒt; NAmE -kɑːt/) *noun* (*biology* 生) a plant whose seeds form EMBRYOS that produce two leaves 双子叶植物 ➲ COMPARE MONOCOTYLEDON

Dicta·phone™ /ˈdɪktəfəʊn; NAmE -foʊn/ *noun* a small machine used to record people speaking, so that their words can be played back later and written down 口述录音机

dic·tate *verb, noun*

■ *verb* /dɪkˈteɪt; NAmE ˈdɪkteɪt/ **1** [T, I] ~ (**sth**) (**to sb**) to say words for sb else to write down 口述：*He dictated a letter to his secretary.* 他向秘书口授信稿。 **2** [T] to tell sb what to do, especially in an annoying way （尤指以令人厌烦的方式）指使，强行规定：~ **sth** (**to sb**) *They are in no position to* ***dictate terms*** (= tell other people what to do). 他们没有资格发号施令。◇ ~ **how, what, etc.…/that…** *What right do they have to dictate how we live our lives?* 他们有什么权利强行规定我们该怎样生活？ **3** [T, I] to control or influence how sth happens 支配；摆布；决定 SYN **determine**：~ (**sth**) *When we take our vacations is very much dictated by Greg's work schedule.* 我们什么时候休假在很大程度上取决于格雷格的工作时间安排。◇ ~ **where, what, etc.…** *It's generally your job that dictates where you live now.* 一般说来，你住在什么地方是由你的工作决定的。◇ ~ **that…** *The social conventions of the day dictated that she should remain at home with her parents.* 那时的社会习俗规定她应该留在家里，与她父母在一起。

PHR V **dicˈtate to sb** [often passive] to give orders to sb, often in a rude or aggressive way 任意指使某人；向某人发号施令：*She refused to be dictated to by anyone.* 她不愿受任何人摆布。

■ *noun* /ˈdɪkteɪt/ [usually pl.] (*formal*) an order or a rule that you must obey 命令；规定：*to follow the dictates of fashion* 赶时髦

dic·ta·tion /dɪkˈteɪʃn/ *noun* **1** [U] the act of speaking or reading so that sb can write down the words 口述 **2** [C, U] a test in which students write down what is being read to them, especially in language lessons 听写

dic·ta·tor /dɪkˈteɪtə(r); NAmE ˈdɪkteɪtər/ *noun* (*disapproving*) **1** a ruler who has complete power over a country, especially one who has gained it using military force 独裁者 **2** a person who behaves as if they have complete power over other people, and tells them what to do 发号施令者；专横的人

dic·ta·tor·ial /ˌdɪktəˈtɔːriəl/ *adj.* (*disapproving*) **1** connected with or controlled by a dictator 独裁的；专政的：*a dictatorial ruler* 独裁统治者 ◇ *a dictatorial regime* 独裁政权 **2** using power in an unreasonable way by telling people what to do and not listening to their views or wishes 发号施令的；专横的；盛气凌人的：*dictatorial behaviour* 专横的行为 ▸ **dic·ta·tori·al·ly** /-əli/ *adv.*

dic·ta·tor·ship /ˌdɪkˈteɪtəʃɪp; NAmE -tərʃ-/ *noun* **1** [C, U] government by a dictator 独裁；专政 ➲ COLLOCATIONS AT POLITICS **2** [C] a country that is ruled by a dictator 独裁国家 ➲ WORDFINDER NOTE AT SYSTEM

dic·tion /ˈdɪkʃn/ *noun* [U] **1** the way that sb pronounces words 吐字；发音方式：*clear diction* 清晰的吐字 **2** (*specialist*) the choice and use of words in literature 措辞；用语；用词

dic·tion·ary /ˈdɪkʃənri; NAmE -neri/ *noun* (*pl.* **-ies**) **1** a book that gives a list of the words of a language in alphabetical order and explains what they mean, or gives a word for them in a foreign language 词典；字典；辞书：*a Spanish-English dictionary* 西班牙语－英语词典

> **WORDFINDER** 联想词： alphabetical, definition, entry, example, headword, meaning, part of speech, **pronunciation**, register

2 a book that explains the words that are used in a particular subject 专业术语大全；专业词典：*a dictionary of mathematics* 数学词典 **3** a list of words in electronic form, for example stored in a computer's SPELLCHECKER 电子词典 ➲ **WORDFINDER NOTE** AT WORD

dic·tum /ˈdɪktəm/ *noun* (*pl.* **dicta** /-tə/ or **dic·tums**) (*formal*) a statement that expresses sth that people believe is always true or should be followed 名言；格言

did /dɪd/ ➲ DO¹ *v.*

di·dac·tic /daɪˈdæktɪk/ *adj.* (*formal*) **1** designed to teach people sth, especially a moral lesson 道德说教的；教诲的；教导的：*didactic art* 道德说教艺术 **2** (*usually disapproving*) telling people things rather than letting them find out for themselves 说教似的；好教训人的 ▸ **di·dac·tic·al·ly** /-kli/ *adv.*

did·dle /ˈdɪdl/ *verb* **~ sb (out of sth)** (*BrE, informal*) to get money or some advantage from sb by cheating them 欺骗；哄骗；骗取 **SYN** **cheat**

diddly /ˈdɪdli/ (*also* ˌ**diddly-ˈsquat**) *noun* (*NAmE, informal*) (used in negative sentences 用于否定句) not anything; nothing 一点也不；毫不；根本不：*She doesn't know diddly about it.* 她根本不知道这事儿。

did·dums /ˈdɪdəmz/ *exclamation, noun* (*BrE, informal*)
■ ***exclamation*** used for showing sympathy, especially in a way which is not sincere（表示同情，尤指不真心地）好啦，乖
■ ***noun*** used when addressing sb to show sympathy, especially when you are not being sincere（用作称呼以示同情，尤指不真心地）小可怜，小乖乖：*Is Diddums OK?* 小可怜没事了吧？

diddy /ˈdɪdi/ *adj.* (*BrE, informal*) very small 很小的；袖珍的：*a diddy little camera* 袖珍照相机

didg·eri·doo /ˌdɪdʒəriˈduː/ *noun* (*pl.* **-oos**) an Australian musical instrument consisting of a long wooden tube which you blow through to produce a variety of deep sounds 狄洁里都号角（澳大利亚土著用的低沉音木管乐器）

didi /ˈdiːdiː/ *noun* (*IndE*) **1** an older sister 姐姐：*Didi taught me how to read.* 姐姐教我读书。 **2** used after the name of an older female cousin of the same generation（用于堂、表姐名字后）姐 **3** used when speaking to an older female who is not related to you, as a title showing respect（尊称比自己年龄大的女子）姐：*Didi, could you help me with this bag?* 大姐，帮我抬一下这个袋子好吗？

didn't /ˈdɪdnt/ *short form* did not

die /daɪ/ *verb, noun*
■ ***verb*** (**dies**, **dying**, **died**, **died**) **1** [I, T] to stop living 死；死亡；凋谢：*Her husband died suddenly last week.* 她的丈夫上周猝死。◇ *That plant's died.* 那植物已经枯萎。◇ **~ of/from sth** *to die of/from cancer* 死于癌症 ◇ **~ for sth** *He died for his beliefs.* 他为自己的信仰献身。◇ *I'll never forget it to my **dying day*** (= until I die). 这件事我终生难忘。◇ (*informal*) ***I nearly died*** *when I saw him there* (= it was very embarrassing). 看到他在那里我简直无地自容。◇ **~ sth** *to die a violent/painful/natural, etc. death* 横死、痛苦地死去、尽其天年等 ◇ **+ adj.** *She died young.* 她年纪轻轻就死了。◇ *At least they died happy.* 至少他们死时很幸福。◇ **+ noun** *He died a poor man.* 他在贫困中死去。

> **WORDFINDER** 联想词： ashes, cemetery, coffin, cremation, funeral, grave, hearse, morgue, mourn

2 [I] to stop existing; to disappear 消失；消亡；灭亡：*The old customs are dying.* 旧的习俗正在消亡。◇ *His secret died with him* (= he never told anyone). 他的秘密随同他一起进了坟墓。◇ *The words died on my lips* (= I stopped speaking). 我话到嘴边又缩回去了。 **3** [I] (of a machine 机器) to stop working 停止运转：*The engine spluttered and died.* 发动机噼噼啪啪响了一阵后便熄火了。◇ *My car just **died on me**.* 我的汽车我怎么也发动不了。
IDM **be ˈdying for sth/to do sth** (*informal*) to want sth or want to do sth very much 渴望；极想：*I'm dying for a glass of water.* 我真想喝杯水。◇ *I'm dying to know what happened.* 我很想知道发生了什么事儿。 **die a/the ˈdeath** (*BrE, informal*) to fail completely 彻底失败；完全消失：*The play got terrible reviews and quickly died a death.* 这出戏被批得一无是处，很快就收场了。 **die in your ˈbed** to die because you are old or ill/sick 寿终正寝 **die ˈlaughing** to find sth extremely funny 可笑极了；笑死人：*I nearly died laughing when she said that.* 她说那话时，我差点儿给笑死。 **old ˌhabits, traˌditions, etc. die ˈhard** used to say that things change very slowly（旧习惯、传统等）难以改变，根深蒂固 **to ˈdie for** (*informal*) if you think sth is **to die for**, you really want it, and would do anything to get it 就是去死也要；不管怎么样都要：*She was wearing a dress to die for.* 她穿了一条漂亮得要命的连衣裙。 ➲ MORE AT CROSS *v.*, FLY *n.*, SAY *v.*
PHR V ˌ**die aˈway** to become gradually weaker or fainter and finally disappear 逐渐减弱；逐渐模糊；逐渐消失：*The sound of their laughter died away.* 他们的笑声渐渐消失了。 ˌ**die ˈback** if a plant **dies back**, it loses its leaves but remains alive（植物）叶凋而不死 ˌ**die ˈdown** to become gradually less strong, loud, noticeable, etc. 逐渐变弱；逐渐平息；逐渐暗淡：*The flames finally died down.* 火焰终于逐渐减弱了。◇ *When the applause had died down, she began her speech.* 掌声平息后她便开始演讲了。 ˌ**die ˈoff** to die one after the other until there are none left 相继死去；先后死去 ˌ**die ˈout** to stop existing 灭绝；消失：*This species has nearly died out because its habitat is being destroyed.* 因栖息地正受到破坏，这一物种已濒于灭绝。
■ ***noun*** **1** a block of metal with a special shape, or with a pattern cut into it, that is used for shaping other pieces of metal such as coins, or for making patterns on paper or leather 模具；冲模；压模 **2** (*especially NAmE*) = DICE
IDM **the die is cast** (*saying*) used to say that an event has happened or a decision has been made that cannot be changed 事已成定局；木已成舟

ˈdie-cast *adj.* (of a metal object 金属物品) made by pouring liquid metal into a MOULD and allowing it to cool 压铸成形的

die·hard /ˈdaɪhɑːd; NAmE -hɑːrd/ *adj.* strongly opposing change and new ideas 顽固的；因循守旧的；死硬的：*diehard supporters of the exiled king* 顽固支持流亡国王的人 ▸ **die·hard** *noun*：*A few diehards are trying to stop the reforms.* 几个顽固分子试图阻止改革。

die·sel /ˈdiːzl/ *noun* **1** (*also* ˈ**die·sel fuel**, ˈ**die·sel oil**) [U] a type of heavy oil used as a fuel instead of petrol/gas 柴油：*a **diesel engine*** (= one that burns diesel) 柴油机 ◇ ***diesel cars/locomotives/trains*** 柴油汽车 / 机车 / 火车 ➲ COMPARE PETROL **2** [C] a vehicle that uses diesel fuel 柴油车；内燃机车：*Our new car is a diesel.* 我们的新车是柴油车。

diet /ˈdaɪət/ *noun, verb*
■ ***noun*** **1** [C, U] the food that you eat and drink regularly 日常饮食；日常食物：*to have a **healthy, balanced diet*** 有健康和均衡的饮食 ◇ *the Japanese diet of rice, vegetables and fish* 米饭、蔬菜和鱼这些日本人常吃的食物 ◇ *to receive advice on diet* 接受饮食建议 ➲ **WORDFINDER NOTE** AT EAT **2** [C] a limited variety or amount of food that you eat for medical reasons or because you want to lose weight; a time when you only eat this limited variety or amount 规定饮食（为健康或减肥等目的）；规定饮食的时期：*a **low-fat, salt-free diet*** 低脂肪无盐的饮食 ◇ ***diet drinks*** (= with fewer CALORIES than normal) 低热量饮料 ◇ *I decided to **go on a diet*** (= to lose weight) *before my holiday.* 我决

定在休假前节食。➲ WORDFINDER NOTE AT FIT **3** [sing.] **a ~ of sth** (*disapproving*) a large amount of a restricted range of activities 大量单调的活动；大量单一的东西： *Children today are brought up on a diet of television cartoons and soap operas.* 如今的孩子是看电视上的动画片和肥皂剧长大的。▶ **diet·ary** /ˈdaɪətəri; *NAmE* -teri/ *adj.* [usually before noun]: *dietary advice/changes/habits* 饮食建议 / 变化 / 习惯 ◇ *dietary fibre* 膳食纤维

■ *verb* [I] to eat less food or only food of a particular type in order to lose weight 节食；进行规定饮食 SYN **be on a diet**: *She's always dieting but she never seems to lose any weight.* 她总是在节食，但体重好像并未减少。

diet·er /ˈdaɪətə(r)/ *noun* a person who is trying to lose weight on a diet 节食者；限制饮食的人

diet·et·ics /ˌdaɪəˈtetɪks/ *noun* [U] the scientific study of diet and healthy eating 饮食营养学 ▶ **diet·et·ic** *adj.*: *dietetic advice* 饮食建议

diet·itian (*also* **diet·ician**) /ˌdaɪəˈtɪʃn/ *noun* a person whose job is to advise people on what kind of food they should eat to keep healthy 饮食营养学家

dif·fer /ˈdɪfə(r)/ *verb* **1** [I] to be different from sb/sth 相异；有区别；不同于： *They hold differing views.* 他们持有不同的观点。◇ **A ~s from B** *French differs from English in this respect.* 在这方面法语不同于英语。◇ **A and B ~ (from each other)** *French and English differ in this respect.* 在这方面法语和英语不同。◇ **~ between A and B** *Ideas on childcare may differ considerably between the parents.* 在抚育子女方面父母的观点可能迥然不同。➲ LANGUAGE BANK AT CONTRAST **2** [I] to disagree with sb 意见相左；持不同看法；不同意： **~ (with sb) (about/on/over sth)** *I have to differ with you on that.* 在那一点上我不能同意你的看法。◇ **~ (as to sth)** *Medical opinion differs as to how to treat the disease.* 关于如何治疗这种疾病医学界有不同的看法。IDM SEE AGREE, BEG

dif·fer·ence /ˈdɪfrəns/ *noun* **1** [C, U] **~ (between A and B) | ~ (in sth)** the way in which two people or things are not like each other; the way in which sb/sth has changed 差别；差异；不同（之处）；变化（之处）： *There are no significant differences between the education systems of the two countries.* 这两国的教育制度没有大的差别。◇ *He was studying the complex similarities and differences between humans and animals.* 他在研究人和动物之间错综复杂的相似与不同之处。◇ *There's no difference in the results.* 结果没有差别。◇ *I can never* **tell the difference** (= distinguish) *between the twins.* 我从来都分不清这对双胞胎。◇ *She noticed a* **marked difference** *in the children on her second visit.* 她第二次来访时注意到孩子们发生了明显的变化。◇ *There's* **a world of difference** *between liking someone and loving them.* 喜欢一个人和爱一个人有天壤之别。◇ ***What a difference!*** *You look great with your hair like that.* 真是判若两人！你梳这种发型显得太好看了。OPP **similarity** ➲ LANGUAGE BANK AT CONTRAST **2** [sing., U] **~ (in sth) (between A and B)** the amount that sth is greater or smaller than sth else 差；差额： *There's not much difference in price between the two computers.* 这两种计算机价格上没有多大的差别。◇ *There's an age difference of six years between the boys* (= one is six years older than the other). 这两个男孩的年龄相差六岁。◇ *I'll lend you £500 and you'll have to find the difference* (= the rest of the money that you need). 我借给你 500 英镑，其余的你自己解决。◇ *We measured the difference in temperature.* 我们测量了温度的变化。 **3** [C] a disagreement between people 意见分歧；不和： *We* **have our differences***, but she's still my sister.* 我们之间虽然不和，但她仍旧是我的妹妹。◇ *Why don't you* **settle your differences** *and be friends again?* 你们为什么不消除隔阂，言归于好呢？◇ *There was* **a difference of opinion** *over who had won.* 在谁获胜的问题上发生了争执。

IDM **make a, no, some, etc. difference (to/in sb/sth)**

▼ COLLOCATIONS 词语搭配

Diet and exercise 节食和锻炼

Weight 体重

- **put on**/**gain**/**lose** weight/a few kilos/a few pounds 增加 / 减少体重 / 几公斤 / 几磅
- **watch**/**control**/**struggle with** your weight 关注 / 控制体重；努力减肥
- **be**/**become** seriously overweight/underweight 已经 / 变得严重超重 / 体重不足
- **be**/**become** clinically/morbidly obese 已经是 / 变成临床 / 病态肥胖
- **achieve**/**facilitate**/**promote**/**stimulate** weight loss 达到减轻体重的目的；促进减肥
- **slim down to** 70 kilos/(*BrE*) 11 stone/(*especially NAmE*) 160 pounds 减肥到 70 公斤 / 11 英石 / 160 磅
- **combat**/**prevent**/**tackle**/**treat** obesity 遏制 / 防止 / 解决 / 治疗肥胖
- **develop**/**have**/**suffer from**/**struggle with**/**recover from** anorexia/bulimia/an eating disorder 患上 / 对抗 / 治愈厌食症 / 贪食症 / 饮食失调症
- **be on**/**go on**/**follow** a crash/strict diet 采用快速减肥食谱；严格节食
- **have**/**suffer from** a negative/poor body image 有不好的身体形象
- **have**/**develop** a positive/healthy body image 具有 / 达到好的 / 健康的身体形象

Healthy eating 健康的饮食

- **eat** a balanced diet/healthily/sensibly 吃得均衡 / 健康 / 合理
- **get**/**provide**/**receive** adequate/proper nutrition 获得 / 提供 / 得到充足的 / 合适的营养
- **contain**/**get**/**provide** essential nutrients/vitamins/minerals 含有 / 得到 / 提供必需的营养素 / 维生素 / 矿物质
- **be high**/**low in** calories/fat/fibre/(*especially US*) fiber/protein/vitamin D/Omega-3 fatty acids 热量 / 脂肪 / 纤维素 / 蛋白质 / 维生素 D / 欧米加 3 脂肪酸含量高 / 低
- **contain** (**no**)/**use**/**be full of**/**be free from** additives/chemical preservatives/artificial sweeteners （不）含 / 使用 / 含有大量 / 不含添加剂 / 化学防腐剂 / 人工甜味剂
- **avoid**/**cut down on**/**cut out** alcohol/caffeine/fatty foods 避免摄取 / 减少 / 戒酒 / 咖啡因 / 高脂食物
- **stop**/**give up**/(*especially NAmE*) **quit** smoking 戒烟

Exercise 锻炼

- (*BrE*) **take** regular exercise 经常锻炼
- **do** moderate/strenuous/vigorous exercise 做适度 / 剧烈运动
- **play** football/hockey/tennis 玩足球 / 曲棍球 / 网球
- **go** cycling/jogging/running 骑自行车；慢跑；跑步
- **go to**/**visit**/(*especially NAmE*) **hit**/**work out at** the gym 去健身房锻炼
- **strengthen**/**tone**/**train** your stomach muscles 增强 / 锻炼腹肌
- **contract**/**relax**/**stretch**/**use**/**work** your lower-body muscles 收缩 / 放松 / 伸展 / 使用 / 锻炼下肢的肌肉
- **build** (**up**)/**gain** muscle 增强肌肉
- **improve**/**increase** your stamina/energy levels/physical fitness 增强耐力 / 体能 / 体质
- **burn**/**consume**/**expend** calories 消耗热量

Staying healthy 保持健康

- **be**/**get**/**keep**/**stay** healthy/in shape/(*especially BrE*) fit 身体健康；变得 / 保持健康
- **lower** your cholesterol/blood pressure 降低胆固醇 / 血压
- **boost**/**stimulate**/**strengthen** your immune system 增强免疫力
- **prevent**/**reduce the risk of** heart disease/high blood pressure/diabetes/osteoporosis 预防 / 减少患心脏病 / 高血压 / 糖尿病 / 骨质疏松的风险
- **reduce**/**relieve**/**manage**/**combat** stress 缓解 / 控制压力
- **enhance**/**promote** relaxation/physical and mental well-being 有助于身体放松 / 身心健康

to have an effect/no effect on sb/sth 有（或没有、有些等）作用，关系，影响：*The rain didn't make much difference to the game.* 这场雨对比赛没多大影响。◇ *Your age shouldn't make any difference to whether you get the job or not.* 你能否得到这工作应该与你的年龄无关。◇ *Changing schools made a **big difference** to my life.* 转学对我的一生有着重大影响。◇ *What difference will it make if he knows or not?* 他知不知道有什么关系吗？◇ *I don't think it makes **a lot of difference** what colour it is* (= it is not important). 我认为颜色无关紧要。◇ *'Shall we go on Friday or Saturday?' 'It makes no difference (to me).'* "我们星期五还是星期六去？" "（我）无所谓。" **make all the 'difference (to sb/sth)** to have an important effect on sb/sth; to make sb feel better 关系重大；大不相同；使更好受：*A few kind words at the right time make all the difference.* 在适当的时候说几句体贴话效果迥然不同。 **same 'difference** (*informal*) used to say that you think the differences between two things are not important 差不多一样：*'That's not a xylophone, it's a glockenspiel.' 'Same difference.'* "那不是木琴而是钟琴。" "反正都差不多。" **with a 'difference** (*informal*) (after nouns 用于名词后) used to show that sth is interesting or unusual 引人注目；与众不同：*The traditional backpack with a difference—it's waterproof.* 这个传统背包有个与众不同的特点，它能防水。 ➲ MORE AT BURY, SINK *v.*, SPLIT *v.*, WORLD

dif·fer·ent 🔑 /ˈdɪfrənt/ *adj.* **1** 🔑 ~ (**from/to/than sb/sth**) not the same as sb/sth; not like sb/sth else 不同的；有区别的；有差异的：*American English is significantly different from British English.* 美式英语与英式英语有很大差异。◇ (*BrE*) *It's very different to what I'm used to.* 这与我所习惯的大不相同。◇ (*NAmE*) *He saw he was no different than anybody else.* 他认为他与其他人没什么两样。◇ *It's different now than it was a year ago.* 现在同一年前不一样了。◇ *People often give very different accounts of the same event.* 人们对同一件事的叙述常常大为不同。◇ *My son's terribly untidy; my daughter's **no different**.* 我儿子邋遢极了，女儿也不比他强。 OPP **similar** **2** 🔑 [only before noun] separate and individual 分别的；各别的；各种的：*She offered us five different kinds of cake.* 她给我们提供了五种不同的蛋糕。◇ *The programme was about customs in different parts of the country.* 这个节目介绍全国各地的风俗习惯。◇ *They are sold in many different colours.* 这些有多种颜色供选购。◇ *I looked it up in three different dictionaries.* 我分别在三本词典里查找过。 **3** [not usually before noun] (*informal*) unusual; not like other people or things 不平常；与众不同；别致：*'Did you enjoy the play?' 'Well, it was certainly different!'* "你喜欢这出戏吗？" "哦，的确不同凡响！" ➲ MORE LIKE THIS 23, page R27 ▶ **dif·fer·ent·ly** 🔑 *adv.*：*Boys and girls may behave differently.* 男孩儿和女孩儿的表现可能不同。◇ *The male bird has a differently shaped head.* 雄鸟的头形有点特别。

IDM **a different kettle of fish** (*informal*) a completely different situation or person from the one previously mentioned 另一码事；截然不同的人 ➲ MORE AT COMPLEXION, KNOW *v.*, MARCH *v.*, MATTER *n.*, PULL *v.*, SING, TELL

▼ **BRITISH/AMERICAN 英式 / 美式英语**

different from / to / than

- **Different from** is the most common structure in both *BrE* and *NAmE*. **Different to** is also used in *BrE*.
  * different from 在英式英语和美式英语中均为最常用的结构。different to 亦用于英式英语：*Paul's very different from/to his brother.* 保罗与他的哥哥大不一样。◇ *This visit is very different from/to last time.* 这次访问与上一次的大不相同。
- In *NAmE* people also say **different than**. 美式英语亦有 different than 的说法：*Your trains are different than ours.* 你们的火车与我们的不一样。◇ *You look different than before.* 你看上去与从前不一样了。
- Before a clause you can also use **different from** (and **different than** in *NAmE*). 从句前亦可用 different from（美式英语用 different than）：*She looked different from what I'd expected.* ◇ *She looked different than (what) I'd expected.* 她看上去与我想象的不一样。

dif·fer·en·tial /ˌdɪfəˈrenʃl/ *noun, adj.*

■ ***noun*** **1** ~ (**between A and B**) a difference in the amount, value or size of sth, especially the difference in rates of pay for people doing different work in the same industry or profession 差别；差额；差价；（尤指同行业不同工种的）工资级差：***wage/pay/income differentials*** 工资 / 收入差异 **2** (*also* **ˌdifferential ˈgear**) a gear that makes it possible for a vehicle's back wheels to turn at different speeds when going around corners（汽车）差速器

■ ***adj.*** [only before noun] (*formal*) showing or depending on a difference; not equal 差别的；以差别而定的；有区别的：*the differential treatment of prisoners based on sex and social class* 按性别和社会阶层区别对待犯人 ◇ *differential rates of pay* 工资级差

ˌdifferential ˈcalculus *noun* [U] (*mathematics* 数) a type of mathematics that deals with quantities that change in time. It is used to calculate a quantity at a particular moment 微分学 ➲ COMPARE INTEGRAL CALCULUS

diffeˌrential eˈquation *noun* (*mathematics* 数) an EQUATION that involves FUNCTIONS (= quantities that can vary) and their rates of change 微分方程

dif·fer·en·ti·ate AW /ˌdɪfəˈrenʃieɪt/ *verb* **1** [I, T] to recognize or show that two things are not the same 区分；区别；辨别 SYN **distinguish**： ~ (**between**) **A and B** *It's difficult to differentiate between the two varieties.* 这两个品种很难辨别。◇ ~ **A** (**from B**) *I can't differentiate one variety from another.* 我无法将这几个品种区别开来。 **2** [T] ~ **sth** (**from sth**) to be the particular thing that shows that things or people are not the same 表明…间的差别；构成…间差别的特征 SYN **distinguish**： *The male's yellow beak differentiates it from the female.* 雄鸟黄色的喙是与雌鸟相区别的主要特征。 **3** [I] ~ **between A and B** to treat people or things in a different way, especially in an unfair way（尤指不公正地）差别对待，区别对待 SYN **discriminate** ▶ **dif·fer·en·ti·ation** AW /ˌdɪfəˌrenʃiˈeɪʃn/ *noun* [U]

dif·fi·cult 🔑 /ˈdɪfɪkəlt/ *adj.* **1** 🔑 ~ (**for sb**) (**to do sth**) not easy; needing effort or skill to do or to understand 困难的；费力的；难做的；难解的：*a difficult problem/task/exam* 难题；艰巨的任务；很难的考试 ◇ ***It's difficult** for them to get here much before seven.* 他们很难在七点以前早早地来到这里。◇ *It's really difficult to read your writing.* 你的笔迹真是难以辨认。◇ *Your writing is really difficult to read.* 你的笔迹真是难以辨认。◇ *She **finds it** very **difficult** to get up early.* 她觉得很难早起。 ➲ SYNONYMS ON NEXT PAGE **2** 🔑 full of problems; causing a lot of trouble 问题很多的；充满艰难困苦的；麻烦的：*to be in a **difficult position/situation*** 处于困境 ◇ *My boss is **making life** very **difficult for me**.* 我的老板总是给我找麻烦。◇ *13 is a difficult age.* * 13 岁是个容易出问题的年龄。 **3** 🔑 (of people 人) not easy to please; not helpful 难以讨好的；难以取悦的；不愿帮助的 SYN **awkward**： *a difficult child/customer/boss* 难哄的孩子；难对付的顾客；难讨好的老板 ◇ *Don't pay any attention to her—she's just being difficult.* 别理她，她不过是在故意刁难。 IDM SEE JOB, LIFE

dif·fi·culty 🔑 /ˈdɪfɪkəlti/ *noun* (*pl.* **-ies**) **1** 🔑 [C, usually pl., U] a problem; a thing or situation that causes problems 困难；难题；难事；困境：*the difficulties of English syntax* 英语句法的难点 ◇ *children with severe learning difficulties* 学习上有严重困难的孩子 ◇ *We've **run into difficulties/difficulty** with the new project.* 我们在这项新工程中遇到了难题。◇ *He **got into difficulties** while swimming and had to be rescued.* 他游泳时遇险，只好靠人营救。◇ *The bank is **in difficulty/difficulties**.* 这家银行处境困难。◇ *It was a time fraught with difficulties and frustration.* 这是一个充满困难和挫折的时期。 **2** 🔑 [U] the state or quality of being hard to do or to understand; the effort that sth involves 艰难；困难；费劲；辛苦：*I had considerable difficulty (in) persuading her to leave.* 我费了好大的劲说服她离开。◇ *I had no difficulty (in) making myself understood.* 我毫不费力地表达了自己的意思。◇ *The changes were made with*

D

▼ SYNONYMS 同义词辨析

difficult

hard • challenging • demanding • taxing

These words all describe sth that is not easy and requires a lot of effort or skill to do. 以上各词均形容事情困难、费力、难做。

difficult not easy; needing effort or skill to do or understand 指困难的、费力的、难做的、难懂的： *The exam questions were quite difficult.* 考题相当难。◇ *It is difficult for young people to find jobs around here.* 年轻人要在附近找到工作很难。

hard not easy; needing effort or skill to do or understand 指困难的、费力的、难做的、难懂的： *I always found languages quite hard at school.* 在学校读书时我总觉得语言很难学。◇ *It was one of the hardest things I ever did.* 这是我做过的最难的事情之一。

DIFFICULT OR HARD? 用 difficult 还是 hard?

Hard is slightly less formal than **difficult**. It is used particularly in the structure *hard to believe/say/find/take, etc.*, although **difficult** can also be used in any of these examples. * hard 较 difficult 稍非正式，主要用于 hard to believe/say/find/take 等结构中，不过 difficult 亦可用于上述结构。

challenging (*approving*) difficult in an interesting way that tests your ability 指困难而有意思的、有挑战性的、考验能力的

demanding difficult to do or deal with and needing a lot of effort, skill or patience 指要求高的、需要高技能或耐性的、费力的： *It is a technically demanding piece of music to play.* 演奏这一段音乐需要有很高的技艺。

taxing (often used in negative statements) difficult to do and needing a lot of mental or physical effort （常用于否定句）指繁重的、费力的、伤脑筋的： *This shouldn't be too taxing for you.* 这对你来说不至于太费劲。

PATTERNS

- difficult/hard/challenging/demanding/taxing **for** sb
- difficult/hard **to do sth**
- **physically** difficult/hard/challenging/demanding/taxing
- **technically** difficult/challenging/demanding
- **mentally/intellectually** challenging/demanding/taxing

surprisingly little difficulty. 这些变化几乎没有遇到阻力，简直不可思议。◇ *He spoke slowly and with great difficulty.* 他话说得很慢，而且很吃力。◇ *We found the house **without difficulty**.* 我们轻而易举就找到了这栋房子。◇ *They discussed the difficulty of studying abroad.* 他们讨论了到国外学习的困难。HELP You cannot say 'have difficulty to do sth'. 不能说 have difficulty to do sth: ~~*I had difficulty to persuade her to leave.*~~ **3** [U] how hard sth is 困难程度；难度: *varying levels of difficulty* 不同的难度 ◇ *questions of increasing difficulty* 难度不断增加的问题

dif·fi·dent /ˈdɪfɪdənt/ *adj.* ~ (**about sth**) not having much confidence in yourself; not wanting to talk about yourself 缺乏自信的；胆怯的；羞怯的 SYN **shy**: *a **diffident** manner/smile* 畏首畏尾的态度；羞怯的一笑 ◇ *He was modest and diffident about his own success.* 他很谦虚，不愿谈及自己的成功。▶ **dif·fi·dence** /-dəns/ *noun* [U]: *She overcame her natural diffidence and spoke with great frankness.* 她克服了胆怯的毛病，非常坦率地说出了自己的想法。**dif·fi·dent·ly** *adv.*

dif·fract /dɪˈfrækt/ *verb* ~ **sth** (*physics* 物) to break up a stream of light into a series of dark and light bands or into the different colours of the SPECTRUM（使光束）衍射 ▶ **dif·frac·tion** /dɪˈfrækʃn/ *noun* [U]

dif·fuse *adj.*, *verb*

■ ***adj.*** /dɪˈfjuːs/ **1** spread over a wide area 弥漫的；扩散的；漫射的: *diffuse light* 漫射光 ◇ *a diffuse community* 居住分散的社群 **2** not clear or easy to understand, using a lot of words 不清楚的；难解的；冗长的；啰嗦的: *a diffuse style of writing* 冗赘的文体 ▶ **dif·fuse·ly** *adv.* **dif·fuse·ness** *noun* [U]

■ ***verb*** /dɪˈfjuːz/ **1** [T, I] ~ (**sth**) (*formal*) to spread sth or become spread widely in all directions 传播；普及；使分散；散布: *The problem is how to diffuse power without creating anarchy.* 问题在于如何将权力分散而不造成无政府状态。◇ *Technologies diffuse rapidly.* 技术普及非常快。**2** [I, T] ~ (**sth**) (*specialist*) if a gas or liquid **diffuses** or **is diffused** in a substance, it becomes slowly mixed with that substance（使气体或液体）扩散，弥漫，渗透 **3** [T] ~ **sth** (*formal*) to make light shine less brightly by spreading it in many directions（使光）模糊，漫射，漫散: *The moon was fuller than the night before, but the light was diffused by cloud.* 月亮比头一天晚上更圆，但因云层遮掩而月光朦胧。▶ **dif·fu·sion** /dɪˈfjuːʒn/ *noun* [U]

dif·fu·ser /dɪˈfjuːzə(r)/ *noun* **1** a device used in photography to avoid dark shadows or areas which are too bright（摄影用的）漫射体，柔光镜 **2** a part that is attached to a HAIRDRYER to spread the hot air around the head and dry the hair more gently（吹风机的）散风嘴

dig /dɪɡ/ *verb*, *noun*

■ ***verb*** (**dig·ging**, **dug**, **dug** /dʌɡ/) **1** [I, T] to make a hole in the ground or to move soil from one place to another using your hands, a tool or a machine 掘（地）；凿（洞）；挖（土）: ~ (**for sth**) *to dig for coal/gold/Roman remains* 挖煤；采掘黄金；掘地探寻古罗马遗迹 ◇ *They dug deeper and deeper but still found nothing.* 他们越挖越深却仍然一无所获。◇ *I think I'll **do some digging** in the garden.* 我想我该给花园松松土了。◇ ~ **sth** *to dig a ditch/grave/hole/tunnel* 挖沟；挖坟；挖洞；挖隧道 ◇ (*BrE*) *I've been digging the garden.* 我一直在花园松土。**2** [T] ~ **sth** to remove sth from the ground with a tool 掘得；（采）掘出: *I'll dig some potatoes for lunch.* 我要挖点土豆做午餐。**3** [I] (+ **adv./prep.**) to search in sth in order to find an object in sth 寻找，搜寻（物品）: *I dug around in my bag for a pen.* 我在包里到处翻找笔。**4** [T] ~ **sth** (*old-fashioned, slang*) to approve of or like sth very much 赞成；看中；喜欢

IDM **dig 'deep (into sth)** **1** to search thoroughly for information 探究；搜集；细查: *You'll need to dig deep into the records to find the figures you want.* 你必须仔细查阅档案才能找到你需要的数字。**2** to try hard to provide the money, equipment, etc. that is needed 尽力提供（所需金钱、设备等）: *We're asking you to dig deep for the earthquake victims.* 我们请求你们尽力为地震灾民提供财物。**dig your 'heels/'toes in** to refuse to do sth or to change your mind about sth 拒不让步；固执己见: *They dug in their heels and would not lower the price.* 他们说什么也不肯降价。**dig (deep) in/into your pocket(s), savings, etc.** to spend a lot of your own money on sth 慷慨解囊；花费；掏腰包 **dig sb in the 'ribs** to push your finger or your elbow into sb's side, especially to attract their attention（尤指为引起注意用手指或胳膊肘）捅某人一下 **dig yourself into a 'hole** to get yourself into a bad situation that will be very difficult to get out of 使自己陷入困境；使自己处境尴尬 **dig your own 'grave** | **dig a 'grave for yourself** to do sth that will have very harmful results for you 自掘坟墓；自取灭亡；自己害自己

PHR V **,dig 'in** (*informal*) **1** used to tell sb to start to eat 开始吃吧: *Help yourselves, everybody! Dig in!* 请大家随意，开始吃吧！**2** to wait, or deal with a difficult situation, with great patience 耐心等待；忍耐；忍受: *There is nothing we can do except dig in and wait.* 我们除了耐心等待别无他法。**,dig sth↔'in** **1** to mix soil with another substance by digging the two substances together（把…）掺进土中，混入土壤: *The manure should be well dug in.* 肥料应均匀地混入土壤。**2** to push sth into sth else（把…）戳进，插入: *He dug his fork into the steak.* 他把餐叉叉进牛排。**,dig yourself 'in** (of soldiers 士兵) to protect yourself against an attack by making a safe place in the ground 掘壕防守；挖掩体隐蔽 **,dig 'into sth** **1** (*informal*) to start to eat food with enthusiasm 开始津津有味地吃；开始贪婪地吃: *She dug into her bowl of*

pasta. 她津津有味地吃着碗里的面条。 **2** to push or rub against your body in a painful or uncomfortable way 挤痛，磨痛，碰痛（身体部位）: *His fingers dug painfully into my arm.* 他的手指把我的手臂给抓痛了。 **3** to find out information by searching or asking questions 探究；探寻；探询: *Will you dig a little into his past and see what you find?* 你稍微探究一下他的过去看看能发现什么，好吗？
ˌdig sth ˈinto sth **1** to mix soil with another substance by digging the two substances together（把…）掺进土中，混入土壤 **2** to push or press sth into sth else（把…）戳进，插入，压入: *She dug her hands deeper into her pockets.* 她把两手深深地插进衣服口袋里。 **ˌdig sb/sth↔ ˈout (of sth)** **1** to remove sb/sth from somewhere by digging the ground around them or it 挖掘出: *More than a dozen people were dug out of the avalanche alive.* 十多个埋在雪崩下的人被挖了出来，仍然活着。 **2** to find sth that has been hidden or forgotten for a long time 找出，发掘，发现（藏着的或被遗忘的东西）: *I went to the attic and dug out Grandad's medals.* 我到阁楼里找到了祖父的勋章。 **ˌdig sth↔ˈover** to prepare ground by digging the soil to remove stones, etc. 翻（地）；翻挖；刨（地） **ˌdig sth↔ˈup** **1** to break the ground into small pieces before planting seeds, building sth, etc.（在播种或建筑等前）掘地，平整土地: *They are digging up the football field to lay a new surface.* 他们正在把足球场挖开铺一层新地面。 **2** to remove sth from the ground by digging 掘起；挖掘出: *An old Roman vase was dug up here last month.* 上个月在此地出土了一个古罗马花瓶。 **3** to discover information about sb/sth 发现；搜集；查明 SYN **unearth**: *Tabloid newspapers love to dig up scandal.* 通俗小报都热衷于挖丑闻。
■ ***noun*** ➲ SEE ALSO DIGS **1** a small push with your finger or elbow（用手指或肘部）轻碰，轻戳，轻推: *She gave him **a dig in the ribs**.* 她轻轻地戳了一下他的肋部。 **2** ~ **(at sb/sth)** a remark that is intended to annoy or upset sb 挖苦；嘲讽: *He kept making sly little digs at me.* 他总是拐弯抹角地挖苦我。◇ ***to have a dig at sb/sth*** 嘲讽某人 / 某事 **3** an occasion when an organized group of people dig in the ground to discover old buildings or objects, in order to find out more about their history 考古发掘 SYN **excavation**: *to go on a dig* 进行考古发掘 ◇ *an archaeological dig* 一次考古发掘

the dig·er·ati /ˌdɪdʒəˈrɑːti/ *noun* [pl.] (*humorous*) people who are very good at using computers or who use computers a lot 电脑高手；电脑专家 ➲ COMPARE LITERATI

di·gest *verb, noun*
■ ***verb*** /daɪˈdʒest; dɪ-/ **1** [T, I] ~ (sth) when you **digest** food, or it **digests**, it is changed into substances that your body can use 消化: *Humans cannot digest plants such as grass.* 人不能消化草类植物。◇ *You should allow a little time after a meal for the food to digest.* 饭后你应该留点时间让食物消化。 ➲ WORDFINDER NOTE AT EAT **2** [T] ~ **sth** to think about sth so that you fully understand it 领会；领悟；理解: *He paused, waiting for her to digest the information.* 他停了一会儿，等她慢慢领会这一信息。
■ ***noun*** /ˈdaɪdʒest/ a short report containing the most important facts of a longer report or piece of writing; a collection of short reports 摘要；概要；文摘；汇编: *a monthly news digest* 每月新闻摘要

di·gest·ible /daɪˈdʒestəbl; dɪ-/ *adj.* easy to digest; pleasant to eat or easy to understand 易消化的；口感好的；易理解的；可领会的 OPP **indigestible**

di·ges·tion /daɪˈdʒestʃən; dɪ-/ *noun* **1** [U] the process of digesting food 消化 ➲ COMPARE INDIGESTION **2** [C, usually sing.] the ability to digest food 消化能力: *to have a **good/poor digestion*** 消化能力强 / 弱

di·gest·ive /daɪˈdʒestɪv; dɪ-/ *adj.* [only before noun] connected with the digestion of food 消化的；和消化有关的: *the **digestive system/tract*** 消化系统；消化道 ◇ *digestive problems* 消化问题

diˈgestive biscuit (*also* **digestive**) *noun* (*BrE*) a round sweet biscuit made from WHOLEMEAL flour, sometimes covered with chocolate 消化饼干；全麦饼干: *a packet of chocolate digestives* 一包巧克力全麦饼干

diˈgestive system *noun* the series of organs inside the body that digest food 消化系统

dig·ger /ˈdɪɡə(r)/ *noun* **1** a large machine that is used for digging up the ground 挖掘机 **2** a person or an animal that digs 挖掘者；有挖掘习性的动物 ➲ SEE ALSO GOLD-DIGGER **3** (*AustralE, NZE, old-fashioned, informal*) a man 男人；家伙；老兄

digit /ˈdɪdʒɪt/ *noun* **1** any of the numbers from 0 to 9（从 0 到 9 的任何一个）数字，数位: *The number 57306 contains five digits.* 数字 57 306 是个五位数。◇ *a four-digit number* 四位数 **2** (*anatomy* 解) a finger, thumb or toe 手指；拇指；脚趾

digit·al /ˈdɪdʒɪtl/ *adj., noun*
■ ***adj.*** **1** using a system of receiving and sending information as a series of the numbers one and zero, showing that an electronic signal is there or is not there 数字信息系统的；数码的；数字式的；数位的: *a digital camera* 数码相机 ◇ *digital terrestrial and digital satellite broadcasting* 数字陆上广播和数字卫星广播 ◇ ***born digital*** (= not converted from print or ANALOGUE form) 原生数字化的 **2** (of clocks, watches, etc. 钟表等) showing information by using figures, rather than with HANDS that point to numbers 数字显示的: *a **digital clock/watch*** 数字钟；数字表 ➲ PICTURE AT CLOCK ➲ COMPARE ANALOGUE *adj.* ▶ **digit·al·ly** /-təli/ *adv.*: *digitally remastered audio* 以数字方式转录的音频
■ ***noun*** [U] digital television 数字电视: *How long have you had digital?* 你们有数字电视多长时间了？ ◇ *With digital you can choose the camera angle you want.* 有了数字电视你就可以选择你想要的摄像角度。

ˌdigital ˈimmigrant *noun* a person who was born or grew up before the use of digital technology became common 数字移民，数码移民（在数字技术普及之前出生或长大的人） ➲ SEE ALSO DIGITAL NATIVE

digi·talis /ˌdɪdʒɪˈteɪlɪs; *NAmE also* -ˈtælɪs/ *noun* [U] (*medical* 医) a drug made from the FOXGLOVE plant, that helps the heart muscle to work 洋地黄（一种强心剂）

digit·al·ize (*BrE also* **-ise**) /ˈdɪdʒɪtəlaɪz/ *verb* = DIGITIZE ▶ **digit·al·iza·tion, -isa·tion** /ˌdɪdʒɪtəlaɪˈzeɪʃn; *NAmE* -ləˈz-/ *noun* [U] = DIGITIZATION

ˌdigital ˈnative *noun* a person who was born or has grown up since the use of digital technology became common and so is familiar and comfortable with computers and the Internet 数字原生代，数码原住民（在数字技术普及之后出生或长大的人，对计算机和互联网十分熟悉且应付自如） ➲ SEE ALSO DIGITAL IMMIGRANT

ˌdigital ˈpublishing *noun* [U] the business of publishing materials that are distributed online 数字出版: *Digital publishing challenges traditional concepts of books.* 数字出版对于传统的图书观念带来冲击。

ˌdigital reˈcording *noun* [C, U] a recording in which sounds or pictures are represented by a series of numbers showing that an electronic signal is there or is not there; the process of making a recording in this way 数字录制品；数字录制

ˌdigital ˈsignature *noun* (*computing* 计) a code that is added to an electronic file that proves that it was created by a particular person and that it has not been changed 数字签名

ˌdigital ˈtelevision *noun* **1** [U] the system of broadcasting television using digital signals 数字电视（系统） **2** [C] a television set that can receive digital signals 数字电视机

digit·ize (*BrE also* **-ise**) /ˈdɪdʒɪtaɪz/ (*also* **digit·al·ize** /ˈdɪdʒɪtəlaɪz/) *verb* ~ **sth** to change data into a digital form that can be easily read and processed by a computer（使数据）数字化: *a digitized map* 一张数字化地图 ▶ **digit·iza·tion, -isa·tion** /ˌdɪdʒɪtaɪˈzeɪʃn; *NAmE* -təˈz-/

(*also* **digit·al·iza·tion**, **-isa·tion** /ˌdɪdʒɪtəlaɪˈzeɪʃn; *NAmE* -ləˈz-/) *noun* [U]

di·glos·sia /daɪˈɡlɒsiə; *NAmE* -ˈɡlɔːs-; -ˈɡlɑːs-/ *noun* [U] (*linguistics* 语言) a situation in which two languages or two forms of a language are used under different conditions in a community 双语现象，双重语体（两种语言或一种语言的两种变体并存于一个语言集体中）▶ **di·glos·sic** *adj.*

D

dig·ni·fied /ˈdɪɡnɪfaɪd/ *adj.* calm and serious and deserving respect 庄重的；庄严的；有尊严的：*a dignified person/manner/voice* 有尊严的人；庄重的举止；庄严的声音 ◇ *Throughout his trial he maintained a dignified silence.* 在整个审讯过程中，他始终沉默以保持尊严。 OPP **undignified**

dig·nify /ˈdɪɡnɪfaɪ/ *verb* (**dig·ni·fies**, **dig·ni·fy·ing**, **dig·ni·fied**) (*formal*) **1** ~ **sb/sth** to make sb/sth seem impressive 使有尊严；使崇高；使显贵；使增辉：*The mayor was there to dignify the celebrations.* 市长的光临为庆祝活动增辉。 **2** ~ **sth** to make sth appear important when it is not really 使显得堂皇；抬高…的身价；美化：*I'm not going to dignify his comments by reacting to them.* 我才不会理睬他的评论以抬高其身价呢。

dig·ni·tary /ˈdɪɡnɪtəri; *NAmE* -teri/ *noun* (*pl.* **-ies**) a person who has an important official position 显贵；要人；达官贵人 SYN **VIP**

dig·nity /ˈdɪɡnəti/ *noun* [U] **1** a calm and serious manner that deserves respect 庄重；庄严；尊严：*She accepted the criticism with quiet dignity.* 她大度地接受了批评。 **2** the fact of being given honour and respect by people 尊贵；高贵；高尚：*the dignity of work* 工作的光荣 ◇ *The terminally ill should be allowed to die with dignity.* 应该允许垂危病人死得有尊严。 **3** a sense of your own importance and value 自豪；自尊；自重：*It's difficult to preserve your dignity when you have no job and no home.* 一个无家无业的人难以保持自己的尊严。

IDM **beˌneath your ˈdignity** below what you see as your own importance or worth 有失尊严；有失身份；有失体面 **ˌstand on your ˈdignity** (*formal*) to demand to be treated with the respect that you think that you deserve 要求受到应有的礼遇；保持尊严

di·graph /ˈdaɪɡrɑːf; *NAmE* -ɡræf/ *noun* a combination of two letters representing one sound, for example 'ph' and 'sh' in English 合成符（两个相连字母表达单个音素）

di·gress /daɪˈɡres/ *verb* [I] (*formal*) to start to talk about sth that is not connected with the main point of what you are saying 离题；偏离主题 ▶ **di·gres·sion** /daɪˈɡreʃn/ *noun* [C, U]: *After several digressions, he finally got to the point.* 说了几句题外话后，他终于言归正传。

digs /dɪɡz/ *noun* [pl.] (*old-fashioned, informal*) a room or rooms that you rent to live in 租住的住所；住处 SYN **lodgings**

dike *noun* = DYKE

dik·tat /ˈdɪktæt; *NAmE* dɪkˈtæt/ *noun* [C, U] (*disapproving*) an order given by a government, for example, that people must obey 强制执行的命令；勒令：*an EU diktat from Brussels* 来自布鲁塞尔欧盟总部的命令 ◇ *government by diktat* 用专制手段统治

di·lapi·dated /dɪˈlæpɪdeɪtɪd/ *adj.* (of furniture and buildings 家具和建筑物) old and in very bad condition 破旧的；破烂的；年久失修的 SYN **ramshackle** ▶ **di·lapi·da·tion** /dɪˌlæpɪˈdeɪʃn/ *noun* [U]: *in a state of dilapidation* 处于破旧状态

dila·ta·tion /ˌdaɪləˈteɪʃn; ˌdɪlə-; *BrE also* ˌdaɪleɪ-/ *noun* [U] (*medical* 医) the process of becoming wider (= of becoming dilated), or the action of making sth become wider 扩张；扩大；膨胀

di·late /daɪˈleɪt/ *verb* [I, T] to become or to make sth larger, wider or more open 扩大；（使）膨胀，扩张：*Her eyes dilated with fear.* 她吓得瞪大了眼睛。 ◇ ~ **sth** *dilated pupils/nostrils* 扩大了的瞳孔；张大了的鼻孔 ◇ *Red wine can help to dilate blood vessels.* 红葡萄酒有助于扩张血管。 OPP **contract** ▶ **dila·tion** /daɪˈleɪʃn/ *noun* [U, C]

dila·tory /ˈdɪlətəri; *NAmE* -tɔːri/ *adj.* ~ (**in doing sth**) (*formal*) not acting quickly enough; causing delay 拖拉的；拖延的；延误的：*The government has been dilatory in dealing with the problem of unemployment.* 政府迟迟未解决失业问题。

dildo /ˈdɪldəʊ; *NAmE* -doʊ/ *noun* (*pl.* **dildos** *or* **dildoes**) an object shaped like a PENIS that is used for sexual pleasure 人造阴茎；假阳具；女子性快乐器

di·lemma /dɪˈlemə; daɪ-/ *noun* a situation which makes problems, often one in which you have to make a very difficult choice between things of equal importance （进退两难的）窘境，困境 SYN **predicament**: *to face a dilemma* 面临左右为难的困境 ◇ *to be in a dilemma* 处于进退两难的境地 IDM SEE HORN *n.*

dil·et·tante /ˌdɪləˈtænti/ *noun* (*pl.* **dil·et·tanti** /-tiː/ *or* **dil·et·tan·tes**) (*disapproving*) a person who does or studies sth but is not serious about it and does not have much knowledge 浅薄的涉猎者；浅尝辄止者；半吊子；半瓶醋 ▶ **dil·let·tante** *adj.*: *a dilettante artist* 粗通艺术的人

dili·gence /ˈdɪlɪdʒəns/ *noun* [U] (*formal*) careful and thorough work or effort 勤勉；勤奋；用功：*She shows great diligence in her schoolwork.* 她上学非常用功。

dili·gent /ˈdɪlɪdʒənt/ *adj.* (*formal*) showing care and effort in your work or duties 孜孜不倦的；勤勉的；刻苦的：*a diligent student/worker* 勤奋的学生 / 工人 ▶ **dili·gent·ly** *adv.*

dill /dɪl/ *noun* [U] a plant with yellow flowers whose leaves and seeds have a strong taste and are used in cooking as a HERB. Dill is often added to vegetables kept in VINEGAR. 莳萝，土茴香（味冲，用作佐料）：*dill pickles* 加了土茴香的泡菜 ➲ VISUAL VOCAB PAGE V35

dilly-dally /ˈdɪli dæli/ *verb* (**dilly-dallies**, **dilly-dallying**, **dilly-dallied**, **dilly-dallied**) [I] (*old-fashioned, informal*) to take too long to do sth, go somewhere or make a decision 磨蹭；犹豫 SYN **dawdle** ➲ MORE LIKE THIS 11, page R26

di·lute /daɪˈluːt; *BrE also* -ˈljuːt/ *verb, adj.*

■ ***verb*** **1** ~ **sth** (**with sth**) to make a liquid weaker by adding water or another liquid to it 稀释；冲淡 SYN **water down**: *The paint can be diluted with water to make a lighter shade.* 这颜料可用水稀释以使色度淡一些。 ➲ WORDFINDER NOTE AT LIQUID **2** ~ **sth** to make sth weaker or less effective 削弱；降低；使降低效果 SYN **water down**: *Large classes dilute the quality of education that children receive.* 大班上课会降低孩子所受教育的质量。 ▶ **di·lu·tion** /daɪˈluːʃn; *BrE also* -ˈljuːʃn/ *noun* [U]: *the dilution of sewage* 污水的稀释处理 ◇ *This is a serious dilution of their election promises.* 这使他们竞选时许下的诺言大打折扣。

■ ***adj.*** (*also* **di·luted**) (of a liquid 液体) made weaker by adding water or another substance 稀释了的；冲淡了的：*a **dilute acid/solution*** 稀释酸液 / 溶液

dim /dɪm/ *adj., verb*

■ ***adj.*** (**dim·mer**, **dim·mest**)

• LIGHT 光线 **1** not bright 暗淡的；昏暗的；微弱的：*the dim glow of the fire in the grate* 壁炉里微弱的火光 ◇ *This light is too dim to read by.* 这光线太暗，看不了书。

• PLACE 地方 **2** where you cannot see well because there is not much light 不明亮的；光线暗淡的；昏暗的：*a dim room/street* 昏暗的房间 / 街道

• SHAPE 形状 **3** that you cannot see well because there is not much light 不分明的；不清楚的；朦胧的；隐约的：*the dim outline of a house in the moonlight* 月光下影影绰绰的房子的轮廓 ◇ *I could see a dim shape in the doorway.* 我模模糊糊看见门口有个人影。

• EYES 眼睛 **4** not able to see well 看不清的；视力差的；模糊的：*His eyesight is getting dim.* 他的视力越来越差。

• MEMORIES 记忆 **5** that you cannot remember or imagine clearly 不清晰的；模糊的 SYN **vague**: *dim memories* 模糊的记忆 ◇ *She had a dim recollection of the visit.* 她依稀记得那次访问。 ◇ (*humorous*) *in the **dim and distant past*** 在遥远模糊的过去

• PERSON 人 **6** (*informal, especially BrE*) not intelligent 迟钝的；愚笨的；愚蠢的：*He's very dim.* 他很迟钝。
• SITUATION 境况 **7** not giving any reason to have hope; not good 不明朗的；不乐观的：*Her future career prospects look dim.* 她的前程看来很暗淡。
▸ **dim·ness** *noun* [U]: *It took a while for his eyes to adjust to the dimness.* 过了好一阵他的眼睛才适应了这昏暗的地方。 ➲ SEE ALSO DIMLY

IDM **take a dim view of sb/sth** to disapprove of sb/sth; to not have a good opinion of sb/sth 对…持不赞成（或怀疑）态度；对…没有好感：*She took a dim view of my suggestion.* 她对我的建议持否定态度。

■ *verb* (-mm-)
• LIGHT 光线 **1** [I, T] ~ (**sth**) if a light **dims** or if you **dim** it, it becomes or you make it less bright（使）变暗淡，变微弱，变昏暗：*The lights in the theatre dimmed as the curtain rose.* 幕布升起，剧场内的灯光暗了下来。
• FEELING/QUALITY 感觉；品质 **2** [I, T] ~ (**sth**) if a feeling or quality **dims**, or if sth **dims** it, it becomes less strong（使）减弱，变淡漠，失去光泽：*Her passion for dancing never dimmed over the years.* 这些年来她对跳舞的热情一直不减。

dime /daɪm/ *noun* a coin of the US and Canada worth ten cents（美国、加拿大的）十分硬币，十分钱

IDM **a ˌdime a ˈdozen** (*NAmE*) (*BrE* **ˌtwo/ˌten a ˈpenny**) very common and therefore not valuable 普通得不值钱；（因常见而）价值低

ˈdime novel *noun* (*NAmE, old-fashioned*) a cheap popular novel, usually an exciting adventure or romantic story 一角钱小说，廉价通俗小说（常为刺激历险或爱情小说）

di·men·sion AW /daɪˈmenʃn; dɪ-/ *noun* **1** a measurement in space, for example the height, width or length of sth 维（构成空间的因素）：*We measured the dimensions of the kitchen.* 我们测量了厨房的尺寸。◇ *computer design tools that work in three dimensions* 计算机三维设计工具 ➲ SEE ALSO FOURTH DIMENSION **2** [usually pl.] the size and extent of a situation 规模；程度；范围：*a problem of considerable dimensions* 一个涉及面相当广的问题 **3** an aspect, or way of looking at or thinking about sth 方面；侧面：*Her job added a new dimension to her life.* 她的工作为她的生活增添了新的内容。◇ *the social dimension of unemployment* 失业的社会层面

-dimensional AW /daɪˈmenʃənl; dɪ-/ *combining form* (in adjectives 构成形容词) having the number of dimensions mentioned …维的：*a multidimensional model* 多维模型 ➲ SEE ALSO MULTIDIMENSIONAL, THREE-DIMENSIONAL, TWO-DIMENSIONAL

ˈdime store *noun* (*old-fashioned, NAmE*) = FIVE-AND-DIME

di·min·ish AW /dɪˈmɪnɪʃ/ *verb* **1** [I, T] ~ (**sth**) to become or to make sth become smaller, weaker, etc. 减少；（使）减弱，缩减；降低 SYN **decrease**: *The world's resources are rapidly diminishing.* 世界资源正在迅速减少。◇ *His influence has diminished with time.* 随着时间的推移，他的影响已不如从前了。◇ *Our efforts were producing **diminishing returns*** (= we achieved less although we spent more time or money). 我们不断投入，收益却在递减。 **2** [T] ~ **sb/sth** to make sb/sth seem less important than they really are 贬低；贬损；轻视 SYN **belittle**: *I don't wish to diminish the importance of their contribution.* 我并不想贬低他们所作贡献的重要性。

diˌminished responsiˈbility *noun* [U] (*BrE, law* 律) a state in which a person who is accused of a crime is not considered to be responsible for their actions, because they are mentally ill（因精神失常）减轻责任：*He was found not guilty of murder on the grounds of diminished responsibility.* 他未被判谋杀罪是基于精神失常而减轻了刑事责任。

di·minu·endo /dɪˌmɪnjuˈendəʊ; *NAmE* -doʊ/ *noun* (*pl.* **-os**) [C, U] (*music* 音, *from Italian*) a gradual decrease in how loudly a piece of music is played or sung 渐弱 OPP **crescendo**

dim·in·ution AW /ˌdɪmɪˈnjuːʃn; *NAmE* -ˈnuːʃn/ *noun* ~ (**of/in sth**) (*formal*) **1** [U] the act of reducing sth or of being reduced 减少；缩减；降低：*the diminution of political power* 政权的削弱 **2** [C, usually sing.] a reduction; an amount reduced 缩小；减少；缩小量；减少量：*a diminution in population growth* 人口增长幅度的缩小

di·minu·tive /dɪˈmɪnjətɪv/ *adj., noun*
■ *adj.* (*formal*) very small 极小的；特小的；微小的：*She was a diminutive figure beside her husband.* 她同丈夫比起来就像个侏儒。
■ *noun* **1** a word or an ending of a word that shows that sb/sth is small, for example *piglet* (= a young pig), *kitchenette* (= a small kitchen) 指小词，指小词缀（如 piglet 小猪，kitchenette 小厨房） **2** a short informal form of a word, especially a name（单词，尤指名字的）非正式缩略形式：*'Nick' is a common diminutive of 'Nicholas'.* * Nick 是 Nicholas 的常用简称。

dimly /ˈdɪmli/ *adv.* not very brightly or clearly 暗淡地；昏暗地；模糊地：*a dimly lit room* 灯光昏暗的房间 ◇ *I was **dimly aware*** (= only just aware) *of the sound of a car in the distance.* 我隐隐约约听到远处有汽车的声音。◇ *I did remember, but only dimly.* 我的确记得，只是记不太清楚了。

ˈdimmer switch (*also* **dim·mer**) *noun* **1** a switch that allows you to make an electric light brighter or less bright 调光器；调光开关；亮度调节开关 **2** (*NAmE*) (*BrE* **ˈdip switch**) a switch that allows you to make the front lights on a car point downwards（汽车的）前灯变光开关

dimple /ˈdɪmpl/ *verb, noun*
■ *noun* **1** a small hollow place in the skin, especially in the cheek or chin 酒窝；笑靥：*She had a dimple which appeared when she smiled.* 她一笑就现出酒窝。 **2** any small hollow place in a surface 浅凹；小凹；小坑：*a pane of glass with a dimple pattern* 带浅凹形图案的窗玻璃
▸ **dimpled** /ˈdɪmpld/ *adj.*: *a dimpled chin* 有酒窝的脸
■ *verb* [I] to make a hollow place appear on each of your cheeks, especially by smiling 现酒窝；现笑靥

dim sum /ˌdɪm ˈsʌm/ (*also* **dim sim** /ˌdɪm ˈsɪm/) *noun* [U] (*from Chinese*) a Chinese dish or meal consisting of small pieces of food wrapped in sheets of DOUGH 点心（中国食品）

ˌdim-ˈwitted *adj.* (*informal*) stupid 愚笨的；傻的：*a dim-witted child* 傻孩子 ▸ **dim·wit** /ˈdɪmwɪt/ *noun*

din /dɪn/ *noun* [sing.] a loud, unpleasant noise that lasts for a long time 喧嚣声；嘈杂声；吵闹声 SYN **racket**: *The children were making an awful din.* 孩子们吵得厉害。

dinar /ˈdiːnɑː(r)/ *noun* a unit of money in Serbia and various countries in the Middle East and N Africa 第纳尔（塞尔维亚以及中东和北非多国的货币单位）

din-dins /ˈdɪn dɪnz/ (*BrE*) (*NAmE* **din-din** /ˈdɪn dɪn/) *noun* [U] (*humorous*) (used when talking to a baby or a pet 对儿童或宠物的用语) food 食物；好吃的

dine /daɪn/ *verb* [I] (*formal*) to eat dinner 进餐；用饭：*We dined with my parents at a restaurant in town.* 我们同我父母在镇里一家餐馆吃饭。 ➲ COLLOCATIONS AT RESTAURANT

PHR V **ˈdine on sth** (*formal*) to have a particular type of food for dinner 正餐吃…；以…作正餐 **ˌdine ˈout** to eat dinner in a restaurant or sb else's home 下馆子；外出进餐 **ˌdine ˈout on sth** (*informal*) to tell other people about sth that has happened to you, in order to make them interested in you 将（经历等）作为谈资 IDM SEE WINE *v.*

diner /ˈdaɪnə(r)/ *noun* **1** a person eating a meal, especially in a restaurant（尤指餐馆的）就餐者：*a restaurant capable of seating 100 diners* 可容纳 100 人就餐的餐馆 **2** (*especially NAmE*) a small, usually cheap, restaurant（常指较便宜的）小餐馆，小饭店：*a roadside diner* 路边小餐馆

din·ero /dɪˈneərəʊ; *NAmE* dɪˈneroʊ/ *noun* [U] (*informal, especially NAmE, from Spanish*) money 钱

din·ette /daɪˈnet/ *noun* (*especially NAmE*) a small room or part of a room for eating meals 小饭厅；小餐室

ding /dɪŋ/ *noun, verb*

■ *noun* **1** (*NAmE*) a blow, especially one that causes slight damage to a car, etc. （尤指造成汽车上的凹痕、划痕等的）一击：*I got a ding in my rear fender.* 我汽车后面的挡泥板撞瘪了一处。 **2** used to represent the sound made by a bell 叮当；丁零：*The lift came to a halt with a loud 'ding'.* 电梯叮一声停下了。

■ *verb* **1** [I] to make a sound like a bell 叮当（或丁零）作响：*The computer just dings when I press a key.* 我一按键，电脑就发出叮的一声。 **2** [T] ~ **sth** (*NAmE*) to cause slight damage to a car, etc. 使（汽车等）轻微受损：*I dinged my passenger door.* 我把乘客门撞坏了一点。 **3** [T] ~ **sb** (*NAmE*) to hit sb 打：(*figurative*) *My department got dinged by the budget cuts.* 因预算缩减，我的部门受到一定的影响。

ding·bat /ˈdɪŋbæt/ *noun* (*NAmE, slang*) a stupid person 笨蛋；蠢货；傻瓜

ding-dong /ˈdɪŋ dɒŋ; *NAmE* dɔːŋ/ *noun* **1** [U] used to represent the sound made by a bell （钟、铃声）叮当：*I rang the doorbell. Ding-dong! No answer.* 我按了按门铃。叮当！可没有人应门。 **2** (*BrE, informal*) an argument or a fight 辩论；争吵：*They were having a real ding-dong on the doorstep.* 他们在门前大吵起来。 ➲ MORE LIKE THIS 3, page R25

din·ghy /ˈdɪŋi; ˈdɪŋgi/ *noun* (*pl.* **-ies**) **1** a small open boat that you sail or ROW[1] 小艇；敞篷小船；小舢板：*a sailing dinghy* 小帆船 ➲ VISUAL VOCAB PAGE V59 ➲ COMPARE YACHT **2** = RUBBER DINGHY

dingo /ˈdɪŋgəʊ; *NAmE* -goʊ/ *noun* (*pl.* **-oes**) a wild Australian dog 澳洲野犬

dingy /ˈdɪndʒi/ *adj.* (**din·gier**, **din·gi·est**) dark and dirty 又黑又脏的；昏暗的；肮脏的：*a dingy room/hotel* 又黑又脏的房间 / 旅馆 ◇ *dingy curtains/clothes* 脏得发黑的窗帘 / 衣服 ▶ **din·gi·ness** *noun* [U]

ˈdining car (*BrE also* **ˈrestaurant car**) *noun* a coach/car on a train in which meals are served （火车的）餐车

ˈdining room *noun* a room that is used mainly for eating meals in 餐厅；饭厅 ➲ VISUAL VOCAB PAGE V23

ˈdining table *noun* a table for having meals on 餐桌 ➲ COMPARE DINNER TABLE ➲ VISUAL VOCAB PAGE V23

dink /dɪŋk/ *noun* (*also* **ˈdrop shot**) (in TENNIS 网球) a soft hit that makes the ball land on the ground without BOUNCING much 吊球 ▶ **dink** *verb* ~ **sth**

din·kum /ˈdɪŋkəm/ *adj.* (*AustralE, NZE, informal*) (of an article or a person) real or genuine （物品或人）真实的；真正的：*If you're dinkum, I'll help you.* 如果你的身份真实，我就帮你。 ➲ SEE ALSO FAIR DINKUM

dinky /ˈdɪŋki/ *adj.* (*informal*) **1** (*BrE, approving*) small and neat in an attractive way 小巧的；小而精致的：*What a dinky little hat!* 多么漂亮的小帽子啊！ **2** (*NAmE, disapproving*) too small 微不足道的；不起眼的；无足轻重的：*I grew up in a dinky little town that didn't even have a movie theater.* 我生长在一个无名小镇，那里连个电影院都没有。

din·ner 🔑 /ˈdɪnə(r)/ *noun* **1** 🔑 [U, C] the main meal of the day, eaten either in the middle of the day or in the evening （中午或晚上吃的）正餐，主餐：*It's time for dinner.* 该吃饭了。 ◇ *When do you have* **dinner**? 你们什么时间吃主餐？ ◇ *What time do you serve dinner?* 你们什么时候供应主餐？ ◇ *Let's invite them to dinner tomorrow.* 我们明天请他们吃饭吧。 ◇ *What shall we have* **for dinner** *tonight?* 我们今晚吃什么好呢？ ◇ *It's your turn to cook dinner.* 该你做饭了。 ◇ *She didn't eat much dinner.* 她没吃多少饭。 ◇ *I never eat a big dinner.* 我向来饭量不大。 ◇ *Christmas dinner* 圣诞大餐 ◇ *a three-course dinner* 三道菜的正餐 ◇ *I'd like to take you out* **to dinner** *tonight.* 今天晚上我想带你出去吃饭。 ◇ (*BrE*) ***school dinners*** (= meals provided at school in the middle of the day) 学校午餐 ➲ COLLOCATIONS AT RESTAURANT ➲ NOTE AT MEAL **2** 🔑 [C] a large formal social gathering at which dinner is eaten 宴会：*The club's annual dinner will be held on 3 June.* 俱乐部一年一度的宴会将于 6 月 3 日举行。 ➲ SEE ALSO DINNER PARTY

IDM ˌ**done like a ˈdinner** (*AustralE, NZE, informal*) completely defeated 彻底被打败；一败涂地 ➲ MORE AT DOG *n.*

ˈdinner dance *noun* a social event in the evening that includes a formal meal and dancing 晚宴舞会

ˈdinner jacket (*also* **tux·edo**) *noun* a black or white jacket worn with a BOW TIE at formal occasions in the evening （男式，配蝶形领结的）晚礼服上衣，无尾礼服上衣 ➲ COMPARE TAIL *n.* (6)

ˈdinner lady (*BrE*) (*US* **ˈlunch lady**) *noun* a woman whose job is to serve meals to children in schools （学校里照顾孩子吃饭的）女膳食服务员

ˈdinner party *noun* a social event at which a small group of people eat dinner at sb's house （在家里举行的）宴会；家宴

ˈdinner service *noun* a set of matching plates, dishes, etc. for serving a meal 成套餐具

ˈdinner suit (*BrE*) (*also* **tux·edo** *NAmE, BrE*) *noun* a DINNER JACKET and trousers/pants, worn with a BOW TIE at formal occasions in the evening （男式，配蝶形领结的）成套无尾晚礼服

ˈdinner table *noun* (*often* **the dinner table**) [usually sing.] the table at which people are eating dinner; an occasion when people are eating together 餐桌；同一桌进餐：*conversation at the dinner table* 席间交谈 ➲ COMPARE DINING TABLE

ˈdinner theater *noun* (*NAmE*) a restaurant where you see a play after your meal 餐馆剧院（餐后有戏剧表演）

ˈdinner time *noun* [U, C] the time at which dinner is normally eaten 正餐时间

din·ner·ware /ˈdɪnəweə(r); *NAmE* ˈdɪnərwer/ *noun* [U] (*NAmE*) plates, dishes, etc. used for serving a meal 餐具

dino·saur /ˈdaɪnəsɔː(r)/ *noun* **1** an animal that lived millions of years ago but is now EXTINCT (= it no longer exists). There were many types of dinosaur, some of which were very large. 恐龙 **2** (*disapproving*) a person or thing that is old-fashioned and cannot change in the changing conditions of modern life 守旧落伍的人；过时落后的东西

dint /dɪnt/ *noun*

IDM **by dint of sth/of doing sth** (*formal*) by means of sth 借助；凭借；由于：*He succeeded by dint of hard work.* 他靠艰苦的努力获得了成功。

dio·cese /ˈdaɪəsɪs/ *noun* (*pl.* **dio·ceses** /ˈdaɪəsiːz/) (in the Christian Church 基督教会) a district for which a BISHOP is responsible 教区；主教辖区 ▶ **dio·cesan** /daɪˈɒsɪsn; *NAmE* -ˈɑːs-/ *adj.*

diode /ˈdaɪəʊd; *NAmE* -oʊd/ *noun* (*specialist*) an electronic device in which the electric current passes in one direction only, for example a SILICON CHIP （电子）二极管

di·optre (*especially US* **di·opter**) /daɪˈɒptə(r); *NAmE* -ˈɑːp-/ *noun* (*physics* 物) a unit for measuring the power of a LENS to REFRACT light (= make it change direction) 屈光度（透镜的折射能力单位）

di·op·trics /daɪˈɒptrɪks; *NAmE* -ˈɑːp-/ *noun* [U] (*physics* 物) the scientific study of REFRACTION (= the way light changes direction when it goes through glass, etc.) 折射光学 ▶ **di·op·tric** /daɪˈɒptrɪk; *NAmE* -ˈɑːp-/ *adj.*

dio·rama /ˌdaɪəˈrɑːmə; *NAmE also* -ˈræmə/ *noun* a model representing a scene with figures, especially in a museum 透景画（博物馆广泛使用）

di·ox·ide /daɪˈɒksaɪd; *NAmE* -ˈɑːks-/ *noun* [U, C] (*chemistry* 化) a substance formed by combining two atoms of OXYGEN and one atom of another chemical element 二氧化物 ➲ SEE ALSO CARBON DIOXIDE

di·oxin /daɪˈɒksɪn; *NAmE* -ˈɑːks-/ *noun* a chemical used in industry and farming. Most dioxins are poisonous. 二噁英；二氧（杂）芑

dip /dɪp/ *verb, noun*

■ ***verb*** (**-pp-**) **1** [T] to put sth quickly into a liquid and take it out again 蘸；浸：**~ sth (into sth)** *He dipped the brush into the paint.* 他拿画笔蘸了蘸颜料。◇ **~ sth (in)** *Dip your hand in to see how hot the water is.* 把手伸进去看看水有多热。◇ *The fruit had been dipped in chocolate.* 这水果蘸过巧克力酱。 **2** [I, T] to go downwards or to a lower level; to make sth do this （使）下降，下沉 **SYN** **fall**：**(+ adv./prep.)** *The sun dipped below the horizon.* 太阳落到地平线下了。◇ *Sales for this quarter have dipped from 38.7 million to 33 million.* 本季度销售额从 3 870 万下降到 3 300 万。◇ *The road dipped suddenly as we approached the town.* 我们向镇里驶近时道路陡然下斜。◇ **~ sth (+ adv./prep.)** *The plane dipped its wings.* 机翼向下倾斜。➲ WORDFINDER NOTE AT TREND **3** [T] **~ sth** (*BrE*) if you **dip** your HEADLIGHTS when driving a car at night, you make the light from them point down so that other drivers do not have the light in their eyes 把（汽车前灯的）远光调为近光 **4** [T] **~ sth** when farmers **dip** animals, especially sheep, they put them in a bath of a liquid containing chemicals in order to kill insects, etc. 给（牲畜，尤指绵羊）洗药浴

IDM **dip into your ˈpocket** (*informal*) to spend some of your own money on sth 花钱；掏腰包 **dip a ˈtoe in/into sth** | **dip a ˈtoe in/into the water** (*informal*) to start doing sth very carefully to see if it will be successful or not 涉足试试；试做

PHR V **ˌdip ˈinto sth** **1** to put your hand into a container to take sth out 把手伸进（…里取东西）：*She dipped into her purse and took out some coins.* 她从钱包里掏出一些硬币。 **2** to read or watch only parts of sth 浏览；略为过目；涉猎：*I have only had time to dip into the report.* 这份报告我来不及细看，只是草草浏览了一遍。 **3** to take an amount from money that you have saved 提取（款项）；动用（存款）：*We took out a loan for the car because we didn't want to dip into our savings.* 因为不想动用存款，我们申请了一笔贷款买汽车。

■ ***noun*** **1** [C] (*informal*) a quick swim 游一游；泡一泡：*Let's go for a dip before breakfast.* 我们早饭前去游一会儿泳吧。 **2** [C] a decrease in the amount or success of sth, usually for only a short period （通常指暂时的）减少，下降，衰退 **SYN** **fall**：*a sharp **dip in** profits* 利润急剧下降 **3** [C] a place where a surface suddenly drops to a lower level and then rises again 凹陷处；低洼处：*a dip in the road* 路上的凹陷处 ◇ *Puddles had formed in the dips.* 低洼处形成了一个个水坑。 **4** [C, U] a thick mixture into which pieces of food are dipped before being eaten 调味酱（用食物来蘸着吃） **5** [U, C] a liquid containing a chemical into which sheep and other animals can be dipped in order to kill insects on them 药浴液，清洗液（用于绵羊或其他牲畜洗浴以杀死身上的虫子） **6** [sing.] **~ into sth** a quick look at sth 浏览；草草翻阅：*A brief dip into history serves to confirm this view.* 随便翻阅一下历史就足以证实这种观点。 **7** [C, usually sing.] a quick movement of sth down and up （降而复升的）一动：*He gave a dip of his head.* 他点了点头。➲ SEE ALSO LUCKY DIP

diph·theria /dɪfˈθɪəriə; *NAmE* -ˈθɪriə; dɪp-/ *noun* [U] a serious infectious disease of the throat that causes difficulty in breathing 白喉

diph·thong /ˈdɪfθɒŋ; ˈdɪp-; *NAmE* -θɑːŋ; -θɔːŋ/ *noun* (*phonetics* 语音) a combination of two vowel sounds or vowel letters, for example the sounds /aɪ/ in *pipe* /paɪp/ or the letters *ou* in *doubt* 二合元音；复元音；双元音；双元音字母组合 ➲ WORDFINDER NOTE AT PRONUNCIATION ▸ **diph·thong·al** /dɪfˈθɒŋgl; dɪp-; *NAmE* -ˈθɑːŋgl; -ˈθɔːŋgl/ *adj.*

dip·lod·ocus /dɪˈplɒdəkəs; ˌdɪpləˈdəʊkəs; *NAmE* -ˈplɑːd-; -ˈdoʊk-/ *noun* a very large DINOSAUR with a long thin neck and tail 梁龙（颈部和尾巴细长的大恐龙）

dip·loid /ˈdɪplɔɪd/ *adj.* (*biology* 生) (of a cell 细胞) containing two complete sets of CHROMOSOMES, one from each parent 二倍体的（含有两套染色体）➲ COMPARE HAPLOID

dip·loma /dɪˈpləʊmə; *NAmE* -ˈploʊ-/ *noun* **1** (*BrE*) a course of study at a college or university 文凭课程：*a two-year diploma course* 二年制的文凭课程 ◇ *She is taking a diploma in management studies.* 她在攻读管理学文凭课程。 **2** a document showing that you have completed a course of study or part of your education 毕业文凭：*a High School diploma* 高中毕业文凭

D

dip·lo·macy /dɪˈpləʊməsi; *NAmE* -ˈploʊ-/ *noun* [U] **1** the activity of managing relations between different countries; the skill in doing this 外交；外交技巧；外交手腕：*international diplomacy* 国际外交 ◇ *Diplomacy is better than war.* 采取外交手段胜于诉诸战争。➲ COLLOCATIONS AT INTERNATIONAL **2** skill in dealing with people in difficult situations without upsetting or offending them （处理人际关系的）手腕，手段，策略 **SYN** **tact** ➲ SEE ALSO SHUTTLE DIPLOMACY

dip·lo·mat /ˈdɪpləmæt/ *noun* **1** (*also old-fashioned* **dip·lo·ma·tist**) a person whose job is to represent his or her country in a foreign country, for example, in an EMBASSY 外交官 ➲ WORDFINDER NOTE AT ALLY **2** a person who is skilled at dealing with other people 善于交际的人；通权达变的人；圆通的人；有手腕的人

dip·lo·mat·ic /ˌdɪpləˈmætɪk/ *adj.* **1** connected with managing relations between countries (= DIPLOMACY) 外交的；从事外交的：*a diplomatic crisis* 外交危机 ◇ *Attempts are being made to settle the dispute by diplomatic means.* 正在努力通过外交途径解决争端。◇ *to **break off/establish/restore diplomatic relations** with a country* 与某国断绝 / 建立 / 恢复外交关系 **2** having or showing skill in dealing with people in difficult situations 有手腕的；灵活变通的；策略的；圆通的 **SYN** **tactful**：*a diplomatic answer* 圆通的回答 ▸ **dip·lo·mat·ic·al·ly** /-kli/ *adv.*：*The country remained diplomatically isolated.* 这个国家在外交上仍然受到孤立。◇ *'Why don't we take a break for coffee?' she suggested diplomatically.* "我们何不停下来喝杯咖啡呢？"她婉转地提议道。

ˌdiploˌmatic ˈbag (*BrE*) (*US* **ˌdiploˌmatic ˈpouch**) *noun* a container that is used for sending official letters and documents between a government and its representatives in another country and that cannot be opened by customs officers 外交邮袋，外交信袋（海关官员不能拆封）

ˌdiploˈmatic corps *noun* (*usually* **the diplomatic corps**) [C+sing./pl. v.] (*pl.* **diplomatic corps**) all the DIPLOMATS who work in a particular city or country 外交使团

ˌdiploˌmatic imˈmunity *noun* [U] special rights given to diplomats working in a foreign country which mean they cannot be arrested, taxed, etc. in that country 外交豁免权；外交特权

the ˌDiploˈmatic Service (*especially BrE*) (*NAmE usually* **the ˈForeign Service**) *noun* [sing.] the government department concerned with representing a country in foreign countries 外交部门

dip·lo·ma·tist /dɪˈpləʊmətɪst; *NAmE* -ˈploʊ-/ *noun* (*old-fashioned*) = DIPLOMAT

di·pole /ˈdaɪpəʊl; *NAmE* -poʊl/ *noun* (*physics* 物) a pair of separated POLES, one positive and one negative 偶极子

dip·per /ˈdɪpə(r)/ *noun* a bird that lives near rivers 河乌 ➲ SEE ALSO BIG DIPPER

dippy /ˈdɪpi/ *adj.* (*informal*) stupid; crazy 笨的；傻的；脑子有问题的

dipso·maniac /ˌdɪpsəˈmeɪniæk/ *noun* a person who has a strong desire for alcoholic drink that they cannot control 嗜酒狂；间发性酒狂 **SYN** **alcoholic**

dip·stick /ˈdɪpstɪk/ *noun* **1** a long straight piece of metal used for measuring the amount of liquid in a container, especially the amount of oil in an engine 浸量尺；（尤指发动机的）油尺 **2** (*informal*) a stupid person 笨蛋；傻瓜

D

ˈ**dip switch** (*BrE*) (*NAmE* ˈ**dim·mer switch**) *noun* a switch that allows you to make the front lights on a car point downwards （汽车的）前灯变光开关

dip·tych /ˈdɪptɪk/ *noun* (*specialist*) a painting, especially a religious one, with two wooden panels that can be closed like a book （尤指宗教的）对折画，双联画

dire /ˈdaɪə(r)/ *adj.* (**direr**, **dir·est**) **1** [usually before noun] (*formal*) very serious 极其严重的；危急的：*living in dire poverty* 生活赤贫 ◇ ***dire warnings/threats*** 严重的警告 / 威胁 ◇ *Such action may have* ***dire consequences****.* 这种行为可能产生严重后果。◇ *We're* ***in dire need of*** *your help.* 我们急需你的帮助。◇ *The firm is* ***in dire straits*** (= in a very difficult situation) *and may go bankrupt.* 这家公司已陷入极度困境之中，可能会破产。 **2** (*BrE, informal*) very bad 极糟的；极差的：*The acting was dire.* 这表演糟透了。

dir·ect /dəˈrekt; dɪ-; daɪ-/ *adj., verb, adv.*

■ ***adj.***

• **NOBODY/NOTHING IN BETWEEN** 直接 **1** [usually before noun] happening or done without involving other people, actions, etc. in between 直接的；亲自的；亲身的：*They are in direct contact with the hijackers.* 他们与劫机者直接联系。◇ *His death was a direct result of your action.* 他的死是你的行为直接造成的后果。◇ *We are looking for somebody with direct experience of this type of work.* 我们在寻找对这种工作有过亲身体验的人。◇ *This information has a* ***direct bearing on*** (= it is closely connected with) *the case.* 这一信息与此情况有直接关系。 OPP **indirect**

• **JOURNEY/ROUTE** 旅程；路线 **2** going in the straightest line between two places without stopping or changing direction 笔直的；径直的；最近的：*the most* ***direct route/course*** 最直接的路线 / 航线 ◇ *a* ***direct flight*** (= a flight that does not stop) 直飞航班 ◇ *There's a* ***direct train*** *to Leeds* (= it may stop at other stations but you do not have to change trains). 有一班直达利兹的火车。◇ *a* ***direct hit*** (= a hit that is accurate and does not touch sth else first) 直接命中 OPP **indirect**

• **HEAT/LIGHT** 热；光 **3** [only before noun] with nothing between sth and the source of the heat or light 直射的：*Protect your child from direct sunlight by using a sunscreen.* 给孩子搽点防晒霜以防日光直接照射。

• **SAYING WHAT YOU MEAN** 直爽 **4** saying exactly what you mean in a way that nobody can pretend not to understand 直爽的；直率的；坦率的：*a* ***direct answer/question*** 直截了当的回答；坦率的问题 ◇ *You'll have to get used to his direct manner.* 你可得慢慢习惯他这种直率的方式。 OPP **indirect** ➲ SYNONYMS AT HONEST

• **EXACT** 恰好 **5** [only before noun] exact 正好的；恰好的：*That's the* ***direct opposite*** *of what you told me yesterday.* 那与你昨天告诉我的截然相反。 ◇ *a* ***direct quote*** (= one using a person's exact words) 直接引语

• **RELATIONSHIP** 关系 **6** [only before noun] related through parents and children rather than brothers, sisters, aunts, etc. 直系的；嫡系的：*a direct descendant of the country's first president* 该国第一任总统的嫡系后裔 OPP **indirect**

■ ***verb***

• **AIM** 目标 **1** [T] to aim sth in a particular direction or at a particular person 把…对准（某方向或某人）：**~ sth at sth/sb** *The machine directs a powerful beam at the affected part of the body.* 这种机器将很强的射线对准身体感染部位。◇ *Was that remark directed at me?* 那话是冲着我来的吗？ ◇ **~ sth to/towards sth/sb** *There are three main issues that we need to direct our attention to.* 我们需要注意的主要有三个问题。 ◇ **~ sth against sth/sb** *Most of his anger was directed against himself.* 他主要是生自己的气。

• **CONTROL** 控制 **2** [T] **~ sb/sth** to control or be in charge of sb/sth 管理；监督；指导：*A new manager has been appointed to direct the project.* 已任命一位新经理来管理这项工程。 ◇ *He was asked to take command and* ***direct operations****.* 他奉命统率并指挥作战行动。

• **MOVIE/PLAY/MUSIC** 电影；戏剧；音乐 **3** [I, T] to be in charge of actors in a play, or a film/movie, or musicians in an ORCHESTRA, etc. 导演（戏剧或电影）；指挥（管弦乐队）：*She prefers to act rather than direct.* 她宁愿当演员，不愿当导演。 ◇ **~ sb/sth** *The movie was directed by Steven Spielberg.* 这部电影是由史蒂文・斯皮尔伯格导演的。◇ *She now directs a large choir.* 她目前担任一个大合唱团的指挥。 ➲ COLLOCATIONS AT CINEMA

• **SHOW THE WAY** 指路 **4** [T] **~ sb (to…)** to tell or show sb how to get to somewhere or where to go 给（某人）指路；为（某人）领路：*Could you direct me to the station?* 请问到车站怎么走？ ◇ *A police officer was directing the traffic.* 一名警察在指挥交通。 ➲ SYNONYMS AT TAKE

• **GIVE ORDER** 下达命令 **5** [T] (*formal*) to give an official order 指示；命令 SYN **order**： **~ sb to do sth** *The police officers had been directed to search the building.* 警察奉命搜查这栋大楼。 ◇ **~ that…** *The judge directed that the mother be given custody of the children.* 法官判决孩子由母亲监护。◇ (*BrE also*) *The judge directed that the mother should be given custody of the children.* 法官判决孩子由母亲监护。 ➲ SYNONYMS AT ORDER

• **LETTER/COMMENT** 信函；意见 **6** [T] **~ sth to…** (*formal*) to send a letter, etc. to a particular place or to a particular person 把（信件等）寄至；交予：*Direct any complaints to the Customer Services department.* 将投诉寄至用户服务部。

■ ***adv.***

• **JOURNEY/ROUTE** 旅程；路线 **1** without stopping or changing direction 直接；径直：*We flew direct to Hong Kong.* 我们直飞香港。◇ *The 10.40 goes direct to Leeds.* * 10:40 这班火车直达利兹。

• **NOBODY IN BETWEEN** 亲自 **2** without involving other people 亲自；直接：*I prefer to deal with him direct.* 我更愿意直接跟他打交道。

diˌrect ˈaccess *noun* [U] (*computing* 计) the ability to get data immediately from any part of a computer file 直接存取；随机访问

diˌrect ˈaction *noun* [U, C] the use of strikes, protests, etc. instead of discussion in order to get what you want 直接行动（用罢工、抗议等方式达到目的）

diˌrect ˈcurrent *noun* [C, U] (*abbr.* **DC**) an electric current that flows in one direction only 直流；直流电流 ➲ COMPARE ALTERNATING CURRENT

diˌrect ˈdebit *noun* [U, C] (*BrE*) an instruction to your bank to allow sb else to take an amount of money from your account on a particular date, especially to pay bills 直接借记；直接扣账：*We pay all our bills* ***by direct debit****.* 我们以直接借记方式支付所有账单。 ➲ COMPARE STANDING ORDER

diˌrect deˈposit *noun* [U] (*NAmE*) the system of paying sb's wages straight into their bank account 直接将工资转入银行账户

dir·ec·tion /dəˈrekʃn; dɪ-; daɪ-/ *noun*

• **WHERE TO** 去向 **1** [C, U] the general position a person or thing moves or points towards 方向；方位：*Tom went off* ***in the direction of*** *home.* 汤姆朝家的方向去了。◇ *She glanced* ***in his direction****.* 她朝他那个方向瞥了一眼。◇ *The aircraft was flying in a northerly direction.* 飞机正向北飞去。 ◇ *The road was blocked in both directions.* 这条路往返方向都堵死了。 ◇ *They hit a truck coming in the* ***opposite direction****.* 他们撞上一辆迎面开来的卡车。 ◇ *Has the wind* ***changed direction****?* 风向变了吗？ ◇ *When the police arrived, the crowd scattered* ***in all directions****.* 警察赶到后，人群便向四面八方散开了。◇ *I lost all* ***sense of direction*** (= I didn't know which way to go). 我完全迷失了方向。

• **DEVELOPMENT** 发展 **2** [C, U] the general way in which a person or thing develops 趋势；动向：*The exhibition provides evidence of several new directions in her work.* 这个展览表明她的创作有几个新动向。◇ *I am very unhappy with the direction the club is taking.* 我对俱乐部的发展趋势很不满意。◇ *It's only a small improvement, but at least it's* ***a step in the right direction****.* 虽然这只是小小的改进，但至少是朝正确方向迈出的一步。

• **WHERE FROM** 来自 **3** [C] the general position a person or thing comes or develops from 方面：*Support came from an unexpected direction.* 一个出人意料的来源提供了帮助。 ◇ *Let us approach the subject from a different direction.* 咱们从一个不同的角度来探讨这个题目吧。

• **PURPOSE** 目的 **4** 🔑 [U] a purpose; an aim 目的；目标：*We are looking for somebody with a clear **sense of direction**.* 我们想找一个有明确目标的人。◇ *Once again her life felt lacking in direction.* 她的人生似乎又没了方向。
• **INSTRUCTIONS** 说明 **5** 🔑 [C, usually pl.] instructions about how to do sth, where to go, etc. 用法说明；操作指南；旅行指南：*Let's stop and ask for directions.* 咱们停下来问问路吧。◇ *Simple directions for assembling the model are printed on the box.* 模型装配的简要说明印在盒子上。
• **CONTROL** 控制 **6** 🔑 [U] the art of managing or guiding sb/sth 管理；指导：*All work was produced by the students **under the direction of** John Williams.* 所有作品都是在约翰•威廉斯的指导下由学生创作完成的。
• **FILM/MOVIE** 电影 **7** [U] the instructions given by sb directing a film/movie（电影导演的）指点，指示：*There is some clever direction and the film is very well shot.* 由于导演指导有方，影片拍得非常成功。**IDM** SEE PULL *v.*

dir·ec·tion·al /də'rekʃənl; dɪ-; daɪ-/ *adj.* (*specialist*) **1** producing or receiving signals, sound, etc. better in one particular direction（发出或接收信号、声音等）定向的，指向的：***a directional microphone/aerial*** 定向传声器 / 天线 **2** connected with the direction in which sth is moving 方向的：*directional stability* 方向稳定性

dir·ec·tion·less /də'rekʃnləs; dɪ-; daɪ-/ *adj.* (*formal*) without a direction or purpose 无方向的；无目标的

dir·ect·ive /də'rektɪv; dɪ-; daɪ-/ *noun, adj.*
▪ ***noun*** an official instruction 指示；命令：*The EU has issued a new set of directives on pollution.* 欧盟发布了一系列关于污染的新指令。
▪ ***adj.*** (*formal*) giving instructions 指示的；指导的：*They are seeking a central, directive role in national energy policy.* 他们正寻求在国家能源政策方面起中心指导作用。

dir·ect·ly 🔑 /də'rektli; dɪ-; daɪ-/ *adv., conj.*
▪ ***adv.*** **1** 🔑 in a direct line or manner 直接地；径直地；坦率地：*He drove her directly to her hotel.* 他驾车直接把她送到了她下榻的旅馆。◇ *She looked directly at us.* 她正视着我们。◇ *He's directly responsible to the boss.* 他直接对老板负责。◇ *We have not been directly affected by the cuts.* 我们并未直接受到裁减的影响。**OPP** **indirectly** **2** 🔑 exactly in a particular position 正；正好地；恰好：***directly opposite/below/ahead*** 正对面；正下方；正前方 ◇ *They remain directly opposed to these new plans.* 他们仍旧截然反对这些新方案。**3** immediately 立即；立刻：*She left directly after the show.* 演出一结束，她马上就走了。**4** (*old-fashioned, BrE*) soon 过一会儿；很快 **SYN** **shortly**：*Tell them I'll be there directly.* 告诉他们我一会儿就到。
▪ ***conj.*** (*BrE*) as soon as 一…就…：*I went home directly I had finished work.* 我一干完活就回家了。

di,rect 'mail *noun* [U] advertisements that are sent to people through the post/mail 直接邮寄的广告

di,rect 'marketing *noun* [U] the business of selling products or services directly to customers who order by mail, telephone, or email instead of going to a shop/store 直接营销（通过邮寄、电话或电邮直接向顾客销售产品或推销服务）

di,rect 'message *noun* = DM

the di'rect method *noun* [sing.] a way of teaching a foreign language using only that language and not treating the study of grammar as the most important thing（外语）直接教学法（不以语法为中心）

dir·ect·ness /də'rektnəs; dɪ-; daɪ-/ *noun* [U] the quality of being simple and clear, so that it is impossible not to understand 直接；直截了当；坦率：*'What's that?' she asked with her usual directness.* "那是什么？"她以惯用的坦率语气问道。

di,rect 'object *noun* (*grammar* 语法) a noun, noun phrase or pronoun that refers to a person or thing that is directly affected by the action of a verb 直接宾语：*In 'I met him in town', the word 'him' is the direct object.* 在 I met him in town 中，him 是直接宾语。➲ COMPARE INDIRECT OBJECT

dir·ect·or 🔑 /də'rektə(r); dɪ-; daɪ-/ *noun* **1** 🔑 one of a group of senior managers who run a company 董事；理事；经理：*the **managing director*** 总经理 ◇ ***an executive/non-executive director*** 执行 / 非执行董事 ◇ ***He's on the board of directors.*** 他是董事会成员。➲ WORDFINDER NOTE AT COMPANY **2** 🔑 a person who is in charge of a particular activity or department in a company, a college, etc.（某一活动的）负责人；（公司部门的）主任，经理；（学院的）院长：*the musical director* 音乐总监 ◇ *a regional director* 地区主管 ◇ *the director of education* 教育局长 **3** 🔑 a person in charge of a film/movie or play who tells the actors and staff what to do（电影、戏剧等的）导演 ➲ COMPARE PRODUCER (2) ➲ WORDFINDER NOTE AT FILM, THEATRE

dir·ect·or·ate /də'rektərət; dɪ-; daɪ-/ *noun* **1** a section of a government department in charge of one particular activity（政府）部门：*the environmental directorate* 环境部门 **2** the group of directors who run a company 董事会；理事会 **SYN** **board**

di,rector 'general *noun* (*especially BrE*) the head of a large organization, especially a public organization 署长；局长；（尤指公共机构的）总管：*the director general of the BBC* 英国广播公司总裁

dir·ect·or·ial /,daɪrek'tɔːriəl/ *adj.* [only before noun] connected with the position or work of a director, especially of a director of films/movies 主管的；导演的；指挥的：*The film marks her directorial debut.* 这部电影是她作为导演初露头角的标志。

Di,rector of ,Public Prose'cutions *noun* (*abbr.* **DPP**) (in England and Wales) a public official whose job is to decide whether people who are suspected of a crime should be brought to trial（英格兰和威尔士的）检察官

di'rector's chair *noun* a folding wooden chair with crossed legs, a seat and back made of cloth, and sides on which you can rest your arms 导演椅，轻便折叠椅（木制扶手椅，以帆布作座面、椅背）➲ VISUAL VOCAB PAGE V22

di'rector's cut *noun* a version of a film/movie, usually released some time after the original is first shown, that is exactly how the director wanted it to be（电影的）导演剪辑版

dir·ect·or·ship /də'rektəʃɪp; dɪ-; daɪ-; *NAmE* -tərʃ-/ *noun* the position of a company director; the period during which this is held 董事的职位；董事的任期

dir·ec·tory /də'rektəri; dɪ-; daɪ-/ *noun* (*pl.* **-ies**) **1** a book containing lists of information, usually in alphabetical order, for example people's telephone numbers or the names and addresses of businesses in a particular area 名录；电话号码簿；公司名录：***a telephone/trade directory*** 电话号码簿；商行名录 ◇ *a directory of European Trade Associations* 欧洲同业公会名录 **2** a file containing a group of other files or programs in a computer（计算机文件或程序的）目录

di,rectory en'quiries (*BrE*) (*NAmE* **di,rectory as'sistance**, or *informal* **in·for·ma·tion**) *noun* [U+sing./pl. v.] a telephone service that you can use to find out a person's telephone number 电话号码查询台

di,rect 'rule *noun* [U] government of a region by a central government, when that region has had its own government in the past 直辖

di,rect 'speech *noun* [U] (*grammar* 语法) a speaker's actual words; the use of these in writing 说话者原话；直接引语：*Only direct speech should go inside inverted commas.* 只有直接引语应放在引号内。➲ COMPARE INDIRECT SPEECH, REPORTED SPEECH

di,rect 'tax *noun* (*specialist*) a tax which is collected directly from the person who pays it, for example income tax 直接税（如所得税）➲ COMPARE INDIRECT TAX
▸ **di,rect tax'ation** *noun* [U]

dirge /dɜːdʒ; *NAmE* dɜːrdʒ/ *noun* **1** a song sung in the past at a funeral or for a dead person 哀歌；挽歌 **2** (*informal*, *disapproving*) any song or piece of music that is too slow and sad 惨兮兮的歌曲（或乐曲）

diri·gible /ˈdɪrɪdʒəbl/ *adj., noun*
▪*adj.* (*formal*) able to be guided or steered 可驾驶的；可操纵的：*a dirigible balloon* 飞艇
▪*noun* an AIRSHIP 飞艇

D

dirk /dɜːk; *NAmE* dɜːrk/ *noun* a long heavy pointed knife that was used as a weapon in Scotland in the past（旧时苏格兰人用的）长匕首

dirndl /ˈdɜːndl; *NAmE* ˈdɜːrndl/ *noun* (*from German*) a very full wide skirt, pulled in tightly at the waist; a dress with a skirt like this and a closely fitting top 阿尔卑斯村姑裙（束腰宽摆）；阿尔卑斯村姑式连衣裙（有紧胸褡和束腰宽摆裙）

dirt /dɜːt; *NAmE* dɜːrt/ *noun* [U] **1** any substance that makes sth dirty, for example dust, soil or mud 污物；尘土；烂泥：*His clothes were covered in dirt.* 他的衣服沾满了污垢。◇ *First remove any grease or dirt from the surface.* 先把表面的油污或尘土去掉。**2** (*especially NAmE*) loose earth or soil 松土；泥土；散土：*He picked up a handful of dirt and threw it at them.* 他抓起一把土朝他们扔过去。◇ *Pack the dirt firmly round the plants.* 将植物周围的土培实。◇ *They lived in a shack with a dirt floor.* 他们住在土地板的棚屋里。➲SYNONYMS AT SOIL **3** (*informal*) unpleasant or harmful information about sb that could be used to damage their reputation, career, etc. 丑闻；流言蜚语：*Do you have any dirt on the new guy?* 你知道新来的那个人的丑闻吗？ **4** (*informal*) = EXCREMENT：*dog dirt* 狗屎 IDM SEE DISH *v.*, TREAT *v.*

ˈdirt bike *noun* a motorcycle designed for rough ground, especially for competitions（尤指用于比赛的）越野摩托车 ➲VISUAL VOCAB PAGE V55

ˌdirt ˈcheap *adj., adv.* (*informal*) very cheap 非常便宜（的）：*It was dirt cheap.* 这太便宜了。◇ *I got it dirt cheap.* 我买得非常便宜。

ˈdirt farmer *noun* (*NAmE*) a farmer who has poor land and does not make much money, and who does not pay anyone else to work on the farm 自耕农

ˌdirt ˈpoor *adj.* (*NAmE, informal*) extremely poor 极贫困的；极贫穷的

ˈdirt road (*NAmE also* **ˈdirt track**) *noun* a rough road in the country that is made from hard earth 土路

ˈdirt track *noun* **1** (*NAmE*) = DIRT ROAD **2** a track made of CINDERS, soil, etc. used for motorcycle racing 煤渣跑道（供摩托车比赛用）：*a dirt-track race* 煤渣跑道赛车

dirty /ˈdɜːti; *NAmE* ˈdɜːrti/ *adj., verb, adv.*
▪*adj.* (**dirt·ier**, **dirti·est**)
• **NOT CLEAN** 不洁 **1** not clean 肮脏的；龌龊的；污秽的：*dirty hands/clothes* 脏手；脏衣服 ◇ *a dirty mark* 污迹 ◇ *Try not to get too dirty!* 别把身上弄得太脏！◇ *I always get given the dirty jobs* (= jobs that make you become dirty). 让我干的总是些脏活。
• **OFFENSIVE** 冒犯 **2** [usually before noun] connected with sex in an offensive way 下流的；色情的；黄色的；猥亵的：*a **dirty joke/book*** 下流的笑话；黄色的书 ◇ *He's got **a dirty mind*** (= he often thinks about sex). 他满脑子下流事儿。
• **UNPLEASANT/DISHONEST** 令人不快；不诚实 **3** [usually before noun] (*informal*) unpleasant or dishonest 令人厌恶的；卑鄙的；不诚实的：*a dirty lie* 卑鄙的谎言 ◇ *She's a dirty player.* 她是个没有体育道德的运动员。◇ *He's a great man for doing the dirty jobs* (= jobs which are unpleasant because they involve being dishonest or mean to people). 他这个人最会干伤天害理的事。
• **COLOURS** 颜色 **4** [only before noun] dull 不鲜明的；暗淡的：*a dirty brown carpet* 暗褐色的地毯
• **DRUGS** 毒品 **5** (*NAmE, slang*) using illegal drugs 吸毒的
IDM **be a dirty ˈword** to be a subject or an idea that people think is bad or immoral 犯忌的字眼；犯忌的话题；忌讳的想法；淫秽字眼：*Profit is not a dirty word around here.* 在这里，赢利不是一个犯忌的字眼。 (**do sb's**) **ˈdirty work** (to do) the unpleasant or dishonest jobs that sb else does not want to do （干）没人愿干的事，卑鄙的勾当 **do the ˈdirty on sb** (*BrE, informal*) to cheat sb who trusts you; to treat sb badly or unfairly 欺骗，出卖，亏待：*I'd never do the dirty on my friends.* 我决不出卖朋友。 **give sb a dirty ˈlook** to look at sb in a way that shows you are annoyed with them 厌恶地瞪某人一眼；给某人一个白眼 ➲MORE AT DOWN *adv.*, HAND *n.*, WASH *v.*

▼**SYNONYMS** 同义词辨析

dirty

dusty • filthy • muddy • soiled • grubby • stained

These words all describe sb/sth that is not clean. 以上各词均形容人或事物不干净、肮脏。

dirty not clean; covered with dust, soil, mud, oil, etc. 指肮脏的、龌龊的、污秽的：*If your hands are dirty, go and wash them.* 要是你的手脏了，就去洗一洗。

dusty full of dust; covered with dust 指布满灰尘的、灰尘覆盖的：*There were shelves full of dusty books.* 有些书架上全是布满灰尘的书。

filthy very dirty and unpleasant 指肮脏的、污秽的：*It's absolutely filthy in here.* 这里面脏得不得了。

muddy full of or covered in mud 指沾满泥的、泥泞的：*Don't you come in here with those muddy boots on!* 你不要穿着那双沾满泥浆的靴子进来！

soiled (*rather formal*) dirty, especially with waste from the body 指肮脏的、龌龊的，尤指有人体排泄物的：*soiled nappies/diapers* 脏尿布

grubby (*rather informal*) rather dirty, usually because it has not been washed 通常指因未经洗涤而肮脏的、邋遢的、污秽的：*He hoped she wouldn't notice his grubby shirt cuffs.* 他希望她不会注意到他肮脏的衬衫袖口。

stained (often in compounds) covered with stains; marked with a stain (= a dirty mark that is difficult to remove)（常构成复合词）指污渍斑斑的、沾有污渍的：*a pair of paint-stained jeans* 一条沾满油漆的牛仔裤

PATTERNS
- dirty/dusty/filthy/muddy/soiled/grubby/stained **clothes**
- dirty/dusty/filthy/grubby **hands**
- a dirty/dusty/filthy **room**
- to **get** dirty/dusty/filthy/muddy/stained

▪*verb* (**dirt·ies**, **dirty·ing**, **dirt·ied**, **dirt·ied**) ~ **sth** to make sth dirty 弄脏；使变脏
▪*adv.*
IDM **dirty great/big** (*BrE, informal*) used to emphasize how large sth is 非常大的；很大的：*When I turned round he was pointing a dirty great gun at me.* 我转过身来，他用一支老大的枪对准我。 **play ˈdirty** (*informal*) to behave or play a game in an unfair way 干卑鄙勾当；（比赛）犯规 ➲MORE AT TALK *v.*

ˈdirty bomb *noun* a bomb which contains RADIOACTIVE material "脏弹"；放射性炸弹

ˌdirty old ˈman *noun* (*informal*) an older man whose interest in sex or in sexually attractive young people is considered to be offensive or not natural for sb of his age 老色鬼

ˌdirty ˈtrick *noun* **1** [usually pl.] dishonest, secret and often illegal activity by a political group or other organization that is intended to harm the reputation or success of an opponent 卑鄙伎俩；造谣中伤：*a dirty tricks campaign* 肮脏卑鄙的竞选运动 **2** an unpleasant and dishonest act 卑鄙的勾当；奸诈：*What a dirty trick to play!* 玩的手段太卑鄙了！

ˌdirty weekˈend *noun* (*BrE, humorous*) a weekend spent away with a sexual partner, often in secret 与性伴侣厮混的周末

dis (*also* **diss**) /dɪs/ *verb* (**-ss-**) **~ sb** (*informal, especially NAmE*) to show a lack of respect for sb, especially by saying insulting things to them 看不起，作践（尤指用侮辱性言辞）

dis- /dɪs/ *prefix* (in adjectives, adverbs, nouns and verbs 构成形容词、副词、名词和动词) not; the opposite of 不；非；相反；相对：*dishonest* 不诚实 ◇ *disagreeably* 不合意地 ◇ *disadvantage* 不利条件 ◇ *disappear* 消失 ➲ MORE LIKE THIS 6, page R25

dis·abil·ity /ˌdɪsəˈbɪləti/ *noun* (*pl.* **-ies**) **1** [C] a physical or mental condition that means you cannot use a part of your body completely or easily, or that you cannot learn easily （某种）缺陷，障碍：*a* ***physical/mental disability*** 生理缺陷；心理障碍 ◇ *people with severe learning disabilities* 具有严重学习障碍的人 **2** [U] the state of not being able to use a part of your body completely or easily; the state of not being able to learn easily （指状态、身心、学习等方面的）缺陷，障碍：*He qualifies for help on the grounds of disability.* 他因身有残疾有资格得到帮助。➲ NOTE AT DISABLED

dis·able /dɪsˈeɪbl/ *verb* **1 ~ sb** to injure or affect sb permanently so that, for example, they cannot walk or cannot use a part of their body 使丧失能力；使伤残：*He was disabled in a car accident.* 他在车祸中残废了。◇ *a disabling condition* 导致残障的疾病 **2 ~ sth** to make sth unable to work so that it cannot be used 使无效；使不能运转：*The burglars gained entry to the building after disabling the alarm.* 窃贼破坏警报器后便得以进入大楼。

dis·abled 🔑 /dɪsˈeɪbld/ *adj.* **1** 🔑 unable to use a part of your body completely or easily because of a physical condition, an illness, an injury, etc.; unable to learn easily 丧失能力的；有残疾的；无能力的：***physically/mentally disabled*** 有生理残疾的；精神伤残的 ◇ *severely disabled* 严重伤残 ◇ *He was born disabled.* 他天生残疾。◇ *facilities for disabled people* 残疾人使用的设施 **2 the disabled** *noun* [pl.] people who are disabled 残疾人；伤残者：*caring for the sick, elderly and disabled* 关心老弱病残

> ▼ **WHICH WORD?** 词语辨析
>
> **disabled / handicapped**
>
> - **Disabled** is the most generally accepted term to refer to people with a permanent illness or injury that makes it difficult for them to use part of their body completely or easily. **Handicapped** is slightly old-fashioned and many people now think it is offensive. People also now prefer to use the word **disability** rather than **handicap**. The expression **disabled people** is often preferred to **the disabled** because it sounds more personal.
>   * disabled 是最广为接受的用语，指残疾人或伤残人。handicapped 稍有些过时，现在许多人认为该词含冒犯意。现在人们喜欢用 disability 而非 handicap。disabled people 比 the disabled 更为人所接受，原因是听起来较人性化。
> - **Disabled** and **disability** can be used with other words to talk about a mental condition. * disabled 和 disability 可与其他词连用表示智力状况：*mentally disabled* 精神伤残的 ◇ *learning disabilities* 学习障碍
> - If somebody's ability to hear, speak or see has been damaged but not destroyed completely, they have **impaired hearing/speech/sight** (or **vision**). They can be described as **visually/hearing impaired** or **partially sighted**. 听力、说话能力或视力受到损害但未完全丧失，用 impaired hearing / speech / sight（或 vision）表示，或形容某人为 visually / hearing impaired（视力 / 听力受损的）或 partially sighted（视力有缺陷的）：*The museum has special facilities for blind and partially sighted visitors.* 博物馆有专门设备供失明和视力有缺陷的参观者使用。

dis·able·ment /dɪsˈeɪblmənt/ *noun* [U] (*formal*) the state of being disabled or the process of becoming disabled 残废；伤残；失去能力：*The insurance policy covers sudden death or disablement.* 保险单为突然死亡或伤残保险。

dis·abuse /ˌdɪsəˈbjuːz/ *verb* **~ sb** (**of sth**) (*formal*) to tell sb that what they think is true is, in fact, not true 去掉（某人）的错误想法；使省悟

dis·ad·van·tage 🔑 /ˌdɪsədˈvɑːntɪdʒ; *NAmE* -ˈvæn-/ *noun* [C, U] something that causes problems and tends to stop sb/sth from succeeding or making progress 不利因素；障碍；不便之处：*a* ***serious/severe/considerable disadvantage*** 重大的不利条件 ◇ **~** (**of sth**) *One* ***major disadvantage*** *of the area is the lack of public transport.* 这个地区的一大不便之处就是缺少公共交通工具。◇ **~** (**to sth**) *There are disadvantages to the plan.* 这个计划有诸多不利因素。◇ *What's the* ***main disadvantage?*** 主要的不利条件是什么？◇ *I was* ***at a disadvantage*** *compared to the younger members of the team.* 与队里较年轻的队员相比，我处于不利地位。◇ *The fact that he didn't speak a foreign language* ***put him at a distinct disadvantage.*** 他不会说外语使他处于明显的不利地位。◇ *I hope my lack of experience won't* ***be to my disadvantage.*** 但愿我的经验不足不会使我吃亏。◇ *The advantages of the scheme far* ***outweighed the disadvantages.*** 这个计划的优点远远超过了缺点。◇ *Many children in the class suffered severe social and economic disadvantage.* 班上许多孩子都来自社会地位低下、经济困难的家庭。 OPP advantage ▶ **dis·ad·van·tage** *verb* **~ sb/sth**

dis·ad·van·taged /ˌdɪsədˈvɑːntɪdʒd; *NAmE* -ˈvæn-/ *adj.* **1** not having the things, such as education, or enough money, that people need in order to succeed in life 弱势的；社会地位低下的 SYN **deprived**：***disadvantaged groups/children*** 生活条件差的群体 / 孩子 ◇ *a severely disadvantaged area* 极贫困地区 OPP **advantaged** ➲ SYNONYMS AT POOR **2 the disadvantaged** *noun* [pl.] people who are disadvantaged 下层社会

dis·ad·van·ta·geous /ˌdɪsædvænˈteɪdʒəs/ *adj.* **~** (**to/for sb**) (*formal*) causing sb to be in a worse situation compared to other people 不利的；没有好处的：*The deal will not be disadvantageous to your company.* 这项交易不会对你公司不利。OPP **advantageous**

dis·af·fect·ed /ˌdɪsəˈfektɪd/ *adj.* no longer satisfied with your situation, organization, belief, etc. and therefore not loyal to it 不满的：*Some disaffected members left to form a new party.* 部分不满的成员已脱党另立新党。▶ **dis·af·fec·tion** /ˌdɪsəˈfekʃn/ *noun* [U]: *There are signs of growing disaffection amongst voters.* 选民中出现日渐不满的迹象。

dis·af·fili·ate /ˌdɪsəˈfɪlieɪt/ *verb* [I, T] **~** (**sth**) (**from sth**) to end the link between a group, a company or an organization and a larger one （使）脱离；（使）退出：*The local club has disaffiliated from the National Athletic Association.* 当地俱乐部已退出全国体育联合会。▶ **dis·af·fili·ation** /ˌdɪsəfɪliˈeɪʃn/ *noun* [U]

dis·agree 🔑 /ˌdɪsəˈɡriː/ *verb* **1** 🔑 [I] if two people **disagree** or one person **disagrees** with another about sth, they have a different opinion about it 不同意；持不同意见；有分歧：*Even friends disagree sometimes.* 即便是朋友有时也有分歧。◇ *No, I disagree. I don't think it would be the right thing to do.* 不，我不赞成。我认为这样做不合适。◇ **~** (**with sb**) (**about/on/over sth**) *He disagreed with his parents on most things.* 他在多数事情上都与父母意见不一。◇ *Some people disagree with this argument.* 有些人不同意这一论点。◇ **~ that...** *Few would disagree that students learn best when they are interested in the topic.* 学生对自己感兴趣的题目学得最好，这一点几乎所有人都不会有异议。**2** 🔑 [I] if statements or reports **disagree**, they give different information 不符；不一致 OPP **agree**

PHR V **disaˈgree with sb** if sth, especially food, **disagrees** with you, it has a bad effect on you and makes you feel ill/sick （尤指食物）对（某人）不适宜，使不舒服 **disaˈgree with sth/with doing sth** 🔑 to believe that

D

sth is bad or wrong; to disapprove of sth 不赞成；反对：*I disagree with violent protests.* 我不赞成暴力抗议。

▼ EXPRESS YOURSELF 情景表达

Disagreeing 表达不同意见

In a discussion, you may think that what other people say is wrong, but there are polite ways to convey this. It is common to express support for something that the other person says before expressing disagreement. 在讨论中可用比较礼貌的方式表示不同意别人的说法。在表达不同意见之前通常会对别人的说法表示一定的支持：

- ***I'm sorry, I don't agree/I have to disagree with you there.*** 对不起，在那一点上我跟你有不同看法。
- ***Well, actually, I'm not sure that that's true.*** 嗯，其实我拿不准那是否属实。
- ***I don't think that is exactly right.*** 我认为那不见得完全正确。
- ***I wouldn't agree that*** *that's the best solution.* 我不认为那是最好的解决办法。
- ***I have to say that I don't find*** *that argument very convincing.* 我得说我觉得这个论据不是很有说服力。
- ***I can't go along with that idea.*** 我不同意那个看法。
- ***I take/see your point, but I don't think it would work in*** *practice.* 我明白你的意思，但我认为实际上那是行不通的。
- ***Actually, I think*** *that would make the situation worse.* 实际上，我觉得那会使情况更糟。
- *Actually,* ***I'm not sure*** *that's the best plan.* 事实上我不太肯定那是最好的方案。
- ***I understand where you're coming from, but*** *I think we might want to take a different approach here.* 我明白你为什么这么认为，但我想这里我们可能要采取不同的方法。
- ***I can see why you might feel that way, but*** *I think we need to handle this differently.* 我明白你为什么会这么想，但我认为我们需要以不同的方式处理这件事。

dis·agree·able /ˌdɪsəˈɡriːəbl/ *adj.* (*formal*) **1** not nice or enjoyable 不合意的；令人不快的；讨厌的 **SYN** **unpleasant**：*a disagreeable smell/experience/job* 难闻的气味；令人不快的经历；不合意的工作 **2** (of a person 人) rude and unfriendly 不友善的；难相处的 **SYN** **unpleasant**：*a disagreeable bad-tempered man* 一个脾气不好难以相处的男人 **OPP** **agreeable** ▶ **dis·agree·ably** /-əbli/ *adv.*

dis·agree·ment /ˌdɪsəˈɡriːmənt/ *noun* **1** [U, C] a situation where people have different opinions about sth and often argue 意见不一；分歧；争论：~ (**about/on/over/as to sth**) *Disagreement arose about exactly how to plan the show.* 在如何拟订具体演出计划的问题上出现了分歧。◇ *disagreement on the method to be used* 在要采用的方法上的争论 ◇ *There is considerable disagreement over the safety of the treatment.* 这种疗法是否安全争论很大。◇ ~ (**between A and B**) *It was a source of disagreement between the two states.* 这就是两国纷争的一个根源。◇ ~ (**among...**) *There is disagreement among archaeologists as to the age of the sculpture.* 考古学家在这尊雕塑的年代问题上意见不一。◇ ~ (**with sb**) *They have had several disagreements with their neighbours.* 他们与邻居发生过好几次争吵。**OPP** **agreement** **2** [U, C] ~ **between A and B** a difference between two things that should be the same 不符；不一致：*The comparison shows considerable disagreement between theory and practice.* 这一对比表明理论和实践之间有相当大的出入。

dis·allow /ˌdɪsəˈlaʊ/ *verb* ~ **sth** [often passive] (*formal*) to officially refuse to accept sth because it is not valid 不准许；不接受；驳回：*to* ***disallow a claim/an appeal*** 不接受要求；驳回上诉 ◇ *The second goal was disallowed.* 第二个进球被判无效。➲ COMPARE ALLOW (6)

dis·am·bigu·ate /ˌdɪsæmˈbɪɡjueɪt/ *verb* ~ **sth** (*specialist*) to show clearly the difference between two or more words, phrases, etc. which are similar in meaning 消除歧义；消歧

dis·ap·pear /ˌdɪsəˈpɪə(r); *NAmE* -ˈpɪr/ *verb* **1** [I] (+ **adv./prep.**) to become impossible to see 消失；不见 **SYN** **vanish**：*The plane disappeared behind a cloud.* 飞机消失在云层里。◇ *Lisa watched until the train* ***disappeared from view.*** 莉萨一直看着火车从视线中消失。**2** [I] to stop existing 不复存在；灭绝；消亡 **SYN** **vanish**：*Her nervousness quickly disappeared once she was on stage.* 她一走上台紧张情绪便迅速消失了。◇ *The problem won't just disappear.* 这个问题不会就这样不了了之的。◇ *Our countryside is disappearing at an alarming rate.* 我们的农村地区正在以惊人的速度消亡。**3** [I] to be lost or impossible to find 失踪；丢失 **SYN** **vanish**：*I can never find a pen in this house. They disappear as soon as I buy them.* 我在家里从来找不到一支笔。每次我一买来就不翼而飞。◇ ~ **from sth** *The child disappeared from his home some time after four.* 这孩子四点多的时候就离家不见了。▶ **dis·ap·pear·ance** /-ˈpɪərəns; *NAmE* -ˈpɪr-/ *noun* [U, C]：*the disappearance of many species of plants and animals from our planet* 许多动植物物种从我们这颗行星上的消失 ◇ *Police are investigating the disappearance of a young woman.* 警方正在调查一名年轻女子的失踪案。**IDM** SEE ACT *n.*, FACE *n.*

dis·ap·point /ˌdɪsəˈpɔɪnt/ *verb* **1** [T, I] ~ (**sb**) | (**it disappoints sb that...**) to make sb feel sad because sth that they hope for or expect to happen does not happen or is not as good as they hoped 使失望：*Her decision to cancel the concert is bound to disappoint her fans.* 她决定取消这场音乐会，肯定会使她的歌迷失望。◇ *I hate to disappoint you, but I'm just not interested.* 我不想使你扫兴，但我确实不感兴趣。◇ *The movie had disappointed her* (= it wasn't as good as she had expected). 这部电影使她失望。◇ *His latest novel does not disappoint.* 他最近发表的这部小说没有使人失望。**2** [T] ~ **sth** to prevent sth that sb hopes for from becoming a reality 使破灭；使落空：*The new government had soon disappointed the hopes of many of its supporters.* 新政府不久便使许多支持者的希望破灭了。

dis·ap·point·ed /ˌdɪsəˈpɔɪntɪd/ *adj.* upset because sth you hoped for has not happened or been as good, successful, etc. as you expected 失望的；沮丧的；失意的：~ (**at/by sth**) *They were* ***bitterly disappointed*** *at the result of the game.* 他们对比赛结果极为失望。◇ *I was disappointed by the quality of the wine.* 这酒的质量令我失望。◇ ~ (**in/with sb/sth**) *I'm disappointed in you—I really thought I could trust you!* 你真让我失望，我原以为可以相信你的！◇ *I was very disappointed with myself.* 我对自己感到非常失望。◇ ~ (**to see, hear, etc.**) *He was disappointed to see she wasn't at the party.* 看到她没来参加晚会，他感到很失望。◇ ~ (**that...**) *I'm disappointed* (*that*) *it was sold out.* 全都卖完了，我感到很失望。◇ ~ (**not**) **to be...** *She was disappointed not to be chosen.* 她没有被选中感到很沮丧。

dis·ap·point·ing /ˌdɪsəˈpɔɪntɪŋ/ *adj.* not as good, successful, etc. as you had hoped; making you feel disappointed 令人失望的；令人沮丧的；令人扫兴的：*a disappointing result/performance* 令人失望的结果 / 演出 ◇ *The outcome of the court case was disappointing for the family involved.* 诉讼案的结果使得涉及本案的这家人非常失望。▶ **dis·ap·point·ing·ly** *adv.*：*The room was disappointingly small.* 房间小得令人失望。

dis·ap·point·ment /ˌdɪsəˈpɔɪntmənt/ *noun* **1** [U] sadness because sth has not happened or been as good, successful, etc. as you expected or hoped 失望；沮丧；扫兴：*Book early for the show to avoid disappointment.* 欲看演出，从速订票，以免向隅。◇ ***To our great disappointment****, it rained every day of the trip.* 这次旅行天天下雨，让我们大失所望。◇ *He found it difficult to hide his disappointment when she didn't arrive.* 她没有来，他感到很难掩饰自己内心的沮丧。**2** [C] a person or thing that is disappointing 使人失望的人（或事物）；令人扫兴的人（或事物）：*a* ***bitter/major disappointment*** 令人极度失望 / 大失所望的事 ◇ *That new restaurant was a big disappointment.* 那家新餐馆使人大失所望。◇ ~ **to sb** *I always* *felt I was a disappointment to my father.* 我总觉得我使父亲失望了。

dis·ap·pro·ba·tion /ˌdɪsˌæprəˈbeɪʃn/ *noun* [U] (*formal*) disapproval of sb/sth that you think is morally wrong（对不道德的人或事的）反对，不认可

dis·ap·proval /ˌdɪsəˈpruːvl/ *noun* [U] ~ (**of sb/sth**) a feeling that you do not like an idea, an action or sb's behaviour because you think it is bad, not suitable or going to have a bad effect on sb else 不赞成；反对：*disapproval of his methods* 不赞同他的方法 ◇ *to show/express disapproval* 表明 / 表示反对 ◇ *He shook his head **in disapproval**.* 他摇了摇头，表示反对。◇ *She looked at my clothes **with disapproval**.* 她不满意地看着我的衣服。OPP approval

dis·ap·prove /ˌdɪsəˈpruːv/ *verb* [I, T] to think that sb/sth is not good or suitable; to not approve of sb/sth 不赞成；不同意；反对：*She wants to be an actress, but her parents disapprove.* 她想当演员，可是她父母不同意。◇ **~ of sb/sth** *He **strongly disapproved** of the changes that had been made.* 他强烈反对已进行的变革。◇ **~ sth** (*NAmE*) *A solid majority disapproves the way the president is handling the controversy.* 大多数人都反对总统处理争论的方式。OPP approve

dis·ap·prov·ing /ˌdɪsəˈpruːvɪŋ/ *adj.* showing that you do not approve of sb/sth 不赞成的；表示反对的；不以为然的：*a **disapproving glance/tone/look*** 不以为然的一瞥 / 语气 / 样子 OPP **approving** ▶ **dis·ap·prov·ing·ly** *adv.*：*He looked disapprovingly at the row of empty wine bottles.* 他不以为然地看了看那排空酒瓶。

dis·arm /dɪsˈɑːm; *NAmE* -ˈɑːrm/ *verb* **1** [T] **~ sb** to take a weapon or weapons away from sb 缴（某人）的械；解除（某人）的武装：*Most of the rebels were captured and disarmed.* 大部分叛乱分子被俘获并解除了武装。**2** [I] (of a country or a group of people 国家或集体) to reduce the size of an army or to give up some or all weapons, especially nuclear weapons 裁军；裁减军备（尤指核武器）**3** [T] **~ sb** to make sb feel less angry or critical 消释（某人）的怒气（或批评）：*He disarmed her immediately by apologizing profusely.* 他一再向她道歉，很快便消解了她的怒气。 ⊃ COMPARE ARM *v.*

dis·arma·ment /dɪsˈɑːməmənt; *NAmE* -ˈɑːrm-/ *noun* [U] the fact of a country reducing the size of its armed forces or the number of weapons, especially nuclear weapons, that it has 裁军；裁减军备（尤指核武器）：*nuclear disarmament* 核裁军 ◇ *disarmament talks* 裁军谈判 ⊃ COMPARE ARMAMENT

dis·arm·ing /dɪsˈɑːmɪŋ; *NAmE* -ˈɑːrm-/ *adj.* making people feel less angry or suspicious than they were before 使人消气的；解人疑虑的：*a disarming smile* 使人消气的微笑 ▶ **dis·arm·ing·ly** *adv.*：*disarmingly frank* 坦率得使人放心

dis·ar·range /ˌdɪsəˈreɪndʒ/ *verb* [usually passive] **~ sth** (*formal*) to make sth untidy 使紊乱；弄乱

dis·array /ˌdɪsəˈreɪ/ *noun* [U] a state of confusion and lack of organization in a situation or a place 混乱；紊乱：*The peace talks broke up **in disarray**.* 和谈在混乱中破裂了。◇ *Our plans were **thrown into disarray** by her arrival.* 我们的计划因她的到来而陷入一片混乱。

dis·as·sem·ble /ˌdɪsəˈsembl/ *verb* **1** [T] **~ sth** to take apart a machine or structure so that it is in separate pieces 拆卸；拆开：*We had to completely disassemble the engine to find the problem.* 我们只好把发动机全部拆开以寻找故障原因。OPP **assemble** **2** [T] **~ sth** (*computing* 计) to translate sth from computer code into a language that can be read by humans 反汇编（将计算机编码译成普通语言）**3** [I] (*formal*) (of a group of people 人群) to move apart and go away in different directions 散开；分散：*The concert ended and the crowd disassembled.* 音乐会结束，人群便散去了。

dis·as·sem·bler /ˌdɪsəˈsemblə(r)/ *noun* (*computing* 计) a program used to disassemble (2) computer code 反汇编程序

dis·as·so·ci·ate /ˌdɪsəˈsəʊʃieɪt; -ˈsəʊs-; *NAmE* -ˈsoʊ-/ *verb* = DISSOCIATE

dis·as·ter /dɪˈzɑːstə(r); *NAmE* -ˈzæs-/ *noun* **1** [C] an unexpected event, such as a very bad accident, a flood or a fire, that kills a lot of people or causes a lot of damage 灾难；灾祸；灾害 SYN **catastrophe**：*an air disaster* 空难 ◇ *environmental disasters* 环境灾难 ◇ *Thousands died in the disaster.* 数千人在这场灾祸中丧生。◇ *a **natural disaster*** (= one that is caused by nature) 自然灾害

WORDFINDER 联想词：avalanche, cyclone, earthquake, erupt, flood, hurricane, landslide, tornado, tsunami

2 [C, U] a very bad situation that causes problems 不幸；祸患：*Losing your job doesn't have to be such a disaster.* 丢了工作不一定就是大难临头。◇ ***Disaster struck** when the wheel came off.* 车轮脱落，灾难就来了。◇ *financial disaster* 严重的财政危机 ◇ *Letting her organize the party is a **recipe for disaster*** (= something that is likely to go badly wrong). 让她来组织这次聚会非坏事不可。**3** [C, U] (*informal*) a complete failure 彻底失败的人（或事）：*As a teacher, he's a disaster.* 他当老师压根儿就不称职。◇ *The play's first night was a total disaster.* 这出戏头一晚就彻底演砸了。IDM SEE WAIT *v.*

diˈsaster area *noun* **1** a place where a disaster has happened and which needs special help 灾区 **2** (*informal*) a place or situation that has a lot of problems, is a failure, or is badly organized 问题成堆的地方；灾难性局面

dis·as·trous /dɪˈzɑːstrəs; *NAmE* -ˈzæs-/ *adj.* very bad, harmful or unsuccessful 极糟糕的；灾难性的；完全失败的 SYN **catastrophic, devastating**：*a disastrous harvest/fire/result* 严重歉收 / 火灾；灾难性的结果 ◇ *Lowering interest rates could have disastrous consequences for the economy.* 降低利率可能给经济带来灾难性后果。▶ **dis·as·trous·ly** *adv.*：*How could everything go so disastrously wrong?* 怎么会事事都出这么大的错呢？

dis·avow /ˌdɪsəˈvaʊ/ *verb* **~ sth** (*formal*) to state publicly that you have no knowledge of sth or that you are not responsible for sth/sb 不承认；否认；拒绝对…承担责任：*They disavowed claims of a split in the party.* 他们否认了党内出现分裂的说法。▶ **dis·avowal** /-ˈvaʊəl/ *noun* [C, U]

dis·band /dɪsˈbænd/ *verb* [T, I] ~ (**sb/sth**) to stop sb/sth from operating as a group; to separate or no longer operate as a group 解散；解体；散伙：*They set about disbanding the terrorist groups.* 他们开始解散恐怖主义组织。◇ *The committee formally disbanded in August.* 委员会于八月份正式解散。▶ **dis·band·ment** *noun* [U]

dis·bar /dɪsˈbɑː(r)/ *verb* (**-rr-**) [usually passive] **~ sb** (**from sth/from doing sth**) to stop a lawyer from working in the legal profession, especially because he or she has done sth illegal 取消（某人）的律师资格

dis·be·lief /ˌdɪsbɪˈliːf/ *noun* [U] the feeling of not being able to believe sth 不信；怀疑：*He stared at me **in disbelief**.* 他满腹疑惑地盯着我。◇ *To enjoy the movie you have to **suspend your disbelief*** (= pretend to believe sth, even if it seems very unlikely). 要欣赏这部电影就得暂且相信那明知不大可能的事。⊃ COMPARE BELIEF (3), UNBELIEF

dis·be·lieve /ˌdɪsbɪˈliːv/ *verb* [T, I] (not used in the progressive tenses 不用于进行时) ~ (**sth**) (*formal*) to not believe that sth is true or that sb is telling the truth 不信；怀疑：*Why should I disbelieve her story?* 我为什么要怀疑她的说法呢？▶ **dis·be·liev·ing** *adj.*：*a disbelieving look/smile/laugh* 怀疑的表情 / 微笑 / 笑声 **dis·be·liev·ing·ly** *adv.*

PHR V **disbeˈlieve in sth** to not believe that sth exists 怀疑；不信

dis·burse /dɪsˈbɜːs; *NAmE* -ˈbɜːrs/ *verb* **~ sth** (*formal*) to pay money to sb from a large amount that has been collected for a purpose（从资金中）支付，支出 ▶ **dis·burse·ment** *noun* [U, C]：*the disbursement of funds* 款项的拨付 ◇ *aid disbursements* 援助款项的支出额

disc (*also* **disk** *especially in NAmE*) /dɪsk/ *noun* **1** a thin flat round object 圆盘；圆片：*He wears an identity disc around his neck.* 他脖子上挂着圆形身份牌。 **2** = CD：*This recording is available online or* ***on disc****.* 这录音可在线获取，也可购买激光唱片。 **3** (*BrE*) a disk for a computer（计算机）光碟，光盘 **4** (*old-fashioned*) = RECORD (2) **5** a structure made of CARTILAGE between the bones of the back 椎间盘：*He's been off work with a* ***slipped disc*** (= one that has moved from its correct position, causing pain). 他因椎间盘突出一直未上班。

dis·card *verb, noun*

■ ***verb*** /dɪsˈkɑːd; *NAmE* -ˈkɑːrd/ **1** [T] (*formal*) to get rid of sth that you no longer want or need 丢弃；抛弃：**~ sb/sth** *The room was littered with discarded newspapers.* 房间里到处是乱扔的报纸。◇ *He had discarded his jacket because of the heat.* 因天气炎热他脱掉了夹克。◇ (*figurative*) *She could now discard all thought of promotion.* 她现在可以打消晋升的念头了。◇ **~ sb/sth as sth** *10% of the data was discarded as unreliable.* * 10% 的数据因不可靠而被废弃。 **2** [T, I] **~ (sth)** (in card games 纸牌游戏) to get rid of a card that you do not want 垫（牌）；打出（无用的牌）

■ ***noun*** /ˈdɪskɑːd; *NAmE* -kɑːrd/ a person or thing that is not wanted or thrown away, especially a card in a card game 被抛弃的人（或物）；（尤指纸牌游戏中）垫出的牌

ˈdisc brake *noun* [usually pl.] a BRAKE that works by two surfaces pressing onto a disc in the centre of a wheel 盘型制动

dis·cern /dɪˈsɜːn; *NAmE* -ˈsɜːrn/ *verb* (not used in the progressive tenses 不用于进行时) (*formal*) **1** to know, recognize or understand sth, especially sth that is not obvious 觉察出；识别；了解 **SYN** **detect**：**~ sth** *It is possible to discern a number of different techniques in her work.* 从她的作品中可以辨别出许多不同的创作手法。◇ *He discerned a certain coldness in their welcome.* 他觉察到他们的接待有点冷淡。◇ **~ how, whether, etc.…** *It is often difficult to discern how widespread public support is.* 了解公众支持的广泛程度常常是困难的。◇ **~ that…** *I quickly discerned that something was wrong.* 我很快觉察到出了问题。 **2 ~ sth** to see or hear sth, usually with difficulty（依稀）看出，分辨出，听出 **SYN** **make out**：*We could just discern the house in the distance.* 我们只能勉强分辨出远处的房子。

▶ **dis·cern·ible** *adj.* (*formal*) **SYN** **perceptible**：*There is often no discernible difference between rival brands.* 相互竞争的品牌之间往往看不出明显的区别。◇ *His face was barely discernible in the gloom.* 在黑暗中很难看得清他的脸。

dis·cern·ing /dɪˈsɜːnɪŋ; *NAmE* -ˈsɜːrn-/ *adj.* (*approving*) able to show good judgement about the quality of sb/sth 有识别力的；有眼力的；有洞察力的

dis·cern·ment /dɪˈsɜːnmənt; *NAmE* -ˈsɜːrn-/ *noun* [U] (*formal, approving*) the ability to show good judgement about the quality of sb/sth 识别能力；洞察力 **SYN** **discrimination**：*He shows great discernment in his choice of friends.* 他选择朋友很有眼光。

dis·charge *verb, noun*

■ ***verb*** /dɪsˈtʃɑːdʒ; *NAmE* -ˈtʃɑːrdʒ/ (*formal*)

• **FROM HOSPITAL/JOB** 医院；工作 **1** [T, usually passive] **~ sb (from sth)** to give sb official permission to leave a place or job; to make sb leave a job 准许（某人）离开；解雇：*Patients were being discharged from the hospital too early.* 病人都过早获准出院。◇ *She had discharged herself against medical advice.* 她不听医嘱擅自出院了。◇ *He was discharged from the army following his injury.* 他受伤后就退伍了。◇ *She was discharged from the police force for bad conduct.* 她因行为不端被清除出警察队伍。

• **FROM PRISON/COURT** 监狱；法庭 **2** [T, often passive] **~ sb** to allow sb to leave prison or court 释放：*He was* ***conditionally discharged*** *after admitting the theft.* 他承认偷盗行为后被有条件地释放了。➲ WORDFINDER NOTE AT PRISON

• **GAS/LIQUID** 气体；液体 **3** [I, T] when a gas or a liquid **discharges** or **is discharged**, or sb **discharges** it, it flows somewhere 排出；放出；流出：**~ (into sth)** *The river is diverted through the power station before discharging into the sea.* 这条河改道经水电站后流入大海。◇ **~ sth (into sth)** *The factory was fined for discharging chemicals into the river.* 这家工厂因往河里排放化学物质而被罚款。

• **FORCE/POWER** 力量；电力 **4** [T, I] **~ (sth)** (*specialist*) to release force or power 发（力）；放（电）：*Lightning is caused by clouds discharging electricity.* 闪电是由云层放电产生的。

• **DUTY** 职责 **5** [T] **~ sth** to do everything that is necessary to perform and complete a particular duty 尽（职）；完成；履行：*to* ***discharge your duties/responsibilities/obligations*** 履行职责 / 责任 / 义务 ◇ *to* ***discharge a debt*** (= to pay it) 清偿债务

• **GUN** 枪 **6** [T] **~ sth** to fire a gun, etc. 射出；开火

■ ***noun*** /ˈdɪstʃɑːdʒ; *NAmE* -tʃɑːrdʒ/ (*formal*)

• **OF LIQUID/GAS** 液体；气体 **1** [U, C] the action of releasing a substance such as a liquid or gas; a substance that comes out from inside somewhere 排出（物）；放出（物）；流出（物）：*a ban on the discharge of toxic waste* 禁止有毒废物的排放 ◇ *thunder and lightning caused by electrical discharges* 由放电产生的雷电 ◇ ***nasal/vaginal discharge*** (= from the nose/VAGINA) 鼻涕；阴道分泌物

• **FROM HOSPITAL/JOB** 医院；工作 **2** [U, C] **~ (from sth)** the act of officially allowing sb, or of telling sb, to leave somewhere, especially sb in a hospital or the army 获准离开；免职；出院；退伍

• **OF DUTY** 职责 **3** [U] the act of performing a task or a duty or of paying money that is owed（任务或职责的）履行，执行；（债务的）清偿：*the* ***discharge of debts/obligations*** 债务的清偿；义务的履行

dis·ciple /dɪˈsaɪpl/ *noun* **1** a person who believes in and follows the teachings of a religious or political leader 信徒；门徒；追随者 **SYN** **follower**：*a disciple of the economist John Maynard Keynes* 经济学家约翰·梅纳德·凯恩斯的信徒 **2** (according to the Bible) one of the people who followed Jesus Christ and his teachings when he was living on earth, especially one of the twelve APOSTLES（耶稣的）门徒，十二门徒之一

dis·cip·lin·ar·ian /ˌdɪsəplɪˈneəriən; *NAmE* -ˈner-/ *noun* a person who believes in using rules and punishments for controlling people 严格纪律信奉者；严格执行纪律者：*She's a very strict disciplinarian.* 她执行纪律非常严格。

dis·cip·lin·ary /ˈdɪsəplɪnəri; ˌdɪsəˈplɪnəri; *NAmE* ˈdɪsəpləneri/ *adj.* connected with the punishment of people who break rules 有关纪律的；执行纪律的；惩戒性的：*a disciplinary hearing* (= to decide if sb has done sth wrong) 纪律审讯 ◇ *The company will be taking* ***disciplinary action*** *against him.* 公司将对他进行纪律处分。

dis·cip·line /ˈdɪsəplɪn/ *noun, verb*

■ ***noun*** **1** [U] the practice of training people to obey rules and orders and punishing them if they do not; the controlled behaviour or situation that results from this training 训练；训导；纪律；风纪：*The school has a reputation for high standards of discipline.* 这所学校因纪律严格而名闻遐迩。◇ *Strict discipline is imposed on army recruits.* 新兵受严格的纪律约束。◇ *She keeps good discipline in class.* 她严格执行课堂纪律。 **2** [C] a method of training your mind or body or of controlling your behaviour; an area of activity where this is necessary 训练方法；行为准则；符合准则的行为：*Yoga is a good discipline for learning to relax.* 瑜伽是一种学习放松的有效方法。 **3** [U] the ability to control your behaviour or the way you live, work, etc. 自制力；遵守纪律：*He'll never get anywhere working for himself—he's got no discipline.* 他自己做事是不会有什么成就的 —— 他毫无自制力。➲ SEE ALSO SELF-DISCIPLINE **4** [C] (*formal*) an area of knowledge; a subject that people study or are taught, especially in a university 知识领域；（尤指大学的）学科，科目

■ ***verb*** **1 ~ sb (for sth)** to punish sb for sth they have done 惩罚；处罚：*The officers were disciplined for using racist language.* 这些军官因使用种族歧视性语言而受到惩罚。 **2 ~ sb** to train sb, especially a child, to obey particular rules and control the way they behave 训练；训导；管教：*a guide to the best ways of disciplining your child* 管教子女最佳方法指南 **3** to control the way you behave and make yourself do things that you believe you should do 自我控制；严格要求（自己）： **~ yourself** *Dieting is a matter of disciplining yourself.* 节食是自我控制的问题。◇ **~ yourself to do sth** *He disciplined himself to exercise at least three times a week.* 他规定自己每周至少锻炼三次。▶ **dis·cip·lined** *adj.*： *a disciplined army/team* 纪律严明的军队 / 团队 ◇ *a disciplined approach to work* 严格的工作态度

ˈdisc jockey *noun* (*abbr.* **DJ**) (*also informal* **dee·jay**) a person whose job is to introduce and play recorded popular music, on radio or television or at a club（电台、电视台、夜总会）唱片节目主持人

dis·claim /dɪsˈkleɪm/ *verb* (*formal*) **1 ~ sth** to state publicly that you have no knowledge of sth, or that you are not responsible for sth 公开否认；拒绝承认 **SYN deny**: *She disclaimed any knowledge of her husband's whereabouts.* 她否认知道丈夫的下落。◇ *The rebels disclaimed all responsibility for the explosion.* 叛乱分子否认对这次爆炸事件负有任何责任。**2 ~ sth** to give up your right to sth, such as property or a title 放弃（财产、头衔等的）权利 **SYN renounce**

dis·claim·er /dɪsˈkleɪmə(r)/ *noun* **1** (*formal*) a statement in which sb says that they are not connected with or responsible for sth, or that they do not have any knowledge of it 免责声明 **2** (*law* 律) a statement in which a person says officially that they do not claim the right to do sth 弃权声明（书）

dis·close /dɪsˈkləʊz; *NAmE* -ˈkloʊz/ *verb* (*formal*) **1** to give sb information about sth, especially sth that was previously secret 揭露；透露；泄露 **SYN reveal**: **~ sth (to sb)** *The spokesman refused to disclose details of the takeover to the press.* 发言人拒绝向新闻界透露公司收购的详细情况。◇ **~ that…** *The report discloses that human error was to blame for the accident.* 报告披露这次事故是人为原因造成的。◇ **it is disclosed that…** *It was disclosed that two women were being interviewed by the police.* 据透露，有两个女人当时正接受警方的问话。◇ **~ what, whether, etc.…** *I cannot disclose what we discussed.* 我不能泄露我们讨论的内容。**2 ~ sth** to allow sth that was hidden to be seen 使显露；使暴露 **SYN reveal**: *The door swung open, disclosing a long dark passage.* 门开了，露出一条昏暗的长通道。

dis·clo·sure /dɪsˈkləʊʒə(r); *NAmE* -ˈkloʊ-/ *noun* (*formal*) **1** [U] the act of making sth known or public that was previously secret or private 揭露；透露；公开 **SYN revelation**: *the newspaper's disclosure of defence secrets* 报纸对防务内幕的披露 **2** [C] information or a fact that is made known or public that was previously secret or private 透露的秘闻；公开的事情；暴露的事实 **SYN revelation**: *startling disclosures about his private life* 对他的私生活耸人听闻的披露

disco /ˈdɪskəʊ; *NAmE* ˈdɪskoʊ/ *noun* (*pl.* **-os**) **1** (*also old-fashioned* **disco·theque**) a club or party where people dance to recorded pop music 迪斯科舞厅（或舞会）：*disco music/dancing* 迪斯科乐曲 / 舞 ◇ *the youth club disco* 青年俱乐部迪斯科舞厅 **2** the lights and sound equipment for such an event 迪斯科舞会的灯光及音响设备

disc·og·raphy /dɪsˈkɒɡrəfi; *NAmE* -ˈkɑːɡ-/ *noun* (*pl.* **-ies**) **1** [C] all of the music that has been performed, written or collected by a particular person; a list of this music（某人演唱、创作或收藏的）音乐作品集，音乐作品目录 **2** [U] the study of musical recordings or collections 音乐录音（或作品集）研究

dis·col·or·ation (*BrE also* **dis·col·our·ation**) /ˌdɪsˌkʌləˈreɪʃn/ *noun* **1** [U] the process of becoming discoloured 变色；退色：*discoloration caused by the sun* 因日照引起的退色 **2** [C] a place where sth has become discoloured 变色处；退色处

dis·col·our (*especially US* **dis·color**) /dɪsˈkʌlə(r)/ *verb* [I, T] to change colour, or to make the colour of sth change, in a way that makes it look less attractive（使）变色，退色：*Plastic tends to discolour with age.* 塑料久而久之便会退色。◇ **~ sth** *The pipes were beginning to rust, discolouring the water.* 管子开始生锈，水都变颜色了。

dis·comfit /dɪsˈkʌmfɪt/ *verb* [often passive] **~ sb** (*literary*) to make sb feel confused or embarrassed 使困惑；使窘迫；使尴尬 ▶ **dis·com·fit·ure** /dɪsˈkʌmfɪtʃə(r)/ *noun* [U]: *He was clearly taking delight in her discomfiture.* 他显然以她的窘迫为乐。

dis·com·fort /dɪsˈkʌmfət; *NAmE* -fərt/ *noun, verb*

■*noun* (*formal*) **1** [U] a feeling of slight pain or of being physically uncomfortable 轻微的病痛；不舒服；不适：*You will experience some minor discomfort during the treatment.* 治疗中你会稍感不适。◇ *abdominal discomfort* 腹部不适 **2** [U] a feeling of worry or embarrassment 不安；不自在；尴尬 **SYN unease**: *John's presence caused her considerable discomfort.* 约翰在场使她颇感尴尬。**3** [C] something that makes you feel uncomfortable or causes you a slight feeling of pain 使人不舒服的事物；苦事；痛苦

■*verb* [often passive] **~ sb** (*formal*) to make sb feel anxious or embarrassed 使不舒服；使不安；使尴尬

dis·com·pose /ˌdɪskəmˈpəʊz; *NAmE* -ˈpoʊz/ *verb* **~ sb** (*formal*) to disturb sb and make them feel anxious 扰乱；使不安；使心烦意乱 **SYN disconcert, disturb** ▶ **dis·com·pos·ure** /ˌdɪskəmˈpəʊʒə(r); *NAmE* -ˈpoʊ-/ *noun* [U]

dis·con·cert /ˌdɪskənˈsɜːt; *NAmE* -ˈsɜːrt/ *verb* **~ sb** to make sb feel anxious, confused or embarrassed 使不安；使困惑；使尴尬 **SYN disturb**: *His answer rather disconcerted her.* 他的回答使她颇感难堪。▶ **dis·con·cert·ed** *adj.*： *I was disconcerted to find that everyone else already knew it.* 我发现别人都已知道此事，感到甚是尴尬。**dis·con·cert·ing** *adj.*： *She had the disconcerting habit of saying exactly what she thought.* 她怎么想的就怎么说，这种习惯让人很尴尬。**dis·con·cert·ing·ly** *adv.*

dis·con·nect /ˌdɪskəˈnekt/ *verb* **1** [T] **~ sth (from sth)** to remove a piece of equipment from a supply of gas, water or electricity 切断（燃气、水或电的供应）：*First, disconnect the boiler from the water mains.* 先将锅炉与供水总管断开。**2** [T] **~ sb/sth** [usually passive] to officially stop the supply of telephone lines, water, electricity or gas to a building 切断（电话服务）；停止供应（水、电或燃气）：*You may be disconnected if you do not pay the bill.* 若不付账单就可能停止供应。**3** [T] **~ sth (from sth)** to separate sth from sth 使分离；使脱离：*The ski had become disconnected from the boot.* 滑雪板与靴子脱离了。**4** [T] **~ sb** [usually passive] to break the contact between two people who are talking on the telephone 使（电话线路）中断：*We were suddenly disconnected.* 我们的电话突然断了。**5** [T, I, often passive] to end a connection to the Internet（与互联网）断开：**~ sb (from sth)** *I keep getting disconnected when I'm online.* 我连网时不断掉线。◇ **~ (from sth)** *My computer crashes every time I disconnect from the Internet.* 我每次断网，计算机都会突然死机。**OPP connect** ▶ **dis·con·nec·tion** *noun* [U, C]

dis·con·nect·ed /ˌdɪskəˈnektɪd/ *adj.* **1** not related to or connected with the things or people around 分离的；断开的；无关联的：*disconnected images/thoughts/ideas* 互不相关的形象 / 思想 / 意见 ◇ *I felt disconnected from the world around me.* 我感到已与周围世界隔绝。**2** (of speech or writing 讲话或写作) with the parts not connected in a logical order 不连贯的；无条理的 **SYN disjointed, incoherent**

dis·con·so·late /dɪsˈkɒnsələt; *NAmE* -ˈkɑːn-/ *adj.* (*formal*) very unhappy and disappointed 忧郁的；沮丧的；郁郁寡欢的 **SYN dejected** ▶ **dis·con·so·late·ly** *adv.*

dis·con·tent /ˌdɪskənˈtent/ (*also* **dis·con·tent·ment** /ˌdɪskənˈtentmənt/) *noun* [U, C] **~ (at/over/with sth)** a feeling of being unhappy because you are not satisfied with a particular situation; sth that makes you have this feeling 不满；不满足；不满足的缘由 **SYN dissatisfaction**: *There is widespread discontent among the staff at the proposed changes to pay and conditions.* 员工对改变工资和工作环境的建议普遍不满。➲COMPARE CONTENTMENT

dis·con·tent·ed /ˌdɪskənˈtentɪd/ *adj.* ~ (**with sth**) unhappy because you are not satisfied with your situation 不满的；不满足的 SYN **dissatisfied** OPP **contented** ▶ **dis·con·tent·ed·ly** *adv.*

dis·con·tinue /ˌdɪskənˈtɪnjuː/ *verb* (*formal*) **1** ~ (**doing**) **sth** to stop doing, using or providing sth, especially sth that you have been doing, using or providing regularly 停止；终止；中断：*It was decided to discontinue the treatment after three months.* 决定三个月后终止治疗。 **2** [usually passive] ~ **sth** to stop making a product 停止，终止（生产）：*a sale of discontinued china* 出售已停止生产的瓷器

dis·con·tinu·ity /ˌdɪsˌkɒntɪˈnjuːəti; *NAmE* -ˌkɑːntəˈnuː-/ *noun* (*pl.* **-ies**) (*formal*) **1** [U] the state of not being continuous 不连贯；不连续：*discontinuity in the children's education* 儿童教育的不连贯性 **2** [C] a break or change in a continuous process 中断；间断；停顿：*Changes in government led to discontinuities in policy.* 政府的更迭导致政策缺乏连续性。 OPP **continuity**

dis·con·tinu·ous /ˌdɪskənˈtɪnjuəs/ *adj.* (*formal*) not continuous; stopping and starting again 不连续的；间断的；断续的 SYN **intermittent**

dis·cord /ˈdɪskɔːd; *NAmE* -kɔːrd/ *noun* **1** [U] (*formal*) disagreement; arguing 不一致；不和；纷争：***marital/family discord*** 夫妻 / 家庭不和 ◇ *A note of discord surfaced during the proceedings.* 事件进程中出现了不和的征兆。 OPP **concord** **2** [C, U] (*music* 音) a combination of musical notes that do not sound pleasant together 不协和和弦 ➲ COMPARE HARMONY (2)

dis·cord·ant /dɪsˈkɔːdənt; *NAmE* -ˈkɔːrd-/ *adj.* **1** [usually before noun] (*formal*) not in agreement; combining with other things in a way that is strange or unpleasant 不一致的；不协调的；不和的：*discordant views* 相互冲突的观点 **2** (of sounds 声音) not sounding pleasant together 不和谐的 OPP **harmonious**

disco·theque /ˈdɪskətek/ *noun* (*old-fashioned*) = DISCO

dis·count 🔑 *noun, verb*

■ ***noun*** 🔑 /ˈdɪskaʊnt/ [C, U] an amount of money that is taken off the usual cost of sth 折扣 SYN **reduction**：*to **get/give/offer a discount*** 得到 / 给予 / 提供折扣 ◇ ***discount rates/prices*** 贴现率；折扣价 ◇ ~ (**on/off sth**) *They're offering a 10% discount on all sofas this month.* 本月他们给沙发售价统统打九折。 ◇ *They were selling everything **at a discount*** (= at reduced prices). 他们销售的所有商品都打折。 ◇ *a **discount shop*** (= one that regularly sells goods at reduced prices) 打折商店 ◇ *Do you give any discount?* 你们打折吗？ ➲ WORDFINDER NOTE AT BUY ➲ COLLOCATIONS AT SHOPPING

■ ***verb*** /dɪsˈkaʊnt; *NAmE also* ˈdɪskaʊnt/ **1** (*formal*) to think or say that sth is not important or not true 认为…不重要；对…不全信；低估 SYN **dismiss**：~ **sth** *We cannot **discount the possibility of** further strikes.* 我们不能低估再次发生罢工的可能性。 ◇ ~ **sth as sth** *The news reports were being discounted as propaganda.* 人们认为这些新闻报道不过是为了宣传，不可全信。 **2** ~ **sth** to take an amount of money off the usual cost of sth; to sell sth at a discount 打折扣；打折出售 SYN **reduce**：***discounted prices/fares*** 打折价 / 票价 ➲ MORE LIKE THIS 21, page R27

dis·counter /ˈdɪskaʊntə(r)/ (*also* ˈ**discount store**) *noun* a shop/store that sells things very cheaply, often in large quantities or from a limited range of goods 折扣商店；廉价商店

ˈ**discount rate** *noun* (*finance* 财) **1** the minimum rate of interest that banks in the US and some other countries must pay when they borrow money from other banks（美国及其他一些国家银行之间借款的）贴现率 **2** the amount that the price of a BILL OF EXCHANGE is reduced by when it is bought before it reaches its full value（汇票）贴现率 **3** the rate at which an investment increases in value each year （投资）折现率

dis·cour·age /dɪsˈkʌrɪdʒ, *NAmE* -ˈkɜːr-/ *verb* **1** to try to prevent sth or to prevent sb from doing sth, especially by making it difficult to do or by showing that you do not approve of it 阻拦；阻止；劝阻：~ (**doing**) **sth** *a campaign to discourage smoking among teenagers* 劝阻青少年吸烟的运动 ◇ ~ **sb** *I leave a light on when I'm out to discourage burglars.* 我出门时开着灯以防夜贼闯入。 ◇ ~ **sb from doing sth** *His parents tried to discourage him from being an actor.* 他的父母试图阻止他去当演员。 **2** to make sb feel less confident or enthusiastic about doing sth 使灰心；使泄气；使丧失信心 SYN **dishearten**：~ **sb** *Don't be discouraged by the first failure—try again!* 这才是第一次失败，别灰心丧气，再试一次吧！ ◇ ~ **sb from doing sth** *The weather discouraged people from attending.* 这天气使得人们不愿到场出席。 OPP **encourage** ▶ **dis·cour·aged** *adj.* [not usually before noun] SYN **disheartened**：*Learners can feel very discouraged if an exercise is too difficult.* 如果练习太难，学习者就可能感到很受打击。 **dis·cour·aging** *adj.*：*a **discouraging experience/response/result*** 令人泄气的经历 / 回答 / 结果 **dis·cour·aging·ly** *adv.*

dis·cour·age·ment /dɪsˈkʌrɪdʒmənt; *NAmE* -ˈkɜːr-/ *noun* **1** [U] a feeling that you no longer have the confidence or enthusiasm to do sth 泄气；灰心：*an atmosphere of discouragement and despair* 灰心绝望的气氛 **2** [U] the action of trying to stop sth 阻止；阻拦；劝阻：*the government's discouragement of political protest* 政府对政治抗议的阻拦 **3** [C] a thing that discourages sb from doing sth 使人泄气的事物；挫折：*Despite all these discouragements, she refused to give up.* 尽管遇到这么多挫折，她仍不气馁。

dis·course *noun, verb*

■ ***noun*** /ˈdɪskɔːs; *NAmE* -kɔːrs/ **1** [C, U] (*formal*) a long and serious treatment or discussion of a subject in speech or writing 论文；演讲：*a discourse on issues of gender and sexuality* 关于性别和性行为的论文 ◇ *He was hoping for some lively political discourse at the meeting.* 他希望在会上听到些生动的政治演讲。 **2** [U] (*linguistics* 语言) the use of language in speech and writing in order to produce meaning; language that is studied, usually in order to see how the different parts of a text are connected 语篇；话语：***spoken/written discourse*** 口头 / 书面语篇 ◇ *discourse analysis* 语篇分析

■ ***verb*** /dɪsˈkɔːs; *NAmE* -ˈkɔːrs/

PHR V **disˈcourse on/upon sth** (*formal*) to talk or give a long speech about sth that you know a lot about 讲述；论述

ˈ**discourse marker** *noun* (*grammar* 语法) a word or phrase that organizes spoken language into different parts, for example 'Well…' or 'On the other hand…' 语篇标记；话语标记

dis·cour·teous /dɪsˈkɜːtiəs; *NAmE* -ˈkɜːrt-/ *adj.* (*formal*) having bad manners and not showing respect for other people 不礼貌的；失礼的；粗鲁的 SYN **impolite** OPP **courteous** ➲ SYNONYMS AT RUDE

dis·cour·tesy /dɪsˈkɜːtəsi; *NAmE* -ˈkɜːrt-/ *noun* [U, C] (*pl.* **-ies**) (*formal*) behaviour or an action that is not polite 失礼的行为；粗鲁的举动

dis·cover 🔑 /dɪˈskʌvə(r)/ *verb* **1** 🔑 ~ **sth** to be the first person to become aware that a particular place or thing exists （第一个）发现：*Cook is credited with discovering Hawaii.* 人们把发现夏威夷的功劳归于库克。 ◇ *Scientists around the world are working to discover a cure for AIDS.* 全世界的科学家都在努力寻找治疗艾滋病的方法。 ➲ WORDFINDER NOTE AT EXPLORE **2** 🔑 to find sb/sth that was hidden or that you did not expect to find （出乎意料地）发现，找到，发觉：~ **sb/sth** *Police discovered a large stash of drugs while searching the house.* 警方搜查这栋房子时发现里面藏着一大批毒品。 ◇ *We discovered this beach while we were sailing around the island.* 我们在围绕这个海岛航行时发现了这个海滩。 ◇ ~ **sb/sth doing sth** *He was discovered hiding in a shed.* 人们发现他原来藏在棚屋里。 ◇ ~ **sb/sth + adj.** *She was discovered dead at her home in Leeds.* 人们发现她死在利兹的家里。 **3** 🔑 to find out about sth; to find some information about sth 了解到；认识到；查明：~ **sth** *I've just discovered hang-gliding!* 我刚知道有悬挂式滑翔运动！ ◇ ~ (**that**)… *It was a shock to* *discover (that) he couldn't read.* 得知他不识字真令人震惊。◇ **~ why, how, etc....** *We never did discover why she gave up her job.* 我们一直弄不清楚她为什么辞职。◇ **it is discovered that...** *It was later discovered that the diaries were a fraud.* 后来查明这些日记完全是伪造的。◇ **sb/sth is discovered to be/have...** *He was later discovered to be seriously ill.* 后来才了解到他患了重病。 **4** [often passive] **~ sb** to be the first person to realize that sb is very good at singing, acting, etc. and help them to become successful and famous 发现（人才）: *The singer was discovered while still at school.* 这个歌唱家在上学的时候就受到赏识了。 ▶ **dis·cov·er·er** *noun*: *the discoverer of penicillin* 青霉素的发现者

dis·cover·able /dɪˈskʌvərəbl/ *adj.* that you can find by searching or find easily 可发现的; 可搜寻到的 ▶ **dis·cover·ability** /dɪˌskʌvərəˈbɪləti/ *noun* [U]: *They are working to improve the discoverability of their e-books.* 他们正努力使他们的电子书更容易被查找到。

dis·cov·ery /dɪˈskʌvəri/ *noun* (*pl.* **-ies**) **1** [C, U] an act or the process of finding sb/sth, or learning about sth that was not known about before 发现; 发觉: **~ (of sth)** *the discovery of antibiotics in the 20th century* * 20 世纪抗生素的发现 ◇ *The discovery of a child's body in the river has shocked the community.* 在河里发现一个孩子的尸体，使社区大为震惊。◇ *the discovery of new talent in the art world* 艺术界新秀的发现 ◇ *Researchers in this field have* ***made*** *some important new* ***discoveries****.* 这个领域的研究人员有了一些重大的新发现。◇ *He saw life as a voyage of discovery.* 他把生命看作是一次探索未知世界的航行。◇ **~ (that...)** *She was shocked by the discovery that he had been unfaithful.* 她发觉他不忠时感到非常震惊。 **2** [C] a thing, fact or person that is found or learned about for the first time 被发现的事物（或真相、人）: *The drug is not a new discovery—it's been known about for years.* 这种药并不是什么新发现，多年前便为人所知。

dis·credit /dɪsˈkredɪt/ *verb, noun*

■ ***verb*** **1 ~ sb/sth** to make people stop respecting sb/sth 败坏…的名声; 使丧失信誉; 使丢脸: *The photos were deliberately taken to discredit the President.* 这些蓄意拍摄的照片旨在败坏总统的名声。◇ *a discredited* ***government/policy*** 名声扫地的政府; 失去信誉的政策 **2 ~ sth** to make people stop believing that sth is true; to make sth appear unlikely to be true 使不可信; 使受到怀疑: *These theories are now largely discredited among linguists.* 这些理论现已大多受到语言学家的质疑。

■ ***noun*** [U] (*formal*) damage to sb's reputation; loss of respect 名誉丧失; 信誉丧失; 丢脸: *Violent football fans* ***bring discredit on*** *the teams they support.* 狂暴的足球迷败坏了他们所支持球队的声誉。◇ *Britain,* ***to its discredit,*** *did not speak out against these atrocities.* 英国没有公开反对这些残暴行为，因而名誉扫地。 ➲ COMPARE CREDIT *n.* (7)

dis·cred·it·able /dɪsˈkredɪtəbl/ *adj.* (*formal*) bad and unacceptable; causing people to lose respect 不光彩的; 有损尊严的; 丢脸的

dis·creet /dɪˈskriːt/ *adj.* careful in what you say or do, in order to keep sth secret or to avoid causing embarrassment or difficulty for sb （言行）谨慎的，慎重的; 考虑周到的 SYN **tactful**: *He was always very discreet about his love affairs.* 他对谈恋爱一向十分慎重。◇ *You ought to make a few discreet enquiries before you sign anything.* 你应该审慎地询问清楚再签字。 ▶ **dis·creet·ly** *adv.*: *She coughed discreetly to announce her presence.* 她审慎地咳了一声以让人注意自己在场。

> **WORD FAMILY**
> **discreet** *adj.* (≠ indiscreet)
> **discretion** *noun* (≠ indiscretion)

dis·crep·ancy /dɪsˈkrepənsi/ *noun* (*pl.* **-ies**) [C, U] a difference between two or more things that should be the same 差异; 不符合; 不一致: **~ (in sth)** *wide discrepancies in prices quoted for the work* 这项工作的报价出入很大 ◇ **~ (between A and B)** *What are the reasons for the discrepancy between girls' and boys' performance in school?* 女生和男生在学校表现不同的原因何在呢?

dis·crete AW /dɪˈskriːt/ *adj.* (*formal* or *specialist*) independent of other things of the same type 离散的; 分离的; 各别的 SYN **separate**: *The organisms can be divided into discrete categories.* 有机体可分为许多互不关联的种类。 ▶ **dis·crete·ly** AW *adv.* **dis·crete·ness** *noun* [U]

dis·cre·tion AW /dɪˈskreʃn/ *noun* [U] **1** the freedom or power to decide what should be done in a particular situation 自行决定的自由; 自行决定权: *I'll leave it up to you to* ***use your discretion****.* 我把这件事留给你自己斟酌决定。◇ *How much to tell terminally ill patients is* ***left to the discretion of*** *the doctor.* 晚期病人的病情让本人知道多少由医生自行决定。 **2** care in what you say or do, in order to keep sth secret or to avoid causing embarrassment to or difficulty for sb; the quality of being DISCREET 谨慎; 慎重; 审慎: *This is confidential, but I know that I can rely on your discretion.* 这是机密，不过我知道你靠得住。 ➲ COMPARE INDISCRETION

IDM **at sb's diˈscretion** according to what sb decides or wishes to do 由某人斟酌决定; 按照某人的意愿: *Bail is granted at the discretion of the court.* 由法庭决定准予保释。◇ *There is no service charge and tipping is at your discretion.* 不收服务费，给不给小费由你自行决定。 **diˌscretion is the ˌbetter part of ˈvalour** (*saying*) you should avoid danger and not take unnecessary risks 谨慎即大勇; 慎重为勇敢之本

dis·cre·tion·ary AW /dɪˈskreʃənəri; *NAmE* -neri/ *adj.* [usually before noun] (*formal*) decided according to the judgement of a person in authority about what is necessary in each particular situation; not decided by rules 自行决定的; 酌情行事的; 便宜行事的: *You may be eligible for a discretionary grant for your university course.* 读大学课程可能会有资格获得学校自行决定是否发放的助学金。

dis·crim·in·ate AW /dɪˈskrɪmɪneɪt/ *verb* **1** [I, T] to recognize that there is a difference between people or things; to show a difference between people or things 区别; 辨别; 区分 SYN **differentiate, distinguish**: **~ (between A and B)** *The computer program was unable to discriminate between letters and numbers.* 这计算机程序不能辨别字母与数字。◇ **~ sth** *When do babies learn to discriminate voices?* 婴儿什么时候学会辨别嗓音呢? ◇ **~ A from B** *A number of features discriminate this species from others.* 有些特征使这一物种与其他物种区别开来。 **2** [I] to treat one person or group worse/better than another in an unfair way 区别对待; 歧视; 偏袒: **~ (against sb)** | **~ (in favour of sb)** *practices that discriminate against women and in favour of men* 重男轻女的做法 ◇ **~ (on the grounds of sth)** *It is illegal to discriminate on grounds of race, sex or religion.* 因种族、性别或宗教信仰而实行歧视是非法的。 ➲ **WORDFINDER NOTE AT EQUAL**

dis·crim·in·at·ing /dɪˈskrɪmɪneɪtɪŋ/ *adj.* (*approving*) able to judge the good quality of sth 有识别力的; 有辨别力的; 有鉴赏力的 SYN **discerning**: ***a discriminating audience/customer*** 有鉴赏力的观众 / 顾客

dis·crim·in·ation AW /dɪˌskrɪmɪˈneɪʃn/ *noun* **1** [U] the practice of treating sb or a particular group in society less fairly than others 区别对待; 歧视; 偏袒: ***age/racial/sex/sexual discrimination*** (= because of sb's age, race or sex) 年龄 / 种族 / 性别歧视 ◇ **~ against sb** *discrimination against the elderly* 歧视老人 ◇ **~ in favour of sb** *discrimination in favour of the young* 厚待年轻人 ◇ **~ on the grounds of sth** *discrimination on the grounds of race, gender, or sexual orientation* 按照种族、性别或性取向给予区别对待 ➲ **COLLOCATIONS** AT RACE ➲ SEE ALSO POSITIVE DISCRIMINATION **2** [U] (*approving*) the ability to judge what is good, true, etc. 识别力; 辨别力; 鉴赏力 SYN **discernment**: *He showed great discrimination in his choice of friends.* 他在择友方面颇具慧眼。 **3** (*formal*) [U, C] the ability to recognize a difference between one thing and another; a difference that is recognized 区别; 识别; 辨别: *to learn discrimination between right and wrong* 学会分辨是非 ◇ *fine discriminations* 细微区别

dis·crim·in·atory /dɪˈskrɪmɪnətəri; *NAmE* dɪˈskrɪmɪnətɔːri/ *adj.* unfair; treating sb or one group of people worse than others 区别对待的; 不公正的; 歧视

的：*discriminatory practices/rules/measures* 不公正的做法 / 规定 / 措施 ◇ *sexually/racially discriminatory laws* 性别 / 种族歧视性法律

dis·cur·sive /dɪs'kɜːsɪv; *NAmE* -'kɜːrs-/ *adj.* (*formal*) (of a style of writing or speaking 书面或口头表达方式) moving from one point to another without any strict structure 东拉西扯的；离题的；不着边际的：*the discursive style of the novel* 这部小说的散漫风格

D

▼ **SYNONYMS** 同义词辨析

discussion

conversation • dialogue • talk • debate • consultation • chat • gossip

These are all words for an occasion when people talk about sth. 以上各词均表示交谈、谈论。

discussion a detailed conversation about sth that is considered to be important 指重要事情的讨论、谈论、商讨：*Discussions are still taking place between the two leaders.* 两位领导人仍在进行讨论。

conversation a talk, usually a private or informal one, involving two people or a small group; the activity of talking in this way 通常指私下的或非正式的交谈、谈话：*a telephone conversation* 电话交谈

dialogue conversations in a book, play or film 指书、戏剧或电影中的对话、对白：*The novel has long descriptions and not much dialogue.* 这部小说描述多，对话少。A **dialogue** is also a formal discussion between two groups, especially when they are trying to solve a problem or end a dispute. * dialogue 亦指两个团体间为解决问题或结束争端进行的正式对话、讨论、交换意见：*The President told waiting reporters there had been a constructive dialogue.* 总统告诉等候的记者，刚才进行了一次富有建设性的对话。

talk a conversation or discussion, often one about a problem or sth important for the people involved 常指对有关人员就某个问题或重要的事情进行的交谈、谈话、讨论、商讨：*I had a long talk with my boss about my career prospects.* 我和老板就我的事业前景进行了一次长谈。

debate a formal discussion of an issue at a public meeting or in a parliament. In a debate two or more speakers express opposing views and then there is often a vote on the issue. 指公共集会上或议会里就某问题进行的、常以表决结束的辩论：*a debate on prison reform* 关于监狱制度改革的辩论

consultation a formal discussion between groups of people before a decision is made about sth 指团体间在决策前进行的咨询、商讨、磋商：*There have been extensive consultations between the two countries.* 两国之间进行了广泛磋商。

chat a friendly informal conversation; informal talking 指友好的非正式交谈、聊天 **NOTE** The countable use of **chat** is especially British English. * chat 作可数名词尤用于英式英语：*I just called in for a chat about the kids.* 我只是打电话来随便聊聊孩子的事情。

gossip a conversation about other people and their private lives 指关于他人及其私生活的闲谈、闲聊、说长道短：*We had a good gossip about the boss.* 我们讲了好一会儿老板的闲话。

PATTERNS

- a discussion / conversation / dialogue / talk / debate / consultation / chat / gossip **about** sth
- a discussion / conversation / dialogue / debate / consultation **on** sth
- **in** (**close**) discussion / conversation / dialogue / debate / consultation **with** sb
- to **have** a discussion / conversation / dialogue / talk / debate / consultation / chat / gossip **with** sb
- to **hold** a discussion / conversation / debate / consultation

dis·cus /'dɪskəs/ *noun* **1** [C] a heavy flat round object thrown in a sporting event 铁饼（体育运动用品） **2 the discus** [sing.] the event or sport of throwing a discus as far as possible 掷铁饼；掷铁饼比赛 ➲ VISUAL VOCAB PAGE V50

dis·cuss 🔑 /dɪ'skʌs/ *verb* **1** 🔑 to talk about sth with sb, especially in order to decide sth 讨论；谈论；商量：**~ sth with sb** *Have you discussed the problem with anyone?* 你与谁商量过这个问题吗？◇ **~ sth** *I'm not prepared to discuss this on the phone.* 我不想在电话里谈论此事。◇ **~ when, what, etc....** *We need to discuss when we should go.* 我们需要商量一下什么时候动身。◇ **~ (sb/sth) doing sth** *We briefly discussed buying a second car.* 我们草草商量过再买一辆汽车的事儿。**HELP** You cannot say 'discuss about sth'. 不能说 discuss about sth：~~*I discussed about my problem with my parents.*~~ Look also at **discussion**. 另见 discussion。➲ SYNONYMS AT TALK **2** 🔑 **~ sth | ~ what, how, etc....** to write or talk about sth in detail, showing the different ideas and opinions about it 详述；论述：*This topic will be discussed at greater length in the next chapter.* 这个题目将在下一章里详细论述。➲ LANGUAGE BANK AT ABOUT ➲ SYNONYMS AT EXAMINE

dis·cus·sion 🔑 /dɪ'skʌʃn/ *noun* [U, C] **1** 🔑 the process of discussing sb/sth; a conversation about sb/sth 讨论；商讨：*a* ***topic/subject for discussion*** 讨论的题目 / 主题 ◇ *After considerable discussion, they decided to accept our offer.* 他们经过反复讨论决定接受我们的报价。◇ *The plans have been* ***under discussion*** (= being talked about) *for a year now.* 这些计划至今已讨论一年了。◇ *Discussions are still taking place between the two leaders.* 两位领导仍在进行讨论。◇ **~ (with sb) (about/on sb/sth)** *We* ***had a discussion*** *with them about the differences between Britain and the US.* 我们和他们讨论了英美两国的不同之处。**2** 🔑 **~ (of sth)** a speech or a piece of writing that discusses many different aspects of a subject 详述；论述：*Her article is a discussion of the methods used in research.* 她这篇文章论述的是研究中使用的方法。

dis·dain /dɪs'deɪn/ *noun, verb*

■ ***noun*** [U, sing.] the feeling that sb/sth is not good enough to deserve your respect or attention 鄙视；蔑视；鄙弃 **SYN** **contempt**：*to treat sb* ***with disdain*** 鄙视某人 ◇ **~ for sb/sth** *a disdain for the law* 对法律的藐视

■ ***verb*** (*formal*) **1 ~ sb/sth** to think that sb/sth is not good enough to deserve your respect 鄙视；蔑视；鄙弃：*She disdained his offer of help.* 他提出要帮助，遭到她的鄙弃。**2 ~ to do sth** to refuse to do sth because you think that you are too important to do it 不屑（做某事）：*He disdained to turn to his son for advice.* 他不屑向自己的儿子请教。

dis·dain·ful /dɪs'deɪnfl/ *adj.* **~ (of sb/sth)** showing disdain 轻视的；鄙视的；倨傲的 **SYN** **contemptuous, dismissive**：*She's always been disdainful of people who haven't been to college.* 她总是瞧不起那些没有上过大学的人。▶ **dis·dain·ful·ly** /-fəli/ *adv.*

dis·ease 🔑 /dɪ'ziːz/ *noun* **1** 🔑 [U, C] an illness affecting humans, animals or plants, often caused by infection 病；疾病：***heart/liver/kidney, etc. disease*** 心脏病、肝病、肾病等 ◇ *health measures to prevent the* ***spread of disease*** 预防疾病传播的保健措施 ◇ *an* ***infectious/contagious disease*** (= one that can be passed to sb very easily) 传染病；接触性传染病 ◇ *It is not known what causes the disease.* 这种病的起因不明。◇ *protection against sexually transmitted diseases* 性传播疾病的预防 ◇ *He suffers from a rare blood disease.* 他患有一种罕见的血液病。➲ WORDFINDER NOTE AT CURE ➲ COLLOCATIONS AT ILL

WORDFINDER 联想词：bacteria, epidemic, fever, **illness**, immunity, infection, spread, vaccinate, virus

2 [C] (*formal*) something that is very wrong with people's attitudes, way of life or with society 弊端；恶疾；痼疾：*Greed is a disease of modern society.* 贪婪是现代社会的恶疾。

dis·eased /dɪ'ziːzd/ *adj.* suffering from a disease 有病的；患病的；病态的：*diseased tissue* 有病的组织 ◇ *the diseased social system* 病态的社会制度

▼ SYNONYMS 同义词辨析

disease

illness • disorder • infection • condition • ailment • bug

These are all words for a medical problem. 以上各词均表示健康问题。

disease a medical problem affecting humans, animals or plants, often caused by infection 常指人、动植物感染的病、疾病： *He suffers from a rare blood disease.* 他患有一种罕见的血液病。

illness a medical problem, or a period of suffering from one 指病、疾病或患病期： *She died after a long illness.* 她久病不愈而亡。

DISEASE OR ILLNESS? 用 disease 还是 illness?

Disease is used to talk about more severe physical medical problems, especially those that affect the organs. **Illness** is used to talk about both more severe and more minor medical problems, and those that affect mental health. * disease 指较严重的身体疾病，尤其是影响身体器官的疾病。illness 指重病或小病均可，也可指精神上的疾病： ~~heart/kidney/liver illness~~ ◇ ~~mental disease~~
Disease is not used about a period of illness. * disease 不指患病期： ~~She died after a long disease.~~

disorder *(rather formal)* an illness that causes a part of the body to stop functioning correctly 指失调、紊乱、不适、疾病： *a rare disorder of the liver* 一种罕见的肝病
NOTE A **disorder** is generally not infectious. **Disorder** is used most frequently with words relating to mental problems, for example *psychiatric, personality, mental* and *eating*. When it is used to talk about physical problems, it is most often used with *blood, bowel* and *kidney*, and these are commonly *serious, severe* or *rare*. * disorder 一般不传染，多与有关精神问题的词连用，如 psychiatric/personality/mental/eating disorder（精神错乱；人格障碍；精神紊乱；进食障碍）。谈到身体方面的问题常与下列词连用，如 blood/bowel/kidney disorder（血液病；肠道失调；肾脏疾病），这些疾病一般用 serious、severe 或 rare 等词修饰。

infection an illness that is caused by bacteria or a virus and that affects one part of the body 指由细菌或病毒引起的身体某部位的感染或传染疾病： *a throat infection* 喉部感染

condition a medical problem that you have for a long time because it is not possible to cure it 指因不可治愈而长期患有的疾病： *a heart condition* 心脏病

ailment *(rather formal)* an illness that is not very serious 指轻病、小恙： *childhood ailments* 儿童期小病

bug *(informal)* an infectious illness that is usually fairly mild 指轻微的传染病、小病： *a nasty flu bug* 严重的流感

PATTERNS
- to **have/suffer from** a(n) disease/illness/disorder/infection/condition/ailment/bug
- to **catch/contract/get/pick up** a(n) disease/illness/infection/bug

dis·em·bark /ˌdɪsɪmˈbɑːk; *NAmE* -ˈbɑːrk/ *verb* [I] ~ (**from sth**) *(formal)* to leave a vehicle, especially a ship or an aircraft, at the end of a journey 下（车、船、飞机等） OPP **embark** ▶ **dis·em·bark·ation** /ˌdɪsˌembɑːˈkeɪʃn; *NAmE* -bɑːrˈk-/ *noun* [U]

dis·em·bod·ied /ˌdɪsɪmˈbɒdid; *NAmE* -ˈbɑːdid/ *adj.* [usually before noun] **1** (of sounds 声音) coming from a person or place that cannot be seen or identified 从看不到的人（或地方）发出的： *a disembodied voice* 不见其人的说话声 **2** separated from the body 脱离肉体的： *disembodied spirits* 游魂

dis·em·bowel /ˌdɪsɪmˈbaʊəl/ *verb* (**-ll-**, *especially US* **-l-**) ~ **sb/sth** to take the stomach, BOWELS and other organs out of a person or animal 取出…的内脏；开…的膛

dis·en·chant·ed /ˌdɪsɪnˈtʃɑːntɪd; *NAmE* -ˈtʃænt-/ *adj.* ~ (**with sb/sth**) no longer feeling enthusiasm for sb/sth; not believing sth is good or worth doing 不再着迷的；不再抱幻想的 SYN **disillusioned**: *He was becoming disenchanted with his job as a lawyer.* 他对自己的律师工作渐渐地不抱幻想了。 ▶ **dis·en·chant·ment** *noun* [U]: *a growing* **sense/feeling** *of disenchantment with his job* 对他的工作越来越感到失望

dis·en·fran·chise /ˌdɪsɪnˈfræntʃaɪz/ *verb* ~ **sb** to take away sb's rights, especially their right to vote 剥夺（某人）的权利（尤指选举权） OPP **enfranchise**

dis·en·gage /ˌdɪsɪnˈɡeɪdʒ/ *verb* **1** [T, I] *(formal)* to free sb/sth from the person or thing that is holding them or it; to become free（使）脱离，松开；解脱： **~ yourself** (**from sb/sth**) *She gently disengaged herself from her sleeping son.* 她轻轻地放下怀中熟睡的儿子。 ◇ *(figurative) They wished to disengage themselves from these policies.* 他们希望能摆脱这些政策的束缚。 ◇ ~ (**sth/sb**) (**from sth/sb**) *to disengage the clutch* (= when driving a car)（开车时）松开离合器 ◇ *We saw the booster rockets disengage and fall into the sea.* 我们看到火箭助推器脱落后坠入大海。 **2** [I, T] ~ (**sth**) *(specialist)* if an army **disengages** or sb **disengages** it, it stops fighting and moves away（使）脱离战斗 ➲ COMPARE ENGAGE ➲ WORDFINDER NOTE AT PEACE ▶ **dis·en·gage·ment** *noun* [U]

dis·en·tan·gle /ˌdɪsɪnˈtæŋɡl/ *verb* **1** ~ **sth** (**from sth**) to separate different arguments, ideas, etc. that have become confused 理顺，分清，清理出（混乱的论据、想法等）： *It's not easy to disentangle the truth from the official statistics.* 从官方统计资料中理出真实情况并不容易。 **2** ~ **sth/sb** (**from sth**) to free sb/sth from sth that has become wrapped or twisted around it or them 使解脱；使脱出；使摆脱： *He tried to disentangle his fingers from her hair.* 他竭力将手指从她缠绕的头发中挣脱出来。 ◇ *(figurative) She has just disentangled herself from a painful relationship.* 她刚刚摆脱一段痛苦的感情。 **3** ~ **sth** to get rid of the twists and knots in sth 解开…的结；理顺： *He was sitting on the deck disentangling a coil of rope.* 他坐在甲板上解开一捆绳索。 ➲ COMPARE ENTANGLE

dis·equi·lib·rium /ˌdɪsˌiːkwɪˈlɪbriəm; ˌdɪsˌek-/ *noun* [U] *(formal* or *specialist)* a loss or lack of balance in a situation 不平衡；失衡

dis·es·tab·lish AW /ˌdɪsɪˈstæblɪʃ/ *verb* ~ **sth** *(formal)* to end the official status of a national Church 废除（国教）的法定地位： *a campaign to disestablish the Church of England* 废除英格兰圣公会国教地位的运动 ▶ **dis·es·tab·lish·ment** AW *noun* [U]

dis·favour *(especially US* **dis·favor**) /dɪsˈfeɪvə(r)/ *noun* [U] *(formal)* the feeling that you do not like or approve of sb/sth 不喜欢；不赞成

dis·fig·ure /dɪsˈfɪɡə(r); *NAmE* -ɡjər/ *verb* ~ **sb/sth** to spoil the appearance of a person, thing or place 损毁…的外形；使变丑；毁容： *Her face was disfigured by a long red scar.* 她脸上一条红色的长疤使她破相了。 ▶ **dis·fig·ure·ment** *noun* [U, C]: *He suffered permanent disfigurement in the fire.* 那场火灾永久毁了他的面容。

dis·gorge /dɪsˈɡɔːdʒ; *NAmE* -ˈɡɔːrdʒ/ *verb (formal)* **1** ~ **sth** to pour sth out in large quantities 大量涌出；大量泄出： *The pipe disgorges sewage into the sea.* 这管道将污水排入大海。 **2** ~ **sb/sth** if a vehicle or building **disgorges** people, they come out of it in large numbers（从交通工具、建筑物里）涌出： *The bus disgorged a crowd of noisy children.* 公共汽车上涌下来一群叽叽喳喳的孩子。

dis·grace /dɪsˈɡreɪs/ *noun, verb*
■ *noun* **1** [U] the loss of other people's respect and approval because of the bad way sb has behaved 丢脸；耻辱；不光彩 SYN **shame**: *Her behaviour has* **brought disgrace on** *her family.* 她的行为使家人蒙羞。 ◇ *The swimmer was sent home from the Olympics* **in disgrace**. 这位游泳运动员很不光彩地从奥运会上被遣送回国。 ◇ *There is no disgrace in being poor.* 贫穷不是耻辱。 ◇ *Sam was* **in disgrace with** *his parents.* 萨姆已失宠于他的父母。 **2** [sing.] **a ~** (**to sb/**

sth) a person or thing that is so bad that people connected with them or it feel or should feel ashamed 令人感到羞耻的人（或事）: *Your homework is an absolute disgrace.* 你做的作业太丢人了。◇ *That sort of behaviour is **a disgrace to** the legal profession.* 那种行为是法律界的耻辱。◇ *The state of our roads is a national disgrace.* 我们的道路状况是国家的耻辱。◇ ***It's a disgrace that*** (= it is very wrong that) *they are paid so little.* 他们的报酬如此微薄，太不像话了。

■ ***verb*** **1** to behave badly in a way that makes you or other people feel ashamed 使丢脸；使蒙受耻辱: **~ yourself** *I disgraced myself by drinking far too much.* 我喝酒过多出了洋相。◇ **~ sb/sth** *He had disgraced the family name.* 他玷污了家族的名声。 **2 be disgraced** to lose the respect of people, usually so that you lose a position of power 使名誉扫地；使失势；使失去地位: *He was publicly disgraced and sent into exile.* 他被当众贬谪，放逐异乡。◇ *a disgraced politician/leader* 失势的从政者 / 领导人

dis·grace·ful /dɪsˈɡreɪsfl/ *adj.* very bad or unacceptable; that people should feel ashamed about 不光彩的；可耻的；丢脸的: *His behaviour was absolutely disgraceful!* 他的行为真可耻！◇ *It's disgraceful that none of the family tried to help her.* 家里竟无人肯帮助她，太不像话了。◇ *a disgraceful waste of money* 可耻的金钱浪费 ▶ **dis·grace·ful·ly** /-fəli/ *adv.*

dis·grun·tled /dɪsˈɡrʌntld/ *adj.* annoyed or disappointed because sth has happened to upset you 不满的；不高兴的: *disgruntled employees* 不满的雇员 ◇ **~ at sb/sth** *I left feeling disgruntled at the way I'd been treated.* 我受到如此对待，因而愤然离去。

dis·guise /dɪsˈɡaɪz/ *verb, noun*

■ ***verb*** **1** to change your appearance so that people cannot recognize you 假扮；装扮；伪装: **~ sb** *The hijackers were heavily disguised.* 劫持者伪装得严严实实。◇ **~ sb as sb/sth** *They got in disguised as security guards.* 他们装扮成保安人员混了进去。◇ **~ yourself (as sb/sth)** *She disguised herself as a boy.* 她女扮男装。 **2 ~ sth** to hide sth or change it, so that it cannot be recognized 掩蔽；掩饰 SYN **conceal**: *She made no attempt to disguise her surprise.* 她根本不曾掩饰自己惊奇的心情。◇ *It was a **thinly disguised** attack on the President.* 不难看出这是在攻击总统。◇ *She couldn't **disguise the fact that** she felt uncomfortable.* 她无法掩饰她那不安的心情。 ➲ SYNONYMS AT HIDE

■ ***noun*** **1** [C, U] a thing that you wear or use to change your appearance so that people do not recognize you 伪装物；化装用具: *She wore glasses and a wig as a disguise.* 她用眼镜和假发伪装起来。◇ *The star travelled **in disguise*** (= wearing a disguise). 这位明星化了装去旅行。◇ *A vote for the Greens is just a Labour vote in disguise.* 投绿党的票不过是改头换面投工党的票。 **2** [U] the art of changing your appearance so that people do not recognize you 假扮；装扮；伪装: *He is a master of disguise.* 他是伪装能手。 IDM SEE BLESSING ➲ MORE LIKE THIS 20, page R27

dis·gust 🔑 /dɪsˈɡʌst/ *noun, verb*

■ ***noun*** 🔑 [U] a strong feeling of dislike or disapproval for sb/sth that you feel is unacceptable, or for sth that looks, smells, etc. unpleasant 厌恶；憎恶；反感: **~ (at/with sth)** *She expressed her disgust at the programme by writing a letter of complaint.* 她写了封投诉信，表示对这个节目的反感。◇ **~ (for sb)** *I can only feel disgust for these criminals.* 对这些罪犯我只感到憎恶。◇ *The idea fills me **with disgust**.* 这个想法实在令我恶心。◇ *He walked away **in disgust**.* 他厌恶地走开了。◇ ***Much to my disgust**, they refused to help.* 他们不肯帮忙，令我极其愤慨。◇ *She wrinkled her nose **in disgust** at the smell.* 她闻到那气味，恶心地皱起了鼻子。

■ ***verb*** 🔑 **~ sb** if sth **disgusts** you, it makes you feel shocked and almost ill/sick because it is so unpleasant 使作呕；使厌恶；使反感: *The level of violence in the film really disgusted me.* 影片中的暴力程度实在让我反感。

dis·gust·ed 🔑 /dɪsˈɡʌstɪd/ *adj.* feeling or showing disgust 厌恶的；憎恶的；反感的: **~ (at/by sb/sth)** *I was disgusted at/by the sight.* 我一看就恶心。◇ **~ (with sb/sth/yourself)** *I was disgusted with myself for eating so much.* 我吃得太多，自己也觉得无地自容。◇ **~ (to see, hear, etc....)** *He was disgusted to see such awful living conditions.* 看到如此糟糕的生活环境他觉得很气愤。 ▶ **dis·gust·ed·ly** *adv.*: *'This champagne is warm!', he said disgustedly.* "这香槟酒是温的！"他气愤地说。

dis·gust·ing 🔑 /dɪsˈɡʌstɪŋ/ *adj.* **1** 🔑 extremely unpleasant 极糟的；令人不快的 SYN **revolting**: *The kitchen was in a disgusting state when she left.* 她离开时厨房里一片狼藉。◇ *What a disgusting smell!* 这气味真难闻！ **2** 🔑 unacceptable and shocking 令人厌恶的；令人气愤的 SYN **despicable, outrageous**: *I think it's disgusting that they're closing the local hospital.* 他们要关闭这家地方医院，我认为这太让人气愤了。◇ *His language is disgusting* (= he uses a lot of offensive words). 他的言语不堪入耳。

▼ **SYNONYMS 同义词辨析**

disgusting

foul • revolting • repulsive • offensive • gross

These words all describe sth, especially a smell, taste or habit, that is extremely unpleasant and often makes you feel slightly ill. 以上各词形容某物（尤指气味、味道或习惯）令人很不舒服而且常令人恶心。

disgusting extremely unpleasant and making you feel slightly ill 指令人不快的、使人厌恶的、令人恶心的、使人作呕的： *What a disgusting smell!* 这气味真难闻！

foul dirty, and tasting or smelling bad 指肮脏恶臭的、难闻的、恶心的： *She could smell his foul breath.* 她闻得到他的口臭。

revolting extremely unpleasant and making you feel slightly ill 指令人不快的、使人厌恶的、令人恶心的、使人作呕的： *The stew looked revolting.* 这煨菜看上去令人作呕。

DISGUSTING OR REVOLTING? 用 disgusting 还是 revolting?

Both of these words are used to describe things that smell and taste unpleasant, unpleasant personal habits and people who have them. There is no real difference in meaning, but **disgusting** is more frequent, especially in spoken English. 以上两词均指气味、味道、个人习惯和有这些习惯的人令人恶心、使人厌恶，在含义上没有实质的区别，只是 disgusting 更常用，尤其是在口语中。

repulsive (*rather formal*) extremely unpleasant in a way that offends you or makes you feel slightly ill 指使人厌恶的、令人反感的、十分讨厌的 NOTE **Repulsive** usually describes people, their behaviour or habits, which you may find offensive for physical or moral reasons.
* repulsive 通常指人或其行为习惯刺激感官或有违道德而令人厌恶。

offensive (*formal*) (especially of smells) extremely unpleasant 尤指气味令人不适的、令人恶心的、使人厌恶的

gross (*informal*) (of a smell, taste or personal habit) extremely unpleasant 指气味、味道或个人习惯令人很不舒服的、令人恶心的、使人厌恶的

PATTERNS

- disgusting/repulsive/offensive **to** sb
- to **find sb/sth** disgusting/revolting/repulsive/offensive
- to **smell/taste** disgusting/foul/gross
- a(n) disgusting/foul/revolting/offensive/gross **smell**
- a disgusting/revolting/gross **habit**
- disgusting/offensive/gross **behaviour**
- a disgusting/revolting/repulsive **man/woman/person**

dis·gust·ing·ly /dɪsˈɡʌstɪŋli/ *adv.* **1** (*sometimes humorous*) extremely (in a way that other people feel jealous of) 极其，极端，非常（以致使人忌妒）: *He looked disgustingly healthy when he got back from the Bahamas.* 他从巴哈马群岛回来时看上去健康得令人眼红。 **2** in a disgusting way 令人作呕地；令人厌恶地；讨厌地: *disgustingly dirty* 脏得令人作呕

dish /dɪʃ/ *noun, verb*

■ ***noun*** **1** [C] a flat shallow container for cooking food in or serving it from 碟；盘：*a glass dish* 玻璃盘 ◇ *an ovenproof dish* 耐热盘 ◇ *a baking/serving dish* 烤盘；上食物的盘子 ◇ *They helped themselves from a large dish of pasta.* 他们从一大盘意大利面食中自行取一些吃。➲ VISUAL VOCAB PAGE V23 **2** **the dishes** [pl.] the plates, bowls, cups, etc. that have been used for a meal and need to be washed（待清洗的）餐具：*I'll* ***do the dishes*** (= wash them). 我来洗碗。**3** [C] food prepared in a particular way as part of a meal 一道菜；菜肴：*a vegetarian/fish dish* 一道素菜；一盘鱼 ◇ *This makes an excellent hot* ***main dish.*** 这就是一道绝好的热主菜。◇ *I can recommend the chef's* ***dish of the day.*** 我可推荐今天的主厨特餐。➲ SEE ALSO SIDE DISH **4** [C] any object that is shaped like a dish or bowl 盘状物；碟状物：*a soap dish* 肥皂盘 ➲ VISUAL VOCAB PAGE V25 ➲ SEE ALSO SATELLITE DISH **5** [C] (*informal*) a sexually attractive person 性感的人；对异性有诱惑力的人：*What a dish!* 真性感！

■ ***verb***

IDM ˌ**dish the** ˈ**dirt (on sb)** (*informal*) to tell people unkind or unpleasant things about sb, especially about their private life 说（某人）的闲话；揭（某人）的短 ˌ**dish it** ˈ**out** (*disapproving*) to criticize other people 数落；指责；批评：*He enjoys dishing it out, but he really can't take it* (= cannot accept criticism from other people). 他喜欢指责别人，而自己却一点批评都接受不了。

PHR V ˌ**dish sth**↔ˈ**out** **1** (*informal*) to give sth, often to a lot of people or in large amounts 大量提供；分发：*Students dished out leaflets to passers-by.* 学生向路人散发传单。◇ *She's always dishing out advice, even when you don't want it.* 即使你不想听，她仍然没完没了地建议这建议那。**2** to serve food onto plates for a meal 把（食物）分到盘里（以便用餐）：*Can you dish out the potatoes, please?* 你给大家分一下土豆好吗？ˌ**dish** ˈ**up** | ˌ**dish sth**↔ˈ**up** to serve food onto plates for a meal 把（食物）盛到盘里（以便用餐）ˌ**dish sth**↔ˈ**up** to offer sth to sb, especially sth that is not very good 提供，供给（尤指不太好的东西）

dis·ha·bille /ˌdɪsəˈbiːl; -ˈbiː/ *adj.* = DÉSHABILLÉ

dis·har·mony /dɪsˈhɑːməni; *NAmE* -ˈhɑːrm-/ *noun* [U] (*formal*) a lack of agreement about important things, which causes bad feelings between people or groups of people 不协调；不和谐；不一致：***marital/racial/social disharmony*** 夫妻不和；种族分歧；社会不协调 OPP **harmony**

dish·cloth /ˈdɪʃklɒθ; *NAmE* -klɔːθ/ (*NAmE usually* **dish·rag**) *noun* a cloth for washing dishes 洗碟布；洗碗布 ➲ VISUAL VOCAB PAGE V26

dis·heart·en /dɪsˈhɑːtn; *NAmE* -ˈhɑːrtn/ *verb* **~ sb** to make sb lose hope or confidence 使沮丧；使失去信心；使灰心 SYN **discourage**：*Don't let this defeat dishearten you.* 不要因这次失败而气馁。▸ **dis·heart·ened** *adj.*：*a disheartened team* 丧失信心的团队 **dis·heart·en·ing** /-ˈhɑːtnɪŋ; *NAmE* -ˈhɑːrt-/ *adj.*：*a disheartening experience* 令人沮丧的经历

dish·ev·elled /dɪˈʃevld/ (*especially BrE*) (*NAmE usually* **dish·ev·eled**) *adj.* (of hair, clothes or sb's general appearance 头发、衣着或外表) very untidy 凌乱的；不整洁的；衣冠不整的 SYN **unkempt**：*He looked tired and dishevelled.* 他衣冠不整，显得很疲倦。

dis·hon·est /dɪsˈɒnɪst; *NAmE* -ˈɑːn-/ *adj.* not honest; intending to trick people 不诚实的；骗人的；欺骗性的：*Beware of dishonest traders in the tourist areas.* 在旅游区一定要谨防奸商。◇ *I don't like him, and it would be dishonest of me to pretend otherwise.* 我不喜欢他，如果假装喜欢，那就是我不诚实了。OPP **honest** ▸ **dis·hon·est·ly** *adv.* **dis·hon·esty** *noun* [U]

dis·hon·our (*especially US* **dis·honor**) /dɪsˈɒnə(r); *NAmE* -ˈɑːn-/ *noun, verb*

■ ***noun*** [U] (*formal*) a loss of honour or respect because you have done sth immoral or unacceptable 不名誉；耻辱；丢脸

■ ***verb*** (*formal*) **1** **~ sb/sth** to make sb/sth lose the respect of other people 使丧失名誉；使蒙受耻辱；使丢脸：*You have dishonoured the name of the school.* 你败坏了学校的名声。**2** **~ sth** to refuse to keep an agreement or a promise 违背，违反（协议或诺言）：*He had dishonoured nearly all of his election pledges.* 他几乎违背了所有的竞选诺言。OPP **honour**

dis·hon·our·able (*especially US* **dis·hon·or·able**) /dɪsˈɒnərəbl; *NAmE* -ˈɑːn-/ *adj.* not deserving respect; immoral or unacceptable 不名誉的；不光彩的；可耻的：*It would have been dishonourable of her not to keep her promise.* 她要是不履行诺言就不光彩了。◇ *He was given a* ***dishonourable discharge*** (= an order to leave the army for unacceptable behaviour). 他被开除了军籍。OPP **honourable** ▸ **dis·hon·our·ably** /-nərəbli/ *adv.*

dish·pan /ˈdɪʃpæn/ *noun* (*NAmE*) a bowl for washing plates, etc. in 洗碟盆；洗碗盆

dish·rag /ˈdɪʃræg/ *noun* (*NAmE*) = DISHCLOTH

dish·towel /ˈdɪʃtaʊəl/ (*NAmE*) (*BrE* ˈ**tea towel**, ˈ**tea cloth**) *noun* a small towel used for drying cups, plates, knives, etc. after they have been washed（擦拭已洗餐具的）擦碗布，抹布；茶巾 ➲ VISUAL VOCAB PAGE V26

dish·wash·er /ˈdɪʃwɒʃə(r); *NAmE* -wɔːʃ-; -wɑːʃ-/ *noun* **1** a machine for washing plates, cups, etc. 洗碗碟机：*to* ***load/stack the dishwasher*** 将碗碟放在 / 码在洗碗机里 ➲ VISUAL VOCAB PAGE V26 **2** a person whose job is to wash plates, etc., for example in a restaurant 洗碟工；洗碗工

dish·water /ˈdɪʃwɔːtə(r)/ *noun* [U] water that sb has used to wash dirty plates, etc. 洗过碗碟的水；泔水 IDM SEE DULL *adj.*

dishy /ˈdɪʃi/ *adj.* (**dish·ier**, **dishi·est**) (*old-fashioned, informal, especially BrE*) (of a person 人) physically attractive 性感的；有魅力的

dis·il·lu·sion /ˌdɪsɪˈluːʒn/ *verb* **~ sb** to destroy sb's belief in or good opinion of sb/sth 使醒悟；使不再抱幻想；使幻想破灭：*I hate to disillusion you, but not everyone is as honest as you.* 我实在不愿把实情告诉你，但并非人人都像你那样诚实。▸ **dis·il·lu·sion** *noun* [U] = DISILLUSIONMENT

dis·il·lu·sioned /ˌdɪsɪˈluːʒnd/ *adj.* **~ (by/with sb/sth)** disappointed because the person you admired or the idea you believed to be good and true now seems without value 大失所望的；不再抱幻想的；幻想破灭的 SYN **disenchanted**：*I soon became disillusioned with the job.* 我不久便对这个工作不再抱幻想了。

dis·il·lu·sion·ment /ˌdɪsɪˈluːʒnmənt/ (*also* **dis·il·lu·sion**) *noun* [U, sing.] **~ (with sth)** the state of being disillusioned 醒悟；不再抱幻想；幻想破灭 SYN **disenchantment**：*There is widespread disillusionment with the present government.* 人们对现政府普遍感到失望。

dis·in·cen·tive /ˌdɪsɪnˈsentɪv/ *noun* [C] a thing that makes sb less willing to do sth 起抑制作用的事物；遏制因素 OPP **incentive**

dis·in·clin·ation /ˌdɪsˌɪnklɪˈneɪʃn/ *noun* [sing., U] (*formal*) a lack of willingness to do sth; a lack of enthusiasm for sth 不情愿；不乐意；无意：*There was a general disinclination to return to the office after lunch.* 午饭后人们一般都不乐意回办公室办公。

dis·in·clined /ˌdɪsɪnˈklaɪnd/ *adj.* [not before noun] **~ (to do sth)** (*formal*) not willing 不情愿；不乐意；无意于 SYN **reluctant**：*He was strongly disinclined to believe anything that she said.* 她说什么他都坚决不肯相信。

dis·in·fect /ˌdɪsɪnˈfekt/ *verb* **1** **~ sth** to clean sth using a substance that kills bacteria 给…消毒：*to disinfect a surface/room/wound* 给表面 / 房间 / 伤口消毒 **2** **~ sth** to run a computer program to get rid of a computer virus 查杀（计算机）病毒；扫除（电脑）病毒 ▸ **dis·in·fec·tion** *noun* [U]

D

dis·in·fect·ant /ˌdɪsɪnˈfektənt/ *noun* [U, C] a substance that disinfects 消毒剂；杀菌剂：*a strong smell of disinfectant* 呛人的消毒剂气味

dis·in·for·ma·tion /ˌdɪsˌɪnfəˈmeɪʃn; *NAmE* -fərˈm-/ *noun* [U] false information that is given deliberately, especially by government organizations（尤指政府机构故意发布的）虚假信息，假消息

D

dis·in·genu·ous /ˌdɪsɪnˈdʒenjuəs/ *adj.* [not usually before noun] (*formal*) not sincere, especially when you pretend to know less about sth than you really do 不真诚；不诚实；假装不知道：*It would be disingenuous of me to claim I had never seen it.* 要说我从未看到过，那就是言不由衷了。➲ COMPARE INGENUOUS ▶ **dis·in·genu·ous·ly** *adv.*

dis·in·herit /ˌdɪsɪnˈherɪt/ *verb* ~ **sb** to prevent sb, especially your son or daughter, from receiving your money or property after your death 剥夺（某人）的继承权 ➲ COMPARE INHERIT (1)

dis·in·hibit /ˌdɪsɪnˈhɪbɪt/ *verb* ~ **sb** (*formal*) to help sb to stop feeling shy so that they can relax and show their feelings 使不再拘谨；使不再拘束 ▶ **dis·in·hib·ition** /ˌdɪsɪnhɪˈbɪʃn/ *noun* [U]

dis·in·te·grate /dɪsˈɪntɪɡreɪt/ *verb* **1** [I] to break into small parts or pieces and be destroyed 碎裂；解体；分裂：*The plane disintegrated as it fell into the sea.* 飞机坠入大海时解体了。 **2** [I] to become much less strong or united and be gradually destroyed 衰微；瓦解；崩溃 **SYN** **fall apart**: *The authority of the central government was rapidly disintegrating.* 中央政府的权威在迅速丧失。 ▶ **dis·in·te·gra·tion** /dɪsˌɪntɪˈɡreɪʃn/ *noun* [U]: *the gradual disintegration of traditional values* 传统价值观念的逐渐淡薄

dis·in·ter /ˌdɪsɪnˈtɜː(r)/ *verb* (**-rr-**) (*formal*) **1** ~ **sth** to dig up sth, especially a dead body, from the ground 从地下掘出（尤指尸体） **OPP** **inter** **2** ~ **sth** (**from sth**) to find sth that has been hidden or lost for a long time 发现（隐藏或丢失很久的东西）；使显现

dis·in·ter·est /dɪsˈɪntrəst; -trest/ *noun* [U] **1** ~ (**in sth**) lack of interest 无兴趣；不关心；冷漠：*His total disinterest in money puzzled his family.* 他对金钱毫无兴趣使他的家人感到迷惑不解。 **2** the fact of not being involved in sth 客观；公正

dis·in·ter·est·ed /dɪsˈɪntrəstɪd; -trestɪd/ *adj.* **1** not influenced by personal feelings, or by the chance of getting some advantage for yourself 客观的；无私的；公正的 **SYN** **impartial, objective, unbiased**: *a **disinterested onlooker/spectator*** 不偏不倚的旁观者 / 观众 ◇ *Her advice appeared to be disinterested.* 她的建议似乎是客观公正的。➲ MORE LIKE THIS 23, page R27 **2** (*informal*) not interested 无兴趣的；不关心的；冷漠的 ➲ NOTE AT INTERESTED ▶ **dis·in·ter·est·ed·ly** *adv.*

dis·in·vest /ˌdɪsɪnˈvest/ *verb* [I] ~ (**from sth**) (*business* 商) to stop investing money in a company, an industry or a country; to reduce the amount of money invested 撤资；减少（对…的）投资

dis·in·vest·ment /ˌdɪsɪnˈvestmənt/ *noun* [U] (*finance* 财) the process of reducing the amount of money that you have invested in a particular company, industry, etc. 撤资；减少投资

dis·joint·ed /dɪsˈdʒɔɪntɪd/ *adj.* not communicated or described in a clear or logical way; not connected 不连贯的；支离破碎的；杂乱无章的 **SYN** **disconnected, incoherent**

dis·junc·tion /dɪsˈdʒʌŋkʃn/ (*also less frequent* **dis·junc·ture** /dɪsˈdʒʌŋktʃə(r)/) *noun* ~ (**between A and B**) (*formal*) a difference between two things that you would expect to be in agreement with each other 分离；分裂

disk /dɪsk/ *noun* **1** (*especially NAmE*) = DISC: *Red blood cells are roughly the shape of a disk.* 红细胞大致呈圆盘状。 **2** (*also* **magˌnetic ˈdisk**) (*computing* 计) a device for storing information on a computer, with a MAGNETIC surface that records information received in electronic form 磁盘；盘 ➲ SEE ALSO HARD DISK

ˈdisk drive *noun* a device that passes data between a disk and the memory of a computer or from one disk or computer to another 磁盘驱动器

dis·like /dɪsˈlaɪk/ *verb, noun*

■ *verb* (*rather formal*) to not like sb/sth 不喜爱；厌恶：~ **sb/sth** *Why do you dislike him so much?* 你为什么那么讨厌他呢？◇ *He **disliked it** when she behaved badly in front of his mother.* 他讨厌她在他母亲面前举止失当。◇ ~ **doing sth** *I dislike being away from my family.* 我不喜欢同家人分开。◇ ***Much as she disliked** going to funerals* (= although she did not like it at all), *she knew she had to be there.* 尽管她很不喜欢参加葬礼，但她知道她必须去。◇ ~ **sb/sth doing sth** *He disliked her staying away from home.* 他不愿意让她住在外面。➲ SYNONYMS AT HATE **OPP** **like**

■ *noun* **1** [U, sing.] ~ (**of/for sb/sth**) a feeling of not liking sb/sth 不喜爱；厌恶；反感：*He did not try to hide his dislike of his boss.* 他没有掩饰自己对上司的反感。◇ *She **took an instant dislike to** the house and the neighbourhood.* 她一下子就对那栋房子以及街坊邻里产生了反感。 **2** [C, usually pl.] a thing that you do not like 不喜欢的事物；讨厌的事物：*I've told you all my **likes and dislikes**.* 我喜欢什么，不喜欢什么，都对你说了。

dis·locate /ˈdɪsləkeɪt; *NAmE* -loʊk-; dɪsˈloʊ-/ *verb* **1** ~ **sth** to put a bone out of its normal position in a joint 使（骨头）脱位；使脱臼：*He dislocated his shoulder in the accident.* 他在事故中肩膀脱臼了。◇ *a dislocated finger* 脱臼的手指 ➲ COLLOCATIONS AT INJURY **2** ~ **sth** to stop a system, plan etc. from working or continuing in the normal way 扰乱（制度、计划等）；使混乱；使运转不正常 **SYN** **disrupt** ▶ **dis·loca·tion** /ˌdɪsləˈkeɪʃn; *NAmE* -loʊ-/ *noun* [C, U]: *a dislocation of the shoulder* 肩膀脱臼 ◇ *These policies could cause severe economic and social dislocation.* 这些政策可能引起严重的经济和社会混乱。

dis·lodge /dɪsˈlɒdʒ; *NAmE* -ˈlɑːdʒ/ *verb* (*formal*) **1** ~ **sth** (**from sth**) to force or knock sth out of its position（把某物）强行去除，取出，移动：*The wind dislodged one or two tiles from the roof.* 大风从屋顶上刮下了一两片瓦来。 **2** ~ **sb** (**from sth**) to force sb to leave a place, position or job（把某人）逐出，赶出，驱逐出：*The rebels have so far failed to dislodge the President.* 叛乱分子至今未能把总统赶下台。

dis·loyal /dɪsˈlɔɪəl/ *adj.* ~ (**to sb/sth**) not loyal or faithful to your friends, family, country, etc.（对国家、家庭等）不忠实的，不忠诚的；（对朋友等）不守信义的：*He was accused of being disloyal to the government.* 他被指控对政府不忠。▶ **dis·loy·alty** /-ˈlɔɪəlti/ *noun* [U]

dis·mal /ˈdɪzməl/ *adj.* **1** causing or showing sadness 忧郁的；凄凉的；惨淡的；阴沉的 **SYN** **gloomy, miserable**: *dismal conditions/surroundings/weather* 悲惨的状况；凄凉的环境；阴沉的天气 **2** (*informal*) not skilful or successful; of very low quality 不熟练的；差劲的；不怎么样的：*The singer gave a dismal performance of some old songs.* 那歌手唱了几首老歌，唱得也不怎么样。◇ *Their recent attempt to increase sales has been a **dismal failure**.* 他们最近努力提高销售量，全是白费劲。 ▶ **dis·mal·ly** /-məli/ *adv.*: *I tried not to laugh but failed dismally* (= was completely unsuccessful). 我想尽量忍着不笑，但根本忍不住。

dis·man·tle /dɪsˈmæntl/ *verb* **1** ~ **sth** to take apart a machine or structure so that it is in separate pieces 拆开，拆卸（机器或结构）：*I had to dismantle the engine in order to repair it.* 我得把发动机拆开来修理。◇ *The steel mill was dismantled piece by piece.* 钢厂已经一块块拆散了。 **2** ~ **sth** to end an organization or a system gradually in an organized way（逐渐）废除，取消：*The government was in the process of dismantling the state-owned industries.* 政府正在着手逐步取消国有企业。 ▶ **dis·mant·ling** *noun* [U]

dis·may /dɪsˈmeɪ/ *noun, verb*

■ *noun* [U] a worried, sad feeling after you have received an unpleasant surprise 诧异；惊愕；灰心；丧气：*She could not hide her dismay at the result.* 她无法掩饰自己对

这一结果的惶恐不安。◇ *He looked at her* ***in dismay.*** 他诧异地看着她。◇ ***To her dismay,*** *her name was not on the list.* 使她难过的是，名单上没有她的名字。◇ *The news has been greeted* ***with dismay*** *by local business leaders.* 当地商界领袖听到这消息都感到很丧气。

■ ***verb*** **~ sb** to make sb feel shocked and disappointed 使诧异；使惊愕；使失望：*Their reaction dismayed him.* 他们的反应使他感到惊愕。 ▸ **dis·mayed** *adj.*： **~ (at/by sth)** *He was dismayed at the change in his old friend.* 他对老朋友变化之大感到震惊。◇ *The suggestion was greeted by a dismayed silence.* 大家对这个建议感到惊愕，谁都不吭声。◇ **~ (to find, hear, see, etc....)** *They were dismayed to find that the ferry had already left.* 他们发现渡船已经离开，感到很失望。

dis·mem·ber /dɪs'membə(r)/ *verb* **1 ~ sth** to cut or tear the dead body of a person or an animal into pieces 分割…的躯体；肢解 **2 ~ sth** (*formal*) to divide a country, an organization, etc. into smaller parts 分割；瓜分 ▸ **dis·mem·ber·ment** *noun* [U]

dis·miss /dɪs'mɪs/ *verb* **1** to decide that sb/sth is not important and not worth thinking or talking about 不予考虑；摒弃；对…不屑一提 **SYN** **wave sth↔aside/away**： **~ sb/sth** *I think we can safely dismiss their objections.* 我认为我们对他们的异议完全可以不予理会。◇ **~ sb/sth as sth** *Vegetarians are no longer dismissed as cranks.* 素食主义者不再被当作怪人。◇ *He dismissed the opinion polls as worthless.* 他认为民意测验毫无用处而不予考虑。◇ *The suggestion should not be* ***dismissed out of hand*** (= without thinking about it). 这建议不应当直接就被摒弃。 **2** to put thoughts or feelings out of your mind 去除，消除，摒除（思想、感情等）： **~ sth** *Dismissing her fears, she climbed higher.* 她排除了恐惧，爬得更高了。◇ **~ sb/sth from sth** *He dismissed her from his mind.* 他挥去了对她的思念。 **3 ~ sb (from sth)** to officially remove sb from their job 解雇；免职；开除 **SYN** **fire, sack**： *She claims she was unfairly dismissed from her post.* 她声称自己被无理免职。 ➲ WORDFINDER NOTE AT EMPLOY **4 ~ sb** to send sb away or allow them to leave 让（某人）离开；把（某人）打发走；解散： *At 12 o'clock the class was dismissed.* * 12 点下课了。 **5 ~ sth** (*law* 律) to say that a trial or legal case should not continue, usually because there is not enough evidence 驳回；不受理： *The case was dismissed.* 此案已被驳回。 **6 ~ sb** (in CRICKET 板球) to end the INNINGS of a player or team 使（球员或球队）退场；使出局

dis·missal /dɪs'mɪsl/ *noun* **1** [U, C] the act of dismissing sb from their job; an example of this 解雇；开除；撤职： *He still hopes to win his claim against* ***unfair dismissal.*** 他声称遭无理解雇，仍然希望赢得申诉。◇ *The dismissals followed the resignation of the chairman.* 董事长辞职后紧接着就是解雇人员。 **2** [U] the failure to consider sth as important 不予考虑；不予理会；摒弃： *Her casual dismissal of the threats seemed irresponsible.* 她对这些威胁毫不在乎而不予理会，似乎很不负责任。 **3** [U, C] (*law* 律) the act of not allowing a trial or legal case to continue, usually because there is not enough evidence（诉讼的）驳回，不予受理： *the dismissal of the appeal* 驳回上诉 **4** [U, C] the act of sending sb away or allowing them to leave 解散；打发走 **5** [U, C] (in CRICKET 板球) the end of the INNINGS of a player or team （球员或球队的）退场，出局

dis·mis·sive /dɪs'mɪsɪv/ *adj.* **~ (of sb/sth)** showing that you do not believe a person or thing to be important or worth considering 轻蔑的；鄙视的 **SYN** **disdainful**： *a dismissive gesture/tone* 轻蔑的手势 / 语调 ▸ **dis·mis·sive·ly** *adv.*： *to* ***shrug/wave dismissively*** 轻蔑地耸耸肩 / 挥挥手

dis·mount /dɪs'maʊnt/ *verb* [I] **~ (from sth)** (*formal*) to get off a horse, bicycle or motorcycle 下（马、自行车、摩托车） **OPP** **mount** ➲ WORDFINDER NOTE AT CYCLING

dis·obedi·ence /ˌdɪsə'biːdiəns/ *noun* [U] failure or refusal to obey 不服从；不顺从；违抗 ➲ SEE ALSO CIVIL DISOBEDIENCE **OPP** **obedience**

dis·obedi·ent /ˌdɪsə'biːdiənt/ *adj.* failing or refusing to obey 不服从的；不顺从的；违抗的： *a disobedient child* 不听话的孩子 **OPP** **obedient**

dis·obey /ˌdɪsə'beɪ/ *verb* [T, I] **~ (sb/sth)** to refuse to do what a person, a law, an order, etc. tells you to do; to refuse to obey 不服从；不顺从；违抗： *He was punished for disobeying orders.* 他因违抗命令而受到惩罚。 **OPP** **obey**

dis·obli·ging /ˌdɪsə'blaɪdʒɪŋ/ *adj.* deliberately not helpful 不肯帮忙的；不合作的： *a disobliging manner* 不合作的态度

dis·order /dɪs'ɔːdə(r); *NAmE* -'ɔːrd-/ *noun* **1** [U] (*formal*) an untidy state; a lack of order or organization 杂乱；混乱；凌乱： *His financial affairs were* ***in complete disorder.*** 他的财务完全是一笔糊涂账。◇ *The room was in a state of disorder.* 房间凌乱不堪。 **OPP** **order** **2** [U] (*formal*) violent behaviour of large groups of people 骚乱；动乱： *an outbreak of rioting and* ***public disorder*** 暴乱和公众骚乱的爆发 ➲ COMPARE ORDER *n.* **3** [C, U] (*medical* 医) an illness that causes a part of the body to stop functioning correctly 失调；紊乱；疾病： *a* ***blood/bowel, etc. disorder*** 血液病、闹肚子等 ◇ ***eating disorders*** 进食障碍 ◇ *He was suffering from some form of psychiatric disorder.* 他患有某种类型的精神错乱。 ➲ SYNONYMS AT DISEASE

dis·ordered /dɪs'ɔːdəd; *NAmE* -'ɔːrdərd/ *adj.* **1** showing a lack of order or control 杂乱的；混乱的；凌乱的： *disordered hair* 乱七八糟的头发 ◇ *a disordered state* 混乱状态 **OPP** **ordered** **2** (*specialist*) suffering from a mental or physical disorder（身心）失调的，紊乱的，错乱的： *emotionally disordered children* 有情绪障碍的孩子

dis·or·der·ly /dɪs'ɔːdəli; *NAmE* -'ɔːrdərli/ *adj.* [usually before noun] (*formal*) **1** (of people or behaviour 人或行为) showing lack of control; publicly violent or noisy 难驾驭的；目无法纪的；骚乱的： *disorderly conduct* 目无法纪的行为 ◇ *They were arrested for being* ***drunk and disorderly.*** 他们因醉酒滋事而被捕。 **2** untidy 杂乱的；混乱的；凌乱的： *newspapers in a disorderly pile by the door* 门边乱七八糟的一堆报纸 **OPP** **orderly**

disˌorderly 'house *noun* (*law* 律, *old use*) a BROTHEL (= place where people pay to have sex) 妓院

dis·or·gan·ized (*BrE also* **-ised**) /dɪs'ɔːɡənaɪzd; *NAmE* -'ɔːrɡ-/ (*also less frequent* **un·or·gan·ized**, **-ised**) *adj.* badly planned; not able to plan or organize well 计划不周的；缺乏组织的；杂乱无章的： *It was a hectic disorganized weekend.* 这个周末忙乱得一塌糊涂。◇ *She's so disorganized.* 她太缺乏条理了。 ➲ COMPARE ORGANIZED (2) ▸ **dis·or·gan·iza·tion**, **-isa·tion** /dɪsˌɔːɡənaɪ'zeɪʃn; *NAmE* -ˌɔːrɡənə'z-/ *noun* [U]

dis·orien·tate /dɪs'ɔːriənteɪt/ (*BrE*) (*also* **dis·orient** /dɪs'ɔːrient/ *NAmE*, *BrE*) *verb* **1 ~ sb** to make sb unable to recognize where they are or where they should go 使迷失方向： *The darkness had disorientated him.* 黑暗使他迷失了方向。 **2 ~ sb** to make sb feel confused 使迷惘；使不知所措；使无所适从： *Ex-soldiers can be disorientated by the transition to civilian life.* 退伍军人转而去过平民生活可能会感到茫然。 ➲ COMPARE ORIENT ▸ **dis·orien·tated** (*also* **dis·orient·ed**) *adj.*： *She felt shocked and totally disorientated.* 她感到震惊而茫然不知所措。 **dis·orien·ta·tion** /dɪsˌɔːriən'teɪʃn/ *noun* [U]

dis·own /dɪs'əʊn; *NAmE* -'oʊn/ *verb* **~ sb/sth** to decide that you no longer want to be connected with or responsible for sb/sth 与…断绝关系；否认对…的责任： *Her family disowned her for marrying a foreigner.* 她的家人因她嫁给了外国人而与她断绝关系。

dis·par·age /dɪ'spærɪdʒ/ *verb* **~ sb/sth** (*formal*) to suggest that sb/sth is not important or valuable 贬低；轻视 **SYN** **belittle**： *I don't mean to disparage your achievements.* 我并不想贬低你的成就。 ▸ **dis·par·age·ment** *noun* [U] **dis·para·ging** *adj.*： *disparaging remarks* 贬损的言辞 **dis·para·ging·ly** *adv.*： *He spoke disparagingly of his colleagues.* 他言辞之中很是看不起同事。

dis·par·ate /'dɪspərət/ *adj.* (*formal*) **1** made up of parts or people that are very different from each other 由不同的人（或事物）组成的： *a disparate group of individuals*

三教九流的一帮人 **2** (of two or more things 两种或以上的事物) so different from each other that they cannot be compared or cannot work together 迥然不同的；无法比较的；不相干的

dis·par·ity /dɪ'spærəti/ *noun* [U, C] (*pl.* **-ies**) (*formal*) a difference, especially one connected with unfair treatment（尤指因不公正对待引起的）不同，不等，差异，悬殊：*the wide disparity between rich and poor* 贫富悬殊

dis·pas·sion·ate /dɪs'pæʃənət/ *adj.* (*approving*) not influenced by emotion 不动感情的；冷静的；不带偏见的 SYN **impartial**: *taking a calm, dispassionate view of the situation* 以冷静、客观公正的观点看待形势 ◇ *a dispassionate observer* 冷静的旁观者 ▶ **dis·pas·sion·ate·ly** *adv.*

dis·patch (*BrE also* **des·patch**) /dɪ'spætʃ/ *verb, noun*

■ *verb* **1** ~ **sb/sth** (**to**...) (*formal*) to send sb/sth somewhere, especially for a special purpose 派遣；调遣；派出：*Troops have been dispatched to the area.* 部队已派往那个地区。◇ *A courier was dispatched to collect the documents.* 已派快递员去取文件。**2** ~ **sth** (**to sb/sth**) (*formal*) to send a letter, package or message somewhere 发出，发送（邮件、包裹、信息）：*Goods are dispatched within 24 hours of your order reaching us.* 订单到达我方 24 小时内发货。**3** ~ **sb/sth** (*formal*) to deal or finish with sb/sth quickly and completely 迅速处理；迅速办妥；迅速完成：*He dispatched the younger player in straight sets.* 他连续几盘迅速击败了那位比他年轻的选手。**4** ~ **sb/sth** (*old-fashioned*) to kill a person or an animal 杀死；处决

■ *noun* **1** [U] (*formal*) the act of sending sb/sth somewhere 派遣；调遣；发送：*More food supplies are ready for immediate dispatch.* 更多的食品供应已备妥即刻发运。**2** [C] a message or report sent quickly from one military officer to another or between government officials（军事人员或政府官员之间的）急件，快信 **3** [C] a report sent to a newspaper by a journalist who is working in a foreign country（驻外国记者发给报刊的）新闻报道，电讯：*dispatches from the war zone* 从战区发来的报道

IDM **with di'spatch** (*formal*) quickly and efficiently 迅速而有效

di'spatch box (*also* **de'spatch box**) (*both BrE*) *noun* **1** [C] a container for carrying official documents 公文递送箱 **2** **the Dispatch Box** [sing.] a box on a table in the centre of the House of Commons in the British parliament, which ministers stand next to when they speak 下议院案头文箱（置于英国下议院中央的桌子上，大臣站在桌边发言）

dis·patch·er /dɪ'spætʃə(r)/ *noun* **1** a person whose job is to see that trains, buses, planes, etc. leave on time（火车、公交车、飞机等的）调度员 **2** a person whose job is to send emergency vehicles to where they are needed（应急车辆的）调度员

di'spatch rider (*also* **de'spatch rider**) *noun* (*both BrE*) a person whose job is to carry messages or packages by motorcycle（骑摩托车的）通信员，信使

dis·pel /dɪ'spel/ *verb* (**-ll-**) ~ **sth** to make sth, especially a feeling or belief, go away or disappear 驱散，消除（尤指感觉或信仰）：*His speech dispelled any fears about his health.* 他的发言消除了人们对他身体健康的担心。

dis·pens·able /dɪ'spensəbl/ *adj.* [not usually before noun] not necessary; that can be got rid of 不必要；可有可无；不重要：*They looked on music and art lessons as dispensable.* 他们认为音乐课和美术课是可有可无的。OPP **essential, indispensable**

dis·pens·ary /dɪ'spensəri/ *noun* (*pl.* **-ies**) **1** a place in a hospital, shop/store, etc. where medicines are prepared for patients（医院、商店等的）药房，配药处 **2** (*old-fashioned*) a place where patients are treated, especially one run by a charity（尤指慈善机构的）医务室，诊所

dis·pen·sa·tion /ˌdɪspen'seɪʃn/ *noun* **1** [C, U] special permission, especially from a religious leader, to do sth that is not usually allowed or legal（尤指宗教领袖给予的）豁免，宽免：*She needed a special dispensation to remarry.* 她需要得到特准才能再婚。◇ *The sport's ruling body gave him dispensation to compete in national competitions.* 体育运动管理机构特许他参加全国性的体育比赛。**2** [U] (*formal*) the act or process of providing sth, especially by sb in authority 分配；施与；实施：*the dispensation of justice* 执法 **3** [C] (*specialist*) a political or religious system that operates in a country at a particular time（某一国家某一时期的政治、宗教）制度

dis·pense /dɪ'spens/ *verb* **1** ~ **sth** (**to sb**) (*formal*) to give out sth to people 分配；分发：*The machine dispenses a range of drinks and snacks.* 这台机器发售各种饮料和小吃。**2** ~ **sth** (**to sb**) (*formal*) to provide sth, especially a service, for people 施与，提供（尤指服务）：*The organization dispenses free health care to the poor.* 这个机构为穷人提供免费医疗。◇ *to* **dispense justice/advice** 执法；给予忠告 **3** ~ **sth** to prepare medicine and give it to people, as a job 配（药）；发（药）：*to dispense a prescription* 按处方配药 ◇ (*BrE*) *to dispense medicine* 发药 ◇ (*BrE*) *a dispensing chemist* 药剂师 ➲ WORDFINDER NOTE AT MEDICINE

PHR V **di'spense with sb/sth** to stop using sb/sth because you no longer need them or it 摒弃；不再需要；不再用 SYN **do away with**: *Debit cards dispense with the need for cash altogether.* 有借记卡就完全不需要用现金了。◇ *I think we can* **dispense with the formalities** (= speak openly and naturally to each other). 我想我们就免去客套吧。

dis·pens·er /dɪ'spensə(r)/ *noun* a machine or container holding money, drinks, paper towels, etc. that you can obtain quickly, for example by pulling a handle or pressing buttons 自动取款机；自动售货机；自动取物器：*a soap dispenser* 皂液瓶 ➲ VISUAL VOCAB PAGES V25, V71 ➲ SEE ALSO CASH DISPENSER

dis'pensing chemist *noun* (*BrE*) = CHEMIST (1)

dis·pers·al /dɪ'spɜːsl; *NAmE* dɪ'spɜːrsl/ *noun* [U, C] (*formal*) the process of sending sb/sth in different directions; the process of spreading sth over a wide area 分散；疏散；散布：*police trained in crowd dispersal* 在疏散人群方面受过训练的警察 ◇ *the dispersal of seeds* 种子的传播

dis·perse /dɪ'spɜːs; *NAmE* dɪ'spɜːrs/ *verb* **1** [I, T] to move apart and go away in different directions; to make sb/sth do this（使）分散，散开；疏散；驱散：*The fog began to disperse.* 雾开始散了。◇ *The* **crowd dispersed** *quickly.* 人群很快便散开了。◇ ~ **sb/sth** *Police dispersed the protesters with tear gas.* 警察用催泪瓦斯驱散了抗议者。**2** [T, I] ~ (**sth**) to spread or to make sth spread over a wide area 散布；散发；传播 SYN **scatter**: *The seeds are dispersed by the wind.* 这些种子由风传播。

dis·per·sion /dɪ'spɜːʃn; *NAmE* dɪ'spɜːrʒn/ *noun* [U] (*specialist*) the process by which people or things are spread over a wide area 分散；散开；散布

dis·pirited /dɪ'spɪrɪtɪd/ *adj.* having no hope or enthusiasm 气馁的；垂头丧气的；心灰意懒的：*She looked tired and dispirited.* 她显得疲倦而且神情沮丧。➲ COMPARE SPIRITED

dis·pir·it·ing /dɪ'spɪrɪtɪŋ/ *adj.* making sb lose their hope or enthusiasm 令人沮丧的；使人气馁的：*a* **dispiriting experience/failure** 令人沮丧的经历 / 失败

dis·place AW /dɪs'pleɪs/ *verb* [often passive] (*formal*) **1** ~ **sb/sth** to take the place of sb/sth 取代；替代；置换 SYN **replace**: *Gradually factory workers have been displaced by machines.* 工厂的工人已逐渐被机器取代。◇ (*specialist*) *The ship displaces 58 000 tonnes* (= as a way of measuring its size). 这艘轮船的排水量为 58 000 吨。**2** ~ **sb** to force people to move away from their home to another place 迫使（某人）离开家园：*Around 10 000 people have been displaced by the fighting.* 大约 1 万人因战争而背井离乡。**3** ~ **sth** to move sth from its usual position 移动；挪开；转移：*Check for roof tiles that have been displaced by the wind.* 检查一下屋顶上是否有瓦被风刮得挪了位。**4** ~ **sb** (*especially NAmE*) to remove sb from a job or position 撤职；免职；使失业：*displaced workers* 辞退的工人

di͵splaced 'person *noun* (*pl.* **displaced persons**) (*specialist*) a REFUGEE 难民；流亡者

dis·place·ment AW /dɪsˈpleɪsmənt/ *noun* [U] **1** (*formal*) the act of displacing sb/sth; the process of being displaced 取代；替代；移位；免职：*the largest displacement of civilian population since World War Two* 自第二次世界大战以来最大规模的平民迁移 **2** [C] (*physics* 物) the amount of a liquid moved out of place by sth floating or put in it, especially a ship floating in water 排水量：*a ship with a displacement of 10 000 tonnes* 排水量为 1 万吨的船

disˈplacement activity *noun* **1** [U] things that you do in order to avoid doing what you are supposed to be doing 逃避职责的活动 **2** (*biology* 生, *psychology* 心) [U, C] behaviour in animals or humans that seems to have no connection with the situation in which it is performed, resulting from two conflicting urges 替换活动，移代活动（人或动物由于对立的驱力而表现出不相宜的行为）

dis·play AW /dɪˈspleɪ/ *verb, noun*

■ *verb* **1** [T] ~ **sth** (**to sb**) to put sth in a place where people can see it easily; to show sth to people 陈列；展出；展示 SYN **exhibit**：*The exhibition gives local artists an opportunity to display their work.* 这次展览为当地艺术家提供了展示自己作品的机会。◇ *She displayed her bruises for all to see.* 她将自己身上青一块紫一块的伤痕露出来给大家看。 **2** [T] ~ **sth** to show signs of sth, especially a quality or feeling 显示，显露，表现（尤指特性或情感）：*I have rarely seen her display any sign of emotion.* 我难得见到她将喜怒形于色。◇ *These statistics display a definite trend.* 这些统计数据表现出一种明显的趋势。 **3** [T] ~ **sth** (of a computer, etc. 计算机等) to show information 显示：*The screen will display the username in the top right-hand corner.* 屏幕将在右上角显示用户名称。◇ *This column displays the title of the mail message.* 这一栏显示邮件标题。 **4** [I] (*specialist*) (of male birds and animals 雄性的鸟兽) to show a special pattern of behaviour that is intended to attract a female bird or animal （为求偶）炫耀

■ *noun* **1** an arrangement of things in a public place to inform or entertain people or advertise sth for sale 陈列；展览：*a beautiful floral display outside the Town Hall* 市政厅外陈设的美丽的花 ◇ *a window display* 橱窗陈列 ◇ *a display cabinet* 陈列柜 ➲ WORDFINDER NOTE AT SHOP **2** an act of performing a skill or of showing sth happening, in order to entertain 展示；表演：*a firework display* 烟火表演 ◇ *a breathtaking display of aerobatics* 惊险的特技飞行表演 **3** an occasion when you show a particular quality, feeling or ability by the way that you behave （特性、情感或能力的）显示，表现，表露：*a display of affection/strength/wealth* 爱的流露；实力的显示；财富的炫耀 **4** the words, pictures, etc. shown on a computer screen （计算机屏幕上的）显示，显像：*a high resolution colour display* 高分辨率彩色显示 ➲ WORDFINDER NOTE AT COMPUTER ➲ SEE ALSO LIQUID CRYSTAL DISPLAY

IDM **on disˈplay** put in a place where people can look at it 陈列；展出 SYN **show**：*Designs for the new sports hall are on display in the library.* 新体育馆的设计图展示在图书馆里。◇ *to put sth on* ***temporary/permanent display*** 临时 / 长期展出某物

disˈplay bin (*BrE also* **ˈdump bin**) *noun* a box in a shop/store for displaying goods, especially goods whose prices have been reduced （商店）陈列柜；（尤指）减价货品柜

dis·please /dɪsˈpliːz/ *verb* ~ **sb** (*formal*) to make sb feel upset, annoyed or not satisfied 使恼怒；使生气；使不悦 OPP **please** ▸ **dis·pleased** *adj.*：~ (**with sb/sth**) *Are you displeased with my work?* 你对我的工作不满意吗？◇ ~ (**at sth**) *She was not displeased at the effect she was having on the young man.* 她并没有为自己对那个年轻人产生的影响而感到不快。 **dis·pleas·ing** *adj.*：~ (**to sb/sth**) *His remarks were clearly not displeasing to her.* 他的话显然并没使她不快。

dis·pleas·ure /dɪsˈpleʒə(r)/ *noun* [U] ~ (**at/with sb/sth**) (*formal*) the feeling of being upset and annoyed 烦恼；生气；不悦 SYN **annoyance**：*She made no attempt to hide her displeasure at the prospect.* 她没有掩饰自己对前景并不乐观。 ➲ COMPARE PLEASURE

dis·port /dɪˈspɔːt; *NAmE* dɪˈspɔːrt/ *verb* ~ **yourself** (*old-fashioned* or *humorous*) to enjoy yourself by doing sth active 作乐；自娱自乐

dis·pos·able AW /dɪˈspəʊzəbl; *NAmE* -ˈspoʊ-/ *adj.* [usually before noun] **1** made to be thrown away after use 用后即丢弃的；一次性的：*disposable gloves/razors* 一次性手套 / 剃刀 ◇ (*BrE*) *disposable nappies* 一次性尿布 ◇ (*NAmE*) *disposable diapers* 一次性尿布 **2** (*finance* 财) available for use 可动用的；可自由支配的：***disposable assets/capital/resources*** 可支配资产 / 资本 / 资源 ◇ *a person's* ***disposable income*** (= money they are free to spend after paying taxes, etc.) 个人可支配收入

dis·pos·ables /dɪˈspəʊzəblz; *NAmE* -ˈspoʊ-/ *noun* [pl.] items such as NAPPIES/DIAPERS and CONTACT LENSES that are designed to be thrown away after use 用后即丢弃的物品，一次性物品（如尿布、隐形眼镜片）

dis·posal AW /dɪˈspəʊzl; *NAmE* -ˈspoʊ-/ *noun* **1** [U] the act of getting rid of sth 去掉；清除；处理：*a bomb disposal squad* 炸弹清除小组 ◇ *sewage disposal systems* 污水处理系统 ◇ *the disposal of nuclear waste* 核废料的处理 **2** [C] (*business* 商) the sale of part of a business, property, etc. （企业、财产等的）变卖，让与 **3** [C] (*NAmE*) = WASTE-DISPOSAL UNIT

IDM **at your/sb's disposal** available for use as you prefer/sb prefers 任某人处理；供某人任意使用；由某人自行支配：*He will have a car at his disposal for the whole month.* 他将有一辆汽车归他使用一个月。◇ *Well, I'm at your disposal* (= I am ready to help you in any way I can). 好吧，我听候你的吩咐。

dis·pose AW /dɪˈspəʊz; *NAmE* dɪˈspoʊz/ *verb* (*formal*) **1** ~ **sth/sb + adv./prep.** to arrange things or people in a particular way or position 排列；布置；安排 **2** ~ **sb to/toward(s) sth** | ~ **sb to do sth** to make sb behave in a particular way 使倾向于；使有意于；使易于：*a drug that disposes the patient towards sleep* 使病人想睡觉的药

PHR V **diˈspose of sb/sth** **1** to get rid of sb/sth that you do not want or cannot keep 去掉；清除；销毁：*the difficulties of disposing of nuclear waste* 处理核废料的困难 ◇ *to dispose of stolen property* 销赃 **2** to deal with a problem, question or threat successfully 应付；解决；处理：*That seems to have disposed of most of their arguments.* 这样就似乎把他们的大部分论点都驳倒了。 **3** to defeat or kill sb 击败；杀死：*It took her a mere 20 minutes to dispose of her opponent.* 她仅用了 20 分钟就击败了对手。

dis·posed AW /dɪˈspəʊzd; *NAmE* dɪˈspoʊzd/ *adj.* [not before noun] (*formal*) **1** ~ (**to do sth**) willing or prepared to do sth 倾向于；有意于；乐意：*I'm not disposed to argue.* 我无意争论。◇ *You're most welcome to join us if you feel so disposed.* 你若有意参加，我们非常欢迎。◇ *being naturally disposed towards speculation* 天生喜欢猜测 **2** (following an adverb 用于副词后) ~ **to/towards sb/sth** having a good/bad opinion of a person or thing 对…有好感（或恶感）：*She seems favourably disposed to the move.* 她似乎对这一行动持赞同态度。 ➲ SEE ALSO ILL-DISPOSED, WELL DISPOSED

dis·pos·ition /ˌdɪspəˈzɪʃn/ *noun* **1** [C, usually sing.] (*formal*) the natural qualities of a person's character 性格；性情 SYN **temperament**：*to have a cheerful disposition* 性情开朗 ◇ *people of a nervous disposition* 神经质的人 **2** [C, usually sing.] ~ **to/towards sth** | ~ **to do sth** (*formal*) a tendency to behave in a particular way 倾向；意向：*to* ***have/show a disposition*** *towards violence* 有 / 表现出暴力倾向 **3** [C, usually sing.] (*formal*) the way sth is placed or arranged 排列；布置；安排 SYN **arrangement** **4** [C, U] (*law* 律) a formal act of giving property or money to sb （财产、金钱的）处置，让与

dis·pos·sess /ˌdɪspəˈzes/ *verb* [usually passive] ~ **sb** (**of sth**) (*formal*) to take sb's property, land or house away from them 剥夺，夺去（某人的财产、土地、房屋） ▸ **dis·pos·ses·sion** /ˌdɪspəˈzeʃn/ *noun* [U]

the dis·pos·sessed /ˌdɪspəˈzest/ *noun* [pl.] people who have had property taken away from them 被剥夺财产者

dis·pro·por·tion AW /ˌdɪsprəˈpɔːʃn; *NAmE* -ˈpɔːrʃn/ *noun* [U, C] (*formal*) the state of two things not being at an equally high or low level; an example of this 不相称；不均衡；不成比例；不相称（或不均衡、不成比例）的东西：~ (**between A and B**) *the disproportion between the extra responsibilities and the small salary increase* 额外的责任与小幅增加的薪金之间的不相称 ◇ ~ (**of A to B**) *a profession with a high disproportion of male to female employees* 男女雇员比例严重失调的职业

D

dis·pro·por·tion·ate AW /ˌdɪsprəˈpɔːʃənət; NAmE -ˈpɔːrʃ-/ *adj.* ~ (**to sth**) too large or too small when compared with sth else 不成比例的；不相称的；太大（或太小）的：*The area contains a disproportionate number of young middle-class families.* 这一区年轻的中产阶级家庭特别多。➲ COMPARE PROPORTIONATE ▸ **dis·pro·por·tion·ately** AW *adv.*：*The lower-paid spend a disproportionately large amount of their earnings on food.* 低工资者将收入花在食物上的比例很大。

dis·prove /ˌdɪsˈpruːv/ *verb* ~ **sth** to show that sth is wrong or false 证明…是错误（或虚假）的：*The theory has now been disproved.* 这一理论现已证明是错误的。OPP **prove**

dis·put·able /dɪˈspjuːtəbl/ *adj.* (*formal*) that can or should be questioned or argued about 可质疑的；有争辩余地的；可商榷的 ➲COMPARE INDISPUTABLE

dis·pu·ta·tion /ˌdɪspjuˈteɪʃn/ *noun* [C, U] (*formal*) a discussion about sth that people cannot agree on 争论；辩论；讨论

dis·pute *noun, verb*

■*noun* /dɪˈspjuːt; ˈdɪspjuːt/ [C, U] an argument or a disagreement between two people, groups or countries; discussion about a subject where there is disagreement 争论；辩论；争端；纠纷：~ (**between A and B**) *a dispute between the two countries about the border* 两国间的边界争端 ◇ ~ (**over/about sth**) *the latest dispute over fishing rights* 最近关于捕鱼权的争端 ◇ ***industrial/pay disputes*** 劳资 / 工资纠纷 ◇ *The union is **in dispute with** management over working hours.* 工会与资方在工时问题上发生纠纷。◇ *The cause of the accident was still **in dispute*** (= being argued about). 事故的原因仍在争议之中。◇ *The matter was settled **beyond dispute** by the court judgment* (= it could no longer be argued about). 此问题已由法庭判决，不容争辩。◇ *His theories are **open to dispute*** (= can be disagreed with). 他的理论值得商榷。

■*verb* /dɪˈspjuːt/ **1** [T] to question whether sth is true and valid 对…提出质询；对…表示异议（或怀疑）：~ **sth** *These figures have been disputed.* 有人对这些数字提出了质疑。◇ *to **dispute a decision/claim*** 对某项决定 / 权利要求提出异议 ◇ *The family wanted to dispute the will.* 家属想对遗嘱提出质疑。◇ ~ **that…** *No one is disputing that there is a problem.* 没有人否认现在有问题。◇ ~ **whether, how, etc.…** | **it is disputed whether, how, etc.…** *It is disputed whether the law applies in this case.* 有人对这项法律是否适用于这个案例提出质疑。 **2** [T, I] ~ (**sth**) to argue or disagree strongly with sb about sth, especially about who owns sth 争论；辩论；争执：*disputed territory* 有争议的领土 ◇ *The issue remains **hotly disputed**.* 这个问题至今仍在激烈的辩论中。 **3** [T] ~ **sth** to fight to get control of sth or to win sth 争夺；竞争：*On the last lap three runners were disputing the lead.* 在最后一圈，三名赛跑者在争夺领先地位。

dis·qual·ify /dɪsˈkwɒlɪfaɪ; NAmE -ˈkwɑːl-/ *verb* (**dis·quali·fies**, **dis·quali·fy·ing**, **dis·quali·fied**, **dis·quali·fied**) to prevent sb from doing sth because they have broken a rule or are not suitable 使不合格；使不适合；取消（某人）的资格 SYN **bar**：~ **sb** (**from sth**) *He was disqualified from the competition for using drugs.* 他因使用违禁药被取消比赛资格。◇ ~ **sb** (**from doing sth**) (*BrE*) *You could be disqualified from driving for up to three years.* 你可能会被取消驾驶资格达三年之久。◇ ~ **sb** (**for sth**) *A heart condition disqualified him for military service.* 心脏病使他不符合服兵役的条件。 ➲ WORDFINDER NOTE AT COMPETITION ▸ **dis·quali·fi·ca·tion** /dɪsˌkwɒlɪfɪˈkeɪʃn; NAmE -ˌkwɑːl-/ *noun* [C, U]：*Any form of cheating means automatic disqualification.* 任何形式的作弊都意味着自动取消资格。

dis·quiet /dɪsˈkwaɪət/ *noun* [U] ~ (**about/over sth**) (*formal*) feelings of worry and unhappiness about sth 不安；忧虑；烦恼 SYN **unease**：*There is considerable public disquiet about the safety of the new trains.* 公众对新型列车的安全深感忧虑。

dis·quiet·ing /dɪsˈkwaɪətɪŋ/ *adj.* (*formal*) causing worry and unhappiness 令人不安的；使人忧虑的

dis·quisi·tion /ˌdɪskwɪˈzɪʃn/ *noun* (*formal*) a long complicated speech or written report on a particular subject 专题演讲；专题论文；专题报告

dis·re·gard /ˌdɪsrɪˈɡɑːd; NAmE -ˈɡɑːrd/ *verb, noun*

■*verb* ~ **sth** (*formal*) to not consider sth; to treat sth as unimportant 不理会；不顾；漠视 SYN **ignore**：*The board completely disregarded my recommendations.* 董事会完全无视我的建议。◇ *Safety rules were disregarded.* 安全规定被忽视了。

■*noun* [U] ~ (**for/of sb/sth**) (*formal*) the act of treating sb/sth as unimportant and not caring about them/it 漠视；忽视：*She shows a total disregard for other people's feelings.* 她丝毫不顾及别人的感受。

dis·re·pair /ˌdɪsrɪˈpeə(r); NAmE -ˈper/ *noun* [U] a building, road, etc. that is in a state of **disrepair** has not been taken care of and is broken or in bad condition 失修；破败；破损：*The station quickly **fell into disrepair** after it was closed.* 车站关闭后很快便破败不堪。

dis·rep·ut·able /dɪsˈrepjətəbl/ *adj.* that people consider to be dishonest and bad 名声不好的；不名誉的；不光彩的：*She spent the evening with her disreputable brother Stefan.* 她同声名狼藉的弟弟斯蒂芬一起度过了这个晚上。◇ *a disreputable area of the city* 城里名声不好的地方 OPP **respectable** ➲COMPARE REPUTABLE

dis·re·pute /ˌdɪsrɪˈpjuːt/ *noun* [U] (*formal*) the fact that sb/sth loses the respect of other people 丧失名誉；坏名声：*The players' behaviour on the field is likely to **bring** the game **into disrepute**.* 球员在赛场上的表现很可能使这场比赛臭名远扬。

dis·re·spect /ˌdɪsrɪˈspekt/ *noun, verb*

■*noun* [U, C] ~ (**for/to sb/sth**) a lack of respect for sb/sth 不尊敬；无礼；轻蔑：*disrespect for the law/the dead* 藐视法律；对死者的不敬 ◇ ***No disrespect intended**, sir. It was just a joke.* 先生，绝无不敬之意。这不过是个玩笑而已。▸ **dis·res·pect·ful** /-fl/ *adj.* ~ (**to sb/sth**) **dis·res·pect·ful·ly** /-fəli/ *adv.*

■*verb* ~ **sb/sth** (*informal*) to speak about or treat sb/sth without respect 不尊敬；对…无礼：*They were accused of disrespecting the country's flag.* 他们被控亵渎国旗。HELP Some people consider that it is not correct to use **disrespect** as a verb, and that you should use the noun instead, especially in formal and written English. 有人认为 disrespect 用作动词不恰当，应作名词使用，尤其在正式和书面英语中：*They were accused of treating the country's flag with disrespect.* 他们被控亵渎国旗。

dis·robe /dɪsˈrəʊb; NAmE -ˈroʊb/ *verb* [I, T] ~ (**sb**) (*formal* or *humorous*) to take off your or sb else's clothes; to take off clothes worn for an official ceremony 脱去（某人）的衣服；脱衣服；脱去制服（或礼服）：*She went behind the screen to disrobe.* 她到屏风后面去换装。

dis·rupt /dɪsˈrʌpt/ *verb* ~ **sth** to make it difficult for sth to continue in the normal way 扰乱；使中断；打乱：*Demonstrators succeeded in disrupting the meeting.* 示威者成功地扰乱了会议。◇ *Bus services will be disrupted tomorrow because of the bridge closure.* 明日公共汽车服务将因大桥停止通行而受影响。 ▸ **dis·rup·tion** /dɪsˈrʌpʃn/ *noun* [U, C]：*We aim to help you move house with minimum disruption to yourself.* 我们的宗旨是帮您搬家，并且尽量减少给您带来的不便。◇ *disruptions to rail services* 对铁路交通的干扰 ◇ *The strike caused serious disruptions.* 罢工造成了严重的混乱。

dis·rup·tive /dɪsˈrʌptɪv/ *adj.* causing problems, noise, etc. so that sth cannot continue normally 引起混乱的；扰乱性的；破坏性的：*She had a disruptive influence on the rest of the class.* 她搅扰了班上其他学生。

diss = DIS

dis·sat·is·fac·tion /ˌdɪsˌsætɪsˈfækʃn/ *noun* **1** [U] ~ (**with/at sb/sth**) a feeling that you are not pleased and satisfied 不快；不悦；不满意：*Many people have expressed their dissatisfaction with the arrangement.* 许多人表示对这一安排不满。OPP **satisfaction** **2** [C, usually pl.] something that causes you to feel dissatisfied 令人不满之事

dis·sat·is·fied /dɪsˈsætɪsfaɪd; dɪˈsæt-/ *adj.* not happy or satisfied with sb/sth（对…）不满的，不高兴的，不满意的：*dissatisfied customers* 不满的顾客 ◇ ~ **with sb/sth** *If you are dissatisfied with our service, please write to the manager.* 对于服务如有不满，请函告经理。OPP **satisfied** ➲ COMPARE UNSATISFIED

dis·sect /dɪˈsekt; daɪ-/ *verb* **1** ~ **sth** to cut up a dead person, animal or plant in order to study it 解剖（人或动植物） **2** ~ **sth** to study sth closely and/or discuss it in great detail 仔细研究；详细评论；剖析：*Her latest novel was dissected by the critics.* 评论家对她最近出版的一部小说作了详细剖析。 **3** ~ **sth** to divide sth into smaller pieces, areas, etc. 把…分成小块：*The city is dissected by a network of old canals.* 古老的运河网将这座城市分割开来。 ▶ **dis·sec·tion** /dɪˈsekʃn; daɪ-/ *noun* [U, C]: *anatomical dissection* 解剖分析 ◇ *Your enjoyment of a novel can suffer from too much analysis and dissection.* 对一部小说过多的剖析可能会影响你阅读的乐趣。

dis·sem·ble /dɪˈsembl/ *verb* [I, T] ~ (**sth**) (*formal*) to hide your real feelings or intentions, often by pretending to have different ones 掩盖，掩饰（真实感情或意图）：*She was a very honest person who was incapable of dissembling.* 她是一个非常诚实的人，不会伪装。

dis·sem·in·ate /dɪˈsemɪneɪt/ *verb* ~ **sth** (*formal*) to spread information, knowledge, etc. so that it reaches many people 散布，传播（信息、知识等）：*Their findings have been* ***widely disseminated***. 他们的研究成果已经广为传播。 ▶ **dis·sem·in·ation** /dɪˌsemɪˈneɪʃn/ *noun* [U]

dis·sen·sion /dɪˈsenʃn/ *noun* [U] (*formal*) disagreement between people or within a group 意见分歧；（派性）纷争；不和：*dissension within the government* 政府内部的意见分歧

dis·sent /dɪˈsent/ *noun, verb*

■ ***noun*** (*formal*) **1** [U] the fact of having or expressing opinions that are different from those that are officially accepted（与官方的）不同意见，异议：***political/religious dissent*** 政治观点 / 宗教信仰上的分歧 **2** [C] (*NAmE*) a judge's statement giving reasons why he or she disagrees with a decision made by the other judges in a court case（诉讼案中某法官对其他法官判决的）异议，不同意见

■ ***verb*** [I] ~ (**from sth**) (*formal*) to have or express opinions that are different from those that are officially accepted（对官方意见）不同意，持异议：*Only two ministers dissented from the official view.* 只有两位部长与官方持不同的观点。 ▶ **dis·sent·ing** *adj.*：***dissenting groups/voices/views/opinion*** 持不同意见的团体；反对的声音；不同的观点；异议

dis·sent·er /dɪˈsentə(r)/ *noun* a person who does not agree with opinions that are officially or generally accepted（对官方或普遍认可的意见）持异议者，持不同意见者

dis·ser·ta·tion /ˌdɪsəˈteɪʃn; *NAmE* -sərˈt-/ *noun* ~ (**on sth**) a long piece of writing on a particular subject, especially one written for a university degree 专题论文；（尤指）学位论文 ➲ WORDFINDER NOTE AT UNIVERSITY

dis·ser·vice /dɪsˈsɜːvɪs; dɪˈsɜː-; *NAmE* -ˈsɜːrv-/ *noun* [sing.]
IDM **do sb a disˈservice** to do sth that harms sb and the opinion that other people have of them 损害；伤害；危害；中伤

dis·si·dent /ˈdɪsɪdənt/ *noun* a person who strongly disagrees with and criticizes their government, especially in a country where this kind of action is dangerous 持不同政见者 ▶ **dis·si·dence** /ˈdɪsɪdəns/ *noun* [U] **dis·si·dent** *adj.*

dis·simi·lar AW /dɪˈsɪmɪlə(r)/ *adj.* ~ (**from/to sb/sth**) (*formal*) not the same 不一样的；不同的；不相似的：*These wines are* ***not dissimilar*** (= are similar). 这些葡萄酒都差不多。OPP **similar** ▶ **dis·simi·lar·ity** /ˌdɪsɪmɪˈlærəti/ *noun* [C, U] (*pl.* **-ies**)

dis·simu·late /dɪˈsɪmjuleɪt/ *verb* [T, I] ~ (**sth**) (*formal*) to hide your real feelings or intentions, often by pretending to have different ones 掩盖，掩饰（真实感情或意图） SYN **dissemble** ▶ **dis·simu·la·tion** /dɪˌsɪmjuˈleɪʃn/ *noun* [U]

dis·si·pate /ˈdɪsɪpeɪt/ *verb* (*formal*) **1** [I, T] to gradually become or make sth become weaker until it disappears（使）消散，消失；驱散：*Eventually, his anger dissipated.* 他的愤怒终于平息了。◇ ~ **sth** *Her laughter soon dissipated the tension in the air.* 她的笑声很快消除了紧张气氛。 **2** [T] ~ **sth** to waste sth, such as time or money, especially by not planning the best way of using it 挥霍，浪费，消磨（时间、金钱等） SYN **squander**

dis·si·pated /ˈdɪsɪpeɪtɪd/ *adj.* (*disapproving*) enjoying activities that are harmful such as drinking too much alcohol 放荡的；花天酒地的

dis·si·pa·tion /ˌdɪsɪˈpeɪʃn/ *noun* [U] (*formal*) **1** the process of disappearing or of making sth disappear 消散；驱散：*the dissipation of energy in the form of heat* 以热量形式耗散的能量 **2** the act of wasting money or spending money until there is none left 挥霍；浪费：*concerns about the dissipation of the country's wealth* 对挥霍国家财富的忧虑 **3** (*disapproving*) behaviour which is enjoyable but has a harmful effect on you 放荡；纵情遂欲

dis·so·ci·ate /dɪˈsəʊʃieɪt; -ˈsəʊs-; *NAmE* -ˈsoʊ-/ *verb* **1** (*also* **dis·as·so·ci·ate**) ~ **yourself/sb from sb/sth** to say or do sth to show that you are not connected with or do not support sb/sth; to make it clear that sth is not connected with a particular plan, action, etc. 否认同…有关系；声明不支持；表明无关：*He tried to dissociate himself from the party's more extreme views.* 他极力表明自己并不赞成该党较为偏激的观点。◇ *They were determined to dissociate the UN from any agreement to impose sanctions.* 他们决心阻止联合国同意实施制裁。 **2** ~ **sb/sth** (**from sth**) (*formal*) to think of two people or things as separate and not connected with each other 把…分开（或看作是无关联的）：*She tried to dissociate the two events in her mind.* 她试图从思想上将这两件事分开。OPP **associate** ▶ **dis·so·ci·ation** /dɪˌsəʊʃiˈeɪʃn; -ˌsəʊs-; *NAmE* -ˌsoʊ-/ *noun* [U]

dis·sol·ute /ˈdɪsəluːt/ *adj.* (*formal, disapproving*) enjoying immoral activities and not caring about behaving in a morally acceptable way 放纵的；放荡的；道德沦丧的

dis·sol·ution /ˌdɪsəˈluːʃn/ *noun* [U] ~ (**of sth**) (*formal*) **1** the act of officially ending a marriage, a business agreement or a parliament（婚姻关系的）解除；（商业协议的）终止；（议会的）解散 **2** the process in which sth gradually disappears 消失；消亡：*the dissolution of barriers of class and race* 阶级和种族隔阂的消除 **3** the act of breaking up an organization, etc. 解体；瓦解；分裂

dis·solve /dɪˈzɒlv; *NAmE* -ˈzɑːlv/ *verb* **1** [I] ~ (**in sth**) (of a solid 固体) to mix with a liquid and become part of it 溶解：*Salt dissolves in water.* 盐溶解于水。◇ *Heat gently until the sugar dissolves.* 慢慢加热直到糖溶解为止。➲ WORDFINDER NOTE AT LIQUID **2** [T] ~ **sth** (**in sth**) to make a solid become part of a liquid 使（固体）溶解：*Dissolve the tablet in water.* 把药片溶于水中。 **3** [T] ~ **sth** to officially end a marriage, business agreement or parliament 解除（婚姻关系）；终止（商业协议）；解散（议会）：*Their marriage was dissolved in 1999.* 他们于 1999 年解除了婚姻关系。◇ *The election was announced and parliament was dissolved.* 宣布选举后，议会解散了。 **4** [I, T] to disappear; to make sth disappear 消除；（使）消失，消散：*When the ambulance had gone, the crowd dissolved.* 救护车离开后人群便散开了。◇ ~ **sth** *His calm response dissolved her anger.* 他平静的回答化解了她的怒气。 **5** [I] ~ **into laughter, tears, etc.** to suddenly start laughing, crying, etc. 禁不住（笑起来或哭起来等）：*When the teacher looked up, the children dissolved into giggles.* 教师抬头看时，孩子们不禁咯咯地笑起来。◇ *Every time she heard his name, she dissolved into tears.* 每当听到他的名

D

字时，她都禁不住泪流满面。 **6** [T, I] to remove or destroy sth, especially by a chemical process; to be destroyed in this way（尤以化学手段）除去，毁掉；（被）破坏： **~ sth (away)** *a new detergent that dissolves stains* 新型去污洗涤剂 ◇ **~ (away)** *All the original calcium had dissolved away.* 所有原始钙都被破坏了。

D

dis·son·ance /ˈdɪsənəns/ *noun* **1** [C, U] (*music* 音) a combination of musical notes that do not sound pleasant together 不协和和弦 **OPP** **consonance** **2** [U] (*formal*) lack of agreement 不和谐；不协调；不一致 ▶ **dis·son·ant** /ˈdɪsənənt/ *adj.*： **dissonant voices/notes** 刺耳的声音；不协和音符

dis·suade /dɪˈsweɪd/ *verb* **~ sb (from sth/from doing sth)** to persuade sb not to do sth 劝（某人）勿做（某事）；劝阻： *I tried to dissuade him from giving up his job.* 我劝过他不要放弃自己的工作。◇ *They were going to set off in the fog, but were dissuaded.* 他们原打算在雾中出发，但被劝阻了。

dis·taff /ˈdɪstɑːf; *NAmE* ˈdɪstæf/ *noun* a stick that was used in the past for holding wool when it was spun by hand（旧时手工纺纱用的）纺纱杆，绕线杆

IDM **on the distaff side** (*old-fashioned*) on the woman's side of the family 母方家族的；母系的

dis·tal /ˈdɪstl/ *adj.* (*anatomy* 解) located away from the centre of the body or at the far end of sth 远端的；末梢的： *the distal end of the tibia* 胫骨远端

dis·tance /ˈdɪstəns/ *noun, verb*

■ ***noun*** **1** [C, U] the amount of space between two places or things 距离；间距： *a* ***short/long distance*** 短距离；长距离 ◇ *the distance of the earth from the sun* 太阳到地球的距离 ◇ ***a distance of 200 kilometres*** * 200 公里的距离 ◇ *What's the distance between New York City and Boston/from New York City to Boston?* 纽约市离波士顿有多远？◇ *In the US, distance is measured in miles.* 在美国，测量距离以英里作单位。◇ *The beach is* ***within walking distance*** *of my house* (= you can walk there easily). 海滩离我家很近，走几步路就到了。◇ *Paul has to drive very long distances as part of his job.* 保罗不得不长途驾车，这是他工作的一部分。◇ *Our parents live some* ***distance away*** (= quite far away). 我们的父母住的地方相当远。 ➲ SEE ALSO LONG-DISTANCE, MIDDLE DISTANCE, OUTDISTANCE **2** [U] being far away in space or in time（空间的）遥远；（时间的）久远，间隔： *Distance is no problem on the Internet.* 在互联网上距离根本不是问题。 **3** [sing.] a point that is a particular amount of space away from sth else 远方；远处： *You'll never get the ball in from that distance.* 你绝不可能从那么远的地方把球投进去。 **4** [C, usually sing., U] a difference or lack of a connection between two things（两事物之间的）差异，无关： *The distance between fashion and art remains as great as ever.* 时尚与艺术之间的差别之大依然如故。◇ *The government is keen to* ***put some distance between*** *itself and these events* (= show that there is no connection between them). 政府急于表示自身与这些事件无关。◇ (*BrE*) *Eddie is,* ***by some distance*** (= by a great amount), *the funniest character in the show.* 埃迪显然是这个节目中最有趣的人物。 **5** [U, C] a situation in which there is a lack of friendly feelings or of a close relationship between two people or groups of people 冷淡；疏远： *The coldness and distance in her voice took me by surprise.* 她话语中透出的冷淡和疏远使我感到意外。

IDM **at/from a ˈdistance** from a place or time that is not near; from far away 离一段距离；从远处；遥远地；久远地： *She had loved him at a distance for years.* 她曾经暗恋他好多年。 **go the (full) ˈdistance** to continue playing in a competition or sports contest until the end（比赛）打完全场，赛足全局： *Nobody thought he would last 15 rounds, but he went the full distance.* 谁都以为他坚持不到15个回合，可是他却打完了全场。 **in/into the ˈdistance** far away but still able to be seen or heard 在远处；在远方： *We saw lights in the distance.* 我们看到了远处的点点灯光。◇ *Alice stood staring into the distance.* 艾丽斯站着凝视远方。 **keep sb at a ˈdistance** to refuse to be friendly with sb; to not let sb be friendly towards you 对…冷淡；同…疏远；与…保持一定距离 **keep your ˈdistance (from sb/sth)** **1** to make sure you are not too near sb/sth（与…）保持距离 **2** to avoid getting too friendly or involved with a person, group, etc. 疏远；避免（与…）亲近；避免介入： *She was warned to keep her distance from Charles if she didn't want to get hurt.* 有人告诫她说，如果不想受到伤害，就离查尔斯远一点。 ➲ MORE AT SHOUTING, SPIT *v.*, STRIKE *v.*

■ ***verb*** **~ yourself/sb/sth (from sb/sth)** to become, or to make sb/sth become, less involved or connected with sb/sth 拉开距离；与…疏远： *When he retired, he tried to distance himself from politics.* 退休后，他便尽量使自己置身于政治之外。◇ *It's not always easy for nurses to distance themselves emotionally.* 对护士来说，使自己不动感情有时并不容易。

ˈdistance learning *noun* [U] a system of education in which people study at home with the help of special Internet sites and television and radio programmes, and send or email work to their teachers 远程教育；远程学习 ➲ WORDFINDER NOTE AT STUDY

dis·tant /ˈdɪstənt/ *adj.* **1** far away in space or time 遥远的；远处的；久远的： *the distant sound of music* 远处的音乐声 ◇ *distant stars/planets* 遥远的恒星 / 行星 ◇ *The time we spent together is now a distant memory.* 我们一起度过的时光现已成为久远的记忆。◇ (*formal*) *The airport was about 20 kilometres distant.* 机场在大约 20 公里远的地方。◇ *a star 30 000 light years distant from the Earth* 离地球 3 万光年远的恒星 ◇ (*figurative*) *Peace was just a distant hope* (= not very likely). 和平只是遥不可及的希望而已。 **2 ~ (from sth)** not like sth else 不相似的；不同的 **SYN** **remote**: *Their life seemed utterly distant from his own.* 他们的生活与他自己的生活似乎完全不同。 **3** [only before noun] (of a person 人) related to you but not closely 远亲的；远房的： ***a distant cousin/aunt/relative*** 远房堂兄弟 / 姑母 / 亲戚 **4** not friendly; not wanting a close relationship with sb 不友好的；冷淡的；疏远的： *Pat sounded very cold and distant on the phone.* 从电话里听起来帕特非常冷淡和疏远。 **5** not paying attention to sth but thinking about sth completely different 心不在焉的；恍惚的；出神的： *There was a distant look in her eyes; her mind was obviously on something else.* 她眼神恍惚，显然心里在想着别的什么事儿。 ▶ **dis·tant·ly** *adv.*： *Somewhere, distantly, he could hear the sound of the sea.* 他能听到在远处某个地方的海浪声。◇ *We're distantly related.* 我们是远亲。◇ *Holly smiled distantly.* 霍利恍惚地笑了笑。

IDM **the (ˌdim and) ˌdistant ˈpast** a long time ago 很久以前；遥远的过去： *stories from the distant past* 很久以前的故事 **in the not too ˌdistant ˈfuture** not a long time in the future but fairly soon 在不久的将来

dis·taste /dɪsˈteɪst/ *noun* [U, sing.] a feeling that sb/sth is unpleasant or offensive 不喜欢；反感；厌恶： *He looked around the filthy room in distaste.* 他厌恶地环视着这肮脏的房间。◇ **~ for sb/sth** *a distaste for politics of any sort* 对任何形式的政治的反感

dis·taste·ful /dɪsˈteɪstfl/ *adj.* (*formal*) unpleasant or offensive 使人不愉快的；令人反感的；讨厌的

dis·tem·per /dɪˈstempə(r)/ *noun* [U] **1** an infectious disease of animals, especially cats and dogs, that causes fever and coughing 瘟热（动物，尤指猫、狗的传染病） **2** (*BrE*) a type of paint that is mixed with water and used on walls 刷墙水粉；水浆涂料；水性墙漆

dis·tend /dɪˈstend/ *verb* [I, T] **~ (sth)** (*formal* or *medical* 医) to swell or make sth swell because of pressure from inside（使）膨胀，肿胀： *starving children with huge distended bellies* 鼓着浮肿肚子的挨饿儿童 ▶ **dis·ten·sion** /dɪˈstenʃn/ *noun* [U]： *distension of the stomach* 胃胀

dis·til (*NAmE* **dis·till**) /dɪˈstɪl/ *verb* (**-ll-**) **1 ~ sth (from sth)** to make a liquid pure by heating it until it becomes a gas, then cooling it and collecting the drops of liquid that form 蒸馏；用蒸馏法提取： *to distil fresh water from sea water* 用蒸馏法从海水中提取淡水 ◇ *distilled water* 蒸馏水 **2 ~ sth** to make sth such as a strong alcoholic drink in this way 用蒸馏法制造（酒等）： *The factory distils and bottles whisky.* 这家工厂用蒸馏法酿造瓶装威士忌酒。 **3 ~**

sth (**from/into sth**) (*formal*) to get the essential meaning or ideas from thoughts, information, experiences, etc. 吸取…的精华；提炼；浓缩： *The notes I made on my travels were distilled into a book.* 我的旅行笔记精选汇编成了一本书。 ▶ **dis·til·la·tion** /ˌdɪstɪˈleɪʃn/ *noun* [C, U]: *the distillation process* 蒸馏过程

dis·til·late /ˈdɪstɪleɪt/ *noun* [U, C] (*specialist*) a substance which is formed by distilling a liquid 馏出液；馏出物；馏分

dis·til·ler /dɪˈstɪlə(r)/ *noun* a person or company that produces SPIRITS (= strong alcoholic drinks) such as WHISKY by distilling them（采用蒸馏法的）酿酒者，酿酒公司

dis·til·lery /dɪˈstɪləri/ *noun* (*pl.* **-ies**) a factory where strong alcoholic drink is made by the process of distilling（采用蒸馏法的）酿酒厂

dis·tinct AW /dɪˈstɪŋkt/ *adj.* **1** easily or clearly heard, seen, felt, etc. 清晰的；清楚的；明白的；明显的： *There was a distinct smell of gas.* 有一股明显的煤气味。 ◇ *His voice was quiet but every word was distinct.* 他说话声音不大，但字字清晰。 **2** clearly different or of a different kind 截然不同的；有区别的；不同种类的： *The results of the survey fell into two distinct groups.* 调查结果分为截然不同的两组。 ◇ **~ from sth** *Jamaican reggae music is quite distinct from North American jazz or blues.* 牙买加的雷盖音乐完全不同于北美的爵士乐或布鲁斯音乐。 ◇ *rural areas,* ***as distinct from*** *major cities* 完全不同于大城市的农村地区 **3** [only before noun] used to emphasize that you think an idea or situation definitely exists and is important 确定无疑的；确实的；确切的 SYN **definite**: *Being tall gave Tony a distinct advantage.* 托尼个子高是个明显的优势。 ◇ *I had the distinct impression I was being watched.* 我确实感到有人在监视我。 ◇ *A strike is now a distinct possibility.* 目前罢工确有可能发生。 ▶ **dis·tinct·ly** AW *adv.*: *I distinctly heard someone calling me.* 我清楚地听到有人在叫我。 ◇ *a distinctly Australian accent* 明显的澳大利亚口音 ◇ *He could remember everything very distinctly.* 他什么事都能记得清清楚楚。 **dis·tinct·ness** *noun* [U]

dis·tinc·tion AW /dɪˈstɪŋkʃn/ *noun* **1** [C] **~ (between A and B)** a clear difference or contrast especially between people or things that are similar or related 差别；区别；对比： *distinctions between traditional and modern societies* 传统社会和现代社会的差别 ◇ *Philosophers did not use to* ***make a distinction*** *between arts and science.* 哲学家过去不把人文科学和自然科学区别开来。 ◇ *We need to* ***draw a distinction*** *between the two events.* 我们得把两起事件区别开来。 **2** [U] the quality of being excellent or important 优秀；杰出；卓越： *a writer of distinction* 优秀作家 **3** [sing.] the quality of being sth that is special 特质；特点；不同凡响： *She* ***had the distinction of*** *being the first woman to fly the Atlantic.* 她不同凡响，是第一个飞越大西洋的女子。 **4** [U] **~ (between A and B)** the separation of people or things into different groups 区分；分清；辨别： *The new law* ***makes no distinction*** *between adults and children* (= treats them equally). 这项新法规对成人和孩子同样适用。 ◇ *All groups are entitled to this money* ***without distinction.*** 所有团体一律有权得到这笔款项。 **5** [C, U] a special mark/grade or award that is given to sb, especially a student, for excellent work （尤指给学生的）优等评分，荣誉，奖赏： *Naomi got a distinction in maths.* 娜奥米的数学得了优等。 ◇ *He graduated* ***with distinction.*** 他以优异成绩毕业。

dis·tinct·ive AW /dɪˈstɪŋktɪv/ *adj.* having a quality or characteristic that makes sth different and easily noticed 独特的；特别的；有特色的 SYN **characteristic**: *clothes with a distinctive style* 式样独特的衣服 ◇ *The male bird has distinctive white markings on its head.* 雄鸟的头上有明显的白色斑纹。 ▶ **dis·tinct·ive·ly** AW *adv.*: *a distinctively nutty flavour* 特别的坚果味道

dis·tin·guish /dɪˈstɪŋɡwɪʃ/ *verb* **1** [I, T] to recognize the difference between two people or things 区分；辨别；分清 SYN **differentiate**: **~ between A and B** *At what age are children able to distinguish between right and wrong?* 儿童到什么年龄才能明辨是非？ ◇ **~ A from B** *It was hard to distinguish one twin from the other.* 很难分辨出一对孪生儿谁是谁。 ◇ **~ A and B** *Sometimes reality and fantasy are hard to distinguish.* 有时候现实和幻想很难区分。 **2** [T] (not used in the progressive tenses 不用于进行时) **~ A (from B)** to be a characteristic that makes two people, animals or things different 成为…的特征；使具有…的特色；使有别于： *What was it that distinguished her from her classmates?* 是什么使得她有别于班上其他同学呢？ ◇ *The male bird is distinguished from the female by its red beak.* 雄鸟喙红色，有别于雌鸟。 ◇ *Does your cat have any distinguishing marks?* 你的猫有什么特殊斑纹吗？ **3** [T] (not used in the progressive tenses 不用于进行时) **~ sth** to be able to see or hear sth 看清；认出；听出 SYN **differentiate, make out**: *I could not distinguish her words, but she sounded agitated.* 我听不清她说的话，但听得出她很激动。 **4** [T] **~ yourself** (**as sth**) to do sth so well that people notice and admire you 使出众；使著名；使受人青睐： *She has already distinguished herself as an athlete.* 作为运动员她已享有盛名。 ▶ **dis·tin·guish·able** /dɪˈstɪŋɡwɪʃəbl/ *adj.*: **~ (from sb/sth)** *The male bird is easily distinguishable from the female.* 这种鸟很容易辨认雌雄。 ◇ *The coast was barely distinguishable in the mist.* 在雾中很难看清海岸。

dis·tin·guished /dɪˈstɪŋɡwɪʃt/ *adj.* **1** very successful and admired by other people 卓越的；杰出的；著名的： *a distinguished career in medicine* 在医学领域的辉煌生涯 **2** having an appearance that makes sb look important or that makes people admire or respect them 显得重要的；高贵的；有尊严的： *I think grey hair makes you look very distinguished.* 我认为灰白的头发使你看上去特别可敬。

dis·tort AW /dɪˈstɔːt; *NAmE* dɪˈstɔːrt/ *verb* **1 ~ sth** to change the shape, appearance or sound of sth so that it is strange or not clear 使变形；扭曲；使失真： *a fairground mirror that distorts your shape* 露天游乐场的哈哈镜 ◇ *The loudspeaker seemed to distort his voice.* 他的声音从喇叭里传出来好像失真了。 **2 ~ sth** to twist or change facts, ideas, etc. so that they are no longer correct or true 歪曲；曲解： *Newspapers are often guilty of distorting the truth.* 报章常犯歪曲事实的错误。 ◇ *The article gave a distorted picture of his childhood.* 这篇文章对他的童年作了歪曲的描述。 ▶ **dis·tor·tion** AW /dɪˈstɔːʃn; *NAmE* dɪˈstɔːrʃn/ *noun* [C, U]: *modern alloys that are resistant to wear and distortion* 耐磨、防变形的新型合金 ◇ *a distortion of the facts* 对事实的歪曲

dis·tract /dɪˈstrækt/ *verb* **~ sb/sth (from sth)** to take sb's attention away from what they are trying to do 转移（注意力）；分散（思想）；使分心 SYN **divert**: *You're distracting me from my work.* 你使我不能专心工作。 ◇ *Don't talk to her—she's very easily distracted.* 不要同她讲话，她的注意力很容易分散。 ◇ *It was another attempt to* ***distract attention*** *from the truth.* 这又是企图分散人们对事实真相的注意力。 ▶ **dis·tract·ing** *adj.*: *distracting thoughts* 令人分心的想法 ◇ *a distracting noise* 使人心烦意乱的嘈杂声

dis·tract·ed /dɪˈstræktɪd/ *adj.* **~ (by sb/sth)** unable to pay attention to sb/sth because you are worried or thinking about sth else 注意力分散的；思想不集中的 ▶ **dis·tract·ed·ly** *adv.*

dis·trac·tion /dɪˈstrækʃn/ *noun* **1** [C, U] a thing that takes your attention away from what you are doing or thinking about 分散注意力的事物；使人分心的事物： *I find it hard to work at home because there are too many distractions.* 我发觉在家里工作很难，因为使人分心的事太多。 ◇ *cinema audiences looking for distraction* 寻求解闷的电影观众 **2** [C] an activity that amuses or entertains you 娱乐；消遣

IDM **to diˈstraction** so that you become upset, excited or angry, and not able to think clearly 到心烦意乱（或激动、气愤）的地步： *The children are* ***driving me to distraction*** *today.* 今天孩子们闹得我心烦意乱。

dis·trac·tor /dɪˈstræktə(r)/ *noun* **1** a person or thing that takes your attention away from what you should be doing 使分心的人（或事物） **2** one of the wrong answers in a MULTIPLE-CHOICE test （多项选择题中的）干扰项

D

dis·traught /dɪˈstrɔːt/ *adj.* extremely upset and anxious so that you cannot think clearly 心烦意乱的；心急如焚的；发狂的

dis·tress /dɪˈstres/ *noun, verb*

■ ***noun*** [U] **1** a feeling of great worry or unhappiness; great suffering 忧虑；悲伤；痛苦：*The newspaper article caused the actor considerable distress.* 报上的文章给这位演员带来极大的痛苦。◇ *She was obviously* ***in distress*** *after the attack.* 她受到攻击后显然很痛苦。◇ *deep emotional distress* 感情上的深深痛苦 **2** suffering and problems caused by not having enough money, food, etc. 贫困；窘迫；困苦 **SYN** **hardship**：***economic/financial distress*** 经济拮据；财政困难 **3** a situation in which a ship, plane, etc. is in danger or difficulty and needs help（船、飞机等）遇难，遇险：***a distress signal*** (= a message asking for help) 求救信号 ◇ *It is a rule of the sea to help another boat* ***in distress***. 救助别的遇难船是海上的规则。**IDM** SEE DAMSEL

■ ***verb*** to make sb feel very worried or unhappy 使忧虑；使悲伤；使苦恼：**~ sb** *It was clear that the letter had deeply distressed her.* 这封信显然使她极为悲伤。◇ **~ yourself** *Don't distress yourself* (= don't worry). 你别犯愁了。

dis·tressed /dɪˈstrest/ *adj.* **1** upset and anxious 烦恼的；忧虑的；苦恼的：*He was too distressed and confused to answer their questions.* 他非常苦恼而困惑，无法回答他们的问题。**2** suffering pain; in a poor physical condition 痛苦的；身体虚弱的：*When the baby was born, it was blue and distressed.* 这婴儿出生时全身发青，非常虚弱。**3** (of a piece of clothing or furniture 衣服或家具) made to look older and more worn than it really is 刻意磨损以显老旧的；做旧的：*a distressed leather jacket* 做旧的皮夹克 **4** (*formal* or *business* 商) having problems caused by lack of money 贫困的；窘迫的；受经济困扰的：*They buy up financially distressed companies.* 他们收购陷入财务危机的公司。◇ *The charity helps kids in distressed situations.* 这个慈善机构帮助处于困境的儿童。

dis·tress·ing /dɪˈstresɪŋ/ *adj.* making you feel extremely upset, especially because of sb's suffering 使人痛苦的；令人苦恼的 ▸ **dis·tress·ing·ly** *adv.*

dis·trib·ute 🔑 **AW** /dɪˈstrɪbjuːt; ˈdɪstrɪbjuːt/ *verb* **1** 🔑 to give things to a large number of people; to share sth between a number of people 分发；分配：**~ sth** *The newspaper is distributed free.* 本报免费派发。◇ **~ sth to sb/sth** *The organization distributed food to the earthquake victims.* 这个机构向地震灾民分发了食品。◇ **~ sth among sb/sth** *The money was distributed among schools in the area.* 这笔款项是在本地区的学校中分配的。**2** 🔑 **~ sth** to send goods to shops/stores and businesses so that they can be sold 分销：*Who distributes our products in the UK?* 谁在英国经销我们的产品？**3** 🔑 [often passive] **~ sth** to spread sth, or different parts of sth, over an area 使散开；使分布；分散：*Make sure that your weight is evenly distributed.* 要确保你的重量分布均匀。

dis·tri·bu·tion 🔑 **AW** /ˌdɪstrɪˈbjuːʃn/ *noun* **1** 🔑 [U, C] the way that sth is shared or exists over a particular area or among a particular group of people 分配；分布：*the unfair distribution of wealth* 财富分配不公 ◇ *The map shows the distribution of this species across the world.* 地图上标明了这一物种在全世界的分布情况。◇ *They studied the geographical distribution of the disease.* 他们研究了这种疾病的地域分布情况。**2** 🔑 [U] the act of giving or delivering sth to a number of people 分发；分送：*the distribution of food and medicines to the flood victims* 向遭受洪灾的难民分发食品和药物 ◇ *He was arrested on drug distribution charges.* 他被指犯传播毒品罪而遭逮捕。**3** 🔑 [U] (*business* 商) the system of transporting and delivering goods（商品）运销，经销，分销：*distribution costs* 经销成本 ◇ *worldwide distribution systems* 全球经销系统 ◇ *marketing, sales and distribution* 营销、销售和经销 ▸ **dis·tri·bu·tion·al** **AW** /-ʃənl/ *adj.*

distriˈbution board *noun* (*BrE, physics* 物) a board that contains the connections for several electrical CIRCUITS 配电板；配电盘

dis·tribu·tive **AW** /dɪˈstrɪbjətɪv/ *adj.* [usually before noun] (*business* 商) connected with distribution of goods 经销的；分销的

dis·tribu·tor **AW** /dɪˈstrɪbjətə(r)/ *noun* **1** a person or company that supplies goods to shops/stores, etc. 经销商；分销商：*Japan's largest software distributor* 日本最大的软件分销公司 **2** a device in an engine that sends electric current to the SPARK PLUGS（发动机的）分电器

dis·trict 🔑 /ˈdɪstrɪkt/ *noun* **1** 🔑 an area of a country or town, especially one that has particular features 地区；区域：*the City of London's financial district* 伦敦市中心的金融区 **2** 🔑 one of the areas which a country, town or state is divided into for purposes of organization, with official BOUNDARIES (= borders) 区；管区；行政区：***a tax/postal district*** 税务区；邮政区 ◇ *a school district* 学区 ◇ *congressional districts* 议会选区 ◇ *district councils* 区议会

ˌdistrict aˈttorney *noun* (*abbr.* **DA**) (in the US) a lawyer who is responsible for bringing criminal charges against sb in a particular area or state（美国）地方检察官

ˌdistrict ˈcourt *noun* (in the US) a court that deals with cases in a particular area（美国）地区法院

ˌdistrict ˈnurse *noun* (in Britain) a nurse who visits patients in their homes（英国上门护理的）片区护士

dis·trust /dɪsˈtrʌst/ *noun, verb*

■ ***noun*** [U, sing.] a feeling of not being able to trust sb/sth 不信任；怀疑：*They looked at each other with distrust.* 他们心怀戒备地看着对方。◇ **~ of sb/sth** *He has a deep distrust of all modern technology.* 他对所有现代技术都深表怀疑。▸ **dis·trust·ful** /-fl/ *adj.*：*distrustful of authority* 不相信权威

■ ***verb*** **~ sb/sth** to feel that you cannot trust or believe sb/sth 不信任；怀疑：*She distrusted his motives for wanting to see her again.* 她怀疑他想再见她一面是别有用心。➲ NOTE AT DISTRUST ➲ COMPARE MISTRUST *v.*

> **▼ WHICH WORD? 词语辨析**
>
> **distrust / mistrust**
>
> • There is very little difference between these two words, but **distrust** is more common and perhaps slightly stronger. If you are sure that someone is acting dishonestly or cannot be relied on, you are more likely to say that you **distrust** them. If you are expressing doubts and suspicions, on the other hand, you would probably use **mistrust**. 这两个词意义差别很小，但 distrust 更通用，或许语气稍强。确信某人不诚实或不可信较常用 distrust，而表示猜疑、疑虑、不信任则大概要用 mistrust。

dis·turb 🔑 /dɪˈstɜːb; *NAmE* -ˈstɜːrb/ *verb* **1** 🔑 **~ sb/sth** to interrupt sb when they are trying to work, sleep, etc. 打扰；干扰；妨碍：*I'm sorry to disturb you, but can I talk to you for a moment?* 对不起，打扰你一下，我能跟你谈一会儿吗？◇ *If you get up early, try not to disturb everyone else.* 如果你起得早，尽量不要打扰别人。◇ ***Do not disturb*** (= a sign placed on the outside of the door of a hotel room, office, etc.) 请勿打扰（旅馆房间、办公室等门上的提示牌）◇ *She awoke early after a disturbed night.* 她被闹腾了一夜，很早就醒了。**2** 🔑 **~ sth** to move sth or change its position 搅乱；弄乱；搞乱：*Don't disturb the papers on my desk.* 别把我写字台上的文件弄乱。**3** 🔑 to make sb worry 使焦虑；使不安；使烦恼：**~ sb** *The letter shocked and disturbed me.* 这封信使我感到震惊和不安。◇ **it disturbs sb to do sth** *It disturbed her to realize that she was alone.* 她意识到自己孤单一人，心里感到很不安。

dis·turb·ance /dɪˈstɜːbəns; *NAmE* -ˈstɜːrb-/ *noun* **1** [U, C, usually sing.] actions that make you stop what you are doing, or that upset the normal state that sth is in; the act of disturbing sb/sth or the fact of being disturbed （受）打扰，干扰，妨碍：*The building work is creating constant noise, dust and disturbance.* 建筑施工不断制造噪音、灰尘和干扰。◇ *a disturbance in the usual pattern of events* 对平常事情发展状况的干扰 ◇ *the disturbance of the local wildlife by tourists* 游客对当地野生动物的滋扰 **2** [C] a situation in which people behave violently in a public place 骚乱；骚动；动乱：*serious disturbances in the streets* 街上的严重骚乱 ◇ *He was charged with causing a disturbance after the game.* 他被指控在比赛结束后制造骚乱。 **3** [U, C] a state in which sb's mind or a function of the body is upset and not working normally 障碍；失调；紊乱：*emotional disturbance* 情绪失常

dis·turbed /dɪˈstɜːbd; *NAmE* -ˈstɜːrbd/ *adj.* **1** mentally ill, especially because of very unhappy or shocking experiences 有精神病的；心理不正常的；精神紊乱的：*a special school for emotionally disturbed children* 为精神异常儿童开办的特殊学校 ➲ SYNONYMS AT MENTALLY **2** unhappy and full of bad or shocking experiences 不幸的；多灾多难的；坎坷的：*The killer had a disturbed family background.* 那名杀手出身于一个坎坷不幸的家庭。 **3** very anxious and unhappy about sth 心神不安的；心烦意乱的；烦恼的：*I was deeply disturbed and depressed by the news.* 这消息使我深感不安和沮丧。➲ COMPARE UNDISTURBED

dis·turb·ing /dɪˈstɜːbɪŋ; *NAmE* -ˈstɜːrb-/ *adj.* making you feel anxious and upset or shocked 引起烦恼的；令人不安的；引起恐慌的：*a disturbing piece of news* 一则令人不安的消息 ▶ **dis·turb·ing·ly** *adv.*

dis·unite /ˌdɪsjuˈnaɪt/ *verb* [usually passive] **~ sb/sth** (*formal*) to make a group of people unable to agree with each other or work together 使不统一；使不和；使纷争：*a disunited political party* 四分五裂的政党

dis·unity /dɪsˈjuːnəti/ *noun* [U] (*formal*) a lack of agreement between people 不统一；不团结；不和：*disunity within the Conservative party* 保守党内部的不统一 OPP **unity**

dis·use /dɪsˈjuːs/ *noun* [U] a situation in which sth is no longer being used 不用；废弃：*The factory* ***fell into disuse*** *twenty years ago.* 这家工厂二十年前就废弃了。

dis·used /ˌdɪsˈjuːzd/ *adj.* [usually before noun] no longer used 不再使用的；废弃的：*a disused station* 废弃的车站 ➲ COMPARE UNUSED[1]

ditch /dɪtʃ/ *noun, verb*

■ ***noun*** a long channel dug at the side of a field or road, to hold or take away water 沟；渠 ➲ VISUAL VOCAB PAGE V3

■ ***verb*** **1** [T] **~ sth/sb** (*informal*) to get rid of sth/sb because you no longer want or need it/them 摆脱；抛弃；丢弃：*The new road building programme has been ditched.* 新的道路建设计划已废弃。◇ *He ditched his girlfriend.* 他把女朋友给甩了。 **2** [T, I] **~ (sth)** if a pilot **ditches** an aircraft, or if it **ditches**, it lands in the sea in an emergency 使（飞机）在海上紧急降落；（在海上）迫降 **3** [T] **~ school** (*NAmE, informal*) to stay away from school without permission 逃学；旷课

ditch·water /ˈdɪtʃwɔːtə(r)/ *noun* [U] IDM SEE DULL *adj.*

dither /ˈdɪðə(r)/ *verb, noun*

■ ***verb*** [I] to hesitate about what to do because you are unable to decide 犹豫不决；踌躇：*Stop dithering and get on with it.* 别再犹豫了，继续干吧。◇ **~ over sth** *She was dithering over what to wear.* 她拿不定主意穿什么好。

■ ***noun*** [sing.] (*informal*) **1** a state of not being able to decide what you should do 犹豫不决；踌躇：*I'm* ***in a dither*** *about who to invite.* 我拿不定主意邀请谁。 **2** a state of excitement or worry 紧张；焦虑；慌乱：*Don't get yourself* ***in a dither*** *over everything.* 不要什么事都紧张兮兮。

di·tran·si·tive /daɪˈtrænsətɪv; -ˈtrænz-/ *adj.* (*grammar* 语法) (of verbs 动词) used with two objects. In the sentence 'I gave her the book', for example, the verb 'give' is ditransitive and 'her' and 'the books' are both objects. 双及物的；（后接）双宾语的

ditsy = DITZY

ditto /ˈdɪtəʊ; *NAmE* -toʊ/ *noun, adv.*

■ ***noun*** (*abbr.* **do.**) (*symb.* **"**) used, especially in a list, underneath a particular word or phrase, to show that it is repeated and to avoid having to write it again （尤用于序列中）同上，同前

■ ***adv.*** (*informal*) used instead of a particular word or phrase, to avoid repeating it（代替某一词语以免重复）同样，也一样：*The waiters were rude and unhelpful, the manager ditto.* 这些服务员态度生硬，服务不周，经理也一样。

ditty /ˈdɪti/ *noun* (*pl.* **-ies**) (*often humorous*) a short simple song 小曲；小调

ditzy (*also* **ditsy**) /ˈdɪtsi/ *adj.* (*informal, especially NAmE*) (usually of a woman 通常指女性) silly; not able to be trusted to remember things or to think in an organized way 傻的；愚蠢的；忘性大的；糊涂的

di·ur·et·ic /ˌdaɪjuˈretɪk/ *noun* (*medical* 医) a substance that causes an increase in the flow of URINE 利尿药 ▶ **di·ur·et·ic** *adj.*：*diuretic drugs/effects* 利尿药；利尿效果

di·ur·nal /daɪˈɜːnl; *NAmE* -ˈɜːrnl/ *adj.* **1** (*biology* 生) (of animals 动物) active during the day 日间活动的；昼行性的 OPP **nocturnal** **2** (*astronomy* 天) taking one day 周日的：*the diurnal rotation of the earth* 地球的周日自转

Div. *abbr.* (in writing 书写形式) DIVISION 部门；级；师：*League Div. 1* (= in football/SOCCER) 甲级联赛（足球）

diva /ˈdiːvə/ *noun* a famous woman singer, especially an OPERA singer 著名女歌唱家（尤指歌剧女主角）➲ WORDFINDER NOTE AT OPERA

Di·vali = DIWALI

divan /dɪˈvæn; *NAmE* ˈdaɪvæn/ *noun* **1** (*also* **diˌvan ˈbed**) (*both BrE*) a bed with a thick base and a MATTRESS 厚垫睡榻 ➲ VISUAL VOCAB PAGE V24 **2** a long low soft seat without a back or arms （无靠背和扶手的）矮长沙发

dive /daɪv/ *verb, noun*

■ ***verb*** (**dived, dived**, *NAmE also* **dove** /dəʊv; *NAmE* doʊv/, **dived**)

• **JUMP INTO WATER** 跳水 **1** [I] **~ (from/off sth) (into sth)** | **~ (in)** to jump into water with your head and arms going in first 跳水（头和双臂先入水）：*We dived into the river to cool off.* 我们一头跳进河里，凉快一下。➲ WORDFINDER NOTE AT SWIM

• **UNDERWATER** 水下 **2** (*usually* **go diving**) [I] to swim underwater wearing breathing equipment, collecting or looking at things （戴呼吸装备）潜水：*to dive for pearls* 潜水采珠 ◇ *The main purpose of his holiday to Greece was to go diving.* 他到希腊度假的主要目的就是去潜水。➲ SEE ALSO DIVING (2) **3** [I] to go to a deeper level underwater 下潜；潜到更深的水下：*The whale dived as the harpoon struck it.* 鲸被鱼叉击中后下潜。

• **OF BIRDS/AIRCRAFT** 鸟；飞机 **4** [I] to go steeply down through the air 俯冲：*The seagulls soared then dived.* 海鸥翱翔着，然后俯冲下来。➲ SEE ALSO NOSEDIVE *v.* (2)

• **OF PRICES** 价格 **5** [I] to fall suddenly 突然下降；暴跌 SYN **plunge**：*The share price dived from 75p to an all-time low of 50p.* 股价从 75 便士暴跌到 50 便士的历史新低。

• **MOVE/JUMP/FALL** 移动；跳跃；跌下 **6** [I] (*informal*) to move or jump quickly in a particular direction, especially to avoid sth, to try to catch a ball, etc. 扑，冲，奔（以避开某物、接球等）：**~ for sth** *We heard an explosion and* ***dived for cover*** (= got into a place where we would be protected). 我们听到一声爆炸便伏身找掩护。◇ *The goalie dived for the ball, but missed it.* 守门员一个鱼跃向球扑去，可是没有扑到。◇ **+ adv./prep.** *It started to rain so we dived into the nearest cafe.* 天下起雨来，我们立即钻进一家最近的咖啡馆。 **7** [I] (in football (SOCCER), HOCKEY, etc. 足球、曲棍球等) to fall deliberately when sb TACKLES you, so that the REFEREE awards a FOUL（对方阻截时）假摔

PHR V **ˈdive into sth** (*informal*) to put your hand quickly into sth such as a bag or pocket 迅速将手伸入（包或口

袋里）：*She dived into her bag and took out a couple of coins.* 她立即将手伸进包里拿出几枚硬币。

■ *noun*

- **JUMP INTO WATER** 跳水 **1** a jump into deep water with your head first and your arms in front of you（头和双臂先入水的）跳水：*a spectacular high dive* (= from high above the water) 精彩的高台跳水
- **UNDERWATER** 水下 **2** an act of going underwater and swimming there with special equipment （戴呼吸装备的）潜水：*a dive to a depth of 18 metres* 潜到 18 米水深处
- **OF BIRDS/AIRCRAFT** 鸟；飞机 **3** an act of suddenly flying downwards 扑；冲；俯冲
- **BAR/CLUB** 酒吧；夜总会 **4** (*informal*) a bar, music club, etc. that is cheap, and perhaps dark or dirty 下等酒吧；低级夜总会
- **FALL** 跌倒 **5** (in football (SOCCER), HOCKEY, etc. 足球、曲棍球等) a deliberate fall that a player makes when sb TACKLES them, so that the REFEREE awards a FOUL（遇到阻截时的）假摔，故意跌倒

IDM **make a 'dive (for sth)** to suddenly move or jump forward to do sth or reach sb/sth 迅速移动；猛然一跳；扑跃：*The goalkeeper made a dive for the ball.* 守门员一个鱼跃向球扑去。 **take a 'dive** (*informal*) to suddenly get worse 突然下降；暴跌：*Profits really took a dive last year.* 去年利润确实跌得很厉害。

'dive-bomb *verb* **~ sb/sth** (of an aircraft, a bird, etc. 飞机、鸟等) to dive steeply through the air and attack sb/sth 俯冲轰炸；俯冲攻击

diver /ˈdaɪvə(r)/ *noun* **1** a person who works underwater, usually with special equipment（通常有专用装备的）潜水员：*a deep-sea diver* 深海潜水员 ➲ COMPARE FROGMAN **2** a person who jumps into the water with their head first and their arms in front of them 跳水者；跳水运动员

di·verge /daɪˈvɜːdʒ; *NAmE* -ˈvɜːrdʒ/ *verb* (*formal*) **1** [I] to separate and go in different directions 分叉；岔开：*The parallel lines appear to diverge.* 这些平行线像是岔开了。◇ *We went through school and college together, but then our paths diverged.* 我们从小学到大学一直在一起，但后来就分道扬镳了。◇ **~ from sth** *The coastal road diverges from the freeway just north of Santa Monica.* 沿海公路与这条高速公路就在圣莫尼卡以北处岔开。◇ *Many species have diverged from a single ancestor.* 许多物种都是同宗演变而来的。 **2** [I] **~ (from sth)** (*formal*) (of opinions, views, etc. 意见、观点等) to be different 分歧；相异：*Opinions diverge greatly on this issue.* 在这个问题上意见分歧很大。 **3** [I] **~ from sth** to be or become different from what is expected, planned, etc. 偏离；背离；违背：*to diverge from the norm* 与常态不符 ◇ *He diverged from established procedure.* 他违背了既定程序。 **OPP** **converge** ▸ **di·ver·gence** /daɪˈvɜːdʒəns; *NAmE* -ˈvɜːrdʒ-/ *noun* [C, U]：*a wide divergence of opinion* 严重的意见分歧 **di·ver·gent** /-dʒənt/ *adj.*：***divergent paths/opinions*** 岔路；歧见

di·vers /ˈdaɪvəz; *NAmE* -vərz/ *adj.* [only before noun] (*old use*) of many different kinds 各种各样的；不同种类的；形形色色的

di·verse **AW** /daɪˈvɜːs; *NAmE* -ˈvɜːrs/ *adj.* very different from each other and of various kinds 不同的；相异的；多种多样的；形形色色的：*people from diverse cultures* 不同文化背景的人 ◇ *My interests are very diverse.* 我的兴趣非常广泛。

di·ver·sify **AW** /daɪˈvɜːsɪfaɪ; *NAmE* -ˈvɜːrs-/ *verb* (**di·ver·si·fies, di·ver·si·fy·ing, di·ver·si·fied, di·ver·si·fied**) **1** [I, T] **~ (sth) (into sth)** (especially of a business or company 尤指企业或公司) to develop a wider range of products, interests, skills, etc. in order to be more successful or reduce risk 增加…的品种；从事多种经营；扩大业务范围 **SYN** **branch out**：*Farmers are being encouraged to diversify into new crops.* 目前正鼓励农民兼种新的作物。 **2** [I, T] to change or to make sth change so that there is greater variety（使）多样化，变化，不同：*Patterns of family life are diversifying.* 家庭生活模式正在变得多样化。◇ **~ sth** *The culture has been diversified with the arrival of immigrants.* 随着外来移民的到来，这里的文化变得多元化了。 ▸ **di·ver·si·fi·ca·tion** **AW** /daɪˌvɜːsɪfɪˈkeɪʃn; *NAmE* -ˌvɜːrs-/ *noun* [U]

di·ver·sion /daɪˈvɜːʃn; *NAmE* -ˈvɜːrʒn/ *noun* **1** [C, U] the act of changing the direction that sb/sth is following, or what sth is used for 转向；转移；偏离：*a river diversion project* 河流改道工程 ◇ *We made a short diversion to go and look at the castle.* 我们绕了一小段路去参观城堡。◇ *the diversion of funds from the public to the private sector of industry* 资金从公有企业向私有企业的转移 **2** [C] something that takes your attention away from sb/sth while sth else is happening 转移视线（或注意力）的事物：*For the government, the war was a welcome diversion from the country's economic problems.* 政府欢迎这场战争，因为它转移了人们对国家经济问题的注意力。◇ *A smoke bomb* ***created a diversion*** *while the robbery took place.* 劫案发生时，一枚烟雾弹转移了人们的视线。 **3** [C] (*BrE*) (*NAmE* **de·tour**) a road or route that is used when the usual one is closed 临时绕行路；分流路：*Diversions will be signposted.* 临时绕行路都将设置路标。 ➲ WORDFINDER NOTE AT ROAD **4** [C] (*formal*) an activity that is done for pleasure, especially because it takes your attention away from sth else 消遣；娱乐 **SYN** **distraction**：*The party will make a pleasant diversion.* 这个聚会将是一个很不错的消遣活动。◇ *The city is full of diversions.* 城市里各种娱乐活动比比皆是。

di·ver·sion·ary /daɪˈvɜːʃənəri; *NAmE* -ˈvɜːrʒəneri/ *adj.* intended to take sb's attention away from sth 转移注意力的

di·ver·sity **AW** /daɪˈvɜːsəti; *NAmE* -ˈvɜːrs-/ *noun* **1** [U, C, usually sing.] a range of many people or things that are very different from each other 差异（性）；不同（点） **SYN** **variety**：*the biological diversity of the rainforests* 热带雨林的生物多样性 ◇ ***a great/wide/rich diversity*** *of opinion* 意见纷纭 **2** [U] the quality or fact of including a range of many people or things 多样性；多样化：*There is a need for greater diversity and choice in education.* 教育方面需要更加多元化和更大的选择性。 ➲ COLLOCATIONS AT RACE

di·vert /daɪˈvɜːt; *NAmE* -ˈvɜːrt/ *verb* **~ sb/sth (from sth) (to sth)** **1** to make sb/sth change direction 使转向；使绕道；转移：*Northbound traffic will have to be diverted onto minor roads.* 北行车辆将不得不绕次要道路行驶。 **2 ~ sth** to use money, materials, etc. for a different purpose from their original purpose 改变（资金、材料等）的用途 **3 ~ sth** to take sb's thoughts or attention away from sth 转移（某人）的注意力；使分心 **SYN** **distract**：*The war diverted people's attention away from the economic situation.* 战争把民众的注意力从经济状况上移开了。 **4 ~ sb** (*formal*) to entertain people 娱乐；供消遣：*Children are easily diverted.* 孩子们很容易被逗乐。

di·vert·ing /daɪˈvɜːtɪŋ; *NAmE* -ˈvɜːrt-/ *adj.* (*formal*) entertaining and amusing 娱乐的；消遣性的；有趣的

di·vest /daɪˈvest/ *verb* (*formal*) **1 ~ sb/yourself of sth** to remove clothes 使（某人）脱去（衣服）：*He divested himself of his jacket.* 他脱去了短上衣。 **2 ~ yourself of sth** to get rid of sth 处理掉；丢弃：*The company is divesting itself of some of its assets.* 公司正在处理掉它的部分资产。 **3 ~ sb/sth of sth** to take sth away from sb/sth 使解除；使摆脱：*After her illness she was divested of much of her responsibility.* 她生病后便给解除了许多责任。

di·vest·ment /daɪˈvestmənt/ *noun* [U, C] (*finance* 财) the act of selling the shares you have bought in a company or of taking money away from where you have invested it 转让股份；撤销投资

div·ide 🔑 /dɪˈvaɪd/ *verb*, *noun*

> **WORD FAMILY**
> **divide** *verb, noun*
> **division** *noun*
> **divisive** *adj.*

■ *verb*

- **SEPARATE** 分开 **1** 🔑 [I, T] to separate or make sth separate into parts （使）分开，分散，分割，分成… **SYN** **split up**： **~ (up) (into sth)** *The cells began to divide rapidly.* 细胞开始迅速分裂。◇ **~ sth (up) (into sth)** *A sentence can be divided up into* *meaningful segments.* 一个句子可以划分成有意义的若干部分。 **2** [T] to separate sth into parts and give a share to each of a number of different people, etc. 分配；分享；分担 SYN **share**: **~ sth (up/out)** *Jack divided up the rest of the cash.* 杰克把余下的现金分了。◇ **~ sth (up/out) between/among sb** *We divided the work between us.* 我们共同分担这项工作。 **3** [T] **~ sth (between A and B)** to use different parts of your time, energy, etc. for different activities, etc. 把（时间、精力等）分别用于：*He divides his energies between politics and business.* 他把精力一部分用在政治上，一部分用在生意上。 **4** [T] **~ A from B** (*formal*) to separate two people or things 使分离；使分开：*Can it ever be right to divide a mother from her child?* 让母子分离难道还有对的时候？ **5** [T] **~ sth (off) | ~ A from B** to be the real or imaginary line or barrier that separates two people or things 是…的分界线；分隔；把…隔开 SYN **separate**: *A fence divides off the western side of the grounds.* 一道篱笆把庭院的西面隔开。 **6** [I] (of a road 道路) to separate into two parts that lead in different directions 分岔：*Where the path divides, keep right.* 来到岔口就靠右行。

- **CAUSE DISAGREEMENT** 引起分歧 **7** [T] **~ sb/sth** to make two or more people disagree 使产生分歧；使意见不一 SYN **split**: *The issue has divided the government.* 这个问题在政府中引起了意见分歧。
- **MATHEMATICS** 数学 **8** [T, I] **~ (sth) by sth** to find out how many times one number is contained in another 除以：*30 divided by 6 is 5* (= 30 ÷ 6 = 5). * 30 除以 6 等于 5。 **9** [I, T] **~ (sth) into sth** to be able to be multiplied to give another number 除：*5 divides into 30 6 times.* * 5 除 30 等于 6。

IDM **di͵vide and ˈrule** to keep control over people by making them disagree with and fight each other, therefore not giving them the chance to unite and oppose you together 分而治之：*a policy of divide and rule* 分而治之的政策 ➲ MORE AT MIDDLE *n.*

■ ***noun*** [usually sing.]

- **DIFFERENCE** 不同 **1** a difference between two groups of people that separates them from each other 不同；差异；分歧：*the* ***North/South divide*** 南北分歧 ◇ **~ between A and B** *the divide between Catholics and Protestants in Northern Ireland* 北爱尔兰的天主教徒和新教徒之间的分歧
- **BETWEEN RIVERS** 河流之间 **2** (*especially NAmE*) a line of high land that separates two systems of rivers 分水岭；分水线 SYN **watershed** IDM SEE BRIDGE *v.*

di·vid·ed /dɪˈvaɪdɪd/ *adj.* (of a group or an organization 团体或组织) split by disagreements or different opinions 分裂的；有分歧的：*The government is divided on this issue.* 政府在这个问题上意见不统一。◇ *a deeply divided society* 四分五裂的社会 ◇ *The regime is profoundly* ***divided against itself.*** 这一政权内部彻底分裂了。

di͵vided ˈhighway (*NAmE*) (*BrE* **͵dual ˈcarriageway**) *noun* a road with a strip of land in the middle that divides the lines of traffic moving in opposite directions （中央有分隔带的）双幅车行道，双向车道

divi·dend /ˈdɪvɪdend/ *noun* **1** an amount of the profits that a company pays to people who own shares in the company 红利；股息；股利：*dividend payments of 50 cents a share* 每股 50 分的股息支付 ➲ **WORDFINDER NOTE** AT INVEST **2** (*BrE*) a money prize that is given to winners in the FOOTBALL POOLS （足球彩票的）彩金 **3** (*mathematics* 数) a number which is to be divided by another number 被除数 ➲ COMPARE DIVISOR IDM SEE PAY *v.*

di·vider /dɪˈvaɪdə(r)/ *noun* **1** [C] a thing that divides sth 分隔物；分开物：*a room divider* (= a screen or door that divides a room into two parts) 房间分隔板（屏风或门） **2** **dividers** [pl.] an instrument made of two long thin metal parts joined together at the top, used for measuring lines and angles 分线规；两脚规：*a pair of dividers* 一副分线规

diˈviding line *noun* [usually sing.] **1** something that marks the separation between two things or ideas （两种事物或思想的）分界线，界限：*There is no clear dividing line between what is good and what is bad.* 是非之间没有明确的界限。 **2** a place that separates two areas （分隔两个地区的）地界，分界线：*The river was chosen as a dividing line between the two districts.* 两个地区以这条河流为界。

div·in·ation /͵dɪvɪˈneɪʃn/ *noun* [U] the act of finding out and saying what will happen in the future 占卜；预测；预言

di·vine /dɪˈvaɪn/ *adj.*, *verb*

■ ***adj.*** **1** [usually before noun] coming from or connected with God or a god 天赐的；上帝的；神的：***divine law/love/will*** 天道；上帝的慈爱；天意 ◇ ***divine intervention*** (= help from God to change a situation) 上帝之佑 **2** (*old-fashioned*) wonderful; beautiful 绝妙的；非凡的；极美的 ▸ **di·vine·ly** *adv.*

■ ***verb*** **1** [T] **~ what, whether, etc.... | ~ sth** (*formal*) to find out sth by guessing 猜到；领悟：*She could divine what he was thinking just by looking at him.* 她一看就知道他在想什么。 **2** [T, I] **~ (sth)** to search for underground water using a stick in the shape of a Y, called a **divining rod** （用丫形杖）探测（地下水）

di͵vine ˈright *noun* [U, sing.] **1** (in the past) the belief that the right of a king or queen to rule comes directly from God rather than from the agreement of the people （旧时的）君权神授说 **2** a right that sb thinks they have to do sth, without needing to ask anyone else （自认为）应有的权利，天赋的权利：*No player has a divine right to be in this team.* 没有哪名选手天生就有权待在这个队里。

div·ing /ˈdaɪvɪŋ/ *noun* [U] **1** the sport or activity of diving into water with your head and arms first 跳水；跳水运动：*a diving competition* 跳水比赛 **2** the activity of swimming underwater using special breathing equipment （戴呼吸装备的）潜水：*I'd love to* ***go diving*** *in the Aegean.* 我很想到爱琴海去潜水。◇ *a diving suit* 潜水服 ➲ SEE ALSO SKIN-DIVING

ˈdiving bell *noun* a container that has a supply of air and that is open at the bottom, in which a person can be carried down to the deep ocean 潜水钟（内贮空气，底部有开口，潜入深海用）

ˈdiving board *noun* a board at the side of or above a swimming pool from which people can jump or DIVE into the water （游泳池的）跳水板

div·in·ity /dɪˈvɪnəti/ *noun* (*pl.* **-ies**) **1** [U] the quality of being a god or like God 神性：*the divinity of Christ* 基督的神性 **2** [C] a god or GODDESS 神；女神：*Roman/Greek/Egyptian divinities* 罗马 / 希腊 / 埃及神祇 **3** [U] the study of the nature of God and religious belief 神学 SYN **theology**: *a doctor of Divinity* 神学博士

div·is·ible /dɪˈvɪzəbl/ *adj.* [not usually before noun] **~ (by sth)** that can be divided, usually with nothing remaining 可除；可除尽：*8 is divisible by 2 and 4, but not by 3.* * 8 可被 2 和 4 除尽，但不能被 3 除尽。 OPP **indivisible**

div·ision /dɪˈvɪʒn/ *noun*

- **INTO SEPARATE PARTS** 分成若干部分 **1** [U, sing.] the process or result of dividing into separate parts; the process or result of dividing sth or sharing it out 分开；分隔；分配；（分出来的）部分：*cell division* 细胞分裂 ◇ **~ of sth** *a fair division of time and resources* 时间和资源的合理分配 ◇ **~ of sth between A and B** *the division of labour between the sexes* 男女分工 ◇ **~ (of sth) into sth** *the division of the population into age groups* 把人口分成不同的年龄组
- **MATHEMATICS** 数学 **2** [U] the process of dividing one number by another 除（法）：*the division sign* (÷) 除号 ➲ COMPARE MULTIPLICATION ➲ SEE ALSO LONG DIVISION
- **DISAGREEMENT/DIFFERENCE** 不一致；差异 **3** [C, U] a disagreement or difference in opinion, way of life, etc., especially between members of a society or an organization 分歧；不和；差异：**~ (in/within sth)** *There are deep* ***divisions*** *in the party over the war.* 党内对于这场战争存在着严重的分歧。◇ *the work of healing the divisions within society* 弥合社会内部分歧的工作 ◇ **~ (between A and B)** *divisions between rich and poor* 贫富差异 ◇ ***social/class divisions*** 社会分化；阶级对立

- **PART OF ORGANIZATION** 部门 **4** [C+sing./pl. v.] (*abbr.* **Div.**) a large and important unit or section of an organization （机构的）部门： *the company's sales division* 公司销售部
- **IN SPORT** 体育运动 **5** [C+sing./pl. v.] (*abbr.* **Div.**) (in Britain) one of the group of teams that a sport competition is divided into, especially in football (SOCCER) （英国体育运动，尤指足球比赛的）级： *the **first division/division one*** 甲级 ◇ *a first-division team* 甲级队
- **PART OF ARMY** 军队编制 **6** [C+sing./pl. v.] (*abbr.* **Div.**) a unit of an army, consisting of several BRIGADES or REGIMENTS 师： *the Guards Armoured Division* 禁卫装甲师
- **BORDER** 边界 **7** [C] a line that divides sth 分界线： *A hedge forms the division between their land and ours.* 他们的土地与我们的土地之间以一道树篱隔开。
- **IN PARLIAMENT** 议会 **8** [C] (*specialist*) the separation of members of the British parliament into groups to vote for or against sth （英国议会的）分组表决： *The Bill was read without a division.* 议案未经分组表决就宣读通过了。

div·ision·al /dɪˈvɪʒənl/ *adj.* [only before noun] belonging to or connected with a DIVISION (= a section of the army or department of an organization) 部门的；师的： ***the divisional commander/headquarters*** 师长；师部

di'vision bell *noun* a bell which is rung in the British parliament when it is time for a DIVISION (8) （英国议会的）分组表决钟

di'vision lobby *noun* one of the two halls in the British parliament to which members go when there is a DIVISION (8) （英国议会的）分组表决厅

div·isive /dɪˈvaɪsɪv/ *adj.* (*disapproving*) causing people to be split into groups that disagree with or oppose each other 造成不和的；引起分歧的；制造分裂的： *He believes that unemployment is socially divisive.* 他认为失业会引起社会分化。 ➲ SEE ALSO DIVIDE ▶ **div·isive·ly** *adv.* **div·isive·ness** *noun* [U]

div·isor /dɪˈvaɪzə(r)/ *noun* (*mathematics* 数) a number by which another number is divided 除数；除子 ➲ COMPARE REMAINDER *n.* (2)

di·vorce 🔑 /dɪˈvɔːs; *NAmE* dɪˈvɔːrs/ *noun, verb*

■ ***noun*** **1** 🔑 [U, C] the legal ending of a marriage 离婚： *The marriage **ended in divorce** in 1996.* 这桩婚姻在 1996 年以离婚告终。 ◇ *an increase in the **divorce rate*** (= the number of divorces in a year) 离婚率的增长 ◇ *They have agreed to **get a divorce**.* 他们已同意离婚。 ◇ ***Divorce proceedings*** (= the legal process of divorce) *started today.* 今日已提起离婚诉讼。 ➲ COLLOCATIONS AT MARRIAGE ➲ COMPARE SEPARATION (3) **2** [C, usually sing.] (*formal*) ~ (**between A and B**) a separation; the ending of a relationship between two things 分离；脱离： *the divorce between religion and science* 宗教与科学的分裂

■ ***verb*** **1** 🔑 [T, I] ~ (**sb**) to end your marriage to sb legally 与（某人）离婚；判（某人）离婚： *They're **getting divorced**.* 他们要离婚了。 ◇ *She's divorcing her husband.* 她与丈夫在闹离婚。 ◇ *I'd heard they're divorcing.* 我听说他们要离婚了。 **2** [T, often passive] ~ **sb/sth from sth** (*formal*) to separate a person, an idea, a subject, etc. from sth; to keep two things separate 使分离；使脱离： *They believed that art should be divorced from politics.* 他们认为艺术应该与政治分开。

di·vorcé /dɪˌvɔːˈseɪ; *NAmE* dɪˌvɔːrˈseɪ/ *noun* (*NAmE*) a man whose marriage has been legally ended 离婚男子

di·vorced 🔑 /dɪˈvɔːst; *NAmE* -ˈvɔːrst/ *adj.* **1** 🔑 no longer married 离婚的；离异的： *Many divorced men remarry and have second families.* 许多离婚的男子再婚组成了新的家庭。 ◇ *My parents are divorced.* 我的父母离婚了。 ➲ COLLOCATIONS AT MARRIAGE **2** ~ **from sth** (*formal*) appearing not to be affected by sth; separate from sth 表现得不受影响的；脱离…的： *He seems completely divorced from reality.* 他似乎完全脱离了现实。

di·vor·cee /dɪˌvɔːˈsiː; *NAmE* dɪˌvɔːrˈseɪ/ *noun* (*BrE*) a person whose marriage has been legally ended, especially a woman 离婚的人（尤指女子）

di·vorcée /dɪˌvɔːˈseɪ; *NAmE* dɪˌvɔːrˈseɪ/ *noun* (*NAmE*) a woman whose marriage has been legally ended 离婚女子；离异女子

divot /ˈdɪvət/ *noun* a piece of grass and earth that is dug out by accident, for example by a CLUB when sb is playing GOLF （打高尔夫球等时不小心削起的）一块草皮和泥土

di·vulge /daɪˈvʌldʒ/ *verb* ~ **sth** (**to sb**) | ~ **what, whether, etc.…** (*formal*) to give sb information that is supposed to be secret 泄露，透露（秘密） SYN **reveal**： *Police refused to divulge the identity of the suspect.* 警方拒绝透露嫌疑犯的身份。

divvy /ˈdɪvi/ *verb* (**div·vies**, **divvy·ing**, **div·vied**, **div·vied**)
PHR V **ˌdivvy sth↔ˈup** (*informal*) to divide sth, especially money into two or more parts 分，分摊，分享（尤指金钱）

Di·wali (*also* **Di·vali**) /diːˈwɑːli/ (*also* **Dee·pa·vali**) *noun* [U] a Hindu festival that is held in the autumn/fall, celebrated by lighting CANDLES and CLAY lamps, and with FIREWORKS 排灯节（印度教秋季节日）

Dix·ie /ˈdɪksi/ *noun* [U] an informal name for the south-eastern states of the US 迪克西（美国东南部各州的非正式统称）

Dixie·land /ˈdɪksilænd/ *noun* [U] a type of traditional JAZZ 迪克西兰爵士乐 ➲ SEE ALSO TRAD

DIY /ˌdiː aɪ ˈwaɪ/ *noun* [U] the abbreviation for 'do-it-yourself' (the activity of making, repairing or decorating things in the home yourself, instead of paying sb to do it) 自己动手（全写为 do-it-yourself，相对于雇人做）： *a DIY store* * DIY 商店 ➲ COLLOCATIONS AT DECORATE ➲ VISUAL VOCAB PAGE V21

di·zyg·ot·ic twin /ˌdaɪzaɪˌɡɒtɪk ˈtwɪn; *NAmE* -ˌɡɑːtɪk/ (*also* **di·zyg·ous twin** /daɪˌzaɪɡəs ˈtwɪn/) *noun* (*specialist*) = FRATERNAL TWIN ➲ COMPARE MONOZYGOTIC TWIN

dizzy /ˈdɪzi/ *adj.* (**diz·zier**, **diz·zi·est**) **1** feeling as if everything is spinning around you and that you are not able to balance 头晕目眩的；眩晕的 SYN **giddy**： *Climbing so high made me **feel dizzy**.* 爬那么高使我感到头晕目眩。 ◇ *I suffer from **dizzy spells*** (= short periods when I am dizzy). 我患有阵发性头晕。 **2** making you feel dizzy; making you feel that a situation is changing very fast 使人眩晕的；使人头昏眼花的；使人感到变化太快的 SYN **giddy**： *the dizzy descent from the summit* 从山顶陡然而下，令人目眩 ◇ *the dizzy pace of life in Hong Kong* 香港令人目眩的生活节奏 **3** (*informal, especially NAmE*) silly or stupid 愚蠢的；笨的 SYN **giddy**： *a dizzy blonde* 金发傻妞 ▶ **diz·zily** *adv.* **diz·zi·ness** *noun* [U]
IDM **the dizzy ˈheights** (**of sth**) (*informal*) an important or impressive position 重要的职位；显赫的地位： *She dreamed of reaching the dizzy heights of stardom.* 她梦想达到巨星的显赫地位。

dizzy·ing /ˈdɪziɪŋ/ *adj.* making you feel dizzy 使人眩晕的；使人头昏眼花的： *The car drove past at a dizzying speed.* 汽车风驰电掣地驶过。

DJ /ˈdiː dʒeɪ/ *noun, verb*

■ ***noun*** **1** the abbreviation for DISC JOCKEY （电台、电视台、夜总会）唱片节目主持人（全写为 disc jockey） **2** (*BrE*) the abbreviation for DINNER JACKET （男式）晚礼服，无尾礼服（全写为 dinner jacket）

■ ***verb*** (**DJ's**, **DJ'ing**, **DJ'd**, **DJ'd**) [I] to perform as a DISC JOCKEY, especially in a club 做音乐节目主持人（尤指在夜总会）

djibba (*also* **djib·bah**) *noun* = JIBBA

djinn /dʒɪn/ *noun* (in Arabian stories) a spirit with magic powers （阿拉伯神话）神怪，神灵，精灵 SYN **genie**

DLitt (*NAmE* **D.Litt**) /ˌdiː ˈlɪt/ *noun* the abbreviation for 'Doctor of Letters' (a university degree at the highest level, awarded for a long record of academic research, or as an HONORARY degree to recognize sb's contribution to society) 文学博士（全写为 Doctor of Letters，大学最高学位或荣誉学位）

DM /ˌdiː ˈem/ *abbr.* direct message (a private message that you send on TWITTER™, that will only be seen by the person you send it to) 私信，密信（全写为 direct message，在推特上一对一发送的私人信息）

DMA /ˌdiː em ˈeɪ/ *noun* [U] the abbreviation for 'direct memory access' (a system that allows a device attached to a computer to take data from the computer's memory without using the CENTRAL PROCESSING UNIT) 直接存储器存取，直接内存存取（全写为 direct memory access，无须使用中央处理器）

DMs /ˌdiː ˈemz/ *noun* [pl.] (*informal*) = DR MARTENS™

DNA /ˌdiː en ˈeɪ/ *noun* [U] (*chemistry* 化) the abbreviation for 'deoxyribonucleic acid' (the chemical in the cells of animals and plants that carries GENETIC information and is a type of NUCLEIC ACID) 脱氧核糖核酸（全写为 deoxyribonucleic acid，动植物的细胞中带有基因信息的化学物质）：*a DNA test* * DNA 测试 ➲ **WORDFINDER NOTE** AT BIOLOGY

ˌDNA ˈfingerprinting *noun* [U] = GENETIC FINGERPRINTING

do¹ 🔑 /də; du; *strong form* duː/ *verb, auxiliary verb, noun* ➲ IRREGULAR VERBS at page R4 ➲ SEE ALSO DO²

■ ***verb***

• **ACTION** 行为 **1** 🔑 [T] **~ sth** used to refer to actions that you do not mention by name or do not know about 做，干，办（某事）：*What are you doing this evening?* 你今晚打算做什么？ ◇ *We will do what we can to help.* 我们会尽力帮助。◇ *Are you doing anything tomorrow evening?* 你明晚有事吗？ ◇ *The company ought to do something about the poor service.* 公司应该对差劲的服务采取点措施。◇ *What have you done to your hair?* 你的头发是怎么搞的？ ◇ *There's **nothing to do*** (= no means of passing the time in an enjoyable way) *in this place.* 这地方没什么好玩的。◇ *There's **nothing we can do** about it* (= we can't change the situation). 这种事情我们毫无办法。◇ ***What can I do for you*** (= how can I help)? 我能为您做点什么？

• **BEHAVE** 表现 **2** [I] to act or behave in the way mentioned （以某种方式）做，行动，表现：**~ as…** *Do as you're told!* 叫你怎么做你就怎么做！ ◇ *They are free to do as they please.* 他们想怎么做就怎么做。◇ **+ adv./prep.** *You would **do well to*** (= I advise you to) *consider all the options before buying.* 你购买之前最好对各种选择都考虑一下。

• **SUCCEED/PROGRESS** 顺利进行；进展 **3** 🔑 [I] **+ adv./prep.** used to ask or talk about the success or progress of sb/sth（问询或谈论时用）进展，进行：*How is the business doing?* 生意好吗？ ◇ *She **did well** out of* (= made a big profit from) *the deal.* 她从这笔交易中赚了不少钱。◇ *He's **doing very well** at school* (= his work is good). 他在学校里学习很不错。◇ *Both mother and baby are **doing well*** (= after the birth of the baby). 母子平安。◇ (*informal*) ***How are you doing*** (= how are you)? 你好吗？

• **TASK/ACTIVITY** 任务；活动 **4** 🔑 [T] **~ sth** to work at or perform an activity or a task 从事（工作）；进行（活动）；执行（任务）：*I'm doing some research on the subject.* 我正就这一课题进行研究。◇ *I have a number of things to do today.* 我今天有些事情要做。◇ *I do aerobics once a week.* 我每周做一次有氧健身运动。◇ *Let's do* (= meet for) *lunch.* 咱们一起吃顿午饭吧。◇ (*informal*) *Sorry. I don't do funny* (= I can't be funny). 对不起。我可不是开玩笑。 **5** [T] **~ sth** used with nouns to talk about tasks such as cleaning, washing, arranging, etc.（与名词连用，表示打扫、清洗、整理等）：*to do* (= wash) *the dishes* 洗碗碟 ◇ *to do* (= arrange) *the flowers* 插花 ◇ *I like the way you've done your hair.* 我喜欢你梳的发式。 **6** [T] to perform the activity or task mentioned 做；从事：**~ the ironing, cooking, shopping, etc.** *I like listening to the radio when I'm doing the ironing.* 我喜欢边熨衣服边听收音机。◇ **~ some, a little, etc. acting, writing, etc.** *She did a lot of acting when she was at college.* 她在大学时演过很多戏。

• **JOB** 职业 **7** 🔑 [T] **~ sth** (usually used in questions 通常用于疑问句) to work at sth as a job 从事（职业）：***What do you do*** (= what is your job)? 你干什么工作？ ◇ *What does she want to do when she leaves school?* 她毕业后想干什么？ ◇ *What did she **do for a living**?* 她过去干哪一行为生？ ◇ *What's Tom doing these days?* 汤姆最近在干什么？

• **STUDY** 学习 **8** [T] **~ sth** to learn or study sth 学习；攻读；研究：*I'm doing physics, biology and chemistry.* 我在学物理、生物和化学。◇ *Have you done any* (= studied anything by) *Keats?* 你读过济慈的作品吗？

• **SOLVE** 解决 **9** [T] **~ sth** to find the answer to sth; to solve sth 解答；解决：*I can't do this sum.* 我不会做这道算术题。◇ *Are you good at doing crosswords?* 你擅长填纵横字谜吗？

• **MAKE** 制作 **10** 🔑 [T] to produce or make sth 做出；制作：**~ sth** *to do a drawing/painting/sketch* 画画；绘画；画素描 ◇ *Does this pub do* (= provide) *lunches?* 这家酒馆供应午餐吗？ ◇ *Who's doing* (= organizing and preparing) *the food for the wedding reception?* 谁在承办婚宴的酒席？ ◇ **~ sth for sb** *I'll do a copy for you.* 我将为你复印一份。◇ **~ sb sth** *I'll do you a copy.* 我将复印一份给你。 ➲ **SYNONYMS** AT MAKE

• **PERFORM** 演出 **11** [T] **~ sth** to perform or produce a play, an OPERA, etc. 演出，编排（戏剧、歌剧等）：*The local dramatic society is doing 'Hamlet' next month.* 地方戏剧社准备下月演出《哈姆雷特》。

• **COPY SB** 仿效 **12** [T] **~ sb/sth** to copy sb's behaviour or the way sb speaks, sings, etc., especially in order to make people laugh 仿效，模仿，扮演（尤为逗乐）：*He does a great Elvis Presley.* 他把埃尔维斯·普雷斯利模仿得惟妙惟肖。◇ *Can you do a Welsh accent?* 你能模仿威尔士口音吗？

• **FINISH** 完成 **13** [I, T] to finish sth 完成；做完：**have/be done** *Sit there and wait till I've done.* 坐在那儿等到我做完。◇ **have/be done doing sth** *I've done talking—let's get started.* 我的说话完了，咱们开始吧。◇ **get sth done** *Did you get your article done in time?* 你的论文按时完成了吗？

• **TRAVEL** 旅行 **14** [T] **~ sth** to travel a particular distance 走过，旅行过（一段路程）：*How many miles did you do during your tour?* 你走了多少英里的旅程？ ◇ *My car does 40 miles to the gallon* (= uses one gallon of petrol/gas to travel 40 miles). 我的汽车每耗一加仑汽油可行驶 40 英里。 **15** [T] **~ sth** to complete a journey/trip 走完，完成（旅程）：*We did the round trip in two hours.* 我们两小时打了个来回。

• **SPEED** 速度 **16** [T] **~ sth** to travel at or reach a particular speed 以…速度行进；达到…速度：*The car was doing 90 miles an hour.* 汽车以每小时 90 英里的速度行驶。

• **VISIT** 参观 **17** [T] **~ sth** (*informal*) to visit a place as a tourist 参观；游览；在…观光：*We did Tokyo in three days.* 我们在东京游览了三天。

• **SPEND TIME** 度过 **18** 🔑 [T] **~ sth** to spend a period of time doing sth 度过（一段时间）：*She did a year at college, but then dropped out.* 她在大学读了一年书，但后来就辍学了。◇ *He did six years* (= in prison) *for armed robbery.* 他因持械抢劫罪服了六年刑。

• **DEAL WITH** 处理 **19** [T] **~ sb/sth** to deal with or attend to sb/sth 处理；照料：*The hairdresser said she could do me* (= cut my hair) *at three.* 理发师说她三点钟可以给我理发。

• **BE SUITABLE/ENOUGH** 适合；足够 **20** [I, T] to be suitable or be enough for sb/sth 适合；足够：*'Can you lend me some money?' 'Sure—will $20 do?'* "你能借给我一点钱吗？" "当然可以，20 美元够吗？" ◇ **~ for sb/sth** *These shoes **won't do** for the party.* 这双鞋聚会时穿不合适。◇ **~ as sth** *The box will **do fine as** a table.* 这个箱子用作桌子还蛮不错。◇ **~ sb** (**+ adv./prep.**) (*especially BrE*) *This room **will do me** nicely, thank you* (= it has everything I need). 这房间对我很合适，谢谢你。

• **COOK** 烹调 **21** [T] **~ sth** to cook sth 烹制；煮；烧；煎：*How would you like your steak done?* 你的牛排要几成熟？

• **CHEAT** 欺骗 **22** [T, usually passive] **~ sb** (*BrE, informal*) to cheat sb 欺骗：*This isn't a genuine antique—you've been done.* 这不是真正的古董，你上当了。

• **PUNISH** 惩罚 **23** [T] **~ sb** (**for sth**) (*BrE, informal*) to punish sb 惩罚；处罚：*They did him for tax evasion.* 他们因他逃税而处罚了他。◇ *She **got done** for speeding.* 她因超速行驶而受到处罚。

• **STEAL** 偷窃 **24** [T] **~ sth** (*informal*) to steal from a place

（从某地方）盗窃；抢劫（某地方）: *The gang did a warehouse and a supermarket.* 那帮匪徒抢劫了一个仓库和一家超级市场。

• **TAKE DRUGS** 吸毒 **25** [T] ~ sth (*informal*) to take an illegal drug 吸（毒）: *He doesn't smoke, drink or* **do drugs**. 他不抽烟，不喝酒，也不吸毒。

• **HAVE SEX** 性交 **26** [T] ~ it (*slang*) to have sex 性交

D

IDM **HELP** Most idioms containing **do** are at the entries for the nouns and adjectives in the idioms, for example **do a bunk** is at **bunk**. 大多数含 do 的习语，都可在该等习语中的名词及形容词相关词条找到，如 do a bunk 在词条 bunk 下。 **be/have to do with sb/sth** 🔑 to be about or connected with sb/sth 关于；与…有关系（或有联系）: *'What do you want to see me about?' 'It's to do with that letter you sent me.'* "你想见我有什么事？""是关于你写给我的那封信。" **have (got) something, nothing, a lot, etc. to do with sb/sth** used to talk about how much sb/sth is connected with sb/sth 与…有些（毫无、有很大等）关系: *Her job has something to do with computers.* 她的工作与计算机有些关系。◇ *'How much do you earn?' 'What's it got to do with you?'* "你挣多少钱？""这跟你有什么关系？"◇ *Hard work has a lot to do with* (= is an important reason for) *her success.* 努力工作是她成功的重要原因。◇ *We don't have very much to do with our neighbours* (= we do not speak to them very often). 我们与邻居没什么来往。◇ *I'd have nothing to do with him, if I were you.* 如果我是你，我就不会跟他有任何瓜葛。 **it won't 'do** (*especially BrE*) used to say that a situation is not acceptable and should be changed or improved （表示情况不令人满意、需要改变或改进）那不行，这不合适: *This is the third time you've been late this week; it simply won't do.* 这是你本周第三次迟到了，这可不行啊。 **not 'do anything/a lot/much for sb** (*informal*) used to say that sth does not make sb look attractive 并不使某人漂亮一些 / 很多: *That hairstyle doesn't do anything for her.* 那种发型并不使她更漂亮。 **,nothing 'doing** (*informal*) used to refuse a request （拒绝请求）不行，办不到: *'Can you lend me ten dollars?' 'Nothing doing!'* "你能借给我十块钱吗？""不行！" **no you 'don't** (*informal*) used to show that you intend to stop sb from doing sth that they were going to do 不，你办不到；不，我不许你这样做；你敢: *Sharon went to get into the taxi. 'Oh no you don't,' said Steve.* 沙伦走过去要上出租车。"喔，不，你不许走。"史蒂夫说道。 **that 'does it** (*informal*) used to show that you will not accept sth any longer （表示不愿再接受）行了，得了，够了: *That does it, I'm off. I'm not having you swear at me like that.* 够了，我就要不客气了。我不能容忍你那样跟我骂骂咧咧的。 **that's 'done it** (*informal*) used to say that an accident, a mistake, etc. has spoiled or ruined sth 这下可糟了；这下可完了: *That's done it. You've completely broken it this time.* 这下可完了。你这回是把它彻底弄坏了。 **that will 'do** used to order sb to stop doing or saying sth （制止行动或说话）行啦，够啦: *That'll do, children—you're getting far too noisy.* 行啦，孩子们，你们简直吵死人了。 **what do you do for sth?** used to ask how sb manages to obtain the thing mentioned 你是怎么设法获得…的: *What do you do for entertainment out here?* 你在这里有什么消遣? **what is sb/sth doing...?** used to ask why sb/sth is in the place mentioned 为什么在…地方: *What are these shoes doing on my desk?* 这些鞋怎么在我的书桌上呢?

PHR V **,do a'way with sb/yourself** (*informal*) to kill sb/yourself 杀死，干掉（某人）；自杀 **,do a'way with sth** (*informal*) to stop doing or having sth; to make sth end 废除；取消；结束 **SYN** **abolish**: *He thinks it's time we did away with the monarchy.* 他认为我们该废除君主制了。 **,do sb/sth 'down** (*BrE, informal*) to criticize sb/sth unfairly 诋毁；说…的坏话 **'do for sb/sth** [usually passive] (*informal*) to ruin, destroy or kill sb/sth 毁灭；破坏；杀死: *Without that contract, we're done for.* 要是没有那份合同，我们就完蛋了。 **,do sb/yourself 'in** (*informal*) **1** to kill sb/yourself 杀死，干掉（某人）；自杀 **2** [usually passive] to make sb very tired 使筋疲力尽；使疲乏至极: *Come and sit down—you look done in.* 过来坐坐吧，你看样子累坏了。 **,do sth↔'in** (*informal*) to injure a part of the body 伤害（身体某部位）: *He did his back in lifting heavy furniture.* 他抬重家具时扭伤了腰。 **,do sb 'out of sth** (*informal*) to unfairly prevent sb from having what they ought to have （用不正当手段）阻止某人拥有，剥夺: *She was done out of her promotion.* 她受人算计而未获得提升。 **,do sb 'over** (*informal, especially BrE*) to attack and beat sb severely 猛击；痛打；毒打；狠揍: *He was done over by a gang of thugs.* 他被一群暴徒毒打了一顿。 **,do sth↔'over 1** to clean or decorate sth again 重新清理；重新装饰: *The paintwork will need doing over soon.* 需要尽快重新油漆一遍。 **2** (*NAmE*) to do sth again 重做；重复；再做一遍: *She insisted that everything be done over.* 她坚持全部返工。 **3** (*BrE, informal*) to enter a building by force and steal things 入室盗窃: *He got home to find that his flat had been done over.* 他到家后发现公寓里被盗了。 **,do 'up** to be fastened 固定住；扣上；绑紧: *The skirt does up at the back.* 这条裙子在后面系扣。 **,do sth↔'up 1** 🔑 to fasten a coat, skirt, etc. 扣上（外套、裙子等）: *He never bothers to do his jacket up.* 他向来都懒得扣外衣。 **OPP** **undo 2** to make sth into a package 包起来；扎起来 **SYN** **wrap**: *She was carrying a package done up in brown paper.* 她提着一个牛皮纸包。 **3** to repair and decorate a house, etc. 修缮，整修，装饰（房屋等）: *He makes money by buying old houses and doing them up.* 他靠买旧房整修翻新赚钱。 **,do yourself 'up** (*informal*) to make yourself more attractive by putting on MAKE-UP, attractive clothes, etc. 梳妆，打扮（自己） **'do sth with sb/sth** 🔑 (used in negative sentences and questions with *what* 用于否定句和与 what 连用的疑问句): *I don't know what to do with* (= how to use) *all the food that's left over.* 我不知道怎样处理这么多剩饭剩菜。◇ *What have you done with* (= where have you put) *my umbrella?* 你把我的伞弄到哪里去了？◇ *What have you been doing with yourselves* (= how have you been passing the time)? 你们这一向是怎么过的？ ➲ SEE ALSO CAN'T BE DOING WITH SB/STH/SB DOING STH at CAN[1], COULD DO WITH STH at COULD **,do with'out (sb/sth)** 🔑 to manage without sb/sth 没有…也行；没有…而设法对付过去: *She* ***can't do without*** *a secretary.* 她不能没有秘书。◇ *If they can't get it to us in time, we'll just have to do without.* 如果他们不能及时给我们拿来，我们就只好将就了。◇ **do without doing sth** (*ironic*) *I* ***could have done without*** *being* (= I wish I had not been) *woken up at three in the morning.* 其实用不着在凌晨三点钟就把我叫醒。

▼ VOCABULARY BUILDING 词汇扩充

Household jobs: do or make? 家务活：用 do 还是 make?

- To talk about jobs in the home you can use such phrases as **wash the dishes**, **clean the kitchen floor**, **set the table**, etc. In conversation the verb **do** is often used instead. 做家务活可用下列短语表示：wash the dishes（洗餐具）、clean the kitchen floor（擦洗厨房地板）、set the table（摆餐具）等，在口语中常用动词 do 取代: *Let me do the dishes.* 我来洗碗吧。◇ *Michael said he would do the kitchen floor.* 迈克尔说他来擦洗厨房地板。◇ *It's your turn to do the table.* 轮到你摆餐具了。 **Do** is often used with nouns ending in *-ing*. * do 常与以 -ing 结尾的名词连用: *to do the shopping/cleaning/ironing/vacuuming* 买东西；打扫卫生；熨衣服；用吸尘器吸尘
- The verb **make** is used especially in the phrase **make the beds** and when you are talking about preparing or cooking food. 动词 make 尤用于短语 make the beds（铺床）以及谈论烹调: *He makes a great lasagne.* 他做的宽面条真好吃。◇ *I'll make breakfast while you're having a shower.* 你淋浴时我就做早餐。 You can also say **get**, **get ready** and, especially in *NAmE*, **fix** for preparing meals. 做饭亦可用 get、get ready 和 fix（尤用于美式英语）等词: *Can you get dinner while I put the kids to bed?* 我照料孩子们上床睡觉时你做饭行吗？◇ *Sit down—I'll fix supper for you.* 坐下吧，我给你做晚饭。

■ ***auxiliary verb*** (**does** /dʌz/, **did** /dɪd/, **done** /dʌn/) **1** 🔑 used before a full verb to form negative sentences and questions（用于实义动词前构成否定句和疑问句）：*I don't like fish.* 我不喜欢鱼。◇ *They didn't go to Paris.* 他们没去巴黎。◇ *Don't forget to write.* 别忘了写信。◇ *Does she speak French?* 她会说法语吗？ **2** used to make QUESTION TAGS (= short questions at the end of statements)（构成附加疑问句）：*You live in New York, don't you?* 你住在纽约，不是吗？◇ *She doesn't work here, does she?* 她不在这里工作，对吧？ **3** used to avoid repeating a full verb（代替实义动词以避免重复）：*He plays better than he did a year ago.* 他的球比一年前打得好了。◇ *She works harder than he does.* 她工作比他努力。◇ *'Who won?' 'I did.'* "谁赢了？" "我赢了。" ◇ *'I love peaches.' 'So do I.'* "我爱吃桃子。" "我也爱吃。" ◇ *'I don't want to go back.' 'Neither do I.'* "我不想回去。" "我也不想。" **4** used when no other auxiliary verb is present, to emphasize what you are saying（句中无其他助动词时，用以加强语气）：*He does look tired.* 他的确显得很疲倦。◇ *She did at least write to say thank you.* 她至少还写了信道谢。◇ (*BrE*) *Do shut up!* 把嘴给我闭上！ **5** used to change the order of the subject and verb when an adverb is moved to the front（副词移置句首时，用以改变主语和动词的语序）：*Not only does she speak Spanish, she's also good with computers.* 她不仅会说西班牙语，还精通计算机。

■*noun* /duː/ (*pl.* **dos** or **do's** /duːz/) (*informal*) a party; a social event 社交聚会；社交活动：*Are you having a big do for your birthday?* 你打算举行大型生日宴会吗？

IDM **dos and don'ts** (*also* **do's and don'ts**) (*informal*) rules that you should follow 规则；注意事项：*Here are some dos and don'ts for exercise during pregnancy.* 这是妊娠期间锻炼的一些注意事项。➲ MORE AT FAIR *adj.*

do² /dəʊ; *NAmE* doʊ/ *noun* = DOH ➲ SEE ALSO DO¹

do. *abbr.* DITTO 同上；同前

DOA /ˌdiː əʊ ˈeɪ; *NAmE* oʊ/ *abbr.* = DEAD ON ARRIVAL

do·able /ˈduːəbl/ *adj.* (*informal*) **1** [not usually before noun] able to be done 可做；可行：*It's not doable by Friday.* 这事星期五之前做不了。➲ COMPARE FEASIBLE **2** (*BrE*) sexually attractive 性感的

D.O.B. *abbr.* date of birth 出生日期

dob /dɒb; *NAmE* dɑːb/ *verb* (**-bb-**) (*BrE, informal*)

PHR V **ˌdob sb ˈin (to sb) for sth/for doing sth** to tell sb about sth that another person has done wrong 向（某人）告发另一人：*Sue dobbed me in to the teacher.* 休向老师告了我一状。

Do·ber·mann (pin·scher) (*also* **Do·ber·man (pin·scher)** *especially in NAmE*) /ˌdəʊbəmən ˈpɪnʃə(r); *NAmE* ˌdoʊbərmən/ *noun* a large dog with short dark hair, often used for guarding buildings 杜宾狗

doc /dɒk; *NAmE* dɑːk/ *noun* (*informal, especially NAmE*) a way of addressing or talking about a doctor（称呼或谈论时用语）医生，大夫

do·cent /ˈdəʊsnt; *NAmE* ˈdoʊ-/ *noun* (*NAmE*) a person whose job is to show tourists around a museum, etc. and talk to them about it（博物馆等场所的）讲解员，向导

do·cile /ˈdəʊsaɪl; *NAmE* ˈdɑːsl/ *adj.* quiet and easy to control 驯服的；易驾驭的；易控制的：*a docile child/horse* 听话的孩子；温驯的马 ▶ **do·cile·ly** /-saɪlli; *NAmE* -səli/ *adv.* **do·cil·ity** /dəʊˈsɪləti; *NAmE* dɑːˈs-/ *noun* [U]

dock /dɒk; *NAmE* dɑːk/ *noun, verb*

■*noun* **1** [C] a part of a port where ships are repaired, or where goods are put onto or taken off them 船坞；船埠；码头：*dock workers* 码头工人 ◇ *The ship was **in dock**.* 船泊在船坞。➲ SEE ALSO DRY DOCK **2 docks** [pl.] a group of docks in a port and the buildings around them that are used for repairing ships, storing goods, etc. 港区 **3** [C] (*NAmE*) = JETTY **4** [C] (*NAmE*) a raised platform for loading vehicles or trains（供运货汽车或铁路货车装卸货物的）月台 **5** [C] the part of a court where the person who has been accused of a crime stands or sits during a trial（法庭的）被告席：*He's been **in the dock** (= on trial for a crime) several times already.* 他已受审几次。➲ COLLOCATIONS AT JUSTICE **6** [U] a wild plant of northern Europe with large thick leaves that can be rubbed on skin that has been stung by NETTLES to make it less painful 酸模（北欧阔叶野草，可用来揉擦被荨麻刺伤的皮肤以止痛）：*dock leaves* 酸模叶 **7** = DOCKING STATION

■*verb* **1** [I, T] ~ (**sth**) if a ship **docks** or you **dock** a ship, it sails into a HARBOUR and stays there（使船）进港，停靠码头，进入船坞：*The ferry is expected to dock at 6.* 渡船预计在 6 点停靠码头。 **2** [I, T] ~ (**sth**) if two SPACECRAFT **dock**, or **are docked**, they are joined together in space（使航天器在外层空间）对接：*Next year, a technology module will be docked on the space station.* 明年将有一个技术舱与航天站对接。➲ WORDFINDER NOTE AT SPACE **3** [T] to take away part of sb's wages, etc. 扣除（部分工资等）：**~ sth** *If you're late, your wages will be docked.* 如果你迟到了，就要扣你的工资。◇ **~ sth from/off sth** *They've docked 15% off my pay for this week.* 本周他们扣掉了我 15% 的工资。 **4** [T] **~ sth** (*computing* 计) to connect a computer to a DOCKING STATION 入坞（将电脑连接到扩展坞） OPP **undock** **5** [T] **~ sth** to cut an animal's tail short 剪短（动物的尾巴）

dock·er /ˈdɒkə(r); *NAmE* ˈdɑːk-/ *noun* a person whose job is moving goods on and off ships 码头工人

Dock·ers™ /ˈdɒkəz; *NAmE* ˈdɑːkərz/ *noun* [pl.] a US make of trousers/pants made of cotton（美国）道克斯全棉长裤

docket /ˈdɒkɪt; *NAmE* ˈdɑːk-/ *noun* **1** (*business* 商) a document or label that shows what is in a package, which goods have been delivered, which jobs have been done, etc.（载明包裹、发货、完工等情况的）单据，标签 **2** (*NAmE*) (*also* **ˈdocket sheet**) a list of cases to be dealt with in a particular court 备审案件目录表；法院积案清单 **3** (*NAmE*) a list of items to be discussed at a meeting 议程

ˈdocking station (*also* **dock**) *noun* (*computing* 计) a piece of equipment to which a PORTABLE device, for example a LAPTOP computer, can be connected so that it can be used with a printer, a keyboard, speakers, etc.（便携式设备的）扩展坞：*an iPod docking station* 苹果播放器基座 ➲ VISUAL VOCAB PAGE V22

dock·land /ˈdɒklænd; *NAmE* ˈdɑːk-/ *noun* [U] (*also* **dock·lands** [pl.]) (*BrE*) the district near DOCKS (= the place where ships are loaded and unloaded in a port) 港区陆域；码头区：*plans to further redevelop Bristol's docklands* 进一步开发布里斯托尔港区陆域的方案

dock·side /ˈdɒksaɪd; *NAmE* ˈdɑːk-/ *noun* [sing.] the area around the DOCKS (= the place where ships are loaded and unloaded) in a port 码头边；码头邻区；坞边

dock·yard /ˈdɒkjɑːd; *NAmE* ˈdɑːkjɑːrd/ *noun* an area with DOCKS (= the place where ships are loaded and unloaded in a port) and equipment for building and repairing ships 造船厂；修船厂

ˌDoc ˈMartens *noun* (*informal*) = DR MARTENS™

doc·tor /ˈdɒktə(r); *NAmE* ˈdɑːk-/ *noun, verb*

■*noun* (*abbr.* **Dr**) **1** a person who has been trained in medical science, whose job is to treat people who are ill/sick or injured 医生；大夫：*You'd better **see a doctor** about that cough.* 你最好找医生治治你的咳嗽。◇ *Doctor Staples* (= as a title/form of address) 斯特普尔斯医生 ➲ WORDFINDER NOTE AT HOSPITAL

> WORDFINDER 联想词：**cure**, **examine**, **medicine**, patient, practice, prescribe, receptionist, **specialist**, surgeon

2 **doctor's** a place where a doctor sees patients 诊所：*an appointment at the doctor's* 诊所的预约门诊 ➲ MORE LIKE THIS 34, page R29 **3** a person who has received the highest university degree 博士：*a Doctor of Philosophy/Law* 哲学 / 法学博士 ◇ *Doctor Franks* (= as a title/form of address) 弗兰克斯博士 **4** (*especially NAmE*) used as a title or form of address for a dentist（用作头衔或称呼）牙医

IDM **just what the doctor ˈordered** (*humorous*) exactly what sb wants or needs 正是所需之物

■*verb* **1** **~ sth** to change sth in order to trick sb 篡改；伪造 SYN **falsify**：*He was accused of doctoring the figures.* 他被指控篡改数字。 **2** **~ sth** to add sth harmful to food or drink 将有害物掺入（食物或饮料）中：*The wine had been doctored.* 这葡萄酒里掺入了有害物质。 **3 ~ sth** (*informal*) to remove part of the sex organs of an animal 阉割（动物） **SYN neuter**

doc·tor·al /ˈdɒktərəl; *NAmE* ˈdɑːk-/ *adj.* [only before noun] connected with a doctorate 博士的；博士学位的：(*BrE*) *a doctoral thesis* 博士学位论文 ◇ (*NAmE*) *a doctoral dissertation* 博士学位论文

D

doc·tor·ate /ˈdɒktərət; *NAmE* ˈdɑːk-/ *noun* the highest university degree 博士学位：*She's studying for her doctorate.* 她正在攻读博士学位。

doc·trin·aire /ˌdɒktrɪˈneə(r); *NAmE* ˌdɑːktrəˈner/ *adj.* (*disapproving*) strictly following a theory in all circumstances, even if there are practical problems or disagreement 空谈理论的；脱离实际的；教条主义的：*a doctrinaire conservative* 一个看重教条的保守分子 ◇ ***doctrinaire attitudes/beliefs/policies*** 教条主义的态度 / 信条 / 政策

doc·tri·nal /dɒkˈtraɪnl; *NAmE* ˈdɑːktrənl/ *adj.* (*formal*) relating to a doctrine or doctrines 教义的；学说的；主义的：*the doctrinal position of the English church* 英格兰教会教义的立场 ◇ (*disapproving*) *a rigidly doctrinal approach* 硬搬教条的方法 ▶ **doc·tri·nal·ly** *adv.*

doc·trine /ˈdɒktrɪn; *NAmE* ˈdɑːk-/ *noun* **1** [C, U] a belief or set of beliefs held and taught by a Church, a political party, etc. 教义；主义；学说；信条：*the doctrine of parliamentary sovereignty* 议会主权学说 ◇ *Christian doctrine* 基督教教义 **2 Doctrine** [C] (*US*) a statement of government policy （政府政策的）正式声明：*the Monroe Doctrine* 门罗主义

docu·drama /ˈdɒkjudrɑːmə; *NAmE* ˈdɑːk-/ *noun* a film/movie, usually made for television, in which real events are shown in the form of a story 纪实电影；纪实电视剧；文献影片（或电视片）

docu·ment 🔑 **AW** *noun, verb*

■ ***noun*** /ˈdɒkjumənt; *NAmE* ˈdɑːk-/ **1** 🔑 an official paper or book that gives information about sth, or that can be used as evidence or proof of sth 文件；公文；文献；证件：*legal documents* 法律文件 ◇ *travel documents* 旅行证件 ◇ *Copies of the relevant documents must be filed at court.* 有关文件副本必须送交法院备案。 ◇ *One of the documents leaked to the press was a memorandum written by the head of the security police.* 泄露给报界的文件中有一份是秘密警察局长写的备忘录。

WORDFINDER 联想词：agreement, binding, certificate, clause, deed, draft, draw up, subsection, witness

2 🔑 a computer file that contains text that has a name that identifies it （计算机）文档，文件：*Save the document before closing.* 在关闭文档前存盘。 ➲ VISUAL VOCAB PAGE V74

■ ***verb*** /ˈdɒkjument; *NAmE* ˈdɑːk-/ **1 ~ sth** to record the details of sth 记录，记载（详情）：*Causes of the disease have been well documented.* 这种疾病的起因已有完备的记载。 **2 ~ sth** to prove or support sth with documents 用文件证明（或证实）：*documented evidence* 有文件证明的证据

docu·men·tary /ˌdɒkjuˈmentri; *NAmE* ˌdɑːk-/ *noun, adj.*

■ ***noun*** (*pl.* **-ies**) a film or a radio or television programme giving facts about sth 纪录片；纪实广播（或电视）节目：*a television documentary about/on the future of nuclear power* 关于核能前景的纪实电视片 ➲ WORDFINDER NOTE AT PROGRAMME ➲ COLLOCATIONS AT TELEVISION

■ ***adj.*** [only before noun] **1** consisting of documents 文件的；文献的；由文件（或文献）组成的：***documentary evidence/sources/material*** 书面证据；文件来源；文献资料 **2** giving a record of or report on the facts about sth, especially by using pictures, recordings, etc. of people involved 纪录的；纪实的：*a documentary film about the war* 关于那场战争的纪录片

docu·men·ta·tion **AW** /ˌdɒkjumenˈteɪʃn; *NAmE* ˌdɑːk-/ *noun* [U] **1** the documents that are required for sth, or that give evidence or proof of sth 必备资料；证明文件：*I couldn't enter the country because I didn't have all the necessary documentation.* 我不能入境是因为我证明文件不齐备。 **2** the act of recording sth in a document; the state of being recorded in a document 文件记载；文献记录；归档：*the documentation of an agreement* 协议的归档

ˈdocument case *noun* a soft flat case without a handle, usually made from leather, plastic, etc., and used for holding and carrying documents 公文包；文件套

docu·soap /ˈdɒkjusəʊp; *NAmE* ˈdɑːkjusoʊp/ *noun* (*BrE*) a television programme about the lives of real people, presented as entertainment 纪实肥皂剧；纪实电视娱乐节目 ➲ SEE ALSO SOAP OPERA ➲ MORE LIKE THIS 1, page R25

DOD /ˌdiː əʊ ˈdiː; *NAmE* oʊ/ *abbr.* Department of Defense (the government department in the US that is responsible for defence) （美国）国防部

dod·der·ing /ˈdɒdərɪŋ; *NAmE* ˈdɑːd-/ (*BrE also* **dod·dery** /ˈdɒdəri; *NAmE* ˈdɑːd-/) *adj.* weak, slow and not able to walk in a steady way, especially because you are old （尤指因年迈）衰弱而步履蹒跚的

dod·dle /ˈdɒdl; *NAmE* ˈdɑːdl/ *noun* [sing.] (*BrE, informal*) a task or an activity that is very easy 轻而易举的事 **SYN cinch**：*The first year of the course was an absolute doddle.* 第一年的课程简直太容易了。 ◇ *The machine is a doddle to set up and use.* 这机器的安装和使用都很简单。

do·deca·he·dron /ˌdəʊdekəˈhiːdrən; -ˈhed-; *NAmE* ˌdoʊ-/ *noun* (*geometry* 几何) a solid figure with twelve flat sides 十二面体

do·deca·phon·ic /ˌdəʊdekəˈfɒnɪk; *NAmE* ˌdoʊdekəˈfɑːnɪk/ *adj.* (*music* 音) = TWELVE-NOTE

dodge /dɒdʒ; *NAmE* dɑːdʒ/ *verb, noun*

■ ***verb*** **1** [T, I] to move quickly and suddenly to one side in order to avoid sb/sth 闪开；躲开；避开：**~ sth** *He ran across the road, dodging the traffic.* 他躲开来往的车辆跑过马路。 ◇ **(+ adv./prep.)** *The girl dodged behind a tree to hide from the other children.* 这女孩闪身躲到树后不让其他孩子看见。 **2** [T] (*rather informal*) to avoid doing sth, especially in a dishonest way （尤指不诚实地）逃避：**~ sth** *He dodged his military service.* 他弄虚作假逃避了服兵役。 ◇ **~ doing sth** *She tried to dodge paying her taxes.* 她想方设法逃税。

■ ***noun*** (*informal*) a clever and dishonest trick, played in order to avoid sth 推脱的计策；逃避的诡计；骗人的伎俩：*a tax dodge* 逃税花招 ◇ *When it comes to getting off work, he knows all the dodges.* 说到请假歇班，他什么花招都想得出。

dodge·ball /ˈdɒdʒbɔːl; *NAmE* ˈdɑːdʒ-/ *noun* [U] (*NAmE*) a game in which teams of players form circles and try to hit other teams with a large ball 躲球游戏，躲避球（参加者围成一个圈，以一大球投掷圈中人）

dodgem /ˈdɒdʒəm; *NAmE* ˈdɑːdʒəm/ *noun* (*BrE*) **1 the dodgems** [pl.] a ride at a FUNFAIR in which people drive small electric cars around a track, trying to chase and hit the other cars 开碰碰车：*The kids wanted to go on the dodgems.* 孩子们想去玩碰碰车。 **2** (*also* **ˈdodgem car**) (*also* **ˈbumper car** *NAmE, BrE*) one of the small electric cars that you drive in the dodgems 碰碰车

dodger /ˈdɒdʒə(r); *NAmE* ˈdɑːdʒ-/ *noun* (*informal*) a person who dishonestly avoids doing sth 逃避者；回避者；躲避者：*tax dodgers* 逃税者 ◇ *a crackdown on fare dodgers on trains* 对火车逃票者的严厉打击 ➲ SEE ALSO DRAFT DODGER

dodgy /ˈdɒdʒi; *NAmE* ˈdɑːdʒi/ *adj.* (*BrE, informal*) (**dodgi·er, dodgi·est**) **1** seeming or likely to be dishonest 狡猾的；狡诈的；可疑的 **SYN suspicious**：*He made a lot of money, using some very dodgy methods.* 他采用一些极其狡诈的手段赚了许多钱。 ◇ *I don't want to get involved in anything dodgy.* 我不想牵连进任何欺骗勾当。 **2** not working well; not in good condition 有毛病的；运转不良的；状况不佳的：*I can't play—I've got a dodgy knee.* 我不能玩了，我的膝盖出了毛病。 ◇ *The marriage had been distinctly dodgy* *for a long time.* 这桩婚姻长期以来明显有问题。 **3** involving risk, danger or difficulty 冒险的；危险的；困难的： *If you get into any dodgy situations, call me.* 如果你遇上什么难事，给我打电话。

dodo /ˈdəʊdəʊ; *NAmE* ˈdoʊdoʊ/ *noun* (*pl.* **-os**) **1** a large bird that could not fly and that is now EXTINCT (= no longer exists) 渡渡鸟（不能飞行，现已灭绝） **2** (*NAmE*) a stupid person 笨人；蠢人 **IDM** SEE DEAD *adj.*

DOE /ˌdiː əʊ ˈiː; *NAmE* oʊ/ *abbr.* Department of Energy (the US government department that plans and controls the development of the country's sources of energy) （美国）能源部

doe /dəʊ; *NAmE* doʊ/ *noun* a female DEER, RABBIT or HARE 雌鹿；雌兔 ⊃COMPARE BUCK *n.* (2), HIND *n.*, STAG

doer /ˈduːə(r)/ *noun* (*approving*) a person who does things rather than thinking or talking about them 实干的人；身体力行者；实行者： *We need fewer organizers and more doers.* 我们需要的是少些组织者，多些实干者。

does /dʌz/ ⊃DO¹ *v.*

doesn't /ˈdʌznt/ *short form* does not

dof /dɒf; *NAmE* dɑːf/ *adj.* (**dofer**, **dofest**) (*SAfrE*) (*informal*) stupid, lacking knowledge 笨的；傻的；无知的： *Sometimes our guys appear a bit dof!* 有时我们的人显得有点傻！

doff /dɒf; *NAmE* dɑːf; dɔːf/ *verb, adj.*
■ ***verb*** **~ sth** (*old-fashioned*) to take off your hat, especially to show respect for sb/sth 脱（帽）致意
■ ***adj.*** (*SAfrE*, *informal*) stupid 笨的；愚昧无知的

dog /dɒg; *NAmE* dɔːg/ *noun, verb*
■ ***noun*** **1** [C] an animal with four legs and a tail, often kept as a pet or trained for work, for example hunting or guarding buildings. There are many types of dog, some of which are wild. 狗；犬： *I took the dog for a walk.* 我遛狗去了。◇ *I could hear a dog barking.* 我听到狗的叫声。◇ *dog food* 狗粮 ◇ *guard dogs* 看家狗 ◇ *a dog and her puppies* 母狗和它的崽儿 ⊃SEE ALSO GUIDE DOG, GUN DOG, HEARING DOG, LAPDOG, PRAIRIE DOG, SHEEPDOG, SNIFFER DOG, TRACKER DOG **2** [C] a male dog, FOX or WOLF 公狗；公狐；公狼 ⊃COMPARE BITCH *n.* (1) **3 the dogs** [pl.] (*BrE, informal*) GREYHOUND racing 赛狗；灵猩赛 **4** [C] (*informal, especially NAmE*) a thing of low quality; a failure 蹩脚货；失败： *Her last movie was an absolute dog.* 她最近的一部影片彻底砸锅了。 **5** [C] (*informal*) an offensive way of describing a woman who is not considered attractive 丑女人 **6** [C] (*informal, disapproving*) used, especially after an adjective, to describe a man who has done sth bad （尤用于形容词后）家伙，小人，无赖： *You dirty dog!* 你这个下流坯！ ⊃SEE ALSO HOT DOG, SHAGGY-DOG STORY, TOP DOG, WATCHDOG
IDM **a ˌdog and ˈpony show** (*NAmE, informal, disapproving*) an event that is planned only in order to impress people so that they will support or buy sth （为公关或促销而举行的）造势活动 **(a case of) ˌdog eat ˈdog** a situation in business, politics, etc. where there is a lot of competition and people are willing to harm each other in order to succeed 残酷无情的竞争；损人利己的角逐；相互残杀： *I'm afraid in this line of work it's a case of dog eat dog.* 恐怕在这种行业中竞争是残酷无情的。◇ *We're operating in a dog-eat-dog world.* 我们是在一个残酷竞争的世界里经营。 **a ˌdog in the ˈmanger** a person who stops other people from enjoying what he or she cannot use or does not want 占马槽的狗 **a dog's ˈbreakfast/ˈdinner** (*BrE, informal*) a thing that has been done badly 乱七八糟；一团糟 **SYN** mess： *He's made a real dog's breakfast of these accounts.* 他把这些账目搞得简直一塌糊涂。 **a ˈdog's life** an unhappy life, full of problems or unfair treatment 悲惨的生活；牛马不如的生活 **every dog has his/its ˈday** (*saying*) everyone has good luck or success at some point in their life 人人皆有得意时 **give a dog a bad ˈname** (*saying*) when a person already has a bad reputation, it is difficult to change it because others will continue to blame or suspect him/her 恶名难洗；名声一毁，万难挽回 **go to the ˈdogs** (*NAmE also* **go to hell in a ˈhandbasket**) (*informal*) to get into a very bad state 败落；大不如前： *This firm's gone to the dogs since the new management took over.* 这家公司自新的管理人员接手以来日渐衰败。 **not have a ˈdog's chance** to have no chance at all 毫无机会；绝无可能： *He hasn't a dog's chance of passing the exam.* 他根本不可能通过这次考试。 **why keep a ˌdog and bark yourˈself?** (*informal, saying*) if sb can do a task for you, there is no point in doing it yourself 既然有人代劳，何必自己操劳 ⊃MORE AT HAIR, RAIN *v.*, SICK *adj.*, SLEEP *v.*, TAIL *n.*, TEACH
■ ***verb*** (**-gg-**) **1 ~ sb/sth** (of a problem or bad luck 问题或不幸) to cause you trouble for a long time （长期）困扰，折磨，纠缠： *He had been dogged by ill health all his life.* 他一生多病，备受折磨。 **2 ~ sb/sth** to follow sb closely 跟踪；尾随： *She had the impression that someone was dogging her steps.* 她感觉到有人在尾随她。

ˈdog biscuit *noun* a small hard biscuit fed to dogs 狗粮饼干

dog·box /ˈdɒgbɒks; *NAmE* ˈdɔːgbɑːks/ *noun*
IDM **be in the ˈdogbox** (*SAfrE*) = BE IN THE DOGHOUSE

dog·catch·er /ˈdɒgkætʃə(r); *NAmE* ˈdɔːg-/ (*NAmE, becoming old-fashioned*) (*NAmE, formal* **ˌanimal conˈtrol officer**, *BrE* **ˈdog warden**) *noun* a person whose job is to catch dogs and cats that are walking freely in the streets and do not seem to have a home 捕狗员（负责捕捉街上的流浪猫狗）

ˈdog collar *noun* **1** a COLLAR for a dog 狗项圈 **2** (*informal*) a stiff white COLLAR fastened at the back and worn by some Christian priests （圣职人员穿的）白色硬领；牧师领

ˈdog days *noun* [pl.] the hottest period of the year 三伏天；酷暑期

ˈdog-eared *adj.* (of a book 书) used so much that the corners of many of the pages are turned down 卷角的；翻旧了的

ˌdog-ˈend *noun* (*BrE, informal*) the end of a cigarette that has been smoked 烟头；香烟屁股

dog·fight /ˈdɒgfaɪt; *NAmE* ˈdɔːg-/ *noun* **1** a fight between aircraft in which they fly around close to each other （战斗机的）近距离空战 **2** a struggle between two people or groups in order to win sth 争斗；格斗；混战 **3 dog fight** a fight between dogs, especially one that is arranged illegally, for entertainment 狗打架；（尤指非法的）斗狗
▸ **dog·fight·ing** *noun* [U]

dog·fish /ˈdɒgfɪʃ; *NAmE* ˈdɔːg-/ *noun* (*pl.* **dog·fish**) a small SHARK (= an aggressive sea fish with very sharp teeth) 狗鲨（小型鲨鱼，极富攻击性）

dog·ged /ˈdɒgɪd; *NAmE* ˈdɔːg-/ *adj.* [usually before noun] (*approving*) showing determination; not giving up easily 顽强的；坚持不懈的 **SYN** **tenacious**： ***dogged determination/persistence*** 顽强的决心 / 毅力 ◇ *their dogged defence of the city* 他们对城市的严防死守 ⊃MORE LIKE THIS 22, page R27 ▸ **dog·ged·ly** *adv.* **SYN** **tenaciously** **dog·ged·ness** *noun* [U] **SYN** **tenacity**

dog·gerel /ˈdɒgərəl; *NAmE* ˈdɔːg-; ˈdɑːg-/ *noun* [U] poetry that is badly written or ridiculous, sometimes because the writer has not intended it to be serious 蹩脚诗；打油诗；歪诗

doggo /ˈdɒgəʊ; *NAmE* ˈdɔːgoʊ/ *adv.* **lie ~** (*old-fashioned, informal*) to lie still and quiet, so that other people will not notice you 隐蔽地；隐伏着

dog·gone /ˈdɒgɒn; *NAmE* ˈdɔːggɔːn/ *adj.* [only before noun], *adv., exclamation* (*NAmE, informal*) used to show that you are annoyed or surprised （表示恼怒或惊讶）该死的，讨厌的，他妈的： *Where's the doggone key?* 这该死的钥匙上哪儿去了？ ◇ *Don't drive so doggone fast.* 别他妈开这么快呀。◇ *Well, doggone it!* 唉，真该死！

doggy /ˈdɒgi; *NAmE* ˈdɔːgi/ *noun, adj.*
■ ***noun*** (*also* **dog·gie**) (*pl.* **-ies**) (*informal*) a child's word for a dog （儿语）小狗，狗狗，汪汪

■ *adj.* [only before noun] of or like a dog 狗的；像狗一样的：*a doggy smell* 一股狗骚味

ˈ**doggy bag** (*also* ˈ**doggie bag**) *noun* (*informal*) a bag for taking home any food that is left after a meal in a restaurant 剩菜袋（餐馆装剩菜回家用的袋子）

ˈ**doggy-paddle** *noun* = DOG-PADDLE

ˈ**dog handler** *noun* a police officer who works with a trained dog 警犬训练员

dog·house /ˈdɒghaʊs; *NAmE* ˈdɔːg-/ (*NAmE*) (*BrE* **ken·nel**) *noun* a small shelter for a dog to sleep in 狗窝；犬舍

IDM **be in the doghouse** (*informal*, *NAmE*, *BrE*) if you are **in the doghouse**, sb is annoyed with you because of sth that you have done 受冷落；失体面；丢脸

dogie /ˈdəʊgi; *NAmE* ˈdoʊgi/ *noun* (*NAmE*) a young cow that has lost its mother 孤犊（失去母亲的小牛犊）

ˈ**dog-leg** *noun* a sharp bend, especially in a road or on a GOLF COURSE（道路的）急转弯；（高尔夫球场有大幅拐角的）狗腿球道

dogma /ˈdɒgmə; *NAmE* ˈdɔːgmə/ *noun* [U, C] (*often disapproving*) a belief or set of beliefs held by a group or organization, which others are expected to accept without argument 教义；教理；信条；教条：***political/religious/party dogma*** 政治 / 宗教 / 政党信条 ◇ *one of the central dogmas of the Church* 这个教会的核心教义之一

dog·mat·ic /dɒgˈmætɪk; *NAmE* dɔːg-/ *adj.* (*disapproving*) being certain that your beliefs are right and that others should accept them, without paying attention to evidence or other opinions 教条的；武断的；自以为是的：*a* ***dogmatic approach*** 武断的方法 ◇ *There is a danger of becoming too dogmatic about teaching methods.* 在教学方法上存在着过分教条主义的危险。 ▶ **dog·mat·ic·al·ly** /-kli/ *adv.*

dog·ma·tism /ˈdɒgmətɪzəm; *NAmE* ˈdɔːg-/ *noun* [U] (*disapproving*) behaviour and attitudes that are dogmatic 教条主义；独断论；武断

ˌ**do-ˈgooder** *noun* (*informal*, *disapproving*) a person who tries to help other people but who does it in a way that is annoying 帮倒忙的人；帮忙不得法的人

ˈ**dog-paddle** (*also* ˈ**doggy-paddle**) *noun* [U] a simple swimming stroke, with short quick movements like those of a dog in the water 狗爬式（游泳）

dogs·body /ˈdɒgzbɒdi; *NAmE* ˈdɔːgzbɑːdi/ *noun* (*pl.* **-ies**) (*BrE*, *informal*) a person who does all the boring jobs that nobody else wants to do, and who is treated as being less important than other people 勤杂工；干杂活的人

dog·sled /ˈdɒgsled; *NAmE* ˈdɔːg-/ *noun* (*NAmE*) a SLEDGE (= a vehicle that slides over snow) pulled by dogs, used especially in Canada and Alaska（尤用于加拿大和阿拉斯加的）狗拉雪橇

ˈ**dog tag** *noun* (*NAmE*, *slang*) a small piece of metal that US soldiers wear round their necks with their name and number on it（美国士兵挂在颈部的）身份识别牌

ˌ**dog-ˈtired** *adj.* [not usually before noun] (*informal*) very tired 极度疲乏；累极了 SYN **exhausted**

ˈ**dog warden** (*BrE*) (*NAmE*, *becoming old-fashioned* **dog·catch·er**, *formal* **animal control officer**) *noun* a person whose job is to catch dogs and cats that are walking freely in the streets and do not seem to have a home 捕狗员（负责捕捉街上的流浪猫狗）

dog·wood /ˈdɒgwʊd; *NAmE* ˈdɔːg-/ *noun* [U, C] a bush or small tree with red or pink BERRIES and red STEMS, that grows in northern regions; the hard wood of this tree 株木；株木的木材

doh (*also* **do**) /dəʊ; *NAmE* doʊ/ *noun* (*music* 音) the 1st and 8th note of a MAJOR SCALE 大调音阶的第 1 音和第 8 音

d'oh /dəʊ; *NAmE* doʊ/ *exclamation* (*informal*) used when you have just said or done sth that you know is stupid 唉，哦（用以表示自己言行失当）：*D'oh! That was the biggest mistake ever.* 唉！那是我犯过的最大错误。 ➲ MORE LIKE THIS 2, page R25 ORIGIN Used by Homer Simpson in *The Simpsons* television series. 源自电视剧《辛普森一家》中霍默·辛普森的用语。

DOI /ˌdiː əʊ ˈaɪ; *NAmE* oʊ/ *abbr.* **1** (*computing* 计) digital object identifier (a series of numbers and letters that identifies a particular text or document published in electronic form on the Internet) 数字对象识别码（用以识别在互联网上发表的电子文本或文档的数字和字母序列）**2** Department of the Interior (the US government department responsible for protecting the country's environment)（美国）内务部（负责国内环保事务）

doily /ˈdɔɪli/ *noun* (*pl.* **-ies**) **1** a small circle of paper or cloth with a pattern of very small holes in it, that you put on a plate under a cake or SANDWICHES（糕点盘上的）网眼纸垫圈，网眼布垫圈 **2** (*NAmE*) a small decorative MAT that you put on top of a piece of furniture（置于家具上的）装饰小垫

doing /ˈduːɪŋ/ *noun* [C, usually pl., U] a thing done or caused by sb 所做的事；发生的事；所作所为：*I've been hearing a lot about your doings recently.* 我最近不断听到很多关于你的所作所为。◇ *I promise you this was none of my doing* (= I didn't do it). 我向你保证这不是我干的。

IDM **take some ˈdoing | take a lot of ˈdoing** to be hard work; to be difficult 费劲；有困难：*Getting it finished by tomorrow will take some doing.* 要在明天完成有点难度。

ˌ**do-it-yourˈself** *noun* [U] (*especially BrE*) = DIY：*The materials you need are available from any good do-it-yourself store.* 所需材料可以从任何好的 DIY 商店买到。

dojo /ˈdəʊdʒəʊ; *NAmE* ˈdoʊdʒoʊ/ *noun* (*pl.* **-os**) (*from Japanese*) a hall or school where JUDO or other similar MARTIAL ARTS (= fighting sports) are practised 柔道馆；柔道学校；武术学校

Dolby™ /ˈdɒlbi; ˈdəʊlbi; *NAmE* ˈdɔːlbi; ˈdoʊlbi/ *noun* [U] a system for reducing background noise in sound recordings 杜比降噪系统

dol·drums /ˈdɒldrəmz; *NAmE* ˈdoʊl-/ *noun* [pl.] (*usually* **the doldrums**) **1** the state of feeling sad or depressed 忧郁；郁闷；消沉；没精打采：*He's been* ***in the doldrums*** *ever since she left him.* 自从她离开他以来，他一直很消沉。 **2** a lack of activity or improvement 无生气；停滞；萧条：*The bond market normally revives after the summer doldrums.* 债券市场通常在夏天萧条期后开始复苏。◇ *Despite these measures, the economy remains* ***in the doldrums.*** 尽管采取了这些措施，经济仍然停滞不前。ORIGIN From the place in the ocean near the equator where there are sudden periods of calm. A sailing ship caught in this area can be stuck there because of a lack of wind. 源自近赤道海洋上的无风带，帆船到此可能因无风而无法航行。

dole /dəʊl; *NAmE* doʊl/ *noun*, *verb*

■ ***noun*** [sing.] (*usually* **the dole**) (*BrE*, *informal*) money paid by the state to unemployed people 失业救济金：*He's been* ***on the dole*** (= without a job) *for a year.* 他领失业救济金已一年了。◇ *The government is changing the rules for claiming dole.* 政府正在修改申领失业救济金的规定。◇ *lengthening dole queues* 排队领取失业救济金人数的不断增多 ◇ *We could all be* ***in the dole queue*** *on Monday* (= have lost our jobs). 我们都可能在星期一站在领取失业救济金的队伍里。 ➲ COLLOCATIONS AT UNEMPLOYMENT

■ ***verb***

PHR V ˌ**dole sth**↔ˈ**out** (**to sb**) (*informal*) to give out an amount of food, money, etc. to a number of people in a group 发放，发给（食物、钱等）；施舍

dole·ful /ˈdəʊlfl; *NAmE* ˈdoʊlfl/ *adj.* very sad 忧郁的；悲伤的 SYN **mournful**：***a doleful expression/face/song*** 忧郁的表情；愁苦的脸；令人悲伤的歌 ◇ *a doleful looking man* 哭丧着脸的男人 ▶ **dole·ful·ly** /-fəli/ *adv.*

doll /dɒl; *NAmE* dɑːl/ *noun*, *verb*

■ ***noun*** **1** a child's toy in the shape of a person, especially a baby or a child 玩偶；玩具娃娃：*a rag doll* (= one made out of cloth) 布娃娃 **2** (*old-fashioned, informal, especially NAmE*) a word used to describe a pretty or attractive woman, now often considered offensive 俊妞，甜妞儿，美人儿（现多认为意含冒犯）: *She's quite a doll.* 她真是个美人儿。

■ ***verb***

PHR V **ˌdoll sb/yourself ˈup** (*informal*) to make sb/yourself look attractive for a party, etc., with fashionable clothes （把…）打扮得花枝招展，装扮得漂漂亮亮: *Are you getting dolled up for the party?* 你要把自己打扮起来去参加聚会吗？

dol·lar /ˈdɒlə(r); *NAmE* ˈdɑːl-/ *noun* **1** [C] (*symb.* **$**) the unit of money in the US, Canada, Australia and several other countries 元（美国、加拿大、澳大利亚等国的货币单位）: *You will be paid in American dollars.* 你的报酬将以美元支付。 ➲ COMPARE BUCK *n.* (1) ➲ SEE ALSO TOP DOLLAR **2** [C] a BANKNOTE or coin worth one dollar 一元（纸币或硬币）: *Do you have a dollar?* 你有一元钱吗？ ◇ *a dollar bill* 一元钞票 **3 the dollar** [sing.] (*finance* 财) the value of the US dollar compared with the value of the money of other countries 美元（币值）: *The dollar closed two cents down.* 美元收跌两美分。 IDM SEE BET *v.*, MILLION

dol·lar·ize (*BrE also* **-ise**) /ˈdɒləraɪz; *NAmE* ˈdɑːl-/ *verb* [T, I] ~ (sth) (of a country 国家) to start using the US dollar as its own CURRENCY （使）美元化 ▶ **dol·lar·iza·tion, -isa·tion** /ˌdɒləraɪˈzeɪʃn; *NAmE* ˌdɑːlərəˈz-/ *noun* [U]

doll·house /ˈdɒlhaʊs; *NAmE* ˈdɑːl-/ (*NAmE*) (*BrE* **ˈdoll's house**) *noun* a toy house with small furniture and sometimes DOLLS in it for children to play with （儿童放玩偶的）玩具小屋，娃娃屋 ➲ VISUAL VOCAB PAGE V41

dol·lop /ˈdɒləp; *NAmE* ˈdɑːləp/ *noun* (*informal*) **1** a lump of soft food, often dropped from a spoon 一团，一块（从勺中掉落的软食）: *a dollop of whipped cream* 一团搅打的奶油 **2** an amount of sth 少量；些许；一点儿: *A dollop of romance now and then is good for everybody.* 时而来点儿浪漫对每个人都是好事。

ˈdoll's house (*BrE*) (*NAmE* **doll·house**) *noun* a toy house with small furniture and sometimes DOLLS in it for children to play with （儿童放玩偶的）玩具小屋，娃娃屋 ➲ VISUAL VOCAB PAGE V41

dolly /ˈdɒli; *NAmE* ˈdɑːli; ˈdɔːli/ *noun* (*pl.* **-ies**) **1** a child's word for a DOLL（儿语）娃娃，洋娃娃 **2** (*especially NAmE*) a low platform on wheels for moving heavy objects （搬运重物的）台车，滑动台架

ˈdolly bird *noun* (*old-fashioned, BrE, informal*) a way of referring to a young woman who is considered attractive but not very intelligent 傻美妞

dol·men /ˈdɒlmen; *NAmE* ˈdoʊl-/ *noun* a pair or group of vertical stones with a large flat stone on top, built in ancient times to mark a place where sb was buried 石室冢墓（在一组竖石顶端置大石板）

dol·or·ous /ˈdɒlərəs; *NAmE* ˈdoʊl-/ *adj.* [usually before noun] (*literary*) feeling or showing great sadness 悲痛的；悲哀的

dol·phin /ˈdɒlfɪn; *NAmE* ˈdɑːl-/ *noun* a sea animal (a MAMMAL) that looks like a large fish with a pointed mouth. Dolphins are very intelligent and often friendly towards humans. There are several types of dolphin. 海豚: *a school of dolphins* 一群海豚 ➲ COMPARE PORPOISE

dol·phin·arium /ˌdɒlfɪˈneəriəm; *NAmE* ˌdɑːlfɪˈneriəm/ *noun* (*pl.* **dol·phin·ariums** or **dol·phin·aria** /-riə/) a building with a pool where people can go to see dolphins, especially ones who have been trained to do tricks 海豚（表演）馆

dolt /dəʊlt; *NAmE* doʊlt/ *noun* (*disapproving*) a stupid person 笨蛋；傻瓜 SYN **idiot** ▶ **dolt·ish** *adj.*

-dom *suffix* (in nouns 构成名词) **1** the condition or state of （表示状况或状态）: *freedom* 自由 ◇ *martyrdom* 殉难 **2** the rank of; an area ruled by （表示职位、地位、领域）: *kingdom* 王国 **3** the group of （表示群体、集体）: *officialdom* 官员 ➲ MORE LIKE THIS 7, page R25

do·main AW /dəˈmeɪn; dəʊ-; *NAmE* doʊ-/ *noun* **1** an area of knowledge or activity; especially one that sb is responsible for （知识、活动的）领域，范围，范畴: *Financial matters are her domain.* 财务问题是她的专业领域。 ◇ *Physics used to be very much a male domain.* 物理学曾在很大程度上是男性占据的领域。 ➲ SEE ALSO PUBLIC DOMAIN **2** lands owned or ruled by a particular person, government, etc., especially in the past （尤指旧时个人、国家等所拥有或统治的）领土，领地，势力范围: *The Spice Islands were within the Spanish domains.* 香料群岛曾是西班牙的领地。 **3** (*computing* 计) a set of websites on the Internet which end with the same group of letters, for example '.com', '.org' 域；论域；定义域: *top-level domains* 顶级域 ➲ WORDFINDER NOTE AT WEBSITE **4** (*mathematics* 数) the range of possible values of a particular VARIABLE 区域；定义域

doˈmain name *noun* (*computing* 计) a name which identifies a website or group of websites on the Internet 域名

dome /dəʊm; *NAmE* doʊm/ *noun* **1** a round roof with a CIRCULAR base 穹顶: *the dome of St Paul's Cathedral* 圣保罗大教堂的穹顶 ➲ VISUAL VOCAB PAGES V3, V14 **2** a thing or a building shaped like a dome 圆顶状物；穹状建筑物: *his bald dome of a head* 他圆溜溜的秃顶 **3** (*NAmE*) (in names 用于名称) a sports STADIUM whose roof is shaped like a dome 圆顶体育场: *the Houston Astrodome* 休斯敦阿斯托洛圆顶运动场

domed /dəʊmd; *NAmE* doʊmd/ *adj.* [usually before noun] having or shaped like a dome 有圆顶的；圆顶状的；半球形的: ***a domed forehead/ceiling*** 隆起的前额；圆顶篷

do·mes·tic AW /dəˈmestɪk/ *adj.*, *noun*

■ ***adj.*** **1** [usually before noun] of or inside a particular country; not foreign or international 本国的；国内的: ***domestic affairs/politics*** 国内事务 / 政治 ◇ ***domestic flights*** (= to and from places within a country) 国内航班 ◇ *Output consists of both exports and sales on the domestic market.* 产量包括出口和国内市场销售两部分。 OPP **foreign** **2** [only before noun] used in the home; connected with the home or family 家用的；家庭的；家务的: *domestic appliances* 家用器具 ◇ *domestic chores* 家务琐事 ◇ *the growing problem of* ***domestic violence*** (= violence between members of the same family) 日趋严重的家庭暴力问题 ◇ ***domestic service*** (= the work of a servant in a large house) 家政服务 **3** liking home life; enjoying or good at cooking, cleaning the house, etc. 喜爱家庭生活的；享受家庭乐趣的；乐于操持家务的: *I'm not a very domestic sort of person.* 我不是那种很喜欢待在家里的人。 **4** (of animals 动物) kept on farms or as pets; not wild 驯养的；作宠物饲养的；非野生的 ▶ **do·mes·tic·al·ly** AW /-kli/ *adv.*: *domestically produced goods* 本国产品

■ ***noun*** **1** (*also* **ˌdomestic ˈhelp**, **ˌdomestic ˈworker**) a servant who works in sb's house, doing the cleaning and other jobs 家佣；佣人 **2** (*BrE, informal*) a fight between two members of the same family 家庭纠纷；家庭矛盾: *The police were called to sort out a domestic.* 已叫警察来解决家庭纠纷。

do·mes·ti·cate AW /dəˈmestɪkeɪt/ *verb* **1** ~ **sth** to make a wild animal used to living with or working for humans 驯养，驯化（动物） **2** ~ **sth** to grow plants or crops for human use, especially for the first time 培育（植物）；栽培（农作物） **3** ~ **sb** (*often humorous*) to make sb good at cooking, caring for a house, etc.; to make sb enjoy home life 使精于家务；使喜家居: *Some men are very hard to domesticate.* 有些男人很难做好家务活。 ▶ **do·mes·ti·cated** AW *adj.*: *domesticated animals* 驯养的动物 ◇ *They've become a lot more domesticated since they got married.* 他们婚后恋家多了。 **do·mes·ti·ca·tion** /dəˌmestɪˈkeɪʃn/ *noun* [U]: *the domestication of cattle* 牛的驯养

do·mes·ti·city /ˌdəʊmeˈstɪsəti; ˌdɒm-; *NAmE* ˌdoʊ-; ˌdɑːm-/ *noun* [U] home or family life 家庭生活: *an atmosphere of happy domesticity* 幸福的家庭生活气氛

do,mestic 'science *noun* (*old-fashioned, BrE*) = HOME ECONOMICS

'dome tent *noun* a tent which forms the shape of a dome 圆顶帐篷 ➲ COMPARE FRAME TENT, RIDGE TENT

domi·cile /'dɒmɪsaɪl; *NAmE* 'dɑːm-; 'doʊm-/ *noun* (*formal* or *law* 律) the place where sb lives, especially when it is stated for official or legal purposes（尤指正式或法律意义的）住处，住所，定居地

domi·ciled /'dɒmɪsaɪld; *NAmE* 'dɑːm-; 'doʊm-/ *adj.* [not before noun] (*formal* or *law* 律) living in a particular place 定居；在固定住所生活：*to be domiciled in the United Kingdom* 在英国定居

domi·cil·iary /,dɒmɪ'sɪliəri; *NAmE* ,dɑːmə'sɪlieri; ,doʊ-/ *adj.* [only before noun] (*formal*) in sb's home 在住所的；在家中的：*a* ***domiciliary visit*** (= for example, by a doctor) 家访 ◇ ***domiciliary care/services/treatment*** 入户护理 / 诊治

dom·in·ant AW /'dɒmɪnənt; *NAmE* 'dɑːm-/ *adj.* **1** more important, powerful or noticeable than other things 首要的；占支配地位的；占优势的；显著的：*The firm has achieved a dominant position in the world market.* 这家公司在国际市场上占有举足轻重的地位。◇ *The dominant feature of the room was the large fireplace.* 这间屋子要数那个大壁炉最显眼了。 **2** (*biology* 生) a **dominant** GENE causes a person to have a particular physical characteristic, for example brown eyes, even if only one of their parents has passed on this GENE（基因）显性的，优势的 ➲ COMPARE RECESSIVE ▸ **dom·in·ance** AW /'dɒmɪnəns; *NAmE* 'dɑː-/ *noun* [U]: *to achieve/assert dominance over sb* 取得对某人的支配地位 ◇ *political/economic dominance* 政治 / 经济上的优势

dom·in·ate 🔑 AW /'dɒmɪneɪt; *NAmE* 'dɑːm-/ *verb* **1** 🔑 [T, I] ~ (**sb/sth**) to control or have a lot of influence over sb/sth, especially in an unpleasant way 支配；控制；左右；影响：*As a child he was dominated by his father.* 他小时候由父亲主宰一切。◇ *He tended to dominate the conversation.* 他往往左右着交谈的内容。◇ *She always says a lot in meetings, but she doesn't dominate.* 她在会上总是滔滔不绝，但她的话没什么影响。 **2** 🔑 [T] ~ **sth** to be the most important or noticeable feature of sth 在…中具有最重要（或明显）的特色：*The train crash dominated the news.* 火车相撞事故成了最重要的新闻。 **3** [T] ~ **sth** to be the largest, highest or most obvious thing in a place 在…中最显眼的位置；俯视；高耸于：*The cathedral dominates the city.* 大教堂俯视全城。 **4** [T, I] ~ (**sth**) (*sport* 体育) to play much better than your opponent in a game（在比赛中）占有优势，占据主动，控制战局：*Arsenal dominated the first half of the match.* 阿森纳队在上半场比赛中占据上风。 ▸ **dom·in·ation** AW /,dɒmɪ'neɪʃn; *NAmE* ,dɑː-/ *noun* [U]: *political domination* 政治上的支配 ◇ *companies fighting for domination of the software market* 争取控制软件市场的各家公司

dom·in·atrix /,dɒmɪ'neɪtrɪks; *NAmE* ,dɑːm-/ *noun* (*pl.* **dom·in·atri·ces** /,dɒmɪ'neɪtrɪsiːz; *NAmE* ,dɑːm-/, **dom·in·atrixes**) a woman who controls a man during sex, often using violence to give sexual pleasure 虐恋女主人（性生活中常以性虐待等制伏男子）

dom·in·eer·ing /,dɒmɪ'nɪərɪŋ; *NAmE* ,dɑːmə'nɪr-/ *adj.* (*disapproving*) trying to control other people without considering their opinions or feelings 专断的；盛气凌人的：*a cold and domineering father* 冷漠而专制的父亲 ◇ *a domineering manner* 专断的态度

Do·min·ic·an /də'mɪnɪkən/ *noun* a member of a Christian group of MONKS or NUNS following the rules of St Dominic 多明我会修士 ▸ **Do·min·ic·an** *adj.*

do·min·ion /də'mɪniən/ *noun* **1** [U] ~ (**over sb/sth**) (*literary*) authority to rule; control 统治（权）；管辖；支配：*Man has dominion over the natural world.* 人类拥有对自然界的统治权。◇ *Soon the whole country was under his sole dominion.* 不久，他便独揽了整个国家的大权。 **2** [C] (*formal*) an area controlled by one ruler 领土；版图：*the vast dominions of the Roman Empire* 罗马帝国的辽阔疆域 **3** (*often* **Dominion**) [C] (in the past 旧时) any of the countries of the British Commonwealth that had their own government（英联邦）自治领 ➲ COMPARE COLONY, PROTECTORATE (1)

dom·ino /'dɒmɪnəʊ; *NAmE* 'dɑːmənoʊ/ *noun* (*pl.* **-oes**) **1** [C] a small flat block, often made of wood, marked on one side with two groups of dots representing numbers, used for playing games 多米诺骨牌 ➲ VISUAL VOCAB PAGE V42 **2** **dominoes** [U] a game played with a set of dominoes, in which players take turns to put them onto a table 多米诺骨牌游戏

'domino effect *noun* [usually sing.] a situation in which one event causes a series of similar events to happen one after the other 多米诺（骨牌）效应；连锁反应

dom·pas /'dɒmpʌs; *NAmE* 'dɔːm-/ *noun* (*SAfrE, informal, disapproving*) (in South Africa in the past) the official document that black people had to carry with them to prove their identity and where they could live or work（旧时南非黑人的）身份证，居住证

don /dɒn; *NAmE* dɑːn/ *noun, verb*

■ ***noun*** **1** (*BrE*) a teacher at a university, especially Oxford or Cambridge（尤指牛津大学和剑桥大学的）大学教师 ➲ SEE ALSO DONNISH **2** (*informal*) the leader of a group of criminals involved with the Mafia 黑手党头目

■ ***verb*** (-nn-) ~ **sth** (*formal*) to put clothes, etc. on 披上；穿上；戴上：*He donned his jacket and went out.* 他穿上短上衣出去了。

do·nate /dəʊ'neɪt; *NAmE* 'doʊneɪt/ *verb* **1** ~ **sth** (**to sb/sth**) to give money, food, clothes, etc. to sb/sth, especially a charity（尤指向慈善机构）捐赠，赠送：*He donated thousands of pounds to charity.* 他向慈善事业捐款数千英镑。 **2** ~ **sth** (**to sb/sth**) to allow doctors to remove blood or a body organ in order to help sb who needs it 献（血）；捐献（器官）：*All donated blood is tested for HIV and other infections.* 对所有捐献的血液都会进行艾滋病病毒和其他传染病病毒的检测。

do·na·tion /dəʊ'neɪʃn; *NAmE* doʊ-/ *noun* [C, U] something that is given to a person or an organization such as a charity, in order to help them; the act of giving sth in this way 捐赠物；捐赠；赠送：~ (**to sb/sth**) *to make a* ***donation*** *to charity* 向慈善事业捐赠 ◇ *a* ***generous/large/small donation*** 慷慨 / 大量 / 少量捐助 ◇ ~ (**of…**) *a donation of £200/a £200 donation* * 200 英镑的捐款 ◇ *The work of the charity is funded by voluntary donations.* 这家慈善机构工作所需资金是人们自愿捐赠的。◇ ***organ donation*** (= allowing doctors to use an organ from your body in order to save a sick person's life) 器官捐献 ➲ WORDFINDER NOTE AT CHARITY

doncha /'dəʊntʃə; *NAmE* 'doʊ-/ *short form* (*non-standard* or *humorous*) don't you（don't you 的非正式形式）：*The yearbook came out pretty good, doncha think?* 年鉴做出来还不错，你说呢？ ➲ MORE LIKE THIS 5, page R25

done /dʌn/ *adj., exclamation* ➲ SEE ALSO DO[1] *v.*

■ ***adj.*** [not before noun] **1** finished; completed 完毕；了结；结束：*When you're done, perhaps I can say something.* 等你说完，也许我可以说点什么。◇ ~ **with** *I'll be glad when this job is over and done with.* 这个工作彻底完成后我就高兴了。 **2** (of food 食物) cooked enough 煮熟；熟了：*The meat isn't quite done yet.* 这肉还不太熟。 **3** socially acceptable, especially among people who have a strict set of social rules 合乎礼仪；合乎规矩；得体：*At school, it simply wasn't done to show that you cared for anything except cricket.* 在学校里，你对什么都显得关心，就是不关心板球，这显然不对。

IDM **be 'done for** (*informal*) to be in a very bad situation; to be certain to fail 处境艰难；注定完蛋；肯定不行：*Unless we start making some sales, we're done for.* 如果我们还卖不出去，那我们就完了。◇ *When he pointed the gun at me, I thought I was done for* (= about to die). 他把枪对准我时，我以为我死定了。 **be/get 'done for sth/for doing sth** (*BrE, informal*) to be caught and punished for doing sth illegal but not too serious 因轻微违法行为受罚：*I got* *done for speeding on my way back.* 我在返回的路上因超速行驶而受罚。 **be done 'in** (*informal*) to be extremely tired 累得够受；精疲力竭 **SYN exhausted** **be the ˌdone 'thing** (*BrE*) to be socially acceptable behaviour 是合乎礼仪的行为；是得体的行为 **be/have 'done with sth** to have finished dealing with sb, or doing or using sth 与（某人）断绝关系；做完（某事）；用完（某物）：*If you've done with that magazine, can I have a look at it?* 如果你已看完那本杂志，给我看看行吗？ **a ˌdone 'deal** an agreement or a plan that has been finally completed or agreed 达成的协议；决定了的计划：*The merger is by no means a done deal yet.* 合并之事远未成定局。 **done and 'dusted** (*BrE, informal*) completely finished 完全结束；彻底完成：*That's my article for the magazine done and dusted.* 这就是我为该杂志写的文章，已经脱稿。 ➲ MORE LIKE THIS 13, page R26 **have 'done with it** (*BrE*) to do sth unpleasant as quickly as possible, so that it is finished 赶快了结，尽快做完（令人不愉快的事）：*Why not tell her you're quitting and have done with it?* 为什么不告诉她你打算辞职，尽快把这件事了结呢？ ➲ MORE AT EASY *adv.*, HARD *adv.*, SOON

■ ***exclamation*** used to show that you accept an offer（接受提议）行，好：*'I'll give you £800 for it.' 'Done!'* "我出 800 英镑买它。" "成交！"

doner kebab /ˌdɒnə krˈbæb; *NAmE* ˌdoʊnər/ *noun* (*BrE*) thin slices of cooked meat, usually served with PITTA bread 烤肉串，烤羊肉串（通常夹入面包中食用）➲ SEE ALSO KEBAB

donga /ˈdɒŋgə; *NAmE* ˈdɑːŋgə; ˈdɔːŋgə/ *noun* (*SAfrE*) a deep channel in the ground that is formed by the action of water（水流冲出的）深沟；陡岸干沟：*The car slid into a donga at the side of the road.* 汽车滑进了路旁边的深沟。

don·gle /ˈdɒŋgl; *NAmE* ˈdɑːŋgl; ˈdɔːŋgl/ *noun* (*computing* 计) a small device that is used with a computer, especially to access protected software or the Internet 软件保护器；软件狗；硬件锁

Don Juan /ˌdɒn ˈdʒuən; ˌdɒn ˈhwɑːn; *NAmE* ˌdɑːn/ *noun* (*informal*) a man who has sex with a lot of women 唐璜；风流浪荡子；滥交的男子 ➲ MORE LIKE THIS 17, page R27 **ORIGIN** From the name of a character from Spanish legend who was skilled at persuading women to have sex with him. 源自西班牙传说中人物的姓名，此人擅长勾引女人和其发生关系。

don·key /ˈdɒŋki; *NAmE* ˈdɔːŋ-; ˈdɑːŋ-/ *noun* an animal of the horse family, with short legs and long ears. People ride donkeys or use them to carry heavy loads. 驴
IDM **'donkey's years** (*BrE, informal*) a very long time 很长时间：*We've known each other for donkey's years.* 我们已认识多年。 ➲ MORE AT TALK *v.*

'donkey jacket *noun* (*BrE*) a thick short coat, usually dark blue, worn especially by people working outside（尤指野外作业工人穿的深蓝色）短厚外衣

'donkey work *noun* [U] (*informal*) the hard boring part of a job or task 单调的苦差事

don·nish /ˈdɒnɪʃ; *NAmE* ˈdɑːn-/ *adj.* (*BrE*) (usually of a man 通常指男人) serious and concerned with academic rather than practical matters 学究式的：*He has a somewhat donnish air about him.* 他身上有点学究气。

donor /ˈdəʊnə(r); *NAmE* ˈdoʊ-/ *noun* **1** a person or an organization that makes a gift of money, clothes, food, etc. to a charity, etc. 捐赠者；捐赠机构：*international aid donors* (= countries which give money, etc. to help other countries) 国际援助国 ◇ *She is one of the charity's main donors.* 她是这一慈善机构的主要捐赠者之一。 **2** a person who gives blood or a part of his or her body to be used by doctors in medical treatment 献血者；器官捐献者：*a blood donor* 献血者 ◇ *The heart transplant will take place as soon as a suitable donor can be found.* 一找到合适的捐献者即可进行心脏移植手术。 ◇ *donor organs* 捐献的器官 ◇ *a donor card* (= a card that you carry giving permission for doctors to use parts of your body after your death) 器官捐献卡（持有者同意死后将器官捐献）

don't /dəʊnt; *NAmE* doʊnt/ *short form* do not

ˌdon't-'know *noun* a person who does not have a strong opinion about a question which they are asked in an OPINION POLL（回答问卷）没有明确意见的人：*A quarter of all the people surveyed were don't-knows.* 参加问卷调查的所有人中有四分之一没有表示明确意见。

donut *noun* (*especially NAmE*) = DOUGHNUT

doo·dah /ˈduːdɑː/ (*BrE*) (*NAmE* **doo·dad** /ˈduːdæd/) *noun* (*informal*) a small object whose name you have forgotten or do not know（忘掉名称或叫不出名目的）小装置，小玩意儿

doo·dle /ˈduːdl/ *verb* [I] to draw lines, shapes, etc., especially when you are bored or thinking about sth else（尤指厌烦或心不在焉时）乱涂，胡写乱画：*I often doodle when I'm on the phone.* 我打电话时常常信手乱画。 ▶ **doo·dle** *noun*

doo·fus /ˈduːfəs/ *noun* (*NAmE, informal*) a stupid person 蠢人；笨蛋

doo·hickey /ˈduːhɪki/ *noun* (*NAmE, informal*) a small object whose name you have forgotten or do not know, especially part of a machine 那玩意儿（尤指忘掉名称或叫不出名目的机器部件）

doo·lal·ly /duːˈlæli/ *adj.* [not before noun] (*BrE, informal*) crazy 发疯；疯了：*The poor chap's gone doolally.* 这可怜的家伙疯了。

doom /duːm/ *noun, verb*

■ ***noun*** [U] death or destruction; any terrible event that you cannot avoid 死亡；毁灭；厄运；劫数：***to meet your doom*** 死亡 ◇ *She had **a sense of impending doom*** (= felt that sth very bad was going to happen). 她预感到厄运已经逼近。
IDM **ˌdoom and 'gloom | ˌgloom and 'doom** a general feeling of having lost all hope, and of PESSIMISM (= expecting things to go badly) 悲观失望；无望；前景暗淡：*Despite the obvious setbacks, it is not all doom and gloom for the England team.* 尽管明显受挫，但对英格兰队来说绝非胜利无望。 ➲ MORE LIKE THIS 12, page R26 **ˌprophet of 'doom | 'doom merchant** a person who predicts that things will go very badly 末日预言者：*The prophets of doom who said television would kill off the book were wrong.* 认为电视会扼杀书籍的悲观预言家完全错了。

■ ***verb*** [usually passive] **~ sb/sth (to sth) | ~ sb/sth to do sth** to make sb/sth certain to fail, suffer, die, etc. 使…注定失败（或遭殃、死亡等）：*The plan was **doomed to failure**.* 这个计划注定要失败。 ◇ *The marriage was **doomed from the start**.* 这桩婚姻从一开始就注定要破裂。

'doom-laden *adj.* [usually before noun] predicting or leading to death or destruction 预示灭亡的；导致毁灭的：*doom-laden economic forecasts* 经济注定要崩溃的预报

doom·sayer /ˈduːmseɪə(r)/ (*especially NAmE*) (*BrE also* **doom·ster** /ˈduːmstə(r)/) *noun* a person who says that sth very bad is going to happen 凶事预示者；预言灾难者

dooms·day /ˈduːmzdeɪ/ *noun* [sing.] the last day of the world when Christians believe that everyone will be judged by God 最后审判日，世界末日（基督教认为在这一天世人都将接受上帝的审判）
IDM **till 'doomsday** (*informal*) a very long time; for ever 直到世界末日；很长时间；永远：*This job's going to take me till doomsday.* 这项工作要花去我一生一世的心血。

doomy /ˈduːmi/ *adj.* (**doom·ier**, **doomi·est**) suggesting disaster and unhappiness 显示灾难（或厄运）的；令人沮丧的：*doomy predictions* 不祥的预测 ◇ *Their new album is their doomiest.* 他们的新专辑是他们最失败的作品。

Doona™ /ˈduːnə/ *noun* (*AustralE*) a large cloth bag that is filled with feathers or other soft material and that you have on top of you in bed to keep yourself warm 多纳（羽绒）被；棉被 **SYN duvet**

D

door /dɔː(r)/ *noun* **1** [C] a piece of wood, glass, etc. that is opened and closed so that people can get in and out of a room, building, car, etc.; a similar thing in a cupboard/closet 门：*a knock on the door* 敲门 ◇ *to open/shut/close/slam/lock/bolt the door* 开门；关门；砰地关上门；锁门；闩门 ◇ *to answer the door* (= to go and open it because sb has knocked on it or rung the bell) 应门（听到敲门或门铃响后去开门）◇ *the front/back door* (= at the entrance at the front/back of a building) 前门；后门 ◇ *the bedroom door* 卧室门 ◇ *the door frame* 门框 ◇ *a four-door saloon car* 四门轿车 ◇ *the fridge door* 冰箱门 ◇ *Shut the door!* 把门关上！◇ *Close the door behind you, please.* 请随手关门。◇ *The door closed behind him.* 他一出门，门就关上了。➲ VISUAL VOCAB PAGES V26, V56 ➲ SEE ALSO BACK-DOOR, FIRE DOOR, FRENCH DOOR, OPEN DOOR *n.*, REVOLVING DOOR, SLIDING DOOR, STABLE DOOR, STAGE DOOR, SWING DOOR, TRAPDOOR **2** [C] the space when a door is open 出入口；门口：*Marc appeared through a door at the far end of the room.* 马克从房间另一端的门口出现。◇ (*informal*) *She's just arrived—she's just* **come in the door**. 她刚到，刚踏进门。◇ (*informal*) *He walked* **out the door**. 他出门去了。**3** [C] the area close to the entrance of a building 门边；门旁：*There's somebody* **at the door** (= at the front door of a house). 门口有人。◇ *'Can I help you?' asked the man at the door.* "我能为您效劳吗？"门边的男子问道。➲ SEE ALSO DOORWAY **4** [C] a house, room, etc. that is a particular number of houses, rooms, etc. away from another 栋；住户；人家：*the family that lives three doors up from us* 住在与我们相隔三户的那户人家 ◇ *Our other branch is just a few doors down the road.* 我们的另一家分店沿路过几个门面就到。➲ SEE ALSO NEXT DOOR *n.* **5** [U] (*BrE*) the amount of money made by selling tickets for an event 票房收入 SYN **gate**: *50% of the door will go to the Red Cross.* * 50% 的票房收入将捐给红十字会。

IDM **be on the door** to work at the entrance to a theatre, club, etc., for example collecting tickets from people as they enter 把门（在戏院、夜总会等门口做检票等工作）**close/shut the 'door on sth** to make it unlikely that sth will happen 使不可能；拒…于门外；把…的门堵死：*She was careful not to close the door on the possibility of further talks.* 她小心翼翼不让进一步谈判的大门关上。**(from) ˌdoor to 'door** from building to building 从一栋房子到另一栋房子；从一处到另一处；挨家挨户：*The journey takes about an hour door to door.* 全程大约要花一个小时。◇ *a door-to-door salesman* 走家串户的推销员 **(open) the door to sth** (to provide) the means of getting or reaching sth; (to create) the opportunity for sth （为…提供）达到目的的手段；（为…创造）机会：*The agreement will open the door to increased international trade.* 此协议将会提供增长国际贸易的机会。◇ *Our courses are the door to success in English.* 我们的课程是通向掌握英语的成功之路。**lay sth at sb's 'door** (*formal*) to say that sb is responsible for sth that has gone wrong 把…归咎于某人；认为某人应对…负责 **leave the door 'open (for sth)** to make sure that there is still the possibility of doing sth 不把门堵死；保留可能性 **out of 'doors** not inside a building 在户外；露天：*You should spend more time out of doors in the fresh air.* 你应多花点时间在户外呼吸新鲜空气。**shut/slam the door in sb's face 1** to shut a door hard when sb is trying to come in 将某人拒之门外；让某人吃闭门羹 **2** to refuse to talk to sb or meet them, in a rude way 拒绝同某人谈话；拒绝见某人 **to sb's door** directly to sb's house 直接到某人的家：*We promise to deliver to your door within 48 hours of you ordering.* 我们承诺在接到订单后 48 小时内送货上门。➲ MORE AT BACK DOOR, BARN, BEAT *v.*, CLOSE[1] *v.*, CLOSED, DARKEN, DEATH, FOOT *n.*, OPEN *v.*, SHOW *v.*, STABLE DOOR, WOLF *n.*

door·bell /ˈdɔːbel; *NAmE* ˈdɔːrbel/ *noun* a bell with a button outside a house that you push to let the people inside know that you are there 门铃：*to ring the doorbell* 按门铃

ˌdo-or-ˈdie *adj.* having or needing great determination 一往无前的；破釜沉舟的：*a do-or-die attitude* 孤注一掷的态度

ˈdoor furniture *noun* [U] (*BrE, specialist*) the handles, KNOCKERS, etc. on a door 门配件

door·keeper /ˈdɔːkiːpə(r); *NAmE* ˈdɔːrk-/ *noun* a person who guards the entrance to a large building, especially to check on people going in 看门人；守门人

door·knob /ˈdɔːnɒb; *NAmE* ˈdɔːrnɑːb/ *noun* a type of round handle for a door, that you turn in order to open the door 球形门拉手

ˈdoor knocker *noun* = KNOCKER

door·man /ˈdɔːmən; *NAmE* ˈdɔːrmən/ *noun* (*pl.* **-men** /-mən/) a man, often in uniform, whose job is to stand at the entrance to a large building such as a hotel or a theatre, and open the door for visitors, find them taxis, etc.（旅馆、剧院等门口身着制服的）门厅侍者 ➲ COMPARE PORTER (3)

door·mat /ˈdɔːmæt; *NAmE* ˈdɔːrmæt/ *noun* **1** a small piece of strong material near a door that people can clean their shoes on 门口地垫；门口擦鞋垫 **2** (*informal*) a person who allows other people to treat them badly but usually does not complain 逆来顺受的可怜虫；受气包

door·nail /ˈdɔːneɪl; *NAmE* ˈdɔːrn-/ *noun* IDM SEE DEAD *adj.*

door·step /ˈdɔːstep; *NAmE* ˈdɔːrs-/ *noun, verb*

■ *noun* **1** a step outside a door of a building, or the area that is very close to the door 门阶：*The police turned up on their doorstep at 3 o'clock this morning.* 今天凌晨 3 点，警察出现在他们的住所门前。➲ VISUAL VOCAB PAGE V18 **2** (*BrE, informal*) a thick piece of bread, usually one that is made into a SANDWICH（常用以做三明治的）厚面包片

IDM **on the/your 'doorstep** very close to where a person lives 在某人的住所旁：*The nightlife is great with bars and clubs right on the doorstep.* 有这些酒吧和夜总会在家门口，夜生活真是棒极了。

■ *verb* (**-pp-**) [T, I] ~ (**sb**) (*BrE*) when a journalist **doorsteps** sb, he or she goes to the person's house to try to speak to them, even if they do not want to say anything（记者）登门采访，蹲守

door·stop /ˈdɔːstɒp; *NAmE* ˈdɔːrstɑːp/ *noun* a thing that is used to stop a door from closing or to prevent it from hitting and damaging a wall when it is opened（防止门关闭的）制门器；（防止门开时撞墙的）门碰头

door·way /ˈdɔːweɪ; *NAmE* ˈdɔːrweɪ/ *noun* an opening into a building or a room, where the door is 门口；门道；出入口：*She stood* **in the doorway** *for a moment before going in.* 她在门口站了一会儿才进去。◇ *homeless people sleeping in shop doorways* 露宿商店门口无家可归的人

doo·zy (*also* **doo·zie**) /ˈduːzi/ *noun* (*pl.* **-ies**) (*NAmE, informal*) something that is very special or unusual 异乎寻常的东西；独特的事物

dop /dɒp; *NAmE* dɑːp/ *noun, verb* (*SAfrE, informal*)

■ *noun* an alcoholic drink 酒：*Let's have a dop.* 咱们喝杯酒吧。

■ *verb* (**-pp-**) **1** [I, T] ~ (**sth**) to drink alcohol, especially in large amounts （尤指大量地）喝酒；狂饮：*They lay around dopping all day.* 他们一整天无所事事都在狂饮。**2** [T] ~ **sth** (*slang*) to not pass a test or an exam; to not be successful in completing a period of study at a school, university, etc. 考试不及格；学期（或学年）成绩不合格：*I dopped my first year at varsity.* 我在大学的第一年学习很糟糕。

dopa·mine /ˈdəʊpəmiːn; *NAmE* ˈdoʊ-/ *noun* [U] a chemical produced by nerve cells which has an effect on other cells 多巴胺（神经细胞产生的一种作用于其他细胞的化学物质）

dope /dəʊp; *NAmE* doʊp/ *noun, verb*

■ *noun* **1** [U] (*informal*) a drug that is taken illegally for pleasure, especially CANNABIS or, in the US, HEROIN 麻醉剂，毒品（尤指大麻，在美国尤指海洛因） **2** [U] a drug that is taken by a person or given to an animal to affect their performance in a race or sport 兴奋剂：*The athlete failed a* ***dope test*** (= a medical test showed that he had taken such drugs). 这个运动员未能通过药检。 **3** [C] (*informal*) a stupid person 笨蛋；呆子；蠢货 SYN **idiot** **4** [U] **the ~** (**on sb/sth**) (*informal*) information on sb/sth, especially details that are not generally known 内幕消息；情报：*Give me the dope on the new boss.* 把新上司的底细告诉我吧。

■ *verb* **1 ~ sb/sth** to give a drug to a person or an animal in order to affect their performance in a race or sport 给…用兴奋剂 **2 ~ sb/sth** to give sb a drug, often in their food or drink, in order to make them unconscious; to put a drug in food, etc. 给…服麻醉剂；在（食物、饮料）中掺麻醉剂：*Thieves doped a guard dog and stole $10 000 worth of goods.* 盗贼将看门狗麻醉后偷走了价值 1 万美元的东西。◇ *The wine was doped.* 这酒掺有麻醉药。 **3** [usually passive] **~ sb** (**up**) (*informal*) if sb is **doped** or **doped up**, they cannot think clearly or act normally because they are under the influence of drugs 给…用麻醉药；使昏昏沉沉；使药力发作

dopey /ˈdəʊpi; *NAmE* ˈdoʊpi/ *adj.* (*informal*) (**dopi·er, dopi·est**) **1** rather stupid 愚笨的；迟钝的；呆头呆脑的：*a dopey grin* 龇牙咧嘴的傻笑 **2** not fully awake or thinking clearly, sometimes because you have taken a drug 被麻醉的；迷迷糊糊的；昏昏沉沉的：*I felt dopey and drowsy after the operation.* 手术后我感到迷迷糊糊，昏昏欲睡。

dop·pel·gän·ger /ˈdɒplɡæŋə(r); -ɡeŋ-; *NAmE* ˈdɑːpl-/ *noun* (*from German*) a person's **doppelgänger** is another person who looks exactly like them 相貌一样的人

the Dop·pler ef·fect /ˈdɒplə ɪfekt; *NAmE* ˈdɑːplər/ *noun* [sing.] (*physics* 物) the way that sound waves, light waves, etc. change according to the direction that the source is moving in with relation to the person who is observing 多普勒效应（即声波、光波等按声源、光源等相对于观察者的传播方向的变化而变化）

Dop·pler shift /ˈdɒplə ʃɪft; *NAmE* ˈdɑːplər/ *noun* (*physics* 物) the change in sound, colour, etc. caused by the Doppler effect 多普勒频移（多普勒效应引起的声、色等的变化）

Dorian Gray /ˌdɔːriən ˈɡreɪ/ *noun* [usually sing.] a person who continues to look young and beautiful, even though they are growing older or behaving in an immoral way（不受年龄增长或行为不端影响）永远年轻貌美的人：*He's a real Dorian Gray, apparently untouched by the ageing process.* 他像是不受衰老过程的影响，青春永驻。 ➲ MORE LIKE THIS 17, page R27 ORIGIN From the story by Oscar Wilde, *The Picture of Dorian Gray*, in which Dorian Gray is a beautiful young man who behaves in an immoral way. He secretly keeps a painting of himself, which gradually changes, making him look older and more evil in it. Dorian himself continues to look young and beautiful. 源自奥斯卡·王尔德的小说《道林·格雷的肖像》，主人公道林·格雷年轻俊美但品行不端。在他秘密收藏的一幅画像中，他的形象逐渐变得更加衰老与丑恶，而他本人却一直年轻俊美如昔。

Doric /ˈdɒrɪk; *NAmE* ˈdɔːrɪk; ˈdɑːrɪk/ *adj.* [usually before noun] (*architecture* 建) used to describe the oldest style of ARCHITECTURE in ancient Greece that has thick plain columns and no decoration at the top 多立克柱式的（古希腊建筑风格，柱身和柱头形式简朴）：*a Doric column/temple* 多立克柱式圆柱 / 庙宇

dork /dɔːk; *NAmE* dɔːrk/ *noun* (*informal*) a stupid or boring person that other people laugh at（受人嘲笑的）呆子，无聊乏味之人 ▸ **dorky** *adj.* (**dork·ier, dorki·est**)

dorm /dɔːm; *NAmE* dɔːrm/ *noun* (*informal*) = DORMITORY

dor·mant /ˈdɔːmənt; *NAmE* ˈdɔːrm-/ *adj.* not active or growing now but able to become active or to grow in the future 休眠的；蛰伏的；暂停活动的 SYN **inactive**：*a dormant volcano* 休眠火山 ◇ *During the winter the seeds* ***lie dormant*** *in the soil.* 冬天，种子在土壤中休眠。 OPP **active** ▸ **dor·mancy** /ˈdɔːmənsi; *NAmE* ˈdɔːrm-/ *noun* [U]

ˌdormer ˈwindow (*also* **dormer**) *noun* a vertical window in a room that is built into a sloping roof 老虎窗；（建在斜屋顶上的竖式）屋顶窗，天窗 ➲ VISUAL VOCAB PAGE V18

dor·mi·tory /ˈdɔːmətri; *NAmE* ˈdɔːrmətɔːri/ *noun* (*pl.* **-ies**) (*also informal* **dorm**) **1** a room for several people to sleep in, especially in a school or other institution 集体宿舍；学生宿舍 **2** (*NAmE*) (*BrE* ˌ**hall of ˈresidence**, **hall**) a building for university or college students to live in（大学）学生宿舍

ˈdormitory town (*BrE*) (*NAmE* ˈ**bedroom community**, ˈ**bedroom suburb**) *noun* a town that people live in and from where they travel to work in a bigger town or city 郊外住宅区

dor·mouse /ˈdɔːmaʊs; *NAmE* ˈdɔːrm-/ *noun* (*pl.* **dor·mice** /-maɪs/) a small animal like a mouse, with a tail covered in fur 睡鼠

dorp /dɔːp; *NAmE* dɔːrp/ *noun* (*SAfrE, informal*) a small town or village in the country 小镇；村庄

dor·sal /ˈdɔːsl; *NAmE* ˈdɔːrsl/ *adj.* [only before noun] (*specialist*) on or connected with the back of a fish or an animal（鱼或动物）背部的，背上的，背侧的：*a shark's dorsal fin* 鲨鱼的背鳍 ➲ VISUAL VOCAB PAGE V12

dory /ˈdɔːri/ *noun* (*pl.* **-ies**) a narrow fish that has a deep body and that can open its mouth very wide 海鲂

DOS /dɒs; *NAmE* dɔːs/ *abbr.* (*computing* 计) disk operating system 磁盘操作系统；DOS 系统

dosa /ˈdəʊsə; *NAmE* ˈdoʊ-/ *noun* a southern Indian PANCAKE made with rice flour 多莎饼（印度南部的一种米粉薄饼）

dos·age /ˈdəʊsɪdʒ; *NAmE* ˈdoʊ-/ *noun* [usually sing.] an amount of sth, usually a medicine or a drug, that is taken regularly over a particular period of time（通常指药的）剂量：*a* ***high/low dosage*** 大剂量；小剂量 ◇ *to* ***increase/reduce the dosage*** 增加 / 减少剂量 ◇ *Do not exceed the* ***recommended dosage.*** 切勿超过规定剂量。

dos and don'ts ➲ DO[1] *n.*

dose /dəʊs; *NAmE* doʊs/ *noun, verb*

■ *noun* **1** an amount of a medicine or a drug that is taken once, or regularly over a period of time（药的）一剂，一服：*a* ***high/low/lethal dose*** 大 / 小 / 致死剂量 ◇ *Repeat the dose after 12 hours if necessary.* 如果需要，12 小时后再服一剂。 ➲ WORDFINDER NOTE AT MEDICINE **2** (*informal*) an amount of sth 一份；一次；一点：*A dose of flu kept me off work.* 一场感冒使得我上不了班。◇ *Workers at the nuclear plant were exposed to high doses of radiation.* 核电站的工作人员受到大量辐射。◇ *I can cope with her* ***in small doses*** (= for short amounts of time). 我只能跟她应付片刻。

IDM **like a dose of ˈsalts** (*old-fashioned, BrE, informal*) very fast and easily 迅速轻易地；一下子 ➲ MORE AT MEDICINE

■ *verb* **~ sb/yourself** (**up**) (**with sth**) to give sb/yourself a medicine or drug 给（某人）服药：*She dosed herself up with vitamin pills.* 她给自己服了一些维生素片。◇ *He was heavily dosed with painkillers.* 他服用了大量止痛药。

dosh /dɒʃ; *NAmE* dɑːʃ/ *noun* [U] (*BrE, slang*) money 钱

doss /dɒs; *NAmE* dɑːs/ *verb, noun*

■ *verb* (*BrE, slang*) **1** [I] **~** (**down**) to sleep somewhere, especially somewhere uncomfortable or without a real bed（尤指在不舒适或简陋的地方）睡觉，过夜：*You can doss down on my floor.* 你可以在我的地板上睡。 **2** [I] **~** (**about/around**) to spend your time not doing very much 混时间：*We were just dossing about in lessons today.* 今天我们只是在课堂上混时间。

■ *noun* (*BrE*) something that does not need much effort 轻松的事；不费力的事

doss·er /ˈdɒsə(r); *NAmE* ˈdɑːs-/ *noun* (*BrE*) **1** a person who has no permanent home and who lives and sleeps on the streets or in cheap HOSTELS 流浪者；露宿街头者；住廉价旅馆者 **2** (*informal*) a person who is very lazy 懒人

doss·house /ˈdɒshaʊs; *NAmE* ˈdɑːs-/ (*BrE*) (*NAmE* **flop·house**) *noun* (*informal*) a cheap place to stay for people who have no home（供流浪者投宿的）廉价客店

dos·sier /ˈdɒsieɪ; *NAmE* ˈdɔːs-; ˈdɑːs-/ *noun* (*formal*) a collection of documents that contain information about a person, an event or a subject 材料汇编；卷宗；档案 SYN **file**: *to* ***assemble/compile a dossier*** 汇编材料 ◇ **~ on sb/sth** *We have a dossier on him.* 我们有他的档案。

dot /dɒt; *NAmE* dɑːt/ *noun, verb*

■ ***noun*** **1** a small round mark, especially one that is printed 点；小点；小圆点：*There are dots above the letters i and j.* 字母 i 和 j 上面都有一点。◇ *Text and graphics are printed at 300 dots per inch.* 文字和插图按 300 点每英寸的精度打印。◇ *The helicopters appeared as two black dots on the horizon.* 直升机像两个小黑点出现在地平线上。➲ SYNONYMS AT PATCH ➲ **WORDFINDER NOTE** AT PATTERN **2** (*computing* 计) a symbol like a full stop/period used to separate parts of a DOMAIN NAME, a URL or an email address 点（用以分隔域名、统一资源地址、电子邮件地址的组成部分）

IDM **on the ˈdot** (*informal*) exactly on time or at the exact time mentioned 准时；在指定时刻：*The taxi showed up on the dot.* 出租车准时到了。◇ *Breakfast is served at 8 on the dot.* * 8 点整开早饭。➲ MORE AT YEAR

■ ***verb*** (**-tt-**) **1 ~ sth** to put a dot above or next to a letter or word 在（字母上方、字母或单词旁边）加点：*Why do you never dot your i's?* 你为什么从不在字母 i 上加点呢？ **2** [usually passive] **~ sth** to spread things or people over an area; to be spread over an area 星罗棋布于；遍布：*The countryside was* ***dotted with*** *small villages.* 乡间有星罗棋布的小村庄。◇ *Small villages dot the countryside.* 小村庄星罗棋布于乡间。◇ *There are lots of Italian restaurants* ***dotted around*** *London.* 伦敦到处都有意大利餐馆。 **3** to put very small amounts of sth in a number of places on a surface 使布满；点缀：**~ A on/over B** *Dot the cream all over your face.* 将乳霜均匀地搽在脸上。◇ **~ B with A** *Dot your face with the cream.* 将乳霜搽在脸上。

IDM **dot your ˌi's and cross your ˈt's** to pay attention to the small details when you are finishing a task（完成任务时）一丝不苟，注重细节

dot·age /ˈdəʊtɪdʒ; *NAmE* ˈdoʊ-/ *noun*

IDM **be in your dotage** to be old and not always able to think clearly 年老昏聩；年老糊涂

dot-com (*also* **dot·com**) /ˌdɒt ˈkɒm; *NAmE* ˌdɑːt ˈkɑːm/ *noun* a company that sells goods and services on the Internet, especially one whose address ends '.com'（尤指网址末尾为 .com 的）网络公司：*The weaker dot-coms collapsed.* 实力较弱的网络公司倒闭了。◇ *a dot-com millionaire* 一位网络公司富翁

dote /dəʊt; *NAmE* doʊt/ *verb*

PHR V **ˈdote on/upon sb** to feel and show great love for sb, ignoring their faults 溺爱；宠爱；过分喜爱：*He dotes on his children.* 他溺爱他的孩子。➲ SYNONYMS AT LOVE

dot·ing /ˈdəʊtɪŋ; *NAmE* ˈdoʊtɪŋ/ *adj.* [only before noun] showing a lot of love for sb, often ignoring their faults 溺爱的；宠爱的

ˌdot ˈmatrix printer *noun* a machine that prints letters, numbers, etc. formed from very small dots 点阵打印机

dot·ted /ˈdɒtɪd; *NAmE* ˈdɑːt-/ *adj.* **1** covered in dots 有斑点的；星罗棋布的 **2** [only before noun] (*music* 音) (of a musical note 音符) followed by a dot to show that it is one and a half times the length of the same note without the dot 加附点的

ˌdotted ˈline *noun* a line made of dots 点线；虚线：*Country boundaries are shown on this map as dotted lines.* 这张地图上国界以虚线标出。◇ *Fold along the dotted line.* 沿虚线折叠。◇ *Write your name on the dotted line.* 把名字填在虚线上。IDM SEE SIGN *v.*

dotty /ˈdɒti; *NAmE* ˈdɑːti/ *adj.* (**dot·tier**, **dot·ti·est**) (*old-fashioned, BrE, informal*) **1** slightly crazy or silly 疯疯癫癫的；半痴的；低能的 SYN **eccentric** **2 ~ about sb/sth** having romantic feelings for sb; being enthusiastic about sth 迷恋；充满热情；着迷

double /ˈdʌbl/ *adj., det., adv., noun, verb*

■ ***adj.*** [usually before noun]

• **TWICE AS MUCH/MANY** 两倍 **1** twice as much or as many as usual 两倍的；加倍的：*a double helping* 一客双份的食物 ◇ *two double whiskies* 两杯双份的威士忌酒

• **WITH TWO PARTS** 成双 **2** having or made of two things or parts that are equal or similar 双的；成双的；成对的：*double doors* 双扇门 ◇ *a double-page advertisement* 双页广告 ◇ *'Otter' is spelt with a double t.* * otter 一词中有两个 t。◇ *My extension is two four double 0 (2400).* 我的分机号是 2400。

• **FOR TWO PEOPLE** 双人 **3** made for two people or things 供两者用的；双人的：*a* ***double bed/room*** 双人床；双人房间 ➲ **VISUAL VOCAB** PAGE V24 ➲ COMPARE SINGLE *adj.* (4)

• **COMBINING TWO THINGS** 双重 **4** combining two things or qualities 双重的：*a* ***double meaning/purpose/aim*** 双重意义 / 目的 / 目标 ◇ *It has the double advantage of being both easy and cheap.* 它具有既方便又便宜的双重优点。

■ ***det.*** **TWICE AS MUCH/MANY** 两倍 twice as much or as many as 两倍的；双倍的：*His income is double hers.* 他的收入是她的两倍。◇ *He earns double what she does.* 他挣的钱是她的两倍。◇ *We need double the amount we already have.* 我们需要现有数量的两倍。

■ ***adv.*** **IN TWO PARTS** 成双 in twos or in two parts 双双地；成对地：*I thought I was* ***seeing double*** (= seeing two of sth). 我以为我是看到重影了。◇ *Fold the blanket double.* 把毯子对折起来。◇ *I had to* ***bend double*** *to get under the table.* 我必须弓着身子才能钻到桌子底下。

■ ***noun***

• **TWICE AS MUCH/MANY** 两倍 **1** [U] twice the number or amount 两倍；两倍数；两倍量：*He gets paid double for doing the same job I do.* 他与我做同样的工作，但报酬却比我多一倍。

• **ALCOHOLIC DRINK** 酒精饮料 **2** [C] a glass of strong alcoholic drink containing twice the usual amount 一杯双份的烈酒：*Two Scotches, please—and make those doubles, will you?* 请来两杯苏格兰威士忌，两杯都要双份的，好吗？

• **PERSON/THING** 人；物 **3** [C] a person or thing that looks exactly like another 酷似的人；极相似的对应物：*She's the double of her mother.* 她和她母亲长得一模一样。 **4** [C] an actor who replaces another actor in a film/movie to do dangerous or other special things （电影中的）替身演员 ➲ SEE ALSO BODY DOUBLE

• **BEDROOM** 卧室 **5** [C] = DOUBLE ROOM：*Is that a single or a double you want?* 你要的是单人房间还是双人房间？ ➲

▼ **WHICH WORD?** 词语辨析

double / dual

These adjectives are frequently used with the following nouns. 这两个形容词常与下列名词连用：

double ~	**dual ~**
bed	purpose
doors	function
figures	role
standards	approach
thickness	citizenship

• **Dual** describes something that has two parts, uses or aspects. * dual 描述有两个部分、两种用途或两个方面的事物。

• **Double** can be used with a similar meaning, but when it is used to describe something that has two parts, the two parts are usually the same or very similar. * double 具有相似的意思，但所描述事物的两个部分通常是相同或相似的。

• **Double**, but not **dual**, can describe something that is made for two people or things, or is twice as big as usual. 指供给两人或两事物的东西或较平常大一倍的东西用 double，不用 dual。

COMPARE SINGLE *n.* (3)

• **IN SPORT** 体育运动 **6 doubles** [U+sing./pl. v.] a game, especially of TENNIS, in which one pair plays another 双打（尤指网球）: *mixed doubles* (= in which each pair consists of a man and a woman) 混合双打 ➲ COMPARE SINGLES at SINGLE *n.* (6) **7 the double** [sing.] the fact of winning two important competitions or beating the same player or team twice, in the same season or year（在同一赛季或年份）两场大赛获胜，两次打败同一对手

IDM **at the 'double** (*BrE*) (*NAmE* **on the 'double**) (*informal*) quickly; hurrying 迅速地；尽快地；赶紧 **,double or 'quits** (*BrE*) (*NAmE* **,double or 'nothing**) (in gambling 赌博) a risk in which you could win twice the amount you pay, or you could lose all your money 要么赢双倍，要么输得精光

■ *verb*

• **BECOME TWICE AS MUCH/MANY** 加倍 **1** 🔑 [I, T] to become, or make sth become, twice as much or as many（使）加倍；是…的两倍：*Membership almost doubled in two years.* 两年内会员数目几乎翻了一番。◇ **~ sth** *Double all the quantities in the recipe to make enough for eight people.* 把菜谱上的量都增加一倍以够八人用餐。

• **FOLD** 折叠 **2** [T] **~ sth (over)** to bend or fold sth so that there are two layers 把…对折；折叠：*She doubled the blanket and put it under his head.* 她把毯子折叠起来给他做枕头。

• **IN BASEBALL** 棒球 **3** [I] to hit the ball far enough for you to get to second BASE 击出二垒安打：*He doubled to left field.* 他将球击向左外场而跑上了二垒。

PHR V **'double as sth | ,double 'up as sth** to have another use or function as well as the main one 兼任；兼作：*The kitchen doubles as a dining room.* 这厨房兼做饭厅。 **,double 'back** to turn back and go in the direction you have come from 循原路折回 **,double 'up (on sth/with sb)** (*informal*) to form a pair in order to do sth or to share sth（两人）合用，共享：*We'll have to double up on books; there aren't enough to go around.* 因为书不够人手一册，我们只好两人合用了。◇ *They only have one room left: you'll have to double up with Peter.* 他们只剩下一个房间，你只好与彼得合住了。 **,double 'up/'over | ,double sb 'up/'over** to bend or to make your body bend over quickly, for example because you are in pain（使）弯腰，弓身：*Jo doubled up with laughter.* 乔笑弯了腰。◇ *I was doubled over with pain.* 我痛得直不起身子。

'double act *noun* two people who work together, usually to entertain an audience 双人戏；双簧

,double-'action *adj.* [usually before noun] **1** working in two ways 双效的；双功能的：*double-action tablets* 双效药片 **2** (of a gun 枪) needing two separate actions for preparing to fire and firing 双动式的（准备射击和射击需分别进行的）

,double 'agent *noun* a person who is a SPY for a particular country, and also for another country which is an enemy of the first one 双重间谍

,double 'bar *noun* (*music* 音) a pair of vertical lines at the end of a piece of music 复纵线（划分段落或结束乐曲时用）

,double-'barrelled (*especially US* **,double-'barreled**) *adj.* [usually before noun] **1** (of a gun 枪) having two BARRELS (= places where the bullets come out) 双管的 **2** (*BrE*) (of a family name 姓) having two parts, sometimes joined by a hyphen, for example 'Day-Lewis' 由两部分组成的 **3** (of a plan, etc. 计划等) having two parts, and therefore likely to be effective 双重目的的；双作用的

,double 'bass (*also* **bass**) *noun* the largest musical instrument in the VIOLIN family, that plays very low notes 低音提琴；低音大提琴 ➲ VISUAL VOCAB PAGE V38

,double 'bill (*NAmE also* **,double 'feature**) *noun* two films/movies, television programmes, etc. that are shown one after the other 连场，双场（两场电影、两个电视节目等连续播放）

,double 'bind *noun* [usually sing.] a situation in which it is difficult to choose what to do because whatever you choose will have negative results 两难境地

,double-'blind *adj.* [only before noun] (of a test) conducted so that neither the organizer nor any other people involved know any information which might influence the results（测试）双盲的（研究人员和参与者都不知道可能影响结果的信息）：*A randomized double-blind study was carried out to test the drug's effectiveness.* 进行了随机双盲研究以测试药效。

,double 'bluff *noun* a way of trying to trick sb by telling them the truth while hoping that they think you are lying 虚实并用的诈骗（以实相告而期望对方以为有诈）

,double-'book *verb* [often passive] **~ sth** to promise the same room, seat, table, etc. to two different people at the same time 重复预订（将同一房间、座位、餐桌等同时预订给不同的人）➲ COMPARE OVERBOOK ▶ **,double-'booking** *noun* [C, U]

,double-'breast·ed *adj.* a **double-breasted** jacket or coat has two front parts so that one part covers the other when the buttons are done up, and two rows of buttons can be seen（上衣、外套）双排纽扣的 ➲ COMPARE SINGLE-BREASTED

,double-'check *verb* [T, I] **~ (sth) | ~ (that)...** to check sth for a second time or with great care 复核；复查；仔细审核：*I'll double-check the figures.* 我将对这些数字进行复核。▶ **,double-'check** *noun*

,double 'chin *noun* a fold of fat under a person's chin, that looks like another chin 双下巴

,double-'click *verb* [I, T] **~ (on) sth** (*computing* 计) to choose a particular function or item on a computer screen, etc. by pressing one of the buttons on a mouse twice quickly 双击

,double 'cream *noun* [U] (*BrE*) thick cream which contains a lot of fat and can be mixed so that it is no longer liquid 浓奶油 ➲ COMPARE SINGLE CREAM

,double-'cross *verb* **~ sb** to cheat or trick sb who trusts you (usually in connection with sth illegal or dishonest) 欺骗；叛卖；出卖：*He double-crossed the rest of the gang and disappeared with all the money.* 他骗了其他同伙，携款潜逃了。▶ **,double-'cross** *noun* [usually sing.]

,double 'date *noun* an occasion when two couples go out together on a DATE 双约会，四人约会（两对情侣一同赴约）▶ **,double-'date** *verb* [I]

,double-'dealer *noun* (*informal*) a dishonest person who cheats other people 两面派；口是心非者 ▶ **,double-'dealing** *noun* [U]

,double-'decker *noun* **1** a bus with two floors, one on top of the other 双层公共汽车 ➲ VISUAL VOCAB PAGE V62 ➲ COMPARE SINGLE-DECKER **2** (*NAmE*) a SANDWICH made from three pieces of bread with two layers of food between them 双层三明治

,double-'density *adj.* (*computing* 计) (of a computer disk 计算机磁盘) able to hold twice the amount of data as other older disks of the same size 倍密度的；双倍容量的

,double 'digits *noun* [pl.] (*NAmE*) = DOUBLE FIGURES ▶ **,double-'digit** *adj.* (*NAmE*) = DOUBLE-FIGURE

,double 'Dutch *noun* [U] (*BrE, informal*) speech or writing that is impossible to understand, and that seems to be nonsense 晦涩的言语（或文字）；莫名其妙的话

,double-'edged *adj.* **1** (of a knife, etc. 刀等) having two cutting edges 双刃的 **2** (of a remark, comment, etc. 言语、评论等) having two possible meanings 意义双关的；可有两种解释的；模棱两可的 **SYN** **ambiguous** **3** having two different parts or uses, often parts that contrast with each other 有双重效果的，有双重作用的（常指形成鲜明对比的两部分）：*the double-edged quality of life in a small town—security and boredom* 小城镇生活的双重性——安全但乏味

IDM **be a double-edged 'sword/'weapon** to be sth that

has both advantages and disadvantages 既有优点也有缺点；是一把双刃剑

double en·ten·dre /ˌduːbl ɒ̃ˈtɒ̃drə; *NAmE* ɑ̃ːˈtɑ̃ːdrə/ *noun* (*from French*) a word or phrase that can be understood in two different ways, one of which usually refers to sex （通常带有猥亵含义的）双关语

D

ˌdouble-entry ˈbookkeeping *noun* [U] (*business* 商) a system of keeping financial records in which each piece of business is recorded as a CREDIT in one account and a DEBIT in another 复式记账法，复式簿记（将每个账项分别登入贷记和借记）

ˌdouble ˈfault *noun* (in TENNIS 网球) the loss of a point caused by a player not SERVING correctly twice 双发失误；双误（因两次发球失误输掉的一分） ▶ **ˌdouble-ˈfault** *verb* [I]

ˌdouble ˈfeature *noun* (*NAmE*) = DOUBLE BILL

ˌdouble ˈfigures (*especially BrE*) (*NAmE usually* **ˌdouble ˈdigits**) *noun* [pl.] used to describe a number that is not less than 10 and not more than 99 两位数：*Inflation is **in double figures**.* 通货膨胀率达两位数。 ▶ **ˌdouble-ˈfigure** (*especially BrE*) (*NAmE usually* **ˌdouble-ˈdigit**) *adj.* [only before noun]: *a double-figure pay rise* 两位数的工资涨幅

ˌdouble ˈglazing *noun* [U] (*especially BrE*) windows that have two layers of glass with a space between them, designed to make the room warmer and to reduce noise 双层玻璃窗 ⊃ COLLOCATIONS AT DECORATE ▶ **ˌdouble-ˈglaze** *verb* ~ sth **ˌdouble-ˈglazed** *adj.*: *double-glazed windows* 双层玻璃窗

ˌdouble-ˈheader *noun* (*NAmE*) (in BASEBALL 棒球) two games that are played on the same day, traditionally on a Sunday, and usually by the same two teams 一日连赛两场（传统上在星期日，通常为相同的两个队）

ˌdouble ˈhelix *noun* (*biology* 生) the structure of DNA, consisting of two connected long thin pieces that form a SPIRAL shape 双螺旋（脱氧核糖核酸的结构）

ˌdouble ˈjeopardy *noun* [U] (in US law) the fact of taking sb to court twice for the same crime, or punishing sb twice for the same reason. This is not allowed under the Fifth AMENDMENT of the US CONSTITUTION. （美国法律）重复起诉（对同一罪行的重复起诉或定罪，这种情况为美国宪法第五修正案所禁止）

ˌdouble-ˈjointed *adj.* having joints in your fingers, arms, etc. that allow you to bend them both backwards and forwards 有双关节的；关节能前后弯曲的

ˌdouble ˈlife *noun* a life of a person who leads two different lives which are kept separate from each other, usually because one of them involves secret, often illegal or immoral, activities 双重人格的生活（常指其中一重人格涉及非法或不道德行为）: *to **live/lead a double life*** 过着双重人格的生活

ˌdouble ˈnegative *noun* (*grammar* 语法) a negative statement containing two negative words. 'I didn't say nothing' is a double negative because it contains two negative words, 'n't' and 'nothing'. This use is not considered correct in standard English. 双重否定（I didn't say nothing 是双重否定句，包含 n't 和 nothing 两个否定词，此用法在标准英语中被视为不正确）

ˌdouble-ˈpark *verb* [T, I, usually passive] ~ (**sth**) to park a car or other vehicle beside one that is already parked in a street 并排停放（将车停在已停放于路边的车辆旁）: *A car stood double-parked almost in the middle of the road.* 一辆车并排停在路边另一辆车旁，几乎占据了路的中央。◇ *I'll have to rush—I'm double-parked.* 我得赶紧点，我这是并排停车。

ˌdouble ˈplay *noun* (*NAmE*) (in BASEBALL 棒球) a situation in which two players are put out (= made to finish their attempt at scoring a RUN) 双杀

ˌdouble ˈquick *adv.* (*BrE, informal*) very quickly 飞快；快极了 ▶ **ˌdouble-ˈquick** *adj.* [only before noun]: *The TV was repaired in **double-quick time**.* 这电视机一会儿就修好了。

ˌdouble ˈrhyme *noun* [U] (in poetry 诗歌) a pair of words which have two parts ending with the same sounds, for example 'reading' and 'speeding' 双重韵律，双韵（有两处末尾发音相同的两个词，如 reading 和 speeding）

ˌdouble ˈroom (*also* **double**) *noun* a bedroom for two people 双人房间

double·speak /ˈdʌblspiːk/ (*also* **ˈdouble·talk**) *noun* [U] language that is intended to make people believe sth which is not true, or that can be understood in two different ways 欺人之谈；模棱两可的用词；含糊其词的说法

ˌdouble ˈstandard *noun* a rule or moral principle that is unfair because it is used in one situation, but not in another, or because it treats one group of people in a way that is different from the treatment of another 双重标准；双重道德标准

doub·let /ˈdʌblət/ *noun* a short, tightly fitting jacket worn by men from the 14th to the 17th century （14–17 世纪男子穿的）紧身短上衣：*dressed in **doublet and hose*** 穿着紧身衣裤

ˌdouble ˈtake *noun* if you **do a double take**, you wait for a moment before you react to sth that has happened, because it is very surprising 愣了一会儿才恍然大悟的反应

ˈdouble-talk *noun* [U] = DOUBLESPEAK

double·think /ˈdʌblθɪŋk/ *noun* [U] the act of holding two opposite opinions or beliefs at the same time; the ability to do this 双重思想，双重思考（同时保持两种矛盾的看法或信仰）；双重思考能力

ˌdouble ˈtime *noun* [U] twice sb's normal pay, that they earn for working at times which are not normal working hours （付给加班者的）双倍工资

ˌdouble ˈvision *noun* [U] if you have **double vision**, you can see two things where there is actually only one 复视（将一个物体看成两个影像）

doub·loon /dʌˈbluːn/ *noun* (in the past) a Spanish gold coin 达布隆（西班牙旧时的金币）

doubly /ˈdʌbli/ *adv.* (used before adjectives 置于形容词前) **1** more than usual 更加；越发；倍加：***doubly difficult/hard/important*** 越发困难 / 艰难 / 重要 ◇ *I made doubly sure I locked all the doors when I went out.* 我一再查看所有的门都锁好后才出门。 **2** in two ways; for two reasons 在两方面；由于双重原因：*I was doubly attracted to the house—by its size and its location.* 我喜欢这房子有两方面的原因 —— 大小合适而且地点好。

doubt 🔑 /daʊt/ *noun, verb*

■ ***noun*** 🔑 [U, C] a feeling of being uncertain about sth or not believing sth 疑惑；疑问；不确定；不相信：*a feeling of doubt and uncertainty* 迟疑不定的感受 ◇ ~ (**about sth**) *There is **some doubt** about the best way to do it.* 这件事怎么做才是最佳办法有点吃不准。◇ *The article **raised doubts** about how effective the new drug really was.* 这篇文章对这种新药的实效有多大提出了疑问。◇ ~ (**that...**) *There is **no doubt at all** that we did the right thing.* 毫无疑问我们做得对。◇ ~ (**as to sth**) *If you are **in any doubt as to** whether you should be doing these exercises, consult your doctor.* 如果你拿不准是否应进行这些运动，咨询一下医生好了。◇ *New evidence has **cast doubt on** the guilt of the man jailed for the crime.* 新的证据使人们对这个因罪入狱的男子是否有罪产生了怀疑。◇ *She knew **without a shadow of a doubt** that he was lying to her.* 她十分清楚他在对她撒谎。◇ *Whether he will continue to be successful in future is **open to doubt**.* 他今后能否继续获得成功值得怀疑。 ⊃ LANGUAGE BANK AT IMPERSONAL ⊃ MORE LIKE THIS 20, page R27

IDM **beyond** (**any**) **ˈdoubt** in a way that shows that sth is completely certain 无疑；确实：*The research showed beyond doubt that smoking contributes to heart disease.* 这项研究确实表明吸烟会导致心脏病。◇ (*law* 律) *The prosecution was able to establish **beyond reasonable doubt** that the woman had been lying.* 控方能够确切无疑地证实这个女

人一直在撒谎。 **be in 'doubt** ⚷ to be uncertain 不肯定；不确定；拿不准：*The success of the system is not in doubt.* 这种制度的成功确定无疑。 **have your 'doubts (about sth)** to have reasons why you are not certain about whether sth is good or whether sth good will happen（有理由）不相信；对（某事）持怀疑态度：*I've had my doubts about his work since he joined the firm.* 自从他加入公司以来，我对他的工作一直持有怀疑。◇ *It may be all right. Personally, I have my doubts.* 这或许行，但我个人持怀疑态度。 **if in 'doubt** used to give advice to sb who cannot decide what to do 如果没把握；如果拿不准：*If in doubt, wear black.* 拿不定主意就穿黑色衣服。 **ˌno 'doubt 1** ⚷ used when you are saying that sth is probable 无疑；很可能：*No doubt she'll call us when she gets there.* 她到达那里时必定会给我们打电话。 **2** ⚷ used when you are saying that sth is certainly true 无疑；确实地：*He's made some great movies. There's **no doubt about it**.* 他拍了一些非常出色的影片，这一点是毫无疑问的。 **without/beyond 'doubt** ⚷ used when you are giving your opinion and emphasizing the point that you are making 毫无疑问；的确：*This meeting has been, without doubt, one of the most useful we have had so far.* 这无疑是我们迄今为止最有用的一次会议。 ➲ MORE AT BENEFIT *n.*

■ ***verb* 1** ⚷ to feel uncertain about sth; to feel that sth is not true, will probably not happen, etc. 怀疑；无把握；不能肯定；认为…未必可能： **~ sth** *There seems no reason to doubt her story.* 似乎没有理由怀疑她所说的话。◇ *'Do you think England will win?'—'I doubt it.'* "你认为英格兰队会取胜吗？" "不一定。" ◇ **~ (that)...** *I never doubted (that) she would come.* 我从未怀疑过她会来。◇ **~ whether, if, etc....** *I doubt whether/if the new one will be any better.* 我不敢肯定这个新的是否会好些。 **2 ~ sb/sth** to not trust sb/sth; to not believe sb 怀疑；不相信；不信任：*I had no reason to doubt him.* 我没有理由不相信他。
▶ **doubt·er** *noun*

doubt·ful /ˈdaʊtfl/ *adj.* **1** (of a person 人) not sure; uncertain and feeling doubt 拿不定主意；不确定；怀疑 SYN **dubious**: **~ (about sth)** *Rose was doubtful about the whole idea.* 罗斯对整个设想持怀疑态度。◇ **~ (about doing sth)** *He was doubtful about accepting extra work.* 他拿不定主意是否接受额外工作。 **2** unlikely; not probable 未必；难说；不大可能： **~ (if...)** *It's doubtful if this painting is a Picasso.* 这未必就是毕加索的画。◇ **~ (that...)** *With her injuries it's doubtful that she'll ever walk again.* 她多处受伤，今后能否行走还很难说。◇ **~ (whether...)** *It's doubtful whether the car will last another year.* 这辆汽车未必还能用上一年。◇ **~ (for sth)** *He is injured and is doubtful for the game tomorrow* (= unlikely to play). 他受了伤，明天未必能参赛。 **3** [not usually before noun] (of a thing 事情) uncertain and likely to get worse 不明朗，悬而未定（可能变糟）：*At the beginning of the war things were looking very doubtful.* 战争刚开始时，形势看上去很不明朗。 **4** [only before noun] of low value; probably not genuine or of a quality that you can rely on 低劣的；未必是真的；靠不住的 SYN **dubious**: *This wine is of doubtful quality.* 这酒的质量有问题。 ▶ **doubt·ful·ly** /-fəli/ *adv.*

doubt·ing Thomas /ˌdaʊtɪŋ ˈtɒməs; *NAmE* ˈtɑːm-/ *noun* [sing.] (*old-fashioned*) a person who is unlikely to believe sth until they see proof of it 怀疑一切的人；多疑的人；有证据才相信的人 ORIGIN From St Thomas in the Bible, who did not believe that Jesus Christ had risen from the dead until he saw and touched his wounds. 源自《圣经》中的多马，他直到看见和触摸到耶稣基督的伤口才相信耶稣已复活。

doubt·less /ˈdaʊtləs/ *adv.* (*also less frequent* **doubt·less·ly**) almost certainly 多半；几乎肯定地 SYN **without/beyond doubt**: *He would doubtless disapprove of what Kelly was doing.* 他多半不会赞同凯利做的事。

douche /duːʃ/ *noun* a method of washing inside a woman's VAGINA using a stream of water（妇女阴道）冲洗法，灌洗法 ▶ **douche** *verb* [I, T] **~ (sth)**

dough /dəʊ; *NAmE* doʊ/ *noun* **1** [U, sing.] a mixture of flour, water, etc. that is made into bread and PASTRY（用于制面包和糕点的）生面团：*Knead the dough on a floured surface.* 在撒了面粉的案板上揉面团。 **2** [U] (*old-fashioned, slang*) money 钱

dough·nut (*also* **donut** *especially in NAmE*) /ˈdəʊnʌt; *NAmE* ˈdoʊ-/ *noun* a small cake made of fried dough, usually in the shape of a ring, or round and filled with jam/jelly, fruit, cream, etc. 炸面圈，甜甜圈（常含果酱、水果、奶油等）

doughty /ˈdaʊti/ *adj.* (*old-fashioned*) brave and strong 勇敢强悍的

doula /ˈduːlə/ *noun* (*NAmE*) a woman whose role is to provide emotional support to a woman who is giving birth 产妇陪护（给产妇以心理支持） ➲ COMPARE MIDWIFE

dour /ˈdaʊə(r); dʊə(r); *NAmE also* dʊr/ *adj.* **1** (of a person 人) giving the impression of being unfriendly and severe 冷酷的；严厉的 **2** (of a thing, a place, or a situation 事物、地方或情况) not pleasant; with no features that make it lively or interesting 令人不快的；无生气的：*The city, drab and dour by day, is transformed at night.* 这座城市白天死气沉沉、单调乏味，晚上就完全变了样。◇ *The game proved to be a dour struggle, with both men determined to win.* 这次比赛结果成为一场恶战，因为两个人都志在必得。
▶ **dour·ly** *adv.*

douse (*also* **dowse**) /daʊs/ *verb* **1 ~ sth (with sth)** to stop a fire from burning by pouring water over it; to put out a light 浇灭（火）；熄（灯） **2 ~ sb/sth (in/with sth)** to pour a lot of liquid over sb/sth; to SOAK sb/sth in liquid 往…上泼水；把…浸在液体里：*The car was doused in petrol and set alight.* 这辆汽车被浇上汽油点燃了。

dove¹ /dʌv/ *noun* **1** a bird of the PIGEON family. The white dove is often used as a symbol of peace. 鸽子（白鸽常作为和平的象征）：*A dove cooed softly.* 一只鸽子轻柔地咕咕叫。◇ *He wore a dove-grey suit.* 他穿了一套鸽灰色西装。 ➲ SEE ALSO TURTLE DOVE **2** a person, especially a politician, who prefers peace and discussion to war 鸽派人物，温和派人物（尤指愿意和平与谈判而不愿战争的从政者） OPP **hawk**

dove² /dəʊv; *NAmE* doʊv/ (*NAmE*) PAST TENSE OF DIVE

dove·cote /ˈdʌvkɒt; ˈdʌvkəʊt; *NAmE* -kɑːt; -koʊt/ (*also* **dove·cot** /ˈdʌvkɒt; *NAmE* -kɑːt/) *noun* a small building for DOVES OR PIGEONS to live in 鸽房；鸽舍；鸽棚

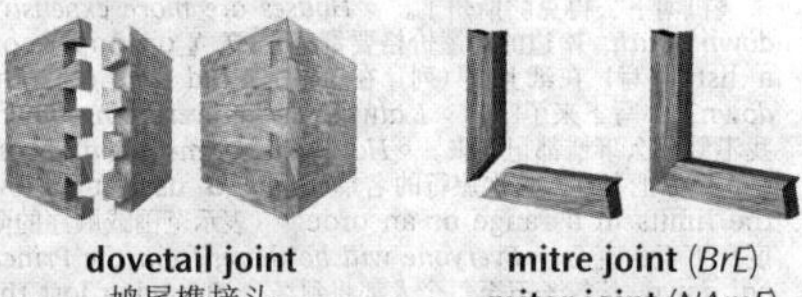

dovetail joint 鸠尾榫接头

mitre joint (*BrE*) **miter joint** (*NAmE*) 斜接头

dove·tail /ˈdʌvteɪl/ *verb, noun*

■ ***verb*** [I, T] (*formal*) **~ (sth) (with/into sth)** if two things **dovetail** or if one thing **dovetails** with another, they fit together well 吻合；与…吻合：*My plans dovetailed nicely with hers.* 我的计划与她的计划正好吻合。

■ ***noun*** (*also* **ˌdovetail ˈjoint**) a joint for fixing two pieces of wood together 燕尾榫接合；鸠尾榫（接头）

dov·ish /ˈdʌvɪʃ/ *adj.* preferring to use peaceful discussion rather than military action in order to solve a political problem 温和派的；鸽派的 OPP **hawkish**

dow·ager /ˈdaʊədʒə(r)/ *noun* **1** a woman of high social rank who has a title from her dead husband（具有亡夫头衔的）孀居贵妇：*the dowager Duchess of Norfolk* 诺福克公爵遗孀 **2** (*informal*) an impressive, usually rich, old woman 气度不凡的老年贵妇人

dowdy /ˈdaʊdi/ *adj.* (**dow·dier**, **dow·di·est**) **1** (of a woman 女人) not attractive or fashionable 缺乏魅力的；不时髦的；过时的 **2** (of a thing 物件) dull or boring and not attractive 单调的；不雅致的；不美观的 SYN **drab**: *a dowdy dress* 单调的连衣裙

dow·el /ˈdaʊəl/ (*also* **ˈdowel rod**) *noun* a small piece of wood, plastic, etc. in the shape of a CYLINDER, used to fix larger pieces of wood, plastic, etc. together 暗榫

dowel·ling (*BrE*) (*US* **dowel·ing**) /ˈdaʊəlɪŋ/ *noun* [U] short pieces of wooden, metal or plastic ROD that are used for holding parts of sth together 榫钉

the Dow Jones Index /ˌdaʊ ˈdʒəʊnz ɪndeks; *NAmE* ˈdʒoʊnz/ (*also* **ˌDow ˈJones average, the ˈDow**) *noun* [sing.] a list of the share prices of 30 US industrial companies that can be used to compare the prices to previous levels 道琼斯（平均）指数

down /daʊn/ *adv., prep., verb, adj., noun*

■ ***adv.*** HELP For the special uses of **down** in phrasal verbs, look at the entries for the verbs. For example **climb down** is in the phrasal verb section at **climb**. * down 在短语动词中的特殊用法见有关动词词条。如 climb down 在词条 climb 的短语动词部分。 **1** to or at a lower place or position 向下；朝下；在下面：*She jumped down off the chair.* 她跳下椅子。◇ *He looked down at her.* 他低头看着她。◇ *We watched as the sun went down.* 我们看着夕阳西沉。◇ *She bent down to pick up her glove.* 她俯身去捡手套。◇ *Mary's not down yet* (= she is still upstairs). 玛丽还没下楼呢。◇ *The baby can't keep any food down* (= in her body). 这婴儿吃什么吐什么。 **2** from a standing or vertical position to a sitting or horizontal one（坐、倒、躺）下：*Please sit down.* 请坐。◇ *He had to go and lie down for a while.* 他不得不去躺一会儿。 **3** at a lower level or rate 在较低水平；下降；下跌：*Prices have gone down recently.* 最近物价下降了。◇ *We're already two goals down* (= the other team has two goals more). 我们已落后对方两球。 ➲ LANGUAGE BANK AT FALL **4** used to show that the amount or strength of sth is lower, or that there is less activity（数量、力量、活动等）减少，减弱，降低：*Turn the music down!* 把音乐声关小点！◇ *The class settled down and she began the lesson.* 全班安静下来她便开始上课了。 **5** (in a CROSSWORD 纵横填字游戏) reading from top to bottom, not from side to side 由上至下：*I can't do 3 down.* 我填不出第 3 个竖行。 **6** to or in the south of a country 向南方；在南方：*They flew down to Texas.* 他们乘飞机南下去得克萨斯州了。◇ *Houses are more expensive down south.* 南边的房屋价格要贵些。 **7** on paper; on a list （写）在纸上；（列）在表格上：*Did you get that down?* 你写下来了吗？◇ *I always write everything down.* 我不管什么事情都记下来。◇ *Have you got me down for the trip?* 你把我列入这次旅行的名单了吗？ **8** used to show the limits in a range or an order （表示范围或顺序的限度）下至，直至：*Everyone will be there, from the Principal down.* 从校长下至每个人都将到场。 **9** having lost the amount of money mentioned 失去（钱数）：*At the end of the day we were £20 down.* 一天下来我们少了 20 英镑。 **10** if you pay an amount of money **down**, you pay that to start with, and the rest later （钱）先付，预付 **11** (*informal*) used to say how far you have got in a list of things you have to do 已完成数量（或进度）：*Well, I've seen six apartments so far. That's six down and four to go!* 好啦，到目前为止我已看了六套公寓房。看完六套还有四套要去看呢！ **12** (*informal*) to or at a local place such as a shop/store, pub, etc. 到，去，在（当地的商店、酒馆等地方）：*I'm just going down to the post office.* 我正要到邮局去。◇ *I saw him down at the shops.* 我刚才看到他在那边的商店里。 HELP In informal British English, **to** and **at** are often left out after **down** in this sense. 在非正式的英式英语中，down 作此义时后面的 to 和 at 经常省略：*He's gone down the shops.* 他到商店去了。

IDM **be down to sb** (*informal*) to be the responsibility of sb 是某人的责任；由某人负责：*It's down to you to check the door.* 检查门是否关好是你的事。 **be down to sb/sth** to be caused by a particular person or thing 由…引起（或造成）：*She claimed her problems were down to the media.* 她声称她的问题是媒体造成的。 **be down to sth** to have only a little money left 只剩下（一点儿钱）：*I'm down to my last dollar.* 我只剩下最后一美元了。 **be/go down with sth** to have or catch an illness 患…病；得…病 **ˌdown and ˈdirty** (*NAmE, informal*) **1** behaving in an unfair or aggressive way, especially because you want to win 不择手段地：*The candidate again got down and dirty with his rival.* 这名候选人再一次用下作的手段对付他的竞争对手。 **2** rude and shocking 粗鲁无礼地；恶劣地：*The singer got down and dirty at the club last night and made headlines again.* 这个歌手昨晚在俱乐部的无耻行为使他又上了报纸的头条。 ➲ MORE LIKE THIS 13, page R26 **down through sth** (*formal*) during a long period of time 在（相当长的一段）时间内：*Down through the years this town has seen many changes.* 多年来这座城镇发生了许多变化。 **down to the last, smallest, final, etc. sth** including every small part or detail of sth 非常详尽地：*She organized everything down to the last detail.* 她每件事情都安排得滴水不漏。 **down ˈunder** (*informal*) to or in Australia and/or New Zealand 到，向，在（澳大利亚和／或新西兰） **down with sb/sth** used to say that you are opposed to sth, or to a person 打倒：*The crowds chanted 'Down with NATO!'* 人群有节奏地反复高喊"打倒北约！" **have/get sth ˈdown** to be able to do sth easily or well 对…游刃有余；能轻易驾驭：*She's young and she hasn't really got it down yet.* 她很年轻，为人处事还不够练达沉稳。 ➲ MORE AT MAN *n.*

■ ***prep.*** **1** from a high or higher point on sth to a lower one（从高处）向下，往下：*The stone rolled down the hill.* 石头滚下山坡。◇ *Tears ran down her face.* 泪水顺着她的脸庞流下来。◇ *Her hair hung down her back to her waist.* 她的长发披在背上直垂腰际。 **2** along; towards the direction in which you are facing 沿着；顺着；朝着：*He lives just down the street.* 他就住在街那头。◇ *Go down the road till you reach the traffic lights.* 沿着这条路一直走到红绿灯处。◇ *There's a bridge a mile down the river from here.* 从这里沿河而下一英里处有座桥。 **3** all through a period of time 贯穿…时间；遍及…时期：*an exhibition of costumes down the ages* (= from all periods of history) 历代服装展览

■ ***verb*** (*informal*) **1 ~ sth** to finish a drink or eat sth quickly （一下子）喝下，吃下，咽下：*We downed our coffees and left.* 我们一口气喝完咖啡就离开了。 **2 ~ sb/sth** to force sb/sth down to the ground 使倒下；击倒：*to down a plane* 击落一架飞机

IDM **ˌdown ˈtools** (*BrE*) (of workers 工人) to stop work; to go on strike 撂下工作；罢工

■ ***adj.*** [not before noun] **1** (*informal*) sad or depressed 悲哀；沮丧；情绪低落：*I feel a bit down today.* 我今天有点闷闷不乐。 **2** (of a computer or computer system 计算机或计算机系统) not working 停机；停止运行：*The system was down all morning.* 这系统整个上午都停机。 ➲ SEE ALSO DOWNTIME (1) IDM SEE HIT *v.*, KICK *v.*, LUCK *n.*, MOUTH *n.*

■ ***noun*** ➲ SEE ALSO DOWNS **1** [U] the very fine soft feathers of a bird（鸟的）绒羽，绒毛：*duck down* 鸭绒 **2** [U] fine soft hair 绒毛；软毛；汗毛 ➲ SEE ALSO DOWNY **3** [C] (in AMERICAN FOOTBALL 美式足球) one of a series of four chances to carry the ball forward ten yards that a team is allowed. These series continue until the team loses the ball or fails to go forward ten yards in four downs. 档（进攻方每轮进攻共有 4 次机会向前累计推进 10 码，每次称 1 档。如果推进 10 码成功，则进攻方继续获得进攻机会；丢球或未能推进 10 码，则攻守互易）

IDM **have a ˈdown on sb/sth** (*BrE, informal*) to have a bad opinion of a person or thing 对…评价不好；瞧不起；厌恶 ➲ MORE AT UP *n.*

ˌdown and ˈout *adj.* (of a person 人) **1** without money, a home or a job, and living on the streets 穷困潦倒；一无所有：*a novel about being down and out in London* 一部以伦敦的流浪生活为题材的小说 **2** certain to be defeated 必输无疑的；必定失败的

ˈdown-and-out *noun* a person without money, a home or a job, who lives on the streets 穷困潦倒的人；无家可归的人

ˌdown at ˈheel *adj.* looking less attractive and fashionable than before, usually because of a lack of money 潦倒的；寒酸的：*The town has become very down at heel.*

这座城镇已变得破败不堪。◇ *a down-at-heel hotel* 寒酸的旅馆

down·beat /ˈdaʊnbiːt/ *adj.* (*informal*) **1** dull or depressing; not having much hope for the future 沉闷的；令人沮丧的；悲观的：*The overall mood of the meeting was downbeat.* 整个会场的气氛是沉闷的。**OPP upbeat** **2** not showing strong feelings or enthusiasm 不强烈的；消沉的；无热情的

down·cast /ˈdaʊnkɑːst; *NAmE* -kæst/ *adj.* **1** (of eyes 眼睛) looking down 向下的；低垂的：*Eyes downcast, she continued eating.* 她低垂双眼，继续吃。**2** (of a person or an expression 人或表情) sad or depressed 悲哀的；沮丧的；垂头丧气的 **SYN dejected**：*A group of downcast men stood waiting for food.* 一群人垂头丧气地站在那儿等着吃饭。

down·draught (*BrE*) (*NAmE* **down·draft**) /ˈdaʊndrɑːft; *NAmE* -dræft/ *noun* a downward movement of air, for example down a CHIMNEY 下曳气流；(烟囱等的) 倒灌风

down·er /ˈdaʊnə(r)/ *noun* (*informal*) **1** [usually pl.] a drug, especially a BARBITURATE, that relaxes you or makes you want to sleep 镇静药，抑制药（尤指巴比妥类）➲ COMPARE UPPER *n.* (2) **2** an experience that makes you feel sad or depressed 令人悲哀（或沮丧）的经历：*Not getting the promotion was a real downer.* 未得到提升真让人很沮丧。◇ *He's really* ***on a downer*** (= very depressed). 他确实很郁闷。

down·fall /ˈdaʊnfɔːl/ *noun* [sing.] the loss of a person's money, power, social position, etc.; the thing that causes this 衰落；衰败；垮台；衰落（或衰败、垮台）的原因：*The sex scandal finally led to his downfall.* 这桩绯闻最终使他身败名裂。◇ *Greed was her downfall.* 贪得无厌就是她堕落的缘由。

down·grade /ˌdaʊnˈɡreɪd/ *verb* **1 ~ sb/sth (from sth) (to sth)** to move sb/sth down to a lower rank or level 使降职；使降级：*She's been downgraded from principal to vice-principal.* 她已从校长降职为副校长。**2 ~ sth/sb** to make sth/sb seem less important or valuable than it/they really are 贬低；降低；低估 ➲ COMPARE UPGRADE ▶ **down·grad·ing** *noun* [U, C]：*a downgrading of diplomatic relations* 外交关系降格

down·heart·ed /ˌdaʊnˈhɑːtɪd; *NAmE* -ˈhɑːrtɪd/ *adj.* [not before noun] feeling depressed or sad 情绪低落；垂头丧气；悲哀：*We're disappointed by these results but we're not downhearted.* 我们对这些结果感到失望，但是并未丧失信心。

down·hill *adv., adj., noun*

■ ***adv.*** /ˌdaʊnˈhɪl/ towards the bottom of a hill; in a direction that goes down 向山下；向下：*to* ***run/walk/cycle downhill*** 跑／走／骑车下山 **OPP uphill**

IDM **go down'hill** to get worse in quality, health, etc. (质量、健康等) 每况愈下，走下坡路，恶化 **SYN deteriorate**：*Their marriage went downhill after the first child was born.* 自第一个孩子出生后他们的婚姻便开始走下坡路了。

■ ***adj.*** /ˌdaʊnˈhɪl/ going or sloping towards the bottom of a hill 下山的；下坡的；下斜的：*a downhill path* 下山的路 **OPP uphill**

IDM **be (all) downhill | be ˌdownhill all the ˈway** (*informal*) **1** to be easy compared to what came before (与前面的相比较) 容易：*It's all downhill from here. We'll soon be finished.* 从这以后就容易了。我们很快就会结束。**2** to become worse or less successful 每况愈下；走下坡路；不断恶化：*It's been all downhill for his career since then, with four defeats in five games.* 从那时起他的战绩便江河日下，五场比赛输掉了四场。◇ *I started work as a journalist and it was downhill all the way for my health.* 我开始当记者后，身体每况愈下。

■ ***noun*** /ˈdaʊnhɪl/ [U] the type of SKIING in which you go directly down a mountain; a race in which people SKI down a mountain 高山速降（比赛）➲ VISUAL VOCAB PAGE V52 ➲ COMPARE CROSS-COUNTRY *n.*

ˌdown-ˈhome *adj.* (*NAmE*) used to describe a person or thing that reminds you of a simple way of life, typical of the country, not the town 淳朴的；乡村的；有乡土味的

Down·ing Street /ˈdaʊnɪŋ striːt/ *noun* [sing.] (not used with *the* 不与 the 连用) a way of referring to the British prime minister and government, taken from the name of the street where the prime minister lives 唐宁街，英国首相，英国政府（英国首相官邸所在街道的名称）：*Downing Street issued a statement late last night.* 昨天深夜唐宁街发表了一项声明。➲ MORE LIKE THIS 19, page R27

down·light·er /ˈdaʊnlaɪtə(r)/ (*also* **down·light** /ˈdaʊnlaɪt/) *noun* a light on a wall which shines downwards (安装于墙壁上的) 下照灯具，下射灯 ➲ COMPARE UPLIGHTER

down·link /ˈdaʊnlɪŋk/ *noun* a communications link by which information is received from space or from an aircraft 下行链路，下链（从太空或飞行器接收信号的通信方式）▶ **down·link** *verb*：**~ sth** *Any organization can downlink the program without charge.* 任何机构都可以免费下载这一程序。

down·load *verb, noun*

■ ***verb*** /ˌdaʊnˈləʊd; *NAmE* -ˈloʊd/ **~ sth** (*computing* 计) to get data from another computer, usually using the Internet (通常经互联网) 下载 **OPP upload** ➲ COLLOCATIONS AT EMAIL ➲ COMPARE LOAD *v.* (5)

■ ***noun*** **1** /ˈdaʊnləʊd; *NAmE* -loʊd/ [C] (*computing* 计) data which is downloaded from another computer system 已下载的数据资料 **2** [U] (*computing* 计) the act or process of downloading data from another computer system 下载：*available for download* 可供下载 ▶ **down·load·able** /ˌdaʊnˈləʊdəbl; *NAmE* -ˈloʊd-/ *adj.*

down·low /ˈdaʊnləʊ; *NAmE* -loʊ/ *noun, adj.*

■ ***noun*** **the downlow** [sing.] (*informal*) **~ on (sb/sth)** the true facts about sb/sth, especially those considered most important to know (有关…的) 实情，重要事实 **SYN low-down**：*the website that gives you the downlow on the best movies* 为您提供最优秀电影情报的网站

IDM **on the ˈdownlow** secretly; not wanting other people to discover what you are doing 秘密地；暗中

■ ***adj.*** [only before noun] (*slang*) used to refer to a man who appears to be HETEROSEXUAL, but secretly has sex with men (男人) 隐秘同性恋的

down·mark·et /ˌdaʊnˈmɑːkɪt; *NAmE* -ˈmɑːrkɪt/ (*BrE*) (*NAmE* **down·scale**) *adj.* (*disapproving*) cheap and of poor quality 价廉质劣的；下品的；低档的：*The company wants to break away from its downmarket image.* 这家公司想摆脱它面向低消费阶层的形象。**OPP upmarket** ▶ **down·mark·et** *adv.*：*To get more viewers the TV station was forced to go* ***downmarket***. 为了争取更多观众，电视台不得不迎合低收入阶层。

ˌdown ˈpayment *noun* a sum of money that is given as the first part of a larger payment (分期付款的) 首期付款；预付金；订金：*We are saving for a down payment on a house.* 我们正攒钱支付买房的首付金。➲ COLLOCATIONS AT HOUSE

down·pipe /ˈdaʊnpaɪp/ (*BrE*) (*US* **ˈfall-pipe**) *noun* a pipe for carrying water from a roof down to the ground or to a DRAIN (从屋顶到地面的) 雨水管

down·play /ˌdaʊnˈpleɪ/ *verb* **~ sth** to make people think that sth is less important than it really is 淡化；对…轻描淡写 **SYN play down**：*The coach is downplaying the team's poor performance.* 教练试图淡化这个队的拙劣表现。

down·pour /ˈdaʊnpɔː(r)/ *noun* [usually sing.] a heavy fall of rain that often starts suddenly 倾盆大雨；暴雨；骤雨 ➲ WORDFINDER NOTE AT RAIN

down·right /ˈdaʊnraɪt/ *adj.* [only before noun] used as a way of emphasizing sth negative or unpleasant (强调负面的或令人不快的事物) 彻头彻尾的，十足的，完全的：*There was suspicion and even downright hatred between them.* 他们之间相互怀疑甚至极度仇恨。▶ **down·right** *adv.*：*She couldn't think of anything to say that wasn't downright rude.* 她除了破口大骂之外再也说不出什么。◇

It's not just stupid—it's downright dangerous. 这岂止是愚蠢，简直是危险。

down·river /ˌdaʊnˈrɪvə(r)/ *adv.* = DOWNSTREAM

downs /daʊnz/ *noun* **the downs** [pl.] an area of open land with low hills, especially in southern England（尤指英格兰南部的）开阔丘陵地

down·scale /ˌdaʊnˈskeɪl/ (*NAmE*) (*BrE* **down·mark·et**) *adj.* (*disapproving*) cheap and of poor quality 价廉质劣的；下品的；低档的 **OPP** **upscale** ▶ **down·scale** *adv.*

down·shift /ˈdaʊnʃɪft/ *verb* **1** [I] (*NAmE*) to change to a lower gear in a vehicle（车辆）调到低速挡，换低挡 **2** [I] to change to a job or style of life where you may earn less but which puts less pressure on you and involves less stress 减慢节奏（为减轻压力而更换工作或生活方式）➲ COLLOCATIONS AT TOWN ▶ **down·shift** *noun* [C, U]

down·side /ˈdaʊnsaɪd/ *noun* [sing.] the disadvantages or less positive aspects of sth 缺点；不利方面 **OPP** **upside**

down·size /ˈdaʊnsaɪz/ *verb* [I, T] ~ (**sth**) (*business* 商) to reduce the number of people who work in a company, business, etc. in order to reduce costs（公司、企业等）裁员，精减 ➲ SYNONYMS AT CUT ▶ **down·siz·ing** *noun* [U]

down·spout /ˈdaʊnspaʊt/ *noun* (*NAmE*) = DRAINPIPE (1)

ˈ**Down's syndrome** (*NAmE usually* ˈ**Down syndrome**) *noun* [U] a medical condition, caused by a fault with one CHROMOSOME, in which a person is born with particular physical characteristics and a mental ability that is below average 唐氏综合征

down·stage /ˈdaʊnsteɪdʒ/ *adv.* towards the front of the stage in a theatre 向舞台前部 ▶ **down·stage** *adj.* **OPP** **upstage**

down·stairs /ˌdaʊnˈsteəz; *NAmE* -ˈsterz/ *adv.*, *noun*

■ *adv.* down the stairs; on or to a floor of a house or building lower than the one you are on, especially the one at ground level 顺楼梯而下；在楼下；往楼下：*She rushed downstairs and burst into the kitchen.* 她冲下楼闯进厨房。◇ *Wait downstairs in the hall.* 在楼下大厅里等着。**OPP** **upstairs** ▶ **down·stairs** *adj.* [only before noun]: *a downstairs bathroom* 楼下的盥洗室

■ *noun* [sing.] the lower floor of a house or building, especially the one at ground level 楼下（尤指地面的一层）：*We're painting the downstairs.* 我们在粉刷底层。**OPP** **upstairs**

down·stream /ˌdaʊnˈstriːm/ *adv.*, *adj.*

■ *adv.* (*also less frequent* **down·river**) ~ (**of/from sth**) in the direction in which a river flows 顺流而下；在下游方向：*to* ***drift/float downstream*** 顺水漂流 / 漂浮而下 ◇ *downstream of/from the bridge* 桥的下游方向 **OPP** **upstream** ➲ WORDFINDER NOTE AT RIVER

■ *adj.* **1** (*also less frequent* **down·river**) in a position along a river which is nearer the sea 在下游的：*downstream areas* 下游地区 **OPP** **upstream** **2** happening as a consequence of sth that has happened earlier 引发的；导致的：*downstream effects* 随之产生的后果

down·swing /ˈdaʊnswɪŋ/ *noun* [usually sing.] **1** ~ (**in sth**) a situation in which sth gets worse or decreases over a period of time 恶化趋势；向下走势；下降：*the current downswing in the airline industry* 航空业目前的滑坡状况 ◇ *He is on a career downswing.* 他在事业上正走下坡路。**OPP** **upswing** **2** (in GOLF) the downward movement of a CLUB when a player is about to hit the ball（高尔夫球）下挥杆

ˈ**Down syndrome** *noun* [U] (*NAmE*) = DOWN'S SYNDROME

down·tick /ˈdaʊntɪk/ *noun* [C, usually sing.] (*NAmE*, *economics* 经) a small decrease in the level or value of sth, especially in the price of shares（尤指股价的）微跌，微落：*The shares were bought* ***on a downtick***. 这些股票是在小幅下跌时买进的。**OPP** **uptick**

down·time /ˈdaʊntaɪm/ *noun* [U] **1** the time during which a machine, especially a computer, is not working（尤指计算机的）停机时间，停止运行时间 ➲ COMPARE UPTIME **2** (*especially NAmE*) the time when sb stops working and is able to relax 停工；休息：*Everyone needs a little downtime.* 大家都需要休息一下。

ˌ**down to ˈearth** *adj.* (*approving*) sensible and practical, in a way that is helpful and friendly 务实的；切合实际的

down·town /ˌdaʊnˈtaʊn/ *adv.* (*especially NAmE*) in or towards the centre of a city, especially its main business area 在市中心，往市中心（尤指商业中心区）：*to go/work downtown* 到商业中心区去；在商业中心区工作 ➲ COLLOCATIONS AT TOWN ➲ COMPARE MIDTOWN, TOWN CENTRE, UPTOWN *adv.* ▶ ˈ**down·town** *adj.* [only before noun]: *a downtown store* 闹市区的商店 ˈ**down·town** *noun* [U]: *a hotel in the heart of downtown* 市区中心的旅馆

down·trend /ˈdaʊntrend/ *noun* [sing.] a situation in which business activity or performance decreases or becomes worse over a period of time（经济活动或运作情况的）下降趋势 **OPP** **uptrend**

down·trod·den /ˈdaʊntrɒdn; *NAmE* -trɑːdn/ *adj.* **downtrodden** people are treated so badly by the people with authority and power that they no longer have the energy or ability to fight back 受欺压的；被蹂躏的；被践踏的

down·turn /ˈdaʊntɜːn; *NAmE* -tɜːrn/ *noun* [C, U] ~ (**in sth**) a fall in the amount of business that is done; a time when the economy becomes weaker（商业经济的）衰退，下降，衰退期：*the recent economic downturns* 最近的经济下滑 ◇ *a* ***downturn in sales/trade/business*** 销量 / 贸易 / 营业额下降 ◇ *the economic downturn of 2008/2009* * 2008 / 2009 年的经济衰退 **OPP** **upturn**

down·ward /ˈdaʊnwəd; *NAmE* -wərd/ *adj.* [usually before noun] moving or pointing towards a lower level 下降的；向下的：*the downward slope of a hill* 向下的山坡 ◇ *the downward trend in inflation* 通货膨胀的下降趋势 ◇ *She was trapped in a* ***downward spiral*** *of personal unhappiness.* 她陷入了个人不幸的漩涡难以自拔。**OPP** **upward** ▶ **down·ward·ly** *adv.*

down·wards /ˈdaʊnwədz; *NAmE* -wərdz/ (*also* **down·ward** *especially in NAmE*) *adv.* towards the ground or towards a lower level 向下：*She was lying* ***face downwards*** *on the grass.* 她俯卧在草地上。◇ *The garden sloped gently downwards to the river.* 花园向河边呈缓坡倾斜。◇ *It was a policy welcomed by world leaders from the US president downwards.* 这一政策受到了美国总统乃至全世界领导人的欢迎。**OPP** **upwards** ➲ LANGUAGE BANK AT FALL

down·wind /ˌdaʊnˈwɪnd/ *adv.*, *adj.* in the direction in which the wind is blowing 顺风地；在下风处：*sailing downwind* 顺风航行 ◇ ~ **of sth** *Warnings were issued to people living downwind of the fire to stay indoors.* 已经向住在火势下风处的人们发出不要出门的警告。**OPP** **upwind**

downy /ˈdaʊni/ *adj.* covered in sth very soft, especially hair or feathers 绒毛覆盖的；长着绒毛的；毛茸茸的 ➲ SEE ALSO DOWN *n.* (1), (2)

dowry /ˈdaʊri/ *noun* (*pl.* **-ies**) **1** money and/or property that, in some societies, a wife or her family must pay to her husband when they get married（新娘家给新郎的）嫁妆，陪嫁 **2** money and/or property that, in some societies, a husband must pay to his wife's family when they get married（新郎给新娘家的）彩礼，财礼

dowse /daʊz/ *verb* **1** [I] to look for underground water or minerals by using a special stick or long piece of metal that moves when it comes near water, etc. 用探测杆探寻（地下水或矿藏）**2** = DOUSE ▶ **dow·ser** *noun*

ˈ**dowsing rod** *noun* a stick used when dowsing for water or minerals underground（探测地下水或矿藏的）探测杆

doxy /ˈdɒksi; *NAmE* ˈdɑːksi/ *noun* (*pl.* **-ies**) (*old use*) **1** a woman who is sb's lover 情妇 **2** a PROSTITUTE 妓女

doyen /ˈdɔɪən/ (*NAmE usually* **dean**) *noun* the most respected or most experienced member of a group or profession（某团体或职业中的）老前辈，资格最老者，元

老：*Richard Dawkins, the doyen of evolutionary biologists* 理查德·道金斯——进化生物学家的泰斗

doy·enne /dɔɪˈen/ *noun* the most respected or most experienced woman member of a group or profession 地位最高的女子；资格最老的女子：*Martha Graham, the doyenne of American modern dance* 玛莎·格雷厄姆——美国现代舞之母

doz. *abbr.* (in writing 书写形式) DOZEN（一）打；十二个：*2 doz. eggs* 两打鸡蛋

doze /dəʊz; *NAmE* doʊz/ *verb, noun*

■ *verb* [I] to sleep lightly for a short time 打瞌睡；打盹儿；小睡 ➲ SYNONYMS AT SLEEP ➲ WORDFINDER NOTE AT SLEEP

PHR V ˌ**doze ˈoff** to go to sleep, especially during the day（尤指在日间）打瞌睡，打盹儿：*She dozed off in front of the fire.* 她在炉火前打起盹儿来。

■ *noun* [sing.] a short period of sleep, usually during the day（通常在日间的）瞌睡，小睡：*I had a doze on the train.* 我在火车上打了个盹儿。

dozen /ˈdʌzn/ *noun, det.* (*pl.* **dozen**) **1** [C] (*abbr.* **doz.**) a group of twelve of the same thing（一）打；十二个：*Give me a dozen, please.* 请给我来一打。◇ *two dozen eggs* 两打鸡蛋 ◇ *three dozen red roses* 三打红玫瑰 ➲ SEE ALSO BAKER'S DOZEN **2** [C] a group of approximately twelve people or things 十来个；十几个；十多个：*several dozen/a few dozen people* 数十 / 几十个人 ◇ *The company employs no more than* ***a couple of dozen*** *people.* 这家公司顶多雇用了几十个人。◇ *Only about* ***half a dozen*** *people turned up.* 只有六七个人到场。◇ *There was only space for a* ***half-dozen*** *tables.* 只有摆六张桌子的地方。 **3** **dozens** [pl.] (*informal*) a lot of people or things 许多；很多：*They arrived* ***in dozens*** (= in large numbers). 他们大批到达了。◇ **~ of sth** *I've been there dozens of times.* 我到过那里很多次了。 IDM SEE NINETEEN, PENNY, SIX

dozy /ˈdəʊzi; *NAmE* ˈdoʊzi/ *adj.* (*informal*) **1** not looking or feeling awake 想睡的；昏昏欲睡的；困倦的 **2** (*BrE*) stupid; not intelligent 愚笨的；不聪明的

DPhil /ˌdiː ˈfɪl/ *noun* (*BrE*) the abbreviation for 'Doctor of Philosophy' 哲学博士（全写为 Doctor of Philosophy）：*to be/have/do a DPhil* 是哲学博士；有 / 攻读哲学博士学位 ◇ *James Mendelssohn DPhil* 哲学博士詹姆斯·门德尔松

dpi /ˌdiː piː ˈaɪ/ *abbr.* (*computing* 计) dots per inch (a measure of how clear the images produced by a printer, SCANNER, etc. are) 点每英寸（打印机、扫描仪等的清晰度参数）

DPP /ˌdiː piː ˈpiː/ *noun* = DIRECTOR OF PUBLIC PROSECUTIONS

Dr (*BrE*) (*also* **Dr.** *NAmE, BrE*) *abbr.* **1** (in writing 书写形式) Doctor 医生；博士：*Dr (Jane) Walker*（简·）沃克博士 **2** (in street names) DRIVE（用于街道名）路，大道

drab /dræb/ *adj.* (**drab·ber**, **drab·best**) without interest or colour; dull and boring 单调乏味的；无光彩的；无生气的：*a cold drab little office* 冷冰冰的小办公室 ◇ *drab women, dressed in browns and greys* 身着棕灰二色衣服毫无光彩的女人 ➲ MORE LIKE THIS 35, page R29 ▶ **drab·ness** *noun* [U]

drabs /dræbz/ *noun* IDM SEE DRIBS

drachma /ˈdrækmə/ *noun* (*pl.* **drachmas** or **drachmae** /ˈdrækmiː/) the former unit of money in Greece (replaced in 2002 by the euro) 德拉克马（希腊货币单位，于 2002 年为欧元所取代）

dra·co·nian /drəˈkəʊniən; *NAmE* -ˈkoʊ-/ *adj.* (*formal*) (of a law, punishment, etc. 法律、惩罚等) extremely cruel and severe 德拉古式的；严酷的；残忍的 ORIGIN From **Draco**, a legislator in ancient Athens who gave severe punishments for crimes, especially the punishment of being killed. 源自古雅典立法者德拉古，他严惩犯罪，尤其是施以死刑。

Drac·ula /ˈdrækjələ/ *noun* a character in many horror films who is a VAMPIRE. Vampires appear at night and suck the blood of their victims. 吸血鬼德古拉 ORIGIN From the novel *Dracula* by Bram Stoker. 源自布拉姆·斯托克的小说《吸血鬼德古拉》（Dracula）。

draft AW /drɑːft; *NAmE* dræft/ *noun, adj., verb*

■ *noun* **1** [C] a rough written version of sth that is not yet in its final form 草稿；草案；草图：*I've made a* ***rough draft*** *of the letter.* 我已经写好这封信的草稿。◇ *This is only the first draft of my speech.* 这只是我演讲的初稿。◇ *the* ***final draft*** (= the final version) 定稿 ◇ *The legislation is still* ***in draft form***. 这条法规还只是项草案。◇ *a* ***draft constitution/treaty/agreement*** 宪法 / 条约 / 协议草案 ➲ WORDFINDER NOTE AT MESSAGE **2** [C] (*finance* 财) a written order to a bank to pay money to sb 汇票：*Payment must be made* ***by bank draft*** *drawn on a UK bank.* 付款必须用英国银行承兑的汇票。 **3** **the draft** [sing.] (*especially US*) = CONSCRIPTION **4** [sing.] (*NAmE*) a system in which professional teams in some sports choose players each year from among college students 选秀，运动员选拔制（某些职业运动队每年在大学生中选拔新队员） **5** [C] (*NAmE*) = DRAUGHT：*Can you shut the door? There's a draft in here.* 你关上门好吗？这里有穿堂风。

■ *adj.* (*NAmE*) = DRAUGHT

■ *verb* (*also* **draught** *especially in BrE*) **1** **~ sth** to write the first rough version of sth such as a letter, speech or book 起草；草拟：*to* ***draft a constitution/contract/bill*** 起草宪法 / 合同 / 法案 ◇ *I'll draft a letter for you.* 我来为你草拟一封信。 ➲ WORDFINDER NOTE AT DOCUMENT **2** **~ sb + adv./prep.** to choose people and send them somewhere for a special task 选派；抽调：*Extra police are being drafted in to control the crowds.* 现正在另外抽调警察去控制人群。 **3** [usually passive] **~ sb** (*NAmE*) = CONSCRIPT：*They were drafted into the army.* 他们应征入伍。

ˈ**draft dodger** *noun* (*NAmE, disapproving*) a person who illegally tries to avoid doing military service 逃避兵役者 ➲ COMPARE CONSCIENTIOUS OBJECTOR

draft·ee /ˌdrɑːfˈtiː; *NAmE* ˌdræfˈtiː/ *noun* (*US*) = CONSCRIPT

draft·er /ˈdrɑːftə(r); *NAmE* ˈdræftər/ *noun* **1** a person who prepares a rough version of a plan, document, etc.（计划、文件等的）起草人，拟稿者 **2** (*NAmE*) = DRAFTSMAN (2)

drafts·man /ˈdrɑːftsmən; *NAmE* ˈdræftsmən/, **drafts·woman** /ˈdrɑːftswʊmən; *NAmE* ˈdræftswʊmən/ *noun* (*pl.* **-men** /-mən/, **-women** /-wɪmɪn/) **1** (*NAmE*) = DRAUGHTSMAN, DRAUGHTSWOMAN **2** (*NAmE also* **drafter**) a person who writes official or legal documents（正式或法律文件的）起草人：*the draftsmen of the constitution* 宪法起草人

drafts·man·ship (*NAmE*) = DRAUGHTSMANSHIP

drafts·pers·on /ˈdrɑːftspɜːsn; *NAmE* ˈdræftspɜːrsn/ *noun* (*NAmE*) = DRAUGHTSPERSON

drafty (*NAmE*) = DRAUGHTY

drag /dræɡ/ *verb, noun*

■ *verb* (**-gg-**)

• **PULL** 拉 **1** [T] (+ **adv./prep.**) to pull sb/sth along with effort and difficulty（使劲而吃力地）拖，拉，拽，扯：*I dragged the chair over to the window.* 我把椅子拖到了窗口那边。◇ *They dragged her from her bed.* 他们把她从床上拽了起来。 ➲ SYNONYMS AT PULL

• **MOVE SLOWLY** 缓慢移动 **2** [T, I] to move yourself slowly and with effort 缓慢而费力地移动（或行进）：**~ yourself + adv./prep.** *I managed to drag myself out of bed.* 我总算硬撑着从床上爬了起来。◇ **+ adv./prep.** *She always drags behind when we walk anywhere.* 我们每去什么地方她都慢慢腾腾吃力地跟在后面。

• **PERSUADE SB TO GO** 劝人走 **3** [T] **~ sb/yourself + adv./prep.** to persuade sb to come or go somewhere they do not really want to come or go to 生拉硬拽；劝人勉强来（或去）：*I'm sorry to drag you all this way in the heat.* 对不起，这么热的天硬拉着你跑了那么远。◇ *The party was so good I couldn't drag myself away.* 这聚会太好玩了，我舍不得离开。

• **OF TIME** 时间 **4** [I] (of time or an event 时间或活动) to pass very slowly 过得很慢；拖沓地进行：*Time dragged terribly.* 时间过得真慢。◇ *The meeting really dragged.* 这会议开得真拖拉。 ➲ SEE ALSO DRAG ON at DRAG

D

D

- **TOUCH GROUND** 触到地上 **5** [I, T] to move, or make sth move, partly touching the ground （使）在地上拖着移动: *This dress is too long—it drags on the ground when I walk.* 这条连衣裙太长了，我走路时会拖在地上。◇ **~ sth** *He was dragging his coat in the mud.* 他的外套拖在泥里。
- **SEARCH RIVER** 在河中搜索 **6** [T] **~ sth (for sb/sth)** to search the bottom of a river, lake, etc. with nets or hooks 用网（或钩）搜索（河或湖底）: *They dragged the canal for the murder weapon.* 他们用拖网沿运河打捞凶器。
- **COMPUTING** 计算机技术 **7** [T] **~ sth + adv./prep.** to move some text, an ICON, etc. across the screen of a computer using the mouse（用鼠标）拖动 ➲ **WORDFINDER NOTE** AT COMMAND ➲ **MORE LIKE THIS** 36, page R29

IDM **drag your 'feet/'heels** to be deliberately slow in doing sth or in making a decision 故意拖拉；故意延迟（作出决定） ➲ MORE AT BOOTSTRAP

PHR V **,drag 'by** (of time 时间) to pass very slowly 过得很慢；拖沓地进行: *The last few weeks of the summer really dragged by.* 夏天最后的几个星期过得真是慢啊。**,drag sb↔'down** to make sb feel weak or unhappy 使虚弱（或不愉快）**,drag sb/sth↔'down (to sth)** to bring sb/sth to a lower social or economic level, a lower standard of behaviour, etc. 使社会地位（或经济地位、行为标准等）下降: *If he fails, he'll drag us all down with him.* 要是他失败了，我们大家都会受到连累。**,drag sth/sb 'into sth | ,drag sth/sb↔'in 1** to start to talk about sth/sb that has nothing to do with what is being discussed 把毫不相干的事（或人）插入谈论；毫无必要地扯到: *Do you have to drag politics into everything?* 你什么事都非要把政治扯进去吗？ **2** to try to get sb who is not connected with a situation involved in it 硬让毫无关系的人卷入；硬把…拉进去: *Don't drag the children into our argument.* 不要硬让孩子也卷入我们的争论。**,drag 'on** (*disapproving*) to go on for too long 拖得太久；持续太久: *The dispute has dragged on for months.* 这场争论已没完没了地持续了数月。**,drag sth↔'out** to make sth last longer than necessary 不必要地拖延；使持续过久 SYN **prolong**: *Let's not drag out this discussion—we need to reach a decision.* 别让这场讨论拖得太久，我们得作出决定。**,drag sth 'out of sb** to make sb say sth they do not want to say 强迫某人说出；套某人的话: *We dragged a confession out of him.* 我们硬逼着他招了供。**,drag sth↔'up** to mention an unpleasant story, fact, etc. that people do not want to remember or talk about 提起（别人不愿回忆或谈论的事）: *Why do you have to keep dragging up my divorce?* 你为什么非要老提我离婚的事呢？

■ ***noun***

- **BORING PERSON/THING** 令人厌烦的人 / 事 **1** [sing.] (*informal*) a boring person or thing; sth that is annoying 令人厌烦的人；乏味无聊的事: *He's such a drag.* 他真惹人讨厌。◇ *Walking's a drag—let's drive there.* 步行太累了，咱们开车去吧。◇ *Having to work late every day is a drag.* 每天都得晚下班可真讨厌。
- **SB/STH STOPPING PROGRESS** 阻碍前进的人 / 事物 **2** [sing.] **a ~ on sb/sth** (*informal*) a person or thing that makes progress difficult 累赘；拖累；绊脚石: *He came to be seen as a drag on his own party's prospects.* 他逐渐被看成是阻碍自己的党走向未来的绊脚石。
- **ON CIGARETTE** 香烟 **3** [C] (*informal*) an act of breathing in smoke from a cigarette, etc. 抽一口；吸一口 SYN **draw**: *She took a long drag on her cigarette.* 她长长地抽了一大口烟。
- **WOMEN'S CLOTHES** 女装 **4** [U] (*informal*) clothes that are usually worn by the opposite sex (usually women's clothes worn by men) 异性服装（通常指男子穿的女装）: *He performed in drag.* 他身着女装演出。◇ ***a drag queen*** (= a man who dresses in women's clothes, usually in order to entertain people) 男扮女装者（通常以娱乐他人为目的）
- **PHYSICS** 物理 **5** [U] the force of the air that acts against the movement of an aircraft or other vehicle（作用于飞机或其他交通工具的）（空气）阻力 ➲ COMPARE LIFT *n.* (5) ➲ SEE ALSO MAIN DRAG

,drag-and-'drop *adj.* (*computing* 计) relating to the moving of ICONS, etc. on a screen using the mouse（鼠标）拖放的

dra·gée /ˈdrɑːʒeɪ; *NAmE* drɑːˈʒeɪ/ *noun* **1** a sweet with a hard covering 糖衣夹心糖 **2** a very small silver or gold-coloured ball, used for decorating cakes（装饰蛋糕的）小银珠（或小金珠）

drag·net /ˈdræɡnet/ *noun* **1** a net which is pulled through water to catch fish, or along the ground to catch animals（捕鱼的）拖网；捕猎网 ➲ **WORDFINDER NOTE** AT FISHING **2** a thorough search, especially for a criminal 彻底搜查；（尤指对罪犯的）拉网式搜捕

dragon /ˈdræɡən/ *noun* **1** (in stories) a large aggressive animal with wings and a long tail, that can breathe out fire（传说中的）龙 **2** (*disapproving, especially BrE*) a woman who behaves in an aggressive and frightening way 悍妇；母夜叉

'dragon boat *noun* a long narrow boat of traditional Chinese design that is used for racing and that is moved through the water by a lot of people using PADDLES. It is decorated to look like a dragon. 龙舟；龙船

dragon·fly /ˈdræɡənflaɪ/ *noun* (*pl.* **-ies**) an insect with a long thin body, often brightly coloured, and two pairs of large transparent wings. Dragonflies are often seen over water. 蜻蜓 ➲ **VISUAL VOCAB** PAGE V13

drag·oon /drəˈɡuːn/ *noun, verb*

■ ***noun*** a soldier in the past who rode a horse and carried a gun（旧时的携枪）骑兵

■ ***verb***

PHR V **dra'goon sb into sth/into doing sth** (*formal*) to force or persuade sb to do sth that they do not want to do 迫使就范；勉强人做（不愿做的事） SYN **coerce**

'drag race *noun* a race between specially adapted cars over a short distance（汽车）直线加速赛 ▶ **'drag racing** *noun* [U]

drag·ster /ˈdræɡstə(r)/ *noun* a car that is used in a drag race 直线加速赛赛车

drain /dreɪn/ *verb, noun*

■ ***verb*** **1** [T, I] **~ (sth)** to make sth empty or dry by removing all the liquid from it; to become empty or dry in this way 排空；（使）流光；放干: *Drain and rinse the pasta.* 把通心粉过一过水。◇ *The marshes have been drained.* 沼泽地里的水已排干。◇ *You will need to drain the central heating system before you replace the radiator.* 你得先把中央供暖系统的水排净再更换散热器。◇ *The swimming pool drains very slowly.* 游泳池里的水排得很慢。◇ *Leave the dishes to drain.* 把碟子控干。➲ **COLLOCATIONS** AT COOKING **2** [T, I] to make liquid flow away from sth; to flow away（使）流走，流出: **~ sth (from/out of sth)** *We had to drain the oil out of the engine.* 我们必须把发动机里的机油全部放掉。◇ **~ sth away/off** *Drain off the excess fat from the meat.* 把肉里面多余的油沥掉。◇ **~ away/off** *She pulled out the plug and the water drained away.* 她拔掉塞子，让水流走了。◇ (*figurative*) *My anger slowly drained away.* 我的怒火慢慢平息下来。◇ **~ into sth** *The river drains into a lake.* 这条河流入湖中。◇ **~ from/out of sth** *All the colour drained from his face when I told him the news.* 我把这消息告诉他时他脸色变得煞白。◇ **~ of sth** *His face drained of colour.* 他的脸上血色全无。 **3** [T] **~ sth** to empty a cup or glass by drinking everything in it 喝光；喝干: *In one gulp, he drained the glass.* 他一口喝干了杯中的水。◇ *She quickly drained the last of her drink.* 她一下子就把最后一点儿酒喝掉了。 **4** [T] to make sb/sth weaker, poorer, etc. by using up their/its strength, money, etc. 使（精力、金钱等）耗尽: **~ sb/sth** *My mother's hospital expenses were slowly draining my income.* 我母亲的住院开销把我的收入渐渐耗光了。◇ *an exhausting and draining experience* 令人精疲力竭的一段经历 ◇ **~ sb/sth of sth** *I felt drained of energy.* 我感到筋疲力尽。

■ ***noun*** **1** [C] a pipe that carries away dirty water or other liquid waste 下水道；排水管: *We had to call in a plumber to unblock the drain.* 我们只得叫个管子工来疏通下水道。◇ *The drains* (= the system of pipes) *date from the beginning of the century.* 下水道排水系统是本世纪初修的。

➲ WORDFINDER NOTE AT WASTE **2** [C] (*BrE*) (*US* **grate**, **'sewer grate**) a frame of metal bars over the opening to a drain in the ground 下水道孔盖 **3** (*US*) (*BrE* **plug·hole**) [C] a hole in a bath/BATHTUB, SINK, etc. where the water flows away and into which a plug fits （浴缸、水池等的）排水孔，渗水孔，漏眼 ➲ VISUAL VOCAB PAGE V25 **4** [sing.] **a ~ on sb/sth** a thing that uses a lot of the time, money, etc. that could be used for sth else 消耗；耗竭；耗费：*Military spending is a huge drain on the country's resources.* 军费开支是对国家资源的巨大耗费。➲ SEE ALSO BRAIN DRAIN

IDM (**go**) **down the 'drain** (*BrE also* (**go**) **down the 'plug-hole**) (*informal*) (to be) wasted; (to get) very much worse （被）浪费掉；（变得）非常糟糕：*It's just money down the drain, you know.* 你要知道，这是白白丢钱。◇ *Safety standards have gone down the drain.* 安全标准根本不管用了。➲ MORE AT LAUGH *v.*

drain·age /'dreɪnɪdʒ/ *noun* [U] **1** the process by which water or liquid waste is drained from an area 排水；放水：*a **drainage system/channel/ditch*** 排水系统 / 渠 / 沟 ◇ *The area has good natural drainage.* 这个地区有良好的天然排水系统。**2** a system of drains 排水系统

drained /dreɪnd/ *adj.* [not usually before noun] very tired and without energy 精疲力竭；无精打采：*She suddenly felt totally drained.* 她突然感到精疲力竭。◇ *The experience left her **emotionally drained**.* 这次经历使得她心灰意懒。

'draining board (*BrE*) (*NAmE* **'drain·board** /'dreɪnbɔːd; *NAmE* -bɔːrd/) *noun* the area next to a kitchen SINK where cups, plates, etc. are put for the water to run off, after they have been washed （厨房洗涤池边控干洗过的杯、碟等的）滴水板 ➲ VISUAL VOCAB PAGE V26 ➲ MORE LIKE THIS 9, page R26

drain·pipe /'dreɪnpaɪp/ *noun* **1** (*NAmE also* **down·spout**) a pipe that carries RAINWATER from the roof of a building to a DRAIN （把雨水从屋顶输送到下水道的）雨水管，排水管 ➲ VISUAL VOCAB PAGE V18 ➲ PICTURE AT PIPE **2** a pipe that carries dirty water or other liquid waste away from a building （排放建筑物内污水的）排水管，泄水管

drake /dreɪk/ *noun* a male DUCK 公鸭 ➲ SEE ALSO DUCKS AND DRAKES

dram /dræm/ *noun* (*especially ScotE*) a small amount of an alcoholic drink, especially WHISKY 少量的酒（尤指威士忌）

drama AW /'drɑːmə/ *noun* **1** [C] a play for the theatre, television or radio 戏；剧：*a **costume/historical, etc. drama*** 古装、历史等剧 ➲ WORDFINDER NOTE AT PLAY, PROGRAMME

> WORDFINDER 联想词：**comedy**, denouement, dialogue, dramatic irony, **play**, scene, set, soliloquy, speech

2 [U] plays considered as a form of literature 戏剧文学；戏剧艺术；戏剧：***classical/Elizabethan/modern, etc. drama*** 古典戏剧、伊丽莎白时代的戏剧、现代戏剧等 ◇ *a drama critic* 戏剧评论家 ◇ *drama school* 戏剧学校 ◇ *a drama student* 学习戏剧艺术的学生 ◇ *I studied English and Drama at college.* 我在大学学的是英语和戏剧。➲ WORDFINDER NOTE AT WRITE **3** [C] an exciting event 戏剧性事件；戏剧性情节：*A powerful human drama was unfolding before our eyes.* 一个极富人情味的戏剧性事件在我们的眼前上演了。**4** [U] the fact of being exciting 激动；兴奋；刺激：*You couldn't help being thrilled by the drama of the situation.* 这充满激情的场面令人不禁激动不已。

IDM **make a drama out of sth** to make a small problem or event seem more important or serious than it really is 小题大做；大惊小怪

'drama queen *noun* (*informal, disapproving*) a person who behaves as if a small problem or event is more important or serious than it really is 大惊小怪的人；小题大做的人

dra·mat·ic AW /drə'mætɪk/ *adj.* **1** (of a change, an event, etc. 变化、事情等) sudden, very great and often surprising 突然的；巨大的；令人吃惊的：*a **dramatic increase/fall/change/improvement*** 暴涨；暴跌；巨变；巨大的改进 ◇ ***dramatic results/developments/news*** 出人意料的结果；突飞猛进的发展；令人吃惊的消息 ◇ *The announcement had a **dramatic effect** on house prices.* 这项公告对房屋价格产生了巨大的影响。**2** exciting and impressive 激动人心的；令人兴奋难忘的：*a dramatic victory* 激动人心的胜利 ◇ *They watched dramatic pictures of the police raid on TV.* 他们在电视上看到了警察突击搜捕的激动人心的画面。➲ SYNONYMS AT EXCITING **3** [usually before noun] connected with the theatre or plays 戏剧的；有关戏剧的；戏剧艺术的：*a local dramatic society* 地方戏剧协会 **4** exaggerated in order to create a special effect and attract people's attention 戏剧性的；戏剧般的；夸张做作的：*He flung out his arms in a **dramatic gesture**.* 他夸张地张开双臂。◇ *Don't be so dramatic!* 别那么夸张做作！▸ **dra·mat·ic·al·ly** AW /-kli/ *adv.*：*Prices have fallen dramatically.* 价格突然暴跌。◇ *Events could have developed in a dramatically different way.* 事情本来可以发展成另一种局面。◇ *'At last!' she cried dramatically.* "终于成功了！" 她激动地叫起来。

dra,matic 'irony *noun* [U] a situation in a play when a character's words carry an extra meaning to the audience because they know more than the character, especially about what is going to happen 戏剧性讽示（指观众比剧中人更能领会其台词的言外之意）➲ WORDFINDER NOTE AT DRAMA

dra·mat·ics /drə'mætɪks/ *noun* [pl.] behaviour that does not seem sincere because it is exaggerated or too emotional 夸张的行为；做作的感情表露 ➲ SEE ALSO AMATEUR DRAMATICS

drama·tis per·sonae /ˌdræmətɪs pɜː'səʊnaɪ; *NAmE* pɜːr'soʊ-/ *noun* [pl.] (*from Latin, formal*) all the characters in a play in the theatre 全体剧中人物；（统称）一出戏的演员

drama·tist AW /'dræmətɪst/ *noun* a person who writes plays for the theatre, television or radio 剧作家；编剧 SYN **playwright**：*a TV dramatist* 电视剧编剧

drama·tize AW (*BrE also* **-ise**) /'dræmətaɪz/ *verb* **1** [T] **~ sth** to present a book, an event, etc. as a play or a film/movie 将…改编成剧本；将…搬上（舞台或银幕）**2** [T, I] **~ (sth)** to make sth seem more exciting or important than it really is 使戏剧化；戏剧性地表现；夸张：*Don't worry too much about what she said—she tends to dramatize things.* 别太在意她说的话，她往往言过其实。▸ **drama·tiza·tion, -isa·tion** AW /ˌdræmətaɪ'zeɪʃn; *NAmE* -tə'z-/ *noun* [U, C]：*a television dramatization of the trial* 根据那次审判改编成的电视剧

drama·turgy /'dræmətɜːdʒi; *NAmE* -tɜːrdʒi/ *noun* [U] (*formal*) the study or activity of writing dramatic texts 编剧研究；编剧

dram·edy /'drɑːmədi; *NAmE* 'dræm-/ *noun* (*pl.* **-ies**) (*NAmE*) a television programme that is intended to be both humorous and serious 正喜剧（融合幽默与严肃成分的电视剧）

drank PAST TENSE OF DRINK

drape /dreɪp/ *verb, noun*

■ *verb* **1 ~ sth around/over/across, etc. sth** to hang clothes, materials, etc. loosely on sb/sth 将（衣服、织物等）悬挂，披：*She had a shawl draped around her shoulders.* 她肩上披着一条围巾。◇ *He draped his coat over the back of the chair.* 他把外衣搭在座椅背上。◇ *She draped a cover over the old sofa.* 她把套子罩在旧沙发上。**2 ~ sb/sth in/with sth** to cover or decorate sb/sth with material 遮盖；盖住；装饰：*walls draped in ivy* 长满常春藤的墙 **3 ~ sth around/round/over, etc. sth** to allow part of your body to rest on sth in a relaxed way 使（身体部位）放松地搭在…上：*His arm was draped casually around her shoulders.* 他随意地将手臂搭在她的双肩上。

■ *noun* (*especially NAmE*) (*NAmE also* **dra·pery**) [usually pl.] a long thick curtain （厚长的）帘子，帷帘，帷幕：*blue velvet drapes* 蓝色丝绒帷帘

D

draper /ˈdreɪpə(r)/ *noun* (*old-fashioned, BrE*) **1** a person who owns or manages a shop that sells cloth, curtains, etc. 布商；布料零售商；纺织品商 **2 draper's** (*pl.* **drapers**) a shop/store that sells cloth, curtains, etc. 布店；纺织品店

dra·pery /ˈdreɪpəri/ *noun* (*pl.* **-ies**) **1** [U] (*also* **dra·per·ies** [pl.]) cloth or clothing hanging in loose folds 垂褶：*a cradle swathed in draperies and blue ribbon* 扎着打褶装饰织物和蓝色缎带的摇篮 **2** [C, usually pl.] (*NAmE*) = DRAPE **3** [U] (*old-fashioned*) cloth and materials for sewing sold by a draper（布商出售的）织物，布料 ➲ COMPARE DRY GOODS

dras·tic /ˈdræstɪk; *BrE also* ˈdrɑːs-/ *adj.* extreme in a way that has a sudden, serious or violent effect on sth 极端的；急剧的；严厉的；猛烈的：***drastic measures/changes*** 严厉的措施；剧烈的变化 ◇ *The government is threatening to **take drastic action**.* 政府警告说要采取断然措施。◇ *a drastic shortage of food* 食物的极度短缺 ◇ *Talk to me before you do anything drastic.* 你采取任何重大行动之前要跟我谈谈。▶ **dras·tic·al·ly** /-kli/ *adv.*：*Output has been drastically reduced.* 产量已急剧下降。◇ *Things have started to go drastically wrong.* 情况开始急转直下，急剧恶化。

drat /dræt/ *exclamation* (*old-fashioned, informal*) used to show that you are annoyed（表示厌烦）见鬼，讨厌，该死，倒霉：*Drat! I forgot my key.* 真见鬼！我忘带钥匙了。▶ **drat·ted** *adj.* [only before noun] (*old-fashioned, BrE, informal*)：*This dratted pen won't work.* 这该死的笔写不出字来。

draught /drɑːft; *NAmE* dræft/ (*BrE*) (*NAmE* **draft**) *noun, adj., verb*

■ ***noun* 1** [C] a flow of cool air in a room or other confined space 穿堂风；通风气流；通风：*There's a draught in here.* 这儿有一股冷风。◇ *A cold draught of air blew in from the open window.* 一股寒气从敞开的窗户吹了进来。◇ *I was sitting **in a draught**.* 我坐在风口上。 **2** [C] (*formal*) one continuous action of swallowing liquid; the amount swallowed 一饮（的量）：*He took a deep draught of his beer.* 他喝了一大口啤酒。 **3** [C] (*old use* or *literary*) medicine in a liquid form 药水；饮剂：*a sleeping draught* (= one that makes you sleep) 一服安眠饮剂 **4 draughts** (*BrE*) (*NAmE* **check·ers**) [U] a game for two players using 24 round pieces on a board marked with black and white squares 国际跳棋；西洋跳棋 **5** [C] (*BrE*) (*NAmE* **check·er**) one of the round pieces used in a game of draughts（国际跳棋的）棋子；（西洋跳棋的）棋子

IDM **on ˈdraught** (*BrE*) (of beer 啤酒) taken from a large container (= a BARREL) 从桶中汲取的；散装的：*This beer is not available on draught* (= it is available only in bottles or cans). 这种啤酒不卖散装。

■ ***adj.* 1** [usually before noun] served from a large container (= a BARREL) rather than in a bottle 零售的；散装的：*draught beer* 散装啤酒 **2** [only before noun] used for pulling heavy loads 拖曳重载用的：*a draught horse* 役马

■ ***verb*** (*especially BrE*) = DRAFT

draught·board /ˈdrɑːftbɔːd; *NAmE* ˈdræftbɔːrd/ (*BrE*) (*NAmE* **ˈcheck·er·board**) *noun* a board with black and white squares, used for playing DRAUGHTS/CHECKERS 国际跳棋棋盘；西洋跳棋棋盘

ˈdraught excluder (*BrE*) (*NAmE* **ˈweather strip**) *noun* [C, U] a piece of material that helps to prevent cold air coming through a door, window, etc.（门窗等的）密封条

draughts·man (*BrE*) (*NAmE* **drafts·man**) /ˈdrɑːftsmən; *NAmE* ˈdræft-/ *noun* (*pl.* **-men** /-mən/) **1** a person whose job is to draw detailed plans of machinery, buildings, etc. 制图员 **2** a person who draws 绘画者：*He's a poor draughtsman.* 他不擅长绘画。➲ SEE ALSO DRAUGHTSWOMAN, DRAUGHTSPERSON

draughts·man·ship (*BrE*) (*NAmE* **drafts·man·ship**) /ˈdrɑːftsmənʃɪp; *NAmE* ˈdræfts-/ *noun* [U] the ability to draw well 画图才能；绘画天赋：*You have to admire her superb draughtsmanship.* 你不得不佩服她那一流的绘画才能。

draughts·person (*BrE*) (*NAmE* **drafts·person**) /ˈdrɑːftspɜːsn; *NAmE* ˈdræftspɜːrsn/ *noun* a draughtsman or a draughtswoman 制图员；绘画者

draughts·woman (*BrE*) (*NAmE* **drafts·woman**) /ˈdrɑːftswʊmən; *NAmE* ˈdræft-/ *noun* (*pl.* **-women** /-wɪmɪn/) **1** a woman whose job is to draw detailed plans of machinery, buildings, etc. 女制图员 ➲ NOTE AT GENDER **2** a woman who draws 女绘画者 ➲ SEE ALSO DRAUGHTSMAN

draughty /ˈdrɑːfti; *NAmE* ˈdræfti/ (*BrE*) (*NAmE* **drafty**) *adj.* (**draught·ier**, **draughti·est**) (of a room, etc. 房间等) uncomfortable because cold air is blowing through 有过堂风的；有冷风吹过的：*a draughty room/corridor* 有过堂风的房间 / 走廊

Dra·vid·ian /drəˈvɪdiən/ *adj.* connected with a group of languages spoken in southern India and in Sri Lanka, or with the people who speak these languages（印度南部和斯里兰卡）达罗毗荼诸语的，达罗毗荼人的

draw /drɔː/ *verb, noun*

■ ***verb*** (**drew** /druː/, **drawn** /drɔːn/)

• **MAKE PICTURES** 绘画 **1** [I, T] to make pictures, or a picture of sth, with a pencil, pen or CHALK (but not paint)（用铅笔、钢笔或粉笔）画，描绘，描画：*You draw beautifully.* 你的画画得真好。◇ **~ sth** ***to draw a picture/diagram/graph*** 画画；画示意图；画曲线图 ◇ *She drew a house.* 她画了一栋房屋。◇ *He drew a circle in the sand with a stick.* 他用枝条在沙地上画了一个圆。◇ (*figurative*) *The report drew a grim picture of inefficiency and corruption.* 这份报告描绘了一幅办事效率低下和贪污腐化的可怕景象。➲ COLLOCATIONS AT ART

• **PULL** 拖；拉 **2** [T] **~ sth/sb + adv./prep.** to move sth/sb by pulling it or them gently 拖（动）；拉（动）；牵引：*He drew the cork out of the bottle.* 他把瓶塞拔了出来。◇ *I drew my chair up closer to the fire.* 我把椅子向火旁拉近了点。◇ *She drew me onto the balcony.* 她把我拉到阳台上。◇ *I tried to **draw him aside*** (= for example where I could talk to him privately). 我试图把他拉到一边。◇ (*figurative*) *My eyes were drawn to the man in the corner.* 角落里的那个男人引起了我的注意。➲ SYNONYMS AT PULL **3** [T] **~ sth** (of horses, etc. 马匹等) to pull a vehicle such as a CARRIAGE 拉，拖（车）：*The Queen's coach was drawn by six horses.* 女王的御驾是由六匹马拉的。◇ *a horse-drawn carriage* 马车

• **CURTAINS** 窗帘 **4** [T] **~ sth** to open or close curtains, etc. 拉（窗帘、帘子）：*The blinds were drawn.* 窗帘拉上了。◇ *It was getting dark so I switched on the light and drew the curtains.* 天快黑了，我便打开灯，拉上了窗帘。◇ *She drew back the curtains and let the sunlight in.* 她拉开窗帘让阳光照进来。

• **MOVE** 移动 **5** [I] **+ adv./prep.** to move in the direction mentioned（向某个方向）移动，行进：*The train drew into the station.* 火车徐徐驶入车站。◇ *The train drew in.* 火车进站了。◇ *The figures in the distance seemed to be drawing closer.* 远处的人影好像越来越近。◇ *Their car **drew alongside** ours.* 他们的汽车与我们的并排行驶。◇ (*figurative*) *Her retirement is drawing near.* 她快退休了。◇ (*figurative*) *The meeting was **drawing to a close**.* 会议快结束了。

• **WEAPON** 武器 **6** [T, I] **~ (sth) (on sb)** to take out a weapon, such as a gun or a SWORD, in order to attack sb 拔出；抽出；掏出：*She drew a revolver on me.* 她拔出左轮手枪对准我。◇ *He came towards them with his sword drawn.* 他手持出鞘的剑向他们走来。

• **ATTRACT** 吸引 **7** [T] to attract or interest sb 吸引；招引；使感兴趣：**~ sb** *The movie is drawing large audiences.* 这部影片吸引着大批观众。◇ *The course draws students from all over the country.* 这课程吸引着来自全国各地的学生。◇ **~ sb to sth** *Her screams drew passers-by to the scene.* 她的惊叫声把过路人吸引到了现场。

• **GET REACTION** 引起反应 **8** [T] to produce a reaction or response 产生，引起，激起（反应或回应）：**~ sth** *The plan has drawn a lot of criticism.* 这个计划引来众多批评。◇ **~ sth from sb** *The announcement drew loud applause from the audience.* 公告博得观众的热烈掌声。

• **MAKE SB TALK** 使人说话 **9** [T] **~ sb (about/on sth)** [often passive] to make sb say more about sth 使说出；使吐露：*Spielberg refused to be drawn on his next movie.* 斯皮尔伯格拒绝透露他下一部影片的任何消息。

- **CONCLUSION** 结论 **10** [T] **~ sth (from sth)** to have a particular idea after you have studied sth or thought about it 获取；得出；推断出：*What conclusions did you draw from the report?* 你从这个报告中得出了什么结论？◇ *We can draw some lessons for the future from this accident.* 我们可以从这起事故中为今后吸取教训。
- **COMPARISON** 比较 **11** [T] **~ sth** to express a comparison or a contrast 进行，作（比较或对比）：*to **draw an analogy/a comparison/a parallel/a distinction** between two events* 对两件事进行类比/比较；找出两件事之间的相似之处/区别
- **CHOOSE** 选择 **12** [I, T] to decide sth by picking cards, tickets or numbers by chance 抽（签、牌）；抓（阄）：*We drew for partners.* 我们抓阄决定搭档。◇ **~ sth** *They had to **draw lots** to decide who would go.* 他们只得抽签决定谁去。◇ *He drew the winning ticket.* 他抽到中彩券了。◇ *Names were drawn from a hat for the last few places.* 从帽子里抽签来决定最后几个名额。◇ *Italy has been drawn against Spain in the first round.* 第一轮比赛的抽签结果是意大利队对西班牙队。◇ **~ sb/sth to do sth** *Italy has been drawn to play Spain.* 抽签结果是意大利队对西班牙队。
- **GAME** 比赛 **13** [I, T] to finish a game without either team winning 以平局结束；不分胜负：*England and France drew.* 英格兰队和法国队打平。◇ *England and France drew 3–3.* 英格兰队与法国队打成三平。◇ **~ with/against sb** *England drew with/against France.* 英格兰队与法国队打成平局。◇ **~ sth** *England drew their game against France.* 英格兰队与法国队战平了。
- **MONEY** 钱 **14** [T] to take money or payments from a bank account or post office 提取；领取；支取 **SYN** **withdraw**: **~ sth out (of sth)** *I drew out £200.* 我取了 200 英镑。◇ *Can I draw $80 out of my account?* 我可以从我的账户上提取 80 美元吗？◇ **~ sth (from sth)** *She went to the post office to draw her pension.* 她到邮局去领取她的养老金。◇ **~ sth on sth** *The cheque was drawn on his personal account.* 这张支票从他的个人账户中支付。
- **LIQUID/GAS** 液体；气体 **15** [T] **~ sth (+adv./prep.)** to take or pull liquid or gas from somewhere 抽出；吸出：*to draw water from a well* 从井中抽水 ◇ *The device draws gas along the pipe.* 这装置将气体顺着管子抽出来。
- **SMOKE/AIR** 烟；空气 **16** [I, T] to breathe in smoke or air 抽（烟）；吸（气）：**~ at/on sth** *He drew thoughtfully on his pipe.* 他若有所思地抽着烟斗。◇ **~ sth in** *She breathed deeply, drawing in the fresh mountain air.* 她深深地呼吸着山上的新鲜空气。

IDM **draw a 'blank** to get no response or result 无回音；无结果；无收获：*So far, the police investigation has drawn a blank.* 到目前为止警方的调查毫无结果。 **draw 'blood** to make sb BLEED 使流血 **draw 'breath** (*BrE*) (*US* **draw a 'breath**) **1** to stop doing sth and rest 停下来歇口气：*She talks all the time and hardly stops to draw breath.* 她一直滔滔不绝，几乎没停下来喘口气。 **2** (*literary*) to live; to be alive 生存；活着：*He was as kind a man as ever drew breath.* 他是世上少有的大善人。 **draw sb's 'fire** to make sb direct their anger, criticism, etc. at you, so that others do not have to face it（为掩护他人）吸引…的火力，转移…的视线 **draw a 'line under sth** (*BrE*) to say that sth is finished and not worth discussing any more 到…为止；就…打住 **draw the 'line (at sth/at doing sth)** to refuse to do sth; to set a limit 拒绝做；给…定界限：*I don't mind helping, but I draw the line at doing everything myself.* 我帮忙倒无所谓，但可不能什么事都让我做。◇ *We would have liked to invite all our relatives, but you have to draw the line somewhere.* 我们本倒是愿意邀请所有亲戚的，但你总得有个限度呀。 **draw the 'line (between sth and sth)** to distinguish between two closely related ideas 划界线；区分（两个密切相关的思想）：*Where do you draw the line between genius and madness?* 天才和疯狂之间如何划界呢？ **ˌdraw the short 'straw** (*BrE*) (*NAmE* **get the ˌshort end of the 'stick**) to be the person in a group who is chosen or forced to perform an unpleasant duty or task 抽到倒霉签；被派做苦差事：*I drew the short straw and had to clean the toilets.* 我抽到了下下签，只得打扫厕所了。 **ˌdraw 'straws (for sth)** to decide on sb to do or have sth, by choosing pieces of paper, etc. 抽签（决定某事）：*We drew straws for who went first.* 我们抽签决定谁先去。 ➲ MORE AT BATTLE *n.*, BEAD, DAGGER, HEIGHT, HORN *n.*, LOT *n.*, SIDE *n.*

PHR V **ˌdraw 'back** to move away from sb/sth 移开；后退：*He came close but she drew back.* 他靠近，而她却向后退。 **ˌdraw 'back (from sth/from doing sth)** to choose not to take action, especially because you feel nervous 退缩；撤销；撤回：*We drew back from taking our neighbours to court.* 我们撤回了对邻居的起诉。 **ˌdraw sth↔'down | ˌdraw 'down** (*especially NAmE*) to reduce a supply of sth that has been created over a period of time; to be reduced 减少；下降：*There are many life events that can unexpectedly draw down savings.* 生活中许多意想不到的事情都可能会花费存款。◇ *If we don't cut costs our reserves will draw down.* 如果我们不削减开支，储备金就会减少。 ➲ RELATED NOUN DRAWDOWN **ˌdraw sth↔'down (from sth) | ˌdraw 'down on sth** (*especially NAmE*) (*BrE usually* **draw**) (*finance* 财) to take money from a fund that a bank, etc. has made available 提取，动用（资金）：*The company has already drawn down €600 million of its €725 million credit line.* 公司已从 7.25 亿欧元的授信额度中动用了 6 亿欧元。◇ *They can draw down on the loan at any time.* 他们可以随时提取这笔贷款。 ➲ RELATED NOUN DRAWDOWN **'draw sth from sb/sth** to take or obtain sth from a particular source （从…中）得到，获得：*to **draw support/comfort/strength** from your family* 从家人那里得到支持/安慰/力量 ◇ *She drew her inspiration from her childhood experiences.* 她从儿时的经历中获得灵感。 **ˌdraw 'in** to become dark earlier in the evening as winter gets nearer （天黑）渐早；（白昼）渐短：*The nights/days are drawing in.* 天黑得越来越早了。 **'draw sb into sth/into doing sth | ˌdraw sb↔'in** to involve sb or make sb take part in sth, although they may not want to take part at first 使卷入；使参与：*youngsters drawn into a life of crime* 身不由己卷入犯罪活动的年轻人 ◇ *The book starts slowly, but it gradually draws you in.* 这本书开始时情节展开得很慢，但渐渐地就把你给完全吸引住了。 **ˌdraw sth↔'off** to remove some liquid from a larger supply 抽出；排掉：*The doctor drew off some fluid to relieve the pressure.* 医生排掉了一些液体以缓解压力。 **ˌdraw 'on** if a time or a season **draws on**, it passes（时光）渐渐过去，荏苒：*Night was drawing on.* 夜渐深了。 **'draw on/upon sth** to use a supply of sth that is available to you 凭借；利用；动用：*I'll have to draw on my savings.* 我只得动用我的存款了。◇ *The novelist draws heavily on her personal experiences.* 这位小说家在很大程度上以她的亲身经历为素材。 **ˌdraw 'out** to become lighter in the evening as summer gets nearer （天黑）渐晚；（白昼）渐长：*The **days/evenings** are drawing out.* 白昼越来越长了。 **ˌdraw sb↔'out** to encourage sb to talk or express themselves freely 使畅所欲言 **ˌdraw sth↔'out** to make sth last longer than usual or necessary 拖延；拉长：*She drew the interview out to over an hour.* 她拖拖沓沓采访了一个多小时。 ➲ SEE ALSO LONG-DRAWN-OUT **ˌdraw 'up** if a vehicle **draws up**, it arrives and stops （车辆）到达某处停下，停止：*The cab drew up outside the house.* 出租车在房子外面停了下来。 **ˌdraw sth↔'up** to make or write sth that needs careful thought or planning 拟订；制订；起草：*to draw up a contract/list* 拟订合同/名单 ➲ WORDFINDER NOTE AT DOCUMENT

■ ***noun***

- **CHOOSING** 选择 **1** (*US also* **draw·ing**) [usually sing.] **~ (for sth)** the act of choosing sth, for example the winner of a prize or the teams who play each other in a competition, usually by taking pieces of paper, etc. out of a container without being able to see what is written on them 抽彩；抽奖；抽签：*the draw for the second round of the Champions League* 欧洲冠军联赛第二轮抽签 ◇ *The draw for the raffle takes place on Saturday.* 星期六进行抽彩。
- **SPORTS/GAMES** 体育运动；比赛 **2** (*especially BrE*) a game in which both teams or players finish with the same number of points 平局；和局；不分胜负：*The match ended in a two-all draw.* 比赛以二平结束。◇ *He managed to hold Smith to a draw* (= to stop him from winning when he seemed likely to do so). 他总算与史密斯打了个

D

平局。➲ COMPARE TIE *n.* (5) **3** (*NAmE usually* **draw·ing**) a competition in which the winners are chosen in a draw 抽奖：*a prize draw* 抽奖 ➲ COMPARE LOTTERY (1) **4** (*BrE*) a sports match for which the teams or players are chosen in a draw 由抽签决定对手的比赛：*Liverpool have an away draw against Manchester United.* 利物浦队抽的签是在客场与曼彻斯特联队进行比赛。 **5** [usually sing.] a set of matches for which the teams or players are chosen in a draw 由抽签决定对手的系列比赛：*There are only two seeded players left in the top half of the draw.* 在抽签系列比赛的上半区就只剩下两名种子选手了。

• ATTRACTION 吸引力 **6** a person, a thing or an event that attracts a lot of people 有吸引力的人（或事物） SYN **attraction**: *She is currently one of the biggest draws on the Irish music scene.* 她是目前爱尔兰音乐界最受欢迎的人物之一。

• SMOKE 烟 **7** an act of breathing in the smoke from a cigarette 吸烟 SYN **drag**

IDM **be quick/fast on the 'draw 1** (*informal*) to be quick to understand or react in a new situation 领悟敏捷；反应迅速：*You can't fool him—he's always quick on the draw.* 你骗不了他，他脑筋一向很快。 **2** to be quick at pulling out a gun in order to shoot it 拔枪迅速 ➲ MORE AT LUCK *n.*

draw·back /ˈdrɔːbæk/ *noun* ~ (**of/to sth**) | ~ (**of/to doing sth**) a disadvantage or problem that makes sth a less attractive idea 缺点；不利条件 SYN **disadvantage, snag**: *The main drawback to it is the cost.* 它的主要缺点是成本高。◇ *This is the one major drawback of the new system.* 这是新系统的一大弊端。

draw·bridge /ˈdrɔːbrɪdʒ/ *noun* a bridge that can be pulled up, for example to stop people from entering a castle or to allow ships to pass under it 活动桥；开合桥；开启桥

draw·down /ˈdrɔːdaʊn/ *noun* [C, U] ~ (**on sth**) **1** the act of reducing a supply of sth that has been created over a period of time; the amount used 消耗；消耗量；泄降：*The cold winter has led to a larger-than-expected draw-down on oil stocks.* 寒冬使石油储备消耗量高出预料。 **2** (*finance* 财) the act of using money that is available to you; the amount used 动用资金；动用资金额：*a draw-down of cash from the company's reserves* 从公司储备金中支取的一笔钱

drawer 🔑 *noun* **1** 🔑 /drɔː(r)/ a part of a piece of furniture such as a desk, used for keeping things in. It is shaped like a box and has a handle on the front for pulling it out. 抽屉：*in the* ***top/middle/bottom drawer*** *of the desk* 写字台的上层 / 中层 / 下层抽屉 ➲ VISUAL VOCAB PAGES V23, V24, V26 ➲ SEE ALSO CHEST OF DRAWERS, TOP DRAWER **2** /ˈdrɔːə(r)/ (*formal*) a person who writes a cheque 开票人；出票人

drawers /drɔːz; *NAmE* drɔːrz/ *noun* [pl.] (*old-fashioned*) KNICKERS or UNDERPANTS, especially ones that cover the upper parts of the legs（长）内裤

draw·ing 🔑 /ˈdrɔːɪŋ/ *noun* **1** 🔑 [C] a picture made using a pencil or pen rather than paint 图画；素描画：*a* ***pencil/charcoal drawing*** 铅笔画；炭笔画 ◇ *a drawing of a yacht* 游艇素描画 ◇ *He* ***did/made a drawing*** *of the old farmhouse.* 他画了一幅古老农舍的素描。 ➲ SYNONYMS AT PICTURE ➲ COLLOCATIONS AT ART **2** 🔑 [U] the art or skill of making pictures, plans, etc. using a pen or pencil 绘画（艺术）；制图（技巧）：*I'm not very good at drawing.* 我不擅长绘画。◇ *technical drawing* 工艺制图 **3** (*NAmE*) = DRAW (1), (3)

'drawing board *noun* a large flat board used for holding a piece of paper while a drawing or plan is being made 绘画板；图画板；制图板

IDM (**go**) **back to the 'drawing board** to start thinking about a new way of doing sth after a previous plan or idea has failed（失败后）另起炉灶，从头开始 **on the 'drawing board** being prepared or considered 在筹划阶段；在设计中：*It's just one of several projects on the drawing board.* 这只是正在筹划的几个项目中的一个。

'drawing pin (*BrE*) (*NAmE* **thumb·tack**, **tack**) *noun* a short pin with a large round flat head, used especially for fastening paper to a board or wall 图钉 ➲ VISUAL VOCAB PAGE V71

'drawing power (*NAmE*) (*BrE* **'pulling power**) *noun* [U] the ability of sb/sth to attract people 吸引力；诱惑力

'drawing room *noun* (*formal* or *old-fashioned*) a room in a large house in which people relax and guests are entertained 起居室；客厅 ➲ COMPARE LIVING ROOM

drawl /drɔːl/ *verb* [T, I] + **speech** | ~ (**sth**) to speak or say sth slowly with vowel sounds that are longer than usual（拉长调子）慢吞吞地说：*'Hi there!' she drawled lazily.* "喂，你好！"她拖着长腔懒洋洋地说。◇ *He had a smooth drawling voice.* 他说起话来油嘴滑舌，带着拖腔。 ▶ **drawl** *noun* [sing.]: *She spoke in a slow southern drawl.* 她带着南方的拖腔慢条斯理地讲话。

drawn /drɔːn/ *adj.* (of a person or their face 人或人脸) looking pale and thin because the person is ill/sick, tired or worried（因身体不适、疲倦或忧虑）憔悴的，苍白的 ➲ SEE ALSO DRAW *v.*

ˌdrawn-'out *adj.* = LONG-DRAWN-OUT

draw·string /ˈdrɔːstrɪŋ/ *noun* a piece of string sewn inside the material at the top of a bag, pair of trousers/pants, etc. that can be pulled tighter in order to make the opening smaller（穿在袋口、裤腰上等的）拉绳，拉带，束带：*They fasten with a drawstring.* 它们是用拉绳系紧的。 ➲ VISUAL VOCAB PAGE V68

dray /dreɪ/ *noun* a low flat vehicle pulled by horses and used in the past for carrying heavy loads, especially BARRELS of beer 平板马车（旧时运重载如桶装啤酒）

dread /dred/ *verb, noun*

■ ***verb*** to be very afraid of sth; to fear that sth bad is going to happen 非常害怕；极为担心： **~ sth** *This was the moment he had been dreading.* 这是他一直最担心的时刻。◇ **~ doing sth** *I dread being sick.* 我特别害怕生病。◇ **~ sb doing sth** *She dreads her husband finding out.* 她生怕丈夫察觉出来。◇ **~ to do sth** *I* ***dread to think*** *what would happen if there really was a fire here.* 我不敢想象假如这儿真的发生火灾会是什么情景。◇ **~ that…** *I both hoped and dreaded that he would come.* 我既希望又害怕他来。

■ ***noun*** [U, C, usually sing.] a feeling of great fear about sth that might or will happen in the future; a thing that causes this feeling 恐惧；令人惧怕的事物：*The prospect of growing old* ***fills me with dread.*** 想到人会一天天老下去便使我充满恐惧。◇ *She has an irrational dread of hospitals.* 她对医院有莫名的恐惧。◇ *The committee members* ***live in dread of*** (= are always worried about) *anything that may cause a scandal.* 委员会成员整天提心吊胆，生怕有什么事会引起流言蜚语。◇ *My greatest dread is that my parents will find out.* 我最担心的就是父母会察觉出来。

dread·ed /ˈdredɪd/ (*also formal* **dread**) *adj.* [only before noun] causing fear 令人害怕的；可怕的：*The dreaded moment had finally arrived.* 可怕的时刻终于来到了。◇ (*humorous*) *Did I hear the dreaded word 'homework'?* 我是不是听到"家庭作业"这可怕的字眼了？

dread·ful /ˈdredfl/ *adj.* (*especially BrE*) **1** very bad or unpleasant 糟糕透顶的；讨厌的；令人不快的：*What dreadful weather!* 多么讨厌的天气！ ◇ *What a dreadful thing to say!* 话说得太难听了！ ◇ *It's dreadful the way they treat their staff.* 他们对待雇员的方式糟糕透了。◇ *How dreadful!* 多讨厌啊！ ◇ *Jane* ***looked dreadful*** (= looked ill or tired). 简看上去脸色很不好。 ➲ SYNONYMS AT TERRIBLE **2** [only before noun] used to emphasize how bad sth is（强调糟糕的程度）极其的，极坏的 SYN **terrible**: *She's making a dreadful mess of things.* 她把事情搞得一塌糊涂。◇ *I'm afraid there's been a dreadful mistake.* 恐怕是出了大错。 **3** [usually before noun] causing fear or suffering 可怕的；令人畏惧的；使人痛苦的 SYN **terrible**: *a dreadful accident* 可怕的事故 ◇ *They suffered dreadful injuries.* 他们严重受伤。

dread·ful·ly /ˈdredfəli/ *adv.* (*especially BrE*) **1** extremely; very much 极其；极端；非常：*I'm dreadfully sorry.* 我感到非常抱歉。◇ *I miss you dreadfully.* 我非常想念你。**2** very badly 糟糕地；厉害地；严重地：*They suffered dreadfully during the war.* 他们在战争中遭受了巨大的痛苦。

dread·locks /ˈdredlɒks; *NAmE* -lɑːks/ (*also informal* **dreads** /dredz/) *noun* [pl.] hair that is twisted into long thick pieces that hang down from the head, worn especially by RASTAFARIANS（尤指拉斯塔法里教派成员蓄的）长发绺，脏辫 ➲ VISUAL VOCAB PAGE V65

dread·nought /ˈdrednɔːt/ *noun* a type of ship used in war in the early 20th century（20 世纪初期的）无畏舰

dream /driːm/ *noun, verb*

■ ***noun*** **1** [C] a series of images, events and feelings that happen in your mind while you are asleep 梦；睡梦：*I had a vivid dream about my old school.* 我做了一个非常逼真的梦，梦见了我的母校。◇ *I thought someone came into the bedroom, but it was just a dream.* 我还以为有人进了卧室，原来只是一场梦。◇ *'Goodnight. Sweet dreams.'* "晚安。祝你做个好梦。" ➲ COMPARE NIGHTMARE (1) ➲ SEE ALSO WET DREAM ➲ WORDFINDER NOTE AT SLEEP **2** [C] a wish to have or be sth, especially one that seems difficult to achieve 梦想；理想；愿望：*Her lifelong dream was to be a famous writer.* 她的毕生愿望就是成为名作家。◇ *He wanted to be rich but it was an impossible dream.* 他想发财，然而这是不可能实现的梦想。◇ *If I win, it will be a* **dream come true**. 如果我赢了，那就是梦想成真。◇ *She tried to turn her dream of running her own business into reality.* 她努力实现经营自己企业的梦想。◇ *a* **dream car/house/job, etc.** 梦寐以求的汽车、房子、工作等 ◇ *I've finally found the man* **of my dreams**. 我终于找到了理想中的男人。◇ *a chance to* **fulfil a** childhood **dream** 实现童年梦想的机会 ◇ *It was the end of all my hopes and dreams.* 我的希望和梦想全都破灭了。➲ SEE ALSO PIPE DREAM **3** [sing.] a state of mind or a situation in which things do not seem real or part of normal life 梦幻状态；恍惚；出神：*She walked around* **in a dream** *all day.* 她整天都在梦游似的到处转悠。➲ SEE ALSO DAYDREAM **4** [sing.] (*informal*) a beautiful or wonderful person or thing 梦一般美妙的人（或事物）；极美好的人（或事物）：*That meal was an absolute dream.* 那顿饭真是太棒了。

IDM **go/work like a ˈdream** **1** to work very well 性能极佳；十分有效：*My new car goes like a dream.* 我的新汽车性能好极了。**2** to happen without problems, in the way that you had planned 毫无困难；非常顺利；完美 **in your ˈdreams** (*informal*) used to tell sb that sth they are hoping for is not likely to happen 你妄想；你在做梦：*'I'll be a manager before I'm 30.' 'In your dreams.'* "我要在 30 岁前当经理。" "你做梦。" **like a bad ˈdream** (of a situation 处境) so unpleasant that you cannot believe it is true 噩梦般令人难以置信：*In broad daylight the events of the night before seemed like a bad dream.* 在大白天里，前一天夜里发生的事情就像噩梦般令人难以置信。➲ MORE AT WILD *adj.*

■ ***verb*** (**dreamt**, **dreamt** /dremt/ or **dreamed**, **dreamed**) **1** [I, T] to experience a series of images, events and feelings in your mind while you are asleep 做梦；梦见：*Did I talk in my sleep? I must have been dreaming.* 我说梦话了吗？我肯定是在做梦。◇ **~ of/about sb/sth** *I dreamt about you last night.* 我昨晚梦见你了。◇ **~ sth** *Did it really happen or did I just dream it?* 这是真的吗？还是我在做梦？◇ **~ (that)…** *I dreamt (that) I got the job.* 我梦见自己得到了那份工作。**2** [I, T] to imagine and think about sth that you would like to happen 想象；梦想：**~ of/about sth** *She dreams of running her own business.* 她梦想自己开公司。◇ *It was the kind of trip most of us only dream about.* 对我们大多数人来说，这样的旅行只是梦想。◇ **~ of/about doing sth** (*informal*) *I wouldn't dream of going without you* (= I would never go without you). 你不去，我绝对不会去。◇ **~ sth** *Who'd have dreamt it? They're getting married.* 谁会料到？他们要结婚了。◇ **~ (that)…** *I never dreamt (that) I'd actually get the job.* 我做梦也没想到会真的得到这份工作。

PHR V **ˌdream sth aˈway** to waste time just thinking about things you would like to do without actually doing anything 梦幻似的度过；在遐想中虚度 **ˌdream ˈon** (*informal*) you say **dream on** to tell sb that an idea is not practical or likely to happen 痴心妄想 **ˌdream sth↔ˈup** (*informal*) to have an idea, especially a very unusual or silly one 凭空想出，虚构出（尤指荒诞不经的事）SYN **think up**：*Trust you to dream up a crazy idea like this!* 你这个人就是会想出这种荒唐的主意来！

dream·boat /ˈdriːmbəʊt; *NAmE* -boʊt/ *noun* (*old-fashioned, informal*) a man who is very attractive 富有魅力的男子；迷人的男子

dreamcatcher 捕梦网

dream·catch·er /ˈdriːmkætʃə(r)/ *noun* a ring containing a decorated net, originally made by Native Americans, and thought to give its owner good dreams 捕梦网（最初由美洲土著制作的一种带装饰网兜的圆环，据信能给主人带来好梦）

dream·er /ˈdriːmə(r)/ *noun* **1** (*sometimes disapproving*) a person who has ideas or plans that are not practical or realistic 梦想家；空想家；不切实际的人 **2** (*usually disapproving*) a person who does not pay attention to what is happening around them, but thinks about other things instead 做白日梦的人；出神的人；神不守舍的人 **3** a person who dreams 做梦的人：*Dreamers do not always remember their dreams.* 做梦的人并不总能记住自己的梦。

dream·land /ˈdriːmlænd/ *noun* [U] (*especially BrE, disapproving*) a pleasant but not very realistic situation that only exists in your mind 梦境；幻想世界；理想世界：*You must be living in dreamland if you think he'll change his mind.* 如果你认为他会改变主意，那你一定是在做梦。

dream·less /ˈdriːmləs/ *adj.* (of sleep 睡眠) without dreams; deep and peaceful 无梦的；酣畅安宁的

dream·like /ˈdriːmlaɪk/ *adj.* as if existing or happening in a dream 似在梦中的；如梦的；梦幻（般）的

ˈdream team *noun* the best possible combination of people for a particular competition or activity 梦之队；最佳阵容；最佳组合

ˈdream ticket *noun* [sing.] (used especially in newspapers about candidates for an election) a combination of people who, together, are considered to be the best（尤用于报章，指大选的候选人）梦幻组合，最佳组合，最佳阵容

Dream·time /ˈdriːmtaɪm/ *noun* [U] = ALCHERINGA

dream·world /ˈdriːmwɜːld; *NAmE* -wɜːrld/ *noun* a world that is not like the real world; a person's idea of reality that is not realistic 幻想世界；理想世界；不现实的想法：*If he thinks it's easy to get a job, he's* **living in a dreamworld**. 如果他认为找工作容易，那他就是在白日做梦。

dreamy /ˈdriːmi/ *adj.* (**dream·ier**, **dreami·est**) **1** looking as though you are thinking about other things and not paying attention to what is happening around you 做白日梦的；心不在焉的：*She had a dreamy look in her* *eyes*. 她眼里带着心不在焉的神色。 **2** (of a person or an idea 人或想法) having a lot of imagination, but not very realistic 爱幻想的（不切实际）: *Paul was dreamy and not very practical.* 保罗喜欢幻想，不太讲究实际。 **3** as if you are in a dream or asleep 似在梦中的；模糊的；朦胧的；恍惚的: *He moved in the dreamy way of a man in a state of shock.* 他惊魂未定，恍恍惚惚。 **4** (*informal*) pleasant and gentle; that makes you feel relaxed 怡然的；恬静的；轻松的: *a slow, dreamy melody* 缓慢柔和的旋律 **5** (*informal*) beautiful; wonderful 漂亮的；美妙的；极好的: *What's he like? I bet he's really dreamy.* 他长得如何？我敢说他一定很俊。 ▶ **dream·ily** /-ɪli/ *adv.* **dreami·ness** *noun* [U]

dreary /ˈdrɪəri; *NAmE* ˈdrɪri/ *adj.* (**drear·ier**, **dreari·est**) that makes you feel sad; dull and not interesting 令人沮丧的；沉闷的；枯燥无味的 SYN **dull**: *a dreary winter's day* 阴沉的冬日 ◇ *a* ***dreary film*** 枯燥无味的影片 ◇ *a long and dreary journey on the train* 火车上漫长而乏味的旅程 ▶ **drear·ily** /ˈdrɪərəli; *NAmE* ˈdrɪr-/ *adv.* **dreari·ness** *noun* [U]

dreck /drek/ *noun* [U] (*slang, especially NAmE*) something that you think is of very bad quality 极低劣的东西；蹩脚货: *The movie is utter dreck.* 那电影完全是垃圾。

dredge /dredʒ/ *verb* **1** [T, I] ~ (**sth**) (**for sth**) to remove mud, stones, etc. from the bottom of a river, CANAL, etc. using a boat or special machine, to make it deeper or to search for sth 疏浚；清淤；挖掘: *They're dredging the harbour so that larger ships can use it.* 他们正在疏浚港湾以便大船驶入。 ◇ *They dredge the bay for gravel.* 他们在挖掘海湾沙砾。 **2** [T] ~ **sth** (**up**) (**from sth**) to bring sth up from the bottom of a river, etc. using a boat or special machine 打捞；采捞；捞取: *waste dredged (up) from the seabed* 从海底打捞出的废物 **3** [T] ~ **sth in/with sth** to cover food lightly with sugar, flour, etc.（用糖、面粉等）撒，涂: *Dredge the top of the cake with icing sugar.* 把糖霜撒在蛋糕面上。

PHR V ˌ**dredge sth↔ˈup** **1** (*usually disapproving*) to mention sth that has been forgotten, especially sth unpleasant or embarrassing 重提，翻出（已遗忘的令人不快的往事）: *The papers keep trying to dredge up details of his past love life.* 这些报纸老是翻出他以往爱情生活的琐事。 **2** to manage to remember sth, especially sth that happened a long time ago 追忆；回忆: *Now she was dredging up memories from the depths of her mind.* 这时，她回忆起内心深处的往事。

dredger /ˈdredʒə(r)/ *noun* a boat or machine that is used to clear mud, etc. from the bottom of a river, or to make the river wider 挖泥船；疏浚船；挖泥机

dregs /dregz/ *noun* [pl.] **1** the last drops of a liquid, mixed with little pieces of solid material that are left in the bottom of a container 残渣；沉淀物: *coffee dregs* 咖啡渣 **2** the worst and most useless parts of sth 渣滓；糟粕: *the dregs of society* 社会渣滓 **3** (*literary*) the last parts of sth 残余: *the last dregs of daylight* 最后的余晖

dreich /driːx/ *adj.* (*ScotE*) dull and depressing 沉闷阴郁的: *dreich weather on the Scottish coast* 苏格兰沿海地区阴郁的天气

drench /drentʃ/ *verb* [often passive] to make sb/sth completely wet 使湿透 SYN **soak**: ~ **sb/sth** *We were caught in the storm and got drenched to the skin.* 我们遇上了暴雨，淋得浑身透湿。 ◇ ~ **sb/sth in/with sth** *His face was drenched with sweat.* 他满头大汗。 ◇ (*figurative*) *She drenched herself in perfume.* 她浑身洒满香水。 ➲ SYNONYMS AT WET

dress 🔑 /dres/ *noun, verb*

■ *noun* **CLOTHES** 衣服 **1** 🔑 [C] a piece of women's clothing that is made in one piece and covers the body down to the legs, sometimes reaching to below the knees, or to the ankles 连衣裙: *a long white dress* 白色的长连衣裙 ◇ *a wedding dress* 婚纱 ➲ VISUAL VOCAB PAGE V66 ➲ SEE ALSO COCKTAIL DRESS, EVENING DRESS, SUNDRESS **2** 🔑 [U] clothes for either men or women 衣服: *to wear* ***casual/formal dress*** 穿便服；穿正装 ◇ *He has no* ***dress sense*** (= no idea of how to dress well). 他毫无服装品味。 ➲ SEE ALSO EVENING DRESS, FANCY DRESS, HEADDRESS, MORNING DRESS

■ *verb*

• **CLOTHES** 衣服 **1** 🔑 [I, T] to put clothes on yourself/sb 穿衣服；给（某人）穿衣服: ~ (**in sth**) *I dressed quickly.* 我很快穿好了衣服。 ◇ ~ **sb** (**in sth**) *She dressed the children in their best clothes.* 她给孩子们穿上了最漂亮的衣服。 ◇ *Get up and* ***get dressed!*** 起床穿衣服了！ OPP **undress** ➲ COLLOCATIONS AT FASHION **2** 🔑 [I, T] to wear a particular type or style of clothes 穿…的服装: *to* ***dress well/badly/fashionably/comfortably*** 穿得好 / 不好 / 时髦 / 舒适 ◇ ~ **for/in/as sth** *You should dress for cold weather today.* 你今天应该穿防寒的衣服。 ◇ *She always dressed entirely in black.* 她一向全身黑色装束。 ◇ ~ **sb** (**for/in/as sth**) *He was dressed as a woman* (= he was wearing women's clothes). 他打扮得像个女人。 ➲ SYNONYMS AT CLOTHES ➲ COLLOCATIONS AT FASHION **3** [I] to put on formal clothes 穿正式服装: *Do they expect us to dress for dinner?* 他们要求我们穿正式服装赴宴吗？ **4** [T] ~ **sb** to provide clothes for sb 为…提供服装: *He dresses many of Hollywood's most famous young stars.* 他为好莱坞许多最著名的年轻明星提供服装。

• **WOUND** 伤口 **5** [T] ~ **sth** to clean, treat and cover a wound 清洗包扎，敷裹（伤口）: *The nurse will dress that cut for you.* 护士将为你包扎那个伤口。

• **FOOD** 食物 **6** [T] ~ **sth** to prepare food for cooking or eating（烹调前）准备，处理；（食用前）给…加调味酱: *to* ***dress a salad*** (= put oil or VINEGAR, etc. on it) 给色拉加调味酱（放油、醋等） ◇ *to* ***dress a chicken*** (= take out the parts you cannot eat) 给鸡去毛开膛

• **DECORATE** 装饰 **7** [T] ~ **sth** (*formal*) to decorate or arrange sth 装饰；布置: *to dress a shop window* (= arrange a display of clothes or goods in it) 布置橱窗

• **STONE/WOOD/LEATHER** 石头；木材；皮革 **8** [T] ~ **sth** to prepare a material such as stone, wood, leather, etc. for use 加工；处理；修整 IDM SEE MUTTON, PART *n.*

PHR V ˌ**dress ˈdown** to wear clothes that are more informal than those you usually wear, for example in an office（与平时比较）穿着随便 ˌ**dress sb ˈdown** to criticize or be angry with sb because they have done sth wrong 训斥；责骂 ➲ RELATED NOUN DRESSING-DOWN ˌ**dress ˈup** 🔑 to wear clothes that are more formal than those you usually wear 穿上盛装；穿上正装 ˌ**dress ˈup** | ˌ**dress sb ˈup** 🔑 to put on special clothes, especially to pretend to be sb/sth different 装扮；乔装打扮: *Kids love dressing up.* 孩子们都喜欢装扮成别人玩儿。 ◇ *The boys were all dressed up as pirates.* 这些男孩子都装扮成了海盗。 ◇ (*BrE*) *dressing-up clothes* 孩子装扮成别人玩的服装 ◇ (*NAmE*) *dress-up clothes* 孩子装扮成别人玩的服装 ˌ**dress sth ˈup** to present sth in a way that makes it seem better or different 装饰；修饰；掩饰: *However much you try to dress it up, office work is not glamorous.* 无论你怎样夸饰，办公室工作都不令人向往。

dress·age /ˈdresɑːʒ/ *noun* [U] a set of controlled movements that a rider trains a horse to perform; a competition in which these movements are performed 盛装舞步；花样骑术

ˌ**dress ˈcircle** (*especially BrE*) (*NAmE usually* ˌ**first ˈbalcony**) *noun* the first level of seats above the ground floor in a theatre（剧院）楼厅前座，二楼正座

ˈ**dress code** *noun* rules about what clothes people should wear at work（工作时的）着装规定: *The company has a strict dress code—all male employees are expected to wear suits.* 公司有严格的着装规定：所有男职员都要穿西服。

dressed 🔑 /drest/ *adj.* [not before noun] **1** 🔑 wearing clothes and not naked or wearing clothes for sleeping 穿着衣服: *Hurry up and* ***get dressed.*** 快点穿上衣服。 ◇ *fully dressed* 穿戴整齐的 ◇ *I can't go to the door—I'm not dressed yet.* 我没法去开门，我还没穿好衣服呢。 **2** 🔑 wearing clothes of a particular type 穿着…服装: *smartly dressed* 衣着讲究 ◇ ~ **in…** *The bride was dressed in white.* 新娘身穿白色礼服。 ◇ *He was casually dressed in jeans and a T-shirt.* 他穿着很随便的牛仔裤和 T 恤衫。

IDM **dressed to 'kill** (*informal*) wearing the kind of clothes that will make people notice and admire you 打扮得引人注目；穿着华丽夺目 **dressed (up) to the 'nines** (*informal*) wearing very elegant or formal clothes 衣饰华丽；穿着讲究 ➲ MORE AT MUTTON

dress·er /ˈdresə(r)/ *noun* **1** (*also* ˌ**Welsh 'dresser**) (*BrE*) a large piece of wooden furniture with shelves in the top part and cupboards below, used for displaying and storing cups, plates, etc. 食具橱；碗橱 **2** (*NAmE*) = CHEST OF DRAWERS **3** (used with an adjective 与形容词连用) a person who dresses in the way mentioned 穿着…的人；衣着…者：*a snappy dresser* 穿着漂亮的人 **4** (in a theatre 剧院) a person whose job is to take care of an actor's clothes for a play and help him/her to get dressed 服装员；服装师 ➲ WORDFINDER NOTE AT PERFORMANCE

dress·ing /ˈdresɪŋ/ *noun* **1** (*also* **'salad dressing**) [C, U] a thin sauce used to add flavour to salads, usually made from oil, VINEGAR, salt, pepper, etc. （拌制色拉用的）调料 ➲ SEE ALSO FRENCH DRESSING **2** [U] (*NAmE*) = STUFFING (1) **3** [C] a piece of soft material placed over a wound in order to protect it（保护伤口的）敷料 **4** [U] the act of putting on clothes 穿衣；穿戴：*Many of our patients need help with dressing.* 我们的许多病人需要有人帮助穿衣。 ➲ SEE ALSO CROSS-DRESSING, POWER DRESSING, WINDOW DRESSING

ˌ**dressing-'down** *noun* [sing.] (*old-fashioned, informal*) an occasion when sb speaks angrily to a person because they have done sth wrong 训斥；责骂

'**dressing gown** (*BrE*) (*NAmE* **bath·robe, robe**) *noun* a long loose piece of clothing, usually with a belt, worn indoors over night clothes, for example when you first get out of bed 晨衣，晨袍（起床后套于睡衣外在室内穿的宽松长罩衫，通常有束带） ➲ VISUAL VOCAB PAGE V68

'**dressing room** *noun* **1** a room for changing your clothes in, especially one for actors or, in British English, for sports players（演员的）化装间；（在英式英语中指运动员的）更衣室 **2** a small room next to a bedroom in some large houses, in which clothes are kept and people get dressed 梳妆室 **3** (*NAmE*) = FITTING ROOM

'**dressing table** (*also* '**vanity table**, *NAmE also* **van·ity**) *noun* a piece of bedroom furniture like a table with drawers and a mirror on top 梳妆台 ➲ VISUAL VOCAB PAGE V24

dress·maker /ˈdresmeɪkə(r)/ *noun* a person who makes women's clothes, especially as a job（女装）裁缝 ▸ **dress·mak·ing** *noun* [U]

ˌ**dress re'hearsal** *noun* the final practice of a play in the theatre, using the clothes and lights that will be used for the real performance 彩排：(*figurative*) *The earlier protests had just been dress rehearsals for full-scale revolution.* 早期的抗议仅仅是大革命开始前的预演。

'**dress shirt** *noun* **1** a white shirt worn on formal occasions with a BOW TIE and suit（白色、打蝶形领结的）西服衬衫，礼服衬衫 **2** (*NAmE*) a smart shirt with long sleeves, which can be worn with a tie（可打领带的）长袖正装衬衫

'**dress uniform** *noun* [U] a uniform that army, navy, etc. officers wear for formal occasions and ceremonies 军礼服

dressy /ˈdresi/ *adj.* (**dress·ier, dressi·est**) **1** (of clothes 衣服) elegant and formal 漂亮雅致的；讲究的；正式的 **2** (of people 人) liking to wear elegant or fashionable clothes 衣着讲究的；穿着时髦的

drew PAST TENSE OF DRAW

drey /dreɪ/ *noun* the home of a SQUIRREL 松鼠窝

drib·ble /ˈdrɪbl/ *verb, noun*

■ *verb* **1** [I, T] ~ (**sth**) to let SALIVA or another liquid come out of your mouth and run down your chin 流口水；垂涎 SYN **drool 2** [I] + **adv./prep.** to fall in small drops or in a thin stream 一点一滴地落下；细流：*Melted wax dribbled down the side of the candle.* 熔化了的蜡一滴滴从蜡烛边上流下。 **3** [T] ~ **sth** (**into/over/onto sth**) to pour sth slowly, in drops or a thin stream 使滴出；使成细流 SYN **drizzle, trickle**: *Dribble a little olive oil over the salad.* 在色拉上面滴少许橄榄油。 **4** [T, I] ~ (**sth**) (+ **adv./prep.**) (in football (SOCCER) and some other sports 足球及其他某些体育运动) to move the ball along with several short kicks, hits or BOUNCES 运球；带球；盘球：*She dribbled the ball the length of the field.* 她带球从后场跑到前场。 ◊ *He dribbled past two defenders and scored a magnificent goal.* 他带球越过两个防守队员，射入非常精彩的一球。

■ *noun* **1** [C] a very small amount of liquid, in a thin stream 涓滴；细流：*a dribble of blood* 一丝血流 ◊ *Add just a dribble of oil.* 只加一点点油。 **2** [U] (*especially BrE*) SALIVA (= liquid) from a person's mouth 口水：*There was dribble all down the baby's front.* 这婴儿胸前淌满了口水。 **3** [C] the act of dribbling the ball in a sport 运球；带球；盘球

dribs /drɪbz/ *noun* [pl.]

IDM **in ˌdribs and 'drabs** (*informal*) in small amounts or numbers over a period of time 少量；一点一滴；零零星星：*She paid me in dribs and drabs, not all at once.* 她一点一点地付给我钱，而不是一次付清。 ➲ MORE LIKE THIS 13, page R26

dried PAST TENSE, PAST PART. OF DRY

ˌ**dried 'fruit** *noun* [U, C] fruit (for example, CURRANTS or RAISINS) that has been dried to be used in cooking or eaten on its own 干果，果干儿（如葡萄干）

drier = DRYER ➲ SEE ALSO DRY *adj.*

dri·est ➲ DRY *adj.*

drift /drɪft/ *noun, verb*

■ *noun*

• **SLOW MOVEMENT** 缓缓流动 **1** [sing., U] a slow steady movement from one place to another; a gradual change or development from one situation to another, especially to sth bad 流动；趋势；逐渐变化（尤指向坏的方面）：*a population drift away from rural areas* 农村地区的人口外流 ◊ *attempts to halt the drift towards war* 制止逐步走上战争道路的努力

• **OF SHIP** 船舶 **2** [U] the movement of a ship or plane away from its direction because of currents or wind（船只或飞机的）偏航，航差

• **OF SEA/AIR** 海水；空气 **3** [U, C] the movement of the sea or air 水流；气流；流动 SYN **current**: *the general direction of drift on the east coast* 东海岸海水的总体流向 ◊ *He knew the hidden drifts in that part of the river.* 他对那段河道中的暗流非常清楚。

• **OF SNOW** 雪 **4** [C] a large pile of sth, especially snow, made by the wind 吹聚物；雪堆：*The road was blocked by deep drifts of snow.* 道路被风吹来的厚厚积雪阻塞。 ➲ SEE ALSO SNOWDRIFT ➲ WORDFINDER NOTE AT SNOW

• **OF FLOWERS** 花 **5** [C] a large mass of sth, especially flowers 大丛的花；丛生的植物：*Plant daffodils in informal drifts.* 随便种几丛黄水仙。

• **MEANING** 意义 **6** [sing.] the general meaning of what sb says or writes 大意；主旨；要点 SYN **gist**: *Do you catch my drift?* 你大概明白我的意思吗？ ◊ *My German isn't very good, but I got the drift of what she said.* 我的德语不太好，但我大致明白她说的意思。 ➲ SEE ALSO CONTINENTAL DRIFT

■ *verb*

• **MOVE SLOWLY** 缓缓流动 **1** [I] (+ **adv./prep.**) to move along smoothly and slowly in water or air 漂流；漂移；飘：*Clouds drifted across the sky.* 朵朵浮云在空中飘过。 ◊ *The empty boat drifted out to sea.* 空船向海上漂去。 **2** [I] + **adv./prep.** to move or go somewhere slowly 缓缓移动；缓慢行走：*The crowd drifted away from the scene of the accident.* 人群渐渐从事故现场散去。 ◊ *Her gaze drifted around the room.* 她的目光缓缓扫视了一下室内。

• **WITHOUT PURPOSE** 漫无目的 **3** [I] (+ **adv./prep.**) to happen or change, or to do sth without a particular plan or purpose 无意间发生；无目的地转变；顺其自然地做：*I didn't intend to be a teacher—I just drifted into it.* 我并没打算过当老师，只是顺其自然就当了。 ◊ *He hasn't decided what to do yet—he's just drifting.* 他还没决定做什么，只

是顺其自然。◇ *The conversation drifted onto politics.* 谈话不知不觉就转到政治方面来了。

• **INTO STATE/SITUATION** 状态；情况 **4** [I] **~ in/into sth** to go from one situation or state to another without realizing it 无意间进入；不知不觉陷入：*Finally she drifted into sleep.* 最后她不知不觉地睡着了。◇ *The injured man tried to speak but soon drifted into unconsciousness.* 受伤的男人想说点什么，但一会儿就不省人事了。

D

• **OF SNOW/SAND** 雪；沙 **5** [I] to be blown into large piles by the wind 吹积；堆积：*drifting sand* 堆积的沙 ◇ *Some roads are closed because of drifting.* 有些道路因积雪而封闭。

• **FLOAT** 漂浮 **6** [T] **+ adv./prep.** to make sth float somewhere 使漂流；使漂浮：*The logs are drifted downstream to the mill.* 原木顺流而下漂到木材加工厂。

PHR V **ˌdrift aˈpart** to become less friendly or close to sb 逐渐疏远：*As children we were very close, but as we grew up we just drifted apart.* 孩提时我们亲密无间，但随着年龄的增长我们就逐渐疏远了。**ˌdrift ˈoff (to sleep)** to fall asleep 入睡；睡着：*I didn't hear the storm. I must have drifted off by then.* 我没有听见暴风雨，那时一定是睡着了。

drift·er /ˈdrɪftə(r)/ *noun* (*disapproving*) a person who moves from one job or place to another with no real purpose 漂泊者；盲流

ˈdrift net *noun* a very large net used by fishing boats. The net has weights at the bottom and FLOATS at the top and is allowed to hang in the sea. 流网；漂网

drift·wood /ˈdrɪftwʊd/ *noun* [U] wood that the sea carries up onto land, or that floats on the water 浮木，漂流木（海水冲上岸或在水中漂流的木头）

drill /drɪl/ *noun, verb*

■ ***noun*** **1** [C] a tool or machine with a pointed end for making holes 钻；钻头；钻床；钻机：*an electric drill* 电钻 ◇ *a pneumatic drill* 风钻 ◇ *a hand drill* 手钻 ◇ *a dentist's drill* 牙钻 ◇ *a drill bit* (= the pointed part at the end of the drill) 钻头 ➲ WORDFINDER NOTE AT DENTIST ➲ VISUAL VOCAB PAGE V21 **2** [C, U] a way of learning sth by means of repeated exercises 练习；训练 **3** [C, U] a practice of what to do in an emergency, for example if there is a fire（应对紧急情况的）演习：*a fire drill* 消防演习 **4** [U] military training in marching, the use of weapons, etc. 军事训练；操练：*rifle drill* 步枪操练 **5 the drill** [sing.] (*old-fashioned*) the correct or usual way to do sth 正确的步骤；常规；程序 SYN **procedure**：*What's the drill for claiming expenses?* 报销费用的手续是什么？ **6** [U] a type of strong cotton cloth 粗斜纹布 **7** [C] a machine for planting seeds in rows 条播机

■ ***verb*** **1** [T, I] to make a hole in sth, using a drill 钻（孔）；打（眼）：**~ sth** *Drill a series of holes in the frame.* 在构架上钻一串孔。◇ **~ (for sth)** *They're* ***drilling for oil*** *off the Irish coast.* 他们在爱尔兰沿海钻井采油。◇ **~ (through sth)** *He drilled through the wall by mistake.* 他误将墙壁钻穿了。 **2** [T] to teach sb to do sth by making them repeat it a lot of times 培训；训练：**~ sb to do sth** *The children were drilled to leave the classroom quickly when the fire bell rang.* 孩子们接受了如何在火警铃拉响时迅速离开教室的训练。◇ **~ sb** *a well-drilled team* 训练有素的队伍 ◇ **~ sb in sth** *Recruits are drilled in basic techniques over the five-day course.* 新兵接受为期五天的基本技能训练。 **3** [T] **~ sb** to train soldiers to perform military actions 进行军事训练；操练

PHR V **ˌdrill ˈdown** (*computing* 计 or *business* 商) to go to deeper levels of an organized set of data in order to find more detail, especially on a computer or a website 自顶向下搜索；向下钻取：*Navigation is good and there's a display to show how far you've drilled down.* 导航很好，可以显示你正在看哪一级信息。 **ˈdrill sth into sb** to make sb remember or learn sth by repeating it often 反复训练某人；向某人反复灌输：*It was drilled into us at an early age never to drop litter.* 我们从小就被叮嘱绝不能乱扔垃圾。

drily (*also* **dryly**) /ˈdraɪli/ *adv.* ➲ SEE ALSO DRY *adj.* **1** if sb speaks **drily**, they are being humorous, but not in an obvious way 幽默而不形于色地：*'That's a lovely purple suit you're wearing,' she said drily.* "你穿的这件紫色套装真好看。"她不动声色地打趣说。 **2** in a way that shows no emotion 冷冰冰地；冷淡地；不动感情地：*He smiled drily and leaned back in his chair.* 他冷冷地笑了笑，随即靠在椅背上。 **3** in a way that shows that there is no liquid present 干燥地：*She coughed drily.* 她干咳着。◇ *He swallowed drily and nodded.* 他干咽了一下，然后点了点头。

drink 🔑 /drɪŋk/ *noun, verb*

■ ***noun*** **1** 🔑 [C, U] a liquid for drinking; an amount of a liquid that you drink 饮料；一杯，一份，一口（饮料）：*Can I* ***have a drink****?* 给我来一杯饮料好吗？◇ *soft drinks* (= cold drinks without alcohol) 软饮料（不含酒精）◇ *a drink of water* 一杯水 ◇ *food and drink* 食物和饮料 ◇ *She took a drink from the glass and then put it down.* 她喝了一口饮料，然后放下杯子。 **2** 🔑 [C, U] alcohol or an alcoholic drink; sth that you drink on a social occasion 酒；酒精饮料：*They went* ***for a drink****.* 他们去喝酒了。◇ *The drinks are on me* (= I'll pay for them). 酒钱由我付。◇ *I need* ***a stiff drink*** (= a very strong drink). 我要一杯烈酒。◇ (*BrE*) *He's got* ***a drink problem****.* 他有贪杯的毛病。◇ (*NAmE*) *He has a* ***drinking problem****.* 他有贪杯的毛病。◇ (*humorous*) *The children are enough to* ***drive me to drink****.* 这些孩子足以逼得我酗起酒来。◇ (*BrE*) *They came home* ***the worse for drink*** (= drunk). 他们喝得酩酊大醉地回到家里。◇ *She* ***took to drink*** (= often drank too much alcohol) *after her marriage broke up.* 婚姻破裂后，她染上了酗酒的恶习。 **3 drinks** [pl.] a social occasion where you have alcoholic drinks 酒宴；酒会：*Would you like to come for drinks on Sunday?* 星期天来参加酒宴好吗？◇ *a drinks party* 酒会

IDM SEE DEMON, MEAT

■ ***verb*** (**drank** /dræŋk/, **drunk** /drʌŋk/) **1** 🔑 [T, I] **~ (sth)** to take liquid into your mouth and swallow it 喝；饮：*What would you like to drink?* 你想喝点什么？◇ *In hot weather, drink plenty of water.* 天热时要多喝水。◇ *I don't drink coffee.* 我不喝咖啡。◇ *He was drinking straight from the bottle.* 他直接对着酒瓶喝酒。 **2** 🔑 [I, T] to drink alcohol, especially when it is done regularly 喝酒；（尤指）酗酒：*He doesn't drink.* 他不喝酒。◇ *Don't* ***drink and drive*** (= drive a car after drinking alcohol). 切勿酒后驾车。◇ *She's been drinking heavily since she lost her job.* 她失业后便常常酗酒。◇ **~ sth** *I drank far too much last night.* 我昨天晚上喝得酩酊大醉。◇ **~ yourself + adj.** *He had drunk himself unconscious on vodka.* 他喝伏特加酒喝得不省人事。 ➲ SEE ALSO DRUNK

IDM **drink sb's ˈhealth** (*BrE*) to wish sb good health as you lift your glass, and then drink from it 为某人的健康干杯 **drink like a ˈfish** to drink a lot of alcohol regularly（习惯性）饮酒过度，酗酒，豪饮 **ˌdrink sb under the ˈtable** (*informal*) to drink more alcohol than sb else without becoming as drunk as they are（拼酒量）喝倒某人；喝到使某人醉倒 ➲ MORE AT EAT, HORSE *n.*

PHR V **ˌdrink sth↔ˈin** to look at or listen to sth with great interest and enjoyment 尽情地欣赏；如饥似渴地倾听；陶醉于：*We just stood there drinking in the scenery.* 我们就站在那儿尽情欣赏景色。 **ˈdrink to sb/sth** to wish sb good luck, health or success as you lift your glass and then drink from it 为…干杯（或祝酒）SYN **toast**：*All raise your glasses and drink to Katie and Tom!* 大家举起杯为凯蒂和汤姆祝福吧！ **ˌdrink ˈup | ˌdrink (sth)↔ˈup** to drink all of sth（把…）喝完：*Drink up and let's go.* 喝完了咱们走吧。◇ *Come on, drink up your juice.* 快，把果汁喝完。

drink·able /ˈdrɪŋkəbl/ *adj.* **1** clean and safe to drink 可饮用的 **2** pleasant to drink 好喝的：*a very drinkable wine* 很好喝的葡萄酒

ˌdrink-ˈdriver (*BrE*) (*also* **ˌdrunk ˈdriver** *NAmE, BrE*) *noun* a person who drives a vehicle after drinking too much alcohol 酒后驾车者

ˌdrink-ˈdriving (*also* **ˌdrunken ˈdriving**) (*both BrE*) (*also* **ˈdrunk driving** *NAmE, BrE*) *noun* [U] driving a vehicle after drinking too much alcohol 酒后驾车

drink·er /ˈdrɪŋkə(r)/ *noun* **1** a person who drinks alcohol regularly, especially sb who drinks too much 饮酒者；（尤指）酗酒者，酒徒：*a heavy/moderate drinker* 酒鬼；有节制的饮酒者 **2** (after a noun 置于名词后) a person who regularly drinks the particular drink mentioned 常饮…酒者；常喝…饮料者：*a coffee drinker* 常喝咖啡的人

drink·ing /ˈdrɪŋkɪŋ/ *noun* [U] the act of drinking alcohol 喝酒；饮酒：*Drinking is not advised during pregnancy.* 建议妊娠期不要饮酒。◊ *There are tough penalties for drinking and driving.* 酒后驾车处罚很重。

ˈdrinking box *noun* (*CanE*) a small cardboard box of juice, etc. that has a drinking straw with it that can be pushed through a small hole in the top（带吸管的）盒装饮料

ˈdrinking chocolate *noun* [U] (*BrE*) a sweet chocolate powder or a hot drink made from this powder mixed with hot milk and/or water 甜巧克力粉；巧克力热饮 ➲ COMPARE COCOA

ˈdrinking fountain (*especially BrE*) (*NAmE usually* **ˈwater fountain**) *noun* a device that supplies water for drinking in public places（设于公共场所的）喷泉式饮水器

ˈdrinking straw *noun* = STRAW (3)

ˌdrinking-ˈup time *noun* [U] (*BrE*) in Britain, the time between when a pub stops serving drinks and when it closes, when people are allowed to finish drinks that they bought earlier（在英国酒吧停止售酒后打烊前留给顾客的）饮完残酒时间

ˈdrinking water *noun* [U] water that is safe for drinking 饮用水 ➲ **MORE LIKE THIS** 9, page R26

drip /drɪp/ *verb, noun*

■ ***verb*** (**-pp-**) **1** [I] (+ **adv./prep.**) (of liquid 液体) to fall in small drops 滴下：*She was hot and sweat dripped into her eyes.* 她很热，汗水滴入双眼。◊ *Water was dripping down the walls.* 水从墙上滴落下来。 **2** [I, T] to produce drops of liquid 滴出；滴水：*The tap was dripping.* 龙头在滴水。◊ **+ adv./prep.** *Her hair dripped down her back.* 她头发上的水顺着后背滴落下来。◊ **~ sth** (**+adv./prep.**) *Be careful, you're dripping paint everywhere!* 小心点，你把颜料滴得到处都是！ **3** [I, T] to contain or hold a lot of sth 含有；充满；充溢：**~ with sth** *The trees were dripping with fruit.* 树上挂满了果子。◊ **~ sth** *His voice dripped sarcasm.* 他的话语中充满了讥讽。

■ ***noun*** **1** [sing.] the sound or action of small drops of liquid falling continuously 滴落；滴水声；滴答声：*The silence was broken only by the steady drip, drip of water from the roof.* 只有屋顶上滴答滴答持续不断的滴水声打破了寂静。 **2** [C] a small drop of liquid that falls from sth 水滴；滴液：*We put a bucket under the hole in the roof to catch the drips.* 我们在屋顶漏洞下放了一个水桶接水滴。 **3** (*NAmE also* **IV**) [C] (*medical* 医) a piece of equipment that passes liquid food, medicine or blood very slowly through a tube into a patient's VEIN（静脉）滴注：*She's been put on a drip.* 她一直在输液。 **4** [C] (*informal, becoming old-fashioned*) a boring or stupid person with a weak personality 怯懦讨厌的人；愚蠢胆怯的人 SYN **wimp**：*Don't be such a drip—come and join in the fun!* 别犯傻了，过来一起玩吧！

ˌdrip-ˈdry *adj.* made of a type of cloth that will dry quickly without CREASES when you hang it up wet（衣服）快速滴干的，滴干免熨的

ˈdrip-feed *verb* (**drip-fed, drip-fed**) **~ sb/sth** to give sb sth in separate small amounts 喂饲；以少量点滴给予 ▸ **ˈdrip feed** *noun* [U, C]：*the steady drip feed of leaked documents in the papers* 泄露的文件一点点接连在报纸上出现

drip·ping /ˈdrɪpɪŋ/ *adj., noun*

■ ***adj.*** **~** (**with sth**) very wet 湿淋淋的：*Her face was dripping with sweat.* 她脸上汗水淋淋。◊ *His clothes were still **dripping wet**.* 他的衣服还是湿淋淋的。◊ (*figurative*) *His wife came in, dripping with diamonds.* 他的妻子浑身珠光宝气地走了进来。

■ ***noun*** [U] fat that comes out of meat when it is cooked, often kept for frying other food in（烤肉时渗出的）油

drip·py /ˈdrɪpi/ *adj.* (**drip·pier, drip·pi·est**) (*informal*) **1** boring, stupid and weak or SENTIMENTAL 愚懦脆弱的；婆婆妈妈的：*her drippy boyfriend* 她那婆婆妈妈的男朋友 **2** in a liquid state, and likely to fall in drops 湿漉漉的；滴水的：*drippy paint* 湿淋淋的油漆 ◊ *a drippy nose* (= with drops of liquid falling from it) 淌鼻涕的鼻子

drive /draɪv/ *verb, noun*

■ ***verb*** (**drove** /drəʊv; *NAmE* droʊv/, **driven** /ˈdrɪvn/)

• **VEHICLE** 交通工具 **1** [I, T] to operate a vehicle so that it goes in a particular direction 驾驶；开车：*Can you drive?* 你会开车吗？◊ *Don't drive so fast!* 别开得那么快！◊ *I drove to work this morning.* 我今天早上开车去上班。◊ *Shall we drive* (= go there by car) *or go by train?* 我们开车去还是乘火车去？◊ **~ sth** *He drives a taxi* (= that is his job). 他是开出租车的。 ➲ **COLLOCATIONS AT DRIVING** **2** [T] **~ sb** (**+ adv./prep.**) to take sb somewhere in a car, taxi, etc. 驾车送（人）：*Could you drive me home?* 你可以开车送我回家吗？ ➲ **SYNONYMS AT TAKE** **3** [T] **~ sth** to own or use a particular type of vehicle 拥有（或驾驶）…汽车：*What car do you drive?* 你开什么车？

• **MACHINE** 机器 **4** [T, usually passive] **~ sth** to provide the power that makes a machine work 驱动；推动：*a steam-driven locomotive* 蒸汽机车

• **MAKE SB DO STH** 使人做某事 **5** [T] **~ sb** (**+ adv./prep.**) to force sb to act in a particular way 迫使；驱使：*The urge to survive drove them on.* 求生的欲望驱使他们继续下去。◊ *You're driving yourself too hard.* 你把自己弄得太累了。 **6** [T] to make sb very angry, crazy, etc. or to make them do sth extreme 迫使（某人生气、发疯或做出极端事情）：**~ sb + adj.** *to **drive sb crazy/mad/insane*** 把某人逼得发疯 / 发狂 / 失去理智 ◊ **~ sb to do sth** *Hunger drove her to steal.* 饥饿迫使她去偷窃。◊ **~ sb to sth** *Those kids are driving me to despair.* 那些孩子让我都快绝望了。◊ (*humorous*) *It's enough to **drive you to drink*** (= to make you start drinking too much alcohol). 这种事足以逼得人拼命喝酒。

• **MAKE SB/STH MOVE** 使移动 **7** [T] **~ sb/sth + adv./prep.** to force sb/sth to move in a particular direction 驱赶；赶走；驱逐：*to drive sheep into a field* 把羊群赶到田野里 ◊ *The enemy was driven back.* 敌人被击退了。

• **CAUSE STH TO MAKE PROGRESS** 推动 **8** [T] **~ sth** to influence sth or cause it to make progress 激励；促进；推进：*This is the main factor driving investment in the area.* 这是推动在这个地区投资的主要因素。

• **HIT/PUSH** 击；推 **9** [T] **~ sth + adv./prep.** to force sth to go in a particular direction or into a particular position by pushing it, hitting it, etc. 击；打；敲；推：*to drive a nail into a piece of wood* 把钉子钉进一块木头

• **MAKE A HOLE** 打洞 **10** [T] **~ sth + adv./prep.** to make an opening in or through sth by using force 凿；挖掘：*They drove a tunnel through the solid rock.* 他们凿出一条穿过坚固岩石的隧道。

• **IN SPORT** 体育运动 **11** [T, I] **~** (**sth**) (**+ adv./prep.**) to hit a ball with force, sending it forward 猛抽，猛击（球）：*to drive the ball into the rough* (= in GOLF) 将球击入长草区（高尔夫球）

• **WIND/WATER** 风；水 **12** [T] **~ sth** (**+ adv./prep.**) to carry sth along 吹；卷；刮；冲：*Huge waves drove the yacht onto the rocks.* 巨浪将快艇冲到岩石上。 **13** [I] (**+ adv./prep.**) to fall or move rapidly and with great force 猛落；急速驱进：*The waves drove against the shore.* 波浪冲击着岸边。

IDM **drive a coach and ˈhorses through sth** to spoil sth, for example a plan 毁掉，糟蹋，破坏（计划等） **drive sth ˈhome** (**to sb**) to make sb understand or accept sth by saying it often, loudly, angrily, etc. 把…讲透彻；阐明；使充分理解：*You will really need to drive your point home.* 你的确需要把你的观点阐释清楚。 **what sb is ˈdriving at** (*informal*) the thing sb is trying to say 某人的用意；某人话中的意思：*I wish I knew what they were driving at.* 我要是知道他们的用意就好了。 ➲ MORE AT GROUND *n.*, HARD *adj.*, SNOW *n.*

PHR V **ˌdrive aˈway** | **ˌdrive sb/sth aˈway** to leave in a vehicle; to take sb away in a vehicle 驱车离开；驾车送走：*We heard him drive away.* 我们听到他驱车离去了。◇ *Someone drove the car away in the night.* 有人夜里把车开走了。 **ˌdrive sb aˈway** 🔑 to make sb not want to stay or not want to go somewhere 使离去；使不愿久留；使不想去（某地）：*Her constant nagging drove him away.* 她不断的唠叨把他给赶跑了。◇ *Terrorist threats are driving away tourists.* 恐怖分子的威胁吓跑了观光客。 **ˌdrive ˈoff** **1** 🔑 (of a driver, car, etc. 驾驶者、汽车等) to leave 驱车离去；驶去：*The robbers drove off in a stolen vehicle.* 劫匪驾驶着一辆偷来的汽车逃跑了。 **2** (in GOLF 高尔夫球) to hit the ball to begin a game 开（球） **ˌdrive sb/sth↔ˈoff** to force sb/sth to go back or away 击退；赶走：*The defenders drove off each attack.* 防守队员击退了每一次进攻。 **ˌdrive ˈon** to continue driving 驱车继续行驶：*Don't stop—drive on!* 不要停，继续往前开！ **ˌdrive sb/sth↔ˈout (of sth)** to make sb/sth disappear or stop doing sth 驱散；消除；使停止：*New fashions drive out old ones.* 新款式服装使旧的款式不再流行。 **ˌdrive sth↔ˈup/ˈdown** to make sth such as prices rise or fall quickly 抬高（或压低）；使上升（或下跌）

■ ***noun***

• **IN/OF VEHICLE** 交通工具 **1** 🔑 [C] a journey in a car or other vehicle 驱车旅行；驾车路程：***Let's go for a drive.*** 咱们开车去兜兜风吧。◇ *It's a three-hour drive to London.* 到伦敦要三小时的车程。 **2** [C, U] the equipment in a vehicle that takes power from the engine to the wheels 传动（或驱动）装置：*the drive shaft* 驱动轴 ◇ *a car with four-wheel drive* 四轮驱动汽车 ◇ *a **left-/right-hand drive** car* (= a car where the driver and the controls are on the left/right) 左 / 右座驾驶的汽车

• **OUTSIDE HOUSE** 住宅外面 **3** (*also* **drive·way**) [C] a wide hard path or a private road that leads from the street to a house（从街道通向住宅的宽阔或私人的）车道：*There were two cars parked **in/on** the drive.* 车道上停了两辆汽车。➲ VISUAL VOCAB PAGE V18

• **EFFORT** 努力 **4** [C] an organized effort by a group of people to achieve sth （团体为达到某目的而进行的）有组织的努力，运动：*a **recruitment/export/economy drive*** 征兵 / 出口 / 节约运动 ◇ **~ for sth** *a drive for greater efficiency* 为提高效率而进行的运动 ◇ **~ to do sth** *the government's drive to reduce energy consumption* 政府为减少能源消耗而发起的运动 ➲ SYNONYMS AT CAMPAIGN

• **DESIRE/ENERGY** 欲望；精力 **5** [C, U] a strong desire or need in people（人的）强烈欲望，本能需求：*a strong sexual drive* 强烈的性欲 **6** [U] (*approving*) a strong desire to do things and achieve sth; great energy 冲劲；干劲；精力：*He'll do very well—he has tremendous drive.* 他会干得很出色的，他干劲十足。

• **IN SPORT** 体育运动 **7** [C] a long hard hit or kick 猛击；猛踢：*She has a strong forehand drive* (= in TENNIS). 她正手击球强而有力。◇ *He scored with a brilliant 25-yard drive.* 他在 25 码外一脚劲射入球得分。

• **COMPUTING** 计算机技术 **8** [C] the part of a computer that reads and stores information on disks or tapes 驱动器：*a 750GB hard drive* * 750 吉字节的硬盘 ◇ *a CD drive* 光盘驱动器 ➲ WORDFINDER NOTE AT COMPUTER ➲ VISUAL VOCAB PAGE V73 ➲ SEE ALSO DISK DRIVE

• **GAMES** 游戏 **9** [C] (*BrE*) a social occasion when a lot of people compete in a game such as WHIST or BINGO（惠斯特或宾戈纸牌游戏）比赛；玩纸牌的聚会

▼ **COLLOCATIONS** 词语搭配

Driving 驾驶

Having a car 拥有一辆汽车

- **have/own/**(*BrE*) **run** a car 有一辆汽车
- **ride** a motorcycle/motorbike 骑摩托车
- **drive/prefer/use** an automatic/a manual/(*NAmE, informal*) a stick shift 开 / 喜欢 / 用自动挡 / 手动挡汽车
- **have/get** your car **serviced/fixed/repaired** 给汽车做一次保养 / 维修一下 / 修理一下
- **buy/sell** a used car/(*especially BrE*) a second-hand car 买 / 卖二手车
- **take/pass/fail** a (*BrE*) driving test/(*both NAmE*) driver's test/road test 参加 / 通过 / 未通过驾照考试 / 道路考试
- **get/obtain/have/lose/carry** a/your (*BrE*) driving licence/(*NAmE*) driver's license 得到 / 拥有 / 丢失 / 携带驾照

Driving 驾驶

- **put on/fasten/**(*NAmE*) **buckle/wear/undo** your seat belt/safety belt 系上 / 解开安全带
- **put/turn/leave** the key in the ignition 把钥匙插进点火开关；转动钥匙点火；把钥匙留在点火开关
- **start** the car/engine 发动汽车 / 引擎
- (*BrE*) **change**/(*NAmE*) **shift/put sth into** gear 换挡；挂上挡
- **press/put your foot on** the brake pedal/clutch/accelerator 踩刹车 / 离合器 / 油门
- **release** the clutch/(*especially BrE*) the handbrake/(*both NAmE*) the emergency brake/the parking brake 松开离合器 / 手刹
- **drive/park/reverse** the car 驾车；停车；倒车
- (*BrE*) **indicate** left/right 示意左转 / 右转
- (*especially NAmE*) **signal** that you are turning left/right 示意左转 / 右转
- **take/miss** (*BrE*) the turning/(*especially NAmE*) the turn 拐弯；错过拐弯处
- **apply/hit/slam on** the brake(s) 踩刹车；猛踩刹车
- **beep/honk/**(*especially BrE*) **toot/**(*BrE*) **sound** your horn 按喇叭

Problems and accidents 问题及事故

- a car **skids/crashes (into sth)/collides (with sth)** 车打滑 / 撞上（某物）/（与某物）相撞
- **swerve to avoid** an oncoming car/a pedestrian 猛地转弯以避开迎面来的车 / 行人
- **crash/lose control of** the car 撞车；车失控
- **have/be in/be killed in/survive** a car crash/a car accident/(*NAmE*) a car wreck/a hit-and-run 出车祸 / 肇事逃逸事故；在车祸 / 肇事逃逸事故中丧生；幸免于车祸 / 肇事逃逸事故
- **be run over/knocked down by** a car/bus/truck 被汽车 / 公交车 / 大卡车轧过 / 撞倒
- **dent/hit** (*BrE*) the bonnet/(*NAmE*) the hood 撞凹 / 撞上引擎盖
- **break/crack/shatter** (*BrE*) the windscreen/(*NAmE*) the windshield 打碎挡风玻璃
- **blow**/(*especially BrE*) **burst/puncture** (*BrE*) a tyre/(*NAmE*) a tire 爆胎；扎破轮胎
- **get/have** (*BrE*) a flat tyre/a flat tire/a puncture 胎瘪了；轮胎被扎破了
- **inflate/change/fit/replace/check** a tyre/tire 给轮胎充气；更换 / 安装 / 更换 / 检查轮胎

Traffic and driving regulations 交通法规

- **be caught in/get stuck in/sit in** a traffic jam 遇上堵车
- **cause** congestion/tailbacks/traffic jams/gridlock 引起交通堵塞
- **experience/face** lengthy delays 经历 / 面临长时间的延误
- **beat/avoid** the traffic/the rush hour 避开交通高峰时段
- **break/observe**/(*NAmE*) **drive** the speed limit 超速行驶；遵守速度限制；限速行驶
- **be caught on** (*BrE*) a speed camera 被测速摄像机逮住
- **stop sb for/pull sb over for**/(*BrE, informal*) **be done for** speeding 因超速被要求停车 / 停靠路边 / 被逮住
- (*both informal*) **run**/(*BrE*) **jump** a red light/the lights 闯红灯
- **be arrested for/charged with** (*BrE*) drink-driving/(*both US*) driving under the influence (DUI)/driving while intoxicated (DWI) 因酒后驾车 / 醉酒驾车被逮捕 / 起诉
- **be banned**/(*BrE*) **disqualified** from driving 被禁止驾车；被取消驾驶资格

• **ANIMALS/ENEMY** 动物；敌人 **10** [C] an act of chasing animals or the enemy and making them go into a smaller area, especially in order to kill or capture them 驱赶；赶拢；（尤指）围攻，围歼

• **ROAD** 路 **11 Drive** (*abbr.* **Dr**) used in the names of roads（用于路名）路，大道：*21 Island Heights Drive* 艾兰海茨路 21 号

'drive bay *noun* (*computing* 计) a space inside a computer for a DISK DRIVE （磁盘）驱动器槽

'drive-by *adj.* (*NAmE*) [only before noun] a **drive-by** shooting, etc. is done from a moving car（枪击等）飞车而过发射的：*a drive-by killing* 从行驶汽车上开枪杀人 ▶ **'drive-by** *noun* (*pl.* **drive-bys**)

'drive-in *noun* a place where you can watch films/movies, eat, etc. without leaving your car "免下车"电影院（或餐馆等）：*We stopped at a drive-in for a hamburger.* 我们在一家"免下车"餐馆停下来吃汉堡包。◇ *drive-in movies* "免下车"露天电影院

drivel /'drɪvl/ *noun, verb*

■ *noun* [U] (*informal, disapproving*) silly nonsense 蠢话；傻话；废话：*How can you watch that drivel on TV?* 你怎么能看电视上那种胡说八道的东西？

■ *verb* (**-ll-**, *US* **-l-**) [I] ~ (**on**) (**about sth**) (usually used in the progressive tenses 通常用于进行时) to keep talking about silly or unimportant things 老是说傻话；喋喋不休地说无聊话

driven /'drɪvn/ *adj.* **1** (of a person 人) determined to succeed, and working very hard to do so 奋发努力的；发愤图强的 **2 -driven** (in compounds 构成复合词) influenced or caused by a particular thing 受…影响的；由…造成的：*a market-driven economy* 市场导向的经济 ◇ *a character-driven movie* 以人物为主的电影 ➲ SEE ALSO DRIVE *v.*

driver /'draɪvə(r)/ *noun* **1** a person who drives a vehicle 驾驶员；司机；驾车者：*a bus/a train/an ambulance/a taxi driver* 公共汽车 / 火车 / 救护车 / 出租车司机 ◇ *She climbed into the driver's seat.* 她爬上了驾驶座。◇ (*BrE*) *a* ***learner driver*** (= one who has not yet passed a driving test) 学开车的人 ◇ (*NAmE*) *a* ***student driver*** 学开车的人 ◇ *The car comes equipped with a driver's airbag.* 这辆汽车装有驾驶员安全气囊。➲ SEE ALSO BACK-SEAT DRIVER **2** (in GOLF 高尔夫球) a CLUB with a wooden head 开球杆 **3** (*computing* 计) software that controls the sending of data between a computer and a piece of equipment that is attached to it, such as a printer 驱动程序 **4** one of the main things that influence sth or cause it to make progress 驱动因素：*Housing is a key driver of the economy.* 住房是个促使经济增长的主要因素。IDM SEE SEAT *n.*

'driver's license (*NAmE*) (*BrE* **'driving licence**) *noun* an official document that shows that you are qualified to drive 驾驶执照；驾照

drive·shaft /'draɪvʃɑːft; *NAmE* -ʃæft/ *noun* a long thin part of a machine that turns round and round and sends power from the engine to another part of the machine（机器的）传动轴，驱动轴

'drive-through (*also* **'drive-thru**) *noun* (*NAmE*) a restaurant, bank, etc. where you can be served without having to get out of your car 不必下车即可得到服务的餐馆（或银行等）

'drive time *noun* [U] a time during the day when many people are driving their cars, for example to or from work（如上下班交通高峰的）开车时间 ▶ **'drive-time** *adj.* [only before noun]：*a drive-time radio show* 驾车时间广播节目

drive·way /'draɪvweɪ/ *noun* = DRIVE (3)：*There was a car parked* ***in/on*** *the driveway.* 有一辆汽车停在车道上。

driv·ing /'draɪvɪŋ/ *noun, adj.*

■ *noun* [U] the way that sb drives a vehicle; the act of driving 行车的方式；驾驶；行车：*dangerous driving* 危险驾驶 ◇ *driving lessons* 驾驶课程 IDM SEE SEAT *n.* ➲ WORDFINDER NOTE AT CAR

■ *adj.* [only before noun] **1** strong and powerful; having a strong influence in making sth happen 强有力的；起推动作用的；推动的：*Who was* ***the driving force*** (= the person with the strongest influence) *in the band?* 谁是乐队的主力？ **2** (of rain, snow, etc. 雨、雪等) falling very fast and at an angle 猛烈的；倾泻而下的

'driving licence (*BrE*) (*NAmE* **'driver's license**) *noun* an official document that shows that you are qualified to drive 驾驶执照；驾照

'driving range *noun* a place where people can practise hitting GOLF balls 高尔夫球练习场

'driving school *noun* a business that gives people lessons in how to drive a car, etc. 驾驶学校

'driving test (*NAmE also* **'road test**) *noun* a test that must be passed before you are qualified to drive a car, etc. 驾照考试

,driving under the 'influence *noun* [U] (*abbr.* **DUI**) (*US*) (in some states in the US 美国某些州) the crime of driving a vehicle after drinking too much alcohol. It is a less serious crime than 'driving while intoxicated'. 酒后驾车罪（较酒醉驾车罪轻）

,driving while in'toxicated *noun* [U] (*abbr.* **DWI**) (*US*) the crime of driving a vehicle after drinking too much alcohol 酒醉驾车罪

driz·zle /'drɪzl/ *verb, noun*

■ *verb* **1** [I] when **it is drizzling**, it is raining lightly 下毛毛雨；下蒙蒙细雨 **2** [T] ~ **sth** (**over sth**) to pour a small amount of liquid over the surface of sth（毛毛雨似的）洒落 SYN **dribble**

■ *noun* [U, sing.] light fine rain 毛毛细雨 ▶ **driz·zly** /'drɪzli/ *adj.*：*a dull, drizzly morning* 阴雨蒙蒙的早上

DRM /ˌdiː ɑːr 'em/ *abbr.* (*computing* 计) digital rights management (actions and devices that are used by the owners of software or information to prevent people from copying it from the Internet) 数字版权管理（指软件或信息拥有者为防止互联网盗版行为所采用的措施或装置）

Dr Mar·tens™ /ˌdɒktə 'mɑːtɪnz; *NAmE* ˌdɑːktər 'mɑːrtnz/ (*also informal* **Doc Martens**, **DMs**) *noun* [pl.] a type of comfortable heavy boot or shoe with LACES 马丁鞋，马丁靴（舒适的系带厚靴或鞋子）

drogue /drəʊg; *NAmE* droʊg/ *noun* a small PARACHUTE, used to pull a larger one from its bag 引导伞，拖曳伞（将大降落伞从袋子中拉出的小型降落伞）

droit de sei·gneur /ˌdrwʌ də sen'jɜː(r)/ *noun* [U] (*from French*) the right of a lord to have sex with a woman of lower social rank on her wedding night, said to exist in the Middle Ages（据传中世纪领主对其封臣新娘的）初夜权

droll /drəʊl; *NAmE* droʊl/ *adj.* (*old-fashioned* or *ironic*) amusing, but not in a way that you expect 离奇可笑的；滑稽古怪的

drom·ed·ary /'drɒmədəri; *NAmE* 'drɑːməderi/ *noun* (*pl.* **-ies**) an animal of the CAMEL family, with only one HUMP, that lives in desert countries 单峰驼

drone /drəʊn; *NAmE* droʊn/ *noun, verb*

■ *noun* **1** [usually sing.] a continuous low noise 嗡嗡声：*the distant drone of traffic* 远处车辆往来发出的嗡嗡声 **2** [usually sing.] a continuous low sound made by some musical instruments, for example the BAGPIPES, over which other notes are played or sung; the part of the instrument that makes this noise 持续低音（如风笛等发出的持续音）；持续音音管（或弦等） **3** a male BEE that does not work 雄蜂 ➲ COMPARE QUEEN BEE (1), WORKER (4) **4** a person who is lazy and gives nothing to society while others work（不劳动，依赖他人为生的）寄生虫 **5** an aircraft without a pilot, controlled from the ground 无人驾驶飞机 ➲ WORDFINDER NOTE AT AIRCRAFT

■ *verb* [I] to make a continuous low noise 嗡嗡叫；嗡嗡响：*A plane was droning in the distance.* 飞机在远处嗡嗡地响。◇ *a droning voice* 嗡嗡的响声

PHR V ˌdrone ˈon (about sth) to talk for a long time in a boring way 唠唠叨叨地说

drongo /ˈdrɒŋɡəʊ; NAmE ˈdrɑːŋɡoʊ/ noun (pl. -os or -oes) **1** a shiny black bird with a long tail 卷尾（毛色光亮的长尾黑鸟） **2** (AustralE, NZE, slang) a stupid person 傻瓜；笨蛋

drool /druːl/ verb **1** [I] to let SALIVA (= liquid) come out of your mouth 垂涎；淌口水 SYN **dribble**: *The dog was **drooling at the mouth**.* 狗嘴里淌着口水。 **2** [I] ~ (over sb/sth) (disapproving) to show in a silly or exaggerated way that you want or admire sb/sth very much （对…）垂涎欲滴，过分痴迷： *teenagers drooling over photos of movie stars* 对电影明星照片如痴如醉的青少年

droop /druːp/ verb **1** [I] to bend, hang or move downwards, especially because of being weak or tired （尤指因衰弱或疲劳）低垂，垂落，垂下： *She was so tired, her eyelids were beginning to droop.* 她太疲倦了，眼睑开始往下垂。 **2** [I] to become sad or depressed 沮丧；消沉；垂头丧气： *Our spirits drooped when we heard the news.* 听到这消息，我们情绪低落下来。 ▶ **droop** noun [sing.]: *the slight droop of her mouth* 她的嘴角微微下垂 **droopy** adj. : *a droopy moustache* 耷拉着的小胡子

drop /drɒp; NAmE drɑːp/ verb, noun

■ *verb* (-pp-)

• **FALL** 落下 **1** [I, T] to fall or allow sth to fall by accident （意外地）落下，掉下，使落下： *The climber slipped and dropped to his death.* 攀登者一失足掉下去摔死了。◇ ~ **sth** *Be careful not to drop that plate.* 小心别把那盘子摔了。 **2** [I, T] to fall or make sth fall deliberately （故意）降下，使降落，使落下： **+ adv./prep.** *He staggered in and dropped into a chair.* 他蹒跚着走进来，一屁股坐在椅子上。 ◇ **~ sth (+ adv./prep.)** *Medical supplies are being dropped into the stricken area.* 正在向灾区空投医药用品。 ◇ (BrE) *He dropped his trousers* (= undid them and let them fall). 他松开腰带，让裤子掉下去。 ◇ (NAmE) *He dropped his pants.* 他松开腰带，裤子掉下去。 **3** [I] (informal) to fall down or be no longer able to stand because you are extremely tired 累倒；累垮： *I feel **ready to drop**.* 我感到快累垮了。◇ *She expects everyone to work till they drop.* 她巴不得人人都干到累垮为止。

• **BECOME WEAKER/LESS** 变弱；减少 **4** [I, T] to become or make sth weaker, lower or less （使）变弱，降低，减少 SYN **fall**: *The temperature has dropped considerably.* 温度已大大降低。◇ *At last the wind dropped.* 风势终于减弱了。◇ *His **voice dropped** to a whisper.* 他的声音已放低到轻声细语了。◇ *The Dutch team have dropped to fifth place.* 荷兰队已降至第五名。 ◇ *The price of shares dropped by 14p.* 股价下跌了 14 便士。 ◇ *Shares **dropped in price** by 14p.* 股价下跌了 14 便士。 ◇ **~ sth** *She **dropped her voice** dramatically.* 她突然压低了声音。 ◇ *You must drop your speed in built-up areas.* 在楼房密集区必须放慢速度。 ➲ LANGUAGE BANK AT FALL 下降

• **EYES** 眼睛 **5** [I, T] **your eyes/gaze ~ | ~ your eyes/gaze** (formal) to look down 垂下（眼睛）；垂视： *Her eyes dropped to her lap.* 她双目低垂，看着自己的腿。

• **SLOPE DOWNWARDS** 向下倾斜 **6** [I] ~ (away) (from sth) to slope steeply downwards 急剧倾斜而下： *In front of them the valley dropped sharply away from the road.* 他们前面的山谷从路旁急剧倾斜而下。

• **DELIVER/SEND** 运送；发送 **7** [T] to stop so that sb can get out of a car, etc.; to deliver sth on the way to somewhere else 中途卸客；中途卸货： **~ sb/sth** *Can you drop me near the bank?* 你可以让我在银行附近下车吗？ ◇ **~ sb/sth off** *You left your jacket, but I can drop it off on my way to work tomorrow.* 你忘了拿你的短上衣，不过我可以在明天上班的路上顺便捎给你。 **8** [T] **~ sb a line/note** to send a short letter to sb 寄，送，写（信）： *Drop me a line when you get there.* 你到那儿后给我写封信。

• **LEAVE OUT** 略去 **9** [T] **~ sb/sth (from sth)** to leave sb/sth out by accident or deliberately 遗漏；省略；不予考虑： *She's been dropped from the team because of injury.* 她因受伤而未被列入队员名单。 ◇ *He spoke with a cockney accent and **dropped his aitches*** (= did not pronounce the letter 'h' at the start of words). 他讲话带着伦敦东区的口音，把词首的 h 音给吞掉了。

• **FRIENDS** 朋友 **10** [T] **~ sb** to stop seeing sb socially 不再与（某人）往来；同（某人）断绝联系： *She's dropped most of her old friends.* 她已与多数老朋友停止了来往。

• **STOP** 停止 **11** [T] **~ sth** to stop doing or discussing sth; to not continue with sth 停止；终止；放弃： *I dropped German* (= stopped studying it) *when I was 14.* 我 14 岁后就没再学德语。◇ ***Drop everything** and come at once!* 放下所有事情赶快来吧！ ◇ *Look, can we just **drop it*** (= stop talking about it)? 喂，这事儿能不能就谈到这儿？ ◇ *I think we'd better **drop the subject**.* 我认为我们最好不要谈这个话题。◇ *Let's drop the formalities—please call me Mike.* 咱们不必拘礼，叫我迈克好了。◇ *The police decided to drop the charges against her.* 警方决定撤回对她的指控。

• **HINT** 暗示 **12** [T] **~ a hint** to say or do sth in order to show sb, in an indirect way, what you are thinking 暗示；透露

• **IN KNITTING** 编织 **13** [T] **~ a stitch** to let a STITCH go off the needle 漏，脱，掉（针）

IDM **drop the ˈball** (NAmE, informal) to make a mistake and spoil sth that you are responsible for 犯错；处理失当 **drop a ˈbrick/ˈclanger** (BrE, informal) to say sth that offends or embarrasses sb, although you did not intend to 失言伤人；出言不慎 **drop ˈdead 1** (informal) to die suddenly and unexpectedly 暴死；突然死去；猝死 **2** (informal) used to tell sb, rudely, to stop annoying you, INTERFERING, etc. 别烦人；别打扰；别捣乱 ➲ SEE ALSO DROP-DEAD **drop sb ˈin it** (BrE, informal) to put sb in an embarrassing situation, especially by telling a secret that you should not have told （尤指因泄露秘密）使尴尬，使狼狈不堪 **drop ˈnames** to mention famous people you know or have met in order to impress others 提及自己认识或见过的名人以抬高身价 ➲ RELATED NOUN NAME-DROPPING **ˌdrop your ˈbundle** (AustralE, NZE, informal) to suddenly not be able to think clearly; to act in a stupid way because you have lost control over yourself 突然发蒙；失态 **let sb/sth ˈdrop 1** to do or say nothing more about sb/sth 不再提起；放弃： *I suggest we let the matter drop.* 我建议咱们别再提及此事。 **2** to mention sb/sth in a conversation, by accident or as if by accident （好像是）无意中说出： *He **let it drop that** the Prime Minister was a close friend of his.* 他有意无意地提起首相是他的密友。 ➲ MORE AT BOTTOM n., FLY n., HEAR, JAW n., LAP n., PENNY

PHR V **ˌdrop aˈway** to become weaker or less 减弱；减少： *She could feel the tension drop away.* 她感到紧张气氛缓和了下来。 **ˌdrop ˈback/beˈhind | ˌdrop beˈhind sb** to move or fall into position behind sb else 后退；落后；落在…后面： *We cannot afford to drop behind our competitors.* 我们可担当不起落后于竞争对手的后果。 **ˌdrop ˈby/ˈin/ˈround | ˌdrop ˈin on sb | ˌdrop ˈinto sth** to pay an informal visit to a person or a place 顺便访问；顺便进入： *Drop by sometime.* 有空儿来坐坐。◇ *I thought I'd drop in on you while I was passing.* 我曾想路过时顺便来看看你。◇ *Sorry we're late—we dropped into the pub on the way.* 对不起，我们迟到了。我们半路上顺便到酒馆坐了坐。 **ˌdrop ˈoff** (informal) **1** to fall into a light sleep 打盹儿；小睡： *I dropped off and missed the end of the film.* 我打了个盹儿，错过了影片的结尾。 **2** to become fewer or less 减少；下降： *Traffic in the town has dropped off since the bypass opened.* 自从这条旁道通车后，城里来往的车辆就减少了。 **ˌdrop ˈout (of sth) 1** to no longer take part in or be part of sth 不再参加；退出；脱离： *He has dropped out of active politics.* 他已不再积极参政了。◇ *a word that has dropped out of the language* 该语言中已废弃的一个词 **2** to leave school, college, etc. without finishing your studies 退学；辍学： *She started a degree but dropped out after only a year.* 她在攻读学位仅一年后就退学了。 ➲ RELATED NOUN DROPOUT (1) **3** to reject the ideas and ways of behaving that are accepted by the rest of society 拒绝传统社会 ➲ RELATED NOUN DROPOUT (2)

■ *noun*

• **OF LIQUID** 液体 **1** [C] a very small amount of liquid that forms a round shape 滴；水珠： *drops of rain* 雨滴 ◇ *a drop of blood* 一滴血 ➲ SEE ALSO RAINDROP, TEARDROP **2** [C, usually sing.] a small quantity of a liquid 少量；微量；一点点： *Could I have a drop more milk in my* *coffee, please?* 请给我在咖啡里多加点牛奶好吗？ ◇ *I haven't touched a drop* (= drunk any alcohol) *all evening.* 整个晚上我滴酒未沾。

- **FALL** 下降 **3** [C, usually sing.] ~ (**in sth**) a fall or reduction in the amount, level or number of sth 下降；下跌；减少：*a **drop in prices/temperature, etc.*** 价格、温度等下降 ◇ *a **dramatic/sharp drop** in profits* 利润大幅度 / 急剧下降 ◇ *a five per cent drop* 下跌百分之五 ➲ LANGUAGE BANK AT FALL
- **DISTANCE** 距离 **4** [sing.] a distance down from a high point to a lower point 下落的距离；落差：*There was a sheer drop of fifty metres to the rocks below.* 距下面的岩石有五十米的垂直距离。◇ *a twenty-foot drop* 二十英尺的落差
- **MEDICINE** 药 **5 drops** [pl.] a liquid medicine that you put one drop at a time into your eyes, ears or nose 滴剂：*eye drops* 眼药水
- **DELIVERING** 运送 **6** [C] the act of delivering sb/sth in a vehicle or by plane; the act of dropping sth 运送；空投：*Aid agencies are organizing food drops to civilians in the war zone.* 援助机构正组织向战区平民运送食品。◇ *a parachute drop* 降落伞空投
- **SWEET/CANDY** 糖果 **7** [C] a small round sweet/candy of the type mentioned 球状糖果：*fruit drops* 水果糖 ◇ *cough drops* (= sweets/candy to help a cough) 止咳糖

IDM **at the ˌdrop of a ˈhat** immediately; without hesitating 立即；毫不迟疑：*The company can't expect me to move my home and family at the drop of a hat.* 公司不可能指望我立即搬家。 **a ˌdrop in the ˈocean** (*BrE*) (*NAmE* **a ˌdrop in the ˈbucket**) an amount of sth that is too small or unimportant to make any real difference to a situation 沧海一粟；九牛一毛

ˈdrop cloth (*NAmE*) (*BrE* **ˈdust sheet**) *noun* a large sheet that is used to protect floors, furniture, etc. from dust or paint （地板、家具等的）防尘罩，苫布

ˌdrop-ˈdead *adv.* (*informal*) used before an adjective to emphasize that sb/sth is attractive in a very noticeable way （用于形容词前，强调非常引人注目）以令人绝倒的方式，极其，非常：*a drop-dead gorgeous Hollywood star* 美得令人瞠目的好莱坞明星

ˌdrop-down ˈmenu *noun* (*computing* 计) a menu that appears on a computer screen when you choose it, and that stays there until you choose one of the functions on it 下拉式选单 ➲ VISUAL VOCAB PAGE V74

ˈdrop goal *noun* (in RUGBY 橄榄球) a goal scored by dropping the ball onto the ground and kicking it over the CROSSBAR as it BOUNCES 落踢射门

ˌdrop ˈhandlebars *noun* [pl.] low curved handles on a bicycle 赛车车把

ˈdrop-in *adj.* [only before noun] able to be visited without arranging a fixed time first 可随时造访的；无须预约的：*a drop-in centre* 开放式中心

ˈdrop kick *noun* (in RUGBY 橄榄球) a kick made by dropping the ball onto the ground and kicking it as it BOUNCES 踢落地球 ▸ **ˈdrop-kick** *verb* **~ sth**

drop·let /ˈdrɒplət; *NAmE* ˈdrɑːp-/ *noun* a small drop of a liquid 小滴

drop·out /ˈdrɒpaʊt; *NAmE* ˈdrɑːp-/ *noun* **1** a person who leaves school or college before they have finished their studies 辍学者；退学者：*college dropouts* 大学肄业生 ◇ *a university with a high dropout rate* 退学率高的大学 **2** a person who rejects the ideas and ways of behaving that are accepted by the rest of society 拒绝传统社会的人

drop·per /ˈdrɒpə(r); *NAmE* ˈdrɑːp-/ *noun* a short glass tube with a hollow rubber end used for measuring medicine or other liquids in drops 滴管 ➲ VISUAL VOCAB PAGE V72

drop·pings /ˈdrɒpɪŋz; *NAmE* ˈdrɑːp-/ *noun* [pl.] the solid waste matter of birds and animals (usually small animals) （鸟、小动物的）粪

ˈdrop shot *noun* = DINK

dropsy /ˈdrɒpsi; *NAmE* ˈdrɑːpsi/ *noun* [U] (*old-fashioned*) = OEDEMA

ˈdrop zone *noun* the area in which sb/sth should land after being dropped from an aircraft 空投区；空降区

dros·oph·ila /drɒˈsɒfɪlə; *NAmE* drəˈsɑːfɪlə/ (*pl.* **dros·oph·ila**) *noun* a small fly that feeds on fruit and is often used in scientific research 果蝇（常用于实验）

dross /drɒs; *NAmE* drɔːs; drɑːs/ *noun* [U] **1** (*especially BrE*) something of very low quality; the least valuable part of sth 劣质品；糟粕：*mass-produced dross* 成批生产的劣质品 ◇ *The well-written dialogue separates this film from the usual teenage dross.* 精心撰写的对白将这部电影与一般的劣质青春片区分开来。 **2** (*specialist*) a waste substance, especially that separated from a metal when it is melted 废料；（尤指金属熔化的）浮渣

drought /draʊt/ *noun* [U, C] a long period of time when there is little or no rain 久旱；旱灾：*two years of severe drought* 两年的严重旱灾 ◇ *one of the worst droughts on record* 有记载以来最严重的旱灾之一 ➲ WORDFINDER NOTE AT RAIN

drove /drəʊv; *NAmE* droʊv/ *noun* [usually pl.] a large number of people or animals, often moving or doing sth as a group （移动的）人群，畜群：*droves of tourists* 成群的游客 ◇ *People were leaving the countryside **in droves** to look for work in the cities.* 一批一批的人离开农村到城里找工作。 ➲ SEE ALSO DRIVE *v.*

drover /ˈdrəʊvə(r); *NAmE* ˈdroʊv-/ *noun* a person who moves groups of cows or sheep from one place to another, especially to market 赶牛羊牲畜者；赶畜群上市者

drown /draʊn/ *verb* **1** [I, T] to die because you have been underwater too long and you cannot breathe; to kill sb in this way （使）淹死，溺死：*Two children drowned after falling into the river.* 两个孩子掉进河里淹死了。◇ *He had attempted to rescue the drowning man.* 他曾试图去救那个溺水的男人。◇ **~ sb/sth/yourself** *She tried to drown herself.* 她试图投水自杀。◇ *He was drowned at sea.* 他淹死在海里。◇ *They had drowned the unwanted kittens.* 他们把没人要的小猫淹死了。 **2** [T] **~ sth** (**in sth**) to make sth very wet; to completely cover sth in water or another liquid 浸透；淹没；浸泡 SYN **drench**：*The fruit was drowned in cream.* 水果在奶油里泡过。 **3** [T] **~ sb/sth** (**out**) (of a sound 声音) to be louder than other sounds so that you cannot hear them 压过；盖没；淹没：*She turned up the radio to drown out the noise from next door.* 她开大了收音机的音量以压过隔壁房间的吵闹声。 ▸ **drown·ing** *noun* [U, C]: *death by drowning* 溺水身亡 ◇ *Alcohol plays a part in an estimated 30% of drownings.* 估计有 30% 的溺水是酒精的作用所致。

IDM **drown your ˈfears/ˈloneliness/ˈsorrows, etc.** (*especially humorous*) to get drunk in order to forget your problems 借酒壮胆、解寂寞、浇愁等

drowse /draʊz/ *verb* [I] to be in a light sleep or almost asleep 打瞌睡；打盹；假寐

drowsy /ˈdraʊzi/ *adj.* (**drows·ier**, **drowsi·est**) **1** tired and almost asleep 困倦的；昏昏欲睡的 SYN **sleepy**：*The tablets may make you feel drowsy.* 这些药片可能会使你昏昏欲睡。 ➲ WORDFINDER NOTE AT SLEEP **2** making you feel relaxed and tired 使人松弛的；令人疲乏的；使人困倦的：*a drowsy afternoon in the sunshine* 阳光照耀下使人困倦的下午 ▸ **drows·ily** /-ɪli/ *adv.* **drow·si·ness** *noun* [U]: *The drugs tend to cause drowsiness.* 这些药常常使人昏昏欲睡。

drub·bing /ˈdrʌbɪŋ/ *noun* (*informal*) (in a sport) a situation where one team easily beats another （体育运动）轻取，轻易战胜：*We gave them a drubbing in the match on Saturday.* 我们在星期六的比赛中轻而易举地打败了他们。

drudge /drʌdʒ/ *noun* a person who has to do long hard boring jobs 苦工；做繁重无聊工作的人

drudg·ery /ˈdrʌdʒəri/ *noun* [U] hard boring work 单调乏味的苦差事；繁重无聊的工作

drug 🔑 /drʌg/ *noun, verb*
■ *noun* **1** 🔑 an illegal substance that some people smoke, INJECT, etc. for the physical and mental effects it has 毒品：*He does not smoke or* ***take drugs****.* 他既不抽烟也不吸毒。◇ *teenagers experimenting with drugs* 试用毒品的青少年 ◇ *I found out Steve was* ***on drugs*** (= regularly used drugs). 我发现史蒂夫已吸毒成瘾。◇ *drug and alcohol abuse* 吸毒和酗酒 ◇ *a* ***hard*** (= very harmful) ***drug*** *such as heroin* 海洛因之类的硬毒品（毒性很大）◇ *a* ***soft drug*** (= one that is not considered very harmful) 软毒品（毒性不太大）◇ *Drugs have been seized with a street value of two million dollars.* 黑市价值二百万美元的毒品已被查获。◇ *She was a* ***drug addict*** (= could not stop using drugs). 她是个吸毒成瘾的人。◇ *He was charged with* ***pushing drugs*** (= selling them). 他被控贩毒。◇ (*informal*) *I don't* ***do drugs*** (= use them). 我不吸毒。◇ *drug rehabilitation* 吸毒者的康复训练

WORDFINDER 联想词： abuse, addict, deal, dependence, detoxification, hallucinate, overdose, rehab, withdrawal

2 🔑 a substance used as a medicine or used in a medicine 药；药物：*prescribed drugs* 处方药 ◇ *The doctor put me on a course of pain-killing drugs.* 医生让我服一个疗程的止痛药。◇ *drug companies* 药品公司 ◇ *The drug has some bad side effects.* 这种药有些严重的副作用。➲ WORDFINDER NOTE AT CURE ➲ COLLOCATIONS AT ILL ➲ SEE ALSO DESIGNER DRUG
■ *verb* (**-gg-**) **1** ~ **sb/sth** to give a person or an animal a drug, especially to make them unconscious, or to affect their performance in a race or competition 使服麻醉药；用药麻醉；使服兴奋剂：*He was drugged and bundled into the back of the car.* 他被麻醉后塞入汽车后座。◇ *It's illegal to drug horses before a race.* 比赛前给马服用兴奋剂是违法的。**2** ~ **sth** to add a drug to sb's food or drink to make them unconscious or SLEEPY（在食物或饮料中）投放麻醉药，下麻醉药：*Her drink must have been drugged.* 她的饮料中肯定被掺了麻醉药。➲ MORE LIKE THIS 36, page R29
IDM **be drugged up to the 'eyeballs** to have taken or been given a lot of drugs 已服用大量毒品

'drug dealer *noun* a person who sells illegal drugs 毒品贩子

drug·gie (*BrE also* **drug·gy**) /ˈdrʌgi/ *noun* (*pl.* **-ies**) (*informal*) a person who takes illegal drugs regularly 吸毒者；有毒瘾的人

drug·ging /ˈdrʌgɪŋ/ *noun* [U] the act of taking a drug, especially an illegal one 服药；（尤指）吸毒：*They were feeling the effects of drinking and drugging all night.* 他们酗酒吸毒，整夜恍惚迷离。

drug·gist /ˈdrʌgɪst/ *noun* (*NAmE, old-fashioned*) **1** (*also* **chem·ist, dis'pensing chemist** *both BrE*) a person whose job is to prepare and sell medicines, and who works in a shop 药剂师；药商 **2** = PHARMACIST (1)

drug·gy /ˈdrʌgi/ *adj., noun*
■ *adj.* (**drug·gier, drug·gi·est**) (*informal*) using or involving illegal drugs 吸毒的；毒品的
■ *noun* (*BrE*) = DRUGGIE

'drug peddler *noun* = PEDDLER

drug·store 🔑 /ˈdrʌgstɔː(r)/ *noun* (*NAmE*) a shop/store that sells medicines and also other types of goods, for example COSMETICS（兼售化妆品等的）药房 ➲ COMPARE PHARMACY (1) ➲ SEE ALSO CHEMIST (2)

Druid /ˈdruːɪd/ *noun* a priest of an ancient Celtic religion 德鲁伊特（古代凯尔特人的祭司）

drum 🔑 /drʌm/ *noun, verb*
■ *noun* **1** 🔑 a musical instrument made of a hollow round frame with plastic or skin stretched tightly across one or both ends. You play it by hitting it with sticks or with your hands. 鼓：*a bass drum* 大鼓 ◇ *Tony Cox on drums* 鼓手托尼・考克斯 ◇ *to play the drums* 击鼓 ◇ *a regular drum beat* 节奏均匀的击鼓声 ➲ VISUAL VOCAB PAGE V37 **2** a large container for oil or chemicals, shaped like a CYLINDER（装油或化学剂的）大桶：*a 50 gallon drum* 容积为 50 加仑的桶 ◇ *an oil drum* 油桶 **3** a thing shaped like a drum, especially part of a machine 鼓状物；（尤指机器上的）鼓轮，滚筒：*The mixture flows to a revolving drum where the water is filtered out.* 混合剂流过旋转着的滚筒时水分便从中滤出。
IDM **beat/bang the 'drum (for sb/sth)** (*especially BrE*) to speak with enthusiasm in support of sb/sth（为…）竭力鼓吹，摇旗呐喊 ➲ MORE AT MARCH *v.*
■ *verb* (**-mm-**) **1** [I] to play a drum 打鼓；击鼓 **2** [T, I] ~ **(sth) on sth** to make a sound by hitting a surface again and again 连续敲击…使发出咚咚声；不停地击打：*Impatiently, he* ***drummed his fingers*** *on the table.* 他不耐烦地用手指嗒嗒地敲击桌子。
IDM **'drum sth into sb's head** = DRUM STH INTO SB
PHR V **'drum sth into sb** to make sb remember sth by repeating it a lot of times 向某人反复灌输；对某人反复讲述：*We had it drummed into us that we should never talk to strangers.* 我们曾被反复叮嘱千万不要与陌生人讲话。**ˌdrum sb 'out (of sth)** [usually passive] to force sb to leave an organization as a punishment for doing sth wrong 开除；轰走；驱逐 **ˌdrum sth↔'up** to try hard to get support or business 竭力争取（支持）；兜揽（生意）：*He had flown to the north of the country to drum up support for the campaign.* 他已乘飞机到国家的北方去努力争取对这一运动的支持。

ˌdrum and 'bass (*also* **ˌdrum 'n' 'bass**) *noun* [U] a type of electronic dance music developed in Britain in the early 1990s, which has a fast drum beat and a strong slower BASS[1] (1) beat 鼓与贝司，鼓打贝司（20 世纪 90 年代初兴起于英国的一种电子舞曲，以快速的鼓点节拍和稍缓慢的重低音节奏为特点）

drum·beat /ˈdrʌmbiːt/ *noun* the sound that a beat on a drum makes 击鼓声

'drum kit *noun* a set of drums 架子鼓 ➲ VISUAL VOCAB PAGE V37

drum·lin /ˈdrʌmlɪn/ *noun* (*geology* 地) a very small hill formed by the movement of a GLACIER (= a large moving mass of ice)（冰川形成的）鼓丘

'drum machine *noun* an electronic musical instrument that produces the sound of drums 电子鼓

ˌdrum 'major *noun* the leader of a marching band of musicians, especially in the army（尤指军乐队的）行进乐队指挥

ˌdrum majo'rette (*especially BrE*) (*NAmE usually* **ma·jor·ette**) *noun* a girl in special brightly coloured clothes who walks in front of a marching band, spinning, throwing and catching a long stick (called a BATON)（行进乐队中身着艳丽服装、舞动抛接指挥棒的）女领队

drum·mer /ˈdrʌmə(r)/ *noun* a person who plays a drum or drums 鼓手 **IDM** SEE MARCH *v.*

drum·ming /ˈdrʌmɪŋ/ *noun* [U, sing.] **1** the act of playing a drum; the sound of a drum being played 击鼓；鼓声 **2** a continuous sound or feeling like the beats of a drum 击鼓似的咚咚声；似击鼓一样连续不停的感觉：*the steady drumming of the rain on the tin roof* 雨点打在铁皮屋顶上发出的有节奏的嗒嗒声

ˌdrum 'n' 'bass *noun* = DRUM AND BASS

drum·stick /ˈdrʌmstɪk/ *noun* **1** a stick used for playing a drum 鼓槌 ➲ VISUAL VOCAB PAGE V37 **2** the lower part of the leg of a chicken or other bird that is cooked and eaten as food 熟鸡（或家禽）腿下段；下段鸡（或家禽）腿肉：***a chicken/turkey drumstick*** 鸡 / 火鸡腿下段

drunk 🔑 /drʌŋk/ *adj., noun* ➲ SEE ALSO DRINK *v.*
■ *adj.* **1** 🔑 [not usually before noun] having drunk so much alcohol that it is impossible to think or speak clearly（酒）醉：*She was too drunk to remember anything about the party.* 她喝得酩酊大醉，聚会上的事什么都记不得了。◇ *His only way of dealing with his problems was to go out and* ***get drunk****.* 他解决烦心事的唯一办法就是出去喝个烂醉。◇ *They got drunk on vodka.* 他们喝伏特加酒醉倒

了。◇ *Police arrested him for being **drunk and disorderly** (= violent or noisy in a public place because of being drunk).* 他因醉酒妨害治安被警方逮捕。 OPP sober **2 ~ with sth** (*formal*) in a great state of excitement because of a particular emotion or situation 陶醉；沉醉；飘飘然；忘乎所以：*drunk with success* 因成功而飘飘然

IDM **(as) drunk as a 'lord** (*BrE*) (*NAmE* **(as) drunk as a 'skunk**) (*informal*) very drunk 烂醉如泥 ➲ MORE AT BLIND *adv.*, ROARING

■ ***noun*** a person who is drunk or who often gets drunk 醉汉；酒鬼；酗酒者

drunk·ard /ˈdrʌŋkəd; *NAmE* -ərd/ *noun* (*old-fashioned*) a person who gets drunk very often 酒鬼；酢鬼 SYN **alcoholic**

ˌdrunk ˈdriver (*especially NAmE*) (*BrE also* **ˌdrink-ˈdriver**) *noun* a person who drives a vehicle after drinking too much alcohol 酒后驾车者

ˈdrunk driving (*especially NAmE*) (*BrE also* **ˌdrink-ˈdriving**, **ˌdrunken ˈdriving**) *noun* [U] driving a vehicle after drinking too much alcohol 酒后驾车

drunk·en /ˈdrʌŋkən/ *adj.* [only before noun] **1** drunk or often getting drunk 醉的；常醉的；酗酒的：*a drunken driver* 喝醉的司机 ◇ *She was often beaten by her drunken husband.* 她常常遭到酗酒丈夫的毒打。 **2** showing the effects of too much alcohol; involving people who are drunk 酒醉引起的；醉汉的：*He came home to find her in a drunken stupor.* 他回到家里，发现她喝得醉醺醺的。◇ *a drunken brawl* 酒后闹事 ▶ **drunk·en·ly** *adv.*：*He staggered drunkenly to his feet.* 他醉醺醺地摇晃着站起来。 **drunk·en·ness** *noun* [U]

ˌdrunken ˈdriving *noun* [U] (*BrE*) = DRINK-DRIVING

ˈdrunk tank *noun* (*informal, humorous, especially NAmE*) a place where people are put by the police because they are drunk 醉汉监禁室：*He spent the night in the drunk tank.* 他在酒鬼监禁室过了一夜。

dry /draɪ/ *adj., verb*

■ ***adj.*** (**drier**, **dri·est**)

• NOT WET 干 **1** not wet, damp or sticky; without water or MOISTURE 干的；干燥的：*Is my shirt dry yet?* 我的衬衣干了吗？◇ *Store onions in a cool dry place.* 把洋葱存放在凉爽干燥的地方。◇ *I'm afraid this cake has turned out very dry.* 恐怕这个蛋糕烤得太干。◇ *Her mouth felt **as dry as a bone*** (= completely dry). 她感到口干舌燥。◇ *When the paint is completely dry, apply another coat.* 油漆干透后再涂上一层。◇ *It was high summer and the rivers were dry* (= had no water in them). 正值盛夏，河流都干涸了。 ➲ SEE ALSO BONE DRY OPP **wet**

• LITTLE RAIN 雨少 **2** with very little rain 雨少的；干旱的；干燥的：*weeks of hot **dry weather*** 连续几周炎热干燥的天气 ◇ *the **dry season*** 旱季 ◇ *I hope it **stays dry** for our picnic.* 希望我们野餐的时候别下雨。◇ *Rattlesnakes occur in the warmer, drier parts of North America.* 响尾蛇出现在北美温暖干燥的地区。 OPP **wet**

• SKIN/HAIR 皮肤；头发 **3** without the natural oils that makes it soft and healthy 干性的；无水分的：*a shampoo for dry hair* 适合干性发质的洗发水

• COUGH 咳嗽 **4** that does not produce any PHLEGM (= the thick liquid that forms in the nose and throat) 干咳的：*a dry hacking cough* 猛烈的干咳

• BREAD 面包 **5** eaten on its own without any butter, jam, etc. 无黄油（或果酱等）的：*Breakfast consisted of dry bread and a cup of tea.* 早餐有不涂黄油的面包和一杯茶。

• WINE 葡萄酒 **6** not sweet 无甜味的；干的：*a crisp dry white wine* 爽口的干白葡萄酒 ◇ *a dry sherry* 干雪利酒 OPP **sweet**

• HUMOUR 幽默 **7** (*approving*) very clever and expressed in a quiet way that is not obvious; often using IRONY 机敏的；不形于色的；不露声色的：*He was a man of few words with a delightful dry sense of humour.* 他话不多，却富有不形于色的幽默感，让人很愉快。

• WITHOUT EMOTION 无感情 **8** not showing emotion 不动感情的；冷冰冰的：*a dry voice* 冷冰冰的声音

• BORING 乏味 **9** not interesting 干巴巴的；枯燥乏味的：*Government reports tend to make dry reading.* 政府报告读起来往往枯燥无味。

• WITHOUT ALCOHOL 无酒 **10** without alcohol; where it is illegal to buy, sell or drink alcohol 无酒的；禁酒的；戒酒的：*We had a dry wedding* (= no alcoholic drinks were served). 我们举行了一个无酒的婚礼。◇ *a dry county/state* 禁酒的郡 / 州

• THIRSTY 口渴 **11** (*informal, especially BrE*) thirsty; that makes you thirsty 口渴的；令人口渴的：*I'm a bit dry.* 我有点渴。◇ *This is dry work.* 这是使人觉得口渴的工作。

▶ **dryly** *adv.* = DRILY **dry·ness** *noun* [U]

IDM **milk/suck sb/sth ˈdry** to get from sb/sth all the money, help, information, etc. they have, usually giving nothing in return 榨干…的钱财；耗尽…的精力；掏尽…的信息 **not a dry eye in the ˈhouse** (*humorous*) used to say that everyone was very emotional about sth 全场无人不流泪；全场无不为之动容：*There wasn't a dry eye in the house when they announced their engagement.* 他们宣布订婚时大伙眼睛全湿了。 **run ˈdry** to stop supplying water; to be all used so that none is left 干涸；枯竭；耗尽：*The wells in most villages in the region have run dry.* 这个地区多数村庄的水井都已干涸。◇ *Vaccine supplies started to run dry as the flu outbreak reached epidemic proportions.* 由于流感爆发已大肆流行，疫苗供应开始消耗殆尽。 ➲ MORE AT BLEED, HIGH *adj.*, HOME *adv.*, POWDER *n.*, SQUEEZE *v.*

■ ***verb*** (**dries**, **dry·ing**, **dried**, **dried**) [I, T] to become dry; to make sth dry （使）变干；（把…）弄干：*Be careful. The paint hasn't dried yet.* 小心点，油漆还没有干。◇ *You wash the dishes and I'll dry.* 你洗盘子，我来擦干。◇ **~ sth** *Use this towel to dry your hands.* 用这条毛巾擦手。◇ *dry your hair* 弄干头发 ◇ *to **dry your eyes/tears*** (= stop crying) 擦干眼睛 / 眼泪

PHR V **ˌdry ˈoff** | **ˌdry sb/sth↔ˈoff** to become dry or make sth dry （使）变干；弄干：*We went swimming and then lay in the sun to dry off.* 我们去游泳了，然后就躺在太阳下晒干。◇ *We dried our boots off by the fire.* 我们把靴子放在火旁烘干。 **ˌdry ˈout** | **ˌdry sb↔ˈout** (*informal*) to stop drinking alcohol after you have continuously been drinking too much; to cure sb of drinking too much alcohol （使）戒酒瘾：*He went to an expensive clinic to dry out.* 他到一家费用昂贵的诊所戒酒瘾。 **ˌdry ˈout** | **ˌdry sth↔ˈout** to become or to allow sth to become dry, in a way that is not wanted （使）变干，干透：*Water the plant regularly, never letting the soil dry out.* 经常给植物浇水，别让土壤干透了。◇ *Hot sun and cold winds can soon dry out your skin.* 火辣辣的太阳和寒风可使你的皮肤很快变干燥。 **ˌdry ˈup 1** (of rivers, lakes, etc. 河流、湖泊等) to become completely dry 干涸：*During the drought the river dried up.* 旱灾期间，河流都干涸了。 **2** if a supply of sth **dries up**, there is gradually less of it until there is none left 枯竭；耗尽：*As she got older, offers of modelling work began to dry up.* 随着她年龄渐长，邀请她做模特儿的工作已越来越少。 **3** to suddenly stop talking because you do not know what to say next（因不知该说什么而）突然住口，突然说不出话来 **ˌdry ˈup** | **ˌdry sth↔ˈup** (*BrE*) to dry dishes with a towel after you have washed them 擦干（刚洗的盘子）：*I'll wash and you can dry up.* 我洗盘子，你来擦干。

dryad /ˈdraɪæd/ *noun* (in stories) a female spirit who lives in a tree （传说中的）林中女仙，树精

ˌdry ˈcell *noun* the type of cell in a **dry battery** which contains chemicals only in solid form 干电池

ˌdry-ˈclean (*also* **clean**) *verb* **~ sth** to clean clothes using chemicals instead of water 干洗：*This garment must be dry-cleaned only.* 这件衣服只可干洗。 ➲ SYNONYMS AT CLEAN ▶ **ˌdry-ˈcleaning** *noun* [U]

ˌdry-ˈcleaner's *noun* = CLEANER'S

ˌdry ˈdock *noun* [C, U] an area in a port from which the water can be removed, used for building or repairing ships 干船坞

dryer (*also* **drier**) /ˈdraɪə(r)/ *noun* (especially in compounds 尤用于构成复合词) a machine for drying sth 烘干

机；脱水机；干燥机：*a hairdryer* 吹风机 ➲ SEE ALSO SPIN DRYER, TUMBLE DRYER

ˌdry-ˈeyed *adj.* [not before noun] not crying 不哭；无泪；哭不出：*She remained dry-eyed throughout the trial.* 整个审讯过程中她没掉一滴眼泪。

ˈdry goods *noun* [pl.] **1** (*BrE*) types of food that are solid and dry, such as tea, coffee and flour 干货 **2** (*old-fashioned*, *NAmE*) cloth and things that are made out of cloth, such as clothes and sheets 纺织品（如衣服、被单等）：*a dry goods store* 纺织品商店 ➲ COMPARE DRAPERY

ˌdry ˈice *noun* [U] solid CARBON DIOXIDE used for keeping food, etc. cold or for producing special effects in the theatre 干冰；固态二氧化碳

ˌdry ˈland *noun* [U] land, rather than sea 陆地（有别于海洋） SYN **terra firma**: *It was a great relief to be back on* ***dry land*** *after such a rough crossing.* 渡过汹涌澎湃的大海回到陆地后使人感到如释重负。

dryly = DRILY

ˌdry ˈmilk (*US*) (*BrE* **ˈmilk powder**, **ˌpowdered ˈmilk**) *noun* [U] dried milk in the form of a powder 奶粉

ˌdry-ˈroasted *adj.* cooked in an oven without adding oil or fat 干烤的，干焙的（不加油脂）：*dry-roasted peanuts* 干烤花生

ˌdry ˈrot *noun* [U] **1** wood that has decayed and turned to powder（木材）干腐病，干朽 **2** any FUNGUS that causes this decay 干腐菌

ˌdry ˈrun *noun* [usually sing.] a complete practice of a performance or way of doing sth, before the real one 排练；演习 SYN **dummy run**

ˈdry slope (*also* **ˈdry-ski slope**) *noun* a steep slope with a special surface for practising SKIING（练习用）人造滑雪斜坡

dry·stone wall /ˌdraɪstəʊn ˈwɔːl; *NAmE* -stoʊn/ *noun* (*BrE*) (*NAmE* **ˈdry wall**) a stone wall built without MORTAR (= a substance used in building to hold bricks or stones together) between the stones 干砌石墙

dry·suit /ˈdraɪsuːt; *BrE also* -sjuːt/ *noun* a piece of clothing that fits the whole body closely and keeps water out, worn by people swimming underwater or sailing 潜水衣 ➲ COMPARE WETSUIT

drywall /draɪwɔːl/ *noun* [U] (*NAmE*) **1** = PLASTERBOARD **2** (*BrE* **dry·stone wall**) a stone wall built without MORTAR (= a substance used in building to hold bricks or stones together) between the stones 干砌石墙

DSL /ˌdiː es ˈel/ *abbr.* (*computing* 计) digital subscriber line (a way of sending electronic data at high speed along ordinary telephone lines, used for supplying the Internet to homes, businesses, etc.) 数字用户线

DST /ˌdiː es ˈtiː/ *abbr.* DAYLIGHT SAVING TIME 夏令时

DT /ˌdiː ˈtiː/ *noun* [U] (*BrE*) the abbreviation for ‘design and technology’ (a school subject in which students learn about the role of technology in modern life and also design and make things for themselves) 设计与科技（全写为 design and technology，学校科目，讲授技术在现代生活中的作用以及实用设计技巧）

DTP /ˌdiː tiː ˈpiː/ *abbr.* DESKTOP PUBLISHING 桌面出版，桌上排版（用微型电脑和打印机从事出版业务）

DTs (*BrE*) (*US* **D.T.'s**) /ˌdiː ˈtiːz/ *noun* [pl.] the abbreviation for ‘delirium tremens’ (a physical condition in which people who drink too much alcohol feel their body shaking and imagine that they are seeing things that are not really there) 震颤性谵妄（全写为 delirium tremens，喝酒太多导致身体震颤和出现幻觉）

dual /ˈdjuːəl; *NAmE* ˈduːəl/ *adj.* [only before noun] having two parts or aspects 两部分的；双重的；双的：*his dual role as composer and conductor* 他兼任作曲家和指挥的双重角色 ◇ *She has* ***dual nationality*** (= is a citizen of two different countries). 她具有双重国籍。◇ *The piece of furniture serves a dual purpose as a cupboard and as a table.* 这件家具有两个用途，既作橱柜也作饭桌。➲ NOTE AT DOUBLE ➲ SEE ALSO DUAL-PURPOSE

ˌdual ˈcarriageway (*BrE*) (*NAmE* **diˌvided ˈhighway**) *noun* a road with a strip of land in the middle that divides the lines of traffic moving in opposite directions（中央有分隔带的）双幅车行道，双向车道

ˌdual conˈtrols *noun* [pl.] two sets of instruments for controlling a vehicle or aircraft, so that a teacher, for example, can take control from the driver（车辆或飞机的）复式控制装置，复式操纵装置 ▶ **ˌdual conˈtrol** *adj.*：*a dual-control vehicle* 有复式操纵装置的汽车

dual·ism /ˈdjuːəlɪzəm; *NAmE* ˈduː-/ *noun* [U] **1** (*philosophy* 哲) the theory that there are two opposite principles in everything, for example good and evil 二元论 **2** (*formal*) the state of having two parts 双重性；二元性 ▶ **dual·ist**, **dual·ist·ic** *adj.* **dual·ist** *noun*

dual·ity /djuːˈæləti; *NAmE* duː-/ *noun* [U, C] (*pl.* **-ies**) (*formal*) the state of having two parts or aspects 双重性；二元性

ˌdual-ˈpurpose *adj.* that can be used for two different purposes 双重目的的；两用的：*a dual-purpose vehicle* (= for carrying passengers or goods) 两用汽车（载客或载货）

dub /dʌb/ *verb*, *noun*

■ *verb* (**-bb-**) **1** **~ sb + noun** to give sb/sth a particular name, often in a humorous or critical way 把…戏称为；给…起绰号：*The Belgian actor Jean-Claude Van Damme has been dubbed ‘Muscles from Brussels’.* 比利时演员尚格•云顿一直被戏称为“布鲁塞尔的肌肉”。 **2** **~ sth (into sth)** to replace the original speech in a film/movie or television programme with words in another language 为（影片或电视节目）配音；译制：*an American movie dubbed into Italian* 用意大利语配音的美国影片 ➲ COMPARE SUBTITLE *v.* ➲ **WORDFINDER NOTE** AT FILM **3** **~ sth** (*especially BrE*) to make a piece of music by mixing sounds from different recordings 混声录制，混录（音乐） ➲ **MORE LIKE THIS** 36, page R29

■ *noun* [U] a type of West Indian music or poetry with a strong beat（西印度群岛的）强节奏音乐，强节拍诗歌

du·bi·ety /ˌdjuːˈbaɪəti; *NAmE* ˌduː-/ *noun* [U] (*formal*) the fact of being uncertain 犹豫；怀疑；疑惑

du·bi·ous /ˈdjuːbiəs; *NAmE* ˈduː-/ *adj.* **1** [not usually before noun] **~ (about sth)/(about doing sth)** (of a person 人) not certain and slightly suspicious about sth; not knowing whether sth is good or bad 怀疑；无把握；拿不准 SYN **doubtful**: *I was rather dubious about the whole idea.* 我对这整个想法持怀疑态度。 **2** (*disapproving*) probably not honest 可疑的；不可信的；靠不住的；不诚实的 SYN **suspicious**: *They indulged in some highly dubious business practices to obtain their current position in the market.* 他们采取了一些极为可疑的商业手段以取得目前在市场上的地位。 **3** that you cannot be sure about; that is probably not good 不确定的；不一定好的：*They consider the plan to be of dubious benefit to most families.* 他们认为这项计划对大多数家庭不一定有好处。◇ (*ironic*) *She had the dubious honour of being the last woman to be hanged in England* (= it was not an honour at all). 她成为英格兰最后一个受绞刑的女子，这也算是一种荣幸吧。 ▶ **du·bi·ous·ly** *adv.*

ˌDublin Bay ˈprawn *noun* = LANGOUSTINE

dub·nium /ˈdʌbniəm; *NAmE* ˈduːb-/ *noun* [U] (*symb.* **Db**) a RADIOACTIVE chemical element. Dubnium is produced when atoms COLLIDE (= crash into each other). 钳（人造化学放射性元素）

dub·step /ˈdʌbstep/ *noun* [U] a type of electronic dance music, developed in England in the late 1990s, that has a strong BASS[1] beat and drum patterns that are repeated many times, and that sometimes contains singing 回响贝斯（一种电子舞曲，20 世纪 90 年代末兴起于英格兰，有重复性的重低音节奏和鼓点节拍，有时含歌唱）

ducal /ˈdjuːkl; *NAmE* ˈduːkl/ *adj.* [only before noun] of or belonging to a DUKE 公爵的；公爵领地的

ducat /ˈdʌkət/ *noun* (in the past) a gold coin used in many European countries 达克特（旧时在多个欧洲国家通用的金币）

duch·ess /ˈdʌtʃəs/ *noun* **1** the wife of a DUKE 公爵夫人：*the Duchess of York* 约克公爵夫人 **2** a woman who has the rank of a DUKE 女公爵

duchy /ˈdʌtʃi/ *noun* (*pl.* **-ies**) (*also* **duke·dom**) an area of land that is owned and controlled by a DUKE or DUCHESS 公爵领地

duck /dʌk/ *noun, verb*

■ *noun* **1** (*pl.* **ducks** or **duck**) [C] a common bird that lives on or near water and has short legs, WEBBED feet (= feet with thin pieces of skin between the toes) and a wide beak. There are many types of duck, some of which are kept for their meat or eggs. 鸭：*wild ducks* 野鸭 ◇ *duck eggs* 鸭蛋 ➲ VISUAL VOCAB PAGE V12 **2** [C] a female duck 母鸭 ➲ COMPARE DRAKE **3** [U] meat from a duck 鸭肉：*roast duck with orange sauce* 烤鸭蘸橘子酱 **4** (*also* **duckie, ducks, ducky**) [C, usually sing.] (*BrE, informal*) a friendly way of addressing sb（表示友好的称呼）乖乖，宝贝儿：*Anything else, duck?* 还有别的事吗，宝贝儿？ ➲ COMPARE DEAR *n.*, LOVE *n.* (5) **5 a duck** [sing.] (in CRICKET 板球) a BATSMAN'S score of zero 零分：*He was out for a duck.* 他因得了零分而出局。 ➲ SEE ALSO LAME DUCK, SITTING DUCK

IDM **get/have (all) your ˌducks in a ˈrow** (*especially NAmE*) to have made all the preparations needed to do sth; to be well organized 为某事做充分准备；把事情安排得井井有条 **(take to sth) like a ˌduck to ˈwater** (to become used to sth) very easily, without any problems or fears 像鸭子入水般容易，轻而易举，毫不困难，毫无畏惧（习惯于某事）：*She has taken to teaching like a duck to water.* 她教起书来驾轻就熟。 ➲ MORE AT DEAD *adj.*, WATER *n.*

■ *verb* **1** [I, T] to move your head or body downwards to avoid being hit or seen 低下头，弯下身（以免被打中或看见）：*He had to duck as he came through the door.* 他穿过门口时得弯下身来。 ◇ **~ (down) (behind/under sth)** *We ducked down behind the wall so they wouldn't see us.* 我们弓身躲在墙后不让他们看见。 ◇ *He just managed to* **duck** *out of sight.* 他总算躲开了别人的视线。 ◇ **~ sth** *She ducked her head and got into the car.* 她低着头进了汽车。 **2** [T] **~ sth** to avoid sth by moving your head or body out of the way 躲闪；躲避 SYN **dodge**：*He ducked the first few blows then started to fight back.* 他躲开最先几拳后便开始反击。 **3** [I] **+ adv./prep.** to move somewhere quickly, especially in order to avoid being seen 迅速行进，飞快行走（以免被看见）：*She ducked into the adjoining room as we came in.* 我们进来时她转身躲进了隔壁房间。 **4** [I, T] (*rather informal*) to avoid a difficult or unpleasant duty or responsibility 逃避，回避，推脱，推诿（职责或责任）：**~ out of sth** *It's his turn to cook dinner, but I bet he'll try to duck out of it.* 轮到他做饭了，但我敢打赌他会想方设法逃避的。 ◇ **~ sth** *The government is ducking the issue.* 政府在回避这个问题。 **5** (*especially NAmE* **dunk**) [T] **~ sb** to push sb underwater and hold them there for a short time 把…按入水中：*The kids were ducking each other in the pool.* 孩子们在池塘里相互把对方按入水中。

ˌduck-billed ˈplatypus *noun* = PLATYPUS

duck·boards /ˈdʌkbɔːdz; *NAmE* -bɔːrdz/ *noun* [pl.] long narrow wooden boards used to make a path over wet ground（用窄长木板做铺在湿地上的）铺道板，垫路板

duck·ling /ˈdʌklɪŋ/ *noun* [C, U] a young duck; the meat of a young duck 小鸭；幼鸭；小鸭肉 ➲ SEE ALSO UGLY DUCKLING

ˌducks and ˈdrakes *noun* [U] (*BrE*) a game in which you make flat stones BOUNCE across the surface of water 打水漂（游戏）

ˌduck ˈsoup *noun* [U] (*NAmE, informal*) a problem that is easy to deal with, or an opponent who is easy to defeat 容易处理的问题；容易打败的对手

duck·weed /ˈdʌkwiːd/ *noun* [U] a very small plant that grows on the surface of still water 浮萍

ducky /ˈdʌki/ *noun, adj.*

■ *noun* (*pl.* **duck·ies**) (*BrE, informal*) = DUCK (4)

■ *adj.* (**duck·ier, ducki·est**) (*NAmE, old-fashioned* or *humorous*) very pleasant 顺心如愿的；令人十分愉快的：*Everything is just ducky.* 一切顺顺当当的。

duct /dʌkt/ *noun* **1** a pipe or tube carrying liquid, gas, electric or telephone wires, etc.（传送液体、气体、电线、电话线等的）管道，管子：*a heating/ventilation duct* 暖气导管；通风道 **2** a tube in the body or in plants through which liquid passes（人体或植物体内输送液体的）管，导管：*the bile duct* 胆管

duc·tile /ˈdʌktaɪl/ *adj.* (*specialist*) (of a metal 金属) that can be made into a thin wire 可拉成细丝的；可延展的；有延性的

duct·ing /ˈdʌktɪŋ/ *noun* [U] **1** a system of ducts 管道（或导管）系统 **2** material in the form of a duct or ducts 管状材料：*a short piece of ducting* 一小截管状材料

ˈduct tape *noun* [U] (*NAmE*) very strong cloth tape that is sticky on one side, often used for repairing things or covering holes in pipes 强力胶布（常用于维修或粘贴管道漏洞）

dud /dʌd/ *noun, adj.*

■ *noun* **1** [C] (*informal*) a thing that is useless, especially because it does not work correctly 不中用的东西；废物：*Two of the fireworks in the box were duds.* 盒子里的烟火有两个是点不着的废品。 **2 duds** [pl.] (*slang*) clothes 衣裳

■ *adj.* [only before noun] useless; that does not work correctly 无用的；不中用的；出故障的：*a dud battery* 废电池 ◇ *a dud cheque* (= written by sb who has not enough money in their bank account) 空头支票

dude /duːd; *BrE also* djuːd/ *noun* (*slang, especially NAmE*) a man 男人：*He's a real cool dude.* 他真是个帅哥。 ◇ *Hey, dude, what's up?* 喂，哥们儿，怎么啦？

ˈdude ranch *noun* an American RANCH (= a large farm) where people can go on holiday/vacation and do the sort of activities that COWBOYS do（美国的）度假牧场，度假农场 ORIGIN From an old meaning of the word *dude*, a man from the city who wears fashionable clothes. 源自 dude 一词的旧义，指衣着时髦的城市男人。

dudgeon /ˈdʌdʒən/ *noun* IDM SEE HIGH *adj.*

due /djuː; *NAmE* duː/ *adj., noun, adv.*

■ *adj.*

• **CAUSED BY** 由于 **1** [not before noun] **~ to sth/sb** caused by sb/sth; because of sb/sth 由于；因为：*The team's success was largely due to her efforts.* 这个队的成功主要是她努力的结果。 ◇ *Most of the problems were due to human error.* 多数问题都是人为错误造成的。 ◇ *The project had to be abandoned due to a lack of government funding.* 这项工程由于缺乏政府的资助而不得不放弃。 ➲ LANGUAGE BANK AT BECAUSE HELP Some people think that it is more correct to use **owing to** to mean 'because of' after a verb or at the beginning of a clause, as **due** is an adjective. 有人认为在动词之后或从句之首用 owing to 表示"因为"更合适，因为 due 是形容词。

• **EXPECTED** 预期 **2** [not before noun] arranged or expected 预定；预期；预计：*When's the baby due?* 宝宝什么时候出世？ ◇ *The next train is due in five minutes.* 下一班火车预定在五分钟后抵达。 ◇ (*especially NAmE*) *My essay's due next Friday* (= it has to be given to the teacher by then). 我的论文下周五必须交。 ◇ **~ to do sth** *Rose is due to start school in January.* 罗斯一月份就要开始上学了。 ◇ **~ for sth** *The band's first album is due for release later this month.* 这个乐队的第一张唱片预定在本月下旬发行。

• **OWED** 欠款 **3** [not usually before noun] when a sum of money is **due**, it must be paid immediately 到期：*Payment is due on 1 October.* 付款期限为 10 月 1 日。 **4** [not before noun] **~ (to sb)** owed to sb as a debt, because it is their right or because they have done sth to deserve it

D

应支付；应给予；应归于：*Have they been paid the money that is due to them?* 他们应得的钱付给他们了吗？◇ *Our thanks are due to the whole team.* 我们要向全队致谢。 **5** [not before noun] owed sth; deserving sth 应有；应得到：**~ sth** *I'm still due 15 days' leave.* 我还应有 15 天的休假。◇ **~ for sth** *She's due for promotion soon.* 她很快该晋升了。
• **SUITABLE/RIGHT** 适当；合适 **6** [only before noun] (*formal*) that is suitable or right in the circumstances 适当的；恰当的；合适的：*After due consideration, we have decided to appoint Mr Davis to the job.* 经过适当考虑之后，我们决定委任戴维斯先生负责这项工作。◇ *to make due allowance for sth* 适当考虑某事 ◇ (*BrE*) *He was charged with driving without **due care and attention**.* 他被控鲁莽驾驶。➲ COMPARE UNDUE

IDM **in ˌdue ˈcourse** at the right time and not before 在适当的时候；到一定的时候：*Your request will be dealt with in due course.* 你的要求将在适当的时候予以处理。➲ MORE AT RESPECT *n.*

■ ***noun*** **1 your/sb's ~** [U] a thing that should be given to sb by right 应有的权利；应得到的东西：*He received a large reward, which was no more than his due* (= than what he deserved). 他得到重赏，这也是他应该得到的。◇ *She's a slow worker, but **to give her her due*** (= to be fair to her), *she does try very hard.* 她做事很慢，但说句公道话，她确实很尽力。 **2 dues** [pl.] charges, for example to be a member of a club 应缴款（如俱乐部会费）：*to pay your dues* 缴纳会费

■ ***adv.*** **~ north/south/east/west** exactly; in a straight line 正向；正对着：*to sail due east* 向正东航行 ◇ *The village lies five miles due north of York.* 这个村庄位于约克正北五英里处。

ˌdue ˈdate *noun* [usually sing.] the date on or by which sth, especially a sum of money, is owed or expected（尤指欠款的）到期日，满期日

duel /ˈdjuːəl; *NAmE* ˈduːəl/ *noun* **1** a formal fight with weapons between two people, used in the past to settle a disagreement, especially over a matter of honour（旧时为解决纷争的）决斗：*to **fight/win a duel*** 进行 / 赢得决斗 ◇ *to **challenge sb to a duel*** 要求与某人决斗 **2** a competition or struggle between two people or groups（双方的）竞争，斗争：*a verbal duel* 舌战 ▸ **duel** *verb* (**-ll-**, *US* **-l-**) [I]: *The two men duelled to the death.* 两个男人决斗到直至一个人丧命。

du·el·ling (*US* **du·el·ing**) /ˈdjuːəlɪŋ; *NAmE* ˈduːəlɪŋ/ *noun* [U] the practice of fighting duels 决斗

ˌdue ˈprocess of law (*also* **ˌdue ˈprocess**) *noun* [U] (*law* 律) (in the US) the right of a citizen to be treated fairly, especially the right to a fair trial 正当法律程序（美国公民得到公正待遇的权利，尤指得到公正审判）

duet /djuˈet; *NAmE* duˈet/ (*also less frequent* **duo**) *noun* a piece of music for two players or singers 二重奏（曲）；二重唱（曲）：*a piano duet* 钢琴二重奏曲 ➲ COMPARE SOLO *n.* (1), TRIO (3)

duff /dʌf/ *adj., noun, verb*

■ ***adj.*** (*BrE, informal*) useless; that does not work as it should 无用的；失灵的；出故障的：*He sold me a duff radio.* 他卖给我一台不响的收音机。

■ ***noun*** (*NAmE, informal*) a person's bottom 屁股

IDM **up the ˈduff** (*BrE, slang*) pregnant 怀孕：*He got her up the duff.* 他使她怀孕了。

■ ***verb***

PHR V **ˌduff sb↔ˈup** (*BrE, informal*) to hit or kick sb severely 痛击；猛踢；毒打 **SYN** **beat up**

duf·fel bag (*also* **duf·fle bag**) /ˈdʌfl bæɡ/ *noun* **1** a bag made out of cloth, shaped like a tube and closed by a string around the top. It is usually carried over the shoulder. 筒状帆布包（或旅行包） **2** (*NAmE*) (*BrE* **hold·all**) a large bag made of strong cloth or soft leather, used when you are travelling for carrying clothes, etc.（用帆布或软皮制造的）大旅行袋 ➲ VISUAL VOCAB PAGE V69

duf·fel coat (*also* **duf·fle coat**) /ˈdʌfl kəʊt; *NAmE* koʊt/ *noun* a heavy coat made of wool, that usually has a HOOD and is fastened with TOGGLES 粗呢外衣（常连帽及用棒形套扣）

duf·fer /ˈdʌfə(r)/ *noun* (*BrE, informal*) a person who is stupid or unable to do anything well 笨蛋；傻瓜；不中用的人

dug PAST TENSE, PAST PART. OF DIG

du·gong /ˈduːɡɒŋ; ˈdjuː-; *NAmE* ˈduːɡɑːŋ; -ɡɔːŋ/ *noun* a large sea animal with thick greyish skin, which lives mainly in the Indian Ocean and eats plants 儒艮，海牛（主要生活于印度洋的大型银灰色厚皮海洋动物）

dug·out /ˈdʌɡaʊt/ *noun* **1** a rough shelter made by digging a hole in the ground and covering it, used by soldiers 防空洞；地下掩体 **2** a shelter by the side of a football (SOCCER) or BASEBALL field where a team's manager, etc. can sit and watch the game 球员席（足球或棒球场边供球队教练、候补队员等就座观赛） **3** (*also* **ˌdugout caˈnoe**) a CANOE (= type of light narrow boat) made by cutting out the inside of a tree TRUNK 独木舟

DUI /ˌdiː juː ˈaɪ/ *abbr.* (*NAmE*) DRIVING UNDER THE INFLUENCE 酒后驾车罪

du jour /duː ˈʒʊə(r); *NAmE* duː ˈʒʊr/ *adj.* [after noun] (*informal, humorous*) very popular or important now 流行的；热门的；当下重要的：*This age group is the target group du jour.* 这个年龄组是眼下受关注的目标组。◇ *What is the Internet phenomenon du jour?* 当前互联网的时髦现象是什么？ **ORIGIN** From French, meaning 'of the day'. 源自法语，意思是"当今的"。

duke /djuːk; *NAmE* duːk/ *noun, verb*

■ ***noun*** **1** a NOBLEMAN of the highest rank 公爵：*the Duke of Edinburgh* 爱丁堡公爵 **2** (in some parts of Europe, especially in the past) a male ruler of a small independent state（尤指旧时欧洲部分地区小公国的）君主 ➲ SEE ALSO ARCHDUKE, DUCHESS, DUCHY, GRAND DUKE

■ ***verb***

IDM **duke it out** (*NAmE, informal*) to fight or argue until an argument has been settled（打斗或争论）拼个高低

duke·dom /ˈdjuːkdəm; *NAmE* ˈduːk-/ *noun* **1** the rank or position of a duke 公爵的爵位；公爵的地位 **2** = DUCHY

dulce /ˈdʌlseɪ/ *noun* [C, U] (*US*) a sweet food or drink, especially a sweet or jam 甜食；甜饮料

dul·cet /ˈdʌlsɪt/ *adj.* [only before noun] (*humorous* or *ironic*) sounding sweet and pleasant 甜美的；悦耳动听的；美妙的：*I thought I recognized your **dulcet tones*** (= the sound of your voice). 我想我听出了你那甜美的嗓音。

dul·ci·mer /ˈdʌlsɪmə(r)/ *noun* **1** a musical instrument that you play by hitting the metal strings with two HAMMERS 大扬琴；洋琴 **2** a musical instrument with strings, popular in American traditional music, that you lay on your knee and play with your fingers 杜西莫琴（美国传统拨弦乐器）

dull /dʌl/ *adj., verb*

■ ***adj.*** (**dull·er, dull·est**)

• **BORING** 乏味 **1** not interesting or exciting 枯燥无味的；沉闷的；无聊的 **SYN** **dreary**: *Life in a small town could be deadly dull.* 小城镇的生活可能会非常没意思。◇ *The first half of the game was pretty dull.* 上半场比赛打得十分沉闷。◇ *There's **never a dull moment** when John's around.* 只要约翰在就不会有沉闷的时候。➲ SYNONYMS AT BORING

• **LIGHT/COLOURS** 光；色彩 **2** not bright or shiny 不明亮的；不鲜明的；无光泽的：*a dull grey colour* 暗灰色 ◇ *dull, lifeless hair* 无光泽、无弹性的头发 ◇ *Her eyes were dull.* 她目光呆滞。

• **WEATHER** 天气 **3** not bright, with a lot of clouds 阴沉的；昏暗的 **SYN** **overcast**: *It was a dull, grey day.* 那是一个阴沉昏暗的日子。

• **SOUNDS** 声音 **4** not clear or loud 不清晰的；隐约的；低沉的：*The gates shut behind him with a dull thud.* 他走出后，大门砰的一声闷响关上了。

• **PAIN** 疼痛 **5** not very severe, but continuous 隐隐约约的：*a **dull ache/pain*** 隐隐的疼痛

• **PERSON** 人 **6** slow in understanding 迟钝的；愚笨的 **SYN** **stupid**: *a dull pupil* 脑子迟钝的小学生
• **TRADE** 贸易 **7** (*especially NAmE*) not busy; slow 萧条的；不景气的；呆滞的：*Don't sell into a dull market.* 不要到萧条的市场去推销。
▶ **dull·ness** *noun* [U] **dully** /ˈdʌlli/ *adv.*：*'I suppose so,' she said dully.* "我看是这样。"她木然说道。◇ *His leg ached dully.* 他的腿隐隐作痛。

IDM **(as) dull as ˈditchwater** (*BrE*) (*US* **(as) dull as ˈdishwater**) extremely boring 索然无味；无聊透顶 ➲ MORE LIKE THIS 14, page R26 ➲ MORE AT WORK *n.*

■ *verb*
• **PAIN** 疼痛 **1** [T, I] ~ (sth) (of pain or an emotion 疼痛或感情) to become or be made weaker or less severe 减轻；（使）变麻木：*The tablets they gave him dulled the pain for a while.* 他们给他的药片暂时缓解了疼痛。
• **PERSON** 人 **2** [T] **~ sb** to make a person slower or less lively 使迟钝；使不活泼：*He felt dulled and stupid with sleep.* 他睡得迷迷糊糊，昏头昏脑。
• **COLOURS/SOUNDS** 色彩；声音 **3** [I, T] to become or to make sth less bright, clean or sharp （使）变得无光泽，变模糊，变低沉：*His eyes dulled and he slumped to the ground.* 他眼前一黑重重地倒在地上。◇ **~ sth** *The endless rain seemed to dull all sound.* 连绵不断的阴雨似乎使所有的声音都变得沉闷起来。

dull·ard /ˈdʌlɑːd; *NAmE* -lɑːrd/ *noun* (*old-fashioned*) a stupid person with no imagination （毫无想象力的）笨蛋，蠢人

dulls·ville /ˈdʌlzvɪl/ *noun* [U] (*NAmE, informal*) a place or situation which is extremely boring 沉闷乏味的地方（或状况）

ˌdull-ˈwitted *adj.* (*old-fashioned*) not understanding quickly or easily 悟性低的；理解力差的 **SYN** **stupid**

duly /ˈdjuːli; *NAmE* ˈduːli/ *adv.* **1** (*formal*) in the correct or expected manner 适当地；恰当地：*The document was duly signed by the inspector.* 这份文件已由检查员签妥。 **2** at the expected and correct time 按时地；准时地；适时地：*They duly arrived at 9.30 in spite of torrential rain.* 尽管下着倾盆大雨，他们仍在 9:30 准时到达了。➲ COMPARE UNDULY

dumb /dʌm/ *adj., verb*
■ *adj.* (**dumb·er, dumb·est**) **1** (*old-fashioned, sometimes offensive*) unable to speak 哑的；不能说话的：*She was born **deaf and dumb**.* 她天生又聋又哑。**HELP** **Dumb** used in this meaning is old-fashioned and can be offensive. It is better to use **speech-impaired** instead. * dumb 用于此义是过时用法，可能含冒犯意，最好以 speech-impaired 代之。 **2** temporarily not speaking or refusing to speak 一时说不出话的；不肯开口的：*We were all **struck dumb** with amazement.* 我们都惊讶得说不出话来。◇ *We sat there in dumb silence.* 我们坐在那里，默然无语。 **3** (*informal, especially NAmE*) stupid 愚蠢的；傻的；笨的：*That was a pretty dumb thing to do.* 做那样的事太愚蠢了。◇ *If the police question you, **act dumb*** (= pretend you do not know anything). 如果警察盘问，你就装傻。◇ *In her early movies she played a **dumb blonde**.* 在她早期的电影中，她扮演傻乎乎的金发女郎。 ▶ **dumb·ly** *adv.*：*'Are you all right?' Laura nodded dumbly.* "你身体好吗？"劳拉默默地点了点头。 **dumb·ness** *noun* [U]
■ *verb*
PHR V **ˌdumb ˈdown | ˌdumb sth↔ˈdown** (*disapproving*) to make sth less accurate or EDUCATIONAL, and of worse quality, by trying to make it easier for people to understand （为使公众更易理解而）降低…的标准，减少…的专业性教育内容 ▶ **ˌdumbing ˈdown** *noun* [U]

ˌdumb ˈanimal *noun* [usually pl.] (*BrE*) an animal, especially when seen as deserving pity （尤指可怜巴巴的）哑巴牲口

ˈdumb-ass *adj.* [only before noun] (*NAmE, taboo, slang*) stupid 愚蠢的；笨头笨脑的

ˈdumb-bell *noun* **1** a short bar with a weight at each end, used for making the arm and shoulder muscles stronger 哑铃 ➲ VISUAL VOCAB PAGE V46 **2** (*NAmE, informal*) a stupid person 笨蛋；蠢货；傻瓜

dumb·found /dʌmˈfaʊnd/ *verb* **~ sb** to surprise or shock sb so much that they are unable to speak 使惊呆：*His reply dumbfounded me.* 他的回答使我哑然。

dumb·found·ed /dʌmˈfaʊndɪd/ (*also less frequent* **dumb·struck** /ˈdʌmstrʌk/) *adj.* unable to speak because of surprise 惊呆了的：*The news left her dumbfounded.* 这消息把她惊呆了。

D

dumbo /ˈdʌmbəʊ; *NAmE* -boʊ/ *noun* (*pl.* **-oes**) (*informal*) a stupid person 笨蛋；蠢货；呆子

ˌdumb ˈwaiter *noun* a small lift/elevator for carrying food and plates from one floor to another in a restaurant （餐厅楼层间运送食物和餐具的）升降架

dum·dum /ˈdʌmdʌm/ (*also* **ˌdumdum ˈbullet**) *noun* a bullet that spreads out and breaks into many pieces when it hits sb 达姆弹（击入目标体内后爆开） **ORIGIN** It is named after the factory at Dumdum near Calcutta in India, where such bullets were originally made. They are now illegal. 源自于印度加尔各答附近的达姆达姆，这种子弹起初在此生产。现在达姆弹属于非法。

dummy /ˈdʌmi/ *noun, adj., verb*
■ *noun* (*pl.* **-ies**) **1** [C] a model of a person, used especially when making clothes or for showing them in a shop window （尤指缝制或陈列服装用的）人体模型：*a tailor's dummy* 裁缝店的模型人 ➲ SEE ALSO MANNEQUIN (1) **2** [C] a thing that seems to be real but is only a copy of the real thing 仿制品；仿造物 **3** [C] (*NAmE, informal*) a stupid person 笨蛋；蠢货：*Don't just stand there, you dummy.* 别在那儿干站着，你这个蠢货。 **4** [C] (in some sports 某些体育运动) an occasion when you pretend to make a particular move and then do not do so 假动作 **5** [C] (*BrE*) (*NAmE* **paci·fier**) a specially shaped rubber or plastic object for a baby to suck 安抚奶嘴 ➲ WORDFINDER NOTE AT BABY **6** [U] (in card games, especially BRIDGE 纸牌游戏，尤指桥牌) the cards which are placed facing upwards on the table and which can be seen by all the players 明手牌
■ *adj.* [only before noun] made to look real, although it is actually a copy which does not work 假的 **SYN** **replica**: *a dummy bomb* 空包弹
■ *verb* [T, I] (in football (SOCCER) 足球) to pretend to make a particular move in order to confuse your opponent 做假动作：**~ sth** *She dummied a shot that brought the goalie to her knees.* 她一个假射门使守门员双膝跪到地上。◇ **+ adv./prep.** *He dummied past five defenders, then shot at the near post.* 他以假动作晃过五个防守队员，接着把球射向近门柱。

ˌdummy ˈrun *noun* (*BrE*) a practice attack, performance, etc. before the real one 演习；试演 **SYN** **dry run**

dump 🔑 /dʌmp/ *verb, noun*
■ *verb*
• **GET RID OF** 丢弃 **1** 🔑 **~ sth** to get rid of sth you do not want, especially in a place which is not suitable （尤指在不合适的地方）丢弃，扔掉，倾倒：*Too much toxic waste is being dumped at sea.* 太多的有毒废料在向大海里倾倒。◇ *The dead body was just dumped by the roadside.* 这具死尸就扔在路边。 ➲ WORDFINDER NOTE AT WASTE **2** **~ sb/sth (on sb)** (*informal*) to get rid of sb/sth or leave them for sb else to deal with 丢下；抛弃；推卸：*He's got no right to keep dumping his problems on me.* 他没有权利总是把他的问题推到我身上。 **3** **~ sth** (*business* 商) to get rid of goods by selling them at a very low price, often in another country （常向国外）倾销，抛售
• **PUT DOWN** 放下 **4** **~ sth** to put sth down in a careless or untidy way 随便堆放；乱放：*Just dump your stuff over there—we'll sort it out later.* 就把你的东西堆在那儿吧，我们以后再整理。
• **END RELATIONSHIP** 断绝关系 **5** **~ sb** (*informal*) to end a romantic relationship with sb 与（某人）结束恋爱关系：*Did you hear he's dumped his girlfriend?* 他已把女朋友给甩了，你听说了吗？
• **COMPUTING** 计算机技术 **6** **~ sth** to copy information and

move it somewhere to store it 转储，转存（信息）IDM SEE LAP *n.*

PHR V **'dump on sb** (*informal, especially NAmE*) to criticize sb severely or treat them badly 非难；亏待

■ ***noun*** ➲ SEE ALSO DUMPS

• **FOR WASTE** 垃圾 **1** 🔑 a place where waste or rubbish/garbage is taken and left 垃圾场；废物堆：(*BrE*) *a* ***rubbish dump*** 垃圾场 ◇ (*NAmE*) *a* ***garbage dump*** 垃圾场 ◇ *the municipal dump* 市政垃圾场 ◇ *a toxic/nuclear* ***waste dump*** 有毒 / 核废料堆 **2** (*also* **'mine dump**) (*SAfrE*) a hill that is formed when waste sand from the production of gold is piled in one place over a period of time 废渣堆；尾矿堆

• **DIRTY PLACE** 脏地方 **3** (*informal, disapproving*) a dirty or unpleasant place 脏地方；邋遢场所；令人讨厌的地方：*How can you live in this dump?* 你怎么会住在这种肮脏地方？

• **FOR WEAPONS** 武器 **4** a temporary store for military supplies 军需品临时存放处：*an ammunition dump* 弹药临时堆积处

• **COMPUTING** 计算机技术 **5** an act of copying data stored in a computer; a copy or list of the contents of this data 转储；转存；转储数据 ➲ SEE ALSO SCREEN DUMP

• **WASTE FROM BODY** 粪便 **6** [C] (*slang*) an act of passing waste matter from the body through the BOWELS 拉屎：*to have a dump* 拉屎

'dump bin (*BrE*) (*also* **dis'play bin** *US, BrE*) *noun* a box in a shop/store for displaying goods, especially goods whose prices have been reduced（商店）陈列柜；（尤指）减价货品柜

dump·er /ˈdʌmpə(r)/ *noun* (*especially NAmE*) a person who throws away dangerous or harmful things, especially in the wrong place 乱扔危险（或有害）物品者

'dumper truck (*BrE*) (*NAmE* **'dump truck**) *noun* a vehicle for carrying earth, stones, etc. in a container which can be lifted up for the load to fall out 自卸货车；翻斗车 ➲ VISUAL VOCAB PAGE V63

dump·ing /ˈdʌmpɪŋ/ *noun* [U] the act or practice of dumping sth, especially dangerous substances（尤指危险物质的）倾倒，倾卸：*a ban on the dumping of radioactive waste at sea* 禁止向海里倾倒放射性废物

'dumping ground *noun* [usually sing.] a place where sth that is not wanted is dumped 垃圾倾倒场

dump·ling /ˈdʌmplɪŋ/ *noun* **1** a small ball of DOUGH (= a mixture of flour, fat and water) that is cooked and served with meat dishes 小面团；汤团；饺子：*chicken with herb dumplings* 香草鸡肉饺子 **2** a small ball of PASTRY, often with fruit in it, eaten as a DESSERT 水果布丁：*apple dumplings* 苹果布丁

dumps /dʌmps/ *noun* [pl.]

IDM **down in the 'dumps** (*informal*) feeling unhappy 闷闷不乐；沮丧 SYN **depressed**

Dump·ster™ /ˈdʌmpstə(r)/ (*NAmE*) (*BrE* **skip**) *noun* a large open container for putting old bricks, rubbish/garbage, etc. in. The Dumpster is then loaded on a lorry/truck and taken away. 大垃圾桶（装工地废料、垃圾等，由卡车拖走）

'dump truck (*NAmE*) (*BrE* **'dumper truck**) *noun* a vehicle for carrying earth, stones, etc. in a container which can be lifted up for the load to fall out 自卸货车；翻斗车 ➲ VISUAL VOCAB PAGE V63

dumpy /ˈdʌmpi/ *adj.* (especially of a person 尤指人) short and fat 矮胖的

dun /dʌn/ *adj.* greyish-brown in colour 棕灰色的；灰褐色的；暗褐色的 ▶ **dun** *noun* [U]

dunce /dʌns/ *noun* (*old-fashioned*) a person, especially a child at school, who is stupid or slow to learn 愚笨的人；（尤指）迟钝的学生

ˌdunce's 'cap (*NAmE also* **'dunce cap**) *noun* a pointed hat that was sometimes given in the past to a child in a class at school who was slow to learn（旧时有时给学习迟缓学生戴的）笨蛋圆锥帽

Dun·dee cake /dʌnˈdiː keɪk/ *noun* [C, U] a fruit cake, usually decorated with ALMONDS (= a type of nut) 邓迪水果杏仁蛋糕

dun·der·head /ˈdʌndəhed; *NAmE* ˈdʌndər-/ *noun* (*informal*) a silly or stupid person 傻瓜；笨蛋

dune /djuːn; *NAmE* duːn/ (*also* **'sand dune**) *noun* a small hill of sand formed by the wind, near the sea or in a desert（风吹积成的）沙丘 ➲ WORDFINDER NOTE AT COAST ➲ VISUAL VOCAB PAGE V5

'dune buggy *noun* = BEACH BUGGY

dung /dʌŋ/ *noun* [U] solid waste from animals, especially from large ones（尤指大型动物的）粪 SYN **manure**：*cow dung* 牛粪

dun·garees /ˌdʌŋɡəˈriːz/ *noun* [pl.] **1** (*BrE*) (*NAmE* **over·alls**, **'bib overalls**) a piece of clothing that consists of trousers/pants with an extra piece of cloth covering the chest, held up by strips of cloth over the shoulders 工装裤；背带工作服：*a pair of dungarees* 一条工装裤 ◇ *His dungarees were covered in grease.* 他的工装裤上沾满了油污。➲ PICTURE AT OVERALL **2** (*NAmE*) heavy cotton trousers/pants for working in 粗布工作裤；劳动布工装裤

dun·geon /ˈdʌndʒən/ *noun* a dark underground room used as a prison, especially in a castle（尤指城堡中的）地牢，土牢

dung·heap /ˈdʌŋhiːp/ (*also* **dung·hill** /ˈdʌŋhɪl/) *noun* a large pile of dung, especially on a farm（尤指农庄上的）粪堆

dunk /dʌŋk/ *verb* **1** [T] **~ sth (in/into sth)** to put food quickly into liquid before eating it（吃前将食物放入液体中）浸一浸，泡一泡：*She sat reading a magazine, dunking cookies in her coffee.* 她坐着一边看杂志一边将曲奇饼在咖啡里蘸一下再吃。**2** [T] **~ sb/sth** (*especially NAmE*) to push sb underwater for a short time, as a joke; to put sth into water（开玩笑地将某人按入水中）浸一下；浸，泡（某物）：*The camera survived being dunked in the river.* 这照相机在河里泡了一下还没坏。**3** [I, T] **~ (sth)** (in BASKETBALL 篮球) to jump very high and put the ball through the BASKET with great force from above 把（球）扣入篮内；扣篮；灌篮

dunno /dəˈnəʊ; *NAmE* dəˈnoʊ/ (*non-standard*) a way of writing the informal spoken form of 'I don't know' 我不知道（I don't know 的非正式写法）➲ MORE LIKE THIS 5, page R25

dunny /ˈdʌni/ *noun* (*pl.* **-ies**) (*AustralE, NZE, informal*) a toilet 厕所；茅厕

dunt /dʌnt/ *verb* **~ sth (+ adv./prep.)** (*ScotE*) to hit or knock sb or sth 击打；敲击 ▶ **dunt** *noun*

duo /ˈdjuːəʊ; *NAmE* ˈduːoʊ/ *noun* (*pl.* **-os**) **1** two people who perform together or are often seen or thought of together 一对表演者；搭档：*the comedy duo Laurel and Hardy* 劳莱和哈代这对喜剧搭档 ➲ COMPARE TRIO **2** = DUET

duo·de·num /ˌdjuːəˈdiːnəm; *NAmE* ˌduːə-/ *noun* (*pl.* **duo·de·nums** or **duo·dena** /-ˈdiːnə/) (*anatomy* 解) the first part of the small INTESTINE, next to the stomach 十二指肠 ➲ VISUAL VOCAB PAGE V64 ➲ COMPARE ILEUM, JEJUNUM ▶ **duo·denal** /ˌdjuːəˈdiːnl; *NAmE* ˌduːə-/ *adj.*：*a duodenal ulcer* 十二指肠溃疡

du·op·oly /djuːˈɒpəli; *NAmE* duːˈɑː-/ *noun* (*pl.* **-ies**) (*business* 商) **1** a right to trade in a particular product or service, held by only two companies or organizations（商品或服务的）两强垄断 **2** a group of two companies or organizations who hold a duopoly 两强垄断集团 ➲ COMPARE MONOPOLY (1)

the DUP /ˌdiː juː ˈpiː/ *abbr.* the Democratic Unionist Party (a political party in Northern Ireland that wants it to remain a part of the United Kingdom) 民主统一党（主张北爱尔兰归属联合王国的北爱尔兰政党）

du·patta /dʊˈpʌtə/ *noun* a long piece of material worn around the head and neck by women in S Asia, usually with a SALWAR OR GHAGRA （南亚女子戴的）围巾，头巾

dupe /djuːp; *NAmE* duːp/ *verb, noun*
- ■ ***verb*** to trick or cheat sb 诈骗；哄骗；欺骗：**~ sb** *They soon realized they had been duped.* 他们很快便意识到自己上当了。◇ **~ sb into doing sth** *He was duped into giving them his credit card.* 他上当受骗把信用卡交给了他们。
- ■ ***noun*** (*formal*) a person who is tricked or cheated 上当受骗者

du·plex /ˈdjuːpleks; *NAmE* ˈduː-/ *noun* (*especially NAmE*) **1** a building divided into two separate homes 二联式住宅；双拼房屋 ➲ VISUAL VOCAB PAGE V16 **2** a flat/apartment with rooms on two floors （占两层楼的）复式住宅；跃层公寓

du·pli·cate *verb, adj., noun*
- ■ ***verb*** /ˈdjuːplɪkeɪt; *NAmE* ˈduː-/ **1** [often passive] **~ sth** to make an exact copy of sth 复制；复印；复写：*a duplicated form* 复制的表格 **2 ~ sth** to do sth again, especially when it is unnecessary （尤指不必要时）重复，再做一次：*There's no point in duplicating work already done.* 重复别人已经做过的工作毫无意义。 ▸ **du·pli·ca·tion** /ˌdjuːplɪˈkeɪʃn; *NAmE* ˌduː-/ *noun* [U, C]
- ■ ***adj.*** /ˈdjuːplɪkət; *NAmE* ˈduː-/ [only before noun] exactly like sth else; made as a copy of sth else 完全一样的；复制的；副本的：*a duplicate invoice* 发票副本
- ■ ***noun*** /ˈdjuːplɪkət; *NAmE* ˈduː-/ one of two or more things that are the same in every detail 完全一样的东西；复制品；副本 SYN **copy**: *Is this a duplicate or the original?* 这是副本还是正本？ ➲ **MORE LIKE THIS** 21, page R27

IDM **in duplicate** (of documents, etc. 文件等) as two copies that are exactly the same in every detail 一式两份的：*to prepare a contract in duplicate* 准备一式两份的合同 ➲ COMPARE TRIPLICATE

du·pli·city /djuːˈplɪsəti; *NAmE* duː-/ *noun* [U] (*formal*) dishonest behaviour that is intended to make sb believe sth which is not true 欺骗，奸诈（行为） SYN **deceit** ▸ **du·pli·ci·tous** /djuːˈplɪsɪtəs; *NAmE* duː-/ *adj.*

dur·able /ˈdjʊərəbl; *NAmE* ˈdʊr-/ *adj.* likely to last for a long time without breaking or getting weaker 耐用的；持久的：*durable plastics* 耐用塑料 ◇ *negotiations for a durable peace* 为持久和平而进行的谈判 ▸ **dur·abil·ity** /ˌdjʊərəˈbɪləti; *NAmE* ˌdʊr-/ *noun* [U]: *the durability of gold* 金子的耐久性 ➲ SEE ALSO CONSUMER DURABLES

ˌdurable ˈgoods (*NAmE*) (*BrE* **conˌsumer ˈdurables**) *noun* [pl.] (*business* 商) goods which are expected to last for a long time after they have been bought, such as cars, televisions, etc. 耐用消费品（如汽车、电视机等）

dur·ation AW /djuˈreɪʃn; *NAmE* du-/ *noun* [U] (*formal*) the length of time that sth lasts or continues 持续时间；期间：*The school was used as a hospital for the duration of the war.* 战争期间这所学校用作医院。◇ *a contract of three years' duration* 三年期的合同

IDM **for the duration** (*informal*) until the end of a particular situation 直到…结束；在整个…期间

dura·tive /ˈdjʊərətɪv; *NAmE* ˈdʊr-/ *adj.* (*grammar* 语法) (of a verb tense, a word, etc. 动词时态、词语等) describing an action that continues for some time 持续（性）的；延续的

dur·ess /djuˈres; *NAmE* du-/ *noun* [U] (*formal*) threats or force that are used to make sb do sth 胁迫；强迫：*He signed the confession **under duress**.* 他被迫在供状上签了字。

Durex™ /ˈdjʊəreks; *NAmE* ˈdjʊr-/ *noun* (*pl.* **Durex**) (*BrE*) a CONDOM 杜蕾斯避孕套

dur·ian /ˈdʊəriən; *NAmE* ˈdʊr-/ *noun* a large tropical fruit with a strong unpleasant smell but a sweet flavour 榴莲 ➲ **VISUAL VOCAB** PAGE V33

dur·ing 🔑 /ˈdjʊərɪŋ; *NAmE* ˈdʊr-/ *prep.* **1** 🔑 all through a period of time 在…期间：*during the 1990s* 在 20 世纪 90 年代 ◇ *There are extra flights to Colorado during the winter.* 冬季有飞往科罗拉多的增开航班。◇ *Please remain seated during the performance.* 演出期间请不要站起来。 **2** 🔑 at some point in a period of time 在…期间的某个时候：*He was taken to the hospital during the night.* 他在夜间被送到医院。◇ *I only saw her once during my stay in Rome.* 我在罗马逗留期间只见过她一次。 HELP **During** is used to say when something happens; **for** answers the question 'how long?'. * during 表示某事发生的时间，for 则回答 how long 的问题：*I stayed in London for a week.* 我在伦敦待了一个星期。◇ ~~*I stayed in London during a week.*~~

durrie *noun* = DHURRIE

durum /ˈdjʊərəm; *NAmE* ˈdʊrəm/ (*also* **ˌdurum ˈwheat**) *noun* [U] a type of hard WHEAT, used to make PASTA 硬质小麦（用于制作意大利面食）

dusk /dʌsk/ *noun* [U] the time of day when the light has almost gone, but it is not yet dark 黄昏；傍晚 SYN **twilight**: *The street lights go on **at dusk**.* 街灯在黄昏时分亮起来。 ➲ COMPARE DAWN *n.* (1)

dusky /ˈdʌski/ *adj.* (*literary*) not very bright; dark or soft in colour 昏暗的；暗淡的；（颜色）暗的，柔和的：*the dusky light inside the cave* 洞中昏暗的光线 ◇ *dusky pink* 暗粉红色

dust 🔑 /dʌst/ *noun, verb*
- ■ ***noun*** **1** 🔑 [U] a fine powder that consists of very small pieces of sand, earth, etc. 沙土；尘土：*A cloud of dust rose as the truck drove off.* 卡车开过时扬起一片灰尘。◇ *The workers wear masks to avoid inhaling the dust.* 工人们戴着面罩避免吸入尘土。 ➲ SEE ALSO COSMIC DUST ➲ **SYNONYMS** AT SOIL **2** 🔑 the fine powder of dirt that forms in buildings, on furniture, floors, etc.（建筑物内、家具或地板等上的）灰尘，尘埃：*The books were all covered with dust.* 书上积满了灰尘。◇ *There wasn't a **speck of dust** anywhere in the room.* 屋子里处处一尘不染。◇ *That guitar's been sitting **gathering dust** (= not being used) for years now.* 那把吉他现已尘封多年。 **3** a fine powder that consists of very small pieces of a particular substance 粉尘；粉末：***coal/gold dust*** 煤粉；金粉 ➲ SEE ALSO DUSTY

IDM **leave sb in the ˈdust** (*NAmE*) to leave sb far behind 把某人远远抛在后面；使望尘莫及 **let the dust settle | wait for the dust to settle** to wait for a situation to become clear or certain 待尘埃落定；待形势明朗 ➲ MORE AT BITE *v.*

- ■ ***verb*** **1** 🔑 [I, T] to clean furniture, a room, etc. by removing dust from surfaces with a cloth 擦去…的灰尘；擦灰：*I broke the vase while I was dusting.* 我擦灰尘时将花瓶打碎了。◇ **~ sth** *Could you dust the sitting room?* 你把起居室擦一擦好吗？ **2** [T] **~ sth (+ adv./prep.)** to remove dirt from sb/sth/yourself with your hands or a brush 掸去；擦去；刷去：*She dusted some ash from her sleeve.* 她掸去袖子上的灰末。 **3** [T] **~ sth (with sth)** to cover sth with fine powder 把（粉末）撒于；撒（粉）：*Dust the cake with sugar.* 把糖撒在蛋糕上。 IDM SEE DONE *adj.*

PHR V **ˌdust sb/sth↔ˈdown** (*especially BrE*) to remove dust, dirt, etc. from sb/sth 除去…的灰尘：*Mel stood up and dusted herself down.* 梅尔站起来拍掉了身上的尘土。
ˌdust sb/sth↔ˈoff to remove dust, dirt, etc. from sb/sth 除去…的灰尘：(*figurative*) *For the concert, he dusted off some of his old hits.* 为了这次音乐会，他重新捡起了他的一些曾红极一时的老歌。

dust·ball /ˈdʌstbɔːl/ (*also* **ˈdust bunny**) *noun* (*NAmE*) a mass of dust and small pieces of thread, hair, material, etc.（由灰尘和细小线段、毛发、布料等形成的）尘球，尘埃团

dust·bin /ˈdʌstbɪn/ (*BrE*) (*NAmE* **ˈgarbage can, ˈtrash can**) *noun* a large container with a lid, used for putting rubbish/garbage in, usually kept outside the house （常置于房外的）垃圾桶，垃圾箱 ➲ NOTE AT RUBBISH

ˈdust bowl *noun* an area of land that has been turned into desert by lack of rain or too much farming 干旱尘暴区；风沙侵蚀区

'dust bunny *noun* (*NAmE, informal*) a DUSTBALL 尘球；尘埃团

dust·cart /'dʌstkɑːt; *NAmE* -kɑːrt/ (*BrE*) (*NAmE* **'garbage truck**) *noun* a vehicle for collecting rubbish/garbage from outside houses, etc. 垃圾车

D

'dust cover *noun* **1** = DUST JACKET **2** a hard or soft plastic cover on a piece of equipment, etc. that protects it when it is not being used 防尘罩；防尘套

'dust devil *noun* a small column of dust over land, caused by the wind 尘卷风

dust·er /'dʌstə(r)/ *noun* **1** a cloth for removing dust from furniture 抹布；擦布；掸子 ➲ VISUAL VOCAB PAGE V21 **2** (*old-fashioned, NAmE*) a piece of clothing that you wear over your other clothes when you are cleaning the house, etc.（打扫清洁时穿的）防尘罩衫 **3** (*NAmE*) a long coat that was worn by COWBOYS（牛仔穿的）防尘长外衣

'dust jacket (*also* **'dust cover**) *noun* a paper cover on a book that protects it but that can be removed（书的）护封，包封

dust·man /'dʌstmən/ *noun* (*pl.* **-men** /-mən/) (*also informal* **bin·man**, *formal* **'refuse collector**) (*all BrE*) (*NAmE* **'garbage man**) a person whose job is to remove waste from outside houses, etc. 垃圾清运工 ➲ NOTE AT RUBBISH

'dust mite (*also* **'house dust mite**) *noun* a very small creature that lives in houses and can cause ALLERGIES 尘螨（可引起过敏）

dust·pan /'dʌstpæn/ *noun* a small flat container with a handle into which dust is brushed from the floor 簸箕 ➲ VISUAL VOCAB PAGE V21

'dust sheet (*BrE*) (*NAmE* **'drop cloth**) *noun* a large sheet that is used to protect floors, furniture, etc. from dust or paint（地板、家具等的）防尘罩，苫布

'dust storm *noun* a storm that carries clouds of dust in the wind over a wide area 尘暴

'dust-up *noun* (*BrE, informal*) an argument or a fight 吵架；争吵；打架

dusty /'dʌsti/ *adj.* (**dust·ier**, **dusti·est**) **1** full of dust; covered with dust 布满灰尘的；灰尘覆盖的：*a dusty road* 尘土飞扬的路 ◇ *piles of dusty books* 一摞一摞布满灰尘的书 ➲ SYNONYMS AT DIRTY **2** (of a colour 颜色) not bright; dull 土灰色的；灰暗的；无光泽的：*dusty pink* 土灰粉红色

Dutch /dʌtʃ/ *adj.* of or connected with the Netherlands, its people or its language 荷兰的；荷兰人的；荷兰语的
IDM **go Dutch (with sb)** to share the cost of sth with sb（同某人）各付各的账，平摊费用

,Dutch 'auction *noun* a sale in which the price of an item is reduced until sb offers to buy it 荷兰式拍卖（把价格逐步降低到有人愿买为止）

,Dutch 'barn *noun* (*BrE*) a farm building without walls that has a roof supported on poles, and is used for storing HAY (= dried grass), etc.（无墙的）干草棚

,Dutch 'courage *noun* [U] (*BrE, informal*) the false courage or confidence that a person gets from drinking alcohol 酒后之勇

,Dutch 'door (*NAmE*) (*BrE* **,stable 'door**) *noun* a door which is divided into two parts so that the top part can be left open while the bottom part is kept shut 马厩式两截门（上下两部分可分别开关）

,Dutch 'elm disease *noun* [U] a disease that kills ELM trees 荷兰榆病；榆枯萎病

duti·ful /'djuːtɪfl; *NAmE* 'duː-/ *adj.* doing everything that you are expected to do; willing to obey and to show respect 尽职的；顺从的；恭敬的 **SYN** **obedient**: *a dutiful daughter/son/wife* 孝顺的女儿 / 儿子；贤惠的妻子 ▸ **duti·ful·ly** /-fəli/ *adv.*

duty 🔑 /'djuːti; *NAmE* 'duːti/ *noun* (*pl.* **-ies**) **1** 🔑 [C, U] something that you feel you have to do because it is your moral or legal responsibility 责任；义务；本分：*It is my duty to report it to the police.* 把这事报告给警方是我的责任。◇ *Local councillors **have a duty to** serve the community.* 地方议员有义务为社区服务。◇ *I don't want you to visit me simply out of **a sense of duty**.* 我希望你不只是出于责任感才来看我。◇ *your duties as a parent* 你作为父母的责任 ◇ *to **do your duty** for your country* 为祖国尽己任 **2** 🔑 [U] the work that is your job 上班；值班：***Report for duty** at 8 a.m.* 早上 8 点钟报到上班。➲ SEE ALSO NIGHT DUTY **3** 🔑 **duties** [pl.] tasks that are part of your job 职责；任务：*I spend a lot of my time on administrative duties.* 我在行政管理事务上花了大量时间。◇ *Your duties will include setting up a new computer system.* 你的职责将包括建立一个新的计算机系统。➲ SEE ALSO HEAVY-DUTY **4** 🔑 [C, U] a tax that you pay on things that you buy, especially those that you bring into a country 税；（尤指进口货品）关税：***customs/excise/import duties*** 关税；消费税；进口税 ◇ **~ on sth** *duty on wine and beer* 葡萄酒和啤酒税 ➲ SYNONYMS AT TAX ➲ SEE ALSO DEATH DUTY, STAMP DUTY
IDM **on/off duty** 🔑 (of nurses, police officers, etc. 护士、警察等) working/not working at a particular time 值（或下）班；值（或不值）勤：*Who's on duty today?* 今天谁值班？◇ *What time do you go off duty?* 你什么时候下班？➲ SEE ALSO OFF-DUTY ➲ MORE AT BOUNDEN, LINE *n.*

,duty-'bound *adj.* [not before noun] (*formal*) having to do sth because it is your duty 责无旁贷；义不容辞：*I felt duty-bound to help him.* 我觉得帮助他责无旁贷。

,duty-'free *adj.* (of goods 商品) that you can bring into a country without paying tax on them 免关税的：*duty-free cigarettes* 免税香烟 ▸ **,duty-'free** *adv.* **,duty-'free** *noun* (*BrE, informal*): *We bought a load of duty-frees* (= duty-free goods) *at the airport.* 我们在机场买了许多免税商品。

,duty-'free shop (*also* **,duty-'free**) *noun* a shop/store in an airport or on a ship, etc. that sells goods such as cigarettes, alcohol, PERFUME, etc. without tax on them（机场内、船上等的）免税商店

'duty officer *noun* the officer, for example in the police, army, etc., who is on duty at a particular time in a particular place（警察、军队等的）值勤官，值班员

duvet /'duːveɪ; *NAmE also* duː'veɪ/ (*BrE also* **quilt**) *noun* a large cloth bag that is filled with feathers or other soft material and that you have on top of you in bed to keep yourself warm 羽绒被：*a **duvet cover*** (= a cover that you can wash, that you put over a duvet) 羽绒被套 ➲ VISUAL VOCAB PAGE V24

'duvet day *noun* (*BrE, informal*) a day when you stay at home instead of going to work because you feel tired and want to rest but are not ill 羽绒被拥卧日；偷懒假日；偷闲日 ➲ COMPARE PERSONAL DAY

dux /dʌks/ *noun* (*ScotE, AustralE*) the top pupil in a school or class 尖子生；成绩最好的学生

DVD 🔑 /,diː viː 'diː/ *noun* the abbreviation for 'digital versatile disc' or 'digital videodisc' (a disk on which large amounts of information, especially photographs and video, can be stored, for use on a computer or **DVD player**) 数字影碟，数码（多功能）光碟（全写为 digital versatile disc 或 digital videodisc）：*a DVD drive* * DVD 驱动器 ◇ *Is it available on DVD yet?* 这个现在有 DVD 版了吗？➲ COLLOCATIONS AT CINEMA ➲ VISUAL VOCAB PAGE V73

DVD-A /,diː viː diː 'eɪ/ *noun* the abbreviation for 'digital versatile disc audio' (a type of DVD that stores sound of very high quality) 音频 DVD（全写为 digital versatile disc audio）

,DV'D burner (*also* **,DV'D writer**) *noun* a piece of equipment used for recording from a computer onto a DVD * DVD 刻录机；光碟刻录机

DVD-R /,diː viː diː 'ɑː(r)/ *noun* the abbreviation for 'digital versatile disc recordable' (a type of DVD that you can use only once to record data) 一次写入式 DVD，可写入光碟（全写为 digital versatile disc recordable）

DVD-ROM /ˌdiː viː diː ˈrɒm; *NAmE* ˈrɑːm/ *noun* the abbreviation for 'digital versatile disc read-only memory' (a type of DVD that allows you to store data but not to record it) 只读型 DVD，只读光碟（全写为 digital versatile disc read-only memory）

DVD-RW /ˌdiː viː diː ɑː ˈdʌbljuː; *NAmE* ɑːr/ *noun* the abbreviation for 'digital versatile disc rewritable' (a type of DVD that you can use many times to record data) 可擦写 DVD，可重写光碟（全写为 digital versatile disc rewritable）

DVR /ˌdiː viː ˈɑː(r)/ *noun* a device that records video onto a hard disk or other memory device, using digital technology (the abbreviation for 'digital video recorder') 数字视频录像机（全写为 digital video recorder） SYN PVR

DVT /ˌdiː viː ˈtiː/ *abbr.* DEEP VEIN THROMBOSIS 深静脉血栓形成

DW /ˌdiː ˈdʌbljuː/ *abbr.* (*informal*) **1** (especially in TEXT MESSAGES, emails, etc.) darling wife 亲爱的老婆（全写为 darling wife，尤用于短信、电邮等） **2** (especially in TEXT MESSAGES, emails, etc.) don't worry 别担心（全写为 don't worry，尤用于短信、电邮等）

dwaal /dwɑːl/ *noun* (*SAfrE*) a confused or very relaxed state of mind 迷惑；茫然：*I was in a complete dwaal.* 我一片茫然。

dwarf /dwɔːf; *NAmE* dwɔːrf/ *noun, adj., verb*

■ ***noun*** (*pl.* **dwarfs** or **dwarves** /dwɔːvz; *NAmE* dwɔːrvz/) **1** (in stories) a creature like a small man, who has magic powers and who is usually described as living and working under the ground, especially working with metal（神话中会魔法的）小矮人 **2** (*sometimes offensive*) an extremely small person, who will never grow to a normal size because of a physical problem; a person suffering from DWARFISM 矮子；侏儒 HELP There is no other word that is generally considered more acceptable. 没有公认的比这更易于接受的用词。

■ ***adj.*** [only before noun] (of a plant or an animal 植物或动物) much smaller than the normal size 矮小的：*dwarf conifers* 矮小的针叶树

■ ***verb*** ~ **sth** to make sth seem small or unimportant compared with sth else 使显得矮小；使相形见绌：*The old houses were dwarfed by the huge new tower blocks.* 这些旧房子在新建的高楼大厦的映衬下显得十分矮小。

dwarf·ism /ˈdwɔːfɪzəm; *NAmE* ˈdwɔːrf-/ *noun* the medical condition of being a dwarf. People who suffer from this condition are very short and often have short arms and legs. 侏儒

ˌdwarf ˈplanet *noun* a round object in space that goes around the sun but is not as large as a planet and does not clear other objects from its path 矮行星（以轨道绕着太阳的球状天体，体积不及行星，未能清除在轨迹上的其他天体）：*the dwarf planets Pluto, Ceres, Eris, Makemake and Haumea* 冥王星、谷神星、阋神星、鸟神星和妊神星等五颗矮行星 ➲ COMPARE PLUTOID

dweeb /dwiːb/ *noun* (*slang, especially NAmE*) a person, especially a boy or a man, who does not have good social skills and is not fashionable（尤指男孩或男人）不合群的人，不合时尚的人，怪人

dwell /dwel/ *verb* (**dwelt**, **dwelt** or **dwelled**, **dwelled**) [I] + **adv./prep.** (*formal* or *literary*) to live somewhere 居住；栖身：*For ten years she dwelled among the nomads of North America.* 她在北美游牧民中生活了十年。

PHR V **ˈdwell on/upon sth 1** to think or talk a lot about sth, especially sth it would be better to forget 老是想着，唠叨（尤指最好应忘记的事）：*So you made a mistake, but there's no need to dwell on it.* 你是错了，不过不必老是想着这事儿。 **2** to look at sth for a long time 细看；凝视

dwell·er /ˈdwelə(r)/ *noun* (especially in compounds 尤用于构成复合词) a person or an animal that lives in the particular place that is mentioned 居民；居住者；栖身者：*apartment dwellers* 公寓房客

dwell·ing /ˈdwelɪŋ/ *noun* (*formal*) a house, flat/apartment, etc. where a person lives 住宅；住所；公寓：*The development will consist of 66 dwellings and a number of offices.* 新建楼区将由 66 套住房和一些办公室组成。

ˈdwelling house *noun* (*BrE, law* 律) a house that people live in, not one that is used as an office, etc. 住宅

ˈdwelling place *noun* (*old-fashioned*) the place where sb lives 住处

DWI /ˌdiː dʌbljuː ˈaɪ/ *abbr.* (*US*) DRIVING WHILE INTOXICATED 醉酒驾车罪

dwin·dle /ˈdwɪndl/ *verb* [I] to become gradually less or smaller（逐渐）减少，变小，缩小：*dwindling audiences* 越来越少的观众 ◇ ~ (**away**) (**to sth**) *Support for the party has dwindled away to nothing.* 支持这个党派的力量渐渐化为乌有。◇ ~ (**from sth**) (**to sth**) *Membership of the club has dwindled from 70 to 20.* 俱乐部会员人数已从 70 减少到 20。

DWP /ˌdiː dʌbljuː ˈpiː/ *abbr.* (in Britain) Department for Work and Pensions（英国）就业和退休保障部

dyad /ˈdaɪæd/ *noun* **1** (*specialist*) something that consists of two parts 二分体；二联体：*the mother-child dyad* 母子二分体 **2** (*mathematics* 数) an OPERATOR which is the combination of two VECTORS 并矢 ▸ **dyad·ic** /daɪˈædɪk/ *adj.*

dye /daɪ/ *verb, noun*

■ ***verb*** (**dyes**, **dye·ing**, **dyed**, **dyed**) to change the colour of sth, especially by using a special liquid or substance 给…染色；染：~ **sth** *to dye fabric* 染织物 ◇ ~ **sth + adj.** *She dyed her hair blonde.* 她把头发染成了金黄色。 ➲ SEE ALSO TIE-DYE

■ ***noun*** [C, U] a substance that is used to change the colour of things such as cloth or hair 染料；染液：*black dye* 黑色染料 ◇ *hair dye* 染发液 ◇ ***natural/chemical/vegetable dyes*** 天然 / 化学 / 植物染料

ˌdyed in the ˈwool *adj.* [usually before noun] (*usually disapproving*) having strong beliefs or opinions that are never going to change（信仰、观念等）根深蒂固的：*dyed-in-the-wool traditionalists* 彻头彻尾的传统主义者 ORIGIN From the idea that wool which was dyed in its raw state gave a more even and lasting colour. 源自染羊毛的方法，即给未加工的羊毛染色，使颜色更均匀、持久。

dying /ˈdaɪɪŋ/ *adj.* **1** [only before noun] connected with or happening at the time of sb's death 临终的；临死的；垂死的：*I will remember it to my **dying day**.* 我至死都不会忘记此事。◇ *her **dying wishes/words*** 她的临终遗愿 / 遗言 **2 the dying** *noun* [pl.] people who are dying 垂死者；临终者：*doctors who care for the dying* 照看临终病人的医生 IDM SEE BREATH ➲ MORE LIKE THIS 24, page R28 ➲ SEE ALSO DIE *v.*

dyke (*also* **dike**) /daɪk/ *noun* **1** a long thick wall that is built to stop water flooding onto a low area of land, especially from the sea 堰；堤；坝 **2** (*especially BrE*) a channel that carries water away from the land 渠；沟；壕沟 SYN ditch **3** (*taboo, slang*) a word for a LESBIAN, that is usually offensive 女同性恋者（常意含冒犯）

dy·nam·ic AW /daɪˈnæmɪk/ *noun, adj.*

■ ***noun* 1 dynamics** [pl.] the way in which people or things behave and react to each other in a particular situation（人或事物）相互作用的方式，动态：*the dynamics of political change* 政治变化动态 ◇ ***group dynamics*** (= the way in which members of a group react to each other) 小组成员的互动 **2 dynamics** [U] the science of the forces involved in movement 力学；动力学：*fluid dynamics* 流体力学 ➲ COMPARE STATIC *n.* (3) **3** [sing.] (*formal*) a force that produces change, action or effects 动力 **4 dynamics** [pl.] (*music* 音) changes in volume in music 力度；力度变化

■ ***adj.* 1** (*approving*) (of a person 人) having a lot of energy and a strong personality 充满活力且个性鲜明的：*a dynamic leader* 一位活力充沛富有个性的领导者 **2** (of a process

过程) always changing and making progress 动态的；发展变化的 **OPP static** **3** (*physics* 物) (of a force or power 力或动力) producing movement 力的；动力的 **OPP static** **4** (*linguistics* 语言) (of verbs 动词) describing an action rather than a state. **Dynamic** verbs (for example *eat, grow, knock, die*) can be used in the progressive tenses. 动态的 ➲ COMPARE STATIVE ▶ **dy·nam·ic·al·ly** AW /-kli/ *adv.*

D

dyna·mism /ˈdaɪnəmɪzəm/ *noun* [U] energy and enthusiasm to make new things happen or to make things succeed 精力；活力；劲头

dyna·mite /ˈdaɪnəmaɪt/ *noun, verb*

■ *noun* [U] **1** a powerful EXPLOSIVE 黄色炸药；甘油炸药；达纳炸药：*a stick of dynamite* 一根达纳炸药 **2** a thing that is likely to cause a violent reaction or a lot of trouble 具有爆炸性的事物；（可能）引起轰动的事物；具有隐患的事物：*The abortion issue is political dynamite.* 堕胎问题在政治上是个爆炸性的议题。 **3** (*informal, approving*) an extremely impressive or exciting person or thing 轰动一时的人（或事物）：*Their new album is dynamite.* 他们的新唱片引起轰动。

■ *verb* ~ sth to destroy or damage sth using dynamite 炸毁；爆破

dy·namo /ˈdaɪnəməʊ; *NAmE* -moʊ/ *noun* (*pl.* **-os**) **1** a device for turning MECHANICAL energy (= energy from movement) into electricity; a GENERATOR 发电机 **2** (*informal*) a person with a lot of energy 精力充沛的人：*the team's midfield dynamo* 这个队的中场活跃分子 ◇ *She's a **human dynamo**.* 她是个精力充沛的人。

dyn·asty /ˈdɪnəsti; *NAmE* ˈdaɪ-/ *noun* (*pl.* **-ies**) **1** a series of rulers of a country who all belong to the same family 王朝；朝代：*the Nehru-Gandhi dynasty* 尼赫鲁－甘地王朝 ➲ WORDFINDER NOTE AT RELATION **2** a period of years during which members of a particular family rule a country 朝；代 ▶ **dyn·as·tic** /dɪˈnæstɪk; *NAmE* daɪ-/ *adj.* [usually before noun]: *dynastic history* 王朝统治史

dys·en·tery /ˈdɪsəntri; *NAmE* -teri/ *noun* [U] an infection of the BOWELS that causes severe DIARRHOEA with loss of blood 痢疾

dys·func·tion /dɪsˈfʌŋkʃn/ *noun* [U, C] **1** (*medical* 医) the fact of a part of the body not working normally（身体）功能障碍：*He's suffering from sexual dysfunction caused by depression.* 他因抑郁而患上性功能障碍。 **2** the situation when the relationships within a society, family, etc. are not working normally（社会、家庭等内部的）关系失衡：*a tale of loneliness and family dysfunction* 一个关于孤独与家庭关系失衡的故事

dys·func·tion·al /dɪsˈfʌŋkʃənl/ *adj.* (*specialist*) not working normally or properly 机能失调的；功能障碍的：*children from dysfunctional families* 有缺陷家庭的子女

dys·lexia /dɪsˈleksiə/ *noun* [U] a slight DISORDER of the brain that causes difficulty in reading and spelling, for example, but does not affect intelligence 诵读困难 ▶ **dys·lex·ic** /dɪsˈleksɪk/ *adj.*：*He's dyslexic.* 他患诵读困难症。 **dys·lex·ic** /dɪsˈleksɪk/ *noun*：*writing courses for dyslexics* 为诵读困难患者开设的写作班

dys·mor·phia /dɪsˈmɔːfiə; *NAmE* -ˈmɔːrf-/ *noun* [U] (*medical* 医) a condition in which a part of the body grows larger than normal 畸形，变形（身体部位的过度增长） ▶ **dys·morph·ic** /dɪsˈmɔːfɪk; *NAmE* -ˈmɔːrf-/ *adj.*

dys·pep·sia /dɪsˈpepsiə; *NAmE* dɪsˈpepʃə/ *noun* [U] (*medical* 医) pain caused by difficulty in DIGESTING food 消化不良 **SYN indigestion**

dys·pep·tic /dɪsˈpeptɪk/ *adj.* **1** (*medical* 医) connected with or suffering from dyspepsia 消化不良的；患消化不良的 **2** (*formal*) bad-tempered 脾气坏的；暴躁的

dys·phoria /dɪsˈfɔːriə/ *noun* [U] (*medical* 医) a state of worry or general unhappiness 病理性心境恶劣 ➲ COMPARE EUPHORIA ▶ **dys·phor·ic** /dɪsˈfɒrɪk; *NAmE* -ˈfɔːr-/ *adj.*

dys·prax·ia /dɪsˈpræksiə/ *noun* [U] a condition of the brain which causes children to have difficulties, for example with physical movement, with writing neatly, and with organizing themselves （儿童）运用障碍

dys·pro·sium /dɪsˈprəʊziəm; *NAmE* -ˈproʊ-/ *noun* [U] (*symb.* **Dy**) a chemical element. Dysprosium is a soft silver-white metal used in nuclear research. 镝（用于核研究）

dys·to·pia /dɪsˈtəʊpiə; *NAmE* -ˈtoʊ-/ *noun* an imaginary place or state in which everything is extremely bad or unpleasant 反乌托邦，反面假想国，敌托帮（极度恶劣的假想处境或状况） ➲ COMPARE UTOPIA ▶ **dys·to·pian** /dɪsˈtəʊpiən; *NAmE* -ˈtoʊ-/ (*also* **dys·top·ic** /dɪsˈtɒpɪk; *NAmE* -ˈtɑːp-/) *adj.*

dys·trophy ➲ MUSCULAR DYSTROPHY

Ee

E /iː/ *noun, abbr.*

■ ***noun*** (*also* **e**) [C, U] (*pl.* **Es, E's, e's** /iːz/) **1** the fifth letter in the English alphabet 英语字母表的第 5 个字母：*'Egg' begins with (an) E/'E'.* * egg 一词以字母 e 开头。**2 E** (*music* 音) the third note in the SCALE of C MAJOR * E 音（C 大调的第 3 音或音符） **3 E** the fifth highest mark/grade that a student can get for a piece of work, showing that it is very bad （学业成绩）第五等，劣：*He got an E* ***in/for*** *French.* 他的法语成绩得 E 级。➲ SEE ALSO E-NUMBER

■ ***abbr.* 1** East; Eastern 东方（的）；东部（的）：*E Asia* 东亚 **2** (*slang*) the drug ECSTASY 摇头丸；迷幻药：*She had taken an E.* 她吃了一颗摇头丸。

e- /iː/ *combining form* (in nouns and verbs 构成名词和动词) connected with the use of electronic communication, especially the Internet, for sending information, doing business, etc. 电子的；电子通信的：*e-commerce* 电子商务 ◇ *e-business* 电子商务 ➲ SEE ALSO E-FIT™, EMAIL

each 🔑 /iːtʃ/ *det., pron., adv.* used to refer to every one of two or more people or things, when you are thinking about them separately （两个或以上的人或物中）各自，各个，每个：*Each answer is worth 20 points.* 每题为 20 分。◇ *Each of the answers is worth 20 points.* 每题为 20 分。◇ *The answers are worth 20 points each.* 这些答题每题为 20 分。◇ *'Red or blue?' 'I'll take one of each, please.'* "红的还是蓝的？""请一样给我一个。"◇ *We each have our own car.* 我们各人都有自己的汽车。◇ *There aren't enough books for everyone to have one each.* 没有足够的书给每人发一本。◇ *They lost $40 each.* 他们每人损失了 40 美元。◇ *Each day that passed he grew more and more desperate.* 一天天过去，他变得越来越绝望。

▼ **GRAMMAR POINT 语法说明**

each / every

- **Each** is used in front of a singular noun and is followed by a singular verb. * each 用于单数名词前，后接单数动词：*Each student has been given his or her own email address.* 每个学生都得到一个自己的电子邮件地址。The use of *his* or *her* sometimes sounds slightly formal and it is becoming more common to use the plural pronoun *their.* 有时候 his 或 her 听起来有点正式，故日渐普遍使用复数代词 their：*Each student has been given their own email address.* 每个学生都得到一个自己的电子邮件地址。
- When **each** is used after a plural subject, it has a plural verb. * each 用于复数主语后，谓语动词用复数：*They each have their own email address.* 他们每个人都有自己的电子邮件地址。
- **Every** is always followed by a singular verb. * every 后总是接单数动词：*Every student in the class is capable of passing the exam.* 班上每个同学都有能力通过这次考试。
- **Each of**, **each one of** and **every one of** are followed by a plural noun or pronoun, but the verb is usually singular. * each of、each one of 与 every one of 后接复数名词或代词，但谓语动词通常用单数：*Each (one) of the houses was slightly different.* 每座房子都稍有不同。◇ *I bought a dozen eggs and every one of them was bad.* 我买了一打鸡蛋，个个都是坏的。A plural verb is more informal. 用复数动词则较非正式。

each 'other 🔑 *pron.* used as the object of a verb or preposition to show that each member of a group does sth to or for the other members （用作动词或介词的宾语）互相，彼此：*Don and Susie really loved each other* (= he loved her and she loved him). 唐和苏茜确实相亲相爱。◇ *They looked at each other and laughed.* 他们彼此看了看便笑了起来。◇ *We can wear each other's clothes.* 我们可以相互换着衣服穿。

ˌeach 'way *adv., adj.* (*BrE*) if you bet money **each way** on a race, you win if your horse, etc. comes first, second or third in the race （赛马等）一注三赢（指投注的赛马等位列前三即赢）：*She put £5 each way on the favourite.* 她在热门马上押了 5 英镑的一注三赢赌注。◇ *an each-way bet* 一注三赢的赌注

eager /ˈiːɡə(r)/ *adj.* very interested and excited by sth that is going to happen or about sth that you want to do 热切的；渴望的；渴求的 **SYN** **keen**：*eager crowds outside the stadium* 体育场外急不可耐的人群 ◇ **~ for sth** *She is eager for* (= wants very much to get) *her parents' approval.* 她渴望得到父母的赞许。◇ **~ to do sth** *Everyone in the class seemed eager to learn.* 班上每个人似乎都热爱学习。◇ *They're* ***eager to please*** (= wanting to be helpful). 他们竭力讨好。▸ **eager·ly** *adv.*：*the band's eagerly awaited new CD* 人们热切等待着的乐队的新唱片 **eager·ness** *noun* [U, sing.]：*I couldn't hide my eagerness to get back home.* 我无法掩饰想回家的渴望。

ˌeager 'beaver *noun* (*informal*) an enthusiastic person who works very hard 干活特别卖力的人；对工作极有热忱的人

eagle /ˈiːɡl/ *noun* **1** a large BIRD OF PREY (= a bird that kills other creatures for food) with a sharp curved beak and very good sight 雕：*eagles soaring overhead* 在上空翱翔的雕 ➲ SEE ALSO BALD EAGLE, GOLDEN EAGLE **2** (in GOLF 高尔夫球) a score of two strokes less than the standard score for a hole (= two under PAR) 鹰击（比标准杆少打两杆） ➲ COMPARE BIRDIE (2), BOGEY (4)

ˌeagle 'eye *noun* [usually sing.] if sb has an **eagle eye**, they watch things carefully and are good at noticing things 敏锐的眼光；锐利的目光：*Nothing escaped our teacher's eagle eye.* 任何事情都逃不过我们老师那锐利的目光。▸ **ˌeagle-'eyed** *adj.* **SYN** **hawk-eyed**：*An eagle-eyed tourist found the suspicious package.* 一位眼尖的游客发现了可疑的包裹。

eag·let /ˈiːɡlət/ *noun* a young eagle 雏雕；小雕

EAL /ˌiː eɪ ˈel/ *abbr.* (in the UK and Ireland) English as an additional language (refers to the teaching of English in schools to children whose first language is not English) （英国和爱尔兰）作为附加语言的英语（教学对象为第一语言非英语的中小学生） ➲ COMPARE EFL, ESL, ESOL

EAP /ˌiː eɪ ˈpiː/ *abbr.* ENGLISH FOR ACADEMIC PURPOSES 学术英语教学（对象为第一语言非英语者）

ear 🔑 /ɪə(r); *NAmE* ɪr/ *noun* **1** 🔑 [C] either of the organs on the sides of the head that you hear with 耳；耳朵：*an ear infection* 耳朵感染 ◇ *the* ***inner/outer ear*** 内耳；外耳 ◇ *She whispered something in his ear.* 她对他耳语了几句。◇ *He put his hands over his ears.* 他用双手捂住耳朵。◇ *She's had her ears pierced.* 她扎了耳朵眼儿。◇ *The elephant flapped its ears.* 大象拍打着双耳。◇ *He was always there with a sympathetic ear* (= a willingness to listen to people). 他总是愿意倾听别人的心声。➲ VISUAL VOCAB PAGE V64 ➲ SEE ALSO CAULIFLOWER EAR, GLUE EAR, MIDDLE EAR **2 -eared** (in adjectives 构成形容词) having the type of ears mentioned 有…耳朵的；耳朵…的：*a long-eared owl* 长耳鸮 ➲ MORE LIKE THIS 8, page R25 **3** [sing.] an ability to recognize and copy sounds well 灵敏的听力；辨音力：*You need a good ear to master the piano.* 弹好钢琴需要有敏锐的辨音能力。**4** [C] the top part of a grain plant, such as WHEAT, that contains the seeds （谷类植物的）穗：*ears of corn* 玉米穗 ➲ VISUAL VOCAB PAGE V35

IDM **be all 'ears** (*informal*) to be waiting with interest to hear what sb has to say 全神贯注地听；聚精会神地听：*'Do you know what he said?' 'Go on—I'm all ears.'* "你知道他说什么了吗？""讲吧，我洗耳恭听。" **be out on your 'ear** (*informal*) to be forced to leave (a job, etc.) 被迫离开（工作岗位等）；被撵出去 **be up to your ears in sth** to have a lot of sth to deal with 深陷于；埋头于；忙于：

We're up to our ears in work. 我们工作忙得不可开交。 **sth comes to/reaches sb's 'ears** somebody hears about sth, especially when other people already know about it 传到…的耳朵里： *News of his affair eventually reached her ears.* 他的绯闻终于传到她耳朵里。 **sb's 'ears are burning** a person thinks that other people are talking about them, especially in an unkind way （感到有人议论自己，尤指说闲话而）耳朵发热： *'I bumped into your ex-wife last night.' 'I thought I could feel my ears burning!'* "我昨天晚上偶然遇到你的前妻。""怪不得我好像觉得耳朵发热呢！" **sb's 'ears are flapping** (*BrE, informal*) a person is trying to listen to sb else's conversation 某人正竖着耳朵听 **go in 'one ear and out the 'other** (*informal*) (of information, etc. 消息等) to be forgotten quickly 一只耳朵进另一只耳朵出；被当作耳边风： *Everything I tell them just goes in one ear and out the other.* 我无论对他们说什么都只被当作耳边风。 **have sth coming out of your 'ears** (*informal*) to have a lot of sth, especially more than you need 有的是某物（形容大量拥有，甚至超过所需） **have sb's ear | have the ear of sb** to be able to give sb advice, influence them, etc. because they trust you 在某人那里说得上话；使某人听得进去： *He had the ear of the monarch.* 他在君主那里说得上话。 **keep/have your ear to the 'ground** to make sure that you always find out about the most recent developments in a particular situation 注意看动向；掌握最新发展情况 **play (sth) by 'ear** to play music by remembering how it sounds rather than by reading it 凭记忆演奏；不看乐谱弹奏 **play it by 'ear** (*informal*) to decide how to deal with a situation as it develops rather than by having a plan to follow 见机行事；随机应变；根据情况需要行动： *I don't know what they'll want when they arrive—we'll have to play it by ear.* 我不知道他们到达时想要什么，我们只有见机行事了。 **shut/close your 'ears to sth** to refuse to listen to sth （对…）充耳不闻，置之不理： *She decided to shut her ears to all the rumours.* 她拿定主意对所有的谣言置之不理。 **smile/grin/beam from ear to 'ear** to be smiling, etc. a lot because you are very pleased about sth 眉开眼笑；笑得合不拢嘴 **with half an 'ear** without giving your full attention to what is being said, etc. 心不在焉地听 ➲ MORE AT BELIEVE, BEND *v.*, BOX *n.*, BOX *v.*, COCK *v.*, DEAF, EASY *adj.*, FEEL *v.*, FLEA, LEND, MUSIC, OPEN *adj.*, PIG *n.*, PRICK *v.*, RING² *v.*, SILK, THICK *adj.*, WALL *n.*, WET *adj.*, WORD *n.*

ear·ache /'ɪəreɪk; *NAmE* 'ɪr-/ *noun* [U, C] pain inside the ear 耳痛： *to have (an) earache* 患耳痛

ear·bash·ing /'ɪəbæʃɪŋ; *NAmE* 'ɪr-/ *noun* [sing.] (*BrE, informal*) an occasion where sb criticizes a person in an angry way 对某人的愤怒指责

ear·bud /'ɪəbʌd; *NAmE* 'ɪr-/ *noun* [usually pl.] a very small HEADPHONE that is worn inside the ear 耳塞 ➲ **VISUAL VOCAB PAGE V73**

'ear drops *noun* [pl.] liquid medicine that can be put into the ears 滴耳药水；滴耳剂

ear·drum /'ɪədrʌm; *NAmE* 'ɪr-/ *noun* the piece of thin tightly stretched skin inside the ear which is moved by sound waves, making you able to hear 耳膜；鼓膜： *a perforated eardrum* 鼓膜穿孔

ear·ful /'ɪəfʊl; *NAmE* 'ɪrfʊl/ *noun* [sing.] (*informal*) if sb gives you an **earful**, they tell you for a long time how angry they are about sth 长时间的斥责（或牢骚）

ear·hole /'ɪəhəʊl; *NAmE* 'ɪrhoʊl/ *noun* (*informal*) the outer opening of the ear 耳孔

earl /ɜːl; *NAmE* ɜːrl/ *noun* a NOBLEMAN of high rank 伯爵： *the Earl of Essex* 埃塞克斯伯爵 ➲ SEE ALSO COUNTESS

,Earl 'Grey *noun* [U] a type of tea flavoured with BERGAMOT （格雷）伯爵茶（用香柠檬调味）

earli·est /'ɜːlɪɪst; *NAmE* 'ɜːrl-/ *noun* [sing.] **the earliest** the time before which sth cannot happen 最早；最早时间： *The earliest we can finish is next Friday.* 我们最早能在下星期五完成。 ◇ *We can't finish before next Friday **at the earliest**.* 我们最早也要到下星期五才能完成。

ear·lobe /'ɪələʊb; *NAmE* 'ɪrloʊb/ (*also* **lobe**) *noun* the soft part at the bottom of the ear 耳垂

early 🔑 /'ɜːli; *NAmE* 'ɜːrli/ *adj., adv.*

■ ***adj.*** (**earl·ier, earli·est**) **1** 🔑 near the beginning of a period of time, an event etc. 早期的；初期的；早先的： *the early morning* 清晨 ◇ *my earliest memories* 我最早的记忆 ◇ *The project is still in the early stages.* 这个项目仍处于初期阶段。 ◇ *the early 1990s* * 20 世纪 90 年代初 ◇ *in **the early days of** space exploration* (= when it was just beginning) 在太空探索初期 ◇ *The earliest possible date I can make it is the third.* 我最早也要到三号才有时间出席。 ◇ *He's in his early twenties.* 他二十出头。 ◇ *Mozart's early works* (= those written at the beginning of his career) 莫扎特的早期作品 ◇ *Early booking is essential, as space is limited.* 座位有限，务必早日预订。 **2** 🔑 arriving, or done before the usual, expected or planned time 早到的；提前的；提早的： *You're early! I wasn't expecting you till seven.* 你来得真早！我还以为你七点钟才能到呢。 ◇ *The bus was ten minutes early.* 公共汽车早到了十分钟。 ◇ *an early breakfast* 很早的早餐 ◇ *Let's **make an early start** tomorrow.* 咱们明天一早就出发吧。 ◇ *She's an **early riser*** (= she gets up early in the morning). 她是个习惯于早起的人。 ◇ *He learnt to play the piano at an **early age**.* 他早年就学会了弹钢琴。 ◇ *early potatoes* (= that are ready to eat at the beginning of the season) 早下来的土豆 **OPP** late

▸ **earli·ness** *noun* [U]

IDM **an 'early bird** (*humorous*) a person who gets up, arrives, etc. very early 早起者；早到者；赶早者；捷足先登者 **at your earliest con'venience** (*business* 商) as soon as possible 尽早；尽快： *Please telephone at your earliest convenience.* 请尽早打电话。 **the ,early bird catches the 'worm** (*saying*) the person who takes the opportunity to do sth before other people will have an advantage over them 捷足先登；捷足先得 **it's early 'days (yet)** (*BrE*) used to say that it is too soon to be sure how a situation will develop 为时尚早；言之过早 ➲ MORE AT BRIGHT *adj.*, HOUR, NIGHT

■ ***adv.*** (**earl·ier, earli·est**) **1** 🔑 near the beginning of a period of time, an event, a piece of work, etc. 在早期；在初期；在开始阶段： ***early in the week/year/season/morning*** 一周开始时；年初；季度初；一大早 ◇ *The best rooms go to those who book earliest.* 最早预订者可得最好的房间。 ◇ *We arrived early the next day.* 我们第二天很早就到达了。 ◇ *He started writing music as early as 1989.* 他早在 1989 年就开始作曲了。 **OPP** late **2** 🔑 before the usual, expected or planned time 提早；提前： *The bus came five minutes early.* 公共汽车早到了五分钟。 ◇ *I woke up early this morning.* 我今天早上醒得早。 ◇ *The baby arrived earlier than expected.* 婴儿早产了。 **OPP** late **3** 🔑 **earlier** before the present time or the time mentioned 先前；早些时候；…之前： *As I mentioned earlier…* 正如我先前所提到的… ◇ *a week earlier* 一周前 ◇ *She had seen him earlier in the day.* 她在那天早些时候已见过他。 **OPP** later

IDM **early 'on** 🔑 at an early stage of a situation, relationship, period of time, etc. 在初期；在开始阶段；早先： *I knew quite early on that I wanted to marry her.* 我老早就知道我想娶她。

,early 'closing *noun* [U] (*BrE*) the practice of closing shops on a particular afternoon every week (now no longer very common) 提早打烊，提前停止营业（指商店每周的某个下午不开门，现已不常见）

,early 'warning *noun* [U, sing.] a thing that tells you in advance that sth serious or dangerous is going to happen 预先警报： *an early warning of heart disease* 心脏病的早期症状 ◇ *an early warning system* (= of enemy attack) 预警系统

ear·mark /'ɪəmɑːk; *NAmE* 'ɪrmɑːrk/ *verb, noun*

■ ***verb*** [usually passive] to decide that sth will be used for a particular purpose, or to state that sth will happen to sb/sth in the future 指定…的用途；预先安排，确定（未来发生的事情）： **~ sb/sth (for sb/sth)** *The money had been earmarked for spending on new school buildings.* 这笔款项已指定用于新校舍建设。 ◇ *The factory has been* *earmarked for closure.* 这家工厂已被指定关闭。◇ **~ sb/sth (as sb/sth)** *She was earmarked early as a possible champion.* 人们早就认定她有可能夺冠。

■ ***noun*** [usually pl.] (*NAmE*) a feature or quality that is typical of sb/sth 标记；特征：*The incident has all the earmarks of a terrorist attack.* 这一事件具有恐怖袭击的所有特征。

ear·muffs /ˈɪəmʌfs; *NAmE* ˈɪrmʌfs/ *noun* [pl.] a pair of coverings for the ears connected by a band across the top of the head, and worn to protect the ears, especially from cold （尤指御寒用的）耳罩，耳套，护耳：*a pair of earmuffs* 一副耳套

earn /ɜːn; *NAmE* ɜːrn/ *verb* **1** [T, I] to get money for work that you do 挣得；赚得；挣钱：**~ (sth)** *He earns about $40 000 a year.* 他一年大约挣 4 万美元。◇ *She* ***earned a living*** *as a part-time secretary.* 她靠做兼职秘书为生。◇ *She must* ***earn a fortune*** (= earn a lot of money). 她准是挣了一大笔钱。◇ *All the children are earning now.* 所有子女都在挣钱了。◇ **~ sb sth** *His victory in the tournament earned him $50 000.* 他在这次锦标赛中获胜，挣得了 5 万美元。➲ WORDFINDER NOTE AT PAY ➲ COLLOCATIONS AT FINANCE **2** [T] **~ sth** to get money as profit or interest on money you lend, have in a bank, etc. 生（利）；获（利）：*Your money would earn more in a high-interest account.* 你的钱放在高利息账户里可获利更多。 **3** [T] to get sth that you deserve, usually because of sth good you have done or because of the good qualities you have 应得；博得；赢得：**~ sth** *He earned a reputation as an expert on tax law.* 他赢得了税法专家的美名。◇ *As a teacher, she had earned the respect of her students.* 作为教师，她赢得了学生的尊敬。◇ *I need a rest. I think I've earned it, don't you?* 我需要休息一下。我觉得应该让我歇一歇，你说是不是？◇ *She's having a well-earned rest this week.* 她本周休假，这完全是应当的。◇ **~ sb sth** *His outstanding ability earned him a place on the team.* 他非凡的能力为他在队中赢得了一席之地。

IDM ˌ**earn a/your ˈcrust** (*BrE, informal*) to earn enough money to live on 挣钱糊口；谋生 ˌ**earn your ˈkeep 1** to do useful or helpful things in return for being allowed to live or stay somewhere 挣口饭吃；为有栖身之处而工作 **2** to be worth the amount of time or money that is being spent 值得所花的时间（或金钱）：*He felt he no longer deserved such a high salary. He just wasn't earning his keep.* 他认为他不应再得到那么高的薪金了。他根本不配拿那么多钱。➲ MORE AT SPUR *n.*

ˌ**earned ˈrun** *noun* (in BASEBALL 棒球) a RUN scored without the help of errors by the opposing team 投手责任失分

earn·er /ˈɜːnə(r); *NAmE* ˈɜːrn-/ *noun* **1** a person who earns money for a job that they do 挣钱者；挣工资者：***high/low earners*** 高薪／低薪的人 ➲ SEE ALSO WAGE EARNER **2** an activity or a business that makes a profit 赢利活动；赚钱的生意：*Tourism is the country's biggest foreign currency earner.* 旅游业是这个国家赚取外汇最多的行业。◇ (*BrE, informal*) *Her new business has turned out to be a* ***nice little earner***. 她新开的商店结果还真有点赚钱呢。

earn·est /ˈɜːnɪst; *NAmE* ˈɜːrn-/ *adj.* very serious and sincere 非常认真的；真诚的：*an earnest young man* 非常认真的年轻人 ◇ *Despite her earnest efforts, she could not find a job.* 尽管她已尽心竭力，但是仍然找不到工作。 ▶ **earn·est·ly** *adv.* **earn·est·ness** *noun* [U]

IDM **in ˈearnest 1** more seriously and with more force or effort than before （更加）严肃地，认真地，坚定地：*The work on the house will* ***begin in earnest*** *on Monday.* 这栋房子的修建工作将在星期一正式开始。 **2** very serious and sincere about what you are saying and about your intentions; in a way that shows that you are serious 郑重其事；当真：*You may laugh but I'm in* ***deadly earnest***. 你可以笑，不过我可是正经八百的。◇ *I could tell she spoke in earnest.* 我看得出她是郑重其事地说的。

earn·ings /ˈɜːnɪŋz; *NAmE* ˈɜːrn-/ *noun* [pl.] **1** the money that you earn for the work that you do 薪水；工资；收入：*a rise in average earnings* 平均收入的增加 ◇ *compensation for loss of earnings caused by the accident* 由于事故造成收入损失的赔偿 ➲ SYNONYMS AT INCOME **2** the profit that a company makes 利润；收益；赢利：*earnings per share* 每股收益 ◇ *export earnings* 出口利润 ➲ COLLOCATIONS AT BUSINESS

ˌ**earnings-reˈlated** *adj.* (*BrE*) (of payments, etc. 付款等) connected to and changing according to the amount of money that you earn 与收入挂钩的；按收益计算的：*an earnings-related pension scheme* 与收入挂钩的退休金计划

ear·phones /ˈɪəfəʊnz; *NAmE* ˈɪrfoʊnz/ *noun* [pl.] = HEADPHONES

ear·piece /ˈɪəpiːs; *NAmE* ˈɪrpiːs/ *noun* the part of a telephone or piece of electrical equipment that you hold next to or put into your ear so that you can listen （电话）听筒；耳机；耳塞

ˈ**ear-piercing** *adj., noun*

■ ***adj.*** [only before noun] very high, loud and unpleasant 刺耳的；尖厉的：*an ear-piercing scream* 一声刺耳的尖叫

■ ***noun*** [U] the practice of making small holes in sb's ears so jewellery can be put in them 穿耳洞；扎耳朵眼儿

ear·plug /ˈɪəplʌɡ; *NAmE* ˈɪrp-/ *noun* [usually pl.] a piece of soft material that you put into your ear to keep out noise or water 耳塞（用以挡噪音、防水）

ear·ring /ˈɪərɪŋ; *NAmE* ˈɪrɪŋ/ *noun* a piece of jewellery that you fasten in or on your ear 耳环；耳饰：*a pair of earrings* 一对耳环 ➲ VISUAL VOCAB PAGE V70

ear·set /ˈɪəset; *NAmE* ˈɪrset/ *noun* a piece of equipment that fits into your ear and has a MICROPHONE attached to it. It is connected to a telephone and allows you to use the telephone without using your hands. （电话）耳麦

ear·shot /ˈɪəʃɒt; *NAmE* ˈɪrʃɑːt/ *noun*

IDM **out of ˈearshot (of sb/sth)** too far away to hear sb/sth or to be heard 在听力范围之外：*We waited until Ted was safely out of earshot before discussing it.* 我们一直等到特德保准听不见时才讨论这事。 **within ˈearshot (of sb/sth)** near enough to hear sb/sth or to be heard 在听力范围之内：*As she came within earshot of the group, she heard her name mentioned.* 她刚走近到能听见这群人说话声时便听到有人提她的名字。

ˈ**ear-splitting** *adj.* extremely loud 极响的；震耳欲聋的 ➲ MORE LIKE THIS 10, page R26

earth /ɜːθ; *NAmE* ɜːrθ/ *noun, verb*

■ ***noun*** **1** (*also* **Earth, the Earth**) [U, sing.] the world; the planet that we live on 世界；地球：*the* ***planet Earth*** 行星地球 ◇ *the history of* ***life on earth*** 地球上的生命史 ◇ *the earth's ozone layer* 地球的臭氧层 ◇ *The earth revolves around the sun.* 地球绕着太阳转。◇ *I must be the happiest person* ***on earth!*** 我一定是世界上最幸福的人！

> WORDFINDER 联想词：**climate**, equator, equinox, hemisphere, International Date Line, latitude, map, planet, tropic

2 [U, sing.] land; the hard surface of the world that is not the sea or the sky; the ground 陆地；地面；大地：*After a week at sea, it was good to feel the earth beneath our feet again.* 出海一周后，重新踏上陆地感到很愉快。◇ *You could feel the earth shake as the truck came closer.* 卡车开近时会感觉到地面在震动。➲ SYNONYMS AT FLOOR **3** [U] the substance that plants grow in 土；泥；泥土：*a* ***clod/lump/mound of earth*** 一块土；一团泥；一堆土 ➲ SYNONYMS AT SOIL **4** [C] the hole where an animal, especially a FOX, lives 兽穴；（尤指狐狸栖息的）洞穴 **5** (*BrE*) (*NAmE* **ground**) [C, usually sing.] a wire that connects an electric CIRCUIT with the ground and makes it safe （接）地线

IDM **charge, cost, pay, etc. the ˈearth** (*BrE, informal*) to charge, etc. a lot of money 收（或花、付等）很多钱 **come back/down to ˈearth (with a ˈbang/ˈbump) | bring sb (back) down to ˈearth (with a ˈbang/ˈbump)** (*informal*) to return, or to make sb return, to a normal way of thinking or behaving after a time when they have been very excited, not very practical, etc.（使）从幻想中清醒过来，回到现实中来 ➲ SEE ALSO DOWN TO EARTH **go to 'earth/'ground** (*BrE*) to hide, especially to escape from sb who is chasing you 躲藏起来（以免被捉住） **how, why, where, who, etc. on 'earth** (*informal*) used to emphasize the question you are asking when you are surprised or angry or cannot think of an obvious answer（加强疑问句的语气）到底，究竟：*What on earth are you doing?* 你究竟在干什么？◇ *How on earth can she afford that?* 她怎么可能负担得起呢？ **be, feel, look, taste, etc. like nothing on 'earth** (*informal*) to be, feel, look, taste, etc. very bad 感到（或显得、尝起来等）非常糟糕，非常难受 **on 'earth** used after negative nouns or pronouns to emphasize what you are saying（用于否定名词或代词之后表示强调）在世界上，在人世间：*Nothing on earth would persuade me to go with him.* 无论什么都不能说服我跟他一块儿走。 **run sb/sth to 'earth/'ground** (*BrE*) to find sb/sth after looking hard for a long time（长期搜寻后）终于找到 ➲ MORE AT END *n.*, FACE *n.*, MOVE *v.*, PROMISE *v.*, SALT *n.*, WIPE *v.*

■ ***verb*** (*BrE*) (*NAmE* **ground**) [usually passive] **~ sth** to make electrical equipment safe by connecting it to the ground with a wire 把（电气设备）接地

earth·bound /'ɜːθbaʊnd; *NAmE* 'ɜːrθ-/ *adj.* **1** unable to leave the surface of the earth（只在）地球上的，陆地的，地面上的：*birds and their earthbound predators* 鸟和地面上捕食它们的动物 **2** (*literary*) not spiritual or having much imagination 世俗的；物质世界的；缺乏想象力的

earth·en /'ɜːθn; *NAmE* 'ɜːrθn/ *adj.* [only before noun] **1** (of floors or walls 地面或墙) made of earth 泥土做的；土制的 **2** (of objects 物体) made of baked CLAY 陶制的：*earthen pots* 陶罐

earth·en·ware /'ɜːθnweə(r); *NAmE* 'ɜːrθnwer/ *adj.* made of very hard baked CLAY 陶制的：*an earthenware bowl* 陶碗 ▶ **earth·en·ware** *noun* [U]

earth·ling /'ɜːθlɪŋ; *NAmE* 'ɜːrθ-/ *noun* (in SCIENCE FICTION stories) a word used by creatures from other planets to refer to a person living on the earth（科幻小说中外星人用语）地球人

earth·ly /'ɜːθli; *NAmE* 'ɜːrθ-/ *adj.* [usually before noun] **1** (*literary*) connected with life on earth and not with any spiritual life 人间的；尘世的；世俗的：*the sorrows of this earthly life* 尘世的悲哀 **2** (often used in questions and negatives for emphasis 常用于疑问句或否定句以加强语气) possible 可能的：*There's* ***no earthly reason*** *why you shouldn't go.* 你完全没有理由不去。◇ *What earthly difference is my opinion going to make?* 我的意见会有什么作用呢？◇ *He didn't have an earthly chance of getting the job.* 他根本就不可能得到这份工作。

'earth mother *noun* **1** (*also* **Earth Mother**) a GODDESS who represents the earth as the source of life; a GODDESS of FERTILITY（象征生命之源的）大地母亲；（主生殖繁衍的）女神 **2** (*informal*) a woman who seems very suited to being a mother 天生的母亲

'earth mover *noun* a vehicle or machine that digs up large quantities of soil 推土机；挖土车

earth·quake /'ɜːθkweɪk; *NAmE* 'ɜːrθ-/ (*also informal* **quake**) *noun* a sudden, violent shaking of the earth's surface 地震 ➲ WORDFINDER NOTE AT DISASTER

'earth science *noun* [C, U] a science concerned with studying the earth or part of it. Geography and GEOLOGY are both earth sciences. 地球科学，地学（涵盖地理学和地质学） ➲ COMPARE LIFE SCIENCES, NATURAL SCIENCE

'earth-shatter·ing *adj.* having a very great effect and of great importance 震撼世界的；影响深远的；极其重大的：*an earth-shattering discovery* 惊天动地的发现

earth·work /'ɜːθwɜːk; *NAmE* 'ɜːrθwɜːrk/ *noun* [usually pl.] a large bank of earth that was built long ago in the past and used as a defence 土垒（旧时防御用的工事）

earth·worm /'ɜːθwɜːm; *NAmE* 'ɜːrθwɜːrm/ *noun* a common long thin WORM that lives in soil 蚯蚓

earthy /'ɜːθi; *NAmE* 'ɜːrθi/ *adj.* (**earth·ier**, **earthi·est**) **1** concerned with the body, sex, etc. in an open and direct way that some people find rude or embarrassing 粗俗的；庸俗的；不文雅的：*an earthy sense of humour* 粗俗的幽默感 **2** of or like earth or soil 泥土的；泥土似的；有泥土气息的：*earthy colours* 泥土的颜色 ▶ **earthi·ness** *noun* [U]

'ear trumpet *noun* a device shaped like a TRUMPET, used in the past by people who could not hear well（旧时的）号角状助听器

ear·wax /'ɪəwæks; *NAmE* 'ɪrwæks/ *noun* [U] the yellow substance produced inside the ear to protect it 耵聍；耳垢

ear·wig /'ɪəwɪg; *NAmE* 'ɪrwɪg/ *noun* a small brown insect with a long body and two curved pointed parts called PINCERS that stick out at the back end of its body 蠼螋；地蜈蚣；土蚣

ear·worm /'ɪəwɜːm; *NAmE* 'ɪrwɜːrm/ *noun* a song or tune that stays in your head for a long time after you have heard it 耳虫（听过后长久萦绕在头脑中的歌或旋律）

ease 🔑 /iːz/ *noun, verb*

■ ***noun*** [U] **1** 🔑 lack of difficulty 容易；轻易；不费劲：*He passed the exam* ***with ease***. 他轻而易举地通过了考试。◇ *The ease with which she learns languages is astonishing.* 她学习语言之轻松令人惊讶。◇ *This computer is popular for its good design and* ***ease of use***. 这种计算机因设计巧妙、简单易用而广受欢迎。◇ *All important points are numbered* ***for ease of reference*** (= so that you can find them easily). 全部重点均编了号码以便查阅。 **2** the state of feeling relaxed or comfortable without worries, problems or pain 舒适；安逸；自在；无忧无虑：*In his retirement, he lived a life of ease.* 他退休后过着悠闲舒适的生活。

IDM **(stand) at 'ease** used as a command to soldiers to tell them to stand with their feet apart and their hands behind their backs（对士兵的命令用语）稍息 ➲ COMPARE ATTENTION *n.* (5) **at (your) 'ease** relaxed and confident and not nervous or embarrassed 舒适；自由自在；无拘无束：*I never feel completely at ease with him.* 我跟他在一起总感到不是很自在。 **put sb at (their) 'ease** to make sb feel relaxed and confident, not nervous or embarrassed 使舒适；使自在；使不受拘束 ➲ MORE AT ILL *adj.*, MIND *n.*

■ ***verb*** **1** 🔑 [I, T] to become or to make sth less unpleasant, painful, severe, etc.（使）宽慰；减轻；缓解 SYN **alleviate**：*The pain immediately eased.* 疼痛立刻减轻了。◇ **~ sth** *This should help ease the pain.* 这该有助于减轻痛楚。◇ *The plan should ease traffic congestion in the town.* 这项计划对城里的交通拥挤状况应该有所缓解。◇ *It would* ***ease my mind*** (= make me less worried) *to know that she was settled.* 知道她已安顿下来会使我放心些。 **2** [I, T] to move, or to move sb/sth, slowly and carefully（使）小心缓缓地移动：**+ adv./prep.** *He eased slowly forwards.* 他缓缓向前移动。◇ **~ sb/sth + adv./prep.** *She eased herself into a chair.* 她轻手轻脚地坐到椅子上。◇ *He eased off* (= took off) *his shoes.* 他小心翼翼地脱下鞋子。 **3** [T] **~ sth** to make sth easier 使…容易些：*Ramps have been built to ease access for the disabled.* 为方便残疾人的出入修建了坡道。 **4** [T, I] **~ (sth)** to make sth or to become less tight and more relaxed（使）缓和，放松 SYN **relax**：*Ease your grip on the wheel a little.* 握方向盘的手放松一点。 **5** [I, T] **~ (sth)** to become or make sth lower in price or value 降低；（使）贬值 SYN **reduce**：*Share prices eased back from yesterday's levels.* 股价从昨天的水平上回落了。

PHR V **'ease into sth | 'ease yourself/sb into sth** to become or help sb to become familiar with sth new, especially a new job 熟悉，使熟悉（新事物，尤指新工作） **,ease 'off | ,ease 'off sth** to become or make sth become less strong, unpleasant, etc. 减轻；放松：*We* waited until the traffic had eased off. 我们一直等到交通缓解。◇ Ease off the training a few days before the race. 比赛前几天要减轻训练强度。 ˌ**ease sb↔ˈout (of sth)** to force sb to leave a job or position of authority, especially by making it difficult or unpleasant for them over a period of time （尤指故意为难）迫使某人离开（管理岗位等） ˌ**ease ˈup 1** to reduce the speed at which you are travelling 放慢速度 **2** to become less strong, unpleasant, etc. 减轻；缓和；放松

ease·ful /ˈiːzfl/ *adj.* (*literary*) that provides comfort or peace 舒适的；安闲的

easel /ˈiːzl/ *noun* a wooden frame to hold a picture while it is being painted 画架 ➲ VISUAL VOCAB PAGE V45

ease·ment /ˈiːzmənt/ *noun* [U] **1** (*law* 律) the right to cross or use sb's land for a particular purpose 地役权（穿越或征用某人土地的权利） **2** (*literary*) a state or feeling of peace or happiness 安逸；安乐

eas·ily /ˈiːzəli/ *adv.* **1** without problems or difficulty 容易地；轻易地；不费力地： *I can easily finish it tonight.* 我今晚能毫不费力地把它完成。◇ *The museum is easily accessible by car.* 开车可以方便地到达博物馆。 **2** very probably; very likely 很可能；多半： *Are you sure you locked the gate? You could easily have forgotten.* 你肯定锁上大门了吗？你很可能是忘了。◇ *The situation might* ***all too easily*** *have become a disaster.* 这形势本来是极有可能成为一场大灾难的。 **3 ~ the best, nicest, etc.** without doubt; definitely 无疑；肯定： *It's easily the best play I've seen this year.* 这无疑是我今年看过的最好的一出戏。 **4** quickly; more quickly than is usual 一会儿；不多久： *I get bored easily.* 我易生厌倦。◇ *He's easily distracted.* 他注意力很容易分散。

east /iːst/ *noun, adj., adv.*
■ ***noun*** [U, sing.] (*abbr.* **E**) **1** (*usually* **the east**) the direction that you look towards to see the sun rise; one of the four main points of the COMPASS 东；东方： *Which way is east?* 哪边是东？◇ *A gale was blowing from the east.* 大风从东面吹来。◇ *a town* ***to the east of*** (= further east than) *Chicago* 芝加哥以东的一个城镇 ➲ PICTURE AT COMPASS ➲ COMPARE NORTH *n.*, SOUTH *n.*, WEST *n.* **2** (*also* **East**) the eastern part of a country, region or city 东部；东边： *I was born in the East, but now live in San Francisco.* 我出生在东部，但现住在旧金山。 **3 the East** the countries of Asia, especially China, Japan and India 亚洲国家，东方国家（尤指中国、日本和印度） **4 the East** (in the past) the Communist countries of Central and Eastern Europe （旧时）中欧和东欧共产主义国家： *East-West relations* 东西方关系
■ ***adj.*** [only before noun] **1** (*also* **East**) (*abbr.* **E**) in or towards the east 东方的；向东的；东部的： *East Africa* 东非 ◇ *They live on the east coast.* 他们住在东海岸。 **2** an east wind blows from the east 东风的；东方吹来的 ➲ COMPARE EASTERLY *adj.*
■ ***adv.*** towards the east 向东；朝东： *The house faces east.* 房子朝东。

east·bound /ˈiːstbaʊnd/ *adj.* travelling or leading towards the east 东行的；向东的： *eastbound traffic* 东行交通 ◇ *the eastbound carriageway of the motorway* 高速公路的东行车道

ˌ**East Coast ˈFever** *noun* [U] a disease that cows in Africa can get by being bitten by a TICK (= a small insect), and which can kill them 东海岸热（病）（非洲牛被蜱叮咬引起的疾病，可导致死亡）

the ˌEast ˈEnd *noun* an area of East London traditionally connected with working people 伦敦东区（传统上为工人居住区） ▸ ˌ**East ˈEnder** *noun* : *He's a real East Ender.* 他是一个地道的伦敦东区人。

Easter /ˈiːstə(r)/ *noun* **1** [U, C] (*also* ˌ**Easter ˈDay**, ˌ**Easter ˈSunday**) (in the Christian religion) a Sunday in March or April when Christians remember the death of Christ and his return to life 复活节（纪念耶稣复活，在三月或四月的一个星期日） **2** (*also* **East·er·time**) the period that includes Easter Day and the days close to it 复活节期间： *the Easter holidays/vacation* 复活节假期

ˈ**Easter egg** *noun* **1** an egg made of chocolate that is given as a present and eaten at Easter 复活节巧克力蛋 **2** an egg with a shell that is painted and decorated at Easter 复活节彩蛋（复活节时彩绘或装饰的蛋）

east·er·ly /ˈiːstəli; *NAmE* -ərli/ *adj., noun*
■ ***adj.*** [only before noun] **1** in or towards the east 东方的；向东的；东部的： *travelling in an easterly direction* 向东旅行 **2** [usually before noun] (of winds 风) blowing from the east 从东方吹来的： *a cold easterly wind* 寒冷的东风 ➲ COMPARE EAST *adj.*
■ ***noun*** (*pl.* **-ies**) a wind that blows from the east 东风

east·ern /ˈiːstən; *NAmE* -ərn/ *adj.* **1** (*also* **Eastern**) (*abbr.* **E**) [only before noun] located in the east or facing east 东方的；向东的；东部的： *eastern Spain* 西班牙东部 ◇ *Eastern Europe* 东欧 ◇ *the eastern slopes of the mountain* 东山坡 **2** (*usually* **Eastern**) connected with the part of the world that is to the east of Europe （欧洲以东的）亚洲国家的，东方国家的： *Eastern cookery* 东方烹饪

ˌ**Eastern ˈDaylight Time** *noun* [U] (*abbr.* **EDT**) the time used in the summer in the eastern US and Canada, which is four hours behind UTC 东部夏令时间（美国东部和加拿大东部的夏季时间，比协调世界时晚四个小时）

east·ern·er /ˈiːstənə(r); *NAmE* ˈiːstərnər/ *noun* a person who comes from or lives in the eastern part of a country, especially the US 东部人；（尤指）美国东部人

east·ern·most /ˈiːstənməʊst; *NAmE* -ərnmoʊst/ *adj.* furthest east 最东的；最东端的；最东部的： *the easternmost city in Europe* 欧洲最东边的城市

the ˌEastern ˌOrthodox ˈChurch *noun* = ORTHODOX CHURCH

ˌ**Eastern ˈStandard Time** *noun* [U] (*abbr.* **EST**) (*also* **Eastern time**) the time used in the winter in the eastern US and Canada, which is five hours behind UTC 东部标准时间，东部冬令时间（美国东部和加拿大东部的冬季时间，比协调世界时晚五个小时）

ˈ**Eastern time** *noun* [U] the standard time in the eastern US and parts of Canada 东部时间（美国东部和加拿大部分地区的标准时间）

East·er·time /ˈiːstətaɪm; *NAmE* ˈiːstərt-/ *noun* [U, C] = EASTER (2)

ˌ**east-north-ˈeast** *noun* [sing.] (*abbr.* **ENE**) the direction at an equal distance between east and north-east 东东北；东北东 ▸ ˌ**east-north-ˈeast** *adv.*

ˌ**east-south-ˈeast** *noun* [sing.] (*abbr.* **ESE**) the direction at an equal distance between east and south-east 东东南；东南东 ▸ ˌ**east-south-ˈeast** *adv.*

east·wards /ˈiːstwədz; *NAmE* -wərdz/ (*also* **east·ward**) *adv.* towards the east 向东；朝东： *to go/look/turn eastwards* 向东走 / 看 / 转 ▸ **east·ward** *adj.* : *in an eastward direction* 向东

easy /ˈiːzi/ *adj., adv.*
■ ***adj.*** (**eas·ier**, **easi·est**) **1** not difficult; done or obtained without a lot of effort or problems 容易的；轻易的；不费力的： *an easy exam/job* 容易的考试 / 工作 ◇ *He didn't make it easy for me to leave.* 他并没有轻易让我离开。◇ *Their house isn't the easiest place to get to.* 他们的房子可不容易到。◇ *vegetables that are easy to grow* 容易种植的蔬菜 ◇ *Several schools are* ***within easy reach*** (= not far away). 几所学校都在附近不远处。◇ *It can't be easy for her, on her own with the children.* 她一个人带着这些孩子绝非易事。◇ *It's easy for you to tell me to keep calm, but you're not in my position.* 你叫我保持冷静当然容易，那是你没到我这份儿上。 OPP **hard** **2** comfortable, relaxed and not worried 舒适的；安逸的；安心的： *I'll agree to anything for an easy life.* 只要有安逸舒适的生活我什么都同意。◇ *I don't feel easy about letting the kids go out alone.* 让孩子们单独出去我不放心。 OPP **uneasy** **3** [only before noun]

open to attack; not able to defend yourself 易受攻击的；无自卫能力的；容易吃亏的： *She's an easy target for their criticisms.* 她很容易成为他们抨击的目标。◇ *The baby fish are easy prey for birds.* 这些小鱼很容易被鸟类捕食。 **4** [only before noun] pleasant and friendly 随和的；平易近人的 **SYN** **easy-going**： *He had a very easy manner.* 他很容易相与。 **OPP** **awkward** **5** [not usually before noun] (*informal, disapproving*) (of women 女人) willing to have sex with many different people 水性杨花；轻浮；放荡 ➲ SEE ALSO EASILY ▶ **easi·ness** *noun* [U]

IDM **as ˌeasy as ˈanything/as ˈpie/as ABˈC/as falling off a ˈlog** (*informal*) very easy or very easily 十分容易；极容易；轻而易举 **ˌeasy ˈmoney** money that you get without having to work very hard for it 来得容易的钱 **ˌeasy on the ˈear/ˈeye** (*informal*) pleasant to listen to or look at 好听 / 好看的；悦耳 / 悦目的 **have an easy ˈtime (of it)** to have no difficulties or problems 日子好过；过得舒适；毫无困难 **I'm ˈeasy** (*informal*) used to say that you do not have a strong opinion when sb has offered you a choice 我随便；我好办；我无所谓： *'Do you want to watch this or the news?' 'Oh, I'm easy. It's up to you.'* "你想看这个节目还是看新闻？" "噢，我随便。你决定吧。" **of easy ˈvirtue** (*old-fashioned*) (of a woman 女人) willing to have sex with anyone 水性杨花；轻浮；放荡 **on ˈeasy street** enjoying a comfortable way of life with plenty of money 环境舒适；生活优裕；安定富足 **take the easy way ˈout** to end a difficult situation by choosing the simplest solution even if it is not the best one 以最简单的方法解决难题；快刀斩乱麻 ➲ MORE AT FREE *adj.*, OPTION *n.*, REACH *n.*, RIDE *n.*, TOUCH *n.*

■ *adv.* (**eas·ier**, **easi·est**) used to tell sb to be careful when doing sth 小心；慢些；轻点： *Easy with that chair—one of its legs is loose.* 小心那椅子，有一条腿松了。

IDM **breathe/rest ˈeasy** to relax and stop worrying 安下心；松口气： *You can rest easy—I'm not going to tell anyone.* 你尽管放心，我不会告诉任何人的。 **be ˌeasier ˌsaid than ˈdone** (*saying*) to be much more difficult to do than to talk about 说时容易做时难；谈何容易： *'Why don't you get yourself a job?' 'That's easier said than done.'* "你怎么不给自己找个工作呢？" "那谈何容易呀。" **ˌeasy ˈcome, ˌeasy ˈgo** (*saying*) used to mean that sb does not care very much about money or possessions especially if they spend it or lose sth 来得容易去得快；易得则易失 **ˌeasy ˈdoes it** (*informal*) used to tell sb to do sth, or move sth, slowly and carefully 小心些；别急；悠着点 **go ˈeasy on sb** (*informal*) used to tell sb to treat a person in a gentle way and not to be too angry or severe 对某人温和（或宽容）些： *Go easy on her—she's having a really hard time at the moment.* 对她宽容些吧，她目前的处境真是很艰难。 **go ˈeasy on/with sth** (*informal*) used to tell sb not to use too much of sth 省着点；少用些；别浪费： *Go easy on the sugar.* 糖要省着点用。 **not come ˈeasy (to sb)** to be difficult for sb to do （对某人来说）并非易事： *Talking about my problems doesn't come easy to me.* 要讲自己的问题，对我来说并不容易。 **ˌstand ˈeasy** used as a command to soldiers who are already STANDING AT EASE to tell them that they can stand in an even more relaxed way （对士兵的命令用语）原地休息 **ˌtake it ˈeasy** (*informal*) used to tell sb not to be worried or angry 别急；沉住气；从容点： *Take it easy! Don't panic.* 沉住气！不要惊慌。 **ˌtake it/things ˈeasy** to relax and avoid working too hard or doing too much 放松；休息；别过分劳累： *The doctor told me to take it easy for a few weeks.* 医生叫我休息几周。

ˈeasy-care *adj.* (of clothes or cloth 衣服或布料) not needing to be ironed after washing 免熨烫的

ˌeasy ˈchair *noun* a large comfortable chair 安乐椅： *to sit in an easy chair* 坐在安乐椅上

ˌeasy-ˈgoing *adj.* relaxed and happy to accept things without worrying or getting angry 悠闲的；随和的；不慌不忙的

ˌeasy ˈlistening *noun* [U] music that is pleasant and relaxing but that some people think is not very interesting （不用费神欣赏的）悦耳乐曲

easy-peasy /ˌiːzi ˈpiːzi/ *adj.* (*BrE, informal*) (used especially by children 尤为儿语) very easy 简单得很；容易极了

eat 🔑 /iːt/ *verb* (**ate** /et; eɪt/, **eaten** /ˈiːtn/) **1** 🔑 [I, T] to put food in your mouth, chew it and swallow it 吃： *I was too nervous to eat.* 我紧张得饭都吃不下。◇ *She doesn't eat sensibly* (= doesn't eat food that is good for her). 她饮食不合理。◇ **~ sth** *I don't eat meat.* 我不吃肉。◇ *Would you like something to eat?* 你想吃点什么吗？◇ *I couldn't eat another thing* (= I have had enough food). 我再也吃不下了。 ➲ COLLOCATIONS AT DIET **2** 🔑 [I] to have a meal 吃饭；用餐： *Where shall we eat tonight?* 我们今晚在哪儿吃饭？◇ *We ate at a pizzeria in town.* 我们在城里一家比萨饼店用餐。

WORDFINDER 联想词： binge, calorie, **diet**, digest, fattening, food, **meal**, **restaurant**, **taste**

IDM **ˌeat sb aˈlive** (*informal*) **1** to criticize or punish sb severely because you are extremely angry with them （对某人极为气愤而）尖锐批评，严厉惩罚，横加指责 **2** to defeat sb completely in an argument, a competition, etc. （辩论、比赛等中）大败某人，完全战胜某人： *The defence lawyers are going to eat you alive tomorrow.* 辩护律师明天一定会彻底打败你们。 **3** [usually passive] (of insects, etc. 昆虫等) to bite sb many times （多次）叮，蜇： *I was being eaten alive by mosquitoes.* 蚊子要把我活活吃了。 **ˌeat, drink and be ˈmerry** (*saying*) said to encourage sb to enjoy life now, while they can, and not to think of the future 行乐要及时 **eat your ˈheart out!** (*informal*) used to compare two things and say that one of them is better （比较两事物）比…还好： *Look at him dance! Eat your heart out, Fred Astaire* (= he dances even better than Fred Astaire). 看看他跳的舞！比弗雷德 · 阿斯泰尔跳得还好。 **eat your ˈheart out (for sb/sth)** (*especially BrE*) to feel very unhappy, especially because you want sb/sth you cannot have （尤因愿望无法达成而）极度不快 **eat humble ˈpie** (*NAmE also* **eat ˈcrow**) to say and show that you are sorry for a mistake that you made 认错；道歉；赔罪 **ORIGIN** From a pun on the old word **umbles**, meaning 'offal', which was considered to be food for poor people. 源自古词 umbles 的双关谐音，意为"内脏"，被认为是穷人的食物。 **eat like a ˈhorse** (*informal*) to eat a lot 吃得很多： *She may be thin, but she eats like a horse.* 她或许是瘦了点，但吃得却很多。 **eat out of your/sb's ˈhand** to trust sb and be willing to do what they say 甘愿听命于某人；顺从某人： *She'll have them eating out of her hand in no time.* 她很快就会让他们俯首帖耳的。 **eat sb out of ˌhouse and ˈhome** (*informal, often humorous*) to eat a lot of sb else's food 把某人吃穷 ➲ MORE LIKE THIS 13, page R26 **eat your ˈwords** to admit that what you said was wrong 收回前言；承认说错 **I could eat a ˈhorse** (*informal*) used to say that you are very hungry 我饿极了 **I'll eat my ˈhat** (*informal*) used to say that you think sth is very unlikely to happen （认为某事不可能发生）我才不信，那才怪，绝不可能： *If she's here on time, I'll eat my hat!* 她要是准时到这儿那才怪咧！ **what's eating him, etc?** (*informal*) used to ask what sb is annoyed or worried about （某人）为何苦恼（或担忧） ➲ MORE AT CAKE *n.*, DOG *n.*

PHR V **ˌeat sth↔aˈway** to reduce or destroy sth gradually 侵蚀；腐蚀；逐渐破坏 **SYN** **erode**： *The coastline is being eaten away year by year.* 海岸线年复一年地被侵蚀着。 **ˌeat aˈway at sth/sb** **1** to reduce or destroy sth gradually 侵蚀；腐蚀；逐渐破坏： *Woodworm had eaten away at the door frame.* 木蛀虫将门框一点点蛀坏了。◇ *His constant criticism ate away at her self-confidence.* 他不断的批评使她逐渐丧失了自信心。 **2** to worry sb over a period of time （一段时间内）使某人苦恼，使某人担心 **ˈeat into sth** **1** to use up a part of sth, especially sb's money or time 消耗，花掉，耗费（尤指金钱或时间）： *Those repair bills have really eaten into my savings.* 那些修理账单已经耗掉我相当一部分积蓄。 **2** to destroy or damage the surface of sth 腐蚀，损坏（物体表面）： *Rust had eaten into the metal.* 这金属已经锈坏。 **ˌeat ˈout** 🔑 to have a meal in a restaurant, etc. rather than at home 上馆子吃饭；在外用餐： *Do you feel like eating out tonight?*

你今晚想下馆子吗？ ˌ**eat ˈup** | ˌ**eat sth↔ˈup** to eat all of sth 吃完；吃光： *Eat up! We've got to go out soon.* 都吃光！我们得马上出去。◇ *Come on. Eat up your potatoes.* 快点儿。把土豆都吃掉。ˌ**eat sb ˈup** [usually passive] to fill sb with a particular emotion so that they cannot think of anything else （情感）使沉迷，使焦虑，使纠缠： *She was eaten up by regrets.* 她后悔不已。ˌ**eat sth↔ˈup** to use sth in large quantities （大量地）耗费，花费，损耗： *Legal costs had eaten up all the savings she had.* 诉讼费耗掉了她所有的积蓄。

eat·able /ˈiːtəbl/ *adj.* good enough to be eaten 可吃的；可食用的 ➲ SEE ALSO EDIBLE

eater /ˈiːtə(r)/ *noun* (usually after an adjective or a noun 通常用于形容词或名词后) a person or an animal that eats a particular thing or in a particular way （以某种方式）吃…的人，吃…的动物： *We're not great meat eaters.* 我们肉吃得不多。◇ *He's a big eater* (= he eats a lot). 他饭量很大。

eat·ery /ˈiːtəri/ (*pl.* **-ies**) *noun* (*informal, especially NAmE*) a restaurant or other place that serves food 餐馆；饮食店

ˈ**eat-in** *adj.* [only before noun] (of a kitchen 厨房) big enough for eating in as well as cooking in 可供用餐的

eat·ing /ˈiːtɪŋ/ *noun* [U] the act of eating sth 吃；饮食： *healthy eating* 有益健康的饮食 IDM SEE PROOF *n.*

ˈ**eating apple** *noun* any type of apple that can be eaten raw 可生吃的苹果 ➲ COMPARE COOKING APPLE ➲ MORE LIKE THIS 9, page R26

ˈ**eating disorder** *noun* an emotional DISORDER that causes eating habits that are not normal, for example ANOREXIA 饮食功能失调（如厌食）

eats /iːts/ *noun* [pl.] (*informal*) food, especially at a party （尤指聚会上的）小吃

eau de cologne /ˌəʊ də kəˈləʊn; *NAmE* ˌoʊ də kəˈloʊn/ *noun* [U] = COLOGNE

eau de toilette /ˌəʊ də twɑːˈlet; *NAmE* ˌoʊ/ *noun* [C, U] PERFUME that contains a lot of water and does not smell very strong 淡香水

eaves /iːvz/ *noun* [pl.] the lower edges of a roof that stick out over the walls 屋檐： *birds nesting under the eaves* 在屋檐下筑巢的鸟 ➲ VISUAL VOCAB PAGE V18

eaves·drop /ˈiːvzdrɒp; *NAmE* -drɑːp/ *verb* (**-pp-**) [I] ~ (**on sb/sth**) to listen secretly to what other people are saying 偷听，窃听（其他人谈话）： *We caught him eavesdropping outside the window.* 我们撞见他正在窗外偷听。▸ **eaves·drop·per** *noun*

eaves·trough /ˈiːvztrɒf; *NAmE* -trɔːf; -trɑːf/ *noun* (*CanE*) = GUTTER (1)

eBay™ /ˈiːbeɪ/ *noun* [U] a website on the Internet where people can AUCTION goods (= sell them to the person who offers the most money for them) （电子湾）拍卖网站： *He buys rare baseball cards on eBay.* 他从拍卖网站上购买珍稀的棒球卡。▸ **eBay** *verb* ~ **sth**

ebb /eb/ *noun, verb*

■ *noun* **the ebb** [usually sing.] the period of time when the sea flows away from the land 落潮；退潮： *the ebb tide* 退潮

IDM **the** ˌ**ebb and** ˈ**flow** (**of sth/sb**) the repeated, often regular, movement from one state to another; the repeated change in level, numbers or amount 涨落；盛衰；起伏；消长： *the ebb and flow of the seasons* 四时更迭 ◇ *She sat in silence enjoying the ebb and flow of conversation.* 她默默地坐在那儿，饶有兴致地听着时高时低的谈话声。➲ MORE AT LOW *adj.*

■ *verb* **1** [I] (*formal*) (of the TIDE in the sea 海潮) to move away from the land 退；落 SYN **go out** OPP **flow** **2** [I] ~ (**away**) to become gradually weaker or less 衰弱；衰退；减退 SYN **decrease**: *The pain was ebbing.* 疼痛逐渐减轻了。◇ *As night fell, our enthusiasm began to ebb away.* 我们的热情随着夜晚的降临而渐渐低落下来。

ˈ**e-bike** *noun* a type of bicycle that you can ride by pushing the PEDALS with your feet or by using a small electric motor 电动自行车；电动脚踏车

Ebola fever /iːˈbəʊlə fiːvə(r); əˈbəʊlə; *NAmE* -ˈboʊlə fiːvər/ *noun* [U] a very serious disease, caused by a virus, which causes internal parts of the body to lose blood and usually ends in death 埃博拉热病（致命出血热，由病毒引起）

Eb·on·ics /eˈbɒnɪks; *NAmE* -ˈbɑːn-/ *noun* [U] a type of English spoken by many African Americans that has been considered by some people to be a separate language 乌语，美国黑人英语（有些人认为是一种语言而非方言）

ebony /ˈebəni/ *noun, adj.*

■ *noun* [U] the hard black wood of various tropical trees 乌木；黑檀： *an ebony carving* 一件乌木雕刻

■ *adj.* black in colour 乌黑的： *ebony skin* 黝黑的皮肤

ˈ**e-book** *noun* a book that is displayed on a computer screen or on an electronic device that is held in the hand, instead of being printed on paper 电子书 ➲ COMPARE P-BOOK

ebul·li·ent /ɪˈbʌliənt; -ˈbʊl-/ *adj.* (*formal*) full of confidence, energy and good humour 充满自信的；精力充沛的；热情洋溢的： *The Prime Minister was in ebullient mood.* 首相兴致勃勃。▸ **ebul·li·ence** /-əns/ *noun* [U] **ebul·li·ent·ly** *adv.*

ˈ**e-card** *noun* a message that is like a card that you send to sb on their birthday, etc., but that is displayed on a computer screen instead of being printed on paper and usually opened through a HYPERLINK in an email 电子贺卡

ˈ**e-cash** *noun* [U] a system for sending and receiving payments using the Internet 电子现金（互联网付费和收费系统）

ec·cen·tric /ɪkˈsentrɪk/ *adj.* considered by other people to be strange or unusual 古怪的；异乎寻常的： *eccentric behaviour/clothes* 古怪的行为；奇装异服 ◇ *an eccentric aunt* 怪僻的大姊 ➲ WORDFINDER NOTE AT BEHAVIOUR ▸ **ec·cen·tric** *noun*: *Most people considered him a harmless eccentric.* 多数人都认为他是一个无伤大雅的怪人。**ec·cen·tric·al·ly** /-kli/ *adv.*

ec·cen·tri·city /ˌeksenˈtrɪsəti/ (*pl.* **-ies**) *noun* **1** [U] behaviour that people think is strange or unusual; the quality of being unusual and different from other people 古怪行为；反常： *As a teacher, she had a reputation for eccentricity.* 她身为教师，以行为古怪而出名。◇ *Arthur was noted for the eccentricity of his clothes.* 阿瑟以穿奇装异服而闻名。 **2** [C, usually pl.] an unusual act or habit 怪行；怪癖： *We all have our little eccentricities.* 我们都有些小怪癖。

Ec·cles cake /ˈeklz keɪk/ *noun* a small flat cake made from PASTRY with RAISINS inside 埃克尔斯葡萄干小饼

ec·cle·si·as·tic /ɪˌkliːziˈæstɪk/ *noun* (*formal*) a priest or minister in the Christian Church （基督教）教士，圣职人员

ec·cle·si·as·tic·al /ɪˌkliːziˈæstɪkl/ *adj.* [usually before noun] connected with the Christian Church 基督教会的；与基督教会有关的

ECG /ˌiː siː ˈdʒiː/ (*NAmE also* **EKG**) *noun* the abbreviation for 'electrocardiogram' (a medical test that measures and records electrical activity of the heart) 心电图，心动电流图（全写为 electrocardiogram）

ech·elon /ˈeʃəlɒn; *NAmE* -lɑːn/ *noun* **1** [usually pl.] a rank or position of authority in an organization or a society 职权的等级；阶层： *the lower/upper/top/higher echelons of the Civil Service* 公务员的低层 / 上层 / 最高层 / 高层 **2** an arrangement of soldiers, planes, etc. in which each one is behind and to the side of the one in front （士兵、飞机等的）梯形编队，梯队

ech·idna /ɪˈkɪdnə/ (*also* ˌ**spiny ˈanteater**) *noun* an Australasian animal which has a long nose, sharp CLAWS on its feet, and sharp SPINES on its body, and which eats insects 针鼹，针食蚁兽（澳大拉西亚长吻食蚁兽）

ech·in·acea /ˌekɪˈneɪsiə; -ʃə/ *noun* [U, C] a plant similar to a DAISY, that is thought to help the body heal itself and fight infection 松果菊属植物，紫锥菊（类似雏菊，据信有助于身体自愈及抗感染）

echo /ˈekəʊ; *NAmE* ˈekoʊ/ *noun, verb*

■ ***noun*** (*pl.* **-oes**) **1** the reflecting of sound off a wall or inside a confined space so that a noise appears to be repeated; a sound that is reflected back in this way 回响；回声；回音：*There was an echo on the phone and I couldn't hear clearly.* 电话里有回音，我听不清楚。◇ *The hills sent back a faint echo.* 座座山丘传来微弱的回声。◇ *the echo of footsteps running down the corridor* 沿走廊跑的脚步回声 **2** the fact of an idea, event, etc. being like another and reminding you of it; sth that reminds you of sth else 映现；暗示；启示；反响：*Yesterday's crash has grim echoes of previous disasters.* 昨天的撞车事故使人想起之前那些令人痛心的灾难。 **3** an opinion or attitude that agrees with or repeats one already expressed or thought 共鸣；附和；重复：*His words were an echo of what she had heard many times before.* 他的话她以往听过许多次。◇ *The speech* ***found an echo*** *in the hearts of many of the audience* (= they agreed with it). 这次演讲在许多听众的心中引起共鸣。

■ ***verb*** (**echoes, echo·ing, echoed, echoed**) **1** [I] if a sound echoes, it is reflected off a wall, the side of a mountain, etc. so that you can hear it again 回响；回荡 **SYN** **reverberate**：*Her footsteps echoed in the empty room.* 她的脚步声在空荡荡的屋子里回响着。◇ *The gunshot echoed through the forest.* 枪炮声在林中回荡。 **2** [I, T] to send back and repeat a sound; to be full of a sound 发出回声；产生回响；充满回声 **SYN** **reverberate**：*The whole house echoed.* 整个房子充满回声。◇ **~ to/with sth** *The street echoed with the cries of children.* 街上回荡着孩子的哭声。◇ **~ sth** (**back**) *The valley echoed back his voice.* 山谷里回荡着他的声音。 **3** [T] **~ sth** to repeat an idea or opinion because you agree with it 重复，附和（想法或看法）：*This is a view echoed by many on the right of the party.* 这是党内许多右翼分子都重复过的观点。 **4** [T] **+ speech | ~ sth** to repeat what sb else has just said, especially because you find it surprising （尤因感到意外而）重复…话，模仿：*'He's gone!' Viv echoed.* "他去了！" 维夫重复道。

echo·loca·tion /ˌekəʊləʊˈkeɪʃn; *NAmE* ˌekoʊloʊ-/ *noun* [U] the use of reflected sound waves for finding things, especially by creatures such as DOLPHINS and BATS （尤指海豚、蝙蝠等动物的）回声定位

echt /ext/ *adj.* (*from German*) genuine and typical 真正的；典型的；十足的 ▶ **echt** *adv.*：*echt Viennese cream cakes* 真正的维也纳奶油蛋糕

ˈ**e-cigarette** *noun* = ELECTRONIC CIGARETTE

eclair /ɪˈkleə(r); *NAmE* ɪˈkler/ *noun* a long thin cake for one person, made of light PASTRY, filled with cream and usually with chocolate on top （巧克力）长形泡芙；奶油松饼；奶油酥饼

eclamp·sia /ɪˈklæmpsiə/ *noun* [U] a condition in which a pregnant woman has high blood pressure and CONVULSIONS, which can be dangerous to the woman and the baby 子痫（怀孕引起的高血压和惊厥，对产妇母子造成威胁） ➲ COMPARE PRE-ECLAMPSIA

eclec·tic /ɪˈklektɪk/ *adj.* (*formal*) not following one style or set of ideas but choosing from or using a wide variety 不拘一格的；兼收并蓄的：*She has very eclectic tastes in literature.* 她在文学方面的兴趣非常广泛。 ▶ **eclec·tic·al·ly** /-tɪkli/ *adv.* **eclec·ti·cism** /ɪˈklektɪsɪzəm/ *noun* [U]

eclipse /ɪˈklɪps/ *noun, verb*

■ ***noun*** **1** [C] an occasion when the moon passes between the earth and the sun so that you cannot see all or part of the sun for a time; an occasion when the earth passes between the moon and the sun so that you cannot see all or part of the moon for a time 日食；月食：*an eclipse of the sun/moon* 日食；月食 ◇ *a* ***total/partial*** *eclipse* 全食；偏食 ➲ WORDFINDER NOTE AT SUN **2** [sing., U] a loss of importance, power, etc. especially because sb/sth else has become more important, powerful, etc. （重要性、权势等的）丧失，黯然失色，暗淡：*The election result marked the eclipse of the right wing.* 选举结果标志着右翼的失势。◇ *Her work was* ***in eclipse*** *for most of the 20th century.* 她的作品在 20 世纪大部分时间里都湮没无闻。

■ ***verb*** **1** [often passive] **~ sth** (of the moon, the earth, etc. 月球、地球等) to cause an eclipse 遮住…的光 **2** **~ sb/sth** to make sb/sth seem dull or unimportant by comparison 使失色；使相形见绌；使丧失重要性 **SYN** **outshine, overshadow**：*Though a talented player, he was completely eclipsed by his brother.* 他虽是个天才运动员，但与他的哥哥相比就黯然失色了。

eco- /ˈiːkəʊ; *NAmE* ˈiːkoʊ/ *combining form* (in nouns, adjectives and adverbs 构成名词、形容词和副词) connected with the environment 环境的；生态的：*eco-friendly* 环保的 ◇ *eco-warriors* (= people who protest about damage to the environment) 生态保护斗士 ◇ *eco-terrorism* (= the use of force or violent action in order to protest about damage to the environment) 过激环保行为（用暴力行动来抗议对环境的破坏）

ˈ**eco-chic** *adj.* (of design or clothing) fashionable and designed or produced with concern for the environment （设计或服装）环保时尚的，生态时尚的 ▶ **eco-chic** *noun* [U]

ˌ**eco-ˈfriend·ly** *adj.* not harmful to the environment 对环境无害的；环保的：*eco-friendly products* 环保型产品

E. coli /ˌiː ˈkəʊlaɪ; *NAmE* ˈkoʊ-/ *noun* [U] a type of bacteria that lives inside humans and some animals, some forms of which can cause FOOD POISONING 大肠杆菌

eco·logic·al /ˌiːkəˈlɒdʒɪkl; *NAmE* -ˈlɑːdʒ-/ *adj.* **1** connected with the relation of plants and living creatures to each other and to their environment 生态的；生态学的：*We risk upsetting the ecological balance of the area.* 我们有可能破坏这个地区的生态平衡。◇ *an ecological disaster* (= one that alters the whole balance of ecology in an area) 生态灾难 **2** interested in and concerned about the ecology of a place 关注生态环境的；主张生态保护的：*the ecological movement* 生态保护运动 ▶ **eco·logic·al·ly** /-kli/ *adv.*：*The system is both practical and ecologically* ***sound***. 这个系统不但切合实际，从生态学观点来看也是合理的。

ecoˌlogical ˈfootprint *noun* a measure of the amount of the earth's resources used by a person or a population that lives in a particular way 生态足迹（测定个人或群体生活所消耗地球资源的指标）：*the ecological footprint of the average Canadian* 普通加拿大人的生态足迹

ecolo·gist /iˈkɒlədʒɪst; *NAmE* iˈkɑːl-/ *noun* **1** a scientist who studies ecology 生态学家 **2** a person who is interested in ecology and believes the environment should be protected 生态保护论者

ecol·ogy /iˈkɒlədʒi; *NAmE* iˈkɑːl-/ *noun* [U] the relation of plants and living creatures to each other and to their environment; the study of this 生态；生态学：***plant/animal/human ecology*** 植物 / 动物 / 人类生态学 ◇ *the ecology movement* 生态保护运动 ◇ *Oil pollution could damage the* ***fragile ecology*** *of the coral reefs.* 石油污染可能破坏珊瑚礁脆弱的生态环境。

eco·nom·ic 🔑 **AW** /ˌiːkəˈnɒmɪk; ˌekə-; *NAmE* -ˈnɑːm-/ *adj.* **1** 🔑 [only before noun] connected with the trade, industry and development of wealth of a country, an area or a society 经济的；经济上的；经济学的：*social, economic and political issues* 社会、经济和政治问题 ◇ ***economic growth/cooperation/development/reform*** 经济增长 / 合作 / 发展 / 改革 ◇ *the government's economic policy*

政府的经济政策 ◇ *economic history* 经济史 ◇ *the current economic climate* 目前的经济形势 **2** (of a process, a business or an activity 工序、业务或活动) producing enough profit to continue 有利可图的；可赚钱的；合算的 **SYN** **profitable** **OPP** **uneconomic** ➲ SYNONYMS AT SUCCESSFUL

▼ **SYNONYMS** 同义词辨析

economic

financial • commercial • monetary • budgetary

These words all describe activities or situations that are connected with the use of money, especially by a business or country. 以上各词尤用于企业或国家的经济活动或状况。

economic connected with the trade, industry and development of wealth of a country, an area or a society 指国家、地区或社会经济的、经济上的、经济学的： *This book deals with the social, economic and political issues of the period.* 这本书论及了那个时期的社会、经济和政治问题。

financial connected with money and finance 指财政的、财务的、金融的： *She had got into financial difficulties.* 她陷入了财务困境。◇ *Tokyo is a major financial centre.* 东京是主要的金融中心。

commercial connected with the buying and selling of goods and services 指贸易的、商业的

monetary (*formal* or *finance*) connected with money, especially all the money in a country 指货币的、钱的，尤指一国的货币： *closer European monetary union* 更为紧密的欧洲货币联盟

budgetary (*finance*) connected with a budget (= the money available or a plan of how it will be spent) 指财政预算的

PATTERNS
- economic/financial/commercial/monetary/budgetary **affairs/decisions**
- the economic/financial/commercial/budgetary **climate**
- the economic/financial/commercial **side** of sth
- a(n) economic/financial/commercial **centre**

eco·nom·ic·al AW /ˌiːkəˈnɒmɪkl; ˌekə-; *NAmE* -ˈnɑːm-/ *adj.* **1** providing good service or value in relation to the amount of time or money spent 经济的；实惠的： *an economical car to run* (= one that does not use too much petrol/gas) 节油型汽车 ◇ *It would be more economical to buy the bigger size.* 买尺寸大点的更实惠。 **OPP** **uneconomical** **2** using no more of sth than is necessary 节俭的；节约的；简洁的： *an economical use of space* 节约利用空间 ◇ *an economical prose style* (= one that uses no unnecessary words) 简练的散文文体 **OPP** **uneconomical**

▼ **WHICH WORD?** 词语辨析

economic / economical

- **Economic** means 'connected with the economy of a country or an area, or with the money that a society or an individual has'. * economic 意为与国家、地区、社会或个人经济有关的： *the government's economic policy* 政府的经济政策 ◇ *the economic aspects of having children* 生育孩子在经济方面的问题

➲ SEE ALSO ECONOMY (1)

- **Economical** means 'spending money or using something in a careful way that avoids waste'. * economical 意为经济实惠的、节俭的、节约的： *It is usually economical to buy washing powder in large quantities.* 大量购买洗衣粉通常要省钱些。

➲ SEE ALSO ECONOMY (3)

3 not spending more money than necessary 精打细算的；省钱的 **SYN** **frugal**: *He was economical in all areas of his life.* 他在生活的各个方面都精打细算。

IDM **economical with the 'truth** a way of saying that sb has left out some important facts, when you do not want to say that they are lying 没把实话全讲出来（婉指某人隐瞒了一些重要事实）

eco·nom·ic·al·ly AW /ˌiːkəˈnɒmɪkli; ˌekə-; *NAmE* -ˈnɑːm-/ *adv.* **1** in a way connected with the trade, industry and development of wealth of a country, an area or a society 在经济上；在经济学上： *The factory is no longer economically viable.* 这家工厂在经济上已经维持不下去了。◇ *Economically, the centre of Spain has lost its dominant role.* 西班牙中部在经济上已失去了其主导地位。 ◇ *the* ***economically active/inactive*** *population* (= those who are employed or available for work/those who are not) 经济活动/非经济活动人口 **2** in a way that provides good service or value in relation to the amount of time or money spent 经济地；实惠地： *I'll do the job as economically as possible.* 我一定尽可能高效率地工作。 **3** in a way that uses no more of sth than is necessary 节俭地；节约地；节省地；简洁地： *The design is intended to use space as economically as possible.* 这个设计方案是为了尽可能节省空间。◇ *She writes elegantly and economically.* 她写作典雅而简练。

ˌeconomic ˈmigrant *noun* a person who moves from their own country to a new country in order to find work or have a better standard of living 经济移民（以找工作或寻求更高生活水平为目的）： *They claimed they were political refugees and not economic migrants.* 他们宣称自己是政治难民，不是经济移民。

eco·nom·ics AW /ˌiːkəˈnɒmɪks; ˌekə-; *NAmE* -ˈnɑːm-/ *noun* **1** [U] the study of how a society organizes its money, trade and industry 经济学： *He studied politics and economics at Yale.* 他曾在耶鲁大学学习政治学和经济学。◇ *Keynesian/Marxist economics* 凯恩斯主义/马克思主义经济学 ➲ SEE ALSO HOME ECONOMICS **2** [pl., U] the way in which money influences, or is organized within, an area of business or society 经济情况；经济因素；经济意义： *The economics of the project are very encouraging.* 这项工程的经济情况非常令人鼓舞。

econo·mist AW /ɪˈkɒnəmɪst; *NAmE* ɪˈkɑːn-/ *noun* a person who studies or writes about economics 经济学家；经济专家

econo·mize (*BrE also* **-ise**) /ɪˈkɒnəmaɪz; *NAmE* ɪˈkɑːn-/ *verb* [I] ~ (**on sth**) to use less money, time, etc. than you normally use 节省；节约；节俭： *Old people often try to economize on heating, thus endangering their health.* 老年人常常想方设法节约用暖气，结果损害了他们的健康。 ➲ SYNONYMS AT SAVE

econ·omy AW /ɪˈkɒnəmi; *NAmE* ɪˈkɑːn-/ *noun* (*pl.* **-ies**) **1** (*often* **the economy**) [C] the relationship between production, trade and the supply of money in a particular country or region 经济；经济情况；经济结构： *The economy is in recession.* 经济处于衰退之中。◇ *the world economy* 世界经济 ◇ *a market economy* (= one in which the price is fixed according to both cost and demand) 市场经济 ➲ WORDFINDER NOTE AT MONEY **2** [C] a country, when you are thinking about its economic system （就经济体制而言）国家；经济制度： *Ireland was one of the fastest-growing economies in Western Europe in the 1990s.* 在20世纪90年代爱尔兰是西欧经济发展最快的国家之一。 **3** [C, U] the use of the time, money, etc. that is available in a way that avoids waste 节约；节省；节俭： *We need to make substantial economies.* 我们需要厉行节约。 ◇ *It's a* ***false economy*** *to buy cheap clothes* (= it seems cheaper but it is not really since they do not last very long). 买便宜衣服实际上划不来。 ◇ *She writes with a great economy of words* (= using only the necessary words). 她写作文字非常简练。◇ (*BrE*) *We're on an* ***economy drive*** *at home* (= trying to avoid waste and spend as little money as possible). 我们正在家里实行勤俭节约。 ◇

*Buy the large **economy pack*** (= the one that gives you better value for money). 买大包的实惠装吧。◇ *to fly **economy** (**class**)* (= by the cheapest class of air travel) 乘坐经济舱 ◇ *an economy fare* (= the cheapest) 经济舱票价

e'conomy class syndrome *noun* [U] the fact of a person suffering from DEEP VEIN THROMBOSIS after they have travelled on a plane. This condition is thought to be more common among people who travel in the cheapest seats because they do not have space to move their legs much. 经济舱综合征，经济舱症候群（乘坐飞机导致深静脉血栓形成，被认为在经济舱乘客中更常见）

eco·sys·tem /'iːkəʊsɪstəm; *NAmE* 'iːkoʊ-/ *noun* all the plants and living creatures in a particular area considered in relation to their physical environment 生态系统 ➲ COLLOCATIONS AT ENVIRONMENT

eco·ter·ror·ism /'iːkəʊterərɪzəm; *NAmE* 'iːkoʊ-/ *noun* [U] **1** violent activities which are done in order to draw attention to issues relating to the environment 过激环保行为（为引起对环境问题的关注而实施暴力行动）**2** deliberate damage to the environment, done in order to draw attention to a political issue 生态恐怖主义（为引起对某政治问题的关注而蓄意破坏环境）▶ **eco·ter·ror·ist** *noun*

eco·tour·ism /'iːkəʊtʊərɪzəm; -tɔːr-; *NAmE* 'iːkoʊtʊr-/ *noun* [U] organized holidays/vacations that are designed so that the tourists damage the environment as little as possible, especially when some of the money they pay is used to protect the local environment and animals 生态旅游 ▶ **eco·tour·ist** /'iːkəʊtʊərɪst; -tɔːr-; *NAmE* 'iːkoʊtʊr-/ *noun*

eco·type /'iːkəʊtaɪp; *NAmE* 'iːkoʊ-/ *noun* (*biology* 生) the type or race of a plant or an animal that has adapted to live in particular local conditions 生态型（已适应特定局部条件的植物或动物种类）

ecru /'eɪkruː; 'ekruː/ *noun* a light brown or cream colour 淡褐色；米色

ec·stasy /'ekstəsi/ *noun* (*pl.* **-ies**) **1** [U, C] a feeling or state of very great happiness 狂喜；陶醉；入迷 SYN **bliss** **2 Ecstasy** [U] (*abbr.* **E**) an illegal drug, taken especially by young people at parties, clubs, etc. 摇头丸；迷幻药

ec·stat·ic /ɪk'stætɪk/ *adj.* very happy, excited and enthusiastic; feeling or showing great enthusiasm 狂喜的；热情极高的 SYN **delighted**: *Sally was ecstatic about her new job.* 萨莉对她的新工作高兴得发狂。◇ ***ecstatic applause/praise/reviews*** 狂热的鼓掌 / 赞美 / 评论 ➲ SYNONYMS AT EXCITED ▶ **ec·stat·ic·al·ly** /-kli/ *adv.*

-ec·tomy *combining form* (in nouns 构成名词) a medical operation in which part of the body is removed 切除术；截除：*appendectomy* (= removal of the APPENDIX) 阑尾切除术

ec·top·ic /ek'tɒpɪk; *NAmE* -'tɑːp-/ *adj.* (*medical* 医) in an **ectopic** PREGNANCY, the baby starts to develop outside the mother's WOMB （妊娠）异位的，子宫外的

ecto·plasm /'ektəʊplæzəm; *NAmE* 'ektoʊ-/ *noun* [U] **1** (*biology* 生, *old-fashioned*) the outer layer of the jelly-like substance inside cells 外质（细胞的外胚层质）➲ COMPARE ENDOPLASM **2** a substance which is said to come from the body of sb who is communicating with the spirit of a dead person, allowing the spirit to have a form 外质（据信为通灵者身上渗出的物质，可令亡灵成形）

ecu·men·ic·al /ˌiːkjuː'menɪkl; ˌekjuː-/ *adj.* involving or uniting members of different branches of the Christian Church 基督宗教合一的；大公的

ecu·men·ism /ɪ'kjuːmənɪzəm/ *noun* [U] the principle or aim of uniting different branches of the Christian Church （基督教）合一运动精神，大公主义

ec·zema /'eksmə; *NAmE* ɪg'ziːmə/ *noun* [U] a skin condition in which areas of skin become red, rough and ITCHY 湿疹

▼ COLLOCATIONS 词语搭配

The economy 经济

Managing the economy 管理经济

- **handle/run/manage** the economy 管理经济
- **boost** investment/spending/employment/growth 促进投资 / 支出 / 就业 / 增长速度
- **stimulate** demand/the economy/industry 刺激需求 / 经济 / 工业
- **cut/reduce** investment/spending/borrowing 削减投资 / 支出 / 借贷
- **reduce/curb/control/keep down** inflation 减少 / 遏制通货膨胀
- **create/fuel** growth/demand/a boom/a bubble 创造 / 刺激增长 / 需求 / 繁荣 / 泡沫
- **encourage/foster/promote/stimulate/stifle** innovation/competition 鼓励 / 促进 / 刺激 / 抑制创新 / 竞争
- **encourage/work with/compete with** the private sector 鼓励私营部门；与私营部门合作 / 竞争
- **increase/boost/promote** US/agricultural exports 增加 / 促进美国 / 农业出口
- **ban/restrict/block** cheap/foreign imports 禁止 / 限制 / 阻止廉价 / 国外进口产品
- the economy **grows/expands/shrinks/contracts/slows (down)/recovers/improves/is booming** 经济增长 / 扩张 / 收缩 / 萎缩 / 放缓 / 复苏 / 改善 / 繁荣
- **enjoy** an economic/housing/property boom 享受经济 / 住房 / 房地产的繁荣期

Economic problems 经济问题

- **push up/drive up** prices/costs/inflation 抬高价格 / 成本；加剧通货膨胀
- **damage/hurt/destroy** industry/the economy 破坏工业 / 经济
- **cause/lead to/go into/avoid/escape** recession 引起 / 导致 / 进入 / 避开经济衰退
- **experience/suffer** a recession/downturn 经历 / 遭受经济衰退
- **fight/combat** inflation/deflation/unemployment 抵抗通货膨胀 / 通货紧缩 / 失业
- **cause/create** inflation/poverty/unemployment 导致 / 造成通货膨胀 / 贫穷 / 失业
- **create/burst** a housing/stock market bubble 造成 / 引爆住房 / 股票市场泡沫
- **cause/trigger** a stock market crash/the collapse of the banking system 引起股市崩盘 / 银行系统崩溃
- **face/be plunged into** a financial/an economic crisis 面临 / 陷入财政 / 经济危机
- **be caught in/experience** cycles of boom and bust 陷入 / 经历周期性繁荣与萧条

Public finance 公共财政

- **cut/reduce/slash/increase/double** the defence/(*especially US*) defense/education/aid budget 削减 / 大幅削减 / 增加 / 加倍国防 / 教育 / 援助预算
- **increase/boost/slash/cut** public spending 增加 / 大幅削减 / 削减公共支出
- **increase/put up/raise/cut/lower/reduce** taxes 提高 / 降低税收
- **raise/cut/lower/reduce** interest rates 提高 / 降低利率
- **ease/loosen/tighten** monetary policy 放宽 / 收紧货币政策
- **balance** the (state/federal) budget 平衡（州 / 联邦）预算
- **achieve/maintain** a balanced budget 达到 / 保持预算平衡
- **run** a ($4 trillion) budget deficit/surplus 有（4 万亿美元的）预算赤字 / 盈余

➲ COLLOCATIONS AT POLITICS, VOTE

---

ed. (*also* **Ed.**) *abbr.* (in writing 书写形式) EDITED (BY), EDITION, EDITOR (由…) 编纂；版本；编者：*'Eighteenth Century Women Poets', Ed. Lonsdale* 朗斯代尔主编的《十八世纪女诗人》◇ *7th ed.* 第七版

-ed, **-d** *suffix* **1** (in adjectives 构成形容词) having; having the characteristics of 有…的；有…特征的；以…为特征的：*talented* 天才的 ◇ *bearded* 长胡须的 ◇ *diseased* 患病的 **2** (makes the past tense and past participle of regular verbs 构成规则动词的过去式和过去分词)：*hated* 恨 ◇ *walked* 走路 ◇ *loved* 爱

Edam /ˈiːdæm/ *noun* [U, C] a type of round yellow Dutch cheese that is covered with red WAX 埃丹干酪（荷兰球形干酪，色黄，外涂红蜡）

eddy /ˈedi/ *noun, verb*

■ ***noun*** (*pl.* **-ies**) a movement of air, dust or water in a circle （空气、灰尘或水的）旋涡，涡流

■ ***verb*** (**ed·dies**, **eddy·ing**, **ed·died**, **ed·died**) [I] (of air, dust, water, etc. 空气、灰尘、水等) to move around in a circle 起旋涡；旋转 SYN **swirl**：*The waves swirled and eddied around the rocks.* 波浪翻滚着在岩石周围打漩。

edema (*NAmE*) (*BrE* **oe·dema**) /ɪˈdiːmə/ *noun* [U] (*medical* 医) a condition in which liquid collects in the spaces inside the body and makes it swell 水肿

Eden /ˈiːdn/ (*also* **the ˌGarden of ˈEden**) *noun* [sing.] (in the Bible 《圣经》) the beautiful garden where Adam and Eve, the first humans, lived before they did sth God had told them not to and were sent away, often seen as a place of happiness and INNOCENCE 伊甸园

edge /edʒ/ *noun, verb*

■ ***noun*** **1** [C] the outside limit of an object, a surface or an area; the part furthest from the centre 边；边缘；边线；边沿：*He stood **on the edge of** the cliff.* 他站在悬崖边上。◇ *a big house **on/at the edge of town*** 城边的一栋大房子 ◇ *Don't put that glass so near the edge of the table.* 别把那只玻璃杯放在离桌边太近的地方。◇ *I sat down at the water's edge.* 我在水边坐了下来。◇ *Stand the coin on its edge.* 让硬币竖起来。➲ SEE ALSO LEADING EDGE **2** [C] the sharp part of a blade, knife or SWORD that is used for cutting 刀口；刀刃；利刃：*Be careful—it has a sharp edge.* 小心点，这刀刃很锋利。➲ VISUAL VOCAB PAGE V27 ➲ SEE ALSO KNIFE-EDGE **3** (*usually* **the edge**) [sing.] the point at which sth, especially sth bad, may begin to happen （尤指灾难的）边缘 SYN **brink, verge**：*They had brought the country to the edge of disaster.* 他们使国家濒临灾难。➲ SEE ALSO CUTTING EDGE **4** [sing.] a slight advantage over sb/sth （微弱的）优势：*The company needs to improve its **competitive edge**.* 公司需要提高它的竞争力。◇ **~ on/over sb/sth** *They have the edge on us.* 他们略胜我们一筹。**5** [sing.] a strong, often exciting, quality 锐利；敏锐；尖锐：*Her show now has a hard political edge to it.* 她现在的表演具有强烈的政治性。**6** [sing.] a sharp tone of voice, often showing anger 尖刻的声调；愤怒的语气：*He did his best to remain calm, but there was a distinct edge to his voice.* 尽管他竭力保持镇静，话音里仍明显带有怒气。**7 -edged** (in adjectives 构成形容词) having the type of edge or edges mentioned 有…边的；有…棱的；有…锋的：*a lace-edged handkerchief* 有网眼花边的手绢 ➲ SEE ALSO GILT-EDGED

IDM **be on ˈedge** to be nervous, excited or bad-tempered 紧张不安；激动；烦躁 ➲ SYNONYMS AT NERVOUS **on the edge of your ˈseat** very excited and giving your full attention to sth 异常兴奋；极为激动；有浓厚兴趣：*The game had the crowd on the edge of their seats.* 这场比赛使观众兴奋不已。**take the ˈedge off sth** to make sth less strong, less bad, etc. 减弱；使变钝；挫伤…的锐气：*The sandwich took the edge off my appetite.* 这份三明治使我食欲大减。➲ MORE AT FRAY *v.*, RAZOR, ROUGH *adj.*, TEETER, TOOTH

■ ***verb*** **1** [I, T] to move or to move sth slowly and carefully in a particular direction （使）徐徐移动，渐渐移动：**+ adv./prep.** *She edged a little closer to me.* 她慢慢地向我靠近了一些。◇ *I edged nervously past the dog.* 我紧张地从狗旁边慢慢走过去。◇ **~ sth + adv./prep.** *Emily edged her chair forward.* 埃米莉把椅子慢慢地向前挪动。**2** [T, usually passive] **~ sth (with/in sth)** to put sth around the edge of sth 给…加边：*The handkerchief is edged with lace.* 这条手绢镶着网眼花边。**3** [I] **+ adv./prep.** to increase or decrease slightly 略为增加（或减少）：*Prices edged up 2% in the year to December.* 到十二月为止的年度价格上涨了2%。

PHR V **ˌedge sb/sth↔ˈout (of sth)** to move sb from their position or job gradually, especially when they are not fully aware of what is happening 逐渐将…排挤出：*She was edged out of the company by the new director.* 新上任的经理一步步把她排挤出了公司。

ˌedge ˈcity *noun* (*NAmE*) a large area of buildings on the edge of a city, usually near a main road 边缘城市，卫星城（通常位于主干公路旁）

edge·ways /ˈedʒweɪz/ (*BrE*) (*NAmE* **edge·wise** /-waɪz/) *adv.* with the edge upwards or forwards; on one side 边向上（或向前）；侧着；斜着：*You'll only get the desk through the door if you turn it edgeways.* 你要把书桌侧着才能搬过这道门。IDM SEE WORD *n.*

edging /ˈedʒɪŋ/ *noun* [U, C] something that forms the border or edge of sth, added to make it more attractive, etc. 边缘；饰边；缘饰

edgy /ˈedʒi/ *adj.* (*informal*) (**edgi·er**, **edgi·est**) **1** nervous, especially about what might happen 紧张的；烦躁不安的：*She's been very edgy lately.* 她近来一直烦躁不安。◇ *After the recent unrest there is an edgy calm in the capital.* 最近的骚乱之后，首都平静得令人不安。**2** (of a film/movie, book, piece of music, etc. 电影、书籍、乐曲等) having a sharp exciting quality 紧张的；激动人心的：*a clever, edgy film* 一部情节巧妙、扣人心弦的电影 ▶ **edgi·ly** *adv.*：*'I'm not sure I can make it tomorrow,' he said edgily.* "我不敢肯定明天能到。"他紧张不安地说。**edgi·ness** *noun* [U, sing.]

EDI /ˌiː diː ˈaɪ/ *noun* [U] (*computing* 计) the abbreviation for 'electronic data interchange' (a system that is used in business for sending information between different companies' computer systems) 电子数据交换（全写为electronic data interchange，公司间局域网信息传送系统）

ed·ible /ˈedəbl/ *adj.* fit or suitable to be eaten; not poisonous 适宜食用的；（无毒而）可以吃的：*The food at the hotel was barely edible.* 这家旅馆的食物简直不能入口。◇ *edible fungi/snails/flowers* 可食用的真菌 / 蜗牛 / 花

edict /ˈiːdɪkt/ *noun* [U, C] (*formal*) an official order or statement given by sb in authority 法令；命令；敕令 SYN **decree**

edi·fi·ca·tion /ˌedɪfɪˈkeɪʃn/ *noun* [U] (*formal* or *humorous*) the improvement of sb's mind or character 教化；启迪；陶冶：*The books were intended for the edification of the masses.* 这些书旨在教化民众。

edi·fice /ˈedɪfɪs/ *noun* (*formal*) a large impressive building 大厦；宏伟建筑：*an imposing edifice* 一座宏伟的建筑 ◇ (*figurative*) *an edifice of lies* 谎话连篇

edify /ˈedɪfaɪ/ *verb* (**edi·fies**, **edify·ing**, **edi·fied**, **edi·fied**) [I, T] **~ sb** (*formal*) to improve people's minds or characters by teaching them about sth 教化；启迪；教诲

edify·ing /ˈedɪfaɪɪŋ/ *adj.* (*formal* or *humorous*) likely to improve your mind or your character 启迪的；有启发意义的；起教化作用的

edit AW /ˈedɪt/ *verb* **1** [T, I] ~ (**sth**) to prepare a piece of writing, a book, etc. to be published by correcting the mistakes, making improvements to it, etc. 编辑，编纂，校订（文章、书籍等）：*I know that this draft text will need to be edited.* 我知道这篇草稿需要校订。◇ *This is the edited version of my speech* (= some parts have been taken out). 这是我的演讲稿选编本。 **2** [T] ~ **sth** to prepare a book to be published by collecting together and arranging pieces of writing by one or more authors 编选；编纂；编集：*He's editing a book of essays by Isaiah Berlin.* 他正在编辑一本以赛亚·伯林的散文集。 **3** [T, I] ~ (**sth**) (*computing* 计) to make changes to text or data on screen 编辑：*You can download the file and edit it on your computer.* 你可以把文件下载，在计算机上编辑。 **4** [T] ~ **sth** when sb **edits** a film/movie, television programme, etc. they take what has been filmed or recorded and decide which parts to include and in which order 剪辑，剪接（影片、电视节目等）：*They're showing the* ***edited highlights*** *of last month's game.* 他们正在放映上月比赛的精彩片段剪辑。 ➲ COLLOCATIONS AT CINEMA **5** [T] ~ **sth** to be responsible for planning and publishing a newspaper, magazine, etc. (= to be the EDITOR) 主编（报纸、杂志等）：*She used to edit a women's magazine.* 她曾主编过一本女性杂志。 ▸ **edit** *noun*：*I had time to do a quick edit of my essay before handing it in.* 我呈交论文之前有点时间，很快地校订了一遍。

PHR V ˌ**edit sth**↔ˈ**out** (**of sth**) to remove words, phrases or scenes from a book, programme, etc. before it is published or shown （从书、节目等中）删除，删掉，删节 SYN **cut out**：*They edited out references to her father in the interview.* 他们删掉了采访中提到她父亲的部分。

edit·able /ˈedɪtəbl/ *adj.* (*computing* 计) (of text or software 文本或软件) that can be EDITED by the user （用户）可编辑的：*an editable document* 可编辑文档

edi·tion 🔑 AW /ɪˈdɪʃn/ *noun* **1** 🔑 the form in which a book is published 版本（出版形式）：*a* ***paperback/hardback edition*** 平装本；精装本 ◇ *She collects* ***first editions*** *of Victorian novels.* 她收集维多利亚时代的初版小说。◇ *the online edition of 'The Guardian'* 《卫报》的网络版 **2** 🔑 a particular newspaper or magazine, or radio or television programme, especially one in a regular series （报纸、杂志的）一份；（广播、电视节目的）一期，一辑：*Tonight's edition of 'Panorama' looks at unemployment.* 今晚这辑《全景》探讨的是失业问题。 **3** 🔑 (*abbr.* **ed.**) the total number of copies of a book, newspaper or magazine, etc. published at one time （书、报纸、杂志等的）一版印刷总数，版次：*The dictionary is now in its ninth edition.* 本词典现在是第九版。◇ *The article appeared in the evening edition of 'The Mercury'.* 这篇文章刊登在《信使报》的晚间版上。 ➲ SEE ALSO LIMITED EDITION ➲ COMPARE IMPRESSION (7)

edi·tor 🔑 AW /ˈedɪtə(r)/ *noun* **1** 🔑 a person who is in charge of a newspaper, magazine, etc., or part of one, and who decides what should be included （报纸、杂志等的）主编，编辑：*the editor of 'The Washington Post'* 《华盛顿邮报》的主编 ◇ *the* ***sports/financial/fashion, etc. editor*** 体育、财经、时尚等编辑 ➲ WORDFINDER NOTE AT JOURNALIST **2** 🔑 a person who prepares a book to be published, for example by checking and correcting the text, making improvements, etc. （书籍的）编辑，校订者，审校者 ➲ SEE ALSO COPY EDITOR, SUBEDITOR ➲ WORDFINDER NOTE AT BOOK **3** a person who prepares a film/movie, radio or television programme for being shown or broadcast by deciding what to include, and what order it should be in （影片、广播或电视节目的）剪辑员，剪接师 **4** a person who works as a journalist for radio or television reporting on a particular area of news （广播或电视新闻报道的）记者，编辑：*our economics editor* 本台经济新闻的记者 **5** a person who chooses texts written by one or by several writers and prepares them to be published in a book （书籍的）编者：*She's the editor of a new collection of ghost stories.* 她编了一部新版鬼故事集。 **6** (*computing* 计) a program that allows you to change stored text or data 编辑程序 ▸ **edit·or·ship** *noun* [U]：*the editorship of 'The Times'* 《泰晤士报》的编辑工作

edi·tor·ial AW /ˌedɪˈtɔːriəl/ *adj., noun*

■ ***adj.*** [usually before noun] connected with the task of preparing sth such as a newspaper, a book or a television or radio programme, to be published or broadcast 编辑的；编者的；主编的：*the magazine's editorial staff* 杂志的全体编辑人员 ◇ *an editorial decision* 稿件取舍决定

■ ***noun*** (*BrE also* **lead·er**, ˌ**leading ˈarticle**) an important article in a newspaper, that expresses the editor's opinion about an item of news or an issue; in the US also a comment on radio or television that expresses the opinion of the STATION or network （报章的）社论；（美国电台或电视台的）评论 ➲ WORDFINDER NOTE AT NEWSPAPER

edi·tor·ial·ize (*BrE also* **-ise**) /ˌedɪˈtɔːriəlaɪz/ *verb* **1** [I] to express your opinions rather than just reporting the news or giving the facts （在报道中）加入意见：*He accused the BBC of editorializing in its handling of the story.* 他指责英国广播公司在报道这则新闻时掺杂了主观评论。 **2** [I] (*NAmE*) to express an opinion in an editorial 发表社论：*Yesterday the 'Washington Post' editorialized on this subject.* 昨天《华盛顿邮报》就这一主题发表了社论。

ˈ**edit suite** *noun* a room containing electronic equipment for EDITING material recorded on video 录像编辑室；影像制作室

EDT /ˌiː diː ˈtiː/ *abbr.* EASTERN DAYLIGHT TIME 东部夏令时间

edu·cate 🔑 /ˈedʒukeɪt/ *verb* **1** 🔑 [often passive] ~ **sb** to teach sb over a period of time at a school, university, etc. （在学校）教育：*She was educated in the US.* 她是在美国受的教育。◇ *He was educated at his local comprehensive school and then at Oxford.* 他先在地方综合学校上学，然后在牛津大学接受教育。 **2** 🔑 to teach sb about sth or how to do sth 教导；教养；训练：~ **sb** (**in/on sth**) *Children need to be educated on the dangers of drug-taking.* 有必要教导儿童吸毒的危害。◇ ~ **sb to do sth** *The campaign is intended to educate the public to respect the environment.* 这一运动旨在教育公众爱护环境。

edu·cated 🔑 /ˈedʒukeɪtɪd/ *adj.* **1** 🔑 **-educated** having had the kind of education mentioned; having been to the school, college or university mentioned 受过…教育（或训练）的；上过…学校的：*privately educated children* 上过私立学校的孩子 ◇ *a British-educated lawyer* 受过英国教育的律师 ◇ *He's a Princeton-educated Texan.* 他是受过普林斯顿大学教育的得克萨斯人。 **2** 🔑 having had a high standard of education; showing a high standard of education 受过良好教育（或训练）的；有教养的：*an educated and articulate person* 有教养而且善于表达的人 ◇ *the educated elite* 受过良好教育的精英 ◇ *He spoke in an educated voice.* 他说话很斯文。

IDM **an** ˌ**educated ˈguess** a guess that is based on some degree of knowledge, and is therefore likely to be correct 基于一定知识的猜测

edu·ca·tion 🔑 /ˌedʒuˈkeɪʃn/ *noun* **1** 🔑 [U, sing.] a process of teaching, training and learning, especially in schools or colleges, to improve knowledge and develop skills （尤指学校）教育：*primary/elementary education* 初等 / 基础教育 ◇ *secondary education* 中等教育 ◇ *further/higher/post-secondary education* 继续 / 高等 / 中学后教育 ◇ *students in full-time education* 接受全日制教育的学生 ◇ *adult education classes* 成人教育班 ◇ *a college/university education* 大学教育 ◇ *the state education system* 国家教育体制 ◇ *a man of little education* 没受过多少教育的人 ◇ *She completed her formal education in 1995.* 她在 1995 年完成正规学业。 ➲ WORDFINDER NOTE AT STUDY, UNIVERSITY **2** 🔑 [U, sing.] a particular kind of teaching or training 教育；培养；训练：*health education* 健康教育 **3** 🔑 (*also* **Education**) [U] the institutions or people involved in teaching and training 教育机构；教育界人

士： *the Education Department* 教育部 ◇ *the Department of Health, Education and Welfare* 卫生、教育和福利部 ◇ *There should be closer links between education and industry.* 教育界与产业界之间应该有更紧密的联系。 **4** (*usually* **Education**) [U] the subject of study that deals with how to teach 教育学： *a College of Education* 教育学院 ◇ *a Bachelor of Education degree* 教育学学士 ◇ *She's an education major.* 她主修教育学。 **5** [sing.] (*often humorous*) an interesting experience that teaches you sth 有教益的经历： *The rock concert was quite an education for my parents!* 这场摇滚音乐会真让我父母大受教益！

edu·ca·tion·al /ˌedʒuˈkeɪʃənl/ *adj.* connected with education; providing education 教育的；有关教育的；有教育意义的： *children with special educational needs* 需要特殊教育的孩子 ◇ *an educational psychologist* 教育心理学家 ◇ *an educational visit* 教育访问 ◇ ***educational games/toys*** (= that teach you sth as well as amusing you) 寓教于乐的游戏 / 玩具 ◇ *Watching television can be very educational.* 看电视可以使人受到很多教益。 ▸ **edu·ca·tion·al·ly** /-ʃənəli/ *adv.* ： *Children living in inner-city areas may be educationally disadvantaged.* 居住在内城区的孩子在教育方面可能处于不利的地位。 ◇ (*old-fashioned*) *educationally subnormal* 教育上低于正常标准的

edu·ca·tion·al·ist /ˌedʒuˈkeɪʃənəlɪst/ (*also* **edu·ca·tion·ist** /ˌedʒuˈkeɪʃənɪst/) *noun* a specialist in theories and methods of teaching 教育家；教育学家

edu·ca·tive /ˈedjukətɪv/ *adj.* (*formal*) that teaches sth 教育的；有教育作用的： *the educative role of the community* 社区的教育作用

edu·ca·tor /ˈedʒukeɪtə(r)/ *noun* (*formal*) **1** a person whose job is to teach or educate people 教育工作者；教师： *adult educators* (= who teach adults) 成人教育教师 **2** (*especially NAmE*) a person who is an expert in the theories and methods of education 教育学家；教育家 ➲ SEE ALSO EDUCATIONALIST

edu·tain·ment /ˌedjuˈteɪnmənt/ *noun* [U] products such as books, television programmes and especially computer software that both educate and entertain 寓教于乐型产品（指教育兼娱乐的书籍、电视节目，尤其是电脑软件等） ➲ **MORE LIKE THIS** 1, page R25

Ed·ward·ian /edˈwɔːdiən; *NAmE* -ˈwɔːrd-/ *adj.* from the time of the British king Edward VII (1901–1910) 英王爱德华七世时代的（1901–1910）： *an Edwardian terraced house* 一座爱德华七世时代的排房 ▸ **Ed·ward·ian** *noun*

-ee *suffix* (in nouns 构成名词) **1** a person affected by an action 受动者；受益者： *employee* 雇员 ➲ COMPARE -ER, -OR **2** a person described as or concerned with 称为…的人；与…有关的人： *absentee* 缺席者 ◇ *refugee* 难民 ➲ **MORE LIKE THIS** 7, page R25

EEG /ˌiː iː ˈdʒiː/ *noun* the abbreviation for 'electroencephalogram' (a medical test that measures and records electrical activity in the brain) 脑电图（全写为 electroencephalogram）

eejit /ˈiːdʒɪt/ *noun* (*informal, IrishE, ScotE, disapproving*) a way of saying IDIOT which represents the way it is pronounced by some people 白痴，傻瓜（代表一些人对 idiot 的读音方式）

eek /iːk/ *exclamation* used to express fear or surprise （表示害怕或惊讶）呀，咦： *Eek! It moved!* 咦！它动了！ ➲ **MORE LIKE THIS** 2, page R25

eel /iːl/ *noun* [C, U] a long thin sea or FRESHWATER fish that looks like a snake. There are several types of eel,

▼ **COLLOCATIONS** 词语搭配

Education 教育

Learning 学习

- **acquire/get/lack** (an) education/training/(*BrE*) (some) qualifications 获得 / 缺少教育 / 培训 / 资格
- **receive/provide sb with** training/tuition 得到 / 给某人提供培训 / 指导
- **develop/design/plan** a curriculum/(*especially BrE*) course/(*NAmE*) program/syllabus 制订课程方案 / 教学大纲
- **give/go to/attend** a class/lesson/lecture/seminar 讲课；上课；举办 / 参加 / 出席研讨会
- **hold/run/conduct** a class/seminar/workshop 办班；举办研讨会 / 讲习班
- **sign up for/take** a course/classes/lessons 报名参加 / 修读课程

School 学校

- **go to/start** preschool/kindergarten/nursery school 上学前班 / 幼儿园 / 托儿所
- **be in the first, second, etc.** (*NAmE*) grade/(*especially BrE*) year (at school) 在读一年级、二年级等
- **study/take/drop** history/chemistry/German, etc. 修读 / 放弃修历史课 / 化学课 / 德语课等
- (*BrE*) **leave/finish/drop out of**/ (*NAmE*) **quit** school 离校；完成学业；辍学；退学
- (*NAmE*) **graduate** high school/college 高中 / 大学毕业

Problems at school 在学校遇到的问题

- **be the victim/target of** bullying 成为被欺负的受害者 / 对象
- (*BrE*) **play truant from**/ (*both BrE, informal*) **bunk off/skive off** school (= not go to school when you should) 逃学
- (*both especially NAmE*) **skip/cut** class/school 逃课；逃学
- (*BrE*) **cheat** in/(*NAmE*) **cheat** on an exam/a test 考试作弊
- **get/be given** a detention (for doing sth) （因做了某事）被罚放学后留校
- **be expelled from/be suspended from** school 被学校开除 / 暂时停学

Work and exams 功课和考试

- **do** your homework/(*BrE*) revision/a project on sth 做家庭作业；复习功课；对…做专题研究
- **work on/write/do/submit** an essay/a dissertation/a thesis/an assignment/(*NAmE*) a paper 写 / 提交文章 / 学位论文 / 毕业论文 / 作业 / 论文
- **finish/complete** your dissertation/thesis/studies/coursework 完成学位论文 / 毕业论文 / 学业 / 课程作业
- **hand in**/ (*NAmE*) **turn in** your homework/essay/assignment/paper 提交家庭作业 / 文章 / 作业 / 论文
- **study/prepare**/ (*BrE*) **revise**/ (*NAmE*) **review**/ (*NAmE, informal*) **cram** for a test/an exam 为应考而学习 / 准备 / 复习 / 临时死记硬背
- **take**/ (*both BrE*) **do/sit** a test/an exam 参加考试
- (*especially BrE*) **mark**/ (*especially NAmE*) **grade** homework/a test 给作业 / 考试打分
- (*BrE*) **do well in**/ (*NAmE*) **do well on**/ (*informal, especially NAmE*) **ace** a test/an exam 在考试中取得好成绩
- **pass/fail**/ (*informal, especially NAmE*) **flunk** a test/an exam/a class/a course/a subject 测验 / 考试 / 课程 / 学科及格 / 不及格

University 大学

- **apply to/get into/go to/start** college/(*BrE*) university 申请 / 上 / 开始上大学
- **leave/graduate from** law school/college/(*BrE*) university (with a degree in computer science) 离开 / 毕业于法学院；离开大学；大学毕业（取得计算机科学的学位）
- **study for/take**/ (*BrE*) **do/complete** a law degree/a degree in physics 攻读 / 读完法学学位 / 物理学位课程
- (*both NAmE*) **major/minor** in biology/philosophy 主修 / 辅修生物学 / 哲学
- **earn/receive/be awarded/get/have/hold** a master's degree/a bachelor's degree/a PhD in economics 获得 / 被授予 / 拿到 / 拥有经济学硕士学位 / 学士学位 / 博士学位

some of which are used for food. 鳗；鳗鲡：*jellied eels* 鳗鱼冻

e'en /iːn/ *adv.* (*literary*) = EVEN

e'er /eə(r); *NAmE* er/ *adv.* (*literary*) = EVER

-eer *suffix* **1** (in nouns 构成名词) a person concerned with 与…有关的人：*auctioneer* 拍卖商 ◊ *mountaineer* 登山运动员 **2** (in verbs 构成动词) (*often disapproving*) to be concerned with 与…有关：*profiteer* 牟取暴利 ◊ *commandeer* 强占

eerie /ˈɪəri; *NAmE* ˈɪri/ *adj.* strange, mysterious and frightening 怪异的；神秘的；恐怖的 **SYN** **uncanny**：*an eerie yellow light* 诡异的黄灯 ◊ *I found the silence underwater really eerie.* 我发觉水下的寂静很恐怖。 ▶ **eer·ily** /ˈɪərəli; *NAmE* ˈɪr-/ *adv.* **eeri·ness** *noun* [U]

eff /ef/ *verb*

IDM **eff and 'blind** (*BrE, informal*) to use swear words 咒骂；诅咒：*There was a lot of effing and blinding going on.* 咒骂声没完没了。

PHR V **ˌeff 'off** (*taboo, BrE*) a rude way of telling sb to go away, used instead of 'fuck off' 滚蛋，滚开（代替 fuck off） ➲ SEE ALSO EFFING

ef·face /ɪˈfeɪs/ *verb* ~ **sth** (*formal*) to make sth disappear; to remove sth 消除；抹去；擦掉 ➲ SEE ALSO SELF-EFFACING

ef·fect 🔑 /ɪˈfekt/ *noun, verb*

■ ***noun*** **1** 🔑 [C, U] ~ (**on sb/sth**) a change that sb/sth causes in sb/sth else; a result 效应；影响；结果：*the effect of heat on metal* 热对金属产生的效应 ◊ ***dramatic/long-term effects*** 巨大的影响；长期效应 ◊ *to learn to distinguish between* ***cause and effect*** 学会分清因果 ◊ *the beneficial effects of exercise* 锻炼的好处 ◊ *Modern farming methods can have an* ***adverse effect*** *on the environment.* 现代农业耕作方法可能对环境造成负面影响。 ◊ *Her criticisms* ***had the effect of*** *discouraging him completely.* 她批评的结果是使他完全丧失了信心。 ◊ *Despite her ordeal, she seems to have suffered no* ***ill effects.*** 她尽管备受磨难，但好像并未受到不利影响。 ◊ *I can certainly* ***feel the effects of*** *too many late nights.* 我当然能感觉到熬夜太多产生的影响。 ◊ *'I'm feeling really depressed.' 'The winter here has that effect sometimes.'* "我真感到抑郁。" "这儿的冬天有时候就会产生这种影响。" ◊ *I tried to persuade him, but with little or no effect.* 我试图说服他，但却无济于事。 ➲ LANGUAGE BANK AT CONSEQUENTLY ➲ NOTE AT AFFECT ➲ SEE ALSO GREENHOUSE EFFECT, KNOCK-ON, SIDE EFFECT **2** 🔑 [C, U] a particular look, sound or impression that sb, such as an artist or a writer, wants to create （艺术家或作家等所要创造的特定）外观，声响，印象，效果：*The overall effect of the painting is overwhelming.* 这幅画的总体效果气势磅礴。 ◊ *The stage lighting gives the effect of a moonlit scene.* 这种舞台灯光能产生月下景色的效果。 ◊ *Add a scarf for a casual effect.* 再围上一条围巾以显得随意些。 ◊ *He only behaves like that* ***for effect*** (= in order to impress people). 他那样表现不过是为了哗众取宠。 ➲ SEE ALSO SOUND EFFECT, SPECIAL EFFECTS **3 effects** [pl.] (*formal*) your personal possessions （个人）财产，所有物，财物 **SYN** **belongings**：*The insurance policy covers all baggage and personal effects.* 这份保险单为全部行李和个人财产提供保险。

IDM **bring/put sth into ef'fect** 🔑 to cause sth to come into use 使生效；实行；实施：*The recommendations will soon be put into effect.* 这些建议即将付诸实施。 **come into ef'fect** 🔑 to come into use; to begin to apply 生效；开始实施：*New controls come into effect next month.* 下月开始实施新的管制措施。 **in ef'fect 1** used when you are stating what the facts of a situation are 实际上；事实上：*In effect, the two systems are identical.* 实际上，这两种系统完全一样。 ◊ *His wife had, in effect, run the government for the past six months.* 过去的六个月实际上是他的妻子在执政。 **2** (of a law or rule 法律或规则) in use 在实施中；有效：*These laws are in effect in twenty states.* 这些法律在二十个州有效。 **take ef'fect 1** to start to produce the results that are intended 开始起作用；见效：*The aspirins soon take effect.* 阿司匹林药片很快见效。 **2** to come into use; to begin to apply 生效；开始实施：*The new law takes effect from tomorrow.* 新法律明日起生效。 **to the effect that... | to this/that ef'fect** used to show that you are giving the general meaning of what sb has said or written rather than the exact words 大意是；意思是；有这个（或那个）意思：*He left a note to the effect that he would not be coming back.* 他留下一张字条，大意是他不回来了。 ◊ *She told me to get out—or* ***words to that effect.*** 她叫我滚开，或说了类似的话。 **to good, great, dramatic, etc. ef'fect** producing a good, successful, dramatic, etc. result or impression 富有成效；效果良好 **to no ef'fect** not producing the result you intend or hope for 毫无效果；毫无成效；不起作用：*We warned them, but to no effect.* 我们曾告诫过他们，但没起任何作用。 **with immediate effect | with effect from...** (*formal*) starting now; starting from... 立即生效；从…起开始生效：*The government has cut interest rates with effect from the beginning of next month.* 政府已削减利率，从下月初开始生效。

■ ***verb*** ~ **sth** (*formal*) to make sth happen 使发生；实现；引起：*to* ***effect*** *a cure/change/recovery* 产生疗效；引起变化；实现复苏 ➲ NOTE AT AFFECT

ef·fect·ive 🔑 /ɪˈfektɪv/ *adj.* **1** 🔑 producing the result that is wanted or intended; producing a successful result 产生预期结果的；有效的：*Long prison sentences can be a very effective deterrent for offenders.* 判处长期监禁可对违法者起到强有力的威慑作用。 ◊ *Aspirin is a simple but highly effective treatment.* 阿司匹林药片治疗方法简便，效果却非常显著。 ◊ *drugs that are effective against cancer* 治疗癌症的有效药物 ◊ *I admire the effective use of colour in her paintings.* 我很欣赏她绘画作品中的色彩效果。 **OPP** **ineffective** ➲ SEE ALSO COST-EFFECTIVE **2** [only before noun] in reality, although not officially intended 实际的；事实上的：*the effective, if not the actual, leader of the party* 虽未居其位却实际上是党的领导人 ◊ *He has now taken effective control of the country.* 他目前已实际上控制了这个国家。 **3** (*formal*) (of laws and rules 法律和规则) coming into use 生效的；起作用的：*The new speed limit on this road becomes effective from 1 June.* 这条路的新限速规定自 6 月 1 日起生效。 ▶ **ef·fect·ive·ness** (*also less frequent* **ef·fect·iv·ity** /ˌɪfekˈtɪvəti/) *noun* [U]：*to check the effectiveness of the security system* 检查安全系统的有效性

ef·fect·ive·ly 🔑 /ɪˈfektɪvli/ *adv.* **1** 🔑 in a way that produces the intended result or a successful result 有效地：*The company must reduce costs to compete effectively.* 公司要有效地参与竞争必须降低成本。 ◊ *You dealt with the situation very effectively.* 你应付这种局面很有一套。 **OPP** **ineffectively** **2** used when you are saying what the facts of a situation are 实际上；事实上：*He was very polite but effectively he was telling me that I had no chance of getting the job.* 他彬彬有礼，但实际上却是在告诉我，我不可能得到这份工作。

ef·fect·or /ɪˈfektə(r)/ *noun* (*biology* 生) an organ or a cell in the body that is made to react by sth outside the body 效应物，效应器（对外界刺激做出反应的身体器官或细胞）

ef·fec·tual /ɪˈfektʃuəl/ *adj.* (*formal*) (of things, not people 指物，不指人) producing the result that was intended 有效的；奏效的 **SYN** **effective**：*an effectual remedy* 有效的疗法 ➲ COMPARE INEFFECTUAL ▶ **ef·fec·tual·ly** *adv.*

ef·fec·tu·ate /ɪˈfektʃueɪt/ *verb* ~ **sth** (*formal*) to make sth happen 使发生；实现 **SYN** **cause**

ef·fem·in·ate /ɪˈfemɪnət/ *adj.* (*disapproving*) (of a man or a boy 男人或男孩) looking, behaving or sounding like a woman or a girl 女人气的 ▶ **ef·fem·in·acy** /ɪˈfemɪnəsi/ *noun* [U]

ef·fer·ves·cent /ˌefəˈvesnt; *NAmE* ˌefərˈv-/ *adj.* **1** (*approving*) (of people and their behaviour 人及其行为) excited, enthusiastic and full of energy 兴高采烈的；热情洋溢的；充满活力的 **SYN** **bubbly** **2** (of a liquid 液体) having or producing small bubbles of gas 冒泡的；起沫的 **SYN** **fizzy** ▶ **ef·fer·ves·cence** /ˌefəˈvesns; *NAmE* ˌefərˈv-/ *noun* [U]

ef·fete /ɪˈfiːt/ *adj.* (*disapproving*) **1** weak; without the power that it once had 衰弱的；衰败的；丧失权力的 **2** (of a man 男人) without strength; looking or behaving like a woman 软弱的；女人气的

ef·fi·ca·cious /ˌefɪˈkeɪʃəs/ *adj.* (*formal*) (of things, not of people 指物，不指人) producing the result that was wanted or intended 有效的；奏效的；灵验的 **SYN** **effective**: *They hope the new drug will prove especially efficacious in the relief of pain.* 他们希望这种新药能在缓解疼痛方面产生特效。

ef·fi·cacy /ˈefɪkəsi/ *noun* [U] (*formal*) the ability of sth to produce the results that are wanted 功效；效验；效力 **SYN** **effectiveness**

ef·fi·ciency /ɪˈfɪʃnsi/ *noun* **1** [U] the quality of doing sth well with no waste of time or money 效率；效能；功效：*improvements in efficiency at the factory* 工厂效率的提高 ◇ *I was impressed by the efficiency with which she handled the crisis.* 她应对危机效率之高给我留下了深刻的印象。 **2 efficiencies** [pl.] ways of wasting less time and money or of saving time or money 提高功效的方法：*We are looking at our business to see where savings and efficiencies can be made.* 我们正在研究我们的经营情况，看是否有可以节约和提高功效的地方。 **3** [U] (*specialist*) the relationship between the amount of energy that goes into a machine or an engine, and the amount that it produces （机器等的）效率 **4** [C] = EFFICIENCY APARTMENT

efˈficiency apartment (*also* **efˈficiency unit**, **ef·fi·ciency**) *noun* (*NAmE*) a small flat/apartment with one main room for living, cooking and sleeping in and a separate bathroom 一厅小套房，简易小寓房（起居室、厨房和寝区在同一个房间里，有独立盥洗室）

ef·fi·cient 🔑 /ɪˈfɪʃnt/ *adj.* doing sth well and thoroughly with no waste of time, money or energy 效率高的；有功效的：*an efficient secretary* 效率高的秘书 ◇ *efficient heating equipment* 效能好的供暖设备 ◇ *the efficient use of energy* 能源的有效利用 ◇ *As we get older, our bodies become less efficient at burning up calories.* 随着一天天衰老，我们的身体消耗热量的功能逐渐减弱。 ◇ *fuel-efficient cars* (= that do not use much fuel) 节能汽车 **OPP** **inefficient** ▸ **ef·fi·cient·ly** 🔑 *adv.*：*a very efficiently organized event* 组织效率极高的活动

ef·figy /ˈefɪdʒi/ *noun* (*pl.* **-ies**) **1** a statue of a famous person, a SAINT or a god （名人、圣人或神的）雕像，塑像：*stone effigies in the church* 教堂里的石雕像 **2** a model of a person that makes them look ugly （丑化人的）模拟像，画像：*The demonstrators burned a crude effigy of the president.* 示威者焚毁了总统的丑化像。

eff·ing (*also* **f-ing**) /ˈefɪŋ/ *adj.* [only before noun] (*taboo*, *slang*) a swear word that many people find offensive that is used to emphasize a comment or an angry statement; used instead of saying 'fucking' 该死的，他妈的（避而不说 fucking）

ef·flor·es·cence /ˌefləˈresns/ *noun* [U, C] **1** (*formal*) the most developed stage of sth 全盛期；最高潮期 **2** (*chemistry* 化) the powder which appears on the surface of bricks, rocks, etc. when water EVAPORATES （砖、岩石等表面的）风化物

ef·flu·ent /ˈefluənt/ *noun* [U, C] (*formal*) liquid waste, especially chemicals produced by factories, or SEWAGE 流出物，流出液（尤指工厂排出的化学废料） ➲ WORDFINDER NOTE AT WASTE

ef·fort 🔑 /ˈefət; *NAmE* ˈefərt/ *noun* **1** 🔑 [U, C] the physical or mental energy that you need to do sth; sth that takes a lot of energy 气力；努力；费力的事：*You should put more **effort into** your work.* 你应该更加努力地工作。 ◇ *A lot of effort has gone into making this event a success.* 为使这次活动成功费了很大的劲。 ◇ *It's a long climb to the top, but well worth the effort.* 爬到顶上路程很长，虽然费力却很值得。 ◇ *Getting up this morning was quite an effort* (= it was difficult). 今天早上起床相当费力。 ◇ (*BrE*) ***With** (**an**) **effort*** (= with difficulty) *she managed to stop herself laughing.* 她好不容易才忍住了笑。 **2** 🔑 [C] an attempt to do sth especially when it is difficult to do 艰难的尝试；试图；尽力：*a **determined/real/special effort*** 坚决的 / 真正的 / 特别的努力 ◇ *to **make an effort*** 作出努力 ◇ *I didn't really feel like going out, but I am glad I **made the effort**.* 我当时并不很想出去，不过我很庆幸还是出去了。 ◇ ~ (**to do sth**) *The company has laid off 150 workers **in an effort to** save money.* 公司为节省资金遣散了 150 名工人。 ◇ *The local clubs are **making every effort** to interest more young people.* 地方俱乐部正在尽一切努力来吸引更多的年轻人。 ◇ *We need to make a **concerted effort** to finish on time.* 我们需要通力合作才能按时完成。 ◇ *I spent hours cleaning the house, but there isn't much to show **for all my efforts**.* 我花了几个小时来打扫房子，但费了这么大力气却看不到多少效果。 ◇ *With an **effort of will** he resisted the temptation.* 他凭自己的意志顶住了这一诱惑。 ◇ *The project was a **joint/group** effort.* 这项工程是共同 / 集体努力的结果。 **3** [C] (usually after a noun 通常置于名词后) a particular activity that a group of people organize in order to achieve sth 有组织的活动：*the Russian space effort* 俄罗斯航天计划 ◇ *the United Nations' peacekeeping effort* 联合国的维和行动 **4** [C] the result of an attempt to do sth 努力的结果；成就：*I'm afraid this essay is a poor effort.* 很抱歉，这篇文章写得不好。 **IDM** SEE BEND *v.*

ef·fort·less /ˈefətləs; *NAmE* ˈefərt-/ *adj.* needing little or no effort, so that it seems easy 不需费力的；容易的：*She dances with effortless grace.* 她跳舞动作优美，轻松自如。 ◇ *He made playing the guitar look effortless.* 他弹起吉他来显得轻松自如。 ▸ **ef·fort·less·ly** *adv.* **ef·fort·less·ness** *noun* [U]

ef·front·ery /ɪˈfrʌntəri/ *noun* [U] (*formal*) behaviour that is confident and very rude, without any feeling of shame 厚颜无耻的行为；傲慢鲁莽的举止 **SYN** **nerve**

ef·ful·gent /ɪˈfʌldʒənt/ *adj.* (*literary*) shining brightly 灿烂的；光辉的 ▸ **ef·ful·gence** /ɪˈfʌldʒəns/ *noun* [U]

ef·fu·sion /ɪˈfjuːʒn/ *noun* [C, U] **1** (*specialist*) something, especially a liquid, that flows out of sb/sth; the act of flowing out 流出（物）；溢出（物）；泻流 **2** (*formal*) the expression of feelings in an exaggerated way; feelings that are expressed in this way （感情）过分流露，迸发，倾泻；过分流露的感情

ef·fu·sive /ɪˈfjuːsɪv/ *adj.* showing much or too much emotion 感情过分流露的；太动感情的；奔放的：*an effusive welcome* 非常热烈的欢迎 ◇ *He was effusive in his praise.* 他极尽溢美之词。 ▸ **ef·fu·sive·ly** *adv.*

E-fit™ /ˈiː fɪt/ *noun* (*BrE*) a picture of a person who is wanted by the police, made using a computer program that puts together and makes changes to pictures of different features of faces, based on information that is given by sb who has seen the person （根据目击者的描述用计算机拼合成的）通缉犯画像 ➲ COMPARE IDENTIKIT™, PHOTOFIT

EFL /ˌiː ef ˈel/ *abbr.* (*BrE*) English as a foreign language (refers to the teaching of English to people for whom it is not the first language) 非母语的英语教学；作为外语的英语教学 ➲ COMPARE EAL, EAP, ESL, ESOL

ˈe-float *noun* [U] (in Kenya) money that exists in an account that you can access to make payments, transfer money, etc. on your mobile/cell phone, and that you can add to or exchange for cash by visiting an agent （肯尼亚）电子流通资金（可用于手机支付、转账等，通过代理商充值或提现）

ˈe-friend *noun* = E-PAL

EFTA /ˈeftə/ *abbr.* European Free Trade Association (an economic association of some European countries) 欧洲自由贸易联盟

e.g. 🔑 /ˌiː ˈdʒiː/ *abbr.* for example (from Latin 'exempli gratia') 例如（源自拉丁文 exempli gratia）：*popular pets, e.g. cats and dogs* 大众喜爱的宠物，如猫和狗 ➲ LANGUAGE BANK ON NEXT PAGE

E

▼ LANGUAGE BANK 用语库

e.g.

Giving examples 举例

- *The website has a variety of interactive exercises (**e.g.** matching games, crosswords and quizzes).* 这个网站有各种各样的互动练习（比如：配对游戏、纵横填字游戏和智力测试）。
- *The website has a variety of interactive exercises, **including** matching games, crosswords and quizzes.* 这个网站有各种各样的互动练习，包括配对游戏、纵横填字游戏和智力测试。
- *Web 2.0 technologies, **such as** wikis, blogs and social networking sites, have changed the way that people use the Internet.* * Web 2.0 技术，比如维基、博客及社交网站，改变了人们使用互联网的方式。
- *Many websites now allow users to contribute information. **A good example of this is** the 'wiki', a type of website that anyone can edit.* 现在许多网站都允许用户撰写信息。维基就是一个很好的例子，它是一种任何人都可以编辑的网站。
- *Wikis vary in how open they are. **For example**, some wikis allow anybody to edit content, while others only allow registered users to do this.* 各维基网的开放程度不同。比如，有些维基网允许任何人编辑内容，另一些则只允许注册用户进行内容编辑。
- *Wikis vary in how open they are. Some wikis, **for example/for instance**, allow anybody to edit content, while others only allow registered users to do this.* 各维基网的开放程度不同。比如，有些维基网允许任何人编辑内容，另一些则只允许注册用户进行内容编辑。
- *More and more people read their news on the Internet. **To take one example**, over 14 million people now read the online version of 'The Oxford Herald'.* 越来越多的人在网上阅读新闻。举个例子来说，现在有超过 1 400 万人阅读《牛津先驱报》的网络版。
- *Online newspapers are now more popular than paper ones. 'The Oxford Herald' **is a case in point**. Its print circulation has fallen in recent years, while its website attracts millions of users every month.* 现在，网络报纸比纸质报纸更受欢迎。《牛津先驱报》就是一个很好的例子。近年来，其印刷版发行量趋于减少，但其网站每个月却吸引上千万的用户。

➲ NOTE AT EXAMPLE

➲ LANGUAGE BANK AT ADDITION, ARGUE, EVIDENCE, ILLUSTRATE

egali·tar·ian /iˌgælɪˈteəriən; *NAmE* -ˈter-/ *adj.* based on, or holding, the belief that everyone is equal and should have the same rights and opportunities 主张人人平等的；平等主义的 ▶ **egali·tar·ian** *noun* : *He described himself as 'an egalitarian'.* 他自称为"平等主义者"。 **egali·tar·ian·ism** /-ɪzəm/ *noun* [U]

egg /eg/ *noun, verb*

■ ***noun*** **1** [C] a small OVAL object with a thin hard shell produced by a female bird and containing a young bird; a similar object produced by a female fish, insect, etc.（鸟类的）蛋；（鱼、昆虫等的）卵：*The female sits on the eggs until they hatch.* 雌鸟伏在蛋上直到其孵化。◇ *The fish lay thousands of eggs at one time.* 这种鱼一次产卵数千个。◇ *crocodile eggs* 鳄鱼蛋 ➲ COLLOCATIONS AT LIFE ➲ VISUAL VOCAB PAGES V12, V13 **2** [C, U] a bird's egg, especially one from a chicken, that is eaten as food （用作食物的）禽蛋；（尤指）鸡蛋：*a **boiled egg*** 煮蛋 ◇ *bacon and eggs* 熏肉加煎蛋 ◇ ***fried/poached/scrambled eggs*** 煎蛋；荷包蛋；炒蛋 ◇ *Bind the mixture together with a little beaten egg.* 用少许打匀的蛋液将混合料搅拌在一起。◇ *You've got some egg on your shirt.* 你的衬衣上沾了些蛋。◇ ***egg yolks/whites*** 蛋黄；蛋白 ◇ *egg noodles* 鸡蛋面 ◇ *ducks'/quails' eggs* 鸭蛋；鹌鹑蛋 ◇ *a chocolate egg* (= made from chocolate in the shape of an egg) 巧克力蛋 ➲ SEE ALSO EASTER EGG, SCOTCH EGG **3** [C] (in women and female animals 妇女和雌性动物) a cell that combines with a SPERM to create a baby or young animal 卵子；卵细胞 SYN **ovum**: *The male sperm fertilizes the female egg.* 雄性的精子使雌性的卵子受精。◇ *an egg donor* 卵子捐献者 ➲ SEE ALSO NEST EGG

IDM **a 'good egg** (*old-fashioned, informal*) a person who you can rely on to behave well 好人；正人君子 **have/be left with 'egg on/all over your face** (*informal*) to be made to look stupid 使显得愚蠢；出丑；丢脸：*They were left with egg on their faces when only ten people showed up.* 只有十人到场，他们感到很丢面子。 **put all your eggs in one 'basket** to rely on one particular course of action for success rather than giving yourself several different possibilities 寄希望于一件事情上 ➲ MORE AT CHICKEN *n.*, CURATE[1], KILL *v.*, OMELETTE, SURE *adv.*, TEACH

■ ***verb***

PHR V **ˌegg sb↔'on** (*informal*) to encourage sb to do sth, especially sth that they should not do 鼓动；怂恿；煽动：*He hit the other boy again and again as his friends egged him on.* 他在朋友的煽动下一次又一次地打了另一个男孩。

ˌegg-and-'spoon race *noun* (*BrE*) a race, usually run by children, in which those taking part have to hold an egg balanced in a spoon 汤匙盛蛋赛跑（通常为儿童比赛，赛跑者须手持盛鸡蛋的汤匙）

'egg cup *noun* a small cup for holding a boiled egg （盛放煮蛋的）蛋杯 ➲ VISUAL VOCAB PAGE V23

egg·head /ˈeghed/ *noun* (*informal, disapproving* or *humorous*) a person who is very intelligent and is only interested in studying 学究

egg·nog /ˈegnɒg; *NAmE* -nɑːg; -nɔːg/ (*BrE also* **'egg flip**) *noun* [U, C] an alcoholic drink made by mixing beer, wine, etc. with eggs and milk 蛋奶酒（用啤酒、葡萄酒等和蛋、牛奶搅拌而成）

egg·plant /ˈegplɑːnt; *NAmE* -plænt/ (*NAmE*) (*BrE* **au·ber·gine**) *noun* [C, U] a vegetable with shiny dark purple skin and soft white flesh 茄子 ➲ VISUAL VOCAB PAGE V33

ˌegg 'roll *noun* (*NAmE*) a type of SPRING ROLL in which the PASTRY is made with eggs 炸蛋卷；蛋皮春卷

egg·shell /ˈegʃel/ *noun* **1** [C, U] the hard thin outside of an egg 蛋壳 **2** [U] a type of paint that is smooth but not shiny when it dries 蛋壳漆（干后平滑无光）

'egg timer *noun* a device that you use to measure the time needed to boil an egg 煮蛋计时器

ego /ˈiːgəʊ; ˈegəʊ; *NAmE* ˈiːgoʊ/ *noun* (*pl.* **-os**) **1** your sense of your own value and importance 自我价值感：*He has the biggest ego of anyone I've ever met.* 他是我见过的最自负的人。◇ *Winning the prize really **boosted her ego**.* 获得这个奖项大大增强了她的自尊心。 **2** (*psychology* 心) the part of the mind that is responsible for your sense of who you are (= your identity) 自我 ➲ COMPARE ID, SUPEREGO ➲ SEE ALSO ALTER EGO

ego·cen·tric /ˌegəʊˈsentrɪk; ˌiːg-; *NAmE* ˌiːgoʊ-/ *adj.* thinking only about yourself and not about what other people need or want 以自我为中心的；自私自利的 SYN **selfish**

ego·ism /ˈegəʊɪzəm; ˈiːg-; *NAmE* -goʊ-/ (*also* **ego·tism** /ˈegətɪzəm; ˈiːg-/) *noun* [U] (*disapproving*) the fact of thinking that you are better or more important than anyone else 利己主义；自高自大；自负；自我主义 ▶ **ego·is·tic** /ˌegəʊˈɪstɪk; ˌiːg-; *NAmE* -goʊ-/ (*also* **ego·tis·tic·al** /ˌegəˈtɪstɪkl; ˌiːgə-/, **ego·tis·tic** /ˌegəˈtɪstɪk; ˌiːgə-/) *adj.* **ego·tis·tic·al·ly** /-kli/ *adv.*

ego·ist /ˈegəʊɪst; ˈiːg-; *NAmE* ˈiːgoʊ-/ (*also* **ego·ist** /ˈegətɪst; ˈiːgə-/) *noun* (*disapproving*) a person who thinks that he or she is better than other people and who thinks and talks too much about himself or herself 利己主义者；自高自大者；自我主义者

ego·mania /ˌeɡəʊˈmeɪniə; ˌiːɡəʊ-; *NAmE* ˌiːɡoʊ-/ *noun* [U] a mental condition in which sb is interested in themselves or concerned about themselves in a way that is not normal 极端利己；病态自我中心主义 ▸ **ego·maniac** /ˌeɡəʊˈmeɪniæk; ˌiːɡəʊ-; *NAmE* ˌiːɡoʊ-/ *noun* **ego·ma·ni·acal** /ˌeɡəʊməˈnaɪəkl; ˌiːɡəʊ-; *NAmE* ˌiːɡoʊ-/ *adj.*

ˈ**ego-surfing** *noun* [U] (*often humorous*) the activity of searching the Internet to find places where your own name has been mentioned 自我冲浪，自我搜寻（在互联网上搜索提及自己名字的网页）

ˈ**ego trip** *noun* (*usually disapproving*) an activity that sb does because it makes them feel good and important 自我表现；自我满足的行为

egre·gious /ɪˈɡriːdʒiəs/ *adj.* (*formal*) extremely bad 极糟的；极坏的

e·gress /ˈiːɡres/ *noun* [U] (*formal*) the act of leaving a place 离开；外出 ➲ COMPARE ACCESS *n.* (1), INGRESS

egret /ˈiːɡrət/ *noun* a bird of the HERON family, with long legs and long white tail feathers 白鹭

Egypt·ology /ˌiːdʒɪpˈtɒlədʒi; *NAmE* -ˈtɑːl-/ *noun* [U] the study of the language, history and culture of ancient Egypt 埃及学（研究古埃及的语言、历史和文化）▸ **Egypt·olo·gist** /ˌiːdʒɪpˈtɒlədʒɪst; *NAmE* -ˈtɑːl-/ *noun*

eh /eɪ/ *exclamation* (*BrE*) (*NAmE usually* **huh**) **1** the sound that people make when they want sb to repeat sth（请对方再说一遍）嗯，什么：*'I'm not hungry.' 'Eh?' 'I said I'm not hungry.'*“我不饿。”“嗯？”“我说我不饿。”**2** the sound that people make when they want sb to agree or reply（征求对方同意或答复）是吗，好吗，嗯：*So what do you think, eh?* 那你是怎么想的，嗯？ **3** the sound people make when they are surprised（表示惊奇）啊：*Another new dress, eh!* 呵，又是一件新连衣裙！ ➲ MORE LIKE THIS 2, page R25

Eid (*also* **Id**) /iːd/ *noun* one of the two main Muslim festivals, either **Eid ul-Fitr** /ˌiːd ʊl ˈfɪtrə/ at the end of Ramadan, or **Eid ul-Adha** /ˌiːd ʊl ˈɑːdə/ which celebrates the end of the PILGRIMAGE to Mecca and Abraham's SACRIFICE of a sheep（伊斯兰教）开斋节，宰牲节（开斋节在斋月结束后第一天，宰牲节纪念易卜拉欣以羊献祭，庆祝麦加朝觐结束）

ei·der·down /ˈaɪdədaʊn; *NAmE* -dərd-/ *noun* (*BrE*) a thick, warm cover for a bed, filled with feathers or other soft material, and usually placed on top of a sheet and BLANKETS 羽绒被；（用轻软物作芯子的）软被

eider duck /ˈaɪdə dʌk; *NAmE* ˈaɪdər/ *noun* a large DUCK with soft feathers, that lives in northern countries 绒鸭（生活在北方国家）

eight 🔑 /eɪt/ **1** 🔑 *number* 8 八 HELP There are examples of how to use numbers at the entry for **five**. 数词用法示例见 five 条。**2** *noun* a team of eight people who ROW¹ a long narrow boat in races; the boat they row¹ 八人赛艇队；八人赛艇 ➲ SEE ALSO FIGURE OF EIGHT

eight·een 🔑 /ˌeɪˈtiːn/ *number* 18 十八 ▸ **eight·eenth** 🔑 /ˌeɪˈtiːnθ/ *ordinal number, noun* HELP There are examples of how to use ordinal numbers at the entry for **fifth**. 序数词用法示例见 fifth 条。

eighth 🔑 /eɪtθ/ *ordinal number, noun*
■ ***ordinal number*** 🔑 8th 第八 HELP There are examples of how to use ordinal numbers at the entry for **fifth**. 序数词用法示例见 fifth 条。
■ ***noun*** 🔑 each of eight equal parts of sth 八分之一

ˈ**eighth note** (*NAmE*) (*BrE* **qua·ver**) *noun* (*music* 音) a note that lasts half as long as a CROTCHET/QUARTER NOTE 八分音符 ➲ PICTURE AT MUSIC

eighty 🔑 /ˈeɪti/ **1** 🔑 *number* 80 八十 **2** *noun* **the eight·ies** [pl.] numbers, years or temperatures from 80 to 89 八十几；八十年代 ▸ **eight·ieth** 🔑 /ˈeɪtiəθ/ *ordinal number, noun* HELP There are examples of how to use ordinal numbers at the entry for **fifth**. 序数词用法示例见 fifth 条。

IDM **in your eighties** between the ages of 80 and 89 * 80 多岁

eina /ˈeɪnɑː/ *exclamation* (*SAfrE*) used to express sudden pain（突然疼痛时发出的声音）哎唷，啊：*Eina! That was sore!* 哎唷！好痛！

ein·stein·ium /aɪnˈstaɪniəm/ *noun* [U] (*symb.* **Es**) a chemical element. Einsteinium is a RADIOACTIVE element produced artificially from PLUTONIUM and other elements. 锿（放射性化学元素）

ei·stedd·fod /aɪˈsteðvɒd; *NAmE* -vɑːd/ *noun* (*WelshE*) a type of festival, held in Wales, in which there are singing, music and poetry competitions 艾斯特福德节（威尔士的一种节日，有歌唱、音乐和诗歌比赛）

ei·ther 🔑 /ˈaɪðə(r); ˈiːðə(r)/ *det., pron., adv.*
■ ***det., pron.*** **1** 🔑 one or the other of two; it does not matter which（两者中的）任何一个：*You can park on either side of the street.* 这条街两边都可停车。◇ *You can keep one of the photos. Either of them—whichever you like.* 你可以保留一张照片。两张里任选一张，你喜欢的就行。◇ *There are two types of qualification—either is acceptable.* 有两种资格证明，任何一种都可以接受。➲ NOTE AT NEITHER **2** 🔑 each of two（两者中的）每个，各方：*The offices on either side were empty.* 两边的办公室都是空的。◇ *There's a door at either end of the corridor.* 走廊两端各有一道门。
■ ***adv.*** **1** 🔑 used after negative phrases to state that a feeling or situation is similar to one already mentioned（用于否定词组后）也：*Pete can't go and I can't either.* 皮特不能去，我也不能。◇ (*NAmE, informal*) *'I don't like it.' 'Me either.'* (= Neither do I). “我不喜欢这个。”“我也不喜欢。”**2** 🔑 used to add extra information to a statement（补充时说）而且：*I know a good Italian restaurant. It's not far from here, either.* 我知道一家很好的意大利餐馆，而且离这儿不远。**3** 🔑 **either... or...** used to show a choice of two things（对两事物的选择）要么…要么，不是…就是，或者…或者：*Well, I think she's either Czech or Slovak.* 嗯，我看她不是捷克人就是斯洛伐克人。◇ *I'm going to buy either a camera or a DVD player with the money.* 我打算用这笔钱买一台照相机或者 DVD 机。◇ *Either he could not come or he did not want to.* 他要么是不能来，要么就是不想来。 ➲ NOTE AT NEITHER ➲ COMPARE OR (1)

ejacu·late /iˈdʒækjuleɪt/ *verb* **1** [I, T] ~ (**sth**) when a man or a male animal **ejaculates**, SEMEN comes out through the PENIS 射精 **2** [T] + **speech** (*old-fashioned*) to say or shout sth suddenly 突然说出；突然喊出；突然喊叫 SYN **exclaim**

ejacu·la·tion /iˌdʒækjuˈleɪʃn/ *noun* **1** [C, U] the act of ejaculating; the moment when SPERM comes out of a man's PENIS 射精：*premature ejaculation* 早泄 **2** [C] (*formal*) a sudden shout or sound that you make when you are angry or surprised（愤怒或吃惊时）突然喊出，叫喊 SYN **exclamation**

eject /iˈdʒekt/ *verb* **1** [T] ~ **sb** (**from sth**) (*formal*) to force sb to leave a place or position 驱逐；逐出；赶出 SYN **throw sb↔out** (**of...**): *Police ejected a number of violent protesters from the hall.* 警察将一些暴力抗议者赶出了会议厅。 **2** [T] ~ **sth** (**from sth**) to push sth out suddenly and with a lot of force 喷出；喷射；排出：*Used cartridges are ejected from the gun after firing.* 空弹壳在射击后从枪里弹出。 **3** [I] (of a pilot) to escape from an aircraft that is going to crash, sometimes using an EJECTOR SEAT（飞行员在飞机坠毁前从航空器）弹出 **4** [T, I] ~ (**sth**) when you **eject** a disk, tape, etc., or when it **ejects**, it comes out of the machine after you have pressed a button（按键后磁带、磁盘等）弹出；使弹出 ▸ **ejec·tion** /iˈdʒekʃn/ *noun* [U, C]

eject·or seat /iˈdʒektə siːt; *NAmE* -tər/ (*US also* **ejec·tion seat**) *noun* a seat that allows a pilot to be thrown out of an aircraft in an emergency（飞行员在紧急情况下从飞机中弹出用的）弹射座椅

eke /iːk/ *verb*

PHR V **ˌeke sth↔ˈout 1** to make a small supply of sth such as food or money last longer by using only small amounts of it （靠节省用量）使…的供应持久；节约使用： *She managed to eke out her student loan till the end of the year.* 她想方设法节约用钱使学生贷款维持到了年底。 **2 eke out a living, etc.** to manage to live with very little money 竭力维持生计；勉强度日

EKG /ˌiː keɪ ˈdʒiː/ *noun* (*NAmE*) = ECG

elab·or·ate *adj.*, *verb*

■ ***adj.*** /ɪˈlæbərət/ [usually before noun] very complicated and detailed; carefully prepared and organized 复杂的；详尽的；精心制作的： *elaborate designs* 精心的设计 ◇ *She had prepared a very elaborate meal.* 她做了一顿精美的饭菜。 ◇ *an elaborate computer system* 精密的计算机系统 ▶ **elab·or·ate·ly** *adv.* : *an elaborately decorated room* 精心装饰的房间 **elab·or·ate·ness** *noun* [U]

■ ***verb*** /ɪˈlæbəreɪt/ **1** [I, T] to explain or describe sth in a more detailed way 详尽阐述；详细描述： **~ (on/upon sth)** *He said he was resigning but did not elaborate on his reasons.* 他说他准备辞职但未详细说明原因。 ◇ **~ sth** *She went on to elaborate her argument.* 她进而详尽阐述了她的论点。 **2** [T] **~ sth** to develop a plan, an idea, etc. and make it complicated or detailed 详细制订；精心制作： *In his plays he takes simple traditional tales and elaborates them.* 他在剧本里采用了一些简单的传统故事并加以发挥。 ▶ **elab·or·ation** /ɪˌlæbəˈreɪʃn/ *noun* [U, C]: *The importance of the plan needs no further elaboration.* 这个计划的重要性无须赘述。

elan /eɪˈlɒ̃; eɪˈlæn; *NAmE* eɪˈlɑ̃ː/ *noun* [U] (*from French, literary*) great enthusiasm and energy, style and confidence 活力和风格

eland /ˈiːlənd/ *noun* (*pl.* **eland** or **elands**) a large African ANTELOPE with curled horns 大角斑羚

elapse /ɪˈlæps/ *verb* [I] (not usually used in the progressive tenses 通常不用于进行时) (*formal*) if a period of time **elapses**, it passes （时间）消逝，流逝 SYN **go by**: *Many years elapsed before they met again.* 过了许多年他们才再次相见。

eˌlapsed ˈtime *noun* [U] (*specialist*) used to describe the time that passes between the start and end of a project or a computer operation, in contrast to the actual time needed to do a particular task which is part of the project （一项工程的）实耗时间；（计算机一次操作的）运行时间

elas·tic /ɪˈlæstɪk/ *noun*, *adj.*

■ ***noun*** [U] material made with rubber, that can stretch and then return to its original size 橡皮圈（或带）；松紧带： *This skirt needs some new elastic in the waist.* 这条裙子需要换一根松紧腰带。

■ ***adj.*** **1** made with elastic 橡皮圈（或带）的： *an elastic headband* 松紧头箍 **2** able to stretch and return to its original size and shape 有弹性的；有弹力的： *elastic materials* 弹性材料 **3** that can change or be changed 灵活的；可改变的；可伸缩的： *Our plans are fairly elastic.* 我们的计划有相当大的灵活性。

elas·ti·cated /ɪˈlæstɪkeɪtɪd/ (*BrE*) (*NAmE* **elas·ti·cized** /ɪˈlæstɪsaɪzd/) *adj.* (of clothing, or part of a piece of clothing 衣服或衣服某部分) made using elastic material that can stretch 弹性物质织成的；织入橡皮筋的；有松紧带的： *a skirt with an elasticated waist* 有松紧腰带的裙子

eˌlastic ˈband *noun* (*BrE*) = RUBBER BAND ➲ VISUAL VOCAB PAGE V71

elas·ti·city /ˌiːlæˈstɪsəti; ˌelæ-; ɪˌlæ-/ *noun* [U] the quality that sth has of being able to stretch and return to its original size and shape (= of being elastic) 弹性；弹力

elas·tin /ɪˈlæstɪn/ *noun* [U] (*biology* 生) a natural substance that stretches easily, found in the skin, the heart and other body TISSUES 弹性蛋白（存在于皮肤、心脏等身体组织）

elasto·mer /ɪˈlæstəmə(r)/ *noun* (*chemistry* 化) a natural or artificial chemical that behaves like rubber 高弹体；弹性体

elated /iˈleɪtɪd/ *adj.* **~ (at/by sth)** very happy and excited because of sth good that has happened, or will happen 兴高采烈的；欢欣鼓舞的；喜气洋洋的： *They were elated at the result.* 他们对这一结果感到欢欣鼓舞。 ◇ *I was elated by the prospect of the new job ahead.* 我为眼前新工作的前景所鼓舞。 ➲ SYNONYMS AT EXCITED

ela·tion /iˈleɪʃn/ *noun* [U] a feeling of great happiness and excitement 兴高采烈；欢欣鼓舞；喜气洋洋

elbow 🔑 /ˈelbəʊ; *NAmE* -boʊ/ *noun*, *verb*

■ ***noun*** **1** 🔑 the joint between the upper and lower parts of the arm where it bends in the middle 肘；肘部： *She jabbed him with her elbow.* 她用胳膊肘捅他。 ◇ *He's fractured his elbow.* 他肘部骨折。 ➲ VISUAL VOCAB PAGE V64 **2** 🔑 the part of a piece of clothing that covers the elbow （衣服的）肘部： *The jacket was worn at the elbows.* 这件夹克衫的肘部磨破了。 **3** a part of a pipe, CHIMNEY, etc. where it bends at a sharp angle （管子、烟囱等的）弯处，弯头

IDM **get the ˈelbow** (*BrE, informal*) to be told by sb that they no longer want to have a relationship with you; to be told to go away 被排斥；被甩；被撵走 **give sb the ˈelbow** (*BrE, informal*) to tell sb that you no longer want to have a relationship with them; to tell sb to go away 排斥；甩掉；撵走 ➲ MORE AT KNOW *v.*, POWER *n.*, RUB *v.*

■ ***verb*** **~ sb/sth (+adv./prep.)** to push sb with your elbow, usually in order to get past them 用肘推；用肘挤： *She elbowed me out of the way to get to the front of the line.* 她用肘部把我推开朝队伍前面挤。 ◇ *He elbowed his way through the crowd.* 他用手肘从人群中挤了过去。

ˈelbow grease *noun* [U] (*informal*) the effort used in physical work, especially in cleaning or polishing sth 苦干；（尤指费劲的）清洁，擦拭

ˈelbow room *noun* [U] (*informal*) enough space to move or walk in 足够的活动空间

elder /ˈeldə(r)/ *adj.*, *noun*

■ ***adj.*** **1** [only before noun] (of people, especially two members of the same family 指人，尤指同一家庭里两个成员中) older 年纪较长的： *my elder brother* 我的哥哥 ◇ *his elder sister* 他的姐姐 **2 the elder** used without a noun immediately after it to show who is the older of two people （后面不紧跟名词，指两者中的）较年长者： *the elder of their two sons* 他们的两个儿子中年纪较大的那个 **3 the elder** (*formal*) used before or after sb's name to show that they are the older of two people who have the same name （用于人名前或后，指同名的两个人中）年龄较大的一个： *the elder Pitt* 老皮特 ◇ *Pitt the elder* 老皮特 ➲ NOTE AT OLD ➲ COMPARE THE YOUNGER

■ ***noun*** **1 elders** [pl.] people of greater age, experience and authority 长者；长辈；元老： *Children have no respect for their elders nowadays.* 现今的孩子对长辈一点儿也不尊敬。 ◇ *the village elders* (= the old and respected people of the village) 村里德高望重的长辈 **2 my, etc. elder** [sing.] (*formal*) a person older than me, etc. 比…年长的人： *He is her elder by several years.* 他比她年长几岁。 **3** [C] an official in some Christian churches （某些基督教会中的）长老 **4** [C] a small tree with white flowers with a sweet smell (**elderflowers**) and bunches of small black BERRIES (**elderberries**) 接骨木

IDM **your ˌelders and ˈbetters** people who are older and wiser than you and whom you should respect 前辈；长者

ˈelder abuse *noun* [U] the crime of harming or stealing from an old person, committed by sb who is trusted to care for or help them 虐待老人；虐老

elder·berry /ˈeldəberi; *NAmE* ˈeldərb-/ *noun* (*pl.* **-ies**) a small black BERRY that grows in bunches on an elder tree 接骨木果

elder·care /ˈeldəkeə(r); *NAmE* ˈeldərker/ *noun* [U] (*especially NAmE*) help for old people, especially services such as special homes and medical care 老年保健（尤指老年照护及医疗）: *nursing homes and other eldercare facilities* 养老院等老年护理设施

elder·flower /ˈeldəflaʊə(r); *NAmE* ˈeldərf-/ *noun* the flower of the elder tree, used to make wines and other drinks 接骨木花（用于制作果酒等饮料）

eld·er·ly /ˈeldəli; *NAmE* -ərli/ *adj.* **1** (of people 人) used as a polite word for 'old' 年纪较大的，上了年纪的（婉辞，与 old 同义）: *an elderly couple* 一对老年夫妇 ◇ *elderly relatives* 年老的亲戚 ➲ SYNONYMS AT OLD **2 the elderly** *noun* [pl.] people who are old 老人；上了年纪的人 ➲ MORE LIKE THIS 24, page R28 ➲ WORDFINDER NOTE AT AGE

ˌelder ˈstatesman *noun* **1** an old and respected politician or former politician whose advice is still valued because of his or her long experience 政界元老 **2** any experienced and respected person whose advice or work is valued 资深前辈；德高望重的老前辈: *an elder statesman of golf* 高尔夫球的元老

eld·est /ˈeldɪst/ *adj.* **1** (of people, especially of three or more members of the same family 指人，尤指同一家庭里三个或三个以上成员中) oldest 年龄最大的: *Tom is my eldest son.* 汤姆是我的长子。 **2 the eldest** used without a noun immediately after it to show who is the oldest of three or more people（后面不紧跟名词，指三个或三个以上的人中）年龄最大的人: *the eldest of their three children* 他们的三个子女中最大的那个 ➲ NOTE AT OLD

eld·ritch /ˈeldrɪtʃ/ *adj.* [usually before noun] (*literary*) strange and frightening 怪异可怕的；骇人的: *an eldritch screech* 骇人的怪叫声

ˈe-learning *noun* [U] a system of learning which uses electronic media, typically over the Internet 电子学习；在线学习: *We use e-learning to deliver online training to our employees.* 我们使用电子学习系统为员工提供在线培训。 ◇ *an e-learning course/module/platform* 电子学习课程／课程单元／平台 ➲ COMPARE DISTANCE LEARNING, M-LEARNING

elect /ɪˈlekt/ *verb*, *adj.*

■ ***verb*** **1** to choose sb to do a particular job by voting for them 选举；推选: **~ sb/sth** *an elected assembly/leader/representative* 选出的议会／领导人／代表 ◇ *the newly elected government* 新选的政府 ◇ **~ sb to sth** *She became the first black woman to be elected to the Senate.* 她成为第一个被选进参议院的黑人妇女。 ◇ **~ sb (as) sth** | **~ sb + noun** *He was elected (as) MP for Oxford East.* 他被选为牛津东区的议员。 ➲ COLLOCATIONS AT VOTE **2 ~ to do sth** (*formal*) to choose to do sth 选择，决定（做某事）: *Increasing numbers of people elect to work from home nowadays.* 现在越来越多的人选择在家工作。

■ ***adj.*** **1** used after nouns to show that sb has been chosen for a job, but is not yet doing that job（用于名词后）当选而尚未就职的，候任的: *the president elect* 候任总统 **2 the elect** *noun* [pl.] (*religion* 宗) people who have been chosen to be saved from punishment after death 上帝的选民

elec·tion /ɪˈlekʃn/ *noun* **1** [U, C] the process of choosing a person or a group of people for a position, especially a political position, by voting 选举，推选（尤指从政）: ***election campaigns/results*** 竞选运动；选举结果 ◇ (*especially BrE*) *How many candidates are* ***standing for election***? 有多少候选人参加竞选？ ◇ (*especially NAmE*) *to* ***run for election*** 参加竞选 ◇ *to* ***win/lose an election*** 在选举中获胜／失败 ◇ *to* ***fight an election*** 参加竞选 ◇ *to* ***vote in an election*** 参加投票选举 ◇ *In America, presidential* ***elections are held*** *every four years.* 美国每四年举行一次总统选举。 ◇ *The prime minister is about to* ***call*** (= announce) ***an election***. 首相即将宣布举行大选。 ➲ COLLOCATIONS AT VOTE **2** [U] the fact of having been chosen by election 当选: **~ (as sth)** *We welcome his election as president.* 我们欢迎他当选总统。 ◇ **~ (to sth)** *a year after her election to the committee* 她获选进入该委员会之后一年 ➲ SEE ALSO BY-ELECTION, GENERAL ELECTION ➲ WORDFINDER NOTE AT DEMOCRACY, PARLIAMENT

▼ **SYNONYMS 同义词辨析**

election

vote • poll • referendum • ballot

These are all words for an event in which people choose a representative or decide sth by voting. 以上各词均表示选举或投票表决。

election an occasion on which people officially choose a political representative or government by voting 指选举、推选，尤指政治选举: *Who did you vote for in the last election?* 上次选举中你把票投给了谁？

vote an occasion on which a group of people vote for sb/sth 指投票、选举、表决: *They took a vote on who should go first.* 他们以投票方式决定谁先走。

poll (*journalism*) the process of voting in an election（新闻）指选举投票、计票: *They suffered a defeat* ***at the polls***. 他们在投票选举中惨遭失败。

referendum an occasion on which all the adults in a country can vote on a particular issue 指全民投票、全民公决

ballot the system of voting by marking an election paper, especially in secret; an occasion on which a vote is held 尤指无记名投票选举、投票表决: *The leader will be chosen by secret ballot.* 领导人将通过无记名投票选举产生。 NOTE **Ballot** is usually used about a vote within an organization rather than an occasion on which the public vote. * ballot 通常用于机构内部的选举，而非公众的投票选举。

PATTERNS

- a **national**/**local** election/vote/poll/referendum/ballot
- to **have**/**hold**/**conduct** a(n) election/vote/poll/referendum/ballot

elec·tion·eer·ing /ɪˌlekʃəˈnɪərɪŋ; *NAmE* -ˈnɪr-/ *noun* [U] the activity of making speeches and visiting people to try to persuade them to vote for a particular politician or political party in an election 竞选活动；拉选票

elect·ive /ɪˈlektɪv/ *adj.*, *noun*

■ ***adj.*** [usually before noun] (*formal*) **1** using or chosen by election 选举的；由选举产生的；选任的: *an elective democracy* 民主选举的国家 ◇ *an elective assembly* 由选举产生的大会 ◇ *an elective member* 选任的成员 ◇ *He had never held elective office* (= a position which is filled by election). 他从未担任过经选举获得的职务。 **2** having the power to elect 有选举权的: *an elective body* 有选举权的机构 **3** (of medical treatment 医疗) that you choose to have; that is not urgent 可选择的；非急需的 SYN **optional**: *elective surgery* 非急需施行的手术 **4** (of a course or subject 课程或科目) that a student can choose 可选择的；选修的 SYN **optional**

■ ***noun*** (*especially NAmE*) a course or subject at a college or school which a student can choose to do 选修课程；选修科目

elect·or /ɪˈlektə(r)/ *noun* a person who has the right to vote in an election 有选举权的人；选民

elect·or·al /ɪˈlektərəl/ *adj.* [only before noun] connected with elections 有关选举的: *electoral systems/reforms* 选举制度／改革 ▸ **elect·or·al·ly** /-rəli/ *adv.*: *an electorally effective campaign* 富有成效的竞选运动

eˌlectoral ˈcollege *noun* **1 the Electoral College** (in the US) a group of people who come together to elect the President and Vice-President, based on the votes of people in each state 总统选举团（在美国由各州选民投票推选组成，集中在一起选举总统和副总统） ➲ WORDFINDER NOTE AT CONGRESS **2** (*BrE*) a group of people who are chosen to represent the members of a political party, etc. in the election of a leader 领袖选举团（经推选组成，代表政党党员选举领导人）

e,lectoral 'register (*also* **e,lectoral 'roll**) *noun* (in Britain) the official list of people who have the right to vote in a particular area （英国）选民登记册

elect·or·ate /ɪ'lektərət/ *noun* **1** [C+sing./pl. v.] the people in a country or an area who have the right to vote, thought of as a group （一国或一地区的）全体选民： *Only 60% of the electorate voted in the last election.* 上次选举只有 60% 的选民参加了投票。 ➲ COLLOCATIONS AT VOTE **2** [C] (*AustralE, NZE*) = CONSTITUENCY (1)

elec·tric /ɪ'lektrɪk/ *adj., noun*

■ ***adj.*** **1** [usually before noun] connected with electricity; using, produced by or producing electricity 电的；用电的；电动的；发电的： *an electricmotor* 电动机 ◇ *an **electric light/guitar, etc.*** 电灯、电吉他等 ◇ *an **electric current/charge*** 电流；电荷 ◇ *an electric generator* 发电机 ◇ *an **electric plug/socket/switch*** (= that carries electricity) 电源插头／插座／开关 ➲ SEE ALSO ELECTRIC SHOCK, ELECTRICAL STORM **2** full of excitement; making people excited 充满刺激的；令人激动的 SYN **electrifying**: *The atmosphere was electric.* 气氛很热烈。

▼ **WHICH WORD?** 词语辨析

electric / electrical

These adjectives are frequently used with the following nouns. 这两个形容词常与下列名词连用：

electric ~	electrical ~
light	equipment
guitar	wiring
drill	signal
chair	engineer
shock	shock

- **Electric** is usually used to describe something that uses or produces electricity. You use **electrical** with more general nouns such as *equipment* and *wiring* and things that are concerned with electricity. * electric 通常指使用或产生电力的。electrical 与更笼统的名词如 equipment（电气设备）和 wiring（供电线路），以及与电有关的事物搭配： *an electrical fault* 电路故障 However, the distinction is not always so clear now. 不过现在两者的区别并不总是如此明显： *an electric/electrical company* 电力公司 ◇ *an electric/electrical current* 电流 ◇ *an electric/electrical shock* 触电

■ ***noun*** [U] (*informal*) used to refer to the supply of electricity to a building 供电： *The electric will be off tomorrow.* 明天停电。

elec·tric·al /ɪ'lektrɪkl/ *adj.* connected with electricity; using or producing electricity 电的；用电的；发电的： *an electrical fault in the engine* 发动机的电路故障 ◇ ***electrical equipment/appliances*** 电气设备；电器 ◇ ***electrical power/energy*** 电力；电能 ▸ **elec·tric·al·ly** /-kli/ *adv.*： *a car with electrically operated windows* 带电动窗的汽车 ◇ *electrically charged particles* 带电粒子

e,lectrical engi'neering *noun* [U] the design and building of machines and systems that use or produce electricity; the study of this subject 电工；电气工程；电气工程学 ▸ **e,lectrical engi'neer** *noun*

e,lectrical 'storm (*BrE also* **e,lectric 'storm**) *noun* a violent storm in which electricity is produced in the atmosphere 电暴；雷暴

e,lectric 'blanket *noun* a BLANKET for a bed that is heated by electricity passing through the wires inside it (usually used under the bottom sheet of the bed) 电热毯

e,lectric 'blue *noun* [U] a bright or METALLIC blue colour 钢青色；铁蓝色 ➲ MORE LIKE THIS 15, page R26

e,lectric 'chair (*usually* **the electric chair**) (*also informal* **the chair**) *noun* [sing.] (especially in the US) a chair in which criminals are killed by passing a powerful electric current through their bodies; the method of EXECUTION which uses this chair （尤指美国处决犯人的）电椅，电刑： *He was sent to the electric chair.* 他被送上电椅处决。 ◇ *They face death by the electric chair.* 他们面临着被电刑处死。

e,lectric 'fence *noun* a wire fence through which an electric current can be passed 电篱笆；电铁丝网

elec·tri·cian /ɪ,lek'trɪʃn/ *noun* a person whose job is to connect, repair, etc. electrical equipment 电工；电气技师

elec·tri·city /ɪ,lek'trɪsəti/ *noun* **1** [U] a form of energy from charged ELEMENTARY PARTICLES, usually supplied as electric current through cables, wires, etc. for lighting, heating, driving machines, etc. 电；电能： *a waste of electricity* 浪费电 ◇ *The electricity is off* (= there is no electric power supply). 停电了。

WORDFINDER 联想词： battery, charge, conduct, connect, generate, insulate, power, switch, wire

2 [U, sing.] a feeling of great emotion, excitement, etc. 强烈的感情；激动；兴奋

e,lectric 'razor *noun* = SHAVER

elec·trics /ɪ'lektrɪks/ *noun* [pl.] (*BrE, informal*) the system of electrical wires in a house, car or machine （房屋、汽车或机器的）电力系统，电路： *There's a problem with the electrics.* 电路有问题。

e,lectric 'shock (*also* **shock**) *noun* a sudden painful feeling that you get when electricity passes through your body 电休克；触电；电击

elec·tri·fi·ca·tion /ɪ,lektrɪfɪ'keɪʃn/ *noun* [U] the process of changing sth so that it works by electricity 电气化

elec·trify /ɪ'lektrɪfaɪ/ *verb* (**elec·tri·fies, elec·tri·fy·ing, elec·tri·fied, elec·tri·fied**) **1** [usually passive] **~ sth** to make sth work by using electricity; to pass an electrical current through sth 使电气化；使通电；使带电： *The railway line was electrified in the 1950s.* 这条铁路线在 20 世纪 50 年代实现了电气化。 ◇ *He had all the fences around his home electrified.* 他把房子周围的铁丝网都通了电。 **2 ~ sb** to make sb feel very excited and enthusiastic about sth 使激动；使兴奋： *Her performance electrified the audience.* 她的表演使观众兴奋不已。

elec·tri·fy·ing /ɪ'lektrɪfaɪɪŋ/ *adj.* very exciting 令人激动的；使人兴奋的： *The dancers gave an electrifying performance.* 舞蹈演员们的表演激动人心。

elec·tro- /ɪ'lektrəʊ; *NAmE* -troʊ/ *combining form* (in nouns, adjectives, verbs and adverbs 构成名词、形容词、动词和副词) connected with electricity 电的： *electromagnetism* 电磁学

elec·tro·car·dio·gram /ɪ,lektrəʊ'kɑːdiəʊgræm; *NAmE* ɪ,lektroʊ'kɑːrdioʊ-/ *noun* = ECG

elec·tro·con·vul·sive ther·apy /ɪ,lektrəʊkən'vʌlsɪv θerəpi; *NAmE* -troʊ-/ (*also* **elec·tro·shock ther·apy**) *noun* [U] a medical treatment of mental illness that passes electricity through the patient's brain 电休克治疗

elec·tro·cute /ɪ'lektrəkjuːt/ *verb* [usually passive] **~ sb** to injure or kill sb by passing electricity through their body 使触电受伤（或死亡）；用电刑处死： *The boy was electrocuted when he wandered onto a railway track.* 那名男孩闲逛时踩到铁轨上触电死亡。 ◇ *He was electrocuted* *in Virginia in 2006* (= punished by being killed in the electric chair). 他于 2006 年在弗吉尼亚州被电刑处死。 ▸ **elec·tro·cu·tion** /ɪˌlektrəˈkjuːʃn/ *noun* [U]: *Six people were drowned; five died from electrocution.* 六人淹死，五人触电身亡。◇ *He was sentenced to death by electrocution.* 他被判电刑处死。

elec·trode /ɪˈlektrəʊd; *NAmE* -troʊd/ *noun* either of two points (or TERMINALS) by which an electric current enters or leaves a battery or other electrical device 电极 ➲ SEE ALSO ANODE, CATHODE

elec·tro·dynam·ics /ɪˌlektrəʊdaɪˈnæmɪks; *NAmE* -troʊ-/ *noun* [U] (*physics* 物) the study of the way that electric currents and MAGNETIC FIELDS affect each other 电动力学

elec·tro·enceph·alo·gram /ɪˌlektrəʊɪnˈsefələɡræm; -ˈkefələ-; *NAmE* -troʊm'sef-/ *noun* = EEG

elec·troly·sis /ɪˌlekˈtrɒləsɪs; *NAmE* -ˈtrɑːl-/ *noun* [U] **1** the destruction of the roots of hairs by means of an electric current, as a beauty treatment 电解（除毛）术（美容方法） **2** (*chemistry* 化) the separation of a liquid (or electrolyte) into its chemical parts by passing an electric current through it 电解

elec·tro·lyte /ɪˈlektrəlaɪt/ *noun* (*chemistry* 化) a liquid that an electric current can pass through, especially in an electric cell or battery 电解液；电解质 ▸ **elec·tro·ly·tic** /ɪˌlektrəˈlɪtɪk/ *adj.*

elec·tro·mag·net /ɪˈlektrəʊmæɡnət; *NAmE* -troʊ-/ *noun* (*physics* 物) a piece of metal which becomes MAGNETIC when electricity is passed through it 电磁体；电磁铁

elec·tro·mag·net·ic /ɪˌlektrəʊmæɡˈnetɪk; *NAmE* -troʊ-/ *adj.* (*physics* 物) having both electrical and MAGNETIC characteristics (or PROPERTIES) 电磁的：*an electromagnetic wave/field* 电磁波；电磁场

elec·tro·mag·net·ism /ɪˌlektrəʊˈmæɡnətɪzəm; *NAmE* -troʊ-/ *noun* [U] (*physics* 物) the production of a MAGNETIC FIELD by means of an electric current, or of an electric current by means of a MAGNETIC FIELD 电磁学

elec·tron /ɪˈlektrɒn; *NAmE* -trɑːn/ *noun* (*physics* 物) a very small piece of matter (= a substance) with a negative electric charge, found in all atoms 电子 ➲ SEE ALSO NEUTRON, PROTON ➲ **WORDFINDER NOTE** AT ATOM

elec·tron·ic 🔑 /ɪˌlekˈtrɒnɪk; *NAmE* -ˈtrɑːnɪk/ *adj.* [usually before noun] **1** 🔑 (of a device 装置) having or using many small parts, such as MICROCHIPS, that control and direct a small electric current 电子的；电子器件的：*an electronic calculator* 电子计算器 ◇ *electronic music* 电子音乐 ◇ *This dictionary is available in electronic form.* 本词典有电子版。 **2** 🔑 concerned with electronic equipment 电子设备的；电子器件的：*an electronic engineer* 电子工程师

elec·tron·ic·al·ly /ɪˌlekˈtrɒnɪkli; *NAmE* -ˈtrɑːn-/ *adv.* in an electronic way, or using a device that works in an electronic way 用电子方法；用电子装置：*to process data electronically* (= using a computer) 进行电子数据处理

ˌelectronic ˌcigaˈrette (*also* **ˈe-cigarette**) *noun* an electronic device, shaped like a cigarette, that contains NICOTINE that you can take into your lungs through your mouth, and that produces VAPOUR that looks like cigarette smoke 电子香烟；电子烟

ˌelectronic ˈmail *noun* [U] (*formal*) = EMAIL (1)

ˌelectronic ˈpublishing *noun* [U] the business of publishing books in a form that can be read on a computer, for example as CD-ROMs 电子出版

elec·tron·ics /ɪˌlekˈtrɒnɪks; *NAmE* -ˈtrɑːn-/ *noun* **1** [U] the branch of science and technology that studies electric currents in electronic equipment 电子学 **2** [U] the use of electronic technology, especially in developing new equipment 电子技术的应用：*the electronics industry* 电子工业 **3 electronics** [pl.] the electronic CIRCUITS and COMPONENTS (= parts) used in electronic equipment 电子电路；电子器件：*a fault in the electronics* 电子电路故障

ˌelectronic ˈsignature *noun* (*also* **ˈe-signature**) symbols or other text used instead of a signature on a document that is sent electronically to sb 电子签名

elecˌtronic ˈtagging *noun* [U] the system of attaching an electronic device to a person so that the police, etc. know where the person is 电子标识跟踪系统（附于人体，以便警方等知道其行踪）

eˌlectron ˈmicroscope *noun* a very powerful MICROSCOPE that uses ELECTRONS instead of light 电子显微镜

elec·tro·plate /ɪˈlektrəpleɪt/ *verb* [usually passive] **~ sth** to cover sth with a thin layer of metal using ELECTROLYSIS 电镀

elec·tro·shock ther·apy /ɪˈlektrəʊʃɒk θerəpi; *NAmE* -troʊʃɑːk/ *noun* = ELECTROCONVULSIVE THERAPY

elec·tro·stat·ic /ɪˌlektrəʊˈstætɪk; *NAmE* -troʊ-/ *adj.* (*physics* 物) used to talk about electric charges that are not moving, rather than electric currents 静电的

ele·gant 🔑 /ˈelɪɡənt/ *adj.* **1** 🔑 (of people or their behaviour 人或行为) attractive and showing a good sense of style 优美的；文雅的 **SYN** **stylish**: *She was tall and elegant.* 她身材修长，优雅大方。 **2** 🔑 (of clothes, places and things 衣服、地方和物品) attractive and designed well 漂亮雅致的；陈设讲究的；精美的 **SYN** **stylish**: *an elegant dress* 高雅的连衣裙 ◇ *an elegant room/restaurant* 雅致的房间 / 餐厅 **3** (of a plan or an idea 计划或想法) clever but simple 简练的；简洁的；简明的：*an elegant solution to the problem* 解决这个问题的简要方法 ▸ **ele·gance** /ˈelɪɡəns/ *noun* [U]: *She dresses with casual elegance.* 她的穿着随意而不失雅致。◇ *His writing combines elegance and wit.* 他的文章典雅而风趣。 **ele·gant·ly** *adv.*: *elegantly dressed* 穿着考究 ◇ *elegantly furnished* 布置精美

ele·giac /ˌelɪˈdʒaɪək/ *adj.* (*formal* or *literary*) expressing sadness, especially about the past or people who have died 挽歌的；哀悼的；伤感的

elegy /ˈelədʒi/ *noun* (*pl.* **-ies**) a poem or song that expresses sadness, especially for sb who has died 挽诗；挽歌；哀歌

elem·ent 🔑 **AW** /ˈelɪmənt/ *noun*
- **PART/AMOUNT** 部分；数量 **1** 🔑 [C] **~ (in/of sth)** a necessary or typical part of sth 要素；基本部分；典型部分：*Cost was a **key element** in our decision.* 成本是我们决策时考虑的一个重要因素。◇ *The story has all the elements of a soap opera.* 这个故事有肥皂剧的所有要素。◇ *Customer relations is an important element of the job.* 与客户的关系是这个工作的重要部分。 **2** 🔑 [C, usually sing.] **~ of surprise, risk, truth, etc.** a small amount of a quality or feeling 少量；有点；有些：*We need to preserve the element of surprise.* 我们得保留一些使人感到意外的东西。◇ *There appears to be an element of truth in his story.* 他的话似乎有点事实根据。
- **GROUP OF PEOPLE** 集团 **3** [C, usually pl.] a group of people who form a part of a larger group or society（大团体或社会中的）一组，一群，一伙：***moderate/radical elements** within the party* 党内的温和派 / 激进派 ◇ *unruly elements in the school* 学校里难管教的一伙人
- **CHEMISTRY** 化学 **4** 🔑 [C] a simple chemical substance that consists of atoms of only one type and cannot be split by chemical means into a simpler substance. Gold, OXYGEN and CARBON are all elements. 元素（如金、氧、碳） ➲ COMPARE COMPOUND *n.* (2)
- **EARTH/AIR/FIRE/WATER** 土；空气；火；水 **5** [C] one of the four substances: earth, air, fire and water, which people used to believe everything else was made of 要素（旧时认为土、空气、火和水是构成一切物质的四大要素）
- **WEATHER** 天气 **6 the elements** [pl.] the weather, especially bad weather（尤指恶劣的）天气：*Are we going to brave the elements and go for a walk?* 我们要冒着风雨去散步吗？◇ *to be exposed to the elements* 经受风吹雨打
- **BASIC PRINCIPLES** 基本原理 **7 elements** [pl.] the basic principles of a subject that you have to learn first（学科

的）基本原理，基础，纲要 SYN **basics**: *He taught me the elements of map-reading.* 他教我看地图的基本方法。

• ENVIRONMENT 环境 **8** [C, usually sing.] a natural or suitable environment, especially for an animal （尤指动物的）自然环境，适宜的环境： *Water is a fish's natural element.* 水是鱼的天然生活环境。

• ELECTRICAL PART 电器元件 **9** [C] the part of a piece of electrical equipment that gives out heat 电热元件；电热丝： *The kettle needs a new element.* 这个壶需要一根新电热丝。

IDM **in your 'element** doing what you are good at and enjoy 如鱼得水；得心应手： *She's really in her element at parties.* 她在聚会上真是如鱼得水。 **out of your 'element** in a situation that you are not used to and that makes you feel uncomfortable 处于不适应的环境；不得其所

elem·en·tal /ˌelɪˈmentl/ *adj.* [usually before noun] (*formal*) **1** wild and powerful; like the forces of nature 狂暴的；猛烈的；似自然力的： *the elemental fury of the storm* 暴风雨的肆虐 **2** basic and important 基本的；主要的；重要的： *an elemental truth* 基本事实

elem·en·tary /ˌelɪˈmentri/ *adj.* **1** in or connected with the first stages of a course of study 初级的；基础的： *an elementary English course* 基础英语课程 ◇ *a book for elementary students* 初学者课本 ◇ *at an elementary level* 处于初级水平 ⊃ COMPARE PRIMARY *adj.*, SECONDARY **2** of the most basic kind 基本的： *the elementary laws of economics* 基本经济法则 ◇ *an elementary mistake* 基本错误 **3** very simple and easy 简单的；容易的： *elementary questions* 简单的问题

ˌelementary ˈparticle *noun* (*physics* 物) any of the different types of very small pieces of matter (= a substance) smaller than an atom 基本粒子

ˌeleˈmentary school (*also informal* **'grade school**) *noun* (in the US) a school for children between the ages of about 6 and 12 （美国）小学

ele·phant /ˈelɪfənt/ *noun* a very large animal with thick grey skin, large ears, two curved outer teeth called TUSKS and a long nose called a TRUNK. There are two types of elephant, the African and the Asian. 象： *herds of elephants/elephant herds* 象群 ◇ *a baby elephant* 幼象 ⊃ SEE ALSO WHITE ELEPHANT

IDM **the ˌelephant in the ˈroom** a problem or question that everyone knows about but does not mention because it is easier not to discuss it 明摆着的难题；众所周知却避而不谈的事： *The elephant in the room was the money that had to be paid in bribes.* 难题明摆着，就是要出钱行贿。

ele·phant·ia·sis /ˌelɪfənˈtaɪəsɪs/ *noun* [U] (*medical* 医) a condition in which part of the body swells and becomes very large because the LYMPHATIC system is blocked 象皮肿（因淋巴系统阻塞而引起的身体肿胀）

ele·phant·ine /ˌelɪˈfæntaɪn; *NAmE* -tiːn/ *adj.* (*formal* or *humorous*) very large and CLUMSY; like an elephant 庞大的；笨重的；似大象的

ele·vate /ˈelɪveɪt/ *verb* **1** (*formal*) to give sb/sth a higher position or rank, often more important than they deserve 提拔，晋升，提升（到不应有的位置） SYN **raise, promote**: **~ sb/sth (to sth)** *He elevated many of his friends to powerful positions within the government.* 他将许多朋友都提拔到政府部门的要职上。 ◇ **~ sth (into sth)** *It was an attempt to elevate football to a subject worthy of serious study.* 这是试图将足球拔高成一门学科来进行严肃的研究。 **2 ~ sth** (*specialist* or *formal*) to lift sth up or put sth in a higher position 举起；抬起： *It is important that the injured leg should be elevated.* 将受伤的腿抬高是很重要的。 **3 ~ sth** (*specialist*) to make the level of sth increase 提高；使升高： *Smoking often elevates blood pressure.* 抽烟常常使血压升高。 **4 ~ sth** (*formal*) to improve a person's mood, so that they feel happy 使情绪高昂；使精神振奋；使兴高采烈： *The song never failed to elevate his spirits.* 这首歌总使他精神振奋。

ele·vated /ˈelɪveɪtɪd/ *adj.* [usually before noun] **1** high in rank 高贵的；职位高的： *an elevated status* 高贵的身份 **2** (*formal*) having a high moral or INTELLECTUAL level 高尚的；睿智的： *elevated language/sentiments/thoughts* 高尚的语言 / 情操 / 思想 **3** higher than the area around; above the level of the ground 高的；升高的；高出地面的： *The house is in an elevated position, overlooking the town.* 这栋房子地势较高，可以俯瞰全镇。 ◇ *an* ***elevated highway/railway/road*** (= one that runs on a bridge above the ground or street) 高架公路 / 铁路 / 道路 **4** (*specialist*) higher than normal 偏高的： *elevated blood pressure* 血压偏高

ele·vat·ing /ˈelɪveɪtɪŋ/ *adj.* making people think about serious and interesting subjects 发人深思的；启发思考的；有趣的： *Reading this essay was an elevating experience.* 阅读这篇短文很有启发。

ele·va·tion /ˌelɪˈveɪʃn/ *noun* **1** [U] (*formal*) the process of sb getting a higher or more important rank 提拔；晋级；提升： *his elevation to the presidency* 他提升到主席的职位 **2** [C, usually sing.] (*specialist*) the height of a place, especially its height above sea level （某地方的）高程；（尤指）海拔： *The city is at an elevation of 2 000 metres.* 这座城市海拔 2 000 米。 **3** [C] (*formal*) a piece of ground that is higher than the area around 高地；高处 **4** [C] (*architecture* 建) one side of a building, or a drawing of this by an ARCHITECT （建筑物的）外立面，立面图： *the* ***front/rear/side elevation*** *of a house* 房子的正面 / 后面 / 侧面立面图 ⊃ COMPARE PLAN *n.* (4) **5** [U, sing.] (*specialist*) an increase in the level or amount of sth （水平或数量的）提高，升高，增加： *elevation of blood sugar levels* 血糖升高

ele·va·tor 🔑 /ˈelɪveɪtə(r)/ *noun* **1** 🔑 (*NAmE*) (*BrE* **lift**) a machine that carries people or goods up and down to different levels in a building or a mine 电梯；升降机： *It's on the fifth floor, so we'd better take the elevator.* 那是在六楼上，我们最好乘电梯。 **2** a place for storing large quantities of grain 谷仓；粮仓 **3** a part in the tail of an aircraft that is moved to make it go up and down （航空器的）升降舵 ⊃ VISUAL VOCAB PAGE V57

eleven 🔑 /ɪˈlevn/ **1** 🔑 *number* 11 十一 **2** *noun* a team of eleven players for football (SOCCER), CRICKET or HOCKEY （足球、板球或曲棍球）十一人队： *She was chosen for the first eleven.* 她被选派首发上场。 ▸ **elev·enth** 🔑 /ɪˈlevnθ/ *ordinal number, noun* HELP There are examples of how to use ordinal numbers at the entry for **fifth**. 序数词用法示例见 fifth 条。

IDM **at the eˌleventh ˈhour** at the last possible moment; just in time 在最后时刻；刚好来得及

eˌleven-ˈplus *noun* (*usually* **the eleven-plus**) [sing.] an exam that all children used to take in Britain at the age of eleven to decide which type of SECONDARY SCHOOL they should go to. It is still taken in a few areas. 十一岁儿童入学考试（英国旧时举行的升中学甄别考试，现仍在少数地区实行）

elev·enses /ɪˈlevnzɪz/ *noun* [U] (*old-fashioned, BrE, informal*) a very small meal, for example biscuits with tea or coffee, that people sometimes have at about eleven o'clock in the morning （上午十一时左右吃的）午前茶点

ELF /elf/ *abbr.* (*linguistics* 语言) English as a lingua franca 作为共同语言的英语；通用英语

elf /elf/ *noun* (*pl.* **elves** /elvz/) (in stories) a creature like a small person with pointed ears, who has magic powers （故事中的）精灵，小妖精

elfin /ˈelfɪn/ *adj.* (of a person or their features 人或容貌) small and delicate 小巧玲珑的： *an elfin face* 小巧清秀的脸庞

elicit /iˈlɪsɪt/ *verb* **~ sth (from sb)** (*formal*) to get information or a reaction from sb, often with difficulty 引出；探出；诱出： *I could elicit no response from him.* 我从他那里套不出任何反应。 ◇ *Her tears elicited great sympathy from her audience.* 她的眼泪博得观众的无限同情。 ▸ **elicit·ation** /iˌlɪsɪˈteɪʃn/ *noun* [U]

elide /iˈlaɪd/ *verb* **~ sth** (*phonetics* 语音) to leave out the sound of part of a word when you are pronouncing it 省略（词的部分）发音：*The 't' in 'often' may be elided.* * often 中的 t 可以不发音。➔ SEE ALSO ELISION ➔ WORDFINDER NOTE AT PRONUNCIATION

eli·gible /ˈelɪdʒəbl/ *adj.* **1** a person who is **eligible** for sth or to do sth, is able to have or do it because they have the right qualifications, are the right age, etc. 有资格的；合格的；具备条件的：**~ (for sth)** *Only those over 70 are eligible for the special payment.* 只有 70 岁以上的人才有资格领取这项专款。◇ **~ (to do sth)** *When are you eligible to vote in your country?* 在你们国家几岁才有资格投票选举呢？ **OPP** **ineligible** **2** an **eligible** young man or woman is thought to be a good choice as a husband/wife, usually because they are rich or attractive（指作为结婚对象）合意的，合适的，中意的 ▸ **eli·gi·bil·ity** /ˌelɪdʒəˈbɪləti/ *noun* [U]

elim·in·ate **AW** /ɪˈlɪmɪneɪt/ *verb* **1** to remove or get rid of sth/sb 排除；清除；消除：**~ sth/sb** *Credit cards eliminate the need to carry a lot of cash.* 有了信用卡就用不着携带很多现金。◇ **~ sth/sb from sth** *The police have eliminated two suspects from their investigation.* 警方通过调查已经排除了两名嫌疑犯。◇ *This diet claims to eliminate toxins from the body.* 这种饮食号称具有排除体内毒素的作用。**2** **~ sb (from sth)** [usually passive] to defeat a person or a team so that they no longer take part in a competition, etc.（比赛中）淘汰 **SYN** **knock out**：*All the English teams were eliminated in the early stages of the competition.* 所有英格兰队伍在比赛初期就被淘汰了。**3** **~ sb** (*formal*) to kill sb, especially an enemy or opponent 消灭，杀死（尤指敌人或对手）：*Most of the regime's left-wing opponents were eliminated.* 这个政权的左翼反对派多数已被除掉。▸ **elim·in·ation** **AW** /ɪˌlɪmɪˈneɪʃn/ *noun* [U, C]：*the **elimination of disease/poverty/crime*** 消除疾病 / 贫困 / 犯罪 ◇ *There were three eliminations in the first round of the competition.* 比赛第一轮淘汰了三个队。◇ *the elimination of toxins from the body* 排除体内毒素

eli·sion /ɪˈlɪʒn/ *noun* [U, C] (*phonetics* 语音) the act of leaving out the sound of part of a word when you are pronouncing it, as in *we'll, don't* and *let's* 省音，省略部分读音（如 we'll、don't 和 let's）➔ SEE ALSO ELIDE

elite /eɪˈliːt; ɪˈliːt/ *noun* [C+sing./pl. v.] a small group of people in a society, etc. who are powerful and have a lot of influence, because they are rich, intelligent, etc. 上层集团；（统称）掌权人物，社会精英：*a member of the **ruling/intellectual elite*** 上层统治集团的成员；知识界的精英 ◇ *Public opinion is influenced by the small elite who control the media.* 舆论为少数控制着新闻媒介的上层人士所左右。◇ *In these countries, only the elite can afford an education for their children.* 在这些国家，只有上层人士才供得起子女上学。➔ WORDFINDER NOTE AT SOCIETY ▸ **elite** *adj.* [only before noun]：*an elite group of senior officials* 一批出类拔萃的高级官员 ◇ *an elite military academy* 精英军事学院

elit·ism /eɪˈliːtɪzəm; ɪ-/ *noun* [U] (*often disapproving*) **1** a way of organizing a system, society, etc. so that only a few people (= an elite) have power or influence 精英统治；精英主义：*Many people believe that private education encourages elitism.* 许多人认为私立教育助长精英主义。**2** the feeling of being better than other people that being part of an elite encourages 高人一等的优越感 ▸ **elit·ist** *adj.*：*an elitist model of society* 精英统治的社会模式 ◇ *She accused him of being elitist.* 她指责他自以为高人一等。**elit·ist** *noun*

elixir /ɪˈlɪksə(r); -sɪə(r); *NAmE* ɪˈlɪksər/ *noun* (*literary*) a magic liquid that is believed to cure illnesses or to make people live for ever 圣水；灵丹妙药；长生不老药：*the **elixir of life/youth*** 长生不老 / 永葆青春药

Eliza·bethan /ɪˌlɪzəˈbiːθn/ *adj.* connected with the time when Queen Elizabeth I was queen of England (1558–1603) 伊丽莎白女王一世时代的 ▸ **Eliza·bethan** *noun*：*Shakespeare was an Elizabethan.* 莎士比亚是伊丽莎白女王一世时代的人。

elk (*BrE*) / moose (*NAmE*) 驼鹿

wapiti (*NAmE also* elk) 美洲赤鹿

elk /elk/ *noun* (*pl.* **elk** or **elks**) **1** (*BrE*) a large DEER that lives in the north of Europe, Asia and N America. In N America it is called a MOOSE. 驼鹿，犴（生活于北欧、亚洲和北美洲，北美洲称 moose）**2** (*NAmE*) = WAPITI **3** **Elk** a member of the Benevolent and Protective Order of Elks, a US social organization that gives money to charity（美国）厄尔克思慈善互助会会员（捐款给慈善机构）

ell /el/ *noun* a unit used in the past for measuring cloth, equal to about 45 inches or 115 centimetres 埃尔（旧时量布的长度单位，相当于大约 45 英寸或 115 厘米）

el·lipse /ɪˈlɪps/ *noun* (*specialist*) a regular OVAL shape, like a circle that has been squeezed on two sides 椭圆 ➔ PICTURE AT CONIC SECTION

el·lip·sis /ɪˈlɪpsɪs/ *noun* (*pl.* **el·lip·ses** /-siːz/) [C, U] **1** (*grammar* 语法) the act of leaving out a word or words from a sentence deliberately, when the meaning can be understood without them（词在句子中的）省略 **2** three dots (...) used to show that a word or words have been left out 省略号

el·lip·tic·al /ɪˈlɪptɪkl/ *adj.* **1** (*grammar* 语法) with a word or words left out of a sentence deliberately 省略的；隐晦的：*an elliptical remark* (= one that suggests more than is actually said) 隐晦的话 **2** (*also less frequent* **el·lip·tic** /ɪˈlɪptɪk/) (*geometry* 几何) connected with or in the form of an ELLIPSE 椭圆的；椭圆形的 ▸ **el·lip·tic·al·ly** /-kli/ *adv.*：*to speak/write elliptically* 说得 / 写得晦涩难懂

elm /elm/ *noun* **1** [C, U] (*also* **'elm tree**) a tall tree with broad leaves 榆树：*a line of stately elms* 一排雄伟壮观的榆树 ◇ *The avenue was planted with elm.* 大道边上种着榆树。**2** [U] the hard wood of the elm tree 榆木

El Niño /ˌel ˈniːnjəʊ; *NAmE* -joʊ/ *noun* [U] a set of changes in the weather system near the coast of northern Peru and Ecuador that happens every few years, causing the surface of the Pacific Ocean there to become warmer and having severe effects on the weather in many parts of the world 厄尔尼诺现象，圣婴现象（南美洲西海岸每隔数年一次的海温升高现象，导致太平洋水温上升，严重影响全球多处气候）➔ COMPARE LA NIÑA

elo·cu·tion /ˌeləˈkjuːʃn/ *noun* [U] the ability to speak clearly and correctly, especially in public and pronouncing the words in a way that is considered to be socially acceptable 演讲技巧；演说术

elong·ate /ˈiːlɒŋgeɪt; *NAmE* ɪˈlɔːŋ-; ɪˈlɑːŋ-/ *verb* [I, T] **~ (sth)** to become longer; to make sth longer（使）变长，伸

E

长；拉长 SYN lengthen ▸ **elonga·tion** /ˌiːlɒŋˈɡeɪʃn; NAmE ˌiːlɔːŋ-; ˌiːlɑːŋ-/ *noun* [U]: *the elongation of vowel sounds* 元音拖长

elong·ated /ˈiːlɒŋɡeɪtɪd; NAmE ɪˈlɔːŋ-; ɪˈlɑːŋ-/ *adj.* long and thin, often in a way that is not normal 细长的；拉得又细又长的：*Modigliani's women have strangely elongated faces.* 莫迪里阿尼画中的妇女都长着奇长无比的脸。

elope /ɪˈləʊp; NAmE ɪˈloʊp/ *verb* [I] ~ (**with sb**) to run away with sb in order to marry them secretly 私奔 ▸ **elope·ment** *noun* [C, U]

elo·quent /ˈeləkwənt/ *adj.* **1** able to use language and express your opinions well, especially when you are speaking in public 雄辩的；有口才的；流利的：*an eloquent speech/speaker* 雄辩的演讲 / 演讲人 **2** (of a look or movement 表情或动作) able to express a feeling 传神的：*His eyes were eloquent.* 他的眼睛很传神。▸ **elo·quence** /ˈeləkwəns/ *noun* [U]: *a speech of passionate eloquence* 热情洋溢的演讲 ◇ *the eloquence of his smile* 他意味深长的微笑 **elo·quent·ly** *adv.*: *She spoke eloquently on the subject.* 她讲起这个题目来滔滔不绝。◇ *His face expressed his grief more eloquently than any words.* 他那张脸比任何言语都更清楚地表达了他的忧伤。

else /els/ *adv.* (used in questions or after *nothing, nobody, something, anything,* etc. 用于疑问句或nothing、nobody、something、anything 等之后) **1** in addition to sth already mentioned 其他的；别的：*What else did he say?* 他还说了些什么？◇ *I don't want anything else, thanks.* 我不要别的东西了，谢谢。◇ *I'm taking a few clothes and some books, not much else.* 我带了几件衣服和一些书，别的就没什么了。**2** different 另外的；不同的：*Ask somebody else to help you.* 另请个人来帮帮你吧。◇ *Haven't you got anything else to wear?* 你没有其他穿的了吗？◇ *Why didn't you come? Everybody else was there.* 你为什么没来呢？其他所有的人都来了。◇ *Yes I did give it to her. What else could I do?* 是的，我的确给她了。我还能怎么办呢？

IDM **or else 1** if not 要不然；否则 SYN **otherwise**: *Hurry up or else you'll be late.* 快点，否则你就要迟到了。◇ *They can't be coming or else they'd have called.* 他们不会来，不然他们就打电话了。**2** used to introduce the second of two possibilities（表示另一种可能）或者，也许：*He either forgot or else decided not to come.* 他或许忘了，或许决定不来。**3** (*informal*) used to threaten or warn sb（威胁或警告）否则的话，要不然的话：*Just shut up, or else!* 住口，不然的话，哼！

else·where /ˌelsˈweə(r); NAmE -ˈwer/ *adv.* in, at or to another place 在（或去、到）别处：*The answer to the problem must be sought elsewhere.* 这个问题的答案必须在别处寻找。◇ *Our favourite restaurant was closed, so we had to go elsewhere.* 我们最喜欢的餐馆已关门了，所以我们只好到别处去。◇ *Elsewhere, the weather today has been fairly sunny.* 今天其他地方的天气都比较晴朗。◇ *Prices are higher here than elsewhere.* 这里的价格比其他地方高。

ELT /ˌiː el ˈtiː/ *abbr.* (*BrE*) English Language Teaching (the teaching of English to people for whom it is not the first language)（对英语为非第一语言者的）英语教学

elu·ci·date /iˈluːsɪdeɪt/ *verb* [T, I] (*formal*) to make sth clearer by explaining it more fully 阐明；解释；说明 SYN **explain**: ~ (**sth**) *He elucidated a point of grammar.* 他解释了一个语法要点。◇ *Let me elucidate.* 让我来说明一下吧。◇ ~ **what, how, etc.…** *I will try to elucidate what I think the problems are.* 我将尽力阐明我认为的问题所在。▸ **elu·ci·da·tion** /iˌluːsɪˈdeɪʃn/ *noun* [U, C]: *Their objectives and methods require further elucidation.* 他们的目标和方法都需要进一步阐明。

elude /iˈluːd/ *verb* **1** ~ **sb/sth** to manage to avoid or escape from sb/sth, especially in a clever way（尤指机敏地）避开，逃避，躲避：*The two men managed to elude the police for six weeks.* 这两个男人想方设法逃避警方追捕达六个星期。**2** ~ **sb** if sth **eludes** you, you are not able to achieve it, or not able to remember or understand it 使达不到；使不记得；使不理解：*He was extremely tired but sleep eluded him.* 他累极了，却睡不着。◇ *They're a popular band but chart success has eluded them so far.* 他们是一支很受欢迎的乐队，但到目前为止还未能在流行唱片排行榜上取得佳绩。◇ *Finally he remembered the tiny detail that had eluded him the night before.* 他终于想起了前一天晚上想不起来的细节。

elu·sive /iˈluːsɪv/ *adj.* difficult to find, define or achieve 难找的；难以解释的；难以达到的：*Eric, as elusive as ever, was nowhere to be found.* 埃里克总是这样神出鬼没，哪儿也找不着。◇ *the elusive concept of 'literature'* "文学"这一难以解释的概念 ◇ *A solution to the problem of toxic waste is **proving elusive**.* 有毒废料这个问题证明难以解决。▸ **elu·sive·ly** *adv.* **elu·sive·ness** *noun* [U]

elver /ˈelvə(r)/ *noun* a young EEL 幼鳗

elves PL. OF ELF

Elys·ian /ɪˈlɪziən; NAmE ɪˈliːʒən/ *adj.* (*literary*) relating to heaven or to a place of perfect happiness 天堂的；乐土的；埃律西昂的

IDM **the ˌElysian ˈFields** (in ancient Greek stories 古希腊神话) a wonderful place where some people were taken by the gods after death 埃律西昂田野，埃律西昂（受神灵庇护的人死后所去的乐园）

em- ➔ EN-

'em /əm/ *pron.* (*informal*) = THEM: *Don't let 'em get away.* 别让他们跑掉。➔ MORE LIKE THIS 5, page R25

ema·ci·ated /ɪˈmeɪʃieɪtɪd; ɪˈmeɪs-/ *adj.* thin and weak, usually because of illness or lack of food（常指因疾病或缺少食物而）消瘦的，憔悴的，瘦弱的 ▸ **ema·ci·ation** /ɪˌmeɪsiˈeɪʃn/ *noun* [U]: *She was very thin, almost to the point of emaciation.* 她很瘦，几乎到了憔悴的地步。

email (*also* **e-mail**) /ˈiːmeɪl/ *noun, verb*

■ *noun* **1** (*also formal* ˌ**electronic** ˈ**mail**) [U] a way of sending messages and data to other people by means of computers connected together in a network 电子邮件（通信方式）：*to send a message by email* 用电邮发送一条信息 **2** [C, U] a message sent by email 电子邮件 ➔ WORDFINDER NOTE AT MESSAGE

■ *verb* [T, I] to send a message to sb by email（给…）发电子邮件；用电邮发送：~ (**sb**) *Patrick emailed me yesterday.* 帕特里克昨天给我发电邮了。◇ ~ **sth** (**to sb**) *I'll email the documents to her.* 我将用电邮把这些文件发送给她。◇ ~ **sb sth** *I'll email her the documents.* 我将用电邮把这些文件发送给她。

em·an·ate /ˈeməneɪt/ *verb* ~ **sth** (*formal*) to produce or show sth 产生；表现；显示：*He emanates power and confidence.* 他表现出力量和信心。▸ **em·an·ation** /ˌeməˈneɪʃn/ *noun* [C, U]

PHR V **ˈemanate from sth** to come from sth or somewhere 发源于；从…发出 SYN **issue from**: *The sound of loud music emanated from the building.* 喧闹的音乐声是从那栋楼房里传出来的。◇ *The proposal originally emanated from the UN.* 这个建议最初是由联合国提出的。

eman·ci·pate /ɪˈmænsɪpeɪt/ *verb* [often passive] ~ **sb** (**from sth**) (*formal*) to free sb, especially from legal, political or social restrictions 解放；使不受（法律、政治或社会的）束缚 SYN **free**: *Slaves were not emancipated until 1863 in the United States.* 美国奴隶直到 1863 年才获得自由。▸ **eman·ci·pated** *adj.*: *Are women now fully emancipated* (= with the same rights and opportunities as men)? 现在女性已经彻底解放了吗？◇ *an emancipated young woman* (= one with modern ideas about women's place in society) 一位思想解放的年轻女士 **eman·ci·pa·tion** /ɪˌmænsɪˈpeɪʃn/ *noun* [U]: *the emancipation of slaves* 奴隶的解放

emas·cu·late /iˈmæskjuleɪt/ *verb* [often passive] (*formal*) **1** ~ **sb/sth** to make sb/sth less powerful or less effective 削弱；使无力；使失去效力 **2** ~ **sb** to make a man feel that he has lost his male role or qualities 使（男人）柔弱；使无男子气 ▸ **emas·cu·la·tion** /iˌmæskjuˈleɪʃn/ *noun* [U]

em·balm /ɪmˈbɑːm/ *verb* **~ sth** to prevent a dead body from decaying by treating it with special substances to preserve it 对（尸体）进行防腐处理 ▶ **em·balm·er** /ɪmˈbɑːmə(r)/ *noun*

em·bank·ment /ɪmˈbæŋkmənt/ *noun* **1** a wall of stone or earth made to keep water back or to carry a road or railway/railroad over low ground 堤；堤岸；堤围；（公路或铁路）路堤 **2** a slope made of earth or stone that rises up from either side of a road or railway/railroad （公路或铁路两侧的）护坡

em·bargo /ɪmˈbɑːgəʊ; *NAmE* ɪmˈbɑːrgoʊ/ *noun, verb*

■ *noun* (*pl.* **-oes**) an official order that bans trade with another country 禁止贸易令；禁运 SYN **boycott**: *an arms embargo* 武器禁运 ◇ **~ (on sth)** *an embargo on arms sales to certain countries* 禁止向某些国家出售武器的法令 ◇ *a* ***trade embargo*** *against certain countries* 对某些国家的贸易禁运 ◇ *to* ***impose/enforce/lift an embargo*** 实行 / 实施 / 取消贸易禁令 ➲ WORDFINDER NOTE AT TRADE ➲ COLLOCATIONS AT INTERNATIONAL

■ *verb* (**em·bar·goes**, **em·bargo·ing**, **em·bar·goed**, **em·bar·goed**) **~ sth** to place an embargo on sth 禁止…的贸易；禁运 SYN **boycott**: *There have been calls to embargo all arms shipments to the region.* 曾有人呼吁禁止所有武器运往这个地区。

em·bark /ɪmˈbɑːk; *NAmE* ɪmˈbɑːrk/ *verb* [I, T] (*formal*) to get onto a ship; to put sth onto a ship 上船；装船: *We stood on the pier and watched as they embarked.* 我们站在突码头上目送他们登船。 ◇ **~ sb/sth** *They embarked the troops by night.* 他们让部队在夜里上了船。 OPP **disembark** ▶ **em·bark·ation** /ˌembɑːˈkeɪʃn/ *noun* [U, C]: *Embarkation will be at 14:20 hours.* 上船时间是 14:20。

PHR V **emˈbark on/upon sth** (*formal*) to start to do sth new or difficult 从事，着手，开始（新的或艰难的事情）: *She is about to embark on a diplomatic career.* 她即将开始外交生涯。

em·bar·rass 🔑 /ɪmˈbærəs/ *verb* **1** 🔑 to make sb feel shy, awkward or ashamed, especially in a social situation （尤指在社交场合）使窘迫，使尴尬: **~ sb** *Her questions about my private life embarrassed me.* 她询问我的私生活使我感到很尴尬。 ◇ *I didn't want to embarrass him by kissing him in front of his friends.* 我并不想当着他的朋友吻他而使他感到难堪。 ◇ **it embarrasses sb to do sth** *It embarrassed her to meet strange men in the corridor at night.* 夜里在走廊上遇见陌生男人使她感到很不好意思。 **2** 🔑 **~ sb** to cause problems or difficulties for sb 使困惑；使为难；使陷入困境: *The speech was deliberately designed to embarrass the prime minister.* 这个发言是故意为难首相。

em·bar·rassed 🔑 /ɪmˈbærəst/ *adj.* **1** 🔑 (of a person or their behaviour 人或行为) shy, awkward or ashamed, especially in a social situation （尤指在社交场合）窘迫的，尴尬的，害羞的: *I've never felt so embarrassed in my life!* 我一生中从未感到如此难堪过！ ◇ *Her remark was followed by an embarrassed silence.* 她的话讲完后，接下来便是难堪的沉默。 ◇ **~ about sth** *She's embarrassed about her height.* 她因自己的身高而困窘。 ◇ **~ at sth** *He felt embarrassed at being the centre of attention.* 他因自己成为众人注目的中心而感到很尴尬。 ◇ **~ to do sth** *Some women are too embarrassed to consult their doctor about the problem.* 有些妇女太害羞，不愿就这个问题向医生咨询。 ➲ NOTE AT ASHAMED ➲ WORDFINDER NOTE AT SORRY **2** **financially ~** (*informal*) not having any money; in a difficult financial situation 拮据的；经济困难的

em·bar·rass·ing 🔑 /ɪmˈbærəsɪŋ/ *adj.* **1** 🔑 making you feel shy, awkward or ashamed 使人害羞的（或难堪的、惭愧的）: *an* ***embarrassing mistake/question/situation*** 令人难堪的错误 / 问题 / 处境 ◇ *It can be embarrassing for children to tell complete strangers about such incidents.* 让孩子们向素不相识的人讲述这样的事情可能是难为了他们。 ◇ *It was so embarrassing having to sing in public.* 非得在众人面前唱歌太令人难为情了。 **2** 🔑 causing sb to look stupid, dishonest, etc. 使显得愚蠢的（或不诚实的等）: *The report is likely to prove highly embarrassing to the government.* 这份报告可能会让政府非常尴尬。 ▶ **em·bar·rass·ing·ly** *adv.*: *The play was embarrassingly bad.* 这出戏很糟，令人难堪。

▼ **COLLOCATIONS** 词语搭配

Email and the Internet 电子邮件和互联网

Email 电子邮件

- **receive/get/open** an email 收到 / 打开电邮
- **write/send/answer/forward/delete** an email 写 / 发送 / 回复 / 转发 / 删除电邮
- **check/read/access** your email 查收 / 阅读 / 读取电邮
- **block/filter (out)** junk/spam/unsolicited email 阻止 / 过滤垃圾 / 不请自来的电邮
- **exchange** email addresses 交换电邮地址
- **open/check** your inbox 打开 / 查看收件箱
- junk mail **fills/floods/clogs** your inbox 垃圾电邮塞满收件箱
- **have/set up** an email account 拥有 / 创建电邮账号
- **open/send/contain** an attachment 打开 / 发送 / 包含附件
- **sign up for/receive** email alerts 注册使用 / 收到电邮提醒

Connecting to the Internet 连接到互联网

- **use/access/log onto** the Internet/the Web 使用 / 登录互联网
- **go** online/on the Internet 上网
- **have** a high-speed/dial-up/broadband/wireless (Internet) connection 有高速 / 拨号 / 宽带 / 无线网络连接
- **access/connect to/locate** the server 登录 / 连接到 / 定位服务器
- **use/open/close/launch** a/your web browser 使用 / 打开 / 关闭 / 开启网页浏览器
- **browse/surf/search/scour** the Internet/the Web 上网浏览 / 搜索
- **send/contain/spread/detect** a (computer/email) virus 发送 / 含有 / 传播 / 发现（电脑 / 电邮）病毒
- **update** your anti-virus software 升级杀毒软件
- **install/use/configure** a firewall 安装 / 使用 / 设置防火墙
- **accept/enable/block/delete** cookies 接受 / 启用 / 阻止 / 删除网站饼干

Using the Internet 使用互联网

- **visit/check** a website/an Internet site/sb's blog 访问 / 查看网站 / 互联网站点 / 某人的博客
- **create/design/launch** a website/social networking site 创建 / 设计 / 启用一个网站 / 社交网站
- **start/write/post/read** a blog 创建 / 写 / 发布 / 读博客
- **update** your blog/a website 更新博客 / 网站内容
- **be in/meet sb in/go into/enter** an Internet chat room 在 / 遇见某人在 / 进入网络聊天室
- **download/upload** music/software/a song/a podcast/a file/a copy of sth 下载 / 上传音乐 / 软件 / 一首歌 / 一个播客 / 一个文件 / 一个…的备份
- **share** information/data/files 共享信息 / 数据 / 文件
- **post** a comment/message on a(n) website/online message board/web forum/Internet chat room 在网站上 / 网络留言板上 / 网络论坛上 / 网络聊天室里发布评论 / 信息
- **stream** video/audio/music/content over the Internet 在互联网上流播视频 / 音频 / 音乐 / 内容
- **join/participate in/visit/provide** a(n) (web-based/web/online/Internet/discussion) forum 加入 / 访问 / 提供（网络）论坛
- **generate/increase/monitor** Internet traffic 产生 / 增加 / 监管网络流量

em·bar·rass·ment /ɪmˈbærəsmənt/ *noun* **1** [U] shy, awkward or guilty feelings; a feeling of being embarrassed 害羞；窘迫；愧疚；难堪：*I nearly died of embarrassment when he said that.* 他说那话差点儿把我给难堪死了。◇ *I'm glad you offered—it saved me the embarrassment of having to ask.* 你提出帮忙我很高兴，省得我厚着脸皮来问你。◇ *Much* **to her embarrassment** *she realized that everybody had been listening to her singing.* 她意识到大家一直在听她唱歌，感到很不好意思。 **2** [C] ~ **(to/for sb)** a situation which causes problems for sb 使人为难的处境；困境：*Her resignation will be a severe embarrassment to the party.* 她的辞职将使党处于极度的困境。 **3** [C] ~ **(to sb)** a person who causes problems for another person or other people and makes them feel embarrassed 令人为难（或难堪、尴尬）的人

IDM **an embarrassment of ˈriches** so many good things that it is difficult to choose just one 好东西多得难以选择

em·bassy /ˈembəsi/ *noun* (*pl.* **-ies**) **1** a group of officials led by an AMBASSADOR who represent their government in a foreign country 大使馆；（统称）使馆官员：*embassy officials* 大使馆官员 ◇ *to inform the embassy of the situation* 向大使馆报告形势 **2** the building in which an embassy works 大使馆（指馆舍）：*a demonstration outside the Russian Embassy* 在俄罗斯大使馆外的示威游行 ➲ COMPARE CONSULATE, HIGH COMMISSION ➲ WORDFINDER NOTE AT ALLY

em·bat·tled /ɪmˈbætld/ *adj.* **1** surrounded by problems and difficulties 被困扰的；处境艰难的；危机四伏的：*the embattled party leader* 处境艰难的党的领导人 **2** (of an army, a city, etc. 军队、城市等) involved in war; surrounded by the enemy 卷入战争的；被敌人包围的

embed (*also* **imbed**) /ɪmˈbed/ *verb* (**-dd-**) [usually passive] **1** ~ **sth (in sth)** to fix sth firmly into a substance or solid object 把…牢牢地嵌入（或插入、埋入）：*an operation to remove glass that was embedded in his leg* 取出扎入他腿部玻璃的手术 ◇ *The bullet embedded itself in the wall.* 子弹射进了墙里。◇ (*figurative*) *These attitudes are deeply embedded in our society* (= felt very strongly and difficult to change). 这些看法在我们这个社会中根深蒂固。 **2** ~ **sb** to send a journalist, photographer, etc. to an area where there is fighting, so that he or she can travel with the army and report what is happening 派遣（战地记者、摄影记者等）：*embedded reporters in the war zone* 战区特派记者 **3** ~ **sth** (*linguistics* 语言) to place a sentence inside another sentence. In the sentence 'I'm aware that she knows', *she knows* is an embedded sentence. 嵌入（在 I'm aware that she knows 句中，she knows 为内嵌句）

em·bel·lish /ɪmˈbelɪʃ/ *verb* (*formal*) **1** ~ **sth** to make sth more beautiful by adding decorations to it 美化；装饰；布置 SYN **decorate** **2** ~ **sth** to make a story more interesting by adding details that are not always true 对…加以渲染（或发挥）；润饰；对…添枝加叶 SYN **embroider** ▸ **em·bel·lish·ment** *noun* [U, C]: *Good fresh food needs very little embellishment.* 优质新鲜的食物基本不需调味。◇ *a 16th century church with 18th century embellishments* 增添了具有 18 世纪装饰艺术的 16 世纪教堂

ember /ˈembə(r)/ *noun* [usually pl.] a piece of wood or coal that is not burning but is still red and hot after a fire has died 余火未尽的木块（或煤块）

em·bez·zle /ɪmˈbezl/ *verb* [T, I] ~ **(sth)** to steal money that you are responsible for or that belongs to your employer 盗用，挪用，贪污，侵吞（款项）：*He was found guilty of embezzling $150 000 of public funds.* 他被判犯有盗用 15 万美元公款罪。 ▸ **em·bezzle·ment** *noun* [U]: *She was found guilty of embezzlement.* 她被判犯有贪污罪。 **em·bez·zler** /ɪmˈbezlə(r)/ *noun*

em·bit·ter /ɪmˈbɪtə(r)/ *verb* ~ **sb** to make sb feel angry or disappointed about sth over a long period of time 使怨愤；使沮丧；使苦恼 ▸ **em·bit·tered** *adj.*：*a sick and embittered old man* 身患疾病、牢骚满腹的老人 ◇ *an embittered laugh* 苦笑

em·bla·zon /ɪmˈbleɪzn/ (*also* **bla·zon**) *verb* [usually passive] to decorate sth with a design, a symbol or words so that people will notice it easily （用图案、符号或文字醒目地）装饰：~ **A with B** *baseball caps emblazoned with the team's logo* 饰有球队标识的棒球帽 ◇ ~ **B on, across, etc. A** *The team's logo was emblazoned on the baseball caps.* 球队标识醒目地印在棒球帽上。

em·blem /ˈembləm/ *noun* ~ **(of sth)** **1** a design or picture that represents a country or an organization （代表国家或组织的）徽章，标记，图案：*America's national emblem, the bald eagle* 美国的国徽 —— 白头鹫 ◇ *the club emblem* 俱乐部的徽章 **2** something that represents a perfect example or a principle 象征；标志：*The dove is an emblem of peace.* 鸽子是和平的象征。

em·blem·at·ic /ˌembləˈmætɪk/ *adj.* ~ **(of sth)** (*formal*) **1** that represents or is a symbol of sth 标志的；象征（性）的 SYN **representative** **2** that is considered typical of a situation, an area of work, etc. 特有的；典型的；有代表性的 SYN **typical**: *The violence is emblematic of what is happening in our inner cities.* 这种暴力行为正标示了我们市中心贫民区的状况。

em·bodi·ment /ɪmˈbɒdimənt; *NAmE* -ˈbɑːd-/ *noun* [usually sing.] ~ **of sth** (*formal*) a person or thing that represents or is a typical example of an idea or a quality （体现一种思想或品质的）典型，化身 SYN **epitome**: *He is the embodiment of the young successful businessman.* 他是成功青年企业家的典型。

em·body /ɪmˈbɒdi; *NAmE* ɪmˈbɑːdi/ *verb* (**em·bodies, em·body·ing, em·bodied, em·bodied**) **1** to express or represent an idea or a quality 具体表现，体现，代表（思想或品质） SYN **represent**: ~ **sth** *a politician who embodied the hopes of black youth* 代表黑人青年希望的政治家 ◇ **be embodied in sth** *the principles embodied in the Declaration of Human Rights* 体现在《人权宣言》中的原则 **2** ~ **sth** (*formal*) to include or contain sth 包括；包含；收录：*This model embodies many new features.* 这种型号具有许多新特点。

em·bold·en /ɪmˈbəʊldən; *NAmE* -ˈboʊl-/ *verb* **1** [usually passive] (*formal*) to make sb feel braver or more confident 使增加勇气；使更有胆量；使更有信心：~ **sb** *Emboldened by the wine, he went over to introduce himself to her.* 他借酒壮胆，走上前去向她作自我介绍。◇ ~ **sb to do sth** *With such a majority, the administration was emboldened to introduce radical new policies.* 政府有了这大多数人的支持，才敢推行激进的新政策。 **2** ~ **sth** (*specialist*) to make a piece of text appear in BOLD print 将（文本）变成粗体

em·bol·ism /ˈembəlɪzəm/ *noun* (*medical* 医) a condition in which a BLOOD CLOT or air bubble blocks an ARTERY in the body 栓塞（动脉被栓子堵塞）

em·bolus /ˈembələs/ *noun* (*pl.* **em·boli** /-laɪ; -liː/) (*medical* 医) a BLOOD CLOT, air bubble, or small object that causes an embolism 栓子（造成动脉栓塞的血块、气泡或小团块）

em·boss /ɪmˈbɒs; *NAmE* ɪmˈbɔːs; ɪmˈbɑːs/ *verb* [usually passive] to put a raised design or piece of writing on paper, leather, etc. 压印浮凸字体（或图案）；凹凸印：~ **A with B** *stationery embossed with the hotel's name* 凸印旅馆名称的信笺 ◇ ~ **B on A** *The hotel's name was embossed on the stationery.* 旅馆的名字凸印在信笺上。 ▸ **em·bossed** *adj.*：*embossed stationery* 有凸起图案的文具

em·bouch·ure /ˌɒmbʊˈʃʊə(r); *NAmE* ˌɑːmbʊˈʃʊr/ *noun* (*music* 音, *from French*) **1** the shape of the mouth when playing a WIND INSTRUMENT 置唇法（吹奏管乐器时的口型） **2** the MOUTHPIECE of a FLUTE （长笛的）吹口

em·brace /ɪmˈbreɪs/ *verb* (*formal*) **1** [I, T] to put your arms around sb as a sign of love or friendship 抱；拥抱 SYN **hug**: *They embraced and promised to keep in touch.* 他们互相拥抱，许诺将保持联系。◇ ~ **sb** *She embraced her son warmly.* 她热情地拥抱儿子。 **2** [T] ~ **sth** to accept an idea, a proposal, a set of beliefs, etc., especially when it is done with enthusiasm 欣然接受，乐意采纳（思想、建议等）；信奉（宗教、信仰等）：*to embrace democracy/*

feminism/Islam 信奉民主 / 女权主义 / 伊斯兰教 **3** [T] **~ sth** to include sth 包括；包含：*The talks embraced a wide range of issues.* 这些谈话涉及的问题非常广泛。
▸ **em·brace** *noun* [C, U]: *He held her in a warm embrace.* 他热情地拥抱她。◇ *There were tears and embraces as they said goodbye.* 他们分别时又是流泪，又是拥抱。◇ *the country's eager embrace of modern technology* 这个国家对现代技术的热切欢迎

em·bras·ure /ɪmˈbreɪʒə(r)/ *noun* (*architecture* 建) an opening in a wall for a door or window, wider on the inside than on the outside 斜面门（或窗）洞（两侧向内渐宽）

em·bro·ca·tion /ˌembrəˈkeɪʃn/ *noun* [U] a liquid for rubbing on sore muscles to make them less painful, for example after too much exercise 擦剂（用于缓解因运动量过大等造成的肌肉酸痛）

em·broi·der /ɪmˈbrɔɪdə(r)/ *verb* **1** [T, I] to decorate cloth with a pattern of STITCHES usually using coloured thread 刺绣：**~ A on B** *She embroidered flowers on the cushion covers.* 她在这些靠垫套上绣了花。◇ **~ B with A** *She embroidered the cushion cover with flowers.* 她在靠垫套上绣了花。◇ **~ (sth)** *an embroidered blouse* 绣花女衬衫 ◇ *She sat in the window, embroidering.* 她坐在窗前绣花。**2** [T] **~ sth** to make a story more interesting by adding details that are not always true 加以渲染（或润饰）；对…添枝加叶 **SYN** **embellish**

em·broi·dery /ɪmˈbrɔɪdəri/ *noun* **1** [U, C] patterns that are sewn onto cloth using threads of various colours; cloth that is decorated in this way 绣花；刺绣图案；刺绣品：*a beautiful piece of embroidery* 一件美丽的刺绣品 ◇ *Indian embroideries* 印度刺绣品 **2** [U] the skill or activity of decorating cloth in this way 刺绣技法；刺绣 ➲ **WORDFINDER NOTE** AT SEW ➲ **VISUAL VOCAB** PAGE V45

em·broil /ɪmˈbrɔɪl/ *verb* [often passive] **~ sb/yourself (in sth)** (*formal*) to involve sb/yourself in an argument or a difficult situation 使卷入（纠纷）；使陷入（困境）；使纠缠于：*He became embroiled in a dispute with his neighbours.* 他与邻居们发生了争执。◇ *I was reluctant to embroil myself in his problems.* 我不愿意卷入到他的问题中去。

em·bryo /ˈembriəʊ; *NAmE* -brioʊ/ *noun* (*pl.* **-os**) a young animal or plant in the very early stages of development before birth, or before coming out of its egg or seed, especially a human egg in the first eight weeks after FERTILIZATION 胚；胚胎；（尤指受孕后八周内的）人类胚胎：*human embryos* 人的胚胎 ◇ (*figurative*) *the embryo of an idea* 一种想法的雏形 ◇ *an embryo politician* (= one who is not yet very experienced) 尚未成熟的政治家

IDM **in embryo** existing but not yet fully developed 在胚胎阶段；在萌芽时期；尚未成熟：*The idea already existed in embryo in his earlier novels.* 这个想法在他早期的小说中已初见端倪。

em·bry·ology /ˌembriˈɒlədʒi; *NAmE* -ˈɑːl-/ *noun* [U] the scientific study of the development of embryos 胚胎学
▸ **em·bryo·logic·al** /ˌembriəˈlɒdʒɪkl; *NAmE* -ˈlɑːdʒ-/ *adj.* **em·bry·olo·gist** /ˌembriˈɒlədʒɪst; *NAmE* -ˈɑːl-/ *noun*

em·bry·on·ic /ˌembriˈɒnɪk; *NAmE* -ˈɑːnɪk/ *adj.* [usually before noun] **1** (*formal*) in an early stage of development 胚胎期的；萌芽期的；未成熟的：*The plan, as yet, only exists in embryonic form.* 这个计划迄今为止还只是在酝酿之中。**2** (*specialist*) of an embryo 胚的；胚胎的：*embryonic cells* 胚胎细胞

emcee /emˈsiː/ *noun* (*NAmE, informal*) **1** a person who introduces guests or entertainers at a formal occasion 司仪；（演出的）主持人 **SYN** **master of ceremonies** **2** an MC (3) at a club or party（夜总会或聚会的）说唱歌手
▸ **emcee** *verb* [I, T] **~ (sth)**

emend /iˈmend/ *verb* **~ sth** (*formal*) to remove the mistakes in a piece of writing, especially before it is printed 校订，校改，修改（文稿）**SYN** **correct**

emend·ation /ˌiːmenˈdeɪʃn/ *noun* [C, U] (*formal*) a letter or word that has been changed or corrected in a text; the act of making changes to a text 校订的内容；修改的意见；校订；修改

em·er·ald /ˈemərəld/ *noun* **1** [C, U] a bright green PRECIOUS STONE 祖母绿；绿宝石；翡翠：*an emerald ring* 绿宝石戒指 **2** (*also* ˌ**emerald** ˈ**green**) [U] a bright green colour 翡翠绿；绿宝石色 ➲ **MORE LIKE THIS** 15, page R26
▸ **em·er·ald** (*also* ˌ**emerald** ˈ**green**) *adj.*

the ˌ**Emerald** ˈ**Isle** *noun* [sing.] (*literary*) a name for Ireland 绿宝石岛（爱尔兰的别称）

emerge 🔑 **AW** /iˈmɜːdʒ; *NAmE* iˈmɜːrdʒ/ *verb* **1** 🔑 [I] to come out of a dark, confined or hidden place（从隐蔽处或暗处）出现，浮现，露出：**~ (from sth)** *The swimmer emerged from the lake.* 游泳者从湖水中浮出来。◇ *She finally emerged from her room at noon.* 中午，她终于从房间里出来了。◇ **~ (into sth)** *We emerged into bright sunlight.* 我们来到明媚的阳光下。**2** 🔑 [I, T] (of facts, ideas, etc. 事实、意见等) to become known 暴露；露出真相；被知晓 **SYN** **transpire**：*No new evidence emerged during the investigation.* 调查过程中未发现新证据。◇ **it emerges that…** *It emerged that the company was going to be sold.* 事已清楚，这家公司将被出售。**3** 🔑 [I] to start to exist; to appear or become known 露头；显现；显露：*After the elections opposition groups began to emerge.* 选举以后反对派开始露头。◇ *the emerging markets of South Asia* 正在兴起的南亚市场 ◇ **~ as sth** *He emerged as a key figure in the campaign.* 他已初露头角，成为这次运动的主要人物。**4** [I] **~ (from sth)** to survive a difficult situation or experience（从困境或苦难经历中）幸存下来，摆脱出来：*She emerged from the scandal with her reputation intact.* 丑闻过后她安然无恙，名声丝毫未受影响。▸ **emer·gence** **AW** /-dʒəns/ *noun* [U]: *the island's emergence from the sea 3 000 years ago* * 3 000 年前这个岛从大海中露出 ◇ *the emergence of new technologies* 新技术的出现

emer·gency 🔑 /iˈmɜːdʒənsi; *NAmE* iˈmɜːrdʒ-/ *noun* (*pl.* **-ies**) [C, U] a sudden serious and dangerous event or situation which needs immediate action to deal with it 突发事件；紧急情况：*The government has declared a* ***state of emergency*** *following the earthquake.* 地震发生后政府已宣布进入紧急状态。◇ *This door should only be used* ***in an emergency****.* 这道门只能在紧急情况下使用。◇ *the emergency exit* (= to be used in an emergency) 紧急出口 ◇ *The government had to take emergency action.* 政府只得采取紧急措施。◇ *The pilot made an emergency landing in a field.* 飞行员在一片农田里应急着陆。◇ *I always have some extra cash with me* ***for emergencies****.* 我总是随身多带点现金以备急需。◇ *The government has been granted emergency powers* (= to deal with an emergency). 政府已被授予应急权力。

eˈmergency brake *noun* (*NAmE*) **1** = HANDBRAKE ➲ **VISUAL VOCAB** PAGE V56 **2** a BRAKE on a train that can be pulled in an emergency（火车的）紧急刹车

eˈmergency room (*NAmE*) (*abbr.* **ER**) (*BrE* ˌ**accident and eˈmergency**) *noun* the part of a hospital where people who need urgent treatment are taken（医院）急诊室

eˈmergency services *noun* [pl.] (*BrE*) the public organizations that deal with emergencies: the police, fire, ambulance and COASTGUARD services 应急服务机构（治安、消防、救护和海岸警卫）➲ **COMPARE** FIRST RESPONDER

emer·gent **AW** /iˈmɜːdʒənt; *NAmE* iˈmɜːrdʒ-/ *adj.* [usually before noun] new and still developing 新兴的；处于发展初期的：***emergent nations/states*** 新兴民族 / 国家

emeri·tus /iˈmerɪtəs/ *adj.* (*often* **Emeritus**) used with a title to show that a person, usually a university teacher, keeps the title as an honour, although he or she has stopped working（常指大学教师）退休后保留头衔的，荣誉退休的：*the Emeritus Professor of Biology* 荣誉退休的生物学教授 **HELP** In *NAmE* the form **Emerita**

E

/iˈmerɪtə/ is used for women. 在美式英语中 Emerita 用于女性：*Professor Emerita Mary Judd* 荣誉退休教授玛丽•贾德女士

emery /ˈeməri/ *noun* [U] a hard mineral used especially in powder form for polishing things and making them smooth 金刚砂，刚玉粉（尤以粉末状用作磨料）

ˈemery board *noun* a small strip of wood or cardboard covered in emery, used for shaping your nails 指甲砂锉 ➲ VISUAL VOCAB PAGE V25

E

emet·ic /iˈmetɪk/ *noun* (*medical* 医) a substance that makes you VOMIT (= bring up food from the stomach) 催吐药；催吐剂 ▸ **emet·ic** *adj.*

emi·grant /ˈemɪɡrənt/ *noun* a person who leaves their country to live in another 移居外国的人；移民：*emigrant workers* 移居国外的工人 ◇ *emigrants to Canada* 移居加拿大的人 ➲ COMPARE IMMIGRANT

emi·grate /ˈemɪɡreɪt/ *verb* [I] ~ (**from**...) (**to**...) to leave your own country to go and live permanently in another country 移居国外；移民 ➲ COMPARE IMMIGRATE ▸ **emi·gra·tion** /ˌemɪˈɡreɪʃn/ *noun* [U, C]: *the mass emigration of Jews from Eastern Europe* 犹太人从东欧往其他地区的大批移居 ➲ COMPARE IMMIGRATION

émi·gré /ˈemɪɡreɪ/ *noun* (*from French*) a person who has left their own country, usually for political reasons（通常因政治原因移居外国的）流亡者，逃亡者 **SYN** **exile**

emi·nence /ˈemɪnəns/ *noun* **1** [U] (*formal*) the quality of being famous and respected, especially in a profession（尤指在某专业中）卓越，著名，显赫：*a man of political eminence* 政坛上出类拔萃的人 **2** [C] **His/Your Eminence** a title used in speaking to or about a CARDINAL (= a priest of the highest rank in the Roman Catholic Church)（天主教中对枢机主教的尊称）最可敬的枢机：*Their Eminences will see you now.* 最可敬的枢机现在要见你。 **3** [C] (*old-fashioned* or *formal*) an area of high ground 高地；山丘

emi·nent /ˈemɪnənt/ *adj.* [usually before noun] **1** (of people 人) famous and respected, especially in a particular profession（尤指在某专业中）卓越的，著名的，显赫的：*an eminent architect* 著名的建筑师 **2** (of good qualities 良好品质) unusual; excellent 非凡的；杰出的：*a man of eminent good sense* 极其明智的人

ˌeminent doˈmain *noun* [U] (*NAmE, law* 律) the right to force sb to sell land or a building if it is needed by the government（对私有财产的）国家征用权

emi·nent·ly /ˈemɪnəntli/ *adv.* (*formal*) (used to emphasize a positive quality 强调良好品质) very; extremely 非常；特别；极其：*She seems eminently suitable for the job.* 她看来非常适合这个工作。

emir (*also* **amir**) /eˈmɪə(r); ˈeɪmɪə(r); *NAmE* eˈmɪr; eɪˈmɪr/ *noun* the title given to some Muslim rulers 埃米尔（对某些穆斯林首领的尊称）：*the Emir of Kuwait* 科威特的埃米尔

emir·ate /ˈemɪərət; ˈemɪrət; *NAmE* ˈemərət/ *noun* **1** the position of an emir 埃米尔的职位 **2** an area of land that is ruled over by an emir 埃米尔的管辖地；酋长国：*the United Arab Emirates* 阿拉伯联合酋长国 **3** the period of time that an emir rules 埃米尔统治期

emis·sary /ˈemɪsəri; *NAmE* -seri/ *noun* (*pl.* **-ies**) (*formal*) a person who is sent to deliver an official message, especially from one country to another, or to perform a special task 特使；密使 **SYN** **envoy**

emis·sion /iˈmɪʃn/ *noun* **1** [U] (*formal*) the production or sending out of light, heat, gas, etc.（光、热、气等的）发出，射出，排放：*the emission of carbon dioxide into the atmosphere* 向大气排放二氧化碳 ◇ *emission controls* 排放管制 **2** [C] gas, etc. that is sent out into the air 排放物；散发物：*The government has pledged to clean up industrial emissions.* 政府已保证要清除工业排放物。 ➲ COLLOCATIONS AT ENVIRONMENT

eˈmissions trading *noun* = CARBON TRADING

emit /iˈmɪt/ *verb* (**-tt-**) ~ **sth** (*formal*) to send out sth such as light, heat, sound, gas, etc.发出，射出，散发（光、热、声音、气等）：*The metal container began to emit a clicking sound.* 金属容器开始发出咔嗒咔嗒的声音。◇ *Sulphur gases were emitted by the volcano.* 硫黄气体由火山喷发出来。

Emmy /ˈemi/ *noun* (*pl.* **-ies**) one of the awards given every year in the US for achievement in the making of television programmes 艾美奖（美国每年颁发的电视节目及演出奖项之一）

emo /ˈiːməʊ; *NAmE* ˈiːmoʊ/ *noun* (*pl.* **emos**) **1** [U] a style of rock music that developed from PUNK, but has more complicated musical arrangements and deals with more emotional subjects 情感核摇滚乐，情感核（基于朋克摇滚乐，音乐编排更复杂，主题更富于情感） **2** [C] a person who likes emo music and often follows emo fashion, wearing tight jeans and having long black hair. Emos are typically supposed to be emotional and sensitive and full of ANGST. 情感核乐迷（常追随情感核时尚，穿紧身牛仔裤，蓄黑色长发，以冲动、敏感、忧虑为特征）

emol·li·ent /iˈmɒliənt; *NAmE* iˈmɑːl-/ *adj., noun*
■ *adj.* (*formal*) **1** making a person or situation calmer in the hope of keeping relations peaceful 使平静的；使缓和的 **SYN** **soothing**: *an emollient reply* 息事宁人的回答 **2** (*specialist*) used for making your skin soft or less painful 润肤的；护肤的 **SYN** **soothing**: *an emollient cream* 润肤霜
■ *noun* [C, U] (*specialist*) a liquid or cream that is used to make the skin soft 润肤剂；润肤霜

emolu·ment /ɪˈmɒljumənt; *NAmE* ɪˈmɑːl-/ *noun* [usually pl.] (*formal*) money paid to sb for work they have done, especially to sb who earns a lot of money（尤指付给高收入者的）酬金，薪水，工资

emote /ɪˈməʊt; *NAmE* ɪˈmoʊt/ *verb* [I] to show emotion in a very obvious way 强烈地表现（或表露）感情

emoti·con /ɪˈməʊtɪkɒn; *NAmE* ɪˈmoʊtɪkɑːn/ *noun* (*computing* 计) a short set of keyboard symbols that represents the expression on sb's face, used in email, etc. to show the feelings of the person sending the message. For example :-) represents a smiling face (when you look at it sideways). 表情符号，情感符号（如 :-) 表示笑脸） ➲ WORDFINDER NOTE AT MESSAGE

emo·tion 🔑 /ɪˈməʊʃn; *NAmE* ɪˈmoʊʃn/ *noun* [C, U] a strong feeling such as love, fear or anger; the part of a person's character that consists of feelings 强烈的感情；激情；情感；情绪：*He lost control of his emotions.* 他对自己的情绪失去了控制。 ◇ *They expressed mixed emotions at the news.* 他们对这个消息表现出复杂的感情。◇ ***Emotions are running high*** (= people are feeling very excited, angry, etc.). 群情激昂。◇ *The decision was based on emotion rather than rational thought.* 这个决定不是基于理性的思考而是基于感情作出的。◇ *She showed no emotion at the verdict.* 她对这一裁定无动于衷。 ◇ *Mary was overcome with emotion.* 玛丽激动得不能自持。

emo·tion·al 🔑 /ɪˈməʊʃənl; *NAmE* ɪˈmoʊ-/ *adj.* **1** 🔑 [usually before noun] connected with people's feelings (= with the emotions) 感情的；情感的；情绪的：***emotional problems/needs*** 情感问题 / 需求 ◇ *emotional stress* 情绪紧张 ◇ *a child's emotional and intellectual development* 儿童的情感和智力发育 ◇ *Mothers are often the ones who provide **emotional support** for the family.* 母亲通常是家庭的情感支柱。 **2** 🔑 causing people to feel strong emotions 激起感情的；有感染力的；激动人心的 **SYN** **emotive**: *emotional language* 有感染力的语言 ◇ *abortion and other **emotional issues*** 堕胎和其他使人情绪激动的问题 **3** 🔑 (*sometimes disapproving*) showing strong emotions, sometimes in a way that other people think is unnecessary 情绪激动的；感情冲动的：*an **emotional outburst/response/reaction*** 感情爆发；情绪激动的回答 / 反应 ◇ *They made an emotional appeal for help.* 他们情绪激动地恳求救助。 ◇ *He tends to **get emotional** on these occasions.* 他在这些场合往往容易感情冲动。 ▸ **emo·tion·al·ly** 🔑 /-ʃənəli/ *adv.*：*emotionally disturbed children* 情绪异常的孩子 ◇ *I try not to become emotionally involved.*

我尽量不要感情用事。◇ *They have suffered physically and emotionally.* 他们遭受了肉体上和情感上的折磨。◇ *an emotionally charged atmosphere* 群情激昂的气氛

e,motional in'telligence *noun* [U] the ability to understand your emotions and those of other people and to behave appropriately in different situations 情绪智力（指理解情感、在不同场合下举止得体的能力）

emo·tion·less /ɪˈməʊʃənləs; *NAmE* ɪˈmoʊ-/ *adj.* not showing any emotion 没有感情的；冷漠的：*an emotionless voice* 冷漠的声音

emo·tive /iˈməʊtɪv; *NAmE* iˈmoʊ-/ *adj.* causing people to feel strong emotions 激起感情的；有感染力的；激动人心的 **SYN** **emotional**: ***emotive language/words*** 有感染力的语言 / 话语 ◇ *Capital punishment is a highly **emotive issue**.* 死刑是极易引起激烈争论的问题。

em·panel = IMPANEL

em·pa·thize (*BrE also* **-ise**) /ˈempəθaɪz/ *verb* [I] **~ (with sb/sth)** to understand another person's feelings and experiences, especially because you have been in a similar situation 有同感；产生共鸣；同情

em·pathy /ˈempəθi/ *noun* [U] the ability to understand another person's feelings, experience, etc. 同感；共鸣；同情：**~ (with sb/sth)** *the writer's imaginative empathy with his subject* 作者在想象中与笔下的人物情感共鸣 ◇ **~ (for sb/sth)** *empathy for other people's situations* 对他人所处境况的同情 ◇ **~ (between A and B)** *The empathy between the two women was obvious.* 显然这两个女人心灵相通。

em·peror /ˈempərə(r)/ *noun* the ruler of an empire 皇帝：*the Roman emperors* 古罗马皇帝 ◇ *the Emperor Napoleon* 拿破仑皇帝 ➲ SEE ALSO EMPRESS

IDM **the ,emperor has no 'clothes** used to describe a situation in which everybody suddenly realizes that they were mistaken in believing that sb/sth was very good, important, etc. 原来皇帝没有穿衣服；恍然大悟；如梦初醒：*Soon investors will realize that the emperor has no clothes and there will be a big sell-off in stocks.* 投资者很快会了解事实真相，股票将被大肆抛售。**ORIGIN** From the story of *The Emperor's New Clothes* by Hans Christian Andersen, in which the emperor is tricked into thinking he is wearing beautiful new clothes and everyone pretends to admire them, until a little boy points out that he is naked. 这句话源自汉斯・克里斯蒂安・安徒生的童话《皇帝的新装》。在这个童话中，皇帝被欺骗，以为自己穿上了美丽的新衣，所有人都假装赞赏其衣服光彩耀人，直至一个小男孩说出他赤身裸体的真相时才恍然大悟。

em·phasis 🔑 **AW** /ˈemfəsɪs/ *noun* (*pl.* **em·phases** /-siːz/) [U, C] **1** 🔑 special importance that is given to sth 强调；重视；重要性 **SYN** **stress**: **~ (on/upon sth)** *The emphasis is very much on learning the spoken language.* 重点主要放在学习口语上。◇ *to **put/lay/place emphasis** on sth* 强调 / 重视某事 ◇ *We provide all types of information, **with an emphasis on** legal advice.* 我们提供各种信息服务，尤其是法律咨询。◇ *There has been **a shift of emphasis** from manufacturing to service industries.* 重点已经从制造业向服务行业转移。◇ *The course has a vocational emphasis.* 这门课程着重职业培训。◇ *The examples we will look at have quite different emphases.* 我们将要研究观察的例子所强调的重点很不相同。**2** 🔑 the extra force given to a word or phrase when spoken, especially in order to show that it is important; a way of writing a word (for example drawing a line underneath it) to show that it is important （对某个词或短语的）强调，加重语气，重读 **SYN** **stress**: *'I can assure you,' she added with emphasis, 'the figures are correct.'* "我可以向你保证，" 她加重语气补充道，"这些数字是正确的。"

em·pha·size 🔑 **AW** (*BrE also* **-ise**) /ˈemfəsaɪz/ *verb* **1** 🔑 to give special importance to sth 强调；重视；着重 **SYN** **stress**: **~ sth** *His speech emphasized the importance of attracting industry to the town.* 他的发言强调了将工业吸引到这个城镇的重要性。◇ **~ that…** *She emphasized that their plan would mean sacrifices and hard work.* 她强调说他们的计划意味着牺牲和辛勤工作。◇ **~ how, what, etc.…** *He emphasized how little was known about the disease.* 他着重指出对这种疾病所知甚少。◇ **it must/should be emphasized that…** *It should be emphasized that this is only one possible explanation.* 应该强调的是，这只是一种可能的解释。◇ **+ speech** *'This must be our top priority,' he emphasized.* "这必须成为我们的当务之急。" 他强调说。➲ LANGUAGE BANK AT EMPHASIS **2** 🔑 **~ sth** to make sth more noticeable 使突出；使明显：*She swept her hair back from her face to emphasize her high cheekbones.* 她把头发朝脸后拢，使高高的颧骨显得更为突出。**3** 🔑 **~ sth** to give extra force to a word or phrase when you are speaking, especially to show that it is important 重读，强调（词或短语）；加强…的语气 ➲ SYNONYMS AT STRESS

em·phat·ic **AW** /ɪmˈfætɪk/ *adj.* **1** an **emphatic** statement, answer, etc. is given with force to show that it is important 强调的；有力的：***an emphatic denial/rejection*** 断然的否认 / 拒绝 **2** (of a person 人) making it very clear what you mean by speaking with force 明确表示的；加强语气的：*He was emphatic that he could not work with her.* 他强调他不能与她共事。**3** an **emphatic** victory, win, or defeat is one in which one team or player wins by a large amount （胜负）明显的，突出的，显著的 ▸ **em·phat·ic·al·ly** **AW** /-kli/ *adv.*: *'Certainly not,' he replied emphatically.* "当然不。" 他断然回答道。◇ *She is emphatically opposed to the proposals.* 她坚决反对这些建议。◇ *He has always emphatically denied the allegations.* 他一直断然否认这些指控。◇ *The proposal was emphatically defeated.* 这个建议已被断然否决。

em·phy·se·ma /ˌemfɪˈsiːmə/ *noun* [U] (*medical* 医) a condition that affects the lungs, making it difficult to breathe 肺气肿

em·pire 🔑 /ˈempaɪə(r)/ *noun* **1** 🔑 a group of countries or states that are controlled by one ruler or government 帝国：*the Roman empire* 罗马帝国 **2** 🔑 a group of commercial organizations controlled by one person or company 大企业；企业集团：*a business empire* 大型企业集团

▼ **LANGUAGE BANK** 用语库

emphasis

Highlighting an important point 强调重点

- *This case **emphasizes/highlights** the importance of honest communication between managers and employees.* 这个事例凸显出经理与员工之间坦诚交流的重要性。
- *Effective communication skills are **essential/crucial/vital**.* 有效的交流技巧是至关重要的。
- ***It should be noted that** this study considers only verbal communication. Non-verbal communication is not dealt with here.* 应该注意的是本研究只考查了言语交流，在此没有涉及非言语交流。
- ***It is important to remember that/An important point to remember is that** non-verbal communication plays a key role in getting your message across.* 非言语交流在传递信息过程中起着重要的作用，记住这一点非常重要。
- *Communication is not only about the words you use but also your body language and, **especially/above all**, the effectiveness with which you listen.* 交流不仅涉及使用的词语，同时也涉及身体语言，尤其与能否有效听取对方的话有关。
- *I would like to **draw attention to** the role of listening in effective communication.* 我想让大家注意倾听在有效交流中扮演的角色。
- *Choose your words carefully: **in particular**, avoid confusing and ambiguous language.* 注意用词，特别是避免使用令人费解和有歧义的语言。
- *Finally, and perhaps **most importantly**, you must learn to listen as well as to speak.* 最后，也许是最重要的，你不仅要学会说还要学会听。

➲ NOTE AT ESSENTIAL

➲ LANGUAGE BANK AT VITAL

'empire-building *noun* [U] (*usually disapproving*) the process of obtaining extra land, authority, etc. in order to increase your own power or position （为增加自己的权力或地位）扩展疆土（或加强权力等）；营造帝国

'Empire line *noun* a style of women's dress with the WAISTLINE positioned just below the breasts and a low-cut neck （连衣裙的）帝政高腰款式

E

em·pir·ic·al AW /ɪm'pɪrɪkl/ *adj.* [usually before noun] (*formal*) based on experiments or experience rather than ideas or theories 以实验（或经验）为依据的；经验主义的：*empirical evidence/knowledge/research* 实践经验的证明；从实际经验中获得的知识；以实验为基础的研究 ◇ *an* ***empirical study*** 经验式研究 OPP **theoretical** ▶ **em·pir·ic·al·ly** AW /-kli/ *adv.*：*Such claims need to be tested empirically.* 这类断言需要实践来检验。

em·piri·cism AW /ɪm'pɪrɪsɪzəm/ *noun* [U] (*philosophy* 哲) the use of experiments or experience as the basis for your ideas; the belief in these methods 经验主义；经验论；实证论 ▶ **em·piri·cist** /-sɪst/ *adj.*：*an empiricist theory* 经验主义理论 **em·piri·cist** /-sɪst/ *noun*：*the English empiricist, John Locke* 英格兰经验主义者约翰·洛克

em·place·ment /ɪm'pleɪsmənt/ *noun* (*specialist*) a position that has been specially prepared so that a large gun can be fired from it 炮台；炮位

em·ploy /ɪm'plɔɪ/ *verb, noun*

■ *verb* **1** to give sb a job to do for payment 雇用：**~ sb** *How many people does the company employ?* 这家公司雇用了多少人？ ◇ **~ sb as sth** *For the past three years he has been employed as a firefighter.* 三年来他一直受雇当消防员。◇ **~ sb to do sth** *A number of people have been employed to deal with the backlog of work.* 已雇来一些人处理积压的工作。 ➲ WORDFINDER NOTE AT COMPANY ➲ COLLOCATIONS AT JOB ➲ SEE ALSO SELF-EMPLOYED, UNEMPLOYED

WORDFINDER 联想词：**apply**, appoint, contract, dismiss, **job**, **pay**, retire, **work**, workforce

2 **~ sth** (*formal*) to use sth such as a skill, method, etc. for a particular purpose 应用；运用；使用：*He criticized the repressive methods employed by the country's government.* 他指责了这个国家政府采取的镇压手段。◇ *The police had to employ force to enter the building.* 警察不得不强行进入大楼。

IDM **be employed in doing sth** if a person or their time is **employed in doing sth**, the person spends time doing that thing 从事，忙于（做某事）：*She was employed in making a list of all the jobs to be done.* 她忙着把要做的所有工作列一个清单。

■ *noun* [U]

IDM **in sb's em'ploy | in the em'ploy of sb** (*formal*) working for sb; employed by sb 替某人工作；为某人所雇用

em·ploy·able /ɪm'plɔɪəbl/ *adj.* having the skills and qualifications that will make sb want to employ you 具备受雇条件的；适宜雇用的

em·ploy·ee /ɪm'plɔɪiː/ *noun* a person who is paid to work for sb 受雇者；雇工；雇员：*The firm has over 500 employees.* 这家公司有500多名雇员。◇ *government employees* 政府雇员 ◇ ***employee rights/relations*** 雇员权利 / 关系

em·ploy·er /ɪm'plɔɪə(r)/ *noun* a person or company that pays people to work for them 雇用者；雇主；老板：*They're very good employers* (= they treat the people that work for them well). 他们是非常好的雇主。◇ *one of the largest employers in the area* 这个地区最大的雇主之一

em·ploy·ment /ɪm'plɔɪmənt/ *noun* **1** [U, C] work, especially when it is done to earn money; the state of being employed 工作；职业；受雇：*to be in* ***paid employment*** 有拿工资的工作 ◇ ***full-time/part-time employment*** 全职 / 兼职工作 ◇ ***conditions/terms of employment*** 雇用条件 / 条款 ◇ *Graduates are finding it more and more difficult to find employment.* 毕业生感到找工作越来越难。◇ *pensions from previous employments* 以前工作的退休金 ➲ SYNONYMS AT WORK ➲ COLLOCATIONS AT JOB, UNEMPLOYMENT **2** [U] the situation in which people have work 就业：*The government is aiming at* ***full employment.*** 政府在力求实现充分就业。◇ *Changes in farming methods have badly affected employment in the area.* 耕作方法的改变严重影响了这个地区的就业。OPP **unemployment** **3** [U] the act of employing sb 雇用：*The law prevented the employment of children under ten in the cotton mills.* 法律禁止棉纺厂雇用十岁以下的童工。 **4** [U] **~ (of sth)** (*formal*) the use of sth 使用；利用：*the employment of artillery in the capture of the town* 在攻城时使用大炮

em'ployment agency *noun* a business that helps people to find work and employers to find workers 职业介绍所

em,ployment tri'bunal (*also* **in,dustrial tri'bunal**) *noun* (*BrE*) a type of court that can decide on disagreements between employees and employers 劳资裁判庭；劳资仲裁庭：*She took her case to an employment tribunal.* 她向劳资裁判庭提起诉讼。

em·por·ium /em'pɔːriəm/ *noun* (*pl.* **em·por·iums** or **em·poria** /-riə/) **1** (*old-fashioned*) a large shop/store 大百货商店；大型商场 **2** a shop/store that sells a particular type of goods 专门店：*an arts and crafts emporium* 工艺品商店

em·power /ɪm'paʊə(r)/ *verb* [often passive] **1** **~ sb (to do sth)** (*formal*) to give sb the power or authority to do sth 授权；给（某人）…的权力 SYN **authorize**: *The courts were empowered to impose the death sentence for certain crimes.* 法院有权因某些罪行判处罪犯死刑。 **2** **~ sb (to do sth)** to give sb more control over their own life or the situation they are in 增加（某人的）自主权；使控制局势：*The movement actively empowered women and gave them confidence in themselves.* 这场运动使女性更能主动掌握自己的命运，对自己充满信心。 ▶ **em·power·ment** *noun* [U]: *the empowerment of the individual* 让个人掌握自己的命运

emp·ress /'emprəs/ *noun* **1** a woman who is the ruler of an empire 女皇：*the Empress of Egypt* 埃及女皇 **2** the wife of an EMPEROR 皇后

emp·ties /'emptiz/ *noun* [pl.] empty bottles or glasses 空瓶；空玻璃杯

emp·ti·ness /'emptinəs/ *noun* [U, sing.] **1** a feeling of being sad because nothing seems to have any value 空虚：*There was an aching emptiness in her heart.* 她的内心有一种隐隐作痛的空虚感。 **2** the fact that there is nothing or nobody in a place 空无；空旷：*The silence and emptiness of the house did not scare her.* 房子的空寂并未使她感到害怕。 **3** (*formal*) a place that is empty 空地：*He stared out at the vast emptiness that was the sea.* 他放眼向辽阔无际的海洋望去。

empty /'empti/ *adj., verb*

■ *adj.* (**emp·tier**, **emp·ti·est**) **1** with no people or things inside 空的：*an empty box/glass* 空盒；空杯 ◇ *empty hands* (= not holding anything) 空手 ◇ *an empty plate* (= with no food on it) 空盘子 ◇ *The theatre was* ***half empty.*** 剧场空了一半。 ◇ *an empty house/room/bus* 空着的房子 / 房间 / 公共汽车 ◇ *Is this an empty chair* (= a chair that nobody else is using)? 这张椅子没人坐吗？ ◇ *The house had been* ***standing empty*** (= without people living in it) *for some time.* 这房子已经有一段时间没人住了。◇ *It's not good to drink alcohol* ***on an empty stomach*** (= without having eaten something). 空腹饮酒不好。 ◇ **~ of sth** (*formal*) *The room was empty of furniture.* 房间里什么家具都没有。 **2** [usually before noun] (of sth that sb says or does 言语或行动) with no meaning; not meaning what is said 空洞的；说话不算数的；无诚意的 SYN **hollow**：*empty words* 空话 ◇ *an empty promise* 兑现不了的承诺 ◇ *an empty gesture aimed at pleasing the crowds* 旨在取悦观众的装腔作势 **3** (of a person, or a person's life 人或其生活) unhappy because life does not seem to have a purpose, usually after sth sad has happened 空虚的；无意义的；无目的的：*Three months after his death, she still felt empty.* 他死后三个月她仍然感到心里空落落的。◇ *My life seems empty without you.* 没有你，我的生活似乎就没有了意义。 **4 ~ of sth** without a quality that you would expect to be there 没有；缺乏；无：*words that were empty of meaning* 无意义的话 ▶ **emp·ti·ly** *adv.*：*She stood staring emptily into space.* 她站着茫然地凝视前方。

■ *verb* (**emp·ties, empty·ing, emp·tied, emp·tied**) **1** [T] to remove everything that is in a container, etc. 倒空；腾空；掏空：**~ sth** *He emptied the ashtrays, washed the glasses and went to bed.* 他倒掉烟灰缸里的灰，洗完杯子就上床睡觉了。◇ *He emptied his glass and asked for a refill.* 他干了一杯，又要求再斟满一杯。◇ **~ sth out** *I emptied out my pockets but could not find my keys.* 我把口袋里的东西都掏了出来，仍然找不到我的钥匙。◇ **~ sth out of sth** *She emptied the water out of the vase.* 她把水从花瓶里倒了出来。◇ **~ sth of sth** *The room had been emptied of all furniture.* 房间里所有的家具都搬走了。◇ (*figurative*) *She emptied her mind of all thoughts of home.* 她打消了想家的所有念头。 **2** [I] to become empty 变空：*The streets soon emptied when the rain started.* 雨下起来时街上很快便空无一人。◇ **~ out** *The tank empties out in five minutes.* 水箱五分钟就空了。 **3** [T] **~ sth** (**out**) to take out the contents of sth and put them somewhere else 把…移出，把…腾出（置于别处）：*She emptied the contents of her bag onto the table.* 她把包里的东西全倒在了桌子上。◇ *Many factories emptied their waste into the river.* 许多工厂都将废料倒进了这条河里。 **4** [T] **~ sth** to make sure that everyone leaves a room, building, etc. （把…）撤出，撤离；撤空 SYN **evacuate**：*Police had instructions to empty the building because of a bomb threat.* 由于炸弹的威胁，警方奉命将所有人撤离这栋大楼。 **5** [I] to flow or move out from one place to another 流入；涌进：**~ into/onto sth** *The Rhine empties into the North Sea.* 莱茵河流入北海。◇ **~ out into/onto sth** *Fans emptied out onto the streets after the concert.* 音乐会结束后，乐迷涌到大街上。

ˌempty-ˈhanded *adj.* [not usually before noun] without getting what you wanted; without taking sth to sb 一无所获；空手：*The robbers fled empty-handed.* 抢劫犯一无所获地逃走了。◇ *She visited every Sunday and never arrived empty-handed.* 她每个星期天都来拜访，没有哪一次不带礼物。

ˌempty-ˈheaded *adj.* (*disapproving*) unable to think or behave in an intelligent way 没头脑的；傻的；无知的

the ˌempty ˈnest *noun* [sing.] the situation that parents are in when their children have grown up and left home 空巢（子女长大离家后父母独守家中）

ˌempty ˈnester *noun* [usually pl.] a parent whose children have grown up and left home 空巢父母

EMS /ˌiː em ˈes/ *noun* **1** [U] the abbreviation for 'enhanced message service' (a system for sending pictures, music and long written messages from one mobile/cell phone to another) 增强型消息业务（全写为 enhanced message service，手机传送图片、音乐和长条信息的系统） **2** [C] a message sent by EMS 增强型消息；音画信息；增强型短消息

EMU /ˌiː em ˈjuː/ *abbr.* Economic and Monetary Union (of the European Union) （欧盟）经济和货币联盟

emu /ˈiːmjuː/ *noun* a large Australian bird that can run fast but cannot fly 鸸鹋（澳洲大型鸟，善跑但不会飞）

emu·late /ˈemjuleɪt/ *verb* **1 ~ sb/sth** (*formal*) to try to do sth as well as sb else because you admire them 努力赶上；向…看齐：*She hopes to emulate her sister's sporting achievements.* 她希望在运动成绩方面赶上她姐姐。 **2 ~ sth** (*computing* 计) (of a computer program, etc. 计算机程序等) to work in the same way as another computer, etc. and perform the same tasks 仿真；模仿 ▶ **emu·la·tion** /ˌemjuˈleɪʃn/ *noun* [U, C]

emu·la·tor /ˈemjuleɪtə(r)/ *noun* (*computing* 计) a device or piece of software that makes it possible to use programs, etc. on one type of computer even though they have been designed for a different type 仿真器；仿真程序

emul·si·fier /ɪˈmʌlsɪfaɪə(r)/ *noun* (*chemistry* 化) a substance that is added to food to make the different substances in them combine to form a smooth mixture （食品）乳化剂

emul·sify /ɪˈmʌlsɪfaɪ/ *verb* (**emul·si·fies, emul·si·fy·ing, emul·si·fied, emul·si·fied**) [I, T] **~ (sth)** (*specialist*) if two liquids of different thicknesses **emulsify** or **are emulsified**, they combine to form a smooth mixture （使）乳化

emul·sion /ɪˈmʌlʃn/ *noun* [C, U] **1** any mixture of liquids that do not normally mix together, such as oil and water 乳状液；乳剂 **2** (*also* **eˈmulsion paint**) (*BrE*) a type of paint used on walls and ceilings that dries without leaving a shiny surface 乳胶漆（干后无光泽） **3** (*specialist*) a substance on the surface of PHOTOGRAPHIC film that makes it sensitive to light （照相）乳胶

en- /ɪn/ HELP Before 'b', 'm', or 'p', the form is **em-** /ɪm/. 在以字母 b、m 或 p 开头的单词前为 em-。
prefix (in verbs 构成动词) **1** to put into the thing or condition mentioned 置于…之中；使处于…状态；赋予：*encase* 置于箱中 ◇ *endanger* 使遭遇危险 ◇ *empower* 授权 **2** to cause to be 使；使成为：*enlarge* 扩大 ◇ *embolden* 使更有胆量 ➲ MORE LIKE THIS 6, page R25

-en *suffix* **1** (in verbs 构成动词) to make or become 使；使成为；变得：*blacken* 使变黑 ◇ *sadden* 使悲伤 **2** (in adjectives 构成形容词) made of; looking like 由…制成（或构成）的；像…一样的：*wooden* 木制的 ◇ *golden* 金的

en·able AW /ɪˈneɪbl/ *verb* **1 ~ sb to do sth** to make it possible for sb to do sth 使能够；使有机会 SYN **allow**：*The software enables you to create your own DVDs.* 这个软件可用来自制 DVD。◇ *a new programme to enable older people to study at college* 使老年人有机会在大学学习的新方案 **2** to make it possible for sth to happen or exist by creating the necessary conditions 使成为可能；使可行；使实现 SYN **allow**：**~ sth to do sth** *Insulin enables the body to use and store sugar.* 胰岛素使人体能够利用和贮存糖分。◇ **~ sth** *a new train line to enable easier access to the stadium* 到体育场更为便捷的新列车线路 ➲ LANGUAGE BANK AT PROCESS[1]

-enabled /ɪˈneɪbld/ *adj.* (in compound adjectives 构成复合形容词) (*computing* 计) that can be used with a particular system or technology, especially the Internet 能与某一系统（或技术）使用的：*Internet-enabled devices* 具有上网功能的设备

eˈnabling act *noun* a law which allows a person or an organization to do sth, especially to make rules 授权法

enact /ɪˈnækt/ *verb* **1** [often passive] **~ sth | it is enacted that...** (*law* 律) to pass a law 通过（法律）：*legislation enacted by parliament* 由议会通过的法律 **2** [often passive] **~ sth** (*formal*) to perform a play or act a part in a play 扮演；担任…角色；演出：*scenes from history enacted by local residents* 由当地居民演出的历史场面 **3 be enacted** (*formal*) to take place 发生；进行；举行 SYN **play out**：*They seemed unaware of the drama being enacted a few feet away from them.* 他们对于正在咫尺之外上演的戏剧性事件似乎浑然不知。 **4 ~ sth** to put sth into practice 把…付诸实践；实施：*This involves identifying problems and enacting solutions.* 这需要找出问题并解决问题。

en·act·ment /ɪˈnæktmənt/ *noun* [U, C] (*law* 律) the process of a law becoming official; a law which has been made official （法律、法案、法令的）制定，通过，颁布；法律；法规

en·amel /ɪˈnæml/ *noun* **1** [U, C] a substance that is melted onto metal, pots, etc. and forms a hard shiny surface to protect or decorate them; an object made from enamel 搪瓷；珐琅；搪瓷制品：*a chipped enamel bowl* 掉瓷的搪瓷碗 ◇ *a handle inlaid with enamel* 有珐琅镶饰的把手 ◇ *an exhibition of enamels and jewellery* 搪瓷艺术品和珠宝首饰展览 **2** [U] the hard white outer

E

layer of a tooth （牙齿的）珐琅质，釉质 **3** (*also* **e,namel 'paint**) [U, C] a type of paint that dries to leave a hard shiny surface 瓷漆；瓷釉

en·am·elled (*especially US* **en·am·eled**) /ɪˈnæmld/ *adj.* [usually before noun] covered or decorated with enamel 上了瓷漆（或瓷釉）的；用搪瓷（或珐琅）装饰的

en·am·oured (*especially US* **en·amored**) /ɪˈnæməd; *NAmE* -ərd/ *adj.* **1** (*formal*) (often in negative sentences 常用于否定句) liking sth a lot 爱好；喜欢： **~ of sth** *He was less than enamoured of the music.* 他不大爱好这种音乐。◇ **~ with sth** (*humorous*) *I'm not exactly enamoured with the idea of spending a whole day with them.* 我不是很喜欢一整天都跟他们待在一起的想法。 **2 ~ of/with sb** (*literary*) in love with sb 迷恋，倾心（于某人）

en bloc /ˌɒ̃ ˈblɒk; *NAmE* ˌɑ̃ː ˈblɑːk/ *adv.* (*from French*) as a group rather than separately 整体；全部；一起；统统： *There are reports of teachers resigning en bloc.* 有一些关于教师集体辞职的报道。

enc. = ENCL.

en·camp /ɪnˈkæmp/ *verb* [I, T] (*formal*) if a group of people **encamp** or **are encamped** somewhere, they set up a camp or have set up a camp there （使）扎营，露营

en·camp·ment /ɪnˈkæmpmənt/ *noun* a group of tents, HUTS, etc. where people live together, usually for only a short period of time （常指临时居住的）营房，营地： *a military encampment* 军营

en·cap·su·late /ɪnˈkæpsjuleɪt/ *verb* **~ sth (in sth)** (*formal*) to express the most important parts of sth in a few words, a small space or a single object 简述；概括；压缩 **SYN sum up**: *The poem encapsulates many of the central themes of her writing.* 这首诗概括了她许多著作的核心主题。 ▸ **en·cap·su·la·tion** *noun* [U, C]

en·case /ɪnˈkeɪs/ *verb* [often passive] **~ sth (in sth)** (*formal*) to surround or cover sth completely, especially to protect it 把…装箱（或围住、包起）： *The reactor is encased in concrete and steel.* 核反应堆由钢筋混凝土围封住。

en·cash /ɪnˈkæʃ/ *verb* **~ sth** (*BrE, formal*) to exchange a cheque, etc. for money 把（支票等）兑现；把…变为现钱 **SYN cash** ▸ **en·cash·ment** *noun* [U, C]

-ence ➲ -ANCE

en·ceph·al·itis /enˌsefəˈlaɪtəs; -ˌkefə-/ *noun* [U] (*medical* 医) a condition in which the brain becomes swollen, caused by an infection or ALLERGIC reaction 脑炎

en·ceph·al·op·athy /enˌsefəˈlɒpəθi; -ˌkefə-; *NAmE* -ˈlɑːp-/ *noun* [U] (*medical* 医) a disease in which the functioning of the brain is affected by infection, BLOOD POISONING, etc. 脑病 ➲ SEE ALSO BSE

en·chant /ɪnˈtʃɑːnt; *NAmE* -ˈtʃænt/ *verb* **1 ~ sb** (*formal*) to attract sb strongly and make them feel very interested, excited, etc. 使着迷；使陶醉 **SYN delight** **2 ~ sb/sth** to place sb/sth under a magic SPELL (= magic words that have special powers) 使着魔；对…施魔法（或念咒语） **SYN bewitch**

en·chant·ed /ɪnˈtʃɑːntɪd; *NAmE* -ˈtʃæntɪd/ *adj.* **1** placed under a SPELL (= magic words that have special powers) 中魔法的；着了魔的；施过魔法的： *an* ***enchanted forest/kingdom*** 被施了魔法的森林 / 王国 **2** (*formal*) filled with great pleasure 狂喜的；极乐的 **SYN delighted**: *He was enchanted to see her again after so long.* 与她久别重逢，他欣喜不已。

en·chant·er /ɪnˈtʃɑːntə(r); *NAmE* -ˈtʃæn-/ *noun* (in stories) a man who has magic powers that he uses to control people （故事中）施魔法的人，巫师

en·chant·ing /ɪnˈtʃɑːntɪŋ; *NAmE* -ˈtʃæntɪŋ/ *adj.* attractive and pleasing 迷人的；令人陶醉的；使人喜悦的 **SYN delightful**: *an enchanting view* 迷人的景色 ▸ **en·chant·ing·ly** *adv.*

en·chant·ment /ɪnˈtʃɑːntmənt; *NAmE* -ˈtʃænt-/ *noun* **1** [U] (*formal*) a feeling of great pleasure 狂喜；陶醉 **2** [U] the state of being under a magic SPELL 中魔法；着魔： *It was a place of deep mystery and enchantment.* 这是一个极其神秘和迷人的地方。 **3** [C] (*literary*) = SPELL (3)： *They had been turned to stone by an enchantment.* 他们被魔咒变成了石头。

en·chant·ress /ɪnˈtʃɑːntrəs; *NAmE* -ˈtʃæn-/ *noun* **1** (in stories) a woman who has magic powers that she uses to control people （故事中）施魔法的女人，巫婆 **2** (*literary*) a woman that men find very attractive and interesting 迷人的女子

en·chil·ada /ˌentʃɪˈlɑːdə/ *noun* (*from Spanish*) a Mexican dish consisting of a TORTILLA filled with meat and covered with a spicy sauce （墨西哥）辣肉馅玉米卷

IDM **the whole enchil'ada** (*informal*) the whole thing; everything 整个；全部；所有 ➲ MORE AT BIG *adj.*

en·cir·cle /ɪnˈsɜːkl; *NAmE* ɪnˈsɜːrkl/ *verb* **~ sb/sth** (*formal*) to surround sb/sth completely in a circle 环绕；围绕；包围： *Jack's arms encircled her waist.* 杰克的双臂搂着她的腰。◇ *The island is encircled by a coral reef.* 这个岛周围都是珊瑚礁。 ▸ **en·circle·ment** *noun* [U]

encl. (*also* **enc.**) *abbr.* (*business* 商) enclosed (used on business letters to show that another document is being sent in the same envelope) 随函附上的，附上的（用于商业信函）

en·clave /ˈenkleɪv/ *noun* an area of a country or city where the people have a different religion, culture or NATIONALITY from those who live in the country or city that surrounds it 飞地（某国或某市境内隶属外国或外市，具有不同宗教、文化或民族的领土）

en·close /ɪnˈkləʊz; *NAmE* ɪnˈkloʊz/ *verb* **1** [usually passive] **~ sth (in/with sth)** to build a wall, fence, etc. around sth （用墙、篱笆等）把…围起来： *The yard had been enclosed with iron railings.* 院子用铁栅栏围了起来。◇ *The land was enclosed in the seventeenth century* (= in Britain, when public land was made private property). 这块地在 17 世纪被圈为私有。◇ (*figurative*) *All translated words should be enclosed in brackets.* 所有译文都应用括号括起来。 **2 ~ sth** (especially of a wall, fence, etc. 尤指墙、篱笆等) to surround sth 围住： *Low hedges enclosed the flower beds.* 矮树篱把花坛围了起来。 ◇ (*figurative*) *She felt his arms enclose her.* 她感到他双臂搂住了她。 **3 ~ sth (with sth)** to put sth in the same envelope, package, etc. as sth else 附入；随函（或包裹等）附上： *Please return the completed form, enclosing a recent photograph.* 请将填好的表格寄回，并附上近照一张。

en·closed /ɪnˈkləʊzd; *NAmE* ɪnˈkloʊzd/ *adj.* **1** with walls, etc. all around （用墙等）围住的，封闭的： *Do not use this substance in an enclosed space.* 切勿在封闭空间使用此物质。 **2** (*abbr.* **encl.**) sent with a letter, etc. 随函附上的；附上的： *Please complete the enclosed application form.* 请填好随函所附的申请表。 ◇ *Please* ***find enclosed*** *a cheque for £100.* 随函附上 100 英镑支票一张。 **3** (of religious communities 宗教团体) having little contact with the outside world 与外界隔绝的

en·clos·ure /ɪnˈkləʊʒə(r); *NAmE* -ˈkloʊ-/ *noun* **1** [C] a piece of land that is surrounded by a fence or wall and is used for a particular purpose 圈占地；圈用地；围场： *a wildlife enclosure* 野生动物围场 **2** [U, C] the act of placing a fence or wall around a piece of land 圈地： *the enclosure of common land in the seventeenth century* * 17 世纪对公用地的圈占 **3** [C] something that is placed in an envelope with a letter （信中）附件

en·code /ɪnˈkəʊd; *NAmE* ɪnˈkoʊd/ *verb* **1 ~ sth** to change ordinary language into letters, symbols, etc. in order to send secret messages 把…译成电码（或密码） **2 ~ sth** (*computing* 计) to change information into a form that can be processed by a computer 把…编码 **3 ~ sth** (*linguistics* 语言) to express the meaning of sth in a foreign language 把…译成外语 ➲ COMPARE DECODE

en·co·mium /enˈkəʊmiəm; *NAmE* -ˈkoʊm-/ *noun* (*pl.* **en·co·miums** or **en·co·mia** /enˈkəʊmiə; *NAmE* -ˈkoʊm-/) (*formal*) a speech or piece of writing that praises sb or sth highly 高度赞扬的话（或文章）；颂词

en·com·pass /ɪnˈkʌmpəs/ *verb* (*formal*) **1 ~ sth** to include a large number or range of things 包含，包括，涉及（大量事物）： *The job encompasses a wide range of responsibilities.* 这项工作涉及的职责范围很广。 ◇ *The group encompasses all ages.* 这个小组各种年龄的人都有。 **2 ~ sth** to surround or cover sth completely 包围；围绕；围住： *The fog soon encompassed the whole valley.* 大雾很快笼罩了整个山谷。

en·core /ˈɒŋkɔː(r); *NAmE* ˈɑːŋ-/ *noun, exclamation*
■ ***noun*** an extra short performance given at the end of a concert or other performance; a request for this made by an audience calling out （音乐会或其他演出结束时）加演的节目；（观众要求的）再演一个；安可： *She played a Chopin waltz as an encore.* 她应听众的要求又加演了一首肖邦的圆舞曲。 ◇ *The group got three encores.* 乐团三次得到观众“再来一个”的请求。
■ ***exclamation*** an audience calls out **encore!** at the end of a concert to ask the performer to play or sing another piece of music （在音乐会结束时观众喊的）再来一个，再唱一首，再奏一曲

en·coun·ter 🔑 AW /ɪnˈkaʊntə(r)/ *verb, noun*
■ ***verb*** **1** 🔑 **~ sth** to experience sth, especially sth unpleasant or difficult, while you are trying to do sth else 遭遇，遇到（尤指令人不快或困难的事） SYN **meet, run into**: *We encountered a number of difficulties in the first week.* 我们在第一周遇到了一些困难。 ◇ *I had never encountered such resistance before.* 我以前从未遇到过这么大的阻力。 **2** 🔑 **~ sb/sth** (*formal*) to meet sb, or discover or experience sth, especially sb/sth new, unusual or unexpected 偶然碰到；意外地遇见；与…邂逅 SYN **come across**: *She was the most remarkable woman he had ever encountered.* 她是他所见到过的最出色的女性。
■ ***noun*** **1** 🔑 a meeting, especially one that is sudden, unexpected or violent （尤指突然、意外或暴力的）相遇，邂逅，遭遇，冲突： **~ (with sb/sth)** *Three of them were killed in the subsequent encounter with the police.* 他们中有三个人后来在与警察的冲突中被杀死。 ◇ **~ (between A and B)** *The story describes the extraordinary encounter between a man and a dolphin.* 这个故事描述了一个男人与一只海豚之间的奇遇。 ◇ *a chance encounter* 偶然相遇 ◇ *I've had a number of* **close encounters** (= situations that could have been dangerous) *with bad drivers.* 我好几次都险些与技术不佳的司机相撞。 ◇ *It was his first sexual encounter* (= first experience of sex). 那是他的第一次性经历。 **2** a sports match against a particular player or team （体育）比赛，交锋： *She has beaten her opponent in all of their previous encounters.* 她在以前的所有交锋中都击败了这个对手。 **3** (*IndE*) an incident in which police shoot dead a suspected criminal 警察击毙嫌疑犯事件

enˈcounter group *noun* a group of people who meet regularly in order to help each other with emotional and PSYCHOLOGICAL problems 交心心理治疗团体，会心团体（成员定期聚集）

en·cour·age 🔑 /ɪnˈkʌrɪdʒ; *NAmE* -ˈkɜːr-/ *verb* **1** 🔑 to give sb support, courage or hope 支持；鼓励；激励： **~ sb in sth** *My parents have always encouraged me in my choice of career.* 在我选择职业时父母总是鼓励我。 ◇ **~ sb** *We were greatly encouraged by the positive response of the public.* 公众所持的肯定态度给了我们极大的鼓舞。 **2** 🔑 **~ sb to do sth | ~ doing sth** to persuade sb to do sth by making it easier for them and making them believe it is a good thing to do 鼓动；劝告；怂恿： *Banks actively encouraged people to borrow money.* 银行积极鼓动人们贷款。 **3** 🔑 to make sth more likely to happen or develop 促进；助长；刺激： **~ sth (in sb/sth)** *They claim that some computer games encourage violent behaviour in young children.* 他们声称有些电脑游戏助长儿童的暴力行为。 ◇ **~ sb to do sth** *Music and lighting are used to encourage shoppers to buy more.* 音乐和灯光用于刺激购物者买更多的东西。 ◇ **~ doing sth** *Technology encourages multitasking.* 技术进步促进多任务处理。 OPP **discourage**
▸ **en·cour·aging** *adj.* [not usually before noun]: *This month's unemployment figures are not very encouraging.* 这个月的失业统计数字不太乐观。 ◇ *You could try being a little more encouraging!* 你可以试着多给人一些鼓励嘛！ **en·cour·aging·ly** *adv.*: *to smile encouragingly* 表示鼓励地微微一笑 ◇ *The attendance was encouragingly high.* 出席人数之多令人振奋。

en·cour·age·ment 🔑 /ɪnˈkʌrɪdʒmənt; *NAmE* -ˈkɜːr-/ *noun* [U, C, usually sing.] the act of encouraging sb to do sth; something that encourages sb 鼓舞；鼓励；起激励作用的事物： *a few words of encouragement* 几句鼓励的话 ◇ *He needs all the support and encouragement he can get.* 他需要所能得到的一切支持和鼓励。 ◇ *With a little encouragement from his parents he should do well.* 只要父母给点鼓励，他应该会干得很好。 ◇ **~ (to sb) (to do sth)** *She was given every encouragement to try something new.* 她得到充分的鼓励去尝试新事物。 ◇ *Her words were a great encouragement to them.* 她的话对他们是极大的鼓舞。 OPP **discouragement**

en·croach /ɪnˈkrəʊtʃ; *NAmE* ɪnˈkroʊtʃ/ *verb* (*formal*) **1** [I] **~ (on/upon sth)** (*disapproving*) to begin to affect or use up too much of sb's time, rights, personal life, etc. 侵占（某人的时间）；侵犯（某人的权利）；扰乱（某人的生活）： *I won't encroach on your time any longer.* 我不会再占用你的时间了。 ◇ *He never allows work to encroach upon his family life.* 他从不让工作扰乱他的家庭生活。 **2** [I] **~ (on/upon sth)** to slowly begin to cover more and more of an area 侵蚀，蚕食（地区）： *The growing town soon encroached on the surrounding countryside.* 这个不断扩大的城镇不久便将周围的农村变成了市区。 ◇ *the encroaching tide* (= that is coming in) 不断涌向陆地的潮水
▸ **en·croach·ment** *noun* [U, C]: **~ (on/upon sth)** *the regime's many encroachments on human rights* 这个政权种种侵犯人权的行为

en·crust·ation /ˌenkrʌˈsteɪʃn/ *noun* = INCRUSTATION

en·crust·ed /ɪnˈkrʌstɪd/ *adj.* **~ (with/in sth)** covered with a thin hard layer of sth; forming a thin hard layer on sth 硬壳覆盖的；形成硬外层的： *a crown encrusted with diamonds* 镶满钻石的王冠 ◇ *encrusted blood* 已凝结的血

en·crypt /ɪnˈkrɪpt/ *verb* **~ sth** (*computing* 计) to put information into a special code, especially in order to prevent people from looking at it without authority 把…加密（或编码） OPP **decrypt** ▸ **en·cryp·tion** /ɪnˈkrɪpʃn/ *noun* [U] OPP **decryption**

en·cum·ber /ɪnˈkʌmbə(r)/ *verb* [usually passive] (*formal*) **1 ~ sb/sth (with sth)** to make it difficult for sb to do sth or for sth to happen 妨碍；阻碍；拖累： *The police operation was encumbered by crowds of reporters.* 警方的行动被成群的记者所妨碍。 **2 ~ sb/sth (with sth)** to be large and/or heavy and make it difficult for sb to move 大（或重）得难以移动；使负担沉重： *The frogmen were encumbered by their diving equipment.* 沉重的潜水装备使蛙人行动困难。

en·cum·brance /ɪnˈkʌmbrəns/ *noun* (*formal*) a person or thing that prevents sb from moving easily or from doing what they want 妨碍者；累赘；障碍物 SYN **burden**: *I felt I was being an encumbrance to them.* 我感到自己成了他们的累赘。

-ency ⊃ -ANCY

en·cyc·lic·al /ɪnˈsɪklɪkl/ *noun* an official letter written by the Pope and sent to all Roman Catholic BISHOPS 教皇通谕

en·cyc·lo·pe·dia (*BrE also* **-pae·dia**) /ɪnˌsaɪkləˈpiːdiə/ *noun* a book or set of books giving information about all areas of knowledge or about different areas of one particular subject, usually arranged in alphabetical order; a similar collection of information on a website or CD-ROM （纸质、网络或光盘版）百科全书；（某一学科的）专科全书： ***an online encyclopedia*** 一部网络百科全书

E

en·cyclo·pe·dic (*BrE also* **-pae·dic**) /ɪnˌsaɪkləˈpiːdɪk/ *adj.* **1** connected with encyclopedias or the type of information found in them 百科全书的；百科知识的： *encyclopedic information* 百科知识 ◇ *an encyclopedic dictionary* 百科词典 **2** having a lot of information about a wide variety of subjects; containing complete information about a particular subject 包含各种学科知识的；知识渊博的；博学的： *She has an encyclopedic knowledge of natural history.* 她具有广博的自然史知识。

E

end /end/ *noun, verb*

■ *noun*

• **FINAL PART** 最后部分 **1** the final part of a period of time, an event, an activity or a story （时间、事件、活动或故事的）终止，终结，结局，结尾： ***at the end of the week*** 在周末 ◇ *We didn't leave until the* ***very end.*** 我们直到最后才离开。 ◇ *the end of the book* 书的末尾 ◇ *We had to hear about the whole journey* ***from beginning to end.*** 我们只好从头到尾把整个旅行情况听完。 ◇ *It's the end of an era.* 这是一个时代的终结。

• **FURTHEST PART** 末端 **2** the part of an object or a place that is the furthest away from its centre 末端；尽头；末梢： *Turn right at the end of the road.* 在路的尽头向右转。 ◇ *I joined the end of the queue.* 我站在了这队伍的最后。 ◇ *Go to the end of the line!* 到这条队的最后去！ ◇ *You've got something on the end of your nose.* 你的鼻尖上有点东西。 ◇ *Tie the ends of the string together.* 把绳子两端系在一起。 ◇ *That's his wife sitting at* ***the far end*** *of the table.* 坐在桌子远端的那位就是他妻子。 ◇ *These two products are from opposite ends of the price range.* 这两种产品一种是价格最高的，一种是价格最低的。 ◇ *We've travelled from one end of Mexico to the other.* 我们从墨西哥的一端旅行到了另一端。 ◇ *They live in the end house.* 他们住在最后的那座房子里。 ➲ SEE ALSO BIG END, DEAD END, EAST END, SPLIT END, TAIL END

• **FINISH** 结束 **3** a situation in which sth does not exist any more 结束；破灭： *the end of all his dreams* 他所有梦想的破灭 ◇ *The meeting* ***came to an end*** (= finished). 会议结束了。 ◇ *The war was finally* ***at an end.*** 战争终于结束了。 ◇ *The coup* ***brought*** *his corrupt regime* ***to an end.*** 政变结束了他的腐败统治。 ◇ ***There's no end in sight*** *to the present crisis.* 目前的危机无望结束。 ◇ *They have* ***called for an end to*** *violence.* 他们呼吁停止暴力。 ◇ *That was by no means the end of the matter.* 事情绝不可能到此为止。

• **AIM** 目的 **4** an aim or a purpose 目的；目标： *They are prepared to use violence in pursuit of their ends.* 他们准备使用暴力来达到目的。 ◇ *She is exploiting the current situation for her own ends.* 她在利用目前的形势来达到自己的目的。 ◇ ***With this end in view*** (= in order to achieve this) *they employed 50 new staff.* 为了达到这个目标他们雇用了 50 名新职员。 ◇ *We are willing to make any concessions necessary* ***to this end*** (= in order to achieve this). 为达到此目的我们愿作出任何必要的让步。 ➲ SYNONYMS AT TARGET

• **PART OF ACTIVITY** 部分活动 **5** [usually sing.] a part of an activity with which sb is concerned, especially in business （尤指经营活动的）部分，方面： *We need somebody to handle the marketing end of the business.* 我们需要有人来处理业务的推广。 ◇ *Are there any problems at your end?* 你那边有什么问题吗？ ◇ *I have kept my end of the bargain.* 我已履行了我的协议条件。

• **OF TELEPHONE LINE/JOURNEY** 电话线；旅程 **6** [usually sing.] either of two places connected by a telephone call, journey, etc. 端点；终点： *I answered the phone but there was no one* ***at the other end.*** 我接了电话，但线路的另一端没人说话。 ◇ *Jean is going to meet me at* ***the other end.*** 琼打算在那边终点站接我。

• **OF SPORTS FIELD** 运动场 **7** one of the two halves of a sports field 半边球场： *The teams changed ends at half-time.* 上半场结束时双方交换了场地。

• **PIECE LEFT** 剩余物 **8** (*BrE*) a small piece that is left after sth has been used 剩余物；残余；残片： *a cigarette end* 烟蒂 ➲ SEE ALSO FAG END, LOOSE END, ODDS AND ENDS

• **DEATH** 死亡 **9** [usually sing.] a person's death. People say 'end' to avoid saying 'death'. 辞世，过世（婉辞，与 death 同义）： *She came to* ***an untimely end*** (= died young). 她英年早逝。 ◇ *I was with him at the end* (= when he died). 他临终时我在他身边。 ◇ (*literary*) *He* ***met his end*** (= died) *at the Battle of Waterloo.* 他在滑铁卢战役中阵亡。

IDM **at the ˌend of the ˈday** (*informal*) used to introduce the most important fact after everything has been considered （考虑到所有情况后引出最重要的事实）最终，到头来： *At the end of the day, he'll still have to make his own decision.* 最终，他还得自己拿主意。 **a bad/sticky ˈend** (*BrE*) something unpleasant that happens to sb, for example punishment or a violent death, usually because of their own actions 不愉快的结局；可悲的下场： *He'll* ***come to a sticky end*** *one of these days if he carries on like that.* 如果他继续那样下去，总有一天会落得个可悲的下场。 **be at the end of sth** to have almost nothing left of sth 所剩无几；到…的尽头（或极限）： *I'm at the end of my patience.* 我已忍无可忍。 ◇ *They are at the end of their food supply.* 他们的食物储备快要消耗殆尽。 **be at the ˌend of your ˈtether** (*BrE*) (*NAmE* **be at the ˌend of your ˈrope**) to feel that you cannot deal with a difficult situation any more because you are too tired, worried, etc. 筋疲力尽；智穷力竭；山穷水尽 **be the ˈend** (*BrE, informal*) when you say that people or situations are **the end**, you mean that you are annoyed with them 令人讨厌；惹人烦恼；让人无法容忍 **an ˌend in itˈself** a thing that is itself important and not just a part of sth more important 本身重要的事 **the end justifies the ˈmeans** (*saying*) bad or unfair methods of doing sth are acceptable if the result of that action is good or positive 只要目的正当，可以不择手段 **(reach) the end of the ˈline/ˈroad** (to reach) the point at which sth can no longer continue in the same way （达到）尽头，极限；穷途末路： *A defeat in the second round marked the end of the line for last year's champion.* 第二局的失利表明去年的冠军得主已卫冕无望。 **end of ˈstory** (*informal*) (*BrE also* **end ˈof...**) used when you are stating that there is nothing more that can be said or done about sth 情况就是这样；就这么办 **ˌend to ˈend** in a line, with the ends touching 首尾相接连成一行： *They arranged the tables end to end.* 他们将桌子连接起来排成一行。 **get/have your ˈend away** (*BrE, slang*) to have sex 性交 **go to the ˌends of the ˈearth** to do everything possible, even if it is difficult, in order to get or achieve sth 走遍天涯海角；历尽千辛万苦： *I'd go to the ends of the earth to see her again.* 哪怕走遍天涯海角我也要再见她一面。 **in the ˈend** **1** after a long period of time or series of events 最后；终于： *He tried various jobs and in the end became an accountant.* 他尝试过各种各样的工作，最后当上了会计。 **2** after everything has been considered 到头来；最终： *You can try your best to impress the interviewers but in the end it's often just a question of luck.* 你可以尽最大的努力给主持面试的人留下深刻的印象，不过最终常常要看运气。 **keep your ˈend up** (*BrE, informal*) to continue to be cheerful in a difficult situation （在困境中）不泄气，保持乐观 **make (both) ends ˈmeet** to earn just enough money to be able to buy the things you need 使收支相抵；勉强维持生计： *Many families struggle to make ends meet.* 许多家庭只能勉强维持生计。 **no ˈend** (*informal*) very much 极其；非常： *It upset me no end to hear they'd split up.* 听说他们已离婚，我感到非常不安。 **no ˈend of sth** (*informal*) a lot of sth 无数；大量；许多： *We had no end of trouble getting them to agree.* 我们费了九牛二虎之力才使他们同意。 **not the end of the ˈworld** (*informal*) not the worst thing that could happen to sb 天不会塌下来；不是灭顶之灾： *Failing one exam is not the end of the world.* 一次考试不及格并非世界末日。 **on ˈend** **1** in a vertical position 竖着；直立着： *It'll fit if you stand it on end.* 如果把它竖着就放得进去了。 **2** for the stated length of time, without stopping 连续地；不断地： *He would disappear for* ***weeks on end.*** 他常常是连续几周不见人影。 **put an ˈend to yourself | put an ˈend to it all** to kill yourself 自杀；一了百了 ➲ MORE AT BEGINNING, BITTER *adj.*, BURN *v.*, DEEP *adj.*, HAIR, HEAR, LIGHT *n.*, LOOSE END, MEANS, RECEIVE, ROUGH *adj.*, SHARP *adj.*, SHORT *adj.*, THIN *adj.*, WIT, WRONG *adj.*

■ ***verb*** 🔑 [I, T] to finish; to make sth finish 结束；终止：*The road ends here.* 这条路到此为止。◇ *How does the story end?* 这个故事结局如何？◇ *The speaker ended by suggesting some topics for discussion.* 演讲者最后给出了几个讨论话题。◇ **~ with sth** *Her note ended with the words: 'See you soon.'* 她的便条以"再见"结束。◇ **~ sth** *They decided to end their relationship.* 他们决定断绝关系。◇ **~ sth with sth** *They ended the play with a song.* 他们以一首歌曲结束了这出戏。◇ **+ speech** *'And that was that,' she ended.* "就这样了。"她最后说。➲ EXPRESS YOURSELF AT FINISH

▼ EXPRESS YOURSELF 情景表达

Ending a conversation 结束谈话

When you stop talking to someone, there are polite ways to end a conversation. 结束与别人的谈话可用比较礼貌的方式：

- ***It's been lovely/so nice/good talking to you.*** 和你谈谈很开心。
- ***I'm so glad we got to talk.*** 我们有机会谈话，我很高兴。
- ***I'm sorry, I have to rush off.*** 抱歉，我得赶紧走了。
- ***It was nice to meet you.*** *I'm sorry I have to go now.* 很高兴见到你。对不起，我现在得走了。
- ***Will you excuse me?*** *There's someone I've got to speak to.* 失陪了，我得跟一个人说几句。

IDM **a/the sth to end all sths** used to emphasize how large, important, exciting, etc. you think sth is 最大（或最重要、最激动人心等）的…：*The movie has a car chase to end all car chases.* 这部影片的汽车追逐场面非常刺激。**ˌend your ˈdays/ˈlife (in sth)** to spend the last part of your life in a particular state or place （在某种状态下或某处）度过余生，安度晚年：*He ended his days in poverty.* 他在贫穷中度过余生。**ˌend in ˈtears** (*BrE, informal*) if you say that sth will **end in tears**, you are warning sb that what they are doing will have an unhappy or unpleasant result （告诫时说）以痛苦而告终，结局悲惨 **ˈend it all | ˌend your ˈlife** to kill yourself 自杀；一了百了

PHR V **ˈend in sth** [no passive] **1** 🔑 to have sth as an ending 以…结尾；末端是：*The word I'm thinking of ends in '-ous'.* 我想到的这个词以 ous 结尾。**2** 🔑 to have sth as a result 以…为结果；以…告终：*Their long struggle ended in failure.* 他们的长期努力以失败告终。◇ *The debate ended in uproar.* 那场辩论最后以大吵大闹收场。**ˌend ˈup** 🔑 to find yourself in a place or situation that you did not intend or expect to be in 最终成为；最后处于：**end up doing sth** *I ended up doing all the work myself.* 结果所有的活儿都是我一个人干了。◇ **+ adv./prep.** *If you go on like this you'll end up in prison.* 如果你继续这样，早晚得进监狱。◇ **+ adj.** *If he carries on driving like that, he'll end up dead.* 如果他继续那样开车，总有一天会把命都丢掉。

en·dan·ger /ɪnˈdeɪndʒə(r)/ *verb* **~ sb/sth** to put sb/sth in a situation in which they could be harmed or damaged 使遭危险；危及；危害：*The health of our children is being endangered by exhaust fumes.* 我们孩子的健康正受到废气损害。◇ *That one mistake seriously endangered the future of the company.* 仅那一个失误就严重地危及了公司的未来。➲ WORDFINDER NOTE AT GREEN

en·dan·gered /ɪnˈdeɪndʒəd; *NAmE* -dʒərd/ *adj.* (used about groups of animals, plants, etc.) at risk of no longer existing （动植物群落等）濒临灭绝的，濒危的：*14% of primate species are highly endangered.* * 14% 的灵长目动物处于高度濒危状态。◇ *The sea turtle is an* ***endangered species****.* 海龟是濒危物种。

en·dear /ɪnˈdɪə(r); *NAmE* -ˈdɪr/ *verb*

PHR V **enˈdear sb/yourself to sb** to make sb/yourself popular 使受欢迎（或喜爱、爱慕）：*Their policies on taxation didn't endear them to voters.* 他们的税收政策并没使他们受到选民的欢迎。◇ *She was a talented teacher who endeared herself to all who worked with her.* 她是一位深受同事喜爱的有才华的教师。

en·dear·ing /ɪnˈdɪərɪŋ; *NAmE* -ˈdɪr-/ *adj.* causing people to feel affection 令人爱慕的；惹人喜爱的；讨人喜欢的 **SYN** **lovable**：*an endearing habit* 讨人喜欢的习惯 ▸ **en·dear·ing·ly** *adv.*

en·dear·ment /ɪnˈdɪəmənt; *NAmE* -ˈdɪrm-/ *noun* [C, U] a word or an expression that is used to show affection 表示爱慕的话语；亲热的表示：*They were whispering endearments to each other.* 他们彼此低声倾吐着爱慕之情。◇ *'Darling' is a term of endearment.* "亲爱的"是一种昵称。

en·deav·our (*especially US* **en·deavor**) /ɪnˈdevə(r)/ *noun, verb*

■ ***noun*** [U, C] (*formal*) an attempt to do sth, especially sth new or difficult （尤指新的或艰苦的）努力，尝试：*Please make every endeavour to arrive on time.* 请尽全力按时到达。◇ *advances in the field of scientific endeavour* 在科学探索领域的进步 ◇ *The manager is expected to use his or her best endeavours to promote the artist's career.* 经纪人应以最大的努力来推动艺人的事业发展。

■ ***verb*** **~ to do sth** (*formal*) to try very hard to do sth 努力；尽力；竭力 **SYN** **strive**：*I will endeavour to do my best for my country.* 我将竭尽全力报效祖国。

en·dem·ic /enˈdemɪk/ *adj.* regularly found in a particular place or among a particular group of people and difficult to get rid of 地方性的；（某地或某集体中）特有的，流行的，难摆脱的：**~ (in…)** *Malaria is endemic in many hot countries.* 疟疾是许多气候炎热国家的流行病。◇ *Corruption is endemic in the system.* 腐败在这种制度下普遍存在。◇ **~ (among…)** *an attitude endemic among senior members of the profession* 此行业中的资深者普遍持有的看法 ◇ **~ (to…)** *species endemic to* (= only found in) *Madagascar* 马达加斯加特有的物种 ◇ *the endemic problem of racism* 普遍存在的种族主义问题 ➲ COMPARE PANDEMIC

end·game /ˈendgeɪm/ *noun* **1** the final stage of a game of CHESS （棋赛的）尾盘，残局 **2** the final stage of a political process （政治进程的）最后阶段

end·ing 🔑 /ˈendɪŋ/ *noun* **1** 🔑 the last part of a story, film/movie, etc. （故事、电影等的）结尾，结局：*His stories usually have a* ***happy ending****.* 他的故事通常有一个美满的结局。**OPP** **opening** ➲ WORDFINDER NOTE AT PLOT **2** 🔑 the act of finishing sth; the last part of sth 结束；终结；最后部分：*the anniversary of the ending of the Pacific War* 太平洋战争结束的周年纪念日 ◇ *It was the perfect ending to the perfect day.* 那是美好一天的圆满结束。**3** 🔑 the last part of a word, that is added to a main part 词尾；字尾：*verb endings* 动词词尾 ◇ *a* ***masculine/feminine ending*** 阳性 / 阴性词尾

en·dive /ˈendaɪv; -dɪv/ *noun* [C, U] **1** (*BrE*) (*NAmE also* **chic·ory**, **ˌcurly ˈendive**, **fri·sée** [U]) a plant with green curly leaves that are eaten raw as a vegetable （卷叶）欧洲菊苣 **2** (*NAmE*) (*BrE* **chic·ory**) a small pale green plant with bitter leaves that are eaten raw or cooked as a vegetable. The root can be dried and used with or instead of coffee. 菊苣（根干燥后可与咖啡同饮或作其代用品）

end·less /ˈendləs/ *adj.* **1** very large in size or amount and seeming to have no end 无止境的；无垠的；无穷无尽的；不计其数的 **SYN** **limitless**：*endless patience* 无限的耐心 ◇ *endless opportunities for making money* 无数挣钱的机会 ◇ *The possibilities are endless.* 存在着无限的可能性。◇ *an endless list of things to do* 列不完的要做的事 ◇ *We don't have an endless supply of money, you know.* 你要知道，我们没有源源不竭的资金供给。**2** continuing for a long time and seeming to have no end 永久的；不断的；无休止的：*an endless round of parties and visits* 没完没了一个又一个的社交聚会和访问 ◇ *The journey seemed endless.* 旅程似乎没有尽头。◇ *I've had enough of their endless arguing.* 我听够了他们无休止的争吵。**3** (*specialist*) (of a LOOP, etc. 环状物) having the ends joined together so it forms one piece 两端连接的；环状的：*an endless loop of tape* 环状带 ▸ **end·less·ly** *adv.*：*She talks endlessly about her* *problems.* 她喋喋不休地谈论着自己的问题。◇ *an endlessly repeated pattern* 不断重复的模式

end·note /ˈendnəʊt; *NAmE* -noʊt/ *noun* a note printed at the end of a book or section of a book （书末或章节末的）尾注

endo·crine /ˈendəʊkrɪn; -kraɪn; *NAmE* ˈendəkrɪn/ *adj.* (*biology* 生) connected with GLANDS that put HORMONES and other products directly into the blood 内分泌的；内分泌腺的： *the endocrine system* 内分泌系统 ➲ COMPARE EXOCRINE

E

endo·crin·ology /ˌendəʊkrɪˈnɒlədʒi; *NAmE* ˌendoʊkrəˈnɑːl-/ *noun* [U] (*medical* 医) the part of medicine concerning the endocrine system and HORMONES 内分泌学 ▸ **endo·crin·olo·gist** /-dʒɪst/ *noun*

en·dog·amy /enˈdɒgəmi; *NAmE* -ˈdɑːg-/ *noun* [U] (*specialist*) the custom of marrying only people from your local community 族内婚，内婚制（只在一个群体内部通婚的风俗） ➲ COMPARE EXOGAMY

en·dogen·ous /enˈdɒdʒənəs; *NAmE* -ˈdɑːdʒ-/ *adj.* (*medical* 医) (of a disease or SYMPTOM 疾病或症状) having a cause that is inside the body 内源性的；内生的 ➲ COMPARE EXOGENOUS

endo·plasm /ˈendəʊplæzəm; *NAmE* ˈendoʊ-/ *noun* [U] (*biology* 生, *old-fashioned*) the more liquid inner layer of the jelly-like substance inside cells （细胞）内质 ➲ COMPARE ECTOPLASM (1)

en·dor·phin /enˈdɔːfɪn; *NAmE* -ˈdɔːrf-/ *noun* (*biology* 生) a HORMONE produced in the brain that reduces the feeling of pain 内啡肽（内分泌激素，有镇痛作用）

en·dorse /ɪnˈdɔːs; *NAmE* ɪnˈdɔːrs/ *verb* **1** ~ **sth** to say publicly that you support a person, statement or course of action （公开）赞同，支持，认可： *I wholeheartedly endorse his remarks.* 我真诚地赞同他的话。◇ *Members of all parties endorsed a ban on land mines.* 各党派成员都赞同禁用地雷。 **2** ~ **sth** to say in an advertisement that you use and like a particular product so that other people will want to buy it （在广告中）宣传，代言（某一产品） **3** ~ **sth** to write your name on the back of a cheque so that it can be paid into a bank account （在支票背面）签名，背书 **4** [usually passive] ~ **sth** (*BrE*) to record details of a driving offence on sb's DRIVING LICENCE （在驾驶执照上）记录违章事项： *You risk having your licence endorsed.* 你这样做驾照可能被记录违章。

en·dorse·ment /ɪnˈdɔːsmənt; *NAmE* -ˈdɔːrs-/ *noun* [C, U] **1** a public statement or action showing that you support sb/sth （公开的）赞同，支持，认可： *The election victory is a clear endorsement of their policies.* 竞选成功显然是对他们政策的支持。◇ *a letter of endorsement* 认可证书 **2** a statement made in an advertisement, usually by sb famous or important, saying that they use and like a particular product （通常由名人或要人在广告中为某一产品的）宣传，代言 **3** (*BrE*) details of a driving offence recorded on sb's DRIVING LICENCE （驾驶执照上的）违章记录

en·do·scope /ˈendəskəʊp; *NAmE* -skoʊp/ *noun* an instrument used in medical operations which consists of a very small camera on a long thin tube which can be put into a person's body so that the parts inside can be seen 内镜；内窥镜；内腔镜

en·dos·co·py /enˈdɒskəpi; *NAmE* -ˈdɑːsk-/ *noun* [C, U] (*pl.* **-ies**) (*medical* 医) a medical operation in which an endoscope is put into a person's body so that the parts inside can be seen 内镜检查术；内窥镜检查

endo·skel·eton /ˈendəʊskelɪtn; *NAmE* ˈendoʊ-/ *noun* (*anatomy* 解) the bones inside the body of an animal that give it shape and support 内骨骼（动物体内的支撑骨架） ➲ COMPARE EXOSKELETON

endo·sperm /ˈendəʊspɜːm; *NAmE* ˈendoʊspɜːrm/ *noun* [U] (*biology* 生) the part of the plant seed that provides food for the EMBRYO 胚乳

endo·ther·mic /ˌendəʊˈθɜːmɪk; *NAmE* ˌendoʊˈθɜːrmɪk/ *adj.* (*chemistry* 化) (of a chemical reaction 化学反应) needing heat in order to take place 吸热的 ➲ COMPARE EXOTHERMIC

endow /ɪnˈdaʊ/ *verb* ~ **sth** to give a large sum of money to a school, a college or another institution to provide it with an income （向学校等机构）捐钱，捐赠，资助
PHR V **be en'dowed with sth** (*formal*) to naturally have a particular feature, quality, etc. 天生赋有，生来具有（某种特性、品质等）： *She was endowed with intelligence and wit.* 她天资聪颖。 ➲ SEE ALSO WELL ENDOWED **en'dow sb/sth with sth** (*formal*) **1** to believe or imagine that sb/sth has a particular quality 认为…具有某种品质： *She had endowed Marcus with the qualities she wanted him to possess.* 她认为马库斯具有她所期望的品质。 **2** to give sth to sb/sth 给予；赋予： *to endow sb with a responsibility* 赋予某人以责任

en·dow·ment /ɪnˈdaʊmənt/ *noun* (*formal*) **1** [C, U] money that is given to a school, a college or another institution to provide it with an income; the act of giving this money 捐款；捐赠；资助 **2** [C, usually pl.] a quality or an ability that you are born with 天赋；天资；才能

en'dowment mortgage *noun* (*BrE*) a type of MORTGAGE (= money borrowed to buy property) in which money is regularly paid into an endowment policy. At the end of a particular period of time this money is then used to pay back the money that was borrowed. 定期人寿保险按揭；两全人寿保险按揭 ➲ COMPARE REPAYMENT MORTGAGE

en'dowment policy *noun* (*BrE*) a type of life insurance in which a person regularly pays money to an insurance company, and receives a sum of money from them at the end of a particular period of time 定期人寿保险，两全人寿保险（保险期满或保险期内死亡均可得到保险金）

end·paper /ˈendpeɪpə(r)/ *noun* (*specialist*) a blank or decorated page stuck inside the front or back cover of a book 衬页

'end product *noun* something that is produced by a particular activity or process 制成品

ˌend re'sult *noun* [usually sing.] the final result of a particular activity or process 最终结果

'end run *noun* (in AMERICAN FOOTBALL 美式足球) an attempt by the person carrying the ball to run around the end of the line of defending players 迂回进攻（持球绕过防守线一端向前推进）

en·dur·ance /ɪnˈdjʊərəns; *NAmE* -ˈdʊr-/ *noun* [U] the ability to continue doing sth painful or difficult for a long period of time without complaining 忍耐力；耐久力： *He showed remarkable endurance throughout his illness.* 他在整个生病期间表现出非凡的忍耐力。◇ *They were humiliated* ***beyond endurance****.* 他们被羞辱到忍无可忍的地步。◇ *This event tests both physical and mental endurance.* 该比赛项目既是对体力也是对心理承受力的考验。◇ *powers of endurance* 耐力 ◇ *The party turned out to be more of an* ***endurance test*** *than a pleasure.* 这次聚会结果成了一次耐力测试，而不是一件乐事。

en·dure /ɪnˈdjʊə(r); *NAmE* -ˈdʊr/ *verb* (*formal*) **1** [T] to experience and deal with sth that is painful or unpleasant, especially without complaining 忍耐；忍受 **SYN** **bear**： ~ **sth** *They had to endure a long wait before the case came to trial.* 在此案审理前他们只得忍受长时间的等待。◇ *She could not endure the thought of parting.* 一想到分别她就无法忍受。 ◇ *The pain was almost too great to endure.* 痛苦得几乎难以忍受。 ◇ (*formal*) *a love that endures all things and never fails* 可经受一切考验的永不凋谢的爱情 ◇ ~ **doing sth** *He can't endure being defeated.* 他无法忍受失败。◇ ~ **to do sth** *He can't endure to be defeated.* 他无法忍受失败。 **2** [I] to continue to exist for a long time 持续；持久 **SYN** **last**[1]： *a success that will endure* 将会持续的成功 ▸ **en·dur·able** /ɪnˈdjʊərəbl;

NAmE -'dʊr-/ *adj.* : *I felt that life was no longer endurable.* 我感到生活再也无法忍受。 OPP **unendurable**

en·dur·ing /ɪn'djʊərɪŋ; *NAmE* -'dʊr-/ *adj.* lasting for a long time 持久的；耐久的： *enduring memories* 永存的记忆 ◇ *What is the reason for the game's enduring appeal?* 这种游戏为什么具有经久不衰的吸引力呢？ ▶ **en·dur·ing·ly** *adv.* : *an enduringly popular style* 一直流行的式样

ˌend 'user *noun* a person who actually uses a product rather than one who makes or sells it, especially a person who uses a product connected with computers（尤指计算机产品的）最终用户，直接用户，终端用户

end·ways /'endweɪz/ (*also* **end·wise** /-waɪz/) *adv.* **1** (*also* **ˌendways/ˌendwise 'on**) (of an object 物体) with one end facing up, forwards, or towards the person who is looking at it 末端朝上（或向前）地；竖着： *We turned the table endways to get it through the doors.* 我们把桌子竖起来以便挪进门。◇ *The first picture was taken from the side of the building, and the second one endways on.* 第一张照片照的是楼房侧面，第二张照的是楼房正面。 **2** with the end of one thing touching the end of another 首尾相连地；两端相接地： *The stones are laid down endways to make a path.* 石头一块接一块地铺成小路。

'end zone *noun* the area at the end of an AMERICAN FOOTBALL field into which the ball must be carried or passed in order to score points（美式足球的）端区，球门区

enema /'enəmə/ *noun* a liquid that is put into a person's RECTUM (= the opening through which solid waste leaves the body) in order to clean out the BOWELS, especially before a medical operation; the act of cleaning out the bowels in this way 灌肠剂；（尤指手术前的）灌肠

enemy 🔑 /'enəmi/ *noun* (*pl.* **-ies**) **1** 🔑 [C] a person who hates sb or who acts or speaks against sb/sth 敌人；仇人；反对者： *He has a lot of enemies in the company.* 他在公司里有很多对头。 ◇ *After just one day, she had already* ***made an enemy of*** *her manager.* 刚过一天她就已经与经理为敌了。◇ *It is rare to find a prominent politician with few* ***political enemies.*** 没有什么政敌的杰出从政者是罕见的。 ◇ *The state has a duty to protect its citizens against external enemies.* 国家有义务保护本国公民不受外敌侵犯。 ◇ *Birds are the* ***natural enemies*** *of many insect pests* (= they kill them). 鸟类是许多害虫的天敌。 ➲ SEE ALSO ENMITY **2** 🔑 **the enemy** [sing.+sing./pl. v.] a country that you are fighting a war against; the soldiers, etc. of this country 敌国；敌军；敌兵： *The enemy was/were forced to retreat.* 敌军被迫撤退了。 ◇ ***enemy forces/aircraft/territory*** 敌军；敌机；敌方领土 ◇ ***behind enemy lines*** (= the area controlled by the enemy) 在敌后 ➲ COLLOCATIONS AT WAR **3** 🔑 [C] **~ (of sth)** (*formal*) anything that harms sth or prevents it from being successful 危害物；大敌： *Poverty and ignorance are the enemies of progress.* 贫穷和愚昧阻碍进步。 IDM SEE WORST *adj.*

en·er·get·ic AW /ˌenə'dʒetɪk; *NAmE* ˌenər'dʒ-/ *adj.* having or needing a lot of energy and enthusiasm 精力充沛的；充满活力的；需要能量的；积极的： *He knew I was energetic and dynamic and would get things done.* 他知道我精力充沛、生气勃勃，会把事情办成的。◇ *an energetic supporter* 热情支持者 ◇ *The heart responds well to energetic exercise.* 心脏对剧烈运动反应良好。 ◇ *For the more energetic* (= people who prefer physical activities), *we offer windsurfing and diving.* 我们为喜欢运动的人准备了帆板和潜水运动。 ◇ *I think I'd prefer something a little less energetic.* 我想我更喜欢不太剧烈的活动。 ▶ **en·er·get·ic·al·ly** AW /-kli/ *adv.*

en·er·gize (*BrE also* **-ise**) /'enədʒaɪz; *NAmE* 'enərdʒ-/ *verb* **1 ~ sb** to make sb enthusiastic about sth 使充满热情 **2 ~ sb** to give sb more energy, strength, etc. 给（某人）增添能量（或精力、活力、干劲）： *a refreshing and energizing fruit drink* 提神并增加能量的果汁饮料 **3 ~ sth** (*specialist*) to supply power or energy to a machine, an atom, etc. 为…提供电力（或能量）；使通电

en·ergy 🔑 AW /'enədʒi; *NAmE* -ərdʒi/ *noun* **1** 🔑 [U] the ability to put effort and enthusiasm into an activity, work, etc. 精力；活力；干劲： *It's a waste of time and energy.* 那是浪费时间和精力。◇ *She's always* ***full of energy.*** 她总是充满活力。 ◇ ***nervous energy*** (= energy produced by feeling nervous) 精神紧张而产生的精力 **2 energies** [pl.] the physical and mental effort that you use to do sth 精力；力量： *She put all her energies into her work.* 她把全部精力都投入到工作中去了。 ◇ ***creative/destructive energies*** 创造力；毁灭力 **3** 🔑 [U] a source of power, such as fuel, used for driving machines, providing heat, etc. 能源： ***solar/nuclear energy*** 太阳能；核能 ◇ *It is important to conserve energy.* 节省能源十分重要。 ◇ *an energy crisis* (= for example when fuel is not freely available) 能源危机 ➲ COLLOCATIONS AT ENVIRONMENT

> **WORDFINDER** 联想词： fossil fuel, fracking, fuel, hydroelectric, nuclear, oil, power station, solar, wind farm

4 [U] (*physics* 物) the ability of matter or RADIATION to work because of its mass, movement, electric charge, etc. 能；能量： ***kinetic/potential, etc. energy*** 动能、势能等 ➲ WORDFINDER NOTE AT PHYSICS

ener·vate /'enəveɪt; *NAmE* 'enərv-/ *verb* **~ sb** (*formal*) to make sb feel weak and tired 使感到衰弱（或虚弱、无力）： *an enervating disease/climate* 使人衰弱的疾病；使人感到乏力的气候 ▶ **en·er·va·tion** /ˌenə'veɪʃn; *NAmE* ˌenər'v-/ *noun* [U]

en·fant ter·rible /ˌɒ̃fɒ̃ te'riːbl; *NAmE* ˌɑ̃ːfɑ̃ː/ *noun* (*pl.* **en·fants ter·ribles** /ˌɒ̃fɒ̃ te'riːbl; *NAmE* ˌɑ̃ːfɑ̃ː/) (*from French*) a person who is young and successful and whose behaviour and ideas may be unusual and may shock or embarrass other people 少年得志肆无忌惮的人

en·fee·ble /ɪn'fiːbl/ *verb* **~ sb/sth** (*formal*) to make sb/sth weak 使衰弱；使虚弱；使无力 ▶ **en·fee·bled** *adj.*

en·fold /ɪn'fəʊld; *NAmE* ɪn'foʊld/ *verb* (*literary*) **1 ~ sb/sth (in sth)** to hold sb in your arms in a way that shows affection 拥抱；搂抱 SYN **embrace**: *She lay quietly, enfolded in his arms.* 她静静地躺在他怀里。 **2 ~ sb/sth (in sth)** to surround or cover sb/sth completely 包起；围住；裹住： *Darkness spread and enfolded him.* 黑暗弥漫开来，将他笼罩。

en·force AW /ɪn'fɔːs; *NAmE* ɪn'fɔːrs/ *verb* **1 ~ sth (on/against sb/sth)** to make sure that people obey a particular law or rule 强制执行，强行实施（法律或规定）： *It's the job of the police to enforce the law.* 警察的工作就是执法。 ◇ *The legislation will be difficult to enforce.* 这一法规将难以实施。◇ *United Nations troops enforced a ceasefire in the area.* 联合国军队在该地区强制执行停火命令。 **2 ~ sth (on sb)** to make sth happen or force sb to do sth 强迫；迫使： *You can't enforce cooperation between the players.* 队员间的配合不能靠强迫。 ▶ **en·force·able** /-əbl/ *adj.* : *A gambling debt is not legally enforceable.* 赌债不能通过法律手段强制偿还。 **en·force·ment** AW *noun* [U]: *strict enforcement of regulations* 规章的严格执行 ◇ ***law enforcement officers*** 执法官员

en·forced AW /ɪn'fɔːst; *NAmE* ɪn'fɔːrst/ *adj.* that sb is forced to do or experience without being able to control it 强迫的；强制性的： *a period of enforced absence* 不得不离开的一段时间

en·for·cer /ɪn'fɔːsə(r); *NAmE* -'fɔːrs-/ *noun* a person whose responsibility is to make sure that other people perform the actions they are supposed to, especially in a government 实施者；强制执行者

en·fran·chise /ɪn'fræntʃaɪz/ *verb* [usually passive] **~ sb** (*formal*) to give sb the right to vote in an election 给（某人）选举权 OPP **disenfranchise** ▶ **en·fran·chise·ment** /ɪn'fræntʃɪzmənt/ *noun* [U]

eng. *abbr.* (*BrE*) (in writing 书写形式) engineer; engineering 工程师；工程；工程学

E

en·gage /ɪnˈɡeɪdʒ/ *verb* **1** [T] **~ sth** (*formal*) to succeed in attracting and keeping sb's attention and interest 吸引住（注意力、兴趣）: *It is a movie that engages both the mind and the eye.* 这是一部令人赏心悦目的影片。 **2** [T] **~ sb (as sth) | ~ sth | ~ sb to do sth** (*formal*) to employ sb to do a particular job 雇用；聘用: *He is currently engaged as a consultant.* 他现在受雇为顾问。 **3** [I] **~ (with sth/sb)** to become involved with and try to understand sth/sb 与…建立密切关系；尽力理解: *She has the ability to engage with young minds.* 她能够与年轻人心意相通。 **4** [T, I] **~ (sb)** (*formal*) to begin fighting with sb 与（某人）交战；与（某人）开战: *to engage the enemy* 与敌人交战 **5** [I, T] when a part of a machine **engages**, or when you **engage** it, it fits together with another part of the machine and the machine begins to work（使）衔接，啮合: *The cogwheels are not engaging.* 齿轮未啮合在一起。 ◇ **~ with sth** *One cogwheel engages with the next.* 齿轮一个个啮合在一起。 ◇ **~ sth** *Engage the clutch before selecting a gear.* 先踩离合器再挂挡。 **OPP disengage**

PHR V **enˈgage in sth | enˈgage sb in sth** (*formal*) to take part in sth; to make sb take part in sth（使）从事，参加: *Even in prison, he continued to engage in criminal activities.* 他甚至在监狱里还继续从事犯罪活动。◇ *She tried desperately to* ***engage him in conversation.*** 她用尽办法要他跟她谈话。

en·gaged /ɪnˈɡeɪdʒd/ *adj.* **1** (*formal*) busy doing sth 忙于；从事于: **~ (in sth)** *They are engaged in talks with the Irish government.* 他们正忙着与爱尔兰政府谈判。◇ *They were engaged in conversation.* 他们正谈得来劲。◇ **~ (on sth)** *He is now engaged on his second novel.* 他正埋头写他的第二部小说。 ◇ *I can't come to dinner on Tuesday—I'm* ***otherwise engaged*** (= I have already arranged to do something else). 我星期二不能来参加宴会，我有别的安排。 **2** having agreed to marry sb 已订婚: *When did you get* ***engaged****?* 你们什么时候订的婚？ ◇ *an engaged couple* 已订婚的一对 ◇ **~ to sb** *She's engaged to Peter.* 她与彼得订了婚。 ◇ *They are engaged to be married* (= to each other). 他们已经订婚。 ⊃ WORDFINDER NOTE AT WEDDING ⊃ COLLOCATIONS AT MARRIAGE **3** (*BrE*) (*NAmE* **busy**) (of a telephone line 电话线) being used 被占用的；使用中的: *I couldn't get through—the line's engaged.* 我打不通电话，线路忙。 ◇ *I phoned earlier but you were engaged* (= using your phone). 我早先打过电话，但你那边占线。 ◇ *the* ***engaged tone/signal*** 忙音；占线信号 ⊃ WORDFINDER NOTE AT CALL ⊃ COLLOCATIONS AT PHONE **4** (*BrE*) (of a public toilet/bathroom 公共卫生间) being used 占用着；使用中 **OPP vacant**

en·gage·ment /ɪnˈɡeɪdʒmənt/ *noun*

• **BEFORE MARRIAGE** 婚前 **1** [C] an agreement to marry sb; the period during which two people are engaged 订婚；订婚期间: *Their engagement was announced in the local paper.* 他们订婚的消息已在当地报纸上公布。 ◇ **~ (to sb)** *She has* ***broken off her engagement*** *to Charles.* 她已解除同查尔斯的婚约。 ◇ *an engagement party* 订婚宴会 ◇ *a long/short engagement* 长 / 短婚约期

• **ARRANGEMENT TO DO STH** 约定 **2** [C] an arrangement to do sth at a particular time, especially sth official or sth connected with your job（尤指正式的或与工作有关的）约定，约会，预约: *an* ***engagement book/diary*** 预约簿 / 日志 ◇ *He has a number of social engagements next week.* 他下周有几次社交约会。 ◇ *It was her first* ***official engagement****.* 那是她第一次正式约会。 ◇ *I had to refuse because of a* ***prior engagement****.* 我因为已经有预约只好拒绝了。

• **FIGHTING** 战斗 **3** [C, U] (*specialist*) fighting between two armies, etc. 战斗；交战: *The general tried to avoid an engagement with the enemy.* 将军竭力避免与敌军交火。

• **BEING INVOLVED** 联系 **4** [U] **~ (with sb/sth)** (*formal*) being involved with sb/sth in an attempt to understand them/it（与…的）密切关系；（对…的）了解: *Her views are based on years of engagement with the problems of the inner city.* 她的观点是以多年对内城区问题的了解为基础的。

• **EMPLOYMENT** 雇用 **5** [U, C] (*BrE*) an arrangement to employ sb; the process of employing sb 雇用；聘用: *The terms of engagement are to be agreed in writing.* 聘用条款应有书面协议。

enˈgagement ring *noun* a ring that a man gives to a woman when they agree to get married 订婚戒指

en·gaging /ɪnˈɡeɪdʒɪŋ/ *adj.* interesting or pleasant in a way that attracts your attention 有趣的；令人愉快的；迷人的: *an engaging smile* 迷人的微笑 ► **en·ga·ging·ly** *adv.*

en·gen·der /ɪnˈdʒendə(r)/ *verb* **~ sth** (*formal*) to make a feeling or situation exist 产生，引起（某种感觉或情况）: *The issue engendered controversy.* 这个问题引起了争论。

en·gine /ˈendʒɪn/ *noun* **1** the part of a vehicle that produces power to make the vehicle move 发动机；引擎: *a* ***diesel/petrol engine*** 柴油 / 汽油发动机 ◇ *My car had to have a new engine.* 我的汽车得换一个新发动机。 ◇ *engine trouble* 发动机故障 ◇ ***I switched/turned the engine off.*** 我关掉了发动机。 ⊃ VISUAL VOCAB PAGE V55 ⊃ SEE ALSO INTERNAL-COMBUSTION ENGINE, JET ENGINE, TRACTION ENGINE **2** (*also* **loco·mo·tive**) a vehicle that pulls a train 火车头；机车 ⊃ VISUAL VOCAB PAGE V63 **3 -engined** (in adjectives 构成形容词) having the type or number of engines mentioned 有…型发动机的；有…个引擎的: *a twin-engined speedboat* 双引擎快艇 ⊃ SEE ALSO FIRE ENGINE, SEARCH ENGINE

ˈengine driver (*BrE, becoming old-fashioned*) (*NAmE* **en·gin·eer**) *noun* a person whose job is driving a railway/railroad engine 火车司机；机车司机

en·gin·eer /ˌendʒɪˈnɪə(r); *NAmE* -ˈnɪr/ *noun, verb*

■ *noun* **1** a person whose job involves designing and building engines, machines, roads, bridges, etc. 工程师；设计师 ⊃ SEE ALSO CHEMICAL ENGINEER at CHEMICAL ENGINEERING, CIVIL ENGINEER at CIVIL ENGINEERING, ELECTRICAL ENGINEER at ELECTRICAL ENGINEERING, LIGHTING ENGINEER, MECHANICAL ENGINEER at MECHANICAL ENGINEERING, SOFTWARE ENGINEER, SOUND ENGINEER **2** a person who is trained to repair machines and electrical equipment 机修工；技师；技工: *They're sending an engineer to fix the phone.* 他们会派一名技师来安装电话。 **3** a person whose job is to control and repair engines, especially on a ship or an aircraft（船上的）轮机手；（飞机上的）机械师: *a flight engineer* 空勤机械师 ◇ *the chief engineer on a cruise liner* 游轮的轮机长 **4** (*NAmE*) (*BrE* **ˈengine driver**) a person whose job is driving a railway/railroad engine 火车司机；机车司机 **5** a soldier trained to design and build military structures 工兵

■ *verb* **1 ~ sth** (*often disapproving*) to arrange for sth to happen or take place, especially when this is done secretly in order to give yourself an advantage 密谋策划 **SYN contrive**: *She engineered a further meeting with him.* 她精心安排又和他见了一面。 **2** [usually passive] **~ sth** to design and build sth 设计制造: *The car is beautifully engineered and a pleasure to drive.* 这辆汽车设计完美，工艺精良，开起来过瘾。 **3 ~ sth** to change the GENETIC structure of sth 改变…的基因（或遗传）结构: *genetically engineered crops* 转基因农作物

en·gin·eer·ing /ˌendʒɪˈnɪərɪŋ; *NAmE* -ˈnɪr-/ *noun* [U] **1** the activity of applying scientific knowledge to the design, building and control of machines, roads, bridges, electrical equipment, etc. 工程: *The bridge is a triumph of modern engineering.* 这座桥是现代工程的一大成就。 ⊃ COMPARE REVERSE ENGINEERING **2** (*also* **ˌengineering ˈscience**) the study of engineering as a subject 工程学: *a degree in engineering* 工程学学位 ⊃ SEE ALSO CHEMICAL ENGINEERING, CIVIL ENGINEERING, ELECTRICAL ENGINEERING, GENETIC ENGINEERING, MECHANICAL ENGINEERING, SOCIAL ENGINEERING

ˈengine room *noun* **1** the part of a ship where the engines are（船舶）机舱 **2** the part of an organization where most of the important activity takes place or important decisions are made（机构的）决策部门

Eng·lish /ˈɪŋglɪʃ/ *noun, adj.*
■ ***noun*** **1** [U, C] the language, originally of England, now spoken in many other countries and used as a language of international communication throughout the world 英语；英文：*She speaks good English.* 她英语说得很好。◇ *I need to improve my English.* 我需要提高我的英语水平。◇ *world Englishes* 世界各地的英语 **2** [U] English language or literature as a subject of study （作为一门学科的）英语语言文学；英语学科：*a degree in English* 英语学位 ◇ *English is my best subject.* 英语是我学得最好的一门科目。 **3 the English** [pl.] the people of England (sometimes wrongly used to mean the British, including the Scots, the Welsh and the Northern Irish) 英格兰人（有时误用以指包括苏格兰、威尔士和北爱尔兰人在内的英国人） IDM SEE PLAIN *adj.*
■ ***adj.*** connected with England, its people or its language 英格兰的；英格兰人的；英语的：*the English countryside* 英格兰乡村 ◇ *an English man/woman* 英格兰男人 / 女人 ◇ *typically English attitudes* 典型的英格兰式态度 ◇ *an English dictionary* 英语词典 ➲ NOTE AT BRITISH

ˌEnglish ˈbreakfast *noun* [C, U] a large breakfast, usually consisting of CEREAL (= food made from grain), cooked BACON and eggs, TOAST and tea or coffee 英式早餐（通常包括麦片类、熏猪肉片、鸡蛋、烤面包片以及茶或咖啡） ➲ COMPARE CONTINENTAL BREAKFAST

ˌEnglish for ˌAcademic ˈPurposes (*abbr.* **EAP**) *noun* [U] the teaching of English for people who are using English for study, but whose first language is not English 学术英语教学（对象为第一语言非英语者）

ˌEnglish ˈhorn *noun* (*especially NAmE*) = COR ANGLAIS

Eng·lish·man /ˈɪŋglɪʃmən/ *noun* (*pl.* **-men** /-mən/) a man from England 英格兰（男）人
IDM **an ˌEnglishman's ˌhome is his ˈcastle** (*BrE*) (*US* **a ˌman's ˌhome is his ˈcastle**) (*saying*) a person's home is a place where they can be private and safe and do as they like 人之住宅即其城堡；人在家中，自成一统

ˌEnglish ˈmuffin (*NAmE*) (*BrE* **muf·fin**) *noun* a type of round flat bread roll, usually TOASTED and eaten hot with butter 英格兰松饼（通常烤热加黄油吃）

ˌEnglish ˈrose *noun* an attractive girl with fair skin and an appearance that is thought to be typical of English people 英格兰玫瑰少女（皮肤白皙、有典型英格兰人长相的美丽少女）

Eng·lish·woman /ˈɪŋglɪʃwʊmən/ *noun* (*pl.* **-women** /-wɪmɪn/) a woman from England 英格兰女人

en·gorge /ɪnˈɡɔːdʒ; *NAmE* ɪnˈɡɔːrdʒ/ *verb* **~ sth** (*specialist*) to cause sth to become filled with blood or another liquid and to swell 使充血；使涨满液体

en·grave /ɪnˈɡreɪv/ *verb* [often passive] to cut words or designs on wood, stone, metal, etc. 在…上雕刻（字或图案）：**~ A (with B)** *The silver cup was engraved with his name.* 银杯上刻有他的名字。◇ **~ B on A** *His name was engraved on the silver cup.* 他的名字刻在了银杯上。
IDM **be engraved on/in your ˈheart, ˈmemory, ˈmind, etc.** to be sth that you will never forget because it affected you so strongly 牢记，铭记，深深印入（心中、记忆中、头脑中等）

en·graver /ɪnˈɡreɪvə(r)/ *noun* a person whose job is to cut words or designs on wood, stone, metal, etc. 雕刻师；雕刻工；镌版工

en·grav·ing /ɪnˈɡreɪvɪŋ/ *noun* **1** [C] a picture made by cutting a design on a piece of metal and then printing the design on paper 版画；雕版印刷品 **2** [U] the art or process of cutting designs on wood, stone, metal, etc. 雕刻（术）；镌版术 ➲ COLLOCATIONS AT ART

en·gross /ɪnˈɡrəʊs; *NAmE* -ˈɡroʊs/ *verb* **~ sb** if sth engrosses you, it is so interesting that you give it all your attention and time 使全神贯注；占去（某人的）全部注意力和时间 ▸ **en·gross·ing** /ɪnˈɡrəʊsɪŋ; *NAmE* -ˈɡroʊs-/ *adj.*：*an engrossing problem* 引人关注的问题

en·grossed /ɪnˈɡrəʊst; *NAmE* -ˈɡroʊst/ *adj.* **~ (in/with sth)** so interested or involved in sth that you give it all your attention 全神贯注的；聚精会神的；专心致志的：*She was engrossed in conversation.* 她聚精会神地谈话。

en·gulf /ɪnˈɡʌlf/ *verb* (*formal*) **1 ~ sb/sth** to surround or to cover sb/sth completely 包围；吞没；淹没：*He was engulfed by a crowd of reporters.* 他被一群记者团团围住。◇ *The vehicle was* ***engulfed in flames.*** 汽车被大火吞没。 **2 ~ sb/sth** to affect sb/sth very strongly 严重影响：*Fear engulfed her.* 她陷入深深的恐惧之中。

en·hance AW /ɪnˈhɑːns; *NAmE* -ˈhæns/ *verb* **~ sth** to increase or further improve the good quality, value or status of sb/sth 提高；增强；增进：*This is an opportunity to enhance the reputation of the company.* 这是提高公司声誉的机会。◇ *the skilled use of make-up to enhance your best features* 熟练地利用化妆以突出容貌的优点 ▸ **en·hanced** AW *adj.*：*enhanced efficiency* 提高了的效率 **en·hance·ment** AW *noun* [U, C]：*equipment for the enhancement of sound quality* 音质提升设备 ◇ *software enhancements* 软件增强设备

en·hancer /ɪnˈhɑːnsə(r); *NAmE* -ˈhæns-/ *noun* (*specialist*) a substance or device that is designed to improve sth 增强剂；促进剂：*flavour enhancers* 增味剂

en·igma /ɪˈnɪɡmə/ *noun* a person, thing or situation that is mysterious and difficult to understand 神秘的人；费解的事物；令人困惑的处境 SYN **mystery, puzzle**

en·ig·mat·ic /ˌenɪɡˈmætɪk/ *adj.* mysterious and difficult to understand 神秘的；费解的；令人困惑的：*an enigmatic smile* 神秘的笑 ▸ **en·ig·mat·ic·al·ly** /-kli/ *adv.*：*'I might,' he said enigmatically.* "我也许会的。" 他神秘地说道。

en·jambe·ment (*also* **en·jamb·ment**) /ɪnˈdʒæmbmənt/ *noun* [U, C] (*from French, specialist*) the fact of a sentence continuing beyond the end of a line of poetry without a pause （诗句的）跨行 ➲ COMPARE CAESURA

en·join /ɪnˈdʒɔɪn/ *verb* **1** [often passive] **~ sb to do sth | ~ sth** (*formal*) to order or strongly advise sb to do sth; to say that a particular action or quality is necessary 命令；责令；嘱咐 **2 ~ sb from doing sth** (*law* 律) to legally prevent sb from doing sth, for example with an INJUNCTION 禁止

enjoy 🔑 /ɪnˈdʒɔɪ/ *verb* **1** 🔑 [T] to get pleasure from sth 享受…的乐趣；欣赏；喜爱：**~ sth** *We thoroughly enjoyed our time in New York.* 我们在纽约的时间过得十分快活。◇ *Thanks for a great evening. I really* ***enjoyed it.*** 非常感谢你，我今晚玩得很开心。◇ **~ doing sth** *I enjoy playing tennis and squash.* 我喜欢打网球和壁球。 ➲ MORE LIKE THIS 27, page R28 **2** 🔑 [T] **~ yourself** to be happy and get pleasure from what you are doing 过得快活；玩得痛快；得到乐趣：*They all enjoyed themselves at the party.* 他们在聚会上都玩得非常痛快。 **3** [T] **~ sth** (*formal*) to have sth good that is an advantage to you 享有；享受：*People in this country enjoy a high standard of living.* 这个国家的人民享有很高的生活水平。◇ *He's always enjoyed good health.* 他一直都很健康。 **4** [I] **enjoy!** (*informal*) used to say that you hope sb gets pleasure from sth that you are

▼ **GRAMMAR POINT 语法说明**

enjoy

Note the following patterns. 注意下列句型：

- *I enjoyed myself at the party.* 我在聚会上玩得很开心。
  ◇ ~~*I enjoyed at the party.*~~
- *Thanks. I really enjoyed it.* 谢谢，我真的很开心。
  ◇ ~~*Thanks. I really enjoyed.*~~
- *I enjoy playing basketball.* 我喜欢打篮球。
  ◇ ~~*I enjoy to play basketball.*~~
- *I enjoy reading very much.* 我非常喜欢阅读。
  ◇ ~~*I enjoy very much reading.*~~
- *I hope you enjoy your trip.* 祝你旅途愉快。
  ◇ ~~*I hope you enjoy with your trip.*~~

giving them or recommending to them （祝愿时说）玩痛快些，过愉快些，好好欣赏：*Here's that book I promised you. Enjoy!* 这就是我答应给你的那本书。好好欣赏吧！

en·joy·able /ɪnˈdʒɔɪəbl/ *adj.* giving pleasure 有乐趣的；使人快乐的；令人愉快的：*an enjoyable weekend/experience* 令人愉快的周末／经历 ◇ ***highly/really/thoroughly/very enjoyable*** 令人非常愉快 ▶ **en·joy·ably** /-əbli/ *adv.*：*The evening passed enjoyably.* 这个晚上过得很愉快。

E

en·joy·ment /ɪnˈdʒɔɪmənt/ *noun* **1** [U] the pleasure that you get from sth 愉快；快乐；乐趣：*He spoiled my enjoyment of the game by talking all through it.* 他一直在讲话，破坏了我看比赛的兴致。◇ *The rules are there to ensure everyone's safety and enjoyment.* 这些规定是为了保证每个人的安全和快乐。◇ *Children seem to have lost their enjoyment in reading.* 孩子们似乎已失去阅读的乐趣。◇ *I get a lot of enjoyment from my grandchildren.* 我从孙辈那儿得到很多乐趣。➲ SYNONYMS AT FUN **2** [C] something that gives you pleasure 乐事；令人愉快的事：*Children like to share interests and enjoyments with their parents.* 孩子们喜欢同父母一起分享各种兴趣和乐事。**3** [U] **~ of sth** (*formal*) the fact of having and using sth 享有；享受：*the enjoyment of equal rights* 平等权利的享有

en·large /ɪnˈlɑːdʒ; *NAmE* -ˈlɑːrdʒ/ *verb* **1** [T, I] **~ (sth)** to make sth bigger; to become bigger 扩大；扩充；扩展；增大：*There are plans to enlarge the recreation area.* 已经有了扩大娱乐场地的计划。◇ *Reading will enlarge your vocabulary.* 阅读能扩大词汇量。**2** [T, usually passive] **~ sth** to make a bigger copy of a photograph or document 放大（照片或文件）：*We're going to have this picture enlarged.* 我们准备将这张照片放大。▶ **en·larged** *adj.*：*an enlarged heart* 肥大的心脏

PHR V **enˈlarge on/upon sth** (*formal*) to say or write more about sth that has been mentioned 详述；细说 SYN **elaborate**

en·large·ment /ɪnˈlɑːdʒmənt; *NAmE* -ˈlɑːrdʒ-/ *noun* **1** [U, sing.] **~ (of sth)** the process or result of sth becoming or being made larger 扩大；扩充；扩展；增大：*the enlargement of the company's overseas business activities* 公司海外业务的扩展 ◇ *There was widespread support for **EU enlargement*** (= the fact of more countries joining). 欧盟扩大得到了广泛的支持。**2** [C] something that has been made larger, especially a photograph 扩大物，放大物（尤指照片）：*If you like the picture I can send you an enlargement of it.* 如果你喜欢这照片，我可以给你寄一张放大的。OPP **reduction**

en·lar·ger /ɪnˈlɑːdʒə(r); *NAmE* -ˈlɑːrdʒ-/ *noun* a piece of equipment for making photographs larger or smaller （照片）放大机，缩放机

en·light·en /ɪnˈlaɪtn/ *verb* **~ sb** (*formal*) to give sb information so that they understand sth better 启发；开导；向…阐明：*She didn't enlighten him about her background.* 她未向他讲明自己的出身背景。▶ **en·light·en·ing** *adj.*：*It was a very enlightening interview.* 那次面谈让人很受启发。

en·light·ened /ɪnˈlaɪtnd/ *adj.* [usually before noun] (*approving*) having or showing an understanding of people's needs, a situation, etc. that is not based on old-fashioned attitudes and PREJUDICE 开明的；有见识的；摆脱偏见的：***enlightened opinions/attitudes/ideas*** 开明的见解／态度／想法

en·light·en·ment /ɪnˈlaɪtnmənt/ *noun* **1** [U] knowledge about and understanding of sth; the process of understanding sth or making sb understand it 启迪；启发；开导；开明：*The newspapers provided little enlightenment about the cause of the accident.* 报章对事故原因并未解释清楚。◇ *spiritual enlightenment* 心灵启迪 ➲ COLLOCATIONS AT RELIGION **2 the Enlightenment** [sing.] the period in the 18th century when many writers and scientists began to argue that science and reason were more important than religion and tradition （18 世纪欧洲的）启蒙运动

en·list /ɪnˈlɪst/ *verb* **1** [T] to persuade sb to help you or to join you in doing sth 争取，谋取（帮助、支持或参与）：**~ sth/sb (in sth)** *They hoped to **enlist the help of** the public in solving the crime.* 他们希望寻求公众协助破案。◇ **~ sb (as sth)** *We were enlisted as helpers.* 我们应邀协助。◇ **~ sb to do sth** *We were enlisted to help.* 我们应邀协助。**2** [I, T] to join or to make sb join the armed forces （使）入伍；征募；从军 SYN **call up, conscript, draft**：*They both enlisted in 1915.* 他俩都是 1915 年入伍的。◇ **~ as sth** *to enlist as a soldier* 入伍当兵 ◇ **~ sb (in/into/for/as sth)** *He was enlisted into the US Navy.* 他应征加入了美国海军。▶ **en·list·ment** *noun* [U]：*the enlistment of expert help* 寻求专家的帮助 ◇ *his enlistment in the Royal Air Force* 他应征加入皇家空军

en·list·ed /ɪnˈlɪstɪd/ *adj.* (*especially US*) (of a member of the army, etc. 部队等的一员) having a rank that is below that of an officer 士兵的：*enlisted men and women* 男兵和女兵 ◇ *enlisted personnel* 应征入伍人员

en·liven /ɪnˈlaɪvn/ *verb* **~ sth** (*formal*) to make sth more interesting or more fun 使更有生气（或乐趣）

en masse /ˌɒ̃ ˈmæs; *NAmE* ˌɑː/ *adv.* (*from French*) all together, and usually in large numbers 一起；全体

en·mesh /ɪnˈmeʃ/ *verb* [usually passive] **~ sb/sth (in sth)** (*formal*) to involve sb/sth in a bad situation that it is not easy to escape from 使陷入，使卷入（困境）

en·mity /ˈenməti/ *noun* [U, C] (*pl.* **-ies**) feelings of hatred towards sb 敌意；敌对；仇恨：*personal enmities and political conflicts* 个人仇恨和政治冲突 ◇ *Her action earned her the enmity of two or three colleagues.* 她的行动激起了两三个同事对她的怨恨。◇ **~ between A and B** *the traditional problem of the enmity between Protestants and Catholics* 新教徒和天主教徒之间互相仇视的传统问题 ➲ SEE ALSO ENEMY (1)

en·noble /ɪˈnəʊbl; *NAmE* ɪˈnoʊbl/ *verb* (*formal*) **1** [usually passive] **~ sb** to make sb a member of the NOBILITY 封（某人）为贵族 **2 ~ sb/sth** to give sb/sth a better moral character 使更崇高；使更高尚；使更尊贵：*In a strange way she seemed ennobled by her grief.* 奇怪的是，忧伤使她显得更加高贵。▶ **en·noble·ment** *noun* [U]

ennui /ɒnˈwiː; *NAmE* ɑːn-/ *noun* [U] (*from French, literary*) feelings of being bored and not satisfied because nothing interesting is happening 无聊；厌倦；倦怠

en·ol·ogy (*US*) (*BrE* **oen·ology**) /iːˈnɒlədʒi; *NAmE* -ˈnɑːl-/ *noun* [U] (*specialist*) the study of wine 葡萄酿酒学；葡萄酒酿造学

eno·phile (*US*) (*BrE* **oeno·phile**) /ˈiːnəfaɪl/ *noun* (*formal*) a person who knows a lot about wine 葡萄酒行家

enor·mity AW /ɪˈnɔːməti; *NAmE* ɪˈnɔːrm-/ *noun* (*pl.* **-ies**) **1** [U] **the ~ of sth** (of a problem, etc. 问题等) the very great size, effect, etc. of sth; the fact of sth being very serious 巨大；深远影响；严重性：*the enormity of the task* 任务的艰巨性 ◇ *People are still coming to terms with the enormity of the disaster.* 人们仍在逐渐适应忍受这一灾难带来的严重恶果。◇ *The full enormity of the crime has not yet been revealed.* 这一罪行的严重性还没有充分揭示出来。**2** [C, usually pl.] (*formal*) a very serious crime 滔天罪行；罪大恶极：*the enormities of the Hitler regime* 希特勒政权的滔天罪行

enor·mous AW /ɪˈnɔːməs; *NAmE* ɪˈnɔːrməs/ *adj.* extremely large 巨大的；庞大的；极大的 SYN **huge, immense**：*an enormous house/dog* 巨大的房子；大狗 ◇ *an **enormous amount** of time* 大量的时间 ◇ *enormous interest* 浓厚的兴趣 ◇ *The problems facing the President are enormous.* 总统面临的问题是巨大的。

enor·mous·ly AW /ɪˈnɔːməsli; *NAmE* ɪˈnɔːrm-/ *adv.* very; very much 非常；极其：***enormously rich/powerful/grateful*** 非常富有／强大／感激 ◇ *The price of wine varies enormously depending on where it comes from.* 不同产地的葡萄酒价格差别很大。◇ *She was looking forward to the meeting enormously.* 她急切期待着这次会面。

enough 🔑 /ɪ'nʌf/ *det., pron., adv.*

■ ***det.*** 🔑 used before plural or uncountable nouns to mean 'as many or as much as sb needs or wants'（用于复数或不可数名词前）足够的，充足的，充分的 **SYN sufficient**: *Have you made enough copies?* 你复印的份数够吗？ ◇ *Is there enough room for me?* 有足够的地方给我吗？ ◇ *I didn't have enough clothes to last a week.* 我的衣服不够一周穿的。 ◇ *Don't ask me to do it. I've got enough problems as it is.* 别让我做这件事。我目前的问题已够多了。 ◇ (*old-fashioned*) *There was food enough for all.* 所有人都有足够的食物。 **HELP** Although **enough** after a noun now sounds old-fashioned, **time enough** is still fairly common. 尽管 enough 置于名词后现在似乎有些过时，但 time enough 仍然相当常用：*There'll be time enough to relax when you've finished your work.* 你完成工作后会有足够的时间来放松。

■ ***pron.*** 🔑 as many or as much as sb needs or wants 足够；充分；充足：*Six bottles should be enough.* 六瓶应该够了。 ◇ *Have you had enough* (= to eat)*?* 你吃饱了吗？ ◇ *If enough of you are interested, we'll organize a trip to the theatre.* 如果你们中有足够多的人感兴趣，我们就组织去看一场戏。 ◇ *There was* ***nowhere near enough*** *for everybody.* 根本不够所有人。 ◇ *We've nearly run out of paper. Do you think there's enough for today?* 我们的纸差不多已用完了。你看够今天用的吗？

IDM **e'nough already** (*informal, especially NAmE*) used to say that sth is annoying or boring and that you want it to stop 行了；早已够了 **e,nough is e'nough** (*saying*) used when you think that sth should not continue any longer（认为不应再继续）够了，行了，适可而止 **e,nough 'said** used to say that you understand a situation and there is no need to say any more 无须再讲；不必多说：*'He's a politician, remember.' 'Enough said.'* "记住，他是一个政客。" "不用多说了。" **have had e'nough (of sth/sb)** used when sth/sb is annoying you and you no longer want to do, have or see it or them 对…已厌烦透了；再也忍受不住；受够了：*I've had enough of driving the kids around.* 我已受够了开车带孩子们到处去。

■ ***adv.*** (used after verbs, adjectives and adverbs 用于动词、形容词和副词后) **1** 🔑 to the necessary degree 足够地；充分地；充足地：*I hadn't trained enough for the game.* 为这次比赛我训练得不够。 ◇ *This house isn't big enough for us.* 这房子对我们来说不够大。 ◇ *She's old enough to decide for herself.* 她已到自己作决定的年龄了。 ◇ *We didn't leave early enough.* 我们离开得不够早。 ◇ *Tell them it's just* ***not good enough****.* 告诉他们这确实不够好。 **2** 🔑 to an acceptable degree, but not to a very great degree 相当；尚：*He seemed pleasant enough to me.* 他对我似乎已相当和气了。 **3** 🔑 to a degree that you do not wish to get any greater 十分；很：*I hope my job's safe. Life is hard enough as it is.* 希望我的工作安稳。生活照现在这样已经够苦了。

IDM **,curiously, ,funnily, ,oddly, ,strangely, etc. e'nough** used to show that sth is surprising（表示惊奇）奇怪的是，说来也奇怪：*Funnily enough, I said the same thing myself only yesterday.* 奇怪的是，就在昨天我自己也说过同样的话。 ➲ MORE AT FAIR *adj.*, FAR *adv.*, LIKE *adv.*, MAN *n.*, NEAR *adv.*, RIGHT *adj.*, SURE *adv.*

en passant /,ɒ̃ 'pæsɒ̃; *NAmE* ,ɑːn pɑː'sɑːn/ *adv.* (*from French*) while talking about sth else and without giving much information 顺便；附带地：*He mentioned en passant that he was going away.* 他顺便提到他要离开。

en·quire (*especially BrE*) (*also* **in·quire** *NAmE, BrE*) /ɪn'kwaɪə(r)/ *verb* [I, T] (*rather formal*) to ask sb for some information 询问；打听：**~ (about sb/sth)** *I called the station to enquire about train times.* 我打电话到车站询问火车时刻。 ◇ **~ (as to sb/sth)** *She enquired as to your whereabouts.* 她打听你的下落。 ◇ **~ why, where, etc....** *Might I enquire why you have not mentioned this until now?* 请问你为什么直到现在才提及此事呢？ ◇ **~ sth** *He enquired her name.* 他打听她的姓名。 ◇ **+ speech** *'What is your name?' he enquired.* "您叫什么名字？" 他询问道。 ➲ SYNONYMS AT ASK **HELP** In British English people sometimes distinguish between **enquire** and **inquire**, using **enquire** for the general meaning of 'ask for information' and **inquire** for the more particular meaning of 'officially investigate'. 在英式英语中，人们有时会区分 enquire 和 inquire 的用法，用 enquire 表示一般意义上的询问、打听，用 inquire 表示特别意义上的探究、查询、调查：*I called to enquire about train times.* 我打电话询问火车时刻表。 ◇ *A committee will inquire into the allegations.* 一个委员会将调查这些指控。However, you can use either spelling in either meaning. In American English **inquire** is usually used in both meanings. 不过两种拼写用于两个意思均可。在美式英语中，通常两种意思均用 inquire。

PHR V **en'quire after sb** (*formal*) to ask for information about sb, especially about their health or about what they are doing 向某人问好（或问候） **en'quire into sth** to find out more information about sth 调查；查究；查问 **SYN investigate**: *A committee was appointed to enquire into the allegations.* 一个委员会已受命调查这些指控。 **en'quire sth of sb** (*formal*) to ask sb sth 向某人打听（或询问、了解）：(**+ speech**) *'Will you be staying for lunch?' she enquired of Charles.* "留下吃午饭好吗？" 她向查尔斯问道。

en·quir·er (*especially BrE*) (*also* **in·quir·er** *NAmE, BrE*) /ɪn'kwaɪərə(r)/ *noun* (*formal*) a person who asks for information 询问者；调查者

en·quir·ing (*also* **in·quir·ing** *especially in NAmE*) /ɪn'kwaɪərɪŋ/ *adj.* [usually before noun] **1** showing an interest in learning new things 爱探索的；好奇的；好问的：*a child with an enquiring mind* 有好奇心的孩子 **2** asking for information 探询的；探究的：*an enquiring look* 探询的神色 ► **en·quir·ing·ly** (*also* **in·quir·ing·ly** *especially in NAmE*) *adv.*

en·quiry 🔑 (*especially BrE*) (*also* **in·quiry** *NAmE, BrE*) /ɪn'kwaɪəri; *NAmE usually* 'ɪŋkwəri/ *noun* (*pl.* **-ies**) **1** 🔑 [C] an official process to find out the cause of sth or to find out information about sth 调查；查究；查问：*a* ***murder enquiry*** 谋杀案调查 ◇ **~ into sth** ***a public enquiry*** *into the environmental effects of the proposed new road* 拟建新路对环境影响的公开调查 ◇ *to* ***hold/order an enquiry*** *into the affair* 对此事进行调查；责令调查此事 ➲ COLLOCATIONS AT CRIME **2** 🔑 [C] a request for information about sb/sth; a question about sb/sth 询问；打听：*a telephone enquiry* 电话查询 ◇ **~ (from sb) (about sb/sth)** *We received over 300 enquiries about the job.* 我们收到 300 多个关于这项工作的查询。 ◇ *enquiries from prospective students* 有意来求学的学生的咨询 ◇ *I'll have to* ***make a few enquiries*** (= try to find out about it) *and get back to you.* 我得打听打听再给你答复。 ◇ (*BrE*) *Two men have been* ***helping police with their enquiries*** (= are being questioned about a crime, but have not been charged with it). 两名男子一直在配合警方的问询调查。 **3** [U] the act of asking questions or collecting information about sb/sth 查询；探究；探索：*scientific enquiry* 科学探索 ◇ *The police are following several* ***lines of enquiry****.* 警方正沿着几条线索进行调查。 ◇ *a committee of enquiry* 调查委员会 **4 enquiries** [pl.] (*BrE*) a place where you can get information 问讯处：*Ask at enquiries to see if your bag has been handed in.* 到问讯处看看是否有人交来了你的包。 ➲ SEE ALSO DIRECTORY ENQUIRIES **HELP** In British English people sometimes distinguish between **enquiry** and **inquiry**, using **enquiry** for the general meaning of 'a request for information' and **inquiry** for the more particular meaning of 'official investigation'. 在英式英语中，人们有时会区分 enquiry 和 inquiry 的用法，用 enquiry 表示一般意义上的询问、打听，用 inquiry 表示特别意义上的探究、查询、调查：*enquiries from prospective students* 有意来求学的学生的咨询 ◇ *a murder inquiry* 谋杀案调查 However, you can use either spelling in either meaning. In American English **inquiry** is usually used in both meanings. 不过两种拼写用于两个意思均可。在美式英语中，通常两种意思均用 inquiry。

en·rage /ɪn'reɪdʒ/ *verb* [usually passive] **~ sb** to make sb very angry 使异常愤怒；激怒；触怒 **SYN infuriate**

en·rap·ture /ɪn'ræptʃə(r)/ *verb* [usually passive] **~ sb** (*formal*) to give sb great pleasure or joy 使欣喜若狂；使兴高采烈 **SYN enchant**

en·rap·tured /ɪnˈræptʃəd; *NAmE* -ərd/ *adj.* (*formal*) filled with great pleasure or joy 狂喜的；欣喜万分的；陶然的 SYN **enchanted**

en·rich /ɪnˈrɪtʃ/ *verb* **1** to improve the quality of sth, often by adding sth to it 充实；使丰富；使饱含（某物）: **~ sth** *The study of science has enriched all our lives.* 科学研究丰富了我们的整个生活。◇ **~ sth with sth** *Most breakfast cereals are enriched with vitamins.* 多数谷类早餐食物都添加了维生素。 **2 ~ sb/sth** to make sb/sth rich or richer 使富有；使富裕： *a nation enriched by oil revenues* 靠石油收入富裕起来的国家 ◇ *He used his position to enrich himself.* 他利用职务之便敛财。 ▶ **en·rich·ment** *noun* [U]

enrol /ɪnˈrəʊl; *NAmE* -ˈroʊl/ (*especially US* **en·roll**) *verb* (**-ll-**) [I, T] to arrange for yourself or for sb else to officially join a course, school, etc. （使）加入；注册；登记： *You need to enrol before the end of August.* 你必须在八月底前注册。◇ (*BrE*) *to enrol on a course* 注册学习一门课程 ◇ (*NAmE*) *to enroll in a course* 注册学习一门课程 ◇ **~ sb** *The centre will soon be ready to enrol candidates for the new programme.* 中心将很快为新课程的招生做好准备。 ➲ MORE LIKE THIS 36, page R29

en·rol·lee /ɪnˌrəʊˈliː; *NAmE* ɪnˌroʊ-/ *noun* (*NAmE*) a person who has officially joined a course, an organization, etc. 入学者；被录用者；入会者

en·rol·ment (*especially US* **en·roll·ment**) /ɪnˈrəʊlmənt; *NAmE* -ˈroʊl-/ *noun* [U, C] the act of officially joining a course, school, etc.; the number of people who do this 入学，注册，登记（人数）： *Enrolment is the first week of September.* 九月份的第一周注册。◇ *School enrolments are currently falling.* 目前学校的注册人数在减少。

en route /ˌɒ̃ ˈruːt; ˌɒn; *NAmE* ˌɑ̃ː; ˌɑːn/ *adv.* (*from French*) on the way; while travelling from/to a particular place 在途中；在路上： *We stopped for a picnic en route.* 我们在途中停下来野餐。◇ **~ (from…) (to…)** *The bus broke down en route from Boston to New York.* 公共汽车在从波士顿到纽约的途中抛锚了。◇ (*BrE*) **~ (for…)** *a plane en route for Heathrow* 在飞往希思罗机场途中的飞机

en·sconce /ɪnˈskɒns; *NAmE* -ˈskɑːns/ *verb* **be ensconced (+adv./prep.)** | **~ yourself (+adv./prep.)** (*formal*) if you **are ensconced** or **ensconce yourself** somewhere, you are made or make yourself comfortable and safe in that place or position 安置；使安顿；使安坐

en·sem·ble /ɒnˈsɒmbl; *NAmE* ɑːnˈsɑːmbl/ *noun* **1** [C+sing./pl. v.] a small group of musicians, dancers or actors who perform together 乐团，剧团，舞剧团（全体成员）： *a* ***brass/wind/string, etc. ensemble*** 铜管乐器、管乐器、弦乐器等合奏组 ◇ *The ensemble is/are based in Lyons.* 这个乐团总部设在里昂。 **2** [C, usually sing.] (*formal*) a number of things considered as a group 全体；整体 **3** [C, usually sing.] a set of clothes that are worn together 全套服装

en·shrine /ɪnˈʃraɪn/ *verb* [usually passive] **~ sth (in sth)** (*formal*) to make a law, right, etc. respected or official, especially by stating it in an important written document 把（法律、权利等）奉为神圣；把…庄严地载入： *These rights are enshrined in the country's constitution.* 这些权利已庄严地载入国家宪法。

en·shroud /ɪnˈʃraʊd/ *verb* **~ sth** (*literary*) to cover or surround sth completely so that it cannot be seen or understood 掩盖；遮蔽；笼罩

en·sign /ˈensən/ *noun* **1** a flag flown on a ship to show which country it belongs to （表明国籍的）舰旗，船旗： *the White Ensign* (= the flag of the British Navy) 英国海军旗 **2** an officer of low rank in the US navy （美国）海军少尉： *Ensign Marshall* 马歇尔海军少尉

en·slave /ɪnˈsleɪv/ *verb* [usually passive] **1 ~ sb** to make sb a SLAVE 使成为奴隶；奴役 **2 ~ sb/sth (to sth)** (*formal*) to make sb/sth completely depend on sth so that they cannot manage without it 使受控制；征服；制伏 ▶ **en·slave·ment** *noun* [U]

en·snare /ɪnˈsneə(r); *NAmE* -ˈsner/ *verb* **~ sb/sth** (*formal*) to make sb/sth unable to escape from a difficult situation or from a person who wants to control them 使入陷阱（或圈套、困境） SYN **trap**: *young homeless people who become ensnared in a life of crime* 陷入犯罪活动的无家可归的年轻人

ensue /ɪnˈsjuː; *NAmE* -ˈsuː/ *verb* [I] (*formal*) to happen after or as a result of another event 接着发生；因而产生 SYN **follow**: *An argument ensued.* 紧接着的是一场争论。 ▶ **en·su·ing** *adj.*: *He had become separated from his parents in the ensuing panic.* 在随后的慌乱中他便与父母分散了。

en suite /ˌɒ̃ ˈswiːt; *NAmE* ˌɑ̃ː/ *adj., adv.* (*BrE, from French*) (of a bathroom 浴室) joined onto a bedroom and for use only by people in that bedroom 与卧室配套的： *Each bedroom in the hotel has a bathroom en suite/an en suite bathroom.* 旅馆里每间卧室都带浴室。◇ *an en suite bedroom* (= a bedroom with an en suite bathroom) 带浴室的卧室 ◇ *en suite facilities* 与卧室配套的设备 ➲ VISUAL VOCAB PAGE V24 ▶ **en-suite** *noun*: *The en-suite has a power shower.* 卧室的配套浴室有电泵淋浴器。◇ *Both bedrooms have tiled en-suites.* 两间卧室都带有铺瓷砖的浴室。

en·sure 🔑 AW (*also* **in·sure** *especially in NAmE*) /ɪnˈʃʊə(r); ɪnˈʃɔː(r); *NAmE* ɪnˈʃʊr/ *verb* to make sure that sth happens or is definite 保证；担保；确保： **~ sth** *The book ensured his success.* 这本书确保了他的成功。◇ **~ sb sth** *Victory ensured them a place in the final.* 战胜对手让他们晋级决赛。◇ **~ (that)**… *Please ensure (that) all lights are switched off.* 请确保将所有灯都关掉。

ENT /ˌiː en ˈtiː/ *abbr.* ear, nose and throat (as a department in a hospital) （医院的）耳鼻喉科

-ent ➲ -ANT

en·tail /ɪnˈteɪl/ *verb* to involve sth that cannot be avoided 牵涉；需要；使必要 SYN **involve**: **~ sth** *The job entails a lot of hard work.* 这工作需要十分艰苦的努力。◇ **be entailed in sth** *The girls learn exactly what is entailed in caring for a newborn baby.* 姑娘们学的是怎样照看新生儿。◇ **~ (sb) doing sth** *It will entail driving a long distance every day.* 这意味着每天都要长途开车。

en·tan·gle /ɪnˈtæŋɡl/ *verb* [usually passive] **1 ~ sb/sth (in/with sth)** to make sb/sth become caught or twisted in sth 使纠缠；缠住；套住： *The bird had* ***become entangled*** *in the wire netting.* 那只小鸟被铁丝网缠住了。 **2** to involve sb in a difficult or complicated situation 使卷入；使陷入： **~ sb in sth** *He* ***became entangled*** *in a series of conflicts with the management.* 他卷入了与管理层的一系列冲突之中。◇ **~ sb with sb** *She didn't want to* ***get entangled*** (= emotionally involved) *with him.* 她不想与他有瓜葛。

en·tangle·ment /ɪnˈtæŋɡlmənt/ *noun* **1** [C] a difficult or complicated relationship with another person or country 瓜葛；牵连 **2** [U] the act of becoming entangled in sth; the state of being entangled 纠缠；缠住： *Many dolphins die each year from entanglement in fishing nets.* 每年都有许多海豚被捕鱼网缠绕致死。 **3 en·tangle·ments** [pl.] (*specialist*) barriers made of BARBED WIRE, used to stop an enemy from getting close 铁丝网（用以阻止敌人靠近）

en·tente /ɒnˈtɒnt; *NAmE* ɑːnˈtɑːnt/ *noun* [U, sing.] (*from French*) a friendly relationship between two countries （国家间的）友好关系： *the Franco-Russian entente* 法俄友好关系

en·tente cor·di·ale /ˌɒntɒnt ˌkɔːdiˈɑːl; *NAmE* ɑːnˌtɑːnt ˌkɔːrd-/ *noun* [U, sing.] (*from French*) a friendly relationship between two countries, especially between Britain and France （尤指英法两国间的）友好关系

enter 🔑 /ˈentə(r)/ *verb*

• **COME/GO IN** 进来；进去 **1** 🔑 [I, T] (not usually used in the passive 通常不用于被动语态) (*formal*) to come or go into sth 进来；进去；进入： *Knock before you enter.* 进来前先敲门。◇ **~ sth** *Someone entered the room behind me.* 有人跟着我进了房间。◇ *Where did the bullet enter the body?* 子弹从哪个部位进入身体的？◇ (*figurative*) *A note of* *defiance entered her voice.* 她的声音里带有蔑视的口气。◇ (*figurative*) *It never* ***entered my head*** (= I never thought) *that she would tell him about me.* 我从未想到过她会把我的事告诉他。

- **JOIN INSTITUTION/START WORK** 加入机构；开始从事 **2** [T, no passive] **~ sth** (*formal*) to become a member of an institution; to start working in an organization or a profession 成为…的一员；加入；开始从事：***to enter a school/college/university*** 考入学校 / 学院 / 大学 ◇ ***to enter politics*** 开始从政 ◇ ***to enter Parliament*** (= become an MP) 成为英国议会议员 ◇ ***to enter the Church*** (= become a priest) 成为神职人员
- **BEGIN ACTIVITY** 开始活动 **3** [T] **~ sth** to begin or become involved in an activity, a situation, etc. 开始参加；开始进入；着手进行：***to enter a relationship/conflict/war*** 建立关系；发生冲突；参战 ◇ *Several new firms have now entered the market.* 有几家新公司已打入市场。◇ *The investigation has entered a new phase.* 调查已进入新阶段。◇ *The strike is entering its fourth week.* 罢工正进入第四周。
- **EXAM/COMPETITION** 考试；比赛 **4** [T, I] to put your name on the list for an exam, a race, a competition, etc.; to do this for sb 报名参加，为…报名参加（考试、比赛等）：**~ sth** *1 000 children entered the competition.* * 1 000 名孩子报名参加了比赛。◇ **~ sb/sth in sth** *Irish trainers have entered several horses in the race.* 爱尔兰驯马师让好几匹马参加了比赛。◇ **~ sb/sth for sth** *How many students have been entered for the exam?* 让多少学生参加了考试？◇ **~ (for sth)** *Only four British players have entered for the championship.* 只有四名英国运动员报名参加锦标赛。
- **WRITE INFORMATION** 记录信息 **5** [T] to put names, numbers, details, etc. in a list, book or computer 登记，录入，输入（姓名、号码、详细资料等）：**~ sth (in sth)** *Enter your name and occupation in the boxes* (= on a form). 将姓名和职业填入（表格的）方框里。◇ **~ sth (into sth)** *to enter data into a computer* 将数据输入计算机 ◇ **~ sth (on sth)** *to enter figures on a spreadsheet* 将数字输入电脑表格 ➲ WORDFINDER NOTE AT COMMAND
- **SAY OFFICIALLY** 正式说 **6** [T] **~ sth** (*formal*) to say sth officially so that it can be recorded （正式）提出：*to* ***enter a plea*** *of not guilty* (= at the beginning of a court case) （在诉讼案件开始时）提出无罪的抗辩 ◇ *to enter an offer* 报价 ➲ SEE ALSO ENTRANCE[1], ENTRY **IDM** SEE FORCE *n.*, NAME *n.*

PHR V **'enter into sth** (*formal*) **1** to begin to discuss or deal with sth 开始讨论；着手处理：*Let's not enter into details at this stage.* 咱们现阶段不要讨论细节问题。**2** to take an active part in sth 积极参加；投入：*They* ***entered into the spirit*** *of the occasion* (= began to enjoy and feel part of it). 他们开始感受到了节庆的气氛。**3** [no passive] to form part of sth or have an influence on sth 成为…的一部分；影响：*This possibility never entered into our calculations.* 我们从未估计到这种可能性。◇ *Your personal feelings shouldn't enter into this at all.* 这根本就不应该掺杂进你个人的感情。**'enter into sth (with sb)** to begin sth or become involved in sth 开始；进入；参与：*to enter into an agreement* 订立协议 ◇ *to enter into negotiations* 开始谈判 **'enter on/upon sth** (*formal*) to start to do sth or become involved in it 开始；着手；参与：*to enter on a new career* 开始新的职业生涯

en·ter·ic /en'terɪk/ *adj.* (*medical* 医) connected with the INTESTINES 肠的

en·ter·itis /ˌentə'raɪtəs/ *noun* [U] (*medical* 医) a painful infection in the INTESTINES that usually causes DIARRHOEA 小肠炎 ➲ SEE ALSO GASTROENTERITIS

en·ter·prise /'entəpraɪz; *NAmE* -tərp-/ *noun* **1** [C] a company or business 公司；企业：*an enterprise with a turnover of $26 billion* 营业额 260 亿美元的公司 ◇ ***state-owned/public enterprises*** 国有企业；国营企业 ◇ *small and medium-sized enterprises* 中小型企业 **2** [C] a large project, especially one that is difficult （尤指艰巨而重大的）规划，事业 **SYN** **venture**：*his latest business enterprise* 他最新的企业规划 ◇ *a* ***joint enterprise*** 共同事业 **3** [U] the development of businesses by the people of a country rather than by the government 企业发展；企业经营；企业活动：*grants to encourage enterprise in the region* 鼓励这个地区企业发展的拨款 ◇ *an enterprise culture* (= in which people are encouraged to develop small businesses) 经商文化（鼓励发展小型企业）➲ SEE ALSO FREE ENTERPRISE, PRIVATE ENTERPRISE **4** [U] (*approving*) the ability to think of new projects and make them successful 事业心；进取心；创业精神 **SYN** **initiative**：*a job in which enterprise is rewarded* 对事业进取精神有所回报的工作

en·ter·pris·ing /'entəpraɪzɪŋ; *NAmE* -tərp-/ *adj.* (*approving*) having or showing the ability to think of new projects or new ways of doing things and make them successful 有事业心的；有进取心的；有创业精神的

en·ter·tain /ˌentə'teɪn; *NAmE* -tər't-/ *verb* **1** [I, T] to invite people to eat or drink with you as your guests, especially in your home （尤指在自己家中）招待，款待：*The job involves a lot of entertaining.* 这项工作需要经常设宴招待客人。◇ **~ sb** *Barbecues are a favourite way of entertaining friends.* 户外烧烤是特别受人喜爱的待客方式。**2** [T, I] **~ (sb) (with sth)** to interest and amuse sb in order to please them 使有兴趣；使快乐；娱乐：*He entertained us for hours with his stories and jokes.* 他讲故事说笑话，逗我们乐了好几个小时。◇ *The aim of the series is both to entertain and inform.* 这套系列节目是为了寓教于乐。**3** [T] (not used in the progressive tenses 不用于进行时) **~ sth** (*formal*) to consider or allow yourself to think about an idea, a hope, a feeling, etc. 心存，怀有（想法、希望、感觉等）：*He had* ***entertained hopes*** *of a reconciliation.* 他曾对和解抱有希望。◇ ***to entertain a doubt/suspicion*** 持怀疑态度

en·ter·tain·er /ˌentə'teɪnə(r); *NAmE* -tər't-/ *noun* a person whose job is amusing or interesting people, for example, by singing, telling jokes or dancing （歌唱、说笑话、舞蹈等的）演员，表演者，艺人

en·ter·tain·ing /ˌentə'teɪnɪŋ; *NAmE* -tər't-/ *adj.* interesting and amusing 有趣的；娱乐的；使人愉快的：*an entertaining speech/evening* 妙趣横生的演讲；令人开心的晚上 ◇ *I found the talk both informative and entertaining.* 我认为这次演讲知识与趣味并重。◇ *She was always so funny and entertaining.* 她总是那么风趣，令人愉快。➲ SYNONYMS AT FUNNY ▸ **en·ter·tain·ing·ly** *adv.*

en·ter·tain·ment /ˌentə'teɪnmənt; *NAmE* -tər't-/ *noun* **1** [U, C] films/movies, music, etc. used to entertain people; an example of this 娱乐片；文娱节目；表演会；娱乐活动：*radio, television and other forms of entertainment* 广播、电视和其他形式的娱乐活动 ◇ *There will be* ***live entertainment*** *at the party.* 联欢会上将有现场表演节目。◇ *It was typical* ***family entertainment***. 这是典型的家庭娱乐活动。◇ *The entertainment was provided by a folk band.* 这个文娱节目由民歌乐队演出。◇ *Local entertainments are listed in the newspaper.* 本地的娱乐活动刊登在报上。◇ *The show was good* ***entertainment value***. 这场演出有很大的娱乐价值。➲ SYNONYMS ON NEXT PAGE **2** [U] the act of entertaining sb 招待；款待；娱乐：*a budget for the entertainment of clients* 用于招待客户的专项预算

en·thral (*BrE*) (*NAmE* **en·thrall**) /ɪn'θrɔːl/ *verb* (**-ll-**) [T, I, usually passive] **~ (sb)** if sth **enthrals** you, it is so interesting, beautiful, etc. that you give it all your attention 迷住；吸引住 **SYN** **entrance**[2]：*The child watched, enthralled by the bright moving images.* 这孩子看着那明亮的移动的影像，被迷住了。▸ **en·thral·ling** *adj.*：*an enthralling performance* 迷人的表演

en·throne /ɪn'θrəʊn; *NAmE* ɪn'θroʊn/ *verb* [usually passive] **~ sb** when a king, queen or important member of a Church is **enthroned**, they sit on a THRONE (= a special chair) in a ceremony to mark the beginning of their rule 使登基；使即位 ▸ **en·throne·ment** *noun* [U, C]

en·thuse /ɪn'θjuːz; *NAmE* -'θuːz/ *verb* **1** [I, T] to talk in an enthusiastic and excited way about sth 充满热情地说；热烈地讲：**~ (about/over sth/sb)** *The article enthused about the benefits that the new system would bring.* 本文热情阐述了新制度将带来的好处。◇ **+ speech** *'It's a wonderful idea', he enthused.* "这真是个绝妙的主意。"他

充满热情地说。◇ **~ that…** *The organizers enthused that it was their most successful event yet.* 组织者充满热情地说这是他们迄今为止最成功的活动。 **2** [usually passive] **~ sb (with sth)** to make sb feel very interested and excited 使热衷；使热心；使激动：*Everyone present was enthused by the idea.* 在场的每一个人都为这种想法感到激动。

en·thu·si·asm /ɪnˈθjuːziæzəm; *NAmE* -ˈθuː-/ *noun* **1** [U] a strong feeling of excitement and interest in sth and a desire to become involved in it 热情；热心；热忱：**~ (for sth)** *I can't say I share your enthusiasm for the idea.* 我可不像你那样，对这个想法那样热心。◇ *He had a real enthusiasm for the work.* 他的确热衷于这项工作。◇ **~ (for doing sth)** *She never lost her enthusiasm for teaching.* 她从未失去过教书的热忱。◇ *The news was greeted with a lack of enthusiasm by those at the meeting.* 与会者对这消息未表现出多少兴趣。◇ *'I don't mind,' she said, without much enthusiasm.* "我不在乎。"她不冷不热地说。◇ *full of enthusiasm* 充满热情 **2** [C] (*formal*) something that you are very interested in and spend a lot of time doing 热衷的事物；激发热情的事物 ➲ WORDFINDER NOTE AT ADVENTURE

▼ **SYNONYMS 同义词辨析**

entertainment

fun • recreation • relaxation • play • pleasure • amusement

These are all words for things or activities used to entertain people when they are not working. 以上各词均指休闲、娱乐或相关活动。

entertainment films, television, music, etc. used to entertain people 指娱乐片、文娱节目、表演会等：*There are three bars, with live entertainment seven nights a week.* 有三家酒吧每周七个晚上都有现场文艺节目。

fun (*rather informal*) behaviour or activities that are not serious but come from a sense of enjoyment 指嬉戏、逗乐、玩笑：*It wasn't serious—it was all done in fun.* 那不是认真的，全是闹着玩的。◇ *We didn't mean to hurt him. It was just **a bit of fun**.* 我们并非有意要伤害他，只不过是开个玩笑罢了。◇ *The lottery provides **harmless fun** for millions.* 彩票抽奖为数百万人提供无伤大雅的娱乐。

recreation (*rather formal*) things people do for enjoyment when they are not working 指娱乐、消遣：*His only form of recreation is playing football.* 他唯一的娱乐就是踢足球。

relaxation (*rather formal*) things people do to rest and enjoy themselves when they are not working; the ability to relax 指休闲活动、消遣：*I go hill-walking for relaxation.* 我要是想放松放松，就到山上走走。

RECREATION OR RELAXATION? 用 recreation 还是 relaxation?

Both these words can be used for a wide range of activities, physical and mental, but **relaxation** is sometimes used for gentler activities than **recreation**. 以上两词均可指各种体力和精神活动，但 relaxation 有时指较 recreation 轻松的活动：*I play the flute in a wind band for recreation.* 我在管乐队吹长笛消遣。◇ *I listen to music for relaxation.* 我听音乐放松心情。

play things that people, especially children, do for enjoyment rather than as work 尤指孩子游戏、玩耍、娱乐：*the happy sounds of children **at play*** 儿童嬉戏的欢闹声

pleasure the activity of enjoying yourself, especially in contrast to working 指玩乐、休闲，尤与工作相对：*Are you in Paris **for business or pleasure**?* 你来巴黎公干还是游玩？

amusement the fact of being entertained by sth 指娱乐、消遣、游戏：*What do you do for amusement round here?* 你在这儿以什么消遣？

PATTERNS

- to do sth **for** entertainment/fun/recreation/relaxation/pleasure/amusement
- **to provide** entertainment/fun/recreation/relaxation/amusement

en·thu·si·ast /ɪnˈθjuːziæst; *NAmE* -ˈθuː-/ *noun* **1 ~ (for/of sth)** a person who is very interested in sth and spends a lot of time doing it 热衷于…的人；热心者；爱好者：*a football enthusiast* 足球爱好者 ◇ *an enthusiast of jazz* 爵士乐爱好者 **2 ~ (for/of sth)** a person who approves of sth and shows enthusiasm for it 热烈支持者；热情赞成者：*enthusiasts for a united Europe* 热烈赞成建立统一欧洲的人

en·thu·si·as·tic /ɪnˌθjuːziˈæstɪk; *NAmE* -ˌθuː-/ *adj.* feeling or showing a lot of excitement and interest about sb/sth 热情的；热心的；热烈的；满腔热忱的：*an enthusiastic supporter* 热心的支持者 ◇ *an enthusiastic welcome* 热烈欢迎 ◇ **~ about sb/sth** *You don't sound very enthusiastic about the idea.* 你好像对这个想法不太感兴趣。◇ **~ about doing sth** *She was even less enthusiastic about going to Spain.* 她对去西班牙更是不感兴趣。▸ **en·thu·si·as·tic·al·ly** /-kli/ *adv.*

en·tice /ɪnˈtaɪs/ *verb* to persuade sb/sth to go somewhere or to do sth, usually by offering them sth 诱使；引诱 **SYN** **persuade**：**~ sb/sth (+ adv./prep.)** *The bargain prices are expected to entice customers away from other stores.* 低廉的价格意在把顾客从其他商店吸引过来。◇ *The animal refused to be enticed from its hole.* 那只动物怎么引诱也不肯出洞。◇ **~ sb into doing sth** *He was not enticed into parting with his cash.* 他没有因为诱惑而掏钱。◇ **~ sb to do sth** *Try and entice the child to eat by offering small portions of their favourite food.* 给孩子少许爱吃的食物，设法诱使他们吃饭。▸ **en·tice·ment** *noun* [C, U]：*The party is offering low taxation as its main enticement.* 这个党正提出低税收，以此作为其主要的吸引人的手段。

en·ticing /ɪnˈtaɪsɪŋ/ *adj.* something that is **enticing** is so attractive and interesting that you want to have it or know more about it 有诱惑力的；诱人的；有吸引力的：*The offer was too enticing to refuse.* 这提议太有诱惑力，使人难以拒绝。▸ **en·ticing·ly** *adv.*

en·tire /ɪnˈtaɪə(r)/ *adj.* [only before noun] (used when you are emphasizing that the whole of sth is involved 用以强调) including everything, everyone or every part 全部的；整个的；完全的 **SYN** **whole**：*The entire village was destroyed.* 整个村庄都给毁了。◇ *I wasted an entire day on it.* 我为此浪费了整整一天。◇ *I have never in my entire life heard such nonsense!* 我一生中从未听到过这样的胡话！◇ *The disease threatens to wipe out the entire population.* 这种疾病有可能毁灭整个族群。

en·tire·ly /ɪnˈtaɪəli; *NAmE* ɪnˈtaɪərli/ *adv.* in every way possible; completely 全部地；完整地；完全地：*I entirely agree with you.* 我完全同意你的看法。◇ *I'm not entirely happy about the proposal.* 我对这个建议并不十分满意。◇ *That's an entirely different matter.* 那完全是另一码事。◇ *The audience was almost entirely female.* 观众几乎全是女性。

en·tir·ety /ɪnˈtaɪərəti/ *noun* [sing.] (*formal*) **the ~ of sth** the whole of sth 全部；全体；整体

IDM **in its/their en'tirety** as a whole, rather than in parts 作为整体；整个地；全面地：*The poem is too long to quote in its entirety.* 这首诗太长，不能全部引用。

en·title /ɪnˈtaɪtl/ *verb* **1** [often passive] to give sb the right to have or to do sth 使享有权利；使符合资格：**~ sb to sth** *You will be entitled to your pension when you reach 65.* 你到 65 岁就有资格领取养老金。◇ *Everyone's entitled to their own opinion.* 人人都有权发表自己的意见。◇ **~ sb to do sth** *This ticket does not entitle you to travel first class.* 你拿这张票不能坐头等舱。 **2** [usually passive] **~ sth + noun** to give a title to a book, play, etc. 给…命名（或题名）：*He read a poem entitled 'Salt'.* 他朗诵了一首题为《盐》的诗。

en·title·ment /ɪnˈtaɪtlmənt/ *noun* (*formal*) **1** [U] **~ (to sth)** the official right to have or do sth （拥有某物或做某事的）权利，资格：*This may affect your entitlement to* *compensation.* 这可能影响你索赔的权利。 **2** [C] something that you have an official right to; the amount that you have the right to receive 有权得到的东西；应得的数额：*Your contributions will affect your pension entitlements.* 你缴纳的养老金分摊额将会影响你领取养老金的数额。 **3** [C] (*NAmE*) a government system that provides financial support to a particular group of people （以特定群体为对象的）政府津贴制： *a reform of entitlements* 政府津贴制度的改革 ◇ *Medicaid, Medicare and other entitlement programs* 医疗补助制度、老年保健医疗制度以及其他政府津贴计划

en·tity AW /'entəti/ *noun* (*pl.* **-ies**) (*formal*) something that exists separately from other things and has its own identity 独立存在物；实体： *The unit has become part of a larger department and no longer exists as a* ***separate entity.*** 这个单位已附属于一个大的部门，不再作为一个实体独立存在。 ◇ *These countries can no longer be viewed as a* ***single entity.*** 这些国家不能再被看成是一个单独的实体。

en·tomb /ɪn'tuːm/ *verb* [usually passive] (*formal*) **1** ~ **sb/sth** (**in sth**) to bury or completely cover sb/sth so that they cannot get out, be seen, etc. 掩埋；埋葬 **2** ~ **sb/sth** (**in sth**) to put a dead body in a TOMB 把（尸体）葬入坟墓

en·to·mol·ogy /ˌentə'mɒlədʒi; *NAmE* -'mɑːl-/ *noun* [U] the scientific study of insects 昆虫学 ▶ **en·to·mo·logic·al** /ˌentəmə'lɒdʒɪkl; *NAmE* -'lɑːdʒ-/ *adj.* **en·to·molo·gist** /ˌentə'mɒlədʒɪst; *NAmE* -'mɑːl-/ *noun*

en·tou·rage /'ɒntʊrɑːʒ; *NAmE* 'ɑːn-/ *noun* [C+sing./pl. v.] a group of people who travel with an important person （统称）随行人员，随从

en·tr'acte /'ɒntrækt; 'ɒ̃t-; *NAmE* 'ɑːntrækt; ɑːn'trækt/ *noun* (*from French*) **1** (*formal*) the time between the different parts of a play, show, etc. （戏剧、演出等的）幕间休息 SYN **interval** **2** a short performance between the different parts of a play, show, etc. 幕间插演的节目；幕间表演

en·trails /'entreɪlz/ *noun* [pl.] the organs inside the body of a person or an animal, especially their INTESTINES 内脏；（尤指）肠 SYN **innards, inside**

en·trance[1] /'entrəns/ *noun* ➲ SEE ALSO ENTRANCE[2]

• **DOOR/GATE** 门 **1** [C] ~ (**to sth**) a door, gate, passage, etc. used for entering a room, building or place 大门（口）；入口（处）；入口通道： *the entrance to the museum/the museum entrance* 博物馆入口处 ◇ *A lighthouse marks the entrance to the harbour.* 灯塔是进入海港的标志。 ◇ *the* ***front/back/side entrance*** *of the house* 房子的前门 / 后门 / 侧门 ◇ *an* ***entrance hall/lobby*** 门厅 ◇ *I'll meet you at the* ***main entrance.*** 我在正门和你碰面。 ➲ COMPARE EXIT *n.* (1)

• **GOING IN** 进入 **2** [C, usually sing.] the act of entering a room, building or place, especially in a way that attracts the attention of other people 进入；出场；登场： *His sudden entrance took everyone by surprise.* 他的突然出场使所有人都感到意外。 ◇ *A fanfare signalled the entrance of the king.* 响亮的喇叭声是国王驾到的信号。 ◇ *She* ***made her entrance*** *after all the other guests had arrived.* 她在其他所有客人都到达后才入场。 ◇ *The hero* ***makes his entrance*** (= walks onto the stage) *in Scene 2.* 男主角在第 2 场出场。 ➲ WORDFINDER NOTE AT PLAY **3** [U] ~ (**to sth**) the right or opportunity to enter a building or place 进入权；进入机会： *They were refused entrance to the exhibition.* 他们被拒于展览会门外。 ◇ *The police were unable to* ***gain entrance*** *to the house.* 警方未能得到进入这栋房子的许可。 ◇ *an* ***entrance fee*** (= money paid to go into a museum, etc.) 入场费

• **BECOMING INVOLVED** 卷入 **4** [C] ~ (**into sth**) the act of becoming involved in sth 卷入；参与： *The company made a dramatic entrance into the export market.* 这家公司戏剧性地打入了出口市场。

• **TO CLUB/INSTITUTION** 俱乐部；机构 **5** [U] permission to become a member of a club, society, university, etc. （俱乐部、社团、大学等的）准许加入，进入许可： *a university entrance exam* 大学入学考试 ◇ *entrance requirements* 入学要求 ◇ ~ (**to sth**) *Entrance to the golf club is by sponsorship only.* 只有通过赞助才能加入这个高尔夫球俱乐部。 ➲ COMPARE ENTRY

en·trance[2] /ɪn'trɑːns; *NAmE* -'træns/ *verb* [usually passive] ~ **sb** (*formal*) to make sb feel great pleasure and admiration so that they give sb/sth all their attention 使狂喜；使入迷 SYN **enthral**: *He listened to her, entranced.* 他听她讲话听得出了神。 ➲ SEE ALSO ENTRANCE[1] ▶ **en·tran·cing** *adj.*: *entrancing music* 令人陶醉的音乐

'entrance hall *noun* (*especially BrE*) a large room inside the entrance of a large or public building 门厅

en·trant /'entrənt/ *noun* **1** ~ (**to sth**) a person who has recently joined a profession, university, etc. 新职员；新生；新会员；新成员： *new women entrants to the police force* 新加入警察部队的女警察 ◇ *university entrants* 大学新生 **2** ~ (**to sth**) a person or an animal that enters a race or a competition; a person that enters an exam 参赛者（或动物）；考生

en·trap /ɪn'træp/ *verb* (**-pp-**) [often passive] (*formal*) **1** ~ **sb/sth** to put or catch sb/sth in a place or situation from which they cannot escape 使入陷阱（或圈套、困境等） SYN **trap** **2** ~ **sb** (**into doing sth**) to trick sb, and encourage them to do sth, especially to commit a crime, so that they can be arrested for it 诱捕；诱骗

en·trap·ment /ɪn'træpmənt/ *noun* [U] (*law* 律) the illegal act of tricking sb into committing a crime so that they can be arrested for it （非法）诱捕，诱人犯罪

en·treat /ɪn'triːt/ *verb* (*formal*) to ask sb to do sth in a serious and often emotional way 恳求；乞求 SYN **beg, implore**: ~ **sb** *Please help me, I entreat you.* 请帮帮我吧，求你了。 ◇ ~ **sb to do sth** *She entreated him not to go.* 她恳求他不要走。 ◇ ~ (**sb**) + **speech** *'Please don't go,' she entreated (him).* "请不要走。" 她恳求（他）说。

en·treaty /ɪn'triːti/ *noun* (*pl.* **-ies**) [C, U] (*formal*) a serious and often emotional request 恳求；乞求

en·trée /'ɒntreɪ; *NAmE* 'ɑːn-/ *noun* (*from French*) **1** [C] (in a restaurant or at a formal meal) the main dish of the meal or a dish served before the main course （餐厅里或正式宴会上的）主菜，前菜 **2** [U, C] ~ (**into/to sth**) (*formal*) the right or ability to enter a social group or institution 入场权；进入许可；进入资格

en·trench (*also* **in·trench**) /ɪn'trentʃ/ *verb* [usually passive] ~ **sth** (*sometimes disapproving*) to establish sth very firmly so that it is very difficult to change 使处于牢固地位；牢固确立： *Sexism is* ***deeply entrenched*** *in our society.* 性别歧视在我们这个社会根深蒂固。 ◇ ***entrenched attitudes/interests/opposition*** 顽固的态度；固有的利益；顽固的反对

en·trench·ment /ɪn'trentʃmənt/ *noun* **1** [U] the fact of sth being firmly established 牢固确立；根深蒂固 **2** [C, usually pl.] a system of TRENCHES (= long narrow holes dug in the ground by soldiers to provide defence) 堑壕；战壕

entre·pôt /'ɒntrəpəʊ; *NAmE* 'ɑːntrəpoʊ/ *noun* (*from French*) a port or other place where goods are brought for import and export 转口港；转运口岸

entre·pre·neur /ˌɒntrəprə'nɜː(r); *NAmE* ˌɑːn-/ *noun* a person who makes money by starting or running businesses, especially when this involves taking financial risks 创业者，企业家（尤指涉及财务风险的） ➲ WORDFINDER NOTE AT BUSINESSMAN ▶ **en·tre·pre·neur·ial** /-'nɜːriəl/ *adj.*: *entrepreneurial skills* 办企业的能力 **entre·pre·neur·ship** *noun* [U]

en·tropy /'entrəpi/ *noun* [U] **1** (*specialist*) a way of measuring the lack of order that exists in a system 无序状态测量法 **2** (*physics* 物) (*symb.* **S**) a measurement of the energy that is present in a system or process but is not available to do work 熵（物质系统中不能用来做功的能量的度量） **3** a complete lack of order 无序状态： *In the business world, entropy rules.* 在商业世界中，无序是常态。 ▶ **en·trop·ic** /en'trɒpɪk; -'trəʊp-; *NAmE* -'trɑːp-/ *adj.* **en·trop·ical·ly** /-kli/ *adv.*

en·trust /ɪn'trʌst/ *verb* (*formal*) to make sb responsible for doing sth or taking care of sb 委托；交托；托付：**~ A (to B)** *He entrusted the task to his nephew.* 他把这任务托付给了他的侄儿。◇ **~ B with A** *He entrusted his nephew with the task.* 他把这任务托付给了他的侄儿。

entry /'entri/ *noun* (*pl.* **-ies**)
• GOING IN 进入 **1** [C, U] an act of going into or getting into a place 进入（指行动）：*She **made her entry** to the sound of thunderous applause.* 她在雷鸣般的掌声中走了进来。◇ *The children were surprised by the sudden entry of their teacher.* 老师突然进来使孩子们感到意外。◇ **~ (into sth)** *How did the thieves **gain entry** into the building?* 窃贼是怎样进入大楼的？ **2** [U] the right or opportunity to enter a place 进入（指权利、机会）：***No Entry*** (= for example, on a sign) 禁止入内 ◇ **~ (to/into sth)** *Entry to the museum is free.* 这座博物馆免费参观。◇ *to **be granted/refused entry** into the country* 准予 / 禁止入境
• JOINING GROUP 加入集体 **3** [U] **~ (into sth)** the right or opportunity to take part in sth or become a member of a group 参与，加入（指权利、机会）：*countries seeking entry into the European Union* 寻求加入欧盟的国家 ◇ *the entry of women into the workforce* 妇女加入劳动大军
• IN COMPETITION 比赛 **4** [C] something that you do, write or make to take part in a competition, for example answering a set of questions 参赛作品；竞赛答题：*There have been some impressive entries in the wildlife photography section* (= impressive photographs). 野生动物摄影部分已有一些上佳参赛作品。◇ *The closing date for entries is 31 March.* 递交参赛作品的截止日期是3月31日。◇ *The sender of the first correct entry drawn will win a weekend for two in Venice.* 抽中的第一个寄来正确答案的竞赛答题者将获得威尼斯周末双人游的机会。 **5** [U] the act of taking part in a competition, race, etc. 参赛：*Entry is open to anyone over the age of 18.* * 18 岁以上的人均可参赛。◇ *an entry form* 参赛表格 **6** [sing.] the total number of people who are taking part in a competition, race, etc. 参赛人数：*There's a record entry for this year's marathon.* 参加本年度马拉松比赛的人数创下最高纪录。
• WRITTEN INFORMATION 书面资料 **7** [C] an item, for example a piece of information, that is written or printed in a dictionary, an account book, a diary, etc. （词典等的）条目；词条；账目；记录：*an encyclopedia entry* 百科全书的一个条目 ◇ **~ (in sth)** *There is no entry in his diary for that day.* 他的日记里没有那天的记录。➲ WORDFINDER NOTE AT DICTIONARY **8** [U] the act of recording information in a computer, book, etc. 登记；登录；录入
• DOOR/GATE 门 **9** (*also* **entry·way** /'entriweɪ/) (*both NAmE*) [C] a door, gate or passage where you enter a building; an entrance hall 大门；入口处；通道；门厅：*You can leave your umbrella in the entry.* 你可以把伞放在入口处。

'entry-level *adj.* [usually before noun] **1** (of a product 产品) basic and suitable for new users who may later move on to a more advanced product 适合初级用户的；入门级的：*an entry-level computer* 供初学者使用的计算机 **2** (of a job 工作) at the lowest level in a company （公司中）最初级的

Entry·phone™ /'entrifəʊn; *NAmE* -foʊn/ *noun* (*BrE*) a type of telephone on the wall next to the entrance to a building enabling a person inside the building to speak to a person outside before opening the door 应门对讲机

en·twine /ɪn'twaɪn/ *verb* [usually passive] **1 ~ sth (with/in/around sth)** to twist or wind sth around sth else 盘绕；缠绕：*They strolled through the park, with arms entwined.* 他们挽着胳膊漫步穿过公园。 **2 be entwined (with sth)** to be very closely involved or connected with sth 与…密切相关（或紧密相联）：*Her destiny was entwined with his.* 她与他的命运紧密相联。

'E-number *noun* (*BrE*) a number beginning with the letter E that is printed on packs and containers to show what artificial flavours and colours have been added to food and drink; an artificial flavour, colour, etc. added to food and drink * E 数（干包装上注明食品或饮料中添加剂的含量）；食品添加剂：*This sauce is full of E-numbers.* 这种调味汁尽是人造香料和色素。

enu·mer·ate /ɪ'nju:məreɪt; *NAmE* ɪ'nu:-/ *verb* **~ sth** (*formal*) to name things on a list one by one 列举；枚举 ▸ **enu·mer·ation** /ɪˌnju:mə'reɪʃn; *NAmE* ɪˌnu:-/ *noun* [U, C]

enun·ci·ate /ɪ'nʌnsieɪt/ *verb* **1** [T, I] **~ (sth) | + speech** to say or pronounce words clearly 清楚地念（字）；清晰地发（音）：*She enunciated each word slowly and carefully.* 她每个字都念得又慢又仔细。 **2** [T] **~ sth** (*formal*) to express an idea clearly and exactly 清楚地表明；阐明：*He enunciated his vision of the future.* 他阐明了自己对未来的看法。 ▸ **enun·ci·ation** /ɪˌnʌnsi'eɪʃn/ *noun* [U, C]

en·ur·esis /ˌenjʊə'ri:sɪs; *NAmE* ˌenjʊ'ri:-/ *noun* [U] (*medical* 医) URINATION (= letting waste liquid flow from the body) that is not under sb's control, especially in the case of a child who is asleep 遗尿（症）；（尤指儿童）尿床

en·velop /ɪn'veləp/ *verb* **~ sb/sth (in sth)** (*formal*) to wrap sb/sth up or cover them or it completely 包住；裹住；盖住：*She was enveloped in a huge white towel.* 她裹在一条白色大毛巾里。◇ *Clouds enveloped the mountain tops.* 云雾笼罩着山顶。 ▸ **en·velop·ment** *noun* [U]

en·vel·ope /'envələʊp; 'ɒn-; *NAmE* 'envəloʊp; 'ɑ:n-/ *noun* **1** a flat paper container used for sending letters in 信封：*writing paper and envelopes* 信纸和信封 ◇ ***an airmail/a padded/a prepaid envelope*** 航空 / 有垫料夹层的 / 预付邮资信封 ➲ VISUAL VOCAB PAGE V71 ➲ SEE ALSO PAY ENVELOPE, SAE, SASE **2** a flat container made of plastic for keeping papers in 塑料封套；塑料封皮 IDM SEE PUSH *v.*

en·vi·able /'enviəbl/ *adj.* something that is **enviable** is the sort of thing that is good and that other people want to have too 令人羡慕的；引起忌妒的：*He is in **the enviable position** of having two job offers to choose from.* 他有两份工作可选，真让人羡慕。 OPP **unenviable** ▸ **en·vi·ably** /-bli/ *adv.*：*an enviably mild climate* 温和得让人羡慕的气候

▼ SYNONYMS 同义词辨析

environment

setting • surroundings • background

These are all words for the type of place in which sb/sth exists or is situated. 以上各词均指人或事物生存或所处的环境。

environment the conditions in a place that affect the behaviour and development of sb/sth 指影响人或事物的行为或发展的环境：*An unhappy **home environment** can affect children's behaviour.* 不幸的家庭环境可能对孩子的行为造成影响。◇ *a pleasant **working environment*** 令人愉快的工作环境

setting a place or situation of a particular type, in which sth happens or exists 指事物所处的环境或发生的背景：*The island provided an idyllic setting for the concert.* 这岛为音乐会提供了优美的田园布景。

surroundings everything that is around or near sb/sth 指周围的环境：*The huts blend in perfectly with their surroundings.* 这些棚屋与周围的环境浑然一体，非常和谐。

background the things or area behind or around the main objects or people that are in a place or picture 指对主要人物、事物起衬托作用的事物、背景：*The mountains in the background were capped with snow.* 远处的山峦白雪覆盖。

PATTERNS
- **in** (a/an) environment/setting/surroundings
- (a/an) **new/unfamiliar** environment/setting/surroundings
- sb/sth's **immediate** environment/surroundings
- (a) **dramatic** setting/background

en·vi·ous /ˈenviəs/ *adj.* ~ (**of sb/sth**) wanting to be in the same situation as sb else; wanting sth that sb else has 羡慕的；忌妒的：*Everyone is so envious of her.* 人人都那么羡慕她。◇ *They were envious of his success.* 他们忌妒他的成功。◇ *He saw the envious look in the other boy's eyes.* 他看到了另一个男孩眼里那羡慕的目光。▶ **en·vi·ous·ly** *adv.*：*They look enviously at the success of their European counterparts.* 他们看着欧洲同行的成功，羡慕不已。➲ SEE ALSO ENVY

en·vir·on·ment 🔑 AW /ɪnˈvaɪrənmənt/ *noun* **1** 🔑 [C, U] the conditions that affect the behaviour and development of sb/sth; the physical conditions that sb/sth exists in （影响个体行为或事物发展的）环境；客观环境：*a pleasant* ***working/learning environment*** 令人愉快的工作 / 学习环境 ◇ *An unhappy* ***home environment*** *can affect a child's behaviour.* 不幸的家庭环境可能对孩子的行为造成影响。◇ *They have created an environment in which productivity should flourish.* 他们创造了一种可以大大提高生产力的环境。◇ *the political environment* 政治环境 ◇ *tests carried out in a controlled environment* 在受控环境下进行的试验 **2** 🔑 **the environment** [sing.] the natural world in which people, animals and plants live 自然环境；生态环境：*the Department of the Environment* 环境事务部 ◇ *measures to protect the environment* 保护环境的措施 ◇ *pollution of the environment* 环境污染 ◇ *damage to the environment* 对环境的破坏 ➲ WORDFINDER NOTE AT GREEN ➲ VISUAL VOCAB PAGES V6-9 **3** [C] (*computing* 计) the complete structure within which a user, computer or program operates （运行）环境：*a desktop development environment* 桌面开发环境

en·vir·on·men·tal 🔑 AW /ɪnˌvaɪrənˈmentl/ *adj.* [usually before noun] **1** 🔑 connected with the natural conditions in which people, animals and plants live; connected with the environment 自然环境的；生态环境的；有关环境的：*the environmental impact of pollution* 污染对环境的影响 ◇ ***environmental issues/problems*** 环境问题 ◇ *an* ***environmental group/movement*** (= that aims to improve or protect the natural environment) 环境保护组织 / 运动 ◇ *environmental damage* 环境破坏 **2** 🔑 connected with the conditions that affect the behaviour and development of sb/sth （影响个体或事物行为或发展）环境的：*environmental influences* 环境影响 ◇ *an environmental health officer* 环境卫生检查官员 ▶ **en·vir·on·men·tal·ly** AW /-təli/ *adv.*：*an environmentally sensitive area* (= one that is easily damaged or that contains rare animals, plants, etc.) 生态环境脆弱的地区 ◇ *environmentally damaging* 对环境有害的

en·vir·on·men·tal·ist AW /ɪnˌvaɪrənˈmentəlɪst/ *noun* a person who is concerned about the natural environment and wants to improve and protect it 环境保护论者 ▶ **en·vir·on·ment·al·ism** *noun* [U]

enˌvironmentally ˈfriendly (*also* **enˌvironment-ˈfriendly**) *adj.* (of products 产品) not harming the environment 环保的；不损害环境的：*environmentally friendly packaging* 环保包装

en·vir·ons /ɪnˈvaɪrənz/ *noun* [pl.] (*formal*) the area surrounding a place 周围地区：*Berlin and its environs* 柏林及其周围地区 ◇ *people living in the immediate environs of a nuclear plant* 居住在核电站附近地区的人

▼ **COLLOCATIONS 词语搭配**

The environment 环境

Environmental damage 环境破坏

- **cause/contribute to** climate change/global warming 引起气候变化 / 全球变暖
- **produce** pollution/CO_2/greenhouse (gas) emissions 产生污染 / 二氧化碳 / 温室气体排放
- **damage/destroy** the environment/a marine ecosystem/the ozone layer/coral reefs 破坏环境 / 海洋生态系统 / 臭氧层 / 珊瑚礁
- **degrade** ecosystems/habitats/the environment 使生态系统 / 栖息地 / 环境退化
- **harm** the environment/wildlife/marine life 危害环境 / 野生动物 / 海洋生物
- **threaten** natural habitats/coastal ecosystems/a species with extinction 构成对自然栖息地 / 沿海生态系统 / 物种灭绝的威胁
- **deplete** natural resources/the ozone layer 大量损耗自然资源 / 臭氧层
- **pollute** rivers and lakes/waterways/the air/the atmosphere/the environment/oceans 污染河流湖泊 / 航道 / 空气 / 大气层 / 环境 / 海洋
- **contaminate** groundwater/the soil/food/crops 污染地下水 / 土壤 / 食物 / 庄稼
- **log** forests/rainforests/trees 采伐森林 / 热带雨林 / 树木

Protecting the environment 保护环境

- **address/combat/tackle** the threat/effects/impact of climate change 设法解决 / 防止 / 应对气候变化带来的威胁 / 影响 / 冲击
- **fight/take action on/reduce/stop** global warming 对抗 / 采取行动应对 / 减缓 / 阻止全球变暖
- **limit/curb/control** air/water/atmospheric/environmental pollution 控制空气 / 水 / 大气 / 环境污染
- **cut/reduce** pollution/greenhouse gas emissions 减少污染 / 温室气体排放
- **offset** carbon/CO_2 emissions 抵消碳 / 二氧化碳的排放
- **reduce** (the size of) your carbon footprint 减少碳足迹（量）
- **achieve/promote** sustainable development 实现 / 促进可持续发展
- **preserve/conserve** biodiversity/natural resources 保持生物多样性；保护自然资源
- **protect** endangered species/a coastal ecosystem 保护濒危物种 / 沿海生态系统
- **prevent/stop** soil erosion/overfishing/massive deforestation/damage to ecosystems 防止 / 阻止水土流失 / 过度捕捞 / 大面积森林砍伐 / 对生态系统的破坏
- **raise** awareness of environmental issues 增强环境意识
- **save** the planet/the rainforests/an endangered species 拯救地球 / 热带雨林 / 濒危物种

Energy and resources 能源和资源

- **conserve/save/consume/waste** energy 保护 / 节约 / 消耗 / 浪费能源
- **manage/exploit/be rich in** natural resources 管理 / 开发 / 有丰富的自然资源
- **dump/dispose of** hazardous/toxic/nuclear waste 倾倒 / 处理有害 / 有毒 / 核废料
- **dispose of/throw away** litter/(*especially BrE*) rubbish/(*especially NAmE*) garbage/(*NAmE*) trash/sewage 处理 / 扔掉垃圾 / 废物；排放污水
- **use/be made from** recycled/recyclable/biodegradable material 使用回收 / 可回收 / 可生物降解材料；由回收 / 可回收 / 可生物降解材料制成
- **recycle** bottles/packaging/paper/plastic/waste 回收瓶子 / 包装材料 / 纸 / 塑料 / 废品
- **promote/encourage** recycling/sustainable development/the use of renewable energy 促进 / 鼓励回收利用 / 可持续发展 / 使用可再生能源
- **develop/invest in/promote** renewable energy 研发 / 投资 / 推动可再生能源
- **reduce** your dependence/reliance on fossil fuels 减少对化石燃料的依赖
- **get/obtain/generate/produce** electricity from wind, solar and wave power/renewable sources 利用风、太阳能、潮汐 / 可再生能源发电
- **build/develop** a (50-megawatt/offshore) wind farm 修建一座（50 兆瓦 / 海上）风力发电站
- **install/be fitted with/be powered by** solar panels 安装太阳能板；由太阳能板提供动力

en·vis·age /ɪnˈvɪzɪdʒ/ (*especially BrE*) (*NAmE usually* **en·vi·sion**) *verb* to imagine what will happen in the future 想象；设想；展望： **~ sth** *What level of profit do you envisage?* 你预计会有什么样的利润水平？ ◇ **~ (sb) doing sth** *I can't envisage her coping with this job.* 我无法设想她如何应付这个工作。 ◇ **it is envisaged that…** *It is envisaged that the talks will take place in the spring.* 谈判预期在春季举行。 ◇ **~ that…** *I envisage that the work will be completed next year.* 我预计这项工作将在明年完成。 ◇ **~ how, where, etc.…** *It is difficult to envisage how people will react.* 很难设想人们将有什么反应。 ➲ SYNONYMS AT IMAGINE

E

en·vi·sion /ɪnˈvɪʒn/ *verb* **1** **~ sth** (*formal*) to imagine what a situation will be like in the future, especially a situation you intend to work towards 展望；想象： *They envision an equal society, free of poverty and disease.* 他们向往一个没有贫穷和疾病的平等社会。 ➲ SYNONYMS AT IMAGINE **2** (*especially NAmE*) = ENVISAGE： *They didn't envision any problems with the new building.* 他们没想到这栋新楼会有什么问题。

envoy /ˈenvɔɪ/ *noun* a person who represents a government or an organization and is sent as a representative to talk to other governments and organizations 使者；使节；（谈判等的）代表 SYN **emissary**

envy /ˈenvi/ *noun, verb*

■ ***noun*** [U] the feeling of wanting to be in the same situation as sb else; the feeling of wanting sth that sb else has 羡慕；忌妒 SYN **jealousy**： **~ (of sb)** *He couldn't conceal his envy of me.* 他掩饰不住对我的忌妒。 ◇ **~ (at/of sth)** *She felt a pang of envy at the thought of his success.* 她想到他的成功便感到一阵忌妒的痛苦。 ◇ *They looked* ***with envy*** *at her latest purchase.* 他们羡慕地看着她最近买到的东西。 ◇ *Her colleagues were* ***green with envy*** (= they had very strong feelings of envy). 她的同事都非常眼红。

IDM **be the envy of sb/sth** to be a person or thing that other people admire and that causes feelings of envy 成为羡慕（或忌妒）的对象： *British television is the envy of the world.* 英国电视节目令世人羡慕。 ➲ SEE ALSO ENVIABLE, ENVIOUS

■ ***verb*** (**en·vies**, **envy·ing**, **en·vied**, **en·vied**) **1** to wish you had the same qualities, possessions, opportunities, etc. as sb else 羡慕；忌妒： **~ sb** *He envied her—she seemed to have everything she could possibly want.* 他羡慕她，她似乎要什么有什么。 ◇ **~ sth** *She has always envied my success.* 她一直忌妒我的成功。 ◇ **~ sb sth** *I envied him his good looks.* 我羡慕他的英俊。 ◇ **~ sb doing sth** *I envy you having such a close family.* 我羡慕你有这么一个关系紧密的家庭。 **2** to be glad that you do not have to do what sb else has to do 庆幸（不必做别人非做不可的事）： **not ~ sb** *It's a difficult situation you're in. I don't envy you.* 你的处境很困难，万幸不是我摊上。 ◇ **not ~ sb sth** *I don't envy her that job.* 我庆幸没做她那样的工作。

en·zyme /ˈenzaɪm/ *noun* (*biology* 生) a substance, produced by all living things, which helps a chemical change happen or happen more quickly, without being changed itself 酶 ➲ SEE ALSO PROTEIN

eo·lian (*NAmE*) (*especially BrE* **ae·olian**) /iːˈəʊliən; *NAmE* iːˈoʊ-/ *adj.* (*specialist*) connected with or caused by the action of the wind 风的；风成的；风积的

eon (*especially NAmE*) (*BrE usually* **aeon**) /ˈiːən/ *noun* **1** (*formal*) an extremely long period of time; thousands of years 极漫长的时间；千万年 **2** (*geology* 地) a major division of time, divided into ERAS 宙（地质学上的年代分期，下分代）： *eons of geological history* 数以亿万年计的地质史

ˈe-pal (*also* **ˈe-friend**) *noun* a person that you make friends with by sending emails, often sb you have never met 网友（通过电子邮件交流）

ep·aul·ette (*especially BrE*) (*NAmE usually* **ep·aulet**) /ˈepəlet/ *noun* a decoration on the shoulder of a coat, jacket, etc., especially when part of a military uniform （尤指军服上的）肩章，肩饰

épee /ˈepeɪ; ˈepeɪ/ *noun* **1** [C] a SWORD used in the sport of FENCING 重剑（击剑运动用） **2** [U] (*NAmE*) the sport of FENCING with an épée 重剑（运动项目）

ephem·era /ɪˈfemərə/ *noun* [pl.] things that are important or used for only a short period of time 只在短期内有用的事物： *a collection of postcards, tickets and other ephemera* 明信片、票证和其他短时效物品的收藏系列

ephem·eral /ɪˈfemərəl/ *adj.* (*formal*) lasting or used for only a short period of time 短暂的；瞬息的 SYN **short-lived**

epic /ˈepɪk/ *noun, adj.*

■ ***noun*** **1** [C, U] a long poem about the actions of great men and women or about a nation's history; this style of poetry 史诗： *one of the great Hindu epics* 伟大的印度教史诗之一 ◇ *the creative genius of Greek epic* 富有创造力的希腊史诗天才 ➲ COMPARE LYRIC *n.* (1) **2** [C] a long film/movie or book that contains a lot of action, usually about a historical subject 史诗般的电影（或书） **3** [C] (*sometimes humorous*) a long and difficult job or activity that you think people should admire 壮举；惊人之举： *Their four-hour match on Centre Court was an epic.* 他们在中心球场历时四个小时的比赛是一个壮举。

■ ***adj.*** [usually before noun] **1** having the features of an epic 具有史诗性质的；史诗般的： *an epic poem* 史诗 ➲ COMPARE LYRIC *adj.* (1) **2** taking place over a long period of time and involving a lot of difficulties 漫长而艰难的；艰苦卓绝的： *an* ***epic journey/struggle*** 漫长而艰难的旅程；艰苦卓绝的斗争 **3** very great and impressive 宏大的；壮丽的；给人深刻印象的： *a tragedy* ***of epic proportions*** 巨大的不幸 **4** (*informal*) very good, impressive or enjoyable 极好的；令人印象深刻的；令人愉快的： *The party was epic!* 聚会棒极了！ ◇ *I went to an epic festival last summer.* 去年夏天我参加了一个非常棒的庆典。

epi·cene /ˈepɪsiːn/ *adj.* **1** (*formal*) having characteristics of both the male and female sex or of neither sex in particular 兼具男女两性特征的；缺乏性特征的： *epicene beauty* 兼具阳刚和阴柔之美 **2** (*grammar* 语法) (of a word 词) having one form to represent male and female 通性的： *You can write* ***'s/he'*** *as an* ***epicene*** *pronoun when you are not referring to men or women in particular.* 不特指男性或女性时可以写成 s/he 表示通性代词。

epi·centre (*especially US* **epi·cen·ter**) /ˈepɪsentə(r)/ *noun* **1** the point on the earth's surface where the effects of an EARTHQUAKE are felt most strongly （地震的）震中 **2** (*formal*) the central point of sth 中心；焦点；集中点

epi·cure /ˈepɪkjʊə(r); *NAmE* -kjʊr/ *noun* (*formal*) a person who enjoys food and drink of high quality and knows a lot about it 讲究饮食的人；美食家

epi·cur·ean /ˌepɪkjʊəˈriːən; *NAmE* ˌepɪkjʊˈr-/ *adj.* (*formal*) devoted to pleasure and enjoying yourself 享乐的；吃喝玩乐的

epi·dem·ic /ˌepɪˈdemɪk/ *noun* **1** a large number of cases of a particular disease happening at the same time in a particular community 流行病： *the outbreak of a flu epidemic* 流感的爆发 ◇ *an epidemic of measles* 麻疹的流行 ➲ **WORDFINDER NOTE** AT DISEASE **2** a sudden rapid increase in how often sth bad happens （坏事迅速的）泛滥，蔓延： *an epidemic of crime in the inner cities* 内城区犯罪活动盛行 ▶ **epi·dem·ic** *adj.*： *Car theft is now reaching* ***epidemic proportions.*** 汽车偷盗现已近泛滥成灾。 ➲ COMPARE PANDEMIC

epi·demi·ology /ˌepɪˌdiːmiˈɒlədʒi; *NAmE* -ˈɑːl-/ *noun* [U] the scientific study of the spread and control of diseases 流行病学 ▶ **epi·demi·ologic·al** /ˌepɪˌdiːmiəˈlɒdʒɪkl; *NAmE* -ˈlɑːdʒ-/ *adj.* **epi·demi·olo·gist** /ˌepɪˌdiːmiˈɒlədʒɪst; *NAmE* -ˈɑːl-/ *noun*

epi·der·mis /ˌepɪˈdɜːmɪs; *NAmE* -ˈdɜːrm-/ *noun* [sing., U] (*anatomy* 解) the outer layer of the skin 表皮

epi·dural /ˌepɪˈdjʊərəl; *NAmE usually* -ˈdʊr-/ *noun* (*medical* 医) an ANAESTHETIC that is put into the lower part of the back so that no pain is felt below the waist 硬膜外阻滞；硬膜外麻醉： *Some mothers choose to have an epidural when giving birth.* 有些母亲分娩时选择硬膜外阻滞。

epi·glot·tis /ˌepɪˈɡlɒtɪs; *NAmE* -ˈɡlɑːtɪs/ *noun* (*anatomy* 解) a thin piece of TISSUE behind the tongue that prevents food or drink from entering the lungs 会厌

epi·gram /ˈepɪɡræm/ *noun* a short poem or phrase that expresses an idea in a clever or amusing way 诙谐短诗；警句；隽语 ▸ **epi·gram·mat·ic** /ˌepɪɡrəˈmætɪk/ *adj.*

epi·graph /ˈepɪɡrɑːf; *NAmE* -ɡræf/ *noun* a line of writing, short phrase, etc. on a building or statue, or as an introduction to part of a book （建筑物或雕塑的）刻文，铭文；（书籍卷首或章节前的）引言，题词

epi·lepsy /ˈepɪlepsi/ *noun* [U] a DISORDER of the nervous system that causes a person to become unconscious suddenly, often with violent movements of the body 癫痫；羊角风 ▸ **epi·lep·tic** /ˌepɪˈleptɪk/ *adj.*：*an epileptic fit* 癫痫发作 **epi·lep·tic** /ˌepɪˈleptɪk/ *noun*：*Is she an epileptic?* 她是癫痫病患者吗？

epi·logue /ˈepɪlɒɡ; *NAmE* -lɔːɡ; -lɑːɡ/ *noun* a speech, etc. at the end of a play, book, or film/movie that comments on or acts as a conclusion to what has happened （剧本、电影的）收场白，尾声；（书籍的）后记，跋 ➲ COMPARE PROLOGUE

Epiph·any /ɪˈpɪfəni/ *noun* a Christian festival, held on the 6 January, in memory of the time when the MAGI came to see the baby Jesus at Bethlehem 显现节，主显节（1 月 6 日，纪念贤士朝拜耶稣）

epis·copacy /ɪˈpɪskəpəsi/ *noun* [U] government of a church by BISHOPS 主教制（以主教为主体管理教会）

epis·cop·al /ɪˈpɪskəpl/ *adj.* **1** connected with a BISHOP or BISHOPS 主教的：*episcopal power* 主教管辖权 **2** (*usually* **Episcopal**) (*also* **Epis·co·pa·lian**) (of a Christian Church 基督教) that is governed by BISHOPS 主教制的：*the Episcopal Church* (= the Anglican Church in Scotland and the US) （苏格兰和美国的）圣公会

Epis·co·pa·lian /ɪˌpɪskəˈpeɪliən/ *noun* a member of the Episcopal Church （苏格兰和美国的）圣公会教徒

epis·co·pate /ɪˈpɪskəpət/ *noun* [usually sing.] (*religion* 宗) **1 the episcopate** the BISHOPS of a particular church or area 主教团（统称某教会或地区的主教） **2** the job of BISHOP or the period of time during which sb is bishop 主教职位；主教任期

episi·otomy /ɪˌpiːsiˈɒtəmi; *NAmE* -ˈɑːtəmi/ *noun* (*pl.* **-ies**) (*medical* 医) a cut that is sometimes made at the opening of a woman's VAGINA to make the birth of a baby easier or safer 会阴切开术

epi·sode /ˈepɪsəʊd; *NAmE* -soʊd/ *noun* **1** an event, a situation, or a period of time in sb's life, a novel, etc. that is important or interesting in some way （人生的）一段经历；（小说的）片段，插曲 SYN **incident**：*I'd like to try and forget the whole episode.* 我倒想尽量把那段经历全部忘掉。◇ *One of the funniest episodes in the book occurs in Chapter 6.* 书中最有趣的片段之一在第 6 章。**2** one part of a story that is broadcast on television or radio in several parts （电视连续剧或广播剧的）一集

epi·sod·ic /ˌepɪˈsɒdɪk; *NAmE* -ˈsɑːd-/ *adj.* (*formal*) **1** happening occasionally and not at regular intervals 偶尔发生的；不定期的 **2** (of a story, etc. 故事等) containing or consisting of many separate and different events 由松散片段组成的；有许多片段的：*My memories of childhood are hazy and episodic.* 我儿时的回忆是一些朦朦胧胧的零散片段。

epi·stem·ic /ˌepɪˈstiːmɪk; -ˈstem-/ *adj.* (*formal*) relating to knowledge 知识的；认识的

epis·te·mol·ogy /ɪˌpɪstəˈmɒlədʒi; *NAmE* -ˈmɑːl-/ *noun* [U] the part of philosophy that deals with knowledge 认识论

epis·tle /ɪˈpɪsl/ *noun* **1 Epistle** any of the letters in the New Testament of the Bible, written by the first people who followed Christ 使徒书信，宗徒书信（《圣经·新约》书卷）：*the Epistles of St Paul* 圣保罗书信 **2** (*formal* or *humorous*) a long, serious letter on an important subject （文体郑重、内容重要、篇幅较长的）书信

epis·tol·ary /ɪˈpɪstələri; *NAmE* -leri/ *adj.* (*formal*) written or expressed in the form of letters 书信的；用书信表达的；书信体的：*an epistolary novel* 书信体小说

epi·taph /ˈepɪtɑːf; *NAmE* -tæf/ *noun* **1** words that are written or said about a dead person, especially words on a GRAVESTONE 悼文；祭文；（尤指）墓志铭，碑文 **2** ~ (**to sb/sth**) something which is left to remind people of a particular person, a period of time or an event 遗物；遗存；遗迹：*These slums are an epitaph to the housing policy of the 1960s.* 这些贫民窟是 20 世纪 60 年代住房政策的遗迹。

epi·thet /ˈepɪθet/ *noun* **1** an adjective or phrase that is used to describe sb/sth's character or most important quality, especially in order to give praise or criticism （尤用于褒贬人或事物特征或性质的）表述形容词，修饰语：*The film is long and dramatic but does not quite earn the epithet 'epic'.* 这部影片篇幅长，戏剧性强，不过还不能誉为"史诗"。 **2** (*especially NAmE*) an offensive word or phrase that is used about a person or group of people 别称；绰号；诨名：*Racial epithets were scrawled on the walls.* 墙上涂写着一些带有种族歧视的称谓。

epit·ome /ɪˈpɪtəmi/ *noun* [sing.] **the ~ of sth** (*formal*) a perfect example of sth 典型；典范 SYN **embodiment**：*He is the epitome of a modern young man.* 他是现代青年男子的典范。◇ *clothes that are the epitome of good taste* 典型的高品味服装

epit·om·ize (*BrE also* **-ise**) /ɪˈpɪtəmaɪz/ *verb* **~ sth** to be a perfect example of sth 成为…的典范（或典型）：*The fighting qualities of the team are epitomized by the captain.* 这个队的战斗精神从队长身上体现出来。◇ *These movies seem to epitomize the 1950s.* 这些影片似乎就是 20 世纪 50 年代的缩影。

epoch /ˈiːpɒk; *NAmE* ˈepək/ *noun* (*formal* or *literary*) **1** a period of time in history, especially one during which important events or changes happen 时代；纪元；时期 SYN **era**：*The death of the emperor marked the end of an epoch in the country's history.* 皇帝驾崩标志着该国历史上一个时代的结束。 **2** (*geology* 地) a length of time which is a division of a PERIOD 世（地质年代，纪下分世）：*geological epochs* 地质世

ˈepoch-making *adj.* (*formal*) having a very important effect on people's lives and on history 划时代的；开创新纪元的；意义重大的

ep·onym /ˈepənɪm/ *noun* (*specialist*) a person or thing, or the name of a person or thing, from which a place, an invention, a discovery, etc. gets its name 名祖（姓名或名称被用以命名地方、发明、发现等的人或物）

epony·mous /ɪˈpɒnɪməs; *NAmE* ɪˈpɑːn-/ *adj.* [only before noun] the **eponymous** character of a book, play, film/movie, etc. is the one mentioned in the title （主人公与标题）同名的 SYN **titular**：*Don Quixote, eponymous hero of the great novel by Cervantes* 堂吉诃德 —— 塞万提斯巨著中与书同名的主人公

epoxy /ɪˈpɒksi; *NAmE* ɪˈpɑːksi/ *noun* [U, C] (*pl.* **-ies**) (*also* **eˌpoxy ˈresin**) a type of strong glue 环氧树脂

ep·si·lon /ˈepsɪlɒn; epˈsaɪlɒn; *NAmE* ˈepsɪlɑːn/ *noun* the fifth letter of the Greek alphabet (E, ϵ) 希腊字母表的第 5 个字母

Epsom salts /ˌepsəm ˈsɔːlts/ *noun* [pl.] a white powder that can be mixed with water and used as a medicine or LAXATIVE 泻盐

equ·able /ˈekwəbl/ *adj.* (*formal*) **1** calm and not easily upset or annoyed 宁静的；平和的；不易恼怒的：*an equable temperament* 平和的性情 **2** (of weather 天气) keeping a steady temperature with no sudden changes 稳定的；变化小的；温差小的 ▸ **equ·ably** /ˈekwəbli/ *adv.*

equal /ˈiːkwəl/ *adj., noun, verb*

■ *adj.* **1** the same in size, quantity, value, etc. as sth else（大小、数量、价值等）相同的，同样的；相等的：*There is an equal number of boys and girls in the class.* 这个班男女生人数相等。◇ *two pieces of wood equal in length/of equal length* 两块长度相同的木头 ◇ **~ to sb/sth** *One unit of alcohol is equal to half a pint of beer.* 一酒精单位相当于半品脱啤酒。 HELP You can use **exactly**, **precisely**, **approximately**, etc. with **equal** in this meaning. * equal 作此义可与 exactly、precisely、approximately 等词连用。 **2** having the same rights or being treated the same as other people, without differences such as race, religion or sex being considered 平等的；同等的：***equal rights/pay*** 平等的权利；同酬 ◇ *The company has an **equal opportunities** policy* (= gives the same chances of employment to everyone). 这家公司的政策是人人机会均等。◇ *the desire for a more equal society* (= in which everyone has the same rights and chances) 对更平等的社会的向往 HELP You can use **more** with **equal** in this meaning. * equal 作此义可与 more 连用。

WORDFINDER 联想词：bias, discriminate, feminism, homophobia, human right, marginalize, persecute, **race**, **society**

3 **~ to sth** (*formal*) having the necessary strength, courage and ability to deal with sth successfully（力气、勇气、能力）相当的；能胜任的；能应付的：*I hope that he proves equal to the challenge.* 我希望他最后能应对这一挑战。 ➲ SEE ALSO EQUALLY

IDM **on ˌequal ˈterms (with sb)** having the same advantages and disadvantages as sb else（与某人）处于平等的地位：*Can our industry compete on equal terms with its overseas rivals?* 我们的工业能与海外对手以平等的地位竞争吗？ ➲ MORE AT THING

■ *noun* a person or thing of the same quality or with the same status, rights, etc. as another 同等的人；相等物：*She treats the people who work for her as her equals.* 她以平等的身份对待为她工作的人。◇ *Our cars are the equal of those produced anywhere in the world.* 我们的汽车可与世界上任何地方生产的汽车媲美。

IDM **be without ˈequal | have no ˈequal** (*formal*) to be better than anything else or anyone else of the same type 无与伦比；无敌；无比：*He is a player without equal.* 他是个无与伦比的运动员。 **ˌsome (people, members, etc.) are more equal than ˈothers** (*saying*) although the members of a society, group, etc. appear to be equal, some, in fact, get better treatment than others 有些（人、成员等）比其他的更平等 ORIGIN This phrase is used by one of the pigs in the book 'Animal Farm' by George Orwell: 'All animals are equal but some animals are more equal than others.' 本短语来自乔治 • 奥威尔所著的《动物庄园》中一头猪所说的话："所有的动物都平等，但有些动物比其他的动物更平等。" ➲ MORE AT FIRST *n.*

■ *verb* (**-ll-**, *US* **-l-**) **1** *linking verb* **+ noun** to be the same in size, quantity, value, etc. as sth else（大小、数量、价值等）与…相等，等于：*2x plus y equals 7* (= 2x+y=7) * 2x 加 y 等于 7。◇ *A metre equals 39.38 inches.* * 1 米等于 39.38 英寸。 **2** **~ sth** to be as good as sth else or do sth to the same standard as sb else 比得上；敌得过：*This achievement is unlikely ever to be equalled.* 这一成就可能永远无可匹敌。◇ *Her hatred of religion is equalled only by her loathing for politicians.* 只有对政客的厌恶才能与她对宗教的憎恨相比。◇ *With his last jump he equalled the world record.* 凭借最后一跳，他平了世界纪录。 **3** **~ sth** to lead to or result in sth 导致；结果为：*Cooperation equals success.* 合作意味着成功。 ➲ MORE LIKE THIS 36, page R29

equal·ity /iˈkwɒləti; *NAmE* iˈkwɑː-/ *noun* [U] the fact of being equal in rights, status, advantages, etc. 平等；均等；相等：***racial/social/sexual equality*** 种族 / 社会 / 男女平等 ◇ *equality of opportunity* 机会均等 ◇ *the principle of equality before the law* (= the law treats everyone the same) 法律面前人人平等的原则 ◇ *Don't you believe in equality between men and women?* 难道你不相信男女平等吗？ OPP inequality ➲ WORDFINDER NOTE AT SOCIETY ➲ COLLOCATIONS AT RACE

equal·ize (*BrE also* **-ise**) /ˈiːkwəlaɪz/ *verb* **1** [T] **~ sth** to make things equal in size, quantity, value, etc. in the whole of a place or group 使平等；使均等；使相等：*a policy to equalize the distribution of resources throughout the country* 使资源在全国分配均衡的政策 **2** [I] (*BrE*) (especially in football (SOCCER) 尤指足球) to score a goal that makes the score of both teams equal 扳平比分：*Rooney equalized early in the second half.* 鲁尼在下半场比赛开始后不久将比分扳平。 ▸ **equal·iza·tion, -isa·tion** /ˌiːkwəlaɪˈzeɪʃn; *NAmE* -ləˈz-/ *noun* [U]

equal·izer (*BrE also* **-iser**) /ˈiːkwəlaɪzər/ *noun* [usually sing.] (*BrE*) (especially in football (SOCCER) 尤指足球) a goal hat makes the score of both teams equal 扳平比分的得分：*Rooney scored the equalizer.* 鲁尼进了一球，扳平了比分。

equal·ly /ˈiːkwəli/ *adv.* **1** to the same degree; in the same or in a similar way 平等地；同样地：*Diet and exercise are equally important.* 饮食和锻炼同样重要。◇ *This job could be done **equally well** by a computer.* 这个工作用计算机同样可以做得很好。◇ *We try to treat every member of staff equally.* 我们尽可能平等对待每一位工作人员。 **2** in equal parts, amounts, etc. 平均地；相等地；均等地：*The money was divided equally among her four children.* 这笔钱在她的四个孩子中平分了。◇ *They share the housework equally.* 他们平均分担家务。 **3** used to introduce another phrase or idea that adds to and is as important as what you have just said（引出同样重要的内容）同样，此外，也：*I'm trying to do what is best, but equally I've got to consider the cost.* 我在尽力做到最好，但同时我也得考虑费用。

ˈequals sign (*also* **ˈequal sign**) *noun* the symbol (=), used in mathematics 等号

equa·nim·ity /ˌekwəˈnɪməti/ *noun* [U] (*formal*) a calm state of mind which means that you do not become angry or upset, especially in difficult situations（尤指处于困境时的）镇静，沉着，冷静：*She accepted the prospect of her operation **with equanimity**.* 她心情平静地接受了动手术的可能性。

equate AW /iˈkweɪt/ *verb* **~ sth (with sth)** to think that sth is the same as sth else or is as important 同等看待；使等同：*Some parents equate education with exam success.* 有些父母认为教育就是考试成绩优秀。◇ *I don't see how you can equate the two things.* 我不明白你怎么能把这两件事等同起来。

PHR V **eˈquate to sth** to be equal to sth else 相当于；等于：*A $5 000 raise equates to 25%.* 加薪 5 000 美元相当于增加了 25%。

equa·tion AW /ɪˈkweɪʒn/ *noun* **1** [C] (*mathematics* 数) a statement showing that two amounts or values are equal, for example 2x + y = 54 方程；方程式；等式 ➲ WORDFINDER NOTE AT MATHS **2** [U, sing.] the act of making sth equal or considering sth as equal (= of equating them) 相等；等同看待：*The equation of wealth with happiness can be dangerous.* 把财富与幸福等同起来可能是危险的。 **3** [C, usually sing.] a problem or situation in which several things must be considered and dealt with（多种因素的）平衡，综合体：*When children **enter the equation**, further tensions may arise within a marriage.* 有了孩子以后，可能会使夫妻关系更加紧张。

equa·tor /ɪˈkweɪtə(r)/ (*usually* **the equator**) *noun* [sing.] an imaginary line around the earth at an equal distance from the North and South Poles 赤道 ➲ WORDFINDER NOTE AT EARTH

equa·tor·ial /ˌekwəˈtɔːriəl/ *adj.* near the equator or typical of a country that is near the equator 赤道的；赤道附近的；赤道地区特有的：*equatorial rainforests* 赤道地区的雨林 ◇ *an equatorial climate* 赤道气候 ➲ WORDFINDER NOTE AT CLIMATE

equerry /ɪˈkweri; ˈekwəri/ *noun* (*pl.* **-ies**) a male officer who acts as an assistant to a member of a royal family 王室侍从官

eques·trian /ɪˈkwestriən/ *adj.* [usually before noun] connected with riding horses, especially as a sport 马术的： *equestrian events at the Olympic Games* 奥林匹克运动会的马术比赛项目 ➲ VISUAL VOCAB PAGE V51

eques·tri·an·ism /ɪˈkwestriənɪzəm/ *noun* [U] **1** the skill or sport of riding horses 马术 **2** an Olympic sport consisting of SHOWJUMPING, DRESSAGE and THREE-DAY EVENTING 马术（运动项目）

equi- /ˈiːkwɪ-; ˈekwɪ-/ *combining form* (in nouns, adjectives and adverbs 构成名词、形容词和副词) equal; equally 相等的；相等地： *equidistant* 等距 ◇ *equilibrium* 平衡

equi·dis·tant /ˌiːkwɪˈdɪstənt; ˌek-/ *adj.* [not before noun] **~ (from sth)** (*formal*) equally far from two or more places 等距离；等距： *All points on a circle are equidistant from the centre.* 圆周上各点离圆心的距离相等。

equi·lat·eral tri·angle /ˌiːkwɪˌlætərəl ˈtraɪæŋɡl/ *noun* (*geometry* 几何) a triangle whose three sides are all the same length 等边三角形 ➲ PICTURE AT TRIANGLE

equi·lib·rium /ˌiːkwɪˈlɪbriəm; ˌek-/ *noun* [U, sing.] **1** a state of balance, especially between opposing forces or influences 平衡；均衡；均势： *The point at which the solid and the liquid are* ***in equilibrium*** *is called the freezing point.* 固体和液体的平衡点叫做冰点。 ◇ *Any disturbance to the body's state of equilibrium can produce stress.* 对身体平衡状态的任何干扰都可能产生压力。 ◇ *We have achieved an equilibrium in the economy.* 我们已在经济上达到平衡。 **2** a calm state of mind and a balance of emotions （心情、情绪）平静，安宁；心理平衡： *He sat down to try and recover his equilibrium.* 他坐了下来，努力恢复平静。

equine /ˈekwaɪn; ˈiːk-; *NAmE* ˈiːk-/ *adj.* (*formal*) connected with horses; like a horse 马的；马科的；似马的

equi·noc·tial /ˌiːkwɪˈnɒkʃl; ˌek-; *NAmE* -ˈnɑːk-/ *adj.* connected with an equinox 二分点的；昼夜平分时的；春分（或秋分）的

equi·nox /ˈiːkwɪnɒks; ˈek-; *NAmE* -nɑːks/ *noun* one of the two times in the year (around 20 March and 22 September) when the sun is above the EQUATOR and day and night are of equal length 二分时刻；昼夜平分时；春分；秋分： *the* ***spring/autumn equinox*** 春分；秋分 ➲ WORDFINDER NOTE AT EARTH, SUN

equip AW /ɪˈkwɪp/ *verb* (**-pp-**) **1** to provide yourself/sb/sth with the things that are needed for a particular purpose or activity 配备；装备 SYN **kit out/up**: **~ sth** *to be* ***fully/poorly equipped*** 装备齐全 / 简陋 ◇ *She got a bank loan to rent and equip a small workshop.* 她向银行贷款，为成立一个小工作室租地方和买设备。 ◇ **~ yourself/sb/sth (with sth) (for sth)** *He equipped himself with a street plan.* 他随身带着一张街道平面图。 ◇ *The centre is* ***well equipped*** *for canoeing and mountaineering.* 中心配有齐全的划船和登山设备。 **2 ~ sb (for sth) | ~ sb (to do sth)** to prepare sb for an activity or task, especially by teaching them what they need to know 使有所准备；使有能力： *The course is designed to equip students for a career in nursing.* 此课程旨在使学生能够胜任护理工作。

equip·ment 🔑 AW /ɪˈkwɪpmənt/ *noun* [U] **1** 🔑 the things that are needed for a particular purpose or activity 设备；器材： *a useful* ***piece of equipment*** *for the kitchen* 一件有用的厨房设备 ◇ *office equipment* 办公室设备 ◇ *new equipment for the sports club* 体育俱乐部的新器材 ➲ VISUAL VOCAB PAGE V72 **2** the process of providing a place or person with necessary things 配备；装备： *The equipment of the photographic studio was expensive.* 这个照相馆的装备花费巨大。 ➲ MORE LIKE THIS 28, page R28

equi·poise /ˈiːkwɪpɔɪz; ˈek-/ *noun* [U] (*formal*) a state of balance 平衡；均势

equit·able /ˈekwɪtəbl/ *adj.* (*formal*) fair and reasonable; treating everyone in an equal way 公平合理的；公正的 SYN **fair** OPP **inequitable** ▶ **equit·ably** /-bli/ *adv.*

equity /ˈekwəti/ *noun* **1** [U] (*finance* 财) the value of a company's shares; the value of a property after all charges and debts have been paid （公司的）股本；资产净值 ➲ SEE ALSO NEGATIVE EQUITY ➲ WORDFINDER NOTE AT INVEST **2 equities** [pl.] (*finance* 财) shares in a company which do not pay a fixed amount of interest （公司的）普通股 **3** [U] (*formal*) a situation in which everyone is treated equally 公平；公正 SYN **fairness** OPP **inequity** **4** [U] (*law* 律, *especially BrE*) a system of natural justice allowing a fair judgement in a situation which is not covered by the existing laws 衡平法

equiva·lent 🔑 AW /ɪˈkwɪvələnt/ *adj., noun*

■ ***adj.*** 🔑 equal in value, amount, meaning, importance, etc. （价值、数量、意义、重要性等）相等的，相同的： *250 grams or an equivalent amount in ounces* * 250 克或与之等量的盎司 ◇ **~ to sth** *Eight kilometres is roughly equivalent to five miles.* 八公里约等于五英里。 ▶ **equiva·lence** AW /-ləns/ *noun* [U] (*formal*)： *There is no straightforward equivalence between economic progress and social well-being.* 经济进步与社会福利之间绝非轻易等同。

■ ***noun*** 🔑 a thing, amount, word, etc. that is equivalent to sth else 相等的东西；等量；对应词： *Send €20 or the equivalent in your own currency.* 寄 20 欧元或等值的贵国货币。 ◇ **~ of/to sth** *Creutzfeldt-Jakob disease, the human equivalent of BSE* 克罗伊茨费尔特 – 雅各布病，相当于疯牛病的人类疾病 ◇ *Breathing such polluted air is the equivalent of* (= has the same effect as) *smoking ten cigarettes a day.* 呼吸污染这么严重的空气等于每天抽十支烟。 ◇ *The German 'Gymnasium' is the closest equivalent to the grammar school in England.* 德语 Gymnasium 基本上相当于英格兰的文法学校。

▼ **SYNONYMS** 同义词辨析

equipment

material • gear • kit • apparatus

These are all words for the things that you need for a particular purpose or activity. 以上各词均指特定目的或活动所需的材料、设备、器材。

equipment the things that are needed for a particular purpose or activity 指特定目的或活动所需的设备、器材： *camping equipment* 野营装备 ◇ *a piece of equipment* 一件设备

material things that are needed for a particular activity 指特定活动所需的材料： *household cleaning materials* 家用清洁剂 ◇ *teaching material* 教学材料

EQUIPMENT OR MATERIAL? 用 equipment 还是 material?

Equipment is usually solid things, especially large ones. **Materials** may be liquids, powders or books, CDs, etc. containing information, as well as small solid items. * equipment 通常指固体材料，尤其是大型设备器材；material 除指小型固体材料外，还可指液体、粉末、书籍、信息光盘等。

gear the equipment or clothes needed for a particular activity 指某种活动所需的设备、用具、衣服： *Skiing gear can be expensive.* 滑雪装备有时会很昂贵。

kit a set of tools or equipment that you use for a particular purpose 指用于特定目的的成套工具、成套设备： *a first-aid kit* 一套急救用品 ◇ *a tool kit* 一套工具

apparatus the tools or other pieces of equipment that are needed for a particular activity or task 指特定活动或任务所需的仪器、器械、装置： *breathing apparatus for firefighters* 消防员用的呼吸器 ◇ *laboratory apparatus* 实验室仪器 NOTE **Apparatus** is used especially for scientific, medical or technical purposes. * apparatus 尤具有科学、医学或技术等方面的用途。

PATTERNS

- **electrical/electronic** equipment/gear/apparatus
- **sports** equipment/gear/kit
- **camping** equipment/gear
- a **piece of** equipment/apparatus

E

equivo·cal /ɪˈkwɪvəkl/ *adj.* (*formal*) **1** (of words or statements 言语或陈述) not having one clear or definite meaning or intention; able to be understood in more than one way 模棱两可的；意义双关的；含糊其词的 SYN **ambiguous**: *She gave an equivocal answer, typical of a politician.* 她的回答模棱两可，是典型的政客口吻。 **2** (of actions or behaviour 行动或行为) difficult to understand or explain clearly or easily 难以理解的；难以解释清楚的：*The experiments produced equivocal results.* 这些实验产生的结果难以理解。 ➲ SEE ALSO UNEQUIVOCAL

equivo·cate /ɪˈkwɪvəkeɪt/ *verb* [I, T] (+ **speech**) (*formal*) to talk about sth in a way that is deliberately not clear in order to avoid or hide the truth （故意）含糊其词，支吾，搪塞

equivo·ca·tion /ɪˌkwɪvəˈkeɪʃn/ *noun* [C, U] (*formal*) a way of behaving or speaking that is not clear or definite and is intended to avoid or hide the truth 含糊其词；支吾；搪塞

ER /ˌiː ˈɑː(r)/ *abbr.* EMERGENCY ROOM （医院）急诊室

er /ɜː(r)/ (*also* **erm**) *exclamation* (*BrE*) the sound that people make when they are deciding what to say next （思索接着说什么时发出的声音）哦，嗯：*'Will you do it?' 'Er, yes, I suppose so.'* "你会干这事儿吗？" "哦，会的，我想我会。" ➲ MORE LIKE THIS 2, page R25

-er *suffix* **1** (in nouns 构成名词) a person or thing that …的人（或物）：*lover* 情人 ◇ *computer* 计算机 ➲ COMPARE -EE, -OR **2** (in nouns 构成名词) a person or thing that has the thing or quality mentioned 具有…的人（或物）：*three-wheeler* 三轮车 ◇ *foreigner* 外国人 **3** (in nouns 构成名词) a person concerned with 与…有关的人：*astronomer* 天文学家 ◇ *philosopher* 哲学家 **4** (in nouns 构成名词) a person belonging to 属于…的人：*New Yorker* 纽约人 **5** (makes comparative adjectives and adverbs 构成形容词和副词的比较级)：*wider* 较宽 ◇ *bigger* 较大 ◇ *happier* 更幸福 ◇ *sooner* 更早 ➲ COMPARE -EST ➲ MORE LIKE THIS 7, page R25

era /ˈɪərə; *NAmE* ˈɪrə; ˈerə/ *noun* **1** a period of time, usually in history, that is different from other periods because of particular characteristics or events 时代；年代；纪元：*the Victorian/modern/post-war era* 维多利亚女王 / 当今 / 战后时代 ◇ *When she left the firm, it was the* ***end of an era*** (= things were different after that). 她离开公司后，一个时代结束了（后来的情况就大不一样了）。 **2** (*geology* 地) a length of time which is a division of an AEON 代（地质年代，宙下分代）

eradi·cate /ɪˈrædɪkeɪt/ *verb* to destroy or get rid of sth completely, especially sth bad 根除；消灭；杜绝 SYN **wipe out**: **~ sth** *Diphtheria has been virtually eradicated in the United States.* 在美国白喉几乎已经绝迹。 ◇ **~ sth from sth** *We are determined to eradicate racism from our sport.* 我们决心要杜绝体育竞技活动中的种族歧视现象。 ▶ **eradi·ca·tion** /ɪˌrædɪˈkeɪʃn/ *noun* [U]

erase /ɪˈreɪz; *NAmE* ɪˈreɪs/ *verb* **1** to remove sth completely 清除；消除；消灭：**~ sth** *She tried to* ***erase the memory*** *of that evening.* 她试图忘却那天晚上的事。 ◇ **~ sth from sth** *All doubts were suddenly* ***erased from his mind***. 他心中所有的疑虑突然一扫而空了。 ◇ *You cannot erase injustice from the world.* 任何人都不可能让不公平的现象从世界上消失。 **2 ~ sth** to make a mark or sth you have written disappear, for example by rubbing it, especially in order to correct it 擦掉，抹掉（笔迹等）：*He had erased the wrong word.* 他擦去了写错的字。 ◇ *All the phone numbers had been erased.* 所有的电话号码都被抹掉了。 **3 ~ sth** to remove a recording from a tape or information from a computer's memory 抹去，清洗（磁带上的录音或存储器中的信息）：*Parts of the recording have been erased.* 部分录音已被抹掉。

eraser /ɪˈreɪzə(r); *NAmE* ɪˈreɪsər/ (*NAmE* or *formal*) (*BrE also* **rub·ber**) *noun* a small piece of rubber or a similar substance, used for removing pencil marks from paper; a piece of soft material used for removing CHALK marks from a BLACKBOARD 橡皮；黑板擦 ➲ VISUAL VOCAB PAGE V71

eras·ure /ɪˈreɪʒə(r)/ *noun* [U] (*formal*) the act of removing or destroying sth 擦掉；抹掉；消除；删除：*the accidental erasure of important computer files* 计算机上重要文件的意外删除

er·bium /ˈɜːbiəm; *NAmE* ˈɜːrb-/ *noun* [U] (*symb.* **Er**) a chemical element. Erbium is a soft silver-white metal. 铒

ere /eə(r); *NAmE* er/ *conj.*, *prep.* (*old use* or *literary*) before 在…之前：*Ere long* (= soon) *they returned.* 他们不久就回来了。

ˈe-reader *noun* a small device on which you can store and read texts taken from the Internet; an APPLICATION on a device that enables you to do this 电子书阅读器；电子书阅读应用软件；电子书阅读应用程序

erect /ɪˈrekt/ *adj.*, *verb*

■ ***adj.*** **1** (*formal*) in a vertical position 垂直的；竖直的；直立的 SYN **straight**: *Stand with your arms by your side and your head erect.* 手放两边，昂首站立。 **2** (of the PENIS OR NIPPLES 阴茎或乳头) larger than usual, stiff and standing up because of sexual excitement （因性兴奋）勃起的，坚挺的

■ ***verb*** (*formal*) **1 ~ sth** to build sth 建立；建造：*The church was erected in 1582.* 此教堂建于 1582 年。 ➲ SYNONYMS AT BUILD **2 ~ sth** to put sth in position and make it stand vertical 竖立；搭起 SYN **put up**: *Police had to erect barriers to keep crowds back.* 警察得设立路障来阻截人群。 ◇ *to erect a tent* 搭帐篷 ➲ SYNONYMS AT BUILD **3 ~ sth** to create or establish sth 创立；设立：*to erect trade barriers* 设置贸易壁垒

erect·ile /ɪˈrektaɪl; *NAmE also* ɪˈrektl/ *adj.* (*biology* 生) (of a part of the body 身体部位) able to become stiff and stand up 能勃起的：*erectile tissue* 勃起组织

erec·tion /ɪˈrekʃn/ *noun* **1** [C] if a man has an **erection**, his PENIS is hard and stands up because he is sexually excited （阴茎）勃起：*to* ***get/have an erection*** 勃起 **2** [U] (*formal*) the act of building sth or putting it in a vertical position 建造；竖立：*the erection of scaffolding around the building* 建筑物周围鹰架的搭建 **3** [C] (*formal*) a structure or building, especially a large one （尤指大型）结构，建筑物

erf /ɜːf; *NAmE* ɜːrf/ *noun* (*pl.* **erfs** or **erven** /ˈɜːvn; *NAmE* ˈɜːrvn/) (*SAfrE*) a plot of land 小块土地

erg /ɜːg; *NAmE* ɜːrg/ *noun* a unit of work or energy 尔格（功或能量单位）

erga·tive /ˈɜːgətɪv; *NAmE* ˈɜːrg-/ *adj.* (*grammar* 语法) (of verbs 动词) able to be used in both a TRANSITIVE and an INTRANSITIVE way with the same meaning, where the object of the transitive verb is the same as the subject of the intransitive verb 作格的（可在不改变词义的情况下同时用作及物和不及物的动词，作及物动词时的宾语与作不及物动词时的主语一致）：*The verb 'grow' is ergative because you can say 'She grew flowers in her garden' or 'Flowers grew in her garden'.* * grow 为作格动词，因为既可以说 She grew flowers in her garden，也可以说 Flowers grew in her garden。 ➲ COMPARE CAUSATIVE (2), INCHOATIVE

ergo /ˈɜːgəʊ; *NAmE* ˈɜːrgoʊ/ *adv.* (*from Latin*, *formal* or *humorous*) therefore 因此；所以

er·go·nom·ic /ˌɜːgəˈnɒmɪk; *NAmE* ˌɜːrgəˈnɑːm-/ *adj.* designed to improve people's working conditions and to help them work more efficiently 工效学的；人类工程学的：*ergonomic design* 提高工效的设计 ▶ **er·go·nom·ic·al·ly** *adv.*：*The layout is hard to fault ergonomically.* 这一设计从工效学方面看几乎无懈可击。

er·go·nom·ics /ˌɜːgəˈnɒmɪks; *NAmE* ˌɜːrgəˈnɑːm-/ *noun* [U] the study of working conditions, especially the design of equipment and furniture, in order to help people work more efficiently 工效学（研究如何改善工作条件，提高工作效率）

erm /ɜːm/ *exclamation* (*BrE*) = ER : *'Shall we go?' 'Erm, yes, let's.'* "咱们走吧?" "喔，好的，咱们走。"

er·mine /'ɜːmɪn; *NAmE* 'ɜːrmɪn/ *noun* [U] the white winter fur of the STOAT, used especially to decorate the formal clothes of judges, kings, etc. 白色鼬皮（尤用于法官、国王等的服饰）

erode AW /ɪ'rəʊd; *NAmE* ɪ'roʊd/ *verb* [often passive] **1** [T, I] to gradually destroy the surface of sth through the action of wind, rain, etc.; to be gradually destroyed in this way 侵蚀；腐蚀；风化 SYN **wear away**: **~ sth (away)** *The cliff face has been steadily eroded by the sea.* 峭壁表面逐渐被海水侵蚀。◇ **~ (away)** *The rocks have eroded away over time.* 这些岩石随着时间的推移逐渐风化了。 **2** [T, I] **~ (sth)** to gradually destroy sth or make it weaker over a period of time; to be destroyed or made weaker in this way 逐渐毁坏；削弱；损害: *Her confidence has been slowly eroded by repeated failures.* 她的自信心因屡屡失败慢慢消磨掉了。◇ *Mortgage payments have been eroded* (= decreased in value) *by inflation.* 偿还的按揭贷款因通货膨胀而降值。 ▶ **ero·sion** AW /ɪ'rəʊʒn; *NAmE* ɪ'roʊʒn/ *noun* [U]: *the erosion of the coastline by the sea* 海水对海岸线的侵蚀 ◇ *soil erosion* 水土流失 ◇ *the erosion of her confidence* 她信心的削弱

er·ogen·ous zone /ɪ'rɒdʒənəs zəʊn; *NAmE* ɪ'rɑːdʒənəs zoʊn/ *noun* an area of the body that gives sexual pleasure when it is touched 性欲发生区；性敏感区；性感带

Eros /'ɪərɒs; *NAmE* 'ɪrɑːs; 'erɑːs/ *noun* [U] (*formal*) sexual love or desire 性爱；性欲

erot·ic /ɪ'rɒtɪk; *NAmE* ɪ'rɑːtɪk/ *adj.* showing or involving sexual desire and pleasure; intended to make sb feel sexual desire 性欲的；性爱的；色情的: *erotic art* 色情艺术 ◇ *an erotic fantasy* 性幻想 ▶ **erot·ic·al·ly** /-kli/ *adv.*

erot·ica /ɪ'rɒtɪkə; *NAmE* ɪ'rɑːt-/ *noun* [U] books, pictures, etc. that are intended to make sb feel sexual desire 色情书画；色情作品

eroti·cism /ɪ'rɒtɪsɪzəm; *NAmE* ɪ'rɑːt-/ *noun* [U] the fact of expressing or describing sexual feelings and desire, especially in art, literature, etc.（尤指艺术、文学作品等中的）色情描写

err /ɜː(r); *NAmE* er/ *verb* [I] (*old-fashioned, formal*) to make a mistake 犯错误；做错事；出差错: *To err is human…* 犯错人皆难免…

IDM **err on the side of sth** to show too much of a good quality 过于；偏向于（好的特质）: *I thought it was better to **err on the side of caution*** (= to be too careful rather than take a risk). 我认为宁可过于谨慎也不要冒风险。

er·rand /'erənd/ *noun* a job that you do for sb that involves going somewhere to take a message, to buy sth, deliver goods, etc. 差使；差事: *He often **runs errands** for his grandmother.* 他经常给他的祖母跑腿儿。◇ *Her boss sent her **on an errand** into town.* 老板派她进城办事去了。 ➲ SEE ALSO FOOL'S ERRAND

er·rant /'erənt/ *adj.* [only before noun] (*formal* or *humorous*) **1** doing sth that is wrong; not behaving in an acceptable way 犯错误的；行为不当的；出格的 **2** (of a husband or wife 丈夫或妻子) not sexually faithful 对配偶不忠的；出轨的

er·rat·ic /ɪ'rætɪk/ *adj., noun*

■ ***adj.*** (*often disapproving*) not happening at regular times; not following any plan or regular pattern; that you cannot rely on 不规则的；不确定的；不稳定的；不可靠的 SYN **unpredictable**: *The electricity supply here is quite erratic.* 这里的电力供应相当不稳定。◇ *She had learnt to live with his sudden changes of mood and erratic behaviour.* 她已经学会适应他那变幻莫测的情绪和难以捉摸的行为。◇ *Mary is a gifted but erratic player* (= she does not always play well). 玛丽是一名有天赋的运动员，但发挥不太稳定。 ▶ **er·rat·ic·al·ly** /-kli/ *adv.*: *He was obviously upset and was driving erratically.* 他显然心烦意乱，开起车来摇晃不定。

■ ***noun*** (*also* **er,ratic 'block**, **er,ratic 'boulder**) (*geology* 地) a large rock that is different from the rock around and was left behind when a large mass of ice melted 漂砾；漂石

er·ratum /e'rɑːtəm/ *noun* [usually pl.] (*pl.* **er·rata** /-tə/) (*specialist*) a mistake in a book (shown in a list at the back or front)（书刊中的）错误（复数 errata 为勘误表，列于书前或书后）；误符

er·ro·ne·ous AW /ɪ'rəʊniəs; *NAmE* ɪ'roʊ-/ *adj.* (*formal*) not correct; based on wrong information 错误的: ***erroneous conclusions/assumptions*** 错误的结论 / 假设 ▶ **er·ro·ne·ous·ly** AW *adv.*

error 🔑 AW /'erə(r)/ *noun* [C, U] a mistake, especially one that causes problems or affects the result of sth 错误；差错；谬误: *No payments were made last week because of a computer error.* 由于计算机出错，上周未付任何款项。◇ **~ in sth** *There are too many errors in your work.* 你的工作失误太多。◇ **~ in doing sth** *I think you have made an error in calculating the total.* 我想你在计算总数时出了差错。◇ *A simple **error of judgement** meant that there was not enough food to go around.* 一个简单的判断错误就意味着食物不够每人一份。◇ *a **grave error*** (= a very serious mistake) 严重错误 ◇ *a **glaring error*** (= a mistake that is very obvious) 明显的错误 ◇ *The delay was due to **human error*** (= a mistake made by a person rather than by a machine). 延误是人为错误造成的。◇ *The computer system was switched off **in error*** (= by mistake). 计算机系统被错误关闭。◇ *There is no **room for error** in this job.* 这项工作决不允许出差错。 ➲ SYNONYMS AT MISTAKE ➲ SEE ALSO MARGIN OF ERROR

IDM **see, realize, etc. the ,error of your 'ways** (*formal* or *humorous*) to realize or admit that you have done sth wrong and decide to change your behaviour 知过即改；承认自己的做法不对并决心改正 ➲ MORE AT TRIAL *n.*

'error message *noun* (*computing* 计) a message that appears on a computer screen which tells you that you have done sth wrong or that the program cannot do what you want it to do 错误信息（在计算机屏幕上出现，表示有错误）

er·satz /'eəzæts; *NAmE* 'ersɑːts/ *adj.* artificial and not as good as the real thing or product 人造的，代用的，合成的（因而质量不如真品）: *ersatz coffee* 咖啡替代品

Erse /ɜːs; *NAmE* ɜːrs/ *noun* [U] (*old-fashioned*) the Scottish or Irish Gaelic language 苏格兰（或爱尔兰）盖尔语；埃尔斯语 ➲ COMPARE GAELIC, IRISH *n.* (1)

erst·while /'ɜːstwaɪl; *NAmE* 'ɜːrst-/ *adj.* [only before noun] (*formal*) former; that until recently was the type of person or thing described but is not any more 以前的；先前的；过去的；往昔的: *an erstwhile opponent* 以前的对手 ◇ *His erstwhile friends turned against him.* 他先前的朋友转而与他作对。

eru·dite /'erudaɪt/ *adj.* (*formal*) having or showing great knowledge that is gained from academic study 博学的；有学问的 SYN **learned**

eru·di·tion /,eru'dɪʃn/ *noun* [U] (*formal*) great academic knowledge 博学；学问

erupt /ɪ'rʌpt/ *verb* **1** [I, T] when a VOLCANO **erupts** or burning rocks, smoke, etc. **erupt** or **are erupted**, the burning rocks, etc. are thrown out from the volcano （火山）爆发；（岩浆、烟等）喷出: *The volcano could erupt at any time.* 这座火山随时可能爆发。◇ **~ from sth** *Ash began to erupt from the crater.* 火山灰开始从火山口喷出。◇ **~ sth** *An immense volume of rocks and molten lava was erupted.* 大量岩石和熔岩喷发出来。 ➲ SYNONYMS AT EXPLODE **2** [I] to start happening, suddenly and violently 突然发生；爆发 SYN **break out**: *Violence erupted outside the embassy gates.* 大使馆门外突然发生了暴乱。◇ **~ into sth** *The unrest erupted into revolution.* 动乱爆发为革命。 **3** [I, T] to suddenly express your feelings very strongly, especially by shouting loudly 突然发出（尤指叫喊）:

When Davis scored for the third time the crowd erupted. 戴维斯第三次得分，观众欢声雷动。◇ ~ in/into sth My father just erupted into fury. 我父亲勃然大怒。◇ + speech 'How dare you?' she erupted. "你竟敢这样？" 她突然大声叫道。 4 [I] (of spots, etc. 斑点等) to suddenly appear on your skin 突然（在皮肤上）出现： A rash had erupted all over his chest. 他的胸部突然出满疹子。 ▶ erup·tion /ɪ'rʌpʃn/ noun [C, U]: a major volcanic eruption 火山大爆发 ◇ an eruption of violent protest 暴力抗议的爆发 ◇ skin rashes and eruptions 皮疹和疹子 ➲ WORDFINDER NOTE AT DISASTER

erup·tive /ɪ'rʌptɪv/ adj. relating to or produced by the ERUPTION of a VOLCANO 火山爆发的；火山喷发的

erven PL. OF ERF

-ery, -ry suffix (in nouns 构成名词) 1 the group or class of …群体（或类）的事物： greenery 绿色植物 ◇ gadgetry 小巧装置 2 the state or character of …状态（或性质）： bravery 勇气 ◇ rivalry 竞争 3 the art or practice of …的艺术（或技术）： cookery 烹饪 ◇ archery 射箭 4 a place where sth is made, grows, lives, etc. 做（或生长、住等）…的地方： bakery 面包店 ◇ orangery 柑橘园

eryth·ro·cyte /ɪ'rɪθrəsaɪt/ noun (biology 生) = RED BLOOD CELL

es·cal·ate /'eskəleɪt/ verb [I, T] to become or make sth greater, worse, more serious, etc. （使）逐步扩大，不断恶化，加剧： ~ (into sth) The fighting escalated into a full-scale war. 这场交战逐步扩大为全面战争。◇ the escalating costs of health care 逐渐增加的医疗费用 ◇ ~ sth (into sth) We do not want to escalate the war. 我们不想让战争升级。 ▶ es·cal·ation /ˌeskə'leɪʃn/ noun [C, U]: an escalation in food prices 食品价格的不断上涨 ◇ further escalation of the conflict 冲突的进一步加剧

es·cal·ator /'eskəleɪtə(r)/ noun moving stairs that carry people between different floors of a large building 自动扶梯；电扶梯；滚梯

es·cal·ope /'eskəlɒp; e'skæləp; NAmE ɪ'skɑːləp; ɪ'skæ-/ noun a thin slice of meat with no bones in it, often covered with BREADCRUMBS and fried 薄肉片（常裹以面包屑油炸）： escalopes of veal 小牛肉片

es·cap·ade /ˌeskə'peɪd; 'eskəpeɪd/ noun an exciting adventure (often one that people think is dangerous or stupid) （常指危险或愚蠢的）冒险行为，恶作剧： Isabel's latest romantic escapade 伊莎贝尔最近的恋爱闹剧 ➲ WORDFINDER NOTE AT ADVENTURE

es·cape 🔑 /ɪ'skeɪp/ verb, noun

■ verb 1 🔑 [I] to get away from a place where you have been kept as a prisoner or not allowed to leave （从监禁或管制中）逃跑，逃走，逃出： Two prisoners have escaped. 两名犯人逃走了。 ◇ ~ from sb/sth He escaped from prison this morning. 他今天早上从监狱里逃跑了。 2 🔑 [I, T] to get away from an unpleasant or dangerous situation （从不愉快或危险处境中）逃脱，摆脱，逃避： ~ (from sth) She managed to escape from the burning car. 她设法从燃烧的汽车里逃了出来。 ◇ ~ (into sth) (figurative) As a child he would often escape into a dream world of his own. 小时候他常常躲进自己的梦幻世界中。 ◇ ~ sth They were glad to have escaped the clutches of winter for another year. 他们很高兴又一年躲过了寒冬的魔爪。 3 🔑 [T, no passive] to avoid sth unpleasant or dangerous 避开，避免（不愉快或危险的事物）： ~ sth She was lucky to escape punishment. 她逃脱惩罚真是幸运。 ◇ The pilot escaped death by seconds. 这名飞行员数秒之内死里逃生。 ◇ There was no escaping the fact that he was overweight. 他身体超重这一事实是无法回避的。 ◇ ~ doing sth He narrowly escaped being killed. 他险些丧命。 ➲ MORE LIKE THIS 27, page R28 4 🔑 [I] to suffer no harm or less harm than you would expect （没有受伤或只受了一点伤害而）逃脱，幸免于难： ~ (with sth) I was lucky to escape with minor injuries. 我只受了一点轻伤逃出来真是万幸。 ◇ + adj. Both drivers escaped unhurt. 两个驾驶员都幸免于难，安然无恙。 5 [T, no passive] ~ sb/sth to be forgotten or not noticed 被忘掉；被忽视；未被注意： Her name escapes me (= I can't remember it). 我记不起她的名字了。 ◇ It might have escaped your notice, but I'm very busy at the moment. 也许你没注意到，可我此刻忙得不可开交。 6 [I] (of gases, liquids, etc. 气体、液体等) to get out of a container, especially through a hole or crack 漏出；泄漏；渗出： Put a lid on to prevent heat escaping. 盖上盖子，以免热气跑了。 ◇ toxic waste escaping into the sea 流入大海的有毒废料 7 [T, I] ~ (sth) (of a sound 声音) to come out from your mouth without you intending it to （不自觉地）由…发出： A groan escaped her lips. 她不由得发出一声呻吟。

■ noun 1 🔑 [C, U] ~ (from sth) the act or a method of escaping from a place or an unpleasant or dangerous situation 逃跑；逃脱；逃避： an escape from a prisoner of war camp 从战俘营中逃出 ◇ I had a narrow escape (= I was lucky to have escaped). 我是死里逃生。 ◇ There was no hope of escape from her disastrous marriage. 她无望从不幸的婚姻中解脱出来。 ◇ He took an elaborate escape route from South Africa to Britain. 他周密安排了一条路线从南非逃往英国。 ◇ As soon as he turned his back, she would make her escape. 他一转身，她就逃跑。 ➲ SEE ALSO FIRE ESCAPE 2 🔑 [sing., U] a way of forgetting sth unpleasant or difficult for a short time 逃避现实；（暂时的）解脱，消遣： For her, travel was an escape from the boredom of her everyday life. 对她来说，旅行是为了从乏味的日常生活中暂时解脱出来。 3 [C] the fact of a liquid, gas, etc. coming out of a pipe or container by accident; the amount that comes out 漏出，溢出，渗出（量）： an escape of gas 漏气 4 [U] (also e'scape key [C]) (computing 计) a button on a computer keyboard that you press to stop a particular operation or leave a program * Esc 键；退出键： Press escape to get back to the menu. 按 Esc 键，退回到菜单。 ➲ WORDFINDER NOTE AT KEYBOARD

IDM make ˌgood your e'scape (formal) to manage to escape completely 成功地逃脱 ➲ MORE AT STABLE DOOR

es'cape clause noun a part of a contract which states the conditions under which the contract may be broken （合约的）免责条款，例外条约

es·caped /ɪ'skeɪpt/ adj. [only before noun] having escaped from a place 逃跑了的： an escaped prisoner/lion 逃犯；脱逃的狮子

es·capee /ɪˌskeɪ'piː/ noun (formal) a person or an animal that has escaped from somewhere, especially sb who has escaped from prison 逃亡者；脱逃的动物；（尤指）逃犯

es·cap·ism /ɪ'skeɪpɪzəm/ noun [U] an activity, a form of entertainment, etc. that helps you avoid or forget unpleasant or boring things 逃避现实；解脱方法： the pure escapism of adventure movies 惊险电影的纯娱乐性 ◇ For John, books are a form of escapism. 对约翰来说，看书是一种消遣形式。 ▶ es·cap·ist /-pɪst/ adj.

es·cap·olo·gist /ˌeskə'pɒlədʒɪst; NAmE -'pɑːl-/ noun a performer who escapes from ropes, chains, boxes, etc. 脱逃术表演者（擅长表演从捆扎的绳索或箱子等中脱身的魔术演员）

es·carp·ment /ɪ'skɑːpmənt; NAmE ɪ'skɑːrp-/ noun a steep slope that separates an area of high ground from an area of lower ground 陡坡；悬崖；峭壁

ES cell /ˌiː 'es sel/ noun (biology 生) the abbreviation for 'embryonic stem cell' (a STEM CELL taken from an EMBRYO soon after it is formed) 胚胎干细胞（全写为 embryonic stem cell，从形成之初的胚胎上提取的干细胞）

eschat·ology /ˌeskə'tɒlədʒi; NAmE -'tɑːl-/ noun [U] (religion 宗) the part of THEOLOGY concerned with death and judgement 末世论（神学中关于死亡和审判的论述） ▶ eschat·ologic·al /eˌskætə'lɒdʒɪkl; NAmE -'lɑːdʒ-/ adj.

es·chew /ɪs'tʃuː/ verb ~ sth (formal) to deliberately avoid or keep away from sth （有意地）避开，回避，避免

es·cort noun, verb

■ noun /'eskɔːt; NAmE 'eskɔːrt/ 1 [C, U] a person or group of people or vehicles that travels with sb/sth in order to protect or guard them 护送者；护卫队；护卫舰（或车队、飞机）： Armed escorts are provided for visiting heads *of state.* 来访的国家元首由武装卫队护送。◇ *Prisoners are taken to court* ***under police escort.*** 囚犯由警察押送带上法庭。 **2** [C] (*formal* or *old-fashioned*) a person, especially a man, who takes sb to a particular social event 陪同某人参加社交活动的人（尤指男人） **3** [C] a person, especially a woman, who is paid to go out socially with sb 受雇陪同某人外出社交的人（尤指女人）： *an escort service/agency* 社交陪伴服务社

■ ***verb*** /ɪ'skɔːt; *NAmE* ɪ'skɔːrt/ **~ sb (+ adv./prep.)** to go with sb to protect or guard them or to show them the way 护卫；护送： *The President arrived, escorted by twelve soldiers.* 总统在十二名卫兵的护送下到达。 ➲ SYNONYMS AT TAKE

es·cudo /e'skuːdəʊ; *NAmE* -doʊ/ *noun* (*pl.* **-os**) the unit of money in Cape Verde, and formerly in Portugal (replaced in Portugal in 2002 by the euro) 埃斯库多（佛得角货币单位，以及葡萄牙原货币单位，在葡萄牙于2002年为欧元所取代）

es·cut·cheon /ɪ'skʌtʃn/ *noun* **1** a flat piece of metal around a KEYHOLE, door handle, or light switch 孔罩；锁眼盖；门把手盖板；电灯开关板 **2** a SHIELD that has a COAT OF ARMS on it 盾形饰牌

-ese *suffix* **1** (in adjectives and nouns 构成形容词和名词) of a country or city; a person who lives in a country or city; the language spoken there …国（或城市）的；…国（或城市）的人；…国（或城市）的语言： *Chinese* 中国的 ◇ *Viennese* 维也纳的 **2** (in nouns 构成名词) (*often disapproving*) the style or language of …文体（或用语）： *journalese* 新闻文体 ◇ *officialese* 公文用语 ➲ MORE LIKE THIS 7, page R25

'e-signature *noun* = ELECTRONIC SIGNATURE

esker /'eskə(r)/ *noun* (*geology* 地) a long narrow area of small stones and earth that has been left by a large mass of ice that has melted 蛇形丘（由冰川融化后留下的沙砾和土形成的狭长脊）

Es·kimo /'eskɪməʊ; *NAmE* -moʊ/ *noun* (*pl.* **Es·kimo** or **Es·kimos**) (*sometimes offensive*) a member of a race of people from northern Canada, and parts of Alaska, Greenland and Siberia. Some of these people prefer to use the name Inuit. 爱斯基摩人（有些人喜欢 Inuit（因纽特人）这个名称） ➲ COMPARE INUIT

Esky™ /'eski/ *noun* (*pl.* **-ies**) (*AustralE*) a bag or box which keeps food or drinks cold and which can be used for a PICNIC 埃斯基冷藏袋（或盒）（可用于野餐）

ESL /ˌiː es 'el/ *abbr.* (in the US and Canada) English as a second language (refers to the teaching of English as a foreign language to people who are living in a country in which English is either the first or second language) （美国和加拿大）作为第二语言的英语（指对生活在英语为第一或第二语言的国家的人的英语教学） ➲ COMPARE EAL, EFL, ESOL

ESOL /'iːsɒl; *NAmE* -sɑːl/ *abbr.* (in the UK and Ireland) English for speakers of other languages (refers to the teaching of English as a foreign language to people who are living in a country in which English is either the first or second language) （英国和爱尔兰）操其他语言者的英语（指对生活在英语为第一或第二语言的国家的人的英语教学） ➲ COMPARE EAL, EFL, ESL

esopha·gus (*NAmE*) (*BrE* **oe·sopha·gus**) /i'sɒfəgəs; *NAmE* i'sɑː-/ *noun* (*pl.* **-pha·guses** or **-ph·agi** /-gaɪ/) (*anatomy* 解) the tube through which food passes from the mouth to the stomach 食道；食管 **SYN gullet** ➲ VISUAL VOCAB PAGE V64

eso·ter·ic /ˌesə'terɪk; ˌiːsə-/ *adj.* (*formal*) likely to be understood or enjoyed by only a few people with a special knowledge or interest 只有内行才懂的；难领略的

ESP /ˌiː es 'piː/ *abbr.* **1** English for specific/special purposes (the teaching of English for scientific, technical, etc. purposes to people whose first language is not English) （科技等方面的）专业英语，专门用途英语（教学对象第一语言并非英语） **2** extrasensory perception (the ability to know things without using the senses of sight, hearing, etc., for example to know what people are thinking or what will happen in the future) 超感知觉

esp. *abbr.* (in writing 书写形式) especially 尤其；特别

es·pa·drille /'espədrɪl/ *noun* a light shoe made of strong cloth with a SOLE made of rope 帆布便鞋（鞋底用绳子编织而成）

es·pal·ier /ɪ'spæliə(r)/ *noun* **1** a tree or SHRUB that is grown flat along a wooden or wire frame on a wall 棚树；墙树；树篱 **2** the frame that such a tree grows along 花木架；攀架

es·pe·cial /ɪ'speʃl/ *adj.* [only before noun] (*formal*) greater or better than usual; special in some way or for a particular group 格外的；特别的；特殊的： *a matter of especial importance* 特别重要的事情 ◇ *The lecture will be of especial interest to history students.* 学历史的学生会对这个讲座特别有兴趣。 ➲ COMPARE SPECIAL *adj.*

es·pe·cial·ly /ɪ'speʃəli/ *adv.* (*abbr.* **esp.**) **1** more with one person, thing, etc. than with others, or more in particular circumstances than in others 尤其；特别；格外 **SYN particularly**: *The car is quite small, especially if you have children.* 这辆汽车很小，如果有孩子就尤其显得小。◇ *Teenagers are very fashion conscious, especially girls.* 青少年，尤其是女孩，很注重时尚。◇ *I love Rome, especially in the spring.* 我喜爱罗马，尤其是春天的罗马。 ➲ LANGUAGE BANK AT EMPHASIS **2** for a particular purpose, person, etc. 专门；特地： *I made it especially for you.* 这是我特地为你做的。 **3** very much; to a particular degree 十分；非常： *I wasn't feeling especially happy that day.* 那天我并不十分高兴。◇ *'Do you like his novels?' 'Not especially.'* "你喜欢他的小说吗？" "不十分喜欢。"

▼ **WHICH WORD?** 词语辨析

especially / specially

- **Especially** usually means 'particularly'. * especially 通常表示尤其、特别： *She loves all sports, especially swimming.* 她喜爱各种运动，尤其是游泳。 It is not placed first in a sentence. 该词不用于句首： *I especially like sweet things.* 我特别喜欢吃甜食。◇ ~~*Especially I like sweet things.*~~
- **Specially** usually means 'for a particular purpose' and is often followed by a past participle, such as *designed*, *developed* or *made*. * specially 通常表示特意地、专门地，其后常接 designed、developed 或 made 等过去分词： *a course specially designed to meet your needs* 为满足你们的需要专门开设的课程 ◇ *She has her clothes specially made in Paris.* 她的衣服是特意在巴黎定做的。
- In *BrE*, **especially** and **specially** are often used in the same way and it can be hard to hear the difference when people speak. **Specially** is less formal. 在英式英语中，especially 和 specially 常具有相同的用法，说话时很难听出其区别。specially 较非正式： *I bought this especially/specially for you.* 这是我特意为你买的。◇ *It is especially/specially important to remember this.* 记住这一点尤为重要。
- The adjective for both **especially** and **specially** is usually **special**. * especially 和 specially 的形容词通常为 special。

Es·per·anto /ˌespə'ræntəʊ; *NAmE* -toʊ/ *noun* [U] an artificial language invented in 1887 as a means of international communication, based on the main European languages but with easy grammar and pronunciation 世界语（1887年创制的一种人造国际语言，以欧洲主要语言为基础）

es·pi·on·age /'espiənɑːʒ/ *noun* [U] the activity of secretly getting important political or military information about another country or of finding out another company's secrets by using SPIES 间谍活动；谍报活动；刺探活动

SYN spying: *Some of the commercial activities were a cover for espionage.* 有些商业活动是为间谍活动提供掩护。◇ *She may call it research; I call it industrial espionage.* 她可以称之为研究，可我称它为产业情报刺探。➲ SEE ALSO COUNTER-ESPIONAGE

es·plan·ade /ˌespləˈneɪd/ *noun* a level area of open ground in a town for people to walk along, often by the sea or a river （常指城镇中海滨、河畔供人散步的）广场，空地

es·pouse /ɪˈspaʊz/ *verb* **~ sth** (*formal*) to give your support to a belief, policy, etc. 支持，拥护，赞成（信仰、政策等）: *They espoused the notion of equal opportunity for all in education.* 他们赞同在教育方面人人机会均等的观念。▸ **es·pousal** /ɪˈspaʊzl/ *noun* [U, sing.]: **~ of sth** *his recent espousal of populism* 他最近对民粹主义的支持

es·presso /eˈspresəʊ; *NAmE* -soʊ/ *noun* (*pl.* **-os**) **1** [U] strong black coffee made by forcing steam or boiling water through GROUND coffee 浓缩咖啡（让蒸汽或开水通过磨碎的咖啡豆制成的浓咖啡） **2** [C] a cup of espresso 一杯浓缩咖啡

es·prit de corps /eˌspriː də ˈkɔː(r)/ *noun* [U] (*from French*) feelings of pride, care and support for each other, etc. that are shared by the members of a group 集体荣誉感；团队精神

espy /eˈspaɪ/ *verb* (**espies**, **espy·ing**, **espied**, **espied**) **~ sb/sth** (*literary*) to see sb/sth suddenly 突然看见 SYN **sight**, **spy**

Esq. *abbr.* **1** (*old-fashioned, especially BrE*) Esquire (a polite title written after a man's name, especially on an official letter addressed to him. If Esq. is used, Mr. is not then used.) 先生（写信时用于男子名后的尊称。如果用了 Esq.，便不再用 Mr.）: *Edward Smith, Esq.* 爱德华·史密斯先生 **2** (*NAmE*) used as a title after the name of a male or female lawyer （对男、女律师的称谓）…律师

-esque *suffix* (in adjectives 构成形容词) in the style of … 风格（或样式）的: *statuesque* 雕像般的 ◇ *Kafkaesque* 卡夫卡风格的 ➲ MORE LIKE THIS 7, page R25

-ess *suffix* (in nouns 构成名词) female 女…；雌…；母…: *lioness* 母狮子 ◇ *actress* 女演员 ➲ NOTE AT GENDER ➲ MORE LIKE THIS 7, page R25

essay 🔑 *noun, verb*

■ ***noun*** /ˈeseɪ/ **1** 🔑 **~ (on sth)** a short piece of writing by a student as part of a course of study （作为课程作业，学生写的）文章，短文: *an essay on the causes of the First World War* 关于第一次世界大战起因的文章 **2** 🔑 **~ (on sth)** a short piece of writing on a particular subject, written in order to be published （用来刊登的）论说文，小品文 **3** **~ (in sth)** (*formal*) an attempt to do sth 企图；尝试: *His first essay in politics was a complete disaster.* 他初次涉足政坛便碰得头破血流。

■ ***verb*** /eˈseɪ/ **~ sth** (*literary*) to try to do sth 企图；试图

es·say·ist /ˈeseɪɪst/ *noun* a person who writes essays to be published 论说文（或小品文）作者

es·sence /ˈesns/ *noun* **1** [U] **~ (of sth)** the most important quality or feature of sth, that makes it what it is 本质；实质；精髓: *His paintings capture the essence of France.* 他的画描绘出法国的神韵。◇ ***In essence*** (= when you consider the most important points), *your situation isn't so different from mine.* 从本质上讲，你我的情况并非相差很远。 **2** [U, C] a liquid taken from a plant, etc. that contains its smell and taste in a very strong form 香精；精油: *essence of rose* 玫瑰精油 ◇ (*BrE*) ***coffee/vanilla/almond essence*** 咖啡 / 香草 / 杏仁香精 ➲ SEE ALSO EXTRACT *n.* (2)

IDM **of the ˈessence** necessary and very important 必不可少；非常重要: *In this situation* ***time is of the essence*** (= we must do things as quickly as possible). 在这种情况下，时间是至关重要的。

es·sen·tial 🔑 /ɪˈsenʃl/ *adj., noun*

■ ***adj.*** **1** 🔑 completely necessary; extremely important in a particular situation or for a particular activity 完全必要的；必不可少的；极其重要的 SYN **vital**: ***an essential part/ingredient/component of sth*** 某事物必不可少的一部

▼ SYNONYMS 同义词辨析

essential

vital • crucial • critical • decisive • indispensable

These words all describe sb/sth that is extremely important and completely necessary because a particular situation or activity depends on them. 以上各词均表示极其重要、完全必要、必不可少。

essential extremely important and completely necessary, because without it sth cannot exist, be made or be successful 指极其重要的、完全必要的、必不可少的: *Experience is essential for this job.* 对于这个工作，经验是非常重要的。

vital essential 指极其重要的、完全必要的、必不可少的: *The police play a vital role in our society.* 警察在我们的社会中起着极其重要的作用。

ESSENTIAL OR VITAL? 用 essential 还是 vital?

These words have the same meaning but there can be a slight difference in tone. **Essential** is used to state a fact or opinion with authority. **Vital** is often used when there is some anxiety felt about sth, or a need to persuade sb that a fact or opinion is true, right or important. **Vital** is less often used in negative statements. 以上两词意义相同，但语气稍有区别。essential 用以说明事实或表明权威意见，vital 常用于对某事感到急迫或需要使人信服某一事实或意见确实、正确或重要等情况。vital 较少用于否定句: *It was vital to show that he was not afraid.* 最重要的是要表现出他毫无畏惧。◇ ~~*Money is not vital to happiness.*~~

crucial extremely important because a particular situation or activity depends on it 指至关重要的、关键的: *It is crucial that we get this right.* 我们把这个问题弄明白是极其重要的。

critical extremely important because a particular situation or activity depends on it 指至关重要的、关键的: *Your decision is critical to our future.* 你的决定对我们的将来至关重要。

CRUCIAL OR CRITICAL? 用 crucial 还是 critical?

These words have the same meaning but there can be a slight difference in context. **Critical** is often used in technical matters of business or science; **crucial** is often used to talk about matters that may cause anxiety or other emotions. 以上两词意义相同，但使用场合稍有区别。critical 常用于商业或科学的技术问题，crucial 常用于可能引起焦虑或其他情感方面的问题。

decisive of the greatest importance in affecting the final result of a particular situation 指决定性的、关键的: *She has played a decisive role in the peace negotiations.* 她在和谈中起了关键作用。

indispensable essential; too important to be without 指必需的、不可或缺的: *Cars have become an indispensable part of our lives.* 汽车已成了我们生活中必不可少的一部分。

PATTERNS

- essential/vital/crucial/critical/decisive/indispensable **for** sth
- essential/vital/crucial/critical/indispensable **to** sth
- essential/vital/crucial/critical **that…**
- essential/vital/crucial/critical **to do sth**
- a(n) essential/vital/crucial/critical/decisive/indispensable **part/factor**
- **of** vital/crucial/critical/decisive **importance**
- **absolutely** essential/vital/crucial/critical/decisive/indispensable

分 / 成分 / 组成部分 ◇ *essential services such as gas, water and electricity* 诸如燃气、水、电等基本公共事业 ◇ *The museum is closed while essential repairs are being carried out.* 博物馆正在进行大修，在此期间暂停开放。 ◇ *Even in small companies, computers are an essential tool.* 即使在小公司里，计算机也是必不可少的工具。 ◇ **~ to sth** *Money is not essential to happiness.* 金钱对于幸福并非必不可少。 ◇ **~ for sth** *Experience is essential for this job.* 对于这个工作，经验是非常重要的。 ◇ **it is essential to do sth** *It is essential to keep the two groups separate.* 将这两组分开是完全必要的。 ◇ **it is essential that...** *It is essential that you have some experience.* 你必须要有些经验。 ➲ COMPARE INESSENTIAL, NON-ESSENTIAL **OPP** **dispensable** ➲ LANGUAGE BANK AT EMPHASIS, VITAL **2** [only before noun] connected with the most important aspect or basic nature of sb/sth 本质的；基本的；根本的 **SYN** **fundamental**: *The essential difference between Sara and me is in our attitude to money.* 我与萨拉的根本区别在于我们对金钱的态度。 ◇ *The essential character of the town has been destroyed by the new road.* 这个城镇的主要特色被这条新公路毁了。

■ ***noun*** [usually pl.] **1** something that is needed in a particular situation or in order to do a particular thing 必不可少的东西；必需品：*I only had time to pack the **bare essentials*** (= the most necessary things). 我只来得及装上最基本的必需品。 ◇ *The studio had all the essentials like heating and running water.* 工作室里具备所有的基本设施，如暖气和自来水。 **2** an important basic fact or piece of knowledge about a subject 要点；要素；实质：*the essentials of English grammar* 英语语法基础

es·sen·tial·ly /ɪˈsenʃəli/ *adv.* when you think about the true, important or basic nature of sb/sth 本质上；根本上；基本上 **SYN** **basically, fundamentally**: *There are three **essentially different** ways of tackling the problem.* 解决这个问题有三种本质上完全不同的方法。 ◇ *The pattern is **essentially the same** in all cases.* 这种模式在所有情况下基本相同。 ◇ *Essentially, what we are suggesting is that the firm needs to change.* 说到底，我们的建议是公司必须思变。 ◇ *He was, essentially, a teacher, not a manager.* 他本质上来说是个教师而不是经理。 ◇ *The article was essentially concerned with her relationship with her parents* (= it dealt with other things, but this was the most important). 本文主要是关于她与父母的关系。

es,sential 'oil *noun* an oil taken from a plant, used because of its strong smell for making PERFUME and in AROMATHERAPY 精油

Essex girl /ˈesɪks ɡɜːl/ *noun* (*BrE, humorous, disapproving*) a name used especially in jokes to refer to a type of young woman who is not intelligent, dresses badly, talks in a loud and ugly way, and is very willing to have sex 埃塞克斯女郎（尤用于笑话，指愚笨、邋遢、讲话没修养、随便与人发生关系的女子）

EST /ˌiː es ˈtiː/ *abbr.* EASTERN STANDARD TIME 东部标准时间；东部冬令时间

-est *suffix* (makes superlative adjectives and adverbs 构成形容词和副词的最高级)：*widest* 最宽 ◇ *biggest* 最大 ◇ *happiest* 最幸福 ◇ *soonest* 最早 ➲ COMPARE -ER

es·tab·lish **AW** /ɪˈstæblɪʃ/ *verb* **1** **~ sth** to start or create an organization, a system, etc. that is meant to last for a long time 建立；创立；设立 **SYN** **set up**: *The committee was established in 1912.* 这个委员会创立于 1912 年。 ◇ *The new treaty establishes a free trade zone.* 新条约设立了自由贸易区。 **2** **~ sth** to start having a relationship, especially a formal one, with another person, group or country 建立（尤指正式关系）：*The school has established a successful relationship with the local community.* 这所学校与当地社区建立了良好的关系。 **3** **~ sb/sth/yourself (in sth) (as sth)** to hold a position for long enough or succeed in sth well enough to make people accept and respect you 确立；使立足；使稳固：*By then she was established as a star.* 那时她作为明星的地位已经确立。 ◇ *He has just set up his own business but it will take him a while to **get established**.* 他刚建立起自己的公司，但要站稳脚跟还得花上一段时间。 **4** **~ sth** to make people accept a belief, claim, custom etc. 使…获得接受；使…得到认可：*It was this campaign that established the paper's reputation.* 正是这场运动确立了这家报纸的声誉。 ◇ *Traditions get established over time.* 传统是随着时间的推移而得到认可的。 **5** to discover or prove the facts of a situation 查实；确定；证实 **SYN** **ascertain**: **~ sth** *Police are still trying to establish the cause of the accident.* 警方仍在努力确定事故的原因。 ◇ **~ that...** *They have established that his injuries were caused by a fall.* 他们已经证实他是摔伤的。 ◇ **~ where, what, etc....** *We need to establish where she was at the time of the shooting.* 我们需要查实枪击发生时她在何处。 ◇ **it is established that...** *It has since been established that the horse was drugged.* 此后便证实那匹马被注射了兴奋剂。

es·tab·lished **AW** /ɪˈstæblɪʃt/ *adj.* [only before noun] **1** respected or given official status because it has existed or been used for a long time 已确立的；已获确认的；确定的：*They are an established company with a good reputation.* 他们是一家地位稳固、信誉良好的公司。 ◇ *This unit is now an established part of the course.* 这个单元现在为本课程既定的一部分。 ➲ SEE ALSO WELL ESTABLISHED **2** (of a person 人) well known and respected in a job, etc. that they have been doing for a long time 著名的；成名的；公认的：*an established actor* 著名演员 **3** (of a Church or a religion 教会或宗教) made official for a country 成为国教的

es·tab·lish·ment **AW** /ɪˈstæblɪʃmənt/ *noun* **1** [C] (*formal*) an organization, a large institution or a hotel 机构；大型机关；企业；旅馆：*an educational establishment* 教育机构 ◇ *a research establishment* 研究机构 ◇ *The hotel is a comfortable and well-run establishment.* 这家旅馆舒适宜人，管理到位。 **2** (*usually* **the Establishment**) [sing.+sing./pl. v.] (*often disapproving*) the people in a society or a profession who have influence and power and who usually do not support change （通常反对变革的）当权派，权势集团；（统称）权威人士：*the **medical/military/political, etc. establishment*** 医学界、军界、政界等当权派 ◇ *young people rebelling against the Establishment* 反对当权者的年轻人 **3** [U] the act of starting or creating sth that is meant to last for a long time 建立；创立；确立：*The speaker announced the establishment of a new college.* 发言人宣布了新学院的成立。 ◇ *the establishment of diplomatic relations between the countries* 国家间外交关系的建立

es·tate **AW** /ɪˈsteɪt/ *noun* **1** [C] a large area of land, usually in the country, that is owned by one person or family （通常指农村的）大片私有土地，庄园 **2** [C] (*BrE*) an area of land with a lot of houses or factories of the same type on it 住宅区；工业区；工厂区：*She lives in a tower block on an estate in London.* 她住在伦敦某住宅区的一栋高楼里。 ➲ SEE ALSO COUNCIL ESTATE, HOUSING ESTATE, INDUSTRIAL ESTATE, TRADING ESTATE **3** (*law* 律) [C, U] all the money and property that a person owns, especially everything that is left when they die 个人财产；（尤指）遗产：*Her estate was left to her daughter.* 她的遗产全部留给了女儿。 **4** [C] (*BrE*) = ESTATE CAR

e'state agent (*BrE*) (*NAmE* **Real·tor™**, **'real estate agent**) *noun* a person whose job is to sell houses and land for people 房地产经纪人 ➲ COLLOCATIONS AT HOUSE

e'state car (*also* **estate**) (*both BrE*) (*NAmE* **'station wagon**) *noun* a car with a lot of space behind the back seats and a door at the back for loading large items 旅行轿车；客货两用小汽车 ➲ VISUAL VOCAB PAGE V56

e'state sale *noun* (*NAmE*) a sale of the possessions of a person who has died or is moving to another house 遗物出售；（搬迁户的）旧物变卖

e'state tax *noun* [U] (*NAmE*) = INHERITANCE TAX

es·teem /ɪˈstiːm/ *noun, verb*

■ ***noun*** [U] (*formal*) great respect and admiration; a good opinion of sb 尊重；敬重；好评：*She is **held in high esteem** by her colleagues.* 她深受同事们的敬重。 ◇ *Please* accept this small gift as a token of our esteem. 小小礼物，聊表敬意，请笑纳。➲ SEE ALSO SELF-ESTEEM

■ **verb** (*formal*) (not used in the progressive tenses 不用于进行时) **1** [usually passive] **~ sb/sth** to respect and admire sb/sth very much 尊重；敬重：*a* ***highly esteemed*** *scientist* 深受敬重的科学家 **2 ~ sb/sth + noun** (*old-fashioned, formal*) to think of sb/sth in a particular way 把…看作；认为：*She was esteemed the perfect novelist.* 她被认为是完美的小说家。

ester /ˈestə(r)/ *noun* (*chemistry* 化) a sweet-smelling substance that is formed from an ORGANIC acid and an alcohol 酯（由有机酸和醇形成的芳香物质）

es·thete, es·thet·ic (*NAmE*) = AESTHETE, AESTHETIC

es·tim·able /ˈestɪməbl/ *adj.* (*old-fashioned* or *formal*) deserving respect and admiration 值得尊重的；值得敬佩的

es·ti·mate AW *noun, verb*

■ **noun** /ˈestɪmət/ **1** a judgement that you make without having the exact details or figures about the size, amount, cost, etc. of sth（对大小、数量、成本等的）估计；估价：*I can give you a* ***rough estimate*** *of the amount of wood you will need.* 我可以粗略估计一下你所需要的木材量。◇ *a* ***ballpark estimate*** (= an approximate estimate) 大致相近的估计 ◇ *official government estimates of traffic growth over the next decade* 政府对今后十年交通增长的官方估计 ◇ *At least 5 000 people were killed, and that's a* ***conservative estimate*** (= the real figure will be higher). 至少 5 000 人丧生，这还是个保守的估计。 **2** a statement of how much a piece of work will probably cost 估计的成本；估价

■ **verb** /ˈestɪmeɪt/ [often passive] to form an idea of the cost, size, value etc. of sth, but without calculating it exactly 估计；估价；估算：**~ sth (at sth)** *The satellite will cost an estimated £400 million.* 这颗卫星估计要耗资 4 亿英镑。◇ *Police estimate the crowd at 30 000.* 警方估计聚集的人有 3 万。◇ **~ sth to do sth** *The deal is estimated to be worth around $1.5 million.* 这笔交易估计价值 150 万美元左右。◇ **~ (that)…** *We estimated (that) it would cost about €5 000.* 我们估计要花费大约 5 000 欧元。◇ **it is estimated (that)…** *It is estimated (that) the project will last four years.* 据估计，这项工程将用时四年。◇ **~ how many, large, etc.…** *It is hard to estimate how many children suffer from dyslexia.* 很难估计有多少孩子受诵读困难的困扰。➲ MORE LIKE THIS 21, page R27

es·ti·ma·tion AW /ˌestɪˈmeɪʃn/ *noun* (*formal*) **1** [sing.] a judgement or opinion about the value or quality of sb/sth 判断；评价；看法：*Who is the best candidate* ***in your estimation****?* 你认为谁是最佳人选？◇ *Since he left his wife he's certainly* ***gone down in my estimation*** (= I have less respect for him). 他离弃妻子后我对他的看法便不如以前了。◇ *She* ***went up in my estimation*** (= I have more respect for her) *when I discovered how much charity work she does.* 我发现她做了这么多慈善工作，我就比以前更尊敬她了。 **2** [C] a judgement about the levels or quantity of sth（对水平、数量的）估计：*Estimations of our total world sales are around 50 million.* 我们在全世界的总销售量估计在 5 000 万左右。

es·tranged /ɪˈstreɪndʒd/ *adj.* (*formal*) **1** [usually before noun] no longer living with your husband or wife（夫妻）分居的：*his estranged wife Emma* 他分居的妻子埃玛 **2 ~ (from sb)** no longer friendly, loyal or in contact with sb（与某人）疏远的，分手的：*He became estranged from his family after the argument.* 那场争吵后他便与家人疏远了。 **3 ~ (from sth)** no longer involved in or connected with sth, especially sth that used to be important to you（尤指与过去某重要事物）脱离的，决裂的：*She felt estranged from her former existence.* 她感到自己已脱离了过去的生活方式。

es·trange·ment /ɪˈstreɪndʒmənt/ *noun* [U, C] (*formal*) the state of being estranged; a period of being estranged 疏远（的一段时间）；分居（期）：**~ (from sb/sth)** *a period of estrangement from his wife* 他与妻子分居期间 ◇ **~ (between A and B)** *The misunderstanding had caused a seven-year estrangement between them.* 这场误会使得他们七年互不往来。

es·tro·gen (*NAmE*) (*BrE* **oes·tro·gen**) /ˈiːstrədʒən; *NAmE* ˈes-/ *noun* [U] a HORMONE produced in women's OVARIES that causes them to develop the physical and sexual features that are characteristic of females and that causes them to prepare their body to have babies 雌激素 ➲ COMPARE PROGESTERONE, TESTOSTERONE

es·trus (*NAmE*) (*BrE* **oes·trus**) /ˈiːstrəs; *NAmE* ˈestrəs/ *noun* [U] (*specialist*) a period of time in which a female animal is ready to have sex（雌性动物的）动情期

es·tu·ary /ˈestʃuəri; *NAmE* -eri/ (*pl.* **-ies**) *noun* the wide part of a river where it flows into the sea（江河入海的）河口，河口湾：*the Thames estuary* 泰晤士河河口 ➲ WORDFINDER NOTE AT RIVER ➲ VISUAL VOCAB PAGE V5

ˌEstuary ˈEnglish *noun* [U] a way of speaking which has features of standard English and of the type of English that is typical of London, used by many people in the south-east of England 港湾英语（兼具标准英语和伦敦英语的特点，多为英格兰东南部人使用）

ETA /ˌiː tiː ˈeɪ/ *abbr.* estimated time of arrival (the time at which an aircraft, a ship, etc. is expected to arrive)（航班等的）预计到达时间 ➲ COMPARE ETD

eta /ˈiːtə/ *noun* the 7th letter of the Greek alphabet (Η, η) 希腊字母表的第 7 个字母

ˈe-tailing *noun* [U] the business of selling goods to the public over the Internet 网上零售；网络零售：*E-tailing in the US broke all records last year.* 去年美国的网上零售业打破了所有纪录。▶ **ˈe-tailer** *noun*：*America's leading e-tailers* 美国主要的网上零售商

et al. /ˌet ˈæl/ *abbr.* (used especially after names) and other people or things (from Latin 'et alii/alia') 等人，等物，等等（尤置于名称后，源自拉丁文 et alii / alia）：*research by West et al., 2012* 韦斯特等人 2012 年所做的研究

etc. /ˌet ˈsetərə; ˌɪt/ *abbr.* used after a list to show that there are other things that you could have mentioned (the abbreviation for 'et cetera') 以及诸如此类；以及其他；等等：*Remember to take some paper, a pen, etc.* 记住带些纸、笔等东西。◇ *We talked about the contract, pay, etc.* 我们讨论了合同、工资等问题。

et cet·era /ˌet ˈsetərə; ˌɪt/ = ETC.

etch /etʃ/ *verb* **1** [T, I] to cut lines into a piece of glass, metal, etc. in order to make words or a picture 蚀刻，凿出（玻璃、金属等上的文字或图画）：**~ (A) (in/into/on B)** *a glass tankard with his initials etched on it* 刻有他姓名首字母的玻璃大酒杯 ◇ **~ B (with A)** *a glass tankard etched with his initials* 刻有他姓名首字母的玻璃大酒杯 **2** [T, usually passive] (*literary*) if a feeling is **etched** on sb's face, or sb's face is **etched** with a feeling, that feeling can be seen very clearly（脸上）流露出：**~ A in/into/on B** *Tiredness was etched on his face.* 从他的脸上可以看出他疲惫不堪。◇ **~ B with A** *His face was etched with tiredness.* 从他的脸上可以看出他疲惫不堪。 **3** [T, usually passive] **~ sth (+ adv./prep.)** to make a strong clear mark or pattern on sth 铭刻；画出…的轮廓：*a mountain etched* (= having a clear outline) *against the sky* 在天空映衬下轮廓清晰的山
IDM **be etched on your ˈheart/ˈmemory/ˈmind** if sth is **etched** on your memory, you remember it because it has made a strong impression on you 铭记在心；永志不忘；牢记心头

etch·ing /ˈetʃɪŋ/ *noun* [C, U] a picture that is printed from an etched piece of metal; the art of making these pictures 蚀刻画；蚀刻术；蚀刻法

ETD /ˌiː tiː ˈdiː/ *abbr.* estimated time of departure (the time at which an aircraft, ship, etc. is expected to leave)（航班等的）预计离开时间 ➲ COMPARE ETA

eter·nal /ɪˈtɜːnl; *NAmE* ɪˈtɜːrnl/ *adj.* **1** without an end; existing or continuing forever 不朽的；永久的；永恒的：*the promise of eternal life in heaven* 在天国永生的

许诺 ◇ *She's an eternal optimist* (= she always expects that the best will happen). 她是个永远的乐观主义者。◇ *eternal truths* (= ideas that are always true and never change) 永恒的真理 **2** [only before noun] (*disapproving*) happening often and seeming never to stop 无休止的；永不停止的；没完没了的 SYN **constant**: *I'm tired of your eternal arguments.* 我烦透了你们那没完没了的争论。▶ **eter·nal·ly** /ɪˈtɜːnəli; *NAmE* -ˈtɜːrn-/ *adv.*: *I'll be eternally grateful to you for this.* 我将为此永远感激你。◇ *women trying to look eternally young* 试图永葆青春的女人 IDM SEE HOPE *n.*

eˌternal ˈtriangle *noun* a situation where two people are in love with or having a sexual relationship with the same person 三角恋爱

eˌternal ˈverity *noun* [usually pl.] (*formal*) an essential basic moral principle 基本道德原则

eter·nity /ɪˈtɜːnəti; *NAmE* ɪˈtɜːrn-/ *noun* **1** [U] (*formal*) time without end, especially life continuing without end after death 永恒；永生；不朽: *There will be rich and poor for all eternity.* 贫富将永远存在。◇ *They believed that their souls would be condemned to burn in hell for eternity.* 他们相信他们的灵魂会受到惩罚，在地狱里永受烈焰焚烧。**2 an eternity** [sing.] (*informal*) a period of time that seems to be very long or to never end （似乎）无穷无尽的一段时间: *After what* ***seemed like an eternity*** *the nurse returned with the results of the test.* 过了漫长的一段时间后护士才拿着检验结果回来。

eth /eð/ *noun* (*phonetics* 语音) the letter ð that was used in Old English to represent the sounds /θ/ and /ð/ and later written as *th*. This letter is now used as a PHONETIC symbol for the sound /ð/, as in *this*. * ð（古英语中用以表示 /θ/ 和 /ð/ 音的字母，后写作 th）

eth·ane /ˈiːθeɪn/ *noun* [U] (*symb.* C_2H_6) (*chemistry* 化) a gas that has no colour or smell and that can burn. Ethane is found in natural gas and mineral oil. 乙烷（无色无味的可燃气体）

etha·nol /ˈeθənɒl; *NAmE* -nɔːl; -nɑːl/ (*also* **ˌethyl ˈalcohol**) *noun* [U] (*chemistry* 化) the type of alcohol in alcoholic drinks, also used as a fuel or SOLVENT 乙醇

eth·ene /ˈeθiːn/ *noun* [U] = ETHYLENE

ether /ˈiːθə(r)/ *noun* [U] **1** a clear liquid made from alcohol, used in industry as a SOLVENT and, in the past, in medicine to make people unconscious before an operation 醚；乙醚 **2 the ether** (*old use* or *literary*) the upper part of the sky 苍穹；苍天；太空: *Her words disappeared into the ether.* 她的话消失在九霄云外。**3 the ether** the air, when it is thought of as the place in which radio or electronic communication takes place 以太

ether·eal /iˈθɪəriəl; *NAmE* iˈθɪr-/ *adj.* (*formal*) extremely delicate and light; seeming to belong to another, more spiritual, world 优雅的；轻飘的；缥缈的；超凡的: *ethereal music* 优雅的音乐 ◇ *her ethereal beauty* 她飘逸的美

Ether·net /ˈiːθənet; *NAmE* ˈiːθərnet/ *noun* [sing.] (*computing* 计) a system for connecting a number of computer systems to form a network 以太网

ethic AW /ˈeθɪk/ *noun* **1 ethics** [pl.] moral principles that control or influence a person's behaviour 道德准则；伦理标准: ***professional/business/medical ethics*** 职业 / 商业道德；医德 ◇ *to* ***draw up a code of ethics*** 拟定一份道德规范 ◇ *He began to question the ethics of his position.* 他开始对他的立场是否符合道德准则提出质疑。**2** [sing.] a system of moral principles or rules of behaviour 道德体系；行为准则: *a strongly defined work ethic* 明确规定的工作守则 ◇ *the Protestant ethic* 新教伦理 **3 ethics** [U] the branch of philosophy that deals with moral principles 伦理学；道德学

eth·ic·al AW /ˈeθɪkl/ *adj.* **1** connected with beliefs and principles about what is right and wrong （有关）道德的；伦理的: ***ethical issues/standards/questions*** 有关道德的问题；道德标准 / 问题 ◇ *the* ***ethical problems*** *of human embryo research* 人类胚胎研究的伦理问题 **2** morally correct or acceptable 合乎道德的: *Is it ethical to promote cigarettes through advertising?* 通过广告推销香烟合乎道德吗？◇ ***ethical investment*** (= investing money in businesses that are considered morally acceptable) 合乎道德的投资 ▶ **eth·ic·al·ly** AW /-kli/ *adv.*: *The committee judged that he had not behaved ethically.* 委员会裁定他的行为违背了道德标准。

eth·nic AW /ˈeθnɪk/ *adj., noun*

■ ***adj.*** **1** connected with or belonging to a nation, race or people that shares a cultural tradition 民族的；种族的: ***ethnic groups/communities*** 族群；种族社区 ◇ ***ethnic strife/tensions/violence*** (= between people from different races or peoples) 种族冲突 / 紧张形势 / 暴力 ◇ *ethnic Albanians living in Germany* 生活在德国的阿尔巴尼亚族人 **2** typical of a country or culture that is very different from modern Western culture and therefore interesting for people in Western countries 具有民族特色的；异国风味的: ***ethnic clothes/jewellery/cooking*** 具有民族特色的服装 / 珠宝首饰 / 烹调 ▶ **eth·nic·al·ly** /-kli/ *adv.*: *an ethnically divided region* 种族分裂地区

■ ***noun*** (*especially NAmE*) a person from an ETHNIC MINORITY 少数民族的人

ˌethnic ˈcleansing *noun* [U] (used especially in news reports) the policy of forcing the people of a particular race or religion to leave an area or a country （尤用于新闻报道）种族清洗 ⊃ COLLOCATIONS AT WAR

eth·ni·city AW /eθˈnɪsəti/ *noun* [U] (*specialist*) the fact of belonging to a particular race 民族性；种族渊源；种族特点: *Many factors are important, for example class, gender, age and ethnicity.* 许多因素都很重要，如阶级、性别、年龄和种族。

ˌethnic miˈnority *noun* a group of people from a particular culture or of a particular race living in a country where the main group is of a different culture or race 少数民族

ethno·cen·tric /ˌeθnəʊˈsentrɪk; *NAmE* ˌeθnoʊ-/ *adj.* based on the ideas and beliefs of one particular culture and using these to judge other cultures 种族（或民族）中心主义的；种族（或民族）优越感的: *a white, ethnocentric school curriculum* 以白种人为中心的学校课程 ▶ **ethno·cen·trism** *noun* [U]

eth·nog·raph·er /eθˈnɒɡrəfə(r); *NAmE* -ˈnɑːɡ-/ *noun* a person who studies different races and cultures 民族志（或民族学）研究者

eth·nog·raphy /eθˈnɒɡrəfi; *NAmE* -ˈnɑːɡ-/ *noun* [U] the scientific description of different races and cultures 民族志；民族学 ▶ **ethno·graph·ic** /ˌeθnəˈɡræfɪk/ *adj.*: *ethnographic research* 民族志研究

eth·no·logy /eθˈnɒlədʒi; *NAmE* -ˈnɑːl-/ *noun* [U] the scientific study and comparison of human races 人种学；民族学 ▶ **ethno·logic·al** /ˌeθnəˈlɒdʒɪkl; *NAmE* -ˈlɑːdʒ-/ *adj.* **eth·nolo·gist** /eθˈnɒlədʒɪst; *NAmE* -ˈnɑːl-/ *noun*

ethos /ˈiːθɒs; *NAmE* ˈiːθɑːs/ *noun* [sing.] (*formal*) the moral ideas and attitudes that belong to a particular group or society （某团体或社会的）道德思想，道德观: *an ethos of public service* 公益服务的道德意识

ethyl /ˈeθɪl; ˈiːθaɪl/ *adj.* [only before noun] (*chemistry* 化) containing the group of atoms C_2H_5, formed from ETHANE 含乙基的: *ethyl acetate* 乙酸乙酯

ˌethyl ˈalcohol *noun* [U] (*chemistry* 化) = ETHANOL

ethyl·ene /ˈeθɪliːn/ (*also* **eth·ene**) *noun* [U] (*symb.* C_2H_4) (*chemistry* 化) a gas which is present in coal, CRUDE OIL, and NATURAL GAS 乙烯

eth·yne /ˈiːθaɪn; *NAmE* ˈeθ-/ *noun* [U] (*symb.* C_2H_2) the chemical name for ACETYLENE 乙炔

ˈe-ticket (*US* **ˈE-ticket™**) *noun* a ticket, for example a plane ticket, that you buy over the Internet and receive by email. Your purchase details are stored on computer so you do not need a paper ticket. 电子票

eti·ol·ated /ˈiːtiəleɪtɪd/ *adj.* **1** (*biology* 生) if a plant is etiolated it is pale because it does not receive enough light（植物因吸收光线不足而）黄化的 **2** (*formal*) lacking force and energy 无力的；虚弱的

eti·ology (*NAmE*) (*BrE* **aeti·ology**) /ˌiːtiˈɒlədʒi; *NAmE* -ˈɑːl-/ *noun* [U] (*medical* 医) the scientific study of the causes of disease 病因学；病理学

E

eti·quette /ˈetɪket; -kət/ *noun* [U] the formal rules of correct or polite behaviour in society or among members of a particular profession（社会或行业中的）礼节，礼仪，规矩：*advice on etiquette* 在礼节方面的忠告 ◇ ***medical/legal/professional etiquette*** 医学界的 / 法律界的 / 行业规矩 ➲ WORDFINDER NOTE AT BEHAVIOUR ➲ SEE ALSO NETIQUETTE

ˈ**e-toll** (*also* ˈ**etoll**) *noun* (*SAfrE*) **1** [U] ˈ**e-tolls** [pl.] the system of collecting TOLLS (= money that you pay to use a particular road) automatically using equipment that recognizes vehicles through electronic TAGS 电子收费系统（通过识别车辆上的电子标签来自动收取过路费） **2** [C] the charge for using this system （经电子收费系统收取的）过路费：*Motorists are fined if they fail to pay their e-tolls within a week.* 驾车者如果一周内不支付电子过路费，将被处以罚款。 ▸ ˈ**e-tolling** *noun* [U]：*the e-tolling system* 电子收费系统

Eton·ian /iːˈtəʊniən; *NAmE* -ˈtoʊ-/ *noun* a person who is or was a student at the English private school Eton College （英国）伊顿公学学生，伊顿公学校友

-ette *suffix* (in nouns 构成名词) **1** small 小：*kitchenette* 小厨房 **2** female 女性：*usherette* 女引座员

étude /ˈeɪtjuːd; *NAmE also* -tuːd/ (*especially NAmE*) (*BrE also* **study**) *noun* (*music* 音, *from French*) a piece of music designed to give a player practice in technical skills 练习曲

ety·mol·ogy /ˌetɪˈmɒlədʒi; *NAmE* -ˈmɑːl-/ *noun* (*pl.* **-ies**) **1** [U] the study of the origin and history of words and their meanings 词源学 **2** [C] the origin and history of a particular word 词源 ▸ **etymo·logic·al** /ˌetɪməˈlɒdʒɪkl; *NAmE* -ˈlɑːdʒ-/ *adj.*：*an etymological dictionary* 词源词典

EU /ˌiː ˈjuː/ *abbr.* EUROPEAN UNION 欧洲联盟；欧盟

eu·ca·lyp·tus /juːkəˈlɪptəs/ *noun* [C, U] (*pl.* **eu·ca·lyp·tuses** or **eu·ca·lyp·ti** /-taɪ/) (*also* **eucaˈlyptus tree**, ˈ**gum tree**) a tall straight tree with leaves that produce an oil with a strong smell, that is used in medicine. There are several types of eucalyptus and they grow especially in Australasia. 桉树（尤产于澳大拉西亚） ➲ VISUAL VOCAB PAGE V12

Eu·char·ist /ˈjuːkərɪst/ *noun* [sing.] a ceremony in the Christian Church during which people eat bread and drink wine in memory of the last meal that Christ had with his DISCIPLES; the bread and wine taken at this ceremony （基督教）圣祭礼，圣餐，圣体血 ➲ SEE ALSO COMMUNION (1), MASS (1)

Eu·clid·ean geom·etry /juːˌklɪdiən dʒiˈɒmətri; *NAmE* -ˈɑːm-/ *noun* [U] the system of GEOMETRY based on the work of Euclid 欧几里得几何

eu·gen·ics /juːˈdʒenɪks/ *noun* [U] the study of methods to improve the mental and physical characteristics of the human race by choosing who may become parents 优生学 ▸ **eu·gen·ic** *adj.* **eu·gen·ist** /juːˈdʒiːnɪst/ (*also* **eu·geni·cist** /juːˈdʒenɪsɪst/) *noun*

eu·lo·gize (*BrE also* **-ise**) /ˈjuːlədʒaɪz/ *verb* ~ **sb/sth** (**as sth**) (*formal*) to praise sb/sth very highly 称赞；颂扬；赞颂：*He was eulogized as a hero.* 他被赞誉为英雄。 ▸ **eu·lo·gis·tic** /ˌjuːləˈdʒɪstɪk/ *adj.*

eu·logy /ˈjuːlədʒi/ *noun* [C, U] (*pl.* **-ies**) **1** ~ (**of/to sb/sth**) a speech or piece of writing praising sb/sth very much 颂词；颂文：*a eulogy to marriage* 婚礼颂词 **2** ~ (**for/to sb**) a speech given at a funeral praising the person who has died （颂扬死者的）悼词，悼文

eu·nuch /ˈjuːnək/ *noun* **1** a man who has been CASTRATED, especially one who guarded women in some Asian countries in the past 阉人；太监；宦官 **2** (*formal*) a person without power or influence 无权力（或影响）的人：*a political eunuch* 政治"阉人"

eu·phem·ism /ˈjuːfəmɪzəm/ *noun* ~ (**for sth**) an indirect word or phrase that people often use to refer to sth embarrassing or unpleasant, sometimes to make it seem more acceptable than it really is 委婉语；委婉说法：*'Pass away' is a euphemism for 'die'.* "去世"是"死"的委婉语。◇ *'User fees' is just a politician's euphemism for taxes.* "用户费"不过是政治家对"税款"的委婉说法。 ➲ WORDFINDER NOTE AT IMAGE ▸ **eu·phem·is·tic** /ˌjuːfəˈmɪstɪk/ *adj.*：*euphemistic language* 委婉的语言 **eu·phem·is·tic·al·ly** /ˌjuːfəˈmɪstɪkli/ *adv.*：*The prison camps were euphemistically called 'retraining centres'.* 战俘营被委婉地称作"再训练中心"。

eu·pho·ni·ous /juːˈfəʊniəs; *NAmE* -ˈfoʊ-/ *adj.* (*formal*) (of a sound, word, etc. 声音、词等) pleasant to listen to 悦耳的；动听的；和谐的 ▸ **eu·pho·ny** /ˈjuːfəni/ *noun* [U]

eu·pho·nium /juːˈfəʊniəm; *NAmE* -ˈfoʊ-/ *noun* a large BRASS musical instrument like a TUBA 尤风宁号

eu·phoria /juːˈfɔːriə/ *noun* [U] an extremely strong feeling of happiness and excitement that usually lasts only a short time （通常指持续时间较短的）极度愉快的心情，极度兴奋的情绪 ▸ **eu·phor·ic** /juːˈfɒrɪk; *NAmE* -ˈfɔːr-/ *adj.*：*My euphoric mood could not last.* 我兴奋的心情持久不了。 ➲ SYNONYMS AT EXCITED

Eur·asian /juˈreɪʒn; -ˈreɪʃn/ *adj.*, *noun*

■ ***adj.*** **1** of or connected with both Europe and Asia 欧亚的：*the Centre for Russian and Eurasian Studies* 俄罗斯和欧亚研究中心 **2** having one Asian parent and one parent who is white or from Europe 欧亚混血儿的

■ ***noun*** a person with one Asian parent and one parent who is white or from Europe 欧亚混血儿：*Singapore Eurasians* 新加坡的欧亚混血儿

eur·eka /juˈriːkə/ *exclamation* used to show pleasure at having found sth, especially the answer to a problem （因找到某物，尤指问题的答案而高兴）我发现了，我找到了

euˈreka moment *noun* the moment when you suddenly understand sth important, have a great idea, or find the answer to a problem 顿悟时刻；突发灵感的一刻

eu·rhyth·mics (*BrE*) (*NAmE usually* **eu·ryth·mics**) /juˈrɪðmɪks/ *noun* [U] a form of exercise which combines physical movement with music and speech 韵律（体）操

Euro /ˈjʊərəʊ; *NAmE* ˈjʊroʊ/ *adj.* (*informal*) (used especially in newspapers) connected with Europe, especially the European Union （尤用于报章）欧洲的，欧盟的：*Euro rules* 欧盟条例

euro 🔑 /ˈjʊərəʊ; *NAmE* ˈjʊroʊ/ *noun* (*symb.* €) (*pl.* **euros** or **euro**) the unit of money of some countries of the European Union 欧元（欧盟中某些国家的货币单位）：*The price is given in dollars or euros.* 价格用美元或欧元标出。◇ *I paid five euros for it.* 买这我花了五欧元。◇ *10 million euro* * 1 000 万欧元 ◇ *a 30-million-euro deal* * 3 000 万欧元的交易 ◇ *the value of the euro against the dollar* 欧元对美元的比值

Euro- /ˈjʊərəʊ; *NAmE* ˈjʊroʊ/ *combining form* (in nouns and adjectives 构成名词和形容词) connected with Europe or the European Union 欧洲的；欧盟的：*a Euro-MP* 欧洲议会议员 ◇ *Euro-elections* 欧盟选举

Euro·land /ˈjʊərəʊlænd; *NAmE* ˈjʊroʊ-/ *noun* [U] = EUROZONE

Eur·ope /ˈjʊərəp; *NAmE* ˈjʊrəp/ *noun* [U] **1** the continent next to Asia in the east, the Atlantic Ocean in the west, and the Mediterranean Sea in the south 欧洲：***western/eastern/central Europe*** 西欧；东欧；中欧 **2** the European Union 欧盟：*countries wanting to join Europe* 想加入欧盟的国家 ◇ *He's very pro-Europe.* 他非常支持欧盟。 **3** (*BrE*) all of Europe except for Britain （除不列颠

群岛以外的）欧洲：*British holidaymakers in Europe* 在欧洲大陆度假的英国人

Euro·pean /ˌjʊərəˈpiːən; *NAmE* jʊr-/ *adj., noun*

- ***adj.*** **1** of or connected with Europe 欧洲的；全欧的：*European languages* 欧洲的语言 **2** of or connected with the European Union 欧盟的：*European law* 欧盟的法律 ◇ *our European partners* 我们的欧盟伙伴
- ***noun*** **1** a person from Europe, or whose ANCESTORS came from Europe 欧洲人；祖籍欧洲的人；欧洲人的后裔 **2** (*BrE*) a person who supports the principles and aims of the European Union 欧盟支持者；欧盟拥护者：*a good European* 欧盟的坚定拥护者

the ˌEuropean Comˈmission *noun* [sing.] the group of people who are responsible for the work of the European Union and for suggesting new laws 欧盟委员会，欧盟执委会（负责欧盟工作和新法规的提出）

Euro·pean·ize (*BrE also* **-ise**) /ˌjʊərəˈpiːənaɪz; *NAmE* jʊr-/ *verb* **1** ~ **sb/sth** to make sb/sth feel or seem European 欧化；使具有欧洲风味：*a Europeanized American* 一名欧化的美国人 **2** ~ **sth** to put sth under the control of the European Union 使受欧盟管辖 ▸ **Euro·pean·iza·tion, -isa·tion** /ˌjʊərəpiːənaɪˈzeɪʃn; *NAmE* jʊrəpiːənəˈz-/ *noun* [U]

the ˌEuropean ˈParliament *noun* [sing.] the group of people who are elected in the countries of the European Union to make and change its laws 欧洲议会（由欧盟各国选举产生，负责法律的制定和修改）

ˌEuropean ˈplan *noun* [sing.] (*NAmE*) a system of charging for a hotel room only, without meals 欧式旅馆收费制（只收客房费，不含餐饮）➲ COMPARE BED AND BREAKFAST (1), FULL BOARD, HALF BOARD

the ˌEuropean ˈUnion *noun* [sing.] (*abbr.* **EU**) an economic and political organization, based in Brussels, that many European countries belong to 欧洲联盟，欧盟（总部设在布鲁塞尔）

euro·pium /jʊəˈrəʊpiəm; *NAmE* jʊˈroʊ-/ *noun* [U] (*symb.* **Eu**) a chemical element. Europium is a silver-white metal used in colour television screens. 铕（用于彩电屏幕）

Euro·scep·tic /ˈjʊərəʊˈskeptɪk; ˈjʊərəʊskeptɪk; *NAmE* jʊroʊ-; ˈjʊroʊ-/ *noun* a person, especially a British politician, who is opposed to closer links with the European Union （尤指英国政界）反欧盟化的人 ▸ **Euro·scep·tic** *adj.*

the Euro·zone /ˈjʊərəʊzəʊn; *NAmE* ˈjʊroʊzoʊn/ *noun* [sing.] (*also* **Euro·land**) the countries in the European Union that use the euro as a unit of money 欧元区

Eus·ta·chian tube /juːˈsteɪʃn tjuːb/ *noun* (*anatomy* 解) a narrow tube that joins the throat to the middle ear 咽鼓管；耳咽管

eu·tha·nasia /ˌjuːθəˈneɪziə; *NAmE* -ˈneɪʒə/ *noun* [U] the practice (illegal in most countries) of killing without pain a person who is suffering from a disease that cannot be cured 安乐死 SYN **mercy killing**: *They argued in favour of legalizing **voluntary euthanasia*** (= people being able to ask for euthanasia themselves). 他们据理力争让自愿安乐死合法化。

eu·than·ize (*BrE also* **-ise**) /ˈjuːθənaɪz/ *verb* ~ **sb/sth** (*especially NAmE*) to kill a sick or injured animal or person by giving them drugs so that they die without pain 使（人或动物）安乐死 SYN **put down, put to sleep**

eu·troph·ic /juːˈtrɒfɪk; *NAmE* -ˈtrɑːf-/ *adj.* (*specialist*) (of a lake, river, etc. 湖、河等) containing too many food substances that encourage plants to grow, which then kill animal life by using too much OXYGEN from the water 富营养的

eu·trophi·ca·tion /juːtrəfɪˈkeɪʃn/ *noun* [U] (*specialist*) the process of too many plants growing on the surface of a river, lake, etc., often because chemicals that are used to help crops grow have been carried there by rain （常因雨水带来的化肥造成水体的）富营养化

EV /ˌiː ˈviː/ *noun* (*especially NAmE*) the abbreviation for 'electric vehiclek' (= a vehicle that uses one or more electric motors) 电动车（全写为 electric vehicle）

evacu·ate /ɪˈvækjueɪt/ *verb* **1** [T] to move people from a place of danger to a safer place （把人从危险的地方）疏散，转移，撤离：~ **sth** *Police evacuated nearby buildings.* 警方已将附近大楼的居民疏散。◇ ~ **sb** (**from**…) (**to**…) *Children were evacuated from London to escape the bombing.* 为躲避轰炸，孩子们都撤离了伦敦。 **2** [T, I] ~ (**sth**) to move out of a place because of danger, and leave the place empty （从危险的地方）撤出，搬出，撤空：*Employees were urged to evacuate their offices immediately.* 已敦促各雇员立即从办公室撤出。◇ *Locals were told to evacuate.* 当地居民已收到撤离的通知。 **3** [T] ~ **sth** (*formal*) to empty your BOWELS 排空（胃肠）；排泄（粪便） ▸ **evacu·ation** /ɪˌvækjuˈeɪʃn/ *noun* [U, C]: *the emergency evacuation of thousands of people after the earthquake* 地震后数千人的紧急疏散

evac·uee /ɪˌvækjuˈiː/ *noun* a person who is sent away from a place because it is dangerous, especially during a war （尤指战时）被疏散者，撤离者

evade /ɪˈveɪd/ *verb* **1** ~ (**doing**) **sth** to escape from sb/sth or avoid meeting sb 逃脱；躲开；躲避：*For two weeks they evaded the press.* 他们有两周一直避而不见记者。◇ *He managed to **evade capture**.* 他设法逃脱了抓捕。 **2** ~ (**doing**) **sth** to find a way of not doing sth, especially sth that legally or morally you should do 逃避，规避（尤指法律或道德责任）：*to evade payment of taxes* 逃税 ◇ *She is trying to **evade all responsibility** for her behaviour.* 她在试图逃避应为自己的行为承担的所有责任。 **3** to avoid dealing with or talking about sth 回避，避开（处理或谈论某事）：~ **sth** *Come on, don't you think you're **evading the issue**?* 得了吧，你不认为你是在回避这个问题吗？◇ ~ **doing sth** *to evade answering a question* 避而不答某一问题 **4** ~ **sb** (*formal*) to not come or happen to sb 使达不到；未发生在（某人）身上 SYN **elude**: *The answer evaded him* (= he could not think of it). 他答不上来。➲ SEE ALSO EVASION, EVASIVE

evalu·ate AW /ɪˈvæljueɪt/ *verb* to form an opinion of the amount, value or quality of sth after thinking about it carefully 估计；评价；评估 SYN **assess**: ~ **sth** *Our research attempts to evaluate the effectiveness of the different drugs.* 我们的研究试图对不同药物的疗效进行评估。◇ ~ **how, whether, etc.…** *We need to evaluate how well the policy is working.* 我们需要对这一政策产生的效果作出评价。➲ WORDFINDER NOTE AT SCIENCE ▸ **evalu·ation** AW /ɪˌvæljuˈeɪʃn/ *noun* [C, U]: *an evaluation of the health care system* 对保健制度的评价 **evalu·ative** AW /ɪˈvæljuətɪv/ *adj.*

evan·es·cent /ˌiːvəˈnesnt; *NAmE usually* ˌev-/ *adj.* (*literary*) disappearing quickly from sight or memory 瞬息即逝的；迅速遗忘的 ▸ **evan·es·cence** *noun* [U]

evan·gel·ic·al /ˌiːvænˈdʒelɪkl/ *adj., noun*

- ***adj.*** **1** of or belonging to a Christian group that emphasizes the authority of the Bible and the importance of people being saved through faith 基督教福音派的：*They're evangelical Christians.* 他们是福音派基督徒。 **2** wanting very much to persuade people to accept your views and opinions 热衷于传播自己观点的：*He delivered his speech with evangelical fervour.* 他发表演说时热烈鼓吹自己的思想。 ▸ **evan·gel·ic·al·ism** *noun* [U]
- ***noun*** a member of the evangelical branch of the Christian Church 基督教福音派教徒

evan·gel·ist /ɪˈvændʒəlɪst/ *noun* **1** a person who tries to persuade people to become Christians, especially by travelling around the country holding religious meetings or speaking on radio or television （基督教）布道者 ➲ SEE ALSO TELEVANGELIST **2** **Evangelist** one of the four writers (Matthew, Mark, Luke, John) of the books called the GOSPELS in the Bible 福音作者，圣史（写作《圣经》中四福音的人） ▸ **evan·gel·ism** *noun* [U] **evan·gel·ist·ic** /ɪˌvændʒəˈlɪstɪk/ *adj.*: *an evangelistic meeting* 布道会

evan·gel·ize (*BrE also* **-ise**) /ɪˈvændʒəlaɪz/ *verb* ~ **sb** to try to persuade people to become Christians 传播福音；使皈依基督教

E

evap·or·ate /ɪˈvæpəreɪt/ *verb* **1** [I, T] if a liquid **evaporates** or if sth **evaporates** it, it changes into a gas, especially steam （使）蒸发，挥发： *Heat until all the water has evaporated.* 加热直至水全部蒸发。 ◇ **~ sth** *The sun is constantly evaporating the earth's moisture.* 太阳使地球上的湿气不断蒸发。 ➲ WORDFINDER NOTE AT LIQUID **2** [I] to disappear, especially by gradually becoming less and less （逐渐）消失，消散，衰减： *Her confidence had now completely evaporated.* 她的信心已消失殆尽。 ▶ **evap·or·ation** /ɪˌvæpəˈreɪʃn/ *noun* [U]

eˌvaporated ˈmilk *noun* [U] thick sweet milk sold in cans, often served with fruit instead of cream （罐装）甜炼乳

eˈvaporating dish *noun* (*specialist*) a dish in which scientists heat a liquid, so that it leaves a solid when it has disappeared 蒸发皿 ➲ VISUAL VOCAB PAGE V72

eva·sion /ɪˈveɪʒn/ *noun* [C, U] **1** the act of avoiding sb or of avoiding sth that you are supposed to do 躲避；规避；逃避；回避： *His behaviour was an evasion of his responsibilities as a father.* 他的行为是逃避为父之责。 ◇ *She's been charged with* ***tax evasion***. 她被控逃税。 **2** a statement that sb makes that avoids dealing with sth or talking about sth honestly and directly 遁词；借口；托辞： *His speech was full of evasions and half-truths.* 他的发言尽是些遁词和真假参半的说法。 ➲ SEE ALSO EVADE

eva·sive /ɪˈveɪsɪv/ *adj.* not willing to give clear answers to a question 回避提问的；推托的；推诿的 SYN **cagey**: ***evasive answers/comments/replies*** 含糊其词的回答 / 意见 / 答复 ◇ *Tessa was evasive about why she had not been at home that night.* 特萨对她那天晚上不在家的原因避而不谈。 ▶ **eva·sive·ly** *adv.*： *'I'm not sure,' she replied evasively.* "我不敢确定。" 她躲躲闪闪地答道。 **eva·sive·ness** *noun* [U]

IDM **take evasive action** to act in order to avoid danger or an unpleasant situation 采取回避行动（以避免危险或不愉快的处境）

eve /iːv/ *noun* **1** the day or evening before an event, especially a religious festival or holiday （尤指宗教节假日的）前夜，前夕： *Christmas Eve* (= 24 December) 圣诞前夕（12 月 24 日）。◇ *a New Year's Eve party* (= on 31 December) 除夕晚会◇ ***on the eve of the election*** 在选举前夕 **2** (*old use* or *literary*) evening 傍晚；黄昏

even /ˈiːvn/ *adv., adj., verb*

■ *adv.* **1** used to emphasize sth unexpected or surprising （强调出乎意料）甚至，连，即使： *He never even opened the letter* (= so he certainly didn't read it). 他根本没打开过那封信。 ◇ *It was cold there even in summer* (= so it must have been very cold in winter). 那儿即使夏天也很冷。 ◇ *Even a child can understand it* (= so adults certainly can). 这就连小孩子也能理解。 ◇ *She didn't even call to say she wasn't coming.* 她甚至没打电话来说一声她不来了。 **2** used when you are comparing things, to make the comparison stronger （用以加强比较）甚至更，愈加，还： *You know even less about it than I do.* 你对此事的了解甚至还不如我。 ◇ *She's even more intelligent than her sister.* 她甚至比她姐姐还聪明。 **3** used to introduce a more exact description of sb/sth （引出更精确的说法）甚至可以说，其实，实际上： *It's an unattractive building, ugly even.* 这栋建筑毫不美观，甚至可以说难看。 ➲ NOTE AT ALTHOUGH

IDM **even as** (*formal*) just at the same time as sb does sth or as sth else happens 正当；恰好在…时候： *Even as he shouted the warning the car skidded.* 他正在高喊注意时，汽车就打滑了。 **even if/though** despite the fact or belief that; no matter whether 即使；纵然；虽然： *I'll get there, even if I have to walk.* 我就是走也要走到那儿去。 ◇ *I like her, even though she can be annoying at times.* 尽管她有时可能很烦人，我还是喜欢她。 ➲ NOTE AT ALTHOUGH **ˌeven ˈnow/ˈthen 1** despite what has/had happened 甚至到现在（或那时）；即便是这样（或那样）；尽管如此（或那样）： *I've shown him the photographs but even now he won't believe me.* 我把照片给他看了，即便是这样他仍然不相信我。 ◇ *Even then she would not admit her mistake.* 甚至到那时她还是不肯认错。 **2** (*formal*) at this or that exact moment 恰好在这时（或那时）： *The troops are even now preparing to march into the city.* 部队此刻正在准备向城里开进。 **ˌeven ˈso** despite that 尽管如此；即使那样： *There are a lot of spelling mistakes; even so, it's quite a good essay.* 尽管有许多拼写错误，它仍不失为一篇佳作。 ➲ MORE AT LESS *adv.*

■ *adj.*
- **SMOOTH/LEVEL** 平滑；平 **1** smooth, level and flat 平滑的；平的；平坦的： *You need an even surface to work on.* 你需要有个平面在上面工作。 OPP **uneven**
- **NOT CHANGING** 不变 **2** not changing very much in amount, speed, etc. （数量、速度等）变化不大的，均匀的，平稳的： *an even temperature all year* 常年温度变化不大 ◇ *Children do not learn at an even pace.* 孩子学东西有快有慢。 OPP **uneven**
- **EQUAL** 相等 **3** (of an amount of sth 数量) equal or the same for each person, team, place, etc. 相等的；均等的： *Our scores are now even.* 我们的比分现在相等。 ◇ *the even distribution of food* 食物的平均分配 OPP **uneven 4** (of two people or teams 两人或两队) equally balanced or of an equal standard 均衡的；不相上下的；同一水平的： *an even contest* 势均力敌的竞赛 ◇ *The two players were pretty even.* 这两个运动员不分上下。 OPP **uneven**
- **NUMBERS** 数目 **5** that can be divided exactly by two 双数的；偶数的： *4, 6, 8, 10 are all* ***even numbers***. * 4、6、8、10 都是偶数。 OPP **odd**
- **SAME SIZE** 大小相同 **6** equally spaced and the same size 匀称的；均匀的；同样大小的： *even features/teeth* 匀称的面容；整齐的牙齿 OPP **uneven**
- **CALM** 平静 **7** calm; not changing or becoming upset 镇静的；稳重的；平和的，温和的： *She has a very even temperament.* 她的性情非常平和。 ◇ *He spoke in a steady, even voice.* 当时他说话的声音平稳而镇静。

▶ **even·ness** /ˈiːvənnəs/ *noun* [U]

IDM **be ˈeven** (*informal*) to no longer owe sb money or a favour 了账；扯平；两清；两抵 **be/get ˈeven (with sb)** (*informal*) to cause sb the same amount of trouble or harm as they have caused you （向某人）报复；（跟某人）算账，扯平： *I'll get even with you for this, just you wait.* 这事我会找你算账的，等着瞧吧。 **break ˈeven** to complete a piece of business, etc. without either losing money or making a profit 收支平衡；不赔不赚： *The company just about broke even last year.* 这家公司去年接近收支平衡。 **have an even ˈchance (of doing sth)** to be equally likely to do or not do sth （做某事）有一半的机会；正反各半的可能性： *She has more than an even chance of winning tomorrow.* 她明天多半会赢。 **on an even ˈkeel** living, working or happening in a calm way, with no sudden changes, especially after a difficult time （生活、工作等经历困难后）平稳下来，顺顺当当 ➲ MORE AT HONOUR *n.*

■ *verb*

IDM **ˌeven the ˈscore** to harm or punish sb who has harmed or cheated you in the past 结清宿怨；摆平

PHR V **ˌeven ˈout** to become level or steady, usually after varying a lot （在多变之后）变平坦，稳定下来： *House prices keep rising and falling but they should eventually even out.* 房价一直时涨时落，但最终应该会趋于平稳。 **ˌeven sth↔ˈout** to spread things equally over a period of time or among a number of people 平均分配；平均分摊： *He tried to even out the distribution of work among his employees.* 他尽量把工作平均分配给雇员。 **ˌeven sth↔ˈup** to make a situation or a competition more equal 使拉平；使相等；使平衡

ˌeven-ˈhanded *adj.* completely fair, especially when dealing with different groups of people 不偏不倚的；公正的；公平的

even·ing /ˈiːvnɪŋ/ *noun* **1** [C, U] the part of the day between the afternoon and the time you go to bed 晚上；傍晚： *I'll see you tomorrow evening.* 我明天晚上来看你。 ◇ *Come over on Thursday evening.* 星期四晚上过来。 ◇ *What do you usually do* ***in the evening***? 你晚上通常干什么？ ◇ *She's going to her sister's* ***for the evening***. 她打算晚上到姐姐家去。 ◇ *the long winter evenings* 冬季漫长的夜晚

◇ *the evening performance* 晚上的演出 ➲ SEE ALSO GOOD EVENING **2** [C] an event of a particular type happening in the evening 晚会；晚间活动： *a musical evening at school* (= when music is performed) 学校的音乐晚会 ▸ **even·ings** *adv.* (*especially NAmE*)： *He works evenings.* 他晚上工作。 IDM SEE OTHER

ˈevening class *noun* a course of study for adults in the evening 夜校课程： *an evening class in car maintenance* 夜校的汽车维修课程 ◇ *to go to/attend evening classes* 上夜校

ˈevening dress *noun* **1** [U] elegant clothes worn for formal occasions in the evening 晚礼服： *Everyone was in evening dress.* 人人都身着晚礼服。 **2** [C] a woman's long formal dress 女装晚礼服

ˌevening ˈprimrose *noun* [C, U] a plant with yellow flowers that open in the evening, sometimes used as a medicine 月见草（晚间开黄花，有时作药用）

the ˌevening ˈstar *noun* [sing.] the planet Venus, when it is seen in the western sky after the sun has set 昏星（即太阳落山后出现于西方天空的金星）

even·ly /ˈiːvnli/ *adv.* **1** in a smooth, regular or equal way 平滑地；有规律地；均匀地；相等地： *Make sure the paint covers the surface evenly.* 要确保油漆均匀地涂在表面上。◇ *She was fast asleep, breathing evenly.* 她睡熟了，呼吸很平稳。◇ ***evenly spaced** at four cm apart* 以四厘米的间隔均匀分布 **2** with equal amounts for each person or in each place 平均地；均等地： ***evenly distributed/divided*** 平均分配 / 分开 ◇ *Incidence of the disease is fairly **evenly spread** across Europe.* 这种疾病的发生率在欧洲各地相当平均。◇ *The two teams are very **evenly matched*** (= are equally likely to win). 这两个队势均力敌。 **3** calmly; without showing any emotion 平静地；镇静地；平和地： *'I warned you not to phone me,' he said evenly.* “我告诫过你不要给我打电话。”他平静地说。

ˌeven ˈmoney *noun* (*BrE also* **evens** [pl.]) (in betting 赌博) ODDS that give an equal chance of winning or losing and that mean a person has the chance of winning the same amount of money that he or she has bet 同额赌注；均等的输赢机会

even·song /ˈiːvnsɒŋ; *NAmE* -sɔːŋ; -sɑːŋ/ *noun* [U] the service of evening prayer in the Anglican Church（圣公会的）晚祷 ➲ COMPARE MATINS, VESPERS

event 🔑 /ɪˈvent/ *noun* **1** 🔑 a thing that happens, especially sth important 发生的事情；（尤指）重要事情，大事： *The election was the main event of 2008.* 那次选举是 2008 年的重大事件。◇ *In the light of later events the decision was proved right.* 从后来发生的事看，这一决定证明是正确的。◇ *The decisions we take now may influence **the course of events*** (= the way things happen) *in the future.* 我们现在作出的决定可能会对未来事情的发展产生影响。◇ *Everyone was frightened by the strange **sequence of events**.* 人人都因接二连三发生的怪事感到惊恐。◇ ***In the normal course of events*** (= if things had happened as expected) *she would have gone with him.* 要是事情发展顺利的话，她已同他一块儿走了。 **2** 🔑 a planned public or social occasion 公开活动；社交场合： *a fund-raising event* 筹款活动 ◇ *the social event of the year* 本年度最重要的社交活动 **3** one of the races or competitions in a sports programme （体育运动的）比赛项目： *The 800 metres is the fourth event of the afternoon.* * 800 米赛是下午的第四项比赛。 ➲ SEE ALSO FIELD EVENT, TRACK EVENT

IDM **after the eˈvent** (*BrE*) after sth has happened 事情发生后；事后： *Anyone can be wise after the event.* 事后聪明谁都会。 **in ˈany event | at ˈall events** used to emphasize or show that sth is true or will happen in spite of other circumstances 不管怎样；无论如何 SYN **in any case**： *I think she'll agree to do it but in any event, all she can say is 'no'.* 我想她会同意做的，但无论怎样，她只能说“不”。 **in the eˈvent** when the situation actually happened 结果；到头来： *I got very nervous about the exam, but in the event, I needn't have worried; it was really easy.* 我对考试提心吊胆，但其实我本不必担心，这次考试的确很容易。 **in the event of sth | in the event that sth happens** 🔑 if sth happens 如果…发生；万一；倘若： *In the event of an accident, call this number.* 万一发生事故就拨这个号码。◇ *Sheila will inherit everything in the event of his death.* 他一旦故去，所有财产都由希拉继承。 **in ˈthat event** if that happens 如果是那样的话；如果那种事情发生： *In that event, we will have to reconsider our offer.* 如果是那样的话，我们就得重新考虑我们的建议。 ➲ MORE AT HAPPY, WISE *adj.*

ˌeven-ˈtempered *adj.* not easily made angry or upset 性情平和的

event·ful /ɪˈventfl/ *adj.* full of things that happen, especially exciting, important or dangerous things 充满大事的；多事故的；多变故的： *an eventful day/life/journey* 不平凡的一天；多姿多彩的一生 / 旅程

even·tide /ˈiːvntaɪd/ *noun* [U] (*old use* or *literary*) evening 黄昏；薄暮

event·ing /ɪˈventɪŋ/ (*also* **ˌthree-day eˈventing**) *noun* [U] the sport of taking part in competitions riding horses. These are often held over three days and include riding across country, jumping and DRESSAGE. 马术三项赛，马术三日赛（包括越野赛、障碍赛和盛装舞步）

even·tual AW /ɪˈventʃuəl/ *adj.* [only before noun] happening at the end of a period of time or of a process 最后的；最终的；结果的： *the eventual winner of the tournament* 锦标赛的最终胜利者 ◇ *It is impossible to predict what the eventual outcome will be.* 无法预测最终结果会怎么样。◇ *The village school may face eventual closure.* 这所乡村学校可能面临最后被关闭。 ➲ MORE LIKE THIS 32, page R28

even·tu·al·ity AW /ɪˌventʃuˈæləti/ *noun* (*pl.* **-ies**) (*formal*) something that may possibly happen, especially sth unpleasant （尤指令人不快的）可能发生的事情，可能出现的结果： *We were prepared for **every eventuality**.* 我们已做好准备应付任何可能出现的情况。◇ *The money had been saved **for just such an eventuality**.* 钱积攒下来就是为应付这样的意外。

even·tu·al·ly 🔑 AW /ɪˈventʃuəli/ *adv.* at the end of a period of time or a series of events 最后；终于： *Our flight eventually left five hours late.* 我们的班机最终晚了五个小时起飞。◇ *I'll get round to mending it eventually.* 我最后会抽出时间来修理它的。◇ *She hopes to get a job on the local newspaper and eventually work for 'The Times'.* 她希望先在当地报社找一份工作，而最终到《泰晤士报》工作。 HELP Use **finally** for the last in a list of things. 列举事物中的最后一项用 finally。

even·tu·ate /ɪˈventʃueɪt/ *verb* [I] (*formal*) to happen as a result of sth 导致；最终造成

ever 🔑 /ˈevə(r)/ *adv.* **1** 🔑 used in negative sentences and questions, or sentences with *if* to mean 'at any time' （用于否定句和疑问句，或与 if 连用的句子）在任何时候，从来： *Nothing ever happens here.* 这儿从未发生过任何事。◇ *Don't you ever get tired?* 难道你从来不累吗？ ◇ *If you're ever in Miami, come and see us.* 你要是什么时候到了迈阿密，就来看看我们吧。 ◇ *'Have you ever thought of changing your job?' 'No, never/No I haven't.'* “你想过换一下工作吗？”“没有，从未想过。”◇ *'Have you ever been to Rome?' 'Yes, I have, actually. Not long ago.'* “你去过罗马吗？”“是的，我确实去过，就在不久前。”◇ *She **hardly ever*** (= almost never) *goes out.* 她几乎从不出门。 ◇ *We see them very seldom, **if ever**.* 我们难得见到他们。 ◇ (*informal*) *I'll **never ever** do that again!* 我再也不会干那种事了！ **2** 🔑 used for emphasis when you are comparing things （进行比较时用以加强语气）以往任何时候，曾经： *It was raining harder than ever.* 当时下着前所未有的大雨。◇ *It's my **best ever** score.* 这是我得到过的最好分数。 **3** (*rather formal*) all the time or every time; always 不断地；总是；始终： *Paul, ever the optimist, agreed to try again.* 保罗这个永远的乐观主义者答应再试一次。 ◇ *She married the prince and they **lived happily ever after**.* 她与王子成了婚，从此过着幸福的生活。◇ *He said he would love her **for ever*** (***and ever***). 他说会永远爱她。 ◇ *Their debts grew ever* larger (= kept increasing). 他们的债务不断增加。◇ *the ever-growing problem* 日趋严重的问题 ◇ *an ever-present danger* 始终存在的危险 **4** used after *when*, *why*, etc. to show that you are surprised or shocked（用于 when、why 等之后表示惊讶）究竟，到底：*Why ever did you agree?* 你究竟为什么要同意？

IDM **all sb ever does is**... used to emphasize that sb does the same thing very often, usually in an annoying way 某人只会 / 就知道做某事：*All he ever does is grumble about things.* 他只会抱怨。 **did you 'ever (...)!** (*old-fashioned, informal*) used to show that you are surprised or shocked（表示惊讶）你曾…过吗：*Did you ever hear anything like it?* 你听到过这种事吗？ **ever since (...)** continuously since the time mentioned 自从；自…以后；从…起：*He's had a car ever since he was 18.* 他从 18 岁起就有汽车了。◇ *I was bitten by a dog once and I've been afraid of them ever since.* 我曾被狗咬过，自那以后就一直害怕狗。 **'ever so/'ever such a** (*informal, especially BrE*) very; really 非常；很；确实；的确：*He looks ever so smart.* 他样子很帅。◇ *She's ever such a nice woman.* 她是个非常好的女人。◇ *It's ever so easy.* 这非常容易。 **if ˌever there 'was (one)** (*informal*) used to emphasize that sth is certainly true（用以加强语气）确实，无可置疑，真正地：*That was a disaster if ever there was one!* 那确实是场灾难！ **was/is/does, etc. sb 'ever!** (*informal, especially NAmE*) used to emphasize sth you are talking about 确实如此；千真万确；一点儿不差：*'You must have been upset by that.' 'Was I ever!'* "你一定曾为那事而心烦了。" "可不是嘛！" **yours 'ever/ever 'yours** sometimes used at the end of an informal letter, before you write your name（有时用于非正式书信末尾署名前）你的永远的朋友

ever·green /ˈevəgriːn; *NAmE* ˈevərg-/ *noun* a tree or bush that has green leaves all through the year 常青树；常绿树 ➲ VISUAL VOCAB PAGE V10 ➲ COMPARE CONIFER, DECIDUOUS ▶ **ever·green** *adj.*：*evergreen shrubs* 常青灌木 ◇ (*figurative*) *a new production of Rossini's evergreen* (= always popular) *opera* 经久不衰的罗西尼歌剧的重新制作

ever·last·ing /ˌevəˈlɑːstɪŋ; *NAmE* ˌevərˈlæstɪŋ/ *adj.* **1** continuing for ever; never changing 永久的；永恒的；经久不变的 SYN **eternal**：*everlasting life/love* 永生；永恒的爱 ◇ *an everlasting memory of her smile* 她的微笑留下的永久回忆 ◇ ***To his everlasting credit**, he never told anyone what I'd done.* 值得永远称赞的是他从未把我做的事告诉过任何人。 **2** (*disapproving*) continuing too long; repeated too often 冗长的；持续过长的；重复太多的 SYN **constant, interminable, never-ending**：*I'm tired of your everlasting complaints.* 我讨厌你没完没了的抱怨。 ▶ **ever·last·ing·ly** *adv.*

ever·more /ˌevəˈmɔː(r); *NAmE* ˌevərˈm-/ (*also* **for ever'more**) *adv.* (*literary*) always 始终；永远

every /ˈevri/ *det.* **1** used with singular nouns to refer to all the members of a group of things or people（与单数名词连用，指整体中的）每一个，每个：*She knows every student in the school.* 她认识学校里的每一个学生。◇ *I could hear every word they said.* 他们说的每句话我都能听见。◇ *We enjoyed every minute of our stay.* 我们逗留期间每一分钟都过得很愉快。◇ *Every day seemed the same to him.* 对他来说似乎天天都一样。◇ ***Every single** time he calls, I'm out.* 他每次打电话来我都不在家。◇ *I read **every last** article in the newspaper* (= all of them). 报纸上的每一篇文章我都读。◇ *They were watching her every movement.* 他们注视着她的每一个动作。◇ *Every one of their CDs has been a hit.* 他们的每一张激光唱片都曾经非常流行。 ➲ NOTE AT EACH **2** all possible 所有可能的；完全可能的：*We wish you every success.* 我们祝你万事如意。◇ *He had every reason to be angry.* 他完全有理由感到愤怒。 **3** used to say how often sth happens or is done（表示发生的频率）每，每逢，每隔：*The buses go every 10 minutes.* 公共汽车每隔 10 分钟发一班车。◇ *We had to stop every few miles.* 我们每走几英里就得停一停。◇ *One in every three marriages ends in divorce.* 三分之一的婚姻都以离婚告终。◇ *He has every third day off* (= he works for two days, then has one day off, then works for two days and so on). 他每隔两天休息一天。◇ *We see each other **every now and again**.* 我们偶尔相见。◇ ***Every now and then** he regretted his decision.* 他有时为自己的决定后悔。

IDM **every other** each ALTERNATE one (= the first, third, fifth, etc. one, but not the second, fourth, sixth, etc.) 每隔一个：*They visit us every other week.* 他们隔周来看我们一次。

every·body /ˈevribɒdi; *NAmE* -bɑːdi; -bʌdi/ *pron.* = EVERYONE：*Everybody knows Tom.* 人人都认识汤姆。◇ *Have you asked everybody?* 你每个人都问了吗？◇ *Didn't you like it? **Everybody else** did.* 你不喜欢吗？其他所有人都喜欢。

every·day /ˈevrideɪ/ *adj.* [only before noun] used or happening every day or regularly; ordinary 每天的；每日发生的；日常的：*everyday objects* 日常物品 ◇ *The Internet has become part of **everyday life**.* 互联网已成为日常生活的一部分。◇ *a small dictionary for everyday use* 常用小词典

Every·man /ˈevrimæn/ *noun* [sing.] an ordinary or typical person 普通人；常人：*a story of Everyman* 寻常百姓的故事

every·one /ˈevriwʌn/ (*also* **every·body**) *pron.* every person; all people 每人；人人；所有人：*Everyone cheered and clapped.* 人人都鼓掌欢呼。◇ *Everyone has a chance to win.* 每个人都有机会赢。◇ *Everyone brought their partner to the party.* 所有人都携伴参加聚会。◇ (*formal*) *Everyone brought his or her partner to the party.* 每个人都携伴参加聚会。◇ *The police questioned everyone in the room.* 警方盘问了房间里的每一个人。◇ *The teacher commented on everyone's work.* 老师对每个人的作业都给了评语。◇ ***Everyone else** was there.* 其他所有人都在那儿。

every·place /ˈevripleɪs/ *adv.* (*NAmE*) = EVERYWHERE

every·thing /ˈevriθɪŋ/ *pron.* (with a singular verb 与单数动词连用) **1** all things 每件事；所有事物；一切：*Everything had gone.* 一切都过去了。◇ *When we confronted him, he denied everything.* 我们与他当面对质时，他什么都不承认。◇ *Take this bag, and leave **everything else** to me.* 把这个包拿走，其他所有东西都给我留下。◇ *She seemed to **have everything**—looks, money, intelligence.* 她似乎什么都有了 —— 美貌、金钱和智慧。 **2** the situation now; life generally 形势；情况；生活：*Everything in the capital is now quiet.* 目前首都的形势很平静。◇ *'How's everything with you?' 'Fine, thanks.'* "你一切都好吗？" "很好，谢谢。" **3** the most important thing 最重要的东西；最要紧的事情：*Money isn't everything.* 金钱不是最重要的。◇ *My family **means everything** to me.* 对我来说家庭意味着一切。

IDM **and everything** (*informal*) and so on; and other similar things 以及其他；等等：*Have you got his name and address and everything?* 你知道他的名字、地址及其他情况吗？◇ *She told me about the baby and everything.* 她向我讲了小宝宝和其他的情况。

every·where /ˈevriweə(r); *NAmE* -wer/ (*NAmE also* **every·place**) *adv., pron., conj.* in, to or at every place; all places 处处；到处；各个地方；所有地方：*I've looked everywhere.* 我各处都看过了。◇ *He follows me everywhere.* 我无论去哪儿他都跟着我。◇ *We'll have to eat here—**everywhere else** is full.* 我们只好在这儿吃饭了，其他地方都客满。◇ *Everywhere we went was full of tourists.* 我们所到之处游客人头攒动。

'eve-teasing *noun* [U] (*IndE*) physical contact, comments about sex, etc. by a man to a woman in a public place, that the woman finds annoying and offensive（男性在公共场所对女性）性骚扰，性挑逗 ➲ COMPARE SEXUAL HARASSMENT ▶ **'eve-teaser** *noun*

evict /ɪˈvɪkt/ *verb* ~ **sb (from sth)** to force sb to leave a house or land, especially when you have the legal right to do so（尤指依法从房屋或土地上）驱逐，赶出，逐出：*A number of tenants have been evicted for not paying the rent.* 一些房客因没付房租被赶了出来。 ▶ **evic·tion** /ɪˈvɪkʃn/ *noun* [U, C]：*to face eviction from your home* 面临着被赶出家门

evi·dence 🔑 AW /ˈevɪdəns/ *noun, verb*

■ ***noun*** **1** 🔑 [U] the facts, signs or objects that make you believe that sth is true 根据；证明；证据： **~ (of sth)** *There is convincing evidence of a link between exposure to sun and skin cancer.* 有可靠证据表明日光暴晒与皮肤癌之间有联系。◇ *The room bore evidence of a struggle.* 房间里有搏斗过的痕迹。◇ **~ (for sth)** *We found further scientific evidence for this theory.* 我们找到了进一步证实这种理论的科学根据。◇ **~ (that…)** *There is* ***not a shred of evidence*** *that the meeting actually took place.* 没有丝毫证据表明确实有过这次会面。◇ **~ (to suggest, show, etc.)** *Have you any evidence to support this allegation?* 你有证据支持这种说法吗？ ◇ ***On the evidence of*** *their recent matches, it is unlikely the Spanish team will win the cup.* 从西班牙队最近的比赛情况看，他们不太可能夺冠。 ➲ WORDFINDER NOTE AT SCIENCE **2** 🔑 [U] the information that is used in court to try to prove sth （法庭上的）证据，证词，人证，物证： *I was asked to* ***give evidence*** (= to say what I knew, describe what I had seen, etc.) *at the trial.* 我被要求审讯时出庭作证。◇ *He was released when the judge ruled there was no evidence against him.* 法官裁决没有证明他有罪的证据，他获得释放了。 ➲ WORDFINDER NOTE AT TRIAL ➲ COLLOCATIONS AT JUSTICE ➲ SEE ALSO CIRCUMSTANTIAL

IDM **(be) in ˈevidence** present and clearly seen 显眼；显而易见： *The police were much in evidence at today's demonstration.* 在今天的示威集会上警察随处可见。 **turn King's/Queen's ˈevidence** (*BrE*) (*US* **turn state's ˈevidence**) to give information against other criminals in order to get a less severe punishment 提供同犯的罪证，揭发其他案犯（以减轻所受惩罚） ➲ COMPARE PLEA BARGAINING ➲ MORE AT BALANCE *n.*

■ ***verb*** [usually passive] **~ sth** (*formal*) to prove or show sth; to be evidence of sth 证明；表明；作为…的证据 SYN **testify to**: *The legal profession is still a largely male world,* ***as evidenced by*** *the small number of women judges.* 法律界在很大程度上仍然是男人的世界，这一点从女法官的人数屈指可数即可得到证实。

▼ **LANGUAGE BANK 用语库**

evidence

Giving proof 提供证据

- ***There is clear evidence that*** *TV advertising influences what children buy.* 有明确的证据表明电视广告影响儿童的购买行为。
- ***It is clear*** *from numerous studies* ***that*** *TV advertising influences what children buy.* 众多研究清楚地表明电视广告影响儿童的购买行为。
- *Recent research* ***demonstrates*** *that TV advertising influences children's spending habits.* 最近的研究表明电视广告影响儿童的消费习惯。
- *Many parents think that TV advertising influences their children. This view* ***is supported by*** *the findings of a recent study, which* ***show*** *a clear link between television advertisements and children's spending habits.* 许多家长认为电视广告对他们的孩子会产生影响。这一观点得到近期研究结果的支持，即电视广告和儿童消费习惯之间有明显的关联。
- *The findings also* ***reveal*** *that most children are unaware of the persuasive purpose of advertising.* 这些研究结果还显示大多数儿童没有意识到广告的说服意图。
- ***There is little evidence that*** *children understand the persuasive intent of advertising.* 几乎没有证据表明儿童能够理解广告的说服意图。
- *The results* ***contradict*** *claims that advertising is unrelated to children's spending habits.* 这些研究结果否定了广告与儿童消费习惯无关的说法。
- *Manufacturers argue that it is difficult to* ***prove*** *that advertising alone influences what children buy.* 生产厂商争辩说，很难证明单凭广告就能影响儿童的购买行为。

➲ LANGUAGE BANK AT ARGUE, E.G., ILLUSTRATE

evi·dent AW /ˈevɪdənt/ *adj.* clear; easily seen 清楚的；显而易见的；显然的 SYN **obvious**: *The orchestra played with evident enjoyment.* 管弦乐队演奏得兴致勃勃。◇ **~ (to sb) (that…)** *It has now become evident to us that a mistake has been made.* 我们现已清楚知道出了差错。◇ **~ in/from sth** *The growing interest in history is clearly evident in the number of people visiting museums and country houses.* 从参观博物馆和乡村住宅的人数明显看出人们对历史越来越感兴趣。 ➲ SYNONYMS AT CLEAR ➲ SEE ALSO SELF-EVIDENT

evi·den·tial AW /ˌevɪˈdenʃl/ *adj.* [usually before noun] (*formal*) providing or connected with evidence 提供证据的；作证的： *The necessary evidential basis for her claim is lacking.* 她的诉求缺乏必要的基本凭据。

evi·dent·ly AW /ˈevɪdəntli/ *adv.* **1** clearly; that can be seen or understood easily 明显地；显然地 SYN **obviously**: *She walked slowly down the road, evidently in pain.* 她沿路慢慢地走着，显然很痛苦。◇ *'I'm afraid I couldn't finish the work last night.' 'Evidently not.'* "对不起，昨天晚上我没能完成工作。" "显然完不成。" **2** according to what people say 据说 SYN **apparently**: *Evidently, she had nothing to do with the whole affair.* 据说，她与整件事情毫无关系。

evil 🔑 /ˈiːvl; ˈiːvɪl/ *adj., noun*

■ ***adj.*** **1** 🔑 (of people 人) enjoying harming others; morally bad and cruel 恶毒的；邪恶的： *an evil man* 恶棍 ◇ *an evil grin* 狞笑 **2** 🔑 having a harmful effect on people; morally bad 有害的；道德败坏的： *evil deeds* 恶行 ◇ *the evil effects of racism* 种族主义的恶劣影响 **3** 🔑 connected with the DEVIL and with what is bad in the world 恶魔的；罪恶的： *evil spirits* 邪灵 **4** extremely unpleasant 讨厌的；令人作呕的；使人不舒服的： *an evil smell* 难闻的气味

IDM **the evil ˈhour/ˈday/ˈmoment** (*often humorous*) the time when you have to do sth difficult or unpleasant 倒霉的时候（或日子、时刻） ➲ MORE AT BREW *n.*, GENIUS

■ ***noun*** (*formal*) **1** 🔑 [U] a force that causes bad things to happen; morally bad behaviour 邪恶；罪恶；恶行： *the eternal struggle between good and evil* 善与恶永不休止的斗争 ◇ *the forces of evil* 邪恶势力 ◇ *You cannot pretend there's no evil in the world.* 你不能睁着眼睛瞎说世界上没有罪恶。 OPP **good** **2** 🔑 [C, usually pl.] a bad or harmful thing; the bad effect of sth 害处；坏处；弊端： ***the evils of drugs/alcohol*** 毒品 / 酒的害处 ◇ *social evils* 社会弊端 IDM SEE LESSER, NECESSARY

ˈevil-doer *noun* (*formal*) a person who does very bad things 作恶的人；坏人

the ˌevil ˈeye *noun* [sing.] the magic power to harm sb by looking at them 恶毒的眼光，恶目（传说能伤人）

evil·ly /ˈiːvəli/ *adv.* in a morally bad or very unpleasant way 邪恶地；阴险地： *to grin evilly* 狞笑 ◇ *to look evilly at sb* 邪恶地看着某人

evince /ɪˈvɪns/ *verb* **~ sth** (*formal*) to show clearly that you have a feeling or quality 表明，表现，显示（感情或品质）： *He evinced a strong desire to be reconciled with his family.* 他表现出与家人和好的强烈愿望。

evis·cer·ate /ɪˈvɪsəreɪt/ *verb* **~ sth** (*formal*) to remove the inner organs of a body 切除内脏；切除…的内部器官 SYN **disembowel**

evoca·tive /ɪˈvɒkətɪv; *NAmE* ɪˈvɑːk-/ *adj.* making you think of or remember a strong image or feeling, in a pleasant way 引起记忆的；唤起感情的： ***evocative smells/sounds/music*** 引起回忆的气味 / 声音 / 音乐 ◇ **~ of sth** *Her new book is wonderfully evocative of village life.* 她的新书唤起人们对乡村生活的美好感情。 ▶ **evoca·tive·ly** *adv.*

evoke /ɪˈvəʊk; *NAmE* ɪˈvoʊk/ *verb* **~ sth** (*formal*) to bring a feeling, a memory or an image into your mind 引起，唤起（感情、记忆或形象）： *The music* ***evoked*** *memories of her youth.* 这乐曲勾起了她对青年时代的回忆。◇ *His case is unlikely to evoke public sympathy.* 他的情况不大可能引起公众的同情。 ▶ **evo·ca·tion** /ˌiːvəʊˈkeɪʃn; *NAmE* ˌiːvoʊ-/ *noun* [C, U]: *a brilliant evocation of childhood in the 1940s* 唤起对 20 世纪 40 年代童年生活的美好回忆

E

evo·lu·tion AW /ˌiːvəˈluːʃn; ˌev-/ *noun* [U] **1** (*biology* 生) the gradual development of plants, animals, etc. over many years as they adapt to changes in their environment 进化: *the evolution of the human species* 人类的进化 ◇ *Darwin's theory of evolution* 达尔文的进化论 **2** the gradual development of sth 演变；发展；渐进: *In politics Britain has preferred evolution to revolution* (= gradual development to sudden violent change). 英国在政治上宁愿渐进而不愿革命。

evo·lu·tion·ary AW /ˌiːvəˈluːʃənri; ˌev-; *NAmE* -neri/ *adj.* connected with evolution; connected with gradual development and change 进化的；演变的；逐渐发展的: *evolutionary theory* 进化论 ◇ *evolutionary change* 逐渐演变 ▶ **evo·lu·tion·ar·ily** *adv.*

evo·lu·tion·ist AW /ˌiːvəˈluːʃnɪst; ˌev-/ *noun, adj.*
■ *noun* a person who believes in the theories of EVOLUTION and NATURAL SELECTION 进化论者
■ *adj.* relating to the theories of EVOLUTION and NATURAL SELECTION 进化论的 ▶ **evo·lu·tion·ism** /ˌiːvəˈluːʃnɪzəm; ˌev-/ *noun* [U]

evolve AW /iˈvɒlv; *NAmE* iˈvɑːlv/ *verb* **1** [I, T] to develop gradually, especially from a simple to a more complicated form; to develop sth in this way （使）逐渐形成，逐步发展，逐渐演变: ~ **(from sth) (into sth)** *The idea evolved from a drawing I discovered in the attic.* 这种想法是从我在阁楼里发现的一幅画得到启发的。◇ *The company has evolved into a major chemical manufacturer.* 这家公司已逐步发展成一家大型的化工厂。◇ ~ **sth (from sth)** *Each school must evolve its own way of working.* 每所学校必须发展出自己的办学方式。 **2** [I, T] (*biology* 生) (of plants, animals, etc. 动植物等) to develop over time, often many generations, into forms that are better adapted to survive changes in their environment 进化；演化: ~ **(from sth)** *The three species evolved from a single ancestor.* 这三种生物从同一祖先进化而来。◇ ~ **sth** *The dolphin has evolved a highly developed jaw.* 海豚已经进化出高度发达的下颌。

ewe /juː/ *noun* a female sheep 母羊；雌羊；牝羊 ➲ COMPARE RAM *n.* (1)

ewer /ˈjuːə(r)/ *noun* a large JUG used in the past for carrying water （旧时提水用的）大口水壶，大口水罐

eww (*also* **ew**) /ˈiːuː/ *exclamation* the way of writing the sound /ˈiːuː/ that people make when they think that sth is disgusting or unpleasant 唷，呃，咦呀（书写形式，表示恶心或厌恶时发出的声音）: *Eww! There's a fly in my lemonade!* 呃！我的柠檬水里有只苍蝇！ ➲ MORE LIKE THIS 2, page R25

ex /eks/ *noun, prep.*
■ *noun* (*pl.* **exes**) (*informal*) a person's former wife, husband or partner 前妻；前夫；以前的性伴侣: *The children are spending the weekend with my ex and his new wife.* 孩子们与我的前夫及其新夫人在一起度周末。
■ *prep.* (*BrE*) not including sth 不包括；除…之外: *The price is £1 500 ex VAT.* 价格为 1 500 英镑，不含增值税。

ex- 🔑 /eks/ *prefix* (in nouns 构成名词) former 前任: *ex-wife* 前妻 ◇ *ex-president* 前总裁 ➲ MORE LIKE THIS 6, page R25

ex·acer·bate /ɪɡˈzæsəbeɪt; *NAmE* ɪɡˈzæsərb-/ *verb* ~ **sth** (*formal*) to make sth worse, especially a disease or problem 使恶化；使加剧；使加重 SYN **aggravate**: *The symptoms may be exacerbated by certain drugs.* 这些症状可能会因为某些药物而加重。 ▶ **ex·acer·ba·tion** *noun* [U, C]

exact 🔑 /ɪɡˈzækt/ *adj., verb*
■ *adj.* **1** 🔑 correct in every detail 精确的；准确的 SYN **precise**: *She gave an exact description of the attacker.* 她对袭击者的特征作了精确的描述。◇ *an exact copy/replica of the painting* 那幅画的精确复制品 ◇ *We need to know the exact time the incident occurred.* 我们需要了解事情发生的确切时间。◇ *What were his exact words?* 他的原话是什么？◇ *She's in her mid-thirties—thirty-six* ***to be exact.*** 她三十五岁左右，确切地说是三十六岁。◇ *The colours were an exact match.* 颜色极为协调。◇ *He started to phone me at the exact moment I started to phone him* (= at the same time). 他给我拨电话时，我也正好在给他拨电话。◇ *Her second husband was* ***the exact opposite*** *of her first* (= completely different). 她的第二任丈夫与第一任截然不同。 **2** 🔑 (of people 人) very accurate and careful about details 严谨的；严格的；一丝不苟的 SYN **meticulous, precise** **3** (of a science 科学) using accurate measurements and following set rules 精密的；严密的 SYN **precise**: *Assessing insurance risk can never be an exact science.* 估定承保的风险永远不会成为一门精确的科学。 ▶ **exact·ness** *noun* [U]
■ *verb* (*formal*) **1** ~ **sth (from sb)** to demand and get sth from sb 要求；索取: *She was determined to exact a promise from him.* 她决意要他作出许诺。 **2** to make sth bad happen to sb 迫使；强迫；强求: ~ **sth** *He exacted* (= took) *a terrible revenge for their treatment of him.* 他因受他们的虐待而痛加报复。◇ ~ **sth from sb** *Stress can exact a high price from workers* (= can affect them badly). 压力可能迫使工人付出昂贵的代价。 ▶ **exac·tion** /ɪɡˈzækʃn/ *noun* [C, U] (*formal*)

exact·ing /ɪɡˈzæktɪŋ/ *adj.* needing or demanding a lot of effort and care about details 严谨细致的；要求小心仔细的；要求严格的 SYN **demanding**: *exacting work* 艰巨的工作 ◇ *products designed to meet the exacting standards of today's marketplace* 为符合当今市场严格的标准而设计的产品 ◇ *He was an exacting man to work for.* 他对手下的人要求极为严格。

exac·ti·tude /ɪɡˈzæktɪtjuːd; *NAmE* -tuːd/ *noun* [U] (*formal*) the quality of being very accurate and exact 精确性；准确性；严密性

exact·ly 🔑 /ɪɡˈzæktli/ *adv.* **1** 🔑 used to emphasize that sth is correct in every way or in every detail 精确地；准确地；确切地 SYN **precisely**: *I know exactly how she felt.* 我完全清楚她的感受。◇ *Do exactly as I tell you.* 严格按照我说的办。◇ *It happened almost exactly a year ago.* 这事情发生差不多正好一年了。◇ *It's exactly nine o'clock.* 现在是九点整。◇ *You haven't changed at all—you still look* ***exactly the same.*** 你一点没变，看上去依然是老样子。◇ *His words had* ***exactly the opposite*** *effect.* 他的话产生了截然相反的效果。◇ *Your answer is exactly right.* 你的回答完全正确。◇ *It was a warm day, if not exactly hot.* 这一天即使算不上热，也是一个暖和的日子。 **2** 🔑 (*informal*) used to ask for more information about sth （要求得到更多信息）究竟，到底: *Where exactly did you stay in France?* 你究竟待在法国什么地方？◇ (*disapproving*) *Exactly what are you trying to tell me?* 你到底想对我说什么？ **3** 🔑 used as a reply, agreeing with what sb has just said, or emphasizing that it is correct （答语，表示赞同或强调正确）一点不错，正是如此，完全正确: *'You mean somebody in this room must be the murderer?' 'Exactly.'* "你的意思是这屋子里肯定有人是凶手？""正是。"
IDM **not exactly** (*informal*) **1** 🔑 used when you are saying the opposite of what you really mean （说反话时用）根本不，决不，一点也不: *He wasn't exactly pleased to see us—in fact he refused to open the door.* 他根本不愿见我们，事实上他连门都不开。◇ *It's not exactly beautiful, is it?* (= it's ugly) 这一点也不美，是吗？ **2** 🔑 used when you are correcting sth that sb has said （纠正对方刚说过的话）不完全: *'So he told you you'd got the job?' 'Not exactly, but he said they were impressed with me.'* "如此看来，他对你说你得到这份工作了？""不完全是这样，不过他说我给他们留下了深刻的印象。"

ex·ag·ger·ate 🔑 /ɪɡˈzædʒəreɪt/ *verb* [I, T] to make sth seem larger, better, worse or more important than it really is 夸张；夸大；言过其实: *The hotel was really filthy and I'm not exaggerating.* 我不是夸张，这旅店真的很脏。◇ ~ **sth** *He tends to exaggerate the difficulties.* 他往往夸大困难。◇ *I'm sure he exaggerates his Irish accent* (= tries to sound more Irish than he really is). 我肯定他故意把爱尔兰口音说得很重。◇ *Demand for the product has been greatly exaggerated.* 对这项产品的需求给过分夸大了。

ex·ag·ger·ated /ɪɡ'zædʒəreɪtɪd/ *adj.* **1** made to seem larger, better, worse or more important than it really is or needs to be 夸张的；夸大的；言过其实的： *to make **greatly/grossly/wildly exaggerated** claims* 提出极为过分的索偿 ◇ *She has an exaggerated sense of her own importance.* 她自视过高。 **2** (of an action 行为) done in a way that makes people notice it 故作姿态的；矫揉造作的： *He looked at me with exaggerated surprise.* 他故作吃惊地看着我。 ▶ **ex·ag·ger·ated·ly** *adv.*

ex·ag·ger·ation /ɪɡˌzædʒə'reɪʃn/ *noun* [C, usually sing., U] a statement or description that makes sth seem larger, better, worse or more important than it really is; the act of making a statement like this 夸张；夸大；言过其实： *a **slight/gross/wild exaggeration*** 有点 / 明显的 / 过于夸张 ◇ *It would be an exaggeration to say I knew her well—I only met her twice.* 说我非常了解她不免言过其实，我只见过她两次。 ◇ *It's no exaggeration to say that most students have never read a complete Shakespeare play.* 说大多数同学从未读过一部完整的莎士比亚戏剧一点也不夸张。 ◇ *He told his story simply and without exaggeration.* 他简单扼要、毫不夸张地讲述了自己的故事。

exalt /ɪɡ'zɔːlt/ *verb* (*formal*) **1 ~ sb (to sth)** to make sb rise to a higher rank or position, sometimes to one that they do not deserve 提拔，提升（有时指不该得到的职位） **2 ~ sb/sth** to praise sb/sth very much 表扬；褒扬；高度赞扬

exalt·ation /ˌeɡzɔːl'teɪʃn/ *noun* [U] (*formal*) **1** a feeling of very great joy or happiness 兴奋；兴高采烈 **2** an act of raising sth/sb to a high position or rank 提高；晋升；提拔： *the exaltation of emotion above logical reasoning* 把情感提高到逻辑推理之上

exalt·ed /ɪɡ'zɔːltɪd/ *adj.* **1** (*formal* or *humorous*) of high rank, position or great importance 地位高的；高贵的；显赫的： *She was the only woman to rise to such an exalted position.* 她是唯一升到如此显赫位置的女人。 ◇ *You're moving in very exalted circles!* 你这是出入于显贵要人的圈子呀！ **2** (*formal*) full of great joy and happiness 兴奋的；兴高采烈的： *I felt exalted and newly alive.* 我感到兴高采烈，充满新的活力。

exam /ɪɡ'zæm/ (*also formal* **exam·in·ation**) *noun* **1** a formal written, spoken or practical test, especially at school or college, to see how much you know about a subject, or what you can do （笔头、口头或操作）考试： *to **take an exam*** 参加考试 ◇ *to **pass/fail an exam*** 考试合格 / 不合格 ◇ *an **exam paper*** 试卷 ◇ *I got my **exam results** today.* 我今天得到了考试成绩。 ◇ *A lot of students suffer from **exam nerves**.* 许多学生考试怯阵。 ◇ (*BrE*) *I hate **doing exams**.* 我不喜欢考试。 ◇ (*BrE, formal*) *to **sit an exam*** 参加考试 ◇ (*BrE*) *to **mark an exam*** 阅卷评分 ◇ (*NAmE*) *to **grade an exam*** 阅卷评分 ◇ (*BrE*) *She did well **in her exams**.* 她考试考得好。 ◇ (*NAmE*) *She did well **on her exams**.* 她考试考得好。 ➲ WORDFINDER NOTE AT STUDY ➲ COLLOCATIONS AT EDUCATION

> **WORDFINDER** 联想词： candidate, grade, invigilate, mark, oral, paper, practical, resit, revise

2 (*NAmE*) a medical test of a particular part of the body （对身体特定部位进行的）检查；体检： *an eye exam* 眼睛检查

> ▼ **MORE ABOUT ...** 补充说明
>
> **exams**
>
> - **Exam** is the usual word for a written, spoken or practical test at school or college, especially an important one that you need to do in order to get a qualification. **Examination** is a very formal word. A **test** is something that students might be given in addition to, or sometimes instead of, regular exams, to see how much they have learned. A very short informal test is called a **quiz** in *NAmE*. **Quiz** in both *NAmE* and *BrE* also means a contest in which people try to answer questions. * exam 为常用词，指学校的笔试、口试或操作考试，尤指为取得学历必须参加的重要考试。examination 是很正式的词。test 指对学生所学知识的测验，是正规考试的补充，有时也取代正规考试。在美式英语中非正规的小测验称为 quiz；在美式英语和英式英语中 quiz 亦指问答竞赛： *a trivia quiz* 难题问答竞赛 ◇ *a quiz show* 问答竞赛节目

exam·in·ation /ɪɡˌzæmɪ'neɪʃn/ *noun* **1** [C] (*formal*) = EXAM： *to sit an examination in mathematics* 参加数学考试 ◇ *successful candidates in GCSE examinations* 通过普通中等教育证书考试的考生 ◇ *Applicants are selected for jobs on the results of a competitive examination.* 竞聘者按遴选考试结果择优录用。 **HELP** Use: ***take/do/sit an examination*** not: ~~*write an examination*~~. 可以说 take/do/sit an examination，不作 write an examination。 **2** [U, C] the act of looking at or considering sth very carefully 审查；调查；考查；考察： *Careful examination of the ruins revealed an even earlier temple.* 仔细考察这片废墟后发现了一座更为古老的庙宇。 ◇ ***On closer examination** it was found that the signature was not genuine.* 经过进一步认真检查发现签名是伪造的。 ◇ *Your proposals are still **under examination**.* 你的提议仍在审查之中。 ◇ *The issue needs **further examination**.* 这个问题需要进一步考查。 ◇ *The chapter concludes with a brief examination of some of the factors causing family break-up.* 本章结束时简要考查了引起家庭破裂的某些因素。 **3** [C] a close look at sth/sb, especially to see if there is anything wrong or to find the cause of a problem （仔细的）检查，检验： *a medical examination* 体格检查 ◇ *a post-mortem examination* 验尸 ➲ SEE ALSO CROSS-EXAMINATION at CROSS-EXAMINE

exam·ine /ɪɡ'zæmɪn/ *verb* **1** to consider or study an idea, a subject, etc. very carefully 审查；调查；考查；考察： **~ sth** *These ideas will be examined in more detail in Chapter 10.* 这些观点将在第 10 章作更为详细的探讨。 ◇ **~ how, what, etc.…** *It is necessary to examine how the proposals can be carried out.* 有必要调查一下怎样才能实施这些方案。 ➲ SYNONYMS ON NEXT PAGE ➲ LANGUAGE BANK AT ABOUT **2** to look at sb/sth closely, to see if there is anything wrong or to find the cause of a problem （仔细地）检查，检验： **~ sb/sth** *The doctor examined her but could find nothing wrong.* 医生给她做了检查，但没发现什么问题。 ◇ **~ sth/sb for sth** *The goods were examined for damage on arrival.* 货物到达时检查是否有破损。 ➲ WORDFINDER NOTE AT DOCTOR ➲ SYNONYMS AT CHECK

> **WORDFINDER** 联想词： biopsy, diagnose, sample, scan, swab, symptom, test, ultrasound, X-ray

3 ~ sb (in/on sth) (*formal*) to give sb a test to see how much they know about a subject or what they can do 考，测验（某人）： *The students will be examined in all subjects at the end of term.* 期末时学生须要参加所有学科的考试。 ◇ *You are only being examined on this semester's work.* 现在只考你在本学期学的课程。 **4 ~ sb** (*law* 律) to ask sb questions formally, especially in court （尤指在法庭上）审问，查问 ➲ SEE ALSO CROSS-EXAMINE **IDM** SEE NEED *v.*

exam·inee /ɪɡˌzæmɪ'niː/ *noun* a person who is being tested to see how much they know about a subject or what they can do; a person who is taking an exam 应试人；参加考试者

exam·in·er /ɪɡ'zæmɪnə(r)/ *noun* **1** a person who writes the questions for, or marks/grades, a test of knowledge or ability 主考人；考官： *The papers are sent to **external examiners*** (= ones not connected with the students' school or college). 试卷送到校外主考人那里。 **2** (*especially NAmE*) a person who has the official duty to check that things are being done correctly and according to the rules of an organization; a person who officially examines sth 审查人；检查人 ➲ SEE ALSO MEDICAL EXAMINER

▼ SYNONYMS 同义词辨析

examine

analyse • review • study • discuss

These words all mean to think about, study or describe sb/sth carefully, especially in order to understand them, form an opinion of them or make a decision about them. 以上各词均含思量、审查、调查、研究之义。

examine to think about, study or describe an idea, subject or piece of work very carefully 指审查、调查、考查、考察： *These ideas will be examined in more detail in Chapter 10.* 这些观点将在第 10 章作更为详细的探讨。

analyse/analyze to examine the nature or structure of sth, especially by separating it into its parts, in order to understand or explain it 指分析： *The job involves gathering and analysing data.* 这项工作需要搜集和分析资料。◇ *He tried to analyse his feelings.* 他试图分析自己的感情。

review to examine sth again, especially so that you can decide if it is necessary to make changes 指复查、检讨，以做必要的修改： *The government will review the situation later in the year.* 政府将在今年晚些时候重新检讨形势。

study to examine sb/sth in order to understand them or it 指研究、调查： *We will study the report carefully before making a decision.* 我们将认真研究这份报告，然后再作决定。

EXAMINE OR STUDY? 用 examine 还是 study?

You **examine** sth in order to understand it or to help other people understand it, for example by describing it in a book; you **study** sth in order to understand it yourself. 为理解或帮助别人理解某事，如在书中探讨，用 examine；为使自己理解某事，用 study。

discuss to write or talk about sth in detail, showing the different ideas and opinions about it 指详述、论述： *This topic will be discussed at greater length in the next chapter.* 这个主题将在下一章里详细论述。

PATTERNS

- to examine/analyse/review/study/discuss **what/how/whether...**
- to examine/analyse/review/study/discuss the **situation/evidence**
- to examine/analyse/review/study/discuss sth **carefully/critically/systematically/briefly**

ex·ample /ɪɡˈzɑːmpl; *NAmE* -ˈzæmpl/ *noun* **1** ~ (**of sth**) something such as an object, a fact or a situation that shows, explains or supports what you say 实例；例证；例子： *Can you give me an example of what you mean?* 你能给我举个实例来解释你的意思吗？ ◇ *This dictionary has many examples of how words are used.* 这部词典有许多关于词语用法的示例。◇ *Just to give you an example of his generosity—he gave me his old car and wouldn't take any money for it.* 且给你举个例子来说明他的慷慨吧 —— 他把他的旧汽车给了我，而且分文不取。◇ *It is important to cite examples to support your argument.* 重要的是引用实例来证明你的论点。 ➲ LANGUAGE BANK AT E.G. ➲ WORDFINDER NOTE AT DICTIONARY **2** ~ (**of sth**) a thing that is typical of or represents a particular group or set 典型；范例；样品： *This is a good example of the artist's early work.* 这是这位艺术家早期作品的范例。◇ *It is a **perfect example** of a medieval castle.* 这是最典型的中世纪城堡。◇ *Japan is often quoted as the **prime example** of a modern industrial nation.* 人们经常举例把日本作为现代工业国家的典范。 ◇ *It is a **classic example** of how not to design a new city centre.* 这对于如何设计新市中心是个绝佳的反面教材。 **3** a person or their behaviour that is thought to be a good model for others to copy 榜样；楷模；模范： ~ (**to sb**) *Her courage is an example to us all.* 她的勇气是我们大家的榜样。 ◇ *He **sets an example** to the other students.* 他为其他同学树立了榜样。 ◇ ~ (**of sth**) *She is a **shining example** of what people with disabilities can achieve.* 她为残疾人有所作为树立了光辉的榜样。◇ *He is a captain who **leads by example**.* 他是个以身作则的队长。 **4** a person's behaviour, either good or bad, that other people copy 样板；榜样： *It would be a mistake to **follow his example**.* 仿效他的做法是错误的。

IDM **for example** (*abbr.* **e.g.**) used to emphasize sth that explains or supports what you are saying; used to give an example of what you are saying 例如；譬如： *There is a similar word in many languages, for example in French and Italian.* 在许多语言，譬如法语和意大利语中都有相似的词。 ◇ *The report is incomplete; it does not include sales in France, for example.* 这份报告不完整，例如在法国的销售情况就没包括进去。◇ *It is possible to combine Computer Science with other subjects, for example Physics.* 将计算机科学与其他学科，如物理学，结合起来是可能的。 ➲ LANGUAGE BANK AT E.G. **make an example of sb** to punish sb as a warning to others not to do the same thing 惩罚某人以儆戒他人；用某人来杀一儆百

▼ SYNONYMS 同义词辨析

example

case • instance • specimen • illustration

These are all words for a thing or situation that is typical of a particular group or set, and is sometimes used to support an argument. 以上各词均指事例、实例、例证。

example something such as an object, a fact or a situation that shows, explains or supports what you say; a thing that is typical of or represents a particular group or set 指实例、例证、典型、范例、样品： *Can you give me an example of what you mean?* 你能给我举个实例来解释你的意思吗？

case a particular situation or a situation of a particular type; a situation that relates to a particular person or thing 指具体情况、事例、实例、特定情况： *In some cases people have had to wait several weeks for an appointment.* 在某些情况下，人们必须等上好几周才能得到约见。

instance (*rather formal*) a particular situation or a situation of a particular type 指例子、事例、实例： *The report highlights a number of instances of injustice.* 这篇报道重点列举了一些不公正的实例。

specimen an example of sth, especially an animal or plant 尤指动植物的样品、实例： *The aquarium has some interesting specimens of unusual tropical fish.* 水族馆里有一些罕见的热带鱼，很有趣。

illustration (*rather formal*) a story, an event or an example that clearly shows the truth about sth 指说明事实的故事、实例、示例： *The statistics are a clear illustration of the point I am trying to make.* 这些统计数字清楚地阐明了我要陈述的要点。

EXAMPLE OR ILLUSTRATION? 用 example 还是 illustration?

An **illustration** is often used to show that sth is true. An **example** is used to help to explain sth. * illustration 常用以表示事物的真实性，example 用以解释说明。

PATTERNS

- a(n) example/case/instance/specimen/illustration **of** sth
- **in** a particular case/instance
- **for** example/instance

ex·as·per·ate /ɪɡˈzæspəreɪt; *BrE also* -ˈzɑːsp-/ *verb* ~ **sb** to annoy or irritate sb very much 使烦恼；使恼怒；激怒 SYN **infuriate** ▶ **ex·as·per·ation** /ɪɡˌzæspəˈreɪʃn; *BrE also* -ˌzɑːsp-/ *noun* [U]: *He shook his head in exasperation.* 他恼怒地摇了摇头。 ◇ *a groan/look/sigh of exasperation* 恼怒的哼声 / 样子 / 叹息声

ex·as·per·ated /ɪɡˈzæspəreɪtɪd; *BrE also* -ˈzɑːsp-/ *adj.* extremely annoyed, especially if you cannot do anything to improve the situation 恼怒的；烦恼的；愤怒的 **SYN** **infuriate**: *'Why won't you answer me?' he asked in an exasperated voice.* "你为什么不愿意回答我？"他愤怒地问道。◇ *She was becoming exasperated with all the questions they were asking.* 她开始对他们问的所有问题感到恼火。▶ **ex·as·per·ated·ly** *adv.*

ex·as·per·at·ing /ɪɡˈzæspəreɪtɪŋ; *BrE also* -ˈzɑːsp-/ *adj.* extremely annoying 使人恼怒的；惹人生气的 **SYN** **infuriating**

ex·cav·ate /ˈekskəveɪt/ *verb* **1** to dig in the ground to look for old buildings or objects that have been buried for a long time; to find sth by digging in this way 发掘，挖出（古建筑或古物）：**~ sth** *The site has been excavated by archaeologists.* 这个遗址已被考古学家发掘出来。◇ **~ sth from sth** *pottery and weapons excavated from the burial site* 从墓地挖掘出的陶器和兵器 **2 ~ sth** (*formal*) to make a hole, etc. in the ground by digging 挖掘，开凿，挖空（洞、隧道等）：*The body was discovered when builders excavated the area.* 建筑工人挖地时发现了这具尸体。

ex·cav·ation /ˌekskəˈveɪʃn/ *noun* **1** [C, U] the activity of digging in the ground to look for old buildings or objects that have been buried for a long time （对古建筑或古物的）发掘，挖掘 **2** [C, usually pl.] a place where people are digging to look for old buildings or objects 发掘现场：*The excavations are open to the public.* 发掘现场对公众开放。**3** [U] the act of digging, especially with a machine 挖掘；开凿；挖土

ex·cav·ator /ˈekskəveɪtə(r)/ *noun* **1** a large machine that is used for digging and moving earth 挖掘机；挖土机 ➲ **VISUAL VOCAB** PAGE V63 **2** a person who digs in the ground to look for old buildings and objects 发掘者

ex·ceed **AW** /ɪkˈsiːd/ *verb* (*formal*) **1 ~ sth** to be greater than a particular number or amount 超过（数目或数量）：*The price will not exceed £100.* 价格不会超过 100 英镑。◇ *His achievements have* ***exceeded expectations.*** 他的成就出乎预料。**2 ~ sth** to do more than the law or an order, etc. allows you to do 超越（法律、命令等）的限制：*She was exceeding the speed limit* (= driving faster than is allowed). 当时她超速驾驶。◇ *The officers had exceeded their authority.* 这些官员超越了他们的权限。➲ SEE ALSO EXCESS

ex·ceed·ing·ly /ɪkˈsiːdɪŋli/ *adv.* (*formal, becoming old-fashioned*) extremely; very; very much 极其；非常；很 **SYN** **exceptionally**

excel /ɪkˈsel/ *verb* (**-ll-**) **1** [I] to be very good at doing sth 擅长；善于；突出：**~ (in/at sth)** *She has always excelled in foreign languages.* 她的外语从来都是出类拔萃。◇ *As a child he excelled at music and art.* 他小时候擅长音乐和美术。◇ **~ (at doing sth)** *The team excels at turning defence into attack.* 这个队善于打防守反击。**2** [T] **~ yourself** (*BrE*) to do extremely well and even better than you usually do 胜过平时：*Rick's cooking was always good but this time he really excelled himself.* 里克的烹饪技术一直不错，但这次简直是好上加好。➲ **MORE LIKE THIS** 36, page R29

ex·cel·lence /ˈeksələns/ *noun* [U] the quality of being extremely good 优秀；杰出；卓越：*a reputation for academic excellence* 因学术上的杰出成就而获得的声誉 ◇ **~ in sth** *The hospital is recognized as* ***a centre of excellence*** *in research and teaching.* 这所医院已被确认为成就卓著的教学和研究中心。➲ SEE ALSO PAR EXCELLENCE

Ex·cel·lency /ˈeksələnsi/ *noun* **His/Her/Your Excellency** (*pl.* **-ies**) a title used when talking to or about sb who has a very important official position, especially an AMBASSADOR （对身居要职的人，尤其是大使的尊称）阁下：*Good evening, your Excellency.* 晚上好，阁下。◇ *their Excellencies the French and Spanish Ambassadors* 法国和西班牙大使阁下

ex·cel·lent /ˈeksələnt/ *adj.* **1** extremely good 优秀的；杰出的；极好的：*an excellent meal* 一顿美味佳肴 ◇ *excellent service* 优质服务 ◇ *At $300 the bike is* ***excellent value.*** 这辆自行车 300 美元太合算了。◇ *She speaks excellent French.* 她法语说得好极了。◇ (*informal*) *It was absolutely excellent.* 这简直太好了。**2** used to show that you are very pleased about sth or that you approve of sth （用以表示愉快或赞同）好极了，妙极了：*You can all come? Excellent!* 你们都能来？太好了！▶ **ex·cel·lent·ly** *adv.*

▼ **SYNONYMS** 同义词辨析

excellent

outstanding • perfect • superb

These words all describe sth that is extremely good. 以上各词均形容某事物极好。

excellent extremely good 指优秀的、杰出的、极好的 **NOTE** **Excellent** is used especially about standards of service or of sth that sb has worked to produce. * excellent 尤用于修饰服务或产品的质量标准：*The rooms are excellent value at $20 a night.* 这些房间一晚 20 美元太合算了。◇ *He speaks excellent English.* 他英语说得棒极了。**NOTE** **Excellent** is also used to show that you are very pleased about sth or that you approve of sth. * excellent 亦用以表示愉快或赞同：*You can all come? Excellent!* 你们都能来？太好了！

outstanding extremely good 指优秀的、杰出的、出色的 **NOTE** **Outstanding** is used especially about how well sb does sth or how good sb is at sth. * outstanding 尤指在做某事上或某方面杰出：*an outstanding achievement* 杰出的成绩

perfect extremely good 指极好的、很好的 **NOTE** **Perfect** is used especially about conditions or how suitable sth is for a purpose. * perfect 尤指条件状况极好或很合适：*Conditions were perfect for walking.* 散步的环境再好不过了。◇ *She came up with the perfect excuse.* 她想出了极好的借口。

superb (*informal*) extremely good or impressive 指极佳的、卓越的、出色的：*The facilities at the hotel are superb.* 旅馆的设施棒极了。

PATTERNS

- a(n) excellent/outstanding/perfect/superb **job/performance**
- a(n) excellent/outstanding/superb **achievement**
- **really/absolutely/quite** excellent/outstanding/perfect/superb

---

ex·cept /ɪkˈsept/ *prep., conj., verb*

■ ***prep.*** (*also* **ex'cept for**) used before you mention the only thing or person about which a statement is not true （用于所言不包括的人或事物前）除…之外 **SYN** **apart from**：*We work every day except Sunday.* 我们除星期天外每天都工作。◇ *They all came except Matt.* 除马特外他们都来了。◇ *I had nothing on except for my socks.* 我除了短袜什么都还没穿。➲ NOTE AT BESIDES ➲ **LANGUAGE BANK** ON NEXT PAGE

■ ***conj.*** **~ (that)**… used before you mention sth that makes a statement not completely true 除了；只是：*I didn't tell him anything except that I needed the money.* 我什么都没告诉他，只是说我需要钱。◇ *Our dresses were the same except mine was red.* 我们的连衣裙是一样的，只是我的那件是红色。

■ ***verb*** [usually passive] (*formal*) to not include sb/sth 不包括；不计；把…除外：**~ sb/sth** *The sanctions ban the sale of any products excepting medical supplies and food.* 国际制裁禁止销售医药用品和食物以外的任何产品。◇ *Tours are arranged all year round (January excepted).* 全年都提供观光旅游（一月份除外）。◇ **~ sb/sth from sth** *Children under five are excepted from the survey.* 五岁以下的儿童不在调查之列。**IDM** SEE PRESENT *adj.*

E

▼ LANGUAGE BANK 用语库

except

Making an exception 说明例外的情况

- *She wrote all of the songs on the album* ***except for*** *the final track.* 除最后一首歌外，这张专辑中所有歌曲都是她写的。
- ***Apart from / aside from*** *the final track, all of the songs on the album were written by her.* 除最后一首歌外，这张专辑中所有歌曲都是她写的。
- *The songwriting—**with a few minor exceptions**—is of a very high quality.* 除了几首歌美中不足以外，歌曲创作质量非常高。
- *With only **one or two exceptions**, the songwriting is of a very high quality.* 歌曲创作质量非常高，仅有一两首歌例外。
- *The majority of the compositions are less than three minutes long, **with the notable exception of** the title track.* 大多数曲目的长度都不超过三分钟，只有与专辑同名的曲目是明显的例外。
- ***With the exception of** the title track, this album is a huge disappointment.* 这张专辑令人大失所望，只有与专辑同名的曲目还过得去。
- *Here is a list of all the band's CDs, **excluding** unofficial 'bootleg' recordings.* 这是这个乐队所有 CD 的清单，未经批准非法录制的那些没有计算在内。

ex·cep·tion 🔑 /ɪk'sepʃn/ *noun* **1** 🔑 a person or thing that is not included in a general statement 一般情况以外的人（或事物）；例外： *Most of the buildings in the town are modern, but the church is an exception.* 城里大多是现代建筑，不过教堂是个例外。 ◇ *With very few exceptions, private schools get the best exam results.* 私立学校的考试成绩是最好的，很少有例外情况。 ◇ *Nobody had much money at the time and I was **no exception**.* 那时候谁都没有很多钱，我也不例外。 ➲ LANGUAGE BANK AT EXCEPT **2** 🔑 a thing that does not follow a rule 规则的例外；例外的事物： *Good writing is unfortunately **the exception rather than the rule*** (= it is unusual). 可惜优秀的文字作品真是可遇不可求。 ◇ *There are always a lot of exceptions to grammar rules.* 语法规则总是有很多例外。

IDM **the exception that proves the 'rule** (*saying*) people say that sth is **the exception that proves the rule** when they are stating sth that seems to be different from the normal situation, but they mean that the normal situation remains true in general 反证规律的例外；足以证明普遍性的例外： *Most electronics companies have not done well this year, but ours is the exception that proves the rule.* 今年多数电子公司都不景气，而我们公司却是普遍中的例外。 **make an ex'ception** 🔑 to allow sb not to follow the usual rule on one occasion 允许有例外；让…成为例外： *Children are not usually allowed in, but I'm prepared to make an exception in this case.* 儿童一般不允许入内，不过这次我可以破例。 **take ex'ception to sth** to object strongly to sth; to be angry about sth （强烈地）反对；生…的气： *I take great exception to the fact that you told my wife before you told me.* 你还没告诉我就先对我妻子讲了，为此我非常生气。 ◇ *No one could possibly take exception to his comments.* 任何人都不可能对他的意见提出异议。 **with the ex'ception of sb/sth** 🔑 except; not including 除…之外；不包括…在内： *All his novels are set in Italy with the exception of his last.* 他的小说除最后一部外全是以意大利为背景。 ➲ LANGUAGE BANK AT EXCEPT **without ex'ception** 🔑 used to emphasize that the statement you are making is always true and everyone or everything is included 一律；无一例外： *All students without exception must take the English examination.* 所有学生都必须参加英语考试，无一例外。

ex·cep·tion·al /ɪk'sepʃənl/ *adj.* **1** unusually good 杰出的；优秀的；卓越的 SYN **outstanding**: *At the age of five he showed exceptional talent as a musician.* 他五岁时就表现出非凡的音乐才能。 ◇ *The quality of the recording is **quite exceptional**.* 录音质量相当不错。 **2** very unusual 异常的；特别的；罕见的： *This deadline will be extended only **in exceptional circumstances**.* 只有在特殊情况下才会延长最后期限。 OPP **unexceptional**

ex·cep·tion·al·ly /ɪk'sepʃənəli/ *adv.* **1** used before an adjective or adverb to emphasize how strong or unusual the quality is （用于形容词和副词之前表示强调）罕见，特别，非常： *The weather, even for January, was exceptionally cold.* 这种天气即使在一月份也算得上非常寒冷。 ◇ *I thought Bill played exceptionally well.* 我认为比尔的球打得特别好。 **2** only in unusual circumstances 只有在特殊情况下；例外地： *Exceptionally, students may be accepted without formal qualifications.* 在特殊情况下，也可能接受无正式文凭的学生。

ex·cerpt /'eksɜːpt; *NAmE* -sɜːrpt/ *noun* **~ (from sth)** a short piece of writing, music, film, etc. taken from a longer whole 摘录；节选；（音乐、电影的）片段 ▶ **ex·cerpt** *verb* : **~ sth (from sth)** *The document was excerpted from an unidentified FBI file.* 此文件摘自来源不明的联邦调查局档案。

ex·cess *noun, adj.*

■ ***noun*** /ɪk'ses/ **1** [sing., U] more than is necessary, reasonable or acceptable 超过；过度；过分： *You can throw away any excess.* 凡多余的你都可以扔掉。 ◇ **~ of sth** *Are you suffering from an excess of stress in your life?* 你生活中的压力太大吗？ ◇ *In an excess of enthusiasm I agreed to work late.* 我一时热情过度答应了加班。 ◇ *He started drinking **to excess** after losing his job.* 他失业后便开始酗酒了。 ◇ *The increase will not be **in excess of*** (= more than) *two per cent.* 增加幅度不会超过百分之二。 **2** [C, U] an amount by which sth is larger than sth else 过多的量；超过的量： *We cover costs up to £600 and then you pay the excess.* 我们最多支付 600 英镑的费用，超出的部分由你支付。 **3** [C, usually sing.] (*BrE*) (*NAmE* **de·duct·ible**) the part of an insurance claim that a person has to pay while the insurance company pays the rest 免赔额；自负额： *There is an excess of £100 on each claim under this policy.* 本保险单每次索赔均有 100 英镑的免赔额。 ➲ WORDFINDER NOTE AT INSURANCE **4 excesses** [pl.] extreme behaviour that is unacceptable, illegal or immoral 放肆行为；越轨行为： *the worst excesses committed by the occupying army* 占领军犯下的残忍暴行

■ ***adj.*** /'ekses/ [only before noun] in addition to an amount that is necessary, usual or legal 超额的；额外的；附加的；过度的： *Excess food is stored as fat.* 多余的食物作为脂肪贮存起来。 ◇ *Driving with excess alcohol in the blood is a serious offence.* 血液里酒精含量过高时驾车是严重的违法行为。

ˌexcess 'baggage *noun* [U] bags, cases, etc. taken on to a plane that weigh more than the amount each passenger is allowed to carry without paying extra （需另收运费的）超重行李

ex·ces·sive /ɪk'sesɪv/ *adj.* greater than what seems reasonable or appropriate 过分的；过度的： *They complained about the excessive noise coming from the upstairs flat.* 他们抱怨楼上发出的噪音太大。 ◇ *The amounts she borrowed were not excessive.* 她借的数量没有超额。 ◇ *Excessive drinking can lead to stomach disorders.* 酗酒可能引起胃病。 ▶ **ex·ces·sive·ly** *adv.* : *excessively high prices* 过高的价格

ex·change 🔑 /ɪks'tʃeɪndʒ/ *noun, verb*

■ ***noun***

• **GIVING AND RECEIVING** 交换 **1** 🔑 [C, U] an act of giving sth to sb or doing sth for sb and receiving sth in return 交换；互换；交流；掉换： *The exchange of prisoners took place this morning.* 今天早上交换了俘虏。 ◇ *We need to promote an open exchange of ideas and information.* 我们需要促进思想和信息的公开交流。 ◇ *an **exchange of glances/insults*** 互换眼色；相互侮辱 ◇ *an **exchange of fire*** (= between enemy soldiers) 交火 ◇ *I buy you lunch and you fix my computer. Is that a **fair exchange**?* 我请你吃午饭，你给我修计算机，这算是公平交易吧？ ◇ *Would you like my old TV **in exchange for** this camera?* 用我的旧电视机换这架照相机，你愿意吗？ ◇ *I'll type your report if* *you'll babysit **in exchange**.* 如果你愿意代我照看孩子，我就把这个报告给你打出来。 ➲ SEE ALSO PART EXCHANGE

• **CONVERSATION/ARGUMENT** 交谈；争论 **2** [C] a conversation or an argument 交谈；对话；争论： *There was only time for a brief exchange.* 只有简短的交谈时间。 ◇ *The Prime Minister was involved in a **heated exchange** with Opposition MPs.* 首相参与了和反对党议员的激烈争论。

• **OF MONEY** 金钱 **3** 🔑 [U] the process of changing an amount of one CURRENCY (= the money used in one country) for an equal value of another 兑换；汇兑： *currency exchange facilities* 货币兑换服务 ◇ *Where can I find the best **exchange rate/rate of exchange**?* 在什么地方才能获得最好的兑换价？ ➲ SEE ALSO FOREIGN EXCHANGE

• **BETWEEN TWO COUNTRIES** 两国之间 **4** 🔑 [C] an arrangement when two people or groups from different countries visit each other's homes or do each other's jobs for a short time （不同国家人或团体之间的）交流，互访： *Our school does an exchange with a school in France.* 我们学校与法国的一所学校进行交流。 ◇ *Nick went on the French exchange.* 尼克到法国去作互访了。 ◇ *trade and cultural exchanges with China* 与中国的贸易和文化交流

• **BUILDING** 建筑物 **5** (*often* **Exchange**) [C] (in compounds 构成复合词) a building where business people met in the past to buy and sell a particular type of goods 交易所： *the old Corn Exchange* 古老的谷物交易所 ➲ SEE ALSO STOCK EXCHANGE

• **TELEPHONE** 电话 **6** [C] = TELEPHONE EXCHANGE

■ *verb*

• **GIVE AND RECEIVE** 交换 **1** 🔑 to give sth to sb and at the same time receive the same type of thing from them 交换；交流；掉换： **~ sth** *to **exchange ideas/news/information*** 交流思想；互通消息；交流信息 ◇ *Juliet and David **exchanged glances*** (= they looked at each other). 朱丽叶和戴维相互看了看对方。 ◇ *Everyone in the group exchanged email addresses.* 所有的组员都相互交换了电子邮件地址。 ◇ **~ sth with sb** *I shook hands and exchanged a few words with the manager.* 我和经理握了握手，交谈了几句。 ◇ *The two men **exchanged blows*** (= hit each other). 两个男人相互殴打起来。

• **MONEY/GOODS** 金钱；商品 **2** 🔑 to give or return sth that you have and get sth different or better instead 兑换；交易；更换 **SYN** **change**: **~ sth** *If it doesn't fit, take it back and the store will exchange it.* 如果不合适就把它拿回来，商店将给你更换。 ◇ **~ A for B** *You can exchange your currency for dollars in the hotel.* 你可在旅馆把你的钱兑换成美元。

• **CONTRACTS** 契约 **3 ~ contracts** (*especially BrE*) to sign a contract with the person that you are buying sth from, especially a house or land （尤指房屋或土地买卖时）订立契约 **IDM▸** SEE WORD *n.*

ex·change·able /ɪks'tʃeɪndʒəbl/ *adj.* that can be exchanged 可交换的；可交易的；可兑换的；可更换的： *These tokens are exchangeable for DVDs only.* 这些赠券只能换 DVD 盘。

ex·chequer /ɪks'tʃekə(r)/ *noun* [sing.] **1** (*often* **the Exchequer**) (in Britain) the government department that controls public money （英国）财政部 **SYN** **treasury** ➲ SEE ALSO CHANCELLOR OF THE EXCHEQUER **2** the public or national supply of money 公共财源；国库；金库： *This resulted in a considerable loss to the exchequer.* 这使国库遭受了重大损失。

ex·cise[1] /'eksaɪz/ *noun* [U] a government tax on some goods made, sold or used within a country 国内货物税；消费税： *new excise duties on low-alcohol drinks* 低酒精饮料新的消费税 ◇ *a sharp increase in vehicle excise* 机动车消费税的剧增 ◇ *an excise officer* (= an official whose job is to collect excise[1]) 国内消费税务官 ➲ COMPARE CUSTOMS (3)

ex·cise[2] /ɪk'saɪz/ *verb* **~ sth (from sth)** (*formal*) to remove sth completely 切除；删除： *Certain passages were excised from the book.* 书中某些段落已删去。

ex·ci·sion /ɪk'sɪʒn/ *noun* [U, C] (*formal* or *specialist*) the act of removing sth completely from sth; the thing removed 切除（术）；切离；切除物

ex·cit·able /ɪk'saɪtəbl/ *adj.* (of people or animals 人或动物) likely to become easily excited 易激动的；易兴奋的： *a class of excitable ten-year-olds* 一群易兴奋的十岁儿童 ▸ **ex·cit·abil·ity** /ɪkˌsaɪtə'bɪləti/ *noun* [U]

ex·cite 🔑 /ɪk'saɪt/ *verb* **1** 🔑 **~ sb** to make sb feel very pleased, interested or enthusiastic, especially about sth that is going to happen 使激动；使兴奋： *The prospect of a year in India greatly excited her.* 有望在印度待上一年使她激动万分。 **2** to make sb nervous or upset and unable to relax 刺激；使紧张不安： **~ sb** *Try not to excite your baby too much before bedtime.* 睡觉前尽量别使宝宝太兴奋。 ◇ **~ yourself** *Don't excite yourself* (= keep calm). 别激动。 **3** to make sb feel a particular emotion or react in a particular way 激发；引发；引起 **SYN** **arouse**: **~ sth** *to **excite attention/criticism/curiosity*** 引起注意 / 批评 / 好奇心 ◇ *The news has certainly **excited comment*** (= made people talk about it). 这消息已经使人们议论纷纷了。 ◇ **~ sth in sb** *The European Parliament is not an institution which excites interest in voters.* 欧洲议会是个激不起选民兴趣的机构。 **4 ~ sb** to make sb feel sexual desire 激发（性欲） **SYN** **arouse** **5 ~ sth** (*formal*) to make a part of the body or part of a physical system more active 使（身体部位或身体系统某部分）活动；刺激…的活动 **SYN** **stimulate**

ex·cited 🔑 /ɪk'saɪtɪd/ *adj.* **1** 🔑 feeling or showing happiness and enthusiasm 激动的；兴奋的： **~ (about sth)** *The children were excited about opening their presents.* 孩子们兴奋不已，想打开礼物。 ◇ **~ (at sth)** *I'm really excited at the prospect of working abroad.* 我对有希望到国外工作着实很激动。 ◇ **~ (by sth)** *Don't get too excited by the sight of your name in print.* 不要一看到你的名字出现在出版物中就过分激动。 ◇ **~ (to do sth)** *He was very excited to be asked to play for Wales.* 入选威

▼ SYNONYMS 同义词辨析

excited

ecstatic • elated • euphoric • rapturous • exhilarated

These words all describe feeling or showing happiness and enthusiasm. 以上各词均指激动、兴奋。

excited feeling or showing happiness and enthusiasm 指激动的、兴奋的： *The kids were excited about the holiday.* 孩子们对假期兴奋不已。

ecstatic very happy, excited and enthusiastic; showing this enthusiasm 指狂喜的、热情极高的： *Sally was ecstatic about her new job.* 萨莉对她的新工作高兴得发狂。

elated happy and excited because of sth good that has happened or will happen 指兴高采烈的、欢欣鼓舞的、喜气洋洋的： *I was elated with the thrill of success.* 我为成功的喜悦所鼓舞。

euphoric very happy and excited, but usually only for a short time 指极度愉快的、兴奋的，通常持续时间较短： *My euphoric mood could not last.* 我兴奋的心情持久不了。

rapturous expressing extreme pleasure or enthusiasm 指兴高采烈的、狂喜的、热烈的： *He was greeted with rapturous applause.* 他受到热烈的鼓掌欢迎。

exhilarated happy and excited, especially after physical activity 尤指身体活动后感到高兴的、兴奋的、激动的： *She felt exhilarated with the speed.* 这种速度令她兴奋不已。

PATTERNS

- to **feel** excited / elated / euphoric / exhilarated
- to be excited / ecstatic / elated / euphoric **at** sth
- to be excited / ecstatic / elated **about** sth
- to be excited / elated / exhilarated **by** sth
- to be ecstatic / elated / exhilarated **with** sth

E

尔士队使他非常兴奋。◇ *The new restaurant is* ***nothing to get excited about*** (= not particularly good). 这家新餐馆没什么值得特别激动的地方。◇ *An excited crowd of people gathered around her.* 一群激动的人聚集在她周围。**2** nervous or upset and unable to relax 受刺激的；紧张不安的：*Some horses become excited when they're in traffic.* 有些马在车流中会受惊。**3** feeling sexual desire 性兴奋的 SYN **aroused** ▸ **ex·cited·ly** *adv.*：*She waved excitedly as the car approached.* 汽车开近时她激动地挥着手。

E

ex·cite·ment /ɪk'saɪtmənt/ *noun* **1** [U] the state of feeling excited 激动；兴奋；刺激：*The news caused great excitement among her friends.* 这消息使她的朋友们兴奋不已。◇ *to feel a* ***surge/thrill/shiver of excitement*** 感到一阵激动 ◇ *He was flushed* ***with excitement*** *at the thought.* 他想到这就激动得满脸通红。◇ *The dog leapt and wagged its tail* ***in excitement.*** 狗兴奋得摇着尾巴跳来跳去。◇ ***In her excitement*** *she dropped her glass.* 她一激动把杯子摔了。**2** [C] (*formal*) something that you find exciting 令人激动（或兴奋）的事：*The new job was not without its excitements.* 这个新工作并非枯燥无味。➲ WORDFINDER NOTE AT ADVENTURE

ex·cit·ing /ɪk'saɪtɪŋ/ *adj.* causing great interest or excitement 令人激动的；使人兴奋的：*one of the most exciting developments in biology in recent years* 近年来生物学上最令人振奋的进展之一 ◇ *They waited and waited for something exciting to happen.* 他们等啊等啊，等待着激动人心的事情发生。◇ *an* ***exciting prospect/possibility*** 令人激动的前景 / 可能性 ◇ *an* ***exciting story/discovery*** 激动人心的故事 / 发现 ▸ **ex·cit·ing·ly** *adv.*

ex·claim /ɪk'skleɪm/ *verb* [I, T] to say sth suddenly and loudly, especially because of strong emotion or pain （尤因强烈的情感或痛苦而）惊叫，呼喊：*She opened her eyes and exclaimed in delight at the scene.* 看到这情景，她瞪着眼睛，高兴得大叫起来。◇ **+ speech** *'It isn't fair!', he exclaimed angrily.* "这不公平！"他气愤地喊道。◇ **~ that...** *She exclaimed that it was useless.* 她大叫说这是无效的。➲ SYNONYMS AT CALL

ex·clam·ation /ˌekskləˈmeɪʃn/ *noun* a short sound, word or phrase spoken suddenly to express an emotion. *Oh!, Look out!* and *Ow!* are exclamations. 感叹；感叹语；感叹词：*He gave an exclamation of surprise.* 他发出一声惊叹。

excla'mation mark (*especially BrE*) (*NAmE usually* **excla'mation point**) *noun* the mark (!) that is written after an exclamation 感叹号

ex·clama·tory /ɪk'sklæmətri; ek-; *NAmE* -tɔːri/ *adj.* (*formal*) (of language 语言) expressing surprise or strong feelings 表示感叹的；惊叹的

ex·clude AW /ɪk'skluːd/ *verb* **1** **~ sth (from sth)** to deliberately not include sth in what you are doing or considering 不包括；不放在考虑之列：*The cost of borrowing has been excluded from the inflation figures.* 通胀数字未包括借贷费用。◇ *Try excluding fat from your diet.* 平时用餐时试一试不吃含脂肪的食物。◇ *Buses run every hour, Sundays excluded.* 公共汽车每小时一班，星期天除外。OPP **include** **2** **~ sb/sth (from sth)** to prevent sb/sth from entering a place or taking part in sth 防止…进入；阻止…参加；把…排斥在外：*Women are still excluded from some London clubs.* 伦敦有些俱乐部仍然拒绝妇女参加。◇ (*BrE*) *Concern is growing over the number of children excluded from school* (= not allowed to attend because of bad behaviour). 大批儿童遭学校开除，人们对此越来越表关注。◇ *She felt excluded by the other girls* (= they did not let her join in what they were doing). 她感到自己受到其他女孩子的排斥。**3** **~ sth** to decide that sth is not possible 排除（…的可能性）；认为…不可能：*We should not* ***exclude the possibility*** *of negotiation.* 我们不应该排除谈判的可能性。◇ *The police have excluded theft as a motive for the murder.* 警方已排除这起谋杀案中有偷窃的动机。OPP **include**

ex·clud·ing AW /ɪk'skluːdɪŋ/ *prep.* not including 不包括；除…外：*Lunch costs £10 per person, excluding drinks.* 午餐每人 10 英镑，酒水除外。➲ LANGUAGE BANK AT EXCEPT

ex·clu·sion AW /ɪk'skluːʒn/ *noun* **1** [U] **~ (of sb/sth) (from sth)** the act of preventing sb/sth from entering a place or taking part in sth 排斥；排除在外：*He was disappointed with his exclusion from the England squad.* 他对自己没有入选英格兰队感到失望。◇ *Exclusion of air creates a vacuum in the bottle.* 瓶子里的空气排除后就产生真空。◇ *Memories of the past filled her mind* ***to the exclusion of*** *all else.* 她满脑子全是对过去的回忆，其他事情都不想了。OPP **inclusion** **2** [C] a person or thing that is not included in sth 不包括在内的人（或事物）；被排除在外的人（或事物）：*Check the list of exclusions in the insurance policy.* 检查一下保险单上的除外责任清单。**3** [U] **~ (of sth)** the act of deciding that sth is not possible 排除；认为不可能：*the exclusion of robbery as a motive* 排除抢劫动机 **4** [U, C] (*BrE*) a situation in which a child is banned from attending school because of bad behaviour 开除学籍：*the exclusion of disruptive students from school* 把捣蛋的学生开除出学校 ◇ *Two exclusions from one school in the same week is unusual.* 一所学校在一周内就有两起开除学生的事是少有的。

▼ SYNONYMS 同义词辨析

exciting

dramatic • heady • thrilling • exhilarating

These words all describe an event, experience or feeling that causes excitement. 以上各词均指事情、经历或感受令人激动、兴奋。

exciting causing great interest or excitement 指令人激动的、使人兴奋的：*This is one of the most exciting developments in biology in recent years.* 这是近年来生物学上最令人振奋的进展之一。

dramatic (of events or scenes) exciting and impressive （指事情或情景）激动人心的、引人注目的、给人印象深刻的：*They watched dramatic pictures of the police raid on TV.* 他们在电视上看到了警察突击搜捕的激动人心的画面。

heady having a strong effect on your senses; making you feel excited and hopeful 指强烈作用于感官的、使兴奋的、使抱有希望的：*the heady days of youth* 令人陶醉的年轻时代

thrilling exciting and enjoyable 指惊险的、紧张的、扣人心弦的、令人兴奋不已的：*Don't miss next week's thrilling episode!* 别错过下周扣人心弦的那一集！

exhilarating very exciting and enjoyable 指使人兴奋的、令人激动的、令人高兴的：*My first parachute jump was an exhilarating experience.* 我第一次跳伞的经历很令人激动。

EXCITING, THRILLING OR EXHILARATING? 用 exciting、thrilling 还是 exhilarating?

Exhilarating is the strongest of these words and **exciting** the least strong. **Exciting** is the most general and can be used to talk about any activity, experience, feeling or event that excites you. **Thrilling** is used especially for contests and stories where the ending is uncertain. **Exhilarating** is used especially for physical activities that involve speed and/or danger. 在这组词中 exhilarating 语气最强，exciting 语气最弱。exciting 最宽泛，可用于任何令人激动的活动、经历、感受或事情；thrilling 尤用于结局难测的比赛和故事；exhilarating 尤用于涉及高速度或危险的体育活动。

PATTERNS

- a(n) exciting/dramatic/heady/thrilling/exhilarating **experience/moment**
- a(n) exciting/dramatic/heady **atmosphere**
- a(n) exciting/dramatic/thrilling **finish/finale/victory/win**

ex·clu·sion·ary AW /ɪk'sklu:ʒənri/ *adj.* (*formal*) designed to prevent a particular person or group of people from taking part in sth or doing sth 排斥（性）的；排除在外的

ex'clusion order *noun* (*BrE*) an official order not to go to a particular place（进入某场所的）禁令：*The judge placed an exclusion order on him, banning him from city centre shops.* 法官给他下了禁令，禁止他进入市中心的店铺。

ex'clusion zone *noun* an area where people are not allowed to enter because it is dangerous or is used for secret activities 禁区

ex·clu·sive AW /ɪk'sklu:sɪv/ *adj., noun*
■ ***adj.*** **1** only to be used by one particular person or group; only given to one particular person or group（个人或集体）专用的，专有的，独有的，独占的：*The hotel has exclusive access to the beach.* 这家旅馆有通向海滩的专用通道。◇ *exclusive rights to televise the World Cup* 世界杯赛的独家电视播放权 ◇ *His mother has told 'The Times' about his death in an exclusive interview* (= not given to any other newspaper). 他的母亲在接受《泰晤士报》的独家采访时谈到他的死亡。➲ WORDFINDER NOTE AT JOURNALIST **2** (of a group, society, etc. 团体、社团等) not very willing to allow new people to become members, especially if they are from a lower social class 排外的；不愿接收（较低社会阶层）新成员的：*He belongs to an exclusive club.* 他参加的是一个不轻易吸收新会员的俱乐部。**3** of a high quality and expensive and therefore not often bought or used by most people 高档的；豪华的；高级的：*an exclusive hotel* 高级酒店 ◇ *exclusive designer clothes* 高档名牌服装 **4** not able to exist or be a true statement at the same time as sth else 排斥的；排他的：*The two options are not* ***mutually exclusive*** (= you can have them both). 这两种选择并不相互排斥。**5 ~ of sb/sth** not including sb/sth 不包括；不算；除…外：*The price is for accommodation only, exclusive of meals.* 此价只包括住宿，饭费除外。OPP **inclusive** ▸ **ex·clu·sive·ly** AW *adv.*：*a charity that relies almost exclusively on voluntary contributions* 几乎全靠自愿捐赠的慈善机构 **ex·clu·sive·ness** *noun* [U]
■ ***noun*** an item of news or a story about famous people that is published in only one newspaper or magazine 独家新闻；独家专文；独家报道

ex·clu·siv·ity /ˌeksklu:'sɪvəti/ (*also* **ex·clu·sive·ness** /ɪk'sklu:sɪvnəs/) *noun* [U] the quality of being exclusive 排他性；专有权；独特性：*The resort still preserves a feeling of exclusivity.* 这个度假胜地仍然保持着特有的情调。◇ *a designer whose clothes have not lost their exclusiveness* 设计的服装不失独特风格的设计师

ex·com·mu·ni·cate /ˌekskə'mju:nɪkeɪt/ *verb* **~ sb (for sth)** to punish sb by officially stating that they can no longer be a member of a Christian Church, especially the Roman Catholic Church（尤指天主教）绝罚（开除教籍） ▸ **ex·com·mu·ni·ca·tion** /ˌekskəˌmju:nɪ'keɪʃn/ *noun* [U, C]

ex·cori·ate /ˌeks'kɔ:rieɪt/ *verb* **1 ~ sth** (*medical* 医) to irritate a person's skin so that it starts to come off 擦破，擦伤，剥落（皮肤） **2 ~ sb/sth** (*formal*) to criticize sb/sth severely 严厉指责；痛斥 ▸ **ex·cori·ation** *noun* [U, C]

ex·cre·ment /'ekskrɪmənt/ *noun* [U] (*formal*) solid waste matter that is passed from the body through the BOWELS 粪便；排泄物 SYN **faeces**：*the pollution of drinking water by untreated human excrement* 未经处理的人体排泄物对饮用水的污染 ▸ **ex·cre·men·tal** *adj.*

ex·cres·cence /ɪk'skresns/ *noun* (*formal*) an ugly lump that has grown on a part of an animal's body or on a plant 赘生物；赘疣；瘤：(*figurative*) *The new office block is an excrescence* (= it is very ugly). 这座新办公楼很是煞风景。

ex·creta /ɪk'skri:tə/ *noun* [U] (*formal*) solid and liquid waste matter passed from the body（身体的）排泄物：*human excreta* 人体排泄物

ex·crete /ɪk'skri:t/ *verb* [I] (*specialist*) to pass solid or liquid waste matter from the body 排泄 ▸ **ex·cre·tion** /ɪk'skri:ʃn/ *noun* [U, C]

ex·cre·tory /ɪks'kri:təri; *NAmE* 'ekskrətɔ:ri/ *adj.* (*biology* 生) connected with getting rid of waste matter from the body 排泄的；有排泄功能的：*the excretory organs* 排泄器官

ex·cru·ci·at·ing /ɪk'skru:ʃieɪtɪŋ/ *adj.* extremely painful or bad 极痛苦的；极坏的；糟糕透顶的：*The pain in my back was excruciating.* 我的背疼痛难忍。◇ *She groaned at the memory, suffering all over again the excruciating embarrassment of those moments.* 她在回忆中呻吟，又一次饱尝那时所经历的极度困窘。➲ SYNONYMS AT PAINFUL ▸ **ex·cru·ci·at·ing·ly** *adv.*：*excruciatingly uncomfortable* 极不舒服 ◇ ***excruciatingly painful/boring/embarrassing*** 极其痛苦／乏味／难堪

ex·cul·pate /'ekskʌlpeɪt/ *verb* **~ sb** (*formal*) to prove or state officially that sb is not guilty of sth 证明（或宣布）无罪；为（某人）开脱 ▸ **ex·cul·pa·tion** /ˌekskʌl'peɪʃn/ *noun* [U]

ex·cur·sion /ɪk'skɜ:ʃn; *NAmE* ɪk'skɜ:rʒn/ *noun* **1** a short journey made for pleasure, especially one that has been organized for a group of people（尤指集体）远足，短途旅行：*They've gone* ***on an excursion*** *to York.* 他们到约克旅游去了。➲ SYNONYMS AT TRIP ➲ WORDFINDER NOTE AT JOURNEY **2 ~ into sth** (*formal*) a short period of trying a new or different activity（短期的）涉足，涉猎：*After a brief excursion into drama, he concentrated on his main interest, which was poetry.* 他短暂涉猎过戏剧之后便把全部精力投入到他的主要兴趣——诗歌中去了。

ex·cus·able /ɪk'skju:zəbl/ *adj.* [not usually before noun] that can be excused 可原谅；可谅解 SYN **forgivable**：*Doing it once was just about excusable—doing it twice was certainly not.* 这种事干一次还可以原谅，干两次就绝对不能了。OPP **inexcusable**

ex·cuse *noun, verb*
■ ***noun*** /ɪk'skju:s/ **1** a reason, either true or invented, that you give to explain or defend your behaviour 借口；理由；辩解：*Late again! What's your excuse this time?* 又迟到了！你这次有什么借口？◇ **~ (for sth)** *There's* ***no excuse for*** *such behaviour.* 这种行为说不过去。◇ **~ (for doing sth)** *His excuse for forgetting her birthday was that he had lost his diary.* 他辩解说因为日记本丢了才忘了她的生日。◇ *You don't have to* ***make excuses*** *for her* (= try to think of reasons for her behaviour). 你不必为她辩解了。◇ *It's late. I'm afraid I'll have to* ***make my excuses*** (= say I'm sorry, give my reasons and leave). 时间不早了。很抱歉，我得告辞了。➲ SYNONYMS AT REASON **2** a good reason that you give for doing sth that you want to do for other reasons（正当的）理由，借口：**~ (for sth/for doing sth)** *It's just an excuse for a party.* 这只是聚会的一个借口。◇ **~ (to do sth)** *It gave me an excuse to take the car.* 这使我有理由开车去。**3** a very bad example of sth 拙劣样品；蹩脚货：*Why get involved with that pathetic excuse for a human being?* 为什么要与那个讨厌的家伙混在一起？**4** (*NAmE*) a note written by a parent or doctor to explain why a student cannot go to school or sb cannot go to work 假条（家长或医生写明请假或给假理由）
■ ***verb*** /ɪk'skju:z/ **1** to forgive sb for sth that they have done, for example not being polite or making a small mistake 原谅；宽恕：**~ sth** *Please excuse the mess.* 这里凌乱不堪，请见谅。◇ **~ sb** *You must excuse my father—he's not always that rude.* 你一定要原谅我父亲，他并不总是那样粗暴无礼。◇ **~ sb for sth/for doing sth** *I hope you'll excuse me for being so late.* 我来得这么晚，希望你能原谅。◇ (*BrE*) *You* ***might be excused for*** *thinking that Ben is in charge* (= he is not, but it is an easy mistake to make). 你误以为是本在负责，这是情有可原的。◇ **~ sb doing sth** (*formal*) *Excuse my interrupting you.* 对不起，打扰你一下。**2 ~ sth | ~ sb/yourself (for sth/for doing sth)** to make your or sb else's behaviour seem less offensive by finding reasons for it 为…辩解（或找理由） SYN **justify**：*Nothing can excuse such rudeness.* 如此粗暴无礼不能原谅。**3 ~ sb/yourself (from sth)** to

E

allow sb to leave; to say in a polite way that you are leaving 准许…离开；请求准予离开；（离开前）请求原谅： *Now if you'll excuse me, I'm a very busy man.* 如果可以，我先行一步了。我很忙。◇ *She excused herself and left the meeting early.* 她说了声"请原谅"就提前离开了会场。 **4** [usually passive] **~ sb (from sth/from doing sth) | ~ sb sth** to allow sb to not do sth that they should normally do 同意免除；同意免做： *She was excused from giving evidence because of her age.* 因年龄关系她获准不予作证。

E

IDM **ex'cuse me** **1** used to politely get sb's attention, especially sb you do not know （引起尤其是陌生人的注意）劳驾，请原谅： *Excuse me, is this the way to the station?* 劳驾，这是去车站的路吗？ **2** used to politely ask sb to move so that you can get past them （客气地请人让路）对不起，劳驾，借光： *Excuse me, could you let me through?* 对不起，能让我过去吗？ **3** used to say that you are sorry for interrupting sb or behaving in a slightly rude way （因打扰别人或失礼表示歉意）对不起，请原谅： *Guy sneezed loudly. 'Excuse me,' he said.* 盖伊大声打了个喷嚏，然后说了声"对不起"。 **4** used to disagree politely with sb （婉转地表示不赞成）对不起，请原谅，很抱歉： *Excuse me, but I don't think that's true.* 很抱歉，我认为这不是真的。 **5** used to politely tell sb that you are going to leave or talk to sb else （婉转地要求离开或要与另外的人讲话）对不起，请原谅，抱歉： *'Excuse me for a moment,' she said and left the room.* 她说了声"很抱歉，失陪一会儿"就离开了房间。 **6** (*especially NAmE*) used to say sorry for pushing sb or doing sth wrong （因挤着别人或做错了事表示歉意）对不起，请原谅，很抱歉： *Oh, excuse me. I didn't see you there.* 啊呀，对不起，我没看到你在那里。 **7** **excuse me?** (*NAmE*) used when you did not hear what sb said and you want them to repeat it （没听清楚，请对方再说一遍）对不起，请再说一遍 ➲ MORE AT FRENCH *n.*

,ex-di'rectory *adj.* (*BrE*) (of a person or telephone number 人或电话号码) not listed in the public telephone book, at the request of the owner of the telephone. The telephone company will not give ex-directory numbers to people who ask for them. 未列入电话号码簿的（经用户要求电话公司不向询问人提供其电话号码）： *an ex-directory number* 未列入电话簿的电话号码 ◇ *She's ex-directory.* 她的名字未列入电话号码簿。 ➲ SEE ALSO UNLISTED (2)

exeat /'eksiæt/ *noun* (*BrE*) permission from an institution such as a BOARDING SCHOOL to be away from it for a period of time （寄宿学校等机构的）短期外出许可，短假许可

exec /ɪg'zek/ *noun* (*informal*) an executive in a business （公司的）经理，管理人员

exe·crable /'eksɪkrəbl/ *adj.* (*formal*) very bad 糟糕的；拙劣的；极坏的 SYN **terrible**

exe·cut·able /ɪg'zekjətəbl/ *adj.* (*computing* 计) (of a file or program 文件或程序) that can be run by a computer 可执行的

exe·cute /'eksɪkju:t/ *verb* **1** [usually passive] **~ sb (for sth)** to kill sb, especially as a legal punishment （尤指依法）处决，处死： *He was* ***executed*** *for treason.* 他因叛国罪被处死。◇ *The prisoners were executed by firing squad.* 这些犯人已由行刑队枪决。 ➲ WORDFINDER NOTE AT ATTACK **2** **~ sth** (*formal*) to do a piece of work, perform a duty, put a plan into action, etc. 实行；执行；实施： *They drew up and executed a plan to reduce fuel consumption.* 他们制订并实施了一项降低燃料消耗的计划。◇ *The crime was very cleverly executed.* 这一犯罪活动实施得非常巧妙。◇ *Check that the computer has executed your commands.* 检查一下计算机是否已执行指令。 **3** **~ sth** (*formal*) to successfully perform a skilful action or movement 成功地完成（技巧或动作）： *The pilot executed a perfect landing.* 飞行员完成了一个非常娴熟的着陆动作。 **4** **~ sth** (*formal*) to make or produce a work of art 制作，做成（艺术品）： *Picasso also executed several landscapes at Horta de San Juan.* 毕加索还在奥尔塔–德圣胡安画了几幅风景画。 **5** **~ sth** (*law* 律) to follow the instructions in a legal document; to make a document legally valid 执行（法令）；使（法律文件）生效

exe·cu·tion /,eksɪ'kju:ʃn/ *noun* **1** [U, C] the act of killing sb, especially as a legal punishment 处决： *He faced execution by hanging for murder.* 他因谋杀罪要以绞刑处死。◇ *Over 200 executions were carried out last year.* 去年执行了 200 多起死刑。 **2** [U] (*formal*) the act of doing a piece of work, performing a duty, or putting a plan into action 实行；执行；实施： *He had failed in the execution of his duty.* 他未能履行职责。◇ *The idea was good, but the execution was poor.* 这个主意倒不错，可实施情况不理想。 **3** [U] (*formal*) skill in performing or making sth, such as a piece of music or work of art 表演；（乐曲的）演奏；（艺术品的）制作： *Her execution of the piano piece was perfect.* 她把那段钢琴曲演奏得非常完美。 **4** [U] (*law* 律) the act of following the instructions in a legal document, especially those in sb's WILL （尤指遗嘱的）执行 IDM SEE STAY *n.*

exe·cu·tion·er /,eksɪ'kju:ʃənə(r)/ *noun* a public official whose job is to execute criminals 行刑者；死刑执行者

ex·ecu·tive /ɪg'zekjətɪv/ *noun, adj.*

■ ***noun*** **1** [C] a person who has an important job as a manager of a company or an organization （公司或机构的）经理，主管领导，管理人员： ***advertising/business/sales, etc. executives*** 广告、业务、销售等主管 ◇ ***a chief/senior/top executive*** *in a computer firm* 一家计算机公司的总裁 / 资深主管 / 高层主管 ➲ WORDFINDER NOTE AT BUSINESSMAN **2** [C+sing./pl. v.] a group of people who run a company or an organization （统称公司或机构的）行政领导，领导层： *The union's executive has/have yet to reach a decision.* 工会领导层尚未作出决策。 **3** **the executive** [sing.+sing./pl. v.] the part of a government responsible for putting laws into effect （政府的）行政部门 ➲ COMPARE JUDICIARY, LEGISLATURE

■ ***adj.*** [only before noun] **1** connected with managing a business or an organization, and with making plans and decisions 经营管理的；经理的；决策的： *She has an executive position in a finance company.* 她在一家金融公司担任主管。◇ ***executive decisions/duties/jobs/positions*** 经营管理的决策 / 职责 / 工作 / 职位 ◇ *the executive dining room* 管理人员食堂 **2** having the power to put important laws and decisions into effect 有执行权的；实施的；行政的： *executive authority* 行政当局 ◇ *an* ***executive board/body/committee/officer*** 执行董事会；行政机构；执行委员会；行政长官 ◇ *Executive power is held by the president.* 执行权由董事长掌握。 **3** expensive; for the use of sb who is considered important 高级的；供重要人物使用的： *an* ***executive car/home*** 高级汽车 / 住宅 ◇ *an* ***executive suite*** (= in a hotel) （旅馆的）贵宾套房 ◇ *an* ***executive lounge*** (= at an airport) （机场的）贵宾休息室

the e'xecutive branch *noun* [sing.] (in the US) the part of the government that is controlled by the President （美国）政府行政部门（由总统掌管）

e,xecutive 'privilege *noun* [U] (in the US) the right of the President and the executive part of the government to keep official documents secret 行政特权，总统特权（美国总统和政府行政部门对官方文件保密的特权）

e,xecutive 'summary (*also* **,management 'summary**) *noun* a short statement that gives the important facts, conclusions and suggestions of a report, usually printed at the beginning of a report 报告摘要，内容撮要（常印在报告开头的简短说明或总结）

ex·ecu·tor /ɪg'zekjətə(r)/ *noun* (*specialist*) a person, bank, etc. that is chosen by sb who is making their WILL to follow the instructions in it 遗嘱执行人（或银行等）

exe·gesis /,eksɪ'dʒi:sɪs/ *noun* [U, C] (*pl.* **exe·geses** /-si:z/) (*formal*) the detailed explanation of a piece of writing, especially religious writing （尤指宗教著作的）诠释；解经；释经

ex·em·plar /ɪg'zemplɑ:(r)/ *noun* (*formal*) a person or thing that is a good or typical example of sth 模范；榜样；典型；范例 SYN **model**

ex·em·plary /ɪɡˈzempləri/ *adj.* **1** providing a good example for people to copy 典范的；可作榜样的；可作楷模的： *Her behaviour was exemplary.* 她的行为堪作楷模。◇ *a man of exemplary character* 一个具有模范品德的人 **2** [usually before noun] (*law* 律 or *formal*) (of punishment 惩罚) severe; used especially as a warning to others 严厉的；儆戒性的；惩戒性的

ex·em·plify /ɪɡˈzemplɪfaɪ/ *verb* (**ex·em·pli·fies, ex·em·pli·fy·ing, ex·em·pli·fied, ex·em·pli·fied**) [often passive] (*formal*) **1** ~ **sth** to be a typical example of sth 是…的典型（或典范、榜样）： *Her early work is exemplified in her book, 'A Study of Children's Minds'.* 她的《儿童思维研究》一书是她早期的代表作。◇ *His food exemplifies Italian cooking at its best.* 他的菜肴体现了意大利烹饪的精髓。 **2** ~ **sth** to give an example in order to make sth clearer 举例说明；例证；例示 SYN **illustrate**: *She exemplified each of the points she was making with an amusing anecdote.* 她的每一个论点都用一个逸闻趣事来说明。 ▶ **ex·em·pli·fi·ca·tion** /ɪɡˌzemplɪfɪˈkeɪʃn/ *noun* [U, C]

ex·empt /ɪɡˈzempt/ *adj., verb*

■ ***adj.*** [not before noun] ~ (**from sth**) if sb/sth is **exempt** from sth, they are not affected by it, do not have to do it, pay it, etc. 免除（责任、付款等）；获豁免： *The interest on the money is exempt from tax.* 这笔钱的利息免税。◇ *Some students are exempt from certain exams.* 有些学生可免除某些考试。 ▶ **-exempt** (in compounds, forming adjectives 构成复合形容词): *tax-exempt donations to charity* 给慈善机构的免税捐款

■ ***verb*** ~ **sb/sth** (**from sth/from doing sth**) (*formal*) to give or get sb's official permission not to do sth or not to pay sth they would normally have to do or pay 免除；豁免： *His bad eyesight exempted him from military service.* 他因视力不好而免服兵役。◇ *Charities were exempted from paying the tax.* 慈善团体免付税款。

ex·emp·tion /ɪɡˈzempʃn/ *noun* **1** [U, C] ~ (**from sth**) official permission not to do sth or pay sth that you would normally have to do or pay 免除；豁免： *She was given exemption from the final examination.* 她已获准期末免试。 **2** [C] a part of your income that you do not have to pay tax on （部分收入的）免税： *a tax exemption on money donated to charity* 给慈善机构的捐款免税

ex·er·cise 🔑 /ˈeksəsaɪz; *NAmE* -sərs-/ *noun, verb*

■ ***noun***

• **ACTIVITY/MOVEMENTS** 活动；运动 **1** 🔑 [U] physical or mental activity that you do to stay healthy or become stronger （身体或脑力的）活动，锻炼，运动： *Swimming is good exercise.* 游泳是有益的运动。◇ *I don't **get much exercise** sitting in the office all day.* 我整天坐在办公室很少运动。◇ *The mind needs exercise as well as the body.* 大脑同身体一样需要锻炼。◇ ***vigorous/gentle exercise*** 剧烈的 / 平和的运动 ◇ (*BrE*) *to take exercise* 锻炼 ➲ WORDFINDER NOTE AT FIT ➲ COLLOCATIONS AT DIET **2** 🔑 [C] a set of movements or activities that you do to stay healthy or develop a skill （保持健康或培养技能的）一套动作，训练活动，练习： ***breathing/relaxation/stretching exercises*** 呼吸 / 放松 / 伸展运动 ◇ *exercises for the piano* 钢琴练习 ◇ *Repeat the exercise ten times on each leg.* 每条腿重复做十次这种动作。

• **QUESTIONS** 问题 **3** 🔑 [C] a set of questions in a book that tests your knowledge or practises a skill 习题；练习： *grammar exercises* 语法练习 ◇ *Do exercise one for homework.* 家庭作业做习题一。

• **USE OF POWER/RIGHT/QUALITY** 权力 / 权利的行使；品质的运用 **4** [U] ~ **of sth** the use of power, a skill, a quality or a right to make sth happen 行使；运用；使用： *the exercise of power by the government* 政府权力的行使 ◇ *the exercise of discretion* 自行决定权的行使

• **FOR PARTICULAR RESULT** 为某结果 **5** [C] an activity that is designed to achieve a particular result （为达到特定结果的）活动： *a communications exercise* 通信演习 ◇ *In the end it proved a pointless exercise.* 这最终证明是一项毫无意义的活动。◇ ~ **in sth** *an exercise in public relations* 公关活动 ◇ *Staying calm was an exercise in self-control.* 保持镇定是一种自我控制活动。

• **FOR SOLDIERS** 士兵 **6** [C, usually pl.] a set of activities for training soldiers （士兵的）操练，演习，演练： *military exercises* 军事演习

• **CEREMONIES** 仪式 **7 exercises** [pl.] (*NAmE*) ceremonies 典礼；仪式： *college graduation exercises* 大学毕业典礼

■ ***verb***

• **USE POWER/RIGHT/QUALITY** 行使权力 / 权利；运用品质 **1** 🔑 [T] ~ **sth** (*formal*) to use your power, rights or personal qualities in order to achieve sth 行使；使用；运用： *When she appeared in court she exercised her right to remain silent.* 她出庭时行使了自己保持沉默的权利。◇ *He was a man who exercised considerable influence over people.* 他是个对别人有相当影响的人。

• **DO PHYSICAL ACTIVITY** 体力锻炼 **2** 🔑 [I, T] to do sports or other physical activities in order to stay healthy or become stronger; to make an animal do this 锻炼；训练；操练： *an hour's class of exercising to music* 音乐伴奏下的一小时健身操课 ◇ *How often do you exercise?* 你多长时间锻炼一次？ ◇ ~ **sth** *Horses need to be exercised regularly.* 马需要有规律的训练。 **3** [T] ~ **sth** to give a part of the body the movement and activity it needs to keep strong and healthy 锻炼（身体某部位）： *These movements will exercise your arms and shoulders.* 这些动作将锻炼你的手臂和肩膀。

• **BE ANXIOUS** 焦虑 **4** [usually passive] ~ **sb/sth** (**about sth**) (*formal*) if sb is **exercised** about sth, they are very anxious about it 使焦虑；使不安；使烦恼

ˈexercise ball (*also* **ˈSwiss ball™**) *noun* a large ball that you can sit on when doing exercises to make your muscles work in a different way 健身球

ˈexercise bike *noun* a bicycle that does not move forward but is used for getting exercise indoors （室内使用的）健身脚踏车 ➲ VISUAL VOCAB PAGE V46

ˈexercise book *noun* **1** (*BrE*) (*NAmE* **note·book**) a small book for students to write their work in 练习本 ➲ VISUAL VOCAB PAGE V72 **2** = WORKBOOK

exert /ɪɡˈzɜːt; *NAmE* ɪɡˈzɜːrt/ *verb* **1** ~ **sth** to use power or influence to affect sb/sth 运用；行使；施加： *He exerted all his authority to make them accept the plan.* 他利用他的所有权力让他们接受这个计划。◇ *The moon exerts a force on the earth that causes the tides.* 月球对地球的吸引力引起潮汐。 **2** ~ **yourself** to make a big physical or mental effort 努力；竭力： *In order to be successful he would have to exert himself.* 他必须努力才能成功。

ex·er·tion /ɪɡˈzɜːʃn; *NAmE* -ˈzɜːrʃ-/ *noun* **1** [U] (*also* **exertions** [pl.]) physical or mental effort; the act of making an effort 努力；尽力；费力： *She was hot and breathless from the exertion of cycling uphill.* 她骑车上山累得全身发热，喘不过气来。◇ *He needed to relax after the exertions of a busy day at work.* 他忙碌工作了一天后需要休息。 **2** [sing.] the use of power to make sth happen 行使；运用；施加： *the **exertion** of force/strength/authority* 使用武力；使劲；行使权力

exe·unt /ˈeksiʌnt/ *verb* [I] (*from Latin*) used in a play as a written instruction that tells two or more actors to leave the stage （剧本中的说明，两个或以上演员）退场，下场 ➲ COMPARE EXIT *v.* (3)

ex·foli·ate /eksˈfəʊlieɪt; *NAmE* -ˈfoʊ-/ *verb* [I, T] ~ (**sth**) to remove dead cells from the surface of skin in order to make it smoother 使死皮剥脱 ▶ **ex·foli·ation** *noun* [U]

ex gra·tia /ˌeks ˈɡreɪʃə/ *adj.* (*from Latin*) given or done as a gift or favour, not because there is a legal duty to do it 作为礼物的；作为恩惠的： *ex gratia payments* 通融付款 ▶ **ex gra·tia** *adv.*: *The sum was paid ex gratia.* 这是所付的一笔特惠款。

ex·hale /eksˈheɪl/ *verb* [I, T] (*formal*) to breathe out the air or smoke, etc. in your lungs 呼出，吐出（肺中的空气、烟等）；呼气： *He sat back and exhaled deeply.* 他仰坐着深深地呼气。◇ ~ **sth** *She exhaled the smoke through her nose.* 她从鼻子里喷出烟雾。 OPP **inhale** ▶ **ex·hal·ation** /ˌekshəˈleɪʃn/ *noun* [U, C]

E

ex·haust /ɪɡˈzɔːst/ *noun, verb*

■ ***noun*** **1** [U] waste gases that come out of a vehicle, an engine or a machine（车辆、发动机或机器排出的）废气：*car **exhaust fumes/emissions*** 汽车排出的废气；汽车排放物 ➲ VISUAL VOCAB PAGE V6 **2** (*also* **exˈhaust pipe**) (*also* **tail·pipe** *especially in NAmE*) [C] a pipe through which exhaust gases come out 排气管：*My car needs a new exhaust.* 我的汽车需要一个新排气管。➲ VISUAL VOCAB PAGE V56

■ ***verb*** **1** to make sb feel very tired 使筋疲力尽；使疲惫不堪 **SYN** **wear out**: **~ sb** *Even a short walk exhausted her.* 走不了几步她就会疲惫不堪。◇ **~ yourself** *There's no need to exhaust yourself clearing up—we'll do it.* 你不必筋疲力尽地收拾，我们会做的。 **2 ~ sth** to use all of sth so that there is none left 用完；花光；耗尽：*Within three days they had exhausted their supply of food.* 他们在三天之内就把所有粮食吃光了。◇ *Don't give up until you have exhausted all the possibilities.* 只要还有可能就别放弃。 **3 ~ sth** to talk about or study a subject until there is nothing else to say about it 详尽讨论（或研究）：*I think we've exhausted that particular topic.* 我认为我们已把那个题目讨论透彻了。

ex·haust·ed /ɪɡˈzɔːstɪd/ *adj.* **1** very tired 筋疲力尽的；疲惫不堪的：*I'm exhausted!* 我累死了！◇ *to feel **completely/utterly exhausted*** 感到筋疲力尽 ◇ *The exhausted climbers were rescued by helicopter.* 筋疲力尽的登山者由直升机营救出来。 **2** completely used or finished 用完的；耗尽的；枯竭的：*You cannot grow crops on exhausted land.* 地力耗尽的土地上种不了庄稼。

ex·haust·ing /ɪɡˈzɔːstɪŋ/ *adj.* making you feel very tired 使人疲惫不堪的；令人筋疲力尽的：*an exhausting day at work* 工作得筋疲力尽的一天 ◇ *I find her exhausting—she never stops talking.* 我发现她真累人 —— 她总是说个不停。

ex·haus·tion /ɪɡˈzɔːstʃən/ *noun* [U] **1** the state of being very tired 筋疲力尽；疲惫不堪：*suffering from **physical/mental/nervous exhaustion*** 身体 / 精神 / 神经衰弱 ◇ *Her face was grey with exhaustion.* 她疲惫得脸色发白。 **2** (*formal*) the act of using sth until it is completely finished 耗尽；用尽；枯竭：*the exhaustion of natural resources* 自然资源的枯竭

ex·haust·ive /ɪɡˈzɔːstɪv/ *adj.* including everything possible; very thorough or complete 详尽的；彻底的；全面的：***exhaustive research/tests*** 彻底的研究；全面的测试 ◇ *This list is not intended to be exhaustive.* 这份清单不求详尽无遗。 ▶ **ex·haust·ive·ly** *adv.*：*Every product is exhaustively tested before being sold.* 每件产品销售前都经过全面检验。

exˈhaust pipe *noun* = EXHAUST (2)

ex·hibit 🔑 **AW** /ɪɡˈzɪbɪt/ *verb, noun*

■ ***verb*** **1** 🔑 [T, I] to show sth in a public place for people to enjoy or to give them information 展览；展出：**~ sth (at/in…)** *They will be exhibiting their new designs at the trade fairs.* 他们将在商品交易会上展出他们新的设计。◇ **~ (at/in…)** *He exhibits regularly in local art galleries.* 他经常在当地的画廊举办画展。 **2** [T] **~ sth** (*formal*) to show clearly that you have or feel a particular feeling, quality or ability 表现，显示，显出（感情、品质或能力）**SYN** **display**: *The patient exhibited signs of fatigue and memory loss.* 病人表现出疲劳和记忆力丧失的迹象。

■ ***noun*** **1** 🔑 an object or a work of art put in a public place, for example a museum, so that people can see it（一件）展览品，陈列品 **2** a thing that is used in court to prove that sb is guilty or not guilty（在法庭上出示的）物证，证据：*The first exhibit was a knife which the prosecution claimed was the murder weapon.* 当庭出示的第一件物证就是原告称为杀人凶器的一把刀。 **3** 🔑 (*NAmE*) = EXHIBITION (1)：*The new exhibit will tour a dozen US cities next year.* 这批新展品明年将在美国十几个城市巡回展出。

ex·hib·ition 🔑 **AW** /ˌeksɪˈbɪʃn/ *noun* **1** 🔑 (*especially BrE*) (*NAmE usually* **ex·hibit**) [C] a collection of things, for example works of art, that are shown to the public（一批）展览品：*Have you seen the Picasso exhibition?* 你看过毕加索的画展吗？◇ *an exhibition of old photographs* 老照片展 ➲ WORDFINDER NOTE AT CONFERENCE, PAINTING ➲ COLLOCATIONS AT ART **2** [U] **~ of sth** the act of showing sth, for example works of art, to the public 展览；展出：*She refused to allow the exhibition of her husband's work.* 她拒不允许展出她丈夫的作品。 **3** [sing.] **an ~ of sth** (*formal*) the act of showing a skill, a feeling, or a kind of behaviour（技能、感情或行为的）表现，显示，表演：*We were treated to an exhibition of the footballer's speed and skill.* 足球运动员表现出的速度和技术，真让我们大饱眼福。◇ *an appalling exhibition of bad manners* 极其恶劣无礼的行为 **4** [C] (*BrE*) an amount of money that is given as a prize to a student 奖学金

IDM **make an exhiˈbition of yourself** (*disapproving*) to behave in a bad or stupid way in public 出洋相；当众出丑

ex·hib·ition·ism /ˌeksɪˈbɪʃənɪzəm/ *noun* [U] **1** (*disapproving*) behaviour that is intended to make people notice or admire you 表现癖；表现狂；出风头 **2** (*psychology* 心) the mental condition that makes sb want to show their sexual organs in public 露阴癖；露阴狂；裸露癖

ex·hib·ition·ist /ˌeksɪˈbɪʃənɪst/ *noun* (*usually disapproving*) a person who likes to make other people notice him or her 好出风头者；好表现者：*Children are natural exhibitionists.* 儿童天生好表现自己。

ex·hib·it·or /ɪɡˈzɪbɪtə(r)/ *noun* a person or a company that shows their work or products to the public 参展者；参展商

ex·hil·ar·ate /ɪɡˈzɪləreɪt/ *verb* **~ sb** to make sb feel very happy and excited 使高兴；使兴奋；使激动：*Speed had always exhilarated him.* 速度总让他感到兴奋。 ▶ **ex·hil·ar·ated** *adj.*：*I felt exhilarated after a morning of skiing.* 我滑了一上午的雪兴奋不已。 ➲ SYNONYMS AT EXCITED **ex·hil·ar·ation** /ɪɡˌzɪləˈreɪʃn/ *noun* [U]：*the exhilaration of performing on stage* 在舞台上演出的激动心情

ex·hil·ar·at·ing /ɪɡˈzɪləreɪtɪŋ/ *adj.* very exciting and enjoyable 使人兴奋的；令人激动的；令人高兴的：*My first parachute jump was an exhilarating experience.* 我第一次跳伞的经历很令人激动。➲ SYNONYMS AT EXCITING

ex·hort /ɪɡˈzɔːt; *NAmE* ɪɡˈzɔːrt/ *verb* (*formal*) to try hard to persuade sb to do sth 规劝；敦促；告诫 **SYN** **urge**: **~ sb to do sth** *The party leader exhorted his members to start preparing for government.* 该党领袖敦促党员着手准备筹建政府的工作。◇ **~ sb to sth** *They had been exhorted to action.* 已经告诫他们采取行动。◇ **~ (sb) + speech** *'Come on!' he exhorted (them).* "快点！"他敦促（他们）道。 ▶ **ex·hort·ation** /ˌeɡzɔːˈteɪʃn; *NAmE* -zɔːrˈt-/ *noun* [C, U]

ex·hume /eksˈhjuːm; ɪɡˈzjuːm; *NAmE* ɪɡˈzuːm/ *verb* [usually passive] **~ sth** (*formal*) to remove a dead body from the ground especially in order to examine how the person died（为检查死因）掘出（尸首）**SYN** **dig up** ▶ **ex·hum·ation** /ˌekshjuːˈmeɪʃn/ *noun* [U]

exi·gency /ˈeksɪdʒənsi; ɪɡˈzɪdʒ-/ *noun* [C, usually pl., U] (*pl.* **-ies**) (*formal*) an urgent need or demand that you must deal with 急切需要；迫切要求 **SYN** **demand**

ex·igu·ous /eɡˈzɪɡjuəs/ *adj.* (*formal*) very small in size or amount; hardly enough 微小的；稀少的；不够的

exile /ˈeksaɪl; ˈeɡzaɪl/ *noun, verb*

■ ***noun*** **1** [U, sing.] the state of being sent to live in another country that is not your own, especially for political reasons or as a punishment 流放；流亡；放逐：*to be/live **in exile*** 在流放中；过流放生活 ◇ *to be forced/sent **into exile*** 被流放 ◇ *to go **into exile*** 流亡 ◇ *a place of exile* 流放地 ◇ *He returned after 40 years of exile.* 他流放 40 年后归来。 **2** [C] a person who chooses, or is forced to live away from his or her own country 流亡国外者；被流放者；离乡背井者：*political exiles* 政治流亡者 ◇ *a **tax exile*** (= a rich person who moves to another country where taxes are lower) 迁居低税国家的富人

■ ***verb*** [usually passive] **~ sb** (**from…**) to force sb to leave their country, especially for political reasons or as a punishment; to send sb into exile 流放；放逐：*the party's exiled leaders* 该党的流亡领袖

exist /ɪɡˈzɪst/ *verb* **1** [I] (not used in the progressive tenses 不用于进行时) to be real; to be present in a place or situation 存在；实际上有：*Does life exist on other planets?* 其他行星上有生命吗？◇ *The problem only exists in your head, Jane.* 这个问题不过是你的想象，简。◇ *Few of these monkeys still exist in the wild.* 这些野生的猴子已为数不多了。◇ *On his retirement the post will* **cease to exist**. 他退休后这个职位将不复存在。◇ *The charity exists to support victims of crime.* 设立这个慈善机构是为了援助罪案受害者。 **2** [I] ~ (**on sth**) to live, especially in a difficult situation or with very little money（尤指在困境或贫困中）生活，生存：*We existed on a diet of rice.* 我们靠吃大米过活。◇ *They can't exist on the money he's earning.* 他们靠他挣的那点钱无法维持生活。

ex·ist·ence /ɪɡˈzɪstəns/ *noun* **1** [U] the state or fact of being real or living or of being present 存在；实有：*I was unaware of his existence until today.* 直到今天我才知道有他这么个人。◇ *This is the oldest Hebrew manuscript* **in existence**. 这是现存最古老的希伯来文手稿。◇ *Pakistan* **came into existence** *as an independent country in 1947.* 巴基斯坦在 1947 年成为了独立国家。◇ *a crisis that threatens the industry's continued existence* 对这一行业的继续生存构成威胁的危机 **2** [C] a way of living especially when this is difficult or boring（尤指艰难或无聊的）生活，生活方式：*The family endured a miserable existence in a cramped apartment.* 这家人在狭小的公寓里艰难度日。◇ *We led a poor but happy enough existence as children.* 我们儿时的生活虽然贫穷却过得很愉快。◇ *They eke out a precarious existence* (= they have hardly enough money to live on). 他们勉强维持着朝不保夕的生活。◇ *The peasants depend on a good harvest for their* **very existence** (= in order to continue to live). 农民靠丰收才能活命。

ex·ist·ent /ɪɡˈzɪstənt/ *adj., noun*
- **adj.** (*formal*) existing; real 存在的；实有的：*creatures existent in nature* 自然界中现存的生物 OPP **non-existent**
- **noun** (*philosophy* 哲) a thing that is real and exists 存在（或实有）的事物：*The self is the only knowable existent.* 自我是唯一可知的存在物。

ex·ist·en·tial /ˌeɡzɪˈstenʃəl/ *adj.* [only before noun] **1** (*formal*) connected with human existence 关于人类存在的；与人类存在有关的 **2** (*philosophy* 哲) connected with the theory of existentialism（关于）存在主义的

ex·ist·en·tial·ism /ˌeɡzɪˈstenʃəlɪzəm/ *noun* [U] (*philosophy* 哲) the theory that humans are free and responsible for their own actions in a world without meaning 存在主义 ▸ **ex·ist·en·tial·ist** /-ʃəlɪst/ *noun*：*Sartre was an existentialist.* 萨特是个存在主义者。 **ex·ist·en·tial·ist** /-ʃəlɪst/ *adj.*：*existentialist theory* 存在主义理论

ex·ist·ing /ɪɡˈzɪstɪŋ/ *adj.* [only before noun] found or used now 现存的；现行的：*New laws will soon replace existing legislation.* 新法即将取代现行法规。

exit /ˈeksɪt; ˈeɡzɪt/ *noun, verb*
- **noun 1** a way out of a public building or vehicle 出口；通道；太平门：*Where's the exit?* 出口在哪儿？◇ *There is a* **fire exit** *on each floor of the building.* 这栋建筑每层楼都有个消防通道。◇ *The* **emergency exit** *is at the back of the bus.* 紧急出口在公共汽车的尾部。 ➲ COMPARE ENTRANCE[1] **2** an act of leaving, especially of an actor from the stage 退出；离去；（尤指演员）退场：*The heroine* **made her exit** *to great applause.* 女主角在热烈的掌声中退场。◇ *He made a quick exit to avoid meeting her.* 他迅速离去以避免见到她。◇ *an* **exit visa** (= a stamp in a passport giving sb permission to leave a particular country) 出境签证 ➲ WORDFINDER NOTE AT PLAY **3** a place where vehicles can leave a road to join another road（车辆可以从一道路驶出进入另一道路的）出口，出路：*Leave the roundabout at the second exit.* 在第二个出口处驶离环岛。◇ *Take the exit for Brno.* 从通往布尔诺的出口驶出。
- **verb 1** [I, T] (*formal*) to go out; to leave a building, stage, vehicle, etc. 出去；离去；退场：(**+ adv./prep.**) *The bullet entered her back and exited through her chest.* 子弹从她背部射入，穿胸而出。◇ *We exited via a fire door.* 我们从防火安全门走了出去。◇ **~ sth** *As the actors exited the stage the lights went on.* 演员们退场时灯光便亮了起来。 **2** [I, T] to finish using a computer program 退出（计算机程序）：**~ (from sth)** *To exit from this page, press the return key.* 退出本页面按返回键。◇ **~ sth** *I exited the database and switched off the computer.* 我退出数据库后关掉了计算机。 **3** [I] **exit…** used in the instructions printed in a play to say that an actor must leave the stage（剧本里的指示）退场，退下 ➲ COMPARE EXEUNT

ˈexit exam (*also formal* **ˈexit examination**) *noun* (*especially NAmE*) an exam that you take at the end of the last year in school or at the end of a period of training 毕业考试；结业考试：*a high school exit exam* 中学毕业考试

ˈexit poll *noun* in an **exit poll** immediately after an election, people are asked how they voted, in order to predict the result of the election 出口民调；投票后民调

ex libris /ˌeks ˈlɪbrɪs; ˈliːb-/ *adv.* (*from Latin*) written in the front of a book before the name of the person the book belongs to（写于书前页的藏书者姓名前）…的藏书，…的藏本：*ex libris David Harries* 戴维•哈里斯藏书

exo·crine /ˈeksəʊkraɪn; -krɪn; *NAmE* ˈeksəkrɪn; -kriːn/ *adj.* (*biology* 生) connected with GLANDS that do not put substances directly into the blood but export their product through tubes for use outside the body 外分泌的；外分泌腺的：*exocrine glands* 外分泌腺 ➲ COMPARE ENDOCRINE

exo·dus /ˈeksədəs/ *noun* [sing.] ~ (**from…**) (**to…**) (*formal* or *humorous*) a situation in which many people leave a place at the same time（大批人同时）离开，外出，出去：*the* **mass exodus** *from Paris to the country in the summer* 夏日大批人离开巴黎到乡村

ex of·fi·cio /ˌeks əˈfɪʃiəʊ; *NAmE* -ʃioʊ/ *adj.* (*from Latin, formal*) included or allowed because of your job, position or rank 出于工作（或职位、职权）的；（由于工作、职位或职权而成为的）当然的：*an ex officio member of the committee* 委员会的当然委员 ▸ **ex of·fi·cio** *adv.*

ex·og·amy /ekˈsɒɡəmi; *NAmE* -ˈsɑːɡ-/ *noun* [U] (*specialist*) marriage outside your family or CASTE (= division of society) 族外婚；外婚制 ➲ COMPARE ENDOGAMY ▸ **ex·og·am·ous** /ekˈsɒɡəməs; *NAmE* -ˈsɑːɡ-/ *adj.*

ex·ogen·ous /ekˈsɒdʒənəs; ɪk-; *NAmE* ekˈsɑːdʒ-/ *adj.* (*medical* 医) (of a disease or SYMPTOM 疾病或症状) having a cause that is outside the body 外源性的 ➲ COMPARE ENDOGENOUS

ex·on·er·ate /ɪɡˈzɒnəreɪt; *NAmE* -ˈzɑːn-/ *verb* **~ sb** (**from sth**) (*formal*) to officially state that sb is not responsible for sth that they have been blamed for 宣布（某人）无罪；免除责任：*The police report exonerated Lewis from all charges of corruption.* 警方的报告免除了对刘易斯贪污的所有指控。 ▸ **ex·on·er·ation** /ɪɡˌzɒnəˈreɪʃn; *NAmE* -ˌzɑːnə-/ *noun* [U]

ex·or·bi·tant /ɪɡˈzɔːbɪtənt; *NAmE* -ˈzɔːrb-/ *adj.* (*formal*) (of a price 价格) much too high 过高的；高得离谱的：***exorbitant costs/fares/fees/prices/rents*** 过高的花费 / 交通费 / 收费 / 价格 / 租金 ▸ **ex·or·bi·tant·ly** *adv.*：*Prices are exorbitantly high in this shop.* 这家商店的价格高得离谱。

ex·or·cise (*also* **-ize**) /ˈeksɔːsaɪz; *NAmE* -sɔːrs-/ *verb* **1 ~ sth** (**from sb/sth**) to make an evil spirit leave a place or sb's body by special prayers or magic（用祈祷或法术）祛除（邪恶），驱（魔） **2 ~ sth** (**from sth**) (*formal*) to remove sth that is bad or painful from your mind 消除，除去（不好的或痛苦的想法）：*She had managed to exorcise these unhappy memories from her mind.* 她终于把这些不愉快的记忆从头脑中抹掉了。

ex·or·cism /ˈeksɔːsɪzəm; *NAmE* -sɔːrs-/ *noun* [U, C] **1** the act of getting rid of an evil spirit from a place or a person's body by prayers or magic; a ceremony where this is done（用祈祷或法术）驱魔，驱邪，驱邪的仪式 **2** (*formal*) the act of making yourself forget a bad experience or memory（不愉快的经历或记忆的）消除，忘掉

ex·or·cist /ˈeksɔːsɪst; *NAmE* -sɔːrs-/ *noun* a person who makes evil spirits leave a place or a person's body by prayers or magic （用祈祷或法术）驱邪的法师，驱魔者

exo·skel·eton /ˈeksəʊskelɪtn; *NAmE* ˈeksoʊ-/ *noun* (*biology* 生) a hard outer covering that protects the bodies of certain animals, such as insects （昆虫等动物的）外骨骼 ➲ COMPARE ENDOSKELETON

exo·ther·mic /ˌeksəʊˈθɜːmɪk; *NAmE* ˌeksoʊˈθɜːrmɪk/ *adj.* (*chemistry* 化) (of a chemical reaction 化学反应) producing heat 放热的 ➲ COMPARE ENDOTHERMIC

exot·ic /ɪɡˈzɒtɪk; *NAmE* ɪɡˈzɑːtɪk/ *adj.* from or in another country, especially a tropical one; seeming exciting and unusual because it is connected with foreign countries 来自异国（尤指热带国家）的；奇异的；异国情调的；异国风味的： *brightly-coloured **exotic flowers/plants/birds*** 色彩鲜艳的异国花卉 / 植物 / 鸟儿 ◇ *She travels to all kinds of exotic locations all over the world.* 她走遍了全世界所有具有奇异风情的地方。 ▶ **exot·ic·al·ly** *adv.*: *rainbows of exotically coloured blooms* 奇异的七彩花彩虹

exot·ica /ɪɡˈzɒtɪkə; *NAmE* ɪɡˈzɑːt-/ *noun* [U] unusual and exciting things, especially from other countries （尤指来自异国的）奇异事物，异族事物

eˌxotic ˈdancer *noun* an entertainer who dances with very few clothes on, or who removes clothes while dancing 脱衣舞女；艳舞女郎

exoti·cism /ɪɡˈzɒtɪsɪzəm; *NAmE* ɪɡˈzɑːt-/ *noun* [U] (*formal*) the quality of being exciting and unusual that sth has because it is connected with foreign countries 异国情调；外国风情

ex·pand 🔑 AW /ɪkˈspænd/ *verb* **1** 🔑 [I, T] to become greater in size, number or importance; to make sth greater in size, number or importance 扩大，增加，增强（尺码、数量或重要性）： *Metals expand when they are heated.* 金属受热会膨胀。 ◇ *Student numbers are expanding rapidly.* 学生人数在迅速增加。 ◇ *A child's vocabulary expands through reading.* 孩子的词汇量通过阅读得到扩大。 ◇ *The waist expands to fit all sizes.* 腰部可松可紧，适合任何尺码。 ◇ **~ sth** *In breathing the chest muscles expand the rib cage and allow air to be sucked into the lungs.* 呼吸时胸部肌肉使胸廓扩大让空气吸入肺部。 ◇ *The new system expanded the role of family doctors.* 新体制扩大了家庭医生的作用。 ◇ *There are no plans to expand the local airport.* 目前没有扩建地方机场的计划。 OPP **contract** **2** 🔑 [I, T] if a business **expands** or **is expanded**, new branches are opened, it makes more money, etc. 扩展，发展（业务）： *an expanding economy* (= with more businesses starting and growing) 不断发展的经济 ◇ **~ sth** *We've expanded the business by opening two more stores.* 我们增开了两家商店以扩展业务。 **3** [I] to talk more; to add details to what you are saying 细谈；详述；详细阐明： *I repeated the question and waited for her to expand.* 我把问题重复了一遍，等着她详细回答。

PHR V **exˈpand on/upon sth** to say more about sth and add some details 详述；充分叙述；详细阐明： *Could you expand on that point, please?* 请你把那一点详细说明一下好吗？

ex·pand·able /ɪkˈspændəbl/ *adj.* (*specialist*) that can be expanded 可扩张的；可扩充的；可膨胀的： *an expandable briefcase* 可伸缩公文包 ◇ **~ to sth** *The system has 1GB RAM, expandable to 4GB.* 这个系统的内存为 1 千兆字节，可扩充到 4 千兆字节。

ex·panse /ɪkˈspæns/ *noun* ~ (**of sth**) a wide and open area of sth, especially land or water 一大片，广阔，宽广，浩瀚（尤指陆地或海洋）： *a **wide/vast expanse** of blue sky* 广阔的蓝天 ◇ *flat expanses of open farmland* 平坦而辽阔的农田

ex·pan·sion AW /ɪkˈspænʃn/ *noun* [U, C] an act of increasing or making sth increase in size, amount or importance 扩张；扩展；扩大；膨胀： *a period of rapid economic expansion* 经济迅猛发展期 ◇ *Despite the recession the company is confident of further expansion.* 尽管经济衰退，公司对进一步扩展仍充满信心。 ◇ *The book is an expansion of a series of lectures given last year.* 本书是去年举行的系列讲座的扩充。

ex·pan·sion·ary /ɪkˈspænʃənri/ *adj.* (*formal*) encouraging economic expansion 刺激经济扩张的： *This budget will have a net expansionary effect on the economy.* 本预算对经济的发展最终会有促进作用。

exˈpansion card (*also* **ˈadd-in**) *noun* (*computing* 计) a CIRCUIT BOARD that can be put into a computer to give it more memory or make it able to do more things 扩展卡

ex·pan·sion·ism AW /ɪkˈspænʃənɪzəm/ *noun* [U] (*sometimes disapproving*) the belief in and process of increasing the size and importance of sth, especially in a country or a business 扩张主义；扩张政策： *the economic expansionism of America* 美国的经济扩张主义 ◇ ***military/territorial expansionism*** 军事 / 领土扩张主义 ▶ **ex·pan·sion·ist** /-ʃənɪst/ *adj.*: *expansionist policies* 扩张主义政策 **ex·pan·sion·ist** /-ʃənɪst/ *noun*: *He was a ruthless expansionist.* 他是个残酷的扩张主义者。

ex·pan·sive AW /ɪkˈspænsɪv/ *adj.* **1** covering a large amount of space 广阔的；辽阔的；浩瀚的： *She opened her arms wide in an expansive gesture of welcome.* 她展开双臂以示欢迎。 ◇ *landscape with expansive skies* 以辽阔蓝天为背景的风景 **2** covering a large subject area, rather than trying to be exact and use few words 广泛的；全面的： *We need to look at a more expansive definition of the term.* 我们需要考虑这个用语所包含的更广泛意义。 ◇ *The piece is written in his usual expansive style.* 这篇文章是以他惯常的洋洋洒洒的风格写成的。 **3** friendly and willing to talk a lot 友善健谈的；开朗的： *She was clearly relaxed and in an expansive mood.* 她显然悠闲自在，心情豁朗。 **4** (especially of a period of time 尤指一段时间) encouraging economic EXPANSION 刺激经济扩展的： *In the expansive 1990s bright graduates could advance rapidly.* 在经济发展快速的 20 世纪 90 年代，有才华的大学毕业生可以发展很快。 ▶ **ex·pan·sive·ly** *adv.*: *He waved his arms expansively.* 他豪爽地挥舞着双臂。 **ex·pan·sive·ness** *noun* [U]

ex·pati·ate /ɪkˈspeɪʃieɪt/ *verb*

PHR V **exˈpatiate on/upon sth** (*formal*) to write or speak in detail about a subject 详述；细说；阐述

ex·patri·ate /ˌeksˈpætriət; *NAmE* -ˈpeɪt-/ (*also informal* **expat** /ˌeksˈpæt/) *noun* a person living in a country that is not their own 居住在国外的人；侨民： *American expatriates in Paris* 居住在巴黎的美国人 ▶ **ex·patri·ate** *adj.* [only before noun]: *expatriate Britons in Spain* 居住在西班牙的英国人 ◇ *expatriate workers* 在国外工作的人

ex·pect 🔑 /ɪkˈspekt/ *verb* **1** 🔑 [T] to think or believe that sth will happen or that sb will do sth 预料；预期；预计： **~ sth** *We are expecting a rise in food prices this month.* 我们预计这个月的食物价格会上涨。 ◇ **~ sth from sb/sth** *Don't expect sympathy from me!* 休想得到我的同情！ ◇ **~ sth of sb/sth** *That's not the sort of behaviour I expect of you!* 我不敢相信你竟有那样的行为！ ◇ **~ to do sth** *You can't expect to learn a foreign language in a few months.* 不要指望在几个月内就能学会一门外语。 ◇ *I looked back, **half expecting** to see someone following me.* 我回过头去，预计可能看到有人跟踪我。 ◇ **~ sb/sth to do sth** *House prices are expected to rise sharply.* 预计房价会急剧上涨。 ◇ *Do you really expect me to believe you?* 你真以为我会相信你吗？ ◇ **~ (that)**… *Many people were expecting (that) the peace talks would break down.* 许多人预料和平谈判会破裂。 ◇ **it is expected that**… *It is expected that the report will suggest some major reforms.* 预计这个报告会提出一些重大的改革。 ➲ MORE LIKE THIS 26, page R28 **2** 🔑 [T] (often used in the progressive tenses 常用于进行时) to be waiting for sb/sth to arrive, as this has been arranged 等待；期待；盼望： **~ sb/sth** *to expect a visit/call/letter from sb* 等待某人的来访 / 电话 / 来信 ◇ *Are you expecting visitors?* 你在等客人吗？ ◇ *We were expecting him yesterday.* 我们昨天一直在等他。 ◇ **~ sb to do sth** *We were expecting him to arrive yesterday.* 我们一直盼望着他昨天到达。 **3** 🔑 [T] to demand that sb will do sth because it is their duty or responsibility 要求；期望；指望：**~ sth (from sb)** *Her parents expected high standards from her.* 她的父母对她的期望很高。◇ *He's still getting over his illness, so don't expect too much from him.* 他仍处于康复期，所以不要对他期望过高。◇ **~ sth (of sb)** *Are you clear what is expected of you?* 你清楚大家对你的期望吗？◇ **~ sb to do sth** *They expected all their children to be high achievers.* 他们期望自己所有的孩子都大有作为。◇ **~ to do sth** *I expect to be paid promptly for the work.* 我希望立即给付工钱。➲ SYNONYMS AT DEMAND **4** [I, T] (*informal, especially BrE*) (not used in the progressive tenses 不用于进行时) used when you think sth is probably true 猜想；认为；料想：*'Will you be late?' 'I expect so.'* "你会迟到吗？""我想会的。"◇ *'Are you going out tonight?' 'I don't expect so.'* "你今晚要出去吗？""我想不会吧。"◇ **~ (that...)** *'Who's eaten all the cake?' 'Tom, I expect/I expect it was Tom.'* "谁把蛋糕都吃光了？""我想是汤姆吧。" HELP 'That' is nearly always left out. * that 几乎总是被省略。➲ COMPARE UNEXPECTED

IDM **be expecting a baby/child** (*informal*) to be pregnant 怀孕；怀胎：*Ann's expecting a baby in June.* 安六月份要生孩子。 **be (only) to be ex'pected** to be likely to happen; to be quite normal 可能发生；可以预料；相当正常：*A little tiredness after taking these drugs is to be expected.* 服用这些药后有点倦意是正常的。 **what (else) do you ex'pect?** (*informal*) used to tell sb not to be surprised by sth 那有什么大惊小怪的；那还用得着惊奇吗；那还用说吗：*She swore at you? What do you expect when you treat her like that?* 她用粗话骂你了？你那样待她那还用说吗？

▼ **LANGUAGE BANK 用语库**

expect

Discussing predictions 谈论预测

- *The number of people using mobile phones to purchase goods and services is* ***expected/likely*** *to more than double by the end of 2015.* 到 2015 年年底，使用手机购买商品和服务的人数预计 / 可能会是现在的两倍多。
- *Experts have* ***predicted/forecast*** *that the number of people using their mobile phones to pay for goods and services should exceed 190 million in 2015.* 专家已经预言，到 2015 年使用手机支付商品和服务费用的人数将超过 1.9 亿。
- *This figure* ***is set to*** *reach 200 million by 2016.* 到 2016 年这个数字可能会达到 2 亿。
- *By 2015, 800 million mobile phone users worldwide* ***will*** *be participating in social networks via their phone.* 到 2015 年，全球将有 8 亿手机用户通过手机参与社交网络。
- *Sales of mobile phones in 2009 were lower* ***than expected.*** * 2009 年的手机销量低于预期。
- *The company's announcement of 1.26 billion handsets sold for the year is* ***in line with predictions.*** 公司宣布本年度手机销量为 12.6 亿部，符合预期。

➲ LANGUAGE BANK AT FALL, ILLUSTRATE, INCREASE, PROPORTION

ex·pect·ancy /ɪk'spektənsi/ *noun* [U] the state of expecting or hoping that sth, especially sth good or exciting, will happen 预料；预期；期待；盼望：*There was* ***an air of expectancy*** *among the waiting crowd.* 等待的人群心怀期盼。➲ SEE ALSO LIFE EXPECTANCY

ex·pect·ant /ɪk'spektənt/ *adj.* **1** hoping for sth, especially sth good and exciting 期待的；预期的；期望的：*children with expectant faces waiting for the fireworks to begin* 带着期盼的神情等待烟火表演的孩子们 ◇ *A sudden roar came from the expectant crowd.* 期待的人群中突然欢声雷动。 **2 ~ mother/father/parent** used to describe sb who is going to have a baby soon or become a father 准（母亲、父亲、父母） ▶ **ex·pect·ant·ly** *adv.*：*She looked at him expectantly.* 她满怀期望地看着他。◇ *waiting expectantly* 满怀期望地等待

ex·pect·ation /ˌekspek'teɪʃn/ *noun* **1** [U, C] a belief that sth will happen because it is likely 预料；预期；期待：**~ (of sth)** *We are confident in our expectation of a full recovery.* 我们满怀信心地期待着完全康复。◇ **~ (that...)** *There was a general expectation that he would win.* 普遍认为他会获胜。◇ *The expectation is that property prices will rise.* 预计地产价格会上涨。◇ *I applied for the post more in hope than expectation.* 我申请这个职位是希望多于期待。◇ ***Contrary to expectations,*** *interest rates did not rise.* 出乎意料的是利率并未上升。◇ ***Against all expectations,*** *she was enjoying herself.* 完全没想到她过得非常快活。 **2** [C, usually pl., U] a hope that sth good will happen 希望；盼望：*She went to college with great expectations.* 她满怀希望地进入大学。◇ *There was an air of expectation and great curiosity.* 有着一种期待和强烈好奇的气氛。◇ *The results exceeded our expectations.* 结果比我们希望的还好。◇ *The numbers attending fell short of expectations.* 出席的人数比预期的要少。◇ *The event did not* ***live up to expectations.*** 这项活动有负众望。 **3** [C, usually pl.] a strong belief about the way sth should happen or how sb should behave 期望；指望：*Some parents have unrealistic expectations of their children.* 有些父母对孩子的指望不切实际。◇ *Unfortunately the new software has failed to* ***meet expectations.*** 遗憾的是新软件并不理想。

ˌexpectation of 'life *noun* [U] = LIFE EXPECTANCY

ex·pect·ed /ɪk'spektɪd/ *adj.* that you think will happen 预料的；预期的：*Double the expected number of people came to the meeting.* 出席会议的人数比预期的多一倍。◇ *this year's expected earnings* 今年的预计收入 ➲ COMPARE UNEXPECTED

ex·pec·tor·ant /ɪk'spektərənt/ *noun* (*medical* 医) a cough medicine that helps you to get rid of thick liquid (= PHLEGM) from the lungs 祛痰药

ex·pec·tor·ate /ɪk'spektəreɪt/ *verb* [I] (*formal*) to cough and make PHLEGM come up from your lungs into your mouth so you can SPIT it out 咳出（痰） ▶ **ex·pec·tor·ation** /ɪkˌspektə'reɪʃn/ *noun* [U]

ex·pe·di·ent /ɪk'spiːdiənt/ *noun, adj.*

■ ***noun*** an action that is useful or necessary for a particular purpose, but not always fair or right 权宜之计；应急办法：*The disease was controlled* ***by the simple expedient of*** *not allowing anyone to leave the city.* 采取了禁止所有人出城的简单应急办法，使疾病得到了控制。

■ ***adj.*** [not usually before noun] (of an action 行动) useful or necessary for a particular purpose, but not always fair or right 得当；可取；合宜；权宜之计：*The government has clearly decided that a cut in interest rates would be politically expedient.* 政府显然认为削减利率是政治上的权宜之计。 OPP **inexpedient** ▶ **ex·pe·di·ency** /-ənsi/ *noun* [U]：*He acted out of expediency, not principle.* 他的行为是出于权宜之计而非原则。 **ex·pe·di·ent·ly** *adv.*

ex·ped·ite /'ekspədaɪt/ *verb* **~ sth** (*formal*) to make a process happen more quickly 加快；加速 SYN **speed up**：*We have developed rapid order processing to expedite deliveries to customers.* 我们已开发了快速处理订单的方法以便迅速将货物交给顾客。

ex·ped·ition /ˌekspə'dɪʃn/ *noun* **1** an organized journey with a particular purpose, especially to find out about a place that is not well known 远征；探险；考察：*to plan/lead/go on an expedition to the North Pole* 计划 / 带队 / 去北极探险 **2** the people who go on an expedition 远征队；探险队；考察队：*Five members of Scott's expedition made it to the South Pole.* 斯科特考察队的五名成员成功到达南极。 **3** (*sometimes humorous*) a short trip that you make when you want or need sth （短途的）旅行，出行：*a shopping expedition* 外出购物 ➲ SYNONYMS AT TRIP ➲ WORDFINDER NOTE AT JOURNEY

ex·ped·ition·ary force /ˌekspə'dɪʃənri fɔːs; *NAmE* -neri fɔːrs/ *noun* [C+sing./pl. v.] a group of soldiers who are sent to another country to fight in a war （派往国外参战的）远征军

ex·pe·di·tious /ˌekspəˈdɪʃəs/ *adj.* (*formal*) that works well without wasting time, money, etc. 迅速而有效的；迅速完成的 SYN **efficient** ▸ **ex·pe·di·tious·ly** *adv.*

expel /ɪkˈspel/ *verb* (-**ll**-) **1** ~ **sb** (**from sth**) to officially make sb leave a school or an organization 把…开除（或除名）：*She was expelled from school at 15.* 她 15 岁时被学校开除了。◇ *Olympic athletes expelled for drug-taking* 因服禁药被取消比赛资格的奥运会运动员 ➲ COLLOCATIONS AT EDUCATION **2** ~ **sb** (**from sth**) to force sb to leave a country 驱逐出境：*Foreign journalists are being expelled.* 外国记者被驱逐出境。**3** ~ **sth** (**from sth**) (*specialist*) to force air or water out of a part of the body or from a container 排出；喷出：*to expel air from the lungs* 用力呼出肺里的气 ➲ SEE ALSO EXPULSION

ex·pend /ɪkˈspend/ *verb* ~ **sth** (**in/on sb**) | ~ **sth** (**in/on/doing sth**) (*formal*) to use or spend a lot of time, money, energy, etc. 花费；消费；耗费：*She expended all her efforts on the care of home and children.* 她把所有精力都花在照顾家庭和孩子上。

ex·pend·able /ɪkˈspendəbl/ *adj.* (*formal*) if you consider people or things to be **expendable**, you think that you can get rid of them when they are no longer needed, or think it is acceptable if they are killed or destroyed 可牺牲的；可消耗的；可毁灭的 SYN **dispensable**

ex·pend·iture /ɪkˈspendɪtʃə(r)/ *noun* [U, C] **1** the act of spending or using money; an amount of money spent 花费；消费；费用；开支：*a reduction in* ***public/government/military expenditure*** 公共 / 政府 / 军费开支的削减 ◇ *plans to increase expenditure on health* 增加医疗保健开支的计划 ◇ *The budget provided for a total expenditure of £27 billion.* 预算案规定支出总额为 270 亿英镑。➲ SYNONYMS AT COST **2** the use of energy, time, materials, etc. （精力、时间、材料等的）耗费，消耗：*the expenditure of emotion* 感情耗费 ◇ *This study represents a major expenditure of time and effort.* 这项研究意味着要耗费大量的时间和精力。➲ COMPARE INCOME

ex·pense 🔑 /ɪkˈspens/ *noun* **1** 🔑 [U] the money that you spend on sth 费用；价钱：*The garden was transformed* ***at great expense***. 花园改建花了一大笔费用。◇ ***No expense was spared*** (= they spent as much money as was needed) *to make the party a success.* 为使聚会成功多大费用都在所不惜。◇ *He's arranged everything,* ***no expense spared***. 他不惜代价把一切安排得井井有条。◇ *She always travels first-class regardless of expense.* 无论费用多高她总是乘头等舱。◇ *The results are well worth the expense.* 有这些结果花的钱很值。➲ WORDFINDER NOTE AT MONEY ➲ SYNONYMS AT PRICE **2** 🔑 [C, usually sing.] something that makes you spend money 花钱的东西；开销：*Running a car is a big expense.* 养一辆车开销很大。**3** 🔑 **expenses** [pl.] money spent in doing a particular job, or for a particular purpose 开支；花费；费用：***living/household/medical/legal, etc. expenses*** 生活费用；家庭开支；医疗、律师等费用 ◇ *Can I give you something towards expenses?* 在开支方面我能为你做点什么吗？◇ *financial help to meet the expenses of an emergency* 供紧急情况下开支的经济援助 ◇ *The payments he gets barely cover his expenses.* 他几乎是入不敷出。➲ SYNONYMS AT COST **4** 🔑 **expenses** [pl.] money that you spend while you are working and which your employer will pay back to you later （向雇主报销的）费用，开支，花销，业务费用：*You can claim back your* ***travelling/travel*** *expenses.* 你可以报销差旅费。◇ (*BrE*) *to take a client out for a meal* ***on expenses*** 用业务费请客户外出就餐 ◇ *an* ***all-expenses-paid*** *trip* 费用全数报销的公差 ➲ SYNONYMS AT COST

IDM **at sb's expense** **1** paid for by sb 由某人付钱；由某人负担费用：*We were taken out for a meal at the company's expense.* 公司出钱请我们外出就餐。**2** if you make a joke **at sb's expense**, you laugh at them and make them feel silly 在某人受损的情况下；以某人为代价；跟某人开玩笑 **at the expense of sb/sth** with loss or damage to sb/sth 在牺牲（或损害）…的情况下：*He built up the business at the expense of his health.* 他以自己的健康为代价逐步建立起这个企业。**go to the expense of sth/of doing sth** | **go to a lot of, etc. expense** to spend money on sth 把钱用在…上；花钱于：*They went to all the expense of redecorating the house and then they moved.* 他们不惜一切代价重新装饰这房子，可后来又搬走了。**put sb to the expense of sth/of doing sth** | **put sb to a lot of, etc. expense** to make sb spend money on sth 使某人花钱（于…）；使某人负担费用：*Their visit put us to a lot of expense.* 他们的来访使我们破费不小。➲ MORE AT OBJECT *n.*

exˈpense account *noun* an arrangement by which money spent by sb while they are at work is later paid back to them by their employer; a record of money spent in this way 报销账目；费用账户

ex·pen·sive 🔑 /ɪkˈspensɪv/ *adj.* costing a lot of money 昂贵的；花钱多的；价格高的：*an expensive car/restaurant/holiday* 昂贵的汽车；高档的餐馆；花费大的假日 ◇ *Art books are expensive to produce.* 美术书籍制作成本高。◇ *I can't afford it, it's too expensive.* 我买不起，太贵了。◇ *Making the wrong decision could* ***prove expensive***. 错误的决策可能会付出昂贵的代价。◇ *That dress was an* ***expensive mistake***. 那件连衣裙看走眼买贵了。OPP **inexpensive** ▸ **ex·pen·sive·ly** *adv.*：*expensively dressed/furnished* 穿着 / 陈设华贵 ◇ *There are other restaurants where you can eat less expensively.* 还有其他一些餐馆价钱稍微便宜些。

▼ **SYNONYMS** 同义词辨析

expensive

costly • **overpriced** • **pricey** • **dear**

These words all describe sth that costs a lot of money. 以上各词均表示昂贵、花钱多。

expensive costing a lot of money; charging high prices 指昂贵的、花钱多的、价格高的：*I can't afford it—it's just too expensive for me.* 我买不起，对我来说这太贵了。◇ *an expensive restaurant* 高档餐馆

costly (*rather formal*) costing a lot of money, especially more than you want to pay 指昂贵的、花钱多的、价钱比愿意付的为高：*You want to avoid costly legal proceedings if you can.* 如果能够的话你希望避免昂贵的法律诉讼。

overpriced too expensive; costing more than it is worth 指价格太高的、过于昂贵的：*ridiculously overpriced designer clothes* 贵得离谱的名牌衣服

pricey (*informal*) expensive 指昂贵的、价格高的：*Houses in the village are now too pricey for local people to afford.* 如今该村镇的房价太高，当地人根本买不起。

dear [not usually before noun] (*BrE*) expensive 指昂贵、价格高：*Everything's so dear now, isn't it?* 现在什么东西都那么贵，是不是？ NOTE This word is starting to become rather old-fashioned. 这词已开始有些过时了。

PATTERNS

- expensive/costly/overpriced/pricey **for** sb/sth
- expensive/costly **to do sth**
- **very/too/fairly/quite/pretty** expensive/costly/pricey

ex·peri·ence 🔑 /ɪkˈspɪəriəns; *NAmE* -ˈspɪr-/ *noun, verb*

■ ***noun*** **1** 🔑 [U] the knowledge and skill that you have gained through doing sth for a period of time; the process of gaining this （由实践得来的）经验；实践：*to have over ten years' teaching experience* 有十多年教学经验 ◇ *Do you have any* ***previous experience*** *of this type of work?* 你以前干过这种工作吗？◇ *a doctor with* ***experience in*** *dealing with patients suffering from stress* 在治疗心理应激的病人方面很有经验的医生 ◇ *My lack of* ***practical experience*** *was a disadvantage.* 我缺少实际经验是个不利条件。◇ *She didn't get paid much but it was all* ***good experience***. 她得到的报酬虽然不高，但有极好的体验。◇ *He gained valuable experience whilst working on the project.* 从事这项工程使他获得了宝贵的经验。◇ ***We all learn by experience***. 我们都从经验中学习。➲ SEE ALSO WORK EXPERIENCE ➲ WORDFINDER NOTE AT APPLY **2** 🔑 [U] the things that have happened to you that influence the way you think and behave 经历；阅历：*Experience has taught me that life can be very unfair.* 经历使我懂得人生有时是很不公平的。◇ *It is important to try and* ***learn from experience.*** 努力从经验中学习是重要的。◇ ***In my experience,*** *very few people really understand the problem.* 据我的经验看，真正理解这个问题的人很少。◇ *She knew* ***from past experience*** *that Ann would not give up easily.* 她凭以往的经验知道安是不会轻易放弃的。◇ *The book is based on* ***personal experience.*** 本书是以个人经历为基础的。◇ ***direct/first-hand experience*** *of poverty* 对贫穷的直接 / 亲身感受 **3** [C] an event or activity that affects you in some way（一次）经历，体验：*an enjoyable/exciting/unusual/unforgettable, etc. experience* 愉快、激动人心、异乎寻常、难以忘记等的经历 ◇ **~ (of sth)** *It was her first experience of living alone.* 那是她第一次体验单独生活。◇ *Living in Africa was very different from home and* ***quite an experience*** (= unusual for us). 生活在非洲完全不同于在家里，那真是一次不同寻常的经历。◇ *I had a bad experience with fireworks once.* 我放烟火有过一次不愉快的遭遇。◇ *He seems to have had some sort of religious experience.* 他似乎有某种宗教体验。 **4 the… experience** [sing.] events or knowledge shared by all the members of a particular group in society, that influences the way they think and behave 传统：*musical forms like jazz that emerged out of the Black American experience* 诸如爵士乐这类起源于美国黑人传统的音乐形式

IDM **put sth down to ex'perience** (*also* **chalk sth up to ex'perience**) used to say that sb should think of a failure as being sth that they can learn from 从…中吸取教训：*We lost a lot of money, but we just put it down to experience.* 我们损失了很多钱，只当是吃一堑长一智了。

■ ***verb*** **1** **~ sth** to have a particular situation affect you or happen to you 经历；经受；遭受：*The country experienced a foreign currency shortage for several months.* 这个国家经历了几个月的外汇短缺。◇ *Everyone experiences these problems at some time in their lives.* 每个人在人生的某个阶段都会经历这些问题。 **2** **~ sth** to have and be aware of a particular emotion or physical feeling 感受；体会；体验：*to experience pain/pleasure/unhappiness* 感受痛苦 / 愉快 / 不幸 ◇ *I experienced a moment of panic as I boarded the plane.* 我上飞机时曾一度感到恐慌。

ex·peri·enced /ɪk'spɪəriənst; *NAmE* -'spɪr-/ *adj.* **1** having knowledge or skill in a particular job or activity 有经验的；熟练的：*an experienced teacher* 经验丰富的教师 ◇ **~ in sth/in doing sth** *He's very experienced in looking after animals.* 他养动物很有经验。 **2** having knowledge as a result of doing sth for a long time, or having had a lot of different experiences 有阅历的；有见识的；老练的：*She's very young and not very experienced.* 她很年轻，还不太老练。◇ *an experienced traveller* (= sb who has travelled a lot) 阅历丰富的旅行者 **OPP** **inexperienced**

ex·peri·en·tial /ɪk,spɪəri'enʃl; *NAmE* -,spɪr-/ *adj.* (*formal* or *specialist*) based on or involving experience 经验得来的；来自经验的；经验的：*experiential knowledge* 由经验得来的知识 ◇ *experiential learning methods* 由经验得来的学习方法

ex·peri·ment /ɪk'sperɪmənt/ *noun, verb*

■ ***noun*** [C, U] **1** a scientific test that is done in order to study what happens and to gain new knowledge 实验；试验：*to* ***do/perform/conduct an experiment*** 做实验 ◇ *proved* ***by experiment*** 经过实验证明 ◇ *laboratory experiments* 实验室实验 ◇ *Many people do not like the idea of experiments on animals.* 许多人不赞成在动物身上做试验。➲ WORDFINDER NOTE AT SCIENCE ➲ COLLOCATIONS AT SCIENTIFIC **2** a new activity, idea or method that you try out to see what happens or what effect it has 尝试；实践：*I've never cooked this before so it's an experiment.* 我以前从未做过这种菜，所以这是一个尝试。◇ **~ in sth** *the country's brief experiment in democracy* 这个国家对民主的短暂尝试

■ ***verb*** **1** [I] **~ (on sb/sth)** | **~ (with sth)** to do a scientific experiment or experiments 做试验；进行实验：*Some people feel that experimenting on animals is wrong.* 有人觉得利用动物做试验是不道德的。 **2** [I] **~ (on sb/sth)** | **~ (with sth)** to try or test new ideas, methods, etc. to find out what effect they have 尝试；试用：*I experimented until I got the recipe just right.* 我不断地尝试，直至找到正合适的烹饪法为止。◇ *He wanted to experiment more with different textures in his paintings.* 他想在自己的绘画中更多地尝试不同的纹理结构。▶ **ex·peri·ment·er** *noun*

ex·peri·men·tal /ɪk,sperɪ'mentl/ *adj.* **1** based on new ideas, forms or methods that are used to find out what effect they have 以实验（或试验）为基础的；实验性的；试验性的：*experimental teaching methods* 试验性教学方法 ◇ ***experimental theatre/art/music*** 实验戏剧 / 艺术 / 音乐 ◇ *The equipment is still at the experimental stage.* 这种设备仍处于试验阶段。 **2** connected with scientific experiments 科学实验的；科学试验的：***experimental conditions/data/evidence*** 实验环境 / 数据 / 证据 ▶ **ex·peri·men·tal·ly** /-təli/ *adv.*：*This theory can be confirmed experimentally.* 这种理论可通过实验得到证实。◇ *The new drug is being used experimentally on some patients.* 这种新药正由某些病人试用。◇ *He moved his shoulder experimentally to see if it still hurt.* 他试着动了动肩看看还疼不疼。

ex·peri·men·ta·tion /ɪk,sperɪmen'teɪʃn/ *noun* [U] (*formal*) the activity or process of experimenting 实验；试验：*experimentation with new teaching methods* 用新的教学方法实验 ◇ *Many people object to experimentation on embryos.* 许多人反对用胚胎做实验。

ex·pert **AW** /'ekspɜːt; *NAmE* -pɜːrt/ *noun, adj.*

■ ***noun*** a person with special knowledge, skill or training in sth 专家；行家；能手：*a computer/medical expert* 计算机 / 医学专家 ◇ **~ (at/in/on sth)** *an expert in child psychology* 儿童心理学家 ◇ *an expert on modern literature* 现代文学研究专家 ◇ **~ (at/in/on doing sth)** *He's an expert at getting his own way.* 他在如何达到自己的目的方面很在行。◇ *Don't ask me—I'm no expert!* 不要问我，我不是行家！

■ ***adj.*** done with, having or involving great knowledge or skill 熟练的；内行的；专家的；经验（或知识）丰富的：*to* ***seek expert advice/an expert opinion*** 征求专家意见 ◇ *an expert driver* 技术高超的驾驶员 ◇ *We need some expert help.* 我们需要一些内行的帮助。◇ **~ (at/in sth)** *They are all expert in this field.* 他们都是这个领域的行家。◇ **~ (at/in doing sth)** *She's expert at making cheap but stylish clothes.* 她擅长做便宜但雅致的服装。➲ COMPARE INEXPERT ▶ **ex·pert·ly** **AW** *adv.*：*The roads were icy but she stopped the car expertly.* 道路结了冰，可她却非常熟练地把车停了下来。◇ *The music was expertly performed.* 乐曲演奏得非常娴熟。

ex·pert·ise **AW** /,ekspɜː'tiːz; *NAmE* -pɜːr't-/ *noun* [U] expert knowledge or skill in a particular subject, activity or job 专门知识；专门技能；专长：***professional/scientific/technical, etc. expertise*** 专业、科学、技术等知识 ◇ *We have the expertise to help you run your business.* 我们有帮助你经营自己企业的专门知识。◇ **~ in sth/in doing sth** *They have considerable expertise in dealing with oil spills.* 他们在解决溢油问题方面非常在行。

,expert 'system *noun* (*computing* 计) a computer system that can provide information and expert advice on a particular subject. The program asks users a series of questions about their problem and gives them advice based on its store of knowledge.（计算机）专家系统

ex·pi·ate /'ekspieɪt/ *verb* **~ sth** (*formal*) to accept punishment for sth that you have done wrong in order to show that you are sorry 为（所犯罪过）接受惩罚；赎（罪）：*He had a chance to confess and expiate his guilt.* 他有认错和赎罪的机会。▶ **ex·pi·ation** /,ekspi'eɪʃn/ *noun* [U, sing.]

ex·pir·ation /,ekspə'reɪʃn/ *noun* [U] (*NAmE, formal*) = EXPIRY

expi'ration date *noun* (*NAmE*) (*BrE* **ex'piry date**) the date after which an official document, agreement, etc. is no longer valid, or after which sth should not be used or eaten（文件、协议等的）到期日，截止日期；（物品、食品等的）有效期：*Check the expiration date on your passport.* 检查一下你护照上的有效期。◇ *The expiration date on this yogurt was November 20.* 这酸奶的食用期限到11月20日。

E

ex·pire /ɪk'spaɪə(r)/ *verb* **1** [I] (of a document, an agreement, etc. 文件、协议等) to be no longer valid because the period of time for which it could be used has ended （因到期而）失效，终止；到期 SYN **run out**：*When does your driving licence expire?* 你的驾照什么时候到期？ **2** [I] (of a period of time, especially one during which sb holds a position of authority 任期等) to end 届满：*His term of office expires at the end of June.* 他的任期六月底届满。 **3** [I] (*literary*) to die 逝世；去世；故去 ▸ **ex·pired** *adj.*：*an expired passport* 过期的护照 ➲ SEE ALSO UNEXPIRED

ex·piry /ɪk'spaɪəri/ (*especially BrE*) (*NAmE usually, formal* **ex·pir·ation**) *noun* [U] an ending of the period of time when an official document can be used, or when an agreement is valid （文件、协议等的）满期，届期，到期：*the expiry of a fixed-term contract* 定期合同的满期 ◇ *The licence can be renewed on expiry.* 执照期满时可延期。

ex'piry date (*BrE*) (*NAmE* **expi'ration date**) *noun* the date after which an official document, agreement, etc. is no longer valid, or after which sth should not be used or eaten （文件、协议等的）到期日，截止日期；（物品、食品等的）有效期：*Check the expiry date of your credit cards.* 查看一下你的信用卡的有效期。

ex·plain 🔑 /ɪk'spleɪn/ *verb* **1** 🔑 [T, I] to tell sb about sth in a way that makes it easy to understand 解释；说明；阐明：~ (**sth**) (**to sb**) *First, I'll explain the rules of the game.* 首先我要说明一下游戏规则。 ◇ *It was difficult to explain the problem to beginners.* 对初学者解释这个问题很难。 ◇ *'Let me explain!' he added helpfully.* "让我来说明一下！" 他热心地补充道。 ◇ ~ **that…** *I explained that an ambulance would be coming soon.* 我解释说救护车很快就到。 ◇ ~ **who, how, etc.…** *He explained who each person in the photo was.* 他一一介绍了照片里的人。 ◇ ~ **to sb who, how, etc.…** *She explained to them what to do in an emergency.* 她向他们说明了紧急情况下应采取的行动。 ◇ + **speech** *'It works like this,' she explained.* "它是这样工作的。" 她解释道。 ◇ **it is explained that…** *It was explained that attendance was compulsory.* 所给的解释是必须到场。 **2** 🔑 [I, T] to give a reason, or be a reason, for sth 说明（…的）原因；解释（…的）理由：*She tried to explain but he wouldn't listen.* 她试图说明一下原因，可他根本不听。 ◇ ~ **that…** *Alex explained that his car had broken down.* 亚历克斯解释说他的汽车出了毛病。 ◇ ~ **why, how, etc.…** *Well, that doesn't explain why you didn't phone.* 嗳，那不是你不打电话的理由。 ◇ ~ **sth** (**to sb**) *scientific findings that help explain the origins of the universe* 有助于解释宇宙起源的科学发现 ◇ *The government now has to explain its decision to the public.* 政府现在必须向公众解释决策的理由。 ◇ (*informal*) *Oh well then, that* ***explains it*** (= I understand now why sth happened). 噢，原来是这么回事。 HELP You cannot say 'explain me, him, her, etc.'. 不能说 explain me / him / her 等：*Can you explain the situation to me?* 你能给我说明一下情况吗？ ◇ ~~*Can you explain me the situation?*~~ ◇ *I'll explain to you why I like it.* 我会向你解释我为什么喜欢它。 ◇ ~~*I'll explain you why I like it.*~~

> **WORD FAMILY**
> explain *verb*
> explanation *noun*
> explanatory *adj.*
> explicable *adj.*
> (≠ inexplicable)

IDM **ex'plain yourself** **1** 🔑 to give sb reasons for your behaviour, especially when they are angry or upset because of it 为自己的行为作说明（或解释）：*I really don't see why I should have to explain myself to you.* 我真不明白我为什么非要向你解释我的行为不可。 **2** 🔑 to say what you mean in a clear way 把自己的意思解释清楚：*Could you explain yourself a little more—I didn't understand.* 请把你的意思说得更清楚一点，我还是不明白。

PHR V **ex,plain sth↔a'way** to give reasons why sth is not your fault or why sth is not important 为…作辩解

> **▼ EXPRESS YOURSELF 情景表达**
>
> **Asking for clarification 请求澄清**
>
> When you are given some information or asked to do something, you may need to check that you have understood correctly. Here are some ways of asking people to clarify what they said. 别人告知一些信息或提出要求时需要核实自己的理解是否正确。以下是一些请求他人澄清事由的方式：
>
> - ***I'm sorry, I didn't quite understand.*** 对不起，我不太明白。
> - ***Would you mind explaining that again?*** *I'm not sure that I've understood correctly.* 请你再解释一遍行吗？我拿不准我理解得对不对。
> - ***Sorry, I don't quite follow (you).*** 抱歉，我没太听懂（你的话）。
> - ***Can I just check that I've got this right?*** 我核实一下我的理解是否正确好吗？
> - ***I'm not quite/exactly clear about/really sure*** *what I'm supposed to do.* 我不太清楚 / 不太肯定该做什么。
> - ***Sorry, could you repeat that?*** *I didn't hear what you said.* 对不起，你能再说一遍吗？你刚才说的我没听到。
> - ***Sorry, would you mind repeating what you just said?*** 对不起，请你把刚才说的话重复一遍好吗？
> - ***If I understand you correctly,*** *you want me to phone the customer and apologise?* 如果我的理解没错，你是要我打电话给客户道歉？
> - ***Do you mean (to say)*** *that the deal's off?* 你的意思是（说）交易取消了？
> - ***What exactly are you saying?*** 你到底在说什么？
> - ***So you're saying that*** *the meeting's cancelled?* 那么你是说会议取消了？
> - ***Sorry, did you mean that*** *I should wait here or come back later?* 抱歉，你的意思是我该在这里等，还是一会儿再过来？
> - ***Can you just confirm*** *your date of birth for me, please?* 请您帮我确认一下您的出生日期好吗？

ex·plan·ation 🔑 /ˌekspləˈneɪʃn/ *noun* **1** 🔑 [C, U] a statement, fact, or situation that tells you why sth happened; a reason given for sth 解释；说明；阐述：*The most likely explanation is that his plane was delayed.* 最可能的解释是他的飞机晚点了。 ◇ *to* ***offer/provide an explanation*** 给予解释 ◇ ~ (**for sth**) *I can't think of any possible explanation for his absence.* 我想不出他缺席的任何理由。 ◇ ~ (**for doing sth**) *She didn't* ***give an adequate explanation*** *for being late.* 她没有给出充分的理由说明迟到的原因。 ◇ ~ (**of sth**) *The book opens with an explanation of why some drugs are banned.* 本书在开篇阐述了禁用某些药物的原因。 ◇ ~ (**as to why…**) *an explanation as to why he had left early* 关于他提早离开的原因说明 ◇ *She left the room abruptly* ***without explanation.*** 她未作解释就突然离开了房间。 ◇ *'I had to see you,' he said, by way of explanation.* "我当时必须来找你。" 他解释道。 ➲ SYNONYMS AT REASON **2** 🔑 [C] a statement or piece of writing that tells you how sth works or makes sth easier to understand 解释性说法；说明性文字：*For a full explanation of how the machine works, turn to page 5.* 关于机器工作原理的详细说明，请翻阅第 5 页。

ex·plana·tory /ɪk'splænətri; *NAmE* -tɔːri/ *adj.* [usually before noun] giving the reasons for sth; intended to describe how sth works or to make sth easier to understand 解释的；说明的；阐述的：*There are explanatory notes at the back of the book.* 书后有注解。 ➲ SEE ALSO SELF-EXPLANATORY

ex·ple·tive /ɪk'spliːtɪv; *NAmE* 'eksplətɪv/ *noun* (*formal*) a word, especially a rude word, that you use when you are angry, or in pain （愤怒或痛苦时用的）秽语，咒骂语，感叹语 SYN **swear word**

ex·plic·able /ɪk'splɪkəbl; 'eksplɪkəbl/ *adj.* [not usually before noun] (*formal*) that can be explained or understood 可解释；可说明；可理解：*His behaviour is only explicable in terms of* (= because of) *his recent illness.* 他的行为只能用他最近患病来解释。 OPP **inexplicable**

ex·pli·cate /ˈeksplɪkeɪt/ *verb* ~ **sth** (*formal*) to explain an idea or a work of literature in a lot of detail 详细解释，详细分析（想法或文学作品）▶ **ex·pli·ca·tion** /ˌeksplɪˈkeɪʃn/ *noun* [C, U]

ex·pli·cit AW /ɪkˈsplɪsɪt/ *adj.* **1** (of a statement or piece of writing 陈述或文章) clear and easy to understand 清楚明白的；易于理解的：*He gave me very explicit directions on how to get there.* 他清楚地向我说明了去那儿的路线。 **2** (of a person 人) saying sth clearly, exactly and openly（说话）清晰的，明确的；直言的；坦率的 SYN **frank**: *She was quite explicit about why she had left.* 她对自己离开的原因直言不讳。 **3** said, done or shown in an open or direct way, so that you have no doubt about what is happening 直截了当的；不隐晦的；不含糊的：*The reasons for the decision should be made explicit.* 应该直截了当给出决定的理由。◇ *She made some very explicit references to my personal life.* 她毫不隐讳地谈到了我的私生活。◇ *a sexually explicit film* 一部有露骨性爱场面的影片 ➲ COMPARE IMPLICIT ▶ **ex·pli·cit·ly** AW *adv.*: *The report states explicitly that the system was to blame.* 报告明确指出问题出在制度上。 ➲ COMPARE IMPLICITLY at IMPLICIT **ex·pli·cit·ness** *noun* [U]: *He didn't like the degree of sexual explicitness in the film.* 他不喜欢那部电影里性爱露骨的程度。

ex·plode 🔑 /ɪkˈspləʊd; *NAmE* ɪkˈsploʊd/ *verb*

> **WORD FAMILY**
> explode *verb*
> explosion *noun*
> explosive *adj., noun*
> unexploded *adj.*

• **BURST VIOLENTLY** 爆炸 **1** 🔑 [I, T] to burst or make sth burst loudly and violently, causing damage 爆炸；爆破；爆裂 SYN **blow up**: *Bombs were exploding all around the city.* 城里到处都响起炸弹的爆炸声。◇ ~ **sth** *There was a huge bang as if someone had exploded a rocket outside.* 突然一声巨响，仿佛有人在外面引爆了火箭似的。◇ *Bomb disposal experts exploded the device under controlled conditions.* 炸弹销毁专家对这个装置实施了可控引爆。 ➲ COMPARE IMPLODE
• **GET ANGRY/DANGEROUS** 变得愤怒 / 危急 **2** [I, T] (of a person or situation 人或形势) to suddenly become very angry or dangerous 勃然（大怒）；大发（雷霆）；突然发生（危险）：~ (**with sth**) *Suddenly Charles exploded with rage.* 查尔斯勃然大怒。◇ ~ (**into sth**) *The protest exploded into a riot.* 抗议爆发成一场暴乱。◇ **+ speech** *'Of course there's something wrong!' Jem exploded.* "当然是出了毛病！" 杰姆大发雷霆道。
• **EXPRESS EMOTION** 表达感情 **3** [I] ~ (**into/with sth**) to suddenly express an emotion 突然爆发，迸发（感情）：*We all exploded into wild laughter.* 我们都一下子大笑起来。
• **MOVE SUDDENLY** 突然行动 **4** [I] ~ (**into sth**) to suddenly and quickly do sth; to move suddenly with a lot of force 突然做起…来；突然活跃起来：*After ten minutes the game exploded into life.* 比赛在十分钟后突然激烈起来。
• **MAKE LOUD NOISE** 发出巨响 **5** [I] to make a sudden very loud noise 突然发出巨响：*Thunder exploded overhead.* 雷声在头顶上炸开。
• **INCREASE QUICKLY** 激增 **6** [I] to increase suddenly and very quickly in number 突增；激增：*the exploding world population* 迅猛增长的世界人口
• **SHOW STH IS NOT TRUE** 推翻 **7** [T] ~ **sth** to show that sth is not true, especially sth that people believe 推翻；驳倒；破除：*At last, a women's magazine to explode the myth that thin equals beautiful.* 终于有一家女性杂志起来推翻瘦就是美的迷思。

> ▼ **SYNONYMS** 同义词辨析
>
> **explode**
>
> **blow up • go off • burst • erupt • detonate**
>
> These are all words that can be used when sth bursts apart violently, causing damage or injury. 以上各词均可表示爆炸、爆破、爆裂。
>
> **explode** to burst loudly and violently, causing damage; to make sth burst in this way 指爆炸、爆破、爆裂、引爆：*The jet smashed into a hillside and exploded.* 喷气式飞机撞上山坡爆炸了。◇ *The bomb was exploded under controlled conditions.* 对炸弹实施了可控引爆。
>
> **blow (sth) up** to be destroyed by an explosion; to destroy sth by an explosion 指爆炸、（被）炸毁：*A police officer was killed when his car blew up.* 一名警员在其汽车爆炸时遇难。
>
> **go off** (of a bomb) to explode; (of a gun) to be fired 指（炸弹）爆炸、（枪）开火：*The bomb went off in a crowded street.* 炸弹在挤满人的大街上爆炸了。 **NOTE** When used about guns, the choice of **go off** (instead of 'be fired') can suggest that the gun was fired by accident. 用 go off（而非 be fired）可指枪支走火。
>
> **burst** to break open or apart, especially because of pressure from inside; to make sth break in this way 指（使）爆裂、胀开：*That balloon's going to burst.* 那气球马上要爆了。
>
> **erupt** (of a volcano) to throw out burning rocks and smoke; (of burning rocks and smoke) to be thrown out of a volcano 指（火山）爆发、（岩浆、烟）喷出
>
> **detonate** (*rather formal*) (of a bomb) to explode; to make a bomb explode 指（炸弹）爆炸、使（炸弹）爆炸、引爆、起爆：*Two other bombs failed to detonate.* 另外两枚炸弹没有爆炸。
>
> **PATTERNS**
> • a **bomb** explodes/blows up/goes off/bursts/detonates
> • a **car/plane/vehicle** explodes/blows up
> • a **firework/rocket** explodes/goes off

ex·ploded /ɪkˈspləʊdɪd; *NAmE* -ˈsploʊ-/ *adj.* (*specialist*) (of a drawing or diagram 图样或图表) showing the parts of sth separately but also showing how they are connected to each other 分解的 ➲ COMPARE UNEXPLODED

ex·ploit AW *verb, noun*

■ *verb* /ɪkˈsplɔɪt/ **1** ~ **sth** (*disapproving*) to treat a person or situation as an opportunity to gain an advantage for yourself 利用（…为自己谋利）：*He exploited his father's name to get himself a job.* 他利用他父亲的名声为自己找到一份工作。◇ *She realized that her youth and inexperience were being exploited.* 她意识到因为自己少不更事而受人利用了。 **2** ~ **sb** (*disapproving*) to treat sb unfairly by making them work and not giving them much in return 剥削；压榨：*What is being done to stop employers from exploiting young people?* 目前有什么措施制止雇主剥削年轻人呢？ **3** ~ **sth** to use sth well in order to gain as much from it as possible 运用；利用；发挥：*She fully exploits the humour of her role in the play.* 她在剧中把她那个角色的幽默发挥得淋漓尽致。 **4** to develop or use sth for business or industry 开发；开采；开拓：~ **sth** *No minerals have yet been exploited in Antarctica.* 南极洲的矿藏还未开采。◇ ~ **sth for sth** *countries exploiting the rainforests for hardwood* 为获取硬木而开发热带雨林的国家 ▶ **ex·ploit·er** *noun*

■ *noun* /ˈeksplɔɪt/ [usually pl.] a brave, exciting or interesting act 英勇（或激动人心、引人注目）的行为：*the daring exploits of Roman heroes* 古罗马英雄的英勇壮举

ex·ploit·ation AW /ˌeksplɔɪˈteɪʃn/ *noun* [U] **1** (*disapproving*) a situation in which sb treats sb else in an unfair way, especially in order to make money from their work 剥削；榨取：*the exploitation of children* 对儿童的剥削 **2** the use of land, oil, minerals, etc. 利用；开发；开采：*commercial exploitation of the mineral resources in Antarctica* 南极洲矿物资源的商业开采 **3** (*disapproving*) the fact of using a situation in order to get an advantage for yourself （出于私利的）利用：*exploitation of the situation for his own purposes* 利用这种局势达到他自己的目的

ex·ploit·ative /ɪkˈsplɔɪtətɪv/ (*NAmE also* **ex·ploit·ive** /ɪkˈsplɔɪtɪv/) *adj.* treating sb unfairly in order to gain an advantage or to make money 剥削的；榨取的

ex·plor·ation /ˌekspləˈreɪʃn/ *noun* [C, U] **1** the act of travelling through a place in order to find out about it or look for sth in it 勘探；勘查；探索：*the exploration of space* 对宇宙空间的探索 ◇ *oil exploration* (= searching for oil in the ground) 石油勘探 **2** an examination of sth in order to find out about it 探究；研究；探测：*the book's explorations of the human mind* 本书对人类思维的研究

ex·plora·tory /ɪkˈsplɒrətri; *NAmE* ɪkˈsplɔːrətɔːri/ *adj.* done with the intention of examining sth in order to find out more about it 探索的；探究的；探测的；勘探的：*exploratory surgery* 探索性手术 ◇ *exploratory drilling for oil* 钻井勘探石油

E

ex·plore 🔑 /ɪkˈsplɔː(r)/ *verb* **1** 🔑 [T, I] to travel to or around an area or a country in order to learn about it 勘探；勘查；探索；考察：**~ sth (for sth)** *The city is best explored on foot.* 最好是徒步探索这个城市。◇ *They explored the land to the south of the Murray River.* 他们勘查了墨累河以南的地区。◇ **~ (for sth)** *As soon as we arrived on the island we were eager to explore.* 我们一来到岛上就急不可耐地开始探胜。◇ *companies exploring for* (= searching for) *oil* 石油勘探公司 ⊃ WORDFINDER NOTE AT ADVENTURE

> **WORDFINDER 联想词**：colonize, discover, pioneer, reconnaissance, scout, settle, terrain, territory, voyage

2 🔑 [T] **~ sth** to examine sth completely or carefully in order to find out more about it 探究；调查研究；探索；探讨 SYN **analyse**：*These ideas will be explored in more detail in chapter 7.* 这些想法将在第 7 章里作更详细的探讨。⊃ LANGUAGE BANK AT ABOUT **3** [T] **~ sth** to feel sth with your hands or another part of the body （用手或其他部位）触摸，探查：*She explored the sand with her toes.* 她用脚趾触探沙子。⊃ SEE ALSO UNEXPLORED

ex·plorer /ɪkˈsplɔːrə(r)/ *noun* a person who travels to unknown places in order to find out more about them 探险者；勘探者；考察者

Exˈplorer Scout (*US*) (*BrE* **ˈVenture Scout**) *noun* a member of the senior branch of the SCOUT ASSOCIATION for young people between the ages of 14 and 18 深资童军，奋进童子军（14 岁至 18 岁）

ex·plo·sion 🔑 /ɪkˈspləʊʒn; *NAmE* -ˈsploʊ-/ *noun* **1** 🔑 [C, U] the sudden violent bursting and loud noise of sth such as a bomb exploding; the act of deliberately causing sth to explode 爆炸，爆破，爆裂（声）：***a bomb/nuclear/gas explosion*** 炸弹 / 核 / 气体爆炸 ◇ *There were two loud explosions and then the building burst into flames.* 两声巨响之后建筑物便燃烧起来。◇ *Bomb Squad officers carried out a* ***controlled explosion*** *of the device.* 炸弹处理小组人员对该装置实施了可控引爆。◇ *300 people were injured in the explosion.* 有 300 人在爆炸中受伤。**2** 🔑 [C] a large, sudden or rapid increase in the amount or number of sth 突增；猛增；激增：*a population explosion* 人口激增 ◇ *an explosion of interest in learning Japanese* 学习日语的兴趣陡然上升 **3** [C] (*formal*) a sudden, violent expression of emotion, especially anger （感情，尤指愤怒的）突然爆发，迸发 SYN **outburst**

ex·plo·sive /ɪkˈspləʊsɪv; -zɪv; *NAmE* -ˈsploʊ-/ *adj., noun*

■ ***adj.*** **1** easily able or likely to explode 易爆炸的；可能引起爆炸的：*an* ***explosive device*** (= a bomb) 爆炸装置（炸弹）◇ *an explosive mixture of chemicals* 易爆化学混合物 **2** likely to cause violence or strong feelings of anger or hatred 易爆发的；可能引起冲动的；爆炸性的：*a potentially explosive situation* 可能引起爆炸性反应的形势 **3** often having sudden violent or angry feelings 暴躁的：*an explosive temper* 暴躁的脾气 **4** increasing suddenly and rapidly 突增的；猛增的；激增的：*the explosive growth of the export market* 出口市场的急剧扩大 **5** (of a sound 声音) sudden and loud 爆发的 ▸ **ex·plo·sive·ly** *adv.*

■ ***noun*** [C, U] a substance that is able or likely to cause an explosion 炸药；爆炸物：*plastic explosives* 塑性炸药 ◇ *The bomb was packed with several pounds of* ***high explosive.*** 这枚炸弹装有几磅烈性炸药。

ex·po·nent /ɪkˈspəʊnənt; *NAmE* -ˈspoʊ-/ *noun* **1** a person who supports an idea, theory, etc. and persuades others that it is good （观点、理论等的）拥护者，鼓吹者，倡导者 SYN **proponent**：*She was* ***a leading exponent*** *of free trade during her political career* 她从政期间是自由贸易的主要倡导者。**2** a person who is able to perform a particular activity with skill （某种活动的）能手，大师：*the most famous exponent of the art of mime* 最著名的哑剧表演艺术大师 **3** (*mathematics* 数) a raised figure or symbol that shows how many times a quantity must be multiplied by itself, for example the figure 4 in a^4 指数

ex·po·nen·tial /ˌekspəˈnenʃl/ *adj.* **1** (*mathematics* 数) of or shown by an exponent 指数的；由指数表示的：*2^4 is an exponential expression.* * 2^4 是个指数式。◇ *an* ***exponential curve/function*** 指数曲线 / 函数 **2** (*formal*) (of a rate of increase 增长率) becoming faster and faster 越来越快的：***exponential growth/increase*** 越来越快的增长 ▸ **ex·po·nen·ti·al·ly** /-ʃəli/ *adv.*：*to increase exponentially* 呈指数增长

ex·port 🔑 AW *verb, noun*

■ ***verb*** /ɪkˈspɔːt; *NAmE* ɪkˈspɔːrt/ **1** 🔑 [T, I] **~ (sth) (to sb)** to sell and send goods to another country 出口；输出：*The islands export sugar and fruit.* 这些岛出口糖和水果。◇ *90% of the engines are exported to Europe.* * 90% 的发动机都出口到欧洲。**2** [T] **~ sth (+ adv./prep.)** to introduce an idea or activity to another country or area 传播，输出（思想或活动）：*American pop music has been exported around the world.* 美国流行音乐已传播到世界各地。**3** [T] **~ sth** (*computing* 计) to send data to another program, changing its form so that the other program can read it 输出；移出；调出 OPP **import**

■ ***noun*** /ˈekspɔːt; *NAmE* ˈekspɔːrt/ **1** 🔑 [U] the selling and transporting of goods to another country 出口；输出：*a ban on the export of live cattle* 禁止活牛出口 ◇ *Then the fruit is packaged* ***for export.*** 然后水果便包装出口。◇ *export earnings* 出口收益 ◇ *an export licence* 出口许可证 **2** 🔑 [C, usually pl.] a product that is sold to another country 出口产品；输出品：*the country's major exports* 该国的主要出口产品 ◇ *a fall in the value of exports* 出口产品值的下跌 OPP **import** ⊃ COLLOCATIONS AT ECONOMY ⊃ MORE LIKE THIS 21, page R27

ex·port·ation /ˌekspɔːˈteɪʃn; *NAmE* ˌekspɔːrˈt-/ *noun* [U] the process of sending goods to another country for sale 出口；输出 OPP **importation**

ex·port·er AW /ekˈspɔːtə(r); *NAmE* ekˈspɔːrt-/ *noun* a person, company or country that sells goods to another country 出口商；出口公司；出口国：*the world's* ***largest/major/leading exporter*** *of cars* 世界上最大的 / 重要的 / 主要的汽车输出国 ◇ *The country is now a* ***net exporter*** *of fuel* (= it exports more than it imports). 目前这个国家是燃料净输出国。OPP **importer**

ex·pose 🔑 AW /ɪkˈspəʊz; *NAmE* ɪkˈspoʊz/ *verb*

• **SHOW STH HIDDEN** 使显露 **1** 🔑 to show sth that is usually hidden 暴露；显露；露出 SYN **reveal**：**~ sth** *He smiled suddenly, exposing a set of amazingly white teeth.* 他突然一笑，露出一口雪白的牙齿。◇ *Miles of sand are exposed at low tide.* 在低潮时数英里的沙滩就会显现出来。◇ *My job as a journalist is to expose the truth.* 我作为记者的职责就是揭露真相。◇ **~ sth to sb** *He did not want to expose his fears and insecurity to anyone.* 他不想向任何人显露他的恐惧与不安。

• **SHOW TRUTH** 揭露事实 **2** 🔑 **~ sb/sth (as sth)** to tell the true facts about a person or a situation, and show them/it to be immoral, illegal, etc. 揭露；揭穿：*She was exposed as a liar and a fraud.* 她说谎和欺骗的面目被揭穿了。◇ *He threatened to expose the racism that existed within the police force.* 他扬言要把警队内部存在的种族歧视公之于众。

• **TO STH HARMFUL** 有害事物 **3** 🔑 **~ sb/sth/yourself (to sth)** to put sb/sth in a place or situation where they are not protected from sth harmful or unpleasant 使面临，使遭受（危险或不快）：*to expose yourself to ridicule* 让自己受到嘲笑 ◇ *Do not expose babies to strong sunlight.* 不要让婴孩受到强烈的阳光照射。

• **GIVE EXPERIENCE** 给予经验 **4 ~ sb to sth** to let sb find out about sth by giving them experience of it or showing them what it is like 使接触；使体验：*We want to expose the kids to as much art and culture as possible.* 我们想让孩子们尽量受到艺术和文化熏陶。
• **FILM IN CAMERA** 照相机胶片 **5 ~ sth** to allow light onto the film inside a camera when taking a photograph 曝光
• **YOURSELF** 自己 **6 ~ yourself** a man who **exposes** himself, shows his sexual organs in public in a way that is offensive to other people 当众露阴茎 ➲SEE ALSO EXPOSURE

ex·posé /ek'spəʊzeɪ; *NAmE* ˌekspoʊ'zeɪ/ *noun* an account of the facts of a situation, especially when these are shocking or have deliberately been kept secret （尤指对令人震惊或故意保密的事实的）陈述，阐述，揭露

ex·posed AW /ɪk'spəʊzd; *NAmE* ɪk'spoʊzd/ *adj.* **1** (of a place 地方) not protected from the weather by trees, buildings or high ground 无遮蔽的；不遮挡风雨的 **2** (of a person 人) not protected from attack or criticism 易受攻击（或批评）的；无保护的：*She was left feeling exposed and vulnerable.* 她感到自己孤立无助，非常脆弱。**3** (*finance* 财) likely to experience financial losses 风险高的；很可能遭受经济损失的

ex·pos·ition /ˌekspə'zɪʃn/ *noun* (*formal*) **1** [C, U] a full explanation of a theory, plan, etc. （理论、计划等的）解释，说明，阐述：*a clear and detailed exposition of their legal position* 对他们的法律地位清楚而详尽的说明 **2** [C] an event at which people, businesses, etc. show and sell their goods; a TRADE FAIR （产品的）展销；商品交易会；产品博览会

ex·posi·tory /ɪk'spɒzətri; *NAmE* ɪk'spɑːzətɔːri/ *adj.* (*formal*) intended to explain or describe sth 阐述的；解释的；说明性的：*The film suffers from too much expository dialogue.* 这部影片的败笔在于论说性对话过多。

ex·pos·tu·late /ɪk'spɒstʃuleɪt; *NAmE* ɪk'spɑːs-/ *verb* [I, T] (**+ speech**) (*formal*) to argue, disagree or protest about sth 争论；争执；抗议 ▸ **ex·pos·tu·la·tion** /ɪkˌspɒstʃu'leɪʃn; *NAmE* ɪkˌspɑːs-/ *noun* [U, C]

ex·pos·ure AW /ɪk'spəʊʒə(r); *NAmE* -'spoʊ-/ *noun*
• **TO STH HARMFUL** 有害事物 **1** [U] ~ (**to sth**) the state of being in a place or situation where there is no protection from sth harmful or unpleasant 面临，遭受（危险或不快）：*prolonged exposure to harmful radiation* 长时间接触有害辐射 ◇ (*finance* 财) *the company's exposure on the foreign exchange markets* (= to the risk of making financial losses) 公司面对外汇市场的风险
• **SHOWING TRUTH** 揭露事实 **2** [U] the state of having the true facts about sb/sth told after they have been hidden because they are bad, immoral or illegal 揭露：*his exposure as a liar and a fraud* 他那谎话连篇的骗子的面目被揭露 ◇ *the exposure of illegal currency deals* 对非法交易货币的揭露
• **ON TV/IN NEWSPAPERS, ETC.** 电视、报章等 **3** [U] the fact of being discussed or mentioned on television, in newspapers, etc. （在电视、报纸等上的）亮相，被报道 SYN **publicity**：*Her new movie has had a lot of exposure in the media.* 她的新电影媒体有很多报道。
• **MEDICAL CONDITION** 身体状况 **4** [U] a medical condition caused by being out in very cold weather for too long without protection 挨冻；受寒：*Two climbers were brought in suffering from exposure.* 两名登山者因冻僵被带了进来。
• **FILM IN CAMERA** 照相机胶片 **5** [C] a length of film in a camera that is used to take a photograph （照一张照片的）软片，底片，胶片：*There are three exposures left on this roll of film.* 这卷胶卷还有三张没拍。**6** [C] the length of time for which light is allowed to reach the film when taking a photograph 曝光时间：*I used a long exposure for this one.* 我这张照片用的曝光时间长。
• **SHOWING STH HIDDEN** 使暴露 **7** [U] the act of showing sth that is usually hidden 暴露；显露 ➲SEE ALSO INDECENT EXPOSURE

ex·pound /ɪk'spaʊnd/ *verb* [T, I] (*formal*) to explain sth by talking about it in detail 详解；详述；阐述：**~ sth** (**to sb**) *He expounded his views on the subject to me at great length.* 他详细地向我阐述了他在这个问题上的观点。◇ **~ on sth** *We listened as she expounded on the government's new policies.* 我们听她详细讲解了政府的新政策。

ex·press /ɪk'spres/ *verb, adj., adv., noun*
■*verb* **1** to show or make known a feeling, an opinion, etc. by words, looks or actions 表示；表达；表露：**~ sth** *Teachers have expressed concern about the changes.* 教师对这些变化表示忧虑。◇ *His views have been expressed in numerous speeches.* 他已在无数次发言中表达了自己的观点。◇ *to **express fears/doubts/reservations*** 表示担心 / 怀疑 / 保留意见 ◇ *to **express interest/regret/surprise*** 表示关注 / 遗憾 / 惊讶 ◇ **~ how, what, etc….** *Words cannot express how pleased I am.* 言语无法表达我的愉快心情。➲SEE ALSO UNEXPRESSED **2** to speak, write or communicate in some other way what you think or feel 表达（自己的思想感情）：**~ yourself** *Teenagers often have difficulty expressing themselves.* 十来岁的孩子在表达思想方面常常有困难。◇ **~ yourself + adv./prep.** *Perhaps I have not expressed myself very well.* 我大概未把自己的意思表达清楚。◇ *She expresses herself most fully in her paintings.* 她把自己的感情在画作中表现得淋漓尽致。◇ (*formal*) **~ yourself + adj.** *They expressed themselves delighted.* 他们表示他们很高兴。**3 ~ itself** (**+ adv./prep.**) (*formal*) (of a feeling 感觉) to become obvious in a particular way 显而易见；不言自明：*Their pleasure expressed itself in a burst of applause.* 他们的喜悦从一阵热烈的掌声中表现出来。**4** (*mathematics* 数) to represent sth in a particular way, for example by symbols （用符号等）表示，代表：**~ sth as sth** *The figures are expressed as percentages.* 这些数字用百分数表示。◇ **~ sth in sth** *Educational expenditure is often expressed in terms of the amount spent per student.* 教育经费通常以用于每个学生的开支表示。**5 ~ sth** (**from sth**) to remove air or liquid from sth by pressing it 压榨，挤压出（空气或液体）：*Coconut milk is expressed from grated coconuts.* 椰子汁是从擦碎的椰肉里榨出来的。**6 ~ sth** (**to sb/sth**) (*NAmE*) to send sth by express post 快递邮寄（或发送）：*As soon as I receive payment I will express the book to you.* 我一收到款就把书用快递给你寄去。
■*adj.* [only before noun] **1** travelling very fast; operating very quickly 特快的；快速的；快递的：*an **express bus/coach/train*** 特快公共汽车 / 长途汽车 / 列车 ◇ *express delivery services* 快递服务 **2** (of a letter, package, etc. 信件、包裹等) sent by express service 用快递寄送的：*express mail* 特快邮件 **3** (*NAmE*) (of a company that delivers packages 邮递公司) providing an express service 提供快递服务的：*an air express company* 航空快递公司 **4** (*formal*) (of a wish or an aim 愿望或目的) clearly and openly stated 明确的；明白表示的 SYN **definite**：*It was his **express wish** that you should have his gold watch after he died.* 他明确表示死后把金表留给你。◇ *I came here with the **express purpose** of speaking with the manager.* 我特意来这里与经理面谈。➲MORE LIKE THIS 32, page R28
■*adv.* using a special fast service 使用快速服务：*I'd like to send this express, please.* 劳驾，我要寄快递。
■*noun* **1** (*also* **ex'press train**) [C] a fast train that does not stop at many places 特快列车：*the 8.27 express to Edinburgh* * 8:27 开往爱丁堡的特快列车 ◇ *the Trans-Siberian Express* 横穿西伯利亚的特快列车 **2** (*BrE also* ˌ**special de'livery**) [U] a service for sending or transporting things quickly 快件服务；快递服务；快运服务

ex·pres·sion /ɪk'spreʃn/ *noun*
• **SHOWING FEELINGS/IDEAS** 表达感情 / 思想 **1** [U, C] things that people say, write or do in order to show their feelings, opinions and ideas 表示；表达；表露：***Freedom of expression*** (= freedom to say what you think) *is a basic human right.* 言论自由是基本的人权。◇ (*formal*) *The poet's anger **finds expression in*** (= is shown in) *the last verse of the poem.* 诗人的愤怒在诗的最后一节表达出来。◇ *Only in his dreams does he **give expression to** his fears.* 只有在梦里他的恐惧才能得以表露。◇ *an expression of support* 表示支持 ◇ *Expressions of sympathy flooded in from all over the country.* 同情之意潮水般地从全国各地涌来。
• **ON FACE** 脸上 **2** [C] a look on a person's face that shows their thoughts or feelings 表情；神色 SYN **look**：*There*

E

was a worried expression on her face. 她脸上流露出担心的神色。◇ an **expression of amazement/disbelief/horror** 惊讶 / 不相信 / 恐怖的神色 ◇ His expression changed from surprise to one of amusement. 他的神情由惊变喜。◇ The expression in her eyes told me something was wrong. 她的眼神告诉我出事了。◇ facial expressions 面部表情

WORDFINDER 联想词：beam, frown, grimace, grin, leer, scowl, smirk, sneer, wince

- **WORDS** 词语 **3** [C] a word or phrase 词语；措辞；表达方式：an old-fashioned expression 陈旧的表达方式 ◇ (informal) He's a pain in the butt, **if you'll pardon the expression**. 请原谅我这么说，他是一个讨厌透顶的家伙。➲ SYNONYMS AT WORD
- **IN MUSIC/ACTING** 音乐；表演 **4** [U] a strong show of feeling when you are playing music, speaking, acting, etc.（演奏乐曲、说话、表演等时流露的）感情，表情：Try to put a little more expression into it! 尽量注入更多的感情！
- **MATHEMATICS** 数学 **5** [C] a group of signs that represent an idea or a quantity 式；表达式

ex·pres·sion·ism (also **Expressionism**) /ɪk'spreʃənɪzəm/ noun [U] a style and movement in early 20th century art, theatre, cinema and music that tries to express people's feelings and emotions rather than showing events or objects in a realistic way 表现主义 ▶ **ex·pres·sion·ist** /-ʃənɪst/ (also **Expressionist**) noun, adj.

ex·pres·sion·less /ɪk'spreʃənləs/ adj. not showing feelings, thoughts, etc. 无表情的；呆板的：an **expressionless face/tone/voice** 呆板的面孔 / 声调 / 声音 ➲ COMPARE EXPRESSIVE (1)

ex·pres·sive /ɪk'spresɪv/ adj. **1** showing or able to show your thoughts and feelings 富于表情的；有表现力的；意味深长的：She has wonderfully expressive eyes. 她有一双会说话的眼睛。◇ the expressive power of his music 他的音乐的表现力 ➲ COMPARE EXPRESSIONLESS **2** [not before noun] **~ of sth** (formal) showing sth; existing as an expression of sth 表现；表达；表示：Every word and gesture is expressive of the artist's sincerity. 这位艺术家的真诚从一言一行中表现出来。▶ **ex·pres·sive·ly** adv. **ex·pres·sive·ness** noun [U]

ex'press lane noun (NAmE) **1** part of a road on which certain vehicles can travel faster because there is less traffic 快车道 **2** a place in a shop/store where customers can pay without having to wait for a long time（购物场所收银结账的）快速通道：Customers with ten items or less can use the express lane. 购买十件以内商品的顾客可使用快速购物通道。➲ COMPARE CHECKOUT (1), TILL n. (2)

ex·press·ly /ɪk'spresli/ adv. (formal) **1** clearly; definitely 清楚地；明确地；确切地：She was expressly forbidden to touch my papers. 已经明确禁止她动我的文件。**2** for a special and deliberate purpose 特意；专程 SYN **especially**: The rule was introduced expressly for this purpose. 这项规则是为此特意设置的。

ex·press·way /ɪk'spresweɪ/ noun (in the US) a wide road that allows traffic to travel fast through a city or other area where many people live （美国）高速公路

ex·pro·pri·ate /eks'prəʊprieɪt; NAmE -'proʊ-/ verb **1 ~ sth** (formal or law 律) (of a government or an authority 政府或权力机构) to officially take away private property from its owner for public use 征用，没收（私有财产）**2 ~ sth** (formal) to take sb's property and use it without permission 侵占（他人财产）▶ **ex·pro·pri·ation** /ˌeks-ˌprəʊpri'eɪʃn; NAmE -ˌproʊ-/ noun [U]

ex·pul·sion /ɪk'spʌlʃn/ noun **1** [U, C] **~ (from…)** the act of forcing sb to leave a place; the act of EXPELLING sb 驱逐；逐出：These events led to the expulsion of senior diplomats from the country. 这些事件导致一些高级外交官被驱逐出境。**2** [U, C] **~ (from…)** the act of sending sb away from a school or an organization, so that they can no longer belong to it; the act of EXPELLING sb 开除；除名：The headteacher threatened the three girls with expulsion. 校长以开除来威胁这三名女学生。◇ The club faces expulsion from the football league. 这家俱乐部面临被足协开除。**3** [U] **~ (from…)** (formal) the act of sending or driving a substance out of your body or a container 排出

ex·punge /ɪk'spʌndʒ/ verb **~ sth (from sth)** (formal) to remove or get rid of sth, such as a name, piece of information or a memory, from a book or list, or from your mind 抹去；除去；删去 SYN **erase**: Details of his criminal activities were expunged from the file. 他犯罪活动的详细情况已从档案中删去。◇ What happened just before the accident was expunged from his memory. 事故前一刻发生的事他都记不得了。

ex·pur·gate /'ekspəgeɪt; NAmE -pərg-/ verb **~ sth** [usually passive] (formal) to remove or leave out parts of a piece of writing or a conversation when printing or reporting it, because you think those parts could offend people 删除…中的不当之处；略去…中的不雅之处

ex·quis·ite /ɪk'skwɪzɪt; 'ekskwɪzɪt/ adj. **1** extremely beautiful or carefully made 精美的；精致的：exquisite craftsmanship 精美的工艺 **2** (formal) (of a feeling 感觉) strongly felt 剧烈的；强烈的 SYN **acute**: **exquisite pain/pleasure** 剧烈的疼痛；极大的快乐 **3** (formal) delicate and sensitive 雅致的；敏锐的：The room was decorated in exquisite taste. 这个房间的装饰情趣高雅。◇ an exquisite sense of timing 时间安排上恰到好处的感觉 ▶ **ex·quis·ite·ly** adv.

ˌex-'service adj. (BrE) having previously been a member of the army, navy, etc. 退役的；退伍的：ex-service personnel 退伍人员

ex-service·man /ˌeks 'sɜːvɪsmən; NAmE 'sɜːrvɪs-/, **ˌex-'service·woman** /-wʊmən/ noun (pl. **-men** /-mən/, **-women** /-wɪmɪn/) (BrE) a person who used to be in the army, navy, etc. 退役军人；复员军人

ext. abbr. (used as part of a telephone number) EXTENSION（用于电话号码）电话分机线，分机号码：Ext. 4299 分机号码 4299

ex·tant /ek'stænt; 'ekstənt/ adj. (formal) (of sth very old 古老的东西) still in existence 尚存的；现存的：extant remains of the ancient wall 尚存的古城墙遗迹

ex·tem·pore /ek'stempəri/ adj. (formal) spoken or done without any previous thought or preparation 即席的；即兴的；无准备的 SYN **impromptu** ▶ **ex·tem·pore** adv.

ex·tem·por·ize (BrE also **-ise**) /ɪk'stempəraɪz/ verb [I] (formal) to speak or perform without preparing or practising 即席发言；即兴表演 SYN **improvise** ▶ **ex·tem·por·iza·tion, -isa·tion** /ɪkˌstempəraɪ'zeɪʃn; NAmE -rə'z-/ noun [U]

ex·tend /ɪk'stend/ verb

- **MAKE LONGER/LARGER/WIDER** 延长；扩大；扩展 **1** [T] **~ sth** to make sth longer or larger 使伸长；扩大；扩展：to extend a fence/road/house 扩建护栏 / 公路 / 房子 ◇ There are plans to extend the no-smoking area. 现已有扩大无烟区的计划。**2** [T] **~ sth** to make sth last longer 延长；使延期：to **extend a deadline/visa** 延长最后期限 / 签证 ◇ The show has been extended for another six weeks. 展览会又延长了六周。◇ Careful maintenance can **extend the life** of your car. 精心保养可延长汽车寿命。**3** [T] **~ sth** to make a business, an idea, an influence, etc. cover more areas or operate in more places 扩大…的范围（或影响）：The company plans to extend its operations into Europe. 公司打算将业务扩展到欧洲。◇ The school is extending the range of subjects taught. 学校正在拓宽授课学科的范围。
- **INCLUDE** 包括 **4** [I] **+ adv./prep.** to relate to or include sb/sth 适用于；包括：The offer does not extend to employees' partners. 这项优惠不包括雇员的伴侣。◇ His willingness to help did not extend beyond making a few phone calls. 他帮助的诚意只限于打几个电话罢了。
- **COVER AREA/TIME/DISTANCE** 涉及范围 / 时间 / 距离 **5** [I] **+ adv./prep.** to cover a particular area, distance or length of time 涉及（范围）；延伸（距离）；延续（时间）：Our land extends as far as the river. 我们的土地一直延伸到河边。◇ His writing career extended over a period of 40

years. 他的写作生涯超过了 40 年。 **6** [I] **+ adv./prep.** to make sth reach sth or stretch 使达到；使延伸： *to extend a rope between two posts* 在两根柱子间拉根绳子

- **PART OF BODY** 身体部位 **7** [T] **~ sth** to stretch part of your body, especially an arm or a leg, away from yourself 伸展，舒展，展开（尤指手臂或腿）： *He extended his hand to* (= offered to shake hands with) *the new employee.* 他伸出手来与新雇员握手。◇ (*figurative*) *to* ***extend the hand of friendship*** *to* (= try to have good relations with) *another country* 向另一个国家伸出友谊之手
- **OFFER/GIVE** 提供；给予 **8** [T] (*formal*) to offer or give sth to sb 提供；给予： **~ sth to sb** *I'm sure you will join me in extending a very warm welcome to our visitors.* 我肯定你们会同我一起向来访者表示热烈的欢迎。◇ *to extend hospitality to overseas students* 殷勤款待外国留学生 ◇ *The bank refused to extend credit to them* (= to lend them money). 银行拒绝向他们提供信贷。◇ **~ sb sth** *to extend sb an invitation* 向某人发出邀请
- **USE EFFORT/ABILITY** 努力；尽力 **9** [T, often passive] **~ sb/sth/yourself** to make sb/sth use all their effort, abilities, supplies, etc. 使竭尽全力： *Jim didn't really have to extend himself in the exam.* 吉姆大可不必为这次考试那么拼命。◇ *Hospitals were already fully extended because of the epidemic.* 这场流行病已使各医院疲于奔命。 ➲ SEE ALSO EXTENSION, EXTENSIVE

ex·tend·able (*also* **ex·tend·ible**) /ɪk'stendəbl/ *adj.* that can be made longer, or made valid for a longer time 可延长的；可延伸的；可延期的： *an extendable ladder* 伸缩梯 ◇ *The visa is for 14 days, extendable to one month.* 此签证有效期为 14 天，可延期到一个月。

ex·tend·ed /ɪk'stendɪd/ *adj.* [only before noun] long or longer than usual or expected 延长了的；扩展了的： *an extended lunch hour* 延长了的午餐时间

ex,tended 'family *noun* [C+sing./pl. v.] a family group with a close relationship among the members that includes not only parents and children but also uncles, aunts, grandparents, etc. 大家庭（几代同堂的家庭） ➲ COMPARE NUCLEAR FAMILY

ex·ten·sion 🔑 /ɪk'stenʃn/ *noun*

- **INCREASING INFLUENCE** 扩大影响 **1** 🔑 [U, C] **~ (of sth)** the act of increasing the area of activity, group of people, etc. that is affected by sth 扩大；延伸： *the extension of new technology into developing countries* 新技术向发展中国家的传播 ◇ *a gradual extension of the powers of central government* 中央政府权力的逐渐扩大 ◇ *The bank plans various extensions to its credit facilities.* 银行计划多方面扩展信贷服务。
- **OF BUILDING** 建筑 **2** 🔑 [C] **~ (to sth)** (*NAmE also* **add·ition**) a new room or rooms that are added to a house 增加的房间 ➲ COLLOCATIONS AT DECORATE **3** 🔑 [C] a new part that is added to a building 扩建部分；增建部分： *a planned two-storey extension to the hospital* 计划在医院增建一栋两层的楼
- **EXTRA TIME** 增加的时间 **4** 🔑 [C] **~ (of sth)** an extra period of time allowed for sth 延期；延长期；放宽的期限： *He's been granted an extension of the contract for another year.* 他的合同获得延期一年。◇ *a visa extension* 延长签证 ◇ (*BrE*) *The pub had an extension* (= was allowed to stay open longer) *on Christmas Eve.* 这家酒吧已获准在圣诞前夕延长营业时间。
- **TELEPHONE** 电话 **5** 🔑 [C] (*abbr.* **ext.**) an extra telephone line connected to a central telephone in a house or to a SWITCHBOARD in a large building. In a large building, each extension usually has its own number. 电话分机线；分机号码： *We have an extension in the bedroom.* 我们的卧室里有一个分机。◇ *What's your extension number?* 你的分机号码是多少？ ◇ *Can I have extension 4332 please?* 请接 4332 号分机。
- **MAKING STH LONGER/LARGER** 延伸；扩大 **6** [U, C] the act of making sth longer or larger; the thing that is made longer and larger 延长；扩大；延长（或扩大）的事物： *The extension of the subway will take several months.* 扩建地铁需用几个月时间。 ◇ *extensions to the original railway track* 原有铁路线的若干延伸路线 ◇ ***hair extensions*** (= pieces of artificial hair that are added to your hair to make it longer) 接长的假发
- **COLLEGE/UNIVERSITY** 学院；大学 **7** [C] a part of a college or university that offers courses to students who are not studying FULL-TIME; a programme of study for these students （为非全日制学生开设的）进修部，进修课： *La Salle Extension University* 拉萨尔大学进修部 ◇ *extension courses* 大学进修课程
- **COMPUTING** 计算机技术 **8** [C] the set of three letters that are placed after a dot at the end of the name of a file and that show what type of file it is 扩展名
- **ELECTRICAL** 电的 **9** [C] (*BrE*) = EXTENSION LEAD

IDM **by ex'tension** (*formal*) taking the argument or situation one stage further 引申；再则： *The blame lies with the teachers and, by extension, with the Education Service.* 应受指责的是教师，再则就是教育机构。

ex'tension agent *noun* (in the US) a person who works for a state university in a country area, and whose job is to give advice to farmers, do research into farming, etc. （美国州立大学乡村的）农业技术推广研究员

extension lead /ɪk'stenʃn li:d/ (*also* **extension**) (*both BrE*) (*NAmE* **ex'tension cord**) *noun* an extra length of electric wire, used when the wire on an electrical device is not long enough 接长线路，延长线（电器上的电线加长部分）

ex·ten·sive 🔑 /ɪk'stensɪv/ *adj.* **1** 🔑 covering a large area; great in amount 广阔的；广大的；大量的： *The house has extensive grounds.* 这栋房子有宽敞的庭院。◇ *The fire caused extensive damage.* 火灾造成了巨大的损失。◇ *She suffered extensive injuries in the accident.* 她在事故中受了重伤。◇ *Extensive repair work is being carried out.* 大规模的修缮工作正在进行。◇ *an extensive range of wines* 各种各样的葡萄酒 **2** 🔑 including or dealing with a wide range of information 广泛的；广博的 **SYN** **far-reaching**: *Extensive research has been done into this disease.* 对这种疾病已进行了广泛研究。 ◇ *His knowledge of music is extensive.* 他音乐知识很广博。 ▶ **ex·ten·sive·ly** *adv.* : *a spice used extensively in Eastern cooking* 东方烹饪广泛使用的香料 ◇ *She has travelled extensively.* 她游历甚广。

ex·ten·sor /ɪk'stensə(r); *BrE also* ek's-; *NAmE* ɪk'stensɔ:r/ (*also* **ex'tensor muscle**) *noun* (*anatomy* 解) a muscle that allows you to make part of your body straight or stretched out 伸肌 ➲ COMPARE FLEXOR

ex·tent 🔑 /ɪk'stent/ *noun* [sing., U] **1** 🔑 how large, important, serious, etc. sth is 程度；限度： *It is difficult to assess the* ***full extent*** *of the damage.* 损失情况难以全面估计。◇ *She was exaggerating the* ***true extent*** *of the problem.* 她夸大了问题的严重性。◇ *I was amazed at the extent of his knowledge.* 他知识之渊博令我惊奇。 **2** the physical size of an area 大小；面积；范围： *You can't see the* ***full extent*** *of the beach from here.* 从这儿不能看到海滩全貌。

IDM **to... extent** 🔑 used to show how far sth is true or how great an effect it has 到…程度；在…程度上： *To a* ***certain extent****, we are all responsible for this tragic situation.* 我们都在一定程度上对这悲惨的局面负有责任。◇ *He had changed* ***to such an extent*** (= so much) *that I no longer recognized him.* 他变得我简直认不出了。◇ ***To some extent*** *what she argues is true.* 她的论证在某种程度上是符合事实的。 ◇ *The pollution of the forest has seriously affected plant life and,* ***to a lesser extent****, wildlife.* 森林污染严重影响了植物的生存，其次也对野生动物造成了影响。◇ ***To what extent*** *is this true of all schools?* 这在多大程度上符合所有学校的实际情况？ ◇ *The book discusses the* ***extent to which*** (= how much) *family life has changed over the past 50 years.* 本书论述了近 50 年来家庭生活的变化程度。 ➲ LANGUAGE BANK AT GENERALLY

ex·tenu·at·ing /ɪk'stenjueɪtɪŋ/ *adj.* [only before noun] (*formal*) showing reasons why a wrong or illegal act, or a bad situation, should be judged less seriously or excused 情有可原的；可减轻的： *There were* ***extenuating circumstances*** *and the defendant did not receive a prison sentence.* 因为有可减轻罪行的情节，所以被告未被判刑。

ex·ter·ior /ɪk'stɪəriə(r); *NAmE* -'stɪr-/ *noun, adj.*

■***noun*** **1** [C] the outside of sth, especially a building（尤指建筑物的）外部，外观，表面，外貌：*The exterior of the house needs painting.* 房子外墙需要油漆。**OPP interior** **2** [sing.] the way that sb appears or behaves, especially when this is very different from their real feelings or character（人的）外貌，外表：*Beneath his confident exterior, he was desperately nervous.* 他表面上自信，内心极度紧张。

■***adj.*** [usually before noun] on the outside of sth; done or happening outdoors 外面的；外部的；外表的；户外的：***exterior walls/surfaces*** 外墙；外层表面 ◇ *The filming of the exterior scenes was done on the moors.* 外景是在高沼地拍摄的。**OPP interior**

ex·ter·min·ate /ɪk'stɜːmɪneɪt; *NAmE* -'stɜːrm-/ *verb* **~ sb/sth** to kill all the members of a group of people or animals 灭绝；根除；消灭；毁灭 **SYN wipe out** ▶ **ex·ter·min·ation** /ɪkˌstɜːmɪ'neɪʃn; *NAmE* -ˌstɜːrm-/ *noun* [U]

ex·tern /'ekstɜːn; *NAmE* -tɜːrn/ *noun* (*US*) a person who works in an institution but does not live there, especially a doctor or other worker in a hospital 不住机构内的工作人员；（尤指）非住院医生，非住院的医院员工

ex·ter·nal AW /ɪk'stɜːnl; *NAmE* ɪk'stɜːrnl/ *adj.* **1** connected with or located on the outside of sth/sb 外部的；外面的：*the external walls of the building* 建筑物的外墙 ◇ *The lotion is* ***for external use*** *only* (= only for the skin and must not be swallowed). 此洗剂仅限外用。 **2** happening or coming from outside a place, an organization, your particular situation, etc. 外界的；外来的；在外的：*A combination of internal and external factors caused the company to close down.* 内外因结合导致了公司的倒闭。◇ *external pressures on the economy* 外部因素对经济的压力 ◇ *Many external influences can affect your state of mind.* 许多外在因素都可能影响人的心情。 **3** coming from or arranged by sb from outside a school, a university or an organization 来自（学校或机构）以外的；外来的：(*BrE*) ***external examiners/assessors*** 校外主考人 / 评定人 ◇ *An external auditor will verify the accounts.* 外部审计员将核实这些账目。 **4** connected with foreign countries 与外国有关的；对外的：*The government is committed to reducing the country's external debt.* 政府决心减少国家的外债。◇ *the Minister of State for External Affairs* 外交大臣 **OPP internal** ▶ **ex·ter·nal·ly** AW /ɪk'stɜːnəli; *NAmE* -'stɜːrn-/ *adv.* : *The building has been restored externally and internally.* 这栋建筑内外均已修复。◇ *The university has many externally funded research projects.* 这所大学有许多外界资助的研究项目。

exˌternal 'ear *noun* (*anatomy* 解) the parts of the ear outside the EARDRUM 外耳

ex·ter·nal·ity AW /ˌekstɜː'næləti; *NAmE* -stɜːr'n-/ *noun* **1** [C] (*economics* 经) a consequence of an industrial or commercial activity which affects other people or things without this being reflected in market prices 外部性，界外效应（工商业活动所产生的影响，但不通过市场价格反映）：*Pollution is a negative externality that imposes a cost—reduced happiness—on the victims.* 污染是一种负面外部效应，使部分人的幸福被牺牲而成为受害者。 **2** [U] (*philosophy* 哲) the fact of existing outside the person or thing that is aware of it 外在性；客观性：*man's externality to an indifferent natural world* 相对于冷漠自然界的人类外在性

ex·ter·nal·ize AW (*BrE also* **-ise**) /ɪk'stɜːnəlaɪz; *NAmE* -'stɜːrn-/ *verb* **~ sth** (*formal*) to show what you are thinking and feeling by what you say or do（以言行）表达；使（思想、感情）表露出来 ➲ COMPARE INTERNALIZE ▶ **ex·ter·nal·iza·tion, -isation** AW /ɪkˌstɜːnəlaɪ'zeɪʃn; *NAmE* -ˌstɜːrnələ'z-/ *noun* [U]

ex·ter·nals /ɪk'stɜːnlz; *NAmE* -'stɜːrn-/ *noun* [pl.] (*formal*) the outer appearance of sth 外表；外观；外貌

ex·tinct /ɪk'stɪŋkt/ *adj.* **1** (of a type of plant, animal, etc. 某种植物、动物等) no longer in existence 不再存在的；已灭绝的；绝种的：*an extinct species* 已灭绝的物种 ◇ *to become extinct* 绝种 ➲ WORDFINDER NOTE AT GREEN **2** (of a type of person, job or way of life 某种类型的人、工作或生活方式) no longer in existence in society 绝迹的；消亡了的；废除了的：*Servants are now almost extinct in modern society.* 在现代社会里奴仆已近乎不复存在。 **3** (of a VOLCANO 火山) no longer active 不再活跃的；死的 **OPP active**

ex·tinc·tion /ɪk'stɪŋkʃn/ *noun* [U, C] a situation in which a plant, an animal, a way of life, etc. stops existing（植物、动物、生活方式等的）灭绝，绝种，消亡：*a tribe* ***threatened with extinction/in danger of extinction*** 面临消亡威胁 / 有消亡危险的部落 ◇ *The mountain gorilla is* ***on the verge of extinction.*** 山地大猩猩已濒临灭绝。◇ *We know of several mass extinctions in the earth's history.* 我们知道地球历史上出现过几次大规模的灭绝。

ex·tin·guish /ɪk'stɪŋgwɪʃ/ *verb* (*formal*) **1 ~ sth** to make a fire stop burning or a light stop shining 熄灭；扑灭 **SYN put out**: *Firefighters tried to extinguish the flames.* 消防队员奋力救火。◇ *All lights had been extinguished.* 所有灯光都熄灭了。 **2 ~ sth** to destroy sth 毁灭；消灭；使破灭：*News of the bombing extinguished all hope of peace.* 轰炸的消息使和平的希望全部破灭。

ex·tin·guish·er /ɪk'stɪŋgwɪʃə(r)/ *noun* = FIRE EXTINGUISHER

ex·tirp·ate /'ekstəpeɪt; *NAmE* -tərp-/ *verb* **~ sth** (*formal*) to destroy or get rid of sth that is bad or not wanted 消灭，根除，除掉（坏的或不需要的事物） ▶ **ex·tir·pa·tion** /ˌekstə'peɪʃn; *NAmE* -tər'p-/ *noun* [U]

extol /ɪk'stəʊl; *NAmE* ɪk'stoʊl/ *verb* (**-ll-**) (*formal*) to praise sb/sth very much 赞扬；颂扬；称赞：**~ sb/sth** *Doctors often* ***extol the virtues*** *of eating less fat.* 医生常常宣扬少吃脂肪的好处。◇ **~ sb/sth as sth** *She was extolled as a genius.* 她被誉为天才。

ex·tort /ɪk'stɔːt; *NAmE* ɪk'stɔːrt/ *verb* **~ sth (from sb)** to make sb give you sth by threatening them 敲诈；勒索；强夺：*The gang extorted money from over 30 local businesses.* 这帮歹徒向当地 30 多家企业勒索过钱财。 ▶ **ex·tor·tion** /ɪk'stɔːʃn; *NAmE* ɪk'stɔːrʃn/ *noun* [U, C]: *He was arrested and charged with extortion.* 他因敲诈勒索罪被拘捕和控告。

ex·tor·tion·ate /ɪk'stɔːʃənət; *NAmE* -'stɔːrʃ-/ *adj.* (*rather informal, disapproving*) (of prices, etc. 价格等) much too high 过于昂贵的；过高的 **SYN excessive, outrageous**: *They are offering loans at extortionate rates of interest.* 他们在放高利贷。 ▶ **ex·tor·tion·ate·ly** *adv.* : *extortionately priced* 价格过于昂贵的

extra 🔑 /'ekstrə/ *adj., noun, adv.*

■***adj.*** 🔑 more than is usual, expected, or than exists already 额外的；分外的；外加的；附加的 **SYN additional**: *Breakfast is provided at no extra charge.* 供应早餐，不另收费。◇ *The conference is going to be a lot of extra work.* 这次会议将有很多额外工作。◇ *an extra pint of milk* 外加的一品脱牛奶 ◇ *The government has promised an extra £1 billion for health care.* 政府承诺为医疗保健再拨款 10 亿英镑。◇ *Take extra care on the roads this evening.* 今晚在路上要格外小心。➲ SEE ALSO EXTRA TIME

■***noun*** **1** 🔑 a thing that is added to sth that is not usual, standard or necessary and that costs more 额外的事物；另外收费的事物：*The monthly fee is fixed and there are no* ***hidden extras*** (= unexpected costs). 月费是固定的，没有未言明的额外开支。◇ (*BrE*) *Metallic paint is* ***an optional extra*** (= a thing you can choose to have or not, but must pay more for if you have it). 喷金属漆是自由选择的，要额外收费。 **2** a person who is employed to play a very small part in a film/movie, usually as a member of a crowd（电影里的）临时演员，群众演员

■***adv.*** **1** 🔑 in addition; more than is usual, expected or exists already 额外；另外；外加：*to* ***charge/pay/cost extra*** 另外收费；另付；额外花费 ◇ *I need to earn a bit extra this month.* 我这个月需要挣点外快。◇ *The rate for a room is £60, but breakfast is extra.* 一个房间收费 60 英镑，不含早餐。 **2** 🔑 (with an adjective or adverb 与形容词或副词连用) more than usually 特别；格外；分外：

You need to be extra careful not to make any mistakes. 你要格外小心，别犯错误。◇ *an extra large T-shirt* 一件特大号的 T 恤衫 ◇ *She tried extra hard.* 她特别努力。

extra- /ˈekstrə/ *prefix* (in adjectives 构成形容词) **1** outside; beyond 在…之外；超出；越出：*extramarital sex* 婚外性行为 ◇ *extraterrestrial beings* 外星人 **2** (*informal*) very; more than usual 非常；格外；十分：*extra-thin* 特别瘦 ◇ *extra-special* 十分特别 ➲ MORE LIKE THIS 6, page R25

ex·tract AW *noun, verb*

■ ***noun*** /ˈekstrækt/ **1** [C] **~ (from sth)** a short passage from a book, piece of music, etc. that gives you an idea of what the whole thing is like 摘录；选录；选曲；节录：*The following extract is taken from her new novel.* 下面一段摘自她的新小说。 **2** [U, C] a substance that has been obtained from sth else using a particular process 提取物；浓缩物；精；汁：*yeast extract* 酵母萃 ◇ *face cream containing natural plant extracts* 含有天然植物提取物的面霜 ◇ (*NAmE*) *vanilla extract* 香草精 ➲ SEE ALSO ESSENCE (2)

■ ***verb*** /ɪkˈstrækt/ **1 ~ sth (from sb/sth)** to remove or obtain a substance from sth, for example by using an industrial or a chemical process 提取；提炼：*a machine that extracts excess moisture from the air* 抽湿机 ◇ *to extract essential oils from plants* 从植物中提取香精油 **2 ~ sth (from sb/sth)** to obtain information, money, etc., often by taking it from sb who is unwilling to give it 索取，设法得到（对方不愿提供的信息、钱财等）：*Journalists managed to extract all kinds of information about her private life.* 记者们终于得到了有关她私生活的各种信息。 **3 ~ sth (from sb/sth)** to choose information, etc. from a book, a computer, etc. to be used for a particular purpose 选取；摘录；选录：*This article is extracted from his new book.* 本文选自他的新书。 **4 ~ sth (from sb/sth)** (*formal* or *specialist*) to take or pull sth out, especially when this needs force or effort （用力）取出，拔出：*The dentist may decide that the wisdom teeth need to be extracted.* 牙医可能会认为智齿需要拔掉。 ◇ *He rifled through his briefcase and extracted a file.* 他在公文包内搜索一番，取出一份文件。 ➲ WORDFINDER NOTE AT DENTIST **5 ~ sth (from sb/sth)** (*formal*) to get a particular feeling or quality from a situation 获得，得到（某种感觉或品质） SYN **derive**：*They are unlikely to extract much benefit from the trip.* 他们不大可能从这次旅行中获得多大益处。 ➲ MORE LIKE THIS 21, page R27

ex·trac·tion AW /ɪkˈstrækʃn/ *noun* **1** [U, C] the act or process of removing or obtaining sth from sth else 提取；提炼；拔出；开采：***oil/mineral/coal, etc. extraction*** 石油、矿物、煤等的开采 ◇ *the extraction of salt from the sea* 从海水中提取盐 **2** [U] **of... extraction** (*formal*) having a particular family origin （有…）血统；族裔：*an American of Hungarian extraction* 匈牙利血统的美国人 **3** [C] (*specialist*) the removal of a tooth 拔牙

ex·tract·ive /ɪkˈstræktɪv; ek-/ *adj.* (*specialist*) relating to the process of removing or obtaining sth, especially minerals 提取的；提炼的；（尤指矿物）冶炼的：*extractive industries* 冶金工业

ex·tract·or /ɪkˈstræktə(r)/ *noun* **1** (*also* **exˈtractor fan**) a device that removes hot air, unpleasant smells, etc. from a room 排气扇；抽油烟机 **2** a device or machine that removes sth from sth else 提取器；抽出器：*a juice extractor* 榨汁机

ˌextra-curˈricu·lar *adj.* [usually before noun] not part of the usual course of work or studies at a school or college 课外的；课程以外的：*She's involved in many* ***extra-curricular activities.*** 她参加了许多课外活动。

extra·dite /ˈekstrədaɪt/ *verb* **~ sb (to...) (from...)** to officially send back sb who has been accused or found guilty of a crime to the country where the crime was committed 引渡（嫌犯或罪犯）：*The British government attempted to extradite the suspects from Belgium.* 英国政府试图从比利时引渡犯罪嫌疑人。 ▸ **extra·di·tion** /ˌekstrəˈdɪʃn/ *noun* [U, C]：*the extradition of terrorist suspects* 对恐怖分子嫌疑犯的引渡 ◇ *an extradition treaty* 引渡条约 ◇ *to start extradition proceedings* 启动引渡程序

extra·judi·cial /ˌekstrədʒuˈdɪʃl/ *adj.* happening outside the normal power of the law 未按法律程序的；法庭以外的

extra·mar·it·al /ˌekstrəˈmærɪtl/ *adj.* happening outside marriage 婚外的：*an extramarital affair* 婚外情

extra·mural /ˌekstrəˈmjʊərəl; *NAmE* -ˈmjʊrəl/ *adj.* [usually before noun] **1** (*BrE*) arranged by a university, college, etc. for people who only study PART-TIME 校外的（高等院校为非全日制学生而设的）：***extramural education/studies/departments*** 校外教育 / 学习 / 课程部 ➲ SEE ALSO EXTENSION (7) **2** (*formal*) happening or existing outside or separate from a place, an organization, etc. （地方、机构等）之外的，外部的，以外的：*The hospital provides extramural care to patients who do not need to be admitted.* 这家医院对无须住院的病人提供院外护理。

ex·tra·ne·ous /ɪkˈstreɪniəs/ *adj.* (*formal*) not directly connected with the particular situation you are in or the subject you are dealing with 没有直接联系的；无关的 SYN **irrelevant**：*We do not want any extraneous information on the page.* 我们不希望这一页上有任何无关的信息。 ◇ **~ to sth** *We shall ignore factors extraneous to the problem.* 我们应该撇开与此问题无直接联系的因素。

extra·or·din·aire /ɪkˌstrɔːdɪˈneə(r); *NAmE* ɪkˌstrɔːrdɪˈner/ *adj.* (*from French, approving, often humorous*) used after nouns to say that sb is a good example of a particular kind of person （用于名词后）卓越的，杰出的，非凡的：*Houdini, escape artist extraordinaire* 胡迪尼——擅长表演脱身术的杰出魔术师

extra·or·din·ary /ɪkˈstrɔːdnri; *NAmE* ɪkˈstrɔːrdəneri/ *adj.* **1** unexpected, surprising or strange 意想不到的；令人惊奇的；奇怪的 SYN **incredible**：*It's extraordinary that he managed to sleep through the party.* 真想不到他竟然从聚会开始一直睡到结束。 ◇ *What an extraordinary thing to say!* 真是咄咄怪事！ **2** not normal or ordinary; greater or better than usual 不平常的；不一般的；非凡的；卓越的：*an extraordinary achievement* 卓越的成就 ◇ *She was a truly extraordinary woman.* 她是位非常杰出的女性。 ◇ *They went to extraordinary lengths to explain their behaviour.* 他们竭力为自己的行为辩解。 ➲ COMPARE ORDINARY **3** [only before noun] (*formal*) (of a meeting, etc. 会议等) arranged for a special purpose and happening in addition to what normally or regularly happens 特别的；临时的：*An extraordinary meeting was held to discuss the problem.* 举行了特别会议讨论这个问题。 **4** (following nouns 紧接名词之后) (*specialist*) (of an official 官员) employed for a special purpose in addition to the usual staff 特派的；特命的：*an envoy extraordinary* 特使 ▸ **extra·or·din·ar·ily** /ɪkˈstrɔːdnrəli; *NAmE* ɪkˌstrɔːrdəˈnerəli/ *adv.*：*He behaves extraordinarily for someone in his position.* 对他那种地位的人来说，他的行为很特别。 ◇ *extraordinarily difficult* 特别困难 ◇ *She did extraordinarily well.* 她干得特别好。

exˌtraordinary renˈdition *noun* = RENDITION (2)

ex·trapo·late /ɪkˈstræpəleɪt/ *verb* [I, T] (*formal*) to estimate sth or form an opinion about sth, using the facts that you have now and that are valid for one situation and supposing that they will be valid for the new one 推断；推知；外推：**~ (from/to sth)** *The figures were obtained by extrapolating from past trends.* 这些数字是从过去的趋势推断出来的。 ◇ **~ sth (from/to sth)** *We have extrapolated these results from research done in other countries.* 我们从其他国家所作的研究中推断出这些结果。 ▸ **ex·trapo·la·tion** /ɪkˌstræpəˈleɪʃn/ *noun* [U, C]：*Their age can be determined by extrapolation from their growth rate.* 它们的年龄可从其生长速度来推定。

extra·sens·ory per·cep·tion /ˌekstrəˌsensəri pəˈsepʃn; *NAmE* pərˈs-/ *noun* [U] = ESP (2)

extra·solar /ˌekstrəˈsəʊlə(r); *NAmE* -ˈsoʊlər/ *adj.* [usually before noun] (*specialist*) (of a planet, etc. 行星等) located outside our SOLAR SYSTEM 在太阳系之外的

E

extra·ter·res·trial /ˌekstrətəˈrestriəl/ *noun, adj.*
■ ***noun*** (in stories) a creature that comes from another planet; a creature that may exist on another planet （故事中的）天外来客，外星人，外星生物
■ ***adj.*** connected with life existing outside the planet Earth 地球外的；外星球的；宇宙的： ***extraterrestrial beings/life*** 外星生命

extra·ter·ri·tor·ial /ˌekstrəterəˈtɔːriəl/ *adj.* (of a law 法律) valid outside the country where the law was made 治外法权的

ˌextra ˈtime (*BrE*) (*NAmE* **over·time**) *noun* [U] (*sport* 体育) a set period of time that is added to the end of a sports game, etc., if there is no winner at the end of the normal period （体育比赛等的）加时，加时赛： *They won by a single goal after extra time.* 他们凭借加时赛中的一个进球而获胜。

ex·trava·gance /ɪkˈstrævəɡəns/ *noun* **1** [U] the act or habit of spending more money than you can afford or than is necessary 奢侈；挥霍；铺张浪费 **2** [C] something that you buy although it costs a lot of money, perhaps more than you can afford or than is necessary 奢侈品： *Going to the theatre is our only extravagance.* 去剧院看戏是我们唯一的奢侈享受。 **3** [C, U] something that is impressive or noticeable because it is unusual or extreme 富丽堂皇；豪华；奢华： *the extravagance of Strauss's music* 施特劳斯音乐作品的富丽堂皇

ex·trava·gant /ɪkˈstrævəɡənt/ *adj.* **1** spending a lot more money or using a lot more of sth than you can afford or than is necessary 奢侈的；挥霍的；铺张浪费的： *I felt very extravagant spending £100 on a dress.* 我觉得花 100 英镑买一条连衣裙太奢侈了。◇ *She's got very extravagant tastes.* 她有很奢侈的嗜好。◇ *Residents were warned not to be* ***extravagant with*** *water, in view of the low rainfall this year.* 鉴于今年降雨量少，居民被告诫不得浪费用水。 **2** costing a lot more money than you can afford or is necessary 过于昂贵的： *an extravagant present* 昂贵的礼物 **3** (of ideas, speech or behaviour 想法或言行) very extreme or impressive but not reasonable or practical 无节制的；过分的；放肆的；不切实际的 **SYN** **exaggerated**: *the* ***extravagant claims/promises*** *of politicians* 政客的夸大其词 / 不切实际的承诺 ▶ **ex·trava·gant·ly** *adv.*： *extravagantly expensive* 极为昂贵 ◇ *extravagantly high hopes* 奢望

ex·trava·ganza /ɪkˌstrævəˈɡænzə/ *noun* a large, expensive and impressive entertainment 铺张华丽的娱乐表演

ex·tra·vert = EXTROVERT

ˌextra ˈvirgin *adj.* used to describe good quality oil obtained the first time that OLIVES are pressed （橄榄油）优质初榨的： *extra virgin olive oil* 优质初榨橄榄油

ex·treme 🔑 /ɪkˈstriːm/ *adj., noun*
■ ***adj.*** **1** 🔑 [usually before noun] very great in degree 极度的；极大的： *We are working under extreme pressure at the moment.* 目前我们正在极大的压力下工作。◇ *people living in extreme poverty* 生活在极度贫困中的人 ◇ *The heat in the desert was extreme.* 沙漠中极其炎热。 **2** 🔑 not ordinary or usual; serious or severe 异乎寻常的；严重的；严厉的： *Children will be removed from their parents only* ***in extreme circumstances.*** 只有在极端情况下才会让孩子离开父母。◇ *Don't go doing anything extreme like leaving the country.* 千万不要做出诸如离开国家之类的极端行为。◇ *It was the most* ***extreme example*** *of cruelty to animals I had ever seen.* 这是我见过的最严重的虐待动物的事例。◇ *extreme weather conditions* 极端恶劣的天气状况 **3** 🔑 (of people, political organizations, opinions, etc. 人、政治组织、意见等) far from what most people consider to be normal, reasonable or acceptable 极端的；偏激的；过分的： ***extreme left-wing/right-wing*** *views* 极左 / 极右观点 **OPP** **moderate** **4** [only before noun] as far as possible from the centre, the beginning or in the direction mentioned 远离中心的；末端的；尽头的： *Kerry is in the extreme west of Ireland.* 凯里位于爱尔兰的最西端。◇ *She sat on the extreme edge of her seat.* 她坐在座位最边上。
■ ***noun*** **1** a feeling, situation, way of behaving, etc. that is as different as possible from another or is opposite to it 极端不同的感情（或境况、行为方式等）；完全相反的事物： *extremes of love and hate* 爱和恨两种截然不同的感情 ◇ *He used to be very shy, but now he's gone to* ***the opposite extreme*** (= changed from one extreme kind of behaviour to another). 他以前很腼腆，现在却走向了另一个极端。 **2** the greatest or highest degree of sth 极端；极度；极限： *extremes of cold, wind or rain* 严寒、狂风、暴雨
IDM **go, etc. to exˈtremes | take sth to exˈtremes** to act or be forced to act in a way that is far from normal or reasonable 走极端；被迫采取极端行为： *It's embarrassing the extremes he'll go to in order to impress his boss.* 他为了给上司留下深刻印象，不惜走极端，真令人难堪。◇ *Taken to extremes, this kind of behaviour can be dangerous.* 这种行为如果走向极端则可能是非常危险的。 **in the exˈtreme** (*formal*) to a great degree 极度；极端；非常： *The journey would be dangerous in the extreme.* 这段旅程将会是极其危险的。

exˈtreme fighting *noun* [U] = ULTIMATE FIGHTING™

ex·treme·ly 🔑 /ɪkˈstriːmli/ *adv.* (usually with adjectives and adverbs 通常与形容词和副词连用) to a very high degree 极其；极端；非常： *extremely important/useful/complicated* 极为重要 / 有用 / 复杂 ◇ *She found it extremely difficult to get a job.* 她发觉找工作极其困难。

exˌtreme ˈsports *noun* [pl.] sports that are extremely exciting to do and often dangerous, for example SKY-DIVING and BUNGEE JUMPING 极限运动 ➲ VISUAL VOCAB PAGES V53-54

exˌtreme ˈunction *noun* [U] (*religion* 宗, *old use*) in the Catholic Church, the ceremony of BLESSING sick or dying people 终傅圣事（天主教为病人或临终者做的圣事）： *He was given extreme unction.* 他接受了终傅圣事。

ex·tre·mis ➲ IN EXTREMIS

ex·trem·ism /ɪkˈstriːmɪzəm/ *noun* [U] political, religious, etc. ideas or actions that are extreme and not normal, reasonable or acceptable to most people 极端主义；过激论： *political extremism* 政治上的极端主义

ex·trem·ist /ɪkˈstriːmɪst/ *noun* (*usually disapproving*) a person whose opinions, especially about religion or politics, are extreme, and who may do things that are violent, illegal, etc. for what they believe 极端主义者；极端分子；过激分子： ***left-wing/right-wing/political/religious extremists*** 左翼 / 右翼 / 政治 / 宗教极端主义者 ➲ WORDFINDER NOTE AT ATTACK ▶ **ex·trem·ist** *adj.* [usually before noun]: ***extremist attacks/groups/policies*** 过激分子的攻击；极端分子组织；极端主义政策

ex·trem·ity /ɪkˈstreməti/ *noun* (*pl.* **-ies**) **1** [C] the furthest point, end or limit of sth 末端；端点；尽头： *The lake is situated at the eastern extremity of the mountain range.* 湖位于山脉最东端。 **2** [C, U] the degree to which a situation, a feeling, an action, etc. is extreme, difficult or unusual 极端；极度；极限： *the extremities/extremity of pain* 极度疼痛 **3 extremities** [pl.] (*formal*) the parts of your body that are furthest from the centre, especially your hands and feet （人体的）四肢，手足

ex·tri·cate /ˈekstrɪkeɪt/ *verb* (*formal*) **1 ~ sb/sth/yourself (from sth)** to escape or enable sb to escape from a difficult situation （使）摆脱，脱离，脱出： *He had managed to extricate himself from most of his official duties.* 他终于摆脱了大部分公务。 **2 ~ sb/sth/yourself (from sth)** to free sb/sth or yourself from a place where they/it or you are trapped 解救；救出；挣脱： *They managed to extricate the pilot from the tangled control panel.* 他们设法把困在控制盘里的飞行员救了出来。

ex·trin·sic /eksˈtrɪnsɪk; -zɪk/ *adj.* (*formal*) not belonging naturally to sb/sth; coming from or existing outside sb/sth rather than within them 非固有的；非本质的；外在的；外来的： *extrinsic factors* 外在因素 ➲ COMPARE INTRINSIC

ex·tro·vert (*also less frequent* **ex·tra·vert**) /ˈekstrəvɜːt; *NAmE* -vɜːrt/ *noun* a lively and confident person who enjoys being with other people 性格外向者；活泼自信的

人 OPP introvert ▸ **ex·tro·ver·sion** (*also* **ex·tra·ver·sion**) *noun* [U] **ex·tro·vert·ed** (*BrE also* **ex·tro·vert**) *adj.*

ex·trude /ɪk'stru:d/ *verb* **1** [T, I] ~ (**sth**) (**from sth**) (*formal*) to force or push sth out of sth; to be forced or pushed in this way （被）挤压出，排出，喷出： *Lava is extruded from the volcano.* 熔岩从火山中喷出。 **2** [T] ~ **sth** (*specialist*) to shape metal or plastic by forcing it through a hole （把金属或塑料）挤压成，压制 ▸ **ex·tru·sion** /ɪk'stru:ʒn/ *noun* [U]

ex·tru·sive /ɪk'stru:sɪv/ *adj.* (*geology* 地) (of rock 岩石) that has been pushed out of the earth by a VOLCANO （火山）喷出的

ex·uber·ant /ɪɡ'zju:bərənt; *NAmE* -'zu:-/ *adj.* **1** full of energy, excitement and happiness 精力充沛的；热情洋溢的；兴高采烈的： *She gave an exuberant performance.* 她的表演热情洋溢。 ◇ *an* ***exuberant personality/imagination*** 充满活力的个性；丰富的想象力 ◇ *a picture painted in exuberant reds and yellows* 用鲜艳的红黄两色画的画 **2** (of plants, etc. 植物等) strong and healthy; growing quickly and well 繁茂的；茂盛的；茁壮的 ▸ **ex·uber·ance** /-rəns/ *noun* [U]: *We can excuse his behaviour as youthful exuberance.* 年轻人精力旺盛，所以他的行为我们可以原谅。 **ex·uber·ant·ly** *adv.*

exude /ɪɡ'zju:d; *NAmE* -'zu:d/ *verb* **1** [T, I] ~ (**sth**) | ~ (**from sb**) if you **exude** a particular feeling or quality, or it **exudes** from you, people can easily see that you have it 流露，显露（感觉或品质）；（感觉或品质）显现： *She exuded confidence.* 她显得信心十足。 **2** [T, I] if sth **exudes** a liquid or smell, or a liquid or smell **exudes** from somewhere, the liquid, etc. comes out slowly 流出，渗出（液体）；散发出（气味）；（从某处）渗出，散发出来： ~ **sth** *The plant exudes a sticky fluid.* 这种植物分泌出一种黏液。 ◇ ~ (**from sth**) *An awful smell exuded from the creature's body.* 这个动物身上发出难闻的气味。

exult /ɪɡ'zʌlt/ *verb* [I, T] (*formal*) to feel and show that you are very excited and happy because of sth that has happened 欢欣鼓舞；兴高采烈；喜形于色： ~ (**at/in sth**) *He leaned back, exulting at the success of his plan.* 他向后一靠，为自己计划的成功而得意扬扬。 ◇ + **speech** *'We won!' she exulted.* "我们赢了！" 她欣喜若狂道。

ex·ult·ant /ɪɡ'zʌltənt/ *adj.* ~ (**at sth**) (*formal*) feeling or showing great pride or happiness especially because of sth exciting that has happened 欢欣鼓舞的；兴高采烈的；得意扬扬的 SYN **triumphant** ▸ **ex·ult·ant·ly** *adv.*

ex·ult·ation /ˌeɡzʌl'teɪʃn/ *noun* [U] (*formal*) great pride or happiness, especially because of sth exciting that has happened 得意；欢悦；兴高采烈

-ey ➲ -Y

eye /aɪ/ *noun, verb*

■ *noun*

• **PART OF BODY** 身体部位 **1** [C] either of the two organs on the face that you see with 眼睛： *The suspect has dark hair and green eyes.* 嫌疑犯有着一头黑发和一双绿眼睛。 ◇ *to* ***close/open your eyes*** 闭上 / 睁开眼睛 ◇ *to* ***drop/lower your eyes*** (= to look down) 眼睛朝下看 ◇ *There were tears in his eyes.* 他眼里噙着泪水。 ◇ *I have something in my eye.* 我的眼睛里进了什么东西。 ◇ *to* ***make/avoid eye contact*** *with sb* (= to look/avoid looking at them at the same time as they look at you) 与 / 避免与某人目光接触 ◇ ***All eyes were on*** *him* (= everyone was looking at him) *as he walked on to the stage.* 他走上台时所有的目光都注视着他。 ➲ COLLOCATIONS AT PHYSICAL ➲ VISUAL VOCAB PAGE V64 ➲ SEE ALSO BLACK EYE, COMPOUND EYE, LAZY EYE, SHUT-EYE **2 -eyed** (in adjectives 构成形容词) having the type or number of eyes mentioned 有…眼睛的；有…只眼的： *a blue-eyed blonde* 蓝眼睛的金发女郎 ◇ *a one-eyed monster* 独眼怪物 ➲ MORE LIKE THIS 8, page R25

• **ABILITY TO SEE** 视力 **3** [sing.] the ability to see 视力；眼力： *A surgeon needs a good eye and a steady hand.* 做外科医生眼要准，手要稳。 ➲ SEE ALSO EAGLE EYE

• **WAY OF SEEING** 眼光 **4** [C, usually sing.] a particular way of seeing sth 眼光；视角： *He looked at the design* ***with the eye of*** *an engineer.* 他以工程师的眼光看这个设计。 ◇ *She viewed the findings with a critical eye.* 她以批判的眼光看待这些研究结果。 ◇ ***To my eye****, the windows seem out of proportion.* 在我看来，这些窗子似乎不成比例。

• **OF NEEDLE** 针 **5** [C] the hole in the end of a needle that you put the thread through 针鼻儿；针眼

• **ON CLOTHES** 衣服 **6** [C] a small thin piece of metal curved round, that a small hook fits into, used for fastening clothes （钩眼扣的）扣眼；金属环眼： *It fastens with a* ***hook and eye****.* 它是用钩眼扣扣上的。 ➲ VISUAL VOCAB PAGE V68

• **OF STORM** 风暴 **7** [sing.] **the ~ of a/the storm, tornado, hurricane, etc.** a calm area at the centre of a storm, etc. 风眼（风暴等的中心平静区）

• **ON POTATO** 马铃薯 **8** [C] a dark mark on a potato from which another plant will grow 芽眼 ➲ SEE ALSO BULLSEYE, CATSEYE™, EVIL EYE, FISHEYE LENS, RED-EYE

IDM **be all 'eyes** to be watching sb/sth carefully and with a lot of interest 极注意地看；留神地看；全神贯注地看；目不转睛 **before/in front of sb's (very) eyes** in sb's presence; in front of sb 当着某人的面；就在某人的眼皮底下： *He had seen his life's work destroyed before his very eyes.* 他曾看到他毕生的劳动成果就在自己的眼前毁于一旦。 **be up to your eyes in sth** to have a lot of sth to deal with 忙于；埋头于；深陷于： *We're up to our eyes in work.* 我们工作忙得不可开交。 **cast/run an eye/your eyes over sth** to look at or examine sth quickly 用眼光瞥（或扫）；匆匆查看；粗略地看一看： *Could you just run your eyes over this report?* 你就粗略地看一下这报告可以吗？ **clap/lay/set eyes on sb/sth** (*informal*) (usually used in negative sentences 通常用于否定句) to see sb/sth 看见；注意到： *I haven't clapped eyes on them for weeks.* 我几周没见到他们了。 ◇ *I hope I never set eyes on this place again!* 我希望永远不再见到这个地方！ **an ˌeye for an 'eye (and a ˌtooth for a 'tooth)** (*saying*) used to say that you should punish sb by doing to them what they have done to you or to sb else 以眼还眼；以牙还牙 **sb's eyes are bigger than their 'stomach** used to say that sb has been GREEDY by taking more food than they can eat （表示贪吃）眼大肚皮小，眼馋肚饱 **for sb's eyes 'only** to be seen only by a particular person 只供某人读（或看）： *I'll lend you the letters but they're for your eyes only.* 我会把这些信借给你，但只准你一个人看。 **get your 'eye in** (*BrE*) (in ball games 球类运动) to practise so that you are able to judge more clearly how fast and where the ball is going 能进行准确判断（球的速度和方向） **have an eye for sth** to be able to judge if things look attractive, valuable, etc. 对…有鉴赏力（或识别力、眼力）： *I've never had much of an eye for fashion.* 我对时装从来没多少鉴赏力。 ◇ *She has an eye for a bargain.* 她善识便宜货。 **have eyes in the back of your 'head** to be aware of everything that is happening around you, even things that seem difficult or impossible to see 脑后长眼；眼光敏锐；什么都能觉察到 **have (got) eyes like a 'hawk** to be able to notice or see everything 洞察一切；眼尖： *She's bound to notice that chipped glass. The woman has eyes like a hawk!* 她一定会注意到那只破损的玻璃杯。这个女人的眼睛尖着呢！ **have one eye/half an eye on sth** to look at or watch sth while doing sth else, especially in a secret way so that other people do not notice 做另一件事的同时（悄悄）注意： *During his talk, most of the delegates had one eye on the clock.* 他讲话时大部分代表边听边悄悄看钟。 **have your 'eye on sb 1** to be watching sb carefully, especially to check that they do not do anything wrong 密切注视；盯住；监视 **2** to be thinking about asking sb out, offering sb a job, etc. because you think they are attractive, good at their job, etc. 看中；看上： *He's got his eye on the new girl in your class.* 他看中了你们班上新来的那个女孩。 **have your 'eye on sth** to be thinking about buying sth 想得到；想买到 **in the eyes of the 'law, 'world, etc.** according to the law, most people in the world, etc. 从（法律、世人等）的观点看；就…而言 **in 'sb's eyes** (*BrE also* **to 'sb's eyes**) in sb's opinion or according to the way that they see the situation 按某人的意见；在某人眼里；依某人看： *She can do no wrong in her father's eyes.* 在她父亲看来，她不可能做坏事。 **keep an eye on sb/sth** to take care of sb/sth and make sure that they are not harmed, damaged, etc. 照看；留神；留意： *We've asked the neighbours to keep an eye on the house for us while we are away.* 我们已请邻居在我们外出时帮我们照看一下房子。 **keep an eye open/out (for sb/sth)** to look for sb/sth while you are doing other things 密切注意；提防；警觉： *Police have asked residents to keep an eye out for anything suspicious.* 警方要求居民密切注意一切可疑的情况。 **keep your eye on the 'ball** to continue to give your attention to what is most important 眼睛盯着大事；密切注意关键问题 **keep your 'eyes peeled/skinned (for sb/sth)** to look carefully for sb/sth 留心；注意；仔细查找： *We kept our eyes peeled for any signs of life.* 我们注意寻找任何生命的迹象。 **look sb in the 'eye(s)/'face** (usually used in negative sentences and questions 通常用于否定句和疑问句) to look straight at sb without feeling embarrassed or ashamed （坦然或问心无愧地）直视某人，正视某人： *Can you look me in the eye and tell me you're not lying?* 你能问心无愧地看着我说你没撒谎吗？ ◇ *I'll never be able to look her in the face again!* 我再也不能坦然地面对她了！ **make 'eyes at sb | give sb the 'eye** to look at sb in a way that shows that you find them sexually attractive 向某人送秋波；向某人抛媚眼： *He's definitely giving you the eye!* 他肯定是在向你眉目传情！ **,my 'eye!** (*old-fashioned, informal*) used to show that you do not believe sb/sth （表示不相信）： *'It's an antique.' 'An antique, my eye!'* "这是件文物。" "是文物才怪！" **not see eye to 'eye with sb (on sth)** to not share the same views as sb about sth 与某人看法不一致（或意见不尽相同）；与…不敢苟同 **not (be able to) take your 'eyes off sb/sth** to find sb/sth so interesting, attractive, etc. that you watch them all the time 目不转睛地盯着；始终注视着 **one in the eye (for sb/sth)** (*informal*) a result, action, etc. that represents a defeat or disappointment for sb/sth 失败；挫折；失望： *The appointment of a woman was one in the eye for male domination.* 任命女性担任这个职位是对男权统治的严重打击。 **only have eyes for/have eyes only for sb** to be in love with only one particular person 只钟情于某人；只爱某人： *He's only ever had eyes for his wife.* 他始终只爱自己的妻子。 **see, look at, etc. sth through sb's eyes** to think about or see sth the way that another person sees it 从别人的角度看： *Try looking at it through her eyes for a change.* 试试设身处地站在她的角度想想这事吧。 **shut/close your eyes to sth** 🔑 to pretend that you have not noticed sth so that you do not have to deal with it （对…）视而不见，熟视无睹，置若罔闻 **take your eye off the 'ball** to stop giving your attention to what is most important 不再关注重要问题 **under the (watchful) eye of sb** being watched carefully by sb 在某人的密切注视下；在某人的监视下： *The children played under the watchful eye of their father.* 孩子们在父亲悉心看护下玩耍。 **what the eye doesn't 'see (the heart doesn't 'grieve over)** (*saying*) if a person does not know about sth that they would normally disapprove of, then it cannot hurt them 眼不见（心不烦）；眼不见为净： *What does it matter if I use his flat while he's away? What the eye doesn't see…!* 我趁他外出时用他的公寓有什么关系呢？反正他又看不见！ **with an eye for/on/to the main chance** (*BrE, usually disapproving*) with the hope of using a particular situation in order to gain some advantage for yourself 瞅机会捞一把 **with an eye to sth/to doing sth** with the intention of doing sth 着眼于；目的在于；试图： *He bought the warehouse with an eye to converting it into a hotel.* 他买这个仓库是为了将它改建成一家旅馆。 **with your eyes 'open** fully aware of the possible problems or results of a particular course of action 明知后果如何；明知有问题；心中有数： *I went into this with my eyes open so I guess I only have myself to blame.* 我是明明知道做这事的后果的，所以我想只能责怪我自己。 **with your eyes 'shut/'closed** having enough experience to be able to do sth easily 轻车熟路；毫不费力： *I've made this trip so often, I could do it with my eyes shut.* 我经常走这条路，闭着眼睛都能找到。 ➲ MORE AT APPLE, BAT *v.*, BEAUTY, BELIEVE, BIRD *n.*, BLIND *adj.*, BLINK *n.*, CATCH *v.*, CLOSE² *adj.*, COCK *v.*, CORNER *n.*, DRY *adj.*, EASY *adj.*, FAR *adv.*, FEAST *v.*, HIT *v.*, MEET *v.*, MIND *n.*, NAKED, OPEN *adj.*, OPEN *v.*, PLEASE *v.*, PUBLIC *adj.*, PULL *v.*, ROVING, SIGHT *n.*, TWINKLING, WEATHER *n.*

■ *verb* (**eye·ing, eying, eyed, eyed**) ~ **sb/sth (+ adv./prep.)** to look at sb/sth carefully, especially because you want sth or you are suspicious of sth 注视；审视；细看： *to eye sb suspiciously* 怀疑地注视着某人 ◇ *He couldn't help eyeing the cakes hungrily.* 他饥不可耐地盯着蛋糕。 ◇ *They eyed us with alarm.* 他们警觉地注视着我们。

PHR V **,eye sb ↔ 'up** (*informal*) to look at sb in a way that shows you have a special interest in them, especially a sexual interest 色眯眯地打量着某人

eye·ball /ˈaɪbɔːl/ *noun, verb*

■ *noun* the whole of the eye, including the part inside the head that cannot be seen 眼球；眼珠 ➲ VISUAL VOCAB PAGE V64

IDM **,eyeball to 'eyeball (with sb)** very close to sb and looking at them, especially during an angry conversation, meeting, etc. （与某人）面对面，怒目相视，对峙： *The protesters and police stood eyeball to eyeball.* 抗议者与警察剑拔弩张。 ◇ *an eyeball-to-eyeball confrontation* 面对面的对抗 **be up to your eyeballs in sth** to have a lot of sth to deal with 忙于；埋头于；深陷于： *They're up to their eyeballs in work.* 他们的工作忙得不可开交。 ➲ MORE AT DRUG *v.*

■ *verb* ~ **sb/sth** (*informal*) to look at sb/sth in a way that is very direct and not always polite or friendly 瞪着；逼视；盯住

eye·bath /ˈaɪbɑːθ; *NAmE* -bæθ/ *noun* a small container that you put a liquid in to wash your eye with 洗眼杯

eye·brow /ˈaɪbraʊ/ (*also* **brow**) *noun* [usually pl.] the line of hair above the eye 眉；眉毛 ➲ COLLOCATIONS AT PHYSICAL ➲ VISUAL VOCAB PAGE V64

IDM **be up to your eyebrows in sth** to have a lot of sth to deal with 忙于；埋头于；深陷于： *He's in it* (= trouble) *up to his eyebrows.* 他深陷于困境之中。 ➲ MORE AT RAISE *v.*

'eyebrow pencil *noun* a type of make-up in the form of a pencil, used for emphasizing or improving the shape of the EYEBROWS 眉笔

'eye candy *noun* [U] (*informal*) a person or thing that is attractive but not intelligent or useful 有魅力但不聪明的人；中看不中用的东西

'eye-catching *adj.* (of a thing 事物) immediately noticeable because it is particularly interesting, bright or attractive 惹人注意的；引人注目的： *an eye-catching advertisement* 醒目的广告

eye·ful /ˈaɪfʊl/ *noun* **1** an amount of sth such as liquid or dust that has been thrown, or blown into your eye 满眼 **2** (*informal*) a person or thing that is beautiful or interesting to look at 悦目的人（或物）；美人；好看的东西

IDM **have/get an eyeful (of sth)** (*BrE, informal*) to look carefully at sth that is interesting or unusual 一饱眼福；好好看一看

eye·glass /ˈaɪɡlɑːs; *NAmE* -ɡlæs/ *noun* **1** a LENS for one eye used to help you see more clearly with that eye 镜片；单片眼镜 **2 eyeglasses** (*NAmE*) = GLASSES

eye·lash /ˈaɪlæʃ/ (*also* **lash**) *noun* [usually pl.] one of the hairs growing on the edge of the EYELIDS 睫；睫毛： *false eyelashes* 假睫毛 ◇ *She just **flutters her eyelashes** and the men come running!* 她只要眨一下眼睫毛，男人们便忙不迭地跑过来！ ➲ COLLOCATIONS AT PHYSICAL ➲ VISUAL VOCAB PAGE V64 IDM SEE BAT *v.*

eye·let /ˈaɪlət/ *noun* a hole with a metal ring around it in a piece of cloth or leather, normally used for passing a rope or string through （供穿绳、线用的）圆孔眼

'eye level *noun* [U] the height of a person's eyes 视线的水平高度： *Computer screens should be at eye level.* 计算机屏幕应该与眼睛齐平。 ◇ *an eye-level grill* 与眼睛齐平的铁栅栏

eye·lid /ˈaɪlɪd/ (*also* **lid**) *noun* either of the pieces of skin above and below the eye that cover it when you BLINK or close the eye 眼睑；眼皮 ➲ VISUAL VOCAB PAGE V64 IDM SEE BAT *v.*

eye·line /ˈaɪlaɪn/ *noun* the direction that sb is looking in 视线

eye·liner /ˈaɪlaɪnə(r)/ (*also* **liner**) *noun* [U] a type of make-up, usually black, that is put around the edge of the eyes to make them more noticeable and attractive （化妆的）眼线；眼线笔 ➲ **WORDFINDER NOTE** AT MAKE-UP ➲ **VISUAL VOCAB** PAGE V65

ˈ**eye-opener** *noun* [usually sing.] an event, experience, etc. that is surprising and shows you sth that you did not already know 使人大开眼界的事情（或经历等）：*Travelling around India was a real eye-opener for me.* 周游印度真让我开了眼界。

eye·patch /ˈaɪpætʃ/ *noun* a piece of material worn over one eye, usually because the eye is damaged 眼罩（通常因眼睛受伤而戴）

eye·piece /ˈaɪpiːs/ *noun* the piece of glass (= a LENS) at the end of a TELESCOPE or MICROSCOPE that you look through （望远镜或显微镜的）目镜 ➲ PICTURE AT BINOCULARS ➲ **VISUAL VOCAB** PAGE V72

ˈ**eye-popping** *adj.* so exciting, large or impressive that it is very surprising or difficult to believe; amazing 令人瞠目的；令人大为惊奇的；令人惊叹的：*The special effects in the film were truly eye-popping.* 影片的特效实在令人叹为观止。➲ **MORE LIKE THIS** 10, page R26

ˈ**eye-rolling** *noun, adj.*
- ***noun*** [U] the action of rolling your eyes, usually because you are annoyed or you do not believe or approve of sth 翻白眼（通常因为恼火、不相信或不赞成）：*There's been a lot of eye-rolling in the office about the latest announcements.* 办公室里有很多人对最近的这些公告大翻白眼。
- ***adj.*** causing sb to roll their eyes, usually because they are annoyed or they don't believe or approve of sth 使人翻白眼的；令人不以为然的：*There were a few eye-rolling moments during the presentation.* 在演示过程中几度让人忍不住翻白眼。▶ ˈ**eye-rollingly** *adv.*

eye·shadow /ˈaɪʃædəʊ; *NAmE* -doʊ/ *noun* [C, U] a type of coloured make-up that is put on the skin above the eyes (= the EYELIDS) to make them look more attractive 眼影 ➲ **WORDFINDER NOTE** AT MAKE-UP ➲ **VISUAL VOCAB** PAGE V65

eye·sight /ˈaɪsaɪt/ *noun* [U] the ability to see 视力；目力：*to have* ***good/bad/poor eyesight*** 视力好/不好/差 ◇ *an eyesight test* 视力测试

eye·sore /ˈaɪsɔː(r)/ *noun* a building, an object, etc. that is unpleasant to look at 碍眼的建筑；丑陋的东西；令人厌恶的东西：*That old factory is a real eyesore!* 那老工厂实在碍眼！

ˈ**eye strain** *noun* [U] a condition of the eyes caused, for example, by a long period of reading or looking at a computer screen 眼疲劳

ˈ**eye teeth** *noun* [pl.]
IDM **give your eye teeth for sth/to do sth** (*BrE, informal*) used when you are saying that you want sth very much 迫切想要；巴不得有：*I'd give my eye teeth to own a car like that.* 我巴不得有一辆那样的汽车。

eye·wall /ˈaɪwɔːl/ *noun* (*specialist*) a thick ring of cloud around the EYE (= calm area at the centre) of a HURRICANE （飓风）眼壁

eye·wash /ˈaɪwɒʃ; *NAmE* -wɔːʃ; -wɑːʃ/ *noun* [U] (*old-fashioned, informal*) words, promises, etc. that are not true or sincere 空话；假话；口惠

ˈ**eye-watering** *adj.* (*informal, especially BrE*) so high or extreme that it is difficult or painful to think about it （高得）难以想象的；令人心痛的；催人落泪的：*eye-watering fare increases* 超乎想象的交通票价飙升 ▶ **eye-wateringly** *adv.*：*eye-wateringly high interest rates* 难以承受的高利率

eye·wear /ˈaɪweə(r); *NAmE* -wer/ *noun* [U] (*formal*) things worn on the eyes such as glasses or CONTACT LENSES （隐形）眼镜

eye·wit·ness /ˈaɪwɪtnəs/ *noun* a person who has seen a crime, accident, etc. and can describe it afterwards 目击者；见证人：*an eyewitness account of the suffering of the refugees* 目击者对难民苦难遭遇的叙述 ➲ **SYNONYMS** AT WITNESS ➲ SEE ALSO WITNESS *n.* (1)

eyrie (*especially BrE*) (*NAmE usually* **aerie**) /ˈɪəri; ˈeəri; ˈaɪəri; *NAmE* ˈɪri; ˈeri/ *noun* **1** a nest that is built high up among rocks by a BIRD OF PREY (= a bird that kills other creatures for food) such as an EAGLE （在岩石高处筑的）猛禽巢，鹰巢 **2** a room or building in a high place, especially one that is difficult to reach and from which sb can see what is happening below （尤指难以接近的）高处的房屋

ˈ**e-zine** *noun* a magazine published in electronic form on the Internet 电子杂志

F /ef/ *noun, abbr.*

■ ***noun*** (*also* **f**) [C, U] (*pl.* **Fs, F's, f's** /efs/) **1** the 6th letter of the English alphabet 英语字母表的第 6 个字母：*'Fox' begins with (an) F/'F'.* * fox 一词以字母 f 开头。 **2 F** (*music* 音) the fourth note in the SCALE of C MAJOR * F 音（C 大调的第 4 音或音符） **3** the 6th highest mark/grade that a student can get for a piece of work, showing that it is very bad and the student has failed（学业成绩）第六等，不及格：*He got* **(an)** *F/'F'* **in/for** *Chemistry.* 他的化学成绩不及格。 ➲ SEE ALSO F-WORD

■ ***abbr.*** **1** FAHRENHEIT 华氏度：*Water freezes at 32°F.* 水在 32 华氏度结冰。 **2** (*BrE*) (in academic titles 学术头衔) FELLOW (4) of 会员：*FRCM* (= Fellow of the Royal College of Music) 皇家音乐学院研究员 **3** FARAD 法拉（电容单位）

f /ef/ (*also* **f.**) *abbr.* **1** female 女的；女性的 **2** (*grammar* 语法) feminine 阴性的；女性的 **3** (*music* 音) loudly (from Italian 'forte')（演奏或歌唱）强，强有力（源自意大利语 forte）

F-1 visa /ˌef wʌn ˈviːzə/ *noun* a document that allows sb from another country to enter the US as a student （美国）外国学生签证

F2F /ˌef tuː ˈef/ *abbr.* (*informal*) face to face (= involving people who are close together and looking at each other) 面对面（全写为 face to face）：*F2F communication* 面对面的交流

FA /ˌef ˈeɪ/ *abbr.* [sing.] **the FA** Football Association (the organization that controls the sport of football (SOCCER) in England and Wales)（英格兰和威尔士的）足球协会（全写为 Football Association）

fa = FAH

fab /fæb/ *adj.* (*BrE, informal*) extremely good 极好的

fable /ˈfeɪbl/ *noun* **1** [C, U] a traditional short story that teaches a moral lesson, especially one with animals as characters; these stories considered as a group 寓言；寓言故事：*Aesop's Fables* 伊索寓言 ◇ *a land rich in fable* 寓言之乡 **2** [U, C] a statement, or an account of sth, that is not true 谎言；不实之词；无稽之谈

fabled /ˈfeɪbld/ *adj.* (*literary* or *humorous*) famous and often talked about, but rarely seen 传说中的 SYN **legendary**：*a fabled monster* 传说中的怪物 ◇ *For the first week he never actually saw the fabled Jack.* 第一周他实际上没见到传闻已久的杰克。

fab·ric /ˈfæbrɪk/ *noun* **1** [U, C] material made by WEAVING wool, cotton, silk, etc., used for making clothes, curtains, etc. and for covering furniture 织物；布料：*cotton fabric* 棉织物 ◇ *furnishing fabrics* 室内装饰织品 **2** [sing.] **the ~ (of sth)** (*formal*) the basic structure of a society, an organization, etc. that enables it to function successfully （社会、机构等的）结构：*a trend which threatens the very* ***fabric of society*** 威胁社会基本结构的趋势 ➲ SYNONYMS AT STRUCTURE **3** [sing.] **the ~ (of sth)** the basic structure of a building, such as the walls, floor and roof （建筑物的）结构（如墙、地面、屋顶）

fab·ri·cate /ˈfæbrɪkeɪt/ *verb* [often passive] **1 ~ sth** to invent false information in order to trick people 编造；捏造 SYN **make up**：*The evidence was totally fabricated.* 这个证据纯属伪造。 **2 ~ sth** (*specialist*) to make or produce goods, equipment, etc. from various different materials 制造；装配；组装 SYN **manufacture** ▶ **fab·ri·ca·tion** /ˌfæbrɪˈkeɪʃn/ *noun* [C, U] (*formal*)：*Her story was a complete fabrication from start to finish.* 她的叙述从头至尾都是编造出来的。

fabu·list /ˈfæbjəlɪst/ *noun* (*formal*) a person who invents or tells stories 寓言作家；讲故事的人；说谎者

fabu·lous /ˈfæbjələs/ *adj.* **1** (*informal*) extremely good 极好的；绝妙的：*a fabulous performance* 精彩的表演 ◇ *Jana is a fabulous cook.* 詹娜的厨艺堪称一绝。 ➲ SYNONYMS AT GREAT **2** (*formal*) very great 很大的；巨大的：***fabulous wealth/riches/beauty*** 大量财产；非常美丽 **3** [only before noun] (*literary*) appearing in FABLES 寓言中的；神话似的：*fabulous beasts* 传说中的野兽

fabu·lous·ly /ˈfæbjələsli/ *adv.* (*formal*) extremely 极其；非常：***fabulously wealthy/rich*** 极为富有

fa·cade /fəˈsɑːd/ *noun* **1** the front of a building（建筑物的）正面 **2** [usually sing.] the way that sb/sth appears to be, which is different from the way sb/sth really is（虚假的）表面，外表：*She managed to maintain a facade of indifference.* 她设法继续装作漠不关心的样子。 ◇ *Squalor and poverty lay behind the city's glittering facade.* 表面的繁华掩盖了这座城市的肮脏和贫穷。

face /feɪs/ *noun, verb*

■ ***noun***

• **FRONT OF HEAD** 头的正面 **1** the front part of the head between the FOREHEAD and the chin 脸；面孔：*a pretty/round/freckled face* 漂亮的 / 圆的 / 有雀斑的面孔 ◇ *He buried his face in his hands.* 他双手掩面。 ◇ *You should have seen the look* ***on her face*** *when I told her!* 我告诉她的时候你真该看到她的脸色！ ◇ *The expression on his face never changed.* 他的面部表情总是一成不变。 ➲ VISUAL

▼ **SYNONYMS** 同义词辨析

fabric

cloth • material • textile

These are all words for woven or knitted cotton, silk, wool, etc., used for making things such as clothes and curtains, and for covering furniture. 以上各词均指织物、布料。

fabric woven or knitted cotton, silk, wool, etc., used for making things such as clothes and curtains, and for covering furniture 指织物、布料：*cotton fabric* 棉织物 ◇ *furnishing fabrics* 室内装饰织物 NOTE **Fabric** is often fairly strong material, and is often used when talking about covering furniture or making curtains. * fabric 常指较结实的材料，常用于指盖家具、做窗帘的织物。

cloth fabric made by weaving or knitting cotton, wool, silk, etc. 指织物、布料：*His bandages had been made from strips of cloth.* 他的绷带是用布条做的。 NOTE **Cloth** is often fairly light material, especially in a form that has not been printed, treated, or prepared for use in any way. **Cloth** is frequently used in talking about buying and selling woven material. * cloth 常指较轻的材料，尤指尚未印花、处理或加工的织物。cloth 常指买卖的织物、布料。

material fabric used for making clothes, curtains, etc. 指布料：*'What material is this dress made of?' 'Cotton.'* "这条裙子是用什么料子做的？" "棉布。" NOTE **Material** is a more general word than **fabric** or **cloth** as it has the related meaning of 'a substance that things can be made from'. It is not used when it might not be clear which type of material is meant. * material 较 fabric 或 cloth 含义更广，因为该词含材料、原料等相关意义。不清楚布料类型就不用该词：~~*furnishing material*~~ ◇ ~~*the material industry*~~ ◇ ~~*a material manufacturer*~~

textile any type of fabric made by weaving or knitting 指纺织品：*He owns a factory producing a range of textiles.* 他拥有一家工厂，生产一系列纺织品。 ◇ *the textile industry* 纺织工业 NOTE **Textile** is used mostly when talking about the business of making woven materials. The industry of making textiles is called **textiles**. * textile 多用来表示织物生产活动，纺织业叫 textiles：*He got a job in textiles.* 他在纺织行业找到一份工作。

PATTERNS

- **woven/cotton/woollen** fabric/cloth/material/textiles
- **synthetic** fabric/material/textiles
- **printed** fabric/cloth/textiles
- **furnishing/curtain/dress** fabric/material

VOCAB PAGE V64

- **EXPRESSION** 表情 **2** 🔑 an expression that is shown on sb's face 面部表情： *a sad/happy/smiling face* 悲哀/幸福的面容；笑脸 ◇ *Her **face lit up*** (= showed happiness) *when she spoke of the past.* 她讲到往事时就面露喜色。◇ *His **face fell*** (= showed disappointment, sadness, etc.) *when he read the headlines.* 他读大标题时脸沉了下来。◇ *Sue's **face was a picture*** (= she looked very surprised, angry, etc.) *as she listened to her husband's speech.* 休听她丈夫讲话时，脸上露出又惊又气的表情。
- **-FACED** 面容… **3** 🔑 (in adjectives 构成形容词) having the type of face or expression mentioned 有…面容的；有…表情的： *pale-faced* 面色苍白的 ◇ *grim-faced* 表情严肃的 ➲ MORE LIKE THIS 8, page R25
- **PERSON** 人 **4** 🔑 (in compounds 构成复合词) used to refer to a person of the type mentioned（某类型的）人： *She looked around for a **familiar face**.* 她环顾四周想找个熟人。◇ *a well-known face on our television screens* 电视屏幕上的一位名人 ◇ *It's nice to see some **new faces** here this evening.* 今晚在这儿见到一些新面孔真是太好了。◇ *I'm fed up of seeing the **same old faces** every time we go out!* 每次参加社交活动都只见到那些旧面孔，我都腻了。
- **SIDE/SURFACE** 面；表面 **5** 🔑 a side or surface of sth（某物的）面，表面： *the north face of the mountain* 山的北坡 ◇ *The birds build their nests in the rock face.* 这些鸟在岩壁上筑巢。◇ *How many faces does a cube have?* 立方体有几个面？ ➲ PICTURE AT SOLID ➲ SEE ALSO COALFACE
- **FRONT OF CLOCK** 钟面 **6** the front part of a clock or watch 钟面；表盘 ➲ PICTURE AT CLOCK
- **CHARACTER/ASPECT** 特征；方面 **7** **~ of sth** the particular character of sth（事物的某种）特征： *the changing face of Britain* 大不列颠变化中的特征 **8** **~ of sth** a particular aspect of sth 方面： *the unacceptable face of capitalism* 资本主义不可接受的方面 ➲ SEE ALSO IN-YOUR-FACE, TYPEFACE, VOLTE-FACE

IDM **disappear/vanish off the face of the 'earth** to disappear completely 完全消失；消逝得无影无踪： *Keep looking—they can't just have vanished off the face of the earth.* 继续找，他们不可能就从此消失得无影无踪的。 **sb's face doesn't fit** used to say that sb will not get a particular job or position because they do not have the appearance, personality, etc. that the employer wants, even when this should not be important 长相不合格；性格不合适： *It doesn't matter how well qualified you are, if your face doesn't fit, you don't stand a chance.* 资历多好也没用，如果人家看你不顺眼，你就不会有机会。 **sb's face is like 'thunder | sb has a face like 'thunder** somebody looks very angry 某人怒气冲冲；某人满面怒容 **ˌface to 'face (with sb)** 🔑 close to and looking at sb（与某人）面对面： *The two have never met face to face before.* 两个人过去从未见过面。 **ˌface to 'face with sth** 🔑 in a situation where you have to accept that sth is true and deal with it 面对某种处境： *She was at an early age brought face to face with the horrors of war.* 她年幼时就面临战争的恐怖。 **ˌface 'up/'down** **1** 🔑 (of a person 人) with your face and stomach facing upwards/downwards 面朝上/朝下： *She lay face down on the bed.* 她俯卧在床上。 **2** 🔑 with the front part or surface facing upwards/downwards 正面朝上/朝下；表面冲上/冲下： *Place the card face up on the pile.* 把纸牌正面朝上放在这一叠的上面。 **have the 'face to do sth** (*BrE, informal*) to do sth that other people think is rude or shows a lack of respect, without feeling embarrassed or ashamed 居然有脸干某事；恬不知耻做某事 **in sb's 'face** (*NAmE, informal*) annoying sb by criticizing them or telling them what to do all the time 批评某人，支使某人（使人恼火） **in the face of 'sth** **1** despite problems, difficulties, etc. 即使面对（问题、困难等）： *She showed great courage in the face of danger.* 面对危险她表现出了巨大的勇气。 **2** as a result of sth 由于；因为： *He was unable to deny the charges in the face of new evidence.* 面对新的证据，他无法否认这些指控。 **lose 'face** to be less respected or look stupid because of sth you have done 丢脸；失面子 **on the 'face of it** (*informal*) used to say that sth seems to be good, true, etc. but that this opinion may need to be changed when you know more about it 表面上看： *On the face of it, it seems like a great deal.* 表面上看来好像很多。 **pull/make 'faces/a 'face (at sb)** 🔑 to produce an expression on your face to show that you do not like sb/sth or in order to make sb laugh（对某人）耷拉着脸，板着脸，做鬼脸： *What are you pulling a face at now?* 你干吗板着脸？ **put your 'face on** (*informal*) to put on MAKE-UP 化妆 **set your face against sb/sth** (*especially BrE*) to be determined to oppose sb/sth 坚决反对某人/事物： *Her father had set his face against the marriage.* 她的父亲坚决反对这门亲事。 **to sb's 'face** if you say sth **to sb's face**, you say it to them directly rather than to other people 当着某人的面 ➲ COMPARE BEHIND SB'S BACK at BACK *n.* **'what's his/her face** (*informal*) used to refer to a person whose name you cannot remember（指记不起姓名的人）叫…的人： *Are you still working for what's her face?* 你还在为那个叫什么的女人干活？ ➲ MORE AT BLOW *v.*, BLUE *adj.*, BRAVE *adj.*, DOOR, EGG *n.*, EYE *n.*, FEED *v.*, FLAT *adv.*, FLY *v.*, LAUGH *v.*, LONG *adj.*, NOSE *n.*, PLAIN *adj.*, PRETTY *adj.*, SAVE *v.*, SHOW *v.*, SHUT *v.*, SLAP *n.*, STARE *v.*, STRAIGHT *adj.*, WIPE *v.*, WRITE

■ ***verb***

- **BE OPPOSITE** 面对 **1** 🔑 [T, I] to be opposite sb/sth; to have your face or front pointing towards sb/sth or in a particular direction 面对；面向；正对： **~ sb/sth** *She turned and faced him.* 她转过身来面对着他。◇ *Most of the rooms face the sea.* 多数房间朝海。◇ **+ adv./prep.** *The terrace faces south.* 露台朝南。◇ *a north-facing wall* 面北的墙 ◇ *Stand with your feet apart and your hands facing upwards.* 两脚叉开站着，双手向上。◇ *Which direction are you facing?* 你面朝哪个方向？
- **SB/STH DIFFICULT** 难对付的人/事物 **2** 🔑 [T] if you **face** a particular situation, or it **faces** you, you have to deal with it 面临，必须对付（某情况）： **~ sth** *the problems faced by one-parent families* 单亲家庭面对的问题 ◇ *The company is facing a financial crisis.* 公司正面临财政危机。◇ **be faced with sth** *She's faced with a difficult decision.* 她眼前有一项难作的决定。 **3** 🔑 [T] **~ sth** to accept that a difficult situation exists, although you would prefer not to 承认，正视（现实）： *It's not always easy to face the truth.* 承认事实并不总是一件容易的事。◇ *She had to **face the fact that** her life had changed forever.* 她得正视她的生活已永远改变了这一事实。◇ ***Face facts**—she isn't coming back.* 面对现实吧，她不会回来了。◇ ***Let's face it**, we're not going to win.* 我们得承认，我们赢不了啦。 **4** 🔑 [T] if you **can't face** sth unpleasant, you feel unable or unwilling to deal with it（感到不能）对付；（不愿）处理： **~ sth** *I just can't face work today.* 我今天就是没法工作。◇ **~ doing**

▼ **VOCABULARY BUILDING** 词汇扩充

Expressions on your face 面部表情

- To **beam** is to have a big happy smile on your face. * beam 指笑逐颜开。
- To **frown** is to make a serious, angry or worried expression by bringing your eyebrows closer together so that lines appear on your forehead. * frown 指皱眉、蹙额。
- To **glare** or **glower** is to look in an angry, aggressive way. * glare 和 glower 指怒目而视、咄咄逼人地瞪眼。
- To **grimace** is to make an ugly expression with your face to show pain, disgust, etc. * grimace 指因痛苦、厌恶等面目扭曲。
- To **scowl** is to look at someone in an angry or annoyed way. * scowl 指怒视。
- To **smirk** is to smile in a silly or unpleasant way that shows that you are pleased with yourself, know something that other people do not know, etc. * smirk 指傻笑、得意地笑，以示自鸣得意、知他人所不知等。
- To **sneer** is to show that you have no respect for someone by turning your upper lip upwards. * sneer 指翘起上唇嗤笑、讥笑，以示轻蔑。

These words can also be used as nouns. 以上各词亦可作名词： *She looked up with a puzzled frown.* 她抬起头来，困惑地皱着眉头。◇ *He gave me an icy glare.* 他冷冰冰地怒视着我。◇ *a grimace of pain* 痛得扭曲的脸

F

sth *I can't face seeing them.* 我真不愿意见到他们。 **5** [T] **~ sb** to talk to or deal with sb, even though this is difficult or unpleasant（明知不好办而）交谈，应付：*How can I face Tom? He'll be so disappointed.* 我怎样才能和汤姆谈呢？他会很失望的。

• COVER SURFACE 覆盖表面 **6** [T, usually passive] **~ sth with sth** to cover a surface with another material（以另一物）覆盖表面：*a brick building faced with stone* 石料贴面的砖建筑物

IDM **face the 'music** (*informal*) to accept and deal with criticism or punishment for sth you have done 接受批评（或惩罚）：*The others all ran off, leaving me to face the music.* 其他人都跑掉了，留下我来挨罚。

F

PHR V **,face sb↔'down** to oppose or beat sb by dealing with them directly and confidently （威风凛凛地）把某人压制下去 **,face 'off** (*especially NAmE*) **1** to start a game such as ICE HOCKEY（冰球等）开球：*Both teams are ready to face off.* 两队都准备好了开球。 **2** to argue, fight or compete with sb, or to get ready to do this 跟人辩论（或战斗、比赛）；准备好辩论（或战斗、比赛）：*The candidates are preparing to face off on TV tonight.* 今夜候选人准备在电视上进行辩论。 ➲ RELATED NOUN FACE-OFF **,face 'up to sth** 🔑 to accept and deal with sth that is difficult or unpleasant 敢于面对，勇于正视（困难或不快之事）：*She had to face up to the fact that she would never walk again.* 她必须敢于面对现实：她再也不能走路了。

Face·book™ /ˈfeɪsbʊk/ *noun* a SOCIAL NETWORKING website 脸谱，脸书（社交网站）

'face card (*especially NAmE*) (*BrE also* **'court card**) *noun* a PLAYING CARD with a picture of a king, queen or JACK on it 人头牌，花牌（纸牌的 K、Q 或 J） ➲ VISUAL VOCAB PAGE V42

face·cloth /ˈfeɪsklɒθ; *NAmE* -klɔːθ/ *noun* (*BrE*) = FLANNEL (2)

'face cream *noun* [U, C] a thick cream that you put on your face to clean the skin or keep it soft 面霜；雪花膏

face·less /ˈfeɪsləs/ *adj.* [usually before noun] (*disapproving*) having no noticeable characteristics or identity 无个性的；缺乏特征的；身份不明的：*faceless bureaucrats* 千人一面的官僚主义者 ◇ *faceless high-rise apartment blocks* 千篇一律的高层公寓大楼

face·lift /ˈfeɪslɪft/ *noun* [usually sing.] **1** a medical operation in which the skin on a person's face is made tighter in order to make them look younger 去皱整容手术；面部拉皮手术：*to have a facelift* 接受去皱整容手术 **2** changes made to a building or place to make it look more attractive（建筑物、地方的）翻新，整修：*The town has recently been given a facelift.* 该镇最近进行了整修。

'face-off *noun* **1** (*informal, especially NAmE*) an argument or a fight 辩论；搏斗：*a face-off between the presidential candidates* 总统候选人之间的辩论 **2** the way of starting play in a game of ICE HOCKEY（冰球赛的）开球

'face pack *noun* (*BrE*) a substance that you put on your face and take off after a short period of time, used to clean your skin 面膜（洁净面部皮肤用）

'face powder *noun* powder that you put on your face to make it look less shiny 扑面粉；敷面粉

'face-saving *adj.* [only before noun] intended to protect sb's reputation and to avoid embarrassment 保全面子的：*a face-saving compromise* 体面的妥协

facet /ˈfæsɪt/ *noun* **1 ~ (of sth)** a particular part or aspect of sth （事物的）部分，方面：*Now let's look at another facet of the problem.* 现在咱们看问题的另一面。 **2** one of the flat sides of a JEWEL （宝石的）小平面，琢面

'face time *noun* [U] (*NAmE, informal*) time that you spend talking face-to-face (= in person) to people you work with, rather than speaking on the phone or sending emails （与同事等的）面对面（交流）时间

fa·cetious /fəˈsiːʃəs/ *adj.* trying to appear amusing and intelligent at a time when other people do not think it is appropriate, and when it would be better to be serious 乱引人发笑的；不分场合要聪明的 SYN **flippant**：*a* ***facetious comment/remark*** 不分场合要聪明的议论 ◇ *Stop being facetious; this is serious.* 别乱开玩笑，这是个严肃的事。 ▶ **fa·cetious·ly** *adv.* **fa·cetious·ness** *noun* [U]

,face-to-'face *adj.* involving people who are close together and looking at each other 面对面的：*a face-to-face conversation* 面谈 ◇ *I deal with customers on the phone and rarely meet them face-to-face.* 我用电话和客户打交道，很少和他们见面。 ▶ **face-to-face** *adv.*：*He opened the door and* ***came face-to-face with*** *a burglar.* 他打开门和窃贼打了个照面。 ◇ (*figurative*) *She was brought face-to-face with the horrors of war.* 她直面了战争的恐怖。

,face 'value *noun* [U, sing.] the value of a stamp, coin, ticket, etc. that is shown on the front of it （邮票、钱币、票等的）票面价值，面值

IDM **take sth at face 'value** to believe that sth is what it appears to be, without questioning it 相信表面：*Taken at face value, the figures look very encouraging.* 若只看表面，数字很令人鼓舞。 ◇ *You shouldn't take anything she says at face value.* 她的话你绝对不能只看表面。

fa·cia = FASCIA

fa·cial /ˈfeɪʃl/ *adj., noun*

▪ ***adj.*** [usually before noun] connected with a person's face; on a person's face 面部的：*a facial expression* 面部表情 ◇ *facial hair* 面部毫毛 ▶ **fa·cial·ly** /ˈfeɪʃəli/ *adv.*：*Facially the two men were very different.* 这两个男人的脸型迥异。

▪ ***noun*** a beauty treatment in which a person's face is cleaned using creams, steam, etc. in order to improve the quality of the skin 面部护理；美容

fa·cile /ˈfæsaɪl; *NAmE* ˈfæsl/ *adj.* (*disapproving*) **1** produced without effort or careful thought 轻率作出的；不动脑筋的 SYN **glib**：*a* ***facile remark/generalization*** 信口开河；随意概括 **2** [only before noun] (*formal*) obtained too easily and having little value 轻易可得的；得来容易的：*a facile victory* 唾手可得的胜利

fa·cili·tate AW /fəˈsɪlɪteɪt/ *verb* **~ sth** (*formal*) to make an action or a process possible or easier 促进；促使；使便利：*The new trade agreement should facilitate more rapid economic growth.* 新贸易协定应当会加快经济发展。◇ *Structured teaching facilitates learning.* 有条理的教导有利于学习。 ▶ **fa·cili·ta·tion** AW /fə,sɪlɪˈteɪʃn/ *noun* [U, sing.]

fa·cili·ta·tor AW /fəˈsɪlɪteɪtə(r)/ *noun* **1** a person who helps sb do sth more easily by discussing problems, giving advice, etc. rather than telling them what to do 引导者：*The teacher acts as a facilitator of learning.* 教师是学习的引导者。 **2** (*formal*) a thing that helps a process take place 促进（或推动）…的事物

fa·cil·ity 🔑 AW /fəˈsɪləti/ *noun* **1** 🔑 **facilities** [pl.] buildings, services, equipment, etc. that are provided for a particular purpose 设施；设备：***sports/leisure facilities*** 体育 / 休闲设施 ◇ *conference facilities* 会议设施 ◇ ***shopping/banking/cooking facilities*** 商店 / 银行设施；炊事设备 ◇ *The hotel has special facilities for welcoming disabled people.* 这家旅馆有专供残疾人使用的设施。 ◇ *All rooms have* ***private facilities*** (= a private bathroom). 每一个房间都有独立的浴室。 **2** [C] a special feature of a machine, service, etc. that makes it possible to do sth extra（机器等的）特别装置；（服务等的）特色：*a bank account with an overdraft facility* 提供透支服务的银行账户 ◇ *a facility for checking spelling* 检查拼写的设备 **3** [C] a place, usually including buildings, used for a particular purpose or activity（供特定用途的）场所：*the world's largest nuclear waste facility* 世界最大的核废料处理场 ◇ *a new health care facility* 新保健中心 **4** [sing., U] **~ (for sth)** a natural ability to learn or do sth easily（学习、做事的）天资，才能，天赋：*She has a facility for languages.* 她有语言天赋。

fa·cing /ˈfeɪsɪŋ/ *noun* **1** [C, U] a layer of brick, stone, etc. that covers the surface of a wall to make it look more attractive （建筑物的）饰面，面层 **2** [C, U] a layer of stiff material sewn around the inside of the neck, ARMHOLES, etc. of a piece of clothing to make them stronger 领口

衬里，袖口贴边，镶边（使衣服耐穿） **3 facings** [pl.] the COLLAR, CUFFS, etc. of a piece of clothing that are made in a different colour or material （不同质地或颜色的）领子（或袖口等）

fac·sim·ile /fæk'sɪməli/ *noun* **1** [C] an exact copy of sth 摹本；传真本；复制本：*a facsimile edition* 摹本版 ◇ *a manuscript reproduced **in facsimile*** 精确复制的手稿 **2** [C, U] (*formal*) = FAX：*a facsimile machine* 传真机

fact /fækt/ *noun* **1** [sing.] ~ (**that**...) used to refer to a particular situation that exists 现实；实际情况：*I could no longer ignore the fact that he was deeply unhappy.* 我再不能对他深感不快这个事实不闻不问了。◇ ***Despite the fact that** she was wearing a seat belt, she was thrown sharply forward.* 尽管她系了安全带，还是被猛然前抛。◇ ***Due to the fact that** they did not read English, the prisoners were unaware of what they were signing.* 这些囚犯由于看不懂英语，不知道自己在签什么。◇ *She was happy **apart from the fact that** she could not return home.* 除了不能回家之外，她很快活。◇ *Voluntary work was particularly important **in view of the fact that** women were often forced to give up paid work on marriage.* 鉴于妇女一结婚就常常被迫放弃有报酬工作的事实，义务工作尤其重要。◇ *How do you account for the fact that unemployment is still rising?* 你如何解释失业人数仍在增加这个现实？◇ ***The fact remains** that we are still two teachers short.* 实际情况是我们还缺少两名教师。◇ *The mere fact of being poor makes such children criminals in the eyes of the police.* 只因为贫穷就使得这群儿童成为警方眼中的罪犯。➲ LANGUAGE BANK AT HOWEVER **2** [C] a thing that is known to be true, especially when it can be proved （可证实的）事实，真相：*Isn't it a fact that the firm is losing money?* 公司正在亏本，这难道不是事实吗？◇ (*informal*) *I haven't spoken to anyone in English for days **and that's a fact**.* 我有好多天没和任何人说英语了，事实就是这样。◇ ***I know for a fact*** (= I am certain) *that she's involved in something illegal.* 我肯定她卷入了非法活动。◇ *The judge instructed both lawyers to **stick to the facts** of the case.* 法官责令双方律师要紧扣案情。◇ *First, some basic facts about healthy eating!* 首先，说说健康饮食的几点基本事实！◇ *The report is based on **hard facts*** (= information that can be proved to be true). 这个报告是以铁的事实为根据的。◇ *If you're going to make accusations, you'd better **get your facts right*** (= make sure your information is correct). 你要是打算控告最好把证据弄确凿。◇ *It's about time you learnt to **face** (**the**) **facts*** (= accepted the truth about the situation). 现在该是你学会正视现实的时候了。**3** [U] things that are true rather than things that have been invented 真实的事物；真实情况：*The story is based on fact.* 这个故事是根据真人真事写的。◇ *It's important to distinguish fact from fiction.* 区别真实和虚构是重要的。

IDM **ˌafter the 'fact** after sth has happened or been done, when it is too late to prevent it or change it 事后：*On some vital decisions employees were only informed after the fact.* 有一些重大决策雇员只在事后才获悉。**the fact (of the matter) is (that)...** used to emphasize a statement, especially one that is the opposite of what has just been mentioned（用以强调，尤其与刚提到的相反）事实上是，实际情况是：*A new car would be wonderful but the fact of the matter is that we can't afford one.* 有新车好是好，不过实际情况是我们买不起。**a ˌfact of 'life** a situation that cannot be changed, especially one that is unpleasant 生活的（不快）现实 **ˌfacts and 'figures** accurate and detailed information 准确的信息；精确的资料；确实的情报：*I've asked to see all the facts and figures before I make a decision.* 我已要求在看到所有的确切信息后再作决定。➲ MORE LIKE THIS 13, page R26 **the ˌfacts of 'life** the details about sex and about how babies are born, especially as told to children （尤指对儿童讲的）性知识 **the facts speak for them'selves** it is not necessary to give any further explanation about sth because the information that is available already proves that it is true 事实足以说明一切 **in (actual) fact 1** used to give extra details about sth that has just been mentioned（补充细节）确切地说：*I used to live in France; in fact, not far from where you're going.* 我曾在法国住过；确切地说，离你要去的地方不远。**2** used to emphasize a statement, especially one that is the opposite of what has just been mentioned（用以强调，尤其与刚提到的相反）事实上，实际上：*I thought the work would be difficult. In actual fact, it's very easy.* 我原以为这工作会很难，事实上却很容易。➲ LANGUAGE BANK AT HOWEVER **Is that a 'fact?** (*informal*) used to reply to a statement that you find interesting or surprising, or that you do not believe（回答认为有趣、惊奇或不相信的说法）是真的吗：*'She says I'm one of the best students she's ever taught.' 'Is that a fact?'* "她说我是她教过的最好的学生之一。""真的是这样吗？" ➲ MORE AT MATTER *n.*, POINT *n.*

'fact-finding *adj.* [only before noun] done in order to find out information about a country, an organization, a situation, etc. 实情调查的：*a **fact-finding mission/visit*** 实情调查团；查访

fac·tion /'fækʃn/ *noun* **1** [C] a small group of people within a larger one whose members have some different aims and beliefs to those of the larger group（大团体中的）派系，派别，小集团：*rival factions within the administration* 政府中的对立派别 ➲ COLLOCATIONS AT POLITICS **2** [U] opposition, disagreement, etc. that exists between small groups of people within an organization or political party 派系斗争；内讧：*a party divided by faction and intrigue* 因派系和阴谋诡计搞得四分五裂的政党 **3** [U] films/movies, books, etc. that combine fact with FICTION (= imaginary events) 纪实与虚构相结合的电影（或书等）

fac·tion·al /'fækʃənl/ *adj.* [only before noun] connected with the factions of an organization or political party 派系的；派别的：*factional conflict* 派系冲突 ▶ **fac·tion·al·ism** *noun* [U]

fac·ti·tious /fæk'tɪʃəs/ *adj.* (*formal*) not genuine but created deliberately and made to appear to be true 人为的；虚假的

fac·toid /'fæktɔɪd/ *noun* **1** something that is widely accepted as a fact, although it is probably not true 仿真陈述（很可能不真实但使人信以为真） **2** a small piece of interesting information, especially about sth that is not very important 有趣消息（尤指有关不太重要事情的）：*Here's a pop factoid for you.* 告诉你一个广为流传的趣闻。

fac·tor AW /'fæktə(r)/ *noun, verb*

■ ***noun*** **1** [C] one of several things that cause or influence sth 因素；要素：*economic factors* 经济因素 ◇ *The closure of the mine was the **single most important** factor in the town's decline.* 矿山的关闭是这个镇衰落的唯一重要的因素。◇ *the **key/crucial/deciding factor*** 关键的 / 至关重要的 / 决定性的因素 ➲ LANGUAGE BANK AT CAUSE **2** [C] (*mathematics* 数) a number that divides into another number exactly 因子；因数：*1, 2, 3, 4, 6 and 12 are the factors of 12.* *1、2、3、4、6 和 12 是 12 的因子。**3** [C] the amount by which sth increases or decreases（增或减的）数量，倍数：*The real wage of the average worker has increased by a factor of over ten in the last 70 years.* 近 70 年来工人的实际工资平均增长超过了十倍。**4** [C] a particular level on a scale of measurement 系数：*a suntan lotion with a protection factor of 10* 防护系数为 10 的防晒油 ◇ *The wind-chill factor will make it seem colder.* 风寒系数大，会使人觉得比实际温度更冷一些。**5** [U] (*medical* 医) a substance in the blood that helps the CLOTTING process. There are several types of this substance. 凝血因子：*Haemophiliacs have no factor 8 in their blood.* 血友病患者的血液中缺乏凝血因子 Ⅷ。IDM SEE FEEL-GOOD

■ ***verb***

PHR V **ˌfactor sth↔in | factor sth into sth** (*specialist*) to include a particular fact or situation when you are thinking about or planning sth 把…因素包括进去：*Remember to factor in staffing costs when you are planning the project.* 规划该项目时，记住要把雇人费用这个因素考虑进去。

fac·tor VIII (*also* **factor 8, factor eight**) /ˌfæktər 'eɪt/ *noun* [U] (*biology* 生) a substance in the blood that helps it to CLOT (= become thick) 因子 Ⅷ；凝血因子 Ⅷ

fac·tor·ial /fæk'tɔːriəl/ *noun* (*mathematics* 数) the result when you multiply a whole number by all the numbers below it 阶乘：*5!* (= factorial 5) *is 120* (=*5×4×3×2×1*). * 5!（5 的阶乘）为 120（即 5 × 4 × 3 × 2 × 1）。

fac·tor·ize (*BrE also* **-ise**) /ˈfæktəraɪz/ *verb* **~ sth** (*mathematics* 数) to express a number in terms of its FACTORS 因数分解；因式分解；将…分解成因子

fac·tory /ˈfæktri; -təri/ *noun* (*pl.* **-ies**) a building or group of buildings where goods are made 工厂；制造厂：*a car factory* 汽车制造厂 ◇ *factory workers* 工厂工人

WORDFINDER 联想词：assembly line, capacity, foreman, plant, process, production, shift, shop floor, workforce

▼ **SYNONYMS** 同义词辨析

factory

plant • mill • works • yard • workshop • foundry

These are all words for buildings or places where things are made or where industrial processes take place. 以上各词均指工厂、车间、工场、制造厂。

factory a building or group of buildings where goods are made 指工厂、制造厂：*a chocolate/cigarette/clothing factory* 巧克力厂；香烟厂；制衣厂

plant a factory or place where power is produced or an industrial process takes place 指发电厂、工厂：*a nuclear power plant* 核电厂 ◇ *a manufacturing plant* 制造厂

mill a factory that produces a particular type of material 指（生产特定材料的）工厂、制造厂：*a cotton/paper/textile/woollen mill* 棉纺厂；造纸厂；纺织厂；毛纺厂

works (often in compounds) a place where things are made or an industrial process takes place （常构成复合词）指工厂、制造厂：*a brickworks* 砖厂 ◇ *a steelworks* 炼钢厂 ◇ *Raw materials were carried to the works by barge.* 原材料由驳船运到工厂。

yard (usually in compounds) an area of land used for building sth （通常构成复合词）指建造某物的区域、场地：*a shipyard* 船坞

workshop a room or building in which things are made or repaired using tools or machinery 指车间、工场、作坊：*a car repair workshop* 汽车修理厂

foundry a factory where metal or glass is melted and made into different shapes or objects 指铸造厂、玻璃厂：*an iron foundry* 铸铁厂

PATTERNS

- a **car/chemical/munitions** factory/plant
- an **engineering** plant/works
- to **manage/run** a factory/plant/mill/works/yard/workshop/foundry
- to **work in/at** a factory/plant/mill/yard/workshop/foundry
- factory/mill/foundry **owners/managers/workers**

ˈ**factory farm** *noun* a type of farm in which animals are kept inside in small spaces and are fed special food so that a large amount of meat, milk, etc. is produced as quickly and cheaply as possible 工厂化农场 ➲ COMPARE BATTERY FARM ▶ ˈ**factory farming** *noun* [U]

ˌ**factory ˈfloor** *noun* (*often* **the factory floor**) [sing.] the part of a factory where the goods are actually produced 厂房；车间：*Jobs are at risk, not just on the factory floor* (= among the workers, rather than the managers) *but throughout the business.* 职位不保，不仅对车间工人如此，而且危及整个行业。

ˈ**factory ship** *noun* a large ship used for catching fish, that has equipment for cleaning and freezing the fish on board 捕鱼加工船（有加工冰冻设备）

ˈ**factory shop** (*BrE*) (*also* ˈ**factory store**, ˈ**factory outlet** *NAmE, BrE*) *noun* a shop/store in which goods are sold directly by the company that produces them at a cheaper price than normal 厂家直销店；工厂直营店

fac·to·tum /fækˈtəʊtəm; *NAmE* -ˈtoʊ-/ *noun* (*formal* or *humorous*) a person employed to do a wide variety of jobs for sb 勤杂工；事务总管

ˈ**fact sheet** *noun* a piece of paper or an electronic document giving information about a subject, especially (in Britain) one discussed on a radio or television programme（尤指英国广播或电视节目中有关讨论题目的）资料页，资料电子文件

fac·tual /ˈfæktʃuəl/ *adj.* based on or containing facts 根据事实的；事实的；真实的：*a factual account of events* 事件的如实报道 ◇ *factual information* 事实信息 ◇ *The essay contains a number of factual errors.* 文章中有一些与事实不符的错误。▶ **fac·tu·al·ly** /-tʃuəli/ *adv.*：*factually correct* 与事实相符

fac·ulty /ˈfæklti/ *noun* (*pl.* **-ies**) **1** [C, usually pl.] any of the physical or mental abilities that a person is born with 官能；天赋：*the faculty of sight* 视觉 ◇ *She retained her mental faculties* (= the ability to think and understand) *until the day she died.* 她直到去世那天一直保持着思维和理解能力。◇ *to be **in full possession of your faculties*** (= be able to speak, hear, see, understand, etc.) 拥有一切官能（能够说、听、看见、理解等）**2** [sing.] **~ of/for** (**doing**) **sth** (*formal*) a particular ability for doing sth 才能；能力：*the faculty of understanding complex issues* 理解复杂问题的能力 ◇ *He had a faculty for seeing his own mistakes.* 他具有看到自己错误的能力。 **3** [C] a department or group of related departments in a college or university（高等院校的）系，院：*the Faculty of Law* 法学院 ◇ *the Arts Faculty* 文学院 **4** [C+sing./pl. v.] all the teachers in a faculty of a college or university（高等院校中院、系的）全体教师：*the Law School faculty* 法学院全体教师 ◇ *a faculty meeting* 全体教师会议 ◇ *faculty members* 全系教师 **5** [C, U] (*often* **the faculty**) (*NAmE*) all the teachers of a particular university or college（某高等院校的）全体教师：*faculty members* 全系教师

fad /fæd/ *noun* something that people are interested in for only a short period of time 一时的风尚；短暂的狂热 SYN **craze**：*the **latest/current fad*** 最新 / 当前的时尚 ◇ *a fad for physical fitness* 一阵健身狂热 ◇ *Rap music proved to be more than just a **passing fad**.* 事实证明，说唱音乐并不是昙花一现。

faddy /ˈfædi/ *adj.* (*BrE, informal, disapproving*) liking some things and not others, especially food, in a way that other people think is unreasonable 口味不寻常的；（尤指）挑食的，偏食的：*a faddy eater* 过分挑食的人 ▶ **fad·di·ness** *noun* [U]

fade /feɪd/ *verb* **1** [I, T] to become or to make sth become paler or less bright （使）变淡，变暗：*The curtains had faded in the sun.* 窗帘已经给晒退了色。◇ **~ from sth** *All colour had faded from the sky.* 天上的颜色都退去了。◇ **~ sth** *The sun had faded the curtains.* 太阳把窗帘晒退了色。◇ *He was wearing faded blue jeans.* 他穿着退色的蓝牛仔裤。 **2** [I] to disappear gradually 逐渐消逝；逐渐消失：*Her smile faded.* 她的笑容逐渐消失。 ◇ **~ away** *Hopes of reaching an agreement seem to be fading away.* 达成协议的希望看来已逐渐渺茫。◇ *The laughter faded away.* 笑声逐渐消逝。 ◇ **~ to/into sth** *His voice faded to a whisper* (= gradually became quieter). 他的声音越来越小，变成了耳语。◇ *All other issues **fade into insignificance** compared with the struggle for survival.* 与挣扎求存相比，所有其他问题都显得不重要了。 **3** [I] if a sports player, team, actor, etc. **fades**, they stop playing or performing as well as they did before（运动员、运动队、演员等）走下坡路，衰退，衰落：*Black faded on the final bend.* 布莱克在最后一个弯道处速度慢了下来。 IDM SEE WOODWORK

PHR V ˌ**fade aˈway** (of a person 人) to become very weak or ill/sick and die 衰弱；病重死亡：*In the last weeks of her life she simply faded away.* 她在生命的最后几个星期已是草枯灯油尽了。ˌ**fade ˈin/ˈout** to become clearer or louder/less clear or quieter（画面）淡入 / 淡出，渐显 / 渐隐；（声音）渐强 / 渐弱：*George saw the monitor black* *out and then a few words faded in.* 乔治看见屏幕变暗，接着出现了几个字。ˌ**fade sth ˈin/ˈout** to make a picture or a sound clearer or louder/less clear or quieter 使（画面）淡入 / 淡出；使渐显 / 渐隐；使（声音）渐强 / 渐弱：*Fade out the music at the end of the scene.* 在这个场景的末尾把音乐减弱。

ˈ**fade-out** *noun* [U, C] (in cinema, broadcasting, etc. 电影、广播等) the process of making a sound or an image gradually disappear; an occasion when this happens（画面）淡出，渐隐；（声音的）渐弱

fader /ˈfeɪdə(r)/ *noun* (*specialist*) a piece of equipment used to make sounds or images gradually appear or disappear 音量控制器；光量控制器

fae·ces (*BrE*) (*NAmE* **feces**) /ˈfiːsiːz/ *noun* [pl.] (*formal*) solid waste material that leaves the body through the ANUS 粪便 **SYN** **excrement** ▶ **fae·cal** (*BrE*) (*NAmE* **fecal**) /ˈfiːkl/ *adj.* [only before noun]

faff /fæf/ *verb, noun* (*BrE, informal*)

■ *verb*

PHR V ˌ**faff aˈbout/aˈround** to spend time doing things in a way that is not well organized and that does not achieve much 胡乱做事：*Stop faffing about and get on with it!* 别瞎摆弄了，干正事！

■ *noun* [U, sing.] a lot of activity that is not well organized and that may cause problems or be annoying 忙乱：*There was the usual faff of finding somewhere to park the car.* 找地方停车照例又是一番忙乱。

fag /fæg/ *noun* **1** [C] (*BrE, informal*) = CIGARETTE **2** (*also* **fag·got**) [C] (*NAmE, taboo, slang*) an offensive word for a male HOMOSEXUAL（蔑称）男同性恋者 **3** [sing.] (*BrE, informal*) something that is boring and tiring to do 苦工；苦差事：*It's too much of a fag to go out.* 外出活动真叫人吃不消。 **4** [C] (*BrE*) (especially in the past) a boy at a PUBLIC SCHOOL who has to do jobs for an older boy（尤指旧时）公学中受高年级男生使唤的低年级男生

ˌ**fag ˈend** *noun* (*BrE, informal*) **1** [C] the last part of a cigarette that is left after it has been smoked 烟蒂；香烟头 **2** [sing.] **the ~ of sth** the last part of sth, especially when it is less important or interesting（尤指不重要或索然无味的）结尾，末尾：*I only caught the fag end of their conversation.* 我仅听到他们谈话的结尾。

fagged /fægd/ (*also* ˌ**fagged ˈout**) *adj.* [not before noun] (*BrE, informal*) very tired 筋疲力尽；累得要死 **SYN** **exhausted**

IDM **I can't be ˈfagged (to do sth)** used to say that you are too tired or bored to do sth（让我做某事）我可吃不消

fag·got /ˈfægət/ *noun* **1** (*BrE*) a ball of finely chopped meat mixed with bread, baked or fried and eaten hot 烤肉丸；炸肉丸 **2** (*NAmE*) = FAG (2) **3** a bunch of sticks tied together, used for burning on a fire 柴把；柴捆

ˈ**fag hag** *noun* (*slang, offensive*) a woman who likes to spend time with HOMOSEXUAL men 喜欢与男同性恋者交往的女性

fah (*also* **fa**) /fɑː/ *noun* (*music* 音) the fourth note of a MAJOR SCALE 大调音阶的第 4 音

ˈ**fah-fee** *noun* [U] (*SAfrE*) an illegal game in which you risk money on a particular number being chosen 推筒子，押宝（一种对所选点数押钱赌博的游戏）

Fahr·en·heit /ˈfærənhaɪt/ *adj.* (*abbr.* **F**) of or using a scale of temperature in which water freezes at 32° and boils at 212° 华氏温度计的，华氏的（冰点为 32 度，沸点为 212 度）：*fifty degrees Fahrenheit* 五十华氏度 ▶ **Fahr·en·heit** *noun* [U]: *to give the temperature in Fahrenheit* 以华氏表示温度

fail /feɪl/ *verb, noun*

■ *verb*

• **NOT SUCCEED** 不成功 **1** [I, T] to not be successful in achieving sth 失败；未能（做到）：*Many diets fail because they are boring.* 许多规定饮食因单调乏味都不奏效。◇ *a failing school* 一所失败的学校 ◇ **~ in sth** *I failed in my attempt to persuade her.* 我未能说服她。◇ **~ to do sth** *She failed to get into art college.* 她未能进入艺术学院。◇ *The song* ***can't fail*** *to be a hit* (= definitely will be a hit). 这首歌不可能不流行起来。

• **NOT DO STH** 未做某事 **2** [I] to not do sth 未做；未履行（某事）：**~ to do sth** *He failed to keep the appointment.* 他未履约。◇ *She never fails to email every week.* 每周她必定发电子邮件。◇ ***I fail to see*** (= I don't understand) *why you won't even give it a try.* 我不懂为什么你连试一试都不愿意。◇ **~ in sth** *He felt he would be failing in his duty if he did not report it.* 他认为如果不报告就是他失职。➲ MORE LIKE THIS 26, page R28

• **TEST/EXAM** 测验；考试 **3** [T, I] to not pass a test or an exam; to decide that sb/sth has not passed a test or an exam 不及格；评定不及格：**~ (sth)** *He failed his driving test.* 他驾驶执照考试不及格。◇ *She was disqualified after failing a drugs test.* 她药检未通过，被取消了资格。◇ *What will you do if you fail?* 如果你考试失败打算干什么？◇ **~ sb** *The examiners failed over half the candidates.* 主考人员评定，半数以上考生不及格。 **OPP** **pass**

• **OF MACHINES/PARTS OF BODY** 机器；身体部位 **4** [I] to stop working 出故障；失灵：*The brakes on my bike failed half way down the hill.* 我的自行车下山至中途车闸失灵了。

• **OF HEALTH/SIGHT** 健康；视力 **5** [I] (especially in the progressive tenses 尤用于进行时) to become weak 衰退：*Her eyesight is failing.* 她的视力日渐衰退。◇ *His last months in office were marred by failing health.* 由于健康恶化，他最后几个月的公职工作受到了影响。

• **DISAPPOINT SB** 使失望 **6** [T] **~ sb** to disappoint sb; to be unable to help when needed 使失望；有负于；无能为力：*When he lost his job, he felt he had failed his family.* 他失去工作以后，感到辜负了家庭。◇ *She tried to be brave, but her courage failed her.* 她想勇敢，但却鼓不起勇气。◇ (*figurative*) ***Words fail me*** (= I cannot express how I feel). 我无法表达自己的感受。

• **NOT BE ENOUGH** 不足 **7** [I] to not be enough when needed or expected 不足；缺乏：*The crops failed again last summer.* 上个夏季庄稼又歉收了。◇ *The rains had failed and the rivers were dry.* 雨量不足，河流干涸。

• **OF COMPANY/BUSINESS** 公司；企业 **8** [I] to be unable to continue 倒闭；破产：*Several banks failed during the recession.* 经济衰退期间有几家银行倒闭了。

IDM **if all else ˈfails** used to suggest sth that sb can do if nothing else they have tried is successful 实在不行的话（还可以…）：*If all else fails, you can always sell your motorbike.* 如果所有别的办法都不行，你总还可以卖掉摩托车。

■ *noun* **1** the result of an exam in which a person is not successful（考试）不及格：*I got three passes and one fail.* 我考试三门及格，一门不及格。 **OPP** **pass** **2** (*informal*) a mistake or lack of success in doing sth 失误；失败：*The show was an* ***epic fail.*** 这场演出惨不忍睹。

▼ **GRAMMAR POINT** 语法说明

fail / failure

This use of **fail** as a noun instead of **failure** in a sense that does not just apply to exams has become more common in informal language in the 21st century. A similar case is **reveal**. * fail 取代 failure 用作名词不只限于描述考试，这种用法在 21 世纪的非正式用语中已经越来越普遍。类似的情况还有 reveal：*We have to wait for the final chapter for the big reveal.* 我们得等到最后一章才能看到大结局。

IDM **without ˈfail** **1** when you tell sb to do sth **without fail**, you are telling them that they must do it 务必；一定：*I want you here by two o'clock without fail.* 我要你两点钟务必来到这里。 **2** always 总是；必定：*He emails every week without fail.* 他每周必定发电子邮件。

failed /feɪld/ *adj.* [only before noun] not successful 失败的；不成功的：*a failed writer* 不成功的作家 ◇ *a failed coup* 流产政变

ˌfailed ˈstate *noun* a country in which the government is so weak that it has lost control of the structures of the state and other groups have more power 失败国家（政府软弱无能，而其他团体拥有更多权力）

fail·ing /ˈfeɪlɪŋ/ *noun, prep.*

■ ***noun*** [usually pl.] a weakness or fault in sb/sth 弱点；缺点：*She is aware of her own failings.* 她了解自己的弱点。◇ *The inquiry acknowledges failings in the judicial system.* 这次调查承认司法制度有缺陷。

■ ***prep.*** used to introduce a suggestion that could be considered if the one just mentioned is not possible 如果不能；如果没有：*Ask a friend to recommend a doctor or, **failing that**, ask for a list in your local library.* 请朋友推荐一位医生，如果办不到就向当地图书馆要一份名单。

F

ˈfail-safe *adj.* [usually before noun] (of machinery or equipment 机器或设备) designed to stop working if anything goes wrong 有自动保险装置的；具有自动防止故障性能的：*a **fail-safe device/mechanism/system*** 故障保护装置 / 机械装置 / 系统

fail·ure 🔑 /ˈfeɪljə(r)/ *noun*

• **NOT SUCCESSFUL** 不成功 **1** 🔑 [U] lack of success in doing or achieving sth 失败：*The success or failure of the plan depends on you.* 这项计划的成败取决于你。◇ *The attempt was **doomed to failure**.* 这项尝试注定失败。◇ *All my efforts **ended in failure**.* 我的一切努力最后都无济于事。◇ *the problems of economic failure and increasing unemployment* 经济失败和失业人数增加的问题 ◇ *She is still coming to terms with the failure of her marriage.* 她还在努力适应婚姻失败的事实。OPP **success** **2** 🔑 [C] a person or thing that is not successful 失败的人（或事物）：*The whole thing was a complete failure.* 整个事情彻底失败了。◇ *He was a failure as a teacher.* 他当教师并不成功。OPP **success**

• **NOT DOING STH** 未做某事 **3** 🔑 [U, C] **~ to do sth** an act of not doing sth, especially sth that you are expected to do 未做，未履行（应做之事）：*the failure of the United Nations to maintain food supplies* 联合国未能维持粮食供应 ◇ *Failure to comply with the regulations will result in prosecution.* 不遵守规章制度将被起诉。

• **OF MACHINE/PART OF BODY** 机器；身体部位 **4** 🔑 [U, C] the state of not working correctly or as expected; an occasion when this happens 故障；失灵：*patients suffering from **heart/kidney, etc. failure*** 心脏、肾等衰竭的病人 ◇ *A power failure plunged everything into darkness.* 停电使一切陷入黑暗。◇ *The cause of the crash was given as engine failure.* 撞车事故的原因被认定是发动机故障。

• **OF BUSINESS** 企业 **5** [C, U] **business ~** a situation in which a business has to close because it is not successful 倒闭

• **OF CROP/HARVEST** 庄稼；收成 **6** [U, C] **crop/harvest ~** a situation in which crops do not grow correctly and do not produce food 歉收

fain /feɪn/ *adv.* (*old use*) willingly or with pleasure 欣然；乐意地：*I would fain do as you ask.* 听候你的吩咐。

faint 🔑 /feɪnt/ *adj., verb, noun*

■ ***adj.*** (**faint·er**, **faint·est**) **1** 🔑 that cannot be clearly seen, heard or smelt（光、声、味）微弱的，不清楚的：*a **faint glow/glimmer/light*** 微弱的光亮 / 闪光 / 光 ◇ *a faint smell of perfume* 淡淡的香水味 ◇ *We could hear their voices growing fainter as they walked down the road.* 他们沿路走远时我们听见他们的说话声逐渐模糊。◇ *His breathing became faint.* 他的呼吸变得微弱了。 **2** 🔑 very small; possible but unlikely 微小的；可能性不大的 SYN **slight**：*There is still a faint hope that she may be cured.* 她的病还有一点点希望可以治愈。◇ *They don't have the faintest chance of winning.* 他们毫无获胜的可能。**3** not enthusiastic 不热情的；不积极的：*a faint show of resistance* 软弱无力装模作样的抵抗 ◇ *a faint smile* 淡淡一笑 **4** 🔑 [not before noun] feeling weak and tired and likely to become unconscious 昏眩；快要昏厥：*She suddenly felt faint.* 她突然感到快要昏倒。◇ *The walkers were faint from hunger.* 那些走路的人饿得头昏眼花。 ▶ **faint·ly** 🔑 *adv.*：*She smiled faintly.* 她淡淡地笑了一下。◇ *He looked faintly embarrassed.* 他显得有点难堪。

IDM **not have the ˈfaintest (idea)** (*informal*) to not know anything at all about sth 完全不知道：*I didn't have the faintest idea what you meant.* 我一点也不明白你的意思。 ➲ MORE AT DAMN *v.*

■ ***verb*** [I] to become unconscious when not enough blood is going to your brain, usually because of the heat, a shock, etc. 昏厥 SYN **pass out**：*to faint from hunger* 饿昏过去 ◇ *Suddenly the woman in front of me fainted.* 我面前的女人突然昏倒了。◇ (*informal*) *I almost fainted* (= I was very surprised) *when she told me.* 她告诉我时我吃惊得差点儿昏过去。

■ ***noun*** [sing.] the state of becoming unconscious 昏厥：*He fell to the ground in a dead faint.* 他跌倒在地，昏死过去。

ˌfaint-ˈhearted *adj., noun*

■ ***adj.*** lacking confidence and not brave; afraid of failing 胆怯的；怯懦的 SYN **cowardly**

■ ***noun***

IDM **ˌnot for the ˌfaint-ˈhearted** not suitable for people who lack confidence or who get frightened easily 不适合缺乏信心的人；不适合胆怯之人：*The climb is **not for the faint-hearted*** (= is only for people who are brave). 攀岩绝不是胆小的人做的事。

faint·ness /ˈfeɪntnəs/ *noun* [U] the state of feeling weak and tired and likely to become unconscious 眩晕；虚弱；近乎昏厥

fair 🔑 /feə(r); *NAmE* fer/ *adj., adv., noun*

■ ***adj.*** (**fair·er**, **fair·est**)

• **ACCEPTABLE/APPROPRIATE** 可接受；恰当 **1** 🔑 acceptable and appropriate in a particular situation 合理的；恰当的；适当的：*a fair deal/wage/price/question* 公平交易；合理的工资；公道的价格；恰当的问题 ◇ *The punishment was very fair.* 这个处罚很公正。◇ **~ to sb (to do sth)** *Was it really fair to him to ask him to do all the work?* 要他做所有的工作对他真的公平吗？◇ **~ on sb (to do sth)** *It's not fair on the students to keep changing the timetable.* 不断改动时间表，这样对待学生不恰当。◇ **~ to do sth** ***It's only fair*** *to add that they were not told about the problem until the last minute.* 要补充说明以下情况才合理，即他们是最后一刻才获知这个问题。◇ *I think **it is fair to say that** they are pleased with this latest offer.* 我认为恰当地说，他们对最新的这一次提议很满意。◇ **~ that...** *It seems only fair that they should give us something in return.* 似乎他们应该给我们点什么作为回报才像话。◇ ***To be fair**, she behaved better than we expected.* 说句公道话，她表现得比我们预期的要好。◇ (*especially BrE*) *'You should really have asked me first.' 'Right, okay, **fair comment**.'* "你本来应该先问我。" "对，是的，是这样。" OPP **unfair**

• **TREATING PEOPLE EQUALLY** 一视同仁 **2** 🔑 treating everyone equally and according to the rules or law（按法律、规定）平等待人的，秉公办事的，公正的：*She has always been scrupulously fair.* 她总是一丝不苟地秉公办事。◇ *demands for a fairer distribution of wealth* 更加公平分配财富的要求 ◇ **~ (to sb)** *We have to be fair to both players.* 我们必须公正对待双方运动员。◇ *to receive a fair trial* 得到公正审判 ◇ *free and fair elections* 自由公正的选举 ◇ ***It's not fair!** He always gets more than me.* 这不公平！他得到的总比我多。◇ *The new tax is fairer than the old system.* 新税制比旧税制公正。OPP **unfair**

• **QUITE LARGE** 相当大 **3** 🔑 [only before noun] quite large in number, size or amount（数量、大小）相当大的：*A fair number of people came along.* 有相当多的人来了。◇ *a fair-sized town* 一座不小的市镇 ◇ *We've still got **a fair bit*** (= quite a lot) *to do.* 我们还有相当多的事要做。

• **QUITE GOOD** 相当好 **4** (*especially BrE*) quite good 相当好的；不错的：*There's **a fair chance** that we might win this time.* 这次我们可能胜算很大。◇ *It's a fair bet that they won't turn up.* 我敢打赌，他们不会露面。◇ *I have a fair idea of what happened.* 我相当了解发生的事。◇ *His knowledge of French is only fair.* 他的法语知识还算可以。

• **HAIR/SKIN** 头发；皮肤 **5** 🔑 pale in colour 浅色的；白皙的：*a fair complexion* 白皙的肤色 ◇ *She has long fair hair.* 她有一头浅色长发。◇ *All her children are fair* (= they all have fair hair). 她的孩子们都长着淡色的头发。OPP **dark** ➲ WORDFINDER NOTE AT BLONDE

• **WEATHER** 天气 **6** 🔑 bright and not raining 晴朗的 SYN **fine**：*a fair and breezy day* 风和日丽的日子 **7** (*literary*) (of winds 风) not too strong and blowing in the right direction 顺风的：*They set sail with the first fair wind.* 顺风一起他们就扬帆出航了。

• BEAUTIFUL 美丽 **8** (*literary* or *old use*) beautiful 美丽的：*a fair maiden* 美丽的少女

IDM **ˌall's ˌfair in ˌlove and ˈwar** (*saying*) in some situations any type of behaviour is acceptable to get what you want 在情场和战场上可以不择手段 **be ˈfair!** (*informal*) used to tell sb to be reasonable in their judgement of sb/sth 要讲道理：*Be fair! She didn't know you were coming.* 要讲道理！她不知道你要来。 **by fair means or ˈfoul** using dishonest methods if honest ones do not work 不择手段 **a fair crack of the ˈwhip** (*BrE, informal*) a reasonable opportunity to show that you can do sth（做某事的）适当机会：*I felt we weren't given a fair crack of the whip.* 我觉得我们没有得到适当的机会。 **fair eˈnough** (*informal, especially BrE*) used to say that an idea or suggestion seems reasonable（指想法、建议）有道理，说得对，行：*'We'll meet at 8.' 'Fair enough.'* "我们 8 点钟见。" "行。" ◇ *If you don't want to come, fair enough, but let Bill know.* 你要是不想来，可以，不过要让比尔知道。 **fair's ˈfair** (*informal*) (*BrE also* **fair ˈdos/ˈdo's**) used, especially as an exclamation, to say that you think that an action, decision, etc. is acceptable and appropriate because it means that everyone will be treated fairly（尤用作感叹词，表示认为行动、决定等可以接受）彼此都要公平，应该公正才是：*Fair's fair—you can't expect them to cancel everything just because you can't make it.* 彼此都要公平，不可能就因为你不能出席就指望他们取消一切。 **(give sb) a fair ˈhearing** (to allow sb) the opportunity to give their opinion of sth before deciding if they have done sth wrong, often in court（给某人）申辩机会；（让某人接受）公平审讯：*I'll see that you get a fair hearing.* 我务必使你有说明观点的机会。 **(give sb/get) a fair ˈshake** (*NAmE, informal*) (to give sb/get) fair treatment that gives you the same chance as sb else（给某人 / 得到）公平待遇 **(more than) your fair share of sth** (more than) an amount of sth that is considered to be reasonable or acceptable（超过）合理的数量，恰当的数量：*He has more than his fair share of problems.* 他的问题过多。 ◇ *I've had my fair share of success in the past.* 过去我已经取得了应有的成功。 **fair to ˈmiddling** (*old-fashioned*) not particularly good or bad 一般水平；不过不失 **it's a fair ˈcop** (*BrE, informal, humorous*) used by sb who is caught doing sth wrong, to say that they admit that they are wrong（当场被抓获时说）这是罪有应得，抓得有理

■ *adv.* according to the rules; in a way that is considered to be acceptable and appropriate 按照规则；公正地；公平合理地：*Come on, you two, fight fair!* 得了，你们俩，要按规则比赛！ ◇ *They'll respect you as long as you* ***play fair*** (= behave honestly). 只要为人正直，别人就会尊敬你。

IDM **fair and ˈsquare | fairly and ˈsquarely** **1** honestly and according to the rules 诚实；光明正大：*We won the election fair and square.* 我们光明正大地竞选获胜。 **2** (*BrE*) in a direct way that is easy to understand 直截了当：*I told him fair and square to pack his bags.* 我直截了当让他收拾好行李走人。 **3** (*BrE*) exactly in the place you were aiming for 不偏不斜：*I hit the target fair and square.* 我不偏不斜正中靶子。 ➲ MORE LIKE THIS 12, page R26 **set fair (to do sth/for sth)** (*BrE*) having the necessary qualities or conditions to succeed 有成功的素质；具备成功的条件：*She seems set fair to win the championship.* 她似乎具备夺冠的条件。 ◇ *Conditions were set fair for stable economic development.* 形势适合经济稳定发展。 ➲ MORE AT SAY *v.*

■ *noun*

• ENTERTAINMENT 娱乐 **1** (*BrE also* **fun·fair**) (*NAmE also* **car·ni·val**) a type of entertainment in a field or park at which people can ride on large machines and play games to win prizes 露天游乐场：*Let's take the kids to the fair.* 咱们带孩子们到游乐场吧。 ◇ *all the fun of the fair* 露天游乐园的一切乐趣 **2** (*NAmE*) a type of entertainment in a field or park at which farm animals and products are shown and take part in competitions（评比农畜产品的）集市：*the* ***county/state fair*** 县 / 州农畜产品集市 **3** (*BrE*) = FETE (1)

• BUSINESS 商业 **4** an event at which people, businesses, etc. show and sell their goods 商品交易会；展销会：*a world trade fair* 世界交易会 ◇ *a craft/a book/an antique fair* 工艺品展销会；书市；古玩交易会

• ANIMAL MARKET 牲畜市场 **5** (*BrE*) (in the past) a market at which animals were sold（旧时）牲畜市场：*a horse fair* 马市

• JOBS 工作 **6 job/careers ~** an event at which people who are looking for jobs can get information about companies who might employ them 职业介绍会；就业展览会

ˌfair ˈcopy *noun* (*BrE*) a neat version of a piece of writing 誊清本；清稿

ˌfair ˈdinkum *adj., adv.* (*AustralE, NZE, informal*) **1** used to emphasize that sth is genuine or true, or to ask whether it is（强调或询问真实性）：*It's a fair dinkum Aussie wedding.* 那是地道的澳大利亚婚礼。 ◇ *'Burt's just told me he's packing up in a month.' 'Fair dinkum?'* "伯特刚才跟我说，再过一个月他就收拾行李走人。" "真的吗？" **2** used to emphasize that behaviour is acceptable（强调行为可接受）：*They were asking a lot for the car, but fair dinkum considering how new it is.* 他们这辆车的要价很高，但考虑到车子很新，还是可以接受的。

the ˌfairer ˈsex *noun* = FAIR SEX

ˌfair ˈgame *noun* [U] if a person or thing is said to be **fair game**, it is considered acceptable to play jokes on them, criticize them, etc. 可开玩笑（或嘲弄、作弄）的对象：*The younger teachers were considered fair game by most of the kids.* 多数小孩认为年轻教师是可作弄的对象。

fair·ground /ˈfeəɡraʊnd; *NAmE* ˈferɡ-/ *noun* **1** an outdoor area where a FAIR with entertainments is held 露天游乐场 **2** [usually pl.] (*NAmE*) a place where a FAIR showing farm animals, farm products, etc. is held 农畜产品集市场地：*the Ohio State Fairgrounds* 俄亥俄州农畜产品集市场地 **3** [usually pl.] (*NAmE*) a place where companies and businesses hold a FAIR to show their products 商品交易会场址；展销会场地：*the Milan trade fairgrounds* 米兰交易会场址

ˌfair-ˈhaired *adj.* with light or blonde hair 浅色头发的；金发的

fair·ly 🔑 /ˈfeəli; *NAmE* ˈferli/ *adv.* **1** 🔑 (before adjectives and adverbs 用于形容词和副词前) to some extent but not very 一定地；相当地：*a fairly easy book* 一本相当浅易的书 ◇ *a fairly typical reaction* 相当典型的反应 ◇ *I know him fairly well, but I wouldn't say we were really close friends.* 我相当了解他，但并不是说我们是真正的密友。 ◇ *I go jogging fairly regularly.* 我基本上经常慢跑锻炼。 ◇ *We'll have to leave fairly soon* (= before very long). 我们不久得离开。 ◇ *I'm fairly certain I can do the job.* 我有相当把握能干这项工作。 ◇ *The report was fairly incomprehensible.* 这份报告相当难懂。 ◇ *I think you'll find it fairly difficult* (= you do not want to say that it is very difficult). 我认为你会觉得它相当难。 ➲ NOTE AT QUITE **2** 🔑 in a fair and reasonable way; honestly 公平合理地；公正地：*He has always treated me very fairly.* 他待我一直很公正。 ◇ *Her attitude could fairly be described as hostile.* 公平而论，她的态度可以说是怀有敌意。 **3** (*old-fashioned*) used to emphasize sth that you are saying（用以强调）简直，竟然：*The time fairly raced by.* 时间过得真快。

IDM **fairly and squarely** = FAIR AND SQUARE

ˌfair-ˈminded *adj.* (of people 人) looking at and judging things in a fair and open way 公正的；不偏不倚的

fair·ness /ˈfeənəs; *NAmE* ˈfernəs/ *noun* [U] **1** the quality of treating people equally or in a way that is reasonable 公正性；公平合理性：*the fairness of the judicial system* 司法制度的公正性 **2** a pale colour of skin or hair（皮肤）白皙；（头发）浅色：*A tan emphasized the fairness of her hair.* 晒黑的皮肤更加衬托出了她那浅色的头发。

IDM **in (all) fairness (to sb)** used to introduce a statement that defends sb who has just been criticized, or that explains another statement that may seem unreasonable 要公正对待，不能怪（某人）：*In all fairness to him, he did try to stop her leaving.* 不能怪他，他确实曾设法阻止她离开。

ˌfair ˈplay *noun* [U] the fact of playing a game or acting honestly, fairly and according to the rules 按规则比赛；公平办事：*a player admired for his **sense of fair play*** 因公正比赛而受人尊敬的运动员 ◇ *The task of the organization is to **ensure fair play** when food is distributed to the refugees.* 该组织的任务就是保证把粮食分给难民时要公平合理。
IDM **fair ˈplay to sb** (*BrE, informal*) used to express approval when sb has done sth that you think is right or reasonable（表示赞许）做得对，公道，公平合理

the ˌfair ˈsex (*also* **the ˌfairer ˈsex**) *noun* [sing.+sing./pl. v.] (*old-fashioned*) women 女性；妇女

F

ˌfair-ˈtrade *adj.* involving trade which supports producers in developing countries by paying fair prices and making sure that workers have good working conditions and fair pay 公平贸易的（尤指支持发展中国家在价格、工人工资等方面实行公平政策）

fair·way /ˈfeəweɪ; *NAmE* ˈferweɪ/ *noun* (in GOLF 高尔夫球) the long strip of short grass that you must hit the ball along before you get to the GREEN and the hole 球道 ➲ VISUAL VOCAB PAGE V44 ➲ COMPARE ROUGH *n.* (1)

ˈfair-weather *adj.* [only before noun] (*disapproving*) (of people 人) behaving in a particular way or doing a particular activity only when it is pleasant for them 同甘不共苦的；只在顺境中的：***a fair-weather friend*** (= sb who stops being a friend when you are in trouble) 不能共患难的朋友

fairy /ˈfeəri; *NAmE* ˈferi/ *noun* (*pl.* **-ies**) **1** (in stories) a creature like a small person, who has magic powers（故事中的）小仙人，仙子，小精灵：*a **good/wicked fairy*** 善良的仙子；邪恶的精灵 ➲ SEE ALSO TOOTH FAIRY **2** (*slang, disapproving*) an offensive word for a HOMOSEXUAL man 兔子（男同性恋者）

ˈfairy cake (*BrE*) (*also* **cup·cake** *NAmE, BrE*) *noun* a small cake, baked in a paper container shaped like a cup and often with ICING on top（常撒有糖霜的）纸杯蛋糕

ˌfairy ˈgodmother *noun* a person who rescues you when you most need help 恩人；救星

fairy·land /ˈfeərilænd; *NAmE* ˈferi-/ *noun* **1** [U] the home of FAIRIES 仙国；仙界 **2** [sing.] a beautiful, special or unusual place 仙境；奇境：*The toyshop is a fairyland for young children.* 玩具店是孩子们的仙境。

ˈfairy lights *noun* [pl.] (*BrE*) small coloured electric lights used for decoration, especially on a tree at Christmas（尤指挂在圣诞树上的）彩色小灯

ˈfairy tale (*also* **ˈfairy story**) *noun* **1** a story about magic or FAIRIES, usually for children 童话（故事） **2** a story that sb tells that is not true; a lie 不实之词；谎言：*Now tell me the truth: I don't want any more of your fairy stories.* 现在跟我说实话：我不想再听你胡编乱诌了。

ˈfairy-tale *adj.* typical of sth in a fairy tale 童话的；童话式的：*a fairy-tale castle on an island* 岛上的一座神奇城堡 ◇ *a fairy-tale wedding in the cathedral* 在大教堂举行的童话般的婚礼

fait ac·com·pli /ˌfeɪt əˈkɒmpliː; *NAmE* əˈkɑːm-/ *noun* [usually sing.] (*pl.* **faits ac·com·plis** /ˌfeɪz əˈkɒmpliː; *NAmE* əˈkɑːm-/) (*from French*) something that has already happened or been done and that you cannot change 既成事实

faith 🔑 /feɪθ/ *noun* **1** 🔑 [U] ~ (**in sb/sth**) trust in sb's ability or knowledge; trust that sb/sth will do what has been promised 信任；相信；信心：*I have great faith in you—I know you'll do well.* 我对你有信心，我知道你会干好的。◇ *We've **lost faith** in the government's promises.* 我们不再相信政府的承诺。◇ *Her friend's kindness has **restored her faith** in human nature.* 朋友的善意使她恢复了对人性的信心。◇ *He has **blind faith*** (= unreasonable trust) *in doctors' ability to find a cure.* 他盲目相信医生有妙手回春的能力。**2** 🔑 [U, sing.] strong religious belief 宗教信仰：*to lose your faith* 失去信仰 ◇ *Faith is stronger than reason.* 信仰比理智更有力。➲ COLLOCATIONS AT RELIGION **3** 🔑 [C] a particular religion（某一）宗教：*the Christian faith* 基督教 ◇ *The children are learning to understand people of different faiths.* 孩子们在学着理解不同宗教信仰的人。 **4** [U] **good ~** the intention to do sth right 诚意；善意：*They handed over the weapons as a gesture of good faith.* 他们交出武器以示诚意。
IDM **break/keep faith with sb** to break/keep a promise that you have made to sb; to stop/continue being loyal to sb 对某人不守信用 / 守信用；不忠诚 / 忠诚于某人 **in bad ˈfaith** knowing that what you are doing is wrong 存心不良；背信弃义地 **in good ˈfaith** believing that what you are doing is right; believing that sth is correct 真诚；诚心诚意：*We printed the report in good faith but have now learnt that it was incorrect.* 我们好意印发了这份报告，但现在才知道它并不正确。➲ MORE AT PIN *v.*

faith·ful 🔑 /ˈfeɪθfl/ *adj.* **1** 🔑 staying with or supporting a particular person, organization or belief 忠实的；忠诚的 SYN **loyal**：***a faithful servant/friend/dog*** 忠诚的仆人 / 朋友 / 狗 ◇ *She was rewarded for her 40 years' faithful service with the company.* 她为公司忠诚服务了 40 年，因而获得奖赏。◇ *I have been a faithful reader of your newspaper for many years.* 我是贵报多年来的忠实读者。◇ **~ to sb/sth** *He **remained faithful** to the ideals of the party.* 他对党的理想坚贞不移。 **2 the faithful** *noun* [pl.] people who believe in a religion; the loyal supporters of a political party （宗教的）忠实信徒；（政党的）忠诚支持者：*The president will keep the support of the **party faithful**.* 总统将继续获得忠诚党员的拥护。➲ MORE LIKE THIS 24, page R28 **3** 🔑 (of a wife, husband or partner 夫妻或性伴侣) ~ (**to sb**) not having a sexual relationship with anyone else 忠诚的；忠贞的 OPP **unfaithful** **4** true and accurate; not changing anything 如实的；丝毫不变的：***a faithful copy/account/description*** 精确的副本；如实的叙述 / 描述 ◇ **~ to sth** *His translation manages to be faithful to the spirit of the original.* 他的译文做到了忠于原文的精神。**5** [only before noun] able to be trusted; that you can rely on 可信任的；可信赖的：*my faithful old car* 我那可靠的老爷车 ▸ **faith·ful·ness** *noun* [U]：*faithfulness to tradition* 对传统的恪守 ◇ *She had doubts about his faithfulness.* 她怀疑他的忠诚。

faith·ful·ly 🔑 /ˈfeɪθfəli/ *adv.* **1** 🔑 accurately; carefully 准确地；如实地；仔细地：*to follow instructions faithfully* 严格遵循指示 ◇ *The events were faithfully recorded in her diary.* 这些事件在她的日记中如实地记录了下来。**2** 🔑 in a loyal way; in a way that you can rely on 忠实地；忠诚地：*He had supported the local team faithfully for 30 years.* 他忠实地支持当地球队 30 年。◇ *She promised faithfully not to tell anyone my secret.* 她保证恪守诺言，不把我的秘密告诉任何人。
IDM **Yours faithfully** 🔑 (*BrE*) used at the end of a formal letter before you sign your name, when you have addressed sb as 'Dear Sir/Dear Madam, etc.' and not by their name（正式信末署名前的套语）

ˈfaith healing *noun* [U] a method of treating a sick person through the power of belief and prayer 信仰医治（通过信心、祈祷治疗病人） ▸ **ˈfaith healer** *noun*

faith·less /ˈfeɪθləs/ *adj.* (*formal*) not loyal; that you cannot rely on or trust 不忠诚的；不可信任的；不可信赖的：*a faithless friend* 不忠实的朋友

ˈfaith school *noun* (*BrE*) a school especially for children of a particular religion 信众学校（为某种宗教的儿童信仰者特设）：*He called for new faith schools to be created.* 他呼吁设立新的信众学校。➲ COMPARE PAROCHIAL SCHOOL

fa·jitas /fəˈhiːtəs/ *noun* [pl.] (*from Spanish*) a Mexican dish of strips of meat and/or vegetables wrapped in a soft TORTILLA and often served with sour cream（墨西哥）肉丝蔬菜玉米卷饼（常佐以酸奶油）

fake /feɪk/ *adj., noun, verb*
■ ***adj.*** **1** (*disapproving*) not genuine; appearing to be sth it is not 假的 SYN **counterfeit**：*fake designer clothing* 冒牌的名设计师服装 ◇ *a fake American accent* 伪装的美国口音 **2** made to look like sth else 冒充的；伪造的 SYN **imitation**：*a jacket in fake fur* 人造毛皮短上衣 ◇ *Don't*

go out in the sun—get a fake tan from a bottle. 别到外面晒太阳了，擦点儿美黑霜装装样子就行了。➲ SYNONYMS AT ARTIFICIAL

■ *noun* **1** an object such as a work of art, a coin or a piece of jewellery that is not genuine but has been made to look as if it is 假货；赝品：*All the paintings proved to be fakes.* 所有这些画结果证实都是赝品。**2** a person who pretends to be what they are not in order to cheat people 冒充者

■ *verb* **1** [T] ~ **sth** to make sth false appear to be genuine, especially in order to cheat sb 伪造；冒充：*She faked her mother's signature on the document.* 她伪造了母亲在文件上的签字。◇ *He arranged the accident in order to fake his own death.* 他策划了这次事故以便造成自己死亡的假象。**2** [T, I] ~ (**sth**) to pretend to have a particular feeling, illness, etc. 假装，佯装，装出（某种感情、有病等）：*She's not really sick—she's just* ***faking it.*** 她并不是真的病了，不过是假装的。◇ *He faked a yawn.* 他装着打了一个哈欠。

▶ **faker** *noun*

fakie /ˈfeɪki/ *noun* (*informal*) a movement backwards on a SKATEBOARD or SNOWBOARD（用滑板或滑雪板的）倒滑，倒溜

fakir (*also* **faquir**) /ˈfeɪkɪə(r); *NAmE* fəˈkɪr/ *noun* a Muslim (or sometimes a Hindu) who lives without possessions and survives by receiving food and money from other people（伊斯兰教或印度教乞讨度日的）托钵僧

fala·fel (*also* **fela·fel**) /fəˈlæfl/ *noun* [U, C] (*pl.* **fala·fel** or **fala·fels**) a Middle Eastern dish consisting of small balls formed from crushed CHICKPEAS, usually eaten with flat bread; one of these balls 炸豆丸子（中东食品，用鹰嘴豆泥制成，常与面包一起吃）

fal·con /ˈfɔːlkən; *NAmE* ˈfælkən/ *noun* a BIRD OF PREY (= a bird that kills other creatures for food) with long pointed wings 隼

fal·con·er /ˈfɔːlkənə(r); *NAmE* ˈfælkənər/ *noun* a person who keeps and trains falcons, often for hunting（为狩猎活动）养隼者；训练隼者

fal·con·ry /ˈfɔːlkənri; *NAmE* ˈfæl-/ *noun* [U] the art or sport of breeding falcons and training them to hunt other birds or animals 鹰猎 ➲ WORDFINDER NOTE AT HUNT

fall 🔑 /fɔːl/ *verb, noun*

■ *verb* (**fell** /fel/, **fall·en** /ˈfɔːlən/)

• **DROP DOWN** 落下 **1** 🔑 [I] to drop down from a higher level to a lower level 落下；下落；掉落；跌落：*September had come and the leaves were starting to fall.* 已到九月了，树叶开始凋落。◇ *They were injured by falling rocks.* 他们被落石砸伤了。◇ **+ adv./prep.** *Several of the books had fallen onto the floor.* 这些书有几本掉到了地上。◇ *One of the kids fell into the river.* 小孩中有一个掉进了河里。◇ *The handle had fallen off the drawer.* 抽屉的拉手掉了。◇ *He fell 20 metres onto the rocks below.* 他掉到下面 20 米处的岩石上。◇ *The rain was falling steadily.* 雨不停地下着。

• **STOP STANDING** 倒下 **2** 🔑 [I] to suddenly stop standing 突然倒下；跌倒；倒塌：*She slipped on the ice and fell.* 她在冰上滑了一跤。◇ **+ adv./prep.** *I* ***fell over*** *and cut my knee.* 我摔倒了，划破了膝盖。◇ *The house looked as if it was about to fall down.* 房子看起来好像就要倒塌似的。➲ SEE ALSO FALLEN

• **OF HAIR/MATERIAL** 毛发；材料 **3** 🔑 [I] **+ adv./prep.** to hang down 下垂；低垂：*Her hair fell over her shoulders in a mass of curls.* 她的鬈发披肩。

• **SLOPE DOWNWARDS** 向下倾斜 **4** 🔑 [I] ~ (**away/off**) to slope downwards 向下倾斜：*The land falls away sharply towards the river.* 地势向河边陡然倾斜。

• **DECREASE** 减少 **5** 🔑 [I] to decrease in amount, number or strength（数量）减少，下降；（强度）减小：*Their profits have fallen by 30 per cent.* 他们的利润减少了 30%。◇ *Prices continued to fall on the stock market today.* 今天股票市场价格继续下跌。◇ *The temperature fell sharply in the night.* 夜间温度陡降。◇ *falling birth rates* 下降的出生率 ◇ *Her voice fell to a whisper.* 她的声音变小，成了耳语。◇ **+ noun** *Share prices fell 30p.* 股价下跌了 30 便士。 OPP **rise**

• **BE DEFEATED** 被打败 **6** [I] to be defeated or captured 被打败；沦陷；失守：*The coup failed but the government fell shortly afterwards.* 政变虽然流产，但是不久以后政府便垮台了。◇ ~ **to sb** *Troy finally fell to the Greeks.* 特洛伊城最终被希腊人攻陷。

• **DIE IN BATTLE** 阵亡 **7** [I] (*literary*) to die in battle; to be shot 阵亡；被击毙：*a memorial to those who fell in the two world wars* 两次世界大战阵亡将士纪念碑

• **BECOME** 变成 **8** 🔑 [I] to pass into a particular state; to begin to be sth 进入（某状态）；开始变成（某事物）：**+ adj.** *He had fallen asleep on the sofa.* 他在沙发上睡着了。◇ *The book fell open at a page of illustrations.* 书翻开在有插图的那一页。◇ *The room had fallen silent.* 整个房间都变得静悄悄的。◇ *She fell ill soon after and did not recover.* 不久后她就病倒了，而且未能痊愈。◇ ~ **into sth** *I had fallen into conversation with a man on the train.* 在火车上我和一个男人攀谈起来。◇ *The house had fallen into disrepair.* 这栋房子已年久失修。◇ **+ noun** *She knew she must not fall prey to his charm.* 她清楚自己绝不可以被他迷住。

• **HAPPEN/OCCUR** 发生 **9** [I] (*literary*) to come quickly and suddenly 突然来到；突然出现 SYN **descend**：*A sudden silence fell.* 突然一片鸦雀无声。◇ *Darkness falls quickly in the tropics.* 在热带地区夜幕降临迅速。◇ ~ **on sb/sth** *An expectant hush fell on the guests.* 客人们即时安静了下来，期待着将要发生的事。**10** [I] **+ adv./prep.** to happen or take place 发生：*My birthday falls on a Monday this year.* 今年我的生日适逢星期一。**11** [I] **+ adv./prep.** to move in a particular direction or come in a particular position（向某方向）移动；落（在某位置上）：*My eye fell on* (= I suddenly saw) *a curious object.* 我突然见到了一样奇怪的东西。◇ *Which syllable does the stress fall on?* 重音在哪个音节？◇ *A shadow fell across her face.* 一片阴影掠过她的脸庞。

• **BELONG TO GROUP** 属于群体 **12** [I] **+ adv./prep.** to belong to a particular class, group or area of responsibility 属于（某类、群体、责任范围）：*Out of over 400 staff there are just 7 that fall into this category.* * 400 多个职员中只有 7 人属于这一类。◇ *This case falls outside my jurisdiction.* 这个案件不属于我的管辖范围。◇ *This falls under the heading of scientific research.* 这一项属于科研类目。

IDM HELP Idioms containing **fall** are at the entries for the nouns and adjectives in the idioms, for example **fall by the wayside** is at **wayside**. 含 fall 的习语，都可在该等习语中的名词及形容词相关词条找到，如 fall by the wayside 在词条 wayside 下。

PHR V **ˌfall aˈbout** (*BrE, informal*) to laugh a lot 捧腹大笑；笑得前仰后合：**fall about doing sth** *We all fell about laughing.* 我们都笑得前仰后合。

ˌfall aˈpart 1 to be in very bad condition so that parts are breaking off 破碎；破裂：*My car is falling apart.* 我

▼ **LANGUAGE BANK** 用语库

fall

Describing a decrease 描述下降

- *Car crime in Oxford* ***fell significantly*** *last year.* 去年牛津的汽车犯罪显著下降。
- *Car crime* ***fell*** *by about a quarter over a 12-month period.* * 12 个月内汽车犯罪下降了约四分之一。
- *The number of stolen vehicles* ***dropped*** *from 1 013 to 780,* ***a fall of*** *26 per cent.* 被盗汽车数量从 1 013 辆减少到 780 辆，下降了 26%。
- *According to this data, 780 vehicles were stolen, 26%* ***down*** *on the previous year.* 根据这份数据，780 辆车被盗，比去年下降了 26%。
- *There was an 11%* ***drop*** *in reported thefts from motor vehicles, from 1 971 to 1 737.* 机动车财物盗窃案件数量下降了 11%，从 1 971 下降到 1 737。
- *These figures show that, as far as car crime is concerned,* ***the main trend is downwards.*** 这些数据表明，就汽车犯罪而言，大趋势是下降的。

➲ LANGUAGE BANK AT EXPECT, ILLUSTRATE, INCREASE, PROPORTION

的汽车要散架了。 **2** to have so many problems that it is no longer possible to exist or function 破裂；崩溃： *Their marriage finally fell apart.* 他们的婚姻终于破裂了。◇ *The deal fell apart when we failed to agree on a price.* 我们在价格上未能达成一致意见，生意吹了。

ˌfall aˈway to become gradually fewer or smaller; to disappear（逐渐）减少，减小；消失；消散： *His supporters fell away as his popularity declined.* 随着他的名望下降，他的支持者渐渐离他而去。◇ *The market for their products fell away to almost nothing.* 他们产品的市场几乎萎缩到零。◇ *All our doubts fell away.* 我们的一切疑虑都烟消云散。◇ *The houses fell away as we left the city.* 随着我们离城市越来越远，房屋也逐渐在视线中消失了。

ˌfall ˈback 1 to move or turn back 后退；撤退；退却 **SYN** **retreat**: *The enemy fell back as our troops advanced.* 我军向前挺进，敌军向后撤退。 **2** to decrease in value or amount（价值）降低；（数量）减少 **ˌfall ˈback on sb/sth** [no passive] to go to sb for support; to have sth to use when you are in difficulty 求助于；借助于；转而依靠： *I have a little money in the bank to fall back on.* 我在银行还有一点钱，需要时可以动用。◇ *She fell back on her usual excuse of having no time.* 她以惯用的借口推说没有时间。 ➲RELATED NOUN FALLBACK

ˌfall beˈhind (sb/sth) to fail to keep level with sb/sth 落后；落在…后面： *She soon fell behind the leaders.* 她很快就落在领先者的后面。 **ˌfall beˈhind with sth** (*also* **ˌfall beˈhind on sth** *especially in NAmE*) to not pay or do sth at the right time 拖欠（付款）；没有及时做： *They had fallen behind on their mortgage repayments.* 他们拖欠了按揭还款。◇ *He's fallen behind with his school work again.* 他又没有按时做学校作业。

ˌfall ˈdown to be shown to be not true or not good enough 不实；不能令人满意；不够好： *And that's where the theory falls down.* 这就是该理论的不足之处。 ➲ SEE ALSO FALL *v.*

ˈfall for sb [no passive] (*informal*) to be strongly attracted to sb; to fall in love with sb 爱上；倾心于： *They fell for each other instantly.* 他俩一见钟情。 **ˈfall for sth** [no passive] (*informal*) to be tricked into believing sth that is not true 信以为真： *I'm surprised you fell for that trick.* 我感到惊奇，你竟中了那个诡计。

ˌfall ˈin if soldiers **fall in**, they form lines 集合；列队： *The sergeant ordered his men to fall in.* 中士命令士兵集合。 **ˌfall ˈin with sb/sth** [no passive] (*BrE*) to agree to sth 同意；赞成： *She fell in with my idea at once.* 她立刻同意了我的主意。

ˈfall into sth to be able to be divided into sth 可以分为；能够分成： *My talk falls naturally into three parts.* 我的讲话可以自然分成三个部分。

ˌfall ˈoff to decrease in quantity or quality 数量减少；质量下降： *Attendance at my lectures has fallen off considerably.* 听我讲课的学生大大减少了。 **OPP** **rise**

ˈfall on/upon sb/sth [no passive] (*especially BrE*) **1** to attack or take hold of sb/sth with a lot of energy and enthusiasm 袭击；向…进攻；扑向；抓住： *They fell on him with sticks.* 他们用棍棒袭击他。◇ *The children fell on the food and ate it greedily.* 孩子们扑向食物，狼吞虎咽地吃起来。 **2** to be the responsibility of sb（责任）落在…身上；由…负担： *The full cost of the wedding fell on us.* 整个婚礼费用由我们负担了。

ˌfall ˈout 1 to become loose and drop 掉落；脱落： *His hair is falling out.* 他的头发在脱落。 **2** if soldiers **fall out**, they leave their lines and move away 原地解散；离开队列 **ˌfall ˈout (with sb)** to have an argument with sb so that you are no longer friendly with them（与某人）吵翻，闹翻

ˌfall ˈover (*informal*) (of a computer or program 计算机或程序) to stop working suddenly（突然）发生故障，不运转，死机： *My spreadsheet keeps falling over.* 我的电子表格程序不断出故障。 **ˌfall ˈover sb/sth** [no passive] to hit your foot against sth when you are walking and fall, or almost fall 被…绊倒；几乎被…绊倒 **SYN** **trip**: *I rushed for the door and fell over the cat in the hallway.* 我冲向门口，在过道被猫绊了一跤。 ➲ SEE ALSO FALL *v.* (2) **ˌfall ˈover yourself to do sth** (*informal*) to try very hard or want very much to do sth 特别卖力；迫不及待；煞费苦心；不遗余力： *He was falling over himself to be nice to me.* 他尽力对我友好。

ˌfall ˈthrough to not be completed, or not happen 落空；失败；成为泡影： *Our plans fell through because of lack of money.* 我们的计划由于缺钱而落空了。

ˈfall to sb to become the duty or responsibility of sb（职责、责任）落在…身上；应由…做： *With his partner away, all the work now fell to him.* 他的搭档走了以后，工作现在全落在他的身上。◇ **it falls to sb to do sth** *It fell to me to inform her of her son's death.* 把她儿子死讯通知她的差事落在了我的头上。 **ˈfall to sth** (*literary*) to begin to do sth 开始做；干起来： **fall to doing sth** *She fell to brooding about what had happened to her.* 她开始愤愤地思忖着自己的遭遇。

■ ***noun***

• **ACT OF FALLING** 落下 **1** [C] an act of falling 落下；下落；跌落；掉落： *I had a bad fall and broke my arm.* 我重重地跌了一跤，摔断了手臂。◇ *She was killed in a fall from a horse.* 她从马背上掉下来摔死了。

• **OF SNOW/ROCKS** 雪；岩石 **2** [C] **~ (of sth)** an amount of snow, rocks, etc. that falls or has fallen（雪、岩石等的）降落： *a heavy fall of snow* 一场大雪◇ *a rock fall* 岩崩

• **WAY STH FALLS/HAPPENS** 下落；发生 **3** [sing.] **~ of sth** the way in which sth falls or happens 下落；发生： *the fall of the dice* 骰子的掷出◇ *the dark fall of her hair* (= the way her hair hangs down) 她那垂泻的黑发

• **OF WATER** 水 **4 falls** [pl.] (especially in names 尤用于名称) a large amount of water falling down from a height 瀑布 **SYN** **waterfall**: *The falls upstream are full of salmon.* 上游瀑布一带盛产鲑鱼。◇ *Niagara Falls* 尼亚加拉瀑布

• **AUTUMN** 秋 **5** [C] (*NAmE*) = AUTUMN: *in the fall of 2009* 在 2009 年的秋天◇ *last fall* 去年秋天◇ *fall weather* 秋季天气

• **DECREASE** 减少 **6** [C] **~ (in sth)** a decrease in size, number, rate or level（大小）减小；（数量）减少；（比率、水平）降低： *a steep fall in profits* 利润的骤降◇ *a big fall in unemployment* 失业人数的大大减少 **OPP** **rise**

• **DEFEAT** 失败 **7** [sing.] **~ (of sth)** a loss of political, economic, etc. power or success; the loss or defeat of a city, country, etc. in war（政权的）垮台；（经济的）崩溃；（城市、国家的）沦陷，灭亡： *the fall of the Roman Empire* 罗马帝国的灭亡◇ *the **rise and fall** of British industry* 英国工业的兴衰◇ *the fall of Berlin* 柏林的沦陷

• **LOSS OF RESPECT** 丧失尊敬 **8** [sing.] a situation in which a person, an organization, etc. loses the respect of other people because they have done sth wrong（威信的）骤降： *the TV preacher's spectacular **fall from grace*** 电视布道者威信的遽降

• **IN BIBLE** 《圣经》 **9 the Fall** [sing.] the occasion when Adam and Eve did not obey God and had to leave the Garden of Eden 人类堕落（指亚当和夏娃违背上帝意旨而被逐离开伊甸园）

IDM **break sb's ˈfall** to stop sb from falling onto sth hard 缓和某人的跌势；防止某人跌得很重： *Luckily, a bush broke his fall.* 幸亏有灌木接着，他摔得不重。 **take the ˈfall (for sb/sth)** (*informal, especially NAmE*) to accept responsibility or punishment for sth that you did not do, or did not do alone 替…承担责任；成为…的替罪羊： *He took the fall for his boss and resigned.* 他成了老板的替罪羊，辞职了。 ➲ MORE AT PRIDE *n.*, RIDE *v.*

fal·la·cious /fəˈleɪʃəs/ *adj.* (*formal*) wrong; based on a false idea 谬误的： *a fallacious argument* 谬误的论证

fal·lacy /ˈfæləsi/ *noun* (*pl.* **-ies**) **1** [C] a false idea that many people believe is true 谬见；谬论；谬误： ***It is a fallacy** to say that the camera never lies.* 说照相机绝不骗人，这是谬见。 **2** [U, C] a false way of thinking about sth 思维方式谬误；谬误推理： *He detected the fallacy of her argument.* 他发觉她论据中的推理谬误。 ➲SEE ALSO PATHETIC FALLACY

fall·back /ˈfɔːlbæk/ *noun* a plan or course of action that is ready to be used in an emergency if other things fail 应变计划；退路： *What's our fallback if they don't come up with the money?* 要是他们拿不出钱，我们如何应变？◇ *We need a **fallback position** if they won't do the job.* 如果他们不干这个工作，我们就需要一个应变的方案。

fall·en /ˈfɔːlən/ *adj.* [only before noun] **1** lying on the ground, after falling 倒下的；落下的；落在地上的： *a fallen tree* 倒下的树 **2** (*formal*) (of a soldier 士兵) killed in a war 阵亡的 ➲SEE ALSO FALL *v.*

ˌfallen ˈwoman *noun* (*old-fashioned*) a way of describing a woman in the past who had a sexual relationship with sb who was not her husband 堕落的妇女（旧时指有奸情的）

ˈfall guy *noun* (*especially NAmE*) a person who is blamed or punished for sth wrong that another person has done 代人受过者；替罪羊 SYN **scapegoat**

fall·ible /ˈfæləbl/ *adj.* able to make mistakes or be wrong 会犯错误的： *Memory is selective and fallible.* 记忆有选择性而且会出错。◇ *All human beings are fallible.* 人人都难免犯错误。 OPP **infallible** ▸ **fal·li·bil·ity** /ˌfæləˈbɪləti/ *noun* [U]: *human fallibility* 人的易错性

ˈfalling-off *noun* [sing.] (*BrE*) = FALL-OFF

ˌfalling-ˈout *noun* (*informal*) [sing.] a situation where people are no longer friends, caused by a disagreement or an argument 失和；闹翻： *Dave and I **had a falling-out**.* 戴夫和我闹翻了。

ˌfalling ˈstar *noun* = SHOOTING STAR

ˈfall-off (*BrE also*, *less frequent* **ˈfalling-off**) *noun* [sing.] ~ **(in sth)** a reduction in the number, amount or quality of sth （数量的）减少；（质量的）降低： *a recent fall-off in sales* 近来销售量的减少

fal·lo·pian tube /fəˌləʊpiən ˈtjuːb; *NAmE* fəˈloʊpiən tuːb/ *noun* (*anatomy* 解) one of the two tubes in the body of a woman or female animal along which eggs pass from the OVARIES to the UTERUS 输卵管

fall·out /ˈfɔːlaʊt/ *noun* [U] **1** dangerous RADIOACTIVE dust that is in the air after a nuclear explosion （核爆炸后的）放射性沉降物 **2** the bad results of a situation or an action 后果；余波

fal·low /ˈfæləʊ; *NAmE* -loʊ/ *adj.* **1** (of farm land 农田) not used for growing crops, especially so that the quality of the land will improve 休耕的；休闲的： *Farmers are now paid to let their land **lie fallow**.* 如今农民让土地休耕能得到回报。 ➲ WORDFINDER NOTE AT FARM **2** (of a period of time 一段时期) when nothing is created or produced; not successful 休闲的；休眠的；不成功的： *Contemporary dance is coming onto the arts scene again after a long fallow period.* 当代舞蹈经过一段长时期销声匿迹以后现在又回到了艺术舞台。

ˈfallow deer *noun* a small European DEER with white spots on its back 黇鹿（有白色斑点）

ˈfall-pipe (*US*) (*BrE* **down·pipe**) *noun* a pipe for carrying water from a roof down to the ground or to a DRAIN （从房顶到地面排水的）雨水管

false 🔑 /fɔːls/ *adj.*

- **NOT TRUE** 不真实 **1** 🔑 wrong; not correct or true 错误的；不正确的；不真实的： *A whale is a fish. True or false?* 鲸鱼是鱼，对还是错？◇ *Predictions of an early improvement in the housing market proved false.* 认为房屋市场很快就好转的预测结果证明是错误的。 ◇ *She gave false information to the insurance company.* 她向保险公司提供了不真实的资料。◇ *He used a false name to get the job.* 他用假名得到了这份工作。
- **NOT NATURAL** 非天生 **2** 🔑 not natural 非天生的；人造的；假的 SYN **artificial**: *false teeth/eyelashes* 假牙；假睫毛◇ *a false beard* 假胡子 ➲SYNONYMS AT ARTIFICIAL
- **NOT GENUINE** 伪造 **3** 🔑 not genuine, but made to look real to cheat people 假的；伪造的： *a false passport* 假护照
- **NOT SINCERE** 不真诚 **4** (of people's behaviour 人的行为) not real or sincere 表里不一的；不真诚的： *false modesty* 假谦虚◇ *She flashed him a false smile of congratulation.* 她向他虚情假意地微微一笑表示祝贺。
- **WRONG/MISTAKEN** 错误 **5** 🔑 [usually before noun] wrong or mistaken, because it is based on sth that is not true or correct 错误的： *a **false argument/assumption/belief*** 错误的论据 / 假设 / 信念◇ *to give a **false impression** of wealth* 给人以富有的错觉◇ *to lull sb into a **false sense of security*** (= make sb feel safe when they are really in danger) 哄某人产生虚假的安全感◇ *They didn't want to raise any **false hopes**, but they believed her husband had escaped capture.* 他们并不想让人心存奢望，但是他们相信她的丈夫已逃脱追捕。◇ *Buying a cheap computer is a **false economy*** (= will not actually save you money). 买廉价计算机看似省钱，但其实并不划算。
- **NOT FAITHFUL** 不忠实 **6** (*literary*) (of people 人) not faithful 不忠实的；不忠诚的： *a false lover* 不忠诚的情人

▸ **false·ly** *adv.* : *to be falsely accused of sth* 被诬告某事◇ *She smiled falsely at his joke.* 她听了他的笑话假装笑了。

IDM **by/under/on false preˈtences** by pretending to be sth that you are not, in order to gain some advantage for yourself 靠欺诈手段；以虚假的借口： *She was accused of obtaining money under false pretences.* 她被控诈骗钱财。 ➲MORE AT RING² *v.*

ˌfalse aˈlarm *noun* a warning about a danger that does not happen; a belief that sth bad is going to happen, when it is not 假警报；虚惊： *The fire service was called out but it was a false alarm.* 消防人员接到报警后出动，但这是假报火警。

ˌfalse beˈginner *noun* a person who has a basic knowledge of a language, but has started to study it again from the beginning 二次初学者，非真实初学者（对某一语言虽已有基本知识但又从头学习）

ˌfalse ˈdawn *noun* [usually sing.] (*formal*) a situation in which you think that sth good is going to happen but it does not 假曙光；虚幻的希望： *a false dawn for the economy* 经济复苏的假象

ˌfalse ˈfriend *noun* **1** a person who seems to be your friend, but who is not loyal and cannot be trusted 不忠实的朋友 **2** a word in a foreign language that looks similar to a word in your own language, but has a different meaning （与某外国语的）同形异义词： *The English word 'sensible' and the French word 'sensible' are false friends.* 英语的 sensible 一词和法语的 sensible 一词同形异义。

false·hood /ˈfɔːlshʊd/ *noun* (*formal*) **1** [U] the state of not being true; the act of telling a lie 虚假；说谎： *to test the truth or falsehood of her claims* 检验她陈述的真伪 **2** [C] a statement that is not true 不实之词；谎言 SYN **lie²**

ˌfalse imˈprisonment *noun* [U] (*law* 律) the crime of illegally keeping sb as a prisoner somewhere 私禁；非法拘禁；非法拘留

ˌfalse ˈmemory *noun* (*psychology* 心) a memory of sth that did not actually happen （对事实上并未发生的事情的）伪记忆

ˌfalse ˈmove *noun* [usually sing.] an action that is not allowed or not recommended and that may cause a bad result （可能引起不良后果的）不允行为，不明智行动： ***One false move** and the bomb might blow up.* 一步弄错，炸弹就可能会爆炸。

ˌfalse ˈrib *noun* = FLOATING RIB

ˌfalse ˈstart *noun* **1** an attempt to begin sth that is not successful 不成功的开端；起步失误： *After a number of false starts, she finally found a job she liked.* 她起初失败了几次，之后终于找到了喜欢的工作。 **2** (*sport* 体育) a situation when sb taking part in a race starts before the official signal has been given 起跑犯规；抢跑

ˌfalse ˈteeth *noun* [pl.] a set of artificial teeth used by sb who has lost their natural teeth （整副的）假牙 ➲ COMPARE DENTURES

fal·setto /fɔːlˈsetəʊ; *NAmE* -toʊ/ *noun* (*pl.* **-os**) an unusually high voice, especially the voice that men use to sing very high notes （尤指男高音的）假声

fal·sies /ˈfɔːlsiz/ *noun* [pl.] (*informal*) pieces of material used inside a BRA to make a woman's breasts seem larger 胸罩衬垫；衬垫义乳

F

fal·si·fy /ˈfɔːlsɪfaɪ/ *verb* (**fal·si·fies**, **fal·si·fy·ing**, **fal·si·fied**, **fal·si·fied**) ~ **sth** (*formal*) to change a written record or information so that it is no longer true 篡改，伪造（文字记录、信息）▶ **fal·si·fi·ca·tion** /ˌfɔːlsɪfɪˈkeɪʃn/ *noun* [U, C]: *the deliberate falsification of the company's records* 对公司记录的蓄意篡改

fal·sity /ˈfɔːlsəti/ *noun* [U] the state of not being true or genuine 虚假；不真实；错误 OPP **truth**

Fal·staff·i·an /fɔːlˈstɑːfiən; *NAmE* -ˈstæf-/ *adj.* (*literary*) fat, cheerful and eating and drinking a lot 福斯塔夫式的（源于莎士比亚笔下人物，外形肥胖且喜狂欢闹饮）：*My uncle was a Falstaffian figure.* 我的叔叔是个福斯塔夫式的人物。➲ MORE LIKE THIS 17, page R27 ORIGIN From Sir John Falstaff, a character in several plays by William Shakespeare. 源自莎士比亚笔下几部戏剧中的人物福斯塔夫（Sir John Falstaff）。

fal·ter /ˈfɔːltə(r)/ *verb* **1** [I] to become weaker or less effective 衰弱；衰退；衰落 SYN **waver**: *The economy shows no signs of faltering.* 经济没有衰退的迹象。◇ *Her courage never faltered.* 她从未气馁过。**2** [I, T] (+ **speech**) to speak in a way that shows that you are not confident（嗓音）颤抖；结巴地说；支吾其词：*His voice faltered as he began his speech.* 他开始演讲时说话结结巴巴。**3** [I] to walk or behave in a way that shows that you are not confident 蹒跚；摇晃；犹豫；畏缩：*She walked up to the platform without faltering.* 她健步走上了讲台。◇ *He never faltered in his commitment to the party.* 他对党始终忠贞不渝。▶ **fal·ter·ing** /ˈfɔːltərɪŋ/ *adj.*：*the faltering peace talks* 一波三折的和平谈判 ◇ *the baby's first faltering steps* 婴儿学步时摇摇晃晃的脚步

fame 🔑 /feɪm/ *noun* [U] the state of being known and talked about by many people 名声；声誉；名气：*to* ***achieve/win*** *instant* ***fame*** 立即获得 / 迅即赢得名声 ◇ *to* ***rise/shoot to fame*** *overnight* 一夜之间成名 ◇ *Andrew Lloyd Webber of 'Cats' fame* (= famous for 'Cats') 以《猫》闻名的安德鲁·劳埃德·韦伯 ◇ *The town's only* ***claim to fame*** *is that there was once a riot there.* 这个镇唯一出名之处就是那里有过一次暴乱。◇ *She went to Hollywood in search of* ***fame and fortune.*** 她为追逐名利去了好莱坞。➲ SEE ALSO FAMOUS

famed /feɪmd/ *adj.* ~ (**for sth**) very well known 著名的 SYN **renowned**: *Las Vegas, famed for its casinos* 以赌场著名的拉斯韦加斯 ◇ *a famed poet and musician* 一位大名鼎鼎的诗人和音乐家 ➲ SEE ALSO FAMOUS

fa·mil·ial /fəˈmɪliəl/ *adj.* [only before noun] (*formal*) **1** related to or typical of a family 家庭的；家族的 **2** (*medical* 医) (of diseases, conditions, etc. 疾病、情况等) affecting several members of a family 家族性的；家庭遗传的：*familial left-handedness* 家族遗传的左撇子

fa·mil·iar 🔑 /fəˈmɪliə(r)/ *adj.* **1** 🔑 well known to you; often seen or heard and therefore easy to recognize 熟悉的；常见到的；常听说的：*to* ***look/sound/taste familiar*** 看 / 听 / 尝起来熟悉 ◇ *He's a familiar figure in the neighbourhood.* 他在这个地区是大家熟悉的人物。◇ *Something about her voice was vaguely familiar.* 她的声音有点耳熟。◇ ~ **to sb** *The smell is very familiar to everyone who lives near a bakery.* 住在面包店附近的人都很熟悉这种气味。◇ *Violent attacks are becoming* ***all too familiar*** (= sadly familiar). 暴力攻击变成了司空见惯的现象。OPP **unfamiliar** **2** 🔑 ~ **with sth** knowing sth very well 通晓；熟悉：*an area with which I had been familiar since childhood* 我自幼就了若指掌的一个地区 ◇ *Are you familiar with the computer software they use?* 你熟悉他们使用的计算机软件吗？OPP **unfamiliar** **3** ~ (**with sb**) (of a person's behaviour 人的行为) very informal, sometimes in a way that is unpleasant 随便的：*You seem to be on very familiar terms with your tutor.* 你似乎和你的导师之间很随便。◇ *After a few drinks her boss started getting too familiar for her liking.* 老板几杯酒下肚以后就开始令她觉得过分亲昵。

fa·mil·iar·ity /fəˌmɪliˈærəti/ *noun* [U] **1** ~ (**with sth**) | ~ (**to sb**) the state of knowing sb/sth well; the state of recognizing sb/sth 熟悉；通晓；认识：*His familiarity with the language helped him enjoy his stay.* 他通晓这种语言，所以逗留期间过得很惬意。◇ *When she saw the house, she had a feeling of familiarity.* 她见到这座房子就有一种熟悉的感觉。**2** a friendly informal manner 友好随便；亲近：*She addressed me with an easy familiarity that made me feel at home.* 她和我谈话亲切随和，使我不感到拘束。
IDM **familiarity breeds conˈtempt** (*saying*) knowing sb/sth very well may cause you to lose admiration and respect for them/it 过分亲密就会有所侮慢

fa·mil·iar·ize (*BrE also* **-ise**) /fəˈmɪliəraɪz/ *verb* ~ **yourself/sb** (**with sth**) to learn about sth or teach sb about sth, so that you/they start to understand it（使）熟悉，了解，通晓 SYN **acquaint**: *You'll need time to familiarize yourself with our procedures.* 你需要时间熟悉我们的程序。▶ **fa·mil·iar·iza·tion**, **-isa·tion** /fəˌmɪliəraɪˈzeɪʃn; *NAmE* -rəˈz-/ *noun* [U]

fa·mil·iar·ly /fəˈmɪliəli; *NAmE* -ərli/ *adv.* **1** in a friendly and informal manner, sometimes in a way that is too informal to be pleasant 友好随便地；亲昵地：*John Hunt, familiarly known to his friends as Jack* 约翰·亨特，朋友昵称他为杰克 ◇ *He touched her cheek familiarly.* 他亲昵地碰了碰她的面颊。**2** in the way that is well known to people 人们熟悉地：*The elephant's nose or, more familiarly, trunk, is the most versatile organ in the animal kingdom.* 象的鼻子，俗称为 trunk，是动物界中功能最多的器官。

fam·ily 🔑 /ˈfæməli/ *noun, adj.*
■ ***noun*** (*pl.* **-ies**) **1** 🔑 [C+sing./pl. v.] a group consisting of one or two parents and their children 家，家庭（包括父母子女）：*the other members of my family* 我家的其他成员 ◇ *Almost every family in the country owns a television.* 这个国家几乎家家都有一台电视机。◇ *All my family enjoy skiing.* 我们全家都喜欢滑雪。◇ ***one-parent/single-parent families*** 单亲家庭 ◇ *a family of four* 四口之家 ◇ *families with young children* 有小孩的家庭 ➲ SEE ALSO BLENDED FAMILY, NUCLEAR FAMILY

WORDFINDER 联想词：adopt, child, generation, heir, in-laws, parent, relation, stepfamily, surrogate mother

2 🔑 [C+sing./pl. v., U] a group consisting of one or two parents, their children and close relations（大）家庭（包括父母子女及近亲）；亲属：*All our family came to Grandad's eightieth birthday party.* 我们所有亲属都来参加了祖父的八十寿宴。◇ *The support of* ***family and friends*** *is vital.* 亲友的支持极为重要。◇ *We've only told the* ***immediate family*** (= the closest relations). 我们只告诉了直系亲属。◇ *the* ***Royal Family*** (= the children and close relations of the king or queen) 王室 ◇ *I always think of you as* ***one of the family.*** 我一直把你当成自家人。◇ (*informal*) *She's family* (= she is a relation). 她是我们家的人。➲ SEE ALSO EXTENDED FAMILY **3** 🔑 [C+sing./pl. v.] all the people who are related to each other, including those who are now dead 家族：*Some families have farmed in this area for hundreds of years.* 有些家族在这个地区务农有几百年了。◇ *This painting has* ***been in our family*** *for generations.* 这幅画是我们家的传家宝。**4** 🔑 [C+sing./pl. v., U] a couple's or a person's children, especially young children 子女；（尤指）年幼子女：*They have a large family.* 他们的子女成群。◇ *I addressed it to Mr and Mrs Jones and family.* 我以此致琼斯伉俪及子女。◇ *Do they plan to* ***start a family*** (= have children)? 他们打算生孩子吗？◇ *to* ***bring up/raise a family*** 抚育 / 抚养孩子 ➲ COLLOCATIONS AT CHILD **5** 🔑 [C] a group of related animals and plants; a group of related things, especially languages（动植物）科；（尤指语言）语族：*Lions belong to the cat family.* 狮属于猫科。◇ *the Germanic family of languages* 日耳曼语族
IDM (**be/get**) **in the ˈfamily way** (*old-fashioned, informal*) (to be/become) pregnant 怀孕；有喜 **run in the ˈfamily** to be a common feature in a particular family 为一家人所共有；世代相传：*Heart disease runs in the family.* 这家人都有心脏病。
■ ***adj.*** [only before noun] **1** 🔑 connected with the family or a particular family 家庭的：*family life* 家庭生活 ◇ *your family background* 你的家庭背景 **2** 🔑 owned by a family 一家所有的：*a family business* 家庭企业 **3** 🔑 suitable for

all members of a family, both adults and children 适合全家人的：*a family show* 家庭节目

the ˈFamily Division *noun* [sing.] in the UK, the part of the High Court which deals with cases that affect families, for example when people get divorced or adopt a child（英国高等法院的）家事法庭

ˌfamily ˈdoctor *noun* (*informal, especially BrE*) = GENERAL PRACTITIONER

ˈfamily man *noun* a man who has a wife or partner and children; a man who enjoys being at home with his wife or partner and children 有妻室儿女的人；恋家的男人；喜欢在家享受天伦之乐的男人：*I see he's become a family man.* 我发觉他已变得很恋家。◇ *a devoted family man* 忠于家庭的男人

ˈfamily name *noun* the part of your name that shows which family you belong to 姓 ➲ COMPARE SURNAME

ˌfamily ˈplanning *noun* [U] the process of controlling the number of children you have by using CONTRACEPTION 计划生育；家庭计划

ˌfamily ˈpractitioner *noun* (*especially BrE*) = GENERAL PRACTITIONER

ˈfamily room *noun* **1** (*NAmE*) a room in a house where the family can relax, watch television, etc. 家庭娱乐室 **2** a room in a hotel for three or four people to sleep in, especially parents and children（旅馆的）家庭间 **3** (in Britain) a room in a pub where children are allowed to sit（英国酒吧里的）儿童休息室

ˌfamily ˈtree *noun* a diagram that shows the relationship between members of a family over a long period of time 家谱；家谱图：*How far back can you trace your family tree?* 你的家谱可以追溯到多少代？➲ **WORDFINDER NOTE** AT RELATION

fam·ine /ˈfæmɪn/ *noun* [C, U] a lack of food during a long period of time in a region 饥荒：*a severe famine* 严重饥荒 ◇ *disasters such as floods and famine* 水灾和饥荒这一类灾难 ◇ *the threat of* ***widespread famine*** *in the area* 这一地区内大范围的饥荒威胁 ◇ *to raise money for* ***famine relief*** 为赈济饥荒筹款

fam·ished /ˈfæmɪʃt/ *adj.* [not usually before noun] (*informal, becoming old-fashioned*) very hungry 很饿 **SYN** **starve**：*When's lunch? I'm famished!* 什么时候吃午饭？我饿得要死了！

fam·ous 🔑 /ˈfeɪməs/ *adj.* known about by many people 著名的；出名的：*a famous artist/hotel* 著名的艺术家 / 旅馆 ◇ *the most famous lake in Italy* 意大利最著名的湖 ◇ *One day, I'll be* ***rich and famous***. 总有一天我会名利双收。◇ **~ for sth** *He became internationally famous for his novels.* 他以小说享誉国际。◇ **~ as sth** *She was more famous as a writer than as a singer.* 她作为作家比作为歌手名声要大。➲ SEE ALSO FAME, INFAMOUS, NOTORIOUS, WORLD-FAMOUS ➲ **MORE LIKE THIS** 23, page R27

IDM **ˌfamous ˌlast ˈwords** (*saying*) people sometimes say **Famous last words!** when they think sb is being too confident about sth that is going to happen 吹牛，胡扯（表示某人盲目乐观）：*'Everything's under control.' 'Famous last words!'* "一切都在掌握之中。" "净吹牛！" **ORIGIN** This phrase refers to a collection of quotations of the dying words of famous people. 这个短语原指名人临终遗言语录选编。

fam·ous·ly /ˈfeɪməsli/ *adv.* in a way that is famous 著名地；出名地：*Some newspapers, most famously the New York Times, refused to print the word Ms.* 有些报纸拒不刊用 Ms 这个词，其中最著名的是《纽约时报》。

IDM **get on/along ˈfamously** (*informal, becoming old-fashioned*) to have a very good relationship 和睦相处；相处极好

fan 🔑 /fæn/ *noun, verb*

■ ***noun*** **1** 🔑 a person who admires sb/sth or enjoys watching or listening to sb/sth very much 迷；狂热爱好者；狂热仰慕者：*movie fans* 电影迷 ◇ *crowds of football fans* 一群群足球迷 ◇ *a big fan of Rihanna* 蕾哈娜的狂热仰慕者 ◇ ***fan mail*** (= letters from fans to the person they admire) 狂热仰慕者的来信 **2** 🔑 a machine with blades that go round to create a current of air 风扇：*to switch on the electric fan* 开电扇 ◇ *a fan heater* 风扇式加热器 ➲ SEE ALSO EXTRACTOR (1) **3** a thing that you hold in your hand and wave to create a current of cool air 扇子 **IDM** SEE SHIT *n.*

fans 扇

■ ***verb*** (**-nn-**) **1 ~ sb/sth/yourself** to make air blow onto sb/sth by waving a fan, your hand, etc. 扇（风）：*He fanned himself with a newspaper to cool down.* 他用一张报纸给自己扇凉。**2 ~ sth** to make a fire burn more strongly by blowing on it 扇，吹（使火更旺）：*Fanned by a westerly wind, the fire spread rapidly through the city.* 火借助西风迅速蔓延全城。**3 ~ sth** (*literary*) to make a feeling, an attitude, etc. stronger 煽起；激起 **SYN** **fuel**：*His reluctance to answer her questions simply fanned her curiosity.* 他不爽快地回答她的问题，这就激起了她的好奇心。

IDM **fan the ˈflames (of sth)** to make a feeling such as anger, hatred, etc. worse 煽风点火；煽动（情绪）：*His writings fanned the flames of racism.* 他的写作煽起了种族主义情绪。

PHR V **ˌfan ˈout** | **ˌfan sth↔ˈout** to spread out or spread sth out over an area（使）展开，散开，成扇形散开：*The police fanned out to surround the house.* 警察散开包围了这座房子。◇ *The bird fanned out its tail feathers.* 这只鸟把尾羽展成扇形。

fan·at·ic /fəˈnætɪk/ *noun* **1** (*informal*) a person who is extremely enthusiastic about sth 入迷者 **SYN** **enthusiast**：*a* ***fitness/crossword, etc. fanatic*** 热衷于健美、纵横填字游戏等的人 **2** (*disapproving*) a person who holds extreme or dangerous opinions 极端分子；狂热信徒 **SYN** **extremist**：*religious fanatics* 宗教极端分子 ▸ **fan·at·ic·al** /-kl/ *adj.*：*a fanatical supporter* 狂热的支持者 ◇ *fanatical anti-royalists* 狂热的反君主制度者 ◇ *a fanatical interest in football* 对足球入迷 ◇ *She's fanatical about healthy eating.* 她对健康饮食着了迷。**fan·at·ic·al·ly** /-kli/ *adv.*：*fanatically devoted to exercise* 极其热衷于锻炼

fan·ati·cism /fəˈnætɪsɪzəm/ *noun* [U] (*disapproving*) extreme beliefs or behaviour, especially in connection with religion or politics（尤指宗教、政治上的）狂热，入迷 **SYN** **extremism**

ˈfan belt *noun* a belt that operates the machinery that cools a car engine（带动冷却汽车引擎散热器的）风扇皮带

fan·boy /ˈfænbɔɪ/ *noun* (*informal*) a person, especially a boy or young man, who is extremely interested in sth such as a particular type of music or software 迷（尤指痴迷某种音乐、软件等的男孩或年轻男子）：*a Nintendo fanboy* 任天堂电玩迷 ◇ *Linux fanboys* * Linux 操作系统迷

F

fan·ci·able /ˈfænsiəbl/ *adj.* (*BrE, informal*) sexually attractive 性感的

fan·cier /ˈfænsiə(r)/ *noun* (usually in compounds 通常构成复合词) (*especially BrE*) a person who has a special interest in sth, especially sb who keeps or breeds birds, animals or plants 爱好者；（尤指）饲养迷，园艺迷：*a pigeon fancier* 喜欢养鸽子的人

fan·ci·ful /ˈfænsɪfl/ *adj.* **1** (*disapproving*) based on imagination and not facts or reason 空想的；想象的 **2** (of things 物件) decorated in an unusual style that shows imagination 装饰独出心裁的；式样奇特的；花哨的：*a fanciful gold border* 别出心裁的金色镶边 ▶ **fan·ci·ful·ly** /-fəli/ *adv.*

ˈfan club *noun* an organization that a person's fans belong to and that sends them information, etc. about that person …迷俱乐部；影迷（或歌迷、球迷等）会

fancy /ˈfænsi/ *verb, noun, adj.*

■ ***verb*** (**fan·cies**, **fancy·ing**, **fan·cied**, **fan·cied**) **1** [T] (*BrE, informal*) to want sth or want to do sth 想要；想做 SYN **feel like**：**~ sth** *Fancy a drink?* 想喝一杯吗？◇ *She didn't fancy* (= did not like) *the idea of going home in the dark.* 她不想在黑夜里回家。◇ **~ doing sth** *Do you fancy going out this evening?* 今晚你想不想外出？ **2** [T] **~ sb** (*BrE, informal*) to be sexually attracted to sb 对…有性幻想；倾慕：*I think she fancies me.* 我觉得她对我动心了。 **3** [T] **~ yourself** (*BrE, informal, disapproving*) to think that you are very popular, attractive or intelligent 自负；自命不凡：*He started to chat to me and I could tell that he really fancied himself.* 他和我聊起天来，我看得出他确实自以为了不起。 **4** [T] (*BrE*) to like the idea of being sth or to believe, often wrongly, that you are sth 自认为是；自命为：**~ yourself** (**as**) **sth** *She fancies herself* (*as*) *a serious actress.* 她自以为是严肃的演员。◇ **~ yourself + adv./prep.** **5** [I, T] **Fancy!** (*informal, becoming old-fashioned*) used to show that you are surprised or shocked by sth（表示惊奇或震惊）真想不到，竟然：*Fancy! She's never been in a plane before.* 真想不到！她竟然从未坐过飞机。◇ **~ doing sth** *Fancy meeting you here!* 竟然在这儿遇到你！◇ **~ sth** *'She remembered my name after all those years.' 'Fancy that!'* "过了那么多年她还记得我的名字。""真是不可思议！" **6** [T] (*BrE*) **~ sb/sth** to think that sb/sth will win or be successful at sth, especially in a race 认为…会成功；（尤指速度竞赛）认为…要赢：*Which horse do you fancy in the next race?* 下一轮赛马你认为哪匹马会赢？◇ *He's hoping to get the job but I don't **fancy his chances**.* 他希望得到那份工作，不过我认为他的机会不大。 **7** [T] **~ (that)...** (*literary*) to believe or imagine sth 认为；想象：*She fancied* (*that*) *she could hear footsteps.* 她觉得好像听到了脚步声。

■ ***noun*** (*pl.* **-ies**) **1** [C, U] something that you imagine; your imagination 想象的事物；想象（力） SYN **fantasy**：*night-time fancies that disappear in the morning* 在早上逝去的夜间幻觉 ◇ *a child's wild **flights of fancy*** 孩子的异想天开 **2** [sing.] a feeling that you would like to have or to do sth 想要；爱好 SYN **whim**：*She said she wanted a dog but it was only a passing fancy.* 她说想要一条狗，但这不过是一时心血来潮。 **3** [C, usually pl.] (*BrE*) a small decorated cake 花色小蛋糕

IDM **as/whenever, etc. the fancy ˈtakes you** as/whenever, etc. you feel like doing sth 当（或无论何时等）想做某事时：*We bought a camper van so we could go away whenever the fancy took us.* 我们买了一辆野营车，所以我们啥时想去野营就可以去。 **catch/take sb's ˈfancy** to attract or please sb 吸引某人；中某人的意：*She looked through the hotel advertisements until one of them caught her fancy.* 她仔细查看旅馆广告，终于有一家中了她的意。 **take a ˈfancy to sb/sth** (*especially BrE*) to start liking sb/sth, often without an obvious reason 喜欢上，爱上（常指没有明显原因） ➲ MORE AT TICKLE *v.*

■ ***adj.*** (**fan·cier**, **fan·ci·est**) **1** unusually complicated, often in an unnecessary way; intended to impress other people 异常复杂的；太花哨的：*a kitchen full of fancy gadgets* 有各式各样小器具的厨房 ◇ *They added a lot of fancy footwork to the dance.* 他们给这个舞蹈增加了许多复杂的舞步。◇ *He's always using fancy legal words.* 他总是使用异常复杂的法律词语。 OPP **simple** **2** [only before noun] (especially of small things 尤指小物件) with a lot of decorations or bright colours 精致的；有精美装饰的；绚丽的；花哨的：*fancy goods* (= things sold as gifts or for decoration) 饰物礼品 ➲ COMPARE PLAIN *adj.* (3) **3** (*sometimes disapproving*) expensive or connected with an expensive way of life 昂贵的；奢华的：*fancy restaurants with fancy prices* 价格昂贵的豪华餐厅 ◇ *Don't come back with any fancy ideas.* 别又说什么美妙的空想。 **4** (*NAmE*) (of food 食物) of high quality 优质的；高档的

ˌfancy ˈdress *noun* [U] (*BrE*) clothes that you wear, especially at parties, to make you appear to be a different character 化装服；化装舞会服：*guests **in fancy dress*** 身着化装服的客人们 ◇ *a fancy-dress party* 化装晚会 ➲ SEE ALSO COSTUME, MASQUERADE *n.* (2)

ˌfancy-ˈfree *adj.* free to do what you like because you are not emotionally involved with anyone 无拘束的；逍遥自在的：*I was still **footloose and fancy-free*** (= free to enjoy myself) *in those days.* 当时我仍然毫无牵挂、逍遥自在呢。

ˈfancy man, **ˈfancy woman** *noun* (*old-fashioned, informal, disapproving*) the man/woman with whom a person is having a romantic relationship, especially when one or both of them is married to sb else（尤指一方或双方已婚的）情夫，情妇

fan·dango /fænˈdæŋgəʊ; *NAmE* -goʊ/ *noun* (*pl.* **fan·dan·goes** or **fan·dangos**) [C] a lively Spanish dance; a piece of music for this dance 凡丹戈舞（节奏欢快的西班牙舞蹈）；凡丹戈舞曲

fan·fare /ˈfænfeə(r); *NAmE* -fer/ *noun* **1** [C] a short loud piece of music that is played to celebrate sb/sth important arriving 号角花彩，号角齐鸣（欢迎仪式等上奏的响亮短曲） **2** [U, C] a large amount of activity and discussion on television, in newspapers, etc. to celebrate sb/sth（为庆祝而在媒体上的）喧嚷：*The product was launched amid much fanfare worldwide.* 这个产品在世界各地隆重推出。

ˈfan fiction *noun* [U] a type of literature, usually written on the Internet, by people who admire a particular novel, film/movie, etc., with characters taken from these stories 同人小说（由某小说、电影等的爱好者创作，人物取自原作，常为网络文学）

fang /fæŋ/ *noun* [usually pl.] either of two long sharp teeth at the front of the mouths of some animals, such as a snake or dog 尖牙；犬齿；（蛇的）毒牙 ➲ VISUAL VOCAB PAGE V13

ˈF angles *noun* [pl.] = CORRESPONDING ANGLES

fan·light /ˈfænlaɪt/ (*NAmE also* **tran·som**) *noun* a small window above a door or another window 气窗（门或窗上方的小窗）

Fanny /ˈfæni/ *noun* IDM SEE SWEET *adj.*

fanny /ˈfæni/ *noun* (*pl.* **-ies**) **1** (*BrE, taboo, slang*) the female sex organs 女性生殖器；阴部 **2** (*informal, especially NAmE*) a person's bottom 屁股

ˈfanny pack (*NAmE*) (*BrE* **bum-bag**) *noun* (*informal*) a small bag attached to a belt and worn around the waist, to keep money, etc. in（围在腰间，放钱物的）腰包 ➲ VISUAL VOCAB PAGE V69

fan·ta·sia /fænˈteɪziə/ *noun* a piece of music in a free form, often based on well-known tunes 幻想曲

fan·ta·size (*BrE also* **-ise**) /ˈfæntəsaɪz/ *verb* [I, T] **~ (about sth)** | **~ (that...)** to imagine that you are doing sth that you would like to do, or that sth that you would like to happen is happening, even though this is very unlikely 想象；幻想；做白日梦：*He sometimes fantasized about winning the gold medal.* 他有时幻想赢得金牌的情景。 ▶ **fan·ta·sist** /ˈfæntəsɪst/ *noun*

fan·tas·tic /fænˈtæstɪk/ *adj.* **1** (*informal*) extremely good; excellent 极好的；了不起的 SYN **great**, **brilliant**：*a fantastic beach in Australia* 澳大利亚旖旎的海滩 ◇ *a fantastic achievement* 了不起的成就 ◇ *The weather was absolutely* *fantastic.* 天气十分宜人。◇ *You've got the job? Fantastic!* 你得到那工作了？太好了！➲ SYNONYMS AT GREAT **2** (*informal*) very large; larger than you expected 很大的；大得难以置信的 SYN **enormous, amazing**: *The response to our appeal was fantastic.* 我们的呼吁引起十分强烈的反应。◇ *The car costs a fantastic amount of money.* 这轿车的价钱贵得吓人。**3** (*also less frequent* **fan·tas·tic·al**) [usually before noun] strange and showing a lot of imagination 怪诞的；荒诞不经的；富于想象的 SYN **weird**: *fantastic dreams of forests and jungles* 关于森林和热带丛林的怪梦 **4** impossible to put into practice 不切实际的；无法实现的：*a* ***fantastic scheme/project*** 不切实际的计划 / 方案 ▶ **fan·tas·tic·al·ly** /fæn'tæstɪkli/ *adv.*: *fantastically successful* 极其成功 ◇ *a fantastically shaped piece of stone* 一块奇形怪状的石头

fan·tasy /'fæntəsi/ *noun* (*pl.* **-ies**) **1** [C] a pleasant situation that you imagine but that is unlikely to happen 幻想；想象：*his childhood fantasies about becoming a famous football player* 他儿时想成为著名足球运动员的幻想 **2** [C] a product of your imagination 想象的产物；幻想作品：*Her books are usually escapist fantasies.* 她的书通常是逃避现实的幻想作品。 **3** [U] the act of imagining things; a person's imagination 幻想；想象：*a work of fantasy* 幻想作品 ◇ *Stop living in a* ***fantasy world.*** 别再生活在幻想世界中了。

ˌfantasy 'football *noun* [U] a competition in which you choose players to make your own imaginary team, and score points according to the performance of the real players 梦幻足球（虚幻比赛方式，组成想象中的球队，根据球员的实际比赛表现计算得分）

fan·zine /'fænziːn/ *noun* a magazine that is written and read by fans of a musician, sports team, etc.（音乐、体育等方面的）爱好者杂志

fao *abbr.* (*BrE*) used in writing to mean 'for the attention of' (written on a document or letter to say who should deal with it)（书写形式）请…注意；（文件或书信用语）由…处理，由…办理 ➲ SEE ALSO ATTN

FAQ /ˌef eɪ 'kjuː/ *abbr.* used in writing to mean 'frequently asked questions' 常问问题（全写为 frequently asked questions，书写形式）

fa·quir = FAKIR

far /fɑː(r)/ *adv., adj.*

■ ***adv.*** (**far·ther, far·thest** or **fur·ther, fur·thest**)

• **DISTANCE** 距离 **1** a long distance away 远：*We didn't go far.* 我们没有走远。◇ *Have you come far?* 你是远道来的吗？◇ *It's not far to the beach.* 到海滩不远。◇ *There's not far to go now.* 现在离得不远了。◇ ~ (**from, away, below, etc.**) *The restaurant is not far from here.* 餐厅离这儿不远。◇ *countries as far apart as Japan and Brazil* 像日本和巴西这样相隔遥远的国家 ◇ *He looked down at the traffic far below.* 他俯视远在下方行驶的车辆。◇ *Far away in the distance, a train whistled.* 远处有一辆火车鸣笛。◇ *The farther north they went, the colder it became.* 他们愈往北去，天气就变得愈冷。◇ *a concert of music from* ***near and far*** 来自四面八方的音乐的演奏会 HELP In positive sentences it is more usual to use **a long way**. 肯定句较常用 a long way: *We went a long way.* 我们走了很长的路。◇ ~~*We went far.*~~ ◇ *The restaurant is a long way from here.* 餐馆离这儿很远。 **2** used when you are asking or talking about the distance between two places or the distance that has been travelled or is to be travelled（问到或谈及距离时说）有多远，远（至）：*How far is it to your house from here?* 从这儿到你家有多远？◇ *How much further is it?* 还有多远？◇ *We'll go by train* ***as far as*** *London, and then take a bus.* 我们坐火车到伦敦，然后转乘公共汽车。◇ *We didn't go* ***as far as*** *the others.* 我们不如其他人走得远。◇ *I'm not sure I can walk* ***so far.*** 我没有把握能步行这么远。

• **TIME** 时间 **3** a long time from the present; for a large part of a particular period of time 久；远：~ **back** *The band made their first record as far back as 1990.* 这个乐队早在 1990 年就录制了他们的第一张唱片。◇ ~ **ahead** *Let's try to plan further ahead.* 咱们尽量计划得更长远些。◇ ~ **into sth** *We worked far into the night.* 我们工作到深夜。

• **DEGREE** 程度 **4** very much; to a great degree 非常；很大程度上；远远；大大：*That's a far better idea.* 那个主意好得多。◇ *There are* ***far more*** *opportunities for young people than there used to be.* 现在年轻人的机会比过去多得多。◇ *It had been a success* ***far beyond*** *their expectations.* 成功之大远远超过他们的预期。◇ *He's fallen far behind in his work.* 他的工作大大落后了。◇ *She always gives us* ***far too much*** *homework.* 她总是让我们做多得不得了的家庭作业。 **5** used when you are asking or talking about the degree to which sth is true or possible（问到或谈及程度时说）有多大，直（至）：*How far can we trust him?* 我们能够信任他到什么程度？◇ *His parents supported him* ***as far as*** *they could.* 他的父母全力支持他。◇ *Plan your route in advance, using main roads* ***as far as possible.*** 预先安排好你的路线，尽量走大路。

• **PROGRESS** 进展 **6** used to talk about how much progress has been made in doing or achieving sth 进展程度：*How far have you got with that report?* 你那个报告写得怎么样了？◇ *I read* ***as far as*** *the third chapter.* 我读到了第三章。➲ NOTE AT FARTHER

IDM **as far as the eye can/could 'see** to the HORIZON (= where the sky meets the land or sea) 极目所尽：*The bleak moorland stretched on all sides as far as the eye could see.* 荒凉的旷野向四面伸展开去，一望无际。**as far as I 'know | as far as I can re'member, 'see, 'tell, etc.** used to say that you think you know, remember, understand, etc. sth but you cannot be completely sure, especially because you do not know all the facts 就我所知；尽我所记得的；依我看：*As far as we knew, there was no cause for concern.* 就我们所知，没有什么需要担心的。◇ *As far as I can see, you've done nothing wrong.* 依我看，你没有做错任何事。◇ *She lived in Chicago, as far as I can remember.* 据我所记得的，她过去住在芝加哥。**as/so far as 'I am concerned** used to give your personal opinion on sth 就我而言：*As far as I am concerned, you can do what you like.* 就我而言，你想干什么就可以干什么。**as/so far as sb/sth is concerned | as/so far as sb/sth goes** used to give facts or an opinion about a particular aspect of sth 就…而言 **as/so far as it 'goes** to a limited degree, usually less than is sufficient 在一定程度上（通常指不足）：*It's a good plan as far as it goes, but there are a lot of things they haven't thought of.* 这计划还算不错，不过还有很多事情没有考虑到。**by 'far** (used with comparative or superlative adjectives or adverbs 与形容词、副词的比较级或最高级连用) by a great amount 大大地；…得多：*The last of these reasons is by far the most important.* 这些理由中最后一条比其他的重要得多。◇ *Amy is the smartest by far.* 埃米显然最聪明。 **carry/take sth too 'far** to continue doing sth beyond reasonable limits 做得过分 **far and a'way** (followed by comparative or superlative adjectives 后接形容词比较级或最高级) by a very great amount 远为；大大地：*She's far and away the best player.* 她是当之无愧的最佳选手。 **far and 'wide** over a large area 到处；各处；广泛：*They searched far and wide for the missing child.* 他们四处搜寻失踪的小孩。 **far be it from me to do sth (but...)** (*informal*) used when you are just about to disagree with sb or to criticize them and you would like them to think that you do not really want to do this（要表示不同意和批评但又希望对方感到自己并非真正想要这样做）：*Far be it from me to interfere in your affairs but I would like to give you just one piece of advice.* 我绝不想干涉你的事，我只不过想给你一个忠告。**far from sth/from doing sth** almost the opposite of sth or of what is expected 几乎相反；远非：*It is far from clear (= it is not clear) what he intends to do.* 他打算怎样做一点都不清楚。◇ *Computers, far from destroying jobs, can create employment.* 计算机远非破坏就业，而是能创造就业。**far 'from it** (*informal*) used to say that the opposite of what sb says is true 完全相反；绝非；远非如此：*'You're not angry then?' 'Far from it. I've never laughed so much in my life.'* "那么你不生气？""非但没有生气，我一生中还没有这样笑过呢。" **go 'far** (of people 人) to be very successful in the future 有远大前程：*She is very talented and should go far.* 她天赋很高，会很有出息。 **go far enough** (used in questions and negative sentences 用于疑问句和否定句) to achieve all that is wanted 达到目的：*The new legislation is welcome but does not go far enough.*

新法规受到欢迎，但力度还不够大。◇ *Do these measures go far enough?* 这些措施能不能解决问题？◇ (*disapproving*) *Stop it now. The joke has gone far enough* (= it has continued too long). 行啦，这玩笑开得太久了。 **go so/as far as to…** to be willing to go to extreme or surprising limits in dealing with sth 竟然；甚至：*I wouldn't go as far as to say that he's a liar* (= but I think he may be slightly dishonest). 我倒不想说他是个骗子（不过我认为他可能有点不老实）。 **go too ˈfar | go ˈthis/ˈthat far** to behave in an extreme way that is not acceptable 走得太远；做得过分：*He's always been quite crude, but this time he's gone too far.* 他一向很粗鲁，但这次太过分了。◇ *I never thought she'd go this far.* 我绝没有想到她会做得这么过分。 **in so/as ˈfar as** to the degree that 到…程度；在…范围：*That's the truth, in so far as I know it.* 就我所知，那是真实情况。 **not far ˈoff/ˈout/ˈwrong** (*informal*) almost correct 几乎正确：*Your guess wasn't far out at all.* 你猜得几乎一点不错。 **not go ˈfar 1** (of money 钱) to not be enough to buy a lot of things 不够买，买不了（许多东西）：*Five pounds doesn't go very far these days.* 这年头五英镑买不了多少东西。 **2** (of a supply of sth 某物的供应) to not be enough for what is needed 不充足；不够用：*Four bottles of wine won't go far among twenty people.* 四瓶酒不够二十人喝。 **ˈso far | ˈthus far** 🔑 until now; up to this point 到目前为止；迄今为止；到这点为止：*What do you think of the show so far?* 到目前为止你觉得这场演出怎么样？◇ *Detectives are so far at a loss to explain the reason for his death.* 至今侦探仍茫然无法解释他的死因。 **ˌso ˈfar** 🔑 (*informal*) only to a limited degree 仅到一定程度；只在有限范围内：*I trust him only so far.* 我只相信他到这个程度。 **ˌso far, so ˈgood** (*saying*) used to say that things have been successful until now and you hope that they will continue to be successful, but you know that the task, etc. is not finished yet 到目前为止，一切还算顺利 ➲ MORE AT AFIELD, FEW *det.*, NEAR *adv.*

■ ***adj.*** (**far·ther, far·thest** or **fur·ther, fur·thest**) [only before noun] **1** 🔑 at a greater distance away from you 较远的：*I saw her on the **far side** of the road.* 我看见她在马路那头。◇ *at the **far end** of the room* 在房间的另一头 ◇ *They made for an empty table in the **far corner**.* 他们走向远处那个角落的空桌子。 **2** 🔑 at the furthest point in a particular direction（某方向的）最远的，远端的：*the **far north** of Scotland* 苏格兰的最北边 ◇ *Who is that on the **far left** of the photograph?* 相片上最左边的那个人是谁？◇ *She is on the **far right** of the party* (= holds extreme RIGHT-WING political views). 她是党内的极右分子。 **3** (*old-fashioned* or *literary*) a long distance away 远的；远方的；遥远的：*a far country* 远方的国家

IDM **a far cry from sth** a very different experience from sth 和…相去甚远；与…大相径庭 **SYN** **remote**

Farad /ˈfæræd/ *noun* (*abbr.* **F**) (*physics* 物) a unit for measuring CAPACITANCE 法拉（电容单位）

far·away /ˈfɑːrəweɪ/ *adj.* [only before noun] **1** a long distance away 远的；远方的；遥远的 **SYN** **distant**：*a war in a faraway country* 在一个远方国家发生的战争 **2** **a ~ look/expression** an expression on your face that shows that your thoughts are far away from your present surroundings 心不在焉的；恍惚的；出神的 **SYN** **distant**

farce /fɑːs; *NAmE* fɑːrs/ *noun* **1** [C, U] a funny play for the theatre based on ridiculous and unlikely situations and events; this type of writing or performance 滑稽戏（剧本）；闹剧（剧本）；笑剧（剧本）：*a bedroom farce* (= a funny play about sex) 床上笑剧 **2** [C] a situation or an event that is so unfair or badly organized that it becomes ridiculous 荒唐的事情；闹剧：*The trial was a complete farce.* 这次审判完全是一场闹剧。

far·ci·cal /ˈfɑːsɪkl; *NAmE* ˈfɑːrs-/ *adj.* ridiculous and not worth taking seriously 荒唐的；荒谬的；可笑的：*It was a farcical trial.* 那是一次荒唐的审判。◇ *a situation verging on the farcical* 近乎荒唐的场面

fare /feə(r); *NAmE* fer/ *noun, verb*

■ ***noun*** **1** [C, U] the money that you pay to travel by bus, plane, taxi, etc. 车费；船费；飞机票价：***bus/taxi fares*** 公共汽车费；出租汽车费 ◇ ***train/rail fares*** 火车票价 ◇ *Children travel (at) half fare.* 儿童交通费减半。◇ *When do they start paying full fare?* 他们什么时候开始买全票？➲ SEE ALSO AIRFARE ➲ **SYNONYMS** AT RATE **2** [C] a passenger in a taxi 出租车乘客：*The taxi driver picked up a fare at the station.* 出租车司机在车站接了一名乘客。 **3** [U] (*old-fashioned* or *formal*) food that is offered as a meal 饭菜：*The restaurant provides good traditional fare.* 这家餐厅提供传统风味佳馔。

■ ***verb*** [I] **~ well, badly, better, etc.** to be successful/unsuccessful in a particular situation 成功（或不成功、更好等） **SYN** **get on**：*The party fared very badly in the last election.* 该党上次竞选情况很糟。

the ˌFar ˈEast *noun* China, Japan and other countries of E and SE Asia 远东（中国、日本等东亚及东南亚诸国）➲ COMPARE MIDDLE EAST ▸ **ˌFar ˈEastern** *adj.*

fare·well /ˌfeəˈwel; *NAmE* ˌferˈwel/ *noun, exclamation, verb*

■ ***noun*** [C, U] the act of saying goodbye to sb 告别；辞行：*She said her farewells and left.* 她告别后就离开了。◇ *a **farewell party/drink, etc.*** 欢送会、惜别酒会等

■ ***exclamation*** (*old use* or *formal*) goodbye 再见；再会

■ ***verb*** **~ sb** (*AustralE*) to arrange a ceremony or party for sb because they are leaving 为…举行送别仪式（或宴会）：*The troops were farewelled at a ceremony in Darwin.* 为军队举办的送别仪式在达尔文举行。

ˌfar-ˈfetched *adj.* very difficult to believe 难以置信的；牵强的：*The whole story sounds very far-fetched.* 整个叙述听起来很难以置信。➲ **WORDFINDER NOTE** AT STORY

ˌfar-ˈflung *adj.* [usually before noun] (*literary*) **1** a long distance away 遥远的：*expeditions to the far-flung corners of the world* 去世界偏远地方的探险 **2** spread over a wide area 分布广的；广泛的：*a newsletter that helps to keep all our far-flung graduates in touch* 使我们分布在各地的毕业生保持联系的通讯

ˌfar ˈgone *adj.* [not before noun] (*informal*) very ill/sick, crazy or drunk 病重；精神失常；烂醉：*She was too far gone to understand anything we said to her.* 她已神志不清，听不懂我们对她说的任何话。

farm 🔑 /fɑːm; *NAmE* fɑːrm/ *noun, verb*

■ ***noun*** **1** 🔑 an area of land, and the buildings on it, used for growing crops and/or keeping animals 农场：*a 200-hectare farm* 一个200公顷的农场 ◇ *a **farm worker/labourer*** 农场工人 ◇ ***farm buildings/machinery*** 农场建筑物；农业机械 ◇ *to **live/work on a farm*** 在农场居住 / 工作 ➲ **COLLOCATIONS** AT FARMING ➲ **VISUAL VOCAB** PAGE V3

WORDFINDER 联想词：arable, barn, **crop**, cultivate, dairy, fallow, graze, livestock, tractor

2 🔑 (*also* **farm·house**) the main house on a farm, where the farmer lives 农舍 **3** (especially in compounds 尤用于构成复合词) a place where particular fish or animals are bred 养殖场；饲养场：*a trout/mink/pig farm* 鳟鱼养殖场；水貂饲养场；养猪场 ➲ SEE ALSO BATTERY FARM, COLLECTIVE FARM, DAIRY *n.* (1), FACTORY FARM, FUNNY FARM, HEALTH FARM, TRUCK FARM, WIND FARM **IDM** SEE BET *v.*

■ ***verb*** [I, T] to use land for growing crops and/or keeping animals 务农；种田；从事畜牧业：*The family has farmed in Kent for over two hundred years.* 这个家族在肯特务农两百多年了。◇ **~ sth** *They farm dairy cattle.* 他们饲养奶牛。◇ *He farmed 200 acres of prime arable land.* 他耕种了200英亩良田。◇ *organically farmed produce* 有机种植农产品

IDM SEE BUY *v.*

PHR V **ˌfarm sb↔ˈout (to sb)** (*disapproving*) to arrange for sb to be cared for by other people 托（别人）照看某人 **ˌfarm sth↔ˈout to sb** to send out work for other people to do 把工作包给（某人）：*The company farms out a lot of work to freelancers.* 这家公司把大量工作包给了自由职业者。

ˈfarm belt *noun* (*US*) an area where there are a lot of farms 农场密集地区

farm·er 🔑 /ˈfɑːmə(r); *NAmE* ˈfɑːrm-/ *noun* a person who owns or manages a farm 农场主；农人

'farmers' market *noun* a place where farmers sell food directly to the public 农产品直销市场；农贸市场

farm·hand /ˈfɑːmhænd; *NAmE* ˈfɑːrm-/ (*NAmE also* **'field hand**) *noun* a person who works for a farmer 农场工人

farm·house /ˈfɑːmhaʊs; *NAmE* ˈfɑːrm-/ *noun* the main house on a farm, where the farmer lives 农场住宅，农舍（农场主的主要住房） ➲ VISUAL VOCAB PAGE V3

farm·ing 🔑 /ˈfɑːmɪŋ; *NAmE* ˈfɑːrmɪŋ/ *noun* [U] the business of managing or working on a farm 务农；农场经营：*to take up farming* 从事农业 ◇ ***sheep/fish, etc. farming*** 牧羊、养鱼等 ◇ *organic farming* 有机耕作 ◇ *modern farming methods* 现代耕作方法 ◇ *a farming community* 农业社区

▼ COLLOCATIONS 词语搭配

Farming 农场经营

Growing food and raising animals 种植粮食和饲养动物

- **plant** trees/seeds/crops/vines/barley 植树；播种；种庄稼；种植葡萄树；种大麦
- **grow/produce** corn/wheat/rice/fruit 种植 / 生产玉米 / 小麦 / 大米 / 水果
- **plough/** (*NAmE*) **plow** land/a field 耕地；犁田
- **sow/harvest** seeds/crops/fields 播种 / 收获谷粒 / 农作物 / 庄稼
- **spread** manure/fertilizer on sth 给…施撒粪肥 / 肥料
- **cultivate/irrigate/water/contaminate** crops/plants/fields/land 耕作 / 灌溉 / 浇灌 / 污染庄稼 / 植物 / 田地 / 土地
- **damage/destroy/lose** your crop 损害 / 毁坏 / 损失农作物
- **ripen/pick** fruit/berries/grapes 催熟 / 采摘水果 / 浆果 / 葡萄
- **press/dry/ferment** grapes 压榨 / 晾干 / 发酵葡萄
- **grind/thresh** grain/corn/wheat 磨 / 打谷物 / 玉米 / 小麦
- **raise/rear/keep** chickens/poultry/cattle/pigs 饲养鸡 / 家禽 / 牛 / 猪
- **raise/breed/feed/graze** livestock/cattle/sheep 饲养 / 喂养 / 放养家畜 / 牛 / 羊
- **kill/slaughter** livestock 屠宰家畜
- **preserve/smoke/cure/salt** meat 防腐保存 / 熏 / 加工贮藏 / 用盐腌制肉

Modern farming 现代农场经营

- **run** a fish farm/an organic dairy 经营养鱼场 / 有机乳品场
- **engage in/be involved in** intensive (pig/fish) farming 从事集约型（生猪 / 渔业）养殖
- **use/apply** (chemical/organic) fertilizer/insecticides/pesticides 使用（化学 / 有机）肥料 / 杀虫剂
- **begin/do/conduct** field trials of GM (= genetically modified) crops 开始 / 进行转基因作物的田间试验
- **grow/develop** GM crops/seeds/plants/foods 种植 / 研发转基因作物 / 种子 / 植物 / 粮食
- **fund/invest in** genetic engineering/research 资助 / 投资基因工程 / 研究
- **improve/increase** crop yields 提高 / 增加粮食产量
- **face/suffer from/alleviate** food shortages 面临 / 遭受 / 缓解食物短缺
- **label** food that contains GMOs (= genetically modified organisms) 给含有转基因生物的食品贴标签
- **eliminate/reduce** farm subsidies 取消 / 减少农业补贴
- **oppose/be against** factory farming/GM food 反对工厂化养殖 / 转基因食品
- **promote/encourage/support** organic/sustainable farming 促进 / 鼓励 / 支持有机 / 可持续农耕

farm·land /ˈfɑːmlænd; *NAmE* ˈfɑːrm-/ *noun* [U, pl.] land that is used for farming 农田；耕地：*250 acres of farmland* * 250 英亩耕地 ◇ *the prosperous farmlands of Picardy* 皮卡第的富饶农田

farm·stead /ˈfɑːmsted; *NAmE* ˈfɑːrm-/ *noun* (*NAmE* or *formal*) a FARMHOUSE and the buildings near it 农舍及附近建筑物

farm·yard /ˈfɑːmjɑːd; *NAmE* ˈfɑːrmjɑːrd/ *noun* an area that is surrounded by farm buildings 农家庭院 ➲ VISUAL VOCAB PAGE V3

'far-off *adj.* [only before noun] **1** a long distance away 遥远的 SYN **distant, faraway, remote**：*a far-off land* 一个遥远的国度 **2** a long time ago 很久以前的；久远的 SYN **distant**：*memories of those far-off days* 久远往昔的回忆

far·rago /fəˈrɑːgəʊ; *NAmE* -goʊ/ *noun* [usually sing.] (*pl.* **-oes** or **-os**) (*formal, disapproving*) a confused mixture of different things 大杂烩；混杂物 SYN **hotchpotch**

ˌfar-'reaching *adj.* likely to have a lot of influence or many effects 影响深远的；广泛的：***far-reaching consequences/implications*** 影响深远的后果；意味深长 ◇ ***far-reaching changes/reforms*** 意义深远的变革 / 改革

far·rier /ˈfæriə(r)/ *noun* a person whose job is making and fitting HORSESHOES for horses' feet 蹄铁工

far·row /ˈfærəʊ; *NAmE* -roʊ/ *noun, verb*

■ ***noun*** **1** a group of baby pigs that are born together to the same mother（同时生出的）一窝子猪 SYN **litter** **2** an act of giving birth to pigs 产子猪

■ ***verb*** [I] (of a female pig 母猪) to give birth 产子猪

Farsi /ˈfɑːsiː; *NAmE* ˈfɑːrsiː/ *noun* [U] = PERSIAN (2)

ˌfar-'sighted (*NAmE* **far·sighted**) *adj.* **1** having or showing an understanding of the effects in the future of actions that you take now, and being able to plan for them 有远见的；深谋远虑的：*the most far-sighted of politicians* 最有远见的政治家 ◇ *a far-sighted decision* 有远见的决定 **2** (*especially NAmE*) = LONG-SIGHTED ▸ **ˌfar-'sighted·ness** *noun* [U]

fart /fɑːt; *NAmE* fɑːrt/ *verb, noun*

■ ***verb*** [I] (*taboo, slang*) to let air from the BOWELS come out through the ANUS, especially when it happens loudly 放屁；（尤指）放响屁 HELP A more polite way of expressing this is 'to break wind'. 较为礼貌的说法是 to break wind。

PHR V **ˌfart a'round** (*BrE also* **ˌfart a'bout**) (*taboo, slang*) to waste time by behaving in a silly way 闲荡；浪荡

■ ***noun*** (*taboo, slang*) **1** an act of letting air from the BOWELS come out through the ANUS, especially when it happens loudly 放屁；（尤指）放响屁 **2** an unpleasant, boring or stupid person 讨厌的人；令人厌烦的人；蠢人

far·ther 🔑 /ˈfɑːðə(r); *NAmE* ˈfɑːrðə-/ *adv., adj.*

■ ***adv.*** 🔑 (comparative of *far* * far 的比较级) at or to a greater distance in space or time（时间或空间上）更远，

▼ WHICH WORD? 词语辨析

farther / further / farthest / furthest

- These are the comparative and superlative forms of **far**. 以上为 far 的比较级和最高级形式。
- To talk about distance, use either **farther**, **farthest** or **further**, **furthest**. In *BrE*, **further**, **furthest** are the most common forms and in *NAmE*, **further** and **farthest**. 表示距离既可用 farther、farthest，也可用 further、furthest。英式英语最常用 further、furthest，美式英语最常用 further、farthest：*I have to travel further/farther to work now.* 现在我得走更远的路去上班。
- To talk about the degree or extent of something, **further/furthest** are usually preferred. 表示事物的程度或幅度通常宜用 further / furthest：*Let's consider this point further.* 让我们更深入地考虑这一点。
- **Further**, but not **farther**, can also mean 'more' or 'additional'. * further 亦可表示更加或进一步，farther 则无此意：*Are there any further questions?* 还有什么问题吗？This sounds very formal in *NAmE*. 这在美式英语中是很正式的用法。

较远：*farther north/south* 再往北 / 南 ◇ ***farther along** the road* 沿路继续往前 ◇ *I can't go **any farther**.* 我再也走不动了。◇ *As a family we grew **farther and farther** apart.* 我们一家人越来越疏远了。◇ *We watched their ship moving gradually **farther away**.* 我们望着他们的船渐渐远去。◇ *How much farther is it?* 还有多远？◇ *They hadn't got any farther with the work* (= they had made no progress). 他们的工作毫无进展。 IDM SEE AFIELD

■***adj.*** (comparative of *far* * far 的比较级) at a greater distance in space, direction or time（空间、方向或时间上）更远的，较远的：*the farther shore of the lake* 湖的彼岸

F

far·thest /ˈfɑːðɪst; *NAmE* ˈfɑːrð-/ (*also* **fur·thest**) *adv., adj.*

■***adv.*** (superlative of *far* * far 的最高级) at or to the greatest distance in space or time（空间或时间上）最远，最久：*the house **farthest away** from the road* 离这条路最远的那栋房子 ◇ *a competition to see who could throw (the) farthest* 掷远比赛

■***adj.*** (superlative of *far* * far 的最高级) at the greatest distance in space, direction or time（空间、方向或时间上）最远的，最久的：*the farthest point of the journey* 旅程的最远端 ◇ *the part of the garden farthest from the house* 花园离房子最远的那部分

far·thing /ˈfɑːðɪŋ; *NAmE* ˈfɑːrðɪŋ/ *noun* in the past, a British coin worth one quarter of an old penny 法寻（英国旧硬币，值¼旧便士）

fa·scia /ˈfeɪʃə/ *noun* **1** (*BrE*) (*also* **facia**) = DASHBOARD (1) **2** (*also* **ˈfascia board**) a board on the roof of a house, at the end of the RAFTERS 封檐板；挑口板 **3** (*BrE also* **facia**) a board above the entrance of a shop/store, with the name of the shop on it（商店入口上方的）招牌 **4** (*BrE also* **facia**) the hard cover on a mobile/cell phone 手机盖

fas·cin·ate /ˈfæsɪneɪt/ *verb* [T, I] ~ (**sb**) to attract or interest sb very much 深深吸引；迷住：*China has always fascinated me.* 中国一直令我心驰神往。◇ *It was a question that had fascinated him since he was a boy.* 这是他自幼就着迷的问题。◇ *The private lives of movie stars never fail to fascinate.* 电影明星的私生活总让人津津乐道。 ⊃ MORE LIKE THIS 20, page R27

fas·cin·ated /ˈfæsɪneɪtɪd/ *adj.* very interested 入迷的；极感兴趣的：*The children watched, fascinated, as the picture began to appear.* 电影开始以后孩子们入迷地观看着。◇ ~ **by sth** *I've always been fascinated by his ideas.* 我总是对他的想法极感兴趣。◇ ~ **to see, learn, etc.** *They were fascinated to see that it was similar to one they had at home.* 他们发现这个和他们家中的那个相似，极感兴趣。

fas·cin·at·ing /ˈfæsɪneɪtɪŋ/ *adj.* extremely interesting and attractive 极有吸引力的；迷人的：*a fascinating story/subject* 迷人的故事；趣味无穷的话题 ◇ *The results of the survey made fascinating reading.* 调查结果令人读起来饶有兴味。◇ *It's **fascinating to see** how different people approach the problem.* 看到不同的人怎样处理这个问题真是有趣极了。◇ *I fail to see what women find so fascinating about him.* 我就看不出他哪一点使女人神魂颠倒。 ⊃ SYNONYMS AT INTERESTING ▶ **fas·cin·at·ing·ly** *adv.*

fas·cin·ation /ˌfæsɪˈneɪʃn/ *noun* **1** [C, usually sing.] a very strong attraction, that makes sth very interesting 魅力；极大的吸引力：*Water **holds a fascination for** most children.* 水对多数孩子都有极大的吸引力。◇ *The fascination of the game lies in trying to guess what your opponent is thinking.* 这个游戏的魅力就在于要努力去猜对手在想什么。 **2** [U, sing.] the state of being very attracted to and interested in sb/sth 入迷；着迷：*The girls listened **in fascination** as the story unfolded.* 故事情节逐渐展开，小女孩都入迷地听着。◇ ~ **for/with sb/sth** *the public's enduring fascination with the Royal Family* 公众对王室的经久不衰的兴趣

fas·cin·ator /ˈfæsɪneɪtə(r)/ *noun* a light decorative ACCESSORY for women that is worn on the head on special occasions and made from feathers, artificial flowers, etc. 装饰帽，羽饰花帽（女性在特殊场合佩戴的头饰，用羽毛、假花等制成）

fas·cism (*also* **Fas·cism**) /ˈfæʃɪzəm/ *noun* [U] an extreme RIGHT-WING political system or attitude which is in favour of strong central government and which does not allow any opposition 法西斯主义 ⊃ WORDFINDER NOTE AT SYSTEM

fas·cist (*also* **Fas·cist**) /ˈfæʃɪst/ *noun* **1** a person who supports fascism 法西斯主义者 **2** a way of referring to sb that you disapprove of because they have RIGHT-WING attitudes 极右分子 ▶ **fas·cist** *adj.*: *a fascist state* 法西斯国家 ◇ *fascist sympathies* 极右分子的支持

fash·ion /ˈfæʃn/ *noun, verb*

■***noun*** **1** [U, C] a popular style of clothes, hair, etc. at a particular time or place; the state of being popular（衣服、发式等的）流行款式，时兴式样：*dressed in the latest fashion* 穿着入时 ◇ *the new season's fashions* 新一季的流行款式 ◇ *Long skirts have **come into fashion** again.* 长裙又时兴起来了。◇ *Jeans are still **in fashion**.* 牛仔裤仍然流行。◇ *Some styles never **go out of fashion**.* 有些款式永远不会过时。 **2** [C] a popular way of behaving, doing an activity, etc.（行为、活动等的）时尚，时兴：*The fashion at the time was for teaching mainly the written language.* 那时教学时兴的主要是书面语。◇ *Fashions in art and literature come and go.* 文艺的潮流总是昙花一现。 **3** [U] the business of making or selling clothes in new and different styles 时装业：*a **fashion designer/magazine/show*** 时装设计师 / 杂志 / 表演 ◇ *the world of fashion* 时装界 ◇ *the fashion industry* 时装业 ⊃ WORDFINDER NOTE AT STORE

IDM **after a ˈfashion** to some extent, but not very well 还过得去；还算可以：*I can play the piano, after a fashion.* 我会弹钢琴，不过马马虎虎。 **after the fashion of sb/sth** (*formal*) in the style of sb/sth 模仿…的式样；像…的风格：*The new library is very much after the fashion of Nash.* 这座新图书馆很像纳什的风格。 **in (a)... ˈfashion** (*formal*) in a particular way 以…方式：*How could they behave in such a fashion?* 他们的态度怎么会这样呢？◇ *She was proved right, in dramatic fashion, when the whole department resigned.* 整个部门的人都辞了职，戏剧性地证明她是对的。 **like it's going out of ˈfashion** (*informal*) used to emphasize that sb is doing sth or using sth a lot 做得很多；大量使用；大肆花费：*She's been spending money like it's going out of fashion.* 她花钱一直大手大脚。 ⊃ SEE ALSO PARROT-FASHION

■***verb*** to make or shape sth, especially with your hands（尤指用手工）制作，使成形，塑造：~ **A (from/out of B)** *She fashioned a pot from the clay.* 她用黏土制成一个罐。◇ ~ **B (into A)** *She fashioned the clay into a pot.* 她用黏土制成一个罐。

fash·ion·able /ˈfæʃnəbl/ *adj.* **1** following a style that is popular at a particular time 流行的；时兴的；时髦的：*fashionable clothes/furniture/ideas* 时髦的服装 / 家具 / 思想 ◇ *It's becoming fashionable to have long hair again.* 现在又开始流行蓄长发了。◇ *Such thinking is fashionable among right-wing politicians.* 在政界右翼人士中这种想法很流行。 **2** used or visited by people following a current fashion, especially by rich people 时髦人物使用的；（尤指）有钱人常光顾的：*a fashionable address/resort/restaurant* 时髦人物常去的地点 / 度假地 / 餐馆 ◇ *She lives in a very fashionable part of London.* 她住在伦敦一个高级住宅区。 OPP **unfashionable** ⊃ COMPARE OLD-FASHIONED ▶ **fash·ion·ably** /-əbli/ *adv.*: *fashionably dressed* 穿着时髦 ◇ *His wife was blonde and fashionably thin.* 他的妻子一头金发，苗条入时。

ˈfashion-conscious *adj.* aware of the latest fashions and wanting to follow them 赶时髦的；讲究时髦的：*fashion-conscious teenagers* 赶时髦的青少年

ˈfashion designer *noun* a person who designs fashionable clothes 时装设计师

ˈfashion-forward *adj.* more modern than the current fashion 超时尚的；超时髦的；超前于流行款式的：*We tend to be traditional rather than fashion-forward in our designs.* 我们的设计倾向于传统而非超前于流行款式。

fash·ion·ista /ˌfæʃn'iːstə/ *noun* (used especially in newspapers 尤用于报章) a fashion DESIGNER, or a person who is always dressed in a fashionable way 时装设计师；穿着入时的人

'fashion show *noun* an occasion where people can see new designs of clothes being worn by fashion models 时装表演

'fashion statement *noun* something that you wear or own that is new or unusual and is meant to draw attention to you 时尚宣言（为引人注目而穿戴或拥有的奇装异服）: *This shirt is great for anyone who wants to* ***make a fashion statement.*** 要求着装别树一帜的人穿这件衬衫最合适。

'fashion victim *noun* a person who always wears the newest fashions even if they do not suit him or her 时尚受害者（盲目赶时髦的人）

fast /fɑːst; *NAmE* fæst/ *adj., adv., verb, noun*

■ ***adj.*** (**fast·er, fast·est**)

• **QUICK** 快速 **1** moving or able to move quickly 快的；迅速的；敏捷的: *a fast car/horse* 速度快的汽车 / 马 ◇ *the world's fastest runner* 世界最快的赛跑运动员 **2** happening in a short time or without delay 迅速发生的；立即发生的: *the fastest rate of increase for years* 多年来最高的增长率 ◇ *a fast response time* 迅速的反应时间 **3** able to do sth quickly 动作迅速的；头脑灵活的: *a fast learner* 领悟快的学习者

• **SURFACE** 物体表面 **4** producing or allowing quick movement 可供快速运动的: *a* ***fast road/pitch*** 快车道；快速投球 ➲ SEE ALSO FAST LANE

• **WATCH/CLOCK** 钟表 **5** [not before noun] showing a time later than the true time 走得快: *I'm early—my watch must be fast.* 我早了，我的表肯定快了。◇ *That clock's ten minutes fast.* 那座钟快十分钟。

• **PHOTOGRAPHIC FILM** 照相胶片 **6** (*specialist*) very sensitive to light, and therefore useful when taking photographs in poor light or of sth that is moving very quickly 感光快的

• **FIRMLY FIXED** 牢牢固定 **7** (of a boat, etc. 船等) firmly fixed and safe 系牢的；稳固的: *He* ***made*** *the boat* ***fast.*** 他把船系牢了。

• **COLOURS IN CLOTHES** 衣服颜色 **8** not likely to change or to come out when washed 不退色的 **HELP** There is no noun related to **fast**. Use **speed** in connection with vehicles, actions, etc.; **quickness** is used about thinking. * fast 没有派生的名词。关于交通工具、行动等的速度用 speed，关于思维则用 quickness。

IDM **fast and 'furious** (of films/movies, shows, etc. 电影、演出等) full of rapid action and sudden changes 情节节奏快且变化多端: *In his latest movie, the action is fast and furious.* 在他的最新电影中，情节起伏跌宕。➲ MORE LIKE THIS 13, page R26 **a fast 'talker** a person who can talk very quickly and easily, but who cannot always be trusted 快嘴快舌但不可信赖的人 **a fast 'worker** (*informal*) a person who knows how to get what they want quickly, especially when beginning a sexual relationship with sb 善于迅速达到目的的人；（尤指恋爱方面）善于一下子获得青睐的人 ➲ MORE AT BUCK *n.*, DRAW *n.*, HARD *adj.*, PULL *v.*

■ ***adv.*** (**fast·er, fast·est**)

• **QUICKLY** 快速 **1** quickly 快；快速；迅速: *Don't drive so fast!* 别把车开得这么快！◇ *How fast were you going?* 当时你们走得有多快？◇ *I can't go any faster.* 我不能走得更快了。◇ *The water was rising fast.* 水迅猛上涨。◇ *Her heart beat faster.* 她的心跳加快。◇ (*formal*) *Night was fast approaching.* 黑夜迅速降临。◇ *a fast-flowing stream* 湍急的溪流 ➲ NOTE AT QUICK **2** in a short time; without delay 不久；立即: *Children grow up so fast these days.* 如今孩子们长得真快。◇ *Britain is* ***fast becoming*** *a nation of fatties.* 英国不久就要变成一个胖子国了。◇ *The police said that they had reacted as fast as they could.* 警方说他们已尽快作出了反应。

• **FIRMLY** 牢固 **3** firmly; completely 牢固地；完全地: *Within a few minutes she was* ***fast asleep*** (= sleeping deeply). 几分钟后她就沉睡了。◇ *The boat was* ***stuck fast*** (= unable to move) *in the mud.* 船深陷在淤泥里动弹不得。**HELP** There is no noun related to **fast**. Use **speed** in connection with vehicles, actions, etc.; **quickness** is used about thinking. * fast 没有派生的名词。关于交通工具、行

▼ **COLLOCATIONS** 词语搭配

Clothes and fashion 服装与时尚

Clothes 衣服

- **be wearing** a new outfit/bright colours/fancy dress/fur/uniform 穿着一身新衣裳 / 鲜艳的服装 / 化装舞会服 / 毛皮衣服 / 制服
- **be** (**dressed**) **in** black/red/jeans and a T-shirt/your best suit/leather/silk/rags (= very old torn clothes) 穿着黑色衣服 / 红色衣服 / 牛仔裤和 T 恤 / 最好的西服 / 皮衣 / 丝绸衣服 / 破衣烂衫
- **be dressed for** work/school/dinner/a special occasion 穿好衣服准备上班 / 上学 / 赴晚宴 / 出席特殊场合
- **be dressed as** a man/woman/clown/pirate 打扮成男人 / 女人 / 小丑 / 海盗
- **wear/dress in** casual/designer/second-hand clothes 穿休闲服 / 名牌服装 / 二手衣服
- **wear** jewellery/(*especially US*) jewelry/accessories/a watch/glasses/contact lenses/perfume 佩戴珠宝首饰 / 饰品 / 手表 / 眼镜 / 隐形眼镜；喷香水
- **have** a cowboy hat/red dress/blue suit **on** 戴着牛仔帽；穿着红色连衣裙 / 蓝色西服
- **put on/take off** your clothes/coat/shoes/helmet 穿上 / 脱下衣服 / 外套 / 鞋子；戴上 / 取下头盔
- **pull on/pull off** your coat/gloves/socks 穿上 / 脱下外套；戴上 / 脱下手套；穿上 / 脱下袜子
- **change into/get changed into** a pair of jeans/your pyjamas/(*especially US*) your pajamas 换上牛仔裤 / 睡衣

Appearance 外貌

- **change/enhance/improve** your appearance 改变 / 提升 / 改善形象
- **create/get/have/give sth** a new/contemporary/retro look 塑造 / 获得 / 拥有 / 给某物以新的 / 现代的 / 复古的外貌
- **brush/comb/shampoo/wash/blow-dry** your hair 梳 / 用洗发剂洗 / 洗 / 吹头发
- **have/get** a haircut/your hair cut/a new hairstyle 理发；换一个新发型
- **have/get** a piercing/your nose pierced 穿孔；穿鼻孔
- **have/get** a tattoo/a tattoo done (on your arm)/a tattoo removed 有纹身；在（胳膊上）刺花纹；去除纹身
- **have/get** a makeover/cosmetic surgery 做整容手术
- **use/wear/apply/put on** make-up/cosmetics 使用化妆品；化妆

Fashion 时尚

- **follow/keep up with** (the) fashion/the latest fashions 追求时尚；赶时髦
- **spend/waste money on** designer clothes 把钱花在 / 浪费在名牌服装上
- **be** fashionably/stylishly/well **dressed** 衣着时尚 / 新潮 / 考究
- **have** good/great/terrible/awful **taste** in clothes 着装很有品味 / 品味很差
- **update/revamp** your wardrobe 更新服装
- **be in/come into/go out of** fashion 流行；开始流行；不再流行
- **be** (**back/very much**) in vogue （又开始 / 非常）流行
- **create** a style/trend/vogue for sth 为…创造了一种风格 / 趋势 / 潮流
- **organize/put on** a fashion show 策划 / 举办时装秀
- **show/unveil** a designer's spring/summer collection 展示 / 首次推出一位设计师的春 / 夏装系列
- **sashay/strut** down the catwalk/(*NAmE also*) runway 走 T 型台
- **be on/do** a photo/fashion shoot 做专业摄影 / 时装摄影

动等的速度用 speed；关于思维则用 quickness。

IDM **as fast as your ˌlegs can ˈcarry you** as quickly as you can 尽快 **hold ˈfast to sth** (*formal*) to continue to believe in an idea, etc. despite difficulties 坚持（某种思想等）**play fast and ˈloose (with sb/sth)** (*old-fashioned*) to treat sb/sth in a way that shows that you feel no responsibility or respect for them 反复无常；若即若离；玩弄 **stand ˈfast/ˈfirm** to refuse to move back; to refuse to change your opinions 坚定不移；不让步；不改变主张 ➲ MORE AT THICK *adv.*

■ ***verb*** [I] to eat little or no food for a period of time, especially for religious or health reasons（因宗教或健康原因）节食，禁食，斋戒：*Muslims fast during Ramadan.* 伊斯兰教徒在斋月期间斋戒。

■ ***noun*** a period during which you do not eat food, especially for religious or health reasons 禁食期；斋戒期：*to go on a fast* 开始禁食 ◇ *to break* (= end) *your fast* 开斋

▼ WHICH WORD? 词语辨析

fast / quick / rapid

These adjectives are frequently used with the following nouns. 这些形容词常与下列名词连用：

fast ~	quick ~	rapid ~
car	glance	change
train	look	growth
bowler	reply	increase
pace	decision	decline
lane	way	progress

- **Fast** is used especially to describe a person or thing that moves or is able to move at great speed. * fast 尤用以描述高速运动的人或事物。
- **Quick** is more often used to describe something that is done in a short time or without delay. * quick 较常用以描述迅速或立即完成的事。
- **Rapid**, **swift** and **speedy** are more formal words. * rapid、swift 和 speedy 较正式。
- **Rapid** is most commonly used to describe the speed at which something changes. It is not used to describe the speed at which something moves or is done. * rapid 最常用于描述事物变化的速度，而非运动或完成的速度：~~*a rapid train*~~ ◇ ~~*We had a rapid coffee.*~~
- **Swift** usually describes something that happens or is done quickly and immediately. * swift 通常指事物发生或完成的速度快而及时：*a swift decision* 迅即作出的决定 ◇ *The government took swift action.* 政府立即采取了行动。
- **Speedy** has a similar meaning. * speedy 与 swift 意思相近：*a speedy recovery* 迅速康复 It is used less often to talk about the speed at which something moves. 该词较少指事物运动速度快：~~*a speedy car*~~
- For the use of **fast** and **quick** as adverbs, ➲ NOTE AT QUICK. 关于 fast 和 quick 作副词的用法，见词条 quick 的用法说明。

fast·ball /ˈfɑːstbɔːl; *NAmE* ˈfæst-/ *noun* (in BASEBALL 棒球) a ball that is thrown at the PITCHER'S fastest speed（投手投出的）快速球

ˌfast ˈbowler (*also* **ˌpace ˈbowler, pace·man**) *noun* (in CRICKET 板球) a person who BOWLS very fast 快速球投手

ˌfast ˈbreeder (*also* **ˌfast ˌbreeder reˈactor**) *noun* a REACTOR in a nuclear power station in which the reaction that produces energy is not made slower 快堆；快中子增殖反应堆

fas·ten 🔑 /ˈfɑːsn; *NAmE* ˈfæsn/ *verb* **1** 🔑 [T, I] to close or join together the two parts of sth; to become closed or joined together（使两部分）系牢，扎牢，结牢，扣紧 SYN **do up**：**~ sth** *Fasten your seat belts, please.* 请系好安全带。◇ **~ sth up** *He fastened up his coat and hurried out.* 他扣好大衣就匆匆出去了。◇ **~ (up)** *The dress fastens at the back.* 这件连衣裙是在后背系扣的。OPP **unfasten** **2** 🔑 [T, I] **~ (sth)** to close sth firmly so that it will not open; to be closed in this way（使）关紧，盖好：*Fasten the gates securely so that they do not blow open.* 把大门闩好以免被风吹开。◇ *The window wouldn't fasten.* 这扇窗子关不严。OPP **unfasten** **3** 🔑 [T] **~ sth + adv./prep.** to fix or place sth in a particular position, so that it will not move 使牢固；使固定：*He fastened back the shutters.* 他把活动护窗拉开系紧。**4** 🔑 [T] **~ A to B | ~ A and B (together)** to attach or tie one thing to another thing（使两物）系牢，扎牢，结牢，扣牢：*He fastened the papers together with a paper clip.* 他用回形针别好了文件。**5** [T, I] if you **fasten** your arms around sb, your teeth into sth, etc., or if your arms, teeth, etc. **fasten** around, into, etc. sb/sth, you hold the person/thing firmly with your arms, etc. 握住；抓牢；咬住：**~ sth + adv./prep.** *The dog fastened its teeth in his leg.* 狗死死咬着他的腿。◇ **+ adv./prep.** *His hand fastened on her arm.* 他用手牢牢抓住她的胳膊。**6** [T, I] **~ (sth) (on sb/sth)** if you **fasten** your eyes on sb/sth or your eyes **fasten** on sb/sth, you look at them for a long time 盯住：*He fastened his gaze on her face.* 他盯着她的脸。➲ MORE LIKE THIS 20, page R27

PHR V **ˈfasten on(to) sb/sth** to choose or follow sb/sth in a determined way 抓住；对…锲而不舍；坚决跟随；纠缠 SYN **latch on(to)**

fas·ten·er /ˈfɑːsnə(r); *NAmE* ˈfæs-/ (*also* **fas·ten·ing**) *noun* a device, such as a button or a ZIP/ZIPPER, used to close a piece of clothing; a device used to close a window, suitcase, etc. tightly 纽扣；拉链；扣件 ➲ VISUAL VOCAB PAGE V68

fas·ten·ing /ˈfɑːsnɪŋ; *NAmE* ˈfæs-/ *noun* **1** = FASTENER **2** the place where sth, especially a piece of clothing, fastens; the way sth fastens（尤指衣服的）扣处，扣法：*The trousers have a fly fastening.* 这条裤子是前开口的。

ˌfast ˈfood *noun* [U] hot food, such as HAMBURGERS and chips/fries, that is served very quickly and can be taken away to be eaten in the street 快餐；速食：*fast-food restaurants* 快餐店 ➲ COMPARE SLOW FOOD

ˌfast-ˈforward *verb* **1** [T, I] **~ (sth)** to move a recording forwards to a later point without playing it（使录音或录像）快进 **2** [I] **~ to sth | + adv./prep.** to move quickly forwards in time, especially to a later point in a story（尤指故事情节）迅速进入：*The action then fast-forwards to Ettore as a young man.* 情节很快发展到埃多勒的青年时代。▶ **ˌfast ˈforward** *noun* [U]: *Press fast forward to advance the tape.* 按下快进键向前转带子。◇ *the fast-forward button* 快进按钮

fas·tidi·ous /fæˈstɪdiəs/ *adj.* **1** being careful that every detail of sth is correct 一丝不苟的；严谨的 SYN **meticulous**：*Everything was planned in fastidious detail.* 样样都一丝不苟地计划好了。◇ *He was fastidious in his preparation for the big day.* 他认真仔细地准备着这个盛大的日子。**2** (*sometimes disapproving*) not liking things to be dirty or untidy 讲究整洁的；有洁癖的：*She wasn't very fastidious about personal hygiene.* 她不过分讲究个人卫生。▶ **fas·tidi·ous·ly** *adv.* **fas·tidi·ous·ness** *noun* [U]

ˈfast lane *noun* [sing.] the part of a major road such as a MOTORWAY or INTERSTATE where vehicles drive fastest（高速公路或州际公路上的）快车道

IDM **in the ˈfast lane** where things are most exciting and where a lot is happening 在生活的快车道上；享受丰富多彩的生活：*He had a good job, plenty of money and he was enjoying life in the fast lane.* 他有份好工作，钱又多，尽情享受着丰富多彩的生活。

fast·ness /ˈfɑːstnəs; *NAmE* ˈfæs-/ *noun* (*literary*) a place that is thought to be safe because it is difficult to get to or easy to defend 要塞；堡垒 SYN **stronghold**

ˈfast track *noun* [sing.] a quick way to achieve sth, for example a high position in a job 快速晋升之道；迅速成功

之路 ▶ ˈ**fast-track** *adj.*: *the fast-track route to promotion* 快速晋升之道 ◇ *fast-track graduates* 快速获得学位者

ˈ**fast-track** *verb* **~ sb/sth** to make sb's progress in achieving sth, for example a high position in a job, quicker than usual 加速…的进程

fat /fæt/ *adj., noun*

WORD FAMILY
fat *adj.*
fatty *adj.*
fatten *verb*
fattening *adj.*

■ ***adj.*** (**fat·ter**, **fat·test**) **1** (of a person's or an animal's body 人或动物的身体) having too much flesh on it and weighing too much 肥的；肥胖的：*a big fat man/woman* 大胖男人/女人 ◇ *You'll* ***get fat*** *if you eat so much chocolate.* 你如果吃这么多巧克力是会发胖的。◇ *He grew fatter and fatter.* 他愈来愈胖了。◇ *fat flabby legs* 肥胖松弛的双腿 OPP **thin** **2** thick or wide 厚的；宽大的：*a fat volume on American history* 厚厚的一册美国史 **3** [only before noun] (*informal*) large in quantity; worth a lot of money 大量的；值钱的：*a* ***fat sum/profit*** 一大笔款子；丰厚的利润 ◇ *He gave me a nice fat cheque.* 他给了我一张大额支票。 ⇨ MORE LIKE THIS 35, page R29 ▶ **fat·ness** *noun* [U]: *Fatness tends to run in families.* 肥胖往往有遗传性。

IDM (**a**) **fat ˈchance** (**of sth/doing sth**) (*informal*) used for saying that you do not believe sth is likely to happen 不大可能发生：*'They might let us in without tickets.' 'Fat chance of that!'* "他们也许会让我们免票入场。""别痴心妄想了！" **a fat lot of good, use, etc.** (*informal*) not at all good or useful 差极了；毫无用处：*Paul can't drive so he was a fat lot of use when I broke my arm.* 保罗不会开车，所以我手臂骨折时他一点忙也没帮上。 **it's not ˌover until the fat lady ˈsings** (*saying*) used for saying that a situation may still change, for example that a contest, election, etc. is not finished yet, and sb still has a chance to win it 最后才能见输赢；不到最后，结果难料

■ ***noun*** **1** [U] a white or yellow substance in the bodies of animals and humans, stored under the skin 脂肪；肥肉：*excess body fat* 多余的体内脂肪 ◇ *This ham has too much fat on it.* 这块火腿肥肉太多。 ⇨ COLLOCATIONS AT DIET **2** [C, U] a solid or liquid substance from animals or plants, treated so that it becomes pure for use in cooking（烹调用的）动植物油：*Cook the meat in shallow fat.* 用少许油煎肉。 **3** [C, U] animal and vegetable fats, when you are thinking of them as part of what a person eats （人体摄入的动植物）脂肪：*You should cut down on fats and carbohydrates.* 你应该减少摄入脂肪和碳水化合物。◇ *foods which are* ***low in fat*** 低脂肪食物 ◇ *reduced-fat margarines* 低脂人造黄油 IDM SEE CHEW *v.*, LIVE[1]

▼ VOCABULARY BUILDING 词汇扩充

Saying that somebody is fat 形容人肥胖

- **Fat** is the most common and direct word, but it is not polite to say to someone that they are fat. * fat 最常用，意思最直接，但当面说某人 fat 不礼貌：*Does this dress make me look fat?* 我穿这连衣裙显胖吗？◇ ~~*You're looking fat now.*~~
- **Overweight** is a more neutral word. * overweight 是比较中性的词：*I'm a bit overweight.* 我有点超重。 It can also mean too fat, especially so that you are not fit. 这词亦含过胖之义，尤指身体不健康。
- **Large** or **heavy** is less offensive than **fat**. 与 fat 相比，large 或 heavy 含冒犯意较少：*She's a rather large woman.* 她是个大块头。 **Big** describes someone who is tall as well as fat. * big 指人又高又胖：*Her sister is a big girl, isn't she?* 她姐姐块头挺大的，是吗？
- **Plump** means slightly fat in an attractive way, often used to describe women. * plump 常用于形容女性丰满。
- **Chubby** is used mainly to describe babies and children who are fat in a pleasant, healthy-looking way. * chubby 主要用以形容婴儿和孩子健康可爱、胖乎乎的样子：*the baby's chubby cheeks* 婴儿胖乎乎的脸蛋
- **Tubby** (*informal*) is used in a friendly way to describe people who are short and round, especially around the stomach. * tubby（非正式）用于善意地描述矮胖的人，尤指肚子圆滚滚的。
- **Stocky** is a neutral word and means fairly short, broad and strong. * stocky 是中性词，意为矮壮。
- **Stout** is often used to describe older people who have a round and heavy appearance. * stout 常用以描述圆胖壮实的较年长者：*a short stout man with a bald head* 一个矮壮秃顶男人
- **Flabby** describes flesh that is fat and loose. * flabby 指肌肉肥胖松弛，有冒犯意：*exercises to firm up flabby thighs* 使大腿松弛肌肉结实的锻炼
- **Obese** is used by doctors to describe people who are so fat that they are unhealthy. It is also used in a general way to mean 'really fat'. * obese 是医学用语，指患肥胖症，亦可泛指十分肥胖。

Note that although people talk a lot about their own size or weight, it is generally not considered polite to refer to a person's large size or their weight when you talk to them. 注意：虽然人们常谈论自己的身材和体重，但一般认为与人谈话时提及对方的胖大身材或体重是不礼貌的。

⇨ NOTE AT THIN

fatal /ˈfeɪtl/ *adj.* **1** causing or ending in death 致命的：*a* ***fatal accident/blow/illness*** 致命的事故/一击/疾病 ◇ *a* ***potentially fatal*** *form of cancer* 潜在致死型癌症 ◇ *If she gets ill again it could* ***prove fatal.*** 如果她再患病，就会有性命之忧。 ⇨ COMPARE MORTAL *adj.* (2) **2** causing disaster or failure 灾难性的；毁灭性的；导致失败的：*a* ***fatal error/mistake*** 灾难性的错误 ◇ *Any delay would be fatal.* 任何延误都可能导致失败。◇ *There was a* ***fatal flaw*** *in the plan.* 计划中有一个致命的缺陷。◇ *It'd be fatal to try and stop them now.* 现在要试图制止他们就会导致灾难性后果。 ▶ **fa·tal·ly** /-təli/ *adv.*: ***fatally injured/wounded*** 受致命伤 ◇ *The plan was* ***fatally flawed*** *from the start.* 这个计划一开始就有致命的缺陷。

fa·tal·ism /ˈfeɪtəlɪzəm/ *noun* [U] the belief that events are decided by FATE and that you cannot control them; the fact of accepting that you cannot prevent sth from happening 宿命论 ▶ **fa·tal·ist** *noun*: *I'm a fatalist.* 我是宿命论者。

fa·tal·is·tic /ˌfeɪtəˈlɪstɪk/ *adj.* showing a belief in FATE and feeling that you cannot control events or stop them from happening 宿命论的；听天由命的 ▶ **fa·tal·is·tic·al·ly** /ˌfeɪtəˈlɪstɪkəli/ *adv.*

fa·tal·ity /fəˈtæləti/ *noun* (*pl.* **-ies**) **1** [C] a death that is caused in an accident or a war, or by violence or disease（事故、战争、疾病等中的）死亡：*Several people were injured, but there were no fatalities.* 有几个人受伤，但没有人死亡。 **2** [U] the fact that a particular disease will result in death （疾病的）致命性：*to reduce the fatality of certain types of cancer* 降低某些癌症的致命性 ◇ *Different forms of cancer have different fatality rates.* 不同类型的癌症死亡率也不同。 **3** [U] the belief or feeling that we have no control over what happens to us 宿命；听天由命；天数：*A sense of fatality gripped her.* 一种命中注定的意识控制着她。

ˈ**fat camp** *noun* [U, C] an organized holiday/vacation for fat children during which they are helped to lose weight 儿童减肥假期训练营

ˈ**fat cat** *noun* (*informal, disapproving*) a person who earns, or who has, a lot of money (especially when compared to people who do not earn so much) 大亨；阔佬

fate /feɪt/ *noun* **1** [C] the things, especially bad things, that will happen or have happened to sb/sth 命中注定的事（尤指坏事）；命运的安排：***The fate of*** *the three men is unknown.* 这三个人命运未卜。◇ *She sat outside, waiting to find out her fate.* 她坐在外面，等待命运对她作出的安排。◇ *The court will* ***decide our fate/fates.*** 法庭将决定我们的命运。◇ *Each of the managers* ***suffered the same fate.*** 每一个经理命运都是如此。◇ *The government had* ***abandoned*** *the refugees* ***to their fate.*** 政府抛弃了难民，让他们听天由命。◇ *From that moment* ***our fate was sealed*** (= our future was decided). 从那时起我们的命运就已经注定了。

2 [U] the power that is believed to control everything that happens and that cannot be stopped or changed 命运；天数；定数；天意：*Fate was kind to me that day.* 那天我很幸运。◇ *By a strange* ***twist of fate****, Andy and I were on the same plane.* 由于命运的奇特安排，我和安迪乘坐了同一架飞机。➲ SYNONYMS AT LUCK ➲ WORDFINDER NOTE AT LUCK

IDM **a fate worse than 'death** (*often humorous*) a terrible thing that could happen（可能发生的）极可怕的事 ➲ MORE AT TEMPT

fated /ˈfeɪtɪd/ *adj.* **1** ~ (**to do sth**) unable to escape a particular fate; certain to happen because everything is controlled by fate 命中注定的；命运决定的 SYN **destined**: *We were fated never to meet again.* 我们注定了永远不能再相见。◇ *He believes that everything in life is fated.* 他相信生命中的一切都是注定的。 **2** = ILL-FATED

fate·ful /ˈfeɪtfl/ *adj.* [usually before noun] having an important, often very bad, effect on future events 对未来有重大（负面）影响的：*She looked back now to* ***that fateful day*** *in December.* 她现在回顾十二月里那决定性的一天。

ˌfat 'finger *noun* [U, sing.] (*informal*) used to refer to mistakes that are made when typing, usually because one finger hits two keys at the same time "胖手指"，打字错误（通常因一指同时击两键造成）：*The data was all wrong—it must have been a case of fat finger!* 数据全错了 —— 这一定是"胖手指"造成的！◇ *The document was full of fat-finger mistakes.* 文件中打字错误比比皆是。 ▶ **'fat-finger** *verb* **~ sth**: *I couldn't enter the site because I kept fat-fingering my password.* 我无法进入网站，因为我老是输错密码。 **'fat-fingered** *adj.*

ˌfat-'free *adj.* not containing any fat 不含脂肪的：*fat-free yogurt* 脱脂酸奶

father /ˈfɑːðə(r)/ *noun, verb*

■ ***noun*** **1** a male parent of a child or an animal; a person who is acting as the father to a child 父亲；爸爸：*Ben's a wonderful father.* 本是个极好的父亲。◇ *You've been* ***like a father*** *to me.* 你对我一直像父亲一样。◇ *Our new boss is a* ***father of three*** (= he has three children). 我们的新老板是三个孩子的父亲。◇ *He was a wonderful father to both his natural and adopted children.* 他对亲生的和领养的子女都很好。◇ (*old-fashioned*) *Father, I cannot lie to you.* 爸爸，我不能对你说谎。➲ SEE ALSO GODFATHER, GRANDFATHER, STEPFATHER **2 fathers** [pl.] (*literary*) a person's ANCESTORS (= people who are related to you who lived in the past) 祖先：*the land of our fathers* 我们祖先的土地 ➲ SEE ALSO FOREFATHER **3** ~ (**of sth**) the first man to introduce a new way of thinking about sth or of doing sth 创始人；奠基者；先驱；鼻祖：*Henry Moore is considered to be the father of modern British sculpture.* 亨利·穆尔被认为是现代英国雕塑之父。 ➲ SEE ALSO FOUNDING FATHER **4 Father** used by Christians to refer to God 天父；上帝：*Father, forgive us.* 天父，宽恕我们吧。◇ *God the Father* 天父 **5 Father** (*abbr.* **Fr**) the title of a priest, especially in the Roman Catholic Church and the Orthodox Church（尤指天主教和东正教的）神父：*Father Dominic* 多米尼克神父 ➲ SEE ALSO HOLY FATHER

IDM **from ˌfather to 'son** from one generation of a family to the next 从父到子；世代相传 **like ˌfather, like 'son** (*saying*) used to say that a son's character or behaviour is similar to that of his father 有其父必有其子 ➲ MORE AT OLD, WISH *n.*

■ ***verb*** **1 ~ sb** to become the father of a child by making a woman pregnant 成为父亲；做父亲：*He claims to have fathered over 20 children.* 他声称有 20 多个亲生子女。 **2 ~ sth** to create new ideas or a new way of doing sth 创立（新思想）；创造，发明（新方法）

ˌFather 'Christmas *noun* (*BrE*) = SANTA CLAUS

'father figure *noun* an older man that sb respects because he will advise and help them like a father 父亲般的人；受尊敬的人；长者

father·hood /ˈfɑːðəhʊd; *NAmE* -ðərhʊd/ *noun* [U] the state of being a father 父亲的地位（或身份）

'father-in-law *noun* (*pl.* **fathers-in-law**) the father of your husband or wife 岳父；外父；公公 ➲ COMPARE MOTHER-IN-LAW

father·land /ˈfɑːðəlænd; *NAmE* -ðərlænd/ *noun* [usually sing.] (*old-fashioned*) (used especially about Germany) the country where a person, or their family, was born, especially when they feel very loyal towards it 祖国（尤用以指德国）

father·less /ˈfɑːðələs; *NAmE* -ðərləs/ *adj.* [usually before noun] without a father, either because he has died or because he does not live with his children 没有父亲的：***fatherless children/families*** 没有父亲的孩子 / 家庭

father·ly /ˈfɑːðəli; *NAmE* -ðərli/ *adj.* typical of a good father 父亲的；慈父般的：*fatherly advice* 慈父般的忠告 ◇ *He keeps a fatherly eye on his players.* 他像父亲一样照管着他的球员。

'Father's Day *noun* a day when fathers receive cards and gifts from their children, usually the third Sunday in June 父亲节（通常为六月的第三个星期日）

ˌFather 'Time *noun* an imaginary figure who represents time and looks like an old man carrying a SCYTHE and an HOURGLASS 时间老人（手拿镰刀和沙漏、象征时间的虚构人物）

fathom /ˈfæðəm/ *verb, noun*

■ ***verb*** to understand or find an explanation for sth 理解；彻底了解；弄清真相：**~ sb/sth (out)** *It is hard to fathom the pain felt at the death of a child.* 丧子之痛是难以体会的。◇ **~ (out) what, where, etc.…** *He couldn't fathom out what the man could possibly mean.* 他弄不清这个男人的意思。

■ ***noun*** a unit for measuring the depth of water, equal to 6 feet or 1.8 metres 英寻（计量水深的单位，合 6 英尺或 1.8 米）：*The ship sank in 20 fathoms.* 船沉在水下 20 英寻处。◇ (*figurative*) *She kept her feelings hidden fathoms deep.* 她把感情深深地隐藏在心中。

fa·tigue /fəˈtiːɡ/ *noun* **1** [U] a feeling of being extremely tired, usually because of hard work or exercise 极度疲劳；极度劳累 SYN **exhaustion, tiredness**: *physical and mental fatigue* 精疲力竭 ◇ *Driver fatigue was to blame for the accident.* 这个事故是驾驶员疲劳所致。◇ *I was dropping with fatigue and could not keep my eyes open.* 我快要累倒了，眼睛也睁不开了。 **2** [U] (usually after another noun 通常置于另一名词后) a feeling of not wanting to do a particular activity any longer because you have done too much of it 厌倦：*battle fatigue* 战斗疲劳 **3** [U] weakness in metal or wood caused by repeated bending or stretching（金属或木材的）疲劳：*The wing of the plane showed signs of* ***metal fatigue****.* 机翼显示出金属疲劳的迹象。 **4 fatigues** [pl.] loose clothes worn by soldiers（士兵穿的）工作服 **5 fatigues** [pl.] (*especially NAmE*) duties, such as cleaning and cooking, that soldiers have to do, especially as a punishment 士兵杂役（尤指作为惩罚，如做打扫、帮厨）

fa·tigued /fəˈtiːɡd/ *adj.* [not usually before noun] (*formal*) very tired, both physically and mentally 身心交瘁；精疲力竭 SYN **exhausted**

fa·tiguing /fəˈtiːɡɪŋ/ *adj.* (*formal*) very tiring, both physically and mentally 令人身心交瘁的；劳心劳力的 SYN **exhausting**

fatso /ˈfætsəʊ; *NAmE* -soʊ/ *noun* (*pl.* **-oes**) = FATTY

fat·ten /ˈfætn/ *verb* [T, I] **~ (sb/sth) (up)** to make sb/sth fatter, especially an animal before killing it for food; to become fatter（使）长胖，长肥；（尤指动物宰杀前）育肥：*The piglets are taken from the sow to be fattened for market.* 这些小猪被从母猪身边带走，好育肥上市。◇ *She's very thin after her illness—but we'll soon fatten her up.* 她病后瘦得很，不过我们会使她迅速胖起来的。

fat·ten·ing /ˈfætnɪŋ/ *adj.* (of food 食物) likely to make you fat 要使人发胖的：*fattening cakes* 吃了会发胖的蛋糕 ➲ WORDFINDER NOTE AT EAT

fat·tism /ˈfætɪzəm/ *noun* [U] unfair treatment of people because of their large body size 胖人歧视 ▸ **fat·tist** *adj.*

fatty /ˈfæti/ *adj., noun*
■ ***adj.*** (**fat·tier**, **fat·ti·est**) containing a lot of fat; consisting of fat 富含脂肪的；肥胖的；脂肪的：*fatty foods* 高脂食物 ◇ *fatty tissue* 脂肪组织
■ ***noun*** (*pl.* **-ies**) (*also* **fatso**) (*informal, disapproving*) a fat person 胖子：*Britain is fast becoming a nation of fatties.* 英国很快就会变成胖子国。

ˌfatty ˈacid *noun* (*chemistry* 化) an acid that is found in fats and oils 脂肪酸

fatu·ous /ˈfætʃuəs/ *adj.* (*formal*) stupid 愚蠢的；愚昧的：*a fatuous comment/grin* 愚蠢的话语；龇牙咧嘴的傻笑 ▸ **fatu·ous·ly** *adv.*

fatwa /ˈfætwɑː/ *noun* a decision or order made under Islamic law 法特瓦（伊斯兰律法的裁决或教令）

fau·cet 🔑 /ˈfɔːsɪt/ (*NAmE*) (*especially BrE* **tap**) *noun* a device that controls the flow of water from a pipe 龙头；旋塞：*the **hot/cold faucet*** 热水 / 冷水龙头 ◇ *to **turn a faucet on/off*** 开 / 关龙头 ➲ PICTURE AT PLUG ➲ **VISUAL VOCAB** PAGES V25, V26

fault 🔑 /fɔːlt/ *noun, verb*
■ ***noun***
• **RESPONSIBILITY** 责任 **1** 🔑 [U] the responsibility for sth wrong that has happened or been done 责任；过错；过失：*Why should I say sorry when it's not **my fault**?* 不是我的错为什么要我道歉？◇ *It's nobody's fault.* 谁都没有错。◇ **~ (that...)** *It was **his fault** that we were late.* 我们迟到责任在他。◇ **~ (for doing sth)** *It's **your own fault** for being careless.* 你粗心大意是你自己的过失。◇ *Many people live in poverty **through no fault of their own**.* 很多人生活贫困并非他们自己有什么过错。◇ *I think the owners are **at fault** (= responsible) for not warning us.* 我认为业主没有提醒我们是有责任的。
• **IN SB'S CHARACTER** 人品 **2** 🔑 [C] a bad or weak aspect of sb's character 弱点；缺点 **SYN** **shortcoming**：*He's proud of his children and blind to their faults.* 他为孩子们感到自豪，对他们的缺点视而不见。◇ *I love her **for all her faults** (= in spite of them).* 尽管她有这么多缺点，我还是爱她。
• **STH WRONG** 错事 **3** 🔑 [C] something that is wrong or not perfect; something that is wrong with a machine or system that stops it from working correctly 缺陷；毛病；故障 **SYN** **defect**：*The book's virtues far outweigh its faults.* 这本书优点远远大于缺点。◇ *The system, **for all its faults**, is the best available at the moment.* 这个系统虽然缺点不少，却是现有最好的一个。◇ *a major fault in the design* 设计中的一个重大失误 ◇ *a structural fault* 结构缺陷 ◇ *an electrical fault* 电路故障
• **IN TENNIS** 网球 **4** [C] a mistake made when SERVING 发球失误：*He has served a number of **double faults** in this set.* 他在这盘发球出现了一些双误。
• **GEOLOGY** 地质 **5** [C] a place where there is a break that is longer than usual in the layers of rock in the earth's CRUST（地壳岩层的）断层：*the San Andreas fault* 圣安德烈亚斯断层 ◇ *a fault line* 断层线

IDM **to a ˈfault** used to say that sb has a lot, or even too much, of a particular good quality（良好品质）过分，过度：*She is generous to a fault.* 她过分慷慨。➲ MORE AT FIND *v.*

■ ***verb*** **~ sb/sth** (often used in negative sentences with *can* and *could* 常与 can 和 could 连用于否定句) to find a mistake or a weakness in sb/sth 发现错误；找出缺点 **SYN** **criticize**：*Her colleagues could not fault her dedication to the job.* 她的同事认为她的敬业精神是无可挑剔的。◇ *He had always been polite—she couldn't fault him on that.* 他总是彬彬有礼，在这方面她对他无可指摘。

ˈfault-finding *noun* [U] the act of looking for faults in sb/sth 找岔子；挑剔

fault·less /ˈfɔːltləs/ *adj.* having no mistakes 没有错误的；无缺点的；完美无缺的 **SYN** **perfect**：*faultless English* 完美的英语 ▸ **fault·less·ly** *adv.*

faulty /ˈfɔːlti/ *adj.* **1** not perfect; not working or made correctly 不完美的；有错误的；有缺陷的 **SYN** **defective**：*Ask for a refund if the goods are faulty.* 商品如有缺陷，可要求退款。◇ *faulty workmanship* 不完美的做工 ◇ *an accident caused by a faulty signal* 错误信号造成的事故 **2** (of a way of thinking 思想方法) wrong or containing mistakes, often resulting in bad decisions 错误的；有错误的：*faulty reasoning* 错误推理

faun /fɔːn/ *noun* (in ancient Roman stories) a god of the woods, with a man's face and body and a GOAT'S legs and horns 农牧神（见于古罗马故事，呈人面人身羊腿羊角）

fauna /ˈfɔːnə/ *noun* [U, C] all the animals living in an area or in a particular period of history（某地区或某时期的）动物群，动物区系：*the local **flora and fauna** (= plants and animals)* 当地动植物群 ◇ (*specialist*) *land and marine faunas* 陆地和海洋动物区系

Faust·ian /ˈfaʊstiən/ *adj.* (*formal*) **~ bargain/pact/agreement** an agreement in which sb agrees to do sth bad or dishonest, in return for money, success or power 浮士德式的（交易或协议）（为获得财富、成功或权力而不择手段）**ORIGIN** From **Faust**, who, according to the German legend, sold his soul to the Devil in return for many years of power and pleasure. 源自德国传说中的人物浮士德（Faust），他将灵魂出卖给了魔鬼，以换取多年的权力和享乐。

faute de mieux /ˌfəʊt də ˈmjɜː; *NAmE* ˌfoʊt/ *adv.* (*from French*) because there is nothing else that is better 因无更好的：*We were obliged, faute de mieux, to drink the local beverage.* 因为没有更好的饮料，我们只好将就着喝当地的。

Fauve /fəʊv; *NAmE* foʊv/ *noun* a member of a group of French painters who were important in Fauvism（法国）野兽派核心画家

Fauv·ism /ˈfəʊvɪzəm; *NAmE* ˈfoʊv-/ *noun* [U] (*art* 美术) a style of painting that uses bright colours and in which objects and people are represented in a non-realistic way. It was popular in Paris for a short period from 1905. 野兽派，野兽主义（一种绘画风格，以鲜明色彩和非现实主义方式表现物体和人物，从 1905 年起在巴黎流行一时）

faux /fəʊ; *NAmE* foʊ/ *adj.* artificial, but intended to look or seem real 人造的；仿制的：*The chairs were covered in faux animal skin.* 椅子套是人造兽皮的。◇ *His accent was so faux.* 他的口音听上去很假。

faux pas /ˌfəʊ ˈpɑː; *NAmE* ˌfoʊ/ *noun* (*pl.* **faux pas** /ˌfəʊ ˈpɑːz; *NAmE* ˌfoʊ/) (*from French*) an action or a remark that causes embarrassment because it is not socially correct 有失检点；失态；失礼；失言

fava bean /ˈfɑːvə biːn/ (*NAmE*) (*especially BrE* **ˌbroad ˈbean**) *noun* a type of round, pale green BEAN. Several fava beans grow together inside a fat POD. 蚕豆

fave /feɪv/ *noun* (*informal*) a favourite person or thing 特别喜爱的人（或事物）：*That song is one of my faves.* 这是我特别喜爱的歌曲之一。▸ **fave** *adj.* [only before noun]：*her fave TV show* 她特别喜爱的电视节目

fa·vela /fæˈvelə/ *noun* (*from Portuguese*) a poor area in or near a Brazilian city, with many small houses that are close together and in bad condition（巴西城市或边缘的）棚户区，贫民窟 ➲ COMPARE SHANTY TOWN

favi·con /ˈfævɪkɒn; *NAmE* ˈfevɪkɑːn; *BrE also* ˈfeɪv-/ *noun* an ICON (1) (= a small symbol) associated with a website, that usually appears in the line near the top of a page on an Internet BROWSER (1) where the address for that website is also displayed 网页图标，网站头像（通常出现在浏览器页面顶端的网址框）

fa·vour 🔑 (*especially US* **favor**) /ˈfeɪvə(r)/ *noun, verb*
■ ***noun***
• **HELP** 帮助 **1** 🔑 [C] a thing that you do to help sb 帮助；好事；恩惠：*Could you **do me a favour** and pick up Sam from school today?* 今天你能帮我个忙去学校接萨姆吗？◇ *Can I **ask a favour**?* 请帮个忙行吗？◇ *I would never ask for*

any favours from her. 我再也不会请她帮任何忙了。◇ *I'm going **as a favour** to Ann, not because I want to.* 我去是给安一个面子，而不是我想去。◇ *I'll ask Steve to take it. He **owes me a favour**.* 我要让史蒂夫接受，他欠我一个人情。◇ *Thanks for helping me out. I'll **return the favour*** (= help you because you have helped me) *some time.* 多谢你帮了我个大忙。总有一天我会报答你的。◇ ***Do yourself a favour*** (= help yourself) *and wear a helmet on the bike.* 要照顾自己，骑车戴上头盔。➲ EXPRESS YOURSELF AT PERMISSION

• **APPROVAL** 赞同 **2** 🔑 [U] approval or support for sb/sth 赞同；支持：*The suggestion to close the road has **found favour with*** (= been supported by) *local people.* 关闭这条路的建议已得到当地人的支持。◇ *The programme has **lost favour** with viewers recently.* 近来这个节目已不受观众欢迎。◇ *an athlete who **fell from favour** after a drugs scandal* 在毒品丑闻以后不再受人喜爱的运动员 ◇ (*formal*) *The government **looks with favour upon*** (= approves of) *the report's recommendations.* 政府赞同报告所提出的建议。◇ *She's not **in favour with*** (= supported or liked by) *the media just now.* 目前她没有媒体的捧场。◇ *It seems Tim is **back in favour** with the boss* (= the boss likes him again). 看来蒂姆又赢得了老板的好感。

• **BETTER TREATMENT** 优惠 **3** [U] treatment that is generous to one person or group in a way that seems unfair to others 特别照顾；偏袒；偏爱 **SYN** **bias**：*As an examiner, she showed no favour to any candidate.* 作为主考人她没有偏袒任何应试者。

• **PARTY GIFT** 聚会小礼物 **4 favors** [pl.] (*NAmE*) = PARTY FAVORS

• **SEX** 性 **5 favours** [pl.] (*old-fashioned*) agreement to have sex with sb 同意性交：*demands for sexual favours* 对性交的要求

IDM **do sb no 'favours** to do sth that is not helpful to sb or that gives a bad impression of them 无助于某人；给某人留下坏印象：*You're not doing yourself any favours, working for nothing.* 你干活不取报酬，对自己没有任何好处。◇ *The orchestra did Beethoven no favours.* 这个交响乐团没有把贝多芬的乐曲演奏好。 **do me a 'favour!** (*informal*) used in reply to a question that you think is silly（回答认为是愚蠢的问题）得了吧：*'Do you think they'll win?' 'Do me a favour! They haven't got a single decent player.'* "你认为他们会赢吗？" "得了吧！他们连一个像样的运动员都没有。" **in favour (of sb/sth) 1** 🔑 if you are **in favour** of sb/sth, you support and agree with them/it 赞同；支持：*He argued in favour of a strike.* 他据理力争主张罢工。◇ *There were 247 votes in favour (of the motion) and 152 against.* 有 247 票赞成（动议），152 票反对。◇ *I'm **all in favour of*** (= completely support) *equal pay for equal work.* 我完全支持同工同酬。◇ *Most of the 'don't knows' in the opinion polls **came down in favour of*** (= eventually chose to support) *the Democrats.* 在民意测验中多数未作决定的选民最终决定支持民主党人。**2** in exchange for another thing (because the other thing is better or you want it more) 为获得（更好或更需要的事物）：*He abandoned teaching in favour of a career as a musician.* 他弃教从事音乐。 **in sb's favour 1** if sth is **in sb's favour**, it gives them an advantage or helps them 有利于某人；有助于某人：*The exchange rate is in our favour at the moment.* 目前汇率对我们有利。◇ *She was willing to bend the rules in Mary's favour.* 她愿意放宽规定以有利于玛丽。**2** a decision or judgement that is **in sb's favour** benefits that person or says that they were right（决定）对某人有利；（判决）判某人正确 ➲ MORE AT CURRY *v.*, FEAR *n.*, STACKED

■ ***verb***

• **PREFER** 较喜欢 **1 ~ sth | ~ (sb) doing sth** to prefer one system, plan, way of doing sth, etc. to another 较喜欢；选择：*Many countries favour a presidential system of government.* 很多国家选择总统制政府。

• **TREAT BETTER** 优惠 **2 ~ sb** to treat sb better than you treat other people, especially in an unfair way 优惠；特别照顾；偏袒：*The treaty seems to favour the US.* 这项条约似乎偏向美国。

• **HELP** 帮助 **3 ~ sth** to provide suitable conditions for a particular person, group, etc. 有助于；有利于：*The warm climate favours many types of tropical plants.* 温暖的气候对多种热带植物生长有利。

• **LOOK LIKE PARENT** 外貌像父母 **4 ~ sb** (*old-fashioned* or *NAmE*) to look like one of your parents or older relations 外貌像，长得像（父母或长辈）：*She definitely favours her father.* 她酷似她父亲。

fa·vour·able (*especially US* **fa·vor·able**) /ˈfeɪvərəbl/ *adj.* **1** making people have a good opinion of sb/sth 给人好印象的：*She **made a favourable impression** on his parents.* 她给他的父母留下了好印象。◇ *The biography shows him in a favourable light.* 传记刻画出了他的正面形象。 **2** positive and showing your good opinion of sb/sth 肯定的；赞同的；支持的：*favourable comments* 好评 **3 ~ (to/for sb/sth)** good for sth and making it likely to be successful or have an advantage 有利的；有助于…的 **SYN** **advantageous**：*The terms of the agreement are favourable to both sides.* 协议条款对双方都有利。◇ *favourable economic conditions* 有利的经济环境 **4** fairly good and not too expensive 好而不贵的；优惠的：*They offered me a loan on very **favourable terms**.* 他们提出以十分优惠的条件贷款给我。 **OPP** **unfavourable** ▶ **fa·vour·abil·ity** (*especially US* **fa·vor·abil·ity**) /ˌfeɪvərəˈbɪləti/ *noun* [U] **fa·vour·ably** (*especially US* **fa·vor·ably**) /-əbli/ *adv.*：*He speaks very favourably of your work.* 他对你的工作十分赞赏。◇ *These figures compare favourably with last year's.* 这些数字比去年的要好。◇ *I was very favourably impressed with her work.* 她的工作给我留下了很好的印象。

fa·voured (*especially US* **favored**) /ˈfeɪvəd; *NAmE* -vərd/ *adj.* **1** treated in a special way or receiving special help or advantages in a way that may seem unfair 受到宠爱的；得到偏爱的；获得优惠的：*a member of the President's favoured circle of advisers* 总统宠爱的顾问班子中的一员 **2** preferred by most people 大众喜爱的：*the favoured candidate* 公众喜爱的候选人 **3** (*formal*) particularly pleasant and worth having 称心如意的；中意的：*Their house is in a very favoured position near the park.* 他们的房子在公园附近一个很惬意的地段。

fa·vour·ite 🔑 (*especially US* **fa·vor·ite**) /ˈfeɪvərɪt/ *adj.*, *noun*

■ ***adj.*** 🔑 liked more than others of the same kind 特别受喜爱的：*It's one of my favourite movies.* 这是我特别喜欢的电影之一。◇ *Who is your favourite writer?* 谁是你特别喜欢的作家？◇ *January is my least favourite month.* 一月是我最不喜欢的月份。➲ SYNONYMS AT CHOICE

IDM **sb's favourite 'son 1** a performer, politician, sports player, etc., who is popular where they were born 故乡的骄子（可指演员、政治家、运动员等） **2** (in the US) a candidate for president who is supported by his or her own state in the first part of a campaign（美国大选第一阶段）本州支持的总统候选人

■ ***noun* 1** 🔑 a person or thing that you like more than the others of the same type 特别喜爱的人（或事物）：*These biscuits are great favourites with the children.* 孩子们特别喜欢这种饼干。◇ *This song is a **particular favourite** of mine.* 我尤其喜爱这首歌曲。◇ *The band played all my **old favourites**.* 乐队演奏了所有我最喜欢的老曲子。◇ *Which one's your favourite?* 你最喜欢哪一个？◇ *The programme has become a **firm favourite** with young people.* 这个节目已着实赢得了年轻人的喜爱。 **2** 🔑 a person who is liked better by sb and receives better treatment than others 受宠的人；得到偏爱的人：*She loved all her grandchildren but Ann was her favourite.* 她爱所有的孙儿孙女，但最宠安。 **3** (*computing* 计) a record of a section of an APP or the address of a website that enables you to find it quickly（收藏应用程序或网址的）我的最爱，收藏夹：*Add the website as a favourite.* 将这个网站加到收藏夹。➲ COMPARE BOOKMARK (2) **4** the horse, runner, team, etc. that is expected to win（比赛中）被认为最有希望的获胜者：*The favourite came third.* 那个有望夺魁者得了第三名。◇ **~ (for sth)** *Her horse is the **hot favourite** for the race.* 她的马在这次赛马中夺魁的呼声最高。◇ **~ (to do sth)** *AC Milan, the hot favourites to win the Champions League* * AC 米兰队，欧洲冠军联赛的夺标大热门 **5** the person who is expected by most people to get a particular job or position（取得职位等的）最有希望者：**~ (for sth)** *She's the favourite for the job.* 她最有希望得到这份工作。◇ **~ (to do** sth) *She's the favourite to succeed him as leader.* 她最有希望接替他成为领导人。

fa·vour·it·ism (*especially US* **fa·vor·it·ism**) /ˈfeɪvərɪtɪzəm/ *noun* [U] (*disapproving*) the act of unfairly treating one person better than others because you like them better 偏爱；偏袒：*The students accused the teacher of favouritism.* 学生指责老师偏心。

fawn /fɔːn/ *adj., noun, verb*
■ ***adj.*** light yellowish-brown in colour 浅黄褐色的：*a fawn coat* 浅黄褐色外套
■ ***noun*** **1** [C] a DEER less than one year old（不足一岁的）幼鹿 **2** [U] a light yellowish-brown colour 浅黄褐色
■ ***verb*** [I] ~ (**on/over sb**) (*disapproving*) to try to please sb by praising them or paying them too much attention 恭维；讨好；巴结

fax /fæks/ *noun, verb*
■ ***noun*** (*also formal* **fac·sim·ile**) **1** (*also* **ˈfax machine**) [C] a machine that sends and receives documents in an electronic form along telephone wires and then prints them 传真机：*Do you have a fax?* 你有传真机吗？**2** [U] a system for sending documents using a fax machine 传真（系统）：*Can you send it to me* ***by fax****?* 你能用传真把它发给我吗？◇ *What is your fax number?* 你的传真号码是多少？ **3** [C] a letter or message sent by fax 传真信件；传真电文；明电：*Did you get my fax?* 你收到我的传真信件没有？◇ *You can send faxes by email from your computer.* 你可以通过计算机用电子邮件发送传真信件。 ➲ COLLOCATIONS AT PHONE
■ ***verb*** to send sb a document, message, etc. by fax 传真（文档、信件等）：**~ sb sth** *Could you fax me the latest version?* 你可不可以把最新版本传真给我？◇ **~ sth to sb** *Could you fax it to me?* 你能把它传真给我吗？◇ **~ sth** *I faxed the list of hotels through to them.* 我把旅馆名单传真给了他们。

faze /feɪz/ *verb* **~ sb** [often passive] (*informal*) to make you feel confused or shocked, so that you do not know what to do 使慌乱；使惊慌失措；使困窘 SYN **disconcert**：*She wasn't fazed by his comments.* 她并没有因他的话而惊慌失措。◇ *He looked as if nothing could faze him.* 他显得镇静自若，遇事不惊。

FBI /ˌef biː ˈaɪ/ *abbr.* Federal Bureau of Investigation (the police department in the US that is controlled by the national government and that is responsible for dealing with crimes that affect more than one state)（美国）联邦调查局

FC /ˌef ˈsiː/ *abbr.* (*BrE*) football club 足球俱乐部：*Liverpool FC* 利物浦足球俱乐部

FCE /ˌef siː ˈiː/ *noun* [U] the abbreviation for 'First Certificate in English' (a British test now called 'Cambridge English: First', that measures a person's ability to speak and write English as a foreign language at an UPPER-INTERMEDIATE level) 第一英语证书考试，剑桥英语第三级认证（全写为 First Certificate in English，现称 Cambridge English: First，英国考试，检测英语作为外语者的中高级口语和写作能力）

FCO /ˌef siː ˈəʊ; *NAmE* ˈoʊ/ *abbr.* FOREIGN AND COMMONWEALTH OFFICE 外交和联邦事务部

FDA /ˌef diː ˈeɪ/ *abbr.* Food and Drug Administration (the US government department that is responsible for making sure that food and drugs are safe to be sold)（美国）食品及药物管理局

FE /ˌef ˈiː/ *abbr.* (in Britain) FURTHER EDUCATION （英国）继续教育，进修教育

fealty /ˈfiːəlti/ *noun* [U] (*old use*) a promise to be loyal to sb, especially a king or queen （尤指对君主的）效忠宣誓

fear 🔑 /fɪə(r); *NAmE* fɪr/ *noun, verb*
■ ***noun*** 🔑 [U, C] the bad feeling that you have when you are in danger, when sth bad might happen, or when a particular thing frightens you 害怕；惧怕；担忧：*Her eyes showed no fear.* 她的眼神无丝毫畏惧。◇ *The child was shaking* ***with fear****.* 小孩吓得发抖。◇ ~ (**of sb/sth**) (*a*) ***fear of the dark/spiders/flying, etc.*** 害怕黑暗、蜘蛛、坐飞机等 ◇ *We lived* ***in constant fear of*** *losing our jobs.* 我们一直生活在担心失去工作的阴影里。◇ ~ (**for sb/sth**) *her fears for her son's safety* 她对儿子安全的担忧 ◇ *Alan spoke of his* ***fears for the future****.* 艾伦谈到了他对未来的担忧。◇ ~ (**that...**) *the fear that he had cancer* 他对患癌症的恐惧 ◇ *The doctor's report confirmed our worst fears.* 医生的报告证实了我们最大的担忧。

IDM **for fear of sth/of doing sth | for fear (that)...** to avoid the danger of sth happening 唯恐，以免（发生危险）：*We spoke quietly for fear of waking the guards.* 我们悄悄说话，以免惊醒警卫。◇ *I had to run away for fear (that) he might one day kill me.* 我只好逃走，生怕他有一天把我杀了。 **in ˌfear of your ˈlife** feeling frightened that you might be killed 害怕会丧生；为生命安全担忧 **ˌno ˈfear** (*BrE, informal*) used to say that you definitely do not want to do sth（表示决不愿做某事）绝不，当然不：*'Are you coming climbing?' 'No fear!'* "你来爬山吗？""当然不！" **put the fear of ˈGod into sb** to make sb very frightened, especially in order to make them do sth 恐吓；（尤指）威胁某人服从 **without fear or ˈfavour** (*formal*) in a fair way 公正地；不偏不倚 ➲ MORE AT FOOL *n.*, STRIKE *v.*

▼ **SYNONYMS** 同义词辨析

fear

terror • panic • alarm • fright

These are all words for the bad feeling you have when you are afraid. 以上各词均表示害怕时的恐慌情绪。

fear the bad feeling that you have when you are in danger, when sth bad might happen, or when a particular thing frightens you 指害怕、惧怕、担忧：*(a) fear of flying* 害怕坐飞机 ◇ *She showed no fear.* 她毫无惧色。

terror a feeling of extreme fear 指惊恐、恐惧、惊骇：*Her eyes were wild with terror.* 她的眼睛里充满了恐惧。

panic a sudden feeling of great fear that cannot be controlled and prevents you from thinking clearly 指惊恐、恐慌：*I had a sudden moment of panic.* 我突然一阵惊慌。

alarm fear or worry that sb feels when sth dangerous or unpleasant might happen 指惊恐、惊慌、恐慌：*The doctor said there was* ***no cause for alarm****.* 医生说不必惊慌。

fright a feeling of fear, usually sudden 通常指突如其来的惊吓、恐怖：*She cried out in fright.* 她吓得大声叫喊。

FEAR OR FRIGHT? 用 fear 还是 fright?
Fright is a reaction to sth that has just happened or is happening now. Use **fear**, but not **fright**, to talk about things that always frighten you and things that may happen in the future. * fright 指对刚刚发生或正在发生的事情的反应。对一直使人害怕的事物和对未来可能发生的事情感到担忧应该用 fear，而不能用 fright：~~*I have a fright of spiders.*~~ ◇ ~~*his fright of what might happen*~~

PATTERNS
- a fear/terror **of** sth
- **in** fear/terror/panic/alarm/fright
- fear/terror/panic/alarm **that...**
- to be **filled with** fear/terror/panic/alarm
- a **feeling of** fear/terror/panic/alarm

■ ***verb*** **1** 🔑 [T] to be frightened of sb/sth or frightened of doing sth 害怕；畏惧；惧怕：**~ sb/sth** *All his employees fear him.* 他的雇员都怕他。◇ *to fear death/persecution/the unknown* 怕死；害怕遭迫害 / 未知的事物 ◇ *Don't worry, you have* ***nothing to fear from*** *us.* 别担心，你一点也不必害怕我们。◇ **~ to do sth** (*formal*) *She feared to tell him the truth.* 她不敢把真相告诉他。◇ **~ doing sth** (*formal*) *She feared going out at night.* 她不敢晚上出去。 **2** 🔑 [T, I] to feel that sth bad might have happened or might happen in the future 担心；担忧：**~ sth** *She has been missing for* three days now and police are beginning to *fear the worst* (= think that she is dead). 现在她已经失踪三天了，警方担心发生了最坏的情况（认为她已死亡）。◇ **~ sb/sth + adj.** *Hundreds of people are feared dead.* 好几百人恐遭不测。◇ **be feared to be/have sth** *Women and children are feared to be among the victims.* 大家担心受害者中有妇女儿童。◇ **it is feared (that)...** *It is feared (that) he may have been kidnapped.* 人们担心他可能被绑架了。◇ **~ (that)...** *She feared (that) he might be dead.* 她担心他可能死了。◇ ***Never fear/Fear not*** (= Don't worry), *I shall return.* 别担心，我会回来的。**3 I fear** [I] (*formal*) used to tell sb that you think that sth bad has happened or is true（引出不好的事情）恐怕：*They are unlikely to get here on time, I fear.* 恐怕他们不大可能准时到达这里。◇ *'He must be dead then?' 'I fear so.'* "那么他肯定死了？" "恐怕是这样。" ◇ *'She's not coming back?' 'I fear not.'* "她不打算回来了？" "我想是的。"

PHR V **'fear for sb/sth** to be worried about sb/sth 为…担心（或担忧）：*We fear for his safety.* 我们担心他的安全。◇ *He feared for his mother, left alone on the farm.* 他为独自一人留在农场的母亲担忧。

fear·ful /ˈfɪəfl; *NAmE* ˈfɪrfl/ *adj.* **1** (*formal*) nervous and afraid 担心；担忧；忧虑：**~ (for sb)** *Parents are ever fearful for their children.* 父母总是为子女担忧。◇ **~ (of sth/of doing sth)** *fearful of an attack* 担心遭到袭击 ◇ **~ (that...)** *She was fearful that she would fail.* 她生怕失败。**2** [only before noun] (*formal*) terrible and frightening 可怕的；吓人的；恐惧的 **3** (*old-fashioned, informal*) extremely bad 极坏的；极糟的：*We made a fearful mess of the room.* 我们把房间弄得一团糟。▶ **fear·ful·ly** /-fəli/ *adv.*: *We watched fearfully.* 我们忧心忡忡地看着。◇ *fearfully* (= extremely) *expensive* 贵得吓人 **fear·ful·ness** *noun* [U]

fear·less /ˈfɪələs; *NAmE* ˈfɪrləs/ *adj.* (*approving*) not afraid, in a way that people admire 不怕的；无畏的；大胆的：*a fearless mountaineer* 无畏的登山运动员 ▶ **fear·less·ly** *adv.* **fear·less·ness** *noun* [U]

fear·some /ˈfɪəsəm; *NAmE* ˈfɪrsəm/ *adj.* (*formal*) making people feel very frightened 很可怕的；十分吓人的

feas·ible /ˈfiːzəbl/ *adj.* that is possible and likely to be achieved 可行的；行得通的 **SYN** **practicable**: *a feasible plan/suggestion/idea* 可行的计划 / 建议 / 想法 ◇ *It's just not feasible to manage the business on a part-time basis.* 兼职管理业务是搞不好的。**OPP** **unfeasible** ▶ **feasi·bil·ity** /ˌfiːzəˈbɪləti/ *noun* [U]: *a* ***feasibility study*** *on the proposed new airport* 关于建议中新机场的可行性研究 ◇ *I doubt the feasibility of the plan.* 我怀疑这个计划的可行性。

feast /fiːst/ *noun, verb*

■ ***noun*** **1** a large or special meal, especially for a lot of people and to celebrate sth 盛宴；宴会：*a wedding feast* 婚筵 **2** a day or period of time when there is a religious festival（宗教的）节日，节期：*the feast of Christmas* 圣诞佳节 ◇ *a feast day* 一个宗教节日 **3** [usually sing.] a thing or an event that brings great pleasure 使人欢快的事物（或活动）：*a feast of colours* 五彩缤纷 ◇ *The evening was a real feast for music lovers.* 这个晚会真是让音乐爱好者大饱耳福。

■ ***verb*** [I] **~ (on sth)** to eat a large amount of food, with great enjoyment 尽情享用（美味佳肴）

IDM **feast your 'eyes (on sb/sth)** to look at sb/sth and get great pleasure 尽情欣赏；大饱眼福；赏心悦目

ˌFeast of 'Tabernacles *noun* [U] = SUCCOTH

ˌFeast of 'Weeks *noun* [U] = SHAVUOTH

feat /fiːt/ *noun* (*approving*) an action or a piece of work that needs skill, strength or courage 技艺；武艺；功绩；英勇事迹：*The tunnel is a brilliant feat of engineering.* 这条隧道是工程方面的光辉业绩。◇ *to* ***perform/attempt/achieve*** *astonishing* ***feats*** 表演惊人的技艺；争取 / 取得惊人的功绩 ◇ *That was* ***no mean feat*** (= it was difficult to do). 那是伟大的成就。

fea·ther 🔑 /ˈfeðə(r)/ *noun, verb*

■ ***noun*** 🔑 one of the many soft light parts covering a bird's body 羽毛；翎毛：*a peacock feather* 孔雀羽毛 ◇ *a feather pillow* (= one containing feathers) 羽绒枕头 ➲ VISUAL VOCAB PAGE V12

IDM **a 'feather in your cap** an action that you can be proud of 可引以自豪的行为 **ORIGIN** This idiom comes from the Native American custom of giving a feather to sb who had been very brave in battle. 此习语源自美国土著的风俗，把一根羽毛奖赏给在战斗中表现英勇的人。➲ MORE AT BIRD *n.*, KNOCK *v.*, RUFFLE *v.*, SMOOTH *v.*

■ ***verb***

IDM **feather your (own) 'nest** to make yourself richer, especially by spending money on yourself that should be spent on sth else 中饱私囊 ➲ MORE AT TAR *v.*

ˌfeather-'bed *verb* (**-dd-**) **~ sb/sth** (*BrE*) to make things easy for sb, especially by giving them money or good conditions of work（尤指提供金钱或良好条件）使安逸，使轻松，娇养，溺爱

ˌfeather 'boa (*also* **boa**) *noun* a long thin piece of clothing like a SCARF, made of feathers and worn over the shoulders by women, especially in the past（旧时女用）羽毛围巾

'feather-brained *adj.* (*informal, disapproving*) very silly 浑头浑脑的

ˌfeather 'duster *noun* a stick with feathers on the end of it that is used for cleaning 羽毛掸子 ➲ VISUAL VOCAB PAGE V21

fea·thered /ˈfeðəd; *NAmE* -ðərd/ *adj.* covered with feathers or having feathers 覆盖着羽毛的；有羽毛的

fea·ther·weight /ˈfeðəweɪt; *NAmE* ˈfeðərw-/ *noun* a BOXER weighing between 53.5 and 57 kilograms, heavier than a BANTAMWEIGHT 次轻量级拳击手，羽量级拳击手（体重 53.5 至 57 公斤）

fea·thery /ˈfeðəri/ *adj.* light and soft; like feathers 轻软的；羽毛似的

fea·ture 🔑 **AW** /ˈfiːtʃə(r)/ *noun, verb*

■ ***noun*** [C] **1** 🔑 something important, interesting or typical of a place or thing 特色；特征；特点：*An interesting feature of the city is the old market.* 这座城市的一个有趣特征就是古老的市场。◇ *Teamwork is a* ***key feature*** *of the training programme.* 团队合作是这项训练计划的重要特点。◇ *Which features do you look for when choosing a car?* 你挑选轿车时要着重哪些特点？◇ *The software has no particular* ***distinguishing*** *features.* 这个软件没有明显的特点。◇ *geographical features* 地势 ➲ SEE ALSO WATER FEATURE **2** 🔑 [usually pl.] a part of sb's face such as their nose, mouth and eyes 面容的一部分（如鼻、口、眼）：*his strong handsome features* 他轮廓分明的英俊面孔 ◇ *Her eyes are her most* ***striking feature.*** 她容貌中最引人注目的是她的双眼。**3** 🔑 **~ (on sb/sth)** (in newspapers, on television, etc.) a special article or programme about sb/sth（报章、电视等的）特写，专题节目：*a special feature on education* 关于教育的专题文章 ➲ WORDFINDER NOTE AT NEWSPAPER **4** (*old-fashioned*) the main film/movie in a cinema programme （电影的）正片，故事片

■ ***verb*** **1** 🔑 [T] to include a particular person or thing as a special feature 以…为特色；是…的特征：**~ sb/sth as sb/sth** *The film features Cary Grant as a professor.* 这部电影由卡里 · 格兰特饰演一位教授。◇ **~ sb/sth** *The latest model features alloy wheels and an electronic alarm.* 最新款式的特色是合金车轮和电子报警器。◇ *Many of the hotels featured in the brochure offer special deals for weekend breaks.* 小册子列举的多家旅馆都有周末特别优惠。**2** 🔑 [I] **~ (in sth)** to have an important part in sth 起重要作用；占重要地位：*Olive oil and garlic feature prominently in his recipes.* 橄榄油和大蒜在他的食谱中是重要的材料。

'feature film *noun* a main film/movie with a story, rather than a DOCUMENTARY, etc. 故事片

'feature-length *adj.* [usually before noun] of the same length as a typical film/movie（影片）达到正片应有长度的

fea·ture·less /ˈfiːtʃələs; *NAmE* -tʃərl-/ *adj.* without any qualities or noticeable characteristics 没有特色的；平淡无

奇的： *The countryside is flat and featureless.* 这乡村一马平川，平淡无奇。

'feature phone *noun* a mobile/cell phone that can do some important things such as connect to the Internet, play and store music, etc. but does not have all the functions of a SMARTPHONE 功能手机（具备多项重要功能，如上网、播放和存储音乐等，但不具备智能手机的所有功能）

fe·brile /'fi:braɪl; *NAmE also* 'feb-/ *adj.* **1** (*formal*) nervous, excited and very active 狂热的： *a product of her febrile imagination* 她狂想的产物 **2** (*medical* 医) (of an illness 疾病) caused by fever 发热引起的；热性的；发热的

Feb·ru·ary /'februəri; *NAmE* -ueri/ *noun* [U, C] (*abbr.* **Feb.**) the 2nd month of the year, between January and March 二月 HELP To see how **February** is used, look at the examples at **April**. * February 的用法见词条 April 下的示例。

feces (*NAmE*) (*BrE* **fae·ces**) /'fi:si:z/ *noun* [pl.] (*formal*) solid waste material that leaves the body through the ANUS 粪便 SYN **excrement** ▶ **fecal** (*NAmE*) (*BrE* **fae·cal**) /'fi:kl/ *adj.* [only before noun]

feck·less /'fekləs/ *adj.* having a weak character; not behaving in a responsible way 品格差的；不负责任的： *Her husband was a charming, but lazy and feckless man.* 她的丈夫讨人喜欢，但却是个懒惰没有出息的人。 ▶ **feck·less·ness** *noun* [U]

fe·cund /'fi:kənd; 'fek-/ *adj.* (*formal*) **1** able to produce a lot of children, crops, etc. 生殖力旺盛的；多产的 SYN **fertile** **2** producing new and useful things, especially ideas 有发明创造力的；（尤指）能提出新颖想法的 ▶ **fe·cund·ity** /fɪ'kʌndəti/ *noun* [U]

Fed /fed/ *noun* (*US, informal*) **1** [C] an officer of the FBI or another federal organization（美国）联邦调查局官员，联邦政府官员 **2** **the Fed** [sing.] = FEDERAL RESERVE SYSTEM

fed PAST TENSE, PAST PART. OF FEED

fed·eral AW /'fedərəl/ *adj.* **1** having a system of government in which the individual states of a country have control over their own affairs, but are controlled by a central government for national decisions, etc. 联邦制的： *a federal republic* 联邦共和国 **2** (within a federal system, for example the US and Canada) connected with national government rather than the local government of an individual state（在美国、加拿大等联邦制下）联邦政府的： *a federal law* 联邦法 ◇ *state and federal income taxes* 州政府和联邦政府征收的所得税 ➲ WORDFINDER NOTE AT GOVERNMENT ▶ **fed·er·al·ly** *adv.* : *federally funded health care* 由联邦政府拨款的医疗

the ˌFederal ˌBureau of Investi'gation *noun* [sing.] = FBI

fed·er·al·ist /'fedərəlɪst/ *noun* a supporter of a federal system of government 联邦主义者 ▶ **fed·er·al·ism** /'fedərəlɪzəm/ *noun* [U]: *European federalism* 欧洲联邦主义 **fed·er·al·ist** *adj.* : *a federalist future in Europe* 欧洲联邦主义的未来

the ˌFederal Re'serve System (*also* **the Federal Reserve**) *noun* (*abbr.* **the FRS**) (*also informal* **the Fed**) [sing.] the organization that controls the supply of money in the US（美国）联邦储备系统

fed·er·ate /'fedəreɪt/ *verb* [I] (*specialist*) (of states, organizations, etc. 州、组织、机构等) to unite under a central government or organization while keeping some local control 结成联邦；组成同盟

fed·er·ation AW /ˌfedə'reɪʃn/ *noun* **1** [C] a country consisting of a group of individual states that have control over their own affairs but are controlled by a central government for national decisions, etc. 联邦： *the Russian Federation* 俄罗斯联邦 **2** [C] a group of clubs, trade/labor unions, etc. that have joined together to form an organization（俱乐部、工会等的）联合会： *the International Tennis Federation* 国际网球联合会 **3** [U] the act of forming a federation 联邦；同盟；联盟： *Many MPs are against federation in Europe.* 许多议会议员反对欧洲结成联邦。

fe·dora /fɪ'dɔ:rə/ *noun* a low soft hat with a curled BRIM 浅顶卷檐软呢帽

ˌfed 'up *adj.* [not before noun] (*informal*) bored or unhappy, especially with a situation that has continued for too long 厌烦；厌倦；不愉快： *You look fed up. What's the matter?* 你满脸不高兴的样子。怎么啦？ ◇ **~ with sb/sth** *People are fed up with all these traffic jams.* 总是交通堵塞，让人受够了。 ◇ *In the end, I just* **got fed up with** *his constant complaining.* 他不停地发牢骚，终于使我厌烦了。 ◇ *I wish he'd get a job. I'm* **fed up with it** (= with the situation). 但愿他能找到工作。这样下去我都烦死了。 ◇ **~ with doing sth** *I'm fed up with waiting for her.* 我等她等烦了。 HELP Some people say 'fed up of sth' in informal British English, but this is not considered correct in standard English. 非正式英式英语中，有人说 fed up of sth，但在规范英语中，此用法被视为不正确。

fee AW /fi:/ *noun* **1** an amount of money that you pay for professional advice or services 专业服务费；咨询费；报酬： *legal fees* 律师费 ◇ *Does the bank* **charge a fee** *for setting up the account?* 在这家银行开立账户要收费吗？ ◇ *fee-paying schools* (= that you have to pay to go to) 收费学校 ➲ SYNONYMS AT RATE **2** an amount of money that you pay to join an organization, or to do sth（加入组织或做某事付的）费： *membership fees* 会费 ◇ *There is no* **entrance fee** *to the gallery.* 这个美术陈列馆不收门票。

fee·ble /'fi:bl/ *adj.* (**fee·bler** /'fi:blə(r)/, **feeb·lest** /'fi:blɪst/) **1** very weak 虚弱的；衰弱的： *a feeble old man* 衰弱的老人 ◇ *The heartbeat was feeble and irregular.* 心搏无力，心律不齐。 **2** not effective; not showing determination or energy 无效的；缺乏决心的；无力的： *a feeble argument/excuse/joke* 无力的证据；站不住脚的借口；不好笑的笑话 ◇ *a feeble attempt to explain* 无力的试图解释 ◇ *Don't be so feeble! Tell her you don't want to go.* 别那么软弱了！告诉她你不想去。 ▶ **feeble·ness** *noun* [U] **feebly** /'fi:bli/ *adv.*

ˌfeeble-'minded *adj.* **1** (*old use, offensive*) having less than usual intelligence 弱智的；低能的；愚笨的 **2** weak and unable to make decisions 意志薄弱的；优柔寡断的；无决断的

feed /fi:d/ *verb, noun*

■ *verb* (**fed, fed** /fed/)

• **GIVE/EAT FOOD** 提供 / 吃食物 **1** [T] to give food to a person or an animal 给（人或动物）食物；喂养；饲养： **~ sb/sth/yourself** *Have you fed the cat yet?* 你喂了猫没有？ ◇ *The baby can't feed itself yet* (= can't put food into its own mouth). 这个婴儿还不能自己吃东西。 ◇ **~ sb/sth (on) sth** *The cattle are fed (on) barley.* 牛要喂大麦。 ◇ **~ sth to sb/sth** *The barley is fed to the cattle.* 牛喂的是大麦。 ➲ WORDFINDER NOTE AT BABY **2** [I] (of a baby or an animal 婴儿或动物) to eat food 进食： *Slugs and snails feed at night.* 蛞蝓和蜗牛夜间进食。 ➲ SEE ALSO FEED ON/OFF STH at FEED **3** [T] **~ sb** to provide food for a family or group of people 养，养活（全家、一群人）： *They have a large family to feed.* 他们要养活一大家人。 ◇ *There's enough here to feed an army.* 这儿的东西足以养活一支军队。

• **PLANT** 植物 **4** [T] **~ sth** to give a plant a special substance to make it grow 施（肥等）： *Feed the plants once a week.* 每星期要给这些花草施一次肥。

• **GIVE ADVICE/INFORMATION** 提供意见 / 信息 **5** [T] to give advice, information, etc. to sb/sth 提供（意见或信息等）；灌输： **~ sb sth** *We are constantly fed gossip and speculation by the media.* 媒体不断给我们灌输流言蜚语和猜测臆断。 ◇ **~ sth to sb** *Gossip and speculation are constantly fed to us by the media.* 媒体不断把流言蜚语和猜测臆断灌输给我们。

• **SUPPLY** 供给 **6** [T] to supply sth to sb/sth 供给；供应： *The electricity line is fed with power through an underground cable.* 这条电线的电源是通过地下电缆传输的。 ◇ **~ B into A** *Power is fed into the electricity line through an underground cable.* 电力通过地下电缆传输到这条电线。

• **PUT INTO MACHINE** 放进机器中 **7** [T] to put or push sth

F

into or through a machine 把…放进机器；将…塞进机器：**~ A (with B)** *He fed the meter with coins.* 他把硬币投入停车计时收费器。◇ **~ B into A** *He fed coins into the meter.* 他把硬币投入停车计时收费器。◇ **~ sth into/through sth** *The fabric is fed through the machine.* 布料放进了机器。

• SATISFY NEED 满足需要 **8** [T] **~ sth** to satisfy a need, desire, etc. and keep it strong 满足（需要、愿望、欲望等）：*For drug addicts, the need to feed the addiction takes priority over everything else.* 对于吸毒者来说满足毒瘾胜过一切。

IDM ˌ**feed your ˈface** (*informal, usually disapproving*) to eat a lot of food or too much food 大吃一顿；吃得过饱 ➲ MORE AT BITE *v.*

PHR V ˌ**feed ˈback (into/to sth)** to have an influence on the development of sth by reacting to it in some way 反过来影响（事物的发展）：*What the audience tells me feeds back into my work.* 观众给我提的意见反过来对我的作品起到了促进作用。ˌ**feed (sth)↔ˈback (to sb)** to give information or opinions about sth, especially so that it can be improved 反馈，反应（信息或意见）：*Test results will be fed back to the schools.* 测验的成绩将反馈给各学校。ˈ**feed into sth** to have an influence on the development of sth 对…的发展产生影响：*The report's findings will feed into company policy.* 公司的政策将会考虑到报告的调研结果。ˈ**feed on/off sth 1** (of an animal 动物) to eat sth 以…为食：*Butterflies feed on the flowers of garden plants.* 蝴蝶以园林中草木的花为食。**2** (*often disapproving*) to become stronger because of sth else 因…而壮大；从…中得到滋养：*Racism feeds on fear.* 恐惧心理会助长种族主义。ˌ**feed ˈthrough (to sb/sth)** to reach sb/sth after going through a process or system 最终得以提供给：*It will take time for the higher rates to feed through to investors.* 需要时日投资者才能最终得到较高的回报率。ˌ**feed sb↔ˈup** (*BrE*) to give a lot of food to sb to make them fatter or stronger（用大量食物）养肥，养壮

■ ***noun***

• MEAL FOR BABY/ANIMAL 婴儿 / 动物的食物 **1** [C] a meal of milk for a young baby; a meal for an animal（婴儿的）一次喂奶，一餐；（动物的）一次喂给的饲料：*her morning feed* 她早上的一次喂奶

• FOR ANIMALS/PLANTS 动植物 **2** [U, C] food for animals or plants 动物的饲料；植物的肥料：*winter feed for the horses* 马的冬季饲料

• FOR MACHINE 机器 **3** [U] material supplied to a machine（机器的）进料 **4** [C] a pipe, device, etc. which supplies a machine with sth（机器的）进料装置，进料器：*the cold feed to the water cylinder* 水缸的冷进水管 ◇ *The printer has an automatic paper feed.* 这台打印机有自动进纸装置。

• LARGE MEAL 丰盛膳食 **5** [C] (*informal*) a large meal 丰盛的一餐：*They needed a bath and a good feed.* 他们需要洗个澡，饱餐一顿。

• TELEVISION PROGRAMMES 电视节目 **6** [U] (*NAmE*) television programmes that are sent from a central station to other stations in a network; the system of sending out these programmes（电视中心台）网络供给节目（系统）：*network feed* 网络供给节目系统

• WEBSITE 网站 **7** a special feature on a BLOG, news website, SOCIAL NETWORKING website, etc. that allows you to see new information that has been added without having to visit the website, usually using a FEED READER (= a piece of software that displays this information)（博客、新闻网站、社交网站等的）信息推送，信息订阅功能：*an RSS feed* 简易信息聚合订阅

feed·back /ˈfiːdbæk/ *noun* [U] **1** advice, criticism or information about how good or useful sth or sb's work is 反馈的意见（或信息）：*I'd appreciate some feedback on my work.* 如果有人对我的工作提出意见我将感激不尽。◇ *The teacher will* ***give you feedback*** *on the test.* 老师会对你的测验提供反馈信息。◇ *We need both positive and negative feedback from our customers.* 我们需要顾客正反两方面的反馈意见。**2** the unpleasant noise produced by electrical equipment such as an AMPLIFIER when some of the power returns to the system（电器的）反馈噪音 ➲ MORE LIKE THIS 28, page R28

feed·bag /ˈfiːdbæg/ (*NAmE*) (*BrE* **nose·bag**) *noun* a bag containing food for a horse, that you hang from its head（挂在马头上的）饲料袋

feed·er /ˈfiːdə(r)/ *noun, adj.*

■ ***noun* 1** (used with an adjective or a noun 与形容词或名词连用) an animal or plant that eats a particular thing or eats in a particular way（动植物）进某种食物者，以…方式进食者：*plankton feeders* 以浮游生物为食者 **2** a part of a machine that supplies sth to another part of the machine（机器的）进料器，供给装置 **3** a container filled with food for birds or animals 鸟食罐；饲料槽

■ ***adj.*** [only before noun] **1** (of roads, rivers, etc. 道路、河流等) leading to a bigger road, etc. 汇入主干道（或河等）的：*a* ***feeder road*** *to the motorway/freeway* 汇入高速公路的支路 **2** supplying goods, services, etc. to a large organization（向大机构）供应商品的，提供服务的 **3** (*NAmE*) (of animals on a farm 饲养场中的动物) kept to be killed and used for meat 育肥备宰的；供肉食的

ˈ**feeder school** *noun* (*BrE*) a school from which most of the children go to a particular SECONDARY SCHOOL or college in the same area 直属学校（学生毕业后大多进入本地区特定中学或高校）

feed·ing /ˈfiːdɪŋ/ *noun* [U] the act of giving food to a person, an animal or a plant 喂食；饲养；施肥：*breast/bottle feeding* 母乳 / 奶瓶喂养

ˈ**feeding bottle** *noun* (*BrE*) a plastic bottle with a rubber top which a baby or young animal can suck milk through 奶瓶

ˈ**feeding frenzy** *noun* **1** an occasion when a group of SHARKS or other fish attack sth（鲨鱼等鱼群的）疯狂捕食 **2** a situation in which a lot of people compete with each other in an excited way because they want to get sth（对某物的）集体狂热追求，疯狂竞争

the Feeding of the Five ˈThousand *noun* [sing.] a situation in which a lot of people need to be given food 众人求食的场面：*I made breakfast for all my son's friends—it was like the Feeding of the Five Thousand.* 我为儿子的所有朋友做了早餐，就像供应食物给五千人一样。

ORIGIN From the Bible story in which Jesus is said to have fed 5 000 people with five loaves of bread and two fish. 源自《圣经》中耶稣用五个饼和两条鱼让 5 000 人吃饱的故事。

ˈ**feed reader** *noun* a piece of software that you use to see new information that has been added on a BLOG, news website, SOCIAL NETWORKING website, etc. without having to visit the website 推送阅读器，订阅器（用户无须访问网站便可看到博客、新闻网站、社交网站等的更新信息）

feed·stuff /ˈfiːdstʌf/ *noun* [U] (*also* **feed·stuffs** [pl.]) food for farm animals, especially food that has been processed（尤指经加工的）饲料 SYN **feed** ➲ COMPARE FOODSTUFF

feel /fiːl/ *verb, noun*

■ ***verb*** (**felt, felt** /felt/)

• WELL/SICK/HAPPY/SAD, ETC. 健康、不适、愉快、悲伤等 **1** *linking verb* to experience a particular feeling or emotion 觉得；感到；体会到：**+ adj.** *The heat made him feel faint.* 炎热使他觉得快要晕倒了。◇ *She sounded more confident than she felt.* 她的语气听起来比她本人的感觉要有信心。◇ *I was feeling guilty.* 我感到歉疚。◇ *You'll feel better after a good night's sleep.* 你晚上睡个好觉就会觉得舒服些。◇ *She felt betrayed.* 她感到被出卖了。◇ *I feel sorry for him.* 我为他感到可惜。◇ **+ adv./prep.** *How are you feeling today?* 你今天觉得怎么样？◇ *I know exactly how you feel* (= I feel sympathy for you). 我完全理解你的心情。◇ *Luckily I was feeling in a good mood.* 幸好我当时情绪好。◇ **~ sth** *He seemed to feel no remorse at all.* 他当时似乎一点也不感到懊悔。◇ **+ noun** *Standing there on stage I felt a complete idiot.* 我站在舞台上觉得简直是一个大傻瓜。◇ **~ like sth** *I felt like a complete idiot.* 我感到完全像个傻瓜。

• BE/BECOME AWARE 发觉；意识到 **2** [T] (not usually used in the progressive tenses 通常不用于进行时) to notice or be aware of sth because it is touching you or having a physical effect on you（通过触觉）注意到，意识到，感觉

到 SYN **sense**: **~ sth** *I could feel the warm sun on my back.* 我背上感受到了阳光的温暖。◇ *She could not feel her legs.* 她的双腿失去了知觉。◇ *He felt a hand on his shoulder.* 他感到有只手在他肩上。◇ **~ sb/sth/yourself doing sth** *He felt a hand touching his shoulder.* 他感到有只手在触摸他的肩膀。◇ *She could feel herself blushing.* 她可以感到脸都红了。◇ **~ sb/sth/yourself do sth** *I felt something crawl up my arm.* 我觉得有个东西顺着手臂往上爬。◇ *We felt the ground give way under our feet.* 我们感觉到脚下的土地下陷了。 **3** [T] (not usually used in the progressive tenses 通常不用于进行时) **~ sth** to become aware of sth even though you cannot see it, hear it, etc. 感到，感觉到（抽象事物） SYN **sense**: *Can you feel the tension in this room?* 你能感觉到这房间里的紧张气氛吗？

• **GIVE IMPRESSION** 留下印象 **4** *linking verb* (not used in the progressive tenses 不用于进行时) to give you a particular feeling or impression 给…感觉；有印象；感受到：**+ adj.** *It felt strange to be back in my old school.* 我回到母校有一种生疏的感觉。◇ *My mouth felt completely dry.* 我感到口干舌燥。◇ **~ like sth** *The interview only took ten minutes, but it felt like hours.* 面试只用了十分钟，但觉得像几个小时似的。◇ *It* ***feels like rain*** (= seems likely to rain). 好像快要下雨了。◇ **~ as if/though...** *Her head felt as if it would burst.* 她觉得头要爆裂了。◇ *It felt as though he had run a marathon.* 他感到好像跑了一个马拉松似的。◇ *How does it feel to be alone all day?* 整天独自一个人的感受如何？ HELP In spoken English people often use **like** instead of **as if** or **as though** in this meaning, especially in *NAmE*. 英语口语中，尤其是美式英语，常用 like 代替 as if 或 as though 表示此义：*He felt like he'd run a marathon.* 他感到好像跑了一个马拉松似的。This is not considered correct in written *BrE*. 书面英式英语中，此用法被视为不正确。

• **TOUCH** 触摸 **5** *linking verb* (not used in the progressive tenses 不用于进行时) to have a particular physical quality which you become aware of by touching 摸起来；手感：**+ adj.** *The water feels warm.* 这水摸着很暖。◇ *Its skin feels really smooth.* 它的皮摸起来真光滑。◇ **~ like sth** *This wallet feels like leather.* 这个钱包摸上去像是皮的。 **6** [T] to deliberately move your fingers over sth in order to find out what it is like 触；摸：**~ sth** *Can you feel the bump on my head?* 你能摸到我头上那个肿块吗？◇ *Try to tell what this is just by feeling it.* 凭手摸摸说出这是什么东西。◇ **~ how, what, etc....** *Feel how rough this is.* 摸摸这有多粗糙。

• **THINK/BELIEVE** 认为；相信 **7** [T, I] (not usually used in the progressive tenses 通常不用于进行时) to think or believe that sth is the case; to have a particular opinion or attitude 以为；认为；相信：**~ (that)...** *We all felt (that) we were unlucky to lose.* 我们都认为我们输了是运气不好。◇ *I felt (that) I had to apologize.* 我以为我得道歉。◇ **~ it to be sth** *She felt it to be her duty to tell the police.* 她认为她有责任报警。◇ **~ it + noun** *She felt it her duty to tell the police.* 她认为报警是她的义务。◇ **~ it + adj.** *I felt it advisable to do nothing.* 我觉得最好不要作出行动。◇ (**+ adv./prep.**) *This is something I feel strongly about.* 这事令我感触颇深。◇ *This decision is,* ***I feel****, a huge mistake.* 我认为这个决定是个天大的错误。 ⊃ SYNONYMS AT THINK

• **BE STRONGLY AFFECTED** 强烈影响 **8** [T] **~ sth** to experience the effects or results of sth, often strongly 受（强烈）影响；（深深）体验到：*He feels the cold a lot.* 他很怕冷。◇ *Cathy was really feeling the heat.* 凯茜真的感到很热。◇ *She felt her mother's death very deeply.* 她深感丧母之痛。◇ *The effects of the recession are being felt everywhere.* 经济衰退的影响无所不在。◇ *We all felt the force of her arguments.* 我们都体会到了她的论据的分量。

• **SEARCH WITH HANDS** 用手摸索 **9** [I] **~ (in sth/about/around, etc.) (for sth)** to search for sth with your hands, feet, etc. （用手、足等）摸索，寻找，探索：*He felt in his pockets for some money.* 他在口袋里摸着想找一些钱。◇ *I had to feel about in the dark for the light switch.* 我得在黑暗中摸索寻找电灯开关。

IDM **,feel your 'age** to realize that you are getting old, especially compared with people you are with who are younger than you （尤指与较年轻者比）感到自己上年纪了，意识到自己老了 **feel your 'ears burning** to think or imagine that other people are talking about you 觉得耳朵在发烧（认为或猜测别人在说自己） **feel 'free (to do sth)** (*informal*) used to tell sb that they are allowed to do sth（表示允许）可以随便做某事：*Feel free to ask questions if you don't understand.* 你要是不懂，可以随便提问。◇ *'Can I use your phone?' 'Feel free.'* "我能用你的电话吗？" "随便用吧。" **feel 'good** to feel happy, confident, etc. 感到愉快（或有信心等）：*It makes me feel good to know my work is appreciated.* 我知道我的工作得到赏识后感到很高兴。 **feel (it) in your 'bones (that...)** to be certain about sth even though you do not have any direct proof and cannot explain why you are certain 心中感到；本能预感到；直觉确信：*I know I'm going to fail this exam—I can feel it in my bones.* 我知道这次考试我过不了关，我有这种直觉。 **feel like sth/like doing sth** (*informal*) to want to have or do sth 想要某物；想做某事：*I feel like a drink.* 我想喝一杯。◇ *We all felt like celebrating.* 我们都想庆祝一番。◇ *We'll go for a walk if you feel like it.* 要是你愿意，我们去散散步。 **feel the 'pinch** (*informal*) to not have enough money 手头拮据；经济困难：*Lots of people who have lost their jobs are starting to feel the pinch.* 大量失业者开始感到日子不好过了。 **feel 'sick** (*especially BrE*) to feel as though you will VOMIT soon 觉得要呕吐；想吐：*Mum! I feel sick.* 妈妈！我觉得恶心。 **feel ,sick to your 'stomach** (*NAmE*) to feel as though you will VOMIT soon 觉得要呕吐；想吐 **feel your 'way 1** to move along carefully, for example when it is dark, by touching walls, objects, etc.（如在黑暗中）摸索着走动 **2** to be careful about how you do things, usually because you are in a situation that you are not familiar with（在新环境中）谨慎行事：*She was new in the job, still feeling her way.* 她对这项工作不熟悉，还在摸索着干。 **not feel your'self** to not feel healthy and well 觉得身体不好；感到身体不舒服 ⊃ MORE AT DEATH, FLATTER, HARD *adv.*, HONOUR *n.*, HONOUR *v.*, JELLY, MARK *n.*, MILLION, PRESENCE, SMALL *adj.*

PHR V **'feel for sb** to have sympathy for sb 同情，怜悯（某人）：*I really felt for her when her husband died.* 她的丈夫去世，我确实同情她。◇ *I do feel for you, honestly.* 说真的，我确实同情你。 **,feel sb↔'up** (*informal*) to touch sb sexually, especially when they do not want you to 对某人动手动脚 SYN **grope** **,feel 'up to sth** to have the strength and energy to do or deal with sth 觉得有精力（做某事）；感到有能力（处理某事）：*Do we have to go to the party? I really don't feel up to it.* 我们是不是一定得去参加这次聚会？我实在没有精力应付了。◇ **feel up to doing sth** *After the accident she didn't feel up to driving.* 事故过后，她开车已力不从心。

■ *noun* [sing.]

• **TOUCH** 触摸 **1 the feel** the feeling you get when you touch sth or are touched 触觉；手感：*You can tell it's silk by the feel.* 你一摸就知道这是丝绸。◇ *She loved the feel of the sun on her skin.* 她喜欢太阳照在皮肤上的感觉。 **2** an act of feeling or touching 触摸；摸：*I had a feel of the material.* 我摸了一下这种布料。

• **IMPRESSION** 印象 **3** the impression that is created by a place, situation, etc.; atmosphere（场所、情况等给人的）印象，感受；气氛：*It's a big city but it has the feel of a small town.* 这是座大城市，却给人小城镇的印象。◇ *The room has a comfortable feel to it.* 这个房间令人感到舒适。

IDM **get the feel of sth/of doing sth** to become familiar with sth or with doing sth 开始熟悉，开始熟悉做（某事）：*I haven't got the feel of the brakes in this car yet.* 我还没有掌握这辆车的刹车性能。 **have a feel for sth** to have an understanding of sth or be naturally good at doing it 善于理解某事物；有…的天才：*She has a real feel for languages.* 她有语言天才。

feel·er /ˈfiːlə(r)/ *noun* [usually pl.] either of the two long thin parts on the heads of some insects and of some animals that live in shells that they use to feel and touch things with（某些昆虫和贝壳动物的）触角，触须 SYN **antenna**

IDM **put out 'feelers** (*informal*) to try to find out what people think about a particular course of action before you do it 试探

'feel-good *adj.* making you feel happy and pleased about life 使人愉悦的：*a feel-good movie* 令人愉悦的电影

IDM **the 'feel-good factor** (*BrE*) (used especially in newspapers, etc.) the feeling of confidence in the future that is shared by many people（尤用于报章等）前景美好的氛围

feel·ing /'fi:lɪŋ/ *noun*
- **STH THAT YOU FEEL** 感觉 **1** [C] ~ (**of sth**) something that you feel through the mind or through the senses（内心和感官的）感觉，感触：*a* ***feeling of hunger/excitement/sadness, etc.*** 饥饿、兴奋、悲伤等的感觉 ◇ *guilty feelings* 内疚感 ◇ *I've got a tight feeling in my stomach.* 我觉得胃部胀痛。◇ (*informal*) *'I really resent the way he treated me.' '**I know the feeling** (= I know how you feel).'* "我实在气愤他如此待我。""我理解你的感受。" ◇ *'I'm going to miss you.' '**The feeling's mutual** (= I feel exactly the same).'* "我会想念你的。""我也是。"
- **IDEA/BELIEF** 想法；信念 **2** [sing.] the idea or belief that a particular thing is true or a particular situation is likely to happen 想法；看法；信念 SYN **impression**：~ (**of sth**) *He suddenly had the feeling of being followed.* 他突然觉得被跟踪了。◇ ~ (**that...**) *I got the feeling that he didn't like me much.* 我的感觉是他并不很喜欢我。◇ *I had a nasty feeling that we were lost.* 我有个不祥的预感：我们迷路了。
- **ATTITUDE/OPINION** 态度；意见 **3** [U, C] an attitude or opinion about sth 态度；意见：*The general feeling of the meeting was against the decision.* 会议上普遍的意见是反对这个决定。◇ ~ (**about/on sth**) *I don't have any strong feelings about it one way or the other.* 我对此既不特别喜欢，也不特别讨厌。◇ *She **had mixed feelings** about giving up her job.* 她对辞去工作感到又喜又忧。◇ *My own feeling is that we should buy the cheaper one.* 我个人的意见是我们应该买较便宜的那个。◇ *Public feeling is being ignored by the government.* 公众的意见遭到了政府忽视。
- **EMOTIONS** 情感 **4** **feelings** [pl.] a person's emotions rather than their thoughts or ideas 情感；感情：*He hates talking about his feelings.* 他讨厌谈他的感情。◇ *I didn't mean to **hurt your feelings*** (= offend you). 我不是故意伤害你的感情。**5** [U, C] strong emotion 激动；激情；强烈情绪：*She spoke **with feeling** about the plight of the homeless.* 她激动地讲述了无家可归者的困境。◇ ***Feelings are running high*** (= people are very angry or excited). 群情激奋。
- **UNDERSTANDING** 理解 **6** [U] the ability to understand sb/sth or to do sth in a sensitive way 理解力；领悟力；敏感：*He played the piano with great feeling.* 他钢琴弹得很有感觉。◇ ~ **for sb/sth** *She has a wonderful feeling for colour.* 她的色感特强。
- **SYMPATHY/LOVE** 同情；爱 **7** [U, pl.] ~ (**for sb/sth**) sympathy or love for sb/sth 同情；爱：*You have no feeling for the sufferings of others.* 你对他人的痛苦毫无同情心。◇ *I still **have feelings** for her* (= feel attracted to her in a romantic way). 我仍然爱她。
- **PHYSICAL** 身体 **8** [U] the ability to feel physically 身体感觉；知觉：*I've lost all feeling in my legs.* 我的双腿已完全失去知觉。
- **ATMOSPHERE** 气氛 **9** [sing.] the atmosphere of a place, situation, etc.（场所、情况等的）气氛：*They have managed to recreate the feeling of the original theatre.* 他们设法再现了老戏院原来的气氛。

IDM **bad/ill 'feeling** (*also* **bad/ill 'feelings** *especially in NAmE*) anger between people, especially after an argument or disagreement 恶感；不满；反感：*There was a lot of bad feeling between the two groups of students.* 这两群学生互怀敌意。➲ MORE AT HARD *adj.*, SINK *v.*, SPARE *v.*

feel·ing·ly /'fi:lɪŋli/ *adv.* with strong emotion 激情地；激动地 SYN **emotionally**：*He spoke feelingly about his dead father.* 他谈起他死去的父亲时激动不已。

feet PL. OF FOOT

feign /feɪn/ *verb* ~ **sth** | ~ **to do sth** (*formal*) to pretend that you have a particular feeling or that you are ill/sick, tired, etc. 假装，装作，佯装（有某种感觉或生病、疲倦等）：*He survived the massacre by feigning death.* 他装死才在大屠杀中死里逃生。◇ *'Who cares?' said Alex, feigning indifference.* "有谁在乎？"亚历克斯佯作漠不关心地说。

feint /feɪnt/ *noun, verb*
- ***noun*** (especially in sport) a movement that is intended to make your opponent think you are going to do one thing when you are really going to do sth else（尤指体育运动中的）假动作，佯攻，虚晃
- ***verb*** [I] (especially in sport 尤用于体育运动) to confuse your opponent by making them think you are going to do one thing when you are really going to do sth else 做假动作；佯攻；虚晃

feisty /'faɪsti/ *adj.* (**feist·ier**, **feisti·est**) (*informal, approving*) (of people 人) strong, determined and not afraid of arguing with people 坚决而据理力争的

fela·fel = FALAFEL

feld·spar /'feldspɑ:(r)/ *noun* [U, C] a type of white or red rock 长石

fe·lici·tous /fə'lɪsɪtəs/ *adj.* (*formal* or *literary*) (especially of words 尤指言辞) chosen well; very suitable; giving a good result 贴切的；恰当的；妥帖的 SYN **apt**, **happy**：*a felicitous turn of phrase* 贴切的措辞 ▶ **fe·lici·tous·ly** *adv.*

fe·li·city /fə'lɪsəti/ *noun* (*pl.* **-ies**) (*formal* or *literary*) **1** [U] great happiness 幸福；十分快乐 **2** [U] the quality of being well chosen or suitable 贴切；恰当；得体 **3 felicities** [pl.] well-chosen or successful features, especially in a speech or piece of writing （尤指讲话或文章中的）精彩之处，言辞巧妙，措辞恰当

fe·line /'fi:laɪn/ *adj., noun*
- ***adj.*** like a cat; connected with an animal of the cat family 猫似的；猫科动物的：*She walks with feline grace.* 她步履如猫般轻盈。
- ***noun*** (*formal*) a cat; an animal of the cat family 猫；猫科动物

fell /fel/ *noun, verb, adj.* ➲ SEE ALSO FALL *verb*
- ***noun*** a hill or an area of hills in northern England（英格兰北部的）小山，丘陵地区
- ***verb*** **1** ~ **sth** to cut down a tree 砍伐（树木） **2** ~ **sb** (*literary*) to make sb fall to the ground 击倒，打倒（某人）：*He felled his opponent with a single blow.* 他一拳击倒了对手。
- ***adj.*** (*literary*) very evil or violent 邪恶的；残暴的

IDM **at/in one fell swoop** all at the same time; in a single action, especially a sudden or violent one 一下子；一举

fella (*also* **fell·er**) /'felə(r)/ *noun* (*informal*) **1** an informal way of referring to a man 伙伴；伙计；哥们儿 **2** an informal way of referring to sb's boyfriend 男朋友：*Have you met her new fella?* 你见到她的新男朋友没有？

fel·late /fə'leɪt; *NAmE also* 'feleɪt/ *verb* ~ **sb** (*formal*) to perform FELLATIO on a man 吮吸…的阴茎；为…口交

fel·la·tio /fə'leɪʃiəʊ; *NAmE* -ʃioʊ/ *noun* [U] (*formal*) the practice of touching a man's PENIS with the tongue and lips to give sexual pleasure 吮吸阴茎；口交

fel·low /'feləʊ; *NAmE* 'feloʊ/ *noun, adj.*
- ***noun*** **1** (*informal, becoming old-fashioned*) a way of referring to a man or boy 男人；男孩；家伙；哥们儿：*He's a nice old fellow.* 他这位老兄人不错。➲ SEE ALSO FELLA **2** [usually pl.] a person that you work with or that is like you; a thing that is similar to the one mentioned 同事；同辈；同类；配对物：*She has a very good reputation among her fellows.* 她在同事中的口碑甚佳。◇ *Many caged birds live longer than their fellows in the wild.* 许多笼中鸟比野外同类鸟的寿命长。**3** (*BrE*) a senior member of some colleges or universities（某些学院或大学的）董事：*a fellow of New College, Oxford* 牛津大学新学院董事 **4** a member of an academic or professional organization （学术或专业团体的）会员：*a fellow of the Royal College of Surgeons* 皇家外科医生学会会员 **5** (*especially NAmE*) a GRADUATE student who holds a FELLOWSHIP（接受奖学金的）研究生：*a graduate fellow* 接受奖学金的研究生 ◇ *a teaching fellow* 兼任教学的研究生
- ***adj.*** [only before noun] used to describe sb who is the same as you in some way, or in the same situation 同类的；同事的；同伴的；同情况的：***fellow members/citizens/workers*** 同一组织的成员；同胞；同事 ◇ *my **fellow passengers** on the train* 和我同火车的旅伴

ˌ**fellow ˈfeeling** *noun* [U, C] a feeling of sympathy for sb because you have shared similar experiences（遭遇相同而产生的）同情，同感；同病相怜

fel·low·ship /ˈfeləʊʃɪp; *NAmE* -loʊ-/ *noun* **1** [U] (*formal*) a feeling of friendship between people who do things together or share an interest 伙伴关系；友谊；交情 **2** [C] an organized group of people who share an interest, aim or belief（具有共同利益、目的或信仰的）团体，协会，联谊会 **3** [C] (*especially BrE*) the position of being a senior member of a college or university（学院或大学的）董事职位 **4** [C] an award of money to a GRADUATE student to allow them to continue their studies or to do research 研究生奖学金 **5** [C, U] the state of being a member of an academic or professional organization（学术或专业团体的）会员资格：*to be elected to fellowship of the British Academy* 当选为英国人文社会科学院的院士

ˌ**fellow-ˈtraveller** *noun* **1** a person who is travelling to the same place as another person 旅伴 **2** a person who agrees with the aims of a political party, especially the Communist party, but is not a member of it 同路人（政党的支持者，尤指赞同共产党的党外人）

felon /ˈfelən/ *noun* (*especially NAmE, law* 律) a person who has committed a felony 重罪犯

fe·loni·ous /fəˈləʊniəs; *NAmE* -ˈloʊ-/ *adj.* (*formal*) relating to or involved in crime 罪行的；犯罪的

fel·ony /ˈfeləni/ *noun* [C, U] (*pl.* **-ies**) (*US* or *old-fashioned, law* 律) the act of committing a serious crime such as murder or RAPE; a crime of this type 重罪；重刑罪：*a charge of felony* 对犯重罪的指控 ➲ COMPARE MISDEMEANOUR (2)

felt /felt/ *noun* [U] a type of soft thick cloth made from wool or hair that has been pressed tightly together 毛毡：*a felt hat* 毡帽 ➲ SEE ALSO FEEL *v.*

ˌ**felt-tip ˈpen** (*also* **ˈfelt tip**, ˌ**felt-tipped ˈpen**) *noun* a pen that has a point made of felt 毡头笔

fe·male 🔑 /ˈfiːmeɪl/ *adj., noun*

■ *adj.* **1** 🔑 being a woman or a girl 女的；女性的：*a female student/employee/artist* 女学生；女雇员；女艺术家 ◇ *Two of the candidates must be female.* 候选人中必须有两名是女性。 **2** 🔑 of the sex that can lay eggs or give birth to babies 雌的；母的：*a female cat* 母猫 **3** 🔑 of women; typical of women; affecting women 女性的；妇女的；女性特有的：*female characteristics* 女性特征 ◇ *the female role* 妇女的角色 ➲ COMPARE FEMININE *adj.* (1) **4** (*biology* 生) (of plants and flowers 植物和花) that can produce fruit 能结果实的；雌性的；有雌蕊的 **5** (*specialist*) (of electrical equipment 电气设备) having a hole that another part fits into 阴的；内孔的；凹的：*a female plug* 内孔插头 OPP **male**

■ *noun* **1** 🔑 an animal that can lay eggs or give birth to babies; a plant that can produce fruit 雌性动物；雌性植物；雌株 **2** 🔑 (*formal*) a woman or a girl 女子：*More females than males are employed in the factory.* 这家工厂雇用的女性比男性多。 OPP **male**

femi·nine /ˈfemənɪn/ *adj., noun*

■ *adj.* **1** having the qualities or appearance considered to be typical of women; connected with women（指气质或外貌）女性特有的，女性的，妇女的：*That dress makes you look very feminine.* 那件衣服你穿起来很有女人味儿。 ◇ *He had delicate, almost feminine, features.* 他面目清秀，五官很像女性。 ◇ *the traditional feminine role* 传统的女性角色 ➲ COMPARE FEMALE *adj.* (3), MASCULINE *adj.* (1) **2** (*grammar* 语法) belonging to a class of words that refer to female people or animals and often have a special form 阴性的：*Some people prefer not to use the feminine form 'actress' and use the word 'actor' for both sexes.* 有些人不喜欢使用 actress 这一阴性形式，而用 actor 一词代表两种性别。 **3** (*grammar* 语法) (in some languages 用于某些语言) belonging to a class of nouns, pronouns or adjectives that have feminine GENDER, not MASCULINE or NEUTER（指名词、代词或形容词）阴性的：*The French word for 'table' is feminine.* 法语的 table 一词是阴性。

■ *noun* (*grammar* 语法) **1 the feminine** [sing.] the feminine GENDER (= form of nouns, adjectives and pronouns) 阴性（指名词、形容词和代词的形式） **2** [C] a feminine word or word form 阴性词（形式） ➲ COMPARE MASCULINE, NEUTER

femi·nin·ity /ˌfeməˈnɪnəti/ *noun* [U] the fact of being a woman; the qualities that are considered to be typical of women 女子气质；女子气；阴柔

femi·nism /ˈfemənɪzəm/ *noun* [U] the belief and aim that women should have the same rights and opportunities as men; the struggle to achieve this aim 女权主义；女性主义；女权运动 ➲ WORDFINDER NOTE AT EQUAL

femi·nist /ˈfemənɪst/ *noun* a person who supports the belief that women should have the same rights and opportunities as men 女权主义者；女性主义者；女权运动者 ▸ **femi·nist** *adj.* [usually before noun]: *feminist demands/ideas/theories* 女权主义要求 / 思想 / 理论 ◇ *the feminist movement* 女权运动

femi·nize (*BrE also* **-ise**) /ˈfemənaɪz/ *verb* **1 ~ sb** to make sb more like a woman 使女性化；使更像女人 **2 ~ sth** to make sth involve more women 增加…中的女性成员：*Offices became increasingly feminized during the 1960s.* * 20 世纪 60 年代期间办公室的女职员越来越多。

femme /fem/ *adj.* (*sometimes offensive*) (of a HOMOSEXUAL person) having qualities typical of a woman（同性恋者）女人气的，脂粉气的 ➲ COMPARE BUTCH

femme fa·tale /ˌfæm fəˈtɑːl; *NAmE* ˌfem fəˈtæl/ *noun* (*pl.* **femmes fa·tales** /ˌfæm fəˈtɑːl; -z; *NAmE* ˌfem fəˈtæl/) (*from French*) a very beautiful woman that men find sexually attractive but who brings them trouble or unhappiness 祸水红颜

femto- /ˈfemtəʊ; *NAmE* -toʊ/ *combining form* (*specialist*) (in units of measurement 用于计量单位) 10^{-15} 飞（母托）；毫微微；千万亿分之一：*a femtosecond* 毫微微秒

femur /ˈfiːmə(r)/ *noun* (*pl.* **fe·murs** or **fem·ora** /ˈfemərə/) (*anatomy* 解) the THIGH BONE 股骨 ➲ VISUAL VOCAB PAGE V64 ▸ **fem·oral** /ˈfemərəl/ *adj.* [only before noun]

fen *noun* an area of low, flat, wet land, especially in the east of England （尤指英格兰东部）低位沼泽，沴泽

fence 🔑 /fens/ *noun, verb*

■ *noun* **1** 🔑 a structure made of wood or wire supported with posts that is put between two areas of land as a BOUNDARY, or around a garden/yard, field, etc. to keep animals in, or to keep people and animals out 栅栏；篱笆；围栏 ➲ VISUAL VOCAB PAGES V3, V20 **2** a structure that horses must jump over in a race or a competition（障碍赛马中的）障碍物 **3** (*informal*) a criminal who buys and sells stolen goods 买卖赃物者；销赃犯 IDM SEE GRASS *n.*, MEND *v.*, SIDE *n.*, SIT

■ *verb* **1** [T] **~ sth** to surround or divide an area with a fence（用栅栏、篱笆或围栏）围住，隔开：*His property is fenced with barbed wire.* 他的房产四周围有带刺的铁丝网。 ➲ SEE ALSO UNFENCED **2** [I] to take part in the sport of FENCING 参加击剑运动 **3** [I] **~ (with sb)** to speak to sb in a clever way in order to gain an advantage in the conversation 搪塞；支吾；回避

PHR V ˌ**fence sb/sth↔ˈin** [often passive] **1** to surround sb/sth with a fence（用栅栏、篱笆或围栏）围住，关住 **2** to restrict sb's freedom 限制自由 SYN **hem in**: *She felt fenced in by domestic routine.* 她感到被日常家务束缚住了。 ˌ**fence sth↔ˈoff** [often passive] to divide one area from another with a fence （用栅栏、篱笆、围栏）隔开

ˈ**fence-mending** *noun* [U] an attempt to improve relations between two people or groups and to try to find a solution to a disagreement between them 友好关系的修复；修好

fen·cer /ˈfensə(r)/ *noun* a person who takes part in the sport of FENCING 击剑运动员

fen·cing /ˈfensɪŋ/ *noun* [U] **1** the sport of fighting with long thin SWORDS 击剑运动 ➲ VISUAL VOCAB PAGE V52 **2** fences; wood, wire, or other material used for making fences 栅栏；篱笆；围栏；筑栅栏用的材料：*The factory is surrounded by electric fencing.* 工厂有电网围着。

fend /fend/ *verb*

PHR V **,fend for your'self** to take care of yourself without help from anyone else 照料自己；自谋生计：*His parents agreed to pay the rent for his apartment but otherwise left him to fend for himself.* 他的父母同意替他付房租，其他的则让他自己解决。 **,fend sth/sb↔'off 1** to defend or protect yourself from sth/sb that is attacking you 抵挡，挡开，避开（攻击）SYN **fight off, ward off**: *The police officer fended off the blows with his riot shield.* 那名警察用防暴盾牌抵挡攻击。 **2** to protect yourself from difficult questions, criticisms, etc., especially by avoiding them 避开，回避（难题、批评等）SYN **ward off**: *She managed to fend off questions about new tax increases.* 她设法避开了关于新增赋税的问题。

fend·er /'fendə(r)/ *noun* **1** (*NAmE*) (*BrE* **wing**) a part of a car that is above a wheel（汽车的）挡泥板；翼子板 ➲ VISUAL VOCAB PAGE V56 **2** (*NAmE*) (*BrE* **mud·guard**) a curved cover over a wheel of a bicycle（自行车的）挡泥板 **3** a frame around a FIREPLACE to prevent burning coal or wood from falling out 壁炉的栅栏 **4** a soft solid object such as an old tyre or a piece of rope that is hung over the side of a boat so the boat is not damaged if it touches another boat, a wall, etc. 护舷材（悬挂在船舷的轮胎、绳子等，起防碰损作用）

'fender bender *noun* (*NAmE, informal*) a car accident in which there is not a lot of damage 不严重的撞车事故；轻微车祸

feng shui /ˌfeŋ 'ʃuːi; ˌfʊŋ 'ʃweɪ/ *noun* [U] (*from Chinese*) a Chinese system for deciding the right position for a building and for placing objects inside a building in order to make people feel comfortable and happy 风水

Fen·ian /'fiːniən/ *noun* **1** a member of an organization formed in the 1850s in the US and Ireland in order to end British rule in Ireland 芬尼运动成员（19 世纪 50 年代在美国和爱尔兰成立组织，致力于争取爱尔兰脱离英国统治） **2** (*informal, taboo*) (especially in Northern Ireland) an offensive word for a Catholic（尤用于北爱尔兰）芬尼亚人（对天主教徒的蔑称）

fen·land /'fenlænd; -lənd/ *noun* [U, C] an area of low, flat, wet land in the east of England（英格兰东部的）沼泽地带

fen·nel /'fenl/ *noun* [U] a vegetable that has a thick round STEM with a strong taste. The seeds and leaves are also used in cooking. 茴香（茎作蔬菜，籽和叶亦用于烹调）➲ VISUAL VOCAB PAGE V33

fenu·greek /'fenjʊɡriːk/ *noun* [U] a plant with hard yellow-brown seeds that are used in S Asian cooking as a spice 葫芦巴（种子用于南亚食物调味）

feral /'ferəl/ *adj.* (of animals 动物) living wild, especially after escaping from life as a pet or on a farm 野生的（尤指喂养后逃脱的）：*feral cats* 野猫

fe·ring·hee /fə'rɪŋɡi/ *noun* a word used in some Asian countries for any person with a white skin, especially a European or an American（一些亚洲国家用词，尤指欧洲或美洲的）白人

fer·mata /fɜː'mɑːtə; *NAmE* fɜːr'm-/ *noun* (*music* 音, *from Italian, especially NAmE*) = PAUSE (2)

fer·ment *verb, noun*

■ *verb* /fə'ment; *NAmE* fər'm-/ [I, T] to experience a chemical change because of the action of YEAST or bacteria, often changing sugar to alcohol; to make sth change in this way（使）发酵：*Fruit juices ferment if they are kept for too long.* 果汁存放过久就会发酵。◇ (*figurative*) *A blend of emotions fermented inside her.* 她百感交集，激动不已。◇ ~ **sth** *Red wine is fermented at a higher temperature than white.* 红葡萄酒发酵的温度比白葡萄酒高。▶ **fer·men·ta·tion** /ˌfɜːmen'teɪʃn; *NAmE* ˌfɜːrm-/ *noun* [U]

■ *noun* /'fɜːment; *NAmE* 'fɜːrm-/ [U, sing.] (*formal*) a state of political or social excitement and confusion（政治或社会上的）动乱，骚动，纷扰：*The country is in ferment.* 这个国家动荡不安。

fer·mium /'fɜːmiəm; *NAmE* 'fɜːrm-/ *noun* [U] (*symb.* **Fm**) a chemical element. Fermium is a very rare RADIOACTIVE metal. 镄（罕有的放射性化学元素）

fern /fɜːn; *NAmE* fɜːrn/ *noun* [C, U] a plant with large delicate leaves and no flowers that grows in wet areas or is grown in a pot. There are many types of fern. 蕨；蕨类植物 ➲ VISUAL VOCAB PAGE V11 ▶ **ferny** *adj.*

fer·ocious /fə'rəʊʃəs; *NAmE* -'roʊ-/ *adj.* very aggressive or violent; very strong 凶猛的；残暴的；猛烈的 SYN **savage**: *a ferocious beast/attack/storm* 猛兽；猛烈的进攻；狂风暴雨 ◇ *a man driven by ferocious determination* 为强烈的决心所驱使的人 ◇ *ferocious opposition to the plan* 对这个计划激烈的反对 ▶ **fer·ocious·ly** *adv.*

fer·ocity /fə'rɒsəti; *NAmE* -'rɑːs-/ *noun* [U] violence; aggressive behaviour 残暴；凶猛；凶恶：*The police were shocked by the ferocity of the attack.* 警方对那起攻击的凶残感到震惊。

fer·ret /'ferɪt/ *noun, verb*

■ *noun* a small aggressive animal with a long thin body, kept for chasing RABBITS from their holes, killing RATS, etc. 雪貂（身体细长，饲养用于驱兔灭鼠）

■ *verb* **1** [I] ~ (**about/around**) (**for sth**) (*informal*) to search for sth that is lost or hidden among a lot of things 搜索，四处搜寻，翻找（丢失或藏匿的东西）：*She opened the drawer and ferreted around for her keys.* 她打开抽屉，翻找她的钥匙。 **2** [I] to hunt RABBITS, RATS, etc. using ferrets 用雪貂猎兔（或捕鼠等）

PHR V **,ferret sb/sth↔'out** (*informal*) to discover information or to find sb/sth by searching thoroughly, asking a lot of questions, etc. 搜索出；搜寻出；查获

Fer·ris wheel /'ferɪs wiːl/ (*especially NAmE*) (*BrE also* **,big 'wheel**) *noun* a large wheel which stands in a vertical position at an AMUSEMENT PARK, with seats hanging at its edge for people to ride in（游乐场的）摩天轮，大转轮

fer·rite /'feraɪt/ *noun* [U] **1** a chemical containing iron, used in electrical devices such as AERIALS/ANTENNAS 铁氧体（用于制作天线等电气设备） **2** a form of pure iron that is found in steel which contains low amounts of CARBON（存在于钢中的）铁素体

ferro·mag·net·ic /ˌferəʊmæɡ'netɪk; *NAmE* ˌferoʊ-/ *adj.* (*physics* 物) having the kind of MAGNETISM which iron has 铁磁的

fer·rous /'ferəs/ *adj.* [only before noun] (*specialist*) containing iron; connected with iron 含铁的；铁的

fer·rule /'feruːl; *NAmE* 'ferəl/ *noun* a piece of metal or rubber that covers the end of an umbrella or a stick to protect it（棍杖、伞顶端的）金属包箍，橡皮包头

ferry /'feri/ *noun, verb*

■ *noun* (*pl.* **-ies**) a boat or ship that carries people, vehicles and goods across a river or across a narrow part of the sea 渡船；摆渡；轮渡：*the cross-channel ferry service* 横渡海峡轮渡服务 ◇ *We caught the ferry at Ostend.* 我们在奥斯坦德赶上了渡船。◇ *the Dover-Calais ferry crossing* 多佛尔－加来轮渡 ◇ *the Staten Island ferry* 往返斯塔滕岛的渡船 ➲ COLLOCATIONS AT TRAVEL ➲ VISUAL VOCAB PAGE V59

■ *verb* (**fer·ries, ferry·ing, fer·ried, fer·ried**) [T, I] ~ (**sb/sth**) (+ **adv./prep.**) to carry people or goods in a boat or other vehicle from one place to another, often for a short distance and as a regular service 渡运；摆渡：*He offered to ferry us across the river in his boat.* 他提出坐他的船载我们渡河。◇ *The children need to be ferried to and from school.* 孩子们上学放学需要摆渡。

'ferry boat *noun* a boat that is used as a ferry 渡船

ferry·man /'ferimən/ *noun* (*pl.* **-men** /-mən/) a person in charge of a ferry across a river 渡船船工；渡船主

fer·tile /'fɜːtaɪl; *NAmE* 'fɜːrtl/ *adj.* **1** (of land or soil 土地或土壤) that plants grow well in 肥沃的；富饶的：*a fertile region* 富饶的地区 OPP **infertile** ➲ WORDFINDER NOTE AT

LANDSCAPE **2** (of people, animals or plants 人或动植物) that can produce babies, young animals, fruit or new plants 能生育的；可繁殖的；能结果的：*The treatment has been tested on healthy fertile women under the age of 35.* 这个疗法已对 35 岁以下能生育的健康妇女进行了试验。**OPP infertile** **3** [usually before noun] that produces good results; that encourages activity 能产生好结果的；促进的：*a fertile partnership* 有成效的合伙关系 ◇ *The region at the time was* ***fertile ground*** *for revolutionary movements* (= there were the necessary conditions for them to develop easily). 当时该地区是革命运动的沃土。**4** [usually before noun] (of a person's mind or imagination 人的思想或想象力) that produces a lot of new ideas 点子多的；想象力丰富的：*the product of a* ***fertile imagination*** 想象力丰富的产物 ➲ COMPARE STERILE

fer·til·ity /fəˈtɪləti; *NAmE* fərˈt-/ *noun* [U] the state of being fertile 富饶；丰产；能生育性；可繁殖性；想象力丰富：*the fertility of the soil/land* 土壤的肥沃；土地的丰饶 ◇ *a god of fertility* 丰收之神 ◇ *fertility treatment* (= medical help given to a person to help them have a baby) 不孕症治疗 **OPP infertility**

fer·til·ize (*BrE also* **-ise**) /ˈfɜːtəlaɪz; *NAmE* ˈfɜːrt-/ *verb* **1 ~ sth** to put POLLEN into a plant so that a seed develops; to join SPERM with an egg so that a baby or young animal develops 使受粉；使受精；使受胎；使受孕：*Flowers are often fertilized by bees as they gather nectar.* 花常在蜜蜂采蜜时受粉。◇ *a fertilized egg* 受精卵 **2 ~ sth** to add a substance to soil to make plants grow more successfully 施肥于 ▸ **fer·til·iza·tion, -isation** /ˌfɜːtəlaɪˈzeɪʃn; *NAmE* ˌfɜːrtələˈz-/ *noun* [U]：*Immediately after fertilization, the cells of the egg divide.* 卵受精后细胞立即开始分裂。◇ *the fertilization of soil with artificial chemicals* 给土壤施人工化肥

fer·til·izer (*BrE also* **-iser**) /ˈfɜːtəlaɪzə(r); *NAmE* ˈfɜːrt-/ *noun* [C, U] a substance added to soil to make plants grow more successfully 肥料：***artificial/chemical fertilizers*** 人工 / 化学肥料 ➲ COLLOCATIONS AT FARMING

fer·vent /ˈfɜːvənt; *NAmE* ˈfɜːrv-/ *adj.* [usually before noun] having or showing very strong and sincere feelings about sth 热情的；热忱的；热诚的；热烈的 **SYN ardent**：*a* ***fervent admirer/believer/supporter*** 热诚的仰慕者；虔诚的信徒；热情的支持者 ◇ *a* ***fervent belief/hope/desire*** 虔诚的信仰；热望；强烈的愿望 ▸ **fer·vent·ly** *adv.*

fer·vid /ˈfɜːvɪd; *NAmE* ˈfɜːrvɪd/ *adj.* (*formal*) feeling sth too strongly; showing feelings that are too strong 情感异常强烈的；激昂的；充满激情的 ▸ **fer·vid·ly** *adv.*

fer·vour (*especially US* **fer·vor**) /ˈfɜːvə(r); *NAmE* ˈfɜːrv-/ *noun* [U] very strong feelings about sth 热情；热忱；热诚；热烈 **SYN enthusiasm**：*She kissed him with unusual fervour.* 她特别热烈地吻着他。◇ *religious/patriotic fervour* 宗教狂热；爱国热忱

fess /fes/ *verb*
PHR V ˌ**fess ˈup** (*informal*) to admit that you have done sth wrong 供认；坦白 **SYN own up**

-fest /fest/ *combining form* (in nouns 构成名词) a festival or large meeting involving a particular activity or with a particular atmosphere 节日；联欢；大型聚会：*a jazzfest* 爵士音乐节 ◇ *a talkfest* (= a session involving long discussions) 漫谈会 ◇ (*usually disapproving*) *a lovefest* (= an event in which people show too much affection for each other that may not be genuine) 爱筵

fes·ter /ˈfestə(r)/ *verb* **1** [I] (of a wound or cut 伤口或破口) to become badly infected 化脓；溃烂：***festering sores/wounds*** 脓疮；化脓伤口 **2** [I] (of bad feelings or thoughts 不快的情感或思想) to become much worse because you do not deal with them successfully 更加苦恼；愈益恶化

fes·ti·val 🔑 /ˈfestɪvl/ *noun* **1** 🔑 a series of performances of music, plays, films/movies, etc., usually organized in the same place once a year; a series of public events connected with a particular activity or idea（音乐、戏剧、电影等的）会演，节：*the Edinburgh festival* 爱丁堡艺术节 ◇ *the Cannes film festival* 戛纳电影节 ◇ *a beer festival* 啤酒节 ◇ *a rock festival* (= where bands perform, often outdoors and over a period of several days) 摇滚音乐节 **2** 🔑 a day or period of the year when people stop working to celebrate a special event, often a religious one 节日；喜庆日；节期 ➲ SEE ALSO HARVEST FESTIVAL

fes·tive /ˈfestɪv/ *adj.* **1** typical of a special event or celebration 节日的；喜庆的；欢乐的：*a festive occasion* 喜庆场合 ◇ *The whole town is in* ***festive mood.*** 全城喜气洋洋。**2** (*BrE*) connected with the period when people celebrate Christmas 圣诞节的：*the* ***festive season/period*** 圣诞节期间 ◇ *festive decorations* 圣诞节装饰

fes·tiv·ity /feˈstɪvəti/ *noun* **1 festivities** [pl.] the activities that are organized to celebrate a special event 庆祝活动 **2** [U] the happiness and enjoyment that exist when people celebrate sth 欢乐；喜庆：*The wedding was an occasion of great festivity.* 这个婚礼是喜庆盛事。◇ *an air of festivity* 欢庆的气氛 ➲ WORDFINDER NOTE AT CELEBRATE

fes·toon /feˈstuːn/ *verb, noun*
■ ***verb*** [usually passive] **~ sb/sth (with sth)** to decorate sb/sth with flowers, coloured paper, etc., often as part of a celebration 给…饰以花彩；结彩于；张灯结彩
■ ***noun*** a chain of lights, coloured paper, flowers, etc., used to decorate sth 彩灯；花彩

Fest·schrift /ˈfestʃrɪft/ *noun* (*from German*) a collection of articles published in honour of a SCHOLAR（纪念某学者的）纪念文集

feta cheese /ˌfetə ˈtʃiːz/ (*also* **feta**) *noun* [U] a type of Greek cheese made from sheep's milk（希腊的）羊奶干酪

fetal (*BrE also* **foe·tal**) /ˈfiːtl/ *adj.* [only before noun] connected with a fetus; typical of a fetus 胎儿的；胎的：*fetal abnormalities* 胎儿异常 ◇ *She lay curled up in a* ***fetal position.*** 她像胎儿一样蜷曲地躺着。

ˌfetal ˈalcohol syndrome *noun* [U] (*medical* 医) a condition in which a child's mental and physical development are damaged because the mother drank too much alcohol while she was pregnant 胎儿酒精综合征

fetch 🔑 /fetʃ/ *verb* **1** 🔑 (*especially BrE*) to go to where sb/sth is and bring them/it back （去）拿来；（去）请来：**~ sb/sth** *to fetch help/a doctor* 去请人帮忙；去请医生 ◇ *The inhabitants have to walk a mile to fetch water.* 居民得走一英里路去取水。◇ *She's gone to fetch the kids from school.* 她去学校接孩子了。◇ **~ sb sth** *Could you fetch me my bag?* 你能帮我去取我的包吗？ **2 ~ sth** to be sold for a particular price 售得，卖得（某价）**SYN sell**：*The painting is expected to fetch $10 000 at auction.* 这幅画预计拍卖可得 10 000 美元。

IDM **fetch and ˈcarry (for sb)** to do a lot of little jobs for sb as if you were their servant （为某人）打杂，当听差，跑腿

PHR V ˌ**fetch ˈup** (*informal, especially BrE*) to arrive somewhere without planning to 偶然来到；意外到达：*And then, a few years later, he somehow fetched up in Rome.* 后来，过了几年，他不知怎么到了罗马。

fetch·ing /ˈfetʃɪŋ/ *adj.* (*informal*) (especially of a person or their clothes 尤指人或穿的衣服) attractive 吸引人的；迷人的；动人的 ▸ **fetch·ing·ly** *adv.*

fete (*also* **fête**) /feɪt/ *noun, verb*
■ ***noun*** **1** (*also* **fair**) (*both BrE*) (*NAmE* **car·ni·val**) an outdoor entertainment at which people can play games to win prizes, buy food and drinks, etc., usually arranged to make money for a special purpose 露天游乐会；义卖游乐会：*the* ***school/village/church fete*** 学校 / 村庄 / 教堂义卖会 **2** (*NAmE*) a special occasion held to celebrate sth 庆祝活动：*a charity fete* 慈善庆典
■ ***verb*** [usually passive] **~ sb** (*formal*) to welcome, praise or entertain sb publicly 盛宴款待；热情招待；表彰

fetid (*BrE, less frequent* **foe·tid**) /ˈfetɪd; ˈfiːt-/ *adj.* [usually before noun] (*formal*) smelling very unpleasant 恶臭的 **SYN stinking**

fet·ish /ˈfetɪʃ/ *noun* **1** (*usually disapproving*) the fact that a person spends too much time doing or thinking about a particular thing or thinks that it is more important than it really is 迷恋；癖：*She has a fetish about cleanliness.* 她有洁癖。◇ *He makes a fetish of his work.* 他迷上了他的工作。**2** the fact of getting sexual pleasure from a particular object（从某物获得性快感的）恋物：*to have a leather fetish* 有恋皮革癖 **3** an object that some people worship because they believe that it has magic powers 奉若神明之物；物神 ▶ **fet·ish·ism** *noun* [U]：*a magazine specializing in rubber fetishism* 专登橡胶恋物的杂志 ◇ *the importance of animal fetishism in the history of Egypt* 动物崇拜在埃及史上的重要性 **fet·ish·ist** *noun*：*a leather fetishist* 有恋皮革癖者 **fet·ish·is·tic** /ˌfetɪˈʃɪstɪk/ *adj.*

fet·ish·ize (*BrE also* **-ise**) /ˈfetɪʃaɪz/ *verb* **1 ~ sth** to spend too much time thinking about or doing sth 迷恋于；沉迷于 **2 ~ sth** to get sexual pleasure from thinking about or looking at a particular thing 对…有恋物癖

fet·lock /ˈfetlɒk; *NAmE* -lɑːk/ *noun* the part at the back of a horse's leg, just above its HOOF, where long hair grows 球节（马蹄上面有丛毛的部分）

fet·ter /ˈfetə(r)/ *verb, noun*

■ *verb* [usually passive] **1 ~ sb** (*literary*) to restrict sb's freedom to do what they want 束缚；限制，抑制（某人的自由）**2 ~ sb** to put chains around a prisoner's feet 给（囚犯）上脚镣 SYN **shackle**

■ *noun* **1** [usually pl.] (*literary*) something that stops sb from doing what they want 束缚；桎梏；羁绊：*They were at last freed from the fetters of ignorance.* 他们终于从愚昧无知的束缚中解脱出来。**2 fetters** [pl.] chains that are put around a prisoner's feet 脚镣 SYN **chain, shackles**

fet·tle /ˈfetl/ *noun*

IDM **in fine/good ˈfettle** (*old-fashioned, informal*) healthy; in good condition 健康；身心俱佳；状况良好

fetus (*BrE also* **foe·tus**) /ˈfiːtəs/ *noun* a young human or animal before it is born, especially a human more than eight weeks after 胎儿；胎 ⊃ WORDFINDER NOTE AT PREGNANT

feud /fjuːd/ *noun, verb*

■ *noun* an angry and bitter argument between two people or groups of people that continues over a long period of time 长期不和；争吵不休；世仇；夙怨：~ (**between A and B**) *a long-running feud between the two artists* 两个艺术家之间的夙怨 ◇ ~ (**with sb**) *a feud with the neighbours* 与邻不睦 ◇ *a family feud* (= within a family or between two families) 家族世仇 ◇ ~ (**over sb/sth**) *a feud over money* 为钱争吵不休

■ *verb* [I] ~ (**with sb**) to have an angry and bitter argument with sb over a long period of time 长期争斗；争吵不休；世代结仇 ▶ **feud·ing** *noun* [U]：*stories of bitter feuding between rival drug dealers* 势不两立的毒贩之间疯狂争斗的故事

feu·dal /ˈfjuːdl/ *adj.* [usually before noun] connected with or similar to feudalism 封建（制度）的：*the feudal system* 封建制度

feu·dal·ism /ˈfjuːdəlɪzəm/ *noun* [U] the social system that existed during the Middle Ages in Europe in which people were given land and protection by a NOBLEMAN, and had to work and fight for him in return 封建制度；封建主义 ▶ **feu·dal·ist·ic** /ˌfjuːdəˈlɪstɪk/ *adj.*

fever 🔑 /ˈfiːvə(r)/ *noun* **1** 🔑 [C, U] a medical condition in which a person has a temperature that is higher than normal 发烧；发热：*He has a high fever.* 他发高烧。◇ *Aspirin should help reduce the fever.* 阿司匹林应该可以退烧。⊃ WORDFINDER NOTE AT DISEASE ⊃ COLLOCATIONS AT ILL ⊃ COMPARE TEMPERATURE (2) **2** 🔑 [C, U] (*old-fashioned*) (used mainly in compounds 主要用于构成复合词) a particular type of disease in which sb has a high temperature 热（病）：*She caught a fever on her travels in Africa, and died.* 她在非洲旅行时患热病而死。⊃ SEE ALSO GLANDULAR FEVER, HAY FEVER, RHEUMATIC FEVER, SCARLET FEVER, YELLOW FEVER **3** [sing.] ~ (**of sth**) a state of nervous excitement 激动不安；兴奋紧张：*He waited for her arrival in a fever of impatience.* 他焦急不安地等待她的到来。**4** [U] (especially in compounds 尤用于构成复合词) great interest or excitement about sth 狂热：*election fever* 选举热

ˈfever blister *noun* (*NAmE*) = COLD SORE

fe·vered /ˈfiːvəd; *NAmE* -vərd/ *adj.* [only before noun] **1** showing great excitement or worry 非常激动的；焦虑不安的：***fevered excitement/speculation*** 兴奋异常；焦急不安的猜测 ◇ *a **fevered imagination/mind*** (= that imagines strange things) 驰骋的想象力；奇想联翩 **2** suffering from a fever 发烧的；发热的：*She mopped his **fevered brow**.* 她擦了擦他那发烧的前额。

fever·few /ˈfiːvəfjuː; *NAmE* ˈfiːvər-/ *noun* [U] a plant of the DAISY family, sometimes used as a medicine 小白菊（可作药用）

fe·ver·ish /ˈfiːvərɪʃ/ *adj.* **1** [usually before noun] showing strong feelings of excitement or worry, often with a lot of activity or quick movements 激动的；焦虑不安的：*The whole place was a scene of **feverish activity**.* 整个地方都是一片紧张匆忙的景象。◇ *a state of feverish excitement* 异常激动的状态 ◇ *feverish with longing* 十分渴望 **2** suffering from a fever; caused by a fever 发烧的；发烧引起的：*She was aching and feverish.* 她疼痛发烧。◇ *a feverish cold/dream* 伴有发烧的感冒；发烧引起的梦 ▶ **fe·ver·ish·ly** *adv.*：*The team worked feverishly to the November deadline.* 整个团队抢在十一月最后期限前拼命工作。◇ *Her mind raced feverishly.* 她思潮起伏。

ˈfever pitch *noun* [U, C] a very high level of excitement or activity 高度兴奋；极为激动；狂热：*Speculation about his future had **reached fever pitch**.* 关于他的前途的猜测达到了狂热的地步。◇ *Excitement has been **at fever pitch** for days.* 狂热的兴奋持续了好些日子。

few 🔑 /fjuː/ *det., adj., pron.*

■ *det., adj.* (**fewer, few·est**) **1** 🔑 used with plural nouns and a plural verb to mean 'not many'（与复数名词和复数动词连用）不多，很少：*Few people understand the difference.* 很少有人了解这个差别。◇ *There seem to be fewer tourists around this year.* 今年来访的旅游者似乎少了。◇ *Very few students learn Latin now.* 现在学拉丁语的学生少得很。**2** 🔑 (*usually* **a few**) used with plural nouns and a plural verb to mean 'a small number', 'some'（与复数名词和复数动词连用）有些，几个：*We've had a few replies.* 我们已得到了一些答复。◇ *I need a few things from the store.* 我需要从商店买些东西。◇ ***Quite a few** people are going to arrive early.* 相当多的人打算早到。◇ *I try to visit my parents **every few weeks**.* 我尽量每隔几个星期看望一次父母。

IDM **ˌfew and ˌfar beˈtween** not frequent; not happening often 稀少；稀疏；不常发生

■ *pron.* **1** 🔑 not many people, things or places 很少人（或事物、地方）：*Very few of his books are worth reading.* 他的书值得读的太少了。◇ *You can pass with **as few as** 25 points.* 只需要 25 分就可以及格。◇ (*formal*) *Few will argue with this conclusion.* 很少有人会不同意这个结论。**2** 🔑 **a few** a small number of people, things or places; some 有些（人、事物、地方）；一些：*I recognized a few of the other people.* 我认出了一些其他的人。◇ *I've seen most of his movies. Only a few are as good as his first one.* 他的电影多数我都看过。只有少数几部能与他的第一部媲美。◇ *Could you give me a few more details?* 你能再给我提供一些详情吗？**3** 🔑 **fewer** not as many as 不和…一般多；少于：*Fewer than 20 students passed all the exams.* 不到 20 个学生考试全部及格。◇ *There are **no fewer than** 100 different species in the area.* 这个地区有不少于 100 个不同物种。HELP Look at the note at **less**. 参看 less 词条下的注释。**4 the few** used with a plural verb to mean 'a small group of people'（与复数动词连用）少数人：*Real power belongs to the few.* 真正的权力掌握在少数人手中。◇ *She was one of **the chosen few*** (= the small group with special rights). 她属于少数享有特权的人。

IDM **quite a ˈfew** 🔑 (*BrE also* **a good ˈfew**) a fairly large number 相当多；不少：*I've been there quite a few times.*

我去过那里好多次了。**have 'had a few** (*informal*) to have had enough alcohol to make you drunk 喝醉了；已醉

fey /feɪ/ *adj.* (*literary, sometimes disapproving*) (usually of a person 通常指人) sensitive and rather mysterious or strange; not acting in a very practical way 古怪易冲动的；有点故弄玄虚的；不讲求实际的

fez /fez/ *noun* (*pl.* **fezzes**) a round red hat with a flat top and a TASSEL but no BRIM, worn by men in some Muslim countries（一些伊斯兰国家男人戴的平顶有缨无檐）红圆帽

ff *abbr.* (*music* 音) very loudly (from Italian 'fortissimo')（演奏或歌唱）很强（源自意大利语 fortissimo）

ff. *abbr.* written after the number of a page or line to mean 'and the following pages or lines' 及以后各页（或各行）：*See pp. 96 ff.* 见 96 页及以后各页。

fi·ancé /fiˈɒnseɪ; -ˈɑːns-; *NAmE* ˌfiːɑːnˈseɪ/ *noun* the man that a woman is engaged to 未婚夫：*Linda and her fiancé were there.* 琳达和她的未婚夫在那里。➲ COLLOCATIONS AT MARRIAGE

fi·an·cée /fiˈɒnseɪ; *NAmE* ˌfiːɑːnˈseɪ/ *noun* the woman that a man is engaged to 未婚妻：*Paul and his fiancée were there.* 保罗和他的未婚妻在那里。➲ COLLOCATIONS AT MARRIAGE

Fianna Fáil /ˌfiænə ˈfɔɪl/ *noun* [sing.+sing./pl. v.] one of the two main political parties in the Republic of Ireland 共和党（爱尔兰共和国两大政党之一）➲ COMPARE FINE GAEL

fi·asco /fiˈæskəʊ; *NAmE* fiˈæskoʊ/ *noun* (*pl.* **-os**, *NAmE also* **-oes**) (*informal*) something that does not succeed, often in a way that causes embarrassment 惨败；可耻的失败；尴尬的结局 **SYN** **disaster**: *What a fiasco!* 真是使人下不了台！

fiat /ˈfiːæt; ˈfaɪæt/ *noun* [C, U] (*formal*) an official order given by sb in authority（当权者的）法令，命令，谕 **SYN** **decree**

fib /fɪb/ *noun, verb*

■ *noun* (*informal*) a statement that is not true; a lie about sth that is not important 谎言；（无关紧要的）小谎，瞎话：*Stop **telling fibs**.* 别再撒谎了。

■ *verb* (**-bb-**) [I] (*informal*) to tell a lie, usually about sth that is not important 撒谎；说瞎话：*Come on, don't fib! Where were you really last night?* 得了吧，不要撒谎了！昨夜你到底在哪儿？ ▶ **fib·ber** *noun*：*You fibber!* 你骗人！

Fi·bo·nacci ser·ies /ˌfɪbəˈnɑːtʃi sɪəriːz; *NAmE* sɪriːz/ *noun* (*mathematics* 数) a series of numbers in which each number is equal to the two numbers before it added together. Starting from 1, the series is 1,1,2,3,5,8,13, etc. 斐波那契数列（其中每数等于前面两数之和）

fibre (*especially US* **fiber**) /ˈfaɪbə(r)/ *noun* **1** [U] the part of food that helps to keep a person healthy by keeping the BOWELS working and moving other food quickly through the body（食物中的）纤维素 **SYN** **roughage**: ***dietary fibre*** 饮食纤维素 ◇ *Dried fruits are especially **high in fibre**.* 干水果的纤维素含量尤其高。◇ *a **high-/low-fibre diet*** 纤维素含量高 / 低的饮食 **2** [C, U] a material such as cloth or rope that is made from a mass of natural or artificial threads（织物或绳等）纤维制品：*nylon and other **man-made fibres*** 尼龙和其他人造纤维制品 **3** [C] one of the many thin threads that form body TISSUE, such as muscle, and natural materials, such as wood and cotton（人或动物身体组织及天然物质的）纤维：***cotton/wood/nerve/muscle fibres*** 棉 / 木 / 神经 / 肌肉纤维 ◇ (*literary*) *She loved him with every fibre of her being.* 她一心一意地爱他。➲ SEE ALSO MORAL FIBRE, OPTICAL FIBRE

fibre·board (*especially US* **fiber·board**) /ˈfaɪbəbɔːd; *NAmE* ˈfaɪbərbɔːrd/ *noun* [U] a building material made of wood or other plant fibres pressed together to form boards 纤维板

fibre·glass (*especially US* **fiber·glass**) /ˈfaɪbəglɑːs; *NAmE* ˈfaɪbərglæs/ (*BrE also* ˌ**glass 'fibre**) (*US also* ˌ**glass 'fiber**) *noun* [U] a strong light material made from glass fibres and plastic, used for making boats, etc. 玻璃纤维

ˌ**fibre 'optics** (*especially US* ˌ**fiber 'optics**) *noun* [U] the use of thin fibres of glass, etc. for sending information in the form of light signals 光导纤维；光纤 ▶ ˌ**fibre-'optic** (*especially US* ˌ**fiber-'optic**) *adj.* [usually before noun]：*fibre-optic cables* 光缆

fi·brin /ˈfaɪbrɪn; ˈfɪb-/ *noun* [U] (*biology* 生) a PROTEIN that stops blood from flowing or being lost from a wound 纤维蛋白，血纤蛋白（有凝血作用）

fi·brino·gen /faɪˈbrɪnədʒən; fɪˈb-/ *noun* [U] (*biology* 生) a PROTEIN in the blood from which fibrin is produced 凝血因子 I；血纤蛋白原

fibro /ˈfaɪbrəʊ; *NAmE* -oʊ/ *noun* (*pl.* **-os**) (*AustralE*) **1** [U] a mixture of sand, CEMENT, and plant FIBRES, used as a building material 石棉水泥（以沙子、水泥及植物纤维混合而成的建筑材料） **2** [C] a house that is built mainly of such material 石棉水泥房

fi·broid /ˈfaɪbrɔɪd/ *noun* (*medical* 医) a mass of cells that form a lump, usually found in the wall of a woman's UTERUS（通常长在子宫壁上的）纤维瘤；平滑肌瘤

fi·broma /faɪˈbrəʊmə; *NAmE* -ˈbroʊ-/ *noun* (*medical* 医) a harmless lump that grows inside the body（体内生长的）纤维瘤

fi·brous /ˈfaɪbrəs/ *adj.* [usually before noun] (*specialist*) made of many fibres; looking like fibres 纤维构成的；纤维状的：*fibrous tissue* 纤维组织

fib·ula /ˈfɪbjələ/ *noun* (*pl.* **fibu·lae** /ˈfɪbjəliː/ or **fibu·las**) (*anatomy* 解) the outer bone of the two bones in the lower part of the leg between the knee and the ankle 腓骨 ➲ VISUAL VOCAB PAGE V64 ➲ SEE ALSO TIBIA

fickle /ˈfɪkl/ *adj.* (*disapproving*) **1** changing often and suddenly 易变的；无常的：*The weather here is notoriously fickle.* 这里的天气出了名的变化无常。◇ *the fickle world of fashion* 千变万化的时装界 **2** (of a person 人) often changing their mind in an unreasonable way so that you cannot rely on them 反复无常的：*a fickle friend* 靠不住的朋友 ▶ **fickle·ness** *noun* [U]：*the fickleness of the English climate* 英国气候的变幻不定

fic·tion /ˈfɪkʃn/ *noun* **1** [U] a type of literature that describes imaginary people and events, not real ones 小说：*a work of popular fiction* 通俗小说作品 ◇ *historical/romantic fiction* 历史 / 言情小说 **OPP** **non-fiction** ➲ COLLOCATIONS AT LITERATURE ➲ SEE ALSO SCIENCE FICTION ➲ WORDFINDER NOTE AT WRITE **2** [C, U] a thing that is invented or imagined and is not true 虚构的事；假想之物：*For years he managed to keep up the fiction that he was not married.* 多年来他设法一直给人一种未婚的假象。**IDM** SEE TRUTH

fic·tion·al /ˈfɪkʃənl/ *adj.* not real or true; existing only in stories; connected with fiction 虚构的；小说（中）的：*fictional characters* 虚构的人物 ◇ *a fictional account of life on a desert island* 对荒岛生活的虚构描述 ◇ *fictional techniques* 小说技巧 **OPP** **real-life**

fic·tion·al·ize (*BrE also* **-ise**) /ˈfɪkʃənəlaɪz/ *verb* [usually passive] ~ **sth** to write a book or make a film/movie about a true story, but changing some of the details, characters, etc. 把（真人真事）改编成小说（或电影）：*a fictionalized account of his childhood* 关于他童年的小说式描述

fic·ti·tious /fɪkˈtɪʃəs/ *adj.* invented by sb rather than true 虚构的；虚假的：*All the places and characters in my novel are fictitious* (= they do not exist in real life). 我小说中的人物和地点纯属虚构。

fid·dle /ˈfɪdl/ *verb, noun*

■ *verb* **1** [I] ~ (**with sth**) to keep touching or moving sth with your hands, especially because you are bored or nervous（尤指厌烦或紧张地）不断摸弄，不停摆弄：*He was fiddling with his keys while he talked to me.* 和我谈话时他不停地摆弄钥匙。 **2** [T] ~ **sth** (*informal*) to change the details or figures of sth in order to try to get money dishonestly, or gain an advantage 篡改；伪造；对…做手脚：*to fiddle the accounts* 篡改账目 ◇ *She **fiddled the books*** (= changed a company's financial records) *while working as an accountant.* 她当会计时对账簿做了手脚。 **3** [I] (*informal*) to play music on the VIOLIN 拉小提琴

PHR V **,fiddle a'bout/a'round** to spend your time doing things that are not important 虚度光阴；瞎混 **,fiddle a'bout/a'round with sth | 'fiddle with sth 1** to keep touching sth or making small changes to sth because you are not satisfied with it 不断摆弄；不停对…做小修小改：*I've been fiddling about with this design for ages.* 我不断地修改这个设计已经好长时间了。 **2** to touch or move the parts of sth in order to try to change it or repair it 拨弄，摆弄（为改变或修理某物）：*Who's been fiddling with the TV again?* 谁又在摆弄电视机了？

■ ***noun*** (*informal*) **1** [C] = VIOLIN **2** [C] (*BrE*) something that is done dishonestly to get money 欺诈；骗钱行为；骗局 SYN **fraud**：*an **insurance/tax, etc. fiddle*** 保险、纳税等骗局 **3** [sing.] (*BrE*) an act of moving sth or adjusting sth in order to make it work 修理；调整；摆弄 **4** [sing.] (*BrE*) something that is difficult to do 难事

IDM **be on the 'fiddle** (*BrE*) to be doing sth dishonest to get money 搞骗钱勾当 **play second 'fiddle (to sb/sth)** to be treated as less important than sb/sth; to have a less important position than sb/sth else 当二把手；当副手；居次要地位 ➲ MORE AT FIT *adj.*

fid·dler /ˈfɪdlə(r)/ *noun* a person who plays the VIOLIN, especially to play FOLK MUSIC 小提琴手（尤指演奏民间音乐者）

fiddle·sticks /ˈfɪdlstɪks/ *exclamation* (*old-fashioned, informal*) used to say that you disagree with sb（表示不同意）胡扯，废话

fid·dling /ˈfɪdlɪŋ/ *adj.* [usually before noun] (*informal*) small, unimportant and often annoying 琐碎的；繁琐的

fid·dly /ˈfɪdli/ *adj.* (**fid·dlier, fid·dli·est**) (*BrE, informal*) difficult to do or use because small objects are involved 微小难弄的；需要手巧的；精巧难使用的：*Changing a fuse is one of those fiddly jobs I hate.* 换保险丝是我不愿干的麻烦事之一。

fi·del·ity /fɪˈdeləti/ *noun* [U] **1 ~ (to sth)** (*formal*) the quality of being loyal to sb/sth 忠诚；忠实；忠贞：*fidelity to your principles* 对原则的忠诚不移 **2 ~ (to sb)** the quality of being faithful to your husband, wife or partner by not having a sexual relationship with anyone else（对丈夫、妻子或性伴侣的）忠贞，忠实，忠诚：***marital/sexual fidelity*** 婚姻 / 性的忠贞 OPP **infidelity** **3 ~ (of sth) (to sth)** (*formal*) the quality of being accurate 准确性；精确性：*the fidelity of the translation to the original text* 对原文翻译的准确性 ➲ SEE ALSO HIGH FIDELITY

fidget /ˈfɪdʒɪt/ *verb, noun*

■ ***verb*** [I] **~ (with sth)** to keep moving your body, your hands or your feet because you are nervous, bored, excited, etc. 坐立不安；烦躁：*Sit still and stop fidgeting!* 坐好，不要动来晃去的！

■ ***noun*** a person who is always fidgeting 坐立不安的人

fidgety /ˈfɪdʒɪti/ *adj.* (*informal*) (of a person 人) unable to remain still or quiet, usually because of being bored or nervous 坐立不安的 SYN **restless**

fidu·ciary /fɪˈdjuːʃəri; *NAmE also* fɪˈduːʃieri/ *adj., noun* (*law* 律)

■ ***adj.*** involving trust, especially in a situation where a person or company controls money or property belonging to others 信托的；信用的；（尤指）受委托的，受信托的：*the company's fiduciary duty to its shareholders* 公司对股东负有的受托责任

■ ***noun*** (*pl.* **-ies**) a person or company that is in a position of trust, especially when it involves controlling money or property belonging to others（尤指财产）受信托人（或公司）

fief /fiːf/ (*also* **fief·dom** /ˈfiːfdəm/) *noun* **1** (*law* 律, *old use*) an area of land, especially a rented area for which the payment is work, not money 土地；（尤指）采邑，封地 **2** an area or a situation in which sb has control or influence 领域；势力范围：*She considers the office as her own private fiefdom.* 她把办公室视为她的私人领地。

field 🔑 /fiːld/ *noun, verb*

■ ***noun***

• **AREA OF LAND** 田地 **1** 🔑 [C] an area of land in the country used for growing crops or keeping animals in, usually surrounded by a fence, etc. 田；地；牧场：*People were working in the fields.* 人们在田间劳动。 ◇ *a ploughed field* 已耕地 ◇ *a field of wheat* 麦田 ◇ *We camped in a field near the village.* 我们在靠近村庄的地里露营。 ➲ COLLOCATIONS AT FARMING ➲ VISUAL VOCAB PAGE V3 **2** [C] (usually in compounds 通常构成复合词) an area of land used for the purpose mentioned（作某种用途的）场地：*a landing field* 降落场 ◇ *a medal for bravery in the field (of battle)* 作战英勇奖章 ➲ SEE ALSO AIRFIELD, BATTLEFIELD, MINEFIELD **3** 🔑 [C] (usually in compounds 通常构成复合词) a large area of land covered with the thing mentioned; an area from which the thing mentioned is obtained（覆盖…的或有…的）大片地方：*ice fields* 冰原 ◇ *gas fields*（天然）气田 ➲ SEE ALSO COALFIELD, GOLDFIELD, OILFIELD, SNOWFIELD

• **SUBJECT/ACTIVITY** 学科；活动 **4** 🔑 [C] a particular subject or activity that sb works in or is interested in 专业；学科；界；领域 SYN **area**：*famous **in the field of** music* 音乐界著名的 ◇ *All of them are experts in their chosen field.* 他们在各自选定的专业中都是专家。 ◇ *This discovery has opened up a whole new field of research.* 这个发现开辟了一个崭新的研究领域。

• **PRACTICAL WORK** 实地工作 **5** [C] (usually used as an adjective 通常用作形容词) the fact of people doing practical work or study, rather than working in a library or laboratory 实地；野外：*a **field study/investigation*** 实地研究 / 调查 ◇ ***field research/methods*** 野外研究；实习方法 ◇ *essential reading for those working **in the field*** 实地工作者必备读物 ➲ SEE ALSO FIELD TRIP, FIELDWORK

• **IN SPORT** 体育运动 **6** 🔑 (*BrE also* **pitch**) [C] (usually in compounds 通常构成复合词) an area of land used for playing a sport on 运动场：*a **baseball/rugby/football, etc. field*** 棒球、橄榄球、足球等场地 ◇ *a sports field* 运动场 ◇ *Today they **take the field*** (= go on to the field to play a game) *against county champions Essex.* 今天他们登场与郡冠军队埃塞克斯队比赛。 ➲ SEE ALSO PLAYING FIELD **7** [sing.+sing./pl. v.] (in CRICKET and BASEBALL 板球和棒球) the team that is trying to catch the ball rather than hit it 守队 **8** [sing.+sing./pl. v.] all the people or animals competing in a particular sports event（比赛项目的）全体参赛者：*The field includes three world-record holders.* 参赛运动员中有三位世界纪录的保持者。

• **IN BUSINESS** 商业 **9** [sing.+sing./pl. v.] all the people or products competing in a particular area of business 行业：*They **lead the field** in home entertainment systems.* 他们在家庭娱乐设备行业中居领先地位。

• **PHYSICS** 物理学 **10** [C] (usually in compounds 通常构成复合词) an area within which the force mentioned has an effect 场：*the earth's gravitational field* 地球引力场 ◇ *an electro-magnetic field* 电磁场

• **COMPUTING** 计算机技术 **11** [C] part of a record that is a separate item of data 字段；信息组；栏：*You will need to create separate fields for first name, surname and address.* 名字、姓氏和地址要各自编成单独的字段。

IDM **leave the field 'clear for sb | leave sb in possession of the 'field** to enable sb to be successful in a particular area of activity because other people or groups have given up competing with them 为…的胜利铺平道路；为…的成功扫清障碍 **play the 'field** (*informal*) to have sexual relationships with a lot of different people 性滥交；乱搞男女关系

■ ***verb***

• **CANDIDATE/TEAM** 候选人；队 **1** [T] **~ sb/sth** to provide a candidate, speaker, team, etc. to represent you in an election, a competition, etc. 使参加竞选；使参加比赛：*Each of the main parties fielded more than 300 candidates.* 每个主要政党都选派出 300 多个候选人。 ◇ *England fielded a young side in the World Cup.* 英格兰派出了一支年轻的队伍参加世界杯赛。

• **IN CRICKET/BASEBALL** 板球；棒球 **2** [I] to be the person or the team that catches the ball and throws it back after sb has hit it 担任守场员；任守方：*He won the toss and chose to field first.* 他在掷硬币时猜中了，选择先作守方。**3** [T] **~ sth** to catch the ball and throw it back 接守；接防：*He fielded the ball expertly.* 他熟练地接住球，防守成功。

• QUESTIONS 问题 **4** [T] **~ sth** to receive and deal with questions or comments 处理，应付（问题或意见）：*The BBC had to field more than 300 phone calls after last night's programme.* 英国广播公司在昨夜的节目播出以后，不得不答复了 300 多个电话。

'field day (*NAmE*) (*BrE* **'sports day**) *noun* a special day at school when there are no classes and children compete in sports events（学校的）运动会

IDM **have a 'field day** (*NAmE, BrE*) to be given the opportunity to do sth that you enjoy, especially sth that other people do not approve of 有展现本领的机会，有机会大干一番（尤指他人不赞同的事）：*The tabloid press had a field day with the latest government scandal.* 这家小报利用最近的政府丑闻大做文章。

field·er /'fi:ldə(r)/ *noun* (*BrE also* **fields·man**) (in CRICKET and BASEBALL 板球和棒球) a member of the team that is trying to catch the ball rather than hit it 守场员

'field event *noun* [usually pl.] a sport done by ATHLETES that is not a race, for example jumping or throwing the JAVELIN 田赛项目（如跳高或掷标枪）➲ VISUAL VOCAB PAGE V50 ➲ COMPARE TRACK EVENT

'field glasses *noun* [pl.] (*specialist*) = BINOCULARS

'field goal *noun* **1** (in AMERICAN FOOTBALL or RUGBY 美式足球或橄榄球) a goal scored by kicking the ball over the bar of the goal 越过球门横木得分的球 **2** (in BASKETBALL 篮球) a goal scored by throwing the ball through the net during normal play（除罚球外的）投篮得分

'field hand *noun* (*NAmE*) = FARMHAND

'field hockey (*NAmE*) (*also* **hockey**) *noun* [U] a game played on a field by two teams of 11 players, with curved sticks and a small hard ball. Teams try to hit the ball into the other team's goal. 曲棍球 ➲ VISUAL VOCAB PAGE V48

'field hospital *noun* a temporary hospital near a BATTLEFIELD 野战医院

'field house *noun* (*NAmE*) **1** a building at a sports field where people can change their clothes, have a shower, etc.（有更衣室、淋浴间等的）运动场附属设施楼 **2** a building where sports events are held, with seats for people to watch（比赛用）室内运动场，体育馆

field·ing /'fi:ldɪŋ/ *noun* [U] (in CRICKET and BASEBALL 板球和棒球) the activity of catching and returning the ball 接守；接防

,field 'marshal *noun* (*abbr.* **FM**) an officer of the highest rank in the British army（英国）陆军元帅：*Field Marshal Montgomery* 蒙哥马利陆军元帅

'field officer *noun* **1** a person in a company or other organization whose job involves practical work in a particular area or region（公司等的）派驻地区工作人员，地区工作人员 **2** an officer of high rank in the army (= a MAJOR, LIEUTENANT COLONEL or COLONEL) 陆军校官

,field of 'fire *noun* (*pl.* **fields of fire**) the area that you can hit when shooting from a particular position 射界

,field of 'vision (*also* **,field of 'view**, or *specialist* **,visual 'field**) *noun* (*pl.* **fields of vision/view, visual fields**) the total amount of space that you can see from a particular point without moving your head 视野；视界

fields·man /'fi:ldzmən/ *noun* (*pl.* **-men** /-mən/) (*BrE*) = FIELDER

'field sports *noun* [pl.] (*BrE*) outdoor sports such as hunting, fishing and shooting 野外运动（如打猎、钓鱼、射击）

'field-test *verb* **~ sth** to test sth, such as a piece of equipment, in the place where it will be used 对（设备等）做现场试验 ▶ **'field test** *noun*：*Laboratory and field tests have been conducted.* 已进行实验室试验和现场试验。

'field trip *noun* a journey made by a group of people, often students, to study sth in its natural environment（常指学生进行的）野外考察，实地考察：*We went on a geology field trip.* 我们去进行地质野外考察。

field·work /'fi:ldwɜ:k; *NAmE* -wɜ:rk/ *noun* [U] research or study that is done in the real world rather than in a library or laboratory 实地研究；野外考察 ▶ **field·worker** *noun*

fiend /fi:nd/ *noun* **1** a very cruel or unpleasant person 恶魔般的人；残忍的人；令人憎恶的人 **2** (*informal*) (used after another noun 用于另一名词后) a person who is very interested in the thing mentioned …迷；…狂；爱好者 SYN **fanatic**：*a crossword fiend* 纵横填字游戏爱好者 **3** an evil spirit 魔鬼；恶魔

fiend·ish /'fi:ndɪʃ/ *adj.* [usually before noun] **1** cruel and unpleasant 恶魔般的；残忍的；令人憎恶的：*a fiendish act* 残忍的行为 ◇ *shrieks of fiendish laughter* 恶魔般的尖笑声 **2** (*informal*) extremely clever and complicated, often in an unpleasant way（常令人不快地）巧妙复杂的：*a puzzle of fiendish complexity* 深奥复杂的谜 ◇ *a fiendish plan* 巧妙复杂的计划 **3** (*informal*) extremely difficult 极其困难的：*a fiendish problem* 大难题

fiend·ish·ly /'fi:ndɪʃli/ *adv.* (*informal*) very; extremely 很；极其：***fiendishly clever/complicated*** 极其巧妙 / 复杂

fierce /fɪəs; *NAmE* fɪrs/ *adj.* (**fier·cer, fier·cest**) **1** (especially of people or animals 尤指人或动物) angry and aggressive in a way that is frightening 凶猛的；凶狠的；凶残的：*a fierce dog* 恶狗 ◇ *Two fierce eyes glared at them.* 一双凶狠的眼睛瞪着他们。◇ *He suddenly looked fierce.* 他突然面露凶相。◇ *She spoke in a fierce whisper.* 她恶狠狠地低声说话。**2** (especially of actions or emotions 尤指动作或情感) showing strong feelings or a lot of activity, often in a way that is violent 狂热的；强烈的；猛烈的：*fierce loyalty* 极度的忠诚 ◇ *the scene of fierce fighting* 激烈战斗的场面 ◇ *He launched a fierce attack on the Democrats.* 他对民主党人发动了猛烈的攻击。◇ *Competition from abroad became fiercer in the 1990s.* * 20 世纪 90 年代，来自国外的竞争加剧。**3** (of weather conditions or temperatures 天气或温度) very strong in a way that could cause damage 狂暴的；恶劣的：*fierce wind* 狂风 ◇ *the fierce heat of the flames* 火焰的炽热高温 ▶ **fierce·ly** *adv.*：*'Let go of me,' she said fiercely.* "放开我。" 她极为气愤地说道。◇ *fiercely competitive* 竞争激烈的 ◇ *The aircraft was burning fiercely.* 飞机猛烈地燃烧着。**fierce·ness** *noun* [U]

IDM **something 'fierce** (*NAmE, informal*) very much; more than usual 十分；特别：*I sure do miss you something fierce!* 我真的非常想念你！

fiery /'faɪəri/ *adj.* [usually before noun] (**fier·ier, fieri·est**) **1** looking like fire; consisting of fire 火一般的；火的：*fiery red hair* 火红的头发 ◇ *The sun was now sinking, a fiery ball of light in the west.* 西边的太阳像一个发光的火球正在下沉。**2** quickly or easily becoming angry 暴躁的；易怒的：*She has a **fiery temper**.* 她脾气暴躁。◇ *a fiery young man* 动辄发怒的年轻人 **3** showing strong emotions, especially anger 充满激情的；（尤指）怒气冲冲的 SYN **passionate**：*a fiery look* 怒容满面 **4** (of food or drink 食物或饮料) causing a part of your body to feel as if it is burning 辣的：*a fiery Mexican dish* 味辣的墨西哥菜肴

fi·esta /fi'estə/ *noun* (*from Spanish*) a public event when people celebrate and are entertained with music and dancing, usually connected with a religious festival in countries where the people speak Spanish（通常指说西班牙语国家的）宗教节日，节日

FIFA /'fi:fə/ *abbr.* (*from French*) Fédération Internationale de Football Association (the international organization that controls the sport of football (SOCCER)) 国际足联；国际足球联合会

fife /faɪf/ *noun* a musical instrument like a small FLUTE that plays high notes and is used with drums in military music 小横笛（用于军乐中，与鼓合奏）

fif·teen /ˌfɪfˈtiːn/ **1** *number* 15 十五 **2** *noun* a team of RUGBY UNION players 十五人制橄榄球队；联合会橄榄球队：*He's in the first fifteen.* 他是联合会橄榄球队首发队员。▶ **fif·teenth** /ˌfɪfˈtiːnθ/ *ordinal number, noun* HELP There are examples of how to use ordinal numbers at the entry for **fifth**. 序数词用法示例见 fifth 条。

fifth /fɪfθ/ *ordinal number, noun*

■ ***ordinal number*** 5th 第五：*Today is the fifth (of May).* 今天是（五月）五号。◇ *the fifth century BC* 公元前五世纪 ◇ *It's her fifth birthday.* 这是她五岁生日。◇ *My office is on the fifth floor.* 我的办公室在六楼。◇ *It's the fifth time that I've been to America.* 这是我第五次去美国了。◇ *Her mother had just given birth to another child, her fifth.* 她的母亲刚又生了孩子，她的第五个孩子。◇ *the world's fifth-largest oil exporter* 世界第五大石油输出国◇ *He finished fifth in the race.* 他赛跑得了第五名。◇ *Edward V* (= Edward the Fifth) 爱德华五世

■ ***noun*** each of five equal parts of sth 五分之一：*She cut the cake into fifths.* 她把蛋糕切成五块。◇ *He gave her a fifth of the total amount.* 他给了她总数的五分之一。

IDM **take/plead the 'fifth** (*US*) to make use of the right to refuse to answer questions in court about a crime, because you may give information which would make it seem that you are guilty（在法庭上）拒绝回答，避而不答 ORIGIN From the **Fifth Amendment** of the US Constitution, which guarantees this right. 源自《美国宪法》第五条修正案，该条文保障这种权利。

ˌfifth 'column *noun* a group of people working secretly to help the enemy of the country or organization they are in 第五纵队（为所在国家或组织的敌人秘密工作的一群人）▶ **ˌfifth 'columnist** *noun*

fifth·ly /ˈfɪfθli/ *adv.* used to introduce the fifth of a list of points you want to make in a speech or piece of writing（用于列举）第五：*Fifthly, we need to consider the effect on the local population.* 第五，我们必须考虑对当地居民的影响。

fifty /ˈfɪfti/ **1** *number* 50 五十 **2** *noun* **the fifties** [pl.] numbers, years or temperatures from 50 to 59 五十几；五十年代：*She was born in the fifties.* 她是五十年代出生的。▶ **fif·ti·eth** /ˈfɪftiəθ/ *ordinal number, noun* HELP There are examples of how to use ordinal numbers at the entry for **fifth**. 序数词用法示例见 fifth 条。

IDM **in your 'fifties** between the ages of 50 and 59 * 50 多岁：*He retired in his fifties.* 他在五十多岁时退休了。

ˌfifty-'fifty *adj., adv.* (*informal*) divided equally between two people, groups or possibilities 对半（的）；各半（的）；平分（的）；二一添作五：*Costs are to be shared on **a fifty-fifty basis** between the government and local businesses.* 费用由政府和当地企业均摊。◇ *She has **a fifty-fifty chance** of winning* (= an equal chance of winning or losing). 她获胜的可能性是百分之五十。◇ *Let's split this fifty-fifty.* 咱们把这平分了吧。

ˌfifty 'pence (*also* **ˌfifty pence 'piece, 50p** /ˌfɪfti ˈpiː/) *noun* a British coin worth 50 pence（英国硬币）50 便士：*Put a fifty pence in the machine.* 把一枚 50 便士硬币投进机器。◇ *Have you got a 50p?* 你有没有 50 便士的硬币？

fig /fɪɡ/ *noun* a soft sweet fruit that is full of small seeds and often eaten dried 无花果：*a fig tree* 无花果树 ➲ VISUAL VOCAB PAGE V32

IDM **not care/give a 'fig (for sb/sth)** (*old-fashioned, BrE, informal*) not to care at all about sth; to think that sth is not important 对…丝毫不在乎；完全不把…放在心上；认为…毫无价值

fig. *abbr.* **1** (in writing 书写形式) FIGURE 图；表：*See fig. 3.* 见图表 3。**2** (in writing 书写形式) FIGURATIVE (1) 比喻的；譬如说

fight /faɪt/ *verb, noun*

■ ***verb*** (**fought, fought** /fɔːt/)

• **IN WAR/BATTLE** 战争；战斗 **1** [I, T] to take part in a war or battle against an enemy 打仗；战斗；作战：*soldiers trained to fight* 受过作战训练的士兵 ◇ *He fought in Vietnam.* 他在越南打过仗。◇ **~ against sb** *My grandfather fought against the Fascists in Spain.* 我的祖父曾经在西班牙与法西斯分子作战。◇ **~ sb/sth** *to fight a war/battle* 打仗；作战 ◇ *They gathered soldiers to fight the invading army.* 他们召集士兵对抗入侵的军队。➲ COLLOCATIONS AT WAR

• **STRUGGLE/HIT** 搏斗；打击 **2** [I, T] **~ (sb)** to struggle physically with sb 搏斗；打斗；打架：*My little brothers are always fighting.* 我的小弟弟们总在打架。◇ *She'll **fight like a tiger** to protect her children.* 她为了保护孩子，可以凶得像只老虎。

• **IN CONTEST** 竞赛 **3** [T, I] to take part in a contest against sb 参加（竞赛）；竞争：**~ sb/sth (for sth)** *to fight an **election/a campaign*** 参加竞选 / 争取权益的运动◇ **~ for sth** *She's fighting for a place in the national team.* 她正努力争取加入国家队。

• **OPPOSE** 反对 **4** [T, I] **~ (sth)** to try hard to stop, deal with or oppose sth bad 极力反对；与…作斗争：*to fight **racism/corruption/poverty, etc.*** 与种族主义、腐败、贫困等作斗争 ◇ *Workers are fighting the decision to close the factory.* 工人在极力反对关闭工厂的决定。◇ *The fire crews had problems fighting the blaze.* 消防队员扑灭那场大火困难重重。◇ *We will fight for as long as it takes.* 我们要一直斗争到底。

• **TRY TO GET/DO STH** 争取 **5** [I, T] to try very hard to get sth or to achieve sth 努力争取；为…而斗争：**~ (for sth)** *He's still fighting for compensation after the accident.* 他还在力争事故后的赔偿。◇ **~ your way…** *She gradually fought her way to the top of the company.* 她努力奋斗，逐渐登上公司的高位。◇ **~ to do sth** *Doctors fought for more than six hours to save his life.* 医生抢救了六个多小时来拯救他的生命。➲ SYNONYMS AT CAMPAIGN

• **ARGUE** 争辩 **6** [I] **~ (with sb) (about/over sth)** to have an argument with sb about sth 争辩：*It's a trivial matter and not worth fighting about.* 这是一桩小事，不值得为之争辩。

• **IN BOXING** 拳击 **7** [I, T] **~ (sb)** to take part in a BOXING match 参加拳击比赛：*Doctors fear he may never fight again.* 医生认为他可能再也不能重返拳坛了。

• **LAW** 法律 **8** [T, I] to try to get what you want in court（为…）和某人打官司：**~ (sb) for sth** *He fought his wife for custody of the children.* 他和妻子打官司争取孩子的监护权。◇ **~ sth** *I'm determined to fight the case.* 我决意要打这场官司。

▶ **fight·ing** *noun* [U]: *Fighting broke out in three districts of the city last night.* 昨夜这座城市有三个区发生了战斗。◇ *outbreaks of street fighting* 巷战的爆发

IDM **fight your/sb's 'corner** (*BrE*) to defend your/sb's position against other people 维护地位、立场等 **fight ˌfire with 'fire** to use similar methods in a fight or an argument to those your opponent is using 以眼还眼，以牙还牙 **ˌfight for (your) 'life** to make a great effort to stay alive, especially when you are badly injured or seriously ill（尤指严重伤病时）与死亡作斗争 **a ˌfighting 'chance** a small chance of being successful if a great effort is made 要努力奋斗才有的一线成功机会 **fighting 'fit** extremely fit or healthy 十分健壮；彪悍 **fighting 'spirit** a feeling that you are ready to fight very hard for sth or to try sth difficult 斗志；战斗精神 **fighting 'talk** comments or remarks that show that you are ready to fight very hard for sth 战斗性的言论：*What we want from the management is fighting talk.* 我们要求资方的是发表战斗宣言。 **fight a ˌlosing 'battle** to try to do sth that you will probably never succeed in doing 打一场无望取胜的仗；虽必败无疑犹作奋斗 **fight your own battles** to be able to win an argument or get what you want without anyone's help 独力战胜；独自奋斗成功：*I wouldn't get involved—he's old enough to fight his own battles.* 我不想参与。他已经长大，能独自应付了。 **fight 'shy of sth/of doing sth** to be unwilling to accept sth or do sth, and to try to avoid it 不愿接受（或做）某事；回避；躲避：*Successive governments have fought shy of such measures.* 一届接一届政府均不愿采取这些措施。**fight to the 'death/'finish** to fight until one of the two people or groups is dead, or until one person or group defeats the other 打到有一方倒下；一决雌雄 **fight ˌtooth and 'nail** to fight in a very determined way for what you want 坚决斗争；全

力以赴地斗争：*The residents are fighting tooth and nail to stop the new development.* 居民为制止新的建房开发计划正在全力以赴进行斗争。 ➲ MORE AT LIVE[1]

PHR V ˌ**fight ˈback (against sb/sth)** to resist strongly or attack sb who has attacked you 奋力抵抗；还击：*Don't let them bully you. Fight back!* 别让他们欺侮你。要还击！◇ *It is time to fight back against street crime.* 现在是打击街头犯罪行为的时候了。ˌ**fight sth↔ˈback/ˈdown** to try hard not to do or show sth, especially not to show your feelings 忍住，抑制住（尤指情感）：*I was fighting back the tears.* 我强忍住眼泪。◇ *He fought down his disgust.* 他强忍住心里的厌恶。ˌ**fight sb/sth↔off** to resist sb/sth by fighting against them/it 抵抗；击退：*The jeweller was stabbed as he tried to fight the robbers off.* 珠宝商在试图抵抗强盗时被刺伤了。ˌ**fight ˈout sth** | ˌ**fight it ˈout** to fight or argue until an argument has been settled 以斗争方式解决；辩论出结果：*The conflict is still being fought out.* 仍在通过战斗解决这次冲突。◇ *They hadn't reached any agreement so we left them to fight it out.* 他们未能取得一致意见，所以我们让他们争出个结果。

■ ***noun***

• **STRUGGLE** 搏斗 **1** ⚷ [C] a struggle against sb/sth using physical force 搏斗；打斗；打架：**~ (with sb/sth)** *He got* ***into a fight*** *with a man in the bar.* 他在酒吧里和一个男人斗殴。◇ *a* ***street/gang fight*** 街头 / 帮派打斗 ◇ **~ (between A and B)** *A* ***fight broke out*** *between rival groups of fans.* 比赛双方球迷打了起来。◇ *a world title fight* (= fighting as a sport, especially BOXING) 一场世界冠军争夺战（尤指拳击）

• **TRYING TO GET/DO STH** 争取 **2** ⚷ [sing.] the work of trying to destroy, prevent or achieve sth 斗争：**~ (against sth)** *the fight against crime* 打击犯罪 ◇ **~ (for sth)** *a fight for survival* 为生存而奋斗 ◇ **~ (to do sth)** *Workers won their fight to stop compulsory redundancies.* 工人在阻止强制性裁员的斗争中取得了胜利。

• **COMPETITION** 竞赛 **3** [sing.] a competition or an act of competing, especially in a sport（尤指体育运动）比赛，竞赛：*The team* ***put up a good fight*** (= they played well) *but were finally beaten.* 这个队打得不错，但最后还是输了。◇ *She now* ***has a fight on her hands*** (= will have to play very well) *to make it through to the next round.* 现在她得表现突出才能进入下一轮比赛。 ➲ SYNONYMS AT CAMPAIGN

• **ARGUMENT** 争论 **4** ⚷ [C] **~ (with sb) (over/about sth)** (*especially NAmE*) an argument about sth 争论；争吵：*Did you have a fight with him?* 你和他争辩了？◇ *We had a fight over money.* 我们为钱吵了一架。

• **BATTLE/WAR** 战斗；战争 **5** [C] a battle, especially for a particular place or position 战斗（尤指为夺取某一地方或位置）：*In the fight for Lemburg, the Austrians were defeated.* 在争夺伦贝格的战斗中，奥地利人战败了。

• **DESIRE TO FIGHT** 斗志 **6** [U] the desire or ability to keep fighting for sth 斗志；战斗力：*In spite of many defeats, they still had plenty of fight left in them.* 他们尽管多次失败，但仍然斗志昂扬。

IDM **a fight to the ˈfinish** a sports competition, election, etc. between sides that are so equal in ability that they continue fighting very hard until the end（体育比赛、选举等的）直到最后才能决出胜负的斗争 ➲ MORE AT PICK *v.*, SPOIL *v.*

> ▼ **SYNONYMS 同义词辨析**
>
> **fight**
>
> **clash • brawl • struggle • scuffle**
>
> These are all words for a situation in which people try to defeat each other using physical force. 以上各词均指搏斗、打斗、打架。
>
> **fight** a situation in which two or more people try to defeat each other using physical force 指搏斗、打斗、打架：*He got into a fight with a man in the bar.* 他在酒吧里和一个男人斗殴。
>
> **clash** (*journalism*) a short fight between two groups of people（新闻用语）指两群人之间短暂的打斗、打架、冲突：*Clashes broke out between police and demonstrators.* 警方与示威者发生了冲突。
>
> **brawl** a noisy and violent fight involving a group of people, usually in a public place 通常指一群人在公共场合喧闹、斗殴、闹事：*a drunken brawl in a bar* 在酒吧里酒后闹事
>
> **struggle** a fight between two people or groups of people, especially when one of them is trying to escape, or to get sth from the other 指搏斗、扭打，尤指抢夺、挣扎脱身：*There were no signs of a struggle at the murder scene.* 在谋杀现场没有打斗痕迹。
>
> **scuffle** a short and not very violent fight or struggle 指短暂而不太激烈的扭打、冲突：*He was involved in a scuffle with a photographer.* 他和一名摄影记者发生了肢体冲撞。
>
> **PATTERNS**
>
> - a fight/clash/brawl/struggle/scuffle **over** sth
> - **in** a fight/brawl/struggle/scuffle
> - a **violent** fight/clash/struggle
> - to **be in/get into/be involved in** a fight/clash/brawl/scuffle
> - a fight/clash/brawl/scuffle **breaks out**

fight·back /ˈfaɪtbæk/ *noun* [usually sing.] (*BrE*) an effort by a person, group or team to get back to a strong position that they have lost 回击；反攻

fight·er /ˈfaɪtə(r)/ *noun* **1** (*also* **ˈfighter plane**) a fast military plane designed to attack other aircraft 战斗机；歼击机：*a* ***jet fighter*** 喷气式战斗机 ◇ *a* ***fighter pilot*** 战斗机驾驶员 ◇ *fighter bases* 战斗机基地 ➲ WORDFINDER NOTE AT AIRCRAFT ➲ VISUAL VOCAB PAGE V58 **2** a person who fights 战士；战斗者；拳击手 ➲ SEE ALSO FIREFIGHTER, FREEDOM FIGHTER, PRIZEFIGHTER at PRIZEFIGHT **3** (*approving*) a person who does not give up hope or admit that they are defeated 斗士；奋斗者

ˈfighter-bomber *noun* a military plane that can fight other planes in the air and also drop bombs 战斗轰炸机

ˈfig leaf *noun* **1** a leaf of a FIG tree, traditionally used for covering the sex organs of naked bodies in paintings and on statues 无花果树叶（传统上用作裸体画像或雕像的遮阴物）**2** a thing that is used to hide an embarrassing fact or situation 遮羞布

fig·ment /ˈfɪgmənt/ *noun*

IDM **a figment of sb's imagiˈnation** something that sb has imagined and that does not really exist 凭空想象的事物；臆造的东西；虚构的事

fig·ura·tive /ˈfɪgərətɪv; *NAmE* ˈfɪgjə-/ *adj.* [usually before noun] **1** (of language, words, phrases, etc. 语言、词语等) used in a way that is different from the usual meaning, in order to create a particular mental picture. For example, 'He exploded with rage' shows a figurative use of the verb 'explode'. 比喻的 ➲ COMPARE LITERAL (1), METAPHORICAL **2** (of paintings, art, etc. 绘画、艺术等) showing people, animals and objects as they really look 具象的：*a figurative artist* 具象艺术家 ➲ COMPARE ABSTRACT *adj.* ▶ **fig·ura·tive·ly** *adv.*：*She is, figuratively speaking, holding a gun to his head.* 打个比方说，她正拿枪对着他的脑袋。

fig·ure ⚷ /ˈfɪgə(r); *NAmE* ˈfɪgjər/ *noun, verb*

■ ***noun***

• **NUMBERS** 数 **1** ⚷ [C, usually pl.] a number representing a particular amount, especially one given in official information（代表数量，尤指官方资料中的）数字：*the latest* ***trade/sales/unemployment, etc. figures*** 最新的贸易、销售、失业等数字 ◇ *By 2009, this figure had risen to 14 million.* 到 2009 年为止，这个数字已经增长到 1 400 万。◇ *Experts put the real figure at closer to 75%.* 专家们估计真实的数字较接近于 75%。 **2** ⚷ [C] a symbol rather than a word representing one of the numbers between 0 and 9 数字符号；字码；位数：*Write the figure '7' on the board.* 把数字 7 写在黑板上。◇ *a six-figure salary* (= over 100 000 pounds or dollars) 六位数的薪水（即超

F

过 10 万英镑或美元) ◇ *His salary is now in six figures.* 他的薪水现在是六位数。 ➲ SEE ALSO DOUBLE FIGURES, SINGLE FIGURES **3** 🔑 **fig·ures** [pl.] (*informal*) the area of mathematics that deals with adding, multiplying, etc. numbers 算术 SYN **arithmetic**: *Are you any good at figures?* 你的算术好吗? ◇ *I'm afraid I don't **have a head for figures*** (= I am not good at adding, etc.). 恐怕我没有算术头脑。

• **PERSON** 人 **4** 🔑 [C] a person of the type mentioned 人物; 人士: *a **leading figure** in the music industry* 音乐界一位主要人物 ◇ *a political figure* 政治人物 ◇ *a figure of authority* 当权者 ➲ SEE ALSO FATHER FIGURE, MOTHER FIGURE **5** 🔑 [C] the shape of a person seen from a distance or not clearly (远处人的) 轮廓; (隐约可见的) 人影: *a tall figure in black* 一个黑衣高个子人影

• **SHAPE OF BODY** 体形 **6** 🔑 [C] the shape of the human body, especially a woman's body that is attractive 身材; 体形; (尤指) 身段: *She's always had a good figure.* 她身材一向很好。 ◇ *I'm watching my figure* (= trying not to get fat). 我一直注意保持身材。 ➲ COLLOCATIONS AT PHYSICAL

• **IN PAINTING/STORY** 绘画; 故事 **7** [C] a person or an animal in a drawing, painting, etc., or in a story (绘画或故事中的) 人, 动物: *The central figure in the painting is the artist's daughter.* 画中间那个人是画家的女儿。

• **STATUE** 造像 **8** [C] a statue of a person or an animal (人、动物的) 雕像, 塑像: *a bronze figure of a horse* 一座马的铜像

• **PICTURE/DIAGRAM** 图表 **9** [C] (*abbr.* **fig.**) a picture, diagram, etc. in a book, that is referred to by a number (书中的) 图, 表: *The results are illustrated in figure 3 opposite.* 结果已在对页图表 3 中显示。

• **GEOMETRY** 几何 **10** [C] a particular shape formed by lines or surfaces 图形: *a five-sided figure* 五边形 ◇ *a solid figure* 立体图形

• **MOVEMENT ON ICE** 冰上动作 **11** [C] a pattern or series of movements performed on ice (冰上表演动作的) 花样

IDM **be/become a figure of 'fun** to be/become sb that other people laugh at 是嘲笑的对象; 成为笑柄 **cut a... 'figure** (of a person 人) to have a particular appearance 显出…的样子; 显得: *He cut a striking figure in his white dinner jacket.* 他穿着白色晚礼服显得十分出众。 **put a figure on sth** to say the exact price or number of sth 定价; 说出…的准确数字 ➲ MORE AT FACT

■ *verb*

• **BE IMPORTANT** 重要 **1** 🔑 [I] to be part of a process, situation, etc. especially an important part 是重要部分; 是…的部分 SYN **feature**: *My feelings about the matter didn't seem to figure at all.* 我对这个问题的意见似乎根本无足轻重。 ◇ **~ (as sth) (in/on/among sth)** *Do I still figure in your plans?* 在你的计划中还包括我吗? ◇ *The question of the peace settlement is likely to **figure prominently** in the talks.* 和平解决的问题很可能是这轮谈判的突出重点。 ◇ *It did not figure high on her list of priorities.* 这没有列入她最优先考虑办理的事项。

• **THINK/DECIDE** 认为; 认定 **2** [T] (*informal*) to think or decide that sth will happen or is true 认为, 认定 (某事将发生或属实): **~ (that)...** *I figured (that) if I took the night train, I could be in Scotland by morning.* 我认为, 如果我坐夜班火车, 早上就可以到达苏格兰。 ◇ *We figured the sensible thing to do was to wait.* 我们认为, 明智的做法是等待。 ◇ **~ sth** *That's what I figured.* 这就是我的看法。 ◇ **~ why, whether, etc....** *He tried to figure why she had come.* 他试图弄清楚她为什么来了。

• **CALCULATE** 计算 **3** [T] **~ sth (at sth)** (*NAmE*) to calculate an amount or the cost of sth 计算 (数量或成本): *We figured the attendance at 150 000.* 我们估计有 15 万人参加。

IDM **go 'figure** (*NAmE, informal*) used to say that you do not understand the reason for sth, or that you do not want to give an explanation for sth because you think it is obvious 搞不懂; 明摆着不用解释: *People are more aware of the risks of smoking nowadays, but more young women are smoking than ever. Go figure!* 现在人们更加了解吸烟的危害, 但吸烟的年轻女性倒比以往多了。真让人搞不懂! **it/that figures** used to say that sth was expected or seems logical (表示应该或似乎合乎逻辑) 有道理, 合乎情理: *'John called in sick.' 'That figures, he wasn't feeling well yesterday.'* "约翰打电话来请病假。" "怪不得, 他昨天就感到不舒服。" ◇ (*disapproving*) *'She was late again.' 'Yes, that figures.'* "她又迟到了。" "是呀, 她总是这样。"

PHR V **'figure on sth | 'figure on (sb/sth) doing sth** to plan sth or to do sth; to expect sth (to happen) 计划; 打算; 预料到 SYN **plan**: *I hadn't figured on getting home so late.* 我没有估计到这么晚才回到家。 **ˌfigure sb/sth↔'out** **1** 🔑 to think about sb/sth until you understand them/it 弄懂; 弄清楚; 弄明白 SYN **work out**: *We couldn't figure her out.* 我们摸不透她。 ◇ **figure out how, what, etc....** *I can't figure out how to do this.* 我弄不懂怎样做这件事。 **2** 🔑 to calculate an amount or the cost of sth 计算 (数量或成本) SYN **work out**: **figure out how, what, etc....** *Have you figured out how much the trip will cost?* 旅行要花多少费用你算出来没有?

fig·ured /ˈfɪɡəd; *NAmE* ˈfɪɡjərd/ *adj.* [only before noun] (*specialist*) decorated with a small pattern 饰以图案的: *figured pottery* 绘有图案的陶器

fig·ure·head /ˈfɪɡəhed; *NAmE* -ɡjərh-/ *noun* **1** a person who is in a high position in a country or an organization but who has no real power or authority 有名无实的领导人; 傀儡 **2** a large wooden statue, usually representing a woman, that used to be fixed to the front end of a ship (过去的) 艏饰像

'figure-hugging *adj.* [usually before noun] (of a piece of clothing) tight in an attractive way that shows the shape of a woman's body (女装) 紧身的, 包身的, 烘托线条的

ˌfigure of 'eight (*BrE*) (*NAmE* **ˌfigure 'eight**) *noun* (*pl.* **figures of eight, figure eights**) a pattern or movement that looks like the shape of the number 8 (图案、运动的) 8 字形

ˌfigure of 'speech *noun* (*pl.* **figures of speech**) a word or phrase used in a different way from its usual meaning in order to create a particular mental picture or effect 修辞格; 修辞手段 ➲ WORDFINDER NOTE AT IMAGE

'figure-skating *noun* [U] a type of ICE SKATING in which you cut patterns in the ice and do jumps and spins 花样滑冰 ➲ COMPARE SPEED SKATING

fig·ur·ine /ˈfɪɡəriːn; *NAmE* ˌfɪɡjəˈriːn/ *noun* a small statue of a person or an animal used as a decorative object (人、动物的) 小雕像, 小塑像

fila·ment /ˈfɪləmənt/ *noun* **1** a thin wire in a LIGHT BULB that produces light when electricity is passed through it (电灯泡的) 灯丝; 丝极 **2** (*specialist*) a long thin piece of sth that looks like a thread 细丝; 丝状物: ***glass/metal filaments*** 玻璃丝; 金属丝

fil·bert /ˈfɪlbət; *NAmE* -bərt/ *noun* (*especially NAmE*) = HAZELNUT

filch /fɪltʃ/ *verb* **~ sth** (*informal*) to steal sth, especially sth small or not very valuable 偷 (尤指小的或不贵重的物品) SYN **pinch**

file 🔑 AW /faɪl/ *noun, verb*

■ ***noun*** **1** 🔑 a box or folded piece of card for keeping loose papers together and in order 文件夹; 卷宗: *a box file* 文件箱 ◇ *A stack of files awaited me on my desk.* 我桌上有一堆文件等着我去处理。 ➲ VISUAL VOCAB PAGE V71 **2** 🔑 a collection of information stored together in a computer, under a particular name (计算机的) 文件: ***to access/copy/create/delete/download/save a file*** 存取 / 复制 / 新建 / 删除 / 下载 / 保存文件 ◇ *Every file on the same disk must have a different name.* 同一磁盘上的每一个文件都必须有不同的文件名。 ➲ SEE ALSO PDF

WORDFINDER 联想词: copy, data, delete, folder, icon, menu, open, password, print

3 🔑 a file and the information it contains, for example about a particular person or subject 档案: *secret police files* 警方秘密档案 ◇ *Your application will be kept **on file*** (= in a file, to be used later). 你的申请书将存档。 ◇ **~ on sb** *to have/open/keep a confidential file on sb* 有 / 设立 / 保存某人的机密档案 ◇ *Police have reopened the file* (= have started collecting information again) *on the missing girl.*

警方对失踪的女孩已重新建档调查。 **4** a metal tool with a rough surface for cutting or shaping hard substances or for making them smooth 锉；锉刀 ➲ VISUAL VOCAB PAGE V21 ➲ SEE ALSO NAIL FILE **5** a line of people or things, one behind the other 排成一行的人（或物）： *They set off in file behind the teacher.* 他们跟在教师后面鱼贯出发。

IDM **(in) single 'file** (*also old-fashioned* **(in) Indian file**) (in) one line, one behind the other 一路纵队；单行： *They made their way in single file along the cliff path.* 他们一个接着一个沿悬崖小径前进。

■ *verb* **1** [T] to put and keep documents, etc. in a particular place and in a particular order so that you can find them easily; to put a document into a file 把（文件等）归档： **~ sth (+ adv./prep.)** *The forms should be filed alphabetically.* 这些表格应该按字母顺序归档。◇ *Please file it in my 'Research' file.* 请把它归入我的研究类档案。◇ **~ sth away** *I filed the letters away in a drawer.* 我把信件存放到抽屉里了。 **2** [I, T] (*law* 律) to present sth so that it can be officially recorded and dealt with 提起（诉讼）；提出（申请）；送交（备案）： **~ for sth** *to file for divorce* 提交离婚申请书 ◇ **~ sth** *to file a claim/complaint/petition/lawsuit* 提出索赔 / 申诉；呈交诉状；提起诉讼 ◇ **~ to do sth** *He filed to divorce his wife.* 他提交了与妻子离婚的申请。 **3** [T] **~ sth** (of a journalist 记者) to send a report or a story to your employer 发送（报道给报社） **4** [I] **+ adv./prep.** to walk in a line of people, one after the other, in a particular direction 排成一行行走： *The doors of the museum opened and the visitors began to file in.* 博物馆开门了，参观者鱼贯而入。 **5** [T] **~ sth (away/down, etc.)** to cut or shape sth or make sth smooth using a file 锉平；锉去；锉薄；锉光滑： *to file your nails* 把指甲锉光滑

'file cabinet (*NAmE*) (*especially BrE* **'filing cabinet**) *noun* a piece of office furniture with deep drawers for storing files 文件柜；档案柜 ➲ VISUAL VOCAB PAGE V71

'file clerk (*NAmE*) (*BrE* **'filing clerk**) *noun* a person whose job is to FILE letters, etc. and do general office tasks 档案管理员

file·name /'faɪlneɪm/ *noun* (*computing* 计) a name given to a computer file in order to identify it 文件名

'file sharing *noun* [U] the practice of sharing computer files with other people over the Internet or another computer network 文件共享： *Illegal music file-sharing sites have spread through the Net.* 非法的音乐文件共享网站已遍布互联网。

filet *noun* (*NAmE*) = FILLET

fil·ial /'fɪliəl/ *adj.* [usually before noun] (*formal*) connected with the way children behave towards their parents 子女（对父母）的： ***filial affection/duty*** 子女的亲情 / 孝道

fili·bus·ter /'fɪlɪbʌstə(r)/ *noun* (*especially NAmE*) a long speech made in a parliament in order to delay a vote （议会中为拖延表决的）冗长演说 ▶ **fili·bus·ter** *verb* [I]

fili·gree /'fɪlɪgriː/ *noun* [U] delicate decoration made from gold or silver wire 金银丝饰品

fil·ing /'faɪlɪŋ/ *noun* **1** [U] the act of putting documents, letters, etc. into a file 存档；归档 **2** [C] (*especially NAmE*) something that is placed in an official record 存档档案；归档记录： *a bankruptcy filing* 破产档案 **3 filings** [pl.] very small pieces of metal, made when a larger piece of metal is filed 锉屑： *iron filings* 铁锉屑

'filing cabinet (*NAmE also* **'file cabinet**) *noun* a piece of office furniture with deep drawers for storing files 文件柜；档案柜 ➲ VISUAL VOCAB PAGE V71

'filing clerk (*BrE*) (*NAmE* **'file clerk**) *noun* a person whose job is to FILE letters, etc. and do general office tasks 档案管理员

Fi·li·pino /ˌfɪlɪ'piːnəʊ; *NAmE* -noʊ/ *noun, adj.*

■ *noun* (*pl.* **-os**) **1** [C] a person from the Philippines 菲律宾人 **2** [U] the language of the Philippines 菲律宾语

■ *adj.* connected with the Philippines, its people or their language 菲律宾的；菲律宾人的；菲律宾语的

fill /fɪl/ *verb, noun*

■ *verb*

• **MAKE FULL** 使充满 **1** [T, I] to make sth full of sth; to become full of sth （使）充满，装满，注满，填满： **~ sth** *Please fill this glass for me.* 请把这个杯子给我倒满。◇ *to fill a vacuum/void* 填补真空 / 空间 ◇ *The school is **filled to capacity**.* 这所学校已经满员。◇ *Smoke filled the room.* 房间里烟雾弥漫。◇ *The wind filled the sails.* 风吹帆张。◇ *A Disney film can always fill cinemas* (= attract a lot of people to see it). 迪士尼电影总是让电影院满座。◇ **~ sth with sth** *to fill a hole with earth/a bucket with water* 用泥土把洞填起来；把水桶装满水 ◇ **~ sth + adj.** *Fill a pan half full of water.* 给平底锅装半锅水。◇ **~ (with sth)** *The room was filling quickly.* 房间很快就挤满了人。◇ *Her eyes suddenly filled with tears.* 她的眼里突然噙满了泪水。◇ *The sails filled with wind.* 帆张满了风。

• **BLOCK HOLE** 堵洞 **2** [T] **~ sth (with sth)** to block a hole with a substance 堵塞，填补（洞、孔）： *The crack in the wall had been filled with plaster.* 墙上的裂缝已用灰泥堵上了。◇ *I need to have two teeth filled* (= to have FILLINGS put in them). 我有两颗牙要补。◇ (*figurative*) *The product has **filled a gap** in the market.* 这个产品填补了市场的空白。

• **WITH FEELING** 感情 **3** [T] **~ sb (with sth)** to make sb have a strong feeling 使充满（感情）： *We were all filled with admiration for his achievements.* 我们都十分佩服他的成就。

• **WITH SMELL/SOUND/LIGHT** 气味；声；光 **4** [T] **~ sth (with sth)** if a smell, sound or light **fills** a place, it is very strong, loud or bright and easy to notice 使遍及；弥漫；布满；照满

• **-FILLED** 充满… **5** (in adjectives 构成形容词) full of the thing mentioned 充满…的： *a smoke-filled room* 烟雾弥漫的房间 ◇ *a fun-filled day* 充满欢乐的一天

• **A NEED** 需要 **6** [T] **~ sth** to stop people from continuing to want or need sth 满足： *More nurseries will be built to fill the need for high-quality child care.* 将建立更多的托儿所以满足高质量儿童保育的需要。

• **JOB** 工作 **7** [T] **~ sth** to do a job, have a role or position, etc. 担任；充任： *He fills the post satisfactorily* (= performs his duties well). 他很尽职。◇ *The team needs someone to fill the role of manager very soon.* 该队迫切需要一个人来担任主教练。 **8** [T] **~ sth** to appoint sb to a job 派人担任： *The vacancy has already been filled.* 该空缺已有人接任。

• **TIME** 时间 **9** [T] **~ sth (up)** to use up a particular period of time doing sth 耗去；打发；消磨： *How do you fill your day now that you've retired?* 现在你已退休了，怎样打发你的日子？

• **WITH FOOD** 食物 **10** [T] **~ sb/yourself (up) (with sth)** (*informal*) to make sb/yourself feel unable to eat any more （使）吃饱： *The kids filled themselves with snacks.* 孩子们吃零食吃饱了。

• **AN ORDER** 订单 **11** [T] **~ sth** if sb **fills** an order or a PRESCRIPTION, they give the customer what they have asked for （按订单）供应；交付（订货）；（按药方）配药 ➲ SEE ALSO UNFILLED (4)

IDM **fill your boots** (*informal*) used to invite sb to take as much as they like of sth such as food, drink, etc.; help yourself 尽情享用；随便吃（或喝、用等）；请自便 **fill sb's shoes/boots** to do sb's job in an acceptable way when they are not there 妥善代职 ➲ MORE AT BILL *n.*

PHR V **ˌfill 'in (for sb)** to do sb's job for a short time while they are not there 暂时代替；临时补缺 **ˌfill sth↔'in 1** (*BrE*) to complete a form, etc. by writing information on it 填写（表格等）： *to fill in an application form* 填写申请表 ◇ *To order, fill in the coupon on p 54.* 订货需填写第 54 页上的订货单。 **2** to fill sth completely 填满；塞满： *The hole has been filled in.* 洞已填平。 **3** to spend time doing sth while waiting for sth more important 消磨，打发（时间）： *He filled in the rest of the day watching television.* 他看电视打发了那天余下的时光。 **4** to complete a drawing, etc. by covering the space inside the outline with colour 给（图画等）最后着色 **ˌfill sb 'in (on sth)** to tell sb about sth that has happened 向…提供（情况） **ˌfill**

ˈout to become larger, rounder or fatter 膨胀；扩张；长胖；长肥 ˌ**fill sth↔ˈout** = FILL STH↔IN ˌ**fill ˈup (with sth)** | ˌ**fill sth↔ˈup (with sth)** to become completely full; to make sth completely full 充满；（使）填满；装满：*The ditches had filled up with mud.* 沟渠中积满了淤泥。◇ *to fill up the tank with oil* 把油箱装满油

■ ***noun*** [sing.] **1 your ~ (of sth/sb)** as much of sth/sb as you are willing to accept 填满…的量；足够…的量：*I've had my fill of entertaining for one week.* 我已足足享受了一周的款待。**2 your ~ (of food/drink)** as much as you can eat/drink 吃饱的量；喝足的量

fill·er /ˈfɪlə(r)/ *noun* **1** [U, C] a substance used to fill holes or cracks, especially in walls before painting them 填充物，填料（尤用于漆墙前填孔或缝）**2** [C] (*informal*) something that is not important but is used to complete sth else because nothing better is available 充数的东西；填补空白之物：*The song was originally a filler on their first album.* 这首歌在他们第一张专辑中本来是用来凑时间的。➲ SEE ALSO STOCKING FILLER

ˈfiller cap *noun* a lid for covering the end of the pipe through which petrol/gas is put into a vehicle（汽车）加油口盖，油箱盖，管盖

fil·let /ˈfɪlɪt; *NAmE* fɪˈleɪ/ *noun, verb*

■ ***noun*** (*NAmE also* **filet**) [C, U] a piece of meat or fish that has no bones in it 无骨肉片；去骨鱼片：*plaice fillets* 鲽鱼片 ◇ *a fillet of cod* 一片鳕鱼 ◇ *fillet steak* 无骨牛排

■ ***verb*** **~ sth** to remove the bones from a piece of fish or meat; to cut fish or meat into fillets 剔去（鱼、肉的）骨头；把（鱼、肉）切成片

fill·ing /ˈfɪlɪŋ/ *noun, adj.*

■ ***noun*** **1** [C] a small amount of metal or other material used to fill a hole in a tooth （补牙的）填料：*I had to have two fillings at the dentist's today.* 我今天不得不在牙科诊所补了两颗牙。➲ WORDFINDER NOTE AT DENTIST **2** [C, U] food put inside a SANDWICH, cake, PIE, etc.（糕点等的）馅：*a sponge cake with cream and jam filling* 奶油果酱作馅的海绵蛋糕 ◇ *a wide range of sandwich fillings* 各种各样的三明治馅 **3** [C, U] soft material used to fill CUSHIONS, PILLOWS, etc.（枕头、靠垫等的）填充物，填料

■ ***adj.*** (of food 食物) making your stomach feel full 能填饱肚子的：*This cake is very filling.* 这种饼很能填饱肚子。

ˈfilling station *noun* = GAS STATION, PETROL STATION

fil·lip /ˈfɪlɪp/ *noun* [sing.] **a ~ (to/for sth)** (*formal*) a thing or person that causes sth to improve suddenly 起推动作用的人（或事物）SYN **boost**：*A drop in interest rates gave a welcome fillip to the housing market.* 降低利率给房屋市场带来利好刺激。

ˈfill-up *noun* an occasion when a car is completely filled up with petrol/gas（汽车）加满油

filly /ˈfɪli/ *noun* (*pl.* **-ies**) a young female horse 小牝马 ➲ COMPARE COLT (1), MARE (1)

film /fɪlm/ *noun, verb*

■ ***noun***

• **MOVING PICTURES** 电影 **1** [C] (*especially BrE*) (*NAmE usually* **movie**) a series of moving pictures recorded with sound that tells a story, shown on television or at the cinema/movie theater 电影；影片：*Let's go to the cinema—there's a good film on this week.* 咱们去看电影吧，本周在上映一部好片子。◇ *Let's stay in and watch a film.* 咱们待在家里看电影吧。◇ *a horror/documentary/feature film* 恐怖片；纪录片；故事片 ◇ *a silent film* (= one recorded without sound) 无声电影 ◇ *an international film festival* 国际电影节 ◇ *a film crew/critic/director/producer* 电影摄制组 / 评论家 / 导演 / 制作人 ◇ *the film version of the novel* 由同名小说改编的电影版本 ◇ *to make/shoot a film* 制作 / 拍摄电影 ➲ COLLOCATIONS AT CINEMA

> **WORDFINDER** 联想词：**actor**, cameraman, **cinema**, dialogue, director, dub, location, scenario, sound effect

2 [U] (*especially BrE*) (*NAmE usually* **the movies** [pl.]) (*BrE also* **the cin·ema**) the art or business of making films/movies 电影制作艺术；电影业：*to study film and photography* 学习电影制作和摄影 ◇ *the film industry* 电影业 ➲ COMPARE CINEMA (3) **3** [U] moving pictures of real events, shown for example on television 新闻片 SYN **footage**：*television news film of the riots* 这场暴乱的电视新闻片 ◇ *The accident was captured/caught on film.* 事故已给拍摄下来。

• **IN CAMERAS** 摄影机；摄像机 **4** [U, C] thin plastic that is sensitive to light, used for taking photographs and making films/movies; a roll of this plastic, used in cameras 胶片；胶卷；底片：*a roll of film* 一卷胶卷 ◇ *a 35mm film* *35 毫米胶片 ◇ *She put a new film in her camera.* 她在相机里装上新胶卷。◇ *to have a film developed* 让人冲洗胶卷

• **THIN LAYER** 薄层 **5** [C, usually sing.] **~ (of sth)** a thin layer of sth, usually on the surface of sth else 薄薄的一层；薄膜 SYN **coat, coating, layer**：*Everything was covered in a film of dust.* 所有的东西都蒙上了一层灰尘。➲ SEE ALSO CLING FILM

■ ***verb*** [I, T] to make a film/movie of a story or a real event 拍摄电影：*They are filming in Moscow right now.* 目前他们正在莫斯科拍电影。◇ *The show was filmed on location in New York.* 这次演出是在纽约取景录制的。◇ **~ sb/sth doing sth** *Two young boys were filmed stealing CDs on the security video.* 两个少年偷唱片时被保安录像机拍摄了下来。▶ **film·ing** *noun* [U]：*Filming was delayed because of bad weather.* 由于天气恶劣，拍摄受阻了。

ˈfilm-goer (*especially BrE*) (*NAmE usually* **movie·goer**) (*BrE also* **ˈcinema-goer**) *noun* a person who goes to the cinema/movies, especially when they do it regularly（经常）上电影院的人；爱看电影者

film·ic /ˈfɪlmɪk/ *adj.* [only before noun] (*formal*) connected with films/movies 电影的；与电影有关的

ˈfilm-maker *noun* a person who makes films/movies 电影制作人 ▶ **ˈfilm-making** *noun* [U]

film noir /ˌfɪlm ˈnwɑː(r)/ *noun* (*from French*) **1** [U] a style of making films/movies in which there are strong feelings of fear or evil; films/movies made in this style 黑色电影（充满恐惧、邪恶色彩）**2** [C] (*pl.* **films noirs** /ˌfɪlm ˈnwɑː(r)/) a film made in this style 黑色影片

film·og·raphy /ˌfɪlˈmɒɡrəfi; *NAmE* -ˈmɑːɡ-/ *noun* (*pl.* **-ies**) a list of films/movies made by a particular actor or director, or a list of films/movies that deal with a particular subject（演员、导演或某主题的）电影作品年表，影片目录

ˈfilm star (*especially BrE*) (*NAmE usually* **ˈmovie star**) *noun* a male or female actor who is famous for being in films/movies 电影明星

film·strip /ˈfɪlmstrɪp/ *noun* a series of images on a film, through which light is shone to show them on a screen 幻灯片

filmy /ˈfɪlmi/ *adj.* [usually before noun] thin and almost transparent 薄而几乎透明的 SYN **sheer**：*a filmy cotton blouse* 薄如蝉翼的女棉衬衫

Filo·fax™ /ˈfaɪləʊfæks; *NAmE* -loʊ-/ *noun* a small book with pages that can be added or removed easily, used for writing notes, addresses, etc. in 菲洛法克斯活页记事本 ➲ SEE ALSO PERSONAL ORGANIZER

filo pastry /ˈfiːləʊ ˌpeɪstri; *NAmE* ˈfiːloʊ/ (*also* **filo**) *noun* [U] a type of thin PASTRY, used in layers 油酥千层饼

fil·ter /ˈfɪltə(r)/ *noun, verb*

■ ***noun*** **1** a device containing paper, sand, chemicals, etc. that a liquid or gas is passed through in order to remove any materials that are not wanted 滤器；过滤器：*an air/oil filter* 空气过滤器；滤油器 ◇ *a coffee/water filter* 咖啡过滤器；滤水器 ◇ *filter paper for the coffee machine* 咖啡机滤纸 ◇ *He smokes cigarettes without filters.* 他吸没有过滤嘴的香烟。➲ VISUAL VOCAB PAGES V26, V72 **2** a device that allows only particular types of light or sound to pass through it 滤光器；滤声器；滤波器 **3** (*computing* 计) a program that processes information to exclude the types which are not wanted or that stops certain types of electronic information, email, etc. being sent to a computer

filters 分离装置

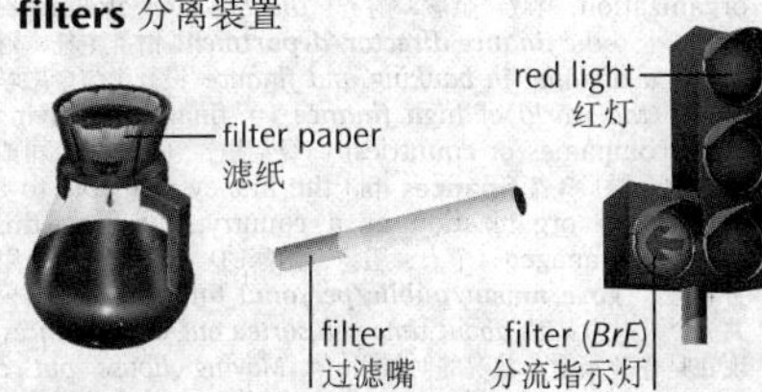

筛选（过滤）程序 **4** (*BrE*) a light on a set of TRAFFIC LIGHTS showing that traffic can turn left or right while traffic that wants to go straight ahead must wait（交通红灯指示不得直行的同时，表示可左转或右转的）分流指示灯

■ ***verb*** **1** [T] **~ sth** to pass liquid, light, etc. through a special device, especially to remove sth that is not wanted 过滤：*All drinking water must be filtered.* 所有饮用水必须经过过滤。◇ *Use a sun block that filters UVA effectively.* 使用能有效滤掉长波紫外线的防晒霜。◇ (*figurative*) *My secretary is very good at filtering my calls* (= making sure that calls that I do not want do not get through). 我的秘书很会替我推掉不相干的电话。➲ SEE ALSO FILTRATION ➲ **WORDFINDER NOTE AT LIQUID** **2** [T] **~ sth** to use a special program to check the content of emails or websites before they are sent to your computer（用程序）筛选，过滤 **3** [I] **+ adv./prep.** (of people 人) to move slowly in a particular direction 缓行：*The doors opened and people started filtering through.* 门开了，人们开始徐徐通过。 **4** [I] **+ adv./prep.** (of information, news, etc. 信息、新闻等) to slowly become known 慢慢传开；走漏：*More details about the crash are filtering through.* 关于这场空难的具体情况慢慢披露了。**5** [I] **+ adv./prep.** (of light or sound 光或声) to come into a place slowly or in small amounts 渗入；透过：*Sunlight filtered in through the curtains.* 阳光从窗帘透了进来。 **6** [I] (*BrE*) (of traffic at traffic lights 交通指示灯处的交通) to turn left at traffic lights while other vehicles wanting to go straight ahead or turn right must wait 仅可左转行驶

PHR V ˌ**filter sth↔ˈout** **1** to remove sth that you do not want from a liquid, light, etc. by using a special device or substance 过滤掉：*to filter out dust particles/light/impurities* 过滤掉尘粒；滤光；过滤掉杂质 **2** to remove sb/sth that you do not want from a large number of people or things using a special system, device, etc.（用专门的系统、装置等）过滤掉，筛除，淘汰掉：*The test is used to filter out candidates who may be unsuitable.* 这个测验是用来淘汰不适合的求职者。◇ *The software filters out Internet sites whose content is not suitable for children.* 这个软件可筛除含儿童不宜内容的互联网网站。

ˈ**filter tip** *noun* a filter at the end of a cigarette that removes some of the harmful substances from the smoke; a cigarette that has this filter（香烟的）过滤嘴；过滤嘴香烟

filth /fɪlθ/ *noun* [U] **1** any very dirty and unpleasant substance 污物；污秽：*The floor was covered in grease and filth.* 地板上满是油垢和污物。 **2** words, magazines, etc. that are connected with sex and that are considered very rude and offensive 下流言辞；淫秽书刊：*How can you read such filth?* 你怎么能看这种淫秽读物？ **3 the filth** [U] (*BrE, slang*) an offensive word for the police （骂人话）警察；雷子

filthy /ˈfɪlθi/ *adj., adv.*

■ ***adj.*** (**filth·ier, filthi·est**) **1** very dirty and unpleasant 肮脏的；污秽的：*filthy rags/streets* 肮脏的破布 / 街道 ◇ *It's filthy in here!* 这里面脏得很！ ➲ **SYNONYMS AT DIRTY** **2** very rude and offensive and usually connected with sex 下流的；淫秽的；猥亵的：***filthy language/words*** 下流的语言 / 言辞 ◇ *He's got a **filthy mind*** (= is always thinking about sex). 他满脑子淫乱思想。 **3** (*informal*) showing anger 气愤的：*He was in a **filthy mood**.* 他气愤不已。◇ *She has a **filthy temper**.* 她脾气暴躁。◇ *Ann gave him a **filthy look**.* 安气愤地瞧了他一眼。 **4** (*BrE, informal*) (of the weather 天气) cold and wet 寒冷潮湿的；恶劣的；糟糕的：*Isn't it a filthy day?* 今天可不是又冷又湿吗？ ▶ **filth·ily** *adv.* **filthi·ness** *noun* [U]

■ ***adv.*** (*informal*) **1 ~ dirty** extremely dirty 极其肮脏的 **2 ~ rich** so rich that you think the person is too rich and you find it offensive 富得流油的

fil·trate /ˈfɪltreɪt/ *noun* (*chemistry* 化) a liquid that has passed through a FILTER 滤液

fil·tra·tion /fɪlˈtreɪʃn/ *noun* [U] (*chemistry* 化) the process of FILTERING a liquid or gas 过滤；滤清；滤除

fin /fɪn/ *noun* **1** a thin flat part that sticks out from the body of a fish, used for swimming and keeping balance（鱼的）鳍 ➲ **VISUAL VOCAB** PAGE V12 **2** a thin flat part that sticks out from the body of a vehicle, an aircraft, etc., used for improving its balance and movement 鳍状物，翼（车辆、航空器等用以保持平衡等的突出窄扁部分）：*tail fins* 垂直尾翼 ➲ **VISUAL VOCAB** PAGE V57

fin·agle /fɪˈneɪgl/ *verb* [T, I] **~ (sth)** (*informal, especially NAmE*) to behave dishonestly or to obtain sth dishonestly 欺诈；骗取：*He finagled some tickets for tonight's big game.* 他骗到了几张今晚大赛的门票。

final 🔑 AW /ˈfaɪnl/ *adj., noun*

■ ***adj.*** **1** 🔑 [only before noun] being or happening at the end of a series of events, actions, statements, etc. 最终的；最后的：*his final act as party leader* 他作为党的领袖所采取的最后行动 ◇ *The referee blew the final whistle.* 裁判吹响了终场的哨声。◇ *The project is in its final stages.* 这个项目到了最后阶段。◇ *I'd like to return to the final point you made.* 我想再谈谈你所说的最后一点。 ➲ **LANGUAGE BANK** AT PROCESS[1] **2** 🔑 [only before noun] being the result of a particular process（指结果）最终的，最后的：*the final product* 成品 ◇ *No one could have predicted the final outcome.* 谁也没有预想到最终结果会是这样。 **3** 🔑 that cannot be argued with or changed 决定性的；不可改变的；最终的：*The judge's **decision is final**.* 法官的判决是最终判决。◇ *Who has the **final say** around here?* 这里谁有最终决定权？◇ *I'll give you $500 for it, and that's my **final offer**!* 我出价 500 美元，不可能再高了！ ◇ *I'm not coming, **and that's final**!* (= I will not change my mind) 我不来，就这么定了！ IDM SEE ANALYSIS, STRAW, WORD *n.*

■ ***noun*** **1** 🔑 [C] the last of a series of games or competitions in which the winner is decided 决赛：*She reached the final of the 100m hurdles.* 她取得了 100 米跨栏的决赛权。◇ *the 2014 World Cup Finals* (= the last few games in the competition) * 2014 年世界杯决赛阶段 ◇ *The winner of each contest goes through to the **grand final**.* 每场比赛的胜者进入最后的决赛。➲ SEE ALSO QUARTER-FINAL, SEMI-FINAL **2 finals** [pl.] (*BrE*) the last exams taken by university students at the end of their final year 大学毕业考试：*to **sit/take your finals*** 参加大学毕业考试 **3** [C] (*NAmE*) an exam taken by school, university or college students at the end of a SEMESTER or QUARTER, usually in a topic that they will not study again 期终考试；期终结业考试

ˌ**final ˈclause** *noun* (*grammar* 语法) a clause that expresses purpose or intention, for example one that follows 'in order that' or 'so that' 目的从句，目的子句（如 in order that、so that 等引导的从句）

fi·nale /fɪˈnɑːli; *NAmE* fɪˈnæli/ *noun* **1** the last part of a show or a piece of music（演出的）终场，结局；（音乐的）终曲，末乐章：*the rousing finale of Beethoven's Ninth Symphony* 贝多芬《第九交响曲》激动人心的末乐章 ◇ *The festival ended with a **grand finale** in Hyde Park.* 节日的压轴活动是在海德公园举行的盛大演出。**2 ~ (to sth)** (after an adjective 置于形容词后) an ending to sth of the type mentioned 结尾：*a fitting finale to the day's events* 当天活动的圆满结束

fi·nal·ist /ˈfaɪnəlɪst/ *noun* a person who takes part in the final of a game or competition 参加决赛者：*an Olympic finalist* 奥运会决赛运动员

fi·nal·ity AW /faɪˈnæləti/ *noun* [U] the quality of being final and impossible to change 终结；定局；不可改变性：*the finality of death* 死亡的不可改变性 ◇ *There was a note of finality in his voice.* 他的话有斩钉截铁的意味。

fi·nal·ize AW (*BrE also* **-ise**) /ˈfaɪnəlaɪz/ *verb* ~ **sth** to complete the last part of a plan, trip, project, etc. 把（计划、旅行、项目等）最后定下来；定案：*to* ***finalize*** *your* ***plans/arrangements*** 把计划 / 安排最后确定下来 ◇ *They met to finalize the terms of the treaty.* 他们会晤确定条约的条款。▶ **fi·nal·iza·tion, -isa·tion** *noun* [U]

F

fi·nal·ly AW /ˈfaɪnəli/ *adv.* **1** after a long time, especially when there has been some difficulty or delay 终于；最终 SYN **eventually**：*The performance finally started half an hour late.* 延迟了半小时以后演出终于开始了。◇ *I finally managed to get her attention.* 我终于设法引起了她的注意。◇ *When they finally arrived it was well past midnight.* 他们最终到达时已是午夜后的凌晨。 **2** used to introduce the last in a list of things （用于列举）最后 SYN **lastly**：*And finally, I would like to thank you all for coming here today.* 最后，我感谢大家今天的光临。➲ LANGUAGE BANK AT FIRST, PROCESS[1] **3** in a way that ends all discussion about sth 彻底地；决定性地：*The matter was not finally settled until later.* 这事后来才得到彻底解决。

fi·nance AW /ˈfaɪnæns; faɪˈnæns; fəˈnæns/ *noun, verb*

■ ***noun*** **1** (*especially BrE*) (*NAmE usually* **fi·nan·cing**) [U] ~ (**for sth**) money used to run a business, an activity or a project 资金：*Finance for education comes from taxpayers.* 教育经费来自纳税人。 **2** [U] the activity of managing money, especially by a government or commercial organization 财政；金融；财务：*the Minister of Finance* 财政部长 ◇ *the* ***finance director/department*** 财务主任；财务科 ◇ *a diploma in banking and finance* 银行学与金融学文凭 ◇ *the world of* ***high finance*** (= finance involving large companies or countries) 高级金融界（关乎大公司或国家的金融） **3** **finances** [pl.] the money available to a person, an organization or a country; the way this money is managed （个人、组织、国家的）财力，财源，财务管理：***government/public/personal finances*** 政府 / 公共 / 个人财力 ◇ *It's about time you sorted out your finances.* 现在是你整顿财务状况的时候了。◇ *Moving house put a severe strain on our finances.* 搬家使我们的经济十分紧张。

➲ WORDFINDER NOTE AT MONEY

■ ***verb*** ~ **sth** to provide money for a project 提供资金 SYN **fund**：*The building project will be financed by the government.* 这个建筑项目将由政府出资。 ◇ *He took a job to finance his stay in Germany.* 他找了一份工作以赚钱支付在德国逗留的费用。

ˈfinance company (*BrE also* **ˈfinance house**) *noun* a company that lends money to people or businesses （向个人或公司贷款的）信贷公司，金融公司

fi·nan·cial AW /faɪˈnænʃl; fəˈnæ-/ *adj.* [usually before noun] **1** connected with money and finance 财政的；财务的；金融的：*financial services* 金融服务 ◇ *to give financial advice* 提供财务咨询 ◇ *to be in* ***financial difficulties*** 处于财务困难之中 ◇ *an independent* ***financial adviser*** 独立财务顾问 ◇ *Tokyo and New York are major* ***financial centres.*** 东京和纽约是主要的金融中心。➲ SYNONYMS AT ECONOMIC **2** (*AustralE, NZE, informal*) having money 有钱的 ▶ **fi·nan·cial·ly** AW /-ʃəli/ *adv.*：*She is still* ***financially dependent*** *on her parents.* 她在经济上仍然依靠父母。◇ *Financially, I'm much better off than before.* 我的经济状况比过去好多了。◇ *Such projects are not* ***financially viable*** *without*

▼ **COLLOCATIONS 词语搭配**

Finance 财务

Income 收入

- **earn** money/cash/(*informal*) a fortune 挣钱；挣一大笔钱
- **make** money/a fortune/(*informal*) a killing on the stock market 在股市上赚钱 / 赚一大笔钱 / 发大财
- **acquire/inherit/amass** wealth/a fortune 获得 / 继承 / 积累财富 / 一大笔钱
- **build up** funds/savings 积累资金 / 存款
- **get/receive/leave** (**sb**) an inheritance/a legacy 得到 /（给某人）留下遗产
- **live on** a low wage/a fixed income/a pension 靠低微的工资 / 固定收入 / 养老金过活
- **get/receive/draw/collect** a pension 领取养老金
- **depend/be dependent on** (*BrE*) benefits/(*NAmE*) welfare/social security 靠福利金 / 社会保障金过活

Expenditure 开支；支出

- **spend** money/your savings/(*informal*) a fortune on… 把钱 / 存款 / 一大笔钱花在…上
- **invest/put** your savings in… 投资 / 把储蓄金用于…
- **throw away/waste**/ (*informal*) **shell out** money on… 把钱浪费 / 花费巨资在…上
- **lose** your money/inheritance/pension 失去钱财 / 遗产 / 养老金
- **use up**/ (*informal*) **wipe out** all your savings 把储蓄用光
- **pay** (**in**) cash 用现金支付
- **use/pay by** a credit/debit card 用信用卡 / 借记卡支付
- **pay by/make out a/write sb a/accept a** (*BrE*) cheque/(*US*) check 用支票支付；开支票；给某人开支票；接受支票
- **change/exchange** money/currency/(*BrE*) traveller's cheques/(*US*) traveler's checks 兑换钱 / 货币 / 旅行支票
- **give/pay/leave** (**sb**) a deposit 预付（某人）订金

Banks 银行

- **have/hold/open/close/freeze** a bank account/an account 持有 / 开立 / 注销 / 冻结银行账户
- **credit/debit/pay sth into/take money out of** your account 记入账户的贷方 / 借方；把钱存入账户 / 从账户中取出
- **deposit** money/funds in your account 往账户里存钱 / 存入资金
- **withdraw** money/cash/£30 from an ATM, etc. 从自动提款机等取钱 / 现金 / 30 英镑
- (*formal*) **make** a deposit/withdrawal 存款；取款
- **find/go to/use** (*especially NAmE*) an ATM/(*BrE*) a cash machine/dispenser 找到 / 去 / 使用自动提款机
- **be** in credit/in debit/in the black/in the red/overdrawn 账面有钱 / 亏空；有盈余；透支

Personal finance 个人理财

- **manage/handle/plan/run**/ (*especially BrE*) **sort out** your finances 管理 / 处理 / 计划 / 经营管理 / 整顿财务问题
- **plan/manage/work out/stick to** a budget 计划 / 管理 / 制订 / 严格执行预算
- **offer/extend** credit (to sb) （给某人）提供贷款
- **arrange/take out** a loan/an overdraft 商定 / 获得贷款 / 透支额
- **pay back/repay** money/a loan/a debt 偿还钱 / 贷款 / 债务
- **pay for sth in** (*especially BrE*) instalments/(*NAmE usually*) installments 以分期付款方式购买某物

Financial difficulties 财务困难

- **get into** debt/financial difficulties 陷入债务 / 财务困难
- **be short of**/ (*informal*) **be strapped for** cash 缺钱
- **run out of/owe** money 钱用光了；欠钱
- **face/get**/ (*informal*) **be landed with** a bill for £… 面对 / 收到一张…英镑的账单
- **can't afford** the cost of…/payments/rent 承担不起…的费用 / 款项 / 房租
- **fall behind with**/ (*especially NAmE*) **fall behind on** the mortgage/repayments/rent 拖欠按揭贷款 / 分期偿还款项 / 房租
- **incur/run up/accumulate** debts 带来 / 积欠 / 累积债务
- **tackle/reduce/settle** your debts 处理 / 减少 / 付清债务

government funding. 没有政府专款，这样的项目在资金上是不可行的。

fiˌnancial ˈaid *noun* [U] (*NAmE*) money that is given or lent to students at a university or college who cannot pay the full cost of their education（高等院校的）助学金，助学贷款：*to apply for financial aid* 申请助学金

the Fiˌnancial Times ˈindex *noun* = FTSE INDEX™

fiˌnancial ˈyear (*BrE*) (*BrE also* **ˈtax year**) (*NAmE* **ˌfiscal ˈyear**) *noun* [usually sing.] a period of twelve months over which the accounts and taxes of a company or a person are calculated 财政年度；会计年度：*the current financial year* 本财政年度

fi·nan·cier AW /faɪˈnænsiə(r); fə-; *NAmE* ˌfɪnənˈsɪr/ *noun* a person who lends large amounts of money to businesses 金融家；理财家

fi·nan·cing /ˈfaɪnænsɪŋ; faɪˈnænsɪŋ; fəˈnænsɪŋ/ *noun* [U] (*NAmE*) = FINANCE: *The project will only go ahead if they can raise the necessary financing.* 只有筹集到必要的资金，这个项目才能得以进行。

finch /fɪntʃ/ *noun* (often in compounds 常构成复合词) a small bird with a short beak. There are several types of finch. 雀；雀科小鸟 ➲ VISUAL VOCAB PAGE V12 ➲ SEE ALSO BULLFINCH, CHAFFINCH, GOLDFINCH

find 🔑 /faɪnd/ *verb, noun*

■ ***verb*** (**found, found** /faʊnd/)

• **BY CHANCE** 偶然 **1** 🔑 [T] to discover sb/sth unexpectedly or by chance（意外或偶然地）发现，碰到：**~ sb/sth** *Look what I've found!* 看我发现了什么！◊ *We've found a great new restaurant near the office.* 我们在办公处附近发现了一家挺好的新餐馆。◊ **~ sb/sth + adj.** *A whale was found washed up on the shore.* 一头鲸被发现冲到了岸上。

• **BY SEARCHING** 通过搜寻 **2** 🔑 [T] to get back sth/sb that was lost after searching for it/them 找到；找回：**~ sth for sb** *Can you find my bag for me?* 你能帮我找我的包吗？◊ **~ sb sth** *Can you find me my bag?* 你能帮我找我的包吗？◊ **~ sb/sth** *I wanted to talk to him but he was* **nowhere to be found**. 我想和他谈谈，但哪儿也找不到他。◊ **~ sb/sth + adj.** *The child was found safe and well.* 小孩找到了，安然无恙。

• **BY STUDYING/THINKING** 通过研究 / 思考 **3** 🔑 [T] to discover sth/sb by searching, studying or thinking carefully（经寻找、研究或思考）发现，查明，找出，求得：**~ sth/sb** *scientists trying to find a cure for cancer* 努力寻找癌症疗法的科学家 ◊ *I managed to find a solution to the problem.* 我设法找出了解决问题的办法。◊ *I'm having trouble finding anything new to say on this subject.* 在这个课题上要提出什么新看法，我有困难。◊ *Have they found anyone to replace her yet?* 他们找到了代替她的人没有？◊ **~ sth for sb** *Can you find a hotel for me?* 你能给我找一家旅馆吗？◊ **~ sb sth** *Can you find me a hotel?* 你能给我找一家旅馆吗？

• **BY EXPERIENCE/TESTING** 通过体验 / 试验 **4** 🔑 [T] to discover that sth is true after you have tried it, tested it or experienced it 发现（某事属实）：**~ (that)...** *I find (that) it pays to be honest.* 我发现老实人不吃亏。◊ *The report found that 30% of the firms studied had failed within a year.* 据报告称，调查过的公司有 30% 一年内倒闭了。◊ **~ sb/sth + adj./noun** *We found the beds very comfortable.* 我们发现这些床非常舒适。◊ **~ sb/sth to be/do sth** *They found him to be charming.* 他们觉得他很招人喜欢。◊ *Her blood was found to contain poison.* 她的血液中发现有毒素。◊ **it is found that...** *It was found that her blood contained poison.* 她的血液中发现有毒素。

• **HAVE OPINION/FEELING** 有意见 / 看法 **5** 🔑 [T] to have a particular feeling or opinion about sth 认为；感到：**~ sth + adj.** *You may find your illness hard to accept.* 你可能觉得难以接受自己患病。◊ *You may* **find it hard** *to accept your illness.* 你可能觉得难以接受自己患病。◊ *I find it amazing that they're still together.* 他们还在一起，这使我大吃一惊。◊ **~ sth + noun** *She* **finds it a strain** *to meet new people.* 她和生人见面总感到局促不安。➲ SYNONYMS AT REGARD

• **HAVE/MAKE AVAILABLE** 现有；使现有 **6** [T] **~ sth** to have sth available so that you can use it 现有（可用）：*I keep meaning to write, but never seem to find (the) time.* 我一直打算写信，但似乎总找不到时间。◊ *How are we going to find £5 000 for a car?* 我们哪里有 5 000 英镑买车呢？

• **IN UNEXPECTED SITUATIONS** 处于意外状况 **7** [T] to discover sb/sth/yourself doing sth or in a particular situation, especially when this is unexpected（尤指意外地）发现，发觉（处于某状态、在做某事）：**~ sb/sth/yourself + adv./prep.** *She woke up and found herself in a hospital bed.* 她醒来发觉自己躺在医院的床上。◊ **~ sb/sth/yourself + adj.** *We came home and found him asleep on the sofa.* 我们回到家发现他在沙发上睡着了。◊ **~ sb/sth/yourself doing sth** *I suddenly found myself running down the street.* 我不知不觉突然在街上跑了起来。◊ **~ (that)...** *I was disappointed to find that they had left already.* 我发现他们已经离开了，觉得很失望。

• **REACH** 达到；到达 **8** [T] **~ sth** (of things 事物) to arrive at sth naturally; to reach sth 自然到达；达到：*Water will always find its own level.* 水总会自行流平。◊ *Most of the money finds its way to the people who need it.* 多数的钱都会辗转传到需要的人的手中。◊ *The criticism found its mark* (= had the effect intended). 批评击中了要害。

• **EXIST/GROW** 存在；生长 **9** [T] **~ sth + adv./prep.** used to say that sth exists, grows, etc. somewhere（在某处）存在，生长：*These flowers are found only in Africa.* 这些花仅见于非洲。◊ *You'll find this style of architecture all over the town.* 全城到处可见这种风格的建筑。

• **IN COURT** 法庭 **10** [T, I] (*formal*) to make a particular decision in a court case 裁决；判决：**~ sb + adj.** *The jury found him guilty.* 陪审团裁决他有罪。◊ *How do you find the accused?* 你如何裁定被告？◊ **~ in sb's favour** *The court found in her favour.* 法庭判决对她有利。

IDM **all ˈfound** (*old-fashioned, BrE*) with free food and accommodation in addition to your wages（工资外）加免费食宿 **find fault (with sb/sth)** to look for and discover mistakes in sb/sth; to complain about sb/sth 找茬儿；挑错；挑剔；抱怨 **find your ˈfeet** to become able to act independently and with confidence 已能独立而有信心地工作；已适应新环境：*I only recently joined the firm so I'm still finding my feet.* 我最近才加入这家公司，所以还在适应过程中。**find it in your heart/yourself to do sth** (*literary*) to be able or willing to do sth 能做某事；愿意干某事：*Can you find it in your heart to forgive her?* 你能够做到宽恕她吗？◊ *He couldn't find it in himself to trust anyone again.* 他再也不愿意相信任何人了。 **find your ˈvoice/ˈtongue** to be able to speak or express your opinion 能说出自己的看法；能表达自己的意见 **find your way (to...)** to discover the right route (to a place) 找到正确的路（去某处）：*I hope you can find your way home.* 希望你能找到回家的路。 **find your/its ˈway (to/into...)** to come to a place or a situation by chance or without intending to 偶然来到；无意中处于：*He eventually found his way into acting.* 他弄到最后竟干起了演艺这一行。**take sb as you ˈfind them** to accept sb as they are without expecting them to behave in a special way or have special qualities 接受某人的现状；承认某人的情况（别无指望）➲ MORE AT BEARING, MATCH *n.*, NOWHERE

PHR V **ˈfind for/against sb** [no passive] (*law* 律) to make a decision in favour of/against sb in a court case 作出对…有利（或不利）的裁决；判…胜诉（或败诉）：*The jury found for the defendant.* 陪审团作出了对被告有利的裁决。**ˌfind ˈout (about sth/sb)** | **ˌfind ˈout sth (about sth/sb)** 🔑 to get some information about sth/sb by asking, reading, etc. 查明，弄清（情况）：*She'd been seeing the boy for a while, but didn't want her parents to find out.* 她和这个男孩约会已有一段时间了，但不想让父母知道。◊ *I haven't found anything out about him yet.* 我还没有发现有关他的什么情况。◊ **find out what, when, etc....** *Can you find out what time the meeting starts?* 你能查清楚会议什么时候开始吗？◊ **find out that...** *We found out later that we had been at the same school.* 后来我们才弄清楚我们是校友。**ˌfind sb ˈout** to discover that sb has done sth wrong 查出（坏人）；识破：*He had been cheating the taxman but it was years before he was found out.* 他过去一直在欺骗税务部门，只是多年以后才被查出来。

■ ***noun*** a thing or person that has been found, especially one that is interesting, valuable or useful 发现物，被发现的人（尤指有趣、有价值或有用者）：*an important*

F

archaeological find 考古的重大发现 ◇ *Our new babysitter is* ***a real find.*** 我们新来的临时保姆是难得的好保姆。

find·er /ˈfaɪndə(r)/ *noun* a person who finds sth 发现者；寻得者 ➲ SEE ALSO VIEWFINDER

IDM **ˌfinders ˈkeepers** (*saying*) (often used by children 儿童常用语) anyone who finds sth has a right to keep it 谁找到是谁的；谁捡到的归谁

fin de siècle /ˌfæ̃ də ˈsjekl/ *adj.* (*from French*) typical of the end of the 19th century, especially of its art, literature and attitudes（尤指文学、艺术、看法）19 世纪末的

find·ing /ˈfaɪndɪŋ/ *noun* **1** [usually pl.] information that is discovered as the result of research into sth 调查发现；调研结果：*The findings of the commission will be published today.* 委员会的调查结果将于今天公布。➲ COLLOCATIONS AT SCIENTIFIC **2** (*law* 律) a decision made by the judge or JURY in a court case 判决；裁决

fine /faɪn/ *adj., adv., noun, verb*

■ ***adj.*** (**finer**, **fin·est**)

• **VERY GOOD** 很好 **1** [usually before noun] of high quality; good 高质量的；美好的：*a very fine performance* 十分精彩的演出 ◇ *fine clothes/wines/workmanship* 漂亮的衣服；美酒；精湛的工艺 ◇ *a particularly fine example of Saxon architecture* 撒克逊式建筑的优秀范例 ◇ *Jim has made a fine job of the garden.* 吉姆把花园拾掇得漂漂亮亮的。◇ *people who enjoy the* ***finer things*** *in life* (= for example art, good food, etc.) 享受生活中美好事物的人 ◇ *He tried to appeal to their* ***finer feelings*** (= feelings of duty, love, etc.). 他试图打动他们更美好的情感（即责任感、爱等）。◇ *It was his* ***finest hour*** (= most successful period) *as manager of the England team.* 那是他作为英格兰队主教练的鼎盛时期。

• **VERY WELL** 很不错 **2** (of a person 人) in good health 健康的；身体很好的：*'How are you?' 'Fine, thanks.'* "你好吗？" "很好，谢谢。" ◇ *I was* ***feeling fine*** *when I got up this morning.* 今天早上我起床时感觉很好。 ➲ SYNONYMS AT WELL

• **ACCEPTABLE/GOOD ENOUGH** 可接受；够好 **3** (also used as an exclamation 亦作感叹词) used to tell sb that an action, a suggestion or a decision is acceptable（指行为、建议、决定）可接受：*'I'll leave this here, OK?' 'Fine.'* "我把这个留在这儿，可以吗？" "可以。" ◇ *'Bob wants to know if he can come too.'* ***'That's fine by me.'*** "鲍勃想知道他是否也能来。" "我认为没问题。" **4** used to say you are satisfied with sth（表示满意）很好，不错，满意：*Don't worry. Your speech was fine.* 别担心。你的讲话挺好的。◇ *You go on without me.* ***I'll be fine.*** 别管我了，你继续吧。我没事的。◇ *'Can I get you another drink?' 'No, thanks.* ***I'm fine.'*** "我可以再给你取一杯吗？" "不，谢谢。我够了。" ◇ (*ironic*) *This is* ***a fine*** (= terrible) ***mess we're in!*** 我们的处境好狼狈啊！◇ (*ironic*) ***You're a fine one to talk!*** (= you are not in a position to criticize, give advice, etc.) 哪有你说话的分儿！

• **ATTRACTIVE** 有吸引力 **5** [usually before noun] pleasing to look at 好看的；漂亮的：*a fine view* 美景 ◇ *a fine-looking woman* 漂亮女人 ◇ *a fine figure of a man* 身材俊美的男人

• **DELICATE** 精致 **6** [usually before noun] attractive and delicate 精巧的；精美的：*fine bone china* 精致的骨瓷 ◇ *She has inherited her mother's fine features* (= a small nose, mouth, etc.). 她遗传了她母亲的清秀面容。

• **WEATHER** 天气 **7** (*especially BrE*) bright and not raining 晴朗的：*a fine day/evening* 晴朗的一天/晚上 ◇ *I hope it* ***stays fine*** *for the picnic.* 我希望野餐那天还是晴天。

• **VERY THIN** 纤细 **8** very thin or narrow 纤细的；很细的：*fine blond hair* 纤细的金发 ◇ *a fine thread* 细线 ◇ *a brush with a fine tip* 笔头尖细的画笔

• **DETAIL/DISTINCTIONS** 细节；差别 **9** [usually before noun] difficult to see or describe 难以看出的；很难描述的 **SYN** **subtle**：*You really need a magnifying glass to appreciate all the fine detail.* 确实需要放大镜才能欣赏到一切细微之处。◇ *There's no need to make such* ***fine distinctions.*** 没有必要区分出如此细微的差别。◇ *There's* ***a fine line*** *between love and hate* (= it is easy for one to become the other). 爱恨只有一线之隔。

• **WITH SMALL GRAINS** 小颗粒 **10** made of very small grains 小颗粒制成的；颗粒细微的：*fine sand* 细沙 ◇ *Use a finer piece of sandpaper to finish.* 用细砂纸最后磨光。 **OPP** **coarse**

• **PERSON** 人 **11** [only before noun] that you have a lot of respect for 值得尊敬的；杰出的：*He was a fine man.* 他是个优秀的人。

• **WORDS/SPEECHES** 词语；话语 **12** sounding important and impressive but unlikely to have any effect 漂亮的；虚饰的；辞藻华丽的：*His speech was full of fine words which meant nothing.* 他的演讲华而不实。

• **METALS** 金属 **13** (*specialist*) containing only a particular metal and no other substances that reduce the quality 纯的；无杂质的：*fine gold* 纯金

IDM **get sth down to a fine ˈart** (*informal*) to learn to do sth well and efficiently 把…学到家；学得非常在行：*I spend so much time travelling that I've got packing down to a fine art.* 我常常旅行，这样便把打点行李学到家了。 **not to put too fine a ˈpoint on it** used to emphasize sth that is expressed clearly and directly, especially a criticism 直截了当地说，不客气地说（尤指批评）：*Not to put too fine a point on it, I think you are lying.* 不客气地说，我认为你在撒谎。➲ MORE AT CHANCE *n.*, FETTLE, LINE *n.*

■ ***adv.*** (*informal*) in a way that is acceptable or good enough 可接受；够好；蛮不错：*Keep going like that—you're* ***doing fine.*** 就这样做下去，你做得蛮不错嘛。◇ *Things were* ***going fine*** *until you showed up.* 你一露面就把事情搞糟了。◇ *That arrangement* ***suits me fine.*** 那种安排对我很合适。◇ (*BrE*) *An omelette will* ***do me fine*** (= will be enough for me). 一份摊鸡蛋我就够了。

IDM **cut it/things ˈfine** (*informal*) to leave yourself just enough time to do sth 把时间扣得很紧；时间上不留余地：*If we don't leave till after lunch we'll be cutting it very fine.* 我们要是午饭以后才走，时间就紧得很了。

■ ***noun*** a sum of money that must be paid as punishment for breaking a law or rule 罚金；罚款：*a parking fine* 违规停车罚款 ◇ *Offenders will be liable to a* ***heavy fine*** (= one that costs a lot of money). 违者须付巨额罚金。◇ *She has already paid over $2 000 in fines.* 她已经付了 2 000 多美元罚金。➲ SYNONYMS AT RATE ➲ COLLOCATIONS AT JUSTICE

■ ***verb*** [often passive] to make sb pay money as an official punishment 对…处以罚款：**~ sb (for sth/for doing sth)** *She was fined for speeding.* 她因超速而被罚款。◇ **~ sb sth (for sth/for doing sth)** *The company was fined £20 000 for breaching safety regulations.* 这家公司因违反安全条例而被罚款 2 万英镑。

fine ˈart *noun* [U] (*also* **fine ˈarts** [pl.]) forms of art, especially painting, drawing and SCULPTURE, that are created to be beautiful rather than useful 美术（尤指绘画和雕塑）

Fine Gael /ˌfiːnə ˈɡeɪl/ *noun* [sing.+sing./pl. v.] the more conservative of the two main political parties in the Republic of Ireland 统一党（爱尔兰共和国两大政党之一，保守党派）➲ COMPARE FIANNA FÁIL

fine·ly /ˈfaɪnli/ *adv.* **1** into very small grains or pieces 成颗粒；细微地；细小地：*finely chopped herbs* 剁得很细的香草 **2** in a beautiful or impressive way 华丽地；优雅地：*a finely furnished room* 陈设雅致的房间 **3** in a very delicate or exact way 精致地；精巧地；精确地：*a finely tuned engine* 精确调整的发动机 ◇ *The match was finely balanced throughout.* 比赛自始至终不分上下。

fine·ness /ˈfaɪnnəs/ *noun* [U] **1** the quality of being made of thin threads or lines very close together 纤细；精细度；细度：*fineness of detail* 详情的细微 **2** (*specialist*) the quality of sth 纯度；成色：*the fineness of the gold* 黄金的成色

the ˌfine ˈprint (*NAmE*) (*especially BrE* **the ˌsmall ˈprint**) *noun* [U] the important details of an agreement or a legal document that are usually printed in small type and are therefore easy to miss（合同或法律文件等中易被忽略但很重要的）小字号的附加条款

fin·ery /ˈfaɪnəri/ *noun* [U] (*formal*) brightly coloured and elegant clothes and jewellery, especially those that are worn for a special occasion 高雅华丽的衣服；精美的饰物

fi·nesse /fɪˈnes/ *noun, verb*

■ ***noun*** [U] great skill in dealing with people or situations, especially in a delicate way 手腕；策略；手段

■ ***verb*** (*especially NAmE*) **1 ~ sth** to deal with sth in a way that is clever but slightly dishonest 用策略对付某事： *to finesse a deal* 略施小计达成一桩交易 **2 ~ sth** to do sth with a lot of skill or style 巧妙地做；派头十足地做

ˌfine-tooth ˈcomb (*also* **ˌfine-toothed ˈcomb**) *noun* a COMB in which the pointed parts are thin and very close together 细齿梳子

IDM **go over/through sth with a fine-tooth/fine-toothed comb** to examine or search sth very carefully 十分认真地检查；非常仔细地搜查

ˌfine-ˈtune *verb* **~ sth** to make very small changes to sth so that it is as good as it can possibly be 对…微调 ▸ **ˌfine-ˈtuning** *noun* [U]: *The system is set up but it needs some fine-tuning.* 该系统已装配好，但需要一些细小调整。

f-ing *adj.* [only before noun] (*taboo, slang*) = EFFING

fin·ger /ˈfɪŋɡə(r)/ *noun, verb*

■ ***noun*** **1** one of the four long thin parts that stick out from the hand (or five, if the thumb is included) 手指: *She **ran her fingers through** her hair.* 她用手指梳理头发。◇ *Hold the material between finger and thumb.* 用拇指和另一指拿住这个材料。◇ *He was about to speak but she raised a finger to her lips.* 他正要说话，但她举起手指放在唇上示意不要说。➲ COLLOCATIONS AT PHYSICAL ➲ SEE ALSO BUTTERFINGERS, FOREFINGER, GREEN FINGERS, INDEX FINGER, LITTLE FINGER, MIDDLE FINGER, RING FINGER **2 -fingered** (in adjectives 构成形容词) having the type of fingers mentioned; having or using the number of fingers mentioned 有…手指的（指类型）；有（或用）…手指的（指数目）: *long-fingered* 长手指的 ◇ *nimble-fingered* 手指灵敏的 ◇ *a four-fingered chord* 四指弹奏的和弦 ➲ SEE ALSO LIGHT-FINGERED ➲ MORE LIKE THIS 8, page R25 **3** the part of a glove that covers the finger （手套的）指部 **4 ~ (of sth)** a long narrow piece of bread, cake, land, etc. 狭长物（如面包、糕饼、土地等）: *a finger of toast* 长条吐司 ◇ *chocolate fingers* 巧克力条 ➲ SEE ALSO FISH FINGER

IDM **the ˌfinger of susˈpicion** if the finger of suspicion points or is pointed at sb, they are suspected of having committed a crime, being responsible for sth, etc. 怀疑对象 **get, pull, etc. your ˈfinger out** (*BrE, informal*) used to tell sb to start doing some work or making an effort 干起来；加把劲: *You're going to have to pull your finger out if you want to pass this exam.* 如果你想通过这次考试就得多加把劲。 **give sb the ˈfinger** (*especially NAmE, informal*) to raise your middle finger in the air with the back part of your hand facing sb, done to be rude to sb or to show them that you are angry 向某人竖起中指（手背向外以表示侮辱） **have a finger in every ˈpie** (*informal*) to be involved in a lot of different activities and have influence over them, especially when other people think that this is annoying 多管闲事；到处干预 **have, etc. your ˈfingers in the till** (*BrE, informal*) to be stealing money from the place where you work 偷自己工作单位的钱；内盗；监守自盗 **have/keep your finger on the ˈpulse (of sth)** to always be aware of the most recent developments in a particular situation 始终了解…的最新情况；掌握…的脉搏 **lay a ˈfinger on sb** (usually used in negative sentences 通常用于否定句) to touch sb with the intention of hurting them physically 触碰，动…的一根毫毛（意欲伤害某人）: *I never laid a finger on her.* 我从来没有碰过她。 **not put your finger on sth** to not be able to identify what is wrong or different about a particular situation 看不出（问题所在）；说不出（差别）: *There was something odd about him but I couldn't put my finger on it.* 他有些古怪，但我说不出到底是什么。 **put/stick two ˈfingers up at sb** (*BrE, informal*) to form the shape of a V with the two fingers nearest your thumb and raise your hand in the air with the back part of it facing sb, done to be rude to them or to show them that you are angry 向某人竖起两指（做出V形手势，手背向外以表示侮辱） ➲ SEE ALSO V-SIGN **work your fingers to the ˈbone** to work very hard 拼命干活 ➲ MORE AT BURN *v.*, COUNT *v.*, CROSS *v.*, LIFT *v.*, POINT *v.*, SLIP *v.*, SNAP *v.*, STICKY *adj.*, THUMB *n.*

■ ***verb*** **1 ~ sth** to touch or feel sth with your fingers 用手指触摸: *Gary sat fingering his beard, saying nothing.* 加里坐着用手捋着胡子，一言不发。 **2 ~ sb (for sth) | ~ sb (as sth)** (*informal, especially NAmE*) to accuse sb of doing sth illegal and tell the police about it 告发；告密: *Who fingered him for the burglaries?* 谁告发他入室盗窃？

finger·board /ˈfɪŋɡəbɔːd; *NAmE* ˈfɪŋɡərbɔːrd/ *noun* a flat strip on the neck of a musical instrument such as a GUITAR or VIOLIN, against which the strings are pressed to play different notes （吉他或小提琴等的）指板

ˈfinger bowl *noun* a small bowl of water for washing your fingers during a meal （用餐时用的）洗指碗

ˈfinger food *noun* [U, C] pieces of food that you can easily eat with your fingers 手取食物（便于用手指取食的食物）

fin·ger·ing /ˈfɪŋɡərɪŋ/ *noun* [U, C] the positions in which you put your fingers when playing a musical instrument （演奏乐器的）指法

fin·ger·mark /ˈfɪŋɡəmɑːk; *NAmE* ˈfɪŋɡərmɑːrk/ *noun* [usually pl.] (*especially BrE*) a mark made by a finger, for example on a clean surface 指痕；指迹

fin·ger·nail /ˈfɪŋɡəneɪl; *NAmE* -ɡərn-/ *noun* the thin hard layer that covers the outer tip of each finger 手指甲 ➲ VISUAL VOCAB PAGE V64

fin·ger·print /ˈfɪŋɡəprɪnt; *NAmE* -ɡərp-/ *noun* a mark made by the pattern of lines on the tip of a person's finger, often used by the police to identify criminals 指纹；指印 ➲ SYNONYMS AT MARK ➲ SEE ALSO GENETIC FINGERPRINT at GENETIC FINGERPRINTING ▸ **fin·ger·print** *verb* **~ sb**

fin·ger·print·ing /ˈfɪŋɡəprɪntɪŋ; *NAmE* -ɡərp-/ *noun* [U] the practice of recording sb's fingerprints, often used by the police to identify criminals 取（罪犯等的）指纹印；盖手印 ➲ SEE ALSO DNA FINGERPRINTING, GENETIC FINGERPRINTING

fin·ger·tip /ˈfɪŋɡətɪp; *NAmE* -ɡərt-/ *noun* [usually pl.] the end of the finger that is furthest from the hand 指尖

IDM **have sth at your ˈfingertips** to have the information, knowledge, etc. that is needed in a particular situation and be able to find it easily and use it quickly 掌握（信息等）；熟悉，精通（知识等）；对…了如指掌；有…随时可供使用 **to your ˈfingertips** (*BrE*) in every way 完全；十足: *She's a perfectionist to her fingertips.* 她是个道道地地的完美主义者。

fin·ial /ˈfɪniəl/ *noun* **1** (*architecture* 建) a decorative part at the top of a roof, wall, etc. （屋顶、墙头等的）顶端饰 **2** a decorative part that fits on the end of a curtain pole （帘杆的）装饰头 ➲ VISUAL VOCAB PAGE V22

fin·icky /ˈfɪnɪki/ *adj.* **1** (*disapproving*) too worried about what you eat, wear, etc.; disliking many things （对衣食等）过分讲究的，过分挑剔的 SYN **fussy**: *a finicky eater* 过分挑食者 **2** needing great care and attention to detail 需认真仔细对待的；需要注意细节的 SYN **fiddly**: *It's a very finicky job.* 这是个很细致的工作。

fin·ish /ˈfɪnɪʃ/ *verb, noun*

■ ***verb*** **1** [T, I] to stop doing sth or making sth because it is complete 完成；做好: **~ (sth)** *Haven't you finished your homework yet?* 难道你还没有完成家庭作业吗？◇ *She finished law school last year.* 她去年毕业于法学院。◇ *I thought you'd never finish!* 我还以为你会完成不了呢！◇ *a beautifully finished piece of furniture* 一件做工精美的家具 ◇ *He **put the finishing touches** to his painting* (= did the things that made it complete). 他在画上作了最后几处润色。◇ **~ doing sth** *Be quiet! He hasn't finished speaking.* 安静！他还没有讲完。◇ **+ speech** *'And that was all,' she finished.* "情况就这些。" 她结束时说。➲ MORE LIKE THIS 27, page R28 **2** [I, T] to come to an end; to bring sth to an end （使）结束: *The play finished at 10.30.* 比赛于 10:30 结束。◇ **~ with sth** *The symphony finishes with a flourish.* 交响乐在响亮的乐曲声中结束。◇ **~ sth** *A cup of coffee finished the meal perfectly.* 饭后一杯咖啡，美餐圆满结束。 **3** [T] **~ sth (off/up)** to eat, drink or use what remains of sth 吃完，喝光，用尽（所剩之物）: *He finished off his drink with one large gulp.* 他一大口喝完了饮料。◇ *We* *might as well finish up the cake.* 我们倒不如把蛋糕吃完。**4** [I] to be in a particular state or position at the end of a race or a competition（赛跑、竞赛）得…名；获…成绩：**+ adj.** *She was delighted to finish second.* 她为竞赛得了第二名而高兴。◇ *The dollar finished the day slightly down.* 当日结束时美元汇率略有下跌。◇ **+ adv./prep.** *He finished 12 seconds outside the world record.* 他的赛跑成绩比世界纪录慢 12 秒。**5** [T] **~ sb (off)** (*informal*) to make sb so tired or impatient that they cannot do any more 使筋疲力尽；使失去耐心：*Climbing that hill really finished me off.* 登那座山真把我累得筋疲力尽。◇ *A lecture from my parents now would just finish me.* 现在父母教训我简直会使我受不了。

F

PHR V **ˌfinish sb/sth↔ˈoff** (*informal*) to destroy sb/sth, especially sb/sth that is badly injured or damaged 杀死，彻底摧毁（已严重受伤或受损的人或事物）：*The hunter moved in to finish the animal off.* 猎人逼到近前，了结了那只动物。**ˌfinish sth↔ˈoff** to do the last part of sth; to make sth end by doing one last thing 收尾；做最后加工：*I need about an hour to finish off this report.* 我需要一小时左右结束这篇报告。◇ *They finished off the show with one of their most famous songs.* 他们用自己的一首最著名的歌曲作演出的压台戏。**ˌfinish ˈup...** (*BrE*) to be in a particular state or at a particular place after a series of events 结果成为；以…终结；最终来到：**+ adj.** *If you're not careful, you could finish up seriously ill.* 你要是不小心，可能到头来会得场大病。**ˈfinish with sb 1** (*BrE*) to end a relationship with sb 与（某人）断绝关系：*She finished with her boyfriend last week.* 上星期她和男友分手了。**2** to stop dealing with a person 停止和（某人）打交道：*He'll regret he ever said it once I've finished with him.* 我不再和他打交道，他就会后悔他说过那句话。**ˈfinish with sth 1** to no longer need to use sth 不再需用（某物）：*When you've finished with the book, can I see it?* 这本书你看完以后我能看吗？**2** (*BrE, informal*) to stop doing sth 不再做（某事）：*I've finished with gambling.* 我已戒赌了。**finish (up) with sth** to have sth at the end 最后得到；以…结束：*We had a five-course lunch and finished up with coffee and mints.* 我们这顿午餐吃了五道菜，最后是咖啡和薄荷糖。◇ *To finish with, we'll listen to a few songs.* 最后我们将听几首歌。

▼ EXPRESS YOURSELF 情景表达

Wrapping up a discussion 结束讨论

In a formal meeting or conference, you may have to bring the session to a close. Here are some ways to get people to stop speaking. 以下是一些在正式会议结束时请求与会人员终止发言的方式：

- ***I'm afraid time is running out/we're running out of time,*** *so we'll have to make this the final question.* 恐怕时间不多了，所以这将是我们最后一个问题了。
- ***We've only got a couple of minutes left,*** *so can we summarize what we've agreed?* 我们只剩下几分钟了，所以概括一下已经达成一致的意见好吗？
- ***I'd like to close the session with a few final remarks...*** 我想最后说几句来结束这次会议…
- ***We'll have to leave it there,*** *but thank you all very much for your input.* 我们就到这儿吧，非常感谢大家的参与。
- ***Well, that's all we have time for today,*** *but we'll meet again on Tuesday.* 好了，我们今天没有时间了，但星期二我们将再次开会。
- ***I'd like to thank you all for coming*** *and for a very productive meeting.* 感谢大家出席这次会议，以及为这次富有成效的会议付出的努力。

■ ***noun* 1** [C, usually sing.] the last part or the end of sth 最后部分；结尾；结局：*a dramatic finish to the race* 赛跑的戏剧性结局 ◇ *It was **a close finish**, as they had predicted.* 正如他们所预料的，比赛结果难分上下。◇ *They won in the end but it was **a tight finish**.* 他们终于赢了，但比分十分接近。◇ *The story was a lie **from start to finish**.* 这样的讲述自始至终都是骗人的。◇ *I want to see the job through **to the finish**.* 我要看到这项工作做完为止。➲ SEE ALSO PHOTO FINISH **2** [C, U] the last covering of paint, polish, etc. that is put onto the surface of sth; the condition of the surface 末道漆；抛光；（漆完抛光后的）成品表面：*a **gloss/matt finish*** 光泽 / 无光表面 ◇ *furniture available in a range of finishes* 有各种光泽处理的家具 **3** [C, U] the final details that are added to sth to make it complete 最后精细加工：*The bows will give a feminine finish to the curtains.* 窗帘最后配上蝴蝶结显出女性的柔美。IDM SEE FIGHT *v.*

fin·ished /ˈfɪnɪʃt/ *adj.* **1** [not before noun] no longer doing sth or dealing with sb/sth 完成；不再与…打交道：*I won't be finished for another hour.* 我还得一小时以后才能完成。◇ **~ with sb/sth** *I'm not finished with you yet.* 你我还得打交道。**2** [not before noun] no longer powerful, effective or able to continue 垮台；失败；完蛋：*If the newspapers find out, he's finished in politics.* 如果报界发现这些问题，他的政治生涯就完了。◇ *Their marriage was finished.* 他们的婚姻破裂了。**3** [usually before noun] fully completed, especially in a particular way 完成了的：*the **finished product/article*** 成品；脱稿的文章 ◇ *a beautifully finished suit* 做工精美的一套西服

fin·ish·er /ˈfɪnɪʃə(r)/ *noun* a person or an animal that finishes a race, etc.（赛跑等的）到达终点者

ˈfin·ish·ing line (*BrE*) (*NAmE* **ˈfinish line**) *noun* the line across a sports track, etc. that marks the end of a race（体育比赛跑道的）终点线：*The two horses crossed the finishing line together.* 两匹马同时越过终点线。

ˈfin·ish·ing school *noun* a private school where young women from rich families are taught how to behave in fashionable society 精修学校（为富家女子学习上流社会行为所办的私立学校）

fi·nite AW /ˈfaɪnaɪt/ *adj.* **1** having a definite limit or fixed size 有限的；有限制的：*a finite number of possibilities* 为数有限的可能 ◇ *The world's resources are finite.* 世界的资源是有限的。OPP **infinite 2** (*grammar* 语法) a **finite** verb form or clause shows a particular tense, PERSON and NUMBER 限定的：*'Am', 'is', 'are', 'was' and 'were' are the finite forms of 'be'; 'being' and 'been' are the non-finite forms.* *am、is、are、was和were是be的限定形式，being和 been 是非限定形式。OPP **non-finite**

fink /fɪŋk/ *noun* (*informal, especially NAmE*) an unpleasant person 讨厌鬼；卑鄙小人

fiord = FJORD

fir /fɜː(r)/ (*also* **ˈfir tree**) *noun* an EVERGREEN forest tree with leaves like needles 枞；冷杉 ➲ VISUAL VOCAB PAGE V10

ˈfir cone (*BrE*) (*also* **cone** *NAmE, BrE*) *noun* the hard fruit of the fir tree 冷杉球果 ➲ VISUAL VOCAB PAGE V10

fire /ˈfaɪə(r)/ *noun, verb*

■ ***noun***

• **STH BURNING** 燃烧的东西 **1** [U] the flames, light and heat, and often smoke, that are produced when sth burns 火：*Most animals are afraid of fire.* 大多数动物怕火。**2** [U, C] flames that are out of control and destroy buildings, trees, etc. 失火；火灾：*The car was now **on fire**.* 小轿车在燃烧。◇ *The warehouse has been badly damaged by fire.* 仓库因失火损毁严重。◇ *Several youths had **set fire to** the police car* (= had made it start burning). 几个年轻人纵火焚烧警车。◇ *A candle had **set** the curtains **on fire**.* 蜡烛把窗帘燃起来了。◇ *These thatched roofs frequently **catch fire*** (= start to burn). 这些茅草屋顶屡屡着火。◇ ***forest fires*** 森林大火 ◇ *Five people died in a house fire last night.* 有五人死于昨夜的住宅火灾。◇ *A small fire had started in the kitchen.* 厨房失火了，燃起了一股小的火苗。◇ ***Fires** were **breaking out** everywhere.* 到处都在发生火灾。◇ *It took two hours to **put out the fire*** (= stop it burning). 用了两小时才把火扑灭。

• **FOR HEATING/COOKING** 取暖；烹饪 **3** [C] a pile of burning fuel, such as wood or coal, used for cooking food or heating a room 炉火；灶火：***to make/build a fire***

生火 ◇ *a **log/coal fire*** 柴火；煤火 ◇ *Sam had **lit a fire** to welcome us home.* 萨姆点燃炉火欢迎我们回家。◇ *Come and get warm by the fire.* 到炉火边来取暖。◇ *We sat in front of a **roaring fire**.* 我们坐在熊熊的炉火面前。➲ SEE ALSO BONFIRE, CAMPFIRE **4** [C] (*especially BrE*) a piece of equipment for heating a room 取暖器；暖气装置：*a **gas/electric fire*** 煤气 / 电取暖器 ◇ *Shall I put the fire on?* 我打开暖气好吗？➲ SEE ALSO HEATER

• **FROM GUNS** 枪支 **5** [U] shots from guns 射击；火力：*a burst of machine-gun fire* 一阵机枪射击 ◇ *to **return fire*** (= to fire back at sb who is shooting at you) 用枪炮还击 ◇ *The gunmen **opened fire on*** (= started shooting at) *the police.* 持枪歹徒向警察开火。◇ *Their vehicle **came under fire*** (= was being shot at). 他们的车遭到射击。◇ *He ordered his men to **hold their fire*** (= not to shoot). 他命令士兵停止射击。◇ *A young girl was **in the line of fire*** (= between the person shooting and what he/she was shooting at). 有一个女孩处于射程之内。

• **ANGER/ENTHUSIASM** 愤怒；热情 **6** [U] very strong emotion, especially anger or enthusiasm 激情；愤怒；热情：*Her eyes were full of fire.* 她的双眼充满激情的火花。

IDM **be/come under 'fire** to be criticized severely for sth you have done 受到严厉批评；遭到猛烈批判：*The health minister has come under fire from all sides.* 卫生部长受到来自各方的责难。**hang/hold 'fire** to delay or be delayed in taking action（使行动）延迟；（使）迟缓：*The project had hung fire for several years for lack of funds.* 这个项目因缺少资金耽搁了好几年。**on 'fire** giving you a painful burning feeling 火辣辣；火烧火燎的：*He couldn't breathe. His chest was on fire.* 他无法呼吸。他的胸部火辣辣地疼痛。**play with 'fire** to act in a way that is not sensible and take dangerous risks 玩火；冒险 ➲ MORE AT BALL *n.*, BAPTISM, DRAW *v.*, FIGHT *v.*, FRYING PAN, HOUSE *n.*, IRON *n.*, SMOKE *n.*, WORLD

■ *verb*

• **SHOOT** 射击 **1** [I, T] to shoot bullets from a gun 射击；开火；开枪：*The officer ordered his men to fire.* 军官下令士兵射击。◇ **~ on sb/sth** *Soldiers fired on the crowd.* 军人朝人群开枪。◇ **~ sth** *They ran away as soon as the first shot was fired.* 第一枪刚响他们就跑了。◇ **~ (sth) (into sth)** *He fired the gun into the air.* 他朝天鸣枪。◇ **~ (sth) (at sb/sth)** *Missiles were fired at the enemy.* 向敌人发射了导弹。➲ COLLOCATIONS AT WAR **2** [I, T] (of a gun 枪) to shoot bullets out 射出（子弹）：*We heard the sound of guns firing.* 我们听见枪炮射击声。◇ **~ sth** *A starter's pistol fires only blanks.* 初学者的手枪发射的只是空弹。**3** [T] **~ sth** to shoot an arrow 射（箭）：*She fired an arrow at the target.* 她瞄准靶子射箭。

• **FROM JOB** 工作 **4** [T] **~ sb** to force sb to leave their job 解雇；开除 **SYN** **sack**：*We had to fire him for dishonesty.* 他不诚实，我们不得不开除他。◇ *She got fired from her first job.* 她第一份工作是被解雇的。◇ *He was responsible for **hiring and firing** staff.* 他负责招聘和解雇职员。➲ COLLOCATIONS AT UNEMPLOYMENT

• **MAKE SB ENTHUSIASTIC** 使充满激情 **5** [T] **~ sb (with sth)** to make sb feel very excited about sth or interested in sth 激励；激起热情；使充满热情：*The talk had fired her with enthusiasm for the project.* 这次谈话激起了她对这个项目的热情。◇ *His imagination had been fired by the film.* 这部电影激发了他的想象力。

• **OF ENGINE** 发动机 **6** [I] when an engine **fires**, an electrical SPARK is produced that makes the fuel burn and the engine start to work 点火；发动

• **-FIRED** 燃…的 **7** (in adjectives 构成形容词) using the fuel mentioned in order to operate 以…为燃料的：*gas-fired central heating* 煤气集中供暖

• **CLAY OBJECTS** 陶器 **8** [T] **~ sth** to heat a CLAY object to make it hard and strong 烧制（陶器、砖等）：*to fire pottery* 烧制陶器 ◇ *to fire bricks in a kiln* 在窑内烧砖

IDM **fire 'questions, 'insults, etc. at sb** to ask sb a lot of questions one after another or make a lot of comments very quickly 对某人发出连珠炮似的问题（或辱骂等）：*The room was full of journalists, all firing questions at them.* 满屋的记者向他们接二连三地提问题。➲ MORE AT CYLINDER

PHR V **ˌfire a'way** (*informal*) used to tell sb to begin to speak or ask a question（让人）开始说，开始问：*'I've got a few questions.' 'OK then, fire away.'* "我有几个问题。" "好，那就问吧。" **ˌfire sth↔'off** **1** to shoot a bullet from a gun 开枪；射击：*They fired off a volley of shots.* 他们举枪齐射。**2** to write or say sth to sb very quickly, often when you are angry（常指愤怒地）连珠炮似的说，奋笔疾书：*He fired off a letter of complaint.* 他奋笔写了一封投诉信。◇ *She spent an hour firing off emails to all concerned.* 她花了一个小时气冲冲地向有关各方发电邮。**ˌfire sb↔'up** to make sb excited or interested in sth 激起热情；使充满激情：*She's all fired up about her new job.* 她对新工作充满热情。**ˌfire sth↔'up** (*informal*) to start a machine, piece of equipment, computer program, etc. 发动（机器）；启动（设备、程序等）：*We need to fire up one of the generators.* 我们需要开动一台发电机。◇ *Let me fire up another window* (= on the computer screen). 让我再打开一个窗口。

'fire alarm *noun* a bell or other device that gives people warning of a fire in a building 火警钟；火警报警器：*Who set off the fire alarm?* 谁拉响了火警报警器？

fire·arm /ˈfaɪərɑːm; *NAmE* -ɑːrm/ *noun* (*formal*) a gun that can be carried（便携式的）枪：*The police were issued with firearms.* 警察都配发了小型枪支。

fire·ball /ˈfaɪəbɔːl; *NAmE* ˈfaɪərb-/ *noun* a bright ball of fire, especially one at the centre of an explosion（尤指在爆炸中心的）火球

fire·bomb /ˈfaɪəbɒm; *NAmE* ˈfaɪərbɑːm/ *noun* a bomb that makes a fire start burning after it explodes 燃烧弹 ▸ **fire·bomb** *verb* **~ sth**

fire·brand /ˈfaɪəbrænd; *NAmE* ˈfaɪərb-/ *noun* a person who is always encouraging other people to take strong political action, often causing trouble 挑动政治争端者；煽动动乱者

fire·break /ˈfaɪəbreɪk; *NAmE* ˈfaɪərb-/ *noun* a thing that stops a fire from spreading, for example a special door or a strip of land in a forest that has been cleared of trees 火障（如防火安全门、防火带、防火线）➲ SEE ALSO FIRE LINE

fire·brick /ˈfaɪəbrɪk; *NAmE* ˈfaɪər-/ *noun* [U, C] (*specialist*) brick which is not destroyed by very strong heat; an individual block of this 耐火砖；耐火砖块

'fire brigade (*also* **'fire service**) (*both BrE*) (*NAmE* **'fire department**) *noun* [C+sing./pl. v.] an organization of people who are trained and employed to put out fires and to rescue people from fires; the people who belong to this organization 消防队；消防队员：*to call out the fire brigade* 叫消防队来 ◇ *The fire brigade were there in minutes.* 几分钟后消防队就到了现场。

fire·bug /ˈfaɪəbʌɡ; *NAmE* ˈfaɪər-/ *noun* (*informal*) a person who deliberately starts fires 放火者；纵火狂 **SYN** **arsonist**

fire·crack·er /ˈfaɪəkrækə(r); *NAmE* ˈfaɪərk-/ *noun* a small FIREWORK that explodes with a loud noise 鞭炮；爆竹

'fire de·part·ment (*NAmE*) (*BrE* **'fire brigade**, **'fire service**) *noun* [usually sing.] an organization of people who are trained and employed to put out fires and to rescue people from fires; the people who belong to this organization 消防队；消防队员

'fire door *noun* a heavy door that is used to prevent a fire from spreading in a building（建筑物内的）防火安全门

'fire drill (*BrE also* **'fire practice**) *noun* [C, U] a practice of what people must do in order to escape safely from a fire in a building 消防演习

'fire-eater *noun* an entertainer who pretends to eat fire 吞火表演者

'fire engine (*NAmE also* **'fire truck**) *noun* a special vehicle that carries equipment for fighting large fires 消防车；救火车

'fire escape *noun* metal stairs or a LADDER on the outside of a building, which people can use to escape from a fire 安全梯，太平梯（在建筑物外部，用以逃离火场） ➲ VISUAL VOCAB PAGE V16

'fire extinguisher (*also* **ex·tin·guish·er**) *noun* a metal container with water or chemicals inside for putting out small fires 灭火器

fire·fight /'faɪəfaɪt; *NAmE* 'faɪərf-/ *noun* (*specialist*) a battle where guns are used, involving soldiers or the police 交火；枪战；炮战

fire·fight·er /'faɪəfaɪtə(r); *NAmE* 'faɪərf-/ *noun* a person whose job is to put out fires 消防队员 ➲SEE ALSO FIREMAN

fire·fight·ing /'faɪəfaɪtɪŋ; *NAmE* 'faɪərf-/ *noun* [U] **1** the job or activity of putting out fires 灭火；救火；消防：*fire-fighting equipment/vehicles* 消防设备 / 车辆 **2** (in business 商业) the practice of dealing with problems as they occur rather than planning carefully to avoid them 处理问题，解决问题（相对于预防问题）

fire·fly /'faɪəflaɪ; *NAmE* 'faɪərf-/ *noun* (*pl.* **-ies**) (*NAmE also* **'lightning bug**) a flying insect with a tail that shines in the dark 萤火虫

fire·guard /'faɪəgɑːd; *NAmE* 'faɪərgɑːrd/ (*NAmE usually* **'fire screen**) *noun* a metal frame that is put in front of a fire in a room to prevent people from burning themselves（室内取暖炉的）炉栏，炉挡

'fire hose *noun* a long tube that is used for directing water onto fires 消防水龙带； 消防水管

fire·house /'faɪəhaʊs; *NAmE* 'faɪərh-/ *noun* (*US*) a FIRE STATION in a small town（小城镇的）消防站

'fire hydrant (*also* **hy·drant**) *noun* a pipe in the street through which water can be sent using a PUMP in order to put out fires or to clean the streets 消防栓；消防龙头

fire·light /'faɪəlaɪt; *NAmE* 'faɪərl-/ *noun* [U] the light that comes from a fire in a room（室内的）炉火光

fire·light·er /'faɪəlaɪtə(r); *NAmE* 'faɪərl-/ (*BrE*) (*NAmE* **'fire-start·er**) *noun* [C, U] a block of material that burns easily and is used to help start a coal or wood fire（生炉子的）引火物

'fire line *noun* (*NAmE*) a strip of land that has been cleared in order to stop a fire from spreading 防火带；防火线 ➲SEE ALSO FIREBREAK

fire·man /'faɪəmən; *NAmE* 'faɪərmən/ *noun* (*pl.* **-men** /-mən/) a person, usually a man, whose job is to put out fires 消防队员 ➲SEE ALSO FIREFIGHTER ➲NOTE AT GENDER

fire·place /'faɪəpleɪs; *NAmE* 'faɪərp-/ *noun* an open space for a fire in the wall of a room 壁炉 ➲VISUAL VOCAB PAGE V22

fire·power /'faɪəpaʊə(r); *NAmE* 'faɪərp-/ *noun* [U] the number and size of guns that an army, a ship, etc. has available （军队、舰船等的）火力：(*figurative*) *The company has enormous financial firepower.* 这家公司财力雄厚。

'fire practice *noun* [C, U] (*BrE*) = FIRE DRILL

fire·proof /'faɪəpruːf; *NAmE* 'faɪərp-/ *adj.* able to resist great heat without burning or being badly damaged 防火的；耐火的：*a fireproof door* 防火门 ◇ *a fireproof dish* (= that can be heated in an oven) 耐火盘

'fire-raiser *noun* (*BrE*) a person who starts a fire deliberately 纵火者；放火者 SYN **arsonist** ▸ **'fire-raising** *noun* [U]

fire-retard·ant /'faɪə rɪˌtɑːdənt; *NAmE* 'faɪər rɪˌtɑːrd-/ (*also* **'flame-retardant**) *adj.* [usually before noun] that makes a fire burn more slowly 阻燃的

'fire sale *noun* **1** a sale at low prices of things that a company or person owns, usually in order to pay debts（抵债）大甩卖：*The company was forced to have a fire sale of its assets.* 公司被迫低价抛售其资产偿还债务。**2** a sale of goods at low prices because they have been damaged by a fire or because they cannot be stored after a fire 火灾后大甩卖

'fire screen *noun* **1** (*NAmE*) = FIREGUARD **2** a screen, often decorative, that is put in front of an open fire in a room to protect people from the heat or from SPARKS, or to hide it when it is not lit 挡火隔板

'fire service *noun* [usually sing.] (*BrE*) = FIRE BRIGADE

fire·side /'faɪəsaɪd; *NAmE* 'faɪərs-/ *noun* [usually sing.] the part of a room beside the fire 炉边：*sitting by the fireside* 坐在炉边

'fire starter (*NAmE*) (*BrE* **fire·light·er**) *noun* a block of material that burns easily and is used to help start a coal or wood fire（生炉子的）引火物

fire·start·er /'faɪəstɑːtə(r); *NAmE* 'faɪərstɑːrtər/ *noun* (*NAmE*) **1** a device that allows you to start a fire, usually by hitting a piece of FLINT (= a hard grey stone) against a piece of steel 打火石点火器具 **2** (*BrE* **fire·light·er**) a block of material that burns easily and is used to help start a coal or wood fire （生炉子的）引火物 **3** a person who commits the crime of deliberately setting fire to sth 纵火犯；蓄意纵火者 SYN **arsonist**

'fire station *noun* a building for a FIRE BRIGADE or FIRE DEPARTMENT and its equipment 消防站

fire·storm /'faɪəstɔːm; *NAmE* 'faɪərstɔːrm/ *noun* a very large fire, usually started by bombs, that is not under control and is made worse by the winds that it causes（尤指爆炸引起的）风暴性大火

'fire trap *noun* a building that would be very dangerous if a fire started there, especially because it would be difficult for people to escape 火焰陷阱（发生火灾时难以逃生的建筑物）

'fire truck *noun* (*NAmE*) = FIRE ENGINE

fire·wall /'faɪəwɔːl; *NAmE* 'faɪərw-/ *noun* (*computing* 计) a part of a computer system that prevents people from reaching information without permission, but still allows them to receive information that is sent to them 防火墙，网盾（防止窃取计算机信息的系统） ➲ COLLOCATIONS AT EMAIL

fire·water /'faɪəwɔːtə(r); *NAmE* 'faɪər-/ *noun* [U] (*informal*) strong alcoholic drink 烈酒；烧酒

fire·wood /'faɪəwʊd; *NAmE* 'faɪərwʊd/ *noun* [U] wood that has been cut into pieces to be used for burning in fires 柴火；木柴

fire·work /'faɪəwɜːk; *NAmE* 'faɪərwɜːrk/ *noun* **1** [C] a small device containing powder that burns or explodes and produces bright coloured lights and loud noises, used especially at celebrations 烟火；烟花：(*BrE*) *to let off a few fireworks* 放几个烟火 ◇ (*NAmE*) *to set off a few fireworks* 放几个烟火 ◇ *a firework(s) display* 烟火表演 **2 fireworks** [pl.] a display of fireworks 烟火表演；烟花表演；放烟火：*When do the fireworks start?* 什么时候开始放烟火？ **3 fireworks** [pl.] (*informal*) strong or angry words; exciting actions 激烈的言辞；愤怒的话语；令人激动的行动：*There'll be fireworks when he finds out!* 他要是发觉了就会大发雷霆！

fir·ing /'faɪərɪŋ/ *noun* **1** [U] the action of firing guns 射击；发射；开枪；开炮：*There was continuous firing throughout the night.* 整夜枪炮不息。**2** [U, C] (*especially NAmE*) the action of forcing sb to leave their job 解雇；开除：*teachers protesting against the firing of a colleague* 因一位同事被开除而抗议的教师们 ◇ *She's responsible for the hirings and firings.* 她负责雇佣和解雇。

'firing line *noun*

IDM **be in the 'firing line** (*BrE*) (*NAmE* **be on the 'firing line**) **1** to be in a position where you can be shot at 处于射程以内 **2** to be in a position where people can criticize or blame you 处于易受批评（或责备）的地位：*The employment secretary found himself in the firing line over recent job cuts.* 劳工部长因近期的工作岗位削减而备受责难。

'firing squad *noun* [C+sing./pl. v., U] a group of soldiers who are ordered to shoot and kill sb who is found guilty of a crime 行刑队（对判死刑的犯人执行枪决）：*He was executed by (a) firing squad.* 他被行刑队执行枪决。

fir·kin /ˈfɜːkɪn; *NAmE* ˈfɜːrkɪn/ *noun* (*old use*) **1** a small BARREL (= a round container with flat ends), used mainly for liquids, butter or fish（盛液体、黄油、鱼等的）小桶 **2** a unit for measuring volume, equal to about 41 litres 桶（容量单位，约相当于 41 升）

firm /fɜːm; *NAmE* fɜːrm/ *noun, adj., adv., verb*

■ ***noun*** a business or company 商行；商号；公司：*an engineering firm* 工程公司 ◊ *a firm of accountants* 会计师事务所 ⊃ COLLOCATIONS AT BUSINESS

■ ***adj.*** (**firm·er**, **firm·est**) **1** fairly hard; not easy to press into a different shape 坚固的；坚硬的；结实的：*a firm bed/mattress* 结实的床 / 床垫 ◊ *These peaches are still firm.* 这些桃子还很硬。◊ *Bake the cakes until they are firm to the touch.* 把糕饼烤到摸起来有硬感为止。**2** not likely to change 坚定的；确定的；坚决的：*a **firm believer** in socialism* 坚定信仰社会主义的人 ◊ *a **firm agreement/date/decision/offer/promise*** 巩固的协议；确定的日期；不能更改的决定；实盘；坚决的保证 ◊ ***firm beliefs/conclusions/convictions/principles*** 坚定不移的信仰；定论；坚定的信念 / 原则 ◊ *She is a **firm favourite with** the children.* 孩子们着实喜欢她。◊ *We have no **firm evidence** to support the case.* 我们没有确凿的证据支持这个论点。◊ *They remained **firm friends**.* 他们依然友情甚笃。**3** strongly fixed in place 牢固的；稳固的 SYN **secure**：*Stand the fish tank on a firm base.* 把鱼缸放在牢固的基座上。◊ *No building can stand without firm foundations, and neither can a marriage.* 没有稳固的基础，建筑就不牢靠，婚姻也是如此。**4** (of sb's voice or hand movements 声音或手势) strong and steady 强有力的；坚决的：*'No,' she repeated, her voice firmer this time.* "不。"她重复说，这次语气较前坚决。◊ *With a **firm grip** on my hand, he pulled me away.* 他紧握我的手把我拉开。◊ *Her handshake was cool and firm.* 她握手镇定而有力。**5** (of sb's behaviour, position or understanding of sth 行为、处境或理解) strong and in control 牢牢控制的；严格的；掌握的：*to exercise **firm control/discipline/leadership*** 实施严格的控制 / 纪律 / 领导 ◊ *Parents must **be firm with** their children.* 父母必须对子女严格。◊ *The company now has a **firm footing** in the marketplace.* 现在这家公司在市场上已站稳了脚跟。◊ *This book will give your students a **firm grasp of** English grammar.* 这本书将使学生牢固地掌握英语语法。◊ *We need to keep a **firm grip** on the situation.* 我们需要牢牢地掌握局面。**6** [usually before noun] ~ (**against sth**) (of a country's money, etc. 货币等) not lower than another 坚挺的：*The euro remained firm against the dollar, but fell against the yen.* 欧元对美元依然坚挺，但对日元的汇率则下跌。⊃ SEE ALSO FIRMLY ▸ **firm·ness** *noun* [U]

IDM **be on firm 'ground** to be in a strong position in an argument, etc. because you know the facts（在辩论等中）立场坚定，对事实确信无疑：*Everyone agreed with me, so I knew I was on firm ground.* 每个人都同意我的意见，所以我知道自己立场稳固了。**a firm 'hand** strong control or discipline 牢固控制；严格纪律；铁腕：*Those children need a firm hand to make them behave.* 那些孩子得严加管教。**take a firm 'line/'stand** (**on/against sth**) to make your beliefs known and to try to make others follow them（对…）采取坚定的立场（或态度）：*We need to take a firm line on tobacco advertising.* 我们需要对烟草广告采取强硬的态度。◊ *They took a firm stand against drugs in the school.* 他们坚决反对校园吸毒现象。

■ ***adv.***

IDM **hold 'firm** (**to sth**) (*formal*) to believe sth strongly and not change your mind 坚信；坚持：*She held firm to her principles.* 她坚持自己的原则。**stand 'fast/'firm** to refuse to move back; to refuse to change your opinions 坚定不移；不让步；坚持自己的观点

■ ***verb*** **1** [T] ~ **sth** to make sth become stronger or harder 使强壮；使坚固；使坚实：*Firm the soil around the plant.* 把植物周围的土弄紧实。◊ *This product claims to firm your body in six weeks.* 这个产品据称能在六周内使身体强壮。**2** [I] ~ (**to/at...**) (*finance* 财) (of shares, prices, etc. 股票、物价等) to become steady or rise steadily 坚挺；稳步上涨：*The company's shares firmed 3p to 696p.* 这家公司的股票涨了 3 便士，升至 696 便士。

PHR V ˌ**firm 'up** to become harder or more solid 变坚固；变坚实：*Put the mixture somewhere cool to firm up.* 把混合物放在一个地方冷却变硬。ˌ**firm sth↔'up 1** to make arrangements more final and fixed 最后落实；敲定：*The company has not yet firmed up its plans for expansion.* 公司的扩大计划尚未最后落实。◊ *The precise details still have to be firmed up.* 准确的细节仍需最后敲定。**2** to make sth harder or more solid 使坚固；使坚硬；使坚实：*A few weeks of aerobics will firm up that flabby stomach.* 几个星期的有氧健身运动将使松弛的腹部结实。

firma·ment /ˈfɜːməmənt; *NAmE* ˈfɜːrm-/ *noun* **the firmament** [sing.] (*old use* or *literary*) the sky 天空；苍穹：(*figurative*) *a rising star in the literary firmament* 文坛上一颗冉冉升起的新星

firm·ly /ˈfɜːmli; *NAmE* ˈfɜːrm-/ *adv.* in a strong or definite way 坚定地；坚固地：*'I can manage,' she said firmly.* "我应付得了。"她坚定地说。◊ *It is now firmly established as one of the leading brands in the country.* 现在它已稳稳地确立为国内主要品牌之一。◊ *Keep your eyes firmly fixed on the road ahead.* 密切注视路的前方。

firm·ware /ˈfɜːmweə(r); *NAmE* ˈfɜːrmwer/ *noun* [U] (*computing* 计) a type of computer software that is stored in such a way that it cannot be changed or lost 固件

first /fɜːst; *NAmE* fɜːrst/ *det., ordinal number, adv., noun*

■ ***det., ordinal number* 1** happening or coming before all other similar things or people; 1st 第一：*his first wife* 他的第一个妻子 ◊ *the first turning on the right* 第一个右转弯 ◊ *It was the first time they had ever met.* 这是他们初次见面。◊ *I didn't take the first bus.* 我没有乘坐首班公共汽车。◊ *students in their first year at college* 大学一年级学生 ◊ *your first impressions* 你的初步印象 ◊ *She resolved to do it at the first* (= earliest) *opportunity.* 她决定一有机会就去做。◊ *King Edward I* (= pronounced 'King Edward the First') 英王爱德华一世 ◊ *the first of May/May 1st* * 5 月 1 日 ◊ *His second book is better than his first.* 他的第二部书比第一部好。**2** the most important or best 最重要的；首要的；最优秀的：*Your first duty is to your family.* 你首先应对家庭尽责。◊ *She won first prize in the competition.* 她在竞赛中获得一等奖。◊ *an issue of the first importance* 最重要的问题

IDM HELP Most idioms containing **first** are at the entries for the nouns and adjectives in the idioms, for example **on first acquaintance** is at **acquaintance**. 大多数含有 first 的习语位于该习语中名词和形容词所在的词条，如 first acquaintance 位于 acquaintance 词条。**there's a first time for everything** (*saying, humorous*) the fact that sth has not happened before does not mean that it will never happen 没有发生的事情并不意味着永远不会发生；什么事情都有第一次

■ ***adv.* 1** before anyone or anything else; at the beginning 首先；第一；最初：*'Do you want a drink?' 'I'll finish my work first.'* "你想喝杯饮料吗？""我要先完成工作。"◊ *First I had to decide what to wear.* 首先我得决定穿什么。◊ *Who **came first** in the race* (= who won)? 赛跑谁第一？◊ *It plunged nose first into the river.* 它一头跳入水中。**2** for the first time 第一次；首次：*When did you first meet him?* 你和他初次见面是何时？**3** used to introduce the first of a list of points you want to make in a speech or piece of writing（列举时用）第一，首先 SYN **firstly**：*This method has two advantages: first it is cheaper and second it is quicker.* 这个方法有两个优点：一是更便宜，二是较快。⊃ LANGUAGE BANK AT PROCESS[1] **4** used to emphasize that you are determined not to do sth（强调不愿意）宁可，宁愿：*She swore that she wouldn't apologize—she'd die first!* 她发誓决不道歉，宁死也不！

IDM **at 'first** at or in the beginning 起初；起先：*I didn't like the job much at first.* 起初我并不很喜欢这个工作。◊ *At first I thought he was shy, but then I discovered he was just not interested in other people.* 起先我以为他腼腆，后来才发现他就是对别人没兴趣。◊ (*saying*) *If at first you don't succeed, try, try again.* 一次不成功就反复尝试。⊃ NOTE AT FIRSTLY **come 'first** to be considered more important than anything else 首要；第一；首先要考虑的：*In any decision she makes, her family always comes first.* 她作任何决定都是家庭第一。**ˌfirst and ˈforemost** more than anything else 首要的是；首先：*He does a little teaching, but first and foremost he's a writer.* 他干一点教学，但首要的是写作。➲ MORE LIKE THIS 13, page R26 **ˌfirst and ˈlast** in every way that is important; completely 从各方面看；完全地：*She regarded herself, first and last, as a musician.* 她认为她自己是一个不折不扣的音乐家。**ˌfirst ˈcome, ˌfirst ˈserved** (*saying*) people will be dealt with, seen, etc. strictly in the order in which they arrive 先来先接待；先到先供应；按先来后到对待：*Tickets are available on a first come, first served basis.* 票先来先买，售完为止。**ˌfirst of ˈall** **1** before doing anything else; at the beginning 第一；首先：*First of all, let me ask you something.* 首先，让我问你一件事。➲ LANGUAGE BANK AT PROCESS[1] **2** as the most important thing 最重要；首先：*The content of any article needs, first of all, to be relevant to the reader.* 任何文章的内容都首先要与读者有关。➲ NOTE AT FIRSTLY **ˌfirst ˈoff** (*informal, especially BrE*) before anything else 首先：*First off, let's see how much it'll cost.* 首先咱们看看这要花多少钱。**ˌfirst ˈup** (*BrE, informal*) to start with; before anything else 第一；首先 **ˌput sb/sth ˈfirst** to consider sb/sth to be more important than anyone/anything else 认为…最重要；把…放在第一位：*She always puts her children first.* 她总是把子女放在第一位。➲ MORE AT FOOT *n.*, HEAD *n.*, SAFETY

■ ***noun*** **1** **the first** (*pl.* **the first**) the person or thing that comes or happens before all other similar people or things 第一个人（或事物）：*I was the first in my family to go to college.* 我是我们家第一个大学生。◇ *Sheila and Jim were the first to arrive.* 希拉和吉姆最先到的。**2 the first** [sing.] the earliest 最早：***The first I heard about*** *the wedding* (= the first time I became aware of it) *was when I saw it in the local paper.* 我最初知道他们结婚的消息是从当地报纸上看到的。◇ *The first I knew of a problem was around 9.30 a.m. last Monday.* 我最早知道有问题是在上星期一上午 9 点 30 分左右。**3 the first** (*pl.* **the first**) the most likely 最有可能：*I'd be **the first to admit*** (= I will most willingly admit) *I might be wrong.* 我非常愿意承认我可能错了。◇ *The poorest will be the first to suffer.* 最贫穷的人受害的可能性最大。**4** [C, usually sing.] an important achievement, event, etc., never done or experienced before 空前的成就；前所未有的事情：*We went on a cruise, a first for both of us.* 我俩都是平生第一次去海上旅游。**5** (*also* **ˌfirst ˈgear**) [U] the lowest gear on a car, bicycle, etc. that you use when you are moving slowly（汽车、自行车等的）一挡，最低挡：*He stuck the car **in first** and revved.* 他挂上了一挡，开动了汽车。**6** [C] **~ (in sth)** the highest level of university degree at British universities（英国大学学位）最高成绩，优等成绩：*She **got a first** in maths at Exeter.* 她在埃克塞特大学毕业，获数学一级优等学位。➲ COMPARE SECOND[1] *n.* (7), THIRD *n.* (2)

IDM **ˌfirst among ˈequals** the person or thing with the highest status in a group 第一把手；首要的事物 **from the (very) ˈfirst** from the beginning 从一开始：*They were attracted to each other from the first.* 他俩一见倾心。**from ˌfirst to ˈlast** from beginning to end; during the whole time 从头至尾；自始至终：*It's a fine performance that commands attention from first to last.* 这是个精彩的演出，自始至终都扣人心弦。

> ▼ **LANGUAGE BANK 用语库**
>
> ### first
>
> Ordering your points 梳理要点
>
> - *This study has **the following** aims: **first**, to investigate how international students in the UK use humour; **second**, to examine how jokes can help to establish social relationships; and, **third**, to explore the role that humour plays in helping overseas students adjust to life in the UK.* 本研究有以下几个目的：第一，调查在英国的留学生如何运用幽默；第二，考察笑话如何帮助建立社交关系；第三，探究幽默对留学生适应英国生活所起的作用。
> - ***Let us begin by** identifying some of the popular joke genres in the UK.* 首先我们来探究一下流行于英国的一些笑话类型。
> - ***Next, let us turn to/Next, let us consider** the question of gender differences in the use of humour.* 接下来，我们来探讨一下运用幽默的性别差异问题。
> - ***Finally/Lastly**, let us briefly examine the role of humour in defining a nation's culture.* 最后，我们来简略地探讨一下幽默在界定民族文化中所起的作用。
>
> ➲ NOTE AT FIRSTLY, LASTLY
> ➲ LANGUAGE BANK AT CONCLUSION, PROCESS[1]

ˌfirst ˈaid *noun* [U] simple medical treatment that is given to sb before a doctor comes or before the person can be taken to a hospital 急救：*to give first aid* 进行急救 ◇ *a first-aid course* 急救课程 ➲ WORDFINDER NOTE AT ACCIDENT

ˌfirst ˈaider *noun* (*BrE*) a person who is trained to give first aid 急救员

the ˌFirst Aˈmendment *noun* [sing.] the statement in the US Constitution that protects freedom of speech and religion and the right to meet in peaceful groups（美国宪法）第一修正案（保障言论、宗教自由及和平集会的权利）

ˌfirst ˈbalcony *noun* (*NAmE*) = DRESS CIRCLE

ˌfirst ˈbase *noun* (in BASEBALL 棒球) the first of the BASES that players must touch 一垒：*He didn't make it past first base.* 他未能跑过一垒。

IDM **not get to first ˈbase (with sth/sb)** (*informal, especially NAmE*) to fail to make a successful start in a project, relationship, etc.; to fail to get through the first stage（工程、关系等）未能顺利开始，未能跨出第一步

first·born /ˈfɜːstbɔːn; *NAmE* ˈfɜːrstbɔːrn/ *noun* (*old-fashioned*) a person's first child 头胎；长子；长女 ▶ **first·born** *adj.* [only before noun]: *their firstborn son* 他们的长子

ˌfirst ˈclass *noun, adv.*

■ ***noun*** [U] **1** the best and most expensive seats or accommodation on a train, plane or ship 头等座位（或车厢、舱）：*There is more room in first class.* 头等舱更宽敞。**2** (in Britain) the class of mail that is delivered most quickly 第一类邮件（在英国投递最快的邮件）：*First class costs more.* 第一类邮件邮资较高。**3** (in the US) the class of mail that is used for letters 第一类邮件（在美国用于投递信件和明信片）**4** the highest standard of degree given by a British university 一级优等学位（英国大学学位等级）

■ ***adv.*** **1** using the best and most expensive seats or accommodation in a train, plane or ship 乘坐头等座位（或车厢、舱）：*to travel first class* 乘头等舱旅行 **2** (in Britain) by the quickest form of mail（英国）按最快投递邮件：*I sent the package first class on Monday.* 我于星期一以最快投递邮件寄出包裹。**3** (in the US) by the class of mail that is used for letters（美国）按第一类邮件

ˌfirst-ˈclass *adj.* **1** [usually before noun] in the best group; of the highest standard 第一流的；一级的；一等的；最优的 **SYN** **excellent**: *a first-class novel* 最佳小说 ◇ *a first-class writer* 一流作家 ◇ *The car was in first-class condition.* 当时车子处于最佳状态。◇ *I know a place where the food is first-class.* 我知道有一个品尝一流美食的地方。**2** [only before noun] connected with the best and most expensive way of travelling on a train, plane or ship（座位、车厢、舱位）头等的：*first-class rail travel* 乘头等车厢旅行 ◇ *a first-class cabin/seat/ticket* 头等舱 / 座位 / 票 **3** [only before noun] (in Britain) connected with letters, packages, etc. that are delivered most quickly, or that cost more to send 第一类的（英国邮件等级，投递最快）：***first-class mail/post/postage/stamps*** 第一类邮件 / 邮资 / 邮票 **4** [only before noun] used to describe a university degree of the highest class from a British university 一级优等的（英国大学学位）：*She was awarded a first-class degree in English.* 她获得一级优等英语学位。

ˈfirst cost *noun* [C, U] (*economics* 经) = PRIME COST

ˌfirst ˈcousin *noun* = COUSIN (1)

ˈ**first degree** *noun* (*especially BrE*) an academic qualification given by a university or college, for example a BA or BSc, that is given to sb who does not already have a degree in that subject（大学的）初级学位，学士学位：*What was your first degree in?* 你的学士学位是什么专业？◇ *to study geography at first-degree level* 攻读地理学学士学位

ˌ**first-deˈgree** *adj.* [only before noun] **1** (*especially NAmE*) **~ murder, assault, robbery, etc.** murder, etc. of the most serious kind 一级（谋杀、人身侵犯或抢劫等罪，最严重）**2 ~ burns** burns of the least serious of three kinds, affecting only the surface of the skin 一度（烧伤）➲ COMPARE SECOND-DEGREE, THIRD-DEGREE

ˌ**first ˈdown** *noun* (in AMERICAN FOOTBALL 美式足球) **1** the first of a series of four DOWNS (= chances to move the ball forward ten yards) 首档，首攻（四次进攻机会中的）**2** the chance to start a new series of four DOWNS because your team has succeeded in going forward ten yards（成功推进十码之后的）新一轮四次十码进攻权

ˌ**first eˈdition** *noun* one of the copies of a book that was produced the first time the book was printed（书籍的）第一版，初版

ˌ**first-ˈever** *adj.* [only before noun] never having happened or been experienced before 首次的：*his first-ever visit to London* 他对伦敦的初次访问 ◇ *the first-ever woman vice-president* 第一位女副总统

the ˌfirst ˈfamily *noun* [sing.] the family of the President of the United States 第一家庭（美国总统的家庭）

ˌ**first ˈfinger** *noun* = INDEX FINGER

ˌ**first ˈfloor** (*usually* **the first floor**) *noun* [sing.] **1** (*BrE*) the level of a building above the ground level 底层以上的一层；二楼：*Menswear is on the first floor.* 男装在第二层。**2** (*NAmE*) (*BrE* **ground ˈfloor**) the floor of a building that is at the same level as the ground outside 底层，底楼，一楼（建筑物与外面地面相平的一层）▶ ˌ**first-ˈfloor** *adj.* [only before noun]: *a first-floor flat/apartment* 二楼的一套公寓 ➲ NOTE AT FLOOR

ˌ**first-ˈfoot** *verb* **~ sb** to be the first person to enter sb's house in the New Year. First-footing is a Scottish custom.（苏格兰风俗）作为新年第一位访客 ▶ ˌ**first-ˈfooter** *noun*

ˈ**first fruit** *noun* [usually pl.] the first result of sb's work or effort（工作、努力的）初步成果，最初收获

ˌ**first geneˈration** *noun* [sing.] **1** people who have left their country to go and live in a new country; the children of these people（移民的）第一代；第一代移民的子女 **2** the first type of a machine or piece of software to be developed（研制的机器或软件的）第一代：*the first generation of personal computers* 第一代个人电脑 ▶ **first-geneˈration** *adj.* [usually before noun]: *first-generation Caribbeans in the UK* 在英国的第一代加勒比海移民

ˌ**first-ˈhand** *adj.* [only before noun] obtained or experienced yourself 第一手的；直接的：*to have first-hand experience of poverty* 亲身体验贫穷 ➲ COMPARE SECOND-HAND ▶ ˌ**first-ˈhand** *adv.*: *to experience poverty first-hand* 亲身体验贫穷

ˌ**First ˈLady** *noun* [usually sing.] **1 the First Lady** (in the US) the wife of the President 第一夫人（美国的总统夫人）**2** (*NAmE*) the wife of the leader of a state 第一夫人（州长的夫人）**3** (*usually* **first lady**) the woman who is thought to be the best in a particular profession, sport, etc.（某行业、体育运动等方面的）巾帼英雄，女杰，女冠军：*the first lady of country music* 乡村音乐最佳女歌手

ˌ**first ˈlanguage** *noun* the language that you learn to speak first as a child; the language that you speak best 母语；第一语言：*His first language is Welsh.* 他的母语是威尔士语。➲ COMPARE SECOND LANGUAGE

ˌ**first lieuˈtenant** *noun* **1** an officer in the navy with responsibility for managing a ship, etc. under the guidance of the captain 舰务官 **2** an officer in the US army and AIR FORCE just below the rank of a captain（美国陆军和空军的）中尉 **3** (*informal*) a person who is the next most important to sb 第二把手

ˌ**first ˈlight** *noun* [U] the time when light first appears in the morning 黎明；破晓；曙光 SYN **dawn, daybreak**: *We left at first light.* 我们黎明时离去。

first·ly /ˈfɜːstli; *NAmE* ˈfɜːrst-/ *adv.* used to introduce the first of a list of points you want to make in a speech or piece of writing（用于列举）第一，首先：*There are two reasons for this decision: firstly…* 作此决定理由有二：第一… ➲ LANGUAGE BANK AT FIRST

▼ **WHICH WORD?** 词语辨析

firstly / first of all / at first

- **Firstly** and **first (of all)** are used to introduce a series of facts, reasons, opinions, etc. * firstly 和 first (of all) 均用以引出一系列事实、理由、意见等：*The brochure is divided into two sections, dealing firstly with basic courses and secondly with advanced ones.* 小册子分为两部分：第一部分涉及基础课程，第二部分涉及高级课程。 **Firstly** is more common in *BrE* than in *NAmE*. * firstly 在英式英语中比在美式英语中更常用。
- **At first** is used to talk about the situation at the beginning of a period of time, especially when you are comparing it with a different situation at a later period. * at first 用以讲述最初阶段的情况，尤指与后来的不同情况相比较：*Maggie had seen him nearly every day at first. Now she saw him much less.* 起初玛吉几乎每天都见到他，现在见到他的次数少得多了。

ˌ**first ˈmate** (*also* ˌ**first ˈofficer**) *noun* the officer on a commercial ship just below the rank of captain or MASTER（商船的）大副

ˌ**first ˈminister** (*also* **First Minister**) *noun* the leader of the ruling political party in some regions or countries, for example in Scotland 首席部长（一些地区或国家中执政党的领袖）

ˈ**first name** (*also* ˈ**given name** *especially in NAmE*) *noun* a name that was given to you when you were born, that comes before your family name 名字：*His first name is Tom and his surname is Green.* 他叫汤姆，姓格林。◇ *Please give all your first names.* 请给出姓以外的全名。◇ (*BrE*) *to be* ***on first-name terms with sb*** (= to call them by their first name as a sign of a friendly informal relationship) 与某人以名字相称（指关系密切）◇ (*NAmE*) *to be* ***on a first-name basis*** 关系密切直呼其名

ˌ**First ˈNations** *noun* [pl.] (*CanE*) the Aboriginal peoples of Canada, not including the Inuit or Metis（加拿大的）原住民，土著居民（不包括因纽特人或米提人）

ˌ**first ˈnight** *noun* **1** the first public performance of a play, film/movie, etc.（戏剧、电影等的）首场，首次上演 **2** (*NAmE*) a public celebration of NEW YEAR'S EVE 新年前夜的公众庆祝活动

ˌ**first ofˈfender** *noun* a person who has been found guilty of a crime for the first time 初犯

ˌ**first ˈofficer** *noun* = FIRST MATE

ˌ**first-ˌpast-the-ˈpost** *adj.* [only before noun] (of a system of elections 选举体制) in which only the person who gets the most votes is elected 得票最多者当选的 ➲ COMPARE PROPORTIONAL REPRESENTATION

the ˌfirst ˈperson *noun* [sing.] **1** (*grammar* 语法) a set of pronouns and verb forms used by a speaker to refer to himself or herself, or to a group including himself or herself 第一人称：*'I am' is the first person singular of the present tense of the verb 'to be'.* * I am 是动词 to be 现在时的第一人称单数形式。◇ *'I', 'me', 'we' and 'us' are first-person pronouns.* * I、me、we 和 us 是第一人称代词。**2** a way of writing a novel, etc. as if one of the characters is telling the story using the word *I* 以第一人称叙述的文体：*a novel written **in the first person*** 以第一人称写作的小说 ➲ COMPARE SECOND PERSON, THIRD PERSON

ˌfirst ˈprinciples *noun* [pl.] the basic ideas on which a theory, system or method is based 基本原理；基本原则：*I think we should go back to first principles.* 我认为我们应该回到基本原则上。

ˌfirst-ˈrate *adj.* of the highest quality 第一流的；质量最优的；优等的 SYN **excellent**：*a first-rate swimmer* 优秀游泳运动员 ◇ *The food here is absolutely first-rate.* 这里的食物绝对是第一流的。

F

ˌfirst reˈfusal *noun* [U] the right to decide whether to accept or refuse sth before it is offered to others 优先取舍权：*Will you give me first refusal on the car, if you decide to sell it?* 如果你决定出售这辆车，给我优先购买权好吗？

first responder /ˌfɜːst rɪˈspɒndə(r); *NAmE* ˌfɜːrst rɪˈspɑːndər/ *noun* (*especially NAmE*) a person such as a member of the police or fire department in a position to arrive first at an emergency, who has been trained to give basic medical treatment 第一反应人员（指接受过培训在紧急情况下首先到达现场施行基本救治的人，如警察或消防队员）➲ COMPARE EMERGENCY SERVICES

ˈfirst school *noun* (in Britain) a school for children between the ages of 5 and 8 or 9（英国）初级学校（学生为 5 至 8、9 岁的儿童）

ˌfirst ˈstrike *noun* an attack on an enemy made before they attack you 先发制人；首先发起攻击

ˈfirst-time *adj.* [only before noun] doing or experiencing sth for the first time 首次的；第一次的：*houses for first-time buyers* 供应给首次购房者的房屋 ◇ *a computer program designed for first-time users* 为初次用户设计的计算机程序

ˌfirst-ˈtimer *noun* a person who does sth for the first time 初次…者：*conference first-timers* 初次与会人员

ˌFirst ˈWorld *noun* [sing.] the rich industrial countries of the world 第一世界（指富有的工业国）➲ COMPARE THIRD WORLD

the ˌFirst World ˈWar (*also* **ˌWorld War ˈI**) *noun* [sing.] the war that was fought mainly in Europe between 1914 and 1918 第一次世界大战（1914 至 1918 年间，主战场在欧洲）

firth /fɜːθ; *NAmE* fɜːrθ/ *noun* (especially in Scottish place names) a narrow strip of the sea that runs a long way into the land, or a part of a river where it flows into the sea （尤用于苏格兰地名）狭长海湾，河流入海口：*the Moray Firth* 马里湾 ◇ *the Firth of Clyde* 克莱德湾

fis·cal /ˈfɪskl/ *adj.* connected with government or public money, especially taxes 财政的；国库的；国家岁入的：***fiscal policies/reforms*** 财政政策 / 改革 ▶ **fis·cal·ly** *adv.* ➲ SEE ALSO PROCURATOR FISCAL

ˌfiscal ˈyear (*NAmE*) (*BrE* **fiˌnancial ˈyear, ˈtax year**) *noun* [usually sing.] a period of twelve months over which the accounts and taxes of a company or a person are calculated 财政年度；会计年度

fish /fɪʃ/ *noun, verb*

■ ***noun*** (*pl.* **fish** or **fishes**) HELP **Fish** is the usual plural form. The older form, **fishes**, can be used to refer to different kinds of fish. * fish 是通常的复数形式，较古老的形式 fishes 可用于表示不同种类的鱼。 **1** [C] a creature that lives in water, breathes through GILLS, and uses FINS and a tail for swimming 鱼：*They caught several fish.* 他们捉到了几条鱼。◇ ***tropical/marine/freshwater fish*** 热带鱼；海鱼；淡水鱼 ◇ ***shoals*** (= groups) ***of fish*** 鱼群 ◇ ***a fish tank/pond*** 鱼缸；鱼池 ◇ *There are about 30 000 species of fish in the world.* 世界上约有 3 万种鱼。◇ *The list of endangered species includes nearly 600 fishes.* 濒临灭绝物种的名单中列有将近 600 种鱼。◇ *Fish stocks in the Baltic are in decline.* 波罗的海的鱼类资源逐渐减少。➲ COLLOCATIONS AT LIFE ➲ VISUAL VOCAB PAGE V12 ➲ SEE ALSO COARSE FISH, FLATFISH, SEA FISH, SHELLFISH, WET FISH **2** [U] the flesh of fish eaten as food 鱼肉：***frozen/smoked/fresh fish*** 冻鱼；熏鱼；鲜鱼 ◇ *fish pie* 鱼肉馅饼

IDM **a ˌfish out of ˈwater** a person who feels uncomfortable or awkward because he or she is in surroundings that are not familiar 离水之鱼；在陌生环境不得其所的人 **have bigger/other fish to fry** to have more important or more interesting things to do 还有更重要的事情要做；另有他图 **neither ˌfish nor ˈfowl** neither one thing nor another 非驴非马；不伦不类 **an odd/a queer ˈfish** (*old-fashioned, BrE*) a person who is slightly strange or crazy 古怪的人；有些荒唐的人 **there are plenty more fish in the ˈsea** there are many other people or things that are as good as the one sb has failed to get 海里的鱼有的是；还有很多一样好的（人或事物）➲ MORE AT BIG *adj.*, COLD *adj.*, DIFFERENT, DRINK *v.*, SHOOT *v.*

■ ***verb*** **1** [I] to try to catch fish with a hook, nets, etc. 钓鱼；捕鱼：*The trawler was fishing off the coast of Iceland.* 拖网渔船在冰岛沿海捕鱼。◇ **~ for sth** *You can fish for trout in this stream.* 你可以在这条小溪钓鳟鱼。 **2** [I] **go fishing** to spend time fishing for pleasure 钓鱼；捕鱼：*Let's go fishing this weekend.* 咱们这个周末去钓鱼吧。 **3** [T] **~ sth (for sth)** to try to catch fish in the area of water mentioned 在…捕鱼（或钓鱼）：*They fished the loch for salmon.* 他们在狭长海湾里钓鲑鱼。 **4** [I] **+ adv./prep.** to search for sth, using your hands 摸找：*She fished around in her bag for her keys.* 她在包里摸找钥匙。

PHR V **ˈfish for sth** to try to get sth, or to find out sth, although you are pretending not to 旁敲侧击地打听；转弯抹角地谋取：*to fish for compliments/information* 转弯抹角地谋取恭维 / 打听情况 **ˌfish sth/sb↔ˈout (of sth)** to take or pull sth/sb out of a place （从…中）取出，拿出，拖出：*She fished a piece of paper out of the pile on her desk.* 她从桌上一大堆纸中抽出了一张。◇ *They fished a dead body out of the river.* 他们从河里捞起了一具尸体。

ˌfish and ˈchips *noun* [U] a dish of fish that has been fried in BATTER served with CHIPS/FRIES, and usually bought in the place where it has been cooked and eaten at home, etc., especially in Britain 炸鱼加土豆条；炸鱼薯条：*Three portions of fish and chips, please.* 请来三份炸鱼薯条。◇ *a fish and chip shop* 炸鱼薯条店

fish·bowl /ˈfɪʃbəʊl; *NAmE* -boʊl/ *noun* = GOLDFISH BOWL

fish·cake /ˈfɪʃkeɪk/ *noun* (*especially BrE*) pieces of fish mixed with MASHED potato made into a flat round shape, covered with BREADCRUMBS and fried 鱼饼（鱼肉拌土豆泥煎成）

fish·er /ˈfɪʃə(r)/ *noun* (*especially NAmE*) = FISHERMAN

fish·er·man /ˈfɪʃəmən; *NAmE* ˈfɪʃərmən/ *noun* (*pl.* **-men** /-mən/) a person who catches fish, either as a job or as a sport 渔民；钓鱼的人 ➲ COMPARE ANGLER

fisher·woman /ˈfɪʃəwʊmən; *NAmE* ˈfɪʃər-/ *noun* (*pl.* **-women** /-wɪmɪn/) a woman who catches fish, either as a job or as a sport 女渔民；渔妇；女钓鱼爱好者 ➲ COMPARE ANGLER ➲ NOTE AT GENDER

fish·ery /ˈfɪʃəri/ *noun* (*pl.* **-ies**) **1** a part of the sea or a river where fish are caught in large quantities 渔场：*a herring fishery* 鲱鱼渔场 ◇ ***coastal/freshwater fisheries*** 沿海 / 淡水渔场 **2** = FISH FARM：*a trout fishery* 鳟鱼养殖场

fish·eye lens /ˌfɪʃaɪ ˈlenz/ *noun* a camera LENS with a wide angle that gives the view a curved shape 鱼眼镜头；超广角镜头

ˈfish farm (*also* **fish·ery**) *noun* a place where fish are bred as a business 养鱼场

ˌfish ˈfinger (*BrE*) (*NAmE* **ˌfish ˈstick**) *noun* a long narrow piece of fish covered with BREADCRUMBS or BATTER, usually frozen and sold in packs 鱼条（裹有面包屑或面糊的鱼肉条，通常冷冻后小包装出售）

ˈfish hook *noun* a sharp metal hook for catching fish, that has a point which curves backwards to make it difficult to pull out 鱼钩；钓钩 ➲ PICTURE AT HOOK

fish·ing 🔑 /ˈfɪʃɪŋ/ *noun* [U] the sport or business of catching fish 钓鱼；捕鱼业（或活动）：*They often* ***go fishing***. 他们常去钓鱼。◇ *deep-sea fishing* 深海捕鱼 ◇ *a fishing boat* 小渔船 ◇ *fishing grounds* 渔场 ◇ *We enjoyed a day's fishing by the river.* 我们在河边享受了一天垂钓之乐。

WORDFINDER 联想词： bait, bite, dragnet, fly, hook, line, net, rod, trawl

ˈfishing line *noun* [C, U] a long thread with a sharp hook attached, that is used for catching fish（带钓钩的）钓线，钓丝

ˈfishing rod (*also* **rod**) (*NAmE also* **ˈfishing pole**) *noun* a long wooden or plastic stick with a fishing line and hook attached, that is used for catching fish 钓竿

ˈfishing tackle *noun* [U] equipment used for catching fish 渔具

ˈfish knife *noun* a knife with a broad blade and without a sharp edge, used for eating fish（吃鱼用的）鱼餐刀 ➲ VISUAL VOCAB PAGE V23

fish·mon·ger /ˈfɪʃmʌŋɡə(r)/ *noun* (*especially BrE*) **1** a person whose job is to sell fish in a shop 鱼贩；鱼商 **2 fish·mon·ger's** (*pl.* **fish·mon·gers**) a shop that sells fish 鱼店 ➲ MORE LIKE THIS 34, page R29

fish·net /ˈfɪʃnet/ *noun* [U] a type of cloth made of threads that produce a pattern of small holes like a net 网眼织物：*fishnet stockings* 网眼长袜

ˈfish slice (*BrE*) (*also* **spat·ula** *NAmE, BrE*) *noun* a kitchen UTENSIL that has a broad flat blade with narrow holes in it, attached to a long handle, used for turning and lifting food when cooking 煎鱼锅铲，漏铲（铲面有细长孔）➲ VISUAL VOCAB PAGE V27

ˌfish ˈstick (*NAmE*) (*BrE* **ˌfish ˈfinger**) *noun* a long narrow piece of fish covered with BREADCRUMBS or BATTER, usually frozen and sold in packs 鱼条（裹有面包屑或面糊的鱼肉条，通常冷冻后小包装出售）

fish·tail /ˈfɪʃteɪl/ *verb* [I] if a vehicle **fishtails**, the back end slides from side to side（车辆）甩尾行驶

fish·wife /ˈfɪʃwaɪf/ *noun* (*pl.* **-wives** /-waɪvz/) (*disapproving*) a woman with a loud voice and bad manners 骂街的泼妇；粗野的女人

fishy /ˈfɪʃi/ *adj.* (**fish·ier**, **fishi·est**) **1** (*informal*) that makes you suspicious because it seems dishonest 可疑的；值得怀疑的 SYN **suspicious**: *There's something fishy going on here.* 这儿有点不大对头。 **2** smelling or tasting like a fish（像）鱼味的；有鱼腥味的：*What's that fishy smell?* 那是什么腥味？

fis·sile /ˈfɪsaɪl; *NAmE* ˈfɪsl/ *adj.* (*physics* 物) capable of nuclear FISSION 易裂变的：*fissile material* 易裂变物质

fis·sion /ˈfɪʃn/ *noun* [U] **1** (*also* **ˌnuclear ˈfission**) (*physics* 物) the act or process of splitting the NUCLEUS (= central part) of an atom, when a large amount of energy is released（核）裂变，分裂 ➲ COMPARE FUSION (2) ➲ WORDFINDER NOTE AT PHYSICS **2** (*biology* 生) the division of cells into new cells as a method of reproducing cells 裂体生殖

fis·sure /ˈfɪʃə(r)/ *noun* (*specialist*) a long deep crack in sth, especially in rock or in the earth（岩石、土地等中深长的）裂缝，裂隙 ▶ **fis·sured** *adj.*

fist /fɪst/ *noun* a hand when it is tightly closed with the fingers bent into the PALM 拳；拳头：*He punched me with his fist.* 他用拳头猛击我。◇ *She* ***clenched her fists*** *to stop herself trembling.* 她紧握双拳，克制颤抖。◇ *He got into a* ***fist fight*** *in the bar.* 他在酒吧与人挥拳斗殴。➲ SEE ALSO HAM-FISTED, TIGHT-FISTED

IDM **make a better, good, poor, etc. fist of sth** (*BrE, old-fashioned, informal*) to make a good, bad, etc. attempt to do sth 试图把（或未能把）某事做得很成功 ➲ MORE AT IRON *adj.*, MONEY

ˈfist bump *noun* (*informal*) a way of saying 'hello' or of showing support or agreement, in which two people raise one FIST (= a hand when it is tightly closed) each and lightly tap them together 击拳，碰拳（表示打招呼、支持或赞同）：*do/give a fist bump* 击拳致意 ▶ **ˈfist-bump** *verb* [T, I] ~ (**sb**): *Several of the politician's supporters fist-bumped him as he left the stage.* 那名政治人物走下舞台时几个支持者跟他碰了碰拳头。

fist·ful /ˈfɪstfʊl/ *noun* a number or an amount of sth that can be held in a fist 一把（的量）：*a fistful of coins* 一把硬币

fisti·cuffs /ˈfɪstɪkʌfs/ *noun* [pl.] (*old-fashioned* or *humorous*) a fight in which people hit each other with their FISTS 拳斗；互殴

ˈfist pump *noun* (*especially NAmE, informal*) an action to celebrate success or victory, or to show support, in which you raise your bent arm with your hand tightly closed and then move it quickly and strongly down towards your body 攥拳（以示庆祝或支持）：*When I saw the final score, I gave a fist pump and shouted out 'YES!'* 看到最终比分，我攥拳大喊"太棒了！" ▶ **ˈfist-pump** *verb* [I]: *They sang, they fist-pumped and they cheered the speakers.* 他们唱歌，攥拳，向演讲者欢呼。**ˈfist-pumping** *noun* [U]

fis·tula /ˈfɪstjʊlə; *NAmE* ˈfɪstʃələ/ *noun* (*medical* 医) an opening between two organs of the body, or between an organ and the skin, that would not normally exist, caused by injury, disease, etc. 瘘；瘘管

fit 🔑 /fɪt/ *verb, adj., noun*

■ *verb* (**fit·ting**, **fit·ted**, **fit·ted**) (*NAmE usually* **fit·ting**, **fit**, **fit**) HELP **Fit** is not used in *NAmE* as the past participle in the passive. 美式英语的被动语态中过去分词不用 fit。

• **RIGHT SIZE/TYPE** 恰当的大小 / 类型 **1** 🔑 [I, T] (not used in the progressive tenses 不用于进行时) to be the right shape and size for sb/sth（形状和尺寸）适合，合身：*I tried the dress on but it didn't fit.* 我试穿了那连衣裙，但不合身。◇ *That jacket fits well.* 那件短上衣很合身。◇ *a close-fitting dress* 紧身连衣裙 ◇ **~ sb/sth** *I can't find clothes to fit me.* 我找不到合身的衣服。◇ *The key doesn't fit the lock.* 这把钥匙打不开这把锁。 **2** 🔑 [I] to be of the right size, type or number to go somewhere（大小、式样、数量适合）可容纳，装进：*I'd like to have a desk in the room but it won't fit.* 我想在房间放一张桌子，但是搁不下。◇ **+ adv./prep.** *All the kids will fit in the back of the car.* 所有的孩子都可以坐到车的后排。**3** [T, often passive] **~ sb (for sth)** to put clothes on sb and make them the right size and shape 试穿（衣服）：*I'm going to be fitted for my wedding dress today.* 今天我要去试穿结婚礼服。

• **PUT STH SOMEWHERE** 安置 **4** 🔑 [T] to put or fix sth somewhere 安置，安装（在某处）：**~ sth + adv./prep.** *They fitted a smoke alarm to the ceiling.* 他们把烟雾报警器安装在天花板上。◇ **~ sth with sth** *The rooms were all fitted with smoke alarms.* 所有的房间都安装了烟雾报警器。**5** 🔑 [I, T] to put or join sth in the right place 合上；盖上；组合；组装：**~ + adv./prep.** *The glass fits on top of the jug to form a lid.* 这个玻璃杯放在大罐口上恰好当个盖子。◇ *How do these two parts* ***fit together***? 这两部分如何拼在一起呢？◇ **~ sth + adv./prep.** *We fitted together the pieces of the puzzle.* 我们把拼图玩具的各部分拼合在了一起。

• **AGREE/MATCH** 一致；相称 **6** 🔑 [I, T] (not used in the progressive tenses 不用于进行时) to agree with, match or be suitable for sth; to make sth do this（使）与…一致，和…相称，符合：*Something doesn't quite fit here.* 这里有点不大协调。◇ **~ into sth** *His pictures don't fit into any category.* 他的画哪一类也算不上。◇ **~ sth** *The facts certainly fit your theory.* 这些事实和你的说法丝毫不差。◇ *The punishment ought to fit the crime.* 罚须当罪。◇ **~ sth to sth** *We should fit the punishment to the crime.* 我们应该根据罪行量刑。

• **MAKE SUITABLE** 使适合 **7** [T] (*especially BrE*) to make sb/sth suitable for a particular job 使适合，使胜任（某工作）：**~ sb/sth for sth** *His experience fitted him perfectly for the* job. 他的经验使他完全胜任这项工作。◇ ~ sb/sth to do sth His experience fitted him to do the job. 他的经验使他适合干这个工作。➲SEE ALSO FITTED

IDM fit (sb) like a 'glove to be the perfect size or shape for sb（大小、形状）完全合适，恰好合身 ➲MORE AT BILL n., DESCRIPTION, FACE n., SHOE n.

PHR V ˌfit sb/sth↔'in | ˌfit sb/sth 'in/'into sth 1 to find time to see sb or to do sth 找到时间（见某人、做某事）：*I'll try and fit you in after lunch.* 我尽量午饭后抽时间见你。◇ *I had to fit ten appointments into one morning.* 我得在一个上午安排十个约见。2 to find or have enough space for sb/sth in a place 找到足够的地方；有足够空间：*We can't fit in any more chairs.* 我们没有地方再摆更多的椅子了。 ˌfit 'in (with sb/sth) to live, work, etc. in an easy and natural way with sb/sth（与…）合得来；适应：*He's never done this type of work before; I'm not sure how he'll fit in with the other people.* 他过去从未干过这种工作，很难说他是否会与其他人配合得好。◇ *Where do I fit in?* 哪里有适合我的地方？◇ *Do these plans fit in with your arrangements?* 这些计划和你的安排有冲突吗？ ˌfit sb/sth ↔'out/'up (with sth) to supply sb/sth with all the equipment, clothes, food, etc. they need 向…提供所需的东西（如设备、衣服、粮食等） SYN equip: *to fit out a ship before a long voyage* 给要远航的轮船提供必需品 ◇ *The room has been fitted out with a stove and a sink.* 这个房间安装有炉子和洗涤槽。 ˌfit sb↔'up (for sth) (*BrE, informal*) to make it look as if sb is guilty of a crime they have not committed 诬陷某人（犯罪） SYN frame: *I didn't do it—I've been fitted up!* 这事不是我干的，我遭到诬陷了！

■ *adj.* (fit·ter, fit·test)

• HEALTHY 健康 1 healthy and strong, especially because you do regular physical exercise 健壮的；健康的：*Top athletes have to be very fit.* 顶级运动员体格必须十分健壮。◇ ~ (to do sth) *He won't be fit to play in the match on Saturday.* 他身体不适，不能在星期六出场比赛。◇ *She tries to* ***keep fit*** *by jogging every day.* 她每天慢跑以保持健康。◇ ~ (for sth) (*BrE*) *He's had a bad cold and isn't fit enough for work yet.* 他得了重感冒，还不能上班。◇ *I feel really fighting fit* (= very healthy and full of energy). 我觉得十分健康，精力充沛。◇ *The government aims to make British industry leaner and fitter* (= employing fewer people and with lower costs). 政府旨在使英国的工业更加简而精。OPP unfit ➲SYNONYMS AT WELL ➲SEE ALSO KEEP-FIT

WORDFINDER 联想词： **diet**, exercise, gym, health spa, nutrition, personal trainer, **sport**, stamina, workout

• SUITABLE 合适 2 suitable; of the right quality; with the right qualities or skills（质量、素质或技能）适合的，恰当的，合格的：~ for sb/sth *The food was not fit for human consumption.* 这食物不适合人吃。◇ *It was a meal* ***fit for a king*** (= of very good quality). 这饭菜够得上御膳。◇ *The children seem to think I'm only fit for cooking and washing!* 孩子们似乎以为我只配做饭洗衣！◇ ~ to do sth *Your car isn't fit to be on the road!* 你的车子还不适合上马路！◇ *He's so angry he's* ***in no fit state*** *to see anyone.* 他气成这个样子，不适合见人。◇ (*formal*) *This is not a fit place for you to live.* 这个地方不适合你居住。OPP unfit

• READY 准备好 3 ~ to do sth (*BrE, informal*) ready or likely to do sth extreme 可能（或准备）做某事至极端程度：*They worked until they were* ***fit to drop*** (= so tired that they were likely to fall down). 他们一直工作到快要累趴下了。◇ *I've eaten so much I'm* ***fit to burst***. 我吃得太多，肚子快要撑破了。◇ *She was laughing* ***fit to burst*** (= very much). 她笑得肚皮都要破了。

• ATTRACTIVE 诱人 4 (*BrE, informal*) sexually attractive 性感迷人的 ➲MORE LIKE THIS 35, page R29

IDM (as) ˌfit as a 'fiddle (*informal*) in very good physical condition 非常健康 ➲MORE LIKE THIS 14, page R26 **fit for purpose** (of an institution, a system, a thing, etc.) suitable for the function or purpose that it was designed for（机构、体系、事物等）符合设计原意的，具有适当功能的 **see/think 'fit (to do sth)** (*formal*) to consider it right or acceptable to do sth; to decide or choose to do sth 认为（做某事）恰当（或适合）；决定，愿意（做某事）：*You must do as you think fit* (= but I don't agree with your decision). 你认为怎么合适就怎么干（但我不同意你的决定）。◇ *The newspaper did not see fit to publish my letter* (= and I criticize it for that). 那份报纸认为我的信件不宜发表（而我批评这种看法）。➲MORE AT SURVIVAL

■ *noun*

• ILLNESS 疾病 1 [C] a sudden attack of an illness, such as EPILEPSY, in which sb becomes unconscious and their body may make violent movements（癫痫等的）突发，发作；昏厥；痉挛 SYN convulsion: *to have an epileptic fit* 癫痫发作 ◇ *Her fits are now controlled by drugs.* 她的病现已用药物控制，没有发作。

• OF COUGHING/LAUGHTER 咳嗽；笑 2 [C] a sudden short period of coughing or of laughing, that you cannot control 一阵（忍不住的咳嗽、笑） SYN bout: *a fit of coughing* 一阵咳嗽 ◇ *He had us all* ***in fits*** *(of laughter) with his jokes.* 他的笑话使我们都笑得前仰后合。

• OF STRONG FEELING 强烈感情 3 [C] a short period of very strong feeling（强烈感情）发作，冲动：*to act in a* ***fit of anger/rage/temper/pique*** 一阵愤怒 / 狂怒 / 怒火 / 恼怒之下采取行动 ➲SEE ALSO HISSY FIT

• OF CLOTHING 衣服 4 [C, U] (often with an adjective 常与形容词连用) the way that sth, especially a piece of clothing, fits（尤指衣服）适合，合身：*a* ***good/bad/close/perfect fit*** 很合身；不合身；贴身；完全合身

• MATCH 匹配 5 [C] ~ (between A and B) the way that two things match each other or are suitable for each other 匹配；相配：*We need to work out the best fit between the staff required and the staff available.* 我们得算出所需人员与现有人员之间的最佳配比。

IDM by/in ˌfits and 'starts frequently starting and stopping again; not continuously 间歇地；一阵一阵地：*Because of other commitments I can only write my book in fits and starts.* 由于还承担着其他任务，我只能断断续续地写书。 **have/throw a 'fit** (*informal*) to be very shocked, upset or angry 大为震惊；非常心烦意乱；大发脾气：*Your mother would have a fit if she knew you'd been drinking!* 要是你母亲知道你一直喝酒，会很生气的！

fit·ful /ˈfɪtfl/ *adj.* happening only for short periods; not continuous or regular 断断续续的；一阵阵的；间歇的：*a fitful night's sleep* 夜间时睡时醒 ▶ **fit·ful·ly** /ˈfɪtfəli/ *adv.*: *to sleep fitfully* 睡睡醒醒

fit·ment /ˈfɪtmənt/ *noun* [usually pl.] (*BrE, specialist*) a piece of furniture or equipment, especially one that is made for and fixed in a particular place（尤指为固定位置定做的）家具，设备

fit·ness /ˈfɪtnəs/ *noun* [U] 1 the state of being physically healthy and strong 健壮；健康：*a magazine on health and fitness* 卫生与健康杂志 ◇ *a* ***fitness instructor/class/test*** 健美教练；健美班；健康合格检查 ◇ *a high level of physical fitness* 高水平体质 ➲COLLOCATIONS AT DIET 2 the state of being suitable or good enough for sth 适合（某事物或做某事）：~ for sth *He convinced us of his fitness for the task.* 他使我们相信他适合做这项工作。◇ ~ to do sth *There were doubts about her fitness to hold office.* 她是否称职还不确定。

'fitness centre (*BrE*) (*NAmE* **'fitness center**) *noun* a place where people go to do physical exercise in order to stay or become healthy and fit 健身中心

fit·ted /ˈfɪtɪd/ *adj.* 1 [only before noun] (*especially BrE*) (of furniture 家具) built to be fixed into a particular space（按放置的地方）定做的 SYN built-in: ***fitted wardrobes/cupboards*** 定做的衣橱 / 橱柜 ➲VISUAL VOCAB PAGE V24 2 [only before noun] (*especially BrE*) (of a room 房间) with matching cupboards and other furniture built for the space and fixed in place 有定做配套家具的：*a* ***fitted kitchen/bedroom*** 整体厨房 / 卧室 3 [only before noun] (of clothes 衣服) made to follow the shape of the body 定做的；合身的：*a fitted jacket* 合身的短上衣 OPP loose 4 ~ for/to sth | ~ to do sth (*especially BrE*) suitable; with the right qualities and skills 合适的；恰当的；胜任的：*She was well fitted to the role of tragic heroine.* 她很适合演悲剧女主角。5 ~ with sth having sth as equipment 有…设备的：*Insurance costs will be reduced for houses fitted with window locks.* 窗户有锁的房子保险费用降低。

ˌ**fitted ˈcarpet** *noun* (*BrE*) a carpet that is cut and fixed to cover the floor of a room completely（房间的）满铺地毯 ➲ VISUAL VOCAB PAGE V24 ➲ SEE ALSO WALL-TO-WALL (1)

fit·ter /ˈfɪtə(r)/ *noun* **1** a person whose job is to put together or repair equipment 装配工；修理工；钳工：*a gas fitter* 煤气设备装修工 **2** a person whose job is to cut and fit clothes or carpets, etc. 试衣裁缝；试样裁缝；地毯安装工

fit·ting /ˈfɪtɪŋ/ *adj., noun*

▪ ***adj.*** **1** (*formal*) suitable or right for the occasion 适合（某场合）的；恰当的 SYN **appropriate**: *The award was a* ***fitting tribute*** *to her years of devoted work.* 这个奖项是对她多年全心全意工作的恰如其分的褒奖。◇ *A fitting end to the meal would be a glass of port.* 餐后最好来一杯波尔图葡萄酒。◇ ***It is fitting that*** *the new centre for European studies should be in a university that teaches every European language.* 新的欧洲研究中心应设在教授所有欧洲语言的大学里才合适。**2 -fitting** (in adjectives 构成形容词) having a particular FIT 合身的；合适的：*a tight-fitting dress* 贴身的连衣裙

▪ ***noun*** **1** [usually pl.] a small part on a piece of equipment or furniture（设备或家具的）小配件，附件：*light fittings* 灯具配件 ◇ *a pine cupboard with brass fittings* 黄铜镶配的松木橱柜 **2** [usually pl.] (*BrE*) items in a house such as a cooker, lights or shelves that are usually fixed but that you can take with you when you move to a new house 可拆除装置，附加设备（如煤气灶、灯、搁架）➲ COMPARE FIXTURE (2) **3** an occasion when you try on a piece of clothing that is being made for you to see if it fits 试衣

ˈ**fitting room** (*NAmE also* ˈ**dressing room**) *noun* a room or CUBICLE in a shop/store where you can put on clothes to see how they look（商店的）试衣室，试衣间 ➲ WORDFINDER NOTE AT SHOP

five 🔑 /faɪv/ *number* 5 五：*There are only five cookies left.* 只剩下五块曲奇了。◇ *five of Sweden's top financial experts* 五个一流的瑞典金融专家 ◇ *Ten people were invited but only five turned up.* 邀请了十人，只有五人出席。◇ *Do you have change for five dollars?* 你有五美元零钱吗？◇ *a five-month contract* 一项为期五个月的合同 ◇ *Look at page five.* 见第五页。◇ *Five and four is nine.* 五加四等于九。◇ *Three fives are fifteen.* 三个五等于十五。◇ *I can't read your writing—is this meant to be a five?* 我看不懂你的笔迹，这个是不是五字？◇ *The bulbs are planted in threes or fives* (= groups of three or five). 这些鳞茎植物是三五株在一起种植的。◇ *We moved to America when I was five* (= five years old). 我五岁时我们移居到美国。◇ *Shall we meet at five* (= at five o'clock), *then?* 那么我们五点钟见面好吗？➲ SEE ALSO HIGH FIVE

IDM ˌ**give sb ˈfive** (*informal*) to hit the inside of sb's hand with your hand as a way of saying hello or to celebrate a victory 与某人击掌问候（或庆祝胜利）：*Give me five!* 咱们击掌相庆吧！➲ MORE AT NINE

ˌ**five-and-ˈdime** (*also* ˈ**dime store**) *noun* (*old-fashioned, NAmE*) a shop/store that sells a range of cheap goods 廉价品店

ˌ**five-a-ˈside** *noun* [U] (*BrE*) a game of football (SOCCER) played indoors with five players on each team（室内）五人制足球

five·fold /ˈfaɪvfəʊld; *NAmE* -foʊld/ *adj., adv.* ➲ -FOLD

ˌ**five o'clock ˈshadow** *noun* [sing.] (*informal*) the dark colour that appears on a man's chin and face when the hair has grown a little during the day（早上刮脸后下午又长出的）胡须楂儿

ˌ**five ˈpence** (*also* ˌ**five pence ˈpiece**, **5p**) *noun* a British coin worth five pence（英国）五便士硬币：*Have you got a five pence?* 你有一枚五便士硬币吗？

fiver /ˈfaɪvə(r)/ *noun* (*informal*) **1** (*BrE*) £5 or a five-pound note * 5 英镑；五英镑钞票：*Can you lend me a fiver?* 你能借我五英镑吗？**2** (*NAmE, old-fashioned*) $5 or a five-dollar bill * 5 美元；五美元钞票

fives /faɪvz/ *noun* [U] a game played especially in British PUBLIC SCHOOLS in which players hit a ball with their hand or a BAT against the walls of a COURT 英式墙手球（用手或球拍对墙击球，流行于英国公学）

ˈ**five-star** *adj.* [usually before noun] **1** having five stars in a system that measures quality. Five stars usually represents the highest quality.（服务质量）五星级的：*a five-star hotel* 五星级宾馆 **2** (*NAmE*) having the highest military rank, and wearing a uniform which has five stars on it（军阶）五星的：*a five-star general* 五星上将

fix 🔑 /fɪks/ *verb, noun*

▪ ***verb***

• **ATTACH** 附；系 **1** 🔑 **~ sth (+ adv./prep.)** (*especially BrE*) to put sth firmly in a place so that it will not move 使固定；安装：*to fix a shelf to the wall* 把搁架固定在墙上。◇ *to fix a post in the ground* 把柱子固定在地上 ◇ (*figurative*) *He noted every detail so as to fix the scene in his mind.* 他留意着每一个细节以便牢记这一幕。

• **ARRANGE** 安排 **2** 🔑 **~ sth** to decide on a date, a time, an amount, etc. for sth 决定，确定（日期、时间、数量等）SYN **set**: *Has the date of the next meeting been fixed?* 下次会议的日期确定了没有？◇ *They fixed the rent at £100 a week.* 他们把租金定为每周 100 英镑。◇ *Their prices are fixed until the end of the year* (= will not change before then). 他们的价格一直到年底固定不变。**3** to arrange or organize sth 安排；组织：**~ sth (for sb)** *I'll fix a meeting.* 我要安排一次会议。◇ **~ sth up (for sb)** *You have to fix visits up in advance with the museum.* 你得预先和博物馆联系安排好参观事宜。◇ **~ sth with sth** (*informal*) *Don't worry, I'll fix it with Sarah.* 别着急，我会和萨拉商量安排好的。◇ **~ (up) (for sb) to do sth** *I've fixed up (for us) to go to the theatre next week.* 我已安排好（我们）下星期去看戏。

• **POSITION/TIME** 位置；时间 **4 ~ sth** to discover or say the exact position, time, etc. of sth 找到，确定，说出（确切位置、时间等）：*We can fix the ship's exact position at the time the fire broke out.* 我们可以确定发生火灾时那艘船的确切位置。

• **REPAIR** 修理 **5** 🔑 **~ sth** to repair or correct sth 修理；校准；校正：*The car won't start—can you fix it?* 这辆车发动不起来了，你能修理一下吗？◇ *I've fixed the problem.* 我已解决了这个问题。

• **FOOD/DRINK** 食物；饮料 **6** (*especially NAmE*) to provide or prepare sth, especially food 提供，准备（尤指食物）：**~ sb sth** *Can I fix you a drink?* 我给你弄杯饮料好吗？◇ **~ sth for sb** *Can I fix a drink for you?* 我给你弄杯饮料好吗？◇ **~ sth** *I'll fix supper.* 我来准备晚餐。

• **HAIR/FACE** 头发；面孔 **7 ~ sth** (*especially NAmE*) to make sth such as your hair or face neat and attractive 梳洗；整理；收拾：*I'll fix my hair and then I'll be ready.* 我梳梳头就准备好了。

• **RESULT** 结果 **8** [often passive] **~ sth** (*informal*) to arrange the result of sth in a way that is not honest or fair 操纵；作弊：*I'm sure the race was fixed.* 我肯定这场比赛有人操纵。

• **PUNISH** 惩罚 **9 ~ sb** (*informal*) to punish sb who has harmed you and stop them doing you any more harm 惩罚；收拾：*Don't worry—I'll fix him.* 别担忧，我会收拾他的。

• **IN PHOTOGRAPHY** 摄影 **10 ~ sth** (*specialist*) to treat film for cameras, etc. with a chemical so that the colours do not change or become less bright 定（影）；定（色）

• **ANIMAL** 动物 **11 ~ sth** (*NAmE, informal*) to make an animal unable to have young by means of an operation 阉割（家畜）➲ SEE ALSO NEUTER *v.* (1)

IDM **fix sb with a ˈlook, ˈstare, ˈgaze, etc.** to look directly at sb for a long time 定睛凝视（某人）：*He fixed her with an angry stare.* 他生气地盯着她。➲ MORE AT AIN'T

PHR V ˈ**fix on sb/sth** to choose sb/sth 选定；决定：*They've fixed on Paris for their honeymoon.* 他们已选定在巴黎度蜜月。ˈ**fix sth on sb/sth** [often passive] if your eyes or your mind are **fixed on** sth, you are looking at or thinking about sth with great attention 集中（目光、注意力、思想等）于 ˌ**fix sth↔ˈup** to repair, decorate or make sth ready 修理；装饰；准备好：*They fixed up the house before they moved in.* 他们把房子装修了以后才迁入。ˌ**fix sb ˈup (with sb)** (*informal*) to arrange for sb to have a meeting with sb who might become a boyfriend or girlfriend 给…介绍（男友、女友）ˌ**fix sb ˈup (with sth)** (*informal*) to arrange for sb to have sth; to provide sb with sth 向某人提供；给某人准备；安顿：*I'll fix you up with a place to stay.* 我会给你安排住处的。

■ ***noun***

• **SOLUTION** 解决 **1** [C] (*informal*) a solution to a problem, especially an easy or temporary one（尤指简单、暂时的）解决方法：*There is no* ***quick fix*** *for the steel industry.* 钢铁工业的问题没有即时解决的办法。

• **DRUG** 毒品 **2** [sing.] (*informal*) an amount of sth that you need and want frequently, especially an illegal drug such as HEROIN（致瘾的东西，尤指毒品的）一次用量：*to get yourself a fix* 给自己注射一剂毒品 ◇ *I need a fix of coffee before I can face the day.* 我总需要喝足咖啡才有精神应付一天的工作。

• **DIFFICULT SITUATION** 困境；窘境 **3** [sing.] a difficult situation 困境；窘境 **SYN** **mess**: *We've got ourselves* ***in a fix*** *about this.* 在这个问题上我们已陷入了困境。

• **ON POSITION** 位置 **4** [sing.] the act of finding the position of a ship or an aircraft（船或飞机的）方位确定，定位：*They managed to* ***get a fix*** *on the yacht's position.* 他们设法确定了快艇的方位。

• **UNDERSTANDING** 理解 **5** [sing.] (*informal*) an act of understanding sth 理解；了解：*He tried to* ***get a fix*** *on the young man's motives, but he just couldn't understand him.* 他努力了解这个年轻人的动机，但就是弄不清楚。

• **DISHONEST RESULT** 不正当结果 **6** [sing.] (*informal*) a thing that is dishonestly arranged; a trick 受操纵的事；勾当；搞鬼：*Her promotion was a fix, I'm sure!* 我肯定她的提升有内幕！

fix·ated /fɪkˈseɪtɪd/ *adj.* [not before noun] **~ (on sb/sth)** always thinking and talking about sb/sth in a way that is not normal（对…）异常依恋，固恋

fix·ation /fɪkˈseɪʃn/ *noun* **1** [C] a very strong interest in sb/sth, that is not normal or natural（对…的）异常依恋，固恋；癖：*a mother fixation* 恋母情结 ◇ **~ with/on sb/sth** *He's got this fixation with cleanliness.* 他有洁癖。 **2** [U] (*specialist*) the process of a gas becoming solid 固定（指气态变成固态的过程）：*nitrogen fixation* 固氮作用

fixa·tive /ˈfɪksətɪv/ *noun* [C, U] **1** a substance that is used to prevent colours or smells from changing or becoming weaker, for example in photography, art or the making of PERFUME 定影剂；固色剂；防（香味）挥发剂 **2** a substance that is used to stick things together or keep things in position 固定剂

fixed /fɪkst/ *adj.* **1** staying the same; not changing or able to be changed 固定的；不变的；不能变的：*fixed prices* 固定价格 ◇ *a fixed rate of interest* 固定利率 ◇ *people living on* ***fixed incomes*** 靠固定收入生活的人们 ◇ *The money has been invested for a* ***fixed period.*** 这笔款项已做定期投资。 ➲ SEE ALSO ABODE **2** (*often disapproving*) (of ideas and wishes 思想和期望) held very firmly; not easily changed 不易改变的；执着的：*My parents had* ***fixed ideas*** *about what I should become.* 父母对我应该成为什么样的人有定见。 **3** [only before noun] (of expressions on sb's face 面部表情) not changing and not sincere 呆板的；不变的：*He greeted all his guests with a fixed smile on his face.* 他对所有的客人都以一贯的笑容相迎。

IDM **how are you, etc. ˈfixed (for sth)?** (*informal*) used to ask how much of sth a person has, or to ask about arrangements 你有多少…；你…的安排如何：*How are you fixed for cash?* 你有多少现金？ ◇ *How are we fixed for Saturday* (= have we arranged to do anything)? 星期六我们有什么安排？

fixed ˈassets *noun* [pl.] (*business* 商) land, buildings and equipment that are owned and used by a company 固定资产

fixed ˈcosts *noun* [pl.] (*business* 商) the costs that a business must pay that do not change even if the amount of work produced changes 固定成本

fix·ed·ly /ˈfɪksɪdli/ *adv.* continuously, without looking away, but often with no real interest 凝视地；目不转睛地：*to stare/gaze fixedly at sb/sth* 目不转睛地盯着某人 / 某物

ˌ**fixed-ˈterm** *adj.* [only before noun] a **fixed-term** contract, etc. is one that only lasts for the agreed period of time 定期的

ˌ**fixed-ˈwing** *adj.* [only before noun] used to describe aircraft with wings that remain in the same position, rather than HELICOPTERS, etc. 固定机翼的

fixer /ˈfɪksə(r)/ *noun* **1** (*informal*) a person who arranges things for other people, sometimes dishonestly（有时用不正当的手段）代人安排者，代人疏通者：*a great political fixer* 一位杰出的政治调停人 **2** a chemical substance used in photography to prevent a photograph from changing and becoming too dark 定影剂；定色剂

ˌ**fixer-ˈupper** *noun* (*NAmE, informal*) a house or flat/apartment that is cheap because it needs a lot of repair work when you buy it 待修廉价房

fix·ings /ˈfɪksɪŋz/ *noun* [pl.] (*NAmE*) **1** = TRIMMING: *a hamburger with all the fixings* 有各种配料的汉堡包 **2** the ingredients necessary to make a dish or meal（菜肴的）配料；预备好的食材：*picnic fixings* 预备好的野餐食物组合

fix·ity /ˈfɪksəti/ *noun* [U] (*formal*) the quality of being firm and not changing 固定性；稳定性

fix·ture /ˈfɪkstʃə(r)/ *noun* **1** (*BrE*) a sports event that has been arranged to take place on a particular date and at a particular place（定期定点举行的）体育活动，体育节：*an annual fixture* 一年一度的体育节 ◇ *Saturday's fixture against Liverpool* 定于星期六与利物浦队的比赛 ◇ *the season's fixture list* 这个季度的体育活动项目表 ➲ WORDFINDER NOTE AT SPORT **2** a thing such as a bath/BATHTUB or a toilet that is fixed in a house and that you do not take with you when you move house 固定设施（如房屋内安装的浴缸或抽水马桶）：(*BrE*) *The price of the house includes* ***fixtures and fittings.*** 房屋价格包括固定装置和附加设备。◇ (*figurative*) *He has stayed with us so long he seems to have become* ***a permanent fixture.*** 他在我们这里待了很久，好像成了我们的固定成员。➲ COLLOCATIONS AT DECORATE ➲ COMPARE FITTING *n.* (2)

fizz /fɪz/ *verb, noun*

■ ***verb*** [I] when a liquid **fizzes**, it produces a lot of bubbles and makes a long sound like an 's' 起泡发嘶嘶声：*Champagne was fizzing in the glass.* 杯里的香槟酒嘶嘶地冒泡。◇ (*figurative*) *Share prices are fizzing.* 股价活力十足。◇ **~ with sth** (*figurative*) *He started to fizz with enthusiasm.* 他开始热情奔放起来。

■ ***noun*** **1** [U, sing.] the small bubbles of gas in a liquid（液体中的）气泡：(*figurative*) *There is plenty of fizz and sparkle in the show.* 演出精彩，妙趣横生。◇ (*figurative*) *The fizz has gone out of the market.* 市场已失去生气。 **2** [U, sing.] the sound that is made by bubbles of gas in a liquid, or a sound similar to this（液体中的）气泡嘶嘶声，嘶嘶声，噼啪声：*the fizz of a firework* 烟火的噼啪声 **3** [U] (*BrE, informal*) a drink that has a lot of bubbles of gas, especially CHAMPAGNE 起泡饮料（尤指香槟）

fizz·er /ˈfɪzə(r)/ *noun* (*AustralE, NZE, informal*) a failure 失败：*The party was a fizzer.* 聚会搞砸了。

fiz·zle /ˈfɪzl/ *verb* [I] when sth, especially sth that is burning, **fizzles**, it makes a sound like a long 's'（火等）发出嘶嘶声 **SYN** **hiss**

PHR V ˌ**fizzle ˈout** (*informal*) to gradually become less successful and end in a disappointing way（顺利开始）结果失败，终成泡影；虎头蛇尾

fizzy /ˈfɪzi/ *adj.* (*BrE*) (**fizz·ier, fizzi·est**) (of a drink 饮料) having bubbles of gas in it 起泡的 **SYN** **sparkling**: *fizzy drinks* 起泡饮料 **OPP** **still**

fjord (*also* **fiord**) /ˈfjɔːd; *NAmE* ˈfjɔːrd/ *noun* a long narrow strip of sea between high CLIFFS, especially in Norway（尤指挪威两岸峭壁间的）峡湾

flab /flæb/ *noun* [U] (*informal, disapproving*) soft, loose flesh on a person's body（人体）松弛的肌肉

flab·ber·gast·ed /ˈflæbəɡɑːstɪd; *NAmE* ˈflæbərɡæstɪd/ *adj.* [not usually before noun] (*informal*) extremely surprised and/or shocked 大吃一惊；目瞪口呆 SYN **astonished**

flabby /ˈflæbi/ *adj.* (*informal, disapproving*) (**flab·bier, flab·bi·est**) **1** having soft, loose flesh; fat（肌肉）松弛的；肥胖的：*flabby thighs* 肥胖的大腿 **2** weak; with no strength or force 软弱的；无力的：*a flabby grip* 无力的一握 ◇ *a flabby argument* 无力的论据

flac·cid /ˈflæsɪd; ˈflæk-/ *adj.* (*formal*) soft and weak; not firm and hard 软弱的；松弛的；不结实的：*flaccid breasts* 松弛的乳房

flack /flæk/ *noun* **1** [U] = FLAK **2** [C] (*NAmE, informal*) = PRESS AGENT

flag /flæɡ/ *noun, verb*

■ *noun* **1** a piece of cloth with a special coloured design on it that may be the symbol of a particular country or organization, or may have a particular meaning. A flag can be attached to a pole or held in the hand. 旗：*the Italian flag* 意大利国旗 ◇ *the flag of Italy* 意大利国旗 ◇ *The hotel* ***flies the*** *European Union* ***flag.*** 这家旅馆悬挂着欧盟的旗帜。◇ *The American* ***flag was flying.*** 美国国旗飘扬。◇ *All the* ***flags were at half mast*** (= in honour of a famous person who has died). 到处都下半旗志哀。◇ *The black and white flag went down, and the race began.* 黑白旗落下，赛跑开始了。➲ VISUAL VOCAB PAGE V3 ➲ SEE ALSO BLUE FLAG (1) **2** used to refer to a particular country or organization and its beliefs and values 旗帜（指某国家或组织及其信仰和价值观）：*to swear allegiance to the flag* 面对旗帜作效忠宣誓 ◇ *He was working under the flag of the United Nations.* 他在联合国工作。**3** a piece of cloth that is attached to a pole and used as a signal or MARKER in various sports（体育运动的）信号旗，标志旗 **4** a flower that is a type of IRIS and that grows near water 菖蒲；鸢尾；香蒲：*yellow flags* 黄菖蒲 **5** = FLAGSTONE

IDM **fly/show/wave the ˈflag** to show your support for your country, an organization or an idea to encourage or persuade others to do the same 表示并号召拥护自己的国家（或某组织、某思想）**keep the ˈflag flying** to represent your country or organization 代表自己的国家（或组织）：*Our exporters keep the flag flying at international trade exhibitions.* 我们的出口商在国际贸易展览会上代表我们的国家参展。➲ MORE AT WAVE *v.*

■ *verb* (**-gg-**) **1** [T] **~ sth** to put a special mark next to information that you think is important 标示（重要处）：*I've flagged the paragraphs that we need to look at in more detail.* 我已用特殊记号标出我们需要更仔细研究的段落。**2** [I] to become tired, weaker or less enthusiastic 疲乏；变弱；热情衰减：*It had been a long day and the children were beginning to flag.* 这一天真漫长，孩子们都累得打起蔫来。◇ *Her confidence had never flagged.* 她的信心从未减弱。◇ ***flagging support/enthusiasm*** 日益减少的支持；渐渐低落的热情 ➲ MORE LIKE THIS 36, page R29

PHRV **ˌflag sb/sth↔ˈdown** to signal to the driver of a vehicle to stop by waving at them 挥旗（或挥手）示意停车 **ˌflag sth↔ˈup** (*BrE*) to draw attention to sth 引起对…的注意：*The report flagged up the dangers of under-age drinking.* 这篇报道引起大众对未成年人饮酒危害的关注。

ˈflag day *noun* **1** (*BrE*) a day when money is collected in public places for a charity, and people who give money receive a small paper STICKER 募捐售旗日 **2 Flag Day** 14 June, the anniversary of the day in 1777 when the Stars and Stripes became the national flag of the United States 美国国旗纪念日（6月14日）

fla·gel·late /ˈflædʒəleɪt/ *verb* **~ sb/yourself** (*formal*) to WHIP yourself or sb else, especially as a religious punishment or as a way of experiencing sexual pleasure 鞭笞（自己或他人，尤作为一种宗教惩罚或为获得性快感）▶ **fla·gel·la·tion** /ˌflædʒəˈleɪʃn/ *noun* [U]

ˌflag ˈfootball *noun* [U] (*NAmE*) a type of AMERICAN FOOTBALL played without the usual form of TACKLING. A TACKLE is made instead by pulling a piece of cloth from an opponent's WAISTBAND.（美式）夺旗橄榄球（擒抱方式不同于一般的美式足球，而是从对方的腰带上拽出一块织物）➲ COMPARE TOUCH FOOTBALL

flagged /flæɡd/ *adj.* covered with large flat stones (called FLAGSTONES) 铺石板的：*a flagged floor* 石板地面

ˌflag of conˈvenience *noun* a flag of a foreign country that is used by a ship from another country for legal or financial reasons 方便旗（指船由于法律或经济上的原因挂外国国旗）

flagon /ˈflæɡən/ *noun* a large bottle or similar container, often with a handle, in which wine, etc. is sold or served 大肚短颈瓶；大酒壶

flag·pole /ˈflæɡpəʊl; *NAmE* -poʊl/ (*also* **flag·staff**) *noun* a tall pole on which a flag is hung 旗杆 ➲ VISUAL VOCAB PAGE V3

fla·grant /ˈfleɪɡrənt/ *adj.* (of an action 行动) shocking because it is done in a very obvious way and shows no respect for people, laws, etc. 骇人听闻的；公然的；罪恶昭彰的 SYN **blatant**：*a flagrant abuse of human rights* 粗暴的践踏人权 ◇ *He showed a flagrant disregard for anyone else's feelings.* 他公然蔑视其他任何人的感情。▶ **fla·grant·ly** *adv.*

fla·grante ➲ IN FLAGRANTE

flag·ship /ˈflæɡʃɪp/ *noun* **1** the main ship in a FLEET of ships in the navy 旗舰 **2** [usually sing.] the most important product, service, building, etc. that an organization owns or produces（某组织机构的）最重要产品，最佳服务项目，主建筑物，王牌：*The company is opening a new flagship store in London.* 这家公司将在伦敦新开一家旗舰店。

flag·staff /ˈflæɡstɑːf; *NAmE* -stæf/ *noun* = FLAGPOLE

flag·stone /ˈflæɡstəʊn; *NAmE* -stoʊn/ (*also* **flag**) *noun* a large flat square piece of stone that is used for floors, paths, etc. 石板（方形，用于铺地面、小径等）

ˈflag-waving *noun* [U] the expression of strong national feelings, especially in a way that people disapprove of 强烈民族情绪；（尤指）沙文主义的表现

flail /fleɪl/ *verb, noun*

■ *verb* **1** [I, T] **~ (sth) (about/around)** to move around without control; to move your arms and legs around without control 乱动；胡乱摆动：*The boys flailed around on the floor.* 男孩子们在地板上手舞足蹈任意地动来动去。◇ *He was running along, his arms flailing wildly.* 他向前跑，拼命摆动双臂。**2** [T] **~ sb/sth** to hit sb/sth very hard, especially with a stick（尤指用棍棒）猛击，猛打

■ *noun* a tool that has a long handle with a stick swinging from it, used especially in the past to separate grains of WHEAT from their dry outer covering, by beating the WHEAT 连枷（旧时长柄脱粒农具）

flair /fleə(r); *NAmE* fler/ *noun* **1** [sing., U] **~ for sth** a natural ability to do sth well 天资；天赋；天分 SYN **talent**：*He* ***has a flair for*** *languages.* 他有学语言的天分。**2** [U] a quality showing the ability to do things in an interesting way that shows imagination 才华；资质：*artistic flair* 艺术魅力 ◇ *She dresses with real flair.* 她衣着甚有品味。

flak (*also* **flack**) /flæk/ *noun* [U] **1** guns on the ground that are shooting at enemy aircraft; bullets from these guns 高射炮；高射炮火 **2** (*informal*) severe criticism 严厉批评；抨击：*He's* ***taken a lot of flak*** *for his left-wing views.* 他的左倾观点受到了强烈指责。◇ *She* ***came in for a lot of flak*** *from the press.* 她遭到报界猛烈抨击。

flake /fleɪk/ *noun, verb*

■ *noun* **1** a small, very thin layer or piece of sth, especially one that has broken off from sth larger 小薄片；（尤指）碎片：***flakes of snow/paint*** 雪花；剥落的片片油漆 ◇ *dried onion flakes* 干洋葱皮片 ➲ SEE ALSO CORNFLAKES, SNOWFLAKE, SOAP FLAKES **2** (*NAmE, informal*) a person who is strange or unusual or who forgets things easily 古怪的人；奇特的人；健忘的人

■ *verb* **1** [I] **~ (off)** to fall off in small thin pieces（成小薄片）脱落，剥落：*You could see bare wood where the paint had flaked off.* 油漆剥落处可以看见光秃秃的木头。◇

His skin was dry and flaking. 他的皮肤干燥，脱皮屑。 **2** [T, I] ~ (**sth**) to break sth, especially fish or other food into small thin pieces; to fall into small thin pieces 把（鱼、食物等）切成薄片；成为薄片：*Flake the tuna and add to the sauce.* 把金枪鱼切成片，加上调味汁。◇ *flaked almonds* 杏仁片

PHR V **,flake 'out** **1** (*informal*) to lie down or fall asleep because you are extremely tired （疲倦得）倒下，睡着：*When I got home he'd already flaked out on the bed.* 我到家时他已累倒在床上。 **2** (*NAmE, informal*) to begin to behave in a strange way 行为古怪起来

F

'flak jacket *noun* a heavy jacket without sleeves that has metal inside it to make it stronger, and is worn by soldiers and police officers to protect them from bullets 防弹背心

flaky /'fleɪki/ *adj.* **1** tending to break into small, thin pieces 易碎成小薄片的；易剥落的：*flaky pastry* 酥饼 ◇ *dry flaky skin* 干燥易脱皮屑的皮肤 **2** (*informal*) (of a person 人) behaving in a strange or unusual way; tending to forget things 行为古怪的；好忘事的 **3** (*especially BrE, informal, computing* 计) that does not work well or often stops working 运行不正常的；经常出问题的：*I found the software a bit flaky.* 我发现这个软件有点问题。 ▸ **flaki·ness** *noun* [U]

flambé /'flɒmbeɪ; *NAmE* flɑːm'beɪ/ *adj.* [after noun] (*from French*) (of food 食物) covered with alcohol, especially BRANDY and allowed to burn for a short time 火焰（浇上白兰地等酒后点燃上桌） ▸ **flambé** *verb* ~ **sth** ➲ VISUAL VOCAB PAGE V28

flam·boy·ant /flæm'bɔɪənt/ *adj.* **1** (of people or their behaviour 人或行为) different, confident and exciting in a way that attracts attention 炫耀的；卖弄的：*a flamboyant gesture/style/personality* 炫耀的手势 / 作风 / 个性 **2** brightly coloured and noticeable 艳丽的；绚丽夺目的：*flamboyant clothes/designs* 艳丽的衣服；华丽的设计 ▸ **flam·boy·ance** /-'bɔɪəns/ *noun* [U] **flam·boy·ant·ly** *adv.*

flame /fleɪm/ *noun, verb*

■ *noun* **1** [C, U] a hot bright stream of burning gas that comes from sth that is on fire 火焰；火舌：*the tiny yellow flame of a match* 火柴小小的黄色火焰 ◇ *The flames were growing higher and higher.* 熊熊火焰越来越高。◇ *The building was **in flames*** (= was burning). 大楼失火了。◇ *The plane **burst into flame(s)*** (= suddenly began burning strongly). 飞机突然起了大火。◇ *Everything **went up in flames*** (= was destroyed by fire). 一切都毁于大火。➲ VISUAL VOCAB PAGE V72 **2** [U] a bright red or orange colour 鲜红色；橘红色；橙黄色：*a flame-red car* 橘红色的汽车 **3** [C] (*literary*) a very strong feeling 强烈的感情；激情：*a flame of passion* 激情的烈火 ➲ SEE ALSO OLD FLAME **4** [C] (*informal*) an angry or insulting message sent to sb by email or on the Internet 火药味电邮（或互联网信息）

IDM SEE FAN *v.*

■ *verb* **1** [I] (+ **adj.**) (*literary*) to burn with a bright flame 燃烧：*The logs flamed on the hearth.* 木柴在壁炉炉床里燃烧。◇ (*figurative*) *Hope flamed in her.* 她满怀希望。 **2** [I, T] (+ **adj.**) | ~ (**sth**) (*literary*) (of a person's face 人脸) to become red as a result of a strong emotion; to make sth become red（因强烈情绪而）变红，使变红：*Her cheeks flamed with rage.* 她愤怒得两颊通红。 **3** [T] ~ **sb** (*informal*) to send sb an angry or insulting message by email or on the Internet 发送火药味电邮（或互联网信息）

fla·menco /flə'meŋkəʊ; *NAmE* -koʊ/ *noun* (*pl.* **-os**) **1** [U, C] a fast exciting Spanish dance that is usually danced to music played on a GUITAR 弗拉门科舞（一种西班牙舞，节奏快而强烈，吉他伴奏）：*flamenco dancing* 跳弗拉门科舞 ◇ *to dance the flamenco* 跳弗拉门科舞 **2** [U] the GUITAR music that is played for this dance 弗拉门科舞吉他乐曲

flame·proof /'fleɪmpruːf/ *adj.* made of or covered with a special material that will not burn easily 耐火的；防火的

flame-retard·ant /'fleɪm rɪ,tɑːdənt; *NAmE* -,tɑːrd-/ *adj.* = FIRE-RETARDANT

flame·throw·er /'fleɪmθrəʊə(r); *NAmE* -θroʊər/ *noun* a weapon like a gun that shoots out burning liquid or flames and is often used for clearing plants from land 喷火器；火焰喷射器

flam·ing /'fleɪmɪŋ/ *adj.* [only before noun] **1** full of anger 满腔怒火的；激动的：*a **flaming argument/temper*** 激烈的争论；暴躁的脾气 **2** burning and covered in flames 燃烧的；冒火焰的：*Flaming fragments were still falling from the sky.* 燃烧着的碎片还在不断地从天而降。 **3** (*BrE, informal*) used to emphasize that you are annoyed（强调恼怒）可恶的，讨厌的：*You flaming idiot!* 你这个讨厌的笨蛋！ **4** bright red or orange in colour 鲜红色的；橙黄色的；橘红色的：*flaming (red) hair* 火焰般的（红）头发 ◇ *a flaming sunset* 嫣红的晚霞

fla·mingo /flə'mɪŋgəʊ; *NAmE* -goʊ/ *noun* (*pl.* **-oes** or **-os**) a large pink bird with long thin legs and a long neck, that lives near water in warm countries 红鹳，火烈鸟，红鹤（热带大涉禽，羽色粉红，腿细长，长颈）

flam·mable /'flæməbl/ (*also* **in·flam·mable** *especially in BrE*) *adj.* that can burn easily 易燃的；可燃的：***highly flammable liquids*** 高度易燃的液体 OPP **non-flammable** ➲ MORE LIKE THIS 23, page R27

flan /flæn/ *noun* [C, U] **1** (*especially BrE*) an open PIE made of PASTRY or cake filled with eggs and cheese, fruit, etc.（蛋糊）果馅饼：*a mushroom/strawberry flan* 蘑菇 / 草莓馅饼 ◇ *Have some more flan.* 再吃一点果馅饼。➲ COMPARE QUICHE, TART *n.* **2** (*NAmE*) (*BrE* **crème caramel**) a cold DESSERT (= a sweet dish) made from milk, eggs and sugar 焦糖蛋奶（冷甜食）

flange /flændʒ/ *noun* an edge that sticks out from an object and makes it stronger or (as in a wheel of a train) keeps it in the correct position 凸缘；法兰；（火车的）轮缘

flank /flæŋk/ *noun, verb*

■ *noun* **1** the side of sth such as a building or mountain（建筑物、山等的）侧面 **2** the left or right side of an army during a battle, or a sports team during a game（军队或运动队的）翼侧，侧面，侧翼 **3** the side of an animal between the RIBS and the hip（动物的）肋腹

■ *verb* **1** **be flanked by sb/sth** to have sb/sth on one or both sides 侧面（或两侧）有：*She left the courtroom flanked by armed guards.* 她在武装警卫护送下离开法庭。 **2** ~ **sth** to be placed on one or both sides of sth 位于…的侧翼；在…侧面：*They drove through the cotton fields that flanked Highway 17.* 他们驾车穿过了 17 号公路边上的棉田。

flank·er /'flæŋkə(r)/ *noun* an attacking player in RUGBY or AMERICAN FOOTBALL（橄榄球或美式足球）边锋

flan·nel /'flænl/ *noun* **1** [U] a type of soft light cloth, containing cotton or wool, used for making clothes 法兰绒：*a flannel shirt* 法兰绒衬衣 ◇ *a grey flannel suit* 一套灰法兰绒西服 **2** (*also* **face·cloth**) (*both BrE*) (*NAmE* **wash·cloth**) [C] a small piece of cloth used for washing yourself（擦洗身体用的）毛巾：*a face flannel* 洗脸毛巾 ➲ VISUAL VOCAB PAGE V25 **3** **flannels** [pl.] trousers/pants made of flannel 法兰绒裤 **4** [U] (*BrE, informal*) words that do not have much meaning and that avoid telling sb what they want to know 兜圈子的话语；应付性言语

flan·nel·ette /,flænə'let/ *noun* [U] a type of soft cotton cloth, used especially for making sheets and NIGHTCLOTHES 绒布，棉法兰绒（尤用于制作床单和睡衣）

flap /flæp/ *noun, verb*

■ *noun*

• **FLAT PIECE OF PAPER, ETC.** 平整的纸等 **1** [C] a flat piece of paper, cloth, metal, etc. that is attached to sth along one side and that hangs down or covers an opening（附于某物的）片状下垂物，封盖，口盖，袋盖：*the flap of an envelope* 信封的封盖 ◇ *I zipped the tent flaps shut.* 我拉上了帐篷门帘的拉链。➲ SEE ALSO CAT FLAP ➲ VISUAL VOCAB PAGE V71

• **MOVEMENT** 动作 **2** [C, usually sing.] a quick often noisy movement of sth up and down or from side to side（上下或左右）拍打，振（翅），拍击：*With a flap of its* *wings, the bird was gone.* 鸟拍打着翅膀飞走了。◇ *the flap of the sails* 风帆的猎猎摆动

- **WORRY/EXCITEMENT** 忧虑；激动 **3** [sing.] (*informal, especially BrE*) a state of worry, confusion and excitement 忧虑；困惑；激动：*She **gets in a flap** over the slightest thing.* 极小的事也能令她不安。
- **PUBLIC DISAGREEMENT** 公众不同意 **4** [sing.] (*NAmE*) public disagreement, anger or criticism caused by sth a public figure has said or done 公众不同意；群众愤怒；大众批评：*the flap about the President's business affairs* 公众对总统公务的批评
- **PART OF AIRCRAFT** 飞行器部分 **5** [C] (*specialist*) a part of the wing of an aircraft, on the rear of the wing, that can be moved up or down to control upward or downward movement（飞机的）襟翼 ➲ VISUAL VOCAB PAGE V57
- **PHONETICS** 语音学 **6** [C] = TAP (6)

■ *verb* (**-pp-**)

- **MOVE QUICKLY** 快速动作 **1** [T, I] ~ (**sth**) if a bird **flaps** its wings, or if its wings **flap**, they move quickly up and down 振（翅）SYN **beat**：*The bird flapped its wings and flew away.* 鸟振翅飞去。◇ *The gulls flew off, wings flapping.* 海鸥拍打着双翅飞走了。**2** [I, T] to move or to make sth move up and down or from side to side, often making a noise（使上下或左右）拍打，拍击，摆动：(+ **adv./prep.**) *The sails flapped in the breeze.* 风帆在微风中摆动。◇ *Two large birds flapped* (= flew) *slowly across the water.* 两只大鸟振翅缓缓飞过水面。◇ **~ sth** *She walked up and down, flapping her arms to keep warm.* 她来回走动，挥动着双臂使身体暖和起来。◇ *A gust of wind flapped the tents.* 一阵风吹动了帐篷。
- **BE WORRIED/EXCITED** 忧虑；激动 **3** [I] (*BrE, informal*) to behave in an anxious or excited way 忧虑；激动：*There's no need to flap—I've got everything under control.* 不必担心，一切都已在我控制之中。
- **PHONETICS** 语音学 **4** [T] **~ sth** = TAP (7) IDM SEE EAR

flap·jack /ˈflæpdʒæk/ *noun* **1** [U, C] (*BrE*) a thick soft biscuit made from OATS, butter, sugar and SYRUP 燕麦甜饼 **2** [C] (*NAmE*) a thick PANCAKE 煎饼；烤饼

flap·per /ˈflæpə(r)/ *noun* a fashionable young woman in the 1920s who was interested in modern ideas and was determined to enjoy herself（20 世纪 20 年代不受传统拘束的）新潮女郎

flare /fleə(r); *NAmE* fler/ *verb, noun*

■ *verb* **1** [I] to burn brightly, but usually for only a short time or not steadily（短暂）烧旺；（摇曳着）燃烧；（火光）闪耀：*The match flared and went out.* 火柴闪亮了一下就熄了。◇ *The fire flared into life.* 火旺了起来。◇ (*figurative*) *Colour flared in her cheeks.* 她两颊泛起了红晕。**2** [I] ~ (**up**) (especially of anger and violence 尤指愤怒和暴力) to suddenly start or become much stronger 突发；加剧 SYN **erupt**：*Violence flared when the police moved in.* 警察逼近时爆发了暴力行为。◇ ***Tempers flared*** *towards the end of the meeting.* 会议快结束时群情激愤。➲ RELATED NOUN FLARE-UP (1) **3** [T, I] (+ **speech**) to say sth in an angry and aggressive way 发怒地说；粗暴地说：*'You should have told me!' she flared at him.* "你应该告诉我的！"她气冲冲地对他说。**4** [I] (of clothes 衣服) to become wider towards the bottom 底部展开；呈喇叭形：*The sleeves are tight to the elbow, then flare out.* 袖子在肘部收紧，接着逐渐展开。**5** [T, I] ~ (**sth**) if a person or an animal **flares** their NOSTRILS (= the openings at the end of the nose), or if their nostrils **flare**, they become wider, especially as a sign of anger（尤指因气愤）使（鼻孔）张开，（鼻孔）张开：*The horse backed away, its nostrils flaring with fear.* 马向后惊退，吓得鼻翼扇动。

PHR V ˌ**flare ˈup** **1** (of flames, a fire, etc. 火焰、火等) to suddenly start burning more brightly 突然旺起来 ➲ RELATED NOUN FLARE-UP (3) **2** (of a person 人) to suddenly become angry 突然发怒 ➲ RELATED NOUN FLARE-UP (1) **3** (of an illness, injury, etc. 疾病、损伤等) to suddenly start again or become worse 复发；突然加剧 ➲ RELATED NOUN FLARE-UP (2)

■ *noun* **1** [usually sing.] a bright but unsteady light or flame that does not last long（短暂的）旺火；（摇曳的）光；（闪耀的）火光：*The flare of the match lit up his face.* 火柴的光照亮了他的脸。**2** a device that produces a bright flame, used especially as a signal; a flame produced in this way 闪光装置；闪光信号灯；照明弹：*The ship sent up distress flares to attract the attention of the coastguard.* 这艘船发出了遇险信号以引起海岸警卫队的注意。**3** a shape that becomes gradually wider 逐渐展开；喇叭形：*a skirt with a slight flare* 下摆略张的裙子 **4** **flares** (*BrE also* ˌ**flared ˈtrousers**) [pl.] (*informal*) trousers/pants that become very wide at the bottom of the legs 喇叭裤：*a pair of flares* 一条喇叭裤

flared /fleəd; *NAmE* flerd/ *adj.* (of clothes 衣服) wider at the bottom edge than at the top 底部展开的；喇叭形的

ˈ**flare-up** *noun* [usually sing.] **1** a sudden expression of angry or violent feeling（怒气、激烈情绪等的）爆发 SYN **outburst**：*a flare-up of tension between the two sides* 双方剑拔弩张 **2** (of an illness 疾病) a sudden painful attack, especially after a period without any problems or pain 突发；（尤指）复发 **3** the fact of a fire suddenly starting to burn again more strongly than before 骤燃；突然燃起更大的火焰：*a flare-up of the bushfires* 林区大火的猛燃

flash 🔑 /flæʃ/ *verb, noun, adj.*

■ *verb*

- **SHINE BRIGHTLY** 照耀 **1** 🔑 [I, T] to shine very brightly for a short time; to make sth shine in this way（使）闪耀，闪光：*Lightning flashed in the distance.* 远处电光闪闪。◇ *the flashing blue lights of a police car* 警车闪烁的蓝灯 ◇ + **adv./prep.** *A neon sign flashed on and off above the door.* 门上方霓虹灯忽明忽暗地闪烁着。◇ **~ sth** *The guide flashed a light into the cave.* 导游用手电筒照射洞穴。
- **GIVE SIGNAL** 发出信号 **2** 🔑 [T, I] to use a light to give sb a signal（向…）用光发出（信号）：**~ sth** (**at sb**) *Red lights flashed a warning at them.* 红灯闪亮向他们发出警告。◇ **~ sb** (**sth**) *Red lights flashed them a warning.* 红灯闪亮向他们发出警告。◇ **~ at sb** *Why is that driver flashing at us?* 那个司机为什么向我们闪灯？
- **SHOW QUICKLY** 快速显示 **3** [T] **~ sth at sb** to show sth to sb quickly（快速地）出示，显示：*He flashed his pass at the security officer.* 他向保安员亮了一下通行证。
- **MOVE QUICKLY** 快速移动 **4** [I] + **adv./prep.** to move or pass very quickly 飞速运动；掠过：*The countryside flashed past the train windows.* 乡村景色从火车窗外飞掠而过。◇ *A look of terror flashed across his face.* 他脸上掠过惊恐的神色。
- **OF THOUGHTS/MEMORIES** 思想；记忆 **5** [I] + **adv./prep.** to come into your mind suddenly 突然想到；猛然想起：*A terrible thought flashed through my mind.* 一个可怕的想法闪过我的脑海。
- **ON SCREEN** 屏幕上 **6** [I, T] to appear on a television screen, computer screen, etc. for a short time; to make sth do this（使）闪现，映出，显示：*A message was flashing on his pager.* 他的寻呼机上闪现出一则信息。◇ **~** (**sth**) (**up**) *His name was flashed up on the screen.* 屏幕上显示出了他的名字。
- **SEND NEWS** 发送消息 **7** [T] **~ sth + adv./prep.** to send information quickly by radio, computer, etc.（通过无线电、计算机等）快速发送（信息）：*News of their triumph was flashed around the world.* 他们胜利的消息迅速传遍了全世界。
- **SHOW EMOTION** 显露情感 **8** [I] (+ **adv./prep.**) (*literary*) to show a strong emotion suddenly and quickly 突然显露（强烈情感）：*Her eyes flashed with anger.* 她眼中闪出怒火。
- **OF A MAN** 男子 **9** [I] (*informal*) if a man **flashes**, he shows his sexual organs in public 当众暴露性器官

IDM **flash sb a ˈsmile, ˈlook, etc.** to smile, look, etc. at sb suddenly and quickly 向…微微一笑（或瞥一眼）

PHR V ˌ**flash sth aˈround** (*disapproving*) to show sth to other people in order to impress them 炫耀（某物）：*He's always flashing his money around.* 他总是在炫耀他的金钱。ˌ**flash ˈback** (**to sth**) **1** if your mind **flashes back** to sth, you remember sth that happened in the past 回忆；回想；回顾：*Her thoughts flashed back to their wedding day.* 她回忆起他们婚礼那一天的情景。➲ RELATED NOUN FLASHBACK (2) **2** if a film/movie **flashes back** to sth, it shows things that happened at an earlier time, for example at an earlier part of sb's life（电影）闪回，倒叙 ➲ RELATED NOUN FLASHBACK (1) **3** to reply very quickly and/or angrily 迅即答复；愤怒回答 **,flash 'by/'past** (of time 时间) to go very quickly 飞逝：*The morning has just flashed by.* 这个上午转眼就过去了。**'flash on sb** (*US, informal*) [no passive] if sth **flashes on you**, you suddenly realize it 使…突然意识到；使…猛然领悟：**it flashes on sb that…** *It flashed on me that he was the man I'd seen in the hotel.* 我突然想起他就是我在旅馆里看到的那个人。**'flash on sth** (*US, informal*) to suddenly remember or think of sth 突然回想起；猛地想到：*I flashed on an argument I had with my sister when we were kids.* 我突然回想起小时候和姐姐的一次争吵。

F

■ *noun*
• **LIGHT** 光 **1** [C] a sudden bright light that shines for a moment and then disappears 闪光；闪耀：*a **flash of lightning*** 一道闪电 ◇ *Flashes of light were followed by an explosion.* 阵阵闪光后就是一声爆炸的巨响。◇ *There was **a blinding flash** and the whole building shuddered.* 一道眩目的闪光过后，整栋大楼颤抖起来。
• **SIGNAL** 信号 **2** [C] the act of shining a light on sth, especially as a signal （尤指信号灯）闪亮
• **IN PHOTOGRAPHY** 摄影 **3** [C, U] a piece of equipment that produces a bright light for a very short time, used for taking photographs indoors, when it is dark, etc.; the use of this when taking a photograph 闪光灯：*a camera with a built-in flash* 有内置闪光灯的照相机 ◇ *I'll need flash for this shot.* 拍这个镜头我需要闪光灯。◇ *flash photography* 闪光摄影术 ➲ VISUAL VOCAB PAGE V45
• **OF BRIGHT COLOUR** 鲜明颜色 **4** [C] **~ of sth** the sudden appearance for a short time of sth bright （明亮的东西）闪现：*a flash of white teeth* 闪露洁白的牙齿 ◇ *On the horizon, she saw a flash of silver—the sea!* 她看见天边闪现一片银色，那是大海！
• **SUDDEN IDEA/EMOTION** 突然的想法；突发的情感 **5** [C] **~ of sth** a particular feeling or idea that suddenly comes into your mind or shows in your face （想法的）突现；（情感的）突发：*a **flash of anger/inspiration, etc.*** 怒上心头、灵感闪现等
• **NEWS** 新闻 **6** [C] = NEWSFLASH
• **ON UNIFORM** 制服 **7** [C] (*BrE*) a band or small piece of cloth worn on a military uniform to show a person's rank （佩戴在军服上的）徽章，肩章，臂章
• **ON BOOK/PACK** 书；小包 **8** [C] a band of colour or writing across a book, pack, etc. 彩条；文字条
• **COMPUTING** 计算机技术 **9 Flash™** [U] a program which creates moving images for websites * Flash 网站动画制作程序

IDM **a ,flash in the 'pan** a sudden success that lasts only a short time and is not likely to be repeated 昙花一现 **in/like a 'flash** very quickly and suddenly 转瞬间；立即 ➲ MORE AT QUICK *adv.*

■ *adj.* (*BrE, informal, disapproving*) attracting attention by being large or expensive, or by having expensive clothes, etc. 庞大的；昂贵的；穿着奢华的：*a flash car* 外表华丽的轿车 ◇ *He's very flash, isn't he?* 他穿着十分奢华，不是吗？

flash·back /ˈflæʃbæk/ *noun* **1** [C, U] a part of a film/movie, play, etc. that shows a scene that happened earlier in time than the main story （电影或戏剧的）闪回，倒叙，倒叙片段：*The events that led up to the murder were shown in a series of flashbacks.* 通过一系列倒叙展现出了导致谋杀的各个情节。◇ *The reader is told the story **in flashback**.* 故事是以倒叙手法向读者讲述的。➲ WORDFINDER NOTE AT PLOT **2** [C] a sudden, very clear, strong memory of sth that happened in the past that is so real you feel that you are living through the experience again （往事的）闪回，回顾

flash·bulb /ˈflæʃbʌlb/ *noun* a small electric BULB that can be attached to a camera to take photographs indoors or when it is dark （照相机的）闪光灯泡

'flash card *noun* a card with a word or picture on it, that teachers use during lessons 教学卡片；识字卡

'flash drive (*also* **US'B drive**, **'pen drive**) (*NAmE also* **'thumb drive**) *noun* (*computing* 计) a small memory device that can be used to store data from a computer and to move it from one computer to another 闪存盘；闪盘；U 盘 SYN **memory stick** ➲ VISUAL VOCAB PAGE V73

flash·er /ˈflæʃə(r)/ *noun* **1** (*informal*) a man who shows his sexual organs in public, especially in order to shock or frighten women （男子）暴露狂 **2** a device that turns a light on and off quickly 闪光装置 **3** (*NAmE*) a light on a vehicle that you can turn on and off quickly as a signal （车用）闪光灯：*four-way flashers* (= four lights that flash together to warn other drivers of possible danger) 四向闪光灯

'flash flood *noun* a sudden flood of water caused by heavy rain （暴雨引起的）暴发洪水 ➲ WORDFINDER NOTE AT RAIN

flash·gun /ˈflæʃgʌn/ *noun* a piece of equipment that holds and operates a bright light that is used to take photographs indoors or when it is dark （摄影用的）闪光枪

flash·ing /ˈflæʃɪŋ/ *noun* [U] (*also* **flashings** [pl.]) a strip of metal put on a roof where it joins a wall to prevent water getting through （房顶与墙交接处的）防雨板，盖片

flash·light /ˈflæʃlaɪt/ (*especially NAmE*) (*BrE also* **torch**) *noun* a small electric lamp that uses batteries and that you can hold in your hand 手电筒

'flash memory *noun* [U] (*computing* 计) computer memory that does not lose data when the power supply is lost 闪速存储器，闪存（断电时不丢失数据）

'flash mob *noun* a large group of people who arrange (by mobile/cell phone or email) to gather together in a public place at exactly the same time, spend a short time doing sth there and then quickly all leave at the same time 快闪族（通过手机或电邮相约同一时间在公共场所速聚速散的一大群人）▶ **'flash mob·ber** *noun* **'flash mob·bing** *noun* [U]

flash·point /ˈflæʃpɔɪnt/ *noun* [C, U] a situation or place in which violence or anger starts and cannot be controlled （暴力或愤怒的）一触即发，危机即将爆发的地点：*Tension in the city is rapidly reaching flashpoint.* 这座城市处于紧张状态，大有一触即发之势。◇ *potential flashpoints in the south of the country* 该国南部潜在的暴力爆发点

flashy /ˈflæʃi/ *adj.* (**flash·ier**, **flashi·est**) (*informal, usually disapproving*) **1** (of things 物品) attracting attention by being bright, expensive, large, etc. 俗艳的；（因昂贵、巨大等）显眼的：*a flashy hotel* 奢华的旅馆 ◇ *I just want a good reliable car, nothing flashy.* 我只要一辆性能可靠的轿车，不要华而不实的那种。**2** (of people 人) attracting attention by wearing expensive clothes, etc. 穿着奢华的 **3** intended to impress by looking very skilful 炫耀技艺的：*He specializes in flashy technique, without much depth.* 他就会些没有深度的花招。▶ **flash·ily** *adv.*: *flashily dressed* 穿着艳俗的

flask /flɑːsk; *NAmE* flæsk/ *noun* **1** a bottle with a narrow top, used in scientific work for mixing or storing chemicals 烧瓶 ➲ VISUAL VOCAB PAGE V72 **2** (*BrE*) = VACUUM FLASK：*a **flask of tea/coffee*** 一保温瓶的茶 / 咖啡 ➲ COMPARE THERMOS™ **3** (*especially NAmE*) (*also* **'hip flask** *NAmE, BrE*) a small flat bottle made of metal or glass and often covered with leather, used for carrying alcohol 小扁酒瓶（用金属或玻璃制成，常带皮套，随身携带）

flat /flæt/ *adj., noun, adv., verb*

■ *adj.* (**flat·ter**, **flat·test**)
• **LEVEL** 平 **1** having a level surface, not curved or sloping 水平的；平坦的：*low buildings with flat roofs* 平顶矮建筑物 ◇ *People used to think the earth was flat.* 人们曾经认为地球是平的。◇ *Exercise is the only way to get a flat stomach after having a baby.* 产后只有通过锻炼才能使腹部收平。◇ *The sails hung limply in the flat calm* (= conditions at sea when there is no wind and the water is completely level). 风平浪静，风帆无力地垂挂着。**2** (of land 土地) without any slopes or hills 平坦的：*The road stretched ahead across the flat landscape.* 公路向前延伸，

经过一片平坦的地。**3** ⚷ (of surfaces 表面) smooth and even; without lumps or holes 平滑的: *I need a flat surface to write on.* 我需要一个平面在上面写字。◇ *We found a large flat rock to sit on.* 我们找了一块可以坐的大而平滑的石头。

- **NOT HIGH** 不高 **4** ⚷ broad but not very high 扁平的: *Chapattis are a kind of flat Indian bread.* * chapatti 是一种印度薄饼。◇ *flat shoes* (= with no heels or very low ones) 平跟鞋; 平底鞋
- **DULL** 枯燥 **5** dull; lacking interest or enthusiasm 枯燥的; 无趣的; 缺乏热情的: *He felt very flat after his friends had gone home.* 他的朋友们回家后, 他感到兴味索然。
- **VOICE** 嗓音 **6** not showing much emotion; not changing much in tone 平淡的; 单调的: *Her voice was flat and expressionless.* 她的声音平淡而呆板。
- **COLOURS/PICTURES** 颜色; 图画 **7** very smooth, with no contrast between light and dark, and giving no impression of depth 色彩单调的; 无反差的; 无景深的: *Acrylic paints can be used to create large, flat blocks of colour.* 丙烯颜料可用来创作单一色调的大幅图块。
- **BUSINESS** 商业 **8** not very successful because very little is being sold 不景气的; 萧条的; 生意清淡的: *The housing market has been flat for months.* 房屋市场已有好几个月处于低迷状态。
- **REFUSAL/DENIAL** 拒绝; 否认 **9** [only before noun] not allowing discussion or argument; definite 断然的; 绝对的: *Her request was met with a flat refusal.* 她的请求被断然拒绝。◇ *He gave a flat 'No!' to one reporter's question.* 他对一名记者的提问直截了当地答复"不!"
- **IN MUSIC** 音乐 **10** used after the name of a note to mean a note a SEMITONE/HALF STEP lower 降音的; 降半音的: *That note should be B flat, not B.* 那个音应该是降B音, 而不是B音。➲ PICTURE AT MUSIC OPP **sharp** ➲ COMPARE NATURAL *adj.* (9) **11** below the correct PITCH (= how high or low a note sounds) 低于标准音高的; 偏低的: *The high notes were slightly flat.* 这些高音略为偏低。OPP **sharp**
- **DRINK** 饮料 **12** no longer having bubbles in it; not fresh 走了气的; 不新鲜的: *The soda was warm and had gone flat.* 这汽水是温的, 已走了气。
- **BATTERY** 电池 **13** (*BrE*) unable to supply any more electricity 电用完了的
- **TYRE** 轮胎 **14** not containing enough air, usually because of a hole 瘪了的; 撒了气的
- **FEET** 足 **15** with no natural raised curves underneath 扁平的; 足弓平坦的 ➲ SEE ALSO FLAT-FOOTED (1) ➲ MORE LIKE THIS 35, page R29

▸ **flat·ness** *noun* [U]

IDM **and ˌthat's 'flat!** (*BrE, informal*) that is my final decision and I will not change my mind 这就是最后决定: *You can't go and that's flat!* 你不能去, 就这样! **as ˌflat as a 'pancake** completely flat 完全平的 ➲ MORE LIKE THIS 14, page R26 ➲ MORE AT BACK *n.*, SPIN *n.*

■ ***noun***

- **ROOMS** 房间 **1** ⚷ [C] (*BrE*) a set of rooms for living in, including a kitchen, usually on one floor of a building 一套房间; 公寓; 单元房: *Do you live in a flat or a house?* 你住的是公寓还是独立住宅? ◇ *They're renting a **furnished flat** on the third floor.* 他们租了四楼一套带家具的公寓。◇ *a ground-floor flat* 一楼的一套单元房 ◇ *a new **block of flats*** 一栋新建的公寓楼 ◇ *Many large old houses have been converted into flats.* 许多大的老房子已改建成单元房。◇ *Children from the flats* (= the block of flats) *across the street were playing outside.* 街对面公寓楼里的儿童正在户外玩耍。➲ COLLOCATIONS AT HOUSE ➲ VISUAL VOCAB PAGE V16 ➲ COMPARE APARTMENT (1)
- **LEVEL PART** 平面部分 **2** [sing.] **the ~ of sth** the flat level part of sth (某物的) 平面部分: *He beat on the door with the flat of his hand.* 他用手掌打门。◇ *the flat of a sword* 剑面
- **LAND** 土地 **3** [C, usually pl.] an area of low flat land, especially near water (尤指水边的) 平地; 低洼地: *salt flats* 盐滩 ➲ SEE ALSO MUDFLAT
- **HORSE RACING** 赛马 **4 the flat, the Flat** [sing.] (*BrE*) the season for racing horses on flat ground with no jumps 无障碍平地赛马季节
- **IN MUSIC** 音乐 **5** [C] a note played a SEMITONE/HALF STEP lower than the note that is named. The written symbol is (♭). 降半音; 降音; 降号: *There are no sharps or flats in the key of C major.* * C 大调中没有升半音和降半音。OPP **sharp** ➲ COMPARE NATURAL *n.* (2)
- **TYRE** 轮胎 **6** [C] (*especially NAmE*) a tyre that has lost air, usually because of a hole 瘪了的轮胎; 撒了气的轮胎: *We got a flat on the way home.* 我们在回家的路上有一个轮胎漏气瘪了。◇ *We had to stop to fix a flat.* 我们只得停车修一下撒了气的轮胎。
- **IN THEATRE** 剧院 **7** [C] (*specialist*) a vertical section of SCENERY used on a theatre stage 平面布景; 布景屏
- **SHOES** 鞋 **8 flats** (*also* **flat·ties**) [pl.] (*informal*) shoes with a very low heel 平跟鞋; 平底鞋: *a pair of flats* 一双平跟鞋 ➲ VISUAL VOCAB PAGE V69

IDM **on the 'flat** (*BrE*) on level ground, without hills or jumps (= for example in horse racing) 在平地上

■ ***adv.*** (*comparative* **flat·ter**, *no superlative*)

- **LEVEL** 水平地 **1** spread out in a level, straight position, especially against another surface (尤指贴着另一表面) 平直地, 平躺地: *Lie flat and breathe deeply.* 平躺做深呼吸。◇ *They pressed themselves flat against the tunnel wall as the train approached.* 火车接近时他们身体紧贴着隧道壁。
- **REFUSING/DENYING** 拒绝; 否认 **2** (*NAmE also* **ˌflat 'out**) (*informal*) in a definite and direct way 断然; 直截了当地: *She told me flat she would not speak to me again.* 她直截了当地跟我说她再不会理我了。◇ *I made them a reasonable offer but they turned it down flat.* 我向他们提出一个合理报价, 但是他们断然拒绝了。
- **IN MUSIC** 音乐 **3** lower than the correct PITCH (= how high or low a note sounds) 低于标准音高: *He sings flat all the time.* 他总是唱低了音。OPP **sharp**

IDM **fall 'flat** if a joke, a story, or an event **falls flat**, it completely fails to amuse people or to have the effect that was intended (笑话、故事、事件等) 完全失败, 根本未达到预期效果 **fall flat on your 'face 1** to fall so that you are lying on your front 摔趴下 **2** to fail completely, usually causing embarrassment (颜面丢尽地) 彻底失败: *His next television venture fell flat on its face.* 他的下一个电视项目丢人现眼, 彻底失败了。 **flat 'broke** (*BrE also* **stony 'broke**) (*informal*) completely BROKE (= without money) 穷得一个子儿也没有; 一贫如洗; 穷得叮当响 **flat 'out** (*informal*) **1** as fast or as hard as possible 全速; 全力以赴: *Workers are working flat out to meet the rise in demand for new cars.* 为满足对新轿车需求的增加, 工人正全力以赴地工作。**2** (*especially NAmE*) in a definite and direct way; completely 直截了当; 断然: *I told him flat out 'No'.* 我斩钉截铁地告诉他"不"。◇ *It's a 30-year mortgage we just flat out can't handle.* 这是一笔我们根本无法还得起的30年按揭贷款。➲ SEE ALSO FLAT-OUT **in… 'flat** (*informal*) used with an expression of time to say that sth happened or was done very quickly, in no more than the time stated (与表达时间的词语连用, 表示发生或做得很快) 才…, 只用了…, 整: *They changed the wheel in three minutes flat* (= in only three minutes). 他们仅用三分钟就换好了轮胎。

■ ***verb*** (**-tt-**) [I] (*AustralE, NZE*) to live in or share a flat/apartment 住公寓; 合住公寓: *My sister Zoe flats in Auckland.* 我妹妹佐伊住在奥克兰的一栋公寓里。

flat·bed /ˈflætbed/ *noun* **1** (*computing* 计) = FLATBED SCANNER **2** (*also* **ˌflatbed 'truck, ˌflatbed 'trailer**) (*especially NAmE*) an open truck or TRAILER without high sides, used for carrying large objects 平板车; 平板拖车

ˌflatbed 'scanner (*also* **flat'bed**) *noun* (*computing* 计) a SCANNER (= device for copying pictures and documents so that they can be stored on a computer) on which the picture or document can be laid flat for copying 平板扫描仪 ➲ VISUAL VOCAB PAGE V71

flat·bread /ˈflætbred/ *noun* [U, C] a type of flat, thin bread made without any YEAST 无酵饼; 死面薄饼

ˌflat 'cap *noun* (*BrE*) = CLOTH CAP

F

F

flat·car /ˈflætkɑː(r)/ *noun* (*NAmE*) a WAGON (1) on a train without a roof or sides, used for carrying goods（铁路）平车，敞车

ˌflat-ˈchested *adj.* (of a woman 妇女) having small breasts 平胸的；乳房小的

flat·fish /ˈflætfɪʃ/ *noun* (*pl.* **flat·fish**) any sea fish with a flat body, for example a PLAICE 比目鱼（扁平海鱼，如鲽）

ˌflat-ˈfooted *adj.* **1** without naturally raised curves (= ARCHES) under the feet 平足的；扁平足的 **2** (*especially NAmE*) not prepared for what is going to happen 无准备的：*They were **caught flat-footed** by the attack.* 他们冷不防遭到了攻击。

flat·head /ˈflæthed/ *adj.* (of a SCREWDRIVER 螺丝刀) with a straight end rather than a cross-shaped end 平头的；一字头的 ➲ COMPARE PHILLIPS

flat·let /ˈflætlət/ *noun* (*BrE*) a very small flat/apartment 公寓小套间；小套房

flat·line /ˈflætlaɪn/ *verb* (*informal*) **1** [I] to die 死；断气 **2** [I] to be at a low level and fail to improve or increase 处于低潮；没有起色

flat·ly /ˈflætli/ *adv.* **1** in a way that is very definite and will not be changed 断然；斩钉截铁地 SYN **absolutely**: *to flatly deny/reject/oppose sth* 断然否认 / 拒绝 / 反对某事 ◇ *I flatly refused to spend any more time helping him.* 我断然拒绝再花时间帮助他。 **2** in a dull way with very little interest or emotion 枯燥地；无趣地；缺乏热情地：*'Oh, it's you,' she said flatly.* "哦，是你。" 她冷冷地说。

flat·mate /ˈflætmeɪt/ (*BrE*) (*NAmE* **room·mate**) *noun* a person who shares a flat/apartment with one or more others 合住公寓套间者；同公寓房客

ˌflat-ˈout *adj.* [only before noun] (*especially NAmE*) definite and direct; complete 直截了当的；完全的：*His story was full of contradictions and flat-out lies.* 他的话充满矛盾和不折不扣的谎言。▶ **ˌflat-ˈout** *adv.*: *She just flat-out hated me.* 她就是恨透了我。➲ SEE ALSO FLAT OUT at FLAT *adv.* (2)

ˈflat-pack *noun* (*BrE*) a piece of furniture that is sold in pieces in a flat box and that you have to build yourself 平板家具（买主自己拼装）

ˌflat-ˈpanel *adj.* = FLAT-SCREEN

ˈflat racing *noun* [U] the sport of horse racing over flat ground with no jumps 无障碍平地赛马 ➲ COMPARE STEEPLECHASE

ˌflat ˈrate *noun* a price that is the same for everyone and in all situations 统一价格；固定收费率：*Interest is charged at a flat rate of 11%.* 利息按标准比率 11% 收取。

ˌflat-ˈscreen (*also* **ˌflat-ˈpanel**) *adj.* [only before noun] ~ **television/TV/computer/monitor, etc.** a type of television or computer monitor that is very thin when compared with the original type（电视或电脑显示器）平面的，平板的，超薄的 ➲ VISUAL VOCAB PAGE V22

ˌflat ˈspin *noun* (*specialist*) a movement of an aircraft in which it goes gradually downwards while flying around in almost horizontal circles（飞机的）平旋，水平螺旋下降，平面旋转下降

IDM **in a flat ˈspin** very confused, worried or excited 慌乱；惊慌失措；紧张激动

flat·ten /ˈflætn/ *verb* **1** [I, T] to become or make sth become flat or flatter（使）变平；把…弄平：*The cookies will flatten slightly while cooking.* 曲奇饼烤时会略微变平。◇ **~ sth** *These exercises will help to flatten your stomach.* 这些身体锻炼有助你腹部变平。◇ *He flattened his hair down with gel.* 他用发胶把头发弄平。**2** [T] **~ sth** to destroy or knock down a building, tree, etc. 摧毁，推倒，弄倒（建筑物、树木等）： *Most of the factory was flattened by the explosion.* 工厂的大部分被爆炸夷为平地。 **3** [T] **~ sb** (*informal*) to defeat sb easily in a competition, an argument, etc. 轻易击败 SYN **smash, thrash**: *Our team was flattened this evening!* 今晚我们队被打得落花流水！ **4** [T] **~ sb** (*informal*) to hit sb very hard so that they fall down 击倒；打倒：*He flattened the intruder with a single punch.* 他一拳就把闯入者打倒在地。◇ *I'll flatten you if you do that again!* 你要再那样我就把你揍趴下！

PHR V **ˌflatten sth/yourself aˈgainst/ˈon sb/sth** to press sth/your body against sb/sth 使平贴；把…紧贴着：*She flattened her nose against the window and looked in.* 她把鼻子紧贴着窗户朝里瞧。◇ *Greg flattened himself against the wall to let me pass.* 格雷格身体紧靠着墙让我通过。 **ˌflatten ˈout 1** to gradually become completely flat 逐渐变平：*The hills first rose steeply then flattened out towards the sea.* 山峦起初拔地而起，然后逐渐平坦，伸向大海。**2** to stop growing or going up 停止生长；不再长高；停止上升：*Export growth has started to flatten out.* 出口增长已逐渐缓了下来。 **ˌflatten sth↔ˈout** to make sth completely flat 使变平

flat·ter /ˈflætə(r)/ *verb* **1** [T] **~ sb** to say nice things about sb, often in a way that is not sincere, because you want them to do sth for you or you want to please them 奉承；讨好；向…谄媚：*Are you trying to flatter me?* 你是想讨好我？ **2** [T] **~ yourself (that…)** to choose to believe sth good about yourself and your abilities, especially when other people do not share this opinion 自命不凡：*'How will you manage without me?' 'Don't flatter yourself.'* "没有我看你怎么办！" "别自以为了不起。" **3** [T] **~ sb** to make sb seem more attractive or better than they really are 使显得更漂亮；使胜过本人：*That colour doesn't flatter many people.* 那种颜色对很多人都不适宜。◇ *The scoreline flattered England* (= they did not deserve to get such a high score). 英格兰队的最终比分大大超过了其实力。 ▶ **flat·ter·er** /ˈflætərə(r)/ *noun*

IDM **be/feel ˈflattered** to be pleased because sb has made you feel important or special 被奉承得高兴；感到荣幸：*He was flattered by her attention.* 她的关注使他感到格外高兴。◇ *I felt flattered at being asked to give a lecture.* 承蒙邀请来演讲，我深感荣幸。 **ˌflatter to deˈceive** (*BrE*) if sth **flatters to deceive**, it appears to be better, more successful, etc. than it really is 显得比实际好；看似比实际成功

flat·ter·ing /ˈflætərɪŋ/ *adj.* **1** making sb look more attractive 使人显得更漂亮的：*a flattering dress* 穿上去使人更漂亮的连衣裙 **2** saying nice things about sb/sth 奉承的；阿谀的；讨好的：*flattering remarks* 奉承话 **3** making sb feel pleased and special 奉承的；使人感到荣幸的：*I found it flattering that he still recognized me after all these years.* 过了这么多年他还认得我，使我觉得荣幸。

flat·tery /ˈflætəri/ *noun* [U] praise that is not sincere, especially in order to obtain sth from sb 奉承；阿谀；讨好；恭维：*You're too intelligent to fall for his flattery.* 你很聪明，不会受他的阿谀奉承所惑。

IDM **flattery will get you ˈeverywhere/ˈnowhere** (*informal, humorous*) praise that is not sincere will/will not get you what you want 阿谀奉承将会使你如愿以偿（或无济于事）

flat·ties /ˈflætiz/ *noun* [pl.] = FLATS

ˈflat-top *noun* a HAIRSTYLE in which the hair is cut short and flat across the top 平顶头，平头（发型）➲ VISUAL VOCAB PAGE V65

flatu·lence /ˈflætjʊləns; *NAmE* -tʃə-/ *noun* [U] an uncomfortable feeling caused by having too much gas in the stomach （肠胃）气胀

flatu·lent /ˈflætjʊlənt; *NAmE* -tʃə-/ *adj.* **1** (*disapproving*) sounding important and impressive in a way that exaggerates the truth or facts 浮夸的；虚夸的 **2** suffering from too much gas in the stomach 患肠胃气胀的

flat·ware /ˈflætweə(r); *NAmE* -wer/ *noun* [U] (*NAmE*) **1** = SILVERWARE **2** flat dishes such as plates and SAUCERS 扁平餐具（如盘子、茶碟等）

flat·worm /ˈflætwɜːm; *NAmE* -wɜːrm/ *noun* a very simple WORM with a flat body 扁形动物；扁虫

flaunt /flɔːnt/ *verb* (*disapproving*) **1 ~ sth** to show sth you are proud of to other people, in order to impress them

炫耀；夸示；夸耀；卖弄：*He did not believe in flaunting his wealth.* 他不赞成摆阔。◇ *She openly flaunted her affair with the senator.* 她公开夸耀与参议员的恋情。**2 ~ yourself** to behave in a confident and sexual way to attract attention （性感地）招摇过市

IDM if you've ˌgot it, ˈflaunt it (*humorous, saying*) used to tell sb that they should not be afraid of allowing other people to see their qualities and abilities 有什么能耐施展出来瞧瞧

flaut·ist /ˈflɔːtɪst; *NAmE* ˈflaʊtɪst/ (*BrE*) (*NAmE usually* **flut·ist**) *noun* a person who plays the FLUTE 长笛手

fla·von·oid /ˈfleɪvənɔɪd/ *noun* (*chemistry* 化) a type of substance that is found in some plants such as tomatoes, which is thought to protect against some types of cancer and heart disease 黄酮类化合物，类黄酮（存在于西红柿等植物中，据信对某些癌症和心脏病有防治作用）

fla·vour (*especially US* **fla·vor**) /ˈfleɪvə(r)/ *noun, verb*

■ ***noun*** **1** [U] how food or drink tastes （食物或饮料的）味道 **SYN taste**: *The tomatoes **give** extra **flavour** to the sauce.* 番茄使调味汁别有风味。◇ *It is stronger **in flavour** than other Dutch cheeses.* 这比其他荷兰干酪的味道要浓。**2** [C] a particular type of taste （某种）味道：*This yogurt comes in ten different flavours.* 这种酸奶有十种不同的味道。◇ *a wine with a delicate fruit flavour* 有淡淡的水果味的葡萄酒 **3** (*NAmE*) = FLAVOURING **4** [sing.] a particular quality or atmosphere 特点；特色；气氛 **SYN ambience**: *the distinctive flavour of South Florida* 南佛罗里达的独特风情 ◇ *Foreign visitors help to **give a** truly international **flavour** to the occasion.* 外国客人使这个场合显出一种真正国际性的气氛。**5** [sing.] **a/the ~ of sth** an idea of what sth is like 像…的想法：*I have tried to convey something of the flavour of the argument.* 我试图传达某种类似论据的东西。**6** (*computing* 计) a particular type of sth, especially computer software 衍生系统

IDM flavour of the ˈmonth (*especially BrE*) a person or thing that is very popular at a particular time 风靡一时的人（或事物）

■ ***verb*** **~ sth (with sth)** to add sth to food or drink to give it more flavour or a particular flavour 给（食物或饮料）调味；加味于

fla·voured (*especially US* **fla·vored**) /ˈfleɪvəd; *NAmE* -vərd/ *adj.* **1 -flavoured** having the type of flavour mentioned 有…味道的：*lemon-flavoured sweets/candy* 柠檬味糖果 **2** having had flavour added to it 添加了味道的：*flavoured yogurt* 有添加味道的酸奶

fla·vour·ing (*especially US* **fla·vor·ing**) /ˈfleɪvərɪŋ/ (*NAmE also* **fla·vor**) *noun* [U, C] a substance added to food or drink to give it a particular flavour 调味品；调味香料：*orange/vanilla flavouring* 橙 / 香草调味香料 ◇ *This food contains no artificial flavourings.* 这种食品不含人工调味品。

fla·vour·less (*especially US* **fla·vor·less**) /ˈfleɪvələs; *NAmE* -ərləs/ *adj.* having no flavour 无味的；没有味道的：*The meat was tough and flavourless.* 这肉咬不动，又没有滋味。

fla·vour·some /ˈfleɪvəsəm; *NAmE* -vərs-/ (*especially US* **fla·vor·ful** /ˈfleɪvəfʊl; *NAmE* -vərf-/) *adj.* having a lot of flavour 多味的；味道丰富的；很有滋味的

flaw /flɔː/ *noun* **1** a mistake in sth that means that it is not correct or does not work correctly 错误；缺点 **SYN defect, fault**: *The argument is full of fundamental flaws.* 这段论述充满根本性的错误。◇ **~ in sth** *The report reveals **fatal flaws** in security at the airport.* 报告揭示了机场安全的致命缺陷。**2 ~ (in sth)** a crack or fault in sth that makes it less attractive or valuable 裂痕；裂隙；瑕疵 **3 ~ (in sb/sth)** a weakness in sb's character （性格上的）弱点，缺点：*There is always a flaw in the character of a tragic hero.* 悲剧主角总有性格上的缺点。

flawed /flɔːd/ *adj.* having a flaw; damaged or spoiled 有错误的；有缺点的；有瑕疵的：***seriously/fundamentally/fatally flawed*** 有严重 / 根本 / 致命缺点 ◇ *a flawed argument* 有错误的论点 ◇ *the book's flawed heroine* 书中有弱点的女主角

flaw·less /ˈflɔːləs/ *adj.* without FLAWS and therefore perfect 完美的；无瑕的 **SYN perfect**: *a flawless complexion/performance* 无瑕疵的面容；完美的表演 ◇ *Her English is almost flawless.* 她的英语几乎无可挑剔。▶ **flaw·less·ly** *adv.*

flax /flæks/ *noun* [U] **1** a plant with blue flowers, grown for its STEM that is used to make thread and its seeds that are used to make LINSEED OIL 亚麻 **2** threads from the STEM of the flax plant, used to make LINEN 亚麻纤维

flax·en /ˈflæksn/ *adj.* (*literary*) (of hair 毛发) pale yellow 浅黄色的；亚麻色的 **SYN blonde**

flax·seed /ˈflækssiːd/ *noun* [U, C] the seeds of the flax plant, eaten as a health food or used to make LINSEED OIL 亚麻籽

ˈflaxseed oil *noun* [U] = LINSEED OIL

flay /fleɪ/ *verb* **1 ~ sth/sb** to remove the skin from an animal or person, usually when they are dead 剥（死人或动物的皮）**2 ~ sb** to hit or WHIP sb very hard so that some of their skin comes off 毒打，狠狠鞭打（直至皮开肉绽）**3 ~ sb/yourself** (*formal*) to criticize sb/yourself severely 严厉批评

flea /fliː/ *noun* a very small jumping insect without wings, that bites animals and humans and sucks their blood 蚤：*The dog has fleas.* 这条狗有跳蚤。➲ VISUAL VOCAB PAGE V13

IDM with a ˈflea in your ear if sb sends a person away **with a flea in their ear**, they tell them angrily to go away 以气愤的言语，以责难（把人轰走）

flea·bag /ˈfliːbæg/ *noun* (*informal*) **1** a person who looks poor and does not take care of their appearance 邋遢的人 **2** an animal that is in poor condition 肮脏的动物 **3** (*especially NAmE*) a hotel that is cheap and dirty 廉价低级旅馆

ˈflea-bitten *adj.* (*informal*) in poor condition and with an unpleasant appearance 邋遢的

ˈflea market *noun* an outdoor market that sells SECOND-HAND (= old or used) goods at low prices 跳蚤市场（廉价出售旧物的露天市场）

flea·pit /ˈfliːpɪt/ *noun* (*old-fashioned, BrE, informal*) an old and dirty cinema or theatre 破旧肮脏的电影院（或剧院）

fleck /flek/ *noun, verb*

■ ***noun*** [usually pl.] **~ (of sth)** **1** a very small area of a particular colour 色斑；斑点：*His hair was dark, with flecks of grey.* 他的黑发间有缕缕银丝。➲ WORDFINDER NOTE AT PATTERN **2** a very small piece of sth 微粒；小片：*flecks of dust/foam/dandruff* 灰尘微粒；泡沫；头皮屑

■ ***verb*** [usually passive] **~ sth (with sth)** to cover or mark sth with small areas of a particular colour or with small pieces of sth 使有斑点；使斑驳：*The fabric was red, flecked with gold.* 织物是红色的，带有金黄色的斑点。◇ *His hair was flecked with paint.* 他的头发上粘有点点油漆。

flec·tion = FLEXION

fled PAST TENSE, PAST PART. OF FLEE

fledged /fledʒd/ *adj.* (of birds 鸟) able to fly 能飞翔的；羽翼已丰的 ➲ SEE ALSO FULLY FLEDGED

fledg·ling (*BrE also* **fledge·ling**) /ˈfledʒlɪŋ/ *noun* **1** a young bird that has just learnt to fly （刚会飞的）幼鸟 **2** (usually before another noun 通常置于另一名词前) a person, an organization or a system that is new and without experience 初出茅庐的人；无经验的组织；新体系：*fledgling democracies* 新兴的民主国家

flee /fliː/ *verb* (**fled**, **fled** /fled/) [I, T, no passive] to leave a person or place very quickly, especially because you are afraid of possible danger 迅速离开；（尤指害怕有危险而）逃避，逃跑：*She burst into tears and fled.* 她突然哭了起来，跑开了。◇ **~ from sb/sth** *a camp for refugees fleeing from the war* 收留战争难民的难民营 ◇ **~ to.../into...**

He fled to London after an argument with his family. 他与家人争吵以后离家去了伦敦。◇ **~ sth** *He was caught trying to flee the country.* 他试图逃离该国时被抓住了。➲ COMPARE FLY *v.* (13)

fleece /fliːs/ *noun, verb*
▪**noun** **1** [C] the wool coat of a sheep; this coat when it has been removed from a sheep (by SHEARING) 羊毛；（一只羊一次剪下的）毛 **2** [U, C] a type of soft warm cloth that feels like sheep's wool; a jacket or SWEATSHIRT that is made from this cloth 羊毛状织物；绒头织物短上衣；绒头织物运动衫：*a fleece lining* 绒头织物衬里 ◇ *a bright red fleece* 鲜红的绒头织物
▪**verb** **~ sb** (*informal*) to take a lot of money from sb by charging them too much 敲诈；敲竹杠：*Some local shops have been fleecing tourists.* 当地有些商店一直在敲游客的竹杠。

fleecy /ˈfliːsi/ *adj.* [usually before noun] made of soft material, like the wool coat of a sheep; looking like this 软如羊毛的；羊毛似的：*a fleecy sweatshirt* 绒毛长袖运动衫 ◇ *a blue sky with fleecy clouds* 飘浮着朵朵白云的蓝色天空

fleet /fliːt/ *noun, adj.*
▪**noun** **1** [C] a group of military ships commanded by the same person 舰队 ➲ WORDFINDER NOTE AT NAVY **2** [C] a group of ships fishing together 捕鱼船队：*a **fishing/whaling fleet*** 捕鱼 / 捕鲸船队 **3 the fleet** [sing.] all the military ships of a particular country（一国的）全部军舰，海军：*a reduction in the size of the British fleet* 英国海军的裁减 **4** [C] **~ (of sth)** a group of planes, buses, taxis, etc. travelling together or owned by the same organization（同一机构或统一调度的）机群，车队：*the company's new fleet of vans* 公司的新客货车队
▪**adj.** (*literary*) able to run fast 跑得快的；快速的：*fleet of foot* 跑得快 ◇ *fleet-footed* 跑得快

ˌ**Fleet ˈAdmiral** (*US*) (*BrE* ˌ**Admiral of the ˈFleet**) *noun* an admiral of the highest rank in the navy（英国）海军元帅；（美国）海军五星上将：*Fleet Admiral William Hunter* 海军五星上将威廉·亨特

fleet·ing /ˈfliːtɪŋ/ *adj.* [usually before noun] lasting only a short time 短暂的；闪现的 SYN **brief**：*a **fleeting glimpse/smile*** 短暂的一瞥；一闪即逝的微笑 ◇ *a **fleeting moment** of happiness* 转瞬即逝的幸福时刻 ◇ *We paid a **fleeting visit** to Paris.* 我们短暂游览了巴黎。▶ **fleet·ing·ly** *adv.*

ˈ**Fleet Street** *noun* [U] a street in central London where many national newspapers used to have their offices (now used to mean British newspapers and journalists in general) 舰队街，弗利特街（位于伦敦中心的一条街道，曾是全国性大报社所在地）；（统称）英国报界，英国新闻界

Flem·ish /ˈflemɪʃ/ *noun* [U] the Dutch language as spoken in northern Belgium 佛兰芒语（比利时北部的荷兰语）

flesh 🔑 /fleʃ/ *noun, verb*
▪**noun** **1** 🔑 [U] the soft substance between the skin and bones of animal or human bodies（动物或人的）肉：*The trap had cut deeply into the rabbit's flesh.* 捕夹深深嵌入了兔子的肉里。◇ *Tigers are **flesh-eating** animals.* 虎是食肉动物。◇ *the smell of rotting flesh* 腐肉的气味 **2** [U] the skin of the human body（人体的）皮肤：*His fingers closed around the soft flesh of her arm.* 他握住了她柔软的手臂。◇ ***flesh-coloured*** (= a light brownish pink colour) 肉色的 **3** 🔑 [U] the soft part of fruit and vegetables, especially when it is eaten 蔬菜的可食部分；果肉 ➲ VISUAL VOCAB PAGES V32-33 **4 the flesh** [sing.] (*literary*) the human body when considering its physical and sexual needs, rather than the mind or soul 肉体；肉欲；情欲：*the pleasures/sins of the flesh* 肌肤之乐；肉欲之罪
IDM ˌ**flesh and ˈblood** when you say that sb is **flesh and blood**, you mean that they are a normal human with needs, emotions and weaknesses 血肉之躯（有常人的需要、感情和缺点）：*Listening to the cries was more than flesh and blood could stand.* 听这种哭喊非常人所能忍受。**your** (ˌ**own**) ˌ**flesh and ˈblood** a person that you are related to 亲骨肉；亲人 **in the ˈflesh** if you see sb **in the flesh**, you are in the same place as them and actually see them rather than just seeing a picture of them 活生生地；亲自；本人 **make your ˈflesh creep** to make you feel afraid or full of disgust 使起鸡皮疙瘩；令人毛骨悚然；使人十分厌恶 **put flesh on** (**the bones of**) **sth** to develop a basic idea, etc. by giving more details to make it more complete 充实；加细节于：*The strength of the book is that it puts flesh on the bare bones of this argument.* 本书的优点是对这个论点的基本事实有翔实的论述。➲ MORE AT POUND *n.*, PRESS *v.*, SPIRIT *n.*, THORN, WAY *n.*
▪**verb**
PHR V ˌ**flesh sth**↔ˈ**out** to add more information or details to a plan, an argument, etc. 充实（计划、论据等的内容）：*These points were fleshed out in the later parts of the speech.* 这几点在演讲的后面部分得到了充实。

flesh·ly /ˈfleʃli/ *adj.* [only before noun] (*literary*) connected with physical and sexual desires 肉欲的；性欲的：***fleshly temptations/pleasures*** 情欲的诱惑；性快感

flesh·pots /ˈfleʃpɒts; *NAmE* -pɑːts/ *noun* [pl.] (*humorous*) places supplying food, drink and sexual entertainment 满足肉欲的场所，红灯区（指提供饮食及性娱乐的场所）

ˈ**flesh wound** *noun* an injury in which the skin is cut but the bones and organs inside the body are not damaged 皮肉之伤（指未伤及骨头和器官）

fleshy /ˈfleʃi/ *adj.* **1** (of parts of the body or people 人体部位或人) having a lot of flesh 多肉的；肥胖的：*fleshy arms/lips* 肥胖的胳膊；厚嘴唇 ◇ *a large fleshy man* 大个子胖男人 **2** (of plants or fruit 植物或水果) thick and soft 肉质的：***fleshy fruit/leaves*** 肉质水果 / 叶子

fleur-de-lis (*also* **fleur-de-lys**) /ˌflɜː də ˈliː; ˈliːs; *NAmE* ˌflɜːr/ *noun* (*pl.* **fleurs-de-lis** or **fleurs-de-lys** /ˌflɜː də ˈliː; ˈliːs; *NAmE* ˌflɜːr/) (*from French*) a design representing a flower with three PETALS joined together at the bottom, often used in COATS OF ARMS 鸢尾花饰，百合花饰（常用作纹章）

flew PAST TENSE OF FLY

flex /fleks/ *verb, noun*
▪**verb** [T, I] **~ (sth)** to bend, move or stretch an arm or a leg, or contract a muscle, especially in order to prepare for a physical activity 屈伸，活动（四肢或肌肉，尤指为准备体力活动）：*to flex your fingers/feet/legs* 活动手指 / 双脚 / 双腿 ◇ *He stood on the side of the pool flexing his muscles.* 他站在游泳池旁活动肌肉。
IDM **flex your ˈmuscles** to show sb how powerful you are, especially as a warning or threat 显示实力，炫耀力量（尤指作为警告或威胁）
▪**noun** (*BrE*) (*also* **cord** *NAmE, BrE*) [C, U] a piece of wire that is covered with plastic, used for carrying electricity to a piece of equipment 花线；皮线：*an electric flex* 一根导电花线 ◇ *a length of flex* 一段花线 ➲ PICTURE AT CORD

flex·ible AW /ˈfleksəbl/ *adj.* **1** (*approving*) able to change to suit new conditions or situations 能适应新情况的；灵活的；可变动的：*a more **flexible approach*** 更灵活的方法 ◇ *flexible working hours* 弹性工作时间 ◇ *Our plans need to be flexible enough to cater for the needs of everyone.* 我们的计划必须足够变通，以满足每个人的需要。◇ *You need to be more flexible and imaginative in your approach.* 你的方法必须更加灵活，更富有想象力。**2** able to bend easily without breaking 柔韧的；可弯曲的；有弹性的：*flexible plastic tubing* 挠性塑料管 OPP **inflexible** ▶ **flexi·bil·ity** AW /ˌfleksəˈbɪləti/ *noun* [U]：*Computers offer a much greater degree of flexibility in the way work is organized.* 利用计算机，工作安排可以灵活得多。◇ *exercises to develop the flexibility of dancers' bodies* 增加跳舞者身体柔软度的训练动作 **flex·ibly** *adv.*

flex·ion (*also* **flec·tion**) /ˈflekʃn/ *noun* [U] the action of bending sth 弯曲；屈曲

flexi·time /ˈfleksitaɪm/ (*especially BrE*) (*NAmE usually* **flex·time** /ˈflekstaɪm/) *noun* [U] a system in which employees work a particular number of hours each week or month but can choose when they start and finish work each day 弹性工作时间制：*She works flexitime.* 她的上班时间是弹性的。

flex·or /ˈfleksə(r); *NAmE also* ˈfleksɔːr/ (*also* ˈ**flexor muscle**) *noun* (*anatomy* 解) a muscle that allows you to bend part of your body 屈肌 ➲ COMPARE EXTENSOR

flib·ber·ti·gib·bet /ˈflɪbətidʒɪbɪt; ˌflɪbətiˈdʒɪbɪt; *NAmE* -bər-/ *noun* (*informal*) a person who is not serious enough or talks a lot about silly things 轻浮的人；饶舌的人

flick /flɪk/ *verb, noun*

■ ***verb*** **1** [T] **~ sth + adv./prep.** to hit sth with a sudden quick movement, especially using your finger and thumb together, or your hand（尤指用手指或手快速地）轻击，轻拍，轻拂，轻弹：*She flicked the dust off her collar.* 她轻轻弹掉了衣领上的灰尘。◇ *The horse was flicking flies away with its tail.* 马轻轻甩动尾巴把苍蝇赶走。◇ *James flicked a peanut at her.* 詹姆斯朝她轻轻弹一颗花生。◇ *Please don't flick ash on the carpet!* 请勿把烟灰弹在地毯上！**2** [I, T] to move or make sth move with sudden quick movements（使）突然快速移动：**+ adv./prep.** *The snake's tongue flicked out.* 蛇伸吐着芯子。◇ *Her eyes flicked from face to face.* 她的眼光扫过人们的脸。◇ **~ sth (+ adv./prep.)** *He lifted his head, flicking his hair off his face.* 他抬起头，拂开了脸上的头发。◇ *The horse moved off, flicking its tail.* 马甩着尾巴走开了。**3** [T] to smile or look at sb suddenly and quickly 向…笑了一下（或瞥了一眼等）：**~ a smile/look, etc. at sb** *She flicked a nervous glance at him.* 她紧张不安地瞟了他一眼。◇ **~ sb a smile/look, etc.** *She flicked him a nervous glance.* 她紧张不安地瞟了他一眼。**4** [T] to press a button or switch quickly in order to turn a machine, etc. on or off（快速地）按（开关），按（键）**SYN flip**：**~ sth** *He flicked a switch and all the lights went out.* 他啪的一声按了下开关，灯全熄了。◇ **~ sth on/off** *She flicked the TV on.* 她轻轻一按打开了电视机。**5** [T] to move sth up and down with a sudden movement so that the end of it hits sth（用…）轻挥，轻打：**~ A (with B)** *He flicked me with a wet towel.* 他用湿毛巾轻打我。◇ **~ B (at A)** *He flicked a wet towel at me.* 他用湿毛巾轻打我。◇ *to flick a whip* 用鞭子抽打 **6** [I, T] **~ (sth)** to move your finger quickly across the screen of an electronic device such as a mobile/cell phone or small computer in order to move text, pictures, etc.（用手指在手机等电子装置屏幕上）快速滑动，快速滑屏：*Flick to the next photo and pinch to zoom in or out.* 滑屏至下一张照片，然后两指开合将照片放大或缩小。◇ *She flicked the screen and searched through her emails.* 她手指在屏幕上快速滑动着查看电邮。➲ COMPARE PINCH *v.* (3), SWIPE *v.* (4), TAP *v.* (1)

PHR V ˌ**flick ˈthrough sth** (*especially BrE*) **1** to turn the pages of a book, etc. quickly and look at them without reading everything 浏览；草草翻阅 **SYN flip through**：*I've only had time to flick through your report but it seems to be fine.* 我的时间不多，只是草草翻阅了一下你的报告，但似乎还不错。**2** to keep changing television channels quickly to see what programmes are on 快速浏览，不停地变换（电视频道）**SYN flip through**：*Flicking through the channels, I came across an old war movie.* 我快速浏览电视频道，发现有一部老的战争片在播放。

■ ***noun*** **1** [C, usually sing.] a small sudden, quick movement or hit, for example with a WHIP or part of the body（用鞭子等的）轻打；（身体部位的）小而快的动作：*Bell's flick into the penalty area helped to create the goal.* 贝尔迅速插进禁区助攻，创造了这次进球的机会。◇ *All this information is available **at the flick of a switch*** (= by simply turning on a machine). 这所有的信息只需按一下开关便可获得。◇ *He threw the ball back with a quick **flick of the wrist**.* 他手腕一抖把球传了回来。**2** [sing.] **a ~ through sth** a quick look through the pages of a book, magazine, etc. 浏览；草草翻阅 **SYN flip**：*I had a flick through the catalogue while I was waiting.* 我等待时浏览了目录。**3** [C] (*old-fashioned, informal*) a film/movie 电影 **4 the flicks** [pl.] (*old-fashioned, BrE, informal*) the cinema 电影院

flicker /ˈflɪkə(r)/ *verb, noun*

■ ***verb*** **1** [I] (of a light or a flame 灯光或火焰) to keep going on and off as it shines or burns 闪烁；闪现；忽隐忽现；摇曳：*The lights flickered and went out.* 灯光闪了闪就熄了。◇ *the flickering screen of the television* 图像在抖动的电视荧光屏 **2** [I] **+ adv./prep.** (of an emotion, a thought, etc. 情绪、思想等) to be expressed or appear somewhere for a short time 闪现；一闪而过：*Anger flickered in his eyes.* 他眼中闪现出一股怒火。**3** [I] to move with small quick movements 快速摆动；颤动；抖动；拍动：*Her eyelids flickered as she slept.* 她睡觉时眼睑不停地抖动。

■ ***noun*** [usually sing.] **~ (of sth) 1** a light that shines in an unsteady way（光）摇曳，闪烁，忽隐忽现：*the flicker of a television/candle* 电视画面的闪动；烛光的摇曳 **2** a small, sudden movement with part of the body（身体部位的）小而快的动作：*the flicker of an eyelid* 眼睑的跳动 **3** a feeling or an emotion that lasts for only a very short time（情感、情绪的）闪现，一闪而过：*a **flicker of hope/doubt/interest*** 希望 / 怀疑 / 兴趣的闪现 ◇ *A flicker of a smile crossed her face.* 她脸上闪过一丝微笑。

ˈ**flick knife** (*BrE*) (*also* **switch·blade** *NAmE, BrE*) *noun* a knife with a blade inside the handle that jumps out quickly when a button is pressed 弹簧刀

flier *noun* = FLYER

flies /flaɪz/ *noun* [pl.] **1** PL. OF FLY **2** (*BrE*) = FLY (3) **3 the flies** the space above the stage in a theatre, used for lights and for storing SCENERY（舞台上方）悬吊布景的空间，吊景区

flight 🔑 /flaɪt/ *noun, verb*

■ ***noun***

• **JOURNEY BY AIR** 空中航行 **1** 🔑 [C] a journey made by air, especially in a plane（尤指乘飞机的）空中航行，航程：*a **smooth/comfortable/bumpy flight*** 平稳 / 舒适 / 颠簸的空中航行 ◇ ***a domestic/an international flight*** 国内 / 国际航班 ◇ *a hot-air balloon flight* 热气球航行 ◇ *We met on a flight from London to Paris.* 我们在从伦敦到巴黎的飞行途中相遇。➲ SEE ALSO IN-FLIGHT

• **PLANE** 飞机 **2** 🔑 [C] a plane making a particular journey 航班飞机；班机：*We're booked on the same flight.* 我们订了同一班机的机票。◇ *Flight BA 4793 is now boarding at Gate 17.* * BA 4793 航班现在正在 17 号登机口登机。◇ *If we leave now, I can catch the earlier flight.* 我们要是现在动身，我就可以赶上早一点的航班。◇ ***mercy/relief flights*** (= planes taking help to countries where there is a war) 急救 / 救援班机（运送救援物资至发生战争的国家）➲ COLLOCATIONS AT TRAVEL

• **FLYING** 飞 **3** 🔑 [U] the act of flying 飞行；飞翔：*the age of supersonic flight* 超声速飞行时代 ◇ *flight safety* 飞行安全 ◇ *The bird is easily recognized **in flight*** (= when it is flying) *by the black band at the end of its tail.* 这种鸟尾部末端有一条黑带，飞翔时很容易认出来。

• **MOVEMENT OF OBJECT** 物体的运动 **4** [U] the movement or direction of an object as it travels through the air（物体的）飞行，飞行方向：*the flight of a ball* 球的飞行

• **OF STEPS** 台阶 **5** [C] a series of steps between two floors or levels 一段楼梯；一段阶梯：*She fell down **a flight of stairs/steps** and hurt her back.* 她从一段楼梯上跌了下来，摔伤了背。

• **RUNNING AWAY** 逃走 **6** [U, sing.] the act of running away from a dangerous or difficult situation（从危险或困境中的）逃避，躲避：*the flight of refugees from the advancing forces* 难民躲避挺进的军队 ◇ *The main character is a journalist in flight from a failed marriage.* 主角是一个逃避失败婚姻的记者。

• **OF FANCY/IMAGINATION** 幻想；想象 **7** [C] **~ of fancy/imagination** an idea or a statement that shows a lot of imagination but is not practical or sensible 异想天开；奇思怪想

• **GROUP OF BIRDS/AIRCRAFT** 鸟群；机群 **8** [C] a group of birds or aircraft flying together（一起飞行的）鸟群（或机群）：*a flight of geese* 一队飞雁 ◇ *an aircraft of the Queen's flight* 女王专机机队中的一架飞机

IDM in the first/top ˈflight among the best of a particular group 名列前茅；佼佼者 ➲ SEE ALSO TOP-FLIGHT **put sb to ˈflight** (*old-fashioned*) to force sb to run away 迫使逃窜 **take ˈflight** to run away 逃走：*The gang took flight when they heard the police car.* 这伙歹徒听见警车声就逃走了。

■ ***verb*** [usually passive] **~ sth** (*BrE, sport* 体育) to kick, hit or throw a ball through the air in a skilful way（熟练地踢、击或掷）使（球）在空中飞行：*He equalized with a beautifully flighted shot.* 他漂亮一击把比分扳平。

F

'flight attendant *noun* a person whose job is to serve and take care of passengers on an aircraft（客机的）乘务员；空乘人员

'flight crew *noun* [C+sing./pl. v.] the people who work on a plane during a flight（统称）机组人员

'flight deck *noun* **1** an area at the front of a large plane where the pilot sits to use the controls and fly the plane（飞机的）驾驶舱 ➲ VISUAL VOCAB PAGE V57 **2** a long flat surface on top of a ship that carries aircraft (= an AIRCRAFT CARRIER) where they take off and land（航空母舰上的）飞行甲板

'flight jacket (*US*) (*BrE* **'flying jacket**) *noun* a short leather jacket with a warm LINING and COLLAR, originally worn by pilots 飞行夹克；翻领皮夹克

flight·less /ˈflaɪtləs/ *adj.* [usually before noun] (of birds or insects 鸟或昆虫) unable to fly 不能飞的

,flight lieu'tenant *noun* (*abbr.* **Flt. Lt.**) an officer of fairly high rank in the British AIR FORCE（英国空军）上尉：*Flight Lieutenant Richard Clarkson* 理查德·克拉克森空军上尉

'flight path *noun* the route taken by an aircraft through the air（飞机的）飞行路径，航迹 ➲ WORDFINDER NOTE AT PLANE

'flight recorder *noun* = BLACK BOX (1)

'flight sergeant *noun* a member of the British AIR FORCE, just below the rank of an officer（英国空军）上士：*Flight Sergeant Bob Andrews* 鲍勃·安德鲁斯空军上士

'flight simulator *noun* a device that reproduces the conditions that exist when flying an aircraft, used for training pilots 飞行模拟器；飞行练习器

flighty /ˈflaɪti/ *adj.* (*informal*) a **flighty** woman is one who cannot be relied on because she is always changing activities, ideas and partners without treating them seriously（女子）反复无常的，轻浮的

flim·flam /ˈflɪmflæm/ *noun* [U] (*old-fashioned, informal*) nonsense 废话；无聊话

flimsy /ˈflɪmzi/ *adj.* (**flim·sier**, **flim·si·est**) **1** badly made and not strong enough for the purpose for which it is used 劣质的；不结实的 SYN **rickety**: *a flimsy table* 不结实的桌子 **2** (of material 材料) thin and easily torn 薄而易损坏的：*a flimsy piece of paper/fabric/plastic* 薄薄的一张纸 / 一块织物 / 一片塑料 **3** difficult to believe 不足信的 SYN **feeble**: *a flimsy excuse/explanation* 站不住脚的借口 / 解释 ◇ *The evidence against him is pretty flimsy.* 对他不利的证据很难站住脚。▶ **flim·sily** *adv.* **flim·si·ness** *noun* [U]

flinch /flɪntʃ/ *verb* [I] to make a sudden movement with your face or body as a result of pain, fear, surprise, etc.（突然）退缩；畏缩：*He met my gaze without flinching.* 他毫不畏缩，跟我对视着。◇ **~ at sth** *He flinched at the sight of the blood.* 他一见到血就往后退。◇ **~ away** *She flinched away from the dog.* 她一下子避开了那条狗。➲ SEE ALSO UNFLINCHING

PHR V **'flinch from sth | 'flinch from doing sth** (often used in negative sentences 常用于否定句) to avoid thinking about or doing sth unpleasant 不想，不做（不愉快的事）；畏缩不前：*He never flinched from facing up to trouble.* 他敢于面对困难，从不退缩。

fling /flɪŋ/ *verb, noun*

■ *verb* (**flung**, **flung** /flʌŋ/) **1 ~ sb/sth + adv./prep.** to throw sb/sth somewhere with force, especially because you are angry（尤指生气地）扔，掷，抛，丢 SYN **hurl**: *Someone had flung a brick through the window.* 有人把一块砖扔进了窗户。◇ *He flung her to the ground.* 他把她推倒在地。◇ *The door was suddenly flung open.* 门突然被推开了。◇ *He had his enemies flung into prison.* 他把敌人投进了监狱。➲ SYNONYMS AT THROW **2 ~ yourself/sth + adv./prep.** to move yourself or part of your body suddenly and with a lot of force 猛动（身体或身体部位）：*She flung herself onto the bed.* 她扑倒在床上。◇ *He flung out an arm to stop her from falling.* 他猛伸手臂扶她，阻止她跌倒。**3 ~ sth (at sb) | + speech** to say sth to sb in an aggressive way 粗暴地（向某人）说；气势汹汹地（对某人）说 SYN **hurl**: *They were flinging insults at each other.* 他们互相辱骂。➲ SEE ALSO FAR-FLUNG

PHR V **'fling yourself at sb** (*informal, disapproving*) to make it too obvious to sb that you want to have a sexual relationship with them（太露骨地）向某人求爱；向（异性）献殷勤 **'fling yourself into sth** to start to do sth with a lot of energy and enthusiasm 投身于；一心扑在…上：*They flung themselves into the preparations for the party.* 他们一心一意地准备聚会。**,fling sth↔'off/'on** (*informal*) to take off or put on clothing in a quick and careless way 匆匆脱下（或穿上）：*He flung off his coat and collapsed on the sofa.* 他随手脱掉大衣，倒在沙发上。**,fling sb↔'out** (*BrE, informal*) to make sb leave a place suddenly 逐出；开除 SYN **throw sb↔out (of...)** **,fling sth↔'out** (*BrE, informal*) to get rid of sth that you do not want any longer 扔掉；丢掉 SYN **throw sth↔out**

■ *noun* [usually sing.] (*informal*) **1** a short period of enjoyment when you do not allow yourself to worry or think seriously about anything 一阵尽情欢乐；一时的放纵：*He was determined to have one last fling before retiring.* 他决心在退休前最后痛痛快快地玩乐一番。**2 ~ (with sb)** a short sexual relationship with sb 短暂的风流韵事 ➲ SEE ALSO HIGHLAND FLING

flint /flɪnt/ *noun* **1** [U, C] a type of very hard grey stone that can produce a SPARK when it is hit against steel 燧石；火石：*prehistoric flint implements* 史前燧石工具 ◇ *His eyes were as hard as flint.* 他的眼神冷酷无情。**2** [C] a piece of flint or hard metal that is used to produce a SPARK 打火石

flint·lock /ˈflɪntlɒk; *NAmE* -lɑːk/ *noun* a gun used in the past that produced a SPARK from a flint when the TRIGGER was pressed（旧时的）燧发机，明火枪

flinty /ˈflɪnti/ *adj.* **1** showing no emotion 冷冷的：*a flinty look/gaze/stare* 冷冷的目光 / 凝视 / 盯视 **2** containing flint 含燧石的：*flinty pebbles/soils* 含燧石的卵石 / 土壤

flip /flɪp/ *verb, noun, adj.*

■ *verb* (**-pp-**) **1** [I, T] to turn over into a different position with a sudden quick movement; to make sth do this（使）快速翻转，迅速翻动：*The plane flipped and crashed.* 飞机猛地翻转，撞毁了。◇ (*figurative*) *She felt her heart flip* (= with excitement, etc.). 她感到心潮澎湃。◇ **~ sth (+ adj.)** *He flipped the lid open and looked inside the case.* 他猛然开盖，朝箱里看。➲ SEE ALSO FLIP OVER at FLIP **2** [T] to press a button or switch in order to turn a machine, etc. on or off 按（开关）；按（按钮）；开（或关）（机器等）SYN **flick**: **~ sth** *to flip a switch* 按开关 ◇ **~ sth on/off** *She reached over and flipped off the light.* 她伸过手去关掉了灯。**3** [T] to throw sth somewhere using your thumb and/or fingers（用手指）轻抛，轻掷 SYN **toss**: **~ a coin** *They flipped a coin to decide who would get the ticket.* 他们掷硬币决定谁得这张票。◇ **~ sth + adv./prep.** *He flipped the keys onto the desk.* 他把钥匙轻抛到桌上。**4** [I] **~ (out)** (*informal*) to become very angry, excited or unable to think clearly 十分气愤；异常激动；神志不清：*She finally flipped under the pressure.* 她在这种压力下终于发疯了。

IDM **,flip your 'lid** (*informal*) to become very angry and lose control of what you are saying or doing 发火；气得丧失自制力；气得发疯

PHR V **,flip 'over** to turn onto the other side or upside down 翻倒；翻转：*The car hit a tree and flipped over.* 汽车撞上一棵树，翻倒了。◇ *He flipped over and sat up.* 他翻了一个身坐了起来。**,flip sth↔'over** to turn sth onto the other side or upside down 使翻倒；使翻转：*The wind flipped over several cars.* 大风吹翻了几辆汽车。**'flip through sth** **1** to turn the pages of a book, etc. quickly and look at them without reading everything 浏览；草草翻阅 SYN **flick through**: *She flipped through the magazine looking for the letters page.* 她浏览杂志寻找读者来信页。**2** (*especially NAmE*) to keep changing television channels quickly to see what shows are on 不断转换（电视频道）

SYN **flick through**: *Flipping through the channels, I came across an old war movie.* 我不停地转换电视频道，偶然发现了一部旧战争片。

■ **noun 1** [C] a small quick hit with a part of the body that causes sth to turn over 轻抛；捻掷：*The whole thing was decided on the **flip of a coin**.* 整个事情都是由掷硬币决定的。**2** [C] a movement in which the body turns over in the air 空翻 SYN **somersault**: *The handstand was followed by a back flip.* 先倒立，接着后空翻。◇ (*figurative*) *Her heart did a flip.* 她心里咯噔了一下子。**3** [sing.] ~ **through sth** a quick look through the pages of a book, magazine, etc. 浏览；草草翻阅 SYN **flick**: *I had a quick flip through the report while I was waiting.* 我等待时迅速浏览了一下报告。

■ **adj.** (*informal*) = FLIPPANT : *a **flip answer/comment*** 轻率的答复；轻浮的话 ◇ *Don't be flip with me.* 不要对我油嘴滑舌。

'flip chart *noun* large sheets of paper fixed at the top to a stand so that they can be turned over, used for presenting information at a talk or meeting 活动挂图；翻页式展示图 ➲ VISUAL VOCAB PAGE V71

'flip-flop *noun, verb*

■ **noun** (*NAmE also* **thong**) a type of SANDAL (= open shoe) that has a piece of leather, etc. that goes between the big toe and the toe next to it 人字拖鞋；夹脚趾拖鞋：*a pair of flip-flops* 一双人字拖鞋 ➲ VISUAL VOCAB PAGE V69

■ **verb** (**-pp-**) [I] ~ (**on sth**) (*informal, especially NAmE*) to change your opinion about sth, especially when you then hold the opposite opinion 改变观点；（尤指）转持相反观点，来一个 180 度的大转弯：*The vice-president was accused of flip-flopping on several major issues.* 副总统受到谴责，说他在几个重大问题上出尔反尔。

'flip-flopper *noun* (*informal, especially NAmE*) a person, especially a politician, who suddenly changes his or her opinion or policy 出尔反尔的人（尤指政客） ➲ SEE ALSO U-TURN

flip·pant /ˈflɪpənt/ (*also informal* **flip**) *adj.* showing that you do not take sth as seriously as other people think you should 轻率的：*a **flippant answer/attitude*** 轻率的回答；轻浮的态度 ◇ *Sorry, I didn't mean to sound flippant.* 对不起，我并不是故意油嘴滑舌的。 ▶ **flip·pancy** /-ənsi/ *noun* [U] **flip·pant·ly** *adv.*

flipped 'classroom *noun* [C, usually sing.] (*also* **flip 'teaching** [U]) a method of teaching in which students study new material at home, for example with videos or over the Internet, and then discuss and practise it with teachers in class, instead of the usual method where teachers present new material in school and students practise at home 翻转课堂，翻转式教学（与通常的教学过程相反，学生在家利用视频或互联网等学习新教材，然后在课堂上跟老师讨论和练习） ➲ SEE ALSO BLENDED LEARNING

flip·per /ˈflɪpə(r)/ *noun* [usually pl.] **1** a flat part of the body of some sea animals such as SEALS and TURTLES, used for swimming （海豹、海龟等的）鳍肢，鳍足 ➲ VISUAL VOCAB PAGE V13 **2** a long flat piece of rubber or plastic that you wear on your foot to help you swim more quickly, especially below the surface of the water （潜水、游泳用的）脚蹼，蛙鞋，鸭脚板，橡皮脚掌 ➲ WORDFINDER NOTE AT SWIM ➲ VISUAL VOCAB PAGE V44

'flip phone *noun* a small mobile/cell phone with a cover that opens upwards 折叠式手机；翻盖手机

flip·ping /ˈflɪpɪŋ/ *adj., adv.* (*BrE, informal*) used as a mild swear word by some people to emphasize sth or to show that they are annoyed 该死；真讨厌；糟透：*I hate this flipping hotel!* 我讨厌这个该死的旅馆！◇ *Flipping kids!* 讨厌的孩子！◇ *It's flipping cold today!* 今天冷得要命！

'flip side *noun* [usually sing.] ~ (**of/to sth**) **1** different and less welcome aspects of an idea, argument or action （想法、论点或行动的）反面，负面 **2** (*old-fashioned*) the side of a record that does not have the main song or piece of music on it 唱片反面（尤指没有主要歌曲或乐曲的一面）

flip 'teaching *noun* [U] = FLIPPED CLASSROOM

flirt /flɜːt; *NAmE* flɜːrt/ *verb, noun*

■ **verb** [I] ~ (**with sb**) to behave towards sb as if you find them sexually attractive, without seriously wanting to have a relationship with them 调情

PHR V **'flirt with sth 1** to think about or be interested in sth for a short time but not very seriously 玩儿似的想做某事：*She flirted with the idea of becoming an actress when she was younger.* 她早些年曾闹着玩似的想过当演员。**2** to take risks or not worry about a dangerous situation that may happen 冒险；不顾危险后果：*to flirt with danger/death/disaster* 冒险；玩儿命；不把灾祸当回事

■ **noun** [usually sing.] a person who flirts with a lot of people 与多人调情的人：*She's a real flirt.* 她是个打情骂俏的老手。

flir·ta·tion /flɜːˈteɪʃn; *NAmE* flɜːrˈt-/ *noun* **1** [C, U] ~ **with sth** a short period of time during which sb is involved or interested in sth, often not seriously 不认真对待；一时的参与；一时兴起；逢场作戏：*a brief and unsuccessful flirtation with the property market* 对房地产市场一时兴起、并不成功的介入 **2** [U] behaviour that shows you find sb sexually attractive but are not serious about them 调情：*Frank's efforts at flirtation had become tiresome to her.* 弗兰克一个劲地打情骂俏已使得她非常厌倦。**3** [C] ~ (**with sb**) a short sexual relationship with sb that is not taken seriously 短暂的风流韵事

flir·ta·tious /flɜːˈteɪʃəs; *NAmE* flɜːrˈt-/ (*also informal* **flirty**) *adj.* behaving in a way that shows a sexual attraction to sb that is not serious 卖弄风情的；打情骂俏的：*a flirtatious young woman* 卖弄风情的年轻女子 ◇ *a flirtatious smile* 卖弄风情的一笑 ▶ **flir·ta·tious·ly** *adv.* **flir·ta·tious·ness** *noun* [U]

flit /flɪt/ *verb, noun*

■ **verb** (**-tt-**) **1** [I] to move lightly and quickly from one place or thing to another 轻快地从一处到另一处；掠过：**~ from A to B** *Butterflies flitted from flower to flower.* 蝴蝶在花丛中飞来飞去。◇ *He flits from one job to another.* 他频繁跳槽。◇ **+ adv./prep.** *A smile flitted across his face.* 他脸上笑容一闪而过。◇ *A thought flitted through my mind.* 我脑海中掠过一个念头。**2** [I] (*ScotE*) to change the place where you live 迁移；迁居；搬家：*I had to change schools every time my parents flitted.* 我父母每次迁居，我都得换学校。

■ **noun**

IDM **do a moonlight/midnight 'flit** (*BrE, informal*) to leave a place suddenly and secretly at night, usually in order to avoid paying money that you owe to sb （通常为了躲债）夜间偷偷逃走

float /fləʊt; *NAmE* floʊt/ *verb, noun*

■ **verb**

• **ON WATER/IN AIR** 水上；空中 **1** [I] + **adv./prep.** to move slowly on water or in the air 浮动；漂流；飘动；飘移 SYN **drift**: *A group of swans floated by.* 一群天鹅缓缓游过。◇ *The smell of new bread floated up from the kitchen.* 厨房里飘出新鲜面包的香味。◇ *Beautiful music came floating out of the window.* 美妙的乐声从窗口传出。◇ (*figurative*) *An idea suddenly floated into my mind.* 我脑海里突然浮现出一个想法。◇ (*figurative*) *People seem to float in and out of my life.* 不同的人在我的生命中出现和消失。**2** [I] to stay on or near the surface of a liquid and not sink 浮；漂浮：*Wood floats.* 木头能浮起来。◇ **~ in/on sth** *A plastic bag was floating in the water.* 一个塑料袋在水中漂浮。◇ *Can you float on your back?* 你能仰浮吗？ **3** [T] to make sth move on or near the surface of a liquid 使浮动；使漂流：**~ sth** *There wasn't enough water to float the ship.* 水不够深，船浮动不起来。◇ **~ sth + adv./prep.** *They float the logs down the river to the towns.* 他们把原木沿河漂运至城镇。

• **WALK LIGHTLY** 飘然走动 **4** [I] + **adv./prep.** (*literary*) to walk or move in a smooth and easy way 轻盈走动；飘然移动 SYN **glide**: *She floated down the steps to greet us.* 她轻盈地下楼来迎接我们。

• **SUGGEST IDEA** 提出想法 **5** [T] ~ **sth** to suggest an idea or a plan for other people to consider 提出，提请考虑（想

法或计划）：*They floated the idea of increased taxes on alcohol.* 他们建议提高酒税。

• **BUSINESS/ECONOMICS** 商业；经济学 **6** [T] **~ sth** (*business* 商) to sell shares in a company or business to the public for the first time（公司或企业）首次公开发行（股票），使上市：*The company was floated on the stock market in 2014.* 这家公司于 2014 年上市。◇ *Shares were floated at 585p.* 股票最初上市价为 5 英镑 85 便士。**7** [T, I] **~ (sth)** (*economics* 经) if a government **floats** its country's money or allows it to **float**, it allows its value to change freely according to the value of the money of other countries（使货币汇率）自由浮动

IDM **float sb's 'boat** (*informal*) to be what sb likes 为某人所喜欢：*You can listen to whatever kind of music floats your boat.* 无论你喜欢哪种音乐，你都可以听。➲ MORE AT AIR *n.*

PHR V **ˌfloat aˈbout/aˈround** (usually used in the progressive tenses 通常用于进行时) if an idea, etc. is **floating around**, it is talked about by a number of people or passed from one person to another（思想等）传播，流传

■ *noun*

• **VEHICLE** 车辆 **1** a large vehicle on which people dressed in special COSTUMES are carried in a festival 彩车：*a carnival float* 狂欢节彩车

• **IN FISHING** 钓鱼 **2** a small light object attached to a FISHING LINE that stays on the surface of the water and moves when a fish has been caught 浮子；鱼漂

• **FOR SWIMMING** 游泳 **3** a light object that floats in the water and is held by a person who is learning to swim to stop them from sinking（学游泳用的）浮板 ➲ WORDFINDER NOTE AT SWIM

• **DRINK** 饮料 **4** (*NAmE*) a drink with ice cream floating in it 加冰淇淋的饮料：*a Coke float* 一杯加冰淇淋的可口可乐

• **MONEY** 钱 **5** (*especially BrE*) a sum of money consisting of coins and notes of low value that is given to sb before they start selling things so that they can give customers change（商店的）备用零钱

• **BUSINESS** 商业 **6** = FLOTATION (1)

float·er /ˈfləʊtə(r); *NAmE* ˈfloʊt-/ *noun* (*medical* 医) a very small object inside a person's eye which they see moving up and down（眼睛中的）悬浮物，飘浮物

float·ing /ˈfləʊtɪŋ; *NAmE* ˈfloʊt-/ *adj.* [usually before noun] not fixed permanently in one particular position or place 不固定的；流动的；浮动的：***floating exchange rates*** 浮动汇率 ◇ *a **floating population*** (= one in which people frequently move from one place to another) 流动人口 ◇ (*medical* 医) *a floating kidney* 游走肾

ˌfloating ˈrib (*also* **ˌfalse ˈrib**) *noun* (*anatomy* 解) any of the lower RIBS which are not attached to the BREASTBONE 浮肋；浮动弓肋

ˌfloating ˈvoter (*BrE*) (*NAmE* **ˈswing voter**) *noun* a person who does not always vote for the same political party and who has not decided which party to vote for in an election 游离选民（不确定投哪个政党的票）

floaty /ˈfləʊti; *NAmE* ˈfloʊti/ *adj.* (of cloth or clothing 布料或衣服) very light and thin 十分轻薄的

flock /flɒk; *NAmE* flɑːk/ *noun, verb*

■ *noun* **1** [C+sing./pl. v.] **~ (of sth)** a group of sheep, GOATS or birds of the same type（羊或鸟）群 ➲ COMPARE HERD *n.* (1) **2** [C+sing./pl. v.] **~ (of sb)** a large group of people, especially of the same type（尤指同类人的）一大群：*a flock of children/reporters* 一大群儿童 / 记者 ◇ *They came in flocks to see the procession.* 他们成群结队来看游行队伍。**3** [C+sing./pl. v.] (*literary*) the group of people who regularly attend the church of a particular priest, etc.（常跟随某圣职人员等做礼拜的）信众；追随者 **4** [U] small pieces of soft material used for filling CUSHIONS, chairs, etc.（填充垫子、椅子等的）小块软填料 **5** [U] small pieces of soft material on the surface of paper or cloth that produce a raised pattern（植绒用的）短绒，绒屑：*flock wallpaper* 植绒墙纸

■ *verb* [I] to go or gather together somewhere in large numbers 群集；聚集；蜂拥：**+ adv./prep.** *Thousands of people flocked to the beach this weekend.* 这个周末有好几千人蜂拥到了海滩。◇ *Huge numbers of birds had flocked together by the lake.* 大群的鸟聚集在湖边。◇ **~ to do sth** *People flocked to hear him speak.* 人们成群结队地去听他演讲。IDM SEE BIRD *n.*

floe /fləʊ; *NAmE* floʊ/ *noun* = ICE FLOE

flog /flɒg; *NAmE* flɑːg/ *verb* (**-gg-**) **1** [often passive] **~ sb** to punish sb by hitting them many times with a WHIP or stick 鞭笞，棒打（作为惩罚）：*He was publicly flogged for breaking the country's alcohol laws.* 他因违犯国家的酒法而被当众处以鞭刑。**2** (*BrE, informal*) to sell sth to sb 出售（某物给某人）：**~ sth (to sb)** *She flogged her guitar to another student.* 她把吉他卖给另一个同学。◇ **~ sth (off)** *We buy them cheaply and then flog them off at a profit.* 我们低价买下这些，然后卖出获利。◇ **~ sb sth** *I had a letter from a company trying to flog me insurance.* 我收到了一家公司的信，向我推销保险。

IDM **ˌflog a dead ˈhorse** (*informal*) to waste your effort by trying to do sth that is no longer possible 鞭策死马；做徒劳无益的事 **ˌflog sth to ˈdeath** (*BrE, informal*) to use an idea, a story, etc. so often that it is no longer interesting 多次重复（想法、故事等）而使人失去兴趣

flog·ging /ˈflɒgɪŋ; *NAmE* ˈflɑːg-/ *noun* [C, U] a punishment in which sb is hit many times with a WHIP or stick（作为惩罚的）鞭笞，棒打：*a public flogging* 当众处以鞭刑

flood /flʌd/ *noun, verb*

■ *noun*

• **WATER** 水 **1** [C, U] a large amount of water covering an area that is usually dry 洪水；水灾：*The heavy rain has caused floods in many parts of the country.* 大雨使全国许多地方泛滥成灾。◇ *flood damage* 洪涝灾害 ◇ *Police have issued **flood warnings** for Nevada.* 警方已经发布了内华达的水灾警告。◇ *The river is **in flood*** (= has more water in it than normal and has caused a flood). 河水泛滥。➲ SEE ALSO FLASH FLOOD ➲ WORDFINDER NOTE AT DISASTER

• **LARGE NUMBER** 大量 **2** [C] **~ (of sth)** a very large number of things or people that appear at the same time 大批，大量（的人或事物）：*a flood of complaints* 大量投诉 ◇ *a flood of refugees* 难民潮 ◇ *The child was **in floods of tears*** (= crying a lot). 小孩哭得泪人儿似的。

■ *verb*

• **FILL WITH WATER** 灌满水 **1** [I, T] if a place **floods** or sth **floods** it, it becomes filled or covered with water（使）灌满水；淹没：*The cellar floods whenever it rains heavily.* 只要一下大雨地窖就淹水。◇ **~ sth** *If the pipe bursts it could flood the whole house.* 要是水管破裂整座房子就会灌满水。

• **OF RIVER** 河 **2** [I, T] to become so full that it spreads out onto the land around it 泛滥；淹没：*When the Ganges floods, it causes considerable damage.* 恒河泛滥时造成严重损害。◇ **~ sth** *The river flooded the valley.* 河水泛滥淹没了河谷。

• **LARGE NUMBERS** 大量 **3** [I] **~ in | ~ into/out of sth** to arrive or go somewhere in large numbers 大量涌入；蜂拥而出 SYN **pour**: *Refugees continue to flood into neighbouring countries.* 难民不断涌入邻国。◇ *Telephone calls **came flooding in** from all over the country.* 全国各地的电话像潮水般打来。**4** [T, usually passive] **~ sb/sth with sth** to send sth somewhere in large numbers 大量送至；挤满；拥满：*The office was flooded with applications for the job.* 办公室堆满了应征该职的求职信。**5** [T] to become or make sth become available in a place in large numbers（使）充斥，充满：**~ sth** *Cheap imported goods are **flooding the market**.* 廉价进口商品充斥着市场。◇ **~ sth with sth** *A man who planned to flood Britain with cocaine was jailed for 15 years.* 一个企图往英国大量运送可卡因的男人被监禁 15 年。

• **OF FEELING/THOUGHT** 思想；感情 **6** [I, T] to affect sb suddenly and strongly 使大受感动；充满：**+ adv./prep.** *A great sense of relief flooded over him.* 他深感宽慰。◇ *Memories of her childhood **came flooding back**.* 她童年的往事涌上心头。◇ **~ sb with sth** *The words flooded him with self-pity.* 这些话使他充满了自怜。

• **OF LIGHT/COLOUR** 光；颜色 **7** [I, T] to spread suddenly into sth; to cover sth 照进；覆盖：**+ adv./prep.** *She drew the curtains and the sunlight flooded in.* 她拉开窗帘，阳

光洒了进来。◇ ~ sth *She looked away as the colour flooded her cheeks.* 她双颊泛出红晕，视线转向别处。◇ **be flooded with sth** *The room was flooded with evening light.* 室内一片暮色。

• ENGINE 发动机 **8** [I, T] ~ (sth) if an engine **floods** or if you **flood** it, it becomes so full of petrol/gas that it will not start （使）溢流

▶ **flood·ed** adj. : *flooded fields* 淹没的田野 **flood·ing** noun [U]: *There will be heavy rain with flooding in some areas.* 将有大雨，有些地方会泛滥成灾。

PHR V ˌ**flood sb↔ˈout** [usually passive] to force sb to leave their home because of a flood 洪水迫使某人背井离乡

flood·gate /ˈflʌdgeɪt/ *noun* [usually pl.] a gate that can be opened or closed to control the flow of water on a river 防洪闸门；泄水闸门：(*figurative*) *If the case is successful, it may* **open the floodgates** *to more damages claims against the industry* (= start sth that will be difficult to stop). 如果本案胜诉，就可能有更多的人向这个产业提出损害索赔，从而一发不可收拾。

flood·light /ˈflʌdlaɪt/ *noun, verb*

■ *noun* [usually pl.] a large powerful lamp, used for lighting sports grounds, theatre stages and the outside of buildings 泛光灯，泛光照明灯（运动场、舞台和建筑物外墙等用）：*a match played* **under floodlights** 泛光灯下进行的比赛 ▶ **flood·light·ing** *noun* [U]: *The floodlighting had been turned off.* 泛光照明已关闭。

■ *verb* (**flood·lit, flood·lit** /-lɪt/) [usually passive] ~ **sth** to light a place or a building using floodlights 用泛光灯照明：*The swimming pool is floodlit in the evenings.* 游泳池晚间有泛光灯照明。◇ *floodlit tennis courts* 泛光灯照明的网球场

flood·plain /ˈflʌdpleɪn/ *noun* an area of flat land beside a river that regularly becomes flooded when there is too much water in the river 洪泛区；泛滥平原；河漫滩

ˈ**flood tide** *noun* a very high rise in the level of the sea as it moves in towards the coast 涨潮 ➲ COMPARE HIGH TIDE

flood·water /ˈflʌdwɔːtə(r); *NAmE also* -wɑːtər/ *noun* [U] (*also* **floodwaters** [pl.]) water that covers land after there has been a flood 洪水：*The floodwaters have now receded.* 洪水现已消退。

floor /flɔː(r)/ *noun, verb*

■ *noun*

• OF ROOM 房间 **1** [C, usually sing.] the surface of a room that you walk on 地板；地面：*a* **wooden/concrete/marble, etc. floor** 木质、水泥、大理石等地面 ◇ *ceramic floor tiles* 陶瓷地板砖 ◇ *The body was lying on the kitchen floor.* 尸体躺在厨房的地上。◇ *The alterations should give us extra floor space.* 这些改动应该使我们有更大的楼面面积。➲ WORDFINDER NOTE AT DANCE

• OF VEHICLE 车辆 **2** (*NAmE also* **floor·board**) [C, usually sing.] the bottom surface of a vehicle（车辆的）地板：*The floor of the car was covered in cigarette ends.* 小轿车地板上满是烟蒂。

• LEVEL OF BUILDING 楼层 **3** [C] all the rooms that are on the same level of a building 楼层：*Her office is* **on the second floor**. 她的办公室在第三层。◇ *the Irish guy who lives two floors above* 住在两层楼上面的爱尔兰人 ◇ *There is a lift to all floors.* 有电梯通往各楼层。◇ *Their house is* **on three floors** (= it has three floors). 他们的房子有三层。➲ NOTE AT STOREY ➲ SEE ALSO GROUND FLOOR

• OF THE SEA/FORESTS 海；森林 **4** [C, usually sing.] the ground at the bottom of the sea, a forest, etc.（海等的）底；（森林等的）地面：*the* **ocean/valley/cave/forest floor** 海底；谷底；洞底；森林的地面

• IN PARLIAMENT, ETC. 议会等 **5 the floor** [sing.] the part of a building where discussions or debates are held, especially in a parliament; the people who attend a discussion or debate 议员席；全体议员；全体与会者：*Opposition politicians registered their protest on the floor of the House.* 反对党从政者在议院的议员席提出了抗议。◇ *We will now take any questions from the floor.* 现在我们将接受会众席上的任何提问。➲ WORDFINDER NOTE AT DEBATE

• AREA FOR WORK 工作区 **6** [C, usually sing.] an area in a building that is used for a particular activity（建筑物内的）场地：*on the floor of the Stock Exchange* (= where trading takes place) 在证券交易所的交易厅 ➲ SEE ALSO DANCE FLOOR, FACTORY FLOOR, SHOP FLOOR, TRADING FLOOR

• FOR WAGES/PRICES 工资；物价 **7** [C, usually sing.] the lowest level allowed for wages or prices（工资或物价的）最低额，底价：*Prices have* **gone through the floor** (= fallen to a very low level). 物价已经探底。➲ COMPARE CEILING (2)

IDM **get/be given/have the ˈfloor** to get/be given/have the right to speak during a discussion or debate（讨论或辩论中）取得发言权 ˌ**hold the ˈfloor** to speak during a discussion or debate, especially for a long time so that nobody else is able to say anything 发言；长篇大论地发言（尤指使他人无法发言）ˌ**take** (**to**) **the ˈfloor** to start

▼ **BRITISH/AMERICAN 英式 / 美式英语**

floor

- In *BrE* the floor of a building at street level is the **ground floor**, the one above it is the **first floor** and the one below it is the **basement**, or **lower ground floor** in a public building. 在英式英语中，地面的楼层叫 ground floor，上面一层叫 first floor，下面一层叫 basement 或在公共建筑中叫 lower ground floor。
- In *NAmE* the floor at street level is usually called the **first floor**, the one above it is the **second floor** and the one below it is the **basement**. In public buildings the floor at street level can also be called the **ground floor**. 在美式英语中，地面的一层通常叫 first floor，上面一层叫 second floor，下面一层叫 basement。在公共建筑中，地面的一层亦可称为 ground floor。

➲ NOTE AT STOREY

▼ **SYNONYMS 同义词辨析**

floor

ground • land • earth

These are all words for the surface that you walk on. 以上各词均指地面。

floor the surface of a room that you walk on 指室内地板、地面：*She was sitting on the floor watching TV.* 她坐在地板上看电视。

ground (often **the ground**) the solid surface of the earth that you walk on（常作 the ground）指室外地、地面：*I found her lying on the ground.* 我发现她躺在地上。◇ *The rocket crashed a few seconds after it* **left the ground**. 火箭离开地面几秒钟便坠毁了。

land the surface of the earth that is not sea 指陆地、大地：*It was good to be back on* **dry land** *again.* 回到陆地上真好。◇ *They fought both at sea and* **on land**. 他们在海上和陆上都打过仗。

earth (often **the earth**) the solid surface of the world that is made of rock, soil, sand, etc.（常作 the earth）指大地、陆地、地面：*You could feel the earth shake as the truck came closer.* 卡车开近时可感觉到地面在震动。

GROUND, LAND OR EARTH? 用 ground、land 还是 earth? **Ground** is the normal word for the solid surface that you walk on when you are not in a building or vehicle. You can use **earth** if you want to draw attention to the rock, soil etc. that the ground is made of. **Land** is only used when you want to contrast it with the sea.

* ground 常指建筑物或车辆外的地面。如果关注的是构成大地的岩石、土壤等可用 earth。land 只在与海相对照时使用：~~the land beneath our feet~~ ◇ ~~feel the land shake~~ ◇ ~~sight ground/earth~~ ◇ ~~travel by ground/earth~~

PATTERNS

- **on/under** the floor/ground/earth
- **bare** floor/ground/earth
- to **drop/fall to** the floor/the ground/(the) earth
- to **reach** the floor/the ground/land

dancing on a DANCE FLOOR（在舞池）开始跳舞：*Couples took the floor for the last dance of the evening.* 双双对对开始跳晚会的最后一支舞。**wipe/mop the 'floor with sb** (*informal*) to defeat sb completely in an argument or a competition（在辩论或竞赛中）彻底打败对手，把对手打得一败涂地 ➲MORE AT GROUND FLOOR

■*verb*

• SURPRISE/CONFUSE 惊奇；困惑 **1 ~ sb** to surprise or confuse sb so that they are not sure what to say or do 使惊奇；使困惑

• HIT 击中 **2** [usually passive] **~ sb** to make sb fall down by hitting them, especially in a sport（尤指体育运动中）击倒，打倒

• BUILDING/ROOM 建筑物；房间 **3** [usually passive] **~ sth** to provide a building or room with a floor 给…安装地板；给…铺设地面

• DRIVING 驾驶 **4 ~ the accelerator** to press the ACCELERATOR pedal of a car hard 把（汽车的油门踏板）踩到底

floor·board /ˈflɔːbɔːd; *NAmE* ˈflɔːrbɔːrd/ *noun* **1** a long flat piece of wood in a wooden floor 木质地板条；木板条：*bare/polished floorboards* 素面 / 打了蜡的木地板 ➲ VISUAL VOCAB PAGE V22 **2** [usually sing.] (*NAmE*) = FLOOR (2)：*a car floorboard* 汽车地板 ◇ *He had his foot to the floorboard* (= was going very fast). 他猛踩油门飞速驾驶。

floor·cloth /ˈflɔːklɒθ; *NAmE* ˈflɔːrklɔːθ/ *noun* (*BrE*) a cloth for cleaning floors 擦地布

floor·ing /ˈflɔːrɪŋ/ *noun* [U] material used to make the floor of a room 铺室内地面的材料：*vinyl/wooden flooring* 乙烯基塑料 / 木地板 ◇ *kitchen/bathroom flooring* 厨房 / 浴室地砖

ˈfloor lamp (*BrE also* **ˈstandard lamp**) *noun* a tall lamp that stands on the floor 落地灯 ➲VISUAL VOCAB PAGE V22

ˈfloor manager *noun* the person responsible for the lighting and other technical arrangements for a television production（电视节目的）现场指导

ˈfloor plan *noun* (*specialist*) a drawing of the shape of a room or building, as seen from above, showing the position of the furniture, etc. 楼层平面图

ˈfloor show *noun* a series of performances by singers, dancers, etc. at a restaurant or club（旅馆或夜总会的）系列表演

floozy (*also* **flooz·ie**) /ˈfluːzi/ *noun* (*pl.* **-ies**) (*old-fashioned, informal, disapproving*) a woman who has sexual relationships with many different men 荡妇

flop /flɒp; *NAmE* flɑːp/ *verb, noun*

■*verb* (**-pp-**) **1** [I] **~ into/on sth | ~ (down/back)** to sit or lie down in a heavy and sudden way because you are very tired（因疲惫而）猛然坐下，沉重地躺下：*Exhausted, he flopped down into a chair.* 他筋疲力尽，一屁股坐到椅子上。**2** [I] **+ adv./prep.** to fall, move or hang in a heavy or awkward way, without control（沉重、笨拙或不由自主地）落下，移动，悬挂：*Her hair flopped over her eyes.* 她的头发耷拉下来遮住了眼睛。◇ *The young man flopped back, unconscious.* 那年轻人仰面倒下，不省人事。◇ *The fish were flopping around in the bottom of the boat.* 鱼在船底扑腾。**3** [I] (*informal*) to be a complete failure 砸锅；完全失败：*The play flopped on Broadway.* 这出戏在百老汇砸了锅。

■*noun* (*informal*) a film/movie, play, party, etc. that is not successful（电影、戏剧、聚会等）失败，不成功 OPP **hit** ➲ SEE ALSO BELLYFLOP

flop·house /ˈflɒphaʊs; *NAmE* ˈflɑːp-/ (*NAmE*) (*BrE* **doss-house**) *noun* (*informal*) a cheap place to stay for people who have no home（供流浪者投宿的）廉价客栈

floppy /ˈflɒpi; *NAmE* ˈflɑːpi/ *adj.* (**flop·pier**, **flop·piest**) hanging or falling loosely; not hard and stiff 松散下垂的；耷拉的；松软的：*a floppy hat* 耷拉着的帽子

flora /ˈflɔːrə/ *noun* [U] (*specialist*) the plants of a particular area, type of environment or period of time（某地区、环境或时期的）植物群，植物区系：*alpine flora* 高山植物群 ◇ *rare species of **flora and fauna*** (= plants and animals) 动植物的罕见物种

floral /ˈflɔːrəl/ *adj.* [usually before noun] **1** consisting of pictures of flowers; decorated with pictures of flowers 绘有花的；饰以花的：*wallpaper with a **floral design/pattern*** 有花卉图案的墙纸 ◇ *a floral dress* 有花卉图案的连衣裙 **2** made of flowers 花的：*a **floral arrangement/display*** 插花；花展 ◇ ***Floral tributes*** *were sent to the church.* 敬献的鲜花已送往教堂。

flor·en·tine /ˈflɒrəntaɪn; -tiːn; *NAmE* ˈflɔːrəntiːn; -tɪn/ *adj., noun*

■*adj.* (of food 食物) served on SPINACH 佛罗伦萨式的；（上桌时）放在菠菜上的：*eggs florentine* 佛罗伦萨式鸡蛋

■*noun* a biscuit/cookie containing nuts and fruit, half covered in chocolate（一面有巧克力的）干果饼干

floret /ˈflɒrət; *NAmE* ˈflɔː-/ *noun* a flower part of some vegetables, for example BROCCOLI and CAULIFLOWER. Each vegetable has several florets coming from one main STEM.（花椰菜等的）花部 ➲VISUAL VOCAB PAGE V33

flori·bunda /ˌflɒrɪˈbʌndə; *NAmE* ˌflɔːr-/ *noun* (*specialist*) a plant, especially a ROSE, with flowers that grow very close together in groups 多花植物；（尤指）多花月季

florid /ˈflɒrɪd; *NAmE* ˈflɔː-; ˈflɑː-/ *adj.* **1** (of a person's face 人脸) red 红润的：*a florid complexion* 红润的脸色 **2** (*usually disapproving*) having too much decoration or detail 过分装饰的；过多修饰的：*florid language* 辞藻堆砌的语言 ▶**florid·ly** *adv.*

florin /ˈflɒrɪn; *NAmE* ˈflɔː-; ˈflɑː-/ *noun* an old British coin worth two SHILLINGS (= now 10p) 弗罗林（英国旧时价值两先令的硬币，相当于现在的 10 便士）

flor·ist /ˈflɒrɪst; *NAmE* ˈflɔː-/ *noun* **1** a person who owns or works in a shop/store that sells flowers and plants 花商 **2 flor·ist's** (*pl.* **flor·ists**) a shop/store that sells flowers and plants 花店：*I've ordered some flowers from the florist's.* 我向花店订购了一些花。➲MORE LIKE THIS 34, page R29

floss /flɒs; *NAmE* flɔːs; flɑːs/ *noun, verb*

■*noun* [U] **1** = DENTAL FLOSS **2** thin silk thread 丝线 ➲SEE ALSO CANDYFLOSS

■*verb* [I, T] **~ (sth)** to clean between your teeth with DENTAL FLOSS 用牙线剔（牙）

flo·ta·tion /fləʊˈteɪʃn; *NAmE* floʊ-/ *noun* **1** (*also* **float**) [C, U] (*business* 商) the process of selling shares in a company to the public for the first time in order to raise money（公司）首次公开发行股票：*plans for (a) flotation on the stock exchange* 在证券市场上发行股票的计划 ◇ *a stock-market flotation* 在股票市场上市 **2** [U] the act of floating on or in water 浮；漂浮

floˈtation tank *noun* a container filled with salt water in which people float in the dark as a way of relaxing 盐水浮力池（解乏用）

flo·tilla /fləˈtɪlə; *NAmE* floʊˈt-/ *noun* a group of boats or small ships sailing together 船队；小型舰队

flot·sam /ˈflɒtsəm; *NAmE* ˈflɑːt-/ *noun* [U] **1** parts of boats, pieces of wood or rubbish/garbage, etc. that are found on land near the sea or floating on the sea; any kind of rubbish/garbage（冲上海岸或漂浮海上的）船只残骸，碎木，零碎杂物；废弃物：*The beaches are wide and filled with interesting **flotsam and jetsam**.* 海滩宽阔，到处是有趣的被冲上岸的零碎杂物。➲COMPARE JETSAM **2** people who have no home or job and who move from place to place, often rejected by society 无家可归者；失业流浪者：*the human flotsam of inner cities* 内城区无家可归的流浪者

flounce /flaʊns/ *verb, noun*

■*verb* [I] (**+ adv./prep.**) to move somewhere in a way that draws attention to yourself, for example because you are angry or upset（因愤怒或烦躁等而）走动，急动，骤动，扭转：*She flounced out of the room.* 她愤愤地冲出房间。

■*noun* **1** a strip of cloth that is sewn around the edge of a skirt, dress, curtain, etc.（衣、裙、窗帘等的）荷叶边 **2** a quick and exaggerated movement that you make when you are angry or want people to notice you（因气愤或想引人注意）猛的一动；故作夸张的动作：*She left the room with a flounce.* 她气冲冲地冲出房间。 ▶ **flounced** *adj.*：*a flounced skirt* 镶荷叶边的裙子

floun·der /ˈflaʊndə(r)/ *verb, noun*
■ ***verb* 1** [I, T] (+ **speech**) to struggle to know what to say or do or how to continue with sth 不知所措；挠头；支吾：*His abrupt change of subject left her floundering helplessly.* 他突然改变话题，使她茫然不知所措。 **2** [I] to have a lot of problems and to be in danger of failing completely 困难重重；艰苦挣扎：*At that time the industry was floundering.* 那时这个行业举步维艰。 **3** [I] (+ **adv./prep.**) to struggle to move or get somewhere in water, mud, etc.（在水、泥等中）挣扎：*She was floundering around in the deep end of the swimming pool.* 她在游泳池深水区挣扎着。
■ ***noun*** (*pl.* **floun·der** or **floun·ders**) a small flat sea fish that is used for food 偏口鱼；比目鱼；鲽

flour 🔑 /ˈflaʊə(r)/ *noun, verb*
■ ***noun*** 🔑 [U] a fine white or brown powder made from grain, especially WHEAT, and used in cooking for making bread, cakes, etc.（尤指小麦的）面粉；（谷物磨成的）粉 ➲ SEE ALSO PLAIN FLOUR, SELF-RAISING FLOUR
■ ***verb*** [usually passive] ~ **sth** to cover sth with a layer of flour 在…上撒（或覆以）面粉：*Roll the dough on a lightly floured surface.* 揉生面团时，案板上要撒点面粉。

flour·ish /ˈflʌrɪʃ; *NAmE* ˈflɜːrɪʃ/ *verb, noun*
■ ***verb* 1** [I] to develop quickly and be successful or common 繁荣；昌盛；兴旺 SYN **thrive**：*Few businesses are flourishing in the present economic climate.* 在目前的经济气候下，很少有企业兴旺发达。 **2** [I] to grow well; to be healthy and happy 茁壮成长；健康幸福 SYN **thrive**：*These plants flourish in a damp climate.* 这些植物在潮湿的气候下长势茂盛。◇ (*especially BrE*) *I'm glad to hear you're all flourishing.* 听说你们都健康幸福，我感到高兴。 **3** [T] ~ **sth** to wave sth around in a way that makes people look at it（为引起注意）挥舞
■ ***noun* 1** [usually sing.] an exaggerated movement that you make when you want sb to notice you（为引起注意的）夸张动作：*He opened the door for her with a flourish.* 他做了一个夸张动作为她开了门。◇ *With a final flourish she laid down her pen.* 最后她做了一个夸张的动作，放下钢笔。 **2** [usually sing.] an impressive act or way of doing sth 给人深刻印象的行动；令人难忘的方式：*The season ended with a flourish for Rooney, when he scored in the final minute of the match.* 鲁尼本赛季华丽收官：他在比赛最后一分钟射进一球。 **3** details and decoration that are used in speech or writing（讲话或文章的）华丽辞藻，修饰：*a speech full of rhetorical flourishes* 满篇华丽辞藻的演讲 **4** a curved line, that is used as decoration, especially in writing（尤指手写体的）装饰曲线，花饰 **5** [usually sing.] a loud short piece of music, that is usually played to announce an important person or event 花彩号声：*a flourish of trumpets* 小号齐鸣

floury /ˈflaʊəri/ *adj.* **1** covered with flour 覆有面粉的：*floury hands* 沾满面粉的双手 **2** like flour; tasting of flour 面粉似的；味道像面粉的：*a floury texture* 粉质 **3** (of potatoes 土豆) soft and light when they are cooked（煮后）很面的

flout /flaʊt/ *verb* ~ **sth** to show that you have no respect for a law, etc. by openly not obeying it 公然藐视，无视（法律等）SYN **defy**：*Motorists regularly* ***flout the law.*** 驾车者经常无视法律。◇ *to* ***flout*** *authority/convention* 公然藐视权威 / 惯例

flow 🔑 /fləʊ; *NAmE* floʊ/ *noun, verb*
■ ***noun*** [C, usually sing., U]
• **CONTINUOUS MOVEMENT** 流动 **1** 🔑 ~ (**of sth/sb**) the steady and continuous movement of sth/sb in one direction 流；流动：*She tried to stop the flow of blood from the wound.* 她试图止住伤口流血。◇ *an endless flow of refugees into the country* 难民源源不断流入这个国家 ◇ *to improve traffic flow* (= make it move faster) 改善交通流量 ◇ *to control the direction of flow* 控制流向
• **PRODUCTION/SUPPLY** 生产；供应 **2** 🔑 ~ (**of sth**) the continuous production or supply of sth 持续生产；不断供应：*the flow of goods and services to remote areas* 商品和服务对边远地区源源不断的供应 ◇ *to encourage the free flow of information* 鼓励信息自由交流 ◇ *data flow* 数据流 ➲ SEE ALSO CASH FLOW
• **OF SPEECH/WRITING** 言语；文字 **3** continuous talk by sb 滔滔不绝：*You've interrupted my flow—I can't remember what I was saying.* 你打断了我的话，我记不得我在说什么了。◇ *As usual, Tom was* ***in full flow.*** 汤姆如常地口若悬河。 **4** ~ **of sth** the way that words and ideas are linked together in speech or writing 连贯；流畅：*Too many examples can interrupt the smooth flow of the text.* 例子太多会使行文不流畅。
• **OF THE SEA** 海 **5** the movement of the sea towards the land 涨潮：***the ebb and flow of the tide*** 潮涨潮落
IDM **go with the ˈflow** (*informal*) to be relaxed and not worry about what you should do 随大溜 ➲ MORE AT EBB *n.*
■ ***verb***
• **MOVE CONTINUOUSLY** 不断移动 **1** 🔑 [I] (of liquid, gas or electricity 液体、气体或电) to move steadily and continuously in one direction 流；流动：*She lost control and the tears began to flow.* 她禁不住泪如泉涌。◇ + **adv./prep.** *It's here that the river flows down into the ocean.* 这条河就在这里汇入海洋。◇ *Blood flowed from a cut on her head.* 血从她头上的伤口处流出来。◇ *This can prevent air from flowing freely to the lungs.* 这可以防止空气任意流入肺部。 **2** 🔑 [I] (+ **adv./prep.**) (of people or things 人或事物) to move or pass continuously from one place or person to another, especially in large numbers or amounts 涌流；流动：*Constant streams of traffic flowed past.* 车流不断通过。◇ *Election results flowed in throughout the night.* 整夜不断传来选举的结果。
• **OF IDEAS/CONVERSATION** 思想；交谈 **3** [I] to develop or be produced in an easy and natural way 流畅：*Conversation flowed freely throughout the meal.* 席间大家一直相谈甚欢。
• **BE AVAILABLE EASILY** 有的是 **4** [I] to be available easily and in large amounts 有的是；大量供应：*It was obvious that money flowed freely in their family.* 显然他们家族有的是钱。◇ *The party got livelier as the drink began to flow.* 开始尽兴畅饮时，聚会的气氛活跃起来。
• **OF FEELING** 感觉 **5** [I] + **adv./prep.** to be felt strongly by sb 被强烈感到：*Fear and excitement suddenly flowed over me.* 我突然感到又恐惧又兴奋。
• **OF CLOTHES/HAIR** 衣服；头发 **6** [I] ~ (**down/over sth**) to hang loosely and freely 飘垂；飘拂：*Her hair flowed down over her shoulders.* 她的头发垂到肩上。◇ *long flowing skirts* 飘逸长裙
• **OF THE SEA** 海 **7** [I] (of the TIDE in the sea/ocean 海潮) to come in towards the land 涨；涨潮 OPP **ebb**
PHR V **ˈflow from sth** (*formal*) to come or result from sth 来自；由…引起

ˈflow chart (*also* **ˈflow diagram**) *noun* a diagram that shows the connections between the different stages of a process or parts of a system 流程图

flower 🔑 /ˈflaʊə(r)/ *noun, verb*
■ ***noun* 1** 🔑 the coloured part of a plant from which the seed or fruit develops. Flowers usually grow at the end of a STEM and last only a short time. 花；花朵：*The plant has a beautiful bright red flower.* 这株植物开了一朵美丽鲜红的花。◇ *The roses are* ***in flower*** *early this year.* 今年玫瑰花开得早。◇ *The crocuses are late* ***coming into flower.*** 番红花开得迟。 ➲ COLLOCATIONS AT LIFE ➲ VISUAL VOCAB PAGE V11 **2** 🔑 a plant grown for the beauty of its flowers 开花植物：*a garden full of flowers* 种满花的花园 ◇ *a* ***flower garden/show*** 花园；花展 **3** 🔑 a flower with its STEM that has been picked as a decoration（已摘）带梗的花：***I picked some flowers.*** 我摘了一些花。◇ ***a bunch of flowers*** 一束花 ◇ *a* ***flower arrangement*** 一组插花 ➲ SEE ALSO BOUQUET (1)
IDM **the flower of sth** (*literary*) the finest or best part of sth（某事物的）最佳部分，精华；精英
■ ***verb* 1** [I] (of a plant or tree 花草树木) to produce flowers 开花 SYN **bloom**：*This particular variety flowers in July.* 这个品种七月开花。◇ *early-flowering spring bulbs* 早开花

的春季鳞茎植物 **2** [I] (*literary*) to develop and become successful 成熟；繁荣；兴旺 SYN **blossom**

'flower arranging *noun* [U] the art of arranging cut flowers in an attractive way 插花

'flower bed *noun* a piece of ground in a garden/yard or park where flowers are grown 花坛 ➲ VISUAL VOCAB PAGE V20

flowered /'flaʊəd; *NAmE* 'flaʊərd/ *adj.* [usually before noun] decorated with patterns of flowers 饰有花卉图案的

flower·ing /'flaʊərɪŋ/ *noun* **1** [U] the time when a plant has flowers 开花时节 **2** [C, usually sing.] **~ of sth** the time when sth, especially a period of new ideas in art, music, science, etc., reaches its most complete and successful stage of development （艺术、音乐、科学等新思潮的）繁荣时期，鼎盛时期

flower·pot /'flaʊəpɒt; *NAmE* 'flaʊərpɑːt/ *noun* a container made of plastic or CLAY for growing plants in 花盆 ➲ VISUAL VOCAB PAGE V20

'flower power *noun* [U] the culture connected with young people of the 1960s and early 1970s who believed in love and peace and were against war 花之力（20 世纪 60 年代和 70 年代初期年轻人信奉爱与和平、反对战争的文化取向）

flowery /'flaʊəri/ *adj.* [usually before noun] **1** covered with flowers or decorated with pictures of flowers 覆盖着花的；饰以花卉图形的 **2** smelling or tasting of flowers 花香的；花味的 **3** (*usually disapproving*) (of speech or writing 言语或文字) too complicated; not expressed in a clear and simple way 过分复杂费解的；华而不实的

flown PAST PART. OF FLY

'flow-on *noun, adj.* (*AustralE, NZE*)
■ ***noun*** an increase in pay or an improvement in working conditions that is made because one has already been given in a similar job 顺势加薪，顺势改善工作条件（因大势所趋）
■ ***adj.*** **flow-on** effects, etc. are ones that happen as a result of sth else（效应等）顺势的

fl oz *abbr.* (*pl.* **fl oz**) (in writing 书写形式) FLUID OUNCE 液量盎司：*Add 8 fl oz water.* 加 8 液量盎司水。

Flt Lt *abbr.* (in writing 书写形式) FLIGHT LIEUTENANT (= an officer of fairly high rank in the British AIR FORCE) （英国）空军上尉：*Flt Lt Richard Clarkson* 空军上尉理查德·克拉克森

flu 🔑 /fluː/ (*often* **the flu**) (*also formal* **in·flu·enza**) *noun* [U] an infectious disease like a very bad cold, that causes fever, pains and weakness 流行性感冒；流感：*The whole family has the flu.* 全家都患流感。◇ (*BrE*) *She's got flu.* 她患上了流感。➲ COLLOCATIONS AT ILL

flub /flʌb/ *verb* (**-bb-**) [T, I] **~ (sth)** (*NAmE, informal*) to do sth badly or make a mistake 搞坏；搞糟；犯错误 SYN **fluff, bungle**：*She flubbed the first line of the song.* 她把第一行歌词唱错了。▶ **flub** *noun*

fluc·tu·ate AW /'flʌktʃueɪt/ *verb* [I] to change frequently in size, amount, quality, etc., especially from one extreme to another （大小、数量、质量等）波动；（在…之间）起伏不定 SYN **vary**：*fluctuating prices* 波动的价格 ◇ **~ between A and B** *During the crisis, oil prices fluctuated between $20 and $40 a barrel.* 在危机时期，每桶石油价格在 20 至 40 美元之间波动。◇ **+ adv./prep.** *Temperatures can fluctuate by as much as 10 degrees.* 温差可达 10 度之多。◇ *My mood seems to fluctuate from day to day.* 我的情绪似乎天天在变。➲ WORDFINDER NOTE AT TREND ▶ **fluc·tu·ation** AW /ˌflʌktʃu'eɪʃn/ *noun* [C, U]: **~ (in/of sth)** *wild fluctuations in interest rates* 利率的疯狂波动

flue /fluː/ *noun* a pipe or tube that takes smoke, gas or hot air away from a fire, a HEATER or an oven 烟道

flu·ency /'fluːənsi/ *noun* [U, sing.] **1** the quality of being able to speak or write a language, especially a foreign language, easily and well（尤指外语）流利，流畅：*Fluency in French is required for this job.* 这个工作要求法语熟练自如。 **2** the quality of doing sth in a smooth and skilful way 熟练自如；流畅：*The team lacked fluency during the first half.* 该队在上半场打得不够流畅。

flu·ent /'fluːənt/ *adj.* **1** **~ (in sth)** able to speak, read or write a language, especially a foreign language, easily and well （尤指外语）流利的，流畅的；熟练的：*She's fluent in Polish.* 她的波兰语很流利。◇ ***a fluent speaker/reader*** 说话流利的人；阅读熟练的人 **2** (of a language, especially a foreign language 语言，尤指外语) expressed easily and well 流利表达的：*He speaks fluent Italian.* 他说一口流利的意大利语。 **3** (of an action 动作) done in a smooth and skilful way 流畅的；技能娴熟的：*fluent handwriting* 流畅的笔迹 ◇ *fluent movements* 技能娴熟的动作 ▶ **flu·ent·ly** *adv.*

fluff /flʌf/ *noun, verb*
■ ***noun*** [U] **1** (*also* **lint**) small pieces of wool, cotton, etc. that gather on clothes and other surfaces（衣服等上的）绒毛，蓬松毛团，尘团 **2** soft animal fur or bird feathers, that is found especially on young animals or birds（禽兽，尤指幼者的）绒毛 **3** (*informal, especially NAmE*) entertainment that is not serious and is not considered to have great value 没多大意义的娱乐
■ ***verb*** **1** **~ sth** (*informal*) to do sth badly or to fail at sth 搞糟；弄砸 SYN **bungle**：*He completely fluffed an easy shot* (= in sport). 一个唾手可得的进球机会被他搞砸了。◇ *Most actors fluff their lines occasionally.* 多数演员都会偶尔说错台词。 **2** **~ sth (out/up)** to shake or brush sth so that it looks larger and/or softer 抖松；使松散：*The female sat on the eggs, fluffing out her feathers.* 母鸟抖开羽毛孵蛋。◇ *Let me fluff up your pillows for you.* 我来把你的枕头拍松。

fluffy /'flʌfi/ *adj.* (**fluf·fier, fluf·fiest**) **1** like fluff; covered in fluff 绒毛般的；覆有绒毛的：*a little fluffy kitten* 毛茸茸的小猫 **2** (of food 食物) soft, light and containing air 松软的：*Beat the butter and sugar until soft and fluffy.* 搅打黄油和糖直到松软为止。 **3** looking as if it is soft and light 轻软状的：*fluffy white clouds* 轻飘飘的白云 **4** (*informal, disapproving*) light and not serious; having no substance, depth or power 轻浮的；空洞的；浅薄的；无说服力的：*a fluffy film/movie* 内容空洞的影片 ◇ *a fluffy argument* 一个无说服力的论据

flu·gel·horn /'fluːglhɔːn; *NAmE* -hɔːrn/ *noun* a BRASS musical instrument like a small TRUMPET 活塞军号（铜管乐器，类似小号）

fluid /'fluːɪd/ *noun, adj.*
■ ***noun*** [C, U] (*formal* or *specialist*) a liquid; a substance that can flow 液体；流体；液：*body fluids* (= for example, blood) 体液（如血液）◇ *The doctor told him to drink plenty of fluids.* 医生要他多喝流食。◇ *cleaning fluid* 清洗液
■ ***adj.*** **1** (*formal*) (of movements, designs, music, etc. 动作、设计、音乐等) smooth and elegant 流畅优美的 SYN **flowing**：*a loose, fluid style of dancing* 灵活流畅优美的舞蹈风格 ◇ *fluid guitar playing* 流畅优美的吉他演奏 ◇ *the fluid lines of the drawing* 图画的流畅线条 **2** (*formal*) (of a situation 形势) likely to change; not fixed 易变的；不稳定的：*a fluid political situation* 不稳定的政治局势 **3** (*specialist*) that can flow freely, as gases and liquids do 流动的；流体的：*a fluid consistency* 流体黏稠度

flu·id·ity /flu'ɪdəti/ *noun* [U] **1** (*formal*) the quality of being smooth and elegant 流畅优美：*She danced with great fluidity of movement.* 她跳舞的动作十分流畅优美。 **2** (*formal*) the quality of being likely to change 易变（性）；不稳定（性）：*the fluidity of human behaviour* 人的行为的易变性 ◇ *social fluidity* 社会的不稳定性 **3** (*specialist*) the quality of being able to flow freely, as gases and liquids do 流动（性）

ˌfluid 'ounce *noun* (*abbr.* **fl oz**) a unit for measuring liquids. There are 20 fluid ounces in a British pint and 16 in an American pint. 液量盎司（液量单位，英制等于 1/20 品脱，美制等于 1/16 品脱）

fluke /fluːk/ *noun* [usually sing.] (*informal*) a lucky or unusual thing that happens by accident, not because of planning or skill 侥幸；偶然；意外：*They are determined to show that their last win was no fluke.* 他们决心证明上一次的胜利绝非侥幸。◇ *a fluke goal* 偶然的进球 ▶ **fluky** (*also* **flukey**) /ˈfluːki/ *adj.*

flume /fluːm/ *noun* **1** a narrow channel made to carry water for use in industry（工业用）渡槽，引水槽，放水沟 **2** a water CHUTE (= a tube for sliding down) at an AMUSEMENT PARK or a swimming pool（游乐园或游泳池的）水滑道

flum·mery /ˈflʌməri/ *noun* [U] nonsense, especially praise that is silly or not sincere 废话；（尤指）无聊（或虚假）的恭维话：*She hated the flummery of public relations.* 她讨厌公关工作中的虚夸恭维。

flum·mox /ˈflʌməks/ *verb* [usually passive] (not used in the progressive tenses 不用于进行时) **~ sb** (*informal*) to confuse sb so that they do not know what to say or do 使困惑；使糊涂：*I was flummoxed by her question.* 她的问题把我弄糊涂了。▶ **flum·moxed** *adj.*

flung PAST TENSE, PAST PART. OF FLING

flunk /flʌŋk/ *verb* (*informal, especially NAmE*) **1** [T, I] **~ (sth)** to fail an exam, a test or a course（考试、测验等）失败，不及格：*I flunked math in second grade.* 我二年级时数学不及格。**2** [T] **~ sb** to make sb fail an exam, a test, or a course by giving them a low mark/grade 给（某人）不及格：*She's flunked 13 of the 18 students.* * 18 个学生她给了 13 个不及格。

PHR V ˌ**flunk ˈout (of sth)** (*NAmE, informal*) to have to leave a school or college because your marks/grades are not good enough（因不及格而）离（校），给开除（学籍），退学

flun·key (*also* **flunky**) /ˈflʌŋki/ *noun* (*pl.* **-eys** or **-ies**) **1** (*disapproving*) a person who tries to please sb who is important and powerful by doing small jobs for them 阿谀奉承者；势利小人；马屁精 **2** (*old-fashioned*) a servant in uniform（穿制服的）男仆

fluor·es·cent /ˌflɔːˈresnt; *BrE also* ˌflʊəˈr-; *NAmE also* ˌflʊˈr-/ *adj.* **1** (of substances 物质) producing bright light by using some forms of RADIATION 发荧光的：*a fluorescent lamp* (= one that uses such a substance) 荧光灯 ◇ *fluorescent lighting* 荧光照明 **2** (of a colour, material, etc. 颜色、材料等) appearing very bright when light shines on it; that can be seen in the dark 强烈反光的；发亮的：*fluorescent armbands worn by cyclists* 骑车人戴的发亮臂章 ➲ SYNONYMS AT BRIGHT ➲ COMPARE PHOSPHORESCENT (1) ▶ **fluor·es·cence** *noun* [U]

fluorid·ation /ˌflɔːrɪˈdeɪʃn; *BrE also* ˌflʊər-; *NAmE also* ˌflʊr-/ *noun* [U] the practice of adding fluoride to drinking water to prevent tooth decay 饮用水氟化（以防止牙齿蛀蚀）

fluor·ide /ˈflɔːraɪd; *BrE also* ˈflʊər-; *NAmE also* ˈflʊr-/ *noun* a chemical containing fluorine that protects teeth from decay and is often added to TOOTHPASTE and sometimes to drinking water 氟化物

fluor·ine /ˈflɔːriːn; *BrE also* ˈflʊər-; *NAmE also* ˈflʊr-/ *noun* [U] (*symb.* **F**) a chemical element. Fluorine is a poisonous pale yellow gas and is very REACTIVE. 氟

flur·ried /ˈflʌrid; *NAmE* ˈflɜːrid/ *adj.* nervous and confused, especially because there is too much to do（尤指因事情过多而）慌乱的 **SYN** **flustered**

flurry /ˈflʌri; *NAmE* ˈflɜːri/ *noun* (*pl.* **-ies**) **1** [usually sing.] an occasion when there is a lot of activity, interest, excitement, etc. within a short period of time 一阵忙乱（或激动、兴奋等）：*a sudden flurry of activity* 突然的频繁活动 ◇ *Her arrival caused a flurry of excitement.* 她的到来引起了一阵轰动。◇ *A flurry of shots rang out in the darkness.* 黑暗中突然发出一阵枪声。**2** a small amount of snow, rain, etc. that falls for a short time and then stops 小阵雪（或雨等）：*snow flurries* 小雪阵阵 ◇ *flurries of snow* 阵阵小雪 ➲ WORDFINDER NOTE AT SNOW **3** a sudden short movement of paper or cloth, especially clothes（纸张、织物，尤指衣服）窸窣：*The ladies departed in a flurry of silks and satins.* 女士们在一片绸缎窸窣声中离去。

flush /flʌʃ/ *verb, noun, adj.*

■ ***verb*** **1** [I, T] (of a person or their face 人或脸) to become red, especially because you are embarrassed, angry or hot 发红；脸红：*She flushed with anger.* 她气得涨红了脸。◇ **+ adj.** *Sam felt her cheeks flush red.* 萨姆感觉自己满脸通红。◇ **~ sth** *A rosy blush flushed her cheeks.* 她面若桃花。**2** [I, T] **~ (sth)** when a toilet **flushes** or you **flush** it, water passes through it to clean it, after a handle, etc. has been pressed 冲（抽水马桶）**3** [T] to clean sth by causing water to pass through it（用水）冲洗干净，冲洗：**~ sth out (with sth)** *Flush the pipe out with clean water.* 用净水冲洗管子。◇ **~ sth through sth** *Flush clean water through the pipe.* 用净水冲洗管子。**4** [T] **~ sth + adv./prep.** to get rid of sth with a sudden flow of water（用水）冲走：*They flushed the drugs down the toilet.* 他们从马桶冲走了毒品。◇ *Drinking lots of water will help to flush toxins out of the body.* 大量饮水有助于清除体内毒素。

PHR V ˌ**flush sb/sth↔ˈout** | ˌ**flush sb/sth ˈout of sth** to force a person or an animal to leave the place where they are hiding 把（人或动物从藏身处）驱赶出来

■ ***noun*** **1** [C, usually sing.] a red colour that appears on your face or body because you are embarrassed, excited or hot 脸红；潮红：*A pink flush spread over his cheeks.* 他满脸通红。➲ SEE ALSO HOT FLUSH **2** [C, usually sing.] a sudden strong feeling; the hot feeling on your face or body caused by this 一阵强烈情感；（流露出的）一阵激情：*a flush of anger/embarrassment/enthusiasm/guilt* 一阵愤怒 / 尴尬 / 热情 / 内疚 **3** [sing.] the act of cleaning a toilet with a sudden flow of water 冲（抽水马桶）：*Give the toilet a flush.* 冲抽水马桶。**4** [C] (in card games 纸牌游戏) a set of cards that a player has that are all of the same SUIT 同花的一手牌

IDM **(in) the first flush of sth** (*formal*) (at) a time when sth is new, exciting and strong（在）新鲜兴奋时刻，初期强盛阶段：*in the first flush of youth/enthusiasm/romance* 在青春活力旺盛时期；在热情高涨阶段；在热恋的初期

■ ***adj.*** [not before noun] **1** (*informal*) having a lot of money, usually for a short time 富有，很有钱（通常为短期的）**2** **~ with sth** (of two surfaces 两个表面) completely level with each other 完全齐平：*Make sure the paving stones are flush with the lawn.* 务必要使铺路石和草坪齐平。

flushed /flʌʃt/ *adj.* (of a person 人) red; with a red face 脸红的：*flushed cheeks* 发红的双颊 ◇ *Her face was flushed with anger.* 她的脸气红了。◇ (*figurative*) *He was* ***flushed with success*** (= very excited and pleased) *after his first novel was published.* 他的第一部小说发表以后，他志得意满。

flus·ter /ˈflʌstə(r)/ *verb, noun*

■ ***verb*** [often passive] **~ sb** to make sb nervous and/or confused, especially by giving them a lot to do or by making them hurry 使忙乱；使慌乱；使紧张 ▶ **flus·tered** *adj.* **SYN** **flurried**：*She arrived late, looking hot and flustered.* 她迟到了，显得火急火燎，局促不安。

■ ***noun*** [sing.] (*BrE*) a state of being nervous and confused 慌乱；慌张

flute /fluːt/ *noun* **1** a musical instrument of the WOODWIND group, shaped like a thin pipe. The player holds it sideways and blows across a hole at one end. 长笛 ➲ VISUAL VOCAB PAGE V38 **2** **champagne ~** a tall narrow glass used for drinking CHAMPAGNE 细长香槟杯（形似长笛）➲ VISUAL VOCAB PAGE V23

fluted /ˈfluːtɪd/ *adj.* (especially of a round object 尤指圆物体) with a pattern of curves cut around the outside 外部有凹槽纹的：*fluted columns* 饰有凹槽纹的柱子 ▶ **flut·ing** *noun* [U]

flut·ist /ˈfluːtɪst/ (*NAmE*) (*especially BrE* **flaut·ist**) *noun* a person who plays the FLUTE 长笛手

flut·ter /ˈflʌtə(r)/ *verb, noun*

■ ***verb*** **1** [I, T] to move lightly and quickly; to make sth

F

move in this way（使）飘动，挥动，颤动：*Flags fluttered in the breeze.* 旗帜在微风中飘扬。◇ *Her eyelids fluttered but did not open.* 她的眼皮动了一下，但没有睁开眼。◇ **~ sth** *He fluttered his hands around wildly.* 他拼命挥舞着双手。◇ *She **fluttered her eyelashes** at him* (= tried to attract him in order to persuade him to do sth). 她向他眨眼睛。 **2** [I, T] **~ (sth)** when a bird or an insect **flutters** its wings, or its wings **flutter**, the wings move lightly and quickly up and down（鸟或昆虫）拍（翅），振（翅），鼓（翼） **3** [I] **+ adv./prep.** (of a bird or an insect 鸟或昆虫) to fly somewhere moving the wings quickly and lightly 飞来飞去；翩翩飞舞：*The butterfly fluttered from flower to flower.* 蝴蝶在花丛中飞来飞去。 **4** [I] (of your heart, etc. 心脏等) to beat very quickly and not regularly 怦怦乱跳；扑腾：*I could feel a fluttering pulse.* 我感到脉搏跳动。◇ (*figurative*) *The sound of his voice in the hall made her heart flutter.* 他在大厅中讲话的声音使她的心怦怦直跳。

■ ***noun*** **1** [C, usually sing.] a quick, light movement 振动；飘动；挥动；颤动：*the flutter of wings* 翅膀的拍动 ◇ *with a flutter of her long, dark eyelashes* 她那长长的黑睫毛扑闪了一下 ◇ (*figurative*) *to feel a flutter of panic in your stomach* 胸中感到一阵恐慌 **2** [C, usually sing.] **~ (on sth)** (*BrE, informal*) a small bet 小赌注：*to have a flutter on the horses* 赛马中下小赌注 **3** [sing.] a state of nervous or confused excitement 紧张兴奋；慌乱：*Her sudden arrival caused quite a flutter.* 她的突然来到引起一片慌乱。 **4** [C] a very fast HEARTBEAT, caused when sb is nervous or excited（心脏的）怦怦乱跳，扑腾：*Her heart gave a flutter when she saw him.* 她见到他时心怦怦乱跳。 **5** [U] (*medical* 医) a medical condition in which you have a fast, unsteady HEARTBEAT 扑动；快速的颤动（或搏动） **6** [U] (*specialist*) rapid changes in the PITCH or volume of recorded sound（重放录音的）颤振 ➲ COMPARE WOW *n.* (2)

flu·vial /ˈfluːviəl/ *adj.* (*specialist*) connected with rivers 河流的；与河流有关的

flux /flʌks/ *noun* **1** [U] continuous movement and change 不断的变动；不停的变化：*Our society is **in a state of flux**.* 我们的社会在不断演变。**2** [C, usually sing., U] (*specialist*) a flow; an act of flowing 通量；流：*a flux of neutrons* 一个中子流

fly 🔑 /flaɪ/ *verb, noun, adj.*

■ ***verb*** (**flies**, **fly·ing**, **flew** /fluː/, **flown** /fləʊn; *NAmE* floʊn/)

HELP In sense 15 **flied** is used for the past tense and past participle. 作第 15 义时过去式和过去分词用 flied。

• **OF BIRD/INSECT** 鸟；昆虫 **1** 🔑 [I] (**+ adv./prep.**) to move through the air, using wings 飞；飞翔：*A stork flew slowly past.* 一只鹳缓缓飞过。◇ *A wasp had flown in through the window.* 一只黄蜂从窗口飞了进来。

• **AIRCRAFT/SPACECRAFT** 航空器；航天器 **2** 🔑 [I] (**+ adv./prep.**) (of an aircraft or a SPACECRAFT 航空器或航天器) to move through air or space（在空中或宇宙）飞行，航行：*They were on a plane flying from London to New York.* 他们在从伦敦飞往纽约的飞机上。◇ *to fly at the speed of sound* 以声速飞行 ◇ *Lufthansa fly to La Paz from Frankfurt.* 汉莎航空公司的飞机从法兰克福飞往拉巴斯。**3** 🔑 [I] to travel in an aircraft or a SPACECRAFT （乘航空器或航天器）航行，飞行：*Is this the first time that you've flown?* 这是你第一次乘飞机吗？ ◇ **~ (from…) (to…)** *I'm flying to Hong Kong tomorrow.* 明天我要乘飞机去香港。◇ **+ noun** *I always fly business class.* 我搭飞机总是坐商务舱。◇ *We're flying KLM.* 我们乘坐荷兰皇家航空公司的飞机。**4** 🔑 [T, I] **~ (sth)** to control an aircraft, etc. in the air 驾驶（飞机等）；操纵（飞行器等）：*a pilot trained to fly large passenger planes* 受过驾驶大型客机训练的飞行员 ◇ *children flying kites* 放风筝的儿童 ◇ *He's learning to fly.* 他在学习驾驶飞机。**5** [T] **+ adv./prep.** to transport goods or passengers in a plane 空运（货物或乘客）：*The stranded tourists were finally flown home.* 滞留的游客终于由飞机送返家园。◇ *He had flowers specially flown in for the ceremony.* 他特地为这个庆典空运鲜花来。**6** [T] **~ sth** to travel over an ocean or area of land in an aircraft 乘飞行器飞越（海洋或陆地）：*to fly the Atlantic* 飞越大西洋

• **MOVE QUICKLY/SUDDENLY** 快速 / 突然移动 **7** 🔑 [I] (**+ adv./prep.**) to go or move quickly 疾驰；疾行；快速移动：*The train was flying along.* 火车飞驰着。◇ *She gasped and her hand flew to her mouth.* 她倒抽了一口气，连忙用手掩着嘴。◇ *It's late—I must fly.* 已经晚了，我得赶快走。**8** 🔑 [I] to move suddenly and with force 猛然移动：(**+ adv./prep.**) *A large stone came flying in through the window.* 一块大石头飞进了窗户。◇ *Several people were hit by flying glass.* 有几个人被飞溅的玻璃击中。◇ **+ adj.** *David gave the door a kick and it flew open.* 戴维踢了门一脚，门一下子开了。

• **OF TIME** 时间 **9** 🔑 [I] to seem to pass very quickly 飞逝：*Doesn't time fly?* 时间过得真快！◇ **~ by/past** *Summer has just flown by.* 夏天一晃就过去了。

• **FLAG** 旗帜 **10** [I, T] if a flag **flies**, or if you **fly** it, it is displayed, for example on a long pole（旗）飘扬；升，悬挂（旗）：*Flags were flying at half mast on all public buildings.* 所有的公共建筑都降半旗。◇ **~ sth** *to fly the Stars and Stripes* 悬挂美国国旗

• **MOVE FREELY** 自由移动 **11** [I] to move around freely 自由移动：*hair flying in the wind* 随风飘拂的头发

• **OF STORIES/RUMOURS** 故事；传闻 **12** [I] to be talked about by many people 流传；四处传播

• **ESCAPE** 逃跑 **13** [T, I] **~ (sth)** (*formal*) to escape from sb/sth（从…）逃走，逃跑：*Both suspects have flown the country.* 两个嫌疑犯都逃到国外了。➲ COMPARE FLEE

• **OF PLAN** 计划 **14** [I] (*NAmE*) to be successful 成功：*It remains to be seen whether his project will fly.* 他的计划能否成功尚需拭目以待。

• **IN BASEBALL** 棒球 **15** (**flies**, **flying**, **flied**, **flied**) [I, T] **~ (sth)** to hit a ball high into the air 将（球）击出飞球

IDM **fly the ˈcoop** (*informal, especially NAmE*) to escape from a place 逃走 **fly ˈhigh** to be successful 成功 **fly in the face of ˈsth** to oppose or be the opposite of sth that is usual or expected 悍然不顾；公然违抗；与…相悖：*Such a proposal is flying in the face of common sense.* 这个建议违反常识。 **fly into a ˈrage, ˈtemper, etc.** to become suddenly very angry 勃然大怒 **(go) fly a/your ˈkite** (*NAmE, informal*) used to tell sb to go away and stop annoying you or INTERFERING 走开；别烦人；别插手 **fly the ˈnest** **1** (of a young bird 幼鸟) to become able to fly and leave its nest 羽翼已丰可离巢 **2** (*informal*) (of sb's child 子女) to leave home and live somewhere else 另立门户 **fly off the ˈhandle** (*informal*) to suddenly become very angry 大发雷霆 **go ˈflying** (*informal*) to fall, especially as a result of not seeing sth under your feet 跌倒；（尤指）绊了一跤：*Someone's going to go flying if you don't pick up these toys.* 你要是不捡起这些玩具，就会绊倒别人。 **let ˈfly (at sb/sth) (with sth)** to attack sb by hitting them or speaking angrily to them（用…）打；（向某人）大发雷霆：*He let fly at me with his fist.* 他挥拳打我。◇ *She let fly with a stream of abuse.* 她破口大骂了一通。➲ MORE AT BIRD *n.*, CROW *n.*, FLAG *n.*, PIG *n.*, SEAT *n.*, TANGENT, TIME *n.*, WINDOW

PHR V **ˈfly at sb** (of a person or an animal 人或动物) to attack sb suddenly 扑向；猛烈攻击

■ ***noun*** (*pl.* **flies**)

• **INSECT** 昆虫 **1** 🔑 [C] a small flying insect with two wings. There are many different types of fly. 蝇；苍蝇：*A fly was buzzing against the window.* 一只苍蝇嗡嗡地飞着，直撞窗子。◇ *Flies rose in thick black swarms.* 苍蝇黑压压地成群飞起。

• **IN FISHING** 钓鱼 **2** [C] a fly or sth made to look like a fly, that is put on a hook and used as BAIT to catch fish（作钓饵的）苍蝇，假蝇：*fly fishing* 用假蝇作饵钓鱼 ➲ WORDFINDER NOTE AT FISHING

• **ON TROUSERS/PANTS** 裤子 **3** [sing.] (*BrE also* **flies**) an opening down the front of a pair of trousers/pants that fastens with a ZIP or buttons and is usually covered over by a strip of material（裤子的）前裆开口：*Your fly is undone!* 你的裤子前裆没拉上！◇ *Your flies are undone!* 你的裤子前裆开着呢！ ➲ VISUAL VOCAB PAGE V68

• **ON TENT** 帐篷 **4** [C] a piece of material that covers the entrance to a tent 门帘 ➲ SEE ALSO FLIES

IDM **die/fall/drop like ˈflies** (*informal*) to die or fall down in very large numbers 大批死亡；大批倒下：*People were dropping like flies in the intense heat.* 酷暑中人们成批死去。 **a/the fly in the ˈointment** a person or thing that spoils a situation or an occasion that is fine in all other ways 扫兴的人；煞风景的事物 **a fly on the ˈwall** a person who watches others without being noticed 不为人觉察的观察者：*I'd love to be a fly on the wall when he tells her the news.* 他把这消息告诉她时，我想悄悄在旁观看。◇ *fly-on-the-wall documentaries* (= in which people are filmed going about their normal lives as if the camera were not there) 纪实影片 **(there are) no flies on 'sb** (*informal*) the person mentioned is clever and not easily tricked 某人精明得不会上当 **not harm/hurt a 'fly** to be kind and gentle and unwilling to cause unhappiness 连一只苍蝇都不肯伤害；心地善良 **on the 'fly** (*informal*) if you do sth **on the fly**, you do it quickly while sth else is happening, and without thinking about it very much 赶紧地；匆忙中

■ ***adj.*** (*informal*) **1** (*BrE*) clever and showing good judgement about people, especially so that you can get an advantage for yourself 机灵的；机警的；不会上当的 **2** (*NAmE, informal*) fashionable and attractive 时髦迷人的；漂亮的

fly agar·ic /ˌflaɪ ˈæɡərɪk/ *noun* [U] a poisonous MUSHROOM with a red top with white spots 捕蝇蕈，毒蝇鹅膏（有毒蘑菇）

fly·away /ˈflaɪəweɪ/ *adj.* (especially of hair 尤指毛发) soft and fine; difficult to keep tidy 细软的；凌乱的；飘拂的

ˈfly ball *noun* (in BASEBALL 棒球) a ball that is hit high into the air 高飞球；腾空球

fly·blown /ˈflaɪbləʊn; *NAmE* -bloʊn/ *adj.* (*BrE*) dirty and in bad condition; not fit to eat 不洁净的；沾有苍蝇卵的；不能食用的

ˈfly boy *noun* (*NAmE, informal*) a pilot, especially one in the AIR FORCE（尤指空军）飞行员

ˈfly-by *noun* (*pl.* **fly-bys**) **1** the flight of a SPACECRAFT near a planet to record data （航天器的）近天体探测飞行 **2** (*also* **ˈfly·over**) (*both NAmE*) (*BrE* **ˈfly-past**) a special flight by a group of aircraft, for people to watch at an important ceremony （飞机编队的）检阅飞行

ˈfly-by-night *adj.* [only before noun] (of a person or business 人或企业) dishonest and only interested in making money quickly 无信用（或不可靠）而唯利是图的 ▶ **ˈfly-by-night** *noun*

fly·catch·er /ˈflaɪkætʃə(r)/ *noun* a small bird that catches insects while it is flying 翔食雀（能在飞行中捕捉昆虫）

ˈfly-drive *adj., noun* (*BrE*)

■ ***adj.*** [only before noun] (of a holiday/vacation 假期) organized by a travel company at a fixed price that includes your flight to a place, a car to drive while you are there and somewhere to stay 半自助的（由旅行社组织，费用包含航班、自行驾车以及住宿）：*a fly-drive break* 半自助旅行休假

■ ***noun*** a fly-drive holiday 半自助旅行假期

flyer (*also* **flier**) /ˈflaɪə(r)/ *noun* **1** (*informal*) a person who flies an aircraft (usually a small one, not a passenger plane)（常指驾驶小飞机而非客机的）飞行员 **2** a person who travels in a plane as a passenger 飞机乘客：*frequent flyers* 航空常旅客 **3** a person who operates sth such as a model aircraft or a KITE from the ground 地面操纵飞行器者（如玩模型飞机或放风筝的人）**4** a thing, especially a bird or an insect, that flies in a particular way 飞行物（尤指飞鸟或昆虫）：*Butterflies can be strong flyers.* 蝴蝶的飞翔力强。**5** a small sheet of paper that advertises a product or an event and is given to a large number of people 小（广告）传单 **6** (*informal*) a person, an animal or a vehicle that moves very quickly 能飞跑的人（或动物）；能疾驰的车辆：*Ford's flashy new flyer* 福特牌新型高速轿车 **7** = FLYING START ➲ SEE ALSO HIGH-FLYER

ˈfly fishing *noun* [U] the sport of fishing in a river or lake using an artificial fly at the end of the line to attract and catch the fish 用假蝇钓鱼

ˌfly ˈhalf *noun* = STAND-OFF HALF

fly·ing 🔑 /ˈflaɪɪŋ/ *adj., noun*

■ ***adj.*** 🔑 [only before noun] able to fly 能飞的：*flying insects* 能飞的昆虫

IDM **with ˌflying ˈcolours** very well; with a very high mark/grade 很好；成绩优异：*She passed the exam with flying colours.* 她以优异成绩通过了考试。**ORIGIN** In the past, a ship returned to port after a victory in battle decorated with flags (= colours). 源自旧时战船凯旋回港用彩旗装饰。

■ ***noun*** [U] **1** 🔑 travelling in an aircraft 乘飞机：*I'm terrified of flying.* 我十分害怕坐飞机。**2** 🔑 operating the controls of an aircraft 飞行；飞行器驾驶：*flying lessons* 飞行驾驶课

ˈflying boat *noun* a large plane that can take off from and land on water 水上飞机

ˌflying ˈbuttress *noun* (*architecture* 建) a half ARCH of brick or stone that supports the outside wall of a large building such as a church 飞扶壁

ˌflying ˈdoctor *noun* (especially in Australia) a doctor who travels in an aircraft to visit patients who live far from a town （尤指澳大利亚乘飞机出诊的）飞行医生：*A flying doctor service operates in remote regions.* 在偏远地区有飞行医生服务。

ˌflying ˈfish *noun* (*pl.* **flying fish**) a tropical sea fish that can rise and move forwards above the surface of the water, using its FINS (= flat parts that stick out from its body) as wings 飞鱼（分布于暖水海洋，有翼状鳍）

ˌflying ˈfox *noun* a large BAT (= an animal like a mouse with wings) that lives in hot countries and eats fruit 狐蝠；飞狐

ˈflying jacket (*BrE*) (*US* **ˈflight jacket**) *noun* a short leather jacket with a warm LINING and COLLAR, originally worn by pilots 飞行夹克；翻领皮夹克

ˌflying ˈleap *noun* a long high jump made while you are running quickly （有助跑的）腾空跳远：*to take a flying leap into the air* 腾空向前一跳

ˈflying machine *noun* an aircraft, especially one that is unusual or was built a long time ago（尤指非同寻常或很久以前造的）飞机，航空器

ˈflying officer *noun* an officer of fairly low rank in the British AIR FORCE（英国）皇家空军中尉：*Flying Officer Ian Wall* 伊恩·沃尔皇家空军中尉

ˌflying ˈpicket *noun* (*BrE*) a worker on strike who can go quickly to other factories, etc. to help persuade the workers there to join the strike 流动罢工鼓动员

ˌflying ˈsaucer *noun* a round SPACECRAFT that some people claim to have seen and that some people believe comes from another planet 飞碟 ➲ COMPARE UFO

ˈflying squad *noun* (*usually* **the Flying Squad**) [C+sing./pl. v.] a group of police officers in Britain who are ready to travel very quickly to the scene of a serious crime（英国）机动警察队，快速特警队

ˌflying ˈsquirrel *noun* a small animal like a SQUIRREL which travels through the air between trees, spreading out the skin between its front and back legs to stop itself from falling too quickly 飞鼠

ˌflying ˈstart (*also less frequent* **flyer**) *noun* [sing.] a very fast start to a race, competition, etc. （赛跑、竞赛等的）快速起动

IDM **get off to a ˌflying ˈstart | get off to a ˈflyer** to make a very good start; to begin sth well 有很好的开端；有良好的起步；开门红

ˈflying suit *noun* a piece of clothing that covers the whole body, worn by the pilot and CREW of a military or light aircraft （连体）飞行服

ˌflying ˈvisit *noun* (*BrE*) a very short visit 短暂访问；闪电式访问

ˈfly kick *noun* the act of kicking a ball while you are running, especially in a game of RUGBY（尤指橄榄球运动中的）跑动踢球，飞踢 ▶ **ˈfly-kick** *verb* ~ sth

fly·leaf /ˈflaɪliːf/ *noun* (*pl.* **fly·leaves**) an empty page at the beginning or end of a book（书籍前后的）空白页，衬页

fly·over /ˈflaɪəʊvə(r); *NAmE* -oʊvər/ *noun* **1** (*BrE*) (*NAmE* **over·pass**) a bridge that carries one road over another one 高架桥；跨线桥；立交桥 **2** (*NAmE*) = FLY-BY

ˈflyover country *noun* [U] (*also* **the ˈflyover states** [pl.]) (*informal, disapproving*) (in the US) the area in the middle of the country between the states on the coasts 飞越之地（指位于美国东、西海岸各州之间的中部地区）：*It's an area most New Yorkers know as flyover country.* 那个地区被大多数纽约人称为飞越之地。

F

fly·paper /ˈflaɪpeɪpə(r)/ *noun* [C, U] a strip of sticky paper that you hang in a room to catch flies 捕蝇纸

ˈfly-past (*BrE*) (*NAmE* **ˈfly-by**, **ˈfly·over**) *noun* a special flight by a group of aircraft, for people to watch at an important ceremony（飞机编队的）检阅飞行

ˈfly-post *verb* [I, T] ~ (**sth**) (*BrE*) to put up pieces of paper that advertise sth in public places, without official permission（未经正式许可）张贴（小广告）▶ **ˈfly-posting** *noun* [U] **ˈfly-poster** *noun*

fly·sheet /ˈflaɪʃiːt/ *noun* (*BrE*) an extra sheet of material on the outside of a tent that keeps the rain out（帐篷外层防雨的）篷盖

ˈfly-tip *verb* (**-pp-**) [I] (*BrE*) to leave waste somewhere illegally 乱倒垃圾 ➲ WORDFINDER NOTE AT WASTE ▶ **ˈfly-tipping** *noun* [U] **ˈfly-tipper** *noun*

fly·weight /ˈflaɪweɪt/ *noun* a BOXER, WRESTLER, etc. of the lightest class, usually weighing between 48 and 51 kilograms 特轻量级拳击手，次最轻量级拳击手，最轻量级摔跤手，蝇量级拳击手（体重 48 至 51 公斤之间）

fly·wheel /ˈflaɪwiːl/ *noun* a heavy wheel in a machine or an engine that helps to keep it working smoothly and at a steady speed 飞轮；惯性轮

FM *abbr.* **1** /ˌef ˈem/ frequency modulation (a method of broadcasting high-quality sound by radio) 调频：*Radio 1 FM* 无线电调频 1 台 **2** (in writing 书写形式) FIELD MARSHAL 陆军元帅

foal /fəʊl; *NAmE* foʊl/ *noun, verb*

■ *noun* a very young horse or DONKEY 驹子；小马驹；小驴驹

IDM **in foal** (of a female horse 母马) pregnant 怀孕的，怀驹的

■ *verb* [I] to give birth to a foal 产驹

foam /fəʊm; *NAmE* foʊm/ *noun, verb*

■ *noun* **1** (*also* ˌ**foam ˈrubber**) [U] a soft light rubber material, full of small holes, that is used for seats, MATTRESSES, etc. 泡沫橡胶；海绵橡胶：*a foam mattress* 泡沫橡胶床垫 ◇ *foam packaging* 泡沫橡胶包装材料 **2** [U] a mass of very small air bubbles on the surface of a liquid 泡沫 SYN **froth**：*a glass of beer with a good head of foam* 一杯表面有厚厚一层泡沫的啤酒 ◇ *The breaking waves left the beach covered with foam.* 浪花四溅，海滩上满是泡沫。➲ VISUAL VOCAB PAGE V5 **3** [U, C] a chemical substance that forms or produces a soft mass of very small bubbles, used for washing, shaving, or putting out fires, for example 泡沫剂（用于洗涤、剃须、灭火等）：*shaving foam* 剃须泡沫膏 ➲ PICTURE AT FROTH

■ *verb* [I] (of a liquid 液体) to have or produce a mass of small bubbles 有泡沫；起泡沫 SYN **froth**

IDM **foam at the ˈmouth 1** (especially of an animal 尤指动物) to have a mass of small bubbles in and around its mouth, especially because it is sick or angry 口吐白沫（尤指因发病或暴怒）**2** (*informal*) (of a person 人) to be very angry 大发雷霆

foamy /ˈfəʊmi; *NAmE* ˈfoʊmi/ *adj.* consisting of or producing a mass of small bubbles; like foam 泡沫的；起泡沫的；泡沫般的

FOB /fɒb; *NAmE* fɑːb/ *noun* (*becoming old-fashioned, informal, offensive, especially NAmE*) the abbreviation for 'fresh off the boat' (a person who has recently come to a country as an IMMIGRANT and does not speak or behave like people who have lived there a long time) 新移民（全写为 fresh off the boat，指其不谙当地语言以及尚未融入当地社会）

fob /fɒb; *NAmE* fɑːb/ *verb, noun*

■ *verb* (**-bb-**)

PHR V ˌ**fob sb↔ˈoff** (**with sth**) **1** to try to stop sb asking questions or complaining by telling them sth that is not true（用不实之词）搪塞，欺骗：*Don't let him fob you off with any more excuses.* 别让他再以任何借口哄骗你了。◇ *She wouldn't be fobbed off this time.* 这次她一定不会上当受骗了。**2** to give sb sth that is not what they want or is of worse quality than they want（把劣质的或不想要的商品）骗售给：*He was unaware that he was being fobbed off with out-of-date stock.* 他没有意识到对方正向他骗售过期存货。

■ *noun* **1** a short chain that is attached to a watch that is carried in a pocket 怀表短链 **2** (*also* **ˈfob watch**) a watch that is attached to a fob 带表链的怀表 **3** a small decorative object that is attached to a KEY RING, etc.（钥匙环等上的）小饰物

f.o.b. /ˌef əʊ ˈbiː; *NAmE* oʊ/ *abbr.* (in writing 书写形式) FREE ON BOARD 离岸价格；船上交货价

focal /ˈfəʊkl; *NAmE* ˈfoʊkl/ *adj.* [only before noun] central; very important; connected with or providing a focus 中心的；很重要的；焦点的；有焦点的

fo·cal·ize (*BrE also* **-ise**) /ˈfəʊkəlaɪz; *NAmE* ˈfoʊ-/ *verb* ~ **sth** (*formal*) to make sth focus or concentrate on a particular thing 使聚焦；使集中 ▶ **fo·cal·iza·tion**, **-isa·tion** /ˌfəʊkəlaɪˈzeɪʃn; *NAmE* ˌfoʊkələˈz-/ *noun* [U, C]

ˌ**focal ˈlength** *noun* (*physics* 物) the distance between the centre of a mirror or a LENS and its FOCUS 焦距

ˈfocal point *noun* **1** a thing or person that is the centre of interest or activity 集中点，焦点（指人或事物）；活动中心：*In rural areas, the school is often the focal point for the local community.* 在农村，学校常常是当地社区的活动中心。◇ *He quickly became the focal point for those who disagreed with government policy.* 他迅速成为不同意政府政策者的中心人物。**2** (*specialist*) = FOCUS (3)

fo'c'sle = FORECASTLE

focus ⚷ AW /ˈfəʊkəs; *NAmE* ˈfoʊ-/ *verb, noun*

■ *verb* (**-s-** or **-ss-**) **1** ⚷ [I, T] to give attention, effort, etc. to one particular subject, situation or person rather than another 集中（注意力、精力等于）：~ (**on/upon sb/sth**) *The discussion focused on three main problems.* 讨论集中在三个主要问题上。◇ *Each exercise focuses on a different grammar point.* 每个练习各有不同的语法重点。◇ ~ **sth** (**on/upon sb/sth**) *The visit helped to focus world attention on the plight of the refugees.* 这次访问促使全世界关注难民的困境。**2** ⚷ [I, T] (of your eyes, a camera, etc. 眼睛、摄影机等) to adapt or be adjusted so that things can be seen clearly; to adjust sth so that you can see things clearly（使）调节焦距：*It took a few moments for her eyes to focus in the dark.* 过了一会儿她的眼睛才适应了黑暗。◇ ~ **on sb/sth** *Let your eyes focus on objects that are further away from you.* 睁大眼睛看清楚离你较远的物体。◇ *In this scene, the camera focuses on the actor's face.* 在这个镜头中，摄影机对准演员的脸部。◇ ~ **sth** (**on sb/sth**) *He focused his blue eyes on her.* 他那蓝色的眼睛注视着她。◇ *I quickly focused the camera on the children.* 我迅速把照相机的镜头对准孩子们。**3** [T] ~ **sth** (**on sth**) (*specialist*) to aim light onto a particular point using a LENS 集中（光束于）；聚焦（于）

■ *noun* (*pl.* **fo·cuses** or **foci** /ˈfəʊsaɪ; *NAmE* ˈfoʊ-/) **1** ⚷ [U, C, usually sing.] the thing or person that people are most interested in; the act of paying special attention to sth and making people interested in it 中心点（指人或事物）；关注；引起关注：*It was the main focus of attention at the meeting.* 这是会议上关注的主要焦点。◇ ~ **for sth** *His comments provided a focus for debate.* 他的评论提供了辩论的重点。◇ ~ **on sth** *We shall maintain our focus on the* *needs of the customer.* 我们将继续重点关注顾客的需要。◇ *In today's lecture the focus will be on tax structures within the European Union.* 今天讲课的重点是欧洲联盟内部的税制结构。◇ *The incident* ***brought*** *the problem of violence in schools* ***into*** *sharp* ***focus***. 这次事件使校园暴力成为焦点问题。◇ *What we need now is a* ***change of focus*** (= to look at things in a different way). 我们现在需要的是改变对事物的看法。**2** [U] a point or distance at which the outline of an object is clearly seen by the eye or through a LENS（眼睛或镜头的）焦距，调焦：*The children's faces are badly* ***out of focus*** (= not clearly shown) *in the photograph.* 照片上孩子们的脸模糊不清。◇ *The binoculars were not* ***in focus*** (= were not showing things clearly). 这副双筒望远镜的焦距不对。 **3** (*also* **'focal point**) [C] (*physics* 物) a point at which waves of light, sound, etc. meet after REFLECTION or REFRACTION; the point from which waves of light, sound, etc. seem to come（光、声等的）焦点，中心点，源 **4** [C] (*geology* 地) the point at which an EARTHQUAKE starts to happen （地震的）震源

fo·cused (*also* **fo·cussed**) /'fəʊkəst; *NAmE* 'foʊ-/ *adj.* with your attention directed to what you want to do; with very clear aims 注意力集中的；目标明确的：*She should do well in her studies this year—she's very focused.* 今年她的功课应该学得好，她的注意力很集中。

'focus group *noun* [C+sing./pl. v.] a small group of people, specially chosen to represent different social classes, etc., who are asked to discuss and give their opinions about a particular subject. The information obtained is used by people doing MARKET RESEARCH, for example about new products or for a political party. 焦点小组（选自各阶层，讨论某专项问题；所得信息常为市场调查人员或某政党所用）

fod·der /'fɒdə(r); *NAmE* 'fɑːd-/ *noun* [U] **1** food for horses and farm animals（马等家畜的）饲料，秣 **2** (*disapproving*) (often after a noun 常置于名词后) people or things that are considered to have only one use（人或东西）只能是…的料：*Without education, these children will end up as factory fodder* (= only able to work in a factory). 不受教育，这些孩子将来只能到工厂干活。◇ *This story will be more fodder for the gossip columnists.* 这个传闻会是闲谈专栏作家的又一素材。➲ SEE ALSO CANNON FODDER

foe /fəʊ; *NAmE* foʊ/ *noun* (*old-fashioned* or *formal*) an enemy 敌人；仇敌

foehn = FÖHN

foe·tal (*BrE*) = FETAL

foe·tid = FETID

foe·tus (*BrE*) = FETUS

fog /fɒg; *NAmE* fɔːg; fɑːg/ *noun, verb*

■***noun*** [U, C] **1** a thick cloud of very small drops of water in the air close to the land or sea, that is very difficult to see through 雾：***Dense/thick fog*** *is affecting roads in the north and visibility is poor.* 浓雾影响了北部的公路，能见度很低。◇ ***freezing fog*** 寒雾 ◇ ***Patches of fog*** *will clear by mid-morning.* 上午十时左右，团团浓雾将散去。◇ *We get heavy fogs on this coast in winter.* 冬天这片海岸雾气很重。◇ *The town was covered in a thick* ***blanket of fog***. 大雾笼罩了这个城镇。◇ *The* ***fog*** *finally* ***lifted*** (= disappeared). 雾终于散了。 ➲ COLLOCATIONS AT WEATHER ➲ COMPARE MIST *n.* (1) **2** a state of confusion, in which things are not clear 迷惘；困惑：*He went through the day with his mind* ***in a fog***. 整整一天，他的头脑都是昏昏沉沉的。

■***verb*** (**-gg-**) **1** [I, T] ~ (**sth**) (**up**) if a glass surface **fogs** or is **fogged** up, it becomes covered in steam or small drops of water so that you cannot see through（使）雾气笼罩 **2** [T] ~ **sth** to make sb/sth confused or less clear 使迷惘；使困惑：*I tried to clear the confusion that was fogging my brain.* 我试图解除使我迷茫的困惑。◇ *The government was trying to* ***fog the real issues*** *before the election.* 政府企图在选举前混淆实质问题。

fog·bound /'fɒgbaʊnd; *NAmE* 'fɔːg-; 'fɑːg-/ *adj.* unable to operate because of fog; unable to travel or to leave a place because of fog 因雾不能运行的；因雾滞留的：*a fogbound airport* 因雾关闭的机场 ◇ *fogbound passengers* 因雾滞留的旅客 ◇ *She spent hours fogbound in Brussels.* 她因雾在布鲁塞尔滞留了好几个小时。

fogey (*also* **fogy**) /'fəʊgi; *NAmE* 'foʊgi/ *noun* (*pl.* **fogeys**, **fo·gies**) a person with old-fashioned ideas that he or she is unwilling to change 老顽固；守旧落伍的人：*He sounds like such an* ***old fogey!*** 他说话听起来真是个老顽固！

foggy /'fɒgi; *NAmE* 'fɔːgi; 'fɑːgi/ *adj.* (**fog·gier**, **fog·gi·est**) not clear because of FOG 有雾的；雾茫茫的：*foggy conditions* 有雾的环境 ◇ *a foggy road* 雾茫茫的道路

IDM **not have the 'foggiest (idea)** (*informal*) to not know anything at all about sth 完全不知道；一无所知；茫无头绪：*'Do you know where she is?' 'Sorry, I haven't the foggiest.'* "你知道她在哪儿吗？" "对不起，我一点也不知道。"

fog·horn /'fɒghɔːn; *NAmE* 'fɔːghɔːrn; 'fɑːg-/ *noun* an instrument that makes a loud noise to warn ships of danger in FOG 雾角，雾喇叭（向雾中的船只发警告）：*He's got a voice like a foghorn* (= a loud unpleasant voice). 他那大嗓门像雾角一样刺耳。

'fog lamp (*BrE*) (*also* **'fog light** *NAmE, BrE*) *noun* a very bright light on the front or back of a car to help the driver to see or be seen in FOG 雾灯（在车头或车尾）

fogy = FOGEY

föhn (*also* **foehn**) /fɜːn/ *noun* (*usually* **the föhn**) [sing.] a hot wind that blows in the Alps（阿尔卑斯山脉的）焚风

foi·ble /'fɔɪbl/ *noun* a silly habit or a strange or weak aspect of a person's character, that is considered harmless by other people（性格上无伤大雅的）怪癖，弱点，小缺点 SYN **idiosyncrasy**：*We have to tolerate each other's little foibles.* 我们得互相容忍对方的小缺点。

,foie 'gras *noun* [U] ➲ PÂTÉ DE FOIE GRAS

foil /fɔɪl/ *noun, verb*

■***noun*** **1** (*BrE also* **,silver 'foil**) [U] metal made into very thin sheets that is used for covering or wrapping things, especially food（尤指包装食物等用的）箔：(*BrE*) *aluminium foil* 铝箔 ◇ (*NAmE*) *aluminum foil* 铝箔 ➲ SEE ALSO TINFOIL **2** [U] paper that is covered in very thin sheets of metal 箔纸（覆有箔的纸）：*The chocolates are individually wrapped in gold foil.* 巧克力用金箔纸一颗颗独立包装。 **3** [C] ~ (**for sb/sth**) a person or thing that contrasts with, and therefore emphasizes, the qualities of another person or thing 陪衬者；陪衬物：*The pale walls provide a perfect foil for the furniture.* 浅色的墙壁完全衬托出家具的特色。 **4** [C] a long thin light SWORD used in the sport of FENCING（击剑运动用的）花剑 ➲ VISUAL VOCAB PAGE V52

■***verb*** [often passive] to stop sth from happening, especially sth illegal; to prevent sb from doing sth 挫败，阻止，制止（非法活动等）SYN **thwart**：~ **sth** *to* ***foil*** *a plan/crime/plot* 挫败计划 / 犯罪 / 阴谋 ◇ *Customs officials foiled an attempt to smuggle the paintings out of the country.* 海关关员阻截了一次企图走私画作出境的阴谋。◇ ~ **sb** (**in sth**) *They were foiled in their attempt to smuggle the paintings.* 他们走私绘画作品的企图未能得逞。

foist /fɔɪst/ *verb*

PHR V **'foist sb/sth on/upon sb** to force sb to accept sb/sth that they do not want 强迫接受；把…强加于：*The title for her novel was foisted on her by the publishers.* 她的小说书名是出版商强加给她的。

fold /fəʊld; *NAmE* foʊld/ *verb, noun*

■***verb*** **1** [T] to bend sth, especially paper or cloth, so that one part lies on top of another part 折叠，对折（纸、织物等）：~ **sth** (**up**) *He folded the map up and put it in his pocket.* 他把地图折叠起来，放进了口袋。◇ *First,* ***fold*** *the paper* ***in half/in two***. 首先，把纸对折起来。◇ ~ **sth** (**back, down, over, etc.**) *The blankets had been folded down.* 毛毯已折叠起来。◇ *a pile of neatly folded clothes* 一摞折叠整齐的衣服 ◇ *The bird folded its wings.* 那只鸟收起了翅膀。OPP **unfold** ➲ SEE ALSO FOLD-UP **2** [T, I] to bend sth so that it becomes smaller or flatter and can be stored or carried more easily; to bend or be able to bend in this way 折小，叠平，可折小，可叠平（以便贮存或携带）：

F

~ sth (away/down/up) *The bed can be folded away during the day.* 这张床在白天可以折叠收起。◇ ~ (away/up) *The table folds up when not in use.* 这桌子不用时可以折叠起来。◇ (*figurative*) *When she heard the news, her legs just folded under her* (= she fell). 她听到这消息时双腿发软（倒在地上）。◇ + adj. *The ironing board folds flat for easy storage.* 烫衣板能够折起来，便于存放。**3** [T] to wrap sth around sb/sth 包；裹：~ A in B *She gently folded the baby in a blanket.* 她轻轻地把婴儿裹在毯子里。◇ ~ B round/over A *She folded a blanket around the baby.* 她用毯子把婴儿裹了起来。**4** [I] (of a company, a play, etc. 公司、戏剧等) to close because it is not successful 倒闭；停演；结束

F

IDM **fold your 'arms** to put one of your arms over the other one and hold them against your body 双臂交叉在胸前 **fold your 'hands** to bring or hold your hands together 十指交叉合拢交叠：*She kept her hands folded in her lap.* 她双手合拢，放在腿上。**fold sb in your 'arms** (*literary*) to put your arms around sb and hold them against your body 拥抱；搂住

PHR V **,fold sth↔'in | ,fold sth 'into sth** (in cooking 烹饪) to add one substance to another and gently mix them together 把…调入；拌入：*Fold in the beaten egg whites.* 调入打好的蛋白。

■ *noun* **1** [C] a part of sth, especially cloth, that is folded or hangs as if it had been folded 褶；褶层；折叠部分：*the folds of her dress* 她的连衣裙上的褶 ◇ *loose folds of skin* 皮肤松垮的褶皱 **2** [C] a mark or line made by folding sth, or showing where sth should be folded 褶痕；褶缝；褶线 **3** [C] an area in a field surrounded by a fence or wall where sheep are kept for safety 羊栏；羊圈 **4 the fold** [sing.] a group of people with whom you feel you belong or who share the same ideas or beliefs 志趣相同的人们；同一信仰的人们：*He called on former Republican voters to return to the fold.* 他号召昔日拥护共和党的选民重新回到支持共和党的行列。**5** [C] (*geology* 地) a curve or bend in the line of the layers of rock in the earth's CRUST（地壳岩石层的）褶皱 **6** [C] (*BrE*) a hollow place among hills or mountains 山坳；山洼；山谷

IDM **a,bove/be,low the 'fold** in/not in a position where you see it first, for example in the top/bottom part of a newspaper page or web page（报纸或网页）最上 / 下面部分，最显眼 / 不显眼部分：*Your ad will be placed above the fold for prominent exposure.* 你们的广告将放在页面上端的醒目位置。➲ COMPARE ABOVE-THE-FOLD, BELOW-THE-FOLD

-fold *suffix* (in adjectives and adverbs 构成形容词和副词) multiplied by; having the number of parts mentioned 乘以；…倍；由…部分组成：*to increase tenfold* 增加到十倍 ➲ MORE LIKE THIS 7, page R25

fold·away /ˈfəʊldəweɪ; *NAmE* ˈfoʊld-/ *adj.* = FOLDING

fold·er /ˈfəʊldə(r); *NAmE* ˈfoʊld-/ *noun* **1** a cardboard or plastic cover for holding loose papers, etc. 文件夹；纸夹 ➲ VISUAL VOCAB PAGE V71 **2** (in some computer systems) a way of organizing and storing computer files（某些计算机系统中的）文件夹 ➲ WORDFINDER NOTE AT FILE

fold·ing /ˈfəʊldɪŋ; *NAmE* ˈfoʊ-/ (*also less frequent* **fold·away**) *adj.* [only before noun] (of a piece of furniture, a bicycle, etc. 家具、自行车等) that can be folded, so that it can be carried or stored in a small space 折叠式的；可折叠的：*a folding chair* 折椅 ◇ *a foldaway bed* 折叠床

'fold-up *adj.* [only before noun] (of an object 物件) that can be made smaller by closing or folding so that it takes up less space 可收拢的；可折叠的

fo·li·age /ˈfəʊliɪdʒ; *NAmE* ˈfoʊ-/ *noun* [U] the leaves of a tree or plant; leaves and branches together（植物的）叶；枝叶：*dense green foliage* 茂密的绿叶 ➲ VISUAL VOCAB PAGE V10

fo·liar /ˈfəʊliə(r); *NAmE* ˈfoʊ-/ *adj.* (*specialist*) relating to leaves 叶的；叶状的：*foliar colour* 叶子的颜色

folic acid /ˌfɒlɪk ˈæsɪd; ˌfəʊ-; *NAmE* ˌfoʊ-/ *noun* [U] a VITAMIN found in green vegetables, LIVER and KIDNEY, needed by the body for the production of red blood cells 叶酸（见于绿色蔬菜、肝、肾的一种维生素，用于造红血球）

folio /ˈfəʊliəʊ; *NAmE* ˈfoʊlioʊ/ *noun* (*pl.* **-os**) **1** a book made with large sheets of paper, especially as used in early printing（尤指早期印刷的）对开本 **2** (*specialist*) a single sheet of paper from a book（书籍的）一页

folk /fəʊk; *NAmE* foʊk/ *noun, adj.*

■ *noun* **1** (*also* **folks** *especially in NAmE*) [pl.] (*informal*) people in general 人们：*ordinary working-class folk* 普通劳动大众 ◇ *I'd like a job working with* **old folk** *or kids.* 我喜欢与老人或小孩打交道的工作。◇ *the folks back home* (= from the place where you come from) 家乡的乡亲父老 **2 folks** [pl.] (*informal*) a friendly way of addressing more than one person 各位；大伙儿：*Well, folks, what are we going to do today?* 喂，伙计们，我们今天要干什么？ **3 folks** [pl.] (*informal, especially NAmE*) the members of your family, especially your parents 亲属；家属；（尤指）爹妈：*How are your folks?* 你爸妈好吗？**4** [pl.] people from a particular country or region, or who have a particular way of life（某国、某地区或某生活方式的）普通百姓：*country folk* 乡下人 ◇ *townsfolk* 城里人 ◇ *farming folk* 农民 **5** (*also* **'folk music**) [U] music in the traditional style of a country or community 民间音乐：*a folk festival/concert* 民间音乐节 / 音乐会

■ *adj.* [only before noun] **1** (of art, culture, etc. 艺术、文化等) traditional and typical of the ordinary people of a country or community 传统民间的；民俗的：*folk art* 民间艺术 ◇ *a folk museum* 民俗博物馆 **2** based on the beliefs of ordinary people 流传民间的；普通百姓的：*folk wisdom* 民间智慧 ◇ *Garlic is widely used in Chinese folk medicine.* 大蒜广泛应用于中国民间医药。

'folk dance *noun* [C, U] a traditional dance of a particular area or country; a piece of music for such a dance 土风舞；民间舞蹈；民间舞曲 ➲ WORDFINDER NOTE AT DANCE

'folk etymology (*also* **,popular ety'mology**) *noun* [U, C] a process by which a word is changed, for example because of a mistaken belief that it is related to another word, or to make a foreign word sound more familiar 民间词源；俗词源学：*Folk etymology has created the cheeseburger and the beanburger, but the first hamburgers were in fact named after the city of Hamburg.* 民间词源创造了 cheeseburger 和 beanburger，但最初 hamburger 一词实际上是以德国汉堡市命名的。

'folk hero *noun* a person that people in a particular place admire because of sth special he or she has done 民间英雄

folk·lore /ˈfəʊklɔː(r); *NAmE* ˈfoʊk-/ *noun* [U] the traditions and stories of a country or community 民间传统；民俗；民间传说：*Irish/Indian folklore* 爱尔兰 / 印度民俗 ◇ *The story rapidly became part of family folklore.* 这个故事很快就成为家族传说的一部分。

folk·lor·ist /ˈfəʊklɔːrɪst; *NAmE* ˈfoʊk-/ *noun* a person who studies folklore, especially as an academic subject 民俗学家；民俗学研究者

,folk 'memory *noun* [C, U] a memory of sth in the past that the people of a country or community never forget 民间共同记忆（一个国家或社群的人不会忘记的事）

'folk music *noun* [U] = FOLK (5)

,folk 'rock *noun* [U] a style of music that combines elements of folk music and rock 民歌摇滚乐

'folk singer *noun* a person who sings folk songs 民歌手；唱民歌者

'folk song *noun* **1** a song in the traditional style of a country or community 民歌；民谣 **2** a type of song that became popular in the US in the 1960s, played on a GUITAR and often about political topics 仿民歌歌曲（美国 20 世纪 60 年代盛行，吉他伴奏，常以政治为题材）

folksy /ˈfəʊksi; *NAmE* ˈfoʊksi/ *adj.* **1** (*especially NAmE*) simple, friendly and informal 淳朴友好自然的；朴实热情

随意的：*They wanted the store to have a folksy small-town image.* 他们希望这家商店具有小城镇那种朴实热情的形象。**2** (*sometimes disapproving*) done or made in a traditional style that is typical of simple customs in the past 有民间传统的；有民间风味的；土里土气的：*a folksy ballad* 有民间风味的歌谣

'folk tale *noun* a very old traditional story from a particular place that was originally passed on to people in a spoken form 民间故事；民间传说

fol·licle /'fɒlɪkl; *NAmE* 'fɑːl-/ *noun* one of the very small holes in the skin which hair grows from（毛）囊

fol·low /'fɒləʊ; *NAmE* 'fɑːloʊ/ *verb*

- **GO AFTER** 跟随 **1** [T, I] ~ (**sb/sth**) to come or go after or behind sb/sth 跟随；跟着：*He followed her into the house.* 他跟随她走进房屋。◇ *Follow me please. I'll show you the way.* 请跟我走。我来给你指路。◇ *I think we're being followed.* 我认为有人跟踪我们。◇ (*figurative*) *She followed her mother into the medical profession.* 她走她母亲的路，从事医务工作。◇ *Wherever she led, they followed.* 她引向哪里，他们就跟到哪里。◇ *Sam walked in, with the rest of the boys following closely behind.* 萨姆走了进来，其他男孩紧跟其后。
- **HAPPEN/DO AFTER** 在…后发生／做 **2** [T, I] ~ (**sth/sb**) to come after sth/sb else in time or order; to happen as a result of sth else（时间或顺序上）在…后发生；因…而发生：*The first two classes are followed by a break of ten minutes.* 上完头两节课，有十分钟的课间休息。◇ *I remember little of the days that followed the accident.* 那次事故以后的日子我记不大清楚了。◇ *A period of unrest followed the president's resignation.* 总统辞职之后有一段时期的动荡。◇ *A detailed news report will follow shortly.* 下面紧接着是详细的新闻报道。◇ ***There followed** a short silence.* 接着沉默了一会儿。◇ *The opening hours are **as follows**...* 营业时间如下…◇ *A new proposal followed on from the discussions.* 讨论之后，出了一个新提案。**3** [T] to do sth after sth else 在…后做：**~ sth with sth** *Follow your treatment with plenty of rest.* 你治疗以后要多休息。◇ **~ sth up with sth** *They follow up their March show with four UK dates next month.* 他们在三月演出以后，就是下个月在英国的四场演出。
- **BE RESULT** 结果 **4** [I, T] (not usually used in the progressive tenses 通常不用于进行时) to be the logical result of sth 是…的必然结果：**~ (from sth)** *I don't see how that follows from what you've just said.* 根据你刚才所说的，我不明白怎么会产生那样的结果。◇ **it follows that...** *If a = b and b = c it follows that a = c.* 设a = b，b = c，则a = c。
- **OF PART OF MEAL** 一餐的部分 **5** [T, I] ~ (**sth**) to come or be eaten after another part 接着是；然后是；下一道是：*The main course was followed by fresh fruit.* 主菜以后是新鲜水果。**HELP** This pattern is usually used in the passive. 此句型通常用于被动语态：*I'll have soup and fish **to follow**.* 我要汤，然后要鱼。
- **ROAD/PATH** 道路；小径 **6** [T] ~ **sth** to go along a road, path, etc. 沿着（道路、小径等）：*Follow this road until you get to the school, then turn left.* 沿着这条路走到学校，然后向左拐。**7** [T] ~ **sth** (of a road, path, etc. 道路、小径等) to go in the same direction as sth or parallel to sth 沿着…伸延；与…平行：*The lane follows the edge of a wood for about a mile.* 小路沿树林边延伸约一英里。
- **ADVICE/INSTRUCTIONS** 忠告；指示 **8** [T] ~ **sth** to accept advice, instructions, etc. and do what you have been told or shown to do 接受，遵循，听从（忠告、指示等）：*to **follow** a **diet/recipe*** 按照规定饮食／菜谱 ◇ *He has trouble **following** simple **instructions**.* 简单的指示他都难以照办。◇ *Why didn't you **follow** my **advice**?* 你为什么不听我的劝告？
- **ACCEPT/COPY** 接受；效仿 **9** [T] ~ **sth** to accept sb/sth as a guide, a leader or an example; to copy sb/sth 接受…为指导（或领导、榜样）；追随；拥护；仿效：*They followed the teachings of Buddha.* 他们信佛教。◇ *He always followed the latest fashions* (= dressed in fashionable clothes). 他总是紧跟着服装潮流。◇ *I don't want you to follow my example and rush into marriage.* 我不希望你走我的老路，匆忙结婚。◇ *The movie follows the book faithfully.* 这部电影忠于原著。
- **UNDERSTAND** 理解 **10** [I, T] to understand an explanation or the meaning of sth 理解，明白（说明或意思）：**~ (sb)** *Sorry, I don't follow.* 对不起，我不明白。◇ *Sorry, I don't follow you.* 对不起，我听不懂你的话。◇ **~ sth** *The plot is almost impossible **to follow**.* 故事情节几乎叫人看不懂。➲ SYNONYMS AT UNDERSTAND
- **WATCH/LISTEN** 注视；听 **11** [T] ~ **sb/sth** to watch or listen to sb/sth very carefully 密切注视；倾听：*The children were following every word of the story intently.* 孩子们一字不漏地专心听故事。◇ *Her eyes followed him everywhere* (= she was looking at him all the time). 她一直在注视着他。
- **BE INTERESTED IN** 兴趣 **12** [T] ~ **sth** to take an active interest in sth and be aware of what is happening 对…产生浓厚兴趣而关注：*Have you been following the basketball championships?* 你是否一直在关注篮球锦标赛的赛程？◇ *Millions of people followed the trial on TV.* 几百万人饶有兴趣地收看了电视转播的审判。**13** to choose to regularly receive messages from a person, company, etc. using a MICROBLOGGING service（在微博客上）关注（人、公司等）：*I don't follow many celebrities on Twitter any more.* 我不再在推特上关注很多名人了。
- **OF BOOK/MOVIE** 书籍；电影 **14** [T] ~ **sth** to be concerned with the life or development of sb/sth 涉及…生活；有关…发展：*The novel follows the fortunes of a village community in Scotland.* 小说叙述了苏格兰一个村落的变迁。
- **PATTERN/COURSE** 模式；进程 **15** [T] ~ **sth** to develop or happen in a particular way 按…方式（或方向）发展；以…方式发生：*The day followed the usual pattern.* 这一天和平常过得一样。

IDM **follow in sb's 'footsteps** to do the same job, have the same style of life, etc. as sb else, especially sb in your family 仿效某人：*She works in television, following in her father's footsteps.* 她步父亲的后尘，在电视台工作。**follow your 'nose 1** to be guided by your sense of smell 凭嗅觉指引 **2** to go straight forward 一直向前走：*The garage is a mile ahead up the hill—just follow your nose.* 汽车修理站在前面一英里处的山坡上，一直往前走就可以到。**3** to act according to what seems right or reasonable, rather than following any particular rules 凭感觉行事；凭直觉办事 **follow 'suit 1** (in card games 纸牌游戏) to play a card of the same SUIT that has just been played 跟牌（跟着别人出同花色的牌）**2** to act or behave in the way that sb else has just done 跟着某人做；仿效某人；照着做 ➲ MORE AT ACT *n.*

PHR V **,follow sb a'round/a'bout** to keep going with sb wherever they go 到处跟随；跟踪：*Will you stop following me around!* 你不要再到处跟着我了！**,follow 'on 1** to go somewhere after sb else has gone there 跟着走；接着来；随后去：*You go to the beach with the kids and I'll follow on when I've finished work.* 你和孩子们去海滨，我办完事随后就来。**2** (of a CRICKET (1) team 板球队) to play a second INNINGS (= a period during which a team is BATTING) immediately after its first, because it has failed to reach a particular score 连打（在第一局得分不足时继续在下一局击球）**,follow 'through** (in TENNIS, GOLF, etc. 网球、高尔夫球等) to complete a stroke by continuing to move the club, RACKET, etc. after hitting the ball（击球后球拍、球棒等）完成顺势动作 ➲ RELATED NOUN FOLLOW-THROUGH (1) **,follow 'through (with sth)** | **,follow sth ↔'through** to finish sth that you have started 把…进行到底；完成（开了头的事）➲ RELATED NOUN FOLLOW-THROUGH (2) **,follow sth↔'up 1** to add to sth that you have just done by doing sth else 对…采取进一步行动；…后接着：*You should follow up your phone call with an email or a letter.* 你打电话后应该接着发一封电子邮件或写封信。**2** to find out more about sth that sb has told you or suggested to you 追查更多情况 **SYN** **investigate**：*The police are following up several leads after their TV appeal for information.* 警方在电视上呼吁提供信息后正沿着几条线索继续追查。➲ RELATED NOUN FOLLOW-UP

fol·low·ee /ˌfɒləʊ'iː; *NAmE* ˌfɑːloʊ'iː/ *noun* a person, company, etc. whose messages on a MICROBLOGGING service people choose to receive regularly（微博客的）关注对象：*I often use Twitter recommendations to select new* *followees*. 我经常利用推特的推荐来选择新的关注对象。 ➲ COMPARE FOLLOWER (4)

fol·low·er /ˈfɒləʊə(r); *NAmE* ˈfɑːloʊ-/ *noun* **1** a person who supports and admires a particular person or set of ideas 拥护者；追随者；信徒：*the followers of Mahatma Gandhi* 圣雄甘地的拥护者 **2** a person who is very interested in a particular activity and follows all the recent news about it 爱好者：*keen followers of football* 足球迷 ◇ *a follower of fashion* 赶时髦者 **3** a person who does things after sb else has done them first 仿效者；追随者：*She is a leader, not a follower.* 她是领导者，不是追随者。 **4** a person who chooses to regularly receive sb's messages using a MICROBLOGGING service （微博客上某人的）关注者：*a celebrity with thousands of followers on Twitter* 一个在推特上有成千上万关注者的名人 ➲ COMPARE FOLLOWEE

fol·low·ing 🔑 /ˈfɒləʊɪŋ; *NAmE* ˈfɑːloʊɪŋ/ *adj.*, *noun*, *prep.*

■ ***adj.* the following... 1** 🔑 next in time （时间上）接着的：*the following afternoon/month/year/week* 第二天下午；第二个月；第二年；第二周 ◇ *They arrived on Monday evening and we got there the following day.* 他们是星期一晚上到的，我们次日也抵达那里。 **2** 🔑 that is/are going to be mentioned next 下述的；下列的：*Answer the following questions.* 回答下列问题。 ➲ LANGUAGE BANK AT FIRST

IDM **a ˌfollowing ˈwind** a wind blowing in the same direction as a ship or other vehicle that helps it move faster 顺风

■ ***noun* 1** 🔑 [usually sing.] a group of supporters （统称）拥护者，追随者：*The band has a huge following in Italy.* 这个乐队在意大利有一大批热心的追随者。 **2** 🔑 **the following** (used with either a singular or a plural verb, depending on whether you are talking about one thing or person or several things or people 动词用单数还是复数取决于后面谈及的人、事物的单复数) the thing or things that you will mention next; the person or people that you will mention next 下述；下列；如下：*The following is a summary of events.* 现将重大事件综述如下。 ◇ *The following have been chosen to take part: Watts, Hodges and Lennox.* 已选定下列人员参加：沃茨、霍奇斯和伦诺克斯。

■ ***prep.*** 🔑 after or as a result of a particular event 在（某事）以后；由于：*He took charge of the family business following his father's death.* 父亲死后他就接管了家族企业。

ˌfollow-ˈon *noun* [sing.] (in CRICKET 板球) a second INNINGS (= a period during which a team is BATTING) that a team is made to play immediately after its first, if it fails to reach a particular score （一局未得到一定分数后的）连打，二局继续击球

ˌfollow-the-ˈleader (*also* **ˌfollow-my-ˈleader**) *noun* [U] a children's game in which people follow the person in front of them in a line, going wherever they go 学样游戏（参加者模仿领头人的动作）

ˌfollow-ˈthrough *noun* **1** [U, sing.] (in TENNIS, GOLF, etc. 网球、高尔夫球等) the final part of a stroke after the ball has been hit （击球后的）随球动作，顺势动作 **2** [U] the actions that sb takes in order to complete a plan （为完成某计划所采取的）后续行动：*The project could fail if there is inadequate follow-through.* 如果缺少恰当的后续行动，该项目可能失败。

ˈfollow-up *noun* [C, U] an action or a thing that continues sth that has already started or comes after sth similar that was done earlier 后续行动；后续事物：*The book is a follow-up to her excellent television series.* 这本书是继她的优秀电视系列片之后的又一力作。 ▶ **ˈfollow-up** *adj.* [only before noun]: *a follow-up study* 进一步的研究

folly /ˈfɒli; *NAmE* ˈfɑːli/ *noun* (*pl.* **-ies**) **1** [U, C] a lack of good judgement; the fact of doing sth stupid; an activity or idea that shows a lack of judgement 愚蠢；愚笨；愚蠢的想法（或事情、行为） **SYN** **stupidity**: *an act of sheer folly* 纯粹愚蠢的行动 ◇ *Giving up a secure job seems to be the height of folly.* 放弃一份稳定的工作似乎愚蠢至极。 ◇ **~ (to do sth)** *It would be folly to turn the offer down.* 拒绝这个建议是愚蠢之举。 ◇ *the follies of youth* 青年时期的愚蠢行为 **2** [C] a building that has no practical purpose but was built in the past for decoration, often in the garden of a large country house （常见于旧时乡间豪宅花园中的）装饰性建筑

fo·ment /fəʊˈment; *NAmE* foʊ-/ *verb* **~ sth** (*formal*) to create trouble or violence or make it worse 挑起，激起，煽动（事端或暴力） **SYN** **incite**: *They accused him of fomenting political unrest.* 他们指控他煽动政治动乱。

fond /fɒnd; *NAmE* fɑːnd/ *adj.* (**fond·er**, **fond·est**) **1 ~ of sb** feeling affection for sb, especially sb you have known for a long time 喜爱（尤指认识已久的人）：*Over the years, I have **grown quite fond of** her.* 经过这么多年，我已相当喜欢她了。 ➲ SYNONYMS AT LOVE **2 ~ of (doing) sth** finding sth pleasant or enjoyable, especially sth you have liked or enjoyed for a long time 喜爱（尤指长期喜爱的事物）：*fond of music/cooking* 喜好音乐 / 烹饪 ◇ *We had **grown fond of** the house and didn't want to leave.* 我们已经喜欢上了这座房子，不想搬家。 ➲ SYNONYMS AT LIKE **3 ~ of (doing) sth** liking to do sth which other people find annoying or unpleasant, and doing it often 喜欢（做令人不快的事）：*Sheila's very fond of telling other people what to do.* 希拉爱对别人指手画脚。 ◇ *He's rather too fond of the sound of his own voice* (= he talks too much). 他太爱讲话了。 **4** [only before noun] kind and loving 深情的；温情的；慈爱的 **SYN** **affectionate**: *a **fond look/embrace/farewell*** 慈爱的目光；温情的拥抱；深情的告别 ◇ *I have very **fond memories** of my time in Spain* (= I remember it with affection and pleasure). 我十分怀念从前在西班牙的时光。 **5** [only before noun] **~ hope** a hope about sth that is not likely to happen （指希望）难以实现的；痴想的：*I waited all day **in the fond hope that** she would change her mind.* 我整天等待，痴心地希望她会回心转意。 ▶ **fond·ness** *noun* [U, sing.]: *He will be remembered by the staff with great fondness.* 全体人员将深挚地怀念他。 ◇ **~ for sb/sth** *a fondness for animals* 喜爱动物 **IDM** SEE ABSENCE

fon·dant /ˈfɒndənt; *NAmE* ˈfɑːn-/ *noun* **1** [U] a thick sweet soft mixture made from sugar and water, used especially to cover cakes 软糖料（尤用于装饰糕点）：*fondant icing* 软糖料糖霜 **2** [C] a soft sweet/candy that melts in the mouth, made of fondant 方旦软糖

fon·dle /ˈfɒndl; *NAmE* ˈfɑːndl/ *verb* **~ sb/sth** to touch and move your hand gently over sb/sth, especially in a sexual way, or in order to show love （尤指示爱或两性间）爱抚，抚摸 **SYN** **caress**

fond·ly /ˈfɒndli; *NAmE* ˈfɑːndli/ *adv.* **1** in a way that shows great affection 深情地；温情地；慈爱地 **SYN** **affectionately**: *He looked at her fondly.* 他深情地望着她。 ◇ *I fondly remember my first job as a reporter.* 我深深地记得我初次工作当记者的情景。 **2** in a way that shows hope that is not reasonable or realistic 天真地；想当然地；一厢情愿地：*I fondly imagined that you cared for me.* 我天真地以为你很喜欢我。

fon·due /ˈfɒndjuː; *NAmE* fɑːnˈduː/ *noun* [C, U] **1** a Swiss dish of melted cheese and wine into which pieces of bread are DIPPED 奶酪火锅（瑞士特色菜，蘸面包片吃） **2** a dish of hot oil into which small pieces of meat, vegetables, etc. are DIPPED 热油火锅（在热油中涮肉片、蔬菜等）

font /fɒnt; *NAmE* fɑːnt/ *noun* **1** a large stone bowl in a church that holds water for the ceremony of BAPTISM 圣洗池（设于教堂中，常为石造） **2** (*specialist*) the particular size and style of a set of letters that are used in printing, etc. 字体；字型

fon·ta·nelle (*US usually* **fon·ta·nel**) /ˌfɒntəˈnel; *NAmE* ˌfɑːn-/ *noun* (*anatomy* 解) a space between the bones of a baby's SKULL, which makes a soft area on the top of the baby's head 囟，囟门（婴儿头顶骨未合缝处）

food 🔑 /fuːd/ *noun* **1** 🔑 [U] things that people or animals eat 食物：***a shortage of food/food shortages*** 粮食短缺 ◇ *food and drink* 饮食 ◇ *the food industry* 食品工业 **2** 🔑 [C, U] a particular type of food （某种）食物：*Do you like Italian food?* 你喜欢意大利食物吗？ ◇ ***frozen foods*** 冷冻食品 ◇ *a can of **dog food*** (= for a dog to eat) 一罐狗粮 ◇ *He's* *off his food* (= he does not want to eat anything). 他不想吃东西。 ➲ SEE ALSO CONVENIENCE FOOD, FAST FOOD, FUNCTIONAL FOOD, HEALTH FOOD, JUNK FOOD, SEAFOOD, SOUL FOOD, WHOLEFOOD ➲ WORDFINDER NOTE AT EAT

IDM **food for 'thought** an idea that makes you think seriously and carefully 引人深思的想法

'food bank *noun* a place where poor people can go to get free food 食物赈济处；食物银行

'food chain *noun* (*usually* **the food chain**) a series of living creatures in which each type of creature feeds on the one below it in the series 食物链：*Insects are fairly low down (on) the food chain.* 在食物链中，昆虫是级别相当低的生物。

foodie /'fu:di/ *noun* (*informal*) a person who is very interested in cooking and eating different kinds of food 美食家

'food mile *noun* a measurement of the distance food has to be transported from the producer to the consumer and the fuel that this uses 食物里程（指食物从产地运送到消费者手中的距离及油耗）：*We keep food miles to a minimum by sourcing products locally.* 我们在当地采购产品，从而将食物里程控制在最低。

'food poisoning *noun* [U] an illness of the stomach caused by eating food that contains harmful bacteria 食物中毒

'food processor *noun* a piece of equipment that is used to mix or cut up food 食物料理机；食物加工器 ➲ VISUAL VOCAB PAGE V26

'food science *noun* [U] the scientific study of food, for example what it is made of, the effects it has on our body, and how to prepare it and store it safely 食品科学（研究食品成分、对身体的作用及加工和贮存方法等）

'food stamp *noun* (*US*) a piece of paper that is given by the government to poor people, for them to buy food with（政府发给贫民的）食物券

food·stuff /'fu:dstʌf/ *noun* [usually pl.] (*specialist*) any substance that is used as food 食物；食品：*basic foodstuffs* 基本食物

'food web *noun* (*specialist*) a system of FOOD CHAINS that are related to and depend on each other 食物网（即相互关联和依存的食物链体系）

fool /fu:l/ *noun, verb, adj.*

■ ***noun*** **1** [C] a person who you think behaves or speaks in a way that lacks intelligence or good judgement 蠢人；傻瓜 SYN **idiot**: *Don't be such a fool!* 别这么傻了！◇ *I felt a fool when I realized my mistake.* 我意识到了自己的错误，觉得自己是个傻瓜。◇ *He told me he was an actor and I was* ***fool enough to*** *believe him.* 他告诉我他是演员，而我真傻，竟相信了他的话。**2** [C] (in the past) a man employed by a king or queen to entertain people by telling jokes, singing songs, etc.（旧时国王或王后豢养供人娱乐的）小丑，弄臣 SYN **jester 3** [U, C] (*BrE*) (usually in compounds 通常构成复合词) a cold light DESSERT (= a sweet dish) made from fruit that is cooked and crushed and mixed with cream or CUSTARD 奶油果泥，蛋奶果泥（甜食）：*rhubarb fool* 奶油大黄泥

IDM **act/play the 'fool** to behave in a stupid way in order to make people laugh, especially in a way that may also annoy them 装傻，扮丑相（以逗人笑，但往往惹人恼怒）：*Quit playing the fool and get some work done!* 别再装傻了，干点实事吧！**any fool can/could...** (*informal*) used to say that sth is very easy to do 任何人都能；容易得很：*Any fool could tell she was lying.* 任何人都可以看出她在撒谎。**be ˌno/ˌnobody's 'fool** to be too intelligent or know too much about sth to be tricked by other people 精明机智；不易上当：*She's nobody's fool when it comes to dealing with difficult patients.* 她对付难缠的病人很有办法。**a ˌfool and his ˌmoney are soon 'parted** (*saying*) a person who is not sensible usually spends money too quickly or carelessly, or is cheated by others 傻瓜口袋漏，有钱留不住；蠢人不积财 **fools rush 'in (where angels fear to 'tread)** (*saying*) people with little experience try to do the difficult or dangerous things which more experienced people would not consider doing（智者却步处）愚者独敢闯 **make a 'fool of sb** to say or do sth deliberately so that people will think that sb is stupid 愚弄某人：*Can't you see she's making a fool of you?* 难道你不明白她是在愚弄你？ ➲ SYNONYMS AT CHEAT **make a 'fool of yourself** to do sth stupid which makes other people think that you are a fool 出丑：*I made a complete fool of myself in front of everyone!* 我当众出了大丑了！**ˌmore fool 'sb (for doing sth)** (*informal*) used to say that you think that sb was stupid to do sth, especially when it causes them problems 蠢极了；犯傻：*'He's not an easy person to live with.' 'More fool her for marrying him!'* "和他共同生活很难。" "她和他结婚真傻！" **(there's) ˌno fool like an 'old fool** (*saying*) an older person who behaves in a stupid way is worse than a younger person who does the same thing, because experience should have taught him or her not to do it 糊涂莫过老糊涂；老糊涂最糊涂 ➲ MORE AT SUFFER

■ ***verb*** **1** [T] to trick sb into believing sth that is not true 欺骗；愚弄：**~ sb** *You don't fool me!* 不要骗我！◇ *She certainly* ***had me fooled****—I really believed her!* 她确实把我骗了，我真的相信了她的话！◇ **~ yourself** *You're fooling yourself if you think none of this will affect you.* 你要是认为此事一点也不会影响你，那就是欺骗自己。◇ **~ sb into doing sth** *Don't be fooled into thinking they're going to change anything.* 别上当受骗，以为他们打算作出任何改变。 **2** [I] to say or do stupid or silly things, often in order to make people laugh 说蠢话，干傻事（常为逗乐）：**~ (about/around)** *Stop fooling around and sit down!* 别干傻事了，坐下来！◇ **~ (about/around) with sth** *If you fool about with matches, you'll end up getting burned.* 如果你玩火柴，最后可能烧到自己。

IDM **you could have fooled 'me** (*informal*) used to say that you do not believe sth that sb has just told you（表示不相信别人的话）休想骗我，说得像真的一样：*'I'm trying as hard as I can!' 'You could have fooled me!'* "我要尽力而为！" "说得像真的似的！"

PHR V **ˌfool a'round 1** (*BrE also* **ˌfool a'bout**) to waste time instead of doing sth that you should be doing 闲耍；虚度光阴 SYN **mess around 2 fool around (with sb)** to have a sexual relationship with another person's partner; to have a sexual relationship with sb who is not your partner（和某人）乱搞男女关系 SYN **mess around**: *She's been fooling around with a married man.* 她一直和一个有妇之夫鬼混。

■ ***adj.*** [only before noun] (*informal*) showing a lack of intelligence or good judgement 傻的；愚蠢的 SYN **silly, stupid, foolish**: *That was a damn fool thing to do!* 干那种事真蠢！

fool·hardy /'fu:lhɑ:di; *NAmE* -hɑ:rdi/ *adj.* (*disapproving*) taking unnecessary risks 莽撞的；有勇无谋的 SYN **reckless**: *It would be foolhardy to sail in weather like this.* 这种天气出航就是瞎冒险。 ▶ **fool·hardi·ness** *noun* [U]

fool·ish /'fu:lɪʃ/ *adj.* **1** (of actions or behaviour 作为或行为) not showing good sense or judgement 愚蠢的；傻的 SYN **silly, stupid**: *She's just a vain, foolish woman.* 她不过是个愚蠢虚荣的女人。◇ *I was foolish enough to believe what Jeff told me.* 我真蠢，竟相信杰夫和我说的话。◇ *The accident was my fault—****it would be foolish*** *to pretend otherwise.* 这次事故是我的过失，装作没有责任那才傻呢。◇ *How could she have been so foolish as to fall in love with him?* 她怎么这么傻，竟爱上了他？ ◇ *a foolish idea/dream/mistake* 荒唐的想法 / 梦 / 错误 ◇ *It was a very foolish thing to do.* 干那种事很蠢。 **2** [not usually before noun] made to feel or look silly and embarrassed 不知所措；出丑；显得尴尬 SYN **silly, stupid**: *I felt foolish and a failure.* 我自觉是个愚蠢的失败者。◇ *He's afraid of looking foolish in front of his friends.* 他怕在朋友面前出丑。 ▶ **fool·ish·ly** *adv.*: *We foolishly thought that everyone would speak English.* 我们真蠢，竟以为人人都会说英语。◇ *Foolishly, I allowed myself to be persuaded to enter the contest.* 我竟傻乎乎地让人说服去参加比赛。 **fool·ish·ness** *noun* [U]: *Jenny had* *to laugh at her own foolishness.* 珍妮只好拿自己的愚蠢解嘲了。

fool·proof /ˈfuːlpruːf/ *adj.* (of a plan, machine, method, etc. 计划、机器、方法等) very well designed and easy to use so that it cannot fail and you cannot use it wrongly 使用简便的；完全可靠的；万无一失的 **SYN** **infallible**: *This recipe is foolproof—it works every time.* 这个食谱绝对管用，每次都万无一失。

fools·cap /ˈfuːlskæp/ *noun* [U] (*BrE*) a large size of paper for writing on （书写纸规格）大裁，大页纸

F

ˌfool's ˈerrand *noun* [sing.] a task that has no hope of being done successfully 徒劳无益的差事：*He sent me **on a fool's errand**.* 他派我去干白费力的事。

ˌfool's ˈgold *noun* [U] **1** a yellow mineral found in rock, which looks like gold but is not valuable, also called **iron pyrites** 愚人金（指黄铁矿） ➲ SEE ALSO PYRITES **2** something that you think is valuable or will earn you a lot of money, but which has no chance of succeeding 虚幻的摇钱树

ˌfool's ˈparadise *noun* [usually sing.] a state of happiness that is based on sth that is false or cannot last although the happy person does not realize it 傻瓜的天堂；虚幻的幸福

foos·ball /ˈfuːzbɔːl/ (*NAmE*) (*BrE* **ˈtable football**) *noun* [U] an indoor game for two people or teams, played by moving rows of small models of football (SOCCER) players in order to move a ball on a board that has marks like a football (SOCCER) field 桌上足球；桌式手动足球；足球机

foot /fʊt/ *noun, verb*

■ ***noun*** (*pl.* **feet** /fiːt/)

• **PART OF BODY** 身体部位 **1** [C] the lowest part of the leg, below the ankle, on which a person or an animal stands （人或动物的）脚，足：*My feet are aching.* 我的脚疼。◇ *to get/rise **to your feet*** (= stand up) 起立 ◇ *I've been **on my feet*** (= standing or walking around) *all day.* 我一整天没歇脚。◇ *We came **on foot*** (= we walked). 我们是走来的。◇ *walking around the house **in bare feet*** (= not wearing shoes or socks) 赤脚在房子里走来走去 ◇ ***Please wipe your feet*** (= your shoes) *on the mat.* 请在垫子上蹭一蹭脚。◇ *a **foot pump*** (= operated using your foot, not your hand) 脚踏泵 ◇ *a **foot passenger*** (= one who travels on a FERRY without a car) 步行旅客（无车上渡船者） ➲ SYNONYMS AT STAND ➲ COLLOCATIONS AT PHYSICAL ➲ VISUAL VOCAB PAGE V64 ➲ SEE ALSO ATHLETE'S FOOT, BAREFOOT, CLUB FOOT, UNDERFOOT

• **-FOOTED** …脚 **2** (in adjectives and adverbs 构成形容词和副词) having or using the type or number of foot/feet mentioned 有…脚（或足的）；有…只脚（的）；用…脚（或足的）：*bare-footed* 赤脚的 ◇ *four-footed* 四足的 ◇ *a left-footed shot into the corner* 踢入球门一角的左脚一记射门 ➲ SEE ALSO FLAT-FOOTED, SURE-FOOTED ➲ MORE LIKE THIS 8, page R25

• **PART OF SOCK** 袜子部分 **3** [C, usually sing.] the part of a sock, STOCKING, etc. that covers the foot （袜子的）足部

• **BASE/BOTTOM** 基础；底部 **4** [sing.] **the ~ of sth** the lowest part of sth; the base or bottom of sth 最下部；基础；底部：*the **foot of the stairs/page/mountain*** 楼梯底部；页末；山脚 ◇ *The nurse hung a chart at the **foot of the bed*** (= the part of the bed where your feet normally are when you are lying in it). 护士在床尾挂了一张表。➲ SYNONYMS AT BOTTOM

• **MEASUREMENT** 计量 **5** (*pl.* **feet** or **foot**) (*abbr.* **ft**) a unit for measuring length equal to 12 inches or 30.48 centimetres 英尺（= 12 英寸或 30.48 厘米）：*a 6-foot high wall* * 6 英尺高的墙 ◇ *We're flying at 35 000 feet.* 我们在 35 000 英尺高空飞行。◇ *'How tall are you?' 'Five foot nine'* (= five feet and nine inches). "你多高？" "五英尺九英寸。"

• **-FOOTER** …英尺高（或长）者 **6** (in compound nouns 构成复合名词) a person or thing that is a particular number of feet tall or long …英尺高的人（或东西）；…英尺长的东西：*His boat is an eighteen-footer.* 他的小船长十八英尺。

• **IN POETRY** 诗歌 **7** [sing.] (*specialist*) a unit of rhythm in a line of poetry containing one stressed syllable and one or more syllables without stress. Each of the four divisions in the following line is a foot. 音步（诗行中的节奏单位，每个音步中有一个重读音节）：*For ˈmen / may ˈcome / and ˈmen / may ˈgo.*（此诗行四个部分有四个音步）

IDM **be rushed/run off your ˈfeet** to be extremely busy; to have too many things to do 忙得不可开交；要做太多的事 **fall/land on your ˈfeet** to be lucky in finding yourself in a good situation, or in getting out of a difficult situation 特别走运；安然脱离困境；幸免于难 **feet ˈfirst 1** with your feet touching the ground before any other part of your body 脚先着地：*He landed feet first.* 他落地时双脚先着地。**2** (*humorous*) if you leave a place **feet first**, you are carried out after you are dead 伸腿离开某地（指死去）：*You'll have to carry me out feet first!* 想把我撵走，除非让我横着出去！ **get/have a/your ˌfoot in the ˈdoor** to manage to enter an organization, a field of business, etc. that could bring you success 设法加入，涉足（某组织、行业等）：*I always wanted to work in TV but it took me two years to get a foot in the door.* 我一直想做电视工作，但花了两年才进了这个圈子。**get/start off on the right/wrong ˈfoot (with sb)** (*informal*) to start a relationship well/badly 开始时关系良好 / 不好：*I seem to have got off on the wrong foot with the new boss.* 看来我和新老板的关系一开头就不好。**get your ˈfeet wet** (*especially NAmE, informal*) to start doing sth that is new for you 初次涉足；开始做（新鲜的事情）：*At that time he was a young actor, just getting his feet wet.* 那时他还是个年轻演员，才初出茅庐。**have feet of ˈclay** to have a fault or weakness in your character 品格上有缺陷（或弱点） **have/keep your ˈfeet on the ground** to have a sensible and realistic attitude to life 实事求是；脚踏实地 **have/keep a foot in both ˈcamps** to be involved in or connected with two different or opposing groups 脚踩两只船 **have ˌone foot in the ˈgrave** (*informal*) to be so old or ill/sick that you are not likely to live much longer 行将就木；命不久矣；大去之期不远 **…my ˈfoot!** (*informal, humorous*) a strong way of saying that you disagree completely with what has just been said（完全不同意对方所说）胡说八道：*'Ian can't come because he's tired.' 'Tired my foot! Lazy more like!'* "伊恩不能来，因为他累了。" "累个屁！说懒还差不多！" **on your ˈfeet** completely well or in a normal state again after an illness or a time of trouble （困境后）恢复，完全复原；（病后）痊愈：*Sue's back on her feet again after her operation.* 休手术后又恢复健康了。◇ *The new chairman hopes to get the company back on its feet within six months.* 新董事长希望在六个月以内使公司恢复元气。➲ SYNONYMS AT STAND **put your best foot ˈforward** to make a great effort to do sth, especially if it is difficult or you are feeling tired 竭尽全力；全力以赴 **put your ˈfeet up** to sit down and relax, especially with your feet raised and supported （尤指架起双腿）坐下休息：*After a hard day's work, it's nice to get home and put your feet up.* 辛劳一天后回家架起双腿休息是很惬意的。**put your ˈfoot down 1** to be very strict in opposing what sb wishes to do 坚决制止；执意反对：*You've got to put your foot down and make him stop seeing her.* 你得坚决制止他再见她。**2** (*BrE*) to drive faster 踩油门；加速行驶：*She put her foot down and roared past them.* 她猛踩油门，从他们旁边呼啸而过。**put your ˈfoot in it** (*BrE*) (*also* **put your foot in your ˈmouth** *NAmE, BrE*) to say or do sth that upsets, offends or embarrasses sb （在语言或行为上）使人不安，冒犯别人，使人尴尬：*I really put my foot in it with Ella—I didn't know she'd split up with Tom.* 我真的冒犯了埃拉，我不知道她和汤姆分手了。**put a foot ˈwrong** (usually used in negative sentences 通常用于否定句) to make a mistake 犯错误；做错事：*In the last two games he has hardly put a foot wrong.* 他在上两局比赛中几乎一点错都没有出。**set ˈfoot in/on sth** to enter or visit a place 进入，访问，参观（某地）：*the first man to set foot on the moon* 第一个登上月球的人 ◇ *I vowed never to set foot in the place again.* 我发誓再不去那个地方了。**set sb/sth on their/its ˈfeet** to make sb/sth independent or successful 使独立；使成功：*His business sense helped* *set the club on its feet again.* 他的经营意识使俱乐部又重振雄风。**stand on your own (two) 'feet** to be independent and able to take care of yourself 自立；独立：*When his parents died he had to learn to stand on his own two feet.* 他的父母去世后他不得不学会自立。**under your 'feet** in the way; stopping you from working, etc. 阻碍，妨碍（工作等）；碍手碍脚：*I don't want you kids under my feet while I'm cooking.* 我做饭时不希望你们这些孩子在我这儿碍手碍脚的。➲ MORE AT BOOT *n.*, COLD *adj.*, DRAG *v.*, FIND *v.*, GRASS *n.*, GROUND *n.*, HAND *n.*, HEAD *n.*, ITCHY, LEFT *adj.*, PATTER *n.*, PULL *v.*, SHOE *n.*, SHOOT *v.*, SIT, STOCKING, SWEEP *v.*, THINK *v.*, VOTE *v.*, WAIT *v.*, WALK *v.*, WEIGHT *n.*, WORLD

■ *verb*

IDM **foot the 'bill** (*informal*) to be responsible for paying the cost of sth 负担费用：*Once again it will be the tax-payer who has to foot the bill.* 这一次掏腰包的又得是纳税人。

foot·age /ˈfʊtɪdʒ/ *noun* [U] part of a film showing a particular event（影片中的）连续镜头，片段：*old film footage of the moon landing* 一段登月的老影片

ˌfoot-and-ˈmouth disease (*NAmE also* **ˌhoof-and-ˈmouth disease**) *noun* [U] a disease of cows, sheep, etc., which causes sore places on the mouth and feet 口蹄疫，口蹄病（牛羊等的疾病，引起口、蹄溃疡）

foot·ball /ˈfʊtbɔːl/ *noun* **1** [U] (*also formal* **Asˌsociation ˈfootball**) (*both BrE*) (*also* **soc·cer** *NAmE, BrE*) (*also BrE, informal* **footy**, **footie**) a game played by two teams of 11 players, using a round ball which players kick up and down the playing field. Teams try to kick the ball into the other team's goal. 足球运动：*to **play football*** 踢足球 ◇ ***a football match/team/stadium*** 足球比赛；足球队；足球场 ➲ VISUAL VOCAB PAGE V48 ➲ SEE ALSO GAELIC FOOTBALL **2** [U] (*NAmE*) = AMERICAN FOOTBALL ➲ VISUAL VOCAB PAGE V48 **3** [C] a large round or OVAL ball made of leather or plastic and filled with air 足球；橄榄球 ➲ VISUAL VOCAB PAGE V48 **4** [C] (always used with an adjective 总是与形容词连用) an issue or a problem that frequently causes argument and disagreement 屡起争议的课题；被踢来踢去的难题：*Health care should not become a political football.* 保健问题不应该成为被踢来踢去的政治皮球。

ˈfootball boot *noun* (*BrE*) a leather shoe with pieces of rubber on the bottom to stop it slipping, worn for playing football (SOCCER) 足球鞋（鞋底有防滑橡胶钉）➲ COMPARE CLEAT (3)

foot·baller /ˈfʊtbɔːlə(r)/ *noun* (*BrE*) a person who plays football (SOCCER), especially as a profession（职业）足球运动员

foot·ball·ing /ˈfʊtbɔːlɪŋ/ *adj.* [only before noun] (*BrE*) connected with the game of football (SOCCER) 足球的；与足球比赛有关的：*footballing skills* 足球技巧

ˈfootball pools (*also* **the pools**) *noun* [pl.] a form of gambling in Britain in which people try to win money by saying what the results of football (SOCCER) matches will be 赌球，足球普尔（猜足球赛结果的赌博）：*They've had a big win on the football pools.* 他们在赌球中赢了一大笔钱。

foot·brake /ˈfʊtbreɪk/ *noun* a BRAKE in a vehicle which is operated using your foot 脚刹车

foot·bridge /ˈfʊtbrɪdʒ/ *noun* a narrow bridge used only by people who are walking 人行桥；步行桥 ➲ VISUAL VOCAB PAGE V3

foot·er /ˈfʊtə(r)/ *noun* **1** a line or block of text that is automatically added to the bottom of every page that is printed from a computer（计算机打印的每页的）页脚，页尾 ➲ COMPARE HEADER (2) **2** a line at the bottom of a page on the Internet（网页的）页脚：*a website footer* 一个网站页脚

foot·fall /ˈfʊtfɔːl/ *noun* **1** [C] (*literary*) the sound of the steps made by sb walking 脚步声 **2** [U] (*BrE, business* 商) the number of people that visit a particular shop/store, shopping centre, etc. over a period of time 客流，人流（商店、购物中心在一段时间内的访客人数）：*a campaign to increase footfall* 旨在增加客流的活动

ˈfoot fault *noun* (in TENNIS 网球) a mistake that is made by not keeping behind the line when SERVING 脚误，脚部犯规（发球踏线）

foot·hill /ˈfʊthɪl/ *noun* [usually pl.] a hill or low mountain at the base of a higher mountain or range of mountains 山麓小丘：*the foothills of the Himalayas* 喜马拉雅山脉山麓丘陵 ➲ WORDFINDER NOTE AT MOUNTAIN ➲ VISUAL VOCAB PAGE V5

foot·hold /ˈfʊthəʊld; *NAmE* -hoʊld/ *noun* **1** a crack, hole or branch where your foot can be safely supported when climbing 立足处（攀登时足可踩的缝、洞、树枝等）**2** [usually sing.] a strong position in a business, profession, etc. from which sb can make progress and achieve success（可以此发展或取得成功的）稳固地位，立足点：*The company is eager to **gain a foothold** in Europe.* 这家公司急于在欧洲取得一席之地。

footie /ˈfʊti/ *noun* [U] (*BrE, informal*) = FOOTBALL (1)

foot·ing /ˈfʊtɪŋ/ *noun* [sing.] **1** the position of your feet when they are safely on the ground or some other surface 立足；站稳：*She **lost her footing*** (= she slipped or lost her balance) *and fell backwards into the water.* 她脚未站稳，向后一仰掉进水中。◇ *I slipped and struggled to regain my footing.* 我滑了一下，但挣扎着站稳了脚跟。**2** the basis on which sth is established or organized 立足点；基础：*The company is now **on a sound financial footing**.* 该公司现在已是资金稳健。◇ *The country has been **on a war footing*** (= prepared for war) *since March.* 自三月份起这个国家就准备要打仗。**3** the position or status of sb/sth in relation to others; the relationship between two or more people or groups 地位；人际关系：*The two groups must meet **on an equal footing**.* 这两个集团必须以平等地位会谈。◇ *They were demanding to be treated **on the same footing** as the rest of the teachers.* 他们要求得到和其他老师同等的待遇。

foot·lights /ˈfʊtlaɪts/ *noun* [pl.] a row of lights along the front of the stage in a theatre 脚灯（舞台前面的一排灯）➲ WORDFINDER NOTE AT STAGE

foot·ling /ˈfuːtlɪŋ/ *adj.* (*old-fashioned, informal*) not important and likely to make you annoyed 无足轻重的；无聊（而烦人）的

foot·loose /ˈfʊtluːs/ *adj.* free to go where you like or do what you want because you have no responsibilities 行动无拘无束的；自由自在的：*Bert was a footloose, unemployed actor.* 伯特是不受雇于任何人的自由演员。◇ *Ah, I was still **footloose and fancy-free*** (= free to enjoy myself) *in those days.* 啊，那些日子我还是自由自在、无忧无虑的。

foot·man /ˈfʊtmən/ *noun* (*pl.* **-men** /-mən/) a male servant in a house in the past, who opened the door to visitors, served food at table, etc.（旧时宅院的）男仆，门房，侍者

foot·note /ˈfʊtnəʊt; *NAmE* -noʊt/ *noun* **1** an extra piece of information that is printed at the bottom of a page in a book 脚注 **2** (of an event or a person 事情或人) that may be remembered but only as sth/sb that is not important 次要者

foot·path /ˈfʊtpɑːθ; *NAmE* -pæθ/ *noun* **1** (*BrE*) a path that is made for people to walk along, especially in the country（尤指乡间的）人行小道：*a public footpath* 人行道 ➲ VISUAL VOCAB PAGE V3 **2** (*AustralE, NZE*) = PAVEMENT

foot·plate /ˈfʊtpleɪt/ *noun* (*BrE*) the part of a steam train's engine where the driver stands（蒸汽机车司机站立的）平台

foot·print /ˈfʊtprɪnt/ *noun* **1** [usually pl.] a mark left on a surface by a person's foot or shoe or by an animal's foot 脚印；足迹：*footprints in the sand* 沙地足迹 ◇ *muddy footprints on the kitchen floor* 厨房地板上的泥脚印 **2** the amount of space that sth fills, for example the amount of space that a computer takes up on a desk（某物所占的）

F

空间量，面积 **3** the area on the earth in which a signal from a communications SATELLITE can be received（通信卫星）覆盖区

foot·rest /ˈfʊtrest/ *noun* a support for your foot or feet, for example on a motorcycle or when you are sitting down 搁脚物

the Foot·sie™ /ˈfʊtsi/ *noun* = FTSE INDEX™

foot·sie /ˈfʊtsi/ *noun* (*informal*)
IDM **play ˈfootsie with sb** to touch sb's feet lightly with your own feet, especially under a table, as an expression of affection or sexual interest（在桌下）与某人脚碰脚调情，脚挨脚爱抚

ˈfoot soldier *noun* **1** a soldier who fights on foot, not on a horse or in a vehicle 步兵 **2** a person in an organization who does work that is important but boring, and who has no power or responsibility（组织中从事乏味工作而不担责任，但又不可或缺的）群众员工

foot·sore /ˈfʊtsɔː(r)/ *adj.* (*formal*) having sore or tired feet, especially after walking a long way（因走远路）脚痛，脚酸

foot·step /ˈfʊtstep/ *noun* [usually pl.] the sound or mark made each time your foot touches the ground when you are walking or running 脚步声；足迹：*the sound of footsteps on the stairs* 楼梯上的脚步声 ◇ *footsteps in the snow* 雪地上的足迹 IDM SEE FOLLOW

foot·stool /ˈfʊtstuːl/ *noun* a low piece of furniture used for resting your feet on when you are sitting 脚凳（坐时搁脚的矮凳）➲ VISUAL VOCAB PAGE V22

foot·sure /ˈfʊtʃʊə(r); ˈfʊtʃɔː(r); *NAmE* -ʃʊr/ *adj.* = SURE-FOOTED

foot·way /ˈfʊtweɪ/ *noun* (*BrE, formal*) a flat part at the side of a road for people to walk on（马路边的）人行道 SYN **pavement, sidewalk**

foot·wear /ˈfʊtweə(r); *NAmE* -wer/ *noun* [U] things that people wear on their feet, for example shoes and boots 鞋类（如鞋和靴）：*Be sure to wear the correct footwear to prevent injuries to your feet.* 一定要穿合适的鞋，以免脚受伤。

foot·work /ˈfʊtwɜːk; *NAmE* -wɜːrk/ *noun* [U] **1** the way in which a person moves their feet when playing a sport or dancing（体育、舞蹈的）步法，脚步动作 **2** the ability to react quickly and skilfully to a difficult situation（应付困境的）策略，应变能力：*It was going to take some deft political footwork to save the situation.* 当时得采取一些巧妙的政治手段以挽回局势。

footy /ˈfʊti/ *noun* [U] (*BrE, informal*) = FOOTBALL (1)

fop /fɒp; *NAmE* fɑːp/ *noun* (*old-fashioned*) a man who is too interested in his clothes and the way he looks 纨绔子弟；花花公子 ▸ **fop·pish** *adj.*

for 🔑 /fə(r); *strong form* fɔː(r)/ *prep., conj.*

■ ***prep.*** HELP For the special uses of **for** in phrasal verbs, look at the entries for the verbs. For example **fall for sb** is in the phrasal verb section at **fall**. * for 在短语动词中的特殊用法见有关动词词条。如 fall for sb 在词条 fall 的短语动词部分。 **1** 🔑 used to show who is intended to have or use sth or where sth is intended to be put（表示对象、用途等）给，对，供：*There's a letter for you.* 有你一封信。◇ *It's a book for children.* 这是本儿童读物。◇ *We got a new table for the dining room.* 我们给饭厅添了一张新桌子。◇ *This is the place for me* (= I like it very much). 这里很适合我。 **2** 🔑 in order to help sb/sth 以帮助；为了：*What can I do for you* (= how can I help you)? 有什么事我可以为你效劳？◇ *Can you translate this letter for me?* 你能为我翻译这封信吗？ ◇ *I took her classes for her while she was sick.* 她生病时我为她代课。◇ *soldiers fighting for their country* 为祖国战斗的军人 **3** 🔑 concerning sb/sth 关于：*They are anxious for her safety.* 他们为她的安全担心。◇ *Fortunately for us, the weather changed.* 我们运气好，天气变了。 **4** 🔑 as a representative of 代表：*I am speaking for everyone in this department.* 我代表这个部门全体人员讲话。 **5** 🔑 employed by 受雇于：*She's working for IBM.* 她在 IBM 公司工作。 **6** 🔑 meaning 意思是：*Shaking your head for 'No' is not universal.* 以摇头表示"不"，并非放诸四海而皆准。 **7** 🔑 in support of sb/sth 支持；拥护：*Are you for or against the proposal?* 你支持还是反对这个建议？◇ *They voted for independence in a referendum.* 他们在全民公决投票中赞成独立。◇ *There's a strong case for postponing the exam.* 有充分理由推迟考试。◇ *I'm* **all for** *people having fun.* 我完全赞成人们尽情享乐。➲ COMPARE AGAINST (2) **8** 🔑 used to show purpose or function（表示目的或功能）：*a machine for slicing bread* 面包切片机 ◇ *Let's go for a walk.* 咱们去散散步。◇ *Are you learning English for pleasure or for your work?* 你学英语是出于消遣还是为了工作？◇ *What did you do that for* (= Why did you do that)? 你为什么干那件事？ **9** 🔑 used to show a reason or cause 因为；由于：*The town is famous for its cathedral.* 这个城镇以大教堂著名。◇ *She gave me a watch for my birthday.* 她送给我一块手表作为生日礼物。◇ *He got an award for bravery.* 他因英勇受奖。◇ *I couldn't speak for laughing.* 我笑得说不出话来。 **10** 🔑 in order to obtain sth 为得到；为获取：*He came to me for advice.* 他来征求我的意见。◇ *For more information, call this number.* 欲知详情，请拨打此电话号码。◇ *There were over fifty applicants for the job.* 有五十多人申请这个工作。 **11** 🔑 in exchange for sth 换取：*Copies are available for two dollars each.* 两美元一份。◇ *I'll swap these two bottles for that one.* 我要拿这两瓶换那一瓶。 **12** 🔑 considering what can be expected from sb/sth 就…而言：*The weather was warm for the time of year.* 在一年的这个时节这天气算是暖和的了。◇ *She's tall for her age.* 从她这个年龄看她个子算是高的。◇ *That's too much responsibility for a child.* 对于一个孩子来说，这责任是太重了。 **13** **better, happier, etc. ~ sth** better, happier, etc. following sth …后（更好、更快乐等）：*You'll feel better for a good night's sleep.* 你晚上睡个好觉就会觉得好些。◇ *This room would look more cheerful for a spot of paint.* 这个房间油漆一下就会显得更加悦目。 **14** 🔑 used to show where sb/sth is going（表示去向）往，向：*Is this the bus for Chicago?* 这辆公共汽车是去芝加哥的吗？◇ *She knew she was destined for a great future.* 她知道她注定要成大器。 **15** 🔑 used to show a length of time（表示一段时间）：*I'm going away for a few days.* 我要离开几天。◇ *That's all the news there is* **for now**. 目前新闻就这么多。 **16** 🔑 used to show that sth is arranged or intended to happen at a particular time（安排或预定）在…时：*an appointment for May 12* * 5 月 12 日的一次约见 ◇ *We're invited for 7.30.* 我们受到邀请，7 点 30 分出席。 **17** 🔑 used to show the occasion when sth happens（表示场合）：*I'm warning you for the last time—stop talking!* 我最后一次警告你，闭嘴！ **18** 🔑 used to show a distance（表示距离）：*The road went on for miles and miles.* 这条道路绵延到很远的地方。 **19** 🔑 used to say how difficult, necessary, pleasant, etc. sth is that sb might do or has done 对（某人）来说（困难、必需、愉快等）：*It's useless* **for** *us* **to** *continue.* 我们继续做下去也无用。◇ *There's no need* **for** *you* **to** *go.* 你不必走。◇ *For her to have survived such an ordeal was remarkable.* 她经历了那样的苦难活下来了，真不简单。 ◇ *The box is* **too** *heavy* **for** *me to lift.* 这只箱子太沉，我搬不动。◇ *Is it clear* **enough for** *you* **to** *read?* 这个你读起来清不清楚？ **20** used to show who can or should do sth（表示谁可以或应该做某事）：*It's not for me to say why he left.* 由我说出他离开的原因不合适。 ◇ *How to spend the money is for you to decide.* 怎样花这笔钱由你决定。

IDM **be ˈin for it** (*BrE also* **be ˈfor it**) (*informal*) to be going to get into trouble or be punished 会惹出麻烦；要受惩罚：*We'd better hurry or we'll be in for it.* 我们最好赶快，不然要受罚的。 **for ˈall 1** despite 尽管；虽然：*For all its clarity of style, the book is not easy reading.* 这本书虽然文体清晰，但读起来并不容易。 **2** used to say that sth is not important or of no interest or value to you/sb（表示对某人不重要、无价值或无所谓）：*For all I know she's still living in Boston.* 据我所知，她还住在波士顿。◇ *You can do what you like, for all I care.* 你想干什么就可以干什么，我才不管呢。 ◇ *For all the good it's done we might as well not have bothered.* 那件事带来的好处不多，我们本不该操心的。 **there's/that's... for you** (*often ironic*) used to say that sth is a typical example of its kind …的典型；…就是

这样：*She might at least have called to explain. There's gratitude for you.* 她本来至少可以来电话解释一下。她就这么表示感谢。

■ *conj.* (*old-fashioned* or *literary*) used to introduce the reason for sth mentioned in the previous statement 因为；由于：*We listened eagerly, for he brought news of our families.* 我们急不可待地听着，因为他带来了我们家人的消息。◇ *I believed her—for surely she would not lie to me.* 我相信她的话，因为她肯定不会向我撒谎。

for·age /ˈfɒrɪdʒ; *NAmE* ˈfɔː-; ˈfɑː-/ *verb, noun*

■ *verb* **1** [I] ~ (**for sth**) (especially of an animal 尤指动物) to search for food 觅（食） **2** [I] ~ (**for sth**) (of a person 人) to search for sth, especially using the hands（尤指用手）搜寻（东西） SYN **rummage**

■ *noun* [U] food for horses and cows（牛马的）饲料：*forage crops/grass* 饲料作物；饲草

foray /ˈfɒreɪ; *NAmE* ˈfɔː-; ˈfɑː-/ *noun* **1** ~ (**into sth**) an attempt to become involved in a different activity or profession（改变职业、活动的）尝试：*the company's first foray into the computer market* 该公司对计算机市场的初次涉足 **2** ~ (**into sth**) a short sudden attack made by a group of soldiers 突袭；闪电式袭击 **3** ~ (**to/into...**) a short journey to find a particular thing or to visit a new place 短途（寻物）；短暂访问（新地方） SYN **expedition**：*weekend shopping forays to France* 周末赴法国购物

for·bade PAST TENSE OF FORBID

for·bear *verb, noun*

■ *verb* /fɔːˈbeə(r); *NAmE* fɔːrˈber/ (**for·bore** /fɔːˈbɔː(r); *NAmE* fɔːrˈbɔːr/, **for·borne** /fɔːˈbɔːn; *NAmE* fɔːrˈbɔːrn/) [I, T] (*formal*) to stop yourself from saying or doing sth that you could or would like to say or do 克制；自制；忍住（不说话或不做某事）：~ (**from sth/from doing sth**) *He wanted to answer back, but he forbore from doing so.* 他想顶嘴，但是忍住了。◇ ~ **to do sth** *She forbore to ask any further questions.* 她克制自己，不再进一步提问。

■ *noun* = FOREBEAR

for·bear·ance /fɔːˈbeərəns; *NAmE* fɔːrˈber-/ *noun* [U] (*formal*) the quality of being patient and sympathetic towards other people, especially when they have done sth wrong 宽容

for·bear·ing /fɔːˈbeərɪŋ; *NAmE* fɔːrˈber-/ *adj.* (*formal*) showing forbearance 宽容的 SYN **patient**：*Thank you for being so forbearing.* 感谢您如此宽宏大量。

for·bid /fəˈbɪd; *NAmE* fərˈb-/ *verb* (**for·bade** /fəˈbæd; fəˈbeɪd; *NAmE* fərˈbæd; fərˈb-/, **for·bid·den** /fəˈbɪdn; *NAmE* fərˈb-/) **1** to order sb not to do sth; to order that sth must not be done 禁止；不准：~ **sb** (**from doing sth**) *He forbade them from mentioning the subject again.* 他不准他们再提这个话题。◇ ~ **sth** *Her father forbade the marriage.* 她的父亲不允许这桩婚事。◇ ~ **sb to do sth** *You are all forbidden to leave.* 你们都不准离开。◇ ~ **sb sth** *My doctor has forbidden me sugar.* 医生禁止我吃糖。◇ ~ (**sb**) **doing sth** *She knew her mother would forbid her going.* 她知道她妈妈是不会让她去的。 OPP **allow**, **permit** **2** ~ **sth** | ~ **sb to do sth** (*formal*) to make it difficult or impossible to do sth 妨碍；阻碍；阻止 SYN **prohibit**：*Lack of space forbids further treatment of the topic here.* 由于篇幅所限，这里不能深入阐述这个问题。

IDM **God/Heaven forˈbid** (**that...**) (*informal*) used to say that you hope that sth will not happen 但愿这事不发生：*'Maybe you'll end up as a lawyer, like me.' 'God forbid!'* "也许你会像我一样，最终成为律师。" "但愿不会这样！" HELP Some people find this use offensive. 有人认为此用法含冒犯意。

▼ EXPRESS YOURSELF 情景表达

Forbidding somebody to do something 禁止某人做某事

When speaking to somebody, we usually use indirect language to ask them not to do something. 要求某人不要做某事通常使用间接的表达方式：

- *I'm sorry, smoking **isn't allowed**./**You're not allowed to** smoke here.* 对不起，不准吸烟。/ 这里不准吸烟。
- ***Would you mind not** talking during the music?* 演奏音乐时请不要说话好吗？
- ***Could I ask you not to** use your phone here, please?* 请不要在这里使用手机好吗？
- ***I'm afraid I have to ask you not to** take pictures here.* 对不起，请你不要在这里拍照。

for·bid·den /fəˈbɪdn; *NAmE* fərˈb-/ *adj.* not allowed 禁止的；不准的：*Photography is **strictly forbidden** in the museum.* 博物馆内禁止摄影。◇ *The conversation was in danger of wandering into forbidden territory* (= topics that they were not allowed to talk about). 谈话很可能离题而涉及禁止讨论的领域。

IDM **for,bidden 'fruit** a thing that is not allowed and that therefore seems very attractive 禁果（唯其禁止，故特别诱人）

for·bid·ding /fəˈbɪdɪŋ; *NAmE* fərˈb-/ *adj.* seeming unfriendly and frightening 冷峻的；令人生畏的：*a **forbidding appearance/look/manner*** 冷峻的样子 / 面孔 / 态度 ◇ *The house looked dark and forbidding.* 房子黑森森的，令人望而生畏。▶ **for·bid·ding·ly** *adv.*

for·bore PAST TENSE OF FORBEAR

for·borne PAST PART. OF FORBEAR

force /fɔːs; *NAmE* fɔːrs/ *noun, verb*

WORD FAMILY
force *noun, verb*
forceful *adj.*
forcefully *adv.*
forced *adj.* (≠ unforced)
forcible *adj.*
forcibly *adv.*
enforce *verb*

■ *noun*

• **VIOLENT ACTION** 暴力行动 **1** [U] violent physical action used to obtain or achieve sth 武力；暴力：*The release of the hostages could not be achieved without the use of force.* 不使用武力不可能使人质获释。◇ *The rioters were taken away **by force**.* 聚众闹事者被强行带走。◇ *The ultimatum contained the threat of military force.* 这份最后通牒含有武力威胁。◇ *We will achieve much more by persuasion than by **brute force**.* 我们通过说服会比使用暴力更有成效。

• **PHYSICAL STRENGTH** 力 **2** [U] the physical strength of sth that is shown as it hits sth else 力；力量：*the **force of the blow/explosion/collision*** 打击力；爆炸力；碰撞力 ◇ *The shopping centre took the **full force** of the blast.* 购物中心承受了全部爆炸力。

• **STRONG EFFECT** 强大效力 **3** [U] the strong effect or influence of sth 强大效力；巨大影响：*They realized the force of her argument.* 他们领悟到了她那论据的威力。◇ *He controlled himself by **sheer force of will**.* 他全凭意志力控制住了自己。◇ *She spoke with force and deliberation.* 她讲话铿锵有力，字斟句酌。

• **SB/STH WITH POWER** 具有力量的人 / 事物 **4** [C] a person or thing that has a lot of power or influence 力量大的人（或事物）；影响大的人（或事物）：***economic/market forces*** 经济 / 市场力量 ◇ *the **forces of good/evil*** 善 / 恶的力量 ◇ *Ron is **the driving force*** (= the person who has the most influence) *behind the project.* 罗恩是这个计划的主心骨。◇ *She's **a force to be reckoned with*** (= a person who has a lot of power and influence and should therefore be treated seriously). 她是个有影响力的人物，需要认真对待。◇ *The expansion of higher education should be a powerful force for change.* 高等教育的发展对变革应该是一个强大的推动力。

• **AUTHORITY** 权威 **5** [U] the authority of sth 权力；效力：*These guidelines do not have **the force of law**.* 这些指导原则不具有法律效力。◇ *The court ruled that these standards have force in English law.* 法院裁定，这些标准在英格兰法律中有效。

• **GROUP OF PEOPLE** 一群人 **6** [C+sing./pl. v.] a group of people who have been organized for a particular purpose（为某目的组织起来的）一群人：*a member of the **sales force*** 销售团队中的一员 ◇ *A large proportion of the* *labour force* (= all the people who work in a particular company, area, etc.) *is unskilled.* 很大一部分劳动力是非熟练工。 ➲SEE ALSO WORKFORCE

• **MILITARY** 武装力量 **7** [C+sing./pl. v.] a group of people who have been trained to protect other people, usually by using weapons 武装部队；部队：*a member of the security forces* 安全部队成员 ◇ ***rebel/government forces*** 反叛 / 政府武装力量 ◇ *a peace-keeping force* 维和部队 ➲ SEE ALSO AIR FORCE, POLICE FORCE, TASK FORCE **8 the forces** [pl.] (*BrE*) the army, navy and AIR FORCE 兵力，武装力量（陆海空三军）：*allied forces* 盟军 ➲ SEE ALSO ARMED FORCES **9 forces** [pl.] the weapons and soldiers that an army, etc. has, considered as things that may be used 武装力量：*strategic nuclear forces* 战略核部队

• **POLICE** 警察 **10 the force** [sing.] the police force 警察部门：*He joined the force twenty years ago.* 他二十年前加入了警队。

• **PHYSICS** 物理 **11** [C, U] an effect that causes things to move in a particular way 力：*The moon exerts a force on the earth.* 月球对地球有引力。◇ *the force of gravity* 重力 ◇ *magnetic/centrifugal force* 磁力；离心力 ➲ WORDFINDER NOTE AT PHYSICS

• **OF WIND** 风 **12** [C, usually sing.] a unit for measuring the strength of the wind 风力；风力等级：*a force 9 gale* * 9 级大风 ◇ *a gale force wind* 一场大风级的风 ➲ WORDFINDER NOTE AT WIND[1] ➲SEE ALSO TOUR DE FORCE

IDM **bring sth into 'force** to cause a law, rule, etc. to start being used（使法律、规则等）开始生效，开始实施：*They are hoping to bring the new legislation into force before the end of the year.* 他们希望在年底前实施新法。 **come/enter into 'force** (of a law, rule, etc. 法律、规则等) to start being used 开始生效；开始实施：*When do the new regulations come into force?* 新规章什么时候开始执行？ **force of 'habit** if you do sth from or out of **force of habit**, you do it automatically and in a particular way because you have always done it that way in the past 习惯力量 **the forces of 'nature** the power of the wind, rain, etc., especially when it causes damage or harm（尤指造成损害的）自然力；大自然的力量 **in 'force 1** (of people 人) in large numbers 大量；众多：*Protesters turned out in force.* 有很多抗议者到场。**2** (of a law, rule, etc. 法律、规则等) being used 已生效；在实施中：*The new regulations are now in force.* 新规章现已生效。 **join/combine 'forces (with sb)** to work together in order to achieve a shared aim（同…）联合；（与…）合作：*The two firms joined forces to win the contract.* 两家公司联合起来争取合同。 ➲MORE AT SPENT

■ *verb*

• **MAKE SB DO STH** 使做某事 **1** [often passive] to make sb do sth that they do not want to do 强迫，迫使（某人做某事） SYN **compel**：**~ sb into doing sth** *The President was forced into resigning.* 总统被迫辞职。◇ **~ sb/yourself to do sth** *The President was forced to resign.* 总统被迫辞职。◇ *I* ***was forced to*** *take a taxi because the last bus had left.* 最后一班公共汽车已经开走，所以我只好叫了一辆出租车。◇ *She forced herself to be polite to them.* 她对他们强装客气。◇ **~ sb into sth** *Ill health forced him into early retirement.* 他由于健康不佳不得不提前退休。◇ **~ sb** *He didn't force me—I wanted to go.* 他没有逼迫我，是我想去的。◇ **~ yourself** (*informal, humorous*) *'I shouldn't really have any more.' 'Go on—force yourself!'* "我确实不应该再吃了。" "接着吃，再努力努力！" ◇ **~ sth** *Public pressure managed to force a change in the government's position.* 公众的压力成功地迫使政府改变了立场。

• **USE PHYSICAL STRENGTH** 用体力 **2** to use physical strength to move sb/sth into a particular position 用力，强行（把…移动）：**~ sth** *to force a lock/window/door* (= to break it open using force) 强行打开锁 / 窗 / 门 ◇ *to force an entry* (= to enter a building using force) 强行进入建筑物 ◇ **~ sth + adv./prep.** *She forced her way through the crowd of reporters.* 她在记者群中挤出一条路。◇ *He tried to force a copy of his book into my hand.* 他硬要把他的一本书往我手里塞。◇ **~ sth + adj.** *The door had been forced open.* 门被强行打开了。

• **MAKE STH HAPPEN** 使发生 **3** to make sth happen, especially before other people are ready 使发生（尤指趁他人尚未准备好）：**~ sth** *He was in a position where he had to force a decision.* 他当时的处境是，不得不强行通过一项决定。◇ **~ sth + adv./prep.** *Building a new road here will force house prices down.* 在这里修建一条新道路将使房价下跌。

• **A SMILE/LAUGH** 微笑；大笑 **4 ~ sth** to make yourself smile, laugh, etc. rather than doing it naturally 强作笑颜；强装欢笑：*She managed to force a smile.* 她勉强笑笑。

• **FRUIT/PLANTS** 果实；植物 **5 ~ sth** to make fruit, plants, etc. grow or develop faster than normal by keeping them in special conditions 人工催长；加速（水果、植物等）生长；催熟：*forced rhubarb* 人工催长的大黄 ◇ (*figurative*) *It is unwise to force a child's talent.* 对儿童的才能拔苗助长是不明智的。

IDM **force sb's 'hand** to make sb do sth that they do not want to do or make them do it sooner than they had intended 迫使某人做某事（或提前行动） **'force the issue** to do sth to make people take a decision quickly 迫使从速决定 **force the 'pace** (*especially BrE*) **1** to run very fast in a race in order to make the other people taking part run faster 迫使（赛跑对手）加速 **2** to make sb do sth faster than they want to 迫使（某人）加快速度：*The demonstrations have succeeded in forcing the pace of change.* 示威成功地促使改革进程加快。 ➲MORE AT THROAT

PHR V **ˌforce sth↔'back** to make yourself hide an emotion 强忍（不表露情感）：*She swallowed hard and forced back her tears.* 她使劲咽了一下口水，强忍住了眼泪。 **ˌforce sth↔'down 1** to make yourself eat or drink sth that you do not really want 强迫咽下（食物或饮料） **2** to make a plane, etc. land, especially by threatening to attack it 迫使（飞机等）降落 **'force sb/sth on/upon sb** to make sb accept sth that they do not want 强迫接受；把…强加给：*to force your attentions/opinions/company on sb* 强行对（某人）献殷勤；把意见强加给（某人）；硬要陪伴（某人） **ˌforce sth 'out of sb** to make sb tell you sth, especially by threatening them 强迫说出（尤其通过威胁）：*I managed to force the truth out of him.* 我设法迫使他说出了实情。

forced /fɔːst; *NAmE* fɔːrst/ *adj.* **1** happening or done against sb's will 被迫的；不得已的：*forced relocation to a job in another city* 不得已迁移至另一城市工作 ◇ *a forced sale of his property* 强制变卖他的财产 **2** not sincere; not the result of genuine emotions 勉强的；不真诚的：*She said she was enjoying herself but her smile was forced.* 她说自己很快活，但是她的笑容很勉强。 ➲ SEE ALSO UNFORCED (2)

ˌforced 'entry *noun* [U, C] an occasion when sb enters a building illegally, using force 强行闯入（建筑物）

ˌforced 'labour (*especially US* **ˌforced 'labor**) *noun* [U] **1** hard physical work that sb, often a prisoner or SLAVE, is forced to do（对囚犯、奴隶等实施的）强制劳动 **2** prisoners or SLAVES who are forced to work 强制劳工（如囚犯或奴隶）：*The mines were manned by forced labour from conquered countries.* 这些矿由来自被征服国家的强制劳工开采。

ˌforced 'landing *noun* an act of having to land an aircraft unexpectedly in order to avoid a crash（航空器的）迫降，强行着陆：*to make a forced landing* 强行着陆

ˌforced 'march *noun* a long march, usually made by soldiers in difficult conditions 强行军

ˌforce-'feed *verb* (**force-fed, force-fed**) **~ sb** to use force to make sb, especially a prisoner, eat or drink, by putting food or drink down their throat 强迫进食（尤指把饮食灌进囚犯等口中）

'force field *noun* (often used in stories about space travel 常用于有关太空旅行的小说) a barrier that you cannot see（无形的）力场，力障碍区

force·ful /ˈfɔːsfl; *NAmE* ˈfɔːrsfl/ *adj.* **1** (of people 人) expressing opinions firmly and clearly in a way that persuades other people to believe them 强有力的；坚强的 SYN **assertive**：*a forceful woman/speaker* 强有力的女人；说话有说服力的人 ◇ *a forceful personality* 坚强的个性

2 (of opinions, etc. 意见等) expressed firmly and clearly so that other people believe them 有说服力的: *a forceful argument/speech* 有说服力的论据 / 演讲 **3** using force 强迫的; 使用武力的: *the forceful suppression of minorities* 对少数族群的武力镇压 ▸ **force·ful·ly** /-fəli/ *adv.*: *He argued his case forcefully.* 他雄辩地阐述了他的立场。 **force·ful·ness** *noun* [U]

force ma·jeure /ˌfɔːs mæˈʒɜː(r); *NAmE* ˌfɔːrs/ *noun* [U] (*from French, law* 律) unexpected circumstances, such as war, that can be used as an excuse when they prevent sb from doing sth that is written in a contract 不可抗力（如战争，常指未能履行合约的原因）

force·meat /ˈfɔːsmiːt; *NAmE* ˈfɔːrs-/ *noun* [U] a mixture of meat or vegetables cut into very small pieces, which is often placed inside a chicken, etc. before it is cooked to give it flavour （常作烹饪填料用的）碎肉，菜末

ˈforce-out *noun* (in BASEBALL 棒球) a situation in which a player running to a BASE is out because a FIELDER is holding the ball at the base 封杀; 封杀出局

for·ceps /ˈfɔːseps; *NAmE* ˈfɔːrs-/ *noun* [pl.] an instrument used by doctors, with two long thin parts for picking up and holding things（医生用的）镊子，钳子: *a pair of forceps* 一把镊子 ◇ ***a forceps delivery*** (= a birth in which the baby is delivered with the help of forceps) 产钳分娩

for·cible /ˈfɔːsəbl; *NAmE* ˈfɔːrs-/ *adj.* [only before noun] involving the use of physical force 强行的; 用暴力的: *forcible repatriation* 强行遣返 ◇ *The police checked all windows and doors for signs of forcible entry.* 警察检查了所有的门窗以寻找强行闯入的痕迹。

for·cibly /ˈfɔːsəbli; *NAmE* ˈfɔːrs-/ *adv.* **1** in a way that involves the use of physical force 用强力; 用武力: *Supporters were forcibly removed from the court.* 支持者都被强行从法庭赶走。 **2** in a way that makes sth very clear 明白地; 清楚地: *It struck me forcibly how honest he'd been.* 我猛然醒悟他是多么的正直。

ford /fɔːd; *NAmE* fɔːrd/ *noun, verb*
▪ ***noun*** a shallow place in a river where it is possible to drive or walk across（可涉过或驶过的）河流浅水处
▪ ***verb*** **~ sth** to walk or drive across a river or stream 涉过，驶过（浅水）

fore /fɔː(r)/ *noun, adj., adv.*
▪ ***noun***
IDM **come to the ˈfore** (*BrE also* **be to the ˈfore**, *NAmE also* **be at the ˈfore**) to be/become important and noticed by people; to play an important part 变得重要（或突出）; 起重要作用: *The problem has come to the fore again in recent months.* 近几个月来这个问题又成为热点。◇ *She has always been to the fore at moments of crisis.* 在危急时刻她总是挺身而出。 **bring sth to the ˈfore** to make sth become noticed by people 使处于显要地位; 使突出
▪ ***adj.*** [only before noun] (*specialist*) located at the front of a ship, an aircraft or an animal 在（船、航空器或动物）前部的; 在头部的 ➲ COMPARE AFT, HIND *adj.*
▪ ***adv.*** **1** at or towards the front of a ship or an aircraft 在（或向）船头; 在（或向）飞行器头部 ➲ COMPARE AFT **2** **Fore!** used in the game of GOLF to warn people that they are in the path of a ball that you are hitting 前方注意，看球（打高尔夫球时警告前面球路中的人以免被击中）

fore- /fɔː(r)/ *combining form* (in nouns and verbs 构成名词和动词) **1** before; in advance 先于; 预先: *foreword* 前言 ◇ *foretell* 预言 **2** in the front of 在…的前部: *the foreground of the picture* 图画的前景

fore·arm¹ /ˈfɔːrɑːm; *NAmE* -ɑːrm/ *noun* the part of the arm between the elbow and the wrist 前臂 ➲ VISUAL VOCAB PAGE V64

fore·arm² /ˌfɔːrˈɑːm; *NAmE* -ˈɑːrm/ *verb* IDM SEE FOREWARN

fore·bear (*also* **for·bear**) /ˈfɔːbeə(r); *NAmE* ˈfɔːrber/ *noun* [usually pl.] (*formal* or *literary*) a person in your family who lived a long time ago 祖先; 祖宗 SYN **ancestor**

fore·bod·ing /fɔːˈbəʊdɪŋ; *NAmE* fɔːrˈboʊ-/ *noun* [U, C] a strong feeling that sth unpleasant or dangerous is going to happen（对不祥或危险事情的）强烈预感: *She had **a sense of foreboding** that the news would be bad.* 她预感到这会是坏消息。◇ *He knew from her face that his forebodings had been justified.* 他从她的脸上看出，自己不祥的预感是正确的。 ▸ **fore·bod·ing** *adj.* [only before noun]: *a foreboding feeling that something was wrong* 出了问题的不祥预感

fore·brain /ˈfɔːbreɪn; *NAmE* ˈfɔːr-/ *noun* (*anatomy* 解) the front part of the brain 前脑

fore·cast 🔑 /ˈfɔːkɑːst; *NAmE* ˈfɔːrkæst/ *noun, verb*
▪ ***noun*** 🔑 a statement about what will happen in the future, based on information that is available now 预测; 预报: *sales forecasts* 销售预测 ◇ *The forecast said there would be sunny intervals and showers.* 预报间晴，有阵雨。 ➲ SEE ALSO WEATHER FORECAST
▪ ***verb*** 🔑 (**fore·cast**, **fore·cast** or **fore·cast·ed**, **fore·cast·ed**) to say what you think will happen in the future based on information that you have now 预测; 预报 SYN **predict**: **~ sth** *Experts are forecasting a recovery in the economy.* 专家预测经济将复苏。◇ *Snow is forecast for tomorrow.* 预报明天有雪。◇ **~ sth to do sth** *Temperatures were forecast to reach 40°C.* 预报温度将达 40 摄氏度。◇ **~ that...** *The report forecasts that prices will rise by 3% next month.* 报告预测下月物价将上涨 3%。◇ **~ how, what, etc....** *It is difficult to forecast how the markets will react.* 很难预测市场会有什么样的反应。 ➲ COLLOCATIONS AT WEATHER ➲ LANGUAGE BANK AT EXPECT

fore·cast·er /ˈfɔːkɑːstə(r); *NAmE* ˈfɔːrkæstər/ *noun* a person who says what is expected to happen, especially sb whose job is to forecast the weather 预测者;（尤指）天气预报员，气象预报员: *a weather forecaster* 天气预报员 ◇ *an economic forecaster* 经济预测专家

fore·castle (*also* **fo'c'sle**) /ˈfəʊksl; *NAmE* ˈfoʊksl/ *noun* the front part of a ship below the DECK, where the sailors live 艏楼

fore·close /fɔːˈkləʊz; *NAmE* fɔːrˈkloʊz/ *verb* **1** [I, T] **~ (on sb/sth)** | **~ sth** (*finance* 财) (especially of a bank 尤指银行) to take control of sb's property because they have not paid back money that they borrowed to buy it（因抵押人未如期还贷）取消（抵押品）赎回权 ➲ COLLOCATIONS AT HOUSE **2** [T] **~ sth** (*formal*) to reject sth as a possibility 排除…的可能 SYN **exclude**

fore·clos·ure /fɔːˈkləʊʒə(r); *NAmE* fɔːrˈkloʊ-/ *noun* [U, C] (*finance* 财) the act of foreclosing on money that has been borrowed; an example of this 抵押品赎回权的取消

fore·court /ˈfɔːkɔːt; *NAmE* ˈfɔːrkɔːrt/ *noun* (*BrE*) a large open space in front of a building, for example a PETROL STATION/GAS STATION or hotel, often used for parking cars on 大片空地（在加油站或旅馆等建筑物前面，常用作停车场）

fore·doomed /fɔːˈduːmd; *NAmE* fɔːrˈd-/ *adj.* **~ (to sth)** (*formal*) that will not be successful, as if FATE has decided this from the beginning 注定（失败）的: *Any attempt to construct an ideal society is foredoomed to failure.* 要构建一个完美无缺的社会，这样的努力注定失败。

fore·father /ˈfɔːfɑːðə(r); *NAmE* ˈfɔːrf-/ *noun* [usually pl.] (*formal* or *literary*) a person (especially a man) in your family who lived a long time ago 祖先，祖宗（尤指男性） SYN **ancestor**

fore·fend = FORFEND (1)

fore·fin·ger /ˈfɔːfɪŋɡə(r); *NAmE* ˈfɔːrf-/ *noun* the finger next to the thumb 食指 SYN **index finger**

fore·foot /ˈfɔːfʊt; *NAmE* ˈfɔːrfʊt/ *noun* (*pl.* **fore·feet** /-fiːt/) either of the two front feet of an animal that has four feet（四足动物的）前足

fore·front /ˈfɔːfrʌnt; *NAmE* ˈfɔːrf-/ *noun* [sing.]
IDM **at/in/to the ˈforefront (of sth)** in or into an important or leading position in a particular group or activity 处于最前列；进入重要地位（或主要地位）：*Women have always been at the forefront of the Green movement.* 妇女总是在环境保护运动的最前列。◇ *The new product took the company to the forefront of the computer software field.* 该新产品使这家公司跻身计算机软件业的前列。◇ *The court case was constantly in the forefront of my mind* (= I thought about it all the time). 这个诉讼案件一直萦系在我的心头。

F

fore·gather (*also* **for·gather**) /ˌfɔːˈɡæðə(r); *NAmE* ˌfɔːrˈɡ-/ *verb* [I] (*formal*) to meet together in a group（一群人）聚会，集合

fore·go = FORGO

fore·going /ˈfɔːɡəʊɪŋ; *NAmE* ˈfɔːrɡoʊɪŋ/ *adj.* [only before noun] (*formal*) **1** used to refer to sth that has just been mentioned 上述的；前述的：*the foregoing discussion* 上述讨论 **2 the foregoing** *noun* [sing.+sing./pl. v.] what has just been mentioned 前面所提到的事物；以上所述 OPP **following**

fore·gone /ˈfɔːɡɒn; *NAmE* ˈfɔːrɡɔːn/ *adj.*
IDM **a ˌforegone conˈclusion** if you say that sth is **a foregone conclusion**, you mean that it is a result that is certain to happen 预料中的必然结局

fore·ground /ˈfɔːɡraʊnd; *NAmE* ˈfɔːrɡ-/ *noun, verb*
■ *noun* **the foreground 1** [C, usually sing.] the part of a view, picture, etc. that is nearest to you when you look at it（景物、图画等的）前景：*The figure* ***in the foreground*** *is the artist's mother.* 图画前景中的人是画家的母亲。➲ WORDFINDER NOTE AT PAINTING ➲ EXPRESS YOURSELF AT DESCRIBE **2** [sing.] an important position that is noticed by people 瞩目地位；重要位置：*Inflation and interest rates will be very much* ***in the foreground of*** *their election campaign.* 通货膨胀和利率将很可能是他们竞选的重点问题。➲ COMPARE BACKGROUND
IDM **in the ˈforeground** (*computing* 计)(of a computer program 计算机程序) being used at the present time and appearing in front of any other programs on the screen 在前台；在前景中 ➲ COMPARE IN THE BACKGROUND at BACKGROUND
■ *verb* ~ **sth** to give particular importance to sth 强调；突出：*The play foregrounds the relationship between father and daughter.* 这部戏剧凸显了父女之间的关系。

fore·hand /ˈfɔːhænd; *NAmE* ˈfɔːrh-/ *noun* [usually sing.] (in TENNIS, etc. 网球等) a way of hitting a ball in which the inner part of the hand (= the PALM) faces the ball as it is hit 正手击球；正手；正拍：*She has a strong forehand.* 她正手击球强劲有力。◇ *a forehand volley* 正手截击球 ◇ *He served to his opponent's forehand.* 他把球发向对方的正手位置。➲ COMPARE BACKHAND

fore·head /ˈfɔːhed; ˈfɒrɪd; *NAmE* ˈfɔːrhed; ˈfɔːred/ *noun* the part of the face above the eyes and below the hair 额；前额 SYN **brow** ➲ COLLOCATIONS AT PHYSICAL ➲ VISUAL VOCAB PAGE V64

for·eign 🔑 /ˈfɒrən; *NAmE* ˈfɔːrən; ˈfɑːrən/ *adj.* **1** 🔑 in or from a country that is not your own 外国的：*a foreign accent/language/student* 外国口音/语言/学生 ◇ *a foreign-owned company* 外资公司 ◇ *foreign holidays* 外国假日 ◇ *You could tell she was foreign by the way she dressed.* 从她的穿着就可以看出她是外国人。**2** 🔑 [only before noun] dealing with or involving other countries 涉外的；外交的：***foreign affairs/news/policy/trade*** 外交事务；外国新闻；对外政策/贸易 ◇ ***foreign aid*** 外援 ◇ *a* ***foreign correspondent*** (= one who reports on foreign countries in newspapers or on television) 驻外记者 OPP **domestic, home 3** ~ **to sb/sth** (*formal*) not typical of sb/sth; not known to sb/sth and therefore seeming strange 非典型的；陌生的：*Dishonesty is foreign to his nature.* 弄虚作假并非他的本性。**4** ~ **object/body** (*formal*) an object that has entered sth by accident and should not be there 异物；异体：*Tears help to protect the eye from potentially harmful foreign bodies.* 眼泪有助于保护眼睛去除可能有害的异物。➲ MORE LIKE THIS 20, page R27 ▶ **for·eign·ness** *noun* [U]

the ˌForeign and ˈCommonwealth Office *noun* [sing.+sing./pl. v.] (*abbr.* **FCO**) the British government department that deals with relations with other countries. It used to be called **the Foreign Office** and it is still often referred to as this. 外交和联邦事务部（英国政府部门，旧称 the Foreign Office，现在仍常见此说法）

for·eign·er /ˈfɒrənə(r); *NAmE* ˈfɔːr-; ˈfɑːr-/ *noun* (*sometimes offensive*) **1** a person who comes from a different country 外国人：*The fact that I was a foreigner was a big disadvantage.* 我是外国人这一事实对我十分不利。**2** a person who does not belong in a particular place 外来人；外地人：*I have always been regarded as a foreigner by the local folk.* 当地人总把我视为外地人。

ˌforeign exˈchange *noun* **1** [U, C] the system of exchanging the money of one country for that of another country; the place where money is exchanged 国际汇兑；外汇市场；外币兑换处：*The euro fell on the foreign exchanges yesterday.* 欧元汇价昨天下跌。**2** [U] money that is obtained using this system 外汇：*our largest source of foreign exchange* 我们外汇的最主要来源

the ˈForeign Office *noun* [sing.+sing./pl. v.] = FOREIGN AND COMMONWEALTH OFFICE

ˌforeign-reˈturned *adj.* (*IndE, informal*) (of a person 人) educated or trained in a foreign country, and having returned to India 学成归国的；海归的

the ˌForeign ˈSecretary *noun* the British government minister in charge of the FOREIGN AND COMMONWEALTH OFFICE（英国）外交大臣

ˈForeign Service *noun* (*NAmE*) = DIPLOMATIC SERVICE

fore·know·ledge /fɔːˈnɒlɪdʒ; *NAmE* fɔːrˈnɑːl-/ *noun* [U] (*formal*) knowledge of sth before it happens 预知；事先知道

fore·land /ˈfɔːlənd; *NAmE* ˈfɔːr-/ *noun* [sing., U] **1** an area of land which lies in front of sth 前陆；前沿地；前方地 **2** an area of land which sticks out into the sea 岬；陆岬

fore·leg /ˈfɔːleɡ; *NAmE* ˈfɔːrleɡ/ (*also* **fore·limb** /ˈfɔːlɪm; *NAmE* ˈfɔːr-/) *noun* either of the two front legs of an animal that has four legs（四足动物的）前足，前腿

fore·lock /ˈfɔːlɒk; *NAmE* ˈfɔːrlɑːk/ *noun* **1** a piece of hair that grows at the front of the head and hangs down over the FOREHEAD 额发 **2** a part of a horse's MANE that grows forwards between its ears（马的）额毛，门鬃
IDM **touch/tug your ˈforelock (to sb)** (*BrE, disapproving*) to show too much respect for sb, especially because you are anxious about what they think of you（对某人）毕恭毕敬 ORIGIN In the past people of the lower classes either took off their hats or pulled on their forelocks to show respect. 源自旧时下层人或者脱掉帽子，或者紧拽额发，以示恭敬。

fore·man /ˈfɔːmən; *NAmE* ˈfɔːrmən/, **fore·woman** /ˈfɔːwʊmən; *NAmE* ˈfɔːrw-/ *noun* (*pl.* **-men** /-mən/, **-women** /-wɪmɪn/) **1** a worker who is in charge of a group of other factory or building workers 领班；工头 ➲ WORDFINDER NOTE AT FACTORY **2** a person who acts as the leader of a JURY in court 陪审团团长 ➲ NOTE AT GENDER

fore·most /ˈfɔːməʊst; *NAmE* ˈfɔːrmoʊst/ *adj., adv.*
■ *adj.* the most important or famous; in a position at the front 最重要的；最著名的；最前的：*the world's foremost authority on the subject* 该学科全世界首屈一指的权威 ◇ *The Prime Minister was foremost among those who condemned the violence.* 首相带头谴责暴力行为。◇ *This question has been foremost in our minds recently.* 近来在我们的心目中这一直是个最重要的问题。
■ *adv.* IDM SEE FIRST *adv.*

fore·name /ˈfɔːneɪm; *NAmE* ˈfɔːrn-/ *noun* (*formal*) a person's first name rather than the name that they share with the other members of their family (= their SURNAME) 名：*Please check that your surname and forenames have been correctly entered.* 请核对你的姓名已正确输入。

fore·noon /ˈfɔːnuːn; *NAmE* ˈfɔːr-/ *noun* (*NAmE, ScotE*) the morning 上午；午前

fo·ren·sic /fəˈrensɪk; -ˈrenzɪk/ *adj.* [only before noun] connected with the scientific tests used by the police when trying to solve a crime 法医的：***forensic evidence/medicine/science/tests*** 法医证据 / 学 / 科学 / 检验 ◊ *the forensic laboratory* 法医检验室 ◊ *a forensic pathologist* 法医病理学家 ➲ COLLOCATIONS AT CRIME

fore·play /ˈfɔːpleɪ; *NAmE* ˈfɔːrp-/ *noun* [U] sexual activity, such as touching the sexual organs and kissing, that takes place before people have sex（性交的）前戏

fore·run·ner /ˈfɔːrʌnə(r)/ *noun* ~ **(of sb/sth)** a person or thing that came before and influenced sb/sth else that is similar; a sign of what is going to happen 先驱；先行者；预兆；前兆：*Country music was undoubtedly one of the forerunners of rock and roll.* 乡村音乐无疑是摇滚乐的先导之一。

fore·sail /ˈfɔːseɪl; ˈfɔːsl; *NAmE* ˈfɔːrseɪl; ˈfɔːrsl/ *noun* [usually sing.] the main sail on the MAST of a ship which is nearest the front (called the **foremast**) 前桅帆；前帆

fore·see /fɔːˈsiː; *NAmE* fɔːrˈsiː/ *verb* (**fore·saw** /fɔːˈsɔː; *NAmE* fɔːrˈsɔː/, **fore·seen** /fɔːˈsiːn; *NAmE* fɔːrˈsiːn/) to think sth is going to happen in the future; to know about sth before it happens 预料；预见；预知 SYN **predict**: ~ **sth** *We do not foresee any problems.* 我们预料不会出任何问题。◊ *The extent of the damage could not have been foreseen.* 损害的程度是无法预见到的。◊ ~ **(that)...** *No one could have foreseen (that) things would turn out this way.* 谁都没有预料到事情的结果会是这样。◊ ~ **how, what, etc....** *It is impossible to foresee how life will work out.* 不可能预知生命将如何发展。◊ ~ **sb/sth doing sth** *I just didn't foresee that happening.* 我只是没预料到会发生那种事。➲ COMPARE UNFORESEEN

fore·see·able /fɔːˈsiːəbl; *NAmE* fɔːrˈs-/ *adj.* that you can predict will happen; that can be foreseen 可预料的；可预见的；可预知的：***foreseeable risks/consequences*** 可预料的风险 / 后果 OPP **unforeseeable**

IDM **for/in the foreseeable ˈfuture** for/in the period of time when you can predict what is going to happen, based on the present circumstances（在）可预见的将来：*The statue will remain in the museum for the foreseeable future.* 短期内这座雕像将留在博物馆。◊ *It's unlikely that the hospital will be closed in the foreseeable future* (= soon). 这家医院不大可能很快就关闭。

fore·shadow /fɔːˈʃædəʊ; *NAmE* fɔːrˈʃædoʊ/ *verb* ~ **sth** (*formal*) to be a sign of sth that will happen in the future 预示；是…的预兆

fore·shore /ˈfɔːʃɔː(r); *NAmE* ˈfɔːrʃ-/ *noun* [C, usually sing., U] **1** (on a beach or by a river) the part of the SHORE between the highest and lowest levels reached by the water（海滩上或河边高潮线和低潮线之间的）前滨，滩头，前滩，滩地 **2** the part of the SHORE between the highest level reached by the water and the area of land that has buildings, plants, etc. on it（最高水位与建筑物或树木等之间的）海滨，水边土地

fore·short·en /fɔːˈʃɔːtn; *NAmE* fɔːrˈʃɔːrtn/ *verb* **1** ~ **sth/sb** (*specialist*) to draw, photograph, etc. objects or people so that they look smaller or closer together than they really are（绘画、摄影等）用透视法缩小（或缩短） **2** ~ **sth** (*formal*) to end sth before it would normally finish 提前结束；缩短；节略 SYN **curtail**: *a foreshortened education* 缩短了的教育

fore·sight /ˈfɔːsaɪt; *NAmE* ˈfɔːrs-/ *noun* [U] (*approving*) the ability to predict what is likely to happen and to use this to prepare for the future 深谋远虑；先见之明：*She had had the foresight to prepare herself financially in case of an accident.* 她有先见之明，经济上作了准备以防万一发生事故。➲ COMPARE HINDSIGHT

fore·skin /ˈfɔːskɪn; *NAmE* ˈfɔːrs-/ *noun* the loose piece of skin that covers the end of a man's PENIS 包皮

for·est 🔑 /ˈfɒrɪst; *NAmE* ˈfɔːr-; ˈfɑːr-/ *noun* **1** 🔑 [C, U] a large area of land that is thickly covered with trees 森林；林区：*a tropical forest* 热带森林 ◊ *a forest fire* 森林火灾 ◊ *Thousands of hectares of forest are destroyed each year.* 每年都有几千公顷的森林遭到破坏。➲ SEE ALSO RAINFOREST ➲ VISUAL VOCAB PAGE V5 **2** [C] ~ **(of sth)** a mass of tall narrow objects that are close together（森林似的）一丛，一片：*a forest of television aerials* 林立的电视天线

IDM **not see the ˌforest for the ˈtrees** (*NAmE*) (*BrE* **not see the ˌwood for the ˈtrees**) to not see or understand the main point about sth, because you are paying too much attention to small details 见树不见林

fore·stall /fɔːˈstɔːl; *NAmE* fɔːrˈs-/ *verb* ~ **sth/sb** (*formal*) to prevent sth from happening or sb from doing sth by doing sth first 防止；在（他人）之前行动；先发制人：*Try to anticipate what your child will do and forestall problems.* 尽量预见你的孩子会干什么，并预先阻止问题发生。

for·ested /ˈfɒrɪstɪd; *NAmE* ˈfɔːr-; ˈfɑːr-/ *adj.* covered in forest 满是森林的；林木覆盖的：***thickly forested*** *hills* 森林密布的丘陵 ◊ *The province is* ***heavily forested*** *and sparsely populated.* 该省森林茂密，人烟稀少。

for·est·er /ˈfɒrɪstə(r); *NAmE* ˈfɔːr-; ˈfɑːr-/ *noun* a person who works in a forest, taking care of the trees, planting new ones, etc. 林务员；护林人

for·est·ry /ˈfɒrɪstri; *NAmE* ˈfɔːr-; ˈfɑːr-/ *noun* [U] the science or practice of planting and taking care of trees and forests 林学；林业

fore·taste /ˈfɔːteɪst; *NAmE* ˈfɔːrt-/ *noun* [sing.] **a** ~ **(of sth)** a small amount of a particular experience or situation that shows you what it will be like when the same thing happens on a larger scale in the future 预先的体验；预示；征象：*They were unaware that the street violence was just a foretaste of what was to come.* 他们没有意识到，这起街头暴力事件预示了后来发生的大规模暴力行为。

fore·tell /fɔːˈtel; *NAmE* fɔːrˈtel/ *verb* (**fore·told**, **fore·told** /fɔːˈtəʊld; *NAmE* fɔːrˈtoʊld/) (*literary*) to know or say what will happen in the future, especially by using magic powers（尤指用魔力）预知，预言：~ **sth** *to foretell the future* 预言未来 ◊ ~ **that...** *The witch foretold that she would marry a prince.* 女巫预言她将嫁给王子。◊ ~ **what, when, etc....** *None of us can foretell what lies ahead.* 我们谁都不能预知未来。

fore·thought /ˈfɔːθɔːt; *NAmE* ˈfɔːrθ-/ *noun* [U] careful thought to make sure that things are successful in the future 深谋远虑：*Some forethought and preparation are necessary before you embark on the project.* 你着手进行这个项目之前必须有所考虑，有所准备。IDM SEE MALICE

fore·told PAST TENSE, PAST PART. OF FORETELL

for·ever 🔑 /fərˈevə(r)/ *adv.* **1** 🔑 (*BrE also* **for ever**) used to say that a particular situation or state will always exist 永远：*I'll love you forever!* 我永远爱你！◊ *After her death, their lives changed forever.* 她死后他们的生活永远改变了。◊ *Just keep telling yourself that it won't last forever.* 要不停地提醒自己，不会一直都是这样的。**2** 🔑 (*BrE also* **for ever**) (*informal*) a very long time 长久地：*It takes her forever to get dressed.* 她穿衣打扮要用好长的时间。**3** (*informal*) used with verbs in the progressive tenses to say that sb does sth very often and in a way that is annoying to other people（与动词进行时连用）老是，没完没了地：*She's forever going on about how poor they are.* 她老是没完没了地讲他们有多穷。

fore·warn /fɔːˈwɔːn; *NAmE* fɔːrˈwɔːrn/ *verb* [often passive] ~ **sb (of sth)** | ~ **sb that...** (*formal*) to warn sb about sth bad or unpleasant before it happens 预先警告；事先告诫：*The commander had been forewarned of the attack.* 指挥官预先得到敌人要发动袭击的警报。▸ **fore·warn·ing** *noun* [U, C]

IDM **foreˌwarned is foreˈarmed** (*saying*) if you know about problems, dangers, etc. before they happen, you can be better prepared for them 预警即预备；有备无患

fore·woman *noun* ➲ FOREMAN

fore·word /ˈfɔːwɜːd; NAmE ˈfɔːrwɜːrd/ *noun* a short introduction at the beginning of a book（书的）前言，序言 ➲ COMPARE PREFACE *n.*

for·feit /ˈfɔːfɪt; NAmE ˈfɔːrfət/ *verb, noun, adj.*

■ ***verb*** **~ sth** to lose sth or have sth taken away from you because you have done sth wrong（因犯错）丧失，被没收：*If you cancel your flight, you will forfeit your deposit.* 乘客取消航班订位，订金概不退还。◇ *He has forfeited his right to be taken seriously.* 他丧失了被认真对待的权利。

■ ***noun*** something that a person has to pay, or sth that is taken from them, because they have done sth wrong 罚金；没收物

■ ***adj.*** [not before noun] (*formal*) taken away from sb as a punishment 被罚；被没收

for·feit·ure /ˈfɔːfɪtʃə(r); NAmE ˈfɔːrfətʃər/ *noun* [U] (*law* 律) the act of forfeiting sth 丧失；没收：*the forfeiture of property* 财产的丧失

for·fend /fɔːˈfend; NAmE fɔːr-/ *verb* **1** (*also* **fore·fend**) **~ sth** (*NAmE*) to prevent sth 防止；阻止 **2** **~ sth** (*old use*) to prevent sth or keep sth away 防止；挡开

IDM **Heaven/God for'fend (that)...** (*humorous* or *old use*) used to say that you are frightened of the idea of sth happening 但愿不要…；千万别…：*Heaven forfend that students are encouraged to think!* 千万不要鼓励学生思考！

for·gather *verb* [I] = FOREGATHER

for·gave PAST TENSE OF FORGIVE

forge /fɔːdʒ; NAmE fɔːrdʒ/ *verb, noun*

■ ***verb*** **1** [T] **~ sth** to put a lot of effort into making sth successful or strong so that it will last 艰苦干成；努力加强：*a move to forge new links between management and workers* 努力建立新劳资关系的措施◇ *Strategic alliances are being forged with major European companies.* 正与欧洲主要公司设法结成战略同盟。◇ *She forged a new career in the music business.* 她在乐坛上另创一番新事业。**2** [T] **~ sth** to make an illegal copy of sth in order to cheat people 伪造；假冒：*to forge a passport/banknote/cheque* 伪造护照 / 钞票 / 支票◇ *He's getting good at forging his mother's signature.* 他把母亲的签名伪造得越来越像了。➲ COLLOCATIONS AT CRIME ➲ COMPARE COUNTERFEIT *v.* **3** [T] **~ sth (from sth)** to shape metal by heating it in a fire and hitting it with a hammer; to make an object in this way 锻造；制作：*swords forged from steel* 用钢锻造的刀剑 **4** [I] **+ adv./prep.** (*formal*) to move forward in a steady but powerful way 稳步前进：*He forged through the crowds to the front of the stage.* 他挤过人群稳步走到台前。◇ *She forged into the lead* (= in a competition, race, etc.). 她（在比赛、赛跑等中）稳步领先。

PHR V **,forge a'head (with sth)** to move forward quickly; to make a lot of progress quickly 迅速向前；进步神速：*The company is forging ahead with its plans for expansion.* 公司的拓展计划正顺利进行。

■ ***noun*** **1** a place where objects are made by heating and shaping pieces of metal, especially one where a BLACKSMITH works 铁匠铺 **2** a large piece of equipment used for heating metals in; a building or part of a factory where this is found 锻铁炉；锻造车间；锻造工厂

for·ger /ˈfɔːdʒə(r); NAmE ˈfɔːrdʒ-/ *noun* a person who makes illegal copies of money, documents, etc. in order to cheat people 伪造者；犯伪造罪的人 ➲ COMPARE COUNTERFEITER

for·gery /ˈfɔːdʒəri; NAmE ˈfɔːrdʒ-/ *noun* **1** [U] the crime of copying money, documents, etc. in order to cheat people 伪造；伪造罪 **SYN** **fake** **2** [C] something, for example a document, piece of paper money, etc., that has been copied in order to cheat people 伪造品；赝品：*Experts are dismissing claims that the painting is a forgery.* 专家排除了这幅画是赝品的说法。➲ COMPARE COUNTERFEIT

for·get 🔑 /fəˈget; NAmE fərˈg-/ *verb* (**for·got** /fəˈgɒt; NAmE fərˈgɑːt/, **for·got·ten** /fəˈgɒtn; NAmE fərˈgɑːtn/)

• **EVENTS/FACTS** 事情；事实 **1** 🔑 [I, T] (not usually used in the progressive tenses 通常不用于进行时) to be unable to remember sth that has happened in the past or information that you knew in the past 忘记；遗忘：**~ (about sth)** *I'd completely forgotten about the money he owed me.* 我完全忘记不得他欠我的钱了。◇ *Before I forget, there was a call from Italy for you.* 趁我还记得，有一个从意大利打来的电话找你。◇ **~ sth** *I never forget a face.* 见过的面孔我从不忘记。◇ *Who could forget his speech at last year's party?* 谁能忘记他去年在聚会上的讲话呢？◇ **~ (that)...** *She keeps forgetting (that) I'm not a child any more.* 她老是忘了我不再是个小孩子了。◇ ***I was forgetting*** (= I had forgotten) *(that) you've been here before.* 我忘了你以前来过这里。◇ **~ where, how, etc....** *I've forgotten where they live exactly.* 我忘记了他们的确切住址。◇ *I forget how much they paid for it.* 我忘了他们用多少钱买的这东西。◇ **~ (sb) doing sth** *I'll never forget hearing this piece of music for the first time.* 我永远不会忘记第一次听到这首曲子的情景。◇ **it is forgotten that...** ***It should not be forgotten that*** *people used to get much more exercise.* 不应忘记的是，人们过去的锻炼要多得多。

• **TO DO STH** 做某事 **2** 🔑 [I, T] to not remember to do sth that you ought to do, or to bring or buy sth that you ought to bring or buy 忘记做（或带、买等）：**~ (about sth)** *'Why weren't you at the meeting?' 'Sorry—I forgot.'* "你为什么没有参加会议？""对不起，我忘了。"◇ **~ to do sth** *Take care, and don't forget to write.* 要保重，别忘了写信。◇ *I forgot to ask him for his address.* 我忘记向他要地址。◇ **~ sth/sb** *I forgot my purse* (= I did not remember to bring it). 我忘了带钱包。◇ *'Hey, don't forget me!'* (= don't leave without me) "喂，走时别落下我！"◇ ***Aren't you forgetting something?*** (= I think you have forgotten to do sth) 你难道没有忘记要做的事吗？ **HELP** You cannot use **forget** if you want to mention the place where you have left something. 把东西忘在某处不用 forget：*I've left my book at home.* 我把书忘在家了。◇ ~~*I've forgotten my book at home.*~~

• **STOP THINKING ABOUT STH** 不再想 **3** 🔑 [I, T] to deliberately stop thinking about sb/sth 不再想；不再把…放在心上：**~ (about sb/sth)** *Try to forget about what happened.* 尽量不再想发生过的事情。◇ *Could you possibly forget about work for five minutes?* 你能不能匀出五分钟来不去想工作？◇ **~ sb/sth** *Forget him!* 别把他放在心上！◇ *Let's forget our differences and be friends.* 咱们别把分歧放在心上，做个朋友吧。◇ **~ (that)...** *Forget (that) I said anything!* 不要把我说的话放在心上！ **4** [I, T] to stop thinking that sth is a possibility 不再考虑…的可能：**~ about sth** *If I lose this job, we can forget about buying a new car.* 要是我丢掉这份工作，我们就别想买新车。◇ **~ sth** *'I was hoping you might be able to lend me the money.' 'You can forget that!'* "我希望你能借钱给我。""打消这个念头吧！"

• **YOURSELF** 自己 **5** [T] **~ yourself** to behave in a way that is not socially acceptable（举止）不得体：*I'm forgetting myself. I haven't offered you a drink yet!* 我真是不成体统。还没有让您喝点什么呢！

IDM **and don't (you) for'get it** (*informal*) used to tell sb how they should behave, especially when they have been behaving in a way you do not like 可别忘了；你可给我记住；你给我老实点：*You're a suspect, not a detective, and don't you forget it.* 你是嫌疑犯，不是侦探，给我记住了。 **for'get it** (*informal*) **1** used to tell sb that sth is not important and that they should not worry about it 没关系；不必在意：*'I still owe you for lunch yesterday.' 'Forget it.'* "昨天午饭我还欠着你呢。""算了吧！" **2** used to tell sb that you are not going to repeat what you said（表示不想重复说过的话）别提它了：*'Now, what were you saying about John?' 'Forget it, it doesn't matter.'* "嗳，你刚才说约翰什么来着？""别提了，那无关紧要。" **3** used to emphasize that you are saying 'no' to sth 休想；不可能：*'Any chance of you helping out here?' 'Forget it, I've got too much to do.'* "这儿你能帮个忙吗？""不可能，我还有一大堆活儿要干呢。" **4** used to tell sb to stop talking about sth because they are annoying you 住嘴；别再烦人地说下去了：*Just forget it, will you!* 闭上嘴，行不行！ **not forgetting...** (*BrE*) used to include sth in the list of things that you have just mentioned 还包括：*I share the house with Jim, Ian and Sam, not forgetting Spike, the dog.* 我和吉姆、伊恩、萨姆共住一所房子，还有这条狗斯派克。➲ MORE AT FORGIVE

for·get·ful /fə'getfl; *NAmE* fər'g-/ *adj.* **1** often forgetting things 健忘的；好忘事的 **SYN** **absent-minded**: *She has become very forgetful in recent years.* 近年来她变得十分健忘。 **2 ~ of sb/sth** (*formal*) not thinking about sb/sth that you should be thinking about 疏忽的；不经心的 ▶ **for·get·ful·ly** /-fəli/ *adv.* **for·get·ful·ness** *noun* [U]

for'get-me-not *noun* a small wild plant with light blue flowers 勿忘我，勿忘草

for·get·table /fə'getəbl; *NAmE* fər'g-/ *adj.* not interesting or special and therefore easily forgotten（因平淡无奇）易被忘记的，容易遗忘的: *an instantly forgettable tune* 转瞬即忘的曲调 **OPP** **unforgettable**

for·giv·able /fə'gɪvəbl; *NAmE* fər'g-/ *adj.* that you can understand and forgive 可原谅的；可宽恕的 **SYN** **excusable**: *His rudeness was forgivable in the circumstances.* 他当时的无理情有可原。 **OPP** **unforgivable**

for·give /fə'gɪv; *NAmE* fər'gɪv/ *verb* (**for·gave** /fə'geɪv; *NAmE* fər'geɪv/, **for·given** /fə'gɪvn; *NAmE* fər'g-/) **1** [T, I] to stop feeling angry with sb who has done sth to harm, annoy or upset you; to stop feeling angry with yourself 原谅；宽恕: **~ sb/yourself (for sth/for doing sth)** *I'll never forgive her for what she did.* 我绝不会原谅她做的事。◇ *I'd never forgive myself if she heard the truth from someone else.* 如果她从别人那里听到了真相，我永远不会原谅自己。◇ **~ (sth)** *I can't forgive that type of behaviour.* 我不能宽恕那种行为。◇ *We all have to learn to forgive.* 我们都得学会宽恕。◇ **~ sb sth** *She'd forgive him anything.* 无论他做了什么，她都会原谅他。 ➲ WORDFINDER NOTE AT SORRY **2** [T] used to say in a polite way that you are sorry if what you are doing or saying seems rude or silly 对不起；请原谅: **~ me** *Forgive me, but I don't see that any of this concerns me.* 对不起，我就看不出这与我有啥关系。◇ **~ me for doing sth** *Forgive me for interrupting, but I really don't agree with that.* 请原谅我打岔，不过我确实不同意那一点。◇ **~ my...** *Forgive my ignorance, but what exactly does the company do?* 请原谅我的无知，这家公司到底是干什么的？◇ **~ my doing sth** *Forgive my interrupting but I really don't agree with that.* 请原谅我打岔，不过我确实不同意那一点。 **3** [T] **~ (sb) sth** (*formal*) (of a bank, country, etc. 银行、国家等) to say that sb does not need to pay back money that they have borrowed 免除（债务）: *The government has agreed to forgive a large part of the debt.* 政府同意免除一大部分债务。

IDM **sb could/might be forgiven for doing sth** used to say that it is easy to understand why sb does or thinks sth, although they are wrong 某人的做法虽错却是可以理解的: *Looking at the crowds out shopping, you could be forgiven for thinking that everyone has plenty of money.* 见到人们成群结队地外出购物，难怪你会以为人人都很富有。 **for,give and for'get** to stop feeling angry with sb for sth they have done to you and to behave as if it had not happened 不念旧恶；不记仇 ➲ MORE LIKE THIS 13, page R26

for·give·ness /fə'gɪvnəs; *NAmE* fər'g-/ *noun* [U] the act of forgiving sb; willingness to forgive sb 原谅；宽恕；宽宏大量: *to pray for God's forgiveness* 祈求上帝宽恕 ◇ *the forgiveness of sins* 对罪的宽恕 ◇ *He begged forgiveness for what he had done.* 他乞求饶恕他的所作所为。

for·giv·ing /fə'gɪvɪŋ; *NAmE* fər'g-/ *adj.* willing to forgive 宽宏大量的；宽容的: *She had not inherited her mother's forgiving nature.* 她没有承袭她母亲的宽厚天性。◇ **~ of sth** *The public was more forgiving of the president's difficulties than the press and fellow politicians.* 公众比报界和总统的政界同人更能体谅他的难处。

forgo (*also* **fore·go**) /fɔː'gəʊ; *NAmE* fɔːr'goʊ/ *verb* (**for·goes** /fɔː'gəʊz; *NAmE* fɔːr'goʊz/, **for·went** /fɔː'went; *NAmE* fɔːr'went/, **for·gone** /fɔː'gɒn; *NAmE* fɔːr'gɔːn/) **~ sth** (*formal*) to decide not to have or do sth that you would like to have or do 放弃，弃绝（想做的事或想得之物）: *No one was prepared to forgo their lunch hour to attend the meeting.* 谁都不愿意放弃午餐时间出席会议。

for·got PAST TENSE OF FORGET

for·got·ten PAST PART. OF FORGET

fork /fɔːk; *NAmE* fɔːrk/ *noun, verb*

■ ***noun*** **1** a tool with a handle and three or four sharp points (called PRONGS), used for picking up and eating food 餐叉: *to eat with a* ***knife and fork*** 用刀叉吃东西 ➲ VISUAL VOCAB PAGE V23 **2** a garden tool with a long or short handle and three or four sharp metal points, used for digging 叉（挖掘用的园艺工具）➲ VISUAL VOCAB PAGE V20 ➲ SEE ALSO PITCHFORK **3** a place where a road, river, etc. divides into two parts; either of these two parts（道路、河流等的）分岔处，分流处，岔口，岔路: *Shortly before dusk they reached a fork and took the left-hand track.* 快到黄昏时，他们来到一个岔路口，沿着左边的小径走去。◇ *Take the right fork.* 走右边的岔路。 **4** a thing shaped like a fork, with two or more long parts 叉状物: *a jagged fork of lightning* 锯齿状闪电 ➲ SEE ALSO TUNING FORK **5** either of two metal supporting pieces into which a wheel on a bicycle or motorcycle is fitted（自行车或摩托车的）车叉子 ➲ VISUAL VOCAB PAGE V55

■ ***verb*** **1** [I] (not used in the progressive tenses 不用于进行时) (**+ adv./prep.**) (of a road, river, etc. 道路、河流等) to divide into two parts that lead in different directions 分岔；岔开两条分支: *The path forks at the bottom of the hill.* 小径在山丘脚下分岔。◇ *The road forks right after the bridge.* 这条路过桥后岔开分成两条。 **2** [I] **+ adv./prep.** (not used in the progressive tenses 不用于进行时) (of a person 人) to turn left or right where a road, etc. divides into two 走岔路中的一条: *Fork right after the bridge.* 过桥后走右边那条岔路。 **3** [T] (**+ adv./prep.**) to move, carry or dig sth using a fork 叉运；叉掘: *Clear the soil of weeds and fork in plenty of compost.* 清除土中的杂草，然后叉入大量堆肥。

PHR V **,fork 'out (for sth)** | **,fork 'out sth (for/on sth)** (*informal*) to spend a lot of money on sth, especially unwillingly（尤指不情愿地）大量花钱，大把掏钱: *Why fork out for a taxi when there's a perfectly good bus service?* 有挺好的公共汽车，干吗要多掏钱坐出租汽车？◇ *We've forked out a small fortune on their education.* 我们在他们的教育上可花了不少钱。

forked /fɔːkt; *NAmE* fɔːrkt/ *adj.* with one end divided into two parts, like the shape of the letter 'Y' 叉状的（形如字母 Y）: *a bird with a forked tail* 有叉形尾羽的鸟 ◇ *the forked tongue of a snake* 蛇的叉形舌 ➲ VISUAL VOCAB PAGE V13

,forked 'lightning *noun* [U] the type of LIGHTNING that is like a line that divides into smaller lines near the ground 叉状闪电 ➲ COMPARE SHEET LIGHTNING

fork·ful /'fɔːkfʊl; *NAmE* 'fɔːrk-/ *noun* the amount that a fork holds 一叉子（的量）

fork·lift truck /,fɔːklɪft 'trʌk; *NAmE* ,fɔːrk-/ (*also* **'fork·lift**) *noun* a vehicle with special equipment on the front for moving and lifting heavy objects 叉车；叉式装卸车；堆高机 ➲ VISUAL VOCAB PAGE V62

for·lorn /fə'lɔːn; *NAmE* fər'lɔːrn/ *adj.* **1** (of a person 人) appearing lonely and unhappy 孤苦伶仃的；孤独凄凉的: *She looked so forlorn, standing there in the rain.* 她站在雨中，显得孤苦伶仃。 **2** (of a place 地方) not cared for and with no people in it 凄凉的；荒芜的: *Empty houses quickly take on a forlorn look.* 空无一人的房屋很快就显得凄凉。 **3** unlikely to succeed, come true, etc. 不大可能成功的；难以实现的: *She waited* ***in the forlorn hope*** *that he would one day come back to her.* 她几乎毫无指望地等待他有一天会回到她的身边。◇ *His father smiled weakly* ***in a forlorn attempt*** *to reassure him that everything was all right.* 他父亲淡淡地一笑，试图安慰他一切都好，却没什么效果。 ▶ **for·lorn·ly** *adv.*

form /fɔːm; *NAmE* fɔːrm/ *noun, verb*

■ ***noun***

• **TYPE** 类型 **1** [C] a type or variety of sth 类型；种类: *forms of transport/government/energy* 运输种类；政体类型；能源种类 ◇ *one of the most common forms of cancer* 最常见的一种癌症 ◇ *all the millions of different life forms on* *the planet today* 当今地球上所有的几百万生命种类 ➲ SEE ALSO ART FORM

• **WAY STH IS/LOOKS** 形式 **2** 🔑 [C, U] the particular way sth is, seems, looks or is presented 形式；外表；样子： *The disease can take several different forms.* 这种疾病可能有几种不同的形式。◇ *Help **in the form of** money will be very welcome.* 欢迎以金钱形式予以资助。◇ *Help arrived **in the form of** two police officers.* 来支援的是两名警察。◇ *The training programme **takes the form of** a series of workshops.* 培训课程采取一系列研讨会的形式。◇ *Most political questions involve morality **in some form or other**.* 多数政治问题牵涉到这样或那样的道义性。◇ *We need to come to **some form of** agreement.* 我们需要达成某种形式的协议。◇ *I'm opposed to censorship **in any shape or form**.* 我反对任何形式的审查。◇ *This dictionary is also available in electronic form.* 这部词典也有电子版本的。

• **DOCUMENT** 文件 **3** 🔑 [C] an official document containing questions and spaces for answers 表格： *an **application/entry/order form*** 申请表；报名表；订货单 ◇ (*especially BrE*) *to **fill in a form*** 填表 ◇ (*especially NAmE*) *to **fill out a form*** 填表 ◇ *I filled in/out a form on their website.* 我在他们的网站上填了一张表。◇ *to complete a form* 填表 ◇ (*BrE*) *a **booking form*** 预订单 ◇ (*NAmE*) *a **reservation form*** 预订单

• **SHAPE** 形状 **4** 🔑 [C] the shape of sb/sth; a person or thing of which only the shape can be seen 形状；体形： *her slender form* 她苗条的身段 ◇ *The human form has changed little over the last 30 000 years.* * 3 万多年以来，人的体形没有多大变化。◇ *They made out a shadowy form in front of them.* 他们认出了前面的模糊人影。

• **ARRANGEMENT OF PARTS** 结构 **5** [U] the arrangement of parts in a whole, especially in a work of art or piece of writing（尤指艺术作品或文章的）结构，形式： *In a novel, form and content are equally important.* 小说的形式和内容同样重要。➲ SYNONYMS AT STRUCTURE

• **BEING FIT/HEALTHY** 健壮；健康 **6** [U] (*BrE*) how fit and healthy sb is; the state of being fit and healthy 体能；良好的健康状态： *After six months' training the whole team is in superb form.* 经过半年的训练，全队状态极佳。◇ *I really need to get back **in form**.* 我实在需要恢复状态。◇ *The horse was clearly **out of form**.* 这匹马显然状态不佳。

• **PERFORMANCE** 表现 **7** [U] how well sb/sth is performing; the fact that sb/sth is performing well 表现状态；良好表现： *Midfielder Elliott has shown disappointing form recently.* 中场队员埃利奥特近来表现令人失望。◇ ***On current/present form** the party is heading for another election victory.* 就该党目前情况来看，下届选举又会胜利。◇ *She signalled her return to form with a convincing victory.* 她令人信服的胜利显示她已恢复状态。◇ *He's right **on form*** (= performing well) *as a crazy science teacher in his latest movie.* 他在最近的一部电影中扮演疯狂的理科教师，表现出色。◇ *The whole team was **on good form** and deserved the win.* 全队表现良好，获胜是理所当然的。◇ *She was **in great form*** (= happy and cheerful and full of energy) *at the wedding party.* 在婚宴上她欢欣雀跃。

• **WAY OF DOING THINGS** 做事方式 **8** [U, C] (*especially BrE*) the usual way of doing sth 惯常做法；常规；习俗： *What's the form when you apply for a research grant?* 申请科研补助金按常规应该怎么办？◇ *conventional social forms* 常规社会习俗 ◇ ***True to form*** (= as he usually does) *he arrived an hour late.* 他和往常一样迟到了一小时。◇ *Partners of employees are invited **as a matter of form**.* 按惯例，雇员的配偶受到了邀请。 **9** [U] **good/bad ~** (*old-fashioned, BrE*) the way of doing things that is socially acceptable/not socially acceptable 礼貌；礼节

• **OF WORD** 单词 **10** [C] a way of writing or saying a word that shows, for example, if it is plural or in a particular tense 词形；形式： *the infinitive form of the verb* 动词不定式

• **IN SCHOOL** 学校 **11** (*BrE, old-fashioned*) a class in a school 年级： *Who's your form teacher?* 你们的年级老师是谁？➲ SEE ALSO SIXTH FORM ➲ COMPARE YEAR (4) **12 -former** (in compounds 构成复合词) (*BrE, old-fashioned*) a student in the form mentioned at school …年级学生： *a third-former* 三年级学生 ➲ SEE ALSO SIXTH-FORMER

IDM **take 'form** (*formal*) to gradually form into a particular shape; to gradually develop 逐渐成形；渐渐发展： *In her body a new life was taking form.* 一个新的生命在她的体内逐渐形成。➲ MORE AT SHAPE *n.*

■ ***verb***

• **START TO EXIST** 开始存在 **1** 🔑 [I, T] (especially of natural things 尤指自然事物) to begin to exist and gradually develop into a particular shape; to make sth begin to exist in a particular shape （使）出现，产生： *Flowers appeared, but fruits failed to form.* 开了花，但没有结果。◇ *Storm clouds are forming on the horizon.* 天边出现了暴雨云。◇ **~ sth** *These hills were formed by glaciation.* 这些山丘是冰川作用形成的。 **2** 🔑 [I, T] to start to exist and develop; to make sth start to exist and develop （使）形成： *A plan formed in my head.* 一个计划在我的头脑中形成。◇ **~ sth** *I formed many close friendships at college.* 我大学时结交了许多密友。◇ *I didn't see enough of the play to form an opinion about it.* 我对这部戏剧了解得不够，说不出什么意见。➲ SYNONYMS AT MAKE

• **MAKE SHAPE/FORM** 使成形 **3** 🔑 [T, often passive] to produce sth in a particular way or make it have a particular shape （使）成形，组成；制作： **~ sth** *Bend the wire so that it forms a 'V'.* 把铁丝弯成 V 形。◇ *Rearrange the letters to form a new word.* 重新排列字母，组成另一单词。◇ *Games can help children learn to form letters.* 游戏可以帮助儿童学会组合字母。◇ *Do you know how to form the past tense?* 你知道怎样构成过去时吗？◇ **~ sth into sth** *Form the dough into balls with your hands.* 用手把生面团揉成一些球儿。◇ **~ sth from/of sth** *The chain is formed from 136 links.* 这根链条由 136 个环组成。**4** 🔑 [T, I] to move or arrange objects or people so that they are in a group with a particular shape; to become arranged in a group like this （使）排列成，排成： **~ sb/sth (up) (into sth)** *to **form a line/queue/circle*** 排成一队 / 圈 ◇ *First get students to form groups of four.* 首先让学生分成四人一组。◇ **~ (up) (into sth)** *Queues were already forming outside the theatre.* 剧院外已经在排队了。◇ *The teams formed up into lines.* 各队已整好了队列。

• **HAVE FUNCTION/ROLE** 功能；作用 **5** 🔑 [T] **~ sth** to have a particular function or pattern 有…功能；有…模式： *The trees form a natural protection from the sun's rays.* 树木起天然的保护作用，遮挡了太阳的光线。 **6** *linking verb* + **noun** to be sth 是；成为： *The castle forms the focal point of the city.* 这座城堡是城市的中心。◇ *The survey **formed part of** a larger programme of research.* 这个调查是研究计划的一部分。◇ *These drawings will **form the basis of** the exhibition.* 这些画作将成为展览的基本部分。

• **ORGANIZATION** 组织 **7** 🔑 [T, I] **~ (sth)** to start a group of people, such as an organization, a committee, etc.; to come together in a group of this kind 组织；建立： *They hope to form the new government.* 他们希望组建新政府。◇ *He formed a band with some friends from school.* 他和学校里的一些朋友组成一支乐队。◇ *a newly-formed political party* 新建立的政党 ◇ *The band formed in 2007.* 这支乐队成立于 2007 年。

• **HAVE INFLUENCE ON** 影响 **8** [T] **~ sth** to have an influence on the way that sth develops 对…的发展有影响 **SYN** **mould**： *Positive and negative experiences form a child's character.* 正反两方面的经历都影响儿童性格的形成。

for·mal 🔑 /ˈfɔːml; *NAmE* ˈfɔːrml/ *adj.* **1** 🔑 (of a style of dress, speech, writing, behaviour, etc. 穿着、言语、行为等) very correct and suitable for official or important occasions 适合正式场合的；正规的；庄重的： *formal evening dress* 晚礼服 ◇ *The dinner was a formal affair.* 这是正式宴会。◇ *He kept the tone of the letter formal and businesslike.* 他使这封信保持正式公文的语气。◇ *She has a very formal manner, which can seem unfriendly.* 她的举止很是郑重其事，有可能会显得不友好。 **OPP** **informal** **2** 🔑 official; following an agreed or official way of doing things 正式的；合乎规矩的： *formal legal processes* 正式法律程序 ◇ *to make a **formal apology/complaint/request*** 正式道歉 / 投诉 / 要求 ◇ *Formal diplomatic relations between the two countries were re-established in December.* 两国于十二月重新建立了正式外交关系。◇ *It is time to put these arrangements on a slightly more formal basis.* 是应该把这些安排做得略为正式一点的时候了。**3** 🔑 (of education or training 学校教育或培训) received in a school, college or university, with lessons, exams, etc., rather than gained just through practical experience 正规的： *He has no* *formal teaching qualifications.* 他没有正规的教学资历证明。◇ *Young children are beginning their formal education sometimes as early as four years old.* 幼儿有时早在四岁时就开始接受正规教育。**4** concerned with the way sth is done rather than what is done 方式上的；做法上的；形式上的：*Getting approval for the plan is a purely formal matter; nobody will seriously oppose it.* 计划报批纯粹是一个形式上的问题，没有人会当真反对的。◇ *Critics have concentrated too much on the formal elements of her poetry, without really looking at what it is saying.* 评论家过多地集中评论她诗歌的形式，而没有真正看其内容。**5** (of a garden, room or building 花园、房间、建筑物) arranged in a regular manner, according to a clear, exact plan 整齐的；布置井然的：*delightful formal gardens, with terraced lawns and an avenue of trees* 精心布置的有片片草坪和林荫道的宜人花园 OPP **informal** ▶ **for·mal·ly** /-məli/ *adv.*：*'How do you do?' she said formally.* "你好！"她很正式地说。◇ *The accounts were formally approved by the board.* 账目已由董事会正式批准。◇ *Although not formally trained as an art historian, he is widely respected for his knowledge of the period.* 虽然他不是科班出身的艺术史学家，但他对这一时期的知识却普遍为人尊重。

for·mal·de·hyde /fɔːˈmældɪhaɪd; *NAmE* fɔːrˈm-/ *noun* [U] **1** (*symb.* CH_2O) a gas with a strong smell 甲醛 **2** (*also specialist* **for·mal·in** /ˈfɔːməlɪn; *NAmE* ˈfɔːrm-/) a liquid made by mixing formaldehyde and water, used for preserving BIOLOGICAL SPECIMENS, making plastics and as a DISINFECTANT 福尔马林；甲醛水溶液

for·mal·ism /ˈfɔːməlɪzəm; *NAmE* ˈfɔːrm-/ *noun* [U] a style or method in art, music, literature, science, etc. that pays more attention to the rules and the correct arrangement and appearance of things than to inner meaning and feelings 形式主义 ▶ **for·mal·ist** /ˈfɔːməlɪst; *NAmE* ˈfɔːrm-/ *noun* **for·mal·ist** /ˈfɔːməlɪst; *NAmE* ˈfɔːrm-/ *adj.* [usually before noun]：*formalist theory* 形式主义理论

for·mal·ity /fɔːˈmæləti; *NAmE* fɔːrˈm-/ *noun* (*pl.* **-ies**) **1** [C, usually pl.] a thing that you must do as a formal or official part of a legal process, a social situation, etc. 正式手续：*to go through all the formalities necessary in order to get a gun licence* 办理取得持枪执照的全部必要手续 ◇ *Let's skip the formalities and get down to business.* 咱们省去繁文缛节，开始讨论实质问题吧。**2** [C, usually sing.] a thing that you must do as part of an official process, but which has little meaning and will not affect what happens 例行公事：*He already knows he has the job so the interview is a mere formality.* 他已知道得到了这个工作，所以面试仅仅是走走过场。**3** [U] correct and formal behaviour 遵守礼节：*Different levels of formality are appropriate in different situations.* 不同规格的礼节适用于不同场合。◇ *She greeted him with stiff formality.* 她拘谨地按礼节向他致意。

for·mal·ize (*BrE also* **-ise**) /ˈfɔːməlaɪz; *NAmE* ˈfɔːrm-/ *verb* **1** ~ **sth** to make an arrangement, a plan or a relationship official 使（安排、计划、关系）成为正式的：*They decided to formalize their relationship by getting married.* 他们决定结婚，正式确定关系。**2** ~ **sth** to give sth a fixed structure or form by introducing rules （通过规则）使有固定体系，使定形：*The college has a highly formalized system of assessment.* 这所学院有一套十分固定的评估体系。▶ **for·mal·iza·tion, -isa·tion** /ˌfɔːməlaɪˈzeɪʃn; *NAmE* ˌfɔːrmələˈz-/ *noun* [U]

for·mat AW /ˈfɔːmæt; *NAmE* ˈfɔːrmæt/ *noun, verb*

■ ***noun*** **1** the general arrangement, plan, design, etc. of sth 总体安排；计划；设计：*The format of the new quiz show has proved popular.* 新的智力竞赛节目的总体安排结果证明很受欢迎。**2** the shape and size of a book, magazine, etc. （出版物的）版式，开本：*They've brought out the magazine in a new format.* 他们用新的版式出版这杂志。**3** (*computing* 计) the way in which data is stored or held to be worked on by a computer 格式

■ ***verb*** (**-tt-**) **1** ~ **sth** to prepare a computer disk so that data can be recorded on it 格式化 **2** ~ **sth** (*specialist*) to arrange text in a particular way on a page or a screen 安排…的版式

for·ma·tion /fɔːˈmeɪʃn; *NAmE* fɔːrˈm-/ *noun* **1** [U] the action of forming sth; the process of being formed 组成；形成：*the formation of a new government* 组建新政府 ◇ *evidence of recent star formation in the galaxy* 银河系新恒星形成的证据 **2** [C] a thing that has been formed, especially in a particular place or in a particular way 组成物；形成物：*rock formations* 岩层 **3** [U, C] a particular arrangement or pattern 编队；队形：*aircraft flying* ***in formation*** 编队飞行的飞机 ◇ *formation flying* 编队飞行 ◇ *The team usually plays in a 4-4-2 formation.* 这支球队比赛通常排出的是 4-4-2 阵形。

for·ma·tive /ˈfɔːmətɪv; *NAmE* ˈfɔːrm-/ *adj.* [only before noun] having an important and lasting influence on the development of sth or of sb's character （对某事物或性格的发展）有持续重大影响的：*the* ***formative years*** *of childhood* 童年性格形成的时期

for·mer /ˈfɔːmə(r); *NAmE* ˈfɔːrm-/ *adj., noun*

■ ***adj.*** [only before noun] **1** that existed in earlier times 以前的 SYN **past**：*in former times* 从前 ◇ *This beautiful old building has been restored to* ***its former glory***. 这座美丽的老建筑物已恢复了昔日的壮观。**2** that used to have a particular position or status in the past 昔日的；前 SYN **previous, one-time**：*former South African president Nelson Mandela* 南非前总统纳尔逊・曼德拉 ◇ *my former boss/colleague/wife* 以前的老板／同事；前妻 ◇ *the countries of the former Soviet Union* 前苏联加盟共和国 **3** **the former...** used to refer to the first of two things or people mentioned （两者中）前者的：*The former option would be much more sensible.* 前一种选择要明智得多。➲ COMPARE LATTER *adj.*

IDM **be a shadow/ghost of your former 'self** to not have the strength, influence, etc. that you used to have 失去昔日的力量（或影响等）；威风不再；不如当年

■ ***noun*** **1** **the former** (*pl.* **the former**) the first of two things or people mentioned （两者中的）前者：*He had to choose between giving up his job and giving up his principles. He chose the former.* 他得在放弃工作和放弃原则二者中择其一。他选择了前者。◇ *However, the former are excluded.* 不过，前者被排除在外。➲ COMPARE LATTER *n.* **2** a person or thing that forms sth 形成者；构成物：*opinion formers and policy makers* 意见领袖和政策制定者

for·mer·ly /ˈfɔːməli; *NAmE* ˈfɔːrmərli/ *adv.* in earlier times 以前；从前 SYN **previously**：*Namibia, formerly known as South West Africa* 纳米比亚，旧称西南非洲 ◇ *I learnt that the house had formerly been an inn.* 我得知这座房子以前是家客栈。◇ *John Marsh, formerly of London Road, Leicester, now living in France* 约翰・马什，以前家在莱斯特市伦敦路，现居住在法国

For·mica™ /fɔːˈmaɪkə; *NAmE* fɔːrˈm-/ *noun* [U] a hard plastic that can resist heat, used for covering work surfaces, etc. 福米加（商标，用作贴面板等的抗热硬塑料）

for·mic acid /ˌfɔːmɪk ˈæsɪd; *NAmE* ˌfɔːrmɪk/ *noun* [U] (*chemistry* 化) an acid made from CARBON MONOXIDE and steam. It is also present in a liquid produced by some ANTS. 甲酸；蚁酸

for·mid·able /ˈfɔːmɪdəbl; fəˈmɪd-; *NAmE* ˈfɔːrm-; fərˈm-/ *adj.* if people, things or situations are **formidable**, you feel fear and/or respect for them, because they are impressive or powerful, or because they seem very difficult 可怕的；令人敬畏的；难对付的：*In debate he was a formidable opponent.* 在辩论中他是位难应付的对手。◇ *She has a formidable list of qualifications.* 她有一长串令人敬畏的资历。◇ *The two players together make a formidable combination.* 这两个选手配对儿，难以对付。◇ *The task was a formidable one.* 这任务非常艰巨。◇ *They had to overcome formidable obstacles.* 他们得克服重重障碍。▶ **for·mid·ably** /-əbli/ *adv.*：*He now has the chance to prove himself in a formidably difficult role.* 现在他的任务十分艰巨，他有机会证明自己的能力了。◇ *She's formidably intelligent.* 她聪明绝顶。

form·less /ˈfɔːmləs; *NAmE* ˈfɔːrm-/ *adj.* without a clear or definite shape or structure 无明确形状的；无定形的；结

构不清的：*formless dreams* 杂乱的梦 ▶ **form·less·ness** *noun* [U]

for·mula 🔑 AW /ˈfɔːmjələ; *NAmE* ˈfɔːrm-/ *noun* (*pl.* **for·mu·las, formulae** /-liː/) HELP **Formulae** is used especially in scientific language. * formulae 尤用于科学语境。 **1** 🔑 [C] (*mathematics* 数) a series of letters, numbers or symbols that represent a rule or law 公式；方程式；计算式：*This formula is used to calculate the area of a circle.* 这个公式用于计算圆的面积。**2** 🔑 [C] (*chemistry* 化) letters and symbols that show the parts of a chemical COMPOUND, etc. 分子式：*CO is the formula for carbon monoxide.* * CO 是一氧化碳的分子式。➲ WORDFINDER NOTE AT CHEMISTRY **3** 🔑 [C] a particular method of doing or achieving sth 方案；方法：*They're trying to work out a peace formula acceptable to both sides in the dispute.* 他们正在设法制定出一个争执双方都可以接受的和平方案。◇ ~ **for sth/for doing sth** *There's no magic formula for a perfect marriage.* 没有一个达到完美婚姻的神奇方法。**4** 🔑 [C] a list of the things that sth is made from, giving the amount of each substance to use 配方；处方；药方：*the secret formula for the blending of the whisky* 调配威士忌的秘方 **5** (*also* **ˈformula milk**) [U, C] (*especially NAmE*) a type of liquid food for babies, given instead of breast milk 配方奶（母乳的替代品）**6** [C] a class of racing car, based on engine size, etc. 方程式（按发动机大小等对赛车的分级）：*Formula One™ racing* 一级方程式赛车 **7** [C] a fixed form of words used in a particular situation（特定场合的）惯用词语，套话：*legal formulae* 法律惯用词语 ◇ *The minister keeps coming out with the same tired formulas.* 这个部长开口便是千篇一律、使人厌倦的套话。

for·mu·la·ic /ˌfɔːmjuˈleɪɪk; *NAmE* ˌfɔːrm-/ *adj.* (*formal*) made up of fixed patterns of words or ideas 由固定套话堆砌的；公式化构思的：*Traditional stories make use of formulaic expressions like 'Once upon a time…'.* 传统故事采用"从前…"一类的套语。

for·mu·late AW /ˈfɔːmjuleɪt; *NAmE* ˈfɔːrm-/ *verb* **1** to create or prepare sth carefully, giving particular attention to the details 制定；规划；构想；准备：**~ sth** *to formulate a policy/theory/plan/proposal* 制定政策；创立理论；构想计划；准备建议 ◇ *The compost is specially formulated for pot plants.* 此混合肥料专门用于盆栽植物。◇ **~ sth to do sth** *This new kitchen cleaner is formulated to cut through grease and dirt.* 这种新的厨房清洁剂能去除油渍和污垢。**2** **~ sth** to express your ideas in carefully chosen words 确切表达；认真阐述：*She has lots of good ideas, but she has difficulty formulating them.* 她有很多好主意，但就是不善于表达。▶ **for·mu·la·tion** AW /ˌfɔːmjuˈleɪʃn; *NAmE* ˌfɔːrm-/ *noun* [U, C]: *the formulation of new policies* 新政策的制定

for·ni·cate /ˈfɔːnɪkeɪt; *NAmE* ˈfɔːrn-/ *verb* [I] (*formal, disapproving*) to have sex with sb that you are not married to 私通；通奸 ▶ **for·ni·ca·tion** /ˌfɔːnɪˈkeɪʃn; *NAmE* ˌfɔːrn-/ *noun* [U] **for·ni·ca·tor** *noun*

for·sake /fəˈseɪk; *NAmE* fərˈs-/ *verb* (**for·sook** /fəˈsʊk; *NAmE* fərˈs-/, **for·saken** /fəˈseɪkən; *NAmE* fərˈs-/) (*literary*) **1** **~ sb/sth (for sb/sth)** to leave sb/sth, especially when you have a responsibility to stay 抛弃，遗弃，离开（尤指不履行责任）SYN **abandon**: *He had made it clear to his wife that he would never forsake her.* 他明确地向妻子说，永远不离开她。**2** **~ sth (for sb/sth)** to stop doing sth, or leave sth, especially sth that you enjoy 摒弃，离开（尤指喜爱的事物）SYN **renounce**: *She forsook the glamour of the city and went to live in the wilds of Scotland.* 她抛开城市的绚烂，去苏格兰荒原居住。➲ SEE ALSO GODFORSAKEN

for·sooth /fəˈsuːθ; *NAmE* fər-/ *adv.* (*old use* or *humorous*) used to emphasize a statement, especially in order to show surprise（用以强调，尤为表示惊讶）实在，确实

for·swear /fɔːˈsweə(r); *NAmE* fɔːrˈswer/ *verb* (**for·swore** /fɔːˈswɔː(r); *NAmE* fɔːrˈs-/, **for·sworn** /fɔːˈswɔːn; *NAmE* fɔːrˈswɔːrn/) **~ sth** (*formal* or *literary*) to stop doing or using sth; to make a promise that you will stop doing or using sth 放弃；发誓戒除 SYN **renounce**: *The group forswears all worldly possessions.* 这个团体放弃一切尘世财物。◇ *The country has not forsworn the use of chemical weapons.* 该国并未保证禁用化学武器。

for·sythia /fɔːˈsaɪθiə; *NAmE* fərˈsɪθiə/ *noun* [U, C] a bush that has small bright yellow flowers in the early spring 连翘，金钟花（灌木，早春开小黄花）

fort /fɔːt; *NAmE* fɔːrt/ *noun* **1** a building or buildings built in order to defend an area against attack 要塞；堡垒；城堡 ➲ VISUAL VOCAB PAGE V15 **2** (*NAmE*) a place where soldiers live and have their training 兵营；军营；营地：*Fort Drum* 德拉姆堡

IDM **hold the ˈfort** (*BrE*) (*NAmE* **hold down the ˈfort**) (*informal*) to have the responsibility for sth or care of sb while other people are away or out 代为负责（某事）；代为照看（某人）：*Why not have a day off? I'll hold the fort for you.* 干吗不休息一天？我来为你代管。

forte /ˈfɔːteɪ; *NAmE* fɔːrt/ *noun, adv.*

■ *noun* [sing.] a thing that sb does particularly well 专长；特长：*Languages were never my forte.* 语言从来就不是我的强项。

■ *adv.* (*music* 音, *from Italian*) played or sung loudly（演奏或歌唱）强，强有力 OPP **piano** ▶ **forte** *adj.*

For·tean /ˈfɔːtiən; *NAmE* ˈfɔːrt-/ *adj.* involving or relating to things that cannot be explained by science 反常现象的；无法用科学解释的；超自然的；神秘莫测的 SYN **paranormal**

forth /fɔːθ; *NAmE* fɔːrθ/ *adv.* (*literary* except in particular idioms and phrasal verbs 文学用语，但在某些习语和短语动词中例外) **1** away from a place; out 离去；外出：*They set forth at dawn.* 他们在黎明时出发。◇ *Huge chimneys belched forth smoke and grime.* 巨大的烟囱冒出烟和灰尘。**2** towards a place; forwards 向某处；向前：*Water gushed forth from a hole in the rock.* 水从岩洞里涌出。➲ SEE ALSO BRING SB/STH↔FORTH at BRING

IDM **from that day/time ˈforth** (*literary*) beginning on that day; from that time 从那天起；从那时以后 ➲ MORE AT BACK *adv.*, SO *adv.*

the ˌForth ˈBridge *noun*

IDM **like painting the Forth ˈBridge** (*BrE*) used to describe a job that never seems to end because by the time you get to the end you have to start at the beginning again 永无止境的工作（快完成时又得重新开始）ORIGIN From the name of a very large bridge over the River Forth in Scotland. 源自苏格兰福斯河（River Forth）上巨型的福斯桥。

forth·com·ing AW /ˌfɔːθˈkʌmɪŋ; *NAmE* ˌfɔːrθ-/ *adj.* **1** [only before noun] going to happen, be published, etc. very soon 即将发生（或出版等）的：*the forthcoming elections* 即将举行的选举 ◇ *a list of forthcoming books* 近期将出版书籍的目录 ◇ *the band's forthcoming UK tour* 乐队即将在英国的巡回演出 **2** [not before noun] ready or made available when needed 现成；随要随有：*Financial support was not forthcoming.* 财政支援尚未到手。**3** [not before noun] willing to give information about sth 乐于提供信息：*She's never very forthcoming about her plans.* 她一直不大愿意说出自己的计划。OPP **unforthcoming**

forth·right /ˈfɔːθraɪt; *NAmE* ˈfɔːrθ-/ *adj.* direct and honest in manner and speech 直率的；直截了当的；坦诚的 SYN **frank**: *a woman of forthright views* 观点明确的女子 ▶ **forth·right·ly** *adv.* **forth·right·ness** *noun* [U]

forth·with /ˌfɔːθˈwɪθ; -ˈwɪð; *NAmE* ˌfɔːrθ-/ *adv.* (*formal*) immediately; at once 立即；马上；立刻：*The agreement between us is terminated forthwith.* 我们之间的协议立即终止。

for·ti·eth ➲ FORTY

for·ti·fi·ca·tion /ˌfɔːtɪfɪˈkeɪʃn; *NAmE* ˌfɔːrt-/ *noun* **1** [C, usually pl.] a tower, wall, gun position, etc. built to defend a place against attack 碉堡；围墙；炮台；防御工事：*the ramparts and fortifications of the Old Town* 旧城区的城墙和城堡 **2** [U] the act of fortifying or making sth stronger 筑城；设防；加强：*plans for the fortification of the city* 城市设防计划

for·tify /ˈfɔːtɪfaɪ; *NAmE* ˈfɔːrt-/ *verb* (**for·ti·fies, for·ti·fy·ing, for·ti·fied, for·ti·fied**) **1 ~ sth (against sb/sth)** to make a place more able to resist attack, especially by building high walls 筑防御工事；（尤指）筑城防御：*a fortified town* 设防的城镇 **2 ~ sb/yourself (against sb/sth)** to make sb/yourself feel stronger, braver, etc.（在物质或精神上）加强，增强：*He fortified himself against the cold with a hot drink.* 他喝了一杯热饮御寒。**3** to make a feeling or an attitude stronger 增强（感觉或态度）：*The news merely fortified their determination.* 这消息只是增强了他们的决心。 **4 ~ sth (with sth)** to increase the strength or quality of food or drink by adding sth to it（加入某物）强化（食品或饮料）；提高（营养价值）：*Sherry is **fortified wine*** (= wine with extra alcohol added). 雪利酒是添加了酒精的葡萄酒。◇ *cereal fortified with extra vitamins* 添加维生素的谷类食物

for·ti·ori ➲ A FORTIORI

for·tis·simo /fɔːˈtɪsɪməʊ; *NAmE* fɔːrˈtɪsɪmoʊ/ *adv.* (*abbr.* **ff**) (*music* 音, *from Italian*) very loudly 很强 OPP **pianissimo** ▸ **for·tis·simo** *adj.*

for·ti·tude /ˈfɔːtɪtjuːd; *NAmE* ˈfɔːrtətuːd/ *noun* [U] (*formal*) courage shown by sb who is suffering great pain or facing great difficulties （在巨大痛苦或困难面前表现出的）勇气，胆量，刚毅 SYN **bravery, courage**

Fort Knox /ˌfɔːt ˈnɒks; *NAmE* ˌfɔːrt ˈnɑːks/ *noun*
IDM **be like/as safe as Fort ˈKnox** (of a building 建筑物) to be strongly built, often with many locks, strong doors, guards, etc., so that it is difficult for people to enter and the things kept there are safe 坚固且戒备森严；固若金汤：*This home of yours is like Fort Knox.* 你这所房子可以说是固若金汤。ORIGIN From the name of the military base in Kentucky where most of the US's store of gold is kept. 源自美国肯塔基州存放美国大部分黄金储备的军事基地名。

fort·night /ˈfɔːtnaɪt; *NAmE* ˈfɔːrt-/ *noun* [usually sing.] (*BrE*) two weeks 两星期：*a fortnight's holiday* 两周的假期 ◇ *a fortnight ago* 两星期以前 ◇ *in a fortnight's time* 在两周的时间内 ◇ *He's had three accidents in the past fortnight.* 在过去两周他出了三次事故。

fort·night·ly /ˈfɔːtnaɪtli; *NAmE* ˈfɔːrt-/ *adj.* (*BrE*) happening once a fortnight 两星期一次的：*Meetings take place at fortnightly intervals.* 每两周开一次会。▸ **fort·night·ly** *adv.*：*The committee meets fortnightly.* 委员会两星期开一次会。

fort·ress /ˈfɔːtrəs; *NAmE* ˈfɔːrt-/ *noun* a building or place that has been made stronger and protected against attack 城堡；堡垒；要塞；设防的地方：*a fortress town enclosed by four miles of ramparts* 由四英里长的城墙围着的设防城镇 ◇ *Fear of terrorist attack has turned the conference centre into a fortress.* 由于害怕恐怖分子袭击，会议中心已变成了堡垒。

for·tuit·ous /fɔːˈtjuːɪtəs; *NAmE* fɔːrˈtuː-/ *adj.* (*formal*) happening by chance, especially a lucky chance that brings a good result 偶然发生的；（尤指）巧合的 ▸ **for·tuit·ous·ly** *adv.*

for·tu·nate /ˈfɔːtʃənət; *NAmE* ˈfɔːrtʃ-/ *adj.* having or bringing an advantage, an opportunity, a piece of good luck, etc. 幸运的；交好运的；吉利的 SYN **lucky**：**~ (to do sth)** *I have been fortunate enough to visit many parts of the world as a lecturer.* 我很有福气，去过世界许多地方作演讲。◇ **~ (in having…)** *I was fortunate in having a good teacher.* 我很幸运，有位好老师。◇ *Remember those less fortunate than yourselves.* 要记住那些不如你们幸运的人。◇ **~ (for sb) (that…)** ***It was very fortunate** for him that I arrived on time.* 算他运气好，我准时到了。OPP **unfortunate**

for·tu·nate·ly /ˈfɔːtʃənətli; *NAmE* ˈfɔːrtʃ-/ *adv.* by good luck 幸运地；交好运地；吉利地 SYN **luckily**：*I was late, but fortunately the meeting hadn't started.* 我迟到了，不过幸好会议还没有开始。◇ *Fortunately for him, he was very soon offered another job.* 他运气好，很快就有人聘请他做另一个工作。OPP **unfortunately**

for·tune 🔑 /ˈfɔːtʃuːn; *NAmE* ˈfɔːrtʃən/ *noun* **1** 🔑 [U] chance or luck, especially in the way it affects people's lives（尤指影响人生的）机会，运气：*I have **had the good fortune to** work with some brilliant directors.* 我有幸与一些卓越的主管人员共事。◇ ***By a stroke of fortune** he found work almost immediately.* 他运气好，几乎立刻找到了工作。◇ ***Fortune smiled on me*** (= I had good luck). 我交了好运。 ➲ WORDFINDER NOTE AT LUCK **2** 🔑 [C] a large amount of money 大笔的钱；巨款：*He **made a fortune** in real estate.* 他在房地产上发了财。◇ *She inherited a share of the family fortune.* 她继承了家庭的一份财产。◇ *A car like that costs **a small fortune**.* 像这样的轿车要花一大笔钱。◇ *You don't have to **spend a fortune** to give your family tasty, healthy meals.* 让家里人吃味道好又健康的餐食并不需要花许多钱。◇ *She is hoping her US debut will be the first step on the road to **fame and fortune**.* 她希望她在美国的首次演出将是她走上名利双收之路的第一步。◇ *That ring must be **worth a fortune**.* 那枚戒指肯定要值好多钱。**3** 🔑 [C, usually pl., U] the good and bad things that happen to a person, family, country, etc.（个人、家庭、国家等的）发展变化的趋势，命运，际遇：*the changing fortunes of the film industry* 电影业的变迁 ◇ *the fortunes of war* 战争的局势 ◇ *a reversal of fortune(s)* 命运的扭转 **4** [C] a person's FATE or future（个人的）命运，前途：*She can **tell your fortune** by looking at the lines on your hand.* 她可凭看手纹替你算命。 IDM SEE HOSTAGE, SEEK ➲ SEE ALSO SOLDIER OF FORTUNE

ˈfortune cookie *noun* a thin hollow biscuit/cookie, served in Chinese restaurants, containing a short message that predicts what will happen to you in the future 签饼（中国餐馆提供的薄脆饼，内有预测命运的小纸条）

ˈfortune hunter *noun* a person who tries to become rich by marrying sb with a lot of money（企图通过跟有钱人结婚）猎财的人，攀龙附凤的人

ˈfortune teller *noun* a person who claims to have magic powers and who tells people what will happen to them in the future 算命先生；给人算命的人

forty 🔑 /ˈfɔːti; *NAmE* ˈfɔːrti/ **1** 🔑 *number* 40 四十 **2** *noun* **the for·ties** [pl.] numbers, years or temperatures from 40 to 49 四十几；四十年代 ▸ **fortieth** 🔑 /ˈfɔːtiəθ; *NAmE* ˈfɔːrtiəθ/ *ordinal number, noun* HELP There are examples of how to use ordinal numbers at the entry for **fifth**. 序数词用法示例见 fifth 条。
IDM **in your forties** between the ages of 40 and 49 * 40 多岁

the ˌforty-ninth ˈparallel *noun* the line on a map that is 49° north of the EQUATOR, thought of as forming the border between western Canada and the US 北纬 49 度纬线（据认为形成加拿大西部和美国之间的边境线）

ˌforty ˈwinks *noun* [pl.] (*informal*) a short sleep, especially during the day（尤指白天）打盹儿，小睡，午睡：*I'll feel much better when I've had forty winks.* 我打个盹儿就会感到好得多。

forum /ˈfɔːrəm/ *noun* **1 ~ (for sth)** a place where people can exchange opinions and ideas on a particular issue; a meeting organized for this purpose 公共讨论场所；论坛；讨论会：*Television is now an important forum for political debate.* 电视现在成了政治辩论的重要平台。◇ *an Internet forum* 互联网论坛 ◇ *to hold an international forum on drug abuse* 举行药物滥用问题国际论坛 ➲ COLLOCATIONS AT EMAIL **2** (in ancient Rome) a public place where meetings were held （古罗马）公共集会场所

for·ward 🔑 /ˈfɔːwəd; *NAmE* ˈfɔːrwərd/ *adv., adj., verb, noun*
■ *adv.* **1** 🔑 (*also* **for·wards** *especially in BrE*) towards a place or position that is in front 向前：*She **leaned forward** and kissed him on the cheek.* 她倾身向前，吻了他的面颊。◇ *He took two steps forward.* 他向前走了两步。◇ *They ran forward to welcome her.* 他们跑向前去欢迎她。OPP **back, backwards 2** 🔑 towards a good result 进展；前进：*We consider this agreement to be an important **step forward**.* 我们认为，这项协定是向前迈出了重要的一步。 ◇ *Cutting our costs is the only **way forward**.* 降低成本是我们发展的

唯一途径。◇ *We are not getting any* ***further forward*** *with the discussion.* 我们的讨论没有取得任何进展。◇ *The project* ***will go forward*** (= continue) *as planned.* 这个项目将按计划继续进行。 OPP **backwards** **3** towards the future; ahead in time 向将来；往后： ***Looking forward,*** *we hope to expand our operations in several of our overseas branches.* 展望未来，我们希望拓展其中几家海外分公司的业务。◇ *The next scene takes the story forward five years.* 下一个场面是描述故事中五年后的情况。◇ (*old use*) *from this day forward* 从今天起 **4** earlier; sooner 提前： *It was decided to bring the meeting forward two weeks.* 已决定把会议提前两周。 **5** (*specialist*) in or towards the front part of a ship or plane 在（或向）船头；在（或向）机首： *The main cabin is situated forward of* (= in front of) *the mast.* 主舱在桅杆的前面。 ➲ SEE ALSO LOOK FORWARD TO STH at LOOK, PUT STH↔FORWARD at PUT

IDM **ˌgoing/ˌmoving ˈforward** (*formal* or *business* 商) in the future, starting from now 将来；以后；从现在起： *We have a very solid financial position going forward.* 今后我们会有非常稳健的财务状况。 ➲ MORE AT BACKWARDS, CLOCK *n.*, FOOT *n.*

▪ ***adj.*** **1** [only before noun] directed or moving towards the front 向前的；前进的： *The door opened, blocking his* ***forward movement.*** 门开了，挡住他前进的路。◇ *a* ***forward pass*** (= in a sports game) 向前传球 **2** [only before noun] (*specialist*) located in front, especially on a ship, plane or other vehicle（尤指船、飞机或其他交通工具）前部的，前面的： *the forward cabins* 前部舱室 ◇ *A bolt may have fallen off the plane's forward door.* 飞机前舱门的一个门闩可能脱落了。 **3** relating to the future 未来的；将来的： *the forward movement of history* 历史的向前发展 ◇ *A little* ***forward planning*** *at the outset can save you a lot of expense.* 一开始就为未来作点打算能节约很多开支。 ◇ *The plans are still* ***no further forward*** *than they were last month.* 计划无丝毫进展，仍是上个月的老样子。 **4** behaving towards sb in a manner which is too confident or too informal 鲁莽的；冒失的；无礼的： *I hope you don't think I'm being too forward.* 我希望你不要认为我太冒失。 ➲ COMPARE BACKWARD

▪ ***verb*** **1** (*formal*) to send or pass goods or information to sb 发送，寄（商品或信息）： **~ sth to sb** *We will be forwarding our new catalogue to you next week.* 我们将于下星期给你寄上新的商品目录。◇ **~ sb sth** *We will be forwarding you our new catalogue next week.* 我们将于下星期给你寄上新的商品目录。◇ **~ sth** *to forward a request/complaint/proposal* 提出要求 / 投诉 / 建议 **2** to send a letter, etc. received at the address a person used to live at to their new address （按新地址）转寄，转投，转交 SYN **send on**: **~ sth (to sb)** *Could you forward any mail to us in New York?* 你能不能把所有信件转寄到纽约给我们？◇ **~ (sth)** *I put 'please forward' on the envelope.* 我在信封上写了"请转递"。 ➲ WORDFINDER NOTE AT MESSAGE **3 ~ sth** (*formal*) to help to improve or develop sth 促进；有助于…的发展；增进 SYN **further**: *He saw the assignment as a way to forward his career.* 他把这项任务看作事业发展的途径。 ➲ SEE ALSO FAST-FORWARD

▪ ***noun*** an attacking player whose position is near the front of a team in some sports（运动队的）前锋 ➲ COMPARE BACK *n.* (8)

ˈforwarding address *noun* a new address to which letters should be sent on from an old address that sb has moved away from （信件应转递的）新地址

ˈforward-looking *adj.* (*approving*) planning for the future; willing to consider modern ideas and methods 向前看的；有远见的；有进步思想的

for·ward·ness /ˈfɔːwədnəs; *NAmE* ˈfɔːrwərd-/ *noun* [U] behaviour that is too confident or too informal 鲁莽；冒失；无礼；孟浪

ˈforward slash *noun* the symbol (/) used in computer commands and in Internet addresses to separate the different parts 正斜杠（用于计算机命令和互联网地址） ➲ COMPARE BACKSLASH

for·went PAST TENSE OF FORGO

fos·sick /ˈfɒsɪk; *NAmE* ˈfɑːs-/ *verb* (*AustralE, NZE, informal*) **1** [I] **~ (through sth)** to search through sth（在…中）搜寻，查找: *He spent ages fossicking through the documents.* 他花了老半天时间在那些文件中搜寻。 **2** [I] to search for gold in mines that are no longer used（在废矿中）淘金

fos·sil /ˈfɒsl; *NAmE* ˈfɑːsl/ *noun* **1** the remains of an animal or a plant which have become hard and turned into rock 化石： *fossils over two million years old* 两百多万年的化石 **2** (*informal, disapproving*) an old person, especially one who is unable to accept new ideas or adapt to changes 老人；（尤指）老顽固，老古董

ˈfossil fuel *noun* [C, U] fuel such as coal or oil, that was formed over millions of years from the remains of animals or plants 化石燃料（如煤或石油） ➲ COMPARE BIOMASS ➲ WORDFINDER NOTE AT ENERGY ➲ VISUAL VOCAB PAGE V6

fos·sil·ize (*BrE also* **-ise**) /ˈfɒsəlaɪz; *NAmE* ˈfɑːs-/ *verb* **1** [T, usually passive, I] **~ (sth)** to become or make sth become a fossil（使）变成化石，石化: *fossilized bones* 成为化石的骨骼 **2** [I, T] **~ (sb/sth)** (*disapproving*) to become, or make sb/sth become, fixed and unable to change or develop（使人或物）僵化 ▸ **fos·sil·iza·tion, -isa·tion** /ˌfɒsəlaɪˈzeɪʃn; *NAmE* ˌfɑːsələˈz-/ *noun* [U]

fos·ter /ˈfɒstə(r); *NAmE* ˈfɔːs-; ˈfɑːs-/ *verb, adj.*

▪ ***verb*** **1** [T] **~ sth** to encourage sth to develop 促进；助长；培养；鼓励 SYN **encourage, promote**: *The club's aim is to foster better relations within the community.* 俱乐部的宗旨是促进团体内部的关系。 **2** [T, I] **~ (sb)** (*especially BrE*) to take another person's child into your home for a period of time, without becoming his or her legal parents 代养，抚育，照料（他人子女一段时间）: *They have fostered over 60 children during the past ten years.* 在过去十年间，他们抚育了 60 多个儿童。◇ *We couldn't adopt a child, so we decided to foster.* 我们不能领养孩子，所以决定代养一个。 ➲ COLLOCATIONS AT CHILD ➲ COMPARE ADOPT (1)

▪ ***adj.*** [only before noun] used with some nouns in connection with the fostering of a child（与某些代养有关的名词连用）: *a* ***foster mother/father/family*** 代养母亲 / 父亲；代养的家庭 ◇ ***foster parents*** 代养父母 ◇ *a* ***foster child*** 代养的小孩 ◇ *a* ***foster home*** 寄养家庭 ◇ ***foster care*** 寄养照管

fought PAST TENSE, PAST PART. OF FIGHT

foul /faʊl/ *adj., verb, noun*

▪ ***adj.*** (**foul·er, foul·est**) **1** dirty and smelling bad 肮脏恶臭的；难闻的: ***foul air/breath*** 污浊难闻的空气 / 气息 ◇ *a* ***foul-smelling*** *prison* 臭烘烘的监狱 ➲ SYNONYMS AT DISGUSTING **2** (*especially BrE*) very unpleasant; very bad 很令人不快的；很坏的: *She's in a* ***foul mood.*** 她的情绪很糟。◇ *His boss has a* ***foul temper.*** 他的老板脾气很坏。◇ *This tastes foul.* 这个味道很差。 **3** (of language 语言) including rude words and swearing 充满脏话的；辱骂性的；下流的 SYN **offensive**: ***foul language*** 脏话 ◇ *I'm sick of her* ***foul mouth*** (= habit of swearing). 我讨厌她一开口就骂人的那张臭嘴。◇ *He called her the foulest names imaginable.* 他用最下流的话辱骂她。 **4** (of weather 天气) very bad, with strong winds and rain 恶劣的；风雨交加的: *a foul night* 风雨交加的夜晚 **5** (*literary*) very evil or cruel 邪恶的；残忍的 SYN **abominable**: *a* ***foul crime/murder*** 邪恶的罪行；恶毒的谋杀 ▸ **foul·ly** /ˈfaʊlli/ *adv.*: *He swore foully.* 他恶毒地诅咒。◇ *She had been foully murdered during the night.* 她在夜间被残忍地谋杀了。 **foul·ness** *noun* [U]: *The air was heavy with the stink of damp and foulness.* 空气中弥漫着一股潮湿的恶臭味。

IDM **fall foul of ˈsb/ˈsth** to get into trouble with a person or an organization because of doing sth wrong or illegal（因做错事或不法行为）与…发生麻烦，与…产生纠葛，冒犯: *to fall foul of the law* 触犯了法律 ➲ MORE AT CRY *v.*, FAIR *adj.*

▪ ***verb*** **1** [T] **~ sb** (in sport 体育运动) to do sth to another player that is against the rules of the game 对（对手）犯规: *He was fouled inside the penalty area.* 在禁区内对方队员对他犯规。 **2** [I, T] **~ (sth)** (in BASEBALL 棒球) to hit the ball outside the playing area 击（球）出界 **3** [T] **~ sth** to make sth dirty, especially with waste matter from the body（尤指用粪便）弄脏，污染：*Do not permit your dog to foul the grass.* 禁止狗在草地便溺。 **4** [T, I] to become caught or twisted in sth and stop it working or moving（被）缠住：**~ sth (up)** *The rope fouled the propeller.* 绳索缠住了螺旋桨。◇ **~ (up)** *A rope fouled up* (= became twisted) *as we pulled the sail down.* 我们收帆时有一根绳索缠住了。

PHR V **,foul 'up** (*informal*) to make a lot of mistakes; to do sth badly 大量出错；搞糟：*I've fouled up badly again, haven't I?* 我又搞砸了，是不是？ ➲ RELATED NOUN FOUL-UP

,foul sth↔'up (*informal*) to spoil sth, especially by doing sth wrong 把…搞糟；弄乱 ➲ RELATED NOUN FOUL-UP

■ ***noun*** (in sport 体育运动) an action that is against the rules of the game 犯规：*It was a clear foul by Ford on the goalkeeper.* 这明显是福特对守门员犯规。◇ (*NAmE*) *to hit a foul* (= in BASEBALL, a ball that is too far left or right, outside the lines that mark the side of the field)（棒球）击球出界 ➲ SEE ALSO PROFESSIONAL FOUL

'foul ball *noun* (in BASEBALL 棒球) a hit that goes outside the allowed area 界外球

'foul line *noun* **1** (in BASEBALL 棒球) either of two lines that show the area inside which the ball must be hit 边线 **2** (in BASKETBALL 篮球) a line from which a player is allowed to try to throw the ball into the BASKET after a foul 罚球线

,foul-'mouthed *adj.* using rude, offensive language 说下流话的；口出恶言的：*a foul-mouthed racist* 口出恶言的种族主义分子

,foul 'play *noun* [U] **1** criminal or violent activity that causes sb's death 谋杀罪行；暴力致死行为：*Police immediately began an investigation, but did not suspect foul play* (= did not suspect that the person had been murdered). 警方立即开始调查，但没有怀疑谋杀。 **2** (*BrE*) dishonest or unfair behaviour, especially during a sports game（尤指体育比赛中的）犯规动作，不公平行为

'foul-up *noun* (*informal*) a problem caused by bad organization or a stupid mistake（因组织不当或愚蠢错误而引起的）混乱，差错

found 🔑 AW /faʊnd/ *verb* **1** 🔑 **~ sth** to start sth, such as an organization or an institution, especially by providing money 创建，创办（组织或机构，尤指提供资金） SYN **establish**：*to found a club/company* 创办俱乐部 / 公司 ◇ *Her family founded the college in 1895.* 她的家族于 1895 年创办了这所学院。 **2** 🔑 **~ sth** to be the first to start building and living in a town or country 建立，兴建（城镇或国家）：*The town was founded by English settlers in 1790.* 这座城镇是英格兰移民于 1790 年建立的。 **3** [usually passive] **~ sth (on sth)** to base sth on sth 把…基于；把…建立在：*Their marriage was founded on love and mutual respect.* 他们的婚姻建立在爱情和互相尊重的基础上。 ➲ SEE ALSO ILL-FOUNDED, UNFOUNDED, WELL FOUNDED **4 ~ sth** (*specialist*) to melt metal and pour it into a MOULD; to make objects using this process 熔铸；铸造 ➲ SEE ALSO FIND *v.*

foun·da·tion 🔑 AW /faʊnˈdeɪʃn/ *noun* **1** 🔑 [C, usually pl.] a layer of bricks, concrete, etc. that forms the solid underground base of a building 地基；房基；基础：*The builders are now beginning **to lay the foundations** of the new school.* 建筑工人正开始给新校舍打地基。◇ *The explosion shook the foundations of the houses nearby.* 爆炸震撼了附近房屋的地基。 ➲ SYNONYMS AT BOTTOM ➲ WORDFINDER NOTE AT CONSTRUCTION **2** 🔑 [C, U] a principle, an idea or a fact that sth is based on and that it grows from 基本原理；根据；基础：*Respect and friendship provide a **solid foundation** for marriage.* 尊重和友爱是婚姻的牢固基础。◇ *The rumour is totally **without foundation*** (= not based on any facts). 这谣传毫无事实根据。◇ *These stories **have no foundation*** (= are not based on any facts). 这些故事纯属虚构。 ➲ SYNONYMS AT BASIS **3** 🔑 [C] an organization that is established to provide money for a particular purpose, for example for scientific research or charity 基金会：*The money will go to the San Francisco AIDS Foundation.* 这笔钱将交给旧金山艾滋病基金会。 **4** 🔑 [U] the act of starting a new institution or organization（机构或组织的）创建，创办 SYN **establishment**：*The organization has grown enormously since its foundation in 1955.* 该组织自 1955 年创建以来已有重大的发展。 **5** [U] a skin-coloured cream that is put on the face underneath other make-up（化妆打底用的）粉底霜 ➲ WORDFINDER NOTE AT MAKE-UP ➲ VISUAL VOCAB PAGE V65

IDM **shake/rock the 'foundations of sth | shake/rock sth to its 'foundations** to cause people to question their basic beliefs about sth 从根本上动摇：*This issue has shaken the foundations of French politics.* 这个问题从根本上动摇了法国的政治。

foun'dation course *noun* (*BrE*) a general course at a college that prepares students for longer or more difficult courses 预科课程

foun'dation stone *noun* a large block of stone that is put at the base of an important new public building in a special ceremony 基石，奠基石（重要公共建筑奠基典礼时放置）：*to lay the foundation stone of the new museum* 为新建博物馆奠基

foun·der /ˈfaʊndə(r)/ *noun, verb*

■ ***noun*** a person who starts an organization, institution, etc. or causes sth to be built（组织、机构等的）创建者，创办者，发起人：*the founder and president of the company* 公司的创办人和总裁

■ ***verb*** (*formal*) **1** [I] **~ (on sth)** (of a plan, etc. 计划等) to fail because of a particular problem or difficulty 失败；破产：*The peace talks foundered on a basic lack of trust.* 由于缺乏基本信任，和平谈判搁浅。 **2** [I] **~ (on sth)** (of a ship 船) to fill with water and sink 沉没：*Our boat foundered on a reef.* 我们的船触礁沉没。

,founder 'member (*BrE*) (*NAmE* **,charter 'member**) *noun* one of the first members of a society, an organization, etc., especially one who helped start it（社团、组织等的）创办人之一，发起人之一，创建人之一

,founding 'father *noun* **1** (*formal*) a person who starts or develops a new movement, institution or idea（运动、机构或思想的）创建人，发起人，元勋 **2 Founding Father** a member of the group of people who wrote the Constitution of the US in 1787（1787 年参加制定美国宪法的）制宪元勋

found·ling /ˈfaʊndlɪŋ/ *noun* (*old-fashioned*) a baby who has been left by its parents and who is found and taken care of by sb else 弃婴；弃儿

foun·dry /ˈfaʊndri/ *noun* (*pl.* **-ies**) a factory where metal or glass is melted and made into different shapes or objects 铸造厂；玻璃厂：*an iron foundry* 铸铁厂 ◇ *foundry workers* 铸造工人 ➲ SYNONYMS AT FACTORY

fount /faʊnt/ *noun* **~ (of sth)** (*literary* or *humorous*) the place where sth important comes from（重要事物的）来源，根源，源泉 SYN **source**：*She treats him as if he were **the fount of all knowledge**.* 她把他当成无所不晓。

foun·tain /ˈfaʊntən; *NAmE* ˈfaʊntn/ *noun* **1** a structure from which water is sent up into the air by a PUMP, used to decorate parks and gardens/yards 人工喷泉；喷水池 ➲ VISUAL VOCAB PAGE V3 ➲ SEE ALSO DRINKING FOUNTAIN **2** a strong flow of liquid or of another substance that is forced into the air 喷泉；（液体或其他物质的）喷射，涌流：*The amplifier exploded in a fountain of sparks.* 放大器爆炸，喷射出火星。 **3** a rich source or supply of sth 丰富来源；源泉：*Tourism is a fountain of wealth for the city.* 旅游业是该市的重要收入来源。

foun·tain·head /ˈfaʊntənhed; *NAmE* -tnhed/ *noun* (*literary*) a source or origin 泉源；根源；来源

'fountain pen *noun* a pen with a container that you fill with ink that flows to a NIB 自来水笔 ➲ VISUAL VOCAB PAGE V71

four 🔑 /fɔː(r)/ **1** 🔑 *number* 4 四 HELP There are examples of how to use numbers at the entry for **five**. 数词用法示例见 five 条。 **2** *noun* a group of four people or things 四个人（或事物）的一组：*to **make up a four** at tennis* 凑成四

个人打网球 ◇ *a coach and four* (= four horses) 四匹马拉的四轮大马车 **3** *noun* (in CRICKET 板球) a shot that scores four RUNS 得四分的一击 **4** *noun* a team of four people who ROW[1] a long narrow boat in races; the boat that they row[1] 四人赛艇队；四人赛艇

IDM **on all 'fours** (of a person 人) bent over with hands and knees on the ground 匍匐着；趴着：*We were crawling around on all fours.* 我们匍匐着四处爬行。**these four 'walls** used when you are talking about keeping sth secret（用于叮嘱保守秘密）到此为止：*Don't let this go further than these four walls* (= Don't tell anyone else who is not in the room now). 走出屋外这事就不要再谈了。

,four-by-'four (*also* **4x4**) *noun* a vehicle with FOUR-WHEEL DRIVE (= a system in which power is given to all four wheels) 四轮驱动汽车

,four-colour 'process *noun* (*specialist*) a way of reproducing natural colours in photographs and printing using COLOUR SEPARATION 四色分色制版法

,four-di'mensional *adj.* having four DIMENSIONS, usually length, width, depth, and time 四维的（包括长、宽、高和时间）；四度空间的

four·fold /'fɔːfəʊld; *NAmE* 'fɔːrfoʊld/ *adj.*, *adv.* ➲ -FOLD

,four-letter 'word *noun* a short word that is considered rude or offensive, especially because it refers to sex or other functions of the body（字母少的）粗俗下流词 SYN **swear word**

,four-poster 'bed (*also* **,four-'poster**) *noun* a large bed with a tall post at each of the four corners, a cover over the top and curtains around the sides 四帷柱大床 ➲ VISUAL VOCAB PAGE V24

four·some /'fɔːsəm; *NAmE* 'fɔːrsəm/ *noun* [C+sing./pl. v.] a group of four people taking part in a social activity or sport together 四人一组，四人参加的活动（指社交活动或体育活动）：*Can you make up a foursome for tennis tomorrow?* 你们明天能凑足四人打网球吗？

,four-'square *adj.* **1** (of a building 建筑物) square in shape, solid and strong 方形坚固的；方方正正的 **2** (of a person 人) firm, steady and determined 坚决果断的；坚定不移的 ▸ **four-'square** *adv.*：*I stand four-square with the President on this issue.* 在这个问题上我坚定不移地和总统站在一起。

'four-star *adj.* [usually before noun] **1** having four stars in a system that measures quality. The highest quality is shown by either four or five stars.（服务质量）四星级的：*a four-star hotel* 四星级宾馆 **2** (*NAmE*) having the second-highest military rank, and wearing a uniform that has four stars on it（军阶）四星的：*a four-star general* 四星上将

'four-stroke *adj.* (*specialist*) (of an engine or vehicle 发动机或机动车) with a PISTON that makes four up and down movements in each power CYCLE 四冲程的 ➲ COMPARE TWO-STROKE

four·teen /,fɔː'tiːn; *NAmE* ,fɔːr't-/ *number* 14 十四 ▸ **four·teenth** /,fɔː'tiːnθ; *NAmE* ,fɔːr't-/ *ordinal number*, *noun* HELP There are examples of how to use ordinal numbers at the entry for **fifth**. 序数词用法示例见 fifth 条。

the ,Fourteenth A'mendment *noun* [sing.] a change made to the US Constitution in 1866 that gave all Americans equal rights and allowed former SLAVES to become citizens 美国宪法第十四修正案（1866 年对美国宪法的修正，授予所有美国人平等权利并允许之前为奴隶的人成为公民）

fourth /fɔːθ; *NAmE* fɔːrθ/ *ordinal number*, *noun*

■ *ordinal number* 4th 第四 HELP There are examples of how to use ordinal numbers at the entry for **fifth**. 序数词用法示例见 fifth 条。

■ *noun* (*especially NAmE*) = QUARTER (1)

the ,fourth di'mension *noun* [sing.] **1** (used by scientists and writers of SCIENCE FICTION) time 第四维，第四度空间（科学家和科幻小说作家用语，即时间）**2** an experience that is outside normal human experience 非常人的体验

the ,fourth e'state *noun* [sing.] newspapers and journalists in general and the political influence that they have 第四等级（指新闻界及其政治影响）SYN **press**

fourth·ly /'fɔːθli; *NAmE* 'fɔːrθ-/ *adv.* used to introduce the fourth of a list of points you want to make in a speech or piece of writing（用于列举）第四

,fourth o'fficial *noun* (in football (SOCCER) 足球) an official who helps the REFEREE (1) before, during and after a match（在比赛前后及比赛期间协助裁判的）第四官员；第四球证

the ,Fourth of Ju'ly *noun* [sing.] a national holiday in the US when people celebrate the anniversary of the Declaration of Independence in 1776 独立日（7 月 4 日，美国节日，庆祝 1776 年美国宣告脱离英国独立）➲ SEE ALSO INDEPENDENCE DAY

,four-way 'stop *noun* (*SAfrE*) a place where two roads cross each other, at which there are signs indicating that all vehicles must stop before continuing 停车前行路口，四岔停车路口（有路标提示车辆先停再行驶）

,four-wheel 'drive (*especially NAmE* **,all-wheel 'drive**) *noun* [U, C] a system in which power is applied to all four wheels of a vehicle, making it easier to control; a vehicle with this system（车辆）四轮驱动；四轮驱动汽车：*a car with four-wheel drive* 四轮驱动轿车 ◇ *We rented a four-wheel drive to get around the island.* 我们租了一辆四轮驱动车作环岛旅游。➲ VISUAL VOCAB PAGE V56 ➲ SEE ALSO FOUR-BY-FOUR

,four-'wheeler (*NAmE*) (*BrE* **'quad bike**) *noun* a motorcycle with four large wheels, used for riding over rough ground, often for fun 四轮摩托车（常用于娱乐）➲ SEE ALSO ATV

fowl /faʊl/ *noun* **1** [C, U] (*pl.* **fowl** or **fowls**) a bird that is kept for its meat and eggs, for example a chicken 家禽：*fowl such as turkeys and ducks* 诸如火鸡和鸭之类的家禽 **2** [C] (*old use*) any bird 鸟 ➲ SEE ALSO GUINEA FOWL, WATERFOWL, WILDFOWL IDM SEE FISH *n.*

fox /fɒks; *NAmE* fɑːks/ *noun*, *verb*

■ *noun* **1** [C] a wild animal of the dog family, with reddish-brown fur, a pointed face and a thick heavy tail 狐；狐狸 ➲ SEE ALSO FLYING FOX, VIXEN (1) **2** [U] the skin and fur of the fox, used to make coats, etc. 狐皮 **3** [C] (*often disapproving*) a person who is clever and able to get what they want by influencing or tricking other people 狡猾的人；老狐狸；老滑头：*He's a wily old fox.* 他是个诡计多端的老狐狸。**4** [C] (*informal*) an attractive young woman 靓女

■ *verb* **~ sb** (*informal, especially BrE*) to be too difficult for sb to understand or solve; to trick or confuse sb 使猜不透；把…难住；使上当；使迷惑：*The last question foxed even our panel of experts.* 最后这个问题甚至把我们的专家小组都难倒了。

foxed /fɒkst; *NAmE* fɑːkst/ *adj.* **1** unable to understand or solve sth 困惑的；迷惑不解的：*I must admit I'm completely foxed.* 我得承认我一点都不懂。**2** (of the paper of old books or prints 旧书书页或图片) covered with brown spots 布满褐色斑点的

fox·glove /'fɒksglʌv; *NAmE* 'fɑːks-/ *noun* [C, U] a tall plant with purple or white flowers shaped like bells growing up its STEM 洋地黄，毛地黄（高棵植物，开紫色或白色钟状花朵）

fox·hole /'fɒkshəʊl; *NAmE* 'fɑːkshoʊl/ *noun* a hole in the ground that soldiers use as a shelter against the enemy or as a place to fire back from 散兵坑 ➲ COMPARE HOLE *n.*

fox·hound /'fɒkshaʊnd; *NAmE* 'fɑːks-/ *noun* a dog with a very good sense of smell, that is trained to hunt FOXES 狐猩；猎狐狗

ˈfox hunting (*BrE also* **hunt·ing**) *noun* [U] a sport in which FOXES are hunted by specially trained dogs and by people on horses. Fox hunting with dogs is now illegal in the UK. 猎狐（一种体育运动，如今在英国用狗猎狐是违法的）：*to go fox hunting* 去猎狐 ▶ **ˈfox hunt** *noun*：*a ban on fox hunts* 禁止猎狐令

ˌfox ˈterrier *noun* a small dog with short hair 猎狐㹴狗

fox·trot /ˈfɒkstrɒt; *NAmE* ˈfɑːkstrɑːt/ *noun* a formal dance for two people together, with both small fast steps and longer slow ones; a piece of music for this dance 狐步舞；狐步舞曲

foxy /ˈfɒksi; *NAmE* ˈfɑːksi/ *adj.* **1** like a FOX in appearance 貌似狐狸的 **2** (*informal, especially NAmE*) (of a woman 女子) sexually attractive 性感的；狐媚的 SYN **sexy** **3** clever at tricking others 狡猾的；奸诈的 SYN **cunning**

foyer /ˈfɔɪeɪ; *NAmE* ˈfɔɪər/ *noun* **1** a large open space inside the entrance of a theatre or hotel where people can meet or wait （剧院或旅馆的）门厅，休息厅 SYN **lobby** ➲ WORDFINDER NOTE AT THEATRE **2** (*NAmE*) an entrance hall in a private house or flat/apartment（私宅或公寓的）前厅，门厅

Fr (*also* **Fr.** *especially in NAmE*) *abbr.* Father (used in front of the name of some Christian priests) 神父（用于姓名前）：*Fr (Paul) O'Connor*（保罗•）奥康纳神父

fra·cas /ˈfrækɑː; *NAmE* ˈfreɪkəs/ *noun* (*pl.* **fra·cas** /-kɑːz/, *NAmE* **fra·cases**) [usually sing.] a noisy argument or fight, usually involving several people （通常有好几个人的）高声争吵，打斗

frack·ing /ˈfrækɪŋ/ (*also formal* or *specialist* **hyˌdraulic ˈfracturing**) *noun* [U] the process of forcing liquid at high pressure into rocks, deep holes in the ground, etc. in order to force open existing cracks and take out oil or gas 水力压裂（开采石油或天然气的方法）➲ WORDFINDER NOTE AT ENERGY

frac·tal /ˈfræktl/ *noun* (*mathematics* 数, *physics* 物) a curve or pattern that includes a smaller curve or pattern which has exactly the same shape 分形

frac·tion /ˈfrækʃn/ *noun* **1** a small part or amount of sth 小部分；少量；一点儿：*Only a small fraction of a bank's total deposits will be withdrawn at any one time.* 任何时候，一家银行的总存款只有少量会被提取。◇ *She hesitated for the merest fraction of a second.* 她略微犹豫了一下。HELP If **fraction** is used with a plural noun, the verb is usually plural. 如 fraction 与复数名词连用，则动词用复数：*Only a fraction of cars in the UK* ***use*** *leaded petrol.* 在英国只有一小部分轿车使用含铅汽油。If it is used with a singular noun that represents a group of people, the verb can be singular or plural in *BrE*, but is usually singular in *NAmE*. 如与表示一群人的单数名词连用，在英式英语中动词用单复数均可，但在美式英语中动词通常用单数：*A tiny fraction of the population never* ***vote/votes.*** 极小部分人从不投票。**2** a division of a number, for example ⅝ 分数；小数 SYN **rational number** ➲ LANGUAGE BANK AT PROPORTION ➲ COMPARE INTEGER ➲ SEE ALSO VULGAR FRACTION

frac·tion·al /ˈfrækʃənl/ *adj.* **1** (*formal*) very small; not important 很小的；很少的；微不足道的 SYN **minimal**：*a fractional decline in earnings* 利润微降 **2** (*mathematics* 数) of or in fractions 分数的；小数的：*a fractional equation* 分式方程

ˌfractional distilˈlation *noun* [U] (*chemistry* 化) the process of separating the parts of a liquid mixture by heating it. As the temperature goes up, each part in turn becomes a gas, which then cools as it moves up a tube and can be collected as a liquid. 分馏

frac·tion·al·ly /ˈfrækʃənəli/ *adv.* to a very small degree 很小；很少：*He was just fractionally ahead at the finishing line.* 在终点线他只是稍微领先。

frac·tious /ˈfrækʃəs/ *adj.* (*especially BrE*) **1** bad-tempered or easily upset, especially by small things 暴躁的；易怒的；动辄烦躁的 SYN **irritable**：*Children often get fractious and tearful when tired.* 孩子们疲倦时易烦躁好哭。**2** (*formal*) making trouble and complaining 捣乱的；惹是生非的：*The six fractious republics are demanding autonomy.* 这六个不安分的加盟共和国要求自治。

frac·ture /ˈfræktʃə(r)/ *noun, verb*

■ ***noun*** **1** [C] a break in a bone or other hard material（指状态）骨折，断裂，折断，破裂：*a fracture of the leg/skull* 腿骨／颅骨骨折 ◇ *a* ***compound/simple fracture*** (= one in which the broken bone comes/does not come through the skin) 复合（开放）骨折；单纯（闭合）骨折 ➲ WORDFINDER NOTE AT HURT ➲ COLLOCATIONS AT INJURY **2** [U] the fact of sth breaking, especially a bone（指事实）骨折，断裂，折断，破裂：*Old people's bones are more prone to fracture.* 老人更易骨折。

■ ***verb*** **1** [I, T] to break or crack; to make sth break or crack （使）断裂，折断，破裂：*His leg fractured in two places.* 他的一条腿有两处骨折。◇ **~ sth** *She fell and fractured her skull.* 她跌倒摔裂了颅骨。◇ *a fractured pipeline* 破裂的管道 **2** [I, T] (*formal*) (of a society, an organization, etc. 团体、组织等) to split into several parts so that it no longer functions or exists; to split a society or an organization, etc. in this way（使）分裂：*Many people predicted that the party would fracture and split.* 很多人预言该党将分崩离析。◇ **~ sth** (**into sth**) *The company was fractured into several smaller groups.* 这家公司被拆分成几家小公司。▶ **frac·tured** *adj.* [usually before noun]：*He suffered a badly fractured arm.* 他的手臂严重骨折。◇ (*figurative*) *They spoke a sort of fractured German.* 他们讲德语结结巴巴。

frae·num·lum (*BrE*) = FRENULUM

fra·gile /ˈfrædʒaɪl; *NAmE* -dʒl/ *adj.* **1** easily broken or damaged 易碎的；易损的：*fragile china/glass/bones* 易碎的瓷器／玻璃制品／骨骼 **2** weak and uncertain; easily destroyed or spoilt 不牢固的；脆弱的：*a* ***fragile alliance/ceasefire/relationship*** 不牢固的联盟；不确定的停火／关系 ◇ *The economy remains extremely fragile.* 经济仍然极其脆弱。**3** delicate and often beautiful 纤巧的；精细的；纤巧美丽的：*fragile beauty* 纤美 ◇ *The woman's fragile face broke into a smile.* 那面孔秀丽的女子粲然一笑。**4** not strong and likely to become ill/sick 虚弱的：*Her father is now 86 and in fragile health.* 她的父亲现在 86 岁，身体虚弱。◇ (*BrE, informal*) *I'm feeling a bit fragile after last night* (= not well, perhaps because of drinking too much alcohol). 昨夜以后我觉得身子有点发虚（可能是纵酒所致）。▶ **fra·gil·ity** /frəˈdʒɪləti/ *noun* [U]：*the fragility of the human body* 人体的脆弱

frag·ment *noun, verb*

■ ***noun*** /ˈfrægmənt/ a small part of sth that has broken off or comes from sth larger 碎片；片段：*Police found fragments of glass near the scene.* 警方在现场附近发现了玻璃碎片。◇ *The shattered vase lay in fragments on the floor.* 打碎的花瓶在地上成了一堆碎片。◇ *I overheard a fragment of their conversation.* 我无意中听到他们谈话的片段。

■ ***verb*** /frægˈment/ [I, T] **~** (**sth**) to break or make sth break into small pieces or parts（使）碎裂，破裂，分裂 ▶ **frag·men·ta·tion** /ˌfrægmenˈteɪʃn/ *noun* [U]：*the fragmentation of the country into small independent states* 该国分裂成一些独立的小国家 **frag·ment·ed** *adj.*：*a fragmented society* 一个四分五裂的社会

frag·men·tary /ˈfrægməntri; *NAmE* -teri/ *adj.* (*formal*) made of small parts that are not connected or complete 残缺不全的；不完整的：*There is only fragmentary evidence to support this theory.* 只有零零星星的证据证实这个理论。

ˌfragmenˈtation grenade (*also* **ˌfragmenˈtation bomb**) *noun* a bomb that breaks into very small pieces when it explodes 杀伤榴弹（爆炸时迸射出大量碎片）

fra·grance /ˈfreɪgrəns/ *noun* **1** [C, U] a pleasant smell 香气；香味；芳香：*The bath oil comes in various fragrances.* 这种沐浴油有不同的香味。**2** [C] a liquid that you put on your skin in order to make yourself smell nice 香水 SYN **perfume**：*an exciting new fragrance from Dior* 迪奥新推出的一款令人惊喜的香水

F

fra·grant /ˈfreɪɡrənt/ *adj.* having a pleasant smell 香的；芳香的：*fragrant herbs/flowers/oils* 芳草；香花；精油 ◇ *The air was fragrant with scents from the sea and the hills.* 空气中荡漾着山和海的芬芳气息。▶ **fra·grant·ly** *adv.*

fraidy cat /ˈfreɪdi kæt/ *noun* (*US, informal, disapproving*) = SCAREDY-CAT

frail /freɪl/ *adj.* (**frail·er, frail·est**) **1** (especially of an old person 尤指老人) physically weak and thin 瘦弱的：*Mother was becoming too frail to live alone.* 母亲已逐渐衰弱到无法独居。➲ WORDFINDER NOTE AT OLD **2** weak; easily damaged or broken 弱的；易损的；易碎的：*the frail stems of the flowers* 柔弱的花茎 ◇ *Human nature is frail.* 人性脆弱。

frailty /ˈfreɪlti/ *noun* (*pl.* **-ies**) **1** [U] weakness and poor health 虚弱；衰弱：*Increasing frailty meant that she was more and more confined to bed.* 日益衰弱意味着她愈来愈需要卧床。**2** [U, C] (*formal*) weakness in a person's character or moral standards（性格或道德上的）弱点，懦弱，软弱：*human frailty* 人性的弱点 ◇ *the frailties of human nature* 人性的种种弱点

frames 框架；构架

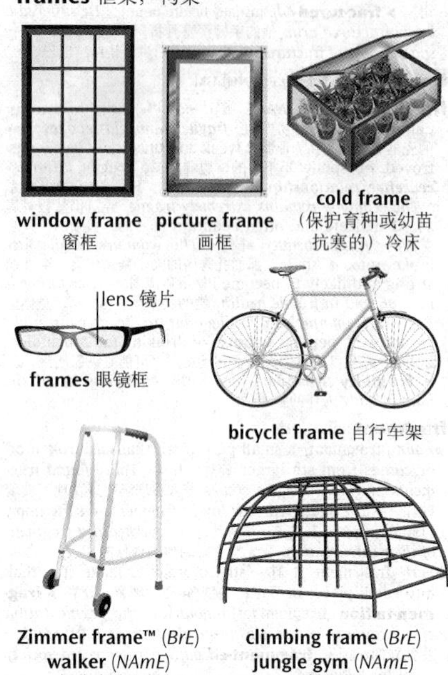

window frame 窗框 | picture frame 画框 | cold frame （保护育种或幼苗抗寒的）冷床 | frames 眼镜框 | bicycle frame 自行车架 | Zimmer frame™ (*BrE*) walker (*NAmE*) 齐默式助行架 | climbing frame (*BrE*) jungle gym (*NAmE*) 攀爬架

frame 🔑 /freɪm/ *noun, verb*

■ *noun*

• **BORDER** 边框 **1** 🔑 [C] a strong border or structure of wood, metal, etc. that holds a picture, door, piece of glass, etc. in position（图画、门、玻璃等的）框架：*a picture frame* 画框 ◇ *aluminium window frames* 铝窗框 ➲ PICTURE AT EDGE

• **STRUCTURE** 结构 **2** 🔑 [C] the supporting structure of a piece of furniture, a building, a vehicle, etc. that gives it its shape（家具、建筑物、车辆等的）构架，支架，骨架：*the frame of an aircraft/a car/a bicycle* 飞机 / 汽车 / 自行车构架 ➲ WORDFINDER NOTE AT PAINTING ➲ VISUAL VOCAB PAGE V55 ➲ SEE ALSO CLIMBING FRAME

• **OF GLASSES** 眼镜 **3** [C, usually pl.] a structure of plastic or metal that holds the LENSES in a pair of glasses 眼镜框：*gold-rimmed frames* 金边眼镜框

• **PERSON/ANIMAL'S BODY** 人 / 动物的身体 **4** [C, usually sing.] the form or structure of a person or animal's body 体形；身材；骨架：*to have a **small/slender/large frame*** 小的 / 苗条的 / 大的体形

• **GENERAL IDEAS** 总的思想 **5** [sing.] the general ideas or structure that form the background to sth（构成某事物背景的）总的思想，体系，体制，模式：*In this course we hope to look at literature in the frame of its social and historical context.* 在本课程中，我们希望从社会和历史背景的整体结构来看文学。➲ SEE ALSO TIME FRAME

• **OF FILM/MOVIE** 电影 **6** [C] one of the single photographs that a film or video is made of 帧头；画格；画面

• **OF PICTURE STORY** 连环画 **7** [C] a single picture in a COMIC STRIP（连环漫画中的）一幅画

• **COMPUTING** 计算机技术 **8** [C] one of the separate areas on an Internet page that you can SCROLL through (= read by using the mouse to move the text up or down) 帧；页帧（框）；图文框

• **IN GARDEN** 花园 **9** [C] = COLD FRAME

• **IN SNOOKER/BOWLING** 斯诺克；保龄球 **10** [C] a single section of play in the game of SNOOKER, etc., or in BOWLING 一轮；一回；一局

IDM **be in/out of the ˈframe (for sth)** (*BrE*) **1** be taking part/not taking part in sth 参加；不参加：*We won our match, so we're still in the frame for the championship.* 我们赢了比赛，所以仍可参加锦标赛。**2** to be wanted/not wanted by the police 被警方通缉；没有被警方通缉：*He was always in the frame for the killing.* 他因杀人一直被警方通缉。

■ *verb*

• **MAKE BORDER** 做边框 **1** 🔑 [usually passive] **~ sth** to put or make a frame or border around sth 给…做框；给…镶边：*The photograph had been framed.* 照片已镶了框。◇ *Her blonde hair framed her face.* 她的金发衬着面庞。◇ *He stood there, head back, framed against the blue sky.* 他站在那里，头向后仰，衬托在蓝天下。

• **PRODUCE FALSE EVIDENCE** 作伪证 **2** [usually passive] **~ sb (for sth)** to produce false evidence against an innocent person so that people think he or she is guilty 作伪证陷害 SYN **fit up**: *He says he was framed.* 他说他是被诬陷的。

• **DEVELOP PLAN/SYSTEM** 拟订计划 / 体系 **3 ~ sth** (*formal*) to create and develop sth such as a plan, a system or a set of rules 制订；拟订

• **EXPRESS STH** 表达 **4 ~ sth** to express sth in a particular way（以某种方式）表达：*You'll have to be careful how you frame the question.* 如何提出这个问题，你得慎重。
▶ **framed** *adj.* (often in compounds 常构成复合词)：*a framed photograph* 装在相框里的相片 ◇ *a timber-framed house* (= with a supporting structure of wood) 木结构房屋

ˌframe of ˈmind *noun* [sing.] the way you feel or think about sth at a particular time 心态；心绪：*We'll discuss this when you're in a better frame of mind.* 你心情好些时我们再讨论这件事。

ˌframe of ˈreference *noun* (*pl.* **frames of reference**) a particular set of beliefs, ideas or experiences that affects how a person understands or judges sth（影响人理解和判断事物的）信仰，准则

ˈframe tent (*BrE*) (*NAmE* **ˈwall tent**) *noun* a large tent with a roof and walls that do not slope much 框架式大帐篷（篷顶和篷壁形成的坡度很小）➲ COMPARE DOME TENT, RIDGE TENT

ˈframe-up *noun* (*informal*) a situation in which false evidence is produced in order to make people think that an innocent person is guilty of a crime 诬陷；陷害

frame·work AW /ˈfreɪmwɜːk; *NAmE* -wɜːrk/ *noun* **1** the parts of a building or an object that support its weight and give it shape（建筑物或物体的）构架，框架，结构 ➲ SYNONYMS AT STRUCTURE **2 ~ (of/for sth)** a set of beliefs, ideas or rules that is used as the basis for making judgements, decisions, etc.（作为判断、决定等基础的）信念，观点，准则：*The report provides a framework for further research.* 报告提供了进一步研究的原则。➲ COLLOCATIONS

AT SCIENTIFIC **3** the structure of a particular system（体系的）结构，机制：*We need to establish a legal framework for the protection of the environment.* 我们需要建立一个法律体制来保护环境。◇ *the basic framework of society* 社会的基本结构

franc /fræŋk/ *noun* the unit of money in Switzerland and several other countries (replaced in 2002 in France, Belgium and Luxembourg by the euro) 法郎（瑞士等国的货币单位，在法国、比利时和卢森堡于 2002 年为欧元所取代）

fran·chise /ˈfræntʃaɪz/ *noun, verb*

■ ***noun*** **1** [C, U] formal permission given by a company to sb who wants to sell its goods or services in a particular area; formal permission given by a government to sb who wants to operate a public service as a business（公司授予的）特许经销权；（国家授予的）特别经营权，特许：*a* ***franchise agreement/company*** 特许经销权协议；特约代销公司 ◇ *a catering/rail franchise* 餐饮 / 铁路经营权 ◇ *In the reorganization, Southern Television lost their franchise.* 在改组过程中南方电视公司失去了特许经营权。◇ *to operate a business* ***under franchise*** 根据特许经营权经营 ➲ COLLOCATIONS AT BUSINESS **2** [C] a business or service run under franchise 获特许权的商业（或服务）机构：*They operate franchises in London and Paris.* 他们在伦敦和巴黎经营专卖店。◇ *a burger franchise* 汉堡包特许经销店 ➲ WORDFINDER NOTE AT COMPANY **3** [U] (*formal*) the right to vote in a country's elections（公民）选举权：*universal adult franchise* 成年人普选权 ➲ SEE ALSO ENFRANCHISE

■ ***verb*** [usually passive] **~ sth (out) (to sb/sth)** to give or sell a franchise *n.* (1) to sb 授予（或出售）特许经销权（或经营权）：*Catering has been franchised (out) to a private company.* 餐饮特许经营权已授予一家私人公司。◇ *franchised restaurants* 获经营权的餐厅 ▶ **fran·chis·ing** *noun* [U]

fran·chisee /ˌfræntʃaɪˈziː/ *noun* a person or company that has been given a franchise 获特许权的人（或公司）；特许经营人（或公司）

fran·chiser (*also* **fran·chisor**) /ˈfræntʃaɪzə(r)/ *noun* a company or an organization that gives sb a franchise 授予（他人）特许权的公司（或组织）

Fran·cis·can /frænˈsɪskən/ *noun, adj.*

■ ***noun*** a member of a religious organization started in 1209 by St Francis of Assisi in Italy 方济各会修士（方济各会于 1209 年由圣方济各创办）

■ ***adj.*** relating to St Francis or to this organization 圣方济各的；方济各会的：*a Franciscan monk* 方济各会修士

fran·cium /ˈfrænsiəm/ *noun* [U] (*symb.* **Fr**) a chemical element. Francium is a RADIOACTIVE metal. 钫（放射性化学元素）

Franco- /ˈfræŋkəʊ; *NAmE* ˈfræŋkoʊ/ *combining form* (in nouns and adjectives 构成名词和形容词) French; France 法国的；法国人的；法国：*the Franco-Prussian War* 普法战争 ◇ *Francophile* 亲法的人

franco·phone /ˈfræŋkəfəʊn; *NAmE* -foʊn/ *adj.* [only before noun] speaking French as the main language 说法语的 ▶ **franco·phone** *noun*：*Canadian francophones* 说法语的加拿大人

fran·gi·pani /ˌfrændʒiˈpæni; -ˈpɑːni/ *noun* **1** [U, C] a tropical American tree or bush with groups of white, pink, or yellow flowers 鸡蛋花树（或灌木）（产于美洲热带）**2** [U] a PERFUME that is made from the frangipani plant 鸡蛋花香水

frank /fræŋk/ *adj., verb*

■ ***adj.*** (**frank·er**, **frank·est**) HELP **More frank** is also common. * more frank 也常用。honest and direct in what you say, sometimes in a way that other people might not like 坦率的；直率的：*a full and frank discussion* 坦诚而充分的讨论 ◇ *a frank admission of guilt* 坦率承认心里有愧 ◇ *He was very frank about his relationship with the actress.* 他对自己和那位女演员的关系直言不讳。◇ ***To be frank with you****, I think your son has little chance of passing the exam.* 坦诚相告，我认为你的儿子不大可能通过考试。➲ SYNONYMS AT HONEST ▶ **frank·ness** *noun* [U]：*They outlined their aims with disarming frankness.* 他们友好坦诚地简述了他们的宗旨。

■ ***verb*** [often passive] **~ sth** to stamp a mark on an envelope, etc. to show that the cost of posting it has been paid or does not need to be paid（在信件上）盖邮资已付印记，盖免付邮资印记

Fran·ken·stein /ˈfræŋkənstaɪn/ *noun* (*also* ˌ**Frankenstein's ˈmonster**, ˌ**Frankenstein ˈmonster**) used to talk about sth that sb creates or invents that goes out of control and becomes dangerous, often destroying the person who created it 失控的受造物（常毁灭创造者）➲ MORE LIKE THIS 17, page R27 ORIGIN From the novel *Frankenstein* by Mary Shelley in which a scientist called Frankenstein makes a creature from pieces of dead bodies and brings it to life. 源自玛丽・雪莱的小说《科学怪人》，其中的科学家弗兰肯斯坦用尸体的不同部位拼成了一个怪物并赋予它生命。

frank·furt·er /ˈfræŋkfɜːtə(r); *NAmE* -fɜːrt-/ (*NAmE also* **wiener**, *informal* **wee·nie**) *noun* a long thin smoked SAUSAGE with a reddish-brown skin, often eaten in a long bread roll as a HOT DOG 法兰克福熏肠（常用于做热狗）

frank·in·cense /ˈfræŋkɪnsens/ *noun* [U] a substance that is burnt to give a pleasant smell, especially during religious ceremonies 乳香（点燃时散发出香味，尤用于宗教礼仪）

ˈ**franking machine** (*especially BrE*) (*NAmE usually* ˈ**postage meter**) *noun* a machine that prints an official mark on a letter to show that the cost of posting it has been paid, or does not need to be paid 邮资机（加盖邮资已付印记）

frank·ly /ˈfræŋkli/ *adv.* **1** in an honest and direct way that people might not like 坦率地；直率地：*He spoke frankly about the ordeal.* 他直率地讲出了苦难的经历。◇ *They frankly admitted their responsibility.* 他们坦率地承认了责任。**2** used to show that you are being honest about sth, even though people might not like what you are saying（表示直言）老实说：*Frankly, I couldn't care less what happens to him.* 说实话，我才不管他出什么事呢。◇ ***Quite frankly****, I'm not surprised you failed.* 老实说，我对你的失败不感到意外。

fran·tic /ˈfræntɪk/ *adj.* **1** done quickly and with a lot of activity, but in a way that is not very well organized 紧张忙乱的；手忙脚乱的 SYN **hectic**：*a* ***frantic dash/search/struggle*** 不顾一切的猛冲；疯狂的搜查 / 斗争 ◇ *They made* ***frantic attempts*** *to revive him.* 他们拼命地努力让他苏醒过来。◇ *Things are frantic in the office right now.* 现在办公室里忙作一团。**2** unable to control your emotions because you are extremely frightened or worried about sth（由于恐惧或担心）无法控制感情的，发狂似的 SYN **beside yourself**：*frantic with worry* 忧虑得要命 ◇ *Let's go back. Your parents must be* ***getting frantic*** *by now.* 咱们回家吧。你的父母现在肯定快要急死了。◇ *The children are driving me frantic* (= making me very annoyed). 孩子们快要使我发疯了。▶ **fran·tic·al·ly** /-kli/ *adv.*：*They worked frantically to finish on time.* 他们拼命工作以按时完成。

frappé /ˈfræpeɪ; *NAmE* fræˈpeɪ/ *adj., noun* (*from French*)

■ ***adj.*** [after noun] (of drinks 饮料) served cold with a lot of ice 加冰（的）；冰镇：*coffee frappé* 加冰咖啡

■ ***noun*** a drink or sweet food served cold with very small pieces of ice 冰镇饮料（或甜食）；碎冰饮料

frat /fræt/ *noun* (*NAmE, informal*) = FRATERNITY (2)：*a frat boy* (= a member of a fraternity)（美国）男大学生联谊会会员

fra·ter·nal /frəˈtɜːnl; *NAmE* -ˈtɜːrnl/ *adj.* [usually before noun] **1** connected with the relationship that exists between people or groups that share the same ideas or interests（指志趣相投者）兄弟般的，亲如手足的：*a fraternal organization/society* 兄弟会组织；共济会 **2** connected with the relationship that exists between brothers 兄弟间的：*fraternal rivalry* 兄弟间的较劲 ▶ **fra·ter·nal·ly** *adv.*

fraˌternal ˈtwin (*also* ˌ**non-iˌdentical ˈtwin**, *specialist* ˌ**dizyˌgotic ˈtwin**) *noun* either of two children or animals born from the same mother at the same time but not from the same egg 二卵双生；异卵双生 ➲ COMPARE IDENTICAL TWIN, MONOZYGOTIC TWIN

fra·ter·nity /frəˈtɜːnəti; NAmE -ˈtɜːrn-/ *noun* (*pl.* **-ies**) **1** [C+sing./pl. v.] a group of people sharing the same profession, interests or beliefs（有相同职业、爱好或信仰的）群体，同人；同好：*members of the medical/banking/racing, etc. fraternity* 医务界、银行界、赛马圈等同仁 **2** (*also NAmE, informal* **frat**) [C] a club for a group of male students at an American college or university（美国男大学生的）联谊会，兄弟会 ➲ COMPARE SORORITY **3** [U] (*formal*) a feeling of friendship and support that exists between the members of a group（团体内的）情谊，兄弟般的友谊，博爱：*the ideals of liberty, equality and fraternity* 自由、平等和博爱的理想

frat·er·nize (*BrE also* **-ise**) /ˈfrætənaɪz; NAmE -tərn-/ *verb* [I] ~ (**with sb**) (*disapproving*) to behave in a friendly manner, especially towards sb that you are not supposed to be friendly with（尤指与不该亲善者）亲善：*She was accused of fraternizing with the enemy.* 她被指责亲敌。 ▸ **frat·er·niza·tion, -isa·tion** /ˌfrætənaɪˈzeɪʃn; NAmE -tərnəˈz-/ *noun* [U]

frat·ri·cide /ˈfrætrɪsaɪd/ *noun* [U, C] (*formal*) **1** the crime of killing your brother or sister; a person who is guilty of this crime 杀害兄弟（或姐妹）罪；杀害兄弟（或姐妹）者 ➲ COMPARE MATRICIDE, PARRICIDE, PATRICIDE **2** the crime of killing people of your own country or group; a person who is guilty of this crime 杀害同胞罪；杀害同胞者 **3** (*especially NAmE*) the accidental killing of your own forces in war（战争中）误致己方伤亡 SYN **friendly fire** ▸ **frat·ri·cidal** /ˌfrætrɪˈsaɪdl/ *adj.*：*to be engaged in a fratricidal struggle* 进行自相残杀的斗争

fraud /frɔːd/ *noun* **1** [U, C] the crime of cheating sb in order to get money or goods illegally 欺诈罪；欺骗罪：*She was charged with credit card fraud.* 她被控告信用卡诈骗罪。◇ *property that has been obtained by fraud* 欺诈所得的财产 ◇ *a $100 million fraud* * 1 亿美元数额的诈骗罪 ➲ COLLOCATIONS AT CRIME **2** [C] a person who pretends to have qualities, abilities, etc. that they do not really have in order to cheat other people 骗子；行骗的人：*He's nothing but a liar and a fraud.* 他只不过是个撒谎者和骗子。◇ *She felt a fraud accepting their sympathy* (= because she was not really sad). 她接受他们的同情时感到自己是在骗人。 **3** [C] something that is not as good, useful, etc. as people claim it is 伪劣品；冒牌货

ˈ**fraud squad** *noun* [sing.+sing./pl. v.] (*BrE*) part of a police force that investigates fraud（警方的）诈骗案调查小组

fraud·ster /ˈfrɔːdstə(r)/ *noun* (*BrE*) a person who commits fraud 犯欺诈罪者；犯欺骗罪者

fraudu·lent /ˈfrɔːdjələnt; NAmE -dʒə-/ *adj.* (*formal*) intended to cheat sb, usually in order to make money illegally 欺骗的；欺诈的：*fraudulent advertising* 虚假不实的广告 ◇ *fraudulent insurance claims* 诈骗性的保险索赔 ▸ **fraudu·lence** /ˈfrɔːdjələns; NAmE -dʒə-/ *noun* [U] **fraudu·lent·ly** /ˈfrɔːdjələntli; NAmE -dʒə-/ *adv.*

fraught /frɔːt/ *adj.* **1** ~ **with sth** filled with sth unpleasant 充满（不愉快事物）的：*a situation* ***fraught with*** *danger/difficulty/problems* 充满危险 / 困难重重 / 问题成堆的局面 **2** (*especially BrE*) causing or feeling worry and anxiety 焦虑的；忧虑的；担心的 SYN **tense**：*She looked/sounded fraught.* 她愁容满面；她的话音显出忧虑。◇ *There was a fraught silence.* 有一阵令人焦虑的沉默。◇ *Things are as fraught as ever in the office.* 办公室的情况和往常一样令人担心。

fray /freɪ/ *verb, noun*

■ ***verb*** **1** [I, T] if cloth **frays** or sth **frays** it, the threads in it start to come apart（使织物边沿）磨损，磨散：*The cuffs of his shirt were fraying.* 他衬衣的袖口磨破了。◇ *This material frays easily.* 这布料容易磨损。◇ ~ **sth** *It was fashionable to fray the bottoms of your jeans.* 曾经时兴把牛仔裤磨毛。 **2** [I, T] ~ (**sth**) if sb's nerves or TEMPER **frays** or sth **frays** them, the person starts to get irritated or annoyed（使）烦躁，恼火：*As the debate went on, tempers began to fray.* 随着辩论的继续，火气就上来了。 ▸ **frayed** *adj.*：*frayed denim shorts* 磨损的牛仔短裤 ◇ *Tempers were getting very frayed.* 脾气变得暴躁起来。

IDM ˌ**fray at/around the ˈedges/ˈseams** to start to come apart or to fail 开始卷边；脱线脚；分崩离析；失败：*Support for the leader was fraying at the edges.* 对这位领导人的拥护已开始瓦解。

■ ***noun*** **the fray** [sing.] a fight, a competition or an argument, especially one that is exciting or seen as a test of your ability 打斗，竞争，争辩（尤指激烈或视为检验能力的）：*They were ready for the fray.* 他们准备好了争斗。◇ *to* ***enter/join the fray*** 加入争辩 ◇ *At 71, he has now retired from the political fray.* 他现年 71 岁，已经退出了政治角逐。

fraz·zle /ˈfræzl/ *noun*

IDM **be burnt, worn, etc. to a ˈfrazzle** (*informal*) to be completely burnt/extremely tired 被烧成灰烬；筋疲力尽

fraz·zled /ˈfræzld/ *adj.* (*informal*) tired and easily annoyed 疲惫而烦躁的：*They finally arrived home, hot and frazzled.* 他们终于回到家，又热又累。

freak /friːk/ *noun, adj., verb*

■ ***noun*** **1** (*informal*) a person with a very strong interest in a particular subject 狂热爱好者：***a health/fitness/jazz, etc. freak*** 对健康、健身、爵士乐等着迷的人 ➲ SEE ALSO CONTROL FREAK **2** (*disapproving*) a person who is considered to be unusual because of the way they behave, look or think（行为、外表、想法）怪异的人；怪人：*She was treated like a freak because she didn't want children.* 她因为不要孩子而被当作怪人。◇ *He's going out with a real freak.* 他和一个真正的怪人在谈恋爱。 **3** (*also* ˌ**freak of ˈnature**) (*sometimes offensive*) a person, an animal, a plant or a thing that is not physically normal（指人、动植物和东西）畸形 **4** a very unusual and unexpected event 怪异的事；不寻常的事：*By some* ***freak of fate*** *they all escaped without injury.* 由于命运之神的奇特安排，他们全都死里逃生，毫发未损。

■ ***adj.*** [only before noun] (of an event or the weather 事情或天气) very unusual and unexpected 不正常的；怪异的：***a freak accident/storm/occurrence*** 反常的事故 / 暴风雨 / 事件 ◇ *freak weather conditions* 反常的天气状况

■ ***verb*** [I, T] (*informal*) if sb **freaks** or if sth **freaks** them, they react very strongly to sth that makes them suddenly feel shocked, surprised, frightened, etc.（使）强烈反应，震惊，畏惧：~ (**out**) *My parents really freaked when they saw my hair.* 我父母看见我的头发时大惊失色。◇ ~ **sb** (**out**) *Snakes really freak me out.* 我一看见蛇便浑身发麻。

freak·ing /ˈfriːkɪŋ/ *adv., adj.* [only before noun] (*NAmE, taboo, slang*) a swear word that many people find offensive, used to emphasize a comment or an angry statement to avoid saying 'fucking'（加强语气，用以替代 fucking）该死的，他妈的

freak·ish /ˈfriːkɪʃ/ *adj.* very strange, unusual or unexpected 怪异的；反常的；意外的：*freakish weather/behaviour* 反常的天气；怪异的行为 ▸ **freak·ish·ly** *adv.*

ˈ**freak show** *noun* **1** a small show at a FAIR, where people pay to see people or animals with strange physical characteristics 畸形（人或动物）展览 **2** (*disapproving*) an event that people watch because it is very strange 人们享受观看的怪事

freaky /ˈfriːki/ *adj.* (*informal*) very strange or unusual 怪异的；反常的

freckle /ˈfrekl/ *noun* [usually pl.] a small, pale brown spot on a person's skin, especially on their face, caused by the sun 雀斑；小斑点 ➲ COMPARE MOLE (2) ▸ **freckled** /ˈfrekld/ *adj.*：*a freckled face/schoolgirl* 有雀斑的脸 / 女学生

free 🔑 /friː/ *adj., verb, adv.*

■ ***adj.*** (**freer** /ˈfriːə(r)/, **freest** /ˈfriːɪst/)

• **NOT CONTROLLED** 不受控制 **1** 🔑 not under the control or in the power of sb else; able to do what you want 能随自己意愿的；随心所欲的：*I have no ambitions other than to have a happy life and be free.* 我没有雄心大志，只求自由自在地过幸福生活。◇ *Students have a free choice of courses* in their final year. 学生在最后一学年可以自由选修课程。◇ **~ to do sth** *You are free to come and go as you please.* 你来去自由。◇ (*informal*) *'Can I use the phone?' 'Please, feel **free** (= of course you can use it).'* "我能用一下电话吗？""请便吧。" **2** not restricted or controlled by anyone else; able to do or say what you want 不受限制的；不受约束的；言行自由的：*A true democracy complete with **free speech** and a free press was called for.* 人们呼吁要有包括言论自由和新闻自由在内的真正民主。◇ *the country's first free election* 该国的第一次自由选举 ◇ *They gave me free access to all the files.* 他们让我自由查阅所有档案资料。

- **NOT PRISONER** 非囚犯 **3** (of a person 人) not a prisoner or SLAVE 自由的（不是囚犯或奴隶）：*He walked out of jail **a free man**.* 他获释出狱，成为自由人。
- **ANIMAL/BIRD** 动物；鸟 **4** not tied up or in a CAGE 未拴住的；非关在笼中的：*The researchers **set** the birds **free**.* 研究人员把鸟放了。
- **NO PAYMENT** 不用付款 **5** costing nothing 不收费的：*Admission is free.* 免费入场。◇ ***free samples/tickets/advice*** 免费样品 / 票 / 咨询 ◇ *We're offering a fabulous **free gift** with each copy you buy.* 购买一册就可以得到一份免费好礼。◇ *You can't expect people to work **for free*** (= without payment). 你不能指望人无偿工作。
- **NOT BLOCKED** 无阻碍 **6** clear; not blocked 无阻碍的；畅通的：*Ensure there is a free flow of air around the machine.* 要确保机器周围空气畅通。
- **WITHOUT STH** 没有 **7** **~ from/of sth** not containing or affected by sth harmful or unpleasant 不含有害物的；不受…伤害（或影响等的）：*free from difficulty/doubt/fear* 没有困难；不怀疑；不害怕 ◇ *free from artificial colours and flavourings* 不含人工色素和人工调味料 ◇ *It was several weeks before he was completely free of pain.* 过了几星期他的疼痛才完全消除。**8** **-free** (in adjectives 构成形容词) without the thing mentioned 没有…的：*virtually fat-free yogurt* 几乎无脂的酸奶 ◇ *tax-free earnings* 免税收入 ◇ *a trouble-free life* 无忧无虑的生活
- **NOT ATTACHED/TRAPPED** 未固定；未缚住 **9** **~ (of sth)** not attached to sth or trapped by sth 未固定的；未缚住的：*Pull gently on the free end of the rope.* 轻拉绳索松开的一端。◇ *They had to be **cut free** from their car after the accident.* 事故后，得破开汽车把他们救出来。◇ *She finally managed to pull herself free.* 她终于设法挣脱了。
- **NOT BEING USED** 未使用 **10** not being used 未使用的；空着的：*He held out his free hand and I took it.* 他伸出空着的一只手，我就抓住了。◇ *Is this seat free?* 这个座位空着吗？
- **NOT BUSY** 不忙 **11** **~ (for sth)** (of a person or time 人或时间) without particular plans or arrangements; not busy 没有安排活动的；空闲的：*If Sarah is free for lunch I'll take her out.* 如果萨拉有空吃午饭，我就带她出去吃。◇ *Keep Friday night free for my party.* 把星期五晚上空出来，参加我的聚会。◇ *What do you like to do in your **free time*** (= when you are not working)? 你闲暇时喜欢干什么？
- **READY TO GIVE** 乐于给予 **12** **~ with sth** (*often disapproving*) ready to give sth, especially when it is not wanted 随便给出的：*He's too free with his opinions.* 他太随便发表意见了。
- **TRANSLATION** 翻译 **13** a free translation is not exact but gives the general meaning 不拘泥原文的；（翻译）根据大意的；意译的 ➲ COMPARE LITERAL (2)

IDM **free and 'easy** informal; relaxed 随便；无拘束；轻松；自由自在：*Life was never going to be so free and easy again.* 生活绝不会再那样无拘无束了。 **get, have, etc. a free 'hand** to get, have, etc. the opportunity to do what you want to do and to make your own decisions 可以全权处理；有自主权：*I was given a free hand in designing the syllabus.* 我获准全权制订教学大纲。 **get, take, etc. a free 'ride** to get or take sth without paying because sb else is paying for it 白白得到好处（因他人已代付款） **it's a free 'country** (*informal*) used as a reply when sb suggests that you should not do sth（有人建议不应做某事时用于回答）这是个自由的国家：*It's a free country; I'll say what I like!* 这是个自由的国家，我想说什么就说什么！ **there's no such ˌthing as a free 'lunch** (*informal*) used to say that it is not possible to get sth for nothing（表示白得东西是不可能的）没有免费的午餐 ➲ MORE AT HOME *adv.*, REIN *n.*

■ ***verb***

- **PRISONER** 囚犯 **1** **~ sb (from sth)** to allow sb to leave prison or somewhere they have been kept against their will 释放；使摆脱 **SYN** **release**：*By the end of May nearly 100 of an estimated 2 000 political prisoners had been freed.* 至五月底，估计 2 000 名政治犯中已经有近 100 人获释。◇ *The hijackers agreed to free a further ten hostages.* 劫持者同意再释放十名人质。
- **SB/STH TRAPPED** 被困住的人 / 物 **2** **~ sb/sth/yourself (from sth)** to move sb/sth that is caught or fixed on sth 释放；使摆脱 **SYN** **release**：*Three people were freed from the wreckage.* 有三人被救出残骸。◇ *She struggled to free herself.* 她挣扎着以求脱身。
- **REMOVE STH** 去除某物 **3** **~ sb/sth of/from sb/sth** to remove sth that is unpleasant or not wanted from sb/sth 解除（或去除、清除） **SYN** **rid**：*These exercises help free the body of tension.* 这些锻炼可使紧张的身体放松。◇ *The police are determined to free the town of violent crime.* 警方决心消灭该城镇的暴力犯罪。◇ *The centre aims to free young people from dependency on drugs.* 这个中心的宗旨是使年轻人解除对毒品的依赖。
- **MAKE AVAILABLE** 使现成可用 **4** **~ sb/sth (up)** to make sb/sth available for a particular purpose 使可用（于某目的）：*We freed time each week for a project meeting.* 我们每周都腾出时间开一次项目会议。◇ *The government has promised to free up more resources for education.* 政府保证调拨更多资源用于教育。**5** **~ sb to do sth** to give sb the extra time to do sth that they want to do 使能腾出时间：*Winning the prize freed him to paint full-time.* 获奖使他能腾出时间整天作画。

■ ***adv.***

- **WITHOUT PAYMENT** 不需付款 **1** (*also* **ˌfree of 'charge**) without payment 免费：*Children under five travel free.* 五岁以下儿童免费乘坐。
- **NOT TRAPPED** 未困住 **2** away from or out of a position in which sb/sth is stuck or trapped 脱离束缚：*The wagon broke free from the train.* 这节货车车厢脱离了列车。 ➲ SEE ALSO SCOT-FREE

IDM **make free with 'sth** (*disapproving*) to use sth a lot, even though it does not belong to you 任意使用他人物品 **run 'free** (of an animal 动物) to be allowed to go where it likes; not tied to anything or kept in a CAGE 四处自由走动；未关起来；未受束缚 ➲ MORE AT WALK *v.*

ˌfree 'agent *noun* a person who can do whatever they want because they are not responsible to or for anyone else 有自主权的人；行动自由的人

free·base /ˈfriːbeɪs/ *noun* [U] (*slang*) a specially prepared form of the powerful illegal drug COCAINE 精炼可卡因

free·bas·ing /ˈfriːbeɪsɪŋ/ *noun* [U] (*slang*) the activity of smoking freebase 吸食精炼可卡因

free·bie /ˈfriːbi/ *noun* (*informal*) something that is given to sb without payment, usually by a company（常指公司提供的）免费品：*He took all the freebies that were on offer.* 他取了可得的全部免费品。◇ *a freebie holiday* 免费度假

free·boot·er /ˈfriːbuːtə(r)/ *noun* a person who takes part in a war in order to steal goods and money 战争掠夺者 ▶ **free·boot·ing** *adj.*, *noun* [U]

free·born /ˈfriːbɔːn; *NAmE* -bɔːrn/ *adj.* [only before noun] (*formal*) not born as a SLAVE 生来自由的；生为自由民的

ˌFree 'Church *noun* a Christian Church that does not belong to the established Church in a particular country 自由教会（不属于国教）

free·dom /ˈfriːdəm/ *noun* **1** [U, C] **~ (of sth)** the right to do or say what you want without anyone stopping you（指权利）自由：***freedom of speech/thought/expression/worship*** 言论 / 思想 / 表达 / 信仰自由 ◇ *a threat to **press/academic, etc. freedom*** 对新闻、学术等自由的威胁 ◇ *rights and freedoms guaranteed by the constitution* 宪法保障的权利和自由 **2** [U, sing.] the state of being able to do what you want, without anything stopping you

F

（指状态）自由：~ (of sth) *freedom of action/choice* 行动 / 选择自由 ◇ *Thanks to the automobile, Americans soon had a freedom of movement previously unknown.* 由于有了汽车，美国人很快就获得了前所未有的行动自由。◇ ~ (to do sth) *complete freedom to do as you wish* 按照自己意愿行事的绝对自由 **3** [U] the state of not being a prisoner or SLAVE 自由民地位（不是囚犯或奴隶）：*He finally won his freedom after twenty years in jail.* 他蹲了二十年监狱以后终于获得了自由。

WORDFINDER 联想词：allow, independence, liberty, oppress, restriction, rule, slave

4 [U] ~ **from sth** the state of not being affected by the thing mentioned 没有…的情况；不受…影响的状态：***freedom from fear/pain/hunger, etc.*** 免于恐惧、痛苦、饥饿等 **5** [sing.] **the ~ of sth** permission to use sth without restriction 自由使用权：*I was given the freedom of the whole house.* 我获得整座房子的自由使用权。

IDM **the freedom of the 'city** (in Britain) an honour that is given to sb by a city as a reward for work they have done（英国）荣誉市民称号 ➲ SEE ALSO FREEMAN IDM ➲ SEE MANOEUVRE *n.*

'freedom fighter *noun* a name used to describe a person who uses violence to try to remove a government from power, by people who support this 自由斗士（支持者用以称呼使用暴力推翻政府的人）➲ COMPARE GUERRILLA *n.*

ˌfreedom of as'sembly *noun* [U] the right to have public meetings which is guaranteed by law in the US 集会自由（受美国法律保障的公开集会权利）

ˌfreedom of associ'ation *noun* [U] the right to meet people and to form organizations without needing permission from the government 结社自由（无须政府批准成立组织的权利）

ˌfreedom of infor'mation *noun* [U] the right to see any information that a government has about people and organizations 信息自由（查阅政府所掌握有关个人及组织的信息的权利）

ˌfree 'enterprise *noun* [U] an economic system in which private businesses compete with each other without much government control 自由企业（体制）➲ COMPARE PRIVATE ENTERPRISE

ˌfree 'fall *noun* [U] **1** the movement of an object or a person falling through the air without engine power or a PARACHUTE（人或物的）自由下落：*a free fall display* 自由下落表演 **2** a sudden drop in the value of sth that cannot be stopped（价值）突降不止：*Share prices have gone into free fall.* 股价猛跌不止。

ˌfree-'floating *adj.* not attached to or controlled by anything 自由浮动的：*a free-floating exchange rate* 自由浮动汇率

Free·fone™ *noun* [U] = FREEPHONE

'free-for-all *noun* [sing.] **1** a situation in which there are no rules or controls and everyone acts for their own advantage 不加管制；自由放任：*The lowering of trade barriers has led to a free-for-all among exporters.* 降低贸易壁垒导致出口商各自为政。**2** a noisy fight or argument in which a lot of people take part 混战；众人激烈争辩；大吵大闹

'free form (*also* **ˌfree 'morpheme**) *noun* (*linguistics* 语言) a unit of language that can be used by itself 自由语素；自由形式；自由形位：*The plural 's' is not a free form, as it must always be attached to a noun.* 表示复数的 s 不是自由语素，必须附着于名词。

'free-form *adj.* [only before noun] (of art or music 美术或音乐) not created according to standard forms or structures 不按传统格式的；独创的：*a free-form jazz improvisation* 自由创作的爵士乐即兴演出

free·gan /ˈfriːɡən/ *noun* a person who only eats food that they can get for free and that would otherwise be thrown out or wasted 免费素食主义者（只吃不要钱的、将要扔掉或浪费的食物）

free·hand /ˈfriːhænd/ *adj.* [only before noun] drawn without using a ruler or other instruments 徒手画的；不用仪器画的：*a freehand drawing* 一幅徒手画 ▶ **free·hand** *adv.*：*to draw freehand* 徒手作画

free·hold /ˈfriːhəʊld; *NAmE* -hoʊld/ *noun* [C, U] (*law* 律, *especially BrE*) the fact of owning a building or piece of land for a period of time that is not limited（房地产）自由保有，完全保有，终身保有 ▶ **free·hold** *adj.*：*a freehold property* 终身保有的财产 **free·hold** *adv.*：*to buy a house freehold* 购买自由保有的房子 ➲ COMPARE LEASEHOLD *n.*

free·hold·er /ˈfriːhəʊldə(r); *NAmE* -hoʊld-/ *noun* (*law* 律, *especially BrE*) a person who owns the freehold of a building or piece of land（房地产的）终身保有者，自由保有者，完全保有者 ➲ COMPARE LEASEHOLDER

ˌfree 'house *noun* (in Britain) a pub that can sell different types of beer because it is not owned and controlled by one particular BREWERY (= a company producing beer)（英国，不受某个啤酒厂约束的）酒吧，酒馆 ➲ COMPARE TIED HOUSE

ˌfree 'kick *noun* (in football (SOCCER) and RUGBY 足球和橄榄球) an opportunity to kick the ball without any opposition, that is given to one team when the other team does sth wrong 任意球：*to take a free kick* 发任意球

free·lance /ˈfriːlɑːns; *NAmE* -læns/ *adj.*, *verb*

▪ ***adj.*** earning money by selling your work or services to several different organizations rather than being employed by one particular organization 特约的；自由职业（者）的：*a freelance journalist* 自由新闻工作者 ◇ *freelance work* 特约工作 ➲ WORDFINDER NOTE AT WORK ➲ COLLOCATIONS AT JOB ▶ **free·lance** *adv.* (*especially BrE*)：*I work freelance from home.* 我是在家中工作的自由职业者。

▪ ***verb*** [I] to earn money by selling your work to several different organizations 做特约工作；从事自由职业

free·lancer /ˈfriːlɑːnsə(r); *NAmE* -lænsər/ (*also* **free·lance**) *noun* a person who works freelance 特约人员；自由职业者

free·load·er /ˈfriːləʊdə(r); *NAmE* -loʊd-/ *noun* (*informal, disapproving*) a person who is always accepting free food and accommodation from other people without giving them anything in exchange 白吃白占的人；寄生虫；爱占便宜的人 ▶ **free·load** *verb* [I] **free·load·ing** *adj.*, *noun* [U]

ˌfree 'love *noun* [U] (*old-fashioned*) the practice of having sex without being married or having several sexual relationships at the same time（无婚约的）自由性爱

free·ly /ˈfriːli/ *adv.* **1** without anyone trying to prevent or control sth 不受限制地；无拘无束地；自由地：*the country's first freely elected president* 该国第一次自由选举出的总统 ◇ *EU citizens can now travel freely between member states.* 欧盟国家的公民现在可以在成员国之间自由旅行。 **2** without anything stopping the movement or flow of sth 无阻碍地；畅通地：*When the gate is raised, the water can flow freely.* 闸门提起时水就可以畅流。◇ *Traffic is now moving more freely following an earlier accident.* 早些时候的交通事故过后，现在交通顺畅些了。◇ *The book is now **freely available** in the shops* (= it is not difficult to get a copy). 现在这本书在商店可以随时买到。◇ (*figurative*) *The wine flowed freely* (= there was a lot of it to drink). 葡萄酒无限量供应。 **3** without trying to avoid the truth even though it might be unpleasant or embarrassing 自愿地；心甘情愿地：*I freely admit that I made a mistake.* 我爽快地承认我犯了错误。**4** in an honest way without worrying about what people will say or do 直率地；坦率地：*For the first time he was able to speak freely without the fear of reprisals against his family.* 他第一次能够直言不讳而不怕家人遭到报复。**5** in a willing and generous way 慷慨地；大方地：*Millions of people gave freely in response to the appeal for the victims of the earthquake.* 为响应救济地震灾民的呼吁，几百万人

慷慨相助。**6** a piece of writing that is translated **freely** is not translated exactly but the general meaning is given 以意译方法；不拘于原文

free·man /ˈfriːmən/ *noun* (*pl.* **-men** /-mən/) **1** (*BrE*) a person who has been given the FREEDOM of a particular city as a reward for the work that they have done 荣誉市民 **2** a person who is not a SLAVE 自由民（非奴隶）

ˌfree ˈmarket *noun* an economic system in which the price of goods and services is affected by supply and demand rather than controlled by a government 自由市场：*She was a supporter of the* ***free market economy.*** 她是自由市场经济的拥护者。

ˌfree markeˈteer *noun* a person who believes that prices should be allowed to rise and fall according to supply and demand and not be controlled by the government 主张自由市场者

Free·mason /ˈfriːmeɪsn/ (*also* **Mason**) *noun* a man belonging to a secret society whose members help each other and communicate using secret signs 共济会成员

Free·mason·ry /ˈfriːmeɪsnri/ *noun* [U] **1** the system and practices of Freemasons 共济会制 **2 freemasonry** the friendship that exists between people who have the same profession or interests 同行情谊；志趣相投：*the freemasonry of actors* 演员的志趣相投

ˌfree ˈmorpheme *noun* (*linguistics* 语言) = FREE FORM

ˌfree on ˈboard *adj.* (*abbr.* **f.o.b.**) (*business* 商) including the cost of putting goods onto a ship in the price 船上交货的；离岸价格的

ˌfree ˈpardon *noun* (*BrE, law* 律) = PARDON (1)

ˌfree ˈperiod *noun* a period of time in a school day when a student or teacher does not have a class 空课时（学生或教师没有课的时候）

Free·phone (*also* **Free·fone™**) /ˈfriːfəʊn; *NAmE* -foʊn/ *noun* [U] (in Britain) a system in which the cost of a telephone call is paid for by the organization being called, rather than by the person making the call（英国）受话方付费电话 ➲ COMPARE TOLL-FREE

ˌfree ˈport *noun* a port at which tax is not paid on goods that have been brought there temporarily before being sent to a different country 自由港

Free·post /ˈfriːpəʊst; *NAmE* -poʊst/ *noun* [U] (in Britain) a system in which the cost of sending a letter is paid for by the organization receiving it, rather than by the person sending it（英国）收件人邮资总付

ˌfree ˈradical *noun* (*chemistry* 化) an atom or group of atoms that has an ELECTRON that is not part of a pair, causing it to take part easily in chemical reactions. Free radicals in the body are thought to be one of the causes of diseases such as cancer. 自由基；游离基 ➲ SEE ALSO ANTIOXIDANT (1)

ˌfree-ˈrange *adj.* [usually before noun] connected with a system of farming in which animals are kept in natural conditions and can move around freely（动物）放养的，散养的：*free-range chickens* 放养的鸡 ◇ *free-range eggs* 放养的鸡产的蛋 ➲ COMPARE BATTERY (4), BATTERY FARM

free·ride /ˈfriːraɪd/ (*also* **ˈfreeride board**) *noun* a type of SNOWBOARD used for riding on all types of snow 全能滑雪板（在各种雪上使用）

ˌfree ˈrunning *noun* [U] the activity or art of moving through a city by running, jumping and climbing under, around and through things in a way that is as elegant as possible 自由跑（指在城市中以尽量优美的方式奔跑、跳跃、攀爬、环绕、穿越的行为或艺术）➲ COMPARE PARKOUR

ˌfree ˈsafety *noun* (in AMERICAN FOOTBALL 美式足球) a defending player who can try to stop any attacking player rather than one particular attacking player 游卫，自由后卫（没有特定防守对象）

free·sia /ˈfriːʒə; ˈfriːziə/ *noun* a plant with yellow, pink, white or purple flowers with a sweet smell, which are also called freesias 小苍兰（花有香味，呈黄、粉红、白或紫色）

ˌfree ˈspirit *noun* a person who is independent and does what they want instead of doing what other people do 独立自主的人；有主见的人

ˌfree-ˈstanding *adj.* **1** not supported by or attached to anything 自力支撑的；无依附的；独立的：*a free-standing sculpture* 独立的雕塑 **2** not a part of sth else 单独的；独立的：*a free-standing adult education service* 自成体系的成人教育服务

free·style /ˈfriːstaɪl/ *noun, verb*

▪ ***noun*** [U] **1** a swimming race in which people taking part can use any stroke they want (usually CRAWL) 自由式游泳竞赛（泳姿不限，参加者常选择爬泳）：*the men's 400 m freestyle* 男子 400 米自由泳 **2** (often used as an adjective 常用作形容词) a sports competition in which people taking part can use any style that they want 自由式体育比赛：*freestyle skiing* 自由式滑雪

▪ ***verb*** [I] to RAP, play music, dance, etc. by inventing it as you do it, rather than by planning it in advance or following fixed patterns 即兴说唱（或奏乐、舞蹈等）**SYN** improvise

free·think·er /ˌfriːˈθɪŋkə(r)/ *noun* a person who forms their own ideas and opinions rather than accepting those of other people, especially in religious teaching（尤指宗教教义的）自由思想者，思想自由的人 ▸ **ˌfree-ˈthink·ing** *adj.* [only before noun]

ˌfree ˈthrow *noun* (in BASKETBALL 篮球) an attempt to throw a ball into the BASKET without any player trying to stop you, that you are allowed after a FOUL 罚球

ˌfree-to-ˈair *adj.* (*BrE*) [usually before noun] (of television programmes 电视节目) that you do not have to pay to watch 免费收视的：*The company provides more than 20 free-to-air channels.* 公司提供 20 多个免费收视频道。

ˌfree ˈtrade *noun* [U] a system of international trade in which there are no restrictions or taxes on imports and exports 自由贸易（制度）➲ COLLOCATIONS AT INTERNATIONAL

ˌfree ˈverse *noun* [U] (*specialist*) poetry without a regular rhythm or RHYME（无固定格律的）自由诗 ➲ COMPARE BLANK VERSE

ˌfree ˈvote *noun* (in Britain) a vote by members of parliament in which they can vote according to their own beliefs rather than following the policy of their political party（英国）自由投票（根据个人信念而非政党政策）

free·ware /ˈfriːweə(r); *NAmE* -wer/ *noun* [U] (*computing* 计) computer software that is offered free for anyone to use 免费软件 ➲ COMPARE SHAREWARE

free·way /ˈfriːweɪ/ (*also* **ex·press·way**) *noun* (in the US) a wide road, where traffic can travel fast for long distances. You can only enter and leave freeways at special RAMPS.（美国）高速公路：*a freeway exit* 高速公路出口 ◇ *an accident on the freeway* 高速公路事故

free·wheel /ˌfriːˈwiːl/ *verb* [I] (**+ adv./prep.**) to ride a bicycle without using the PEDALS（骑自行车）滑行：*I freewheeled down the hill to the village.* 我从山上骑自行车一路滑行至村庄。

free·wheel·ing /ˌfriːˈwiːlɪŋ/ *adj.* [only before noun] (*informal*) not concerned about rules or the possible results of what you do 随心所欲的；无拘无束的：*a freewheeling lifestyle* 自由放纵的生活方式

ˌfree ˈwill *noun* [U] the power to make your own decisions without being controlled by God or FATE 自由意志

IDM **of your own free ˈwill** because you want to do sth rather than because sb has told or forced you to do it 自愿：*She left of her own free will.* 她是自愿离开的。

freeze 🔑 /friːz/ *verb, noun*

▪ ***verb*** (**froze** /frəʊz; *NAmE* froʊz/, **fro·zen** /ˈfrəʊzn; *NAmE*

F

ˈfroʊzn/)

- **BECOME ICE** 结冰 **1** [I, T] to become hard, and often turn to ice, as a result of extreme cold; to make sth do this （使）冻结，结冰：*Water freezes at 0°C.* 水在0摄氏度时结冰。◇ *It's so cold that even the river has frozen.* 天气冷得河都封冻了。◇ **~ sth** *The cold weather had frozen the ground.* 寒冷的天气使地面都冻硬了。◇ **+ adj.** *The clothes* ***froze solid*** *on the washing line.* 衣服在晒衣绳上冻成了硬块。**OPP** thaw
- **OF PIPE/LOCK/MACHINE** 管子；锁；机器 **2** [I, T] if a pipe, lock or machine **freezes**, or sth **freezes** it, it becomes blocked with frozen liquid and therefore cannot be used （使）冻住，冻堵：**~ (up)** *The pipes have frozen, so we've got no water.* 水管已经冻了，我们接不到水。◇ **~ sth (up)** *Ten degrees of frost had frozen the lock on the car.* 零下十摄氏度把轿车上的锁冻住了。
- **OF WEATHER** 天气 **3** [I] when **it freezes**, the weather is at or below 0° Celsius 冰冻；严寒：*It may freeze tonight, so bring those plants inside.* 今夜可能有霜冻，把花草搬进屋来吧。
- **BE VERY COLD** 很冷 **4** [I, T] to be very cold; to be so cold that you die 极冷；（使）冻死：*Every time she opens the window we all freeze.* 每次她开窗户，我们都冷得要死。◇ *Two men* ***froze to death*** *on the mountain.* 两个男子在山上冻死了。◇ **~ sb** *Two men were frozen to death on the mountain.* 两个男子在山上冻死了。
- **FOOD** 食物 **5** [T] **~ sth** to keep food at a very low temperature in order to preserve it 冷冻贮藏；冷藏：*Can you freeze this cake?* 你能不能把这个蛋糕冷藏起来？◇ *These meals are ideal for home freezing.* 这些饭食很适合家庭冷藏。**6** [I] to be able to be kept at a very low temperature 能冷冻贮藏：*Some fruits freeze better than others.* 有些水果比其他的更适宜冷藏。
- **STOP MOVING** 停住 **7** [I] to stop moving suddenly because of fear, etc. （因害怕等）停住不动；惊呆；吓呆：*I froze with terror as the door slowly opened.* 门慢慢开启时我吓呆了。◇ (*figurative*) *The smile froze on her lips.* 她脸上的笑容僵住了。◇ *The police officer shouted 'Freeze!' and the man dropped the gun.* 警察大喊"不许动！"那个男人便放下了枪。
- **COMPUTER** 计算机 **8** [I] when a computer screen **freezes**, you cannot move any of the images, etc. on it, because there is a problem with the system （屏幕）冻结
- **FILM/MOVIE** 电影 **9** [T] **~ sth** to stop a film/movie or video in order to look at a particular picture 使定格：*Freeze the action there!* 把这个画面定格在那里！➲ SEE ALSO FREEZE-FRAME
- **WAGES/PRICES** 工资；物价 **10** [T] **~ sth** to hold wages, prices, etc. at a fixed level for a period of time 使固定不动 **SYN** **peg**: *Salaries have been frozen for the current year.* 今年的工资已冻结。
- **MONEY/BANK ACCOUNT** 现金账；银行账户 **11** [T] **~ sth** to prevent money, a bank account, etc. from being used by getting a court order which bans it 冻结（资金、银行账户等）：*The company's assets have been frozen.* 这家公司的资产已被冻结。

IDM **freeze your 'blood | make your 'blood freeze** to make you extremely frightened or shocked 使人恐惧万分；令人毛骨悚然 ➲ MORE AT TRACK *n.*

PHR V **ˌfreeze sb↔'out (of sth)** (*informal*) to be deliberately unfriendly to sb, creating difficulties, etc. in order to stop or DISCOURAGE them from doing sth or taking part in sth 排挤，排斥（使不能参与…）**ˌfreeze 'over** to become completely covered by ice 冰封：*The lake freezes over in winter.* 这个湖到冬天就全部封冻了。

■ ***noun***

- **OF WAGES/PRICES** 工资；价格 **1** the act of keeping wages, prices, etc. at a particular level for a period of time 冻结：*a wage/price freeze* 工资 / 物价的冻结
- **STOPPING STH** 停止 **2** [usually sing.] **~ (on sth)** the act of stopping sth 停止：*a freeze on imports* 停止进口
- **COLD WEATHER** 寒冷天气 **3** [usually sing.] (*BrE*) an unusually cold period of weather during which temperatures stay below 0° Celsius 冰冻期；严寒期：*Farmers still talk about the* ***big freeze*** *of '99.* 农民至今还在谈论1999年的大严寒。**4** (*NAmE*) a short period of time, especially at night, when the temperature is below 0° Celsius 霜冻：*A freeze warning was posted for Thursday night.* 据警报星期四夜间有霜冻。

'freeze-dry *verb* [usually passive] **~ sth** to preserve food or drink by freezing and drying it very quickly 冷冻干燥保存（食物）

'freeze-frame *noun* [U] the act of stopping a moving film at one particular FRAME (= picture) 定格；定帧

freezer /ˈfriːzə(r)/ (*BrE also* **ˌdeep 'freeze**) (*US also* **ˌdeep 'freezer**) *noun* a large piece of electrical equipment in which you can store food for a long time at a low temperature so that it stays frozen 冷冻柜；冰柜 ➲ SEE ALSO FRIDGE-FREEZER

freez·ing /ˈfriːzɪŋ/ *adj.* **1** extremely cold 极冷的：*It's freezing in here!* 这儿冷得不得了！◇ *I'm freezing!* 我要冻僵了！➲ SYNONYMS AT COLD **2** [only before noun] having temperatures that are below 0° Celsius 冰冻的；冰点以下的：*freezing fog* 冰雾 ◇ *freezing temperatures* 冻结温度 ➲ SYNONYMS AT COLD ► **freez·ing** *adv.* (*informal*)：*It's freezing cold outside.* 外面极为寒冷。

'freezing point *noun* **1** (*also* **freez·ing**) [U] 0° Celsius, the temperature at which water freezes 冰点：*Tonight temperatures will fall well below freezing (point).* 今夜温度将远降至冰点以下。**2** [C, usually sing.] the temperature at which a particular liquid freezes 冻结点；凝固点：*the freezing point of polar sea water* 极地海水的冻结点

freight /freɪt/ *noun, verb*

■ ***noun*** [U] goods that are transported by ships, planes, trains or lorries/trucks; the system of transporting goods in this way （海运、空运或陆运的）货物；货运：*to send goods by air freight* 空运货物 ◇ *a freight business* 货运公司 ◇ *passenger and freight transportation services* 客货运业务

■ ***verb*** **1 ~ sth** to send or carry goods by air, sea or train 寄送，运送（货物）；货运 **2** [usually passive] **~ sth with sth** (*literary*) to fill sth with a particular mood or tone 使充满（某种心情或口气）：*Each word was freighted with anger.* 字字充满愤怒。

'freight car (*NAmE*) (*BrE* **wagon**) *noun* a railway/railroad truck for carrying goods （铁路）货车车厢，车皮

freight·er /ˈfreɪtə(r)/ *noun* a large ship or plane that carries goods 货船；运输飞机

'freight train (*BrE also* **'goods train**) *noun* a train that carries only goods 货运列车 ➲ VISUAL VOCAB PAGE V63

French /frentʃ/ *adj., noun*

■ ***adj.*** of or connected with France, its people or its language 法国的；法国人的；法语的

IDM **take French 'leave** (*BrE*) to leave work without asking permission first 擅离职守

■ ***noun*** the language of France and some other countries 法语

IDM **excuse/pardon my 'French** (*informal*) used to say that you are sorry for swearing 请原谅我说脏话了；不好意思，我骂人了

ˌFrench 'bean *noun* (*BrE*) = GREEN BEAN

ˌFrench 'braid (*NAmE*) (*BrE* **ˌFrench 'plait**) *noun* a HAIRSTYLE for women in which all the hair is gathered into one large PLAIT / BRAID down the back of the head 法式辫子（脑后的一根大辫）➲ VISUAL VOCAB PAGE V65

ˌFrench 'bread *noun* [U] white bread in the shape of a long thick stick 法式面包棒

ˌFrench 'Canada *noun* [U] the part of Canada where most French-speaking Canadians live, especially Quebec 加拿大法语区（尤指魁北克省）

ˌFrench Ca'nadian *noun* a Canadian whose first language is French 母语为法语的加拿大人；法裔加拿大人 ► **ˌFrench Ca'nadian** *adj.*

ˌFrench 'door *noun* (*especially NAmE*) a glass door, often one of a pair, that leads to a room, a garden/yard or a BALCONY（常对开的）落地窗，玻璃门 ➲ VISUAL VOCAB PAGE V18

ˌFrench ˈdressing *noun* [U, C] a mixture of oil, VINEGAR, etc. used to add flavour to a salad 法式色拉调料 SYN **vinaigrette**

ˌFrench ˈfry (*also* **fry**) (*both especially NAmE*) (*BrE also* **chip**) *noun* [usually pl.] a long thin piece of potato fried in oil or fat 油炸土豆条；炸薯条

ˌFrench ˈhorn (*also* **horn** *especially in BrE*) *noun* a BRASS musical instrument that consists of a long tube curled around in a circle with a wide opening at the end（铜管乐器）法国号，圆号 ➲ VISUAL VOCAB PAGE V37

ˌFrench ˈkiss *noun* a kiss during which people's mouths are open and their tongues touch 法式接吻（接触舌头）

ˌFrench ˈletter *noun* (*old-fashioned, BrE, informal*) = CONDOM

ˌFrench ˈloaf *noun* = BAGUETTE (1)

ˌFrench ˈplait (*BrE*) (*NAmE* **ˌFrench ˈbraid**) *noun* a HAIRSTYLE for women in which all the hair is gathered into one large PLAIT / BRAID down the back of the head 法式辫子（脑后的一根大辫）➲ VISUAL VOCAB PAGE V65

ˌFrench ˈpleat (*BrE*) (*NAmE* **ˌFrench ˈtwist**) *noun* a HAIRSTYLE for women in which all the hair is lifted up at the back of the head, twisted and held in place（妇女的）卷筒型发式；法式盘发 ➲ VISUAL VOCAB PAGE V65

ˌFrench ˈpolish *noun* [U] (*BrE*) a type of VARNISH (= transparent liquid) that is painted onto wooden furniture to give it a hard shiny surface 罩光漆；抛光漆 ▶ **ˌFrench ˈpolish** *verb* ~ **sth**

ˌFrench ˈpress (*NAmE*) (*BrE* **cafe·tière**) *noun* a special glass container for making coffee with a metal FILTER that you push down 法式咖啡壶（有活动金属过滤网）➲ VISUAL VOCAB PAGE V26

ˌFrench ˈstick *noun* = BAGUETTE (1) ➲ PICTURE AT STICK

ˌFrench ˈtoast *noun* [U] slices of bread that have been covered with a mixture of egg and milk and then fried 法国吐司（用面包片蘸蛋奶油炸而成）

ˌFrench ˈtwist (*NAmE*) (*BrE* **ˌFrench ˈpleat**) *noun* a HAIRSTYLE for women in which all the hair is lifted up at the back of the head, twisted and held in place（妇女的）卷筒型发式；法式盘发 ➲ VISUAL VOCAB PAGE V65

ˌFrench ˈwindow *noun* [usually pl.] a glass door, usually one of a pair, that leads to a garden/yard or BALCONY（常对开的）落地窗，玻璃门 ➲ VISUAL VOCAB PAGE V18

fre·net·ic /frəˈnetɪk/ *adj.* involving a lot of energy and activity in a way that is not organized 发狂似的；狂乱的：*a scene of frenetic activity* 疯狂活动的场面 ▶ **fre·net·ic·al·ly** /-kli/ *adv.*

frenu·lum /ˈfrenjələm; *BrE also* ˈfriːn-/ (*BrE also* **frae·nu·lum** /ˈfriːn-/) *noun* (*anatomy* 解) a small fold of skin that prevents an organ from moving too much, for example the fold of skin under the tongue 系带

fren·zied /ˈfrenzid/ *adj.* [usually before noun] involving a lot of activity and strong emotions in a way that is often violent or frightening and not under control 疯狂的；狂暴的：*a frenzied attack* 疯狂的进攻 ◇ *frenzied activity* 狂暴的活动 ▶ **fren·zied·ly** *adv.*

frenzy /ˈfrenzi/ *noun* [C, usually sing., U] (*pl.* **-ies**) ~ (**of sth**) a state of great activity and strong emotion that is often violent or frightening and not under control 疯狂；狂乱；狂暴：*in a* ***frenzy of activity/excitement/violence*** 疯狂的活动 / 兴奋 / 暴力 ◇ *The speaker worked the crowd up into a* ***frenzy***. 演讲者把听众煽动得疯狂起来。◇ *an outbreak of patriotic frenzy* 爱国狂热的迸发 ◇ *a killing frenzy* 使人精疲力竭的疯狂 ➲ SEE ALSO FEEDING FRENZY

fre·quency /ˈfriːkwənsi/ *noun* (*pl.* **-ies**) **1** [U, C] the rate at which sth happens or is repeated 发生率；出现率；重复率：*Fatal road accidents have decreased in frequency over recent years.* 近年来致命交通事故发生率已经下降。◇ *a society with a* ***high/low frequency*** (= happening often/not very often) *of stable marriages* 婚姻稳定率高 / 低的社会 ◇ *The program can show us* ***word frequency*** (= how often words occur in a language). 这个程序可给我们显示词频。**2** [U] the fact of sth happening often 频繁：*the alarming frequency of computer errors* 计算机出错的情况惊人的多 ◇ *Objects like this turn up at sales with surprising frequency.* 这样的东西在拍卖会上出人意料地频繁出现。 **3** [C, U] (*specialist*) the rate at which a sound or ELECTROMAGNETIC wave VIBRATES (= moves up and down)（声波或电磁波振动的）频率：*a* ***high/low frequency*** 高频；低频 ➲ WORDFINDER NOTE AT PHYSICS **4** [C, U] (*specialist*) the number of radio waves for every second of a radio signal 频率（无线电信号每秒电波数）：*a frequency band* 频带 ◇ *There are only a limited number of broadcasting frequencies.* 广播频率的数量有限。

fre·quent *adj., verb*

■ ***adj.*** /ˈfriːkwənt/ happening or doing sth often 频繁的；经常发生的：*He is a frequent visitor to this country.* 他常常访问这个国家。◇ *Her calls became less frequent.* 她打电话的次数减少了。◇ *There is a frequent bus service into the centre of town.* 公共汽车有很多班次开往市中心。◇ *How frequent is this word* (= how often does it occur in the language)? 这个单词出现的频率如何？ OPP **infrequent**

■ ***verb*** /friˈkwent/ ~ **sth** (*formal*) to visit a particular place often 常去，常到（某处）：*We met in a local bar much frequented by students.* 我们在学生经常去的一家酒吧里相遇。

fre·quent·ly /ˈfriːkwəntli/ *adv.* often 频繁地；经常：*Buses run frequently between the city and the airport.* 公共汽车频繁地来往于市区与机场之间。◇ *some of the most frequently asked questions about the Internet* 有关互联网的最常见的提问 OPP **infrequently**

fresco /ˈfreskəʊ; *NAmE* -koʊ/ *noun* (*pl.* **-oes** or **-os**) [C, U] a picture that is painted on a wall while the PLASTER is still wet; the method of painting in this way 湿壁画（墙壁灰泥未干时绘）；湿壁画技法 ➲ WORDFINDER NOTE AT PAINTING ➲ COLLOCATIONS AT ART ➲ SEE ALSO AL FRESCO

fresh /freʃ/ *adj., adv.*

■ ***adj.*** (**fresh·er, fresh·est**)

• **FOOD** 食物 **1** (usually of food 通常指食物) recently produced or picked and not frozen, dried or preserved in tins or cans 新鲜的；新产的；刚摘的：*Is this milk fresh?* 这是鲜牛奶吗？◇ *fresh bread/flowers* 刚出炉的面包；鲜花 ◇ *Eat plenty of fresh fruit and vegetables.* 多吃新鲜水果和蔬菜。◇ *vegetables fresh from the garden* 刚从菜园摘的蔬菜 ◇ *Our chefs use only the freshest produce available.* 我们的厨师只用现有最新鲜的农产品。

• **NEW** 新 **2** made or experienced recently 新近的；新近出现的；新近体验的：*fresh tracks in the snow* 雪地上的新脚印 ◇ *Let me write it down while it's still* ***fresh in my mind.*** 趁记忆犹新，我来把它写下来。 **3** [usually before noun] new or different in a way that adds to or replaces sth 新的；不同的：*fresh evidence* 新证据 ◇ *I think it's time we tried a fresh approach.* 我认为是尝试新方法的时候了。◇ *a fresh coat of paint* 刚涂的一层油漆 ◇ *Could we order some fresh coffee?* 我们能点新煮的咖啡吗？ ◇ *This is the opportunity he needs to* ***make a fresh start*** (= to try sth new after not being successful at sth else). 这是他所需要的重振旗鼓的机会。

• **CLEAN/COOL** 清洁；凉爽 **4** [usually before noun] pleasantly clean, pure or cool 清新的；凉爽的：*a toothpaste that leaves a nice fresh taste in your mouth* 在口中留下舒适清凉味道的牙膏 ◇ *Let's go and get some* ***fresh air*** (= go outside where the air is cooler). 咱们出去呼吸点新鲜空气。

• **WATER** 水 **5** [usually before noun] containing no salt 淡的；无盐的：*There is a shortage of fresh water on the island.* 岛上缺少淡水。➲ SEE ALSO FRESHWATER

• **WEATHER** 天气 **6** (of the wind 风) quite strong and cold 凉飕飕的 SYN **brisk**：*a fresh breeze* 凉爽的微风 **7** (*BrE*) quite cold with some wind 清凉的；清爽的：*It's fresh this morning, isn't it?* 今天早上凉飕飕的，是不是？

• **CLEAR/BRIGHT** 洁净；鲜明 **8** looking clear, bright and attractive 洁净的；明净的；亮丽的：*He looked fresh and neat in a clean white shirt.* 他穿上干净的白衬衫显得清爽利落。◇ *a collection of summer dresses in fresh colours* 色

F

彩鲜艳的夏季连衣裙系列 ◇ *a fresh complexion* 白净的肤色

• FULL OF ENERGY 精力充沛 **9** [not usually before noun] full of energy 精力充沛：*Regular exercise will help you feel fresher and fitter.* 经常锻炼会使你感觉更加精力充沛，身体健康。◇ *I managed to sleep on the plane and arrived feeling* ***as fresh as a daisy.*** 我总算在飞机上睡了觉，到达时精神焕发。

• JUST FINISHED 刚结束 **10** ~ **from sth** having just come from a particular place; having just had a particular experience 刚从…来；刚有过…经历：*students fresh from college* 刚刚毕业的大学生 ◇ *fresh from her success at the Olympic Games* 刚从奥运会凯旋归来的她

• RUDE/CONFIDENT 粗鲁；自信 **11** [not before noun] ~ (**with sb**) (*informal*) rude and too confident in a way that shows a lack of respect for sb or a sexual interest in sb 粗鲁；无礼；（对异性）放肆：*Don't get fresh with me!* 别对我无礼！

▶ **fresh·ness** *noun* [U, sing.]: *We guarantee the freshness of all our produce.* 我们保证我们的农产品都是新鲜的。◇ *the cool freshness of the water* 水的清凉 ◇ *I like the freshness of his approach to the problem.* 我喜欢他对这个问题新颖的处理方法。IDM SEE BLOOD *n.*, BREATH, HEART

■ *adv.*

IDM **fresh out of sth** (*informal, especially NAmE*) having recently finished a supply of sth 刚用完（或售完等）：*Sorry, we're fresh out of milk.* 对不起，牛奶我们刚卖完。

fresh·en /ˈfreʃn/ *verb* **1** [T] ~ **sth** (**up**) to make sth cleaner, cooler, newer or more pleasant 使洁净（或凉爽、新鲜、宜人）：*The walls need freshening up with white paint.* 墙壁需要用白漆刷新。◇ *The rain had freshened the air.* 下雨使空气变得清新了。◇ *Using a mouthwash freshens the breath.* 使用漱口液可以使口气清新。 **2** [T] ~ **sth** (**up**) (*especially NAmE*) to add more liquid to a drink, especially an alcoholic one 添加液体于（饮料，尤指酒）之中 ➲ SEE ALSO TOP STH↔UP at TOP **3** [I] (of the wind 风) to become stronger and colder 增强变冷：*The wind will freshen tonight.* 今夜风力将加大，气温下降。

PHR V **ˌfreshen ˈup** | **ˌfreshen yourself ˈup** to wash and make yourself look clean and tidy 梳洗打扮：*I'll just go and freshen up before supper.* 晚饭前我要去梳洗打扮一番。

fresh·ener /ˈfreʃnə(r)/ *noun* [U, C] (often in compounds 常构成复合词) a thing that makes sth cleaner, purer or more pleasant 使清洁（或纯净、清新、宜人）之物：*air freshener* 空气净化剂

fresh·er /ˈfreʃə(r)/ *noun* (*BrE, informal*) a student who has just started his or her first term at a university 大学一年级新生

ˈfresh-faced *adj.* having a young, healthy-looking face 青春而容光焕发的：*fresh-faced kids* 容光焕发的少年

fresh·ly 🔑 /ˈfreʃli/ *adv.* usually followed by a past participle showing that sth has been made, prepared, etc. recently（通常后接过去分词）刚刚，新近：*freshly brewed coffee* 刚煮的咖啡

fresh·man /ˈfreʃmən/ *noun* (*pl.* **-men** /-mən/) **1** (*especially NAmE*) a first-year student at a university or college 大学一年级新生：*college freshmen* 大学一年级新生 ◇ *during my freshman year* 在我大学一年级期间 **2** (*NAmE*) a first-year student at HIGH SCHOOL (1) or JUNIOR HIGH SCHOOL 高中一年级学生；初中一年级学生：*high school freshmen* 高中一年级新生 ➲ COMPARE SOPHOMORE

fresh·water /ˈfreʃwɔːtə(r)/ *adj.* [only before noun] **1** living in water that is not the sea and is not salty 淡水中生长的：*freshwater fish* 淡水鱼 **2** having water that is not salty 淡水的：*freshwater lakes* 淡水湖 ➲ COMPARE SALT WATER

fret /fret/ *verb, noun*

■ *verb* (**-tt-**) [I, T] ~ (**about/over sth**) | ~ (**that…**) (*especially BrE*) to be worried or unhappy and not able to relax 苦恼；烦躁；焦虑不安：*Fretting about it won't help.* 苦恼于事无补。◇ *Her baby starts to fret as soon as she goes out of the room.* 她一走出房间，婴儿就躁动起来。

■ *noun* **1** one of the bars on the long thin part of a GUITAR, etc. Frets show you where to press the strings with your fingers to produce particular sounds.（吉他等指板上定音的）品 ➲ VISUAL VOCAB PAGE V40 **2** (*also* **ˈsea fret**) (*NEngE*) MIST or FOG that comes in from the sea（从海上飘来的）雾气，薄雾，雾

fret·ful /ˈfretfl/ *adj.* behaving in a way that shows you are unhappy or uncomfortable 烦躁的；苦恼的；不舒适的 SYN restless ▶ **fret·ful·ly** *adv.*

fret·saw /ˈfretsɔː/ *noun* a SAW with a thin blade that is used for cutting patterns in wood, metal, etc. 线锯

fret·ted /ˈfretɪd/ *adj.* (*specialist*) (especially of wood or stone 尤指木头或石头) decorated with patterns 回纹饰的

fret·work /ˈfretwɜːk; *NAmE* -wɜːrk/ *noun* [U] patterns cut into wood, metal, etc. to decorate it; the process of making these patterns 回纹饰；回纹饰工序

Freud·ian /ˈfrɔɪdiən/ *adj.* **1** connected with the ideas of Sigmund Freud about the way the human mind works, especially his theories of unconscious sexual feelings 弗洛伊德学说的，与弗洛伊德学说有关的（关于人的内心活动方式，尤指对潜在性感情的理论）**2** (of sb's speech or behaviour 语言或行为) showing your secret thoughts or feelings, especially those connected with sex（尤指性方面）表示出内心思想感情的

ˌFreudian ˈslip *noun* something you say by mistake but which is believed to show your true thoughts 漏嘴，失言（无意中泄露真实思想）ORIGIN This expression is named after Sigmund Freud and his theories of unconscious thought. 源自西格蒙德•弗洛伊德及其潜意识理论。

fri·able /ˈfraɪəbl/ *adj.* (*specialist*) easily broken up into small pieces 脆的；易碎的；易粉碎的：*friable soil* 松散土壤

friar /ˈfraɪə(r)/ *noun* a member of one of several Roman Catholic religious communities of men who in the past travelled around teaching people about Christianity and lived by asking other people for food (= by BEGGING)（天主教）托钵修会会士，修士 ➲ COMPARE MONK

fri·ary /ˈfraɪəri/ *noun* (*pl.* **-ies**) a building in which friars live 托钵修院；会院

fric·as·see /ˈfrɪkəsiː/ *noun* [C, U] a hot dish consisting of small pieces of meat and vegetables that are cooked and served in a thick white sauce 焖肉

frica·tive /ˈfrɪkətɪv/ (*NAmE also* **spir·ant**) *noun* (*phonetics* 语音) a speech sound made by forcing breath out through a narrow space in the mouth with the lips, teeth or tongue in a particular position, for example /f/ and /ʃ/ in *fee* and *she* 摩擦音 ▶ **frica·tive** *adj.* ➲ COMPARE PLOSIVE

fric·tion /ˈfrɪkʃn/ *noun* **1** [U] the action of one object or surface moving against another 摩擦：*Friction between moving parts had caused the engine to overheat.* 活动部件的摩擦使发动机过热。**2** [U] (*physics* 物) the RESISTANCE (= the force that stops sth moving) of one surface to another surface or substance moving over or through it 摩擦力：*The force of friction slows the spacecraft down as it re-enters the earth's atmosphere.* 航天飞船重返地球大气层时因有摩擦力而减慢速度。**3** [U, C] ~ (**between A and B**) disagreement or a lack of friendship among people who have different opinions about sth 争执；分歧；不和 SYN **tension**: *conflicts and frictions that have still to be resolved* 仍有待解决的冲突和摩擦

ˈfriction tape *noun* [U] (*US*) = INSULATING TAPE

Fri·day 🔑 /ˈfraɪdeɪ; -di/ *noun* [C, U] (*abbr.* **Fri.**) the day of the week after Thursday and before Saturday 星期五 HELP To see how **Friday** is used, look at the examples at **Monday**. * Friday 的用法见词条 Monday 下的示例。ORIGIN Originally translated from the Latin for 'day of the planet Venus' *Veneris dies* and named after the Germanic goddess Frigga. 译自拉丁文 Veneris dies，原意为 day of the planet Venus（金星日），以日耳曼女神 Frigga（弗丽嘉）命名。

fridge /frɪdʒ/ (*especially BrE*) (*NAmE* or *formal* **re·friger·ator**) (*US also, old-fashioned* **ice·box**) *noun* a piece of electrical equipment in which food is kept cold so that it stays fresh 冰箱: *This dessert can be served straight from the fridge.* 这种甜食从冰箱里拿出来就可以吃。➲ VISUAL VOCAB PAGE V26

ˌfridge-'freezer *noun* (*BrE*) a piece of kitchen equipment that consists of a fridge/refrigerator and a FREEZER together（有冷藏室和冷冻室的）立式冰箱；双门冰箱

fried PAST TENSE, PAST PART. OF FRY

friend /frend/ *noun*
- **PERSON YOU LIKE** 喜欢的人 **1** a person you know well and like, and who is not usually a member of your family 朋友；友人: *This is my friend Tom.* 这是我的朋友汤姆。◇ *Is he* ***a friend of yours****?* 他是你的朋友吗？◇ *She's an* ***old friend*** (= I have known her a long time). 她是我的老朋友。◇ *He's one of my* ***best friends****.* 他是我最要好的朋友之一。◇ *a* ***close/good friend*** 密友；好友 ◇ *a* ***childhood/family/lifelong friend*** 儿时 / 家庭 / 终生朋友 ◇ *I heard about it through* ***a friend of a friend****.* 我通过朋友的朋友听到这事的。◇ *She has a wide* ***circle of friends****.* 她交游很广。 ➲ SEE ALSO BEFRIEND, BOYFRIEND, FAIR-WEATHER, FALSE FRIEND (1), GIRLFRIEND, PENFRIEND, SCHOOL FRIEND

> **WORDFINDER** 联想词: acquaintance, bond, buddy, companion, comrade, mate, neighbour, platonic, playmate

- **SUPPORTER** 支持者 **2** a person who supports an organization, a charity, etc., especially by giving or raising money; a person who supports a particular idea, etc. 赞助者；支持者: *the Friends of St Martin's Hospital* 圣马丁医院的赞助者 ◇ *a friend of democracy* 维护民主的人
- **NOT ENEMY** 不是敌人 **3** a person who has the same interests and opinions as yourself, and who will help and support you 自己人；同志；同伙；同盟者: *You're among friends here—you can speak freely.* 这儿都是自己人，有话直说吧。
- **SILLY/ANNOYING PERSON** 愚蠢的 / 讨厌的人 **4** (*ironic*) used to talk about sb you do not know who has done sth silly or annoying（指做傻事或烦人的事而说话者不认识的人）: *I wish our friend at the next table would shut up.* 但愿我们邻桌那位仁兄闭嘴。
- **IN PARLIAMENT/COURT** 议会；法庭 **5** (in Britain 英国) used by a member of parliament to refer to another member of parliament or by a lawyer to refer to another lawyer in a court of law（议员间或律师间的一种称呼）朋友，阁下，同人: *my* ***honourable friend****, the member for Henley* (= in the House of Commons) 我尊敬的朋友亨利区议员（下院用语）◇ *my* ***noble friend*** (= in the House of Lords) 我尊贵的朋友（上院用语）◇ *my* ***learned friend*** (= in a court of law) 我博学的同人（法庭用语）
- **IN RELIGION** 宗教 **6 Friend** a member of the Society of Friends（新教）公谊会成员 SYN **Quaker**

IDM **be/make 'friends (with sb)** to be/become a friend of sb 是 / 成为（某人的）朋友: *We've been friends for years.* 我们是多年的朋友了。◇ *They had a quarrel, but they're friends again now.* 他们吵过架，不过现在又和好了。◇ *Simon finds it hard to make friends with other children.* 西蒙感到难以和其他孩子交朋友。 **be (just) good 'friends** used to say that two friends are not having a romantic relationship with each other（无恋爱关系）（只）是好朋友 **a ˌfriend in 'need (is a ˌfriend in'deed)** (*saying*) a friend who gives you help when you need it (is a true friend) 患难的朋友（才是真正的朋友）；患难之交（见真情） **have ˌfriends in high 'places** to know important people who can help you 有位高权重的朋友；有贵人相助 ➲ MORE AT MAN *n.*

friend·less /'frendləs/ *adj.* without any friends 没有朋友的

friend·ly /'frendli/ *adj., noun*

■ *adj.* (**friend·lier**, **friend·li·est**) **1** behaving in a kind and pleasant way because you like sb or want to help them 友爱的；友好的: *a warm and friendly person* 热情友好的人 ◇ **~ to/toward(s) sb** *Everyone was very friendly towards me.* 每个人都对我十分友好。 OPP **unfriendly 2** showing kindness; making you feel relaxed and as though you are among friends 善意的；亲切的；和蔼可亲的: *a friendly smile/welcome* 亲切的微笑；友好的欢迎 ◇ *a small hotel with a friendly atmosphere* 宾至如归的小旅馆 OPP **unfriendly 3** **~ (with sb)** treating sb as a friend 朋友似的: *We soon became friendly with the couple next door.* 我们很快就和隔壁的夫妇友好相处了。◇ *She was* ***on friendly terms*** *with most of the hospital staff.* 她和医院大多数工作人员关系融洽。 **4** (especially of the relationship between countries 尤指国与国之间的关系) not treating sb/sth as an enemy 友好的；和睦的: *to maintain* ***friendly relations*** *with all countries* 与所有国家保持友好关系 OPP **hostile 5** (often in compound adjectives 常构成复合形容词) that is helpful and easy to use; that helps sb/sth or does not harm it 好用的；有用的；无害的: *This software is much friendlier than the previous version.* 这个软件比之前的版本好用得多。◇ *environmentally-friendly farming methods* 环保耕作法 ◇ *ozone-friendly cleaning materials* 对臭氧无害的清洁材料 ➲ SEE ALSO USER-FRIENDLY **6** in which the people, teams, etc. taking part are not seriously competing against each other（比赛）为增进友谊的；非对抗性的: *a friendly argument* 友好的辩论 ◇ *friendly rivalry* 友好竞争 ◇ (*BrE*) *It was only a friendly match.* 这仅是一场友谊赛。 ▶ **friend·li·ness** *noun* [U]

■ *noun* (*pl.* **-ies**) (*also* **'friendly match**) (*both BrE*) a game of football (SOCCER), etc. that is not part of an important competition（足球等的）友谊赛

ˌfriendly 'fire *noun* [U] in a war, if people are killed or injured by **friendly fire**, they are hit by a bomb or weapon that is fired by their own side 误杀，误伤（战争中由己方或友军造成的死伤） SYN **fratricide**

'friendly society *noun* (in Britain) an organization that people pay regular amounts of money to, and which gives them money when they are ill/sick or old（英国）互助会（会员定期交费以备生病或年老之用）

friend·ship /'frendʃɪp/ *noun* **1** [C] a relationship between friends 友谊；朋友关系: *a* ***close/lasting/lifelong friendship*** 亲密的 / 持久的 / 终生的友谊 ◇ *friendships formed while she was at college* 她在大学时建立的友谊 ◇ **~ with sb** *He seemed to have already* ***struck up*** (= begun) ***a friendship*** *with Jo.* 他似乎已经开始和乔交朋友了。◇ **~ between A and B** *It's the story of an extraordinary friendship between a boy and a seal.* 这是一个关于男孩和海豹之间非凡友谊的故事。 **2** [U] the feeling or relationship that friends have; the state of being friends 友情；友谊；友好: *Your friendship is very important to me.* 你的友情对我非常重要。◇ *a conference to promote international friendship* 促进国际友好关系的会议

frier = FRYER

Frie·sian /'friːʒn/ (*BrE*) (*NAmE* **Hol·stein**) *noun* a type of black and white cow that produces a lot of milk 黑白花乳牛，荷兰牛（产奶量很大）

frieze /friːz/ *noun* **1** a border that goes around the top of a room or building with pictures or CARVINGS on it 饰带，带状装饰 **2** a long narrow picture, usually put up in a school, that children have made or that teaches them sth 长条横幅图画（通常校内展示的学生习作或有教育意义的图画）

frig·ate /'frɪgət/ *noun* a small fast ship in the navy that travels with other ships in order to protect them（小型）护卫舰

frig·ging /'frɪgɪŋ/ *adv., adj.* [only before noun] (*taboo, slang*) a swear word that many people find offensive, used to emphasize a comment or an angry statement to avoid saying 'fucking'（避免使用 fucking 而说的粗话）该死地（的），他妈地（的）: *It's frigging cold outside.* 外面真他妈的冷。◇ *Mind your own frigging business!* 别他妈多管闲事!

fright /fraɪt/ *noun* **1** [U] a feeling of fear 惊吓；恐怖: *to cry out* ***in fright*** 吓得大声叫喊 ◇ *He was shaking* ***with fright****.* 他吓得发抖。➲ SYNONYMS AT FEAR ➲ SEE ALSO STAGE FRIGHT **2** [C] an experience that makes you feel fear 使人惊吓的经历；恐怖的经历：*You **gave me a fright** jumping out at me like that.* 你这样跳起来扑向我，把我吓了一大跳。◇ *I got the **fright of my life**.* 我吓得要命。

IDM **look a 'fright** (*old-fashioned, BrE*) to look ugly or ridiculous 模样丑陋；像丑八怪；样子古怪 **take 'fright (at sth)** (*formal*) to be frightened by sth（因某事）受惊吓：*The birds took fright and flew off.* 鸟受惊飞走了。

fright·en /'fraɪtn/ *verb* [T, I] ~ **(sb)** | ~ **sb to do sth** to make sb suddenly feel afraid 使惊吓；使惊恐：*Sorry, I didn't mean to frighten you.* 对不起，我没有吓唬你的意思。◇ *She's not easily frightened.* 她不是能轻易吓倒的。◇ *She **doesn't frighten easily*** (= it is not easy to make her afraid). 她不是能轻易吓倒的。 IDM SEE DAYLIGHTS, DEATH, LIFE

PHR V **,frighten sb/sth↔a'way/'off** | **,frighten sb/sth a'way from sth** **1** to make a person or an animal go away by making them feel afraid 把…吓走（或吓跑）：*He threatened the intruders with a gun and frightened them off.* 他用枪威胁闯入者，把他们吓跑了。**2** to make sb afraid or nervous so that they no longer want to do sth 把…吓得不敢（做某事）：*The high prices have frightened off many customers.* 高价使许多顾客却步。 **'frighten sb into sth/into doing sth** to make sb do sth by making them afraid 把…吓得做某事

▼ SYNONYMS 同义词辨析

frighten

scare • alarm • terrify

These words all mean to make sb afraid. 以上各词均含使害怕、使恐惧之义。

frighten to make sb feel afraid, often suddenly 指（常突如其来地）使惊吓、使惊恐：*He brought out a gun and frightened them off.* 他掏出一把枪，把他们吓跑了。

scare to make sb feel afraid 指使害怕、使恐惧：*They managed to scare the bears away.* 他们设法把那些熊吓跑了。

alarm to make sb anxious or afraid 指使惊恐、使害怕、使担心：*It alarms me that nobody takes this problem seriously.* 谁都不认真对待这个问题，我非常担心。 NOTE **Alarm** is used when sb has a feeling that sth unpleasant or dangerous might happen in the future; the feeling is often more one of worry than actual fear. * alarm 指令人担心不好的事情或危险可能发生，多为忧虑而非真的害怕。

terrify to make sb feel extremely afraid 指使恐惧、使十分害怕、使惊吓：*Flying terrified her.* 她害怕坐飞机。

FRIGHTEN OR SCARE? 用 frighten 还是 scare?

Scare is slightly more informal than **frighten**. * scare 较 frighten 稍非正式。

PATTERNS

- to frighten/scare sb/sth **away/off**
- to frighten/scare/terrify sb **into** doing sth
- **It** frightens/scares/alarms/terrifies me **that...**
- **It** frightens/scares/alarms/terrifies me **to** think, see, etc.

---

fright·ened /'fraɪtnd/ *adj.* afraid; feeling fear 惊吓的；受惊的；害怕的：*a frightened child* 受了惊吓的小孩 ◇ *Don't be frightened.* 别害怕。◇ *He sounded frightened.* 他听起来受了惊。◇ ~ **of sth** *What are you frightened of?* 你怕什么？◇ ~ **of doing sth** *I'm frightened of walking home alone in the dark.* 我害怕在黑夜单独走路回家。◇ ~ **to do sth** *I'm too frightened to ask him now.* 现在我吓得不敢问他了。◇ ~ **that...** *She was frightened that the plane would crash.* 她害怕飞机会坠毁。◇ ~ **for sb** *I'm frightened for him* (= that he will be hurt, etc.). 我为他担惊受怕。◇ (*informal*) *I'd never do that. I'd be **frightened to death**.* 我绝不会干。我会吓死的。 SYNONYMS AT AFRAID IDM SEE SHADOW *n.*, WIT

fright·en·ers /'fraɪtnəz; *NAmE* -nərz/ *noun* [pl.]

IDM **put the 'frighteners on sb** (*BrE, slang*) to threaten sb in order to make them do what you want 威逼，胁迫（某人做某事）

fright·en·ing /'fraɪtnɪŋ/ *adj.* making you feel afraid 引起恐惧的；使惊恐的；骇人的：*a frightening experience/prospect/thought* 可怕的经历／景象／想法 ◇ ***It's frightening** to think it could happen again.* 想到此事可能再次发生就使人不寒而栗。 ▶ **fright·en·ing·ly** *adv.*

fright·ful /'fraɪtfl/ *adj.* (*old-fashioned, especially BrE*) **1** (*informal*) used to emphasize how bad sth is 极坏的；很糟的 SYN **awful, terrible**：*It was absolutely frightful!* 简直糟透了！◇ *This room's in a frightful mess.* 房间里乱七八糟。 **2** very serious or unpleasant 十分严重的；令人很不愉快的 SYN **awful, terrible**：*a frightful accident* 十分严重的事故

fright·ful·ly /'fraɪtfəli/ *adv.* (*old-fashioned, especially BrE*) very; extremely 十分；极其 SYN **awfully, terribly**：*I'm frightfully sorry.* 我非常抱歉。

'fright wig *noun* a WIG with the hair standing up or sticking out, especially worn by a CLOWN（尤指小丑戴的发丝竖立或四散的）滑稽假发

fri·gid /'frɪdʒɪd/ *adj.* **1** (of a woman 女子) not able to enjoy sex 性冷淡的；达不到性高潮的 **2** very cold 寒冷的；严寒的：*frigid air* 冰冷的空气 WORDFINDER NOTE AT CLIMATE **3** not showing any feelings of friendship or kindness 冷淡的 SYN **frosty**：*a frigid voice* 冷冰冰的声音 ◇ *There was a frigid atmosphere in the room.* 房间里一片冷淡的气氛。 ▶ **fri·gid·ly** *adv.*

fri·gid·ity /frɪ'dʒɪdəti/ *noun* [U] (in a woman) the lack of the ability to enjoy sex（女子）性冷淡，性感缺失，性冷感

'frigid zone *noun* [C, usually sing.] (*specialist*) the area inside the Arctic Circle or Antarctic Circle（南、北极圈内的）寒带 COMPARE TEMPERATE ZONE, TORRID ZONE

frill /frɪl/ *noun* **1** [C] a narrow strip of cloth with a lot of folds that is attached to the edge of a dress, curtain, etc. to decorate it（衣服、窗帘等的）饰边，褶边，荷叶边 SYN **ruffle**：*a white blouse with frills at the cuffs* 袖口上有褶边的女衬衫 **2 frills** [pl.] things that are not necessary but are added to make sth more attractive or interesting 不实用的装饰；虚饰：*a simple meal with no frills* 简单的一顿便饭 SEE ALSO NO-FRILLS

frilled /frɪld/ *adj.* (*BrE*) decorated with frills 带饰边的；有褶边的 SYN **ruffled**

frilly /'frɪli/ *adj.* having a lot of frills 多饰边的；多褶边的：*a frilly blouse* 多褶边的女衬衫

fringe /frɪndʒ/ *noun, verb*

■ *noun* **1** [C, usually sing.] (*BrE*) (*NAmE* **bangs** [pl.]) the front part of sb's hair that is cut so that it hangs over their FOREHEAD 额前短垂发；刘海儿 VISUAL VOCAB PAGE V65 **2** [C] a strip of hanging threads attached to the edge of sth to decorate it（某物的）穗，缘饰，流苏 **3** [C] a narrow strip of trees, buildings, etc. along the edge of sth（沿…边缘的）一排（树木、房屋等）：*a fringe of woodland* 一条林带 ◇ *Along the coast, an industrial fringe had already developed.* 沿海岸一片带状工业区已发展起来。 **4** [C] (*BrE*) the outer edge of an area or a group（地区或群体的）边缘：*on the northern fringe of the city* 该市的北部边缘 ◇ *the urban/rural fringe* 市区／农村边缘 ◇ *the fringes of society* 社会的边缘 ◇ *Nina remained on the fringe of the crowd.* 尼娜仍然在人群的边上。 **5** [sing.] (*usually* **the fringe**) groups of people, events and activities that are not part of the main group or activity（指群体、事情或活动）次要部分，外围：*Street musicians have been gathering as part of the festival fringe.* 街头音乐人正聚集起来，为会演作助兴演出。◇ *fringe meetings at the party conference* 党会议的一些分组会议 IDM SEE LUNATIC *adj.*

■ *verb* [usually passive] ~ **sth** to form a border around sth 形成…的边缘：*The beach was fringed by coconut palms.*

沿海岸边长着椰子树。 ▶ **fringed** *adj.*： *a carpet with a fringed edge* 四边有穗子的地毯

ˈ**fringe benefit** *noun* [usually pl.] extra things that an employer gives you as well as your wages（工资外的）额外补贴，附加福利：*The fringe benefits include free health insurance.* 附加福利包括免费健康保险。

ˌ**fringe ˈmedicine** *noun* [U] any type of treatment which is not accepted by many people as being part of Western medicine, for example one using plants instead of artificial drugs 边缘疗法（不为多数人所接受的非西医疗法）

ˌ**fringe ˈtheatre** *noun* [U, C] (*BrE*) plays, often by new writers, that are unusual and question the way people think; a theatre where such plays are performed 边缘戏剧（常由新作家写）；边缘剧院 ➲ COMPARE OFF-BROADWAY

frip·pery /ˈfrɪpəri/ *noun* [C, usually pl., U] (*pl.* **-ies**) (*disapproving, especially BrE*) objects, decorations and other items that are considered unnecessary and expensive 不必要的昂贵饰品（或物件）

Fris·bee™ /ˈfrɪzbi/ *noun* a light plastic object, shaped like a plate, that is thrown from one player to another in a game 弗里斯比飞盘（投掷游戏用的飞碟） ➲ VISUAL VOCAB PAGE V41

fri·sée /ˈfriːzeɪ; *NAmE* friːˈzeɪ/ *noun* = CHICORY (2)

frisk /frɪsk/ *verb* **1** [T] ~ **sb** to pass your hands over sb's body to search them for hidden weapons, drugs, etc. 搜（某人）的身 **2** [I] ~ (**around**) (of animals 动物) to run and jump in a lively and happy way 活蹦乱跳 SYN **gambol, skip**：*Lambs frisked in the fields.* 羊羔在田野里活蹦乱跳。

frisky /ˈfrɪski/ *adj.* (**frisk·ier, friski·est**) **1** (of people or animals 人或动物) full of energy; wanting to play 活泼的；活蹦乱跳的；爱玩要的：*a frisky puppy* 活泼的小狗 **2** (*informal*) wanting to enjoy yourself in a sexual way 有性要求的；性兴奋的

fris·son /ˈfriːsɒ̃; *NAmE* friːˈsoːn/ *noun* [usually sing.] (*from French*) a sudden strong feeling, especially of excitement or fear 强烈兴奋感；恐惧感；震颤

fri·til·lary /frɪˈtɪləri; *NAmE* ˈfrɪtleri/ *noun* (*pl.* **-ies**) **1** a plant with flowers shaped like bells 贝母（花钟状） **2** a BUTTERFLY with orange-brown and black wings 豹纹蛱蝶

frit·ter /ˈfrɪtə(r)/ *verb, noun*

■ *verb*

PHR V ˌ**fritter sth↔aˈway** (**on sth**) to waste time or money on things that are not important 浪费（时间、金钱）；挥霍：*He frittered away the millions his father had left him.* 他挥霍掉了父亲留给他的数百万钱财。

■ *noun* (usually in compounds 通常构成复合词) a piece of fruit, meat or vegetable that is covered with BATTER and fried 油炸馅饼

fritz /frɪts/ *noun*

IDM **on the ˈfritz** (*NAmE, informal*) not working 出故障：*The TV is on the fritz again.* 电视机又出故障了。

fri·vol·ity /frɪˈvɒləti; *NAmE* -ˈvɑːl-/ *noun* (*pl.* **-ies**) (*often disapproving*) [U, C] behaviour that is silly or amusing, especially when this is not suitable 愚蠢的行为；可笑的表现；轻浮的举止：*It was just a piece of harmless frivolity.* 这仅是无恶意的愚蠢行为。◇ *I can't waste time on such frivolities.* 我不能把时间浪费在这种无聊的活动上。

frivo·lous /ˈfrɪvələs/ *adj.* (*disapproving*) **1** (of people or their behaviour 人或行为) silly or amusing, especially when such behaviour is not suitable 愚蠢的；可笑的：***frivolous comments/suggestions*** 愚蠢的话；可笑的建议 ◇ *Sorry, I was being frivolous.* 对不起，我失态了。**2** having no useful or serious purpose 无聊的；不严肃的：***frivolous pastimes/pleasures*** 无聊的消遣 / 娱乐 ▶ **frivo·lous·ly** *adv.*

frizz /frɪz/ *verb, noun*

■ *verb* [I, T] ~ (**sth**) (*informal*) (of hair 头发) to curl very tightly; to make hair do this（使）鬈曲，卷紧 ▶ **frizzy** *adj.* (**friz·zi·er, friz·zi·est**)： *frizzy hair* 鬈发

■ *noun* [U] (*disapproving*) hair that is very tightly curled 鬈发；鬈毛

friz·zle /ˈfrɪzl/ *verb* ~ **sth** to heat sth until it forms curls or until it burns 把…烫卷曲；把…烤焦：*frizzled hair* 鬈发 ◇ *frizzled bacon* 烤熏猪肉

fro /frəʊ; *NAmE* froʊ/ *adv.* IDM SEE TO *adv.*

frock /frɒk; *NAmE* frɑːk/ *noun* (*old-fashioned, especially BrE*) a dress 连衣裙；女装：*a party frock* 女式礼服

ˈ**frock coat** *noun* a long coat worn in the past by men, now worn only for special ceremonies 男长礼服；佛若克男礼服大衣

frog /frɒg; *NAmE* frɔːg; frɑːg/ *noun* **1** a small animal with smooth skin, that lives both on land and in water (= is an AMPHIBIAN). Frogs have very long back legs for jumping, and no tail. 蛙；青蛙：*the croaking of frogs* 蛙鸣 ➲ VISUAL VOCAB PAGE V13 **2 Frog** (*informal*) an offensive word for a French person 法国佬（对法国人的蔑称）

IDM **have, etc. a ˈfrog in your throat** to lose your voice or be unable to speak clearly for a short time（暂时）失音，嗓音嘶哑

frog·ging /ˈfrɒgɪŋ; *NAmE* ˈfrɔːg-; ˈfrɑːg-/ *noun* [U] a decorative fastening on a coat consisting of long wooden buttons and LOOPS 纺锤形纽扣

frog·let /ˈfrɒglət; *NAmE* ˈfrɔːg-; ˈfrɑːg-/ *noun* **1** a type of small frog 小青蛙 **2** a small frog that has recently changed from being a TADPOLE 幼蛙

frog·man /ˈfrɒgmən; *NAmE* ˈfrɔːg-; ˈfrɑːg-/ *noun* (*pl.* **-men** /-mən/) a person who works underwater, wearing a rubber suit, FLIPPERS, and special equipment to help them breathe 蛙人：*Police frogmen searched the lake for the murder weapon.* 警方的蛙人搜索这个湖，寻找谋杀凶器。➲ COMPARE DIVER (1)

frog·march /ˈfrɒgmɑːtʃ; *NAmE* ˈfrɔːgmɑːrtʃ; ˈfrɑːg-/ *verb* ~ **sb + adv./prep.** (*BrE*) to force sb to go somewhere by holding their arms tightly so they have to walk along with you 紧抓双臂押送；挟持而行：*He was grabbed by two men and frogmarched out of the hall.* 他被两个男人紧抓双臂押出大厅。

frog·spawn /ˈfrɒgspɔːn; *NAmE* ˈfrɔːg-; ˈfrɑːg-/ *noun* [U] an almost transparent substance that looks like jelly and contains the eggs of a FROG 蛙卵；蛙的卵块 ➲ VISUAL VOCAB PAGE V13

fro·ing /ˈfrəʊɪŋ; *NAmE* ˈfroʊɪŋ/ *noun* IDM SEE TOING

frolic /ˈfrɒlɪk; *NAmE* ˈfrɑːl-/ *verb, noun*

■ *verb* (**-ck-**) [I] to play and move around in a lively, happy way 嬉戏；嬉闹：*children frolicking on the beach* 在海滩上嬉戏的儿童

■ *noun* [C, U] (*old-fashioned*) a lively and enjoyable activity during which people forget their problems and responsibilities 欢乐的活动：*It was just a harmless frolic.* 那不过是个没有恶意的嬉闹游戏。

frolic·some /ˈfrɒlɪksəm; *NAmE* ˈfrɑːl-/ *adj.* (*especially literary*) playing in a lively happy way 嬉戏的；欢闹的：*frolicsome lambs* 嬉戏的羊羔

from 🔑 /frəm; *strong form* frɒm; *NAmE* frʌm; *strong form* frɑːm/ *prep.* HELP For the special uses of **from** in phrasal verbs, look at the entries for the verbs. For example **keep sth from sb** is in the phrasal verb section at **keep**. * from 在短语动词中的特殊用法见有关动词词条。如 keep sth from sb 在词条 keep 的短语动词部分。**1** 🔑 used to show where sb/sth starts（表示起始点）从…起，始于：*She began to walk away from him.* 她开始离他而去。◇ *Has the train from Bristol arrived?* 从布里斯托尔开来的火车到了没有？ **2** 🔑 used to show when sth starts（表示开始的时间）从…开始：*We're open from 8 a.m. to 7 p.m. every day.* 我们每天从早 8 点至晚 7 点营业。◇ *He was blind from birth.* 他天生失明。 **3** 🔑 used to show who sent or gave sth/sb（表示由某人发出或给出）寄自，得自：*a letter from my* *brother* 我哥哥来的信 ◇ *information from witnesses* 证人提供的信息 ◇ *the man from* (= representing) *the insurance company* 保险公司的人 **4** 🔑 used to show what the origin of sb/sth is（表示来源）来自，源于，出自，从…来：*I'm from Italy.* 我是意大利人。◇ *documents from the sixteenth century* * 16 世纪的文献 ◇ *quotations from Shakespeare* 莎士比亚语录 ◇ *heat from the sun* 太阳热 **5** 🔑 used to show the material that sth is made of（表示所用的原料）由…（制成）：*Steel is made from iron.* 钢是由铁炼成的。 **6** 🔑 used to show how far apart two places are（表示两地的距离）离：*100 metres from the scene of the accident* 离事故现场 100 米 **7** 🔑 used to show sb's position or point of view（表示位置或观点）从：*You can see the island from here.* 从这里可以看见那海岛。◇ *From a financial point of view the project was a disaster.* 从经济观点看，这个项目彻底失败了。 **8** 🔑 **~ sth (to sth)** used to show the range of sth（表示幅度或范围）从…（到）：*The temperature varies from 30 degrees to minus 20.* 温度在 30 度至零下 20 度之间变化。◇ *The store sells everything from shoelaces to computers.* 这家商店出售的商品从鞋带到计算机应有尽有。◇ *Conditions vary from school to school.* 各所学校的情况不同。 **9** 🔑 **~ sth (to sth)** used to show the state or form of sth/sb before a change（表示改变前的状态或形式）从…（到）：*Things have gone* ***from bad to worse.*** 情况越来越糟。◇ *translating from English to Spanish* 从英语译成西班牙语 ◇ *You need a break from routine.* 你需要从日常工作中解脱出来去休息一下。 **10** 🔑 used to show that sb/sth is separated or removed（表示分离或去除）：*The party was ousted from power after eighteen years.* 该党执政十八年后被赶下台。 **11** 🔑 used to show that sth is prevented（表示防止）使免遭，使免受：*She saved him from drowning.* 她救了他一命，使他免遭淹死。**12** 🔑 used to show the reason for sth（表示原因）由于，因为：*She felt sick from tiredness.* 她累得浑身不对劲。 **13** 🔑 used to show the reason for making a judgement（表示进行判断的原因）根据，从…来看：*You can tell a lot about a person from their handwriting.* 根据一个人的笔迹可以了解很多有关他的情况。◇ *From what I heard the company's in deep trouble.* 就我所听到的，这家公司已深陷困境。 **14** 🔑 used when distinguishing between two people or things（区别二者时用）与…（不同）：*Is Portuguese very different from Spanish?* 葡萄牙语与西班牙语区别很大吗？◇ *I can't tell one twin from the other.* 我分不出双胞胎中谁是谁。

IDM **from... on** 🔑 starting at the time mentioned and continuously after that 从…时起：***From now on*** *you can work on your own.* 从现在起你可以独自工作。◇ *She never spoke to him again from that day on.* 从那天起她就再没和他说话。

from·age frais /ˌfrɒmɑːʒ ˈfreɪ; *NAmE* frəˌmɑːʒ/ *noun* [U] (*from French*) a type of very soft cheese, similar to YOGURT 新鲜软干酪（类似酸乳酪）

frond /frɒnd; *NAmE* frɑːnd/ *noun* **1** a long leaf of some plants or trees, especially PALMS or FERNS. Fronds are often divided into parts along the edge.（尤指棕榈类或蕨类的）叶；蕨叶 **2** a long piece of SEAWEED that looks like one of these leaves（海藻长条形的）植物体，叶状体

front 🔑 /frʌnt/ *noun, adj., verb*

■ ***noun***

• **FORWARD PART/POSITION** 前部；前部位置 **1** 🔑 [C, usually sing.] (*usually* **the front**) the part or side of sth that faces forward; the side of sth that you look at first 正面：*The front of the building was covered with ivy.* 大楼的正面爬满了常春藤。◇ *The book has a picture of Rome* ***on the front.*** 书的封面有一张罗马的照片。◇ *The front of the car was badly damaged.* 轿车的前面严重损坏。 ➲ SEE ALSO SHOPFRONT, Y-FRONTS™ **2** 🔑 **the front** [sing.] the position that is in the direction that sb/sth is facing 前面；正前方：*Keep your eyes to the front and walk straight ahead.* 两眼看着正前方径直往前走。◇ *There's a garden* ***at the front of*** *the house.* 房子的前面有一座花园。 **3** 🔑 **the front** [sing.] the part of sth that is furthest forward 前部：*I prefer to travel* ***in the front of*** *the car* (= next to the driver). 我喜欢坐在轿车的前座。◇ *The teacher made me move my seat to the front of the classroom.* 老师把我的座位调到教室的前面。◇ *Write your name in the front of the book* (= the first few pages). 在前面的书页写上你的名字。

• **CHEST** 胸部 **4** 🔑 **sb's front** [sing.] the part of sb's body that faces forwards; sb's chest 身体前部；胸部：*She was lying on her front.* 她俯卧着。◇ *I spilled coffee down my front.* 我把咖啡溅到了前襟上。

• **SIDE OF BUILDING** 建筑物的面 **5** [C] **the west, north, south, east, etc. ~** the side of a large building, especially a church, that faces west, north, etc.（建筑物，尤指教堂朝西、北、东、南等的）面：*the west front of the cathedral* 大教堂的西侧

• **EDGE OF SEA/LAKE** 海边；湖边 **6 the front** [sing.] (*BrE*) the road or area of land along the edge of the sea, a lake or a river 海滨；湖畔；河边；沿海（或湖、河）道路：*Couples walked hand in hand along the front.* 对对情侣手牵手沿河边散步。 ➲ SEE ALSO SEAFRONT

• **IN WAR** 战争 **7** [C, usually sing.] an area where fighting takes place during a war 前线；前方：*More British troops have been sent to the front.* 更多的英国部队已派往前线。◇ *to serve at the front* 在前方服役 ◇ *fighting a war on two fronts* 在两条战线上战斗 ➲ SEE ALSO FRONT LINE, HOME FRONT

• **AREA OF ACTIVITY** 活动领域 **8** [C] a particular area of activity 活动领域；阵线：*Things are looking unsettled on the economic front.* 经济战线上的情况显得不稳定。◇ *Progress has been made* ***on all fronts.*** 各方面都取得了进展。

• **HIDING TRUE FEELINGS** 隐藏感情 **9** [sing.] behaviour that is not genuine, done in order to hide your true feelings or opinions 表面；外表：*Rudeness is just a front for her shyness.* 她的粗鲁只是为了掩饰羞怯。◇ *It's not always easy to* ***put on a*** *brave* ***front*** *for the family.* 常为家人装出勇敢的样子并不容易。◇ *The prime minister stressed the need to* ***present a united front*** (= show people that all members of the group have the same opinion about things). 首相强调必须表现出团结一致。

• **HIDING STH ILLEGAL** 掩盖非法活动 **10** [C, usually sing.] **~ (for sth)** a person or an organization that is used to hide an illegal or secret activity 非法（或秘密）活动掩护者：*The travel company is just a front for drug trafficking.* 这家旅行社不过是毒品交易的掩护场所。

• **POLITICAL ORGANIZATION** 政治组织 **11 Front** [sing.] used in the names of some political organizations（用于政治组织的名称）阵线：*the Animal Liberation Front* 动物解放阵线 ➲ SEE ALSO POPULAR FRONT

• **WEATHER** 天气 **12** [C] the line where a mass of cold air meets a mass of warm air（冷暖空气团接触的）锋：*a* ***cold/warm front*** 冷锋；暖锋

IDM **ˌfront and ˈcenter** (*NAmE*) in or into the most important position 在（或进入）最重要位置 **in ˈfront** *adv.* **1** 🔑 in a position that is further forward than sb/sth but not very far away 在前面：*Their house is the one with the big garden in front.* 他们的房子是前面有大花园的那一座。 **2** 🔑 in first place in a race or competition（赛跑或比赛）领先：*The blue team is currently in front with a lead of six points.* 蓝队目前以六分领先。 **in ˈfront of** *prep.* **1** 🔑 in a position that is further forward than sb/sth but not very far away 在…前面：*The car in front of me stopped suddenly and I had to brake.* 我前面那辆车突然停下来，我也只好刹车。◇ *The bus stops right in front of our house.* 公共汽车就停在我们的房子前面。◇ *He was standing in front of me in the line.* 在队列中他站在我的前面。◇ *She spends all day* ***sitting in front of*** (= working at) *her computer.* 她整天坐在计算机前（工作）。**2** 🔑 if you do sth **in front of** sb, you do it when they are there 当着…的面；在…面前：*Please don't talk about it in front of the children.* 请不要当着孩子们的面谈那件事。**3** 🔑 **~ sb** (of time 时间) still to come; not yet passed 未来；在…前面：*Don't give up. You still have your whole life in front of you.* 不要放弃，你的前面还有一辈子呢。 **out ˈfront 1** in the part of a theatre, restaurant, etc. where the public sits（剧院等）观众席；（餐厅等）座席：*There's only a small audience out front tonight.* 今夜观众席上人很少。**2** (*also BrE, informal* **out the ˈfront**) in the area near to the entrance to a building 在（建筑物）大门外：*I'll wait for you out (the) front.* 我在大门外等你。**up ˈfront** (*informal*) **1** as payment in advance 预付；先付：*We'll pay you half up front and the other half when you've finished the job.* 我们先付一半

给你，工作完成后再付另一半。 **2** (in sports 体育运动) in a forward position 在前锋位置： *to play up front* 担任前锋 ➲ SEE ALSO UPFRONT ➲ MORE AT BACK *n.*, CASH *n.*, EYE *n.*, LEAD[1] *v.*

■ ***adj.*** [only before noun] **1** on or at the front of sth 前面的；前部的；在前的；正面的： *front teeth* 门牙 ◇ *the front wheels of the car* 汽车的前轮 ◇ *We had seats in the front row.* 我们坐在前排座位。 ◇ *an animal's front legs* 动物的前腿 ◇ *Let's go through to the* ***front room*** (= the main room in a house where people sit and entertain guests). 咱们穿过去直到客厅。 ◇ *a front-seat passenger* 前排座位的一个乘客 ➲ COMPARE BACK *adj.* (1), HIND *adj.* **2** (*phonetics* 语音) (of a vowel 元音) produced with the front of the tongue in a higher position than the back, for example /iː/ in English 舌前位发的；舌前的 ➲ COMPARE BACK *adj.* (4), CENTRAL (5)

IDM **on the 'front burner** (*informal, especially NAmE*) (of an issue, a plan, etc. 问题、计划等) being given a lot of attention because it is considered important 处于前列重要地位；受到重视；为当务之急： *Anything that keeps education on the front burner is good.* 任何重视教育的事都是好事。 ➲ COMPARE ON THE BACK BURNER at BACK *adj.*

▼ **WHICH WORD?** 词语辨析

in front of / in the front of

- **In front of** can mean the same as **outside**, but not **opposite**. * in front of 可表示 outside 的词义，但不能表示 opposite 的词义： *I'll meet you in front of/outside your hotel.* 我在你的旅馆前面 / 外面接你。 ◇ *There's a bus stop in front of the house* (= on the same side of the road). 房子前面有一个公共汽车站（在公路的这面）。 ◇ *There's a bus stop opposite the house* (= on the other side of the road). 房子对面有一个公共汽车站（在公路的对面）。
- **In/at the front (of sth)** means 'in the most forward part of something'. * in / at the front (of sth) 表示在某物的最前部分： *The driver sits at the front of the bus.* 驾驶员坐在公共汽车的前端。 ◇ *Put the shortest flowers in the front (of the bunch).* 把最短的花放在花束的靠前位置。

■ ***verb***

- FACE STH 面向 **1** [T, I] to face sth or be in front of sth; to have the front pointing towards sth 面向；在…前面；朝；向： **~ sth** *The cathedral fronts the city's main square.* 大教堂面向城市的主广场。 ◇ **~ onto sth** *The line of houses fronted straight onto the road.* 这排房子正对着马路。
- COVER FRONT 覆盖正面 **2** [T, usually passive] **~ sth** to have the front covered with sth 用…作正面；用…覆盖正面： *a glass-fronted bookcase* 正面是玻璃的书柜
- LEAD GROUP 领导团体 **3** [T] **~ sth** to lead or represent an organization, a group, etc. 领导，代表（团体、组织等）： *He fronts a multinational company.* 他领导一家跨国公司。 ◇ *A former art student fronted the band* (= was the main singer). 乐队的主唱曾是一位艺术院校学生。
- PRESENT TV PROGRAMME 主持电视节目 **4** [T] **~ sth** (*especially BrE*) to present a television programme, a show, etc. 主持（电视节目、演出等）
- GRAMMAR 语法 **5** [T] **~ sth** (*linguistics* 语言) to give more importance to a part of a sentence by placing it at or near the beginning of the sentence, as in 'That I would like to see.' （为强调而）将（句子某一部分）前置

PHR V **'front for sb/sth** to represent a group or an organization and try to hide its secret or illegal activities 为…掩护（秘密、非法活动）： *He fronted for them in several illegal property deals.* 他为他们在几次非法房地产交易中作了掩护。

front·age /ˈfrʌntɪdʒ/ *noun* **1** [C, U] the front of a building, especially when this faces a road or river （建筑物，尤指临街或临河的）正面： *the baroque frontage of Milan Cathedral* 米兰大教堂巴罗克风格的正面 **2** [U] (*especially NAmE*) land that is next to a building, a street or an area of water 临街（或建筑物、河等的）土地： *They bought two miles of river frontage along the Colorado.* 他们买了两英里科罗拉多河沿河的土地。

'frontage road *noun* (*NAmE*) = SERVICE ROAD

front·al /ˈfrʌntl/ *adj.* [only before noun] **1** connected with the front of sth 正面的；前部的： *Airbags protect the driver in the event of a severe frontal impact.* 汽车若遇到正面猛烈撞击，安全气囊可以保护驾车者。 **2** (*also* ˌ**full-'frontal**) a **frontal** attack is very strong and direct （攻击或抨击）正面的，劈头盖脸的，直截了当的： *They launched a frontal attack on company directors.* 他们直截了当地对公司董事进行抨击。 **3** connected with a weather FRONT （天气）锋的： *a cold frontal system* 冷锋系 **4** (*medical* 医) connected with the front part of the head 前额的： *the frontal lobes of the brain* 大脑额叶 ▶ **front·al·ly** /-təli/ *adv.*

ˌfrontal 'lobe *noun* (*anatomy* 解) either of the two parts at the front of the brain that are concerned with behaviour, learning and personality 额叶（与行为、学习和个性有关）

the ˌfront 'bench *noun* [C+sing./pl. v.] the most important members of the government and the opposition in the British parliament, who sit in the front rows of seats 前座议员（英国议会中坐在前排座位的政府和反对党要员的总称）： *an Opposition front-bench spokesman on defence* 一名反对党前座议员国防事务发言人 ➲ COMPARE BACK BENCH

front·bench·er /ˌfrʌntˈbentʃə(r)/ *noun* an important member of the government or the opposition in the British parliament, who sits in the front rows of seats （英国议会中的）前座议员 ➲ COMPARE BACKBENCHER

ˌfront 'desk *noun* the desk inside the entrance of a hotel, an office building, etc. where guests or visitors go when they first arrive （旅馆等处的）前台，总台 ➲ COMPARE RECEPTION (1)

ˌfront 'door *noun* the main entrance to a house, usually at the front 正门；前门： *There's someone at the front door.* 前门有个人。 ➲ VISUAL VOCAB PAGE V18

'front-end *adj.* [only before noun] (*computing* 计) (of a device or program 器件或程序) directly used by a user, and allowing the user to use other devices or programs 前端的；前置的；用户直接调用的 ➲ COMPARE BACK-END (2)

ˌfront-ˌend 'loader *noun* (*especially NAmE*) a large vehicle with machinery for digging worked by a system of HYDRAULICS 前端装载机

fron·tier /ˈfrʌntɪə(r); *NAmE* frʌnˈtɪr/ *noun* **1** [C] a line that separates two countries, etc.; the land near this line 国界；边界；边境： **~ (between A and B)** *the frontier between the land of the Saxons and that of the Danes* 撒克逊人土地和古斯堪的纳维亚人土地的边界 ◇ **~ (with sth)** *a customs post on the frontier with Italy* 与意大利交界的边境上的海关关卡 ◇ *a* ***frontier town/zone/post*** 边陲小镇；边疆地带；边防站 ➲ SYNONYMS AT BORDER **2 the frontier** [sing.] the edge of land where people live and have built towns, beyond which the country is wild and unknown, especially in the western US in the 19th century （尤指 19 世纪美国西部的）开发地区边缘地带，边远地区： *a remote frontier settlement* 边远地区定居点 **3** [C, usually pl.] **~ (of sth)** the limit of sth, especially the limit of what is known about a particular subject or activity （学科或活动的）尖端，边缘： *to* ***push back the frontiers*** *of science* (= to increase knowledge of science) 开拓科学新领域 ◇ *to* ***roll back the frontiers*** *of government* (= to limit the powers of the government) 限制政府权力

fron·tiers·man /ˈfrʌntɪəzmən; *NAmE* frʌnˈtɪrz-/ *noun* (*pl.* **-men** /-mən/) a man living on the frontier especially one who lived in the western US during the 19th century （尤指 19 世纪美国西部的）开拓者，拓荒者，边远地区居民

fron·tis·piece /ˈfrʌntɪspiːs/ *noun* [usually sing.] a picture at the beginning of a book, on the page opposite the page with the title on it （与书名页相对一页上的）卷首插图

the ˌfront ˈline *noun* [sing.] an area where the enemies are facing each other during a war and where fighting takes place 前线：*Tanks have been deployed all along the front line.* 整个前线全都部署了坦克。◇ *front-line troops* 前线部队

IDM in the front line (of sth) doing work that will have an important effect on sth 在最重要的岗位上；在第一线：*a life spent in the front line of research* 在研究的第一线度过的一生

ˌfront-ˈload *verb* **1 ~ sth** (*business* 商) to spread the costs of a project so that more of the money is spent in the earlier stages 将（成本）的大头提前花费：*a need to front-load budget spending* 前期花费大部分预算支出的需要 ◇ *the positive effects of front-loading funds* 前期投入大部分资金的好处 **2 ~ sth** to organize work on a project or information in a document so that the more important work or information is done or placed first 将（项目或文章）的重点前置：*Teach your students to front-load their research.* 教学生从事研究时学会前紧后松。

front·man /ˈfrʌntmæn/ *noun* (*pl.* **-men** /-men/) **1** a person who represents an organization and tries to make its activities seem acceptable to the public, although in fact they may be illegal（某组织的）代表，头面人物；（非法活动的）掩护者：*He acted as a frontman for a drugs cartel.* 他给一个毒品集团当掩护。**2** the leader of a group of musicians 乐队领衔者 **3** (*BrE*) a person who presents a television programme 电视节目主持人

ˌfront ˈoffice *noun* [sing.] (*especially NAmE*) the part of a business concerned with managing things or dealing with the public（企业的）管理部门，与公众打交道的部门

ˌfront-of-ˈhouse *noun* [U] (*BrE*) **1** the parts of a theatre that are used by the audience（剧院的）观众席 **2** (often used as an adjective 常用作形容词) the business of dealing with an audience at a theatre, for example selling tickets and programmes（剧院的）前台事务，观众厅工作

ˌfront ˈpage *noun* the first page of a newspaper, where the most important news is printed（报纸的）头版：*The story was on the front pages of all the tabloids.* 所有小报都在头版报道了这件事。▸ **ˈfront-page** *adj.* [only before noun]：*The divorce made **front-page news**.* 这桩离婚成了头版新闻。

ˌfront ˈrunner *noun* a person, an animal or an organization that seems most likely to win a race or competition（赛跑或竞赛中）最可能获胜者，领先者

ˌfront-wheel ˈdrive *noun* [U] a system in which power from the engine is sent to the front wheels of a vehicle 前轮驱动系统 ⊃ COMPARE REAR-WHEEL DRIVE

frost /frɒst; *NAmE* frɔːst/ *noun, verb*

■ ***noun*** **1** [U, C] a weather condition in which the temperature drops below 0°C (= FREEZING POINT) so that a thin white layer of ice forms on the ground and other surfaces, especially at night 严寒天气；霜冻；冰点以下的温度：*It will be a clear night with some **ground frost**.* 今夜晴，部分地面有霜冻。◇ *a **sharp/hard/severe frost*** 酷寒 ◇ *There were ten degrees of frost* (= the temperature dropped to –10°C) *last night.* 昨夜零下 10 摄氏度。◇ *frost damage* 霜冻害 **2** [U] the thin white layer of ice that forms when the temperature drops below 0°C 霜：*The car windows were covered with frost.* 车窗玻璃结了霜。⊃ SEE ALSO HOAR FROST

■ ***verb*** **1** [T, I] to cover sth or to become covered with a thin white layer of ice（使）蒙上霜，结霜：**~ sth (over/up)** *The mirror was frosted up.* 镜子蒙了一层霜。◇ **~ (over/up)** *The windows had frosted over.* 窗子结满了霜。**2** [T] **~ sth** (*especially NAmE*) to cover a cake with ICING/FROSTING 给（糕饼）覆上糖霜

frost·bite /ˈfrɒstbaɪt; *NAmE* ˈfrɔːst-/ *noun* [U] a medical condition in which parts of the body, especially the fingers and toes, become damaged as a result of extremely cold temperatures 冻伤；冻疮 ▸ **frost·bit·ten** /ˈfrɒstbɪtn; *NAmE* ˈfrɔːst-/ *adj.*

frost·ed /ˈfrɒstɪd; *NAmE* ˈfrɔːstɪd/ *adj.* **1** [only before noun] (of glass 玻璃) that has been given a rough surface, so that it is difficult to see through 毛面的；磨砂的 **2** (*especially NAmE*) (of cakes, etc. 糕饼等) covered with ICING/FROSTING 覆有（或撒有）糖霜的 **3** covered with FROST 结霜的：*the frosted garden* 寒霜覆盖的花园 **4** containing very small shiny pieces 含有闪光小颗粒的：*frosted eye-shadow* 闪光点眼影

frost·ing /ˈfrɒstɪŋ; *NAmE* ˈfrɔːst-/ *noun* [U] **1** (*NAmE*) = ICING **2** (*BrE*) the crime of stealing a vehicle that has been left with the engine running in cold weather so that the engine warms up (冷天趁发动机预热车辆无人看管时下手的）盗窃车辆罪

frosty /ˈfrɒsti; *NAmE* ˈfrɔːsti/ *adj.* (**frost·ier**, **frosti·est**) **1** (of the weather 天气) extremely cold; cold with FROST 严寒的；霜冻的：*a frosty morning* 严寒的早晨 ◇ *He breathed in the frosty air.* 他吸进冰冷的空气。**2** covered with FROST 结霜的：*frosty fields* 结霜的田地 **3** unfriendly, in a way that suggests that sb does not approve of sth 冷淡的；冷若冰霜的：*a **frosty look/reply*** 冷冰冰的样子；冷淡的答复 ◇ *The latest proposals were given a frosty reception.* 对最新的建议反应冷淡。▸ **frost·ily** /-ɪli/ *adv.*：*'No, thank you,' she said frostily.* "不，谢谢你。" 她冷冰冰地说。

froth 泡沫　　foam 泡沫剂

bubble 气泡

bubble 肥皂泡

bubbles 气泡　　blowing bubbles 吹肥皂泡

froth /frɒθ; *NAmE* frɔːθ/ *noun, verb*

■ ***noun*** **1** [U] a mass of small bubbles, especially on the surface of a liquid（尤指液体表面的）泡沫，泡 SYN **foam**：*a glass of beer with thick froth on top* 上面有厚厚一层泡沫的一杯啤酒 **2** [U] ideas, activities, etc. that seem attractive and enjoyable but have no real value 华而不实的思想（或活动等）**3** [sing.] **~ of sth** something that looks like a mass of small bubbles on liquid 泡沫状物：*a froth of black lace* 起泡状的黑色花边

■ ***verb*** **1** [I, T] **~ (sth)** if a liquid **froths**, or if sb/sth **froths** it, a mass of small bubbles appears on the surface（使）起泡沫：*a cup of frothing coffee* 一杯起泡的咖啡 **2** [I] to produce a lot of SALIVA (= liquid in your mouth)（口）吐白沫：*The dog was **frothing at the mouth**.* 这条狗口吐白沫。◇ (*figurative*) *He **frothed at the mouth*** (= was very angry) *when I asked for more money.* 我还要钱时他气得七窍生烟。

frothy /ˈfrɒθi; *NAmE* ˈfrɔːθi/ *adj.* (**froth·ier**, **frothi·est**) **1** (of liquids 液体) having a mass of small bubbles on the surface 有泡沫的；起泡沫的：*frothy coffee* 泡沫咖啡 **2** seeming attractive and enjoyable but having no real value 华而不实的；夸夸其谈的；花架子的：*frothy romantic novels* 轻浮浅薄的浪漫小说 **3** (of clothes or cloth 衣服或布料) light and delicate 轻薄精巧的

frown /fraʊn/ *verb, noun*

■ ***verb*** [I, T] to make a serious, angry or worried expression by bringing your EYEBROWS closer together so that lines appear on your FOREHEAD 皱眉；蹙额：~ (at sb/sth) *What are you frowning at me for?* 你为什么朝我皱眉头？◇ + speech *'I don't understand,' she frowned.* "我不懂。"她皱着眉说。➲ WORDFINDER NOTE AT EXPRESSION

PHR V **'frown on/upon sb/sth** to disapprove of sb/sth 不赞成；不同意；不许可：*In her family, any expression of feeling was frowned upon.* 她家里对任何感情的流露都不以为然。

■ *noun* [usually sing.] a serious, angry or worried expression on a person's face that causes lines on their FOREHEAD 皱眉；蹙额：*She looked up with a puzzled frown on her face.* 她抬头望着，满脸困惑，双眉紧锁。◇ *a slight frown of disapproval/concentration, etc.* 略显不赞成的脸色、全神贯注地微皱眉头等

frow·sty /'fraʊsti/ *adj.* (*BrE*) smelling bad because there is no fresh air 闷热的；不通风的；霉臭的 SYN **fusty**, **musty**：*a small frowsty office* 狭小憋气的办公室

froze PAST TENSE OF FREEZE

fro·zen /'frəʊzn; *NAmE* 'froʊzn/ *adj.* **1** [usually before noun] (of food 食物) kept at a very low temperature in order to preserve it 冷冻的；冷藏的：*frozen peas* 冷冻豌豆 **2** [not usually before noun] (of people or parts of the body 人或身体部位) extremely cold 冻僵；极冷：*I'm absolutely frozen!* 我简直冻僵了！◇ *You look frozen stiff.* 你看来冻僵了。**3** (of rivers, lakes, etc. 河、湖等) with a layer of ice on the surface 冰封的；封冻的；结冰的 **4** (especially of ground 尤指地面) so cold that it has become very hard 冻硬的：*The ground was frozen solid.* 地面冻得硬邦邦的。**5** ~ with/in sth unable to move because of a strong emotion such as fear or horror 吓呆；惊呆：*She stared at him, frozen with shock.* 她惊呆了，直瞪着他。➲ SEE ALSO FREEZE

FRS /ˌef ɑːr 'es/ *abbr.* **1** (*NAmE*) FEDERAL RESERVE SYSTEM（美国）联邦储备系统 **2** (*BrE*) Fellow of the Royal Society (a title given to important British scientists) 皇家学院院士（英国杰出科学家的头衔）

fruc·tose /'frʌktəʊs; -təʊz; *NAmE* -toʊs; -toʊz/ *noun* [U] (*chemistry* 化) a type of sugar found in fruit juice and HONEY 果糖，左旋糖（见于果汁、蜂蜜中）

fru·gal /'fruːgl/ *adj.* **1** using only as much money or food as is necessary（对金钱、食物等）节约的，节俭的：*a frugal existence/life* 俭朴的生活 OPP **extravagant** **2** (of meals 饭菜) small, plain and not costing very much 简单廉价的 SYN **meagre**：*a frugal lunch of bread and cheese* 面包夹奶酪的简单午餐 ▸ **fru·gal·ity** /fru'gæləti/ *noun* [U] **fru·gal·ly** /-gəli/ *adv.*：*to live/eat frugally* 生活 / 吃饭节俭

fruit /fruːt/ *noun, verb*

■ *noun* **1** [C, U] the part of a plant that consists of one or more seeds and flesh, can be eaten as food and usually tastes sweet 水果：*tropical fruits, such as bananas and pineapples* 热带水果，如香蕉和菠萝 ◇ *Eat plenty of fresh fruit and vegetables.* 要多吃新鲜水果和蔬菜。◇ *a piece of fruit* (= an apple, an orange, etc.) 一个水果 ◇ *fruit juice* 果汁 ◇ *fruit trees* 果树 ➲ VISUAL VOCAB PAGES V32-33 ➲ COMPARE VEGETABLE (1) ➲ SEE ALSO DRIED FRUIT, FIRST FRUIT, SOFT FRUIT **2** [C] (*specialist*) a part of a plant or tree that is formed after the flowers have died and in which seeds develop 果实 **3** [C, usually pl.] (*literary*) all the natural things that the earth produces（大地的）产物；农产品 **4** [C] (*offensive*) an offensive word for a HOMOSEXUAL man 男同性恋者

IDM **the fruit/fruits of sth** the good results of an activity or a situation 成果；成效；结果：*to enjoy the fruits of your labours* (= the rewards for your hard work) 享受你艰苦劳动的成果 ◇ *The book is the fruit of years of research.* 这本书是多年研究的成果。➲ MORE AT BEAR *v.*, FORBIDDEN

■ *verb* [I] (*specialist*) (of a tree or plant 树或花草) to produce fruit 结果

fruit·ar·ian /fruː'teəriən; *NAmE* -'ter-/ *noun* a person who eats only fruit 只吃水果的人；果素者 ➲ COMPARE VEGETARIAN

'fruit bat *noun* a BAT (= an animal like a mouse with wings) that lives in hot countries and eats fruit 果蝠（热带大蝙蝠，以水果为食）

'fruit cake *noun* **1** [C, U] a cake containing dried fruit 干果蛋糕 **2 fruitcake** [C] (*informal*) a person who behaves in a strange or crazy way 怪人；疯子：*She's nutty as a fruitcake.* 她古怪得很。

ˌfruit 'cocktail *noun* [U] a mixture of pieces of fruit in liquid, sold in tins （罐装）什锦水果

ˌfruit 'cup *noun* [U, C] **1** (*BrE*) a drink consisting of fruit juices and pieces of fruit 什锦水果杯（用多种果汁和水果混合的饮料）**2** (*NAmE*) = FRUIT SALAD

fruit·er·er /'fruːtərə(r)/ *noun* (*old-fashioned, especially BrE*) a person who owns or manages a shop/store selling fruit 水果商 ➲ COMPARE GREENGROCER (1)

'fruit fly *noun* a small fly that eats plants that are decaying, especially fruit 果蝇；实蝇

fruit·ful /'fruːtfl/ *adj.* **1** producing many useful results 成果丰硕的；富有成效的 SYN **productive**：*a fruitful collaboration/discussion* 富有成效的合作 / 讨论 OPP **fruitless** **2** (*literary*) (of land or trees 土地或树木) producing a lot of crops 富饶的；丰产的 ▸ **fruit·ful·ly** /'fruːtfəli/ *adv.* **fruit·ful·ness** /'fruːtfəlnəs/ *noun* [U]

fruiti·ness /'fruːtinəs/ *noun* [U] (especially of wine 尤指果酒) the quality of tasting or smelling strongly of fruit 果味浓郁

fru·ition /fru'ɪʃn/ *noun* [U] (*formal*) the successful result of a plan, a process or an activity（计划、过程或活动的）完成，实现，取得成果：*After months of hard work, our plans finally came to fruition.* 经过几个月的艰苦工作，我们的计划终于完成了。◇ *His extravagant ideas were never brought to fruition.* 他不切实际的想法从来都没有实现过。

fruit·less /'fruːtləs/ *adj.* producing no useful results 没有成果的；无成效的；徒然的 SYN **unproductive**：*a fruitless attempt/search* 徒然的尝试 / 搜查 ◇ *Our efforts to persuade her proved fruitless.* 我们努力说服她，但毫无成效。OPP **fruitful** ▸ **fruit·less·ly** *adv.*

'fruit machine (*BrE*) (*also* **ˌone-armed 'bandit**, **'slot machine** *NAmE, BrE*) *noun* a gambling machine that you put coins into and that gives money back if particular pictures appear together on the screen 吃角子老虎赌博机；老虎机

ˌfruit 'salad (*NAmE also* **ˌfruit 'cup**) *noun* [U, C] a cold DESSERT (= a sweet dish) consisting of small pieces of different types of fruit 水果色拉

fruity /'fruːti/ *adj.* (**fruit·ier**, **fruiti·est**) **1** smelling or tasting strongly of fruit 果香味浓的：*The wine from this region is rich and fruity.* 这个地区产的葡萄酒浓郁醇香。**2** (of a voice or laugh 嗓音或笑声) deep and pleasant in quality 圆润的 **3** (*NAmE, informal*) (of people 人) slightly crazy 有点疯疯癫癫的；古怪的

frump /frʌmp/ *noun* (*disapproving*) a woman who wears clothes that are not fashionable 衣着老式的女子 ▸ **frumpy** (*also less frequent* **frump·ish**) *adj.*：*frumpy clothes* 过时的衣服 ◇ *a frumpy housewife* 穿着过时的家庭主妇

frus·trate /frʌ'streɪt; *NAmE* 'frʌstreɪt/ *verb* **1** ~ **sb** to make sb feel annoyed or impatient because they cannot do or achieve what they want 使懊丧；使懊恼；使沮丧：*What frustrates him is that there's too little money to spend on the project.* 使他懊恼的是可用于这个项目的资金太少。**2** ~ **sb/sth** to prevent sb from doing sth; to prevent sth from happening or succeeding 阻止；防止；挫败 SYN **thwart**：*The rescue attempt was frustrated by bad weather.* 营救行动因天气恶劣受阻。

frus·trated /frʌ'streɪtɪd; *NAmE* 'frʌstreɪtɪd/ *adj.* **1** feeling annoyed and impatient because you cannot do or achieve what you want 懊丧；懊恼；沮丧：*It's very easy to get frustrated in this job.* 这个工作很容易令人懊恼。◇ ~ **at/with sth** *They felt frustrated at the lack of progress.* 没有进展，他们感到懊丧。**2** (of an emotion 情感) having no effect; not being satisfied 无效的；没有得到满足的：*He stamped his foot in frustrated rage.* 他怒气难消，气得跺脚。◇ *frustrated desires* 没有得到满足的欲望 **3** [only before noun] unable to be successful in a particular career 失意的；不得志的：*a frustrated artist* 不得志的艺术家 **4** not satisfied sexually 性欲没有得到满足的

frus·trat·ing /frʌˈstreɪtɪŋ; *NAmE* ˈfrʌstreɪtɪŋ/ *adj.* causing you to feel annoyed and impatient because you cannot do or achieve what you want 令人懊恼的；令人沮丧的：*It's frustrating to have to wait so long.* 要等这么长时间，真令人懊恼。▶ **frus·trat·ing·ly** *adv.*：*Progress was frustratingly slow.* 进展慢得使人沮丧。

F

frus·tra·tion /frʌˈstreɪʃn/ *noun* **1** [U] the feeling of being frustrated 懊丧；懊恼；沮丧：*Dave thumped the table **in frustration**.* 戴夫懊恼得捶打桌子。◇ *She couldn't stand the frustration of not being able to help.* 她帮不上忙，懊丧得不行。◇ *sexual frustration* 性挫败 **2** [C, usually pl.] something that causes you to feel frustrated 令人懊丧（或懊恼、沮丧）的事物：*Every job has its difficulties and frustrations.* 每个工作都有困难和令人懊恼之处。◇ *She took out her frustrations on the children.* 她把气出在孩子们身上。**3** [U] ~ **of sth** (*formal*) the fact that sth is preventing sth/sb from succeeding 受阻；受挫；阻止；挫败：*the frustration of all his ambitions* 对他所有抱负的打击

fry 🔑 /fraɪ/ *verb, noun*

■*verb* (**fries**, **fry·ing**, **fried**, **fried**) **1** [T, I] ~ (**sth**) to cook sth in hot fat or oil; to be cooked in hot fat or oil 油炸；油煎；油炒：*fried fish* 炸鱼 ◇ *the smell of bacon frying* 煎熏肉的气味 ➲ RELATED NOUN FRY-UP ➲ COLLOCATIONS AT COOKING ➲ VISUAL VOCAB PAGE V28 ➲ SEE ALSO STIR-FRY *v.* **2** [I] (*informal*) to be burnt by the sun（被阳光）灼伤，晒伤：*You'll fry on the beach if you're not careful.* 你在海滩上若不小心会被太阳灼伤的。IDM ➲ SEE FISH *n.*

■*noun* **1** [pl.] very small young fish 鱼苗；鱼秧子 ➲ SEE ALSO SMALL FRY **2** [C] (*usually* **fries** [pl.]) (*especially NAmE*) = FRENCH FRY：*Would you like ketchup with your fries?* 你吃炸薯条要番茄酱吗？

fryer (*also* **frier**) /ˈfraɪə(r)/ *noun* **1** a large deep pan used for frying food in （深底）油炸锅：*a deep-fat fryer* 深油炸锅 **2** (*NAmE*) a young chicken that is suitable for frying （适于炸食的）仔鸡，雏鸡

ˈfrying pan (*NAmE also* **fry·pan**, **skil·let**) *noun* a large shallow pan with a long handle, used for frying food in 长柄平底煎锅 ➲ VISUAL VOCAB PAGE V28

IDM **out of the ˈfrying pan into the ˈfire** (*saying*) from a bad situation to one that is worse 跳出油锅又落火坑；逃出虎口又入狼窝；每况愈下

ˈfry-up *noun* (*BrE, informal*) a meal of fried food, such as BACON and eggs 一份油煎食物（如熏肉和鸡蛋）

FT (*also* **F/T**) *abbr.* (in writing 书写形式) FULL-TIME 全日制（的）；全职（的）：*The course is 1 year FT, 2 years PT.* 该课程全日制学习一年，非全日制学习两年。➲ COMPARE PT

Ft (*also* **Ft.** *especially in NAmE*) *abbr.* FORT 要塞；堡垒；兵营；军营：*Ft William* 威廉堡

ft (*BrE*) (*also* **ft.** *NAmE, BrE*) *abbr.* (in writing measurements) feet; foot（书写形式）英尺：*The room is 12ft × 9ft.* 房间面积是 12 英尺 × 9 英尺。

FTP /ˌef tiː ˈpiː/ *abbr.* file transfer protocol (a set of rules for sending files from one computer to another on the Internet) 文件传送协议（计算机通过互联网传输文件的一系列规则）

the FTSE index™ /ˈfʊtsi ɪndeks/ (*also* **the FT index** /ˌefˈtiː ɪndeks/, **the Fiˌnancial Times ˈindex**, **the Footsie™**) *noun* [sing.] a figure that shows the relative price of shares on the London Stock Exchange《金融时报》指数（伦敦证券交易所股票交易指数）

fuch·sia /ˈfjuːʃə/ *noun* [C, U] a small bush with flowers in two colours of red, purple or white, that hang down 倒挂金钟（灌木，花吊挂，呈红、紫或白色）

fuck /fʌk/ *verb, noun*

■*verb* (*taboo, slang*) **1** [I, T] ~ (**sb**) to have sex with sb 与…性交；肏 **2** [I, T] a swear word that many people find offensive that is used to express anger, disgust or surprise （表示气愤、厌恶、惊奇的粗话）他妈的，见他妈的鬼，滚他妈的蛋：*Oh, fuck! I've lost my keys.* 噢，他妈的！我把钥匙丢了。◇ ~ **sb/sth** *Fuck you—I'm leaving.* 滚你妈的蛋，我要走了。◇ *Fuck it! We've missed the train.* 真他妈的见鬼！我们错过了这趟火车。

IDM **ˌfuck ˈme** used to express surprise （表示惊奇）我他妈的见鬼了

PHR V **ˌfuck aˈround** (*BrE also* **ˌfuck aˈbout**) to waste time by behaving in a silly way 闲混；瞎混 HELP A more polite, informal way of saying this is **mess about** (*BrE*) or **mess around** (*NAmE, BrE*). 较礼貌和非正式的说法是 mess about（英式英语）或 mess around（美式英语、英式英语）。 **ˌfuck sb aˈround** (*BrE also* **ˌfuck sb aˈbout**) to treat sb in a way that is deliberately not helpful to them or wastes their time 瞎糊弄；故意浪费某人的时间 HELP A more polite, informal way of saying this is **mess sb about/around** (*BrE*). 较礼貌和非正式的说法是 mess sb about / around（英式英语）。 **ˌfuck ˈoff** (usually used in orders 通常用于命令) to go away 滚开；走开：*Why don't you just fuck off?* 你干吗不这就滚开？ **ˌfuck ˈup** to do sth badly or make a bad mistake 弄糟；搞坏；出了大错：*You've really fucked up this time!* 你这次确实搞得一塌糊涂！ HELP A more polite way to express this is **mess up**. 较礼貌的说法是 mess up。 **ˌfuck sb↔ˈup** to upset or confuse sb so much that they are not able to deal with problems in their life 使某人的感情受到创伤；完全打乱了某人的生活：*My parents' divorce really fucked me up.* 父母离婚真把我的生活全扰乱了。 HELP A more polite way to express this is **mess sb up**. 较礼貌的说法是 mess sb up。 **ˌfuck sth↔ˈup** to do sth badly or spoil sth 弄糟；搞坏：*I completely fucked up my exams.* 我完全考砸了。 HELP A more polite, informal way of saying this is **mess sth up**. 较礼貌和非正式的说法是 mess sth up。 **ˈfuck with sb** to treat sb badly in a way that makes them annoyed 亏待，恶待（使某人恼怒）：*Don't fuck with him.* 不要激怒他。 HELP A more polite way to express this is **mess with sb**. 较礼貌的说法是 mess with sb。

■*noun* (*taboo, slang*) **1** [C, usually sing.] an act of sex 性交；肏 **2** **the fuck** [sing.] used for emphasis, or to show that you are angry, annoyed or surprised（用于强调或表示气愤、厌恶或惊奇）他妈的：*What the fuck are you doing?* 你他妈的在干啥？ ◇ *Let's get the fuck out of here!* 咱们他妈的走吧！

IDM **not give a ˈfuck (about sb/sth)** to not care at all about sb/sth 毫不在乎；毫不关心 ➲ SEE ALSO F-WORD

ˌfuck ˈall *noun* [U] (*BrE, taboo, slang*) a phrase that many people find offensive, used to mean 'none at all' or 'nothing at all'（冒犯语）他妈的一点没有，他妈的根本没有：*You've done fuck all today.* 你他妈的今天啥也没干。

fuck·er /ˈfʌkə(r)/ *noun* (*taboo, slang*) a very offensive word used to insult sb （冒犯语）笨蛋，浑蛋

fuck·ing /ˈfʌkɪŋ/ *adj., adv.* (*taboo, slang*) a swear word that many people find offensive that is used to emphasize a comment or an angry statement（加强语气）该死的，他妈的：*I'm fucking sick of this fucking rain!* 这该死的雨真他妈的让我心烦！ ◇ *He's a fucking good player.* 他是个他妈的优秀球员。

IDM **ˈfucking well** (*especially BrE*) used to emphasize an angry statement or an order（强调愤怒或命令）：*You're fucking well coming whether you want to or not.* 不管你想不想来，你他妈的也要给我过来。

fud·dled /ˈfʌdld/ *adj.* unable to think clearly, usually as a result of being old or drinking alcohol 头脑糊涂的，思维不清的（常因年老或饮酒）

fuddy-duddy /ˈfʌdi dʌdi/ *noun* (*pl.* **fuddy-duddies**) (*old-fashioned, informal*) a person who has old-fashioned ideas or habits 守旧的人；老顽固；老古董；老古板 ▶ **fuddy-duddy** *adj.* ➲ MORE LIKE THIS 11, page R26

fudge /fʌdʒ/ *noun, verb*

■*noun* **1** [U] a type of soft brown sweet/candy made from sugar, butter and milk 法奇软糖，乳脂软糖（用糖、黄

油和牛奶制成）**2 a fudge** [sing.] (*especially BrE, rather informal*) a way of dealing with a situation that does not really solve the problems but is intended to appear to do so 敷衍，装模作样（没有真正解决问题）：*This solution is a fudge rushed in to win cheers at the party conference.* 这个解决方案是为了在党的会议上赢得赞誉而仓促搞出来的表面文章。

■ ***verb*** [T, I] ~ (**on**) **sth** (*rather informal*) to avoid giving clear and accurate information, or a clear answer 含糊其词；回避：*I asked how long he was staying, but he fudged the answer.* 我问他要待多久，但他含糊其词。◇ *Politicians are often very clever at **fudging the issue**.* 从政者都常常巧妙地回避问题。

fuel 🔑 /ˈfjuːəl/ *noun, verb*

■ ***noun*** **1** 🔑 [U, C] any material that produces heat or power, usually when it is burnt 燃料：***solid fuel*** (= wood, coal, etc.) 固体燃料 ◇ *nuclear fuels* 核燃料 ◇ *a car with high **fuel consumption*** 耗油量大的汽车 ➲ SEE ALSO FOSSIL FUEL ➲ WORDFINDER NOTE AT ENERGY **2** [U] a thing that is said or done that makes sth, especially an argument, continue or get worse（尤指使争论等继续或更加激烈的）刺激性言行：*The new information adds fuel to the debate over safety procedures.* 新信息对于有关安全程序的辩论是火上浇油。◇ *The revelations gave new fuel to angry opponents of the proposed law.* 新披露的情况使反对该法律提案的人更为激愤。◇ *His remarks simply **added fuel to the fire/flames** of her rage.* 他的话只是给她的愤怒火上浇油。

■ ***verb*** (**-ll-**, *US* **-l-**) **1** [T] ~ **sth** to supply sth with material that can be burnt to produce heat or power 给…提供燃料：*Uranium is used to fuel nuclear plants.* 铀用作核电厂的燃料。◇ *oil-fuelled power stations* 燃油发电厂 **2** [T, I] ~ (**sth**) (**up**) to put petrol/gas into a vehicle 给（交通工具）加油：*The helicopter was already fuelled (up) and ready to go.* 直升机已加好油，准备起飞。**3** [T] ~ **sth** to increase sth; to make sth stronger 增加；加强；刺激 SYN **stoke**：*to **fuel speculation/rumours/fears*** 引起猜测 / 谣传 / 恐惧 ◇ *Higher salaries helped to fuel inflation.* 工资提高刺激通货膨胀。➲ MORE LIKE THIS 36, page R29

ˈfuel cell *noun* a device that produces electricity directly from a fuel, such as HYDROGEN, by its reaction with another chemical, such as OXYGEN, without any burning, in order to supply power to a vehicle or machine 燃料电池

ˈfuel injection *noun* [U] a system of putting fuel into the engine of a car under pressure as a way of improving its performance（向汽车发动机的）喷吹燃料

ˈfuel rod *noun* (*specialist*) a long thin piece of fuel used in a nuclear power station（核电站的）燃料棒

fufu /ˈfuːfuː/ *noun* [U] (*WAfrE*) a smooth white food often eaten with soups or STEWS and made by boiling and crushing the roots of plants such as COCOYAMS and CASSAVA 馥馥白糕（将煮熟的芋头或木薯等碾碎制成，常与汤或炖菜一起吃）

fug /fʌɡ/ *noun* [sing.] (*BrE, informal*) air in a room that is hot and smells unpleasant because there are too many people in the room or because people are smoking（室内）闷热污浊的空气

fugal /ˈfjuːɡl/ *adj.* (*music* 音) similar to or related to a FUGUE 赋格式的；赋格曲的

fu·gi·tive /ˈfjuːdʒətɪv/ *noun, adj.*

■ ***noun*** ~ (**from sb/sth**) a person who has escaped or is running away from somewhere and is trying to avoid being caught 逃亡者；逃跑者；亡命者：*a fugitive from justice* 逃犯

■ ***adj.*** [only before noun] **1** trying to avoid being caught 逃亡的；逃跑的：*a fugitive criminal* 逃犯 **2** (*literary*) lasting only for a very short time 短暂的；易逝的 SYN **fleeting**：***a fugitive idea/thought*** 转瞬即逝的想法 / 思想

fugue /fjuːɡ/ *noun* (*music* 音) a piece of music in which one or more tunes are introduced and then repeated in a complicated pattern 赋格曲

-ful *suffix* **1** (in adjectives 构成形容词) full of; having the qualities of; tending to 充满…的；有…性质（或倾向）的：*sorrowful* 悲伤 ◇ *masterful* 专横 ◇ *forgetful* 健忘 **2** (in nouns 构成名词) an amount that fills sth 充满…的量：*handful* 一把 ◇ *spoonful* 一匙 ➲ MORE LIKE THIS 7, page R25

ful·crum /ˈfʊlkrəm; ˈfʌlk-/ *noun* (*pl.* **ful·crums** or **ful·cra** /ˈfʊlkrə; ˈfʌlk-/) **1** (*physics* 物) the point on which a LEVER turns or is supported（杠杆的）支点，支轴 **2** [usually sing.] the most important part of an activity or a situation（活动、情况的）最重要部分，支柱

ful·fil (*BrE*) (*NAmE* **ful·fill**) /fʊlˈfɪl/ *verb* (**ful·fill·ing, ful·filled, ful·filled**) **1** ~ **sth** to do or achieve what was hoped for or expected 实现：*to **fulfil your dream/ambition/potential*** 实现梦想 / 抱负；发挥潜力 **2** ~ **sth** (*formal*) to do or have what is required or necessary 履行；执行；符合；具备：*to **fulfil a duty/an obligation/a promise*** 履行职责 / 义务 / 诺言 ◇ *to **fulfil the terms/conditions** of an agreement* 执行协定条款 / 条件 ◇ *No candidate fulfils all the criteria for this position.* 没有一个候选人完全符合这个职位要求。**3** ~ **sth** to have a particular role or purpose 起…作用；目的是：*Nursery schools should **fulfil the function** of preparing children for school.* 幼儿园应该起到为儿童进小学作准备的作用。**4** ~ **sb/yourself** to make sb feel happy and satisfied with what they are doing or have done 使有成就感；使满足：*I need a job that really fulfils me.* 我需要一份真正令我感到满足的工作。◇ *He was able to fulfil himself through his painting.* 他通过绘画充分发挥了自己的才能。➲ MORE LIKE THIS 36, page R29 ▶ **ful·fil·ment** (*BrE*) (*NAmE* **ful·fill·ment**) *noun* [U]: *the fulfilment of a dream* 梦想的实现 ◇ *to find personal fulfilment* 寻求个人的满足 ➲ SYNONYMS AT SATISFACTION

ful·filled /fʊlˈfɪld/ *adj.* feeling happy and satisfied that you are doing sth useful with your life 感到满足的；觉得满意的；满足的：*He doesn't feel fulfilled in his present job.* 目前的工作未能让他感到满足。OPP **unfulfilled**

ful·fil·ling /fʊlˈfɪlɪŋ/ *adj.* causing sb to feel satisfied and useful 让人感觉有意义的；令人满足的：*a fulfilling experience* 有成就感的经历 OPP **unfulfilling** ➲ SYNONYMS AT SATISFYING

full 🔑 /fʊl/ *adj., adv.*

■ ***adj.*** (**full·er, fullest**)

• **WITH NO EMPTY SPACE** 满 **1** 🔑 ~ (**of sth**) containing or holding as much or as many as possible; having no empty space 满的；充满的；满是…的：*a full bottle of wine* 一满瓶葡萄酒 ◇ *She could only nod, because her mouth was full.* 她只能点点头，因为她嘴里塞满了东西。◇ *My suitcase was full of books.* 我的提箱装满了书。◇ *There were cardboard boxes **stuffed full of** clothes.* 有塞满衣服的一个个纸箱。◇ (*BrE*) *Sorry, the hotel is **full up** tonight.* 对不起，今晚旅馆客满。

• **HAVING A LOT** 大量 **2** 🔑 ~ **of sth** having or containing a large number or amount of sth（有）大量的；（有）许多的；丰富的：*The sky was full of brightly coloured fireworks.* 满天色彩绚丽的烟火。◇ ***Life is full of** coincidences.* 生活中巧合很多。◇ *Our new brochure is **crammed full of** inspirational ideas.* 我们新的小册子中振奋人心的妙计比比皆是。◇ *animals **pumped full of** antibiotics* 注入大量抗生素的动物 ◇ *She was full of admiration for the care she had received.* 她对所受到的关怀照顾赞不绝口。◇ *He smiled, his eyes full of laughter.* 他露出了笑容，双眼也满含着笑意。

• **TALKING A LOT** 话多 **3** ~ **of sth** (of a person 人) thinking or talking a lot about a particular thing（关于某事物）想得很多，谈得很多：*He was full of his new job and everything he'd been doing.* 他滔滔不绝地谈他的新工作和所做的一切。

• **WITH FOOD** 食物 **4** 🔑 (*BrE also* **ˌfull ˈup**) having had enough to eat 吃饱了的：*No more for me, thanks—I'm full up.* 谢谢，我不要了，我已经饱了。◇ *The kids still weren't full, so I gave them an ice cream each.* 孩子们还没有吃饱，所以我给他们每人一份冰淇淋。◇ *You can't run **on a full stomach**.* 饱餐之后不能跑步。

• **COMPLETE** 完全 **5** 🔑 [usually before noun] complete; with nothing missing 完全的；完整的；详尽的：*Full details are available on request.* 详情备索。◇ *I still don't think we've heard **the full story**.* 我还是认为我们未了解全部情况。◇ *a*

F

full English breakfast 全份英式早餐 ◇ *A full refund will be given if the item is faulty.* 如货有瑕疵将退回全部货款。◇ *Fill in your full name and address.* 填写全名和地址。◇ *The country applied for full membership of the European Union.* 这个国家申请成为欧洲联盟的正式成员。

- **AS MUCH AS POSSIBLE** 尽量 **6** [usually before noun] to the highest level or greatest amount possible 最高级的；尽量多的；最大量的 **SYN maximum**: *Many people don't use their computers to their* ***full potential.*** 很多人没有充分利用他们计算机的全部潜在功能。◇ *measures to achieve* ***full employment*** 力求充分就业的措施 ◇ *Students should* ***take full advantage of*** *the university's facilities.* 学生应该充分利用大学的设施。◇ *She came round the corner* ***at full speed.*** 她全速拐过弯道。
- **BUSY** 忙碌 **7** busy; involving a lot of activities 忙的；有很多活动的：*He'd had a very* ***full life.*** 他度过了一个丰富的人生。◇ *Her life was too full to find time for hobbies.* 她的生活太忙碌，没有业余爱好的时间。
- **FOR EMPHASIS** 强调 **8** [only before noun] used to emphasize an amount or a quantity（强调数量）足足的，整整的：*She is a full four inches shorter than her sister.* 她比姐姐足足矮四英寸。
- **MOON** 月亮 **9** appearing as a complete circle 圆的；满的：*The moon was full, the sky clear.* 圆月碧空。➲ SEE ALSO FULL MOON
- **FAT** 肥胖 **10** (of a person or part of the body 人或身体部分) large and round. 'Full' is sometimes used to avoid saying 'fat'. 丰满的；圆鼓鼓的（有时用 full 以避免用 fat）：*He kissed her full sensual lips.* 他吻了她那丰满性感的嘴唇。◇ *They specialize in clothes for women with a fuller figure.* 他们专为体形较丰满的女士做衣服。
- **CLOTHES** 衣服 **11** made with plenty of cloth; fitting loosely 宽松的；肥大的：*a full skirt* 宽裙
- **TONE/VOICE/FLAVOUR** 音调；嗓音；味道 **12** deep, strong and rich 圆浑的；圆润的；浓郁的：*He draws a unique full sound from the instrument.* 他用乐器奏出了独特圆浑的音调。◇ *the full fruity flavour of the wine* 这葡萄酒浓郁的水果味

IDM HELP Most idioms containing **full** are at the entries for the nouns and verbs in the idioms, for example **full of the joys of spring** is at **joy**. 大多数含 full 的习语，都可在该等习语中的名词及动词相关词条找到，如 full of the joys of spring 在词条 joy 下。**'full of it** (*informal, disapproving*) (of a person 指人) not telling the truth; tending to exaggerate things 乱说；夸大其词：*'You are so full of it!' she retorted furiously.* "你胡说！"她生气地反驳道。**'full of yourself** (*disapproving*) very proud; thinking only of yourself 自满；自视甚高；只顾自己 **in full** including the whole of sth 整个；全部：*The address must be printed in full.* 地址必须以印刷体详尽填写。**to the full** (*NAmE usually* **to the fullest**) to the greatest possible degree 达到最大程度；充分：*I've always believed in living life to the full.* 我总是相信生活要尽量充实。

■ *adv.* **~ in/on sth** directly 直接地；径直地：*She looked him full in the face.* 她径直望着他的脸。

'full back (*NAmE* **'fullback**) *noun* **1** [C] one of the defending players in football (SOCCER), HOCKEY or RUGBY whose position is near the goal they are defending（足球、曲棍球或橄榄球）后卫 **2** [C] the attacking player in AMERICAN FOOTBALL whose position is behind the QUARTERBACK and beside the HALF BACKS（美式足球）全卫 **3** [U] the position a full back plays at 后卫位置：*Hunter is at full back.* 亨特担任后卫。

ˌfull 'beam *noun* [U] (*BrE*) the brightest light that a vehicle's HEADLIGHTS can give, usually used when there are no street lights and no other traffic（车前灯的）最强亮度，最强光：*Even with the lights on full beam I couldn't see very far.* 即使把灯打到了最强光我还是看不了多远。

ˌfull-'blooded *adj.* [only before noun] **1** involving very strong feelings or actions; done in an enthusiastic way 感情强烈的；猛烈的；精力旺盛的；热情的：*a full-blooded attack* 猛烈攻击 **2** having parents, grandparents, etc. from only one race or country 全血缘的；纯血统的：*a full-blooded Scotsman* 纯血统的苏格兰人

ˌfull-'blown *adj.* [only before noun] having all the characteristics of sb/sth; fully developed 具所有特征的；成熟的：*full-blown AIDS* 完全型艾滋病 ◇ *The border dispute turned into a full-blown crisis.* 边境争端已演变成全面性的危机。

ˌfull 'board (*BrE*) (*NAmE* **Aˌmerican 'plan**) *noun* [U] a type of accommodation in a hotel, etc. that includes all meals（旅馆的）全食宿：*Do you require full or half board?* 你要全食宿还是半食宿？➲ WORDFINDER NOTE AT HOTEL ➲ COMPARE BED AND BREAKFAST, EUROPEAN PLAN, HALF BOARD

ˌfull-'bodied *adj.* having a pleasantly strong taste or sound（味道）浓郁的，浓烈的；（声音）圆润的，圆浑的：*a full-bodied red wine* 浓郁的红葡萄酒 ◇ *a full-bodied string section* 圆润悦耳的弦乐部

ˌfull-'colour (*especially US* **ˌfull-'color**) *adj.* [only before noun] printed using colours rather than just black and white 彩色的；全色的

ˌfull-court 'press *noun* [sing.] (*NAmE*) **1** (in BASKETBALL 篮球) a way of attacking in which the members of a team stay close to their opponents over the whole area of play 全场紧逼 **2** (*informal*) a strong effort to influence sb or a group of people by putting pressure on them 全面攻势；全面出击

ˌfull-'cream *adj.* (*BrE*) (of milk 牛奶) with none of the fat taken away 全脂的

full·er's earth /ˌfʊləz ˈɜːθ; *NAmE* ˌfʊlərz ˈɜːrθ/ *noun* [U] a type of CLAY used for cleaning cloth and making it thicker 漂白土

ˌfull 'face *adj., adv.* showing the whole of sb's face; not in PROFILE 脸正面的（地）；正脸的（地）：*a full-face view/portrait* 正面面孔 / 肖像

ˌfull-'fat *adj.* [usually before noun] (*especially BrE*) (of milk, cheese, etc. 牛奶、奶酪等) without any of the fat removed 全脂的

ˌfull-'fledged (*especially NAmE*) (*BrE also* **ˌfully 'fledged**) *adj.* completely developed; with all the qualifications necessary for sth 成熟的；完全合格的

ˌfull 'forward *noun* (in AUSTRALIAN RULES football 澳式橄榄球) an attacking player who plays near the opposing team's goal 全前锋

ˌfull-'frontal *adj., noun*

■ *adj.* [only before noun] **1** showing the whole of the front of a person's body 裸露正面的：*full-frontal nudity* 正面全裸 **2** = FRONTAL (2)

■ *noun* a picture or a scene in a film/movie which shows the naked body of a person from the front 正面全裸的照片（或电影镜头）

ˌfull-'grown *adj.* (of people, animals or plants 人或动植物) having reached the greatest size to which they can grow and stopped growing 长足了的；长成的；成熟的

ˌfull 'house *noun* **1** an occasion in a theatre, cinema/movie theater, etc. when there are no empty seats（剧院、电影院等）满座，客满：*They played to a full house.* 他们的演出座无虚席。**2** (in the card game of POKER) three cards of one kind and two of another kind 满堂红（扑克牌游戏中三张点数相同，另两张点数相同的一手牌）

ˌfull-'length *adj., adv.*

■ *adj.* [only before noun] **1** (of a mirror or picture 镜子或相片) showing the whole of a person's body 全身的：*a full-length portrait* 全身肖像 **2** (of a book, play, etc. 书、剧本等) not made shorter; of the usual length 足本的：*a full-length novel* 足本小说 **3** (of curtains or a window 窗帘或窗子) reaching the ground 长及地面的；落地的 **4** (of clothing 衣服) reaching a person's ankles 长及脚踝的：*a full-length skirt* 拖地长裙

■ *adv.* a person who is lying **full-length** is lying flat with their legs straight（身体）伸展开，伸直：*He was* *sprawled full-length across the bed.* 他手脚摊开横躺在床上。

ˌfull ˈmarks *noun* [pl.] (*BrE*) the highest mark/grade in a test, etc. (when you get nothing wrong) (成绩) 满分: *She got full marks in the exam.* 她考试得了满分。◇ (*figurative*) ***Full marks to Bill for an excellent idea!*** (= he deserves praise) 比尔的主意极妙，值得赞扬！

ˌfull ˈmoon *noun* [C, usually sing., U] the moon when it appears as a full circle; a time when this happens 满月；望月；望日 ➲ COMPARE HALF-MOON (1), HARVEST MOON, NEW MOON

full·ness /ˈfʊlnəs/ *noun* [U, sing.] **1** (of the body or part of the body 身体或身体部分) the quality of being large and round 丰满: *the fullness of her lips* 她丰满的双唇 **2** (of colours, sounds and flavours 颜色、声音和味道) the quality of being deep and rich (颜色) 深浓；(声音) 圆浑，圆润；(味道) 浓郁 **3** the quality of being complete and satisfying 完美；完全: *the fullness of life* 生命的圆满

IDM **in the fullness of ˈtime** when the time is appropriate, usually after a long period 在适当时候，时机成熟时 (尤指久待之后)

ˌfull-ˈon *adj.* (*informal*) used to say that sth is done to the greatest possible degree (表示最大程度) 完全的；最强烈的: *It was a full-on night out with the boys.* 这是与男孩们外出玩得最尽兴的一个晚上。

ˌfull-ˈpage *adj.* [only before noun] filling a complete page of a newspaper or magazine (报纸) 整版的；(杂志) 全页的: *a full-page ad* 整版广告

ˌfull ˈpoint *noun* = FULL STOP

ˈfull professor *noun* (*NAmE*) = PROFESSOR (1)

ˌfull-ˈscale *adj.* [only before noun] **1** that is as complete and thorough as possible 全面的；完全的；彻底的: *a full-scale attack* 全面攻击 **2** that is the same size as sth that is being copied 原尺寸的；和实物同样大小的: *a full-scale model* 原尺寸模型

ˌfull-ˈsize (*also* **ˌfull-ˈsized**) *adj.* [usually before noun] not made smaller; of the usual size 原尺寸的；和通常大小一样的: *a full-size model* 原尺寸模型 ◇ *a full-size snooker table* 标准尺寸的斯诺克球台

ˌfull ˈstop *noun, adv.*

■ ***noun*** (*also less frequent* **stop**) (*also* **ˌfull ˈpoint**) (*all BrE*) (*NAmE* **period**) the mark (.) used at the end of a sentence and in some abbreviations, for example *e.g.* 句点；句号

IDM **come to a full ˈstop** to stop completely 完全停止

■ ***adv.*** (*BrE*) (*also* **period** *NAmE, BrE*) (*informal*) used at the end of a sentence to emphasize that there is nothing more to say about a subject (用于句末，强调不再多说) 到此为止，就是这话: *I've already told you—we can't afford it, full stop!* 我已经告诉过你，我们负担不起，不再说了！

ˌfull-ˈterm *adj.* (*specialist*) **1** (of a PREGNANCY 怀胎) lasting the normal length of time 足月的 **2** (of a baby 婴儿) born after a PREGNANCY lasting the normal length of time 足月生的

ˌfull ˈtime *noun* [U] (*BrE*) the end of a sports game (体育运动的) 全场比赛结束时间，终场: *The referee blew his whistle for full time.* 裁判吹响了比赛结束的哨音。◇ *The full-time score was 1–1.* 全场比赛结果为 1:1。➲ COMPARE HALF-TIME

ˌfull-ˈtime *adj., adv.* (*abbr.* **FT**) for all the hours of a week during which people normally work or study, rather than just for a part of it 全日 (制)；全职的 (地)；全日的 (地): *students in full-time education* 全日制学生 ◇ *a full-time employee* 全职雇员 ◇ *a full-time job* 一份全职工作 ◇ *Looking after a child is a full-time job* (= hard work that takes a lot of time). 照管小孩是一天忙到晚的活儿。◇ *She works full-time and still manages to run a home.* 她做全职工作，仍能照管好家庭。➲ COMPARE PART-TIME

ˌfull-ˈtimer *noun* a person who works full-time 全日制工作者；全职人员

ˌfull ˈtoss *noun* (in CRICKET 板球) a ball that reaches the BATSMAN without touching the ground and is easy to hit 未着地的直线球

fully /ˈfʊli/ *adv.* **1** completely 完全地；全部地；充分地: *She had **fully recovered** from the accident.* 事故后她已经完全恢复过来。◇ *We are **fully aware** of the dangers.* 我们充分意识到危险。◇ *I **fully understand** your motives.* 我完全理解你的动机。**2** (*formal*) (used to emphasize an amount 强调数量) the whole of; as much as 整整；足足: *The disease affects fully 30 per cent of the population.* 这种病感染了足足 30% 的人口。

ˌfully ˈfledged (*BrE*) (*also* **ˌfull-ˈfledged** *NAmE, BrE*) *adj.* [usually before noun] completely developed; with all the qualifications necessary for sth 成熟的；完全合格的: *the emergence of a fully fledged market economy* 成熟市场经济的出现 ◇ *She was now a fully fledged member of the teaching profession.* 她现在是完全合格的教师。

ful·mar /ˈfʊlmə(r)/ *noun* a grey and white bird that lives near the sea 暴风鹱 (海鸟)

ful·min·ate /ˈfʊlmɪneɪt; ˈfʌl-/ *verb* [I] **~ against (sb/sth)** (*formal*) to criticize sb/sth angrily 愤怒谴责；怒斥 ▶ **ful·min·ation** /ˌfʊlmɪˈneɪʃn; ˌfʌl-/ *noun* [C, U]

ful·some /ˈfʊlsəm/ *adj.* (*disapproving*) too generous in praising or thanking sb, or in saying sorry, so that you do not sound sincere 过分恭维的；谄媚的；感谢过头的: *a fulsome apology* 低三下四的道歉 ◇ *He was fulsome in his praise of the Prime Minister.* 他称赞首相时有溢美之词。▶ **ful·some·ly** *adv.*

fum·ble /ˈfʌmbl/ *verb, noun*

■ ***verb*** **1** [I, T] to use your hands in an awkward way when you are doing sth or looking for sth 笨手笨脚地做 (某事)；笨拙地摸找 (某物): **~ (at/with/in sth) (for sth)** *She fumbled in her pocket for a handkerchief.* 她在口袋里胡乱摸找手帕。◇ *He fumbled with the buttons on his shirt.* 他笨手笨脚地摆弄衬衣上的纽扣。◇ **~ around** *She was fumbling around in the dark looking for the light switch.* 她摸黑找电灯开关。◇ **~ sth (+ adv./prep.)** *He fumbled the key into the ignition.* 他笨拙地把钥匙插进汽车点火开关。◇ **~ to do sth** *I fumbled to zip up my jacket.* 我笨手笨脚地拉上夹克的拉链。**2** [I, T] to have difficulty speaking clearly or finding the right words to say 笨嘴拙舌地说话；支支吾吾地说: **~ (for sth)** *During the interview, she fumbled helplessly for words.* 面试时她支支吾吾找不出适当的话语。◇ **~ sth** *to fumble an announcement* 结结巴巴地宣告 **3** [T] **~ sth** (especially in sport 尤用于体育运动) to drop a ball or to fail to stop or kick it 失球；接球失误；漏接

■ ***noun*** **1** [sing.] (*also* **fum·bling** [C, usually pl.]) an awkward action using the hands 笨拙的手部动作；乱摸 **2** [C] (*NAmE*) the action of dropping the ball while it is in play in AMERICAN FOOTBALL (美式足球) 失球，接球失误，漏接，掉球 **3** [C] (*NAmE*) the action of failing to pick up a ball that is rolling on the ground in BASEBALL (棒球) 失球，漏球，漏接

fum·bling /ˈfʌmblɪŋ/ *adj.* awkward, uncertain or hesitating 笨拙的；迟疑的: *a fumbling schoolboy* 笨拙的男生

fume /fjuːm/ *verb* **1** [I, T] to be very angry about sth (对…) 大为生气，十分恼火: **~ (at/over/about sb/sth)** *She sat in the car, silently fuming at the traffic jam.* 她坐在汽车里，心中对交通堵塞感到十分恼火。◇ **~ (with sth)** *He was fuming with indignation.* 他愤愤不平。◇ **+ speech** *'This is intolerable!' she fumed.* "这真让人不可容忍！" 她怒气冲冲地说。**2** [I] to produce smoke or fumes 冒烟；冒气

fumes /fjuːmz/ *noun* [pl.] (*also less frequent* **fume** [U]) smoke, gas, or sth similar that smells strongly or is dangerous to breathe in (浓烈的或有害的) 烟，气，汽: ***diesel/petrol/exhaust fumes*** 强烈的柴油味 / 汽油味 / 废气 ◇ *to be overcome by smoke and fumes* 被浓烟熏倒 ◇ *Clouds of toxic fumes escaped in a huge chemical factory blaze.* 从化工厂熊熊烈火中泄漏出团团有毒气体。◇ *The body of a man was found in a **fume-filled** car yesterday.* 昨天在一辆

烟雾弥漫的汽车中发现了一具男尸。 ➲ VISUAL VOCAB PAGE V6

fu·mi·gate /ˈfjuːmɪɡeɪt/ *verb* ~ **sth** to use special chemicals, smoke or gas to destroy the harmful insects or bacteria in a place 烟熏，熏蒸（以灭虫或消毒）: *to fumigate a room* 用熏蒸的方法给房间消毒 ▶ **fu·mi·ga·tion** /ˌfjuːmɪˈɡeɪʃn/ *noun* [U, C]

fun /fʌn/ *noun, adj.*

■ *noun* [U] **1** enjoyment; pleasure; a thing that gives enjoyment or pleasure and makes you feel happy 享乐；乐趣；快乐；享乐的事: *We had a lot of fun at Sarah's party.* 我们在萨拉的聚会上玩得很开心。◇ *Sailing is* ***good fun.*** 帆船运动很有乐趣。◇ ***Have fun!*** (= Enjoy yourself) 尽情地玩吧！◇ *I decided to learn Spanish, just* ***for fun.*** 我决定学西班牙语，只是为了好玩。◇ *I didn't do all that work just* ***for the fun of it.*** 我做这一切并不仅仅是为了好玩。◇ *It's not much fun going to a party on your own.* 独自一人参加聚会没什么意思。◇ *'What fun!' she said with a laugh.* "真开心呀！" 她笑着说。◇ *Walking three miles in the pouring rain is* ***not my idea of fun.*** 顶着倾盆大雨走三英里路，我可不认为是好玩的事。◇ *'What do you say to a weekend in New York?' 'Sounds like fun.'* "在纽约度周末怎么样？" "听起来很惬意。" **2** behaviour or activities that are not serious but come from a sense of enjoyment 嬉戏；逗乐；玩笑: *She's very lively and* ***full of fun.*** 她很活泼，挺有趣的。◇ *We didn't mean to hurt him. It was just* ***a bit of fun.*** 我们并非有意要伤害他，只不过是开个玩笑罢了。◇ *It wasn't serious—it was all done* ***in fun.*** 那不是认真的，全是闹着玩的。 ➲ SYNONYMS AT ENTERTAINMENT

▼ **SYNONYMS 同义词辨析**

fun

pleasure • (a) good time • enjoyment • (a) great time

These are all words for the feeling of enjoying yourself, or activities or time that you enjoy. 以上各词均表示愉快、快乐的事、欢乐的时光。

fun (*rather informal*) the feeling of enjoying yourself; activities that you enjoy 指享乐、乐趣、享乐的事： *We had a lot of fun at Sarah's party.* 我们在萨拉的聚会上玩得很开心。◇ *Sailing is* ***good/great fun.*** 帆船运动很 / 极有乐趣。

pleasure (*rather formal*) the feeling of enjoying yourself or being satisfied 指高兴、快乐、愉快、满意： *Reading for pleasure and reading for study are not the same.* 读书以自娱和读书以学习是不相同的。

(a) **good time** (*rather informal*) a time that you spend enjoying yourself 指欢乐、愉快的时光： *We had a good time in Spain.* 我们在西班牙过得很愉快。

enjoyment (*rather formal*) the feeling of enjoying yourself 指愉快、快乐、乐趣： *I get a lot of enjoyment from music.* 我从音乐中获得很多乐趣。

PLEASURE OR ENJOYMENT? 用 pleasure 还是 enjoyment?

Enjoyment usually comes from an activity that you do; **pleasure** can come from sth that you do or sth that happens. * enjoyment 通常源于活动； pleasure 既可源于所做的事也可源于发生的事： *He beamed with pleasure at seeing her.* 他看到她时喜不自胜。◇ ~~*He beamed with enjoyment at seeing her.*~~

(a) **great time** (*rather informal*) a time that you spend enjoying yourself very much 指非常欢乐、愉快的时光： *We had a really great time together.* 我们一起度过了非常快乐的时光。

PATTERNS

- to do sth **for** fun/pleasure/enjoyment
- **great** fun/pleasure/enjoyment
- to **have** fun/a good time/a great time
- to **get** pleasure/enjoyment **from** sth
- to **spoil** the fun/sb's pleasure/sb's enjoyment

IDM **fun and 'games** (*informal*) activities that are not serious and that other people may disapprove of 嬉戏；欢闹；寻欢作乐 **make 'fun of sb/sth** to laugh at sb/sth or make other people laugh at them, usually in an unkind way 嘲弄；取笑；拿…开玩笑: *It's cruel to make fun of people who stammer.* 嘲笑口吃的人是很不人道的。 ➲ MORE AT FIGURE *n.*, POKE *v.*

■ *adj.* amusing or enjoyable 逗乐的；有趣的；使人快乐的: *She's really fun to be with.* 和她在一起真开心。◇ *This game looks fun!* 这个游戏看来好玩！◇ *There are lots of fun things for young people to do here.* 这里有许多供年轻人玩乐的活动。

func·tion AW /ˈfʌŋkʃn/ *noun, verb*

■ *noun* **1** [C, U] a special activity or purpose of a person or thing 作用；功能；职能；机能: *to* ***fulfil/perform a function*** 发挥功能 ◇ ***bodily functions*** (= for example eating, sex, using the toilet) 身体机能 ◇ *The function of the heart is to pump blood through the body.* 心脏的功能就是把血液输往全身。◇ *This design aims for harmony of form and function.* 这个设计旨在使形式和功能协调一致。 **2** [C] a social event or official ceremony 社交聚会；典礼；宴会: *The hall provided a venue for weddings and other functions.* 大厅可以举办婚礼和其他公开活动。**3** [C] (*mathematics* 数) a quantity whose value depends on the varying values of others. In the statement 2x=y, y is a function of x. 函数: (*figurative*) *Salary is* ***a function of*** *age and experience.* 工资视年龄和经验而定。**4** [C] (*computing* 计) a part of a program, etc. that performs a basic operation 子程序；子例程

■ *verb* [I] (+ **adv./prep.**) (*rather formal*) to work in the correct way 起作用；正常工作；运转 SYN **operate**: *Despite the power cuts, the hospital continued to function normally.* 尽管供电中断，医院继续照常运作。◇ *We now have a functioning shower.* 现在我们有一个功能正常的淋浴器。◇ *Many children can't function effectively in large classes.* 许多孩子在上大课时学习效果不好。

PHRV **'function as sb/sth** to perform the action or the job of the thing or person mentioned 起…作用；具有…功能: *The sofa also functions as a bed.* 这沙发还可当床用。

func·tion·al AW /ˈfʌŋkʃənl/ *adj.* **1** practical and useful; with little or no decoration 实用的 SYN **utilitarian**: *Bathrooms don't have to be purely functional.* 浴室不必完全只为了实用。◇ *The office was large and functional rather than welcoming.* 这间办公室大而实用，但不怎么宜人。 **2** having a special purpose; making it possible for sb to do sth or for sth to happen 作用的；功能的；机能的；职能的: *a functional disorder* (= an illness caused when an organ of the body fails to perform its function) 功能紊乱 ◇ *a functional approach to language learning* 功能语言学习法 ◇ *These units played a key functional role in the military operation.* 这些单位在军事行动中起到了主要的职能作用。 **3** (especially of a machine, an organization or a system 尤指机器、组织、机构或体系) working; able to work （能）起作用的，工作的，运转的: *The hospital will soon be fully functional.* 这家医院将很快全面运作。 ▶ **func·tion·al·ly** AW /-ʃənəli/ *adv.*

ˈfunctional food *noun* [C, U] (*also* **nutra·ceut·ical**) food that has had substances that are good for your health specially added to it 功能食品；保健食品

ˌfunctional 'grammar *noun* [U] (*linguistics* 语言) grammar that analyses how language is used to communicate 功能语法（分析语言如何用于交际的语法）

func·tion·al·ism /ˈfʌŋkʃənəlɪzəm/ *noun* [U] the idea or belief that the most important thing about the style or design of a building or object is how it is going to be used, not how it will look 功能主义，实用建筑主义（主张建筑或物品设计首要的是用途而不是外观） ▶ **func·tion·al·ist** /-ʃənəlɪst/ *noun* **func·tion·al·ist** /-ʃənəlɪst/ *adj.* [usually before noun]

func·tion·al·ity /ˌfʌŋkʃəˈnæləti/ *noun* (*pl.* **-ies**) **1** [U] the quality in sth of being very suitable for the purpose it was designed for 实用；符合实际 SYN **practicality** **2** [U] the purpose that sth is designed for or expected to perform 设计目的；设计功能: *Manufacturing processes may be affected by the functionality of the product.* 生产过程可

能要受到产品设计目的的影响。**3** [U, C] (*computing* 计) the range of functions that a computer or other electronic system can perform（计算机或电子系统的）功能性: *new software with additional functionality* 有附加功能的新软件 ➲WORDFINDER NOTE AT PROGRAM

func·tion·ary /ˈfʌŋkʃənəri; *NAmE* -neri/ *noun* (*pl.* **-ies**) (*often disapproving*) a person with official duties 公职人员；官员 SYN **official**: *party/state/government functionaries* 政党 / 国家 / 政府的官员

ˈ**function key** *noun* (*computing* 计) one of several keys on a computer keyboard, each marked with 'F' and a number, that can be used to do sth, such as save a file or get to the 'help' function in a program 功能键

ˈ**function word** (*also* **func·tor**) *noun* (*grammar* 语法) a word that is important to the grammar of a sentence rather than its meaning, for example 'do' in 'we do not live here' 功能词，虚词（如 we do not live here 中的 do 一词）➲COMPARE CONTENT WORD

func·tor /ˈfʌŋktə(r)/ *noun* **1** (*mathematics* 数) a FUNCTION or a symbol such as + or × 函子 **2** (*grammar* 语法) = FUNCTION WORD

fund AW /fʌnd/ *noun, verb*

▪*noun* **1** [C] an amount of money that has been saved or has been made available for a particular purpose 基金；专款: *a disaster relief fund* 赈灾专款 ◇ *the company's pension fund* 公司的退休基金 ◇ *the International Monetary Fund* 国际货币基金组织 ➲WORDFINDER NOTE AT INVEST **2** **funds** [pl.] money that is available to be spent 资金；现款: *government funds* 政府资金 ◇ *The hospital is trying to raise funds for a new kidney machine.* 这家医院正设法募集资金购买一台新的血液透析器。◇ *The project has been cancelled because of lack of funds* 这个项目因缺乏资金已经撤销。◇ *I'm* ***short of funds*** *at the moment—can I pay you back next week?* 我目前缺钱，下周还你行吗？ ➲COLLOCATIONS AT FINANCE **3** [sing.] **~ of sth** an amount or a supply of sth（相当）数量；储备: *a fund of knowledge* 丰富的知识

▪*verb* **~ sth** to provide money for sth, usually sth official 为…提供资金；拨款给: *a dance festival funded by the Arts Council* 由艺术委员会资助的舞蹈节 ◇ *The museum is privately funded.* 这家博物馆由私人提供资金。◇ *a government-funded programme* 政府资助项目

funda /ˈfʌndə/ *noun* (*IndE*) a fundamental principle that is the basis of sth but that is not always easily noticed（潜在的）根本原则，基本原理: *The artist explained the funda behind her exhibits.* 艺术家解释了她的展品背后的基本原理。

fun·da·men·tal AW /ˌfʌndəˈmentl/ *adj., noun*

▪*adj.* **1** serious and very important; affecting the most central and important parts of sth 十分重大的；根本的 SYN **basic**: *There is a* ***fundamental difference*** *between the two points of view.* 这两个观点有根本区别。◇ *A* ***fundamental change*** *in the organization of health services was required.* 公共医疗在组织上需要一个根本性的变革。◇ *a question of fundamental importance* 首要问题 **2** **~ (to sth)** central; forming the necessary basis of sth 基础的；基本的 SYN **essential**: *Hard work is fundamental to success.* 勤奋工作是成功的基础。**3** [only before noun] (*physics* 物) forming the source or base from which everything else is made; not able to be divided any further 基本的；不能再分的: *a fundamental particle* 基本粒子

▪*noun* [usually pl.] a basic rule or principle; an essential part 基本规律；根本法则；基本原理；基础: *the fundamentals of modern physics* 现代物理学的基本原理 ◇ *He taught me the fundamentals of the job.* 他教给了我这工作的基本知识。

ˌ**fundamental** ˈ**force** *noun* (*specialist*) a force that is a property (= characteristic) of everything in the universe. There are four fundamental forces including GRAVITY and ELECTROMAGNETISM. 基本力（宇宙万物所具有的特性，包括引力和电磁力等四种）

fun·da·men·tal·ism /ˌfʌndəˈmentəlɪzəm/ *noun* [U] **1** the practice of following very strictly the basic rules and teachings of any religion 原教旨主义（认为应严格奉行宗教原则和教义）**2** (in Christianity) the belief that everything that is written in the Bible is completely true（基督教的）基要主义，原教旨主义（强调直解《圣经》） ▸ **fun·da·men·tal·ist** /-ɪst/ *noun* **fun·da·men·tal·ist** /-ɪst/ *adj.*

fun·da·men·tal·ly AW /ˌfʌndəˈmentəli/ *adv.* **1** in every way that is important; completely 根本上；完全地: *The two approaches are fundamentally different.* 这两种方法完全不同。◇ *By the 1960s the situation had changed fundamentally.* 到 20 世纪 60 年代形势已发生了根本的变化。◇ *They remained fundamentally opposed to the plan.* 他们依然从根本上反对这项计划。**2** used when you are introducing a topic and stating sth important about it（引入话题时说）从根本上说，基本上 SYN **basically**: *Fundamentally, there are two different approaches to the problem.* 从根本上说，这个问题有两种不同的处理方法。**3** used when you are saying what is the most important thing about sb/sth（表示最重要的方面）根本上，基本上 SYN **basically**: *She is fundamentally a nice person, but she finds it difficult to communicate.* 她基本上是个好人，但她觉得难以和人沟通。

fun·der AW /ˈfʌndə(r)/ *noun* a person or an organization that provides money for a particular purpose 资金赞助者；资金提供者

fundi /ˈfʊndi:/ *noun* (*SAfrE*) a person who is very skilled at sth or who has gained a lot of knowledge about a particular subject 匠人；行家；专家: *a computer fundi* 电脑高手 ◇ *He's become quite a fundi on wine.* 他成了葡萄酒的行家。

fund·ing AW /ˈfʌndɪŋ/ *noun* [U] money for a particular purpose; the act of providing money for such a purpose 基金；资金；提供基金；提供资金: *There have been large cuts in government funding for scientific research.* 政府提供的科研资金已大幅度削减。

fund·raiser /ˈfʌndreɪzə(r)/ *noun* **1** a person who collects money for a charity or an organization 资金筹集者；募捐者 **2** a social event or an entertainment held in order to collect money for a charity or an organization 募捐会；募捐活动；义演 ➲WORDFINDER NOTE AT CHARITY ▸ **fund·raising** *noun* [U]

fu·neral /ˈfju:nərəl/ *noun* a ceremony, usually a religious one, for burying or CREMATING (= burning) a dead person 葬礼；丧礼；出殡: *Hundreds of people attended the funeral.* 数百人参加了葬礼。◇ *a funeral procession* 送葬队伍 ◇ *a funeral march* (= a sad piece of music suitable for funerals) 丧礼进行曲 ➲WORDFINDER NOTE AT DIE

IDM **it's 'your funeral** (*informal*) used to tell sb that they, and nobody else, will have to deal with the unpleasant results of their own actions 你这是自找麻烦

ˈ**funeral director** *noun* (*formal*) = UNDERTAKER

ˈ**funeral parlour** (*especially US* ˈ**funeral parlor**) (*also* ˈ**funeral home** *NAmE, BrE*) (*NAmE also* **mor·tu·ary**) *noun* a place where dead people are prepared for being buried or CREMATED (= burned) and where visitors can see the body 殡仪馆

fu·ner·ary /ˈfju:nərəri; *NAmE* -reri/ *adj.* [only before noun] (*formal*) of or used at a funeral（用于）葬礼的，丧葬的: *funerary monuments/rites* 墓碑；丧葬仪式

fu·ner·eal /fjuˈnɪəriəl; *NAmE* -ˈnɪr-/ *adj.* (*formal*) suitable for a funeral; sad 适于葬礼的；悲伤的: *a funereal atmosphere* 悲哀肃穆的气氛

fun·fair /ˈfʌnfeə(r); *NAmE* -fer/ *noun* (*BrE*) = FAIR (1)

fung·al /ˈfʌŋgl/ *adj.* of or caused by FUNGUS 真菌的；真菌引起的: *a fungal infection* 真菌感染

fun·gi·cide /ˈfʌngɪsaɪd; ˈfʌndʒɪ-/ *noun* [C, U] a substance that kills fungus 杀真菌剂

fun·goid /ˈfʌŋgɔɪd/ *adj.* (*specialist*) like a FUNGUS 似真菌的；真菌式的: *a fungoid growth* 真菌式赘生物

F

fun·gus /ˈfʌŋɡəs/ *noun* (*pl.* **fungi** /ˈfʌŋɡiː; -ɡaɪ; ˈfʌndʒaɪ/) **1** [C] an ORGANISM (= a living thing) that is similar to a plant without leaves, flowers or green colouring, and that usually grows on plants or on decaying matter. MUSHROOMS and MILDEW are both fungi. 真菌（如蘑菇和霉）➲ COLLOCATIONS AT LIFE **2** [U, C] a covering of MOULD or a similar fungus, for example on a plant or wall 霉；霉菌：*fungus infections* 霉菌感染

fun·house /ˈfʌnhaʊs/ *noun* (*especially NAmE*) a building at an AMUSEMENT PARK containing mirrors that produce strange images, moving floors, and other devices for scaring and amusing people 奇幻屋，欢乐屋（内设哈哈镜、活动地板等惊险有趣的设施）

fu·nicu·lar /fjuːˈnɪkjələ(r)/ (*also* **fu,nicular 'railway**) *noun* a railway on a steep slope, used to transport passengers up and down in special cars by means of a moving cable 缆索铁道 ➲ VISUAL VOCAB PAGE V63

funk /fʌŋk/ *noun, verb*
■ *noun* **1** [U] a type of dance music with a strong rhythm, developed by African American musicians in the 1960s 放克音乐（20 世纪 60 年代美国黑人音乐家创造，节奏感强） **2** (*also* ,**blue 'funk**) [sing.] (*old-fashioned, informal*) a state of fear or anxiety 恐惧；忧虑 **3** [C, usually sing.] (*NAmE*) a strong unpleasant smell 浓烈臭味；恶臭
■ *verb* ~ sth (*BrE, informal*) to avoid doing sth because you are afraid to or find it difficult （因畏惧而）逃避，回避

funky /fʌŋki/ *adj.* (**funk·ier**, **funki·est**) (*informal*) **1** (of pop music 流行音乐) with a strong rhythm that is easy to dance to 节奏强适宜跳舞的：*a funky disco beat* 动感强劲的迪斯科节奏 **2** (*approving*) fashionable and unusual 时髦独特的：*She wears really funky clothes.* 她穿的衣服真是时髦又独特。**3** (*NAmE*) having a strong unpleasant smell 恶臭的

'fun-loving *adj.* (of people 人) liking to enjoy themselves 喜欢玩乐的

fun·nel /ˈfʌnl/ *noun, verb*
■ *noun* **1** a device that is wide at the top and narrow at the bottom, used for pouring liquids or powders into a small opening 漏斗 ➲ VISUAL VOCAB PAGE V72 **2** (*also* **smoke·stack**) a metal CHIMNEY, for example on a ship or an engine, through which smoke comes out（蒸汽机车或轮船上的）烟囱
■ *verb* (**-ll-**, *especially US* **-l-**) [I, T] to move or make sth move through a narrow space, or as if through a funnel（使）流经狭窄空间，经过漏斗形口子：(**+ adv./prep.**) *Wind was funnelling through the gorge.* 风吹过峡谷。◇ **~ sth (+ adv./prep.)** *Huge pipes funnel the water down the mountainside.* 巨大的管道把水沿山坡输送下山。◇ *Barricades funnelled the crowds towards the square.* 设置的路障控制人流涌向广场。◇ (*figurative*) *Some $10 million in aid was funnelled into the country through government agencies.* 约 1 000 万美元援助款已通过政府各部门发放到农村。

the fun·nies /ˈfʌniz/ *noun* [pl.] (*NAmE, informal*) the part of a newspaper where there are several COMIC STRIPS (= series of drawings that tell a funny story)（报章的）滑稽连环漫画，漫画版

fun·nily /ˈfʌnəli/ *adv.* in a strange way 奇怪地
IDM **funnily e'nough** used to show that you expect people to find a particular fact surprising 真奇怪；说来也巧：*Funnily enough, I met her only yesterday.* 说来也巧，昨天我才碰见了她。

funny 🔑 /ˈfʌni/ *adj.* (**fun·nier**, **fun·ni·est**)
• **AMUSING** 好笑 **1** 🔑 making you laugh; amusing 滑稽的；好笑的：*a funny story* 滑稽的故事 ◇ *That's the funniest thing I've ever heard.* 那是我听过的最滑稽可笑的事。◇ *It's not funny! Someone could have been hurt.* 这并不好玩！可能有人已经受到伤害。◇ *I was really embarrassed, but then I saw the* ***funny side of it.*** 我感到非常尴尬，但接着我发现了事情好笑的一面。◇ (*ironic*) *Oh* ***very funny!*** *You expect me to believe that?* 哦，真滑稽！你认为我会相信那个？◇ ***'What's so funny?'*** *she demanded.* "什么事这么好笑？" 她问道。➲ WORDFINDER NOTE AT COMEDY HELP Note that **funny** does not mean 'enjoyable'. 注意 funny 不表示 enjoyable 的意思：*The party was great fun.* 聚会好玩极了。◇ ~~*The party was very funny.*~~
• **STRANGE** 奇怪 **2** 🔑 difficult to explain or understand 奇怪的；难以解释的；难理解的 SYN **strange, peculiar**：*A funny thing happened to me today.* 今天我碰上了一件奇怪的事。◇ ***It's funny how*** *things never happen the way you expect them to.* 真是不懂，事情总是出人意表的。◇ ***That's funny****—he was here a moment ago and now he's gone.* 真怪，他刚才还在这儿，现在就没影了。◇ ***The funny thing is*** *it never happened again after that.* 奇怪的是从那以后这事再也没有发生过。◇ *The engine's making a very funny noise.* 发动机发出一种很怪的声音。◇ *I'm pleased I didn't*

▼ **SYNONYMS** 同义词辨析

funny

amusing • entertaining • witty • humorous • comic • hilarious

These words all describe sb/sth that makes you laugh or smile. 以上各词均用以形容人或事好笑的、滑稽的。

funny that makes you laugh 指好笑的、滑稽的： *a funny story* 滑稽的故事 ◇ *He was a very funny guy.* 他这个人很滑稽。

amusing funny and enjoyable 指逗人笑的、有乐趣的、好笑的： *It's a very amusing game to play.* 这种游戏玩起来非常有趣。

entertaining amusing and interesting 指有趣的、令人开心的、使人愉快的： *It was a very entertaining evening.* 那是一场非常令人开心的晚会。

witty clever and amusing; able to say or write clever and amusing things 指机智的、巧妙的、妙趣横生的、言辞诙谐的： *a witty remark* 机智的话 ◇ *a witty public speaker* 语言幽默的公开演讲人

humorous funny and entertaining; showing a sense of humour 指滑稽有趣的、有幽默感的： *a humorous look at the world of fashion* 对时装界幽默的审视

comic that makes you laugh 指滑稽的、使人发笑的： *Many of the scenes in the book are richly comic.* 这本书里的许多情节都非常滑稽可笑。

hilarious extremely funny 指极其滑稽的

FUNNY, AMUSING, HUMOROUS OR COMIC? 用 funny、amusing、humorous 还是 comic?
Amusing is the most general of these words because it includes the idea of being enjoyable as well as making people laugh and can be used to describe events, activities and occasions. * amusing 在这组词中最通用，既表示逗人笑，也表示好笑、有乐趣，可用以形容事情、活动和场合： *an amusing party/game/evening* 充满乐趣的联欢会 / 游戏 / 晚会 ◇ ~~*a funny/humorous/comic party/game/evening*~~ **Humorous** is more about showing that you see the humour in a situation, than actually making people laugh out loud. **Comic** is used especially to talk about writing and drama or things that are funny in a deliberate and theatrical way. It is not used to describe people (except for *comic writers*). **Funny** can describe people, jokes and stories, things that happen, or anything that makes people laugh. * humorous 更多表示明白情景中的有趣之处，而非实际使人大笑。comic 尤指作品、戏剧、事物等故意营造的戏剧性的滑稽可笑，但不用以描述人（comic writers 除外）。funny 可形容人、笑话、故事、发生的事情以及任何使人发笑的事物。

PATTERNS
• a(n) funny/amusing/entertaining/witty/humorous/comic **story**
• a(n) funny/amusing/entertaining/witty/humorous **speech**
• a(n) funny/entertaining/witty/humorous/comic **writer**
• a(n) funny/amusing/hilarious **joke**
• to **find sth** funny/amusing/entertaining/witty/humorous/hilarious

get that job, in a funny sort of way. 我没有得到那份工作，但我有一种说不清楚的高兴。

- **SUSPICIOUS/ILLEGAL 可疑；非法 3** (*informal*) suspicious and probably illegal or dishonest 可疑的；非法的；不诚实的：*I suspect there may be something funny going on.* 我怀疑可能有某种非法勾当在进行。◇ *If there has been any **funny business**, we'll soon find out.* 如果有任何非法的事，我们会很快发现的。
- **WITHOUT RESPECT 不尊重 4** (*BrE*) humorous in a way that shows a lack of respect for sb 嬉皮笑脸的；放肆的 **SYN** **cheeky**: *Don't you **get funny with me**!* 你不要对我放肆！
- **ILL/SICK 有病；不适 5** (*informal*) slightly ill/sick 小病的；微恙的；稍有不适的：*I feel a bit funny today—I don't think I'll go to work.* 我今天感到有点不舒服，不想去上班了。
- **CRAZY 疯癫 6** (*BrE, informal*) slightly crazy; not like other people 疯疯癫癫的；不很正常的 **SYN** **strange, peculiar**: *That Dave's a funny chap, isn't he?* 那个戴夫疯疯癫癫的，是不是？◇ *She went a bit funny after her husband died.* 丈夫死后她神志就有点不大正常了。
- **MACHINE 机器 7** (*informal*) not working as it should 出故障的：*My computer keeps **going funny**.* 我的计算机老出故障。

IDM **ˌfunny ha-ˈha** (*informal*) used to show that 'funny' is being used with the meaning of 'amusing' 滑稽可笑 **ˌfunny peˈculiar** (*BrE*) (*US* **ˌfunny ˈweird/ˈstrange**) (*informal*) used to show that 'funny' is being used with the meaning of 'strange' 稀奇古怪

ˈfunny bone *noun* [usually sing.] (*informal*) the part of the elbow containing a very sensitive nerve that is painful if you hit it against sth 麻筋儿，鹰嘴突，肘的尺骨端（肘端神经敏感部位）

ˈfunny farm *noun* (*informal, offensive*) a hospital for people who are mentally ill 精神病院

ˌfunny ˈmoney *noun* [U] (*informal, disapproving*) **1** a CURRENCY (= the money used in one country) which is not worth much and whose value can change quickly 币值低（或不稳定）的货币 **2** money that has been FORGED (= is not real) or stolen or that has come from illegal activities 假币；来路不明的钱；黑钱

ˈfun run *noun* (*especially BrE*) an event in which people run a long distance, for fun, and to collect money for charity 募捐公益长跑

fur /fɜː(r)/ *noun* **1** [U] the soft thick mass of hair that grows on the body of some animals（动物浓厚的）软毛 **2** [U] the skin of an animal with the fur still on it, used especially for making clothes（动物的）毛皮：*a fur coat* 毛皮大衣 ◇ *the fur trade* 毛皮贸易 ◇ *a fur farm* (= where animals are bred and killed for their fur) 毛皮动物饲养场 ◇ *The animal is hunted for its fur.* 狩猎这种动物是为了获取其毛皮。◇ *fur-lined gloves* 毛皮衬里手套 **3** [U] an artificial material that looks and feels like fur 人造毛皮 **4** [C] a piece of clothing, especially a coat or jacket, made of real or artificial fur 毛皮衣服，裘皮衣服（尤指大衣或短上衣）：*elegant ladies in furs* 穿着裘皮衣服的高雅贵妇 **5** (*BrE*) = SCALE (9) **6** [U] a greyish-white layer that forms on a person's tongue, especially when they are ill/sick 舌苔 ➲ SEE ALSO FURRED

furi·ous /ˈfjʊəriəs; *NAmE* ˈfjʊr-/ *adj.* **1** very angry 狂怒的；暴怒的：~ (**at sth/sb**) *She was absolutely furious at having been deceived.* 她受了骗，怒不可遏。◇ ~ (**with sb/yourself**) *He was furious with himself for letting things get so out of control.* 他对自己很恼火，怪自己竟让事情变得如此不可收拾。◇ ~ (**that...**) *I'm furious that I wasn't told about it.* 这事没有跟我说，我十分气愤。 **2** with great energy, speed or anger 激烈的；猛烈的；高速的；盛怒的：*a furious debate* 激烈的辩论 ◇ *She drove off at a furious pace.* 她驾车飞驰而去。➲ SEE ALSO FURY ▶ **furi·ous·ly** *adv.*: *furiously angry* 大发雷霆 ◇ *'Damn!' he said furiously.* "该死的！"他十分愤怒地说。◇ *They worked furiously all weekend, trying to get it finished on time.* 整个周末他们拼命工作，以求按时完成这项任务。**IDM** SEE FAST *adj.*

furl /fɜːl; *NAmE* fɜːrl/ *verb* ~ **sth** to roll and fasten sth such as a sail, a flag or an umbrella 卷起，收拢（帆、旗或伞）

fur·long /ˈfɜːlɒŋ; *NAmE* ˈfɜːrlɔːŋ; ˈfɜːrlɑːŋ/ *noun* (especially in horse racing 尤指赛马) a unit for measuring distance, equal to 220 yards or 201 metres; one eighth of a mile 弗隆，浪（长度单位，相当于 220 码、201 米或 ⅛ 英里）

fur·lough /ˈfɜːləʊ; *NAmE* ˈfɜːrloʊ/ *noun* [U, C] **1** permission to leave your duties for a period of time, especially for soldiers working in a foreign country（尤指在国外服役士兵的）休假（许可）**2** (*NAmE*) permission for a prisoner to leave prison for a period of time（犯人的）准假 **3** (*NAmE*) a period of time during which workers are told not to come to work, usually because there is not enough money to pay them（通常因发不出工资而给的）准假 ▶ **fur·lough** *verb* ~ **sb**

fur·nace /ˈfɜːnɪs; *NAmE* ˈfɜːrnɪs/ *noun* **1** a space surrounded on all sides by walls and a roof for heating metal or glass to very high temperatures 熔炉：*It's like a furnace* (= very hot) *in here!* 这里热得像火炉！➲ SEE ALSO BLAST FURNACE **2** (*especially NAmE*) = BOILER

fur·nish /ˈfɜːnɪʃ; *NAmE* ˈfɜːrnɪʃ/ *verb* **1** ~ **sth** to put furniture in a house, room, etc. 在（房屋等）处布置家具：*The room was furnished with antiques.* 房间里摆放了古董。➲ COLLOCATIONS AT DECORATE **2** ~ **sb/sth with sth** | ~ **sth** (*formal*) to supply or provide sb/sth with sth; to supply sth to sb 向（某人或某事物）供应，提供：*She furnished him with the facts surrounding the case.* 她向他提供了与案件有关的事实。

fur·nished /ˈfɜːnɪʃt; *NAmE* ˈfɜːrnɪʃt/ *adj.* (of a house, room, etc. 房屋、房间等) containing furniture 配备家具的：*furnished accommodation* (= to rent complete with furniture) 连家具出租房 ◇ *The house was simply furnished.* 这房子陈设简单。

fur·nish·ings /ˈfɜːnɪʃɪŋz; *NAmE* ˈfɜːrn-/ *noun* [pl.] the furniture, carpets, curtains, etc. in a room or house 家具陈设：*soft furnishings* 织物制成的室内陈设 ◇ *The wallpaper should match the furnishings.* 墙纸应和家具陈设协调。➲ WORDFINDER NOTE AT STORE

fur·ni·ture /ˈfɜːnɪtʃə(r); *NAmE* ˈfɜːrn-/ *noun* [U] objects that can be moved, such as tables, chairs and beds, that are put into a house or an office to make it suitable for living or working in（可移动的）家具：*a **piece of furniture*** 一件家具 ◇ ***garden/office, etc. furniture*** 花园、办公室等处的家具 ◇ *We need to buy some new furniture.* 我们需要买一些新家具。➲ SEE ALSO DOOR FURNITURE, STREET FURNITURE **IDM** SEE PART *n.* ➲ MORE LIKE THIS 28, page R28

ˈfurniture van *noun* (*BrE*) = REMOVAL VAN

fur·ore /fjuˈrɔːri; ˈfjʊərɔː(r); *NAmE* ˈfjʊr-/ (*also* **furor** /ˈfjʊərɔː(r); *NAmE* ˈfjʊr-/ *especially in NAmE*) *noun* [sing.] great anger or excitement shown by a number of people, usually caused by a public event 群情激愤；骚动；轰动 **SYN** **uproar**: ~ (**among sb**) *His novel about Jesus caused a furore among Christians.* 他关于耶稣的小说激起了基督教徒的公愤。◇ ~ (**about/over sth**) *the recent furore over the tax increases* 近来因增税引起的骚动

furphy /ˈfɜːfi; *NAmE* ˈfɜːrfi/ *noun* (*pl.* **-ies**) (*AustralE*) a piece of information or a story that people talk about but that may not be true 传闻；传言 **SYN** **rumour**

fur·red /fɜːd; *NAmE* fɜːrd/ *adj.* covered with fur or with sth that looks like fur 覆盖毛皮的；穿戴毛皮衣物的；长舌苔的：*a furred tongue* 长苔的舌头

fur·rier /ˈfʌriə(r)/ *noun* a person who prepares or sells clothes made from fur 毛皮加工者；皮货商

fur·row /ˈfʌrəʊ; *NAmE* ˈfɜːroʊ/ *noun, verb*

■ ***noun*** **1** a long narrow cut in the ground, especially one made by a PLOUGH for planting seeds in 犁沟；沟；车辙 ➲ VISUAL VOCAB PAGE V3 **2** a deep line in the skin of the face（脸上的）皱纹 **IDM** SEE PLOUGH *v.*

■ ***verb*** **1** [T] ~ **sth** to make a furrow in the earth 犁：*furrowed fields* 犁过的田地 **2** [I, T] ~ (**sth**) (*formal*) if your

BROWS or EYEBROWS **furrow** or **are furrowed**, you pull them together, usually because you are worried, and so produce lines on your face （使）皱（眉），蹙（额）

furry /ˈfɜːri/ *adj.* (**fur·rier**, **fur·ri·est**) **1** covered with fur 覆盖毛皮的：*small furry animals* 毛茸茸的小动物 **2** like fur 毛皮似的；毛一般的：*The moss was soft and furry to the touch.* 苔藓柔软，摸起来像绒毛。

fur·ther /ˈfɜːðə(r); *NAmE* ˈfɜːrð-/ *adv., adj., verb*

■ ***adv.*** **1** (comparative of *far* * far 的比较级) (*especially BrE*) at or to a greater distance（空间距离）较远，更远 SYN **farther**：*We had walked further than I had realized.* 在我不知不觉中我们已走得很远。◇ *Two miles further on we came to a small town.* 我们又走了两英里，来到了一座小镇。◇ *The hospital is further down the road.* 沿这条路走下去就是医院。◇ *Can you stand a bit further away?* 你能不能站远一点？**2** a longer way in the past or the future（过去或未来）较远，更久远：*Think further back into your childhood.* 再往前回想你的童年。◇ *How will the company be doing ten years further on?* 十年以后公司的情况将如何呢？**3** to a greater degree or extent 进一步；在更大程度上；在更大范围内：*The police decided to investigate further.* 警方决定作进一步调查。◇ *My life is further complicated by having to work such long hours.* 我得工作这么长的时间，因此生活中的麻烦事就更多了。◇ *Nothing could be* ***further from the truth***. 绝不是那回事。**4** (*formal*) in addition to what has just been said 此外；而且 SYN **furthermore**：*Further, it is important to consider the cost of repairs.* 此外，重要的是要考虑修理费用。➲ NOTE AT FARTHER

IDM **go ˈfurther** **1** to say more about sth, or make a more extreme point about it 进一步说；提出更极端的意见：*I would go even further and suggest that the entire government is corrupt.* 我甚至进而想要说，整个政府都是腐败的。**2** to last longer; to serve more people 更经久；为更多人服务：*They watered down the soup to make it go further.* 他们往汤里掺水，好让更多的人喝。**go no ˈfurther | not go any ˈfurther** if you tell sb that a secret will **go no further**, you promise not to tell it to anyone else 到此为止；不再传下去 **take sth ˈfurther** to take more serious action about sth or speak to sb at a higher level about it 采取进一步行动；把…向上级反映：*I am not satisfied with your explanation and intend to take the matter further.* 我对你的解释不满意，打算进一步探讨这个问题。➲ MORE AT AFIELD

■ ***adj.*** (comparative of *far* * far 的比较级) more; additional 更多的；更进一步的；附加的：*Cook for a further 2 minutes.* 再煮两分钟。◇ *Have you any further questions?* 你还有问题吗？◇ *For further details call this number.* 欲知详情，请拨打这个电话号码。◇ *We have decided to take no further action.* 我们决定不采取进一步行动。◇ *The museum is closed* ***until further notice*** (= until we say that it is open again). 博物馆现在闭馆，开馆时间另行通知。➲ LANGUAGE BANK AT ADDITION

■ ***verb*** **~ sth** to help sth to develop or be successful 促进；增进：*They hoped the new venture would further the cause of cultural cooperation in Europe.* 他们希望这个新项目将促进欧洲文化合作事业。◇ *She took the new job to further her career.* 她接受了这个新工作以进一步发展她的事业。

fur·ther·ance /ˈfɜːðərəns; *NAmE* ˈfɜːrð-/ *noun* [U] (*formal*) the process of helping sth to develop or to be successful 促进；增进 SYN **advancement**：*He took these actions purely* ***in (the) furtherance of*** *his own career.* 他采取这些行动纯粹是为了促进自己的事业发展。

ˌfurther eduˈcation *noun* [U] (*abbr.* **FE**) (*BrE*) education that is provided for people after leaving school, but not at a university 继续教育，进修教育（为中学毕业后的人举办，但非大学）➲ COMPARE HIGHER EDUCATION ➲ WORDFINDER NOTE AT STUDY

fur·ther·more AW /ˌfɜːðəˈmɔː(r); *NAmE* ˌfɜːrðərˈmɔːr/ *adv.* (*formal*) in addition to what has just been stated. Furthermore is used especially to add a point to an argument. 此外；而且；再者 SYN **moreover**：*He said he had not discussed the matter with her. Furthermore, he had not even contacted her.* 他说他没有和她讨论过这个问题。而且，甚至没有和她联系过。➲ LANGUAGE BANK AT ADDITION

fur·ther·most /ˈfɜːðəməʊst; *NAmE* ˈfɜːrðərmoʊst/ *adj.* (*formal*) located at the greatest distance from sth 最远的：*at the furthermost end of the street* 在街尾

ˈfurther to *prep.* (*formal*) used in letters, emails, etc. to refer to a previous letter, email, conversation, etc.（用于书信、电邮等）关于，至于，考虑到：*Further to our conversation of last Friday, I would like to book the conference centre for 26 June.* 按我们上星期五说过的，我想预约 6 月 26 日使用会议中心。

fur·thest /ˈfɜːðɪst; *NAmE* ˈfɜːrð-/ *adj., adv.* = FARTHEST

fur·tive /ˈfɜːtɪv; *NAmE* ˈfɜːrtɪv/ *adj.* (*disapproving*) behaving in a way that shows that you want to keep sth secret and do not want to be noticed 偷偷摸摸的；鬼鬼祟祟的；遮遮掩掩的 SYN **stealthy**：*She cast a* ***furtive glance*** *over her shoulder.* 她偷偷往背后瞥了一下。◇ *He looked sly and furtive.* 他显得偷偷摸摸，鬼鬼祟祟。▶ **fur·tive·ly** *adv.* **fur·tive·ness** *noun* [U]

fury /ˈfjʊəri; *NAmE* ˈfjʊri/ *noun* **1** [U] extreme anger that often includes violent behaviour 狂怒；暴怒；狂暴；大发雷霆 SYN **rage**：*Her eyes blazed with fury.* 她的双眼迸发出暴怒之火。◇ *Fury over tax increases* (= as a newspaper HEADLINE) 对增税极端愤怒（报纸标题）◇ (*figurative*) *There was no shelter from the fury of the storm.* 那时没有地方可以躲避狂风暴雨。**2** [sing.] a state of being extremely angry about sth 狂怒；暴怒 SYN **rage**：*He flew into a fury when I refused.* 我拒绝，他就勃然大怒。**3 the Furies** [pl.] (in ancient Greek stories) three GODDESSES who punish people for their crimes（古希腊神话）复仇三女神 ➲ SEE ALSO FURIOUS

IDM **like fury** (*informal*) with great effort, power, speed, etc. 拼命；猛烈；迅猛 ➲ MORE AT HELL

furze /fɜːz; *NAmE* fɜːrz/ *noun* [U] (*BrE*) = GORSE

fuse /fjuːz/ *noun, verb*

■ ***noun*** **1** a small wire or device inside a piece of electrical equipment that breaks and stops the current if the flow of electricity is too strong 熔断器；保险丝：*to change a fuse* 换保险丝 ◇ *Check whether a fuse has blown.* 检查一下保险丝是否烧断了。**2** a long piece of string or paper which is lit to make a bomb or a FIREWORK explode 导火线；导火索 **3** (*NAmE also* **fuze**) a device that makes a bomb explode when it hits sth or at a particular time 引信；信管；雷管：*He set the fuse to three minutes.* 他把引信设定为三分钟起爆。◇ *The bombs inside were on a one-hour fuse.* 炸弹内装有一小时起爆的引信。IDM SEE BLOW *v.*, SHORT *adj.*

■ ***verb*** **1** [I, T] (*formal* or *specialist*) when one thing **fuses** with another, or two things **fuse** or **are fused**, they are joined together to form a single thing（使）融合，熔接，结合：**~ (together)** *As they heal, the bones will fuse together.* 骨头愈合时将会连接在一起。◇ **~ (into sth)** *Our different ideas fused into a plan.* 我们不同的想法融合成一项计划。◇ **~ with sth** *The sperm fuses with the egg to begin the process of fertilization.* 精子与卵子结合开始受精过程。◇ **~ sth (into sth)** *The two companies have been fused into a single organization.* 两家公司合并成一个机构。◇ *Atoms of hydrogen are fused to make helium.* 氢原子可熔合成氦。**2** [I, T] **~ (sth)** (*specialist*) when a substance, especially metal, **fuses**, or you **fuse** it, it is heated until it melts（使）熔化 **3** [I, T] **~ (sth)** (*BrE*) to stop working or to make sth stop working because a fuse melts（使保险丝熔断而）停止工作：*The lights have fused.* 保险丝烧断，灯都灭了。◇ *I've fused the lights.* 我把保险丝烧断了，灯都灭了。**4** [T, usually passive] **~ sth** to put a fuse in a CIRCUIT or in a piece of equipment 在（电路或电器）中安装保险丝：*Is this plug fused?* 这个插头有没有安装保险丝？

ˈfuse box *noun* a small box or cupboard that contains the fuses of the electrical system of a building 保险丝盒；熔丝盒

fu·sel·age /ˈfjuːzəlɑːʒ; *NAmE* ˈfjuːs-/ *noun* the main part of an aircraft in which passengers and goods are carried（飞机的）机身 ➲ VISUAL VOCAB PAGE V57

ˈ**fuse wire** *noun* [U] thin wire used in an electrical FUSE 熔丝；保险丝

fu·sil·ier /ˌfjuːzəˈlɪə(r)/ *noun* (in the past) a soldier who carried a light gun（旧时的）燧发枪士兵，明火枪士兵

fu·sil·lade /ˌfjuːzəˈleɪd; *NAmE* -sə-/ *noun* a rapid series of shots fired from one or more guns; a rapid series of objects that are thrown（枪炮的）连发，连续齐射；（某物的）连续投掷 SYN **barrage**: *a* ***fusillade of bullets/stones*** 枪林弹雨；雨点般投掷的石头 ◇ (*figurative*) *He faced a fusillade of questions from the waiting journalists.* 正在等候的记者们向他发出连珠炮似的提问。

fu·sion /ˈfjuːʒn/ *noun* **1** [U, sing.] the process or result of joining two or more things together to form one 融合；熔接；结合：*the fusion of copper and zinc to produce brass* 铜与锌熔合成黄铜 ◇ *The movie displayed a perfect fusion of image and sound.* 这部电影展示了影像与音响的完美结合。**2** (*also* ˌ**nuclear ˈfusion**) [U] (*physics* 物) the act or process of combining the NUCLEI (= central parts) of atoms to form a heavier NUCLEUS, with energy being released 核聚变；热核反应 ➲ COMPARE FISSION (1) **3** [U] music that is a mixture of different styles, especially JAZZ and rock 合成音乐，混合音乐（尤指爵士乐和摇滚乐）**4** [U] cooking that is a mixture of different styles（各种方式的）混合烹调：*French–Thai fusion* 法泰式混合烹饪

ˈ**fusion bomb** *noun* a bomb that gets its energy from nuclear FUSION, especially a HYDROGEN BOMB 聚变弹；热核弹；（尤指）氢弹

fu·sion·ist /ˈfjuːʒənɪst/ *noun* a musician who plays FUSION music 合成音乐演奏者

fuss /fʌs/ *noun, verb*

■ ***noun*** **1** [U, sing.] unnecessary excitement, worry or activity 无谓的激动（或忧虑、活动）；大惊小怪：*He does what he's told without any fuss.* 他不声不响地按照吩咐办事。◇ *All that fuss over a few pounds!* 为几英镑就那么大惊小怪的！◇ *It's a very ordinary movie—I don't know* ***what all the fuss is about*** (= why other people think it is so good). 这是部很普通的电影，我不懂为什么就会轰动。◇ *It was all* ***a fuss about nothing.*** 这完全是瞎折腾。◇ *We'd like a quiet wedding without any fuss.* 我们喜欢静静举行婚礼，不大事铺张。 **2** [sing.] anger or complaints about sth, especially sth that is not important（为小事）大吵大闹，大发牢骚：*I'm sorry for* ***making such a fuss*** *about the noise.* 对不起，我为吵闹声发了这么大的牢骚。◇ *Steve* ***kicks up a fuss*** *every time I even suggest seeing you.* 每次我即使只是提议看望你，史蒂夫就大吵大闹。

IDM **make a fuss of/over sb** to pay a lot of attention to sb, usually to show how much you like them 关爱备至；过分爱护：*They made a great fuss of the baby.* 他们对婴儿呵护备至。◇ *The dog loves being made a fuss of.* 这狗喜欢受到宠爱。

■ ***verb*** **1** [I] to do things, or pay too much attention to things, that are not important or necessary 瞎忙一气；过分关心（枝节小事）：~ (**around**) *Stop fussing around and find something useful to do!* 别瞎忙活了，找点有用的事干！◇ ~ (**with/over sth**) *Don't fuss with your hair!* 不要老摆弄你的头发了！ **2** [I] ~ (**about sth**) to worry about things that are not very important（为小事）烦恼，忧虑：*Don't fuss, Mum, everything is all right.* 别瞎操心了，妈妈，一切都好。

IDM **not be fussed** (**about sth**) (*BrE, informal*) to not mind about sth; to not have feelings about sth 不在意；无所谓；不关心 SYN **not be bothered**: *It'd be good to be there, but I'm not that fussed.* 去那里当然好，不过我无所谓。

PHR V ˈ**fuss over sb** to pay a lot of attention to sb 对…关爱备至；过分关心

fuss·pot /ˈfʌspɒt; *NAmE* -pɑːt/ (*BrE*) (*NAmE* **fuss·budget** /ˈfʌsbʌdʒɪt/) *noun* (*informal*) a person who is often worried about unimportant things and is difficult to please 大惊小怪的人；好挑剔的人；爱吹毛求疵的人

fussy /ˈfʌsi/ *adj.* (**fuss·ier**, **fussi·est**) **1** too concerned or worried about details or standards, especially unimportant ones 无谓忧虑（或担心）的；大惊小怪的；挑剔的：*fussy parents* 瞎操心的父母 ◇ ~ (**about sth**) *Our teacher is very fussy about punctuation.* 我们老师对标点符号十分挑剔。◇ *She's such a fussy eater.* 她太挑食。◇ *'Where do you want to go for lunch?' 'I'm not fussy* (= I don't mind).' "你想去哪儿吃午餐？" "我无所谓。" **2** doing sth with small, quick, nervous movements 紧张不安的：*a fussy manner* 局促不安的举止 ◇ *the quick, fussy movements of her small hands* 她的一双小手快速而紧张不安的动作 **3** having too much detail or decoration 过分琐碎的；装饰太多的：*The costume designs are too fussy.* 这些服装设计过于花哨。▶ **fuss·ily** *adv.* **fussi·ness** *noun* [U]

fus·tian /ˈfʌstiən; *NAmE* -tʃən/ *noun* [U] **1** a thick strong cotton cloth with a slightly rough surface, used in the past for making clothes 纬起绒布（旧时用作衣料）**2** (*literary*) language that sounds impressive but does not mean much 浮夸的言语

fusty /ˈfʌsti/ *adj.* (*disapproving*) **1** smelling old, damp or not fresh 腐臭的；霉湿味的 SYN **musty**: *a dark fusty room* 阴暗霉湿的房间 **2** old-fashioned 过时的；守旧的：*fusty ideas* 守旧的思想 ◇ *a fusty old professor* 古板的老教授

fu·tile /ˈfjuːtaɪl; *NAmE* -tl/ *adj.* having no purpose because there is no chance of success 徒然的；徒劳的；无效的 SYN **pointless**: *a* ***futile attempt/exercise/gesture*** 徒然的尝试 / 练习 / 表示 ◇ *Their efforts to revive him were futile.* 他们努力使他苏醒，但失败了。◇ ***It would be futile to*** *protest.* 抗议也无用。◇ *My appeal proved futile.* 我的申诉白费了。 ▶ **fu·tile·ly** *adv.* **fu·til·ity** /fjuːˈtɪləti/ *noun* [U]: *a sense of futility* 徒劳感 ◇ *the futility of war* 战争的徒劳无益

fu·ton /ˈfuːtɒn; *NAmE* -tɑːn/ *noun* a Japanese MATTRESS, often on a wooden frame, that can be used for sitting on or rolled out to make a bed 日本床垫（折叠可坐，铺开可卧）➲ VISUAL VOCAB PAGE V24

fu·ture 🔑 /ˈfjuːtʃə(r)/ *noun, adj.*

■ ***noun*** **1** 🔑 **the future** [sing.] the time that will come after the present or the events that will happen then 将来；未来：*We need to plan for the future.* 我们需要为将来作好打算。◇ *What will the cities of the future look like?* 未来的城市会是什么样子呢？◇ *The movie is set in the future.* 这部电影以未来为背景。◇ *The exchange rate is likely to fall* ***in the near future*** (= soon). 汇率可能不久就要下跌。◇ *What does the future hold?* 未来将会如何？ **2** 🔑 [C] what will happen to sb/sth at a later time 未来的事；将来发生的事；前景：*Her future is uncertain.* 她前途未卜。◇ *This deal could safeguard the futures of the 2 000 employees.* 这个协议可以保障 2 000 名雇员今后的生活。**3** 🔑 [sing., U] the possibility of being successful or surviving at a later time 前途；前程：*She has* ***a great future*** *ahead of her.* 她前程远大。◇ *I can't see any future in this relationship.* 我看不出这个关系会有什么前途。**4 futures** [pl.] (*finance* 财) goods or shares that are bought at agreed prices but that will be delivered and paid for at a later time 期货：*oil futures* 石油期货 ◇ *the futures market* 期货市场 **5 the future** [sing.] (*grammar* 语法) (*also* **the** ˌ**future** ˈ**tense**) the form of a verb that expresses what will happen after the present（动词的）将来时，将来式

IDM **in future** 🔑 (*BrE*) (*NAmE* **in the future**) from now on 今后；从今以后：*Please be more careful in future.* 今后请多加小心。◇ *In future, make sure the door is never left unlocked.* 从今以后，千万别忘记锁好门。➲ MORE AT DISTANT, FORESEEABLE

■ ***adj.*** 🔑 [only before noun] taking place or existing at a time after the present 将来的；未来的；将来发生的：*future generations* 子孙后代 ◇ *at a future date* 将来某个时候 ◇ *future developments in computer software* 计算机软件的未来发展 ◇ *He met his future wife at law school.* 他在法学院结识了他未来的妻子。

the ˌ**future** ˈ**perfect** (*also* **the** ˌ**future** ˌ**perfect** ˈ**tense**) *noun* [sing.] (*grammar* 语法) the form of a verb that expresses an action completed before a particular point in the future, formed in English with *will have* or *shall have* and the past participle 将来完成时；将来完成式

ˈfuture-proof *adj., verb*

■ ***adj.*** (*business* 商 or *specialist*) designed to continue working or to be effective after changes that may happen in the future 不会过时的：*future-proof website design* 常青而实用的网站设计

■ ***verb*** ~ **sth** to make sth future-proof 使不过时：*The firm claims that it future-proofs its software.* 这家公司声称其软件不会被时间淘汰。

fu·tur·ism /ˈfjuːtʃərɪzəm/ *noun* [U] a movement in art and literature in the 1920s and 30s that did not try to show realistic figures and scenes but aimed to express confidence in the modern world, particularly in modern machines 未来主义（20 世纪 20 和 30 年代的文艺运动，强调对技术时代的赞叹）▶ **fu·tur·ist** *noun* **fu·tur·ist** *adj.*：*futurist poets* 未来主义诗人

fu·tur·is·tic /ˌfjuːtʃəˈrɪstɪk/ *adj.* **1** extremely modern and unusual in appearance, as if belonging to a future time 极其现代的；未来派的：*futuristic design* 未来感设计 **2** imagining what the future will be like 幻想未来的；想象未来情况的：*a futuristic novel* 幻想未来的小说

fu·tur·ity /fjuˈtjʊərəti; *NAmE* -ˈtʊr-/ *noun* [U] (*formal*) the time that will come after the present and what will happen then 将来；未来：*a vision of futurity* 对未来的展望

fu·turo·lo·gist /ˌfjuːtʃəˈrɒlədʒɪst; *NAmE* -ˈrɑːl-/ *noun* a person who is an expert in futurology 未来学家

fu·tur·ology /ˌfjuːtʃəˈrɒlədʒi; *NAmE* -ˈrɑːl-/ *noun* [U] the study of how people will live in the future 未来学

fuze *noun* (*NAmE*) = FUSE (3)

fuzz /fʌz/ *noun* **1** [U] short soft fine hair or fur that covers sth, especially a person's face or arms 茸毛，绒毛（尤指人脸或手臂的）SYN **down** **2** [sing.] a mass of hair in tight curls 鬈发：*a fuzz of blonde hair* 一团金色鬈发 **3 the fuzz** [sing.+sing./pl. v.] (*old-fashioned, slang*) the police 警方 **4** something that you cannot see clearly 模糊的东西 SYN **blur**：*I saw it as a dim fuzz through the binoculars.* 我从双筒望远镜只看见一团模模糊糊的东西。

fuzz·box /ˈfʌzbɒks; *NAmE* -bɑːks/ *noun* a device that is used to change the sound of an electric GUITAR or other instrument by making the notes sound noisier and less clear（电吉他等的）模糊音装置

fuzzy /ˈfʌzi/ *adj.* (**fuzz·ier, fuzzi·est**) **1** covered with short soft fine hair or fur 覆有绒毛的；毛茸茸的 SYN **downy** **2** (of hair 毛发) in a mass of tight curls 紧鬈的；拳曲的 **3** not clear in shape or sound（形状或声音）模糊不清的 SYN **blurred**：*a fuzzy image* 模糊的形象 ◇ *The soundtrack is fuzzy in places.* 这电影声带有些地方模糊不清。**4** confused and not expressed clearly 糊涂的；含混不清的：*fuzzy ideas/thinking* 糊涂的想法 / 思想 ▶ **fuzz·ily** *adv.* **fuzzi·ness** *noun* [U]

ˌfuzzy ˈlogic *noun* [U] (*computing* 计) a type of logic that is used to try to make computers behave like the human brain 模糊逻辑（尝试使计算机模拟人脑）

FWIW *abbr.* (*informal*) used in writing to mean 'for what it's worth' 不论真伪；不论好坏

ˈF-word *noun* [sing.] (*informal*) used to replace a word beginning with F that you do not want to say, especially the offensive swear word 'fuck' * F 开头的词（用以替代不想说出口的以 F 开头的词，尤其是粗俗的骂人话 fuck）：*He was shocked at how often she used the F-word.* 她脏话不离口，使他感到震惊。➲ COMPARE C-WORD

FX /ˌef ˈeks/ *abbr.* **1** a short way of writing SPECIAL EFFECTS 特效（全写为 special effects）**2** a short way of writing FOREIGN EXCHANGE 外汇（全写为 foreign exchange）

-fy ➲ -IFY

FYI *abbr.* used mainly in writing to mean 'for your information' 供参考（for your information 的书写形式）

Gg

G /dʒiː/ *noun, abbr.*

■ ***noun*** (*also* **g**) [C, U] (*pl.* **Gs, G's, g's** /dʒiːz/) **1** the 7th letter of the English alphabet 英语字母表的第 7 个字母：*'Gold' begins with (a) G/'G'.* * gold 一词以字母 g 开头。 **2 G** (*music* 音) the fifth note in the SCALE of C MAJOR * G 音（C 大调的第 5 音或音符）➲ SEE ALSO G AND T, G-STRING

■ ***abbr.*** **1** (*NAmE*) general audience (a label for a film/movie that is suitable for anyone, including children) * G 级，老少咸宜（影片分级用语，表示适合包括儿童在内的任何人观看） **2** (*NAmE, informal*) $1 000 * 1 000 美元

g *abbr.* **1** gram(s) 克：*400g flour* * 400 克面粉 **2** /dʒiː/ (*specialist*) GRAVITY or a measurement of the force with which sth moves faster through space because of GRAVITY 重力；地球引力：*Spacecraft which are re-entering the earth's atmosphere are affected by g forces.* 重返大气层的航天器受到重力的作用。

gab /ɡæb/ *verb, noun*

■ ***verb*** (**-bb-**) (*informal*) [I] to talk for a long time about things that are not important 喋喋不休；啰唆；唠叨

■ ***noun*** IDM SEE GIFT *n.*

gab·ar·dine (*also* **gab·er·dine**) /ˌɡæbəˈdiːn; ˈɡæbədiːn; *NAmE* -bərd-/ *noun* **1** [U] a strong material used especially for making RAINCOATS 华达呢，轧别丁（结实织物，尤用于制雨衣） **2** [C] a coat, especially a RAINCOAT, made of gabardine 华达呢外衣；华达呢雨衣

gab·ble /ˈɡæbl/ *verb, noun*

■ ***verb*** [I, T] (*informal*) to talk quickly so that people cannot hear you clearly or understand you 急促而含混不清地说：*She was nervous and started to gabble.* 她紧张得话都说不清了。◇ **~ on/away** *They were gabbling on about the past.* 他们谈论着过去，声音显得急促而含混不清。◇ **~ sth** *He was gabbling nonsense.* 他在叽里咕噜说废话。◇ **+ speech** *'No, no, not all,' she gabbled.* "不，不，不是所有。"她急促而含糊地说。

■ ***noun*** [sing.] fast speech that is difficult to understand, especially when a lot of people are talking at the same time （尤指许多人同时说话时）急促不清的话

gabby /ˈɡæbi/ *adj.* (*informal, disapproving*) talking a lot, especially about things that are not important 贫嘴的；饶舌的；聒噪的

gab·fest /ˈɡæbfest/ *noun* (*NAmE, informal*) an informal meeting to talk and exchange news; a long conversation 杂谈会；长时间的交谈

ga·bion /ˈɡeɪbiən/ *noun* a large square container made of wire in which rocks are packed. Gabions are used for building structures outdoors, for example to support pieces of ground or control a flow of water. 石笼（筑堤等用的铁丝网）

gable /ˈɡeɪbl/ *noun* the upper part of the end wall of a building, between the two sloping sides of the roof, that is shaped like a triangle 三角墙；山墙 ➲ VISUAL VOCAB PAGE V18

gabled /ˈɡeɪbld/ *adj.* having one or more gables 有山墙的；有三角墙的：***a gabled house/roof*** 有山墙的房子 / 屋顶

ga·boon /ɡəˈbuːn/ (*also* **gaˌboon maˈhogany**) *noun* [U] the hard wood of a tropical African tree, used especially for making parts of musical instruments or small pieces of decoration 加蓬桃花心木（非洲热带硬质木材，尤用于制作乐器部件或小饰物）

gad /ɡæd/ *verb* (**-dd-**)

PHR V **ˌgad aˈbout/aˈround** (*informal, especially BrE*) to visit different places and have fun, especially when you should be doing sth else 闲逛；游荡

gad·about /ˈɡædəbaʊt/ *noun* (*informal, often humorous*) a person who is always going out socially or travelling for pleasure 好社交者；好旅游者

gad·fly /ˈɡædflaɪ/ *noun* (*pl.* **-ies**) (*usually disapproving*) a person who annoys or criticizes other people in order to make them do sth （为使别人做某事而对其进行骚扰或批评的）讨人厌者

gadget /ˈɡædʒɪt/ *noun* a small tool or device that does sth useful 小器具；小装置

gadget·ry /ˈɡædʒɪtri/ *noun* [U] (*sometimes disapproving*) a collection of modern tools and devices（统称）小器具，小装置：*His desk is covered with electronic gadgetry.* 他的书桌上摆满了各种电子玩意儿。

gado·lin·ium /ˌɡædəˈlɪniəm/ *noun* [U] (*symb.* **Gd**) a chemical element. Gadolinium is a soft silver-white metal. 钆

G

gad·zooks /ɡædˈzuːks/ *exclamation* (*old use*) used in the past to show that sb is surprised or annoyed（旧时用语，表示惊讶或恼怒）天哪，哎呀，该死

Gael·ic *noun* [U] **1** /ˈɡælɪk; ˈɡeɪlɪk/ the Celtic language of Scotland（苏格兰的）盖尔语 ➲ COMPARE SCOTS *n.* **2** /ˈɡeɪlɪk/ (*also* **ˌIrish ˈGaelic**) the Celtic language of Ireland（爱尔兰的）盖尔语 ➲ COMPARE ERSE, IRISH *n.* (1) ▶ **Gael·ic** *adj.*

ˌGaelic ˈfootball *noun* [U] a game played mainly in Ireland between two teams of 15 players. The players of one team try to kick or hit a round ball into or over the other team's goal. 盖尔式足球，爱尔兰式足球（两队各 15 人，将球踢进或击进球门或越过门梁得分）

the Gael·tacht /ˈɡeɪltæxt/ *noun* the parts of Ireland and Scotland where Gaelic is spoken by a large part of the population （爱尔兰和苏格兰的）盖尔语地区

gaff /ɡæf/ *noun* **1** a pole with a hook on the end used to pull large fish out of the water（将大鱼拉出水的）挽钩，手钩 **2** (*BrE, slang*) the house, flat/apartment, etc. where sb lives 住所；安乐窝 IDM SEE BLOW *v.*

gaffe /ɡæf/ *noun* a mistake that a person makes in public or in a social situation, especially sth embarrassing 失礼；失态；失言 SYN **faux pas**

gaf·fer /ˈɡæfə(r)/ *noun* **1** (*BrE, informal*) a person who is in charge of a group of people, for example, workers in a factory, a sports team, etc.（工厂的）工头，领班；（运动队等的）领队，负责人 SYN **boss 2** the person who is in charge of the electrical work and the lights when a film/movie or television programme is being made（拍电影或电视节目的）照明电工

ˈgaffer tape *noun* [U] (*BrE*) strong sticky tape with cloth on the back 电工胶布；厚胶布

gag /ɡæɡ/ *noun, verb*

■ ***noun*** **1** a piece of cloth that is put over or in sb's mouth to stop them speaking （使人不能说话的）封口布；塞口布 **2** an order that prevents sth from being publicly reported or discussed 禁刊令（阻止公开报道或讨论某事的法令）：*a press gag* 新闻禁刊令 ◇ ***a gag rule/order*** (= one given by a court of law) 禁止发言规则；限制言论令 **3** (*informal*) a joke or a funny story, especially one told by a professional COMEDIAN（尤指专业喜剧演员的）插科打诨，笑话，噱头 SYN **joke**：***to tell/crack a gag*** 讲笑话 ◇ ***a running gag*** (= one that is regularly repeated during a performance) 重复出现的笑话桥段 **4** (*especially NAmE*) a trick you play on sb 恶作剧；诡计；花招：*It was just a gag—we didn't mean to upset anyone.* 这只是逗着玩，我们没想让人不高兴。

■ ***verb*** (**-gg-**) **1** [T] **~ sb** to put a piece of cloth in or over sb's mouth to prevent them from speaking or shouting 捂住，塞住（某人的嘴）：*The hostages were **bound and gagged**.* 人质被绑起来并被人用东西塞住了嘴。 **2** [T] **~ sb/sth** to prevent sb from speaking freely or expressing their opinion 压制…的言论自由；使缄默：*The new laws are seen as an attempt to gag the press.* 人们认为新法律企图压制新闻界的言论自由。➲ SEE ALSO GAGGING ORDER **3** [I] **~ (on sth)** to have the unpleasant feeling in your mouth and stomach as if you are going to VOMIT 作呕 SYN retch: *She gagged on the blood that filled her mouth.* 她因嘴里充满了血而作呕。

IDM **be gagging for sth/to do sth** (*BrE, slang*) to want sth or want to do sth very much 渴求（某物）；迫切想做（某事） **be 'gagging for it** (*BrE, slang*) to want very much to have sex 欲火中烧

gaga /ˈɡɑːɡɑː/ *adj.* [not usually before noun] (*informal*) **1** (*offensive*) confused and not able to think clearly, especially because you are old 迷糊；（尤因年老）糊涂：*He has gone completely gaga.* 他完全老糊涂了。 **2** slightly crazy because you are very excited about sb/sth, or very much in love 狂热；着迷：*The fans went totally gaga over the band.* 乐迷们对这个乐队完全着迷了。

G

gage (*US*) = GAUGE

'gagging order (*BrE*) (*NAmE* **'gag order**) *noun* an order by a court that prevents people from talking or writing about a particular matter, especially about what is happening in a court case 禁言命令，缄口令，封口令（法院下达禁止谈论或报道庭审案件等的命令）：*to impose/issue/lift/obtain a gagging order* 强制实行 / 发布 / 解除 / 收到禁言令 ➲ SEE ALSO GAG *v.* (2)

gag·gle /ˈɡæɡl/ *noun* **1** a group of noisy people 一群（吵闹的人）：*a **gaggle of** tourists/schoolchildren* 一群喧闹的游客 / 叽叽喳喳的小学生 **2** a group of GEESE 一群（鹅）；（鹅）群

'gag order (*NAmE*) = GAGGING ORDER

Gaia /ˈɡaɪə/ *noun* [sing.] the Earth, considered as a single natural system which organizes and controls itself 盖娅（被视为能进行自我组织与控制的单一自然体系的地球）

gai·ety /ˈɡeɪəti/ *noun* [U] (*old-fashioned*) the state of being cheerful and full of fun 快乐；愉快；高兴：*The colourful flags added to the gaiety of the occasion.* 彩旗增添了盛会的欢乐气氛。 ➲ COMPARE GAYNESS ➲ SEE ALSO GAILY (2), GAY *adj.* (4)

gaily /ˈɡeɪli/ *adv.* **1** in a bright and attractive way 花哨地；艳丽地；华丽地：*a gaily decorated room* 装饰华丽的房间 **2** in a cheerful way 快乐地；欢乐地；喜气洋洋地：*gaily laughing children* 喜笑颜开的孩子 ◇ *She waved gaily to the little crowd.* 她高兴地向这一小群人挥手。 **3** without thinking or caring about the effect of your actions on other people 欠思索地；毫无顾忌地；轻率地：*She gaily announced that she was leaving the next day.* 她不假思索地宣布说她第二天要离开。 ➲ SEE ALSO GAIETY, GAY *adj.* (4)

gain 🔑 /ɡeɪn/ *verb, noun*

■ *verb*

• **OBTAIN/WIN** 获得；赢得 **1** 🔑 [T] to obtain or win sth, especially sth that you need or want 获得；赢得；博得；取得：~ **sth** *to **gain** entrance/entry/access **to** sth* 得以进入 ◇ *The country gained its independence ten years ago.* 这个国家十年前赢得了独立。 ◇ *The party gained over 50% of the vote.* 该党获得超过 50% 的选票。 ◇ ~ **sb sth** *Her unusual talent gained her worldwide recognition.* 她非凡的才能举世公认。 **2** 🔑 [T, I] to obtain an advantage or benefit from sth or from doing sth （从…中）受益，获益；得到（好处）：~ **sth (by/from sth)** *There is **nothing to be gained** from delaying the decision.* 推迟决定得不到任何好处。 ◇ ~ **(by/from sth)** *Who **stands to gain from** this decision?* 谁会从这一决定中受益呢？

• **GET MORE** 增加 **3** 🔑 [T] ~ **sth** to gradually get more of sth 增加；增添；增进；增长：*to **gain** confidence/strength/experience* 增加信心 / 力量 / 经验 ◇ *I've **gained weight** recently.* 最近我的体重增加了。 OPP **lose**

• **OF WATCH/CLOCK** 钟表 **4** [T, I] ~ **(sth)** to go too fast 走得太快；快：*My watch gains two minutes every 24 hours.* 我的表每 24 小时快两分钟。 OPP **lose**

• **OF CURRENCIES/SHARES** 货币；股票 **5** [T, I] to increase in value 增值；升值：~ **sth** *The shares gained 14p to 262p.* 股价上升了 14 便士，收报 262 便士。 ◇ ~ **against sth** *The euro gained against the dollar again today.* 今天欧元兑美元的汇率又上升了。

• **REACH PLACE** 到达某地 **6** [T] ~ **sth** (*formal*) to reach a place, usually after a lot of effort （经过努力）到达：*At last she gained the shelter of the forest.* 她终于到达了森林中的隐蔽处。

IDM **gain 'ground** to become more powerful or successful 变得更强大（或更有成效、更成功）；有进步；获得进展：*Sterling continues to gain ground against the dollar.* 英镑兑美元继续走高。 **gain 'time** to delay sth so that you can have more time to make a decision, deal with a problem, etc. （通过拖延）赢得时间 ➲ MORE AT VENTURE *v.*

PHR V **'gain in sth** to get more of a particular quality 增加；增长：*to gain in confidence* 增加信心 ◇ *His books have gained in popularity in recent years.* 近年来他的书越来越受欢迎。 **'gain on sb/sth** to get closer to sb/sth that you are chasing 接近，逼近（所追逐的人或物）

■ *noun*

• **INCREASE** 增加 **1** 🔑 [C, U] an increase in the amount of sth, especially in wealth or weight （尤指财富、重量的）增值，增加：*a £3 000 gain from our investment* 从我们的投资中获取的 3 000 英镑的收益 ◇ *Regular exercise helps prevent weight gain.* 经常锻炼有助于防止体重增加。

• **ADVANTAGE** 好处 **2** 🔑 [C] an advantage or improvement 好处；利益；改进：*efficiency gains* 效率提高 ◇ *These policies have resulted in great gains in public health.* 这些政策使公共卫生得到极大改进。 ◇ *Our loss is their gain.* 我们之所失即他们之所得。 OPP **loss**

• **PROFIT** 利润 **3** [U] (*often disapproving*) financial profit 利润；经济收益：*He only seems to be interested in personal gain.* 他似乎只在乎个人的收益。 ◇ *It's amazing what some people will do **for gain**.* 有的人为一己之利而干出的事真让人吃惊。 IDM SEE PAIN *n.*

gain·ful /ˈɡeɪnfl/ *adj.* (*formal*) used to describe useful work that you are paid for 有收益的；有报酬的；有利可图的：*gainful employment* 有酬的工作 ▶ **gain·ful·ly** /-fəli/ *adv.*：*gainfully employed* 被有酬雇用

gain·say /ˌɡeɪnˈseɪ/ *verb* (**gain·says** /-ˈsez/, **gain·said**, **gain·said** /-ˈsed/) ~ **sth** (*formal*) (often used in negative sentences 常用于否定句) to say that sth is not true; to disagree with or deny sth 反驳；反对；否认 SYN **deny**: *Nobody can gainsay his claims.* 没人能够反驳他的说法。

gait /ɡeɪt/ *noun* [sing.] a way of walking 步态；步法：*He walked with a rolling gait.* 他走起路来摇摇晃晃。

gai·ter /ˈɡeɪtə(r)/ *noun* [usually pl.] a cloth or leather covering for the leg between the knee and the ankle. Gaiters were worn by men in the past and are now mainly worn by people who go walking or climbing. 绑腿，护腿（旧时为男士所穿，现主要为徒步者或登山者所穿）：*a pair of gaiters* 一副绑腿

gal /ɡæl/ *noun* (*old-fashioned, informal, especially NAmE*) a girl or woman 女孩；姑娘；女子

gal. *abbr.* (in writing 书写形式) gallon(s) 加仑（液量单位）

gala /ˈɡɑːlə; *NAmE* ˈɡeɪlə/ *noun* **1** a special public celebration or entertainment 庆典；盛会；演出：*a charity gala* 慈善义演 ◇ *a **gala** dinner/night* 盛宴；晚会 **2** (*BrE*) a sports competition, especially in swimming 体育运动会，体育竞赛（尤指游泳）：*a swimming gala* 游泳比赛

ga·lac·tic /ɡəˈlæktɪk/ *adj.* relating to a galaxy 银河的；星系的

galah /ɡəˈlɑː/ *noun* (*AustralE, informal*) a stupid person 蠢人；傻瓜

gal·axy /ˈɡæləksi/ *noun* (*pl.* **-ies**) **1** [C] any of the large systems of stars, etc. in outer space 星系 ➲ WORDFINDER NOTE AT UNIVERSE **2 the Galaxy** (*also* **the ˌMilky 'Way**) [sing.] the system of stars that contains our sun and its planets, seen as a bright band in the night sky 银河；银河系 **3** [C] (*informal*) a group of famous people, or people with a particular skill 群英；人才荟萃：*a galaxy of Hollywood stars* 好莱坞影星的荟萃

gale /ɡeɪl/ *noun* an extremely strong wind 大风；飓风：*The gale blew down hundreds of trees.* 大风吹倒了数百棵树。 ◇ ***gale-force** winds* 七到十级的风 ◇ (*BrE*) ***It's blowing a gale** outside* (= a strong wind is blowing). 外面在刮大

风。 ➲ WORDFINDER NOTE AT WIND[1] ➲ COLLOCATIONS AT WEATHER

IDM gale(s) of laughter the sound of people laughing very loudly 一阵（阵）大笑声：*His speech was greeted with gales of laughter.* 人们对他的演讲报以阵阵笑声。

gall /gɔːl/ *noun, verb*

■ ***noun*** **1** rude behaviour showing a lack of respect that is surprising because the person behaving badly is not embarrassed 鲁莽；厚颜无耻 **SYN impudence**：*Then they* ***had the gall to*** *complain!* 而且他们居然还有脸抱怨！ **2** (*formal*) a bitter feeling full of hatred 怨恨；怨愤 **SYN resentment** **3** a swelling on plants and trees caused by insects, disease, etc. 瘿瘤（植物因受病原刺激或虫害而出现的局部增生） **4** (*old-fashioned*) = BILE

■ ***verb*** **~ sb | it galls sb to do sth | it galls sb that…** to make sb feel upset and angry, especially because sth is unfair 使烦恼，使愤怒（尤指因不公平引起）：*It galls me to have to apologize to her.* 非得向她道歉使我感到恼火。 ➲ SEE ALSO GALLING

gal·lant *adj., noun*

■ ***adj.*** /ˈɡælənt/ **1** (*old-fashioned* or *literary*) brave, especially in a very difficult situation（尤指在困境中）勇敢的，英勇的 **SYN heroic**：*gallant soldiers* 勇敢的军人 ◇ *She made a gallant attempt to hide her tears.* 她强忍住泪水。 **2** (of a man 男子) giving polite attention to women 对女子殷勤的 ▸ **gal·lant·ly** *adv.*：*She gallantly battled on alone.* 她单枪匹马继续英勇顽强地战斗。◇ *He bowed and gallantly kissed my hand.* 他鞠了一躬，殷勤地吻了吻我的手。

■ ***noun*** /ɡəˈlænt; ˈɡælənt/ (*old-fashioned*) a fashionable young man, especially one who gives polite attention to women （尤指对女子殷勤的）时髦男子

gal·lant·ry /ˈɡæləntri/ *noun* [U] (*formal*) **1** courage, especially in a battle（尤指在战场上）勇敢，英勇顽强：*a medal for gallantry* 英勇勋章 **2** polite attention given by men to women （男子对女子的）殷勤

ˈgall bladder *noun* an organ attached to the LIVER in which BILE is stored 胆囊 ➲ VISUAL VOCAB PAGE V64

gal·leon /ˈɡæliən/ *noun* a large Spanish sailing ship, used between the 15th and the 17th centuries （15–17 世纪使用的）西班牙大帆船

gal·ler·ied /ˈɡælərid/ *adj.* (of a building 建筑物) having a gallery (3) 有楼座的

gal·lery /ˈɡæləri/ *noun* (*pl.* **-ies**) **1** a room or building for showing works of art, especially to the public（艺术作品的）陈列室，展览馆；画廊：***an art/a picture gallery*** 美术馆 ◇ *the National Gallery* 国家美术馆 ➲ COLLOCATIONS AT ART ➲ SEE ALSO ART GALLERY **2** a small private shop/store where you can see and buy works of art 私家画店 **3** an upstairs area at the back or sides of a large hall where people can sit （大厅的）楼座，楼上旁听席：*Relatives of the victim watched from the public gallery as the murder charge was read out in court.* 法庭宣读谋杀指控时受害者的亲属在公共旁听席观看。 ➲ SEE ALSO PRESS GALLERY **4** the highest level in a theatre where the cheapest seats are （剧场中票价最低的）顶层楼座 **5** a long narrow room, especially one used for a particular purpose 长廊；走廊；柱廊 ➲ SEE ALSO SHOOTING GALLERY **6** a level passage under the ground in a mine or CAVE （矿坑或洞穴中的）水平巷道

IDM play to the ˈgallery to behave in an exaggerated way to attract people's attention 哗众取宠；行为惹人注目

gal·ley /ˈɡæli/ *noun* **1** a long flat ship with sails, usually ROWED by SLAVES or criminals, especially one used by the ancient Greeks or Romans in war（常由奴隶或囚犯划桨的）桨帆船；（古希腊和古罗马的）战舰 **2** the kitchen on a ship or plane（船或飞机上的）厨房

Gal·lic /ˈɡælɪk/ *adj.* connected with or considered typical of France or its people 法国的；法国人的；高卢的；高卢人的：*Gallic charm* 法国的魅力

gall·ing /ˈɡɔːlɪŋ/ *adj.* [not usually before noun] (of a situation or fact 境况或事实) making you angry because it is unfair 令人恼怒；使人烦恼；使人感到屈辱：*It was galling to have to apologize to a man she hated.* 令人恼火的是得向她憎恶的男人道歉。

gal·lium /ˈɡæliəm/ *noun* [U] (*symb.* **Ga**) a chemical element. Gallium is a soft silver-white metal. 镓

gal·li·vant /ˈɡælɪvænt/ *verb* [I] (usually used in the progressive tenses 通常用于进行时) **~ (about/around)** (*old-fashioned, informal*) to go from place to place enjoying yourself 游玩；游览；闲游 **SYN gad**：*You're too old to go gallivanting around Europe.* 你年纪太大，不能到欧洲各地去游逛了。

gal·lon 🔑 /ˈɡælən/ *noun* (*abbr.* **gal.**) a unit for measuring liquid. In the UK, Canada and other countries it is equal to about 4.5 litres; in the US it is equal to about 3.8 litres. There are four QUARTS in a gallon. 加仑（液量单位，在英国、加拿大及其他一些国家约等于 4.5 升，在美国约等于 3.8 升，一加仑为四夸脱）

gal·lop /ˈɡæləp/ *verb, noun*

■ ***verb*** **1** [I] (+ **adv./prep.**) when a horse or similar animal **gallops**, it moves very fast and each STRIDE includes a stage when all four feet are off the ground together （马等）飞奔，奔驰，疾驰 ➲ COMPARE CANTER *v.* ➲ WORDFINDER NOTE AT HORSE **2** [I, T] to ride a horse very fast, usually at a gallop 骑马奔驰；使（马）飞奔：(+ **adv./prep.**) *Jo galloped across the field towards him.* 乔骑马穿过田野向他奔去。◇ **~ sth** (+ **adv./prep.**) *He galloped his horse home.* 他骑着马飞奔回家。 ➲ COMPARE CANTER *v.* **3** [I] (+ **adv./prep.**) (*informal*) (of a person 人) to run very quickly 飞跑；奔跑 **SYN charge**：*She came galloping down the street.* 她沿街飞奔而来。

■ ***noun*** **1** [sing.] the fastest speed at which a horse can run, with a stage in which all four feet are off the ground together（马的）飞奔，奔驰，疾驰：*He rode off* ***at a gallop.*** 他骑马疾驰而去。◇ *My horse suddenly* ***broke into a gallop.*** 我的马突然飞奔起来。 **2** [C] a ride on a horse at its fastest speed 骑马奔驰：*to go for a gallop* 去骑马奔驰一番 **3** [sing.] an unusually fast speed 飞快；高速度

gal·lop·ing /ˈɡæləpɪŋ/ *adj.* [only before noun] increasing or spreading rapidly 迅速增加（或蔓延）的：*galloping inflation* 急剧的通货膨胀

gal·lows /ˈɡæləʊz; *NAmE* -loʊz/ *noun* (*pl.* **gal·lows**) a structure on which people, for example criminals, are killed by hanging 绞刑架；绞台：*to send a man to the gallows* (= to send him to his death by hanging) 把一名男子送上绞刑架

ˌgallows ˈhumour (*especially US* **ˌgallows ˈhumor**) *noun* [U] jokes about unpleasant things like death 绞刑架下的幽默；面临大难时的幽默

gall·stone /ˈɡɔːlstəʊn; *NAmE* -stoʊn/ *noun* a hard painful mass that can form in the GALL BLADDER 胆（结）石

Gal·lup poll™ /ˈɡæləp pəʊl; *NAmE* poʊl/ *noun* a way of finding out public opinion by asking a typical group of people questions 盖洛普民意测验 **ORIGIN** From G H Gallup, who invented it. 源自创始人盖洛普 (G H Gallup) 的名字。

gal·ore /ɡəˈlɔː(r)/ *adj.* [after noun] (*informal*) in large quantities 大量；很多：*There will be games and prizes galore.* 将有很多游戏和奖品。

gal·oshes /ɡəˈlɒʃɪz; *NAmE* -ˈlɑːʃ-/ *noun* [pl.] rubber shoes (no longer very common) that are worn over normal shoes in wet weather 橡胶套鞋（雨天套在平常穿的鞋上，现已不常见）：*a pair of galoshes* 一双橡胶套鞋

gal·umph /ɡəˈlʌmf/ *verb* [I] + **adv./prep.** (*informal*) to move in an awkward, careless or noisy way 笨拙（或懒散）地挪动；脚步声嘈杂地行进

gal·van·ic /ɡælˈvænɪk/ *adj.* **1** (*specialist*) producing an electric current by the action of a chemical on metal （以化学作用）产生电流的 **2** (*formal*) making people react in a sudden and dramatic way 突然的；令人震惊的；使人激动的

gal·van·ize (*BrE also* **-ise**) /ˈɡælvənaɪz/ *verb* **1** ~ **sb** (**into sth/into doing sth**) to make sb take action by shocking them or by making them excited 使震惊；使振奋；激励；刺激：*The urgency of his voice* ***galvanized them into action.*** 他急迫的声音激励他们行动起来。 **2** ~ **sth** (*specialist*) to cover metal with ZINC in order to protect it from RUST 电镀；给（金属）镀锌：*a galvanized bucket* 镀锌桶 ◇ *galvanized steel* 镀锌钢

gam·bit /ˈɡæmbɪt/ *noun* **1** a thing that sb does, or sth that sb says at the beginning of a situation or conversation, that is intended to give them some advantage 开头一招；开局；开场白：*an* ***opening gambit*** (= the first thing you say) 开场白 **2** a move or moves made at the beginning of a game of CHESS in order to gain an advantage later（国际象棋中为获得优势而采取的）开局让棋法

gam·ble /ˈɡæmbl/ *verb, noun*

■ ***verb*** **1** [I, T] to risk money on a card game, horse race, etc.（牌戏、赛马等中）赌博，打赌： ~ (**at/on sth**) *to* ***gamble at cards*** 赌纸牌 ◇ *to* ***gamble on the horses*** 赌马 ◇ ~ **sth** (**at/on sth**) *I gambled all my winnings on the last race.* 我把赢的钱全押在最后一场比赛上了。 **2** [T, I] to risk losing sth in the hope of being successful 冒风险；碰运气；以…为赌注： ~ **sth** (**on sth**) *He's gambling his reputation on this deal.* 他在以自己的声誉为这笔交易作赌注。 ◇ ~ **with/on sth** *It was wrong to gamble with our children's future.* 拿我们孩子的未来冒险是错误的。 ▶ **gam·bler** /ˈɡæmblə(r)/ *noun*：*He was a* ***compulsive gambler*** (= found it difficult to stop). 他嗜赌成癖。

PHR V ˌ**gamble sth↔aˈway** to lose sth such as money, possessions, etc. by gambling 赌掉；赌光 ˈ**gamble on sth/on doing sth** to take a risk with sth, hoping that you will be successful 冒…的风险；碰…的运气：*He gambled on being able to buy a ticket at the last minute.* 他碰运气看能否在最后一刻买到票。

■ ***noun*** [sing.] an action that you take when you know there is a risk but when you hope that the result will be a success 赌博；打赌；冒险：*She knew she was* ***taking a gamble*** *but decided it was worth it.* 她知道是在冒险，但她认为冒这个险值得。 ◇ *They invested money in the company right at the start and* ***the gamble paid off*** (= brought them success). 他们一开始就把资金投到这家公司，结果这一冒险获得了成功。

gam·bling /ˈɡæmblɪŋ/ *noun* [U] the activity of playing games of chance for money and of betting on horses, etc. 赌博；打赌；赌钱：*heavy gambling debts* 沉重的赌债 ➲ WORDFINDER NOTE AT CARD

> WORDFINDER 联想词： bet, casino, chip, croupier, lottery, odds, roulette, stake, streak

gam·bol /ˈɡæmbl/ *verb* (**-ll-**, *US also* **-l-**) [I] (+ **adv./prep.**) to jump or run about in a lively way 跳跃；嬉戏：*lambs gambolling in the meadow* 在草地上蹦蹦跳跳的小羊羔

game /ɡeɪm/ *noun, verb, adj.*

■ ***noun***

• **ACTIVITY/SPORT** 活动；体育运动 **1** [C] an activity or a sport with rules in which people or teams compete against each other （有规则的）游戏，运动，比赛项目：*card games* 纸牌游戏 ◇ *board games* 棋类游戏 ◇ *a game of chance/skill* 靠运气决定胜负 / 凭技巧取胜的游戏 ◇ *ball games, such as football or tennis* 诸如足球或网球等球类运动 ◇ (*NAmE*) *We're going to the ball game* (= BASEBALL game). 我们要去看棒球比赛。 ➲ VISUAL VOCAB PAGES V41-43 ➲ SEE ALSO WAR GAME **2** [C] an occasion of playing a game（一项）游戏，运动，比赛：*to* ***play a game of*** *chess* 下国际象棋 ◇ *Saturday's League game against Swansea* 联赛中星期六对斯旺西队的比赛 ◇ *Let's* ***have a game of*** *table tennis.* 咱们来打场乒乓球赛吧。 ◇ *They're in training for the big game.* 他们正在为大赛进行训练。 **3** [sing.] **sb's ~** the way in which sb plays a game 比赛（或游戏）时用的手法；比赛（或游戏）技巧：*Maguire* ***raised his game*** *to collect the £40 000 first prize.* 马圭尔的比赛技巧有所提高，得到了 4 万英镑的头等奖。 ◇ *Stretching exercises can help you avoid injury and improve your game.* 伸展运动有助于防止身体受伤，并能提高比赛技巧。

• **SPORTS** 体育运动 **4** **games** [pl.] a large organized sports event 运动会：*the Olympic Games* 奥运会 **5** **games** [pl.] (*old-fashioned, BrE*) sport as a lesson or an activity at school（学校的）体育课，体育活动：*I always hated games at school.* 我念书的时候一直不喜欢体育活动。

• **PART OF SPORTS MATCH** 体育比赛的一部分 **6** [C] a section of some games, such as TENNIS, which forms a unit in scoring（网球等比赛的）一局，一场：*two games all* (= both players have won two games) 各赢两局

• **CHILDREN'S ACTIVITY** 儿童活动 **7** [C] a children's activity when they play with toys, pretend to be sb else, etc. 儿童游戏：*a game of cops and robbers* 警察抓强盗的游戏 ➲ SYNONYMS AT INTEREST

• **FUN** 娱乐 **8** [C] an activity that you do to have fun 娱乐；消遣；玩耍：*He was* ***playing games*** *with the dog.* 他在逗着狗玩。 ➲ SYNONYMS AT INTEREST

• **ACTIVITY, BUSINESS** 活动；行业 **9** [C] a type of activity or business 行当；行业；职业： *How long have you been in this game?* 你干这行当多长时间了？ ◇ *the game of politics* 政治活动 ◇ *I'm* ***new to this game*** *myself.* 我本人对这个不熟悉。 ◇ *Getting dirty was* ***all part of the game*** *to the kids.* 对孩子来说弄脏是很正常的事。 ➲ SEE ALSO WAITING GAME

• **SECRET PLAN** 秘密计划 **10** [C] (*informal*) a secret and clever plan; a trick 诡计；策略；花招：*So* ***that's his game*** (= now I know what he has been planning). 原来这就是他的鬼把戏。

• **WILD ANIMALS/BIRDS** 野生鸟兽 **11** [U] wild animals or birds that people hunt for sport or food 猎物；野禽；野味 ➲ VISUAL VOCAB PAGE V12 ➲ WORDFINDER NOTE AT HUNT ➲ SEE ALSO BIG GAME, FAIR GAME

IDM **be a ˈgame** to not be considered to be serious 不当一回事；当儿戏；闹着玩：*For her the whole project was just a game.* 对她来说，整个计划不过是场儿戏而已。 **be on the ˈgame** (*BrE, slang*) to be a PROSTITUTE 卖淫；当"野鸡" **be ˌout of the ˈgame** to no longer have a chance of winning a game or succeeding in an activity that you are taking part in 被淘汰出局 **be ˌstill/ˌback in the ˈgame** to still/once again have a good chance of winning a game or succeeding in an activity that you are taking part in 没有出局；仍有获胜（或成功）的机会： *The team was still in the game, just one goal down.* 这个队还没出局，只落后一球。 **the game is ˈup** (*informal*) said to sb who has done sth wrong, when they are caught and the crime or trick has been discovered （对做坏事被抓或罪行败露者说的话）戏该收场了，别再演戏了 **game ˈon** (*informal*) used after sth has happened that makes it clear that a contest is not yet decided and anyone could still win（赛场局势发生变化后表明）胜负难料：*We were losing 2–0 with ten minutes to go, and then we scored. It was game on!* 离终场还有十分钟，我们以 0:2 落后，随后我们进球了。谁输谁赢还说不定呢！ **give the ˈgame away** to tell a secret, especially by accident; to show sth that should be kept hidden 不慎泄露；露馅；露马脚 **the only game in ˈtown** (*informal*) the most important thing of a particular type, or the only thing that is available 同类中最重要的事物；唯一的选择 **play the ˈgame** to behave in a fair and honest way 办事公道；为人诚实 **play sb's ˈgame** to do sth which helps sb else's plans, especially by accident, when you did not intend to help them（无意中）促成某人的计划 **play** (**silly**) **ˈgames** (**with sb**) not to treat a situation seriously, especially in order to cheat sb（与某人）耍花招，玩鬼把戏： *Don't play silly games with me; I know you did it.* 别跟我兜圈子，我知道是你干的。 **ˈtwo can play at ˈthat game** (*saying*) used to tell sb who has played a trick on you that you can do the same thing to them（表示也会对方要的花招）这一套你会我也会 **what's sb's/your ˈgame?** (*informal*) used to ask why sb is behaving as they are 在干什么；怎么啦 ➲ MORE AT BEAT *v.*, CAT, FUN *n.*, MUG *n.*, NAME *n.*, NUMBER *n.*, RULE *n.*, TALK *v.*, WORTH *adj.*

■ ***verb*** **1** [I] to risk money playing a game of chance 赌博 **2** [I] to play video games 玩电子游戏 **3** [T] ~ **sth** to use sth in a way that is unfair but legal, in order to get what you want 不公平地利用；钻法律空子图利： *Some companies only received a government grant because they gamed the system.* 一些公司钻了这个制度的空子而得到了

政府补助。◇ *The government finance programme is being gamed by some high-profile banks.* 政府财政计划正在被一些备受关注的银行利用。 **4** [T] **~ sb** to treat sb who trusts you in an unfair way in order to get what you want 不公平地对待；利用： *He gamed his publishers, his family and his friends in order to make a success of his autobiography.* 为了使自己的自传成功，他利用了他的出版商、家人和朋友。

■ ***adj.*** **~ (for sth/to do sth)** ready and willing to do sth new, difficult or dangerous 甘愿尝试；有冒险精神： *She's game for anything.* 她什么事都敢试。◇ *We need a volunteer for this exercise. Who's game to try?* 我们需要有人自告奋勇来做这个练习，谁愿意来试试？

'game bird *noun* a bird that people hunt for sport or food 可捕猎的鸟；野禽

'game changer *noun* a person, an idea or an event that completely changes the way a situation develops 游戏规则改变者（指彻底改变事态发展的人、理念或事件） ▶ **'game-changing** *adj.*: *a game-changing technology* 彻底改变行业面貌的技术

game·keep·er /'geɪmkiːpə(r)/ *noun* a person whose job is to take care of and breed wild animals and birds that are kept on private land in order to be hunted （私有猎场的）猎物看守人 IDM SEE POACHER

game·lan /'gæməlæn/ *noun* a traditional group of Indonesian musicians, playing instruments such as XYLOPHONES and GONGS 加美兰乐队（以木琴、大吊锣等乐器为主的印度尼西亚传统乐队）

game·ly /'geɪmli/ *adv.* in a way that seems brave, although a lot of effort is involved 顽强勇敢地；勇于承担地： *She tried gamely to finish the race.* 她顽强地努力跑完比赛。

'game plan *noun* a plan for success in the future, especially in sport, politics or business （尤指体育运动、政治或商业方面的）行动计划，方案，对策

game·play /'geɪmpleɪ/ *noun* [U] the features of a computer game, such as its story or the way it is played, rather than the images or sounds it uses 电脑游戏设定（指游戏的核心内容和玩法等，而非画面或音效）

,game 'point *noun* (especially in TENNIS 尤指网球) a point that, if won by a player, will win them the game 局点

gamer /'geɪmə(r)/ *noun* (*informal*) **1** a person who likes playing computer games 电脑游戏玩家 **2** (*NAmE*) (in sports 体育运动) a player who is enthusiastic and works hard 坚毅的运动员

'game reserve (*also* **'game park**) (*both BrE*) (*NAmE* **'game preserve**) *noun* a large area of land where wild animals can live in safety 禁猎区；野生动物保护区

'games console *noun* = CONSOLE² (2)

'game show *noun* a television programme in which people play games or answer questions to win prizes （电视）游戏节目，有奖竞猜节目 ➲ WORDFINDER NOTE AT PROGRAMME

games·man·ship /'geɪmzmənʃɪp/ *noun* [U] the ability to win games by making your opponent less confident and using rules to your advantage 比赛的战术；比赛策略

gam·ete /'gæmiːt/ *noun* (*biology* 生) a male or female cell that joins with a cell of the opposite sex to form a ZYGOTE (= a single cell that develops into a person, animal or plant) 配子（形成受精卵的精子或卵子）

'game theory *noun* [U] the part of mathematics that deals with situations in which people compete with each other, for example war or business 博弈论；对策论

'game warden *noun* a person whose job is to manage and take care of the wild animals in a GAME RESERVE （野生动物保护区的）看守人，管理员

gamey (*also* **gamy**) /'geɪmi/ *adj.* (of meat that has been hunted 野味) having a strong flavour or smell as a result of being kept for some time before cooking 有变质味道的；有膻味的

gami·fi·ca·tion /ˌgeɪmɪfɪ'keɪʃn; *NAmE* -fə'k-/ *noun* [U] the use of elements of game-playing in another activity, usually in order to make that activity more interesting 游戏化： *The supermarket chain has started using gamification to make food shopping online fun.* 这家连锁超市开始采用游戏化模式，让网购食品变得有趣。 ▶ **gam·ify** *verb* : **~ sth** *We gamified the online survey by awarding virtual rewards at the end of each section.* 我们将在线调查游戏化，在每个部分结束时给予虚拟奖赏。

gam·ine /gæ'miːn/ *adj.* (*formal*) (of a young woman 年轻女子) thin and attractive; looking like a boy 娇小迷人的；男孩子气的 ▶ **gam·ine** *noun*

gam·ing /'geɪmɪŋ/ *noun* [U] **1** (*old-fashioned* or *law* 律) = GAMBLING : *He spent all night at the gaming tables.* 他通宵赌博。 **2** playing computer games 玩电脑游戏 ➲ SEE ALSO WAR GAMING

gamma /'gæmə/ *noun* the third letter of the Greek alphabet (Γ, γ) 希腊字母表的第 3 个字母

gamma globulin /ˌgæmə 'glɒbjʊlɪn; *NAmE* 'glɑːb-/ *noun* (*biology* 生) [U] a type of PROTEIN in the blood that gives protection against some types of diseases 丙种球蛋白；球蛋白

,gamma radi'ation *noun* [U] (*also* **'gamma rays** [pl.]) (*physics* 物) high-energy RAYS of very short WAVELENGTH sent out by some RADIOACTIVE substances 辐射；伽马辐射；γ 射线；伽马射线

gam·mon /'gæmən/ *noun* [U] (*BrE*) meat from the back leg or side of a pig that has been CURED (= preserved using salt or smoke), usually served in thick slices 腌猪后腿；熏腿；熏猪肋肉 ➲ COMPARE BACON, HAM *n.* (1), PORK (1)

gammy /'gæmi/ *adj.* [usually before noun] (*old-fashioned, BrE, informal*) (of a leg or knee 腿或膝) injured 受伤的；受损的

the gamut /'gæmət/ *noun* [sing.] the complete range of a particular kind of thing 全部；全范围： *The network will provide the gamut of computer services to your home.* 这个网络将为家庭提供全方位的计算机服务。◇ *She felt she had* ***run the*** (***whole***) ***gamut of*** *human emotions from joy to despair.* 她觉得自己尝遍了从悲到喜的各种情感。

gamy = GAMEY

Gan /gæn/ *noun* [U] a form of Chinese, spoken mainly in Jiangxi 赣语；赣方言

gan·der /'gændə(r)/ *noun* a male GOOSE (= a bird like a large DUCK) 公鹅

IDM **have/take a 'gander (at sth)** (*informal*) to look at sth 看一看；看一眼 ➲ MORE AT SAUCE

G and T /ˌdʒiː ən 'tiː/ *noun* a drink consisting of GIN mixed with TONIC WATER 掺奎宁水的杜松子酒

gang /gæŋ/ *noun, verb*

■ ***noun*** [C+sing./pl. v.] **1** an organized group of criminals 一帮，一伙（罪犯）： *criminal gang members and drug dealers* 犯罪集团成员和毒品贩子 ◇ *a gang of pickpockets* 扒手集团 ◇ *A four-man gang carried out the robbery.* 这起抢劫是一个四人团伙所为。 **2** a group of young people who spend a lot of time together and often cause trouble or fight against other groups 一帮，一群，一伙（闹事、斗殴的年轻人）： *a gang of youths* 一帮小混混 ◇ *a street gang* 街头流氓团伙 **3** (*informal*) a group of friends who meet regularly 一伙（经常聚在一起的朋友）： *The whole gang will be there.* 大伙儿都将在那儿。 **4** an organized group of workers or prisoners doing work together 一队，一组（一起干活的工人或囚犯） ➲ SEE ALSO CHAIN GANG

■ ***verb***

PHR V **,gang to'gether** (*informal*) to join together in a group in order to have more power or strength 结成一伙；拉帮结伙 **,gang 'up (on/against sb)** (*informal*) to join together in a group to hurt, frighten or oppose sb 结伙，联合起来，拉帮结派（伤害、恐吓或反对某人）：*At school the older boys ganged up on him and called him names.* 在学校读书时那些大男孩联合起来欺负他，辱骂他。

ˈgang bang *noun* (*slang*) **1** an occasion when a number of people have sex with each other in a group 集体淫乱活动 **2** the RAPE of a person by a number of people one after the other 轮奸 ▶ **ˈgang-bang** *verb* **~ sb**

gang·bust·ers /ˈɡæŋbʌstəz; *NAmE* -ərz/ *noun*
IDM **like ˈgangbusters** (*NAmE*, *informal*) with a lot of energy and enthusiasm 干劲十足；满腔热忱

gang·land /ˈɡæŋlænd/ *noun* [sing.] the world of organized and violent crime 盗匪世界；黑社会：*gangland killings* 犯罪集团间的杀戮

G

gan·gling /ˈɡæŋɡlɪŋ/ (*also* **gan·gly** /ˈɡæŋɡli/) *adj.* (of a person 人) tall, thin and awkward in their movements 又高又瘦且动作笨拙的 SYN **lanky**: *a gangling youth/adolescent* 高瘦而笨拙的青年 / 青少年

gan·glion /ˈɡæŋɡliən/ *noun* (*pl.* **gan·glia** /-liə/) (*medical* 医) **1** a mass of nerve cells 神经节 **2** a swelling in a TENDON, often at the back of the hand 腱鞘囊肿（经常出现在手背）

gang·mas·ter /ˈɡæŋmɑːstə(r); *NAmE* -mæs-/ *noun* (*BrE*) a person or company that organizes groups of workers on a temporary basis to do MANUAL work (= physical work using their hands), especially work on farms（大批雇用临时工人从事体力劳动的）雇主，农场雇主

gang·plank /ˈɡæŋplæŋk/ *noun* a board placed between the side of a boat and land so people can get on and off（上下船用的）跳板，步桥

ˈgang rape *noun* [U, C] the RAPE of a person by a number of people one after the other 轮奸 ▶ **ˈgang-rape** *verb* **~ sb**

gan·grene /ˈɡæŋɡriːn/ *noun* [U] the decay that takes place in a part of the body when the blood supply to it has been stopped because of an illness or injury 坏疽：*Gangrene set in and he had to have his leg amputated.* 他的腿生了坏疽，必须截除。▶ **gan·gren·ous** /ˈɡæŋɡrɪnəs/ *adj.*

gang·sta /ˈɡæŋstə/ *noun* **1** [C] (*NAmE*, *slang*) a member of a street GANG 街头流氓；地痞；痞子 **2** (*also* **ˌgangsta ˈrap**) [U] a type of RAP music, typically with words about violence, guns, drugs and sex 冈斯特说唱乐，冈斯特快板歌（歌词内容通常与暴力、枪支、毒品和色情有关）

gang·ster /ˈɡæŋstə(r)/ *noun* a member of a group of violent criminals 匪徒；歹徒；土匪：*Chicago gangsters* 芝加哥的歹徒

gang·way /ˈɡæŋweɪ/ *noun* **1** (*BrE*) a passage between rows of seats in a theatre, an aircraft, etc.（剧场、飞机等的）座间通道 ➲ COMPARE AISLE **2** a bridge placed between the side of a ship and land so people can get on and off（上下船用的）步桥，跳板

ganja /ˈɡændʒə; ˈɡɑːn-/ *noun* [U] (*slang*) = MARIJUANA

gan·net /ˈɡænɪt/ *noun* **1** a large bird that lives near the sea which catches fish by diving 鲣鸟（潜水捕鱼的大海鸟） **2** (*BrE*, *informal*) a person who eats a lot 大胃王；吃得多的人

gan·try /ˈɡæntri/ *noun* (*pl.* **-ies**) a tall metal frame that is used to support a CRANE, road signs, a SPACECRAFT while it is still on the ground, etc.（起重的）龙门架；（道路的）路标架；（发射航天器的）塔架

Gantt chart /ˈɡænt tʃɑːt; *NAmE* tʃɑːrt/ *noun* (*business* 商) a chart used for managing the tasks involved in a project that shows when each stage should start and end and compares the amount of work done with the amount planned 甘特图（用于项目任务管理，显示各阶段的起讫时间，并将已完成工作量和计划工作量进行对比）

gaol, **gaoler** (*BrE*, *old-fashioned*) = JAIL, JAILER

gap 🔑 /ɡæp/ *noun* **~ (in/between sth)** **1** 🔑 a space between two things or in the middle of sth, especially because there is a part missing 开口；豁口；缺口；裂口：*a gap in a hedge* 树篱的豁口 ◇ *Leave a gap between your car and the next.* 在车与车之间留条道。 **2** 🔑 a period of time when sth stops, or between two events 间断；间隔；间隙：*a gap in the conversation* 谈话的间隙 ◇ *They met again after a gap of twenty years.* 他们阔别二十年后又见面了。◇ *There's a big **age gap** between them* (= a big difference in their ages). 他们之间年龄差距很大。 **3** 🔑 a difference that separates people, or their opinions, situation, etc. 分歧；隔阂；差距：*the gap between rich and poor* 贫富之间的差距 ◇ *the gap between theory and practice* 理论与实践的脱节 ➲ SEE ALSO CREDIBILITY, GENERATION GAP **4** 🔑 a space where sth is missing 缺口；空白；漏洞：*His death left an enormous gap in my life.* 他去世给我的生活留下巨大的空白。 ◇ *There were several gaps in my education.* 我受的教育有几个欠缺之处。 ◇ *We think we've identified **a gap in the market*** (= a business opportunity to make or sell sth that is not yet available). 我们认为已经发现了市场上一个尚待填补的空白。 IDM SEE BRIDGE *v.*

gape /ɡeɪp/ *verb* **1** [I] **~ (at sb/sth)** to stare at sb/sth with your mouth open because you are shocked or surprised 张口结舌地看；目瞪口呆地凝视 **2** [I] to be or become wide open 张开；裂开；豁开：*a **gaping** hole/mouth/wound* 豁开的洞；张大的嘴；裂开的伤口 ◇ **~ open** *He stood yawning, his pyjama jacket gaping open.* 他敞开睡衣站着打哈欠。 ▶ **gape** *noun*

gap·per /ˈɡæpə(r)/ *noun* (*BrE*) a young person who is spending a year working or travelling after leaving school and before going to university 空缺年休假者（中学毕业后到上大学前用一年时间实习或旅游）

ˌgap-ˈtoothed *adj.* [usually before noun] having wide spaces between your teeth 齿缝很大的；有齿缝的

ˈgap year *noun* (*BrE*) a year that a young person spends working and/or travelling, often between leaving school and starting university 空缺年（常指中学毕业后上大学前所休的一年假期，用于实习或旅游）：*I'm planning to take a gap year and go backpacking in India.* 我准备休假一年去印度背包旅行。

gar·age 🔑 /ˈɡærɑːʒ; -rɑːdʒ; -rɪdʒ; *NAmE* ɡəˈrɑːʒ; -ˈrɑːdʒ/ *noun*, *verb*
▪ *noun* **1** 🔑 [C] a building for keeping one or more cars or other vehicles in 停车房；车库：(*BrE*) *a house with a built-in garage* 内设车库的房子 ◇ (*NAmE*) *a house with an attached garage* 旁设车库的房子 ◇ *a double garage* (= one for two cars) 停放两辆车的车房 ◇ *a bus garage* 公共汽车车库 ◇ *an underground garage* (= for example under an office building) 地下停车库 ➲ VISUAL VOCAB PAGE V18 **2** 🔑 [C] a place where vehicles are repaired and where you can buy a car or buy petrol/gas and oil（兼营汽车销售、修理及加油的）汽车修理厂：*a garage mechanic* 汽车修理厂的机修工 ➲ SEE ALSO PETROL STATION **3** [U] a type of HOUSE MUSIC 车库音乐，加拉奇音乐（货仓音乐的一种）
▪ *verb* **~ sth** to put or keep a vehicle in a garage 把…送入车库（或修车厂）

ˌgarage ˈrock *noun* [U] a type of rock music played with a lot of energy, often by musicians who are not professionals 车库摇滚乐（充满活力，常为业余乐手演奏）

ˈgarage sale *noun* a sale of used clothes, furniture, etc., held in the garage of sb's house（在私人住宅的车库里进行的）旧物销售

garam masala /ˌɡʌrəm məˈsɑːlə; *NAmE* ˌɡɑːrɑːm/ *noun* [U] a mixture of spices with a strong flavour, used in S Asian cooking （用于南亚烹饪的）辛辣香料粉

garb /ɡɑːb; *NAmE* ɡɑːrb/ *noun* [U] (*formal* or *humorous*) clothes, especially unusual clothes or those worn by a particular type of person（尤指某类人穿的特定）服装，衣服；奇装异服：*prison garb* 囚服

gar·bage 🔑 /ˈɡɑːbɪdʒ; *NAmE* ˈɡɑːrb-/ *noun* [U] **1** 🔑 (*especially NAmE*) waste food, paper, etc. that you throw away

（生活）垃圾；废物：*garbage collection* 垃圾收集 ◇ *Don't forget to take out the garbage.* 别忘了把垃圾拿出去。➲ COLLOCATIONS AT ENVIRONMENT **2** (*especially NAmE*) a place or container where waste food, paper, etc. can be placed 垃圾场；垃圾箱；垃圾桶：*Throw it in the garbage.* 把它扔到垃圾箱里去。 **3** (*informal*) something stupid or not true 废话；无聊的东西 SYN **rubbish** ➲ NOTE AT RUBBISH

IDM **garbage ˌin, garbage ˈout** (*abbr.* **GIGO**) used to express the idea that if wrong or poor quality data is put into a computer, wrong or poor quality data will come out of it（用于计算机）废料输入废料输出，无用输入无用输出

ˈgarbage can (*also* **ˈtrash can**) (*both NAmE*) (*BrE* **dust·bin**) *noun* a large container with a lid, used for putting rubbish/garbage in, usually kept outside the house（常置于室外的）垃圾桶，垃圾箱 ➲ NOTE AT RUBBISH

ˈgarbage disposal *noun* (*NAmE*) = WASTE-DISPOSAL UNIT

ˈgarbage man (*also formal* **ˈgarbage collector**) (*both NAmE*) (*BrE* **dust·man**, *informal* **bin·man**, *formal* **ˈrefuse collector**) *noun* a person whose job is to remove waste from outside houses, etc. 垃圾工 ➲ NOTE AT RUBBISH

ˈgarbage truck (*NAmE*) (*BrE* **dust·cart**) *noun* a vehicle for collecting rubbish/garbage from outside houses, etc. 垃圾车

gar·banzo /gɑːˈbænzəʊ; *NAmE* gɑːrˈbɑːnzoʊ; -ˈbæn-/ (*also* **garˈbanzo ˌbean**) (*both NAmE*) *noun* (*pl.* **-os**) = CHICKPEA

garbed /gɑːbd; *NAmE* gɑːrbd/ *adj.* [not before noun] (*formal*) ~ (**in sth**) dressed in a particular way 以…方式穿着：*brightly garbed* 穿着鲜艳

gar·bled /ˈgɑːbld; *NAmE* ˈgɑːrbld/ *adj.* (of a message or story 信息或叙述) told in a way that confuses the person listening, usually by sb who is shocked or in a hurry 混乱不清的，引起误解的（常因讲述者惊慌或匆忙所致）SYN **confused**：*He gave a garbled account of what had happened.* 他对所发生事情的叙述含混不清。◇ *There was a garbled message from her on my voicemail.* 我的语音信箱里有她含混不清的留言。

garbo /ˈgɑːbəʊ; *NAmE* ˈgɑːrboʊ/ *noun* (*pl.* **-os**) (*AustralE, informal*) a person whose job is to remove waste from outside houses, etc. 垃圾工 SYN **dustman, garbage collector**

Garda /ˈgɑːdə; *NAmE* ˈgɑːrdə/ *noun* **1 the Garda** [U] the police force of the Republic of Ireland（爱尔兰共和国的）警察部门，警察机关 **2** [C] (*also* **garda**) (*pl.* **gardai** /ˈgɑːdiː; *NAmE* ˈgɑːrdiː/) a police officer of the Republic of Ireland （爱尔兰共和国的）警察

gar·den /ˈgɑːdn; *NAmE* ˈgɑːrdn/ *noun, verb*

▪ ***noun*** **1** [C] (*BrE*) (*NAmE* **yard**) a piece of land next to or around your house where you can grow flowers, fruit, vegetables, etc., usually with a LAWN (= an area of grass)（住宅旁或周围的）园圃，花园，果园，菜园：***a front/back garden*** 前 / 后花园 ◇ *children playing in the garden* 在花园里玩耍的孩子 ◇ ***garden flowers/plants*** 园艺花卉 / 植物 ◇ *out in the garden* 在户外的花园里 ◇ *a rose garden* (= where only roses are grown) 玫瑰园 ➲ SEE ALSO KITCHEN GARDEN, MARKET GARDEN, ROCK GARDEN, ROOF GARDEN **2** [C] (*NAmE*) an area in a yard where you grow flowers or plants 庭园；园子 **3** [C] (*usually* **gardens**) a public park 公园：*the botanical gardens in Edinburgh* 爱丁堡的植物园 ➲ SEE ALSO ZOOLOGICAL GARDEN **4 gardens** [sing.] (*abbr.* **Gdns**) (*BrE*) used in the name of streets（用于街名）园，街，广场：*39 Belvoir Gardens* 贝尔沃街 39 号

IDM **everything in the garden is ˈrosy** (*BrE, saying*) everything is fine 一切都好；事事如意 ➲ MORE AT COMMON *adj.*, LEAD[1] *v.*

▪ ***verb*** [I] to work in a garden 做园艺工作；种植花木 ▸ **gar·den·er** /ˈgɑːdnə(r); *NAmE* ˈgɑːrd-/ *noun*：*My wife's a keen gardener.* 我的妻子是个热衷园艺的人。◇ *We employ a gardener two days a week.* 我们雇了个花匠，每周工作两天。**gar·den·ing** /ˈgɑːdnɪŋ; *NAmE* ˈgɑːrd-/ *noun* [U]：*organic gardening* 有机花木种植 ◇ *gardening gloves* 园艺用手套 ◇ *a gardening programme on TV* 电视上的园艺节目 ➲ VISUAL VOCAB PAGE V45

ˈgarden centre (*BrE*) (*especially US* **ˈgarden center**) *noun* a place that sells plants, seeds, garden equipment, etc. 园艺品店

ˌgarden ˈcity, ˌgarden ˈsuburb *noun* (*BrE*) a city or part of a city that has been specially designed to have a lot of open spaces, parks and trees 花园城市（园林化都市或市区）

ˈgarden egg *noun* [C, U] (*WAfrE*) a type of AUBERGINE/EGGPLANT with purple, white or greenish-yellow skin 彩茄；观赏茄子

gar·denia /gɑːˈdiːniə; *NAmE* gɑːrˈd-/ *noun* a bush with shiny leaves and large white or yellow flowers with a sweet smell, also called gardenias 栀子

ˈgardening leave *noun* [U] (*BrE*) a period during which sb does not work but remains employed by a company in order to prevent them working for another company 园艺假（离职后继续受薪但不用上班，以免受雇于另一公司的一段时期）：*She handed in her resignation and was put on three months' gardening leave.* 她递了辞呈，但要休三个月的园艺假。

the ˌGarden of ˈEden *noun* [sing.] = EDEN

ˈgarden party *noun* a formal social event that takes place in the afternoon in a large garden 游园会，园游会（下午在大花园举行）

ˌgarden ˈsalad [U, C] (*NAmE*) a salad containing a variety of raw vegetables, especially LETTUCE 田园色拉（包括各种生食蔬菜，特别是生菜）

ˈgarden-variety (*NAmE*) (*BrE* **ˌcommon or ˈgarden**) *adj.* [only before noun] ordinary; with no special features 普通的；平常的；一般的：*He is not one of your garden-variety criminals.* 他不是个普通的罪犯。

gar·gan·tuan /gɑːˈgæntʃuən; *NAmE* gɑːrˈg-/ *adj.* [usually before noun] extremely large 巨大的；庞大的 SYN **enormous**：***a gargantuan appetite/meal*** 食欲极佳；丰盛的大餐

gar·gle /ˈgɑːgl; *NAmE* ˈgɑːrgl/ *verb, noun*

▪ ***verb*** [I] ~ (**with sth**) to wash inside your mouth and throat by moving a liquid around at the back of your throat and then SPITTING it out 含漱；漱喉

▪ ***noun*** **1** [C, U] a liquid used for gargling（含）漱液：*an antiseptic gargle* 消毒含漱液 **2** [sing.] an act of gargling or a sound like that made when gargling 含漱；漱口；含漱声：*to have a gargle with salt water* 用盐水含漱

gar·goyle /ˈgɑːgɔɪl; *NAmE* ˈgɑːrg-/ *noun* an ugly figure of a person or an animal that is made of stone and through which water is carried away from the roof of a building, especially a church（建筑物，尤指教堂顶上石头怪人或怪兽状的）滴水嘴；滴水兽 ➲ VISUAL VOCAB PAGE V14

gar·ish /ˈgeərɪʃ; *NAmE* ˈgerɪʃ/ *adj.* very brightly coloured in an unpleasant way 俗艳的；花哨的；炫目的 SYN **gaudy**：*garish clothes/colours* 花里胡哨的衣服；过于艳丽的色彩 ▸ **gar·ish·ly** *adv.*：*garishly decorated/lit/painted* 装饰得花里胡哨；照得灯火辉煌；涂得过于鲜艳

gar·land /ˈgɑːlənd; *NAmE* ˈgɑːrl-/ *noun, verb*

▪ ***noun*** a circle of flowers and leaves that is worn on the head or around the neck or is hung in a room as decoration 花环；花冠；环状花饰

▪ ***verb*** [usually passive] ~ **sb/sth** (*literary*) to decorate sb/sth with a garland or garlands 用花环装饰；给…饰以花环（或戴上花冠）

gar·lic /ˈgɑːlɪk; *NAmE* ˈgɑːrlɪk/ *noun* [U] a vegetable of the onion family with a very strong taste and smell, used in cooking to give flavour to food 蒜；大蒜：***a clove of garlic*** (= one section of it) 一瓣蒜 ➲ VISUAL VOCAB PAGE

G

V33 ▶ **gar·licky** *adj.* : *garlicky breath/food* 带大蒜味的气息；加有大蒜的食物

ˌgarlic ˈbread *noun* [U] bread, usually in the shape of a stick, containing melted butter and garlic 蒜蓉面包

gar·ment /ˈɡɑːmənt; *NAmE* ˈɡɑːrm-/ *noun* (*formal*) a piece of clothing（一件）衣服：*a strange shapeless garment that had once been a jacket* 用夹克衫改成的不成形的一件怪衣服 ◇ ***woollen/winter/outer garments*** 毛衣；冬装；外衣 ➲SYNONYMS AT CLOTHES ➲SEE ALSO UNDERGARMENT

gar·ner /ˈɡɑːnə(r); *NAmE* ˈɡɑːrn-/ *verb* **~ sth** (*formal*) to obtain or collect sth such as information, support, etc. 获得，得到，收集（信息、支持等）**SYN** **gather, acquire**

G

gar·net /ˈɡɑːnɪt; *NAmE* ˈɡɑːrn-/ *noun* a clear dark red SEMI-PRECIOUS stone that is fairly valuable 石榴子石

gar·nish /ˈɡɑːnɪʃ; *NAmE* ˈɡɑːrnɪʃ/ *verb, noun*

■ *verb* **~ sth (with sth)** to decorate a dish of food with a small amount of another food（用菜）为（食物）加装饰；加饰菜于 ➲COLLOCATIONS AT COOKING

■ *noun* [C, U] a small amount of food that is used to decorate a larger dish of food （食物上的）装饰菜

gar·otte = GARROTTE

gar·ret /ˈɡærət/ *noun* a room, often a small dark unpleasant one, at the top of a house, especially in the roof 阁楼；顶楼小屋 ➲COMPARE ATTIC ➲SEE ALSO LOFT *n.* (1)

gar·rison /ˈɡærɪsn/ *noun, verb*

■ *noun* [C+sing./pl. v.] a group of soldiers living in a town or FORT to defend it; the buildings these soldiers live in 卫戍部队；守备部队；卫戍区；驻防地：*a garrison of 5 000 troops* 有 5 000 士兵驻守的防地 ◇ *a garrison town* 有驻防的城镇 ◇ *Half the garrison is/are on duty.* 卫戍部队有半数人在执勤。

■ *verb* to put soldiers in a place in order to defend it from attack 驻防；派（兵）驻守： **~ sth** *Two regiments were sent to garrison the town.* 派了两个团驻守在那个城镇。◇ **~ sb + adv./prep.** *100 soldiers were garrisoned in the town.* 派了 100 名士兵在城里驻防。

gar·rotte (*also* **gar·otte**) (*US also* **gar·rote**) /ɡəˈrɒt; *NAmE* ɡəˈrɑːt/ *verb, noun*

■ *verb* **~ sb** to kill sb by putting a piece of wire, etc. around their neck and pulling it tight（用金属丝等）勒死，绞杀，扼杀

■ *noun* a piece of wire, etc. used for garrotting sb 用于绞杀的金属丝（或绳索等）；绞刑刑具

gar·rul·ous /ˈɡærələs; *BrE also* -rjʊl-/ *adj.* talking a lot, especially about unimportant things（尤指在琐事上）饶舌的，唠叨的，喋喋不休的 **SYN** **talkative** ▶ **gar·rul·ous·ly** *adv.*

gar·ter /ˈɡɑːtə(r); *NAmE* ˈɡɑːrt-/ *noun* **1** a band, usually made of ELASTIC, that is worn around the leg to keep up a sock or STOCKING（通常为弹性的）袜带 **2** (*NAmE*) (*BrE* **sus·pend·er**) a short circle of ELASTIC for holding up a sock or STOCKING 吊袜带 **IDM** SEE GUT *n.*

ˈgarter belt (*NAmE*) (*BrE* **suˈspender belt**) *noun* a piece of women's underwear like a belt, worn around the waist, used for holding STOCKINGS up（女用）吊袜腰带

ˈgarter snake *noun* a harmless American snake with coloured lines along its back 带蛇（见于美洲，无毒）

gas 🔑 /ɡæs/ *noun, verb*

■ *noun* (*pl.* **gases** or *less frequent* **gas·ses**)

• **NOT SOLID/LIQUID** 非固体 / 液体 **1** 🔑 [C, U] any substance like air that is neither a solid nor a liquid, for example HYDROGEN and OXYGEN are both gases 气体：*Air is a mixture of gases.* 空气为混合气体。◇ *CFC gases* 含氯氟烃气体 ◇ *a **gas bottle/cylinder*** (= for storing gas) 气瓶；气罐 ➲SEE ALSO GREENHOUSE GAS **2** 🔑 [U] a particular type of gas or mixture of gases used as fuel for heating and cooking 气体燃料；煤气；天然气： *a gas cooker/fire/furnace/oven/ring/stove* 燃气灶；煤气取暖器；煤气锅炉；煤气烤箱；煤气灶火圈；煤气炉 ◇ *a **gas explosion/leak*** 气体爆炸；煤气泄漏 ◇ *gas central heating* 燃气中央供暖系统 ◇ (*BrE*) *Preheat the oven to gas mark 5* (= a particular temperature of a gas oven). 把烤炉预热至 5 挡。➲SEE ALSO CALOR GAS™, COAL GAS, NATURAL GAS **3** [U] a particular type of gas used during a medical operation, to make the patient sleep or to make the pain less（外科手术用）麻醉气：*an anaesthetic gas* 麻醉气体 ◇ *During the birth she was given gas and air.* 她分娩时医生给她吸了麻醉混合气体。➲SEE ALSO LAUGHING GAS **4** [U] a particular type of gas used in war to kill or injure people, or used by the police to control people（战争用）毒气；（警察用）瓦斯：*a gas attack* 毒气攻击 ➲SEE ALSO CS GAS, MUSTARD GAS, NERVE GAS, TEAR GAS

• **IN VEHICLE** 车辆 **5** 🔑 (*also* **gas·oline**) (*both NAmE*) (*BrE* **pet·rol**) [U] a liquid obtained from PETROLEUM, used as fuel in car engines, etc. 汽油：*a gas station* 加油站 ◇ *a gas pump* 加（汽）油泵 ◇ *to fill up the gas tank* 加满油箱 **6 the gas** [sing.] (*especially NAmE*) = GAS PEDAL : ***Step on the gas****, we're late.* 踩油门开快点，我们要迟到了。

• **FUN** 乐趣 **7** [sing.] (*especially NAmE*) a person or an event that is fun 有趣的人（或事物）: *The party was a real gas.* 这次聚会真有趣。

• **IN STOMACH** 胃 **8** (*NAmE*) (*BrE* **wind**) [U] air that you swallow with food or drink; gas that is produced in your stomach or INTESTINES that makes you feel uncomfortable（随食物或饮料）吞下的气；胃气；肠气 **IDM** SEE COOK *v.*

■ *verb* (**-ss-**)

• **KILL/HARM WITH GAS** 用毒气杀死 / 伤害 **1** [T] **~ sb/yourself** to kill or harm sb by making them breathe poisonous gas 用毒气杀伤；使吸入毒气

• **TALK** 谈论 **2** [I] (usually used in the progressive tenses 通常用于进行时) (*old-fashioned, informal*) to talk for a long time about things that are not important 闲聊；空谈；瞎扯 **SYN** **chat**

gas·bag /ˈɡæsbæɡ/ *noun* (*informal, humorous*) a person who talks a lot 夸夸其谈的人；贫嘴子；聒噪的人

ˈgas chamber *noun* a room that can be filled with poisonous gas for killing animals or people 毒气室（用于毒死动物或人）

ˈgas-cooled *adj.* [only before noun] using gas to keep the temperature cool 气冷的；用气体冷却的：*gas-cooled nuclear reactors* 气冷核反应堆

gas·eous /ˈɡæsiəs; ˈɡeɪsiəs/ *adj.* [usually before noun] like or containing gas 似气体的；含气体的：*a gaseous mixture* 气体混合物 ◇ *in gaseous form* 处于气态

ˌgas-ˈfired *adj.* [usually before noun] (*BrE*) using gas as a fuel 燃气的；以煤气为燃料的：*gas-fired central heating* 燃气集中供暖

ˌgas ˈgiant *noun* (*astronomy* 天) a large planet made mostly of the gases HYDROGEN and HELIUM, for example Jupiter or Saturn 气体巨星（主要由氢气和氦气构成，如木星或土星）

ˈgas guzzler (*also* **guz·zler**) *noun* (*informal, especially NAmE*) a car or other vehicle that needs a lot of petrol/gas 高油耗汽车；油老虎 ▶ **ˈgas-guzzling** *adj.* [only before noun]

gash /ɡæʃ/ *noun, verb*

■ *noun* **~ (in/on sth)** a long deep cut in the surface of sth, especially a person's skin 深长的切口（或伤口、划伤）

■ *verb* **~ sth/sb** to make a long deep cut in sth, especially a person's skin 划伤，砍伤（尤指人的皮肤）: *He gashed his hand on a sharp piece of rock.* 他的手在一块尖石头上划了一个大口子。

gas·hold·er /ˈɡæshəʊldə(r); *NAmE* -hoʊl-/ *noun* = GASOMETER

gas·ket /ˈɡæskɪt/ *noun* a flat piece of rubber, etc. placed between two metal surfaces in a pipe or an engine to prevent steam, gas or oil from escaping 垫圈；衬垫；密封垫：*The engine had **blown a gasket*** (= had allowed steam, etc. to escape). 发动机的密封圈漏气了。◇ (*figurative, informal*) *He **blew a gasket** at the news* (= became very angry). 他听到这消息勃然大怒。

ˈ**gas lamp** (*also* **gas·light**) *noun* a lamp in the street or in a house, that produces light from burning gas 煤气灯

gas·light /ˈɡæslaɪt/ *noun* **1** [U] light produced from burning gas 煤气灯光：*In the gaslight she looked paler than ever.* 在煤气灯光下她显得比以往任何时候都苍白。**2** [C] = GAS LAMP

gas·man /ˈɡæsmæn/ *noun* (*pl.* **-men** /-men/) (*informal*) a man whose job is to visit people's houses to see how much gas they have used, or to fit and check gas equipment 煤气抄表员；煤气收费员；煤气设备安装（或检修）工

ˈ**gas mantle** *noun* = MANTLE (4)

ˈ**gas mask** *noun* a piece of equipment worn over the face as protection against poisonous gas 防毒面具

gaso·hol /ˈɡæsəhɒl; *NAmE* -hɔːl; -hɑːl/ *noun* [U] (*NAmE*) a mixture of petrol/gas and alcohol which can be used in cars（汽车用）汽油和酒精混合燃料

ˈ**gas oil** *noun* [U] a type of oil obtained from PETROLEUM which is used as a fuel 瓦斯油；粗柴油

gas·oline 🔑 (*also* **gas·olene**) /ˈɡæsəliːn/ *noun* [U] (*NAmE*) = GAS (5)：*I fill up the tank with gasoline about once a week.* 我大约一个星期加满一箱汽油。◇ ***leaded/unleaded gasoline*** 含铅 / 无铅汽油

gas·om·eter /ɡæˈsɒmɪtə(r); *NAmE* -ˈsɑːm-/ (*also* **gas·hold·er**) *noun* a very large round container or building in which gas is stored and from which it is sent through pipes to other buildings（大型）储燃气罐，储气库

gasp /ɡɑːsp; *NAmE* ɡæsp/ *verb, noun*

■ *verb* **1** [I, T] to take a quick deep breath with your mouth open, especially because you are surprised or in pain（尤指由于惊讶或疼痛而）喘气，喘息，倒抽气：**~ (at sth)** *She gasped at the wonderful view.* 如此美景使她惊讶得倒吸了一口气。◇ *They gasped in astonishment at the news.* 他们听到这消息惊讶得倒吸了一口气。◇ **+ speech** *'What was that noise?' he gasped.* "那是什么声音？"他喘着气问。**2** [I, T] to have difficulty breathing or speaking 透不过气；气喘吁吁地说：**~ (for sth)** *He came to the surface of the water gasping for air.* 他浮出水面急促地喘着气。◇ **~ (sth) (out)** *She managed to gasp out her name.* 她终于气喘吁吁地说出了她的名字。◇ **+ speech** *'Can't breathe,' he gasped.* "透不过气来了。"他气喘吁吁地说。**3 be gasping (for sth)** [I] (*BrE, informal*) to want or need sth very badly, especially a drink or a cigarette 渴望，很想要（尤指饮料或香烟）

■ *noun* a quick deep breath, usually caused by a strong emotion（常指由强烈情感引起的）深吸气，喘息，倒抽气：*to give a* ***gasp of horror/surprise/relief*** 惊恐得 / 吃惊得倒抽一口气；如释重负地松一口气 ◇ *His breath came in short gasps.* 他急促地喘着气。**IDM** SEE LAST[1] *det.*

ˈ**gas pedal** (*especially NAmE*) (*also* **ac·cel·er·ator**) *noun* the PEDAL in a car or other vehicle that you press with your foot to control the speed of the engine（汽车等的）加速装置，油门 ➲ VISUAL VOCAB PAGE V56

ˌ**gas-ˈpermeable** *adj.* allowing gases to pass through 透气的：*gas-permeable contact lenses* 透气隐形眼镜

ˈ**gas ring** *noun* (*especially BrE*) a round piece of metal with holes in it on the top of a gas cooker/stove, where the gas is lit to produce the flame for cooking 煤气灶火圈 ➲ PICTURE AT RING[1] ➲ VISUAL VOCAB PAGE V26

ˈ**gas station** (*NAmE*) (*BrE* ˈ**petrol station**) (*also* ˈ**filling station**, ˈ**service station** *NAmE, BrE*) *noun* a place at the side of a road where you take your car to buy petrol/gas, oil, etc.（汽车）加油站

gassy /ˈɡæsi/ *adj.* **1** (*BrE*) (of drinks 饮料) containing too much gas in the form of bubbles 充满气泡的 **2** (*NAmE*) (of people 人) having a lot of gas in your stomach, etc.（肠胃）胀气的

gas·tric /ˈɡæstrɪk/ *adj.* [only before noun] (*medical* 医) connected with the stomach 胃的；胃部的：*a gastric ulcer* 胃溃疡 ◇ *gastric juices* (= the acids in your stomach that help you to DIGEST food) 胃液（有助于消化的胃酸）

ˌ**gastric ˈband** *noun* a device made of SILICONE that is put around the top of a person's stomach to help them lose weight by reducing the amount of food that they are able to eat 束胃带，胃束带，束胃环（硅胶制，置于胃部顶端，通过减少胃纳助人减肥）

ˌ**gastric ˈflu** *noun* [U] an illness affecting the stomach, which does not last long and is thought to be caused by a virus 胃流感（一种被认为是由病毒引起的短期胃病）

gas·tri·tis /ɡæˈstraɪtɪs/ *noun* [U] (*medical* 医) an illness in which the inside of the stomach becomes swollen and painful 胃炎

gastro·enter·itis /ˌɡæstrəʊˌentəˈraɪtɪs; *NAmE* ˌɡæstroʊ-/ *noun* [U] (*medical* 医) an illness of the stomach and other food passages that causes DIARRHOEA and VOMITING 胃肠炎

gas·tro·intest·inal /ˌɡæstrəʊɪnˈtestɪnl; *NAmE* -roʊ-; *BrE also* ˌɡæstrəʊnteˈstaɪnl/ *adj.* (*medical* 医) of or related to the stomach and INTESTINES 胃肠的

gas·tro·nom·ic /ˌɡæstrəˈnɒmɪk; *NAmE* -ˈnɑːm-/ *adj.* [only before noun] connected with cooking and eating good food 烹饪的；美食的 ▶ **gas·tro·nom·ic·al·ly** /-kli/ *adv.*

gas·tron·omy /ɡæˈstrɒnəmi; *NAmE* -ˈstrɑːn-/ *noun* [U] (*formal*) the art and practice of cooking and eating good food 烹饪法；美食学

gas·tro·pod /ˈɡæstrəpɒd; *NAmE* -pɑːd/ *noun* (*biology* 生) a MOLLUSC such as a SNAIL or SLUG, that moves on one large foot 腹足类；腹足纲软体动物 ➲ VISUAL VOCAB PAGE V13

gas·tro·pub /ˈɡæstrəʊpʌb; *NAmE* -troʊ-/ *noun* (*BrE*) a pub which is well known for serving good food 美食酒吧

gas·works /ˈɡæswɜːks; *NAmE* -wɜːrks/ *noun* (*pl.* **gas·works**) [C+sing./pl. v.] a factory where gas for lighting and heating is made from coal 煤气厂

gate 🔑 /ɡeɪt/ *noun* **1** 🔑 [C] a barrier like a door that is used to close an opening in a fence or a wall outside a building 大门；栅栏门；围墙门：*an iron gate* 铁门 ◇ *He pushed open the garden gate.* 他推开了花园的门。◇ *A crowd gathered at the factory gates.* 一群人聚集在工厂的大门口。◇ *the gates of the city* 城门 ➲ VISUAL VOCAB PAGE V20 ➲ SEE ALSO LYCHGATE, STARTING GATE **2** 🔑 [C] an opening that can be closed by a gate or gates 大门口：*We drove through the palace gates.* 我们驱车驶过重重宫门。**3** [C] a barrier that is used to control the flow of water on a river or CANAL 闸门；阀门：*a* ***lock/sluice gate*** 船闸闸门；水闸 **4** 🔑 [C] a way out of an airport through which passengers go to get on their plane 登机门；登机口：*BA flight 726 to Paris is now boarding at gate 16.* 飞往巴黎的英航 726 号班机在 16 号登机口登机。➲ WORDFINDER NOTE AT AIRPORT **5** [C] the number of people who attend a sports event（体育比赛的）观众人数：*Tonight's game has attracted the largest gate of the season.* 今晚比赛吸引的观众人数创本赛季之最。**6** (*also* ˈ**gate money**) [U] the amount of money made by selling tickets for a sports event（体育比赛的）门票收入：*Today's gate will be given to charity.* 今天的门票收入将捐献给慈善事业。**7 -gate** (forming nouns from the names of people or places; used especially in newspapers 与人名或地名构成名词，尤用于报刊) a political SCANDAL connected with the person or place mentioned（与所提到的人或地方有关的）政治丑闻 **ORIGIN** From **Watergate**, the scandal in the United States that brought about the resignation of President Nixon in 1974. 源自美国的"水门事件"（Watergate），此丑闻导致 1974 年尼克松总统辞职。**8** (*computing* 计) = LOGIC GATE

gat·eau /ˈɡætəʊ; *NAmE* ɡæˈtoʊ/ *noun* [C, U] (*pl.* **gat·eaux** /ˈɡætəʊ; *NAmE* ɡæˈtoʊ/) a large cake filled with cream and usually decorated with fruit, nuts, etc. 奶油水果大蛋糕：*a strawberry gateau* 草莓奶油大蛋糕 ◇ *Is there any gateau left?* 奶油水果大蛋糕有剩的吗？

gate·crash /ˈgeɪtkræʃ/ (*also informal* **crash**) *verb* [T, I] ~ (sth) to go to a party or social event without being invited 未获邀请而参加（或出席）；做（聚会等的）不速之客 ▶ **gate·crash·er** *noun*

gated /ˈgeɪtɪd/ *adj.* [usually before noun] (of a road 道路) having gates that need to be opened and closed by drivers 有门的

ˌ**gated comˈmunity** *noun* a group of houses surrounded by a wall or fence, with an entrance that is guarded 封闭式住宅小区（四周有围墙或栅栏，入口有门卫）

gate·fold /ˈgeɪtfəʊld; *NAmE* -foʊld/ *noun* a large page folded to fit a book or magazine that can be opened out for reading （书籍、杂志的）大张折叠插页，大折页

G

gate·house /ˈgeɪthaʊs/ *noun* a house built at or over a gate, for example at the entrance to a park or castle 门房；门楼

gate·keep·er /ˈgeɪtkiːpə(r)/ *noun* **1** a person whose job is to check and control who is allowed to go through a gate 看门人；守门人；门卫 **2** a person, system, etc. that decides whether sb/sth will be allowed, or allowed to reach a particular place or person 看门人；把关系统：*His secretary acts as a gatekeeper, reading all mail before it reaches her boss.* 老板的秘书负责把关，所有邮件都由她先过目再呈送给老板。

gate·leg table /ˌgeɪtleg ˈteɪbl/ *noun* a table with extra sections that can be folded out to make it larger, supported on legs that swing out from the centre 折叠活腿桌；折叠桌

ˈ**gate money** *noun* [U] = GATE (6)

gate·post /ˈgeɪtpəʊst; *NAmE* -poʊst/ *noun* a post to which a gate is attached or against which it is closed 门柱
IDM **between you, me and the ˈgatepost** (*BrE, informal*) used to show that what you are going to say next is a secret （引出秘密）你我私下说，别对外人讲

gate·way /ˈgeɪtweɪ/ *noun* **1** an opening in a wall or fence that can be closed by a gate 大门口；门道；出入口：*They turned through the gateway on the left.* 他们经左边的出入口通过。 **2** [usually sing.] **~ to/into...** a place through which you can go to reach another larger place （通往其他地区的）门户：*Perth, the gateway to Western Australia* 珀斯——通向西澳大利亚的门户 **3** [usually sing.] **~ to sth** a means of getting or achieving sth 途径；方法；手段：*A good education is the gateway to success.* 良好的教育是通往成功之路。 **4** (*computing* 计) a device that connects two computer networks that cannot be connected in any other way 网关；网间连接器

gather 🔑 /ˈgæðə(r)/ *verb*
• **COME/BRING TOGETHER** 聚集；集合 **1** 🔑 [I, T] to come together, or bring people together, in one place to form a group 聚集；集合；召集：*A crowd soon gathered.* 很快就聚集起了一群人。 ◇ **+ adv./prep.** *His supporters gathered in the main square.* 他的支持者聚集在主广场上。 ◇ *Can you all* ***gather round****? I've got something to tell you.* 你们都围过来好吗？我有事要告诉你们。 ◇ *The whole family* ***gathered together*** *at Ray's home.* 全家人聚集在雷的家中。 ◇ **be gathered + adv./prep.** *They were all* ***gathered round*** *the TV.* 他们都围到电视机旁。 ◇ *A large crowd was gathered outside the studio.* 召集了一大群人在制片厂外面。 ◇ *The kids were* ***gathered together*** *in one room.* 孩子们被聚集在一个房间里。 **2** 🔑 [T] to bring things together that have been spread around 收拢，归拢（分散的东西）：**~ sth** *People slowly gathered their belongings and left the hall.* 人们慢慢地收起他们的随身物品离开了大厅。 ◇ **~ sth together/up** *I waited while he gathered up his papers.* 他整理文件时我就在一旁等待。 ➲ SYNONYMS AT COLLECT
• **COLLECT** 收集 **3** 🔑 [T] **~ sth** to collect information from different sources 搜集，收集（情报）：*Detectives have spent months gathering evidence.* 侦探们花了数月时间搜集证据。 ➲ SYNONYMS AT COLLECT **4** 🔑 [T] **~ sth** to collect plants, fruit, etc. from a wide area 采集（植物、水果等）：*to gather wild flowers* 采集野花
• **CROPS/HARVEST** 庄稼；收成 **5** [T] **~ sth (in)** (*formal* or *literary*) to pick or cut and collect crops to be stored 收割；收获：*It was late August and the harvest had been safely gathered in.* 已是八月下旬，庄稼都妥善收割完毕。
• **BELIEVE/UNDERSTAND** 相信；理解 **6** [T, I] (not used in the progressive tenses 不用于进行时) to believe or understand that sth is true because of information or evidence you have 认为；猜想；推断；理解：**~ (that)...** *I gather (that) you wanted to see me.* 我猜想你想要见我。 ◇ *I gather from your letter that you're not enjoying your job.* 我从信中了解到你并不喜欢你的工作。 ◇ **~ (sth)** *'There's been a delay.' 'I gathered that.'* "已经耽搁了。""那是我预料中的事。" ◇ *'She won't be coming.'* ***'So I gather.'*** "她不会来了。""我也这么认为。" ◇ *You're self-employed, I gather.* 我想你是个体经营吧。 ◇ ***As far as I can gather,*** *he got involved in a fight.* 据我了解，他卷入了一场争斗之中。 ◇ ***From what I can gather,*** *there's been some kind of problem.* 从我了解的情况看，还存在某种问题。
• **INCREASE** 增加 **7** [T] **~ sth** to increase in speed, force, etc. 增加（速度、力量等）：*The truck* ***gathered speed.*** 卡车加快了速度。 ◇ *During the 1980s the green movement* ***gathered momentum.*** * 20 世纪 80 年代期间，绿色运动的势头开始增强。 ◇ *Thousands of these machines are* ***gathering dust*** (= not being used) *in stockrooms.* 数千台这样的机器都尘封在仓库里。
• **OF CLOUDS/DARKNESS** 云层；黑暗 **8** [I] to gradually increase in number or amount 逐渐增加；积聚：*The storm clouds were gathering.* 暴风雨乌云正在聚集。 ◇ *the gathering gloom of a winter's afternoon* 天色越来越暗的一个冬日下午
• **CLOTHING** 衣服 **9** [T] to pull a piece of clothing tighter to your body 收紧，拢起（衣服）：**~ sth around you/sth** *He gathered his cloak around him.* 他用披风把身子裹紧。 ◇ **~ sth up** *She gathered up her skirts and ran.* 她提起裙摆就跑。 **10** [T] **~ sth (in)** to pull parts of a piece of clothing together in folds and sew them in place 给…打褶子：*She wore a skirt gathered (in) at the waist.* 她穿了一条腰部打褶的裙子。
• **HOLD SB** 拉住某人 **11** [T] **~ sb + adv./prep.** to pull sb towards you and put your arms around them 拢；拢住：*She gathered the child in her arms and held him close.* 她把那男孩拢过来紧紧抱在怀里。 ◇ *He gathered her to him.* 他把她拢到身边。
• **PREPARE YOURSELF** 做好准备 **12** [T] **~ sth/yourself** to prepare yourself to do sth that requires effort 攒（动）；使做好准备：*I sat down for a moment to gather my strength.* 我坐下片刻积蓄力量。 ◇ *She was still trying to gather her thoughts together when the door opened.* 门打开时她还努力让自己集中精神。 ◇ *Fortunately the short delay gave him time to gather himself.* 幸运的是，这短暂的拖延给了他喘息的时间。 IDM SEE ROLL *v.*

gath·er·er /ˈgæðərə(r)/ *noun* a person who collects sth 收集者；采集者：*prehistoric hunters and gatherers* 史前的狩猎者和采集者

gath·er·ing /ˈgæðərɪŋ/ *noun* **1** [C] a meeting of people for a particular purpose 聚集；聚会；集会：*a* ***social/family gathering*** 社交 / 家庭聚会 ◇ *a gathering of religious leaders* 宗教领袖的集会 **2** [U] the process of collecting sth 收集；采集；搜集：*methods of information gathering* 信息采集的各种方法

gathers /ˈgæðəz; *NAmE* ˈgæðərz/ *noun* [pl.] small folds that are sewn into a piece of clothing 皱裥；褶裥

ga·tor /ˈgeɪtə(r)/ *noun* (*NAmE, informal*) = ALLIGATOR

gat·vol /xɑːtˈfɒl; *NAmE* -ˈfɑːl/ *adj.* [not usually before noun] (*SAfrE*) (*informal*) disgusted or extremely unhappy or bored with a situation （对境况）厌恶，极端不满，厌烦：**~ (of sb/sth)** *I am gatvol of travelling on a jarring road, picking up punctures.* 我受够了在颠簸的路上开车，轮胎上扎的都是洞。 ◇ **~ (with sb/sth)** *I'm gatvol with this traffic.* 我真受不了这种交通状况。

gauche /gəʊʃ; *NAmE* goʊʃ/ *adj.* awkward when dealing with people and often saying or doing the wrong thing 笨拙的；不善社交的；不老练的：*a gauche schoolgirl/*

manner 不善社交的女生；笨拙的举止 ▶ **gauche·ness** (*also* **gauch·erie** /ˈɡəʊʃəri; *NAmE* ˌɡoʊʃəˈri/) *noun* [U]: *the gaucheness of youth* 青年人的不老练

gau·cho /ˈɡaʊtʃəʊ; *NAmE* -tʃoʊ/ *noun* (*pl.* **-os**) a S American COWBOY 南美牛仔

gaudy /ˈɡɔːdi/ *adj.* (**gaud·ier**, **gaudi·est**) (*disapproving*) too brightly coloured in a way that lacks taste 俗艳的；花哨的 SYN **garish**: *gaudy clothes/colours* 过于花哨的衣服 / 色彩 ▶ **gaud·ily** /ˈɡɔːdɪli/ *adv.*: *gaudily dressed/painted* 穿着 / 涂饰得太俗艳 **gaudi·ness** *noun* [U]

gauge (*US also* **gage**) /ɡeɪdʒ/ *noun*, *verb*

■ *noun* **1** (often in compounds 常构成复合词) an instrument for measuring the amount or level of sth 测量仪器（或仪表）；计量器：*a **fuel/petrol/temperature, etc. gauge*** 燃料表、汽油量表、温度计等 ➲ VISUAL VOCAB PAGE V56 **2** a measurement of the width or thickness of sth 宽度；厚度：*What gauge of wire do we need?* 我们需要多大直径的金属丝？ **3** (*also* **bore** *especially in BrE*) a measurement of the width of the BARREL of a gun（枪管的）口径：*a 12-gauge shotgun* * 12 号猎枪 **4** the distance between the rails of a railway/railroad track or the wheels of a train（铁道的）轨距；（火车的）轮距：***standard gauge*** (= 56½ inches in Britain) 标准轨距（在英国为 56.5 英寸）◇ *a **narrow gauge*** (= narrower than standard) *railway* 窄轨铁路 **5** [usually sing.] **~ (of sth)** a fact or an event that can be used to estimate or judge sth（用于估计或判断的）事实，依据，尺度，标准：*Tomorrow's game against Arsenal will be a good gauge of their promotion chances.* 明天与阿森纳队的比赛是衡量他们能否晋级的很好依据。

■ *verb* **1** to make a judgement about sth, especially people's feelings or attitudes 判定，判断（尤指人的感情或态度）：**~ sth** *They interviewed employees to gauge their reaction to the changes.* 他们与雇员面谈以判定他们的应变能力。◇ *He tried to gauge her mood.* 他试图揣摩她的心情。◇ **~ whether, how, etc....** *It was difficult to gauge whether she was angry or not.* 很难判断她是否在生气。**2** **~ sth** to measure sth accurately using a special instrument （用仪器）测量：*precision instruments that can gauge the diameter to a fraction of a millimetre* 可测出直径为若干分之一毫米的精密仪器 **3** **~ sth** | **~ how, what, etc....** to calculate sth approximately 估计；估算：*We were able to gauge the strength of the wind from the movement of the trees.* 我们可根据树的摇动估算出风力。

gaunt /ɡɔːnt/ *adj.* **1** (of a person 人) very thin, usually because of illness, not having enough food, or worry（常因疾病、饥饿或忧虑而）瘦削憔悴的：*a gaunt face* 憔悴的面容 **2** (of a building 建筑物) not attractive and without any decoration 寒碜的；破败的 ▶ **gaunt·ness** *noun* [U]

gaunt·let /ˈɡɔːntlət/ *noun* **1** a metal glove worn as part of a suit of ARMOUR by soldiers in the Middle Ages（中世纪武士铠甲的）金属手套，铁手套 **2** a strong glove with a wide covering for the wrist, used for example when driving （驾驶等用的）长手套，防护手套：*motorcyclists with leather gauntlets* 戴着皮护手套的摩托车手

IDM **run the ˈgauntlet** to be criticized or attacked by a lot of people, especially a group of people that you have to walk through 受严厉谴责；受夹道攻击：*Some of the witnesses had to run the gauntlet of television cameras and reporters.* 一些证人不得不穿过众多电视摄像机和记者的围堵。 ORIGIN This phrase refers to an old army punishment where a man was forced to run between two lines of soldiers hitting him. 此短语源自古老的军中惩罚，受罚者从两排夹击他的士兵中间跑过。 **take up the ˈgauntlet** to accept sb's invitation to fight or compete 接受挑战；应战 ORIGIN In the Middle Ages a knight threw his gauntlet at the feet of another knight as a challenge to fight. If he accepted the challenge, the other knight would pick up the glove. 在中世纪，一个骑士把铁手套扔在另一个骑士的脚下，以示挑战。如果对方接受挑战，就会捡起铁手套。 **throw down the ˈgauntlet** to invite sb to fight or compete with you 发出挑战

gauze /ɡɔːz/ *noun* **1** [U] a type of light transparent cloth, usually made of cotton or silk 薄纱，纱罗（通常由棉或丝织成） **2** [U] a type of thin cotton cloth used for covering and protecting wounds 纱布（包扎伤口用）：*a gauze dressing* 纱布敷料 **3** [U, C] material made of a network of wire; a piece of this（金属丝制的）网纱，网：*wire gauze* 金属网纱 ➲ VISUAL VOCAB PAGE V72 ▶ **gauzy** *adj.* [usually before noun]: *a gauzy material* 薄纱料

gave PAST TENSE OF GIVE

gavel /ˈɡævl/ *noun* a small hammer used by a person in charge of a meeting or an AUCTION, or by a judge in court, in order to get people's attention（会议主席、拍卖商或法官用的）小槌

ga·vial /ˈɡeɪviəl/ *noun* = GHARIAL

ga·votte /ɡəˈvɒt; *NAmE* ɡəˈvɑːt/ *noun* a French dance that was popular in the past; a piece of music for this dance 加沃特舞（旧时流行于法国）；加沃特舞曲

Gawd /ɡɔːd/ *noun*, *exclamation* (*informal*) used in written English to show that the word 'God' is being pronounced in a particular way to express surprise, anger or fear（书面语中代表发音特别的 God，表示吃惊、气愤或恐惧）上帝，老天爷：*For Gawd's sake hurry up!* 看在上帝的分上，快点吧！

gawk /ɡɔːk/ *verb* [I] **~ (at sb/sth)** (*informal*) to stare at sb/sth in a rude or stupid way 无礼地瞪眼看；呆头呆脑地盯着 SYN **gape**

gawky /ˈɡɔːki/ *adj.* (especially of a tall young person 尤指高个子的年轻人) awkward in the way they move or behave 笨拙的；笨手笨脚的 ▶ **gawk·ily** /ˈɡɔːkɪli/ *adv.* **gawki·ness** *noun* [U]

gawp /ɡɔːp/ *verb* [I] **~ (at sb/sth)** (*BrE, informal*) to stare at sb/sth in a rude or stupid way 无礼地瞪眼看；呆头呆脑地盯着 SYN **gape**

gay /ɡeɪ/ *adj.*, *noun*

■ *adj.* **1** (of people, especially men 人，尤指男性) sexually attracted to people of the same sex 同性恋的 SYN **homosexual**: *gay men* 同性恋的男人 ◇ *I didn't know he was gay.* 我不知道他是同性恋者。◇ *Is she gay?* 她是同性恋者吗？ OPP **straight** **2** [only before noun] connected with people who are gay 与同性恋者有关的：*a **gay club/bar*** 同性恋者俱乐部 / 酒吧 ◇ *the lesbian and gay community* 男女同性恋者群体 **3** [not before noun] (*slang, disapproving, offensive*) (used especially by young people) boring and not fashionable or attractive（尤为年轻人用语）无聊，不时尚，没吸引力：*She didn't like the ringtone—said it was gay.* 她不喜欢那个手机铃声，说它不时尚。◇ *That is so gay!* 那太无聊了！ **4** (**gayer**, **gayest**) (*old-fashioned*) happy and full of fun 愉快的；快乐的；充满乐趣的：*gay laughter* 欢快的笑声 **5** (*old-fashioned*) brightly coloured 鲜艳的；艳丽的：*The garden was gay with red geraniums.* 花园里红色的天竺葵花色彩艳丽。 ➲ SEE ALSO GAIETY, GAILY (2)

IDM **with ˈgay abandon** without thinking about the results or effects of a particular action 不考虑后果；轻率

■ *noun* a person who is HOMOSEXUAL, especially a man 同性恋者（尤指男性）

gay·dar /ˈɡeɪdɑː(r)/ *noun* [U] (*informal*) the ability that a HOMOSEXUAL person is supposed to have to recognize other people who are homosexual 同性恋雷达（同性恋者识别其他同性恋者的能力）

gay·ness /ˈɡeɪnəs/ *noun* [U] the state of being HOMOSEXUAL 同性恋 ➲ COMPARE GAIETY

ˌgay ˈpride *noun* [U] the feeling that HOMOSEXUAL people should not be ashamed of telling people that they are homosexual and should feel proud of themselves 同性恋者尊严

gaze /ɡeɪz/ *verb*, *noun*

■ *verb* [I] **+ adv./prep.** to look steadily at sb/sth for a long time, either because you are very interested or surprised, or because you are thinking of sth else 凝视；注视；盯着 SYN **stare**: *She gazed at him in amazement.* 她惊异地注视着他。◇ *He sat for hours just **gazing into space**.* 他一连

G

几个小时坐在那里茫然地看着前面。➲ SYNONYMS AT STARE
■ **noun** [usually sing.] a long steady look at sb/sth 凝视；注视：*He met her **gaze*** (= looked at her while she looked at him). 他与她凝视的目光相遇。◇ *She **dropped her gaze*** (= stopped looking). 她目光低垂，不再凝视。➲ SYNONYMS AT LOOK

gazebo 观景亭

gaz·ebo /ɡəˈziːbəʊ; *NAmE* -boʊ/ *noun* (*pl.* **-os**) a small building with open sides in a garden/yard, especially one with a view 观景亭；凉亭；眺台

gaz·elle /ɡəˈzel/ *noun* (*pl.* **gaz·elle** or **gaz·elles**) a small ANTELOPE 羚羊

gaz·ette /ɡəˈzet/ *noun* **1** an official newspaper published by a particular organization containing important information about decisions that have been made and people who have been employed （某一组织的）公报 **2 Gazette** used in the titles of some newspapers（用于报刊名）报，报纸：*the Evening Gazette*《晚报》

gaz·et·teer /ˌɡæzəˈtɪə(r); *NAmE* -ˈtɪr/ *noun* a list of place names published as a book or at the end of a book 地名词典；（书末的）地名索引

ga·zil·lion /ɡəˈzɪljən/ *noun* (*NAmE, informal*) a very large number 很大的数目：*gazillion-dollar houses* 高价房子 ◇ *gazillions of copies* 无数册书

gaz·pa·cho /ɡæzˈpætʃəʊ; *NAmE* ɡəzˈpɑːtʃoʊ/ *noun* [U] a cold Spanish soup made with tomatoes, peppers, CUCUMBERS, etc. 西班牙凉菜，西班牙冷汤菜（用番茄、青椒、黄瓜等制成）

gaz·ump /ɡəˈzʌmp/ *verb* [usually passive] **~ sb** (*BrE*) when sb who has made an offer to pay a particular price for a house and who has had this offer accepted is **gazumped**, their offer is no longer accepted by the person selling the house, because sb else has made a higher offer（房价议定后因有人出价更高而向买主）食言毁约 ▶ **gaz·ump·ing** /ɡəˈzʌmpɪŋ/ *noun* [U] ➲ COMPARE GAZUNDER

gaz·un·der /ɡəˈzʌndə(r)/ *verb* [often passive] **~ sb** (*BrE*) to offer a lower price for a house that you have already agreed to buy at a higher price, before the contract is signed（签合同前向卖主）压低房价：*The vendors were gazundered at the last minute.* 卖主在最后一刻被要求降低房价。▶ **gaz·un·der·ing** *noun* [U] ➲ COMPARE GAZUMP

GB *abbr.* **1** /ˌdʒiː ˈbiː/ Great Britain 大不列颠 **2** (in writing 书写形式) GIGABYTE 吉字节，千兆字节（计算机内存或数据单位）：*a 750GB hard drive* * 750 千兆字节的硬盘

Gb (*also* **Gbit**) *abbr.* (in writing 书写形式) GIGABIT 吉比特，千兆比特（计算机内存或数据单位）

GBH /ˌdʒiː biː ˈeɪtʃ/ *abbr.* (*BrE, law* 律) GRIEVOUS BODILY HARM 严重人体伤害（罪）

GCE /ˌdʒiː siː ˈiː/ *noun* [C, U] the abbreviation for 'General Certificate of Education' (a British exam taken by students in England and Wales and some other countries in any of a range of subjects. GCE O levels were replaced in 1988 by GCSE exams.)（英国）普通教育证书（全写为 General Certificate of Education，其中的普通证书考试于 1988 年为普通中等教育证书所取代）➲ COMPARE O LEVEL, A LEVEL

GCSE /ˌdʒiː siː es ˈiː/ *noun* [C, U] the abbreviation for 'General Certificate of Secondary Education' (a British exam taken by students in England and Wales and some other countries, usually around the age of 16. GCSE can be taken in any of a range of subjects.)（英国）普通中等教育证书（全写为 General Certificate of Secondary Education）：*She's got 10 GCSEs.* 她已获得 10 门学科的普通中等教育证书。◇ *He's doing German at GCSE.* 他在学习普通中等教育证书的德语课程。➲ COMPARE A LEVEL

g'day /ɡəˈdeɪ/ *exclamation* (*AustralE, NZE*) hello 喂；你好

Gdns *abbr.* (*BrE*) (used in written addresses) Gardens（用于书写地址）园，街，广场：*7 Windsor Gdns* 温莎街 7 号

GDP /ˌdʒiː diː ˈpiː/ *noun* [U, C, usually sing.] the abbreviation for 'gross domestic product' (the total value of all the goods and services produced by a country in one year) 国内生产总值（全写为 gross domestic product）➲ COMPARE GNP

GDR /ˌdʒiː diː ˈɑː(r)/ *abbr.* German Democratic Republic 德意志民主共和国（前东德）

gear 🔑 /ɡɪə(r); *NAmE* ɡɪr/ *noun, verb*
■ **noun**
• **IN VEHICLE** 车辆 **1** 🔑 [C, usually pl.] machinery in a vehicle that turns engine power (or power on a bicycle) into movement forwards or backwards 排挡；齿轮；传动装置：*Careless use of the clutch may damage the gears.* 离合器使用不慎可能会损坏传动装置。➲ VISUAL VOCAB PAGE V55 **2** 🔑 [U, C] a particular position of the gears in a vehicle that gives a particular range of speed and power 挡：***first/second, etc. gear*** 一挡、二挡等 ◇ ***reverse gear*** 倒挡 ◇ ***low/high gear*** 低速 / 高速挡 ◇ (*BrE*) ***bottom/top gear*** 最低 / 最高挡 ◇ (*BrE*) ***to change gear*** 换挡 ◇ (*NAmE*) ***to shift gear*** 换挡 ◇ *When parking on a hill, leave the car **in gear**.* 在斜坡停车时把汽车挂上挡。◇ *What gear are you in?* 你挂的是几挡？◇ *He drove wildly, crashing through the gears like a maniac.* 他开车很野，发疯似的啪啦啪啦地换挡。➲ COLLOCATIONS AT DRIVING
• **EQUIPMENT/CLOTHES** 设备；衣服 **3** 🔑 [U] the equipment or clothing needed for a particular activity（某种活动的）设备，用具，衣服：***climbing/fishing/sports, etc. gear*** 爬山、钓鱼、运动等用具 ➲ SEE ALSO HEADGEAR, RIOT GEAR ➲ SYNONYMS AT EQUIPMENT **4** [U] (*informal*) clothes 衣服：*wearing the latest gear* 穿着最新款式的衣服 ➲ SYNONYMS AT CLOTHES
• **POSSESSIONS** 所有物 **5** [U] (*informal*) the things that a person owns 所有物；财物：*I've left all my gear at Dave's house.* 我把我所有的东西都留在戴夫家了。
• **MACHINERY** 机器 **6** [U] (often in compounds 常构成复合词) a piece of machinery used for a particular purpose（特定用途的）器械，装置：***lifting/towing/winding, etc. gear*** 起重、牵引、卷扬等装置 ➲ SEE ALSO LANDING GEAR
• **SPEED/EFFORT** 速度 / 努力 **7** [U, C] used to talk about the speed or effort involved in doing sth（做事的）速度，努力：(*BrE*) *The party organization is **moving into top gear** as the election approaches.* 随着选举的临近，这个政党的组织工作正在紧锣密鼓地进行。◇ (*NAmE*) ***to move into high gear*** 进入高速发展 ◇ *Coming out of the final bend, the runner **stepped up a gear** to overtake the rest of the pack.* 那名赛跑选手绕过最后一个弯道后开始加速，以图超越同组的其他选手。
• **DRUGS** 毒品 **8** [U] (*slang*) illegal drugs 毒品
IDM **get into 'gear** | **get sth into 'gear** to start working, or to start sth working, in an efficient way（使）开始工作，进入有效工作状态 **(slip/be thrown) out of 'gear** (of emotions or situations 情绪或形势) (to become) out of control 失去控制：*She said nothing in case her temper slipped out of gear.* 她什么都没说，免得按捺不住情绪。➲ MORE AT ASS

■ *verb*

PHR V **ˈgear sth to/towards sth** [usually passive] to make, change or prepare sth so that it is suitable for a particular purpose 使与…相适应；使适合于：*The course had been geared towards the specific needs of its members.* 课程已作调整，以满足学员的特别需要。 **ˌgear ˈup (for/to sth) | ˌgear sb/sth↔ˈup (for/to sth)** to prepare yourself/sb/sth to do sth（使）为…做好准备：*Cycle organizations are gearing up for National Bike Week.* 自行车组织正在为全国自行车周活动做准备。 ➲ SEE ALSO GEARED

gear·box /ˈɡɪəbɒks; *NAmE* ˈɡɪrbɑːks/ *noun* the part containing the gears of a vehicle 变速箱；齿轮箱

geared /ɡɪəd; *NAmE* ɡɪrd/ *adj.* [not before noun] **1 ~ to/towards sth | ~ to do sth** designed or organized to achieve a particular purpose, or to be suitable for a particular group of people 旨在；适合于：*The programme is geared to preparing students for the world of work.* 本计划旨在为学生进入职场做准备。◇ *The resort is geared towards children.* 这个旅游胜地适合儿童玩耍。 **2 ~ up (for sth) | ~ up (to do sth)** prepared and ready for sth（为…）做好准备，准备好：*We have people on board geared up to help with any problems.* 我们已得到人员支持，准备帮助解决任何问题。

gear·head /ˈɡɪəhed; *NAmE* ˈɡɪrhed/ *noun* (*informal*) a person who is very enthusiastic about cars or new technical devices and equipment 设备发烧友（指对汽车或新科技设备着迷者）：*He's a total gearhead—can't keep away from the race track.* 他是个十足的赛车迷，一刻也离不开赛车道。

gear·ing /ˈɡɪərɪŋ; *NAmE* ˈɡɪrɪŋ/ *noun* [U] **1** (*BrE*) (*NAmE* **le·ver·age**) (*finance* 财) the relationship between the amount of money that a company owes and the value of its shares 资本与负债比率；联动比率 **2** a particular set or arrangement of gears in a machine or vehicle 齿轮机构

ˈgear lever (*also* **ˈgear·stick**) (*both BrE*) (*NAmE* **gearshift, ˈstick shift**) *noun* a handle used to change the gears of a vehicle 变速杆；换挡杆 ➲ VISUAL VOCAB PAGE V56

gear·shift /ˈɡɪəʃɪft; *NAmE* ˈɡɪrʃɪft/ *noun* = STICK SHIFT

gecko /ˈɡekəʊ; *NAmE* ˈɡekoʊ/ *noun* (*pl.* **-os** or **-oes**) a small LIZARD (= a type of REPTILE) that lives in warm countries 壁虎

GED /ˌdʒiː iː ˈdiː/ *noun* (in the US and Canada) the abbreviation for 'general equivalency diploma' or 'general educational development' (an official certificate that people who did not finish high school can get, after taking classes and passing an examination)（美国和加拿大）普通高中同等学历证书（全写为 general equivalency diploma 或 general educational development，为修完课程并通过考试的高中未毕业者颁发的官方证书）

ged·dit? /ˈɡedɪt/ *abbr.* (*informal*) Do you get it? (= Do you understand the joke?)（指笑话）明白了吗

gee /dʒiː/ *exclamation, verb*

■ *exclamation* (*especially NAmE*) a word that some people use to show that they are surprised, impressed or annoyed（表示惊奇、感动或气恼）哇，啊，哎呀：*Gee, what a great idea!* 哇，多好的主意！ ➲ MORE LIKE THIS 2, page R25

■ *verb* (*BrE*)

PHR V **ˌgee sb↔ˈup | ˌgee sb↔ˈon** to encourage sb to work harder, perform better, etc. 激励，鼓励（某人更努力、更好地工作等） **ˌgee ˈup** used to tell a horse to start moving or to go faster（用以吆喝马起行或快走）嘚，驾

ˈgee-gee *noun* (*BrE, informal*) (used especially by and to young children 尤为儿语或对儿童说话时用) a horse 马儿

geek /ɡiːk/ *noun* (*informal*) **1** a person who is boring, wears clothes that are not fashionable, does not know how to behave in social situations, etc. 闷蛋；土包子 SYN **nerd** **2** a person who is very interested in and who knows a lot about a particular subject 极客（对某领域极感兴趣且知之甚多的人）：*a computer geek* 电脑迷 ▸ **geeky** *adj.*

geese PL. OF GOOSE

gee whiz /ˌdʒiː ˈwɪz/ *exclamation* (*old-fashioned, especially NAmE*) = GEE

gee·zer /ˈɡiːzə(r)/ *noun* (*informal*) **1** (*BrE*) a man 男人；家伙：*Some geezer called Danny did it.* 这事是个叫丹尼的家伙干的。 **2** (*NAmE*) an old man, especially one who is rather strange 怪老头；老家伙

Gei·ger count·er /ˈɡaɪɡə kaʊntə(r); *NAmE* ˈɡaɪɡər/ *noun* a device used for finding and measuring RADIOACTIVITY 盖格计数器（用以探测和测量放射性）

gei·sha /ˈɡeɪʃə/ (*also* **ˈgeisha girl**) *noun* a Japanese woman who is trained to entertain men with conversation, dancing and singing 艺伎（陪男子聊天、表演歌舞的日本女子）

gel /dʒel/ *noun, verb*

■ *noun* [U, C] a thick substance like jelly, especially one used in products for the hair or skin 凝胶，冻胶，胶滞体（尤指用于头发或护肤的产品）：***hair/shower gel*** 发胶；沐浴露

■ *verb* (**-ll-**) **1** [I] (*BrE*) (*also* **jell** *NAmE, BrE*) (of two or more people 二人或以上) to work well together; to form a successful group 联手共事；结为一体：*We just didn't gel as a group.* 我们就是不能成为一个集体。 **2** [I] (*BrE*) (*also* **jell** *NAmE, BrE*) (of an idea, a thought, a plan, etc. 主意、想法、计划等) to become clearer and more definite; to work well 变得更清楚；显得更明确；有效；起作用：*Ideas were beginning to gel in my mind.* 各种想法在我头脑里逐渐明朗起来。◇ *That day, everything gelled.* 那天，一切都很顺利。 **3** [I] (*also* **jell** *especially in NAmE*) (*specialist*) (of a liquid 液体) to become thicker and more solid; to form a gel 胶凝；胶化；形成胶体 **4** [T, usually passive] **~ sth** to put gel on your hair 上发胶

gel·atin /ˈdʒelətɪn/ (*also* **gel·atine** /ˈdʒelətiːn/) *noun* [U] a clear substance without any taste that is made from boiling animal bones and is used to make jelly, film for cameras, etc. 明胶

gel·at·in·ous /dʒəˈlætɪnəs/ *adj.* thick and sticky, like a jelly 明胶的；胶状的：*a gelatinous substance* 胶状物质

ˈgelatin paper *noun* [U] paper covered with gelatin, used in photography（照相）明胶相纸

geld /ɡeld/ *verb* **~ sth** (*specialist*) to remove the TESTICLES of a male animal, especially a horse 阉割（雄性动物，尤指马）；给（动物）去势 SYN **castrate**

geld·ing /ˈɡeldɪŋ/ *noun* a horse that has been CASTRATED 阉割的马；去势的马 ➲ COMPARE STALLION

gel·ig·nite /ˈdʒelɪɡnaɪt/ *noun* [U] a powerful EXPLOSIVE 葛里炸药；硝铵炸药；炸胶

gem /dʒem/ *noun* **1** (*also less frequent* **gem·stone** /ˈdʒemstəʊn; *NAmE* -stoʊn/) a PRECIOUS STONE that has been cut and polished and is used in jewellery（经切割打磨的）宝石 SYN **jewel, precious stone**：*a crown studded with gems* 镶有宝石的皇冠 **2** a person, place or thing that is especially good 难能可贵的人；风景优美的地方；美妙绝伦的事物：*This picture is the gem* (= the best) *of the collection.* 这幅画是收藏中的极品。◇ *a gem of a place* 胜地 ◇ *She's a real gem!* 她真是难能可贵！ ➲ COMPARE JEWEL

gemin·ate /ˈdʒemɪneɪt; -nət/ *adj.* (*phonetics* 语音) (of a speech sound 语音) consisting of the same consonant pronounced twice, for example /kk/ in the middle of the word *backcomb* 叠音的（如 backcomb 中的 /kk/）

Gem·ini /ˈdʒemɪnaɪ; -ni/ *noun* **1** [U] the third sign of the ZODIAC, the TWINS 黄道第三宫；双子宫；双子（星）座 **2** [C] a person born when the sun is in this sign, that is between 22 May and 21 June 属双子座的人（约出生于 5 月 22 日至 6 月 21 日）

Gen. /dʒen/ *abbr.* (in writing 书写形式) GENERAL 将军：*Gen.* (*Stanley*) *Armstrong*（斯坦利·）阿姆斯特朗将军

G

gen /dʒen/ *noun, verb*

■ ***noun*** [U] ~ (**on sth**) (*old-fashioned, BrE, informal*) information 消息；情报；资料

■ ***verb*** (-nn-)

PHR V ˌ**gen ˈup** (**on sth**) | ˌ**gen sb/yourself ˈup** (**on sth**) (*old-fashioned, BrE, informal*) to find out or give sb information about sth 了解情况；知道详情；向（某人）提供情报

gen·darme /ˈʒɒndɑːm; *NAmE* ˈʒɑːndɑːrm/ *noun* (*from French*) a member of the French police force（法国的）警察，宪兵

gen·der AW /ˈdʒendə(r)/ *noun* **1** [C, U] the fact of being male or female, especially when considered with reference to social and cultural differences, not differences in biology 性别（尤指社会和文化差异，而非生理差异）：*issues of class, race and gender* 阶级、种族和性别问题 ◇ *traditional concepts of gender* 传统的性别观念 ◇ ***gender differences/relations/roles*** 性别差异/关系/角色 ➲ COMPARE SEX *n.* (1) **2** [C, U] (*grammar* 语法) (in some languages 用于某些语言) each of the classes (MASCULINE, FEMININE and sometimes NEUTER) into which nouns, pronouns and adjectives are divided; the division of nouns, pronouns and adjectives into these different genders. Different genders may have different endings, etc. 性（阳性、阴性和中性，不同的性有不同的词尾等）：*In French the adjective must agree with the noun in number and gender.* 法语中形容词必须在数和性上与名词一致。➲ WORDFINDER NOTE AT GRAMMAR

ˈ**gender bender** *noun* (*informal*) a person who dresses and behaves like a member of the opposite sex 穿着举止像异性的人；假小子；假娘儿们

ˌ**gender reasˈsignment** *noun* [U] the act of changing a person's sex by a medical operation in which parts of their body are changed so that they become like a person of the opposite sex 性别再造手术；变性手术

ˈ**gender-specific** *adj.* connected with women only or with men only 女（或男）性特有的；与某一性别有关的：*The report was redrafted to remove gender-specific language.* 重新起草了这个报告，删除了带有性别特点的语言。

gene /dʒiːn/ *noun* (*biology* 生) a unit inside a cell which controls a particular quality in a living thing that has been passed on from its parents 基因：*a **dominant/recessive gene*** 显性/隐性基因 ◇ *genes that code for the colour of the eyes* 为眼睛的颜色编码的基因 ➲ SEE ALSO GENETIC ➲ WORDFINDER NOTE AT BIOLOGY

IDM **be in the ˈgenes** to be a quality that your parents have passed on to you 基因使然；是遗传的：*I've always enjoyed music—it's in the genes.* 我向来喜欢音乐，这是遗传的。

ge·neal·ogist /ˌdʒiːniˈælədʒɪst/ *noun* a person who studies family history 家谱学者；系谱学家；宗谱学家

ge·neal·ogy /ˌdʒiːniˈælədʒi/ *noun* (*pl.* -**ies**) **1** [U] the study of family history, including the study of who the ANCESTORS of a particular person were 家谱学；系谱学；宗谱学 **2** [C] a particular person's line of ANCESTORS;

▼ **MORE ABOUT ...** 补充说明

gender

Ways of talking about men and women 表示男女的说法

- When you are writing or speaking English it is important to use language that includes both men and women equally. Some people may be very offended if you do not. 说写英语时，重要的是用词要把男女都包括在内，否则可能会冒犯某些人。

The human race 人类

- **Man** and **mankind** have traditionally been used to mean 'all men and women'. Many people now prefer to use **humanity**, **the human race**, **human beings** or **people**. * man 和 mankind 传统上用以指所有男性和女性，不过，现在许多人喜欢用 humanity、the human race、human beings 或 people。

Jobs 职业

- The suffix **-ess** in names of occupations such as **actress**, **hostess** and **waitress** shows that the person doing the job is a woman. Many people now avoid these. Instead you can use **actor** or **host** (although **actress** and **hostess** are still very common), or a neutral word, such as **server** for *waiter* and *waitress*. 后缀 -ess 在职业的名称如 actress、hostess 和 waitress 中表明从事此职业的是女性。目前，许多人避免用这些词。取而代之的是 actor 或 host（尽管 actress 和 hostess 仍然很常见）或用中性词如 server 取代 waiter 和 waitress。
- Neutral words like **assistant**, **worker**, **person** or **officer** are now often used instead of *-man* or *-woman* in the names of jobs. For example, you can use **police officer** instead of *policeman* or *policewoman*, and **spokesperson** instead of *spokesman* or *spokeswoman*. Neutral words are very common in newspapers, on television and radio and in official writing, in both *BrE* and *NAmE*. 现在职业名称常用中性词如 assistant、worker、person 或 officer 取代 -man 或 -woman。例如可用 police officer 代替 policeman 或 policewoman，用 spokesperson 代替 spokesman 或 spokeswoman。在报刊、电视、广播和公文中，英式英语和美式英语都常用中性词。
- When talking about jobs that are traditionally done by the other sex, some people say: **a male secretary/nurse/model** (NOT **man**) or **a woman/female doctor/barrister/driver**. However this is now not usually used unless you need to emphasize which sex the person is, or it is still unusual for the job to be done by a man/woman. 谈及传统上由另一性别干的工作时，有人用 male secretary/nurse/model（不用 man）或 woman/female doctor/barrister/driver 表示。不过现在这种用法不常见，除非要强调此人的性别，或由某性别干此工作仍然少见：*My daughter prefers to see a woman doctor.* 我的女儿喜欢让女医生看病。◇ *They have a male nanny for their kids.* 他们有个男保姆照料孩子。◇ *a female racing driver* 女赛车手

Pronouns 代词

- **He** used to be considered to cover both men and women. * he 过去被认为既指男性也指女性：*Everyone needs to feel he is loved.* 人人都需要有被爱的感觉。 This is not now acceptable. Instead, after **everybody**, **everyone**, **anybody**, **anyone**, **somebody**, **someone**, etc. one of the plural pronouns **they**, **them**, and **their** is often used. 现在此用法不获认同。取而代之的是在 everybody、everyone、anybody、anyone、somebody、someone 等之后常用复数代词 they、them 和 their：*Does everybody know what they want?* 人人都知道自己需要什么吗？◇ *Somebody's left their coat here.* 有人把外衣落在这儿了。◇ *I hope nobody's forgotten to bring their passport with them.* 希望没人忘了随身带上护照。
- Some people prefer to use **he or she**, **his or her**, or **him or her** in speech and writing. 有人在口语和书面语中喜欢用 he or she、his or her 或 him or her：*Everyone knows what's best for him- or herself.* 人人都知道对自己来说什么是最好的。 **He/she** or **(s)he** can also be used in writing. * he/she 或 (s)he 亦可用于书面语中：*If in doubt, ask your doctor. He/she can give you more information.* 如有疑问请向你的医生咨询，他/她会给你更多的信息。(You may find that some writers just use 'she'. 有些人只用 she。) These uses can seem awkward when they are used a lot. It is better to try to change the sentence, using a plural noun. 这种说法用得太多可能显得别扭。最好尽量改动句子，用复数名词。Instead of saying 避免说：*A baby cries when he or she is tired*, you can say 可以说：*Babies cry when they are tired.* 婴儿疲倦时会哭。

a diagram that shows this 家谱（图）；系谱（图）；宗谱（图）➲ WORDFINDER NOTE AT RELATION ▸ **ge·nea·logic·al** /ˌdʒiːniəˈlɒdʒɪkl; *NAmE* -ˈlɑːdʒ-/ *adj.* [only before noun]: *a **genealogical chart/table/tree*** (= a chart with branches that shows a person's ANCESTORS) 系谱图；家谱表；家系树状图

ˈgene pool *noun* (*biology* 生) all of the GENES that are available within breeding populations of a particular SPECIES of animal or plant 基因库（某物种的全部基因）

gen·era PL. OF GENUS

gen·eral 🔑 /ˈdʒenrəl/ *adj., noun*

■ ***adj.***

• **AFFECTING ALL** 涉及全部 **1** 🔑 affecting all or most people, places or things 全体的；普遍的；总的：*The general opinion is that the conference was a success.* 普遍认为这次会议是成功的。◇ *the **general belief/consensus*** 普遍的信念/共识 ◇ *books of **general interest*** (= of interest to most people) 普遍感兴趣的书籍 ◇ *The bad weather has been fairly general* (= has affected most areas). 坏天气影响到的范围相当大。

• **USUAL** 通常 **2** 🔑 [usually before noun] normal; usual 正常的；一般的；常规的：*There is one exception to this general principle.* 这个一般性原则有一例外。◇ ***As a general rule*** (= usually) *he did what he could to be helpful.* 一般情况下他都尽力给予帮助。◇ *This opinion is common among the general population* (= ordinary people). 这是人们普遍的看法。

• **NOT EXACT** 笼统 **3** 🔑 including the most important aspects of sth; not exact or detailed 概括性的；大体的；笼统的 SYN **overall**：*I check the bookings to get a **general idea** of what activities to plan.* 我核查预订情况以便对计划安排些什么活动有个大体的想法。◇ *I know how it works **in general terms**.* 我大致知道其中的运作原理。◇ *They gave a general description of the man.* 他们对这个男人作了大致的描述。 **4 the ~ direction/area** approximately, but not exactly, the direction/area mentioned 大致的，大概的（方向或地区）：*They fired in the general direction of the enemy.* 他们向敌军大致的方向开了枪。

• **NOT LIMITED** 未限定 **5** 🔑 not limited to a particular subject, use or activity 非专门的；一般性的；普通的：*a general hospital* 综合医院 ◇ *general education* 普通教育 ◇ *We shall keep the discussion fairly general.* 我们会保持相当广泛的讨论。 **6** not limited to one part or aspect of a person or thing 整体的；全身的；全面的：*a general anaesthetic* 全身麻醉 ◇ *The building was in a general state of disrepair.* 整座建筑处于失修状态。

• **HIGHEST IN RANK** 最高级别 **7** [only before noun] (*also* **General**) [after noun] highest in rank; chief 首席的；总管的：*the general manager* 总经理 ◇ *the Inspector General of Police* 警察总监 ➲ SEE ALSO ATTORNEY GENERAL, DIRECTOR GENERAL, GOVERNOR GENERAL, SECRETARY GENERAL, SOLICITOR GENERAL, SURGEON GENERAL

IDM **in ˈgeneral 1** 🔑 usually; mainly 通常；大体上：*In general, Japanese cars are very reliable and breakdowns are rare.* 日本汽车通常是很可靠的，发生故障的情况极少。➲ LANGUAGE BANK AT CONCLUSION, GENERALLY **2** 🔑 as a whole 总的说来；从总体上看：*This is a crucial year for your relationships in general and your love life in particular.* 这一年总体上对你们的关系，特别是你们的爱情生活是非常关键的。

■ ***noun*** (*abbr.* **Gen.**) an officer of very high rank in the army and the US AIR FORCE; the officer with the highest rank in the MARINES 将军；（陆军、海军陆战队或美国空军）上将：*a four-star general* 四星上将 ◇ *General Tom Parker* 汤姆·帕克将军 ➲ SEE ALSO BRIGADIER GENERAL, MAJOR GENERAL

ˌGeneral Aˈmerican *noun* [U] the way people speak English in most parts of the US, not including New England, New York, and the South 通用美式英语（除新英格兰、纽约和南方等之外通用于美国大部分地区）

ˌGeneral Cerˌtificate of Eduˈcation *noun* = GCE

ˌGeneral Cerˌtificate of ˌSecondary Eduˈcation *noun* = GCSE

ˌgeneral ˈcounsel *noun* (in the US) the main lawyer who gives legal advice to a company （美国）公司法律总顾问

ˌgeneral deˈlivery (*NAmE*) (*BrE* **poste rest·ante**) *noun* [U] an arrangement in which a post office keeps a person's mail until they go to collect it, used especially when sb is travelling 邮件寄存服务，存局候领（邮局暂为保管以候收件人上门自取）

ˌgeneral eˈlection *noun* an election in which all the people of a country vote to choose a government 大选；普选 ➲ COMPARE BY-ELECTION

ˌgeneral headˈquarters *noun* [U+sing./pl. v.] = GHQ

gen·er·al·ist /ˈdʒenrəlɪst/ *noun* a person who has knowledge of several different subjects or activities 多面手；全才；通才 OPP **specialist**

gen·er·al·ity /ˌdʒenəˈræləti/ *noun* (*pl.* **-ies**) **1** [C, usually pl.] a statement that discusses general principles or issues rather than details or particular examples 概述；概论；通则：*to speak in broad generalities* 泛泛地说 ◇ *As usual, he confined his comments to generalities.* 他和往常一样，只作了笼统的评论。 **2 the generality** [sing.+sing./pl. v.] (*formal*) most of a group of people or things 主体；大多数；大部分：*This view is held by the generality of leading scholars.* 大多数知名学者都持这种观点。 **3** [U] (*formal*) the quality of being general rather than detailed or exact 一般性；普遍性；笼统：*An account of such generality is of little value.* 这种一般性描述没有什么价值。

gen·er·al·iza·tion (*BrE also* **-isa·tion**) /ˌdʒenrəlaɪˈzeɪʃn; *NAmE* -ləˈz-/ *noun* [C, U] a general statement that is based on only a few facts or examples; the act of making such statements 概括；归纳；泛论：*a speech full of **broad/sweeping generalizations*** 通篇大而无当的发言 ◇ ***to make generalizations about sth*** 对某事做出归纳 ◇ *Try to avoid generalization.* 尽量避免泛泛而论。

gen·er·al·ize (*BrE also* **-ise**) /ˈdʒenrəlaɪz/ *verb* **1** [I] **~ (from sth)** to use a particular set of facts or ideas in order to form an opinion that is considered valid for a different situation 概括；归纳：*It would be foolish to generalize from a single example.* 仅从一个事例进行归纳的做法是愚蠢的。 **2** [I] **~ (about sth)** to make a general statement about sth and not look at the details 笼统地讲；概括地谈论：*It is dangerous to generalize about the poor.* 对穷人一概而论是危险的。 **3** [T, often passive] **~ sth (to sth)** (*formal*) to apply a theory, idea, etc. to a wider group or situation than the original one 扩大…的运用；将…类推到（较大的范围）：*These conclusions cannot be generalized to the whole country.* 这些结论不能推及全国。

gen·er·al·ized (*BrE also* **-ised**) /ˈdʒenrəlaɪzd/ *adj.* [usually before noun] not detailed; not limited to one particular area 笼统的；普遍的；概括性的；全面的：*a generalized discussion* 笼统的讨论 ◇ *a **generalized disease/rash*** (= affecting the whole body) 全身性疾病/疹子

ˌgeneral ˈknowledge *noun* [U] knowledge of facts about a lot of different subjects 一般知识；常识：*a general knowledge quiz* 常识问答比赛

gen·er·al·ly 🔑 /ˈdʒenrəli/ *adv.* **1** 🔑 by or to most people 普遍地；广泛地：*The plan was generally welcomed.* 这个计划受到普遍的欢迎。◇ *It is now generally accepted that…* 目前，人们普遍认为… ◇ *The new drug will be generally available from January.* 这种新药从一月份开始将可大量上市。◇ *He was a generally unpopular choice for captain.* 人们普遍不欢迎他当队长。 **2** 🔑 in most cases 一般地；通常；大体上 SYN **as a rule**：*I generally get up at six.* 我一般六点钟起床。◇ *The male is generally larger with a shorter beak.* 雄鸟通常体形较大，喙较短。➲ LANGUAGE BANK ON NEXT PAGE **3** 🔑 without discussing the details of sth 笼统地；概括地；大概：*Let's talk just about investment generally.* 咱们只大概谈谈投资吧。

ˌgeneral ˈpractice *noun* [U, C] **1** (*especially BrE*) the work of a doctor who treats people in the community rather than at a hospital and who is not a specialist in one particular area of medicine; a place where a doctor like this works （医院以外的）综合医疗，全科诊疗；全科诊所：*to* be in general practice 从事普通诊疗 ◇ *She runs a general practice in Hull.* 她在赫尔开了家全科诊所。 **2** (*especially NAmE*) the work of a lawyer who deals with all kinds of legal cases and who is not a specialist in one particular area of law; the place where a lawyer like this works 普通律师业务；普通律师事务所

ˌgeneral pracˈtitioner (*also* **ˌfamily pracˈtitioner**) (*abbr.* **GP**) (*also informal* **ˌfamily ˈdoctor**) (*especially BrE*) *noun* a doctor who is trained in general medicine and who treats patients in a local community rather than at a hospital （医院以外的）全科医生，普通医师

the ˌgeneral ˈpublic *noun* [sing.+sing./pl. v.] ordinary people who are not members of a particular group or organization 普通百姓；大众；公众： *At that time, the general public was/were not aware of the health risks.* 那时，公众对各种危及健康的因素尚不了解。 ◇ *The exhibition is not open to the general public.* 这个展览不对公众开放。

ˌgeneral-ˈpurpose *adj.* [only before noun] having a wide range of different uses 多用途的；多功能的： *a general-purpose farm vehicle* 多功能农用机动车

gen·er·al·ship /ˈdʒenrəlʃɪp/ *noun* [U] the skill or practice of leading an army during a battle 将军才能；将才；将军职能

ˌgeneral ˈstaff (*often* **the general staff**) *noun* [sing.+sing./pl. v.] officers who advise a military leader and help to plan a military operation （军事）参谋

ˌgeneral ˈstore *noun* (*BrE also* **ˌgeneral ˈstores** [pl.]) a shop/store that sells a wide variety of goods, especially one in a small town or village （尤指小城镇或乡村的）杂货店

ˌgeneral ˈstrike *noun* a period of time when most or all of the workers in a country go on strike 总罢工

gen·er·ate 🔑 AW /ˈdʒenəreɪt/ *verb* ~ **sth** to produce or create sth 产生；引起： *to* ***generate electricity/heat/power*** 发电；产生热 / 动力 ◇ *to* ***generate income/profit*** 产生收益 / 利润 ◇ *We need someone to generate new ideas.* 我们需要有人出新主意。 ◇ *The proposal has generated a lot of interest.* 这项建议引起众多的关注。 ➲ WORDFINDER NOTE AT ELECTRICITY ➲ SYNONYMS AT MAKE

▼ LANGUAGE BANK 用语库

generally

Ways of saying 'in general' "通常"的表达方式

- *Women **generally** earn less than men.* 女人通常比男人挣钱少。
- ***Generally speaking**, jobs traditionally done by women are paid at a lower rate than those traditionally done by men.* 一般来说，传统上由妇女干的工作比传统上由男人干的工作报酬低。
- ***In general/By and large**, women do not earn as much as men.* 总的说来，女人不如男人挣钱多。
- *Certain jobs, like nursing and cleaning, are still **mainly** carried out by women.* 有些工作仍然主要由女性做，比如护理和保洁。
- *Senior management posts are **predominantly** held by men.* 高层管理职位大多由男性担任。
- *Most senior management posts **tend to** be held by men.* 大多数高层管理职位通常由男性担任。
- *Women are, **for the most part**, still paid less than men.* 女人的薪水多半仍比男人低。
- *Economic and social factors are, **to a large extent**, responsible for women being concentrated in low-paid jobs.* 经济和社会因素在很大程度上导致女性集中于低报酬工作。

➲ LANGUAGE BANK AT CONCLUSION, EXCEPT, SIMILARLY

gen·er·ation 🔑 AW /ˌdʒenəˈreɪʃn/ *noun* **1** 🔑 [C+sing./pl. v.] all the people who were born at about the same time （统称）一代人，同代人，同辈人： *the* ***younger/older generation*** 年轻的一代；老一辈 ◇ *My generation have grown up without the experience of a world war.* 我这一代人在成长过程中没有经历过世界大战。 ◇ *I often wonder what* ***future generations*** *will make of our efforts.* 我常常想，后代将怎样评价我们所作出的努力。 ➲ WORDFINDER NOTE AT AGE **2** 🔑 [C] the average time in which children grow up, become adults and have children of their own, (usually considered to be about 30 years) 代，一代，一辈（通常认为大约 30 年）： *a generation ago* 一代人以前 ◇ *My family have lived in this house* ***for generations***. 我家祖祖辈辈都住在这房子里。 **3** 🔑 [C, U] a single stage in the history of a family （家史中的）一代，一辈： *stories passed down from generation to generation* 世代相传的故事 ◇ *a* ***first-/second-generation*** *American* (= a person whose family has lived in America for one/two generations) 第一 / 第二代美国人（家人在美国居住了一、二代者） ➲ WORDFINDER NOTE AT FAMILY, RELATION **4** 🔑 [C, usually sing.] a group of people of similar age involved in a particular activity 一批，一届（从事特定活动的同龄人）： *She has inspired a whole generation of fashion school graduates.* 她激励了整整一届时装学校的毕业生。 **5** [C, usually sing.] a stage in the development of a product, usually a technical one （产品发展，尤指技术方面的）代： *fifth-generation computing* 第五代计算机技术 ◇ *a* ***new generation*** *of vehicle* 新一代交通运输工具 **6** [U] the production of sth, especially electricity, heat, etc. （尤指电、热等的）产生： *the generation of electricity* 发电 ◇ *methods of income generation* 产生收益的方法

gen·er·ation·al /ˌdʒenəˈreɪʃənl/ *adj.* [usually before noun] connected with a particular generation or with the relationship between different generations 一代的；代与代之间的： *generational conflict* 两代人之间的冲突

the geneˈration gap *noun* [sing.] the difference in attitude or behaviour between young and older people that causes a lack of understanding 代沟： *a movie that is sure to bridge the generation gap* 肯定能弥合代沟的一部电影

Geneˌration ˈX *noun* [U] the group of people who were born between the early 1960s and the middle of the 1970s, who seem to lack a sense of direction in life and to feel that they have no part to play in society * X 一代（20 世纪 60 年代初至 70 年代中期出生的人，对人生似乎失去方向，对社会感到格格不入）

Geneˌration ˈY *noun* [U] the group of people who were born between the early 1980s and the end of the 1990s, who are mainly the children of the BABY BOOMERS and who are regarded as being very familiar with computers and electronic technology * Y 一代（20 世纪 80 年代初至 90 年代末出生的人，被认为对电脑和电子技术非常熟悉）

gen·era·tive /ˈdʒenərətɪv/ *adj.* (*formal*) that can produce sth 有生产力的；能生产的；有生殖力的： *generative processes* 生产过程

ˌgenerative ˈgrammar *noun* [C, U] (*linguistics* 语言) a type of grammar which describes a language by giving a set of rules which can be used to produce all the possible sentences in that language 生成语法

gen·er·ator /ˈdʒenəreɪtə(r)/ *noun* **1** a machine for producing electricity 发电机： *The factory's emergency generators were used during the power cut.* 工厂应急发电机在停电期间用上了。 ◇ *a wind generator* (= a machine that uses the power of the wind to produce electricity) 风力发电机 **2** a machine for producing a particular substance 发生器： *The museum uses smells and smoke generators to create atmosphere.* 博物馆利用气味和烟雾发生器制造气氛。 ◇ (*figurative*) *The company is a major generator of jobs.* 这家公司创造了相当多的就业机会。 **3** (*BrE*) a company that produces electricity to sell to the public 电力公司： *the UK's major electricity generator* 英国主要的电力公司

gen·er·ic /dʒəˈnerɪk/ *adj.* **1** shared by, including or typical of a whole group of things; not specific 一般的；普通

的；通用的：*'Vine fruit' is the **generic term** for currants and raisins.* * vine fruit 是有核和无核葡萄干的通称。 **2** (of a product, especially a drug 产品，尤指药物) not using the name of the company that made it 无厂家商标的；无商标的：*The doctor offered me a choice of a branded or a generic drug.* 医生让我选择用有商标的还是没有商标的药物。 ▸ **gen·er·ic·al·ly** /-kli/ *adv.*

gen·er·os·ity /ˌdʒenəˈrɒsəti; *NAmE* -ˈrɑːs-/ *noun* [U, sing.] ~ **(to/towards sb)** the fact of being generous (= willing to give sb money, gifts, time or kindness freely) 慷慨；大方；宽宏大量：*He treated them with generosity and thoughtfulness.* 他待他们宽容大度、体贴周到。

gen·er·ous /ˈdʒenərəs/ *adj.* (*approving*) **1** giving or willing to give freely; given freely 慷慨的；大方的；慷慨给予的：*a generous benefactor* 慷慨的捐助者 ◇ ~ **(with sth)** *to be generous with your time* 不吝惜时间 ◇ *to be generous in giving help* 乐于助人 ◇ *a **generous gift/offer*** 丰厚的礼物；慷慨的提议 ◇ *It was **generous of him** to offer to pay for us both.* 他主动为我们俩付钱，真是大方。 OPP **mean** **2** more than is necessary; large 丰富的；充足的；大的 SYN **lavish**：*a generous helping of meat* 一大份肉 ◇ *The car has a generous amount of space.* 这辆汽车的空间很大。 **3** kind in the way you treat people; willing to see what is good about sb/sth 宽厚的；宽宏大量的；仁慈的：*a generous mind* 宽阔的胸怀 ◇ *He wrote a very generous assessment of my work.* 他给我写的工作评价多有赞誉之词。 ▸ **gen·er·ous·ly** *adv.*：*Please give generously.* 请慷慨施与。 ◇ *a dress that is generously cut* (= uses plenty of material) 用料多的连衣裙

gen·esis /ˈdʒenəsɪs/ *noun* [sing.] (*formal*) the beginning or origin of sth 开端；创始；起源

genet /ˈdʒenɪt/ *noun* a wild animal similar to a cat but with a longer tail and body and a pointed head. Genets are found in Africa, southern Europe and Asia and eat insects and small animals. 獛（栖息于非洲、欧洲南部和亚洲）

ˈ**gene therapy** *noun* [U] (*medical* 医) a treatment in which normal GENES are put into cells to replace ones that are missing or not normal 基因疗法；基因治疗

gen·et·ic /dʒəˈnetɪk/ *adj.* connected with GENES (= the units in the cells of a living thing that control its physical characteristics) or GENETICS (= the study of genes) 基因的；遗传学的：*genetic and environmental factors* 遗传和环境因素 ◇ *genetic abnormalities* 基因异常 ▸ **gen·et·ic·al·ly** /-kli/ *adv.*：*genetically engineered/determined/transmitted* 基因工程的；由基因决定的；遗传的

geˌnetically ˈmodified *adj.* (*abbr.* **GM**) (of a plant, etc.) having had its genetic structure changed artificially, so that it will produce more fruit or not be affected by disease （植物等）遗传修饰的，转基因的：*genetically modified foods* (= made from plants that have been changed in this way) 转基因食品 ➲ WORDFINDER NOTE AT CROP ➲ COLLOCATIONS AT FARMING

geˌnetic ˈcode *noun* the arrangement of GENES that controls how each living thing will develop 遗传密码

geˌnetic ˌengiˈneering *noun* [U] the science of changing how a living creature or plant develops by changing the information in its GENES 遗传工程（学）；基因工程

geˌnetic ˈfingerprinting (*also* ˌ**DNA ˈfingerprinting**) *noun* [U] the method of finding the particular pattern of GENES in an individual person, particularly to identify sb or find out if sb has committed a crime 基因指纹分析；遗传指纹法 ▸ **geˌnetic ˈfingerprint** *noun*

gen·eti·cist /dʒəˈnetɪsɪst/ *noun* a scientist who studies genetics 遗传学家

gen·et·ics /dʒəˈnetɪks/ *noun* [U] the scientific study of the ways in which different characteristics are passed from each generation of living things to the next 遗传学 ➲ MORE LIKE THIS 29, page R28

Gen·eva Con·ven·tion /dʒəˌniːvə kənˈvenʃn/ *noun* [sing.] an international agreement which states how PRISONERS OF WAR should be treated 日内瓦公约（有关战俘待遇的国际协定）

Gen·ghis Khan /ˌɡeŋɡɪs ˈkɑːn; ˌdʒeŋ-/ *noun* [usually sing.] a person who is very cruel or has very RIGHT-WING political opinions 非常残酷的人；极右分子：*Her politics are somewhere to the right of Genghis Khan.* 她的政治观点属于极右。 ORIGIN From the name of the first ruler of the Mongol empire, who was born in the 12th century. 源自出生于 12 世纪的蒙古帝国开国君主成吉思汗。

gen·ial /ˈdʒiːniəl/ *adj.* friendly and cheerful 友好的；亲切的；欢快的 SYN **affable**：*a genial person* 和蔼可亲的人 ◇ *a genial smile* 亲切的微笑 ▸ **geni·al·ity** /ˌdʒiːniˈæləti/ *noun* [U]：*an atmosphere of warmth and geniality* 热情友好的气氛 **geni·al·ly** /ˈdʒiːniəli/ *adv.*：*to smile genially* 亲切地微笑

G

genie /ˈdʒiːni/ *noun* (*pl.* **gen·ies** or **genii** /ˈdʒiːniaɪ/) (in Arabian stories) a spirit with magic powers, especially one that lives in a bottle or a lamp（阿拉伯故事中会魔法的妖怪，尤指住在瓶子或灯里的）精灵，镇尼 SYN **djinn**

geni·tal /ˈdʒenɪtl/ *adj.* [only before noun] connected with the outer sexual organs of a person or an animal 生殖的；生殖器的：*the genital area* 生殖区 ◇ *genital infections* 生殖器感染

geni·tals /ˈdʒenɪtlz/ (*also* **geni·talia** /ˌdʒenɪˈteɪliə/) *noun* [pl.] a person's sex organs that are outside their body 外生殖器

geni·tive /ˈdʒenətɪv/ *noun* (*grammar* 语法) (in some languages 用于某些语言) the special form of a noun, a pronoun or an adjective that is used to show possession or close connection between two things 属格；所有格 ➲ COMPARE ABLATIVE, ACCUSATIVE, DATIVE, NOMINATIVE, POSSESSIVE *n.*, VOCATIVE ▸ **geni·tive** *adj.*

ge·nius /ˈdʒiːniəs/ *noun* (*pl.* **ge·niuses**) **1** [U] unusually great intelligence, skill or artistic ability 天才；天资；天赋：*the genius of Shakespeare* 莎士比亚的天才 ◇ *a statesman of genius* 天才的政治家 ◇ *Her idea was **a stroke of genius**.* 她的主意是聪明的一着。 **2** [C] a person who is unusually intelligent or artistic, or who has a very high level of skill, especially in one area 天才人物；（某领域的）天才：*a **mathematical/comic, etc. genius*** 数学、喜剧等天才 ◇ *He's a genius at organizing people.* 他是人员组织方面的天才。 ◇ *You don't have to be a genius to see that they are in love!* 傻子也能看出他们相爱了！ **3** [sing.] ~ **for sth/for doing sth** a special skill or ability（特别的）才能，本领：*He had a genius for making people feel at home.* 他有一种能够使人感觉轻松自在的本领。 ▸ **ge·nius** *adj.* (*informal*)：*a genius idea* 天才的想法

IDM **sb's good/evil ˈgenius** (*especially BrE*) a person or spirit who is thought to have a good/bad influence over you 给人以好（或坏）影响的人；保护（或毁灭）人的神魔

geno·cide /ˈdʒenəsaɪd/ *noun* [U] the murder of a whole race or group of people 种族灭绝；大屠杀 ➲ COLLOCATIONS AT WAR ▸ **geno·cidal** *adj.*

gen·ome /ˈdʒiːnəʊm; *NAmE* -oʊm/ *noun* (*biology* 生) the complete set of GENES in a cell or living thing 基因组；染色体组：*the human genome* 人类基因组

ge·nom·ics /dʒiˈnɒmɪks; *NAmE* -ˈnɑːm-/ *noun* [U] (*biology* 生) the study of the structure, function and development of GENOMES and how they are arranged and organized 基因组学

geno·type /ˈdʒenətaɪp; ˈdʒiːn-/ *noun* (*biology* 生) the combination of GENES that a particular living thing carries, some of which may not be noticed from its appearance 基因型 ➲ COMPARE PHENOTYPE

genre /ˈʒɒ̃rə; ˈʒɒnrə; *NAmE* ˈʒɑːnrə/ *noun* (*formal*) a particular type or style of literature, art, film or music that you can recognize because of its special features（文学、艺

术、电影或音乐的）体裁，类型 ➲ WORDFINDER NOTE AT WRITE

ˈ**genre painting** *noun* [U, C] (*art* 美术) a style of painting showing scenes from ordinary life that is associated with 17th century Dutch and Flemish artists; a painting done in this style 风俗画（与 17 世纪荷兰和佛兰德斯画家有关，取材于日常生活的绘画风格）；风俗画作品

gent /dʒent/ *noun* **1** (*old-fashioned* or *humorous*) a man; a gentleman 男士；绅士；先生：*a gent's hairdresser* 男宾理发师 ◇ *This way please, ladies and gents!* 女士们，先生们，请这边走！ **2 a/the gents**, **a/the Gents** [sing.] (*BrE, informal*) a public toilet/bathroom for men 男厕所；男卫生间；男盥洗室：*Is there a gents near here?* 附近有男厕所吗？ ◇ *Where's the gents?* 男厕所在哪儿？

G

gen·teel /dʒenˈtiːl/ *adj.* (*sometimes disapproving*) **1** (of people and their way of life 人和生活方式) quiet and polite, often in an exaggerated way; from, or pretending to be from, a high social class 显得彬彬有礼的；假斯文的；上流社会的；装体面的；装出绅士派头的：*a genteel manner* 彬彬有礼 ◇ *Her genteel accent irritated me.* 她那矫揉造作的腔调使我感到恼火。 ◇ *He lived in genteel poverty* (= trying to keep the style of a high social class, but with little money). 他摆出一副绅士派头，过的却是穷酸的生活。 **2** (of places 地方) quiet and old-fashioned and perhaps slightly boring 幽静的；古朴单调的 ▸ **gen·teel·ly** /dʒenˈtiːlli/ *adv.*

gen·tian /ˈdʒenʃn/ *noun* [C, U] a small plant with bright blue flowers that grows in mountain areas 龙胆；龙胆草

gen·tile /ˈdʒentaɪl/ (*also* **Gentile**) *noun* a person who is not Jewish 非犹太人；外邦人（犹太人对非犹太人的通称） ▸ **gen·tile** (*also* **Gentile**) *adj.* [only before noun]

gen·til·ity /dʒenˈtɪləti/ *noun* [U] (*formal*) **1** very good manners and behaviour; the fact of belonging to a high social class 文雅；彬彬有礼；高贵的身份：*He took her hand with discreet gentility.* 他温文尔雅地牵着她的手。 ◇ *She thinks expensive clothes are a mark of gentility.* 她认为昂贵的服装是身份高贵的标志。 **2** the fact of being quiet and old-fashioned 幽静古朴：*the faded gentility of the town* 已失去古朴风貌的城镇

gen·tle 🔑 /ˈdʒentl/ *adj.* (**gent·ler** /ˈdʒentlə(r)/, **gent·lest** /ˈdʒentlɪst/) **1** 🔑 calm and kind; doing things in a quiet and careful way 文静的；慈祥的；温柔的；细心的：*a quiet and gentle man* 温文尔雅的男士 ◇ *a gentle voice/laugh/touch* 温柔的声音 / 笑声 / 触摸 ◇ *She was the gentlest of nurses.* 她是个极其和蔼的护士。 ◇ *He lived in a gentler age than ours.* 他生活的时代比我们这个时代更平静祥和。 ◇ *Be gentle with her!* 待她温柔些！ ◇ *She agreed to come, after a little* ***gentle persuasion***. 经过一阵细心劝说，她表示愿意来。 ◇ *He looks scary but he's really a* ***gentle giant***. 他看上去可怕，实际却是个性格温和的巨人。 **2** 🔑 (of weather, temperature, etc. 天气、温度等) not strong or extreme 温和的；徐缓的：*a gentle breeze* 和风 ◇ *the gentle swell of the sea* 缓慢起伏的海浪 ◇ *Cook over a gentle heat.* 要用文火煮。 **3** 🔑 having only a small effect; not strong or violent 平和的；柔和的：*We went for a gentle stroll.* 我们溜达去了。 ◇ *a little* ***gentle exercise*** 少量温和的运动 ◇ *This soap is very gentle on the hands.* 这肥皂擦在手上非常柔和。 **4** 🔑 not steep or sharp 平缓的：*a gentle slope/curve/angle* 平缓的斜坡 / 弯道 / 角度 ➲ SEE ALSO GENTLY ▸ **gentle·ness** *noun* [U]

gentle·folk /ˈdʒentlfəʊk; *NAmE* -foʊk/ *noun* [pl.] (*old-fashioned*) (in the past) people belonging to respected families of the higher social classes（旧时）出身名门世家的人

gentle·man 🔑 /ˈdʒentlmən/ *noun* (*pl.* **-men** /-mən/) **1** 🔑 [C] a man who is polite and well educated, who has excellent manners and always behaves well 彬彬有礼的人；有教养的人；君子：*Thank you—you're a real gentleman.* 谢谢您，您是个真正的君子。 ◇ *He's no gentleman!* 他可不是正人君子！ ➲ COMPARE LADY (2) **2** 🔑 [C, usually pl.] (*formal*) used to address or refer to a man, especially sb you do not know（称呼或指男子，尤其是不认识的）先生：*Ladies and gentlemen! Can I have your attention, please?* 女士们，先生们，请大家注意！ ◇ *Gentlemen of the jury!* 陪审团诸位先生！ ◇ *Can I help you, gentlemen?* 诸位先生，有什么我可以效劳的？ ◇ *There's a gentleman to see you.* 有位先生要见你。 HELP In more informal speech, you could say 非正式谈话中可说：*Can I help you?* 我能为你效劳吗？ ◇ *There's someone to see you.* 有人要见你。 **3** (*NAmE*) used to address or refer to a male member of a LEGISLATURE, for example the House of Representatives（对立法机构男议员的称呼）先生，阁下 **4** (*old-fashioned*) a man from a high social class, especially one who does not need to work 有身份的人；绅士；富绅：*a country gentleman* 乡绅 ◇ *a gentleman farmer* (= one who owns a farm for pleasure, not as his main job) 乡绅（以拥有农场为乐趣，而不作为主业） IDM SEE LEISURE

gentle·man·ly /ˈdʒentlmənli/ *adj.* (*approving*) behaving very well and showing very good manners; like a gentleman 彬彬有礼的；绅士风度的；绅士派头的：*gentlemanly behaviour* 绅士般的举止 ◇ *So far, the election campaign has been a very gentlemanly affair.* 到目前为止，竞选活动都秩序良好。

ˌ**gentleman's aˈgreement** (*also* ˌ**gentlemen's aˈgreement**) *noun* an agreement made between people who trust each other, which is not written down and which has no legal force 君子协定；绅士协定

gentle·woman /ˈdʒentlwʊmən/ *noun* (*pl.* **-women** /-wɪmɪn/) **1** (*old use*) a woman who belongs to a high social class; a woman who is well educated and has excellent manners 贵妇人；有教养的妇女；淑女 **2** (*NAmE*) used to address or refer to a female member of a LEGISLATURE, for example the House of Representatives（对立法机构女议员的称呼）女士，夫人

gent·ly 🔑 /ˈdʒentli/ *adv.* **1** 🔑 in a gentle way 温柔地；温和地；文静地；和缓地：*She held the baby gently.* 她轻轻地抱着婴儿。 ◇ *'You miss them, don't you?' he asked gently.* "你想念他们，是吗？"他温和地问道。 ◇ *Simmer the soup gently for 30 minutes.* 用文火把汤炖 30 分钟。 ◇ *Massage the area* ***gently but firmly***. 推拿此部位要柔中带劲。 ◇ *leaves moving gently in the breeze* 在微风中缓缓飘动的树叶 ◇ *The path ran gently down to the sea.* 这条小路平缓地向大海延伸。 **2 Gently!** (*BrE, informal*) used to tell sb to be careful 注意点；小心点；慢点：*Gently! You'll hurt the poor thing!* 小心点，你会弄痛这可怜的家伙！ ◇ *Don't go too fast—* ***gently does it!*** 别太快，慢点吧！

gen·tri·fy /ˈdʒentrɪfaɪ/ *verb* (**gen·tri·fies**, **gen·tri·fy·ing**, **gen·tri·fied**, **gen·tri·fied**) [usually passive] **~ sth/sb** to change an area, a person, etc. so that they are suitable for, or can mix with, people of a higher social class than before 使（地区、人等）贵族化；对（地区、人等）进行改造以适应较高阶层的人：*Old working-class areas of the city are being gentrified.* 这个城市里劳工阶层居住的老城区正在进行改造以迎合较高阶层人士。 ▸ **gen·tri·fi·ca·tion** /ˌdʒentrɪfɪˈkeɪʃn/ *noun* [U]

gen·try /ˈdʒentri/ *noun* [pl.] (*usually* **the gentry**) (*old-fashioned*) people belonging to a high social class 绅士阶层；上流社会人士：*the local gentry* 当地的绅士阶层 ◇ *the landed gentry* (= those who own a lot of land) 乡绅

genu·flect /ˈdʒenjuflekt/ *verb* (*formal*) **1** [I] to move your body into a lower position by bending one or both knees, as a sign of respect during worship in a church（在教堂礼拜时）跪拜，单膝跪拜 **2** [I] **~ (to sb/sth)** (*disapproving*) to show too much respect to sb/sth 卑躬屈膝 ▸ **genu·flec·tion** (*BrE also* **genu·flex·ion**) /ˌdʒenjuˈflekʃn/ *noun* [C, U]

genu·ine 🔑 /ˈdʒenjuɪn/ *adj.* **1** 🔑 real; exactly what it appears to be; not artificial 真的；名副其实的 SYN **authentic**: *Is the painting a genuine Picasso?* 这幅画是毕加索的真迹吗？ ◇ *Fake designer watches are sold at a fraction of the price of* ***the genuine article***. 伪造的名牌手表以真品若干分之一的价格出售。 ◇ *Only genuine refugees can apply for asylum.* 只有真正的难民才能申请政治避难。 **2** 🔑 sincere and honest; that can be trusted 真诚的；真

心的；可信赖的：*He made a genuine attempt to improve conditions.* 他真心实意地努力改善环境。◇ *genuine concern for others* 对他人真诚的关心 ◇ *a very genuine person* 非常诚实可信的人 ▶ **genu·ine·ly** adv.：*genuinely sorry* 真遗憾 **genu·ine·ness** noun [U]

genus /ˈdʒiːnəs/ noun (pl. **gen·era** /ˈdʒenərə/) (biology 生) a group into which animals, plants, etc. that have similar characteristics are divided, smaller than a family and larger than a SPECIES（动植物等分类的）属 ➲ COMPARE CLASS n. (11), KINGDOM (4), ORDER n. (11), PHYLUM ➲ WORDFINDER NOTE AT BREED ➲ SEE ALSO GENERIC

geo- combining form (in nouns, adjectives and adverbs 构成名词、形容词和副词) of the earth 地球的：*geochemical* 地球化学的 ◇ *geoscience* 地球科学

geo·caching /ˈdʒiːəʊkæʃɪŋ; NAmE ˈdʒiːoʊ-/ noun [U] an activity in which people go out to look for a hidden object (usually a box containing a small item and a record of who has found it) using GPS (= a system that uses signals from satellites to show sb/sth's position on earth) 地理藏宝（利用全球定位系统寻找隐藏物的户外活动）

geo·cen·tric /ˌdʒiːəʊˈsentrɪk; NAmE ˌdʒiːoʊ-/ adj. (specialist) with the earth as the centre 以地球为中心的

geo·des·ic /ˌdʒiːəʊˈdesɪk; -ˈdiːsɪk; NAmE ˌdʒiːoʊ-/ adj. (specialist) relating to the shortest possible line between two points on a curved surface 测地线的，大地线的（曲面上两点间距离最短的线）

ˌgeoˌdesic ˈdome noun (architecture 建) a DOME which is built from panels whose edges form geodesic lines 短程线穹顶 ➲ VISUAL VOCAB PAGE V14

geog·raph·er /dʒiˈɒɡrəfə(r); NAmE -ˈɑːɡ-/ noun a person who studies geography; an expert in geography 地理学研究者；地理学家

geog·raphy /dʒiˈɒɡrəfi; NAmE -ˈɑːɡ-/ noun **1** [U] the scientific study of the earth's surface, physical features, divisions, products, population, etc. 地理（学）：***human/physical/economic/social geography*** 人文 / 自然 / 经济 / 社会地理学 ◇ ***a geography lesson/department/teacher/textbook*** 地理课 / 系 / 教师 / 课本 ◇ *a degree in geography* 地理学学位 **2** [sing.] the way in which the physical features of a place are arranged 地形；地貌；地势：*the geography of New York City* 纽约市的地势 ◇ *Kim knew the geography of the building and strode along the corridor.* 金熟悉这栋建筑物的布局，大步流星地走在走廊上。 **3** [sing.] the way in which a particular aspect of life or society is influenced by geography or varies according to geography 地理环境：*The geography of poverty and the geography of voting are connected.* 贫穷人口的地理分布与选票的地理分布是相联系的。▶ **geo·graph·ic·al** /ˌdʒiːəˈɡræfɪkl/ (also **geo·graph·ic** /ˌdʒiːəˈɡræfɪk/) adj.：*The survey covers a wide **geographical area**.* 此项调查覆盖的地理区域非常广阔。◇ *The importance of the town is due to its **geographical location**.* 这座城镇的重要性在于它的地理位置。 **geo·graph·ic·al·ly** /-kli/ adv.：*geographically remote areas* 地理上的边远地区

geolo·gist /dʒiˈɒlədʒɪst; NAmE -ˈɑːl-/ noun a scientist who studies geology 地质学家

geol·ogy /dʒiˈɒlədʒi; NAmE -ˈɑːl-/ noun **1** [U] the scientific study of the earth, including the origin and history of the rocks and soil of which the earth is made 地质学 **2** [sing.] the origin and history of the rocks and soil of a particular area（某地区的）地质：*the geology of the British Isles* 不列颠群岛的地质 ▶ **geo·logic·al** /ˌdʒiːəˈlɒdʒɪkl; NAmE -ˈlɑːdʒ-/ (also **geo·logic**) adj.：*a geological survey* 地质勘察 **geo·logic·al·ly** /ˌdʒiːəˈlɒdʒɪkli; NAmE -ˈlɑːdʒ-/ adv.

geo·mag·net·ism /ˌdʒiːəʊˈmæɡnətɪzəm; NAmE ˌdʒiːoʊ-/ noun [U] (geology 地) the study of the MAGNETIC characteristics of the earth 地磁学 ▶ **geo·mag·net·ic** /ˌdʒiːəʊmæɡˈnetɪk; NAmE ˌdʒiːoʊ-/ adj.

geo·mancy /ˈdʒiːəʊmænsi; NAmE ˈdʒiːoʊ-/ noun [U] **1** the art of arranging buildings and areas in a good or lucky position 风水；地相术 **2** a method of saying what will happen in the future using patterns on the ground 地卜，泥土占卜（根据地面所呈图迹占卜）

geo·met·ric /ˌdʒiːəˈmetrɪk/ (also less frequent **geo·met·ric·al** /-ɪkl/) adj. of GEOMETRY; of or like the lines, shapes, etc. used in GEOMETRY, especially because of having regular shapes or lines 几何（学）的；（似）几何图形的：*a geometric design* 几何图形设计 ▶ **geo·met·ric·al·ly** /ˌdʒiːəˈmetrɪkli/ adv.

geoˌmetric ˈmean noun the central number in a geometric progression 几何平均；等比中数

geoˌmetric proˈgression (also **geoˌmetric ˈseries**) noun a series of numbers in which each is multiplied or divided by a fixed number to produce the next, for example 1, 3, 9, 27, 81 几何数列；等比数列 ➲ COMPARE ARITHMETIC PROGRESSION

geom·etry /dʒiˈɒmətri; NAmE -ˈɑːm-/ noun **1** [U] the branch of mathematics that deals with the measurements and relationships of lines, angles, surfaces and solids 几何（学） **2** [sing.] the measurements and relationships of lines, angles, etc. in a particular object or shape 几何形状；几何图形；几何结构：*the geometry of a spider's web* 蜘蛛网的几何形状 ➲ WORDFINDER NOTE AT MATHS

geo·phys·ics /ˌdʒiːəʊˈfɪzɪks; NAmE ˌdʒiːoʊ-/ noun [U] the scientific study of the physics of the earth, including its atmosphere, climate and MAGNETISM 地球物理学 ➲ MORE LIKE THIS 29, page R28 ▶ **geo·phys·ic·al** /-ˈfɪzɪkl/ adj.：*geophysical data* 地球物理资料 **geo·physi·cist** /-ˈfɪzɪsɪst/ noun

geo·pol·it·ics /ˌdʒiːəʊˈpɒlətɪks; NAmE ˌdʒiːoʊˈpɑːl-/ noun [U+sing./pl. v.] the political relations between countries and groups of countries in the world; the study of these relations 地缘政治学 ▶ **geo·pol·it·ical** /ˌdʒiːəʊpəˈlɪtɪkl; NAmE ˌdʒiːoʊ-/ adj.

Geor·die /ˈdʒɔːdi; NAmE ˈdʒɔːrdi/ noun (BrE, informal) **1** [C] a person from Tyneside in NE England（英格兰东北部的）泰恩赛德人 **2** [U] a way of speaking, typical of people from Tyneside in NE England（英格兰东北部的）泰恩赛德口音 ▶ **Geor·die** adj.：*a Geordie accent* 泰恩赛德人的口音

geor·gette /ˌdʒɔːˈdʒet; NAmE ˌdʒɔːrˈdʒet/ noun [U] a type of thin silk or cotton cloth, used for making clothes 乔其纱（薄丝或棉织品，用作衣料）

Geor·gian /ˈdʒɔːdʒən; NAmE ˈdʒɔːrdʒən/ adj. (especially of ARCHITECTURE and furniture 尤指建筑和家具) from the time of the British kings George I–IV (1714–1830) 乔治王朝时期的，乔治一世至四世时代的（1714–1830）：*a fine Georgian house* 优雅的乔治王朝时期的房屋

geo·ther·mal /ˌdʒiːəʊˈθɜːml; NAmE ˌdʒiːoʊˈθɜːrml/ adj. (geology 地) connected with the natural heat of rock deep in the ground 地热的：*geothermal energy* 地热能

geo·track·ing (also **geo-tracking**) /ˈdʒiːəʊtrækɪŋ; NAmE ˈdʒiːoʊ-/ noun [U] technology that gives you the ability to find the exact position of a person, vehicle, etc. by obtaining data from their SMARTPHONE or other device 地理位置追踪（通过从智能手机等设备获取数据而定位人、交通工具等的技术）

ge·ra·nium /dʒəˈreɪniəm/ noun a garden plant with a mass of red, pink or white flowers on the end of each STEM 天竺葵；老鹳草

ger·bil /ˈdʒɜːbɪl; NAmE ˈdʒɜːrbɪl/ noun a small desert animal like a mouse, that is often kept as a pet 沙鼠

geri·at·ric /ˌdʒeriˈætrɪk/ noun **1 geriatrics** [U] the branch of medicine concerned with the diseases and care of old people 老年医学 **2** [C] (informal, offensive) an old person, especially one with poor physical or mental health 糟老头子；糟老婆子；老疯子：*I'm not a geriatric yet, you know!* 要知道我还没有老朽！ ➲ WORDFINDER NOTE AT OLD

G

▶ **geri·at·ric** *adj.*: *the geriatric ward* (= in a hospital) 老年病房 ◇ *a geriatric vehicle* (= old and in bad condition) 老爷车

geria·tri·cian /ˌdʒeriəˈtrɪʃn/ *noun* a doctor who studies and treats the diseases of old people 老年病科医师；老年病学专家

germ /dʒɜːm; *NAmE* dʒɜːrm/ *noun* **1** [C, usually pl.] a very small living thing that can cause infection and disease 微生物；细菌；病菌：*Disinfectant kills germs.* 消毒剂可杀菌。◇ *Dirty hands can be a breeding ground for germs.* 脏手可能滋生病菌。 **2** [sing.] ~ **of sth** an early stage of the development of sth 起源；发端；萌芽：*Here was the germ of a brilliant idea.* 一个绝妙的主意就是从这里萌发的。 **3** [C] (*biology* 生) the part of a plant or an animal that can develop into a new one 胚芽；胚原基；芽孢；胚胎 ➲ SEE ALSO WHEATGERM

G

Ger·man /ˈdʒɜːmən; *NAmE* ˈdʒɜːrmən/ *adj., noun*
■ *adj.* from or connected with Germany 德国的
■ *noun* **1** [C] a person from Germany 德国人 **2** [U] the language of Germany, Austria and parts of Switzerland 德语（德国、奥地利和瑞士部分地区的语言）

ger·mane /dʒɜːˈmeɪn; *NAmE* dʒɜːrˈm-/ *adj.* [not usually before noun] ~ (**to sth**) (*formal*) (of ideas, remarks, etc. 想法、言语等) connected with sth in an important or appropriate way 与…有密切关系；贴切；恰当 **SYN** **relevant**: *remarks that are germane to the discussion* 与这次讨论密切相关的评述

Ger·man·ic /dʒɜːˈmænɪk; *NAmE* dʒɜːrˈm-/ *adj.* **1** connected with or considered typical of Germany or its people 德国的；德国人的；有德国（或德国人）特点的：*She had an almost Germanic regard for order.* 她简直像德国人一样讲究条理。 **2** connected with the language family that includes German, English, Dutch and Swedish among others 日耳曼语（族）的

ger·ma·nium /dʒɜːˈmeɪniəm; *NAmE* dʒɜːr-/ *noun* [U] (*symb.* **Ge**) a chemical element. Germanium is a shiny grey element that is similar to a metal (= is a METALLOID). 锗

ˌ**German ˈmeasles** (*also* **ru·bella**) *noun* [U] a mild infectious disease that causes a sore throat and red spots all over the body. It can seriously affect babies born to women who catch it soon after they become pregnant. 德国麻疹；风疹

ˌ**German ˈshepherd** (*especially NAmE*) (*BrE also* **Al·sa·tian**) *noun* a large dog, often trained to help the police, to guard buildings or (especially in the US) to help blind people find their way 德国牧羊犬（常训练成警犬，看家护院，尤其在美国用作导盲犬）

ger·mi·cide /ˈdʒɜːmɪsaɪd; *NAmE* ˈdʒɜːrm-/ *noun* [C, U] a substance which destroys bacteria, etc. 杀菌剂 ▶ **ger·mi·cidal** /ˌdʒɜːmɪˈsaɪdl; *NAmE* ˌdʒɜːrm-/ *adj.*

ger·min·ate /ˈdʒɜːmɪneɪt; *NAmE* ˈdʒɜːrm-/ *verb* [I, T] ~ (**sth**) when the seed of a plant **germinates** or **is germinated**, it starts to grow （使）发芽，萌芽，开始生长：(*figurative*) *An idea for a novel began to germinate in her mind.* 一部小说的构思已经在她的脑海中萌发。 ▶ **ger·min·ation** /ˌdʒɜːmɪˈneɪʃn; *NAmE* ˌdʒɜːrm-/ *noun* [U]

ˌ**germ ˈwarfare** *noun* [U] = BIOLOGICAL WARFARE

ger·on·toc·racy /ˌdʒerənˈtɒkrəsi; *NAmE* -ˈtɑːk-/ *noun* (*pl.* **-ies**) [C, U] a state, society or group governed by old people; government by old people 老人统治的国家（或社会、组织）；老人统治 ▶ **ger·on·to·crat·ic** /dʒəˌrɒntəˈkrætɪk; *NAmE* -ˌrɑːntə-/ *adj.*

ger·ont·olo·gist /ˌdʒerɒnˈtɒlədʒɪst; *NAmE* -rənˈtɑːl-/ *noun* (*especially NAmE*) a person who studies the process of people growing old 老年学专家

ge·ron·tol·ogy /ˌdʒerɒnˈtɒlədʒi; *NAmE* -rənˈtɑːl-/ *noun* [U] the scientific study of OLD AGE and the process of growing old 老年学

ger·ry·man·der (*also* **jer·ry·man·der**) /ˈdʒerimændə(r)/ *verb* ~ **sth** (*disapproving*) to change the size and borders of an area for voting in order to give an unfair advantage to one party in an election 不公正地改划（选区），不公正地划分（选区）（旨在使某政党获得优势） ▶ **ger·ry·man·der·ing** (*also* **jer·ry·man·der·ing**) *noun* [U]

ger·und /ˈdʒerənd/ *noun* (*grammar* 语法) a noun in the form of the present participle of a verb (that is, ending in *-ing*) for example *travelling* in the sentence *I preferred travelling alone.* 动名词

ge·stalt /ɡəˈʃtælt; *NAmE also* -ˈʃtɑːlt/ *noun* (*psychology* 心, *from German*) a set of things, such as a person's thoughts or experiences, that is considered as a single system which is different from the individual thoughts, experiences, etc. within it 格式塔，完形（即有别于其内部个体单位、作为单一体系的一系列思想、经验等）

ges·tate /dʒeˈsteɪt; *NAmE* ˈdʒesteɪt/ *verb* ~ **sth** (*biology* 生 or *medical* 医) to carry a young human or animal inside the WOMB until it is born 怀孕；妊娠；孕育

ges·ta·tion /dʒeˈsteɪʃn/ *noun* **1** [U, sing.] the time that the young of a person or an animal develops inside its mother's body until it is born; the process of developing inside the mother's body 妊娠（期）；怀孕（期）：*a baby born at 38 weeks' gestation* 怀孕 38 周时出生的婴儿 ◇ *The* ***gestation period*** *of a horse is about eleven months.* 马的怀孕期大约为十一个月。 **2** [U] (*formal*) the process by which an idea or a plan develops（想法、计划的）构思，酝酿，孕育 **SYN** **development**

ges·ticu·late /dʒeˈstɪkjuleɪt/ *verb* [I] to move your hands and arms about in order to attract attention or make sb understand what you are saying 做手势；用手势表达；用动作示意：*He* ***gesticulated*** *wildly at the clock.* 他使劲指着钟打手势。 ▶ **ges·ticu·la·tion** /dʒeˌstɪkjuˈleɪʃn/ *noun* [C, U]: ***wild/frantic gesticulations*** 发狂似的手势

ges·ture /ˈdʒestʃə(r)/ *noun, verb*
■ *noun* **1** [C, U] a movement that you make with your hands, your head or your face to show a particular meaning 手势；姿势；示意动作：*He* ***made a rude gesture*** *at the driver of the other car.* 他向另外那辆汽车的司机做了个粗野的手势。◇ *She finished what she had to say with a gesture of despair.* 她用绝望的姿势结束了她不得不讲的话。◇ *They communicated entirely by gesture.* 他们完全用手势交流。 **2** [C] something that you do or say to show a particular feeling or intention（表明感情或意图的）姿态，表示：*They sent some flowers as a gesture of sympathy to the parents of the child.* 他们送了一些花表示对孩子父母的同情。◇ *It was a nice gesture* (= it was kind) *to invite his wife too.* 把他的妻子也请来是友好的表示。◇ *We do not accept responsibility but we will refund the money as a* ***gesture of goodwill.*** 我们不承担责任，不过我们愿意退款以表示我们的善意。◇ *The government has made a gesture towards public opinion* (= has tried to do sth that the public will like). 政府已做出顺应民意的姿态。
■ *verb* [I, T] to move your hands, head, face, etc. as a way of expressing what you mean or want 做手势；用手势表示；用动作示意：(**+ adv./prep.**) *'I see you read a lot,' he said, gesturing at the wall of books.* "看来你读的书很多。"他指着那一墙的书说道。◇ **~ to sb (to do sth) | ~ for sb to do sth** *She gestured for them to come in.* 她示意让他们进来。◇ **~ (to sb) (that)...** *He gestured* (*to me*) *that it was time to go.* 他示意（我）该走了。◇ *They gestured that I should follow.* 他们示意让我跟在后面。

ge·sund·heit /ɡəˈzʊndhaɪt/ *exclamation* (*NAmE, from German*) used when sb has SNEEZED to wish them good health（别人打喷嚏时说）祝你健康

get 🔑 /ɡet/ *verb* (**getting**, **got**, **got** /ɡɒt; *NAmE* ɡɑːt/)
HELP In spoken *NAmE* the past participle **got·ten** /ˈɡɑːtn/ is almost always used. 美式英语口语中过去分词几乎都用 gotten。
• **RECEIVE/OBTAIN** 接到；得到 **1** 🔑 [T, no passive] ~ **sth** to receive sth 收到；接到：*I got a letter from Dave this morning.* 今天早上我收到戴夫的一封来信。◇ *What* (= What presents) *did you get for your birthday?* 你收到什么生日礼物了？◇ *He gets* (= earns) *about $40 000 a year.*

他一年挣 4 万美元左右。◇ *This room gets very little sunshine.* 这个房间几乎照不进阳光。◇ *I got a shock when I saw the bill.* 我看到账单时大吃一惊。◇ *I **get the impression** that he is bored with his job.* 我的印象是他厌倦他的工作。 **2** 🔑 [T, no passive] to obtain sth 获得；得到： **~ sth** *Where did you get (*= buy*) that skirt?* 你在哪儿买的那条裙子？◇ *Did you manage to get tickets for the concert?* 你弄到音乐会的票了吗？◇ *She opened the door wider to get a better look.* 她把门开大些以便看得更清楚。◇ *Try to get some sleep.* 尽量睡会儿吧。◇ *He has just got a new job.* 他刚找到一份新工作。◇ **~ sth for sb** *Did you get a present for your mother?* 给你母亲买礼物了吗？◇ **~ sb/yourself sth** *Did you get your mother a present?* 给你母亲买礼物了吗？◇ *Why don't you get yourself a car?* 你为什么不买辆汽车呢？ **3** 🔑 [T, no passive] **~ sth (for sth)** to obtain or receive an amount of money by selling sth（卖某物）挣得，获得： *How much did you get for your car?* 你的汽车卖了多少钱？

• **BRING** 带来 **4** 🔑 [T] to go to a place and bring sb/sth back 去取（或带来） **SYN** **fetch**： **~ sb/sth** *Quick—go and get a cloth!* 快，去拿块布来！◇ *Somebody get a doctor!* 谁去叫个医生来吧！◇ *I have to go and get my mother from the airport (*= collect her*).* 我得去机场接我的母亲。◇ **~ sth for sb** *Get a drink for John.* 给约翰拿杯饮料来。◇ **~ sb/yourself sth** *Get John a drink.* 给约翰拿杯饮料来。

• **PUNISHMENT** 惩罚 **5** [T, no passive] **~ sth** to receive sth as a punishment 受到；遭到；被判（刑）： *He got ten years (*= was sent to prison for ten years*) for armed robbery.* 他因持枪抢劫被判刑十年。

• **BROADCASTS** 广播 **6** [T, no passive] **~ sth** to receive broadcasts from a particular television or radio station 接收到；收听到；收看到： *We can't get Channel 5 in our area.* 我们地区收不到 5 频道的节目。

• **BUY** 买 **7** [T, no passive] **~ sth** to buy sth, for example a newspaper or magazine, regularly（定期）买，购买 **SYN** **take**： *Which newspaper do you get?* 你订阅什么报纸？

• **MARK/GRADE** 分数；等级 **8** 🔑 [T, no passive] **~ sth** to achieve or be given a particular mark/grade in an exam（考试）获得，达到： *He got a 'C' in Chemistry and a 'B' in English.* 他化学考试得中，英语考试得良。

• **ILLNESS** 疾病 **9** 🔑 [T, no passive] **~ sth** to become infected with an illness; to suffer from a pain, etc. 感染上；患上；遭受…之苦： *I got this cold off (*= from*) you!* 我这感冒是被你传染的！◇ *She gets (*= often suffers from*) really bad headaches.* 她经常头痛得厉害。

• **CONTACT** 联系 **10** [T, no passive] **~ sb** to be connected with sb by telephone 与（某人）电话联系；与（某人）通电话： *I wanted to speak to the manager but I got his secretary instead.* 我想与经理说话，可接电话的却是他的秘书。

• **STATE/CONDITION** 状态；情况 **11** 🔑 *linking verb* to reach a particular state or condition; to make sb/sth/yourself reach a particular state or condition（使）达到，处于： **+ adj.** *to get angry/bored/hungry/fat* 发怒；生厌；饥饿；发胖 ◇ *You'll soon **get used to** the climate here.* 你会很快习惯这儿的气候的。◇ *We ought to go; it's getting late.* 我们该走了，天色越来越晚了。◇ *to **get dressed/undressed** (*= to put your clothes on/take your clothes off*)* 穿上 / 脱下衣服 ◇ *They plan to **get married** in the summer.* 他们打算夏天结婚。◇ *She's upstairs getting ready.* 她在楼上做准备。◇ *I wouldn't go there alone; you might get (*= be*) mugged.* 我不会一个人去那儿，说不准会碰上抢劫的。◇ *My car got (*= was*) stolen at the weekend.* 我的汽车周末被偷了。◇ **~ sb/sth + adj.** *Don't get your dress dirty!* 别把你的连衣裙弄脏了！◇ *He got his fingers caught in the door.* 他的手指给门夹了。◇ *She soon got the children ready for school.* 她很快帮孩子们做好了上学的准备。 ➲ NOTE AT BECOME **12** 🔑 [I] **~ to do sth** to reach the point at which you feel, know, are, etc. sth 开始（感觉到、认识到、成为）；达到…地步（或程度）： *After a time you get to realize that these things don't matter.* 过段时间你会明白这些事情并不要紧。◇ *You'll like her once you **get to know** her.* 你一旦了解了她就会喜欢她的。◇ *His drinking is getting to be a problem.* 他的酗酒越来越成问题了。◇ *She's getting to be an old lady now.* 她现在都快是个老太婆了。

• **MAKE/PERSUADE** 使；让；说服 **13** 🔑 [T] to make, persuade, etc. sb/sth to do sth 使，让（某人或物做某事）；说服（某人做某事）： **~ sb/sth to do sth** *I couldn't get the car to start this morning.* 我今天早上没法让这汽车发动起来。◇ *He got his sister to help him with his homework.* 他让姐姐帮助他做家庭作业。◇ *You'll never get him to understand.* 你永远不会使他明白的。◇ **~ sb/sth doing sth** *Can you really get that old car going again?* 你真能让那老爷车再跑起来吗？◇ *It's not hard to get him talking—the problem is stopping him!* 让他谈话并不难，难的是让他住口！

• **GET STH DONE** 使完成某事 **14** 🔑 [T] **~ sth done** to cause sth to happen or be done 使（某事）发生；使完成（某事）： *I must get my hair cut.* 我得理发了。◇ *I'll never get all this work finished.* 这么多的工作我怎么也干不完。

• **START** 开始 **15** [T] **~ doing sth** to start doing sth 开始；开始做： *I got talking to her.* 我开始与她谈起来。◇ *We need to get going soon.* 我们需要马上出发。

• **OPPORTUNITY** 机会 **16** [I] **~ to do sth** (*informal*) to have the opportunity to do sth 有机会（做某事）；得到（做某事的）机会： *He got to try out all the new software.* 他得以试用了所有的新软件。◇ *It's not fair—I never get to go first.* 这不公平，我从来没有机会先走。

• **ARRIVE** 到达 **17** 🔑 [I] **+ adv./prep.** to arrive at or reach a place or point 抵达，到达（某地或某点）： *We got to San Diego at 7 o'clock.* 我们 7 点钟到达了圣迭戈。◇ *You got in very late last night.* 你昨晚回来得很晚。◇ *What time did you get here?* 你什么时候到达这儿的？◇ *I haven't got very far with the book I'm reading.* 我那本书还没读多少呢。

• **MOVE/TRAVEL** 移动；旅行 **18** 🔑 [I, T] to move to or from a particular place or in a particular direction, sometimes with difficulty; to make sb/sth do this（使）到达，离开，沿…移动，艰难地移动： **+ adv./prep.** *The bridge was destroyed so we couldn't get across the river.* 大桥已经毁坏，我们无法过河了。◇ *She got into bed.* 她上床睡觉了。◇ *He got down from the ladder.* 他从梯子上下来了。◇ *We didn't **get** (*= go*) **to bed** until 3 a.m.* 我们直到凌晨 3 点才上床睡觉。◇ *Where do we **get on** the bus?* 我们在哪儿上公共汽车？◇ *I'm **getting off** (*= leaving the train*) at the next station.* 我在下一站下车。◇ *Where have they **got to** (*= where are they*)?* 他们到什么地方去了？◇ *We must be **getting home**; it's past midnight.* 我们得回家了，已过半夜了。◇ **~ sb/sth + adv./prep.** *The general had to get his troops across the river.* 将军必须让部队过河。◇ *We couldn't get the piano through the door.* 我们无法将钢琴搬过这道门。◇ *We'd better call a taxi and get you home.* 我们最好叫辆出租车送你回家。◇ *I can't get the lid off.* 我打不开盖子。 **19** 🔑 [T, no passive] **~ sth** to use a bus, taxi, plane, etc. 搭乘，乘坐（公共汽车、出租车、飞机等）： *We're going to be late—let's get a taxi.* 我们要迟到了，咱们坐出租车吧。◇ *I usually get the bus to work.* 我通常坐公共汽车上班。

• **MEAL** 饭菜 **20** [T] (*especially BrE*) to prepare a meal 准备，做（饭）： **~ sth** *Who's getting the lunch?* 谁来做午饭？◇ **~ sth for sb/yourself** *I must go home and get tea for the kids.* 我得回家为孩子们准备茶点。◇ **~ sb/yourself sth** *I must go home and get the kids their tea.* 我得回家为孩子们准备茶点。

• **TELEPHONE/DOOR** 电话；门 **21** [T] **~ sth** (*informal*) to answer the telephone or a door when sb calls, knocks, etc. 接（电话）；应（门）： *Will you get the phone?* 你去接一下电话好吗？

• **CATCH/HIT** 抓住；击中 **22** [T] **~ sb** to catch or take hold of sb, especially in order to harm or punish them（尤指为伤害或惩罚）抓住，捉住，逮住： *He was on the run for a week before the police got him.* 他逃跑一周后警方才将他逮住。◇ *to get sb by the arm/wrist/throat* 抓住某人的胳膊 / 手腕；掐住某人的喉咙 ◇ *She fell overboard and the sharks got her.* 她从船上跌入水中被鲨鱼咬了。◇ *He thinks everybody is **out to get him** (*= trying to harm him*).* 他认为所有人都想害他。◇ (*informal*) ***I'll get you for that!*** 这事我跟你没完！ **23** [T] **~ sb + adv./prep.** to hit or wound sb 击中；使受伤： *The bullet got him in the neck.* 子弹击中了他的颈部。

• **UNDERSTAND** 理解 **24** [T, no passive] **~ sb/sth** (*informal*) to understand sb/sth 理解；明白： *I don't get you.* 我搞不懂你的意思。◇ *She didn't get the joke.* 她不明白那笑话的含义。◇ ***I don't get it**—why would she do a thing like that?* 我不明白，她怎么会干那种事？◇ *I **get the message**—you*

don't want me to come. 我明白这意思，你是不希望我来。
➲ SYNONYMS AT UNDERSTAND

• **HAPPEN/EXIST** 发生；存在 **25** [T, no passive] **~ sth** (*informal*) used to say that sth happens or exists（表示发生或存在）：*You get* (= There are) *all these kids hanging around in the street.* 所有这些孩子都在街上闲逛。◇ *They still get cases of typhoid there.* 他们那儿仍有伤寒病发生。

• **CONFUSE/ANNOY** 使困惑 / 烦恼 **26** [T, no passive] **~ sb** (*informal*) to make sb feel confused because they do not understand sth 使困惑；使迷惑；把…难住 SYN **puzzle**: *'What's the capital of Bhutan?' 'You've got me there!'* (= I don't know) "不丹的首都在什么地方？" "你可把我难倒了！" **27** [T, no passive] **~ sb** (*informal*) to annoy sb 使烦恼；使恼火：*What gets me is having to do the same thing all day long.* 使我感到烦恼的是整天都得干同样的事。 HELP **Get** is one of the most common words in English, but some people try to avoid it in formal writing. * get 是英语中最常用的单词之一，但有的人在正式文体中尽量避免使用。
➲ MORE LIKE THIS 33, page R28

IDM HELP Most idioms containing **get** are at the entries for the nouns and adjectives in the idioms, for example **get sb's goat** is at **goat**. 大多数含 get 的习语，都可在该等习语中的名词及形容词相关词条找到，如 get sb's goat 在词条 goat 下。 **be getting 'on** (*informal*) **1** (of a person 人) to be becoming old 变老；上年纪 **2** (of time 时间) to be becoming late 渐晚；渐迟：*The time's getting on—we ought to be going.* 时间越来越晚了，我们该走了。 **be getting on for…** (*especially BrE*) to be nearly a particular time, age or number 接近（某时刻、年龄或数目）：*It must be getting on for midnight.* 一定快到半夜了。◇ *He's getting on for eighty.* 他近八十岁了。 **can't get 'over sth** (*informal*) used to say that you are shocked, surprised, amused, etc. by sth 因…而感到震惊（或惊讶、好笑等）：*I can't get over how rude she was.* 她这么粗鲁真使我感到惊讶。 **get a'way from it all** (*informal*) to have a short holiday/vacation in a place where you can relax（到他处度短假）躲清静 **'get it** (*also* **catch 'hell**) (*both NAmE*) (*BrE* **'catch it**) (*informal*) to be punished or spoken to angrily about sth 受罚；受斥责 **ˌget it 'on (with sb)** (*slang, especially NAmE*) to have sex with sb（与某人）性交 **ˌget it 'up** (*slang*) (of a man 男人) to have an ERECTION 勃起 **get sb 'going** (*informal*) to make sb angry, worried or excited 激怒某人；使某人担忧（或激动） **get sb nowhere/not get sb anywhere** to not help sb make progress or succeed 使无所进展（或成就）；徒劳：*This line of investigation is getting us nowhere.* 这种调查方式不会使我们得到任何结果。◇ *Being rude to me won't get you anywhere.* 你对我撒野也没有用。 **get somewhere/anywhere/nowhere** to make some progress/no progress 有所（或无所）进展：*After six months' work on the project, at last I feel I'm getting somewhere.* 那个项目干了六个月之后我终于感到有了一些进展。◇ *I don't seem to be getting anywhere with this letter.* 我的这封信看样子没什么效果。 **'get there** to achieve your aim or complete a task 达到目的；完成任务；获得成功：*I'm sure you'll get there in the end.* 我相信你最终会成功的。◇ *It's not perfect but we're getting there* (= making progress). 虽然这并非完美无瑕，但我们正朝着目标前进。 **ˌget 'this!** (*informal, especially NAmE*) used to say that you are going to tell sb sth that they will find surprising or interesting 听好了（用于表示要告诉大家令人吃惊或有趣的事情）：*OK, get this guys—there are only two left!* 好吧，听好了，伙计们，只剩两个了！ **how selfish, stupid, ungrateful, etc. can you 'get?** (*informal*) used to express surprise or disapproval that sb has been so selfish, etc.（表示惊奇或不赞成）你怎么这么自私（或愚蠢、忘恩负义等） **there's no getting a'way from sth | you can't get a'way from sth** you have to admit that sth unpleasant is true 不容否认，只好承认（不愉快的事实） **what are you, was he, etc. 'getting at?** (*informal*) used to ask, especially in an angry way, what sb is/was suggesting（尤指气愤地问）你（或他等）这话是什么意思，你（或他等）用意何在：*I'm partly to blame? What exactly are you getting at?* 我应负部分责任？你究竟是什么意思？ **what has got into sb?** (*informal*) used to say that sb has suddenly started to behave in a strange or different way（表示某人突然行为反常起来）…怎么啦：*What's got into Alex? He never used to worry like that.* 亚历克斯怎么啦？他以前从未那样愁过。

PHR V **ˌget a'bout** (*BrE*) = GET AROUND

ˌget a'bove yourself (*especially BrE*) to have too high an opinion of yourself 自以为了不起；自高自大；自视甚高

ˌget a'cross (to sb) | ˌget sth↔a'cross (to sb) to be communicated or understood; to succeed in communicating sth 被传达；被理解；把…讲清楚：*Your meaning didn't really get across.* 你的意思并未真正为别人理解。◇ *He's not very good at getting his ideas across.* 他不太善于清楚地表达自己的思想。

ˌget a'head (of sb) to make progress (further than others have done) 走在（某人的）前面；领先；胜过（某人）：*She wants to get ahead in her career.* 她想在事业上脱颖而出。◇ *He soon got ahead of the others in his class.* 他很快就在班上名列前茅了。

ˌget a'long 1 (usually used in the progressive tenses 通常用于进行时) to leave a place 离开；离去：*It's time we were getting along.* 我们该离开了。 **2** = GET ON

ˌget a'round 1 (*BrE also* **ˌget a'bout**) to move from place to place or from person to person 传播；流传；各处走动：*She gets around with the help of a stick.* 她拄着拐杖四处走动。◇ *News soon got around that he had resigned.* 他已辞职的消息很快传开了。 **2** (*especially NAmE*) = GET ROUND/AROUND SB

'get at sb (usually used in the progressive tenses 通常用于进行时) to keep criticizing sb 一再批评，不断指责，老是数落（某人）：*He's always getting at me.* 他老是责备我。◇ *She feels she's being got at.* 她感到自己总是受人数落。 **'get at sb/sth** to reach sb/sth; to gain access to sb/sth 到达某处；接近某人（或某物）；够得着某物：*The files are locked up and I can't get at them.* 文件资料锁起来了，我取不出来。 **'get at sth** to learn or find out sth 获悉；了解；查明；发现：*The truth is sometimes difficult to get at.* 有时真相很难查明。

ˌget a'way 1 to have a holiday/vacation 度假；休假：*We're hoping to get away for a few days at Easter.* 我们期待着复活节出去休几天假。 ➲ RELATED NOUN GETAWAY **2** (*BrE, informal*) used to show that you do not believe or are surprised by what sb has said（表示不相信或惊奇）别胡扯：*'These tickets didn't cost me a thing.' 'Get away!'* "这些票我一分钱也没花。" "胡说！" **ˌget a'way (from…)** to succeed in leaving a place（得以）离开，脱身：*I won't be able to get away from the office before 7.* 我 7 点钟之前无法离开办公室。 **ˌget a'way (from sb/…)** 🔑 to escape from sb or a place 摆脱（某人）；逃离（某地）

ˌget a'way with sth 1 🔑 to steal sth and escape with it 偷携某物潜逃；偷走：*Thieves got away with computer equipment worth $30 000.* 盗贼偷走了价值 3 万美元的计算机设备。 ➲ RELATED NOUN GETAWAY **2** 🔑 to receive a relatively light punishment 受到从轻发落（轻微惩罚）：*He was lucky to get away with only a fine.* 他算是万幸，只被罚款了事。 **3** 🔑 to do sth wrong and not be punished for it 做（坏事）而未受惩罚：*Don't be tempted to cheat—you'll never get away with it.* 别想着作弊，作弊者一定会受到严惩。◇ **get away with doing sth** *Nobody gets away with insulting me like that.* 任何人那样侮辱我都不会有好果子吃。 **4** to manage with less of sth than you might expect to need 以（比预期少的事物）就能应付：*After the first month, you should be able to get away with one lesson a week.* 第一个月之后，每周上一次课就可以了。

ˌget 'back 🔑 to return, especially to your home 返回；回去；回家：*What time did you get back last night?* 你昨晚什么时候回家的？ ➲ SYNONYMS AT RETURN **ˌget sth↔'back** 🔑 to obtain sth again after having lost it 寻回，找回，重新获得（丢失的东西）：*She's got her old job back.* 她已恢复原职。◇ *I never lend books—you never get them back.* 我的书从不外借，借出去就收不回来。 **ˌget 'back (in)** (of a political party 政党) to win an election after having lost the previous one 重新上台；东山再起 **ˌget 'back at sb** (*informal*) to do sth bad to sb who has done sth bad to you; to get REVENGE on sb 向某人报复：*I'll find a way of getting back at him!* 我会想法报复他的！ **ˌget 'back to sb** (*informal*) to speak or write to sb again later, especially in order to give a reply 以后再答复（或回复）某人：*I'll find out and get back to you.* 我查明之后再答复你。 **ˌget 'back to sth** to return to sth 回到某事上：*Could we get back to* *the question of funding?* 我们回到资金问题上来好吗？ **ˌget back toˈgether (with sb)** to start a relationship with sb again, especially a romantic relationship, after having finished a previous relationship with the same person（与某人，尤指恋人）重归于好，重修旧好：*I just got back together with my ex-girlfriend.* 我刚和前女友重修旧好。

ˌget beˈhind (with sth) to fail to make enough progress or to produce sth at the right time 落后；拖延；拖欠：*I'm getting behind with my work.* 我的工作拖延了。◇ *He got behind with the payments for his car.* 他拖欠了买汽车的车款。

ˌget ˈby (on/in/with sth) 🔑 to manage to live or do a particular thing using the money, knowledge, equipment, etc. that you have（靠…）维持生计，设法过活，勉强应付：*How does she get by on such a small salary?* 她靠这点微薄的工资怎么过活？◇ *I can just about get by in German* (= I can speak basic German). 我用德语只能勉强应付。

ˌget ˈdown (of children 儿童) (*BrE*) to leave the table after a meal（饭后）离开餐桌 **ˌget sb ˈdown** (*informal*) to make sb feel sad or depressed 使悲伤；使沮丧；使忧郁 **ˌget sth↔ˈdown 1** to swallow sth, usually with difficulty（困难地）吞下，咽下 **2** to make a note of sth 记录；记下；写下 **SYN write down**：*Did you get his number down?* 你记下他的号码了吗？ **ˌget ˈdown to sth** to begin to do sth; to give serious attention to sth 开始做某事；开始认真注意（或对待）某事：*Let's get down to business.* 咱们开始干正事吧。◇ *I like to get down to work by 9.* 我喜欢在 9 点之前开始工作。◇ **get down to doing sth** *It's time I got down to thinking about that essay.* 我该认真思考一下那篇论文了。

ˌget ˈin | ˌget ˈinto sth 1 🔑 to arrive at a place 到达：*The train got in late.* 火车晚点到达。◇ *What time do you get into Heathrow?* 你什么时候到达希思罗机场？ **2** 🔑 to win an election 当选：*The Republican candidate stands a good chance of getting in.* 共和党候选人很可能当选。◇ *She first got into Parliament* (= became an MP) *in 2005.* 她 2005 年第一次当选为下议院议员。 **3** 🔑 to be admitted to a school, university, etc. 被录取；被接受入学（或入会等）：*She's got into Durham to study law.* 她被录取到杜伦大学学习法律。 **ˌget sb↔ˈin** to call sb to your house to do a job 请某人来家里做事 **ˌget sth↔ˈin 1** to collect or gather sth 收集；收割：*to get the crops/harvest in* 收获作物 / 庄稼 **2** to buy a supply of sth 购买；买进：*Remember to get in some beers for this evening.* 记住为今天的晚会买些啤酒。 **3** to manage to do or say sth 设法做（或说）：*I got in an hour's work while the baby was asleep.* 我趁孩子睡觉抽空干了一小时的活。◇ *She talks so much it's impossible to get a word in.* 她说起话来滔滔不绝，让人一句话都插不进去。 **ˌget ˈin on sth** to take part in an activity 参加（活动）：*He's hoping to get in on any discussions about the new project.* 他盼望着参加有关这一新项目的任何讨论。

ˌget ˈin with sb (*informal*) to become friendly with sb, especially in order to gain an advantage（尤指为捞取好处与某人）成为朋友，拉关系，套近乎

ˌget ˈinto sth 1 🔑 to put on a piece of clothing, especially with difficulty（尤指费力地）穿上：*I can't get into these shoes—they're too small.* 这双鞋太小，我穿不进去。 **2** 🔑 to start a career in a particular profession 开始从事（某职业）：*What's the best way to get into journalism?* 进入新闻界的最佳途径是什么？ **3** 🔑 to become involved in sth; to start sth 参与，开始（某事）：*I got into conversation with an Italian student.* 我与一位意大利学生谈了起来。◇ *to get into a fight* 参与斗殴 **4** 🔑 to develop a particular habit 养成某种习惯；习惯于：*Don't let yourself get into bad habits.* 别让自己染上恶习。◇ *You should get into the routine of saving the document you are working on every ten minutes.* 你应该养成每十分钟将正在编辑的文件存盘一次的习惯。◇ *How did she get into* (= start taking) *drugs?* 她是怎么染上毒品的？ **5** 🔑 (*informal*) to become interested in sth 对…产生兴趣：*I'm really getting into jazz these days.* 我最近迷上了爵士乐。 **6** to become familiar with sth; to learn sth 开始熟悉；学会：*I haven't really got into my new job yet.* 我还未真正熟悉我的新工作。 **ˌget ˈinto sth | ˌget yourself/sb ˈinto sth** 🔑 to reach a particular state or condition; to make sb reach a particular state or condition（使）陷入，处于，达到：*He got into trouble with the police while he was still at school.* 他还在上学时就曾犯事落入警察手里。◇ *Three people were rescued from a yacht which got into difficulties.* 从遇险的游艇中营救出了三人。◇ *She got herself into a real state* (= became very anxious) *before the interview.* 她面试前格外地焦虑不安。

ˌget ˈoff | ˌget ˈoff sb used especially to tell sb to stop touching you or another person（尤用于告诉别人）别碰，走远点：*Get off me, that hurts!* 放开我，好痛哟！

ˌget ˈoff | ˌget sb ˈoff 1 to leave a place or start a journey; to help sb do this（使某人）离开，出发，动身：*We got off straight after breakfast.* 我们早饭后就立即动身了。◇ *He got the children off to school.* 他打发孩子们上学去了。 **2** (*BrE*) to fall asleep; to make sb do this（使）入睡：*I had great difficulty getting off to sleep.* 我很难入睡。◇ *They couldn't get the baby off till midnight.* 他们直到半夜才把宝宝哄入睡。 **ˌget ˈoff | ˌget ˈoff sth** to leave work with permission（经允许）离开工作，下班：*Could you get off (work) early tomorrow?* 你明天可以提早下班吗？ **ˌget ˈoff sth | ˌget sb ˈoff sth** to stop discussing a particular subject; to make sb do this（使）停止讨论，不再谈论：*Please can we get off the subject of dieting?* 我们别再谈论节食这个话题行吗？◇ *I couldn't get him off politics once he had started.* 他一谈起政治我就没法让他停下。 **ˌget sth ˈoff** to send sth by post/mail 邮寄某物：*I must get these letters off first thing tomorrow.* 我明天首先得把这些信件寄出去。 **ˌget ˈoff on sth** (*informal*) to be excited by sth, especially in a sexual way 因…而兴奋，因…而激动（尤指性兴奋） **ˌget ˈoff (with sth)** to have no or almost no injuries in an accident（在事故中）幸免于难，并无大恙：*She was lucky to get off with just a few bruises.* 她幸免于难，只有几处碰伤。 **ˌget ˈoff (with sth) | ˌget sb ˈoff (with sth)** 🔑 to receive no or almost no punishment; to help sb do this（使）免受处罚，逃脱惩罚：*He was lucky to get off with a small fine.* 他侥幸逃脱惩罚，交了一小笔罚款就了事。◇ *A good lawyer might be able to get you off.* 请位好律师或许能使你脱罪。 **ˌget ˈoff with sb** (*informal, especially BrE*) to have a sexual or romantic experience with sb; to start a sexual relationship with sb（与某人）发生性关系，谈恋爱，开始性关系：*Steve got off with Tracey at the party.* 史蒂夫在聚会上就与特蕾西亲热起来。

ˌget ˈon 1 🔑 (*also* **ˌget aˈlong**) used to talk or ask about how well sb is doing in a particular situation（谈及或问及某人）进展，进步：*He's getting on very well at school.* 他在学校学得很好。◇ ***How did you get on at the interview?*** 你面试的情况怎么样？ **2** 🔑 to be successful in your career, etc. 获得成功；事业有成：*Parents are always anxious for their children to get on.* 父母总是急切地盼望孩子们事业有成。◇ *I don't know how he's going to **get on in life**.* 我不知道他将如何出人头地。 **3** 🔑 (*also* **ˌget aˈlong**) to manage or survive 对付；应付；活下来；过活：*We can get on perfectly well without her.* 没有她我们也能过得很好。◇ *I just can't get along without a secretary.* 没有秘书我简直寸步难行。 **ˌget ˈon to sb 1** to contact sb by telephone, letter or email（用电话、书信或电子邮件）与某人联系：*The heating isn't working; I'll get on to the landlord about it.* 暖气不热，我得与房东联系一下。 **2** to become aware of sb's activities, especially when they have been doing sth bad or illegal 觉察，察觉，识破（某人的不法行为）：*He had been stealing money from the company for years before they got on to him.* 他一直窃取公司的钱，多年后他们才发觉。 **ˌget ˈon to sth** to begin to talk about a new subject 开始讨论，转而谈论（新课题）：*It's time we got on to the question of costs.* 我们该讨论成本问题了。 **ˌget ˈon with sb | ˌget ˈon (together)** 🔑 (*both BrE*) (*also* **ˌget aˈlong with sb, ˌget aˈlong (together)** *NAmE, BrE*) to have a friendly relationship with sb（与某人）和睦相处，关系良好：*She's never really got on with her sister.* 她从未与妹妹真正和睦相处过。◇ *She and her sister have never really got on.* 她与妹妹一直合不来。◇ *We get along just fine together.* 我们相处得还算融洽。 **ˌget ˈon with sth 1** 🔑 (*also* **ˌget aˈlong with sth**) used to talk or ask about how well sb is doing a task（谈及或问及工作情况）进展，进步：*I'm not getting on very fast with this job.* 我这个工作进展不太快。 **2** 🔑 to continue doing sth,

G

especially after an interruption（尤指中断后）继续做某事：*Be quiet and get on with your work.* 安静下来，继续干你的事。◇ *(informal) Get on with it! We haven't got all day.* 继续干吧！我们的时间并不多。

,get 'out to become known 泄露；被人知道：*If this gets out there'll be trouble.* 这事要是被人知道就麻烦了。 **,get sth↔'out 1** to produce or publish sth 生产；发表；出版：*Will we get the book out by the end of the year?* 我们这本书将在年底前出版吗？ **2** to say sth with difficulty 困难地说出；勉强地说：*She managed to get out a few words of thanks.* 她终于勉强说了几句道谢的话。 **,get 'out (of sth)** to leave or go out of a place 离开（某地）；从…出来：*You ought to get out of the house more.* 你应该多到户外去走走。◇ *She screamed at me to get out.* 她冲着我大声喊，让我出去。 **,get 'out of sth 1** 🔑 to avoid a responsibility or duty 逃避，规避，摆脱（责任或义务）：*We promised we'd go—we can't get out of it now.* 我们答应过要去的，现在我们不能食言。◇ **get out of doing sth** *I wish I could get out of going to that meeting.* 但愿我能不去参加那个会。 **2** 🔑 to stop having a particular habit 放弃，戒除，抛弃（习惯）：*I can't get out of the habit of waking at six in the morning.* 我早上六点钟醒的习惯改不了。 **,get sth 'out of sb** to persuade sb to tell or give you sth, especially by force（尤指强行）盘问出，获取：*The police finally got a confession out of her.* 警方最终逼迫她招了供。 **,get sth 'out of sb/sth** to gain or obtain sth good from sb/sth 从…中获得（有益的东西）：*She seems to get a lot out of life.* 她似乎从生活中获益良多。◇ *He always gets the best out of people.* 他总能使人发挥最大的潜力。

,get 'over sth 🔑 to deal with or gain control of sth 解决；克服；控制 SYN **overcome**：*She can't get over her shyness.* 她无法克服羞怯心理。◇ *I think the problem can be got over without too much difficulty.* 我认为这个问题不太难解决。 **,get 'over sth/sb** 🔑 to return to your usual state of health, happiness, etc. after an illness, a shock, the end of a relationship, etc. 从疾病（或震惊、断绝关系等）中恢复常态：*He was disappointed at not getting the job, but he'll get over it.* 他没得到这份工作非常失望，不过他会想得开的。 **,get 'over yourself** *(informal)* to stop thinking that you are so important; to stop being so serious 别自以为是；别太当真了：*Just get over yourself and stop moaning!* 别太当真了，停止抱怨吧！◇ *He needs to grow up a bit and get over himself.* 他需要更成熟一点，不再那么自以为是。 **,get sth↔'over (to sb)** to make sth clear to sb 向（某人）讲清某事；让（某人）明白某事：*He didn't really get his meaning over to the audience.* 他没能把他的意思清楚传递给观众。 **,get sth 'over (with)** *(informal)* to complete sth unpleasant but necessary 完成，结束（令人不快但免不了的事）：*I'll be glad to get the exam **over and done with**.* 考试结束后我就高兴了。

,get 'round/a'round sb to persuade sb to agree or to do what you want, usually by doing nice things for them（常用讨好卖乖的手段）说服某人同意，哄骗某人依顺，笼络某人：*She knows how to get round her dad.* 她知道怎样讨她爸爸的欢心。 **,get 'round/a'round sth** 🔑 to deal with a problem successfully 成功地对付；解决；克服 SYN **overcome**：*A clever lawyer might find a way of getting round that clause.* 高明的律师也许能找到绕过那个条款的办法。 **,get 'round/a'round to sth** 🔑 to find the time to do sth 抽出时间来做某事：*I meant to do the ironing but I didn't get round to it.* 我本想熨衣服的，可就是抽不出时间。◇ **get round/around to doing sth** *I hope to get around to answering your letter next week.* 我希望下周能抽出时间给你回信。

'get through sth 1 🔑 to use up a large amount of sth 消耗掉；用完；耗尽：*We got through a fortune while we were in New York!* 我们在纽约时花掉了一大笔钱！ **2** to manage to do or complete sth（设法）处理，完成：*Let's start—there's a lot to get through.* 咱们开始吧，有很多事要处理呢。 **,get 'through (sth)** *(BrE)* to be successful in an exam, etc. 顺利通过（考试等） **,get sb 'through sth** to help sb to be successful in an exam 帮助某人顺利通过考试：*She got all her students through the exam.* 她帮助她所有的学生顺利通过了考试。 **,get 'through (sth) | ,get sth 'through (sth)** to be officially accepted; to make sth be officially accepted（使）正式通过，获得采纳：*They got the bill through Congress.* 他们使此议案在国会获得通过。 **,get 'through (to sb) 1** 🔑 to reach sb 到达（某人处）：*Thousands of refugees will die if these supplies don't get through to them.* 如果这些供给品运不到，数以千计的难民就会死去。 **2** 🔑 to make contact with sb by telephone（用电话）接通，打通，联系上：*I tried calling you several times but I couldn't get through.* 我试着给你打了几次电话，但都没打通。 **,get 'through (to sth)** (of a player or team 选手或队) to reach the next stage of a competition 进入（下阶段比赛）：*Gulbis has got through to the final.* 古尔比斯已进入决赛。 **,get 'through to sb** to make sb understand or accept what you say, especially when you are trying to help them（尤指在努力帮助某人时）使某人理解，使某人接受（所讲的话）：*I find it impossible to get through to her.* 我发觉根本无法让她听懂。 **,get 'through with sth** to finish or complete a task 结束；完成

'get to sb *(informal)* to annoy or affect sb 使烦恼；使生气；对某人产生影响：*The pressure of work is beginning to get to him.* 工作的压力使他烦恼起来。

,get sb/sth to'gether to collect people or things in one place 召集；聚集；收集；汇集：*I'm trying to get a team together for Saturday.* 我正设法召集一帮人过周六呢。 **,get to'gether (with sb)** *(informal)* to meet with sb socially or in order to discuss sth 举行社交聚会；开会：*We must get together for a drink sometime.* 我们什么时候得聚在一起喝一杯。◇ *Management should get together with the union.* 资方应与工会在一起开个会。 ➲ RELATED NOUN GET-TOGETHER

,get 'up 1 🔑 to stand up after sitting, lying, etc. 站起；起来；起身 SYN **rise**：*The class got up when the teacher came in.* 老师进来时全班起立。 ➲ SYNONYMS AT STAND **2** if the sea or wind **gets up**, it increases in strength and becomes violent （海浪或风）增强，变猛烈 **,get 'up | ,get sb 'up** 🔑 to get out of bed; to make sb get out of bed（使）起床：*He always gets up early.* 他一向起得早。◇ *Could you get me up at 6.30 tomorrow?* 明天你 6:30 叫我起床行吗？ **,get yourself/sb 'up as sth** [often passive] *(BrE)* to dress yourself/sb as sb/sth else（将…）打扮成，化装成，装扮成：*She was got up as an Indian princess.* 她被打扮成了印度公主。 ➲ RELATED NOUN GET-UP **,get sth↔'up** to arrange or organize sth 安排；组织：*We're getting up a party for her birthday.* 我们正在筹备她的生日聚会。 **,get 'up to sth 1** to reach a particular point 到达某一点：*We got up to page 72 last lesson.* 我们上一课学到第 72 页。 **2** to be busy with sth, especially sth surprising or unpleasant 忙于，从事（尤指令人吃惊或不快的事）：*What on earth will he get up to next?* 他下一步究竟要干什么？◇ *She's been getting up to her old tricks again!* 她又在故伎重演了！

get·away /ˈɡetəweɪ/ *noun* [usually sing.] **1** an escape from a difficult situation, especially after committing a crime（尤指犯罪后的）逃跑，逃走：*to **make a quick getaway*** 迅速逃跑 ◇ *a getaway car* 逃跑用的汽车 **2** *(informal)* a short holiday/vacation; a place that is suitable for a holiday/vacation 短假；假日休闲地；适合度假的地方：*a romantic weekend getaway in New York* 在纽约度过的浪漫周末 ◇ *the popular island getaway of Penang* 深受人们喜爱的槟榔屿度假岛

'get-go *noun* *(especially NAmE, informal)* the beginning 开始：*He's covered this case **from the get-go**.* 他从一开始就报道此案。

'get-out *noun* [usually sing.] *(BrE, informal)* a way of avoiding sth, especially a responsibility or duty 回避（责任或义务）的办法；借口：*He said he'd come but he's looking for a get-out.* 他说过他会来，但眼下他又在找借口。◇ *a **get-out clause** in the contract* 合约里的规避条款

get·ting /ˈɡetɪŋ/ *noun* [sing.]

IDM **while the ,getting is 'good** *(NAmE)* *(especially BrE* **while the ,going is 'good***)* before a situation changes and it is no longer possible to do sth 趁形势还未变化时；趁情况还有利时

'get-together *noun* *(informal)* an informal meeting; a party（非正式的）聚会；联欢会

ˌ**get-up** *noun* (*old-fashioned*, *informal*) a set of clothes, especially strange or unusual ones（尤指奇特的）一套衣服，穿戴，装束

ˌ**get-up-and-ˈgo** *noun* [U] (*informal*) energy and determination to get things done 干劲；进取心；魄力；胆量

gew·gaw /ˈɡjuːɡɔː; *NAmE also* ˈɡuː-/ *noun* an object that attracts attention but has no value or use 花哨无用的物品；徒有其表的东西

gey·ser /ˈɡiːzə(r); *NAmE* ˈɡaɪzər/ *noun* **1** a natural SPRING that sometimes sends hot water or steam up into the air 间歇泉 **2** (*BrE*) a piece of equipment in a kitchen or bathroom that heats water, usually by gas（厨房或浴室的）煤气热水器，热水锅炉 **3** (*SAfrE*) a large container in which water is stored and heated, usually by electricity, in order to provide hot water in a building（建筑物的）电热水器，热水锅炉

GF (*also* **gf**) /ˌdʒiː ˈef/ *abbr.* (especially in TEXT MESSAGES, emails, etc.) girlfriend 女朋友（全写为 girlfriend，尤用于短信、电邮等）

ghagra (*also* **ghaghra**) /ˈɡʌɡrɑː/ *noun* a long skirt, worn by women in S Asia（南亚妇女穿的）筒裙

gha·rara /ɡʌˈrɑːrə/ *noun* loose wide trousers, worn with a KAMEEZ and DUPATTA by women in S Asia（南亚妇女配克米兹和围巾穿的）加格拉喇叭裤

ghar·ial /ˈɡæriɑːl; ˌɡʌriˈɑːl; *NAmE* ˈɡeriəl/ (*also* **ga·vial**) *noun* a S Asian CROCODILE 食鱼鳄（栖于南亚）

ghastly /ˈɡɑːstli; *NAmE* ˈɡæstli/ *adj.* (**ghast·lier**, **ghast·li·est**) **1** (of an event 事情) very frightening and unpleasant, because it involves pain, death, etc.（与疼痛、死亡等相关而）恐怖的，可怕的，令人毛骨悚然的 SYN **horrible**: *a ghastly crime/murder* 可怕的罪行 / 谋杀 **2** (*informal*) (of an experience or a situation 经历或形势) very bad; unpleasant 糟透的；令人不快的 SYN **terrible**: *The weather was ghastly.* 天气糟透了。◇ *It's all been a ghastly mistake.* 这是个极其恶劣的错误。 **3** (*informal*) (of a person or thing 人或物) that you find unpleasant and dislike very much 令人恶心的；令人反感的；讨厌的 SYN **horrible**: *her ghastly husband* 她那讨厌的丈夫 ◇ *This lipstick is a ghastly colour.* 这唇膏的颜色令人恶心。 **4** [not usually before noun] ill/sick or upset 有病；不适；苦恼 SYN **terrible**: *I felt ghastly the next day.* 我第二天感到身体很不舒服。 **5** (*literary*) very pale in appearance, like a dead person 死人般苍白的：*His face was ghastly white.* 他的脸色惨白。

ghat /ɡɑːt/ *noun* (*IndE*) **1** [C] steps leading down to a river or lake 河堤（或湖边）的台阶 **2** [C] a road or way over or through mountains 山路；山道 **3 Ghats** [pl.] the mountains near the eastern and western coasts of India 高止山脉（在印度东、西海岸附近）

gha·zal /ˈɡʌzʌl/ *noun* (*IndE*) a type of poem, typically on the theme of love, and normally set to music 厄扎尔（一种抒情诗，一般以爱情为主题，通常谱上曲调）

ghee /ɡiː/ *noun* [U] a type of butter used in S Asian cooking 印度酥油（用牛乳制成）

ghe·rao /ɡeˈraʊ/ *noun* (*pl.* **ghe·raos**) (*IndE*) a protest in which workers prevent employers from leaving a place of work until they are given what they want 挟持雇主（工人阻止雇主离开工作场所，直到要求得到满足）▶ **ghe·rao** *verb* (**ghe·raoes** or **ghe·raos**, **ghe·raoing**, **ghe·raoed**, **ghe·raoed**)：~ **sb** *The protesters are threatening to gherao the vice chancellor.* 抗议者威胁要挟持校长。

gher·kin /ˈɡɜːkɪn; *NAmE* ˈɡɜːrkɪn/ *noun* **1** (*BrE*) (*NAmE* **pickle**) a small CUCUMBER that has been preserved in VINEGAR before being eaten 醋泡小黄瓜 **2** (*NAmE*) a small CUCUMBER 小黄瓜

ghetto /ˈɡetəʊ; *NAmE* ˈɡetoʊ/ *noun* (*pl.* **-os** or **-oes**) **1** an area of a city where many people of the same race or background live, separately from the rest of the population. Ghettos are often crowded, with bad living conditions.（相同种族或背景人的）聚居区；贫民区：*a poor kid growing up in the ghetto* 在贫民区长大的穷孩子 ◇ *The south coast of Spain has become something of a tourist ghetto.* 西班牙南部海岸可以说已经成为旅游者的聚居区。➲ WORDFINDER NOTE AT CITY **2** the area of a town where Jews were forced to live in the past（昔日城镇中的）犹太人居住区：*the Warsaw ghetto* 华沙的犹太人居住区

ˈ**ghetto blaster** (*also* ˈ**boom box** *especially in NAmE*) *noun* (*informal*) a large radio and CD or CASSETTE player that can be carried around, especially to play loud music in public 大型手提式收录机（或激光唱机）

ghil·lie *noun* = GILLIE

ghost /ɡəʊst; *NAmE* ɡoʊst/ *noun*, *verb*

■ *noun* **1** [C] the spirit of a dead person that a living person believes they can see or hear 鬼；鬼魂；幽灵：*Do you believe in ghosts* (= believe that they exist)? 你相信有鬼吗？◇ *the ghost of her father that had come back to haunt her* 回来缠绕她的她父亲的幽灵 ◇ *He looked as if he had seen a ghost* (= looked very frightened). 他那副样子就像是见到鬼一样。 **2** [C] the memory of sth, especially sth bad（尤指可怕事物的）记忆，回忆：*The ghost of anti-Semitism still haunts Europe.* 反犹主义在欧洲仍然阴魂不散。 **3** [sing.] ~ **of sth** a very slight amount of sth that is left behind or that you are not sure really exists 隐约的一点点；（某物残留的）一丝，一点：*There was a ghost of a smile on his face.* 他脸上露出隐隐的一丝微笑。◇ *You don't have a ghost of a chance* (= you have no chance). 你一点儿机会都没有。 **4** [sing.] a second image on a television screen that is not as clear as the first, caused by a fault（电视屏幕上的）重影

IDM **give up the ˈghost** **1** to die 死 **2** (*humorous*) (of a machine 机器) to stop working 报废；不能运转；完蛋：*My car finally gave up the ghost.* 我的汽车终于报废了。➲ MORE AT FORMER *adj.*

■ *verb* **1** = GHOSTWRITE **2** [I] + **adv./prep.** (*literary*) to move without making a sound 悄悄地行进：*They ghosted up the smooth waters of the river.* 他们悄悄地航行在平静的河水上。

ghost·ing /ˈɡəʊstɪŋ; *NAmE* ˈɡoʊ-/ *noun* [U] the appearance of a faint second image next to an image on a television screen, computer screen, etc.（电视、电脑等屏幕上的）重像

ghost·ly /ˈɡəʊstli; *NAmE* ˈɡoʊstli/ *adj.* (**ghost·lier**, **ghost·li·est**) looking or sounding like a ghost; full of ghosts 鬼似的；幽灵般的；鬼魂萦绕的：*a ghostly figure* 鬼影 ◇ *ghostly footsteps* 幽灵般的脚步声 ◇ *the ghostly churchyard* 鬼魂萦绕的教堂墓地

ˈ**ghost story** *noun* a story about ghosts that is intended to frighten you（用来吓唬人的）鬼故事

ˈ**ghost town** *noun* a town that used to be busy and have a lot of people living in it, but is now empty（曾一度繁华的）被废弃城镇

ˈ**ghost train** *noun* (*BrE*) a small train at a FUNFAIR that goes through a dark tunnel full of frightening things（游乐场的）游鬼城小火车

ghost·write /ˈɡəʊstraɪt; *NAmE* ˈɡoʊst-/ (*also* **ghost**) *verb* (**ghost·wrote** /ˈɡəʊstrəʊt; *NAmE* ˈɡoʊstroʊt/, **ghost·written** /ˈɡəʊstrɪtn; *NAmE* ˈɡoʊst-/) [T, often passive, I] ~ (**sth**) to write a book, an article, etc. for another person who publishes it as their own work 代人写作；为人捉刀；代写：*Her memoirs were ghostwritten.* 她的回忆录是由别人代写的。

ghost·writer /ˈɡəʊstraɪtə(r); *NAmE* ˈɡoʊst-/ *noun* a person who writes a book, etc. for another person, under whose name it is then published 代人写作者；代笔者；捉刀人

ghoul /ɡuːl/ *noun* **1** (in stories) an evil spirit that opens graves and eats the dead bodies in them（传说中的）盗墓食尸鬼 **2** (*disapproving*) a person who is too interested in unpleasant things such as death and disaster 对凶残之事兴趣浓厚的人 ▶ **ghoul·ish** /ˈɡuːlɪʃ/ *adj.*：*ghoulish laughter* 狞笑

G

G

GHQ /ˌdʒiː eɪtʃ ˈkjuː/ *abbr.* [U] general headquarters (the main centre of a military organization) 总司令部，统帅部（全写为 general headquarters）: *He was posted to GHQ Cairo.* 他被派往开罗总司令部。

GHz *abbr.* (in writing 书写形式) GIGAHERTZ 千兆赫；吉赫

GI /ˌdʒiː ˈaɪ/ *noun, abbr.*
■ **noun** (*pl.* **GIs**) a soldier in the US armed forces 美国兵
■ **abbr.** GLYCAEMIC INDEX (= a system for measuring the effect of foods containing CARBOHYDRATES on the level of sugar in the blood) 血糖（生成）指数: *The diet is based mainly on low GI foods.* 这种饮食方式主要是以血糖指数低的食物为主。

giant /ˈdʒaɪənt/ *noun, adj.*
■ **noun 1** (in stories) a very large strong person who is often cruel and stupid（故事中常为残酷而愚蠢的）巨人 ➲ SEE ALSO GIANTESS **2** an unusually large person, animal or plant 巨人；巨兽；巨型植物: *He's a giant of a man.* 他是个巨人。 **3** a very large and powerful organization 大公司；强大的组织: *the multinational oil giants* 跨国大石油公司 **4** a person who is very good at sth 伟人；卓越人物: *literary giants* 大文豪
■ **adj.** [only before noun] very large; much larger or more important than similar things usually are 巨大的；特大的；伟大的: *a giant crab* 巨蟹 ◇ *a giant-size box of tissues* 特大的一盒纸巾 ◇ *a giant step towards achieving independence* 朝着独立迈出的巨大的一步

giant·ess /ˌdʒaɪənˈtes/ *noun* (in stories) a female giant（故事中的）女巨人

giant·ism /ˈdʒaɪəntɪzəm/ *noun* [U] = GIGANTISM

ˈgiant-killer *noun* (*BrE*) (especially in sports 尤用于体育运动) a person or team that defeats another much stronger opponent 打败强大对手的人（或队）；强手（或强队）的克星

ˌgiant ˈpanda *noun* = PANDA (1)

ˌgiant ˈslalom *noun* a SLALOM SKIING competition over a long distance, with wide fast turns 大回转滑雪赛；大曲道滑雪赛

GiB *abbr.* (in writing 书写形式) GIBIBYTE 吉字节，千兆字节（二进制计算机内存或数据单位）

Gib (*also* **Gibit**) *abbr.* (in writing 书写形式) GIBIBIT 吉比特，千兆比特（二进制计算机内存或数据单位）

gib·ber /ˈdʒɪbə(r)/ *verb* [I, T] (+ **speech**) to speak quickly in a way that is difficult to understand, often because of fear （常因害怕而）急促不清地说，语无伦次地说: *He cowered in the corner, gibbering with terror.* 他蜷缩在角落里，吓得语无伦次。◇ *By this time I was a* ***gibbering wreck***. 到这时我已是话也说不清的废人了。

gib·ber·ish /ˈdʒɪbərɪʃ/ *noun* [U] (*informal*) words that have no meaning or are impossible to understand 莫名其妙的话；胡话；令人费解的话 SYN **nonsense**: *You were talking gibberish in your sleep.* 你在睡梦里讲着呓语。

gib·bet /ˈdʒɪbɪt/ *noun* (*old-fashioned*) a vertical wooden structure on which criminals used to be hanged 绞刑架；绞台 SYN **gallows**

gib·bon /ˈɡɪbən/ *noun* a small APE (= an animal like a large MONKEY without a tail) with long arms, that lives in SE Asia 长臂猿（栖息于东南亚）

gib·bous /ˈɡɪbəs/ *adj.* (*specialist*) (of the moon 月球) with the bright part bigger than a SEMICIRCLE and smaller than a circle 光亮部分大于半圆的；盈凸的

gibe = JIBE

gibi·bit /ˈɡɪbibɪt/ *noun* (*abbr.* **Gi, Gib, Gibit**) (*computing* 计) = GIGABIT (2)

gibi·byte /ˈɡɪbibaɪt/ *noun* (*abbr.* **GiB**) (*computing* 计) = GIGABYTE (2)

gib·lets /ˈdʒɪbləts/ *noun* [pl.] the inside parts of a chicken or other bird, including the heart and LIVER, that are usually removed before it is cooked （禽类的）内脏

giddy /ˈɡɪdi/ *adj.* (**gid·dier, gid·di·est**) **1** [not usually before noun] feeling that everything is moving and that you are going to fall 头晕；眩晕 SYN **dizzy**: *When I looked down from the top floor, I felt giddy.* 我从顶楼朝下看时感到头晕目眩。 **2** [not usually before noun] ~ (**with sth**) so happy and excited that you cannot behave normally（高兴或激动得）发狂，举止反常: *She was giddy with happiness.* 她高兴得忘乎所以。 **3** [usually before noun] making you feel as if you are about to fall 令人眩晕的；使人头昏眼花的: *The kids were pushing the roundabout at a giddy speed.* 孩子们推动着旋转平台快得令人眩晕。◇ (*figurative*) ***the giddy heights*** *of success* 令人目眩的巨大成功 **4** (*old-fashioned*) (of people 人) not serious 轻率的；轻浮的；不稳重的 SYN **silly**: *Isabel's giddy young sister* 伊莎贝尔轻浮的小妹 ▶ **gid·di·ly** /ˈɡɪdɪli/ *adv.*: *She swayed giddily across the dance floor.* 她飞快地飘过舞池，看得人眼晕。 **gid·di·ness** /ˈɡɪdinəs/ *noun* [U]: *Symptoms include nausea and giddiness.* 症状有恶心和头晕。

ˌgiddy-ˈup *exclamation* used as a command to a horse to make it go faster （赶马的吆喝）驾

GIF /dʒɪf; ɡɪf/ *noun* (*computing* 计) the abbreviation for 'Graphic Interchange Format' (a type of computer file that contains images and is used especially to make them appear to move) * GIF 文件，图形交换格式文件（全写为 Graphic Interchange Format）: *Send it as a GIF.* 把它以 GIF 文件发送。

gift /ɡɪft/ *noun, verb*
■ **noun 1** a thing that you give to sb, especially on a special occasion or to say thank you 礼物；赠品 SYN **present**: *The watch was a gift from my mother.* 这块表是母亲给我的礼物。◇ *Thank you for your generous gift.* 感谢你丰厚的礼物。◇ *a* ***free gift*** *for every reader* 给每位读者的赠品 ◇ *the gift of life* 生命的给予 ◇ (*formal*) *The family* ***made a gift of*** *his paintings to the gallery.* 家人把他的画作赠送给了美术馆。◇ *gifts of toys for the children* 送给孩子们的玩具礼物 **2** a natural ability 天赋；天才；才能 SYN **talent**: ~ (**for sth**) *She has a great gift for music.* 她极有音乐天赋。◇ ~ (**for doing sth**) *He has a gift for making friends easily.* 他天生善交朋友。◇ *She can pick up a tune instantly on the piano. It's a gift.* 她听到曲子就能马上用钢琴弹出来，这是天分。 **3** [usually sing.] (*informal*) a thing that is very easy to do or cheap to buy 轻而易举的事；极便宜的东西: *Their second goal was an absolute gift.* 他们第二个进球简直不费吹灰之力。◇ *At £500 it's a gift.* 只卖500 英镑，真便宜。
IDM **be in the gift of sb | be in sb's ˈgift** (*especially BrE*) if sth such as an important job or a special right or advantage is **in sb's gift**, that person can decide who to give it to 由某人决定；某人有权决定: *All such posts are in the gift of the managing director* (= only given by the managing director). 所有这些岗位都由总经理决定。 **the gift of the ˈgab** (*BrE*) (*US* **a gift for/of ˈgab**) (*informal, sometimes disapproving*) the ability to speak easily and to persuade other people with your words 口才；辩才 **look a gift horse in the ˈmouth** (usually with negatives 通常与否定词连用) (*informal*) to refuse or criticize sth that is given to you for nothing 拒受馈赠；白送的马还看牙口；对礼物吹毛求疵 ➲ MORE AT GOD
■ **verb** (*BrE*) (used especially in JOURNALISM 尤用于新闻报道) to give sth to sb without their having to make any effort to get it 白送；白给: **~ sb sth** *They gifted their opponents a goal.* 他们白送给对方一分。◇ **~ sth to sb** *They gifted a goal to their opponents.* 他们白送给对方一分。

ˈgift certificate (*NAmE*) (*BrE* **ˈgift voucher, ˈgift token**) *noun* a piece of paper that is worth a particular amount of money and that can be exchanged for goods in a shop/store （购物）礼券

gift·ed /ˈɡɪftɪd/ *adj.* **1** having a lot of natural ability or intelligence 有天才的；有天赋的；天资聪慧的: *a gifted musician/player, etc.* 天才的音乐家、运动员等 ◇ *gifted children* 天资聪慧的孩子 **2 ~ with sth** having sth pleasant

具有（令人愉快的特质）： *He was gifted with a charming smile.* 他有迷人的微笑。

ˈgift shop *noun* a shop/store that sells goods that are suitable for giving as presents 礼品店

ˈgift voucher (*also* **ˈgift token**) (*both BrE*) (*NAmE* **ˈgift certificate**) *noun* a piece of paper that is worth a particular amount of money and that can be exchanged for goods in a shop/store （购物）礼券

ˈgift wrap *noun* [U] attractive coloured or patterned paper used for wrapping presents in 礼品包装纸

ˈgift-wrap *verb* (**-pp-**) [often passive] **~ sth** to wrap sth as a present for sb, especially in a shop/store （尤指商店里）将…包装成礼品： *Would you like the chocolates gift-wrapped?* 你需要我们把巧克力包装成礼品吗？ ◇ *The store offers a gift-wrapping service.* 这家商店提供礼品包装服务。

gig /ɡɪɡ/ *noun* **1** a performance by musicians playing popular music or JAZZ in front of an audience; a similar performance by a COMEDIAN （流行音乐或爵士乐）现场演奏会，现场演唱会；现场喜剧表演： *to do a gig* 举行流行音乐演唱会 ◇ *a White Stripes gig* "白色条纹"乐队演奏会 ➲ COLLOCATIONS AT MUSIC **2** (*NAmE, informal*) a job, especially a temporary one （尤指临时的）工作： *a gig as a basketball coach* 临时篮球教练 **3** (*informal*) = GIGABYTE **4** a small light CARRIAGE with two wheels, pulled by one horse 单马双轮轻便马车

giga- /ˈɡɪɡə; ˈdʒɪɡə/ *combining form* (in nouns; used in units of measurement 构成名词，用于计量单位) **1** 10^9, or 1 000 000 000 十亿，吉（咖），千兆（十进制，等于 1 000 000 000）： *gigahertz* 千兆赫 **2** 2^{30}, or 1 073 741 824 吉（咖），千兆（二进制，等于 1 073 741 824）

giga·bit /ˈɡɪɡəbɪt/ *noun* (*abbr.* **Gb**, **Gbit**) (*computing* 计) **1** a unit of computer memory or data, equal to 10^9, or $1\ 000^3$, (= 1 000 000 000) BITS 十亿比特，吉比特，千兆比特（十进制计算机内存或数据单位，等于 1 000 000 000 比特） **2** (*also* **gibi·bit**) a unit of computer memory or data, equal to 2^{30}, or $1\ 024^3$, (= 1 073 741 824) BITS 吉比特，千兆比特（二进制计算机内存或数据单位，等于 1 073 741 824 比特）

giga·byte /ˈɡɪɡəbaɪt/ (*also informal* **gig**) *noun* (*abbr.* **GB**) (*computing* 计) **1** a unit of computer memory or data, equal to 10^9, or $1\ 000^3$, (= 1 000 000 000) BYTES 十亿字节，吉字节，千兆字节（十进制计算机内存或数据单位，等于 1 000 000 000 字节） **2** (*also* **gibi·byte**) a unit of computer memory or data, equal to 2^{30}, or $1\ 024^3$, (= 1 073 741 824) BYTES 吉字节，千兆字节（二进制计算机内存或数据单位，等于 1 073 741 824 字节）

giga·hertz /ˈɡɪɡəhɜːts; ˈdʒɪ-; *NAmE* -hɜːrts/ *noun* (*pl.* **giga·hertz**) (*abbr.* **GHz**) (*computing* 计, *physics* 物) a unit for measuring radio waves and the speed at which a computer operates; 1 000 000 000 HERTZ 十亿赫，吉赫，千兆赫（无线电波频率和计算机运作速度单位，等于 1 000 000 000 赫）

gi·gan·tic /dʒaɪˈɡæntɪk/ *adj.* extremely large 巨大的；庞大的 **SYN** **enormous, huge**

gi·gant·ism /dʒaɪˈɡæntɪzəm; ˈdʒaɪɡæntɪzəm/ (*also* **giant·ism**) *noun* [U] (*medical* 医) a condition in which sb grows to an unusually large size 巨人症

gig·gle /ˈɡɪɡl/ *verb, noun*

■ ***verb*** [I, T] **~ (at/about sb/sth)** | **(+ speech)** to laugh in a silly way because you are amused, embarrassed or nervous （因感到有趣、窘迫或紧张而）咯咯地笑，傻笑： *The girls giggled at the joke.* 女孩子们给这笑话逗得咯咯笑。 ◇ *They giggled nervously as they waited for their turn.* 他们排队等候时紧张地傻笑着。

■ ***noun*** **1** [C] a slight silly repeated laugh 咯咯笑；傻笑： *She gave a nervous giggle.* 她发出紧张的傻笑。 ◇ *Matt collapsed into giggles and hung up the phone.* 马特突然咯咯笑起来，然后挂断了电话。 **2** [sing.] (*BrE, informal*) a thing that you think is amusing 趣事；玩笑；可笑的事： *We only did it **for a giggle**.* 我们做那件事只是开个玩笑而已。 **3 the giggles** [pl.] (*informal*) continuous giggling that you cannot control or stop 止不住的咯咯笑： *I get the giggles when I'm nervous.* 我紧张时就不停地咯咯大笑。 ◇ *She had **a fit of the giggles** and had to leave the room.* 她突然咯咯笑了起来，不得不走出房间。

gig·gly /ˈɡɪɡli/ *adj.* laughing a lot in a silly, nervous way 咯咯傻笑的；紧张得咯咯笑的

GIGO /ˈɡaɪɡəʊ; *NAmE* -ɡoʊ/ ➲ GARBAGE

gig·olo /ˈʒɪɡələʊ; ˈdʒɪ-; *NAmE* -loʊ/ *noun* (*pl.* **-os**) a man who is paid to be the lover of an older woman, usually one who is rich （通常指贵妇人供养的）男伴，面首

gild /ɡɪld/ *verb* **1 ~ sth** (*literary*) to make sth look bright, as if covered with gold 使如金子般生光（或生辉、生色）： *The golden light gilded the sea.* 金色的阳光使大海如金子般闪闪发光。 **2 ~ sth** to cover sth with a thin layer of gold or gold paint 给…镀金；涂金于

IDM **gild the ˈlily** to spoil sth that is already good or beautiful by trying to improve it 画蛇添足；多此一举

gild·ed /ˈɡɪldɪd/ *adj.* [only before noun] **1** covered with a thin layer of gold or gold paint 镀金的；涂金色的 **2** (*literary*) rich and belonging to the upper classes 富贵的；上层阶级的： *the **gilded youth*** (= rich, upper-class young people) *of the Edwardian era* 爱德华时代富贵的年轻人

gild·ing /ˈɡɪldɪŋ/ *noun* [U] a layer of gold or gold paint; the surface that this makes 镀金层；金色涂层；镀金饰面

gilet /ˈʒɪleɪ; ˈʒiː-/ *noun* a light thick jacket without sleeves 厚夹克背心

gill[1] /ɡɪl/ *noun* [usually pl.] one of the openings on the side of a fish's head that it breathes through 鳃 ➲ VISUAL VOCAB PAGE V12

IDM **to the ˈgills** (*informal*) completely full （完全）满了，饱了；满满当当： *I was stuffed to the gills with chocolate cake.* 我吃巧克力蛋糕都撑到嗓子眼儿了。

gill[2] /dʒɪl/ *noun* a unit for measuring liquids. There are four gills in a pint. 及耳（液量单位，等于四分之一品脱）

gil·lie (*also* **ghil·lie**) /ˈɡɪli/ *noun* (*ScotE*) a man or boy who helps sb who is shooting or fishing for sport in Scotland （苏格兰渔猎运动者的）随从，侍童，男仆

gilt /ɡɪlt/ *noun* **1** [U] a thin layer of gold, or sth like gold that is used on a surface for decoration 镀金；金色涂层： *gilt lettering* 烫印的金字 **2 gilts** [pl.] (*BrE, finance* 财) gilt-edged investments 金边证券；绩优证券 **3** [C] (*especially NAmE*) a young female pig 小母猪

IDM **take the gilt off the ˈgingerbread** (*BrE*) to do or be sth that makes a situation or achievement less attractive or impressive 使失去吸引力；令人扫兴；煞风景

ˌgilt-ˈedged *adj.* (*finance* 财) very safe 金边的；安全的；高度可靠的： ***gilt-edged securities/shares/stocks*** (= investments that are considered safe because they have been sold by the government) 金边证券 / 股份 / 股票（由政府发行，安全可靠）

gim·crack /ˈdʒɪmkræk/ *adj.* [only before noun] badly made and of little value 粗制滥造的；劣质的；无价值的 **SYN** **shoddy**

gim·let /ˈɡɪmlət/ *noun* a small tool for making holes in wood to put screws in 螺丝锥；手锥；手钻；木钻： (*figurative*) *eyes like gimlets* (= looking very hard at things and noticing every detail) 锐利如锥的目光

gimme /ˈɡɪmi/ *short form, noun* (*informal*)

■ ***short form*** a way of writing the way that the words 'give me' are sometimes spoken (give me 的一种书写形式，表示此短语某些时候的读法）给我： *Gimme back my bike!* 把自行车还给我！

■ ***noun*** [usually sing.] something that is very easy to do or achieve 轻而易举的事；容易获得的事物

gim·mick /ˈɡɪmɪk/ *noun* (*often disapproving*) an unusual trick or unnecessary device that is intended to attract attention or to persuade people to buy sth （为引人注

G

意或诱人购买而搞的）花招，把戏，噱头：*a promotional/publicity/sales gimmick* 以推销 / 宣传 / 销售为目的的花招 ▸**gim·micky** /ˈɡɪmɪki/ *adj.*：*a gimmicky idea* 鬼主意

gim·mick·ry /ˈɡɪmɪkri/ *noun* [U] (*disapproving*) the use of gimmicks in selling, etc. 玩弄销售伎俩；耍花招

gin /dʒɪn/ *noun* **1** [U, C] an alcoholic drink made from grain and flavoured with JUNIPER BERRIES. Gin is usually drunk mixed with TONIC WATER or fruit juice. 杜松子酒 ➲ SEE ALSO PINK GIN **2** [C] a glass of gin 一杯杜松子酒：*I'll have a gin and tonic, please.* 请来一杯加奎宁水的杜松子酒。 **3** = COTTON GIN

G

gin·ger /ˈdʒɪndʒə(r)/ *noun, adj., verb*
■ ***noun*** [U] **1** the root of the ginger plant used in cooking as a spice 姜：*a teaspoon of ground ginger* 一茶匙姜粉 ◇ (*BrE*) *ginger biscuits* 姜味饼干 ➲ VISUAL VOCAB PAGE V35 **2** a light brownish-orange colour 姜黄色
■ ***adj.*** (*BrE*) light brownish-orange in colour 姜黄色的：*ginger hair* 姜黄色的头发 ◇ *a ginger cat* 姜黄色的猫 ➲ WORDFINDER NOTE AT BLONDE
■ ***verb***
PHR V **ˌginger sth/sb↔ˈup** (*BrE*) to make sth/sb more active or exciting 使有活力；使活跃；使兴奋 SYN **liven up**

ˌginger ˈale *noun* **1** [U, C] a clear FIZZY drink (= with bubbles) that does not contain alcohol, flavoured with ginger, and often mixed with alcoholic drinks 姜味汽水 **2** [C] a bottle or glass of ginger ale 一瓶（或一杯）姜味汽水

ˌginger ˈbeer *noun* **1** [U, C] a FIZZY drink (= with bubbles) that is flavoured with GINGER. Some types of ginger beer contain a small amount of alcohol. 姜汁啤酒 **2** [C] a bottle or glass of ginger beer 一瓶（或一杯）姜汁啤酒

gin·ger·bread /ˈdʒɪndʒəbred; *NAmE* -dʒərb-/ *noun* [U] a sweet cake or soft biscuit/cookie flavoured with GINGER 姜饼；姜味饼干：*a gingerbread man* (= a gingerbread biscuit/cookie in the shape of a person) 人形姜饼 IDM SEE GILT

ˈginger group *noun* (*BrE*) a group of people within a political party or an organization, who work to persuade other members to accept their policies or ideas （政党或组织中的）活跃分子集团，骨干小组

gin·ger·ly /ˈdʒɪndʒəli; *NAmE* -dʒərli/ *adv.* in a careful way, because you are afraid of being hurt, of making a noise, etc. 谨慎地；小心翼翼地；轻手轻脚地：*He opened the box gingerly and looked inside.* 他小心翼翼地打开盒子朝里看。

ˈginger nut (*BrE*) (*also* **ˈginger snap** *NAmE, BrE*) *noun* a hard sweet biscuit/cookie flavoured with GINGER 姜味硬饼干

gin·gery /ˈdʒɪndʒəri/ *adj.* like GINGER in colour or flavour 姜色的；姜味的

ging·ham /ˈɡɪŋəm/ *noun* [U] a type of cotton cloth with a pattern of white and coloured squares 格子棉布：*a blue and white gingham dress* 蓝白格子布连衣裙

gin·gi·vitis /ˌdʒɪndʒɪˈvaɪtəs/ *noun* [U] (*medical* 医) a condition in which the GUMS around the teeth become painful, red and swollen （牙）龈炎

ginkgo /ˈɡɪŋkɡəʊ; *NAmE* -ɡoʊ/ (*also* **gingko** /ˈɡɪŋkəʊ; *NAmE* -koʊ/) *noun* (*pl.* **-os** or **-oes**) a Chinese tree with yellow flowers 银杏（原产中国） SYN **maidenhair tree**

gi·nor·mous /dʒaɪˈnɔːməs; *NAmE* -ˈnɔːrm-/ *adj.* (*BrE, informal*) extremely large 极大的；巨大的

ˌgin ˈrummy *noun* [U] a card game in which players try to get HANDS (= sets of cards) that add up to ten 金拉米纸牌戏（玩牌者争取使手中牌加起来不超过 10 点）

gin·seng /ˈdʒɪnseŋ/ *noun* [U] a medicine obtained from a plant root that some people believe helps you stay young and healthy 人参；西洋参

ˈgin trap *noun* a device for trapping small wild animals or birds （捕小野兽或鸟的）齿夹；捕兽夹

gippy tummy (*also* **gyppy tummy**) /ˌdʒɪpi ˈtʌmi/ *noun* (*old-fashioned, BrE, informal*) DIARRHOEA (= an illness in which waste matter is emptied from the body in liquid form) that affects visitors to hot countries 热带腹泻

Gipsy = GYPSY

gir·affe /dʒəˈrɑːf; *NAmE* -ˈræf/ *noun* (*pl.* **gir·affe** or **gir·affes**) a tall African animal with a very long neck, long legs, and dark marks on its coat 长颈鹿

gird /ɡɜːd; *NAmE* ɡɜːrd/ *verb* ~ **sb/sth** (**with sth**) to surround sth with sth; to fasten sth around sb/sth 束紧；系上；捆上；缠上
IDM **gird** (**up**) **your ˈloins** (*literary* or *humorous*) to get ready to do sth difficult 准备从事（艰苦的工作）；准备行动：*The company is girding its loins for a plunge into the overseas market.* 公司正准备打入海外市场。
PHR V **gird** (**yourself/sb/sth**) (**up**) **for sth** (*literary*) to prepare for sth difficult, especially a fight, contest, etc. 为（战斗、比赛等艰苦工作）做好准备

gird·er /ˈɡɜːdə(r); *NAmE* ˈɡɜːrd-/ *noun* a long strong iron or steel bar used for building bridges and the FRAMEWORK of large buildings （桥或建筑物的）梁，主梁，桁架 ➲ WORDFINDER NOTE AT CONSTRUCTION

gir·dle /ˈɡɜːdl; *NAmE* ˈɡɜːrdl/ *noun, verb*
■ ***noun*** **1** a piece of women's underwear that fits closely around the body from the waist to the top of the legs, designed to make a woman look thinner （女子的）紧身褡 **2** (*literary*) a thing that surrounds sth else 围绕物：*carefully tended lawns set in a girdle of trees* 树木环绕、精心修整的草坪 **3** (*old-fashioned*) a belt or thick string fastened around the waist to keep clothes in position 腰带
■ ***verb*** ~ **sth** (*literary*) to surround sth 围绕；环绕：*A chain of volcanoes girdles the Pacific.* 环绕太平洋的是一连串的火山。

girl 🔑 /ɡɜːl; *NAmE* ɡɜːrl/ *noun* **1** 🔑 [C] a female child 女孩：*a* ***baby girl*** 女婴 ◇ ***a little girl*** *of six* 六岁的小女孩 ◇ *Hello, girls and boys!* 孩子们好！ ➲ SEE ALSO POSTER CHILD **2** 🔑 [C] a daughter 女儿：*Our youngest girl is at college.* 我们的小女儿在大学读书。 **3** 🔑 [C] (*sometimes offensive*) a young woman 年轻女子；女郎：*Alex is not interested in girls yet.* 亚历克斯对女孩子还不感兴趣。 ◇ *He married the girl next door.* 他与隔壁的女孩结婚了。 **4** [C] (usually in compounds 通常构成复合词) (*old-fashioned, offensive*) a female worker 女工；女职员：*an office girl* 女办事员 **5** [C] (*old-fashioned*) a man's girlfriend （男人的）女朋友 **6** **girls** [pl.] (used especially as a form of address by women 女性尤用于称呼) a woman's female friends （女子的）女伴，女友：*I'm having a night out with the girls.* 我今晚要和女友们外出。 ◇ *Good morning, girls!* 姑娘们，早上好！ **7** [sing.] **old** ~ (*often offensive*) an old woman, especially sb's wife or mother 老婆；老母亲；老妇人：*How is the old girl these days?* 老母亲近来好吗？ IDM SEE BIG *adj.*

ˈgirl band (*also* **ˈgirl group**) *noun* a group of attractive young women who sing pop music and dance 少女流行乐队；少女组合

ˌgirl ˈFriday *noun* a girl or a woman who is employed in an office to do several different jobs, helping other people 女助手；女秘书；女助理

girl·friend 🔑 /ˈɡɜːlfrend; *NAmE* ˈɡɜːrl-/ *noun* **1** 🔑 a girl or a woman that sb is having a romantic relationship with 女朋友；女情人 **2** 🔑 (*especially NAmE*) a woman's female friend （女子的）女伴，女友：*I had lunch with a girlfriend.* 我同女友一起吃的午饭。

ˌGirl ˈGuide *noun* (*old-fashioned, BrE*) = GUIDE (6)

ˌGirl ˈGuider *noun* (*BrE*) = GUIDER

girl·hood /ˈɡɜːlhʊd; *NAmE* ˈɡɜːrl-/ *noun* [U] (*old-fashioned*) the time when sb is a girl; the fact of being a girl 少女时期；少女时代；少女

girlie /ˈɡɜːli; *NAmE* ˈɡɜːrli/ *adj., noun* (*informal*)
■ ***adj.*** [only before noun] **1** containing photographs of naked

or nearly naked women, that are intended to make men sexually excited 有裸体或半裸体女人照片的：*girlie magazines* 有女子艳照的杂志 **2** (*disapproving*) suitable for or like girls, not boys 适合少女的；像姑娘一样的：*girlie games* 女孩子的游戏

■ ***noun*** a way of referring to a girl or young woman, that many women find offensive 小妞儿；小娘们儿

girl·ish /ˈɡɜːlɪʃ; *NAmE* ˈɡɜːrlɪʃ/ *adj.* like a girl; of a girl 像女孩子的；女孩子似的；女孩子的：*a girlish giggle* 女孩子气的咯咯笑 ◇ *a girlish figure* 女孩儿的体形

ˈgirl power *noun* [U] the idea that women should take control of their careers and lives 女权（认为女性应主宰自己的事业和生活的观念）

ˌGirl ˈScout (*US*) (*BrE* **Guide**, *old-fashioned* **ˌGirl ˈGuide**) *noun* a member of an organization (called **the Guides** or **the Girl Scouts**) which is similar to the SCOUTS and which trains girls in practical skills and does a lot of activities with them, for example camping 女童子军

girn = GURN

giro /ˈdʒaɪrəʊ; *NAmE* -roʊ/ *noun* (*pl.* **-os**) (*BrE*) **1** [U] (*finance* 财) a system in which money can be moved from one bank or post office account to another by a central computer（银行或邮局）直接转账：*to pay by giro* 用直接转账支付 ◇ *a* ***giro credit/payment/transfer*** 直接转账信贷 / 支付；直接转账 **2** (*also* **ˈgiro cheque**) [C] a cheque that the government pays through the giro system to people who are unemployed or sick, or who have a very small income（政府支付给失业者、病人或低收入者的）直接转账救济支票：*It is easy for families to run out of money before the weekly giro arrives.* 每周直接转账救济支票未到之前钱便花光的情况，许多家庭都容易出现。

girth /ɡɜːθ; *NAmE* ɡɜːrθ/ *noun* **1** [U, C] the measurement around sth, especially a person's waist 围长；干围；腰围：*a man of enormous girth* 腰围很粗的男人 ◇ *a tree one metre in girth/with a girth of one metre* 干围一米的树 **2** [C] a narrow piece of leather or cloth that is fastened around the middle of a horse to keep the seat (called a SADDLE) or a load in place（固定马鞍或驮载的）肚带，腹带

gismo = GIZMO

gist /dʒɪst/ *noun* (*usually* **the gist**) [sing.] **~ (of sth)** the main or general meaning of a piece of writing, a speech or a conversation 要点；主旨；大意：*to get* (= understand) *the gist of an argument* 理解辩论的主旨 ◇ *I missed the beginning of the lecture—can you give me the gist of what he said?* 我错过了讲座的开头，给我讲讲他发言的要点好吗？ ◇ *I'm afraid I don't quite follow your gist* (= what you really mean). 对不起，我还不太明白你的意思。

git /ɡɪt/ *noun* (*BrE, slang*) a stupid or unpleasant man 蠢货；饭桶；讨厌鬼

githeri /ɡɪˈðeri/ *noun* [U] (*EAfrE*) an East African dish of MAIZE and KIDNEY BEANS cooked slowly in liquid and served hot, usually eaten as a main meal 基德哩，玉米炖菜豆（东非的一种主食，用玉米和菜豆慢慢熬煮而成）

give 🔑 /ɡɪv/ *verb, noun*

■ ***verb*** (**gave** /ɡeɪv/, **given** /ˈɡɪvn/)

• **HAND/PROVIDE** 交给；提供 **1** 🔑 [T] to hand sth to sb so that they can look at it, use it or keep it for a time 给；交给：**~ sth to sb** *Give the letter to your mother when you've read it.* 信看完后交给你母亲。 ◇ *She gave her ticket to the woman at the check-in desk.* 她把票递给了登机手续办理处的女工作人员。 ◇ **~ sb sth** *Give your mother the letter.* 把信给你母亲。 ◇ *They were all given a box to carry.* 给了他们每人一个箱子让他们搬。 **2** 🔑 [T, I] to hand sth to sb as a present; to allow sb to have sth as a present 赠送；赠与；送给：**~ sb sth** *What are you giving your father for his birthday?* 你打算送给你父亲什么生日礼物？ ◇ *She was given a huge bunch of flowers.* 有人给她送了一大束花。 ◇ *Did you give the waiter a tip?* 你给服务员小费了吗？ ◇ **~ sth to sb** *We don't usually give presents to people at work.* 我们一般不给在职员工送礼。 ◇ **~ (sth)** *They say it's better to give than to receive.* 人们说施比受有福。 **3** 🔑 [T] to provide sb with sth（为某人）提供，供给，供应：**~ sb sth** *They were all thirsty so I gave them a drink.* 他们都口渴了，所以我给了他们一杯饮料。 ◇ *Give me your name and address.* 把你的名字和地址报给我。 ◇ *We've been given a 2% pay increase.* 我们获得了 2% 的加薪。 ◇ *I was hoping you would give me a job.* 我还盼望着你能给我份工作呢。 ◇ *He was given a new heart in a five-hour operation.* 经过五个小时的手术，给他移植了一颗新的心脏。 ◇ *She wants a job that gives her more responsibility.* 她想得到一份责任更大的工作。 ◇ *Can I give you a ride to the station?* 我开车送你去车站好吗？ ◇ *They couldn't give me any more information.* 他们无法给我提供更多的信息。 ◇ *I'll give you* (= allow you to have) *ten minutes to prepare your answer.* 我会给你十分钟时间准备回答。 ◇ *Don't give me any of that backchat* (= don't be rude). 别跟我顶嘴。 ◇ **~ sth to sb** *He gives Italian lessons to his colleagues.* 他给同事们上意大利语课。 ◇ *The reforms should give a better chance to the less able children.* 这些改革应该给予能力较低的儿童更好的机会。

• **MONEY** 金钱 **4** 🔑 [I, T] to pay money to a charity, etc., to help people 捐助；捐赠；捐款：*We need your help—please give generously.* 我们需要您的帮助，请慷慨解囊吧。 ◇ **~ to sth** *They both gave regularly to charity.* 他俩定期为慈善事业捐款。 ◇ **~ sth (to sth)** *I gave a small donation.* 我给了一点微薄的捐助。 **5** 🔑 [T] to pay in order to have or do sth（为获得某物或做某事而）支付，付款：**~ sb sth (for sth)** *How much will you give me for the car?* 你肯出多少钱买我这辆汽车？ ◇ **~ sth** *I'd give anything to see him again.* 只要能再见他一面我出多少钱都愿意。 ◇ **~ sth for sth** *I gave £50 for the lot.* 我出 50 英镑一下全买了。

• **TREAT AS IMPORTANT** 视为重要 **6** 🔑 [T] to use time, energy, etc. for sb/sth 将（时间、精力等）用于：**~ sb/sth sth** *I gave the matter a lot of thought.* 我反复思考过这个问题。 ◇ **~ sth to sb/sth** *I gave a lot of thought to the matter.* 我反复思考过这个问题。 ◇ *The government has given top priority to reforming the tax system.* 政府优先致力于税制改革。

• **PUNISHMENT** 惩罚 **7** 🔑 [T] to make sb suffer a particular punishment 使受…惩罚：**~ sb sth** *The judge gave him a nine-month suspended sentence.* 法官判处他有期徒刑九个月，缓期执行。 ◇ **~ sth to sb** *We discussed what punishment should be given to the boys.* 我们讨论了该如何惩罚这些男孩。

• **ILLNESS** 疾病 **8** 🔑 [T] to infect sb with an illness 把（疾病）传染给：**~ sb sth** *You've given me your cold.* 你把感冒传染给我了。 ◇ **~ sth to sb** *She'd given the bug to all her colleagues.* 她把这种病毒传染给了所有的同事。

• **PARTY/EVENT** 聚会；活动 **9** 🔑 [T] **~ sth** if you **give** a party, you organize it and invite people 举办；举行 **10** 🔑 [T] **~ sth** to perform sth in public 表演；公开进行：*She gave a reading from her latest volume of poetry.* 她朗诵了她最近出版的诗集里的一首诗。 ◇ *The President will be giving a press conference this afternoon.* 总统今天下午将举行记者招待会。

• **DO/PRODUCE STH** 做；产生 **11** 🔑 [T] used with a noun to describe a particular action, giving the same meaning as the related verb（与名词连用描述某一动作，意义与该名词相应的动词相同）：**~ sth** *She gave a shrug of her shoulders* (= shrugged). 她耸了耸肩。 ◇ *He turned to us and gave a big smile* (= smiled broadly). 他转身对着我们咧开嘴笑。 ◇ *She looked up from her work and gave a yawn* (= yawned). 她停下工作抬起头来打了个哈欠。 ◇ *He gave a loud cry* (= cried out loudly) *and fell to the floor.* 他大叫了一声倒在地板上。 ◇ *Her work has given pleasure to* (= pleased) *millions of readers.* 她的著作给数百万读者带来了欢乐。 ◇ **~ sb sth** *He gave her a kiss* (= kissed her). 他吻了她一下。 ◇ *I have to admit that the news gave us a shock* (= shocked us). 我不得不承认这个消息让我们大为震惊。 ◇ *We'll give you all the help we can* (= help you in every way we can). 我们将尽力帮助你。 **HELP** For other similar expressions, look up the nouns in each. For example, you will find **give your approval** at **approval**. 其他类似词组见有关名词词条。如 give your approval 在词条 approval 下可以查到。 **12** 🔑 [T] **~ sb sth** to produce a particular feeling in sb 使产生（某种感觉）：*All that driving has given me a headache.* 这一路开车让我头都痛了。 ◇ *Go for a walk. It'll give you an appetite.* 去散散步，你就有食欲了。

G

- **TELEPHONE CALL** 电话 **13** [T] ~ **sb sth** to make a telephone call to sb 给（某人）打（电话）：*Give me a call tomorrow.* 明天给我打个电话。◇ *I'll give you a ring.* 我会给你打电话的。
- **MARK/GRADE** 分数；等级 **14** [T] ~ **sb/sth sth** | ~ **sth (to sb/sth)** to judge sb/sth to be of a particular standard 给…评定（等级）：*She had given the assignment an A.* 她给这份作业打了个优。◇ *I give it ten out of ten for originality.* 因其创意我给它打满分。
- **PREDICT HOW LONG** 预计多长时间 **15** [T] ~ **sb/sth sth** to predict that sth will last a particular length of time 预计将持续（…时间）：*That marriage won't last. I'll give them two years, at the outside.* 那桩婚姻不会持久，我看最多两年。
- **IN SPORT** 体育运动 **16** [T] ~ **sb/sth + adj.** to say that a player or the ball is in a particular position 裁定，判（球员或球所处位置）：*The umpire gave the ball out.* 裁判员判球出界。
- **BEND** 弯曲 **17** [I] to bend or stretch under pressure（在压力下）弯曲，伸长：*The branch began to give under his weight.* 他身体的重量把树枝都压弯了。◇ (*figurative*) *We can't go on like this—**something's got to give**.* 我们不能继续这样了，肯定会出事的。 **18** [I] to agree to change your mind or give up some of your demands 让步；妥协：*You're going to have to give a little.* 你可能非得稍做让步不可。 ➲ MORE LIKE THIS 33, page R28

IDM HELP Most idioms containing **give** are at the entries for the nouns and adjectives in the idioms, for example, **give rise to sth** is at **rise** *n.* 大多数含 give 的习语，都可在该等习语中的名词及形容词相关词条找到，如 give rise to sth 在词条 rise 的名词部分。 **don't give me 'that** (*informal*) used to tell sb that you do not accept what they say（表示不相信对方说的话）别跟我来这一套，别以为我会相信你：*'I didn't have time to do it.' 'Oh, don't give me that!'* "我没有时间做这事。""哦，别以为我会相信你的鬼话！" **,give and 'take** to be willing, in a relationship, to accept what sb else wants and to give up some of what you want 互相让步；双方迁就：*You're going to have to learn to give and take.* 你们必须学会互相迁就。 **give as good as you 'get** to react with equal force when sb attacks or criticizes you 回敬；回击；以牙还牙：*She can give as good as she gets.* 她能够给以回击。 **give it up (for sb)** (*informal*) to show your approval of sb by clapping your hands 鼓掌表示支持（某人）：*Give it up for Eddie Murphy!* 给艾迪·墨菲以掌声鼓励！ **'give me sth/sb (any day/time)** (*informal*) used to say that you prefer a particular thing or person to the one that has just been mentioned 我宁愿；我更喜欢；我宁可选择：*We don't go out much. Give me a quiet night in front of the TV any day!* 我们不常出去。我宁愿坐在电视机前安安静静地过一夜！ **give or 'take (sth)** if sth is correct **give or take** a particular amount, it is approximately correct 相差不到；出入至多：*It'll take about three weeks, give or take a day or so.* 这要花大约三周时间，出入不过一天左右。 **give sb to believe/understand (that)...** [often passive] (*formal*) to make sb believe/understand sth 使某人相信；使某人理解：*I was given to understand that she had resigned.* 我得知她已经辞职了。 **I give you...** used to ask people to drink a TOAST to sb 我提议为（某人）干杯：*Ladies and gentlemen, I give you Geoff Ogilby!* 女士们，先生们，我提议为杰夫·奥格尔比干杯！ **I/I'll give you 'that** (*informal*) used when you are admitting that sth is true 我承认这事有理；我承认这是事实 **what 'gives?** (*informal*) what is happening?; what is the news? 发生了什么事；有什么消息

PHR V **,give sb a'way** (in a marriage ceremony 在婚礼上) to lead the BRIDE to the BRIDEGROOM and formally allow her to marry him 将新娘交给新郎：*The bride was given away by her father.* 新娘由父亲交给新郎。 **,give sth↔a'way 1** to give sth as a gift 赠送；捐赠：*He gave away most of his money to charity.* 他把他的大部分钱都捐赠给了慈善事业。◇ (*informal*) *Check out the prices of our pizzas—we're virtually giving them away!* 查看一下我们的比萨饼的价格吧，我们实际上是在白送！ ➲ RELATED NOUN GIVEAWAY **2** to present sth 颁发；分发：*The mayor gave away the prizes at the school sports day.* 市长在学校运动会那天颁发了奖项。 **3** to carelessly allow sb to have an advantage（粗心地）失去，丧失，错失（优势）：*They've given away two goals already.* 他们已白送对手两分了。 **,give sth/sb↔a'way** to make known sth that sb wants to keep secret 泄露；暴露 SYN **betray**：*She gave away state secrets to the enemy.* 她把国家机密泄露给了敌人。◇ *It was supposed to be a surprise but the children **gave the game away**.* 这原本想给人一个惊喜，可孩子们把计划泄露了。◇ *His voice gave him away* (= showed who he really was). 他的声音使他露馅了。 ➲ RELATED NOUN GIVEAWAY **,give sb sth↔'back** | **,give sth↔'back (to sb) 1** to return sth to its owner 归还；送回：*Could you give me back my pen?* 把钢笔还给我好吗？◇ *Could you give me my pen back?* 把钢笔还给我好吗？◇ *I picked it up and gave it back to him.* 我把它捡起来还给了他。◇ (*informal*) *Give it me back!* 把它还给我！ **2** to allow sb to have sth again 使恢复；使重新获得：*The operation gave him back the use of his legs.* 手术使他双腿恢复了功能。 **,give 'in (to sb/sth) 1** to admit that you have been defeated by sb/sth 屈服；认输；投降：*The rebels were forced to give in.* 叛乱分子被迫投降了。 **2** to agree to do sth that you do not want to do 让步；勉强同意：*The authorities have shown no signs of giving in to the kidnappers' demands.* 当局对绑架者的要求没有丝毫让步的迹象。 **,give sth 'in (to sb)** (*BrE*) (*also* **,hand sth↔'in (to sb)** *BrE, NAmE*) to hand over sth to sb in authority 呈上；交上：*Please give your work in before Monday.* 请在星期一之前把作业交上来。 **,give 'off sth** to produce sth such as a smell, heat, light, etc. 发出，放出（气味、热、光等）：*The flowers gave off a fragrant perfume.* 花儿散发出芳香。 **'give on to/onto sth** [no passive] (*BrE*) to have a view of sth; to lead directly to sth 朝向；面向；通向：*The bedroom windows give on to the street.* 卧室的窗户面向街道。◇ *This door gives onto the hall.* 这道门通往大厅。 **,give 'out 1** to come to an end; to be completely used up 用完；耗尽：*After a month their food supplies gave out.* 一个月以后他们的食物储备消耗殆尽。◇ *Her patience finally gave out.* 她最终忍无可忍了。 **2** to stop working 停止运行；停止运转：*One of the plane's engines gave out in mid-air.* 飞机的一个发动机在空中失灵了。◇ *Her legs gave out and she collapsed.* 她腿一软倒了下去。 **,give sth↔'out** to give sth to a lot of people 分发；散发：*The teacher gave out the exam papers.* 老师分发了试卷。 **,give 'out sth 1** to produce sth such as heat, light, etc. 发出，放出（热、光等）：*The radiator gives out a lot of heat.* 散热器释放出大量的热。 **2** [often passive] (*especially BrE*) to tell people or broadcast sth 公布；宣布；播放 **,give 'over** (*BrE, informal*) used to tell sb to stop doing sth 别再…了；到此为止吧；住手：*Give over, Chris! You're hurting me.* 住手，克里斯！你把我弄痛了。◇ **give over doing sth** *Give over complaining!* 别抱怨了！ **,give yourself 'over to sth** (*also* **,give yourself 'up to sth**) to spend all your time doing sth or thinking about sth; to allow sth to completely control your life 致力于；沉溺于 **,give sth↔'over to sth** [usually passive] to use sth for one particular purpose 把…专用作（某种用途）：*The gallery is given over to British art.* 此陈列室专门用于陈列英国艺术品。 **,give 'up** to stop trying to do sth 投降；认输；放弃：*They gave up without a fight.* 他们不战而降。◇ *She doesn't give up easily.* 她不轻易认输。◇ *I give up—tell me the answer.* 我放弃了，把答案告诉我吧。 **,give sb 'up 1** (*also* **,give 'up on sb** *especially in NAmE*) to believe that sb is never going to arrive, get better, be found, etc. 对某人的到来（或康复、能否找到等）不再抱有希望：*There you are at last! We'd given you up.* 你终于来了！我们都以为你不来了呢。◇ *We hadn't heard from him for so long, we'd **given him up for dead**.* 我们这么长时间没有他的音信，都以为他死了。 **2** to stop having a relationship with sb 与某人断绝关系；不再与某人交往：*Why don't you give him up?* 你为什么不与他一刀两断呢？ **,give sth↔'up 1** [no passive] to stop doing or having sth 停止；中止；放弃；抛弃：*She didn't give up work when she had the baby.* 她有孩子后并未放弃工作。◇ *We'd **given up hope** of ever having children.* 我们已放弃生孩子的希望。◇ **give up doing sth** *You ought to give up smoking.* 你应该戒烟。 ➲ MORE LIKE THIS 27, page R28 **2** to spend time on a task that you would normally spend on sth else 把（本该做其他事的时间）耗费于：*I gave up my weekend to help him paint his apartment.* 我耗费了一个周末帮他粉刷公寓。**ˌgive sth↔ˈup (to sb)** to hand sth over to sb else 把…交给（或让与）：*We had to give our passports up to the authorities.* 我们得把护照交给当局。◊ *He gave up his seat to a pregnant woman* (= stood up to allow her to sit down). 他把座位让给了一名孕妇。 **ˌgive yourself/sb ˈup (to sb)** to offer yourself/sb to be captured 自首；投案；投降：*After a week on the run he gave himself up to the police.* 他逃跑一周后向警方投案自首了。 **ˌgive yourself ˈup to sth** = GIVE YOURSELF OVER TO STH **ˌgive ˈup on sb** **1** to stop hoping or believing that sb will change, get better, etc. 对某人不再抱希望（或不再相信）：*His teachers seem to have given up on him.* 他的老师似乎不再对他抱有希望。 **2** (*especially NAmE*) = GIVE SB UP

■ ***noun*** [U] the ability of sth to bend or stretch under pressure 伸展性；弹性：*The shoes may seem tight at first, but the leather has plenty of give in it.* 这鞋刚开始穿时可能显得紧，但皮子的伸展性很好。

IDM **ˌgive and ˈtake** **1** willingness in a relationship to accept what sb else wants and give up some of what you want 双方迁就；相互让步；互相忍让 **2** an exchange of words or ideas 交谈；思想交流：*to encourage a lively give and take* 鼓励活跃的思想交流

give·away /ˈɡɪvəweɪ/ *noun, adj.*

■ ***noun*** (*informal*) **1** something that a company gives free, usually with sth else that is for sale（公司为推销产品搭送的）随赠品 **2** something that makes you guess the real truth about sth/sb 使真相暴露的事物：*She pretended she wasn't excited but the expression on her face was a **dead*** (= obvious) ***giveaway**.* 她假装不为所动，可脸上的表情却将她的心绪暴露无遗。

■ ***adj.*** [only before noun] (*informal*) (of prices 价格) very low 低廉的

give·back /ˈɡɪvbæk/ *noun* (*NAmE*) a situation in which workers agree to accept lower wages or fewer benefits at a particular time, in return for more money or benefits later 福利归还（工人同意在某段时间接受较低工资或较少福利以待日后获得更多补偿）

given /ˈɡɪvn/ *adj., prep., noun*

■ ***adj.*** [usually before noun] **1** already arranged 已经安排好的；规定的：*They were to meet at a given time and place.* 他们要在规定的时间和地点会晤。 **2** that you have stated and are discussing; particular 指定的；所述的；特定的：*We can find out how much money is spent on food in any given period.* 我们可以查明在特定时间内花在食物上的钱有多少。

IDM **be given to sth/to doing sth** (*formal*) to do sth often or regularly 经常做；习惯于：*He's given to going for long walks on his own.* 他有独自长距离步行的习惯。

■ ***prep.*** when you consider sth 考虑到；鉴于：*Given his age* (= considering how old he is), *he's remarkably active.* 考虑到他的年龄，他已是相当活跃的了。◊ *Given her interest in children, teaching seems the right job for her.* 考虑到她喜欢孩子，教书看来是很适合她的工作。 ▸ **given that** *conj.* : *It was surprising the government was re-elected, given that they had raised taxes so much.* 令人惊奇的是，政府把税收提高这么多仍再次当选了。

■ ***noun*** something that is accepted as true, for example when you are discussing sth, or planning sth 认定的事实

ˈgiven name *noun* (*especially NAmE*) = FIRST NAME

giver /ˈɡɪvə(r)/ *noun* (often in compounds 常构成复合词) a person or an organization that gives 给予者；赠与者；捐助机构：*They are very generous givers to charity.* 他们是慈善事业的慷慨捐助者。

gizmo (*also* **gismo**) /ˈɡɪzməʊ; *NAmE* -moʊ/ *noun* (*informal*) (*pl.* **-os**) a general word for a small piece of equipment, often one that does sth in a new and clever way 小玩意儿；小装置

giz·zard /ˈɡɪzəd; *NAmE* -zərd/ *noun* the part of a bird's stomach in which food is broken up into smaller pieces before being DIGESTED（鸟的）砂囊，胗，肫

glacé /ˈɡlæseɪ; *NAmE* ɡlæˈseɪ/ *adj.* [only before noun] (of fruit 水果) preserved in sugar 糖渍的；蜜饯的：*glacé fruits* 蜜饯果 ◊ *glacé cherries* 蜜饯樱桃

gla·cial /ˈɡleɪʃl; ˈɡleɪsiəl/ *adj.* **1** [usually before noun] (*geology* 地) connected with the Ice Age 冰河时代的；冰河期的；冰川期的：*the glacial period* (= the time when much of the northern half of the world was covered by ice) 冰期 **2** (*specialist*) caused or made by glaciers; connected with glaciers 冰川造成的；由冰河形成的；冰河的；冰川的：*a glacial landscape* 由冰河形成的自然景观 ◊ *glacial deposits/erosion* 冰川沉积；冰蚀作用 **3** (*formal*) very cold; like ice 冰冷的；冰一般的 **SYN** **icy**：*glacial winds/temperatures* 刺骨的寒风；极低的温度 **4** (*formal*) (of people 人) cold and unfriendly; not showing feelings 冷若冰霜的；冷冰冰的 **SYN** **icy**：*Her expression was glacial.* 她表情冷淡。◊ *Relations between the two countries had always been glacial.* 这两国间关系一直不好。

gla·ci·ation /ˌɡleɪsiˈeɪʃn/ *noun* [U] (*geology* 地) the process or result of land being covered by glaciers 冰川作用

gla·cier /ˈɡlæsiə(r); *NAmE* ˈɡleɪʃər/ *noun* a large mass of ice, formed by snow on mountains, that moves very slowly down a valley 冰川 ➲ VISUAL VOCAB PAGE V5

glad 🔑 /ɡlæd/ *adj.* **1** 🔑 [not before noun] pleased; happy 高兴；愉快：*'I passed the test!' 'I'm so glad (for you).'* "我考试合格了！" "我真（为你）高兴。" ◊ *She was glad when the meeting was over.* 会议结束时她很高兴。◊ **~ about sth** *'He doesn't need the pills any more.' 'I'm glad about that.'* "他不再需要服那些药片了。" "这真让我高兴。" ◊ **~ to know, hear, see...** *I'm glad to hear you're feeling better.* 听说你感觉好些了，我很高兴。◊ **~ (that)...** *I'm glad (that) you're feeling better.* 你感觉好些了我很高兴。◊ *He was glad he'd come.* 他很高兴他来了。 ◊ *I'm so glad (that) you're safe!* 你安然无恙我真高兴！◊ **~ to do sth** *I'm glad to meet you. I've heard a lot about you.* 很高兴见到你。久闻大名。◊ *I've never been so glad to see anyone in my life!* 我一生中见到谁都未如此高兴过！ **2** grateful for sth 感激；感谢： **~ of sth** *She was very glad of her warm coat in the biting wind.* 在刺骨的寒风中她有温暖的大衣真是谢天谢地。◊ *I'd be glad of your help.* 你若能帮助我，我会非常感激。◊ **~ if...** *I'd be glad if you could help me.* 你若能帮助我，我会非常感激。 ➲ SYNONYMS ON NEXT PAGE **3 ~ to do sth** very willing to do sth 乐意；情愿；愿意：*I'd be glad to lend you the money.* 我很乐意借给你钱。◊ *If you'd like me to help you, I'd **be only too glad to**.* 你若要我帮忙，我非常愿意效劳。 **4** [only before noun] (*old-fashioned*) bringing joy; full of joy 令人愉快的；使人高兴的；充满欢乐的：***glad news/tidings*** 令人愉快的消息；喜讯

IDM **I'm glad to say (that...)** (*informal*) used when you are commenting on a situation and saying that you are happy about it（表示对某种情况感到高兴）我很高兴地说：*Most teachers, I'm glad to say, take their jobs very seriously.* 我很高兴地说，多数老师工作都很认真。

glad·den /ˈɡlædn/ *verb* (*old-fashioned*) to make sb feel pleased or happy 使高兴；使愉快；使喜悦： **~ sth** *The sight of the flowers **gladdened her heart**.* 看到这些花她心花怒放。◊ **it gladdens sb to do sth** *It gladdened him to see them all enjoying themselves.* 见他们都玩得很开心，他非常高兴。

glade /ɡleɪd/ *noun* (*literary*) a small open area of grass in a wood or a forest 林中空地 ➲ VISUAL VOCAB PAGE V5

ˈglad-hand *verb* [I, T] ~ (sb) (especially of a politician 尤指政客) to say hello to sb in a friendly way, especially when this is not sincere 热情招呼（尤指并非出自真心） ▸ **ˈglad-handing** *noun* [U]

gladi·ator /ˈɡlædieɪtə(r)/ *noun* (in ancient Rome) a man trained to fight other men or animals in order to entertain the public（古罗马）角斗士 ▸ **gladia·tor·ial** /ˌɡlædiəˈtɔːriəl/ *adj.* : *gladiatorial combat* 角斗士的格斗

gladi·olus /ˌɡlædiˈəʊləs; *NAmE* -ˈoʊləs/ *noun* (*pl.* **gladi·oli** /-laɪ/) a tall garden plant with long thin leaves and brightly coloured flowers growing up the STEM 唐菖蒲；剑兰；菖兰

glad·ly /ˈɡlædli/ *adv.* **1** willingly 乐意地；情愿地：*I would gladly pay extra for a good seat.* 我很愿意额外付费坐好座位。 **2** happily; with thanks 高兴地；欣然地；感激地：*When I offered her my seat, she accepted it gladly.* 我把座位让给她时，她欣然接受了。IDM SEE SUFFER

glad·ness /ˈɡlædnəs/ *noun* [U] (*literary*) joy; happiness 高兴；愉快；快乐

ˈ**glad rags** *noun* [pl.] (*old-fashioned, informal*) a person's best clothes, worn on a special occasion（某人在特殊场合穿的）最考究的衣服，礼服，盛装

G

glam·or·ize (*BrE also* **-ise**) /ˈɡlæməraɪz/ *verb* **~ sth** (*usually disapproving*) to make sth bad appear attractive or exciting 使有魅力；使有刺激性；美化：*Television tends to glamorize violence.* 电视节目往往渲染暴力。

glam·or·ous /ˈɡlæmərəs/ (*also informal* **glam**) *adj.* especially attractive and exciting, and different from ordinary things or people 特别富有魅力的；富于刺激的；独特的：*glamorous movie stars* 富有魅力的影星 ◇ *a glamorous job* 令人向往的工作 OPP **unglamorous** ▸ **glam·or·ous·ly** *adv.*：*glamorously dressed* 衣着华丽

glam·our (*NAmE also* **glamor**) /ˈɡlæmə(r)/ *noun* [U] **1** the attractive and exciting quality that makes a person, a job or a place seem special, often because of wealth or status 吸引力，魅力，诱惑力（多因财富或地位所致）：*hopeful young actors and actresses dazzled by the glamour of Hollywood* 为好莱坞的魅力神魂颠倒，怀抱希望的年轻演员 ◇ *Now that she's a flight attendant, foreign travel has lost its glamour for her.* 她现在是空中乘务员了，去国外旅行对她已失去吸引力。 **2** physical beauty that also suggests wealth or success（暗示财富或成功的）迷人的美，魅力：*Ireland's top fashion model added a touch of glamour to the event.* 爱尔兰的顶级时装模特为活动增添了一丝魅力。

ˈ**glamour model** *noun* (*especially BrE*) a person, especially a woman, who is photographed wearing very few or no clothes in order to sexually excite the person looking at the photographs （衣着暴露的）魅力模特；性感女模

glamp·ing /ˈɡlæmpɪŋ/ *noun* [U] a type of camping, using tents and other kinds of accommodation, facilities, etc. that are more comfortable and expensive than those usually used for camping 豪华野营；豪华露营 ORIGIN From **glamour** and **camping**. 源自 glamour 和 camping。

glam rock /ˌɡlæm ˈrɒk; *NAmE* ˈrɑːk/ *noun* [U] a style of music popular in the 1970s, in which male singers wore unusual clothes and make-up 魅惑摇滚（流行于 20 世纪 70 年代，男歌手穿着打扮怪异）

glance /ɡlɑːns; *NAmE* ɡlæns/ *verb, noun*

■ ***verb*** **1** [I] **+ adv./prep.** to look quickly at sth/sb 瞥一眼；匆匆一看；扫视：*She glanced at her watch.* 她匆匆看了看表。◇ *He glanced around the room.* 他环视了一下房间。◇ *I glanced up quickly to see who had come in.* 我迅速抬头瞥了一眼看是谁进来了。 **2** [I] **~ at/down/over/through sth** to read sth quickly and not thoroughly 浏览；粗略地看 SYN **scan**：*I only had time to glance at the newspapers.* 我只来得及浏览了一下报纸。◇ *He glanced briefly down the list of names.* 他草草看了一遍名单。◇ *She glanced through the report.* 她浏览了一下报告。

PHR V ˈ**glance on/off sth** (of light 光) to flash on a surface or be reflected off it 在…上闪烁（或闪耀）；从…中反射 ˌ**glance ˈoff** (**sth**) to hit sth at an angle and move off it in a different direction 斜向击中（某物）后改变方向：*The ball glanced off the post into the net.* 球击中门柱后弹入网内。

■ ***noun*** **~ (at sb/sth)** a quick look 匆匆一看；一瞥；扫视：*to* ***take/have a glance*** *at the newspaper headlines* 匆匆看一眼报纸的大标题 ◇ *a* ***cursory/brief/casual/furtive glance*** 草草的 / 短暂的 / 不经意的 / 偷偷的一瞥 ◇ *The sisters* ***exchanged glances*** (= looked at each other). 姐妹俩相互对视了一下。◇ *She shot him a* ***sideways glance***. 她从眼角瞥

▼ SYNONYMS 同义词辨析

glad

happy • pleased • delighted • proud • relieved • thrilled

These words all describe people feeling happy about sth that has happened or is going to happen. 以上各词均形容人对已经发生或将要发生的事感到高兴、愉快。

glad [not usually before noun] happy about sth or grateful for it 指高兴、愉快、感激：*He was glad he'd come.* 他很高兴他来了。◇ *She was glad when the meeting was over.* 会议结束时她很高兴。

happy pleased about sth nice that you have to do or sth that has happened to sb 指对必须做的或发生于某人身上的事感到高兴、快乐：*We are happy to announce the engagement of our daughter.* 我们高兴地宣布，我们的女儿订婚了。

pleased [not before noun] happy about sth that has happened or sth that you have to do 指对已经发生或必须做的事感到高兴、愉快、满意：*She was very pleased with her exam results.* 她对考试成绩非常满意。◇ *You're coming? I'm so pleased.* 你要来呀？我太高兴了。

GLAD, HAPPY OR PLEASED? 用 glad、happy 还是 pleased?

Feeling **pleased** can suggest that you have judged sb/sth and approve of them. Feeling **glad** can be more about feeling grateful for sth. You cannot be 'glad with sb'. * pleased 意味着对人或事作出评判并表示赞同，glad 多指对所发生的事情心怀感激，不能说 glad with sb：~~*The boss should be glad with you.*~~ **Happy** can mean glad, pleased or satisfied. * happy 表示高兴、愉快、满意。

delighted very pleased about sth; very happy to do sth; showing your delight 指高兴的、乐意的、愉快的：*I'm delighted at your news.* 听到你的消息我非常高兴。NOTE **Delighted** is often used to accept an invitation. * delighted 常用于接受邀请：*'Can you stay for dinner?' 'I'd be delighted (to).'* "留下来吃晚饭好吗？""我非常乐意。"

proud pleased and satisfied about sth that you own or have done, or are connected with 指骄傲的、自豪的、得意的、满足的：*proud parents* 自豪的父母 ◇ *He was* ***proud of*** *himself for not giving up.* 他为自己没有放弃而自豪。

relieved feeling happy because sth unpleasant has stopped or has not happened; showing this 指感到宽慰的、放心的、显得开心的：*You'll be relieved to know your jobs are safe.* 现在你们知道工作保住了，可以放心了。

thrilled [not before noun] (*rather informal*) extremely pleased and excited about sth 指非常兴奋、极为激动：*I was thrilled to be invited.* 我获得邀请，感到非常兴奋。

DELIGHTED OR THRILLED? 用 delighted 还是 thrilled?

Thrilled may express a stronger feeling than **delighted**, but **delighted** can be made stronger with *absolutely*, *more than* or *only too*. **Thrilled** can be made negative and ironic with *not exactly* or *less than*. * thrilled 比 delighted 的情感更强烈，但 delighted 可与 absolutely、more than 或 only too 连用以增强语气。thrilled 与 not exactly 或 less than 连用可变为否定或含讽刺意味：*She was* ***not exactly thrilled*** *at the prospect of looking after her niece.* 想到要照料她的侄女，她就高兴不起来了。

PATTERNS

- glad/happy/pleased/delighted/relieved/thrilled **about** sth
- pleased/delighted/relieved/thrilled **at** sth
- glad/happy/pleased/delighted/thrilled **for** sb
- glad/happy/pleased/delighted/proud/relieved/thrilled **that…/to see/hear/find/know…**
- **very** glad/happy/pleased/proud/relieved
- **absolutely** delighted/thrilled

了他一眼。◇ *He walked away **without a backward glance**.* 他头也不回地扬长而去。◇ *She **stole a glance** (= looked secretly) at her watch.* 她偷偷看了看表。➲ SYNONYMS AT LOOK

IDM **at a (single) 'glance** immediately; with only a quick look 立刻；一眼；（只）看一眼：*He could tell at a glance what was wrong.* 他一眼就看出了问题所在。**at first 'glance** when you first look at or think about sth, often rather quickly 乍一看；乍看之下：*At first glance the problem seemed easy.* 乍一看问题似乎很简单。

glan·cing /ˈɡlɑːnsɪŋ; *NAmE* ˈɡlænsɪŋ/ *adj.* [only before noun] hitting sth/sb at an angle, not with full force 斜擦而过的；击偏的：*to strike somebody a **glancing blow*** 以斜击拳击中某人

gland /ɡlænd/ *noun* an organ in a person's or an animal's body that produces a substance for the body to use. There are many different glands in the body. 腺：*a snake's poison glands* 蛇的毒腺 ◇ *Her glands are swollen.* 她的腺体肿胀。➲ SEE ALSO PITUITARY ▶ **glan·du·lar** /ˈɡlændjʊlə(r); *NAmE* -dʒə-/ *adj.* [usually before noun]: *glandular tissue* 腺体组织

ˌglandular 'fever *noun* [U] (*BrE*) = MONONUCLEOSIS

glans /ɡlænz/ (*pl.* **glan·des** /ˈɡlændiːz/) *noun* (*anatomy* 解) the round part at the end of a man's PENIS or a woman's CLITORIS 阴茎头；龟头；阴蒂头

glare /ɡleə(r); *NAmE* ɡler/ *verb, noun*

■ *verb* **1** [I] ~ (**at sb/sth**) to look at sb/sth in an angry way 怒目而视 SYN **glower**: *He didn't shout, he just glared at me silently.* 他没有喊叫，只是默默地怒视着我。**2** [I] to shine with a very bright unpleasant light 发出刺眼的光

■ *noun* **1** [U, sing.] a very bright, unpleasant light 刺眼的光：*the glare of the sun* 炫目的阳光 ◇ *The rabbit was caught in the glare of the car's headlights.* 兔子被耀眼的汽车前灯照射着。◇ *These sunglasses are designed to reduce glare.* 这些太阳镜是为减少刺眼的强光而设计的。◇ (*figurative*) *The divorce was conducted **in the full glare of publicity*** (= with continuous attention from newspapers and television). 这桩离婚案是在媒体的密切关注下进行的。**2** [C] a long, angry look（长久的）怒视，瞪眼：*to give sb a hostile glare* 含敌意地瞪着某人 ➲ SYNONYMS AT LOOK, STARE

glar·ing /ˈɡleərɪŋ; *NAmE* ˈɡler-/ *adj.* **1** [usually before noun] (of sth bad 负面的事物) very easily seen 显眼的；明显的；易见的 SYN **blatant**: *a **glaring error/omission/inconsistency/injustice*** 明显的错误 / 疏漏 / 不一致 / 不公正 ◇ *the most **glaring example** of this problem* 此问题最明显的事例 **2** (of a light 光) very bright and unpleasant 刺眼的；炫目的 **3** angry; aggressive 生气的；愤怒的；富于攻击性的：*glaring eyes* 愤怒的目光 ▶ **glar·ing·ly** *adv.*: *glaringly obvious* 显而易见的

glass /ɡlɑːs; *NAmE* ɡlæs/ *noun, verb*

■ *noun*

• TRANSPARENT SUBSTANCE 透明物质 **1** [U] a hard, usually transparent, substance used, for example, for making windows and bottles 玻璃：*a **sheet/pane of glass*** 一片玻璃；一块窗玻璃 ◇ ***frosted/toughened glass*** 毛 / 钢化玻璃 ◇ *a glass bottle/dish/roof* 玻璃瓶 / 盘 / 屋顶 ◇ *I cut myself on a piece of **broken glass**.* 我被一块碎玻璃划伤了。◇ *The vegetables are grown **under glass*** (= in a GREENHOUSE). 这些蔬菜是在玻璃温室种植的。➲ SEE ALSO CUT GLASS, PLATE GLASS, STAINED GLASS, GLAZIER

• FOR DRINKING 饮用 **2** [C] (often in compounds 常构成复合词) a container made of glass, used for drinking out of 玻璃杯；酒杯：*a sherry glass* 雪利酒杯 ◇ *a wine glass* 葡萄酒杯 ➲ VISUAL VOCAB PAGE V23 **3** [C] the contents of a glass 一杯（的量）：*a **glass of sherry/wine/water, etc.*** 一杯雪利酒、葡萄酒、水等 ◇ *He drank three whole glasses.* 他喝了满满三杯。

• GLASS OBJECTS 玻璃制品 **4** [U] objects made of glass 玻璃制品；玻璃器皿：*We keep all our glass and china in this cupboard.* 我们把所有玻璃器皿和瓷器都放在这个橱里。◇ *She has a fine collection of Bohemian glass.* 她收藏了一批做工精细的波希米亚玻璃制品。**5** [sing.] a protecting cover made of glass on a watch, picture or photograph frame, FIRE ALARM, etc. 玻璃保护面；玻璃（镜）框；（火灾警报器的）玻璃罩：*In case of emergency, break the glass and press the button.* 如遇紧急情况，击碎玻璃罩按下按钮。

• FOR EYES 眼镜 **6** **glasses** (*NAmE also* **eye·glasses**) (*also old-fashioned or formal* **spec·tacles**, *informal* **specs** *especially in BrE*) [pl.] two LENSES in a frame that rests on the nose and ears. People wear glasses in order to be able to see better or to protect their eyes from bright light. 眼镜：***a pair of glasses*** 一副眼镜 ◇ *dark glasses* 墨镜 ◇ ***I wear glasses for driving.*** 我开车时戴眼镜。➲ SEE ALSO FIELD GLASSES, MAGNIFYING GLASS, SUNGLASSES

• MIRROR 镜子 **7** [C, usually sing.] (*old-fashioned*) a mirror 镜子 ➲ SEE ALSO LOOKING GLASS

• BAROMETER 气压表 **8 the glass** [sing.] a BAROMETER 气压表；晴雨表 IDM SEE PEOPLE *n.*, RAISE *v.*

■ *verb* ~ **sb** (*BrE, informal*) to hit sb in the face with a glass 用玻璃杯击（某人）的脸部

PHR V **ˌglass sth 'in/'over** [usually passive] to cover sth with a roof or wall made of glass 给…装玻璃；用玻璃把…盖（或罩、围）住：*a glassed-in pool* 装有玻璃屋顶的游泳池 ➲ COMPARE GLAZE *v.* (2)

'glass-blowing *noun* [U] the art or activity of blowing hot glass into shapes using a special tube 玻璃吹制（术）；吹玻璃 ▶ **'glass-blower** *noun*

ˌglass 'ceiling *noun* [usually sing.] the way in which unfair attitudes can stop women, or other groups, from getting the best jobs in a company, etc. although there are no official rules to prevent them from getting these jobs 玻璃天花板（女性或某些群体的人在职场升迁上遇到的无形限制或障碍）

ˌglass 'fibre (*BrE*) *noun* [U] = FIBREGLASS

glass·ful /ˈɡlɑːsfʊl; *NAmE* ˈɡlæs-/ *noun* the amount that a drinking glass will hold 一玻璃杯（的量）

glass·house /ˈɡlɑːshaʊs; *NAmE* ˈɡlæs-/ *noun* (*BrE*) **1** a building with glass sides and a glass roof, for growing plants in; a type of large GREENHOUSE 玻璃暖房；温室 ➲ VISUAL VOCAB PAGE V15 **2** (*slang*) a military prison 军事监狱

glass·ware /ˈɡlɑːsweə(r); *NAmE* ˈɡlæswer/ *noun* [U] objects made of glass 玻璃器皿；玻璃制品；料器

glassy /ˈɡlɑːsi; *NAmE* ˈɡlæsi/ *adj.* (**glass·ier**, **glassi·est**) **1** like glass; smooth and shiny 像玻璃一样的；光滑透亮的：*a glassy lake* 平静清澈的湖水 ◇ *a glassy material* 玻璃状材料 **2** showing no feeling or emotion 无表情的；木然的；呆滞的：*glassy eyes* 目光呆滞的眼睛 ◇ ***a glassy look/stare*** 呆滞的神色 / 盯视 ◇ *He looked flushed and **glassy-eyed**.* 他看上去满脸通红，目光呆滞。

Glas·we·gian /ɡlæzˈwiːdʒən/ *noun* a person from Glasgow in Scotland（苏格兰的）格拉斯哥人 ▶ **Glas·we·gian** *adj.*

glau·coma /ɡlɔːˈkəʊmə; *NAmE* ɡlaʊˈkoʊmə; ɡlɔː-/ *noun* [U] an eye disease that causes gradual loss of sight 青光眼

glaze /ɡleɪz/ *verb, noun*

■ *verb* **1** [I] ~ (**over**) if a person's eyes **glaze** or **glaze over**, the person begins to look bored or tired（眼睛）变呆滞，发呆：*A lot of people's eyes glaze over if you say you are a feminist.* 如果你说你是女权主义者，好多人都会愣住。◇ *'I'm feeling rather tired,' he said, his eyes glazing.* "我有点累了。"他目光呆滞地说。**2** [T] ~ **sth** to fit sheets of glass into sth 给…安装玻璃：*to glaze a window/house* 给窗户 / 房子安装玻璃 ◇ *a glazed door* 镶着玻璃的门 ➲ COMPARE GLASS *v.* ➲ SEE ALSO DOUBLE GLAZING **3** [T] ~ **sth** (**with sth**) to cover sth with a glaze to give it a shiny surface 给…上釉；使光滑；使光亮：*Glaze the pie with beaten egg.* 在饼的表面刷上打匀的蛋液使它有光泽。◇ *glazed tiles* 釉面砖 ◇ (*NAmE*) *a glazed doughnut* 挂糖浆的炸面圈

■ *noun* [C, U] **1** a thin clear liquid put on CLAY objects such as cups and plates before they are finished, to give them a hard shiny surface 釉；釉料 **2** a thin liquid, made of egg, milk or sugar, for example, that is put on cake, bread, etc. to make it look shiny（浇在糕点上增加光泽的）蛋浆，奶浆，糖浆

glazed /gleɪzd/ *adj.* (especially of the eyes 尤指眼睛) showing no feeling or emotion; dull 木然的；呆滞的：*eyes glazed with boredom* 厌倦无神的眼睛

glaz·ier /ˈgleɪziə(r); *NAmE* -ʒər/ *noun* a person whose job is to fit glass into the frames of windows, etc. 镶玻璃的工人

gleam /gliːm/ *verb, noun*

■ *verb* **1** [I] to shine with a pale clear light 发微光；隐约闪光；闪烁：*The moonlight gleamed on the water.* 月光照在水面上泛起粼粼波光。◇ *Her eyes gleamed in the dark.* 她的眼睛在黑暗中闪着亮光。➲ SYNONYMS AT SHINE **2** [I] to look very clean or bright 显得光洁明亮：~ **(with sth)** *The house was gleaming with fresh white paint.* 房子刚刷过白漆，显得光洁明亮。◇ **+ adj.** *Her teeth gleamed white against the tanned skin of her face.* 她的牙齿在褐色面孔映衬下显得洁白明亮。**3** [I] if a person's eyes **gleam** with a particular emotion, or an emotion **gleams** in a person's eyes, the person shows that emotion（眼睛）表露出，流露出；（在眼中）闪现：~ **(with sth)** *His eyes gleamed with amusement.* 他眼睛里流露出愉悦的神情。◇ ~ **(in sth)** *Amusement gleamed in his eyes.* 他眼睛里流露出愉悦的神情。

■ *noun* [usually sing.] **1** a pale clear light, often reflected from sth 微光（常指反光）：*the gleam of moonlight on the water* 水面上荡漾的月光 ◇ *A few gleams of sunshine lit up the gloomy afternoon.* 几缕阳光使阴暗的下午亮了起来。◇ *I saw the gleam of the knife as it flashed through the air.* 我看见了刀在空中划过时的闪光。**2** a small amount of sth 少量；一丝；一线：*a faint gleam of hope* 微弱的一线希望 ◇ *a serious book with an occasional gleam of humour* 偶有一丝幽默的严肃的书 **3** an expression of a particular feeling or emotion that shows in sb's eyes（感情在眼中的）表露，闪现 SYN **glint**：*a gleam of triumph in her eyes* 她眼里闪烁着胜利的光芒 ◇ *a mischievous gleam in his eye* 他淘气的眼神 ◇ *The gleam in his eye made her uncomfortable* (= as if he was planning sth secret or unpleasant). 他闪烁的眼神令她感到不舒服。

gleam·ing /ˈgliːmɪŋ/ *adj.* shining brightly 闪耀的；明亮的：*gleaming white teeth* 皓齿

glean /gliːn/ *verb* ~ **sth (from sb/sth)** to obtain information, knowledge, etc., sometimes with difficulty and often from various different places 费力地收集，四处搜集（信息、知识等）：*These figures have been gleaned from a number of studies.* 这些数据是通过多次研究收集得来的。

glean·ings /ˈgliːnɪŋz/ *noun* [pl.] information, knowledge, etc., that you obtain from various different places, often with difficulty（费力从多处）收集的信息（或知识等）

glebe /gliːb/ *noun* (*old use*) **1** [C] a piece of land that provided an income for a priest（旧时）作为牧师收入来源的土地 **2** [U] land; fields 土地；田地

glee /gliː/ *noun* [U] a feeling of happiness, usually because sth good has happened to you, or sth bad has happened to sb else 欢喜；高兴；幸灾乐祸 SYN **delight**：*He rubbed his hands* **in glee** *as he thought of all the money he would make.* 他想到自己将赚到那么多钱就高兴得直搓手。◇ *She couldn't disguise her glee at their embarrassment.* 看到他们难堪的样子她不禁喜形于色。

ˈglee club *noun* (*NAmE*) a group of people, usually students, who sing and perform short songs together 歌咏团，合唱团（成员通常为学生）

glee·ful /ˈgliːfl/ *adj.* happy because of sth good you have done or sth bad that has happened to sb else 欢喜的；高兴的；幸灾乐祸的：*a gleeful laugh* 欢快的笑声 ▶**glee·ful·ly** /-fəli/ *adv.*

glen /glen/ *noun* a deep narrow valley, especially in Scotland or Ireland（尤指苏格兰或爱尔兰的）峡谷

glib /glɪb/ *adj.* (*disapproving*) (of speakers and speech 演讲者或演讲) using words that are clever, but are not sincere, and do not show much thought 油腔滑调的；不诚恳的；未经思考的；肤浅的：*a glib salesman* 油嘴滑舌的推销员 ◇ *glib answers* 未经思考的回答 ▶**glib·ly** *adv.*

glide /glaɪd/ *verb, noun*

■ *verb* **1** [I] (+ **adv./prep.**) to move smoothly and quietly, especially as though it takes no effort 滑行；滑动；掠过：*Swans went gliding past.* 天鹅滑行而过。◇ *The skaters were gliding over the ice.* 滑冰者在冰上滑行。**2** [I] (+ **adv./prep.**) (of birds or aircraft 鸟或飞机) to fly using air currents, without the birds moving their wings or the aircraft using the engine 滑翔：*An eagle was gliding high overhead.* 一只鹰在头顶上空翱翔。◇ *The plane managed to glide down to the runway.* 飞机终于成功地滑翔降落在跑道上。

■ *noun* **1** [sing.] a continuous smooth movement 滑行；滑动；滑翔：*the graceful glide of a skater* 滑冰者优美的滑行动作 **2** [C] (*phonetics* 语音) a speech sound made while moving the tongue from one position to another 滑音 ➲ COMPARE DIPHTHONG

glider /ˈglaɪdə(r)/ *noun* a light aircraft that flies without an engine 滑翔机 ➲ VISUAL VOCAB PAGE V58

glid·ing /ˈglaɪdɪŋ/ *noun* [U] the sport of flying in a glider 滑翔运动

glim·mer /ˈglɪmə(r)/ *noun, verb*

■ *noun* **1** a faint unsteady light 微弱的闪光；闪烁的微光：*We could see a glimmer of light on the far shore.* 我们可以看到远处岸上微微闪烁的灯光。**2** (*also* **glim·mer·ing**) a small sign of sth 微弱的迹象；一丝；一线：*a glimmer of hope* 一线希望 ◇ *I caught the* **glimmer of a smile** *in his eyes.* 我看到他眼里闪现出一丝笑意。◇ *the glimmering of an idea* 初露端倪的想法

■ *verb* [I] to shine with a faint unsteady light 隐约地闪烁；发出微弱的闪光：*The candles glimmered in the corner.* 烛光在角落里忽明忽暗地闪烁。◇ (*figurative*) *Amusement glimmered in his eyes.* 他眼里隐约露出愉悦的神情。

glimpse /glɪmps/ *noun, verb*

■ *noun* [usually sing.] **1** ~ **(of sb/sth)** | ~ **(at sb/sth)** a look at sb/sth for a very short time, when you do not see the person or thing completely 一瞥；一看：*He* **caught a glimpse** *of her in the crowd.* 他一眼瞥见她在人群里。◇ *I came up on deck to get my first glimpse of the island.* 我登上甲板第一次看这岛。➲ SYNONYMS AT LOOK, SEE **2** a short experience of sth that helps you to understand it 短暂的感受（或体验、领会）：~ **(into sth)** *a fascinating glimpse into life in the ocean* 对海洋生物的一次短暂而动人心魄的感受 ◇ ~ **(of sth)** *The programme gives us a rare glimpse of a great artist at work.* 这个节目使我们难得地认识到伟大艺术家工作时的情况。

■ *verb* **1** ~ **sb/sth** to see sb/sth for a moment, but not very clearly 瞥见；看一眼 SYN **catch**, **spot**：*He'd glimpsed her through the window as he passed.* 他路过时透过窗户瞥见了她。**2** ~ **sth** to start to understand sth 开始领悟；开始认识到：*Suddenly she glimpsed the truth about her sister.* 她突然开始了解到她姐姐的真实情况。

glint /glɪnt/ *verb, noun*

■ *verb* **1** [I] (+ **adv./prep.**) to produce small bright flashes of light 闪光；闪亮：*The sea glinted in the moonlight.* 月色中海面上波光粼粼。◇ *The sun glinted on the windows.* 太阳照在窗户上闪闪发光。➲ SYNONYMS AT SHINE **2** [I] + **adv./prep.** if a person's eyes **glint** with a particular emotion, or an emotion **glints** in a person's eyes, the person shows that emotion, which is usually a strong one（眼睛）流露出（强烈情感）；（强烈情感在眼中）闪现：*Her eyes glinted angrily.* 她眼睛里闪射着愤怒的目光。◇ *Hostility glinted in his eyes.* 他眼睛里流露出敌意。

■ *noun* **1** a sudden flash of light or colour shining from a bright surface 闪光；闪亮：*the glint of the sun on the water* 太阳照在水上的闪光 ◇ *golden glints in her red hair* 她的红发上闪着的金光 ◇ *She saw a glint of silver in the grass.* 她看到草地上银光闪亮。**2** an expression in sb's eyes showing a particular emotion, often a negative one（眼睛里某种感情，常指负面感情的）闪现：*He had a* *wicked glint in his eye.* 他眼睛里闪着邪恶的神色。◇ *a glint of anger* 愤怒的目光

glis·sando /glɪˈsændəʊ; NAmE -doʊ/ *noun* (*pl.* **glis·san·dos** or **glis·sandi** /-diː/) (*from Italian*) a way of playing a series of notes so that each one slides into the next, making a smooth continuous sound 滑奏

glis·ten /ˈglɪsn/ *verb* [I] (of sth wet 湿物) to shine 闪光；闪亮：*Her eyes were glistening with tears.* 她眼里闪着晶莹的泪花。◇ *Sweat glistened on his forehead.* 他额头上的汗珠晶莹发亮。◇ **+ adj.** *The road glistened wet after the rain.* 雨后的道路润泽闪亮。 ➲ SYNONYMS AT SHINE IDM SEE GOLD *n.*

glis·ter /ˈglɪstə(r)/ *verb* [I] (*literary*) to shine brightly with little flashes of light, like a diamond 闪耀；闪亮；熠熠生辉 SYN **glitter**

glitch /glɪtʃ/ *noun, verb* (*informal*)
■ ***noun*** a small problem or fault that stops sth working successfully 小故障；小毛病；小差错
■ ***verb*** [I] (of a machine or system) to suffer a sudden fault and fail to work correctly （机器或系统）出故障，出毛病

glit·ter /ˈglɪtə(r)/ *verb, noun*
■ ***verb*** **1** [I] to shine brightly with little flashes of light, like a diamond 闪亮；闪耀；光彩夺目 SYN **sparkle**: *The ceiling of the cathedral glittered with gold.* 大教堂的天花板金光闪闪。◇ *The water glittered in the sunlight.* 水面在阳光下闪闪发光。 ➲ SYNONYMS AT SHINE **2** [I] **~ (with sth)** (of the eyes 眼睛) to shine brightly with a particular emotion, usually a strong one 闪现（某种强烈情感）：*His eyes glittered with greed.* 他眼睛里闪现出贪婪的神色。 IDM SEE GOLD *n.*
■ ***noun*** **1** [U] bright light consisting of many little flashes 灿烂的光辉；闪烁；闪耀：*the glitter of diamonds* 钻石的光彩 **2** [sing.] a bright expression in sb's eyes showing a particular emotion（眼睛里某种感情的）闪现，流露 SYN **glint**: *There was a triumphant glitter in his eyes.* 他眼睛里闪烁着胜利的光辉。 **3** [U] the attractive, exciting qualities that sb/sth, especially a rich and famous person or place, seems to have 吸引力；魅力；诱惑力 SYN **glamour**: *the superficial glitter of show business* 演艺业表面上的光彩迷人 **4** [U] very small shiny pieces of thin metal or paper that are stuck to things as a decoration（装饰用的）小发光物：*gold/silver glitter* 金色的 / 银色的闪光装饰物

glit·ter·ati /ˌglɪtəˈrɑːti/ *noun* [pl.] (used in newspapers) fashionable, rich and famous people（报章用语）时髦人物，风云人物，知名人士

glit·ter·ing /ˈglɪtərɪŋ/ *adj.* [usually before noun] **1** very impressive and successful 辉煌的；成功的：*He has a glittering career ahead of him.* 他前程似锦。 **2** very impressive and involving rich and successful people 盛大的；华丽的；众星云集的：*a* ***glittering occasion/ceremony*** 盛会；盛典 ◇ *a glittering array of stars* 众星云集的盛大场面 **3** shining brightly with many small flashes of light 灿烂夺目的；闪闪发光的 SYN **sparkling**: *glittering jewels* 璀璨的宝石

glit·tery /ˈglɪtəri/ *adj.* shining brightly with many little flashes of light 灿烂夺目的；闪闪发光的；华丽的：*a glittery suit* 一套华丽的服装

glitz /glɪts/ *noun* [U] (*sometimes disapproving*) the quality of appearing very attractive, exciting and impressive, in a way that is not always genuine 耀眼；华丽；浮华：*the glitz and glamour of the music scene* 表面光辉灿烂的乐坛 ▶ **glitzy** *adj.*：*a glitzy, Hollywood-style occasion* 好莱坞式的盛大场面

the gloam·ing /ˈgləʊmɪŋ; NAmE ˈgloʊ-/ *noun* [sing.] (*ScotE* or *literary*) the faint light after the sun sets 朦胧的暮色 SYN **twilight, dusk**

gloat /gləʊt; NAmE gloʊt/ *verb* [I] **~ (about/at/over sth)** to show that you are happy about your own success or sb else's failure, in an unpleasant way 扬扬得意；沾沾自喜；幸灾乐祸 SYN **crow**: *She was still gloating over her rival's disappointment.* 她仍在为对手的失望而幸灾乐祸。 ▶ **gloat·ing** *adj.*：*a gloating look* 扬扬得意的样子

glob /glɒb; NAmE glɑːb/ *noun* (*informal*) a small amount of a liquid or substance in a round shape 一小滴；一小团：*thick globs of paint on the floor* 地板上一滴滴黏稠的油漆

global 🔑 AW /ˈgləʊbl; NAmE ˈgloʊbl/ *adj.* [usually before noun] **1** 🔑 covering or affecting the whole world 全球的；全世界的：*global issues* 全球性问题 ◇ *The commission is calling for a global ban on whaling.* 委员会要求全球禁止捕鲸。 ◇ *the company's domestic and global markets* 这家公司在国内外的销售市场 ➲ COLLOCATIONS AT INTERNATIONAL **2** considering or including all parts of sth 整体的；全面的；总括的：*We need to take a more global approach to the problem.* 我们需要更全面地看这个问题。◇ *global searches on the database* 在数据库中的全程检索 ◇ *They sent a global email to all staff.* 他们向全体职员发了一封统一的电邮。 ▶ **glob·al·ly** AW /-bəli/ *adv.*：*We need to start thinking globally.* 我们需着手全面考虑。

glob·al·iza·tion AW (*BrE also* **-isa·tion**) /ˌgləʊbəlaɪˈzeɪʃn; NAmE ˌgloʊbələˈz-/ *noun* [U] the fact that different cultures and economic systems around the world are becoming connected and similar to each other because of the influence of large MULTINATIONAL companies and of improved communication 全球化，全世界化（世界各地的文化和经济体系日益关联） ➲ COLLOCATIONS AT INTERNATIONAL

glob·al·ize (*BrE also* **-ise**) /ˈgləʊbəlaɪz; NAmE ˈgloʊ-/ *verb* [I, T] **~ (sth)** (*economics* 经) if sth, for example a business company, **globalizes** or **is globalized**, it operates all around the world （使）全球化

ˌglobal ˈvillage *noun* [sing.] the whole world, looked at as a single community that is connected by electronic communication systems 地球村（指整个世界作为一个由电子通信系统连接的单一集体）

ˌglobal ˈwarming *noun* [U] the increase in temperature of the earth's atmosphere, that is caused by the increase of particular gases, especially CARBON DIOXIDE 全球（气候）变暖；地球大气层变暖 ➲ COLLOCATIONS AT ENVIRONMENT ➲ COMPARE CLIMATE CHANGE ➲ SEE ALSO GREENHOUSE EFFECT

globe AW /gləʊb; NAmE gloʊb/ *noun* **1** [C] an object shaped like a ball with a map of the world on its surface, usually on a stand so that it can be turned 地球仪 ➲ WORDFINDER NOTE AT MAP **2 the globe** [sing.] the world (used especially to emphasize its size) 地球，世界（尤用以强调其大）：*tourists from every corner of the globe* 来自世界各地的游客 **3** [C] a thing shaped like a ball 球体；球状物

ˌglobe ˈartichoke *noun* = ARTICHOKE (1)

globe·trot·ting /ˈgləʊbtrɒtɪŋ; NAmE ˈgloʊbtrɑːtɪŋ/ *adj.* (*informal*) travelling in many countries all over the world 环球旅行的；周游世界的：*a globetrotting journalist* 环球工作的记者 ▶ **globe·trot·ter** *noun* **globe·trot·ting** *noun* [U]

globu·lar /ˈglɒbjələ(r); NAmE ˈglɑːb-/ *adj.* shaped like a ball, GLOBE or globule; consisting of globules 球形的；球体的；小球状的；由小球组成的

glob·ule /ˈglɒbjuːl; NAmE ˈglɑːb-/ *noun* a very small drop or ball of a liquid or of a solid that has been melted（液体或熔化了的固体的）小滴，小球体：*a globule of fat* 一小滴油

glo·cal /ˈgləʊkl; NAmE ˈgloʊkl/ *adj.* having features or relating to factors that are both local and global 全球本土化的；本土和全球特色兼有的：*As a glocal enterprise, we market different products in different parts of the world.* 作为一家全球本土化企业，我们在世界不同地区营销不同产品。

gloc·al·iza·tion (*BrE also* **-isa·tion**) /ˌgləʊkəlaɪˈzeɪʃn; NAmE ˌgloʊkələˈz-/ *noun* [U] the fact of adapting products or services that are available all over the world to make them suitable for local needs 全球本土化，全球地域一体化，全球地方化（使世界各地的产品或服务适合本地需求）

glock·en·spiel /ˈglɒkənʃpiːl; *NAmE* ˈglɑːk-/ *noun* a musical instrument made of a row of metal bars of different lengths, that you hit with two small HAMMERS 钟琴 ➲ VISUAL VOCAB PAGE V37 ➲ COMPARE XYLOPHONE

glom /glɒm; *NAmE* glɑːm/ *verb* (**-mm-**) **~ sth** (*NAmE, informal*) to steal 盗窃；窃取

PHR V **ˌglom ˈonto sth** **1** to develop a strong interest in sth 对…产生强烈的兴趣： *Kids soon glom onto the latest trend.* 年轻人很快就迷上了最新的款式。 **2** to become attached or stuck to sth 粘住

gloom /gluːm/ *noun* **1** [U, sing.] a feeling of being sad and without hope 忧郁；愁闷；无望 SYN **depression**: *The gloom deepened as the election results came in.* 选举结果陆续传来，失落的情绪越来越重。 **2** [U] (*literary*) almost total DARKNESS 幽暗；黑暗；昏暗： *We watched the boats come back in the gathering gloom.* 我们注视着船只在越来越浓的暮色中返航。 IDM SEE DOOM *n.*, PILE *v.*

gloomy /ˈgluːmi/ *adj.* (**gloom·ier**, **gloomi·est**) **1** nearly dark, or badly lit in a way that makes you feel sad 黑暗的；阴暗的；幽暗的 SYN **depressing**: *a gloomy room/atmosphere* 昏暗的房间；阴沉沉的气氛 ◇ *It was a wet and gloomy day.* 那一天下着雨，阴沉沉的。 **2** sad and without hope 忧郁的；沮丧的；无望的 SYN **glum**: *a gloomy expression* 沮丧的表情 ◇ *We sat in gloomy silence.* 我们郁郁不乐地默默坐着。 **3** without much hope of success or happiness in the future 前景黯淡的；悲观的 SYN **depressing**: *a gloomy picture of the country's economic future* 该国经济前景的黯淡景象 ◇ *Suddenly, the future didn't look so gloomy after all.* 突然感到前途似乎并非如此黯淡。 ▶ **gloom·ily** /-ɪli/ *adv.*: *He stared gloomily at the phone.* 他满脸愁容地盯着电话。 **gloomi·ness** *noun* [U]

gloop /gluːp/ (*BrE*) (*NAmE* **glop** /glɒp; *NAmE* glɑːp/) *noun* [U] (*informal*) a thick wet substance that looks, tastes or feels unpleasant（难看、味道差或令人恶心的）黏稠物 ▶ **gloopy** (*BrE*) (*NAmE* **gloppy**) *adj.*

glop /glɒp; *NAmE* glɑːp/ *noun* [U] (*informal, especially NAmE*) a thick wet substance that looks, tastes or feels unpleasant（难看、味道差或令人恶心的）黏稠物

glori·fied /ˈglɔːrɪfaɪd/ *adj.* [only before noun] making sb/sth seem more important or better than they are 吹捧的；吹嘘的；美化的： *The restaurant was no more than a glorified fast-food cafe.* 这地方美其名曰餐馆，其实只不过是个快餐店而已。

glor·ify /ˈglɔːrɪfaɪ/ *verb* (**glori·fies**, **glori·fy·ing**, **glori·fied**, **glori·fied**) **1 ~ sth** (*often disapproving*) to make sth seem better or more important than it really is 吹捧；吹嘘；美化： *He denies that the movie glorifies violence.* 他否认这部影片美化暴力。 **2 ~ sb** (*formal*) to praise and worship God 颂扬，赞美，崇拜（上帝） ▶ **glori·fi·ca·tion** /ˌglɔːrɪfɪˈkeɪʃn/ *noun* [U]: *the glorification of war* 对战争的颂扬

glori·ous /ˈglɔːriəs/ *adj.* **1** (*formal*) deserving or bringing great fame and success 值得称道的；光荣的；荣耀的： *a glorious victory* 辉煌的胜利 ◇ *a glorious chapter in our country's history* 我国历史上光辉的一页 ➲ COMPARE INGLORIOUS **2** very beautiful and impressive 壮丽的；辉煌的；光辉灿烂的 SYN **splendid**: *a glorious sunset* 瑰丽的晚霞 **3** extremely enjoyable 极其令人愉快的；极为宜人的 SYN **wonderful**: *a glorious trip to Rome* 极为享受的罗马之行 **4** (of weather 天气) hot, with the sun shining 热的；阳光灿烂的；晴朗的： *They had three weeks of glorious sunshine.* 他们度过了三周阳光灿烂的日子。 ▶ **glori·ous·ly** *adv.*

glory /ˈglɔːri/ *noun, verb*

■ *noun* **1** [U] fame, praise or honour that is given to sb because they have achieved sth important 荣誉；光荣；桂冠： *Olympic glory in the 100 metres* 奥林匹克 100 米赛跑的桂冠 ◇ *I do all the work and he gets all the glory.* 活儿都是我干，荣誉都是他得。 ◇ *She wanted to enjoy her moment of glory.* 她希望尽情享受自己的光荣时刻。 ◇ *He came home a rich man, **covered in glory**.* 他发迹还乡，荣归故里。 **2** [U] praise and worship of God（对上帝的）赞颂，赞美，崇拜： *'Glory to God in the highest'* "荣耀归于至高无上的上帝" **3** [U] great beauty 壮丽；辉煌；灿烂： *The city was spread out beneath us **in all its glory**.* 这座城市绚丽多彩地展现在我们下方。 ◇ *The house has now been restored to its **former glory**.* 这栋房子又恢复了它往日的辉煌。 **4** [C] a special cause for pride, respect or pleasure 产生骄傲（或崇敬、愉快）的理由： *The temple is one of the glories of ancient Greece.* 这座神殿是古希腊的一大骄傲。 ◇ *Her long black hair is her **crowning glory*** (= most impressive feature). 她长长的黑发是她的无上荣耀。 ➲ SEE ALSO REFLECTED GLORY

■ *verb* (**glor·ies**, **glory·ing**, **glor·ied**, **glor·ied**)

PHR V **ˈglory in sth** to get great pleasure or enjoyment from sth 因某事而喜悦；为某事而欣喜 SYN **revel**: *She gloried in her new-found independence.* 她为自己刚刚获得的独立而欣喜。

ˈglory days *noun* [pl.] a time in the past which people look back on as being better than the present 往日的美好时光；昔日的辉煌

gloss /glɒs; *NAmE* glɑːs; glɔːs/ *noun, verb*

■ *noun* **1** [U, sing.] a shine on a smooth surface（平滑表面上的）光泽，光亮： *paper with a high gloss on one side* 单面上光纸 ◇ *The gel gives your hair a gloss.* 发胶使你的头发有光泽。 ◇ *You can have the photos with either a gloss or a matt finish.* 你可选择用光面或布面相纸洗这些照片。 **2** [U] (often in compounds 常构成复合词) a substance designed to make sth shiny 用以产生光泽的物质： *lip gloss* 唇彩 **3** (*also* **ˌgloss ˈpaint**) [U] paint which, when dry, has a hard shiny surface 光泽涂料；亮光漆： *two coats of gloss* 两层亮光漆 **4** [U, sing.] an attractive appearance that is only on the surface and hides what is not so attractive 虚假的外表；虚饰： *Beneath the gloss of success was a tragic private life.* 在成功的外表下面却隐藏着悲惨的私人生活。 ◇ *This scandal has taken the gloss off the occasion.* 这丑闻使这次盛会黯然失色。 **5** [C] **~ (on sth)** a way of explaining sth to make it seem more attractive or acceptable 精彩的解释（或阐述）： *The director puts a Hollywood gloss on the civil war.* 导演对内战作了一番好莱坞式的精彩阐述。 **6** [C] **~ (on sth)** a note or comment added to a piece of writing to explain a difficult word or phrase 注释；评注

■ *verb* **~ sth (as sth)** to add a note or comment to a piece of writing to explain a difficult word or idea 在…上作注释（或评注）

PHR V **ˌgloss ˈover sth** to avoid talking about sth unpleasant or embarrassing by not dealing with it in detail 掩饰；掩盖；把…搪塞过去： *to gloss over a problem* 表面上应付问题 ◇ *He glossed over any splits in the party.* 他掩饰了党内出现的任何分裂现象。

gloss·ary /ˈglɒsəri; *NAmE* ˈglɑːs-; ˈglɔːs-/ *noun* (*pl.* **-ies**) a list of technical or special words, especially those in a particular text, explaining their meanings 术语汇编；词汇表

glossy /ˈglɒsi; *NAmE* ˈglɑːsi; ˈglɔːsi/ *adj., noun*

■ *adj.* (**gloss·ier**, **glossi·est**) **1** smooth and shiny 光滑的；光彩夺目的；有光泽的： *glossy hair* 光亮的头发 ◇ *a **glossy brochure/magazine*** (= printed on shiny paper) 用亮光纸印刷的小册子 / 杂志 **2** giving an appearance of being important and expensive 浮华的；虚有其表的；虚饰的： *the glossy world of fashion* 浮华的时装界

■ *noun* (*pl.* **-ies**) (*BrE, informal*) an expensive magazine printed on glossy paper, with a lot of colour photographs, etc. 用亮光纸印刷的杂志

glot·tal /ˈglɒtl; *NAmE* ˈglɑːtl/ *noun* (*phonetics* 语音) a speech sound produced by the glottis 声门音；喉音 ▶ **glot·tal** *adj.*

ˌglottal ˈstop *noun* (*phonetics* 语音) a speech sound made by closing and opening the glottis, which in English sometimes takes the place of a /t/, for example in *butter* 喉塞音；声门闭塞音

glot·tis /ˈglɒtɪs; *NAmE* ˈglɑːt-/ *noun* (*anatomy* 解) the part of the throat that contains the VOCAL CORDS and the narrow opening between them 声门

glove /glʌv/ *noun* a covering for the hand, made of wool, leather, etc. with separate parts for each finger and the thumb（分手指的）手套：*a pair of gloves* 一副手套 ◇ ***rubber gloves*** 胶皮手套 ◇ *gardening gloves* 园艺用手套 ➲ VISUAL VOCAB PAGES V21, V48, V52, V70 ➲ COMPARE MITTEN ➲ SEE ALSO BOXING, OVEN GLOVE
IDM **the gloves are off** used to say that sb is ready for a fight or an argument 准备动手打架；做好战斗（或辩论）准备 ➲ MORE AT FIT *v.*, HAND *n.*, IRON *adj.*, KID *n.*

'glove compartment (*also* **'glove box**) *noun* a small space or shelf facing the front seats of a car, used for keeping small things in（汽车前排座位前放小物件的）杂物箱 ➲ VISUAL VOCAB PAGE V56

gloved /glʌvd/ *adj.* [usually before noun] (of a hand 手) wearing a glove 戴着手套的

'glove puppet (*BrE*) (*NAmE* **'hand puppet**) *noun* a type of PUPPET that you put over your hand and move using your fingers 手偶（套在手上用手指操纵）➲ VISUAL VOCAB PAGE V41

glow /gləʊ; *NAmE* gloʊ/ *verb, noun*
■ *verb* **1** [I] (especially of sth hot or warm 尤指热或微温的物体) to produce a dull, steady light 发出微弱而稳定的光；发出暗淡的光：*The embers still glowed in the hearth.* 余烬仍在炉膛里发出暗淡的光。◇ *The strap has a fluorescent coating that* ***glows in the dark.*** 皮带面上有一层荧光在黑暗中微微发光。◇ **+ adj.** *A cigarette end glowed red in the darkness.* 一个烟头在黑暗中发着红光。➲ SYNONYMS AT SHINE **2** [I] (of a person's body or face 人体或脸) to look or feel warm or pink, especially after exercise or because of excitement, embarrassment, etc.（尤指运动后或因情绪激动、尴尬等而）发红，发热，显得红，感觉热：*Her cheeks were glowing.* 她双颊绯红。◇ **~ with sth** *His face glowed with embarrassment.* 他窘得满脸通红。**3** [I] **~ (with sth)** to look very pleased or satisfied 喜形于色；心满意足：*She was positively glowing with pride.* 她一副踌躇满志的样子。◇ *He gave her a warm glowing smile.* 他给了她一个热情洋溢的微笑。**4** [I] to appear a strong, warm colour 色彩鲜艳；绚丽夺目：**~ (with sth)** *The countryside glowed with autumn colours.* 乡村里秋色绚烂。◇ **+ adj.** *The brick walls glowed red in the late afternoon sun.* 砖墙在夕阳的照耀下闪着红色的光芒。
■ *noun* [sing.] **1** a dull steady light, especially from a fire that has stopped producing flames 微弱稳定的光；暗淡的光：*The city was just a red glow on the horizon.* 城市看上去只是地平线上的一片红光。◇ *There was no light except for the occasional glow of a cigarette.* 除偶尔有香烟的微光外没有一点亮光。**2** the pink colour in your face when you have been doing exercise or feel happy and excited（运动、高兴或激动时）满面红光，容光焕发，满脸通红：*The fresh air had brought a healthy glow to her cheeks.* 新鲜空气使她两颊红润，精神焕发。**3** a gold or red colour 金色；红色：*the glow of autumn leaves* 秋叶红似火 **4** a feeling of pleasure and satisfaction 喜悦；满足的心情：*When she looked at her children, she felt a glow of pride.* 看见自己的孩子，她就感到由衷的自豪。

glow·er /ˈglaʊə(r)/ *verb* [I] **~ (at sb/sth)** to look in an angry, aggressive way 怒视；虎视眈眈；咄咄逼人地盯着 SYN **glare** ▶ **glow·er** *noun*

glow·ing /ˈgləʊɪŋ; *NAmE* ˈgloʊɪŋ/ *adj.* giving enthusiastic praise 热烈赞扬的；热情洋溢的：*a* ***glowing account/report/review*** 热情洋溢的叙述 / 报道 / 评论 ◇ *He spoke of her performance in the film* ***in glowing terms*** (= praising her highly). 他热烈赞扬了她在影片中的表演。▶ **glow·ing·ly** *adv.*

glow·stick /ˈgləʊstɪk; *NAmE* ˈgloʊ-/ (*also* **'light stick**) *noun* a plastic tube filled with chemicals that shines like a lamp when you bend it 荧光棒

'glow-worm *noun* a type of insect. The female has no wings and produces a green light at the end of the tail. 发光虫

glu·cose /ˈgluːkəʊs; -kəʊz; *NAmE* -koʊs; -koʊz/ *noun* [U] a simple type of sugar that is an important energy source in living things and which is a part of many CARBOHYDRATES 葡萄糖；右旋糖

glue /gluː/ *noun, verb*
■ *noun* [U, C] a sticky substance that is used for joining things together 胶；胶水：*a tube of glue* 一管胶水 ◇ *He sticks to her like glue* (= never leaves her). 他形影不离地跟着她。➲ VISUAL VOCAB PAGE V71
■ *verb* to join two things together using glue（用胶水）黏合，粘牢，粘贴 SYN **stick**：**~ A (to/onto B)** *She glued the label onto the box.* 她把标签贴在箱子上。◇ **~ A and B (together)** *Glue the two pieces of cardboard together.* 把这两张硬纸板粘在一起。◇ *Make sure the edges are glued down.* 一定要把边缘粘牢。
IDM **be 'glued to sth** (*informal*) to give all your attention to sth; to stay very close to sth 全神贯注看着某物；离某物很近：*He spends every evening glued to the TV.* 他每天晚上都泡电视。◇ *Her eyes were glued to the screen* (= she did not stop watching it). 她目不转睛地盯着屏幕。 **,glued to the 'spot** not able to move, for example because you are frightened or surprised 动弹不得；吓呆了；惊呆了

,glue 'ear *noun* [U] (*BrE*) a medical condition in which the tubes going from the nose to the ear are blocked with MUCUS 胶耳（咽鼓管由黏液阻塞所致）

'glue-sniffing *noun* [U] the habit of breathing in the gases from some kinds of glue in order to produce a state of excitement; a type of SOLVENT ABUSE 吸胶毒，吸胶（为产生兴奋而吸入某些类胶中气体的习惯）

gluey /ˈgluːi/ *adj.* sticky like glue; covered with glue 胶黏的；涂满胶的

glug /glʌg/ *verb, noun* (*informal*)
■ *verb* (**-gg-**) **1** [I] **+ adv./prep.** (of liquid 液体) to pour out quickly and noisily, especially from a bottle（尤指从瓶中）汩汩地倒出来 **2** [T] **~ sth (down)** to drink sth quickly 大口喝：*She glugged down a glass of water.* 她大口喝下一杯水。
■ *noun* a small amount of a drink or liquid poured out 倒出的少量饮料（或液体）

glum /glʌm/ *adj.* sad, quiet and unhappy 忧郁的；死气沉沉的；闷闷不乐的 SYN **gloomy**：*The players sat there with glum looks on their faces.* 队员们愁眉苦脸地坐在那儿。▶ **glum·ly** *adv.*：*The three of us sat glumly looking out to sea.* 我们三人面向大海闷闷不乐地坐着。

glut /glʌt/ *noun, verb*
■ *noun* [usually sing.] **~ (of sth)** a situation in which there is more of sth than is needed or can be used 供应过剩；供过于求 SYN **surfeit**：*a glut of cheap DVDs on the market* 市场上供过于求的廉价 DVD OPP **shortage**
■ *verb* (**-tt-**) [usually passive] **~ sth (with sth)** to supply or provide sth with too much of sth 超量供应；充斥：*The market has been glutted with foreign cars.* 外国汽车充斥市场。

glu·ten /ˈgluːtn/ *noun* [U] a sticky substance that is a mixture of two PROTEINS and is left when STARCH is removed from flour, especially WHEAT flour 谷蛋白；面筋：*We sell a range of* ***gluten-free*** *products* (= not containing gluten). 我们出售各种无谷蛋白产品。

glutes /gluːts/ *noun* [pl.] (*informal*) the muscles in the BUTTOCKS that move the top of the leg 臀肌

glu·teus /ˈgluːtiəs; *NAmE also* gluːˈtiəs/ (*also* **'gluteus muscle**) *noun* (*anatomy* 解) any of the three muscles in each BUTTOCK 臀肌

glu·tin·ous /ˈgluːtənəs/ *adj.* sticky 黏的；胶质的：*glutinous rice* 糯米

glut·ton /ˈglʌtn/ *noun* **1** (*disapproving*) a person who eats too much 贪吃者；吃得过多的人；饕餮 **2** **~ for punishment/work** a person who enjoys doing difficult or unpleasant tasks 喜欢艰苦工作的人 ▶ **glut·ton·ous** /ˈglʌtənəs/ *adj.* SYN **greedy**

glut·tony /ˈglʌtəni/ *noun* [U] the habit of eating and drinking too much 暴食；暴饮；贪食 SYN **greed**

gly·caem·ic index (*BrE*) (*NAmE* **gly·cem·ic index**) /glaɪˌsiːmɪk ˈɪndeks/ *noun* = GI

gly·cer·ine /ˈɡlɪsəriːn; -rɪn; *NAmE* -rən/ (*especially BrE*) (*US usually* **gly·cerin** /-rɪn; *NAmE* -rən/) *noun* [U] a thick sweet clear liquid made from fats and oils and used in medicines, beauty products and EXPLOSIVES 甘油，丙三醇（用于药物、美容产品和炸药）

glyph /ɡlɪf/ *noun* a symbol CARVED out of stone, especially one from an ancient writing system 石雕符号；象形文字

GM /ˌdʒiː ˈem/ *abbr.* **1** (*BrE*) GENETICALLY MODIFIED 遗传修饰的；转基因的：*GM foods or 'Frankenstein foods' as they are popularly called* 转基因食品或人们常说的"弗兰肯斯坦食品" **2** grant-maintained (used in Britain to describe schools that received money from central, not local, government during the 1990s)（20 世纪 90 年代英国学校）由中央政府出资的，中央政府拨款的

G

gm (*also* **gm.**) *abbr.* (*pl.* **gm** or **gms**) (in writing 书写形式) gram(s) 克

GMAT /ˈdʒiːmæt/ *abbr.* Graduate Management Admissions Test (a test taken by GRADUATE students in the US who want to study for a degree in Business)（美国）企业管理研究生入学考试

GMO /ˌdʒiː em ˈəʊ; *NAmE* ˈoʊ/ *noun* (*pl.* **GMOs**) the abbreviation for 'genetically modified organism' (a plant, etc. that has had its genetic structure changed artificially, so that it will produce more fruit or not be affected by disease) 遗传修饰生物体，转基因生物（全写为 genetically modified organism，人为改变基因结构以求产量更高或抗病的生物）

GMT /ˌdʒiː em ˈtiː/ *abbr.* [U] Greenwich Mean Time (the time at Greenwich in England on the line of 0° LONGITUDE, used in the past for calculating time everywhere in the world) 格林尼治平时，世界时（全写为 Greenwich Mean Time） ➲ COMPARE UTC

gnarled /nɑːld; *NAmE* nɑːrld/ (*also* **gnarly** *NAmE*) *adj.* **1** (of trees 树木) twisted and rough; covered with hard lumps 扭曲的；多节瘤的；疙疙瘩瘩的：*a gnarled oak/branch/trunk* 多节瘤的橡树 / 树枝 / 树干 **2** (of a person or part of the body 人或身体部位) bent and twisted because of age or illness （因年老或疾病）弯曲的，扭曲的：*gnarled hands* 扭曲的手 ➲ MORE LIKE THIS 20, page R27

gnarly /ˈnɑːli; *NAmE* ˈnɑːrli/ *adj.* (*NAmE*) **1** = GNARLED **2** (*slang*) difficult or dangerous 困难的；危险的 **3** (*slang*) very good; excellent 呱呱叫的；极好的：*Wow, man! That's totally gnarly!* 哇，老兄，那真是太好了！

gnash /næʃ/ *verb*

IDM **gnash your ˈteeth** to feel very angry and upset about sth, especially because you cannot get what you want（尤因不获所求而气得）咬牙切齿：*He'll be gnashing his teeth when he hears that we lost the contract.* 他要是听说我们丢了这份合同，准会气得咬牙切齿。 ➲ MORE LIKE THIS 20, page R27

gnash·ers /ˈnæʃəz; *NAmE* -ʃərz/ *noun* [pl.] (*BrE, informal*) teeth 牙齿

gnat /næt/ *noun* a small fly with two wings, that bites 叮人小虫；蚋；蠓 ➲ MORE LIKE THIS 20, page R27

gnaw /nɔː/ *verb* [T, I] to keep biting sth or chewing it hard, so that it gradually disappears 咬；啃；啮：**~ sth** *The dog was gnawing a bone.* 那狗在啃骨头。◇ **~ through sth** *Rats had gnawed through the cable.* 老鼠把电缆咬断了。◇ **~ at/on sth** *She gnawed at her fingernails.* 她咬手指甲。◇ **~ away at/on sth** (*figurative*) *Self-doubt began to gnaw away at her confidence.* 对自己的怀疑渐渐吞噬了她的自信心。 ➲ MORE LIKE THIS 20, page R27

PHR V **ˈgnaw at sb** to make sb feel anxious, frightened or uncomfortable over a long period of time（长时间）折磨某人：*The problem had been gnawing at him for months.* 几个月来这个问题一直折磨着他。

gnaw·ing /ˈnɔːɪŋ/ *adj.* [only before noun] making you feel worried over a period of time（长时间）折磨人的，令人痛苦的，使人苦恼的：*gnawing doubts* 令人痛苦的疑虑

gneiss /naɪs/ *noun* [U] (*geology* 地) a type of METAMORPHIC rock formed at high pressure and temperature deep in the ground 片麻岩（地层深处在高压高温下形成的变质岩）

gnoc·chi /ˈnjɒki; *NAmE* ˈnjɑːki/ *noun* [pl.] an Italian dish consisting of small balls of potato mixed with flour and boiled, usually eaten with a sauce 意大利团子（用面粉和马铃薯做成）

gnome /nəʊm; *NAmE* noʊm/ *noun* **1** (in stories) a creature like a small man with a pointed hat, who lives under the ground and guards gold and TREASURE（神话故事中的）地下宝藏守护神 **2** a plastic or stone figure of a gnome, used to decorate a garden（装饰花园的）守护精灵像 ➲ MORE LIKE THIS 20, page R27

gno·mic /ˈnəʊmɪk; *NAmE* ˈnoʊ-/ *adj.* (*formal*) (of a person or a remark 人或言语) clever and wise but sometimes difficult to understand 喜用格言的；精辟的；深奥的

GNP /ˌdʒiː en ˈpiː/ [U, C, usually sing.] *noun* the abbreviation for 'gross national product' (the total value of all the goods and services produced by a country in one year, including the total income from foreign countries) 国民生产总值（全写为 gross national product） ➲ COMPARE GDP

gnu /nuː; njuː/ *noun* (*pl.* **gnu** or **gnus**) = WILDEBEEST

go 🔑 /ɡəʊ; *NAmE* ɡoʊ/ *verb, noun*

■ *verb* (**goes** /ɡəʊz; *NAmE* ɡoʊz/, **went** /went/, **gone** /ɡɒn; *NAmE* ɡɔːn/) HELP **Been** is used as the past participle of **go** when sb has gone somewhere and come back. 表示去过某地并已回来时，用 been 作 go 的过去分词。

• **MOVE/TRAVEL** 移动；旅行 **1** 🔑 [I] to move or travel from one place to another 去；走：**+ adv./prep.** *She went into her room and shut the door behind her.* 她走进自己的房间，把门关上。◇ *He goes to work by bus.* 他乘公共汽车去上班。◇ *I have to go to Rome on business.* 我得去罗马出差。◇ *She has gone to China* (= is now in China or is on her way there). 她到中国去了。◇ *She has been to China* (= she went to China and has now returned). 她去过中国。◇ *I think you should go to the doctor's.* 我认为你该去看看医生。◇ *Are you going home for Christmas?* 你打算回家过圣诞节吗？◇ **~ to do sth** *She has gone to see her sister this weekend.* 她本周末看她姐姐去了。 HELP In spoken English **go** can be used with **and** plus another verb to show purpose or to tell sb what to do. 口语中，go 可与 and 连用加上另一动词，表示目的或让某人做某事：*I'll go and answer the door.* 我去应门。◇ ***Go and get me a drink!*** 去给我拿杯饮料来！The **and** is sometimes left out, especially in *NAmE*. * and 有时可省略，尤其是美式英语：***Go ask your mom!*** 去问你妈！ **2** 🔑 [I] **~ (to sth) (with sb)** to move or travel, especially with sb else, to a particular place or in order to be present at an event（尤指与某人）去（某处或出席某项活动）：*Are you going to Dave's party?* 你要去参加戴夫的聚会吗？ ◇ *Who else is going?* 还有谁要去？ ◇ *His dog goes everywhere with him.* 他的狗总是跟着他。 **3** 🔑 [I] to move or travel in a particular way or over a particular distance 移动，旅行，行走（指方式或距离）：**+ adv./prep.** *He's going too fast.* 他走得太快。◇ **+ noun** *We had gone about fifty miles when the car broke down.* 我们行驶了约莫五十英里，汽车突然抛锚了。 **4** 🔑 [I] **~ flying, skidding, etc.** (**+ adv./prep.**) to move in a particular way or while doing sth else（以某种方式）移动；在移动中做：*The car went skidding off the road into a ditch.* 汽车打滑冲出公路跌进沟里。◇ *She went sobbing up the stairs.* 她呜咽着上楼去了。◇ *She crashed into a waiter and his tray of drinks went flying.* 她一下子撞到侍者身上，弄得他托盘里的饮料四处飞溅。

• **LEAVE** 离去 **5** 🔑 [I] to leave one place in order to reach another 离开；离去；出发 SYN **depart**：*I must be going now.* 我现在得走了。◇ *They came at six and went at nine.* 他们是六点钟来的，九点钟走的。◇ *Has she gone yet?* 她走了吗？ ◇ *He's been gone an hour* (= he left an hour ago). 他离开一小时了。◇ *When does the train go?* 火车什么时候开？ **6** 🔑 [I] **~ on sth** to leave a place and do sth different 去做（某事）：*to go on a journey/tour/trip/cruise* 去旅

行 / 观光游览 / 短途旅行 / 乘船旅游 ◇ *Richard has gone on leave for two weeks.* 理查德休假去了，为期两周。

• **VISIT/ATTEND** 访问；出席 **7** [I] **~ to sth** to visit or attend a place for a particular purpose（为某目的）去（某处）：(*BrE*) *I have to go to hospital for an operation.* 我得去医院动手术。◇ (*NAmE*) *I have to go to the hospital.* 我得到医院去。◇ *to go to prison* (= to be sent there as punishment for a crime) 进监狱 ◇ *Do you go to church* (= regularly attend church services)? 你经常上教堂吗？ **8** to look at a particular page or website 查看（页面或网站）：*She went on Facebook and changed her relationship status.* 她上脸书更新了她的感情状态。◇ *To find out what the terms mean, go to the glossary.* 要了解这些术语的含义，可查看词汇表。

• **SWIMMING/FISHING/JOGGING, ETC.** 游泳、钓鱼、慢跑等 **9** [I] **~ (for) sth** to leave a place or travel to a place in order to take part in an activity or a sport 去参加，去从事（某项活动或运动）： *to go for a walk/drive/swim/run* 去散步 / 驱车兜风 / 游泳 / 跑步 ◇ *Shall we go for a drink* (= at a pub or bar) *after work?* 我们下班后去（酒吧）喝一杯好吗？ ◇ *I have to go shopping this afternoon.* 我今天下午得去商店买东西。◇ *We're going sailing on Saturday.* 我们打算星期六乘帆船出游。

• **BE SENT** 被发送 **10** [I] (**+ adv./prep.**) to be sent or passed somewhere 被发送；被传递：*I want this memo to go to all managers.* 我想让这份备忘录送交到所有经理手中。

• **LEAD** 通向 **11** [I] **~ (from…) (to…)** to lead or extend from one place to another（从…）通向，延伸到：*I want a rope that will go from the top window to the ground.* 我想要一根可从顶楼窗户垂到地面的绳子。◇ *Where does this road go?* 这条路通到哪里？

• **PLACE/SPACE** 地方；空处 **12** [I] **+ adv./prep.** to have as a usual or correct position; to be placed 被放置，被置于，被安放（在通常或合适的位置）：*This dictionary goes on the top shelf.* 这部词典放在书架最上层。◇ *Where do you want the piano to go* (= be put)? 你想把钢琴放在什么地方？ **13** [I] **will/would not ~ (in/into sth)** used to say that sth does/did not fit into a particular place or space（不）适合；放（不）进：*My clothes won't all go in that one suitcase.* 一个手提箱装不下我所有的衣服。◇ *He tried to push his hand through the gap but it wouldn't go.* 他试着把手伸进豁口，可就是伸不进去。

• **NUMBERS** 数字 **14** [I] if a number will **go into** another number, it is contained in that number an exact number of times 除尽；除：(**+ adj.**) *3 into 12 goes 4 times.* * 3 除 12 得 4。◇ *7 into 15 won't go.* * 7 除 15 除不尽。◇ (*NAmE*) *7 into 15 doesn't go.* * 7 除 15 除不尽。◇ **~ into sth** *7 won't go into 15.* * 7 除不尽 15。

• **PROGRESS** 进展 **15** [I] **+ adv./prep.** used to talk about how well or badly sth makes progress or succeeds（事情）进展，进行：*'How did your interview go?' 'It went very well, thank you.'* “你面试的情况如何？”“非常顺利，谢谢。” ◇ *Did everything go smoothly?* 一切进行得都顺利吗？ ◇ *How's it going* (= is your life enjoyable, successful, etc. at the moment)? 近况可好？ ◇ *The way things are going the company will be bankrupt by the end of the year.* 从事态发展的情况看，到年底公司就得破产。

• **STATE/CONDITION** 状态；状况 **16** [I] used in many expressions to show that sb/sth has reached a particular state/is no longer in a particular state 进入…状态；处于…状况；脱离…状态： **~ to/into sth** *She went to sleep.* 她睡着了。 ◇ **~ out of sth** *That colour has gone out of fashion.* 那种颜色已不时兴了。 **17** *linking verb* **+ adj.** to become different in a particular way, especially a bad way 变成，变为，变得（尤指朝坏的方面）： *to go bald/blind/mad/bankrupt, etc.* 谢顶、失明、发疯、破产等 ◇ *Her hair is going grey.* 她的头发日渐花白。◇ *This milk has gone sour.* 这牛奶馊了。◇ *The children went wild with excitement.* 孩子们欣喜若狂。 ⊃ NOTE AT BECOME **18** [I] **+ adj.** to live or move around in a particular state（在某种状态下）生活，过活，移动：*to go naked/barefoot* 光着身子；赤着脚 ◇ *She cannot bear the thought of children going hungry.* 想到孩子们挨饿她就受不了。 **19** [I] **~ unnoticed, unreported, etc.** to not be noticed, reported, etc. 未被注意到（或报告等）：*Police are worried that many crimes go unreported.* 警方感到不安的是，许多罪行发生后无人报案。

• **SONG/STORY** 歌曲；故事 **20** [I, T] used to talk about what tune or words a song or poem has or what happens in a story（歌曲）唱道；（诗歌）写道；（歌词或故事）内容是：**+ adv./prep.** *How does that song go?* 那首歌怎么唱？ ◇ *I forget how the next line goes.* 我忘记下一句台词怎么说了。◇ **~ that…** *The story goes that she's been married five times.* 据传她结过五次婚。

• **SOUND/MOVEMENT** 声音；动作 **21** [I] to make a particular sound or movement 发出（某种声音）；做（某种动作）： **+ noun** *The gun went 'bang'.* 枪“砰”的一声响了。◇ **+ adv./prep.** *She went like this with her hand.* 她用手这样比画着。 **22** [I] to be sounded as a signal or warning 发出信号（或警告）： *The whistle went for the end of the game.* 比赛结束的哨声响了。

• **SAY** 说 **23** [T] **+ speech** (*informal*) (used when telling a story 讲故事时说) to say 说：*I asked 'How much?' and he goes, 'Fifty' and I go, 'Fifty? You must be joking!'* 我问：“多少钱？”他回答说：“五十。”我又说：“五十？你是在开玩笑吧！”

• **START** 开始 **24** [I] to start an activity 开始（活动）：*I'll say 'One, two, three, go!' as a signal for you to start.* 我喊“一、二、三，开始！”作为你开始的信号。◇ *As soon as he gets here we're ready to go.* 他一到我们就可以开始。

• **MACHINE** 机器 **25** [I] if a machine **goes**, it works 运行；运转；工作：*This clock doesn't go.* 这钟不走了。

• **DISAPPEAR** 消失 **26** [I] to stop existing; to be lost or stolen 不复存在；不见了；丢失；失窃 **SYN** **disappear**: *Has your headache gone yet?* 你还头痛吗？ ◇ *I left my bike outside the library and when I came out again it had gone.* 我把自行车放在图书馆外面，出来时它就不翼而飞了。

• **BE THROWN OUT** 被扔掉 **27** [I] **sb/sth must/has to/can ~** used to talk about wanting to get rid of sb/sth（必须或可以）辞掉（或扔掉、废弃）：*The old sofa will have to go.* 那旧沙发该扔掉了。◇ *He's useless—he'll have to go.* 他毫无用处，得辞掉他。

• **NOT WORK** 不起作用 **28** [I] to get worse; to become damaged or stop working correctly 变坏；损坏；不起作用：*Her sight is beginning to go.* 她的视力开始下降。◇ *His mind is going* (= he is losing his mental powers). 他心智日衰。◇ *I was driving home when my brakes went.* 我正开车回家，突然刹车失灵了。

• **DIE** 死 **29** [I] to die. People say 'go' to avoid saying 'die'. 走（委婉说法，与 die 同义）：*You can't take your money with you when you go.* 你不可能把钱带进棺材。

• **MONEY** 钱 **30** [I] when money **goes**, it is spent or used for sth 用于；花掉：*I don't know where the money goes!* 我不知道钱都花到什么地方去了！ ◇ **~ on sth** *Most of my salary goes on the rent.* 我大部分工资都花在房租上了。◇ **~ to do sth** *The money will go to finance a new community centre.* 这笔钱将用于新的社区活动中心。 **31** [I] **~ (to sb) (for sth)** to be sold 被卖掉；被出售：*We won't let the house go for less than $200 000.* 这房子低于 20 万美元我们是不会卖的。◇ *There was usually some bread **going cheap*** (= being sold cheaply) *at the end of the day.* 在收市前常常有些面包降价出售。 **32** [I] **+ adv./prep.** to be willing to pay a particular amount of money for sth 愿出价购买：*He's offered £3 000 for the car and I don't think he'll go any higher.* 他出价 3 000 英镑买这辆汽车，我看他不会愿意再多付了。◇ *I'll go to $1 000 but that's my limit.* 我愿意出 1 000 美元，这可是最大限度了。

• **HELP** 有助于 **33** [I] **~ to do sth** to help; to play a part in doing sth 有助于；促成；起作用：*This all goes to prove my theory.* 这一切都有助于证明我的说法是对的。◇ *It* (= what has just happened) ***just goes to show*** *you can't always tell how people are going to react.* 这正好说明你不可能总是知道人们会如何反应。

• **BE AVAILABLE** 可得到 **34** **be going** [I] (*informal*) to be available 可得到；可买到；现成可用：*There just aren't any jobs going in this area.* 此地几乎没有工作可找。

• **TIME** 时间 **35** [I] **+ adv./prep.** used to talk about how quickly or slowly time seems to pass 流逝；消逝；过去：*Hasn't the time gone quickly?* 时光过得真快，是不是？ ◇ *Half an hour went past while we were sitting there.* 我们坐在那里，半个小时就这样过去了。

• **USE TOILET** 用厕所 **36** [I] (*informal*) to use a toilet 用厕所；上厕所：*Do you need to go, Billy?* 你要上厕所吗，比利？

G

IDM HELP Most idioms containing **go** are at the entries for the nouns and adjectives in the idioms, for example **go it alone** is at **alone**. 大多数含 go 的习语，都可在该等习语中的名词及形容词相关词条找到，如 go it alone 在词条 alone 下。 **anything goes** (*informal*) anything that sb says or does is accepted or allowed, however shocking or unusual it may be 无奇不有；什么事都不新鲜：*Almost anything goes these days.* 这个年月几乎是无奇不有。 **as people, things, etc. go** in comparison with the average person, thing, etc. 和一般人（或事物等）相比：*As teachers go, he's not bad.* 和一般教师相比，他是不错的。 **be going on (for) sth** (*BrE*) to be nearly a particular age, time or number 接近（或将近、快到）某一年龄（或时间、数字）：*It was going on (for) midnight.* 快半夜了。 **be going to do sth 1** used to show what sb intends to do in the future 打算做某事：*We're going to buy a house when we've saved enough money.* 我们打算攒够钱后买所房子。 **2** used to show that sth is likely to happen very soon or in the future 快要发生某事；某事将要发生：*I think I'm going to faint.* 我看我快昏倒了。◇ *If the drought continues there's going to be a famine.* 如果旱灾继续下去很可能要发生饥荒。 **don't go doing sth** (*informal*) used to tell or warn sb not to do sth（告诉或警告某人）别做某事：*Don't go getting yourself into trouble.* 别惹麻烦。 **enough/something to be going 'on with** (*BrE*) something that is enough for a short time 暂且够用；足以应付一时：*£50 should be enough to be going on with.* * 50 英镑该够应付一时半会儿的了。 **go all 'out for sth | go all out to 'do sth** to make a very great effort to get sth or do sth 竭力获取某物；全力以赴做某事；鼓足干劲做某事 **go and do sth** used to show that you are angry or annoyed that sb has done sth stupid（对某人做了蠢事感到愤怒或烦恼）竟然干出某事，居然干出某事：*Trust him to go and mess things up!* 就知道他会把事情弄得一团糟！◇ *Why did you have to go and upset your mother like that?* 你干吗非得让你母亲那样伤心呢？◇ *You've really gone and done it* (= done sth very stupid) *now!* 你竟然干出这样的事来！ **go 'off on one** (*BrE, informal*) to suddenly become very angry 突然大怒；暴跳如雷 **go 'on (with you)** (*old-fashioned*) used to express the fact that you do not believe sth, or that you disapprove of sth（表示不相信或不赞同）去你的，我才不信呢 **(have) a lot, nothing, etc. 'going for you** (to have) many/not many advantages 有（或没有）很多有利条件：*You're young, intelligent, attractive—you have a lot going for you!* 你年轻、聪明、漂亮，有利条件可多啦！ **,no 'go** (*informal*) not possible or allowed 不可能；不行；不允许：*If the bank won't lend us the money it's no go, I'm afraid.* 如果银行不愿贷款给我们，这恐怕就行不通了。 ➲ SEE ALSO NO-GO AREA **not (even) 'go there** (*informal*) used to say that you do not want to talk about sth in any more detail because you do not even want to think about it 不想细谈；甚至不愿想起：*Don't ask me to choose. I don't want to go there.* 别让我挑选。我连想都不愿想。◇ *'There was a problem with his parents, wasn't there?' 'Don't even go there!'* "他的父母有问题，是不是？" "别往下说了！" **to 'go 1** remaining; still left 剩下的；还有的：*I only have one exam to go.* 我只剩一门考试了。 **2** (*NAmE, informal*) if you buy cooked food **to go** in a restaurant or shop/store, you buy it to take away and eat somewhere else（食品）外卖的；带出餐馆（或商店）吃的：*Two pizzas to go.* 来两份比萨饼，带走。 **what ,goes around 'comes around** (*saying*) **1** the way sb behaves towards other people will affect the way those people behave towards them in the future 你怎么待人，人就怎么待你 **2** something that is not fashionable now will become fashionable again in the future 现在过时的还会再时兴起来 **,where does sb ,go from 'here?** used to ask what action sb should take, especially in order to improve the difficult situation that they are in（尤指为了改变困境而询问）下一步该怎么办，往下怎么做呢 **,who goes 'there?** used by a soldier who is guarding a place to order sb to say who they are（哨兵喝问对方身份用语）谁，什么人：*Halt, who goes there?* 站住，什么人？

PHR V **,go a'bout** (*BrE*) = GO AROUND/ROUND (3) **'go about sth** to continue to do sth; to keep busy with sth 继续做某事；忙于某事：*Despite the threat of war, people went about their business as usual.* 虽然有可能发生战争，人们照常忙着自己的事。 **,go a'bout sth** to start working on sth 着手做某事；开始做某事 SYN **tackle**：*You're not going about the job in the right way.* 你做这事的方法不对。◇ **go about doing sth** *How should I go about finding a job?* 我该怎样着手找工作呢？

,go 'after sb to chase or follow sb 追赶某人；跟在某人后面：*He went after the burglars.* 他追赶那些窃贼。◇ *She left the room in tears so I went after her.* 她流着泪离开了房间，于是我跟着追了出去。 **,go 'after sb/sth** to try to get sb/sth 追求某人；谋求某事（或某物）：*We're both going after the same job.* 我们俩都在谋求同一份工作。

,go a'gainst sb to not be in sb's favour or not to their advantage 对某人不利；不利于某人：*The jury's verdict went against him.* 陪审团的裁定对他不利。 **,go a'gainst sb/sth** to resist or oppose sb/sth 反抗（或反对）某人（或某事）；与…相背：*He would not go against his parents' wishes.* 他不会违背父母的意愿。 **,go a'gainst sth** to be opposed to sth; to not fit or agree with sth 违反；与…不符（或相反）：*Paying for hospital treatment goes against her principles.* 拿钱到医院治病有违她的原则。◇ *His thinking goes against all logic.* 他的想法完全不合情理。

,go a'head 1 to travel in front of other people in your group and arrive before them 走在前面；先走：*I'll go ahead and tell them you're on the way.* 我要先走一步，告诉他们你在路上。 **2** to happen; to be done 发生；进行 SYN **proceed**：*The building of the new bridge will go ahead as planned.* 新桥的修建将按计划进行。 ➲ RELATED NOUN GO-AHEAD **,go a'head (with sth)** to begin to do sth, especially when sb has given permission or has expressed doubts or opposition（尤指经某人允许，或有人表示怀疑或反对后）开始做，着手干：*'May I start now?' 'Yes, go ahead.'* "我现在可以开始了吗？" "可以，开始吧。" ◇ *The government intends to go ahead with its tax cutting plans.* 政府拟开始实施减税计划。

,go a'long 1 to continue with an activity 继续：*He made up the story* **as he went along**. 这个故事是他现编现讲的。 **2** to make progress; to develop 进展；发展：*Things are going along nicely.* 情况进展良好。 **,go a'long with sb/sth** to agree with sb/sth 和某人观点一致；赞同某事：*I don't go along with her views on private medicine.* 在自费医疗的问题上，我不敢苟同她的观点。 ➲ SYNONYMS AT AGREE

,go a'round/'round 1 to spin or turn 旋转；转动：*to go round in a circle* 转圈 **2** to be enough for everyone to have one or some 足够分给每个人；够每人一份：*There aren't enough chairs to go around.* 椅子不够坐。 **3** (*BrE also* **,go a'bout**) to often be in a particular state or behave in a particular way 习惯于（某种状态或行动方式）：*She often goes around barefoot.* 她常常光着脚。◇ **go around/round doing sth** *It's unprofessional to go round criticizing your colleagues.* 总是指责同事，这不符合职业道德。 **4** (*also* **,go a'bout**) to spread from person to person 流传；传播：*There's a rumour going around that they're having an affair.* 谣传他们之间关系暧昧。 **,go a'round/ 'round (to...)** to visit sb or a place that is near 拜访（某人）；访问，参观（附近某处）：*I went round to the post office.* 我到邮局去了一趟。◇ *I'm going around to my sister's* (= her house) *later.* 我打算稍后到姐姐家去看看。

'go at sb to attack sb 攻击某人：*They went at each other furiously.* 他们相互猛烈攻击。 **'go at sth** to make great efforts to do sth; to work hard at sth 拼命干；卖力干：*They went at the job as if their lives depended on it.* 他们干起活来好像性命攸关似的。

,go a'way 1 to leave a person or place 走开；离开：*Just go away!* 走开！◇ *Go away and think about it, then let me know.* 到一边去想一想，然后再告诉我。 **2** to leave home for a period of time, especially for a holiday/vacation 离家外出（尤指度假）：*They've gone away for a few days.* 他们已外出几天了。◇ *I'm going away on business.* 我要出趟差。 **3** to disappear 消失：*The smell still hasn't gone away.* 气味还没散尽。

,go 'back if two people **go back** a period of time (usually a long time), they have known each other for that time 相识，已认识（一段时间）：*Dave and I go back twenty years.* 我和戴夫相识有二十年了。 **,go 'back (to...)**

to return to a place 回到，返回（某地）: *She doesn't want to go back to her husband* (= to live with him again). 她不想回到丈夫的身边了。◇ *This toaster will have to go back* (= be taken back to the shop/store where it was bought)—*it's faulty.* 这烤面包机得退回去，它有毛病。◇ *Of course we want to go back some day—it's our country, our real home.* 我们当然希望有一天能回去，那是我们的祖国，我们真正的家。➲ SYNONYMS AT RETURN **,go 'back (to sth) 1** 🔑 to consider sth that happened or was said at an earlier time 回忆起；回到（原来的话题）: *Can I go back to what you said at the beginning of the meeting?* 我想回到你在会议开始时所提的话题，行吗？◇ *Once you have made this decision, there will be* **no going back** (= you will not be able to change your mind). 你一旦作出这个决定就不能改变。 **2** 🔑 to have existed since a particular time or for a particular period 追溯到；回溯到: *Their family goes back to the time of the Pilgrim Fathers.* 他们家族的渊源可追溯到清教徒前辈移民时代。 **,go 'back on sth** to fail to keep a promise; to change your mind about sth 违约；食言；改变主意: *He never* **goes back on his word** (= never fails to do what he has said he will do). 他从不食言。 **,go 'back to sth** 🔑 to start doing sth again that you had stopped doing 重新开始；重操旧业: *The kids go back to school next week.* 孩子们下周开学。◇ **go back to doing sth** *She's decided to go back to teaching.* 她已决定重新执教。

,go be'fore to exist or happen in an earlier time 居先；先前存在；以往发生: *The present crisis is worse than any that have gone before.* 目前的危机比以往任何一次危机都严重。 **'go before sb/sth** to be presented to sb/sth for discussion, decision or judgement 提交给…讨论（或决定、裁决）: *My application goes before the planning committee next week.* 我的申请下周提交计划委员会审批。

,go be'yond sth to be more than sth 超过（或超出）某事 **SYN** **exceed**: *This year's sales figures go beyond all our expectations* (= are much better than we thought they would be). 今年的销售额大大超过我们的预期。

,go 'by 🔑 (of time 时间) to pass 流逝；过去: *Things will get easier* **as time goes by**. 随着时间的推移情况会有所改善。◇ *The weeks went slowly by.* 时间一周周慢慢地过去了。 **'go by sth** to be guided by sth; to form an opinion from sth 遵循（或依照）某事；以某事来判断: *That's a good rule to go by.* 那是要遵守的好规则。◇ ***If past experience is anything to go by, they'll be late.*** 凭以往的经验看，他们会迟到的。

,go 'down 1 to fall to the ground 倒下；落下；倒在地上: *She tripped and went down with a bump.* 她绊了一下，重重地倒在地上。 **2** if a ship, etc. **goes down**, it disappears below the water（船等）下沉，沉没 **SYN** **sink 3** 🔑 when the sun or moon **goes down**, it disappears below the HORIZON（日、月）落到地平线下，落下 **SYN** **set 4** if food or drink will/will not **go down**, it is easy/difficult to swallow（食物、饮料）被吞下，被咽下，被喝下: *A glass of wine would go down very nicely* (= I would very much like one). 喝一杯葡萄酒就太痛快了。 **5** 🔑 if the price of sth, the temperature, etc. **goes down**, it becomes lower（物价等）下跌；（温度等）下降 **SYN** **fall**: *The price of oil is going down.* 油价正在下跌。◇ *Oil is going down in price.* 油价正在下跌。 **OPP** **go up 6** (*informal*) to get worse in quality（质量）下降: *The neighbourhood has gone down a lot recently.* 近来这一带地方已远不如从前了。 **7** (*computing* 计) to stop working temporarily 暂停作业；暂停运行: *The system is going down in ten minutes.* 这个系统十分钟后要暂停运行。 **8** (*NAmE, informal*) to happen 发生: *You really don't know what's going down?* 你真的不知道发生了什么事？ **,go 'down (from...)** (*BrE, formal*) to leave a university, especially Oxford or Cambridge, at the end of a term or after finishing your studies（大学学期结束或毕业时）离校（尤指牛津或剑桥） **OPP** **go up (to...)** **,go 'down (in sth)** to be written in sth; to be recorded or remembered in sth 被写下；被记下；载入: *It all goes down* (= she writes it all) *in her notebook.* 那些东西全记在她的笔记本上。◇ ***He will go down in history as a great statesman.*** 他将作为伟大的政治家名垂青史。 **,go 'down (on sb)** (*slang*) to perform ORAL sex on sb (= to use the mouth to give sb sexual pleasure)（为某人）进行口交 **,go 'down (to sb)** to be defeated by sb, especially in a game or competition（尤指游戏或比赛中）被击败: *Italy went down to Brazil by three goals to one.* 意大利队以一比三输给了巴西队。 **,go 'down (to...) (from...)** to go from one place to another, especially further south or from a city or large town to a smaller place（从一处）到（另一处）（尤指南下或从城市、大城镇到小地方）: *They've gone down to Brighton for a couple of days.* 他们已南下到布赖顿去待几天。 **OPP** **go up (to...) (from...)** **,go 'down (with sb)** to be received in a particular way by sb 受到（某人的…）对待；被接受: *The suggestion didn't go down very well with her boss.* 她的老板对这个建议不太感兴趣。 **,go 'down with sth** (*especially BrE*) to become ill/sick with sth 患…病；感染上…病 **SYN** **catch**: *Our youngest boy has gone down with chickenpox.* 我们的小儿子染上了水痘。

'go for sb to attack sb 袭击某人；抨击（或攻击）某人: *She went for him with a knife.* 她手持尖刀向他刺去。 **'go for sb/sth 1** to apply to sb/sth 适用于某人（或某事物）: *What I said about Peter goes for you, too.* 我说的关于彼得的话也适用于你。◇ *They have a high level of unemployment—but* **the same goes for** *many other countries.* 他们的失业率很高，不过，其他许多国家也是如此。 **2** to go to a place and bring sb/sth back 去带回某人；去取回某物: *She's gone for some milk.* 她买牛奶去了。 **3** (*informal*) to be attracted by sb/sth; to like or prefer sb/sth 被…所吸引；（更）喜欢某人（或某事物）: *She goes for tall slim men.* 她喜欢瘦高个子的男人。◇ *I don't really go for modern art.* 我并不是很喜欢现代艺术。 **'go for sth 1** to choose sth 选择某物: *I think I'll go for the fruit salad.* 我想要水果色拉。➲ SYNONYMS AT CHOOSE **2** to put a lot of effort into sth, so that you get or achieve sth 努力争取某事物: ***Go for it, John! You know you can beat him.*** 努力争取吧，约翰！你知道你是可以打败他的。◇ *It sounds a great idea.* ***Go for it!*** 这听起来是个极好的主意。努力去实现吧！

,go 'in 1 to enter a room, house, etc. 进入室内；进去: *Let's go in, it's getting cold.* 我们进屋去吧，天冷了。 **2** if the sun or moon **goes in**, it disappears behind a cloud（日、月）被云遮住 **,go 'in for sth 1** (*BrE*) to take an exam or enter a competition 参加考试（或竞赛）: *She's going in for the Cambridge First Certificate.* 她打算参加剑桥初级证书考试。 **2** to have sth as an interest or a hobby 对某事物有兴趣；爱好: *She doesn't go in for team sports.* 她不喜欢团体运动。 **,go 'in with sb** to join sb in starting a business 与某人合伙；与某人联合办企业: *My brothers are opening a garage and they want me to go in with them.* 我的几个兄弟要开办一个汽车修理厂，想让我与他们合伙干。

,go 'into sth 1 🔑 (of a vehicle 交通工具) to hit sth violently 猛烈地撞上某物: *The car skidded and went into a tree.* 汽车打滑，猛地撞到树上。 **2** (of a vehicle or driver 交通工具或驾驶员) to start moving in a particular way 开始某种动作: *The plane went into a nosedive.* 飞机开始俯冲。 **3** 🔑 to join an organization, especially in order to have a career in it 加入某组织；从事某职业: *to go into the Army/the Church/Parliament* 参军；加入教会；当议会议员 ◇ *to go into teaching* 执教 **4** to begin to do sth or behave in a particular way（以某种方式）开始做某事；开始某种表现: *He went into a long explanation of the affair.* 他开始长篇大论地解释起那件事来。 **5** to examine sth carefully 详细调查（或研究）某事: *We need to go into the question of costs.* 我们需要研究一下费用问题。 **6** (of money, time, effort, etc. 金钱、时间、精力等) to be spent on sth or used to do sth 投入某事；用于某事: *More government money needs to go into the project.* 政府需对此工程投入更多的资金。◇ **go into doing sth** *Years of work went into researching the book.* 多年的工夫全花在对这本书的研究上了。

,go 'off 1 to leave a place, especially in order to do sth 离开（尤指去做某事）: *She went off to get a drink.* 她拿饮料去了。 **2** 🔑 to be fired; to explode 开火；爆炸: *The gun went off by accident.* 枪走火了。◇ *The bomb went off in a crowded street.* 炸弹在挤满人群的大街上爆炸了。➲ SYNONYMS AT EXPLODE **3** 🔑 if an alarm, etc. **goes off**, it makes a sudden loud noise（警报器等）突然发出巨响 **4** 🔑 if a light, the electricity, etc. **goes off**, it stops working

G

（电灯）熄灭；（电）中断；停止运行：*Suddenly the lights went off.* 灯突然熄灭了。◇ *The heating goes off at night.* 暖气夜间停止供热。OPP **go on 5** (*BrE, informal*) to fall asleep 入睡；睡着：*Hasn't the baby gone off yet?* 孩子还没睡着吗？ **6** (*BrE*) if food or drink **goes off**, it becomes bad and not fit to eat or drink（食物、饮料）变质，变坏 **7** (*BrE*) to get worse in quality（质量）下降：*Her books have gone off in recent years.* 她近年写的书质量下降了。 **8** to happen in a particular way （以某种方式）发生：*The meeting **went off well**.* 会议进行得很好。 **ˌgo ˈoff (on sb)** (*NAmE, informal*) to suddenly become angry with sb 突然生（某人的）气 **ˌgo ˈoff sb/sth** (*BrE, informal*) to stop liking sb/sth or lose interest in them 不再喜欢某人（或某事物）；失去对…的兴趣：*Jane seems to be going off Paul.* 简好像不再喜欢保罗了。◇ *I've gone off beer.* 我对啤酒已不感兴趣。 **ˌgo ˈoff with sb** to leave your husband, wife, partner, etc. in order to have a relationship with sb else（抛弃原有伴侣等）另寻新欢与（另外的某人）相好；与某人私奔：*He went off with his best friend's wife.* 他和最要好的朋友的妻子走了。 **ˌgo ˈoff with sth** to take away from a place sth that does not belong to you 携他人之物而去：*He went off with $10 000 of the company's money.* 他卷走了公司 1 万美元。

ˌgo ˈon 1 when a performer **goes on**, they begin their performance（演员）上场，出场：*She doesn't go on until Act 2.* 她要到第 2 幕才出场。 **2** (in sport 体育运动) to join a team as a SUBSTITUTE during a game（比赛中）以替补队员身份上场：*Walcott went on in place of Rooney just before half-time.* 就在上半场结束前沃尔科特上场替下了鲁尼。 **3** when a light, the electricity, etc. **goes on**, it starts to work（灯）亮；通（电）；开始运行：*Suddenly all the lights went on.* 突然所有的灯都亮了。OPP **go off 4** (of time 时间) to pass 流逝；过去：*She became more and more talkative as the evening went on.* 夜渐深，她的话越来越多。 **5** (*usually* **be going on**) to happen 发生：***What's going on here?*** 这儿出了什么事？ **6** if a situation **goes on**, it continues without changing（情况、形势）继续下去，持续：*This cannot be allowed to go on.* 决不允许这种情况继续下去。◇ *How much longer will this hot weather go on for?* 这样炎热的天气还会持续多久？◇ ***We can't go on like this***—*we seem to be always arguing.* 我们不能这样继续下去，我们似乎老是争吵不休。 **7** to continue speaking, often after a short pause（常指短暂停顿后）继续说：*She hesitated for a moment and then went on.* 她犹豫了一会儿，然后继续往下说。◇ **+ speech** *'You know,' he went on, 'I think my brother could help you.'* "嗯，"他接着说，"我想我哥哥可以帮助你。" **8** used to encourage sb to do sth （用于鼓励）来吧：*Go on! Have another drink!* 来吧！再喝一杯！◇ *Go on—jump!* 来呀，跳吧！ **ˌgo ˈon (ahead)** to travel in front of sb else 先走一步；先行：*You go on ahead—I'll catch you up in a few minutes.* 你先走，我一会儿就赶上来。 **ˈgo on sth** (used in negative sentences and questions 用于否定句和疑问句) to base an opinion or a judgement on sth 以…为依据；根据…来判断：*The police don't have much to go on.* 警方没多少依据。 **ˌgo ˈon (about sb/sth)** (*informal*) to talk about sb/sth for a long time, especially in a boring or complaining way 唠叨；没完没了地抱怨：*He went on and on about how poor he was.* 他没完没了地哭穷。◇ *She does go on sometimes!* 她有时就是唠叨个没完！ **ˌgo ˈon (at sb)** (*informal, especially BrE*) to complain to sb about their behaviour, work, etc. 埋怨；数落；指责 SYN **criticize**: *She goes on at him continually.* 她老是责备他。 **ˌgo ˈon (with sth)** to continue an activity, especially after a pause or break（尤指停顿或中断之后）继续做（某事）：*That's enough for now—let's go on with it tomorrow.* 现在就到这里，咱们明天再继续吧。 **ˌgo ˈon doing sth** to continue an activity without stopping 不停地做某事：*He said nothing but just went on working.* 他什么都不说，只是不停地干活。 **ˌgo ˈon to sth** to pass from one item to the next 进而转入另外一件事；接着开始另一个项目：*Let's go on to the next item on the agenda.* 咱们接着进行下一项议程吧。 **ˌgo ˈon to do sth** to do sth after completing sth else（完成某事后）接着做另一事：*The book goes on to describe his experiences in the army.* 本书继而描述了他在部队的经历。

ˌgo ˈout 1 to leave your house to go to a social event 出门参加社交活动；外出交际；外出娱乐：*She goes out a lot.* 她经常外出参加社交活动。◇ **go out doing sth** *He goes out drinking most evenings.* 他晚上多半在外喝酒。 **2** when the TIDE **goes out**, it moves away from the land 退潮；落潮 SYN **ebb** OPP **come in 3** to be sent 送出；发出；派出：*Have the invitations gone out yet?* 请柬发出去了吗？ **4** (*BrE*) when a radio or television programme **goes out**, it is broadcast （广播或电视节目）播放，播出 **5** when news or information **goes out**, it is announced or published （新闻或消息）发布，公布，发表：**~ that...** *Word went out that the director had resigned.* 局长已经辞职的消息公开了。 **6** if a fire or light **goes out**, it stops burning or shining（火或灯光）熄灭 **ˌgo ˈout (of sth) 1** to fail to reach the next stage of a competition, etc.（竞赛等中）被淘汰，出局：*She went out of the tournament in the first round.* 她在锦标赛的第一轮比赛中就被淘汰了。 **2** to be no longer fashionable or generally used 过时；不再流行：*Those skirts went out years ago.* 那些裙子多年前就不时兴了。 **ˌgo ˈout of sb/sth** (of a quality or a feeling 品质或情感) to be no longer present in sb/sth; to disappear from sb/sth 在…中不复存在；从…中消失：*All the fight seemed to go out of him.* 他身上的所有斗志似乎都已丧失殆尽。 **ˌgo ˈout to sb** if your thoughts, etc. **go out to sb**, you think about them in a kind way and hope that the difficult situation that they are in will get better 对某人产生同情（及寄予良好的祝愿） **go ˈout with sb** | **ˌgo ˈout (together)** (especially of young people 尤指年轻人) to spend time with sb and have a romantic or sexual relationship with them 与某人谈恋爱（或有性关系）：*Tom has been going out with Lucy for six weeks.* 汤姆与露西相恋六周了。◇ *How long have Tom and Lucy been going out together?* 汤姆和露西相恋多久了？ ⊃ WORDFINDER NOTE AT LOVE

ˌgo ˈover sth 1 to examine or check sth carefully 仔细检查（或审查、查阅）某事：*Go over your work before you hand it in.* 把作业仔细检查后再交。 ⊃ SYNONYMS AT CHECK **2** to study sth carefully, especially by repeating it 反复研究；仔细琢磨：*He went over the events of the day in his mind* (= thought about them carefully). 他心里反复琢磨白天发生的事。 **ˌgo ˈover (to...)** to move from one place to another, especially when this means crossing sth such as a room, town or city 从一处到（另一处）：*He went over and shook hands with his guests.* 他走过去与客人们握手。◇ *Many Irish people went over to America during the famine.* 许多爱尔兰人在饥荒时期迁徙到美国。 **ˌgo ˈover to sb/sth** (in broadcasting 广播) to change to a different person or place for the next part of a broadcast 切换到另一人物（或地点）：*We are now going over to the news desk for an important announcement.* 我们现在转换到新闻部宣布一则重要消息。 **ˌgo ˈover to sth** to change from one side, opinion, habit, etc. to another 转向另一立场（或见解、习惯等）：*Two Conservative MPs have gone over to the Liberal Democrats.* 两名保守党议员已转向自由民主党人一边。 **ˌgo ˈover (with sb)** (*NAmE*) to be received in a particular way by sb 受到（某人的…）对待：*The news of her promotion went over well with her colleagues.* 她晋升的消息一传开，同事都为她高兴。

ˌgo ˈround = GO AROUND/ROUND **ˌgo ˈround (to...)** = GO AROUND/ROUND (TO...)

ˌgo ˈthrough if a law, contract, etc. **goes through**, it is officially accepted or completed（法律、合同等正式）通过，接受，达成：*The deal did not go through.* 这笔交易未谈成。 **go through sth 1** to look at or examine sth carefully, especially in order to find sth 仔细察看某事物；检查某事物；审查某事物：*I always start the day by going through my email.* 我每天第一件事就是看电子邮件。◇ *She went through the company's accounts, looking for evidence of fraud.* 她仔细审查公司的账目，寻找诈骗的证据。 **2** to study or consider sth in detail, especially by repeating it（尤指反复地）详细研究，仔细琢磨：*Let's go through the arguments again.* 咱们再详细研究一下这些论据吧。◇ *Could we go through* (= practise) *Act 2 once more?* 我们把第 2 幕戏再串一次好吗？ **3** to perform a series of actions; to follow a method or procedure 执行某行动；实行某方法；履行某程序：*Certain formalities have to be gone through before you can emigrate.* 必须办理一定的手续方能移居他

国。 **4** 🔑 to experience or suffer sth 经历；遭受： *She's been going through a bad patch recently.* 她最近很不走运。 ◇ *He's amazingly cheerful considering all he's had to go through.* 经历了种种磨难，他还那么乐观，令人惊叹。 **5** to use up or finish sth completely 用完；耗尽： *The boys went through two whole loaves of bread.* 这些男孩把整整两条面包吃得精光。 **ˌgo ˈthrough with sth** 🔑 to do what is necessary to complete a course of action, especially one that is difficult or unpleasant 完成艰难（或令人不快）的事： *She decided not to go through with* (= not to have) *the operation.* 她决定不动手术。

ˈgo to sb/sth 🔑 to be given to sb/sth 由…得到；被授予某人： *Proceeds from the concert will go to charity.* 音乐会的收入将捐赠给慈善事业。 ◇ *All her property went to her eldest son* (= when she died). （她死后）全部财产由她的长子继承了。

ˌgo toˈgether = GO WITH STH (3), (4)

ˈgo towards sth to be used as part of the payment for sth 用于支付…的部分款项；作为对…的部分付款： *The money will go towards a new car.* 这笔钱将用于支付新车的部分款项。 ◇ **go towards doing sth** *Part of my pay cheque went towards buying an MP3 player.* 我的部分工资用于买 MP3 播放器了。

ˌgo ˈunder 1 (of sth that floats 漂浮的东西) to sink below the surface 沉下去；沉没 **2** (*informal*) to become BANKRUPT (= be unable to pay what you owe) 破产： *The firm will go under unless business improves.* 生意若无起色，公司将会倒闭。

ˌgo ˈup 1 to be built 被兴建；被建造： *New office buildings are going up everywhere.* 到处都在兴建新办公楼。 **2** when the curtain across the stage in a theatre **goes up**, it is raised or opened （剧院幕布）升起 **3** to be destroyed by fire or an explosion 被烧毁；被炸毁： *The whole building went up in flames.* 整座楼房在大火中焚毁。 **4** 🔑 if the price of sth, the temperature, etc. **goes up**, it becomes higher （物价等）上涨；（温度等）上升 **SYN** **rise**: *The price of cigarettes is going up.* 香烟价格在上涨。 ◇ *Cigarettes are going up in price.* 香烟在涨价。 **OPP** **go down** **ˌgo ˈup (to…)** (*BrE, formal*) to arrive at a university, especially Oxford or Cambridge, at the beginning of a term or in order to begin your studies （大学开学时）到校上学（尤指牛津和剑桥） **OPP** **go down (from…)** **ˌgo ˈup (to…) (from…)** to go from one place to another, especially further north or to a city or large town from a smaller place （从一处）到（另一处）（尤指北上或从小地方到城市或大城镇）： *When are you next going up to Scotland?* 你下次什么时候北上苏格兰？ ◇ *We went up to London last weekend.* 我们上周末上伦敦去了。 **OPP** **go down (to…) (from…)**

ˈgo with sb 1 (*old-fashioned, informal*) to have a sexual or romantic relationship with sb 与某人有性关系；与某人谈恋爱 **2** (*informal*) to have sex with sb 与某人性交 **ˈgo with sth 1** to be included with or as part of sth 是…的一部分；附属于： *A car goes with the job.* 这份工作配有一辆汽车。 **2** to agree to accept sth, for example a plan or an offer 同意，接受（计划、报价等）： *You're offering £500? I think we can go with that.* 你出价 500 英镑？我想我们可以接受。 **3** 🔑 (*also* **go (together)**) to combine well with sth 与某物相配（或协调、和谐） **SYN** **match**: *Does this jacket go with this skirt?* 这件上衣与这条裙子相配吗？ ◇ *Those colours don't really go (together).* 那些颜色并不十分协调。 **4** 🔑 (*also* **ˌgo toˈgether**) to exist at the same time or in the same place as sth; to be found together 与某事同时（或同地）存在；与某事相伴而生： *Disease often goes with poverty.* 疾病与贫穷常常相伴而生。 ◇ *Disease and poverty often go together.* 疾病与贫穷常常相伴而生。

ˌgo wiˈthout (sth) 🔑 to manage without sth that you usually have or need 没有…而勉强应付；没有…也行： *There wasn't time for breakfast, so I had to go without.* 没有时间吃早饭，我只好不吃了。 ◇ *How long can a human being go* (= survive) *without sleep?* 人不睡觉能活多久？ ◇ **go without doing sth** *She went without eating for three days.* 她三天没吃东西。

■ ***noun*** (*pl.* **goes** /ɡəʊz; *NAmE* ɡoʊz/) **1** [C] (*BrE*) (*also* **turn** *NAmE, BrE*) a person's turn to move or play in a game or an activity （游戏或活动中）轮到的机会： *Whose go is it?* 轮到谁了？ ◇ *It's your go.* 轮到你啦。 ◇ *'How much is it to play?' 'It's 50p a go.'* "玩这游戏多少钱？" "50 便士一回。" ◇ *Can I* ***have a go*** *on your new bike?* 我能骑骑你的新自行车吗？ **2** [C] (*also* **try**) an attempt at doing sth （做某事的）尝试，一番努力： *It took three goes to get it right.* 试了三次才把它弄好。 ◇ *I doubt if he'll listen to advice from me, but* ***I'll give it a go*** (= I'll try but I don't think I will succeed). 我怀疑他是不是会听我劝，不过我想试试看。 **3** [U] (*BrE*) energy and enthusiasm 精力；活力；热情；干劲： *Mary's always got plenty of go.* 玛丽总是精力充沛。 ➲ SEE ALSO GET-UP-AND-GO

IDM **at one ˈgo** (*BrE*) in one single attempt or try 一下子；一举；一口气： *She blew out the candles at one go.* 她一口气把蜡烛全吹灭了。 **be a ˈgo** (*NAmE, informal*) to be planned and possible or allowed 可行；得到允许： *I'm not sure if Friday's trip is a go.* 我说不准星期五是否能成行。 **be all ˈgo** (*BrE, informal*) to be very busy or full of activity 忙得要命；事儿特别多；手忙脚乱： *It was all go in the office today.* 今天办公室里忙得要死。 **be on the ˈgo** (*also* **be on the ˈmove**) (*informal*) to be very active and busy 十分活跃；非常忙碌： *I've been on the go all day.* 我一整天忙得马不停蹄。 ◇ *Having four children keeps her on the go.* 她那四个孩子把她忙得不可开交。 **first, second, etc. ˈgo** (*BrE*) at the first, second, etc. attempt 第一次（或第二次等）尝试： *I passed my driving test first go.* 我考驾照一次就通过了。 **have a ˈgo** (*informal, especially BrE*) to attack sb physically （对身体）攻击，袭击： *There were about seven of them standing round him, all waiting to have a go.* 他们大约有七个人把他围起来，个个都等着下手。 **have a ˈgo (at sth/at doing sth)** to make an attempt to do sth 尝试，试图（做某事）： *'I can't start the engine.' 'Let me have a go.'* "这发动机我发动不起来了。" "让我来试试。" ◇ *I'll have a go at fixing it tonight.* 我今晚试着修一下。 **have a ˈgo at sb** (*informal, BrE*) to criticize sb or complain about sb 指责，数落（某人）： *The boss had a go at me for being late for work.* 我上班迟到，老板剋了我一顿。 **have sth on the ˈgo** (*BrE, informal*) to be in the middle of an activity or a project 正忙于（活动或计划）： *The award-winning novelist often has three or four books on the go at once.* 那位获奖小说家经常是三四部小说同时写的。 **in one ˈgo** (*informal*) all together on one occasion 一举，一下子： *I'd rather do the journey in one go, and not stop on the way.* 我宁愿一次走完全程，中途不停。 ◇ *They ate the packet of biscuits all in one go.* 他们一下子把那包饼干全吃光了。 **make a ˈgo of sth** (*informal*) to be successful in sth 在…方面成功（或有所成就）： *We've had a few problems in our marriage, but we're both determined to make a go of it.* 我们的婚姻有过一些问题，但现在我们俩都决心好好过日子。 ➲ MORE AT LEAVE *v.*, LET *v.*

goad /ɡəʊd; *NAmE* ɡoʊd/ *verb, noun*

■ ***verb*** to keep irritating or annoying sb/sth until they react （不断地）招惹，激怒，刺激： **~ sb/sth** *Goaded beyond endurance, she turned on him and hit out.* 她被气得忍无可忍，于是转身向他猛击。 ◇ **~ sb/sth into sth/into doing sth** *He finally goaded her into answering his question.* 他终于激得她回答了他的问题。

PHR V **ˌgoad sb↔ˈon** to drive or encourage sb to do sth 驱使（或怂恿、激励）某人： *The boxers were goaded on by the shrieking crowd.* 拳击运动员听见观众的喊叫就来劲儿了。

■ ***noun*** **1** a pointed stick used for making cows, etc. move forwards （赶牛等牲畜用的）尖头棒 **2** something that makes sb do sth, usually by annoying them （意在惹恼某人而促其行动的）刺激，激励

ˈgo-ahead *noun, adj.*

■ ***noun*** **the go-ahead** [sing.] (*informal*) permission for sb to start doing sth 批准；许可： *The council has* ***given the go-ahead*** *to start building.* 委员会已批准破土动工。

■ ***adj.*** [usually before noun] willing to try new ideas, methods, etc. and therefore likely to succeed 有进取心的；有开拓精神的： *a go-ahead company* 开拓型公司

goal 🔑 **AW** /ɡəʊl; *NAmE* ɡoʊl/ *noun* **1** 🔑 (in sports 体育运动) a frame with a net into which players must kick or hit the ball in order to score a point 球门： *He* *headed the ball into an open goal* (= one that had nobody defending it). 他把球顶进了空门。◇ *Who is **in goal** (= is the goalkeeper) for Arsenal?* 阿森纳队的守门员是谁？➲ VISUAL VOCAB PAGE V48 **2** the act of kicking or hitting the ball into the goal; a point that is scored for this 射门；进球得分：*The **winning goal** was scored by Hill.* 希尔踢进了致胜的一球。◇ *Liverpool won by three goals to one.* 利物浦队以三比一获胜。◇ *United conceded two goals in the first half.* 联队在上半场被攻入了两球。◇ *a penalty goal* 点球罚中 ➲ SEE ALSO DROP GOAL, GOLDEN GOAL, OWN GOAL **3** something that you hope to achieve 目标；目的 SYN **aim**：*to work towards a goal* 争取达到目标 ◇ *to **achieve/attain a goal*** 达到目标 ◇ *You need to **set yourself** some long-term **goals**.* 你得为自己定一些长期目标。◇ *Our **ultimate goal** must be the preservation of the environment.* 我们的最终目的必须是保护好环境。➲ SYNONYMS AT TARGET

G

goal·keep·er /ˈɡəʊlkiːpə(r); NAmE ˈɡoʊl-/ (*also informal* **goalie** /ˈɡəʊli; NAmE ˈɡoʊli/, *informal* **keeper**, *NAmE also* **goal·tend·er**) *noun* (in football (SOCCER), HOCKEY, etc. 足球、曲棍球等) a player whose job is to stop the ball from going into his or her own team's goal 守门员 ➲ VISUAL VOCAB PAGE V48 ▸ **goal·keep·ing** *noun* [U]: *goalkeeping techniques* 守门的技巧

ˈ**goal kick** *noun* (in football (SOCCER) 足球) a kick taken by one team after the ball has been kicked over their GOAL LINE by the other team without a goal being scored 球门球

goal·less /ˈɡəʊlləs; NAmE ˈɡoʊl-/ *adj.* [usually before noun] without either team scoring a goal 零比零的：(*BrE*) *The match ended in a goalless draw.* 比赛以零比零结束。

ˈ**goal line** *noun* (in football, HOCKEY, etc. 足球、曲棍球等) the line at either end of a sports field on which the goal stands or which the ball must cross to score a goal or TOUCHDOWN 球门线

goal·mouth /ˈɡəʊlmaʊθ; NAmE ˈɡoʊl-/ *noun* the area directly in front of a goal 球门口

ˈ**goal poacher** *noun* = POACHER (3)

goal·post /ˈɡəʊlpəʊst; NAmE ˈɡoʊlpoʊst/ (*also* **post**) *noun* one of the two vertical posts that form part of a goal 球门柱

IDM **move, etc. the ˈgoalposts** (*informal, disapproving*) to change the rules for sth, or conditions under which it is done, so that the situation becomes more difficult for sb 改变规则，改变条件（使某人为难）

goal·scorer /ˈɡəʊlskɔːrə(r); NAmE ˈɡoʊl-/ *noun* a player in a sports game who scores a goal（体育比赛的）得分队员，得分射手，得分者

goal·tend·er /ˈɡəʊltendə(r); NAmE ˈɡoʊl-/ *noun* (*NAmE*) = GOALKEEPER

ˈ**go-around** (*also* ˈ**go-round**) *noun* **1** (*specialist*) a path taken by a plane after an unsuccessful attempt at landing, in order to get into a suitable position to try to land again（飞机降落失败后的）复飞 **2** (*NAmE, informal*) a disagreement or argument 争论；争吵

goat /ɡəʊt; NAmE ɡoʊt/ *noun* **1** an animal with horns and a coat of hair, that lives wild in mountain areas or is kept on farms for its milk or meat 山羊：*a mountain goat* 山羊 ◇ *goat's milk/cheese* 羊奶；羊奶酪 ➲ SEE ALSO BILLY GOAT, KID *n.* (2), NANNY GOAT **2 old ~** (*informal*) an unpleasant old man who is annoying in a sexual way 老色鬼；色狼；好色之徒

IDM **get sb's ˈgoat** (*informal*) to annoy sb very much 使某人大怒 ➲ MORE AT SHEEP

goatee /ɡəʊˈtiː; NAmE ɡoʊ-/ *noun* a small pointed beard (= hair growing on a man's face) that is grown only on the chin（男子下巴上的）山羊胡子 ➲ VISUAL VOCAB PAGE V65

goat·herd /ˈɡəʊthɜːd; NAmE ˈɡoʊthɜːrd/ *noun* a person whose job is to take care of a group of goats 牧羊人；羊倌

goat·skin /ˈɡəʊtskɪn; NAmE ˈɡoʊt-/ *noun* [U] leather made from the skin of a goat 山羊皮革

gob /ɡɒb; NAmE ɡɑːb/ *noun, verb*

■ ***noun*** (*slang*) **1** (*BrE*) a rude way of referring to a person's mouth 嘴（粗俗说法）：*Shut your gob!* (= a rude way of telling sb to be quiet) 闭嘴！ **2** a small amount of a thick wet substance 少许（黏湿的物质）：*Gobs of spittle ran down his chin.* 一滴滴口水顺着他的下巴往下流。 **3** [usually pl.] (*NAmE*) a large amount of sth 大量：*great gobs of cash* 大量现金

■ ***verb*** (**-bb-**) [I] (*BrE, slang*) to blow SALIVA out of your mouth 吐，啐（唾液）SYN **spit**

ˈ**go-bag** *noun* (*especially NAmE*) a bag, packed with essential items, that is kept ready to take away and use if a person needs to leave their home in an emergency 应急撤离包

gob·bet /ˈɡɒbɪt; NAmE ˈɡɑːb-/ *noun* (*old-fashioned*) **~ (of sth)** a small amount of sth 少量；一点点：*gobbets of food* 一点点食物

gob·ble /ˈɡɒbl; NAmE ˈɡɑːbl/ *verb* **1** [T, I] to eat sth very fast, in a way that people consider rude or GREEDY 狼吞虎咽；贪婪地吃 SYN **wolf**：**~ (sth)** *Don't gobble your food like that!* 别那么狼吞虎咽地吃东西！◇ **~ sth up/down** *They gobbled down all the sandwiches.* 他们几口就把三明治全吃光了。 **2** [I] when a TURKEY **gobbles**, it makes a noise in its throat （火鸡）咯咯叫

PHR V **ˌgobble sth↔ˈup** (*informal*) **1** to use sth very quickly 很快耗掉某物：*Hotel costs gobbled up most of their holiday budget.* 旅馆住宿的费用耗掉他们度假预算的一大部分。 **2** if a business company, etc. **gobbles up** a smaller one, it takes control of it（企业等）吞并较小的公司

gobble·de·gook (*also* **gobble·dy·gook**) /ˈɡɒbldiɡuːk; NAmE ˈɡɑːbl-/ *noun* [U] (*informal*) complicated language that is difficult to understand, especially when used in official documents（尤指用于正式文件中的）令人费解的文字，官样文章：*It's all gobbledegook to me.* 这对我来说完全是天书。

ˈ**go-between** *noun* [C, U] a person who takes messages between one person or group and another 中间人：*to act as (a) go-between* 做中间人

gob·let /ˈɡɒblət; NAmE ˈɡɑːb-/ *noun* a cup for wine, usually made of glass or metal, with a STEM and base but no handle（玻璃或金属制）高脚酒杯

gob·lin /ˈɡɒblɪn; NAmE ˈɡɑːb-/ *noun* (in stories) a small ugly creature that likes to trick people or cause trouble（传说中的）小妖精，丑妖怪

gob·shite /ˈɡɒbʃaɪt; NAmE ˈɡɑːb-/ *noun* (*BrE, taboo, slang*) a stupid person who talks nonsense 胡说八道的傻瓜；无聊的蠢人

gob·smacked /ˈɡɒbsmækt; NAmE ˈɡɑːb-/ *adj.* (*BrE, informal*) so surprised that you do not know what to say 瞠目结舌的；目瞪口呆的

gob·stop·per /ˈɡɒbstɒpə(r); NAmE ˈɡɑːbstɑːpər/ (*especially BrE*) (*NAmE* **jaw·break·er**) *noun* a very large hard round sweet/candy 大块圆硬糖

goby /ˈɡəʊbi; NAmE ˈɡoʊ-/ *noun* (*pl.* **goby** or **gob·ies**) a small sea fish with a SUCKER underneath 鰕虎鱼（腹部带吸盘的小海鱼）

ˈ**go-cart** *noun* = GO-KART

god /ɡɒd; NAmE ɡɑːd/ *noun* **1** **God** [sing.] (not used with *the* 不与定冠词连用) (in Christianity, Islam and Judaism 基督教、伊斯兰教和犹太教) the BEING or spirit that is worshipped and is believed to have created the universe 上帝；天主；真主：*Do you **believe in God**?* 你信仰上帝吗？◇ *Good luck and **God bless you**.* 祝你好运，愿上帝保佑你。◇ *the Son of God* (= Christ) 圣子（耶稣基督）➲ COLLOCATIONS AT RELIGION **2** [C] (in some religions) a BEING or spirit who is believed to have power over a particular part of nature or who is believed to represent a particular quality（某些宗教中主宰某个领域的）神：*Mars was the Roman god of war.* 马尔斯是古罗马战神。◇ *the rain god* 雨神 ◇ *Greek gods* 希腊诸神 ➲ SEE ALSO GODDESS **3** [C] a person who is loved or admired very much by other people 极受崇拜的人；被崇拜的偶像：*To her fans she's a god.* 对她的狂热崇拜者来说，她就是偶像。➲ SEE ALSO GODDESS **4** [C] something to which too much importance or attention is given 受到过分崇尚（或推崇）的事物：*Money is his god.* 钱就是他的命。**5 the gods** [pl.] (*BrE, informal*) the seats that are high up at the back of a theatre（剧院中的）顶层楼座，最高楼座

IDM **by 'God!** (*old-fashioned, informal*) used to emphasize a feeling of determination or surprise（强调决心或惊异）老天作证 HELP Some people find this use offensive. 有人认为此用法含冒犯意。**God | God al'mighty | God in 'heaven | good 'God | my 'God | oh (dear) 'God!** (*informal*) used to emphasize what you are saying when you are surprised, shocked or annoyed（惊讶、震惊或烦恼时说）天哪，啊哟，主啊：*God, what a stupid thing to do!* 天啊，这事干得太蠢了！HELP Some people find this use offensive. 有人认为此用法含冒犯意。**God 'bless** used when you are leaving sb, to say that you hope they will be safe, etc.（离别时的祝愿语）愿上帝保佑，祝一路平安：*Goodnight, God bless.* 晚安，上帝保佑。**God ˌrest his/her 'soul | God 'rest him/her** (*old-fashioned, informal*) used to show respect when you are talking about sb who is dead（对死者表示敬意）魂归天国，安息主怀 **God's gift (to sb/sth)** (*ironic*) a person who thinks that they are particularly good at sth or who thinks that sb will find them particularly attractive 上帝（对…）的恩宠；上帝恩赐的人（或物）：*He seems to think he's God's gift to women.* 他似乎认为自己是上帝赐给女人的礼物。**God 'willing** (*informal*) used to say that you hope that things will happen as you have planned and that there will be no problems（希望事情能按计划顺利进行）如系天意，如上帝许可，如一切顺利：*I'll be back next week, God willing.* 如一切顺利，我下星期就回来。**play 'God** to behave as if you control events or other people's lives 俨然如主宰一切的上帝：*It is unfair to ask doctors to play God and end someone's life.* 让医生扮演上帝的角色去结束一个人的生命是不公平的。**to 'God/'goodness/'Heaven** used after a verb to emphasize a particular hope, wish, etc.（用于动词之后，强调希望、愿望等）的确，真：*I wish to God you'd learn to pay attention!* 我真希望你能学会集中注意力！HELP Some people find this use offensive. 有人认为此用法含冒犯意。**ye 'gods!** (*old-fashioned, informal*) used to show surprise, lack of belief, etc.（表示惊讶、不相信等）我的天哪，好家伙 ➲ MORE AT ACT *n.*, FEAR *n.*, FORBID, GRACE *n.*, HELP *v.*, HONEST, KNOW *v.*, LAP *n.*, LOVE *n.*, MAN *n.*, NAME *n.*, PLEASE *v.*, THANK

'God-awful *adj.* [usually before noun] (*informal*) extremely bad 糟糕透顶的；令人憎恶的：*He made a God-awful mess of it!* 他把事情弄得一塌糊涂！HELP Some people find this use offensive. 有人认为此用法含冒犯意。

god·child /'gɒdtʃaɪld; *NAmE* 'gɑːd-/ *noun* (*pl.* **god·chil·dren** /'gɒdtʃɪldrən; *NAmE* 'gɑːd-/) a child that a GODPARENT at a Christian BAPTISM ceremony promises to be responsible for and to teach about the Christian religion 教子（或女）

god·dam (*also* **god·damn**) /'gɒddæm; *NAmE* 'gɑːd-/ (*also* **god·damned** /'gɒddæmd; *NAmE* 'gɑːd-/) *adj., adv.* (*taboo, slang*) a swear word that many people find offensive, used to show that you are angry or annoyed（表示气愤或烦恼的诅咒语，许多人认为此用法含冒犯意）该死，讨厌，十足，极其：*There's no need to be so goddam rude!* 没必要如此粗鲁！◇ *Where's that goddamned pen?* 那该死的笔哪儿去了？

'god-daughter *noun* a female GODCHILD 教女

god·dess /'gɒdes; -əs; *NAmE* 'gɑːdəs/ *noun* **1** a female god 女神：*Diana, the goddess of hunting* 狩猎女神狄安娜 **2** a woman who is loved or admired very much by other people 极受崇拜（或敬慕）的女人：*a screen goddess* (= a female film/movie star) 银幕女神

god·father /'gɒdfɑːðə(r); *NAmE* 'gɑːd-/ *noun* **1** a male GODPARENT 教父 **2** (*often* **Godfather**) a very powerful man in a criminal organization, especially the Mafia（犯罪组织，尤指黑手党的）头面人物，首领 **3 ~ of sth** a person who began or developed sth 发起者；开拓者：*He's the godfather of punk.* 他是朋克摇滚乐的创始人。

'God-fearing *adj.* [usually before noun] (*old-fashioned*) living a moral life based on religious principles 虔诚的；敬畏上帝的

god·for·saken /'gɒdfəseɪkən; *NAmE* 'gɑːdfər-/ *adj.* [only before noun] (of places 地方) boring, depressing and ugly 乏味的；沉闷的；丑陋的：*I can't stand living in this god-forsaken hole.* 住在这么个破地方，我受不了。

'God-given *adj.* [usually before noun] given or created by God 天赋的；天赐的；上帝创造的：*a God-given talent* 天赋的才能 ◇ *What gives you* ***a God-given right*** *to know all my business?* 谁给你权力过问我所有的事了？

god·head /'gɒdhed; *NAmE* 'gɑːd-/ *noun* **the Godhead** [sing.] (*formal*) used in the Christian religion to mean God, including the Father, Son and HOLY SPIRIT（基督教中指上帝，包括圣父、圣子和圣灵）上帝

god·less /'gɒdləs; *NAmE* 'gɑːd-/ *adj.* [usually before noun] not believing in or respecting God 不信神的；不敬上帝的：*a godless generation/world* 无宗教信仰的一代；不信神的世界 ▸ **god·less·ness** *noun* [U]

god·like /'gɒdlaɪk; *NAmE* 'gɑːd-/ *adj.* like God or a god in some quality 上帝般的；如神的；神圣的：*his godlike beauty* 他那天神般的美

godly /'gɒdli; *NAmE* 'gɑːdli/ *adj.* [usually before noun] (*old-fashioned*) living a moral life based on religious principles 虔诚的；敬畏上帝的；高尚的：*a godly man* 虔诚的人 ▸ **god·li·ness** *noun* [U]

'god-man *noun* (*pl.* **god-men**) (*IndE*) (*often disapproving*) a holy man; a religious teacher or leader 圣人；宗教长老；宗教头领：*The god-men in the village claim to have special powers.* 村里的圣人自称有特殊法力。

god·mother /'gɒdmʌðə(r); *NAmE* 'gɑːd-/ *noun* a female GODPARENT 教母 ➲ SEE ALSO FAIRY GODMOTHER

go·down /'gəʊdaʊn; *NAmE* 'goʊ-/ *noun* (*IndE*) a WAREHOUSE (= building where goods are stored) 仓库

god·par·ent /'gɒdpeərənt; *NAmE* 'gɑːdperənt/ *noun* a person who promises at a Christian BAPTISM ceremony to be responsible for a child (= his or her GODCHILD) and to teach them about the Christian religion 教父（或母）

ˌGod ˌSave the 'King/'Queen *noun* [U] the British national ANTHEM (= song)（英国国歌）《天佑吾王》

'God's country *noun* (*NAmE*) a beautiful and peaceful area that people love. Americans often use the expression to mean the US, especially the western states. 人间天堂，乐土（美国人常用以指美国，尤指西部的几个州）

god·send /'gɒdsend; *NAmE* 'gɑːd-/ *noun* [sing.] **~ (for sb/sth) | ~ (to sb/sth)** something good that happens unexpectedly and helps sb/sth when they need help 天赐之物；意外的好运；及时雨：*This new benefit has come as a godsend for low-income families.* 这项新的救济金是低收入家庭的及时雨。

god·son /'gɒdsʌn; *NAmE* 'gɑːd-/ *noun* a male GODCHILD 教子

the 'God squad *noun* [sing.] (*informal, disapproving*) Christians, especially ones who try to make people share their beliefs 上帝部队（指基督教徒，尤指努力传教者）

goer /'gəʊə(r); *NAmE* 'goʊər/ *noun* **1 -goer** (in compounds 构成复合词) a person who regularly goes to the place or event mentioned 常去…的人：*a cinema-goer* 常去看电影的人 ◇ *a moviegoer* 常去看电影的人 **2** (*BrE, informal*) a woman who enjoys having sex frequently, especially with different men 放荡的女人；骚货；破鞋

ˌgo-faster ˈstripes *noun* [pl.] (*informal*) **1** coloured lines that can be stuck on the sides of cars（可贴于车身侧面的）加速彩条 **2** (*disapproving*) features that are added to a product to attract attention but which actually have no practical use（产品的）华而不实的装饰

gofer (*also* **go·pher**) /ˈɡəʊfə(r); *NAmE* ˈɡoʊ-/ *noun* (*informal*) a person whose job is to do small boring tasks for other people in a company 勤杂员；跑腿的办事员 SYN **dogsbody**: *They call me the gofer—go for this, go for that…* 他们称我为跑腿的——一会儿去拿这，一会儿去拿那…

G

ˈgo-getter *noun* (*informal*) a person who is determined to succeed, especially in business（尤指商业上的）实干家，志在必得的人

gogga /ˈxɒxə; ˈxɒxɒ; *NAmE* ˈxɑːxə; ˈxɔːxɔː/ *noun* (*SAfrE, informal*) an insect 虫子；昆虫

gog·gle /ˈɡɒɡl; *NAmE* ˈɡɑːɡl/ *verb* [I] ~ (**at sb/sth**) (*old-fashioned, informal*) to look at sb/sth with your eyes wide open, especially because you are surprised or shocked（尤指由于惊奇而）瞪大眼睛看

ˈgoggle-box *noun* (*BrE, old-fashioned, informal*) a television 电视机

ˌgoggle-ˈeyed *adj.* with your eyes wide open, staring at sth, especially because you are surprised（尤指由于惊奇而）瞪大眼睛的，瞪着眼的

gog·gles /ˈɡɒɡlz; *NAmE* ˈɡɑːɡlz/ *noun* [pl.] a pair of glasses that fit closely to the face to protect the eyes from wind, dust, water, etc. 护目镜；风镜；游泳镜: *a pair of* ***swimming/ski/safety goggles*** 一副游泳 / 滑雪 / 安全护目镜 ➲ WORDFINDER NOTE AT SWIM ➲ VISUAL VOCAB PAGE V52

ˈgo-go *adj.* **1** connected with a style of dancing to pop music in which women dance wearing very few clothes 歌歌舞的（跳舞的女子衣着暴露）: *a go-go dancer* 歌歌舞舞女 **2** (*NAmE, informal*) of a period of time when businesses are growing and people are making money fast 生意兴隆的；赚大钱的: *the go-go years of the 1990s* * 20 世纪 90 年代经济繁荣的岁月

gogo /ˈɡɔːɡɔː/ *noun* (*SAfrE*) **1** a grandmother 祖母；外婆 **2** the title for an older woman that is polite and shows affection（称呼有礼貌、有爱心的年长女士）老婆婆，大娘

going /ˈɡəʊɪŋ; *NAmE* ˈɡoʊɪŋ/ *noun, adj.*

■ ***noun*** **1** [sing.] (*formal*) an act of leaving a place 离去；去；离开 SYN **departure**: *We were all sad at her going.* 我们对她的离去都很难过。 **2** [U] (used with an adjective 与形容词连用) the speed with which sb does sth; how difficult it is to do sth 进展速度；难度: *Walking four miles in an hour is pretty* ***good going*** *for me.* 一小时走四英里对我来说是相当不错了。 ◇ *She had her own company by 25—not* ***bad going!*** 她 25 岁时就有了自己的公司，真了不起！ ◇ *It was* ***hard going*** *getting up at five every morning.* 每天早上五点钟起床太难了。 **3** [U] the condition of the ground, especially in horse racing（尤指赛马场的）地面状况: *The going is good to firm.* 赛马场的地面稍偏硬。 ➲ SEE ALSO OUTGOINGS

IDM **when the ˌgoing gets ˈtough (the ˌtough get ˈgoing)** (*saying*) when conditions or progress become difficult (strong and determined people work even harder to succeed) 当条件变得艰苦时，当进展变得困难时（隐含有志者更勇往直前之意） **while the ˌgoing is ˈgood** (*BrE*) (*NAmE usually* **while the ˌgetting is ˈgood**) before a situation changes and it is no longer possible to do sth 趁形势还未变化时；趁情况还有利时: *Don't you think we should quit while the going is good?* 你不认为我们应该及早脱身吗？ ➲ MORE AT COMING *n.*, HEAVY *adj.*

■ ***adj.*** **-going** (in compounds 构成复合词) going regularly to the place or event mentioned 常去…的: *the theatre-going public* 常去剧院看戏的观众 ➲ SEE ALSO OCEAN-GOING, ONGOING, OUTGOING

IDM **a ˌgoing conˈcern** a business or an activity that is making a profit and is expected to continue to do well 生意兴隆的业务；发展中的事业: *He sold the cafe* ***as a going concern.*** 他把经营得正红火的咖啡馆卖掉了。 **the ˌgoing ˈrate (for sth)** the usual amount of money paid for goods or services at a particular time 现行价格；现行收费标准；现行酬金标准: *They pay slightly more than the going rate.* 他们支付的酬金略高于现行标准。

ˌgoing-ˈover *noun* [sing.] (*informal*) **1** a thorough examination of sb/sth 彻底检查；仔细审查: *The garage gave the car a thorough going-over.* 修车厂对这辆汽车进行了彻底检修。 **2** a serious physical attack on sb 痛打: *The gang gave him a real going-over.* 那帮流氓把他着实毒打了一顿。

ˌgoings-ˈon *noun* [pl.] (*informal*) activities or events that are strange, surprising or dishonest 异常情况；令人吃惊的活动（或事情）；见不得人的勾当: *There were some strange goings-on next door last night.* 昨天夜里隔壁有些异常情况。

goitre (*especially US* **goi·ter**) /ˈɡɔɪtə(r)/ *noun* [U, C] a swelling of the throat caused by a disease of the THYROID GLAND 甲状腺肿

goji berry /ˈɡəʊdʒi beri; *NAmE* ˈɡoʊ-/ *noun* a bright red berry that grows in China and can be eaten, and that is thought to contain a lot of VITAMINS. The two types of bush on which the berries grow are also called goji berries. 枸杞子；枸杞；枸杞树

go-kart (*also* **go-cart**) /ˈɡəʊ kɑːt; *NAmE* ˈɡoʊ kɑːrt/ *noun* a vehicle like a small low car with no roof or doors, used for racing（无篷无门的）微型赛车；卡丁车

gold 🔑 /ɡəʊld; *NAmE* ɡoʊld/ *noun, adj.*

■ ***noun*** **1** 🔑 [U] (*symb.* **Au**) a chemical element. Gold is a yellow PRECIOUS METAL used for making coins, jewellery, decorative objects, etc. 金: ***a gold bracelet/ring/watch, etc.*** 金手镯、金戒指、金表等 ◇ *18-carat gold* * 18 开金 ◇ *the country's gold reserves* 这个国家的黄金储备 ◇ *made of* ***solid/pure gold*** 足金 / 纯金制造 ➲ SEE ALSO FOOL'S GOLD **2** [U] money, jewellery, etc. that is made of gold 金币；金饰品；黄金制品: *His wife was dripping with* (= wearing a lot of) *gold.* 他的妻子穿金戴银。 **3** 🔑 [U, C] the colour of gold 金色；金黄色: *I love the reds and golds of autumn.* 我喜欢秋天的火红色和金黄色。 **4** [U, C] = GOLD MEDAL: *The team look set to win Olympic gold.* 这个队看来可能会拿奥运会金牌。 ◇ *He won three golds and a bronze.* 他获得三枚金牌和一枚铜牌。

IDM **ˌall that ˌglitters/ˌglistens is not ˈgold** (*saying*) not everything that seems good, attractive, etc. is actually good, etc. 闪闪发光的未必都是金子；中看未必中用 **a crock/pot of ˈgold** a large prize or reward that sb hopes for but is unlikely to get 不大可能得到的大笔奖赏（或报酬） **(as) good as ˈgold** (*informal*) behaving in a way that other people approve of 规规矩矩；很乖；表现好: *The kids have been as good as gold all day.* 孩子们一整天都很乖。 ➲ MORE LIKE THIS 14, page R26 ➲ MORE AT HEART, STREET *n.*, STRIKE *v.*, WORTH *adj.*

■ ***adj.*** 🔑 [only before noun] bright yellow in colour, like gold 金色的: *The company name was spelled out in gold letters.* 该公司的名称用烫金字母拼成。

ˈgold brick *noun* (*US, informal*) a person who is lazy and tries to avoid work by pretending to be ill/sick 偷懒的人；（装病）逃避工作的人

gold·brick /ˈɡəʊldbrɪk; *NAmE* ˈɡoʊld-/ *verb* [I] (*US, informal*) to be lazy and try to avoid work by pretending to be ill/sick 偷懒；（装病）逃避工作

ˈgold card *noun* a type of credit card that enables a person to buy more goods and services than a normal card does 信用金卡（信用额度大于普通卡）

gold·crest /ˈɡəʊldkrest; *NAmE* ˈɡoʊld-/ *noun* a very small bird with yellow feathers sticking up from the top of its head 戴菊（头顶有直立的黄羽毛）

ˈgold-digger *noun* (*informal, disapproving*) a person who uses the fact that he or she is attractive to get money from a relationship with sb 以色相骗取钱财的人

ˌgold ˈdisc *noun* a gold record that is given to a singer or group that sells a particularly high number of records 金唱片（颁发给唱片销售量特别大的歌手或乐队）

ˈgold dust *noun* [U] gold in the form of powder 金粉；砂金；金末

IDM **like ˈgold dust** (*BrE*) difficult to find or obtain 难以找到；很难得到：*Tickets for the final are like gold dust.* 决赛票很难弄到。

gold·en /ˈɡəʊldən; *NAmE* ˈɡoʊldən/ *adj.* **1** (*especially literary*) made of gold 金质的；金的：*a golden crown* 金冕 **2** bright yellow in colour like gold 金色的；金黄色的：*golden hair* 金发 ◇ *miles of golden beaches* 数英里长的金色沙滩 **3** special; wonderful 特别的；美好的：*golden memories* 美好的记忆 ◇ *Businesses have a* ***golden opportunity*** *to expand into new markets.* 商界有开拓新市场的良机。◇ *Hollywood's* ***golden boy*** 好莱坞的金牌男星

IDM **be ˈgolden** (*NAmE, informal*) to be in a situation where you are successful or do not have any problems 大功告成；大获成功；一帆风顺：*He thinks once he gets the money he'll be golden.* 他认为只要拿到钱就万事大吉了。➲ MORE AT KILL *v.*, MEAN *n.*, SILENCE *n.*

ˈgolden age *noun* [usually sing.] ~ (**of sth**) a period during which sth is very successful, especially in the past（尤指过去的）黄金时代，鼎盛时期：*the golden age of cinema* 电影的鼎盛时期

ˌgolden ˈager *noun* (*informal*) an old person 老人

ˌgolden anniˈversary *noun* (*US*) **1** (*BrE* **ˌgolden ˈjubilee**) the 50th anniversary of an important event * 50 周年纪念 **2** (*BrE* **ˌgolden ˈwedding**) (*also* **ˌgolden ˈwedding anniversary** *NAmE, BrE*) the 50th anniversary of a wedding 金婚纪念（结婚 50 周年）

ˌgolden ˈeagle *noun* a large BIRD OF PREY (= a bird that kills other creatures for food) of the EAGLE family, with brownish feathers, that lives in northern parts of the world 金雕（猛禽，羽毛呈棕色，分布于北半球）➲ VISUAL VOCAB PAGE V12

ˌgolden ˈgoal *noun* (in some football (SOCCER) competitions 某些足球比赛) the first goal scored during EXTRA TIME, which ends the game and gives victory to the team that scores the goal 金球，黄金入球（打平后加时赛中第一个进球，进球球队即赢得比赛）

ˌgolden ˈgoose *noun* something that provides sb with a lot of money, that they must be very careful with in order not to lose it 产金蛋的鹅（指带来财富但须小心对待以免失去的事物）：*An increase in crime could kill the golden goose of tourism.* 犯罪率的上升可能会扼杀旅游业这只产金蛋的鹅。

ˌgolden ˈhandcuffs *noun* [pl.] a large sum of money and other financial benefits that are given to sb to persuade them to continue working for a company rather than leaving to work for another company 金手铐（诱人安于现职而不另觅高就的一大笔津贴或其他福利）

ˌgolden ˈhandshake *noun* a large sum of money that is given to sb when they leave their job, or to persuade them to leave their job 丰厚的离职金

ˌgolden helˈlo *noun* a large sum of money that is given to sb for accepting a job 见面厚礼（给新员工的厚遇）

ˌgolden ˈjubilee (*BrE*) (*US* **ˌgolden anniˈversary**) *noun* the 50th anniversary of an important event * 50 周年纪念：*Queen Victoria's Golden Jubilee celebrations* 维多利亚女王登基 50 周年庆典 ◇ *a party to mark the company's golden jubilee* 庆祝该公司 50 周年的纪念会 ➲ COMPARE DIAMOND JUBILEE, SILVER JUBILEE

ˌgolden ˈoldie *noun* (*informal*) **1** a song or film/movie that is quite old but still well known and popular 经久不衰的歌曲（或影片）；经典歌曲；经典影片 **2** a person who is no longer young but still successful in their particular career, sport, etc.（在职业、运动生涯等中）老当益壮者；老将

ˌgolden ˈparachute *noun* (*informal*) part of a work contract in which a business person is promised a large amount of money if they have to leave their job 黄金降落伞（规定员工如被解职即可获得大笔补偿金的聘约条款）

ˌgolden ˈraisin (*NAmE*) (*BrE* **sul·tana**) *noun* a small dried GRAPE without seeds, used in cakes, etc. 无核小葡萄干（用于糕点等）

ˌgolden reˈtriever *noun* a large dog with thick yellow hair 金毛拾猎，金毛寻回犬，黄金猎犬（一种有浓密黄毛的大犬）

ˌgolden ˈrule *noun* [usually sing.] an important principle that should be followed when doing sth in order to be successful 成功之重要原则；指导原则：*The golden rule in tennis is to keep your eye on the ball.* 打好网球的重要原则是眼睛要紧盯着球。

ˌgolden ˈsection *noun* (*specialist*) the proportion that is considered to be the most attractive to look at when a line is divided into two 黄金分割

ˌgolden ˈsyrup (*also* **trea·cle**) (*both BrE*) *noun* [U] a very sweet thick yellow liquid made from sugar 金黄色糖浆

ˌgolden ˈwedding (*BrE*) (*US* **ˌgolden anniˈversary**) (*also* **ˌgolden ˈwedding anniversary** *NAmE, BrE*) *noun* the 50th anniversary of a wedding 金婚纪念（结婚 50 周年）：*The couple celebrated their golden wedding in January.* 这对夫妇一月份举行了他们的金婚大庆。➲ COMPARE DIAMOND WEDDING, RUBY WEDDING, SILVER WEDDING

gold·field /ˈɡəʊldfiːld; *NAmE* ˈɡoʊld-/ *noun* an area where gold is found in the ground 金矿区；采金地

gold·finch /ˈɡəʊldfɪntʃ; *NAmE* ˈɡoʊld-/ *noun* a small brightly coloured European bird of the FINCH family, with yellow feathers on its wings 红额金翅（一种色彩艳丽的欧洲小麻雀）

gold·fish /ˈɡəʊldfɪʃ; *NAmE* ˈɡoʊld-/ *noun* (*pl.* **gold·fish**) a small orange or red fish. Goldfish are kept as pets in bowls or PONDS. 金鱼

ˈgoldfish bowl (*also* **fish·bowl**) *noun* **1** a glass bowl for keeping fish in as pets 金鱼缸 **2** a situation in which people can see everything that happens and nothing is private 金鱼缸（指众目睽睽之下毫无隐私的状况）：*Living in this goldfish bowl of publicity would crack the strongest marriage.* 生活在这种全无隐私可言的环境之下，最牢固的婚姻也会破裂。

Goldi·locks /ˈɡəʊldɪlɒks; *NAmE* ˈɡoʊldɪlɑːks/ *adj.* without extremes; just right 适中的；恰到好处的：*The planet is in what astronomers call the Goldilocks zone: neither too hot, nor too cold.* 这颗行星位于天文学家所说的适居带，既不太热，也不太冷。ORIGIN From the story *Goldilocks and the three bears* where a girl finds a house and tries things out until she finds the one that is just right: the chair that is neither too big nor too small, the porridge that is not too hot and not too cold, and the bed that is neither too hard nor too soft. 源自《金发女孩和三只熊》的故事：女孩发现一座房子，试了里面的各种东西，直到找到正合适的，即不大也不小的椅子、不凉也不热的粥和不硬也不软的床。

ˌgold ˈleaf (*also* **ˌgold ˈfoil**) *noun* [U] gold that has been made into a very thin sheet and is used for decoration 金箔；金叶

ˌgold ˈmedal *noun* (*also* **gold**) a MEDAL made of gold that is given to the winner of a race or competition 金牌；金质奖章：*an Olympic gold medal winner* 奥运会金牌得主 ➲ COMPARE BRONZE MEDAL, SILVER MEDAL ▶ **ˌgold ˈmedallist** (*BrE*) (*NAmE* **ˌgold ˈmedalist**) *noun*：*an Olympic gold medallist* 奥运会金牌得主

ˈgold mine *noun* **1** a place where gold is dug out of the ground 金矿 **2** a business or an activity that makes a large profit 财源；宝库：*This restaurant is a potential gold mine.* 这家餐馆很可能是棵摇钱树。

ˌgold ˈplate *noun* [U] **1** dishes, etc. made of gold 金质餐具 **2** a thin layer of gold used to cover another metal; objects made in this way 镀金层；镀金器具

G

ˌgold-ˈplated *adj.* covered with a thin layer of gold 镀金的：*gold-plated earrings* 镀金耳环

ˈgold reserve *noun* [usually pl.] an amount of gold kept by a country's bank in order to support the supply of money（国家银行维持货币供应量的）黄金储备

ˈgold rush *noun* a situation in which a lot of people suddenly go to a place where gold has recently been discovered 淘金热

gold·smith /ˈɡəʊldsmɪθ; *NAmE* ˈɡoʊld-/ *noun* a person who makes, repairs or sells articles made of gold 金匠；金器商

ˈgold standard *noun* **1** (*usually* **the gold standard**) [sing.] an economic system in which the value of money is based on the value of gold 金本位制 **2** [usually sing.] a high level of quality that others try to copy 黄金标准；典范：*Articles like his are the gold standard of news reporting.* 类似他写的文章就是新闻报道的典范。

golem /ˈɡəʊləm; ˈɡɔɪ-; *NAmE* ˈɡoʊ-/ *noun* **1** (in Jewish stories 犹太传说) a figure made of CLAY that comes to life 有生命的泥人 **2** a machine that behaves like a human 机器人

golf /ɡɒlf; *NAmE* ɡɑːlf; ɡɔːlf/ *noun* [U] a game played over a large area of ground using specially shaped sticks to hit a small hard ball (a **golf ball**) into a series of 9 or 18 holes, using as few strokes as possible 高尔夫球运动：*He enjoyed a* ***round of golf*** *on a Sunday morning.* 他喜欢星期天的上午打一场高尔夫球。➲ SEE ALSO CRAZY GOLF, MINIGOLF ➲ VISUAL VOCAB PAGE V44

ˈgolf club *noun* **1** (*also* **club**) a long metal stick with a piece of metal or wood at one end, used for hitting the ball in golf 高尔夫球杆：*a set of golf clubs* 一套高尔夫球杆 ➲ VISUAL VOCAB PAGE V44 **2** an organization whose members play golf; the place where these people meet and play golf 高尔夫球俱乐部（指组织或所在地）：*Pine Ridge Golf Club* 派恩里奇高尔夫球俱乐部 ◇ *We're going for lunch at the golf club.* 我们要去高尔夫球俱乐部吃午餐。

ˈgolf course (*also* **course**) *noun* a large area of land that is designed for playing golf on 高尔夫球场 ➲ VISUAL VOCAB PAGE V44

golf·er /ˈɡɒlfə(r); *NAmE* ˈɡɑːl-; ˈɡɔːl-/ *noun* a person who plays golf 高尔夫球运动员 ➲ VISUAL VOCAB PAGE V44

golf·ing /ˈɡɒlfɪŋ; *NAmE* ˈɡɑːlf-; ˈɡɔːlf-/ *adj.* [only before noun] playing golf; connected with golf 打高尔夫球的；与高尔夫球有关的：*a golfing holiday* 打高尔夫球的假期 ▶ **golf·ing** *noun* [U]：*a week's golfing with friends* 与朋友一起打高尔夫球的一周

ˈgolf links (*also* **links**) *noun* (*pl.* **golf links**) a golf course, especially one by the sea（尤指海边的）高尔夫球场

Gol·iath /ɡəˈlaɪəθ/ *noun* a person or thing that is very large or powerful 巨人；强大的人（或物）：*a Goliath of a man* 巨人一般高大的男子 ◇ *a Goliath of the computer industry* 计算机行业的巨头 ORIGIN From **Goliath**, a giant in the Bible who is killed by the boy David with a stone. 源自《圣经》中被男孩大卫用石子射杀的巨人歌利亚 (Goliath)。

gol·li·wog /ˈɡɒliwɒɡ; *NAmE* ˈɡɑːliwɑːɡ/ (*also informal* **golly** /ˈɡɒli; *NAmE* ˈɡɑːli/ *pl.* **-ies**) *noun* a DOLL (= a model of a person for a child to play with) made of cloth with a black face and short black hair, now often considered offensive to black people 黑脸黑短发布娃娃（现在常被认为会冒犯黑人）

golly /ˈɡɒli; *NAmE* ˈɡɑːli/ *exclamation* (*old-fashioned, informal*) used to express surprise（表示惊奇）天哪，啊：*Golly, you're early!* 天哪，你好早哟！

gonad /ˈɡəʊnæd; *NAmE* ˈɡoʊ-/ *noun* (*anatomy* 解) a male sex organ that produces SPERM; a female sex organ that produces eggs 性腺；生殖腺；睾丸；卵巢

gon·dola /ˈɡɒndələ; *NAmE* ˈɡɑːn-; ɡɑːnˈdoʊlə/ *noun* **1** a long boat with a flat bottom and high parts at each end, used on CANALS in Venice 威尼斯小划船；贡多拉；凤尾船 ➲ VISUAL VOCAB PAGE V60 **2** the part on a CABLE CAR or SKI LIFT where the passengers sit 缆车车厢；缆车座椅 **3** (*especially NAmE*) the part of a hot air BALLOON or AIRSHIP where the passengers sit（热气球、飞船上的）吊舱，吊篮

gon·do·lier /ˌɡɒndəˈlɪə(r); *NAmE* ˌɡɑːndəˈlɪr/ *noun* a person whose job is to move and steer a gondola in Venice 威尼斯小划船船夫 ➲ VISUAL VOCAB PAGE V60

Gon·dwana /ɡɒnˈdwɑːnə; *NAmE* ɡɑːn-/ (*also* **Gon·dwana·land** /ɡɒnˈdwɑːnəlænd; *NAmE* ɡɑːn-/) *noun* [sing.] (*geology* 地) a very large area of land that existed in the southern HEMISPHERE millions of years ago. It was made up of the present Arabia, S America, Antarctica, Australia and India. 冈瓦纳古（大）陆，南方古陆（数百万年前存在于南半球的大片陆地，由如今的阿拉伯半岛、南美洲、南极洲、澳大利亚和印度组成）

gone /ɡɒn; *NAmE* ɡɔːn/ *adj., prep.* ➲ SEE ALSO GO *v.*

■ ***adj.*** [not before noun] **1** (of a thing 物品) used up 用完了；用光了：*'Where's the coffee?' 'It's all gone.'* "咖啡在哪儿？" "喝光了。" **2** (of a person 人) having left a place; away from a place 走了；离开了；不在：*'Is Tom here?' 'No, he was gone before I arrived.'* "汤姆在这儿吗？" "不在，我来之前他就走了。" **3** (*formal*) used to say that a particular situation no longer exists 不复存在；一去不复返：*The days are gone when you could leave your door unlocked at night.* 夜不闭户的时代已经一去不复返了。 **4** (*BrE, informal*) having been pregnant for the length of time mentioned 怀孕…时间了：*She's seven months gone.* 她怀孕七个月了。◇ *How far gone are you?* 你怀孕多久了？

IDM **ˌgoing, ˌgoing, ˈgone** (*also* **going ˈonce, going ˈtwice, ˈsold**) said by an AUCTIONEER to show that an item has been sold（拍卖商用语）一次，两次，成交 ➲ MORE AT DEAD *adj.*

■ ***prep.*** (*BrE, informal*) later than the time mentioned 晚于；已过 SYN **past**：*It's gone six already.* 已经过六点了。

goner /ˈɡɒnə(r); *NAmE* ˈɡɔːn-/ *noun* (*informal*) a person who is going to die soon or who cannot be saved from a dangerous situation 垂死的人；快完蛋的人；无法挽救的人：*We were frantic. We thought you were a goner.* 我们急死了，以为你快没命了。

gong /ɡɒŋ; *NAmE* ɡɑːŋ; ɡɔːŋ/ *noun* **1** a round piece of metal that hangs in a frame and makes a loud deep sound when it is hit with a stick. Gongs are used as musical instruments or to give signals, for example that a meal is ready. 锣 **2** (*BrE, informal*) an award or MEDAL given to sb for the work they have done 奖章；勋章

gonna /ˈɡənə; ˈɡɒnə; *NAmE* ˈɡɔːnə/ (*informal, non-standard*) a way of saying or writing 'going to' in informal speech, when it refers to the future 即将，将要（非正式用语，即 going to）：*What's she gonna do now?* 她现在要干什么？ HELP You should not write this form unless you are copying somebody's speech. 除非转述他人话语，否则不应写成这种形式。➲ MORE LIKE THIS 5, page R25

go·nor·rhoea (*BrE*) (*NAmE* **go·nor·rhea**) /ˌɡɒnəˈrɪə; *NAmE* ˌɡɑːnəˈriːə/ *noun* [U] a disease of the sexual organs, caught by having sex with an infected person 淋病 ➲ SEE ALSO VENEREAL DISEASE

gonzo journalism /ˈɡɒnzəʊ dʒɜːnəlɪzəm; *NAmE* ˈɡɑːnzoʊ dʒɜːrn-/ *noun* [U] (*NAmE, informal*) reporting in newspapers that tries to shock or excite readers rather than to give true information 哗众取宠的新闻报道；新闻炒作

goo /ɡuː/ *noun* [U] (*informal*) any unpleasant sticky wet substance（令人不舒服的）黏稠物质 ➲ SEE ALSO GOOEY

good 🔑 /ɡʊd/ *adj., noun, adv.*

■ ***adj.*** (**bet·ter** /ˈbetə(r)/, **best** /best/)

• **HIGH QUALITY** 高质量 **1** 🔑 of high quality or an acceptable standard 好的；优质的；符合标准的；可接受的：*a good book* 一本好书 ◇ *good food* 符合标准的食品 ◇ *The piano was in good condition.* 这台钢琴状况良好。◇ *Your work is just not good enough.* 你的工作就是不够好。◇ *The results* *were pretty good.* 结果相当不错。◇ *Sorry, my English is not very good.* 对不起，我的英语不太好。◇ *This is **as good a place as any** to spend the night.* 有这么个地方过夜就很好了。◇ *You'll never marry her—she's much too good for you.* 你永远娶不到她，她对你来说高不可攀。

- **PLEASANT** 令人愉快 **2** pleasant; that you enjoy or want 令人愉快的；令人满意的：*Did you have a **good time** in London?* 你在伦敦过得愉快吗？◇ *It's good to see you again.* 再次见到你真高兴。◇ *This is very **good news**.* 这消息真叫人高兴。◇ *Let's hope we have good weather tomorrow.* 希望明天是个好天。◇ *We are still friends, though, which is good.* 不过我们仍然是朋友，这令人感到欣慰。◇ ***It's a good thing*** (= it's lucky) *you came early.* 幸好你来得早。
- **SENSIBLE/STRONG** 合情理；有说服力 **3** sensible, logical or strongly supporting what is being discussed 合情理的；有说服力的；有充分根据的：*Thank you, **good question**.* 谢谢，问题提得好。◇ *Yes, that's a **good point**.* 是的，那是个有说服力的论据。◇ *I have **good reason** to be suspicious.* 我的怀疑有充分理由。◇ *What a **good idea**!* 多好的主意啊！
- **FAVOURABLE** 赞同 **4** showing or getting approval or respect 赞同的；赢得赞许的；令人尊敬的：*The play had good reviews.* 这部戏受到好评。◇ *The hotel has a good reputation.* 这家旅馆声誉良好。◇ *He comes from a good family.* 他出身名门。
- **SKILFUL** 熟练 **5** able to do sth well 能干的；精通的；娴熟的；擅长于…的：*to be a good actor/cook* 是优秀的演员 / 出色的厨师 ◇ **~ at sth** *to be good at languages/your job* 精通多种语言；工作熟练 ◇ **~ at doing sth** *Nick has always been good at finding cheap flights.* 尼克总能找到价格便宜的航班。 **6** **~ with sth/sb** able to use sth or deal with people well 灵巧的；精明的；善于应付…的：*She's good with her hands* (= able to make things, etc.). 她手很巧。◇ *He's very good with children.* 他对孩子很有一套。
- **MORALLY RIGHT** 合乎道德 **7** morally right; behaving in a way that is morally right 符合道德的；正派的；高尚的：*She has tried to lead a **good life**.* 她努力规规矩矩地生活。◇ *a **good deed*** 高尚的行为 ◇ *Giving her that money was a good thing to do.* 把那笔钱给她是做了一件善事。
- **FOLLOWING RULES** 遵守规矩 **8** following strictly a set of rules or principles 循规蹈矩的；守规矩的：*It is **good practice** to supply a written report to the buyer.* 向买主提供书面报告是诚信的做法。◇ *She was a good Catholic girl.* 她是个虔诚的天主教徒。
- **KIND** 善良 **9** willing to help; showing kindness to other people 助人为乐的；心地善良的；好心的：~ **(to sb)** *He was very good to me when I was ill.* 我生病时他对我关怀备至。◇ ~ **(of sb)** **(to do sth)** *It was very good of you to come.* 你能来真是太好了。◇ ~ **(about sth)** *I had to take a week off work but my colleagues were very good about it.* 我得请一周的假，同事们对此非常谅解。

> **▼ VOCABULARY BUILDING** 词汇扩充
>
> **Good and very good**
>
> Instead of saying that something is **good** or **very good**, try to use more precise and interesting adjectives to describe things. 事物好或非常好，除了用 good 或 very good 外，可尽量用更贴切、更有意思的形容词。
>
> - **delicious**/**tasty** food 可口的 / 美味的食物
> - an **exciting**/**entertaining**/**absorbing** movie 激动人心的 / 有趣的 / 引人入胜的影片
> - an **absorbing**/a **fascinating**/an **informative** book 引人入胜的 / 使人着迷的 / 内容丰富的书
> - a **pleasant**/an **enjoyable** trip 令人愉快的旅行
> - a **skilful**/**talented**/**fine** player 娴熟的 / 有天分的 / 优秀的运动员
> - **impressive**/**high-quality** acting 令人赞叹的 / 高质量的表演
> - **useful**/**helpful** advice 有益的 / 有用的忠告
>
> In conversation you can use words like **great**, **super**, **wonderful**, **lovely** and **excellent**. 对话中可用 great、super、wonderful、lovely 和 excellent 等词。
>
> ➲ NOTE AT NICE

- **CHILD** 孩子 **10** behaving well or politely 温顺的；乖的；有礼貌的：*You can stay up late if you're good.* 你要是听话就可以晚一点睡觉。◇ *Get dressed now, there's a good girl.* 现在把衣服穿好，乖孩子。
- **HEALTHY** 健康 **11** healthy or strong 健康的；强健的；健壮的：*Can you speak into my good ear?* 对着我这只没毛病的耳朵说好吗？◇ *I don't feel too good today.* 我今天感觉不太舒服。◇ *'How are you?' 'I'm good.'* (= used as a general reply to a greeting) "你好吗？" "我很好。"
- **USEFUL/HELPFUL** 有用；有益 **12** **~ (for sb/sth)** having a useful or helpful effect on sb/sth（对…）有用，有好处：*Too much sun isn't good for you.* 晒太阳太多对你并没有好处。◇ *It's probably good for you to get some criticism now and then.* 偶尔受点批评或许对你还有好处。◇ (*informal*) *Shut your mouth, **if you know what's good for you*** (= used as a threat). 你不想找麻烦就把嘴闭上。 **13** **no ~ doing sth** | **no ~ to sb** not having a useful or helpful effect 没有用处（或益处）：*It's no good complaining—they never listen.* 抱怨毫无用处，他们根本不听。◇ *This book is no good to me: I need the new edition.* 这本书对我没用，我需要新版本的。
- **SUITABLE** 合适 **14** suitable or appropriate 合适的；适宜的；恰当的；适合…的：*Now is a good time to buy a house.* 现在买房子正是时候。◇ **~ for sth/to do sth** *She would be good for the job.* 她干这工作很合适。◇ **~ for sb** *Can we change our meeting? Monday isn't good* (= convenient) *for me.* 我们把见面时间改改吧，星期一我不方便。
- **SHOWING APPROVAL** 表示赞同 **15** (*informal*) used to show that you approve of or are pleased about sth that has been said or done, or to show that you want to move on to a new topic of conversation （表示赞同、满意或转向新的话题）：*'Dinner's ready.' 'Good—I'm starving.'* "晚饭好了。" "太好了，我正饿得很。" ◇ *'I got the job.' 'Oh, good.'* "我得到这工作了。" "啊，太好了。" ◇ *Good, I think we've come to a decision.* 好的，我们就这样决定吧。 **16** [only before noun] (*informal*) used as a form of praise（用作赞语）：*Good old Jack!* 好心的杰克！◇ *'I've ordered some drinks.' 'Good man!'* "我叫了些饮料。" "真是好人！"
- **IN EXCLAMATIONS** 感叹 **17** (*informal*) used in exclamations（用于感叹句）：*Good heavens!* 天啊！◇ *Good God!* 上帝呀！
- **LARGE** 大 **18** [only before noun] great in number, amount or degree （数量或程度）相当大的，相当多的：*a good many people* 相当多的人 ◇ *The kitchen is a good size.* 这厨房相当大。◇ *We spent a good while* (= quite a long time) *looking for the house.* 我们花了好长时间找这房子。◇ *He devoted **a good deal of*** (= a lot of) *attention to the problem.* 他在这个问题上花了相当多的精力。◇ *There's **a good chance*** (= it is likely) *that I won't be here next year.* 我明年很可能不在这儿。
- **AT LEAST** 至少 **19** not less than; rather more than 不少于；稍多于：*We waited for a good hour.* 我们等了足足一小时。◇ *It's a good three miles to the station.* 到车站至少有三英里。
- **THOROUGH** 彻底 **20** [only before noun] thorough; complete 彻底的；完全的：*We had a good laugh about it afterwards.* 我们后来对此笑了个痛快。◇ *You'll feel better after a good sleep.* 好好睡上一觉你会感觉好些。
- **AMUSING** 有趣 **21** [usually before noun] amusing 有趣的；逗笑的：*a **good story/joke*** 有趣的故事 / 笑话 ◇ (*informal*) *That's a good one!* 那真有意思！
- **FOR PARTICULAR TIME/DISTANCE** 特定的时间 / 距离 **22** **~ for sth** having enough energy, health, strength, etc. to last for a particular length of time or distance（精力、健康、力量等）足以维持…的，能持续…的：*You're good for* (= you will live) *a few years yet.* 你还可以活上几年。 **23** **~ for sth** valid for sth 有效的：*The ticket is good for three months.* 这张票三个月内有效。
- **LIKELY TO PROVIDE** 可能提供 **24** **~ for sth** likely to provide sth 能提供…的：*He's always good for a laugh.* 他总能逗人发笑。◇ *Bobby should be good for a few drinks.* 博比喝上几杯应该是没问题的。

IDM **HELP** Most idioms containing **good** are at the entries for the nouns and verbs in the idioms, for example **(as) good as gold** is at **gold**. 大多数含 good 的习语，都可在该等习语

G

中的名词及动词相关词条找到，如 (as) good as gold 在词条 gold 下。 **as 'good as** very nearly 与…几乎一样；几乎；简直是：*The matter is as good as settled.* 这事实际上可以说解决了。◇ *He as good as called me a coward* (= suggested that I was a coward without actually using the word 'coward'). 他就差说我是懦夫了。 **as ˌgood as it 'gets** used when you are saying that a situation is not going to get any better（形势）不会有什么好转，还是老样子 **a good 'few** several 好几个；一些：*There are still a good few empty seats.* 还有好几个空座位。 **be ˌgood to 'go** (of a thing) to be prepared and ready for use; (of a person) to be prepared and ready to do something（物品）备妥可用；（人）准备好：*By tomorrow afternoon the document will be good to go.* 到明天下午文件就可以备妥。◇ *I've spent several months training for this race so now I'm good to go.* 为了这场比赛我花了几个月的时间训练，现在我准备好了。 **good and...** (*informal*) completely 完全；彻底：*I won't go until I'm good and ready.* 我要完全准备就绪后才走。 **ˌgood for 'you, 'sb, 'them, etc.** (*especially AustralE* **good 'on you, etc.**) (*informal*) used to praise sb for doing sth well（称赞某人）真行，真棒：*'I passed first time.' 'Good for you!'* "我第一次就过了。" "你真行！"

■ ***noun*** ➲ SEE ALSO GOODS

• **MORALLY RIGHT** 合乎道德 **1** 🔑 [U] behaviour that is morally right or acceptable 合乎道德的行为；正直的行为；善行：*the difference between good and evil* 善与恶的区别 ◇ *Is religion always a force for good?* 宗教一向是诲人行善的力量吗？ **2 the good** [pl.] people who live a moral life; people who are admired for the work they do to help other people 有道德的人；高尚的人；好人：*a gathering of the great and the good* 群贤荟萃

• **STH HELPFUL** 益处 **3** 🔑 [U] something that helps sb/sth 用处；好处；益处：*Cuts have been made **for the good of the company**.* 实行裁减是为了公司的利益。◇ *I'm only telling you this **for your own good**.* 我把这事告诉你只是为你好。◇ ***What's the good of*** (= how does it help you) *earning all that money if you don't have time to enjoy it?* 要是没时间去享受，赚那么多钱有什么用？◇ ***What good is it** redecorating if you're thinking of moving?* 如果你打算搬走，那重新装饰有什么用呢？ ➲ SEE ALSO DO-GOODER

IDM **ˌall to the 'good** used to say that if sth happens, it will be good, even if it is not exactly what you were expecting 不失为好事：*If these measures also reduce unemployment, that is all to the good.* 要是这些措施也能降低失业率，那就不失为好事。 **be no 'good | not be any/much 'good 1** 🔑 to not be useful; to have no useful effect 没（或没什么、没多大）用处（或好处）：*This gadget isn't much good.* 这小玩意儿没多大用处。◇ *It's no good trying to talk me out of leaving.* 想说服我不要离开是没用的。◇ *Was his advice ever any good?* 他的建议有过用处吗？ **2** 🔑 to not be interesting or enjoyable 没（或没什么、没多大）乐趣：*His latest film isn't much good.* 他最近拍摄的影片没多大意思。 **do 'good | do sb 'good** 🔑 to have a useful effect; to help sb（对某人）有好处，有用处，有益：*Do you think these latest changes will do any good?* 你认为最近这些变化有什么作用吗？◇ *Don't you think talking to her would do some good?* 你不觉得和她谈一谈会有用吗？◇ *I'm sure a few days off would do you a power of good* (= improve your health). 休息几天肯定对你的身体大有好处。 **for 'good** (*BrE also* **for ˌgood and 'all**) permanently 永远；永久：*This time she's leaving for good* (= she will never return). 她这次走是再也不会回来了。 **to the 'good** used to say that sb now has a particular amount of money that they did not have before 净赚；盈余：*We are £500 to the good.* 我们净赚 500 英镑。 **up to no 'good** (*informal*) doing sth wrong or dishonest 做坏事；做不光彩的事：*Those kids are always up to no good.* 那些孩子尽会恶作剧。 ➲ MORE AT ILL *adj.*, POWER *n.*, WORLD

■ ***adv.*** (*especially NAmE, informal*) well 好：*'How's it going?' 'Pretty good.'* "事情进展如何？" "非常好。" ◇ (*non-standard*) *Now, you listen to me good!* 喂，好好听我说！

> ▼ **WHICH WORD?** 词语辨析
>
> **good / goodness**
>
> • The noun **good** means actions and behaviour that are morally right. You can talk about a person doing **good**. 名词 good 指有道德的行为，指人做好事可用 do good：*The charity does a lot of good.* 这家慈善机构做很多善事。◇ *the difference between good and evil* 善恶之分
>
> • **Goodness** is the quality of being good. You can talk about a person's **goodness**. * goodness 意为善良，可指人的美德：*Her goodness shone through.* 她显然非常善良。

ˌgood after'noon *exclamation* used to say hello politely when people first see each other in the afternoon; in informal use people often just say *Afternoon*（下午见面时用语）下午好，你（们）好（非正式场合常说 Afternoon）

good·bye 🔑 /ˌɡʊdˈbaɪ/ *exclamation, noun* used when you are leaving sb or when sb else is leaving 再见；再会：*Goodbye! It was great to meet you.* 再见！认识你很高兴。◇ *She didn't even **say goodbye** to her mother.* 她甚至没有向母亲道个别。◇ *We **waved** them **goodbye**.* 我们向他们挥手告别。◇ *We've already said our goodbyes.* 我们已经道别了。◇ ***Kiss me goodbye!*** 和我吻别吧！◇ (*figurative*) *Take out our service contract and say goodbye to costly repair bills.* 接受我们的服务合同，告别昂贵的修理费吧。 ➲ COMPARE BYE *exclamation* **IDM** ➲ SEE KISS *v.*

ˌgood 'day *exclamation* (*old-fashioned*) used to say hello or goodbye politely when people first see each other or leave each other during the day（白天见面或分手时用语）白天好，你（们）好，再见：*Good day to you.* 你好。

ˌgood 'evening *exclamation* used to say hello politely when people first see each other in the evening; in informal use people often just say *Evening*（晚上见面时用语）晚上好，你（们）好（非正式场合常说 Evening）

good 'faith *noun* [U] the intention to be honest and helpful 真诚；善意：*a gesture of good faith* 善意的表示 ◇ *He acted **in good faith**.* 他这样做是出于真心诚意。

'good-for-nothing *noun* (*informal*) a person who is lazy and has no skills 懒人；无用之人：*an idle good-for-nothing* 游手好闲的懒虫 ▶ **'good-for-nothing** *adj.* [usually before noun]: *Where's that good-for-nothing son of yours?* 你那没出息的儿子在哪儿？

ˌGood 'Friday *noun* [U, C] the Friday before Easter, the day when Christians remember the Crucifixion of Christ 耶稣受难日（复活节前的星期五）

ˌgood-'hearted *adj.* kind; willing to help other people 善良的；好心的；乐于助人的

ˌgood 'humour (*especially US* **ˌgood 'humor**) *noun* [U, sing.] a cheerful mood 愉快的心情；好脾气：*Everyone admired her patience and unfailing good humour.* 人人都佩服她的耐心和永不衰减的好脾气。 **OPP** **ill humour** ▶ **ˌgood-'humoured** (*especially US* **ˌgood-'humored**) *adj.*: *a good-humoured atmosphere* 令人愉快的气氛 **ˌgood-'humoured·ly** (*especially US* **ˌgood-'humored·ly**) *adv.*

goodie = GOODY

good·ish /ˈɡʊdɪʃ/ *adj.* [only before noun] (*informal*) **1** quite good rather than very good 尚好的；不错的：*'Is the salary good?' 'Goodish.'* "工资还行吧？" "还可以。" **2** quite large in size or amount 相当大的；相当多的：*It'll be a goodish while yet before I've finished.* 我还得花很长时间才能完成。

ˌgood-'looking *adj.* (especially of people 尤指人) physically attractive 漂亮的；好看的：*a good-looking man/couple* 俊美的男子；漂亮的一对 ◇ *She's strikingly good-looking.* 她非常漂亮。 **OPP** **ugly** ➲ SYNONYMS AT BEAUTIFUL

ˌgood 'looks *noun* [pl.] the physical beauty of a person 漂亮的外表；美貌：*an actor famous for his rugged good looks* 以其粗犷美而出名的男演员

good·ly /ˈɡʊdli/ *adj.* [only before noun] **1** (*old-fashioned, formal*) quite large in size or amount 相当大的；相当多的：*a goodly number* 相当大的数目 **2** (*old use*) physically attractive; of good quality 漂亮的；好看的；高质量的

ˌgood ˈmorning *exclamation* used to say hello politely when people first see each other in the morning (in informal use people often just say *Morning* in this case); sometimes also used formally when people leave each other in the morning （上午见面时用语，非正式场合常说 Morning）早上好，上午好，你（们）好；（有时用作上午告别时的正式用语）再见

ˌgood ˈname *noun* [sing.] the good opinion that people have of sb/sth 好名声；好声誉 **SYN** **reputation**: *He told the police he didn't know her, to protect her good name.* 为了维护她的好名声，他对警察说他不认识她。◇ *My election chances are not as important as the good name of the party.* 党的声誉比我当选的机会更重要。

ˌgood ˈnature *noun* [U] the quality of being kind, friendly and patient when dealing with people 善良的品性；和善的本性；温和的性情

ˌgood-ˈnatured *adj.* kind, friendly and patient when dealing with people 本性善良的；和蔼可亲的；友好的：*a good-natured person/discussion* 和蔼可亲的人；友好的讨论 ▸ **ˌgood-ˈnatured·ly** *adv.*: *to smile good-naturedly* 和善地微笑

ˌgood-ˈneighbourliness *noun* [U] (*BrE*) good relations that exist between people who live in the same area or between countries that are near each other 睦邻关系

good·ness /ˈɡʊdnəs/ *noun* [U] **1** the quality of being good 善良；优良；美德：*the essential goodness of human nature* 人性善良的本质 ◇ *evidence of God's goodness* 上帝仁慈的明证 ◇ (*formal*) *At least* ***have the goodness*** (= good manners) *to look at me when I'm talking to you.* 我对你说话时，你至少应该看着我。➲ NOTE AT GOOD **2** the part of sth that has a useful effect on sb/sth, especially sb's health（尤指有益健康的）精华，营养，养分：*These vegetables have had all the goodness boiled out of them.* 这些蔬菜的营养都被煮掉了。

IDM **Goodness!** | **ˌGoodness ˈme!** | **ˌMy ˈgoodness!** | **ˌGoodness ˈgracious!** (*informal*) used to express surprise（表示惊讶）天哪，啊呀：*Goodness, what a big balloon!* 啊，好大的气球呀！◇ *My goodness, you have been busy!* 天哪，你一直在忙！◇ *Goodness me, no!* 天啊，不！ **out of the goodness of your ˈheart** from feelings of kindness, without thinking about what advantage there will be for you 出于好心（不从中捞取好处）：*You're not telling me he offered to lend you the money out of the goodness of his heart?* 你该不是说他是纯粹出于好心才主动借钱给你的吧？ ➲ MORE AT GOD, HONEST, KNOW *v.*, THANK

good·night /ˌɡʊdˈnaɪt/ *exclamation* used when you are saying goodbye to sb late in the evening, or when they or you are going to bed; in informal use people often just say *Night*（晚间道别时或睡前用语）晚安（非正式场合常说 Night）

goodo /ˈɡʊdəʊ; *NAmE* -oʊ/ *adj.* (*AustralE, NZE, informal*) good 好的；令人满意的

ˌgood old ˈboy *noun* (*NAmE, informal*) a man who is considered typical of white men in the southern states of the US 好老弟（美国南方各州的典型白人男子）

goods 🔑 /ɡʊdz/ *noun* [pl.] **1** 🔑 things that are produced to be sold 商品；货品：*cheap/expensive goods* 便宜的/昂贵的商品 ◇ *leather/cotton/paper goods* 皮革/棉织/纸质商品 ◇ *electrical/sports goods* 电器商品；体育器材 ◇ *perishable/durable goods* 易腐/耐用商品 ◇ *increased tax on* ***goods and services*** 增加了的商品及服务税 ➲ SEE ALSO CONSUMER GOODS ➲ SYNONYMS AT PRODUCT **2** 🔑 possessions that can be moved 动产；私人财产：***stolen goods*** 赃物 ◇ *The plastic bag contained all his* ***worldly goods*** (= everything he owned). 这塑料袋里装着他的全部家当。➲ SYNONYMS AT THING **3** (*BrE*) things (not people) that are transported by rail or road（铁路或公路）运载的货物：*a goods train* 货运列车 ◇ *a heavy goods vehicle* 重型货车 ➲ COMPARE FREIGHT *n.*

IDM **be the ˈgoods** (*BrE, informal*) to be very good or impressive 非常好；给人以深刻印象 **deliver the ˈgoods** | **come up with the ˈgoods** (*informal*) to do what you have promised to do or what people expect or want you to do 履行诺言；不负所望：*We expected great things of the England team, but on the day they simply failed to deliver the goods.* 我们本指望英格兰队大获全胜，可那天他们真是有负众望。

ˌgoods and ˈchattels *noun* [pl.] (*BrE, law* 律) personal possessions that are not land or buildings 私人财物；有形动产

ˌgood ˈsense *noun* [U] ~ (**to do sth**) the ability to make the right decision about sth; good judgement 正确的决策力（或判断力）；理智：*a man of honour and good sense* 品德高尚且有头脑的男人 ◇ *Keeping to a low-fat diet* ***makes very good sense*** (= is a sensible thing to do). 坚持低脂饮食是明智的做法。

ˈgoods train *noun* (*BrE*) = FREIGHT TRAIN

ˌgood-ˈtempered *adj.* cheerful and not easily made angry 脾气好的；快活的；和蔼的

ˈgood-time *adj.* [only before noun] only interested in pleasure, and not in anything serious or important 一味追求享乐的；只顾玩乐的：*I was too much of a good-time girl to do any serious studying.* 我过去是个很贪玩的女孩，从来不知道认真学习。

good·will /ˌɡʊdˈwɪl/ *noun* [U] **1** friendly or helpful feelings towards other people or countries 友善；友好；善意；亲善：*a spirit of goodwill in international relations* 国际关系中的亲善精神 ◇ ***a goodwill gesture/a gesture of goodwill*** 友好的表示 **2** the good relationship between a business and its customers that is calculated as part of its value when it is sold 信誉；商誉

goody /ˈɡʊdi/ *noun, exclamation*

■ ***noun*** (*also* **goodie**) [usually pl.] (*pl.* **-ies**) (*informal*) **1** a thing that is very nice to eat 好吃的东西：*a basket of goodies for the children* 给孩子们的一篮好吃的东西 **2** anything that is attractive and that people want to have 诱人的东西；人们渴望得到的东西：*We're giving away lots of free goodies—T-shirts, hats and DVDs!* 我们在赠送大量精美礼品：T 恤衫、帽子，还有 DVD！ **3** a good person, especially in a book or a film/movie（尤指书和电影中的）正面人物，好人：*It's sometimes difficult to tell who are the goodies and who are the baddies.* 好人和坏人有时很难分清。**OPP** **baddy** ➲ WORDFINDER NOTE AT CHARACTER

■ ***exclamation*** (*becoming old-fashioned*) a word children use when they are excited or pleased about sth（儿语）好哇，太好了

ˈgoody bag (*also* **ˈgoodie bag**) *noun* **1** a bag containing sweets/candy and small presents, given to children to take home at the end of a party 糖果礼品袋（聚会结束时送给小孩） **2** a bag containing examples of a company's products, given away in order to advertise them 样品袋（为促销产品而免费赠送）

ˈgoody-goody *noun* (*pl.* **goody-goodies**) (*informal, disapproving*) (used especially by and about children 尤为儿语) a person who behaves very well to please people in authority such as parents or teachers 善于讨好卖乖的人

ˌgoody-ˈtwo-shoes *noun* (*pl.* **goody-two-shoes**) (*informal, disapproving*) a person who always behaves well, and perhaps has a disapproving attitude to people who do not 过于正经的人（对人对己要求很高）

gooey /ˈɡuːi/ *adj.* (*informal*) soft and sticky 软而黏的；黏黏糊糊的：*a gooey mess* 黏糊糊的一团 ◇ *gooey cakes* 黏性甜糕点

goof /ɡuːf/ *verb, noun*

■ ***verb*** [I] (*informal, especially NAmE*) to make a stupid mistake 犯愚蠢的错误：*Sorry, guys. I goofed.* 对不起，各位。我搞砸了。

PHR V **ˌgoof aˈround** (*informal, especially NAmE*) to spend

your time doing silly or stupid things 把时间浪费在荒谬无聊的事情上 SYN **mess around** **,goof 'off** (*NAmE, informal*) to spend your time doing nothing, especially when you should be working 闲荡；混日子；偷懒
■ ***noun*** (*informal, especially NAmE*) **1** a stupid mistake 愚蠢的错误 **2** a silly or stupid person 傻瓜；蠢人

goof·ball /ˈɡuːfbɔːl/ *noun* (*NAmE, informal*) a stupid person 傻瓜；蠢人 ▶ **goof·ball** *adj.* [only before noun]: *This is just another of his goofball ideas.* 这不过是他的又一个愚蠢想法。

ˈgoof-off *noun* (*NAmE, slang*) a person who avoids work or responsibility 逃避工作（或责任）的人；懒汉

goofy /ˈɡuːfi/ *adj.* (*informal, especially NAmE*) silly; stupid 愚蠢的；傻的：*a goofy grin* 龇牙咧嘴的傻笑

goog /ɡʊɡ/ *noun* (*AustralE, NZE, informal*) an egg 蛋

google /ˈɡuːɡl/ *verb* [T, I] ~ (**sb/sth**) (*computing* 计) to type words into the SEARCH ENGINE Google® in order to find information about sb/sth 在谷歌上搜索：*You can google someone you've recently met to see what information is available about them on the Internet.* 你可以在谷歌上搜你最近见过的某人，看看在互联网上能查到什么相关信息。◇ *I tried googling but couldn't find anything relevant.* 我试过用谷歌搜索引擎检索，但找不到任何相关信息。➲ WORDFINDER NOTE AT WEB

googly /ˈɡuːɡli/ *noun* (*pl.* **-ies**) (in CRICKET 板球) a ball that is BOWLED so that it looks as if it will turn in one direction, but that actually turns the opposite way 变向曲线球：(*figurative*) *He bowled the prime minister a googly* (= asked him a difficult question). 他问了首相一个很棘手的问题。

goo·gol /ˈɡuːɡɒl; *NAmE* -ɡɔːl/ *noun* (*mathematics* 数) the number 10^{100}, or 1 followed by 100 zeros 古戈尔（= 10^{100}）；大数

gook /ɡuːk/ *noun* **1** [U] (*informal*) any unpleasant sticky wet substance 黏湿的脏东西 **2** [C] (*NAmE, taboo, slang*) an offensive word for a person from SE Asia（蔑称）东南亚人

goolie (*also* **gooly**) /ˈɡuːli/ *noun* [usually pl.] (*pl.* **-ies**) (*BrE, slang*) a rude word for a man's TESTICLE 睾丸

goon /ɡuːn/ *noun* (*informal*) **1** (*especially NAmE*) a criminal who is paid to frighten or injure people（受雇的）暴徒，流氓，打手 **2** (*old-fashioned, especially BrE*) a stupid or silly person 傻瓜；蠢人

goonda /ˈɡuːndə/ *noun* (*IndE*) a person who is paid to frighten or hurt sb（受雇的）暴徒，流氓，打手：*The politician hired a group of goondas to intimidate rival candidates.* 这政客雇了一伙暴徒去恐吓竞选对手。

goose /ɡuːs/ *noun, verb*
■ ***noun*** (*pl.* **geese** /ɡiːs/) **1** [C] a bird like a large DUCK with a long neck. Geese either live wild or are kept on farms. 鹅 **2** [U] meat from a goose 鹅肉：*roast goose* 烤鹅 **3** [C] a female goose 雌鹅 ➲ COMPARE GANDER **4** [C] (*old-fashioned, informal*) a silly person 傻瓜；笨蛋 ➲ SEE ALSO WILD GOOSE CHASE IDM SEE COOK *v.*, KILL *v.*, SAUCE, SAY *v.*
■ ***verb*** (*informal*) **1 ~ sb** to touch or squeeze sb's bottom 触摸（或捏）（某人）的臀部 **2 ~ sth** (**along/up**) (*NAmE*) to make sth move or work faster 推动；促进；激励

goose·berry /ˈɡʊzbəri; *NAmE* ˈɡuːsberi/ *noun* (*pl.* **-ies**) a small green fruit that grows on a bush with THORNS. Gooseberries taste sour and are usually cooked to make jam, PIES, etc. Children are sometimes told that babies come from 'under the gooseberry bush'. 醋栗：*a gooseberry bush* 醋栗灌木 ➲ VISUAL VOCAB PAGE V33
IDM **play ˈgooseberry** (*BrE*) to be a third person with two people who have a romantic relationship and want to be alone together 当电灯泡（夹在情侣之间，不知趣）

goose·bumps /ˈɡuːsbʌmps/ *noun* [pl.] = GOOSE PIMPLES

ˈgoose egg *noun* (*NAmE, informal*) a score of zero in a game（比赛中的）零分，鸭蛋

ˈgoose pimples *noun* [pl.] (*also less frequent* **goose·flesh** [U]) (*both especially BrE*) (*also* **goose·bumps**) a condition in which there are raised spots on your skin because you feel cold, frightened or excited（由于寒冷、恐惧或激动而起的）鸡皮疙瘩：*It gave me goose pimples just to think about it.* 一想到它我就起鸡皮疙瘩。

ˈgoose-step *noun* [sing.] (*often disapproving*) a way of marching, used by soldiers in some countries, in which the legs are raised high and straight 正步 ▶ **ˈgoose-step** *verb* (**-pp-**) [I]

GOP /ˌdʒiː əʊ ˈpiː; *NAmE* oʊ/ *abbr.* Grand Old Party (the Republican political party in the US) 老大党（美国共和党）

go·pher /ˈɡəʊfə(r); *NAmE* ˈɡoʊ-/ *noun* **1** (*also* **ˈground squirrel**) a N American animal like a RAT, that lives in holes in the ground 囊地鼠；囊鼠 **2** = GOFER

gora /ˈɡɔːrə/ *noun* (*pl.* **goras** or **goray** /ˈɡɔːreɪ/) a word used by people from S Asia for a white person（南亚用语）白人

Gor·dian knot /ˌɡɔːdiən ˈnɒt; *NAmE* ˌɡɔːrdiən ˈnɑːt/ *noun* a very difficult or impossible task or problem 戈尔迪乌姆结；难解的结；难办的事；棘手的问题：*to cut/untie the Gordian knot* (= to solve a problem by taking action) 采取行动解决问题 ORIGIN From the legend in which King Gordius tied a very complicated knot and said that whoever undid it would become the ruler of Asia. Alexander the Great cut through the knot with his sword. 源自传说：戈尔迪乌斯国王打了一个十分难解的结，并称谁能解开便会成为亚洲的统治者，结果亚历山大大帝挥剑将结斩断。

Gor·don Ben·nett /ˌɡɔːdn ˈbenət; *NAmE* ˌɡɔːrd-/ *exclamation* (*BrE*) people sometimes say **Gordon Bennett!** when they are annoyed or surprised about sth（表示恼怒或惊讶）天哪，哎呀 ORIGIN From James Gordon Bennett, an American newspaper owner and financial supporter of sports events. 源自美国报业老板和体育比赛赞助人詹姆斯・戈登・贝内特（James Gordon Bennett）。

gore /ɡɔː(r)/ *verb, noun*
■ ***verb*** **~ sb/sth** (of an animal 动物) to wound a person or another animal with a horn or TUSK（用角或长牙）顶伤，戳伤：*He was gored by a bull.* 他被公牛顶伤。
■ ***noun*** [U] thick blood that has flowed from a wound, especially in a violent situation（尤指在暴力情况下）伤口流出的血，凝固的血：*The movie is not just* ***blood and gore*** (= scenes of violence)*; it has a thrilling story.* 这部影片不光有血淋淋的暴力场面，还有扣人心弦的情节。➲ SEE ALSO GORY

gorge /ɡɔːdʒ; *NAmE* ɡɔːrdʒ/ *noun, verb*
■ ***noun*** a deep narrow valley with steep sides 峡；峡谷 SYN **canyon**：*the Rhine Gorge* 莱茵峡谷 ➲ VISUAL VOCAB PAGE V5
IDM **sb's ˈgorge rises** (*formal*) somebody feels so angry about sth that they feel physically sick 感到烦心（或厌恶）；作呕
■ ***verb*** [T, I] **~ (yourself)** (**on sth**) (*sometimes disapproving*) to eat a lot of sth, until you are too full to eat any more 贪婪地吃；狼吞虎咽 SYN **stuff**

gor·geous /ˈɡɔːdʒəs; *NAmE* ˈɡɔːrdʒəs/ *adj.* **1** (*informal*) very beautiful and attractive; giving pleasure and enjoyment 非常漂亮的；美丽动人的；令人愉快的 SYN **lovely**：*a gorgeous girl/man* 漂亮的女郎；美男子 ◇ *a gorgeous view* 美丽的景色 ◇ *gorgeous weather* (= warm and with a lot of sun) 宜人的天气 ◇ ***You look gorgeous!*** 你真漂亮！◇ *It was* ***absolutely gorgeous.*** 那真是美丽绝伦。➲ SYNONYMS AT BEAUTIFUL **2** [usually before noun] (of colours, clothes, etc. 颜色、衣服等) with very deep colours; impressive 绚丽的；灿烂的；华丽的：*exotic birds with feathers of gorgeous colours* 长着绚丽羽毛的异国的鸟 ▶ **gor·geous·ly** *adv.*

gor·gon /ˈɡɔːɡən; *NAmE* ˈɡɔːrɡən/ *noun* **1** (in ancient Greek stories) one of three sisters with snakes on their heads instead of hair, who can change anyone that looks at them into stone 戈耳工蛇发女怪（古希腊神话中三个蛇发女怪之一，人见之即化为石头） **2** an ugly woman who behaves in an aggressive and frightening way 丑陋凶恶的女人

gor·illa /ɡəˈrɪlə/ *noun* **1** a very large powerful African APE (= an animal like a large MONKEY without a tail) covered with black or brown hair 大猩猩（产于非洲） **2** *(informal)* a large aggressive man 高大凶恶的人

gorm·less /ˈɡɔːmləs; *NAmE* ˈɡɔːrm-/ *adj.* *(BrE, informal)* stupid 愚蠢的；傻的；没头没脑的：*a gormless boy* 呆小子 ◇ *Don't just stand there looking gormless—do something!* 别只是傻乎乎地站在那儿，干点事吧！

ˈgo-round *noun* = GO-AROUND

gorp /ɡɔːp; *NAmE* ɡɔːrp/ *noun* [U] *(NAmE)* a mixture of nuts, dried fruit, etc. eaten between meals to provide extra energy, especially by people on camping trips, etc. 什锦干果果仁

gorse /ɡɔːs; *NAmE* ɡɔːrs/ *(BrE also* **furze***)* *noun* [U] a bush with thin leaves with sharp points and small yellow flowers. Gorse often grows on land that is not used or cared for. 荆豆（叶带刺，开小黄花，长于荒野）

gory /ˈɡɔːri/ *adj.* (**gor·ier**, **gori·est**) **1** *(informal)* involving a lot of blood or violence; showing or describing blood and violence 血淋淋的；残暴的；描述流血和暴力的：*a gory accident* 流血事件 ◇ *the gory task of the pathologist* 病理学家经常与血打交道的工作 ◇ *a gory movie* 充满流血和暴力镜头的电影 ◇ *(humorous) He insisted on telling us all the* **gory details** *about their divorce* (= the unpleasant facts). 他坚持要给我们讲他们离婚的种种惨痛经历。 **2** *(literary)* covered with blood 沾满血污的；血迹斑斑的 SYN **bloodstained**：*a gory figure* 满身是血的人

gosh /ɡɒʃ; *NAmE* ɡɑːʃ/ *exclamation* *(old-fashioned, informal)* people say **'Gosh!'** when they are surprised or shocked（惊奇或惊讶时说）天哪，啊呀：*Gosh, is that the time?* 啊呀，都这会儿啦？

gos·hawk /ˈɡɒshɔːk; *NAmE* ˈɡɑːs-/ *noun* a large HAWK with short wings 苍鹰

gos·ling /ˈɡɒzlɪŋ; *NAmE* ˈɡɑːz-/ *noun* a young GOOSE (= a bird like a large DUCK) 小鹅；幼鹅

ˌgo-ˈslow *(BrE)* *(NAmE* **slow·down***)* *noun* a protest that workers make by doing their work more slowly than usual 怠工 ➲ COMPARE WORK-TO-RULE

gos·pel /ˈɡɒspl; *NAmE* ˈɡɑːspl/ *noun* **1** [C] *(also* **Gospel***)* one of the four books in the Bible about the life and teaching of Jesus 福音（《圣经》中关于耶稣生平和教诲的四福音书之一）：*the Gospel according to St John* 约翰福音 ◇ *St Mark's Gospel* 《马可福音》 **2** [sing.] *(also* **the Gospel***)* the life and teaching of Jesus as explained in the Bible 福音（耶稣的事迹和教诲）：***preaching/spreading the gospel*** 宣讲 / 传布福音 ➲ COLLOCATIONS AT RELIGION **3** [C, usually sing.] a set of ideas that sb believes in and tries to persuade others to accept（个人的）信念，信仰：*He preached a gospel of military strength.* 他鼓吹军事实力主义。 **4** *(also* **ˌgospel ˈtruth***)* [U] *(informal)* the complete truth 绝对真理：*Is that gospel?* 那是绝对真理吗？ ◇ *Don't take his word as gospel.* 别把他的话当作绝对真理。 **5** *(also* **ˈgospel music***)* [U] a style of religious singing developed by African Americans 福音音乐（最初在非裔美国人中间传唱的宗教音乐）：*a gospel choir* 福音唱诗班

gos·samer /ˈɡɒsəmə(r); *NAmE* ˈɡɑːs-/ *noun* [U] **1** the very fine thread made by spiders 蛛丝 **2** *(literary)* any very light delicate material 薄纱；精细织物：*a gown of gossamer silk* 女式丝绸长裙 ◇ *the gossamer wings of a dragonfly* 薄如轻纱的蜻蜓翅膀

gos·sip /ˈɡɒsɪp; *NAmE* ˈɡɑːsɪp/ *noun, verb*

▪ *noun* **1** [U] *(disapproving)* informal talk or stories about other people's private lives, that may be unkind or not true 流言蜚语；闲言碎语：*Don't believe all the gossip you hear.* 别对那些道听途说都信以为真。 ◇ *Tell me all* ***the latest gossip****!* 把最新的小道消息都讲给我听听吧！ ◇ *The gossip was that he had lost a fortune on the stock exchange.* 有小道消息说他在股票交易中赔了一大笔钱。 ◇ *It* ***was common gossip*** (= everyone said so) *that they were having an affair.* 大家议论纷纷说他们之间关系暧昧。 ◇ *She's a great one for* ***idle gossip*** (= she enjoys spreading stories about other people that are probably not true). 她很喜欢说别人闲话。 **2** [C, usually sing.] a conversation about other people and their private lives 闲聊：*I love a good gossip.* 我喜欢闲聊天。 ➲ SYNONYMS AT DISCUSSION **3** [C] *(disapproving)* a person who enjoys talking about other people's private lives 喜欢传播流言蜚语的人；爱说长道短（或说三道四）的人 ➲ SYNONYMS AT SPEAKER ▸ **gos·sipy** /ˈɡɒsɪpi; *NAmE* ˈɡɑːs-/ *adj.*：*a gossipy letter/neighbour* 闲聊式的信；爱说三道四的邻居

▪ *verb* [I] to talk about other people's private lives, often in an unkind way 传播流言蜚语；说三道四；说长道短：*I can't stand here gossiping all day.* 我不能整天站在这儿闲聊啊。 ◇ **~ about sb/sth** *She's been gossiping about you.* 她一直在说你的闲话。

ˈgossip column *noun* a piece of writing in a newspaper about social events and the private and personal lives of famous people 漫谈栏，茶话栏（报刊有关社交活动和名人私生活的专栏） ▸ **ˈgossip columnist** *noun*

got PAST TENSE, PAST PART. OF GET

gotcha /ˈɡɒtʃə; *NAmE* ˈɡɑːtʃə/ *exclamation* *(non-standard)* the written form of the way some people pronounce 'I've got you', which is not considered to be correct（有人用作 I've got you 发音的书写形式，此用法被视为不正确）：*'Gotcha!' I yelled as I grabbed him by the arm* (= used when you have caught sb, or have beaten them at sth). "逮住你了！"我抓住他的胳膊大声喊道。 ◇ *'Don't let go.' 'Yeah, gotcha.'* (= Yes, I understand.) "别松手。" "是，我明白。" HELP You should not write this form unless you are copying somebody's speech. 除非转述他人话语，否则不应写成这种形式。 ➲ MORE LIKE THIS 5, page R25

goth /ɡɒθ; *NAmE* ɡɑːθ/ *noun* **1** [U] a style of rock music, popular in the 1980s, that developed from PUNK music. The words often expressed ideas about the end of the world, death or the DEVIL. 哥特摇滚乐（由朋克摇滚乐发展而来，流行于 20 世纪 80 年代，歌词通常涉及世界末日、死亡或撒旦） **2** [C] a member of a group of people who listen to goth music and wear black clothes and black and white MAKE-UP 哥特派中的一员（听哥特摇滚乐，穿黑色衣服，化黑白色妆） ▸ **goth** *(also* **goth·ic***)* *adj.*

Gotham /ˈɡɒθəm; *NAmE* ˈɡɑːθ-/ *noun* *(informal)* New York City 哥谭镇，傻子村（纽约市的绰号）

Goth·ic /ˈɡɒθɪk; *NAmE* ˈɡɑːθ-/ *adj., noun*

▪ *adj.* **1** connected with the Goths (= a Germanic people who fought against the Roman Empire) 哥特人的，哥特族的，哥特语的 **2** *(architecture* 建*)* built in the style that was popular in western Europe from the 12th to the 16th centuries, and which has pointed ARCHES and windows and tall thin PILLARS 哥特式的，哥特风格的（12 至 16 世纪流行于西欧的建筑风格，以尖拱、尖窗和细长柱为特色）：*a Gothic church* 哥特式教堂 **3** (of a novel, etc. 小说等) written in the style popular in the 18th and 19th centuries, which described romantic adventures in mysterious or frightening surroundings 哥特派的，哥特风格的（流行于 18 至 19 世纪，描述神秘或恐怖气氛中的爱情故事） **4** (of type and printing 字体和印刷字体) having pointed letters with thick lines and sharp angles. German books used to be printed in this style. 哥特体黑体字的（旧时德语书籍常用） **5** connected with goths 哥特派的

▪ *noun* [U] **1** the Gothic style of ARCHITECTURE 哥特式建筑；尖拱式建筑 **2** Gothic printing type or printed letters 哥特体黑体字

ˈgo-to *adj.* [only before noun] *(especially NAmE)* used to refer to the person or place that sb goes to for help, advice or information（指对象）寻求协助的，征询意见的：*He's the president's go-to guy on Asian politics.* 他是总统的亚洲政治智囊。

G

gotta /ˈɡɒtə; NAmE ˈɡɑːtə/ (*informal, non-standard*) the written form of the word some people use to mean '(have) got to' or '(have) got a', which is not considered to be correct（有人用作 (have) got to 和 (have) got a 的书写形式，此用法被视为不正确）：*He's gotta go.* 他得走了。◇ *Gotta cigarette?* 有烟吗？ **HELP** You should not write this form unless you are copying somebody's speech. 除非转述他人话语，否则不应写成这种形式。 ➲ MORE LIKE THIS 5, page R25

got·ten (*NAmE*) PAST PART. OF GET

gou·ache /ɡuˈɑːʃ; ɡwɑːʃ/ *noun* **1** [U] a method of painting using colours that are mixed with water and made thick with a type of glue; the paints used in this method 广告色画法；广告色画颜料 **2** [C] a picture painted using this method 广告色画

gouge /ɡaʊdʒ/ *verb, noun*

■ *verb* **1** ~ **sth** (**in sth**) to make a hole or cut in sth with a sharp object in a rough or violent way 凿：*The lion's claws had gouged a wound in the horse's side.* 狮爪在马身一侧抓了一道深口。◇ *He had gouged her cheek with a screwdriver.* 他用螺丝起子戳她的脸颊。 **2** ~ **sb/sth** (*NAmE*) to force sb to pay an unfairly high price for sth; to raise prices unfairly 敲（某人）的竹杠；诈骗钱财；漫天要价：*Price gouging is widespread.* 漫天要价的情况普遍存在。

PHR V ˌ**gouge sth↔ˈout** (**of sth**) to remove or form sth by digging into a surface 抠出某物；挖出某物：*The man's eyes had gouged out.* 这男人的双眼已被挖了出来。◇ *Glaciers gouged out valleys from the hills.* 冰川把丘陵地带侵蚀出一条条山谷。

■ *noun* **1** a sharp tool for making hollow areas in wood 凿子 **2** a deep, narrow hole or cut in a surface 凿成的槽（或孔、洞）

gou·jons /ˈɡuːdʒənz; ˈɡuːʒ-/ *noun* [pl.] (*BrE, from French*) small pieces of fish or chicken fried in oil 油炸鱼块（或鸡块）

gou·lash /ˈɡuːlæʃ/ *noun* [C, U] a hot spicy Hungarian dish of meat that is cooked slowly in liquid with PAPRIKA 匈牙利红烩牛肉；匈牙利的辣椒炖肉；菜炖牛肉

gourd /ɡʊəd; ɡɔːd; NAmE ɡʊrd; ɡɔːrd/ *noun* a type of large fruit with hard skin and soft flesh. Gourds are often dried and used as containers. 葫芦（晾干后常作容器） ➲ SEE ALSO CALABASH (1)

gour·mand /ˈɡʊəmənd; NAmE ˈɡʊrmɑːnd/ *noun* (*often disapproving*) a person who enjoys eating and eats large amounts of food 大肚子；大肚汉；喜欢吃喝的人

gour·met /ˈɡʊəmeɪ; NAmE ˈɡʊrm-/ *noun* a person who knows a lot about good food and wines and who enjoys choosing, eating and drinking them 美食家；讲究饮食的人；美酒美食品尝家 ▸ **gour·met** *adj.* [only before noun]: *gourmet food* (= of high quality and often expensive) 美味佳肴

gout /ɡaʊt/ *noun* [U] a disease that causes painful swelling in the joints, especially of the toes, knees and fingers 痛风

gov·ern 🔑 /ˈɡʌvn; NAmE ˈɡʌvərn/ *verb* **1** 🔑 [T, I] ~ (**sth**) to legally control a country or its people and be responsible for introducing new laws, organizing public services, etc. 统治；控制；管理；治理：*The country is governed by elected representatives of the people.* 这个国家由民选代表统治。◇ *He accused the opposition party of being unfit to govern.* 他指责反对党无力治理国事。 **2** [T, often passive] ~ **sth** to control or influence sb/sth or how sth happens, functions, etc. 控制；影响；支配：*Prices are governed by market demand.* 价格的高低取决于市场的需求。◇ *All his decisions have been entirely governed by self-interest.* 他的所有决定都受利己之心的支配。◇ *We need changes in the law governing school attendance.* 我们需要对影响就学率的法规做些改动。 **3** [T] ~ **sth** (*grammar* 语法) if a word **governs** another word or phrase, it affects how that word or phrase is formed or used 支配（词或短语的形式或用法）

gov·ern·ance /ˈɡʌvənəns; NAmE -vərn-/ *noun* [U] (*specialist*) the activity of governing a country or controlling a company or an organization; the way in which a country is governed or a company or institution is controlled 统治；管理；统治方式；管理方式

gov·ern·ess /ˈɡʌvənəs; NAmE -vərn-/ *noun* (especially in the past) a woman employed to teach the children of a rich family in their home and to live with them（尤指旧时的）家庭女教师 ➲ COMPARE TUTOR *n.*

gov·ern·ing /ˈɡʌvənɪŋ; NAmE -vərn-/ *adj.* [only before noun] having the right and the authority to control sth such as a country or an institution 统治的；控制的；管理的；治理的：*The Conservatives were then the **governing party**.* 那时是保守党当政。◇ *The school's **governing body*** (= the group of people who control the organization of the school) *took responsibility for the decision.* 学校行政机构对这个决定负责。

gov·ern·ment 🔑 /ˈɡʌvənmənt; NAmE -vərn-/ *noun* **1** 🔑 [C+sing./pl. v.] (*often* **the Government**) (*abbr.* **govt**) the group of people who are responsible for controlling a country or a state 政府；内阁：*to **lead/form a government*** 领导政府；组成内阁 ◇ *the last Conservative government* 上届保守党政府 ◇ *the government of the day* 当时的政府 ◇ *Foreign governments have been consulted about this decision.* 这一决定曾征求过他国政府的意见。◇ *She has resigned from the Government.* 她已辞去内阁职位。◇ *The Government has/have been considering further tax cuts.* 政府一直在考虑进一步减税的问题。◇ ***government policies/officials/ministers*** 政府政策；内阁官员 / 部长 ◇ ***a government department/agency/grant*** 政府部门 / 机构 / 拨款 ◇ ***government expenditure/intervention*** 政府开支 / 干预 ➲ COLLOCATIONS AT POLITICS **2** 🔑 [U] a particular system or method of controlling a country 政体；国家体制：***coalition/communist/democratic/totalitarian, etc. government*** 联合、共产主义、民主、极权主义等政体 ◇ *Democratic government has now replaced military rule.* 民主政体现已取代军事统治。◇ ***central/federal government*** 中央 / 联邦政府 **3** 🔑 [U] the activity or the manner of controlling a country（一国的）统治，治理，统治方式，管理方式：*strong government* 强有力的统治 ◇ *The Democrats are now **in government** in the US.* 美国目前是民主党人执政。 ➲ SEE ALSO BIG GOVERNMENT

WORDFINDER 联想词： cabinet, checks and balances, constitution, federal, minister, the Opposition, **parliament**, **politics**, **system**

gov·ern·men·tal /ˌɡʌvnˈmentl; NAmE ˌɡʌvərn-/ *adj.* connected with government; of a government 统治的；政体的；政府的：*governmental agencies* 政府机构 ◇ *governmental actions* 政府行动

ˌ**government and ˈbinding theory** (*also* ˈ**binding theory**) *noun* [U] (*linguistics* 语言) a theory of grammar based on the idea that a series of conditions relate the parts of a sentence together 支配约束理论，管约理论，管辖约束理论（即基于一系列条件连接起句子各部分的理念的语法理论）

ˌ**government ˈhealth warning** *noun* **1** (in Britain) a notice that must by law appear on a product, especially a pack of cigarettes, that warns people that it is dangerous to their health（在英国于香烟等产品上的）政府健康忠告 **2** (*also* ˈ**health warning**) (*BrE*) a warning that sth should be treated carefully because it may cause problems 需谨慎对待的警告：*These figures should come with a government health warning.* 这些数字该附以谨慎对待的警告。

gov·ern·or 🔑 /ˈɡʌvənə(r); NAmE -vərn-/ *noun* **1** 🔑 (*also* **Governor**) a person who is the official head of a country or region that is governed by another country 统治者；管辖者；总督：*the former governor of the colony* 该殖民地的前总督 ◇ *a provincial governor* 省长 **2** 🔑 (*also* **Governor**) a person who is chosen to be in charge of the government of a state in the US（美国的）州长：*the governor of*

Arizona 亚利桑那州州长 ◇ *the Arizona governor* 亚利桑那州州长 ◇ *Governor Bev Perdue* 贝福•珀杜州长 **3** (*especially BrE*) a member of a group of people who are responsible for controlling an institution such as a school, a college or a hospital（学校、学院、医院等机构的）董事，理事：*a school governor* 学校董事 ◇ *the board of governors of the college* 学院董事会 **4** (*BrE*) a person who is in charge of an institution 主管；机构负责人；总裁：*a prison governor* 监狱长 ◇ *the governor of the Bank of England* 英格兰银行总裁 ◇ (*informal*) *I can't decide. I'll have to ask the governor* (= the man in charge, who employs sb). 我做不了主，我得问问老板。➲ SEE ALSO GUV'NOR

ˌgovernor ˈgeneral *noun* (*pl.* **governors general** or **governor generals**) the official representative in a country of the country that has or had political control over it, especially the representative of the British King or Queen in a Commonwealth country 总督（派驻政治统辖国的官方代表，尤指英国国王或女王派驻英联邦国家的代表）

govt (*also* **govt.** *especially in NAmE*) *abbr.* (in writing 书写形式) government 政府

ˌgo ˈwell *exclamation* (*SAfrE*) used to say goodbye to sb 再见；再会：*I hope you enjoy your holiday. Go well!* 祝你假期玩得愉快。再见！

gown /gaʊn/ *noun* **1** a woman's dress, especially a long one for special occasions（尤指特别场合穿的）女裙，女长服，女礼服：***an evening/a wedding gown*** 女晚礼服；婚纱 **2** a long loose piece of clothing that is worn over other clothes by judges and (in Britain) by other lawyers, and by members of universities (at special ceremonies)（法官、英国律师、大学学生在特别仪式上穿的）长袍，长外衣：*a graduation gown* 毕业礼服 **3** a piece of clothing that is worn over other clothes to protect them, especially in a hospital（尤指在医院穿的）罩衣，外罩：*a surgeon's gown* 外科医生穿的罩衣 ➲ SEE ALSO DRESSING GOWN

gowned /gaʊnd/ *adj.* wearing a gown 穿着长袍（或长服、礼服）的

goy /gɔɪ/ *noun* (*pl.* **goy·im** /ˈgɔɪɪm/ or **goys**) (*informal, often offensive*) a word used by Jewish people for a person who is not Jewish（犹太人用语，含冒犯意）非犹太人，外邦人

GP /ˌdʒiː ˈpiː/ *noun* the abbreviation for 'general practitioner' (a doctor who is trained in general medicine and who works in the local community, not in a hospital) 全科医生，普通医师（全写为 general practitioner，在社区而非在医院工作）：*Go and see your GP as soon as possible.* 尽早去看你的全科医生。◇ *There are four GPs in our local practice.* 在我们地区诊所有四个全科医生。

GPA /ˌdʒiː piː ˈeɪ/ *abbr.* (*NAmE*) GRADE POINT AVERAGE 平均积分点；平均成绩点数：*He graduated with a GPA of 3.8.* 他毕业时各科成绩的平均积分点为 3.8。

Gp Capt *abbr.* GROUP CAPTAIN （英国）空军上校

GPRS /ˌdʒiː piː ɑːr ˈes/ *abbr.* general packet radio services (a way of sending electronic data as radio signals, used especially between mobile/cell phones and the Internet) 通用分组无线业务

GPS /ˌdʒiː piː ˈes/ *noun* the abbreviation for 'global positioning system' (a system by which signals are sent from SATELLITES to a special device, used to show the position of a person or thing on the surface of the earth very accurately) 全球定位系统（全写为 global positioning system）：*The drivers all have GPS in the van.* 这些司机的厢式货车里都装有全球定位系统。➲ COMPARE SATNAV ➲ WORDFINDER NOTE AT MAP

grab /græb/ *verb, noun*

■ *verb* (**-bb-**) **1** [T, I] to take or hold sb/sth with your hand suddenly, firmly or roughly 抓住；攫取 SYN **seize**: **~ (sth)** *She grabbed the child's hand and ran.* 她抓住孩子的手就跑。◇ *He* ***grabbed hold of*** *me and wouldn't let go.* 他抓住我不松手。◇ *Don't grab—there's plenty for everyone.* 别抢，多着呢，人人都有。◇ **~ sth from sb/sth** *Jim grabbed a cake from the plate.* 吉姆从盘子里抓了一块蛋糕。 **2** [I] to try to take hold of sth（试图）抓住，夺得：**~ at sth** *She grabbed at the branch, missed and fell.* 她抓树枝，可没抓着，就跌倒了。◇ **~ for sth** *Kate grabbed for the robber's gun.* 凯特拼命去夺抢劫者的枪。 **3** [T, I] to take advantage of an opportunity to do or have sth 利用，抓住（机会）SYN **seize**: **~ sth** *This was my big chance and I grabbed it with both hands.* 这是我的大好机会，我紧紧抓住。◇ **~ at sth** *He'll grab at any excuse to avoid doing the dishes.* 他会随便找个借口来逃避洗碗。 **4** [T] **~ sth** to have or take sth quickly, especially because you are in a hurry（尤指匆忙地）取，拿，吃，喝：*Let's grab a sandwich before we go.* 咱们赶快吃个三明治就走吧。◇ *I managed to grab a couple of hours' sleep on the plane.* 我在飞机上抓紧时间睡了几个钟头。◇ ***Grab a seat,*** *I won't keep you a moment.* 赶紧找个座位吧，我不会耽误你太多工夫。 **5** [T] **~ sth** to take sth for yourself, especially in a selfish or GREEDY way（尤指自私、贪婪地）捞取，赚取，抢占：*By the time we arrived, someone had grabbed all the good seats.* 我们到达时，所有的好位子都给人占了。 **6** [T] **~ sb/sth** to get sb's attention 引人注意；吸引：*I'll see if I can grab the waitress and get the bill.* 我要看能不能引起服务员的注意，让她拿账单来。◇ *Glasgow's drugs problem has* ***grabbed the headlines tonight*** (= been published as an important story in the newspapers). 格拉斯哥的毒品问题成了今晚报纸的头条新闻。➲ MORE LIKE THIS 36, page R29

IDM **how does...grab you?** (*informal*) used to ask sb whether they are interested in sth or in doing sth 你对…有兴趣吗；你喜欢…吗；你认为…如何：*How does the idea of a trip to Rome grab you?* 你认为去趟罗马这个主意如何？

■ *noun* **1** [usually sing.] **~ (at/for sb/sth)** a sudden attempt to take or hold sb/sth 猛然的抓取；突然的抢夺：*He* ***made a grab for*** *her bag.* 他突然去抢她的手提包。➲ SEE ALSO SMASH-AND-GRAB **2** (*computing* 计) a picture taken from a television or video film, stored as an image on a computer 抓取（或截获、采集）的图像：*a frame grab from CCTV* 从闭路电视抓取的一帧图像 **3** a piece of equipment which lifts and holds goods, for example the equipment that hangs from a CRANE 抓斗；抓具

IDM **up for ˈgrabs** (*informal*) available for anyone who is interested 提供的；可供争夺的：*There are £25 000 worth of prizes up for grabs in our competition!* 在我们的比赛中有价值 25 000 英镑的奖品供人争夺！

ˈgrab bag *noun* (*NAmE*) **1** (*BrE* **ˌlucky ˈdip**) a game in which people choose a present from a container of presents without being able to see what it is going to be 摸彩游戏 **2** (*informal*) a mixed collection of things（各种事物的）混杂，聚合：*He offered a grab bag of reasons for his decision.* 他为自己所作的决定提出了各种理由。

grace /greɪs/ *noun, verb*

■ *noun*

• **OF MOVEMENT** 动作 **1** [U] an attractive quality of movement that is smooth, elegant and controlled 优美；优雅：*She moves with the natural grace of a ballerina.* 她的动作具有芭蕾舞演员自然优雅的丰姿。

• **BEHAVIOUR** 行为 **2** [U] a quality of behaviour that is polite and pleasant and deserves respect 文雅；高雅：*He conducted himself with grace and dignity throughout the trial.* 在整个审讯过程中他表现得文雅而有尊严。 **3 graces** [pl.] (*especially BrE*) ways of behaving that people think are polite and acceptable 风度；体面：*He was not particularly well versed in the* ***social graces.*** 他对社交礼节并不特别熟悉。

• **EXTRA TIME** 额外时间 **4** [U] extra time that is given to sb to enable them to pay a bill, finish a piece of work, etc. 宽限期；延缓期：*They've given me a month's grace to get the money.* 他们宽限我一个月弄到这笔钱。

• **OF GOD** 上帝 **5** [U] the kindness that God shows towards the human race 恩宠；恩典：*It was only by the grace of God that they survived.* 承蒙天恩，他们才幸免于难。➲ COLLOCATIONS AT RELIGION

• **PRAYER** 祈祷 **6** [U, C] a short prayer that is usually said before a meal to thank God for the food（饭前的）谢恩祈

祷：*Let's say grace.* 我们做饭前祷告吧。

• TITLE 称呼 **7 His/Her/Your Grace** [C] used as a title of respect when talking to or about an ARCHBISHOP, a DUKE or a DUCHESS（对大主教、公爵、公爵夫人、女公爵的尊称）大人，阁下，夫人：*Good Morning, Your Grace.* 早上好，阁下。◇ *Their Graces the Duke and Duchess of Kent.* 肯特公爵及公爵夫人阁下。➲ SEE ALSO COUP DE GRÂCE, SAVING GRACE

IDM **be in sb's good 'graces** (*formal*) to have sb's approval and be liked by them 为某人所赞同（或喜爱）；得到某人的欢心 **ˌfall from 'grace** to lose the trust or respect that people have for you, especially by doing sth wrong or immoral（尤指因做了错事或不道德之事而）失去信任，失去尊重，失去恩宠 **sb's ˌfall from 'grace** a situation in which sb loses the trust or respect that people have for them, especially because of sth wrong or immoral that they have done（尤指因做了错事或不道德之事的）失信 **have the (good) grace to do sth** to be polite enough to do sth, especially when you have done sth wrong （尤指犯错后）知趣地做某事，通情达理地做某事：*He didn't even have the grace to look embarrassed.* 他甚至连一丝尴尬的神色都没有。 **there but for the grace of 'God (go 'I)** (*saying*) used to say that you could easily have been in the same difficult or unpleasant situation that sb else is in 若非天助，区区岂能幸免 **with (a) bad 'grace** in an unwilling and/or rude way 勉强地；不情愿地；无礼地：*He handed over the money with typical bad grace.* 他照常不情愿地把钱交出来。 **with (a) good 'grace** in a willing and pleasant way 心甘情愿地；乐意地；高高兴兴地：*You must learn to accept defeat with good grace.* 你必须学会欣然承认失败。➲ MORE AT AIR *n.*, STATE *n.*, YEAR

■ *verb* (*formal*) **1 ~ sth** to make sth more attractive; to decorate sth 为…增色；为…锦上添花；装饰：*The table had once graced a duke's drawing room.* 这张桌子曾一度为公爵的起居室增色不少。 **2** (*usually ironic*) to bring honour to sb/sth; to be kind enough to attend or take part in sth 使荣耀；使生辉；承蒙光临：**~ sb/sth** *She is one of the finest players ever to have graced the game.* 她是曾使这项运动生辉的最杰出的运动员之一。◇ **~ sb/sth with sth** *Will you be **gracing us with your presence** tonight?* 请问您今晚能否赏光？

ˌgrace and 'favour *adj.* [only before noun] (*BrE*) used to describe a house or flat/apartment that a king, queen or government has allowed sb to use（房屋或公寓）君主（或政府当局）准予使用的，钦赐的

grace·ful /ˈɡreɪsfl/ *adj.* **1** moving in a controlled, attractive way or having a smooth, attractive form 优美的；优雅的；雅致的：*The dancers were all tall and graceful.* 这些舞蹈演员都个子高高的，动作十分优雅。◇ *He gave a graceful bow to the audience.* 他优雅地向观众鞠了一躬。◇ *the graceful curves of the hills* 连绵起伏的丘陵美景 **2** polite and kind in your behaviour, especially in a difficult situation （尤指在困境中）得体的，有风度的：*His father had always taught him to be graceful in defeat.* 他父亲总是教导他输了也要有风度。▶ **grace·ful·ly** /-fəli/ *adv.*：*The cathedral's white towers climb gracefully into the sky.* 大教堂白色的塔楼优雅庄重地耸入云霄。◇ *I think we should just give in gracefully.* 我认为我们应该大大方方地认输。 **grace·ful·ness** *noun* [U]

grace·less /ˈɡreɪsləs/ *adj.* **1** not knowing how to be polite and pleasant to other people 不懂礼貌的；粗鲁的；无礼的：*a graceless, angry young man* 一个粗鲁、愤怒的年轻男子 **2** not pleasing or attractive to look at 不优美的；不雅致的；难看的：*the graceless architecture of the 1960s* * 20 世纪 60 年代的丑陋建筑 **3** moving in an awkward way 笨拙的：*She swam with a graceless stroke.* 她游泳的姿势很难看。OPP graceful ▶ **grace·less·ly** *adv.*

ˈgrace note *noun* (*music* 音) an extra note which is not a necessary part of a tune, but which is played before one of the notes of the tune as decoration 装饰音

gra·cious /ˈɡreɪʃəs/ *adj.* **1** (of people or behaviour 人或行为) kind, polite and generous, especially to sb of a lower social position （尤指对社会地位较低者）和蔼的，慈祥的，有礼貌的，宽厚的：*a gracious lady* 好心的女士 ◇ *a gracious smile* 慈祥的微笑 ◇ *He has not yet learned how to be gracious in defeat.* 他还没有学会怎样豁达大度地面对失败。 **2** [usually before noun] showing the comfort and easy way of life that wealth can bring 富贵安逸的：*gracious living* 豪华安逸的生活 **3** [only before noun] (*BrE, formal*) used as a very polite word for royal people or their actions （对王族及其行为的敬语）仁慈的，宽厚的：*her gracious Majesty the Queen* 仁慈的女王陛下 **4 ~ (to sb)** (of God 上帝) showing kindness and MERCY 仁慈的；慈悲的；宽大的：*a gracious act of God* 上帝的慈悲 **5** (*becoming old-fashioned*) used for expressing surprise（表示惊异）天哪，老天爷，啊呀：*Goodness gracious!* 老天爷啊！◇ *'I hope you didn't mind my phoning you.' 'Good gracious, no, of course not.'* "我希望你不会介意我给你打电话。" "啊呀，当然不会。" ▶ **gra·cious·ly** *adv.*：*She graciously accepted our invitation.* 她落落大方地接受了我们的邀请。 **gra·cious·ness** *noun* [U]

grad /ɡræd/ *noun* (*informal, especially NAmE*) = GRADUATE

grad·able /ˈɡreɪdəbl/ *adj.* (*grammar* 语法) (of an adjective 形容词) that can be used in the comparative and superlative forms or be used with words like 'very' and 'less' 可分级的；可分程度的 OPP **non-gradable** ▶ **grad·abil·ity** /ˌɡreɪdəˈbɪləti/ *noun* [U]

grad·ation /ɡrəˈdeɪʃn/ *noun* **1** [C, U] (*formal*) any of the small changes or levels which sth is divided into; the process or result of sth changing gradually 逐渐的变化；层次；阶段；等级：*gradations of colour* 各种层次的颜色 ◇ *gradation in size* 大小等级 **2** (*also* **gradu·ation**) [C] a mark showing a division on a scale 刻度：*the gradations on a thermometer* 温度计上的刻度

grade 🔑 AW /ɡreɪd/ *noun, verb*

■ *noun* **1** 🔑 the quality of a particular product or material （产品、材料的）等级，品级：*All the materials used were of the highest grade.* 使用的材料全是优质品。 **2** 🔑 a level of ability or rank that sb has in an organization （官衔的）级别；职别：*salary grades* (= levels of pay) 工资级别 ◇ *She's still only on a secretarial grade.* 她的职别仍然只是秘书。 **3** 🔑 a mark given in an exam or for a piece of school work 成绩等级；评分等级：(*BrE*) *She got good grades in her exams.* 她考试成绩优良。◇ (*NAmE*) *She got good grades on her exams.* 她考试成绩优良。◇ *70% of pupils got Grade C or above.* * 70% 的小学生成绩都在 C 级或以上。➲ WORDFINDER NOTE AT EXAM **4** 🔑 (in the US school system) one of the levels in a school with children of similar age （美国学制）年级：*Sam is in (the) second grade.* 萨姆读二年级。 **5** (*specialist*) how serious an illness is （疾病的）程度，阶段：***low/high grade fever*** 低烧；高烧 **6** (*especially NAmE*) = GRADIENT (1) **7** (*BrE*) a level of exam in musical skill （音乐考试的）级别，水平

IDM **make the 'grade** (*informal*) to reach the necessary standard; to succeed 达到必要标准；符合要求；成功：*About 10% of trainees fail to make the grade.* 接受培训的人大约有 10% 未达标。

■ *verb* **1** 🔑 [often passive] to arrange people or things in groups according to their ability, quality, size, etc. （按能力、质量、大小等）分级，分等，分类：**~ sth/sb (by/according to sth)** *The containers are graded according to size.* 这些容器按大小分类。◇ **~ sth/sb from… to…** *Eggs are graded from small to extra large.* 鸡蛋从小号到特大号分成不同等级。◇ *Responses were graded from 1 (very satisfied) to 5 (not at all satisfied).* 回答按 1（非常满意）到 5（完全不满意）分类。◇ **~ sth (as) sth** *Ten beaches were graded as acceptable.* 有十个沙滩属于可接受的那一类。 **2** 🔑 (*especially NAmE*) to give a mark/grade to a student or to a piece of their written work 给…评分；给…分数：**~ sb/sth** *I spent all weekend grading papers.* 我整个周末都在评阅试卷。◇ **~ sb/sth + noun** *The best students are graded A.* 最优秀的学生评为甲等。➲ COMPARE MARK *v.* (6)

graded AW /ˈɡreɪdɪd/ *adj.* arranged in order or in groups according to difficulty, size, etc. （按难度、大小等）分级

的：*graded tests for language students* 语言学习者的分级测验 ◇ *graded doses of a drug* 药物的分级剂量

ˈgrade point average *noun* [usually sing.] (*abbr.* **GPA**) the average of a student's marks/grades over a period of time in the US education system（美国教育体制中学生在某一时期内各科成绩的）平均积分点，平均成绩点数

grader /ˈɡreɪdə(r)/ *noun* (*NAmE*) **1 first, second, etc. ~** a student who is in the grade mentioned …年级学生：*The play is open to all seventh and eighth graders.* 所有七、八年级的学生均可观看此剧。 **2** (*BrE* **mark·er**) a person who marks/grades students' work or exam papers 阅卷人；批改作业的人

ˈgrade school *noun* (*informal*) = ELEMENTARY SCHOOL

gra·di·ent /ˈɡreɪdiənt/ *noun* **1** (*also* **grade** *especially in NAmE*) the degree to which the ground slopes, especially on a road or railway（尤指公路或铁路的）坡度，斜率，倾斜度：*a steep gradient* 陡峭的坡度 ◇ *a hill with a gradient of 1 in 4 (or 25%)* 倾斜度为 1:4（或 25%）的小山 **2** (*specialist*) the rate at which temperature, pressure, etc. changes, or increases and decreases, between one region and another （温度、压力等的）变化率，梯度变化曲线

grad·ing /ˈɡreɪdɪŋ/ *noun* [U] (*NAmE*) = MARKING (3)

gra·dio·meter /ˌɡreɪdiˈɒmɪtə(r); *NAmE* -ˈɑːm-/ *noun* **1** (*specialist*) an instrument for measuring the angle of a slope 坡度测量仪 **2** (*physics* 物) an instrument for measuring the changes in an energy field 重力梯度仪

ˈgrad school *noun* (*NAmE, informal*) = GRADUATE SCHOOL

grad·ual 🔑 /ˈɡrædʒuəl/ *adj.* **1** 🔑 happening slowly over a long period; not sudden 逐渐的；逐步的；渐进的：*a gradual change in the climate* 气候的逐渐变化 ◇ *Recovery from the disease is very gradual.* 这种疾病的康复过程非常缓慢。 **OPP sudden** **2** (of a slope 斜坡) not steep 平缓的；不陡的

grad·ual·ism /ˈɡrædʒuəlɪzəm/ *noun* [U] a policy of gradual change in society rather than sudden change or revolution （社会改革上的）渐进主义，渐进主义政策 ▶ **grad·ual·ist** *noun*

grad·ual·ly 🔑 /ˈɡrædʒuəli/ *adv.* slowly, over a long period of time 逐渐地；逐步地；渐进地：*The weather gradually improved.* 天气逐渐好转。◇ *Gradually, the children began to understand.* 孩子们渐渐开始明白。

gradu·ate *noun, verb*

■ *noun* /ˈɡrædʒuət/ (*also informal* **grad** *especially in NAmE*) **1 ~ (in sth)** a person who has a university degree 大学毕业生；学士学位获得者：*a graduate in history* 历史学学士 ◇ *a science graduate* 理学士 ◇ *a graduate of Yale/a Yale graduate* 耶鲁大学毕业生 ◇ *a graduate student/course* 研究生；研究生课程 **2** (*NAmE*) a person who has completed their school studies 毕业生：*a high school graduate* 中学毕业生 ➲ NOTE AT STUDENT

■ *verb* /ˈɡrædʒueɪt/ **1** [I, T] to get a degree, especially your first degree, from a university or college 获得学位（尤指学士）；大学毕业：**~ (in sth)** *Only three students graduated in Czech studies last year.* 去年只有三名学生获得捷克研究学士学位。◇ **~ (from…)** *She graduated from Harvard this year.* 她今年毕业于哈佛大学。◇ *He graduated from York with a degree in Psychology.* 他毕业于约克大学，获心理学学士学位。◇ **~ sth** (*NAmE*) *She graduated college last year.* 她去年大学毕业。 ➲ WORDFINDER NOTE AT UNIVERSITY **2** [I, T] (*NAmE*) to complete a course in education, especially at HIGH SCHOOL 毕业（尤指中学）：**~ (from…)** *Martha graduated from high school two years ago.* 玛莎两年前高中毕业。◇ **~ sth** *Martha graduated high school two years ago.* 玛莎两年前高中毕业。 **3** [T] **~ sb (from sth)** (*NAmE*) to give a degree, DIPLOMA, etc. to sb 授予（某人）学位（或毕业文凭等）：*The college graduated 50 students last year.* 去年这所学院有 50 名毕业生。 **4** [I] **~ (from sth) to sth** to start doing sth more difficult or important than what you were doing before 逐渐发展（或变化、进展、上升）：*She recently graduated from being a dancer to having a small role in a movie.* 她最近从一个舞蹈演员逐步过渡到在电影里扮演小角色。 ➲ WORDFINDER NOTE AT STUDY ➲ COLLOCATIONS AT EDUCATION ➲ MORE LIKE THIS 21, page R27

gradu·ated /ˈɡrædʒueɪtɪd/ *adj.* **1** divided into groups or levels on a scale 分等级的；分层次的：*graduated lessons/tests* 分级课程 / 测验 **2** (of a container or measure 容器或量具) marked with lines to show measurements 标有刻度的 **SYN calibrate**：*a graduated jar* 标有刻度的广口瓶

ˌGraduate ˌManagement Adˈmissions Test ➲ GMAT

ˈgraduate school (*also informal* **ˈgrad school**) (*both NAmE*) *noun* a part of a college or university where you can study for a second or further degree 研究生院

gradu·ation /ˌɡrædʒuˈeɪʃn/ *noun* **1** [U] the act of successfully completing a university degree, or studies at an American HIGH SCHOOL（大学或美国高中的）毕业：*It was my first job after graduation.* 那是我毕业后的第一个工作。 **2** [U, C] a ceremony at which degrees, etc. are officially given out 毕业典礼：*graduation day* 毕业典礼日 ◇ *My whole family came to my graduation.* 我的家人都来参加了我的毕业典礼。 **3** [C] = GRADATION (2)：*The graduations are marked on the side of the flask.* 烧瓶壁标有刻度。

Graeco- (*NAmE usually* **Greco-**) /ˈɡriːkəʊ; *NAmE* ˈɡriːkoʊ/ *combining form* (in adjectives 构成形容词) Greek 希腊的；希腊人的；希腊语的

graf·fiti /ɡrəˈfiːti/ *noun* [U, pl.] drawings or writing on a wall, etc. in a public place（公共场所墙上等处的）涂鸦，胡写乱画：*The subway was covered in graffiti.* 地下通道里涂满了乱七八糟的图画和文字。

graft /ɡrɑːft; *NAmE* ɡræft/ *noun, verb*

■ *noun* **1** [C] a piece cut from a living plant and fixed in a cut made in another plant, so that it grows there; the process or result of doing this 接穗；嫁接 **2** [C] a piece of skin, bone, etc. removed from a living body and placed in another part of the body which has been damaged; the process or result of doing this 移植物，移植片（皮肤或骨骼等）；移植：*a skin graft* 皮移植物 ➲ WORDFINDER NOTE AT OPERATION **3** [U] (*BrE, informal*) hard work 艰苦的工作：*Their success was the result of years of* **hard graft**. 他们的成功是多年艰苦奋斗的结果。 **4** [U] (*especially NAmE*) the use of illegal or unfair methods, especially BRIBERY, to gain advantage in business, politics, etc.; money obtained in this way 行贿；贿赂；受贿；赃款

■ *verb* **1** [T] **~ sth (onto/to/into sth) | ~ sth (on) (from sth)** to take a piece of skin, bone, etc. from one part of the body and attach it to a damaged part 移植（皮肤、骨骼等）：*newly grafted tissue* 新移植的组织 ◇ *New skin had to be grafted on from his back.* 需从他的背部移植新皮肤。 **2** [T] **~ sth (onto sth)** to cut a piece from a living plant and attach it to another plant 嫁接 **3** [T] **~ sth (onto sth)** to make one idea, system, etc. become part of another one 使（思想、制度等）成为（…的一部分）；植根：*Old values are being grafted onto a new social class.* 旧的价值观念正植根于新的社会阶层。 **4** [I] (*BrE, informal*) to work hard 卖力地工作

graham cracker /ˈɡreɪəm krækə(r)/ *noun* (*NAmE*) a slightly sweet RECTANGULAR biscuit/cookie made with WHOLEMEAL flour （格雷厄姆）全麦粉饼干

grail /ɡreɪl/ (*also* **the ˌHoly ˈGrail**) *noun* **1** [sing.] the cup or bowl believed to have been used by Jesus Christ before he died, that became a holy thing that people wanted to find 圣杯（据信为耶稣离世前所用） **2** [C] a thing that you try very hard to find or achieve, but never will 渴望但永远得不到的东西；努力追求但永远不可能实现的目标（或理想）

grain 🔑 /ɡreɪn/ *noun* **1** 🔑 [U, C] the small hard seeds of food plants such as WHEAT, rice, etc.; a single seed of such a plant 谷物；谷粒：*America's grain exports* 美国的谷物出口 ◇ *a few grains of rice* 几粒大米 ➲ WORDFINDER NOTE AT CROP ➲ SEE ALSO WHOLEGRAIN ➲ VISUAL VOCAB

PAGE V35 **2** [C] a small hard piece of particular substances 颗粒；细粒：*a **grain of salt/sand/sugar*** 一粒盐 / 沙 / 砂糖 **3** [C] (used especially in negative sentences 尤用于否定句) a very small amount 少量；微量；一点儿 SYN **iota**: *There isn't **a grain of truth** in those rumours.* 那些谣传一点也不可靠。 **4** [C] a small unit of weight, equal to 0.00143 of a pound or 0.0648 of a gram, used for example for weighing medicines 格令（重量单位，等于 0.00143 磅或 0.0648 克，用于称量药物等） **5** [U] the natural direction of lines in wood, cloth, etc. or of layers of rock; the pattern of lines that you can see（木、织物或石头等的）纹理：*to cut a piece of wood **along/across the grain*** 顺着纹路劈木头；横对纹路把木头拦腰截断 **6** [U, C] how rough or smooth a surface feels（表面的）质地；触感：*wood of **coarse/fine grain*** 质地粗 / 细的木头

G

IDM ▸ **be/go against the 'grain** to be or do sth different from what is normal or natural 违反常理；不正常；不合常情；与…格格不入：*It really goes against the grain to have to work on a Sunday.* 星期天还得上班的确不合常情。

grained /greɪnd/ *adj.* (of wood, stone, etc. 木、石等) **1** having noticeable lines or a pattern on the surface 有纹理的 **2 -grained** having a TEXTURE of the type mentioned 质地…的：*fine-grained stone* 质地细的石头

grainy /'greɪni/ *adj.* (**grain·ier**, **graini·est**) **1** (especially of photographs 尤指照片) not having completely clear images because they look as if they are made of a lot of small dots and marks 有颗粒的；粒状的；有纹的：*The film is shot in grainy black and white.* 这部电影拍成有颗粒感的黑白片。 **2** having a rough surface or containing small bits, seeds, etc. 表面粗糙的；粒面的：*grainy texture* 粒面质地

gram /græm/ *noun* **1** (*BrE also* **gramme**) (*abbr.* **g**, **gm**) a unit for measuring weight. There are 1 000 grams in one kilogram. 克（重量单位，等于 0.001 千克） **2 -gram** a thing that is written or drawn 写（或画）的东西：*telegram* 电报 ◇ *hologram* 全息图

'gram flour (*also* **besan**, **'chickpea flour**) *noun* [U] flour made from CHICKPEAS 鹰嘴豆粉

gram·mar /'græmə(r)/ *noun* **1** [U] the rules in a language for changing the form of words and joining them into sentences 语法；文法：*the basic rules of grammar* 基本语法规则 ◇ *English grammar* 英语语法 ➲ WORDFINDER NOTE AT LANGUAGE ➲ SEE ALSO GENERATIVE GRAMMAR

> WORDFINDER 联想词：case, conjugate, gender, inflect, noun, part of speech, singular, subject, tense

2 [U] a person's knowledge and use of a language（人的）语言知识及运用能力：*His grammar is appalling.* 他运用语言的能力糟透了。◇ *bad grammar* 极差的语言运用能力 **3** [C] a book containing a description of the rules of a language 语法书：*a French grammar* 法语语法书

gram·mar·ian /grə'meəriən; *NAmE* -'mer-/ *noun* a person who is an expert in the study of grammar 语法学家

'grammar school *noun* **1** (in Britain, especially in the past) a school for young people between the ages of 11 and 18 who are good at academic subjects（尤指旧时英国的）文法学校 **2** (*old-fashioned*) = ELEMENTARY SCHOOL

the ˌgrammar trans'lation method *noun* [sing.] (*linguistics* 语言) a traditional way of teaching a foreign language, in which the study of grammar is very important and very little teaching is in the foreign language 语法翻译法（一种传统外语教学方法）

gram·mat·ical /grə'mætɪkl/ *adj.* **1** connected with the rules of grammar 语法的；文法的：*a grammatical error* 语法错误 **2** correctly following the rules of grammar 符合语法规则的；合乎文法的：*That sentence is not grammatical.* 那个句子不合语法。 ▸ **gram·mat·ical·ly** /-kli/ *adv.*：*a grammatically correct sentence* 语法上正确的句子

gramme (*BrE*) = GRAM

Grammy /'græmi/ (*pl.* **Gram·mies** or **Grammys**) one of the awards for achievement in the music industry given every year by the US National Academy of Recording Arts and Sciences 格莱美奖（美国国家录音艺术与科学学会颁发的音乐界年度奖之一）

gramo·phone /'græməfəʊn; *NAmE* -foʊn/ *noun* (*old-fashioned*) = RECORD PLAYER

gran /græn/ *noun* (*BrE, informal*) grandmother 奶奶；姥姥：*Do you want to go to your gran's?* 你想去奶奶家吗？◇ *Gran, can I have some more?* 奶奶，我再吃点儿行吗？

Gran·ary™ /'grænəri/ *adj.* [only before noun] (*BrE*) (of bread 面包) containing whole grains of WHEAT 谷仓牌的（全麦的）

gran·ary /'grænəri/ *noun* (*pl.* **-ies**) a building where grain is stored 谷仓；粮仓

grand /grænd/ *adj., noun*

■ *adj.* (**grand·er**, **grand·est**) **1** impressive and large or important 壮丽的；堂皇的；重大的：*It's not a very grand house.* 这房子并不是十分富丽堂皇。◇ *The wedding was a very grand occasion.* 婚礼场面非常隆重。 **2 Grand** [only before noun] used in the names of impressive or very large buildings, etc.（用于大建筑物等的名称）大：*the Grand Canyon* 大峡谷 ◇ *We stayed at the Grand Hotel.* 我们住在格兰酒店。 **3** needing a lot of effort, money or time to succeed but intended to achieve impressive results 宏大的；宏伟的；有气派的：*a **grand design/plan/strategy*** 宏伟的蓝图；宏大的计划；重大的战略 ◇ *New Yorkers built their city **on a grand scale**.* 纽约人大规模地建造自己的城市。 **4** (of people 人) behaving in a proud way because they are rich or from a high social class 傲慢的；高高在上的 **5** (*dialect* or *informal*) very good or enjoyable; excellent 极好的；快乐的；美妙的；出色的：*I had a grand day out at the seaside.* 我在海边痛痛快快玩了一天。◇ *Thanks. That'll be grand!* 谢谢。那太棒了！◇ *Fred did a grand job of painting the house.* 弗雷德粉刷房子干得很出色。 **6 Grand** used in the titles of people of very high social rank（对上层社会的人的称呼）大：*the Grand Duchess Elena* 大公夫人埃琳娜 ➲ SEE ALSO GRANDEUR ▸ **grand·ly** *adv.*：*He described himself grandly as a 'landscape architect'.* 他自封为"景观建筑师"。 **grand·ness** *noun* [U]

IDM **a/the ˌgrand old 'age (of...)** a great age 高龄：*She finally learned to drive at the grand old age of 70.* 她终于在 70 岁高龄学会了开车。 **a/the ˌgrand old 'man (of sth)** a man who is respected in a particular profession that he has been involved in for a long time 元老；资深前辈；老前辈：*James Lovelock, the grand old man of environmental science* 詹姆斯•洛夫洛克，环境科学的元老

■ *noun* **1** (*pl.* **grand**) (*informal*) \$1 000; £1 000 * 1 000 美元；1 000 英镑：*It'll cost you five grand!* 这要花去你 5 000 块钱！ **2** = GRAND PIANO ➲ SEE ALSO CONCERT GRAND

gran·dad (*also* **grand·dad** *especially in NAmE*) /'grændæd/ *noun* (*informal*) grandfather 爷爷；姥爷

ˌGrand ˌCentral 'Station *noun* (*US*) used to describe a place that is very busy or crowded 非常繁忙（或拥挤）的地方：*My hospital room was like Grand Central Station with everybody coming and going.* 我的病房就像纽约的中央火车站，整天人来人往。 ORIGIN From the name of a very busy train station in New York City. 源自纽约市一个繁忙的火车站站名。 ➲ COMPARE PICCADILLY CIRCUS

grand·child /'græntʃaɪld/ *noun* (*pl.* **grand·chil·dren**) a child of your son or daughter （外）孙子；（外）孙女

grand·daddy (*also* **gran·daddy**) /'grændædi/ *noun* (*pl.* **-ies**) (*NAmE, informal*) **1** = GRANDFATHER **2 the grand·daddy** the first or greatest example of sth（某事物的）老祖宗，祖师爷

grand·daugh·ter /'grændɔːtə(r)/ *noun* a daughter of your son or daughter（外）孙女 ➲ COMPARE GRANDSON

ˌgrand 'duchess *noun* **1** the wife of a grand duke 大公夫人 **2** (in some parts of Europe, especially in the past) a female ruler of a small independent state（尤指旧时欧洲某些地方的）女大公 **3** (in Russia in the past) a daughter of the TSAR（旧时俄国的）公主

ˌgrand ˈduke *noun* **1** (in some parts of Europe, especially in the past) a male ruler of a small independent state（尤指旧时欧洲某些地方的）大公：*The Grand Duke of Tuscany* 托斯卡纳大公 **2** (in Russia in the past) a son of the TSAR（旧时俄国的）王子 ➲ COMPARE ARCHDUKE

gran·dee /ɡrænˈdiː/ *noun* **1** (in the past) a Spanish or Portuguese NOBLEMAN of high rank（旧时西班牙或葡萄牙的）大公 **2** a person of high social rank and importance 大人物；显要人物

grand·eur /ˈɡrændʒə(r); -djə(r)/ *noun* [U] **1** the quality of being great and impressive in appearance 宏伟；壮丽；堂皇 SYN **splendour**：*the grandeur and simplicity of Roman architecture* 古罗马建筑的雄伟和简朴 ◇ *The hotel had an air of faded grandeur.* 这家旅馆给人一种繁华已逝的感觉。 **2** the importance or social status sb has or thinks they have 高贵；显赫；伟大：*He has a sense of grandeur about him.* 他觉得自己很了不起。◇ *She is clearly suffering from **delusions of grandeur*** (= thinks she is more important than she really is). 她显然是犯了妄自尊大的毛病。 ➲ SEE ALSO GRAND *n.*

grand·father /ˈɡrænfɑːðə(r)/ *noun* the father of your father or mother（外）祖父；爷爷；姥爷；外公 ➲ SEE ALSO GRANDAD, GRANDDADDY, GRANDPA ➲ COMPARE GRANDMOTHER

ˌgrandfather ˈclock *noun* an old-fashioned type of clock in a tall wooden case that stands on the floor（置于高木匣中的）落地式大摆钟 ➲ PICTURE AT CLOCK

grand·ilo·quent /ɡrænˈdɪləkwənt/ *adj.* (*formal, disapproving*) using long or complicated words in order to impress people 卖弄辞藻的；言辞浮夸的 SYN **pompous**
▸ **grand·ilo·quence** /-əns/ *noun* [U]

gran·di·ose /ˈɡrændiəʊs; *NAmE* -oʊs/ *adj.* (*disapproving*) seeming very impressive but too large, complicated, expensive, etc. to be practical or possible 华而不实的；浮夸的；不切实际的：*The grandiose scheme for a journey across the desert came to nothing.* 不切实际的穿越沙漠计划已成泡影。◇ *a grandiose opera house* 华而不实的歌剧院

ˌgrand ˈjury *noun* (*law* 律) (in the US) a JURY which has to decide whether there is enough evidence against an accused person for a trial in court（美国）大陪审团

grand·ma /ˈɡrænmɑː/ *noun* (*informal*) grandmother（外）祖母；奶奶；姥姥；外婆

grand mal /ˌɡrɒ̃ ˈmæl; *NAmE* ˌɡræn ˈmɑːl; ˈmæl/ *noun* [U] (*from French, medical* 医) a serious form of EPILEPSY in which sb becomes unconscious for fairly long periods（癫痫）大发作

ˌgrand ˈmaster *noun* a CHESS player of the highest standard 国际象棋大师；棋王；棋圣

grand·mother /ˈɡrænmʌðə(r)/ *noun* the mother of your father or mother（外）祖母；奶奶；姥姥；外婆 ➲ SEE ALSO GRAN, GRANDMA, GRANNY ➲ COMPARE GRANDFATHER IDM SEE TEACH

ˌgrandmother ˈclock *noun* a clock similar to a GRANDFATHER CLOCK but smaller 落地式小摆钟

ˌgrand ˈopera *noun* [U, C] OPERA in which everything is sung and there are no spoken parts 大歌剧

grand·pa /ˈɡrænpɑː/ *noun* (*informal*) grandfather（外）祖父；爷爷；姥爷；外公 ➲ SEE ALSO GRANDAD

grand·par·ent /ˈɡrænpeərənt; *NAmE* -perənt/ *noun* [usually pl.] the father or mother of your father or mother 祖父；祖母；外祖父；外祖母：*The children are staying with their grandparents.* 孩子们与祖父母住在一起。

ˌgrand piˈano (*also* **grand**) *noun* a large piano in which the strings are horizontal 大钢琴；三角钢琴 ➲ VISUAL VOCAB PAGE V40 ➲ COMPARE UPRIGHT PIANO

Grand Prix /ˌɡrɒ̃ ˈpriː; *NAmE* ˌɡrɑ̃ː/ *noun* (*pl.* **Grands Prix** /ˌɡrɒ̃ ˈpriː; *NAmE* ˌɡrɑ̃ː/) one of a series of important international races for racing cars or motorcycles 大奖赛（汽车或摩托车的国际系列大赛中的一场比赛）

ˌgrand ˈslam *noun* **1** (*also* **Grand Slam**) a very important sports event, contest, etc. 大赛；大奖赛：*a Grand Slam **tournament/cup/title*** 锦标大赛；大赛奖杯 / 冠军 **2** the winning of every part of a sports contest or all the main contests in a year for a particular sport 全胜，大满贯（每场皆胜或在全年主要比赛上每战皆胜）：*Will France win the grand slam this year?* (= in RUGBY) 法国队在今年的橄榄球比赛中会大获全胜吗？ **3** (*also* **grand ˌslam home ˈrun**) (in BASEBALL 棒球) a HOME RUN that is worth four points 四分本垒打；满贯本垒打 **4** (in card games, especially BRIDGE 纸牌游戏，尤指桥牌) the winning of all the TRICKS in a single game 大满贯

grand·son /ˈɡrænsʌn/ *noun* a son of your son or daughter 孙子；外孙 ➲ COMPARE GRANDDAUGHTER

grand·stand /ˈɡrænstænd/ *noun* a large covered structure with rows of seats for people to watch sports events 大看台：*The game was played to a packed grandstand.* 比赛时大看台上座无虚席。◇ *From her house, we had a **grandstand view*** (= very good view) *of the celebrations.* 从她的住所望去，我们把整个庆祝活动尽收眼底。

ˌgrandstand ˈfinish *noun* (*BrE*) (in sport 体育运动) a close or exciting finish to a race or competition 相差无几的结局

grand·stand·ing /ˈɡrænstændɪŋ/ *noun* [U] (especially in business, politics, etc. 尤指在商业、政治等方面) the fact of behaving or speaking in a way that is intended to make people impressed in order to gain some advantage for yourself 哗众取宠；炫耀

ˌgrand ˈtotal *noun* the final total when a number of other totals have been added together 总计；共计

ˌgrand ˈtour *noun* **1** (*often humorous*) a visit around a building or house in order to show it to sb 参观，巡视（房屋、住所）：*Steve took us on a grand tour of the house and garden.* 史蒂夫带我们参观了这栋住宅和花园。 **2** (*also* **Grand Tour**) a visit to the main cities of Europe made by rich young British or American people as part of their education in the past 游学旅行（旧时英美富家子弟在欧洲大陆主要城市的观光旅行，是其教育的一部分）

ˌgrand ˈunified theory *noun* (*physics* 物) a single theory that tries to explain all the behaviour of SUBATOMIC PARTICLES 大统一理论（试图解释亚原子粒子的所有活动方式的单一理论）

grange /ɡreɪndʒ/ *noun* (often as part of a name 常作名称的一部分) a country house with farm buildings 农庄；庄园：*Thrushcross Grange* 思拉什克罗斯庄园

gran·ita /ɡrəˈniːtə/ *noun* [U, C] (*from Italian*) a drink or sweet dish made with crushed ice 碎冰饮料；沙冰

gran·ite /ˈɡrænɪt/ *noun* [U] a type of hard grey stone, often used in building 花岗岩；花岗石

granny (*also less frequent* **gran·nie**) /ˈɡræni/ *noun* (*pl.* **-ies**) (*informal*) grandmother 奶奶；姥姥 ➲ SEE ALSO GRANDMA
▸ **granny** (*also less frequent* **gran·nie**) *adj.*：*a pair of granny glasses* 一副老花眼镜

ˈgranny flat *noun* (*BrE*) (*also* **ˈin-law apartment**, **ˈmother-in-law apartment**, **ˈin-law suite** *all NAmE*) (*informal*) a set of rooms for an old person, especially in a relative's house（尤指亲戚家中的）老人套间

ˈgranny knot *noun* an untidy double knot 老奶奶结（不整齐的双环结） ➲ COMPARE REEF KNOT

gran·ola /ɡrəˈnəʊlə; *NAmE* -ˈnoʊ-/ *noun, adj.*
■ *noun* [U] (*especially NAmE*) a type of breakfast CEREAL made of grains, nuts, etc. that have been TOASTED 格兰诺拉麦片（用烘烤过的谷类、坚果等配制成的早餐食品）

G

■ *adj.* [only before noun] (*NAmE, informal*) (of a person 人) eating healthy food, supporting the protection of the environment and having LIBERAL views 讲求身心健康的（吃得健康、支持环保、思想开明）

grant AW /ɡrɑːnt; *NAmE* ɡrænt/ *verb, noun*
■ *verb* **1** [often passive] to agree to give sb what they ask for, especially formal or legal permission to do sth（尤指正式地或法律上）同意，准予，允许： **~ sth** *My request was granted.* 我的请求得到批准。◇ **~ sb sth** *I was granted permission to visit the palace.* 我获准参观宫殿。◇ *She was granted a divorce.* 她获准离婚。◇ *The bank finally granted me a £500 loan.* 银行终于同意给我贷款 500 英镑。◇ **~ sth to sb/sth** *The bank finally granted a £500 loan to me.* 银行终于同意给我贷款 500 英镑。 **2** to admit that sth is true, although you may not like or agree with it（勉强）承认，同意： **~ sb** *She's a smart woman, I grant you, but she's no genius.* 我同意你的观点，她是一个很聪明的女人，但绝不是天才。◇ **~ (sb) (that)...** *I grant you (that) it looks good, but it's not exactly practical.* 我承认你说的，它好看，可并不是很实用。
IDM **take it for 'granted (that...)** to believe sth is true without first making sure that it is 认为…是理所当然： *I just took it for granted that he'd always be around.* 我还想当然地以为他总能随叫随到呢。 **take sb/sth for 'granted** to be so used to sb/sth that you do not recognize their true value any more and do not show that you are grateful（因习以为常）对…不予重视；（因视为当然而）不把…当回事： *Her husband was always there and she just took him for granted.* 她丈夫随时都在身边，她只是认为他理应如此。◇ *We take having an endless supply of clean water for granted.* 我们想当然地认为洁净水的供应是无穷无尽的。
■ *noun* **~ (to do sth)** a sum of money that is given by the government or by another organization to be used for a particular purpose（政府、机构的）拨款： *student grants* (= to pay for their education) 学生助学金 ◇ *He has been awarded a research grant.* 他得到一笔研究经费。

'grant aid *noun* [U] (*BrE*) money given by the government to organizations or local areas（政府对机构或地方的）拨款，资助款 ▸ **,grant-'aided** *adj.* : *a grant-aided school* 受公费补助的学校

grant·ed AW /ˈɡrɑːntɪd; *NAmE* ˈɡræn-/ *adv., conj.*
■ *adv.* used to show that you accept that sth is true, often before you make another statement about it（表示肯定属实，然后再作另一番表述）不错，的确： *'You could have done more to help.' 'Granted.'* "你本可以多给点帮助的。""我承认。" ◇ *Granted, it's not the most pleasant of jobs but it has to be done.* 的确，这不是最令人愉快的工作，但也得做呀。
■ *conj.* **~ (that...)** because of the fact that 因为： *Granted that it is a simple test to perform, it should be easy to get results quickly.* 因为这化验做起来简单，所以应该不难很快得出结果。

,grant-in-'aid *noun* (*pl.* **grants-in-aid**) a sum of money given to a local government or an institution, or to a particular person to allow them to study sth（给地方政府、机构或学者的）拨款，研究资助

,grant-main'tained *adj.* (*abbr.* **GM**) (of a school in Britain 英国学校) receiving financial support from central government rather than local government 由中央政府出资的；中央政府拨款的

granu·lar /ˈɡrænjələ(r)/ *adj.* consisting of small GRANULES; looking or feeling like a collection of GRANULES 由颗粒构成的；含颗粒的；似颗粒状的

granu·lated sugar /ˌɡrænjuleɪtɪd ˈʃʊɡə(r)/ *noun* [U] white sugar in the form of small grains 白砂糖

gran·ule /ˈɡrænjuːl/ *noun* [usually pl.] a small, hard piece of sth; a small grain 颗粒状物；微粒；细粒： *instant coffee granules* 速溶咖啡颗粒

grape /ɡreɪp/ *noun* a small green or purple fruit that grows in bunches on a climbing plant (called a VINE). Wine is made from grapes. 葡萄： *a bunch of grapes* 一串葡萄 ◇ ***black/white grapes*** (= grapes that are actually purple/green in colour) 紫 / 绿葡萄 ➲ VISUAL VOCAB PAGE V32 IDM SEE SOUR *adj.*

grape·fruit /ˈɡreɪpfruːt/ *noun* (*pl.* **grape·fruit** or **grape·fruits**) [C, U] a large round yellow CITRUS fruit with a lot of slightly sour juice 葡萄柚；柚子；西柚 ➲ VISUAL VOCAB PAGE V33

grape·shot /ˈɡreɪpʃɒt; *NAmE* -ʃɑːt/ *noun* [U] a number of small iron balls that are fired together from a CANNON（大炮发射的）葡萄弹

grape·vine /ˈɡreɪpvaɪn/ *noun* a climbing plant that produces GRAPES 葡萄藤；葡萄树
IDM **on/through the 'grapevine** by talking in an informal way to other people 小道消息；传闻： *I heard on the grapevine that you're leaving.* 我听小道消息说你要离开。

graph /ɡræf; *BrE also* ɡrɑːf/ *noun* a planned drawing, consisting of a line or lines, showing how two or more sets of numbers are related to each other 图；图表；曲线图： *Plot a graph of height against age.* 绘制一张身高与年龄对照的曲线图。◇ *The graph shows how house prices have risen since the 1980s.* 此图表明了自 20 世纪 80 年代以来房价上涨的情况。➲ LANGUAGE BANK AT ILLUSTRATE

graph·eme /ˈɡræfiːm/ *noun* (*linguistics* 语言) the smallest unit that has meaning in a writing system 字位，书写单位（语言书写系统的最小有意义单位）➲ COMPARE PHONEME

graph·ene /ˈɡræfiːn/ *noun* [U] a very strong, light form of CARBON (1) 石墨烯；单层石墨

graph·ic /ˈɡræfɪk/ *adj., noun*
■ *adj.* **1** [only before noun] connected with drawings and design, especially in the production of books, magazines, etc. 绘画的；书画的；图样的；图案的： *graphic design* 平面设计 ◇ *a graphic designer* 平面设计人员 **2** (of descriptions, etc. 描述等) very clear and full of details, especially about sth unpleasant（尤指令人不快的事物）形象的，生动的，逼真的 SYN **vivid**： *a **graphic account/description** of a battle* 对战斗的生动叙述 / 描述 ◇ *He kept telling us about his operation, in the most **graphic detail**.* 他不停地向我们绘声绘色地讲述他手术的细节。
■ *noun* a diagram or picture, especially one that appears on a computer screen or in a newspaper or book（尤指电脑荧屏或报纸、书籍上的）图表，图形，图画 ➲ COMPARE GRAPHICS

graph·ic·al /ˈɡræfɪkl/ *adj.* **1** [only before noun] connected with art or computer graphics 图形的；计算机图形的： *The system uses an impressive graphical interface.* 这一系统采用了特别好的图形界面。 **2** in the form of a diagram or graph 用图（或图表）表示的： *a graphical presentation of results* 所得结果的图演

graph·ic·al·ly /ˈɡræfɪkli/ *adv.* **1** in the form of drawings or diagrams 以书画（或图表）形式： *This data is shown graphically on the opposite page.* 对页以图表显示这些数据。 **2** very clearly and in great detail 形象地；生动地；逼真地 SYN **vividly**： *The murders are graphically described in the article.* 这篇文章对几起凶杀案作了血淋淋的描述。

,graphic 'arts *noun* [U] art based on the use of lines and shades of colour, rather than THREE-DIMENSIONAL work 图像艺术；绘画艺术 ▸ **,graphic 'artist** *noun*

,graphic 'equalizer *noun* (*specialist*) an electronic device or computer program that allows you to control the strength and quality of particular sound FREQUENCIES separately 图示均衡器（用以调节声频大小及音质）

,graphic 'novel *noun* a novel in the form of a COMIC STRIP 连环画小说；漫画小说

graph·ics /ˈɡræfɪks/ *noun* **1** [pl.] designs, drawings or pictures that are used especially in the production of books, magazines, etc. 图样；图案；图像： *Text and graphics are prepared separately and then combined.* 文字和图分别编排后再进行混排。 **2** [U] the activity of making these designs, drawings or pictures or the use of these images 绘图；图像运用：*expertise in computer graphics* 计算机制图方面的专业知识

ˈgraphics adapter *noun* (*computing* 计) = VIDEO CARD

ˈgraphics card *noun* (*computing* 计) a CIRCUIT BOARD that allows a computer to show images on its screen 图形卡；图像适配卡；显示卡

graph·ite /ˈɡræfaɪt/ *noun* [U] a soft black mineral that is a form of CARBON. Graphite is used to make pencils, to LUBRICATE machinery and in nuclear REACTORS. 石墨

graph·ology /ɡræˈfɒlədʒi; *NAmE* -ˈfɑːl-/ *noun* [U] the study of HANDWRITING, for example as a way of learning more about sb's character 笔体学，笔迹学（根据笔体推断人的性格）

ˈgraph paper *noun* [U] paper with small squares of equal size printed on it, used for drawing GRAPHS and other diagrams 方格纸；坐标纸；标绘纸

-graphy *combining form* (in nouns 构成名词) **1** a type of art or science 某种艺术（或科学）：*choreography* 编舞艺术 ◇ *geography* 地理学 **2** a method of producing images 产生影像的方法：*radiography* 射线照相术 **3** a form of writing or drawing 写（或画）的形式：*calligraphy* 书法 ◇ *biography* 传记

grappa /ˈɡræpə/ *noun* [U, C] a strong alcoholic drink from Italy, made from GRAPES（意大利）葡萄果渣白兰地

grap·ple /ˈɡræpl/ *verb* **1** [I, T] to take a firm hold of sb/sth and struggle with them 扭打；搏斗：**~ (with sb/sth)** *Passers-by grappled with the man after the attack.* 袭击之后过路人便与这男人扭打起来。◇ **~ sb/sth (+ adv./prep.)** *They managed to grapple him to the ground.* 他们终于把他摔倒在地。 **2** [I] to try hard to find a solution to a problem 努力设法解决：**~ with sth** *The new government has yet to grapple with the problem of air pollution.* 新政府还需尽力解决空气污染问题。◇ **~ to do sth** *I was grappling to find an answer to his question.* 我正在努力想办法解决他的问题。

ˈgrappling iron (*also* **ˈgrappling hook**) *noun* a tool with several hooks attached to a long rope, used for dragging sth along or holding a boat still 多爪钩；多爪锚

grasp /ɡrɑːsp; *NAmE* ɡræsp/ *verb, noun*

■ *verb* **1 ~ sb/sth** to take a firm hold of sb/sth 抓紧；抓牢 SYN **grip**: *He grasped my hand and shook it warmly.* 他热情地抓住我的手握了起来。◇ *Kay grasped him by the wrist.* 凯紧紧抓住他的手腕。➲ SYNONYMS AT HOLD **2** to understand sth completely 理解；领会；领悟；明白：**~ sth** *They failed to grasp the importance of his words.* 他们没有理解他的话的重要性。◇ **~ how, why, etc....** *She was unable to grasp how to do it.* 她弄不明白这事该怎么做。◇ **~ that...** *It took him some time to grasp that he was now a public figure.* 他过了些时候才意识到自己已是个公众人物了。➲ SYNONYMS AT UNDERSTAND **3 ~ a chance/an opportunity** to take an opportunity without hesitating and use it 急忙抓住，毫不犹豫地抓住（机会）：*I grasped the opportunity to work abroad.* 我毫不犹豫地抓住了去国外工作的机会。

IDM **grasp the ˈnettle** (*BrE*) to deal with a difficult situation firmly and without hesitating 果断地处理棘手问题 ➲ MORE AT STRAW

PHR V **ˈgrasp at sth 1** to try to take hold of sth in your hands 尽力抓住某物：*She grasped at his coat as he rushed past her.* 他从她身边冲过去时，她使劲地向他的外衣抓去。 **2** to try to take an opportunity 抓住机会

■ *noun* [usually sing.] **1** a firm hold of sb/sth or control over sb/sth 紧抓；紧握；控制 SYN **grip**: *I grabbed him, but he slipped from my grasp.* 我紧抓着他，可他还是从我手里溜掉了。◇ *She felt a firm grasp on her arm.* 她感到手臂被紧紧地抓住了。◇ *Don't let the situation escape from your grasp.* 别让局面失去控制。 **2** a person's understanding of a subject or of difficult facts 理解（力）；领会：*He has **a good grasp of** German grammar.* 他德语语法掌握得很好。◇ *These complex formulae are **beyond the grasp of** the average pupil.* 这些复杂的公式是一般小学生不能理解的。 **3** the ability to get or achieve sth 能力所及：*Success **was within her grasp**.* 她有把握获得成功。

grasp·ing /ˈɡrɑːspɪŋ; *NAmE* ˈɡræs-/ *adj.* (*disapproving*) always trying to get money, possessions, power, etc. for yourself 一味攫取的；贪婪的；贪心的 SYN **greedy**: *a grasping landlord* 贪婪的地主

grass 🔑 /ɡrɑːs; *NAmE* ɡræs/ *noun, verb*

■ *noun* **1** 🔑 [U] a common wild plant with narrow green leaves and STEMS that are eaten by cows, horses, sheep, etc. 草；青草；牧草：***a blade of grass*** 一片草叶 ◇ *The dry grass caught fire.* 干草着火了。 **2** [C] any type of grass 禾本科植物：*ornamental grasses* 观赏性草 **3** 🔑 [sing., U] (*usually* **the grass**) an area of ground covered with grass 草地；草坪；草场；牧场：*to **cut/mow the grass*** 割草 ◇ *Don't walk on the grass.* 勿践踏草地。◇ ***Keep off the grass.*** (= on a sign) 请勿践踏草地。 **4** [U] (*informal*) MARIJUANA 大麻 **5** [C] (*BrE, informal, usually disapproving*) a person, usually a criminal, who tells the police about sb's criminal activities and plans 向警方告密的人（通常指罪犯）➲ COMPARE SUPERGRASS

IDM **the grass is (always) greener on the other side (of the fence)** (*saying*) said about people who never seem happy with what they have and always think that other people have a better situation than they have 草是那边绿；这山望着那山高 **not let the grass grow under your feet** to not delay in getting things done（做事）不拖拉，不磨洋工 **put sb out to ˈgrass** (*informal*) to force sb to stop doing their job, especially because they are old 迫使（年老者）退休；让某人离职 ➲ MORE AT KICK *v.*, SNAKE *n.*

■ *verb* [I] **~ (on sb)** (*also* **ˌgrass sb↔ˈup**) (*both BrE, informal*) to tell the police about sb's criminal activities（向警方）告密，告发

PHR V **ˌgrass sth↔ˈover** to cover an area with grass 用草覆盖某物；使长满草；在…上种草

ˌgrass ˈcourt *noun* a TENNIS COURT with a grass surface 草地网球场

grass·cutter /ˈɡrɑːskʌtə(r); *NAmE* ˈɡræs-/ (*also* **ˈcutting grass**) *noun* a name used in W Africa for a CANE RAT (= type of large RODENT that is used for food)（西非用语）蔗鼠

grassed /ɡrɑːst; *NAmE* ɡræst/ *adj.* covered with grass 长满草的；被草覆盖的

grass·hop·per /ˈɡrɑːshɒpə(r); *NAmE* ˈɡræshɑːp-/ *noun* an insect with long back legs, that can jump very high and that makes a sound with its legs 蝗虫；蚱蜢；蚂蚱 ➲ VISUAL VOCAB PAGE V13 IDM SEE KNEE-HIGH

grass·land /ˈɡrɑːslænd; *NAmE* ˈɡræs-/ *noun* [U] (*also* **grass·lands** [pl.]) a large area of open land covered with wild grass 草原；草地；草场

ˌgrass ˈroots *noun* [pl.] (*also* **grass·roots**, **the grass roots**) ordinary people in society or in an organization, rather than the leaders or people who make decisions 基层民众；平民百姓；草根：*the grass roots of the party* 党的基层成员 ◇ *We need support at grass-roots level.* 我们需要基层的支持。

ˌgrass ˈskirt *noun* a skirt made of long grass, worn by dancers in the Pacific islands（太平洋岛屿上的跳舞者穿的）草裙

ˈgrass snake *noun* a small harmless snake 游蛇，青草蛇（无毒小蛇）

ˌgrass ˈwidow *noun* a woman whose husband is away from home for long periods of time 活寡妇；守活寡的女子

grassy /ˈɡrɑːsi; *NAmE* ˈɡræsi/ *adj.* (**grass·ier**, **grassi·est**) covered with grass 长满草的；被草覆盖的

grate /ɡreɪt/ *noun, verb*

■ *noun* **1** a metal frame for holding the wood or coal in a FIREPLACE 炉条；炉箅 ➲ VISUAL VOCAB PAGE V22 **2** (*also* **ˈsewer grate**) (*both US*) (*BrE* **drain**) a frame of metal bars over the opening to a DRAIN in the ground 下水道孔盖 ➲ SEE ALSO GRATING *n.*

G

■ *verb* **1** [T] ~ **sth** to rub food against a GRATER in order to cut it into small pieces 擦碎，磨碎（食物）： ***grated apple/carrot/cheese, etc.*** 擦成细丝的苹果、胡萝卜、干酪等 ➲ COLLOCATIONS AT COOKING ➲ VISUAL VOCAB PAGE V30 **2** [I] to irritate or annoy sb 使人烦躁；使人烦恼；使人难受： ~ **(on sb)** *Her voice really grates on me.* 她的声音真叫我难受。◇ ~ **(with sb)** *It grated with him when people implied he wasn't really British.* 当有人暗示他不是地道的英国人时，他很是恼火。 **3** [I, T] when two hard surfaces **grate** as they rub together, they make a sharp unpleasant sound; sb can also make one thing **grate** against another（使）发出刺耳的声音，发出吱吱嘎嘎的摩擦声： *The rusty hinges grated as the gate swung back.* 大门荡了回去，生锈的铰链发出吱嘎吱嘎的刺耳声。◇ ~ **sth (+ adv./prep.)** *He grated his knife across the plate.* 他用刀子划过盘子时发出刺耳的声音。

G

grate·ful 🔑 /ˈɡreɪtfl/ *adj.*

> **WORD FAMILY**
> **grateful** *adj.* (≠ ungrateful)
> **gratefully** *adv.*
> **gratitude** *noun* (≠ ingratitude)

1 🔑 feeling or showing thanks because sb has done sth kind for you or has done as you asked 感激的；表示感谢的： ~ **(to sb) (for sth)** *I am extremely grateful to all the teachers for their help.* 我非常感谢所有老师的帮助。◇ *We would be grateful for any information you can give us.* 如能提供信息我们将感激不尽。◇ ~ **(to do sth)** *She seems to think I should be grateful to have a job at all.* 她似乎认为我有份工作就该谢天谢地了。◇ ~ **(that...)** *He was grateful that she didn't tell his parents about the incident.* 他感到庆幸的是，她未将此事告诉他父母。◇ *Grateful thanks are due to the following people for their help...* 向下列给予过帮助的人表示衷心的感谢…◇ *Kate gave him a grateful smile.* 凯特感激地对他笑了笑。 ➲ EXPRESS YOURSELF AT THANK **2** 🔑 used to make a request, especially in a letter or in a formal situation（尤用于书信或正式场合提出请求）感激不尽，请： ***I would be grateful if you could*** *send the completed form back as soon as possible.* 如能尽快把表格填好寄回，将不胜感激。▸ **grate·ful·ly** /-fəli/ *adv.*： *He nodded gratefully.* 他感激地点了点头。◇ *All donations will be gratefully received.* 如蒙捐助，定将报以衷心的感谢。 IDM SEE SMALL *adj.*

grater /ˈɡreɪtə(r)/ *noun* a kitchen UTENSIL (= a tool) with a rough surface, used for GRATING food into very small pieces 礤床儿，磨碎器（厨房用具）： *a* ***cheese/nutmeg grater*** 奶酪磨碎器；擦肉豆蔻的礤床儿 ➲ VISUAL VOCAB PAGES V27, V30

grat·ifi·ca·tion /ˌɡrætɪfɪˈkeɪʃn/ *noun* [U, C] (*formal*) the state of feeling pleasure when sth goes well for you or when your desires are satisfied; sth that gives you pleasure 满足；满意；快感；令人喜悦的事物 SYN **satisfaction**: *sexual gratification* 性满足 ◇ *A feed will usually provide instant gratification to a crying baby.* 喂食通常可使正在哭闹的婴儿立即得到满足。

grat·ify /ˈɡrætɪfaɪ/ *verb* (**grati·fies, grati·fy·ing, grati·fied, grati·fied**) **1** (*formal*) to please or satisfy sb 使高兴；使满意： **it gratifies sb to do sth** *It gratified him to think that it was all his work.* 他想到这都是他的工作成果，感到十分欣慰。◇ ~ **sb** *I was gratified by their invitation.* 收到他们的邀请，我感到很高兴。 **2** ~ **sth** (*formal*) to satisfy a wish, need, etc. 满足（愿望、需要等）： *He only gave his consent in order to gratify her wishes.* 他只是为满足她的愿望才同意的。 ▸ **grati·fied** *adj.* [not usually before noun]： ~ **(at sth)** | ~ **(to find, hear, see, etc.)** *She was gratified to find that they had followed her advice.* 她看到他们听从了自己的建议，感到很欣慰。

grati·fy·ing /ˈɡrætɪfaɪɪŋ/ *adj.* (*formal*) pleasing and giving satisfaction 令人高兴的；使人满意的： ***It is gratifying*** *to see such good results.* 看到这么好的结果真令人欣慰。 ➲ SYNONYMS AT SATISFYING ▸ **grati·fy·ing·ly** *adv.*

gra·tin /ˈɡrætæn; *NAmE* ˈɡrætn/ *noun* [U] (*from French*) a cooked dish which is covered with a crisp layer of cheese or BREADCRUMBS (1) 脆皮烙菜（表面为干酪或面包屑）

grat·ing /ˈɡreɪtɪŋ/ *noun, adj.*
■ ***noun*** a flat frame with metal bars across it, used to cover a window, a hole in the ground, etc.（窗户、地沟口等的）栅栏，格栅，格子 ➲ SEE ALSO GRATE *n.*
■ ***adj.*** (of a sound or sb's voice 响声或人的声音) unpleasant to listen to 刺耳的

gra·tis /ˈɡrætɪs; ˈɡreɪtɪs/ *adv.* done or given without having to be paid for 免费的；无偿的 SYN **free**: *I knew his help wouldn't be given gratis.* 我知道他的帮助不会是无偿的。 ▸ **gra·tis** *adj.*： *a gratis copy of a book* 一本赠书

grati·tude /ˈɡrætɪtjuːd; *NAmE* -tuːd/ *noun* [U] the feeling of being grateful and wanting to express your thanks 感激之情；感谢： *He smiled at them* ***with gratitude.*** 他向他们笑了笑表示谢意。◇ ~ **(to sb) (for sth)** *I would like to express my gratitude to everyone for their hard work.* 我要对所有辛勤劳动的人表示感谢。◇ *She was presented with the gift* ***in gratitude for*** *her long service.* 这礼物赠送给她以表达对她长期服务的感激之情。◇ *a deep sense of gratitude* 深深的谢意 ◇ ***I owe you a great debt of gratitude*** (= feel extremely grateful). 我对你感激不尽。 OPP **ingratitude**

gra·tuit·ous /ɡrəˈtjuːɪtəs; *NAmE* -ˈtuː-/ *adj.* (*disapproving*) done without any good reason or purpose and often having harmful effects 无正当理由（或目的）的；无谓的 SYN **unnecessary**: *gratuitous violence on television* 电视上无谓的暴力镜头 ▸ **gra·tuit·ous·ly** *adv.*

gra·tu·ity /ɡrəˈtjuːəti; *NAmE* -ˈtuː-/ *noun* (*pl.* **-ies**) **1** (*formal*) money that you give to sb who has provided a service for you 小费；赏钱；报酬 SYN **tip** **2** (*BrE*) money that is given to employees when they leave their job 退职金；遣散费；退休金

grave¹ 🔑 /ɡreɪv/ *noun, adj.* ➲ SEE ALSO GRAVE²
■ ***noun*** **1** 🔑 a place in the ground where a dead person is buried 坟墓；墓穴；坟头： *We visited Grandma's grave.* 我们给祖母扫了墓。◇ *There were flowers on the grave.* 坟上有些花。 **2** [sing.] (*often* **the grave**) (*usually literary*) death; a person's death 死亡；去世；逝世： *Is there life beyond the grave* (= life after death)? 人死后有来生吗？◇ *He followed her to the grave* (= died soon after her). 他紧跟着她离开了人世。◇ *She smoked herself into an early grave* (= died young as a result of smoking). 她因抽烟而早逝。 ➲ WORDFINDER NOTE AT DIE

IDM **turn in his/her ˈgrave** (*BrE*) (*NAmE also* **roll (over) in his/her ˈgrave**) (of a person who is dead 亡者) likely to be very shocked or angry 九泉之下不得安宁： *My father would turn in his grave if he knew.* 我父亲知道的话在九泉之下也会不得安宁的。 ➲ MORE AT CRADLE *n.*, DIG *v.*, FOOT *n.*

■ ***adj.*** (**graver, grav·est**) (*formal*) **1** 🔑 (of situations, feelings, etc. 形势、感情等) very serious and important; giving you a reason to feel worried 严重的；重大的；严峻的；深切的： *The police have expressed grave concern about the missing child's safety.* 警方对失踪孩子的安全深表关注。◇ *The consequences will be very grave if nothing is done.* 如果不采取任何措施，后果将会是非常严重的。◇ *We were in grave danger.* 我们处于极大的危险之中。 **2** (of people 人) serious in manner, as if sth sad, important or worrying has just happened 严肃的；庄严的；表情沉重的： *He looked very grave as he entered the room.* 他进入房间时表情非常严肃。 ➲ SEE ALSO GRAVITY ➲ SYNONYMS AT SERIOUS ▸ **grave·ly** 🔑 *adv.*： *She is gravely ill.* 她病得很重。◇ *Local people are gravely concerned.* 当地人都深感不安。◇ *He nodded gravely as I poured out my troubles.* 我倾诉我的苦恼时他心情沉重地点了点头。

grave² /ɡrɑːv/ (*also* ˌ**grave ˈaccent**) *noun* a mark placed over a vowel in some languages to show how it should be pronounced, as over the *e* in the French word *père* 钝重音符，沉音符，抑音符（标在元音上面表发音） ➲ COMPARE ACUTE ACCENT, CIRCUMFLEX, TILDE (1), UMLAUT ➲ SEE ALSO GRAVE¹

grave·dig·ger /ˈɡreɪvdɪɡə(r)/ *noun* a person whose job is to dig graves 掘墓人

gravel /ˈɡrævl/ *noun* [U] small stones, often used to make the surface of paths and roads 沙砾；砾石；石子： *a* *gravel path* 石子路 ◇ *a **gravel pit*** (= a place where gravel is taken from the ground) 砾石采掘场

grav·elled (*US* **grav·eled**) /ˈɡrævld/ *adj.* (of a road, etc. 道路等) covered with gravel 砾石铺的

grav·el·ly /ˈɡrævəli/ *adj.* **1** full of or containing many small stones 沙砾多的；含沙砾的；含碎石的：*a dry gravelly soil* 多沙砾的干土 **2** (of a voice 嗓音) deep and with a rough sound 低沉沙哑的

gra·ven image /ˌɡreɪvn ˈɪmɪdʒ/ *noun* (*disapproving*) a statue or image which people worship as a god or as if it were a god 神像；偶像

grave·stone /ˈɡreɪvstəʊn; *NAmE* -stoʊn/ *noun* a stone that is put on a grave in a vertical position, showing the name, etc. of the person buried there 墓碑 SYN **headstone** ➲ COMPARE TOMBSTONE

grave·yard /ˈɡreɪvjɑːd; *NAmE* -jɑːrd/ *noun* **1** an area of land, often near a church, where people are buried 墓地，坟场（常在教堂附近） ➲ COMPARE CEMETERY, CHURCHYARD **2** a place where things or people that are not wanted are sent or left 垃圾场；废物堆积处；收容所

ˈgraveyard shift *noun* (*especially NAmE*) a period of time working at night or in the very early morning 大夜班；凌晨班

gravid /ˈɡrævɪd/ *adj.* (*specialist*) pregnant 怀孕的

grav·itas /ˈɡrævɪtɑːs; -tæs/ *noun* [U] (*formal*) the quality of being serious 严肃；庄严 SYN **seriousness**：*a book of extraordinary gravitas* 一本非常严肃的书

gravi·tate /ˈɡrævɪteɪt/ *verb* (*formal*)

PHR V **ˈgravitate to/toward(s) sb/sth** to move towards sb/sth that you are attracted to 被吸引到；受吸引而转向：*Many young people gravitate to the cities in search of work.* 许多年轻人被吸引到城里找工作。

gravi·ta·tion /ˌɡrævɪˈteɪʃn/ *noun* [U] (*physics* 物) a force of attraction that causes objects to move towards each other 引力

gravi·ta·tion·al /ˌɡrævɪˈteɪʃənl/ *adj.* connected with or caused by the force of gravity 引力的；重力引起的：*a gravitational field* 引力场 ◇ *the gravitational pull of the moon* 月球的引力

grav·ity /ˈɡrævəti/ *noun* [U] **1** (*abbr.* **g**) the force that attracts objects in space towards each other, and that on the earth pulls them towards the centre of the planet, so that things fall to the ground when they are dropped 重力；地球引力：*Newton's law of gravity* 牛顿万有引力定律 ➲ SEE ALSO CENTRE OF GRAVITY ➲ WORDFINDER NOTE AT PHYSICS **2** (*formal*) extreme importance and a cause for worry 严重性 SYN **seriousness**：*I don't think you realise the gravity of the situation.* 我认为你没有意识到形势的严重性。◇ *Punishment varies according to the gravity of the offence.* 处罚根据罪行的严重程度而有所不同。 **3** (*formal*) serious behaviour, speech or appearance 严肃；庄严：*They were asked to behave with the gravity that was appropriate in a court of law.* 他们被要求在法庭上表现出应有的严肃态度。 ➲ SEE ALSO GRAVE[1] *adj.*

gravy /ˈɡreɪvi/ *noun* [U] **1** a brown sauce made by adding flour to the juices that come out of meat while it is cooking（调味）肉汁 **2** (*NAmE, informal*) something, especially money, that is obtained when you do not expect it 意外之财；飞来福

ˈgravy boat *noun* a long low JUG used for serving and pouring gravy at a meal 船形肉汁盘

ˈgravy train *noun* (*informal*) a situation where people seem to be making a lot of money without much effort 轻松赚大钱的机会；美差

gray /ɡreɪ/ (*especially NAmE*) = GREY

gray·beard (*especially NAmE*) = GREYBEARD

gray·ish /ˈɡreɪɪʃ/ *adj.* (*especially NAmE*) = GREYISH

gray·scale (*especially NAmE*) = GREYSCALE

graze /ɡreɪz/ *verb, noun*

■ ***verb*** **1** [I, T] (of cows, sheep, etc. 牛、羊等) to eat grass that is growing in a field（在草地上）吃青草：*There were cows grazing beside the river.* 有些牛在河边吃青草。◇ **~ on sth** *The horses were grazing on the lush grass.* 马群正在啃食茂盛的青草。◇ **~ sth** *The field had been grazed by sheep.* 这块地羊已经啃过了。 ➲ WORDFINDER NOTE AT FARM **2** [T] **~ sth** to put cows, sheep, etc. in a field so that they can eat the grass there 放牧；放牛；放羊：*The land is used by local people to graze their animals.* 这块地当地人用来放牧。 ➲ COLLOCATIONS AT FARMING **3** [I] **~ (on sth)** (*informal*) to eat small amounts of food many times during the day, often while doing other things, instead of eating three meals 吃零食（代替正餐）：*I have this really bad habit of grazing on junk food.* 我有个特别不好的习惯，就是吃垃圾食品。 **4** [T] **~ sth (on sth)** to break the surface of your skin by rubbing it against sth rough 擦伤，擦破（皮肤）：*I fell and grazed my knee.* 我摔了一跤擦伤了膝盖。 ➲ COLLOCATIONS AT INJURY **5** [T] **~ sth** to touch sth lightly while passing it（经过时）轻擦，轻触，蹭：*The bullet grazed his cheek.* 子弹从他的脸颊擦过。

■ ***noun*** a small injury where the surface of the skin has been slightly broken by rubbing against sth（表皮）擦伤：*Adam walked away from the crash with just **cuts and grazes**.* 亚当在撞车事故中平安脱险，只受了点划伤和擦伤。

gra·zier /ˈɡreɪziə(r)/ *noun* a farmer who keeps animals that eat grass 牧场主；放牧者

graz·ing /ˈɡreɪzɪŋ/ *noun* [U] land with grass that cows, sheep, etc. can eat 牧场；草场

GRE™ /ˌdʒiː ɑːr ˈiː/ *abbr.* Graduate Record Examination (an examination taken by students who want to study for a further degree in the US)（美国）研究生入学资格考试

grease /ɡriːs/ *noun, verb*

■ ***noun*** [U] **1** any thick OILY substance, especially one that is used to make machines run smoothly 油脂；润滑脂：*Grease marks can be removed with liquid detergent.* 用洗涤液可除去油渍。◇ *Her hands were covered with oil and grease.* 她满手油垢。◇ *the grease in his hair* 他头发上的油 ➲ SEE ALSO ELBOW GREASE **2** animal fat that has been made softer by cooking or heating（炼过的）动物油脂：*plates covered with grease* 油腻的盘子

■ ***verb*** **~ sth** to rub grease or fat on sth 给…加润滑油；在…上涂油（或抹油、擦油）：*to grease a cake tin/pan* 在蛋糕烤盘上抹油

IDM **grease sb's ˈpalm** (*old-fashioned, informal*) to give sb money in order to persuade them to do sth dishonest 向某人行贿；用金钱收买 SYN **bribe** **grease the ˈwheels** (*NAmE*) (*BrE* **oil the ˈwheels**) to help sth to happen easily and without problems, especially in business or politics（尤指在商业上或政治上）起促进作用

grease·ball /ˈɡriːsbɔːl/ *noun* (*NAmE, taboo, slang*) a very offensive word for a person from southern Europe or Latin America 油脂球（指南欧人或拉丁美洲人，极具侮慢性）

ˈgrease gun *noun* a tool for applying GREASE to moving parts of a machine, etc. 滑脂枪；注油枪

ˈgrease monkey *noun* (*informal*) an offensive or humorous word for a person whose job is repairing cars 油猢狲，黑手（指汽车修理工，含侮慢意或幽默）

grease·paint /ˈɡriːspeɪnt/ *noun* [U] a thick substance used by actors as make-up（演员化妆用的）油彩

grease·proof paper /ˌɡriːspruːf ˈpeɪpə(r)/ (*BrE*) (*NAmE* **ˈwax paper**) *noun* [U] paper that does not let GREASE, oil, etc. pass through it, used in cooking and for wrapping food in 防油纸，耐脂纸（烹调和包裹食物用）

greasy /ˈɡriːsi; ˈɡriːzi/ *adj.* (**greas·ier**, **greasi·est**) **1** covered in a lot of GREASE or oil 多油的；油污的；沾油脂的：*greasy fingers/marks/overalls* 沾满油脂的手指；油渍；满是油污的工作服 **2** (*disapproving*) (of food 食物) cooked with too much oil 油腻的：*greasy chips* 油腻的炸薯条 ➲ WORDFINDER NOTE AT CRISP **3** (*disapproving*) (of

G

hair or skin 头发或皮肤) producing too much natural oil 油性的；多脂的：*long greasy hair* 油性长发 **4** (*informal, disapproving*) (of people or their behaviour 人或行为) friendly in a way that does not seem sincere 圆滑的；滑头的；虚情假意的 **SYN smarmy**

IDM the greasy 'pole (*informal*) used to refer to the difficult way to the top of a profession 涂油杆（到达专业之巅的艰难道路）；险峻的职业阶梯

,greasy 'spoon *noun* (*informal, often disapproving*) a small cheap restaurant, usually one that is not very clean or attractive 低档小饭馆（通常不太卫生，装潢简陋，价格低廉）

great /ɡreɪt/ *adj., noun, adv.*

■ *adj.* (**great·er, great·est**)

• **LARGE** 大 **1** [usually before noun] very large; much bigger than average in size or quantity 大的；巨大的；数量大的；众多的：*A great crowd had gathered.* 一大群人聚集在一起。◇ *People were arriving in great numbers.* 人们大批到来。◇ *The **great majority of** (= most) people seem to agree with this view.* 大多数人似乎都同意这种观点。◇ *He must have fallen from a great height.* 他肯定是从很高的地方摔下来的。◇ *She lived to a great age.* 她活了很大岁数。 **2** [only before noun] (*informal*) used to emphasize an adjective of size or quality（强调尺寸、体积或质量）很：*There was a **great big** pile of books on the table.* 桌上有很大一摞书。◇ *He cut himself a great thick slice of cake.* 他给自己切了厚厚的一大块蛋糕。 **3** much more than average in degree or quantity 非常的；很多的；极大的：*a matter of great importance* 非常重要的事 ◇ *The concert had been a great success.* 音乐会非常成功。◇ *Her death was a great shock to us all.* 她的死使我们所有人都感到非常震惊。◇ *It gives me great pleasure to welcome you here today.* 今天能在这里欢迎您是我极大的荣幸。◇ *Take great care of it.* 对此要多加小心。◇ *You've been a great help.* 你帮了大忙。◇ *We are all **to a great extent** the products of our culture.* 我们在很大程度上都是所属文化的产物。 ➲ NOTE AT BIG

• **ADMIRED** 受赞赏 **4** extremely good in ability or quality and therefore admired by many people 伟大的；优秀的；杰出的；卓越的：*He has been described as the world's greatest violinist.* 他被称为世界上最杰出的小提琴手。◇ *Sherlock Holmes, the great detective* 赫赫有名的侦探福尔摩斯 ◇ *Great art has the power to change lives.* 伟大艺术品有着改变人们生活的力量。

• **GOOD** 好 **5** (*informal*) very good or pleasant 美妙的；好极的；使人快乐的：*He's a great bloke.* 他是个大好人。◇ *It's great to see you again.* 很高兴再次见到你。◇ *What a great goal!* 这球进得真妙！◇ *We had a great time in Madrid.* 我们在马德里玩得很开心。◇ *'I'll pick you up at seven.' 'That'll be great, thanks.'* "我七点钟来接你。" "太好了，谢谢。" ◇ (*ironic*) *Oh great, they left without us.* 啊，真绝，他们撇下我们走了。◇ (*ironic*) *You've been a great help, I must say* (= no help at all). 依我看，你真是帮了个大忙啊（指帮倒忙）。

• **IMPORTANT/IMPRESSIVE** 重要；给人深刻印象 **6** [only before noun] important and impressive 重要的；重大的；给人深刻印象的：*The wedding was a great occasion.* 这婚礼可是一大盛典。◇ *As the great day approached, she grew more and more nervous.* 随着这重大日子的临近，她心情越来越紧张。◇ ***The great thing** is to get it done quickly.* 重要的是尽快将它完成。◇ *One great advantage of this metal is that it doesn't rust.* 这种金属的一大优点就是不生锈。

• **WITH INFLUENCE** 有影响 **7** having high status or a lot of influence 地位高的；位高权重的；影响大的：*the great powers* (= important and powerful countries) 大国 ◇ *We can make this country great again.* 我们可以使这个国家再次强大起来。◇ *Alexander the Great* 亚历山大大帝

• **IN GOOD HEALTH** 健康 **8** in a very good state of physical or mental health 身心健康的；心情愉快的：*She seemed in great spirits* (= very cheerful). 她好像心情很不错。◇ *I **feel great** today.* 我今天感觉特别好。◇ *Everyone's in great form.* 每个人的状态都很好。

• **SKILLED** 熟练 **9** [not usually before noun] **~ at (doing) sth** (*informal*) able to do sth well 擅长；精通：*She's great at chess.* 她国际象棋下得很好。

• **USEFUL** 有用 **10 ~ for (doing) sth** (*informal*) very suitable or useful for sth 适合；（对…）有用：*This gadget's great for opening jars.* 这小玩意儿开广口瓶挺好。◇ *Try this cream—it's great for spots.* 试试这种乳霜吧，对皮肤斑点挺有效。

• **FOR EMPHASIS** 强调 **11** [only before noun] used when you are emphasizing a particular description of sb/sth（强调某种情况）：*We are great friends.* 我们是最要好的朋友。◇ *I've never been a great reader* (= I do not read much). 我从来都看书不多。◇ *She's a great talker, isn't she?* 她是个话匣子，对不对？

• **FAMILY** 家庭 **12 great-** added to words for family members to show a further stage in relationship（冠于家庭成员的称呼前，表示更高或更低一辈的亲属关系）：*my great-aunt* (= my father's or mother's aunt) 我的姑婆 / 姨婆 ◇ *her great-grandson* (= the grandson of her son or daughter) 她的曾孙 ◇ *my great-great-grandfather* (= the grandfather of my grandfather) 我的高祖

• **LARGER ANIMALS/PLANTS** 较大的动物 / 植物 **13** [only before noun] used in the names of animals or plants which are larger than similar kinds（用于相似动植物中较大者的名称前）大：*the great tit* 大山雀

• **CITY NAME** 城市名 **14 Greater** used with the name of a city to describe an area that includes the centre of the city and a large area all round it（与城市名连用，指

▼ **SYNONYMS** 同义词辨析

great

cool • fantastic • fabulous • terrific • brilliant • awesome • epic

These are all informal words that describe sb/sth that is very good, pleasant, enjoyable, etc. 以上各词均为非正式用语，表示美妙的、使人快乐的、令人愉快的等。

great (*informal*) very good; giving a lot of pleasure 指美妙的、好极的、使人快乐的：*We had a great time in Madrid.* 我们在马德里玩得很开心。

cool (*informal*) used to show that you admire or approve of sth, often because it is fashionable, attractive or different 指因时髦、漂亮或与众不同而令人钦佩的、绝妙的、顶呱呱的：*I think their new song's really cool.* 我认为他们的新歌棒极了。

fantastic (*informal*) extremely good; giving a lot of pleasure 指极好的、了不起的、非常愉快的：*'How was your holiday?' 'Fantastic!'* "你假期过得好吗？" "棒极了！"

fabulous (*informal*) extremely good 指极好的、绝妙的：*Jane's a fabulous cook.* 简的烹饪技巧堪称一绝。(**Fabulous** is slightly more old-fashioned than the other words in this set. * fabulous 较这组词中的其他词稍显过时。)

terrific (*informal*) extremely good; wonderful 指极好的、绝妙的、了不起的：*She's doing a terrific job.* 她活儿干得真棒。

brilliant (*BrE, informal*) extremely good; wonderful 指极好的、绝妙的、了不起的：*'How was the show?' 'Brilliant!'* "演出怎么样？" "棒极了！"

awesome (*informal, especially NAmE*) very good, impressive, or enjoyable 指极好的、令人惊叹的、极好玩的：*The show was just awesome.* 演出实在棒极了。

epic (*informal*) very good, impressive or enjoyable 极好的；给人深刻印象的；令人愉快的：*The adventure and action are truly epic in scope.* 惊险刺激的动作场面的确壮观。

PATTERNS

- to have a(n) great/cool/fantastic/fabulous/terrific/brilliant/awesome **time**
- to **look/sound** great/cool/fantastic/fabulous/terrific/brilliant/awesome
- **really** great/cool/fantastic/fabulous/terrific/brilliant/awesome
- **absolutely** great/fantastic/fabulous/terrific/brilliant/awesome/epic

包括市区和周围广大地区在内的区域）大：*Greater London* 大伦敦

▸ **great·ness** *noun* [U]

IDM **be going great 'guns** (*informal*) to be doing sth quickly and successfully 做得快；顺利；成功：*Work is going great guns now.* 目前工作很顺利。 **be a 'great one for (doing) sth** to do sth a lot; to enjoy sth 老做，总是做，喜欢做（某事）：*I've never been a great one for writing letters.* 我向来不喜欢写信。◇ *You're a great one for quizzes, aren't you?* 你是智力竞赛老手，不是吗？ **be no great 'shakes** (*informal*) to be not very good, efficient, suitable, etc. 不太出色；不太有效；不怎么合适；不怎么样 **ˌgreat and 'small** of all sizes or types 大小；高低；贵贱：*all creatures great and small* 所有大小生物 **great ˌminds think a'like** (*informal, humorous*) used to say that you and another person must both be very clever because you have had the same idea or agree about sth 英雄所见略同 **the great... in the 'sky** (*humorous*) used to refer to where a particular person is imagined to go when they die or a thing when it is no longer working, similar to the place they were connected with on earth （人死后回到）天上的老家，天国，西天；（东西无用了进）博物馆：*Their pet rabbit had gone to the great rabbit hutch in the sky.* 他们的宠兔已回到西天的兔宫了。➲ MORE AT OAK, PAINS, SUM *n.*

■ ***noun*** [usually pl.] (*informal*) a very well-known and successful person or thing 名人；伟人；伟大的事物：*He was one of boxing's all-time greats.* 他是一位空前的拳击好手。

■ ***adv.*** (*informal, non-standard*) very well 很好地；极好地；很棒地：*Well done. You did great.* 干得好。你干得真棒。

ˌgreat 'ape *noun* [usually pl.] one of the large animals which are most similar to humans (CHIMPANZEES, GORILLAS and ORANG-UTANS) 猩猩科动物

ˌgreat 'auk *noun* a large bird similar to a PENGUIN, that no longer exists 大海雀（类似企鹅，已灭绝）

the ˌGreat 'Bear *noun* [sing.] (*astronomy* 天) = URSA MAJOR

ˌGreat 'Britain *noun* [U] England, Scotland and Wales, when considered as a unit 大不列颠（包括英格兰、苏格兰和威尔士） HELP Sometimes 'Great Britain' (or 'Britain') is wrongly used to refer to the political state, officially called the 'United Kingdom of Great Britain and Northern Ireland' or the 'UK'. 有时 Great Britain 或 Britain 被错误地用来指称政治意义上的英国，其实官方称呼应作 United Kingdom of Great Britain and Northern Ireland（大不列颠及北爱尔兰联合王国）或简写作 UK。

great·coat /ˈgreɪtkəʊt; *NAmE* -koʊt/ *noun* a long heavy coat, especially one worn by soldiers（尤指士兵穿的）厚长大衣

Great Dane /ˌgreɪt ˈdeɪn/ *noun* a very large dog with short hair 丹麦大狗；大丹狗

great·ly 🔑 /ˈgreɪtli/ *adv.* (*formal*) (usually before a verb or participle 常用于动词或分词前) very much 非常；很；大大地：*People's reaction to the film has varied greatly.* 人们对这部影片的反应大不一样。◇ *a greatly increased risk* 大大增加了的风险 ◇ *Your help would be greatly appreciated.* 如蒙帮助，感激不尽。

the ˌGreat 'War *noun* [sing.] (*old-fashioned*) = FIRST WORLD WAR

ˌgreat white 'shark *noun* a large aggressive SHARK with a brown or grey back, found in warm seas 大白鲨，噬人鲨（栖居于温热海域）

the ˌGreat White 'Way *noun* (*informal*) a name for Broadway in New York City that refers to the many bright lights of its theatres 灯光大道，不夜街（指纽约市百老汇）

grebe /griːb/ *noun* a bird like a DUCK, that can also swim underwater 䴙䴘（潜水鸟）：*a great crested grebe* 凤头䴙䴘

Gre·cian /ˈgriːʃn/ *adj.* from ancient Greece or like the styles of ancient Greece 来自古希腊的；古希腊风格的；古希腊式的：*Grecian architecture* 古希腊式建筑

ˌGrecian 'nose *noun* a straight nose that continues the line of the FOREHEAD 希腊式鼻子（鼻梁和额部成一直线）

Greco- *combining form* (*NAmE*) = GRAECO-

greed /griːd/ *noun* [U] (*disapproving*) **1** a strong desire for more wealth, possessions, power, etc. than a person needs 贪婪；贪心；贪欲：*His actions were motivated by greed.* 他的所作所为是受贪婪之心所驱使。◇ **~ for sth** *Nothing would satisfy her greed for power.* 她对权力贪得无厌。 **2** a strong desire for more food or drink when you are no longer hungry or thirsty 贪食；贪吃：*I had another helping of ice cream out of pure greed.* 我纯粹是因为嘴馋贪吃，又吃了一份冰淇淋。

greedy /ˈgriːdi/ *adj.* (**greed·ier, greedi·est**) wanting more money, power, food, etc. than you really need 贪婪的；贪心的；贪吃的：*You greedy pig! You've already had two helpings!* 你这个馋嘴！你已经吃了两份了！◇ *He stared at the diamonds with greedy eyes.* 他眼巴巴地盯着这些钻石。◇ **~ for sth** *The shareholders are greedy for profit.* 股东们都利欲熏心。▸ **greed·ily** *adv.*：*She ate noisily and greedily.* 她吧嗒着嘴狼吞虎咽地吃。

IDM **'greedy guts** (*BrE, informal*) used to refer to sb who eats too much 贪吃的家伙

Greek /griːk/ *noun* **1** [C] a person from modern or ancient Greece 希腊人；古希腊人 **2** [U] the language of modern or ancient Greece 希腊语 **3** [C] (*NAmE*) a member of a FRATERNITY or a SORORITY at a college or university （大学的）学生联谊会会员，女生联谊会会员

IDM **it's all 'Greek to me** (*informal, saying*) I cannot understand it 我全然不懂；我一窍不通：*She tried to explain how the system works, but it's all Greek to me.* 她竭力想解释系统如何运作，可我怎么也弄不明白。

ˌGreek 'cross *noun* a cross with all arms of the same length 希腊式十字架（四臂等长）

ˌGreek 'salad *noun* [C, U] a salad that is made with tomatoes, OLIVES and FETA CHEESE 希腊风味色拉（用番茄、橄榄和羊奶干酪调制而成）

green 🔑 /griːn/ *adj., noun, verb*

■ ***adj.*** (**green·er, green·est**)

• **COLOUR** 颜色 **1** 🔑 having the colour of grass or the leaves of most plants and trees 绿色的；草绿色的：*green beans* 青豆 ◇ *Wait for the light to turn green* (= on traffic lights). 等绿灯亮了再走。

• **COVERED WITH GRASS** 青草覆盖 **2** 🔑 covered with grass or other plants 长满青草的；绿油油的；青葱的：*green fields/hills* 绿油油的农田；青葱翠绿的山丘 ◇ *After the rains, the land was green with new growth.* 雨天过后，大地一片新绿。

• **FRUIT** 果实 **3** 🔑 not yet ready to eat 未成熟的：*green tomatoes* 青西红柿

• **POLITICS** 政治 **4** 🔑 concerned with the protection of the environment; supporting the protection of the environment as a political principle 环境保护的；赞成环保的：*green politics* 主张环保的政见 ◇ *Try to adopt a greener lifestyle.* 尽量采取更环保的生活方式。◇ *the Green Party* 绿党

> **WORDFINDER** 联想词：biodiversity, conservation, endanger, **the environment**, extinct, managed, species, sustainable, toxic

• **PERSON** 人 **5** (*informal*) (of a person 人) young and lacking experience 不成熟的；缺乏经验的；幼稚的：*The new trainees are still very green.* 这些受培训的新学员还很不成熟。 **6** (of a person or their skin 人或其皮肤) being a pale colour, as if the person is going to VOMIT 苍白的；发青的；无血色的：*It was a rough crossing and most of the passengers looked distinctly green.* 渡海时风浪很大，多数乘客看上去脸色发青。

▸ **green·ness** *noun* [U]：*the greenness of the countryside* 乡村的青葱翠绿 ◇ *Supermarkets have started proclaiming the greenness of their products.* 超市已开始宣传他们的产品是绿色环保的。

IDM **ˌgreen with 'envy** very jealous （十分）妒忌的，嫉妒

的，眼红的 ➲ MORE AT GRASS *n.*

■ *noun*

• **COLOUR** 颜色 **1** [U, C] the colour of grass and the leaves of most plants and trees 绿色；草绿色：*the green of the countryside in spring* 春天乡村的青葱翠绿 ◇ *The room was decorated in a combination of greens and blues.* 这房间是把不同的绿色和蓝色搭配起来装饰的。◇ *She was dressed all in green.* 她全身绿装。

• **VEGETABLES** 蔬菜 **2 greens** [pl.] (*especially BrE*) green vegetables 绿色蔬菜；绿叶蔬菜：*Eat up your greens.* 把你那份青菜都吃了吧。

• **AREA OF GRASS** 草地 **3** [C] (*BrE*) an area of grass, especially in the middle of a town or village（尤指城镇或村庄中心的）草地，草坪，公共绿地：*Children were playing on the village green.* 孩子们在村镇公用绿地上玩耍。➲ VISUAL VOCAB PAGE V3 **4** [C] (in GOLF 高尔夫球) an area of grass cut short around a hole on a GOLF COURSE 球穴区，果岭（高尔夫球洞口附近草修得很平整的地区）：*the 18th green* 第 18 洞果岭 ◇ *Did the ball land on the green?* 球落在果岭了吗？➲ VISUAL VOCAB PAGE V44 ➲ SEE ALSO BOWLING GREEN, PUTTING GREEN

• **POLITICS** 政治 **5 the Greens** [pl.] the Green Party (= the party whose main aim is the protection of the environment) 绿党（以保护环境为主要目标）

■ *verb*

• **CREATE PARKS** 绿化 **1** ~ **sth** to create parks and other areas with trees and plants in a city 绿化：*projects for greening the cities* 绿化城市的方案

• **POLITICS** 政治 **2** ~ **sb/sth** to make sb more aware of issues connected with the environment; to make sth appear friendly towards the environment 使增强环境保护意识；使善待环境：*an attempt to green industry bosses* 使企业老板重视环境保护的努力

▸ **green·ing** *noun* [U]: *the greening of British politics* 使英国政界增强环保意识的过程

ˌgreen ˈaudit *noun* an official examination of the effect of a company's business on the environment 绿色审计，环保审计（就某一公司对环境的影响作出的评估）

green·back /ˈgriːnbæk/ *noun* (*NAmE, informal*) an American dollar note 美钞

ˌgreen ˈbean (*BrE also* **ˌFrench ˈbean**) (*NAmE also* **ˌstring ˈbean**) *noun* a type of BEAN which is a long thin green POD, cooked and eaten whole as a vegetable 青刀豆；四季豆 ➲ VISUAL VOCAB PAGE V34

ˌgreen ˈbelt *noun* [U, C, usually sing.] (*especially BrE*) an area of open land around a city where building is strictly controlled（城市周围的）绿化地带：*New roads are cutting into the green belt.* 一条条新路在逐渐吞噬着绿化地带。

ˌGreen Beˈret *noun* a member of the US army Special Forces 绿色贝雷帽（指美国陆军特种部队成员）

ˌgreen ˈcard *noun* **1** a document that legally allows sb from another country to live and work in the US 绿卡（允许外国人在美国居住和工作的法律证件） **2** (*BrE*) an insurance document that you need when you drive your car in another country（在国外开车所需的）绿色保险证

ˌgreen-ˈcollar *adj.* [only before noun] connected with industries that create products and provide services designed to improve and protect the environment 绿领的；环保行业的：*green-collar jobs* 绿领工作

green·ery /ˈgriːnəri/ *noun* [U] attractive green leaves and plants 青枝绿叶；青葱的草木；绿色植物：*The room was decorated with flowers and greenery.* 房间里装点着花卉和绿叶植物。

the ˌgreen-eyed ˈmonster *noun* (*informal*) used as a way of talking about JEALOUSY 绿眼怪兽；嫉妒；妒忌

green·field /ˈgriːnfiːld/ *adj.* [only before noun] used to describe an area of land that has not yet had buildings on it, but for which building development may be planned 未开发地区的；地产发展规划区的；绿色开发区的：*a greenfield site* 待开发区

ˌgreen ˈfingers *noun* [pl.] (*BrE*) (*NAmE* **ˌgreen ˈthumb**) if you have **green fingers**, you are good at making plants grow 园艺技能；种植技能 ▸ **ˌgreen-ˈfingered** *adj.* (*BrE*)

green·fly /ˈgriːnflaɪ/ *noun* [U, C] (*pl.* **green·flies** or **green·fly**) a small flying insect that is harmful to plants 蚜虫：*The roses have got greenfly.* 这些玫瑰花上有蚜虫。

green·gage /ˈgriːngeɪdʒ/ *noun* a small soft green fruit that is a type of PLUM 西洋李；青梅子；青李子：*a greengage tree* 青梅子树

green·gro·cer /ˈgriːngrəʊsə(r); *NAmE* -groʊ-/ *noun* (*especially BrE*) **1** a person who owns, manages or works in a shop/store selling fruit and vegetables 果菜商 ➲ COMPARE FRUITERER **2 green·gro·cer's** (*pl.* **green·gro·cers**) a shop/store that sells fruit and vegetables 蔬菜水果店 ➲ MORE LIKE THIS 34, page R29

green·horn /ˈgriːnhɔːn; *NAmE* -hɔːrn/ *noun* (*informal, especially NAmE*) a person who has little experience and can be easily tricked 新手 SYN **tenderfoot**

green·house /ˈgriːnhaʊs/ *noun* a building with glass sides and a glass roof for growing plants in 温室；暖房 ➲ VISUAL VOCAB PAGE V20

the ˈgreenhouse effect *noun* [sing.] the problem of the gradual rise in temperature of the earth's atmosphere, caused by an increase of gases such as CARBON DIOXIDE in the air surrounding the earth, which trap the heat of the sun 温室效应 ➲ COLLOCATIONS AT ENVIRONMENT ➲ SEE ALSO GLOBAL WARMING

ˌgreenhouse ˈgas *noun* any of the gases that are thought to cause the greenhouse effect, especially CARBON DIOXIDE 温室气体（尤指二氧化碳） ➲ COLLOCATIONS AT ENVIRONMENT

green·ing /ˈgriːnɪŋ/ *noun* [U] ➲ GREEN *n.*

green·ish /ˈgriːnɪʃ/ *adj.* fairly green in colour 带绿色的；浅绿色的

green·keep·er /ˈgriːnkiːpə(r)/ (*NAmE also* **greens·keep·er**) *noun* a person whose job is to take care of a GOLF COURSE 高尔夫球场看管人

ˌgreen ˈlight *noun* [sing.] permission for a project, etc. to start or continue 准许；许可；绿灯 SYN **go-ahead**: *The government has decided to **give the green light** to the plan.* 政府已决定为这项计划开绿灯。

ˌgreen-ˈlight *verb* (**green-lighted**, **green-lighted** or **green-lit**, **green-lit**) ~ **sth** to give permission for a project, etc. to start or continue 为…开绿灯；准许；许可：*A sixth season of the show has been green-lit.* 对开拍第六季节目已经开绿灯了。

ˌgreen maˈnure *noun* [U, C] plants that are dug into the soil in order to improve its quality 绿肥

ˌgreen ˈonion (*also* **scal·lion**) (*both NAmE*) (*BrE* **ˌspring ˈonion**) *noun* a type of small onion with a long green STEM and leaves. Green onions are often eaten raw in salads. 小葱；香葱 ➲ VISUAL VOCAB PAGE V33

ˌGreen ˈPaper *noun* (in Britain) a document containing government proposals on a particular subject, intended for general discussion 绿皮书（英国供讨论的政府提案文件） ➲ COMPARE WHITE PAPER

ˌgreen ˈpepper *noun* a hollow green fruit that is eaten, raw or cooked, as a vegetable 青椒；甜椒；灯笼椒

ˈgreen roof (*also* **ˌliving ˈroof**) *noun* a type of roof that has plants growing on it that help to keep the building cool in summer and warm in winter 绿屋顶，绿化屋顶（种植植物以保持房屋冬暖夏凉）

ˈgreen room *noun* a room in a theatre, television studio, etc. where the performers can relax when they are not performing（剧场、电视演播室等的）演员休息室

ˌgreen ˈsalad *noun* [C, U] a salad that is made with raw green vegetables, especially LETTUCE 绿色拉；生菜色拉：*Serve with a green salad.* 上菜的时候配一份生菜色拉。

greens·keep·er /ˈgriːnzkiːpə(r)/ *noun* (*NAmE*) = GREENKEEPER

greens·ward /ˈgriːnswɔːd; *NAmE* -swɔːrd/ *noun* [U] (*literary*) a piece of ground covered with grass 草坪；草地

ˌgreen ˈtea *noun* [U] a pale tea made from leaves that have been dried but not FERMENTED 绿茶

ˌgreen ˈthumb (*NAmE*) (*BrE* **ˌgreen ˈfingers**) *noun* [sing.] if you have a **green thumb**, you are good at making plants grow 园艺技能；种植技能

ˌgreen ˈvegetable *noun* [C, usually pl.] (*BrE also* **greens** [pl.]) a vegetable with dark green leaves, for example CABBAGE or SPINACH 绿叶蔬菜

green·wash /ˈgriːnwɒʃ; *NAmE* -wɔːʃ/ *noun* [U] (*disapproving*) activities by a company or an organization that are intended to make people think that it is concerned about the environment, even if its real business actually harms the environment 绿色外衣，绿色粉饰，环保幌子，漂绿（指公司或机构假借环保之名进行宣传） ➲ MORE LIKE THIS 1, page R25

Green·wich Mean Time /ˌgrenɪtʃ ˈmiːn taɪm; -nɪdʒ-/ ➲ GMT

greet /griːt/ *verb* **1** to say hello to sb or to welcome them 和（某人）打招呼（或问好）；欢迎；迎接：**~ sb** *He greeted all the guests warmly as they arrived.* 客人到达时他都热情接待。◇ **~ sb with sth** *She greeted us with a smile.* 她微笑着向我们打招呼。➲ SEE ALSO MEET-AND-GREET **2** [usually passive] to react to sb/sth in a particular way（以某种方式）对…作出反应：**~ sb/sth** *Loud cheers greeted the news.* 这消息受到热烈欢呼。◇ **~ sb/sth with sth** *The changes were greeted with suspicion.* 这些变革受到人们的怀疑。◇ **~ sb/sth as sth** *The team's win was greeted as a major triumph.* 这个队获胜被看成是一个重大的胜利。 **3** [usually passive] **~ sb** (of sights, sounds or smells 景象、声音或气味) to be the first thing that you see, hear or smell at a particular time 映入…的眼帘；传入…的耳中（或鼻中）：*When she opened the door she was greeted by a scene of utter confusion.* 她打开门，一片混乱不堪的景象呈现在她的眼前。

greet·er /ˈgriːtə(r)/ *noun* (*especially NAmE*) a person whose job is to meet and welcome people in a public place such as a restaurant or shop/store（餐馆、商店等处的）门迎，迎宾员

greet·ing /ˈgriːtɪŋ/ *noun* **1** [C, U] something that you say or do to greet sb 问候；招呼；迎接；致意：*She waved a friendly greeting.* 她友好地挥手致意。◇ *They* ***exchanged greetings*** *and sat down to lunch.* 他们相互致意后便坐下吃午饭。◇ *He raised his hand* ***in greeting****.* 他举手致意。 **2** **greetings** [pl.] a message of good wishes for sb's health, happiness, etc. 问候的话；祝辞；贺辞：***Christmas/birthday, etc. greetings*** 圣诞、生日等祝辞 ◇ *My mother sends her greetings to you all.* 我母亲向你们各位问好。IDM SEE SEASON *n.*

ˈgreetings card (*BrE*) (*NAmE* **ˈgreeting card**) *noun* a card with a picture on the front and a message inside that you send to sb on a particular occasion such as their birthday 贺卡

gre·gari·ous /grɪˈgeəriəs; *NAmE* -ˈger-/ *adj.* **1** liking to be with other people 爱交际的；合群的 SYN **sociable** **2** (*biology* 生) (of animals or birds 动物或鸟) living in groups 群居的 ▸ **gre·gari·ous·ly** *adv.* **gre·gari·ous·ness** *noun* [U]

Gre·gor·ian calendar /grɪˌgɔːriən ˈkælɪndə(r)/ *noun* [sing.] the system used since 1582 in Western countries of arranging the months in the year and the days in the months and of counting the years from the birth of Christ 格里历，公历，阳历（自 1582 年以来西方国家使用的历法） ➲ COMPARE JULIAN CALENDAR

GreˌGorian ˈchant *noun* [U, C] a type of church music for voices alone, used since the Middle Ages 格里高利圣咏（自中世纪以来教堂演唱的无伴奏圣歌）

grem·lin /ˈgremlɪn/ *noun* an imaginary creature that people blame when a machine suddenly stops working（假想的）捣蛋小精灵（机器出故障时人们常归咎于它）

gren·ade /grəˈneɪd/ *noun* a small bomb that can be thrown by hand or fired from a gun 榴弹；手榴弹；枪榴弹 ➲ SEE ALSO HAND GRENADE

grena·dier /ˌgrenəˈdɪə(r); *NAmE* -ˈdɪr/ *noun* a soldier in the part of the British army known as the **Grenadiers** or **Grenadier Guards** 英国近卫步兵团的士兵

grena·dine /ˈgrenədiːn/ *noun* [U] a sweet red liquid that is made from POMEGRANATES (= a tropical fruit with many seeds). It is drunk mixed with water or alcoholic drinks. 石榴汁饮料（饮用时掺水或酒）

Gretna Green /ˌgretnə ˈgriːn/ *noun* a village in Scotland near the border with England, famous in the past as a place where English couples used to go to get married when they were not allowed to get married in England 格雷特纳格林（临近英格兰边境的苏格兰村庄，旧时一些英格兰情侣因被禁止在本地结婚而跑到此地成婚，因而闻名）

grew PAST TENSE OF GROW

grey 🔑 (*especially BrE*) (*NAmE usually* **gray**) /greɪ/ *adj.*, *noun*, *verb*

■ ***adj.*** **1** 🔑 having the colour of smoke or ASHES 灰色的；烟灰色的；灰白色的：*grey eyes/hair* 灰色的眼睛；灰白的头发 ◇ *wisps of grey smoke* 一缕缕灰色的烟雾 ◇ *a grey suit* 一套灰色西装 ➲ WORDFINDER NOTE AT BLONDE **2** 🔑 [not usually before noun] having grey hair 头发花白；头发灰白：*He's gone very grey.* 他已满头银丝。 **3** 🔑 (of the sky or weather 天空或天气) dull; full of clouds 昏暗的；阴沉的：*grey skies* 昏暗的天空 ◇ *I hate these grey days.* 我讨厌这阴沉沉的天气。 **4** (of a person's skin colour 人的肤色) pale and dull, because they are ill/sick, tired or sad 苍白的 **5** without interest or variety; making you feel sad 单调乏味的；忧郁的；沉闷的：*Life seems grey and pointless without him.* 没有他，生活就显得沉闷而无意义。 **6** (*disapproving*) not interesting or attractive 没趣味的；毫无吸引力的：*The company was full of faceless grey men who all looked the same.* 公司里全是些缺乏个性、毫无吸引力的男人。 **7** [only before noun] connected with old people 老年人的：*the grey vote* 老年人的投票总数 ◇ *grey power* 长者对社会的影响力 ▸ **grey·ness** (*especially BrE*) (*NAmE usually* **gray·ness**) *noun* [U, sing.]

■ ***noun*** **1** 🔑 [U, C] the colour of smoke or ASHES 灰色；烟灰色；灰白色：*the dull grey of the sky* 暗灰色的天空 ◇ *dressed in grey* 身着灰色衣服 **2** [C] a grey or white horse 灰马；白马：*She's riding the grey.* 她骑着一匹灰马。

■ ***verb*** [I] (of hair 头发) to become grey 变灰白；变花白：*His hair was greying at the sides.* 他的两鬓已渐渐斑白。◇ *a tall woman with greying hair* 头发渐白的高个子女人

ˌgrey ˈarea (*especially BrE*) (*NAmE usually* **ˌgray ˈarea**) *noun* an area of a subject or situation that is not clear or does not fit into a particular group and is therefore difficult to define or deal with 灰色地带，中间区域（界线不明、不易归类、难以界定或处理的领域或形势）：*Exactly what can be called an offensive weapon is still a grey area.* 究竟什么可称作攻击性武器仍然难以界定。

grey·beard (*especially BrE*) (*NAmE usually* **gray·beard**) /ˈgreɪbɪəd; *NAmE* -bɪrd/ *noun* (*informal*) an old man 老头儿；老翁：*the greybeards of the art world* 艺术界的老人们

ˌgrey-ˈhaired (*especially BrE*) (*NAmE usually* **ˌgray-ˈhaired**) *adj.* with grey hair 头发灰白的；头发花白的

grey·hound /ˈgreɪhaʊnd/ *noun* a large thin dog with smooth hair and long thin legs, that can run very fast and is used in the sport of **greyhound racing** 灵猩（身细长、腿长、毛滑、善跑的大赛狗）

grey·ish (*especially BrE*) (*NAmE usually* **gray·ish**) /ˈgreɪɪʃ/ *adj.* fairly grey in colour 带灰色的；浅灰色的：*greyish hair* 灰白的头发

ˌgrey ˈmarket (*NAmE usually* **ˌgray ˈmarket**) *noun* [usually sing.] **1** a system in which products are imported into a country and sold without the permission of the company that produced them 灰市，水货市场（未经生产公司授权而进口并销售其产品） **2** (*BrE*) old people, when they are thought of as customers for goods（统称）老年顾客，老年客户

ˈgrey matter (*especially BrE*) (*NAmE usually* **ˈgray matter**) *noun* [U] (*informal*) a person's intelligence（人的）头脑，脑子

grey·scale (*especially BrE*) (*NAmE usually* **gray·scale**) /ˈɡreɪskeɪl/ *adj.* (*specialist*) **1** (of an image 图像) produced using only shades of grey, not colour 灰度的；灰色调的：*I've printed out the pictures* ***in greyscale***. 我已经用灰色调打印出图片。 **2** (of a printer or SCANNER 打印机或扫描仪) producing images using only shades of grey, not colour 灰度的

G

grid /ɡrɪd/ *noun* **1** a pattern of straight lines, usually crossing each other to form squares 网格；方格：*New York's grid of streets* 纽约棋盘式的街道布局 **2** a frame of metal or wooden bars that are parallel or cross each other（金属或木制的）格子，格栅，栅栏 ➲ SEE ALSO CATTLE GRID **3** a pattern of squares on a map that are marked with letters or numbers to help you find the exact position of a place（地图上的）坐标方格：*The* ***grid reference*** *is C8.* 地图上的坐标方格数字为 C8。 ➲ WORDFINDER NOTE AT MAP **4** (*especially BrE*) a system of electric wires or pipes carrying gas, for sending power over a large area （输电线路、天然气管道的）系统网络；输电网；煤气输送网：*the national grid* (= the electricity supply in a country) 国家输电网 **5** (in motor racing 汽车比赛) a pattern of lines marking the starting positions for the racing cars 赛车起跑线 **6** (*often* **the Grid**) [sing.] (*computing* 计) a number of computers that are linked together using the Internet so that they can share power, data, etc. in order to work on difficult problems（利用互联网的）联网，联机

IDM **ˌoff the ˈgrid** (*especially NAmE*) not using the public supplies of electricity, gas, water, etc. 不用水电等公共设施：*The mountain cabin is entirely off the grid.* 这山中小屋完全不用水电等公共设施。 ➲ SEE ALSO OFF-THE-GRID

grid·dle /ˈɡrɪdl/ *noun* a flat round iron plate that is heated on a stove or over a fire and used for cooking 鏊子（圆形平底铁锅）

grid·iron /ˈɡrɪdaɪən; *NAmE* -aɪərn/ *noun* **1** a frame made of metal bars that is used for cooking meat or fish on, over an open fire（烤肉或鱼的）烤架，铁丝格子，铁箅子 **2** (*NAmE*) a field used for AMERICAN FOOTBALL marked with a pattern of parallel lines（标有平行线的）美式足球球场

grid·lock /ˈɡrɪdlɒk; *NAmE* -lɑːk/ *noun* [U] **1** a situation in which there are so many cars in the streets of a town that the traffic cannot move at all 市区交通大堵塞 **2** (usually in politics 通常用于政治) a situation in which people with different opinions are not able to agree with each other and so no action can be taken 僵局（因意见分歧而无法采取行动）：*Congress is in gridlock.* 国会因意见分歧而陷入僵局。 ▸ **grid·locked** *adj.*

grief /ɡriːf/ *noun* **1** [U, C] ~ (**over/at sth**) a feeling of great sadness, especially when sb dies（尤指因某人去世引起的）悲伤，悲痛，伤心：*She was overcome with grief when her husband died.* 丈夫去世时她悲痛欲绝。◇ *They were able to share their common joys and griefs.* 他们做到了同甘共苦。 **2** [C, usually sing.] something that causes great sadness 伤心事；悲痛事：*It was a grief to them that they had no children.* 没有孩子是他们的一块心病。 **3** [U] (*informal*) problems and worry 担心；忧虑：*He caused his parents a lot of grief.* 他没少让父母操心。

IDM **come to ˈgrief** (*informal*) **1** to end in total failure 以彻底失败而告终；惨遭失败 **2** to be harmed in an accident 受伤；遭到不幸；出事故：*Several pedestrians came to grief on the icy pavement.* 好几个人都在结了冰的人行道上摔伤了。 **give sb ˈgrief (about/over sth)** (*informal*) to be annoyed with sb and criticize their behaviour 对某人很生气（或烦恼）；指责某人 **good ˈgrief!** (*informal*) used to express surprise or shock（表示惊奇或震惊）哎呀，天哪：*Good grief! What a mess!* 天哪！好乱哟！

ˈgrief-stricken *adj.* feeling extremely sad because of sth that has happened, especially the death of sb（尤因某人的去世而）极度悲伤的，悲痛欲绝的

griev·ance /ˈɡriːvəns/ *noun* ~ (**against sb**) something that you think is unfair and that you complain or protest about 不平的事；委屈；抱怨；牢骚：*Parents were invited to* ***air their grievances*** (= express them) *at the meeting.* 家长们应邀在会上诉说他们的苦衷。◇ *He had been* ***nursing a grievance against*** *his boss for months.* 他几个月来一直对老板心怀不满。◇ *Does the company have a formal* ***grievance procedure*** (= a way of telling sb your complaints at work)? 公司有正式投诉程序吗？

grieve /ɡriːv/ *verb* **1** [I, T] to feel very sad, especially because sb has died（尤指因某人的去世而）悲伤，悲痛，伤心：~ (**for/over sb/sth**) *They are still grieving for their dead child.* 他们还在为死去的孩子伤心。◇ *grieving relatives* 悲痛欲绝的亲戚 ◇ ~ **sb/sth** *She grieved the death of her husband.* 她为丈夫的去世而悲伤。 **2** [T] (*formal*) to make you feel very sad 使悲伤；使悲痛；使伤心 SYN **pain**: **it grieves sb that…** *It grieved him that he could do nothing to help her.* 他因无法帮助她而伤心。◇ ~ **sb** *Their lack of interest grieved her.* 他们不感兴趣使她很痛心。◇ **it grieves sb to do sth** *It grieved her to leave.* 她要走了，心里很难过。 IDM SEE EYE *n.*

griev·ous /ˈɡriːvəs/ *adj.* (*formal*) very serious and often causing great pain or suffering 极严重的；使人痛苦的；令人伤心的：*He had been the victim of a grievous injustice.* 他曾遭受极不公正的待遇。 ▸ **griev·ous·ly** *adv.*：*grievously hurt/wounded* 受到严重伤害；伤势严重

ˌgrievous ˌbodily ˈharm *noun* [U] (*abbr.* **GBH**) (*BrE, law* 律) the crime of causing sb serious physical injury 严重人体伤害（罪） ➲ COMPARE ACTUAL BODILY HARM

grif·fin /ˈɡrɪfɪn/ (*also* **grif·fon**, **gry·phon** /ˈɡrɪfən/) *noun* (in stories) a creature with a LION'S body and an EAGLE'S wings and head（神话故事中的）狮身鹰首兽；狮鹫

grift·er /ˈɡrɪftə(r)/ *noun* (*especially US*) a person who tricks people into giving them money, etc.（骗取钱财等的）骗子

grill /ɡrɪl/ *noun, verb*

■ ***noun*** **1** (*BrE*) the part of a cooker that directs heat downwards to cook food that is placed underneath it（炊具、烤炉内的）烘烤器 ➲ VISUAL VOCAB PAGE V26 ➲ COMPARE BROILER (2) **2** a flat metal frame that you put food on to cook over a fire（置于火上的）烤架 ➲ SEE ALSO BARBECUE *n.* **3** a dish of grilled food, especially meat 一盘烧烤食物（尤指烤肉） ➲ SEE ALSO MIXED GRILL **4** (especially in names 尤用于名称) a restaurant serving grilled food 烤肉餐馆；烧烤店：*Harry's Bar and Grill* 哈里烤肉酒吧 **5** = GRILLE

■ ***verb*** **1** ~ **sth** (*BrE*) to cook food under or over a very strong heat （在高温下方或上方）烧烤，炙烤：*Grill the sausages for ten minutes.* 把香肠烤十分钟。◇ *grilled bacon* 烤咸肉 ➲ COMPARE BROIL (1) ➲ COLLOCATIONS AT COOKING **2** ~ **sth** (*NAmE*) to cook food over a fire, especially outdoors（在火上，尤指户外）烧，烤，焙：*grilled meat and shrimp* 烤肉和烤虾 **3** ~ **sb** (**about sth**) to ask sb a lot of questions about their ideas, actions, etc., often in an unpleasant way 盘问；追问；审问；责问：*They grilled her about where she had been all night.* 他们盘问她整个晚上去哪里了。 ➲ SEE ALSO GRILLING

grille (*also* **grill**) /ɡrɪl/ *noun* a screen made of metal bars or wire that is placed in front of a window, door or piece of machinery in order to protect it（置于窗、门、机器前面的）铁栅栏，金属网罩：*a radiator grille* (= at the front of a car)（汽车前的）散热器面罩 ◇ *a security grille* 安全保护格栅

grill·ing /ˈɡrɪlɪŋ/ *noun* [usually sing.] a period of being questioned closely about your ideas, actions, etc. 盘问，

责问，审问（的一段时间）：*The minister faced a tough grilling at today's press conference.* 部长在今天的记者招待会上受到了严厉的盘问。

grilse /grɪls/ *noun* a SALMON (= a type of fish) that has returned to a river or lake after spending one winter in the sea（海里过冬后）洄游的鲑鱼

grim /grɪm/ *adj.* (**grim·mer**, **grim·mest**) **1** looking or sounding very serious 严肃的；坚定的；阴冷的：*a grim face/look/smile* 严肃的面孔 / 表情；冷笑 ◇ *She looked grim.* 她表情严肃。◇ *with a look of **grim determination** on his face* 他脸上带有的坚定不移的神态 ◇ *grim-faced policemen* 表情严肃的警察 **2** unpleasant and depressing 令人不快的；令人沮丧的：*grim news* 令人沮丧的消息 ◇ *We face the grim prospect of still higher unemployment.* 我们面临着失业率进一步上升的暗淡前景。◇ *The outlook is pretty grim.* 前景令人甚感忧虑。◇ *Things are **looking grim** for workers in the building industry.* 对建筑业的工人来说，形势看来很不乐观。 **3** (of a place or building 地方或建筑物) not attractive; depressing 无吸引力的；阴森的；凄凉的：*The house looked grim and dreary in the rain.* 这房子在雨中显得阴郁凄凉。◇ *the grim walls of the prison* 令人抑郁的监狱四壁 **4** [not before noun] (*BrE, informal*) ill/sick 生病的；不舒服的：*I feel grim this morning.* 我今天早上感到不舒服。 **5** [not usually before noun] (*BrE, informal*) of very low quality 质量低劣；糟糕：*Their performance was fairly grim, I'm afraid!* 很遗憾，他们的表现真不怎么样！ ▸ **grim·ly** *adv.*：*'It won't be easy,' he said grimly.* "那不会很容易。"他严肃地说。◇ *grimly determined* 坚定不移 **grim·ness** *noun* [U]

IDM **hang/hold on for/like grim 'death** (*BrE*) (*also* **hang/hold on for dear 'life** *NAmE, BrE*) (*informal*) to hold sb/sth very tightly because you are afraid（害怕得）死死抓住不放，紧紧抓住不松手

grim·ace /grɪ'meɪs; 'grɪməs/ *verb, noun*

■ *verb* [I] ~ (**at sb/sth**) to make an ugly expression with your face to show pain, disgust, etc.（因痛苦、厌恶等）做鬼脸，做怪相：*He grimaced at the bitter taste.* 他一尝那苦味，做了个怪相。◇ *She grimaced as the needle went in.* 针扎进去痛得她龇牙咧嘴。 ➲ WORDFINDER NOTE AT EXPRESSION

■ *noun* an ugly expression made by twisting your face, used to show pain, disgust, etc. or to make sb laugh 怪相；鬼脸；脸部扭曲：*to **make/give a grimace** of pain* 做出 / 露出痛苦的表情 ◇ *'What's that?' she asked with a grimace.* "那是什么？"她皱着眉头问道。

grime /graɪm/ *noun* [U] dirt that forms a layer on the surface of sth 一层污垢；尘垢；积垢 SYN **dirt**：*a face covered with grime and sweat* 满是污垢和汗水的脸

the ˌGrim 'Reaper *noun* an imaginary figure who represents death. It looks like a SKELETON, wears a long CLOAK and carries a SCYTHE. 狰狞的收割者（骷髅状的死神形象，身披斗篷，手持长柄大镰刀）

grimy /'graɪmi/ *adj.* (**grimi·er**, **grimi·est**) covered with dirt 沾满污垢的；满是灰尘的 SYN **dirty**：*grimy hands/windows* 沾满污垢的手；满是灰尘的窗户

grin /grɪn/ *verb, noun*

■ *verb* (**-nn-**) [I, T] to smile widely 露齿而笑；咧着嘴笑；粲然而笑：*They grinned with delight when they heard our news.* 他们得知我们的消息时高兴得直咧着嘴笑。◇ *He was **grinning from ear to ear**.* 他笑得合不拢嘴。◇ **~ at sb** *She grinned amiably at us.* 她咧着嘴向我们亲切地笑。◇ **~ sth** *He grinned a wide grin.* 他粲然一笑。 ➲ WORDFINDER NOTE AT EXPRESSION

IDM **grin and 'bear it** (only used as an infinitive and in orders 只用作不定式和用于命令中) to accept pain, disappointment or a difficult situation without complaining 默默忍受；苦笑着忍受：*There's nothing we can do about it. We'll just have to grin and bear it.* 对此我们无能为力，只好默默地忍受。 ➲ MORE AT EAR

■ *noun* a wide smile 露齿的笑；咧着嘴笑：*She gave a **broad grin**.* 她露出大大的笑容。◇ *a wry/sheepish grin* 咧嘴苦笑；尴尬的笑 ◇ *'No,' he said **with a grin**.* "不。"他咧嘴笑了笑说。◇ ***Take that grin off your face!*** 别嬉皮笑脸的！

grind /graɪnd/ *verb, noun*

■ *verb* (**ground**, **ground** /graʊnd/)

• **FOOD/FLOUR/COFFEE** 食物；面粉；咖啡 **1** [T] ~ **sth** (**down/up**) | ~ **sth** (**to/into sth**) to break or crush sth into very small pieces between two hard surfaces or using a special machine 磨碎；碾碎；把…磨成粉：*to grind coffee/corn* 将咖啡 / 谷粒磨成粉 ➲ SEE ALSO GROUND *adj.* **2** [T] ~ **sth** to produce sth such as flour by crushing 磨（粉）：*The flour is ground using traditional methods.* 这面粉是用传统方法磨制而成。 **3** [T] ~ **sth** (*NAmE*) = MINCE (1)

• **MAKE SHARP/SMOOTH** 使锋利 / 光滑 **4** [T] ~ **sth** to make sth sharp or smooth by rubbing it against a hard surface 使锋利；磨快；磨光：*a special stone for grinding knives* 专门磨刀用的石头

• **PRESS INTO SURFACE** 挤压进表层 **5** [T] to press or rub sth into a surface 用力挤压，用力擦（入表层）：**~ sth into sth** *He ground his cigarette into the ashtray.* 他把香烟按在烟灰缸里捻灭。◇ **~ sth in** *The dirt on her hands was ground in.* 她手上的泥渍住了。

• **RUB TOGETHER** 摩擦 **6** [I, T] to rub together, or to make hard objects rub together, often producing an unpleasant noise 摩擦（发出刺耳声）：**~ (together)** *Parts of the machine were grinding together noisily.* 机器零件摩擦发出刺耳的声音。◇ **~ sth (together)** *She **grinds her teeth** when she is asleep.* 她睡觉时磨牙。◇ *He ground the gears on the car.* 他把汽车排挡弄得嘎嘎作响。

• **MACHINE** 机器 **7** [T] ~ **sth** to turn the handle of a machine that grinds sth 摇动手柄（操纵机器）：*to grind a pepper mill* 摇动胡椒磨

IDM **bring sth to a grinding 'halt** to make sth gradually go slower until it stops completely 使渐渐停下来 **grind to a 'halt | come to a grinding 'halt** to go slower gradually and then stop completely 慢慢停下来：*Production ground to a halt during the strike.* 罢工期间生产渐渐陷入瘫痪。 ➲ MORE AT AXE *n.*

PHR V **ˌgrind sb↔'down** to treat sb in a cruel unpleasant way over a long period of time, so that they become very unhappy（长时间）虐待，欺压，折磨（某人）：*Don't let them grind you down.* 别让他们欺压你。◇ *Years of oppression had ground the people down.* 人民年复一年地遭受着压迫。 **ˌgrind 'on** to continue for a long time, when this is unpleasant 令人厌烦地继续下去：*The argument ground on for almost two years.* 这场争论拖拖拉拉持续了近两年。 **ˌgrind sth↔'out** to produce sth in large quantities, often sth that is not good or interesting 大量生产（常指粗制滥造） SYN **churn sth↔out**：*She grinds out romantic novels at the rate of five a year.* 她以一年五部的速度胡乱拼凑低劣的言情小说。

■ *noun*

• **BORING ACTIVITY** 乏味的活动 **1** [sing.] (*informal*) an activity that is tiring or boring and takes a lot of time 令人疲劳（或厌倦）的工作；苦差事：*the **daily grind** of family life* 家庭生活中繁重的家务劳动 ◇ *It's a long grind to the top of that particular profession.* 爬到那种行业的最高位置要经过漫长的艰苦奋斗。

• **OF MACHINES** 机器 **2** [sing.] the unpleasant noise made by machines 刺耳的摩擦声

• **SWOT** 刻苦用功的人 **3** (*US*) (*BrE* **swot**) [C] (*informal*) a person who spends too much time studying 只知一味用功学习的人；书呆子

grind·er /'graɪndə(r)/ *noun* **1** a machine or tool for grinding a solid substance into a powder 碾磨器械：*a coffee grinder* 磨咖啡机 **2** a person whose job is to make knives sharper; a machine which does this 磨刀匠；磨工；磨床 ➲ SEE ALSO ORGAN GRINDER

grind·ing /'graɪndɪŋ/ *adj.* [only before noun] (of a difficult situation 困难的形势) that never ends or improves 没完没了的；无休止的；无改进的：*grinding poverty* 贫困不堪

grind·stone /'graɪndstəʊn; *NAmE* -stoʊn/ *noun* a round stone that is turned like a wheel and is used to make knives and other tools sharp 磨石；砂轮 IDM SEE NOSE *n.*

gringo /ˈgrɪŋgəʊ; *NAmE* -goʊ/ *noun* (*pl.* **-os**) (*informal, disapproving*) used in Latin American countries to refer to a person from the US 美国佬（在拉丁美洲国家使用）

griot /ˈgriːəʊ; *NAmE* ˈgriːoʊ/ *noun* (in W Africa, especially in the past) a person who sings or tells stories about the history and traditions of their people and community （西非，尤指旧时的）部族史（或传统）说唱艺人

grip /grɪp/ *noun, verb*

▪ ***noun***

• **HOLDING TIGHTLY** 紧握 **1** [C, usually sing.] ~ (**on sb/sth**) an act of holding sb/sth tightly; a particular way of doing this 紧握；紧抓 **SYN** **grasp**: *Keep a tight grip on the rope.* 紧紧抓住绳索不放。◇ *to* ***loosen/release/relax your grip*** 松手 ◇ *She tried to* ***get a grip on*** *the icy rock.* 她尽力抓住那冰冷的石头。◇ *The climber slipped and* ***lost her grip.*** 登山女子滑了一下，松开了手。◇ *She struggled from his grip.* 他紧拉住她不放，她奋力挣脱。◇ *Try adjusting your grip on the racket.* 试着调整一下你握球拍的方法。

• **CONTROL/POWER** 控制力；影响力 **2** [sing.] ~ (**on sb/sth**) control or power over sb/sth （对…的）控制，影响力：*The home team took a firm grip on the game.* 主队牢牢控制着比赛的局面。◇ *We need to tighten the grip we have on the market.* 我们得加强对市场的掌控。

• **UNDERSTANDING** 理解 **3** [sing.] ~ (**on sth**) an understanding of sth 理解；了解 **SYN** **grasp**: *I couldn't get a grip on what was going on.* 我无法理解正在发生的事情。◇ *You need to keep a good grip on reality in this job.* 做这个工作你需要充分了解实际情况。

• **MOVING WITHOUT SLIPPING** 不打滑 **4** [U] the ability of sth to move over a surface without slipping 不打滑；走得稳：*These tyres give the bus better grip in slippery conditions.* 这些轮胎可使公共汽车在路滑时行驶得平稳一些。

• **PART OF OBJECT** 物体部位 **5** [C] a part of sth that has a special surface so that it can be held without the hands slipping 把手；手柄；握杆：*the grip on a golf club* 高尔夫球杆的握柄

• **FOR HAIR** 头发 **6** [C] (*BrE*) = HAIRGRIP

• **JOB IN THE MOVIES** 影业工作 **7** [C] a person who prepares and moves the cameras, and sometimes the lighting equipment, when a film/movie is being made （拍摄电影时）摄影机和灯光设备管理人员

• **BAG** 包 **8** [C] (*old-fashioned*) a large soft bag, used when travelling 旅行袋；手提包

IDM **come/get to ˈgrips with sth** to begin to understand and deal with sth difficult 开始理解并着手处理难题：*I'm slowly getting to grips with the language.* 我慢慢开始掌握这种语言。 **get/take a ˈgrip (on yourself)** to improve your behaviour or control your emotions after being afraid, upset or angry 使（自己）镇定下来；控制住（自己的）情绪：*I have to take a grip on myself, he told himself firmly.* 我一定要控制住自己的情绪，他坚定地对自己说。◇ (*informal*) ***Get a grip!*** (= make an effort to control your emotions) 镇静点！ **in the ˈgrip of sth** experiencing sth unpleasant that cannot be stopped 处于不快却无法制止的境遇；受制于某事：*a country in the grip of recession* 陷入衰退的国家 **lose your ˈgrip (on sth)** to become unable to understand or control a situation 失去（对…的）理解（或控制）；驾驭不住：*Sometimes I feel I'm losing my grip.* 有时我感到自己无能为力。

▪ ***verb*** (**-pp-**)

• **HOLD TIGHTLY** 紧握 **1** [T, I] to hold sth tightly 紧握；紧抓 **SYN** **grasp**: **~ sth** *'Please don't go,' he said, gripping her arm.* "请别走。"他紧紧抓住她的手臂说。◇ **~ on to sth** *She gripped on to the railing with both hands.* 她双手紧紧抓住栏杆。 ➲ SYNONYMS AT HOLD

• **INTEREST/EXCITE** 使感兴趣；使激动 **2** [T] **~ sb** to interest or excite sb; to hold sb's attention 使感兴趣；使激动；吸引住（某人）的注意：*The book grips you from start to finish.* 这本书从头至尾扣人心弦。◇ *I was totally gripped by the story.* 我完全被这故事吸引住了。 ➲ SEE ALSO GRIPPING

• **HAVE POWERFUL EFFECT** 具有强烈的影响力 **3** [T] **~ sb/sth** (of an emotion or a situation 情绪或形势) to have a powerful effect on sb/sth 对…产生强有力的影响：*I was gripped by a feeling of panic.* 我惊恐万状。◇ *Terrorism has gripped the country for the past two years.* 两年来恐怖主义一直笼罩着这个国家。

• **MOVE/HOLD WITHOUT SLIPPING** 不打滑；抓牢 **4** [T, I] **~ (sth)** to hold onto or to move over a surface without slipping 抓牢：*tyres that grip the road* 在公路上不打滑的车胎

gripe /graɪp/ *noun, verb*

▪ ***noun*** (*informal*) a complaint about sth 抱怨；怨言；牢骚：*My only gripe about the hotel was the food.* 我对这家旅馆唯一不满的是食物。

▪ ***verb*** [I] **~ (about sb/sth)** (*informal*) to complain about sb/sth in an annoying way 抱怨；发牢骚：*He's always griping about the people at work.* 他老是抱怨共事的人。

ˈGripe Water™ *noun* [U] (*BrE*) medicine that is given to babies when they have stomach pains （缓解婴儿腹痛的）止痛水

grip·ing /ˈgraɪpɪŋ/ *adj.* [only before noun] a **griping** pain is a sudden strong pain in your stomach 肠（或胃）绞痛的

grip·ping /ˈgrɪpɪŋ/ *adj.* exciting or interesting in a way that keeps your attention 激动人心的；吸引人的；扣人心弦的 ➲ SYNONYMS AT INTERESTING ➲ WORDFINDER NOTE AT STORY

grisly /ˈgrɪzli/ *adj.* [usually before noun] (**gris·lier, gris·li·est**) extremely unpleasant and frightening and usually connected with death and violence 令人厌恶的；恐怖的；可怕的：*a grisly crime* 可憎的罪行

grist /grɪst/ *noun*

IDM **(all) grist to the/sb's ˈmill** (*BrE*) (*NAmE* **(all) grist for the/sb's ˈmill**) something that is useful to sb for a particular purpose 对…有用的东西（或有利的事）：*Political sex scandals are all grist to the mill of the tabloid newspapers.* 政界的性丑闻对通俗小报总是多多益善。

gris·tle /ˈgrɪsl/ *noun* [U] a hard substance in meat that is unpleasant to eat （肉中的）软骨：*a lump of gristle* 一块软骨

grit /grɪt/ *noun, verb*

▪ ***noun*** [U] **1** very small pieces of stone or sand 沙粒；沙砾；细沙：*I had a piece of grit in my eye.* 我眼睛里进了一粒沙子。◇ *They were spreading grit and salt on the icy roads.* 他们在结冰的路上撒沙子和盐。 **2** the courage and determination that makes it possible for sb to continue doing sth difficult or unpleasant 勇气；毅力

▪ ***verb*** (**-tt-**) **~ sth** to spread grit, salt or sand on a road that is covered with ice （在结冰的路上）撒沙砾，撒盐，撒沙子

IDM **grit your ˈteeth 1** to bite your teeth tightly together 咬紧牙关：*She gritted her teeth against the pain.* 她咬牙忍痛。◇ *'Stop it!' he said through gritted teeth.* "住手！"他咬牙切齿地说。 **2** to be determined to continue to do sth in a difficult or unpleasant situation 下定决心；鼓起勇气：*It started to rain harder, but* ***we gritted our teeth and carried on.*** 雨开始大起来，可我们鼓起勇气继续进行。

grits /grɪts/ *noun* [pl.] CORN (MAIZE) that is partly crushed before cooking, often eaten for breakfast or as part of a meal in the southern US （美国南部吃的）粗玉米粉，玉米糙子

grit·ter /ˈgrɪtə(r)/ (*BrE*) (*US* **ˈsalt truck**) *noun* a large vehicle used for putting salt, sand or GRIT on the roads in winter when there is ice on them 铺沙机，撒盐车，撒沙车（在结冰的路面上使用）

gritty /ˈgrɪti/ *adj.* (**grit·tier, grit·ti·est**) **1** containing or like GRIT 含沙砾的；沙砾般的：*a layer of gritty dust* 一层沙尘 **2** showing the courage and determination to continue doing sth difficult or unpleasant 坚韧不拔的；坚定的；坚毅的：*gritty determination* 坚定的决心 ◇ *a gritty performance from the British player* 这位英国运动员的坚毅表现 **3** showing sth unpleasant as it really is （对不好事物的描述）逼真的，真实的，活生生的：*a gritty description of urban violence* 对城市暴力的真实描述 ◇ *gritty realism* 活生生的现实 ➲ SEE ALSO NITTY-GRITTY ▸ **grit·tily** *adv.* **grit·ti·ness** *noun* [U]

griz·zle /ˈgrɪzl/ *verb* [I] (*BrE, informal*) (especially of a baby or child 尤指婴儿或小孩) to cry or complain continuously in a way that is annoying 不断地啼哭；哭哭啼啼地缠人

griz·zled /ˈgrɪzld/ *adj.* (*literary*) having hair that is grey or partly grey（头发）灰白的，花白的

griz·zly bear /ˌgrɪzli ˈbeə(r); *NAmE* ˈber/ (*also* **ˈgriz·zly** *pl.* **-ies**) *noun* a large aggressive brown BEAR that lives in N America and parts of Russia 灰熊，银尖熊（生活在北美和俄罗斯部分地区的大型棕熊）

groan /grəʊn; *NAmE* groʊn/ *verb, noun*

■ ***verb*** **1** [I, T] to make a long deep sound because you are annoyed, upset or in pain, or with pleasure 呻吟；叹息；哼哼 SYN **moan**: *He lay on the floor groaning.* 他躺在地板上呻吟。◇ **~ with sth** *to groan with pain/pleasure* 痛苦地呻吟；高兴得直哼哼 ◇ **~ at sth** *We all groaned at his terrible jokes.* 他讲的笑话很糟糕，我们都发出不满的抱怨声。◇ **~ about sth** *They were all* ***moaning and groaning*** (= complaining) *about the amount of work they had.* 他们对工作量都怨声载道。◇ **+ speech** *'It's a complete mess!' she groaned.* "这简直是一团糟！"她叹息道。 **2** [I] to make a sound like a person groaning 发出似呻吟的声音 SYN **moan**: *The trees creaked and groaned in the wind.* 树在风中嘎吱作响。

IDM **groan under the weight of sth** (*formal*) used to say that there is too much of sth 在某物的折磨（或重压）下呻吟；被某物压得喘不过气来（或无法忍受）

PHR V **ˈgroan with sth** (*formal*) to be full of sth 被某物堆满（或摆满、装满、充满）: *tables groaning with food* 摆满食物的桌子

■ ***noun*** a long deep sound made when sb/sth groans 呻吟声；叹息声；哼哼声；嘎吱声 SYN **moan**: *She let out a groan of dismay.* 她发出沮丧的叹息声。◇ *He fell to the floor with a groan.* 他哼了一声倒在地板上。◇ *The house was filled with the cello's dismal squeaks and groans.* 房子里回荡着大提琴低沉而凄厉的声音。

groat /grəʊt; *NAmE* groʊt/ *noun* a silver coin used in Europe in the past 格罗特（欧洲旧时银币）

gro·cer /ˈgrəʊsə(r); *NAmE* ˈgroʊ-/ *noun* **1** a person who owns, manages or works in a shop/store selling food and other things used in the home 食物杂货商 **2 gro·cer's** (*pl.* **gro·cers**) a shop/store that sells these things 食物杂货店 ➲ MORE LIKE THIS 34, page R29

gro·cery 🔑 /ˈgrəʊsəri; *NAmE* ˈgroʊ-/ *noun* (*pl.* **-ies**) **1** 🔑 (*especially BrE*) (*NAmE usually* **ˈgrocery store**) [C] a shop/store that sells food and other things used in the home. In American English 'grocery store' is often used to mean 'supermarket'. 食品杂货店（在美式英语中 grocery store 常用以指 supermarket） **2** 🔑 **groceries** [pl.] food and other goods sold by a grocer or at a supermarket 食品杂货 ➲ COLLOCATIONS AT SHOPPING ▶ **gro·cery** *adj.* [only before noun]: *the grocery bill* 食品杂货账单

grog /grɒg; *NAmE* grɑːg/ *noun* [U] **1** a strong alcoholic drink, originally RUM, mixed with water 格洛格酒（用朗姆酒兑水制成的烈酒） **2** (*informal, AustralE, NZE*) any alcoholic drink, especially beer 酒（尤指啤酒）

groggy /ˈgrɒgi; *NAmE* ˈgrɑːgi/ *adj.* [not usually before noun] (**grog·gier, grog·gi·est**) (*informal*) weak and unable to think or move well because you are ill/sick or very tired（因疾病或疲劳而）昏昏沉沉，眩晕无力，踉踉跄跄

groin /grɔɪn/ *noun* **1** the part of the body where the legs join at the top including the area around the GENITALS (= sex organs) 腹股沟；大腿根儿: *She kicked her attacker in the groin.* 她朝袭击者的下身踢了一脚。◇ *He's been off all season with a groin injury.* 他因腹股沟伤痛休息了整个赛季。 ➲ VISUAL VOCAB PAGE V64 **2** (*especially US*) = GROYNE

grok /grɒk; *NAmE* grɑːk/ *verb* (**-kk-**) **~ sth** (*US, slang*) to understand sth completely using your feelings rather than considering the facts 通过感觉意会: *Children grok this show immediately but their parents take longer to get it.* 孩子很快就通过感觉理解了这一演出，他们的父母却花了更长的时间才理解。

grom·met /ˈgrɒmɪt; *NAmE* ˈgrɑːm-/ *noun* **1** a small metal ring placed around a hole in cloth or leather, to make it stronger（织物或皮革上用以加固扣眼的）金属环，金属圈 **2** (*BrE*) (*NAmE* **tube**) a small tube placed in a child's ear in order to DRAIN liquid from it 鼓室通气管；中耳引流管

groom /gruːm/ *verb, noun*

■ ***verb*** **1 ~ sth** to clean or brush an animal（给动物）擦洗，刷洗: *to groom a horse/dog/cat* 刷洗马／狗／猫 ◇ *The horses are all well fed and groomed.* 这些马都喂得饱饱的，刷洗得干干净净。 **2 ~ sth** (of an animal 动物) to clean the fur or skin of another animal or itself（给自己或其他动物）理毛，梳毛: *a female ape grooming her mate* 为同伴梳毛的母猿 **3** to prepare or train sb for an important job or position 使做好准备；培养；训练: **~ sb (for/as sth)** *Our junior employees are being groomed for more senior roles.* 我们的初级雇员正在接受培训以承担更重要的职责。◇ **~ sb to do sth** *The eldest son is being groomed to take over when his father dies.* 长子正在接受培养，以在父亲过世后接手父业。 **4 ~ sb** (of a person who is sexually attracted to children 恋童癖者) to prepare a child for a meeting, especially using an Internet CHAT ROOM, with the intention of performing an illegal sexual act（尤指利用互联网聊天室）勾引（儿童）

■ ***noun*** **1** a person whose job is to feed and take care of horses, especially by brushing and cleaning them 马夫；马倌；马匹饲养员 **2** = BRIDEGROOM

groomed /gruːmd/ *adj.* (usually following an adverb 通常用于副词之后) used to describe the way in which a person cares for their clothes and hair（描述穿着打扮情况）: *She is always perfectly groomed.* 她总是打扮得干净利落。 ➲ SEE ALSO WELL GROOMED

groom·ing /ˈgruːmɪŋ/ *noun* [U] **1** the things that you do to keep your clothes and hair clean and neat, or to keep an animal's fur or hair clean 打扮；装束；刷洗；（给动物）梳毛: *You should always pay attention to personal grooming.* 你应随时注意个人衣着整洁。 **2** the process in which an adult develops a friendship with a child, particularly through the Internet, with the intention of having a sexual relationship 勾引幼童（尤指通过网络与儿童交友以达到诱奸的目的）

grooms·man /ˈgruːmzmən/ *noun* (*pl.* **-men** /-mən/) (*NAmE*) a friend of the BRIDEGROOM at a wedding, who has special duties 男傧相；伴郎

groove /gruːv/ *noun* **1** a long narrow cut in the surface of sth hard 沟；槽；辙；纹 **2** (*informal*) a particular type of musical rhythm （某种）音乐节奏（或律动）: *a jazz groove* 爵士乐节奏

IDM **be (stuck) in a ˈgroove** (*BrE*) to be unable to change sth that you have been doing the same way for a long time and that has become boring 墨守成规；照惯例行事

grooved /gruːvd/ *adj.* having a groove or grooves 有沟的；有槽的

groovy /ˈgruːvi/ *adj.* (*old-fashioned, informal*) fashionable, attractive and interesting 时髦的；吸引人的；有趣的

grope /grəʊp; *NAmE* groʊp/ *verb, noun*

■ ***verb*** **1** [I] **~ (around) (for sth)** to try and find sth that you cannot see, by feeling with your hands 摸索；搜索；搜寻；探寻: *He groped around in the dark for his other sock.* 他在黑暗中到处摸找另一只袜子。◇ (*figurative*) *'It's so…, so…' I was groping for the right word to describe it.* "它是那么…，那么…" 我想找一个恰当的字眼来描述它。 **2** [T, I] to try and reach a place by feeling with your hands because you cannot see clearly（用手）摸索着往前走: **~ your way + adv./prep.** *He groped his way up the staircase in the dark.* 他摸黑走上楼梯。◇ **+ adv./prep.** *She groped through the darkness towards the doors.* 她摸黑朝门口走去。 **3** [T] **~ sb** (*informal*) to touch sb sexually, especially when they do not want you to 猥亵；摸（某人）

■ ***noun*** (*informal*) an act of groping sb (= touching them sexually) 猥亵；摸

gross /grəʊs; *NAmE* groʊs/ *adj., adv., verb, noun*

■ ***adj.*** (**gross·er, gross·est**) **1** [only before noun] being the total amount of sth before anything is taken away

总的；毛的：*gross weight* (= including the container or wrapping) 毛重 ◇ *gross income/wage* (= before taxes, etc. are taken away)（税前）总收益 / 工资 ◇ *Investments showed a gross profit of 26%.* 投资毛利为 26%。 ➲ COMPARE NET *adj.* (1) **2** [only before noun] (*formal* or *law* 律) (of a crime, etc. 罪行等) very obvious and unacceptable 严重的：*gross indecency/negligence/misconduct* 严重猥亵 / 过失 / 渎职 ◇ *a gross violation of human rights* 严重侵犯人权 **3** (*informal*) very unpleasant 令人不快的；令人恶心的；使人厌恶的 SYN **disgusting**: *'He ate it with mustard.' 'Oh, gross!'* "他用芥末拌着吃。""啊，真恶心！" ➲ SYNONYMS AT DISGUSTING **4** very rude 粗鲁的；不雅的 SYN **crude**: *gross behaviour* 粗鲁的行为 **5** very fat and ugly 肥胖而丑陋的：*She's not just fat, she's positively gross!* 她不只是胖，她简直是五大三粗！ ▶ **gross·ness** *noun* [U]

■*adv.* in total, before anything is taken away 总共；全部：*She earns £25 000 a year gross.* 她一年总收入为 25 000 英镑。 ➲ COMPARE NET

■*verb* ~ **sth** to earn a particular amount of money before tax has been taken off it 总收入为；总共赚得：*It is one of the biggest grossing movies of all time.* 这是票房收入之高创历史纪录的影片之一。

PHR V ˌ**gross sb 'out** (*NAmE, informal*) to be very unpleasant and make sb feel disgusted 使人恶心；令人憎恶；令人作呕 SYN **disgust**: *His bad breath really grossed me out.* 他的口臭实在使我恶心。

■*noun* **1** (*pl.* **gross**) a group of 144 things 一罗（144 个）：*two gross of apples* 两罗苹果 ◇ *to sell sth by the gross* 按罗出售某物 **2** (*pl.* **grosses**) (*especially US*) a total amount of money earned by sth, especially a film/movie, before any costs are taken away（尤指影片的）毛收入，总收入

ˌ**gross doˌmestic 'product** *noun* [sing., U] = GDP

gross·ly /ˈɡrəʊsli; *NAmE* ˈɡroʊsli/ *adv.* (*disapproving*) (used to describe unpleasant qualities 形容令人不快的事物) extremely 极度地；极其；非常：*grossly overweight/unfair/inadequate* 极胖；极不公平；极不充分 ◇ *Press reports have been grossly exaggerated.* 新闻报道过于夸张。

ˌ**gross ˌnational 'product** *noun* [sing., U] = GNP

'**gross-out** *noun* (*especially NAmE, informal*) something disgusting 令人厌恶的东西；倒胃口的东西：*They eat flies? What a gross-out!* 他们吃苍蝇？真恶心！ ▶ '**gross-out** *adj.* [only before noun]: *gross-out movie scenes* 令人作呕的电影镜头

grot /ɡrɒt; *NAmE* ɡrɑːt/ *noun* [U] (*BrE, informal*) something unpleasant, dirty or of poor quality 讨厌（或肮脏、劣质）的东西

gro·tesque /ɡrəʊˈtesk; *NAmE* ɡroʊ-/ *adj., noun*

■*adj.* **1** strange in a way that is unpleasant or offensive 怪诞的；荒唐的；荒谬的：*a grotesque distortion of the truth* 对事实的荒诞歪曲 ◇ *It's grotesque to expect a person of her experience to work for so little money.* 想让她那样有经验的人为这点钱工作真是荒唐。 **2** extremely ugly in a strange way that is often frightening or amusing 丑陋奇异的；奇形怪状的：*a grotesque figure* 奇形怪状的人像 ◇ *tribal dancers wearing grotesque masks* 戴着奇异面具的部落舞者 ▶ **gro·tesque·ly** *adv.*

■*noun* **1** [C] a person who is extremely ugly in a strange way, especially in a book or painting（尤指书画中的）奇形怪状的人，丑陋的人 **2 the grotesque** [sing.] a style of art using grotesque figures and designs 奇异艺术风格

grotto /ˈɡrɒtəʊ; *NAmE* ˈɡrɑːtoʊ/ *noun* (*pl.* **-oes** or **-os**) a small CAVE, especially one that has been made artificially, for example in a garden 洞穴；（尤指园林等中的）石窟

grotty /ˈɡrɒti; *NAmE* ˈɡrɑːti/ *adj.* (*BrE, informal*) (**grot·tier, grot·ti·est**) unpleasant or of poor quality 令人讨厌的；令人不悦的；低劣的：*a grotty little hotel* 条件恶劣的小旅店 ◇ *I'm feeling pretty grotty* (= ill). 我感到身体很不舒服。

grouch /ɡraʊtʃ/ *noun* (*informal*) **1** a person who complains a lot 好抱怨（或发牢骚）的人 **2** a complaint about sth unimportant（对小事的）抱怨，牢骚 ▶ **grouch** *verb* [I]

grouchy /ˈɡraʊtʃi/ *adj.* (*informal*) bad-tempered and often complaining 脾气不好并常发牢骚的；好抱怨的

ground 🔑 /ɡraʊnd/ *noun, verb, adj.* ➲ SEE ALSO GRIND *v.*

■*noun*

• SURFACE OF EARTH 地面 **1** 🔑 (*often* **the ground**) [U] the solid surface of the earth 地；地面：*I found her lying on the ground.* 我发现她躺在地上。 ◇ *He lost his balance and fell to the ground.* 他失去平衡摔倒在地上。 ◇ *2 metres above/below ground* 地上 / 地下 2 米 ◇ *Most of the monkeys' food is found at ground level.* 猴子的食物大多可在地面找到。 ◇ *ground forces* (= soldiers that fight on land, not in the air or at sea) 地面部队 ◇ *Houses and a luxury tourist hotel were burned to the ground* (= completely destroyed, so that there is nothing left). 多间房屋和一家豪华旅游宾馆被大火焚烧殆尽。 ➲ SYNONYMS AT FLOOR

• SOIL 土壤 **2** 🔑 [U] soil on the surface of the earth 土；土地；土壤：*fertile ground for planting crops* 种植农作物的肥沃土壤 ➲ SYNONYMS AT SOIL

• AREA OF LAND 场地 **3** 🔑 [U] an area of open land 开阔地；空旷地：*The kids were playing on waste ground behind the school.* 孩子们在学校后面的荒地上玩耍。 **4** 🔑 [C] (often in compounds 常构成复合词) an area of land that is used for a particular purpose, activity or sport（特定用途的）场地：*a football/recreation/sports, etc. ground* 足球场、娱乐场地、运动场等 ◇ *ancient burial grounds* 古代墓地 ➲ SEE ALSO BREEDING GROUND, DUMPING GROUND, PARADE GROUND, STAMPING GROUND, TESTING GROUND ➲ SYNONYMS AT LAND **5 grounds** [pl.] a large area of land or sea that is used for a particular purpose（某种用途的）地域，水域：*fishing grounds* 渔场 ◇ *feeding grounds for birds* 禽类饲养场

• GARDENS 花园 **6** 🔑 **grounds** [pl.] the land or gardens around a large building（大建筑物周围的）场地，庭院，花园：*the hospital grounds* 医院的院子

• AREA OF KNOWLEDGE/IDEAS 知识 / 思想领域 **7** 🔑 [U] an area of interest, knowledge or ideas（兴趣、知识或思想的）范围，领域：*He managed to cover a lot of ground in a short talk.* 他在简短的谈话中涵盖了许多领域。 ◇ *We had to go over the same ground* (= talk about the same things again) *in class the next day.* 我们得在第二天的课上继续讨论同样的话题。 ◇ *You're on dangerous ground* (= talking about ideas that are likely to offend sb or make people angry) *if you criticize his family.* 你要是批评他的家人可就惹麻烦了。 ◇ *I thought I was on safe ground* (= talking about a suitable subject) *discussing music with her.* 我以为与她一起讨论音乐是稳妥的。 ◇ *He was back on familiar ground, dealing with the customers.* 他又干起了与顾客打交道的老本行。 ◇ *They are fighting the Conservatives on their own ground.* 他们以保守党人自己的逻辑在和他们斗争。 ➲ SEE ALSO COMMON GROUND, MIDDLE GROUND

• GOOD REASON 充分的理由 **8** 🔑 [C, usually pl.] ~ **for sth/for doing sth** a good or true reason for saying, doing or believing sth 充分的理由；根据：*You have no grounds for complaint.* 你没有理由抱怨。 ◇ *What were his grounds for wanting a divorce?* 他要离婚的理由是什么？ ◇ *The case was dismissed on the grounds that there was not enough evidence.* 此案因缺乏足够的证据被驳回。 ◇ *He retired from the job on health grounds.* 他因健康原因退职。 ◇ *Employers cannot discriminate on grounds of age.* 雇主不得有年龄歧视。 ➲ SYNONYMS AT REASON

• IN LIQUID 液体 **9 grounds** [pl.] the small pieces of solid matter in a liquid that have fallen to the bottom 渣滓；沉淀物：*coffee grounds* 咖啡渣

• ELECTRICAL WIRE 电线 **10** (*NAmE*) (*BrE* **earth**) [C, usually sing.] a wire that connects an electric CIRCUIT with the ground and makes it safe （接）地线

• BACKGROUND 背景 **11** [C] a background that a design is painted or printed on（绘画或印刷的）背景，底子：*pink roses on a white ground* 白底粉红玫瑰

IDM **cut the ground from under sb's 'feet** to suddenly spoil sb's idea or plan by doing sth to stop them from continuing with it 挖某人的墙脚；破坏某人的计划；拆某人的台 **gain/make up 'ground (on sb/sth)** to gradually get closer to sb/sth that is moving or making progress in an activity 逼近（正在向前的人或物）: *The police car was gaining ground on the suspects.* 警车渐渐逼近犯罪嫌疑人。◇ *They needed to make up ground on their competitors.* 他们必须穷追猛赶竞争对手。 **get (sth) off the ˈground** to start happening successfully; to make sth start happening successfully（使）顺利开始，开始发生: *Without more money, the movie is unlikely to get off the ground.* 没有更多的资金，这部影片难以顺利开拍。◇ *to get a new company off the ground* 使新公司顺利开张 **give/lose ˈground (to sb/sth)** to allow sb/sth to have an advantage; to lose an advantage for yourself 退让；让步；失利: *They are not prepared to give ground on tax cuts.* 他们不打算在减税方面让步。◇ *The Conservatives lost a lot of ground to the Liberal Democrats at the election.* 在选举中保守党大大失利于自由民主党。 **go to ˈground** (*BrE*) to hide, especially to escape sb who is chasing you 躲藏起来；潜伏下来 **hold/stand your ˈground 1** to continue with your opinions or intentions when sb is opposing you and wants you to change 坚持主张；坚持意图；坚持立场；不让步: *Don't let him persuade you—stand your ground.* 别听他的，坚持自己的主张吧。 **2** to face a situation and refuse to run away 坚守阵地；不撤退；不退却: *It is not easy to hold your ground in front of someone with a gun.* 面对持枪者而不退缩并不容易。 **on the ˈground** in the place where sth is happening and among the people who are in the situation, especially a war 当场；在现场；（尤指）处于战火中: *On the ground, there are hopes that the fighting will soon stop.* 战火中的人都希望战斗尽快结束。◇ *There's a lot of support for the policy on the ground.* 很多在场的人支持这一政策。 **run/drive/work yourself into the ˈground** to work so hard that you become extremely tired 把自己弄得精疲力竭；把自己累垮 **run sb/sth into the ˈground** to make sb work so hard that they are no longer able to work; to use sth so much that it is broken 使某人精疲力竭；耗尽某物；过度使用某物 **thick/thin on the ˈground** (*BrE*) if people or things are **thick/thin on the ground**, there are a lot/not many of them in a place 为数众多（或不多）；数目巨大（或微小）；众多（或稀少）: *Customers are thin on the ground at this time of year.* 一年里这个时节顾客很少。 ➲ MORE AT EAR, FIRM *adj.*, FOOT *n.*, GAIN *v.*, HIT *v.*, MORAL *adj.*, NEUTRAL *adj.*, NEW, PREPARE, RIVET *v.*, SHIFT *v.*, STONY, SUIT *v.*

■ *verb*

- **BOAT** 船 **1** [T, I] ~ (sth) when a boat **grounds** or sth **grounds** it, it touches the bottom of the sea and is unable to move（使）搁浅，触海底: *The fishing boat had been grounded on rocks off the coast of Cornwall.* 渔船在康沃尔海岸外礁石上搁浅了。
- **AIRCRAFT** 飞行器 **2** [T, often passive] ~ **sth** to prevent an aircraft from taking off 使停飞；阻止…起飞: *The balloon was grounded by strong winds.* 热气球因强风停飞。◇ *All planes out of Heathrow have been grounded by the strikes.* 所有由希思罗机场起飞的飞机均因罢工而停飞。
- **CHILD** 孩子 **3** [T, usually passive] ~ **sb** to punish a child or young person by not allowing them to go out with their friends for a period of time 罚（儿童）不准出去玩: *You're grounded for a week!* 罚你一周不准出门！
- **ELECTRICITY** 电 **4** (*NAmE*) (*BrE* **earth**) [T, usually passive] ~ **sth** to make electrical equipment safe by connecting it to the ground with a wire 把（电线）接地 ➲ SEE ALSO GROUNDED, GROUNDING

■ *adj.* [only before noun] (of food 食物) cut, chopped or crushed into very small pieces or powder 磨细的；剁碎的: *ground coffee* 咖啡粉 ◇ (*US*) *ground pork* 猪肉糜 ➲ SEE ALSO HAMBURGER (2)

ˈground ball *noun* = GROUNDER

ˌground ˈbeef *noun* [U] (*NAmE*) = HAMBURGER (2)

ground·break·ing /ˈgraʊndbreɪkɪŋ/ *adj.* [only before noun] making new discoveries; using new methods 开创性的；创新的；革新的: *a groundbreaking piece of research* 富有开拓性的一项研究

ˈground cloth (*US*) (*BrE* **ground·sheet**) *noun* a large piece of material that does not let water through that is placed on the ground inside a tent（帐篷内铺地用的）防潮布

ˈground control *noun* [U] the people and equipment on the ground that make sure that planes or SPACECRAFT take off and land safely 地面控制中心

ˈground cover *noun* [U] plants that cover the soil 地被植物

ˈground crew (*also* **ˈground staff**) *noun* [C+sing./pl. v.] the people at an airport whose job is to take care of aircraft while they are on the ground （统称）地勤人员

ground·ed /ˈgraʊndɪd/ *adj.* having a sensible and realistic attitude to life（对生活）持有理智和现实态度的: *Away from Hollywood, he relies on his family and friends to keep him grounded.* 离开好莱坞之后，他靠家人和朋友使自己保持心态平衡。

IDM **(be) ˈgrounded in/on sth** (to be) based on sth 以…为基础；基于: *His views are grounded on the assumption that all people are equal.* 他的观点建立在人人平等的假设之上。

ground·er /ˈgraʊndə(r)/ (*also* **ˈground ball**) *noun* (in BASEBALL 棒球) a ball that runs along the ground after it has been hit 地滚球

ˌground ˈfloor (*BrE*) (*NAmE* **ˌfirst ˈfloor**) *noun* the floor of a building that is at the same level as the ground outside 底层，底楼，一楼（建筑物与外面地面相平的一层）: *a ground-floor window* 一楼窗户 ◇ *I live on the ground floor.* 我住在一楼。 ➲ NOTE AT FLOOR

IDM **be/get in on the ground ˈfloor** to become involved in a plan, project, etc. at the beginning 在开始时参与

ground·hog /ˈgraʊndhɒg; *NAmE* -hɑːg; -hɔːg/ *noun* = WOODCHUCK

ˈGroundhog Day *noun* **1** (in N America) February 2, when it is said that the groundhog comes out of its hole at the end of winter. If the sun shines and the groundhog sees its shadow, it is said that there will be another six weeks of winter. （北美）土拨鼠日（2 月 2 日，据说是冬末土拨鼠出洞的日子，如果土拨鼠在晴天出洞看到自己的影子，就表示冬天还将持续六个星期） **2** an event that is repeated without changing 原样重复的事情；重复不变的事情: *The Government lost the vote then and it can expect a Groundhog Day next time.* 政府在投票表决中失利，下一次也会是同样的结果。 ORIGIN From the film/movie *Groundhog Day* about a man who lives the same day many times. 源自电影《偷天情缘》，其中的男主人公多次重复同一天的生活。

ground·ing /ˈgraʊndɪŋ/ *noun* **1** [sing.] ~ (**in sth**) the teaching of the basic parts of a subject 基础训练；基础教学: *a good grounding in grammar* 扎实的语法基本功训练 **2** [U, C] the act of keeping a plane on the ground or a ship in a port, especially because it is not in a good enough condition to travel （尤指因机件故障等）（飞机的）留地停飞，（船的）留港停航

ground·less /ˈgraʊndləs/ *adj.* not based on reason or evidence 无理由的；无根据的 SYN **unfounded**: *groundless allegations* 毫无根据的指控 ◇ *Our fears proved groundless.* 我们的担心证明是毫无道理的。 ▶ **ground·less·ly** *adv.*

ground·nut /ˈgraʊndnʌt/ *noun* (*BrE*) = PEANUT

ground·out /ˈgraʊndaʊt/ *noun* (in BASEBALL 棒球) a situation in which a player hits the ball along the ground but a FIELDER touches first BASE with it before the player reaches the base（击球员击出地滚球后的）被杀出局

ˈground plan *noun* **1** a plan of the ground floor of a building（建筑物的）底层平面图 ➲ COMPARE PLAN *n.* (4) **2** a plan for future action 计划；大纲

ˈground rent *noun* [U, C] (in Britain 英国) rent paid by the owner of a building to the owner of the land on which it is built （房产主付给地产主的）地租

ˈground rule *noun* **1** **ground rules** [pl.] the basic rules on which sth is based 基本原则；基本准则: *The new code*

of conduct lays down the ground rules for management-union relations. 新的行为规范确定了资方与工会关系的基本原则。 **2** [C] (*NAmE, sport* 体育) a rule for the playing of a game on a particular field, etc.（某一体育运动场地等的）比赛规则

ground·sel /ˈgraʊnsl/ *noun* [U] a wild plant with yellow flowers, sometimes used as food for animals and birds 千里光，绉叶菊（开黄花，有时用作动物和鸟的饲料）

ground·sheet /ˈgraʊndʃiːt/ (*BrE*) (*US* **ˈground cloth**) *noun* a large piece of material that does not let water through that is placed on the ground inside a tent（帐篷内铺地用的）防潮布

G

grounds·man /ˈgraʊndzmən/ *noun* (*pl.* **-men** /-mən/) (*especially BrE*) a man whose job is to take care of a sports ground or large garden 运动场地（或大花园）管理员

ˈground speed *noun* the speed of an aircraft relative to the ground 地速（飞机相对于地面的速度） ➲ COMPARE AIRSPEED

ˈground squirrel *noun* = GOPHER (1)

ˈground staff *noun* [C+sing./pl. v.] **1** (*BrE*) the people at a sports ground whose job it is to take care of the grass, equipment, etc. 运动场管理员 **2** = GROUND CREW

ground·stroke /ˈgraʊndstrəʊk; *NAmE* -stroʊk/ *noun* (in TENNIS 网球) a hit that is made after the ball has BOUNCED 落地球（球落地弹起之后的一击）

ground·swell /ˈgraʊndswel/ *noun* [sing.] ~ (**of sth**) (*formal*) the sudden increase of a particular feeling among a group of people （群体情绪的）迅速高涨: *a groundswell of support* 拥护的情绪迅速高涨 ◇ *There was a groundswell of opinion that he should resign.* 要求他辞职的呼声越来越高。

ground·water /ˈgraʊndwɔːtə(r)/ *noun* [U] water that is found under the ground in soil, rocks, etc. 地下水

ground·work /ˈgraʊndwɜːk; *NAmE* -wɜːrk/ *noun* [U] ~ (**for sth**) work that is done as preparation for other work that will be done later 基础工作；准备工作: *Officials are **laying the groundwork** for a summit conference of world leaders.* 官员们正在为世界首脑峰会做准备工作。

ˌground ˈzero *noun* [U] **1** the point on the earth's surface where a nuclear bomb explodes（核弹的）爆心投影点 **2 Ground Zero** the site of the Twin Towers in New York, destroyed on 11 September 2001 归零地（2001 年 9 月 11 日炸毁的纽约双子大楼遗址） **3** the beginning; a starting point for an activity 开始；起点

group 🔑 /gruːp/ *noun, verb*

■ *noun* [C+sing./pl. v.] **1** a number of people or things that are together in the same place or that are connected in some way 组；群；批；类；簇: *a group of girls/trees/houses* 一群姑娘；一片树林；一排房子 ◇ *A group of us is/are going to the theatre this evening.* 我们有一帮人今晚要去看戏。 ◇ *Students stood around **in groups** waiting for their results.* 学生们成群地站在周围等待成绩。 ◇ *The residents formed a community action group.* 居民组成了社区行动组。 ◇ *English is a member of the Germanic group of languages.* 英语是日耳曼语族中的一种语言。 ◇ *The proportion of single-parent families varies between different income groups.* 单亲家庭比例在不同收入群体中各不相同。 ◇ *a minority group* 少数群体 ◇ *ethnic groups* 族群 ◇ *a **group activity*** (= done by a number of people working together) 小组活动 ◇ *She asked her students to **get into groups** of four.* 她让学生每四人分为一小组。 ◇ *to **work in groups*** 分组工作 ➲ SEE ALSO SUBGROUP **HELP** There are many other compounds ending in **group**. You will find them at their place in the alphabet. 以 group 结尾的复合词还有很多，可在各字母中的适当位置查到。 **2** (*business* 商) a number of companies that are owned by the same person or organization 集团: *a newspaper group* 报业集团 ◇ *the Burton group* 伯顿集团 ◇ *the group sales director* 集团销售董事 **3** (*rather old-fashioned*) a number of musicians who perform together, especially to play pop music（尤指流行音乐的）演奏组，乐团，乐队: *She sings in a rock group.* 她是摇滚乐队的歌手。

■ *verb* **1** [T, I] to gather into a group; to make sb/sth form a group （使）成群，成组，聚集: **~ sb/sth/yourself** (**round/around sb/sth**) *The children grouped themselves around their teacher.* 孩子们聚集在老师周围。 ◇ **~ round/around sb/sth** *We all grouped around the tree for a photograph.* 我们全体围着这棵树照了张相。 ◇ **~** (**sb/sth**) **together** *The colleges grouped together to offer a wider range of courses.* 这些学院联合在一起，以开设范围更广的课程。 **2** [T] **~ sb/sth** (**together**) to divide people or things into groups of people or things that are similar in some way 将…分类；把…分组: *The books are grouped together by subject.* 这些书按科目分类。 ◇ *Contestants were grouped according to age and ability.* 参赛者按年龄和能力分组。

ˌgroup ˈcaptain *noun* (*abbr.* **Gp Capt**) an officer of high rank in the British AIR FORCE（英国）空军上校: *Group Captain (Jonathan) Sutton*（乔纳森·）萨顿空军上校

groupie /ˈgruːpi/ *noun* a person, especially a young woman, who follows pop or rock musicians or other famous people around and tries to meet them 歌迷；追星少女

group·ing /ˈgruːpɪŋ/ *noun* **1** [C] a number of people or organizations that have the same interests, aims or characteristics and are often part of a larger group 小集团；小团体；小圈子: *These small nations constitute an important grouping within the EU.* 这些小国家是欧盟中的一个重要小集团。 **2** [U] the act of forming sth into a group 分组；归类

ˌgroup ˈpractice *noun* a group of several doctors or other medical workers who work together in the community and use the same building to see patients （社区医务工作者）联合医疗，集体行医

ˌgroup ˈtherapy *noun* [U] a type of PSYCHIATRIC treatment in which people with similar personal problems meet together to discuss them 群体治疗；集体心理治疗

group·ware /ˈgruːpweə(r); *NAmE* -wer/ *noun* [U] (*computing* 计) software that is designed to help a group of people on different computers to work together 群件，协同件，组件，小组软件（协调网络小组工作的软件平台）

ˈgroup work *noun* [U] (*BrE*) work done by a group of people working together, for example students in a classroom 团体工作；小组工作；（课堂的）小组讨论

grouse /graʊs/ *noun, verb*

■ *noun* **1** [C, U] (*pl.* **grouse**) a bird with a fat body and feathers on its legs, which people shoot for sport and food; the meat of this bird 松鸡；松鸡肉: *grouse shooting* 猎捕松鸡 ◇ *grouse moors* 松鸡栖息区 ◇ *roast grouse* 烤松鸡肉 **2** [C] (*informal*) a complaint 怨言；牢骚

■ *verb* [I, T] **~** (**about sb/sth**) | (**+ speech**) (*informal*) to complain about sb/sth in a way that other people find annoying 抱怨；发牢骚 **SYN grumble**

grout /graʊt/ (*also* **grout·ing**) *noun* [U] a substance that is used between the TILES on the walls of kitchens, bathrooms, etc. （用于墙上瓷砖间抹缝的）勾缝剂，薄胶泥 ▸ **grout** *verb* **~ sth**

grove /grəʊv; *NAmE* groʊv/ *noun* **1** (*literary*) a small group of trees 树丛；小树林: *a grove of birch trees* 白桦树丛 **2** a small area of land with fruit trees of particular types on it 果树林；果园: *an olive grove* 橄榄园 **3** used in the names of streets （用于街道名）街，路: *Elm Grove* 埃尔姆街

grovel /ˈgrɒvl; *NAmE* ˈgrɑːvl/ *verb* (**-ll-**, *especially US* **-l-**) **1** [I] **~** (**to sb**) (**for sth**) (*disapproving*) to behave in a very HUMBLE way towards sb who is more important than you or who can give you sth you want 卑躬屈膝；俯首贴耳；奴颜婢膝 **SYN crawl** **2** [I] **+ adv./prep.** to move along the ground on your hands and knees, especially because you are looking for sth 爬行，匍匐（尤指找东西） ▸ **grov·el·ling** (*especially US* **grov·el·ing**) *adj.* [only before noun]: *a grovelling letter of apology* 一封低声下气的道歉信

grow /ɡrəʊ; *NAmE* ɡroʊ/ *verb* (**grew** /ɡruː/, **grown** /ɡrəʊn; *NAmE* ɡroʊn/)

• **INCREASE** 增加 **1** [I] to increase in size, number, strength or quality 扩大；增加；增强：*The company profits grew by 5% last year.* 去年公司的利润增加了 5%。◇ *Fears are growing for the safety of a teenager who disappeared a week ago.* 大家对那一周前失踪少年的安危越来越担忧。◇ **~ in sth** *The family has* ***grown in size*** *recently.* 这家人最近添丁进口了。◇ *She is growing in confidence all the time.* 她的信心在不断增强。◇ **+ adj.** *The company is growing bigger all the time.* 这家公司在不断地扩大。

• **OF PERSON/ANIMAL** 人；动物 **2** [I] to become bigger or taller and develop into an adult 长大；长高；发育；成长：*You've grown since the last time I saw you!* 自从我上次见到你后，你又见长了！◇ *Nick's grown almost an inch in the last month.* 尼克这一个月来长高了差不多一英寸。◇ **+ adj.** *to grow bigger/taller* 长大；长高

• **OF PLANT** 植物 **3** [I, T] to exist and develop in a particular place; to make plants grow（使）生长，发育：*The region is too dry for plants to grow.* 这地区干燥得草木不生。◇ *Tomatoes grow best in direct sunlight.* 西红柿在阳光直射下长得最好。◇ **~ sth** *I didn't know they grew rice in France.* 我本来不知道法国也种稻子。➲ SEE ALSO HOME-GROWN

• **OF HAIR/NAILS** 头发；指甲 **4** [I, T] to become longer; to allow sth to become longer by not cutting it（使）留长，蓄长：*I've decided to let my hair grow.* 我已决定留长发。◇ **~ sth** *I've decided to grow my hair.* 我已决定留长发。◇ *I didn't recognize him—he's grown a beard.* 我没认出他来，他留胡子了。

• **BECOME/BEGIN** 变成；开始 **5** *linking verb* **+ adj.** to begin to have a particular quality or feeling over a period of time 逐渐变得；逐渐成为：*to grow old/bored/calm* 变老；腻烦起来；平静下来 ◇ *As time went on he grew more and more impatient.* 时间长了，他越来越没有耐心。◇ *The skies grew dark and it began to rain.* 天渐渐黑了，又下起雨来。**6** [I] **~ to do sth** to gradually begin to do sth 逐渐开始：*I'm sure you'll grow to like her in time.* 我肯定你慢慢就会喜欢她了。

• **DEVELOP SKILLS** 培养技能 **7** [I] **~ (as sth)** (of a person 人) to develop and improve particular qualities or skills 提升品质；培养技能：*She continues to grow as an artist.* 她作为艺术家不断有所提高。

• **BUSINESS** 业务 **8** [T] **~ sth** to increase the size, quality or number of sth 扩大；扩展；增加：*We are trying to grow the business.* 我们正在努力扩展业务。

IDM **it/money doesn't grow on 'trees** (*saying*) used to tell sb not to use sth or spend money carelessly because you do not have a lot of it 树上长不出钱来，那东西（或钱）来之不易（告诫人不要随便乱用）➲ MORE AT ABSENCE, GRASS *n.*

PHR V **ˌgrow a'part (from sb)** to stop having a close relationship with sb over a period of time（与某人）逐渐疏远，渐渐产生隔阂 **ˌgrow a'way from sb** [no passive] to become less close to sb; to depend on sb or care for sb less 逐渐疏远某人；对某人的依赖（或关心）减少：*When she left school she grew away from her mother.* 她中学毕业后就不再那么依赖母亲了。 **ˌgrow 'back** to begin growing again after being cut off or damaged（砍掉或毁坏后）又生长起来 **ˌgrow 'into sth** [no passive] **1** to gradually develop into a particular type of person over a period of time 逐渐成长为，变为，长成（某种类型的人）**2** (of a child 孩子) to grow big enough to fit into a piece of clothing that used to be too big 长大可以穿以前嫌大的衣服：*The dress is too long for her now but she'll grow into it.* 这件连衣裙她现在穿太长，不过她长大了可以穿。**3** to become more confident in a new job, etc. and learn to do it better 对（新工作等）更有信心；学着做得更好：*She's still growing into her new role as a mother.* 她仍在学着适应她作为母亲的新角色。 **'grow on sb** [no passive] if sb/sth **grows on** you, you start to like them or it more and more 逐渐为某人所喜爱 **ˌgrow 'out** (of a HAIRSTYLE, etc. 发式等) to disappear as your hair grows 因头发长长而消失：*I had a perm a year ago and it still hasn't grown out.* 我一年前烫的发，现在发型依旧。 **ˌgrow sth↔'out** to allow your hair to grow in order to change the style 让头发长长以变换发型：*I've decided to grow my layers out.* 我决定留长发好让层次消失。 **ˌgrow 'out of sth** [no passive] **1** (of a child 孩子) to become too big to fit into a piece of clothing 长得太大而穿不上衣服 **SYN** **outgrow**: *He's already grown out of his school uniform.* 他已长得穿不上他的校服了。 **2** to stop doing sth as you become older 因长大而改掉（或革除、戒除）某习惯 **SYN** **outgrow**: *Most children suck their thumbs but they grow out of it.* 大多数孩子都吮拇指，大了就好了。 **3** to develop from sth 产生于，源于（某事物）：*The idea for the book grew out of a visit to India.* 这本书的构思源于到印度的一次旅行。 **ˌgrow 'up 1** (of a person 人) to develop into an adult 长大；成熟；成长：*She grew up in Boston* (= lived there as a child). 她在波士顿长大。◇ *Their children have all grown up and left home now.* 他们的孩子都已长大成人离开家了。◇ **grow up to do sth** *He grew up to become a famous pianist.* 他长大后成了著名的钢琴家。 ➲ RELATED NOUN GROWN-UP[2] **2** used to tell sb to stop behaving in a silly way 别那么幼稚；别要小孩子脾气；变得老成些：*Why don't you grow up?* 你怎么就长不大呢？◇ *It's time you grew up.* 你该懂事了。 **3** to develop gradually 逐渐发展；形成：*A closeness grew up between the two girls.* 这两个女孩的关系越来越亲密。 **IDM** SEE OAK

grow·bag (*also* **Gro-bag™**) /'ɡrəʊbæɡ; *NAmE* 'ɡroʊ-/ *noun* a large plastic bag full of soil, used for growing plants 栽培袋，植物生长袋（盛满泥土的大塑料袋）

grow·er /'ɡrəʊə(r); *NAmE* 'ɡroʊ-/ *noun* **1** a person or company that grows plants, fruit or vegetables to sell 栽培者；种植商；种植公司：*a tobacco grower* 烟草种植商 ◇ *All our vegetables are supplied by local growers.* 我们所有的蔬菜均由当地菜农供应。 **2** a plant that grows in the way mentioned（以…方式）生长的植物：*a* ***fast/slow grower*** 生长快的 / 慢的植物

grow·ing /'ɡrəʊɪŋ; *NAmE* 'ɡroʊɪŋ/ *adj.* [only before noun] increasing in size, amount or degree 增加的；增长的；增强的：*A* ***growing number*** *of people are returning to full-time education.* 越来越多的人重返学校接受全日制教育。◇ *one of the country's* ***fastest growing*** *industries* 这个国家增长最快的行业之一 ◇ *There is growing concern over the safety of the missing teenager.* 人们对这个失踪少年的安全越来越担心。

'growing pains *noun* [pl.] **1** pains that some children feel in their arms and legs when they are growing（儿童）生长痛，发育期痛 **2** emotional anxieties felt by young people as they grow up 青春期的感情焦虑 **3** problems that are experienced by a company when it begins operating but that are not likely to last（企业）发展初期的困难

'growing season *noun* [usually sing.] the period of the year during which the weather conditions are right for plants to grow（植物的）生长季节

growl /ɡraʊl/ *verb, noun*

■ *verb* **1** [I] **~ (at sb/sth)** (of animals, especially dogs 动物，尤指狗) to make a low sound in the throat, usually as a sign of anger 低声吼叫 **2** [T] to say sth in a low angry voice 发出低沉的怒吼；咆哮：**+ speech (at sb)** *'Who are you?' he growled at the stranger.* "你是谁？" 他向陌生人怒吼道。◇ **~ sth (at sb)** *She growled a sarcastic reply.* 她以讥讽的口吻咬牙切齿地回答。

■ *noun* a deep angry sound made when sb/sth growls 怒吼声；咆哮

grown /ɡrəʊn; *NAmE* ɡroʊn/ *adj.* [only before noun] (of a person 人) mentally and physically an adult 成熟的；成年的；长大的：*It's pathetic that grown men have to resort to violence like this.* 成年人还得这样诉诸暴力，真可悲。➲ SEE ALSO FULL-GROWN, GROW, HOME-GROWN

ˌgrown-'up[1] *adj.* **1** (of a person 人) mentally and physically an adult 成熟的；成年的；长大成人的 **SYN** **adult**: *What do you want to be when you're grown-up?* 你长大成人后想做什么？◇ *She has a grown-up son.* 她有个已成年的儿子。 **2** suitable for or typical of an adult 适合成人

G

的；成人特有的：*The child was clearly puzzled at being addressed in such a grown-up way.* 听到别人用这种成人的方式跟自己说话，那个孩子显然感到不知所措。

'grown-up² *noun* (used especially by and to children 尤为儿语或对儿童说话时用) an adult person 大人 SYN **adult**: *If you're good you can eat with the grown-ups.* 你如果乖一点就可以和大人一起吃饭。

growth /ɡrəʊθ; *NAmE* ɡroʊθ/ *noun* **1** [U] (of people, animals or plants 人、动物或植物) the process of growing physically, mentally or emotionally 发育；成长；生长：*Lack of water will stunt the plant's growth.* 缺水会妨碍植物生长。◇ *Remove dead leaves to encourage new growth.* 去掉枯叶以促进新叶生长。◇ *a concern with personal* (= mental and emotional) *growth and development* 对个人成长和发展的重视 ◇ *growth hormones* (= designed to make sb/sth grow faster) 生长激素 **2** [U] ~ (**in/of sth**) an increase in the size, amount or degree of sth 增加；增长；增强：*population growth* 人口增长 ◇ *the rapid growth in violent crime* 暴力犯罪的迅速增加 **3** [U] an increase in economic activity 经济增长；经济发展：*a disappointing year of little growth in Britain and America* 英美经济增长无几、令人沮丧的一年 ◇ *policies aimed at sustaining economic growth* 旨在保持经济增长的政策 ◇ *an annual growth rate of 10%* * 10% 的年增长率 ◇ *a* ***growth area/industry*** 经济增长的领域 / 行业 ➲ COLLOCATIONS AT ECONOMY **4** [C] a lump caused by a disease that forms on or inside a person, an animal or a plant 赘生物：*a* ***malignant/cancerous growth*** 恶性 / 癌性肿瘤 **5** [U, C] something that has grown 生长物；长成物；产物：*The forest's dense growth provides nesting places for a wide variety of birds.* 森林里茂密的植物为各种各样的鸟儿提供了筑巢的地方。◇ *several days' growth of beard* 长了几天的胡须

'growth ring *noun* a layer of wood, shell or bone developed in one year, or in another regular period of growth, that an expert can look at to find out how old sth is （树木、壳或骨等的）生长轮，年轮

groyne (*especially US* **groin**) /ɡrɔɪn/ *noun* a low wall built out into the sea to prevent it from washing away sand and stones from the beach 丁坝（防止海浪侵蚀海滩砂石的矮墙）

grub /ɡrʌb/ *noun, verb*

■ *noun* **1** [C] the young form of an insect, that looks like a small fat WORM （昆虫的）幼虫；蛆；蛴螬 **2** [U] (*informal*) food 食物：*Grub's up!* (= the meal is ready) 饭好了！◇ *They serve good pub grub there.* 他们那儿供应上好的酒吧食物。

■ *verb* (**-bb-**) [I] ~ (**around/about**) (**for sth**) to look for sth, especially by digging or by looking through or under other things 翻找；搜寻；挖掘寻找：*birds grubbing for worms* 刨虫子的鸟

PHR V **,grub sth↔'up/'out** to dig sth out of the ground 掘出，挖出（某物）

grub·ber /'ɡrʌbə(r)/ *noun* (in CRICKET 板球) a ball that is BOWLED along the ground 地滚球

grubby /'ɡrʌbi/ *adj.* (**grub·bier**, **grub·bi·est**) **1** rather dirty, usually because it has not been washed or cleaned 肮脏的；邋遢的；污秽的：*grubby hands/clothes* 脏手；脏衣服 ➲ SYNONYMS AT DIRTY **2** unpleasant because it involves activities that are dishonest or immoral 卑鄙的；可鄙的 SYN **sordid**: *a grubby scandal* 丑闻 ▶ **grubbi·ness** *noun* [U]

'Grub Street *noun* used to refer to poor writers and journalists as a group, or the life they live 格拉布街（统称潦倒的文人）；潦倒文人的生活 ➲ MORE LIKE THIS 19, page R27 ORIGIN From the name of a street in London where many poor writers lived in the 17th century. 源自 17 世纪伦敦居住着很多穷困作家的格拉布街。

grudge /ɡrʌdʒ/ *noun, verb*

■ *noun* ~ (**against sb**) a feeling of anger or dislike towards sb because of sth bad they have done to you in the past 积怨；怨恨；嫌隙：*I* ***bear him no grudge.*** 我对他不怀任何积怨。◇ *He* ***has a grudge against*** *the world.* 他对社会心存不满。◇ *I don't* ***hold any grudges*** *now.* 我现在没有任何怨恨。◇ *He's a man with a grudge.* 他是一个心怀怨恨的人。◇ *England beat New Zealand in a* ***grudge match*** (= a match where there is strong dislike between the teams). 英格兰队在一场势不两立的比赛中打败了新西兰队。

■ *verb* **1** to do or give sth unwillingly 勉强做；不情愿地给；吝惜 SYN **begrudge**: **~ doing sth** *I grudge having to pay so much tax.* 得付这么多的税，我很不情愿。◇ **~ sth** *He grudges the time he spends travelling to work.* 他不情愿上班花这么多时间在路上。 **2 ~ sb sth** to think that sb does not deserve to have sth 认为…不应得到 SYN **begrudge**: *You surely don't grudge her her success?* 她获得成功，你没有不以为然吧？

grudg·ing /'ɡrʌdʒɪŋ/ *adj.* [usually before noun] given or done unwillingly 勉强的；不情愿的 SYN **reluctant**: *He could not help feeling a grudging admiration for the old lady.* 他不禁感到不得不钦佩这位老太太。 ▶ **grudg·ing·ly** (*also less frequent* **be·grudg·ing·ly**) *adv.*: *She grudgingly admitted that I was right.* 她勉强承认我是对的。

gruel /'ɡruːəl/ *noun* [U] a simple dish made by boiling OATS in milk or water, eaten especially in the past by poor people （尤指旧时穷人吃的）稀粥，燕麦粥

gruel·ling (*especially BrE*) (*NAmE usually* **gruel·ing**) /'ɡruːəlɪŋ/ *adj.* very difficult and tiring, needing great effort for a long time 使人筋疲力尽的；折磨人的 SYN **punishing**: *a* ***gruelling journey/schedule*** 使人筋疲力尽的旅程；累人的日程 ◇ *I've had a gruelling day.* 我一天下来累得筋疲力尽。

grue·some /'ɡruːsəm/ *adj.* very unpleasant and filling you with horror, usually because it is connected with death or injury 令人厌恶的；恐怖的；可怕的：*a gruesome murder* 骇人听闻的谋杀案 ◇ *gruesome pictures of dead bodies* 恐怖的死人照片 ◇ (*humorous*) *We spent a week in a gruesome apartment in Miami.* 我们在迈阿密一套糟糕透顶的公寓里住了一星期。 ▶ **grue·some·ly** *adv.*

gruff /ɡrʌf/ *adj.* **1** (of a voice 声音) deep and rough, and often sounding unfriendly 低沉沙哑的；生硬的 **2** (of a person's behaviour 人的行为) unfriendly and impatient 冷淡的；态度生硬的：*Beneath his gruff exterior, he's really very kind-hearted.* 他外表冷漠，心地却十分善良。 ▶ **gruff·ly** *adv.*

grum·ble /'ɡrʌmbl/ *verb, noun*

■ *verb* **1** [I, T] to complain about sb/sth in a bad-tempered way 咕哝；嘟囔；发牢骚： **~ (at/to sb) (about/at sb/sth)** *She's always grumbling to me about how badly she's treated at work.* 她总是向我抱怨她在工作中如何受亏待。◇ **+ speech** *'I'll just have to do it myself,' he grumbled.* "我只好自己动手了。"他咕哝着说。◇ **~ that...** *They kept grumbling that they were cold.* 他们不停地嘟囔着说冷。 ➲ SYNONYMS AT COMPLAIN **2** [I] to make a deep continuous sound 咕隆；发轰隆声 SYN **rumble**: *Thunder grumbled in the distance.* 远处雷声隆隆。 ▶ **grum·bler** /'ɡrʌmblə(r)/ *noun*

■ *noun* **1 ~ (about sth) | ~ (that...)** something that you complain about because you are not satisfied 嘟囔；牢骚：*My main grumble is about the lack of privacy.* 我最大的抱怨是缺乏私密性。 **2** a long low sound 咕隆声；隆隆声 SYN **rumble**: *a distant grumble of thunder* 远处隆隆的雷声

grum·bling /'ɡrʌmblɪŋ/ *noun* **1** [U] the act of complaining about sth 咕哝；嘟囔；发牢骚：*We didn't hear any grumbling about the food.* 我们没听到过对食物的抱怨。 **2 grumblings** [pl.] protests about sth that come from a number of people but that are not expressed very clearly （集体的）隐隐的不满

grump /ɡrʌmp/ *noun* (*informal*) a bad-tempered person 脾气坏的人

grumpy /'ɡrʌmpi/ *adj.* (**grump·ier**, **grumpi·est**) (*informal*) bad-tempered 脾气坏的；性情暴躁的 ▶ **grump·ily** /'ɡrʌmpɪli/ *adv.*

grunge /ɡrʌndʒ/ *noun* [U] **1** (*informal*) dirt of any kind 脏东西 SYN **grime** **2** (*also* **'grunge rock**) a type of loud rock music, which was popular in the early 1990s 垃圾摇滚乐（流行于 20 世纪 90 年代初） **3** a style of fashion worn by people who like grunge music, usually involving clothes that look untidy 垃圾摇滚风格，垃圾摇滚款式（指迷恋垃圾摇滚乐者的时尚服式，常穿着邋遢的衣服）

grungy /ˈgrʌndʒi/ *adj.* (*informal*) dirty in an unpleasant way 邋遢的；脏的；龌龊的

grunt /grʌnt/ *verb, noun*

■ ***verb*** **1** [I] (of animals, especially pigs 动物，尤指猪) to make a short, low sound in the throat 发出呼噜声 **2** [I, T] (of people 人) to make a short, low sound in your throat, especially to show that you are in pain, annoyed or not interested; to say sth using this sound 发出哼声；咕哝；嘟哝： *He pulled harder on the rope, grunting with the effort.* 他边用力边哼声，使出更大的力气拉绳子。◇ *When I told her what had happened she just grunted and turned back to her book.* 我告诉她出了什么事，她只哼了一声就又看起书来了。◇ **~ sth** *He grunted something about being late and rushed out.* 他嘟哝着说要迟到了便匆匆跑了出去。◇ **+ speech** *'Thanks,' he grunted.* "谢谢。"他咕哝着说。

■ ***noun*** **1** a short, low sound made by a person or an animal (especially a pig) 哼声；咕哝声；嘟哝声；（尤指猪的）呼噜声： *to give a* ***grunt of effort/pain*** 发出费力 / 痛苦的哼声 **2** (*NAmE, informal*) a worker who does boring tasks for low pay 工作乏味收入低的工人 **3** (*NAmE, informal*) a soldier of low rank 步兵；士兵；大兵

ˈgrunt work *noun* [U] (*informal*) hard boring work 乏味的重活： *She has assistants to do the grunt work like research and proofreading.* 她有助手做搜集资料和校对之类的苦差事。

gryphon /ˈgrɪfən/ *noun* = GRIFFIN

GSM /ˌdʒiː es ˈem/ *noun* the abbreviation for 'Global System/Standard for Mobile Communication(s)' (an international system for digital communication by mobile/cell phone) 全球移动通信系统（全写为 Global System / Standard for Mobile Communication(s)）

GSOH *abbr.* good sense of humour (used in personal advertisements) 丰富的幽默感（用于交友广告中）

ˈG spot *noun* a sensitive area inside a woman's VAGINA that is thought to give great sexual pleasure when touched * G 点（女性的性敏感部位）

GST /ˌdʒiː es ˈtiː/ *noun* [U] (*CanE*) goods and services tax (a tax that is added to the price of goods and services) 商品及服务税（附加于价格上）

ˈG-string *noun* a narrow piece of cloth that covers the sexual organs and is held up by a string around the waist * G 带，遮羞布，兜裆布（用绳系于腰部作三角裤用）

Gt (*also* **Gt.** *especially in NAmE*) *abbr.* (in names of places) Great（用于地名）大： *Gt Britain* 大不列颠 ◇ *Gt Yarmouth* 大雅茅斯

gua·ca·mole /ˌgwækəˈməʊleɪ; -li; NAmE -ˈmoʊ-/ *noun* [U] (*from Spanish*) a Mexican dish of crushed AVOCADO mixed with onion, tomatoes, CHILLIES, etc. 墨西哥鳄梨酱（用碾碎的鳄梨加洋葱、番茄、辣椒等调制而成）

guano /ˈgwɑːnəʊ; NAmE -noʊ/ *noun* [U] the waste substance passed from the bodies of birds that live near the sea, used to make plants and crops grow well 海鸟粪（用作肥料）

guanxi /gwænˈʃiː/ *noun* [U] (in China 中国) the system of social networks and the relationships between people that are helpful and useful in business 关系；人脉： *The main reason for his company's success is that he has good guanxi with the authorities.* 他的公司成功的主要原因是他与当局关系好。 ▸ **guanxi** *adj.* [only before noun]

guar·an·tee 🔑 AW /ˌgærənˈtiː/ *noun, verb*

■ ***noun*** **1** 🔑 a firm promise that you will do sth or that sth will happen 保证；担保 SYN **assurance**： *to give a guarantee of good behaviour* 保证行为端正 ◇ *He gave me a guarantee that it would never happen again.* 他向我保证这种事情绝不会再发生。◇ *They are demanding certain guarantees before they sign the treaty.* 他们要求得到某些保证后才签署条约。 **2** 🔑 a written promise given by a company that sth you buy will be replaced or repaired without payment if it goes wrong within a particular period 保修单；保用证书 SYN **warranty**： *We provide a 5-year guarantee against rust.* 我们保证 5 年不生锈。◇ *The watch is still* ***under guarantee***. 这只手表仍在保修期内。◇ *The television comes with a year's guarantee.* 这电视机有一年的保修期。◇ *a money-back guarantee* 退货保证 **3** 🔑 something that makes sth else certain to happen 起保证作用的事物： **~ (of sth)** *Career success is no guarantee of happiness.* 事业成功并不是幸福的保证。◇ **~ (that...)** *There's no guarantee that she'll come* (= she may not come). 不能保证她一定会来。 **4** money or sth valuable that you give or promise to a bank, for example, to make sure that you will do what you have promised 保证金；抵押品： *We had to offer our house as a guarantee when getting the loan.* 我们在贷款时不得不拿房子作抵押。 **5** a written promise to pay back money that sb else owes, or do sth that sb else promised to do, if they cannot do it themselves 担保书： *A close relative, usually a parent, can provide a guarantee for the loan.* 近亲属，通常为父母，可为贷款作担保。

■ ***verb*** **1** 🔑 to promise to do sth; to promise sth will happen 保证；担保；保障： **~ sth** *Basic human rights, including freedom of speech, are now guaranteed.* 现在，包括言论自由在内的基本人权已有了保障。◇ **~ (that)...** *We cannot guarantee (that) our flights will never be delayed.* 我们不能保证我们的所有航班均不误点。◇ **~ sb sth** *The ticket will guarantee you free entry.* 这张票可保证你免费入场。◇ **~ to do sth** *We guarantee to deliver your goods within a week.* 我们保证一周内交货。 **2** 🔑 **~ sth (against sth)** to give a written promise to replace or repair a product free if it goes wrong 提供（产品）保修单（免费掉换或修理有问题的产品）： *This iron is guaranteed for a year against faulty workmanship.* 这种熨斗如有工艺缺陷可保修一年。 **3** 🔑 to make sth certain to happen 使必然发生；确保： **~ sth** *Tonight's victory guarantees the team's place in the final.* 今晚的胜利确保这个队能进入决赛。◇ **~ sb sth** *These days getting a degree doesn't guarantee you a job.* 如今获得学位并不能保证你有工作。 **4** **~ (that)...** to be certain that sth will happen 肯定…必然发生： *You can guarantee (that) the children will start being naughty as soon as they have to go to bed.* 可以肯定孩子一到上床睡觉时就不听话了。 **5** to agree to be legally responsible for sth or for doing sth, especially for paying back money that sb else owes if they cannot pay it back themselves 承诺对…负法律责任；为…作担保： **~ sth** *to guarantee a bank loan* 为银行贷款作保 ◇ **~ to do sth** *to guarantee to pay sb's debts* 为偿还某人的债务作保 ◇ **~ that...** *I guarantee that he will appear in court.* 我保证他会出庭。

IDM **be guaranˈteed to do sth** to be certain to have a particular result 肯定会；必定会： *If we try to keep it a secret, she's guaranteed to find out.* 如果我们试图保密，她肯定会发现。◇ *That kind of behaviour is guaranteed to make him angry.* 那样的行为肯定会让他生气。 ➲ SYNONYMS AT CERTAIN

guar·an·tor /ˌgærənˈtɔː(r)/ *noun* (*formal* or *law* 律) a person who agrees to be responsible for sb or for making sure that sth happens or is done 担保人；保证人： *The United Nations will act as guarantor of the peace settlement.* 联合国将充当和平协议的保证人。

guard 🔑 /gɑːd; NAmE gɑːrd/ *noun, verb*

■ ***noun***

• **PEOPLE WHO PROTECT** 警卫 **1** 🔑 [C] a person, such as a soldier, a police officer or a prison officer, who protects a place or people, or prevents prisoners from escaping 卫兵；警卫员；看守： ***a security guard*** 安全警卫 ◇ ***border guards*** 边防卫士 ◇ *The prisoner slipped past the guards on the gate and escaped.* 犯人从门卫身旁溜出去逃走了。◇ *A guard was posted outside the building.* 建筑物外驻了一名警卫。 ➲ COMPARE WARDER ➲ SEE ALSO BODYGUARD, COASTGUARD, LIFEGUARD **2** [C+sing./pl. v.] a group of people, such as soldiers or police officers, who protect sb/sth （统称）卫兵，警卫，看守： *the captain of the guard* 卫队长 ◇ *the changing of the guard* (= when one

G

group replaces another) 卫队换岗 ◇ *The guard is/are being inspected today.* 今天卫队接受检阅。◇ *Fellow airmen provided a **guard of honour** at his wedding.* 空军战友们为他的婚礼充当仪仗队。◇ *The President always travels with an **armed guard**.* 总统出行总有武装卫队保驾。➲ SEE ALSO NATIONAL GUARD, OLD GUARD, REARGUARD **3** [U] the act or duty of protecting property, places or people from attack or danger; the act or duty of preventing prisoners from escaping 警戒；保卫；保护；看守：*a sentry **on guard*** (= at his or her post, on duty) 执勤哨兵 ◇ *to **do guard duty*** 担任警戒任务 ◇ *The escaped prisoner was brought back **under armed guard**.* 越狱逃犯由武装警卫押回。◇ *The terrorist was kept **under police guard**.* 这名恐怖分子当时在警方的看管之下。◇ *One of the men **kept guard**, while the other broke into the house.* 一人放哨，另一人则闯进了房子里。 **4 the Guards** [pl.] (in Britain and some other countries) special REGIMENTS of soldiers whose original duty was to protect the king or queen（英国和其他一些国家的）禁军，御林军，近卫军

- **AGAINST INJURY** 防止受伤 **5** [C] (often in compounds 常构成复合词) something that covers a part of a person's body or a dangerous part of a machine to prevent injury 防护罩；防护装置；防护用品：*Ensure the guard is in place before operating the machine.* 一定要在防护措施做好后才开机器。➲ SEE ALSO FIREGUARD, MOUTHGUARD, MUDGUARD, SAFEGUARD *n.*, SHIN GUARD ➲ **VISUAL VOCAB** PAGE V52
- **ON TRAIN** 火车 **6** [C] (*BrE, becoming old-fashioned*) = CONDUCTOR (2)
- **IN BOXING/FENCING** 拳击；击剑 **7** [U] a position you take to defend yourself, especially in a sport such as BOXING or FENCING 防御姿势：*to drop/keep up your guard* 放弃 / 保持防御姿势 ◇ (*figurative*) *In spite of the awkward questions the minister never let his guard fall for a moment.* 尽管遇到些令人尴尬的问题，部长从没有放松警惕。
- **IN BASKETBALL** 篮球 **8** [C] one of the two players on a BASKETBALL team who are mainly responsible for staying close to opposing players to stop them from scoring 后卫
- **IN AMERICAN FOOTBALL** 美式足球 **9** [C] one of the two players on an AMERICAN FOOTBALL team who play either side of the CENTRE FORWARD（中锋两侧的）哨锋

IDM **be on your 'guard** to be very careful and prepared for sth difficult or dangerous 警惕；提防；警戒 **mount/stand/keep 'guard (over sb/sth)** to watch or protect sb/sth 守卫；看守；保卫：*Four soldiers stood guard over the coffin.* 有四名士兵守护灵柩。 **off (your) 'guard** not careful or prepared for sth difficult or dangerous 不警惕；不提防；不警戒：*The lawyer's apparently innocent question was designed to **catch** the witness **off** (**his**) **guard**.* 律师看似不经意的问题是为了使证人措手不及。

■ ***verb*** **1** ~ **sb/sth** to protect property, places or people from attack or danger 警卫；守卫；保卫：*The dog was guarding its owner's luggage.* 狗守护着主人的行李。◇ *political leaders guarded by the police* 由警方保卫的政界领袖们 ◇ *You can't get in; the whole place is guarded.* 你进不去，整个地区都戒备森严。◇ (*figurative*) *a closely guarded secret* 严守的秘密 **2** ~ **sb** to prevent prisoners from escaping 看守，监视（囚犯）：*The prisoners were guarded by soldiers.* 犯人由士兵看守。

PHR V **'guard against sth** to take care to prevent sth or to protect yourself from sth 防止，防范，提防（某事）：*to guard against accidents/disease* 防止事故；预防疾病

'guard dog *noun* a dog that is kept to guard a building 看门狗

guard·ed /ˈɡɑːdɪd; *NAmE* ˈɡɑːrdɪd/ *adj.* (of a person or a remark they make 人或其言语) careful; not showing feelings or giving much information 谨慎的；有保留的；不明确表态的 SYN **cautious**：*a guarded reply* 谨慎的回答 ◇ *You should be more guarded in what you say to reporters.* 你对记者说话应更谨慎些。◇ *They gave the news a guarded welcome* (= did not show great enthusiasm about it). 他们对这消息表示谨慎的欢迎。 OPP **unguarded** ▶ **guard·ed·ly** *adv.*

guard·house /ˈɡɑːdhaʊs; *NAmE* ˈɡɑːrd-/ *noun* a building for soldiers who are guarding the entrance to a military camp or for keeping military prisoners in 卫兵室；禁闭室

guard·ian /ˈɡɑːdiən; *NAmE* ˈɡɑːrd-/ *noun* **1** a person who protects sth 保护者；守卫者；保卫者 SYN **custodian**：*Farmers should be guardians of the countryside.* 农民应是农村的守卫者。◇ *The police are guardians of law and order.* 警察是法律和治安的护卫者。 **2** a person who is legally responsible for the care of another person, especially a child whose parents have died（尤指双亲已故孩子的）监护人

ˌguardian ˈangel *noun* a spirit that some people believe protects and guides them, especially when they are in danger 守护天使：(*figurative*) *A delightful guide was my guardian angel for the first week of the tour.* 令人愉快的导游是我第一周旅行的守护神。

guard·ian·ship /ˈɡɑːdiənʃɪp; *NAmE* ˈɡɑːrd-/ *noun* [U] (*formal* or *law* 律) the state or position of being responsible for sb/sth 监护；监护地位；监护人的身份

'guard rail *noun* **1** a rail placed on the edge of a path, a CLIFF or a boat to protect people and prevent them falling over the edge 护栏；扶栏 **2** (*NAmE*) (*BrE* **'crash barrier**) a strong low fence or wall at the side of a road or between the two halves of a major road such as a MOTORWAY or INTERSTATE（高速公路或州际公路上的）防撞护栏，防撞墙

guard·room /ˈɡɑːdruːm; -rʊm; *NAmE* ˈɡɑːrd-/ *noun* a room for soldiers who are guarding the entrance to a building or for keeping military prisoners in 卫兵室；禁闭室

guards·man /ˈɡɑːdzmən; *NAmE* ˈɡɑːrd-/ *noun* (*pl.* **-men** /-mən/) a soldier in the Guards or in the National Guard in the US 禁卫军士兵；（美国）国民警卫队士兵

'guard's van *noun* (*BrE*) the part of a train where the person who is in charge of the train rides 列车车长室；守车

guava /ˈɡwɑːvə/ *noun* the fruit of a tropical American tree, with yellow skin and pink flesh 番石榴（热带美洲水果，黄皮，果肉呈粉红色）

gub·bins /ˈɡʌbɪnz/ *noun* [U] (*old-fashioned, BrE, informal*) various things that are not important 零碎东西：*All the gubbins that came with the computer is still in the box.* 这台电脑的所有零星配件还在箱子里。

gu·ber·na·tor·ial /ˌɡuːbənəˈtɔːriəl; *NAmE* -bərnə-/ *adj.* (*formal*) connected with the job of state governor in the US（美国）州长的，州长职位的：*a gubernatorial candidate* 州长候选人 ◇ *gubernatorial duties* 州长的职责

Guern·sey /ˈɡɜːnzi; *NAmE* ˈɡɜːrnzi/ *noun* **1** a type of cow kept for its rich milk 根西牛（产奶品质好） **2 guernsey** a thick sweater made with dark blue wool that has been specially treated so that it does not let water through, worn originally by FISHERMEN 格恩西防水羊毛衫（深蓝色，原为渔民所穿） **3 guernsey** (*AustralE*) a football sweater, especially one of the type without sleeves worn by Australian Rules players 足球运动衫；（尤指澳大利亚式橄榄球运动员穿的）运动背心

IDM **get a 'guernsey** (*AustralE, informal*) to be recognized as being good (originally meaning to be chosen for a football team) 获得认可；得到承认

guer·rilla (*also* **guer·illa**) /ɡəˈrɪlə/ *noun, adj.*

■ ***noun*** a member of a small group of soldiers who are not part of an official army and who fight against official soldiers, usually to try to change the government 游击队员：*urban guerrillas* (= those who fight in towns) 城市游击队员 ◇ ***guerrilla war/warfare*** (= fought by guerrillas on one or both sides) 游击战 ◇ *a guerrilla movement* 游击运动 ➲ COMPARE FREEDOM FIGHTER

■ ***adj.*** [only before noun] organized in an informal way and without official permission or approval 游击的；非正式的；没有官方认可的：*Guerrilla actors took to the streets in army fatigues to protest against the war.* 非正式演员穿着士兵服走上街头举行反战示威。◇ *guerrilla marketing* (= marketing that uses unusual methods in order to achieve the greatest effect for the smallest amount of money) 游击营销（用不一般的方式以最少金钱取得最大成效）◇ *guerrilla gardening* (= growing plants on land that you do not own to make it more attractive) 游击园艺（在不属于自己的土地上栽种植物以美化环境）

guess /ges/ *verb, noun*
■ ***verb*** **1** [I, T] to try and give an answer or make a judgement about sth without being sure of all the facts 猜测；估计：*I don't really know. I'm just guessing.* 我并不知道，我只是猜测。◇ **~ at sth** *We can only guess at her reasons for leaving.* 对她离去的原因我们只能猜测。◇ **+ adj.** *He* ***guessed right/wrong****.* 他猜对/错了。◇ **~ (that)…** *I'd guess that she's about 30.* 我估计她大约 30 岁。◇ **~ where, who, etc.…** *Can you guess where I've been?* 你能猜出我去什么地方了吗？◇ **~ sth** *Can you guess his age?* 你能猜出他的年龄吗？ ➲ EXPRESS YOURSELF AT SPECULATE **2** [T] to find the right answer to a question or the truth without knowing all the facts 猜对；猜中；猜到：**~ sth** *She guessed the answer straight away.* 她一下子就猜中了答案。◇ **~ what, where, etc.…** ***You'll never guess*** *what she told me.* 你永远猜不到她对我说了什么。◇ **~ (that)…** *You would never guess (that) she had problems. She's always so cheerful.* 你怎么也猜不到她有难以解决的问题。她总是那么乐观。➲ SEE ALSO SECOND-GUESS **3** **I guess** [T, I] **~ (that)…** (*informal, especially NAmE*) to suppose that sth is true or likely 想；以为：*I guess (that) you'll be looking for a new job now.* 我想你现在要找新工作了吧。◇ *'He didn't see me, I guess.'* "我想他没看见我。" ◇ *'Are you ready to go?' 'Yeah, I guess so.'* "你准备好出发了吗？" "是的，应该可以了。" ◇ *'They aren't coming, then?' 'I guess not.'* "这么说，他们不来了？" "我想是吧。" **4** **guess…!** [T] used to show that you are going to say sth surprising or exciting（引出令人惊奇或激动的事）你猜：**~ sth** *Guess what! He's asked me out!* 你猜怎么着！他约我出去了！◇ **~ who, where, etc.…** *Guess who I've just seen!* 你猜我刚才见到谁了！

IDM **keep sb 'guessing** (*informal*) to not tell sb about your plans or what is going to happen next 让某人捉摸不定（或猜不透）：*It's the kind of book that keeps you guessing right to the end.* 这是一本让你从头猜到尾的书。

■ ***noun*** an attempt to give an answer or an opinion when you cannot be certain if you are right 猜测；猜想：**~ (at sth)** (*BrE*) *to* ***have/make a guess*** *(at sth)*（对某事）作猜测 ◇ (*NAmE*) *to* ***take a guess*** 推测 ◇ *Go on! Have a guess!* 继续！猜猜看！◇ **~ (about sth)** *The article is based on guesses about what might happen in the future.* 这篇文章的依据是对未来可能发生什么事情的猜测。◇ *They might be here by 3—but that's just a* ***rough guess*** (= not exact). 他们可能 3 点钟到，不过这只是一个大致的猜测。◇ **~ (that…)** ***My guess is that*** *we won't hear from him again.* 我想我们再不会收到他的消息了。◇ ***At a guess****, there were forty people at the party.* 估计有四十人参加了聚会。◇ *If I might* ***hazard a guess****, I'd say she was about thirty.* 让我来猜的话，我说她大约三十岁。◇ *Who do you think I saw yesterday?* ***I'll give you three guesses.*** 你猜我昨天碰到谁了？我让你猜三次。

IDM **'anybody's/'anyone's guess** (*informal*) something that nobody can be certain about 谁也拿不准的事：*What will happen next is anybody's guess.* 下一步会发生什么事，谁也说不准。 **your ˌguess is as good as 'mine** (*informal*) used to tell sb that you do not know any more about a subject than the person that you are talking to does 我和你一样不知道；我和你一样心中无数：*'Who's going to win?' 'Your guess is as good as mine.'* "谁会赢？" "我和你一样不知道。" ➲ MORE AT EDUCATED, MISS *v.*

'guessing game *noun* **1** a game in which you have to guess the answers to questions 猜谜游戏 **2** a situation in which you do not know what is going to happen or what sb is going to do 捉摸不定的局面

guess·ti·mate (*also* **gues·ti·mate**) /ˈgestɪmət/ *noun* (*informal*) an attempt to calculate sth that is based more on guessing than on information 瞎猜；大致估计 ➲ MORE LIKE THIS 1, page R25

guess·work /ˈgeswɜːk; *NAmE* -wɜːrk/ *noun* [U] the process of trying to find an answer by guessing when you do not have enough information to be sure 猜想；猜测：*It was pure guesswork on our part.* 这纯属我们的猜测。➲ SEE ALSO CONJECTURE *n.*

guest /gest/ *noun, verb*
■ ***noun*** **1** a person that you have invited to your house or to a particular event that you are paying for 客人；宾客：*We have guests staying this weekend.* 这周末我家有客人来住。◇ *more than 100 wedding guests* * 100 多位出席婚礼的宾客 ◇ *I went to the theatre club as Helen's guest.* 海伦请我去戏剧俱乐部看戏了。◇ *He was the* ***guest of honour*** (= the most important person invited to an event). 他是贵宾。◇ *Liz was not on the* ***guest list****.* 利兹不在邀请之列。**2** a person who is staying at a hotel, etc. 旅客；房客：*We have accommodation for 500 guests.* 我们有可供 500 位客人住宿的房间。◇ *a* ***paying guest*** (= a person who is living in a private house, but paying as if they were in a hotel) 寄宿客（付费住在私人家中的人）◇ *Guests should vacate their rooms by 10.30 a.m.* 房客应在上午 10:30 以前腾出房间。 **3** a famous person or performer who takes part in a television show or concert 特别嘉宾；客串演员：*a* ***guest artist/star/singer*** 特约艺人/明星/歌手 ◇ *Our special guest tonight is…* 今晚我们的特别嘉宾是… ◇ *He* ***made a guest appearance*** *on the show.* 他在这个节目里客串出场。 **4** a person who is invited to a particular place or organization, or to speak at a meeting 特邀嘉宾：*The scientists are here as guests of our government.* 出席的科学家是我国政府的贵宾。◇ *a* ***guest speaker*** 特邀演讲人

IDM **be my 'guest** (*informal*) used to give sb permission to do sth that they have asked to do 请便；随便：*'Do you mind if I use the phone?' 'Be my guest.'* "可以用一下电话吗？" "请便。"

■ ***verb*** [I] **~ (on sth)** to take part in a television or radio show, a concert, a game, etc. as a visiting or temporary performer or player 做特邀嘉宾；做客串；做特约演员：*She guested on several chat shows while visiting Britain.* 她访问英国时做过几个访谈节目的特邀嘉宾。

'guest beer *noun* [U, C] (*BrE*) a beer that is not usually available in a particular pub, but which is served there for a limited period, often at a specially reduced price（酒吧里常折价限时供应的）款待啤酒

'guest house *noun* **1** (*BrE*) a small hotel 小旅馆 **2** (*NAmE*) a small house built near a large house, for guests to stay in（大房子旁供客人居住的）客房

gues·ti·mate *noun* = GUESSTIMATE

'guest room *noun* a bedroom that is kept for guests to use 客房；留给客人住的寝室

'guest worker *noun* a person, usually from a poor country, who comes to another richer country in order to work there（通常指来自穷国的）客籍工人，外籍工作人员

guff /gʌf/ *noun* [U] (*informal*) ideas or talk that you think are stupid 胡思乱想；胡说八道；愚蠢的想法；蠢话 SYN **nonsense**

guf·faw /gəˈfɔː/ *verb* [I, T] **(+ speech)** to laugh noisily 大笑；哄笑；狂笑：*They all guffawed at his jokes.* 他们听了他的笑话都一阵狂笑。 ▶ **guf·faw** *noun*：*She let out a loud guffaw.* 她嘎嘎大笑起来。

GUI /ˈguːi; ˌdʒiː juː ˈaɪ/ *noun* (*computing* 计) the abbreviation for 'graphical user interface' (a way of giving instructions to a computer using things that can be seen on the screen such as symbols and menus) 图形用户界面（全写为 graphical user interface）

guid·ance /ˈgaɪdns/ *noun* [U] **1** **~ (on sth)** help or advice that is given to sb, especially by sb older or with more experience 指导；引导；咨询：*guidance for teachers on how to use video in the classroom* 为教师提供的课堂录像教学指导 ◇ *Activities all take place* ***under the guidance of*** *an experienced tutor.* 所有活动都在经验丰富的导师指导下进行。◇ (*NAmE*) *a guidance counselor* (= sb who advises students)（学生）咨询顾问 ➲ SEE ALSO MARRIAGE GUIDANCE **2** the process of controlling the direction of a ROCKET, etc., using electronic equipment（火箭等的）制导，导航：*a missile guidance system* 导弹制导系统

guide /gaɪd/ *noun, verb*

■ *noun*

• **BOOK/MAGAZINE** 书刊 **1** ~ (**to sth**) a book, magazine, etc. that gives you information, help or instructions about sth 指南；手册：*a Guide to Family Health* 家庭健康指南 ◇ *Let's have a look at the TV guide and see what's on.* 咱们看一下节目表，好知道电视上在放些什么。 **2** (*also* **guide·book**) ~ (**to sth**) a book that gives information about a place for travellers or tourists 旅游指南（或手册）：*a guide to Italy* 意大利旅游指南 ◇ *travel guides* 旅行手册 ➲ WORDFINDER NOTE AT TOURIST

• **PERSON** 人 **3** a person who shows other people the way to a place, especially sb employed to show tourists around interesting places 导游；向导： *a tour guide* 导游 ◇ *We hired a local guide to get us across the mountains.* 我们雇了一名当地人做向导带领我们翻山越岭。 **4** a person who advises you on how to live and behave 指导者；指引者：*a spiritual guide* 灵修指导者

• **STH THAT HELPS YOU DECIDE** 指导的事物 **5** something that gives you enough information to be able to make a decision about sth or form an opinion 有指导意义的事物；指导的事物： ***As a rough guide**, allow half a cup of rice per person.* 大致定个标准，就是每人半杯米。◇ *I let my feelings be my guide.* 我是跟着感觉走。

• **GIRL** 女孩 **6 Guide** (*also old-fashioned* ˌ**Girl ˈGuide**) (*both BrE*) (*US* ˌ**Girl ˈScout**) a member of an organization (called **the Guides** or **the Girl Scouts**) which is similar to the SCOUTS and which trains girls in practical skills and does a lot of activities with them, for example camping 女童子军 ➲ COMPARE BROWNIE (3)

■ *verb*

• **SHOW THE WAY** 指路 **1** ~ **sb** (**to/through/around sth**) to show sb the way to a place, often by going with them; to show sb a place that you know well 给某人领路（或导游）；指引： *She guided us through the busy streets to the cathedral.* 她带领我们穿过繁忙的街道去大教堂。◇ *We were guided around the museums.* 我们在导游的带领下参观了博物馆。 ➲ SYNONYMS AT TAKE

• **INFLUENCE BEHAVIOUR** 影响行为 **2** ~ **sb** to direct or influence sb's behaviour 指导，影响（某人的行为）： *He was always guided by his religious beliefs.* 他的言行总是以自己的宗教信仰为依归。

• **EXPLAIN** 阐明 **3** ~ **sb** (**through sth**) to explain to sb how to do sth, especially sth complicated or difficult（向某人）解释，阐明：*The health and safety officer will guide you through the safety procedures.* 健康安全员将把安全规程向你们解释一遍。

• **HELP SB MOVE** 帮助挪动 **4** ~ **sb/sth** (**+ adv./prep.**) to help sb to move in a particular direction; to move sth in a particular direction 搀扶（某人朝…方向）走；（朝…方向）移动（某物）： *She took her arm and guided her across the busy road.* 她挽着她的手臂领她穿过繁忙的公路。◇ *He guided her hand to his face.* 他拉起她的手放到他脸上。 ➲ SEE ALSO GUIDING

guide·book /ˈgaɪdbʊk/ *noun* = GUIDE (2)

guided /ˈgaɪdɪd/ *adj.* [usually before noun] that is led by sb who works as a guide 有指导的；有向导的；有导游的： *a **guided tour/walk*** 有导游的观光 / 步行观光

ˌ**guided ˈmissile** *noun* a MISSILE that can be controlled while in the air by electronic equipment 导弹

ˈ**guide dog** (*NAmE also* ˌ**Seeing ˈEye dog™**) *noun* a dog trained to guide a blind person 导盲犬；领路狗

guide·line AW /ˈgaɪdlaɪn/ *noun* **1 guidelines** [pl.] a set of rules or instructions that are given by an official organization telling you how to do sth, especially sth difficult 指导方针；指导原则；行动纲领；准则： *The government has **drawn up guidelines** on the treatment of the mentally ill.* 政府制订了治疗精神病人的指导方针。 **2** [C] something that can be used to help you make a decision or form an opinion 参考：*The figures are a useful guideline when buying a house.* 买房时这些数据很有参考价值。

Gui·der /ˈgaɪdə(r)/ (*also old-fashioned* ˌ**Girl ˈGuider**) *noun* (*BrE*) an adult leader in the Guides 女童子军指导员

guid·ing /ˈgaɪdɪŋ/ *adj.* [only before noun] giving advice and help; having a strong influence on people 给予指导的；有影响的：*She was inexperienced and needed a **guiding hand**.* 她缺乏经验，需要有人指导。◇ *a guiding force* 有影响的力量

guild /gɪld/ *noun* [C+sing./pl. v.] **1** an organization of people who do the same job or who have the same interests or aims（同一行业、志趣或目的的）协会：*the Screen Actors' Guild* 影视演员协会 **2** an association of skilled workers in the Middle Ages（中世纪的）行会，同业公会

guil·der /ˈgɪldə(r)/ *noun* the former unit of money in the Netherlands (replaced in 2002 by the euro) 荷兰盾（荷兰以前的货币单位，2002 年为欧元所取代）

guild·hall /ˈgɪldhɔːl/ *noun* (*BrE*) a building in which the members of a GUILD used to meet, now often used for meetings and performances（行会或同业公会的）会馆（如今常用作开会或演出的场所）

guile /gaɪl/ *noun* [U] (*formal*) the use of clever but dishonest behaviour in order to trick people 狡诈；欺诈；奸诈 SYN **deceit**

guile·less /ˈgaɪlləs/ *adj.* (*formal*) behaving in a very honest way; not knowing how to trick people 厚道的；老实的；不奸猾的 ▸ **guile·less·ly** *adv.*

guil·le·mot /ˈgɪlɪmɒt; *NAmE* -mɑːt/ *noun* a black and white bird with a long narrow beak that lives near the sea 海鸽（黑白色，喙细长）

guil·lo·tine /ˈgɪlətiːn/ *noun, verb*

■ *noun* **1** [sing.] a machine, originally from France, for cutting people's heads off. It has a heavy blade that slides down a wooden frame. 断头台（源于法国） **2** (*BrE*) (*US* ˈ**paper cutter**) [C] a device with a long blade for cutting paper 裁切机；切纸机 **3** [sing.] (*BrE, politics* 政) the setting of a time limit on a debate in Parliament（议会中）规定截止辩论的时限

■ *verb* **1** ~ **sb** to kill sb by cutting off their head with a guillotine 把（某人）送上断头台 **2** ~ **sth** (*BrE*) to cut paper using a guillotine（用切纸机）切，切断 **3** ~ **sth** (*BrE, politics* 政) to limit the amount of time spent discussing a new law in Parliament（议会中）限制辩论时间：*to guillotine a bill* 限制议案的辩论时间

guilt /gɪlt/ *noun, verb*

■ *noun* [U] **1** ~ (**about sth**) the unhappy feelings caused by knowing or thinking that you have done sth wrong 内疚；悔恨：*She had feelings of guilt about leaving her children and going to work.* 她因离开自己的孩子去工作而感到内疚。◇ *Many survivors were left with **a sense of guilt**.* 许多幸存者都有内疚感。◇ *a **guilt complex*** (= an exaggerated sense of guilt) 内疚情结 **2** the fact that sb has done sth illegal 犯罪；罪行；有罪：*His guilt was proved beyond all doubt by the prosecution.* 他的罪行已被控方证实确凿无疑。◇ *an admission of guilt* 承认有罪 OPP **innocence** **3** blame or responsibility for doing sth wrong or for sth bad that has happened 罪责；责任；罪过： *The investigation will try to find out where the guilt for the disaster really lies.* 此调查将尽力查出灾难的真正责任所在。▸ **guilt·less** *adj.*

IDM **a ˈguilt trip** (*informal*) things you say to sb in order to make them feel guilty about sth 使人内疚的责备：*Don't **lay a guilt trip** on your child about schoolwork.* 别因为功课责备孩子而使他觉得很内疚。

■ *verb*

PHR V **ˈguilt sb into sth/into doing sth** (*informal*) to make sb do sth by persuading them that it is wrong not to do it 诱导某人做某事（使其认为不做不对）：*I only went because she guilted me into it.* 我是受到她的蛊惑才去的。

guilty /ˈgɪlti/ *adj.* (**guilt·ier**, **guilti·est**) HELP **more guilty** and **most guilty** are more common * more guilty 和 most guilty 更常见。 **1** ~ (**about sth**) feeling ashamed because you have done sth that you know is wrong or have not done sth that you should have done 感到内疚

的；感到惭愧的：*I felt guilty about not visiting my parents more often.* 我因没有常去看望父母而感到内疚。◇ *John had a guilty look on his face.* 约翰脸上显出惭愧的表情。◇ *I had a* ***guilty conscience*** *and could not sleep.* 我问心有愧，睡不着觉。 **2** ~ (**of sth**) having done sth illegal; being responsible for sth bad that has happened 犯有罪的；有过失的；有罪责的：*The jury* ***found*** *the defendant* ***not guilty*** *of the offence.* 陪审团裁决被告无罪。◇ *He* ***pleaded guilty*** *to murder.* 他承认犯有谋杀罪。◇ ***the guilty party*** (= the person responsible for sth bad happening) 有罪的一方当事人 ◇ *We've all been guilty of selfishness at some time in our lives.* 我们每个人一生中都有过自私自利的过失。 OPP **innocent** ➲ COLLOCATIONS AT JUSTICE ➲ MORE LIKE THIS 20, page R27 ▶ **guilt·ily** /-ɪli/ *adv.*

IDM **a guilty 'secret** a secret that sb feels ashamed about 见不得人的秘密

guinea /'gɪni/ *noun* an old British gold coin or unit of money worth 21 SHILLINGS (= now £1.05). Prices are sometimes still given in guineas, for example when buying or selling horses. 几尼（英国旧时金币或货币单位，价值 21 先令，现值 1.05 英镑。现时有些价格仍用几尼计算，如马匹买卖）

'guinea fowl *noun* [C, U] (*pl.* **guinea fowl**) a bird of the PHEASANT family, that has dark grey feathers with white spots, and is often used for food; the meat of this bird 珠鸡；珠鸡肉：*roast guinea fowl* 烤珠鸡肉

'guinea pig *noun* **1** a small animal with short ears and no tail, often kept as a pet 天竺鼠，豚鼠（耳小无尾，常作宠物饲养） **2** a person used in medical or other experiments 实验对象：*Students in fifty schools are to act as guinea pigs for these new teaching methods.* 五十所学校的学生将作为这些新教学法的试验对象。

Guin·ness™ /'gɪnɪs/ *noun* [U, C] a type of very dark brown beer, with a white HEAD (= top) on it 健力士黑啤酒（带白色头沫）

guise /gaɪz/ *noun* a way in which sb/sth appears, often in a way that is different from usual or that hides the truth about them/it 表现形式；外貌；伪装；外表：*His speech presented racist ideas* ***under the guise of*** *nationalism.* 他的讲话以民族主义为幌子宣扬种族主义思想。◇ *The story appears in different guises in different cultures.* 这个故事以不同的形式出现在不同的文化中。

gui·tar /gɪ'tɑː(r)/ *noun* a musical instrument that usually has six strings, that you play with your fingers or with a PLECTRUM 吉他：***an acoustic/an electric/a classical, etc. guitar*** 原声吉他、电吉他、古典吉他等 ◇ *a guitar player* 吉他弹奏者 ◇ *Do you* ***play the guitar****?* 你会弹吉他吗？◇ *She plays guitar in a band.* 她在乐队里弹奏吉他。◇ *As he sang, he strummed his guitar.* 他边唱边拨着吉他。 ➲ VISUAL VOCAB PAGE V40 ➲ SEE ALSO AIR GUITAR, BASS[1] *n.* (4)

gui·tar·ist /gɪ'tɑːrɪst/ *noun* a person who plays the guitar 吉他弹奏者；吉他手

Gu·ja·rati (*also* **Gu·je·rati**) /ˌguːdʒə'rɑːti/ *noun* **1** [C] a person from the state of Gujarat in western India（印度西部的）古吉拉特人 **2** [U] the language of Gujarat 古吉拉特语 ▶ **Gu·ja·rati** (*also* **Gu·je·rati**) *adj.*

gulch /gʌltʃ/ *noun* (*especially NAmE*) a narrow valley with steep sides, that was formed by a fast stream flowing through it（两边陡峭的）急流峡谷

gulf /gʌlf/ *noun* **1** [C] a large area of sea that is partly surrounded by land 海湾：*the Gulf of Mexico* 墨西哥湾 **2** **the Gulf** [sing.] the Persian Gulf, the area of sea between the Arabian PENINSULA and Iran 波斯湾：*the Gulf States* (= the countries with coasts on the Gulf) 海湾国家 **3** [C, usually sing.] ~ (**between A and B**) a large difference between two people or groups in the way that they think, live or feel 分歧；鸿沟；隔阂：*The gulf between rich and poor is enormous.* 贫富悬殊。 **4** [C] a wide deep crack in the ground（地面的）裂口，深坑，沟壑 IDM SEE BRIDGE *v.*

the 'Gulf Stream *noun* [sing.] a warm current of water flowing across the Atlantic Ocean from the Gulf of Mexico towards Europe 墨西哥湾流

gull /gʌl/ (*also* **sea·gull**) *noun* a bird with long wings and usually white and grey or black feathers that lives near the sea. There are several types of gull. 海鸥 ➲ VISUAL VOCAB PAGE V12 ➲ SEE ALSO HERRING GULL

Gul·lah /'gʌlə/ *noun* [U] a language spoken by black people living on the coast of South Carolina, that is a combination of English and various W African languages 古勒语（居住在美国南卡罗来纳州沿海地区的黑人所操的一种语言，为英语与多种西非语言的结合）

gul·let /'gʌlɪt/ *noun* the tube through which food passes from the mouth to the stomach 食道；食管 SYN **oesophagus** ➲ VISUAL VOCAB PAGE V64

gul·lible /'gʌləbl/ *adj.* too willing to believe or accept what other people tell you and therefore easily tricked 轻信的；易受骗的；易上当的 SYN **naive** ▶ **gul·li·bil·ity** /ˌgʌlə'bɪləti/ *noun* [U]

gully (*also* **gul·ley**) /'gʌli/ *noun* (*pl.* **gul·lies**, **gul·leys**) **1** a small, narrow channel, usually formed by a stream or by rain 冲沟；溪谷 **2** a deep DITCH 深沟；沟壑

gulp /gʌlp/ *verb, noun*

■ *verb* **1** [T, I] ~ (**sth**) | ~ **sth down** to swallow large amounts of food or drink quickly 狼吞虎咽；大口吞咽；匆匆吞下：*He gulped down the rest of his tea and went out.* 他把剩下的茶一饮而尽便出去了。 **2** [I, T] (+ **speech**) to swallow, but without eating or drinking anything, especially because of a strong emotion such as fear or surprise（尤因害怕或惊讶而）倒吸气：*She gulped nervously before trying to answer.* 她紧张地倒吸了一口气才尽力回答。 **3** [I, T] to breathe quickly and deeply, because you need more air 深呼吸；喘大气；大口大口地吸气：~ (**for sth**) *She came up* ***gulping for air****.* 她气喘吁吁地走上前来。◇ ~ **sth** (**in**) *He leant against the car, gulping in the cold air.* 他倚着汽车大口大口地呼吸冷空气。

PHR V **ˌgulp sth↔'back** to stop yourself showing your emotions by swallowing hard 咽下…（以防止感情的流露）：*She gulped back her tears and forced a smile.* 她忍住泪水，强作笑容。

■ *noun* **1** ~ (**of sth**) an amount of sth that you swallow or drink quickly 吞饮的量；一大口：*He* ***took a gulp*** *of coffee.* 他喝了一大口咖啡。 **2** an act of breathing in or of swallowing sth 吸入；吞咽：*'Can you start on Monday?' Amy gave a gulp. 'Of course,' she said.* “你星期一开始可以吗？”埃米吸了一口气。“当然可以。”她说。◇ *He drank the glass of whisky* ***in one gulp****.* 他将整杯威士忌一饮而尽。

gum /gʌm/ *noun, verb*

■ *noun* **1** [C, usually pl.] either of the firm areas of flesh in the mouth to which the teeth are attached 牙龈；齿龈；牙床：*gum disease* 牙龈病 **2** [U] a sticky substance produced by some types of tree 树胶；树脂 **3** [U] a type of glue used for sticking light things together, such as paper 黏胶，胶质物（用以粘轻东西，如纸等） **4** [U] = CHEWING GUM **5** [C] a firm transparent fruit-flavoured sweet/candy that you chew 透明果味糖：*fruit gums* 水果糖

IDM **by gum!** (*old-fashioned, informal*) used to show surprise（表示惊讶）天啊，老天，啊呀

■ *verb* (**-mm-**) ~ **A to B** | ~ **sth** (**down**) (*rather old-fashioned*) to spread glue on the surface of sth; to stick two things together with glue 在…上涂胶；用黏胶粘：*A large address label was gummed to the package.* 包装袋上贴着一大张地址签条。

PHR V **ˌgum sth↔'up** [usually passive] (*informal*) to cover or fill sth with a sticky substance so that it stops moving or working as it should 黏住（使不能正常工作）

gum·ball /'gʌmbɔːl/ *noun* (*NAmE*) a small ball of CHEWING GUM that looks like a sweet/candy 球形口香糖

gumbo /'gʌmbəʊ; *NAmE* -boʊ/ *noun* [U] a thick chicken or SEAFOOD soup, usually made with the vegetable OKRA 秋葵汤（用秋葵做的鸡汤或海鲜浓汤）

G

gum·boil /ˈɡʌmbɔɪl/ *noun* a small swelling on the GUM in a person's mouth, over an infected area on the root of a tooth 龈脓肿

gum·boot /ˈɡʌmbuːt/ *noun* (*old-fashioned, BrE*) = WELLINGTON

gum·drop /ˈɡʌmdrɒp; *NAmE* -drɑːp/ *noun* a sweet/candy that is like a small firm lump of jelly 胶姆糖；橡皮糖

gummed /ɡʌmd/ *adj.* [usually before noun] (of stamps, paper, etc. 邮票、纸张等) covered with a type of glue that will become sticky when water is put on it 涂胶的；带黏胶的

gummy /ˈɡʌmi/ *adj.* (*informal*) **1** sticky or covered in gum (3) 黏性的；涂有黏胶的 **2** a **gummy** smile shows your teeth and gums （微笑时）露齿龈的

gump·tion /ˈɡʌmpʃn/ *noun* [U] (*old-fashioned, informal*) **1** the intelligence needed to know what to do in a particular situation 机智；老练；精明 **2** courage and determination 勇气；胆力；决心

gum·shield /ˈɡʌmʃiːld/ (*BrE*) (*NAmE* **mouth·guard**) *noun* a cover that a sports player wears in his or her mouth to protect the teeth and GUMS （运动员口中所含的）护齿

gum·shoe /ˈɡʌmʃuː/ *noun* (*old-fashioned, NAmE, informal*) = DETECTIVE (1)

ˈgum tree *noun* a EUCALYPTUS tree 桉树；树胶树
IDM **be up a ˈgum tree** (*BrE, informal*) to be in a very difficult situation 陷入困境；一筹莫展

gun 🔑 /ɡʌn/ *noun, verb*
▪ *noun* **1** 🔑 [C] a weapon that is used for firing bullets or SHELLS 枪；炮：*to fire a gun at sb* 向某人开火 ◇ *a toy gun* 玩具枪 ◇ *anti-aircraft guns* 高射炮 ◇ *Look out, he's got a gun!* 小心，他有枪！◇ *Should police officers **carry guns**?* 警察应该佩枪吗？◇ *He **pointed/aimed the gun** at her head.* 他用枪对准了她的头。◇ *The police officers **drew their guns*** (= took them out so they were ready to use). 警察拔枪。◇ *She **pulled a gun on** me* (= took out a gun and aimed it at me). 她掏出枪来对准了我。◇ *The **gun went off** by accident.* 枪走火了。◇ *a **gun battle** between rival gangs* 对立帮派间的枪战 ➲ SEE ALSO AIRGUN, HANDGUN, MACHINE GUN, SHOTGUN, STUN GUN, SUB-MACHINE GUN, TOMMY GUN **2** [C] a tool that uses pressure to send out a substance or an object 喷射器；喷枪：*a staple gun* * U 形钉枪 ➲ SEE ALSO SPRAY GUN **3 the gun** [sing.] the signal to begin a race, that is made by firing a special gun, called a STARTING PISTOL, into the air 起跑信号；发令枪声 **4** [C] (*informal, especially NAmE*) a person who is paid to shoot sb 受雇杀人的枪手：*a hired gun* 雇用的枪手 ➲ SEE ALSO FLASHGUN, SON OF A GUN
IDM **hold/put a gun to sb's ˈhead** to force sb to do sth that they do not want to do, by making threats 威胁某人；胁迫某人就范 **under the ˈgun** (*NAmE, informal*) experiencing a lot of pressure 承受很大压力：*I'm really under the gun today.* 我今天的压力真大。**(with) all/both guns ˈblazing** (*informal*) with a lot of energy and determination 充满活力；精神抖擞：*The champions came out (with) all guns blazing.* 优胜者们神采奕奕地登场亮相。➲ MORE AT GREAT *adj.*, JUMP *v.*, SPIKE *v.*, STICK *v.*
▪ *verb* (**-nn-**) **1** [I] (*NAmE*) (of an engine 发动机) to run very quickly 快速运转：*a line of motorcycles with their engines gunning* 引擎狂转的一队摩托车 **2** [T] **~ sth + adv./prep.** (*NAmE*) to start driving a vehicle very fast 使（车辆）加速：*He gunned the cab through the red light.* 他猛踩油门，开着出租车闯过了红灯。
PHR V **be ˈgunning for sb** (*informal*) to be looking for an opportunity to blame or attack sb 伺机指责（或攻击）某人 **be ˈgunning for sth** to be competing for or trying hard to get sth 竭力谋求，力图获取，寻求（某物）：*She's gunning for the top job.* 她正竭力谋取最高职位。**ˌgun sb↔ˈdown** [usually passive] to shoot sb, especially killing or seriously injuring them 枪杀，开枪伤害（某人）

gun·boat /ˈɡʌnbəʊt; *NAmE* -boʊt/ *noun* a small ship that is fitted with large guns 护卫艇；炮艇

ˌgunboat diˈplomacy *noun* [U] a way of making another country accept your demands by using the threat of force 炮舰外交（以武力相威胁）

ˈgun carriage *noun* a support on wheels for a large heavy gun 炮架

ˈgun control *noun* [U] (*especially NAmE*) laws that restrict the sale and use of guns 枪支管制（法）

ˈgun dog *noun* a dog trained to help in the sport of shooting, for example by finding birds that have been shot 猎犬

gun·fight /ˈɡʌnfaɪt/ *noun* a fight between people using guns 枪战；炮战 ▶ **gun·fight·er** *noun*

gun·fire /ˈɡʌnfaɪə(r)/ *noun* [U] the repeated firing of guns; the sound of guns firing （接连不断的）炮火，炮火声：*an exchange of gunfire with the police* 与警方的交火 ◇ *I could hear gunfire.* 我可以听到炮声。

gunge /ɡʌndʒ/ (*BrE*) (*also* **gunk** *NAmE, BrE*) *noun* [U] (*informal*) any unpleasant, sticky or dirty substance 肮脏恶心的黏性物质；黏糊糊的东西 ▶ **gungy** *adj.*

gung-ho /ˌɡʌŋ ˈhəʊ; *NAmE* ˈhoʊ/ *adj.* (*informal, disapproving*) too enthusiastic about sth, without thinking seriously about it, especially about fighting and war （尤指对战斗和战争）偏激的，狂热的，莽撞的

gunk /ɡʌŋk/ (*especially NAmE*) (*BrE also* **gunge**) *noun* [U] (*informal*) any unpleasant, sticky or dirty substance 肮脏恶心的黏性物质；黏糊糊的东西 ▶ **gunky** *adj.*

gun·man /ˈɡʌnmən/ *noun* (*pl.* **-men** /-mən/) a man who uses a gun to steal from or kill people 持枪歹徒；持枪杀人者

gun·metal /ˈɡʌnmetl/ *noun* [U] **1** a metal that is a mixture of COPPER, tin and ZINC 炮铜，炮合金（铜、锡和锌的合金） **2** a dull blue-grey colour 炮铜色；暗蓝灰色；铁灰色

gun·nel = GUNWALE

gun·ner /ˈɡʌnə(r)/ *noun* **1** a member of the armed forces who is trained to use large guns 炮手；炮兵 **2** a soldier in the British ARTILLERY (= the part of the army that uses large guns) （英国炮兵部队的）士兵；炮兵

gun·nery /ˈɡʌnəri/ *noun* [U] (*specialist*) the operation of large military guns 重炮射击；枪炮操作

gunny /ˈɡʌni/ *noun* [U] a type of rough cloth used for making SACKS 黄麻袋布；粗麻布

gun·ny·sack /ˈɡʌnisæk/ *noun* (*NAmE*) a large bag made from rough material and used to store flour, potatoes, etc. （装面粉、土豆等的）黄麻袋

gun·point /ˈɡʌnpɔɪnt/ *noun*
IDM **at ˈgunpoint** while threatening sb or being threatened with a gun 用枪威胁；在枪口威胁下：*The driver was robbed at gunpoint.* 司机遭持枪抢劫。

gun·pow·der /ˈɡʌnpaʊdə(r)/ (*also* **pow·der**) *noun* [U] EXPLOSIVE powder used especially in bombs or FIREWORKS 火药

gun·run·ner /ˈɡʌnrʌnə(r)/ *noun* a person who secretly and illegally brings guns into a country 私运军火者；军火走私者 ▶ **gun·run·ning** *noun* [U]

gun·ship /ˈɡʌnʃɪp/ *noun* an armed military HELICOPTER or other aircraft 武装直升机；武装飞机

gun·shot /ˈɡʌnʃɒt; *NAmE* -ʃɑːt/ *noun* **1** [U] the bullets that are fired from a gun （射出的）炮弹，枪弹：*gunshot wounds* 枪弹伤 **2** [C] the firing of a gun; the sound of it being fired 枪炮射击；枪炮声：*I heard the sound of gunshots out in the street.* 我听到外面街上有枪炮声。 **3** [U] the distance that a bullet from a gun can travel （枪炮的）射程：*He was **out of/within gunshot**.* 他在射程之外 / 之内。

gun·sight /ˈɡʌnsaɪt/ *noun* a part of a gun that you look through in order to aim it accurately（枪炮的）瞄准器；射击瞄准具 ➲ SEE ALSO SIGHT *n.* (7)

gun·sling·er /ˈɡʌnslɪŋə(r)/ *noun* (*NAmE*) a person who is paid to kill people, especially in films/movies about the American Wild West（尤指美国西部电影中受人雇用的）杀手

gun·smith /ˈɡʌnsmɪθ/ *noun* a person who makes and repairs guns 造枪工；修枪匠；军械工人

gun·wale (*also* **gun·nel**) /ˈɡʌnl/ *noun* the upper edge of the side of a boat or small ship 舷缘（船舷的上缘）

guppy /ˈɡʌpi/ *noun* (*pl.* **-ies**) a small FRESHWATER fish, commonly kept in AQUARIUMS 虹鳉，孔雀鱼（小型淡水观赏鱼）

gur·dwa·ra /ɡɜːˈdwɑːrə; *NAmE* ɡɜːr-/ *noun* a building in which Sikhs worship 谒师所（锡克教礼拜场所）

gur·gle /ˈɡɜːɡl; *NAmE* ˈɡɜːrɡl/ *verb, noun*

■ ***verb*** **1** [I] to make a sound like water flowing quickly through a narrow space 发汩汩声；发潺潺流水声：*Water gurgled through the pipes.* 水汩汩地从管道中流过。◇ *a gurgling stream* 潺潺溪流 **2** [I] if a baby **gurgles**, it makes a noise in its throat when it is happy（婴儿高兴时）发出咯咯声

■ ***noun*** **1** a sound like water flowing quickly through a narrow space 汩汩声；潺潺声 **2** the sound that babies make in the throat, especially when they are happy（婴儿高兴时发出的）咯咯声

Gur·kha /ˈɡɜːkə; *NAmE* ˈɡɜːrkə/ *noun* one of a group of people from Nepal who are known as good soldiers. Some Gurkhas are members of a REGIMENT in the British army. 廓尔喀士兵（善战的尼泊尔人，有些人服役于英国的一个陆军团）

gurn (*also* **girn**) /ɡɜːn; *NAmE* ɡɜːrn/ *verb* [I] (*especially BrE*) to make a ridiculous or unpleasant face 做俏皮相；扮鬼脸 ▸ **gurn·er** *noun*

gur·ney /ˈɡɜːni; *NAmE* ˈɡɜːrni/ *noun* (*NAmE*) a type of TROLLEY which is used for moving patients in a hospital（医院中推送病人用的）轮床

guru /ˈɡʊruː/ *noun* **1** a Hindu or Sikh religious teacher or leader 古鲁（印度教或锡克教的宗教导师或领袖） **2** (*informal*) a person who is an expert on a particular subject or who is very good at doing sth 专家；权威；大师：*a **management/health/fashion, etc. guru*** 管理、保健、时装等专家

Guru Granth Sahib /ˌɡʊruː ˈɡrʌnt sɑːb; sɑːɪb/ *noun* [sing.] **Adi Granth, the Guru Granth Sahib, the Adi Granth** the main holy book of the Sikh religion, containing songs for worship, religious poetry and teachings《古鲁・格兰特・萨赫布》，《阿迪・格兰特》（锡克教圣典，包含圣歌、圣诗和教义）

gush /ɡʌʃ/ *verb, noun*

■ ***verb*** **1** [I] **~ out of/from/into sth | ~ out/in** to flow or pour suddenly and quickly out of a hole in large amounts（从…中）喷出，涌出，冒出：*blood gushing from a wound* 从伤口冒出的血 ◇ *Water gushed out of the pipe.* 水从管子中涌出。 **2** [T] **~ sth** (of a container/vehicle etc. 容器、车辆等) to suddenly let out large amounts of a liquid 大量涌出，大量泄出（液体）：*The tanker was gushing oil.* 油箱在大量喷油。◇ (*figurative*) *She absolutely gushed enthusiasm.* 她真是热情奔放。 **3** [T, I] (**+ speech**) (*disapproving*) to express so much praise or emotion about sb/sth that it does not seem sincere 过分称赞；夸张地表现对…的感情；装腔作势：*'You are clever,' she gushed.* "你好聪明。" 她夸张地称赞说。

■ ***noun*** [usually sing.] **1 ~ (of sth)** a large amount of liquid suddenly and quickly flowing or pouring out of sth（液体的）喷出，涌出，冒出：*a gush of blood* 血的涌出 **2 ~ (of sth)** a sudden strong expression of feeling（感情的）迸发，爆发，发作：*a gush of emotion* 感情的迸发

gush·er /ˈɡʌʃə(r)/ *noun* **1** (*NAmE*) an OIL WELL where the oil comes out quickly and in large quantities 喷油井；自喷井 **2** a person who gushes 过分恭维而显得不真诚的人；过分表露感情的人

gush·ing /ˈɡʌʃɪŋ/ *adj.* (*disapproving*) expressing so much enthusiasm, praise or emotion that it does not seem sincere 过分热情的；过分赞扬的；夸张地表现感情的 ▸ **gush·ing·ly** *adv.*

gus·set /ˈɡʌsɪt/ *noun* an extra piece of cloth sewn into a piece of clothing to make it wider, stronger or more comfortable（缝在衣服上用以放大、加固等的）衬料

gussy /ˈɡʌsi/ *verb* (**gus·sies**, **gussy·ing**, **gus·sied**, **gus·sied**)
PHR V **ˌgussy ˈup** (*NAmE, informal*) to dress yourself in an attractive way 把自己打扮得漂漂亮亮（或花枝招展） SYN **dress up**: *Even the stars get tired of gussying up for the awards.* 连明星们也厌烦了把自己打扮起来去领奖。

gust /ɡʌst/ *noun, verb*

■ ***noun*** **1** a sudden strong increase in the amount and speed of wind that is blowing 一阵强风；一阵狂风：*A **gust of wind** blew his hat off.* 一阵狂风把他的帽子刮掉了。◇ *The wind was blowing in gusts.* 狂风阵阵刮着。 ➲ WORDFINDER NOTE AT WIND[1] **2** a sudden strong expression of emotion（感情的）迸发，爆发，发作：*a **gust of laughter*** 一阵笑声

■ ***verb*** [I] (of the wind 风) to suddenly blow very hard 猛刮；劲吹：*winds gusting up to 60 mph* 风速达每小时 60 英里的狂风

gusto /ˈɡʌstəʊ; *NAmE* -toʊ/ *noun* [U] enthusiasm and energy in doing sth 热情高涨；兴致勃勃：*They sang **with gusto**.* 他们兴致勃勃地唱歌。

gusty /ˈɡʌsti/ *adj.* [usually before noun] with the wind blowing in GUSTS 有阵风在吹的；刮风的：*a gusty morning* 刮风的早晨 ◇ *gusty winds* 阵阵大风

gut /ɡʌt/ *noun, verb, adj.*

■ ***noun*** **1** [C] the tube in the body through which food passes when it leaves the stomach 肠道；消化道 SYN **intestine** **2 guts** [pl.] the organs in and around the stomach, especially in an animal（尤指动物的）内脏：*I'll only cook fish if the guts have been removed.* 鱼若已收拾干净，我只需烧一下即可。 **3** [C] (*informal*) a person's stomach, especially when it is large（尤指大的）胃，肚子 SYN **belly**: *Have you seen the gut on him!* 你看到他那大肚子了吧！◇ *a **beer gut*** (= caused by drinking beer) 啤酒肚 **4 guts** [pl.] (*informal*) the courage and determination that it takes to do sth difficult or unpleasant 勇气；胆量；决心；魄力：*He **doesn't have the guts** to walk away from a well-paid job.* 他没胆量辞去一份报酬优厚的工作。 **5** [C, usually pl.] the place where your natural feelings that make you react in a particular way are thought to be 内心；直觉；本能：*I had a feeling **in my guts** that something was wrong.* 我本能地感到出了事。 **6 guts** [pl.] the most important part of sth 核心；实质；要点：*the guts of the problem* 问题的实质 **7** [U] = CATGUT

IDM **have sb's ˌguts for ˈgarters** (*BrE, informal*) to be very angry with sb and punish them severely for sth they have done 满腔怒火地严惩（某人） **slog/sweat/work your ˈguts out** (*informal*) to work very hard to achieve sth 拼命工作；拼命干活：*I slogged my guts out for the exam.* 我为这次考试命都豁出去了。 ➲ MORE AT BUST *v.*, GREEDY, HATE *v.*, SPILL *v.*

■ ***verb*** (**-tt-**) **1** [usually passive] **~ sth** to destroy the inside or contents of a building or room 损毁（建筑物或房屋的）内部：*a factory gutted by fire* 内部被火焚毁的工厂 ◇ *The house was completely gutted.* 这房子里的东西全部被毁。 **2 ~ sth** to remove the organs from inside a fish or an animal to prepare it for cooking 取出…的内脏（以便烹饪）

■ ***adj.*** [only before noun] based on feelings and emotions rather than thought and reason 以感情为基础的；非理性的；本能的：*a **gut feeling/reaction*** 本能的感觉 / 反应 ◇ *You have to work on **gut instinct**.* 你得凭借你的直觉工作。

gut·less /ˈɡʌtləs/ *adj.* lacking courage or determination 缺乏勇气的；怯懦的；无魄力的

G

gut·ser /ˈɡʌtsə(r)/ *noun* (*AustralE, NZE, informal*) an occasion when sb/sth falls or knocks into sth 摔跤；跌倒；撞击

IDM **come a ˈgutser** to fail or be defeated 失败；遭挫败

gutsy /ˈɡʌtsi/ *adj.* (**guts·ier**, **gutsi·est**) (*informal*) **1** showing courage and determination 有胆识的；有胆量的；果敢的：*a gutsy fighter/win* 勇敢的战士；用坚强的毅力取得的胜利 **2** having strong and unusual qualities 强劲的；热烈而与众不同的：*a gutsy red wine* 烈性红葡萄酒 ◇ *a gutsy song* 满怀激情的歌

gut·ted /ˈɡʌtɪd/ *adj.* [not before noun] (*BrE, informal*) extremely sad or disappointed 十分伤心；极度失望；非常沮丧：*Disappointed? I was gutted!* 失望？我是伤心透了！

gut·ter /ˈɡʌtə(r)/ *noun, verb*

■ *noun* **1** [C] a long curved channel made of metal or plastic that is fixed under the edge of a roof to carry away the water when it rains 檐沟；天沟：*a blocked/leaking gutter* 堵塞了的 / 漏水的檐沟 ➲ VISUAL VOCAB PAGE V18 **2** [C] a channel at the edge of a road where water collects and is carried away to DRAINS 路旁排水沟；阴沟 **3 the gutter** [sing.] the bad social conditions or low moral standards sometimes connected with the lowest level of society 恶劣的社会环境；（社会最低阶层的）道德沦落：*She rose from the gutter to become a great star.* 她从贫民区一跃而成为大明星。◇ *the language of the gutter* (= using swear words) 粗鄙的语言

■ *verb* [I] (*literary*) (of a flame or CANDLE 火焰或蜡烛) to burn in an unsteady way 忽明忽暗；摇曳不定

gut·ter·ing /ˈɡʌtərɪŋ/ *noun* [U] the system of gutters on a building; the material used to make gutters（建筑物天沟的）排水系统；用于建筑物排水系统的材料：*a length of guttering* 一节沟槽

the ˌgutter ˈpress *noun* [sing.] (*BrE, disapproving*) newspapers that print a lot of shocking stories about people's private lives rather than serious news 低级趣味的报纸

gut·ter·snipe /ˈɡʌtəsnaɪp; *NAmE* -tərs-/ *noun* (*informal, disapproving*) a poor and dirty child 肮脏的穷孩子

gut·tur·al /ˈɡʌtərəl/ *adj.* (of a sound 声音) made or seeming to be made at the back of the throat（似）喉间发出的：*guttural consonants* 腭辅音 ◇ *a low guttural growl* 从喉咙里发出的低沉的吼声

ˈgut-wrenching *adj.* (*informal*) very unpleasant; making you feel very upset 倒胃口的；非常讨厌的；令人厌烦的 ➲ MORE LIKE THIS 10, page R26

guv /ɡʌv/ *exclamation* (*BrE, informal*) used by a man to address another man who is a customer, etc., meaning 'sir'（男人对男顾客等的称呼）先生

guv'nor /ˈɡʌvnə(r)/ *noun* (*BrE, informal*) (often used as a way of addressing sb 常用作称呼) a man who is in a position of authority, for example your employer 老板；头儿：*Do you want me to ask the guv'nor about it?* 你想让我就这事问问老板吗？➲ SEE ALSO GOVERNOR

guy /ɡaɪ/ *noun* **1** [C] (*informal*) a man 男人；小伙子；家伙：*a big/nice/tough guy* 大个子男人；好小伙子；硬汉 ◇ *a Dutch guy* 荷兰男人 ◇ *At the end of the film the bad guy gets shot.* 这坏蛋在影片结尾时被击毙。➲ SEE ALSO FALL GUY, WISE GUY **2 guys** [pl.] (*informal, especially NAmE*) a group of people of either sex 一群男人（或女人）；伙计们；兄弟（或姐妹）们：*Come on, you guys, let's get going!* 快点，伙计们，咱们走吧！ **3** [C] (in Britain) a model of a man dressed in old clothes that is burned on a BONFIRE on 5 November during the celebrations for Bonfire Night 盖伊模拟像（英国每年 11 月 5 日庆祝篝火之夜焚烧的身着古装的人体模型） **4** (*also* **ˈguy rope**) [C] a rope used to keep a pole or tent in a vertical position（立杆子或架帐篷用的）支索，牵索，拉索 IDM SEE MR

Guy Fawkes night /ˈɡaɪ fɔːks naɪt/ *noun* [U, C] Bonfire Night 篝火之夜

guz·zle /ˈɡʌzl/ *verb* [T, I] ~ (**sth**) (*informal, usually disapproving*) to drink sth quickly and in large amounts. In British English it also means to eat food quickly and in large amounts. 狂饮；猛喝；暴饮；（英式英语）狼吞虎咽：*The kids seem to be guzzling soft drinks all day.* 孩子们似乎整天都在猛喝汽水。◇ (*figurative*) *My car guzzles fuel.* 我的汽车很耗油。

guz·zler /ˈɡʌzlə(r)/ *noun* (*informal, especially NAmE*) = GAS GUZZLER

gybe (*especially BrE*) (*NAmE usually* **jibe**) /dʒaɪb/ *verb, noun*

■ *verb* [I] to change direction when sailing with the wind behind you, by swinging the sail from one side of the boat to the other（驾船时）移帆转向；顺风转向

■ *noun* an act of gybing 移帆转向；顺风转向

gym /dʒɪm/ *noun* (*informal*) **1** (*also formal* **gym·na·sium**) [C] a room or hall with equipment for doing physical exercise, for example in a school 健身房；体育馆：*to play basketball in the gym* 在体育馆打篮球 ◇ *The school has recently built a new gym.* 学校最近新建了一个体育馆。 **2** [U] physical exercises done in a gym, especially at school（尤指学校的）体育活动，健身：*I don't enjoy gym.* 我不喜欢做健身锻炼。◇ *gym shoes* 运动鞋 **3** [C] = HEALTH CLUB：*I just joined a gym.* 我刚加入了健身俱乐部。◇ *I work out at the gym most days.* 我多数日子都在健身俱乐部锻炼身体。➲ WORDFINDER NOTE AT FIT ➲ COLLOCATIONS AT DIET

gym·khana /dʒɪmˈkɑːnə/ *noun* (*BrE*) **1** an event in which people riding horses take part in various competitions 赛马会；马术比赛 **2** (*IndE*) a public place with facilities for sports 体育场；运动场

gym·na·sium /dʒɪmˈneɪziəm/ *noun* (*pl.* **gym·na·siums** or **gym·na·sia** /-ziə/) (*formal*) = GYM (1)

gym·nast /ˈdʒɪmnæst/ *noun* a person who performs gymnastics, especially in a competition 体操运动员

gym·nas·tics /dʒɪmˈnæstɪks/ *noun* [U] physical exercises that develop and show the body's strength and ability to move and bend easily, often done as a sport in competitions 体操；体操训练：*a gymnastics competition* 体操比赛 ◇ (*figurative*) ***mental/verbal gymnastics*** (= quick or clever thinking or use of words) 智力 / 表达能力训练 ➲ VISUAL VOCAB PAGE V52 ➲ MORE LIKE THIS 29, page R28 ▶ **gym·nas·tic** *adj.* [only before noun]

ˈgym shoe *noun* (*BrE also* **plim·soll**, **pump**) a light simple sports shoe made of CANVAS (= strong cotton cloth) with a rubber SOLE 橡胶底帆布鞋；体操鞋

gym·slip /ˈdʒɪmslɪp/ *noun* (*BrE*) a dress without sleeves worn over a shirt as a school uniform for girls, especially in the past（尤指旧时女生穿的）无袖连衣裙，无袖制服

gy·nae·colo·gist (*BrE*) (*NAmE* **gyne·colo·gist**) /ˌɡaɪnəˈkɒlədʒɪst; *NAmE* -ˈkɑːl-/ *noun* a doctor who studies and treats the medical conditions and diseases of women, especially those connected with sexual REPRODUCTION 妇科医生；妇科学家 ➲ WORDFINDER NOTE AT SPECIALIST

gy·nae·col·ogy (*BrE*) (*NAmE* **gyne·cology**) /ˌɡaɪnəˈkɒlədʒi; *NAmE* -ˈkɑːl-/ *noun* [U] the scientific study and treatment of the medical conditions and diseases of women, especially those connected with sexual REPRODUCTION 妇科学；妇科 ▶ **gy·nae·co·logic·al** (*BrE*) (*NAmE* **gyne-**) /ˌɡaɪnəkəˈlɒdʒɪkl; *NAmE* -ˈlɑːdʒ-/ *adj.*：*a gynaecological examination* 妇科检查

gyp /dʒɪp/ *noun, verb*

■ *noun* [sing.] (*NAmE, informal*) an act of charging too much money for sth 敲竹杠：*That meal was a real gyp.* 那顿饭真是敲竹杠。

IDM **give sb ˈgyp** (*BrE, informal*) to cause sb a lot of pain 折磨某人；使某人很痛苦：*My back's been giving me gyp lately.* 最近我的后背疼得要命。

■ *verb* (**-pp-**) ~ **sb** (*especially NAmE*) to cheat or trick sb, especially by taking their money 敲诈；诈取；诈骗

gyp·sum /ˈdʒɪpsəm/ *noun* [U] a soft white mineral like CHALK that is found naturally and is used in making PLASTER OF PARIS 石膏

Gypsy (*also* **Gipsy**) /ˈdʒɪpsi/ *noun* (*pl.* **-ies**) (*sometimes offensive*) **1** a member of a race of people, originally from Asia, who traditionally travel around and live in CARAVANS. Many people prefer to use the name Roma or Romani. 吉卜赛人（许多人更喜欢用 Roma 或 Romani 这个名称） **2** = TRAVELLER (2)

gyr·ate /dʒaɪˈreɪt; *NAmE* ˈdʒaɪreɪt/ *verb* [I, T] to move around in circles; to make sth, especially a part of your body, move around 旋转；使（身体部位）旋转，转动：*They began gyrating to the music.* 他们随着音乐的节奏旋转起来。◇ *The leaves gyrated slowly to the ground.* 树叶旋转着慢慢飘落到地上。◇ **~ sth** *As the lead singer gyrated his hips, the crowd screamed wildly.* 当主唱歌手扭摆臀部时，观众发狂似的尖叫起来。 ▶ **gyr·ation** /dʒaɪˈreɪʃn/ *noun* [C, usually pl., U]

gyro·scope /ˈdʒaɪrəskəʊp; *NAmE* -skoʊp/ (*also informal* **gyro** /ˈdʒaɪrəʊ; *NAmE* -roʊ/) *noun* a device consisting of a wheel that spins rapidly inside a frame and does not change position when the frame is moved. Gyroscopes are often used to keep ships and aircraft steady. 陀螺仪；回转仪 ▶ **gyro·scop·ic** /ˌdʒaɪrəˈskɒpɪk; *NAmE* -ˈskɑːpɪk/ *adj.*

G

H (*also* **h**) /eɪtʃ/ *noun, abbr.*

■ ***noun*** [C, U] (*pl.* **Hs, H's, h's** /ˈeɪtʃɪz/) the 8th letter of the English alphabet 英语字母表的第 8 个字母：*'Hat' begins with (an) H/'H'.* * hat 一词以字母 h 开头。 ➲ COMPARE AITCH ➲ SEE ALSO H-BOMB

■ ***abbr.*** (in writing 书写形式) HENRY 亨（利）（电感单位）

ha¹ /hɑː/ *exclamation* **1** (*also* **hah**) the sound that people make when they are surprised or pleased, or when they have discovered sth （惊奇、高兴或有所发现时用）哈：*Ha! It serves you right!* 哈！你活该！◇ *Ha! I knew he was hiding something.* 哈！我就知道他在隐瞒什么。 **2** (*also* **ha! ha!**) the word for the sound that people make when they laugh （笑声）哈 **3** (*also* **ha! ha!**) (*informal, ironic*) used to show that you do not think that sth is funny （认为某事并不可笑）：*Ha! Ha! Very funny! Now give me back my shoes.* 哈！哈！真有意思！把我的鞋还给我。 ➲ MORE LIKE THIS 2, page R25

ha² *abbr.* (in writing 书写形式) HECTARE 公顷

haar /hɑː(r)/ *noun* [sing.] a cold sea FOG on the east coast of England or Scotland 哈雾（英格兰或苏格兰东海岸的冷海雾）

hab·eas cor·pus /ˌheɪbiəs ˈkɔːpəs; *NAmE* ˈkɔːrpəs/ *noun* [U] (*from Latin, law* 律) a law that states that a person who has been arrested should not be kept in prison longer than a particular period of time unless a judge in court has decided that it is right 人身保护法（对被拘禁者的羁押期予以限制）

hab·er·dash·er /ˈhæbədæʃə(r); *NAmE* ˈhæbərd-/ *noun* **1** (*old-fashioned, BrE*) a person who owns or works in a shop/store selling small articles for sewing, for example, needles, pins, cotton and buttons 缝纫用品店店主（或店员） **2** **hab·er·dash·er's** (*pl.* **hab·er·dash·ers**) a shop/store that sells these things 缝纫用品店 **3** (*NAmE*) a person who owns, manages or works in a shop/store that makes and sells men's clothes 男装店店主（或店员等）

hab·er·dash·ery /ˌhæbəˈdæʃəri; *NAmE* ˈhæbərd-/ *noun* (*pl.* **-ies**) **1** [U] (*old-fashioned, BrE*) small articles for sewing, for example needles, pins, cotton and buttons 缝纫用品 **2** [U] (*old-fashioned, NAmE*) men's clothes 男装 **3** [C] a shop/store or part of a shop/store where haberdashery is sold 缝纫用品店（或柜台）；男装店（或柜台）

habit 🔑 /ˈhæbɪt/ *noun* **1** 🔑 [C] a thing that you do often and almost without thinking, especially sth that is hard to stop doing 习惯：*You need to change your eating habits.* 你得改变你的饮食习惯。◇ ***good/bad habits*** 好习惯；恶习 ◇ *He has the irritating habit of biting his nails.* 他有咬指甲的讨厌习惯。◇ *It's all right to borrow money occasionally, but don't* ***let it become a habit.*** 偶尔借点钱倒没关系，但不要养成习惯。◇ *I'd prefer you not to* ***make a habit*** *of it.* 我希望你不要习以为常。◇ *I'm not* ***in the habit of*** *letting strangers into my apartment.* 我不习惯让陌生人进我家。◇ *I've* ***got into the habit of*** *turning on the TV as soon as I get home.* 我习惯了一回家就打开电视。◇ *I'm trying to* ***break the habit*** *of staying up too late.* 我正试图改掉熬夜的习惯。 ➲ WORDFINDER NOTE AT BEHAVIOUR **2** 🔑 [U] usual behaviour 惯常行为；习性：*I only do it* ***out of habit.*** 我这么做只是出于习惯。◇ *I'm a* ***creature of habit*** (= I have a fixed and regular way of doing things). 我这人做事总是凭习惯。 **3** [C] (*informal*) a strong need to keep using drugs, alcohol or cigarettes regularly （吸毒、喝酒、抽烟的）瘾：*He began to finance his habit through burglary.* 他开始靠盗窃来获取可满足他毒瘾的钱。◇ *She's tried to give up smoking but just can't* ***kick the habit.*** 她戒过烟，但就是戒不掉。◇ *a 50-a-day habit* 每天抽 50 根烟的烟瘾 **4** [C] a long piece of clothing worn by a MONK or NUN （修道士或修女穿的）长袍；道袍；道服 **IDM** SEE FORCE *n.*

hab·it·able /ˈhæbɪtəbl/ *adj.* suitable for people to live in 适合居住的：*The house should be habitable by the new year.* 房子到新年时应该就可以住进去了。 **OPP** **uninhabitable**

habi·tat /ˈhæbɪtæt/ *noun* [C, U] the place where a particular type of animal or plant is normally found （动植物的）生活环境，栖息地：*The panda's* ***natural habitat*** *is the bamboo forest.* 大熊猫的天然栖息地是竹林。◇ *the destruction of wildlife habitat* 野生动植物生存环境的破坏 ➲ COLLOCATIONS AT ENVIRONMENT

habi·ta·tion /ˌhæbɪˈteɪʃn/ *noun* **1** [U] the act of living in a place 居住：*They looked around for any signs of habitation.* 他们四处寻找有人居住的迹象。◇ *The houses were* ***unfit for human habitation*** (= not clean or safe enough for people to live in). 那些房子不适合人居住。 **2** [C] (*formal*) a place where people live 住处；住所；聚居地：*The road serves the scattered habitations along the coast.* 这条路连接着海岸线上分散各处的聚居地。

ˈhabit-forming *adj.* a **habit-forming** activity or drug is one that makes you want to continue doing it or taking it 使成习惯的；使上瘾的

ha·bit·ual /həˈbɪtʃuəl/ *adj.* **1** [only before noun] usual or typical of sb/sth 惯常的；典型的：*They waited for his habitual response.* 他们等待着他的一贯反应。◇ (*formal*) *a person's place of habitual residence* 某人通常居住的地方 **2** (of an action 行为) done, often in a way that is annoying or difficult to stop 讨厌的；上瘾的：*habitual complaining* 没完没了的抱怨 ◇ *the habitual use of heroin* 吸食海洛因上瘾 **3** [only before noun] (of a person 人) doing sth that has become a habit and is therefore difficult to stop 习惯性的；积习很深的：***a habitual criminal/drinker/liar, etc.*** 惯犯、嗜酒成性者、习以为常的撒谎者等 **HELP** Some speakers do not pronounce the 'h' at the beginning of **habitual** and use 'an' instead of 'a' before it. This now sounds old-fashioned. 有人说 habitual 时不发 h 音，前面用 an 而不用 a，现在听起来过时了。 ▸ **ha·bit·ual·ly** /-tʃuəli/ *adv.*：*the dark glasses he habitually wore* 他惯常戴的墨镜

ha·bitu·ated /həˈbɪtʃueɪtɪd/ *adj.* ~ (**to sth**) (*formal*) familiar with sth because you have done it or experienced it often 熟悉（某事）的；习惯（于某事）的 **SYN** **accustomed**

ha·bi·tué /hæˈbɪtʃueɪ; æˈbɪ-/ *noun* (*from French, formal*) a person who goes regularly to a particular place or event 常客 **SYN** **regular**：*a(n) habitué of upmarket clubs* 高级俱乐部的常客

ha·ci·enda /ˌhæsiˈendə/ *noun* a large farm in a Spanish-speaking country （讲西班牙语国家的）大庄园，大农场

hack /hæk/ *verb, noun*

■ ***verb*** **1** [T, I] to cut sb/sth with rough, heavy blows 砍；劈：**~ sb/sth + adv./prep.** *I hacked the dead branches off.* 我把枯树枝砍掉了。◇ *They were hacked to death as they tried to escape.* 他们企图逃走时被砍死了。◇ *We had to* ***hack our way*** *through the jungle.* 我们不得不在丛林中辟路穿行。◇ **+ adv./prep.** *We hacked away at the bushes.* 我们劈砍着灌木丛。 **2** [T] **~ sb/sth + adv./prep.** to kick sth roughly or without control 猛踢：*He hacked the ball away.* 他把球一脚踢开。 **3** (*computing* 计) [I, T] to secretly find a way of looking at and/or changing information on sb else's computer system without permission 非法侵入（他人的计算机系统）：**~ into sth** *He hacked into the bank's computer.* 他侵入了这家银行的计算机。◇ **~ sth** *They had hacked secret data.* 他们窃取了保密数据。 **4** (*computing* 计) **~ sth** to work together informally and often quickly with other people to create a program using different technologies （多人合作用不同技术）快速编程 **5** [T] **can/can't hack it** (*informal*) to be able/not able to manage in a particular situation 能/不能应付（某情形）：*Lots of people leave this job because they can't hack it.* 很多人由于应付不了这项工作而放弃了。 **6** [I] (*usually* **go hacking**) (*especially BrE*) to ride a horse for pleasure 骑马消遣 **7** [I] (*NAmE, informal*) to drive a taxi 开出租车

■ *noun* **1** (*disapproving*) a writer, especially of newspaper articles, who does a lot of low quality work and does not get paid much 雇佣文人（尤指廉价受雇撰写报纸庸俗文章者） **2** (*disapproving*) a person who does the hard and often boring work for an organization, especially a politician （受雇于组织，尤其是政客）从事艰苦乏味工作的人；杂务人员： *a party hack* 政党杂务人员 **3** a horse for ordinary riding or one that can be hired 供人骑的马；可出租的马 **4** (*NAmE, informal*) a taxi 出租车 **5** an act of hitting sth, especially with a cutting tool 砍；劈 **6** a piece of computer CODE *n.* (3) that provides a quick solution to a problem by adding to the official function of a program （解决计算机程序问题的）快速修正方法

ˌhacked ˈoff *adj.* [not before noun] (*BrE, informal*) extremely annoyed 极其恼怒 **SYN** **fed up**: *I'm really hacked off.* 我真是很恼火。

hack·er /ˈhækə(r)/ *noun* a person who secretly finds a way of looking at and/or changing information on sb else's computer system without permission 黑客（秘密窥视或改变他人计算机系统信息）

hack·ing /ˈhækɪŋ/ *noun* [U] the action of secretly finding a way of looking at and/or changing information on sb else's computer system without permission 黑客行为： *The government tax website is vulnerable to hacking, putting taxpayers' information at risk.* 政府税收网站容易遭到黑客入侵，使纳税人的信息受到威胁。 ➲ SEE ALSO PHONE HACKING

ˌhacking ˈcough *noun* [sing.] a dry painful cough that is repeated often 频繁的干咳

ˈhacking jacket *noun* a short jacket worn for horse riding 骑马短上装；赛马服

hackles /ˈhæklz/ *noun* [pl.] the hairs on the back of the neck of a dog, cat, etc. that rise when the animal is afraid or angry （狗、猫等害怕或发怒时竖起的）后颈毛
IDM **make sb's ˈhackles rise | raise sb's ˈhackles** to make sb angry 激怒某人 **sb's ˈhackles rise** to become angry 发火；发怒： *Ben felt his hackles rise as the speaker continued.* 随着那人不断地讲下去，本不禁怒火中烧。

hack·ney car·riage /ˈhækni kærɪdʒ/ (*also* **ˈhack·ney cab**) *noun* (*BrE*) a word used in official language for a taxi. In the past hackney carriages were carriages pulled by horses that were used as taxis. 出租车（正式用语，源于旧时的出租马车）

hack·neyed /ˈhæknid/ *adj.* used too often and therefore boring 陈腐的 **SYN** **clichéd**: *a hackneyed phrase/subject* 陈词滥调；老生常谈的话题

hack·saw /ˈhæksɔː/ *noun* a tool with a narrow blade in a frame, used for cutting metal 钢锯，弓锯（用以切割金属） ➲ VISUAL VOCAB PAGE V21

hacky /ˈhæki/ *adj.* (*informal*) **1** not new or interesting; used too often and therefore boring 陈旧无趣的；无聊的；老一套的： *a hacky joke* 无聊的玩笑 **2** (of a piece of computer code) that provides a quick but often badly designed solution to a problem, allowing the user to continue working until a better solution can be provided （计算机代码）供应急之用的，权宜的（往往设计粗陋）： *It's just a hacky workaround.* 这只是应急的权宜办法。

had /həd; əd; *strong form* hæd/ ➲ HAVE *v.*

had·dock /ˈhædək/ *noun* (*pl.* **had·dock**) [C, U] a sea fish like a COD but smaller, with white flesh that is used for food 黑线鳕（肉白色，可食用）： *smoked haddock* 熏黑线鳕

Hades /ˈheɪdiːz/ *noun* [U] (in ancient Greek stories 古希腊神话) the land of the dead 阴间；冥府 **SYN** **hell**

Had·ith /hæˈdiːθ/ *noun* (*pl.* **Had·ith** or **Had·iths**) (in Islam 伊斯兰教) **1** [sing.] a text containing things said by Muhammad and descriptions of his daily life, used by Muslims as a spiritual guide 圣训，哈底斯（穆罕默德言行录） **2** [C] one of the things said by Muhammad, recorded in this text （圣训中的）穆罕默德训词

hadn't /ˈhædnt/ *short form* had not

haem·atite (*BrE*) (*NAmE* **hema·tite**) /ˈhiːmətaɪt/ *noun* [U] (*geology* 地) a dark red rock from which iron is obtained 赤铁矿

haema·tol·ogy (*BrE*) (*NAmE* **hema·tol·ogy**) /ˌhiːməˈtɒlədʒi; *NAmE* -ˈtɑːl-/ *noun* [U] the scientific study of the blood and its diseases 血液学 ► **haem·ato·logic·al** (*BrE*) (*NAmE* **hema·to·logic·al**) /ˌhiːmətəˈlɒdʒɪkl; *NAmE* -ˈlɑːdʒ-/ *adj.* **haema·tolo·gist** (*BrE*) (*NAmE* **hem-**) /ˌhiːməˈtɒlədʒɪst; *NAmE* -ˈtɑːl-/ *noun*

haema·toma (*BrE*) (*NAmE* **hema·toma**) /ˌhiːməˈtəʊmə; *NAmE* -ˈtoʊmə/ *noun* (*medical* 医) a swollen area on the body consisting of blood that has become thick 血肿

haemo- (*BrE*) (*NAmE* **hemo-**) /ˈhiːməʊ; *NAmE* -moʊ/ *combining form* (in nouns and adjectives 构成名词和形容词) connected with blood （有关）血液的： *haemophilia* 血友病

haemo·glo·bin (*BrE*) (*NAmE* **hemo·glo·bin**) /ˌhiːməˈɡləʊbɪn; *NAmE* -ˈɡloʊ-/ *noun* [U] a red substance in the blood that carries OXYGEN and contains iron 血红蛋白

haemo·philia (*BrE*) (*NAmE* **hemo·philia**) /ˌhiːməˈfɪliə/ *noun* [U] a medical condition that causes severe loss of blood from even a slight injury because the blood fails to CLOT normally. It usually affects only men although it can be passed on by women. 血友病

haemo·phil·iac (*BrE*) (*NAmE* **hemo·phil·iac**) /ˌhiːməˈfɪliæk/ *noun* a person who suffers from haemophilia 血友病患者

haem·or·rhage (*BrE*) (*NAmE* **hem·or·rhage**) /ˈhemərɪdʒ/ *noun, verb*
■ **noun** **1** [C, U] a medical condition in which there is severe loss of blood from inside a person's body 体内（大）出血： *a massive **brain/cerebral haemorrhage*** 重度脑溢血 ◇ *He was checked for any signs of haemorrhage.* 他接受检查，以确定是否有出血迹象。 **2** [C, usually sing.] ~ (**of sb/sth**) a serious loss of people, money, etc. from a country, a group or an organization （人、资金等的）大量流失： *Poor working conditions have led to a steady haemorrhage of qualified teachers from our schools.* 工作条件欠佳导致各校大量合格教师不断流失。
■ *verb* **1** [I] to lose blood heavily, especially from the inside of the body; to have a haemorrhage （尤指体内）大出血 **2** [T] ~ **sb/sth** to lose money or people in large amounts at a fast rate 大量快速流失（资金、人等）

haem·or·rhagic (*BrE*) (*NAmE* **hem·or·rhagic**) /ˌheməˈrædʒɪk/ *adj.* (*medical* 医) happening with or caused by haemorrhage 体内出血的；出血引起的： *a haemorrhagic fever* 出血热

haem·or·rhoids (*BrE*) (*NAmE* **hem·or·rhoids**) /ˈhemərɔɪdz/ *noun* [pl.] (*medical* 医) painful swollen VEINS at or near the ANUS 痔；痔疮 **SYN** **piles**

haf·nium /ˈhæfniəm/ *noun* [U] (*symb.* **Hf**) a RADIOACTIVE chemical element. Hafnium is a hard silver-grey metal. 铪（放射性化学元素）

haft /hɑːft; *NAmE* hæft/ *noun* the handle of a knife or weapon （刀或武器的）柄

hag /hæɡ/ *noun* (*offensive*) an ugly and/or unpleasant old woman 丑陋（或讨厌）的老女人 ➲ SEE ALSO FAG HAG

hag·gard /ˈhæɡəd; *NAmE* -ɡərd/ *adj.* looking very tired because of illness, worry or lack of sleep （由于生病、焦虑或睡眠不足）憔悴的，疲惫的 **SYN** **drawn**

hag·gis /ˈhæɡɪs/ *noun* [C, U] a Scottish dish that looks like a large round SAUSAGE made from the heart, lungs and LIVER of a sheep that are finely chopped, mixed with OATS, HERBS, etc. and boiled in a bag that is traditionally made from part of a sheep's stomach （苏格兰）羊杂碎肚（用剁碎的羊的心、肺、肝和燕麦、香料等调成馅，通常包在羊肚中煮成）

H

hag·gle /ˈhæɡl/ *verb* [I] **~ (with sb) (over sth)** to argue with sb in order to reach an agreement, especially about the price of sth 争论；（尤指）讲价：*I left him in the market haggling over the price of a shirt.* 我扔下他自己在市场上就一件衬衫讨价还价。

hagi·og·raph·er /ˌhæɡiˈɒɡrəfə(r); *NAmE* -ˈɑːɡ-/ *noun* (*formal*) **1** a person who writes the life story of a SAINT 圣贤传记作者；圣徒传记作者 **2** a person who writes about another person's life in a way that praises them too much, and does not criticize them 偶像化传记的作者

hagi·og·raphy /ˌhæɡiˈɒɡrəfi; *NAmE* -ˈɑːɡ-/ *noun* (*pl.* **-ies**) [C, U] (*formal*) a book about the life of a person that praises them too much; this style of writing 吹捧性的传记；偶像化（或理想化）传记

H

hah = HA¹ (1)

haiku /ˈhaɪkuː/ *noun* (*pl.* **haiku** or **haikus**) (*from Japanese*) a poem with three lines and usually 17 syllables, written in a style that is traditional in Japan 俳句（日本传统诗体，三行为一首，通常有 17 个音节）

hail /heɪl/ *verb, noun*

■ ***verb*** **1** [T, usually passive] to describe sb/sth as being very good or special, especially in newspapers, etc. 赞扬（或称颂）…为（尤用于报章等）：**~ sb/sth as sth** *The conference was hailed as a great success.* 会议被称颂为一次巨大的成功。◇ **~ sb/sth + noun** *Teenager Matt Brown is being hailed a hero for saving a young child from drowning.* 因救起一名溺水儿童，少年马特·布朗被誉为英雄。**2** [T] **~ sth** to signal to a taxi or a bus, in order to get the driver to stop 招手叫（出租车或公共汽车）：*to hail a taxi/cab* 打手势叫出租车 **3** [T] **~ sb** (*literary*) to call to sb in order to say hello to them or attract their attention 跟…打招呼；向…喊：*A voice hailed us from the other side of the street.* 街对面有个声音招呼我们。**4** [I] when **it hails**, small balls of ice fall like rain from the sky 下雹：*It's hailing!* 正下着冰雹！

PHR V **ˈhail from…** (*formal*) to come from or have been born in a particular place 来自；出生于：*His father hailed from Italy.* 他父亲出生于意大利。

■ ***noun*** **1** [U] small balls of ice that fall like rain 雹；冰雹：*We drove through hail and snow.* 我们顶着冰雹和大雪开车。➲ WORDFINDER NOTE AT SNOW **2** [sing.] **a ~ of sth** a large number or amount of sth that is aimed at sb in order to harm them 一阵像冰雹般袭来的事物；雹子般的一阵：*a hail of arrows/bullets* 一阵乱箭 / 弹雨 ◇ *a hail of abuse* 一顿痛骂

Hail Mary /ˌheɪl ˈmeəri; *NAmE* ˈmeri/ *noun* (*pl.* **Hail Marys**) a Roman Catholic prayer to Mary, the mother of Jesus 万福马利亚（天主教祈祷文）

hail·stone /ˈheɪlstəʊn; *NAmE* -stoʊn/ *noun* [usually pl.] a small ball of ice that falls like rain 雹块；雹子

hail·storm /ˈheɪlstɔːm; *NAmE* -stɔːrm/ *noun* a storm during which hail falls from the sky 雹暴

hair 🔑 /heə(r); *NAmE* her/ *noun* **1** 🔑 [U, C] the substance that looks like a mass of fine threads growing especially on the head; one of these threads growing on the body of people and some animals 毛发；（尤指）头发：*fair/dark hair* 浅色头发；黑发 ◇ *straight/curly/wavy hair* 直发；鬈发；波浪发 ◇ *to comb/brush your hair* 梳头 ◇ (*informal*) *I'll be down in a minute. I'm doing* (= brushing, arranging, etc.) *my hair.* 我马上就下来。我在梳头呢。◇ *I'm having my hair cut this afternoon.* 我今天下午要去理发。◇ *body/facial/pubic hair* 体毛；脸毛；阴毛 ◇ *There's a hair in my soup.* 我的汤里有根毛。◇ *The rug was covered with cat hairs.* 地毯上净是猫毛。➲ WORDFINDER NOTE AT BLONDE ➲ COLLOCATIONS AT FASHION, PHYSICAL ➲ VISUAL VOCAB PAGES V64, V65 ➲ SEE ALSO CAMEL HAIR, HORSEHAIR **2 -haired** (in adjectives 构成形容词) having the type of hair mentioned 有…毛发（或头发）的：*dark-haired* 黑发的 ◇ *long-haired* 长发的 ➲ MORE LIKE THIS 8, page R25 **3** [C] a thing that looks like a fine thread growing on the leaves and STEMS of some plants（植物叶、茎上的）茸毛

IDM **get in sb's ˈhair** (*informal*) to annoy sb by always being near them, asking them questions, etc. 烦扰某人；缠着（提问等） **the hair of the ˈdog (that ˈbit you)** (*informal*) alcohol that you drink in order to make you feel better when you have drunk too much alcohol the night before 用于解宿醉的酒 **keep your ˈhair on** (*BrE, informal*) used to tell sb to stop shouting and become calm when they are angry 冷静下来，别发脾气 **let your ˈhair down** (*informal*) to relax and enjoy yourself, especially in a lively way 放松；轻松一下 **make sb's ˈhair stand on end** to shock or frighten sb 惊吓某人；使某人毛骨悚然：*a chilling tale that will make your hair stand on end* 令人毛骨悚然的故事 **not harm/touch a hair of sb's ˈhead** to not hurt sb physically in any way 不动某人一根头发；丝毫不伤害某人 **not have a ˈhair out of place** (of a person 人) to look extremely clean and neat 显得非常整洁 **not turn a ˈhair** to show no emotion when sth surprising, shocking, etc. happens 面不改色；镇定自若 ➲ MORE AT HANG *v.*, HIDE *n.*, SPLIT *v.*, TEAR¹ *v.*

hair·band /ˈheəbænd; *NAmE* ˈherb-/ *noun* a strip of cloth or curved plastic worn by women in their hair, that fits closely over the top of the head and behind the ears 束发带；发箍

hair·brush /ˈheəbrʌʃ; *NAmE* ˈherb-/ *noun* a brush for making the hair tidy or smooth 发刷；毛刷 ➲ VISUAL VOCAB PAGE V25

hair·cut /ˈheəkʌt; *NAmE* ˈherkʌt/ *noun* **1** the act of sb cutting your hair 理发：*You need a haircut.* 你该理发了。◇ *I see you've had a haircut.* 我看得出你理发了。**2** the style in which sb's hair is cut 发型；发式：*What do you think of my new haircut?* 你觉得我的新发型怎么样？◇ *a trendy haircut* 流行发式 ➲ COLLOCATIONS AT FASHION **3** [sing.] a reduction in an amount of money or in the value of an ASSET (2) 资金量减少；资产价值下降：*The Prime Minister says he'd like to see banks take a bigger haircut from bad loans.* 首相称他希望看到银行以更大力度削减不良贷款。

hair·do /ˈheəduː; *NAmE* ˈherduː/ *noun* (*pl.* **-os**) (*old-fashioned, informal*) the style in which a woman's hair is arranged（女子）发式，发型 SYN **hairstyle**

hair·dress·er 🔑 /ˈheədresə(r); *NAmE* ˈherd-/ *noun* **1** 🔑 a person whose job is to cut, wash and shape hair 理发师；美发师；发型师 **2** 🔑 **hairdresser's** (*pl.* **hair·dress·ers**) a place where you can get your hair cut, washed and shaped 理发店；美发店 ➲ MORE LIKE THIS 34, page R29 ➲ COMPARE BARBER ▶ **hair·dress·ing** *noun* [U]

hair·dryer (*also* **hair·drier**) /ˈheədraɪə(r); *NAmE* ˈherd-/ *noun* a small machine used for drying your hair by blowing hot air over it 吹风机

hair·grip /ˈheəɡrɪp; *NAmE* ˈherɡ-/ (*also* **grip, ˈkirby grip**) (*all BrE*) (*NAmE* **ˈbobby pin**) *noun* a small thin piece of metal or plastic folded in the middle, used by women for holding their hair in place 发夹 ➲ COMPARE HAIRPIN (1)

hair·less /ˈheələs; *NAmE* ˈherləs/ *adj.* without hair 无发的；无毛的；秃的

hair·line /ˈheəlaɪn; *NAmE* ˈherl-/ *noun* **1** the edge of a person's hair, especially at the front（尤指前额的）发际线：*a receding hairline* 渐秃的前额 **2** (often used as an adjective 常用作形容词) a very thin crack or line 很细的裂纹；极细的线：*a hairline crack/fracture* 细小的裂纹 / 裂缝

hair·net /ˈheənet; *NAmE* ˈhernet/ *noun* a net worn over the hair to keep it in place 发网

hair·piece /ˈheəpiːs; *NAmE* ˈherp-/ *noun* a piece of false hair worn to make your own hair look longer or thicker（使头发看上去更长或更浓密的）假发

hair·pin /ˈheəpɪn; *NAmE* ˈherpɪn/ *noun* **1** a small thin piece of wire that is folded in the middle, used by women for holding their hair in place 发夹 ➲ COMPARE HAIRGRIP **2** = HAIRPIN BEND

ˌhairpin ˈbend (*BrE*) (*NAmE* **ˌhairpin ˈcurve**, **ˌhairpin ˈturn**) (*also* **hair·pin** *BrE*, *NAmE*) *noun* a very sharp bend in a road, especially a mountain road （尤指山路的）急转弯

ˈhair-raising *adj.* extremely frightening but often exciting 令人寒毛直竖的；惊险的： *a* ***hair-raising adventure/story*** 紧张刺激的历险 / 故事 ➲ MORE LIKE THIS 10, page R26

ˈhair's breadth *noun* [sing.] a very small amount or distance 细微；极短的距离；毫厘之差： *We won by a hair's breadth.* 我们险胜对手。◇ *They were within a hair's breadth of being killed.* 他们险些丧命。

ˌhair ˈshirt *noun* a shirt made of rough cloth containing hair, worn in the past by people who wished to punish themselves for religious reasons 苦衣，刚毛衬衫（旧时苦修者所穿）

hair·slide /ˈheəslaɪd; *NAmE* ˈhers-/ (*also* **slide**) (*both BrE*) (*NAmE* **bar·rette**) *noun* a small decorative piece of metal or plastic used by women for holding their hair in place （装饰性）小发夹

ˈhair-splitting *noun* [U] (*disapproving*) the act of giving too much importance to small and unimportant differences in an argument 过于强调微不足道的分歧；吹毛求疵 SYN **quibble** IDM SEE SPLIT *v.*

hair·spray /ˈheəspreɪ; *NAmE* ˈhers-/ *noun* [U, C] a substance sprayed onto the hair to hold it in a particular style 发胶；定型剂

ˈhair straighteners (*also* **straighteners**) *noun* [pl.] an electrical tool with two metal or CERAMIC parts that you heat and use to make your hair straight 直发器；直发夹

hair·style /ˈheəstaɪl; *NAmE* ˈhers-/ *noun* the style in which sb's hair is cut or arranged 发型；发式 ➲ COLLOCATIONS AT FASHION

hair·styl·ist /ˈheəstaɪlɪst; *NAmE* ˈhers-/ *noun* a person whose job is to cut, wash and shape hair 理发师；美发师；发型师

hairy /ˈheəri; *NAmE* ˈheri/ *adj.* (**hair·ier**, **hairi·est**) **1** covered with a lot of hair 多毛的： *a* ***hairy chest/monster*** 多毛的胸脯；长满毛的怪兽 ◇ *plants with hairy stems* 茎部有茸毛的植物 **2** (*informal*) dangerous or frightening but often exciting 惊险的；可怕（但刺激）的： *Driving on icy roads can be pretty hairy.* 在结冰的道路上开车很惊险。◇ *a hairy experience* 令人毛骨悚然的经历 ▶ **hairi·ness** *noun* [U]

hajj (*also* **haj**) /hædʒ/ *noun* (*usually* **the Hajj**) [sing.] the religious journey to Mecca that all Muslims try to make at least once in their lives （伊斯兰教徒去麦加的）朝觐

haka /ˈhɑːkə/ *noun* a traditional Maori war dance with singing. New Zealand RUGBY teams perform a version of it before games. 哈卡舞（传统毛利伴歌战舞，新西兰橄榄球队在比赛前跳这种舞）

hake /heɪk/ *noun* [C, U] (*pl.* **hake**) a large sea fish that is used for food 无须鳕（海产鱼，可食用）

ha·kim /həˈkiːm/ *noun* a doctor in India and Muslim countries who uses HERBS and other traditional ways of treating illnesses （印度和伊斯兰国家的）草药医生，郎中

Hakka /ˈhækə/ (*also* **Kejia**) *noun* [U] a form of Chinese spoken by a group of people in SE China 客家话（中国东南部的一种方言）

halal /ˈhælæl/ *adj.* **1** (of meat 肉食) from an animal that has been killed according to Muslim law 按伊斯兰教教法宰杀的： *halal meat* 伊斯兰教的合法畜肉 ◇ *a halal butcher* (= one who sells halal meat) 售卖伊斯兰教合法肉食的肉商 **2** acceptable according to Muslim religious law 符合伊斯兰教教法的 ➲ SEE ALSO HARAM

hal·berd /ˈhælbɜːd; *NAmE* -bərd/ *noun* a weapon used in the past which is a combination of a SPEAR and an AXE 戟（旧时结合长矛和斧头的武器）

hal·cyon /ˈhælsiən/ *adj.* [usually before noun] (*literary*) peaceful and happy 平安幸福的： *the halcyon days of her youth* 她年轻时幸福安宁的日子

hale /heɪl/ *adj.*

IDM **ˌhale and ˈhearty** (especially of an old person 尤指老年人) strong and healthy 健壮的；硬朗的 ➲ MORE LIKE THIS 13, page R26

half 🔑 /hɑːf; *NAmE* hæf/ *noun*, *det.*, *pron.*, *adv.*

■ ***noun*** (*pl.* **halves** /hɑːvz; *NAmE* hævz/) **1** 🔑 either of two equal parts into which sth is or can be divided 一半；半： *two and a half kilos* (= 2½) 两公斤半 ◇ *One and a half hours are allowed for the exam.* 考试时间为一个半小时。◇ *An hour and a half is allowed for the exam.* 考试时间为一个半小时。◇ *The second half of the book is more exciting.* 书的后半部分比较刺激有趣。◇ *I've divided the money* ***in half.*** 我把钱平均分成了两半。◇ *We'll need to reduce the weight* ***by half.*** 我们得把重量减轻一半。 ➲ SEE ALSO HALVE **2** 🔑 either of two periods of time into which a sports game, concert, etc. is divided （比赛、音乐会等的）半场，半局： *No goals were scored in the first half.* 上半场没有得分。 **3** = HALF BACK ➲ SEE ALSO CENTRE HALF, SCRUM HALF **4** (*BrE*, *informal*) half a pint of beer or a similar drink （啤酒等饮料的）半品脱： *Two halves of bitter, please.* 请来两杯半品脱的苦啤酒。 ➲ MORE LIKE THIS 20, page R27

IDM **and a ˈhalf** (*informal*) bigger, better, more important, etc. than usual 更大（或好、重要等）的；非同寻常的；出色的： *That was a game and a half!* 那场比赛真棒！ **do nothing/not do anything by ˈhalves** to do whatever you do completely and thoroughly 做任何事情都完全彻底；善始善终；不半途而废： *You're expecting twins? Well, you never did do anything by halves.* 你怀了对双胞胎？唔，你倒是一步到位。 **go half and ˈhalf | go ˈhalves (with sb)** to share the cost of sth equally with sb （和某人）平均分摊费用： *We go halves on all the bills.* 我们平均分摊所有的费用。 **the ˈhalf of it** used in negative sentences to say that a situation is worse or more complicated than sb thinks （用于否定句）比想象的更糟糕（或更复杂）的部分： *'It sounds very difficult.'* ***'You don't know the half of it.'*** "这事听起来很难。""你还未了解更困难的一面呢。" **how the other half ˈlives** the way of life of a different social group, especially one much richer than you 另一类人的生活方式（尤指比自己富有得多的人） **too clever, etc. by ˈhalf** (*BrE*, *informal*, *disapproving*) clever, etc. in a way that annoys you or makes you suspicious 聪明（等）过头 ➲ MORE AT MIND *n.*, SIX, TIME *n.*

■ ***det.***, ***pron.*** **1** 🔑 an amount equal to half of sth/sb 半数： *half an hour* 半小时 ◇ *Half (of) the fruit was bad.* 水果坏了一半。◇ *Half of the money was mine.* 那些钱有一半是我的。◇ *He has a half share in the company.* 他拥有该公司的一半股份。◇ *Out of 36 candidates, half passed.* * 36 名考生中有半数及格。 ➲ LANGUAGE BANK AT PROPORTION **2 ~ the time, fun, trouble, etc.** the largest part of sth 绝大部分（时间、乐趣、麻烦等）： *Half the fun of gardening is never knowing exactly what's going to come up.* 园艺的最大乐趣是谁也不知道到底会长出什么。◇ *Half the time you don't even listen to what I say.* 你大部分时间甚至没听我说的话。

IDM **half a ˌloaf is better than no ˈbread** (*saying*) you should be grateful for sth, even if it is not as good, much, etc. as you really wanted; something is better than nothing 半块面包比没有面包强；聊胜于无 **half a ˈminute, ˈsecond, etc.** (*informal*) a short time 短时间；一会儿： *Hang on. I'll be ready in half a minute.* 等一下。我马上就准备好了。 **half past ˈone, ˈtwo, etc.** 🔑 (*also BrE*, *informal* **half ˈone, ˈtwo, etc.**) 30 minutes after any hour on the clock 一点（或两点）半等

■ ***adv.*** **1** 🔑 to the extent of half 到一半程度；半： *The glass was half full.* 玻璃杯半满。 **2** 🔑 partly 部分地： *The chicken was only half cooked.* 鸡只煮了半熟。◇ *half-closed eyes* 半睁半闭的眼 ◇ *I'm half inclined to agree.* 我不十分同意。

H

IDM ˌ**half as ˌmany, ˌmuch, etc. aˈgain** (*BrE*) (*US* **half aˈgain as much**) an increase of 50% of the existing number or amount * 50% 的增长： *Spending on health is half as much again as it was in 2009.* 卫生保健方面的开销比 2009 年增加了一半。 ˌ**not ˈhalf** (*BrE, informal*) used to emphasize a statement or an opinion 很；非常： *It wasn't half good* (= it was very good). 这很好。◇ *'Was she annoyed?' 'Not half!'* (= she was extremely annoyed) "她生气了吗？""非常生气！" **not ˈhalf as | not ˈhalf such a** not nearly 远非；差得多： *He is not half such a fool as they think.* 他远不是他们以为的那么傻。 **not half ˈbad** (*informal*) (used to show surprise 表示吃惊) not bad at all; good 一点不坏；很好： *It really isn't half bad, is it?* 这的确很不错，对吗？

H

▼ **GRAMMAR POINT 语法说明**

half / whole / quarter

- **Quarter**, **half** and **whole** can all be nouns. * quarter、half 和 whole 均可作名词： *Cut the apple into quarters.* 把苹果切成四等份。◇ *Two halves make a whole.* 两个一半构成一个整体。
- **Whole** is also an adjective. * whole 亦作形容词： *I've been waiting here for a whole hour.* 我在这儿等了整整一个小时。
- **Half** is also a determiner. * half 亦作限定词： *Half (of) the work is already finished.* 工作已经完成了一半。◇ *They spent half the time looking for a parking space.* 他们花了一半的时间寻找停车位。◇ *Her house is half a mile down the road.* 她的房子在这条路上前面半英里远的地方。 Note that you do not put *a* or *the* in front of **half** when it is used in this way. 注意在此用法中 half 前面不加 a 或 the： *I waited for half an hour.* 我等了半个小时。◇ ~~*I waited for a half an hour.*~~
- **Half** can also be used as an adverb. * half 亦可作副词： *This meal is only half cooked.* 这饭只煮了个半熟。

ˌ**half-and-ˈhalf** *adj., adv., noun*
- *adj.* being half one thing and half another 两种事物各半的： *I was in that half-and-half land where you are not completely asleep nor completely awake.* 我当时半睡半醒。
- *adv.* in a way that is half one thing and half another 各半；对等地
- *noun* [U] (*NAmE*) a mixture of milk and cream that is used in tea and coffee 咖啡伴侣，茶伴侣（一种牛奶与奶油的混合物）

ˌ**half-ˈarsed** (*BrE*) (*NAmE* **ˈhalf-assed**) *adj.* (*slang*) **1** done without care or effort; not well planned 马虎的；草草了事的 **2** stupid 愚蠢的；糊涂的

ˈ**half back** (*also* **half**) (*NAmE* **ˈhalfback**) *noun* **1** [C] one of the defending players in HOCKEY or RUGBY whose position is between those who play at the front of a team and those who play at the back （曲棍球或橄榄球的）前卫 **2** (*also* **tail·back**) [C] one of the two attacking players in AMERICAN FOOTBALL whose position is behind the QUARTERBACK and beside the FULL BACKS （美式橄榄球的）半卫 **3** (*also* **tail·back**) [U] the position a half back plays at 半卫的位置；中场

ˌ**half-ˈbaked** *adj.* [usually before noun] (*informal*) not well planned or considered 计划不完善的；考虑不周的： *a half-baked idea* 不成熟的想法

ˈ**half-bath** *noun* (*NAmE*) a small room in a house, containing a WASHBASIN and a toilet 小盥洗室（内设洗脸盆和抽水马桶） SYN **powder room**

ˌ**half ˈboard** *noun* [U] (*BrE*) a type of accommodation at a hotel, etc. that includes breakfast and an evening meal 半膳宿（旅馆等包括早、晚餐的住宿） ➲ COMPARE AMERICAN PLAN, BED AND BREAKFAST (1), EUROPEAN PLAN, FULL BOARD

ˈ**half-breed** *noun* (*taboo, offensive*) a person whose parents are from different races, especially when one is white and the other is a Native American （尤指白人和美洲土著的）混血儿 ▶ ˈ**half-breed** *adj.* (*taboo, offensive*) HELP It is more acceptable to talk about 'a person **of mixed race**'. 说 a person of mixed race 比较容易让人接受。

ˈ**half-brother** *noun* a person's **half-brother** is a boy or man with either the same mother or the same father as they have 同母异父（或同父异母）的兄弟 ➲ COMPARE STEPBROTHER

ˈ**half-caste** *noun* (*taboo, offensive*) a person whose parents are from different races （不同人种的）混血儿 ▶ ˈ**half-caste** *adj.* (*taboo, offensive*) HELP It is more acceptable to talk about 'a person **of mixed race**'. 说 a person of mixed race 比较容易让人接受。

ˌ**half-ˈcentury** *noun* **1** a period of 50 years 半个世纪；50 年 **2** (in CRICKET 板球) a score of 50 * 50 分

ˌ**half-ˈcock** *noun*

IDM **go off at ˌhalf-ˈcock** (*BrE, informal*) to start before preparations are complete, so that the effect or result is not as it should be 没准备好就开始干，操之过急（因而效果或结果不好）

ˌ**half-ˈcrown** (*also* ˌ**half a ˈcrown**) *noun* an old British coin worth 2½ SHILLINGS (= now 12½ pence) * 2 先令 6 便士硬币（英国旧制硬币，相当于现在 12½ 便士）

ˌ**half ˈday** *noun* a day on which people work only in the morning or in the afternoon 半工作日（只在上午或下午工作）： *Tuesday is her half day.* 星期二她只工作半天。

ˌ**half ˈdollar** *noun* a US coin worth 50 cents （美国的）50 分硬币

ˌ**half-ˈhearted** *adj.* done without enthusiasm or effort 不热心的；不尽力的；冷淡的： *He made a **half-hearted** attempt to justify himself.* 他没有尽力证明自己有理。 ▶ ˌ**half-ˈhearted·ly** *adv.*

ˌ**half ˈhour** (*also* ˌ**half an ˈhour**) *noun* a period of 30 minutes 半小时；30 分钟： *He should arrive within the next half hour.* 他应该会在半小时内到达。◇ *a half-hour drive* 半小时的车程

ˌ**half-ˈhourly** *adj.* happening every 30 minutes 每半小时的： *a half-hourly bus service* 每半小时一班的公共汽车 ▶ ˌ**half-ˈhourly** *adv.* : *The buses run half-hourly.* 公共汽车每半小时一班。

ˈ**half-life** *noun* [C] **1** (*physics* 物) the time taken for the RADIOACTIVITY of a substance to fall to half its original value （放射性物质的）半衰期 **2** the time taken for the concentration of a substance in the body to fall to half its original value （体内物质的）半衰期

ˈ**half-light** *noun* [sing., U] a dull light in which it is difficult to see things 昏暗的光线： *in the grey half-light of dawn* 在黎明的灰暗光线中

ˌ**half ˈmast** *noun*

IDM **at ˌhalf ˈmast** (of a flag 旗) flown at the middle of the MAST as a sign of respect for a person who has just died 降半旗，下半旗（以示哀悼）： *Flags were flown at half mast on the day of his funeral.* 在他葬礼那天降了半旗。

ˌ**half ˈmeasures** *noun* [pl.] a policy or plan of action that is weak and does not do enough 不强硬的折中政策；不彻底的行动计划： *There are **no half measures** with this company.* 这家公司做事绝不会半途而废。

ˌ**half-ˈmoon** *noun* **1** the moon when only half of it can be seen from the earth; the time when this happens 半月；出现半月的时候 ➲ COMPARE FULL MOON, HARVEST MOON, NEW MOON **2** a thing that is shaped like a half-moon 半月形的东西

ˈ**half note** (*NAmE*) (*BrE* **minim**) *noun* (*music* 音) a note that lasts twice as long as a CROTCHET/QUARTER NOTE 二分音符 ➲ PICTURE AT MUSIC

ˈ**half pants** *noun* [pl.] (*IndE, informal*) short trousers/pants 短裤 SYN **shorts**

half·penny *noun* (*pl.* **-ies**) **1** (*also* **ha'penny**) /ˈheɪpni/ a British coin in use until 1971, worth half a penny. There were 480 halfpennies in a pound. 半便士硬币（1971 年前使用的英国硬币，480 半便士硬币为一英镑） **2** /ˈhɑːfpeni/ (*also* **half·pence** /ˌhɑːfpens/) a British coin in use between 1971 and 1984, worth half a penny. There were 200 halfpennies in a pound. 半便士硬币（1971 至 1984 年间使用的英国硬币，200 半便士硬币为一英镑） IDM SEE SPOIL *v.*

ˈ**half-pipe** *noun* a U-shaped structure or a U-shaped channel cut into snow, used for performing complicated movements in SKATEBOARDING, ROLLERBLADING and SNOWBOARDING （滑板、轮滑、滑雪等运动中供人完成复杂动作的）U 字形滑道，半管

ˌ**half-ˈprice** *adj.* costing half the usual price 半价的： *a half-price ticket* 半票 ▸ ˌ**half-ˈprice** *adv.*： *Children aged under four go half-price.* 四岁以下儿童半票。 ˌ**half ˈprice** *noun* [U]： *Many items are at half price.* 许多商品都以半价出售。

ˈ**half-sister** *noun* a person's **half-sister** is a girl or woman who has either the same mother or the same father as them 同母异父（或同父异母）的姐妹 ⊃ COMPARE STEP-SISTER

ˈ**half step** (*also* **half·tone**) (*both NAmE*) (*BrE* **semi·tone**) *noun* (*music* 音) half a TONE on a musical SCALE, for example the INTERVAL between C and C# or between E and F 半音 ⊃ COMPARE STEP *n.* (10)

ˌ**half-ˈterm** *noun* (in British schools) a short holiday/vacation in the middle of each term （英国学校的）期中假： *the* ***half-term break/holiday*** 期中假 ◇ *What are you doing* ***at half-term?*** 你期中假打算干什么？

ˌ**half-ˈtimbered** *adj.* [usually before noun] (of a building 建筑物) having walls that are made from a wooden frame filled with brick, stone, etc. so that the FRAMEWORK can still be seen 露明木架的

ˌ**half-ˈtime** *noun* [U] a short period between the two halves of a sports game during which the players rest （体育比赛上下半场之间的）中场休息时间： *The score at half-time was two all.* 上半场比分为二平。 ◇ *the half-time score* 上半场比分 ⊃ COMPARE FULL TIME

half·tone /ˈhɑːftəʊn; *NAmE* ˈhæftoʊn/ *noun* **1** (*specialist*) a print of a black and white photograph in which the different shades of grey are produced from small and large black dots 网目（凸）版；网版画 **2** (*NAmE, music* 音) = HALF STEP

ˈ**half-truth** *noun* a statement that gives only part of the truth, especially when it is intended to cheat sb 半真半假的陈述（尤指为欺骗人）： *The newspaper reports are a mixture of gossip, lies and half-truths.* 报纸的这些报道尽是些流言蜚语、谎言和真假参半的内容。

ˈ**half-volley** *noun* (in TENNIS and football (SOCCER) 网球和足球) a stroke or kick immediately after the ball has BOUNCED （球反弹当即的）半截击，凌空抽射

half·way /ˌhɑːfˈweɪ; *NAmE* ˌhæf-/ *adv.* **1** at an equal distance between two points; in the middle of a period of time 在…的中间；在中途；到一半： *It's about halfway between London and Bristol.* 它大约位于伦敦和布里斯托尔的中间。 ◇ *He left halfway through the ceremony.* 他在仪式进行到一半时离开了。 ◇ *I'm afraid we're not even* ***halfway there*** *yet.* 恐怕我们连一半的路都还没走完。 **2** ~ **to/towards sth** | ~ **to/towards doing sth** part of the way towards doing or achieving sth 部分地做（或达到）…： *This only goes halfway to explaining what really happened.* 这只是部分地解释了实际发生的事。 **3** ~ **decent** (*informal*) fairly, but not very, good 还不错的；过得去的： *Any halfway decent map will give you that information.* 任何一张还算像样的地图都能提供那些信息。 ▸ **half·way** *adj.*： *the* ***halfway point/stage*** 中间点 / 阶段 IDM SEE MEET *v.*

ˌ**halfway ˈhouse** *noun* **1** [sing.] (*BrE*) something that combines the features of two very different things （两种迥然不同的事物特征的）折中，妥协 **2** [C] a place where prisoners, patients with mental health problems, etc. can stay for a short time after leaving a prison or hospital, before they start to live on their own again 重返社会训练所，中途之家，中途宿舍（为出狱者及离开精神病院的病人而设）

ˈ**halfway line** *noun* a line across a sports field at an equal distance between the ends （球场等的）中线，中场线

half·wit /ˈhɑːfwɪt; *NAmE* ˈhæf-/ *noun* (*informal*) a stupid person 傻瓜；笨蛋 SYN **idiot** ▸ ˌ**half-ˈwitted** *adj.*

ˌ**half-ˈyearly** *adj.* [only before noun] happening every six months; happening after the first six months of the year 每半年一次的；半年度的： *a half-yearly meeting* 每半年举行一次的会议 ◇ *the half-yearly sales figures* 上半年的销售额 ▸ ˌ**half-ˈyearly** *adv.*： *Interest will be paid half-yearly in June and December.* 利息将每半年一次于六月份和十二月份支付。

hali·but /ˈhælɪbət/ *noun* [C, U] (*pl.* **hali·but**) a large flat sea fish that is used for food 圣日比目鱼，大比目鱼（可食用）

hali·tosis /ˌhælɪˈtəʊsɪs; *NAmE* -ˈtoʊ-/ *noun* [U] (*medical* 医) a condition in which the breath smells unpleasant 口臭 SYN **bad breath**

hall /hɔːl/ *noun* **1** (*also* **hall·way**) (*NAmE also* **entry**) a space or passage inside the entrance or front door of a building 门厅；正门过道： *She ran into the hall and up the stairs.* 她跑进门厅，冲上楼梯。 ⊃ SEE ALSO ENTRANCE HALL **2** (*NAmE also* **hall·way**) a passage in a building with rooms down either side （大楼内的）走廊 SYN **corridor**： *I headed for Scott's office down the hall.* 我沿着走廊直奔斯科特的办公室。 **3** a building or large room for public meetings, meals, concerts, etc. 礼堂；大厅： *a* ***concert/banqueting/sports/exhibition, etc. hall*** 音乐厅、宴会厅、体育馆、展厅等 ◇ *There are three dining halls on campus.* 校园里有三个餐厅。 ◇ *The Royal Albert Hall* 皇家艾伯特厅 ◇ (*BrE*) *A jumble sale will be held in the village hall on Saturday.* 星期六将在村礼堂举行义卖。 ⊃ SEE ALSO CITY HALL, DANCE HALL, GUILDHALL, MUSIC HALL, TOWN HALL **4** (*BrE*) = HALL OF RESIDENCE： *She's living* ***in hall(s)***. 她住在学生宿舍。 **5** (*BrE*) (often as part of a name 常作名称的一部分) a large country house 大庄园府邸： *Haddon Hall* 哈登府

hal·le·lu·jah /ˌhælɪˈluːjə/ (*also* **al·le·luia**) *noun* a song or shout of praise to God 哈利路亚（意为赞美上帝） ▸ **hal·le·lu·jah** *exclamation*

hall·mark /ˈhɔːlmɑːk; *NAmE* -mɑːrk/ *noun, verb*

▪ ***noun*** **1** a feature or quality that is typical of sb/sth 特征；特点： *Police said the explosion* ***bore all the hallmarks*** *of a terrorist attack.* 警方称这次爆炸具有恐怖分子袭击的所有特征。 **2** a mark put on gold, silver and PLATINUM objects that shows the quality of the metal and gives information about when and where the object was made 金银纯度印记（打在金、银、铂制品上，表示纯度、生产日期及产地）

▪ ***verb*** ~ **sth** to put a hallmark on metal goods 给…打金银纯度印记

hallo (*BrE*) = HELLO

ˌ**Hall of ˈFame** *noun* (*pl.* **Halls of Fame**) (*especially NAmE*) **1** a place for people to visit, like a museum, with things connected with famous people from a particular sport or activity 名人纪念馆；名人堂： *the Country Music Hall of Fame* 乡村音乐名人堂 **2** [sing.] the group of people who have done a particular activity or sport particularly well（统称体育运动等领域的）代表人物，出类拔萃者，佼佼者

ˌ**hall of ˈresidence** (*also* **hall**) *noun* (*pl.* **halls of resi·dence, halls**) (*both BrE*) (*NAmE* **dor·mi·tory**) a building for university or college students to live in （大学）学生宿舍 ⊃ WORDFINDER NOTE AT UNIVERSITY

hal·loo /hæ'lu:/ *exclamation* **1** used to attract sb's attention （用以引起注意）嘿，喂 **2** used in hunting to tell the dogs to start chasing an animal （打猎时令狗出发追逐猎物）嘿，上 ▶ **hal·loo** *verb* [T, I] ~ (**sb**)

hal·loumi™ /hə'lu:mi/ *noun* [U] a type of firm, white cheese made from the milk of sheep or GOATS, used especially in cooked dishes 哈罗米干酪（用羊奶制成的白色硬奶酪，尤用于烹饪菜肴）

hal·lowed /'hæləʊd; *NAmE* -loʊd/ *adj.* [only before noun] **1** (especially of old things 尤指古老的事物) respected and important 受崇敬的 **SYN** **sacred**: *one of the theatre's most hallowed traditions* 戏院最受尊崇的传统之一 **2** that has been made holy 神圣（化）的 **SYN** **sacred**: *to be buried in hallowed ground* 被安葬在神圣的土地上

Hal·low·een (*also* **Hal·low·e'en**) /ˌhæləʊ'i:n; *NAmE* -loʊ-/ *noun* [C, U] the night of 31st October when it was believed in the past that dead people appeared from their graves, and which is now celebrated in the US, Canada and Britain by children who dress as GHOSTS, WITCHES, etc. 万圣节前夕（10 月 31 日晚，过去认为死人此时会从坟墓中走出来，如今儿童会装鬼玩闹） ➲ SEE ALSO TRICK OR TREAT at TRICK *n.*

hal·lu·cin·ate /hə'lu:sɪneɪt/ *verb* [I] to see or hear things that are not really there because of illness or drugs （由于生病、吸毒）幻视，幻听，产生幻觉 ➲ WORDFINDER NOTE AT DRUG

hal·lu·cin·ation /həˌlu:sɪ'neɪʃn/ *noun* **1** [C, U] the fact of seeming to see or hear sb/sth that is not really there, especially because of illness or drugs 幻觉，幻视，幻听（尤指生病或吸毒所致）: *to have hallucinations* 产生幻觉 ◇ *High temperatures can cause hallucination.* 高烧可使人产生幻觉。 **2** [C] something that is seen or heard when it is not really there 幻视（或幻听）到的东西；幻觉；幻象: *Was the figure real or just a hallucination?* 那个人影是真的呢，还是幻象？ **HELP** Some speakers do not pronounce the 'h' at the beginning of **hallucination** and use 'an' instead of 'a' before it. This now sounds old-fashioned. 有人说 hallucination 时不发 h 音，前面用 an 而不用 a，现在听起来过时了。

hal·lu·cin·atory /hə'lu:sɪnətri; həˌlu:sɪ'neɪtəri; *NAmE* hə'lu:sənətɔ:ri/ *adj.* [only before noun] connected with or causing hallucinations 幻觉的；引起幻觉的: *a hallucinatory experience* 一次幻觉经历 ◇ *hallucinatory drugs* 致幻药

hal·lu·cino·gen /hæ'lu:sɪnədʒən/ *noun* a drug, such as LSD, that affects people's minds and makes them see and hear things that are not really there 致幻剂 ▶ **hal·lu·cino·gen·ic** /həˌlu:sɪnə'dʒenɪk/ *adj.*: *hallucinogenic drugs/effects* 致幻药；致幻作用

hall·way /'hɔ:lweɪ/ *noun* **1** (*especially BrE*) = HALL (1) **2** (*NAmE*) = HALL (2)

halo /'heɪləʊ; *NAmE* -loʊ/ *noun* (*pl.* **-oes** or **-os**) **1** (in paintings, etc.) a circle of light shown around or above the head of a holy person （绘画等中环绕圣人头上的）光环，光轮: *She played the part of an angel, complete with wings and a halo.* 她扮演天使，身上的双翼和头上的光轮一应俱全。 ◇ (*figurative*) *a halo of white frizzy hair* 一圈白色鬈发 **2** (*informal*) = CORONA

halo·gen /'hælədʒən/ *noun* (*chemistry* 化) any of a set of five chemical elements, including FLUORINE, CHLORINE and IODINE, that react with HYDROGEN to form acids from which simple salts can be made. Halogens, in the form of gas, are used in lamps and cookers/stoves. 卤素

halon /'heɪlɒn; *NAmE* -lɑ:n/ *noun* (*chemistry* 化) a gas that is made up of CARBON and one or more halogens, used especially to stop fires 卤化烷（尤用以灭火）

halt /hɔ:lt; *BrE also* hɒlt/ *verb, noun*

■ *verb* [I, T] to stop; to make sb/sth stop （使）停止，停下: *She walked towards him and then halted.* 她向他走去，然后停下。 ◇ *'Halt!' the Major ordered* (= used as a command to soldiers). "立定！"少校发出命令。 ◇ ~ **sb/sth** *The police were halting traffic on the parade route.* 警察正阻止游行路线上的车辆前行。 ◇ *The trial was halted after the first week.* 第一周结束后，审判暂停。 **IDM** SEE TRACK *n.*

■ *noun* **1** [sing.] an act of stopping the movement or progress of sb/sth 停止；阻止；暂停: *Work came to a halt when the machine broke down.* 机器一坏，工作便停了下来。 ◇ *The thought* **brought her to an** *abrupt* **halt**. 她一想到这个便猛地停下了。 ◇ *The car skidded to a halt.* 汽车打滑后停了下来。 ◇ *Strikes have led to* **a halt in** *production.* 罢工已经使生产陷于停顿。 ◇ *They decided it was time to* **call a halt to** *the project* (= stop it officially). 他们决定该叫停这项工程了。 **2** [C] (*BrE*) a small train station in the country that has a platform but no buildings 小火车站（只有站台） **IDM** SEE GRIND *v.*

hal·ter /'hɔ:ltə(r); *BrE also* 'hɒlt-/ *noun* **1** a rope or narrow piece of leather put around the head of a horse for leading it with （马的）笼头，缰绳 **2** (usually used as an adjective 通常用作形容词) a narrow piece of cloth around the neck that holds a woman's dress or shirt in position, with the back and shoulders not covered （女式露背装的）绕颈系带: *She was dressed in a halter top and shorts.* 她穿着三角背心和短裤。

halt·ing /'hɔ:ltɪŋ; *BrE also* 'hɒlt-/ *adj.* [usually before noun] (especially of speech or movement 尤指讲话或动作) stopping and starting often, especially because you are not certain or are not very confident 断断续续的；结结巴巴的 **SYN** **hesitant**: *a halting conversation* 断断续续的谈话 ◇ *a toddler's first few halting steps* 学步幼儿的蹒跚脚步 ▶ **halt·ing·ly** *adv.*: *'Well…' she began haltingly.* "唔…"她开始结结巴巴地讲话。

halve /hɑ:v; *NAmE* hæv/ *verb* **1** [I, T] to reduce by a half; to make sth reduce by a half （使）减半: *The shares have* **halved in value**. 股价已经跌了一半。 ◇ ~ **sth** *The company is halving its prices.* 该公司正将产品半价出售。 **2** [T] ~ **sth** to divide sth into two equal parts 把…对半分 **IDM** SEE TROUBLE *n.*

halves PL. OF HALF

halwa /'hælwɑ:/ *noun* [U] a sweet food from S Asia, made from SEMOLINA or carrots, with ALMONDS and CARDAMOM 哈瓦（用粗面粉或胡萝卜加杏仁和豆蔻干籽制成的南亚甜食）

hal·yard /'hæljəd; *NAmE* -jərd/ *noun* (*specialist*) a rope used for raising or taking down a sail or flag （帆或旗的）升降索

ham /hæm/ *noun, verb*

■ *noun* **1** [C, U] the top part of a pig's leg that has been CURED (= preserved using salt or smoke) and is eaten as food; the meat from this 火腿；火腿肉: *The hams were cooked whole.* 这些火腿是整条烹制的。 ◇ *a slice of ham* 一片火腿 ◇ *a ham sandwich* 火腿三明治 ➲ COMPARE BACON, GAMMON, PORK **2** [C] a person who sends and receives radio messages as a hobby rather than as a job 无线电通讯爱好者: *a radio ham* 无线电通讯爱好者 **3** [C] (*informal*) (often used as an adjective 常用作形容词) an actor who performs badly, especially by exaggerating emotions 拙劣演员（尤指表演过火者）: *a ham actor* 表演过火的演员 **4** [C, usually pl.] (*informal*) the back part of a person's leg above the knee （人的）大腿后部 ➲ SEE ALSO HAMSTRING *n.*

■ *verb* (**-mm-**)

IDM ˌ**ham it 'up** (*informal*) (especially of actors 尤指演员) when people **ham it up**, they deliberately exaggerate their emotions or movements 有意夸张表情（或动作）；表演过火

ham·burg·er /'hæmbɜ:gə(r); *NAmE* -bɜ:rg-/ (*also* **burg·er**) *noun* **1** (*BrE also* **beef·burg·er**) [C] finely chopped beef made into a flat round shape that is then fried, often served in a bread roll 汉堡包；汉堡牛肉饼 **2** (*also* '**hamburger meat**) (*both US*) (*NAmE also* ˌ**ground 'beef**) (*BrE* **mince**) [U] beef that has been finely chopped in a special machine 绞碎的牛肉；牛肉末

ˌham-ˈfisted (*NAmE also* **ˈham-handed**) *adj.* (*informal*) lacking skill when using your hands or when dealing with people 笨手笨脚的；愚笨的 **SYN** **clumsy**: *his ham-fisted efforts to assist her* 他为了帮她做出的笨手笨脚的努力

ham·let /ˈhæmlət/ *noun* a very small village 小村庄

ham·mer /ˈhæmə(r)/ *noun, verb*

■ *noun*

• **TOOL** 工具 **1** [C] a tool with a handle and a heavy metal head, used for breaking things or hitting nails 锤子；榔头：(*figurative*) *The decision is a hammer blow for the steel industry.* 这一决定对于钢铁业是一个沉重的打击。➲ VISUAL VOCAB PAGE V21 ➲ SEE ALSO SLEDGEHAMMER **2** [C] a tool with a handle and a wooden head, used by a person in charge of an AUCTION (= a sale at which things are sold to the person who offers the most money) in order to get people's attention when sth is just being sold （拍卖用的）木槌：*to come/go* ***under the hammer*** (= to be sold at AUCTION) 被拍卖

• **IN PIANO** 钢琴 **3** [C] a small wooden part inside a piano, that hits the strings to produce a sound 音槌

• **IN GUN** 枪炮 **4** [C] a part inside a gun that makes the gun fire 击铁

• **SPORT** 体育运动 **5** [C] a metal ball attached to a wire, thrown as a sport 链球 **6 the hammer** [sing.] the event or sport of throwing the hammer 掷链球（运动）➲ VISUAL VOCAB PAGE V50

IDM **ˌhammer and ˈtongs** if two people are **at it hammer and tongs** or **go at it hammer and tongs**, they argue or fight with a lot of energy and noise 激烈争吵（或打斗）

■ *verb*

• **HIT WITH TOOL** 用工具锤打 **1** [I, T] to hit sth with a hammer （用锤子）敲，锤打：*I could hear somebody hammering next door.* 我听到隔壁有人在锤打东西。◇ **~ sth (in/into/onto sth)** *She hammered the nail into the wall.* 她把钉子钉到墙上。◇ **~ sth + adj.** *He was hammering the sheet of copper flat.* 他正把铜片锤平。

• **HIT MANY TIMES** 连续敲打 **2** [I, T] to hit sth hard many times, especially so that it makes a loud noise 反复敲打，连续击打（尤指发出大声）**SYN** **pound**: *Someone was hammering at the door.* 有人在砰砰地打门。◇ *Hail was hammering down onto the roof.* 冰雹砸得屋顶咚咚响。◇ (*figurative*) *I was so scared my heart was hammering* (= beating very fast) *in my chest.* 我吓得心怦怦直跳。◇ **~ sth** *He hammered the door with his fists.* 他不断地用拳头擂门。➲ SYNONYMS AT BEAT

• **KICK/HIT BALL** 踢球；击球 **3** [T] **~ sth (+ adv./prep.)** (*informal*) to kick or hit a ball very hard 猛踢；猛击：*He hammered the ball into the net.* 他一记猛射，将球踢进网。

• **DEFEAT EASILY** 轻易打败 **4** [T] **~ sb** (*informal*) to defeat sb very easily 轻易打败（对方）：*Our team was hammered 5–1.* 我队以 1:5 的悬殊比分败北。

PHR V **ˌhammer aˈway at sth** to work hard in order to finish or achieve sth; to keep repeating sth in order to get the result that you want 努力干；孜孜以求 **ˌhammer sth↔ˈhome** **1** to emphasize a point, an idea, etc. so that people fully understand it 反复讲透，重点讲清（要点、想法等）**2** to kick a ball hard and score a goal 用力踢球得分；把球猛踢进球门 **ˌhammer sth ˈinto sb** to make sb learn or remember sth by repeating it many times 反复灌输 **ˌhammer ˈout sth** **1** to discuss a plan, an idea, etc. until everyone agrees or a decision is made 反复讨论出（一致意见）；充分研讨出（决定）：*to hammer out a compromise* 反复讨论达成妥协 **2** to play a tune, especially on a piano, loudly and not very well （在钢琴等上）敲打出

ˌhammer and ˈsickle *noun* [sing.] tools representing the people who work in industry and farming, used on the flag of the former Soviet Union and as a symbol of Communism 锤子和镰刀（代表工人和农民，苏联国旗用以象征共产主义）

ham·mered /ˈhæməd; *NAmE* -ərd/ *adj.* [not before noun] (*slang*) very drunk 烂醉

ham·mer·head /ˈhæməhed; *NAmE* -mər-/ (*also* **ˌhammerhead ˈshark**) *noun* a SHARK with flat parts sticking out from either side of its head with eyes at the ends 锤头鲨；双髻鲨

ham·mer·ing /ˈhæmərɪŋ/ *noun* **1** [U, sing.] the sound of sb hitting sth with a hammer or with their FISTS （锤子或拳头的）敲打声，捶打声：*the sound of hammering from the next room* 隔壁传来的敲打声 **2** [C, usually sing.] (*informal*) an act of defeating or criticizing sb severely 挫败；严厉批评：*Our team took a real hammering in the first half.* 上半场我队吃了个大败仗。

ˈhammer price *noun* the last and highest amount offered for sth at an AUCTION which is the price for which it is sold （拍卖）成交价，击槌价

ham·mock /ˈhæmək/ *noun* a type of bed made from a net or from a piece of strong material, with ropes at each end that are used to hang it between two trees, posts, etc. 吊床 ➲ VISUAL VOCAB PAGE V24

Hammond organ™ /ˌhæmənd ˈɔːɡən; *NAmE* ˈɔːrɡ-/ *noun* a type of electronic organ 哈蒙德（电）风琴

hammy /ˈhæmi/ *adj.* (**ham·mier**, **ham·mi·est**) (*informal*) (of a style of acting 演出风格) artificial or exaggerated 做作的；过火的

ham·per /ˈhæmpə(r)/ *verb, noun*

■ *verb* [often passive] **~ sb/sth** to prevent sb from easily doing or achieving sth 妨碍；阻止；阻碍 **SYN** **hinder**

■ *noun* **1** a large BASKET with a lid, especially one used to carry food in （尤指用于盛食物的）带盖大篮子：*a picnic hamper* 野餐篮 ➲ PICTURE AT BASKET **2** (*especially BrE*) a box or package containing food, sent as a gift （作为礼品的）盒装食物，袋装食物：*a Christmas hamper* 圣诞礼品盒 **3** (*NAmE*) a large BASKET that you keep your dirty clothes in until they are washed 盛脏衣服的大篮子

ham·ster /ˈhæmstə(r)/ *noun* an animal like a large mouse, with large cheeks for storing food. Hamsters are often kept as pets. 仓鼠（有颊囊可存放食物，常作宠物）

ham·string /ˈhæmstrɪŋ/ *noun, verb*

■ *noun* **1** one of the five TENDONS behind the knee that connect the muscles of the upper leg to the bones of the lower leg 腘绳肌腱：*a hamstring injury* 腘绳肌腱受伤 ◇ *She's pulled a hamstring.* 她拉伤了一条腘绳肌腱。**2** a TENDON behind the middle joint (= HOCK) of the back leg of a horse and some other animals （马等附关节后部的）后腿肌腱，大肌腱

■ *verb* (**ham·strung**, **ham·strung** /ˈhæmstrʌŋ/) [often passive] **~ sb/sth** to prevent sb/sth from working or taking action in the way that is needed 妨碍；使不能正常工作（或行动）

hand /hænd/ *noun, verb*

■ *noun*

• **PART OF BODY** 身体部位 **1** [C] the part of the body at the end of the arm, including the fingers and thumb 手：*Ian placed a hand on her shoulder.* 伊恩把一只手搭在她的肩上。◇ ***Put your hand up*** *if you know the answer.* 知道答案就举手。◇ *Keep both hands on the steering wheel at all times.* 双手要始终握住方向盘。◇ *She was* ***on*** (***her***) ***hands and knees*** (= CRAWLING on the floor) *looking for an earring.* 她正趴在地板上到处寻找耳环。◇ *Couples strolled past* ***holding hands.*** 一对对恋人手拉手漫步经过。◇ ***Give me your hand*** (= hold my hand) *while we cross the road.* 过马路时拉着我的手。◇ *The crowd* ***threw up their hands*** (= lifted them into the air) *in dismay.* 群众沮丧地举起双手。◇ *He killed the snake* ***with his bare hands*** (= using only his hands). 他徒手杀死了那条蛇。◇ *a* ***hand towel*** (= a small towel for drying your hands on) 擦手的小毛巾 ◇ *a* ***hand drill*** (= one that is used by turning a handle rather than powered by electricity) 手摇钻 ➲ COLLOCATIONS AT PHYSICAL ➲ VISUAL VOCAB PAGE V64 ➲ SEE ALSO LEFT-HAND, RIGHT-HAND

• **-HANDED** …手 **2** (in adjectives 构成形容词) using the hand

H

or number of hands mentioned 用…手的；用…只手的：*a one-handed catch* 单手抓接 ◇ *left-handed scissors* (= intended to be held in your left hand) 供左手使用的剪刀 ➲ MORE LIKE THIS 8, page R25

• HELP 帮助 **3** **a hand** [sing.] (*informal*) help in doing sth 帮助；协助：*Let me **give you a hand** with those bags* (= help you to carry them). 我来帮你拎那些包吧。◇ *Do you **need a hand** with those invoices?* 要不要我帮你处理那些发票？◇ *The neighbours are always willing to **lend a hand**.* 邻居们总是乐于帮忙。

• ROLE IN SITUATION 角色 **4** [sing.] **~ in sth** the part or role that sb/sth plays in a particular situation; sb's influence in a situation 角色；作用；影响：*Early reports suggest the hand of rebel forces in the bombings.* 早期的报道暗示叛乱武装插手了爆炸案。◇ *Several of his colleagues **had a hand in** his downfall.* 他的几个同事促使了他下台。◇ *This appointment was an attempt to **strengthen her hand** in policy discussions.* 这次任命旨在加强她在政策讨论中的作用。

• ON CLOCK/WATCH 钟表 **5** [C] (usually in compounds 通常构成复合词) a part of a clock or watch that points to the numbers 指针 ➲ PICTURE AT CLOCK ➲ SEE ALSO HOUR HAND, MINUTE HAND, SECOND HAND

▼ **VOCABULARY BUILDING 词汇扩充**

Using your hands 用手

Touch 接触

These verbs describe different ways of touching things. 下列动词表示用手接触东西的不同方式：

feel （用手）摸，触摸	*I felt the bag to see what was in it.* 我摸了摸提包，看里面有什么东西。
finger （用手指）摸，触摸	*She fingered the silk delicately.* 她用手指轻轻地摸了摸丝绸。
handle 触碰；拿	*Handle the fruit with care.* 拿水果时小心点。
rub 揉；搓；擦	*She rubbed her eyes wearily.* 她疲倦地揉了揉眼睛。
stroke 轻抚；抚摩	*The cat loves being stroked.* 这猫喜欢被人摩挲。
pat 轻拍	*He patted my arm and told me not to worry.* 他轻轻拍了拍我手臂，叫我别担心。
tap 轻击；轻敲	*Someone was tapping lightly at the door.* 有人在轻轻敲门。
squeeze 挤；捏	*I took his hand and squeezed it.* 我抓住他的手捏了捏。

Hold 拿住

You can use these verbs to describe taking something quickly. 可用下列动词表示迅速抓住：

grab 抓；抢	*I grabbed his arm to stop myself from falling.* 我抓住他的手臂以免自己摔倒。
snatch 一手抓起；一下夺过	*She snatched the letter out of my hand.* 她一把将信从我手上抢走。

These verbs describe holding things tightly. 下列动词表示紧紧握住：

clasp 握紧；抱紧	*Her hands were clasped behind her head.* 她双手紧紧抱住后脑勺。
clutch 抱紧；抓紧	*The child was clutching a doll in her hand.* 女孩手里紧紧抱着一个玩具娃娃。
grasp 抓住	*Grasp the rope with both hands and pull.* 双手抓住绳子拉。
grip 紧抓；紧握	*He gripped his bag tightly and wouldn't let go.* 他紧紧抓住包不松手。

• WORKER 工人 **6** [C] a person who does physical work on a farm or in a factory （农场或工厂的）体力劳动者，工人 ➲ SEE ALSO CHARGEHAND, FARMHAND, HIRED HAND, STAGEHAND

• SAILOR 船员 **7** [C] a sailor on a ship 船员：*All hands on deck!* 全体船员到甲板上集合！ ➲ SEE ALSO DECKHAND

• HAND- 手工 **8** (in compounds 构成复合词) by a person rather than a machine 手工：*hand-painted pottery* 手绘陶器 ◇ *hand-knitted* 手工编织的 ◇ *This item should be hand washed.* 这件物品要用手洗。 ➲ SEE ALSO HANDMADE

• IN CARD GAMES 纸牌游戏 **9** [C] a set of PLAYING CARDS given to one player in a game （分给游戏者的）一手牌：*to be dealt a **good/bad hand*** 拿到一手好牌 / 烂牌 ➲ WORDFINDER NOTE AT CARD ➲ VISUAL VOCAB PAGE V41 **10** [C] one stage of a game of cards （纸牌游戏的）一盘：*I'll have to leave after this hand.* 这一盘打完后我必须走了。

• WRITING 书写 **11** [sing.] (*old use*) a particular style of writing 书法 ➲ SEE ALSO FREEHAND

• MEASUREMENT FOR HORSE 马的测量 **12** [C] a unit for measuring the height of a horse, equal to 4 inches or 10.16 centimetres 一手之宽（测量马的高度的单位，等于 4 英寸或 10.16 厘米） ➲ SEE ALSO DAB HAND, OLD HAND, SECOND-HAND, UNDERHAND

IDM **all ˌhands on ˈdeck** (*also* **all ˌhands to the ˈpump**) (*saying, humorous*) everyone helps or must help, especially in a difficult situation 总动员；全体出动：*There are 30 people coming to dinner tonight, so it's all hands on deck.* 今天晚上有 30 人来吃饭，要全体动员了。 **(close/near) at ˈhand** close to you in time or distance （在时间或距离上）接近：*Help was at hand.* 援助近在咫尺。◇ *The property is ideally located with all local amenities close at hand.* 这处房地产的位置很理想，离当地的生活设施都近。 **at the hands of sb | at sb's hands** (*formal*) if you experience sth **at the hands of sb**, they are the cause of it 某人导致；出自某人之手 **be good with your ˈhands** to be skilful at making or doing things with your hands 技术娴熟 **bind/tie sb hand and ˈfoot 1** to tie sb's hands and feet together so that they cannot move or escape 捆绑住某人的手脚 **2** to prevent sb from doing what they want by creating rules, restrictions, etc. 用条条框框限制某人 **by ˈhand 1** by a person rather than a machine 手工：*The fabric was painted by hand.* 这个织品是手染的。**2** if a letter is delivered **by hand**, it is delivered by the person who wrote it, or sb who is sent by them, rather than by post/mail （信件）亲手交付，由专人递送 **fall into sb's ˈhands/the ˈhands of sb** (*formal*) to become controlled by sb 受制于某人；被某人控制：*The town fell into enemy hands.* 那个小镇落入敌人手里了。◇ *We don't want this document **falling into the wrong hands**.* 我们不希望这份文件落入不当的人手中。 **(at) first ˈhand** by experiencing, seeing, etc. sth yourself rather than being told about it by sb else 第一手；亲自：*The President visited the area to see the devastation at first hand.* 总统亲临该地区视察受损情况。 **get your ˈhands dirty** to do physical work 做体力工作；体力劳动：*He's not frightened of getting his hands dirty.* 他不怕体力劳动。 **sb's ˈhand (in marriage)** (*old-fashioned*) permission to marry sb, especially a woman 答应求婚（尤指女方）：*He asked the general for his daughter's hand in marriage.* 他请求将军把女儿许配给他。 **ˌhand in ˈglove (with sb)** working closely with sb, especially in a secret and/or illegal way 同某人密切合作（尤指勾结） **ˌhand in ˈhand 1** if two people are **hand in hand**, they are holding each other's hand 手拉手 **2** if two things **go hand in hand**, they are closely connected and one thing causes the other 密切关联；相连带：*Poverty and poor health often go hand in hand.* 贫困和健康不良常有连带关系。 **ˌhands ˈdown** (*informal*) easily and without any doubt 容易地；易如反掌地；毋庸置疑地：*They **won hands down**.* 他们轻松取胜。◇ *It is hands down the best movie this year.* 这无疑是今年最好的电影。 ➲ SEE ALSO HANDS-DOWN **(get/take your) ˌhands ˈoff (sth/sb)** (*informal*) used to tell sb not to touch sth/sb （命令）别动某物 / 某人：*Get your hands off my wife!* 不许碰我妻子！◇ *Hey, hands off! That's my drink!* 嘿，别动！那是我的饮料！ **ˌhands ˈup!** (*informal*) **1** used to tell a group of people to raise one hand in the air if they know the answer to a question, etc. 举手（答

问）：*Hands up all those who want to go swimming.* 想去游泳的人举手。**2** used by sb who is threatening people with a gun to tell them to raise both hands in the air 举手（投降） **have your ˈhands full** to be very busy or too busy to do sth else 忙得不可开交；应接不暇：*She certainly has her hands full with four kids in the house.* 家里养着四个孩子，她当然忙得团团转。 **have your ˈhands tied** to be unable to do what you want to do because of rules, promises, etc. 受到制约：*I really wish I could help but my hands are tied.* 我的确想帮忙，但却多有不便。 **hold sb's ˈhand** to give sb support in a difficult situation （困难时）给某人支持；拉某人一把：*Do you want me to come along and hold your hand?* 你想让我过去帮你一把吗？ **hold/put your ˈhands up (to sth)** to admit that you have made a mistake or are responsible for sth bad 承认犯错；承认对坏事负有责任：*I have to hold my hands up and admit that some of the problems have been all my own fault.* 我必须承认有些问题完全是我自己的错。 **in sb's capable, safe, etc. ˈhands** being taken care of or dealt with by sb that you think you can rely on 由可信任的人负责（或处理等）：*Can I leave these queries in your capable hands?* 我能否请你这个能手来解答这些疑问？ **in ˈhand 1** if you have time or money **in hand**, it is left and available to be used 在手头；可供使用 **2** if you have a particular situation **in hand**, you are in control of it 在掌握中；在控制中 **3** the job, question, etc. **in hand** is the one that you are dealing with 正在处理中 **4** if sb works a week, month, etc. **in hand**, they are paid for the work a week, etc. after they have completed it （按星期、月等）领取工资 **in the hands of sb | in sb's ˈhands** 🔑 being taken care of or controlled by sb 受某人照料；受某人控制：*The matter is now in the hands of my lawyer.* 这件事现在正由我的律师处理。◇ *At that time, the castle was in enemy hands.* 那时城堡在敌人手中。 **keep your ˈhand in** to occasionally do sth that you used to do a lot so that you do not lose your skill at it 偶尔操练某事以保持熟练：*She retired last year but still teaches the odd class to keep her hand in.* 她去年退休了，但偶尔还上课，以免技巧生疏。 **lay/get your ˈhands on sb** to catch sb that you are annoyed with 捉住使你不快的人：*Wait till I get my hands on him!* 等我抓住他再说！ **lay/get your ˈhands on sth** to find or get sth 找到 / 得到某物：*I know their address is here somewhere, but I can't lay my hands on it right now.* 我知道他们的地址就放在这块儿，但我一时找不到。 **many hands make light ˈwork** (*saying*) used to say that a job is made easier if a lot of people help 人多好办事；众人拾柴火焰高 **not do a hand's ˈturn** (*old-fashioned*) to do no work 什么活也不干：*She hasn't done a hand's turn all week.* 她闲了整整一星期。 **off your ˈhands** no longer your responsibility 不再由某人负责 **on either/every ˈhand** (*literary*) on both/all sides; in both/all directions 在双方面 / 各个方面；在两个 / 各个方向 **on ˈhand** available, especially to help 现有（尤指帮助）：*The emergency services were on hand with medical advice.* 随时都有急诊服务，并提供医疗咨询。 **on your ˈhands** if you have sb/sth **on your hands**, you are responsible for them or it 由某人负责（某人、某事）：*Let me take care of the invitations—you've enough on your hands with the caterers.* 让我来负责发邀请吧，你负责洽办酒席就够忙了。 **(on the ˈone hand...) on the ˈother (hand)...** used to introduce different points of view, ideas, etc., especially when they are opposites （引出不同的，尤指对立的观点、思想等）一方面…，另一方面…：*On the one hand they'd love to have kids, but on the other, they don't want to give up their freedom.* 一方面，他们想要孩子，但另一方面，他们又不想放弃自由自在的生活。 ➲ LANGUAGE BANK AT CONTRAST **out of ˈhand 1** difficult or impossible to control 难以（或无法）控制：*Unemployment is getting out of hand.* 失业问题越来越难以控制。 **2** if you reject, etc. sth **out of hand**, you do so immediately without thinking about it fully or listening to other people's arguments 不假思索（拒绝等）：*All our suggestions were dismissed out of hand.* 我们的建议均遭到了草率的拒绝。 **ˌout of your ˈhands** no longer your responsibility 不再由某人负责：*I'm afraid the matter is now out of my hands.* 恐怕这件事现已不归我管。 **ˌplay into sb's ˈhands** to do exactly what an enemy, opponent, etc. wants so that they gain the advantage in a particular situation 干敌人（或对手等）所希望的事；做有利于敌人（或对手等）的事；授人以可乘之机：*If we get the police involved, we'll be playing right into the protesters' hands.* 如果出动警察，那将正中抗议者的下怀。 **put your ˌhand in your ˈpocket** (*BrE*) to spend money or give it to sb 掏腰包；出钱；付款：*I've heard he doesn't like putting his hand in his pocket.* 我听说他手很紧。 **(at) second, third, etc. ˈhand** by being told about sth by sb else who has seen it or heard about it, not by experiencing, seeing, etc. it yourself 经过二手三手地；间接地；非亲身经历：*I'm fed up of hearing about these decisions third hand!* 得从别人那里听说这些决定，我受够了！ **ˌtake sb in ˈhand** to deal with sb in a strict way in order to improve their behaviour 管教某人 **take sth into your own ˈhands** to deal with a particular situation yourself because you are not happy with the way that others are dealing with it 亲自处理某事 **throw your ˈhand in** (*informal*) to stop doing sth or taking part in sth, especially because you are not successful （尤指不成功而）放弃，退出 **to ˈhand** that you can reach or get easily 在手边；随时可得到：*I'm afraid I don't have the latest figures to hand.* 恐怕我手头没有最新的数据。 **turn your ˈhand to sth** to start doing sth or be able to do sth, especially when you do it well （尤指成功、顺利地）着手做，能够做：*Jim can turn his hand to most jobs around the house.* 吉姆能担当起家里的大部分杂活。 ➲ MORE AT BIG *adj.*, BIRD *n.*, BITE *v.*, BLOOD *n.*, CAP *n.*, CASH *n.*, CHANGE *v.*, CLOSE[2] *adv.*, COURAGE, DEAD *adj.*, DEVIL, EAT, FIRM *adj.*, FOLD *v.*, FORCE *v.*, FREE *adj.*, HAT, HEAVY *adj.*, HELP *v.*, IRON *adj.*, JOIN *v.*, KNOW *v.*, LAW, LIFE, LIFT *v.*, LIVE[1], MONEY, OFFER *v.*, OVERPLAY, PAIR *n.*, PALM *n.*, PUTTY, RAISE *v.*, SAFE *adj.*, SHOW *n.*, SHOW *v.*, STAY *v.*, TIME *n.*, TRY *v.*, UPPER *adj.*, WAIT *v.*, WASH *v.*, WHIP *n.*, WIN *v.*, WRING

■ ***verb*** 🔑 to pass or give sth to sb 交；递；给：**~ sth to sb** *She handed the letter to me.* 她把信交给我。◇ **~ sb sth** *She handed me the letter.* 她把信交给我。

IDM **hand sth to sb on a ˈplate** (*informal*) to give sth to sb without the person concerned making any effort 把某事物拱手送给某人：*Nobody's going to hand you success on a plate.* 没有人会把胜利白白地送给你的。 **have (got) to ˈhand it to sb** (*informal*) used to say that sb deserves praise for sth （表示某人值得称赞）：*You've got to hand it to her—she's a great cook.* 你没法不佩服她，她的厨艺的确了不起。

PHR V **ˌhand sth↔aˈround/ˈround** 🔑 to offer or pass sth, especially food or drinks, to all the people in a group 传递，分发（尤指食物或饮料） **ˌhand sth ˈback (to sb)** 🔑 to give or return sth to the person who owns it or to where it belongs 归还某物 **ˌhand sth↔ˈdown (to sb) 1** 🔑 [usually passive] to give or leave sth to sb who is younger than you 把某事物传下去；传给（后代） **SYN** **pass down**：*These skills used to be handed down from father to son.* 这些技艺以往都是父子相传。 ➲ RELATED NOUN HAND-ME-DOWN **2** to officially give a decision/statement, etc. 正式宣布；公布 **SYN** **announce**：*The judge has handed down his verdict.* 法官已经宣布了裁决结果。 **ˌhand sth↔ˈin (to sb)** 🔑 (*BrE also* **ˌgive sth ˈin (to sb)**) to give sth to a person in authority, especially a piece of work or sth that is lost 提交，呈交，上交（尤指书面材料或失物）：*You must all hand in your projects by the end of next week.* 你们都必须在下周末前交出研究报告。◇ *I handed the watch in to the police.* 我把那块表交给了警察。◇ ***to hand in your notice/resignation*** (= formally tell your employer that you want to stop working for them) 递交辞呈 **ˌhand sb↔ˈoff** (*BrE*) (*also* **ˌstraight-ˈarm, ˌstiff-ˈarm** *both NAmE*) (in sport 体育运动) to push away a player who is trying to stop you, with your arm straight 伸直手臂挡开（对手） **ˌhand sth↔ˈon (to sb)** to give or leave sth for another person to use or deal with 把某事物交给或留给（某人）使用（或处理） **SYN** **pass on** **ˌhand sth↔ˈout (to sb) 1** 🔑 to give a number of things to the members of a group 分发某物 **SYN** **distribute**：*Could you hand these books out, please?* 请把这些书发给大家好吗？ ➲ RELATED NOUN HANDOUT **2** (*informal*) to give advice, a punishment, etc. 提出，给予（建议、惩罚等）：

H

He's always handing out advice to people. 他总是喜欢给人讲大道理。 ˌ**hand 'over (to sb)** | ˌ**hand sth↔'over (to sb)** to give sb else your position of power or the responsibility for sth 把（权力或责任）移交给（某人）：*She resigned and handed over to one of her younger colleagues.* 她辞职了，由一位比她年轻的同事接任。◇ *He handed over his responsibility for the firm last year.* 他在去年交出了公司的职务。➲ RELATED NOUN HANDOVER ˌ**hand sb 'over to sb** to let sb listen or speak to another person, especially on the telephone or in a news broadcast（尤指打电话时或在新闻广播中）让某人听另一个人讲话或同其谈话：*I'll hand you over to my boss.* 我把你的电话转给我的老板。ˌ**hand sth/sb↔'over (to sb)** to give sth/sb officially or formally to another person 把某事物 / 某人正式交给（某人）：*He handed over a cheque for $200 000.* 他交出了一张 20 万美元的支票。◇ *They handed the weapons over to the police.* 他们把武器交给了警方。➲ RELATED NOUN HANDOVER

H

hand·bag /ˈhændbæɡ/ (*NAmE also* **purse**) *noun* a small bag for money, keys, etc., carried especially by women 手提包；（尤指）坤包 ➲ VISUAL VOCAB PAGE V69

ˈ**hand baggage** *noun* [U] (*especially NAmE*) = HAND LUGGAGE

hand·ball /ˈhændbɔːl/ *noun* **1** [U] (*US also* ˈ**team handball**) a team game for two teams of seven players, usually played indoors, in which players try to score goals by throwing a ball with their hand 手球（比赛两队各七人，通常在室内进行，用手击球或掷球） **2** [U] (*NAmE*) a game in which players hit a small ball against a wall with their hand 墙手球（两人比赛，用手或拳把小球击向墙） **3** [C, U] (in football (SOCCER) 足球) the offence of touching the ball with your hands 手球（用手触球的犯规动作）：*a penalty for handball* 因手球犯规而罚点球

hand·basin /ˈhændbeɪsn/ *noun* (*BrE*) a small bowl that has taps/faucets and is fixed to the wall, used for washing your hands in （固定在墙上有水龙头的）洗手盆

hand·bas·ket /ˈhændbɑːskɪt; *NAmE* -bæs-/ *noun*
IDM **go to hell in a 'handbasket** (*NAmE*) = GO TO THE DOGS

hand·bell /ˈhændbel/ *noun* a small bell with a handle, especially one of a set used by a group of people to play tunes 手摇铃（常指成套摇铃之一，用于小组演奏）

hand·bill /ˈhændbɪl/ *noun* a small printed advertisement that is given to people by hand 传单；小广告

hand·book /ˈhændbʊk/ *noun* a book giving instructions on how to use sth or information about a particular subject 手册；指南 ➲ COMPARE MANUAL *n.*

hand·brake /ˈhændbreɪk/ (*especially BrE*) (*NAmE usually* ˈ**emergency brake**, ˈ**parking brake**) *noun* a BRAKE in a vehicle that is operated by hand, used especially when the vehicle is not moving （车辆的）手闸，手刹：*to put the handbrake on* 拉上手闸 ◇ *to take the handbrake off* 放开手闸 ◇ *Is the handbrake on?* 手闸扳上了吗？➲ COLLOCATIONS AT DRIVING ➲ VISUAL VOCAB PAGE V56

hand·cart /ˈhændkɑːt; *NAmE* -kɑːrt/ *noun* = CART (2)

hand·craft /ˈhændkrɑːft; *NAmE* -kræft/ *noun* (*NAmE*) = HANDICRAFT

hand·craf·ted /ˈhændkrɑːftɪd; *NAmE* -kræft-/ *adj.* skilfully made by hand, not by machine 手工制作的：*a hand-crafted chair* 手工做的椅子

ˈ**hand cream** *noun* [U] cream that you put on your hands to prevent dry skin 护手霜；润手霜

hand·cuff /ˈhændkʌf/ *verb* [usually passive] ~ **sb** to put handcuffs on sb or to fasten sb to sth/sb with handcuffs 用手铐铐住（某人）；把（某人）铐在（某物或某人）上

hand·cuffs /ˈhændkʌfs/ (*also informal* **cuffs**) *noun* [pl.] a pair of metal rings joined by a chain, used for holding the wrists of a prisoner together 手铐：*a pair of handcuffs* 一副手铐 ◇ *She was led away* ***in handcuffs.*** 她被铐住双手带走了。➲ SEE ALSO GOLDEN HANDCUFFS

hand·cycle /ˈhændsaɪkl/ *noun* a vehicle similar to a bicycle, but that has three wheels instead of two and that you ride by pushing the PEDALS with your hands instead of your feet 手动三轮车；手摇三轮车

hand·ful /ˈhændfʊl/ *noun* **1** [C] ~ **(of sth)** the amount of sth that can be held in one hand 一把（的量）；用手抓起的数量：*a handful of rice* 一把米 **2** [sing.] ~ **(of sb/sth)** a small number of people or things 少数人（或物）：*Only a handful of people came.* 只有少数几个人来了。 **3** [sing.] **a ~** (*informal*) a person or an animal that is difficult to control 难以控制的人（或动物）：*Her children can be a real handful.* 她的孩子们有时很难管教。

ˈ**hand grenade** *noun* a small bomb that is thrown by hand 手榴弹

hand·grip /ˈhændɡrɪp/ *noun* **1** a handle for holding sth 把手；柄 **2** a soft bag with handles for carrying things while you are travelling 手提袋

hand·gun /ˈhændɡʌn/ *noun* a small gun that you can hold and fire with one hand 手枪

hand·held /ˌhændˈheld/ *adj.* [usually before noun] small enough to be held in the hand while being used 便携式的；手提式的 ▸ **hand·held** /ˈhændheld/ *noun*：*I prefer to consult a dictionary on a handheld.* 我比较喜欢查便携式词典。

hand·hold /ˈhændhəʊld; *NAmE* -hoʊld/ *noun* something on the surface of a steep slope, wall, etc. that a person can hold when climbing up it 攀缘时手可抓的东西（或地方）

ˈ**hand-hot** *adj.* water that is **hand-hot** is hot, but not too hot to put your hand into （水）热但不烫手的

handi·cap /ˈhændikæp/ *noun, verb*

■ ***noun*** **1** [C, U] (*becoming old-fashioned, sometimes offensive*) a permanent physical or mental condition that makes it difficult or impossible to use a particular part of your body or mind 生理缺陷；弱智；残疾 SYN **disability**：*Despite her handicap, Jane is able to hold down a full-time job.* 简尽管有生理缺陷，却能够保住一份全职工作。◇ ***mental/physical/visual handicap*** 智力 / 生理 / 视力缺陷 ➲ NOTE AT DISABLED **2** [C] something that makes it difficult for sb to do sth 障碍；阻碍 SYN **obstacle**：*Not speaking the language proved to be a bigger handicap than I'd imagined.* 事实证明，不会讲这种语言所造成的障碍比我想象的大。 **3** [C] (*sport* 体育) a race or competition in which the most skilful must run further, carry extra weight, etc. in order to give all those taking part an equal chance of winning; the disadvantage that is given to sb you are competing against in such a race or competition 让赛，让步赛（使参赛者中的优势方跑得较远、增加负重等）；（让步赛中给优势方施加的）障碍，不利条件 **4** [C] (in GOLF 高尔夫球) an advantage given to a weaker player so that competition is more equal when they play against a stronger player. It is expressed as a number related to the number of times a player hits the ball and gets lower as he/she improves. 差点（给弱者减少的杆数，与实际杆数相关，并随参赛者的进度而减少）

■ ***verb*** **(-pp-)** [usually passive] ~ **sb/sth** to make sth more difficult for sb to do 妨碍；阻碍：*British exports have been handicapped by the strong pound.* 英镑强势影响了英国的出口。

handi·capped /ˈhændikæpt/ *adj.* (*becoming old-fashioned, sometimes offensive*) **1** suffering from a mental or physical handicap 有生理缺陷的；残疾的；弱智的 SYN **disabled**：*a visually handicapped child* 弱视儿童 ◇ *The accident left him physically handicapped.* 那次事故使他落下了残疾。➲ SEE ALSO MENTALLY HANDICAPPED **2 the handicapped** *noun* [pl.] people who are handicapped 残疾人；弱智者：*a school for the physically handicapped* 残疾人学校 ➲ NOTE AT DISABLED

han·di·craft /ˈhændikrɑːft; *NAmE* -kræft/ (*NAmE also* **hand·craft**) *noun* [C, usually pl., U] **1** activities such as sewing and making cloth that use skill with your hands and artistic ability to make things 手工艺： *to teach handicrafts* 传授手工艺 ◇ *Her hobbies are music, reading and handicraft.* 她的爱好是音乐、读书和手工。 **2** things made in this way 手工艺品： *traditional handicrafts bought by tourists* 旅游者购买的传统手工艺品

hand·ily /ˈhændɪli/ *adv.* **1** in a way that is HANDY (= convenient) 方便地；便利地： *We're handily placed for the train station.* 我们被安置在去火车站近便的地方。 **2** (*especially NAmE*) easily 容易地；轻松地： *He handily defeated his challengers.* 他轻而易举地打败了向他挑战的人。

han·di·work /ˈhændiwɜːk; *NAmE* -wɜːrk/ *noun* [U] **1** work that you do, or sth that you have made, especially using your artistic skill 手工（艺）；手工（艺）制品： *We admired her exquisite handiwork.* 我们欣赏她精致的手工艺品。 **2** a thing done by a particular person or group, especially sth bad 某人（或团伙）之所为（尤指坏事）： *This looks like the handiwork of an arsonist.* 这看上去像是纵火犯干的。

hand·job /ˈhænddʒɒb; *NAmE* -dʒɑːb/ *noun* (*taboo, slang*) the act of a person rubbing a man's PENIS with their hand to give sexual pleasure （对男性的）手淫

hand·ker·chief /ˈhæŋkətʃɪf; -tʃiːf; *NAmE* -kərtʃ-/ *noun* (*pl.* **hand·ker·chiefs** or **hand·ker·chieves** /-tʃiːvz/) (*also informal* **hanky**, **han·kie**) a small piece of material or paper that you use for blowing your nose, etc. 手帕；纸巾

han·dle 🔑 /ˈhændl/ *verb, noun*

■ *verb*

- **DEAL WITH** 处理 **1** 🔑 [T] to deal with a situation, a person, an area of work or a strong emotion 处理，应付（局势、人、工作或感情）： **~ sth/sb** *A new man was appointed to handle the crisis.* 新指派了一个人来处理这场危机。 ◇ *She's very good at handling her patients.* 她对待病人很有办法。 ◇ *The sale was handled by Adams Commercial.* 亚当斯公司经营这笔买卖。 ◇ *We can handle up to 500 calls an hour at our new offices.* 我们的新办公室每小时可处理 500 通电话。 ◇ *We all have to learn to handle stress.* 我们都得学会应对压力。 ◇ *This matter has been handled very badly.* 这件事处理得很糟糕。 ◇ (*informal*) *'Any problems?' 'Nothing I can't handle.'* "有问题吗？""没有什么我不能对付的。" ◇ (*informal*) *I've got to go. I can't* **handle it** *any more* (= deal with a difficult situation). 我得走了，我已无计可施。 ◇ **~ yourself** (*informal*) *You have to know how to handle yourself in this business* (= know the right way to behave). 你必须知道在这件事上如何自处。
- **TOUCH WITH HANDS** 用手触摸 **2** 🔑 [T] **~ sth** to touch, hold or move sth with your hands （用手）触，拿，搬动： *Our cat hates being handled.* 我们的猫不喜欢被人摸弄。 ◇ *The label on the box said: 'Fragile.* **Handle with care.***'* 箱子上的标签写着："易碎品，小心轻放。"
- **CONTROL** 控制 **3** 🔑 [T] **~ sth** to control a vehicle, an animal, a tool, etc. 控制，操纵（车辆、动物、工具等）： *I wasn't sure if I could handle such a powerful car.* 我没有把握是否能驾驶功率这样大的车。 ◇ *She's a difficult horse to handle.* 那是一匹桀骜不驯的母马。 **4** [I] **~ well/badly** to be easy/difficult to drive or control （容易/难以）驾驶，操纵： *The car handles well in any weather.* 这辆车在任何天气下开起来都很灵便。
- **BUY/SELL** 买卖 **5** [T] **~ sth** to buy or sell sth 买；卖 SYN **deal in**: *They were arrested for* **handling stolen goods.** 他们因收受赃物而遭逮捕。

■ *noun*

- **OF DOOR/DRAWER/WINDOW** 门窗；抽屉 **1** 🔑 the part of a door, drawer, window, etc. that you use to open it 把手；拉手： *She turned the handle and opened the door.* 她转动把手，打开了门。 ➲ VISUAL VOCAB PAGE V56
- **OF CUP/BAG/TOOL** 杯子；包；工具 **2** 🔑 the part of an object, such as a cup, a bag or a tool, that you use to hold it or carry it 柄；把；提梁；把手： *the handle of a knife* 刀柄 ◇ *a broom handle* 扫帚把 ➲ VISUAL VOCAB PAGES V23, V27, V69 ➲ SEE ALSO LOVE HANDLES
- **-HANDLED** 有…柄 **3** (in adjectives 构成形容词) having the number or type of handle mentioned 有…个柄的；有…柄的： *a long-handled spoon* 一把长柄匙
- **NAME** 名字 **4** a name or NICKNAME 名字；绰号 **5** a USERNAME for the Twitter SOCIAL NETWORKING service, sometimes written after the '@' symbol, or the website address for that service, which acts as a link to the user's PROFILE (= a description of that person) and to messages written by or about the user 推特账号；推特用户名： *I added my handle at the top of my blog page so that readers could view my tweets as well as my blog posts.* 我在我的博客页面顶部添加了推特账号，这样读者既能看到我的博客帖子，又可以查看我在推特发送的信息。

IDM **get/have a ˈhandle on sb/sth** (*informal*) to understand or know about sb/sth, especially so that you can deal with it or them later 弄懂；理解；搞明白： *I can't get a handle on these sales figures.* 我搞不懂这些销售数字。 **give sb a ˈhandle (on sth)** (*informal*) to give sb enough facts or knowledge for them to be able to deal with sth （使）弄懂，理解，明白 ➲ MORE AT FLY *v.*

handles 柄；把手

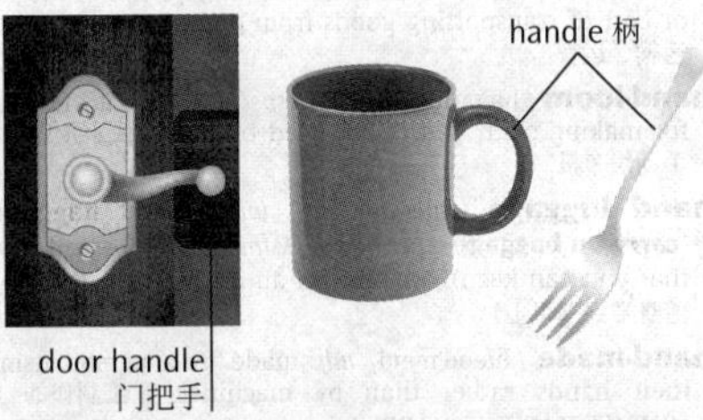

knobs 球形把手；旋钮

buttons 按钮；键

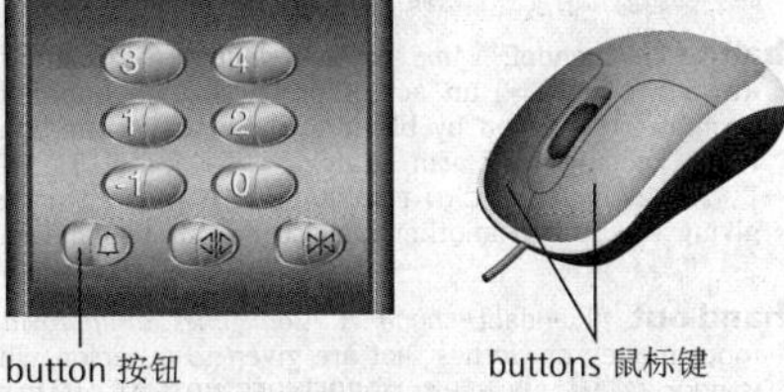

handle·bar /ˈhændlbɑː(r)/ *noun* [C] (*also* **handlebars** [pl.]) a metal bar, with a handle at each end, that you use for steering a bicycle or motorcycle （自行车或摩托车的）把手： *to hold onto the handlebars* 抓紧把手 ➲ WORDFINDER NOTE AT CYCLING ➲ VISUAL VOCAB PAGE V55 ➲ SEE ALSO DROP HANDLEBARS

ˌhandlebar mousˈtache *noun* a MOUSTACHE that is curved upwards at each end 翘八字胡

hand·ler /ˈhændlə(r)/ *noun* (especially in compounds 尤用于构成复合词) **1** a person who trains and controls animals, especially dogs 驯兽员；（尤指）驯犬员 **2** a person who carries or touches sth as part of their job 搬运工；操作者： *airport baggage handlers* 机场行李员 ◇ *food handlers* 食品处理者 **3** (*especially NAmE*) a person who organizes sth or advises sb 组织者；顾问： *the President's campaign handlers* 总统的竞选智囊

hand·ling /ˈhændlɪŋ/ *noun* [U] **1** the way that sb deals with or treats a situation, a person, an animal, etc. （对形势、人、动物等的）处理，对付，对待： *I was impressed by his handling of the affair.* 他对此事的处理方式我甚感佩服。◇ *This horse needs firm handling.* 这匹马需要严加训练。 **2** the action of organizing or controlling sth 组织；控制；管理： *data handling on computer* 计算机的数据处理 **3** the action of touching, feeling or holding sth with your hands （手的）触摸，触摸感觉，握，拿： *toys that can stand up to rough handling* 经得起摔打的玩具 **4** the cost of dealing with an order, delivering goods, booking tickets, etc. （订货、送货、订票等的）费用，手续费： *a small handling charge* 少许的手续费 **5** the way in which a vehicle can be controlled by the driver （车辆的）驾驶，操纵： *a car designed for easy handling* 为驾驶简便而设计的汽车 **6** (*BrE also* **car·riage**) (*formal*) the act or cost of transporting goods from one place to another 运输；运费

H

hand·loom /ˈhændluːm/ *noun* (*especially IndE*) a machine for making cloth that is operated by hand 手摇纺织机；手动织布机

ˈhand luggage (*especially BrE*) (*also* **ˈhand baggage**, **ˈcarry-on baggage** *especially in NAmE*) *noun* [U] small bags that you can keep with you on an aircraft 手提行李（可随身带到飞机上）

hand·made /ˌhændˈmeɪd/ *adj.* made by a person using their hands rather than by machines 手工制作的 ➲ COMPARE MACHINE-MADE

hand·maiden /ˈhændmeɪdn/ (*also* **hand·maid** /ˈhændmeɪd/) *noun* **1** (*old-fashioned*) a female servant 女佣；侍女 **2** (*formal*) something that supports and helps sth else 根基；基础： *Mathematics was once dubbed the handmaiden of the sciences.* 数学曾一度被视为各门科学的基础。

ˈhand-me-down *noun* [usually pl.] (*especially NAmE*) = CAST-OFF： *She hated having to wear her sister's hand-me-downs.* 她讨厌穿她姐姐穿过的旧衣服。 ▶ **ˈhand-me-down** *adj.* (*especially NAmE*) = CAST-OFF

ˈhand-me-up *noun* an item that sb gives to an older member of their family because they no longer use it or because they have bought sth better to replace it （送给年长亲属的）旧东西，替换下的东西

hand·off /ˈhændɒf; *NAmE* -ɔːf; -ɑːf/ *noun* **1** (especially in RUGBY 尤指橄榄球) an act of preventing an opponent from TACKLING you by blocking them with your hand while keeping your arm straight 伸手推开（以防范对手拦截） **2** (in AMERICAN FOOTBALL 美式足球) an act of giving the ball to another player on your team （手递手）传球；递传

hand·out /ˈhændaʊt/ *noun* **1** (*sometimes disapproving*) food, money or clothes that are given to a person who is poor 捐赠品；救济品 ➲ WORDFINDER NOTE AT CHARITY **2** (*often disapproving*) money that is given to a person or an organization by the government, etc., for example to encourage commercial activity 政府拨款（为促进商业活动） **3** a free document that gives information about an event or a matter of public interest, or that states the views of a political party, etc. 传单 ➲ SEE ALSO PRESS RELEASE **4** a document that is given to students in class or people attending a talk, etc. and that contains a summary of the lesson/talk, a set of exercises, etc. （发给学生或参与讨论者等的）讲义，文字材料

hand·over /ˈhændəʊvə(r); *NAmE* -oʊvər/ *noun* [C, U] **1** the act of moving power or responsibility from one person or group to another; the period during which this is done （权力、责任等的）移交，移交期： *the smooth handover of power from a military to a civilian government* 从军政府到文人政府的权力的顺利移交 **2** the act of giving a person or thing to sb in authority （某人或某物的）交出，上交： *the handover of the hostages* 人质的交出

hand·phone /ˈhændfəʊn; *NAmE* -foʊn/ *noun* used in SE Asia as the word for a mobile/cell phone （东南亚用语）手机，移动电话

ˌhand-ˈpicked *adj.* carefully chosen for a special purpose 仔细挑选的；精选的

hand·print /ˈhændprɪnt/ *noun* a mark left by the flat part of someone's hand on a surface 手印

ˈhand puppet (*NAmE*) (*BrE* **ˈglove puppet**) *noun* a type of PUPPET that you put over your hand and move using your fingers 手偶（套在手上用手指操纵） ➲ VISUAL VOCAB PAGE V41

hand·rail /ˈhændreɪl/ *noun* a long narrow bar that you can hold onto for support, for example when you are going up or down stairs （楼梯等的）扶手 ➲ PICTURE AT STAIRCASE

hand·saw /ˈhændsɔː/ *noun* a SAW (= a tool with a long blade with sharp teeth along one edge) that is used with one hand only 手锯 ➲ VISUAL VOCAB PAGE V21

ˌhands-ˈdown *adj.* [only before noun] ~ **winner/favourite/choice** (*informal*) easily the winner of a contest; definitely the one that people prefer 轻易取胜的；首选无疑的： *These kits were hands-down favourites with our testers.* 这套工具绝对是我们的测试者一见倾心的首选。 IDM SEE HAND *n.*

hand·set /ˈhændset/ *noun* **1** the part of a telephone that you hold close to your mouth and ear to speak into and listen 电话听筒 ➲ COMPARE RECEIVER (1) **2** a mobile/cell phone or SMARTPHONE, especially the main part of the phone not including the battery or SIM CARD 手机，智能手机（尤指电话的主体部分，不包括电池和 SIM 卡）： *mobile handsets* 移动电话 ◇ *handset manufacturers* 手机生产商 **3** a device that you hold in your hand to operate a television, etc. （电视等的）遥控器 ➲ SEE ALSO REMOTE CONTROL (2)

ˈhands-free *adj.* (of a telephone, etc. 电话等) able to be used without needing to be held in the hand 免提的

hand·shake /ˈhændʃeɪk/ *noun* an act of shaking sb's hand with your own, used especially to say hello or goodbye or when you have made an agreement 握手 ➲ SEE ALSO GOLDEN HANDSHAKE

ˌhands-ˈoff *adj.* [usually before noun] dealing with people or a situation by not becoming involved and by allowing people to do what they want to 不介入的；放手的： *a hands-off approach to staff management* 不干涉的职员管理方法 ➲ COMPARE HANDS-ON

hand·some /ˈhænsəm/ *adj.* (**hand·somer**, **hand·som·est**) HELP **more handsome** and **most handsome** are more common * more handsome 和 most handsome 更常见。 **1** (of men 男子) attractive 英俊的；漂亮的；有魅力的 SYN **good-looking**： *a handsome face* 英俊的相貌 ◇ *He's the most handsome man I've ever met.* 他是我见过的最俊美的男子。 ◇ *He was aptly described as* ***'tall, dark, and handsome'***. 他被恰如其分地描述为"高大黝黑、相貌堂堂"。 ➲ SYNONYMS AT BEAUTIFUL **2** (of women 女子) attractive, with large strong features rather than small delicate ones 健美的： *a tall, handsome woman* 一位高个头的健美女子 ➲ SYNONYMS AT BEAUTIFUL **3** beautiful to look at 美观的；悦目的： *a handsome horse/house/city* 漂亮的马 / 房子 / 城市 ◇ *The two of them made a* ***handsome couple***. 这对夫妻男俊女靓。 **4** large in amount or quantity 数量大的： *a* ***handsome profit*** 一大笔利润 ◇ *He was elected by a handsome majority* (= a lot of people voted for him). 他以高票当选。 **5** generous 大方的；慷慨的；气量大的： *She paid him a handsome compliment.* 她大大赞扬了他

一番。▶ **hand·some·ly** *adv.*： *a handsomely dressed man* 穿着潇洒的男子 ◇ *a handsomely produced book* 印刷精美的书 ◇ *to be* ***paid/rewarded handsomely*** 得到可观的工资 / 报酬 **hand·some·ness** *noun* [U]

ˌhands-ˈon *adj.* [usually before noun] doing sth rather than just talking about it 动手的；实际操作的： *hands-on computer training* 计算机操作培训 ◇ *to gain* ***hands-on experience*** *of industry* 获得实际的从业经验 ◇ *a hands-on style of management* 事必躬亲的管理方式 ➲ COMPARE HANDS-OFF

hand·spring /ˈhændsprɪŋ/ *noun* a movement in gymnastics in which you jump through the air landing on your hands, then again landing on your feet（体操动作）手翻

hand·stand /ˈhændstænd/ *noun* a movement in which you balance on your hands and put your legs straight up in the air 倒立（动作）

ˌhand-to-ˈhand *adj.* **hand-to-hand** fighting involves physical contact with your opponent 交手的；白刃的；肉搏的

ˌhand-to-ˈmouth *adj.* [usually before noun] if you have a **hand-to-mouth** life, you spend all the money you earn on basic needs such as food and do not have anything left 仅够糊口的；勉强维持生计的 IDM SEE LIVE[1]

hand·writ·ing /ˈhændraɪtɪŋ/ *noun* [U] **1** writing that is done with a pen or pencil, not printed or typed 手写；书写 **2** a person's particular style of writing in this way 笔迹；书法： *I can't read his handwriting.* 我看不懂他写的字。

IDM **the ˌhandwriting on the ˈwall** (*NAmE*) = THE WRITING IS ON THE WALL

hand·writ·ten /ˌhændˈrɪtn/ *adj.* written by hand, not printed or typed 手写的： *a handwritten note* 手写的便条

handy /ˈhændi/ *adj.* (**hand·ier, handi·est**) (*informal*) **1** easy to use or to do 易使用的；容易做的；便利的 SYN **useful**: *a handy little tool* 好用的小工具 ◇ ***handy hints/tips*** *for removing stains* 清除污渍的窍门儿 **2** [not before noun] located near to sb/sth; located or stored in a convenient place 近便；便利： *Always keep a first-aid kit handy.* 手边要常备急救箱。◇ *Have you got a pen handy?* 你手头有笔吗？◇ ~ **(for sth/for doing sth)** (*BrE*) *Our house is very handy for the station.* 我们家离车站很近。 **3** [not before noun] skilful in using your hands or tools to make or repair things 手巧；有手艺： *to be handy around the house* 对家里制作、修理等杂事很在行 ➲ SEE ALSO HANDILY ▶ **handi·ness** *noun* [U]

IDM **ˌcome in ˈhandy** (*informal*) to be useful 有用处： *The extra money came in very handy.* 这笔额外的钱正好派上了用场。◇ *Don't throw that away—it might come in handy.* 别把它扔了，它或许有用。

handy·man /ˈhændimæn/ *noun* (*pl.* **-men** /-men/) a man who is good at doing practical jobs inside and outside the house, either as a hobby or as a job 善于做室内外杂活的人；杂活工

hang /hæŋ/ *verb, noun*

■ ***verb*** (**hung, hung** /hʌŋ/) HELP In sense 4, **hanged** is used for the past tense and past participle. 作第 4 义时过去时和过去分词用 hanged。

• **ATTACH FROM TOP** 悬挂 **1** [T, I] to attach sth, or to be attached, at the top so that the lower part is free or loose 悬挂；吊： ~ **sth + adv./prep.** *Hang your coat on the hook.* 把你的大衣挂在衣钩上。◇ ~ **sth up** *Shall I hang your coat up?* 我把你的大衣挂起来好吗？◇ ~ **sth (out)** (*BrE*) *Have you hung out the washing?* 你把洗好的衣服晾在外面了吗？◇ (*NAmE*) *Have you hung the wash?* 你把洗好的衣服晾了吗？ ◇ ~ **adv./prep.** *There were several expensive suits hanging in the wardrobe.* 衣柜里挂着几套昂贵的套装。

• **FALL LOOSELY** 垂落 **2** [I] ~ **adv./prep.** when sth **hangs** in a particular way, it falls in that way 垂下；垂落： *Her hair hung down to her waist.* 她的长发垂及腰际。◇ *He had lost weight and the suit hung loosely on him.* 他体重减轻了，这套衣服他穿在身上松松垮垮的。

• **BEND DOWNWARDS** 下垂 **3** [I, T] to bend or let sth bend downwards （使）低垂，下垂： ~ **adv./prep.** *The dog's tongue was hanging out.* 狗的舌头耷拉在外面。◇ *Children hung* (= were leaning) *over the gate.* 孩子们趴在门上。◇ *A cigarette hung from her lips.* 她嘴唇上叼着香烟。◇ ~ **sth** *She* ***hung her head*** *in shame.* 她羞愧得垂下了头。

• **KILL SB** 杀人 **4** (**hanged, hanged**) [T, I] ~ **(sb/yourself)** to kill sb, usually as a punishment, by tying a rope around their neck and allowing them to drop; to be killed in this way （被）绞死，施以绞刑： *He was the last man to be hanged for murder in this country.* 他是这个国家中最后一个被处以绞刑的谋杀犯。◇ *She had committed suicide by hanging herself from a beam.* 她悬梁自尽了。◇ *At that time you could hang for stealing.* 那时犯盗窃罪可被绞死。

• **PICTURES** 图画 **5** [T, I] ~ **(sth)** to attach sth, especially a picture, to a hook on a wall; to be attached in this way （使）挂在墙上： *We hung her portrait above the fireplace.* 我们把她的画像挂在壁炉上方。◇ *Several of his paintings hang in the Tate Gallery.* 他的几幅油画挂在泰特美术馆。 **6** [T, usually passive] ~ **sth with sth** to decorate a place by placing paintings, etc. on a wall 挂图画等装饰（某处）： *The rooms were hung with tapestries.* 这些房间装饰着挂毯。

• **WALLPAPER** 壁纸 **7** [T] ~ **sth** to stick WALLPAPER to a wall （在墙上）贴壁纸

• **DOOR/GATE** 门 **8** [T] ~ **sth** to attach a door or gate to a post so that it moves freely 把（门）装在门柱上；装（门）

• **STAY IN THE AIR** 悬在空中 **9** [I] **+ adv./prep.** to stay in the air 悬浮（在空中）： *Smoke hung in the air above the city.* 城市上空烟雾弥漫。

IDM **ˈhang sth** (*BrE, informal*) used to say that you are not going to worry about sth 不在乎；不管： *Oh, let's get two and hang the expense!* 哎呀，我们买两份吧，管它多少钱！ **hang a ˈleft/ˈright** (*NAmE*) to take a left/right turn 向左 / 向右转 **hang by a ˈhair/ˈthread** (of a person's life 人的生命) to be in great danger 命悬一线；气若游丝；危在旦夕 **hang (on) ˈin there** (*informal*) to remain determined to succeed even when a situation is difficult 保持信心；坚持下去；不气馁 **hang on sb's ˈwords/on sb's every ˈword** to listen with great attention to sb you admire 专心致志地听所崇拜的人讲话；洗耳恭听某人的话 **hang ˈtough** (*NAmE*) to be determined and refuse to change your attitude or ideas 立场坚定；态度坚决 **let it all hang ˈout** (*informal*) to express your feelings freely 宣泄情感 ➲ MORE AT BALANCE *n.*, FIRE *n.*, GRIM, HEAVY *adv.*, LOOSE *adj.*, PEG *n.*, WELL *adv.*

PHR V **ˌhang aˈbout** (*BrE, informal*) **1** to wait or stay near a place, not doing very much （在某处附近）等待，逗留，闲荡： *kids hanging about in the streets* 东游西逛的孩子们 **2** to be very slow doing sth 慢悠悠： *I can't hang about—the boss wants to see me.* 我可不能磨磨蹭蹭了，老板要见我。 **3** (*informal*) used to tell sb to stop what they are doing or saying for a short time 停一下；等一等： *Hang about! There's something not quite right here.* 且慢！这儿有点不对头。 **ˌhang aˈbout with sb** (*BrE*) (*NAmE* **ˈhang with sb**) (*informal*) to spend a lot of time with sb （和某人）长时间待在一起，泡在一块儿 **ˌhang aˈround (...)** (*informal*) to wait or stay near a place, not doing very much （在某处附近）等待，逗留，闲荡： *You hang around here in case he comes, and I'll go on ahead.* 你在这附近等着以防万一他来了，我继续往前走。 **ˌhang aˈround with sb** (*informal*) to spend a lot of time with sb （和某人）长时间待在一起，泡在一块儿 **ˌhang ˈback** to remain in a place after all the other people have left 留下；继续留在原处 **ˌhang ˈback (from sth)** to hesitate because you are nervous about doing or saying sth 犹豫；畏缩；吞吞吐吐： *I was sure she knew the answer but for some reason she hung back.* 我敢保证她知道答案，但不知为什么她不敢说出来。 **ˌhang ˈon 1** to hold sth tightly 抓紧： *Hang on tight—we're off!* 抓紧了，我们出发了！ ➲ SYNONYMS AT HOLD **2** (*informal*) used to ask sb to wait for a short time or to stop what they are doing 等一下；停一下： *Hang on—I'm not* quite ready. 等一等，我还没准备好呢。◊ *Now hang on a minute—you can't really believe what you just said!* 等一下，你不可能真的相信你刚才说的话吧！ **3** to wait for sth to happen 等待某事发生；等候：*I haven't heard if I've got the job yet—they've kept me hanging on for days.* 我是否得到了那份工作的事还没消息，他们让我等了好几天了。 **4** (*informal*) used on the telephone to ask sb who is calling to wait until they can talk to the person they want 别挂电话，等一下：*Hang on—I'll just see if he's here.* 等一下，我这就看看他在不在。 **5** to continue doing sth in difficult circumstances （在逆境中）坚持，不放弃：*The team hung on for victory.* 这个队为了胜利坚持不懈。 **ˈhang on sth** to depend on sth 有赖于，取决于（某事物）：*A lot hangs on this decision.* 很多事情都取决于这一决定。 **ˌhang ˈon to sth 1** 🔑 to hold sth tightly 抓紧某物：*Hang on to that rope and don't let go.* 抓紧那根绳子，别松手。 **2** (*informal*) to keep sth, not sell it or give it away 保留；不卖掉；不放弃：*Let's hang on to those old photographs—they may be valuable.* 咱们留着那些旧照片吧，它们或许有价值。 **ˌhang ˈout** (*informal*) to spend a lot of time in a place 常去某处；泡在某处：*The local kids hang out at the mall.* 当地的孩子常在商场闲荡。 ➲ RELATED NOUN HANG-OUT **ˌhang sth↔ˈout** (*especially BrE*) to attach things that you have washed to a piece of thin rope or wire, etc. outside so that they can dry; to attach sth such as a flag outside a window or in the street （把洗好的东西）挂在外面晾干；（把旗子等）挂在外面 **ˌhang ˈover sb** if sth bad or unpleasant is **hanging over** you, you think about it and worry about it a lot because it is happening or might happen 使忧心忡忡；担心可能发生：*The possibility of a court case is still hanging over her.* 可能被告上法庭的阴影依然笼罩在她的心头。 **ˌhang toˈgether 1** to fit together well; to be the same as or CONSISTENT with each other 相符；一致；连贯：*Their accounts of what happened don't hang together.* 他们各人对事情的描述不吻合。 **2** (of people 人) to support or help one another 相互支持；互相帮助；同心协力 **ˌhang ˈup** 🔑 to end a telephone conversation by putting the telephone RECEIVER down or switching the telephone off 挂断电话：*After I hung up I remembered what I'd wanted to say.* 我挂断电话之后才想起来原本想说的话。 **ˌhang sth↔ˈup** (*informal*) to finish using sth for the last time 终止使用某物：*Ruth has hung up her dancing shoes.* 鲁思已挂起舞鞋退出舞台了。 **ˌhang ˈup on sb** (*informal*) to end a telephone call by suddenly and unexpectedly putting the telephone down 突然挂断某人的电话：*Don't hang up on me—we must talk!* 别挂断电话，我们一定得谈谈！ ➲ SEE ALSO HUNG UP **ˈhang with sb** (*NAmE*) (*BrE* **ˌhang aˈbout with sb**) (*informal*) to spend a lot of time with sb 和某人长时间待在一起；和某人一起消磨时间

■ **noun** [sing.] the way in which a dress, piece of cloth, etc. falls or moves （衣服、织物等的）悬挂方式，下垂

IDM **get the ˈhang of sth** (*informal*) to learn how to do or to use sth; to understand sth 掌握…的要领；了解…的用法；找到了诀窍：*It's not difficult once you get the hang of it.* 你掌握了要领就不难了。

hangar /ˈhæŋə(r); ˈhæŋgə(r)/ *noun* a large building in which aircraft are kept 飞机库

hang·dog /ˈhæŋdɒg; *NAmE* -dɔːg; -dɑːg/ *adj.* [only before noun] if a person has a **hangdog** look, they look sad or ashamed 显得难过的；羞愧的

hanger /ˈhæŋə(r)/ (*also* **ˈcoat hanger**, **ˈclothes hanger**) *noun* a curved piece of wood, plastic or wire, with a hook at the top, that you use to hang clothes up on 衣架 ➲ VISUAL VOCAB PAGES V24, V68

ˌhanger-ˈon *noun* (*pl.* **hangers-on**) (*often disapproving*) a person who tries to be friendly with a famous person or who goes to important events, in order to get some advantage 逢迎者；攀附权贵者

ˈhang-glider *noun* **1** the frame used in hang-gliding 悬挂式滑翔机 **2** a person who goes hang-gliding 悬挂式滑翔机运动员

ˈhang-gliding *noun* [U] a sport in which you fly while hanging from a frame like a large KITE which you control with your body movements 悬挂式滑翔运动：*to go hang-gliding* 进行悬挂式滑翔运动 ➲ VISUAL VOCAB PAGE V53

hang·ing /ˈhæŋɪŋ/ *noun* **1** [U, C] the practice of killing sb as a punishment by putting a rope around their neck and hanging them from a high place; an occasion when this happens 绞死；绞刑：*to sentence sb to death by hanging* 判处某人绞刑 ◊ *public hangings* 公开执行的绞刑 **2** [C, usually pl.] a large piece of material that is hung on a wall for decoration 墙幔；帷幔：*wall hangings* 挂在墙上的装饰织物

ˌhanging ˈbasket *noun* a BASKET or similar container with flowers growing in it, that is hung from a building by a short chain or rope 吊花篮；吊花盆 ➲ PICTURE AT BASKET ➲ VISUAL VOCAB PAGE V18

ˌhanging ˈvalley *noun* (*specialist*) a valley which joins a deeper valley, often with a WATERFALL where the two valleys join 悬谷（下接更深的溪谷，连接处常有瀑布）

hang·man /ˈhæŋmən/ *noun* (*pl.* **-men** /-mən/) **1** [C] a man whose job is to hang criminals 执行绞刑的人；刽子手 **2** [U] a game in which one player chooses a word and the other players try to guess it, letter by letter. Each time they guess wrongly, the first person draws one part of a man being hanged. The other players have to guess the word before the drawing is complete. 猜词画人游戏（一个玩家选一个单词，其他玩家设法猜出，每猜错一个字母就画一部分吊着的人的身体，其他玩家须在全部身体画完之前猜出该词。）

hang·nail /ˈhæŋneɪl/ *noun* a piece of skin near the bottom or at the side of your nail that is loose and sore （指甲根部或两侧的）倒刺

ˈhang-out *noun* (*informal*) a place where sb lives or likes to go often 住所；经常去的地方 **SYN** **haunt**

hang·over /ˈhæŋəʊvə(r); *NAmE* -oʊvər/ *noun* **1** the headache and sick feeling that you have the day after drinking too much alcohol 宿醉（过量喝酒后第二天的头痛以及恶心反应）：*She woke up with a terrible hangover.* 她醒来时宿醉反应很厉害。 **2** [usually sing.] **~ (from sth)** a feeling, custom, idea, etc. that remains from the past, although it is no longer practical or suitable 遗留的感觉；沿袭下来的风俗（或思想等）：*the insecure feeling that was a hangover from her childhood* 她儿时留下的不安全感 ◊ *hangover laws from the previous administration* 从上届政府沿袭下来的法律 ➲ SEE ALSO HOLDOVER

the Hang Seng Index /ˌhæŋ ˈseŋ ɪndeks/ *noun* a figure that shows the relative price of shares on the Hong Kong Stock Exchange 恒生指数（香港交易所股票交易指数）

ˈhang-up *noun* (*informal*) **1** **~ (about sth)** an emotional problem about sth that makes you embarrassed or worried 苦恼；难堪；焦虑：*He's got a real hang-up about his height.* 他为他的身高很是苦恼。 **2** (*NAmE*) a problem that delays sth being agreed or achieved （拖延协议等达成的）难题，障碍

hank /hæŋk/ *noun* a long piece of wool, thread, rope, etc. that is wound into a large loose ball （毛线、棉线、绳等的）团

han·ker /ˈhæŋkə(r)/ *verb* [I] to have a strong desire for sth 渴望，渴求（某事物）：**~ after/for sth** *He had hankered after fame all his life.* 他一生追求名望。 ◊ **~ to do sth** *She hankered to go back to Australia.* 她渴望回到澳大利亚。

han·ker·ing /ˈhæŋkərɪŋ/ *noun* [usually sing.] **~ (for/after sth) | ~ (to do sth)** a strong desire （对或做某事的）强烈欲望：*a hankering for a wealthy lifestyle* 渴望过富裕生活

hanky (*also* **han·kie**) /ˈhæŋki/ *noun* (*pl.* **-ies**) (*informal*) = HANDKERCHIEF

hanky-panky /ˌhæŋki ˈpæŋki/ *noun* [U] (*old-fashioned, informal*) **1** sexual activity that is not considered acceptable 不得体的性行为；调戏；不正当性活动 **2** dishonest behaviour 欺骗行为；花招

Han·sard /ˈhænsɑːd; *NAmE* -sɑːrd/ *noun* [U] (in the British, Canadian, Australian, New Zealand or South African parliaments) the official written record of everything that is said in the parliament（英国、加拿大、澳大利亚、新西兰或南非议会的）议会议事录

han·som /ˈhænsəm/ (*also* **ˈhansom cab**) *noun* a CARRIAGE with two wheels, pulled by one horse, used in the past to carry two passengers（旧时由一匹马拉的）双轮双座马车

Ha·nuk·kah (*also* **Cha·nuk·kah, Cha·nuk·ah**) /ˈhænʊkə; ˈxænʊkə/ *noun* an eight-day Jewish festival and holiday in November or December when Jews remember the occasion when the TEMPLE in Jerusalem was DEDICATED again in 165 BC 修殿节，光明节（历时八天的犹太人节日，纪念公元前 165 年重献耶路撒冷圣殿）

ha'·penny = HALFPENNY (1)

hap·haz·ard /hæpˈhæzəd; *NAmE* -zərd/ *adj.* (*disapproving*) with no particular order or plan; not organized well 无秩序的；无计划的；组织混乱的： *The books had been piled on the shelves in a haphazard fashion.* 书架上的书堆放得杂乱无序。◇ *The government's approach to the problem was haphazard.* 政府解决这一问题的方法缺乏计划。▸ **hap·haz·ard·ly** *adv.*

hap·less /ˈhæpləs/ *adj.* [only before noun] (*formal*) not lucky; unfortunate 倒运的；不幸的： *the hapless victims of exploitation* 受到剥削的不幸牺牲品

hap·loid /ˈhæplɔɪd/ *adj.* (*biology* 生) (of a cell 细胞) containing the set of CHROMOSOMES from one parent only 单倍体的 ➲ COMPARE DIPLOID

ha'p'orth /ˈheɪpəθ; *NAmE* -pərθ/ *noun* [sing.] (*old-fashioned, BrE, informal*) a very small amount (in the past, an amount that could be bought for a HALFPENNY) 很少的量，微量（旧时半便士可购买的量） IDM SEE SPOIL *v.*

hap·pen 🔑 /ˈhæpən/ *verb* **1** [I] to take place, especially without being planned （尤指偶然）发生，出现： *You'll never guess what's happened!* 你根本猜不到出了什么事！◇ *Accidents like this happen all the time.* 此类事故经常发生。◇ *Let's see what happens next week.* 咱们等着瞧下一周会怎么样。◇ *I'll be there* ***whatever happens.*** 不管发生什么事我都会到那儿的。◇ *I don't know how this happened.* 我不知道这事怎么发生的。**2** [I] to take place as the result of sth （作为结果）出现，发生： *She pressed the button but nothing happened.* 她按下按钮，但什么反应也没有。◇ *What happens if nobody comes to the party?* 要是没有人来参加聚会，会怎么样呢？◇ *Just plug it in and* ***see what happens.*** 就把插头插上，看看会怎么样。**3** *linking verb* to do or be sth by chance 碰巧；恰好： **~ to be/do sth** *She happened to be out when we called.* 我们打电话时她刚巧不在。◇ *You don't happen to know his name, do you?* 你不会碰巧知道他的名字吧？◇ **it happens that…** *It happened that she was out when we called.* 我们打电话时她刚巧不在。**4** [T] **~ to be/do sth** used to tell sb sth, especially when you are disagreeing with them or annoyed by what they have said （向对方表示异议或不悦等）： *That happens to be my mother you're talking about!* 你们谈论的是我母亲！ ➲ MORE LIKE THIS 26, page R28

IDM **anything can/might ˈhappen** used to say that it is not possible to know what the result of sth will be 什么事都可能发生；结果难以预料 **as it happens/happened** used when you say sth that is surprising, or sth connected with what sb else has just said 令人惊奇的是；恰恰： *I agree with you, as it happens.* 我恰恰和你意见一致。◇ *As it happens, I have a spare set of keys in my office.* 碰巧我在办公室有一套备用钥匙。**it (just) so happens that…** by chance 碰巧；恰好： *It just so happened they'd been invited too.* 他们碰巧也获得邀请。**ˌthese things ˈhappen** used to tell sb not to worry about sth they have done 这类事在所难免；别为做过的事担忧： *'Sorry—I've spilt some wine.' 'Never mind. These things happen.'* "对不起，我弄洒了些酒。""没关系。这种事在所难免。" ➲ MORE AT ACCIDENT, EVENT, SHIT *n.*, WAIT *v.*

PHR V **ˈhappen on sth** (*old-fashioned*) to find sth by chance 偶然发现某物 **ˈhappen to sb/sth** to have an effect on sb/sth 遭到；遇到： *I hope nothing* (= nothing unpleasant) *has happened to them.* 我希望他们没出事。◇ *It's the best thing that has ever happened to me.* 这是我所遇到的最好的事。◇ *What's happened to your car?* 你的车出什么毛病了？◇ *Do you know what happened to Gill Lovecy* (= have you any news about her)? 你有吉尔·洛夫西的消息吗？

hap·pen·ing /ˈhæpənɪŋ/ *noun, adj.*
■ ***noun*** **1** [usually pl.] an event; something that happens, often sth unusual 事件；发生的事情（常指不寻常的）： *There have been strange happenings here lately.* 这儿最近发生了一些怪事。**2** an artistic performance or event that is not planned 即兴艺术表演
■ ***adj.*** [only before noun] (*informal*) where there is a lot of exciting activity; fashionable 热闹的；时髦的： *a happening place* 时髦的地方

hap·pen·stance /ˈhæpənstæns; *BrE also* -stɑːns/ *noun* [U, C] (*literary*) chance, especially when it results in sth good 偶然情况；（尤指）机遇

hap·pily 🔑 /ˈhæpɪli/ *adv.* **1** in a cheerful way; with feelings of pleasure or satisfaction 快乐地；高兴地；满足地： *children playing happily on the beach* 在海滩上嬉戏的孩子们◇ *to be happily married* 婚姻美满◇ *I think we can manage quite happily on our own.* 我想我们自己完全能够应付。◇ ***And they all lived happily ever after*** (= used as the end of a FAIRY TALE). 从此他们都过着幸福美满的生活（用作童话故事的结尾）。**2** by good luck 幸运地 SYN **fortunately**: *Happily, the damage was only slight.* 所幸的是，损伤不大。**3** willingly 欣然；情愿地： *I'll happily help, if I can.* 如果我能帮忙，我倒很乐意。**4** (*formal*) in a way that is suitable or appropriate 合适地；恰当地： *This suggestion did not fit very happily with our existing plans.* 这个建议与我们目前的计划不十分契合。

WORD FAMILY
happy *adj.* (≠ unhappy)
happily *adv.* (≠ unhappily)
happiness *noun* (≠ unhappiness)

happy 🔑 /ˈhæpi/ *adj.* (**hap·pier, hap·pi·est**)
• **FEELING/GIVING PLEASURE** 感到 / 给予快乐 **1** feeling or showing pleasure; pleased 感到（或显得）快乐的；高兴的： *a happy smile/face* 快活的微笑 / 面容◇ *You don't look very happy today.* 你今天好像不太高兴。◇ **~ to do sth** *We are happy to announce the engagement of our daughter.* 我们高兴地宣布，我们的女儿已订婚。◇ **~ for sb** *I'm very happy for you.* 我真为你感到高兴。◇ **~ (that)…** *I'm happy (that) you could come.* 我很高兴你能来。 ➲ SYNONYMS AT GLAD **2** giving or causing pleasure 给予（或带来）快乐的；使人高兴的；幸福的： *a happy marriage/memory/childhood* 幸福的婚姻 / 回忆 / 童年◇ *The story has a* ***happy ending.*** 故事的结局很圆满。◇ *Those were the happiest days of my life.* 那是我一生中最幸福的一段时光。
• **AT CELEBRATION** 祝贺 **3** if you wish sb a **Happy Birthday, Happy New Year**, etc. you mean that you hope they have a pleasant celebration （表示祝愿，如 Happy Birthday 生日快乐、Happy New Year 新年好等）
• **SATISFIED** 满意 **4** satisfied that sth is good or right; not anxious （对事物）满意的，放心的： **~ (with sb/sth)** *Are you happy with that arrangement?* 你对这一安排感到满意吗？◇ *I'm not happy with his work this term.* 我对他这学期的表现不满意。◇ *She was happy enough with her performance.* 她对于自己的表现还算满意。◇ **~ (about sb/sth)** *If there's anything you're not happy about, come and ask.* 你如果有什么不满意的，来说一声。◇ *I'm not too happy about her living alone.* 我不太放心让她一个人住。◇ *I said I'd go just to* ***keep him happy.*** 我说我要去只是为了让他高兴。

• WILLING 情愿 **5** ~ **to do sth** (*formal*) willing or pleased to do sth 情愿，乐意（做某事）：*I'm happy to leave it till tomorrow.* 我愿意把它留到明天再做。◇ *He will be* ***more than happy*** *to come with us.* 他巴不得和我们一起来。

• LUCKY 幸运 **6** lucky; successful 幸运的；成功的 SYN **fortunate**: *By* ***a happy coincidence,*** *we arrived at exactly the same time.* 碰巧运气好，我们恰恰同时到达。◇ *He* ***is in the happy position of*** *never having to worry about money.* 他运气真好，从来不用为金钱操心。

• SUITABLE 合适 **7** (*formal*) (of words, ideas or behaviour 言语、思想或行为) suitable and appropriate for a particular situation 合适的；恰当的：*That wasn't the happiest choice of words.* 那样的措辞并不是十分恰当。

▶ **hap·pi·ness** *noun* [U]: *to* ***find true happiness*** 寻找真正的幸福 ◇ *Her eyes shone with happiness.* 她双眼闪烁着幸福的光芒。 ➲ SYNONYMS AT SATISFACTION

IDM **a ˌhappy eˈvent** the birth of a baby（生孩子）喜事 **a/the happy ˈmedium** something that is in the middle between two choices or two ways of doing sth 折中办法 **many happy reˈturns (of the ˈday)** used to wish sb a happy and pleasant birthday（生日祝福）生日快乐，长命百岁 **not a ˌhappy ˈbunny** (*BrE*) (*NAmE* **not a ˌhappy ˈcamper**) (*informal*) not pleased about a situation 对境况不满意：*She wasn't a happy bunny at all.* 她一点儿都不满意。➲ MORE AT MEAN *n.*

▼ SYNONYMS 同义词辨析

happy

satisfied • content • contented • joyful • blissful

These words all describe feeling, showing or giving pleasure or satisfaction. 以上各词均表示快乐、愉快、满意。

happy feeling, showing or giving pleasure; satisfied with sth or not worried about it 指快乐的、满意的、放心的：*a happy marriage/memory/childhood* 幸福的婚姻 / 回忆 / 童年 ◇ *I said I'd go, just to* ***keep him happy.*** 我说我要去只是为了让他高兴。

satisfied pleased because you have achieved sth or because sth has happened as you wanted it to; showing this satisfaction 指满意的、满足的、欣慰的：*She's never satisfied with what she's got.* 她对自己所得到的从不感到满足。◇ *a satisfied smile* 满意的微笑

content [not before noun] happy and satisfied with what you have 指满意、满足：*I'm perfectly* ***content*** *just to lie in the sun.* 我在阳光下躺着就感到非常满足。

contented happy and comfortable with what you have; showing this 指满意的、满足的、惬意的：*a contented baby* 心满意足的小宝贝 ◇ *a long contented sigh* 惬意的长叹

CONTENT OR CONTENTED? 用 content 还是 contented?

Being **contented** depends more on having a comfortable life; being **content** can depend more on your attitude to your life: you can *have to be content* or *learn to be content.* People or animals can be **contented** but only people can be **content.** * contented 多指因生活舒适而惬意；content 多指对生活的态度，可以用 have to be content（只好知足）或 learn to be content（学会知足）。人和动物均可用 contented，但只有人才能用 content。

joyful (*rather formal*) very happy; making people very happy 指高兴的、快乐的、令人愉快的

blissful making people very happy; showing this happiness 指令人愉快的、极乐的、幸福的：*three blissful weeks away* 无忧无虑的三周假期

JOYFUL OR BLISSFUL? 用 joyful 还是 blissful?

Joy is a livelier feeling; **bliss** is more peaceful. * joy 较活跃和富活力，bliss 则较平和。

PATTERNS

- happy/satisfied/content/contented **with** sth
- a happy/satisfied/contented/blissful **smile**
- a happy/joyful **occasion/celebration**
- to **feel** happy/satisfied/content/contented/joyful
- **very/perfectly/quite** happy/satisfied/content/contented

---

happy-clappy /ˌhæpi ˈklæpi/ *adj.* (*BrE, often disapproving*) connected with a Christian group which worships in a very loud and enthusiastic way, showing a lot of feeling（基督徒在祈祷仪式等）热情过头的

ˌhappy ˈfamilies *noun* [U] a children's card game played with special cards with pictures of family members on them. The aim is to get as many whole families as possible. 快乐家庭游戏（用家人照片作为纸牌的游戏，赢得最多完整家庭纸牌者获胜）

IDM **ˌplay happy ˈfamilies** to do things that normal happy families do, especially when you want it to appear that your family is happy 做快乐家庭所做的事：*I'm not going to play happy families just for the benefit of your parents.* 我不会仅仅为了顾全你父母而装出合家欢的假象。

ˌhappy-go-ˈlucky *adj.* not caring or worrying about the future 无忧无虑的；乐天的：*a happy-go-lucky attitude* 无忧无虑的态度 ◇ *a happy-go-lucky sort of person* 乐天派的人

ˈhappy hour *noun* [usually sing.] (*informal*) a time, usually in the early evening, when a pub or a bar sells alcoholic drinks at lower prices than usual 欢乐时光（酒吧的减价时段）

ˈhappy slapping *noun* (*BrE*) [U] the practice of several people attacking sb while another person in the group makes a film of the attack 开心掌掴（指几人围殴一人，由同伙将袭击画面拍下）

hap·tic /ˈhæptɪk/ *adj.* (*specialist*) relating to or involving the sense of touch 触觉的；与触觉有关的：*Players use a haptic device such as a joystick to control the game.* 玩家用操纵杆之类的触觉设备玩游戏。

hara-kiri /ˌhærə ˈkɪri; *NAmE* ˌherə ˈkeri/ *noun* [U] (*from Japanese*) an act of killing yourself by cutting open your stomach with a SWORD, performed especially by the SAMURAI in Japan in the past, to avoid losing honour 切腹，剖腹自尽（尤指旧时日本武士为免受屈辱而自杀的行为）

haram /hɑːˈrɑːm; *NAmE* ˈherəm; ˈhær-/ *adj.* not permitted by ISLAMIC law 伊斯兰教教法所禁止的：*haram meat* 非清真肉食 OPP **halal**

har·am·bee /həˈræmbiː/ *noun* (*EAfrE*) **1** [C] a meeting that is held in order to collect money for sth, for example a community project（为社区项目等举行的）募捐会，筹款会：*They held a harambee meeting to raise funds for a new classroom.* 他们为筹款建新教室而办了个募捐会。 **2** [U] the act of joining with other people to achieve a difficult task 齐心协力：*the spirit of harambee* 众志成城的精神

har·angue /həˈræŋ/ *verb, noun*

■ *verb* ~ **sb** to speak loudly and angrily in a way that criticizes sb/sth or tries to persuade people to do sth 呵斥；大声谴责；慷慨激昂地劝说

■ *noun* a long loud angry speech that criticizes sb/sth or tries to persuade people to do sth 义愤填膺的谴责；慷慨激昂的劝说

har·ass /ˈhærəs; həˈræs/ *verb* **1** [often passive] ~ **sb** to annoy or worry sb by putting pressure on them or saying or doing unpleasant things to them 侵扰；骚扰：*He has complained of being harassed by the police.* 他投诉受到警方侵扰。◇ *She claims she has been* ***sexually harassed*** *at work.* 她声称在工作中受到性骚扰。 **2** ~ **sb/sth** to make repeated attacks on an enemy 不断攻击（敌人） SYN **harry** ▶ **har·ass·ment** *noun* [U]: ***racial/sexual harassment*** 种族侵扰；性骚扰

har·assed /ˈhærəst; həˈræst/ *adj.* tired and anxious because you have too much to do 疲惫焦虑的：*a harassed-looking waiter* 愁眉苦脸的服务员 ◇ *harassed mothers with their children* 带着孩子的疲惫不堪的母亲们

har·bin·ger /ˈhɑːbɪndʒə(r); *NAmE* ˈhɑːrb-/ *noun* ~ (**of sth**) (*formal* or *literary*) a sign that shows that sth is going to happen soon, often sth bad （常指坏的）预兆，兆头

har·bour (*especially US* **har·bor**) /ˈhɑːbə(r); *NAmE* ˈhɑːrb-/ *noun, verb*

■ ***noun*** [C, U] an area of water on the coast, protected from the open sea by strong walls, where ships can shelter （海）港；港口；港湾：*Several boats lay at anchor in the harbour.* 港湾里停泊着几条船。◇ *to enter/leave harbour* 进入 / 离开港口 ➲ WORDFINDER NOTE AT SEA ➲ VISUAL VOCAB PAGE V5

■ ***verb*** **1** ~ **sb** to hide and protect sb who is hiding from the police 窝藏，庇护（罪犯等）：*Police believe someone must be harbouring the killer.* 警方相信一定有人窝藏了杀人犯。 **2** ~ **sth** to keep feelings or thoughts, especially negative ones, in your mind for a long time 怀有，心怀（尤指反面感情或想法）：*The arsonist may* ***harbour a grudge*** *against the company.* 纵火犯可能对公司怀恨在心。◇ *She began to harbour doubts about the decision.* 她开始对这个决定产生怀疑。 **3** ~ **sth** to contain sth and allow it to develop 包含；藏有：*Your dishcloth can harbour many germs.* 洗碗布中可能藏有很多病菌。

ˈ**harbour master** (*especially US* **har·bor·mas·ter**) *noun* an official in charge of a harbour 港务长

hard 🔑 /hɑːd; *NAmE* hɑːrd/ *adj., adv.*

■ ***adj.*** (**hard·er, hard·est**)

• **SOLID/STIFF** 坚固；坚硬 **1** 🔑 solid, firm or stiff and difficult to bend or break 坚固的；坚硬的；结实的：*Wait for the concrete to go hard.* 等待混凝土凝结。◇ *a hard mattress* 硬床垫 ◇ *Diamonds are the hardest known mineral.* 钻石是已知的最坚硬的矿石。OPP **soft**

• **DIFFICULT** 不易 **2** 🔑 difficult to do, understand or answer 难做的；难懂的；难以回答的：*a hard choice/question* 为难的选择；难以回答的问题 ◇ ~ **to do sth** *It is* ***hard to believe*** *that she's only nine.* 很难相信她只有九岁。◇ *It's* ***hard to see*** *how they can lose.* 很难理解他们怎么会输。◇ *'When will the job be finished?' 'It's* ***hard to say*** (= it is difficult to be certain).' "这项工作什么时候能完成？""难说。"◇ *I find his attitude very* ***hard to take*** (= difficult to accept). 他的态度让我难以接受。◇ *We're finding reliable staff* ***hard to come by*** (= difficult to get). 我们觉得难以找到可靠的职员。◇ ~ **for sb** (**to do sth**) *It's hard for old people to change their ways.* 老年人难以改变他们的习惯。◇ *It must be hard for her, bringing up four children on her own.* 她一个人抚养四个孩子一定很艰难。OPP **easy** **3** 🔑 full of difficulty and problems, especially because of a lack of money 困苦的；艰苦的；艰难的 SYN **tough**：*Times were hard at the end of the war.* 战争后期生活很艰苦。◇ *She's had a hard life.* 她一生艰苦。OPP **easy**

• **NEEDING/USING EFFORT** 费力；用力 **4** 🔑 needing or using a lot of physical strength or mental effort 耗费体力（或脑力）的；辛苦的：*It's* ***hard work*** *shovelling snow.* 铲雪是个苦活儿。◇ *I've had a long hard day.* 我度过了漫长辛苦的一天。➲ SYNONYMS AT DIFFICULT **5** 🔑 (of people 人) putting a lot of effort or energy into an activity 努力的；勤劳的：*She's a very hard worker.* 她工作很卖力。◇ *He's* ***hard at work*** *on a new novel.* 他正努力忙着写一本新小说。◇ *When I left they were all still* ***hard at it*** (= working hard). 我离开的时候他们都还在努力工作。 **6** 🔑 done with a lot of strength or force 用力的；猛烈的：*He gave the door a good hard kick.* 他狠狠踢了一下门。◇ *a hard punch* 砰的一拳

• **WITHOUT SYMPATHY** 缺乏同情心 **7** 🔑 showing no sympathy or affection 冷酷无情的；硬心肠的；苛刻的：*My father was a hard man.* 我父亲是个不讲情面的人。◇ *She gave me a hard stare.* 她狠狠地看了我一眼。◇ *He said some very hard things to me.* 他对我说了些很不近人情的话。

• **NOT AFRAID** 不畏惧 **8** (*informal*) (of people 人) ready to fight and showing no signs of fear or weakness 准备战斗的；不软弱退缩的：*Come and get me if you think you're hard enough.* 你要是觉得自己有种，就冲着我来吧。◇ *You think you're really hard, don't you?* 你是不是以为自己真的很勇猛？

• **FACTS/EVIDENCE** 事实；证据 **9** [only before noun] definitely true and based on information that can be proved 确凿的；可证实的；可靠的：*Is there any* ***hard evidence*** *either way?* 不管正反，有什么确凿证据吗？◇ *The newspaper story is based on* ***hard facts.*** 报纸的这篇报道有可靠的事实根据。

• **WEATHER** 天气 **10** very cold and severe 寒冷的；凛冽的：*It had been a* ***hard winter.*** 那年的冬天特别冷。◇ *There was a* ***hard frost*** *that night.* 那天晚上寒冷多霜。➲ COMPARE MILD *adj.* (2)

• **DRINK** 饮料 **11** [only before noun] strongly alcoholic 酒精浓度高的；烈性的：***hard liquor*** 烈酒 ◇ (*informal*) *a drop of the hard stuff* (= a strong alcoholic drink) 少许烈酒 ➲ COMPARE SOFT DRINK

• **WATER** 水 **12** containing CALCIUM and other mineral salts that make mixing with soap difficult 硬的（含钙及镁等可溶性盐较多）：*a* ***hard water*** *area* 硬水区 ◇ *Our water is very hard.* 我们的水很硬。OPP **soft**

• **CONSONANTS** 辅音 **13** (*phonetics* 语音) used to describe a letter *c* or *g* when pronounced as in 'cat' or 'go', rather than as in 'city' or 'giant' 硬音的（如字母 c 或 g 在 cat 或 go 等词中的发音）OPP **soft**

▸ **hard·ness** *noun* [U]: *water hardness* 水的硬度 ◇ *hardness of heart* 硬心肠

IDM **be ˈhard on sb/sth** **1** 🔑 to treat or criticize sb in a very severe or strict way 严厉对待，严格批评（某人或某事）：*Don't be too hard on him—he's very young.* 别对他太苛刻了，他还很小呢。 **2** 🔑 to be difficult for or unfair to sb/sth 使…为难；对…不公平：*It's hard on people who don't have a car.* 对于没有车的人来说，这不公平。 **3** to be likely to hurt or damage sth 可能损伤，可能损坏（某物）：*Looking at a computer screen all day can be very hard on the eyes.* 成天盯着计算机屏幕可能会对眼睛造成严重损害。 **drive/strike a hard ˈbargain** to argue in an aggressive way and force sb to agree on the best possible price or arrangement 狠狠地杀价 **give sb a hard ˈtime** to deliberately make a situation difficult and unpleasant for sb 给某人找茬儿；使某人不好过：*They really gave me a hard time at the interview.* 面试时他们确实是在难为我。 ˌ**hard and ˈfast** (especially after a negative 尤用于否定词后) that cannot be changed in any circumstances 板上钉钉；不容更改：*There are* ***no hard and fast rules*** *about this.* 这事没有什么硬性的规定。 (**as**) ˌ**hard as ˈnails** showing no sympathy, kindness or fear 冷酷无情；铁石心肠；毫无惧色 ˌ**hard ˈcheese** (*BrE, informal*) used as a way of saying that you are sorry about sth, usually IRONICALLY (= you really mean the opposite) （常作反话）太不幸了，真够倒霉 ˌ**hard ˈgoing** difficult to understand or needing a lot of effort 难懂；费力：*I'm finding his latest novel very hard going.* 我觉得他最近的这部小说很晦涩。 ˌ**hard ˈluck/ˈlines** (*BrE*) used to tell sb that you feel sorry for them （表示惋惜）真遗憾，太不幸了：*'Failed again, I'm afraid.' 'Oh, hard luck.'* "恐怕我又失败了。""哦，太不幸了。" **the ˈhard way** by having an unpleasant experience or by making mistakes 通过痛苦的经历；通过出错：*She won't listen to my advice so she'll just have to* ***learn the hard way.*** 她不肯听我的忠告，所以只好吃了苦头才知道厉害。 **make hard ˈwork of sth** to use more time or energy on a task than is necessary 在某事上耗费过多时间（或精力）；费冤枉力 **no hard ˈfeelings** used to tell sb you have been arguing with or have beaten in a contest that you would still like to be friendly with them （向争论或打败的对方表达善意）别往心里去，别记恨：*It looks like I'm the winner again. No hard feelings, Dave, eh?* 看来我又赢了。你不会不高兴吧，戴夫？ **play hard to ˈget** (*informal*) to make yourself seem more attractive or interesting by not immediately accepting an invitation to do sth 故作姿态；故意摆谱；拿架子 **too much like hard ˈwork** needing too much effort 太费力：*I can't be bothered making a hot meal—it's too much like hard work.* 我懒得做热饭热菜，太麻烦了。➲ MORE AT ACT *n.*, JOB, LONG *adj.*, NUT *n.*, ROCK *n.*

■ ***adv.*** (**hard·er, hard·est**)

• **WITH EFFORT** 努力 **1** 🔑 with great effort; with difficulty 努力地；费力地；艰难地：*to* ***work hard*** 努力工作 ◇ *You must* ***try harder.*** 你得更加努力。◇ *She* ***tried her hardest*** *not to show how disappointed she was.* 她竭力不流露出

H

自己有多失望。◇ *Don't hit it so hard!* 别这么用力打！◇ *He was still breathing hard after his run.* 他跑完步，现在还气喘吁吁的。◇ *Our victory was hard won* (= won with great difficulty). 我们的胜利来之不易。

- **WITH FORCE** 猛力 **2** with great force 猛力地；猛烈地：(*figurative*) *Small businesses have been* ***hit hard/hard hit*** *by the recession.* 小企业受到了经济衰退的沉重打击。
- **CAREFULLY** 仔细 **3** very carefully and thoroughly 彻底认真地：*to think hard* 认真思考 ◇ *We thought* ***long and hard*** *before deciding to move house.* 我们经过长久慎重的考虑之后才决定搬家。
- **A LOT** 大量 **4** heavily; a lot or for a long time 沉重地；大量地；长时间地：*It was* ***raining hard*** *when we set off.* 我们出发时正下着大雨。
- **LEFT/RIGHT** 左；右 **5** at a sharp angle to the left/right 向左（或右）急转弯：*Turn hard right at the next junction.* 在下个路口处向右急转弯。

H

IDM **be/feel hard 'done by** (*informal*) to be or feel unfairly treated 受到不公平待遇；感到委屈：*She has every right to feel hard done by—her parents have given her nothing.* 她完全有理由觉得委屈，她父母什么都没给她。 **be ˌhard 'pressed/'pushed to do sth | be hard 'put (to it) to do sth** to find it very difficult to do sth 很难做某事：*He was hard put to it to explain her disappearance.* 他很难对她的消失作出解释。 **be hard 'up for sth** to have too few or too little of sth 某物匮乏：*We're hard up for ideas.* 我们再想不出主意了。 SEE ALSO HARD UP **'hard on sth** very soon after 紧接着：*His death followed hard on hers.* 她死后不久，他也死了。 **take sth 'hard** to be very upset by sth 为某事很苦恼（或难受）：*He took his wife's death very hard.* 他对妻子的死感到很难过。 MORE AT DIE *v.*, HEEL *n.*

WHICH WORD? 词语辨析

hard / hardly

- The adverb from the adjective **hard** is **hard**. 形容词 hard 的副词为 hard：*I have to work hard today.* 今天我得努力工作。◇ *She has thought very hard about her future plans.* 她曾经苦苦思考将来该怎么办。◇ *It was raining hard outside.* 外面雨下得很大。
- **Hardly** is an adverb meaning 'almost not'. * hardly 为副词，意为几乎不、几乎没有：*I hardly ever go to concerts.* 我很少去听音乐会。◇ *I can hardly wait for my birthday.* 我迫切等待着我的生日。It cannot be used instead of **hard**. 该词不能代替 hard：~~*I've been working hardly today.*~~ ◇ ~~*She has thought very hardly about her future plans.*~~ ◇ ~~*It was raining hardly outside.*~~

NOTE AT HARDLY

---

hard·back /ˈhɑːdbæk; *NAmE* ˈhɑːrd-/ (*also* **hard·cover** *especially in NAmE*) *noun* [C, U] a book that has a stiff cover 精装书：*What's the price of the hardback?* 精装本多少钱？◇ *It was published* ***in hardback*** *last year.* 这书去年以精装本出版。◇ ***hardback books/editions*** 精装书；精装本 COMPARE PAPERBACK

hard·ball /ˈhɑːdbɔːl; *NAmE* ˈhɑːrd-/ *noun* (*NAmE*) **1** the game of BASEBALL (when contrasted with SOFTBALL) 棒球运动（与垒球运动相对） **2** used to refer to a way of behaving, especially in politics, that shows that a person is determined to get what they want 果敢，果决（尤指政治手段）：*I want us to* ***play hardball*** *on this issue.* 我希望我们在这个问题上不手软。◇ *hardball politics* 强硬政治

ˌhard-'bitten *adj.* not easily shocked and not showing emotion, because you have experienced many unpleasant things 久经磨炼而坚强的

hard·board /ˈhɑːdbɔːd; *NAmE* ˈhɑːrdbɔːrd/ *noun* [U] a type of stiff board made by crushing very small pieces of wood together into thin sheets 硬质纤维板（由碎木压成）

ˌhard-'boiled *adj.* **1** (of an egg 鸡蛋) boiled until the inside is hard 煮老的；煮硬的 COMPARE SOFT-BOILED **2** (of people 人) not showing much emotion 不动感情的；不流露情感的

ˌhard 'by *prep.* (*old-fashioned*) very near sth 很接近；临近 ► **ˌhard 'by** *adv.*

ˌhard 'candy (*NAmE*) (*BrE* **ˌboiled 'sweet**) *noun* [U] a hard sweet/candy made from boiled sugar, often with fruit flavours 硬糖（常有水果味）

ˌhard 'cash (*BrE*) (*NAmE also* **ˌcold 'cash**) *noun* [U] money, especially in the form of coins and notes, that you can spend 现金（尤指硬币和纸币）

ˌhard-'charging *adj.* [only before noun] working or performing with a lot of energy and skill 熟练且有干劲的；全力进取的：*He changed from a goofy kid to a hard-charging soldier.* 他从傻乎乎的孩子变成了勇猛干练的士兵。

ˌhard 'cider (*NAmE*) (*BrE* **cider**) *noun* [U, C] an alcoholic drink made from the juice of apples 苹果酒

ˌhard-'code *verb* **~ sth** (*computing* 计) to write data so that it cannot easily be changed 编写硬代码，编写硬编码（编码不会被轻易更改）

ˌhard 'copy *noun* [U, C] (*computing* 计) information from a computer that has been printed on paper 硬拷贝，打印件（打印出的计算机资料） VISUAL VOCAB PAGE V71

ˌhard 'core *noun* (*BrE*) **1** [sing.+sing./pl. v.] the small central group in an organization, or in a particular group of people, who are the most active or who will not change their beliefs or behaviour 核心力量；骨干；中坚力量：*It's really only the hard core that bother(s) to go to meetings.* 也只有那些骨干分子愿意去开会。◇ *A hard core of drivers ignores the law.* 部分顽固的驾车人无视这项法律。 **2** [U] (*usually* **'hardcore**) small pieces of stone, brick, etc. used as a base for building roads on 路基碎砖石；路基垫层

ˌhard-'core *adj.* **1** having a belief or a way of behaving that will not change 中坚的；骨干的：*hard-core party members* 核心党员 **2** showing or describing sexual activity in a detailed or violent way（关于性爱）露骨的，赤裸裸的：*They sell* ***hard-core pornography.*** 他们出售赤裸裸的色情物品。 COMPARE SOFT-CORE

ˌhard 'court *noun* an area with a hard surface for playing TENNIS on, not grass 硬地网球场

hard·cover /ˈhɑːdkʌvə(r); *NAmE* ˈhɑːrd-/ *noun* (*especially NAmE*) = HARDBACK

ˌhard 'currency *noun* [U, C] money that is easy to exchange for money from another country, because it is not likely to lose its value 硬通货（币值稳定，容易兑换）

ˌhard 'disk (*also* **ˌhard 'drive**) *noun* a disk inside a computer that stores data and programs 硬盘；硬磁盘

ˌhard 'disk recorder *noun* a digital recording system that records sound or video directly to a hard disk, without using tape 硬盘录制系统；硬盘录制器（直接将数字音频或视频录制到硬盘）

'hard-drinking *adj.* drinking a lot of alcohol 大量饮酒的；海量的

'hard drive *noun* (*computing* 计) = HARD DISK

ˌhard 'drug *noun* [usually pl.] a powerful illegal drug, such as HEROIN, that some people take for pleasure and can become ADDICTED to 硬性毒品（容易成瘾） COMPARE SOFT DRUG

ˌhard-'earned *adj.* that you get only after a lot of work and effort 辛勤挣来的；来之不易的：*hard-earned cash* 用汗水换来的钱 ◇ *We finally managed a hard-earned draw.* 我们终于追成了平局。

ˌhard-'edged *adj.* powerful, true to life and not affected by emotion 客观逼真的：*the movie's hard-edged realism* 那部电影逼真的现实主义

hard·en /ˈhɑːdn; *NAmE* ˈhɑːrdn/ *verb* **1** [I, T] to become or make sth become firm, stiff or solid （使）变硬，硬化：*The varnish takes a few hours to harden.* 清漆需要几个小时才能干透。◇ **~ sth** *a method for hardening and preserving wood* 硬化和保存木料的方法 **2** [I, T] if your voice, face, etc. **hardens**, or you **harden** it, it becomes more serious or severe （使声音、面孔等）更严肃，更严厉：*Her face hardened into an expression of hatred.* 她的脸沉下来，面带恨意。◇ **~ sth** *He hardened his voice when he saw she wasn't listening.* 看到她没在听他讲话，他声音严厉起来。**3** [I, T] if sb's feelings or attitudes **harden** or sb/sth **hardens** them, they become more fixed and determined （使）更坚定，更强硬：*Public attitudes to the strike have hardened.* 公众对这次罢工所持的态度已强硬起来。◇ *Their suspicions hardened into certainty.* 他们由怀疑变成肯定。◇ **~ sth** *The incident hardened her resolve to leave the company.* 这件事使她更加坚定了离开公司的决心。**4** [T, usually passive] **~ sb/sth/yourself** to make sb less kind or less affected by extreme situations 使变得无情；使不被打动：*Joe sounded different, hardened by the war.* 乔让人觉得变了，因战争变得冷酷无情了。◇ *They were* ***hardened criminals*** (= they showed no regret for their crimes). 他们都是死不悔改的罪犯。◇ *In this job you have to* ***harden your heart*** *to pain and suffering.* 做这项工作面对伤痛和折磨时你得保持沉着冷静。▶ **hard·en·ing** *noun* [U, sing.]: *hardening of the arteries* 动脉硬化 ◇ *a hardening of attitudes towards one-parent families* 对单亲家庭态度的冷漠化

ˌ**hard-ˈfaced** *adj.* (*disapproving*) (of a person 人) showing no feeling or sympathy for other people 缺乏同情心的；麻木不仁的

ˌ**hard-ˈfought** *adj.* that involves fighting very hard 艰苦斗争的；激烈战斗的：*a* ***hard-fought battle/win/victory*** 激烈的战斗；来之不易的胜利

ˌ**hard ˈhat** *noun* a hat worn by building workers, etc. to protect their heads 安全帽（建筑工人等戴）➲ VISUAL VOCAB PAGE V70

ˌ**hard-ˈheaded** *adj.* determined and not allowing your emotions to affect your decisions 坚定而不感情用事的；精明冷静的

ˌ**hard-ˈhearted** *adj.* giving no importance to the feelings or problems of other people 铁石心肠的；无情的 ➲ COMPARE SOFT-HEARTED

ˌ**hard-ˈhitting** *adj.* not afraid to talk about or criticize sb/sth in an honest and very direct way 直言不讳的；单刀直入的：*a hard-hitting speech* 直言不讳的讲话

ˌ**hard ˈlabour** (*especially US* ˌ**hard ˈlabor**) *noun* [U] punishment in prison that involves a lot of very hard physical work 劳役；苦役

ˌ**hard ˈleft** *noun* [sing.+sing./pl. v.] (*especially BrE*) the members of a LEFT-WING political party who have the most extreme opinions 极左派：*hard-left policies* 极左派政策

ˌ**hard ˈline** *noun* [sing.] a strict policy or attitude 强硬政策（或态度）：*the judge's hard line against drug dealers* 法官对待毒品贩子的坚定态度 ◇ *The government* ***took a hard line on*** *the strike.* 政府对罢工采取了强硬态度。

ˌ**hard-ˈline** *adj.* [usually before noun] **1** (of a person 人) having very fixed beliefs and being unlikely or unwilling to change them 有坚定信仰的；不妥协的：*a hard-line conservative* 坚定的保守党支持者 **2** (of ideas 思想) very fixed and unlikely to change 坚定的；坚决的：*a hard-line attitude* 坚定的态度 ▶ **hard·liner** /ˌhɑːdˈlaɪnə(r); *NAmE* ˌhɑːrd-/ *noun*：*a Republican hardliner* 一名共和党的忠实党员

ˌ**hard-ˈluck story** *noun* a story about yourself that you tell sb in order to get their sympathy or help （为博得他人同情或帮助而诉说的）不幸的遭遇

hard·ly 🔑 /ˈhɑːdli; *NAmE* ˈhɑːrd-/ *adv.* **1** 🔑 almost no; almost not; almost none 几乎不；几乎没有：*There's* ***hardly any*** *tea left.* 没有剩什么茶了。◇ *Hardly anyone has bothered to reply.* 几乎没人开口回答。◇ *She* ***hardly ever*** *calls me* (= almost never). 她几乎从未给我来过电话。◇ *We hardly know each other.* 我们彼此还不大认识呢。◇ ***Hardly a day goes by without*** *my thinking of her* (= I think of her almost every day). 我几乎天天想着她。**2** 🔑 used especially after 'can' or 'could' and before the main verb, to emphasize that it is difficult to do sth （尤用于 can 或 could 之后，主要动词之前，强调做某事很难）：*I can hardly keep my eyes open* (= I'm almost falling asleep). 我困得都快睁不开眼了。◇ *I* ***could hardly believe*** *it when I read the letter.* 读到那封信时，我简直不敢相信。**3** 🔑 used to say that sth has just begun, happened, etc. 刚刚；才：*We can't stop for coffee now, we've hardly started.* 现在不能停下来喝咖啡，我们刚刚才开始工作呢。◇ *We had hardly sat down to supper when the phone rang.* 我们刚坐下用晚餐，电话就响了。◇ (*formal*) *Hardly had she spoken than she regretted it bitterly.* 话刚出口，她就后悔不迭。**4** 🔑 used to suggest that sth is unlikely or unreasonable or that sb is silly for saying or doing sth （表示不大可能、不合理或愚蠢）：*He is hardly likely to admit he was wrong.* 他不大可能承认自己错了。◇ *It's* ***hardly surprising*** *she was fired; she never did any work.* 她被解雇了不足为怪，她从来没干过任何工作。◇ *It's* ***hardly the time*** *to discuss it now.* 现在并不是讨论的时候。◇ *You* ***can hardly*** *expect her to do it for free.* 你

▼ **GRAMMAR POINT 语法说明**

hardly / scarcely / barely / no sooner

- **Hardly**, **scarcely** and **barely** can all be used to say that something is only just true or possible. They are used with words like *any* and *anyone*, with adjectives and verbs, and are often placed between *can, could, have, be*, etc. and the main part of the verb. * hardly、scarcely 和 barely 均可指刚刚、几乎不，与 any 和 anyone 等词以及形容词和动词连用，常置于 can、could、have、be 等和动词主要成分之间：*They have sold scarcely any copies of the book.* 这书他们几乎没卖出几本。◇ *I barely recognized her.* 我几乎认不出她了。◇ *His words were barely audible.* 他的话勉强听得见。◇ *I can hardly believe it.* 我几乎不敢相信。◇ ~~*I hardly can believe it.*~~
- **Hardly**, **scarcely** and **barely** are negative words and should not be used with *not* or other negatives. * hardly、scarcely 和 barely 为否定词，不应与 not 或其他否定词连用：~~*I can't hardly believe it.*~~
- You can also use **hardly, scarcely** and **barely** to say that one thing happens immediately after another. 亦可用 hardly、scarcely 和 barely 表示刚…就…：*We had hardly/scarcely/barely sat down at the table, when the phone rang.* 我们刚在桌子旁坐下，电话铃就响了。In formal, written English, especially in a literary style, these words can be placed at the beginning of the sentence and then the subject and verb are turned around. 在正式的书面语中，尤其在文学体中，上述各词可置于句首，然后将主语和动词的位置倒装：*Hardly/Scarcely had we sat down at the table, when the phone rang.* 我们刚在桌子旁坐下，电话铃就响了。Note that you usually use *when* in these sentences, not *than*. You can also use *before*. 注意：在这类句子中通常用 when 而非 than，亦可用 before：*I scarcely had time to ring the bell before the door opened.* 我刚一按门铃，门就开了。**No sooner** can be used in the same way, but is always used with *than*. * no sooner 与上述词用法相同，但总与 than 连用：*No sooner had we sat down at the table than the phone rang.* 我们刚在桌子旁坐下，电话铃就响了。
- **Hardly** and **scarcely** can be used to mean 'almost never', but **barely** is not used in this way. * hardly 和 scarcely 可表示几乎从不、难得，但 barely 不这样用：*She hardly (ever) sees her parents these days.* 这些日子她难得见到她父母。◇ ~~*She barely sees her parents these days.*~~

H

不可能指望她无偿地做这事。◇ *'Couldn't you have just said no?' 'Well, hardly (= of course not), she's my wife's sister.'*"你不能就说声不吗？""喔，不可能，她是我小姨子。"➲ NOTE AT HARD

ˌhard-ˈnosed *adj.* not affected by feelings when trying to get what you want 顽强的；不屈不挠的；不讲情面的：*a hard-nosed journalist* 不屈不挠的记者

ˌhard of ˈhearing *adj.* [not before noun] **1** unable to hear very well 听力弱；耳背 **2 the hard of hearing** *noun* [pl.] people who are unable to hear very well 听力弱的人；耳背的人：*subtitles for the deaf and the hard of hearing* 为耳聋和听力不佳者打出的字幕

ˈhard-on *noun* (*taboo, slang*) an ERECTION (1) (阴茎)勃起

ˌhard ˈporn *noun* [U] (*informal*) films/movies, pictures, books, etc. that show sexual activity in a very detailed and sometimes violent way 色情电影（或图片、书籍等）➲ COMPARE SOFT PORN

ˌhard-ˈpressed *adj.* **1** having a lot of problems, especially too much work, and too little time or money 处于强大压力下的（尤指工作重、时间紧、资金少） **2 ~ to do sth** finding sth very difficult to do 很难（做某事）：*You would be hard-pressed to find a better secretary.* 找一位更好的秘书很难。

ˌhard ˈright *noun* [sing.+sing./pl. v.] (*especially BrE*) the members of a RIGHT-WING political party who have the most extreme opinions 极右派：*hard-right opinions* 极右派观点

ˌhard ˈrock *noun* [U] a type of loud rock music with a very strong beat, played on electric GUITARS 硬摇滚乐（用电吉他演奏，节奏强劲）

hard·scape /ˈhɑːdskeɪp; *NAmE* ˈhɑːrd-/ *noun* [U] (*especially NAmE*) features such as paths and walls that are not natural but that are used to decorate parks and gardens/yards 硬景观，人造景观（公园和庭园里起装饰作用的小径、隔墙等非自然景观）

ˌhard ˈscience *noun* **1** [U] science that is based on the objective measurement and observation of physical facts or events 硬科学（以客观量度和观察物质数据为基础） **2** [C] a science that involves the objective measurement and observation of physical facts or events, such as physics and chemistry 硬科学学科（如物理、化学）

hard·scrab·ble /ˌhɑːdˈskræbl; *NAmE* ˌhɑːrd-/ *adj.* (*NAmE*) not having enough of the basic things you need to live 艰难困苦的；贫困的；勉强维持的：*a* ***hardscrabble life/upbringing*** 贫困的生活；艰苦的成长

ˌhard ˈsell *noun* [sing.] a method of selling that puts a lot of pressure on the customer to buy 强行推销 ➲ COMPARE SOFT SELL

hard·ship /ˈhɑːdʃɪp; *NAmE* ˈhɑːrd-/ *noun* [U, C] a situation that is difficult and unpleasant because you do not have enough money, food, clothes, etc. 艰难；困苦；拮据：***economic/financial, etc. hardship*** 经济、财政等困难 ◇ *People suffered many hardships during that long winter.* 在那个漫长的冬季，人们吃了很多苦头。◇ *It was* ***no hardship*** *to walk home on such a lovely evening.* 在这么一个宜人的傍晚步行回家一点也不辛苦。

ˌhard ˈshoulder (*BrE*) (*US* **ˈbreakdown lane**) *noun* [sing.] a strip of ground with a hard surface beside a major road such as a MOTORWAY or INTERSTATE where vehicles can stop in an emergency 硬路肩（在高速公路旁，可供紧急停车）：*to pull over onto the hard shoulder/into the breakdown lane* 把车开到硬路肩 ➲ WORDFINDER NOTE AT ROAD

hard·top /ˈhɑːdtɒp; *NAmE* ˈhɑːrdtɑːp/ *noun* a car with a metal roof 硬顶小汽车

ˌhard ˈup *adj.* (*informal*) **1** having very little money, especially for a short period of time 拮据的，缺钱的（尤指暂时性的）➲ NOTE AT POOR **2 ~ (for sth)** lacking in sth interesting to do, talk about, etc. 无所事事的；无聊的：*'You could always go out with Steve.' 'I'm not that hard up!'*"你总可以和史蒂夫出去玩玩吧。""我还没无聊到那个地步呢！"

hard·ware /ˈhɑːdweə(r); *NAmE* ˈhɑːrdwer/ *noun* [U] **1** (*computing* 计) the machinery and electronic parts of a computer system 硬件 ➲ COMPARE SOFTWARE **2** (*BrE also* **iron·mon·gery**) tools and equipment that are used in the house and garden/yard （家庭及园艺用）工具，设备，五金制品：*a hardware shop* 五金店 ➲ WORDFINDER NOTE AT STORE **3** the equipment, machinery and vehicles used to do sth 硬件设备；机器；车辆：*tanks and other military hardware* 坦克和其他军事装备

ˈhardware dealer *noun* (*NAmE*) **1** (*BrE, becoming old-fashioned* **iron·mon·ger**) a person who owns or works in a shop/store selling tools and equipment for the house and garden/yard 五金商人 **2** (*BrE* **ironmonger's**) a shop that sells tools and equipment for the house and garden/yard 五金商店

ˌhard-ˈwearing *adj.* (*BrE*) that lasts a long time and remains in good condition 经久耐用的：*a hard-wearing carpet* 耐磨的地毯

hard·wired /ˌhɑːdˈwaɪəd; *NAmE* ˌhɑːrdˈwaɪərd/ *adj.* **1** (*specialist*) (of computer functions 计算机功能) built into the permanent system and not provided by software 硬（布）线的；硬连接的 **2** (of a skill, quality or type of behaviour) present when you are born and not changing during your life （某种技能、品质或行为）与生俱来的，固有的：*Many aspects of morality appear to be hardwired in the brain.* 许多道德观念似乎是人们出生时便根植在脑中的。

ˌhard-ˈwon *adj.* [usually before noun] that you only get after fighting or working hard for it 经奋斗（或努力）得到的；来之不易的：*She was not going to give up her hard-won freedom so easily.* 她不会这么轻易地放弃得来不易的自由。

hard·wood /ˈhɑːdwʊd; *NAmE* ˈhɑːrd-/ *noun* [U, C] hard heavy wood from a BROADLEAVED tree 硬材（阔叶树的木材）➲ COMPARE SOFTWOOD

ˌhard-ˈworking *adj.* putting a lot of effort into a job and doing it well 工作努力的；辛勤的：*hard-working nurses* 辛勤的护士

hardy /ˈhɑːdi; *NAmE* ˈhɑːrdi/ *adj.* (**har·dier**, **har·di·est**) **1** strong and able to survive difficult conditions and bad weather 能吃苦耐劳的；适应力强的：*a hardy breed of sheep* 适应力强的绵羊品种 **2** (of a plant 植物) that can live outside through the winter 耐寒的；能越冬的 ▸ **hardi·ness** *noun* [U]

hare /heə(r); *NAmE* her/ *noun, verb*

■ ***noun*** an animal like a large RABBIT with very strong back legs, that can run very fast 野兔 ➲ PICTURE AT RABBIT IDM SEE MAD

■ ***verb*** [I] + **adv./prep.** (*BrE*) to run or go somewhere very fast 飞跑；疾走

hare·bell /ˈheəbel; *NAmE* ˈherbel/ (*ScotE* **blue·bell**) *noun* a wild plant with delicate blue flowers shaped like bells 圆叶风铃草

ˈhare-brained *adj.* (*informal*) crazy and unlikely to succeed 疯狂的；轻率的：***a hare-brained scheme/idea/theory*** 轻率的计划 / 想法 / 理论

Hare Krishna /ˌhɑːreɪ ˈkrɪʃnə; ˌhæri/ *noun* **1** [U] a religious group whose members wear orange ROBES and use the name of the Hindu god Krishna in their worship 国际黑天觉悟会，哈里·克里希那（宗教派别，崇信印度教黑天神） **2** [C] a member of this religious group 国际黑天觉悟会成员；克里希那教徒

hare·lip /ˈheəlɪp; *NAmE* ˈherlɪp/ *noun* an old-fashioned and now offensive word for CLEFT LIP 兔唇，唇裂（旧式用语，含冒犯意，现称 cleft lip）

harem /ˈhɑːriːm; -rəm; *NAmE* ˈhærəm/ *noun* **1** the women or wives belonging to a rich man, especially in some Muslim societies in the past 哈来姆（尤指旧时某些穆斯林社会中富人的女眷） **2** the separate part of a traditional Muslim house where the women live （穆斯林传统女眷居住的）内室，妇女住房 **3** (*specialist*) a group of female animals that share the same male for reproducing 眷群（和同一雄性动物交配的一群雌性动物）

hari·cot /ˈhærɪkəʊ; *NAmE* -koʊ/ (*also* ˌ**haricot ˈbean**) (*both BrE*) (*NAmE* ˈ**navy bean**) *noun* a type of small white BEAN that is usually dried before it is sold and then left in water before cooking 菜豆；芸豆

hark /hɑːk; *NAmE* hɑːrk/ *verb* [I] (*old use*) used only as an order to tell sb to listen （用于命令）听着，听
PHR V ˈ**hark at sb** (*BrE, informal*) used only as an order to draw attention to sb who has just said sth stupid or who is showing too much pride （仅用作命令）听听某人的蠢话，看某人的傲慢样子： *Just hark at him! Who does he think he is?* 瞧他那副德行！他以为他是谁呀？ ˌ**hark ˈback** (**to sth**) **1** to remember or talk about sth that happened in the past 回忆起，重提（过去的事）： *She's always harking back to how things used to be.* 她总是念叨以前的世道。 **2** to remind you of, or to be like, sth in the past 使想起；和（过去的事物）相似： *The newest styles hark back to the clothes of the Seventies.* 这些最新的款式使人想起 70 年代的服装。

har·ken = HEARKEN

Har·le·quin /ˈhɑːləkwɪn; *NAmE* ˈhɑːrl-/ *noun* an amusing character in some traditional plays, who wears special brightly coloured clothes with a diamond pattern （传统戏剧中穿色彩斑斓菱形花纹服装的）滑稽角色

Har·ley Street /ˈhɑːli striːt; *NAmE* ˈhɑːrli/ *noun* a street in central London in which many private doctors have their offices where they talk to and examine patients 哈利街（伦敦市中心街道，很多私人医生在此设门诊）： *a Harley Street doctor* 哈利街的医生

har·lot /ˈhɑːlət; *NAmE* ˈhɑːrlət/ *noun* (*old use, disapproving*) a PROSTITUTE, or a woman who looks and behaves like one 妓女；荡妇

harm 🔑 /hɑːm; *NAmE* hɑːrm/ *noun, verb*
■ ***noun*** [U] damage or injury that is caused by a person or an event 伤害；损害： *He would never frighten anyone or cause them* ***any harm.*** 他永远不会吓唬或伤害任何人。◇ *He may look fierce, but he* ***means no harm.*** 他可能看上去很凶，但并无恶意。◇ *The court case will* ***do serious harm to*** *my business.* 这起诉讼案件将严重损害我的生意。◇ *The accident could have been much worse; luckily* ***no harm was done.*** 这次事故本来可能糟糕得多；所幸没有造成伤害。◇ *Don't worry, we'll see that the children* ***come to no harm.*** 别担心，我们会保证孩子们安然无恙的。◇ *I can't say I like Mark very much, but I don't* ***wish him any harm.*** 我不能说我很喜欢马克，但我并不愿他受到伤害。◇ *Hard work* ***never did anyone any harm.*** 努力工作对任何人都绝无害处。◇ *Look, we're just going out for a few drinks,* ***where's the harm in that?*** 瞧，我们只不过要出去喝几杯，这有什么坏处？◇ *The treatment they gave him did him* ***more harm than good.*** 他们的治疗对他弊多于利。
IDM **it wouldn't do sb any harm** (**to do sth**) used to suggest that it would be a good idea for sb to do sth （做某事）不会对某人有坏处；不妨： *It wouldn't do you any harm to smarten yourself up.* 你不妨打扮一下。 ˌ**no ˈharm done** (*informal*) used to tell sb not to worry because they have caused no serious damage or injury 没造成严重损害（或伤害） **out of harm's ˈway** in a safe place where sb/sth cannot be hurt or injured or do any damage to sb/sth 在安全的地方；被隔离 **there is no harm in** (**sb's**) **doing sth** | **it does no harm** (**for sb**) **to do sth** used to tell sb that sth is a good idea and will not cause any problems 做某事没有什么坏处： *He may say no, but there's no harm in asking.* 他可能拒绝，但问一问也无妨。◇ *It does no harm to ask.* 问一问也无妨。
■ ***verb*** ~ **sb/sth** to hurt or injure sb or to damage sth 伤害；损害： *He would never harm anyone.* 他永远不会伤害任何人。◇ *Pollution can harm marine life.* 污染会危及海洋生物。◇ *These revelations will harm her chances of winning the election.* 这些揭露的事实将不利于她赢得选举。
IDM SEE FLY *n.*, HAIR ➲ SYNONYMS AT DAMAGE

harm·ful 🔑 /ˈhɑːmfl; *NAmE* ˈhɑːrmfl/ *adj.* (*rather formal*) causing damage or injury to sb/sth, especially to a person's health or to the environment （尤指对健康或环境）有害的，导致损害的： *the harmful effects of alcohol* 酒精的害处 ◇ *the sun's harmful ultra-violet rays* 太阳的有害紫外线 ◇ *Many household products are potentially harmful.* 很多家用产品有潜在的危害。◇ ~ **to sb/sth** *Fruit juices can be harmful to children's teeth.* 果汁可能损坏儿童的牙齿。 ▶ **harm·fully** /-fəli/ *adv.* **harm·ful·ness** *noun* [U]

harm·less 🔑 /ˈhɑːmləs; *NAmE* ˈhɑːrm-/ *adj.* **1** ~ (**to sb/sth**) unable or unlikely to cause damage or harm 无害的；不会导致损伤的： *The bacteria is harmless to humans.* 这种细菌对人类无害。 **2** unlikely to upset or offend anyone 不会引起不快的；无恶意的 SYN **innocuous**: *It's just a bit of harmless fun.* 开个小玩笑罢了，并无恶意的。 ▶ **harm·less·ly** *adv.*: *The missile fell harmlessly into the sea.* 导弹落到了海里，没有造成任何伤害。 **harm·less·ness** *noun* [U]

har·mon·ic /hɑːˈmɒnɪk; *NAmE* hɑːrˈmɑːn-/ *adj., noun*
■ ***adj.*** [usually before noun] (*music* 音) relating to the way notes are played or sung together to make a pleasing sound 和声的
■ ***noun*** [usually pl.] (*music* 音) **1** a note that sounds together with the main note being played and is higher and quieter than that note 泛音（奏法） **2** a high quiet note that can be played on some instruments like the VIOLIN by touching the string very lightly 泛音

har·mon·ica /hɑːˈmɒnɪkə; *NAmE* hɑːrˈmɑːn-/ (*BrE also or NAmE, old-fashioned* ˈ**mouth organ**) *noun* a small musical instrument that you hold near your mouth and play by blowing or sucking air through it 口琴

har·mo·ni·ous /hɑːˈməʊniəs; *NAmE* hɑːrˈmoʊ-/ *adj.* **1** (of relationships, etc. 关系等) friendly, peaceful and without any disagreement 友好和睦的；和谐的 **2** arranged together in a pleasing way so that each part goes well with the others 协调的；和谐的 SYN **pleasing**: *a harmonious combination of colours* 协调的色彩搭配 **3** (of sounds 声音) very pleasant when played or sung together 和谐的；谐调的 ▶ **har·mo·ni·ous·ly** *adv.*: *They worked very harmoniously together.* 他们合作得十分融洽。

har·mo·nium /hɑːˈməʊniəm; *NAmE* hɑːrˈmoʊ-/ *noun* a musical instrument like a small organ. Air is forced through metal pipes to produce the sound and the different notes are played on the keyboard. 簧风琴（键盘乐器，以气流使簧片振动发声）

har·mon·ize (*BrE also* **-ise**) /ˈhɑːmənaɪz; *NAmE* ˈhɑːrm-/ *verb* **1** [I] ~ (**with sth**) if two or more things **harmonize** with each other or one thing **harmonizes** with the other, the things go well together and produce an attractive result （和某事物）协调，和谐： *The new building does not harmonize with its surroundings.* 那栋新楼与周围环境不协调。 **2** [T] ~ **sth** to make systems or rules similar in different countries or organizations 使（不同国家或组织的体制或规则）相一致；使协调： *the need to harmonize tax levels across the European Union* 使欧盟各国的税收标准相一致的必要 **3** [I] ~ (**with sb/sth**) to play or sing music that combines with the main tune to make a pleasing sound 为（主调）配和声 ▶ **har·mon·iza·tion**, **-isa·tion** /ˌhɑːmənaɪˈzeɪʃn; *NAmE* ˌhɑːrmənəˈz-/ *noun* [U, C]

har·mony /ˈhɑːməni; *NAmE* ˈhɑːrm-/ *noun* (*pl.* **-ies**) **1** [U] a state of peaceful existence and agreement 融洽；和睦： *the need to* ***be in harmony with*** *our environment* 同我们的环境协调的必要 ◇ *to live together in perfect harmony* 十分和睦地一同生活 ◇ ***social/racial harmony*** 社会 / 种族融洽 ➲ COMPARE DISCORD (1) **2** [U, C] (*music* 音) the way in which different notes that are played or sung together combine to make a pleasing sound 和声：*to sing in harmony* 用和声唱 ◇ *to study four-part harmony* 研究四部和声 ◇ *passionate lyrics and stunning vocal harmonies* 充满激情的歌词和绝妙的和声演唱 ➲ COMPARE DISCORD (2) ➲ WORDFINDER NOTE AT SING **3** [C, U] a pleasing combination of related things 和谐；协调：*the harmony of colour in nature* 自然界色彩的协调

har·ness /ˈhɑːnɪs; NAmE ˈhɑːrnɪs/ *noun, verb*

■ ***noun*** **1** a set of strips of leather and metal pieces that is put around a horse's head and body so that the horse can be controlled and fastened to a CARRIAGE, etc. 马具；挽具 ➲ WORDFINDER NOTE AT HORSE **2** a set of strips of leather, etc. for fastening sth to a person's body or to keep them from moving off or falling （用于人，起固定或保护作用的）背带，保护带：*a safety harness* 安全带

IDM **in ˈharness** (*BrE*) doing your normal work, especially after a rest or a holiday （尤指休息或假期结束后）做正常工作 **in harness (with sb)** (*BrE*) working closely with sb in order to achieve sth （同某人）联手；密切合作

■ ***verb*** **1** to put a harness on a horse or other animal; to attach a horse or other animal to sth with a harness 给（马等）上挽具；用挽具把…套到…上：**~ sth** *to harness a horse* 给马上挽具 ◇ **~ sth to sth** *We harnessed two ponies to the cart.* 我们把两匹矮种马套到了车上。◇ (*figurative*) *In some areas, the poor feel harnessed to their jobs.* 有些地区的穷人感觉终身被套牢在他们的工作上。 **2 ~ sth** to control and use the force or strength of sth to produce power or to achieve sth 控制，利用（以产生能量等）：*attempts to harness the sun's rays as a source of energy* 利用日光作为能源的尝试 ◇ *We must harness the skill and creativity of our workforce.* 我们必须尽量发挥全体职工的技能和创造力。

harp /hɑːp; NAmE hɑːrp/ *noun, verb*

■ ***noun*** a large musical instrument with strings stretched on a vertical frame, played with the fingers 竖琴 ➲ VISUAL VOCAB PAGE V38 ➲ SEE ALSO JEW'S HARP

■ ***verb***

PHR V **ˌharp ˈon (about sth) | ˈharp on sth** to keep talking about sth in a boring or annoying way 喋喋不休地谈论；唠叨

harp·ist /ˈhɑːpɪst; NAmE ˈhɑːrp-/ *noun* a person who plays the harp 竖琴演奏者

har·poon /hɑːˈpuːn; NAmE hɑːrˈp-/ *noun, verb*

■ ***noun*** a weapon like a SPEAR that you can throw or fire from a gun and is used for catching large fish, WHALES, etc. 渔猎标枪；鱼叉

■ ***verb*** **~ sth** to hit sth with a harpoon 用鱼叉叉

harp·si·chord /ˈhɑːpsɪkɔːd; NAmE ˈhɑːrpsɪkɔːrd/ *noun* an early type of musical instrument similar to a piano, but with strings that are PLUCKED (= pulled), not hit 拨弦键琴；羽管键琴

harp·si·chord·ist /ˈhɑːpsɪkɔːdɪst; NAmE ˈhɑːrpsɪkɔːrd-/ *noun* a person who plays the harpsichord 拨弦键琴演奏者

harpy /ˈhɑːpi; NAmE ˈhɑːrpi/ *noun* (*pl.* **-ies**) **1** (in ancient Greek and Roman stories) a cruel creature with a woman's head and body and a bird's wings and feet 鸟身女妖，哈比（古希腊和古罗马神话中的怪物） **2** a cruel woman 凶残的女子

har·ri·dan /ˈhærɪdən/ *noun* (*old-fashioned* or *literary*) a bad-tempered unpleasant woman 脾气暴躁的讨厌女人；泼妇

har·rier /ˈhæriə(r)/ *noun* a BIRD OF PREY (= a bird that kills other creatures for food) of the HAWK family 鹞（鹰科猛禽）

har·row /ˈhærəʊ; NAmE -roʊ/ *noun* a piece of farming equipment that is pulled over land that has been PLOUGHED to break up the earth before planting 耙 ▶ **har·row** *verb* **~ sth**

har·row·ing /ˈhærəʊɪŋ; NAmE -roʊ-/ *adj.* very shocking or frightening and making you feel very upset 恐怖的；令人肠断的；使人十分难过的

har·rumph /həˈrʌmf/ *verb* [I] (*informal*) to express disagreement or disapproval, especially by making a sound in your throat like a cough （表示不同意而）干咳 ▶ **har·rumph** *noun* [sing.]

harry /ˈhæri/ *verb* (**har·ries, harry·ing, har·ried, har·ried**) (*formal*) **1 ~ sb** to annoy or upset sb by continuously asking them questions or for sth （不断）烦扰；折磨 SYN **harass**：*She has been harried by the press all week.* 整个星期她都受到新闻界的不断烦扰。 **2 ~ sb/sth** to make repeated attacks on an enemy 反复进攻；不断袭击 SYN **harass**

harsh /hɑːʃ; NAmE hɑːrʃ/ *adj.* (**harsh·er, harsh·est**) **1** cruel, severe and unkind 残酷的；严酷的；严厉的：*The punishment was harsh and unfair.* 处罚很重而且不公平。◇ *The minister received some* ***harsh criticism.*** 部长受到了严厉的批评。◇ *the harsh treatment of slaves* 对奴隶的虐待 ◇ *He regretted his harsh words.* 他对自己的刻薄言辞感到后悔。 ◇ *We had to face up to the* ***harsh realities*** *of life sooner or later.* 我们迟早都得正视生活的严酷现实。 **2** (of weather or living conditions 天气或生活环境) very difficult and unpleasant to live in 恶劣的；艰苦的：*a* ***harsh winter/wind/climate*** 寒冷的冬天；凛冽的风；恶劣的气候 ◇ *the harsh conditions of poverty which existed for most people at that time* 那时大多数人所面对的艰苦境况 ➲ WORDFINDER NOTE AT CLIMATE **3** too strong and bright; ugly or unpleasant to look at 强烈刺眼的；丑陋的：*harsh colours* 扎眼的色彩 ◇ *She was caught in the harsh glare of the headlights.* 她遭到车前灯的强光照射。◇ *the harsh lines of concrete buildings* 混凝土建筑物的粗陋线条 OPP **soft** **4** unpleasant to listen to 刺耳的；难听的：*a harsh voice* 刺耳的嗓音 **5** too strong and rough and likely to damage sth 粗糙的；毛糙的；刺激性强的：*harsh detergents* 刺激性强的洗涤剂 ▶ **harsh·ly** *adv.*：*She was treated very harshly.* 她受到了苛刻的对待。◇ *Alec laughed harshly.* 亚历克刺耳地大笑。 **harsh·ness** *noun* [U]

hart /hɑːt; NAmE hɑːrt/ *noun* a male DEER, especially a RED DEER; a STAG 雄鹿（尤指雄赤鹿） ➲ COMPARE BUCK *n.* (2), HIND *n.*

harum-scarum /ˌheərəm ˈskeərəm; NAmE ˌherəm ˈskerəm; ˌhærəm ˈskærəm/ *adj.* (*old-fashioned*) behaving in a wild and sometimes careless way 鲁莽的；莽撞的 ➲ MORE LIKE THIS 11, page R26

har·vest /ˈhɑːvɪst; NAmE ˈhɑːrv-/ *noun, verb*

■ ***noun*** **1** [C, U] the time of year when the crops are gathered in on a farm, etc.; the act of cutting and gathering crops 收获季节；收割；收获：*harvest time* 收获季节 ◇ *Farmers are extremely busy during the harvest.* 农民在收获季节里十分忙碌。 **2** [C] the crops, or the amount of crops, cut and gathered 收成；收获量：*the grain harvest* 谷物的收成 ◇ ***a good/bad harvest*** (= a lot of crops or few crops) 丰收；歉收 ◇ (*figurative*) *The appeal produced a rich harvest of blankets, medicines and clothing.* 呼吁之下，成果颇丰，收到了大批毛毯、药物和衣服。 ➲ WORDFINDER NOTE AT CROP IDM SEE REAP

■ ***verb*** **1** [I, T] **~ (sth)** to cut and gather a crop; to catch a number of animals or fish to eat 收割（庄稼）；捕猎（动物、鱼） ➲ COLLOCATIONS AT FARMING **2** [T] **~ sth** (*medical* 医) to collect cells or TISSUE from sb's body for use in medical experiments or operations 采集（人体的细胞或组织，以供医学实验等）：*She had her eggs harvested and frozen for her own future use.* 她的卵子已经采集下来，冷冻后以备她将来使用。

har·vest·er /ˈhɑːvɪstə(r); NAmE ˈhɑːrv-/ *noun* **1** a machine that cuts and gathers grain 收割机 ➲ SEE ALSO COMBINE *n.* (1) **2** (*old-fashioned*) a person who helps to gather in the crops 收割庄稼的人

ˌharvest ˈfestival *noun* a service held in Christian churches when people thank God for the crops that have been gathered 秋收感恩节 ➲ COMPARE THANKSGIVING (1)

ˌharvest ˈmoon *noun* [sing.] a full moon in the autumn/fall nearest the time when day and night are of equal length 获月（最接近秋分的满月）➲ COMPARE FULL MOON, HALF-MOON (1)

has /həz; əz; *strong form* hæz/ ➲ HAVE *v.*

has-been /ˈhæz biːn/ *noun* (*informal, disapproving*) a person who is no longer as famous, successful or important as they used to be 一度有名（或成功、重要）的人物；曾红极一时的人物；过气名人

hash /hæʃ/ *noun, verb*

■ ***noun* 1** [U, C] a hot dish of cooked meat and potatoes that are cut into small pieces and mixed together（回锅）肉丁土豆 **2** [U] (*informal*) = HASHISH **3** (*also* **ˈhash sign**) (*both BrE*) (*NAmE* **ˈpound sign**) [C] the symbol (#), especially one on a telephone（尤指电话上的）#号

IDM **make a ˈhash of sth** (*informal*) to do sth badly 把某事弄糟：*I made a real hash of the interview.* 我的面试糟透了。

■ ***verb***

PHR V **ˌhash sth↔ˈout** (*informal, especially NAmE*) to discuss sth thoroughly in order to reach an agreement or decide sth 充分讨论（以达成协议或决定）

ˌhash ˈbrowns *noun* [pl.] a dish of chopped potatoes and onions, fried until they are brown 洋葱土豆煎饼

hash·ish /ˈhæʃiːʃ; hæˈʃiːʃ/ (*also informal* **hash**) *noun* [U] a drug made from the RESIN of the HEMP plant, which gives a feeling of being relaxed when it is smoked or chewed. Use of the drug is illegal in many countries. 哈希什，大麻麻醉剂（吸食或咀嚼时有放松感。很多国家的法律禁止服用该毒品）SYN **cannabis**

hash·tag /ˈhæʃtæɡ/ *noun* a word or phrase with the symbol '#' in front of it, included in some messages sent using the Twitter SOCIAL NETWORKING service so that you can search for all messages with the same subject 主题标签，话题标记，题标（推特消息中将#号置于某些词语前，方便用户搜索同一主题的所有消息）：*I often use hashtags to search for trending topics.* 我经常用主题标签搜索热门话题。

Has·id·ism (*also* **Has·sid·ism**) /ˈhæsɪdɪzəm/ *noun* [U] a form of the Jewish religion which has very strict beliefs 哈西德派（犹太教的一支，有严格教义）▶ **Hasid** (*also* **Has·sid**) /ˈhæsɪd/ *noun* **Has·id·ic** (*also* **Has·sid·ic**) /hæˈsɪdɪk/ *adj.*

hasn't /ˈhæznt/ *short form* has not

hasp /hɑːsp; *NAmE* hæsp/ *noun* a flat piece of metal with a long narrow hole in it, used with a PADLOCK to fasten doors, boxes, etc.（门、箱子等挂锁的）搭扣

Has·sid·ism = HASIDISM

has·sium /ˈhæsiəm/ *noun* [U] (*symb.* **Hs**) a chemical element. Hassium is produced when atoms COLLIDE (= crash into each other). 𬭶（化学元素）

has·sle /ˈhæsl/ *noun, verb*

■ ***noun*** [C, U] (*informal*) **1** a situation that is annoying because it involves doing sth difficult or complicated that needs a lot of effort 困难；麻烦：*Send them an email—it's a lot less hassle than phoning.* 给他们发个电邮吧，这比打电话省事多了。◇ *legal hassles* 法律程序的繁复 **2** a situation in which people disagree, argue or annoy you 分歧；争论；烦恼：*Do as you're told and don't give me any hassle!* 告诉你怎么做就怎么做，别跟我顶嘴！

■ ***verb*** **~ sb (for sth/to do sth)** (*informal*) to annoy sb or cause them trouble, especially by asking them to do sth many times（不断）烦扰，麻烦 SYN **bother**: *Don't keep hassling me! I'll do it later.* 别老烦我！我待会儿会做的。

has·sock /ˈhæsək/ *noun* **1** a thick firm CUSHION on which you rest your knees when saying prayers in a church 跪垫（在教堂祈祷时用）**2** (*NAmE*) (*BrE* **pouffe**) a large thick CUSHION used as a seat or for resting your feet on（厚实的）坐垫，脚垫

hast /hæst/ **thou hast** (*old use*) a way of saying 'you have'（you have 的意思）

haste /heɪst/ *noun* [U] (*formal*) speed in doing sth, especially because you do not have enough time 急速；匆忙；仓促 SYN **hurry**: *In her haste to complete the work on time, she made a number of mistakes.* 她急急忙忙想按时完工，结果出了不少错。◇ *The letter had clearly been written in haste.* 这封信明显是在匆忙中写的。◇ *After his first wife died, he married again with almost indecent haste.* 他的第一任妻子死后，他几乎是迫不及待地就再婚了。◇ (*old-fashioned*) *She* ***made haste*** *to open the door.* 她急忙打开门。

IDM **ˌmore ˈhaste, ˌless ˈspeed** (*BrE, saying*) you will finish doing sth sooner if you do not try to do it too quickly because you will make fewer mistakes 欲速则不达 ➲ MORE AT MARRY

has·ten /ˈheɪsn/ *verb* **1** [I] **~ to do sth** to say or do sth without delay 急忙进行；赶紧说（或做）：*She saw his frown and hastened to explain.* 看到他皱起眉头，她赶紧解释。◇ *He has been described as a 'charmless bore'—not by me,* ***I hasten to add.*** 他被说成是"无聊的啰嗦鬼"。不是我说的，我赶忙加了一句。**2** [T] **~ sth** (*formal*) to make sth happen sooner or more quickly 促进；使加快：*The treatment she received may, in fact, have hastened her death.* 实际上，她所接受的治疗可能加快了她的死亡。◇ *News of the scandal certainly hastened his departure from office.* 这一丑闻肯定加速了他的离任。**3** [I] **+ adv./prep.** (*literary*) to go or move somewhere quickly 赶往（某地）SYN **hurry**

hasty /ˈheɪsti/ *adj.* (**hasti·er**, **hasti·est**) **1** said, made or done very quickly, especially when this has bad results 匆忙的；仓促而就的；草率的 SYN **hurried**: *a hasty departure/meal/farewell* 急急忙忙的离去 / 用餐 / 辞别 ◇ *Let's not make any hasty decisions.* 我们不要匆忙作决定。**2 ~ in doing sth** (of a person 人) acting or deciding too quickly, without enough thought 仓促行事；草率作出决定；考虑不周密：*Perhaps I was too hasty in rejecting his offer.* 我拒绝他的提议也许过于草率了。IDM SEE BEAT *v.* ▶ **hasti·ly** /-ɪli/ *adv.*: *Perhaps I spoke too hastily.* 或许我说话太急了些。◇ *She hastily changed the subject.* 她匆匆换了个话题。

hat 🔑 /hæt/ *noun* **1** 🔑 a covering made to fit the head, often with a BRIM (= a flat edge that sticks out), and worn out of doors（常指带檐的）帽子：***a straw/woolly, etc. hat*** 草帽、毛线帽等 ◇ ***to put on/take off a hat*** 戴 / 脱帽子 ➲ VISUAL VOCAB PAGE V70 **2** (*informal*) a position or role, especially an official or professional role, when you have more than one such role（双重的）职位，角色（尤指官职或职业角色）：*I'm wearing two hats tonight—parent and teacher.* 我今晚身兼两职，既是家长又是老师。◇ *I'm telling you this with my lawyer's hat on, you understand.* 你要明白，我是以律师的身份告诉你这事。➲ SEE ALSO OLD HAT

IDM **go hat in ˈhand (to sb)** (*NAmE*) (*especially BrE* **go cap in ˈhand (to sb)**) to ask sb for sth, especially money, in a very polite way that makes you seem less important 谦卑地要，恭敬地讨（尤指钱） **keep sth under your ˈhat** (*informal*) to keep sth secret and not tell anyone else 将某事保密 **ˌmy ˈhat** (*old-fashioned*) used to express surprise（表示惊奇） **out of a/the ˈhat** if sth such as a name is picked **out of a/the hat**, it is picked at RANDOM from a container into which all the names are put, so that each name has an equal chance of being picked, in a competition, etc. 随机抽出 **I take my ˈhat off to sb | hats off to sb** (*both especially BrE*) (*NAmE usually* **I tip my ˈhat to sb**) (*informal*) used to say that you admire sb very much for sth they have done（表示敬佩） **throw your ˈhat into the ring** to announce officially that you are going to compete in an election, a competition, etc. 正式宣布参加竞选（或比赛等）➲ MORE AT DROP *n.*, EAT, KNOCK *v.*, PASS *v.*, PULL *v.*, TALK *v.*

H

hat·band /ˈhætbænd/ *noun* a band of cloth placed around a hat as decoration 帽带（围着帽作装饰）

hat·box /ˈhætbɒks; *NAmE* -bɑːks/ *noun* a round box used for keeping a hat in, to stop it from being crushed or damaged 帽盒

hatch /hætʃ/ *verb, noun*
■ *verb* **1** [I] ~ (**out**) (of a young bird, fish, insect, etc. 小鸟、小鱼、小虫等) to come out of an egg 孵出；出壳：*Ten chicks hatched (out) this morning.* 今早有十只小鸡出壳了。 **2** [I] ~ (**out**) (of an egg 蛋) to break open so that a young bird, fish, insect, etc. can come out 孵化；破壳：*The eggs are about to hatch.* 这些蛋就要孵化了。 ➲ COLLOCATIONS AT LIFE **3** [T] ~ **sth** to make a young bird, fish, insect, etc. come out of an egg 使（小鸟、小鱼、小虫等）孵出：*The female must find a warm place to hatch her eggs.* 母的必须找个温暖的地方孵蛋。 **4** [T] ~ **sth** (**up**) to create a plan or an idea, especially in secret 策划；（尤指）密谋：*Have you been hatching up a deal with her?* 你是不是在和她密谋什么交易？ IDM SEE COUNT *v.*
■ *noun* **1** (*also* **hatch·way**) an opening or a door in the DECK of a ship or the bottom of an aircraft, through which goods to be carried are passed （船甲板或飞机底部装货物的）舱口 **2** an opening in a wall between two rooms, especially a kitchen and a DINING ROOM, through which food can be passed （尤指厨房和餐厅之间供传递食物的）传菜窗口：*a serving hatch* 传递饭菜的窗口 **3** a door in an aircraft or a SPACECRAFT （飞机或航天器的）舱门：*an escape hatch* 紧急出口 **4** an opening or a door in a floor or ceiling （地面或天花板的）开口，门，盖子：*a hatch to the attic* 通阁楼的门
IDM ˌ**down the ˈhatch** (*informal, saying*) used before drinking sth, especially to express good wishes before drinking alcohol 干杯（尤作祝酒辞） ➲ MORE AT BATTEN *v.*

hatch·back /ˈhætʃbæk/ *noun* a car with a sloping door at the back that opens upwards 掀背式汽车 ➲ **VISUAL VOCAB PAGE V56**

hatch·ery /ˈhætʃəri/ *noun* (*pl.* **-ies**) a place for HATCHING eggs as part of a business 孵化处；孵化场：*a trout hatchery* 鳟鱼孵化场

hatchet /ˈhætʃɪt/ *noun* a small AXE (= a tool with a heavy blade for chopping things) with a short handle 短柄小斧 ➲ PICTURE AT AXE IDM SEE BURY

ˈ**hatchet-faced** *adj.* (*disapproving*) (of a person 人) having a long thin face and sharp features 脸瘦削而五官尖细的

ˈ**hatchet job** *noun* [usually sing.] ~ (**on sb/sth**) (*informal*) strong criticism that is often unfair and is intended to harm sb/sth 恶毒攻击；诽谤；诋毁：*The press did a very effective hatchet job on her last movie.* 新闻界对她新近拍摄的电影大加诋毁。

ˈ**hatchet man** *noun* (*informal*) a person employed by an organization to make changes that are not popular with the other people who work there "刀斧手"（受雇进行不受欢迎的改革的人）

hatch·ling /ˈhætʃlɪŋ/ *noun* a baby bird or animal which has just come out of its shell 刚出壳的雏鸟（或小动物）

hatch·way /ˈhætʃweɪ/ *noun* = HATCH (1)

hate 🔑 /heɪt/ *verb, noun*
■ *verb* (not used in the progressive tenses 不用于进行时) **1** 🔑 to dislike sth very much 厌恶，讨厌，憎恶（某事物）： ~ **sth** *I hate spinach.* 我讨厌菠菜。◇ *I hate Monday mornings.* 我讨厌星期一早晨。◇ *I **hate it** when people cry.* 我厌烦别人哭。◇ *He **hated it** in France* (= did not like the life there). 他对法国的生活感到厌恶。◇ *I **hate the way** she always criticizes me.* 我对她不断批评我很反感。◇ ~ **doing sth** *She hates making mistakes.* 她讨厌出错。◇ ~ **to do sth** *He hated to be away from his family.* 他很不愿意离开家。◇ *She's a person who hates to make mistakes.* 她是个讨厌出错的人。◇ *I **hate to think** what would have happened if you hadn't been there.* 我真不敢想要是你不在那里会出什么事。◇ ~ **sb/sth doing sth** *He hates anyone parking in his space.* 他讨厌别人占他的车位停车。◇ ~ **sb/sth to do sth** *She would have hated him to see how her hands shook.* 她会很不愿意让他看到她的双手抖得厉害。◇ *I'd hate anything to happen to him.* 但愿他平安无事。 **2** 🔑 to dislike sb very much 憎恨，憎恶，仇恨（某人）： ~ **sb/yourself** *The two boys hated each other.* 那两个男孩相互仇视。◇ *He was her most hated enemy.* 他是她最恨的人。◇ ~ **sb/yourself for sth/for doing sth** *I hated myself for feeling jealous.* 我恨自己的嫉妒心。 **3** [no passive] ~ **to do sth** used when saying

---

▼ **SYNONYMS 同义词辨析**

hate

dislike • can't stand • despise • can't bear • loathe • detest

These words all mean to have a strong feeling of dislike for sb/sth. 以上各词均含厌恶、讨厌、憎恶之义。

hate to have a strong feeling of dislike for sb/sth 指厌恶、讨厌、憎恶 NOTE Although **hate** is generally a very strong verb, it is also commonly used in spoken or informal English to talk about people or things that you dislike in a less important way, for example a particular type of food. 尽管 hate 通常为语气很强的动词，但亦常用于口语或非正式英语中，谈论不太喜欢的人或物，如某种食物等： *He hates violence in any form.* 他憎恶任何形式的暴力。◇ *I've always hated cabbage.* 我从来都讨厌吃卷心菜。

dislike (*rather formal*) to not like sb/sth 指不喜欢、厌恶 NOTE **Dislike** is a rather formal word; it is less formal, and more usual, to say that you *don't like* sb/sth, especially in spoken English. * dislike 为相当正式的用语，don't like 则较非正式，而且较常用，尤其在英语口语中： *I don't like it when you phone me so late at night.* 我不喜欢你夜里这么晚给我打电话。

can't stand (*rather informal*) used to emphasize that you really do not like sb/sth 强调不喜欢、受不了、不能容忍： *I can't stand his brother.* 他弟弟让我受不了。◇ *She couldn't stand being kept waiting.* 叫她等着，她会受不了。

despise to dislike and have no respect for sb/sth 指鄙视、蔑视、看不起： *He despised himself for being so cowardly.* 他为自己如此怯懦而自惭形秽。

can't bear used to say that you dislike sth so much that you cannot accept or deal with it 指无法承受、应付不了： *I can't bear having cats in the house.* 家里有猫我可受不了。

CAN'T STAND OR CAN'T BEAR? 用 can't stand 还是 can't bear?

In many cases you can use either word, but **can't bear** is slightly stronger and slightly more formal than **can't stand**. 在许多情况下，两个短语可通用，但 can't bear 比 can't stand 语气稍强，而且较正式。

loathe to hate sb/sth very much 指极不喜欢、厌恶： *They loathe each other.* 他们相互讨厌。NOTE **Loathe** is generally an even stronger verb than **hate**, but it can also be used more informally to talk about less important things, meaning 'really don't like'. * loathe 通常比 hate 语气还强，但亦可用于非正式场合指不太重要的事情，意为确实不喜欢： *Whether you **love or loathe** their music, you can't deny their talent.* 无论你是否喜欢他们的音乐，你都无法否认他们的才能。

detest (*rather formal*) to hate sb/sth very much 指厌恶、憎恨、讨厌： *They absolutely detest each other.* 他们完全是相互憎恨。

PATTERNS

- I hate/dislike/can't stand/can't bear/loathe/detest **doing sth**.
- I hate/can't bear **to do sth**.
- I hate/dislike/can't stand/can't bear **it when**...
- I **really** hate/dislike/can't stand/despise/can't bear/detest sb/sth.
- I **absolutely** hate/can't stand/loathe/detest sb/sth.

sth that you would prefer not to have to say, or when politely asking to do sth （表示不愿说某事，或客气地请求）不愿，不想：*I hate to say it, but I don't think their marriage will last.* 我不愿这么说，但我觉得他们的婚姻不会长久。◇ *I hate to trouble you, but could I use your phone?* 我不愿麻烦你，但我能用一下你的电话吗？ ▶ **hater** *noun*：*I'm not a woman hater, I just don't like Joan.* 我并非憎恨女人，只是不喜欢琼。

IDM **hate sb's 'guts** (*informal*) to dislike sb very much 对某人恨之入骨

■ ***noun*** **1** [U] a very strong feeling of dislike for sb 憎恨；厌恶；仇恨 **SYN** **hatred**：*a look of hate* 憎恨的目光 ◇ *a hate campaign* (= cruel comments made about sb over a period of time in order to damage their reputation) 对某人名誉的诋毁 ◇ ***hate mail*** (= letters containing cruel comments) 诋毁信件 **2** [C] (*informal*) a person or thing that you hate 所憎恶的人（或事物）：*Plastic flowers have always been a particular hate of mine.* 我一向特别厌恶塑料花。 **IDM** SEE PET *adj.*

▼ WHICH WORD? 词语辨析

hate / hatred

- These two words have a similar meaning. **Hatred** is more often used to describe a very strong feeling of dislike for a particular person or thing. 这两个词意义相似。hatred 较常指对某人或某事物的强烈仇恨、憎恨：*Her deep hatred of her sister was obvious.* 一眼便能看出她对姐姐恨之入骨。◇ *a cat's hatred of water* 猫对水的憎恨 **Hate** is more often used when you are talking about this feeling in a general way. * hate 较常泛指仇恨、憎恨、厌恶：*a look of pure hate* 充满憎恨的目光 ◇ *people filled with hate* 充满仇恨的人们

'hate crime *noun* **1** [U] violent acts that are committed against people because they are of a different race, because they are HOMOSEXUAL, etc. （因种族、同性恋等歧视引起的）仇恨犯罪，仇恨罪 **2** [C] a single act of this type 仇恨犯罪行为：*the victim of a hate crime* 仇恨犯罪的受害人

hate·ful /'heɪtfl/ *adj.* very unkind or unpleasant 可恶的；十分讨厌的：*a hateful person/place/face* 可恶的人 / 地方 / 面孔 ◇ **~ to sb** *The idea of fighting against men of their own race was hateful to them.* 一想到要跟本族人交战他们就十分难受。

hath /hæθ/ (*old use*) = HAS

hat·pin /'hætpɪn/ *noun* a long pin used for fastening a hat to your hair, especially in the past （尤指旧时的）女帽饰针，帽针

hat·red /'heɪtrɪd/ *noun* [U, C] a very strong feeling of dislike for sb/sth 仇恨；憎恨；厌恶：*He looked at me with intense hatred.* 他满怀敌意地看着我。◇ *There was fear and hatred in his voice.* 他的声音里透露着恐惧和仇恨。◇ **~ (for/of sb/sth)** *She felt nothing but hatred for her attacker.* 她对攻击她的人只有恨。◇ *a profound hatred of war* 对战争的深恶痛绝 ◇ **~ (towards sb)** *feelings of hatred towards the bombers* 对非法放置炸弹者的痛恨 ◇ *racial hatred* (= between people from different races) 种族仇恨 ◇ *The debate simply revived old hatreds.* 这一辩论不过是再次挑起了夙仇。 ➲ NOTE AT HATE

hat·stand /'hætstænd/ *noun* a vertical pole with large hooks around the top, for hanging hats and coats on 立式衣帽架

hat·ter /'hætə(r)/ *noun* (*old-fashioned*) a person who makes and sells hats 制帽者；帽商 **IDM** SEE MAD

'hat-trick *noun* three points, goals, etc. scored by the same player in a particular match or game; three successes achieved by one person （比赛或游戏中）一人连得三分，一人连续三次取胜；帽子戏法：*to score a hat-trick* 上演帽子戏法

haughty /'hɔːti/ *adj.* (**haught·ier**, **haught·iest**) behaving in an unfriendly way towards other people because you think that you are better than them 傲慢的；高傲自大的 **SYN** **arrogant**：*a **haughty face/look/manner*** 自负的面容 / 神态 / 态度 ◇ *He replied with haughty disdain.* 他的回答充满了不屑。 ▶ **haught·ily** /-ɪli/ *adv.* **haughti·ness** *noun* [U]

haul /hɔːl/ *verb, noun*

■ ***verb*** **1** to pull sth/sb with a lot of effort （用力）拖，拉，拽：**~ sth/sb** *The wagons were hauled by horses.* 那些货车是马拉的。◇ **~ sth/sb + adv./prep.** *He reached down and hauled Liz up onto the wall.* 他俯身把利兹拉上墙头。 ➲ SYNONYMS AT PULL **2** **~ yourself up/out of, etc.** to move yourself somewhere slowly and with a lot of effort 用力缓慢挪动到（某处）：*She hauled herself out of bed.* 她费劲地下了床。 **3** **~ sb + adv./prep.** to force sb to go somewhere they do not want to go 强迫（某人）去某处：*A number of suspects have been hauled in for questioning.* 一批嫌疑犯被拘捕接受讯问。 **4** [usually passive] **~ sb (up) before sb/sth** to make sb appear in court in order to be judged 使某人出庭受审；把某人提交法庭：*He was hauled up before the local magistrates for dangerous driving.* 他因危险驾驶而被移交地方法庭审判。

IDM **haul sb over the 'coals** (*BrE*) (*NAmE* **rake sb over the 'coals**) to criticize sb severely because they have done sth wrong 严厉训斥（或斥责）某人

■ ***noun*** **1** a large amount of sth that has been stolen or that is illegal 大批赃物；大量非法物品：*a haul of weapons* 大批非法武器 ◇ *a drugs haul* 一大批毒品 **2** (especially in sport 尤用于体育运动) a large number of points, goals, etc. 很高的得分：*His haul of 40 goals in a season is a record.* 他在一个赛季中得了 40 分，创下了纪录。 **3** [usually sing.] the distance covered in a particular journey 旅行的距离；旅程：*They began the long slow haul to the summit.* 他们踏上了攀登顶峰的漫长行程。◇ *Our camp is only a short haul from here.* 我们的营地离这里很近。◇ *Take the coast road—it'll be less of a haul* (= an easier journey). 走海岸线吧，这样会好走一些。 ➲ SEE ALSO LONG HAUL, SHORT-HAUL **4** a quantity of fish caught at one time 一次捕获的鱼；一网鱼

haul·age /'hɔːlɪdʒ/ *noun* [U] (*BrE*) the business of transporting goods by road or railway; money charged for this （公路或铁路的）货运，货运费：*the road haulage industry* 公路货运业 ◇ *a **haulage firm/contractor*** 陆路货运公司 / 承包人 ◇ *How much is haulage?* 运费是多少？

haul·ier /'hɔːliə(r)/ (*BrE*) (*NAmE* **haul·er** /'hɔːlə(r)/) *noun* a person or company whose business is transporting goods by road or railway/railroad 陆路运输业者；陆路货运承运人；货运公司

haunch /hɔːntʃ/ *noun* **1** **haunches** [pl.] the tops of the legs and BUTTOCKS; the similar parts at the back of the body of an animal that has four legs 臀胯部；（四足动物的）腰腿：*to crouch/squat **on your haunches*** 蹲着 **2** [C] a back leg and LOIN of an animal that has four legs, eaten as food （四足动物可食用的）腰腿肉：*a haunch of venison* 一条鹿腰腿肉

haunt /hɔːnt/ *verb, noun*

■ ***verb*** **1** **~ sth/sb** if the GHOST of a dead person **haunts** a place, people say that they have seen it there （鬼魂）出没：*A headless rider haunts the country lanes.* 一个无头骑士常出没于乡间的小路上。 **2** **~ sb** if sth unpleasant **haunts** you, it keeps coming to your mind so that you cannot forget it （不快的事情）萦绕于脑际，使难以忘却：*The memory of that day still haunts me.* 我的脑海中还常常回想起那天的情景。◇ *For years she was haunted by guilt.* 多年来她一直感到愧疚。 **3** **~ sb** to continue to cause problems for sb for a long time 长期不断地缠扰（某人）：*That decision **came back to haunt him**.* 那个决定对他造成无法摆脱的困扰。

■ ***noun*** a place that sb visits often or where they spend a lot of time 常去的场所；消磨时光的去处：*The pub is a favourite haunt of artists.* 这家酒吧是艺术家最爱光顾的地方。

haunt·ed /ˈhɔːntɪd/ *adj.* **1** (of a building 建筑物) believed to be visited by GHOSTS （被认为）闹鬼的，有鬼魂出没的：*a haunted house* 闹鬼的房子 **2** (of an expression on sb's face 面部表情) showing that sb is very worried 忧心忡忡的；满面愁容的：*There was a haunted look in his eyes.* 他眼中透露出忧虑的神色。

haunt·ing /ˈhɔːntɪŋ/ *adj.* beautiful, sad or frightening in a way that cannot be forgotten 萦绕心头的；使人难忘的：*a **haunting** melody/experience/image* 难以忘怀的优美乐曲；痛苦难忘的经历；吓人难忘的形象 ▸ **haunt·ing·ly** *adv.*

Hausa /ˈhaʊsə; -zə/ *noun* [U] a language spoken by the Hausa people of W Africa, especially in Nigeria and Niger, and also used in other parts of W Africa as a language of communication between different peoples 豪萨语（现通用于尼日利亚、尼日尔和其他一些西非地区）

haute cou·ture /ˌəʊt kuˈtjʊə(r); *NAmE* ˌoʊt kuˈtʊr/ *noun* [U] (*from French*) the business of making fashionable and expensive clothes for women; the clothes made in this business 高档女子时装业；高档女子时装

haute cuis·ine /ˌəʊt kwɪˈziːn; *NAmE* ˌoʊt/ *noun* [U] (*from French*) cooking of a very high standard 高级烹饪 ➲ MORE LIKE THIS 20, page R27

haut·eur /əʊˈtɜː(r); *NAmE* hɔːˈtɜːr; oʊˈt-/ *noun* [U] (*formal*) an unfriendly way of behaving towards other people suggesting that you think that you are better than they are 傲慢；高傲自大

ha·vala /hʌˈveɪlə/ *noun* = HAWALA

have /həv; əv; *strong form* hæv/ *verb, auxiliary verb* ➲ IRREGULAR VERBS at page R4

■ *verb* (In some senses **have got** is also used, especially in British English. 作某些意义时也用 have got，尤其是英式英语。)

• **OWN/HOLD** 拥有；持有 **1** (*also* **have got**) ~ **sth** (not used in the progressive tenses 不用于进行时) to own, hold or possess sth 有；持有；占有：*He had a new car and a boat.* 他有一辆新车和一条船。◇ *Have you got a job yet?* 你有工作了吗？◇ *I don't have that much money on me.* 我身上没带那么多钱。◇ *She's got a BA in English.* 她有英语学士学位。

• **CONSIST OF** 由…组成 **2** (*also* **have got**) ~ **sth** (not used in the progressive tenses 不用于进行时) be made up of 由…组成：*In 2008 the party had 10 000 members.* 这个党在 2008 年时拥有 1 万名党员。

• **QUALITY/FEATURE** 性质；特征 **3** (*also* **have got**) (not used in the progressive tenses 不用于进行时) to show a quality or feature 显示出，带有（性质、特征）：~ **sth** *The ham had a smoky flavour.* 这火腿散发着一种烟熏的香味。◇ *The house has gas-fired central heating.* 这所房子有燃气中央供暖系统。◇ *They have a lot of courage.* 他们勇气十足。◇ ~ **sth + adj.** *He's got a front tooth missing.* 他有一颗门牙掉了。 **4** (*also* **have got**) ~ **sth to do sth** (not used in the progressive tenses 不用于进行时) to show a particular quality by your actions （通过行动）表现出（品质）：*Surely she didn't have the nerve to say that to him?* 她一定没有胆量跟他这样说吧？

• **RELATIONSHIP** 关系 **5** (*also* **have got**) ~ **sb/sth** (not used in the progressive tenses 不用于进行时) used to show a particular relationship （表示关系）有：*He's got three children.* 他有三个孩子。◇ *Do you have a client named Peters?* 你们有一位名叫彼得斯的客户吗？

• **STH AVAILABLE** 可利用 **6** (*also* **have got**) ~ **sth** (not used in the progressive tenses 不用于进行时) to be able to make use of sth because it is available 能用：*Have you got time to call him?* 你有时间给他打电话吗？◇ *We have no choice in the matter.* 我们在这件事上别无选择。

• **SHOULD/MUST** 应该；必须 **7** (*also* **have got**) ~ **sth** (not used in the progressive tenses 不用于进行时) to be in a position where you ought to do sth 有责任（或义务）：*We have a duty to care for the refugees.* 我们有义务关怀这些难民。 **8** (*also* **have got**) (not used in the progressive tenses 不用于进行时) to be in a position of needing to do sth 须要，有必要（做某事）：~ **sth** *I've got a lot of homework tonight.* 我今晚有很多家庭作业要做。◇ ~ **sth to do** *I must go—I have a bus to catch.* 我必须走了，我得去赶公共汽车。

• **HOLD** 抓住 **9** (*also* **have got**) ~ **sb/sth + adv./prep.** (not used in the progressive tenses 不用于进行时) to hold sb/sth in the way mentioned 抓住；握着；支承：*She'd got him by the collar.* 她抓住了他的衣领。◇ *He had his head in his hands.* 他双手抱着脑袋。

• **PUT/KEEP IN A POSITION** 放 / 保持在某位置 **10** (*also* **have got**) ~ **sth + adv./prep.** (not used in the progressive tenses 不用于进行时) to place or keep sth in a particular position 使放在；使保持（在）：*Mary had her back to me.* 玛丽背对着我。◇ *I soon had the fish in a net.* 我不一会儿就网住了那条鱼。

• **FEELING/THOUGHT** 感觉；思想 **11** (*also* **have got**) ~ **sth** (not used in the progressive tenses 不用于进行时) to let a feeling or thought come into your mind 感到；想到：*He had the strong impression that someone was watching him.* 他强烈地感觉到有人在监视他。◇ *We've got a few ideas for the title.* 关于名称，我们有几种想法。◇ (*informal*) ***I've got it!** We'll call it 'Word Magic'.* 我想到了！我们就叫它"文字魔术"吧。

• **ILLNESS** 病 **12** (*also* **have got**) ~ **sth** (not used in the progressive tenses 不用于进行时) to suffer from an illness or a disease 患病；得病；染病：*I've got a headache.* 我头痛。

▼ **BRITISH/AMERICAN** 英式 / 美式英语

have you got? / do you have?

- **Have got** is the usual verb in *BrE* to show possession, etc. in positive statements in the present tense, in negative statements and in questions. 在英式英语中，动词 have got 常用于现在时的肯定句、否定句和疑问句中，表示拥有等：*They've got a wonderful house.* 他们有一所漂亮的房子。◇ *We haven't got a television.* 我们没有电视机。◇ *Have you got a meeting today?* 你今天有会吗？ Questions and negative statements formed with **do** are also common. 以 do 构成疑问句和否定句亦常见：*Do you have any brothers and sisters?* 你有兄弟姐妹吗？◇ *We don't have a car.* 我们没有汽车。
- **Have** is also used but is more formal. 亦可用 have 构成疑问句和否定句，但较正式：*I have no objection to your request.* 我不反对你的请求。◇ *Have you an appointment?* 你有约会吗？ Some expressions with **have** are common even in informal language. 非正式用语中也常见一些带 have 的短语：*I'm sorry, I haven't a clue.* 对不起，我一无所知。
- In the past tense **had** is used in positive statements. In negatives and questions, forms with **did have** are usually used. 在过去时中 had 用于肯定句，而否定句和疑问句通常用 did have：*They had a wonderful house.* 他们曾有一所漂亮的房子。◇ *We didn't have much time.* 我们没有多少时间。◇ *Did she have her husband with her?* 她那时与丈夫在一起吗？
- In *NAmE* **have** and forms with **do/does/did** are the usual way to show possession, etc. in positive statements, negatives and questions. 美式英语通常用 have，以及 have 和 do / does / did 构成的各种形式表示拥有等，用于肯定句、否定句和疑问句：*They have a wonderful house.* 他们有一所漂亮的房子。◇ *We don't have a television.* 我们没有电视机。◇ *Do you have a meeting today?* 你今天有会吗？ **Have got** is not used in questions, but is used in positive statements, especially to emphasize that somebody has one thing rather than another. * have got 不用于疑问句，而用于肯定句中，着重强调某人有某物而非另一物：*'Does your brother have brown hair?' 'No, he's got blond hair.'* "你弟弟的头发是棕色的吗？""不，他有一头金发。"
- In both *BrE* and *NAmE* **have** and forms with **do/does** and **did** are used when you are referring to a habit or routine. 英式英语和美式英语均用 have，以及 have 和 do / does / did 构成的各种形式表示习惯或常规：*We don't often have time to talk.* 我们常常没有时间谈话。

• **EXPERIENCE** 经历 **13** ⚷ **~ sth** to experience sth 经受；经历；经验：*I went to a few parties and had a good time.* 我参加了几次聚会，过得很愉快。◇ *I was having difficulty in staying awake.* 我正困得睁不开眼。◇ *She'll have an accident one day.* 她总有一天会出事的。

• **EVENT** 活动 **14** ⚷ **~ sth** to organize or hold an event 组织；举办：*Let's have a party.* 我们办一次聚会吧。

• **EAT/DRINK/SMOKE** 饮食；吸烟 **15** ⚷ **~ sth** to eat, drink or smoke sth 吃；喝；吸（烟等）：*to **have breakfast/lunch/dinner*** 吃早饭 / 午饭 / 正餐 ◇ *I'll have the salmon* (= for example, in a restaurant). 我要一份鲑鱼。◇ *I had a cigarette while I was waiting.* 我等候时抽了一支烟。

• **DO STH** 做某事 **16** ⚷ **~ sth** to perform a particular action 进行（活动）：*I had a swim to cool down.* 我游了泳，凉快凉快。◇ (*BrE*) *to **have a wash/shower/bath*** 洗一下；冲淋浴；洗澡

• **GIVE BIRTH** 生 **17** ⚷ **~ sb/sth** to give birth to sb/sth 生；生产：*She's going to have a baby.* 她快生孩子了。

• **EFFECT** 效果 **18** ⚷ **~ sth** to produce a particular effect 产生（效果）：*His paintings had a strong influence on me as a student.* 我当学生时，他的画对我产生过强烈的影响。◇ *The colour green has a restful effect.* 绿色使人感到宁静。

• **RECEIVE** 接收 **19** ⚷ **~ sth** (not usually used in the progressive tenses 通常不用于进行时) to receive sth from sb 收到；接到：*I had a letter from my brother this morning.* 我今天早晨收到了弟弟的一封信。◇ ***Can I have the bill, please?*** 请给我账单。 **20** ⚷ **~ sth** to be given sth; to have sth done to you 得到；接受；受到：*I'm having treatment for my back problem.* 我正接受背部疾患的治疗。◇ *How many driving lessons have you had so far?* 你到目前为止上过多少节驾驶课了？ **21** ⚷ (*also* **have got**) **~ sth doing sth** (not used in the progressive tenses 不用于进行时) to experience the effects of sb's actions 接受（某人行为的效果）：*We have orders coming in from all over the world.* 我们接到来自世界各地的订单。

• **HAVE STH DONE** 让某事做成 **22** ⚷ **~ sth done** (used with a past participle 与过去分词连用) to suffer the effects of what sb else does to you 蒙受（他人所为的后果）：*She had her bag stolen.* 她的包被偷了。 **23** ⚷ **~ sth done** (used with a past participle 与过去分词连用) to cause sth to be done for you by sb else 让（他人）为你做（某事）：*You've had your hair cut!* 你理发了！◇ *We're having our car repaired.* 我们的车正在修理。 **24** to tell or arrange for sb to do sth for you 要（或安排）（某人）做（某事）：**~ sb do sth** *He had the bouncers throw them out of the club.* 他叫保安人员把他们轰出了俱乐部。◇ (*informal*) ***I'll have you know*** (= I'm telling you) *I'm a black belt in judo.* 你听着，我可是柔道黑带级高手。◇ **~ sb + adv./prep.** *She's always having the builders in to do something or other.* 她总是让建筑工人到家里来干这干那。

• **ALLOW** 允许 **25** (used in negative sentences, especially after *will not, cannot*, etc. 用于否定句，尤置于 will not、cannot 等之后) to allow sth; to accept sth without complaining 允许；容忍：**~ sth** *I'm sick of your rudeness—I won't have it any longer!* 你的无礼我已经受够了，我不会再容忍下去了！◇ **~ sb/sth doing sth** *We can't have people arriving late all the time.* 我们不能允许有人总是迟到。

• **PUT SB/STH IN A CONDITION** 使处于某状况 **26** ⚷ to cause sb/sth to be in a particular state; to make sb react in a particular way 使处于（某状态）；使做出（某种反应）：**~ sb/sth + adj.** *I want to have everything ready in good time.* 我要求一切都得准时备妥。◇ **~ sb/sth doing sth** *He had his audience listening attentively.* 他抓住了听众的注意力。

• **IN ARGUMENT** 辩论 **27** (*also* **have got**) **~ sb** (*informal*) (not used in the progressive tenses 不用于进行时) to put sb at a disadvantage in an argument 辩过；胜过：***You've got me there.*** *I hadn't thought of that.* 你把我问住了。我没想过这个。

• **SEX** 性 **28** **~ sb** (*slang*) to have sex with sb 同（某人）性交：*He had her in his office.* 他在他的办公室里和她搞上了。

• **TRICK** 欺骗 **29** [usually passive] **~ sb** (*informal*) to trick or cheat sb 欺骗；蒙骗：*I'm afraid you've been had.* 恐怕你上当了。

• **GUESTS** 客人 **30** ⚷ [no passive] **~ sb/sth** to take care of sb/sth in your home, especially for a limited period （尤指短期在自己家中）照料，照看：*We're having the kids for the weekend.* 这个周末孩子们要到我们家来由我们照料。 **31** ⚷ [no passive] **~ sb + adv./prep.** to entertain sb in your home （在家中）招待，款待：*We had some friends to dinner last night.* 我们昨晚请了几位朋友来家里吃饭了。

• **BE WITH** 在一起 **32** ⚷ (*also* **have got**) **~ sb with you** (not used in the progressive tenses 不用于进行时) to be with sb 同（某人）在一起：*She had some friends with her.* 她和几个朋友在一起。

• **FOR A JOB** 工作 **33** [no passive] **~ sb as sth** to take or accept sb for a particular role 让，接受（某人承担职务）：*Who can we have as treasurer?* 我们让谁来主管财务？

IDM **HELP** Most idioms containing **have** are at the entries for the nouns and adjectives in the idioms, for example **have your eye on sb** is at **eye** *n.* 大多数含 have 的习语，都可在该等习语中的名词及形容词相关词条找到，如 have your eye on sb 在词条 eye 的名词部分。 **have 'done with sth** (*especially BrE*) to finish sth unpleasant so that it does not continue 结束（不愉快的事）：*Let's have done with this silly argument.* 我们结束这场无聊的争辩吧。 **have 'had it** (*informal*) **1** to be in a very bad condition; to be unable to be repaired 情形很糟；不能修复：*The car had had it.* 这辆车无法修复了。 **2** to be extremely tired 极度疲乏：*I've had it! I'm going to bed.* 我太困了！我要去睡觉了。 **3** to have lost all chance of surviving sth 毫无幸存机会；完蛋：*When the truck smashed into me, I thought I'd had it.* 那辆卡车撞上我时，我想这下完了。 **4** to be going to experience sth unpleasant 将吃苦头：*Dad saw you scratch the car—you've had it now!* 爸爸看见你把车身划了，这下可有你好受的了！ **5** to be unable to accept a situation any longer 无法继续容忍：***I've had it** (**up to here**) **with him***—*he's done it once too often.* 我受够他了，他这一次太过分了。 **'have it** (**that**...) to claim that it is a fact that... 称…属实；说…是真的：***Rumour has it*** *that we'll have a new manager soon.* 据传我们即将有一位新经理。 **have** (**got**) **it/that 'coming** (**to you**) to be likely to suffer the unpleasant effects of your actions and to deserve to do so 活该；罪有应得：*It was no surprise when she left him—everyone knew he had it coming to him.* 她离开了他，这丝毫不奇怪。大家都知道是他自己造成的。 **have it 'in for sb** (*informal*) to not like sb and be unpleasant to them 跟某人过不去 **have it 'off/a'way** (**with sb**) (*BrE, slang*) to have sex with sb 同（某人）性交 **have it 'in you** (**to do sth**) (*informal*) to be capable of doing sth 有能力（做某事）：*Everyone thinks he has it in him to produce a literary classic.* 大家都认为他有能力写出一部文学名著。◇ *You were great. I didn't know you had it in you.* 你真了不起。我不知道你有这本事。 **have** (**got**) **'nothing on sb/sth** (*informal*) to be not nearly as good as sb/sth 不如；比不上 ➲ SEE ALSO HAVE (GOT) STH ON SB **not 'having any** (*informal*) not willing to listen to or believe sth 不愿听，不愿相信（某事）：*I tried to persuade her to wait but she wasn't having any.* 我竭力劝她等一下，可她不肯听。 **what 'have you** (*informal*) other things, people, etc. of the same kind 诸如此类的事物（或人等）：*There's room in the cellar to store old furniture and what have you.* 地下室有地方存放旧家具之类的东西。

PHR V ˌ**have** (**got**) **sth a'gainst sb/sth** (not used in the progressive tenses 不用于进行时) to dislike sb/sth for a particular reason 因…而讨厌某人 / 某事：*What have you got against Ruth? She's always been good to you.* 你为什么不喜欢鲁思？她一直对你很好。 ˌ**have sb↔'back** to allow a husband, wife or partner that you are separated from to return 和分手的丈夫（或妻子、伴侣）破镜重圆；愿与某人重修旧好 ˌ**have sth 'back** ⚷ to receive sth that sb has borrowed or taken from you 收回被借走（或拿走）的东西：*You can have your files back after we've checked them.* 我们核对完你的文件之后就还给你。 ˌ**have** (**got**) **sth 'in** (not used in the progressive tenses 不用于进行时) to have a supply of sth in your home, etc. 存有某物：*Have we got enough food in?* 我们家里存有足够的食物吗？ ˌ**have sb 'on** (*informal*) to try to make sb believe sth that is not true, usually as a joke 哄骗，欺骗（通常作为玩

笑）：*You didn't really, did you? You're not having me on, are you?* 你真的没有干吧？你不是在哄我吧？**ˌhave (got) sth ˈon** (not used in the progressive tenses 不用于进行时) **1** 🔑 to be wearing sth 穿着；戴着：*She had a red jacket on.* 她穿着件红夹克。◇ *He had nothing (= no clothes) on.* 他没穿衣服。**2** to leave a piece of equipment working 让设备运转着：*She has her TV on all day.* 她一整天都开着电视机。**3** 🔑 to have arranged to do sth 安排（做某事）：*I can't see you this week—I've got a lot on.* 我这个星期不能见你，我安排得很满。**ˌhave (got) sth ˈon sb** [no passive] (*informal*) (not used in the progressive tenses 不用于进行时) to know sth bad about sb, especially sth that connects them with a crime 有某人的把柄，掌握某人的证据（尤指与犯罪有关的）：*I'm not worried—they've got nothing on me.* 我不担心，他们没抓住我什么把柄。**ˌhave sth ˈout** to cause sth, especially a part of your body, to be removed 去除，切除（身体部位等）：*I had to have my appendix out.* 我只好把盲肠切除了。**ˌhave sth ˈout (with sb)** to try to settle a disagreement by discussing or arguing about it openly （与某人）辩论出个结果，把某事讲个明白：*I need to have it out with her once and for all.* 我有必要跟她公开彻底地把话说清楚。**ˌhave sb ˈup (for sth)** (*BrE, informal*) [usually passive] to cause sb to be accused of sth in court （为某事）把某人告上法庭：*He was had up for manslaughter.* 他因误杀罪被送上法庭。

■ ***auxiliary verb*** 🔑 used with the past participle to form perfect tenses （与过去分词连用构成完成时）：*I've finished my work.* 我干完我的活儿了。◇ *He's gone home, hasn't he?* 他回家去了，对吗？◇ *'Have you seen it?' 'Yes, I have/No, I haven't.'* "你看见了吗？""是的，看见了/没有，没看见。"◇ *She'll have had the results by now.* 她现在应该知道结果了。◇ *Had they left before you got there?* 你到那里时他们已经离开了吗？◇ *If I hadn't seen it with my own eyes I wouldn't have believed it.* 要不是亲眼看见了，我不会相信的。◇ (*formal*) *Had I known that* (= if I had known that) *I would never have come.* 要是早知道，我绝不会来的。

haven /ˈheɪvn/ *noun* a place that is safe and peaceful where people or animals are protected 安全的地方；保护区；避难所：*The hotel is a haven of peace and tranquility.* 这家旅馆是一处安宁的去处。◇ *The river banks are a haven for wildlife.* 河的两岸是野生动物的自然栖息地。➲ SEE ALSO SAFE HAVEN, TAX HAVEN

the ˌhave-ˈnots *noun* [pl.] people who do not have money and possessions 一无所有的人；穷人 ➲ COMPARE HAVES

haven't /ˈhævnt/ *short form* have not

hav·er·sack /ˈhævəsæk; *NAmE* -vərs-/ *noun* (*old-fashioned*) a bag that is carried on the back or over the shoulder, especially when walking in the country （尤指野外步行背的）背包，褡裢

the ˈhaves *noun* [pl.] people who have enough money and possessions 有钱人；富人：*the division between the haves and the have-nots* 富人和穷人之间的差异 ➲ COMPARE HAVE-NOTS

have to 🔑 /ˈhæv tə; ˈhæf/ *modal verb* (**has to** /ˈhæz tə; ˈhæs/, **had to, had to** /ˈhæd tə; ˈhæt/) **1** 🔑 (*also* **have got to**) used to show that you must do sth 必须；不得不：*Sorry, I've got to go.* 对不起，我必须走了。◇ *Did she have to pay a fine?* 她非得交罚款吗？◇ *You don't have to knock—just walk in.* 不必敲门，进来就是了。◇ *I haven't got to leave till seven.* 我可以等到七点钟再离开。◇ *First, you have to think logically about your fears.* 首先，你得理性地看待自己的忧虑。◇ ***I have to admit**, the idea of marriage scares me.* 我不得不承认，一想到结婚我就害怕。◇ *Do you have to go?* 你非得走吗？◇ (*especially BrE*) *Have you got to go?* 你非得走吗？**2** 🔑 (*also* **have got to** *especially in BrE*) used to give advice or recommend sth （劝告或建议时用）：*You simply have to get a new job.* 你就是得找份新工作。◇ *You've got to try this recipe—it's delicious.* 你得试试这种烹调法，味道很不错。**3** 🔑 (*also* **have got to** *especially in BrE*) used to say that sth must be true or must happen （表示一定真实或肯定发生）：*There has to be a reason for his strange behaviour.* 他的古怪行为一定事出有因。◇ *This war has got to end soon.* 这场战争必将很快结束。**4** used to suggest that an annoying event happens in order to annoy you, or that sb does sth in order to annoy you （用以暗示麻烦的事或某人有意捣蛋）：*Of course, it had to start raining as soon as we got to the beach.* 可恶的雨，我们一到海滩它就非得下起来。◇ ***Do you have to hum so loudly?*** (= it is annoying) 你非得用这么大嗓门哼唱不可吗？➲ NOTE AT MODAL, MUST

▼ **EXPRESS YOURSELF 情景表达**

Asking about obligation 咨询相关义务

When you are unsure about what is expected of you in a situation, you can ask about obligations. 不确定在某种情境下该做什么时可以询问应履行的义务：

- *What time **do we have to** be home?* 我们必须在什么时候回到家？
- ***Are we supposed to** show our ID cards?* 我们需要出示身份证吗？
- ***Is it necessary to** apply for a visa?* 有必要申请签证吗？
- ***Is there a legal obligation to** wear a bike helmet here?* 在这里骑自行车有没有法律规定要戴头盔？

havoc /ˈhævək/ *noun* [U] a situation in which there is a lot of damage, destruction or confusion 灾害；祸患；浩劫：*The floods caused havoc throughout the area.* 洪水给整个地区带来了灾害。◇ *Continuing strikes are beginning **to play havoc with** the national economy.* 持续的罢工开始严重破坏国家经济。◇ *These insects can **wreak havoc on** crops.* 这些昆虫可严重危害农作物。

haw /hɔː/ *verb* IDM SEE HUM *v.*

Ha·wai·ian shirt /həˌwaɪən ˈʃɜːt; *NAmE* ˈʃɜːrt/ (*also* **aˈloha shirt**) *noun* a loose cotton shirt with a brightly coloured pattern and short sleeves 夏威夷衫，夏威夷衬衫（图案艳丽，短袖）

ha·wala /həˈwɑːlə; *NAmE* həˈv-/ (*also* **ha·vala**) *noun* [U] (in Arab countries and South Asia) a traditional system of transferring money to a person in another country or area, which involves paying money to an agent who then tells another agent in the relevant place to pay that person 哈瓦拉汇款体系（阿拉伯国家和南亚的传统汇款方式，汇款人付钱给一名代理人，后者再告知相关地点的另一名代理人付钱给收款人）

hawk /hɔːk/ *noun, verb*

■ ***noun*** **1** a strong fast BIRD OF PREY (= a bird that kills other creatures for food) 鹰；隼：*He waited, **watching her like a hawk*** (= watching her very closely). 他等待着，用鹰一样锐利的目光紧盯着她。➲ SEE ALSO SPARROWHAWK **2** a person, especially a politician, who supports the use of military force to solve problems 鹰派分子；主战分子 OPP **dove**[1] IDM SEE EYE *n.*

■ ***verb*** **1** [T] ~ **sth** to try to sell things by going from place to place asking people to buy them 沿街叫卖 SYN **peddle** **2** [I, T] ~ **(sth)** to get PHLEGM in your mouth when you cough 咳痰

hawk·er /ˈhɔːkə(r)/ *noun* a person who makes money by hawking goods 沿街叫卖者；小贩

ˌhawk-ˈeyed *adj.* (of a person 人) watching closely and carefully and noticing small details 严密注视的；目光犀利的 SYN **eagle-eyed**

hawk·ish /ˈhɔːkɪʃ/ *adj.* preferring to use military action rather than peaceful discussion in order to solve a political problem 鹰派的；主战的；强硬的 OPP **dovish**

haw·ser /ˈhɔːzə(r)/ *noun* (*specialist*) a thick rope or steel cable used on a ship （船上用的）缆索，钢缆

haw·thorn /ˈhɔːθɔːn; *NAmE* -θɔːrn/ *noun* [U, C] a bush or small tree with THORNS, white or pink flowers and small dark red BERRIES 山楂

hay /heɪ/ *noun* [U] **1** grass that has been cut and dried and is used as food for animals （用作饲料的）干草，草料：*a bale of hay* 一大捆干草 ➲ COMPARE STRAW (1) ➲ VISUAL VOCAB PAGE V3 **2** (*NAmE, informal*) a small amount of money 少量的钱

IDM **make hay while the 'sun shines** (*saying*) to make good use of opportunities, good conditions, etc. while they last 趁有太阳时晒干草；抓紧时机；打铁趁热 ➲ MORE AT HIT *v.*, ROLL *n.*

'hay fever *noun* [U] an illness that affects the nose, eyes and throat and is caused by POLLEN from plants that is breathed in from the air 花粉病，枯草热（由于吸入空气中的花粉而引起的鼻、眼、喉部的过敏症）

hay·loft /'heɪlɒft; *NAmE* -lɔːft/ *noun* a place at the top of a farm building used for storing HAY （农舍顶部的）干草棚；干草顶阁

hay·mak·ing /'heɪmeɪkɪŋ/ *noun* [U] the process of cutting and drying grass to make HAY 制干草

hay·ride /'heɪraɪd/ *noun* (*NAmE*) a ride for pleasure on a CART filled with HAY, pulled by a horse or TRACTOR 乘坐（由马或拖拉机拉的）干草车出游

hay·stack /'heɪstæk/ (*also less frequent* **hay·rick** /'heɪrɪk/) *noun* a large pile of HAY, used as a way of storing it until it is needed 干草堆；干草垛 ➲ VISUAL VOCAB PAGE V3 IDM SEE NEEDLE *n.*

hay·wire /'heɪwaɪə(r)/ *adj.*

IDM **go 'haywire** (*informal*) to stop working correctly or become out of control 出故障；紊乱；失去控制：*After that, things started to go haywire.* 此后事情开始失去控制。

haz·ard /'hæzəd; *NAmE* -ərd/ *noun, verb*

■ ***noun*** a thing that can be dangerous or cause damage 危险；危害：*a fire/safety hazard* 火灾 / 安全隐患 ◇ **~ (to sb/sth)** *Growing levels of pollution represent a serious health hazard to the local population.* 日益严重的污染对当地人民的健康构成了重大威胁。◇ **~ (of sth/of doing sth)** *Everybody is aware of the hazards of smoking.* 大家都明白吸烟的危害。◇ ***hazard lights*** (= flashing lights on a car that warn other drivers of possible danger) （汽车上的）危险报警闪光灯

■ ***verb*** **1** to make a suggestion or guess which you know may be wrong 试着提出；大胆猜测：**~ sth** *Would you like to hazard a guess?* 你想猜猜看吗？◇ **+ speech** *'Is it Tom you're going with?' she hazarded.* "你是要和汤姆一起去吗？"她大胆猜测道。◇ **~ that...** *I would hazard that she is the sole reason we are here.* 我猜想我们来这儿全是因为她。 **2** **~ sth** (*formal*) to risk sth or put it in danger 冒…的风险；使处于危险中 SYN **endanger**：*Careless drivers hazard other people's lives as well as their own.* 粗心大意的驾驶者拿他人和自己的生命冒险。

haz·ard·ous /'hæzədəs; *NAmE* -ərdəs/ *adj.* involving risk or danger, especially to sb's health or safety 危险的；有害的：***hazardous waste/chemicals*** 有害废物 / 化学制品 ◇ *a hazardous journey* 危险的旅程 ◇ *It would be hazardous to invest so much.* 投资这么多会有风险。◇ *a list of products that are potentially hazardous to health* 对健康有潜在危害的产品清单

'hazard pay (*also* **'danger pay**) (*both US*) (*BrE* **'danger money**) *noun* [U] extra pay for doing work that is dangerous 危险工作津贴

haze /heɪz/ *noun, verb*

■ ***noun*** **1** [C, U] air that is difficult to see through because it contains very small drops of water, especially caused by hot weather （尤指热天引起的）薄雾，雾霭：*a heat haze* 热天的雾气 **2** [sing.] air containing sth that makes it difficult to see through it （烟尘等的）雾霭，烟雾：*a **haze of smoke/dust/steam*** 烟雾；尘雾；蒸汽雾 **3** [sing.] a mental state in which your thoughts, feelings, etc. are not clear 迷蒙；迷糊：*an alcoholic haze* 喝醉酒的迷糊

■ ***verb*** **1** [I, T] **~ (sth)** to become covered or to cover sth in a HAZE （使）笼罩在薄雾中 **2** [T] **~ sb** (*NAmE*) to play tricks on sb, especially a new student, or to give them very unpleasant things to do, sometimes as a condition for entering a FRATERNITY or SORORITY 戏弄，刁难（新生等，有时作为加入美国大学生联谊会的条件）

hazel /'heɪzl/ *noun, adj.*

■ ***noun*** [C, U] a small tree that produces small nuts (called hazelnuts) that can be eaten 榛树（其果实榛子可食）

■ ***adj.*** (of eyes 眼睛) greenish-brown or reddish-brown in colour 淡绿褐色的；浅赤褐色的

hazel·nut /'heɪzlnʌt/ (*also* **fil·bert** *especially in NAmE*) *noun* the small brown nut of the HAZEL tree 榛子 ➲ VISUAL VOCAB PAGE V35

hazy /'heɪzi/ *adj.* (**hazi·er**, **hazi·est**) **1** not clear because of HAZE 朦胧的；薄雾蒙蒙的：*a **hazy afternoon/sky*** 雾蒙蒙的下午 / 天空 ◇ ***hazy light/sunshine*** 朦胧的光线 / 阳光 ◇ *The mountains were hazy in the distance.* 远处的山峦在薄雾中若隐若现。 **2** not clear because of a lack of memory, understanding or detail 记不清的；模糊的 SYN **vague**：*a **hazy memory/idea*** 模糊不清的记忆 / 概念 ◇ *What happened next is all very hazy.* 接下来发生的事都记不清楚了。 **3** (of a person 人) uncertain or confused about sth 主意不定的；困惑的：*I'm a little hazy about what to do next.* 我还有点拿不准下一步要做什么。 ▶ **haz·ily** *adv.*：*'Why now?' she wondered hazily.* "为什么是现在？"她困惑地思忖。

'H-bomb *noun* = HYDROGEN BOMB

HCF /ˌeɪtʃ siː 'ef/ *abbr.* (*mathematics* 数) HIGHEST COMMON FACTOR 最大公因数

HCFC /ˌeɪtʃ siː ef 'siː/ *noun* (*chemistry* 化) the abbreviation for 'hydrochlorofluorocarbon', a type of gas used especially in AEROSOLS (= types of container that release liquid in the form of a spray) instead of CFC, as it is less harmful to the earth's OZONE LAYER 氢氯氟烃（全写为 hydrochlorofluorocarbon，因对臭氧层损害较小，替代氯氟烃用于喷雾剂）

HD /ˌeɪtʃ 'diː/ *abbr.* high-definition (used of television, film or video images that are extremely high quality, with very clear, sharp outlines and details) （电视、电影或录像图像）高清晰度，高画质：*The film was shot in HD.* 这部影片是用高清技术拍摄的。

HDMI /ˌeɪtʃ diː em 'aɪ/ *abbr.* the abbreviation for 'high-definition multimedia interface' (a system for connecting audio and video devices to electronic equipment such as a television or computer, in one cable) 高清晰度多媒体接口（全写为 high-definition multimedia interface）：*Your DVDs will look better if connected through the HDMI socket.* 如果连接到高清晰度多媒体接口，DVD 的播放效果会更好。

HDTV /ˌeɪtʃ diː tiː 'viː/ *noun* [U] (*specialist*) the abbreviation for 'high-definition television' (technology that produces extremely clear images on a television screen) 高清晰度电视（技术），高画质电视（技术）（全写为 high-definition television）

HE (*BrE*) (*also* **H.E.** *US, BrE*) *abbr.* **1** Her/His EXCELLENCY 阁下：*HE the Australian Ambassador* 澳大利亚大使阁下 **2** HIGHER EDUCATION 高等教育

he 🔑 /hi; iː; i; *strong form* hiː/ *pron., noun*

■ ***pron.*** (used as the subject of a verb 用作动词主语) **1** 🔑 a male person or animal that has already been mentioned or is easily identified 他；它（指雄性动物）：*Everyone liked my father—he was the perfect gentleman.* 大家都喜欢我父亲，他是真正的绅士。◇ *He* (= the man we are watching) *went through that door.* 他进了那道门。 **2** (*becoming old-fashioned*) a person, male or female, whose sex is not stated or known, especially when referring to sb mentioned earlier or to a group in general 人（指性别未说明或不知道的男性或女性，尤指曾提过的人或泛指某群体）：*Every child needs to know that he is loved.* 每个孩子都需要知道自己是有人爱的。◇ (*saying*) *He who* (= anyone who) *hesitates is lost.* 优柔寡断者坐失良机。 ➲ NOTE AT GENDER **3** **He** used when referring to God （指上帝） ➲ COMPARE HIM

H

■**noun** /hiː/ **1** [sing.] (*informal*) a male 雄性： *What a nice dog—is it a he or a she?* 多好看的狗，它是公的还是母的？ **2 he-** (in compound nouns 构成复合名词) a male animal 雄性动物： *a he-goat* 一头公山羊

head /hed/ *noun, verb*

■**noun**

• **PART OF BODY** 身体部位 **1** [C] the part of the body on top of the neck containing the eyes, nose, mouth and brain 头；头部： *She* ***nodded her head*** *in agreement.* 她点头表示同意。◇ *He* ***shook his head*** *in disbelief.* 他摇头表示不信。◇ *The boys* ***hung their heads*** *in shame.* 男孩子们羞愧地低着头。◇ *The driver suffered head injuries.* 司机头部受伤。◇ *She always* ***has her head in a book*** (= is always reading). 她总是埋头读书。◇ *He still has* ***a good head of hair*** (= a lot of hair). 他的头发依然很多。➲ COLLOCATIONS AT PHYSICAL ➲ VISUAL VOCAB PAGE V64 ➲ SEE ALSO DEATH'S HEAD

• **MIND** 头脑 **2** [C] the mind or brain 头脑；脑筋： *I sometimes wonder what goes on in that head of yours.* 我有时不明白你脑子里想些什么。◇ *I wish you'd* ***use your head*** (= think carefully before doing or saying sth). 我希望你凡事多用用脑子。◇ *The thought* ***never entered my head.*** 我从未有过那种想法。◇ *I can't work it out* ***in my head***—*I need a calculator.* 我没法心算出来，我得用计算器。◇ *I* ***can't get*** *that tune* ***out of my head.*** 我忘不掉那个曲调。◇ *When will you* ***get it into your head*** (= understand) *that I don't want to discuss this any more!* 你何时才能明白我不想再谈论这件事了！◇ *For some reason, she's* ***got it into her head*** (= believes) *that the others don't like her.* 由于某种原因，她有一种感觉，认为其他人都不喜欢她。◇ *Who's been* ***putting*** *such weird ideas* ***into your head*** (= making you believe that)? 是谁让你产生这些怪念头的？◇ *Try to* ***put*** *the exams* ***out of your head*** (= stop thinking about them) *for tonight.* 今晚尽量别想考试的事了。➲ SEE ALSO HOTHEAD

• **MEASUREMENT** 量度 **3 a head** [sing.] the size of a person's or an animal's head, used as a measurement of distance or height （人或动物的）一头长，一头高： *She's a good head taller than her sister.* 她比妹妹足足高出了一个头。◇ *The favourite won* ***by a short head*** (= a distance slightly less than the length of a horse's head). 最被看好的那匹马以不足一马头的优势获胜。

• **PAIN** 疼痛 **4** [C, usually sing.] (*informal*) a continuous pain in your head （持续的）头痛 SYN **headache**： *I woke up with a really bad head this morning.* 我今天早晨醒来时头痛得厉害。

• **OF GROUP/ORGANIZATION** 团体；组织 **5** [C, U] the person in charge of a group of people or an organization 负责人；领导人： *the* ***heads of government/state*** 政府首脑；国家元首 ◇ *She resigned as* ***head of department.*** 她辞去了部门主管的职务。◇ *the* ***crowned heads*** (= the kings and queens) *of Europe* 欧洲各国君主 ◇ *the* ***head gardener/waiter, etc.*** 园艺主管、餐馆服务员领班等 ◇ (*BrE*) *the* ***head boy/girl*** (= a student who is chosen to represent the school) 学校男生 / 女生代表

• **OF SCHOOL/COLLEGE** 学校；学院 **6** [C] (*often* **Head**) (*BrE*) the person in charge of a school or college 校长；院长 SYN **headmaster, headmistress, head teacher**： *I've been called in to see the Head.* 我接到通知去见校长。◇ *the deputy head* 副校长

• **SIDE OF COIN** 硬币的面 **7 heads** [U] the side of a coin that has a picture of the head of a person on it, used as one choice when a coin is TOSSED to decide sth 硬币正面（有人头像） ➲ COMPARE TAIL *n.* (7)

• **END OF OBJECT** 物体一端 **8** [C, usually sing.] ~ (**of sth**) the end of a long narrow object that is larger or wider than the rest of it 较宽大的一端；头： *the head of a nail* 钉子的头 ➲ VISUAL VOCAB PAGE V21 ➲ SEE ALSO BEDHEAD

• **TOP** 顶 **9** [sing.] ~ **of sth** the top or highest part of sth 顶端；上端： *at the head of the page* 在页眉处 ◇ *They finished the season at the head of their league.* 赛季结束时他们在联赛中位居榜首。

• **OF RIVER** 河 **10** [sing.] **the ~ of the river** the place where a river begins （河流）源头 SYN **source**

• **OF TABLE** 桌子 **11** [sing.] **the ~ of the table** the most important seat at a table 上座（桌子旁最重要的座位）： *The President sat at the head of the table.* 总统坐在桌子的上首。

• **OF LINE OF PEOPLE** 人的行列 **12** [sing.] **the ~ of sth** the position at the front of a line of people 领头位置；排头： *The prince rode at the head of his regiment.* 王子骑马走在卫队的前头。

• **OF PLANT** 植物 **13** [C] ~ (**of sth**) the mass of leaves or flowers at the end of a STEM （茎梗顶端的）叶球，头状花序： *Remove the dead heads to encourage new growth.* 把枯萎了的残花除掉以促使新的生长。

• **ON BEER** 啤酒 **14** [sing.] the mass of small bubbles on the top of a glass of beer 啤酒泡沫；酒头

• **OF SPOT** 斑 **15** [C] the part of a spot on your skin that contains a thick yellowish liquid (= PUS) 脓头 ➲ SEE ALSO BLACKHEAD

• **IN TAPE/VIDEO RECORDER** 录音 / 录像机 **16** [C] the part of a TAPE RECORDER or VIDEO RECORDER that touches the tape and changes the electrical signals into sounds and/or pictures 磁头

• **NUMBER OF ANIMALS** 动物数量 **17 ~ of sth** [pl.] used to say how many animals of a particular type are on a farm, in a HERD, etc. （表示农场或牧群等的牲畜的数目）头： *200 head of sheep* * 200 只绵羊

• **OF STEAM** 蒸汽 **18 a ~ of steam** [sing.] the pressure produced by steam in a confined space 蒸汽压力

• **SEX** 性 **19** [U] (*taboo, slang*) ORAL sex (= using the mouth to give sb sexual pleasure) 口交： *to give head* 进行口交

• **LINGUISTICS** 语言学 **20** [C] the central part of a phrase, which has the same GRAMMATICAL function as the whole phrase. In the phrase 'the tall man in a suit', *man* is the head. （短语的）中心成分，中心词，主导词

IDM **a/per 'head** for each person 每人： *The meal worked out at $20 a head.* 这餐饭算下来每人 20 美元。 **bang/knock your/their 'heads together** (*informal*) to force people to stop arguing and behave in a sensible way 强行制止人们争吵并使之恢复理智 **be banging, etc. your head against a brick 'wall** (*informal*) to keep trying to do sth that will never be successful 用头撞墙；徒劳无益；枉费心机： *Trying to reason with them was like banging my head against a brick wall.* 试图和他们讲道理只是白费口舌。 **be/stand head and 'shoulders above sb/sth** to be much better than other people or things 比其他人（或事物）好得多；出类拔萃；鹤立鸡群 **bite/snap sb's 'head off** (*informal*) to shout at sb in an angry way, especially without reason 气愤地对某人大喊大叫；（尤指毫无道理地）呵斥某人 **bring sth to a 'head | come to a 'head** if you **bring** a situation **to a head** or if a situation **comes to a head**, you are forced to deal with it quickly because it suddenly becomes very bad （使）事情达到紧要关头，需要当机立断 **bury/hide your head in the 'sand** to refuse to admit that a problem exists or refuse to deal with it 采取鸵鸟政策；不正视现实；回避问题 **can't make head nor 'tail of sth** to be unable to understand sth 不理解某事；不明白某事： *I couldn't make head nor tail of what he was saying.* 我弄不懂他在说些什么。 **do sb's 'head in** (*BrE, informal*) to make sb feel confused, upset and/or annoyed 使某人困惑（或烦恼、生气）： *Shut up! You're doing my head in.* 闭嘴！你让我烦死了。 **do sth standing on your 'head** (*informal*) to be able to do sth very easily and without having to think too much 做某事不费吹灰之力 **from ˌhead to 'foot/'toe** covering your whole body 从头到脚；遍布全身： *We were covered from head to foot in mud.* 我们浑身是泥。 **get your 'head down** (*informal*) **1** (*BrE*) to sleep 睡觉： *I managed to get my head down for an hour.* 我将就着睡了一小时。 **2** = KEEP/GET YOUR HEAD DOWN **get your 'head round sth** (*BrE, informal*) to be able to understand or accept sth 能够理解；接受得了： *She's dead. I can't get my head round it yet.* 她死了。我仍然无法相信这事。 **give sb their 'head** to allow sb to do what they want without trying to stop them 让某人随心所欲 **go head to 'head** (**with sb**) to deal with sb in a very direct and determined way （与某人）面对面直接谈判 **go to sb's 'head 1** (of alcohol 酒精) to make you feel drunk 上头；使醉： *That glass of wine has gone straight to my head.* 那杯酒一下子就把我弄得头晕脑涨。 **2** (of success, praise, etc. 成功、赞扬等) to make you feel too proud of yourself in a way that other people find annoying 使人过于骄傲；冲昏头脑 **have a good 'head on your shoulders** to be a sensible person 头脑清醒；理智 **have a head for sth 1** to be good at sth 擅长某事：*to have a head for figures/business* 长于算术；有生意头脑 **2** if sb does not **have a head for heights**, they feel nervous and think they are going to fall when they look down from a high place 不惧（高）；无恐（高）症 **have your head in the 'clouds 1** to be thinking about sth that is not connected with what you are doing 心不在焉；走神 **2** to have ideas, plans, etc. that are not realistic 有不切实际的想法（或计划等）；想入非非 **have your 'head screwed on (the right way)** (*informal*) to be a sensible person 头脑清醒；理智 **ˌhead 'first 1** moving forwards or downwards with your head in front of the rest of your body 头在前；头朝下：*He fell head first down the stairs.* 他倒栽葱摔下楼梯。**2** without thinking carefully about sth before acting 未经深思；轻率；鲁莽 **SYN headlong**: *She got divorced and rushed head first into another marriage.* 她离婚后又仓促再婚了。**head over heels in 'love** loving sb very much 深深爱着某人；迷恋：*He's fallen head over heels in love with his boss.* 他深深迷恋上了他的上司。**heads or 'tails?** used to ask sb which side of a coin they think will be facing upwards when it is TOSSED in order to decide sth by chance（掷硬币作决定时说）正面还是反面 **'heads will roll (for sth)** (*informal, usually humorous*) used to say that some people will be punished because of sth that has happened 有些人将（为某事）受到惩罚 **hold your 'head high | hold up your 'head** to be proud of or not feel ashamed about sth that you have done 昂首挺胸；抬起头来：*She managed to hold her head high and ignore what people were saying.* 她勉力昂首挺胸，不理会人家的闲言碎语。**in over your 'head** involved in sth that is too difficult for you to deal with 卷入棘手的事：*After a week in the new job, I soon realized that I was in over my head.* 新工作刚做了一个星期，我便意识到自己做不了。**keep/get your 'head down** to avoid attracting attention to yourself 避免引起注意；保持低姿态 **keep your 'head | keep a clear/cool 'head** to remain calm in a difficult situation（在困境中）保持冷静 **keep your 'head above water** to deal with a difficult situation, especially one in which you have financial problems, and just manage to survive 勉强逃脱困境；设法不举债；挣扎求存 **laugh, scream, etc. your 'head off** (*informal*) to laugh, etc. a lot and very loudly 大笑（或大叫等）**lose your 'head** to become unable to act in a calm or sensible way 慌乱；昏了头；失去理智 **on your (own) head 'be it** used to tell sb that they will have to accept any unpleasant results of sth that they decide to do 你（自己）必须承担任何后果：*Tell him the truth if you want to, but on your own head be it!* 你想把真相告诉他就告诉他吧，但后果自负！**out of/off your 'head** (*BrE, informal*) **1** crazy 发疯 **2** not knowing what you are saying or doing because of the effects of alcohol or drugs （酒后或使用药物后）胡言乱语，行为乖张，神志不清 **over sb's 'head 1** too difficult or complicated for sb to understand 超过某人理解力；过于复杂：*A lot of the jokes went* (= were) *right over my head.* 那些笑话有很多我完全听不懂。**2** to a higher position of authority than sb 职位比某人高；超过某人：*I couldn't help feeling jealous when she was promoted over my head.* 她受到提拔职位超过了我，我不由得感到嫉妒。**put our/your/their 'heads together** to think about or discuss sth as a group 集体思考（或讨论）；集思广益 **stand/turn sth on its 'head** to make people think about sth in a completely different way 使人完全改变思路；使人从反面思考 **take it into your head to do sth** to suddenly decide to do sth, especially sth that other people think is stupid 忽发奇想；心血来潮 **take it into your head that...** to suddenly start thinking sth, especially sth that other people think is stupid 忽发奇想；突然开始想某事 **turn sb's 'head** (of success, praise, etc. 成功、赞扬等) to make a person feel too proud in a way that other people find annoying 使某人得意忘形 **two heads are better than 'one** (*saying*) used to say that two people can achieve more than one person working alone 两人智慧胜一人 ➲ MORE AT BEAR *n.*, BLOCK *n.*, BOTHER *v.*, DRUM *v.*, EYE *n.*, GUN *n.*, HAIR, HEART, HIT *v.*, IDEA, KNOCK *v.*, LAUGH *v.*, NEED *v.*, OLD, PRICE *n.*, REAR *v.*, RING² *v.*, ROOF *n.*, SCRATCH *v.*, THICK *adj.*, TOP *n.*

■ ***verb***

• **MOVE TOWARDS** 移向 **1** 🔑 [I] (*also* **be headed** *especially in NAmE*) **+ adv./prep.** to move in a particular direction 朝（某方向）行进：*Where are we heading?* 我们要往哪儿去？◇ *Where are you two headed?* 你们两个去哪儿？◇ *Let's head back home.* 咱们回家吧。◇ *She headed for the door.* 她朝着门走去。◇ (*figurative*) *Can you forecast where the economy is heading?* 你能预测经济的发展方向吗？

• **GROUP/ORGANIZATION** 团体；机构 **2** 🔑 [T] **~ sth** (*also* **ˌhead sth↔up**) to lead or be in charge of sth 领导；主管：*She has been appointed to head the research team.* 她受命领导研究小组。

• **LIST/LINE OF PEOPLE** 名单；队列 **3** [T] **~ sth** to be at the top of a list of names or at the front of a line of people 位于排行之首；排在前头：*Italy heads the table after two games.* 两场比赛之后意大利队排名榜首。◇ *to* ***head a march/procession*** 在游行队伍 / 队伍前列

• **BE AT TOP** 在顶端 **4** [T, usually passive] **~ sth** to put a word or words at the top of a page or section of a book as a title 在（页或篇章的）顶端加标题：*The chapter was headed 'My Early Life'.* 这一章的标题是"我的早年生活"。

• **FOOTBALL** 足球 **5** [T] **~ sth** to hit a football with your head 用头顶（球）：*Walsh headed the ball into an empty goal.* 沃尔什把球顶进了空门。

PHR V **be 'heading for sth** (*also* **be 'headed for sth** *especially in NAmE*) to be likely to experience sth bad 很可能遭受（不幸）；会招致：*They look as though they're heading for divorce.* 他们看样子会离婚。**ˌhead sb↔'off** to get in front of sb in order to make them turn back or change direction 拦挡某人；使改变方向 **SYN intercept**: *We'll head them off at the bridge!* 我们将在桥头拦截他们！**ˌhead sth↔'off** to take action in order to prevent sth from happening 阻止，防止（某事发生）：*He headed off efforts to replace him as leader.* 他挫败了要取代他的领导地位的企图。**ˌhead sth↔'up** to lead or be in charge of a department, part of an organization, etc. 领导，主管（某部门或机构分支等）➲ SEE ALSO HEAD *v.* (2)

-head /hed/ *suffix* (*informal*) (in nouns 构成名词) a person who is very enthusiastic about a particular thing or is addicted to a particular drug …迷；…瘾君子：*The cybercafe was a nethead's dream.* 网吧是网迷的乐园。◇ *a gearhead* 技术设备发烧友 ◇ *a crackhead* 强效可卡因瘾君子 ◇ *a smackhead* 吸白粉成瘾的人 ◇ *a pothead* 大麻瘾君子

head·ache 🔑 /ˈhedeɪk/ *noun* **1** 🔑 a continuous pain in the head 头痛：*to suffer from headaches* 头痛 ◇ *Red wine gives me a headache.* 我喝红酒会头痛。◇ *I have a* ***splitting headache*** (= a very bad one). 我头痛欲裂。➲ COLLOCATIONS AT ILL **2** (*informal*) a person or thing that causes worry or trouble 令人头痛的人（或事物）；麻烦：*The real headache will be getting the bank to lend you the money.* 真正的麻烦将是设法让银行贷款给你。

head·band /ˈhedbænd/ *noun* a strip of cloth worn around the head, especially to keep hair or sweat out of your eyes when playing sports 头带，束发带（尤指运动时用以固定头发或吸汗）

head·bang·er /ˈhedbæŋə(r)/ *noun* (*informal*) **1** a person who likes to shake their head violently up and down while listening to rock music （听摇滚乐时）拼命摇头者 **2** a stupid or crazy person 愚蠢的人；疯狂的人 ▶ **head-banging** *noun* [U]

head·board /ˈhedbɔːd; *NAmE* -bɔːrd/ *noun* the vertical board at the end of a bed where you put your head 床头板 ➲ VISUAL VOCAB PAGE V24

ˌhead 'boy *noun* (in some British schools) the boy who is chosen each year to represent his school （某些英国学校每年挑选的）男生代表

H

head·butt /'hedbʌt/ *verb* ~ **sb** (*especially BrE*) to deliberately hit sb hard with your head 故意用头撞（人） ▸ **head·butt** *noun*

head·case /'hedkeɪs/ *noun* (*BrE, informal*) a person who behaves in a strange way and who seems to be mentally ill 怪人；神经兮兮的人

head·cheese /'hedtʃiːz/ (*NAmE*) (*BrE* **brawn**) *noun* [U] meat made from the head of a pig or CALF that has been boiled and pressed into a container, served cold in thin slices （罐装）猪头肉，牛犊头肉

head·count /'hedkaʊnt/ *noun* an act of counting the number of people who are at an event, employed by an organization, etc.; the number of people that have been counted in this way 人数统计；统计出的人数： *to do a headcount* 统计人数 ◇ *What's the latest headcount?* 最新统计的人数是多少？

head·dress /'heddres/ *noun* a covering worn on the head on special occasions （特殊场合戴的）头巾，头饰

head·ed /'hedɪd/ *adj.* **1** (of writing paper 信纸) having the name and address of a person, an organization, etc. printed at the top 顶端印有名称和地址的；有信头的： *headed notepaper* 有信头的便笺纸 **2 -headed** (in adjectives 构成形容词) having the type of head or number of heads mentioned 有…头的；有…个头的： *a bald-headed man* 秃顶男子 ◇ *a three-headed monster* 三头怪兽 ➲ SEE ALSO BIG-HEADED, CLEAR-HEADED, COOL-HEADED, EMPTY-HEADED, HARD-HEADED, LEVEL-HEADED, LIGHT-HEADED, PIG-HEADED, WRONG-HEADED ➲ **MORE LIKE THIS** 8, page R25

head·er /'hedə(r)/ *noun* **1** (in football (SOCCER) 足球) an act of hitting the ball with your head 用头顶球；头球 **2** a line or block of text that is automatically added to the top of every page that is printed from a computer （计算机打印时自动加在各页顶端的）标头，首标 ➲ COMPARE FOOTER

head·gear /'hedgɪə(r); *NAmE* -gɪr/ *noun* [U] anything worn on the head, for example a hat 头戴之物；帽子： *protective headgear* 安全帽

ˌhead 'girl *noun* (in some British schools) the girl who is chosen each year to represent her school （某些英国学校每年挑选的）女生代表

head·hunt /'hedhʌnt/ *verb* ~ **sb** to find sb who is suitable for a senior job and persuade them to leave their present job 猎头（物色、延揽高层人员）： *I was headhunted by a marketing agency.* 我被一家销售代理公司物色上了。 ▸ **head·hunt·ing** *noun* [U]

head·hunt·er /'hedhʌntə(r)/ *noun* **1** a person whose job is to find people with the necessary skills to work for a particular company and to persuade them to join this company 猎头者（专门负责延揽人才） **2** a member of a people that collects the heads of the people they kill 猎头部落成员（收集所杀者的人头）

head·ing /'hedɪŋ/ *noun* **1** a title printed at the top of a page or at the beginning of a section of a book （页首或章节开头的）标题： *chapter headings* 篇章标题 **2** the subject of each section of a speech or piece of writing （讲话或作品各章节的）主题： *The company's aims can be grouped under three main headings.* 公司的目标可分成三大类。

head·lamp /'hedlæmp/ *noun* (*especially BrE*) = HEADLIGHT

head·land /'hedlənd; -lænd/ *noun* a narrow piece of high land that sticks out from the coast into the sea 岬，岬角（突入海中的狭长高地） **SYN** **promontory** ➲ **WORDFINDER NOTE** AT COAST ➲ **VISUAL VOCAB** PAGE V5

head·less /'hedləs/ *adj.* [usually before noun] without a head 无头的： *a headless body/corpse* 无头尸体

IDM **run around like a ˌheadless 'chicken** to be very busy and active trying to do sth, but not very organized, with the result that you do not succeed 茫无头绪地瞎忙一通

head·light /'hedlaɪt/ *noun* (*also* **head·lamp** *especially in BrE*) a large light, usually one of two, at the front of a vehicle; the BEAM from this light （车辆的）前灯，头灯，前灯的光束： *He dipped his headlights* (= directed the light downwards) *for the oncoming traffic.* 考虑到迎面而来的车辆，他把自己的前灯调为近光。 ➲ **VISUAL VOCAB** PAGE V56

head·line /'hedlaɪn/ *noun, verb*

■ ***noun*** **1** [C] the title of a newspaper article printed in large letters, especially at the top of the front page （报纸的）大字标题： *They ran the story under the headline 'Home at last!'.* 报纸刊登这个报道的大标题为“终于回家了！”。 ◇ *The scandal was in the headlines for several days.* 这一丑闻连续几天都刊登在头版头条。 ◇ *headline news* 头条新闻 ➲ SEE ALSO BANNER HEADLINE ➲ **WORDFINDER NOTE** AT NEWSPAPER **2 the headlines** [pl.] a short summary of the most important items of news, read at the beginning of a news programme on the radio or television （电台或电视的）新闻摘要

IDM **grab/hit/make the 'headlines** to be an important item of news in newspapers or on the radio or television 成为重要新闻

■ ***verb*** **1** [T, usually passive] ~ **sth + noun** to give a story or article a particular headline 给（报道、文章）加标题： *The story was headlined 'Back to the future'.* 报道的标题是“回到未来”。 **2** [T, I] ~ (**sth**) to be the main performer in a concert or show 是（音乐会或演出的）主角： *The concert is to be headlined by Steve Earle.* 音乐会的主角将是史蒂夫•厄尔。

head·lock /'hedlɒk; *NAmE* -lɑːk/ *noun* (in WRESTLING 摔跤运动) a way of holding an opponent's head so that they cannot move 夹头： *He had him in a headlock.* 他夹住了他的头。

head·long /'hedlɒŋ; *NAmE* -lɔːŋ; -lɑːŋ/ *adv.* **1** with the head first and the rest of the body following 头朝前 **SYN** **head first**: *She fell headlong into the icy pool.* 她倒栽葱掉进了冰冷的水池中。 **2** without thinking carefully before doing sth 轻率地： *The government is taking care not to rush headlong into another controversy.* 政府现在很谨慎，以防不慎陷入另一场争端。 **3** quickly and without looking where you are going 莽撞地；慌慌张张地： *He ran headlong into a police car.* 他一头撞上了一辆警车。 ▸ **head·long** *adj.* [only before noun]: *a headlong dive/rush* 头先入水的跳水；莽撞的向前冲

head·man /'hedmæn; -mən/ *noun* (*pl.* **-men** /-men; -mən/) the leader of a community 头人；首领；酋长 **SYN** **chief**: *the village headman* 村长

head·mas·ter /ˌhed'mɑːstə(r); *NAmE* -'mæs-/, **head·mis·tress** /ˌhed'mɪstrəs/ *noun* (*NAmE usually* **prin·ci·pal**) a teacher who is in charge of a school, especially a private school （尤指私立学校的）校长 ➲ SEE ALSO HEAD TEACHER

ˌhead 'office *noun* [C, U+sing./pl. v.] the main office of a company; the managers who work there 总公司；总部： *Their head office is in New York.* 他们的总部在纽约。 ◇ *I don't know what head office will think about this proposal.* 我不知道总公司对此提议会有何想法。

ˌhead of 'state *noun* (*pl.* **heads of state**) the official leader of a country who is sometimes also the leader of the government 国家元首

ˌhead-'on *adj.* [only before noun] **1** in which the front part of one vehicle hits the front part of another vehicle 迎头相撞的；正面相撞的： *a **head-on** crash/collision* 迎面相撞 **2** in which people express strong views and deal with sth in a direct way 正面反对的；迎头的： *There was a **head-on** confrontation between management and unions.* 资方与工会之间发生了正面冲突。 ▸ **ˌhead-'on** *adv.*: *The cars crashed head-on.* 汽车迎头相撞。 ◇ *We hit the tree head-on.* 我们迎面撞到了树上。 ◇ *to **tackle a problem head-on*** (= without trying to avoid it) 正面处理问题

head·phones /ˈhedfəʊnz; NAmE -foʊnz/ (*also* **ear·phones**) *noun* [pl.] a piece of equipment worn over or in the ears that makes it possible to listen to music, the radio, etc. without other people hearing it 耳机；头戴式受话器：*a pair/set of headphones* 一副耳机

head·quar·tered /ˌhedˈkwɔːtəd; NAmE ˈhedkwɔːrtərd/ *adj.* [not before noun] having headquarters in a particular place 总部在某地：*News Corporation is headquartered in New York.* 新闻集团的总部设在纽约。

head·quar·ters /ˌhedˈkwɔːtəz; NAmE ˈhedkwɔːrtərz/ *noun* [U+sing./pl. v., C] (*pl.* **head·quar·ters**) (*abbr.* **HQ**) a place from which an organization or a military operation is controlled; the people who work there 总部；总公司；大本营；司令部：*The firm's headquarters is/are in London.* 公司总部设在伦敦。◇ *Several companies have their headquarters in the area.* 有几家公司总部设在这个地区。◇ *I'm now based at headquarters.* 我现在在总公司工作。◇ *police headquarters* 警察总局 ◇ *Headquarters in Dublin has/have agreed.* 都柏林总部已经同意了。

head·rest /ˈhedrest/ *noun* the part of a seat or chair that supports a person's head, especially on the front seat of a car （尤指汽车前排座位的）头枕，头垫 ➲ VISUAL VOCAB PAGE V56

head·room /ˈhedruːm; -rʊm/ *noun* [U] **1** the amount of space between the top of a vehicle and an object it drives under （机动车车顶与其上方桥梁等之间的）净空 **2** the amount of space between the top of your head and the roof of a vehicle （机动车内的）头上空间：*There's a lot of headroom for such a small car.* 这么小的一辆汽车的头上空间蛮大的。

ˈhead rush *noun* a thing or an experience that you find very exciting 令人兴奋的事（或经历）：*the physical head rush of being in love* 谈恋爱这一引发身心躁动的经历

head·scarf /ˈhedskɑːf; NAmE -skɑːrf/ *noun* (*pl.* **head·scarves** /-skɑːvz; NAmE -skɑːrvz/) a square piece of cloth tied around the head by women or girls, usually with a knot under the chin （女用）方头巾

head·set /ˈhedset/ *noun* a pair of HEADPHONES, especially one with a MICROPHONE attached to it （尤指带麦克风的）头戴式受话器，耳机 ➲ VISUAL VOCAB PAGE V73

head·ship /ˈhedʃɪp/ *noun* ~ (**of sth**) **1** the position of being in charge of an organization 主管职位：*the headship of the department* 部门领导的职位 **2** (*BrE*) the position of being in charge of a school 校长职位

head·shot /ˈhedʃɒt; NAmE -ʃɑːt/ *noun* **1** a photograph of a person's face or head and shoulders 大头照；脸部正面照：*The casting director looks through hundreds of headshots before selecting actors for auditions.* 选角导演在选定演员试镜之前要翻看数百张候选演员的大头照。**2** a bullet from a gun that is aimed at the head 瞄准头部射击；头部中枪

head·space /ˈhedspeɪs/ *noun* [U] **1** the amount of air or empty space that is left above the contents of a container before it is sealed 顶空，顶隙（密封之前容器内物品上方的空气或空间） **2** (*informal*) the way you think or feel about sth 思维方式；感受方式：*Whenever you read a book, you're entering the writer's headspace.* 读一本书，如同进入了作者的思维空间。 **3** (*informal*) time to think clearly without any pressure （清醒而无压力的）思考时间：*I could do with a bit of headspace just to think about what I'm doing.* 我需要一点独立思考的时间想想我正在做的事。

head·stand /ˈhedstand/ *noun* a position in which a person has their head on the ground and their feet straight up in the air 头倒立

ˌhead ˈstart *noun* [sing.] ~ (**on/over sb**) an advantage that sb already has before they start doing sth 起步前的优势：*Being able to speak French gave her a head start over the other candidates.* 会说法语使她比其他候选人占优势。

head·stone /ˈhedstəʊn; NAmE -stoʊn/ *noun* a piece of stone placed at one end of a grave, showing the name, etc. of the person buried there 墓碑 SYN **gravestone** ➲ COMPARE TOMBSTONE

head·strong /ˈhedstrɒŋ; NAmE -strɔːŋ/ *adj.* (*disapproving*) a **headstrong** person is determined to do things their own way and refuses to listen to advice 固执的；倔强任性的

ˈheads-up *noun* (*pl.* **heads-up** or **heads-ups**) ~ (**about sth**) (*especially NAmE*) a piece of information given in advance of sth or as advice 预先通知；预先劝告：*Send everyone a heads-up about the changes well in advance.* 把这些变化早早通知每个人。

ˌhead ˈtable (*NAmE*) (*BrE* **ˌtop ˈtable**) *noun* the table at which the most important guests sit at a formal dinner （正式宴会上的）主桌

ˌhead ˈteacher *noun* (*BrE*) (*NAmE* **prin·ci·pal**) a teacher who is in charge of a school 校长

ˌhead-to-ˈhead *adj.* [only before noun] in which two people or groups face each other directly in order to decide the result of a disagreement or competition 正面交锋的；面对面的：*a **head-to-head battle/clash/contest*** 正面战斗 / 冲突 / 竞争 ▸ **ˌhead-to-ˈhead** *adv.*：*They are set to meet head-to-head in next week's final.* 他们将在下个星期的决赛中正面交锋。

head·waters /ˈhedwɔːtəz; NAmE -tərz/ *noun* [pl.] streams forming the source of a river 河源；上游

head·way /ˈhedweɪ/ *noun* [U]

IDM **make ˈheadway** to make progress, especially when this is slow or difficult 取得（缓慢的或艰难的）进展：*We are making little headway with the negotiations.* 我们的谈判没有取得什么进展。◇ *The boat was unable to make much headway against the tide.* 船逆着潮水没法开快。

head·wind /ˈhedwɪnd/ *noun* a wind that is blowing towards a person or vehicle, so that it is blowing from the direction in which the person or vehicle is moving 逆风；顶风 ➲ COMPARE TAILWIND

head·word /ˈhedwɜːd; NAmE -wɜːrd/ *noun* (*specialist*) a word that forms a HEADING in a dictionary, under which its meaning is explained （词典中的）词目，首词 ➲ WORDFINDER NOTE AT DICTIONARY

heady /ˈhedi/ *adj.* (**head·ier**, **headi·est**) **1** [usually before noun] having a strong effect on your senses; making you feel excited and confident 强烈作用于感官的；使兴奋的；使有信心的 SYN **intoxicating**：*the heady days of youth* 令人陶醉的年轻时代 ◇ *the heady scent of hot spices* 辣味香料的刺鼻气味 ◇ *a heady mixture of desire and fear* 既期待又害怕的复杂心情 ➲ SYNONYMS AT EXCITING **2** [not before noun] (of a person 人) excited in a way that makes you do things without worrying about the possible results 冲动；冒失：*She felt heady with success.* 成功使她得意忘形。

heal 🔑 /hiːl/ *verb* **1** [I, T] to become healthy again; to make sth healthy again （使）康复，复原：*It took a long time for the wounds to heal.* 伤口过了很长时间才愈合。◇ ~ **up** *The cut healed up without leaving a scar.* 伤口愈合没留下疤痕。◇ ~ **sth** *This will help to heal your cuts and scratches.* 这个会有助于治好割伤和擦伤。◇ (*figurative*) *It was a chance to **heal the wounds** in the party* (= to repair the damage that had been done). 那是个弥合党内创伤的机会。 **2** [T] ~ **sb** (**of sth**) (*old use* or *formal*) to cure sb who is ill/sick; to make sb feel happy again 治疗（病人）；使又愉快起来：*the story of Jesus healing ten lepers of their disease* 耶稣治愈十个麻风病人的故事 ◇ *I felt healed by his love.* 他的爱使我又快乐了起来。 **3** [T, I] ~ (**sth**) to put an end to sth or make sth easier to bear; to end or become easier to bear （使）结束，较容易忍受：*She was never able to heal the rift between herself and her father.* 她一直未能填平和她父亲之间的鸿沟。◇ *The breach between them never really healed.* 他们之间的裂痕从来没有真正弥合。

heal·er /ˈhiːlə(r)/ *noun* **1** a person who cures people of illnesses and disease using natural powers rather than medicine 用自然力（而非药物）治疗别人者：*a* ***faith/spiritual healer*** 实施信仰 / 心灵疗法的人 **2** something that makes a bad situation easier to deal with 缓解情势的事物：*Time is a great healer.* 时间是良药。

heal·ing /ˈhiːlɪŋ/ *noun* [U] the process of becoming or making sb/sth healthy again; the process of getting better after an emotional shock 康复；治疗；（情感创伤的）愈合：*the healing process* 康复过程 ◇ *emotional healing* 感情上的愈合 ➲ SEE ALSO FAITH HEALING

health 🔑 /helθ/ *noun* [U] **1** 🔑 the condition of a person's body or mind 人的身体（或精神）状况；健康：*Exhaust fumes are bad for your health.* 废气对健康有害。◇ ***to be in poor/good/excellent/the best of health*** 健康状况不好 / 好 / 极好 / 好极 ◇ *Smoking can seriously* ***damage your health.*** 吸烟会严重损害健康。◇ ***mental health*** 心理健康 ➲ SEE ALSO ILL HEALTH

WORDFINDER 联想词：acute, **condition**, **medicine**, outbreak, pain, recover, relapse, terminal, **treatment**

2 🔑 the state of being physically and mentally healthy 健康：*He was nursed back to health by his wife.* 他在妻子的照料下恢复了健康。◇ *She was glowing with health and clearly enjoying life.* 她容光焕发，显然生活得很快活。◇ *As long as you have your health, nothing else matters.* 只要身体健康，其他任何事都无关紧要。**3** 🔑 the work of providing medical services 医疗；保健；卫生：*All parties are promising to increase spending on health.* 各政党都在许诺增加医疗开支。◇ *the Health Minister* 卫生部长 ◇ *the Department of Health* 卫生部 ◇ ***health insurance*** 健康保险 ◇ ***health and safety regulations*** (= laws that protect the health of people at work) 健康和安全条例 **4** how successful sth is 状况；牢靠性：*the health of your marriage/finances* 婚姻 / 财政状况 IDM SEE CLEAN *adj.*, DRINK *v.*, PROPOSE, RUDE

ˈ**health care** *noun* [U] the service of providing medical care 医疗（服务）：*the costs of health care for the elderly* 老年人的医疗费用 ◇ ***health care workers/professionals*** 医疗工作人员 / 专家

ˈ**health centre** (*BrE*) (*especially US* ˈ**health center**) *noun* a building where a group of doctors see their patients and where some local medical services have their offices 卫生院；保健中心

ˈ**health club** *noun* (*also* **gym**) a private club where people go to do physical exercise in order to stay or become healthy and fit 健身俱乐部

ˈ**health farm** *noun* (*especially BrE*) = HEALTH SPA

ˈ**health food** *noun* [U, C, usually pl.] food that does not contain any artificial substances and is therefore thought to be good for your health 健康食物；绿色食物

health·ful /ˈhelθfl/ *adj.* [usually before noun] (*formal* or *NAmE*) good for your health 有益于健康的 ▶ **health·ful·ly** *adv.*

ˈ**health service** *noun* a public service providing medical care 公共医疗保健服务 ➲ SEE ALSO NATIONAL HEALTH SERVICE

ˈ**health spa** (*also* ˈ**health farm** *especially in BrE*) *noun* a place where people can stay for short periods of time in order to try to improve their health by eating special food, doing physical exercise, etc. 健身会馆，休闲健身中心（提供特定饮食、身体锻炼等短期休养服务）➲ WORDFINDER NOTE AT FIT

ˈ**health tourism** (*especially NAmE* ˌ**medical** ˈ**tourism**) *noun* [U] the practice of travelling abroad in order to receive medical treatment 医疗旅游（出国接受医疗服务）

ˈ**health visitor** *noun* (in Britain) a trained nurse whose job is to visit people in their homes, for example new parents, and give them advice on some areas of medical care （英国）家访护士

healthy 🔑 /ˈhelθi/ *adj.* (**health·ier**, **healthi·est**) **1** 🔑 having good health and not likely to become ill/sick 健康的；健壮的：*a healthy child/animal/tree* 健康的孩子 / 动物 / 树 ◇ ***Keep healthy*** *by eating well and exercising regularly.* 通过良好饮食和经常性锻炼保持健康。OPP **unhealthy** ➲ SYNONYMS AT WELL **2** 🔑 [usually before noun] good for your health 有益于健康的：*a* ***healthy diet/climate/lifestyle*** 对健康有益的饮食 / 气候 / 生活方式 OPP **unhealthy** **3** 🔑 [usually before noun] showing that you are in good health 反映健康的：*to have a healthy appetite* 胃口好 ◇ *a shampoo that keeps hair looking healthy* 护发洗发剂 **4** normal and sensible 正常合理的：*The child showed a healthy curiosity.* 这孩子的好奇心很正常。◇ *She has a healthy respect for her rival's talents.* 她很有风度地尊重对手的才能。◇ *It's not healthy the way she clings to the past.* 她那种沉湎于过去的态度不明智。OPP **unhealthy** **5** successful and working well 兴旺的；发达的；顺利的：*a healthy economy* 繁荣的经济 ◇ *Your car doesn't sound very healthy.* 你的车听声音好像不很正常。**6** [usually before noun] large and showing success 大而显得成功的；可观的：*a healthy bank balance* 一大笔银行结余 ◇ *a healthy profit* 丰厚的利润 ▶ **health·ily** *adv.*：*to eat healthily* 吃得健康 **healthi·ness** *noun* [U]

heap /hiːp/ *noun, verb*

■ ***noun*** **1** ~ (**of sth**) an untidy pile of sth （凌乱的）一堆：*The building was reduced to a heap of rubble.* 大楼变成了一堆废墟。◇ *a compost heap* 一堆堆肥 ◇ *His clothes lay* ***in a heap*** *on the floor.* 他的衣服堆在地板上。◇ *Worn-out car tyres were stacked* ***in heaps.*** 汽车废轮胎散乱地堆放着。➲ SEE ALSO SCRAPHEAP, SLAG HEAP **2** [usually pl.] (*informal*) a lot of sth 许多；大量：*There's heaps of time before the plane leaves.* 离飞机起飞还有很多时间。◇ (*NAmE*) *I've got a heap of things to do.* 我有一大堆事情要做。**3** (*informal, humorous*) a car that is old and in bad condition 破旧的汽车；老爷车

IDM **at the top/bottom of the ˈheap** high up/low down in the structure of an organization or a society 在（机构或社会的）顶层 / 底层：*These workers are at the bottom of the economic heap.* 这些工人处在经济结构的底层。**collapse, fall, etc. in a ˈheap** to fall down heavily and not move 重重地倒下（不能动） **heaps ˈbetter, ˈmore, ˈolder, etc.** (*BrE, informal*) a lot better, etc. 好（或多、老等）得多：*Help yourself—there's heaps more.* 请随便取用，还多着呢。◇ *He looks heaps better than when I last saw him.* 他看上去比我上回见他时好多了。

■ ***verb*** **1** ~ **sth** (**up**) to put things in an untidy pile 堆积（东西）；堆置：*Rocks were heaped up on the side of the road.* 路边堆积着石头。**2** to put a lot of sth in a pile on sth 在…上放很多（东西）：**~ A on B** *She heaped food on my plate.* 她往我的盘子里放了很多食物。◇ **~ B with A** *She heaped my plate with food.* 她往我的盘子里放了很多食物。**3** to give a lot of sth such as praise or criticism to sb 对（某人）大加赞扬（或批评等）：**~ A on B** *He heaped* ***praise*** *on his team.* 他高度赞扬了他的队。◇ **~ B with A** *He heaped his team with praise.* 他高度赞扬了他的队。IDM SEE SCORN *n.*

heap·ed /hiːpt/ (*especially BrE*) (*NAmE usually* **heap·ing**) *adj.* used to describe a spoon, etc. that has as much in it or on it as it can hold 满满的（一匙等）：*a heaped teaspoon of sugar* 满满一茶匙糖 ◇ *heaping plates of scrambled eggs* 盛得满满的一盘盘炒鸡蛋 ➲ COMPARE LEVEL *adj.* (1)

hear 🔑 /hɪə(r); *NAmE* hɪr/ *verb* (**heard**, **heard** /hɜːd; *NAmE* hɜːrd/) **1** 🔑 [I, T] (not used in the progressive tenses 不用于进行时) to be aware of sounds with your ears 听见；听到：*I can't hear very well.* 我听觉不太好。◇ **~ sth/sb** *She heard footsteps behind her.* 她听到背后有脚步声。◇ **~ sb/sth doing sth** *He could hear a dog barking.* 他听得到狗叫。◇ **~ sb/sth do sth** *Did you hear him go out?* 你听到他出去了吗？◇ **~ what...** *Didn't you hear what I said?* 难道你没有听到我的话？◇ **sb/sth is heard to do sth** *She has been heard to make threats to her former lover.* 有人听见她威胁她先前的恋人。**2** 🔑 [T] (not used in the progressive tenses 不用于进行时) to listen or pay attention to sb/sth 听；注意听；倾听：**~ sth** *Did you hear that play on the* *radio last night?* 你昨晚收听了那出广播剧吗？ ◇ **~ sb/sth/ yourself do sth** *Be quiet—I can't hear myself think!* (= it is so noisy that I can't think clearly) 安静点，我都给吵昏头了！ ◇ **~ what…** *We'd better hear what they have to say.* 我们最好还是听听他们有什么话要说。◇ ***I hear what you're saying*** (= I have listened to your opinion), *but you're wrong.* 我已经听到你的意见了，但你错了。 **3** [I, T] (not usually used in the progressive tenses 通常不用于进行时) to be told about sth 听说；得知：*Haven't you heard? She resigned.* 你还没听说吗？她辞职了。◇ *'I'm getting married.' '**So I've heard.**'* "我要结婚了。" "我听说了。" ◇ *Things are going well **from what I hear**.* 从我所听到的来看，事情进展不错。 ◇ **~ about sb/sth** *I was sorry to hear about your accident.* 获悉你遇到意外，我很难过。 ◇ *I've heard about people like you.* 我听说过像你这样的人。 ◇ **~ sth** *We had heard nothing for weeks.* 我们好几个星期都没得到任何消息了。 ◇ **~ (that)…** *I was surprised to hear (that) he was married.* 听说他结婚了，我很惊讶。 ◇ *I hear you've been away this weekend.* 我听说你这个周末外出了。 ◇ **~ it said (that)…** *I've heard it said (that) they met in Italy.* 我听说他们是在意大利认识的。 ◇ **~ what, how, etc.…** *Did you hear what happened?* 你听说发生什么事了吗？ **4** [T] **~ sth** to listen to and judge a case in court 审理；听审：*The appeal was heard in private.* 这件上诉案不公开审理。 ◇ *Today the jury began to hear the evidence.* 今天陪审团开始听证。

IDM **have you heard the one about…?** used to ask sb if they have heard a particular joke before 你听说过（某笑话）吗？ **ˌhear! 'hear!** used to show that you agree with or approve of what sb has just said, especially during a speech （表示赞同，尤指在听演讲时）对！对！ **hear 'tell (of sth)** (*old-fashioned* or *formal*) to hear people talking about sth 听到人谈论（某事）；听说：*I've often heard tell of such things.* 我常听到人谈起这种事。 **I've heard it all be'fore** (*informal*) used to say that you do not really believe sb's promises or excuses because they are the same ones you have heard before （表示不相信某人的许诺或辩解）这种话我听得多了 **let's hear it for…** (*informal*) used to say that sb/sth deserves praise （表示值得称赞）咱们为…鼓掌，让我们为…喝彩：*Let's hear it for the teachers, for a change.* 咱们变换一下，这回为老师们鼓鼓掌。 **not/never hear the 'end of it** to keep being reminded of sth because sb is always talking to you about it 被人不断纠缠，没完没了：*If we don't get her a dog we'll never hear the end of it.* 我们要是不给她弄条狗来，这事就没完没了。 **you could hear a 'pin drop** it was extremely quiet 鸦雀无声；万籁俱寂：*The audience was so quiet you could have heard a pin drop.* 观众安静得连针落地的声音也听得见。 **(do) you 'hear (me)?** (*informal*) used to tell sb in an angry way to pay attention and obey you （生气地要某人听从）听到我的话没有：*You can't go—do you hear me?* 你不能走，听清楚了吗？ ➲ MORE AT LAST[1] *n.*, THING, VOICE *n.*

PHR V **'hear from sb | 'hear sth from sb** to receive a letter, email, phone call, etc. from sb 收到某人的信件（或电子邮件、电话等）；得到某人的消息：*I look forward to hearing from you.* 盼望着收到你的信。 ◇ *I haven't heard anything from her for months.* 我好几个月都没有她的音信了。 **'hear of sb/sth | 'hear sth of sb/sth** to know about sb/sth because you have been told about them 听说，得知（某人或某事）：*I've never heard of the place.* 我从来没听说过这个地方。 ◇ *She disappeared and was never heard of again.* 她消失了，再也没人听到过她的消息。 ◇ ***The last I heard of** him he was living in Glasgow.* 我最后一次听到他的消息时，他住在格拉斯哥。 ◇ *This is **the first I've heard of it!*** 这可是我第一次听说这件事！ **not 'hear of sth** to refuse to let sb do sth, especially because you want to help them 出于善意拒绝（或不允许）某事：*She wanted to walk home but I wouldn't hear of it.* 她想步行回家，但我就是不允许。 ◇ **not hear of sb doing sth** *He wouldn't hear of my walking home alone.* 他不让我独自一人走回家。 ➲ SEE ALSO UNHEARD-OF **ˌhear sb 'out** to listen until sb has finished saying what they want to say 听某人把话说完

hear·er /ˈhɪərə(r); *NAmE* ˈhɪr-/ *noun* a person who hears sth or who is listening to sb 受话人；听者 **SYN** listener

hear·ing /ˈhɪərɪŋ; *NAmE* ˈhɪr-/ *noun* **1** [U] the ability to hear 听力；听觉：*Her hearing is poor.* 她的听觉不灵。 ◇ *He's **hearing-impaired*** (= not able to hear well). 他听觉受损。 ➲ SEE ALSO HARD OF HEARING **2** [C] an official meeting at which the facts about a crime, complaint, etc. are presented to the person or group of people who will have to decide what action to take 审讯；审理；听审；听证会：*a **court/disciplinary hearing*** 庭审；纪律聆讯 ➲ COLLOCATIONS AT JUSTICE **3** [sing.] an opportunity to explain your actions, ideas or opinions （行为、思想或意见的）解释机会，申辩机会：*to **get/give sb a fair hearing*** 得到 / 给予某人公正的申辩机会 ◇ *His views may be unfashionable but he deserves a hearing.* 他的观点可能不合潮流，但应该给他机会解释。

IDM **in/within (sb's) 'hearing** near enough to sb so that they can hear what is said 在（某人）听得见的范围内 **SYN** **earshot**：*She shouldn't have said such things in your hearing.* 她不应该在你面前说这种事情。 ◇ *I had no reason to believe there was anyone within hearing.* 我不相信周围会有人听得见。 **out of 'hearing** too far away to hear sb/sth or to be heard 离得太远听不见；在听力范围外：*She had moved out of hearing.* 她走远了，已经听不到。

'hearing aid *noun* a small device that fits inside the ear and makes sounds louder, used by people who cannot hear well 助听器：*to **have/wear a hearing aid*** 有 / 戴助听器

'hearing dog *noun* a dog trained to make a deaf person (= person who cannot hear well) aware of sounds such as the ringing of a telephone or a DOORBELL 导聋犬（经训练用来提醒耳聋者如电话铃、门铃等声响）

heark·en (*also* **hark·en**) /ˈhɑːkən; *NAmE* ˈhɑːrkən/ *verb* [I] **~ (to sb/sth)** (*old use*) to listen to sb/sth 倾听；聆听

hear·say /ˈhɪəseɪ; *NAmE* ˈhɪrseɪ/ *noun* [U] things that you have heard from another person but do not (definitely) know to be true 道听途说；传闻：*We can't make a decision based on hearsay and guesswork.* 我们不能根据传言和猜测作决定。 ◇ *hearsay evidence* 传闻的证据

hearse /hɜːs; *NAmE* hɜːrs/ *noun* a long vehicle used for carrying the coffin (= the box for the dead body) at a funeral 灵车；柩车 ➲ WORDFINDER NOTE AT DIE

heart /hɑːt; *NAmE* hɑːrt/ *noun*

- **PART OF BODY** 身体部位 **1** [C] the organ in the chest that sends blood around the body, usually on the left in humans 心；心脏：*The patient's heart stopped beating for a few seconds.* 病人的心跳停顿了几秒钟。 ◇ ***heart trouble/failure*** 心脏病；心力衰竭 ◇ *to have a weak heart* 心脏不好 ◇ *I could feel my heart pounding in my chest* (= because of excitement, etc.). 我能感觉到我的心在胸腔里怦怦直跳。 ➲ VISUAL VOCAB PAGE V64 ➲ SEE ALSO CORONARY, OPEN-HEART SURGERY **2** [C] (*literary*) the outside part of the chest where the heart is 胸部心脏的部位；胸怀：*She clasped the photo to her heart.* 她把相片紧紧地抱在怀里。
- **FEELINGS/EMOTIONS** 感情；心情 **3** [C] the place in a person where the feelings and emotions are thought to be, especially those connected with love 内心；心肠；（尤指）爱心：*She has a kind heart.* 她有一颗善良的心。 ◇ *Have you no heart?* 你没有一点同情心吗？ ◇ *He returned with a **heavy heart*** (= sad). 他心情沉重地回来了。 ◇ *Her novels tend to deal with **affairs of the heart**.* 她的小说往往是有关爱情故事的。 ◇ *The story captured **the hearts and minds** of a generation.* 这部小说准确地传达了一代人的感情和思想。 ➲ SEE ALSO BROKEN HEART
- **-HEARTED** 有…心 **4** (in adjectives 构成形容词) having the type of character or personality mentioned 有…性格（或品格）的：*cold-hearted* 冷酷无情的 ◇ *kind-hearted* 好心肠的 ➲ MORE LIKE THIS 8, page R25
- **IMPORTANT PART** 重要部分 **5** [sing.] **~ (of sth)** the most important part of sth 重点；核心；要点：*the **heart of the matter/problem*** 事情 / 问题的核心 ◇ *The committee's report went to the heart of the government's dilemma.*

委员会的报告直指政府两难困境的要害。 ◇ *The distinction between right and wrong* **lies at the heart of** *all questions of morality.* 是非界限是所有道德问题的核心。

- CENTRE 中心 **6** [C, usually sing.] ~ (**of sth**) the part that is in the centre of sth 中心；中央： *a quiet hotel* **in the very heart of** *the city* 一家位于市中心的安静的旅馆
- OF CABBAGE 卷心菜 **7** [C] the smaller leaves in the middle of a CABBAGE, LETTUCE, etc. 菜心
- SHAPE 形状 **8** [C] a thing shaped like a heart, often red and used as a symbol of love; a symbol shaped like a heart used to mean the verb 'love' 心形物；（常指象征爱的）红心；心形（表示动词"爱"）： *The words 'I love you' were written inside a big red heart.* "我爱你"这几个字写在一个大红心里。 ◇ (*informal*) *I ♥ New York.* 我爱纽约。
- IN CARD GAMES 纸牌游戏 **9 hearts** [pl., U] one of the four sets of cards (called SUITS) in a PACK/DECK of cards, with red heart symbols on them （统称）红桃牌，红心牌： *the queen of hearts* 红桃王后 ◇ *Hearts is/are trumps.* 红桃是主。 ➲ VISUAL VOCAB PAGE V42 **10** [C] one card from the set of hearts （一张）红桃牌，红心牌： *Who played that heart?* 谁打出那张红桃？

IDM **at ˈheart** used to say what sb is really like even though they may seem to be sth different 内心里；本质上： *He's still a socialist at heart.* 他本质上还是个社会主义者。 **break sb's ˈheart** to make sb feel very unhappy 使某人很难过；使心碎： *She broke his heart when she called off the engagement.* 她取消婚约令他心碎。 ◇ *It breaks my heart to see you like this.* 看到你这个样子我很难过。 **by ˈheart** (*BrE also* **off by ˈheart**) using only your memory 单凭记忆；能背诵： *I've dialled the number so many times I know it by heart.* 这个号码我拨了很多次，都记住了。 ◇ *She's learnt the whole speech off by heart.* 她把整篇讲话都背熟了。 **close/dear/near to sb's ˈheart** having a lot of importance and interest for sb 为某人所重视关心；为某人所爱 **from the** (**bottom of your**) **ˈheart** in a way that is sincere 真诚地；从内心（深处）： *I beg you, from the bottom of my heart, to spare his life.* 我诚心诚意地恳求你饶他一命吧。 ◇ *It was clearly an offer that came from the heart.* 那很明显是由衷的提议。 **give sb** (**fresh**) **ˈheart** to make sb feel positive, especially when they thought that they had no chance of achieving sth 激励某人；使某人振作 **give your ˈheart to sb** to give your love to one person 爱上某人；倾心 **have a ˈheart!** (*informal*) used to ask sb to be kind and/or reasonable 发发善心吧；讲点情理吧 **have a heart of ˈgold** to be a very kind person 有金子般的心；心肠很好 **have a heart of ˈstone** to be a person who does not show others sympathy or pity 铁石心肠；冷酷无情 **heart and ˈsoul** with a lot of energy and enthusiasm 满腔热忱干劲十足；全心全意： *They threw themselves heart and soul into the project.* 他们全心全意地投入了这个项目。 **your heart goes ˈout to sb** used to say that you feel a lot of sympathy for sb 十分同情；怜悯： *Our hearts go out to the families of the victims.* 我们很同情那些受害者的家人。 **sb's heart is in their ˈmouth** somebody feels nervous or frightened about sth 提心吊胆；心提到了嗓子眼儿 **sb's heart is in the right ˈplace** used to say that sb's intentions are kind and sincere even though they sometimes do the wrong thing 本意是好的；心眼是好的 **your ˈheart is not in sth** used to say that you are not very interested in or enthusiastic about sth 对某事不很感兴趣（或不热衷） **sb's heart ˈleaps** used to say that sb has a sudden feeling of happiness or excitement 心花怒放 **sb's heart misses a ˈbeat** used to say that sb has a sudden feeling of fear, excitement, etc. （表示突然感到恐惧、兴奋等）心里咯噔一下 **sb's heart ˈsinks** used to say that sb suddenly feels sad or depressed about sth（表示突然感到悲伤或沮丧）心里一沉： *My heart sank when I saw how much work there was left.* 我看到还有那么多活没干时，心顿时沉了下去。 ◇ *She watched him go* **with a sinking heart**. 她心情沉重地看着他走了。 **in good ˈheart** (*BrE*) happy and cheerful 心情舒畅；兴高采烈 **in your ˈheart** (**of ˈhearts**) if you know sth **in your heart**, you have a strong feeling that it is true 在内心深处；内心强烈地感觉到： *She knew in her heart of hearts that she was making the wrong decision.* 她心底里明白她在作出错误的决定。 **it does sb's ˈheart good** (**to do sth**) it makes sb feel happy when they see or hear sth （看到或听到某事时）使人感到高兴，使人心旷神怡： *It does my heart good to see the old place being taken care of so well.* 看到故居被照管得这么好，真叫人高兴。 **let your ˌheart rule your ˈhead** to act according to what you feel rather than to what you think is sensible 感情用事 **lose ˈheart** to stop hoping for sth or trying to do sth because you no longer feel confident 丧失信心；泄气 **lose your ˈheart** (**to sb/sth**) (*formal*) to fall in love with sb/sth 爱上（某人或某事物） **a man/woman after your own ˈheart** a man/woman who likes the same things or has the same opinions as you 趣味相投者；情投意合者 **my heart ˈbleeds** (**for sb**) (*ironic*) used to say that you do not feel sympathy or pity for sb （表示不同情或怜悯）真可怜： *'I have to go to Brazil on business.' 'My heart bleeds for you!'* "我要出差去巴西。" "真够可怜的！" **not have the ˈheart** (**to do sth**) to be unable to do sth because you know that it will make sb sad or upset 不忍心（做某事） **off by ˈheart** (*BrE*) = BY HEART **pour out/open your ˈheart to sb** to tell sb all your problems, feelings, etc. 向某人敞开心扉；倾诉衷肠 **set your ˈheart on sth | have your heart ˈset on sth** to want sth very much 渴望；一心想要 **take ˈheart** (**from sth**) to feel more positive about sth, especially when you thought that you had no chance of achieving sth （由于某事）增强信心；重新振作起来： *The government can take heart from the latest opinion polls.* 政府可以从最近的民意测验中找回信心。 **take sth to ˈheart** to be very upset by sth that sb says or does 对某事感到烦恼；十分介意（某人的话或行为）；耿耿于怀 **ˌtear/ˌrip the ˈheart out of sth** to destroy the most important part or aspect of sth 摧毁…的核心 **to your heart's conˈtent** as much as you want 尽情地；心满意足： *a supervised play area where children can run around to their heart's content* 一处能让孩子们尽情游玩且有人看管的地方 **with all your ˈheart/your whole ˈheart** completely 完全地；全心全意： *I hope with all my heart that things work out for you.* 我衷心希望你一切顺利。 ➲ MORE AT ABSENCE, CHANGE *n.*, CROSS *v.*, EAT, ETCH, EYE *n.*, FIND *v.*, GOODNESS, HOME *n.*, INTEREST *n.*, SICK *adj.*, SOB *v.*, STEAL *v.*, STRIKE *v.*, TEAR[1] *v.*, WARM *v.*, WAY *n.*, WEAR *v.*, WIN *v.*, YOUNG *adj.*

heart·ache /ˈhɑːteɪk; *NAmE* ˈhɑːrt-/ *noun* [U, C] a strong feeling of sadness or worry 痛心；伤心；忧虑： *The relationship caused her a great deal of heartache.* 这段恋情使她非常伤心。 ◇ *the heartaches of being a parent* 为人父母的烦恼

ˈheart attack *noun* a sudden serious medical condition in which the heart stops working normally, sometimes causing death 心脏病发作 ➲ COLLOCATIONS AT ILL ➲ COMPARE CORONARY THROMBOSIS

heart·beat /ˈhɑːtbiːt; *NAmE* ˈhɑːrt-/ *noun* **1** [C, U] the movement or sound of the heart as it sends blood around the body 心跳；心搏；心跳声： *a* **rapid/regular heartbeat** 急速 / 正常的心跳 **2** [sing.] **the ~ of sth** (*NAmE*) an important feature of sth, that is responsible for making it what it is 重要特征；中心： *The candidate said that he understood the heartbeat of the Hispanic community in California.* 这位候选人说他了解加利福尼亚州的拉美裔美国人社区的特点。

IDM **a ˈheartbeat away** (**from sth**) very close to sth （离…）很近；近在咫尺 **in a ˈheartbeat** very quickly, without thinking about it 瞬间；随即： *If I was offered another job, I'd leave in a heartbeat.* 如果能找到另外一份工作，我马上就走。

heart·break /ˈhɑːtbreɪk; *NAmE* ˈhɑːrt-/ *noun* [U, C] a strong feeling of sadness 强烈的悲痛感；心碎： *They suffered the heartbreak of losing a child through cancer.* 他们因癌症夺去了一个孩子而肝肠寸断。 ▶ **ˈheart·break·ing** *adj.*： *a heartbreaking story* 令人心碎的故事 ◇ *It's heartbreaking to see him wasting his life like this.* 看到他如此糟蹋自己的生命真让人心碎。

heart·broken /ˈhɑːtbrəʊkən; *NAmE* ˈhɑːrtbroʊkən/ *adj.* extremely sad because of sth that has happened 极为悲伤的；心碎的 **SYN** **broken-hearted**

heart·burn /'hɑːtbɜːn; *NAmE* 'hɑːrtbɜːrn/ *noun* [U] a pain that feels like sth burning in your chest caused by INDIGESTION （消化不良引起的）胃灼热，烧心

heart·en /'hɑːtn; *NAmE* 'hɑːrtn/ *verb* [usually passive] ~ **sb** to give sb encouragement or hope 激励；鼓舞 OPP **dishearten** ▸ **heart·en·ing** *adj.*： *It is heartening to see the determination of these young people.* 看到这些年轻人如此坚决真令人鼓舞。

'heart failure *noun* [U] a serious medical condition in which the heart does not work correctly 心力衰竭

heart·felt /'hɑːtfelt; *NAmE* 'hɑːrt-/ *adj.* [usually before noun] showing strong feelings that are sincere 衷心的；真诚的 SYN **sincere**： ***a heartfelt apology/plea/sigh*** 真切的道歉 / 恳求 / 叹息 ◇ ***heartfelt sympathy/thanks*** 由衷的同情 / 感谢

hearth /hɑːθ; *NAmE* hɑːrθ/ *noun* **1** the floor at the bottom of a FIREPLACE (= the space for a fire in the wall of a room); the area in front of this 壁炉炉床；壁炉前的地面： *A log fire roared in the open hearth.* 柴火在敞开着的壁炉里熊熊燃烧。◇ *The cat dozed in its favourite spot on the hearth.* 猫躺在壁炉前它最喜欢的地方打盹。➲ VISUAL VOCAB PAGE V22 **2** (*literary*) home and family life 家和家庭生活： *a longing for* ***hearth and home*** 对温暖家庭的渴望

hearth·rug /'hɑːθrʌg; *NAmE* 'hɑːrθ-/ *noun* a RUG (= a small carpet) placed on the floor in front of a FIREPLACE 壁炉前的地毯

heart·ily /'hɑːtɪli; *NAmE* 'hɑːrt-/ *adv.* **1** with obvious enjoyment and enthusiasm 尽情地；关怀地；劲头十足地： *to laugh/sing/eat heartily* 开怀大笑；放声歌唱；大吃 **2** in a way that shows that you feel strongly about sth 强烈地；坚定地： *I heartily agree with her on this.* 在这一点上我十分赞同她。 **3** extremely 极为；极其： *heartily glad/relieved* 极为高兴；愁云尽扫

heart·land /'hɑːtlænd; *NAmE* 'hɑːrt-/ *noun* (*also* **heart·lands** [pl.]) **1** the central part of a country or an area （国家或地区的）腹地，中心区域： *the great Russian heartlands* 广袤的俄罗斯中心地带 **2** an area that is important for a particular activity or political party （活动或政党的）重要场所，核心区域： *the industrial heartland of Germany* 德国的工业中心区 ◇ *the traditional Tory heartland of Britain's boardrooms* 保守党的传统领地：英国的各董事会

heart·less /'hɑːtləs; *NAmE* 'hɑːrt-/ *adj.* feeling no pity for other people 无情的；狠心的 SYN **cruel**： *What a heartless thing to say!* 这么说话太无情了！ ▸ **heart·less·ly** *adv.* **heart·less·ness** *noun* [U]

,heart-'lung machine *noun* a machine that replaces the functions of the heart and lungs, for example during a medical operation on the heart 心肺机（手术等时发挥心肺功能）

'heart-rending *adj.* [usually before noun] causing feelings of great sadness 令人悲痛的 SYN **heartbreaking**： *a heart-rending story* 令人心痛的故事

'heart-searching *noun* [U] the process of examining carefully your feelings or reasons for doing sth 反省；自我检讨

heart·sick /'hɑːtsɪk; *NAmE* 'hɑːrt-/ *adj.* [not usually before noun] (*literary*) extremely unhappy or disappointed 悲痛；伤心失望

'heart-stopping *adj.* [usually before noun] causing feelings of great excitement or worry 使人非常兴奋的；令人十分担忧的： *For one heart-stopping moment she thought they were too late.* 一时间她十分担心他们已经太晚了。

heart·strings /'hɑːtstrɪŋz; *NAmE* 'hɑːrt-/ *noun* [pl.] strong feelings of love or pity 深切的爱（或同情）；心弦： *to* ***tug/pull at sb's heartstrings*** (= to cause such feelings in sb) 动人心弦

'heart-throb *noun* (used especially in newspapers) a famous man, usually an actor or a singer, that a lot of women find attractive （尤用于报章，常指男性演员或歌手）万人迷，大众情人

,heart-to-'heart *noun* [usually sing.] a conversation in which two people talk honestly about their feelings and personal problems 坦诚亲切的交谈；谈心： *to have a heart-to-heart with sb* 和某人谈心 ▸ **,heart-to-'heart** *adj.*： *a heart-to-heart talk* 坦诚亲切的交谈

'heart-warming *adj.* causing feelings of happiness and pleasure 使人幸福愉快的

heart·wood /'hɑːtwʊd; *NAmE* 'hɑːrt-/ *noun* [U] the hard older inner layers of the wood of a tree （树木的）心材 ➲ COMPARE SAPWOOD

hearty /'hɑːti; *NAmE* 'hɑːrti/ *adj., noun*

■ ***adj.*** (**heart·ier**, **hearti·est**) **1** [usually before noun] showing friendly feelings for sb 亲切的；友好的： *a hearty welcome* 热情的欢迎 **2** (*sometimes disapproving*) loud, cheerful and full of energy 喧闹而活泼的；吵闹快活且精力充沛的： *a hearty and boisterous fellow* 活泼爱吵闹的家伙 ◇ *a hearty voice* 响亮的嗓子 **3** [only before noun] (of a meal or sb's APPETITE 饭菜或胃口) large; making you feel full 大的；丰盛的： *a hearty breakfast* 丰盛的早餐 ◇ *to have a hearty appetite* 胃口极好 **4** [usually before noun] showing that you feel strongly about sth 强烈的；尽情的： *He nodded his head in hearty agreement.* 他十分赞同地点了点头。◇ *Hearty congratulations to everyone involved.* 谨向所有有关人员表示热烈的祝贺。◇ *a hearty dislike of sth* 对某事物的强烈反感 IDM SEE HALE ▸ **hearti·ness** *noun* [U]

■ ***noun*** (*pl.* **-ies**) (*BrE, sometimes disapproving*) a person who is loud, cheerful and full of energy, especially one who plays a lot of sport 喧闹、快活而且精力充沛的人（尤指好体育运动的人）

heat /hiːt/ *noun, verb*

■ ***noun***

• **BEING HOT/TEMPERATURE** 热；高温 **1** [U, sing.] the quality of being hot 热： *He could feel the heat of the sun on his back.* 他感觉到太阳照射在背上的热力。◇ *Heat rises.* 热空气向上升。◇ *The fire gave out a fierce heat.* 火焰散发出炽热。➲ SEE ALSO WHITE HEAT **2** [U, C, usually sing.] the level of temperature 温度： *to* ***increase/reduce the heat*** 提高 / 降低温度 ◇ *Test the heat of the water before getting in.* 入水之前先试一试水温。◇ *Set the oven to a* ***low/high/moderate*** *heat.* 把烤箱的温度设定为低 / 高 / 中挡。➲ SEE ALSO BLOOD HEAT **3** [U] hot weather; the hot conditions in a building/vehicle, etc. 炎热天气；（建筑物、车辆等中的）高温，热的环境： *You should not go out* ***in the heat of the day*** (= at the hottest time). 你不应该在天最热的时候外出。◇ *to suffer from the heat* 受暑热之苦 ◇ *the* ***afternoon/midday heat*** 午后 / 正午时分的热浪 ◇ *The heat in the factory was unbearable.* 工厂里的高温令人无法忍受。 ➲ SEE ALSO PRICKLY HEAT

• **FOR COOKING** 烧煮食物 **4** [U] a source of heat, especially one that you cook food on 炉灶；灶眼；炉火： *Return the pan to the heat and stir.* 把锅放回灶上再搅拌。

• **IN BUILDING/ROOM** 建筑物；房间 **5** [U] (*especially NAmE*) = HEATING： *The heat wasn't on and the house was freezing.* 暖气没有开，房子里冰冷。

• **STRONG FEELINGS** 强烈感情 **6** [U] strong feelings, especially of anger or excitement 强烈感情；（尤指）愤怒，激动： *'No, I won't,' he said with heat in his voice.* "不，我绝不。"他怒气冲冲地说。◇ *The chairman tried to* ***take the heat out of the situation*** (= to make people calmer). 主席尽力平息人们的激愤情绪。◇ ***In the heat of the moment*** *she forgot what she wanted to say* (= because she was so angry or excited). 她因为过于激动而忘记了要说的话。◇ *In the heat of the argument he said a lot of things he regretted later.* 他在激烈争吵时说了许多他后来感到后悔的话。

• **PRESSURE** 压力 **7** [U] pressure on sb to do or achieve sth 压力；逼迫： ***The heat is on*** *now that the election is only a week away.* 离选举只有一个星期了，因此大家开始感觉到有压力了。◇ *United* ***turned up the heat on*** *their opponents with a second goal.* 联队进了第二个球，这使对

手感到的压力更大了。◇ *Can she **take the heat** of this level of competition?* 她承受得了这种水平的比赛的压力吗？

• RACE 比赛 **8** [C] one of a series of races or competitions, the winners of which then compete against each other in the next part of the competition 预赛；分组赛：*a qualifying heat* 资格赛 ◇ *She won her heat.* 她在预赛中获胜。◇ *He did well **in the heats**; hopefully he'll do as well in the final.* 他在预赛中成绩很好，且有望在决赛中也有同样出色的表现。➲ SEE ALSO DEAD HEAT

IDM **be on 'heat** (BrE) (NAmE **be in 'heat**) (of a female MAMMAL 雌性哺乳动物) to be in a sexual condition ready to reproduce 处于发情期 **if you can't stand the 'heat (get out of the 'kitchen)** (*informal*) used to tell sb to stop trying to do sth if they find it too difficult, especially in order to suggest that they are less able than other people 如果感到太困难（就别干了）

■ ***verb*** [T, I] ~ (**sth**) to make sth hot or warm; to become hot or warm 加热；变热；（使）变暖：*Heat the oil and add the onions.* 把油烧热后加入洋葱。◇ *The system produced enough energy to heat several thousand homes.* 系统产生的能量足以给几千户人家供暖。➲ COLLOCATIONS AT COOKING

PHR V **,heat 'up 1** to become hot or warm 变热；变暖 SYN **warm**：*The oven takes a while to heat up.* 烤箱得过会儿才能热起来。 **2** (*especially NAmE*) (BrE *also* **,hot 'up**) to become more exciting or to show an increase in activity 激烈起来；更加活跃：*The election contest is heating up.* 选举竞争正趋于白热化。 **,heat sth↔'up** to make sth hot or warm 使变热；使变暖 SYN **warm**：*Just heat up the food in the microwave.* 把食物放在微波炉里热热就行了。

heat·ed /'hiːtɪd/ *adj.* **1** (of a person or discussion 人或讨论) full of anger and excitement 愤怒的；激烈的；十分激动的：*a **heated argument/debate*** 激烈的争论 / 辩论 ◇ *She became very heated.* 她不禁怒火中烧。 **2** (of a room, building, etc. 房间、建筑物等) made warmer using a heater（用加热器）加热了的：*a heated swimming pool* 温水游泳池 OPP **unheated** ▶ **heat·ed·ly** *adv.*：*'You had no right!' she said heatedly.* "你没有权利！"她愤怒地说。

heat·er /'hiːtə(r)/ *noun* a machine used for making air or water warmer 加热器；炉子；热水器：*a gas heater* 煤气炉 ◇ *a water heater* 热水器 ➲ SEE ALSO IMMERSION HEATER, STORAGE HEATER

'heat exchanger *noun* (*specialist*) a device for making heat pass from one liquid to another without allowing the liquids to mix 热交换器，换热器（使热从热流体传递给冷流体）

heath /hiːθ/ *noun* a large area of open land that is not used for farming and is covered with rough grass and other small wild plants（杂草和灌木丛生的）荒地，荒野

hea·then /'hiːðn/ *noun, adj.*

■ ***noun*** (*old-fashioned, offensive*) **1** used by people who have a strong religious belief as a way of referring to a person who has no religion or who believes in a religion that is not one of the world's main religions 无宗教信仰者；异教徒 **2** used to refer to a person who shows lack of education 未开化的人；不文明的人

■ ***adj.*** (*old-fashioned, offensive*) connected with heathens 无宗教信仰的；异教徒的；不文明的：*heathen gods* 异教的神祇 ◇ *He set out to convert **the heathen*** (= people who are heathens). 他决心要使异教徒皈依。

hea·ther /'heðə(r)/ *noun* [U] a low wild plant with small purple, pink or white flowers, that grows on hills and areas of wild open land (= MOORLAND) 帚石楠（低矮野生，开紫、粉红或白色小花）

heath·land /'hiːθlənd; NAmE -lænd/ *noun* [U] **heathlands** [pl.] a large area of heath 大片荒地；荒野

Heath Rob·in·son /,hiːθ 'rɒbɪnsən; NAmE 'rɑːb-/ (BrE) (NAmE **,Rube 'Gold·berg**) *adj.* [only before noun] (*humorous*) (of machines and devices 机器和装置) having a very complicated design, especially when used to perform a very simple task; not practical 结构过于复杂的；不实用的：*a Heath Robinson contraption* 复杂而不实用的装置

heat·ing /'hiːtɪŋ/ *noun* [U] (*especially BrE*) (*also* **heat** *especially in NAmE*) the process of supplying heat to a room or building; a system used to do this 供暖；供暖系统；暖气设备：*Who turned the heating off?* 谁把暖气关掉了？◇ *What type of heating do you have?* 你们用什么供暖？◇ *a gas heating system* 燃气供暖系统 ◇ *heating bills* 暖气账单 ➲ SEE ALSO CENTRAL HEATING

heat·proof /'hiːtpruːf/ *adj.* that cannot be damaged by heat 隔热的；抗热的；耐高温的：*a heatproof dish* 耐高温的盘子

'heat-resistant *adj.* not easily damaged by heat 抗热的；耐热的

'heat-seeking *adj.* [only before noun] (of a weapon 武器) that moves towards the heat coming from the aircraft, etc. that it is intended to hit and destroy 热自导引的；跟踪热源的：*heat-seeking missiles* 热自导引导弹

heat·stroke /'hiːtstrəʊk; NAmE -stroʊk/ *noun* [U] an illness with fever and often loss of CONSCIOUSNESS, caused by being in too great a heat for too long 中暑

heat·wave /'hiːtweɪv/ *noun* a period of unusually hot weather 酷热期；热浪

heave /hiːv/ *verb, noun*

■ ***verb*** **1** [T, I] to lift, pull or throw sb/sth very heavy with one great effort（用力）举起，拖，拉，抛：**~ sth/sb/yourself + adv./prep.** *I managed to heave the trunk down the stairs.* 我用力把箱子弄下楼梯。◇ *They heaved the body overboard.* 他们使劲把尸体从船上抛入水中。◇ **+ adv./prep.** *We all heaved on the rope.* 我们大家一起用力拉绳子。 **2** [I] to rise up and down with strong, regular movements（强烈而有节奏地）起伏：*The boat heaved beneath them.* 小船在他们脚下颠簸着。◇ **~ with sth** *Her shoulders heaved with laughter.* 她笑得双肩抖动。 **3** [T] **~ a sigh, etc.** to make a sound slowly and often with effort（常指吃力地）缓慢发出（声音）：*We all **heaved a sigh of relief**.* 我们都如释重负地舒了一口气。 **4** [I] to experience the tight feeling in your stomach that you get before you VOMIT 恶心：*The thought of it makes me heave.* 一想到那事我就恶心。

IDM **,heave into 'sight/'view** (*formal*) (especially of ships 尤指船) to appear, especially when moving gradually closer from a long way off（从远处）出现；进入视野：*A ship hove into sight.* 远处出现了一条船。 HELP **Hove** is usually used for the past tense and past participle in this idiom. 这个习语通常用 hove 作过去式及过去分词。

PHR V **,heave 'to** (*specialist*) if a ship or its CREW (= the people sailing it) **heave to**, the ship stops moving 停船 HELP **Hove** is usually used for the past tense and past participle in this phrasal verb. 这个短语动词通常用 hove 作过去式及过去分词。

■ ***noun*** **1** [C] an act of lifting, pulling or throwing 举；拖；拉；抛：*With a mighty heave he lifted the sack onto the truck.* 他用劲一举，把大麻袋扔到卡车上。 **2** [U] (*especially literary*) a rising and falling movement 起伏：*the steady heave of the sea* 大海汹涌不断的波涛

heave-ho /,hiːv 'həʊ; NAmE 'hoʊ/ *noun* [sing.]

IDM **give sb the (old) heave-'ho** (*informal*) to dismiss sb from their job; to end a relationship with sb 解雇某人；同某人断绝关系

heaven /'hevn/ *noun* **1** (*also* **Heaven**) [U] (used without *the* 不与 the 连用) (in some religions 某些宗教) the place believed to be the home of God where good people go when they die 天堂；天国：*the kingdom of heaven* 天国 ◇ *I feel like I've died and gone to heaven.* 我仿佛觉得自己已经死了，进了天堂。 **2** [U, C] (*informal*) a place or situation in which you are very happy 极乐之地；极乐：*This isn't exactly my idea of heaven!* 这可不太像我所想象的那么美妙！◇ *It was heaven being away from the office for a week.* 一个星期远离办公室真是快活极了。◇ *The island is truly **a heaven on earth**.* 那个岛堪称人间天堂。 **3 the heavens** [pl.] (*literary*) the sky 天空：*Four tall trees stretched up to the heavens.* 四棵大树参天而立。

IDM (Good) 'Heavens! | ˌHeavens a'bove! (*informal*) used to show that you are surprised or annoyed（表示惊奇或气恼）天哪，我的天：*Good heavens, what are you doing?* 天哪，你在干什么？ **the heavens 'opened** it began to rain heavily 下起了倾盆大雨 **made in 'heaven** (especially of a marriage or other relationship 尤指婚姻或其他关系) seeming to be perfect 天作之合；天造地设 ➲ MORE AT FORBID, GOD, HELP *v.*, HIGH *adj.*, KNOW *v.*, MOVE *v.*, NAME *n.*, SEVENTH *ordinal number*, THANK

heav·en·ly /'hevnli/ *adj.* **1** [only before noun] connected with heaven 天国的；天堂的：*our heavenly Father* (= God) 上帝 ◇ *the heavenly kingdom* 天国 **2** [only before noun] connected with the sky 天空的：***heavenly bodies*** (= the sun, moon, stars and planets) 天体 **3** (*informal*) very pleasant 十分舒适的；很愉快的；美好的 SYN **wonderful**: *a heavenly morning/feeling* 愉快的早晨 / 感觉 ◇ *This place is heavenly.* 这个地方好极了。

ˌheaven-'sent *adj.* [usually before noun] happening unexpectedly and at exactly the right time 天赐的；正合时宜的

heav·en·ward /'hevnwəd; *NAmE* -wərd/ (*also* **heav·en·wards**) *adv.* (*literary*) towards heaven or the sky 朝天上；向天空：*to **cast/raise your eyes heavenward*** (= to show you are annoyed or impatient) 翻白眼（表示生气或不耐烦）

heav·ily 🔑 /'hevɪli/ *adv.* **1** 🔑 to a great degree; in large amounts 在很大程度上；大量地：*It was raining heavily.* 雨下得很大。 ◇ *to **drink/smoke** heavily* 喝酒 / 抽烟很凶 ◇ ***heavily armed*** *police* (= carrying a lot of weapons) 全副武装的警察 ◇ *a **heavily pregnant** woman* (= one whose baby is nearly ready to be born) 临产的孕妇 ◇ *They are both **heavily involved** in politics.* 他们俩都深深卷入政治中。◇ *He **relies heavily** on his parents.* 他极度依赖父母。◇ *She has been **heavily criticized** in the press.* 她受到报界的猛烈抨击。 **2** with a lot of force or effort 以猛力；沉重地：*She fell heavily to the ground.* 她重重地摔倒在地。 **3 ~ built** (of a person 人) with a large, solid and strong body 身材壮实 **4** slowly and loudly 缓慢又高声地：*She was now breathing heavily.* 她喘着粗气。◇ *He was snoring heavily.* 他发着粗重的鼾声。 **5** in a slow way that sounds as though you are worried or sad 缓慢而忧郁地；悲伤地：*He sighed heavily.* 他长叹了一声。 **6** in a way that makes you feel uncomfortable or anxious 令人心情沉重：*Silence hung heavily in the room.* 房间里寂若死灰。◇ *The burden of guilt weighed heavily on his mind.* 愧疚之情压得他透不过气来。 **7 ~ loaded/laden** full of or loaded with heavy things 装满（或装载）重物的；重载的：*a heavily loaded van* 满载重物的货车

heav·ing /'hiːvɪŋ/ *adj.* [not before noun] **~ (with sb/sth)** full of sb/sth 充满（人或事物）：*The place was heaving with journalists.* 那个地方挤满了记者。

heavy 🔑 /'hevi/ *adj., noun, adv.*

■ ***adj.*** **(heav·ier, heavi·est)**

• WEIGHING A LOT 重量大 **1** 🔑 weighing a lot; difficult to lift or move 重的；沉的：*She was struggling with a heavy suitcase.* 她正费力地拎着一只沉重的手提箱。◇ *My brother is much heavier than me.* 我弟弟比我重得多。◇ *He tried to push the heavy door open.* 他试图推开那扇沉重的门。◇ ***How heavy is it*** (= how much does it weigh)? 这东西有多重？ ◇ (*especially NAmE*) *Many young people today are too heavy* (= fat). 现今许多青年人都过于肥胖。◇ (*figurative*) *Her father carried a **heavy burden** of responsibility.* 她父亲肩负着重大责任。 OPP **light**

• WORSE THAN USUAL 比一般严重 **2** 🔑 more or worse than usual in amount, degree, etc.（在数量、程度等方面）超出一般的，比一般严重的：*the noise of **heavy traffic*** 繁忙交通的噪音 ◇ ***heavy frost/rain/snow*** 严重霜冻；暴雨；大雪 ◇ *the effects of **heavy drinking*** 过量饮酒的后果 ◇ *There was heavy fighting in the capital last night.* 昨晚首都发生了激烈战斗。◇ *The penalty for speeding can be a **heavy fine**.* 超速驾驶可能会被处以高额罚款。 ◇ *She spoke with **heavy irony**.* 她的话充满了讽刺。 OPP **light**

• NOT DELICATE 不精致 **3** 🔑 (of sb/sth's appearance or structure 人或物的外表或构造) large and solid; not delicate 大而结实的；不精致的：*big, dark rooms full of heavy furniture* 装满厚实家具、又大又暗的房间 ◇ *He was tall and strong, with heavy features.* 他长得高大壮实，浓眉大眼。

• MATERIAL 材料 **4** 🔑 (of the material or substance that sth is made of 原材料或原料) thick 厚的：*heavy curtains* 厚窗帘 ◇ *a heavy coat* 厚外套 OPP **light**

• FULL OF STH 充满 **5 ~ with sth** (*literary*) full of or loaded with sth 充满，满载（某物）：*trees heavy with apples* 挂满苹果的树 ◇ *The air was heavy with the scent of flowers.* 空气中弥漫着浓郁的花香。 ◇ *His voice was heavy with sarcasm.* 他的语气带着十足的讽刺意味。

• MACHINES 机器 **6** [usually before noun] (of machines, vehicles or weapons 机器、车辆或武器) large and powerful 重型的；大型的：*a wide range of engines and **heavy machinery*** 各种各样的发动机和重型机器 ◇ ***heavy lorries/trucks*** 重型卡车

• BUSY 繁忙 **7** 🔑 [usually before noun] involving a lot of work or activity; very busy 工作（或活动）多的；繁忙的：*a **heavy schedule*** 安排很紧的日程 ◇ *She'd had a heavy day.* 她忙了一天。

• WORK 工作 **8** 🔑 hard, especially because it requires a lot of physical strength 辛苦的；费力的：***heavy digging/lifting*** 费力的挖掘 / 提举

• FALL/HIT 落下；打击 **9** 🔑 falling or hitting sth with a lot of force 沉重的；猛烈的：*a **heavy fall/blow*** 重重的跌落 / 一击

• MEAL/FOOD 餐食；食物 **10** 🔑 large in amount or very solid 量大的；厚实的：*a **heavy lunch/dinner*** 丰盛的午餐 / 正餐 ◇ *a heavy cake* 厚实的蛋糕 OPP **light**

• DRINKER/SMOKER/SLEEPER 喝酒 / 抽烟 / 睡觉的人 **11** 🔑 [only before noun] (of a person 人) doing the thing mentioned more, or more deeply, than usual （做某事）过量的，超出一般的，过度的：*a **heavy drinker/smoker*** 酒瘾 / 烟瘾大的人 ◇ *a heavy sleeper* 睡得很死的人

• SOUND 声音 **12** 🔑 (of a sound that sb makes 人声) loud and deep 响而深沉的：***heavy breathing/snoring*** 沉重的呼吸声 / 鼾声 ◇ ***a heavy groan/sigh*** 深沉的呻吟 / 叹息

• USING A LOT 用很多 **13 ~ on sth** (*informal*) using a lot of sth 使用很多…的；耗费…的：*Older cars are heavy on gas.* 老旧的汽车耗油多。◇ *Don't go so heavy on the garlic.* 别用这么多蒜。

• SERIOUS/DIFFICULT 严肃；困难 **14** (*usually disapproving*) (of a book, programme, style, etc. 书、节目、风格等) serious; difficult to understand or enjoy 严肃的；难懂的；艰涩的：*We found the play very heavy.* 我们觉得这部戏很艰涩。◇ *The discussion got a little heavy.* 讨论变得有点严肃。

• SEA/OCEAN 海；洋 **15** dangerous because of big waves, etc. 危险的；汹涌的：*strong winds and heavy seas* 风急浪高

• AIR/WEATHER 空气；天气 **16** hot and lacking fresh air, in a way that is unpleasant 闷热的；沉闷的：*It's very heavy—I think there'll be a storm.* 天气很闷热，我觉得暴风雨要来了。

• SOIL 泥土 **17** wet, sticky and difficult to dig or to move over 黏重难挖的；泥泞难行的

• STRICT 严厉 **18** (of a person 人) very strict and severe 苛刻的；严厉的：*Don't be so heavy on her—it wasn't her fault.* 别对她这么苛刻，这不是她的过错。

▸ **heavi·ness** *noun* [U]

IDM **get 'heavy** (*informal*) to become very serious, because strong feelings are involved 变得严重；变得激烈：*They started shouting at me. It got very heavy.* 他们开始对我大喊大叫。情势变得很激烈。 **ˌheavy 'going** used to describe sb/sth that is difficult to deal with or understand 难以打交道；难以处理；难以理解：*She's a bit heavy going.* 她有点难缠。 ◇ *I found the course rather heavy going.* 我觉得这门课相当难。 **heavy 'hand** a way of doing sth or of treating people that is much stronger and less sensitive than it needs to be 严厉手段；粗暴方式；暴虐方式：*the heavy hand of management* 粗暴的管理方式 **a heavy 'heart** a feeling of great sadness 悲哀的心情：*She left her children behind with a heavy heart.* 她十分难过地丢下了她的孩子们。 **the 'heavy mob/brigade** (*BrE, informal*) a group of strong, often violent people employed to do sth such as protect sb（雇佣的）打手队，保镖团 **a heavy 'silence/'atmosphere** a situation when

H

people do not say anything, but feel embarrassed or uncomfortable 令人尴尬（或不安）的沉默（或气氛） **make heavy 'weather of sth** to seem to find sth more difficult or complicated than it needs to be 小题大做 ➲ MORE AT CROSS *n.*, TOLL *n.*

■ ***noun*** (*pl.* **-ies**) **1** [C] (*informal*) a large strong man whose job is to protect a person or place, often using violence 保镖；打手 **2** [U] (*ScotE*) strong beer, especially bitter 烈性啤酒；（尤指）苦啤酒：*a pint of heavy* 一品脱烈性啤酒

■ ***adv.***

IDM **hang/lie 'heavy 1** ~ **(on/in sth)** (of a feeling or sth in the air 感情或空气中的东西) to be very noticeable in a particular place in a way that is unpleasant 明显地悬浮于；明显积郁着：*Smoke lay heavy on the far side of the water.* 水面对岸悬浮着黑沉沉的烟雾。◇ *Despair hangs heavy in the stifling air.* 绝望的感觉积压在憋闷的空气中。**2** ~ **on sb/sth** to cause sb/sth to feel uncomfortable or anxious 使不安；使担忧：*The crime lay heavy on her conscience.* 那件罪行使她内疚不安。

ˌheavy 'breather *noun* a person who gets sexual pleasure from calling sb on the telephone and not speaking to them 浊重呼吸者（给人打电话又不说话，从中得到性快感）▶ **ˌheavy 'breathing** *noun* [U]

ˌheavy-'duty *adj.* [only before noun] **1** not easily damaged and therefore suitable for hard physical work or to be used all the time 结实的；重型的；耐用的：*a heavy-duty carpet* 耐磨的地毯 **2** (*informal, especially NAmE*) very serious or great in quantity 严重的；严肃的；大量的：*I think you need some heavy-duty advice.* 我想你需要一些有分量的意见。

ˌheavy 'goods vehicle *noun* (*BrE*) = HGV

ˌheavy-'handed *adj.* **1** not showing a sympathetic understanding of the feelings of other people 缺乏同情心的；冷酷的：*a heavy-handed approach* 冷酷无情的方法 **2** using unnecessary force 强暴的；高压的：*heavy-handed police methods* 警察的高压手段 **3** (of a person 人) using too much of sth in a way that can cause damage 用某物过多的；大手大脚的：*Don't be too heavy-handed with the salt.* 别放太多的盐。

ˌheavy 'hitter *noun* (*informal, especially NAmE*) a person with a lot of power, especially in business or politics （尤指商业或政界的）大亨，要员，大人物

ˌheavy 'industry *noun* [U, C] industry that uses large machinery to produce metal, coal, vehicles, etc. 重工业 ➲ COMPARE LIGHT INDUSTRY

ˌheavy 'lifting *noun* [U] hard or difficult work 重任；重担；艰巨的工作：*The film still has a lot of heavy lifting to do to make $40 million.* 这部电影要想赚 4 000 万美元，还有很多艰苦的工作要做。◇ *Much of the heavy lifting in this report was done by the expert writers.* 这份报告中大部分的繁重工作是由专家作者完成的。

ˌheavy 'metal *noun* **1** [U] a type of rock music with a very strong beat played very loud on electric GUITARS 重金属摇滚乐 **2** [C] (*specialist*) a metal that has a very high DENSITY (= the relation of its weight to its volume), such as gold or LEAD² (1) 重金属

ˌheavy 'petting *noun* [U] sexual activity that does not involve full SEXUAL INTERCOURSE 性爱抚

ˌheavy-'set *adj.* having a broad heavy body 敦实的；壮硕的 SYN **thickset**

'heavy water *noun* [U] (*chemistry* 化) water in which HYDROGEN is replaced by DEUTERIUM, used in nuclear reactions 重水（用于核反应）

heavy·weight /'heviweɪt/ *noun* **1** a BOXER of the heaviest class in normal use, weighing 79.5 kilograms or more 重量级拳击手（体重 79.5 公斤或以上）：*a heavyweight champion* 重量级拳击冠军 **2** a person or thing that weighs more than is usual 特别重的人（或物） **3** a very important person, organization or thing that influences others 有影响力的人（或组织、事物）：*a political heavyweight* 政界要人 ◇ *a heavyweight journal* 有影响力的刊物

Heb·raic /hi'breɪɪk/ *adj.* of or connected with the Hebrew language or people 希伯来语的；希伯来人的：*Hebraic poetry* 希伯来语诗歌

Heb·rew /'hi:bru:/ *noun* **1** a member of an ancient race of people living in what is now Israel and Palestine. Their writings and traditions form the basis of the Jewish religion. 希伯来人 **2** the language traditionally used by the Hebrew people 希伯来语 **3** a modern form of the Hebrew language which is the official language of modern Israel 现代希伯来语（现代以色列的官方语言） ➲ COMPARE YIDDISH ▶ **Heb·rew** *adj.*

heck /hek/ *exclamation, noun* (*informal*) used to show that you are slightly annoyed or surprised （表示略微烦恼或吃惊）：*Oh heck, I'm going to be late!* 见鬼，我要迟到了！◇ *We had to wait **a heck of a** long time!* 我们只好等了很长时间！◇ ***Who the heck** are you?* 你究竟是谁？

IDM **for the 'heck of it** (*informal*) just for pleasure rather than for a reason 只是闹着玩；不为什么 **what the 'heck!** (*informal*) used to say that you are going to do sth that you know you should not do （表示明知不应做某事，却偏要做）：*It means I'll be late for work but what the heck!* 那意味着我上班会迟到，不过管它的呢！

heckle /'hekl/ *verb* [T, I] ~ **(sb)** to interrupt a speaker at a public meeting by shouting out questions or rude remarks （对演说者）责问，诘问，起哄 SYN **barrack**：*He was booed and heckled throughout his speech.* 他的演说自始至终都遭到喝倒彩起哄。▶ **heck·ler** /'heklə(r)/ *noun* **heck·ling** *noun* [U]

hec·tare /'hekteə(r); 'hektɑ:(r); *NAmE* -ter/ *noun* (*abbr.* **ha**) a unit for measuring an area of land; 10 000 square metres or about 2.5 ACRES 公顷（土地丈量单位，等于 1 万平方米或约 2.5 英亩）

hec·tic /'hektɪk/ *adj.* very busy; full of activity 忙碌的；繁忙的：*to lead a hectic life* 生活十分忙碌 ◇ *a hectic schedule* 安排很满的日程表

hecto·litre (*especially US* **hecto·liter**) /'hektəli:tə(r)/ *noun* (*abbr.* **hl**) a unit for measuring volume; 100 litres 百升（容量单位）

hec·tor /'hektə(r)/ *verb* ~ **sb** | + **speech** (*formal*) to try to make sb do sth by talking or behaving in an aggressive way 威逼；威吓 SYN **bully** ▶ **hec·tor·ing** *adj.*：*a hectoring tone of voice* 威逼的口气

he'd /hi:d/ *short form* **1** he had **2** he would

hedge /hedʒ/ *noun, verb*

■ ***noun*** **1** a row of bushes or small trees planted close together, usually along the edge of a field, garden/yard or road 树篱：*a privet hedge* 女贞树篱 ➲ VISUAL VOCAB PAGES V3, V20 **2** ~ **against sth** a way of protecting yourself against the loss of sth, especially money 防止损失（尤指金钱）的手段：*to buy gold as a hedge against inflation* 购买黄金以抵消通货膨胀造成的损失

■ ***verb*** **1** [I] to avoid giving a direct answer to a question or promising to support a particular idea, etc. 避免正面回答；不直接许诺；拐弯抹角：*Just answer 'yes' or 'no'—and stop hedging.* 只要回答"是"或"不是"，别再闪烁其词了。**2** [T] ~ **sth** to put a hedge around a field, etc. 在（田地等）周围植树篱；用树篱围住 **3** [T, usually passive] ~ **sb/sth (about/around) (with sth)** (*formal*) to surround or limit sb/sth 包围；限制：*His religious belief was always hedged with doubt.* 他的宗教信仰一直受到心不诚的局限。◇ *Their offer was hedged around with all sorts of conditions.* 他们的建议附带了各种各样的限制条件。

IDM **ˌhedge your 'bets** to reduce the risk of losing or making a mistake by supporting more than one side in a competition, an argument, etc., or by having several choices available to you （为防止损失或出错）几面下注，有几项选择可选取

PHR V **'hedge against sth** to do sth to protect yourself against problems, especially against losing money 采取保护措施（尤指为避免损失金钱）：*a way of hedging against currency risks* 避免货币风险的保值措施 **ˌhedge sb/sth↔'in** to surround sb/sth with sth 包围；环绕 SYN hem sb/sth↔in: *The cathedral is now hedged in by other buildings.* 大教堂现在被其他建筑物包围着。◇ (*figurative*) *Married life made him feel hedged in and restless.* 婚姻生活使他感觉受到束缚而且心烦。

hedge·hog /'hedʒhɒg; *NAmE* -hɔːg; -hɑːg/ *noun* a small brown animal with stiff parts like needles (called SPINES) covering its back. Hedgehogs are NOCTURNAL (= active mostly at night) and can roll into a ball to defend themselves when they are attacked. 刺猬

hedge·row /'hedʒrəʊ; *NAmE* -roʊ/ *noun* (especially in Britain) a line of bushes planted along the edge of a field or road（尤指英国田边或路边的）矮树篱 ➲ VISUAL VOCAB PAGE V3

he·don·ism /'hedənɪzəm; 'hiːdə-/ *noun* [U] the belief that pleasure is the most important thing in life 享乐主义 ▶ **he·don·is·tic** /ˌhedə'nɪstɪk; ˌhiːdə-/ *adj.*

he·don·ist /'hedənɪst; 'hiːdə-/ *noun* a person who believes that pleasure is the most important thing in life 享乐主义者

the heebie-jeebies /ˌhiːbi 'dʒiːbiz/ *noun* [pl.] (*old-fashioned, informal*) a feeling of nervous fear or worry 忐忑不安；坐立不安

heed /hiːd/ *verb, noun*

■ ***verb*** ~ **sb/sth** (*formal*) to pay careful attention to sb's advice or warning 留心，注意，听从（劝告或警告）SYN **notice**

■ ***noun*** [U]

IDM **give/pay 'heed (to sb/sth)** | **take 'heed (of sb/sth)** (*formal*) to pay careful attention to sb/sth 留心；注意；听从

heed·ful /'hiːdfl/ *adj.* ~ (**of sb/sth**) (*formal*) paying careful attention to sb/sth 留心的；注意的

heed·less /'hiːdləs/ *adj.* [not usually before noun] ~ (**of sb/sth**) (*formal*) not paying careful attention to sb/sth 不加注意；掉以轻心 ▶ **heed·less·ly** *adv.*

hee-haw /'hiː hɔː/ *noun* the way of writing the sound made by a DONKEY 驴叫声

heel 🔑 /hiːl/ *noun, verb*

■ ***noun***

• PART OF FOOT 脚的部位 **1** 🔑 [C] the back part of the foot below the ankle 脚跟；脚后跟 ➲ VISUAL VOCAB PAGE V64

• PART OF SOCK/SHOE 袜子 / 鞋的部分 **2** [C] the part of a sock, etc. that covers the heel（袜子等的）后跟 **3** 🔑 [C] the raised part on the bottom of a shoe, boot, etc. that makes the shoe, etc. higher at the back（鞋、靴子等的）后跟：*shoes with a* ***low/high heel*** 低跟鞋；高跟鞋 ◇ *a stiletto heel* 细高跟 ◇ *The sergeant clicked his heels and walked out.* 中士将鞋跟咔哒一并，走了出去。➲ VISUAL VOCAB PAGE V69 ➲ COMPARE SOLE *n.* (2)

• -HEELED 后跟…的 **4** (in adjectives 构成形容词) having the type of heel mentioned 有…后跟的：*high-heeled shoes* 高跟鞋 ➲ SEE ALSO WELL HEELED

• SHOES 鞋 **5 heels** [pl.] a pair of women's shoes that have high heels 女高跟鞋：*She doesn't often wear heels.* 她不常穿高跟鞋。➲ SEE ALSO KITTEN HEELS

• PART OF HAND 手的部位 **6** [C] ~ **of your hand/palm** the raised part of the inside of the hand where it joins the wrist 手掌根（手掌靠近腕部的隆起部分）

• UNPLEASANT MAN 可恶的人 **7** [C] (*old-fashioned, informal*) a man who is unpleasant to other people and cannot be trusted 卑鄙的家伙；浑蛋 ➲ SEE ALSO ACHILLES HEEL, DOWN AT HEEL

IDM **at/on sb's 'heels** following closely behind sb 紧跟某人：*He fled from the stadium with the police at his heels.* 他逃离了运动场，警察在后面紧追不舍。 **bring sb/sth to 'heel 1** to force sb to obey you and accept discipline 使某人就范；迫使某人服从（纪律） **2** to make a dog come close to you 让狗靠近；唤狗来到身边 **come to 'heel 1** (of a person 人) to agree to obey sb and accept their orders 愿意听从（某人）；顺从 **2** (of a dog 狗) to come close to the person who has called it 走近唤狗人 **(hard/hot) on sb's/sth's 'heels** very close behind sb/sth; very soon after sth 紧跟；紧接在后：*News of rising unemployment followed hard on the heels of falling export figures.* 出口数字下降之后紧接着就是失业率上升的消息。 **ˌtake to your 'heels** to run away from sb/sth 逃走；溜掉 **ˌturn/ˌspin on your 'heel** to turn around suddenly so that you are facing in the opposite direction 急向后转；突然转身 **under the 'heel of sb** (*literary*) completely controlled by sb 完全受某人控制 ➲ MORE AT COOL *v.*, DIG *v.*, DRAG *v.*, HEAD *n.*, KICK *v.*, TREAD *v.*

■ ***verb***

• REPAIR SHOE 修鞋 **1** [T] ~ **sth** to repair the heel of a shoe, etc. 给（鞋等）修理后跟

• OF BOAT 船 **2** [I] ~ (**over**) to lean over to one side 倾侧；倾斜：*The boat heeled over in the strong wind.* 船在狂风中倾侧了。

Heely™ /'hiːli/ *noun* (*pl.* **Heelys**) (*especially BrE*) (*also* **'skate shoe** *especially in NAmE*) a sports shoe that has one or more wheels underneath it 赫利滑轮鞋；暴走鞋；飞行鞋；犀利鞋

heft /heft/ *verb, noun*

■ ***verb* 1** ~ **sth** (+ **adv./prep.**) to lift or carry sth heavy from one position to another 举起，搬动（重物）：*The two men hefted the box into the car.* 两个男子把箱子搬进了汽车。 **2** ~ **sth** to lift or hold sth in order to estimate its weight 掂…的重量：*Anna took the old sword and hefted it in her hands.* 安娜拿起那把古剑掂了掂分量。

■ ***noun*** [U] (*NAmE*) the weight of sb/sth 重量：*She was surprised by the sheer heft of the package.* 那包裹沉甸甸的分量就够她吃惊的了。

hefty /'hefti/ *adj.* (**heft·ier, hefti·est**) **1** (of a person or an object 人或物体) big and heavy 大而重的：*Her brothers were both hefty men in their forties.* 她的两个兄弟都是四十多岁，身高体壮。 **2** (*informal*) (of an amount of money 钱的数额) large; larger than usual or expected 很大的；超出一般的；可观的：*They sold it easily and made a hefty profit.* 他们毫不费力地卖掉了它，得到了一笔可观的利润。 **3** using a lot of force 用力的；猛烈的：*He gave the door a hefty kick.* 他猛踢了一下门。 ▶ **heft·ily** *adv.*

he·gem·ony /hɪ'dʒeməni; -'ge-; 'hedʒɪməni; *NAmE* -moʊni/ *noun* [U, C] (*pl.* **-ies**) (*formal*) control by one country, organization, etc. over other countries, etc. within a particular group 支配权；霸权 ▶ **hege·mon·ic** /ˌhedʒɪ'mɒnɪk; ˌhegɪ-; *NAmE* -'mɑːnɪk/ *adj.*：*hegemonic control* 霸权统治

He·gira (*also* **Hej·ira**) /'hedʒɪrə; hɪ'dʒaɪrə/ (*also* **Hijra**) *noun* [sing.] **1** (*usually* **the Hegira**) the occasion when Muhammad left Mecca to go to Medina in AD 622 希吉拉（意为迁徙，指公元 622 年穆罕默德从麦加前往麦地那） **2** the period which began at this time; the Muslim ERA 伊斯兰纪元（从公元 622 年开始）

heifer /'hefə(r)/ *noun* a young female cow, especially one that has not yet had a CALF（尤指未生育过的）小母牛

height 🔑 /haɪt/ *noun*

• MEASUREMENT 量度 **1** 🔑 [U, C] the measurement of how tall a person or thing is（人或物的）身高，高度：*Height: 210 mm. Width: 57 mm. Length: 170 mm.* 高：210 毫米；宽：57 毫米；长：170 毫米。◇ *Please state your height and weight.* 请说明身高和体重。◇ *It is almost 2 metres* ***in height.*** 它差不多有 2 米高。◇ *She is the same height as her sister.* 她和她姐姐一样高。◇ *to be of* ***medium/average height*** 中等身高 ◇ *You can adjust the height of the chair.* 你可以调节椅子的高度。◇ *The table is available in several different heights.* 这款桌子有几种不同的高度供选择。

• BEING TALL 高 **2** 🔑 [U] the quality of being tall or high 高：*She worries about her height* (= that she is too tall). 她为个子太高而烦恼。◇ *The height of the mountain did not discourage them.* 山高并没有使他们泄气。

• DISTANCE ABOVE GROUND 高度 **3** 🔑 [C, U] a particular distance above the ground 高度：*The plane flew* ***at a height of*** *3 000 metres.* 飞机在 3 000 米的高空飞行。◇ *The stone was dropped* ***from a great height.*** 那块石头是从很

H

高的地方掉落下来的。◇ *The aircraft was gaining height.* 飞机在爬高。◇ *to be at* ***shoulder/chest/waist height*** 齐肩 / 齐胸 / 齐腰高

- **HIGH PLACE** 高处 **4** [C, usually pl.] (often used in names 常用于名称) a high place or position 高地；高处；高位：*Brooklyn Heights* 布鲁克林高地 ◇ *He doesn't have* ***a head for heights*** (= is afraid of high places). 他惧高。◇ *a fear of heights* 恐高 ◇ *We looked out over the city from the heights of Edinburgh Castle.* 我们从爱丁堡城堡所在的高处俯视整个城市。◇ *The pattern of the ancient fields is clearly visible* ***from a height.*** 古战场的布局从高处清晰可见。
- **STRONGEST POINT/LEVEL** 最强点；最高水平 **5** [sing.] the point when sth is at its best or strongest 最佳点；最强点；顶点：*He is at the height of his career.* 他正处于事业的巅峰。◇ *She is still at the* ***height of her powers.*** 她仍然处于最佳状态。◇ *I wouldn't go there* ***in the height of summer.*** 我不会在盛夏时节去那里。◇ *The fire* ***reached its height*** *around 2 a.m.* 大火在半夜两点钟左右烧得最猛。◇ *The crisis was* ***at its height*** *in May.* 危机在五月份到了最严重的关头。 **6 heights** [pl.] a better or greater level of sth; a situation where sth is very good 更好；更高水平；极佳状况：*Their success had reached* ***new heights.*** 他们的成就达到新高水平。
- **EXTREME EXAMPLE** 极端例子 **7** [sing.] **~ of sth** an extreme example of a particular quality 极端；极度：*It would be* ***the height of folly*** (= very stupid) *to change course now.* 现在改变方向可谓愚蠢至极。◇ *She was dressed in the* ***height of fashion.*** 她穿着最时髦的衣服。➲ MORE LIKE THIS 20, page R27

IDM **draw yourself up/rise to your full 'height** to stand straight and tall in order to show your determination or high status 昂首挺胸地站立（以示决心或地位高）➲ MORE AT DIZZY

height·en /'haɪtn/ *verb* [I, T] if a feeling or an effect **heightens**, or sth **heightens** it, it becomes stronger or increases （使）加强，提高，增加 SYN **intensify**：*Tension has heightened after the recent bomb attack.* 最近的炸弹袭击之后，情势更加紧张。◇ **~ sth** *The campaign is intended to heighten public awareness of the disease.* 这场运动的目的是使公众更加了解这种疾病。

hein·ous /'heɪnəs/ *adj.* [usually before noun] (*formal*) morally very bad 极恶毒的；道德败坏的：*a heinous crime* 十恶不赦的罪行 ▸ **hein·ous·ly** *adv.* **hein·ous·ness** *noun* [U]

heir /eə(r); *NAmE* er/ *noun* HELP Use **an**, not **a**, before **heir**. * heir 前不定冠词用 an，不用 a。**~ (to sth) | ~ (of sb) 1** a person who has the legal right to receive sb's property, money or title when that person dies 继承人；后嗣：*to be heir to a large fortune* 是大笔财产的继承人 ◇ *the heir to the throne* (= the person who will be the next king or queen) 王位继承人 ➲ WORDFINDER NOTE AT FAMILY **2** a person who is thought to continue the work or a tradition started by sb else （工作或传统的）继承者，承袭者，传人：*the president's political heirs* 总统的政治继承者 ➲ MORE LIKE THIS 20, page R27

,heir ap'parent *noun* (*pl.* **heirs apparent**) **~ (to sth) 1** an HEIR whose legal right to receive sb's property, money or title cannot be taken away because it is impossible for sb with a stronger claim to be born 当然继承人；法定继承人 **2** a person who is expected to take the job of sb when that person leaves （职位的）确定接替者；确定接班者

heir·ess /'eəres; -rəs; *NAmE* 'er-/ *noun* **~ (to sth)** a female heir, especially one who has received or will receive a large amount of money 女继承人；嗣女 HELP Use **an**, not **a**, before **heiress**. * heiress 前不定冠词用 an，不用 a。

heir·loom /'eəluːm; *NAmE* 'erl-/ *noun, adj.*

■ ***noun*** a valuable object that has belonged to the same family for many years 传家宝；世代相传之物：*a family heirloom* 传家宝 HELP Use **an**, not **a**, before **heirloom**. * heirloom 前不定冠词用 an，不用 a。

■ ***adj.*** [only before noun] (*NAmE*) **heirloom** plants are varieties which were commonly grown in the past but are no longer grown as commercial crops （植物）原种的（通常指过去大量种植，但已不再作为经济作物而种植的植物）

,heir pre'sumptive *noun* (*pl.* **heirs presumptive**) an HEIR who may lose his or her legal right to receive sb's property, money or title if sb with a stronger claim is born 假定继承人（其继承权会因有血统更近的继承人出生而丧失）

heist /haɪst/ *noun, verb*

■ ***noun*** (*informal, especially NAmE*) an act of stealing sth valuable from a shop/store or bank （对商店、银行贵重物、钱的）盗窃 SYN **robbery**：*a bank heist* 银行盗窃案

■ ***verb* ~ sth** (*informal, especially NAmE*) to steal sth valuable from a shop/store or bank （在商店、银行）盗窃（贵重物品）

Hej·ira = HEGIRA

held PAST TENSE, PAST PART. OF HOLD

hel·ic·al /'helɪkl; 'hiːl-/ *adj.* (*specialist*) like a HELIX 螺旋的；螺旋形的

heli·cop·ter /'helɪkɒptə(r); *NAmE* -kɑːp-/ (*also informal* **cop·ter, chop·per**) *noun* an aircraft without wings that has large blades on top that go round. It can fly straight up from the ground and can also stay in one position in the air. 直升机：*He was rushed to the hospital* ***by helicopter.*** 他由直升机火速送到医院。◇ *a police helicopter* 警用直升机 ◇ *a helicopter pilot* 直升机驾驶员 ➲ WORDFINDER NOTE AT AIRCRAFT ➲ VISUAL VOCAB PAGE V57

'helicopter parent *noun* a parent who pays extremely close attention to their child's education, problems, etc. and often makes decisions for the child 直升机父母（对孩子的成长教育极其关注，经常代孩子做决定）

'helicopter view *noun* (*business* 商) a broad general view or description of a problem （对问题的）概览，通观，通盘检视 SYN **overview**

he·lio·cen·tric /,hiːliə'sentrɪk/ *adj.* (*astronomy* 天) with the sun as the centre 日心的：*the heliocentric model of the solar system* 太阳系的日心模型

he·lio·graph /'hiːliəgrɑːf; *NAmE* -græf/ *noun* **1** a device which gives signals by reflecting flashes of light from the sun 日光反射信号器；日光仪 **2** (*also* **he·lio·gram** /'hiːliəgræm/) a message which is sent using signals from a heliograph 日光反射信号 **3** a special camera which takes photographs of the sun （拍摄太阳用的）太阳照相仪

he·lio·trope /'hiːliətrəʊp; *NAmE* -troʊp/ *noun* **1** [C, U] a garden plant with pale purple flowers with a sweet smell 天芥菜（开芳香淡紫色花） **2** [U] a pale purple colour 淡紫色

heli·pad /'helipæd/ (*also* **'helicopter pad**) *noun* a small area where HELICOPTERS can take off and land 直升机停机坪

heli·port /'helipɔːt; *NAmE* -pɔːrt/ *noun* a place where HELICOPTERS take off and land 直升机机场

heli-skiing /'heli skiːɪŋ/ *noun* [U] the sport of flying in a HELICOPTER to a place where there is a lot of snow on a mountain in order to SKI there 直升机滑雪

he·lium /'hiːliəm/ *noun* [U] (*symb.* **He**) a chemical element. Helium is a very light gas that does not burn, often used to fill BALLOONS and to freeze food. 氦；氦气

helix /'hiːlɪks/ *noun* (*pl.* **heli·ces** /'hiːlɪsiːz/) a shape like a SPIRAL or a line curved around a CYLINDER or CONE 螺旋（形）➲ SEE ALSO DOUBLE HELIX

helix 螺旋（形）

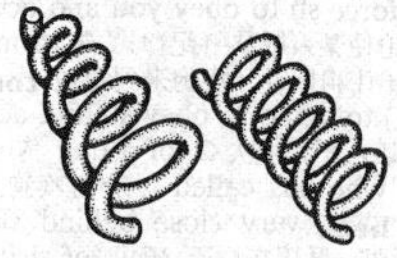

hell 🔑 /hel/ *noun* **1** 🔑[sing.] (*usually* **Hell**) (used without *a* or *the* 不与 a 或 the 连用) in some religions, the place believed to be the home of DEVILS and where bad people go after death 地狱 **2** 🔑[U, sing.] a very unpleasant experience or situation in which people suffer very much 苦难的经历；悲惨的境况：*The last three months have been hell.* 过去的三个月真受罪。◇ *He went* **through hell** *during the trial.* 审讯期间他吃尽了苦头。◇ *Her parents made her life hell.* 她的父母使她生活得很痛苦。◇ *Being totally alone is my idea of* **hell on earth**. 完全的孤独对我而言就是置身人间地狱。 **3** 🔑[U] a swear word that some people use when they are annoyed or surprised or to emphasize sth. Its use is offensive to some people.（有人认为含冒犯意）该死，见鬼：*Oh hell, I've burned the pan.* 真该死，我把锅烧煳了。◇ *What the hell do you think you are doing?* 你到底知不知道自己在干什么？◇ *Go to hell!* 去死吧！◇ *I can't really afford it, but, what the hell* (= it doesn't matter), *I'll get it anyway.* 实在说我是买不起，但管它呢，无论如何我买定了。◇ *He's as guilty as hell.* 他罪孽深重。◇ (*NAmE*) *'Do you understand?' 'Hell, no. I don't.'* "你懂了吗？""懂个鬼。我根本不懂。"

IDM **all 'hell broke loose** (*informal*) suddenly there was a lot of noise, arguing, fighting or confusion 突然喧闹（或争辩、打斗）起来；顿时乱作一团：*There was a loud bang and then all hell broke loose.* 一声巨响之后顿时一片混乱。 **beat/kick (the) 'hell out of sb/sth | knock 'hell out of sb/sth** (*informal*) to hit sb/sth very hard 猛击；狠打：*He was a dirty player and loved to kick hell out of the opposition.* 他是个不讲体育道德的球员，喜欢猛力冲撞对方。 **(just) for the 'hell of it** (*informal*) just for fun; for no real reason 只是闹着玩；没有真正动机：*They stole the car just for the hell of it.* 他们偷这辆汽车只是为了寻求刺激。 **from 'hell** (*informal*) used to describe a very unpleasant person or thing; the worst that you can imagine 十分讨厌；最坏：*They are the neighbours from hell.* 这些邻居太可恶了。 **get the hell 'out (of...)** (*informal*) to leave a place very quickly 迅速离开：*Let's get the hell out of here.* 我们马上离开这里吧。 **give sb 'hell** (*informal*) **1** to make life unpleasant for sb 让某人受罪；使某人不好受：*He used to give his mother hell when he was a teenager.* 他十几岁时常常给他母亲惹麻烦。◇ *My new shoes are giving me hell* (= are hurting me). 我的新鞋磨得我脚疼死了。 **2** to shout at or speak angrily to sb 呵斥；申斥：*Dad will give us hell when he sees that mess.* 爸爸要是看见那乱糟糟的样子会骂我们的。 **go to hell in a 'handbasket** (*NAmE, informal*) = GO TO THE DOGS **hell for 'leather** (*old-fashioned, BrE, informal*) as quickly as possible 尽快：*to ride hell for leather* 拼命快骑 **hell hath no 'fury (like a woman 'scorned)** used to refer to sb, usually a woman, who has reacted very angrily to sth, especially the fact that her husband or lover has been UNFAITHFUL（尤指女人因丈夫或情人不忠而）大发雷霆；醋劲大发 **(come) hell or high 'water** despite any difficulties 无论有什么困难：*I was determined to go, come hell or high water.* 我决心要去，不管有什么困难。 **Hell's 'teeth** (*old-fashioned, BrE, informal*) used to express anger or surprise （表示气愤或吃惊）可恶，天哪 **like 'hell 1** (*informal*) used for emphasis 非常；极其：*She worked like hell for her exams.* 她为了考试而拼命复习。◇ *My broken finger hurt like hell.* 我的手指骨折，痛得要命。 **2** (*informal*) used when you are refusing permission or saying that sth is not true 绝不；不对：*'I'm coming with you.' 'Like hell you are* (= you certainly are not).' "我要和你一起去。""鬼才信呢。" **a/one hell of a... | a/one helluva...** /'heləvə/ (*slang*) used to give emphasis to what a person is saying 极其；非常：*The firm was in a hell of a mess when he took over.* 他接手时公司一团糟。◇ *It must have been one hell of a party.* 那肯定是一次很棒的聚会。◇ *That's one helluva big house you've got.* 你的房子真是大极了。 **play (merry) 'hell with sth/sb** (*BrE, informal*) to affect sth/sb badly 对…造成严重影响；严重损害… **scare, annoy, etc. the 'hell out of sb** (*informal*) to scare, annoy, etc. sb very much 使某人十分恐惧（或恼怒等） **to 'hell and back** (*informal*) used to say that sb has been through a difficult situation 经历过困境；历劫归来：*We'd been to hell and back together and we were still good friends.* 我们曾经患难与共，现在依然是好友。 **to 'hell with sb/sth** (*informal*) used to express anger or dislike and to say that you no longer care about sb/sth and will take no notice of them （表示愤怒或厌恶，不再在乎）见鬼去吧，随便：*'To hell with him,' she thought, 'I'm leaving.'* "让他见鬼去吧，"她想，"我走了。" ➲ MORE AT BAT *n.*, BUG *v.*, CAT, GET, HOPE *n.*, PAY *v.*, RAISE *v.*, ROAD, SNOWBALL *n.*

he'll /hi:l/ *short form* he will

hell-'bent *adj.* **~ on sth/on doing sth** determined to do sth even though the results may be bad 不顾一切：*He seems hell-bent on drinking himself to death.* 他一个劲地喝酒，似乎命都不要了。

hel·le·bore /'helɪbɔ:(r)/ *noun* a poisonous plant with divided leaves and large green, white or purple flowers 鹿食草（有毒）

Hel·lene /'heli:n/ *noun* a person from Greece, especially ancient Greece 希腊人；（尤指）古希腊人

Hel·len·ic /he'lenɪk; -'li:n-/ *adj.* of or connected with ancient or modern Greece 希腊的；古希腊的

Hel·len·is·tic /ˌhelɪ'nɪstɪk/ *adj.* of or connected with the Greek history, language and culture of the 4th–1st centuries BC （公元前 4 至前 1 世纪）希腊化（时期）的

hell·fire /'helfaɪə(r)/ *noun* [U] the fires which are believed by some religious people to burn in hell, where bad people go to be punished after they die 地狱之火

hell·hole /'helhəʊl; *NAmE* -hoʊl/ *noun* (*informal*) a very unpleasant place 非常讨厌的地方

hel·lion /'heliən/ *noun* (*NAmE*) a badly behaved child who annoys other people 调皮捣蛋的孩子

hell·ish /'helɪʃ/ *adj.* (*informal, especially BrE*) extremely unpleasant 极不愉快的

hello 🔑 (*also* **hullo** *especially in BrE*) (*BrE also* **hallo**) /hə'ləʊ; *NAmE* hə'loʊ/ *exclamation, noun* (*pl.* **-os**) **1** 🔑 used as a GREETING when you meet sb, when you answer the

▼ MORE ABOUT ... 补充说明

greetings 打招呼

- **Hello** is the most usual word and is used in all situations, including answering the telephone. * Hello 最为常用，用于所有场合，包括接电话。
- **Hi** is more informal and is now very common. * Hi 较非正式，现在使用很普遍。
- **How are you?** or **How are you doing?** (*very informal*) often follow **Hello** and **Hi**. * How are you? 或 How are you doing?（非常口语化）常用于 Hello 和 Hi 之后：*'Hello, Mark.' 'Oh, hi, Kathy! How are you?'* "马克，你好。""噢，凯西，你好！最近好吗？"
- **Good morning** is often used by members of a family or people who work together when they see each other for the first time in the day. It can also be used in formal situations and on the telephone. In informal speech, people may just say **Morning**. * Good morning 常在家庭成员或同事之间一天中第一次见面时说，亦可用于正式场合和电话中。在非正式谈话中，可只说 Morning。
- **Good afternoon** and **Good evening** are much less common. **Good night** is not used to greet somebody, but only to say goodbye late in the evening or when you are going to bed. * Good afternoon 和 Good evening 少用得多。Good night 只在晚上说再见或上床睡觉前说，不用以打招呼。
- If you are meeting someone for the first time, you can say **Pleased to meet you** or **Nice to meet you** (*less formal*). Some people use **How do you do?** in formal situations. The correct reply to this is **How do you do?** 第一次与人见面时可说 Pleased to meet you 或 Nice to meet you（较非正式）。在正式场合有些人用 How do you do? 正确的回答是 How do you do?。

telephone or when you want to attract sb's attention（用于问候、接电话或引起注意）哈啰，喂，你好：*Hello John, how are you?* 哈啰，约翰，你好吗？◇ *Hello, is there anybody there?* 喂，那里有人吗？◇ ***Say hello** to Liz for me.* 替我向利兹问好。◇ *They exchanged hellos* (= said hello to each other) *and forced smiles.* 他们相互打个招呼，勉强笑笑。 **2** (*BrE*) used to show that you are surprised by sth（表示惊讶）嘿：*Hello, hello, what's going on here?* 嘿，嘿，这是在干吗？ **3** (*informal*) used to show that you think sb has said sth stupid or is not paying attention（认为别人说了蠢话或分心）喂，嘿：*Hello? You didn't really mean that, did you?* 嘿？你不会真是那个意思吧？◇ *I'm like, 'Hello! Did you even listen?'* 我说："嘿！你到底有没有听我说话？" ➲ SEE ALSO GOLDEN HELLO

hell·rais·er /ˈhelreɪzə(r)/ *noun* a person who causes trouble by behaving loudly and often violently, especially when they have drunk too much alcohol 吵闹捣蛋的人；胡打瞎闹的人；（尤指）要酒疯的人

ˌHell's ˈAngel *noun* a member of a group of people, usually men, who ride powerful motorcycles, wear leather clothes and used to be known for their wild and violent behaviour 地狱天使（穿皮衣、骑大马力摩托车横冲直撞，通常为男性）

hel·luva ➲ HELL

helm /helm/ *noun* a handle or wheel used for steering a boat or ship 舵柄；舵轮 ➲ COMPARE TILLER

IDM **at the ˈhelm 1** in charge of an organization, project, etc. 负责；掌管 **2** steering a boat or ship 掌舵 **take the ˈhelm 1** to take charge of an organization, project, etc. 担任领导人；掌管 **2** to begin steering a boat or ship 开始掌舵

hel·met /ˈhelmɪt/ *noun* a type of hard hat that protects the head, worn, for example, by a police officer, a soldier or a person playing some sports 头盔；防护帽 ➲ VISUAL VOCAB PAGES V48, V52, V55 ➲ SEE ALSO CRASH HELMET

hel·met·ed /ˈhelmɪtɪd/ *adj.* [only before noun] wearing a helmet 戴着头盔（或防护帽）的

helms·man /ˈhelmzmən/ *noun* (*pl.* **-men** /-mən/) a person who steers a boat or ship 舵手

help 🔑 /help/ *verb, noun*

■ *verb*

• **MAKE EASIER/BETTER** 使更容易 / 更好 **1** 🔑 [I, T] to make it easier or possible for sb to do sth by doing sth for them or by giving them sth that they need 帮助；协助；援助：*Help, I'm stuck!* 救命，我被卡住了！◇ **~ with sth** *He always helps with the housework.* 他总是帮着做家务。◇ **~ sb** *We must all try and help each other.* 我们都必须努力互相帮助。◇ **~ sb with sth** *Jo will help us with some of the organization.* 乔将帮我们做一部分组织工作。◇ **~ (sb) in doing sth** *I need contacts that could help in finding a job.* 我需要能帮我找到工作的社会关系。◇ **~ sb (to) do sth** *The college's aim is to help students (to) achieve their aspirations.* 大学的目标是帮助学生实现他们的抱负。◇ *This charity aims to help people (to) help themselves.* 这个慈善机构的宗旨是帮助人自力更生。◇ *Come and help me lift this box.* 来帮我抬这个箱子。◇ **~ (to) do sth** *She helped (to) organize the party.* 她协助筹备了晚会。 HELP In verb patterns with a **to** infinitive, the 'to' is often left out, especially in informal or spoken English. 带 to 的不定式动词结构常省略 to，非正式英语和英语口语中尤其如此。 ➲ EXPRESS YOURSELF AT SHALL **2** 🔑 [I, T] to improve a situation; to make it easier for sth to happen 改善状况；促进；促使：***It helped** being able to talk about it.* 能谈谈这件事很有好处。◇ **~ sth** *It doesn't really **help matters** knowing that everyone is talking about us.* 知道大家都在议论我们也于事无补。◇ **~ (to) do sth** *This should help (to) reduce the pain.* 这个应有助于减轻痛楚。

• **SB TO MOVE** 移动某人 **3** 🔑 [T] **~ sb + adv./prep.** to help sb move by letting them lean on you, guiding them, etc. 搀扶；带领：*She helped him to his feet.* 她扶他站了起来。◇ *We were helped ashore by local people.* 我们被当地人救上岸。

• **GIVE FOOD/DRINK** 给食物 / 饮料 **4** 🔑 [T] to give yourself/sb food, drinks, etc. 为（自己或某人）取用：**~ yourself** *If you want another drink, just help yourself.* 你要是想再喝一杯就请自便。◇ **~ yourself/sb to sth** *Can I help you to some more salad?* 再给你来点色拉好吗？

• **STEAL** 偷窃 **5** [T] **~ yourself to sth** (*informal, disapproving*) to take sth without permission 擅自拿走；窃取 SYN **steal**：*He'd been helping himself to the money in the cash register.* 他一直在偷现金出纳机中的钱。

IDM **sb cannot ˈhelp (doing) sth | sb cannot ˈhelp but do sth** 🔑 used to say that it is impossible to prevent or avoid sth 某人忍不住（或无法抑制）做某事；不可能避免某事：*I can't help thinking he knows more than he has told us.* 我总觉得他没把他知道的事全告诉我们。◇ *She couldn't help but wonder what he was thinking.* 她不禁琢磨着他在想些什么。◇ ***It couldn't be helped*** (= there was no way of avoiding it and we must accept it). 这是不可避免的。◇ *I always end up having an argument with her, I don't know why, I just **can't help it**.* 我总是和她意见不合，闹得不欢而散，我不知道为什么，我就是忍不住。◇ *I couldn't help it if the bus was late* (= it wasn't my fault). 公共汽车晚点了，我没办法。◇ *She burst out laughing—she **couldn't help herself*** (= couldn't stop herself). 她突然大笑起来，不能自已。 **give/lend a ˌhelping ˈhand** to help sb 帮助；伸出援助之手 **God/Heaven ˈhelp sb** (*informal*) used to say that you are afraid sb will be in danger or that sth bad will happen to them（表示担心某人将有危险或有难）：*God help us if this doesn't work.* 如果这个行不通，那就要靠上帝了。 HELP Some people find this use offensive. 有人认为此用法含冒犯意。 **so ˈhelp me (God)** used to swear that what you are saying is true, especially in a court of law 我发誓，上帝作证（尤用于法庭）

PHR V **ˌhelp sb ˈoff/ˈon with sth** to help sb take off/put on a piece of clothing 帮某人脱（或穿）衣服：*Let me help you off with your coat.* 我来帮你脱大衣吧。 **ˌhelp ˈout | ˌhelp sb↔ˈout** 🔑 to help sb, especially in a difficult situation 帮助某人摆脱（困境）：*He's always willing to help out.* 他总是急人之难。◇ *When I bought the house, my sister helped me out with a loan.* 我买这所房子时，我姐姐借给了我一笔钱解了急。

▼ **EXPRESS YOURSELF 情景表达**

Asking for help 请求帮助

If you need help, people are more likely to react favourably if you ask politely. 礼貌地求助更有可能让对方答应帮忙：

- ***Could you possibly help me?*** 请问您能帮帮我吗？
- ***I wonder if you could** give me a hand?* 不知道您能否帮我一个忙？
- ***Would you mind** opening the door for me?* 请你帮我开开门好吗？
- ***I wonder if you'd mind** taking a picture of us?* 不知道您是否愿意给我们拍张照片？
- ***Could I ask you to** keep an eye on my luggage for a moment?* 请你帮我照看一下行李好吗？

Responses 回应：

- ***Yes, of course.*** 行，当然可以。
- ***I'm sorry**, I'm in a hurry.* 对不起，我要赶时间。
- ***Sure.*** (*informal* or *NAmE*) 没问题。

■ *noun*

• **MAKING EASIER/BETTER** 使较容易 / 较好 **1** 🔑 [U] the act of helping sb to do sth 帮助；协助；援助：*Thank you for all your help.* 感谢你的一切帮助。◇ **~ (with sth)** *Do you need any help with that?* 这事你需要帮忙吗？◇ *Can I be **of any help** to you?* 我能帮你什么忙吗？◇ *None of this would have been possible without their help.* 如果没有他们的协助，这事没有一样能办成。◇ *She stopped smoking **with the help** of her family and friends.* 她在家人和朋友的帮助下戒了烟。

• **ADVICE/MONEY** 忠告；钱 **2** 🔑 [U] advice, money, etc. that is given to sb in order to solve their problems 有助益的

东西（如忠告、钱等）：*to **seek financial/legal/medical, etc. help*** 寻求经济、法律、医疗等援助 ◊ **~ in doing sth** *The organization offers practical help in dealing with paperwork.* 这个机构提供文件处理方面的实际帮助。◊ **~ with sth** *You should qualify for help with the costs of running a car.* 你应该符合条件得到养车补助。◊ ***a help key/screen*** (= a function on a computer that provides information on how to use the computer) 帮助键 / 屏幕（计算机中提供计算机使用信息的功能）

- **BEING USEFUL** 有用 **3** [U] the fact of being useful 有用：*The map wasn't **much help**.* 这张地图没多大用处。◊ ***With the help of** a ladder, neighbours were able to rescue the children from the blaze.* 邻居们借助一把梯子把孩子们从大火中救了出来。◊ *Just shouting at him isn't going to be a lot of help.* 光是对他大喊大叫不会有多大用处。
- **FOR SB IN DANGER** 对处于危险中的人 **4** [U] the act of helping sb who is in danger 救助：*Quick, get help!* 快，找人援救！◊ *She screamed for help.* 她高声喊救命。
- **PERSON/THING** 人；事物 **5** [sing.] **a ~ (to sb)** a person or thing that helps sb 有帮助的人（或事物）：*She was more of a hindrance than a help.* 她非但没帮上忙，反而碍事。◊ *Your advice was a big help.* 你的建议很有帮助。◊ (*ironic*) *You're a great help, I must say!* 我得说，你可没少帮忙！
- **IN HOUSE** 住宅 **6 the help** [U+sing./pl. v.] (*especially NAmE*) the person or people who are employed by sb to clean their house, etc. 仆人 ➲ SEE ALSO HOME HELP

IDM **there is no 'help for it** (*especially BrE*) it is not possible to avoid doing sth that may harm sb in some way 没办法；别无选择：*There's no help for it. We shall have to call the police.* 没法子了。我们只得叫警察了。

'help desk *noun* a service, usually in a business company, that gives people information and help, especially if they are having problems with a computer（商业公司的）咨询服务，咨询台；（尤指有关电脑问题的）技术支持服务

help·er /ˈhelpə(r)/ *noun* a person who helps sb to do sth 帮手；助手：*a willing helper* 自愿帮忙者

help·ful /ˈhelpfl/ *adj.* **1** able to improve a particular situation 有用的；有益的；有帮助的 SYN **useful**: ***helpful advice/information/suggestions*** 有用的劝告 / 信息 / 建议 ◊ *Sorry I can't be more helpful.* 对不起，我帮不上更多的忙。◊ **~ (for sb) (to do sth)** *It would be helpful for me to see the damage for myself.* 要能亲眼看看造成的破坏会对我有所帮助。◊ **~ in doing sth** *Role-play is helpful in developing communication skills.* 角色扮演有助于提高沟通技巧。◊ **~ to sb** *The booklet should be very helpful to parents of disabled children.* 这本小册子对于残疾儿童的父母会很有用。 **2** (of a person 人) willing to help sb 愿意帮忙的：*I called the police but they weren't very helpful.* 我叫了警察，但他们不太肯帮忙。◊ *The staff couldn't have been more helpful.* 职员们十分愿意帮忙。 OPP **unhelpful** ▸ **help·ful·ly** /-fəli/ *adv.*：*She helpfully suggested that I try the local library.* 她很热心地建议我试试本地的图书馆。 **help·ful·ness** *noun* [U]

help·ing /ˈhelpɪŋ/ *noun* **~ (of sth)** an amount of food given to sb at a meal（进餐时的）一份食物，一客食物 SYN **serving**: ***a small/generous helping*** 一小份 / 一大份食物 ◊ *We all had a **second helping** of pie.* 我们又都吃了一份馅饼。

help·less /ˈhelpləs/ *adj.* **1** unable to take care of yourself or do things without the help of other people 无自理能力的；不能自立的；无助的：*the helpless victims of war* 无助的战争受害者 ◊ *a helpless gesture/look* 无可奈何的姿势 / 表情 ◊ *He lay helpless on the floor.* 他无助地躺在地板上。◊ *It's natural to feel helpless against such abuse.* 对这种虐待感到无能为力是自然的。◊ *The worst part is being helpless to change anything.* 最糟糕的是没有能力改变任何事情。 **2** unable to control a strong feeling 无法抑制的：***helpless panic/rage*** 抑制不住的恐慌 / 愤怒 ◊ **~ with sth** *The audience was **helpless with laughter**.* 观众情不自禁地大笑。 ▸ **help·less·ly** *adv.*：*They watched helplessly as their home went up in flames.* 他们无奈地看着自己的家被大火吞没。 **help·less·ness** *noun* [U]: ***a feeling/sense of helplessness*** 无能为力的感觉

help·line /ˈhelplaɪn/ *noun* a telephone service that provides advice and information about particular problems 服务热线（提供咨询和信息的电话）

help·mate /ˈhelpmeɪt/ (*also* **help·meet** /ˈhelpmiːt/) *noun* (*formal* or *literary*) a helpful partner, especially a wife 得力的伴侣；（尤指）贤内助

helter-skelter /ˌheltə ˈskeltə(r); *NAmE* ˌheltər/ *noun, adj.*

- ***noun*** (*BrE*) a tall tower at a FAIRGROUND that has a path twisting around the outside of it from the top to the bottom for people to slide down（游乐场的）螺旋滑梯
- ***adj.*** [only before noun] done in a hurry and in a way that lacks organization 忙乱的；仓促的：*a helter-skelter dash to meet the deadline* 最后期限到来前的匆忙赶工 ▸ **helter-skelter** *adv.* ➲ MORE LIKE THIS 11, page R26

hem /hem/ *noun, verb*

- ***noun*** the edge of a piece of cloth that has been folded over and sewn, especially on a piece of clothing（衣服等的）褶边，卷边：*to take up the hem of a dress* (= to make the dress shorter) 把连衣裙改短 ➲ WORDFINDER NOTE AT SEW
- ***verb*** (-mm-) **~ sth** to make a hem on sth（给某物）缝边，镶边：*to hem a skirt* 给裙子缝边

IDM **ˌhem and 'haw** (*NAmE*) (*BrE* **ˌhum and 'haw**) (*informal*) to take a long time to make a decision or before you say sth 犹豫不决；支支吾吾；嗯嗯呃呃 ➲ MORE LIKE THIS 13, page R26

PHR V **ˌhem sb/sth↔'in** to surround sb/sth so that they cannot move or grow easily 包围，限制（某人或某事物） SYN **hedge sb/sth↔in**: *The village is hemmed in on all sides by mountains.* 村子四面环山。◊ (*figurative*) *She felt hemmed in by all their petty rules and regulations.* 她觉得受到他们那些琐碎的规章制度的束缚。

'he-man *noun* (*pl.* **he-men**) (*often humorous*) a strong man with big muscles, especially one who likes to show other people how strong he is 强健的男子（尤指好显示其体魄者）

hema·tite (*NAmE*) (*BrE* **haem·atite**) /ˈhiːmətaɪt/ *noun* [U] (*geology* 地) a dark red rock from which iron is obtained 赤铁矿

hema·tol·ogy (*NAmE*) (*BrE* **haema·tol·ogy**) /ˌhiːməˈtɒlədʒi; *NAmE* -ˈtɑːl-/ *noun* [U] the scientific study of the blood and its diseases 血液学 ▸ **hema·to·logic·al** (*NAmE*) (*BrE* **haem-**) /ˌhiːmətəˈlɒdʒɪkl; *NAmE* -ˈlɑːdʒ-/ *adj.* **hema·tolo·gist** (*NAmE*) (*BrE* **haem-**) /ˌhiːməˈtɒlədʒɪst; *NAmE* -ˈtɑːl-/ *noun*

hema·toma (*NAmE*) (*BrE* **haem·atoma**) /ˌhiːməˈtəʊmə; *NAmE* -ˈtoʊmə/ *noun* (*medical* 医) a swollen area on the body consisting of blood that has become thick 血肿

hemi·sphere /ˈhemɪsfɪə(r); *NAmE* -sfɪr/ *noun* **1** one half of the earth, especially the half above or below the EQUATOR（地球的）半球；（尤指）北半球，南半球：*the **northern/southern hemisphere*** 北半球；南半球 ➲ WORDFINDER NOTE AT EARTH **2** either half of the brain（大脑的）半球：*the **left/right cerebral hemisphere*** 大脑左半球 / 右半球 **3** one half of a SPHERE (= a round solid object)（球体的）半球

hemi·spher·ic·al /ˌhemɪˈsferɪkl; *NAmE also* -ˈsfɪr-/ *adj.* shaped like a hemisphere 半球形的

hem·line /ˈhemlaɪn/ *noun* the bottom edge of a dress or skirt; the length of a dress or skirt（衣裙的）底边，下摆；衣裙长度：*Shorter hemlines are back in this season.* 本季又重新时兴较短的衣裙。

hem·lock /ˈhemlɒk; *NAmE* -lɑːk/ *noun* **1** [U, C] a poisonous plant with a mass of small white flowers growing at the end of a STEM that is covered in spots 毒芹 **2** [U] poison made from hemlock 从毒芹提炼的毒药

hemo- (*NAmE*) (*BrE* **haemo-**) /ˈhiːməʊ; *NAmE* -moʊ/ *combining form* (in nouns and adjectives 构成名词和形容词) connected with blood（有关）血液的：*hemophilia* 血友病

H

hemp /hemp/ *noun* [U] a plant which is used for making rope and cloth, and also to make the drug CANNABIS 大麻

hen /hen/ *noun* **1** a female chicken, often kept for its eggs or meat 母鸡：*a small flock of laying hens* 一小群下蛋的母鸡 ◇ *battery hens* 层架式鸡笼饲养的母鸡 **2** (especially in compounds 尤用于构成复合词) any female bird 雌禽：*a hen pheasant* 雌雉 ➲ COMPARE COCK *n.* (1), (2) ➲ SEE ALSO MOORHEN

hence 🔑 AW /hens/ *adv.* (*formal*) for this reason 因此；由此：*We suspect they are trying to hide something, hence the need for an independent inquiry.* 我们怀疑他们在企图隐瞒什么事，因此有必要进行独立调查。➲ LANGUAGE BANK AT THEREFORE

IDM ... **days, weeks, etc. 'hence** (*formal*) a number of days, etc. from now （从现在开始）…天、星期等之后：*The true consequences will only be known several years hence.* 真正的后果只有在几年之后才能知道。

hence·forth /ˌhensˈfɔːθ; *NAmE* -ˈfɔːrθ/ (*also* **hence·for·ward** /ˌhensˈfɔːwəd; *NAmE* -ˈfɔːrwərd/) *adv.* (*formal*) starting from a particular time and at all times in the future 此后；从此以后：*Friday 31 July 1925 henceforth became known as 'Red Friday'.* * 1925 年 7 月 31 日这个星期五从此以后就称为"红色星期五"。

hench·man /ˈhentʃmən/ *noun* (*pl.* **-men** /-mən/) a faithful supporter of a powerful person, for example a political leader or criminal, who is prepared to use violence or become involved in illegal activities to help that person （政治领袖人物或罪犯等的）忠实支持者，亲信，心腹，追随者

hen·deca·syl·lable /ˌhendekəˈsɪləbl/ *noun* (*specialist*) a line of poetry with eleven syllables 十一音节的诗句 ▶ **hen·deca·syl·lab·ic** /ˌhendekəsɪˈlæbɪk/ *adj.*

hen·dia·dys /henˈdaɪədɪs/ *noun* [U] (*grammar* 语法) the use of two words joined with 'and' to express a single idea, for example 'nice and warm' 二词一义，重言法（用 and 连接两个词表达一个意思，如 nice and warm）

henge /hendʒ/ *noun* a circle of large vertical wooden or stone objects built in PREHISTORIC times （史前的）环状直立木（或石）结构

henna /ˈhenə/ *noun* [U] a reddish-brown DYE (= a substance used to change the colour of sth), used especially on the hair and skin 散沫花染剂（棕红色，尤用于染发和涂饰皮肤）

'hen party (*also* **'hen night**) *noun* (*BrE, informal*) a party for women only, especially one held for a woman who will soon get married 准新娘聚会（只有女性参与）➲ COMPARE STAG NIGHT

hen·pecked /ˈhenpekt/ *adj.* (*informal*) a man who people say is **henpecked** has a wife who is always telling him what to do, and is too weak to disagree with her 怕老婆的；惧内的

henry /ˈhenri/ *noun* (*pl.* **hen·ries** or **henrys**) (*abbr.* **H**) a unit for measuring the INDUCTANCE in an electric CIRCUIT 亨（利）（电感单位）

hep·at·ic /hɪˈpætɪk/ *adj.* (*biology* 生) connected with the LIVER 肝的

hepa·titis /ˌhepəˈtaɪtɪs/ *noun* [U] a serious disease of the LIVER. There are three main forms: **hepatitis A** (the least serious, caused by infected food), **hepatitis B** and **hepatitis C** (both very serious and caused by infected blood). 肝炎

hepta·gon /ˈheptəgən; *NAmE* -gɑːn/ *noun* (*geometry* 几何) a flat shape with seven straight sides and seven angles 七边形；七角形 ▶ **hept·agon·al** /hepˈtægənl/ *adj.*

hept·ath·lon /hepˈtæθlən/ *noun* a sporting event, especially one for women, in which people compete in seven different sports （尤指女子）七项全能（运动）➲ COMPARE BIATHLON, DECATHLON, PENTATHLON, TRIATHLON

her 🔑 /hə(r); ɜː(r); ə(r); *strong form* hɜː(r)/ *pron., det.*

▪ *pron.* 🔑 used as the object of a verb, after the verb *be* or after a preposition to refer to a woman or girl who has already been mentioned or is easily identified （用作动词或介词的宾语，或作表语）她：*We're going to call her Sophie.* 我们将给她起名索菲。◇ *Please give her my regards.* 请代我问候她。◇ *The manager will be free soon—you can wait for her here.* 经理很快就有空了，你可以在这里等她。◇ *That must be her now.* 这会儿一定是她了。➲ COMPARE SHE *pron.* ➲ NOTE AT GENDER

▪ *det.* 🔑 (the possessive form of *she* * she 的所有格形式) of or belonging to a woman or girl who has already been mentioned or is easily identified 她的：*Meg loves her job.* 梅格热爱她的工作。◇ *She broke her leg skiing.* 她滑雪时摔断了腿。➲ SEE ALSO HERS

her·ald /ˈherəld/ *verb, noun*

▪ *verb* (*formal*) **1** ~ **sth** to be a sign that sth is going to happen 是（某事）的前兆；预示：*These talks could herald a new era of peace.* 这些谈判可能预示着新的和平时代的来临。 **2** ~ **sb/sth (as sth)** [often passive] to say in public that sb/sth is good or important 宣称（…是好的或重要的）：*The report is being heralded as a blueprint for the future of transport.* 这份报告被宣称是未来运输的蓝图。

▪ *noun* **1** something that shows that sth else is going to happen soon 预兆：*The government claims that the fall in unemployment is the herald of economic recovery.* 政府宣称失业人数减少是经济复苏的先兆。 **2** (in the past) a person who carried messages from a ruler （旧时的）信使，传令官，使者

her·ald·ry /ˈherəldri/ *noun* [U] the study of the COATS OF ARMS and the history of old families 纹章学 ▶ **her·al·dic** /heˈrældɪk/ *adj.*

herb /hɜːb; *NAmE* ɜːrb; hɜːrb/ *noun* **1** a plant whose leaves, flowers or seeds are used to flavour food, in medicines or for their pleasant smell. PARSLEY, MINT and OREGANO are all herbs. 药草；香草：*a herb garden* 芳草园 ◇ (*NAmE*) *an herb garden* 芳草园 ➲ VISUAL VOCAB PAGE V35 **2** (*specialist*) a plant with a soft STEM that dies down after flowering 草本 ➲ MORE LIKE THIS 20, page R27

herb·aceous /hɜːˈbeɪʃəs; *NAmE* ɜːrˈb-; hɜːrˈb-/ *adj.* (*specialist*) connected with plants that have soft STEMS 草本的：*a herbaceous plant* 草本植物

herˌbaceous 'border *noun* a piece of ground in a garden/yard containing plants that produce flowers every year without being replaced （庭园中种植多年生花草的）花坛

herb·age /ˈhɜːbɪdʒ; *NAmE* ˈɜːrb-; ˈhɜːrb-/ *noun* [U] (*specialist*) plants in general, especially grass that is grown for cows, etc. to eat （统称）草本植物；（尤指）牧草

herb·al /ˈhɜːbl; *NAmE* ˈɜːrbl; ˈhɜːrbl/ *adj., noun*

▪ *adj.* connected with or made from HERBS 药草的；香草的：*herbal medicine/remedies* 草药；草药疗法

▪ *noun* a book about HERBS, especially those used in medicines 草本植物志；（尤指）草药志

herb·al·ism /ˈhɜːblɪzəm; *NAmE* ˈɜːrbl-; ˈhɜːrbl-/ *noun* [U] the medical use of plants, especially as a form of ALTERNATIVE MEDICINE 草药疗法（尤指作为替代疗法）➲ WORDFINDER NOTE AT TREATMENT

herb·al·ist /ˈhɜːbəlɪst; *NAmE* ˈɜːrb-; ˈhɜːrb-/ *noun* a person who grows, sells or uses HERBS for medical purposes 药草栽培者；药草商；草药医生

ˌherbal 'tea *noun* [U, C] a drink made from dried HERBS and hot water 草药茶

herbi·cide /ˈhɜːbɪsaɪd; *NAmE* ˈɜːrb-; ˈhɜːrb-/ *noun* [C, U] a chemical that is poisonous to plants, used to kill plants that are growing where they are not wanted 除莠剂；除草剂 ➲ SEE ALSO INSECTICIDE, PESTICIDE

herbi·vore /ˈhɜːbɪvɔː(r); *NAmE* ˈɜːrb-; ˈhɜːrb-/ *noun* any animal that eats only plants 食草动物；草食动物 ➲ COMPARE CARNIVORE, INSECTIVORE, OMNIVORE, VEGETARIAN ▸ **herb·iv·or·ous** /hɜːˈbɪvərəs; *NAmE* ɜːrˈb-; hɜːrˈb-/ *adj.*：*herbivorous dinosaurs* 食草恐龙

Her·cu·lean /ˌhɜːkjuˈliːən; *NAmE* ˌhɜːrk-/ *adj.* [usually before noun] needing a lot of strength, determination or effort 费力的；需要决心的；艰巨的：*a Herculean task* 艰巨的任务 ➲ MORE LIKE THIS 16, page R27 ORIGIN From the Greek myth in which **Hercules** proved his courage and strength by completing twelve very difficult tasks (called the Labours of Hercules). 源自希腊神话。赫拉克勒斯（Hercules）完成了十二项十分艰巨的任务（"赫拉克勒斯的功绩"），由此证明了他的勇气和力量。

herd /hɜːd; *NAmE* hɜːrd/ *noun, verb*
■ ***noun*** **1** a group of animals of the same type that live and feed together 兽群；牧群：***a herd of cows/deer/elephants*** 一群牛／鹿／象 ◇ *a* ***beef/dairy herd*** 肉牛群；奶牛群 ➲ COMPARE FLOCK *n.* (1) **2** (*usually disapproving*) a large group of people of the same type 人群；芸芸众生：*She pushed her way through a herd of lunchtime drinkers.* 她从一群午餐时饮酒的人中间挤了过去。◇ *the* ***common herd*** (= ordinary people) 普通百姓 ◇ *Why* ***follow the herd*** (= do and think the same as everyone else)? 为什么随大溜呢？ IDM SEE RIDE *v.*
■ ***verb*** **1** [I, T] to move or make sb/sth move in a particular direction （使）向…移动：**+ adv./prep.** *We all herded on to the bus.* 我们全都拥上公共汽车。◇ **~ sb/sth + adv./prep.** *They were herded together into trucks and driven away.* 他们被一起赶上卡车拉走了。 **2** [T] **~ sth** to make animals move together as a group 牧放（牲畜、兽群）：*a shepherd herding his flock* 正在放羊的羊倌
IDM **like herding ˈcats** (*informal*) used to describe a very difficult task, especially one that involves organizing people 如牧猫般困难（形容非常难的任务，尤涉及对人的组织管理）：*Managing a political party is a lot like herding cats.* 管理一个政党很像放牧一群猫，极为困难。

herd·er /ˈhɜːdə(r); *NAmE* ˈhɜːrdər/ *noun* a person whose job is to take care of a group of animals such as sheep and cows in the countryside 牧人；牧工

ˈherd instinct *noun* [sing.] the natural tendency in people or animals to behave or think like other people or animals 群体本能（人或动物在行为或思维上从众的自然趋势）

herds·man /ˈhɜːdzmən; *NAmE* ˈhɜːrd-/ *noun* (*pl.* **-men** /-mən/) a man whose job is to take care of a group of animals such as sheep and cows in the countryside 牧人

here /hɪə(r); *NAmE* hɪr/ *adv., exclamation*
■ ***adv.*** **1** used after a verb or preposition to mean 'in, at or to this position or place' （用于动词或介词之后）在这里，向这里：*I live here.* 我住这儿。◇ *Put the box here.* 把箱子放在这里。◇ *Let's get out of here.* 我们离开这里吧。◇ *Come over here.* 过来吧。 **2** now; at this point 现在；在这一点上：*The countdown to Christmas* ***starts here.*** 现在开始圣诞节倒计时。◇ *Here the speaker paused to have a drink.* 讲到这里，演讲人停下来喝了口水。 **3** used when you are giving or showing sth to sb （给某人东西或指出某物时说）：*Here's the money I promised you.* 这是我答应给你的钱。◇ *Here's a dish that is simple and quick to make.* 这是一道简单易做的菜。◇ *Here is your opportunity.* 你的机会来了。◇ ***Here comes*** *the bus.* 公共汽车来了。◇ *I can't find my keys. Oh,* ***here they are.*** 我找不到我的钥匙。哦，原来在这里。◇ ***Here we are*** (= we've arrived). 我们到了。 **4** **~ to do sth** used to show your role in a situation （表示某人的作用）：*I'm here to help you.* 我是来帮助你的。 **5** (used after a noun, for emphasis 用于名词之后，表示强调)：*My friend here saw it happen.* 我的这位朋友目睹了事情的经过。
IDM **by ˈhere** (*WelshE*) here; to here 在这里；到这里：*Come by here now!* 现在到这儿来！ **ˌhere and ˈthere** in various places 在各处；到处：*Papers were scattered here and there on the floor.* 地板上到处散落着文件。 **ˌhere ˈgoes** (*informal*) used when you are telling people that you are just going to do sth exciting, dangerous, etc. （宣称即将开始令人兴奋或危险的活动）看我的 **here's to sb/sth** used to wish sb health or success, as you lift a glass and drink a TOAST （祝酒词）为…的健康（或胜利）干杯：*Here's to your future happiness!* 为你今后的幸福干杯！ **ˌhere, ˌthere and ˈeverywhere** in many different places; all around 在很多地方；四处 **ˌhere we ˈgo** (*informal*) said when sth is starting to happen （某事）开始了：*'Here we go,' thought Fred, 'she's sure to say something.'* "这就开始了。"弗雷德想，"她肯定有话要说。" **ˌhere we go aˈgain** (*informal*) said when sth is starting to happen again, especially sth bad （尤指坏事）又开始了，又一次发生了 **ˌhere you ˈare** (*informal*) used when you are giving sth to sb 给你：*Here you are. This is what you were asking for.* 给你。这就是你一直要的东西。 **ˌhere you ˈgo** (*informal*) used when you are giving sth to sb 给你：*Here you go. Four copies, is that right?* 给你，四本，对吗？ **neither ˈhere nor ˈthere** not important 不重要 SYN **irrelevant**：*What might have happened is neither here nor there.* 曾经发生过什么事已经都不重要了。➲ MORE AT OUT *adv., prep.*
■ ***exclamation*** **1** (*BrE*) used to attract sb's attention （用以引起注意）喂，嘿：*Here, where are you going with that ladder?* 嘿，你要把梯子搬到哪里？ **2** used when offering sth to sb （主动提议时说）：*Here, let me carry that for you.* 来，让我帮你搬吧。

here·abouts /ˌhɪərəˈbaʊts; *NAmE* ˌhɪr-/ (*NAmE also* **here·about**) *adv.* near this place 在这附近：*There aren't many houses hereabouts.* 这一带房子不多。

here·after /ˌhɪərˈɑːftə(r); *NAmE* ˌhɪrˈæf-/ *adv., noun*
■ ***adv.*** **1** (*also* **here·in·after**) (*law* 律) (in legal documents, etc. 用于法律文件等) in the rest of this document 在本文件其余部分；以下 **2** (*formal*) from this time; in future 此后；今后；将来 ➲ COMPARE THEREAFTER **3** (*formal*) after death 死后：*Do you believe in a life hereafter?* 你相信有来世吗？
■ ***noun*** **the hereafter** [sing.] a life believed to begin after death 死后的生命；阴世

here·by /ˌhɪəˈbaɪ; *NAmE* ˌhɪrˈbaɪ/ *adv.* (in legal documents, etc. 用于法律文件等) as a result of this statement, and in a way that makes sth legal 特此；以此

her·edi·tary /həˈredɪtri; *NAmE* -teri/ *adj.* **1** (especially of illnesses 尤指疾病) given to a child by its parents before it is born 遗传的；遗传性的：***a hereditary illness/disease/condition/problem*** 遗传的疾病／问题 ◇ *Epilepsy is hereditary in her family.* 癫痫是她家族的遗传病。 **2** that is legally given to sb's child, when that person dies 世袭的：*a* ***hereditary title/monarchy*** 世袭的头衔／君主制 **3** holding a rank or title that is hereditary 有世袭身份（或头衔）的：***hereditary peers/rulers*** 世袭的贵族／统治者

her·ed·ity /həˈredəti/ *noun* [U] the process by which mental and physical characteristics are passed by parents to their children; these characteristics in a particular person 遗传（过程）；遗传特征：*the debate over the effects of heredity and environment* 有关遗传与环境影响的辩论

here·in /ˌhɪərˈɪn; *NAmE* ˌhɪrˈɪn/ *adv.* (*formal* or *law* 律) in this place, document, statement or fact 在此处；于此文件（或声明、事实）中：*Neither party is willing to compromise and herein lies the problem.* 双方都不愿意妥协，问题就在这里。

here·in·after /ˌhɪərɪnˈɑːftə(r); *NAmE* ˌhɪrɪnˈæf-/ *adv.* (*law* 律) = HEREAFTER (1)

here·of /ˌhɪərˈɒv; *NAmE* ˌhɪrˈʌv; -ˈɑːv/ *adv.* (*law* 律) of this 关于这个；在本文件中：*a period of 12 months from the date hereof* (= the date of this document) 从本文件日期起的 12 个月的时间

her·esy /ˈherəsi/ *noun* [U, C] (*pl.* **-ies**) **1** a belief or an opinion that is against the principles of a particular religion; the fact of holding such beliefs 宗教异端；信奉邪说：*He was burned at the stake for heresy.* 他因为

信奉异端思想而被以火刑处死。◇ *the heresies of the early Protestants* 早期新教徒的异端邪说 ➲ COLLOCATIONS AT RELIGION **2** a belief or an opinion that disagrees strongly with what most people believe 离经叛道的信念（或观点）：*The idea is heresy to most employees of the firm.* 这种想法有悖于公司大多数员工的意见。

her·et·ic /ˈherətɪk/ *noun* a person who is guilty of heresy 犯异端罪者；离经叛道者 ▶ **her·et·ical** /həˈretɪkl/ *adj.*：*heretical beliefs* 异端信仰

here·to /ˌhɪəˈtuː; *NAmE* ˌhɪrˈtuː/ *adv.* (*law* 律) to this 到此为止；至此；于此

here·to·fore /ˌhɪətuˈfɔː(r); *NAmE* ˌhɪrt-/ *adv.* (*law* 律 or *formal*) before this time 在这之前

here·upon /ˌhɪərəˈpɒn; *NAmE* ˌhɪrəˈpɑːn/ *adv.* (*literary*) after this; as a direct result of this situation 此后；于是；随即

H

here·with /ˌhɪəˈwɪð; -ˈwɪθ; *NAmE* ˌhɪrˈw-/ *adv.* (*formal*) with this letter, book or document 随同此信（或书、文件）：*I enclose herewith a copy of the policy.* 我随信附上一份保险单。

her·it·able /ˈherɪtəbl/ *adj.* (*law* 律) (of property 财产) that can be passed from one member of a family to another 可继承的；可传承的

heri·tage /ˈherɪtɪdʒ/ *noun* [usually sing.] the history, traditions and qualities that a country or society has had for many years and that are considered an important part of its character 遗产（指国家或社会长期形成的历史、传统和特色）：*Spain's rich cultural heritage* 西班牙的丰富文化遗产 ◇ *The building is part of our national heritage.* 这个建筑是我们民族遗产的一部分。

ˈheritage centre *noun* (*BrE*) a place where there are exhibitions that people visit to learn about life in the past 遗产保护中心；文化遗产展览馆

herm·aph·ro·dite /hɜːˈmæfrədaɪt; *NAmE* hɜːrˈm-/ *noun* a person, an animal or a flower that has both male and female sexual organs or characteristics 雌雄同体的人（或动物、植物） ▶ **herm·aph·ro·dite** *adj.*

her·men·eut·ic /ˌhɜːməˈnjuːtɪk; *NAmE* ˌhɜːrməˈnjuːtɪk; -ˈnuː-/ *adj.* (*specialist*) relating to the meaning of written texts （对书面文本）解释的，阐释的；解经的

her·men·eut·ics /ˌhɜːməˈnjuːtɪks; *NAmE* ˌhɜːrməˈnjuːtɪks; -ˈnuː-/ *noun* [pl.] (*specialist*) the area of study that analyses and explains written texts （对书面文本的）解释学，阐释学；解经原则

her·met·ic /hɜːˈmetɪk; *NAmE* hɜːrˈm-/ *adj.* **1** (*specialist*) tightly closed so that no air can escape or enter 密封的；不透气的 SYN **airtight** **2** (*formal, disapproving*) closed and difficult to become a part of 封闭的；不受外界影响的：*the strange, hermetic world of the theatre* 神秘、与世隔绝的戏剧世界 ▶ **her·met·ic·al·ly** /-kli/ *adv.*：*a hermetically sealed container* 密封的容器

her·mit /ˈhɜːmɪt; *NAmE* ˈhɜːrmɪt/ *noun* a person who, usually for religious reasons, lives a very simple life alone and does not meet or talk to other people 隐士；隐修者；遁世者

her·mit·age /ˈhɜːmɪtɪdʒ; *NAmE* ˈhɜːrm-/ *noun* a place where a hermit lives or lived 隐居处；修道院

ˈhermit crab *noun* a CRAB (= a sea creature with eight legs and, usually, a hard shell) that has no shell of its own and has to use the empty shells of other sea creatures 寄居蟹

her·nia /ˈhɜːniə; *NAmE* ˈhɜːrniə/ *noun* [C, U] a medical condition in which part of an organ is pushed through a weak part of the body wall 疝；突出

hero /ˈhɪərəʊ; *NAmE* ˈhɪroʊ; ˈhiː-/ *noun* (*pl.* **-oes**) **1** a person, especially a man, who is admired by many people for doing sth brave or good 英雄，豪杰（尤指男性）：*a* ***war hero*** (= sb who was very brave during a war) 战斗英雄 ◇ *The Olympic team were given* ***a hero's welcome*** *on their return home.* 奥运代表队回国时受到了英雄般的欢迎。◇ *one of the country's* ***national heroes*** 这个国家的一位民族英雄 **2** the main male character in a story, novel, film/movie, etc. （故事、小说、电影等的）男主人公，男主角：*The hero of the novel is a ten-year old boy.* 这部小说的主人公是个十岁的男孩。 ➲ WORDFINDER NOTE AT CHARACTER **3** a person, especially a man, that you admire because of a particular quality or skill that they have 崇拜的对象，偶像（尤指男性）：*my childhood hero* 我孩提时的偶像 **4** (*NAmE*) = SUBMARINE (2) ➲ SEE ALSO HEROINE

hero·ic /həˈrəʊɪk; *NAmE* -ˈroʊ-/ *adj.* **1** showing extreme courage and admired by many people 英勇的；英雄的 SYN **courageous**：*a heroic figure* 英雄人物 ◇ *Rescuers made* ***heroic efforts*** *to save the crew.* 救援人员不畏艰险努力营救全体船员。**2** showing great determination to succeed or to achieve sth, especially sth difficult 有必胜决心的；不畏艰难的：*We watched our team's heroic struggle to win back the cup.* 我们目睹了我队为赢回奖杯所付出的不懈努力。**3** that is about or involves a hero （关于）英雄的：*a* ***heroic story/poem*** 英雄故事 / 颂诗 ◇ ***heroic deeds/myths*** 英雄事迹 / 神话 **4** very large or great 非常大的；巨大的：*This was foolishness on a* ***heroic scale.*** 这简直是天大的蠢事。 ▶ **hero·ic·al·ly** /-kli/ *adv.*

heˌroic ˈcouplet *noun* (*specialist*) two lines of poetry one after the other that RHYME and usually contain ten syllables and five stresses 英雄体偶句诗（相互押韵的含有五个抑扬格的二行诗）

hero·ics /həˈrəʊɪks; *NAmE* -ˈroʊ-/ *noun* [pl.] **1** (*disapproving*) talk or behaviour that is too brave or dramatic for a particular situation 哗众取宠的言语（或行为）：*Remember, no heroics, we just go in there and do our job.* 记住，不要大肆宣扬，我们只要到那儿去干我们的活儿就行了。**2** actions that are brave and determined 勇敢果断的行为：*Thanks to Bateman's heroics in the second half, the team won 2–0.* 由于贝特曼在下半场的英勇表现，球队以 2:0 获胜。

her·oin /ˈherəʊɪn; *NAmE* -roʊ-/ *noun* [U] a powerful illegal drug made from MORPHINE, that some people take for pleasure and can become ADDICTED to 海洛因：*a heroin addict* 吸海洛因上瘾的人

hero·ine /ˈherəʊɪn; *NAmE* -roʊ-/ *noun* **1** a girl or woman who is admired by many for doing sth brave or good 女英雄；女豪杰：*the heroines of the revolution* 那场革命中的各位女英雄 **2** the main female character in a story, novel, film/movie, etc. （故事、小说、电影等中的）女主人公，女主角：*The heroine is played by Demi Moore.* 女主角由黛米・摩尔扮演。**3** a woman that you admire because of a particular quality or skill that she has 崇拜的女人；女偶像：*Madonna was her teenage heroine.* 麦当娜是她十几岁时的偶像。

hero·ism /ˈherəʊɪzəm; *NAmE* -roʊ-/ *noun* [U] very great courage 英勇表现；英雄精神

heron /ˈherən/ *noun* a large bird with a long neck and long legs, that lives near water 鹭

ˈhero worship *noun* [U] great admiration for sb because you think they are extremely beautiful, intelligent, etc. 英雄崇拜；个人崇拜

ˈhero-worship *verb* (**-pp-**, *NAmE also* **-p-**) ~ **sb** to admire sb very much because you think they are extremely beautiful, intelligent, etc. 崇拜（某人）

her·pes /ˈhɜːpiːz; *NAmE* ˈhɜːrp-/ *noun* [U] one of a group of infectious diseases, caused by a virus, that cause painful spots on the skin, especially on the face and sexual organs 疱疹

herpes zoster /ˌhɜːpiːz ˈzɒstə(r); *NAmE* ˌhɜːrpiːz ˈzɑːstər/ *noun* [U] (*medical* 医) **1** = SHINGLES **2** a virus which causes SHINGLES and CHICKENPOX 带状疱疹病毒

her·ring /ˈherɪŋ/ *noun* (*pl.* **her·ring** or **her·rings**) [U, C] a N Atlantic fish that swims in very large groups and is used for food 鲱鱼（产于北大西洋，成大群游动，

可食）：*shoals of herring* 鲱鱼群 ◇ *fresh herring fillets* 新鲜鲱鱼片 ◇ *pickled herrings* 腌制的鲱鱼 ➲ SEE ALSO RED HERRING

her·ring·bone /ˈherɪŋbəʊn; *NAmE* -boʊn/ *noun* [U] a pattern used, for example, in cloth consisting of lines of V-shapes that are parallel to each other（织物等的）人字形平行花纹

ˈherring gull *noun* a large N Atlantic bird of the GULL family, with black tips to its wings 银鸥（产于北大西洋，体大，翼端为黑色）

hers /hɜːz; ɜːz; *NAmE* hɜːrz; ɜːrz/ *pron.* of or belonging to her 她的；属于她的：*His eyes met hers.* 他的目光和她的相遇了。◇ *The choice was hers.* 那个选择是她作出的。◇ *a friend of hers* 她的一位朋友 ➲ NOTE AT GENDER

her·self /hɜːˈself; *NAmE* hɜːrˈs-; *weak form* həˈself; *NAmE weak form* hərˈs-/ *pron.* **1** (the reflexive form of *she* * she 的反身形式) used when the woman or girl who performs an action is also affected by it（用作女性的反身代词）她自己，自己：*She hurt herself.* 她弄伤了自己。◇ *She must be very proud of herself.* 她一定非常自豪。**2** used to emphasize the female subject or object of a sentence（强调句中的女性主语或宾语）：*She told me the news herself.* 是她本人告诉我这个消息的。◇ *Jane herself was at the meeting.* 简亲自参加了会议。

IDM **be, seem, etc. herˈself** (of a woman or girl 女性) to be in a normal state of health or happiness; not influenced by other people 身体或心情状况正常；如平时一样；没有受他人影响：*She didn't seem quite herself this morning.* 她今天早上好像有点不太对劲。◇*She needed space to be herself.* 她需要自己的独立空间。**(all) by herˈself** **1** alone; without anyone else（她）独自，单独：*She lives by herself.* 她独自一人生活。**2** without help（她）独立地：*She runs the business by herself.* 她自己经营这项生意。**(all) to herˈself** for only her to have or use 归她自己一人占有（或使用）：*She wants a room all to herself.* 她想要一个完全属于自己的房间。

hertz /hɜːts; *NAmE* hɜːrts/ *noun* (*pl.* **hertz**) (*abbr.* **Hz**) a unit for measuring the FREQUENCY of sound waves 赫，赫兹（声波频率单位）

he's *short form* **1** /hiːz; hiz; ɪz/ he is **2** /hiːz/ he has

hesi·tancy /ˈhezɪtənsi/ *noun* [U] the state or quality of being slow or uncertain in doing or saying sth 犹豫；踌躇；迟疑不决：*I noticed a certain hesitancy in his voice.* 我注意到他的声音有点犹豫。

hesi·tant /ˈhezɪtənt/ *adj.* slow to speak or act because you feel uncertain, embarrassed or unwilling 犹豫的；踌躇的；不情愿的：*a hesitant smile* 勉强的微笑 ◇ *the baby's first few hesitant steps* 婴儿最初的迟疑的几步 ◇ **~ about sth** *She's hesitant about signing the contract.* 她对是否签这个合同还犹豫不决。◇ **~ to do sth** *Doctors are hesitant to comment on the new treatment.* 医生们不愿对新疗法作出评论。▸ **hesi·tant·ly** *adv.*

hesi·tate /ˈhezɪteɪt/ *verb* **1** [I, T] to be slow to speak or act because you feel uncertain or nervous（对某事）犹豫，迟疑不决：*She hesitated before replying.* 她犹豫了一下才回答。◇ **~ about/over sth** *I didn't hesitate for a moment about taking the job.* 我毫不犹豫地接受了那份工作。◇ **+ speech** *'I'm not sure,' she hesitated.* "我不确定。"她犹豫不决地说。**2** [I] **~ to do sth** to be worried about doing sth, especially because you are not sure that it is right or appropriate 顾虑；疑虑：*Please do not hesitate to contact me if you have any queries.* 如果有疑问就请尽管和我联系。➲ MORE LIKE THIS 26, page R28 ▸ **hesi·ta·tion** /ˌhezɪˈteɪʃn/ *noun* [U, C]：*She agreed **without the slightest hesitation**.* 她毫不犹豫地同意了。◇ *I **have no hesitation in** recommending her for the job.* 我毫不犹豫地推荐她做这项工作。◇ *He spoke fluently and without unnecessary hesitations.* 他说得很流畅，毫不支吾。

IDM **he who ˈhesitates (is ˈlost)** (*saying*) if you delay in doing sth you may lose a good opportunity 当断不断，反受其乱；优柔寡断者坐失良机

hes·sian /ˈhesiən; *NAmE* ˈheʃn/ (*especially BrE*) (*NAmE usually* **bur·lap**) *noun* [U] a type of strong rough brown cloth, used especially for making SACKS 棕色粗麻布

hetero- /ˈhetərəʊ; *NAmE* ˈhetəroʊ/ *combining form* (in nouns, adjectives and adverbs 构成名词、形容词和副词) other; different 其他；不同的：*heterogeneous* 由很多种类组成的 ◇ *heterosexual* 异性恋者 ➲ COMPARE HOMO-

het·ero·dox /ˈhetərədɒks; *NAmE* -dɑːks/ *adj.* (*formal*) not following the usual or accepted beliefs and opinions 异端的；非正统的 ➲ COMPARE ORTHODOX (1), UNORTHODOX ▸ **het·ero·doxy** *noun* [U, C] (*pl.* **-ies**)

het·ero·ge·neous /ˌhetərəˈdʒiːniəs/ *adj.* (*formal*) consisting of many different kinds of people or things 由很多种类组成的；各种各样的：*the heterogeneous population of the United States* 由不同族裔组成的美国人口 OPP **homogeneous** ▸ **het·ero·gen·eity** /-dʒəˈniːəti/ *noun* [U]

het·ero·nym /ˈhetərənɪm/ *noun* (*linguistics* 语言) **1** one of two or more words that have the same spelling but different meanings and pronunciation, for example 'tear' meaning 'rip' and 'tear' meaning 'liquid from the eye' 同形异音异义词（如表示"撕裂"的 tear 与表示"眼泪"的 tear）**2** one of two or more words that refer to the same thing, for example 'lift' and 'elevator' 异形同义词（如 lift 和 elevator）

het·ero·sex·ual /ˌhetərəˈsekʃuəl/ *noun* a person who is sexually attracted to people of the opposite sex 异性恋者 ➲ COMPARE BISEXUAL *n.*, HOMOSEXUAL ▸ **het·ero·sex·ual** *adj.*：*a heterosexual relationship* 异性恋关系 **het·ero·sexu·al·ity** /ˌhetərəˌsekʃuˈæləti/ *noun* [U]

het·ero·zy·gote /ˌhetərəˈzaɪgəʊt; *NAmE* -goʊt/ *noun* (*biology* 生) a living thing that has two varying forms of a particular GENE, and whose young may therefore vary in a particular characteristic 杂合子（基因有两种不同形式的生物）▸ **het·ero·zy·gous** /-gəs/ *adj.*

het up /ˌhet ˈʌp/ *adj.* [not before noun] **~ (about/over sth)** (*informal*) anxious, excited or slightly angry 焦虑；兴奋；生气：*What are you getting so het up about?* 什么事让你这么激动？

heur·is·tic /hjuˈrɪstɪk/ *adj.* (*formal*) **heuristic** teaching or education encourages you to learn by discovering things for yourself（教学或教育）启发式的

heur·is·tics /hjuˈrɪstɪks/ *noun* [U] (*formal*) a method of solving problems by finding practical ways of dealing with them, learning from past experience 探索法；启发式

hew /hjuː/ *verb* (**hewed, hewed, hewn** /hjuːn/) **1 ~ sth** (*old-fashioned*) to cut sth large with a tool 砍，劈（大的物体）：*to hew wood* 劈木头 **2 ~ sth (out of sth)** (*formal*) to make or shape sth large by cutting 砍成，劈出（某种形状、某物）：*roughly hewn timber frames* 粗劈成的木架子 ◇ *The statues were hewn out of solid rock.* 这些雕像是在实心岩石上凿出来的。

hex /heks/ *verb* **~ sb** (*NAmE*) to use magic powers in order to harm sb 施魔法以加害（某人）▸ **hex** *noun*：*to put a hex on sb* 施魔法使某人遭殃 ➲ COMPARE CURSE *v.* (3)

hexa- /ˈheksə/ (*also* **hex-**) *combining form* (in nouns, adjectives and adverbs 构成名词、形容词和副词) six; having six 六；有六个的

hexa·deci·mal /ˌheksəˈdesɪml/ (*also* **hex** /heks/) *noun* (*computing* 计) a system for representing pieces of data using the numbers 0–9 and the letters A–F 十六进制的：*The number 107 is represented in hexadecimal as 6B.* * 107 这个数用十六进制表示为 6B。

hexa·gon /ˈheksəgən; *NAmE* -gɑːn/ *noun* (*geometry* 几何) a flat shape with six straight sides and six angles 六边形；六角形 ➲ PICTURE AT POLYGON ▸ **hex·agon·al** /heksˈægənl/ *adj.*

hexa·gram /'heksəgræm/ *noun* (*geometry* 几何) a shape made by six straight lines, especially a star made from two triangles with equal sides 六角星形；六角形

hex·am·eter /hek'sæmɪtə(r)/ *noun* (*specialist*) a line of poetry with six stressed syllables 六音步诗行

hey /heɪ/ *exclamation* (*informal*) **1** used to attract sb's attention or to express interest, surprise or anger（用以引起注意或表示兴趣、惊讶或生气）嘿，喂：*Hey, can I just ask you something?* 嘿，问你点事好吗？◇ *Hey, leave my things alone!* 喂，别碰我的东西！ **2** used to show that you do not really care about sth or that you think it is not important（表示不真正在意或认为不重要）嘿：*That's the third time I've been late this week—but hey!—who's counting?* 那是我这个星期第三次迟到了。不过，嘿，管它多少次呢。 **3** (*SAfrE*) used at the end of a statement, to show that you have finished speaking, or to form a question or invite sb to reply（用于陈述句末尾，表示话已说完，或构成问题或请求回答）就这样，怎么样，你说呢：*Thanks for your help, hey.* 谢谢你的帮助啦。◇ *My new bike's nice, hey?* 我的新自行车挺好，你说呢？ ➲ MORE LIKE THIS 2, page R25

IDM **what the 'hey!** (*NAmE, informal*) used to say that sth does not matter or that you do not care about it 那有什么要紧；没什么；管它呢：*This is probably a bad idea, but what the hey!* 这大概是个馊主意，但管它呢！

hey·day /'heɪdeɪ/ *noun* [usually sing.] the time when sb/sth had most power or success, or was most popular 最为强大（或成功、繁荣）的时期 SYN **prime**：*In its heyday, the company ran trains every fifteen minutes.* 公司在最兴隆时期每隔十五分钟就开出一列火车。◇ *a fine example from the heyday of Italian cinema* 意大利电影业全盛期的一部优秀代表作 ◇ *a picture of Brigitte Bardot in her heyday* 碧姬·芭铎事业鼎盛时的一张照片

ˌ**hey 'presto** *exclamation* (*BrE*) (*NAmE* **presto**) **1** something that people say when they have just done sth so quickly and easily that it seems to have been done by magic 嘿，瞧（变魔术般迅速轻松地做完某事时所说）：*You just press the button and, hey presto, a perfect cup of coffee!* 只要按下按钮，嘿，马上就出来一杯上好的咖啡！ **2** something that people say just before they finish a magic trick 变（变戏法完成之前所说）

HFC /ˌeɪtʃ ef 'siː/ *noun* [C, U] the abbreviation for 'hydrofluorocarbon', a type of gas used especially in AEROSOLS (= types of container that release liquid in the form of a spray). HFCs are not harmful to the earth's OZONE LAYER. 含氢氟烃（全写为 hydrofluorocarbon，尤用于喷雾剂中，对臭氧层无害）

HGV /ˌeɪtʃ dʒiː 'viː/ *noun* (*BrE*) heavy goods vehicle (a large vehicle such as a lorry/truck) 重型货车；大型货运卡车：*You need an HGV licence for this job.* 从事这项工作得有重型货车驾驶执照。

HHS /ˌeɪtʃ eɪtʃ 'es/ *abbr.* Department of Health and Human Services (the US government department responsible for national health programmes and the SOCIAL SERVICES ADMINISTRATION)（美国）卫生与公众服务部

hi 🔑 /haɪ/ *exclamation* (*informal*) used to say hello（用于打招呼）喂，嗨：*Hi guys!* 嗨，伙计们！◇ *Hi, there! How're you doing?* 喂！你好吗？

hia·tus /haɪ'eɪtəs/ *noun* [sing.] (*formal*) **1** a pause in activity when nothing happens 间断；停滞 **2** a space, especially in a piece of writing or in a speech, where sth is missing 空隙；（尤指文章或说话中的）缺漏，漏字，漏句

hi·ber·nate /'haɪbəneɪt; *NAmE* -bərn-/ *verb* [I] (of animals 动物) to spend the winter in a state like deep sleep 冬眠；蛰伏 ➲ COLLOCATIONS AT LIFE ▶ **hi·ber·na·tion** /ˌhaɪbə'neɪʃn; *NAmE* -bər'n-/ *noun* [U]

hi·bis·cus /hɪ'bɪskəs; haɪ-/ *noun* [U, C] (*pl.* **hi·bis·cus**) a tropical plant or bush with large brightly coloured flowers 木槿

hic·cup (*also* **hic·cough**) /'hɪkʌp/ *noun, verb*

■ ***noun*** **1** [C] a sharp, usually repeated, sound made in the throat, that is caused by a sudden movement of the DIAPHRAGM and that you cannot control 嗝；呃逆：*She gave a loud hiccup.* 她打了一个响嗝。 **2** (**the**) **hiccups** [pl.] a series of hiccups 一连串的打嗝：*I ate too quickly and got hiccups.* 我吃得太快，结果不断地打嗝。◇ *He had the hiccups.* 他接连打嗝。 **3** [C] (*informal*) a small problem or temporary delay 小问题；暂时性耽搁：*There was a slight hiccup in the timetable.* 时间安排上出了点小问题。

■ ***verb*** [I] to have hiccups or a single hiccup 打嗝；打呃

hick /hɪk/ *noun* (*informal, especially NAmE*) a person from the country who is considered to be stupid and to have little experience of life 乡巴佬；土里土气的人：*I was just a hick from Texas then.* 那时我不过是从得克萨斯州来的土包子。 ▶ **hick** *adj.*：*a hick town* 小乡镇

hickey /'hɪki/ (*NAmE*) (*BrE* **'love bite**) *noun* a red mark on the skin that is caused by sb biting or sucking their partner's skin when they are kissing 爱痕（在皮肤上吻或咬出的红色痕迹）

hick·ory /'hɪkəri/ *noun* [U] the hard wood of the N American **hickory tree** 山核桃木（产于北美）

ˌ**hidden a'genda** *noun* (*disapproving*) the secret intention behind what sb says or does（言语或行为背后的）隐秘意图，秘密目的：*There are fears of a hidden agenda behind this new proposal.* 人们担心这一新提议的背后有不可告人的目的。

▼ **SYNONYMS 同义词辨析**

hide

conceal • cover • disguise • mask • camouflage

These words all mean to put or keep sb/sth in a place where they/it cannot be seen or found, or to keep the truth or your feelings secret. 以上各词均含藏、隐藏、掩盖、隐瞒之义。

hide to put or keep sb/sth in a place where they/it cannot be seen or found; to keep sth secret, especially your feelings 指藏、隐藏、掩盖（尤指感情）：*He hid the letter in a drawer.* 他把信藏在抽屉里。◇ *She managed to hide her disappointment.* 她设法掩藏了自己的失望。

conceal (*formal*) to hide sb/sth; to keep sth secret 指隐藏、隐瞒、掩盖：*The paintings were concealed beneath a thick layer of plaster.* 那些画藏在厚厚的灰泥层下面。◇ *Tim could barely conceal his disappointment.* 蒂姆几乎掩饰不住自己的失望。 NOTE When it is being used to talk about emotions, **conceal** is often used in negative statements. * conceal 指掩藏感情时常用于否定句。

cover to place sth over or in front of sth in order to hide it 指掩蔽、遮盖：*She covered her face with her hands.* 她双手掩面。

disguise to hide or change the nature of sth, so that it cannot be recognized 指掩蔽、掩饰、伪装，以免被认出：*He tried to disguise his accent.* 他竭力掩饰自己的口音。

mask to hide a feeling, smell, fact, etc. so that it cannot be easily seen or noticed 指掩饰、掩藏（情感、气味、事实等），以免被看出或注意到：*She masked her anger with a smile.* 她用微笑来掩饰她的愤怒。

camouflage to hide sb/sth by making them/it look like the things around, or like sth else 指通过使人或事物与周围环境或其他事物相似而达到伪装、掩饰的目的：*The soldiers camouflaged themselves with leaves and twigs.* 士兵用树叶和树枝来伪装自己。

PATTERNS

- to hide/conceal/disguise/mask/camouflage sth **behind** sth
- to hide/conceal sth **under** sth
- to hide/conceal sth **from** sb
- to hide/conceal/disguise/mask **the truth/the fact that...**
- to hide/conceal/disguise/mask **your feelings**

hide 🔑 /haɪd/ *verb, noun*

■ ***verb*** (**hid** /hɪd/, **hid·den** /ˈhɪdn/) **1** 🔑 [T] to put or keep sb/sth in a place where they/it cannot be seen or found 藏；隐蔽 SYN **conceal**: **~ sb/sth** *He hid the letter in a drawer.* 他把信藏在抽屉里。◇ *I keep my private papers hidden.* 我藏起了我的私人文件。◇ **~ sb/sth from sth** *They hid me from the police in their attic.* 他们把我藏在他们的阁楼上躲避警察。 **2** 🔑 [I, T] to go somewhere where you hope you will not be seen or found 躲避；隐匿：*Quick, hide!* 快，躲起来！◇ **+ adv./prep.** *I hid under the bed.* 我躲在床底下。◇ (*figurative*) *He hid behind a false identity.* 他隐姓埋名。◇ **~ yourself** (**+ adv./prep.**) *She hides herself away in her office all day.* 她成天躲在办公室里。 **3** 🔑 [T] to cover sth so that it cannot be seen 遮住；遮挡 SYN **conceal**: **~ sth + adv./prep.** *He hid his face in his hands.* 他用手捂住了脸。◇ **~ sth** *The house was hidden by trees.* 那所房子被树丛遮住了。◇ *No amount of make-up could hide her age.* 再多的化妆品也遮掩不住她的年龄。 **4** 🔑 [T] **~ sth** to keep sth secret, especially your feelings 掩盖，隐瞒（尤指感情） SYN **conceal**: *She struggled to hide her disappointment.* 她竭力掩饰她的失望。◇ *I have never tried to hide the truth about my past.* 我从未设法隐瞒我的过去。◇ *They claim that they* ***have nothing to hide*** (= there was nothing wrong or illegal about what they did). 他们声称他们没什么可隐瞒的。◇ *She felt sure the letter had some* ***hidden meaning***. 她确信那封信中有言外之意。

IDM **hide your light under a ˈbushel** to not let people know that you are good at sth 不显露才能；不露锋芒 ➲ MORE AT HEAD *n.*, MULTITUDE

■ ***noun*** **1** [C] (*BrE*) a place from which people can watch wild animals or birds, without being seen by them （观看野生动物的）隐蔽处，藏身处 **2** [C, U] an animal's skin, especially when it is bought or sold or used for leather （尤指买卖或用作皮革的）皮，毛皮：*boots made from buffalo hide* 用水牛皮做的靴子 **3** [sing.] (*informal, especially NAmE*) used to refer to sb's life or safety when they are in a difficult situation （困境中的）生命，人身安全：*All he's worried about is his own hide* (= himself). 他所担心的只是他自己的生命安全。

IDM **have/tan sb's ˈhide** (*old-fashioned, informal* or *humorous*) to punish sb severely 严惩某人 **not see hide nor ˈhair of sb/sth** (*informal*) not to see sb/sth for some time （一段时间）不见某人（或某物）的踪影：*I haven't seen hide nor hair of her for a month.* 我有一个月没见过她了。 ➲ MORE AT SAVE *v.*

hide-and-seek /ˌhaɪd n ˈsiːk/ *noun* [U] a children's game in which one player covers his or her eyes while the other players hide, and then tries to find them 捉迷藏游戏

hide·away /ˈhaɪdəweɪ/ *noun* a place where you can go to hide or to be alone 藏身处；退隐处

hide·bound /ˈhaɪdbaʊnd/ *adj.* (*disapproving*) having old-fashioned ideas, rather than accepting new ways of thinking 守旧的；迂腐的 SYN **narrow-minded**

hid·eous /ˈhɪdiəs/ *adj.* very ugly or unpleasant 十分丑陋的；令人厌恶的 SYN **revolting**: *a hideous face/building/dress* 丑陋的面孔／建筑物／衣服 ◇ *Their new colour scheme is hideous!* 他们新的颜色搭配难看极了！◇ *a hideous crime* 骇人听闻的罪行 ◇ *The whole experience had been like some hideous nightmare.* 整个经历就像一场可怕的噩梦。 ▶ **hid·eous·ly** *adv.*: *His face was hideously deformed.* 他的脸严重变形。

hide·out /ˈhaɪdaʊt/ *noun* a place where sb goes when they do not want anyone to find them 藏身处；隐蔽所

hidey-hole (*also* **hidy-hole**) /ˈhaɪdi həʊl; *NAmE* hoʊl/ *noun* (*informal*) a place where sb hides, especially in order to avoid being with other people 躲藏处；隐蔽处；独居处

hid·ing /ˈhaɪdɪŋ/ *noun* **1** [U] the state of being hidden 隐藏；躲藏：*After the trial, she had to* ***go into hiding*** *for several weeks.* 审讯后她不得不躲藏了几个星期。◇ *He only* ***came out of hiding*** *ten years after the war was over.* 战争结束十年之后他才露面。◇ *We spent months* ***in hiding***. 我们躲藏了好几个月。 **2** [C, usually sing.] (*informal, especially BrE*) a physical punishment, usually involving being hit hard many times 体罚；痛打 SYN **beating**: ***to give sb/get a (good) hiding*** 给某人／遭到一顿（狠）揍 ◇ (*figurative*) *The team got a hiding in their last game.* 那支球队在最后一场比赛中被打得一败涂地。

IDM **on a ˌhiding to ˈnothing** (*BrE, informal*) having no chance of success, or not getting much advantage even if you do succeed 毫无成功机会；（即使成功了）也得不到多大好处

ˈhiding place *noun* a place where sb/sth can be hidden 隐藏处；藏身地

hie /haɪ/ *verb* (**hies**, **hying**, **hied**) [I] **+ adv./prep.** (*old use*) to go quickly 快走；急行

hier·arch·ic·al AW /ˌhaɪəˈrɑːkɪkl; *NAmE* -ˈrɑːrk-/ *adj.* arranged in a hierarchy 按等级划分的；等级制度的：***a hierarchical society/structure/organization*** 分等级的社会／结构／组织 ▶ **hier·arch·ic·al·ly** *adv.*

hier·archy AW /ˈhaɪərɑːki; *NAmE* -rɑːrki/ *noun* (*pl.* **-ies**) **1** [C, U] a system, especially in a society or an organization, in which people are organized into different levels of importance from highest to lowest 等级制度（尤指社会或组织）：*the* ***social/political hierarchy*** 社会／政治等级制度 ◇ *She's quite high up in the management hierarchy.* 她位居管理层要职。 **2** [C+sing./pl. v.] the group of people in control of a large organization or institution 统治集团 **3** [C] (*formal*) a system that ideas or beliefs can be arranged into 层次体系：*a hierarchy of needs* 不同层次的需要

hiero·glyph /ˈhaɪərəglɪf/ *noun* a picture or symbol of an object, representing a word, syllable or sound, especially as used in ancient Egyptian and other writing systems 象形文字，象形符号（尤指古埃及等所用的文字） ▶ **hiero·glyph·ic** /ˌhaɪərəˈglɪfɪk/ *adj.*

hieroglyphics
用象形文字书写的东西

hiero·glyph·ics /ˌhaɪərəˈglɪfɪks/ *noun* [pl.] writing that uses hieroglyphs 用象形文字书写的东西

hi-fi /ˈhaɪ faɪ/ *noun* [C, U] equipment for playing recorded music that produces high-quality STEREO sound 高保真音响设备 ▶ **hi-fi** *adj.* [usually before noun]: *a hi-fi system* 高保真系统

higgledy-piggledy /ˌhɪgldi ˈpɪgldi/ *adv.* (*informal*) in an untidy way that lacks any order 杂乱无章；混乱：*Files were strewn higgledy-piggledy over the floor.* 文件乱七八糟地扔了一地。 ▶ **higgledy-piggledy** *adj.*: *a higgledy-piggledy collection of houses* 一片错落杂乱的房屋 ➲ MORE LIKE THIS 11, page R26

high 🔑 /haɪ/ *adj.*, *noun*, *adv.*

> **WORD FAMILY**
> **high** *adj.*, *noun*, *adv.*
> **highly** *adv.*
> **height** *noun*
> **heighten** *verb*

■ ***adj.*** (**high·er**, **high·est**)

• **FROM BOTTOM TO TOP** 从底到顶 **1** 🔑 measuring a long distance from the bottom to the top 高的: *What's the highest mountain in the US?* 美国哪座山最高？◇ *The house has a high wall all the way round it.* 这栋房子的四周围着高墙。◇ *shoes with high heels* 高跟鞋 ◇ *He has a round face with a high forehead.* 他圆脸，高额头。**OPP low** **2** 🔑 used to talk about the distance that sth measures from the bottom to the top 有某高度的: *How high is Mount Aconcagua?* 阿空加瓜山有多高？◇ *It's only a low wall—about a metre high.* 那只不过是一堵矮墙，约一米高。◇ *The grass was waist-high.* 那片草齐腰高。

• **FAR ABOVE GROUND** 离地面远 **3** 🔑 at a level which is a long way above the ground or above the level of the sea（离地面）很高的；海拔很高的: *a high branch/shelf/window* 高处的树枝 / 搁板 / 窗 ◇ *The rooms had high ceilings.* 那些房间的天花板很高。◇ *They were flying at high altitude.* 他们正在高空飞行。◇ *the grasslands of the high prairies* 高地草原 **OPP low**

• **GREATER THAN NORMAL** 超出常规 **4** 🔑 greater or better than normal in quantity or quality, size or degree （数量、质量、体积或程度）高的，超乎寻常的: *a high temperature/speed/price* 高温；高速；高价 ◇ *a high rate of inflation* 高通货膨胀率 ◇ *Demand is high at this time of year.* 一年的这个时期需求很大。◇ *a **high level** of pollution* 严重的污染 ◇ *a **high standard** of craftsmanship* 高水平的手工艺 ◇ ***high-quality** goods* 优质商品 ◇ *A **high degree** of accuracy is needed.* 需要高度的准确性。◇ *The tree blew over in the **high winds**.* 树被大风刮倒了。◇ *We had **high hopes** for the business* (= we believed it would be successful). 我们对这项生意寄予了很大希望。◇ *The cost in terms of human life was high.* 付出了很大的生命代价。➲ COMPARE LOW *adj.* (4)

• **CONTAINING A LOT** 含量多 **5** 🔑 ~ (**in sth**) containing a lot of a particular substance 含某物多: *foods which are high in fat* 高脂肪食物 ◇ *a high potassium content* 高钾含量 ◇ *a **high-fat** diet* 高脂肪的饮食 **OPP low**

• **RANK/STATUS** 等级；地位 **6** (usually before noun 通常用于名词前) near the top in rank or status 上层的；地位高的: *She has held **high office** under three prime ministers.* 她曾在三任首相手下任过要职。◇ *He has friends **in high places*** (= among people of power and influence). 他有位高权重的朋友。**OPP low**

• **VALUABLE** 有价值 **7** of great value 价值高的: *to play for high stakes* 豪赌 ◇ *My highest card is ten.* 我最大的牌是十。

• **IDEALS/PRINCIPLES** 理想；准则 **8** (usually before noun 通常用于名词前) morally good 高尚的；崇高的: *a man of **high ideals/principles*** 有崇高理想 / 道德准则的人

• **APPROVING** 赞同 **9** (usually before noun 通常用于名词前) showing a lot of approval or respect for sb 十分赞同的；非常尊敬的: *She is held in very high regard by her colleagues.* 她很受同事们的敬重。◇ *You seem to have a **high opinion** of yourself!* 你似乎自我评价很高嘛！**OPP low**

• **SOUND** 声音 **10** at the upper end of the range of sounds that humans can hear; not deep or low 高音的: *She has a high voice.* 她嗓音很尖。◇ *That note is definitely too high for me.* 那个音对我来说绝对太高了。**OPP low**

• **OF PERIOD OF TIME** 时段 **11** [only before noun] used to describe the middle or the most attractive part of a period of time 中间的；全盛的: *high noon* 正午 ◇ *high summer* 盛夏

• **FOOD** 食物 **12** (of meat, cheese, etc. 肉、奶酪等) beginning to go bad and having a strong smell 开始变质的；开始发馊的

• **ON ALCOHOL/DRUGS** 喝酒；吸毒 **13** [not before noun] ~ (**on sth**) (*informal*) behaving in an excited way because of the effects of alcohol or drugs 有醉意；表现兴奋

• **PHONETICS** 语音学 **14** (*phonetics* 语音) = CLOSE² (16)

IDM **be/get on your high 'horse** (*informal*) to behave in a way that shows you think you are better than other people 趾高气扬；自命不凡；自以为了不起 **have a 'high old time** (*old-fashioned*, *informal*) to enjoy yourself very much 玩得很开心 **high and 'dry 1** (of a boat, etc. 小船等) in a position out of the water 高出水面；搁浅: *Their yacht was left high and dry on a sandbank.* 他们的帆船搁浅在沙丘上了。**2** in a difficult situation, without help or money 处境艰难；无依无靠；身无分文 ➲ MORE LIKE THIS 12, page R26 **high and 'mighty** (*informal*) behaving as though you think you are more important than other people 趾高气扬；神气活现；自高自大 **high as a 'kite** (*informal*) behaving in a very excited way, especially because of being strongly affected by alcohol or drugs（尤指因酗酒或吸毒）异常兴奋，神情恍惚 **in high 'dudgeon** (*old-fashioned*, *formal*) in an angry or offended mood, and showing other people that you are angry 愤然；怒冲冲: *He stomped out of the room in high dudgeon.* 他愤怒地噔噔走出了屋子。**smell, stink, etc. to high 'heaven** (*informal*) **1** to have a strong unpleasant smell 发出难闻气味；难闻透顶 **2** to seem to be very dishonest or morally unacceptable 很不诚实；不道德 ➲ MORE AT HELL, MORAL *adj.*, ORDER *n.*, PROFILE *n.*, TIME *n.*

> ▼ **WHICH WORD?** 词语辨析
>
> **high / tall**
>
> • **High** is used to talk about the measurement from the bottom to the top of something. * high 用以指从底部到顶部的高度：*The fence is over five metres high.* 这围栏有五米多高。◇ *He has climbed some of the world's highest mountains.* 他攀登过几座世界最高峰。You also use **high** to describe the distance of something from the ground. 亦可用 high 表示离地面的距离：*How high was the plane when the engine failed?* 发动机出故障时飞机离地面多高？
>
> • **Tall** is used instead of **high** to talk about people. 指人用 tall，不用 high：*My brother's much taller than me.* 我哥哥比我高多了。**Tall** is also used for things that are high and narrow such as trees. * tall 亦可指高而窄的事物，如树木：*She ordered cold beer in a tall glass.* 她叫了一杯高玻璃杯装的冰镇啤酒。◇ *tall factory chimneys* 工厂的高烟囱 Buildings can be **high** or **tall**. 建筑物用 high 或 tall 均可。

■ ***noun***

• **LEVEL/NUMBER** 水平；数量 **1** the highest level or number 最高水平；最大数量: *Profits reached an **all-time high** last year.* 去年的利润空前地高。

• **WEATHER** 天气 **2** an area of high air pressure; an ANTICYCLONE 高气压区；反气旋: *A high over southern Europe is bringing fine, sunny weather to all parts.* 欧洲南部上空的高气压正给各地带来阳光灿烂的好天气。**3** the highest temperature reached during a particular day, week, etc. （某天、某星期等的）最高气温: *Highs today will be in the region of 25°C.* 今天的最高气温将为 25 摄氏度左右。

• **FROM DRUGS** 毒品引起 **4** (*informal*) the feeling of extreme pleasure and excitement that sb gets after taking some types of drugs （毒品引致的）快感: *The high lasted all night.* 那种快感持续了一整夜。

• **FROM SUCCESS/ENJOYMENT** 来自成功 / 乐趣 **5** (*informal*) the feeling of extreme pleasure and excitement that sb gets from doing sth enjoyable or being successful at sth 极大欢乐；极度高兴；乐不可支: *He was **on a real high** after winning the competition.* 他赢了那场比赛后高兴极了。◇ *the **highs and lows** of her acting career* 她的演员生涯的大起大落

• **SCHOOL** 学校 **6** used in the name of a high school （用于中学校名）: *He graduated from Little Rock High in 1982.* 他 1982 年毕业于小石城中学。

IDM **on 'high 1** (*formal*) in a high place 在高处: *We gazed down into the valley from on high.* 我们从高处向下眺望山谷。**2** (*humorous*) the people in senior positions in an organization 高层人员: *An order came down from on high that lunchbreaks were to be half an hour and no longer.* 上头指示说午餐休息时间不得超过半小时。**3** in heaven 在天上： *The disaster was seen as a judgement from on high.* 这场灾难被视作上天的惩罚。

■ ***adv.*** (**high·er, high·est**)

• **FAR FROM GROUND/BOTTOM** 远离地面 / 底部 **1** at or to a position or level that is a long way up from the ground or from the bottom 在高处；向高处；高： *An eagle circled high overhead.* 一只鹰在头顶上空盘旋。◇ *I can't jump any higher.* 我没法跳得更高了。◇ *She never got very high in the company.* 她在公司里从未坐到很高的位置。◇ *His desk was **piled high** with papers.* 他的桌子上摞着高高的一堆文件。◇ *She's **aiming high*** (= hoping to be very successful) *in her exams.* 她期望考出优异成绩。

• **VALUE/AMOUNT** 价值；数量 **2** at or to a large cost, value or amount （成本、价值）高；（数量）大： *Prices are expected to rise even higher this year.* 预计今年的价格将涨得更高。

• **SOUND** 声音 **3** at a high PITCH 音调高： *I can't sing that high.* 我唱不了那么高的调子。 **OPP** **low**

IDM **ˌhigh and ˈlow** everywhere 到处；各地： *I've searched high and low for my purse.* 我到处找我的钱包。 **run ˈhigh** (especially of feelings 尤指情绪) to be strong and angry or excited 激愤；激昂： *Feelings ran high as the election approached.* 选举临近，大家情绪都很激动。 ⇨ MORE AT FLY *v.*, HEAD *n.*, RIDE *v.*

ˌhigh and ˈtight *noun* (*US*) a military HAIRSTYLE in which the sides of the head are shaved and the top is cut very short （一种只留头顶寸发的）军人发型

high·ball /ˈhaɪbɔːl/ *noun, verb* (*NAmE*)

■ ***noun*** a strong alcoholic drink, such as WHISKY or GIN, mixed with FIZZY water (= with bubbles) or GINGER ALE, etc. and served with ice 开波酒，冰威士忌苏打（用烈酒掺入汽水等加冰）

■ ***verb*** (*informal*) **1** [I] **+ adv./prep.** to go somewhere very quickly 高速行进： *They highballed out of town.* 他们急匆匆地出了城。 **2** [T] **~ sth** to deliberately make an estimate of the cost, value, etc. of sth that is too high 故意高估…的价值（或成本等）： *He thought she was highballing her salary requirements.* 他认为她的薪金要求过高。 **OPP** **lowball**

ˈhigh beams *noun* [pl.] (*NAmE*) the lights on a car when they are pointing a long way ahead, not down at the road （汽车的）远光灯

ˌhigh-ˈborn *adj.* (*old-fashioned* or *formal*) having parents who are members of the highest social class 出身高贵的 **SYN** **aristocratic** **OPP** **low-born**

high·boy /ˈhaɪbɔɪ/ (*NAmE*) (*BrE* **tall·boy**) *noun* a tall piece of furniture with drawers, used for storing clothes in （带抽屉的）高衣柜

high·brow /ˈhaɪbraʊ/ *adj.* (*sometimes disapproving*) concerned with or interested in serious artistic or cultural ideas 关于正统艺术（或文化）思想的；对正统的艺术（或文化）感兴趣的 **SYN** **intellectual**: *highbrow newspapers* 格调高雅的报纸 ◇ *highbrow readers* 趣味高雅的读者 **OPP** **lowbrow** ⇨ COMPARE MIDDLEBROW

ˈhigh chair *noun* a special chair with long legs and a little seat and table, for a small child to sit in when eating 高脚椅（幼儿进食时坐的，带小饭桌） ⇨ VISUAL VOCAB PAGE V23

ˌHigh ˈChurch *adj.* connected with the part of the Anglican Church that is most similar to the Roman Catholic Church in its beliefs and practices 高派教会的（圣公会的一派，在信仰和礼仪方面与天主教最相似）

ˌhigh-ˈclass *adj.* **1** excellent; of good quality 极好的；高级的： *a high-class restaurant* 一家高级餐厅 ◇ *to stay in high-class accommodation* 住在上好的住所 **2** connected with a high social class 上流社会的： *to come from a high-class background* 出身于上层社会 **OPP** **low-class**

ˌhigh comˈmand *noun* [usually sing.] the senior leaders of the armed forces of a country （全国武装力量的）统帅部，最高指挥部

ˌhigh comˈmission *noun* **1** the office and the staff of an EMBASSY that represents the interests of one Commonwealth country in another （英联邦国家相互派驻的）高级专员公署 **2** a group of people who are working for a government or an international organization on an important project （政府或国际组织的）重大项目工作组；特别事务公署： *the United Nations High Commission for Refugees* 联合国难民事务高级专员公署

ˌHigh Comˈmissioner *noun* **1** a person who is sent by one Commonwealth country to live in another, to protect the interests of their own country （英联邦国家之间互派的）高级专员 **2** a person who is head of an important international project 重大国际项目负责人；高级专员： *the United Nations High Commissioner for Refugees* 联合国难民事务高级专员

ˌhigh-ˈconcept *adj.* (used about an idea in a film/movie or television story) very interesting and unusual but simple to explain and likely to be popular with a wide audience 高概念的（形容电影或电视剧题材新颖有趣，简单易懂，有望大热）： *"Honey, I Shrunk the Kids" is a high-concept comedy about a scientist who accidentally, well, shrinks his kids.* 《亲爱的，我把孩子变小了》是一部高概念喜剧，讲的是一个科学家意外地，嗯，把他的孩子微缩了。

ˌHigh ˈCourt (*also* **ˌHigh Court of ˈJustice**) *noun* **1** a court in England and Wales that deals with the most serious CIVIL cases (= not criminal cases) 高等法院（在英格兰和威尔士审理最严重的民事案件） **2** = SUPREME COURT

ˈhigh day *noun* (*old-fashioned, BrE*) the day of a religious festival 宗教节日

IDM **ˌhigh days and ˈholidays** festivals and special occasions 节日和假日；节庆日

ˌhigh-defiˈnition *adj.* (*abbr.* **HD**) [only before noun] (*specialist*) using or produced by a system that gives very clear detailed images 高清晰度的；高分辨率的： *high-definition television* 高清晰度电视机 ◇ *high-definition displays* 高清晰度显像 ⇨ SEE ALSO HDTV

ˌhigh-ˈend *adj.* expensive and of high quality 高档的；高端的；价高质优的

High·er /ˈhaɪə(r)/ *noun* (in Scotland) an exam that was taken in a particular subject at a higher level than STANDARD GRADE. Highers were usually taken around the age of 17 to 18. （苏格兰）学生高级证书考试（旧时采用，应试年龄一般在 17 至 18 岁） ⇨ SEE ALSO NQ

high·er /ˈhaɪə(r)/ *adj.* [only before noun] at a more advanced level; greater in rank or importance than others 高等级的；级别较高的；较重要的： *The case was referred to a higher court.* 案件转到了上级法院。◇ *higher mathematics* 高等数学 ◇ *My mind was on higher things.* 我那时想着更重要的事。

ˌhigher ˈanimals, ˌhigher ˈplants *noun* [pl.] (*specialist*) animals and plants that have reached an advanced stage of development 高等动物，高等植物（发展到高等进化程度的动植物）

ˌhigher eduˈcation *noun* [U] (*abbr.* **HE**) education and training at college and university, especially to degree level （尤指达到学位水平的）高等教育 ⇨ COMPARE FURTHER EDUCATION ⇨ WORDFINDER NOTE AT STUDY

ˌhigher-ˈup *noun* (*informal*) a person who has a higher rank or who is more senior than you 上级；上司；长官

ˌhighest common ˈfactor *noun* (*abbr.* **HCF**) (*mathematics* 数) the highest number that can be divided exactly into two or more numbers 最大公因数

ˌhigh exˈplosive *noun* [C, U] a very powerful substance that is used in bombs and can damage a very large area 高爆炸药；烈性炸药

high·fa·lu·tin /ˌhaɪfəˈluːtɪn/ *adj.* (*informal*) trying to be serious or important, but in a way that often appears silly and unnecessary 装模作样的；浮夸的；做作的 **SYN** **pretentious**

ˌ**high fiˈdelity** *noun* [U] (*old-fashioned*) = HI-FI

ˌ**high ˈfive** *noun* (*especially NAmE*) an action to celebrate victory or to express happiness in which two people raise one arm each and hit their open hands together 相互高举胳膊击掌（以示庆祝或高兴）：*Way to go! High five!* 好样的！祝贺！

ˌ**high-ˈflown** *adj.* (*usually disapproving*) (of language and ideas 语言和思想) very grand and complicated 浮夸的；故弄玄虚的；说大话的 **SYN** **bombastic**: *His high-flown style just sounds absurd today.* 他的浮夸风格如今听起来真是荒谬。

ˌ**high-ˈflyer** (*also* ˌ**high-ˈflier**) *noun* a person who has the desire and the ability to be very successful in their job or their studies 有抱负有能力的人；有能耐的人：*academic high-flyers* 有学术抱负的人

ˌ**high-ˈflying** *adj.* [only before noun] **1** very successful 十分成功的：*a high-flying career woman* 事业成功的职业女性 **2** that flies very high in the air 在高空飞行的 ➲ MORE LIKE THIS 32, page R28

ˌ**high-ˈgrade** *adj.* [usually before noun] of very good quality 优质的；高级的：*high-grade petrol* 优质汽油

ˈ**high ground** *noun* (*usually* **the high ground**) [sing.] the advantage in a discussion or an argument, etc.（讨论或争论中的）优势，有利条件：*The government is claiming the high ground in the education debate.* 政府在教育辩论中处于有利地位。**IDM** SEE MORAL *adj.*

ˌ**high-ˈhanded** *adj.* (of people or their behaviour 人或行为) using authority in an unreasonable way, without considering the opinions of other people 专横的；高压的 **SYN** **overbearing**

ˈ**high-hat** *noun* = HI-HAT ➲ VISUAL VOCAB PAGE V37

ˌ**high ˈheels** *noun* [pl.] shoes that have very high heels, usually worn by women （女）高跟鞋 ▸ ˌ**high-ˈheeled** *adj.* [only before noun]: ***high-heeled shoes/boots*** 高跟鞋；高跟靴

ˌ**high ˈjinks** (*NAmE also* ˌ**hi-ˈjinks**) *noun* [pl.] (*old-fashioned, informal*) lively and excited behaviour 狂欢作乐；喧闹 **SYN** **fun**

the ˈhigh jump *noun* [sing.] a sporting event in which people try to jump over a high bar that is gradually raised higher and higher 跳高（运动）：*She won a silver medal in the high jump.* 她跳高得了银牌。➲ VISUAL VOCAB PAGE V50

IDM **be for the ˈhigh jump** (*BrE, informal*) to be going to be severely punished 将遭到严厉惩罚

high·land /ˈhaɪlənd/ *adj., noun*

■ ***adj.*** [only before noun] **1** connected with an area of land that has hills or mountains 高地的；高原的；山区的：*highland regions* 高原地区 **2** **Highland** connected with the Highlands of Scotland 苏格兰高地的 ➲ COMPARE LOWLAND *adj.*

■ ***noun*** **1** [C, usually pl.] an area of land with hills or mountains 高地；高原 **2** **the Highlands** [pl.] the high mountain region of Scotland 苏格兰高地 ➲ COMPARE LOWLAND *n.*

ˌ**Highland ˈcattle** *noun* [pl.] cows of a breed with long rough hair and large horns. An individual animal is a **Highland cow.**（统称）高地牛（毛长而粗糙，角长）

ˌ**Highland ˈdress** *noun* [U] traditional clothing worn by men in the Scottish Highlands, which includes a KILT and a SPORRAN (= a small decorated bag worn around the waist that hangs down at the front) 苏格兰高地男装（包括格子呢短裙和毛皮袋）

high·land·er /ˈhaɪləndə(r)/ *noun* **1** a person who comes from an area where there are a lot of mountains 高原地区的人；山地人 **2** **High·land·er** a person who comes from the Scottish Highlands 苏格兰高地人 ➲ COMPARE LOWLANDER

ˌ**Highland ˈfling** *noun* a fast Scottish dance that is danced by one person 高地舞（轻快苏格兰单人舞）

ˌ**Highland ˈGames** *noun* [pl.] a Scottish event with traditional sports, dancing and music 苏格兰高地运动会（包括传统体育运动、跳舞和音乐）

ˌ**high-ˈlevel** *adj.* [usually before noun] **1** involving senior people 级别高的；高层的：***high-level talks/negotiations*** 高层会谈 / 谈判 ◇ *high-level staff* 高级职员 **2** in a high position or place 位置高的；在高处的：*a high-level walk in the hills* 在山地徒步旅行 **3** advanced 高级的；高等的：*a high-level course* 高级课程 **4** (*computing* 计) (of a computer language 计算机语言) similar to an existing language such as English, making it fairly simple to use 高级的 **OPP** **low-level**

ˈ**high life** *noun* (*also* **the high life**) [sing., U] (*also* ˌ**high ˈliving** [U]) (*sometimes disapproving*) a way of life that involves going to parties and spending a lot of money on food, clothes, etc. 豪华的生活；灯红酒绿的生活

high·life /ˈhaɪlaɪf/ *noun* [U] a style of dance and music from W Africa influenced by rock and JAZZ and popular especially in the 1950s and 1960s 强节奏爵士舞，强节奏爵士乐（尤指盛行于 20 世纪 50 年代和 60 年代受摇滚乐、爵士乐和流行音乐影响的源于西非的舞蹈和音乐风格）

high·light 🔑 **AW** /ˈhaɪlaɪt/ *verb, noun*

■ ***verb*** **1** 🔑 **~ sth** to emphasize sth, especially so that people give it more attention 突出；强调：*The report highlights the major problems facing society today.* 报告特别强调了当今社会所面临的主要问题。➲ LANGUAGE BANK AT EMPHASIS **2** **~ sth** to mark part of a text with a special coloured pen, or to mark an area on a computer screen, to emphasize it or make it easier to see 将（文本的某部分）用彩笔做标记；将（计算机屏幕的某区域）增强亮度；使醒目：*I've highlighted the important passages in yellow.* 我用黄色标出了重要段落。 **3** **~ sth** to make some parts of your hair a lighter colour than the rest by using a chemical substance on them 挑染（将部分头发染成浅色）

■ ***noun*** **1** 🔑 the best, most interesting or most exciting part of sth 最好（或最精彩、最激动人心）的部分：*One of the highlights of the trip was seeing the Taj Mahal.* 这次旅行中的最精彩的一件事是参观泰姬陵。◇ *The highlights of the match will be shown later this evening.* 比赛最精彩的片段将于今晚播出。 **2** **highlights** [pl.] areas of hair that are lighter than the rest, usually because a chemical substance has been put on them 挑染的头发 ➲ COMPARE LOWLIGHTS **3** **highlights** [pl.] (*specialist*) the light or bright part of a picture or photograph （图画或照片的）强光部分

high·light·er /ˈhaɪlaɪtə(r)/ *noun* **1** (*also* ˈ**highlighter pen**) a special pen used for marking words in a text in bright colours （颜色鲜亮的）标记笔；荧光笔 ➲ VISUAL VOCAB PAGE V71 **2** a coloured substance that you put above your eyes or on your cheeks to make yourself more attractive （勾画脸、眼的）彩妆

high·ly 🔑 /ˈhaɪli/ *adv.* **1** 🔑 very 很；非常：*highly successful/skilled/intelligent* 十分成功 / 熟练 / 聪明 ◇ *highly competitive/critical/sensitive* 非常有竞争力 / 关键 / 敏感 ◇ *It is **highly unlikely** that she'll be late.* 她不大可能会迟到。 **2** 🔑 at or to a high standard, level or amount 高标准地；高级地；大量地：***highly trained/educated*** 受过高级培训 / 高等教育 ◇ *a **highly paid** job* 高薪工作 **3** 🔑 with admiration or praise 钦佩地；赞赏地：*His teachers **think very highly of him*** (= have a very good opinion of him). 老师们很欣赏他。◇ *She **speaks highly of you.*** 她对你大加称赞。◇ *Her novels are very highly regarded.* 她的小说受到很高的评价。

ˌ**highly ˈstrung** (*BrE*) (*NAmE* ˌ**high-ˈstrung**) *adj.* (of a person or an animal 人或动物) nervous and easily upset 紧张不安的：*a sensitive and highly-strung child* 敏感而脆弱的孩子 ◇ *Their new horse is very highly strung.* 他们的新马很容易受惊。➲ COMPARE NERVOUS (2)

ˌhigh-ˈmaintenance *adj.* needing a lot of attention or effort 耗费精力的；费神费力的：*a high-maintenance girlfriend* 需要操心呵护的女朋友 OPP **low-maintenance**

ˌhigh-ˈminded *adj.* (of people or ideas 人或思想) having strong moral principles 高尚的；高洁的 ▶ **ˌhigh-ˈminded·ness** *noun* [U]

High·ness /ˈhamǝs/ *noun* **His/Her/Your Highness** a title of respect used when talking to or about a member of the royal family（对王室成员的尊称）殿下，阁下 ➲ SEE ALSO ROYAL HIGHNESS

ˌhigh ˈnoon *noun* **1** exactly twelve o'clock in the middle of the day 中午十二点整；正午 **2** (*formal*) the most important stage of sth, when sth that will decide the future happens 最重要的阶段；决定性时刻

ˌhigh-ˈoctane *adj.* [only before noun] **1** (of fuel used in engines 发动机燃料) of very good quality and very efficient 优质的；高辛烷值的 **2** (*informal*) full of energy; powerful 充满活力的；强有力的：*a high-octane athlete* 体力充沛的运动员

ˌhigh-perˈformance *adj.* [only before noun] that can go very fast or do complicated things 高速的；高性能的；功能复杂的：*a high-performance car/computer, etc.* 高性能的汽车、计算机等

ˌhigh-ˈpitched *adj.* (of sounds 声音) very high 很高的；尖利的：*a high-pitched voice/whistle* 尖嗓子；尖锐的口哨声 OPP **low-pitched**

ˈhigh point (*BrE also* **ˈhigh spot**) *noun* the most interesting, enjoyable or best part of sth 最有意思（或最令人愉快、最好）的部分：*It was the high point of the evening.* 那是晚会最精彩的部分。OPP **low point**

ˌhigh-ˈpowered *adj.* **1** (of people 人) having a lot of power and influence; full of energy 有权势的；精力旺盛的：*high-powered executives* 劲头十足的主管们 **2** (of activities 活动) important; with a lot of responsibility 重要的；责任重大的：*a high-powered job* 位高权重的工作 **3** (*also* **ˌhigh-ˈpower**) (of machines 机器) very powerful 大功率的：*a high-powered car/computer, etc.* 大马力的汽车、高性能的计算机等

ˌhigh ˈpressure *noun* [U] **1** the condition of air, gas, or liquid that is kept in a small space by force 高压：*Water is forced through the pipes at **high pressure**.* 水在高压下流过水管。**2** a condition of the air which affects the weather, when the PRESSURE is higher than average 高气压 ➲ COMPARE LOW PRESSURE

ˌhigh-ˈpressure *adj.* [only before noun] **1** that involves aggressive ways of persuading sb to do sth or to buy sth 强力劝说的：*high-pressure sales techniques* 强行推销术 **2** that involves a lot of worry and anxiety 令人焦虑的；非常紧张的；压力大的 SYN **stressful**：*a high-pressure job* 压力很大的工作 **3** using or containing a great force of a gas or a liquid（气体或液体）受到高压的：*a high-pressure water jet* 高压水射流

ˌhigh-ˈpriced *adj.* [usually before noun] expensive 昂贵的；高价的：*high-priced housing/cars* 昂贵的住房 / 汽车 OPP **low**

ˌhigh ˈpriest *noun* **1** the most important priest in the Jewish religion in the past（旧时犹太教的）祭司长 **2** (*feminine* **ˌhigh ˈpriestess**) an important priest in some other non-Christian religions（某些非基督教的）大祭司：(*figurative*) *Janis Joplin was known as the High Priestess of Rock.* 贾尼斯•乔普林就是众所周知的摇滚乐大师。

ˌhigh-ˈprofile *adj.* [usually before noun] receiving or involving a lot of attention and discussion on television, in newspapers, etc. 经常出镜（或见报）的；高姿态的：*a high-profile campaign* 广受关注的运动 ➲ SEE ALSO PROFILE *n.*

ˌhigh-ˈranking *adj.* senior; important 职位高的；显要的：*a high-ranking officer/official* 高级军官 / 官员 ◇ *a high-ranking post* 显要岗位 OPP **low-ranking**

ˌhigh-resoˈlution (*also* **hi-res, high-res**) *adj.* (of a photograph or an image on a computer or television screen 照片或计算机、电视屏幕影像) showing a lot of clear sharp detail 高分辨率的；高清晰度的：*a high-resolution scan* 高清晰度扫描 OPP **low-resolution**

ˈhigh-rise *adj.* [only before noun] (of a building 建筑物) very tall and having a lot of floors 高层的：*high-rise housing* 高层住宅 ➲ WORDFINDER NOTE AT CITY ▶ **ˈhigh-rise** *noun*：*to live in a high-rise* 住在高层楼房里 ➲ COMPARE LOW-RISE *adj.* (1)

ˌhigh-ˈrisk *adj.* [usually before noun] involving a lot of danger and the risk of injury, death, damage, etc. 有高风险的；高危的：*a high-risk sport* 高风险的运动 ◇ *high-risk patients* (= who are very likely to get a particular illness) 高危病人 ➲ COMPARE LOW-RISK

ˈhigh road *noun* [usually sing.] **1** (*old-fashioned*) a main or important road 公路干线；交通要道 **2** ~ (**to sth**) the most direct way 最直接的方式：*This is the high road to democracy.* 这是通向民主的直接途径。

IDM **take the ˈhigh road (in sth)** (*NAmE*) to take the most positive course of action 采取最积极的行动方针：*He took the high road in his campaign.* 他在竞选活动中采取了最积极的方针。

ˌhigh ˈroller *noun* (*NAmE, informal*) a person who spends a lot of money, especially on gambling 挥霍的人；（尤指）豪赌者

ˈhigh school *noun* [C, U] **1** (in the US and some other countries) a school for young people between the ages of 14 and 18（美国和其他一些国家 14 到 18 岁青年的）中学，高中 **2** often used in Britain in the names of schools for young people between the ages of 11 and 18 中学，完全中学（英国常用于为 11 到 18 岁青年开办的学校名称中）：*Worthing High School* 沃辛高中 ➲ COMPARE SECONDARY SCHOOL ➲ COLLOCATIONS AT EDUCATION

the ˌhigh ˈseas *noun* [pl.] (*formal* or *literary*) the areas of sea that are not under the legal control of any one country 公海

ˌhigh ˈseason *noun* [U, sing.] (*especially BrE*) the time of year when a hotel or tourist area receives most visitors（旅馆或旅游地区的）旺季 ➲ COMPARE LOW SEASON

ˌhigh-seˈcurity *adj.* [only before noun] **1** (of buildings and places 建筑或地方) very carefully locked and guarded 戒备森严的；警戒严密的：*a high-security prison* 警备森严的监狱 **2** (of prisoners 囚犯) kept in a prison that is very carefully locked and guarded 关押在警备森严的监狱里的

ˈhigh-sounding *adj.* (*especially BrE, often disapproving*) (of language or ideas 语言或思想) complicated and intended to sound important 夸张的；高调的 SYN **pretentious**

ˌhigh-ˈspeed *adj.* [only before noun] that travels, works or happens very fast 高速的；高效率的；迅速的：*a high-speed train* 高速列车 ◇ *a high-speed car chase* 高速汽车追逐

ˌhigh-ˈspirited *adj.* **1** (of people 人) very lively and active 兴致勃勃的；兴高采烈的：*a high-spirited child* 兴高采烈的孩子 ◇ *high-spirited behaviour* 朝气蓬勃 **2** (of animals, especially horses 动物，尤指马) lively and difficult to control 烈性的；欢蹦乱跳的 OPP **placid** ➲ SEE ALSO SPIRIT

ˈhigh spot *noun* (*BrE*) = HIGH POINT

ˈhigh street (*BrE*) (*NAmE* **ˈmain street**) *noun* (especially in names 尤用于名称) the main street of a town, where most shops/stores, banks, etc. are 大街（城镇的主要街道）：*Peckham High Street* 佩卡姆大街 ◇ *106 High Street, Peckham* 佩卡姆大街 106 号 ◇ ***high-street banks/shops*** 商业区大街上的银行 / 商店 ➲ VISUAL VOCAB PAGE V3

ˌhigh-ˈstrung (*NAmE*) (*BrE* **ˌhighly ˈstrung**) *adj.* (of a person or an animal 人或动物) nervous and easily upset 紧张不安的 ➲ SYNONYMS AT NERVOUS

H

ˌhigh ˈtable *noun* [C, U] (*BrE*) a table on a raised platform, where the most important people at a formal dinner sit to eat 高台餐桌（正式宴会上为显要人士设在高平台上的餐桌）

high·tail /ˈhaɪteɪl/ *verb*
IDM **ˈhightail it** (*informal, especially NAmE*) to leave somewhere very quickly 迅速离开

ˌhigh ˈtea *noun* (*BrE*) a meal consisting of cooked food, bread and butter and cakes, usually with tea to drink, eaten in the late afternoon or early evening instead of dinner 傍晚茶（傍晚前后吃的膳食，通常有茶，代替晚上正餐）

ˌhigh-ˈtech (*also* **ˌhi-ˈtech**) *adj.* (*informal*) **1** using the most modern methods and machines, especially electronic ones 高技术的，高科技的（尤指电子方面）：*high-tech industries* 高科技产业 **2** (of designs, objects, etc. 图案、物体等) very modern in appearance; using modern materials 样式新颖的；用高新技术材料的：*a high-tech table made of glass and steel* 用玻璃和钢制成的现代化桌子 ➲ COMPARE LOW-TECH

ˌhigh techˈnology *noun* [U] the most modern methods and machines, especially electronic ones; the use of these in industry, etc. 高科技，高技术（尤指电子技术）；高科技的运用

ˌhigh-ˈtension *adj.* [only before noun] carrying a very powerful electric current 高（电）压的：***high-tension wires/cables*** 高压电线 / 电缆

ˌhigh ˈtide *noun* [U, C] the time when the sea has risen to its highest level; the sea at this time （海的）高潮时期，高潮，满潮：*You can't walk along this beach **at high tide**.* 高潮时你不能在这个海滩散步。OPP **low tide** ➲ COMPARE FLOOD TIDE, HIGH WATER

ˈhigh-tops *noun* [pl.] (*especially NAmE*) sports shoes that cover the ankle, worn especially for playing BASKETBALL 高帮运动鞋（尤用于篮球运动）▸ **ˈhigh-top** *adj.* [usually before noun]: *high-top sneakers* 高帮运动鞋

ˌhigh ˈtreason *noun* [U] = TREASON

ˈhigh-up *noun* (*BrE, informal*) an important person with a high rank 高官；要员

ˌhigh-visiˈbility *adj.* [usually before noun] (*also informal* **ˌhigh-ˈvis**, **ˌhi-ˈvis**) **1** used to describe clothing made of material that appears very bright and is very easy to see （服装）高能见度的：*cyclists with high-visibility jackets* 身着鲜亮夹克的自行车骑手 ◇ *Hard hats and high-vis vests must be worn on the building site.* 在建筑工地必须头戴安全帽，身着反光背心。**2** used to describe sth that is intended to attract a lot of attention 引人注目的：*a high-visibility ad campaign* 引人注目的广告宣传活动

ˌhigh ˈwater *noun* [U] the time when the sea or the water in a river has risen to its highest level （海、河的）高潮，满潮；高水位：*Fishing is good at high water.* 高水位有利于钓鱼。➲ COMPARE HIGH TIDE IDM SEE HELL

ˌhigh-ˈwater mark *noun* a line or mark showing the highest point that the sea or FLOODWATER has reached 高水位线（海水或洪水所达到的最高水位）：(*figurative*) *the high-water mark of Parisian fashion* (= the most successful time) 巴黎时装最流行的时期 ➲ COMPARE LOW-WATER MARK

high·way /ˈhaɪweɪ/ *noun* **1** (*especially NAmE*) a main road for travelling long distances, especially one connecting and going through cities and towns （尤指城镇间的）公路，干道，交通要道：*an interstate highway* （美国）州际公路 ◇ *Highway patrol officers closed the road.* 公路巡警关闭了这条路。**2** (*BrE, formal*) a public road 公用通道：*A parked car was obstructing the highway.* 一辆停放的汽车堵住了通道。
IDM **ˌhighway ˈrobbery** (*informal, especially NAmE*) = DAYLIGHT ROBBERY ➲ MORE AT WAY *n.*

the ˌHighway ˈCode *noun* [sing.] (in Britain) the official rules for drivers and other users of public roads; the book that contains these rules （英国）公用通道法规，公用通道法规汇编

high·way·man /ˈhaɪweɪmən/ *noun* (*pl.* **-men** /-mən/) a man, usually on a horse and carrying a gun, who stole from travellers on public roads in the past （旧时常骑马持枪的）拦路强盗

ˌhigh ˈwire *noun* [usually sing.] a rope or wire that is stretched high above the ground, and used by CIRCUS performers （杂技演员使用的）高空绳索，空中钢丝 SYN **tightrope**

ˈhi-hat (*also* **ˈhigh-hat**) *noun* a pair of CYMBALS on a set of drums, operated by the foot 踩镲（通过踏板控制）➲ VISUAL VOCAB PAGE V37

hi·jab /hɪˈdʒɑːb/ *noun* **1** [C] a head covering worn in public by some Muslim women （穆斯林妇女出门戴的）头巾，盖头 **2** [U] the religious system which controls the wearing of such clothing 头巾制度（规定戴头巾的宗教制度）

hi·jack /ˈhaɪdʒæk/ *verb* **1** ~ **sth** to use violence or threats to take control of a vehicle, especially a plane, in order to force it to travel to a different place or to demand sth from a government 劫持（交通工具，尤指飞机）：*The plane was hijacked by two armed men on a flight from London to Rome.* 飞机在从伦敦飞往罗马途中遭到两名持械男子劫持。➲ WORDFINDER NOTE AT ATTACK ➲ COLLOCATIONS AT CRIME **2** ~ **sth** (*disapproving*) to use or take control of sth, especially a meeting, in order to advertise your own aims and interests 操纵（会议等，以推销自己的意图）▸ **hi·jack·ing** (*also* **hi·jack**) *noun* [C, U]: *There have been a series of hijackings recently in the area.* 这个地区最近发生了一连串劫持事件。◇ *an unsuccessful hijack* 劫持未遂 ➲ COMPARE CARJACKING

hi·jack·er /ˈhaɪdʒækə(r)/ *noun* a person who hijacks a plane or other vehicle 劫机者；劫持交通工具者；劫持者

hi-jinks (*NAmE*) = HIGH JINKS

Hijra /ˈhɪdʒrə/ *noun* = HEGIRA

hike /haɪk/ *noun, verb*
■ ***noun*** **1** a long walk in the country 远足；徒步旅行：*They went on a ten-mile hike through the forest.* 他们进行了一次穿越森林的十英里徒步旅行。◇ *We could go into town but it's a real hike* (= a long way) *from here.* 我们本可以进城去，但走到那儿实在太远。**2** (*informal*) a large or sudden increase in prices, costs, etc. （价格、花费等的）大幅度提高，猛增：*a **tax/price hike*** 税额 / 价格的大幅度增长 ◇ ~ **in sth** *the latest hike in interest rates* 新近利率的大幅上扬
IDM **take a ˈhike** (*NAmE, informal*) a rude way of telling sb to go away 滚开；走开
■ ***verb*** **1** [I, T] to go for a long walk in the country, especially for pleasure 去…远足；做徒步旅行：*strong boots for hiking over rough country* 适合在崎岖不平的山路徒步旅行用的结实靴子 ◇ ~ **sth** (*NAmE*) *to hike the Rockies* 去落基山脉徒步旅行 **2** [I] **go hiking** to spend time hiking for pleasure 远足；徒步旅行：*If the weather's fine, we'll go hiking this weekend.* 如果天气好，我们这个周末就去远足。**3** [T] ~ **sth** (**up**) to increase prices, taxes, etc. suddenly by large amounts 把（价格、税率等）大幅提高：*The government hiked up the price of milk by over 40%.* 政府把牛奶的价格提高了四成多。
PHR V **ˌhike sth↔ˈup** (*informal*) to pull or lift sth up, especially your clothing 拉起，提起（衣服等）SYN **hitch**: *She hiked up her skirt and waded into the river.* 她提起裙子走进河水中。

hiker /ˈhaɪkə(r)/ *noun* a person who goes for long walks in the country for pleasure 远足者；徒步旅行者 ➲ SEE ALSO HITCHHIKER at HITCHHIKE

hik·ing /ˈhaɪkɪŋ/ *noun* [U] the activity of going for long walks in the country for pleasure 远足；徒步旅行：*to go hiking* 徒步旅行 ◇ *hiking boots* （徒步）旅行靴 ➲ VISUAL VOCAB PAGE V69

hil·ari·ous /hɪˈleəriəs; *NAmE* -ˈler-/ *adj.* extremely funny 极其滑稽的：*a hilarious joke/story* 令人捧腹的笑话 / 故事 ◇ *Lynn found the whole situation hilarious.* 林恩觉得这一切都非常滑稽。◇ *Do you know Pete? He's hilarious.* 你认识皮特吗？他风趣得很。 ➲ SYNONYMS AT FUNNY ▶ **hil·ari·ous·ly** *adv.*：*hilariously funny* 滑稽可笑

hil·ar·ity /hɪˈlærəti/ *noun* [U] a state of great AMUSEMENT which makes people laugh 欢闹；狂欢

hill 🔑 /hɪl/ *noun* **1** 🔑 [C] an area of land that is higher than the land around it, but not as high as a mountain 山丘；小山：*a region of gently rolling hills* 缓缓起伏的丘陵地区 ◇ ***a hill farm/town/fort*** 小山上的农场 / 城镇 / 城堡 ◇ *The house is built **on the side of a hill** overlooking the river.* 房子建在可俯视河流的小山坡上。◇ *I love walking **in the hills*** (= in the area where there are hills). 我喜欢在山中散步。 ➲ VISUAL VOCAB PAGE V3 ➲ SEE ALSO ANTHILL, FOOTHILL, MOLEHILL **2** 🔑[C] a slope on a road（道路的）斜坡：*Always take care when driving down **steep hills**.* 下陡坡时一定要小心驾驶。◇ *a **hill start*** (= the act of starting a vehicle on a slope) 汽车爬坡起步 ➲ SEE ALSO DOWNHILL *n.*, UPHILL **3 the Hill** [sing.] (*NAmE, informal*) = CAPITOL HILL

IDM **a ˌhill of ˈbeans** (*old-fashioned, NAmE, informal*) something that is not worth much 没有多大价值的东西 **ˌover the ˈhill** (*informal*) (of a person 人) old and therefore no longer useful or attractive 老而不中用的；人老珠黄的 ➲ MORE AT OLD

hill·billy /ˈhɪlbɪli/ *noun* (*pl.* **-ies**) (*NAmE, disapproving*) a person who lives in the mountains and is thought to be stupid by people who live in the towns 山区乡巴佬

hil·lock /ˈhɪlək/ *noun* a small hill 小丘

hill·side /ˈhɪlsaɪd/ *noun* the side of a hill 小山坡：*The crops will not grow on exposed hillsides.* 在裸露的山坡上庄稼没法生长。◇ *Our hotel was on the hillside overlooking the lake.* 我们的旅馆位于可俯瞰湖水的小山坡上。

ˈhill station *noun* a small town in the hills, especially in S Asia, where people go to find cooler weather in summer（尤指南亚的）山区避暑小镇

hill·top /ˈhɪltɒp; *NAmE* -tɑːp/ *noun* the top of a hill 小山顶：*the hilltop town of Urbino* 建在小山顶上的乌尔比诺镇

hill·walk·ing /ˈhɪlwɔːkɪŋ/ *noun* [U] the activity of walking on or up hills in the countryside for pleasure 丘陵地带徒步旅行；丘陵远足

hilly /ˈhɪli/ *adj.* (**hill·ier**, **hilli·est**) having a lot of hills 多小山的；多丘陵的：***a hilly area/region*** 丘陵地区

hilt /hɪlt/ *noun* the handle of a SWORD, knife, etc. 刀（或剑等的）柄 ➲ PICTURE AT SWORD

IDM **(up) to the ˈhilt** as much as possible 尽量；尽可能：*We're mortgaged up to the hilt.* 我们已经把什么都抵押了。◇ *They have promised to back us to the hilt.* 他们保证全力支持我们。

him 🔑 /hɪm; ɪm/ *pron.* **1** 🔑 used as the object of a verb, after the verb *be* or after a preposition to refer to a male person or animal that has already been mentioned or is easily identified 他，它（用作动词或介词的宾语，或作表语）：*When did you see him?* 你什么时候见到他的？◇ *He took the children with him.* 他带着孩子。◇ *I'm taller than him.* 我比他高。◇ *It's him.* 是他。 ➲ COMPARE HE *pron.* ➲ NOTE AT GENDER **2 Him** used when referring to God（指上帝）

him·self 🔑 /hɪmˈself/ *pron.* **1** 🔑 (the reflexive form of *he* * he 的反身形式) used when the man or boy who performs an action is also affected by it（用作男性的反身代词）他自己，自己：*He introduced himself.* 他作了自我介绍。◇ *Peter ought to be ashamed of himself.* 彼得应为自己感到羞耻。 **2** 🔑 used to emphasize the male subject or object of a sentence（强调句中的男性主语或宾语）：*The doctor said so himself.* 是医生本人这么说的。◇ *Did you see the manager himself?* 你见到经理本人了吗？

IDM **be, seem, etc. himˈself** (of a man or boy 男性) to be in a normal state of health or happiness; not influenced by other people 一切正常；如平时一般；未受他人影响：*He didn't seem quite himself this morning.* 他今天上午似乎有点不对劲。◇ *He needed space to be himself.* 他需要自己的独立的空间。 **(all) by himˈself 1** alone; without anyone else（他）独自，单独：*He lives all by himself.* 他独自一人生活。 **2** without help（他）独立地：*He managed to repair the car by himself.* 他自己设法修了汽车。 **(all) to himˈself** for only him to have or use 归自己一人占有（或使用）：*He has the house to himself during the week.* 一周之中除周末外他可以一人住这座房子。

hind /haɪnd/ *adj., noun*

■ ***adj.*** [only before noun] the **hind** legs or feet of an animal with four legs are those at the back（四足动物的腿、蹄）后面的：*The horse reared up on its hind legs.* 那匹马后腿直立，站了起来。 OPP **fore, front** IDM SEE TALK *v.*

■ ***noun*** a female DEER, especially a RED DEER; a DOE 雌鹿（尤指雌赤鹿） ➲ COMPARE HART

hind·brain /ˈhaɪndbreɪn/ *noun* (*anatomy* 解) the part of the brain near the base of the head 后脑

hin·der /ˈhɪndə(r)/ *verb* to make it difficult for sb to do sth or for sth to happen 阻碍；妨碍；阻挡 SYN **hamper**：**~ sb/sth** *a political situation that hinders economic growth* 妨碍经济发展的政治局面 ◇ *Some teachers felt hindered by a lack of resources.* 有些教师因资源不足而感到困难重重。◇ **~ sb/sth from sth/from doing sth** *An injury was hindering him from playing his best.* 受伤后他无法发挥出最高水平。 ➲ SEE ALSO HINDRANCE

Hindi /ˈhɪndi/ *noun* [U] one of the official languages of India, spoken especially in northern India 印地语（印度官方语言之一，尤通用于印度北部） ▶ **Hindi** *adj.*

hind·limb /ˈhaɪndlɪm/ *noun* one of the legs at the back of an animal's body（动物的）后肢，后腿

hind·quar·ters /ˌhaɪndˈkwɔːtəz; *NAmE* -ˈkwɔːrtərz/ *noun* [pl.] the back part of an animal that has four legs, including its two back legs（四腿动物的）臀部及后腿

hin·drance /ˈhɪndrəns/ *noun* **1** [C, usually sing.] a person or thing that makes it more difficult for sb to do sth or for sth to happen 造成妨碍的人（或事物）：*To be honest, she was more of a hindrance than a help.* 说实在的，她没帮上忙，反而成了累赘。◇ **~ to sth/sb** *The high price is a major hindrance to potential buyers.* 价格高是使潜在买主却步的主要因素。 **2** [U] (*formal*) the act of making it more difficult for sb to do sth or for sth to happen 妨碍；阻挠：*They were able to complete their journey without further hindrance.* 剩下的旅程他们没再受到阻碍。 ➲ SEE ALSO HINDER IDM SEE LET *n.*

hind·sight /ˈhaɪndsaɪt/ *noun* [U] the understanding that you have of a situation only after it has happened and that means you would have done things in a different way 事后聪明；事后的领悟：***With hindsight** it is easy to say they should not have released him.* 事后才说他们本不应该释放他，这倒容易。◇ *What looks obvious in hindsight was not at all obvious at the time.* 事后一目了然的事在当时根本看不清。◇ *It's easy to criticize **with the benefit of hindsight**.* 事后明白了再评价，这自然容易。 ➲ COMPARE FORESIGHT

Hindu /ˈhɪnduː; ˌhɪnˈduː/ *noun* a person whose religion is Hinduism 印度教教徒 ▶ **Hindu** *adj.*：*a Hindu temple* 印度教庙宇

Hin·du·ism /ˈhɪnduːɪzəm/ *noun* [U] the main religion of India and Nepal which includes the worship of one or more gods and belief in REINCARNATION 印度教（印度和尼泊尔的主要宗教，敬拜一位或多位神祇，相信轮回转世）

Hin·dutva /hɪnˈdʊtvə/ *noun* [U] the belief that Indian culture and the Indian way of life should be based mainly on Hindu values 印度教至上主义（认为印度文化和印度生活方式应以印度教价值观为基础）

hinge /hɪndʒ/ *noun, verb*

■ ***noun*** a piece of metal, plastic, etc. on which a door, lid or gate moves freely as it opens or closes 铰链；合叶：*The door had been pulled off its hinges.* 门从铰链上扯下来了。

■ ***verb*** [usually passive] ~ **sth** to attach sth with a hinge 给（某物）装铰链 ▸ **hinged** *adj.*：*a hinged door/lid* 铰接的门 / 盖

PHR V **'hinge on/upon sth** (of an action, a result, etc. 行动、结果等) to depend on sth completely 有赖于；取决于：*Everything hinges on the outcome of these talks.* 一切都取决于这几次会谈的结果。◇ **hinge on/upon how, what, etc....** *His success hinges on how well he does at the interview.* 他能否成功要看他在面试中的表现。

hinge 铰链

Hing·lish /ˈhɪŋglɪʃ/ *noun* [U] (*informal*) language which is a mixture of ENGLISH and HINDI, especially a type of English that includes many Hindi words 印地英语；印度英语

hint /hɪnt/ *noun, verb*

■ ***noun*** **1** something that you say or do in an indirect way in order to show sb what you are thinking 暗示；提示；示意：*He gave a* **broad hint** (= one that was obvious) *that he was thinking of retiring.* 他几乎明示他正在考虑退休。◇ *Should I* **drop a hint** (= give a hint) *to Matt?* 我应该给马特一点暗示吗？ **2** something that suggests what will happen in the future 征兆；迹象 SYN **sign**：*At the first hint of trouble, they left.* 他们一发现有点不妙的迹象就离开了。 **3** [usually sing.] ~ (**of sth**) a small amount of sth 少许；少量 SYN **suggestion, trace**：*a hint of a smile* 一丝笑意 ◇ *There was more than a hint of sadness in his voice.* 他的声音中流露出了深切的悲伤。◇ *The walls were painted white with a hint of peach.* 墙壁粉刷成了略呈桃红的白色。 **4** [usually pl.] ~ (**on sth**) a small piece of practical information or advice 秘诀；窍门 SYN **tip**：*handy hints on saving money* 省钱妙诀

IDM **take a/the 'hint** to understand what sb wants you to do even though they tell you in an indirect way 领会某人的暗示：*I thought they'd never go—some people just can't take a hint.* 我以为他们永远也不会走的，有些人就是不会看眼色。◇ *Sarah hoped he'd take the hint and leave her alone.* 萨拉希望他能明白她的意思，不来打扰她。

■ ***verb*** [I, T] to suggest sth in an indirect way 暗示；透露；示意：**~ at sth** *What are you hinting at?* 你在暗示什么？ ◇ **~ (that)...** *They hinted (that) there might be more job losses.* 他们暗示说可能会有更多人失业。◇ **+ speech** *'I might know something about it,' he hinted.* "这事我也许知道一些。"他暗示道。

hin·ter·land /ˈhɪntəlænd; *NAmE* -tərl-/ *noun* [usually sing.] the areas of a country that are away from the coast, from the banks of a large river or from the main cities 内陆；腹地；内地：*the rural/agricultural hinterland* 内陆乡下；内地农村

hip 🔑 /hɪp/ *noun, adj., exclamation*

■ ***noun*** **1** 🔑 the area at either side of the body between the top of the leg and the waist; the joint at the top of the leg 臀部；髋：*She stood with her hands on her hips.* 她双手叉腰站着。◇ *These jeans are too tight around the hips.* 这条牛仔裤的臀部太窄。◇ *a hip replacement operation* 髋部复位手术 ◇ *the hip bone* 髋骨 ◇ *She broke her hip in the fall.* 她摔倒时折断了髋骨。 ➲ **COLLOCATIONS** AT **PHYSICAL** ➲ **VISUAL VOCAB PAGE V64** **2 -hipped** (in adjectives 构成形容词) having hips of the size or shape mentioned 臀部…的：*large-hipped* 臀部大的 ◇ *slim-hipped* 臀部窄的 ➲ **MORE LIKE THIS 8, page R25** **3** (*also* **'rose hip**) the red fruit that grows on some types of wild ROSE bush 野蔷薇果 IDM SEE SHOOT *v.*

■ ***adj.*** (**hip·per, hip·pest**) (*informal*) following or knowing what is fashionable in clothes, music, etc.（衣服、音乐等方面）时髦的，赶时髦的

■ ***exclamation***

IDM **hip, hip, hoo'ray!** (*also less frequent* **hip, hip, hur'rah/hur'ray!**) used by a group of people to show their approval of sb. One person in the group says 'hip, hip' and the others then shout 'hooray'. 嘿，嘿，乌拉（或万岁）（集体欢呼声。其中一人说 hip，hip，其他人随后喊 hooray）：*'Three cheers for the bride and groom : Hip, hip...' 'Hooray!'* "向新娘和新郎欢呼三声：嘿，嘿..." "好啊！"

'hip bath *noun* a small bath/BATHTUB that you sit in rather than lie down in 坐式浴盆

'hip flask (*also* **flask**) *noun* a small flat bottle made of metal or glass and often covered with leather, used for carrying alcohol 小扁酒瓶（用金属或玻璃制成，常带皮套，随身携带）

'hip hop *noun* [U] **1** a type of popular music with spoken words and a steady beat played on electronic instruments, originally played by young African Americans 嘻哈音乐（由美国黑人青年兴起，包括说唱和电子乐器演奏） **2** the culture of the young African Americans and others who enjoy this type of music, including special styles of art, dancing, dress, etc. 嘻哈文化（包括艺术、舞蹈、装束等）

'hip-huggers (*NAmE*) (*BrE* **hip·sters**) *noun* [pl.] trousers/pants that cover the hips but not the waist 低腰长裤（裤腰低及臀部） ▸ **'hip-hugger** *adj.* [only before noun]

'hip joint *noun* the joint that connects the leg to the body, at the top of the THIGH bone 髋关节

hip·pie (*also* **hippy**) /ˈhɪpi/ *noun* (*pl.* **-ies**) a person who rejects the way that most people live in Western society, often having long hair, wearing brightly coloured clothes and taking illegal drugs. The hippie movement was most popular in the 1960s. 嬉皮士（拒绝西方主流生活方式的人，常留长发、衣着鲜艳、吸毒。嬉皮士运动在 20 世纪 60 年代最盛行）

hippo /ˈhɪpəʊ; *NAmE* ˈhɪpoʊ/ *noun* (*pl.* **-os**) (*informal*) = HIPPOPOTAMUS

hippo·cam·pus /ˌhɪpəˈkæmpəs/ *noun* (*pl.* **hippo·campi** /-paɪ; -pi/) (*anatomy* 解) either of the two areas of the brain thought to be the centre of emotion and memory 海马（大脑中被认为是感情和记忆中心的部分）

ˌhip 'pocket *noun* a pocket at the back or the side of a pair of trousers/pants or a skirt（裤子或裙子的）后口袋，侧口袋

the Hippo·crat·ic oath /ˌhɪpəkrætɪk ˈəʊθ; *NAmE* ˈoʊθ/ *noun* [sing.] the promise that doctors make to keep to the principles of the medical profession 希波克拉底誓言（医生保证遵守职业道德的誓言）

hip·po·drome /ˈhɪpədrəʊm; *NAmE* -droʊm/ *noun* **1** (*BrE*) used in the names of some theatres and concert halls（用于名称）剧院，音乐厅 **2** (*NAmE*) an ARENA, especially one used for horse shows 竞技场；（尤指）马术表演场 **3** a track in ancient Greece or Rome on which horse races or CHARIOT races took place（古希腊或古罗马的）赛马场，战车竞技场

hippo·pot·amus /ˌhɪpəˈpɒtəməs; *NAmE* -ˈpɑːtə-/ (*also informal* **hippo**) *noun* (*pl.* **hippo·pot·amuses** /-məsɪz/ or **hip·po·pot·ami** /-maɪ/) a large heavy African animal with thick dark skin and short legs, that lives in rivers and lakes 河马

hippy = HIPPIE

hip·ster /ˈhɪpstə(r)/ *noun* (*especially NAmE*) a person who follows what is fashionable in clothes, music, etc. 潮人；时尚达人 ▸ **hip·ster** *adj.* [only before noun]： *a hipster bar* 时尚酒吧

hip·sters /ˈhɪpstəz; *NAmE* -stərz/ (*BrE*) (*NAmE* ˈ**hip-huggers**) *noun* [pl.] trousers/pants that cover the hips but not the waist 低腰长裤（裤腰低及臀部）： *a pair of hipsters* 一条低腰长裤 ▸ **hip·ster** *adj.* [only before noun]： *hipster jeans* 低腰牛仔裤

hira·gana /ˌhɪrəˈɡɑːnə/ *noun* [U] (*from Japanese*) a set of symbols used in Japanese writing （日语中的）平假名 ➲ COMPARE KATAKANA

hire 🔑 /ˈhaɪə(r)/ *verb, noun*

■ *verb* **1** 🔑 [T] ~ **sth** (*especially BrE*) to pay money to borrow sth for a short time 租用；租借： *to hire a car/room/video* 租汽车；租房间；租录像带 ➲ NOTE AT RENT **2** 🔑 [T, I] ~ (**sb**) (*especially NAmE*) to give sb a job 聘用；录用；雇用： *She was hired three years ago.* 她是三年前录用的。◇ *He does the* ***hiring and firing*** *in our company.* 他在我们公司负责员工的聘用和辞退。 ➲ COLLOCATIONS AT JOB **3** 🔑 [T] ~ **sb/sth** to employ sb for a short time to do a particular job 临时雇用： *to hire a lawyer* 聘请律师 ◇ *They hired a firm of consultants to design the new system.* 他们请了一家咨询公司来设计新的系统。

PHR V ˌ**hire sth**↔ˈ**out** 🔑 to let sb use sth for a short time, in return for payment 出租某物 ˌ**hire yourself** ˈ**out** (**to sb**) to arrange to work for sb 为（某人）工作；受聘于；受雇于： *He hired himself out to whoever needed his services.* 他以前打过短工。

■ *noun* **1** 🔑 [U] (*especially BrE*) the act of paying to use sth for a short time 租借；租用；租赁： *bicycles* ***for hire****, £2 an hour* 自行车出租，每小时 2 英镑 ◇ *a* ***hire car*** 供租用的汽车 ◇ *a* ***car hire firm*** 汽车出租公司 ◇ *The price includes the hire of the hall.* 费用包括礼堂租金。◇ *The costumes are* ***on hire from*** *the local theatre.* 戏装可向本地剧院租用。 ➲ NOTE AT RENT **2** [C] (*especially NAmE*) a person who has recently been given a job by a company 新雇员；新员工

IDM SEE PLY *v.*

ˌ**hired** ˈ**hand** *noun* (*NAmE*) a person who is paid to work on a farm 农场雇工

hire·ling /ˈhaɪəlɪŋ; *NAmE* ˈhaɪərlɪŋ/ *noun* (*disapproving*) a person who is willing to do anything or work for anyone as long as they are paid 给钱就什么都愿干的人；有奶就叫娘的人

ˌ**hire** ˈ**purchase** *noun* [U] (*BrE*) (*abbr.* **h.p.**, **HP**) (*NAmE* **in**ˈ**stallment plan**) a method of buying an article by making regular payments for it over several months or years. The article only belongs to the person who is buying it when all the payments have been made. 分期付款购买： *a hire purchase agreement* 分期付款协议 ◇ *We're buying a new cooker* ***on hire purchase****.* 我们以分期付款方式购买一台新炉具。 ➲ COMPARE CREDIT *n.* (1)

hi-res (*also* **high-res**) /ˌhaɪ ˈrez/ *adj.* (*informal*) = HIGH-RESOLUTION

hir·sute /ˈhɜːsjuːt; *NAmE* ˈhɜːrsuːt/ *adj.* (*literary* or *humorous*) (especially of a man 尤指男子) having a lot of hair on the face or body 满脸胡须的；体毛多的 SYN **hairy**

his 🔑 /hɪz; ɪz/ *det., pron.*

■ *det.* (the possessive form of *he* * he 的所有格形式) **1** 🔑 of or belonging to a man or boy who has already been mentioned or is easily identified 他的： *James has sold his car.* 詹姆斯把他的车卖了。◇ *He broke his leg skiing.* 他滑雪时摔断了腿。 **2 His** of or belonging to God 上帝的；属于上帝的

■ *pron.* 🔑 of or belonging to him 他的；属于他的： *He took my hand in his.* 他握住我的手。◇ *The choice was his.* 选择由他作出。◇ *a friend of his* 他的一位朋友 ➲ NOTE AT GENDER

His·pan·ic /hɪˈspænɪk/ *adj., noun*

■ *adj.* of or connected with Spain or Spanish-speaking countries, especially those of Latin America 西班牙的；西班牙语国家（尤指拉丁美洲）的

■ *noun* a person whose first language is Spanish, especially one from a Latin American country living in the US or Canada 母语为西班牙语的人（尤指住在美国或加拿大的拉丁美洲人）

His·pan·o- /hɪˈspænəʊ; *NAmE* -noʊ/ *combining form* (in nouns and adjectives 构成名词和形容词) Spanish 西班牙的： *the Hispano-French border* 西班牙与法国边境 ◇ *Hispanophile* 亲西班牙的

hiss /hɪs/ *verb, noun*

■ *verb* **1** [I] ~ (**at sb/sth**) to make a sound like a long 's' 发嘶嘶声： *The steam escaped with a loud hissing noise.* 蒸汽冒了出来，发出很响的嘶嘶声。◇ *The snake lifted its head and hissed.* 蛇昂起头发出嘶嘶声。 **2** [T, I] ~ (**sb/sth**) | ~ (**sb/sth + adv./prep.**) to make a sound like a long 's' to show disapproval of sb/sth, especially an actor or a speaker 发嘘声（表示不满，尤指对演员或演讲人）： *He was booed and hissed off the stage.* 他在一片倒彩声和嘘声中被轰下台。 **3** [I, T] to say sth in a quiet angry voice 带怒气地低声说出（某事）： ~ **at sb** *He hissed at them to be quiet.* 他生气地低声要他们安静点。◇ **+ speech** *'Leave me alone!' she hissed.* "别烦我！"她生气地低声说。

■ *noun* a sound like a long 's'; this sound used to show disapproval of sb 嘶嘶声；嘘声： *the hiss of the air brakes* 气闸的嘶嘶声 ◇ *the snake's hiss* 蛇发出的嘶嘶声 ◇ *The performance was met with boos and hisses.* 演出换来一片倒彩声和嘘声。 ➲ MORE LIKE THIS 3, page R25

ˈ**hissy fit** *noun* [C, usually sing.] (*informal*) a state of being bad-tempered and unreasonable 坏脾气 SYN **tantrum**: *She* ***threw a hissy fit*** *because her dressing room wasn't painted blue.* 她发脾气是因为她的梳妆室没有漆成蓝色。

his·ta·mine /ˈhɪstəmiːn/ *noun* [U] (*medical* 医) a chemical substance that is given out in the body in response to an injury or an ALLERGY 组胺（遇组织受伤或过敏时释放） ➲ SEE ALSO ANTIHISTAMINE

histo·gram /ˈhɪstəɡræm/ *noun* (*specialist*) a diagram which uses RECTANGLES (= bars) of different heights (and sometimes different widths) to show different amounts, so that they can be compared 直方图，柱形图，条形图（以不同长度或宽度的长方形条块表示不同数量以作比较） ➲ COMPARE BAR CHART

his·tolo·gy /hɪˈstɒlədʒi; *NAmE* -ˈstɑːl-/ *noun* [U] the scientific study of the extremely small structures that form living TISSUE 组织学 ▸ **his·tolo·gist** /hɪˈstɒlədʒɪst; *NAmE* -ˈstɑːl-/ *noun*

histo·path·ology /ˌhɪstəʊpəˈθɒlədʒi; *NAmE* ˌhɪstoʊpəˈθɑːl-/ *noun* [U] the study of changes in cells where disease is present 组织病理学

his·tor·ian /hɪˈstɔːriən/ *noun* a person who studies or writes about history; an expert in history 史学工作者；历史学家 HELP Some speakers do not pronounce the 'h' at the beginning of **historian** and use 'an' instead of 'a' before it. This now sounds old-fashioned. 有人说 historian 时不发 h 音，前面用 an 而不用 a，现在听起来过时了。

his·tor·ic /hɪˈstɒrɪk; *NAmE* -ˈstɔːr-; -ˈstɑːr-/ *adj.* [usually before noun] **1** important in history; likely to be thought of as important at some time in the future 历史上著名（或重要）的；可名垂青史的： *a historic building/monument* 有历史意义的建筑 / 纪念碑 ◇ *The area is of special historic interest.* 这个地区有特别历史意义。◇ *a historic occasion/decision/day/visit/victory* 历史性的时刻 / 决定 / 日子 / 访问 / 胜利 ➲ NOTE ON NEXT PAGE **2** of a period during which history was recorded 有史时期的： *in historic times* 在有史时期 ➲ COMPARE PREHISTORIC HELP Some speakers do not pronounce the 'h' at the beginning of **historic** and use 'an' instead of 'a' before it. This now sounds old-fashioned. 有人说 historic 时不发 h 音，前面用 an 而不用 a，现在听起来过时了。

his·tor·ic·al 🔑 /hɪˈstɒrɪkl; *NAmE* -ˈstɔːr-; -ˈstɑːr-/ *adj.* [usually before noun] **1** 🔑 connected with the past （有关）历史的： *the historical background to the war* 这次

战争的历史背景 ◇ *You must place these events in their **historical context**.* 必须把这些事件同它们的历史环境联系起来看。 **2** connected with the study of history 有关历史研究的；历史学的： ***historical documents/records/research*** 史学文献 / 档案 / 研究 ◇ *The building is of **historical importance**.* 这栋建筑有重要的历史研究价值。 **3** (of a book, film/movie, etc. 书、电影等) about people and events in the past 历史题材的： *a historical novel* 历史小说 ➲ WORDFINDER NOTE AT STORY HELP Some speakers do not pronounce the 'h' at the beginning of **historical** and use 'an' instead of 'a' before it. This now sounds old-fashioned. 有人说 historical 时不发 h 音，前面用 an 而不用 a，现在听起来过时了。 ▶ **his·tor·ic·al·ly** /-kli/ *adv.* : *The book is historically inaccurate.* 这本书与史实不符。 ◇ *Historically, there has always been a great deal of rivalry between the two families.* 这两个家族世世代代对立斗争。

H

▼ **WHICH WORD?** 词语辨析

historic / historical

- **Historic** is usually used to describe something that is so important that it is likely to be remembered. * historic 通常用以表示具有重要历史意义： *Today is a historic occasion for our country.* 今天是我国具有历史意义的日子。 **Historical** usually describes something that is connected with the past or with the study of history, or something that really happened in the past. * historical 通常涉及历史、史学、过去的事实： *I have been doing some historical research.* 我一直在进行史学研究。 ◇ *Was Robin Hood a historical figure?* 罗宾汉是历史人物吗？

his·tori·cism /hɪˈstɒrɪsɪzəm; *NAmE* -ˈstɔːr-; -ˈstɑːr-/ *noun* [U] the theory that cultural and social events and situations can be explained by history 历史决定论；历史主义

the his,toric 'present *noun* [sing.] (*grammar* 语法) the simple present tense used to describe events in the past in order to make the description more powerful 历史现在时（为了表述得更加生动，用一般现在时描述过去的事情）

his·tor·iog·raphy /hɪˌstɒriˈɒɡrəfi; *NAmE* -ˌstɔːriˈɑːɡ-; -ˌstɑːr-/ *noun* [U] the study of writing about history 编史；撰史；历史编纂学 ▶ **his·tori·og·raph·ical** /hɪˌstɒriəˈɡræfɪkl; *NAmE* -ˌstɔːr-; -ˌstɑːr-/ *adj.*

his·tory /ˈhɪstri/ *noun* (*pl.* **-ies**) **1** [U] all the events that happened in the past 历史（指过去发生的所有事情）： *a turning point in human history* 人类历史的一个转折点 ◇ *one of the worst disasters in **recent history*** 近代史上最大的灾难之一 ◇ *a people with no **sense of history*** 一个没有历史感的民族 ◇ *Many people throughout history have dreamt of a world without war.* 历史上有很多人梦想过没有战争的世界。 ◇ *The area was inhabited long before the dawn of **recorded history*** (= before people wrote about events). 早在还没有历史记载的很久以前这个地区就有人居住了。 ◇ *These events changed the **course of history**.* 这些事件改变了历史的进程。 **2** [sing., U] the past events concerned in the development of a particular place, subject, etc. （有关某个地方、主题等的）发展史，历史： *the history of Ireland/democracy/popular music* 爱尔兰 / 民主 / 流行音乐的历史 ◇ *The **local history** of the area is fascinating.* 这个地区的历史很有意思。 ◇ *The school traces its history back to 1865.* 这个学校的历史可以追溯到 1865 年。 **3** [U] the study of past events as a subject at school or university 历史课；历史学： *a **history teacher*** 历史老师 ◇ *a degree in History* 历史学学位 ◇ ***social/economic/political history*** 社会史；经济史；政治史 ◇ ***ancient/medieval/modern history*** 古代史；中世纪史；近代史 ◇ *She's studying **art history**.* 她正在研读艺术史。 ➲ SEE ALSO NATURAL HISTORY **4** [C] a written or spoken account of past events 历史（指历史记载或历史传说）： *She's writing a new history of Europe.* 她正在写一部新的欧洲史。 ◇ *She went on to catalogue a long history of disasters.* 接下来她列举了一长串灾难。 **5** [sing.] **~ (of sth)** a record of sth happening frequently in the past life of a person, family or place; the set of facts that are known about sb's past life （某人的）履历，经历；家族史；（某地的）沿革： *He has a history of violent crime.* 他有暴力犯罪的前科。 ◇ *There is a history of heart disease in my family.* 我家有家族心脏病史。 ◇ *a patient's **medical history*** 病人的病历 ➲ SEE ALSO CASE HISTORY, LIFE HISTORY

IDM **be 'history** (*informal*) to be dead or no longer important 完蛋；已过去了；不再重要；成为历史： *Another mistake like that and you're history.* 要是再犯那种错误你就完了。 ◇ *We won't talk about that—that's history.* 我们不会谈论那件事的，那都已经过去了。 ◇ *That's **past history** now.* 那是以前的事了。 **the 'history books** the record of great achievements in history 历史上重大成就的记载： *She has earned her place in the history books.* 她名垂青史。 **history re'peats itself** used to say that things often happen later in the same way as before 历史时常重演 **make 'history | go down in 'history** to be or do sth so important that it will be recorded in history 载入史册；青史留名；创造历史： *a discovery that made medical history* 载入医学史册的一项重大发现 ➲ MORE AT REST *n.*

'history-sheeter /ˈhɪstri ʃiːtə(r)/ *noun* (*IndE*) a person who has been found guilty of a crime in the past 有犯罪前科者；有案底的人： *He was a history-sheeter who had served two years in jail for his crimes.* 他有犯罪前科，曾入狱两年。

his·tri·on·ic /ˌhɪstriˈɒnɪk; *NAmE* -ˈɑːnɪk/ *adj.* [usually before noun] (*formal, disapproving*) **histrionic** behaviour is very emotional and is intended to attract attention in a way that does not seem sincere 矫揉造作的；装腔作势的 ▶ **his·tri·on·ic·al·ly** /-kli/ *adv.* **his·tri·on·ics** *noun* [pl.]: *She was used to her mother's histrionics.* 她习惯了母亲装腔作势的样子。

hit /hɪt/ *verb, noun*

■ *verb* (**hit·ting, hit, hit**)

- **TOUCH SB/STH WITH FORCE** 打 **1** [T] to bring your hand, or an object you are holding, against sb/sth quickly and with force （用手或器具）击，打： **~ sb/sth** *My parents never used to hit me.* 我的父母以前从来不打我。 ◇ **~ sb/sth with sth** *He hit the nail squarely on the head with the hammer.* 他用锤子正对着钉子敲下去。 ◇ *She hit him on the head with her umbrella.* 她用雨伞打他的头。 **2** [T] **~ sth/sb** to come against sth/sb with force, especially causing damage or injury 碰撞；撞击（造成损伤）： *The bus hit the bridge.* 公共汽车撞到了桥上。 ◇ *I was hit by a falling stone.* 我被一块坠落的石头击中。 **3** [T] **~ sth (on/against sth)** to knock a part of your body against sth 使（身体部位）碰上（某物）： *He hit his head on the low ceiling.* 他的头碰了低矮的天花板。 **4** [T, often passive] **~ sb/sth** (of a bullet, bomb, etc. or a person using them 子弹、炸弹或射击者、抛掷者) to reach and touch a person or thing suddenly and with force 击中；命中： *The town was hit by bombs again last night.* 这个镇子昨晚又一次遭到了轰炸。 ◇ *He was hit by a sniper.* 他被狙击手击中。
- **BALL** 球 **5** [T] **~ sth (+ adv./prep.)** to bring a BAT, etc. against a ball and push it away with force 击（球）： *She hit the ball too hard and it went out of the court.* 她用力过猛，把球打出了场外。 ◇ *We've hit our ball over the fence!* 我们把球击过围栏去了！ **6** [T] **~ sth** (*sport* 体育) to score points by hitting a ball 击球得分： *to hit a home run* 打出本垒打
- **HAVE BAD EFFECT** 有坏影响 **7** [T, I] **~ (sb/sth)** to have a bad effect on sb/sth 产生不良影响；打击；危害： *The tax increases will certainly hit the poor.* 增税肯定会加重穷人的负担。 ◇ *His death didn't really hit me at first.* 他的死起初并没有对我产生影响。 ◇ *Rural areas have been worst hit by the strike.* 这次罢工对农村地区的打击最沉重。 ◇ *Spain was one of the **hardest hit** countries.* 西班牙是遭受打击最严重的国家之一。 ◇ *A tornado hit on Tuesday night.* 星期二晚上发生了一次龙卷风。
- **ATTACK** 攻击 **8** [T, I] **~ (sb/sth)** to attack sb/sth 攻击；进攻；袭击： *We hit the enemy when they least expected it.* 我们在敌人最意想不到的时候发动了进攻。

• **REACH** 到达 **9** [T] **~ sth** (*informal*) to reach a place 到达（某地）： *Follow this footpath and you'll eventually hit the road.* 沿着这条小路走，终会走上大路。◇ *The President **hits town** tomorrow.* 总统明天到镇子上来。 **10** [T] **~ sth** to reach a particular level 达到（某水平）： *Temperatures hit 40° yesterday.* 昨天气温高达 40 度。◇ *The euro hit a record low in trading today.* 今天欧元的兑换价降到了历史最低水平。

• **PROBLEM/DIFFICULTY** 问题；困难 **11** [T] **~ sth** (*informal*) to experience sth difficult or unpleasant 遇到（困难）；经历（不愉快的事情）： *We seem to have hit a problem.* 我们似乎遇到了问题。◇*Everything was going well but then we hit trouble.* 原本一切都进行得很顺利，但后来我们遇到了麻烦。

• **SUDDENLY REALIZE** 突然意识到 **12** [T] **~ sb** (*informal*) to come suddenly into your mind 使突然想起： *I couldn't remember where I'd seen him before, and then it suddenly hit me.* 起初我想不起以前在哪里见过他，后来猛然记起来了。

• **PRESS BUTTON** 按钮 **13** [T] **~ sth** (*informal*) to press sth such as a button to operate a machine, etc. 按，压（按钮等）： *Hit the brakes!* 踩刹车！

IDM **hit (it) 'big** (*informal*) to be very successful 很成功： *The band has hit big in the US.* 乐队在美国大获成功。 **hit the 'buffers** (*informal*) if a plan, sb's career, etc. **hits the buffers**, it suddenly stops being successful （计划、事业等）突然受挫 **hit the 'ceiling/'roof** (*informal*) to suddenly become very angry 勃然大怒；怒气冲天 **hit the 'deck** (*informal*) to fall to the ground 摔倒在地；落到地上 **ˌhit the ground 'running** (*informal*) to start doing sth and continue very quickly and successfully 迅速而顺利地投入某事；一炮打响；一举成功 **hit the 'hay/'sack** (*informal*) to go to bed 上床睡觉 **hit sb (straight/right) in the 'eye** to be very obvious to sb 很显然；一目了然 **'hit it** (*informal*) used to tell sb to start doing sth, such as playing music （要某人开始做某事，如演奏音乐）开始吧： *Hit it, Louis!* 开始吧，路易斯！ **hit it 'off (with sb)** (*informal*) to have a good friendly relationship with sb （和某人）投缘： *We hit it off straight away.* 我们一见如故。 **hit the 'jackpot** to make or win a lot of money quickly and unexpectedly 突然意外赚大钱（或赢大钱）；发大财 **hit the nail on the 'head** to say sth that is exactly right 说到点子上；正中要害 **hit the 'road/'trail** (*informal*) to start a journey/trip 出发；上路 **hit the 'roof** = GO THROUGH THE ROOF (2) **hit the 'spot** (*informal*) if sth **hits the spot** it does exactly what it should do 发挥正当作用；适得其用；恰到好处 **hit the 'streets | hit the 'shops/'stores** (*informal*) to become widely available for sale 大量上市： *The new magazine hits the streets tomorrow.* 新的杂志明天发行。 **hit a/the 'wall** to reach a point when you cannot continue or make any more progress 筋疲力尽；陷入绝境；遇到不可逾越的障碍： *We hit a wall and we weren't scoring.* 我们已经筋疲力尽，得不到分了。 **hit sb when they're 'down** to continue to hurt sb when they are already defeated 落井下石；乘人之危 **hit sb where it 'hurts** to affect sb where they will feel it most 刺着某人痛处；击中要害 ➲ MORE AT HEADLINE *n.*, HOME *adv.*, KNOW *v.*, MARK *n.*, NERVE *n.*, NOTE *n.*, PAY DIRT, SHIT *n.*, SIX, STRIDE *n.*

PHR V **ˌhit 'back (at sb/sth)** to reply to attacks or criticism 回击；反击 SYN **retaliate**: *In a TV interview she hit back at her critics.* 她在电视采访中反驳了那些批评者。 **'hit on sb** (*NAmE, slang*) to start talking to sb to show them that you are sexually attracted to them 开始与某人调情 **'hit on/upon sth** [no passive] (*rather informal*) to think of a good idea suddenly or by chance 突然有个好主意；偶然想到妙点子： *She hit on the perfect title for her new novel.* 她灵机一动，为自己的新小说想了一个绝妙的书名。 **ˌhit 'out (at sb/sth)** to attack sb/sth violently by fighting them or criticizing them 猛烈攻击；狠狠抨击： *I just hit out blindly in all directions.* 我只是漫无目的地四处出击。◇ *In a rousing speech the minister hit out at racism in the armed forces.* 在一次激励人心的讲话中，部长严厉抨击了军中的种族主义。 **ˌhit sb 'up for sth | 'hit sb for sth** (*NAmE, informal*) to ask sb for money 向某人要钱： *Does he always hit you up for cash when he wants new clothes?* 他要买新衣服时是不是总找你要钱？ **'hit sb with sth** (*informal*) to tell sb sth, especially sth that surprises or shocks them （把吓人的事等）告诉某人： *How much is it going to cost, then? Come on, hit me with it!* 那么它究竟要花费多少钱？快点告诉我吧！

▼ **SYNONYMS** 同义词辨析

hit

knock • bang • strike • bump • bash

These words all mean to come against sth with a lot of force. 以上各词均含用力撞击、击打之义。

hit to come against sth with force, especially causing damage or injury 指碰撞、撞击，尤指造成损伤： *The boy was hit by a speeding car.* 男孩被超速行驶的汽车撞倒了。

knock to hit sth so that it moves or breaks; to put sb/sth into a particular state or position by hitting them/it 指打掉、敲动、打破、撞成…： *Someone had knocked a hole in the wall.* 有人在墙上打了个洞。

bang to hit sth in a way that makes a loud noise 指大声地猛敲、砸： *The baby was banging the table with his spoon.* 婴儿用调羹敲打着桌子。

strike (*formal*) to hit sb/sth hard 指猛烈地撞、碰、撞击、碰撞： *The ship struck a rock.* 船触礁了。

bump to hit sb/sth accidentally 指无意地碰、撞： *In the darkness I bumped into a chair.* 我在黑暗中撞上了一把椅子。

bash (*informal*) to hit against sth very hard 指猛击、猛撞： *I braked too late, bashing into the car in front.* 我刹车太晚，撞上了前面的车。

PATTERNS

- to hit/knock/bang/bump/bash **against** sb/sth
- to knock/bang/bump/bash **into** sb/sth
- to hit/strike the **ground/floor/wall**

■ ***noun***

• **ACT OF HITTING** 打 **1** 🔑 an act of hitting sb/sth with your hand or with an object held in your hand 打；击： *Give it a good hit.* 用力打它一下。◇ *He made the winning hit.* 他击出了致胜的一球。 **2** 🔑 an occasion when sth that has been thrown, fired, etc. at an object reaches that object 命中；击中： *The bomber scored a **direct hit** on the bridge.* 轰炸机直接炸中了那座桥。◇ *We finished the first round with a score of two hits and six misses.* 我们在第一轮结束时的分数是两次击中，六次未中。

• **STH POPULAR** 受欢迎的事物 **3** 🔑 a person or thing that is very popular 很受欢迎的人（或事物）： *The duo were a real hit in last year's show.* 这一对搭档在去年的演出中大出风头。◇ *a hit musical* 风靡一时的音乐剧◇ *Her new series is a **smash hit**.* 她的新系列节目极为成功，引起轰动。

• **POP MUSIC** 流行音乐 **4** 🔑 a successful pop song or record 风行一时的流行歌曲（或唱片）： *They are about to release an album of their greatest hits.* 他们即将发行收录他们最热门歌曲的专辑。◇ *She played all her old hits.* 她演奏了她所有曾轰动一时的老曲子。◇ *a **hit record/single*** 风靡一时的唱片 / 单曲唱片

• **OF DRUG** 毒品 **5** (*slang*) an amount of an illegal drug that is taken at one time 毒品的一剂

• **MURDER** 凶杀 **6** (*slang, especially NAmE*) a violent crime or murder 暴力犯罪；凶杀 ➲ SEE ALSO HITMAN

• **COMPUTING** 计算机技术 **7** an occasion on which a web page is displayed or a file is DOWNLOADED from the Internet （网页的）点击；（文件的）下载： *Our website is getting a lot of hits from the USA.* 我们的网站得到很多来自美国的点击。◇ *How many hits did you get?* 你获得了多少点击量？

IDM **be/make a 'hit (with sb)** to be liked very much by sb when they first meet you 给（某人）留下很好的第一印象；使（某人）一见钟情 **take a 'hit** to be damaged or badly affected by sth 遭到破坏；受到严重影响： *The airline industry took a hit last year.* 去年航空业受到了严重冲击。

ˌhit-and-ˈmiss (*also* **ˌhit-or-ˈmiss**) *adj.* not done in a careful or planned way and therefore not likely to be successful 粗制滥造的；时好时坏的

ˌhit-and-ˈrun *adj.* [only before noun] **1** (of a road accident 交通事故) caused by a driver who does not stop to help（驾驶人）肇事后逃逸的： *a **hit-and-run accident/death*** 肇事逃逸的交通事故 / 引起的死亡 ◇ *a **hit-and-run driver*** (= one who causes an accident but drives away without helping) 肇事逃逸的驾驶人 **2** (of a military attack 军事进攻) happening suddenly and unexpectedly so that the people attacking can leave quickly without being hurt 突袭后迅速撤离的： *hit-and-run raids* 打了就撤的袭击 ▶ **ˌhit-and-ˈrun** *noun*: *He was killed in a hit-and-run.* 他被车撞死，车主肇事后逃逸了。

hitch /hɪtʃ/ *verb, noun*

■ ***verb*** **1** [T, I] to get a free ride in a person's car; to travel around in this way, by standing at the side of the road and trying to get passing cars to stop 免费搭车；搭便车： **~ sth** *They **hitched a ride** in a truck.* 他们搭乘了一辆路过的货车。◇ (*BrE also*) *They **hitched a lift**.* 他们搭了便车。◇ **(+ adv./prep.)** *We spent the summer hitching around Europe.* 我们借搭便车在欧洲各地旅行了一个夏天。 ➲ SEE ALSO HITCHHIKE **2** [T] **~ sth (up)** to pull up a piece of your clothing 提起，拉起（衣服） SYN **hike sth↔up**: *She hitched up her skirt and waded into the river.* 她提起裙子，蹚进河里。 **3** [T] **~ yourself (up, etc.)** to lift yourself into a higher position, or the position mentioned 攀上；跃上： *She hitched herself up.* 她爬了上去。◇ *He hitched himself onto the bar stool.* 他一跃坐上酒吧高脚凳。 **4** [T] **~ sth (to sth)** to fix sth to sth else with a rope, a hook, etc. 拴住；套住；钩住： *She hitched the pony to the gate.* 她把小马拴在大门上。

IDM **get ˈhitched** (*informal*) to get married 结婚

■ ***noun*** **1** a problem or difficulty that causes a short delay 暂时的困难（或问题）；故障；障碍： *The ceremony went off **without a hitch**.* 仪式进行得很顺利。◇ *a technical hitch* 技术故障 **2** a type of knot（某种）结： *a clove hitch* 卷结

hitch·hike /ˈhɪtʃhaɪk/ *verb* [I] to travel by asking for free rides in other people's cars, by standing at the side of the road and trying to get passing cars to stop 免费搭便车；搭顺风车： *They hitchhiked around Europe.* 他们一路搭便车周游欧洲。 ➲ SEE ALSO HITCH *v.* (1) ▶ **hitch·hiker** (*also* **hitch·er** /ˈhɪtʃə(r)/) *noun*: *He picked up two hitchhikers on the road to Bristol.* 他在前往布里斯托尔的路上捎带了两个搭便车的人。

ˌhi-ˈtech = HIGH-TECH

hither /ˈhɪðə(r)/ *adv.* (*old use*) to this place 到此处；向此地

IDM **ˌhither and ˈthither** | **ˌhither and ˈyon** (*especially literary*) in many different directions 各处；四处

hith·er·to /ˌhɪðəˈtuː; *NAmE* ˌhɪðərˈtuː/ *adv.* (*formal*) until now; until the particular time you are talking about 迄今；直到某时： *a hitherto unknown species of moth* 迄今仍属未知品种的蛾

ˈhit list *noun* (*informal*) a list of people, organizations, etc. against whom some unpleasant action is being planned 打击对象名单： *Which services are on the government's hit list?* 哪些部门被列入了政府要整顿的机构名单？ ◇ *She was at the top of the terrorists' hit list for over two years.* 她被恐怖分子列为头号谋杀对象长达两年。

hit·man /ˈhɪtmæn/ *noun* (*pl.* **-men** /ˈhɪtmen/) (*informal*) a criminal who is paid to kill sb 受雇充当刺客的人；职业杀手

ˌhit-or-ˈmiss *adj.* = HIT-AND-MISS

ˈhit-out *noun* (in AUSTRALIAN RULES football 澳式橄榄球) a hit of the ball towards a player from your team after it has been BOUNCED by the UMPIRE 争球（将裁判掷地反弹之后的球击向同队队员）；发球

the ˈhit parade *noun* (*old-fashioned*) a list published every week that shows which pop records have sold the most copies（每周）最畅销流行唱片榜

ˈhit squad *noun* a group of criminals who are paid to kill a person 职业杀手团伙；受雇杀人小集团

hit·ter /ˈhɪtə(r)/ *noun* (often in compounds 常构成复合词) **1** (in sports 体育运动) a person who hits the ball in the way mentioned 击球手： *a **big/long/hard hitter*** 很棒的 / 善于长打的 / 打击力强的击球手 **2** (in politics or business 政治或商业) a person who is powerful 要员；大亨： *the **heavy hitters** of Japanese industry* 日本的工业巨子

HIV /ˌeɪtʃ aɪ ˈviː/ *noun* [U] the abbreviation for 'human immunodeficiency virus' (the virus that can cause AIDS) 人体免疫缺损病毒，艾滋病病毒（全写为 human immunodeficiency virus）： *to be infected with HIV* 染上艾滋病病毒 ◇ *to be **HIV-positive/HIV-negative*** (= to have had a medical test which shows that you are/are not infected with HIV) 人体免疫缺损病毒检测呈阳性 / 阴性反应

hive /haɪv/ *noun, verb*

■ ***noun*** **1** (*also* **bee·hive**) [C] a structure made for BEES to live in 蜂房；蜂箱 **2** [C] the BEES living in a hive 一箱蜜蜂；蜂群 **3** [C, usually sing.] **a ~ of activity/industry** a place full of people who are busy 忙碌的场所；繁忙的地方 **4 hives** [U] = URTICARIA

■ ***verb***

PHR V **ˌhive sth↔ˈoff (to/into sth)** [often passive] (*especially BrE*) to separate one part of a group from the rest; to sell part of a business 把一部分分拆出来；卖掉公司的一部分： *The IT department is being hived off into a new company.* 信息技术部正被分拆出来，成立新公司。

hi-vis /ˌhaɪ ˈvɪz/ *adj.* = HIGH-VISIBILITY

hiya /ˈhaɪjə/ *exclamation* used to say hello to sb in an informal way（非正式招呼语）嗨，你好

hl *abbr.* HECTOLITRE 百升

HM (*also* **H.M.**) *abbr.* HIS/HER MAJESTY 陛下： *HM the Queen* 女王陛下 ◇ *HM Customs* 英国海关

HMG *abbr.* (*BrE*) Her Majesty's Government 女王陛下政府；英国政府

hmm (*also* **hm**, **h'm**) /m; hm/ *exclamation* used in writing to show the sound that you make to express doubt or when you are hesitating（书写形式，表示有疑虑或犹豫时发出的声音）唔，嗯，唔，哼

HMRC /ˌeɪtʃ em ɑː ˈsiː; *NAmE* ɑːr/ *abbr.* HM Revenue and Customs 英国海关税务署

ˌHM ˌRevenue and ˈCustoms *noun* [U] (*abbr.* **HMRC**) the government department in Britain that is responsible for collecting taxes. It replaced the INLAND REVENUE and HM CUSTOMS AND EXCISE in 2005. 英国海关税务署（于 2005 年取代了国内税务局和海关与消费局） ➲ COMPARE INTERNAL REVENUE SERVICE

HMS /ˌeɪtʃ em ˈes/ *abbr.* Her/His Majesty's Ship (used before the name of a ship in the British navy) 皇家海军舰艇（用于英国海军舰艇名前）： *HMS Apollo* 皇家海军阿波罗号

HNC /ˌeɪtʃ en ˈsiː/ *noun* the abbreviation for 'Higher National Certificate' (a British university or college qualification, especially in a technical or scientific subject) 国家高级证书（全写为 Higher National Certificate，尤指英国大学科技学科的）： *to do an HNC in electrical engineering* 攻读电机工程国家高级证书

HND /ˌeɪtʃ en ˈdiː/ *noun* the abbreviation for 'Higher National Diploma' (a British university or college qualification, especially in a technical or scientific subject) 国家高级文凭（全写为 Higher National Diploma，尤指英国大学科技学科的）： *to do an HND in fashion design* 攻读时装设计国家高级文凭

ho /həʊ; *NAmE* hoʊ/ *noun* (*pl.* **hos** or **hoes**) (*NAmE, taboo, slang*) **1** a female PROSTITUTE 娼妓；妓女 **2** an offensive word used about a woman, especially one who you think has sex with a lot of men 破鞋 ORIGIN Short form of *whore.* 源自 whore 一词的简约式。

hoagie /ˈhəʊɡi; NAmE ˈhoʊ-/ *noun* (*NAmE*) **1** a long piece of bread filled with meat, cheese and salad （在长条面包中夹肉、干酪、色拉等做成的）大型三明治 **2** a piece of bread used to make a hoagie （用以做大型三明治的）长条面包

hoard /hɔːd; NAmE hɔːrd/ *noun, verb*
- *noun* ~ (**of sth**) a collection of money, food, valuable objects, etc., especially one that sb keeps in a secret place so that other people will not find or steal it （钱、食物、贵重物品等的）贮存，聚藏；（尤指）秘藏
- *verb* [I, T] ~ (**sth**) to collect and keep large amounts of food, money, etc., especially secretly 贮藏；囤积；（尤指）秘藏 ▸ **hoard·er** *noun*

hoard·ing /ˈhɔːdɪŋ; NAmE ˈhɔːrd-/ *noun* **1** (*BrE*) (*also* **bill·board** *NAmE, BrE*) [C] a large board on the outside of a building or at the side of the road, used for putting advertisements on 大幅广告牌 ➲ VISUAL VOCAB PAGE V3 **2** [C] (*BrE*) a temporary fence made of boards that is placed around an area of land until a building has been built （建筑工地用木板搭起的）临时围栏 **3** [U] the act of hoarding things 贮存；聚藏；（尤指）秘藏

hoar frost /ˈhɔː frɒst; NAmE ˈhɔːr frɔːst/ *noun* [U] a layer of small pieces of ice that look like white needles and that form on surfaces outside when temperatures are very low 霜；冰霜

hoarse /hɔːs; NAmE hɔːrs/ *adj.* (of a person or voice 人或嗓音) sounding rough and unpleasant, especially because of a sore throat 嘶哑的；沙哑的：*He shouted himself hoarse.* 他把嗓子喊哑了。◇ *a hoarse cough/cry/scream* 粗哑的咳嗽；嘶哑的哭声 / 尖叫声 ▸ **hoarse·ly** *adv.* **hoarse·ness** *noun* [U]

hoary /ˈhɔːri/ *adj.* [usually before noun] **1** (*old-fashioned*) very old and well known and therefore no longer interesting 陈腐的；老掉牙的；陈旧的：*a hoary old joke* 老掉牙的笑话 **2** (*literary*) (especially of hair 尤指头发) grey or white because a person is old （因年老）灰白的，花白的

hoax /həʊks; NAmE hoʊks/ *noun, verb*
- *noun* an act intended to make sb believe sth that is not true, especially sth unpleasant 骗局；恶作剧：*a bomb hoax* 炸弹骗局 ◇ *hoax calls* 恶作剧电话
- *verb* ~ **sb** to trick sb by making them believe sth that is not true, especially sth unpleasant 作弄；欺骗 ▸ **hoax·er** *noun*

hob /hɒb; NAmE hɑːb/ *noun* **1** (*BrE*) (*NAmE* **stove·top**) the top part of a cooker where food is cooked in pans; a similar surface that is built into a kitchen unit and is separate from the oven 炉盘；厨房烤炉搁架：*an electric/a gas hob* 电炉 / 煤气炉炉盘 **2** a metal shelf at the side of a fire, used in the past for heating pans, etc. on （旧时放在炉侧用于加热锅等的）火炉搁架，壁炉搁架

hob·ble /ˈhɒbl; NAmE ˈhɑːbl/ *verb* **1** [I] (+ **adv./prep.**) to walk with difficulty, especially because your feet or legs hurt 蹒跚；跛行 SYN **limp**：*The old man hobbled across the road.* 老人一瘸一拐地穿过马路。 **2** [T] ~ **sth** to tie together two legs of a horse or other animal in order to stop it from running away 捆绑（马等的）两腿（以防其走失） **3** [T] ~ **sth** to make it more difficult for sb to do sth or for sth to happen 阻止；妨碍

hobby /ˈhɒbi; NAmE ˈhɑːbi/ *noun* (*pl.* **-ies**) an activity that you do for pleasure when you are not working 业余爱好：*Her hobbies include swimming and gardening.* 她爱好游泳和园艺。◇ *I only play jazz as a hobby.* 我弹奏爵士乐只是一种业余爱好。➲ SYNONYMS AT INTEREST ➲ WORDFINDER NOTE AT CLUB ➲ VISUAL VOCAB PAGES V44-46

ˈhobby horse *noun* **1** (*sometimes disapproving*) a subject that sb feels strongly about and likes to talk about 热衷谈论的话题：*to get on your hobby horse* (= talk about your favourite subject) 谈论自己喜爱的话题 **2** a toy made from a long stick that has a horse's head at one end. Children pretend to ride on it. 马头长杆玩具；竹马

hob·by·ist /ˈhɒbiɪst; NAmE ˈhɑːb-/ *noun* (*formal*) a person who is very interested in a particular hobby （业余）爱好者

hob·gob·lin /hɒbˈɡɒblɪn; ˈhɒbɡɒblɪn; NAmE ˈhɑːbɡɑːb-/ *noun* (in stories) a small ugly creature that likes to trick people or cause trouble （传说中的）淘气小妖

hob·nail boot /ˌhɒbneɪl ˈbuːt; NAmE ˌhɑːb-/ (*also* **hob-nailed boot** /-neɪld/) *noun* [usually pl.] a heavy shoe whose SOLE is attached to the upper part with short heavy nails 平头钉靴子

hob·nob /ˈhɒbnɒb; NAmE ˈhɑːbnɑːb/ *verb* (**-bb-**) [I] ~ (**with sb**) (*informal*) to spend a lot of time with sb, especially sb who is rich and/or famous （尤指同有钱有名望的人）过从甚密，亲近；巴结

hobo /ˈhəʊbəʊ; NAmE ˈhoʊboʊ/ *noun* (*pl.* **-os**) (*old-fashioned, especially NAmE*) **1** a person who travels from place to place looking for work, especially on farms 流浪的失业工人；（尤指农场）季节工人，零工 **2** = TRAMP (1)

Hob·son's choice /ˌhɒbsnz ˈtʃɔɪs; NAmE ˌhɑːb-/ *noun* [U] a situation in which sb has no choice because if they do not accept what is offered, they will get nothing 无选择余地的局面；不得已的选择 ➲ MORE LIKE THIS 18, page R27
ORIGIN From Tobias Hobson, a man who hired out horses in the 17th century. He gave his customers the choice of the horse nearest the stable door or none at all. 源自 17 世纪做马匹出租生意的托拜厄斯 • 霍布森 (Tobias Hobson)。他根本不让顾客选择，只租给他们离马厩门最近的马。

hock /hɒk; NAmE hɑːk/ *noun, verb*
- *noun* **1** [C] the middle joint of an animal's back leg （动物后腿的）附关节 **2** [U, C] (*BrE*) a German white wine 莱茵白葡萄酒 **3** [U, C] (*especially NAmE*) = KNUCKLE (2) **4** [U] (*informal*) if sth that you own is in **hock**, you have exchanged it for money but hope to buy it back later 典当；抵押
IDM **be in ˈhock (to sb)** to owe sb sth 欠（某人某物）：*I'm in hock to the bank for £6 000.* 我欠银行 6 000 英镑。
- *verb* ~ **sth** (*informal*) to leave a valuable object with sb in exchange for money that you borrow 典当；抵押 SYN **pawn**

hockey /ˈhɒki; NAmE ˈhɑːki/ *noun* [U] **1** (*BrE*) (*NAmE* **ˈfield hockey**) a game played on a field by two teams of 11 players, with curved sticks and a small hard ball. Teams try to hit the ball into the other team's goal. 曲棍球：*to play hockey* 打曲棍球 ◇ *a hockey stick/player/team* 曲棍球球棍 / 球员 / 球队 **2** (*NAmE*) (*BrE* **ˈice hockey**) a game played on ice, in which players use long sticks to hit a hard rubber disc (called a PUCK) into the other team's goal 冰球运动；冰上曲棍球 ➲ VISUAL VOCAB PAGE V48

hocus-pocus /ˌhəʊkəs ˈpəʊkəs; NAmE ˌhoʊkəs ˈpoʊkəs/ *noun* [U] language or behaviour that is nonsense and is intended to hide the truth from people 骗人的鬼话；花招；骗术 ➲ MORE LIKE THIS 11, page R26

hod /hɒd; NAmE hɑːd/ *noun* an open box attached to a pole, used by building workers for carrying bricks on the shoulder （建筑工人扛砖用的长柄）砖斗

hodge·podge /ˈhɒdʒpɒdʒ; NAmE ˈhɑːdʒpɑːdʒ/ *noun* [sing.] (*NAmE*) = HOTCHPOTCH

Hodg·kin's dis·ease /ˈhɒdʒkɪnz dɪziːz; NAmE ˈhɑːdʒ-/ *noun* [U] a serious disease of the LYMPH NODES, LIVER and SPLEEN 霍奇金病

hoe /həʊ; NAmE hoʊ/ *noun, verb*
- *noun* a garden tool with a long handle and a blade, used for breaking up soil and removing WEEDS (= plants growing where they are not wanted) 锄头 ➲ VISUAL VOCAB PAGE V20
- *verb* (**hoe·ing**, **hoed**, **hoed**) [T, I] ~ (**sth**) to break up soil, remove plants, etc. with a hoe 用锄头锄地（或除草）：*to hoe the flower beds* 用锄头给花坛除草松土

PHR V **hoe 'in** (*AustralE, NZE, informal*) to eat with enthusiasm 痛快地吃

hoe·down /ˈhəʊdaʊn; *NAmE* ˈhoʊ-/ *noun* (*NAmE*) **1** a social occasion when lively dances are performed 热烈的民间舞舞会 **2** a lively dance 热烈的民间舞蹈

hog /hɒɡ; *NAmE* hɔːɡ; hɑːɡ/ *noun, verb*

■ ***noun*** **1** (*especially NAmE*) a pig, especially one that is kept and made fat for eating （尤指喂肥供食用的）猪 **2** (*BrE*) a male pig that has been CASTRATED (= had part of its sex organs removed) and is kept for its meat （供食用的）阉公猪 ➲ COMPARE BOAR (2), SOW[2] ➲ SEE ALSO ROAD HOG, WARTHOG

IDM **go the whole 'hog** (*informal*) to do sth thoroughly or completely 彻底地做某事；贯彻到底

■ ***verb*** (**-gg-**) **~ sth** (*informal*) to use or keep most of sth yourself and stop others from using or having it 多占；独占： *to hog the road* (= to drive so that other vehicles cannot pass) 占着马路中间开车 ◇ *to hog the bathroom* (= to spend a long time in it so that others cannot use it) 长时间占用浴室

Hog·ma·nay /ˈhɒɡmənеɪ; ˌhɒɡməˈneɪ; *NAmE* ˈhɑːɡmənеɪ; ˌhɑːɡməˈneɪ/ *noun* [U] (in Scotland) New Year's Eve (31 December) and the celebrations that happen on that day （苏格兰 12 月 31 日的）除夕以及除夕欢庆活动

hog·wash /ˈhɒɡwɒʃ; *NAmE* ˈhɔːɡwɑːʃ; ˈhɑːɡ-; -wɔːʃ/ *noun* [U] (*informal*) an idea, argument, etc. that you think is stupid 愚蠢的想法（或论点等）；胡言乱语

ho ho /ˌhəʊ ˈhəʊ; *NAmE* ˌhoʊ ˈhoʊ/ *exclamation* **1** used to show the sound of a deep laugh （表示深沉的笑声） **2** used to show surprise （表示惊讶）： *Ho, ho! What have we here?* 嗬嗬！这是什么？ ➲ MORE LIKE THIS 2, page R25

ho-hum /ˌhəʊ ˈhʌm; *NAmE* ˌhoʊ/ *exclamation* used to show that you are bored （表示厌倦） ➲ MORE LIKE THIS 2, page R25

hoick /hɔɪk/ *verb* **~ sth (+ adv./prep.)** (*informal*) to lift or pull sth in a particular direction, especially with a quick sudden movement 猛提；猛拉 SYN **jerk**

the hoi pol·loi /ˌhɔɪ pəˈlɔɪ/ *noun* [pl.] (*disapproving* or *humorous*) an insulting word for ordinary people 寻常百姓；草民；乌合之众

hoist /hɔɪst/ *verb, noun*

■ ***verb*** **~ sth (+ adv./prep.)** to raise or pull sth up to a higher position, often using ropes or special equipment 吊起；提升；拉高： *He hoisted himself onto a high stool.* 他抬身坐上了一张高凳子。 ◇ *The cargo was hoisted aboard by crane.* 货物由起重机吊上了船。 ◇ *to hoist a flag/sail* 升旗；升帆

IDM **be hoist/hoisted by/with your own pe'tard** to be hurt or to have problems as a result of your own plans to hurt or trick others 害人反害己；自食其果

■ ***noun*** a piece of equipment used for lifting heavy things, or for lifting people who cannot stand or walk 起重机；吊车；（残疾人用）升降机

hoity-toity /ˌhɔɪti ˈtɔɪti/ *adj.* (*old-fashioned, informal*) behaving in a way that suggests that you think you are more important than other people 大模大样的；自命不凡的 ➲ MORE LIKE THIS 11, page R26

hokey /ˈhəʊki; *NAmE* ˈhoʊki/ *adj.* (*NAmE, informal*) expressing emotions in a way that seems exaggerated or silly 矫揉造作的；夸张可笑的

hoki /ˈhəʊki; *NAmE* ˈhoʊki/ *noun* (*pl.* **hoki**) a fish found in the seas off New Zealand 福气鱼（见于新西兰附近海域）

hokum /ˈhəʊkəm; *NAmE* ˈhoʊ-/ *noun* [U] (*informal, especially NAmE*) **1** a film/movie, play, etc. that is not realistic and has no artistic qualities 做作的电影（或戏剧等） **2** an idea, argument, etc. that you think is stupid 愚蠢的想法（或论点等）： *What a bunch of hokum!* 真是一派胡言！

hold 🔑 /həʊld; *NAmE* hoʊld/ *verb, noun*

■ ***verb*** (**held, held** /held/)

• **IN HAND/ARMS** 手；双臂 **1** 🔑 [T] **~ sb/sth (+ adv./prep.)** to carry sth; to have sb/sth in your hand, arms, etc. 拿着；抓住；抱住；夹着： *She was holding a large box.* 她提着一只大箱子。 ◇ *I held the mouse by its tail.* 我抓着耗子的尾巴倒提起来。 ◇ *The girl held her father's hand tightly.* 女孩紧紧地拉着她父亲的手。 ◇ *He was holding the baby in his arms.* 他抱着婴儿。 ◇ *The winning captain held the trophy in the air.* 获胜队的队长把奖杯高举到空中。 ◇ *We were **holding hands*** (= holding each other's hands). 我们手拉着手。 ◇ *The lovers held each other close.* 这对恋人紧紧相拥着。 **2** 🔑 [T] **~ sth** to put your hand on part of your body, usually because it hurts 捂住，捂住，按住（受伤的身体部位等）： *She groaned and held her head.* 她呻吟着，用手抱住头。

• **IN POSITION** 位置 **3** 🔑 [T] to keep sb/sth in a particular position 使保持（在某位置）： **~ sth (+ adv./prep.)** *Hold your head up.* 抬起头来。 ◇ *Hold this position for a count of 10.* 保持这个姿势别动，数到 10。 ◇ *The wood is held in position by a clamp.* 这木头用夹钳固定住了。 ◇ *I had to hold my stomach in* (= pull the muscles flat) *to zip up my jeans.* 我得把肚皮收紧才能拉上牛仔裤的拉链。 ◇ **~ sth + adj.** *I'll hold the door open for you.* 我会把门给你开着的。

• **SUPPORT** 支撑 **4** 🔑 [T] **~ sb/sth** to support the weight of sb/sth 支撑…的重量： *I don't think that branch will hold your weight.* 我觉得那根树枝撑不住你的重量。

• **CONTAIN** 容纳；包含 **5** 🔑 [T] **~ sth/sb** to have enough space for sth/sb; to contain sth/sb 容纳；包含： *This barrel holds 25 litres.* 这只桶能盛 25 升。 ◇ *The plane holds about 300 passengers.* 这架飞机可容纳大约 300 名乘客。

• **SB PRISONER** 监禁 **6** 🔑 [T] to keep sb and not allow them to leave 监禁；拘留： **~ sb** *Police are holding two men in connection with last Thursday's bank raid.* 警方拘留了两名与上星期四的银行抢劫案有关的男子。 ◇ **~ sb + noun** *He was **held prisoner** for two years.* 他被囚禁了两年。

• **CONTROL** 控制 **7** [T] **~ sth** to defend sth against attack; to have control of sth 守卫；控制： *The rebels held the radio station.* 叛乱者占据了电台。

• **REMAIN** 保持 **8** [I] to remain strong and safe or in position 承受住；坚持住；保持原位： *They were afraid the dam wouldn't hold.* 他们担心大坝会承受不住。 **9** [I] to remain the same 保持不变： *How long will the fine weather hold?* 好天气会持续多久？ ◇ *If their luck holds, they could still win the championship.* 如果他们的好运持续下去，他们仍能赢得冠军。

• **KEEP** 使持续 **10** 🔑 [T] **~ sth** to keep sb's attention or interest 使（注意力或兴趣）持续不减；吸引住： *There wasn't much in the museum to hold my attention.* 博物馆中没有很多让我感兴趣的东西。 **11** [T] **~ sth (at sth)** to keep sth at the same level, rate, speed, etc. 使保持同样程度（或比率、速度等）： *Hold your speed at 70.* 把速度保持在 70。 **12** 🔑 [T] **~ sth** to keep sth so that it can be used later 保存；存储： *records held on computer* 存在计算机中的记录 ◇ *Our solicitor holds our wills.* 律师保存着我们的遗嘱。 ◇ *We can hold your reservation for three days.* 您的预订我们可以保留三天。

• **OWN** 拥有 **13** 🔑 [T] **~ sth** (*rather formal*) to own or have sth 拥有；持有： *Employees hold 30% of the shares.* 雇员持有 30% 的股份。

• **JOB** 工作 **14** 🔑 [T] **~ sth** to have a particular job or position 担任；任职： *How long has he held office?* 他任职有多久了？

• **RECORD/TITLE** 纪录；称号 **15** 🔑 [T] **~ sth** to have sth you have gained or achieved 获得；赢得： *Who holds the world record for the long jump?* 跳远世界纪录的保持者是谁？ ◇ *She held the title of world champion for three years.* 她保持了三年的世界冠军头衔。

• **OPINION** 意见 **16** [T] to have a belief or an opinion about sb/sth 怀有，持有（信念、意见）： **~ sth** *He holds strange views on education.* 他对教育的看法不同寻常。 ◇ **~ sb/sth + adv./prep./adj.** *She is **held in high regard** by her students* (= they have a high opinion of her). 学生对她评价很高。 ◇ *firmly-held beliefs* 坚定的信念 **17** [T] (*formal*) to consider that sth is true 认为；相信： **~ that...** *I still hold that the government's economic policies are* *mistaken.* 我仍然认为政府的经济政策是错误的。◇ **~ sb/sth + adj.** *Parents will be* ***held responsible*** *for their children's behaviour.* 父母将要对孩子的行为负责。◇ **be held to be sth** *These vases are held to be the finest examples of Greek art.* 这些花瓶被视为希腊艺术的最佳典范。

- **MEETING** 会议 **18** [T, usually passive] **~ sth** to have a meeting, competition, conversation, etc. 召开；举行；进行：*The meeting will be held in the community centre.* 会议将在社区活动中心举行。◇ *It's impossible to hold a conversation with all this noise.* 噪音这么大，根本没法进行交谈。
- **ROAD/COURSE** 道路；路线 **19** [T] **~ the road** (of a vehicle 机动车) to be in close contact with the road and easy to control, especially when driven fast（尤指高速行驶时）平稳行驶 **20** [T] **~ a course** (of a ship or an aircraft 船或飞机) to continue to move in a particular direction 保持航线
- **IN MUSIC** 音乐 **21** [T] **~ sth** to make a note continue for a particular time 延长，继续唱（某音符）

▼ SYNONYMS 同义词辨析

hold

hold on • cling • clutch • grip • grasp • clasp • hang on

These words all mean to have sb/sth in your hands or arms. 以上各词均表示抓住、抱住。

hold to have sb/sth in your hand or arms 指抓住、抱住、托住、夹住：*She was holding a large box.* 她提着一只大箱子。◇ *I held the baby gently in my arms.* 我把婴儿轻轻地抱在怀里。

hold on (to sb/sth) to continue to hold sb/sth; to put your hand on sb/sth and not take your hand away 指抓紧、不放开：*Hold on and don't let go until I say so.* 握紧，我让你松手时才松开。

cling to hold on to sb/sth tightly, especially with your whole body 尤指用身体紧抱、紧握、抓紧：*Survivors* ***clung to*** *pieces of floating debris.* 生还者紧紧抱住漂浮在水面上的残骸。

clutch to hold sb/sth tightly, especially in your hand; to take hold of sth suddenly 尤指用手抓紧、紧握、抱紧、突然抓住：*She stood there, the flowers still clutched in her hand.* 她站在那里，手里仍然紧握着花束。◇ *He felt himself slipping and* ***clutched at*** *a branch.* 他感到自己滑了一下，便一把抓住一根树枝。

grip to hold on to sth very tightly with your hand 指用手紧握、紧抓：*Grip the rope as tightly as you can.* 尽可能紧紧抓住绳子。

grasp to take hold of sth firmly 指抓紧、抓牢：*He grasped my hand and shook it warmly.* 他热情地抓着我的手握了起来。**NOTE** The object of **grasp** is often sb's *hand* or *wrist*. * grasp 的宾语通常为 hand 或 wrist。

clasp (*formal*) to hold sb/sth tightly in your hand or in your arms 指紧握、攥紧、抱紧：*They clasped hands* (= held each other's hands). 他们相互紧握着对方的手。◇ *She clasped the children in her arms.* 她把孩子紧紧地搂在怀里。**NOTE** The object of **clasp** is often your *hands*, sb else's *hand* or another person. * clasp 的宾语通常为 hand 或另一个人。

hang on (to sth) to hold on to sth very tightly, especially in order to support yourself or stop yourself from falling 尤指为支撑自己或防止跌倒而紧紧抓住某物：*Hang on tight. We're off!* 抓紧，我们出发了！

PATTERNS
- to hold/clutch/grip/clasp sth **in your hand/hands**
- to hold/clutch/clasp sb/sth **in your arms**
- to hold/clutch/grip/grasp/clasp/hang **on to** sth
- to hold/cling/hang **on**
- to hold/clutch/clasp sb/sth **to you**
- to hold/hold on to/cling to/clutch/grip/grasp/clasp/hang on to sb/sth **tightly**
- to hold/hold on to/cling to/clutch/grip/grasp/clasp sb/sth **firmly**
- to hold/hold on to/clutch/grip/clasp/hang on to sb/sth **tight**

- **ON TELEPHONE** 电话 **22** [I, T] to wait until you can speak to the person you have telephoned（打电话时）等待，不挂断：*That extension is busy right now. Can you hold?* 分机现在占线。您能等一会吗？◇ **~ the line** *She asked me to hold the line.* 她要我别挂断电话。➲ **WORDFINDER NOTE AT CALL**
- **STOP** 停止 **23** [T] **~ sth** used to tell sb to stop doing sth or not to do sth 停下；不要做：*Hold your fire!* (= don't shoot) 别开枪！◇ *Hold the front page!* (= don't print it until a particular piece of news is available) 把头版暂时空着！◇ (*NAmE, informal*) *Give me a hot dog, but hold the* (= don't give me any) *mustard.* 给我来份热狗，但别加芥末。

IDM **HELP** Most idioms containing **hold** are at the entries for the nouns and adjectives in the idioms, for example **hold the fort** is at **fort**. 大多数含 hold 的习语，都可在该等习语中的名词及形容词相关词条找到，如 hold the fort 在词条 fort 下。**hold 'good** to be true 正确；适用：*The same argument does not hold good in every case.* 同样的论点并非在所有的情况下都适用。**'hold it** (*informal*) used to ask sb to wait, or not to move 稍等；别动：*Hold it a second—I don't think everyone's arrived yet.* 请稍候，我想人还没有到齐。**there is no 'holding sb** a person cannot be prevented from doing sth 阻拦不住某人：*Once she gets on to the subject of politics there's no holding her.* 她一谈起政治就滔滔不绝。

PHR V **,hold sth a'gainst sb** to allow sth that sb has done to make you have a lower opinion of them 因某人的所为而对其评价低：*I admit I made a mistake—but don't hold it against me.* 我承认我做错了，但别因此而看不起我。

,hold sb/sth↔'back 1 to prevent sb/sth from moving forward or crossing sth 拦阻；阻挡：*The police were unable to hold back the crowd.* 警察阻拦不住人群。**2** to prevent the progress or development of sb/sth 妨碍进展：*Do you think that mixed-ability classes hold back the better students?* 你认为把能力参差的学生混在一班会妨碍高水平学生进步吗？ **,hold sth↔'back 1** to not tell sb sth they want or need to know 不透露（情况）；隐瞒：*to hold back information* 隐瞒信息 **2** to stop yourself from expressing how you really feel 抑制，控制（感情等）；不露声色：*She just managed to hold back her anger.* 她勉强压住了自己的怒火。◇ *He bravely held back his tears.* 他勇敢地没让眼泪流出来。**,hold 'back (from doing sth) | ,hold sb 'back (from doing sth)** to hesitate or to make sb hesitate to act or speak（使）犹豫，踌躇：*She held back, not knowing how to break the terrible news.* 她踌躇着，不知如何说出这一可怕的消息。◇ *I wanted to tell him the truth, but something held me back.* 我本想告诉他真实情况，但又开不了口。

,hold sb↔'down 1 to prevent sb from moving, using force 按住某人：*It took three men to hold him down.* 三个人才把他制伏了。**2** to prevent sb from having their freedom or rights 剥夺某人的自由（或权利）：*The people are held down by a repressive regime.* 人民受到了专制政权的压迫。**,hold sth↔'down 1** to keep sth at a low level 使保持低水平：*The rate of inflation must be held down.* 通货膨胀率必须控制在低水平。**2** [no passive] to keep a job for some time 保住（工作、职位）：*He was unable to hold down a job after his breakdown.* 他精神崩溃以后就没能保住工作。**3** [no passive] (*NAmE, informal*) to limit sth, especially a noise 限制（尤指噪音）：*Hold it down, will you? I'm trying to sleep!* 小点声行吗？我要睡觉！

,hold 'forth to speak for a long time about sth in a way that other people might find boring 喋喋不休；大发议论

,hold sth↔'in to not express how you really feel 克制，忍住（真实感情）：*to hold in your feelings/anger* 不流露感情；忍住怒火 **OPP** **let out**

,hold 'off 1 (of rain or a storm 雨或风暴) to not start 不开始；延迟：*The rain held off just long enough for us to have our picnic.* 雨还好，等到我们用完野餐才下起来。**2** to not do sth immediately 推迟：*We could get a new computer now or hold off until prices are lower.* 我们现在就可以买新计算机，不然就等到降价再说。◇ **hold off doing sth** *Could you hold off making your decision for a few days?* 你能推迟几天再作决定吗？ **,hold sb/sth↔'off** to stop sb/sth defeating you 战胜；克服：*She held off all the last-minute challengers and won the race in a new record time.* 她最后一刻甩掉了所有对手，以新的纪录赢得了赛跑冠军。

ˌhold ˈon 1 (*informal*) used to tell sb to wait or stop 等着；停住 SYN **wait**：*Hold on a minute while I get my breath back.* 稍等一下，让我喘口气。◇ *Hold on! This isn't the right road.* 等一下！这条路不对。**2** to survive in a difficult or dangerous situation （在困境或危险中）坚持住，挺住：*They managed to hold on until help arrived.* 他们勉强坚持到救援到来。**3** (*informal*) used on the telephone to ask sb to wait until they can talk to the person they want （电话用语）别挂断，等一下：*Can you hold on? I'll see if he's here.* 等一下行吗？我去看看他在不在。**ˌhold sth↔ˈon** to keep sth in position 固定：*These nuts and bolts hold the wheels on.* 这些螺母和螺栓把轮子固定住了。◇ *The knob is only held on by sticky tape.* 这个旋钮只是用胶带粘住的。**ˌhold ˈon (to sth/sb) | ˌhold ˈon to sth/sb** [no passive] to keep holding sth/sb 抓紧；不放开：*Hold on and don't let go until I say so.* 握紧，等我让你松手时再松开。◇ *He held on to the back of the chair to stop himself from falling.* 他扶住椅子后背，以免摔倒。**ˌhold ˈon to sth | ˌhold ˈonto sth 1** to keep sth that is an advantage for you; to not give or sell sth to sb else 保住（优势）；不送（或不卖）某物：*You should hold on to your oil shares.* 你应该继续保留住你的石油股份。◇ *She took an early lead in the race and held on to it for nine laps.* 赛跑一开始她便冲到了前面，并一直保持领先了九圈。**2** to keep sth for sb else or for longer than usual （替别人或更长时间地）保存某物：*I'll hold on to your mail for you until you get back.* 你回来之前我将一直替你保管邮件。

ˌhold ˈout 1 to last, especially in a difficult situation 维持；坚持：*We can stay here for as long as our supplies hold out.* 我们可以在这里一直待到我们的储备品用完。**2** to resist or survive in a dangerous or difficult situation 抵抗；幸存：*The rebels held out in the mountains for several years.* 反叛分子在山区顽抗了几年。**ˌhold ˈout sth** to offer a chance, hope or possibility of sth 提供机会；给予希望；使有可能：*Doctors hold out little hope of her recovering.* 医生对她的痊愈不抱很大的希望。**ˌhold sth↔ˈout** to put your hand or arms, or sth in your hand, towards sb, especially to give or offer sth 伸出手（或胳膊）；递出东西：*I held out my hand to steady her.* 我伸出手扶住她。◇ *He held out the keys and I took them.* 他伸手把钥匙递过来，我接了。**ˌhold ˈout for sth** [no passive] to cause a delay in reaching an agreement because you hope you will gain sth （为得到利益）拖延达成协议：*The union negotiators are holding out for a more generous pay settlement.* 工会谈判代表拖延着，以期达成较优厚的薪酬协议。**ˌhold ˈout on sb** (*informal*) to refuse to tell or give sb sth 拒绝告诉（或给予）某人

ˌhold sth↔ˈover [usually passive] **1** to not deal with sth immediately; to leave sth to be dealt with later 搁置；推迟 SYN **postpone**：*The matter was held over until the next meeting.* 这件事被推迟到下次会议。**2** to show a film/movie, play, etc. for longer than planned 延长（电影、戏剧等）的上演期：*The movie proved so popular it was held over for another week.* 这部电影十分受欢迎，因此又继续上演了一周。**ˌhold sth ˈover sb** to use knowledge that you have about sb to threaten them or make them do what you want 以某事要挟（或威逼）某人

ˈhold sb to sth 1 to make sb keep a promise 要求某人遵守诺言 **2** to stop an opposing team scoring more points, etc. than you 压住对方；不让对方（的得分等）超过己方：*The league leaders were held to a 0–0 draw.* 联赛积分领先的队伍被逼成了 0:0 的平局。

ˌhold toˈgether | ˌhold sth↔toˈgether 1 to remain, or to keep sth, united （使）保持团结：*A political party should hold together.* 一个政党应当团结一致。◇ *It's the mother who usually holds the family together.* 使全家人凝聚在一起的通常是母亲。**2** (of an argument, a theory or a story 论点、理论或故事) to be logical or CONSISTENT 合乎逻辑；连贯：*Their case doesn't hold together when you look at the evidence.* 你看一下证据就知道他们的论点前后不一致。➲ COMPARE HANG TOGETHER at HANG *v.* **3** if a machine or an object **holds together** or sth **holds it together**, the different parts stay together so that it does not break （机器、物品）完好无损

ˌhold ˈup to remain strong and working effectively 支持住；承受住；支撑得住：*She's holding up well under the pressure.* 她承受住了压力。**ˌhold sb/sth↔ˈup** [often passive] **1** to support sb/sth and stop them from falling 搀扶；支撑；举起；抬起 **2** to delay or block the movement or progress of sb/sth 延迟；阻碍：*An accident is holding up traffic.* 一场事故造成了交通阻塞。◇ *My application was held up by the postal strike.* 我的申请因邮政部门罢工而耽搁了。➲ RELATED NOUN HOLD-UP (1) **3** to use or present sb/sth as an example 举出（例子）；提出（作为榜样）：*She's always holding up her children as models of good behaviour.* 她总是举例说自己的孩子表现如何好。◇ *His ideas were held up to ridicule.* 他的想法被当成了笑料。**ˌhold up ˈsth** to steal from a bank, shop/store, etc. using a gun 持枪抢劫（银行、商店等）➲ RELATED NOUN HOLD-UP (2)

ˈhold with sth [no passive] (used in negative sentences or in questions 用于否定句或疑问句) to agree with sth 同意；赞成 SYN **approve**：*I don't hold with the use of force.* 我不赞成使用武力。◇ **hold with doing sth** *They don't hold with letting children watch as much TV as they want.* 他们不赞成让孩子随心所欲地看太多电视。

■ ***noun***

• **WITH HAND** 用手 **1** [sing., U] the action of holding sb/sth; the way you are holding sb/sth 抓；握；拿；支撑 SYN **grip**：*His hold on her arm tightened.* 他把她的胳膊抓得更紧了。◇ *She tried to* ***keep hold of*** *the child's hand.* 她尽力拉住那孩子的手不放。◇ *Make sure you've got a steady hold on the camera.* 一定要拿稳相机。

• **IN SPORT** 体育运动 **2** [C] a particular way of holding sb, especially in a sport such as WRESTLING or in a fight 持；握；抓；抱；（尤指摔跤、打斗中的）擒拿法：*The wrestler put his opponent into a head hold.* 那位摔跤手给对手来了个头部擒拿。

• **POWER/CONTROL** 权力；控制 **3** [sing.] ~ (**on/over sb/sth**) influence, power or control over sb/sth 影响；权威；控制：*What she knew about his past gave her a hold over him.* 她知道他的过去，所以能够控制他。◇ *He struggled to get a hold of his anger.* 他竭力压制自己的怒火。➲ SEE ALSO STRANGLEHOLD

• **IN CLIMBING** 攀登 **4** [C] a place where you can put your hands or feet when climbing 支撑点（可手攀或脚踏的地方）➲ SEE ALSO FOOTHOLD, HANDHOLD, TOEHOLD

• **ON SHIP/PLANE** 船；飞机 **5** [C] the part of a ship or plane where the goods being carried are stored 货舱 ➲ VISUAL VOCAB PAGE V57

IDM **catch, get, grab, take, etc. (a) ˈhold of sb/sth** to have or take sb/sth in your hands 抓住；拿着；握着；握住：*He caught hold of her wrists so she couldn't get away.* 他抓住她的手腕，使她无法挣脱。◇ *Lee got hold of the dog by its collar.* 李拉住了狗的项圈。◇ *Quick, grab a hold of that rope.* 快，抓住那条绳子。◇ *Gently, she took hold of the door handle and turned it.* 她轻轻地握住门把手扭动了它。**get ˈhold of sb** to contact or find sb 和某人联系；找到某人：*Where have you been? I've been trying to get hold of you all day.* 你去哪了？我一整天都在找你。**get ˈhold of sth 1** to find sth that you want or need 找到所需要的东西：*I need to get hold of Tom's address.* 我需要找到汤姆的地址。◇ *It's almost impossible to get hold of tickets for the final.* 几乎不可能搞到决赛的门票。**2** to learn or understand sth 学会；理解 **ˌno ˌholds ˈbarred** with no rules or limits on what sb is allowed to do 不加约束；没有限制 **on ˈhold 1** delayed until a later time or date 推迟；中断：*She* ***put*** *her career* ***on hold*** *to have a baby.* 她中断了事业以便生孩子。◇ *The project is on hold until more money is available.* 这项工程暂停，等到有更多的资金时再进行。**2** if a person on the telephone is put **on hold**, they have to wait until the person that they want to talk to is free （电话接通后）等某人接电话 **take (a) ˈhold** to begin to have complete control over sb/sth; to become very strong 开始完全控制；变得十分强大：*Panic took hold of him and he couldn't move.* 他突然惊慌得动弹不得。◇ *They got out of the house just before the* *flames took hold.* 他们就在大火吞噬房子之前逃了出来。◇ *It is best to treat the disease early before it takes a hold.* 最好还是病向浅中医。➲MORE AT WRONG *adj.*

hold·all /ˈhəʊldɔːl; *NAmE* ˈhoʊ-/ (*BrE*) (*NAmE* **ˈduffel bag**) *noun* a large bag made of strong cloth or soft leather, used when you are travelling for carrying clothes, etc. 大旅行袋（用帆布或软皮制造）➲VISUAL VOCAB PAGE V69

hold·er /ˈhəʊldə(r); *NAmE* ˈhoʊ-/ *noun* (often in compounds 常构成复合词) **1** a person who has or owns the thing mentioned 持有者；拥有者：*a licence holder* 执照持有人 ◇ *a season ticket holder* 有季票的人 ◇ *the current holder of the world record* 目前的世界纪录保持者 ◇ *holders of high office* 高级官员 ◇ *the holder of a French passport* 持有法国护照者 ➲ SEE ALSO RECORD HOLDER, TITLE-HOLDER **2** a thing that holds the object mentioned 支托（或握持）…之物：*a pen holder* 笔筒 ➲VISUAL VOCAB PAGES V23, V26, V71 ➲SEE ALSO CIGARETTE HOLDER

hold·ing /ˈhəʊldɪŋ; *NAmE* ˈhoʊ-/ *noun* **1 ~ (in sth)** a number of shares that sb has in a company 股份：*She has a 40% holding in the company.* 她持有公司 40% 的股份。**2** an amount of property that is owned by a person, museum, library, etc. 私有财产；（博物馆、图书馆等的）馆藏：*one of the most important private holdings of Indian art* 印度艺术最重要的私人馆藏之一 **3** a piece of land that is rented by sb and used for farming 租种的土地 ➲SEE ALSO SMALLHOLDING

ˈholding company *noun* a company that is formed to buy shares in other companies which it then controls 控股公司

ˈholding operation *noun* a course of action that is taken so that a particular situation stays the same or does not become any worse 维持现状的行动；使局势不致恶化的做法

ˈholding pattern *noun* the route that a plane travels while it is flying above an airport waiting for permission to land 等待航线（飞机在机场上空待降时的飞行路线）

hold·over /ˈhəʊldəʊvə(r); *NAmE* ˈhoʊldoʊvər/ *noun* (*NAmE*) a person who keeps a position of power, for example sb who had a particular position in one ADMINISTRATION and who still has it in the next （在下届政府中）留任的官员

ˈhold-up *noun* **1** a situation in which sth is prevented from happening for a short time 停顿；阻滞；阻碍 SYN **delay**: *What's the hold-up?* 遇到什么障碍了？◇ *We should finish by tonight, barring hold-ups.* 倘若没有延误，我们应该在今晚完工。◇ (*BrE*) *Sorry I'm late. There was a hold-up on the motorway.* 抱歉，我来晚了。公路上堵车了。**2** (*also* **ˈstick-up** *especially in NAmE*) an act of stealing from a bank, etc. using a gun 持枪抢劫 **3 hold-ups** [pl.] (*BrE*) STOCKINGS that are kept up by having a band of material that can stretch at the top 紧口长筒袜

hole /həʊl; *NAmE* hoʊl/ *noun, verb*

■ *noun*

• **HOLLOW SPACE** 空的空间 **1** [C] a hollow space in sth solid or in the surface of sth 洞；孔；坑：*He dug a deep hole in the garden.* 他在花园里挖了个深坑。◇ *The bomb blew a huge hole in the ground.* 炸弹在地上炸了一个大坑。◇ *Water had collected in the holes in the road.* 水积聚在道路的坑洼处。

• **OPENING** 裂口 **2** [C] a space or opening that goes all the way through sth 裂口；开口；孔眼：*to drill/bore/punch/kick a hole in sth* 把某物钻穿/挖穿/冲穿/踢穿 ◇ *There were holes in the knees of his trousers.* 他裤子的膝部有破洞。◇ *The children climbed through a hole in the fence.* 孩子们从栅栏的缺口处爬了过去。◇ *a bullet hole* 枪眼 ◇ *the hole in the ozone layer* 臭氧层空洞 ➲ SEE ALSO OZONE HOLE

• **ANIMAL'S HOME** 动物住处 **3** [C] the home of a small animal 洞穴；巢穴：*a rabbit/mouse, etc. hole* 兔窝、老鼠洞等 ➲COMPARE FOXHOLE, PIGEONHOLE *n.* ➲SEE ALSO BOLTHOLE

• **UNPLEASANT PLACE** 糟糕的地方 **4** [C, usually sing.] (*informal, disapproving*) an unpleasant place to live or be in 糟糕的住所（或处所）SYN **dump**: *I am not going to bring up my child in this hole.* 我不会在这个鬼地方养育孩子的。➲ SEE ALSO HELLHOLE

• **IN GOLF** 高尔夫球 **5** [C] a hollow in the ground that you must get the ball into; one of the sections of a GOLF COURSE with the TEE at the beginning and the hole at the end 球洞；球座到球洞的区域：*The ball rolled into the hole and she had won.* 球滚进了洞，她赢了。◇ *an eighteen-hole golf course* 十八洞高尔夫球场 ◇ *He liked to play a few holes after work.* 他下班后喜欢打几杆高尔夫球。◇ *She won the first hole.* 她在第一洞时领先。➲VISUAL VOCAB PAGE V44

• **FAULT/WEAKNESS** 错误；缺陷 **6** [C, usually pl.] a fault or weakness in sth such as a plan, law or story （计划、法律或报道等的）错误，缺陷，漏洞：*He was found not guilty because of holes in the prosecution case.* 由于起诉案情有破绽，他被判无罪。◇ *I don't believe what she says—her story is full of holes.* 我不相信她的话，她的说法漏洞百出。➲SEE ALSO LOOPHOLE

• **EMPTY PLACE/POSITION** 空缺的地方 / 位置 **7** [sing.] a place or position that needs to be filled because sb/sth is no longer there 空缺的地方（或位置）：*After his wife left, there was a gaping hole in his life.* 妻子离开后，他的人生中出现了一大片空洞。◇ *Buying the new equipment left a big hole in the company's finances.* 购买新设备给公司的财政造成了一个大洞。HELP There are many other compounds ending in **hole**. You will find them at their place in the alphabet. 以 hole 结尾的复合词还有很多，可在各字母中的适当位置查到。

IDM **in a ˈhole** (*informal*) in a difficult situation 处于困境：*He had got himself into a hole and it was going to be difficult to get out of it.* 他使自己陷入了困境，难以摆脱。**in the ˈhole** (*NAmE, informal*) owing money 负债；欠钱；亏空：*We start the current fiscal year $30 million in the hole.* 我们今年的财政年度一开始便负着 3 000 万美元的债。**make a ˈhole in sth** to use up a large amount of sth that you have, especially money 大量耗费（尤指钱）：*School fees can make a big hole in your savings.* 学费会花掉一大笔的储蓄。➲MORE AT ACE *n.*, BURN *v.*, DIG *v.*, PICK *v.*, SQUARE *adj.*

■ *verb*

• **MAKE A HOLE** 打洞 **1** [T, usually passive] **~ sth** to make a hole or holes in sth, especially a boat or ship （尤指在船上）打洞，造成破洞

• **IN GOLF** 高尔夫球 **2** [T, I] to hit a GOLF ball into the hole 击球入洞：**~ sth** *She holed a 25 foot putt.* 她打了一个 25 英尺远的推杆进洞。◇ **~ (out)** *She holed out from 25 feet.* 她在 25 英尺处把球推进洞中。

PHR V **ˌhole ˈup | be ˌholed ˈup** (*informal*) to hide in a place 躲藏：*He'll hole up now and move again tomorrow, after dark.* 他现在会躲起来，等明天天黑以后再动身。◇ *We believe the gang are holed up in the mountains.* 我们认为那帮匪徒躲藏在山里。

ˌhole-and-ˈcorner *adj.* done in secret because you want to avoid being noticed 暗地里的；秘密的：*a hole-and-corner wedding* 悄悄举行的婚礼

hole-in-ˈone *noun* (*pl.* **holes-in-one**) an occasion in GOLF when a player hits the ball from the TEE into the hole using only one shot （高尔夫球）一杆进洞

ˌhole in the ˈheart *noun* (*medical* 医) a condition in which a baby is born with a problem with the wall dividing the parts of its heart, so that it does not get enough OXYGEN in its blood 先天性心室间隔穿孔

ˌhole in the ˈwall *noun* [sing.] (*informal*) **1** (*BrE*) = CASH MACHINE **2** (*NAmE*) a small dark shop/store or restaurant 阴暗小店（或餐馆）▸ **ˌhole-in-the-ˈwall** *adj.* [only before noun]: *hole-in-the-wall cash machines/restaurants* 自动提款机；狭小餐馆

holey /ˈhəʊli; *NAmE* ˈhoʊ-/ *adj.* a **holey** piece of clothing or material has a lot of holes in it 多洞的

holi·day /ˈhɒlədeɪ; *BrE also* -di; *NAmE* ˈhɑːl-/ *noun, verb*

■ *noun* **1** [U] (*also* **holidays** [pl.]) (*both BrE*) (*NAmE* **vac·ation**) a period of time when you are not at work or school 假期： *the* ***school/summer/Christmas, etc. holidays*** 学校假期、暑假、圣诞节等假期 ◇ *I'm afraid Mr Walsh is away* ***on holiday*** *this week.* 很抱歉，沃尔什先生这个星期休假去了。◇ *The package includes 20 days'* ***paid holiday*** *a year.* 这一揽子福利包括每年 20 天的带薪假。◇ ***holiday pay*** 假日薪金 ◇ *a* ***holiday job*** (= done by students during the school holidays) （学生在学校放假时做的）假期工作 **2** [C] (*BrE*) (*NAmE* **vac·ation**) a period of time spent travelling or resting away from home （外出旅游或休闲的）度假期： *a* ***camping/skiing/walking, etc. holiday*** 露营、滑雪、远足等度假 ◇ *a* ***family holiday*** 合家度假 ◇ *a* ***foreign holiday*** 国外度假 ◇ *a* ***holiday cottage/home/resort*** 度假别墅 / 住所 / 胜地 ◇ *the holiday industry* 度假服务业 ◇ *Where are you going* ***for your holidays*** *this year?* 你今年要到哪里休假？ ◇ *They met while* ***on holiday*** *in Greece.* 他们是在希腊度假时认识的。◇ *We* ***went on holiday*** *together last summer.* 去年夏天我们一起去度假了。➲ WORDFINDER NOTE AT HOTEL ➲ COLLOCATIONS AT TRAVEL ➲ SEE ALSO BUSMAN'S HOLIDAY, PACKAGE TOUR

WORDFINDER 联想词： break, camp, cruise, honeymoon, package tour, self-catering, **tourist**, **travel**, visa

3 [C] a day when most people do not go to work or school, especially because of a religious or national celebration 假日，节日（尤指宗教节日或国家庆典日）： *a national holiday* 全国假日 ◇ *Today is a holiday in Wales.* 在威尔士今天是假日。➲ SEE ALSO BANK HOLIDAY, PUBLIC HOLIDAY **4** **holidays** [pl.] (*NAmE*) the time in December and early January that includes Christmas, Hanukkah and New Year 节日假期（从十二月到一月上旬，包括圣诞节、修殿节和新年）： *Happy Holidays!* 节日愉快！

■ *verb* (*BrE*) (*NAmE* **vac·ation**) [I] (**+ adv./prep.**) to spend a holiday somewhere 度假；休假： *She was holidaying with her family in Ireland.* 她当时正和家人在爱尔兰度假。

▼ **BRITISH/AMERICAN** 英式 / 美式英语

holiday / vacation

- You use **holiday** (or **holidays**) in *BrE* and **vacation** in *NAmE* to describe the regular periods of time when you are not at work or school, or time that you spend travelling or resting away from home. * holiday 或 holidays（英式英语）和 vacation（美式英语）均表示休息日、假日、外出休假期： *I get four weeks' holiday/vacation a year.* 我一年有四周休假。◇ *He's on holiday/vacation this week.* 他本周休假。◇ *I like to take my holiday/vacation in the winter.* 我喜欢在冬天休假。◇ *the summer holidays/vacation* 暑假
- In *NAmE* a **holiday** (or a **public holiday**) is a single day when government offices, schools, banks and businesses are closed. 在美式英语中，holiday 或 public holiday 指政府机关、学校、银行和商业机构关门休息的公共假日： *The school will be closed Monday because it's a holiday.* 星期一是公共假日，所以学校不上课。 This is called a **bank holiday** in *BrE*. 在英式英语中，公共假日叫做 bank holiday。
- **The holidays** is used in *NAmE* to refer to the time in late December and early January that includes Christmas, Hanukkah and the New Year. 在美式英语中，the holidays 指十二月下旬至一月上旬，包括圣诞节、修殿节和新年在内的这段时间。
- **Vacation** in *BrE* is used mainly to mean one of the periods when universities are officially closed for the students. 在英式英语中，vacation 主要指大学的放假时期。

ˈ**holiday camp** *noun* (*BrE*) a place that provides accommodation and entertainment for large numbers of people who are on holiday/vacation 度假营地（提供膳宿和娱乐活动）

holi·day·maker /ˈhɒlədeɪmeɪkə(r); *BrE also* -dimeɪ-; *NAmE* ˈhɑːl-/ *noun* (*BrE*) (*NAmE* **vac·ation·er**) a person who is visiting a place on holiday/vacation 度假者

holier-than-thou /ˌhəʊliə ðən ˈðaʊ; *NAmE* ˌhoʊliər/ *adj.* (*disapproving*) showing that you think that you are morally better than other people 自命清高的 SYN **self-righteous**： *I can't stand his holier-than-thou attitude.* 我无法忍受他那种自命不凡的态度。

holi·ness /ˈhəʊlinəs; *NAmE* ˈhoʊ-/ *noun* **1** [U] the quality of being holy 神圣 **2** **His/Your Holiness** [C] a title of respect used when talking to or about the Pope and some other religious leaders 圣座，宗座（对教皇及其他宗教领袖的尊称）： *His Holiness Pope Francis* 教皇圣座方济各

hol·ism /ˈhəʊlɪzəm; ˈhɒl-; *NAmE* ˈhoʊl-; ˈhɑːl-/ *noun* [U] **1** the idea that the whole of sth must be considered in order to understand its different parts 整体论（即必须通过整体理解各部分） ➲ COMPARE ATOMISM **2** the idea that the whole of a sick person, including their body, mind and way of life, should be considered when treating them, and not just the SYMPTOMS (= effects) of the disease 整体观念（治病应全面考量个人的身体、思想和生活方式等）

hol·is·tic /həʊˈlɪstɪk; hɒˈl-; *NAmE* hoʊˈl-; hɑːˈl-/ *adj.* **1** considering a whole thing or being to be more than a collection of parts 整体的；全面的： *a holistic approach to life* 对生命的全面探讨 **2** (*medical* 医) treating the whole person rather than just the SYMPTOMS (= effects) of a disease 功能整体性的： *holistic medicine* 整体医学 ➲ WORDFINDER NOTE AT TREATMENT ▶ **hol·is·tic·al·ly** /-kli/ *adv.*

hol·land·aise sauce /ˌhɒləndeɪz ˈsɔːs; *NAmE* ˌhɑːl-/ *noun* [U] a sauce made with butter, egg YOLKS (= yellow parts) and VINEGAR 荷兰酸酱（由黄油、蛋黄、醋等制成）

hol·ler /ˈhɒlə(r); *NAmE* ˈhɑːl-/ *verb* [I, T] (*informal, especially NAmE*) to shout loudly 叫喊 SYN **yell**： **~ (at sb)** *Don't holler at me!* 别对我大喊大叫的！ ◇ **+ speech** *'Look out!' I hollered.* "当心！"我大喊一声。 ◇ **~ sth** *He hollered something I couldn't understand.* 他大声嚷了一些我不明白的话。

hol·low /ˈhɒləʊ; *NAmE* ˈhɑːloʊ/ *adj., noun, verb*

■ *adj.* **1** having a hole or empty space inside 中空的；空心的： *a hollow ball/centre/tube* 中空的球 / 中心部位 / 管子 ◇ *The tree trunk was hollow inside.* 这树干里面是空的。◇ *Her stomach felt hollow with fear.* 她吓得魂不附体。 **2** (of parts of the face 面部) sinking deeply into the face 凹陷的： ***hollow eyes/cheeks*** 凹陷的双眼 / 双颊 ◇ *hollow-eyed from lack of sleep* 因缺乏睡眠而双眼凹陷的 **3** [usually before noun] (of sounds 声音) making a low sound like that made by an empty object when it is hit 沉闷回荡的；空响的： *a hollow groan* 低沉的呻吟 **4** [usually before noun] not sincere 无诚意的；虚伪的： ***hollow promises/threats*** 空洞的许诺；虚张声势的威胁 ◇ *a hollow laugh* 干笑 ◇ *Their appeals for an end to the violence had a* ***hollow ring***. 他们要求停止使用暴力的呼吁没有诚意。 **5** [usually before noun] without real value 无真正价值的： *to win a* ***hollow victory*** 取得表面胜利 IDM SEE RING[2] *v.* ▶ **hol·low·ly** *adv.*： *to laugh hollowly* 发出干笑 **hol·low·ness** *noun* [U]： *the hollowness of the victory* 那场胜利的了无意义

■ *noun* **1** an area that is lower than the surface around it, especially on the ground 凹陷处；坑洼处： *muddy hollows* 泥泞的洼地 ◇ *The village lay secluded in a hollow of the hills* (= a small valley). 村子坐落在一个幽静的小山谷中。◇ *She noticed the slight hollows under his cheekbones.* 她注意到他颧骨下面的轻微凹陷。 **2** a hole or a confined space in sth 洞；孔；围起来的空间： *The squirrel disappeared into a hollow at the base of the tree.* 松鼠钻进了树根处的一个洞。

■ *verb* [usually passive] **~ sth** to make a flat surface curve in 挖

PHR V ˌ**hollow sth↔ˈout** **1** to make a hole in sth by removing part of it 挖空（某物）；挖出（孔、洞）： *Hollow out the cake and fill it with cream.* 在蛋糕上挖个

洞，填入奶油。 **2** to form sth by making a hole in sth else 挖洞（成某物）： *The cave has been hollowed out of the mountainside.* 窑洞是在半山腰挖成的。

holly /ˈhɒli; *NAmE* ˈhɑːli/ *noun* (*pl.* **-ies**) [U, C] a bush or small tree with hard shiny leaves with sharp points and bright red BERRIES in winter, often used as a decoration at Christmas 冬青： *a sprig of holly* 冬青树枝

hol·ly·hock /ˈhɒlihɒk; *NAmE* ˈhɑːlihɑːk/ *noun* a tall garden plant with white, yellow, red or purple flowers growing up its STEM 蜀葵

Hol·ly·wood /ˈhɒliwʊd; *NAmE* ˈhɑːl-/ *noun* [U] the part of Los Angeles where the film/movie industry is based (used to refer to the US film/movie industry and the way of life that is associated with it) 好莱坞；美国电影业；好莱坞生活方式 ➲ COLLOCATIONS AT CINEMA

ˌHollywood ˈending *noun* (*usually disapproving*) an ending in a film/movie, novel, etc. which happens in the way you expect, is full of exaggerated happiness, pity or love, and may not be very realistic 好莱坞式结尾（指电影、小说等过分渲染的、不太真实的结局）： *The film refuses to sell out and provide a Hollywood ending.* 这部影片拒绝背弃题旨采用好莱坞式的结尾。

hol·mium /ˈhəʊlmiəm; *NAmE* ˈhoʊl-/ *noun* [U] (*symb.* **Ho**) a chemical element. Holmium is a soft silver-white metal. 钬

holo·caust /ˈhɒləkɔːst; *NAmE* ˈhɑːlə-; ˈhoʊlə-/ *noun* **1** [C] a situation in which many things are destroyed and many people killed, especially because of a war or a fire （尤指战争或火灾引起的）大灾难，大毁灭： *a nuclear holocaust* 核灾难 **2 the Holocaust** [sing.] the killing of millions of Jews by the Nazis in the 1930s and 1940s （20 世纪 30 年代和 40 年代纳粹对数百万犹太人的）大屠杀

holo·gram /ˈhɒləɡræm; *NAmE* ˈhɑːl-; ˈhoʊl-/ *noun* a special type of picture in which the objects seem to be THREE-DIMENSIONAL (= solid rather than flat) 全息图

holo·graph /ˈhɒləɡrɑːf; *NAmE* ˈhɑːləɡræf; ˈhoʊl-/ *noun* (*specialist*) a piece of writing that has been written by hand by its author 亲笔文件；手书

holo·graph·ic /ˌhɒləˈɡræfɪk; *NAmE* ˌhɑːl-; ˌhoʊl-/ *adj.* [usually before noun] connected with holograms 全息图的： *a holographic picture* 全息图片

holo·phra·sis /ˌhɒləˈfreɪsɪs; *NAmE* həˈlɑːfrəsɪs/ *noun* [U] (*linguistics* 语言) the expression of a whole idea in a single word, for example a baby saying 'up' for 'I want you to pick me up' 独词表达，独词句（以一个单词表达整句意思，如婴儿用 up 一词表达 I want you to pick me up 的意思） ▸ **holo·phras·tic** /ˌhɒləˈfræstɪk; *NAmE* ˌhɑːlə-; ˌhoʊlə-/ *adj.*

hols /hɒlz; *NAmE* hɑːlz/ *noun* [pl.] (*old-fashioned, BrE, informal*) holidays 假期

Hol·stein /ˈhɒlstaɪn; -stiːn; *NAmE* ˈhoʊl-/ (*NAmE*) (*BrE* **Frie·sian**) *noun* a type of black and white cow that produces a lot of milk 黑白花乳牛，荷兰牛（产奶量很大）

hol·ster /ˈhəʊlstə(r); *NAmE* ˈhoʊ-/ *noun, verb*

■ ***noun*** a leather case worn on a belt or on a narrow piece of leather under the arm, used for carrying a small gun 手枪皮套（挂在腰带或腋下皮带上）

■ ***verb*** **~ sth** to put a gun in a holster 把（枪）放在手枪皮套里

holy 🔑 /ˈhəʊli; *NAmE* ˈhoʊli/ *adj.* (**holi·er, holi·est**) **1** 🔑 [usually before noun] connected with God or a particular religion 与神（或宗教）有关的；神圣的： *the **Holy Bible/Scriptures*** 《圣经》 ◇ *holy ground* 圣地 ◇ *a holy war* (= one fought to defend the beliefs of a particular religion) 圣战 ◇ *the holy city of Mecca* 圣城麦加 ◇ *Islam's holiest shrine* 伊斯兰教最神圣的圣地 OPP **unholy** ➲ SEE ALSO HOLY ORDERS **2** 🔑 good in a moral and religious way 圣洁的： *a holy life/man* 圣洁的生活 / 人 OPP **unholy** **3** [only before noun] (*informal*) used to emphasize that you are surprised, afraid, etc. （强调惊讶、害怕等）： *Holy cow! What was that?* 天哪！那是什么？ ➲ SEE ALSO HOLIER-THAN-THOU, HOLINESS

ˌHoly Comˈmunion *noun* [U] = COMMUNION (1)

the ˌHoly ˈFather *noun* [sing.] the POPE 教皇

the ˌHoly ˈGhost *noun* [sing.] = HOLY SPIRIT

the ˌHoly ˈGrail *noun* [sing.] = GRAIL

the ˌholy of ˈholies *noun* [sing.] **1** the most holy part of a religious building 至圣所（圣殿最神圣的地方） **2** (*humorous*) a special room or building that can only be visited by important people 贵宾室；贵宾楼

ˌholy ˈorders *noun* [pl.] the official position of being a priest 圣秩；圣品： *to take holy orders* (= to become a priest) 领受圣秩

Holy·rood /ˈhɒliruːd; *NAmE* ˈhɑːl-/ *noun* [U] the Scottish parliament and government 苏格兰议会和政府： *elections to Holyrood* 苏格兰议会选举 ➲ MORE LIKE THIS 19, page R27 ORIGIN From the name of the part of Edinburgh where the parliament building is. 源自爱丁堡议会大厦所在地的名称。

the ˌHoly ˈSee *noun* [sing.] **1** the job or authority of the Pope 圣座，宗座（指教皇的职位或权力） **2** the Roman Catholic court at the Vatican in Rome 罗马教廷（设在梵蒂冈）

the ˌHoly ˈSpirit (*also* **the ˌHoly ˈGhost**) *noun* [sing.] (in Christianity 基督教) God in the form of a spirit 圣灵；圣神

ˌholy ˈwater *noun* [U] water that has been BLESSED by a priest 圣水

ˈHoly Week *noun* in the Christian Church, the week before Easter Sunday 圣周（基督教指复活节前的一周）

ˌHoly ˈWrit *noun* [U] (*old-fashioned*) the Bible 《圣经》： (*figurative*) *You shouldn't take what he says as Holy Writ* (= accept that it is true without questioning it). 你不应该把他的话当作圣经。

hom·age /ˈhɒmɪdʒ; *NAmE* ˈhɑːm-/ *noun* [U, C, usually sing.] **~ (to sb/sth)** (*formal*) something that is said or done to show respect for sb 敬辞；表示敬意的举动： *The kings of France **paid homage** to no one.* 法国国王不向任何人致敬。 ◇ *He describes his book as 'a homage to my father'.* 他说他的书是"献给父亲"的。 ◇ *They stood in silent homage around the grave.* 他们恭敬地站在坟墓周围致默哀礼。

hom·bre /ˈɒmbreɪ; *NAmE* ˈɑːmb-/ *noun* (*from Spanish, NAmE, informal*) a man, especially one of a particular type （尤指某类）男人： *Their quarterback is one tough hombre.* 他们的四分卫是个壮汉。

hom·burg /ˈhɒmbɜːɡ; *NAmE* ˈhɑːmbɜːrɡ/ *noun* a man's soft hat with a narrow, curled BRIM 洪堡毡帽（男用软帽，帽边狭窄卷曲）

home 🔑 /həʊm; *NAmE* hoʊm/ *noun, adj., adv., verb*

■ ***noun***

• **HOUSE, ETC.** 房子等 **1** 🔑 [C, U] the house or flat/apartment that you live in, especially with your family 家；住所： *We are not far from my home now.* 我们现在离我家不远了。 ◇ *Old people prefer to stay in their own homes.* 老年人喜欢待在自己家中。 ◇ *She leaves home at 7 every day.* 她每天 7 点钟离家。 ◇ *the family home* 家庭住宅 ◇ *While travelling she missed the comforts of home.* 旅行期间她想念家里的舒适。 ◇ *He **left home** (= left his parents and began an independent life) at sixteen.* 他十六岁时离家独立生活。 ◇ *Nowadays a lot of people **work from home**.* 如今有很多人在家工作。 ◇ *I'll call you from home later.* 我过会儿从家里给你打电话。 ◇ (*figurative*) *We haven't found a home for all our books yet* (= a place where they can be kept). 我们还没找到存放全部书籍的地方。 ◇ *stray dogs needing new homes* 需要新家的流浪狗 ➲ SEE ALSO STAY-AT-HOME *n.* **2** 🔑 [C] a house or flat/apartment, etc., when you think of it as property that can be bought and sold （可买卖的）房子，住宅，寓所： *a **holiday/summer home*** 假日 / 消夏寓所 ◇ *A lot of new homes are being built on the edge of town.* 小镇外围正在兴建很多新房屋。 ◇ *Private*

H

home ownership is increasing faster than ever. 私有房产正以前所未有的速度增长。◇ *They applied for a home improvement loan.* 他们申请了房屋修缮贷款。➲ COLLOCATIONS AT DECORATE, HOUSE ➲ VISUAL VOCAB PAGE V16 ➲ SEE ALSO MOBILE HOME, SECOND HOME, STATELY HOME

WORDFINDER 联想词：accommodation, deed, **house**, lease, let, **location**, mortgage, squat, tenant

• **TOWN/COUNTRY** 城镇；国家 **3** [C, U] the town, district, country, etc. that you come from, or where you are living and that you feel you belong to 家乡；故乡；定居地：*I often think about my friends **back home**.* 我常常想起老家的朋友。◇ *Jane left England and made Greece her home.* 简离开了英国，在希腊安了家。◇ *Jamaica is home to over two million people.* 牙买加是两百多万人的家乡。

• **FAMILY** 家庭 **4** [C] used to refer to a family living together, and the way it behaves 家庭：*She came from a violent home.* 她出身于一个有暴力行为的家庭。◇ *He had always wanted a real home with a wife and children.* 他一直想要一个有妻子和孩子的真正的家庭。➲ SEE ALSO BROKEN HOME

• **FOR OLD PEOPLE/CHILDREN** 老年人；孩子 **5** [C] a place where people who cannot care for themselves live and are cared for by others 养老院；养育院：*a **children's home*** 儿童之家 ◇ *an **old people's home*** 养老院 ◇ *a **retirement home*** 退休疗养院 ◇ *a home for the mentally ill* 精神病院 ◇ *She has lived **in a home** since she was six.* 她从六岁起就在保育院生活。➲ SEE ALSO NURSING HOME, REST HOME

• **FOR PETS** 宠物 **6** [C] a place where pets with no owner are taken care of 收养所：*a **dogs'/cats' home*** 狗 / 猫之家

• **OF PLANT/ANIMAL** 动植物 **7** [sing., U] the place where a plant or an animal usually lives; the place where sb/sth can be found 生息地；栖息地；产地：*This region is the home of many species of wild flower.* 这个地区有很多种类的野花。◇ *The tiger's home is in the jungle.* 老虎栖息在丛林里。◇ *The Rockies are home to bears and mountain lions.* 落基山脉中有熊和美洲狮栖息。

• **WHERE STH FIRST DONE** 发祥地 **8** [sing.] **the ~ of sth** the place where sth was first discovered, made or invented 发源地；发祥地：*New Orleans, the home of jazz* 新奥尔良，爵士乐的发源地 ◇ *Greece, the home of democracy* 希腊，民主的发祥地

IDM **at 'home 1** in a person's own house, flat/apartment, etc. 在家里：*I phoned you last night, but you weren't at home.* 我昨晚给你打电话了，但你不在家。◇ *Oh no, I left my purse at home.* 糟了，我把钱包落在家里了。◇ *He lived at home* (= with his parents) *until he was thirty.* 他一直和父母同住到三十岁。**2** comfortable and relaxed 舒适自在；无拘无束：*Sit down and **make yourself at home**.* 坐下，别拘束。◇ *Simon feels very at home on a horse.* 西蒙骑马得心应手。**3** (used especially in JOURNALISM 尤用于报刊新闻) in sb's own country, not in a foreign country 在本国；在国内：*The president is not as popular at home as he is abroad.* 总统在国内不如在国外受欢迎。**4** if a sports team plays **at home**, it plays in the town, etc. that it comes from （比赛队）在主场：*Leeds are playing at home this weekend.* 本周末利兹队将在主场进行比赛。◇ *Is the match on Saturday at home or away?* 星期六的比赛是在主场还是在客场？**away from 'home 1** away from a person's own house, flat/apartment, etc. 离开家：*He works away from home during the week.* 他除了周末都在外工作。◇ *I don't want to be away from home for too long.* 我不想离家时间太长。**2** if a sports team plays **away from home**, it plays in the town, etc. that its opponent comes from （比赛队）在客场 **a ˌhome from 'home** (*BrE*) (*NAmE* **a ˌhome away from 'home**) a place where you feel relaxed and comfortable as if you were in your own home 像家一样舒适自在的地方 **ˌhome is where the 'heart is** (*saying*) a home is where the people you love are 家乃心之所系 **home sweet 'home** (*often ironic*) used to say how pleasant your home is (especially when you really mean that it is not pleasant at all) 可爱的家；家总是家（有时有反讽意思，指并不愉快）**set up 'home** (*BrE*) (used especially about a couple) to start living in a new place （尤指夫妇）建立家庭，成家：*They got married and set up home together in Hull.* 他们结婚了，一同在赫尔建立了新家。**when he's, it's, etc. at 'home** (*BrE, humorous*) used to emphasize a question about sb/sth （加强疑问语气）到底，究竟：*Who's she when she's at home?* (= I don't know her) 她到底是谁？➲ MORE AT CHARITY, CLOSE² *adj.*, EAT, MAN *n.*, SPIRITUAL *adj.*

■ ***adj.*** [only before noun]

• **WHERE YOU LIVE** 家 **1** connected with the place where you live 家的；家庭的：***home life*** (= with your family) 家庭生活 ◇ *a person's **home address/town*** 家庭地址；家乡 ◇ *We offer customers a free **home delivery** service.* 我们为客户提供免费送货上门的服务。

• **MADE/USED AT HOME** 家里做 / 用 **2** made or used at home 在家里做的；家用的：*home movies* 家庭电影 ◇ *home cooking* 家常饭菜 ◇ *a home computer* 家用电脑

• **OWN COUNTRY** 本国 **3** (*especially BrE*) connected with your own country rather than foreign countries 本国的；国内的 SYN **domestic**：*products for the home market* 为国内市场生产的产品 ◇ ***home news/affairs*** 国内新闻 / 事件 OPP **foreign, overseas**

• **IN SPORT** 体育运动 **4** connected with a team's own sports ground 主场的：*a **home match/win*** 主场比赛 / 胜利 ◇ *the **home team*** 主队 ◇ *Rangers were playing in front of their **home crowd**.* 流浪者队在主场观众面前比赛。➲ COMPARE AWAY (6)

■ ***adv.***

• **WHERE YOU LIVE** 居住地 **1** to or at the place where you live 到家；向家；在家：*Come on, it's time to **go home**.* 快点，该回家了。◇ *What time did you **get home** last night?* 你昨晚什么时间到家的？◇ *The trip has been exhausting and I'll be glad to **be home**.* 这个旅程令人疲惫不堪，要是能回家就好了。◇ *After a month, they went **back home** to America.* 一个月之后，他们返回了美国。◇ *It was a lovely day so I walked home.* 那天天气很好，所以我走路回家了。◇ *Anna will drive me home after work.* 下班后安娜会开车送我回家。◇ *Hopefully the doctors will allow her home tomorrow.* 明天医生可望会允许她回家。◇ (*NAmE*) *I like to **stay home** in the evenings.* 我喜欢晚上待在家里。

• **INTO CORRECT POSITION** 正确位置 **2** into the correct position 到正确的位置：*She leaned on the door and pushed the bolt home.* 她倚在门上，好了门闩。◇ *He drove the ball home* (= scored a goal) *from 15 metres.* 他从 15 米远处劲射破门得分。◇ *The torpedo struck home on the hull of the ship.* 鱼雷正击中船身。

IDM **be home and 'dry** (*BrE*) (*NAmE* **be home 'free**) to have done sth successfully, especially when it was difficult 做成某事（尤指难事）：*I could see the finish line and thought I was home and dry.* 我能看见终点线了，我想我终于成功了。**bring home the 'bacon** (*informal*) to be successful at sth; to earn money for your family to live on 成功；挣到养家糊口的钱 **bring sth 'home to sb** to make sb realize how important, difficult or serious sth is 使某人了解某事的重要性（或艰难、严重程度）：*The television pictures brought home to us the full horror of the attack.* 电视画面使我们充分地了解这次袭击有多么恐怖。**come 'home to sb** to become completely clear to sb, often in a way that is painful 使人（痛苦地）完全明白：*It suddenly came home to him that he was never going to see Julie again.* 他突然明白他再也见不到朱莉了。**sth comes home to 'roost** (*also* **the chickens come home to 'roost**) used to say that if sb says or does sth bad or wrong, it will affect them badly in the future 自食恶果；报应到自己身上 **hit/strike 'home** if a remark, etc. **hits/strikes home**, it has a strong effect on sb, in a way that makes them realize what the true facts of a situation are （言语等）正中要害，说到点子上：*Her face went pale as his words hit home.* 他的话切中要害，她的脸变白了。➲ MORE AT COW *n.*, DRIVE *v.*, LIGHT *n.*, PRESS *v.*, RAM *v.*, ROMP *v.*, WRITE

■ ***verb***

PHR V **ˌhome 'in on sth 1** to aim at sth and move straight towards it 朝向，移向，导向（目标）：*The missile homed in on the target.* 导弹向目标径直飞去。**2** to direct your thoughts or attention towards sth 把（思想、注意力）集中于：*I began to feel I was really homing in on the answer.* 我开始觉得我快找到答案了。

ˌ**home ˈbase** *noun* [sing., U] **1** = HOME PLATE **2** the place where sb/sth usually lives, works or operates from 基地；大本营

home·body /ˈhəʊmbɒdi; *NAmE* ˈhoʊmbɑːdi/ *noun* (*pl.* **-ies**) (*informal, especially NAmE*) a person who enjoys spending time at home 喜欢待在家里的人；恋家的人

home·boy /ˈhəʊmbɔɪ; *NAmE* ˈhoʊm-/ (*also* **homie**) *noun* (*NAmE, informal*) a male friend from the same town as you; a member of your GANG (= a group of young people who go around together) （男）老乡，伙伴

ˌ**home ˈbrew** *noun* [U] **1** beer that sb makes at home 家酿啤酒 **2** something that sb makes at home rather than buying it 自己制作的东西： *The security software he uses is home brew.* 他用的安全软件是自己编写的。 ▸ ˌ**home-ˈbrew** (*also* ˌ**home-ˈbrewed**) *adj.* [only before noun]

home·buy·er /ˈhəʊmbaɪə(r); *NAmE* ˈhoʊm-/ *noun* a person who buys a house, flat/apartment, etc. 购房者

ˌ**home ˈcinema** (*BrE*) (*NAmE* ˌ**home ˈtheater**) *noun* [U] television and video equipment designed to give a similar experience to being in a cinema/movie theater, with high-quality pictures and sound and a large screen 家庭影院

home·com·ing /ˈhəʊmkʌmɪŋ; *NAmE* ˈhoʊm-/ *noun* **1** [C, U] the act of returning to your home after being away for a long time （长时间离家后的）回家，返家，回国 **2** [C] (*NAmE*) a social event that takes place every year at a HIGH SCHOOL, college or university for people who used to be students there （一年一度的）校友返校活动

the ˌ**Home ˈCounties** *noun* [pl.] the counties around London 伦敦周边的郡

ˌ**home ecoˈnomics** *noun* [U] cooking and other skills needed at home, taught as a subject in school 家政学

ˌ**home ˈfront** *noun* [sing.] the people who do not go to fight in a war but who stay in a country to work （战时的）后方民众，大后方

IDM **on the ˈhome front** happening at home, or in your own country 发生在家乡（或本国）

home·girl /ˈhəʊmɡɜːl; *NAmE* ˈhoʊmɡɜːrl/ (*also* **homie**) *noun* (*NAmE, informal*) a female friend from the same town as you; a member of your GANG (= a group of young people who go around together) （女）老乡，伙伴

ˌ**home ˈground** *noun* [sing., U] **1** (*BrE*) a sports ground that a team regularly plays on in their own area or town 主场场地；主队运动场 **2** a place where sb lives or works and where they feel confident, rather than a place that is not familiar to them 自己的家；熟悉的工作地方；自己的地盘： *I'd rather meet him here on my own home ground.* 我宁愿在我自己的地盘上见他。

ˌ**home-ˈgrown** *adj.* **1** (of plants, fruit and vegetables 植物、水果和蔬菜) grown in a person's garden 自家园子里产的： *home-grown tomatoes* 自家种的西红柿 **2** made, trained or educated in your own country, town, etc. 本国（或本地）制造的（或培养的、教育的）： *The team has a wealth of home-grown talent.* 该队有很多自己培养的人才。

ˌ**home ˈhelp** *noun* (*BrE*) a person whose job is to help old or sick people with cooking, cleaning, etc. （给老人或病人料理家务的）佣人

ˌ**home imˈprovement** *noun* [C, U] changes that are made to a house, that increase its value （为增值进行的）房屋修缮，家居装修： *They've spent a lot of money on home improvements.* 他们花了很多钱装修家居。 ◇ *home-improvement products* 家居装修产品 ➲ COLLOCATIONS AT DECORATE

home·land /ˈhəʊmlænd; *NAmE* ˈhoʊm-/ *noun* **1** [usually sing.] the country where a person was born 祖国；家乡： *Many refugees have been forced to flee their homeland.* 很多难民被迫逃离了祖国。 **2** (in the Republic of South Africa under the APARTHEID system in the past) one of the areas with some SELF-GOVERNMENT that were intended for a group of black African people to live in （南非共和国过去在种族隔离制度下设立、有一定自治权的）黑人定居地： *the Transkei homeland* 特兰斯凯黑人定居地

ˌ**Homeland Seˈcurity** *noun* [U] the activities and organizations whose aim is to prevent TERRORIST attacks in the US 国土安全（美国防止恐怖袭击的行动及机构）： *the Department of Homeland Security* 国土安全部

home·less /ˈhəʊmləs; *NAmE* ˈhoʊm-/ *adj.* **1** having no home 无家的： *The scheme has been set up to help homeless people.* 这个计划的目的是帮助无家可归的人。 **2 the homeless** *noun* [pl.] people who have no home 无家可归的人们： *helping the homeless* 帮助无家可归者 ➲ MORE LIKE THIS 24, page R28 ➲ WORDFINDER NOTE AT POOR ▸ **home·less·ness** *noun* [U]

ˌ**home ˈloan** *noun* (*informal*) = MORTGAGE

home·ly /ˈhəʊmli; *NAmE* ˈhoʊm-/ *adj.* (**home·lier**, **home·li·est**) **1** (*BrE, approving*) (of a place 地方) making you feel comfortable, as if you were in your own home 在家一样舒适的；犹如在自家一样的： *The hotel has a lovely homely feel to it.* 那家旅馆给人一种宾至如归的感觉。 **2** (*approving, especially BrE*) simple and good 简单且好的；家常的： *homely cooking* 家常烹调 **3** (*BrE, approving*) (of a woman 女人) warm and friendly and enjoying the pleasures of home and family 热情友好并热衷家庭生活的；亲切喜家的： *His landlady was a kind, homely woman.* 他的房东太太心地善良，待人亲切。 **4** (*NAmE, disapproving*) (of a person's appearance 人的外表) not attractive 相貌平平的 SYN **plain**: *a homely child* 一个相貌普通的孩子

ˌ**home-ˈmade** *adj.* made at home, rather than produced in a factory and bought in a shop/store 自制的；家里做的

home·maker /ˈhəʊmmeɪkə(r); *NAmE* ˈhoʊm-/ *noun* (*especially NAmE*) a person who works at home and takes care of the house and family 料理家务者；操持家务者 ▸ **home·making** *noun* [U]

the ˈHome Office *noun* [sing.+sing./pl. v.] the British government department that deals with the law, the police and prisons, and with decisions about who can enter the country （英国）内政部

ˌ**home ˈoffice** *noun* a room in sb's home that is used for work 家庭办公室

homeo·path (*BrE also* **hom·oeo-**) /ˈhəʊmiəpæθ; ˈhɒmi-; *NAmE* ˈhoʊ-; ˈhɑːm-/ *noun* a person who treats illness using homeopathic methods 顺势疗法医生

hom·eop·athy (*BrE also* **hom·oeo-**) /ˌhəʊmiˈɒpəθi; ˌhɒm-; *NAmE* ˌhoʊmiˈɑːp-; ˌhɑːm-/ *noun* [U] a system of treating diseases or conditions using very small amounts of the substance that causes the disease or condition 顺势疗法 ➲ WORDFINDER NOTE AT TREATMENT ▸ **homeo·path·ic** (*BrE also* **hom·oeo-**) /ˌhəʊmiəˈpæθɪk; ˌhɒm-; *NAmE* ˌhoʊm-; ˌhɑːm-/ *adj.*: *homeopathic medicines/remedies/treatments* 顺势疗法药物；顺势疗法；顺势治疗

homeo·stasis (*BrE also* **hom·oeo-**) /ˌhəʊmiəˈsteɪsɪs; ˌhɒm-; *NAmE* ˌhoʊm-/ *noun* [U] (*biology* 生) the process by which the body reacts to changes in order to keep conditions inside the body, for example temperature, the same 体内稳态，内环境稳定（身体对变化作出自我调整）

home·own·er /ˈhəʊməʊnə(r); *NAmE* ˈhoʊmoʊ-/ *noun* a person who owns their house or flat/apartment 房主

ˈ**home page** *noun* (*computing* 计) **1** the main page created by a company, an organization, etc. on the Internet from which connections to other pages can be made （网站）主页，首页 ➲ VISUAL VOCAB PAGE V74 **2** a page on the Internet that you choose to appear first on your screen whenever you make a connection to the Internet 主页，起始页（上网时首先登录的网页） ➲ WORDFINDER NOTE AT WEBSITE

ˈ**home plate** (*also* ˌ**home ˈbase**) (*NAmE also* **plate**) *noun* (in BASEBALL 棒球) the place where the person hitting

H

the ball stands and where they must return to after running around all the bases 本垒板；本垒

homer /ˈhəʊmə(r); *NAmE* ˈhoʊ-/ *noun* (*NAmE, informal*) = HOME RUN：*He hit a homer.* 他击出了一记本垒打。

home·room /ˈhəʊmruːm; -rʊm; *NAmE* ˈhoʊ-/ *noun* [C, U] (*NAmE*) a room in a school where students go at the beginning of each school day, so that teachers can check who is in school; the time spent in this room 进行课前点名的教室；课前点名教室集合时间

ˌhome ˈrule *noun* [U] the right of a country or region to govern itself, especially after another country or region has governed it （尤指受其他国家或地区统治之后的）地方自治权

ˌhome ˈrun (*also NAmE, informal* **homer**) *noun* (in BASEBALL 棒球) a hit that allows the person hitting the ball to run around all the bases without stopping 本垒打

H

home·school·ing /ˌhəʊmˈskuːlɪŋ; *NAmE* ˌhoʊm-/ *noun* [U] the practice of educating children at home, not in schools （儿童的）在家教育 ▸ **home·school** /ˌhəʊmˈskuːl; *NAmE* ˌhoʊm-/ *verb* ~ **sb**

ˌHome ˈSecretary *noun* the British government minister in charge of the Home Office （英国）内政大臣

ˌhome ˈshopping *noun* [U] the practice of ordering goods by phone or by email and having them delivered to your home 家居购物（通过电话或电子邮件购买）

home·sick /ˈhəʊmsɪk; *NAmE* ˈhoʊm-/ *adj.* sad because you are away from home and you miss your family and friends 思乡的；想家的；患怀乡病的：*I felt homesick for Scotland.* 我思念故乡苏格兰。▸ **home·sick·ness** *noun* [U]

home·spun /ˈhəʊmspʌn; *NAmE* ˈhoʊm-/ *adj.* **1** (especially of ideas 尤指思想) simple and ordinary; not coming from an expert 朴素的；平常的 **2** (of cloth 布) made at home 家纺的；家里制作的

home·stay /ˈhəʊmsteɪ; *NAmE* ˈhoʊm-/ *noun* [C, U] an arrangement that provides accommodation for students or tourists in the home of a family in exchange for payment （为学生或游客提供的）家庭寄宿：*The trip includes a homestay in a traditional village.* 这次旅行包括在一个传统村庄的家庭住宿。◇ *Live with an American family in homestay and learn the language and customs.* 在美国家庭寄宿，学习他们的语言与习俗。

home·stead /ˈhəʊmsted; *NAmE* ˈhoʊm-/ *noun, verb*

■ ***noun*** **1** a house with the land and buildings around it, especially a farm （包括周围土地和附属房屋的）家宅；（尤指）农庄 **2** (in the US in the past) a piece of land given to sb by the government on condition that they lived on it and grew crops on it 宅地（美国旧时由国家分给个人居住并开垦的土地）

■ ***verb*** [I] (*old-fashioned, NAmE*) to live and work on a homestead (2) 在分到的土地上居住并劳作 ▸ **home·stead·er** *noun*

the ˌhome ˈstraight (*especially BrE*) (*also* **the home·stretch** /ˈhəʊmstretʃ; *NAmE* ˈhoʊm-/ *especially in NAmE*) *noun* [sing.] **1** the last part of a race （速度比赛的）最后阶段，冲刺阶段 **2** the last part of an activity, etc. when it is nearly completed （活动等的）最后部分，接近完成的阶段

ˌhome ˈtheater (*NAmE*) (*BrE* **ˌhome ˈcinema**) *noun* [U] television and video equipment designed to give a similar experience to being in a cinema/movie theater, with high-quality pictures and sound and a large screen 家庭影院

home·town /ˈhəʊmtaʊn; *NAmE* ˈhoʊm-/ *noun* the place where you were born or lived as a child 家乡；故乡

ˌhome ˈtruth *noun* [usually pl.] a true but unpleasant fact about a person, usually told to them by sb else 使人不愉快的事实（通常由别人告知）；（关于某人的）大实话：*It's time you told him a few home truths.* 现在你该给他讲点实话了。

ˈhome unit *noun* (*AustralE, NZE*) = UNIT (9)

home·ward /ˈhəʊmwəd; *NAmE* ˈhoʊmwərd/ *adj.* going towards home 回家的；回国的：*the homeward journey* 归家的旅程 ▸ **home·ward** (*also* **home·wards** *especially in BrE*) *adv.*：*Commuters were heading homeward at the end of the day.* 一天结束时上班族正赶着回家。◇ *We drove homewards in silence.* 我们默默地开车回家。◇ *We were* ***homeward bound*** *at last.* 我们终于要回家了。

home·work 🔑 /ˈhəʊmwɜːk; *NAmE* ˈhoʊmwɜːrk/ *noun* [U] **1** 🔑 work that is given by teachers for students to do at home （学生的）家庭作业：*I still haven't done my geography homework.* 我还没做完地理家庭作业呢。◇ *How much homework do you get?* 你有多少家庭作业？◇ *I have to write up the notes* ***for homework.*** 我得完成整理笔记的家庭作业。➲ COLLOCATIONS AT EDUCATION **2** (*informal*) work that sb does to prepare for sth 准备工作：*You could tell that he had really* ***done his homework*** (= found out all he needed to know). 你能看得出他确实做好了充分准备。

home·work·er /ˈhəʊmwɜːkə(r); *NAmE* ˈhoʊmwɜːrk-/ *noun* a person who works at home, often doing jobs that are not well paid such as making clothes for shops/stores 在家工作的人（常做报酬低微的工作）▸ **home·work·ing** *noun* [U]

homey (*also* **homy**) /ˈhəʊmi; *NAmE* ˈhoʊmi/ *adj., noun*

■ ***adj.*** (*informal, especially NAmE*) pleasant and comfortable, like home 愉快舒适的；像家一样的：*The hotel had a nice, homey atmosphere.* 这旅馆有一种舒适美好、宾至如归的气氛。

■ ***noun*** = HOMIE

homi·cidal /ˌhɒmɪˈsaɪdl; *NAmE* ˌhɑːm-/ *adj.* likely to kill another person; making sb likely to kill another person （使）可能会杀人的：*a homicidal maniac* 杀人狂 ◇ *He had clear homicidal tendencies.* 他有明显的杀人倾向。

homi·cide /ˈhɒmɪsaɪd; *NAmE* ˈhɑːm-/ *noun* [C, U] (*especially NAmE, law* 律) the crime of killing sb deliberately （蓄意）杀人罪 SYN **murder** ➲ COMPARE CULPABLE HOMICIDE, MANSLAUGHTER

homie (*also* **homey**) /ˈhəʊmi; *NAmE* ˈhoʊmi/ *noun* (*NAmE, informal*) a HOMEBOY OR HOMEGIRL 老乡；同乡；玩伴

hom·ily /ˈhɒməli; *NAmE* ˈhɑːm-/ (*pl.* **-ies**) *noun* (*formal, often disapproving*) a speech or piece of writing giving advice on the correct way to behave, etc. （有关规矩等的）说教，说教作品：*She delivered a homily on the virtues of family life.* 她进行了一场家庭生活美德方面的说教。

hom·ing /ˈhəʊmɪŋ; *NAmE* ˈhoʊm-/ *adj.* [only before noun] **1** (of a bird or an animal 鸟或动物) trained, or having a natural ability, to find the way home from a long distance away 接受过返回原地训练的；有返回原地本能的：*Many birds have a remarkable* ***homing instinct.*** 很多鸟类具有了不起的返回原地的本能。**2** (of a MISSILE, etc. 导弹等) fitted with an electronic device that enables it to find and hit the place or object it is aimed at 自动寻向的；自导引的：***a homing device*** 自动导引的装置

ˈhoming pigeon *noun* a PIGEON (= a type of bird) that has been trained to find its way home from a long distance away, and that people race against other pigeons for sport 信鸽；赛鸽

hom·in·id /ˈhɒmɪnɪd; *NAmE* ˈhɑːm-/ *noun* (*specialist*) a human, or a creature that lived in the past which humans developed from 人科（包括人及其祖先）

hom·in·oid /ˈhɒmɪnɔɪd; *NAmE* ˈhɑːm-/ *noun* (*specialist*) a human, or a creature related to humans 人猿超科生物

hom·iny /ˈhɒmɪni; *NAmE* ˈhɑːm-/ *noun* [U] dried CORN (MAIZE), boiled in water or milk, eaten especially in the southern states of the US 玉米糁儿（美国南方各州常用水或牛奶煮后食用）

Homo /ˈhɒməʊ; ˈhəʊməʊ; *NAmE* ˈhoʊmoʊ/ *noun* (*from Latin, specialist*) the GENUS (= group) of PRIMATES that includes early and modern humans 人属（灵长目人科的一属，包括早期人和现代人）

homo- /ˈhɒməʊ; ˈhəʊməʊ; *NAmE* ˈhoʊmoʊ/ *combining form* (in nouns, adjectives and adverbs 构成名词、形容词和副词) the same 同样；相同 ➲ COMPARE HETERO-

hom·oe·op·ath (*BrE*) = HOMEOPATH

hom·oe·op·athy (*BrE*) = HOMEOPATHY

hom·oeo·stasis (*BrE*) = HOMEOSTASIS

Homo erectus /ˌhɒməʊ ɪˈrektəs; ˌhəʊməʊ; *NAmE* ˌhoʊmoʊ/ *noun* [U] (*from Latin, specialist*) an early form of human which was able to walk on two legs 直立人（能用腿行走的早期人科成员）

homo·erot·ic /ˌhɒməʊɪˈrɒtɪk; ˌhəʊm-; *NAmE* ˌhoʊmoʊɪˈrɑːtɪk/ *adj.* relating to HOMOSEXUAL sex and sexual desire 同性恋性行为的；同性恋性欲的

homo·gen·eity /ˌhɒmədʒəˈniːəti; *NAmE* ˌhɑːm-/ *noun* [U] (*formal*) the quality of being homogeneous 同种；同质

homo·ge·neous /ˌhɒməˈdʒiːniəs; *NAmE* ˌhoʊm-/ (*also* **homo·gen·ous** /həˈmɒdʒənəs; *NAmE* həˈmɑːdʒənəs/) *adj.* (*formal*) consisting of things or people that are all the same or all of the same type 由同类事物（或人）组成的；同种类的： *a homogeneous group/mixture/population* 相同成分组成的群体 / 混合物；同类人口 OPP **heterogeneous**

hom·ogen·ized (*BrE also* **-ised**) /həˈmɒdʒənaɪzd; *NAmE* həˈmɑːdʒ-/ *adj.* (of milk 牛奶) treated so that the cream is mixed in with the rest 经过均质处理的

homo·graph /ˈhɒməgrɑːf; *NAmE* ˈhɑːməgræf/ *noun* (*grammar* 语法) a word that is spelt like another word but has a different meaning from it, and may have a different pronunciation, for example *bow* /baʊ/, *bow* /bəʊ; *NAmE* boʊ/ 同形异义词（拼写相同，意义不同，读音可能不同）

Homo habilis /ˌhɒməʊ ˈhæbɪlɪs; ˌhəʊməʊ; *NAmE* ˌhoʊmoʊ/ *noun* [U] (*from Latin, specialist*) an early form of human which was able to use tools 能人（能用手准确抓握器物的早期人科成员）

hom·olo·gous /həˈmɒləgəs; *NAmE* hoʊˈmɑːl-; he-/ *adj.* ~ (**with sth**) (*specialist*) similar in position, structure, etc. to sth else （位置、结构等）相应的，类似的；同源的： *The seal's flipper is homologous with the human arm.* 海豹的鳍肢与人类的手臂同源。

homo·nym /ˈhɒmənɪm; *NAmE* ˈhɑːm-; ˈhoʊm-/ *noun* (*grammar* 语法) a word that is spelt like another word (or pronounced like it) but which has a different meaning, for example *can* meaning 'be able' and *can* meaning 'put sth in a container' 同形（同音）异义词（写法或读音相同，但意义不同） ➲ WORDFINDER NOTE AT WORD

homo·pho·bia /ˌhɒməˈfəʊbiə; ˌhəʊm-; *NAmE* ˌhoʊməˈfoʊ-/ *noun* [U] a strong dislike and fear of HOMOSEXUAL people 对同性恋者的厌恶和恐惧 ➲ WORDFINDER NOTE AT EQUAL ▸ **homo·pho·bic** *adj.*

homo·phone /ˈhɒməfəʊn; *NAmE* ˈhɑːməfoʊn/ *noun* (*grammar* 语法) a word that is pronounced like another word but has a different spelling or meaning, for example *some, sum* /sʌm/ 同音异形词，同音异义词（读音相同，写法或意义不同）

hom·oph·onous /həˈmɒfənəs; *NAmE* -ˈmɑːf-/ *adj.* (*linguistics* 语言) (of a word 词语) having the same pronunciation as another word but a different meaning or spelling 同音异义的；同音异形的： *'Bear' and 'bare' are homophonous.* * bear 和 bare 是同音异形词。

Homo sa·pi·ens /ˌhɒməʊ ˈsæpienz; ˌhəʊm-; *NAmE* ˌhoʊmoʊ ˈseɪp-; ˈsæp-/ *noun* [U] (*from Latin, specialist*) the kind or SPECIES of human that exists now 智人（现代人类）

homo·sex·ual /ˌhəʊməˈsekʃuəl; ˌhɒm-; *NAmE* ˌhoʊm-/ *noun* a person, usually a man, who is sexually attracted to people of the same sex 同性恋者（通常指男性）： *a practising homosexual* 有同性恋行为的人 ➲ COMPARE BISEXUAL *n.*, GAY *n.*, HETEROSEXUAL, LESBIAN ▸ **homo·sex·ual** *adj.*： *a homosexual act/relationship* 同性恋行为 / 关系 **homo·sexu·al·ity** /ˌhəʊməˌsekʃuˈæləti; ˌhɒm-; *NAmE* ˌhoʊm-/ *noun* [U]

homo·zy·gote /ˌhɒməˈzaɪgəʊt; *NAmE* ˌhɑːməˈzaɪgoʊt/ *noun* (*biology* 生) a living thing that has only one form of a particular GENE, and whose young are more likely to share a particular characteristic 纯合子（只有某基因的一种形式的生物体） ▸ **homo·zy·gous** /-gəs/ *adj.*

homy = HOMEY

Hon (*also* **Hon.** *especially in NAmE*) /ɒn; *NAmE* ɑːn/ *abbr.* **1** HONORARY (used in official titles of jobs) （用于官方职位头衔）名誉的，义务的： *Hon Treasurer: D Shrimpton* 名誉司库：D. 施林普顿 **2** HONOURABLE 阁下： *the Hon Member for Bolsover* 博尔索弗区议员阁下

hon·cho /ˈhɒntʃəʊ; *NAmE* ˈhɑːntʃoʊ/ *noun* (*pl.* **-os**) (*informal, especially NAmE*) the person who is in charge 主管；老板；头儿 SYN **boss**： *Claude is the studio's **head honcho**.* 克劳德是电影公司的老板。

hone /həʊn; *NAmE* hoʊn/ *verb* **1** to develop and improve sth, especially a skill, over a period of time 磨炼，训练（尤指技艺）： **~ sth** *She honed her debating skills at college.* 她在大学时便练就了辩论技巧。◇ *It was a finely honed piece of writing.* 那是一篇经过仔细推敲写成的文章。◇ **~ sth to sth** *His body was honed to perfection.* 他的身体锻炼得十全十美。 **2 ~ sth** (**to sth**) to make a blade sharp or sharper 磨（刀）；把（刀）磨快 SYN **sharpen**

hon·est 🔑 /ˈɒnɪst; *NAmE* ˈɑːn-/ *adj.* **1** 🔑 always telling the truth, and never stealing or cheating 诚实的；老实的；正直的： *an honest man/woman* 诚实的男人 / 女人 OPP **dishonest** **2** 🔑 not hiding the truth about sth 坦率的；坦诚的： *an honest answer* 坦率的回答 ◇ **~ (about sth)** *Are you being completely honest about your feelings?* 你丝毫没有隐瞒你的感情吗？ ◇ **~ (with sb)** *Thank you for being so honest with me.* 感谢你对我这么坦诚。 ◇ *Give me your honest opinion.* 告诉我你的真实意见。 ◇ ***To be honest*** (= what I really think is), *it was one of the worst books I've ever read.* 说实在的，那是我读过的最差的书之一。 ◇ ***Let's be honest**, she's only interested in Mike because of his money.* 坦率地说吧，她对迈克有好感只不过是因为他有钱。 ➲ SYNONYMS ON NEXT PAGE **3** 🔑 showing an honest mind or attitude 真诚的；显示内心诚意的；表示态度诚恳的： *She's got an honest face.* 她有一张真诚的面孔。 **4** (of work or wages 工作或工资) earned or resulting from hard work 辛勤挣得的；勤劳的： *He hasn't done **an honest day's work** in his life.* 他一辈子从未努力认真干过一天活儿。 ◇ *It's quite a struggle to make **an honest living**.* 要老老实实地过日子是十分辛苦的。 HELP Use **an**, not **a**, before **honest**. * honest 前不定冠词用 an，不用 a。

IDM **honest!** (*informal*) used to emphasize that you are not lying 真的；我发誓： *I didn't mean it, honest!* 我不是有意的，真的！ **honest to 'God/'goodness** used to emphasize that what you are saying is true 老天爷作证；说实话： *Honest to God, Mary, I'm not joking.* 老天爷作证，玛丽，我不是开玩笑。 HELP Some people find this use offensive. 有人认为此用法含冒犯意。 **make an honest 'woman of sb** (*old-fashioned, humorous*) to marry a woman after having had a sexual relationship with her 与跟自己有过性关系的女人结婚

ˌhonest 'broker *noun* a person or country that tries to get other people or countries to reach an agreement or to solve a problem, without getting involved with either side （人际或国际纠纷中的）公正调解者，调停者

hon·est·ly 🔑 /ˈɒnɪstli; *NAmE* ˈɑːn-/ *adv.* **1** 🔑 in an honest way 诚实地；正当地： *I can't believe he got that money honestly.* 我不相信他是靠正当手段弄到那笔钱的。 OPP **dishonestly** **2** 🔑 used to emphasize that what you are saying is true, however surprising it may seem 真的；确实： *I didn't tell anyone, honestly!* 我确实没告诉过任何人！ ◇ *I honestly can't remember a thing about last night.* 我实在想不起昨晚的事了。 ◇ *You can't honestly expect me to believe that!* 你休想指望我相信那种事！ **3** (*informal*) used to show that you disapprove of sth and are irritated by it （表示不赞成并且生气）： *Honestly! Whatever will they think of next?* 真是的！他们接下来还会想出什么？

ˌhonest-to-ˈgoodness *adj.* [only before noun] (*approving*) simple and good 实实在在的；真正的；地道的：*honest-to-goodness country food* 真正的乡下食物

hon·esty /ˈɒnəsti; *NAmE* ˈɑːn-/ *noun* [U] the quality of being honest 诚实；老实；正直：*She answered all my questions with her usual honesty.* 她像平常一样老老实实地回答了我的所有问题。◇ *His honesty is not in question.* 他的诚实是毋庸置疑的。

IDM **in all ˈhonesty** used to state a fact or an opinion which, though true, may seem disappointing 说实话；其实：*The book isn't, in all honesty, as good as I expected.* 说实话，这本书并没有我预期的那么好。

▼ **SYNONYMS** 同义词辨析

honest

frank • direct • open • outspoken • straight • blunt

These words all describe people saying exactly what they mean without trying to hide feelings, opinions or facts. 以上各词均形容人坦率、坦诚。

honest not hiding the truth about sth 指坦率的、坦诚的：*Thank you for being so honest with me.* 感谢你对我这么坦诚。

frank honest in what you say, sometimes in a way that other people might not like 指坦率的、直率的（有时可能不讨人喜欢）：*To be frank with you, I think your son has little chance of passing the exam.* 坦白说，我认为你的儿子不大可能通过考试。

direct saying exactly what you mean in a way that nobody can pretend not to understand 指直接的、直率的、坦率的：*You'll have to get used to his direct manner.* 你得慢慢习惯他这种直率的方式。NOTE Being **direct** is sometimes considered positive but sometimes it is used as a 'polite' way of saying that sb is rude. * direct 有时被认为含褒义，但有时是以礼貌的方式表示某人有些粗鲁。

open (*approving*) (of a person) not keeping thoughts and feelings hidden 指为人诚恳的、坦诚的、直率的：*He was quite open about his reasons for leaving.* 他对离开的原因完全未加隐瞒。

outspoken saying exactly what you think, even if this shocks or offends people 指直率的、坦诚的、直言不讳的：*She was outspoken in her criticism of the plan.* 她对该计划的批评直言不讳。

straight honest and direct 指坦诚的、直率的：*I don't think you're being straight with me.* 我觉得你没跟我坦诚相见。

blunt saying exactly what you think without trying to be polite 指嘴直的、直言不讳的：*She has a reputation for blunt speaking.* 她说话出了名的直截了当。

WHICH WORD? 词语辨析

Honest and **frank** refer to *what* you say as much as *how* you say it. * honest 和 frank 既形容说话方式，也指说话内容：*a(n) honest/frank admission of guilt* 坦承有罪
They are generally positive words, although it is possible to be *too* frank in a way that other people might not like. **Direct**, **outspoken** and **blunt** all describe sb's manner of saying what they think. **Outspoken** suggests that you are willing to shock people by saying what you believe to be right. **Blunt** and **direct** often suggest that you think honesty is more important than being polite. **Open** is positive and describes sb's character. 这两个词通常用作褒义词，但有时也可能指过于直率而使人不快。direct、outspoken 和 blunt 均指说话直截，其中 outspoken 表示宁可冒犯他人也要直抒己见；blunt 和 direct 常表示说话人认为诚实比礼貌重要；open 含褒义，用来形容人的性格：*I'm a very open person.* 我这个人非常坦诚直率。

PATTERNS

- honest/frank/direct/open/outspoken/straight **about** sth
- honest/frank/direct/open/straight/blunt **with** sb
- a(n) honest/direct/straight/blunt **answer**
- a frank/direct/blunt **manner**

honey /ˈhʌni/ *noun* **1** [U] a sweet sticky yellow substance made by BEES that is spread on bread, etc. like jam 蜂蜜 **2** [C] (*informal*) a way of addressing sb that you like or love （爱称）亲爱的，宝贝：*Have you seen my keys, honey?* 你见到我的钥匙了吗，宝贝？ **3** [C] (*informal*) a person that you like or love and think is very kind 可爱的人：*He can be a real honey when he wants to be.* 他高兴的时候挺招人喜欢的。IDM SEE LAND *n.*

honey·bee /ˈhʌnibiː/ *noun* a BEE that makes honey 蜜蜂

honey·comb /ˈhʌnikəʊm; *NAmE* -koʊm/ (*also* **comb**) *noun* [C, U] a structure of cells with six sides, made by BEES for holding their honey and their eggs 蜂巢

honey·combed /ˈhʌnikəʊmd; *NAmE* -koʊmd/ *adj.* ~ (**with sth**) filled with holes, tunnels, etc. 蜂窝状的；多洞的；多孔道的

honey·dew melon /ˌhʌnidjuː ˈmelən; *NAmE* -duː/ *noun* a type of MELON with a pale skin and green flesh 蜜瓜；白兰瓜

hon·eyed /ˈhʌnid/ *adj.* (*literary*) **1** (of words 言辞) soft and intended to please, but often not sincere 柔顺讨好的；甜言蜜语的 **2** tasting or smelling like honey, or having the colour of honey 蜂蜜味的；蜂蜜色的

honey·moon /ˈhʌnimuːn/ *noun, verb*

■ ***noun*** [usually sing.] **1** a holiday/vacation taken by a couple who have just got married 蜜月：*We went to Venice for our honeymoon.* 我们去威尼斯度的蜜月。◇ *They're on **their honeymoon**.* 他们正在度蜜月。➲ WORDFINDER NOTE AT HOLIDAY, WEDDING **2** the period of time at the start of a new activity when nobody is criticized and people feel enthusiastic （新活动之初的）和谐时期：*The **honeymoon period** for the government is now over.* 这届政府的蜜月期现在已经过去了。

■ ***verb*** [I] + **adv./prep.** to spend your honeymoon somewhere （去某处）度蜜月 ▸ **honey·moon·er** *noun*

honey·pot /ˈhʌnipɒt; *NAmE* -pɑːt/ *noun* [usually sing.] (*BrE*) a place, thing or person that a lot of people are attracted to 富有吸引力的地方（或事物、人）

honey·suckle /ˈhʌnisʌkl/ *noun* [U, C] a climbing plant with white, yellow or pink flowers with a sweet smell 忍冬，金银花（蔓生，开白色、黄色或粉红色花，气味芬芳）

ˌhoney-ˈtongued *adj.* (of a person) speaking sweetly or softly, or in a way that is intended to please, often without being sincere; (of a statement, piece of text, etc.) written or spoken in this way 甜言蜜语的；花言巧语的：*As a handsome, honey-tongued politician, he convinced the nation that going to war was a good idea.* 作为一名相貌英俊、巧舌如簧的政客，他使国民相信开战是个好主意。◇ *a honey-tongued lie* 甜言蜜语的谎话 ◇ *His beautiful verses contain echoes of Shakespeare's honey-tongued romantic poetry.* 他美丽的诗句中有对莎士比亚甜蜜恭维的情诗的模仿。

hongi /ˈhɒŋi; *NAmE* ˈhɑːŋi/ *noun* (*NZE*) a traditional Maori GREETING in which people press their noses together 碰鼻礼（毛利人表示欢迎的方式）

honk /hɒŋk; *NAmE* hɑːŋk; hɔːŋk/ *noun, verb*

■ ***noun*** **1** the noise made by a GOOSE 鹅叫声 **2** the noise made by a car horn 汽车喇叭声

■ ***verb*** **1** [I, T] if a car horn **honks** or you **honk** or **honk the horn**, the horn makes a loud noise （使汽车喇叭）鸣响 SYN **hoot**：*honking taxis* 喇叭声大作的出租车 ◇ **~ at sb/sth** *Why did he honk at me?* 他为什么冲我按喇叭？◇ **~ sth** *People honked their horns as they drove past.* 人们开车经过时大按喇叭。 **2** [I] when a GOOSE **honks**, it makes a loud noise （鹅）叫

honky /ˈhɒŋki; *NAmE* ˈhɑːŋ-; ˈhɔːŋ-/ *noun* (*pl.* **-ies**) (*NAmE, slang*) an offensive word for a white person, used by black people （黑人对白人的冒犯称呼）白鬼

honky-tonk /ˈhɒŋki tɒŋk; *NAmE* ˈhɑːŋki tɑːŋk; ˈhɔːŋki tɔːŋk/ *noun* **1** [C] (*NAmE*) a cheap, noisy bar or dance hall 低级嘈杂的酒吧（或舞厅） **2** [U] a type of lively JAZZ played on a piano 杭基汤克音乐，酒吧爵士乐（用钢琴演奏的活泼爵士乐）

honor, **hon·or·able** (*especially US*) = HONOUR, HONOURABLE

hon·or·arium /ˌɒnəˈreəriəm; *NAmE* ˌɑːnəˈrer-/ *noun* (*pl.* **hon·or·aria** /-riə/) (*formal*) a payment made for sb's professional services 酬金；谢礼 **HELP** Use **an**, not **a**, before **honorarium**. * honorarium 前不定冠词用 an，不用 a。

hon·or·ary /ˈɒnərəri; *NAmE* ˈɑːnəreri/ *adj.* (*abbr.* **Hon**) **1** (of a university degree, a rank, etc. 大学学位、级别等) given as an honour, without the person having to have the usual qualifications 荣誉的： *an* ***honorary doctorate/degree*** 荣誉博士学位；荣誉学位 **2** (of a position in an organization 机构中的职位) not paid 无报酬的；义务的： *the honorary president* 名誉校长 ◇ *The post of treasurer is a purely honorary position.* 司库的职位纯属义务性质。 **3** treated like a member of a group without actually belonging to it 被待作…成员的： *She was treated as an honorary man.* 她得到了男子般的待遇。 **HELP** Use **an**, not **a**, before **honorary**. * honorary 前不定冠词用 an，不用 a。

hon·or·ee (*BrE also* **hon·our·ee**) /ˌɒnəˈriː; *NAmE* ˌɑːnəˈriː/ *noun* (*especially NAmE*) a person or thing that wins an award 获奖者；获奖作品： *The author is a Pulitzer Prize honoree.* 这名作者是普利策奖获得者。 **HELP** Use **an**, not **a**, before **honoree**. * honoree 前不定冠词用 an，不用 a。

hon·or·if·ic /ˌɒnəˈrɪfɪk; *NAmE* ˌɑːnə-/ *adj.* (*formal*) showing respect for the person you are speaking to 表示尊敬的： *an honorific title* 尊称 **HELP** Use **an**, not **a**, before **honorific**. * honorific 前不定冠词用 an，不用 a。

hon·oris causa /ɒˌnɔːrɪs ˈkaʊzə; *NAmE* əˌnɔːrəs ˈkɔːzə/ *adv.* (*from Latin*) (especially of a degree 尤指学位) given to a person as a sign of honour and respect, without their having to take an exam 作为荣誉；名誉上： *She was awarded a degree honoris causa.* 她获授名誉学位。

ˈhonor roll *noun* (*especially US*) **1** (*BrE* **ˌroll of ˈhonour**) [usually sing.] a list of people who are being praised officially for sth they have done 荣誉名册；光荣榜 **2** a list of the best students in a college or HIGH SCHOOL （大、中学的）优秀生名单，光荣榜

ˈhonor society *noun* (in the US) an organization for students with the best grades at school or college （美国学校的）优等生联合会

ˈhonor system *noun* [sing.] (*NAmE*) an agreement in which people are trusted to obey rules 诚信制度（信赖人能自动守规则的制度）

hon·our 🔑 (*especially US* **honor**) /ˈɒnə(r); *NAmE* ˈɑːnər/ *noun, verb*

■ ***noun*** **HELP** Use **an**, not **a**, before **honour**. * honour 前不定冠词用 an，不用 a。

• **RESPECT** 尊敬 **1** 🔑 [U] great respect and admiration for sb 尊敬；尊重；崇敬： *the* ***guest of honour*** (= the most important one) 贵宾 ◇ *the* ***seat/place of honour*** (= given to the most important guest) 上座；上席 ◇ *They stood in silence as a mark of honour to her.* 他们肃立以示对她的敬意。 ➲ SEE ALSO MAID OF HONOUR, MATRON OF HONOUR

• **PRIVILEGE** 荣幸 **2** 🔑 [sing.] something that you are very pleased or proud to do because people are showing you great respect 荣幸；光荣 **SYN** **privilege**: *It was a great honour to be invited here today.* 今天承蒙邀请到此，深感荣幸。 ➲ SYNONYMS AT PLEASURE

• **MORAL BEHAVIOUR** 道德品行 **3** 🔑 [U] the quality of knowing and doing what is morally right 正义感；道义；节操： *a man of honour* 品德高尚的人 ◇ *Proving his innocence has become a matter of honour.* 证实他的清白已经成了一件道义上的事。

• **REPUTATION** 名誉 **4** 🔑 [U] a good reputation; respect from other people 荣誉；名誉；他人的尊敬： *upholding the honour of your country* 捍卫祖国的荣誉 ◇ *The family honour is at stake.* 家族名誉岌岌可危。 ➲ COMPARE DISHONOUR *n.* **5** [sing.] **~ to sth/sb** a person or thing that causes others to respect and admire sth/sb 引起尊敬（或尊重、崇敬）的人（或事物）： *She is an honour to the profession.* 她是这一行业的光荣。

• **AWARD** 奖励 **6** 🔑 [C] an award, official title, etc. given to sb as a reward for sth that they have done （为表扬某人的）奖励，荣誉称号，头衔： *the New Year's Honours list* (= in Britain, a list of awards and titles given on January 1 each year) （英国）元旦受勋者名册 ◇ *to win the highest honour* 赢得最高荣誉 ◇ *He was buried* ***with full military honours*** (= with a special military service as a sign of respect). 他以隆重的军葬礼下葬。 ➲ SEE ALSO ROLL OF HONOUR

• **AT UNIVERSITY/SCHOOL** 大学；学校 **7 honours, honors** [pl.] (*abbr.* **Hons**) (often used as an adjective 常用作形容词) a university course that is of a higher level than a basic course (in the US also used to describe a class in school which is at a higher level than other classes) 大学荣誉学位课程；（美国学校的）优等班： *an* ***honours degree/course*** 荣誉学位 / 课程 ◇ *a First Class Honours degree* 一级荣誉学位 ◇ (*NAmE*) *I took an honors class in English.* 我选了一个英语优等班课程。 **8 honours, honors** [pl.] if you pass an exam or GRADUATE from a university or school **with honours**, you receive a special mark/grade for having achieved a very high standard 优异成绩

• **JUDGE/MAYOR** 法官；市长 **9 His/Her/Your Honour** [C] a title of respect used when talking to or about a judge or a US MAYOR 法官大人；（美国）市长阁下： *No more questions, Your Honour.* 没有其他问题了，法官大人。

• **IN CARD GAMES** 纸牌游戏 **10** [C, usually pl.] the cards that have the highest value 最大点数的牌 ➲ MORE LIKE THIS 20, page R27

IDM **do sb an ˈhonour | do sb the ˈhonour (of doing sth)** (*formal*) to do sth to make sb feel very proud and pleased 使增光；赏光；给…带来荣誉： *Would you do me the honour of dining with me?* 你能赏光和我一块吃饭吗？ **do the ˈhonours** to perform a social duty or ceremony, such as pouring drinks, making a speech, etc. 履行社交责任；执行仪式： *Would you do the honours and draw the winning ticket?* 能劳驾为我们抽出获奖的票吗？ **have the ˈhonour of sth/of doing sth** (*formal*) to be given the opportunity to do sth that makes you feel proud and happy 得到某殊荣；有幸做某事： *May I have the honour of the next dance?* 能赏光和我跳下一曲舞吗？ **(there is) honour among ˈthieves** (*saying*) used to say that even criminals have standards of behaviour that they respect 盗亦有道 **(feel) honour-ˈbound to do sth** (*formal*) to feel that you must do sth because of your sense of moral duty （感到）道义上应做某事： *She felt honour-bound to attend as she had promised to.* 她觉得既然答应了就应该出席。 ➲ COMPARE DUTY-BOUND **the honours are ˈeven** no particular person, team, etc. is doing better than the others in a competition, an argument, etc. 势均力敌；不分胜负 **in ˈhonour of sb/sth | in sb's/sth's ˈhonour** in order to show respect and admiration for sb/sth 为向…表示敬意： *a ceremony in honour of those killed in the explosion* 为纪念爆炸中的死难者所举行的仪式 ◇ *A banquet was held in her honour.* 为欢迎她而设宴。 **on your ˈhonour** (*old-fashioned*) **1** used to promise very seriously that you will do sth or that sth is true 用人格担保；以名誉担保： *I swear on my honour that I knew nothing about this.* 我以人格担保我根本不知道这件事。 **2** to be trusted to do sth 受到信任；被信赖： *You're on your honour not to go into my room.* 依你的人格，相信你不会进我的房间。 ➲ MORE AT POINT *n.*

■ ***verb***

• **SHOW RESPECT** 表示敬意 **1 ~ sb (with sth)** to do sth that shows great respect for sb/sth 尊敬，尊重（某人）： *The President honoured us with a personal visit.* 总统亲临，使我们感到荣幸。 ◇ *our honoured guests* 我们的贵宾 ◇ (*ironic*) *I'm glad to see that you've decided to* ***honour us with your presence!*** 很高兴看到你已决定大驾光临！

• **GIVE AWARD** 颁奖 **2 ~ sb/sth (with sth) (for sth)** to give public praise, an award or a title to sb for sth they have done 给予表扬（或奖励、头衔、称号）： *He has been*

H

honoured with a knighthood for his scientific work. 他因科研成就而获授爵士头衔。

• KEEP PROMISE 遵守诺言 **3** ~ sth (*formal*) to do what you have agreed or promised to do 信守，执行（承诺）：*I have every intention of honouring our contract.* 我完全愿意执行我们的合约。◇ *to honour a cheque* (= to keep an agreement to pay it) 承兑支票

IDM **be/feel honoured** (**to do sth**) to feel proud and happy （做某事）感到荣幸：*I was honoured to have been mentioned in his speech.* 他在讲话中提到了我，真是荣幸。

hon·our·able (*especially US* **hon·or·able**) /ˈɒnərəbl; *NAmE* ˈɑːnə-/ *adj.* **1** deserving respect and admiration 可敬的；值得钦佩的：*a long and honourable career in government* 长期光荣的从政生涯 ◇ *They managed an honourable 2–2 draw.* 他们奋力打成了 2:2 平局，值得敬佩。◇ ***With a few honourable exceptions,*** *the staff were found to be incompetent.* 除了几个优秀的人以外，其他职员都不能胜任工作。**2** showing high moral standards 品格高尚的：*an honourable man* 高尚的人 **3** allowing sb to keep their good name and the respect of others 保护声誉的；体面的：*an honourable compromise* 体面的妥协 ◇ *They urged her to* ***do the honourable thing*** *and resign.* 他们力劝她辞职以保全名节。◇ *He received an honourable discharge from the army.* 他获准体面退伍。OPP **dishonourable** **4** **the Honourable** (*abbr.* **Hon**) [only before noun] (in Britain) a title used by a child of some ranks of the NOBILITY （英国某些贵族子女的头衔） **5 the/my Honourable...** (*abbr.* **Hon**) [only before noun] (in Britain) a title used by Members of Parliament when talking about or to another Member during a debate （英国议会议员辩论时相互间的尊称）：*If my Honourable Friend would give me a chance to answer,...* 如果我的朋友阁下能给我答辩的机会… **6** (*abbr.* **Hon**) a title of respect used by an official of high rank （高级官员的尊称）：*the Honorable Alan Simpson, US senator* 美国参议员艾伦・辛普森 ➲ COMPARE RIGHT HONOURABLE HELP Use **an**, not **a**, before **honourable**. * honourable 前不定冠词用 an，不用 a。

▸ **hon·our·ably** (*especially US* **hon·or·ably**) /-əbli/ *adv.*：*to behave honourably* 行为光明磊落

hon·our·ee (*especially US* **hon·or·ee**) /ˌɒnəˈriː; *NAmE* ˌɑːnəˈriː/ *noun* (*especially NAmE*) a person or thing that wins an award 获奖者；获奖作品：*The author is a Pulitzer Prize honouree.* 这名作者是普利策奖获得者。HELP Use **an**, not **a**, before **honouree**. * honouree 前不定冠词用 an，不用 a。

Hons /ɒnz; *NAmE* ɑːnz/ *abbr.* (*BrE*) HONOURS (used after the name of a university degree) 荣誉学位（用于大学学位名称之后）：*Tim Smith BA (Hons)* （荣誉）文学士蒂姆・史密斯

hooch /huːtʃ/ *noun* [U] (*informal, especially NAmE*) strong alcoholic drink, especially sth that has been made illegally （尤指非法酿造的）烈酒

hood /hʊd/ *noun* **1** a part of a coat, etc. that you can pull up to cover the back and top of your head 风帽，兜帽（外衣的一部分，可拉起蒙住头颈）：*a jacket with a detachable hood* 有可拆卸风帽的夹克 ➲ VISUAL VOCAB PAGES V66, V70 **2** a piece of cloth put over sb's face and head so that they cannot be recognized or so that they cannot see （布质）面罩 **3** a piece of coloured silk or fur worn over an academic GOWN to show the kind of degree held by the person wearing it 学位连领帽（表示学位种类） **4** (*especially BrE*) a folding cover over a car, etc. （汽车等的）折叠式车篷：*We drove all the way with the hood down.* 我们一路上敞着车篷开车。➲ PICTURE AT PUSHCHAIR **5** (*NAmE*) (*BrE* **bon·net**) the metal part over the front of a vehicle, usually covering the engine （车辆的）引擎盖 ➲ VISUAL VOCAB PAGE V56 **6** a cover placed over a device or machine, for example, to protect it （设备或机器的）防护罩，罩：*a lens hood* 镜头遮光罩 ◇ *an extractor hood* (= one that removes cooking smells from a kitchen) （厨房）排气罩 ➲ VISUAL VOCAB PAGE V26 **7** (*slang, especially NAmE*) = HOODLUM (1) **8** (*also* **'hood**) (*slang, especially NAmE*) a neighbourhood, especially a person's own neighbourhood 街区；邻里；左邻右舍

-hood *suffix* (in nouns 构成名词) **1** the state or quality of …的状态（或性质）：*childhood* 儿童时期 ◇ *falsehood* 虚假 **2** a group of people of the type mentioned （某类人的）集体：*the priesthood* 司祭团 ➲ MORE LIKE THIS 7, page R25

hood·ed /ˈhʊdɪd/ *adj.* **1** having or wearing a hood 有（或戴）兜帽的：*a hooded jacket* 有兜帽的夹克 ◇ *A hooded figure waited in the doorway.* 一个戴兜帽的人在门口等候。**2** (of eyes 眼睛) having large EYELIDS that always look as if they are partly closed 眼皮耷拉（而状似半睁半闭）的

hood·lum /ˈhuːdləm/ *noun* (*informal*) **1** (*also slang* **hood** *especially in NAmE*) a violent criminal, especially one who is part of a GANG 暴徒，恶棍（尤指属于某团伙者） **2** a violent and noisy young man 小阿飞；小流氓 SYN **hooligan**

hoo·doo /ˈhuːduː/ *noun* (*pl.* **-oos**) (*especially US*) a person or thing that brings or causes bad luck 带来厄运的人；不祥之物

hood·wink /ˈhʊdwɪŋk/ *verb* ~ **sb** (**into doing sth**) to trick sb 欺诈，欺骗（某人）：*She had been hoodwinked into buying a worthless necklace.* 她受骗买了条一文不值的项链。

hoody (*also* **hoodie**) /ˈhʊdi/ *noun* (*pl.* **-ies**) (*informal*) a jacket or a SWEATSHIRT with a HOOD 带兜帽短上衣，连帽短上衣（或运动衫） ➲ VISUAL VOCAB PAGE V68

hooey /ˈhuːi/ *noun* [U] (*informal, especially NAmE*) nonsense; stupid talk 废话；胡说八道

hoof /huːf/ *noun, verb*

▪ ***noun*** (*pl.* **hoofs** or **hooves** /huːvz/) the hard part of the foot of some animals, for example horses （马等动物的）蹄 ➲ VISUAL VOCAB PAGE V12

IDM **on the 'hoof 1** meat that is sold, transported, etc. **on the hoof** is sold, etc. while the cow or sheep is still alive （牲畜等）活着的，待宰的 **2** (*BrE, informal*) if you do sth **on the hoof**, you do it quickly and without giving it your full attention because you are doing sth else at the same time 草草地；顺便

▪ ***verb*** ~ **sth** (*informal*) to kick a ball very hard or a long way 猛踢（球）；把（球）踢出很远

IDM **'hoof it** (*informal*) to go somewhere on foot; to walk somewhere 步行（到某处）：*We hoofed it all the way to 42nd Street.* 我们一路步行到了第 42 街。

hoof-and-'mouth disease *noun* [U] (*NAmE*) = FOOT-AND-MOUTH DISEASE

hoo-ha /ˈhuː hɑː/ *noun* [U, sing.] (*BrE, informal*) noisy excitement, especially about sth unimportant 闹嚷；激动；（尤指）小题大做，大惊小怪 SYN **fuss**

hook 🔑 /hʊk/ *noun, verb*

▪ ***noun*** **1** 🔑 a curved piece of metal, plastic or wire for hanging things on, catching fish with, etc. 钩；钓钩；挂钩；鱼钩：***a picture/curtain/coat hook*** 挂图钩；窗帘钩；挂衣钩 ◇ *a fish hook* 鱼钩 ◇ *Hang your towel* ***on the hook.*** 把你的毛巾挂在钩上。➲ WORDFINDER NOTE AT FISHING ➲ VISUAL VOCAB PAGE V45 ➲ SEE ALSO BOATHOOK **2** (in boxing 拳击运动) a short hard blow that is made with the elbow bent 钩拳：*a left hook to the jaw* 击向下颌的一记左钩拳 **3** (in CRICKET and GOLF 板球及高尔夫球) a way of hitting the ball so that it curves sideways instead of going straight ahead 曲线球 **4** a thing that is used to make people interested in sth 吸引人的事物；诱饵：*The images are used as a hook to get children interested in science.* 这些图像用以吸引孩子们对科学产生兴趣。

IDM **by ˌhook or by 'crook** using any method you can, even a dishonest one 想方设法；不择手段 **get** (**sb**) **off the 'hook** | **let sb off the 'hook** to free yourself or sb else from a difficult situation or a punishment （使）摆脱困境，逃避惩罚 **hook, line and 'sinker** completely 完全地；毫无保留：*What I said was not true, but he fell for it* (= believed it) *hook, line and sinker.* 我的话并非实话，但他完全相信了。**off the 'hook** if you leave or take the telephone **off the hook**, you take the RECEIVER (= the part that you pick up) off the place where it usually rests, so that nobody can call you （为防止电话打进来而使听筒）不挂上 ➲ MORE AT RING[2] *v.*, SLING *v.*

■ ***verb*** **1** [T, I] to fasten or hang sth on sth else using a hook; to be fastened or hanging in this way （使）钩住，挂住： **~ sth + adv./prep.** *We hooked the trailer to the back of the car.* 我们把拖车挂在汽车尾部。◇ **+ adv./prep.** *a dress that hooks at the back* 从后背用钩扣的连衣裙 **2** [T, I] to put sth, especially your leg, arm or finger, around sth else so that you can hold onto it or move it; to go around sth else in this way （尤指用腿、胳膊、手指等）钩住，箍住： **~ sth + adv./prep.** *He hooked his foot under the stool and dragged it over.* 他用脚从底下钩住凳子，把它拖了过去。◇ *Her thumbs were hooked into the pockets of her jeans.* 她的双手拇指钩在牛仔裤袋里。◇ **+ adv./prep.** *Suddenly an arm hooked around my neck.* 突然有一条胳臂箍住了我的脖子。 **3** [T] **~ sth** to catch a fish with a hook 钓（鱼）： *It was the biggest pike I ever hooked.* 那是我钓到的最大的狗鱼。◇ (*figurative*) *She had managed to hook a wealthy husband.* 她成功地嫁给了一个有钱的丈夫。 **4** [T] **~ sth** (especially in GOLF, CRICKET or football (SOCCER) 尤指高尔夫球、板球或足球) to hit or kick a ball so that it goes to one side instead of straight ahead 打曲线球；踢弧线球

PHR V **ˌhook ˈup (to sth)** | **ˌhook sb/sth↔ˈup (to sth)** to connect sb/sth to a piece of electronic equipment, to a power supply or to the Internet 连接到电子设备（或电源、互联网）；接通： *She was then hooked up to an IV drip.* 接着就给她接上了静脉滴注。◇ *Check that the computer is hooked up to the printer.* 检查一下计算机是否与打印机接通。◇ *A large proportion of the nation's households are hooked up to the Internet.* 全国大部分家庭都接通了互联网。 **ˌhook ˈup with sb** (*informal*) **1** to meet sb and spend time with them 与某人来往 **2** to start working with sb 搭档工作 **ˌhook sb ˈup with sb/sth** (*informal*) to put sb in contact with sb who can help them; to get sth for sb that they want 把某人介绍给某人；让某人与某人拉上关系；帮某人搞到某物： *Can you hook me up with someone with a car?* 你能帮我联系到一个有车的人吗？

hooks 钩子；钩拳

picture hooks 挂图钩 | coat hook 挂衣钩 | fish hook 鱼钩

curtain hooks 窗帘钩 | hook and eye 衣服的钩眼扣 | left hook 左钩拳

hoo·kah /ˈhʊkə/ *noun* a long pipe for smoking that passes smoke through a container of water to cool it 水烟袋；水烟筒

ˌhook and ˈeye *noun* (*pl.* **hooks and eyes**) a device for fastening clothes, consisting of a small thin piece of metal curved round, and a hook that fits into it （衣服的）钩眼扣 ➲ PICTURE AT HOOK ➲ VISUAL VOCAB PAGE V68

hooked /hʊkt/ *adj.* **1** curved; shaped like a hook 弯曲的；钩形的： *a hooked nose/beak/finger* 鹰钩鼻子；钩喙；屈指 **2** [not before noun] **~ (on sth)** (*informal*) needing sth that is bad for you, especially a drug 上瘾；（尤指）有毒瘾 **3** [not before noun] **~ (on sth)** (*informal*) enjoying sth very much, so that you want to do it, see it, etc. as much as possible （对某事）着迷 **4** having one or more hooks 有钩的

hook·er /ˈhʊkə(r)/ *noun* **1** the player in a RUGBY team, whose job is to pull the ball out of the SCRUM with his foot （橄榄球并列争球时的）钩球队员 **2** (*informal, especially NAmE*) a PROSTITUTE 卖淫者；妓女

hookey = HOOKY

ˈhook shot *noun* **1** (in BASKETBALL 篮球) a shot in which a player throws the ball towards the BASKET in a wide curve, by stretching their arm out to the side and throwing over their head 勾手投篮 **2** (in CRICKET 板球) a shot in which a player hits the ball to the side by swinging the BAT across their chest 侧飞球

ˈhook-up *noun* a connection between two pieces of equipment, especially electronic equipment used in broadcasting, or computers （广播等的）联播；（计算机之间的）联机： *a satellite hook-up between the major European networks* 欧洲各主要电视网通过卫星的联播

hook·worm /ˈhʊkwɜːm; *NAmE* -wɜːrm/ *noun* **1** [C] a WORM that lives in the INTESTINES of humans and animals 钩虫（寄生于人或动物肠道） **2** [U] a disease caused by hookworms 钩虫病

hooky (*also* **hookey**) /ˈhʊki/ (*old-fashioned, NAmE*)
IDM **play ˈhooky** (*informal*) (*BrE* **play ˈtruant**) to stay away from school without permission 旷课；逃学

hooli·gan /ˈhuːlɪɡən/ *noun* a young person who behaves in an extremely noisy and violent way in public, usually in a group （通常结伙的）阿飞，小流氓： *English football hooligans* 英国足球流氓 ▸ **hooli·gan·ism** /-ɪzəm/ *noun* [U]

hoon /huːn/ *noun* (*AustralE, NZE, informal*) a man who behaves in a rude and aggressive way, especially one who drives in a dangerous way 莽汉；（尤指）危险驾驶的男子，横冲直撞的驾驶员 ▸ **hoon** *verb* [I]

hoop /huːp/ *noun* **1** a large ring of plastic, wood or iron 箍；环；圈： *a barrel bound with iron hoops* 用铁箍箍紧的桶 ◇ *hoop earrings* (= in the shape of a hoop) 耳环 ➲ VISUAL VOCAB PAGE V70 **2** the ring that the players throw the ball through in the game of BASKETBALL in order to score points （篮球）篮圈；篮筐： *Let's shoot some hoops.* 我们投几下篮吧。 ➲ VISUAL VOCAB PAGE V47 **3** a large ring that was used as a children's toy in the past, or for animals or riders to jump through at a CIRCUS （旧时儿童玩的）大环子；（马戏团用的）大圈 **4** = HULA HOOP **5** a small ARCH made of metal or plastic, put into the ground （两端埋在地里的）小铁弓，小塑料弓： *croquet hoops* 槌球戏中的拱门 ◇ *Grow lettuces under plastic stretched over wire hoops.* 在铁弓撑起的塑料棚下种植生菜。 IDM SEE JUMP *v.*

hooped /huːpt/ *adj.* shaped like a hoop 环形的： *hooped earrings* 圈状耳环

hoopla /ˈhuːplɑː/ *noun* **1** [U, sing.] (*informal, especially NAmE*) excitement about sth which gets a lot of public attention 大吹大擂；喧闹 **2** [U] (*BrE*) (*NAmE* **ring·toss**) a game in which players try to throw rings over objects in order to win them as prizes 套圈游戏；投环套物

hoo·poe /ˈhuːpuː; -pəʊ; *NAmE* -poʊ/ *noun* an orange-pink bird with a long beak that curves downwards, black and white wings and a CREST on its head 戴胜（一种鸟，粉红褐色，喙长而下弯，有冠，翅有黑白相间的条斑）

hoo·ray /huˈreɪ/ *exclamation* **1** (*also* **hur·rah**, **hur·ray**) used to show that you are happy or that you approve of sth （表示快乐或赞同）好极了，好哇 **2** (*also* **hoo·roo**) (*AustralE, NZE*) goodbye 再见 IDM SEE HIP *exclamation* ➲ MORE LIKE THIS 2, page R25

Hoo·ray Hen·ry /ˌhuːreɪ ˈhenri/ *noun* (*pl.* **Hoo·ray Hen·rys** or **Hoo·ray Hen·ries**) (*BrE, informal, disapproving*)

H

a young upper-class man who enjoys himself in a loud and silly way 爱喧闹和干蠢事的上流社会年轻人；纨绔子弟 ➲ MORE LIKE THIS 18, page R27

hoo·roo /hə'ruː; hʌ'ruː/ *exclamation* (*AustralE*) = HOORAY (2)

hoot /huːt/ *verb, noun*

■ ***verb*** **1** [I] to make a loud noise 发出大声；喊叫：*He had the audience* ***hooting with laughter****.* 他令观众哄堂大笑。◇ *Some people hooted in disgust.* 有些人厌恶地大声嚷嚷。**2** [I, T] (*BrE*) if a car horn **hoots** or you **hoot** or **hoot the horn**, the horn makes a loud noise （使汽车喇叭）鸣响 SYN **honk**：*hooting cars* 喇叭声大作的汽车 ◇ **~ at sb/sth** *Why did he hoot at me?* 他为什么对着我按喇叭？◇ **~ sth** *Passing motorists hooted their horns.* 路过的驾驶员按响了汽车喇叭。◇ *The train hooted a warning* (= the driver sounded the horn to warn people). 火车鸣笛示警。**3** [I] when an OWL **hoots**, it makes a long calling sound （猫头鹰）鸣叫

■ ***noun*** **1** [C] (*especially BrE*) a short loud laugh or shout 大笑；大喊：*The suggestion was greeted by* ***hoots of laughter****.* 这个建议引起了阵阵哄笑。**2** [sing.] (*informal*) a situation or a person that you find very funny 可笑的事情（或人）：*You ought to meet her—she's a hoot!* 你应该见见她，她笑料十足！**3** the loud sound made by the horn of a vehicle （车辆的）喇叭声 **4** the cry of an OWL （猫头鹰的）鸣叫声

IDM **not care/give a 'hoot | not care/give two 'hoots** (*informal*) not to care at all 丝毫不在乎

hoote·nanny /'huːtnæni/ *noun* (*pl.* **-ies**) (*especially US*) an informal social event at which people play FOLK MUSIC, sing and sometimes dance 民歌演唱会；民间歌舞会

hoot·er /'huːtə(r)/ *noun* **1** (*BrE, rather old-fashioned*) the device in a vehicle, or a factory, that makes a loud noise as a signal （车辆的）喇叭；（工厂的）汽笛 **2** (*BrE, slang*) a person's nose, especially a large one （尤指大的）鼻子 **3** [usually pl.] (*NAmE, slang*) a woman's breast （女人的）乳房

Hoo·ver™ /'huːvə(r)/ *noun* (*BrE*) = VACUUM CLEANER

hoo·ver /'huːvə(r)/ *verb* [T, I] **~ (sth)** (*BrE*) to clean a carpet, floor, etc. with a vacuum cleaner 用真空吸尘器清扫（地毯、地板等）SYN **vacuum**：*to hoover the carpet* 用吸尘器清扫地毯

PHR V **,hoover sth↔'up 1** to remove sth from a carpet, floor, etc. with a VACUUM CLEANER 用真空吸尘器把…清除掉：*to hoover up all the dust* 用吸尘器清除所有的灰尘 **2** (*informal*) to get or collect sth in large quantities 获得大量的（某物）：*The US and Canada usually hoover up most of the gold medals.* 美国和加拿大通常夺得大部分的金牌。▶ **hoo·ver·ing** *noun* [U]：*It's your turn to* ***do the hoovering****.* 该你做吸尘清洁了。

hooves PL. OF HOOF

hop /hɒp; *NAmE* hɑːp/ *verb, noun*

■ ***verb*** (**-pp-**) **1** [I] (**+ adv./prep.**) (of a person 人) to move by jumping on one foot 单脚跳行：*I couldn't put my weight on my ankle and had to hop everywhere.* 我一只脚的脚踝使不上劲，不得不单脚跳来跳去。◇ *kids hopping over puddles* 单足跳过水坑的孩子们 **2** [I] **+ adv./prep.** (of an animal or a bird 动物或鸟) to move by jumping with all or both feet together 齐足（或双足）跳行：*A robin was hopping around on the path.* 一只知更鸟在小路上跳来跳去。**3** [I] **+ adv./prep.** (*informal*) to go or move somewhere quickly and suddenly 突然快速去某处：*Hop in, I'll drive you home.* 快上车吧，我开车送你回家。◇ *to* ***hop into/out of bed*** 一头钻进被窝；猛然起床 ◇ *I hopped on the next train.* 我跳上了下一列火车。◇ *We hopped over to Paris for the weekend.* 我们冲到巴黎去过了个周末。**4** [T] **~ a plane, bus, train, etc.** (*NAmE*) to get on a plane, bus, etc. 登上（飞机、汽车、火车等）**5** [I] **~ (from sth to sth)** to change from one activity or subject to another 换来换去；不断更换：*I like to hop from channel to channel when I watch TV.* 我看电视时喜欢不断地转换频道。

IDM **'hop it** (*old-fashioned, BrE, informal*) usually used in orders to tell sb to go away （用于命令）走开 SYN **go away**：*Go on, hop it!* 快点走开！ **hop 'to it** (*NAmE, informal*) = JUMP TO IT

■ ***noun*** **1** [C] a short jump by a person on one foot 单足短距离跳跃：*He crossed the hall with a hop, skip and a jump.* 他来了一个三级跳远穿过了大厅。**2** [C] a short jump by an animal or a bird with all or both feet together （动物或鸟的）齐足（或双足）短距离跳跃 **3** [C] a short journey, especially by plane （尤指乘飞机的）短途旅行 **4** [C] a tall climbing plant with green female flowers that are shaped like CONES 忽布；啤酒花 **5 hops** [pl.] the green female flowers of the hop plant that have been dried, used for making beer （干的）忽布花，啤酒花 **6** [C] (*old-fashioned, informal*) a social event at which people dance in an informal way （非正式）舞会 ➲ SEE ALSO HIP HOP IDM SEE CATCH *v.*

hope 🔑 /həʊp; *NAmE* hoʊp/ *verb, noun*

■ ***verb*** 🔑 [I, T] to want sth to happen and think that it is possible 希望，期望（某事发生）：**~ (for sth)** *We are hoping for good weather on Sunday.* 我们盼望着星期天天气好。◇ *All we can do now is wait and hope.* 我们现在所能做的就是等候和期待。◇ *'Do you think it will rain?' '****I hope not.****'* "你觉得会下雨吗？" "但愿不会。" ◇ *'Will you be back before dark?' '****I hope so, yes.****'* "你天黑之前能回来吗？" "但愿吧。" ◇ **~ (that)…** *I hope (that) you're okay.* 我希望你平安无事。◇ ***Let's hope*** *we can find a parking space.* 希望咱们能找到个停车位。◇ **it is hoped (that)…** *It is hoped that over £10 000 will be raised.* 希望筹款能超过 1 万英镑。◇ **~ to do sth** *She is hoping to win the gold medal.* 她希望赢得金牌。◇ *We hope to arrive around two.* 我们希望能在两点钟左右到达。 ➲ MORE LIKE THIS 26, page R28 HELP **Hope** can be used in the passive in the form **it is hoped that…**. **For** must always be used with **hope** in other passive sentences. * hope 可用于 it is hoped that... 这一被动句型，其他被动句中 hope 必须与 for 连用：*The improvement that had been hoped for never came.* 人们期待的改进并没有出现。◇ *The hoped-for improvement never came.* 人们期待的改进并没有出现。

IDM **,hope against 'hope (that…)** to continue to hope for sth although it is very unlikely to happen （尤指某事希望渺茫但）依旧抱一线希望 **,hope for the 'best** to hope that sth will happen successfully, especially where it seems likely that it will not 希望某事顺利；寄予最大的希望 **I should hope so/not | so I should hope** (*informal*) used to say that you feel very strongly that sth should/should not happen 希望如此 / 不如此；但愿如此 / 不如此：*'Nobody blames you.' 'I should hope not!'* "没有人责怪你呀。" "但愿没有！" ➲ MORE AT CROSS *v.*

■ ***noun*** **1** 🔑 [U, C] a belief that sth you want will happen 希望；期望：**~ (of sth)** *There is now hope of a cure.* 现在有望治愈了。◇ **~ (for sb/sth)** *Hopes for the missing men are fading.* 找到失踪者的希望逐渐渺茫。◇ **~ (that…)** *There is* ***little hope that*** *they will be found alive.* 活着找到他们的希望很渺茫。◇ **~ (of doing sth)** *They have* ***given up hope*** *of finding any more survivors.* 他们已不抱希望再找到幸存者了。◇ *She* ***has high hopes*** *of winning* (= is very confident about it). 她抱着必胜的信念。◇ *The future is not without hope.* 未来并非没有希望。◇ *Don't* ***raise your hopes*** *too high, or you may be disappointed.* 不要希望过高，否则你可能会失望的。◇ *I'll do what I can, but don't* ***get your hopes up****.* 我会尽力而为的，但别抱太大希望。◇ *There is still a* ***glimmer of hope****.* 仍有一线希望。◇ *The situation is not good but we* ***live in hope*** *that it will improve.* 情况不好，但我们依然希望会好转。**2** 🔑 [C] **~ (of/for sth) | ~ (for sb) | ~ (that…) | ~ (of doing sth)** something that you wish for 希望的东西；期望的事情：*She told me all her hopes, dreams and fears.* 她把一切希望、梦想和担心都告诉了我。◇ *They* ***have high hopes*** *for their children.* 他们对自己的孩子们寄予厚望。**3** [C, usually sing.] **~ (of sth) | ~ (for sb)** a person, a thing or a situation that will help you get what you want 被寄予希望的人（或事物、情况）：*He turned to her in despair and said, 'You're my* ***last hope****.'* 他绝望地向她求助说："你是我最后的希望。" ◇ *The operation was Kelly's* ***only hope of*** *survival.* 那次手术是凯利生存的唯一希望。

IDM **be beyond 'hope (of sth)** to be in a situation where no improvement is possible 毫无希望 **hold out little,** etc. 'hope (of sth/that...) | not hold out any, much, etc. 'hope (of sth/that...) to offer little, etc. reason for believing that sth will happen 不大相信某事会发生：*The doctors did not hold out much hope for her recovery.* 医生们对她的痊愈不抱什么希望。**,hope springs e'ternal** (*saying*) people never stop hoping 人生永远充满希望 **in the hope of sth | in the hope that...** (*NAmE also* **in hopes that...**) because you want sth to happen 抱着…的希望：*I called early in the hope of catching her before she went to work.* 我很早就打了个电话，希望在她上班之前找到她。◇ *He asked her again* ***in the vain hope*** *that he could persuade her to come* (= it was impossible). 他又问了她一次，徒然指望着能说服她来。**not have a 'hope (in 'hell) (of doing sth)** (*informal*) to have no chance at all 毫无机会；不抱希望：*She doesn't have a hope of winning.* 她根本无望取胜。**,some 'hope!** (*BrE, informal*) used to say that there is no chance at all that sth will happen 毫无希望；妄想 ➲ MORE AT DASH *v.*, PIN *v.*

'hope chest *noun* (*NAmE*) items for the house collected by a woman, especially in the past, in preparation for her marriage (and often kept in a large CHEST) （尤指过去未婚女子的）嫁妆 ➲ COMPARE BOTTOM DRAWER

'hoped-for *adj.* [only before noun] wanted and thought possible 期待的；所希望的：*The new policy did not bring the hoped-for economic recovery.* 新政策并没有带来所期待的经济复苏。

hope·ful /'həʊpfl; *NAmE* 'hoʊp-/ *adj., noun*

■ ***adj.*** **1** [not usually before noun] (of a person 人) believing that sth you want will happen 抱有希望；满怀希望 SYN **optimistic**：~ (that...) *I feel hopeful that we'll find a suitable house very soon.* 我对很快找到合适的房子抱有希望。◇ ~ (**about sth**) *He is not very hopeful about the outcome of the interview.* 他对面试的结果不抱很大希望。◇ ~ (**of doing sth**) (*BrE*) *She is hopeful of returning to work soon.* 她希望很快回去工作。OPP **pessimistic** **2** [only before noun] (of a person's behaviour 人的行为) showing hope 表现出希望的：*a hopeful smile* 充满希望的微笑 **3** (of a thing 事物) making you believe that sth you want will happen; bringing hope 给人以希望的 SYN **promising**：*The latest trade figures are a hopeful sign.* 最新贸易数字令人鼓舞。◇ *The future did not seem very hopeful.* 前景似乎不太乐观。▶ **hope·ful·ness** *noun* [U]

■ ***noun*** a person who wants to succeed at sth 希望成功的人；雄心勃勃的人：*50 young hopefuls are trying for a place in the England team.* * 50 名雄心勃勃的年轻人亟欲跻身英格兰队。

hope·ful·ly /'həʊpfəli; *NAmE* 'hoʊp-/ *adv.* **1** used to express what you hope will happen 有希望地；可以指望：*Hopefully, we'll arrive before dark.* 我们有望在天黑前到达。HELP Although this is the most common use of **hopefully**, it is a fairly new use and some people think it is not correct. 尽管这是 hopefully 最常见的用法，但算是相当新的用法，有人认为并不正确。**2** showing hope 抱有希望地：*'Are you free tonight?' she asked hopefully.* "你今晚有空吗？"她抱着希望地问。

hope·less /'həʊpləs; *NAmE* 'hoʊp-/ *adj.* **1** if sth is **hopeless**, there is no hope that it will get better or succeed 没有好转（或成功）希望的；无望的：*a hopeless situation* 无可挽救的局势 ◇ ***It's hopeless*** *trying to convince her.* 想说服她简直是徒劳。◇ *Most of the students are making good progress, but Michael is* ***a hopeless case.*** 大多数学生都很有进步，唯有迈克尔不可救药。◇ *He felt that his life was a hopeless mess.* 他觉得他生活得狼狈不堪。**2** (*BrE, informal*) extremely bad 极差的；糟糕透顶的 SYN **terrible**：*The buses are absolutely hopeless these days!* 如今的公共汽车简直糟透了。**3** (*especially BrE*) (of people 人) very bad (at sth); with no ability or skill 不能胜任的；无能的；缺乏技能的 SYN **terrible**：*a hopeless driver* 无用的司机 ◇ **~ at sth** *I'm hopeless at science.* 我对理科一窍不通。**4** feeling or showing no hope 感到（或显得）无望的：*She felt lonely and hopeless.* 她感到孤独绝望。▶ **hope·less·ly** *adv.*：*hopelessly outnumbered* 数量上被远远超过 ◇ *They were hopelessly lost.* 他们彻底失败了。◇ *to be hopelessly in love* 爱得不能自拔 ◇ *'I'll never manage it,' he said hopelessly.* "我永远也搞不定。"他绝望地说。**hope·less·ness** *noun* [U]：*a sense/feeling of hopelessness* 绝望感

Hopi /'həʊpi; *NAmE* 'hoʊpi/ *noun* (*pl.* **Hopi** or **Hopis**) a member of a Native American people, many of whom live in the US state of Arizona 霍皮人（美洲土著，很多居于美国亚利桑那州）

hop·per /'hɒpə(r); *NAmE* 'hɑːp-/ *noun* a container shaped like a V, that holds grain, coal or food for animals, and lets it out through the bottom * V 形送料斗；漏斗

hop·ping /'hɒpɪŋ; *NAmE* 'hɑːp-/ *adj., adv.*

■ ***adj.*** (*NAmE, informal*) very lively or busy 很活跃的；忙忙碌碌的：*The clubs in town are really hopping.* 城里的俱乐部真够热闹的。

■ ***adv.***

IDM **,hopping 'mad** (*informal*) very angry 愤怒；暴跳如雷

hop·scotch /'hɒpskɒtʃ; *NAmE* 'hɑːpskɑːtʃ/ *noun* [U] a children's game played on a pattern of squares marked on the ground. Each child throws a stone into a square then HOPS (= jumps on one leg) and jumps along the empty squares to pick up the stone again. 跳房子（儿童单足跳格子捡石子的游戏）

horde /hɔːd; *NAmE* hɔːrd/ *noun* (*sometimes disapproving*) a large crowd of people 一大群人：*There are always hordes of tourists here in the summer.* 夏天这里总有成群结队的游客。◇ *Football fans turned up* ***in hordes.*** 来了大批大批的足球迷。

hori·zon /hə'raɪzn/ *noun* **1 the horizon** [sing.] the furthest that you can see, where the sky seems to meet the land or the sea 地平线；海平线：*The sun sank below the horizon.* 太阳落到了地平线下。◇ *A ship appeared on the horizon.* 一艘船出现在地平线上。➲ VISUAL VOCAB PAGE V5 **2** [C, usually pl.] the limit of your desires, knowledge or interests （欲望、知识或兴趣的）范围，眼界：*She wanted to travel to* ***broaden her horizons.*** 她想旅行，以开阔眼界。◇ *The company needs new horizons now.* 公司现在需要开拓新的领域。

IDM **on the ho'rizon** likely to happen soon 很可能即将发生；已露端倪：*There's trouble looming on the horizon.* 可能快要出事了。

hori·zon·tal 🔑 /,hɒrɪ'zɒntl; *NAmE* ,hɔːrə'zɑːntl; ,hɑːr-/ *adj., noun*

■ ***adj.*** 🔑 flat and level; going across and parallel to the ground rather than going up and down 水平的；与地面平行的；横的：*horizontal lines* 横线 ➲ COMPARE VERTICAL *adj.* (1) ▶ **hori·zon·tal·ly** /-təli/ *adv.*：*Cut the cake in half horizontally and spread jam on one half.* 把蛋糕横切成两半，把果酱涂在一面上。

■ ***noun*** **1 the hori·zon·tal** [U] a horizontal position 水平位置：*He shifted his position from the horizontal.* 他从水平姿势变换成其他姿势。**2** [C] a horizontal line or surface 水平线；水平面；横线；横切面

Hor·licks™ /'hɔːlɪks; *NAmE* 'hɔːrl-/ *noun* **1** [U] powder that contains MALT that you mix with hot milk to make a drink 好立克粉（含麦乳精，可与热牛奶混合制作饮料）**2** [U, C] a drink made by mixing Horlicks powder with hot milk 好立克热饮

IDM **make a 'horlicks of sth** (*old-fashioned, BrE, informal*) to do sth badly 弄得一团糟

hor·mone /'hɔːməʊn; *NAmE* 'hɔːrmoʊn/ *noun* a chemical substance produced in the body or in a plant that encourages growth or influences how the cells and TISSUES function; an artificial substance that has similar effects 激素；荷尔蒙：*growth hormones* 生长激素 ◇ *a hormone imbalance* 激素失调 ◇ *Oestrogen is a female sex hormone.* 雌激素是一种雌性荷尔蒙。▶ **hor·mo·nal** /hɔː'məʊnl; *NAmE* hɔːr'moʊnl/ *adj.* [usually before noun]：*the hormonal changes occurring during pregnancy* 妊娠期间的激素变化

,hormone re'placement therapy *noun* [U] = HRT

horn 🔑 /hɔːn; *NAmE* hɔːrn/ *noun, verb*

■ ***noun*** **1** 🔑 [C] a hard pointed part that grows, usually in pairs, on the heads of some animals, such as sheep and cows. Horns are often curved. （羊、牛等动物的）角 ➲ VISUAL VOCAB PAGE V12 **2** [U] the hard substance of which animal horns are made 角质 **3** [C] a simple musical instrument that consists of a curved metal tube that you blow into （乐器）号：*a hunting horn* 猎号 **4** [C] (*especially BrE*) = FRENCH HORN：*a horn concerto* 法国号协奏曲 **5** [C] a device in a vehicle for making a loud sound as a warning or signal （车辆的）喇叭：*to* ***honk your*** *car* ***horn*** 按响汽车喇叭 ◇ (*BrE*) *to* ***sound/toot your horn*** 鸣喇叭 ➲ VISUAL VOCAB PAGE V56 ➲ SEE ALSO FOGHORN

IDM **blow/toot your own 'horn** (*NAmE, informal*) = BLOW YOUR OWN TRUMPET **draw/pull your 'horns in** to start being more careful in your behaviour, especially by spending less money than before 行为检点；（尤指）减少开支 **on the horns of a di'lemma** in a situation in which you have to make a choice between things that are equally unpleasant 进退两难；左右为难 ➲ MORE AT BULL, LOCK *v.*

■ *verb*

PHR V **,horn 'in (on sb/sth)** (*NAmE, informal*) to involve yourself in a situation that does not concern you 干预，介入，插手（与己无关的事）：*I'm sure she doesn't want us horning in on her business.* 我肯定她不希望我们插手她的事。

horn·beam /'hɔːnbiːm; *NAmE* 'hɔːrn-/ *noun* [C, U] a tree with smooth grey BARK and hard wood 鹅耳枥（树皮平滑呈灰色，木质坚韧）

horn·bill /'hɔːnbɪl; *NAmE* 'hɔːrn-/ *noun* a tropical bird with a very large curved beak 犀鸟（热带鸟类）

horned /hɔːnd; *NAmE* hɔːrnd/ *adj.* having horns or having sth that looks like horns 有角的；有角状物的

hor·net /'hɔːnɪt; *NAmE* 'hɔːrnɪt/ *noun* a large WASP (= a black and yellow flying insect) that has a very powerful sting 大黄蜂；马蜂

IDM **a 'hornets' nest** a difficult situation in which a lot of people get very angry 引起公愤的状况；困境：*His letter to the papers* ***stirred up a real hornets' nest.*** 他给报界写的信着实引发了众怒。

,horn of 'plenty *noun* = CORNUCOPIA (1)

horn·pipe /'hɔːnpaɪp; *NAmE* 'hɔːrn-/ *noun* a fast dance for one person, traditionally performed by sailors; the music for the dance 号笛舞（水手传统单人舞）；号笛舞乐

'horn-rimmed *adj.* (of a pair of glasses 眼镜) with frames made of material that looks like horn 角质镜架的

horny /'hɔːni; *NAmE* 'hɔːrni/ *adj.* **1** (*informal*) sexually excited 性兴奋的：*to feel horny* 欲火中烧 **2** (*informal*) sexually attractive 性感的；妖媚的：*to look horny* 外表性感 **3** made of a hard substance like horn 角质的；角质物制的：*the bird's horny beak* 鸟的角质喙 **4** (of skin, etc. 皮肤等) hard and rough 粗硬的；粗糙的：*horny hands* 粗糙的双手

hor·ol·ogy /hɒ'rɒlədʒi; *NAmE* hə'rɑːl-/ *noun* [U] **1** the study and measurement of time 测时法；计时学 **2** the art of making clocks and watches 钟表制造术

horo·scope /'hɒrəskəʊp; *NAmE* 'hɔːrəskoʊp; 'hɑːr-/ *noun* a description of what is going to happen to sb in the future, based on the position of the stars and the planets when the person was born 占星术

hor·ren·dous /hɒ'rendəs; *NAmE* hɔː'r-; hɑː'r-/ *adj.* **1** extremely shocking 令人震惊的；骇人的 SYN **horrific, horrifying**：*horrendous injuries* 可怕的伤势 **2** (*informal*) extremely unpleasant and unacceptable 讨厌得难以容忍的 SYN **terrible**：*horrendous traffic* 糟透了的交通 HELP Some speakers do not pronounce the 'h' at the beginning of **horrendous** and use 'an' instead of 'a' before it. This now sounds old-fashioned. 有人说 horrendous 时不发 h 音，前面用 an 而不用 a，现在听起来过时了。➲ SYNONYMS AT TERRIBLE ▶ **hor·ren·dous·ly** *adv.*：*horrendously expensive* 贵得离谱

hor·rible /'hɒrəbl; *NAmE* 'hɔːr-; 'hɑːr-/ *adj.* **1** (*informal*) very bad or unpleasant; used to describe sth that you do not like 极坏的；十分讨厌的；可恶的：*horrible weather/children/shoes* 糟透了的天气／孩子／鞋 ◇ *The coffee tasted horrible.* 这种咖啡难喝极了。◇ *I've got a horrible feeling she lied to us.* 我有种不快的感觉，觉得她对我们说了谎。➲ SYNONYMS AT TERRIBLE **2** making you feel very shocked and frightened 令人震惊的；恐怖的 SYN **terrible**：*a horrible crime/nightmare* 骇人听闻的罪行；可怕的噩梦 **3** (*informal*) (of people or their behaviour 人或行为) unfriendly, unpleasant or unkind 不友善的；讨厌的；不厚道的 SYN **nasty, obnoxious**：*a horrible man* 讨厌的人 ◇ *My sister was being horrible to me all day.* 我姐姐一整天都对我很凶。◇ *What a horrible thing to say!* 讲这话太不近人情啦！ ▶ **hor·ribly** /-əbli/ *adv.*：*It was horribly painful.* 疼极了。◇ *The experiment went horribly wrong.* 实验弄得一塌糊涂。

hor·rid /'hɒrɪd; *NAmE* 'hɔːr-; 'hɑːr-/ *adj.* (*old-fashioned* or *informal, especially BrE*) very unpleasant or unkind 非常讨厌的；很不友好的 SYN **horrible**：*a horrid child* 很讨人厌的孩子 ◇ *a horrid smell* 恶臭 ◇ *Don't be so horrid to your brother.* 别对你弟弟那么凶。

hor·rif·ic /hə'rɪfɪk/ *adj.* **1** extremely bad and shocking or frightening 极坏的；令人震惊的；令人惊恐的 SYN **horrifying**：*a* ***horrific murder/accident/attack, etc.*** 骇人听闻的谋杀、事故、攻击等 ◇ *Her injuries were horrific.* 她的伤势极为严重。 **2** (*informal*) very bad or unpleasant 极差的；很不愉快的 SYN **horrendous**：*We had a horrific trip.* 我们的旅行糟糕透顶。HELP Some speakers do not pronounce the 'h' at the beginning of **horrific** and use 'an' instead of 'a' before it. This now sounds old-fashioned. 有人说 horrific 时不发 h 音，前面用 an 而不用 a，现在听起来过时了。 ▶ **hor·rif·ic·al·ly** /-kli/ *adv.*

hor·rify /'hɒrɪfaɪ; *NAmE* 'hɔːr-; 'hɑːr-/ *verb* (**hor·ri·fies, hor·ri·fy·ing, hor·ri·fied, hor·ri·fied**) to make sb feel extremely shocked, disgusted or frightened 惊吓；使厌恶；恐吓 SYN **appal**：**~ sb** *The whole country was horrified by the killings.* 全国都对这些凶杀案感到大为震惊。◇ **it horrifies sb to do sth** *It horrified her to think that he had killed someone.* 一想到他杀过人，她就感到毛骨悚然。◇ **it horrifies sb that…** *It horrified her that he had actually killed someone.* 他确实杀过人，这件事使她感到毛骨悚然。 ▶ **hor·ri·fied** *adj.*：*He was horrified when he discovered the conditions in which they lived.* 看到他们的生活状况时，他很震惊。◇ *She gazed at him in horrified disbelief.* 她既惊愕又难以置信地盯着他。

hor·ri·fy·ing /'hɒrɪfaɪɪŋ; *NAmE* 'hɔːr-; 'hɑːr-/ *adj.* making you feel extremely shocked, disgusted or frightened 令人极其震惊的（或厌恶的、恐惧的）SYN **horrific**：*a* ***horrifying sight/experience/story*** 恐怖的景象／经历／故事 ◇ *It's horrifying to see such poverty.* 看到这种贫困状况令人震惊。 ▶ **hor·ri·fy·ing·ly** *adv.*

hor·ror /'hɒrə(r); *NAmE* 'hɔːr-; 'hɑːr-/ *noun* **1** [U] a feeling of great shock, fear or disgust 震惊；恐惧；厌恶：*People watched* ***in horror*** *as the plane crashed to the ground.* 人们惊恐地看着飞机坠落到地面上。◇ *With a look of horror, he asked if the doctor thought he had cancer.* 他惊恐失色地问医生是否认定他患了癌症。◇ *The thought of being left alone filled her with horror.* 想到被孤零零地留下，她就不寒而栗。◇ *She recoiled in horror at the sight of an enormous spider.* 看到一只巨大的蜘蛛，她吓得直退。◇ ***To his horror,*** *he could feel himself starting to cry* (= it upset him very much). 他很恐惧，感到自己都快哭了。◇ *Her eyes were wide with horror.* 她吓得目瞪口呆。 **2** [sing.] a great fear or hatred of sth 对某事物的强烈畏惧（或憎恨）：**~ of sth** *a horror of deep water* 恐惧深水 ◇ **~ of doing sth** *Most people have a horror of speaking in public.* 大多数人都十分害怕当众讲话。 **3** [U] **the ~ of sth** the very unpleasant nature of sth, especially when it is shocking or frightening （某事物）令人厌恶的性质；（尤指）震惊性，恐怖性：***The full horror of*** *the accident was beginning to become clear.* 这次悲惨事故的真相已开始逐渐清晰了。◇ *In his dreams he relives the horror of the attack.* 那次袭击的恐怖景象在他的梦中一再重现。 **4** [C, usually pl.] a very unpleasant or frightening experience

极其不愉快的（或可怕的）经历：*the horrors of war* 战争的恐怖经历 **5** [U] a type of book, film/movie, etc. that is designed to frighten people 恐怖故事（或电影等）：*In this section you'll find horror and science fiction.* 你可以在这一部分找到恐怖和科幻小说。◇ *a* **horror film/movie** 恐怖片 ➲ SEE ALSO HORROR STORY **6** [C] (*BrE, informal*) a child who behaves badly 调皮捣蛋的孩子：*Her son is a little horror.* 她的儿子是个小捣蛋鬼。

IDM **ˌhorror of ˈhorrors** (*humorous* or *ironic*) used to emphasize how bad a situation is 极其糟糕：*I stood up to speak and—horror of horrors—realized I had left my notes behind.* 我站起来讲话，可是，可怕的是，我发现自己忘了带讲稿。➲ MORE AT SHOCK *n.*

ˈhorror story *noun* **1** a story about strange and frightening things that is designed to entertain people 恐怖故事 **2** (*informal*) a report that describes an experience of a situation as very unpleasant 可怕经历的描述；吓人的报道：*horror stories about visits to the dentist* 有关看牙医的种种吓人说法

ˈhorror-struck (*also* **ˈhorror-stricken**) *adj.* suddenly feeling very shocked, frightened or disgusted 突然感到震惊的（或惊恐的、厌恶的）

hors de com·bat /ˌɔː də ˈkɒ̃bɑː; *NAmE* ˌɔːr də koʊmˈbɑː/ *adj.* (*from French, formal*) unable to fight or to take part in an activity, especially because you are injured （尤指因伤）丧失战斗力的，无法参加的

hors d'oeuvre /ˌɔː ˈdɜːv; *NAmE* ˌɔːr ˈdɜːrv/ *noun* [C, U] (*pl.* **hors d'oeuvres** /ˌɔː ˈdɜːv; *NAmE* ˌɔːr ˈdɜːrv/) (*from French*) a small amount of food, usually cold, served before the main part of a meal 开胃小吃；开胃冷盘 ➲ COMPARE STARTER (1) ➲ MORE LIKE THIS 20, page R27

horse /hɔːs; *NAmE* hɔːrs/ *noun, verb*

■ ***noun*** **1** a large animal with four legs, a MANE (= long thick hair on its neck) and a tail. Horses are used for riding on, pulling CARRIAGES, etc. 马：*He mounted his horse and rode off.* 他跨上马骑走了。◇ *a horse and cart* 一辆马车 ➲ SEE ALSO COLT (1), FILLY, FOAL *n.*, GELDING, MARE, STALLION

> **WORDFINDER 联想词：** bridle, gallop, harness, paddock, rein, stable, stirrup, tack, thoroughbred

2 the horses [pl.] (*informal*) horse racing 赛马：*He lost a lot of money on the horses* (= by gambling on races). 他赌赛马输了很多钱。**3** = VAULTING HORSE ➲ SEE ALSO CLOTHES HORSE, HOBBY HORSE, QUARTER HORSE, ROCKING HORSE, SEAHORSE, STALKING HORSE, TROJAN HORSE, WHITE HORSES

IDM **(straight) from the horse's ˈmouth** (*informal*) (of information 信息) given by sb who is directly involved and therefore likely to be accurate 直接的；可靠的 **hold your ˈhorses** (*informal*) used to tell sb that they should wait a moment and not be so excited that they take action without thinking about it first 且慢；请三思 **ˌhorses for ˈcourses** (*BrE*) the act of matching people with suitable jobs or tasks 知人善任 ORIGIN This expression refers to the fact that horses race better on a track that suits them. 含义来自马在合适的跑道上跑得更快。 **a one, two, three, etc. horse ˈrace** a competition or an election in which there are only one, two, etc. teams or candidates with a chance of winning 只有一个（或两个、三个）队（或候选人）有获胜机会的比赛（或竞选） **you can ˌlead/ˌtake a horse to ˌwater, but you ˌcan't make it ˈdrink** (*saying*) you can give sb the opportunity to do sth, but you cannot force them to do it if they do not want to 牵马近水易，逼马饮水难；机会可以给，做不做由人；老牛不饮水，不能强按头 ➲ MORE AT BACK *v.*, CART *n.*, CHANGE *v.*, DARK *adj.*, DRIVE *v.*, EAT, FLOG, GIFT *n.*, HIGH *adj.*, STABLE DOOR, WILD *adj.*, WISH *n.*

■ ***verb***

PHRV **ˌhorse aˈbout/aˈround** (*informal*) to play in a way that is noisy and not very careful so that you could hurt sb or damage sth 胡闹；瞎闹 SYN **fool**

horse·back /ˈhɔːsbæk; *NAmE* ˈhɔːrs-/ *noun, adj.*

■ ***noun***

IDM **on ˈhorseback** sitting on a horse; using horses 骑着马；驾驭着马：*a soldier on horseback* 骑着马的士兵

■ ***adj.*** [only before noun] sitting on a horse 骑着马的：*a horseback tour* 骑马旅行 ▶ **horse·back** *adv.*：*to ride horseback* 骑马

ˈhorseback riding *noun* [U] (*NAmE*) = RIDING (1)

horse·box /ˈhɔːsbɒks; *NAmE* ˈhɔːrsbɑːks/ *noun* (*BrE*) a vehicle for transporting horses in, sometimes pulled behind another vehicle 运马车；运马拖车 ➲ SEE ALSO HORSE TRAILER

ˌhorse ˈchestnut *noun* **1** a large tall tree with spreading branches, white or pink flowers and nuts that grow inside cases which are covered with SPIKES 七叶树；马栗 ➲ VISUAL VOCAB PAGE V10 ➲ SEE ALSO CHESTNUT *n.* **2** the smooth brown nut of the horse chestnut tree 七叶树的坚果 ➲ COMPARE CONKER (1)

ˈhorse-drawn *adj.* [only before noun] (of a vehicle 车辆) pulled by a horse or horses 马拉的

horse·flesh /ˈhɔːsfleʃ; *NAmE* ˈhɔːrs-/ *noun* [U] horses, especially when being bought or sold （尤指买卖的）马匹

horse·fly /ˈhɔːsflaɪ; *NAmE* ˈhɔːrs-/ *noun* (*pl.* **-ies**) a large fly that bites horses and cows 虻

horse·hair /ˈhɔːsheə(r); *NAmE* ˈhɔːrsher/ *noun* [U] hair from the MANE or tail of a horse, used, in the past, for filling MATTRESSES, chairs, etc. 马鬃，马尾毛（旧时用作床垫、椅子等的填料）

horse·man /ˈhɔːsmən; *NAmE* ˈhɔːrs-/ *noun* (*pl.* **-men** /-mən/) a rider on a horse; a person who can ride horses 骑手；骑马的人：*a good horseman* 优秀骑手 ➲ SEE ALSO HORSEWOMAN

horse·man·ship /ˈhɔːsmənʃɪp; *NAmE* ˈhɔːrs-/ *noun* [U] skill in riding horses 马术；骑术

horse·play /ˈhɔːspleɪ; *NAmE* ˈhɔːrs-/ *noun* [U] rough noisy play in which people push or hit each other for fun 打闹嬉戏；玩闹

horse·power /ˈhɔːspaʊə(r); *NAmE* ˈhɔːrs-/ *noun* [C, U] (*pl.* **horse·power**) (*abbr.* **h.p.**) a unit for measuring the power of an engine 马力（功率单位）：*a powerful car with a 170 horsepower engine* 发动机为 170 马力的大功率汽车

ˈhorse race *noun* a race between horses with riders 赛马

ˈhorse racing *noun* [U] a sport in which horses with riders race against each other 赛马运动 ➲ VISUAL VOCAB PAGE V51

horse·rad·ish /ˈhɔːsrædɪʃ; *NAmE* ˈhɔːrs-/ *noun* [U] **1** a hard white root vegetable that has a taste like pepper 辣根 **2** (*also* **ˌhorseradish ˈsauce**) a sauce made from horseradish, that is eaten with meat 辣根酱：*roast beef and horseradish* 烤牛肉加辣根酱

ˈhorse riding *noun* [U] (*BrE*) = RIDING (1)

horse·shoe /ˈhɔːsʃuː; ˈhɔːʃʃuː; *NAmE* ˈhɔːrʃ-; ˈhɔːrs-/ *noun* (*also* **shoe**) **1** a piece of curved iron that is attached with nails to the bottom of a horse's foot. A horseshoe is often used as a symbol of good luck. 马蹄铁，马掌（常用来象征好运） **2** anything shaped like a horseshoe 马蹄铁形物：*a horseshoe bend in the river* 河道中的马蹄形弯曲

ˈhorse-trading *noun* [U] the activity of discussing business with sb using clever or secret methods in order to reach an agreement that suits you 精明的交易；留有一手的交易

ˈhorse trailer *noun* (*NAmE*) a vehicle for transporting horses in, pulled by another vehicle 运马车；运马拖车 ➲ SEE ALSO HORSEBOX

horse·whip /ˈhɔːswɪp; *NAmE* ˈhɔːrs-/ *noun, verb*

■ ***noun*** a long stick with a long piece of leather attached to the end that is used to control or train horses 马鞭

■ ***verb*** (**-pp-**) **~ sb** to beat sb with a horsewhip 用马鞭抽打（人）

horse·woman /ˈhɔːswʊmən; *NAmE* ˈhɔːrs-/ *noun* (*pl.* **-women** /-wɪmɪn/) a woman rider on a horse; a woman who can ride horses well 骑马的女子；女骑手；女骑师：*a good horsewoman* 优秀女骑手

horsey (*also* **horsy**) /ˈhɔːsi; *NAmE* ˈhɔːrsi/ *adj.* **1** interested in and involved with horses or horse racing 爱马的；爱赛马的 **2** connected with horses; like a horse 与马有关的；像马的：*She had a long, horsey face.* 她有一张长长的马脸。

horti·cul·ture /ˈhɔːtɪkʌltʃə(r); *NAmE* ˈhɔːrt-/ *noun* [U] the study or practice of growing flowers, fruit and vegetables 园艺学；园艺：*a college of agriculture and horticulture* 农学与园艺学院 ➲ COMPARE GARDENING at GARDEN *v.* ▶ **horti·cul·tural** /ˌhɔːtɪˈkʌltʃərəl; *NAmE* ˌhɔːrt-/ *adj.*：*a horticultural show* 园艺展览 **horti·cul·tur·al·ist** *noun* **horti·cul·tur·ist** *noun*

hos·anna (*also* **hos·annah**) /həʊˈzænə; *NAmE* hoʊ-/ *exclamation* used in worship to express praise, joy and love for God, especially in the Christian and Jewish religions 和撒那，贺三纳（尤指在基督教和犹太教中对上帝的欢呼之声）▶ **hos·anna** *noun*

hose /həʊz; *NAmE* hoʊz/ *noun, verb*

■ *noun* **1** (*also* **hose·pipe** /ˈhəʊzpaɪp; *NAmE* ˈhoʊz-/) [C, U] a long tube made of rubber, plastic, etc., used for putting water onto fires, gardens, etc.（灭火、浇花等用的）橡皮管，塑料管，水龙带：*a garden hose* 浇花园的软管 ◇ *a length of hose* 一段软管 ➲ VISUAL VOCAB PAGE V20 ➲ SEE ALSO FIRE HOSE **2** [pl.] = HOSIERY **3** [pl.] trousers/pants that fit tightly over the legs, worn by men in the past（旧时的）男式紧身裤：*doublet and hose* 紧身上衣和紧身裤

■ *verb* **~ sth** to wash or pour water on sth using a hose 用软管输水冲洗（或浇水）：*Firemen hosed the burning car.* 消防队员用水龙带向燃烧的汽车喷水。

PHR V **ˌhose sth↔ˈdown** to wash sth using a hose 用喷水软管冲洗某物

ho·siery /ˈhəʊziəri; *NAmE* ˈhoʊʒəri/ (*also* **hose**) *noun* [U] used especially in shops/stores as a word for TIGHTS, STOCKINGS and socks（尤用于商店）袜类：*the hosiery department* 袜类部

hos·pice /ˈhɒspɪs; *NAmE* ˈhɑːs-/ *noun* a hospital for people who are dying 临终安养院：*an AIDS hospice* 艾滋病患者安养院

hos·pit·able /hɒˈspɪtəbl; ˈhɒspɪtəbl; *NAmE* hɑːˈs-; ˈhɑːs-/ *adj.* **1 ~ (to/towards sb)** (of a person 人) pleased to welcome guests; generous and friendly to visitors 好客的；热情友好的；殷勤的 SYN **welcoming**：*The local people are very hospitable to strangers.* 当地人对外来客人十分友好热情。**2** having good conditions that allow things to grow; having a pleasant environment （作物生长条件）适宜的；（环境）舒适的：*a hospitable climate* 宜人的气候 OPP **inhospitable** ▶ **hos·pit·ably** /-əbli/ *adv.*

hos·pital 🔑 /ˈhɒspɪtl; *NAmE* ˈhɑːs-/ *noun* a large building where people who are ill/sick or injured are given medical treatment and care 医院：(*BrE*) *He had to go **to hospital** for treatment.* 他得到医院接受治疗。◇ (*NAmE*) *He had to go **to the hospital** for treatment.* 他得到医院接受治疗。◇ *to **be admitted to** (the) **hospital*** 被接受入院 ◇ *to **be discharged from** (the) **hospital*** 获准出院 ◇ *The injured were **rushed to** (the) **hospital** in an ambulance.* 救护车把伤员火速送往医院。◇ *He died in (the) hospital.* 他在医院里去世。◇ *I'm going to the hospital to visit my brother.* 我要去医院探望我弟弟。◇ *a **psychiatric/mental hospital*** 精神病院 ◇ ***hospital doctors/nurses/staff*** 医院医生 / 护士 / 职工 ◇ *There is an urgent need for more hospital beds.* 医院床位急需增加。➲ SEE ALSO COTTAGE HOSPITAL ➲ WORDFINDER NOTE AT ACCIDENT

▼ BRITISH/AMERICAN 英式 / 美式英语

hospital

- In *BrE* you say **to hospital** or **in hospital** when you talk about somebody being there as a patient. 在英式英语中，去医院看病或住院诊治用 to hospital 或 in hospital：*I had to go to hospital.* 我得去医院看病。◇ *She spent two weeks in hospital.* 她住院两周。
- In *NAmE* you need to use **the**. 美式英语要用定冠词 the：*I had to go to the hospital.* 我得去医院看病。◇ *She spent two weeks in the hospital.* 她住院两周。

WORDFINDER 联想词：A & E, admit, consultant, **doctor**, ICU, inpatient, nurse, **operation**, ward

ˌhospital ˈcorners *noun* [pl.] a way of folding the sheets at the corners of a bed tightly and neatly, in a way that they are often folded in a hospital 医院床单折角法（整齐紧折四角）

hos·pi·tal·ity /ˌhɒspɪˈtæləti; *NAmE* ˌhɑːs-/ *noun* [U] **1** friendly and generous behaviour towards guests 好客；殷勤：*Thank you for your kind hospitality.* 感谢你的友好款待。**2** food, drink or services that are provided by an organization for guests, customers, etc.（款待客人、顾客等的）食物，饮料，服务；款待：*We were entertained in the company's **hospitality suite**.* 公司款待我们住进他们的迎宾套间。◇ *the hospitality industry* (= hotels, restaurants, etc.) 招待性行业（如旅馆、饭店等）

hos·pi·tal·ize (*BrE also* **-ise**) /ˈhɒspɪtəlaɪz; *NAmE* ˈhɑːs-/ *verb* [usually passive] **~ sb** to send sb to a hospital for treatment 送（某人）入院治疗 ▶ **hos·pi·tal·iza·tion**, **-isa·tion** /ˌhɒspɪtəlaɪˈzeɪʃn; *NAmE* ˌhɑːspɪtələˈz-/ *noun* [U]：*a long period of hospitalization* 长期住院

host 🔑 /həʊst; *NAmE* hoʊst/ *noun, verb*

■ *noun* **1** 🔑 [C] a person who invites guests to a meal, a party, etc. or who has people staying at their house 主人：*Ian, our host, introduced us to the other guests.* 主人伊恩把我们介绍给了其他客人。➲ SEE ALSO HOSTESS **2** 🔑 [C] a country, a city or an organization that holds and arranges a special event 东道主；主办国（或城市、机构）：*The college is **playing host to** a group of visiting Russian scientists.* 学院正在接待一批来访的俄罗斯科学家。**3** 🔑 [C] a person who introduces a television or radio show, and talks to guests（电视或广播的）节目主持人 SYN **compère**：*a TV game show host* 电视游戏节目主持人 ➲ SEE ALSO ANNOUNCER (1), PRESENTER **4** [C] (*specialist*) an animal or a plant on which another animal or plant lives and feeds（寄生动植物的）宿主，寄主 **5** [C] **~ of sb/sth** a large number of people or things 许多；大量：*a host of possibilities* 多种可能性 **6** [C] the main computer in a network that controls or supplies information to other computers that are connected to it（计算机网络的）主机，服务机：*transferring files from the host to your local computer* 从主机向你的本地机传送文件 **7 the Host** [sing.] the bread that is used in the Christian service of COMMUNION, after it has been BLESSED 圣饼（基督教圣餐仪式中经过祝祷的面饼）

■ *verb* **1** 🔑 **~ sth** to organize an event to which others are invited and make all the arrangements for them 主办，主持（活动）：*South Africa hosted the World Cup finals.* 南非主办了世界杯决赛。**2** 🔑 **~ sth** to introduce a television or radio programme, a show, etc. 主持（电视或广播节目等）SYN **compère** **3 ~ sth** to organize a party that you have invited guests to 作为主人组织（聚会）；做东：*to host a dinner* 设宴招待客人 **4 ~ sth** to store a website on a computer connected to the Internet, usually in return for payment 为（网站）提供虚拟主机（通常收费）：*a company that builds and hosts e-commerce sites* 为电子商务提供网站创建和虚拟主机服务的公司

hos·tage /ˈhɒstɪdʒ; *NAmE* ˈhɑːs-/ *noun* a person who is captured and held prisoner by a person or group, and who may be injured or killed if people do not do what the person or group is asking 人质：*Three children were **taken hostage** during the bank robbery.* 在银行抢劫案中有三名儿童被扣为人质。◇ *He was **held hostage** for almost a year.* 他被扣为人质几近一年。◇ *The government is negotiating the release of the hostages.* 政府正就释放人质进行谈判。➲ WORDFINDER NOTE AT ATTACK

IDM **a ˌhostage to ˈfortune** something that you have, or have promised to do, that could cause trouble or worry in the future 可能招惹麻烦（或担忧）的东西（或许诺）；造成后患的事物

ˈhostage-taker *noun* a person, often one of a group, who captures sb and holds them prisoner, and who may injure or kill them if people do not do what the person is asking 劫持人质者 ▸ **ˈhostage-taking** *noun* [U]

hos·tel /ˈhɒstl; *NAmE* ˈhɑːstl/ *noun* **1** a building that provides cheap accommodation and meals to students, workers or travellers 宿舍，招待所（提供廉价食宿服务）➲ SEE ALSO YOUTH HOSTEL **2** (*BrE*) (*also* **shel·ter** *NAmE, BrE*) a building, usually run by a charity, where people who have no home can stay for a short time 临时收容所；慈善收容所：*a hostel for the homeless* 流浪者之家 ➲ WORDFINDER NOTE AT POOR

hos·tel·ry /ˈhɒstəlri; *NAmE* ˈhɑːs-/ (*pl.* **-ies**) *noun* (*old use* or *humorous*) a pub or hotel 酒吧；旅店

host·ess /ˈhəʊstəs; -es; *NAmE* ˈhoʊstəs/ *noun* **1** a woman who invites guests to a meal, a party, etc.; a woman who has people staying at her home 女主人；女房东：*Mary was always the perfect hostess.* 玛丽总是最殷勤的女主人。**2** a woman who is employed to welcome and entertain men at a NIGHTCLUB（夜总会的）女招待 **3** a woman who introduces and talks to guests on a television or radio show（电视或广播节目的）女主持人 **SYN** **compère** ➲ NOTE AT GENDER **4** (*NAmE*) a woman who welcomes the customers in a restaurant（餐馆的）女迎宾，女门迎 ➲ SEE ALSO HOST *n.*

hos·tile /ˈhɒstaɪl; *NAmE* ˈhɑːstl; -taɪl/ *adj.* **1** very unfriendly or aggressive and ready to argue or fight 敌意的；敌对的：*The speaker got a hostile reception from the audience.* 演讲人遭到了听众喝倒彩。◇ **~ to/towards sb/sth** *She was openly hostile towards her parents.* 她公然对抗她的父母。**2 ~ (to sth)** strongly rejecting sth 坚决否定；强烈反对 **SYN** **opposed**：*hostile to the idea of change* 强烈反对变革 **3** making it difficult for sth to happen or to be achieved 有阻碍的；不利的：*hostile conditions for plants to grow in* 不利于植物生长的环境 **4** belonging to a military enemy 敌军的；敌人的：*hostile territory* 敌方领土 ➲ WORDFINDER NOTE AT CONFLICT **5** (*business* 商) (of an offer to buy a company, etc. 收购公司等的要约) not wanted by the company that is to be bought 不受（被购公司）欢迎的；敌意的：*a hostile takeover bid* 出价敌意收购

hos·til·ity /hɒˈstɪləti; *NAmE* hɑːˈs-/ *noun* **1** [U] unfriendly or aggressive feelings or behaviour 敌意；对抗：**~ (to/towards sb/sth)** *feelings of hostility towards people from other backgrounds* 对不同背景的人的敌视情绪 ◇ **~ (between A and B)** *There was* **open hostility** *between the two schools.* 这两所学校公开相互敌对。**2** [U] **~ (to/towards sth)** strong and angry opposition towards an idea, a plan or a situation（对思想、计划或情形的）愤怒反对，愤怒反抗：*public hostility to nuclear power* 公众对核动力的愤然反对 **3 hostilities** [pl.] (*formal*) acts of fighting in a war 战争行为：***the start/outbreak of hostilities** between the two sides* 双方之间敌对行为的爆发 ◇ ***a cessation of hostilities*** (= an end to fighting) 战争停止 ➲ COLLOCATIONS AT WAR

host·ler /ˈhɒslə(r); *NAmE* ˈhɑːs-/ *noun* (*NAmE*) = OSTLER

hot 🔑 /hɒt; *NAmE* hɑːt/ *adj., verb*

■ *adj.* (**hot·ter, hot·test**)

• **TEMPERATURE** 温度 **1** 🔑 having a high temperature; producing heat 温度高的；热的：*Do you like this hot weather?* 你喜欢这种炎热的天气吗？◇ *It's hot today, isn't it?* 今天很热，对吗？◇ *It was hot and getting hotter.* 天气很热，而且气温在不断升高。◇ *It was the hottest July on record.* 那是历史记载中最热的七月。◇ *a hot dry summer* 炎热干燥的夏天 ◇ *Be careful—the plates are hot.* 当心，盘子烫手。◇ *All rooms have hot and cold water.* 所有的房间都有冷、热水。◇ *a hot bath* 热水浴 ◇ *a hot meal* (= one that has been cooked) 热的饭菜 ◇ *I couldn't live in a hot country* (= one which has high average temperatures). 我无法在炎热的国家生活。◇ *Cook in a very hot oven.* 放在烤箱里用高温烤。◇ *Eat it while it's hot.* 趁热吃了它吧。◇ *I touched his forehead. He felt hot and feverish.* 我摸了摸他的前额，感到很烫，是在发烧。➲ SEE ALSO BAKING *adj.*, BOILING HOT at BOILING, PIPING HOT, RED-HOT, WHITE-HOT **2** 🔑 (of a person 人) feeling heat in an unpleasant or uncomfortable way 觉得闷（或燥、湿）热：*Is anyone too hot?* 有人觉得太热了吗？◇ *I feel hot.* 我觉得很热。◇ *Her cheeks were hot with embarrassment.* 她的双颊窘得发烫。**3** 🔑 making you feel hot 使人感到热的：*London was hot and dusty.* 伦敦很热而且灰尘多。◇ *a long hot journey* 又远又热的旅行

• **FOOD WITH SPICES** 辣的食物 **4** 🔑 containing pepper and spices and producing a burning feeling in your mouth 辣的；辛辣的：*hot spicy food* 辛辣的食物 ◇ *You can make a curry hotter simply by adding chillies.* 你只需加辣椒就能增加咖喱菜的辣味。◇ *hot mustard* 辣芥末 **OPP** **mild** ➲ WORDFINDER NOTE AT TASTE

• **CAUSING STRONG FEELINGS** 引起强烈感情 **5** involving a lot of activity, argument or strong feelings 活跃的；激动的；强烈的：*Today we enter the hottest phase of the election campaign.* 今天我们进入了竞选活动最激烈的阶段。◇ *The environment has become a very hot issue.* 环境已成为很热门的话题。◇ *Competition is getting hotter day by day.* 竞争日趋白热化。

• **DIFFICULT/DANGEROUS** 艰难；危险 **6** difficult or dangerous to deal with and making you feel worried or uncomfortable 艰难的；棘手的；危险的：*When things got too hot most journalists left the area.* 事态发展到过于严峻时，大多数记者便撤离了这个地区。◇ *They're making life hot for her.* 他们使得她日子难过。

• **POPULAR** 流行 **7** (*informal*) new, exciting and very popular 风行的；风靡一时的；走红的：*This is one of the hottest clubs in town.* 这是市里一家最受欢迎的夜总会。◇ *They are one of this year's hot new bands.* 他们是今年走红的新乐队之一。◇ *The couple are Hollywood's* ***hottest property***. 这一对是好莱坞最炙手可热的人物。

• **NEWS** 新闻 **8** fresh, very recent and usually exciting 最新的，新近的（通常令人兴奋）：*I've got some hot gossip for you!* 我要告诉你一些最新的传闻！◇ *a story that is* ***hot off the press*** (= has just appeared in the newspapers) 刚刚出炉的报道

• **TIP/FAVOURITE** 热门 **9** [only before noun] likely to be successful 有望成功的：*She seems to be the* ***hot favourite*** *for the job.* 她似乎是这份工作最热门的人选。◇ *Do you have any* ***hot tips*** *for today's race?* 你有今天赛马的内部消息吗？

• **GOOD AT STH/KNOWING A LOT** 擅长；熟识 **10** [not before noun] **~ at/on sth** (*informal*) very good at doing sth; knowing a lot about sth 善于（做某事）；（对某事）了解很多：*Don't ask me—I'm* ***not too hot on*** *British history.* 别问我，我不大了解英国历史。

• **ANGER** 愤怒 **11** if sb has a **hot temper** they become angry very easily 易发怒的；（脾气）暴躁的

• **SEXUAL EXCITEMENT** 性激动 **12** feeling or causing sexual excitement 感到（或引起）性激动的：*You were as hot for me as I was for you.* 当时你想要我，我也想要你。◇ *I've got a* ***hot date*** *tonight.* 我今晚有一场令人激动的约会。

• **SHOCKING/CRITICAL** 惊人；严重 **13** containing scenes, statements, etc. that are too shocking or too critical and are likely to cause anger or disapproval（场面、说话等）过激的，过火的：*Some of the nude scenes were regarded as too hot for Broadway.* 有些裸露场面被认为太过火了，不适合在百老汇上演。◇ *The report was highly critical of senior members of the Cabinet and was considered too hot to publish.* 报道中对内阁高级官员的批评被认为过于激烈，不宜发表。➲ SEE ALSO HOT STUFF (4)

• **STRICT** 严格 **14** [not before noun] **~ on sth** thinking that sth is very important and making sure that it always happens or is done 重视，确保（某事发生或完成）：*They're very hot on punctuality at work.* 他们很重视工作守时。

• **MUSIC** 音乐 **15** (of music, especially JAZZ 音乐，尤指爵士乐) having a strong and exciting rhythm 节奏强的

• **GOODS** 货物 **16** stolen and difficult to get rid of because they can easily be recognized 偷来（因容易识别）而难以销赃的：*I'd never have touched those CDs if I'd known they were hot.* 早知道那些光盘是偷来的，我绝不会碰的。

• **IN CHILDREN'S GAMES** 儿童游戏 **17** [not before noun] used in children's games to say that the person playing is very close to finding a person or thing, or to guessing the correct answer 快找到了；快猜中了：*You're getting hot!* 你快猜中了！ ➲ MORE LIKE THIS 35, page R29

IDM **be ˌhot to ˈtrot** (*informal*) **1** to be very enthusiastic about starting an activity 期待（某活动） **2** to be excited in a sexual way 欲火中烧；性欲高涨 **be in/get into hot ˈwater** (*informal*) to be in or get into trouble 有麻烦；惹上麻烦 **go hot and ˈcold** to experience a sudden feeling of fear or anxiety 突然感到害怕（或焦虑）：*When the phone rang I just went hot and cold.* 电话铃响时我吓得一阵冷一阵热。 **go/sell like hot ˈcakes** to sell quickly or in great numbers 畅销 **(all) hot and ˈbothered** (*informal*) in a state of anxiety or confusion because you are under too much pressure, have a problem, are trying to hurry, etc. （因压力过大、有难题、时间紧迫等）焦灼不安，心慌意乱 **hot on sb's/sth's ˈheels** following sb/sth very closely 紧跟着；接踵而至：*He turned and fled with Peter hot on his heels.* 他转身逃跑，彼得紧追不舍。◇ *Further successes came hot on the heels of her first best-selling novel.* 她的第一部畅销小说之后是接二连三的成功。 **hot on sb's/sth's ˈtracks/ˈtrail** (*informal*) close to catching or finding the person or thing that you have been chasing or searching for 快要抓到，即将找到（某人或物） **hot under the ˈcollar** (*informal*) angry or embarrassed 愤怒的；窘迫的：*He got very hot under the collar when I asked him where he'd been all day.* 我问他一整天到哪里去了，他很尴尬。 **in hot purˈsuit (of sb)** following sb closely and determined to catch them （对某人）穷追不舍：*She sped away in her car with journalists in hot pursuit.* 她开车迅速离去，记者们则在后面穷追不舍。 **not so/too ˈhot 1** not very good in quality 质量不大好：*Her spelling isn't too hot.* 她的拼写不太好。 **2** not feeling well 不舒服：*'How are you today?' 'Not so hot, I'm afraid.'* "你今天怎么样？" "很遗憾，不怎么样。" ➲ MORE AT BLOW *v.*, CAT, HEEL *n.*, STRIKE *v.*

■ ***verb*** **(-tt-)**

PHR V **ˌhot ˈup** (*BrE*) (*also* **ˌheat ˈup** *NAmE, BrE*) (*informal*) to become more exciting or to show an increase in activity 激烈起来；更加活跃：*Things are really hotting up in the election campaign.* 竞选活动的确日益激烈了。

ˌhot ˈair *noun* [U] (*informal*) claims, promises or statements that sound impressive but have no real meaning or truth 夸夸其谈；大话；空话

ˌhot-ˈair balloon *noun* = BALLOON (2) ➲ VISUAL VOCAB PAGE V58

hot·bed /ˈhɒtbed; *NAmE* ˈhɑːt-/ *noun* [usually sing.] **~ of sth** a place where a lot of a particular activity, especially sth bad or violent, is happening （坏事、暴力等的）温床：*The area was a hotbed of crime.* 这个地区以前是犯罪活动的温床。

ˌhot-ˈblooded *adj.* (of a person 人) having strong emotions and easily becoming very excited or angry 情感强烈的；血气方刚的；易怒的 SYN **passionate** ➲ COMPARE WARM-BLOODED

ˈhot button *noun* (*NAmE, informal*) a subject or issue that people have strong feelings about and argue about a lot 热点话题：*Race has always been a hot button in this country's history.* 种族一直是这个国家历史上争论不休的问题。◇ *the hot-button issue of nuclear waste disposal* 核废料处理这个热门话题

ˌhot ˈchocolate (*BrE also* **choc·olate**) *noun* [U, C] a drink made by mixing chocolate powder with hot water or milk; a cup of this drink 巧克力热饮；一杯巧克力热饮：*Two coffees and a hot chocolate, please.* 请来两杯咖啡和一杯热巧克力。

hotch·potch /ˈhɒtʃpɒtʃ; *NAmE* ˈhɑːtʃpɑːtʃ/ (*especially BrE*) (*NAmE usually* **hodge·podge**) *noun* [sing.] (*informal*) a number of things mixed together without any particular order or reason 杂乱无章的一堆东西；大杂烩 ➲ MORE LIKE THIS 11, page R26

ˌhot cross ˈbun *noun* a small sweet bread roll that contains CURRANTS and has a pattern of a cross on top, traditionally eaten in Britain around Easter 十字面包

ˌhot-ˈdesking *noun* [U] the practice in an office of giving desks to workers when they are required, rather than giving each worker their own desk 办公桌轮用（非固定分配）

ˈhot dog (*BrE also* **ˌhot ˈdog**) *noun* **1** a hot SAUSAGE served in a long bread roll 热狗（香肠面包） **2** (*NAmE*) a person who performs clever or dangerous tricks while SKIING, SNOWBOARDING or SURFING （滑雪、滑雪板运动或冲浪的）灵巧动作表演者，高难动作表演者：*He's a real hot dog.* 他是个十足的惊险动作运动员。

ˈhot-dog *verb* **(-gg-)** [I] (*NAmE, informal*) to perform clever or dangerous tricks while SKIING, SNOWBOARDING or SURFING （在滑雪、滑雪板运动或冲浪中）表演技巧，表演高难动作

hotel 🔑 /həʊˈtel; *NAmE* hoʊ-/ *noun* **1** a building where people stay, usually for a short time, paying for their rooms and meals 旅馆；旅社：*We stayed at/in a hotel.* 我们住在旅馆里。◇ ***hotel rooms/guests*** 旅馆的房间 / 客人 ◇ *a **two-star/five-star, etc. hotel*** 两星级、五星级等旅馆 ◇ *a **luxury hotel*** 豪华宾馆 ◇ *a friendly, family-run hotel* 一家亲切随和、家庭经营的旅店 ➲ COLLOCATIONS AT TRAVEL

> **WORDFINDER** 联想词：accommodation, book, full board, **holiday**, reception, reservation, room service, suite, vacancy

2 (*AustralE, NZE*) a pub 酒吧；酒馆 **3** (*IndE*) a restaurant 餐馆 HELP Some speakers do not pronounce the 'h' at the beginning of **hotel** and use 'an' instead of 'a' before it. This now sounds old-fashioned. 有人说 hotel 时不发 h 音，前面用 an 而不用 a，现在听起来过时了。

ho·tel·ier /həʊˈteliə(r); -lieɪ; *NAmE* hoʊˈteljər; ˌoʊtelˈjeɪ/ *noun* a person who owns or manages a hotel 旅馆老板；旅馆经理

hot·fix /ˈhɒtfɪks; *NAmE* ˈhɑːt-/ *noun* (*computing* 计) a file that is used to correct a fault in a computer program （电脑的）补丁程序

ˌhot ˈflush (*BrE*) (*NAmE* **ˌhot ˈflash**) *noun* a sudden hot and uncomfortable feeling in the skin, especially experienced by women during the MENOPAUSE 热潮红（皮肤的灼热阵感，尤见于更年期女性）

hot·foot /ˈhɒtfʊt; *NAmE* ˈhɑːt-/ *adv., verb*

■ ***adv.*** moving quickly and in a hurry 急匆匆地；匆忙地：*He had just arrived hotfoot from London.* 他刚从伦敦匆匆赶来。

■ ***verb***

IDM **ˈhotfoot it** (*informal*) to walk or run somewhere quickly 急走，快跑（到某地）：*When the police arrived, they hotfooted it out of there.* 警察到达时，他们匆忙逃离了那里。

hot·head /ˈhɒthed; *NAmE* ˈhɑːt-/ *noun* a person who often acts too quickly, without thinking of what might happen 莽撞的人；急躁的人 ▸ **ˌhot-ˈheaded** *adj.*

hot·house /ˈhɒthaʊs; *NAmE* ˈhɑːt-/ *noun* **1** a heated building, usually made of glass, used for growing delicate plants in 温室；暖房：*hothouse flowers* 温室花卉 **2** a place or situation that encourages the rapid development of sb/sth, especially ideas and emotions 有利于迅速发展的地方（或环境）；（尤指有利于思想感情发展的）温床

ˈhot key *noun* (*computing* 计) a key on a computer keyboard that you can press to perform a set of operations quickly, rather than having to press a number of different keys 热键，快捷键（按下后可迅速进行一系列操作）

hot·line /ˈhɒtlaɪn; *NAmE* ˈhɑːt-/ *noun* **1** a special telephone line that people can use in order to get information or to talk about sth 电话咨询服务专线；热线 **2** a direct telephone line between the heads of government in different countries （各国政府首脑之间通话的）热线

hot·link /ˈhɒtlɪŋk; *NAmE* ˈhɑːt-/ *noun* = LINK (4)

hot·list /ˈhɒtlɪst; *NAmE* ˈhɑːt-/ *noun* a list of popular, fashionable or important people or things 热点（或重要）人物名单；热点（或重要）事物清单

hotly /ˈhɒtli; *NAmE* ˈhɑːtli/ *adv.* **1** done in an angry or excited way or with a lot of strong feeling 愤怒地；激动地；强烈地：*a hotly debated topic* 激烈辩论的话题 ◇ *Recent reports in the press have been hotly denied.* 新闻界最近的报道遭到了坚决否认。◇ *'Nonsense!' he said hotly.* "废话！"他怒气冲冲地说。◇ *The results were hotly disputed.* 结果引起了极大争议。**2** done with a lot of energy and determination 起劲地；坚决地 SYN **closely**: *hotly contested elections* 竞争激烈的选举 ◇ *She ran out of the shop, **hotly pursued** by the store detective.* 她冲出商店，商店保安在后面猛追。

ˈ**hot pants** *noun* [pl.] very short, tight women's SHORTS 女式紧身超短裤；热裤

hot·plate /ˈhɒtpleɪt; *NAmE* ˈhɑːt-/ *noun* a flat, heated metal surface, for example on a cooker/stove, that is used for cooking food or for keeping it hot 烤盘，加热板（置于炉灶等的上面，用于烹调或使食物保温）

hot·pot /ˈhɒtpɒt; *NAmE* ˈhɑːtpɑːt/ *noun* **1** [C, U] (*BrE*) a hot dish of meat, potato, onion, etc. cooked slowly in liquid in the oven 焖罐（内装炖的肉、土豆、洋葱等）**2** [C] (*NAmE*) a small electric pot that you can use to heat water or food 小电热锅（可烧水或热饭）

ˌ**hot poˈtato** *noun* [usually sing.] (*informal*) a problem, situation, etc. that is difficult and unpleasant to deal with 棘手的问题（或情况等）；烫手山芋

ˈ**hot rod** *noun* a car that has been changed and improved to give it extra power and speed 改装的高速汽车

hots /hɒts; *NAmE* hɑːts/ *noun* [pl.]
IDM **get/have the ˈhots for sb** (*informal*) to be sexually attracted to sb 对某人有情欲

the ˈhot seat *noun* [sing.] (*informal*) if sb is **in the hot seat**, they have to take responsibility for important or difficult decisions and actions 责任重大的位置

hot·shot /ˈhɒtʃɒt; *NAmE* ˈhɑːtʃɑːt/ *noun* (*informal*) a person who is extremely successful in their career or at a particular sport 很有成就的人；运动高手 ▸ **hot·shot** *adj.* [only before noun]: *a hotshot lawyer* 业绩非凡的律师

ˈ**hot spot** *noun* (*informal*) **1** a place where fighting is common, especially for political reasons 多事之地；（尤指政治原因的）热点地区 **2** a place where there is a lot of activity or entertainment 活动多的地方；热闹的娱乐场所 **3** (*NAmE*) a place that is very hot and dry, where a fire has been burning or is likely to start 火灾多发地区 **4** (*computing* 计) an area on a computer screen that you can click on to start an operation such as loading a file（屏幕上点击后即可启动程序的）热点区 **5** a place in a hotel, restaurant, airport, etc. that is fitted with a special device that enables you to connect a computer to the Internet without using wires 热点（旅馆、饭店、机场等安装设备可无线上网的地方）

ˌ**hot ˈstuff** *noun* [U] (*informal, especially BrE*) **1** a person who is sexually attractive 性感的人：*She's pretty hot stuff.* 她很性感。**2** a film/movie, book, etc. which is exciting in a sexual way 艳情电影（或书籍等）**3** ~ (**at sth**) a person who is very skilful at sth 技艺很高的人；高手：*She's really hot stuff at tennis.* 她的确是网球高手。**4** something that is likely to cause anger or disagreement 很可能惹人生气（或引起争执）的事物：*These new proposals are proving to be hot stuff.* 这些新的建议结果证明是有争议性的。

ˌ**hot-ˈtempered** *adj.* (*especially BrE*) tending to become very angry easily 易怒的；暴躁的

hot·tie (*also* **hotty**) /ˈhɒti; *NAmE* ˈhɑːti/ *noun* (*informal*) a person who is very sexually attractive 热辣性感的人；帅哥；辣妹

ˈ**hot tub** *noun* a heated bath/BATHTUB, often outside, that several people can sit in together to relax 热水浴池（常置于室外，可供数人坐在里面休息）

ˌ**hot-ˈwater bottle** *noun* a rubber container that is filled with hot water and put in a bed to make it warm 热水袋

ˈ**hot-wire** *verb* ~ **sth** (*informal*) to start the engine of a vehicle by using a piece of wire instead of a key 热线发动，短路点火（不用钥匙而用电线短路方法发动汽车）

Hou·dini /huːˈdiːni/ *noun* a person or an animal that is very good at escaping 善于逃脱的人（或动物）⇨ MORE LIKE THIS 18, page R27 ORIGIN From Harry Houdini, a famous performer in the US who escaped from ropes, chains, boxes, etc. 源自美国著名的脱身魔术演员哈里·胡迪尼（Harry Houdini）。

hou·mous = HUMMUS

hound /haʊnd/ *noun, verb*
■ ***noun*** a dog that can run fast and has a good sense of smell, used for hunting 猎犬；猎狗 ⇨ SEE ALSO AFGHAN HOUND, BLOODHOUND, FOXHOUND, GREYHOUND, WOLFHOUND
■ ***verb*** ~ **sb** to keep following sb and not leave them alone, especially in order to get sth from them or ask them questions 追踪；追逐；纠缠 SYN **harass**: *They were hounded day and night by the press.* 他们日夜遭到新闻界的跟踪。
PHR V ˌ**hound sb ˈout** (**of sth**) | ˈ**hound sb from sth** [usually passive] to force sb to leave a job or a place, especially by making their life difficult and unpleasant 逼迫某人离职（或离开某地）

ˈ**hound dog** *noun* (*NAmE*) (especially in the southern US) a dog used in hunting （尤指美国南部）猎犬

hounds·tooth /ˈhaʊndztuːθ/ *noun* [U] a type of large pattern with pointed shapes, often in black and white, used especially in cloth for jackets and suits （尤指布料上的）犬牙织纹，犬牙花纹

hour 🔑 /ˈaʊə(r)/ *noun* HELP Use **an**, not **a**, before **hour**. * hour 前不定冠词用 an，不用 a。 **1** 🔑 [C] (*abbr.* **hr, hr.**) 60 minutes; one of the 24 parts that a day is divided into 小时：*It will take about an hour to get there.* 到那里大约需要一小时。◇ *The interview lasted half an hour.* 会见持续了半小时。◇ *It was a three-hour exam.* 那是三小时的考试。◇ *I waited **for an hour** and then I left.* 我等了一个小时，然后就走了。◇ *He'll be back **in an hour**.* 他一小时后回来。◇ *We're paid **by the hour**.* 我们是论小时获得报酬的。◇ *The rate of pay is £8.50 **an hour**.* 时薪为 8.5 英镑。◇ *Top speed is 120 miles **per hour**.* 最高时速为 120 英里。◇ *York was within an hour's drive.* 开车到约克不会超过一小时。◇ *Chicago is two hours away* (= it takes two hours to get there). 到芝加哥需要两小时。◇ *We're four hours ahead of New York* (= referring to the time difference). 我们比纽约早四个小时。◇ *We hope to be there **within the hour*** (= in less than an hour). 我们希望一小时内到达那里。**2** 🔑 [C, usually sing.] a period of about an hour, used for a particular purpose 约一小时的时间：*I use the Internet at work, during my **lunch hour**.* 我上班时在午餐时间使用互联网。⇨ SEE ALSO HAPPY HOUR, RUSH HOUR **3** 🔑 **hours** [pl.] a fixed period of time during which people work, an office is open, etc.（工作、办公等的）固定时间：***Opening hours** are from 10 to 6 each day.* 营业时间为每天 10 点到 6 点。◇ *Most people in this kind of job tend to work **long hours**.* 多数从事这种工作的人往往工作时间很长。◇ *What are your **office hours**?* 你的办公时间是几点到几点？◇ *a hospital's **visiting hours*** 医院的探视时间 ◇ *Britain's **licensing hours*** (= when pubs are allowed to open) *used to be very restricted.* 英国的酒吧营业时间从前受到很严格的限制。◇ *This is the only place to get a drink **after hours*** (= after the normal closing time for pubs). 这是酒吧正常关门时间之后唯一能喝一杯的地方。◇ *Clients can now contact us by email **out of hours*** (= when the office is closed). 现在办公时间以外顾客可以用电邮和我们联系。**4** 🔑 **hours** [pl.] a long time 长时间：*It took hours getting there.* 花了好长时间才到那里。◇ *I've been waiting for hours.* 我等了很久了。◇ *'How long did it last?'*

H

'Oh, hours and hours.' "持续了多久？" "噢，很久很久。" **5** [sing.] a particular point in time 某个时间：*You can't turn him away at this hour of the night.* 天这么晚了，你不能把他赶走。 **6** [C, usually sing.] the time when sth important happens 重要时刻：*This was often thought of as the country's **finest hour**.* 一般认为这是该国最美好的一段时光。◇ *She thought her **last hour** had come.* 她以为她生命的最后时刻到了。◇ *Don't desert me in my **hour of need**.* 不要在我困难的时候离开我。 **7 the hour** [sing.] the time when it is exactly 1 o'clock, 2 o'clock, etc. 整点：*There's a bus every hour **on the hour**.* 每小时整点有一班公共汽车。◇ *The clock **struck the hour**.* 钟敲过整点了。 **8 hours** [pl.] used when giving the time according to the 24-hour clock, usually in military or other official language (按 24 小时制给出的时间，通常用于军事或其他官方用语) 点钟：*The first missile was launched at 2300 hours* (= at 11 p.m.). 首枚导弹是在 23 点（晚上 11 点）发射的。HELP This is pronounced '23 hundred hours'. 这要读作 23 hundred hours。 ➲ MORE LIKE THIS 20, page R27

IDM **'all hours** any time, especially a time which is not usual or suitable 任何时间（尤指非正常或不合适的时间）：*He's started staying out **till all hours*** (= until very late at night). 他已经开始在外面待得很晚了。◇ *She thinks she can call me **at all hours of the day and night**.* 她以为她可以不分昼夜随时给我打电话。 **keep ... 'hours** if you keep regular, strange, etc. **hours**, the times at which you do things (especially getting up or going to bed) are regular, strange, etc. 做事（尤指作息）时间有规律（或怪异等） **the 'small/'early hours** (*also especially ScotE* **the wee small 'hours**, *also* **the wee 'hours** *especially in NAmE*) the period of time very early in the morning, soon after midnight 午夜刚过的一段时间；凌晨时分：*We worked well into the small hours.* 我们一直工作到了午夜之后。◇ *The fighting began in the early hours of Saturday morning.* 战斗在星期六凌晨打响了。 ➲ MORE AT ELEVEN, EVIL *adj.*, KILL *v.*, UNEARTHLY, UNGODLY

hour·glass /'aʊəɡlɑːs; *NAmE* 'aʊərɡlæs/ *noun, adj.*

■ ***noun*** a glass container holding sand that takes exactly an hour to pass through a small opening between the top and bottom sections 沙漏（玻璃容器上部的沙子经一小孔漏到下部，全部漏完正好一小时） ➲ COMPARE EGG TIMER

■ ***adj.*** [only before noun] a woman who has an **hourglass** figure, shape, etc. has large breasts and hips and a small waist （女人身材）丰乳肥臀的，上凸下翘的

'hour hand *noun* the small hand on a clock or watch that points to the hour （钟表的）时针 ➲ PICTURE AT CLOCK

hour·ly /'aʊəli; *NAmE* 'aʊərli/ *adj., adv.* HELP Use **an**, not **a**, before **hourly**. * hourly 前不定冠词用 an，不用 a。

■ ***adj.*** [only before noun] **1** done or happening every hour 每小时（一次）的：*an hourly bus service* 每小时一班的公共汽车 ◇ *Trains leave at hourly intervals.* 火车每隔一小时发出一列。 **2** an **hourly wage, fee, rate, etc.** is the amount that you earn every hour or pay for a service every hour （工资、酬金、费用等）按钟点计算的，论小时的：*an hourly rate of $30 an hour* 每小时 30 美元的收费

■ ***adv.*** every hour 每小时（一次）地：*Reapply sunscreen hourly and after swimming.* 每小时以及游泳后重新抹一次防晒霜。◇ *Dressings are changed four hourly* (= every four hours) *to help prevent infection.* 每四小时更换一次敷料，以防感染。

house 🔑 *noun, verb*

■ ***noun*** /haʊs/ (*pl.* **houses** /'haʊzɪz/)

• BUILDING 建筑 **1** 🔑 [C] a building for people to live in, usually for one family 房屋；房子；住宅：*He went into the house.* 他进了房子。◇ *a two-bedroom house* 两居室的住宅 ◇ *Let's have the party **at my house**.* 我们在我家里聚会吧。◇ *house prices* 房价 ◇ *What time do you leave the house in the morning* (= to go to work)? 你早晨几点出门（去上班）？ ◇ (*BrE*) *We're **moving house*** (= leaving our house and going to live in a different one). 我们要搬家了。 ➲ WORDFINDER NOTE AT HOME ➲ COLLOCATIONS AT DECORATE ➲ VISUAL VOCAB PAGE V18 ➲ SEE ALSO PENTHOUSE, SAFE HOUSE, SHOW HOUSE **2** 🔑 [sing.] all the people living in a house 住在一所房子里的人；全家人

▼ COLLOCATIONS 词语搭配

Moving house 搬家

Renting 租房子

- **live in** a rented/(*especially NAmE*) rental property 住在租来的住所里
- **rent/share/move into** a furnished house/(*BrE*) flat/(*especially NAmE*) apartment 租用／合住／搬进配有家具的房屋／公寓
- **rent** a studio/(*BrE*) a studio flat/(*especially NAmE*) a studio apartment/(*BrE*) a bedsit 租一个单间公寓
- **find/get** a housemate/(*BrE*) a flatmate/(*NAmE*) a roommate 找一个室友
- **sign/break** the lease/rental agreement/contract 签署／违反租约／租赁协议／合同
- **extend/renew/terminate** the lease/(*BrE*) tenancy 延长租赁期限；续签／终止租约
- **afford/pay** the rent/the bills/(*NAmE*) the utilities 付得起／支付租金／账单／水电气等杂费
- (*especially BrE*) **fall behind with**/ (*especially NAmE*) **fall behind on** the rent 拖欠租金
- **pay/lose/return** a damage deposit/(*NAmE*) security deposit 支付／失去／退还损坏押金／保证金
- **give/receive** a month's/two-weeks' notice to leave/vacate the property 提前一个月／两周发出／收到离开／腾空住房的通知

Being a landlord 做房东

- **have a flat/apartment/room** (*BrE*) to let/(*especially NAmE*) for rent 有一间公寓／一个房间要出租
- **rent (out)/lease (out)**/ (*BrE*) **let (out)/sublet** a flat/apartment/house/property 出租／转租公寓／房屋／房产
- **collect/increase/raise** the rent 收取／增加／提高房租
- **evict** the existing tenants 赶走现有房客
- **attract/find** new/prospective tenants 吸引／寻找新的／可能的房客
- **invest in** rental property/(*BrE*) property to let/(*BrE*) the buy-to-let market 投资购房用于出租

Buying 购买房子

- **buy/acquire/purchase** a house/(a) property/(*especially NAmE*) (a piece of) prime real estate 购置一栋房子／一处房产／（一块）优质房地产
- **call/contact/use** (*BrE*) an estate agent/(*NAmE*) a Realtor™/(*NAmE*) a real estate agent/broker 电话联系／联系／任用房地产经纪人
- **make**/ (*BrE*) **put in** an offer on a house 提供房子的报价
- **put down/save for** (*BrE*) a deposit on a house 支付／存钱付房屋订金
- **make/put/save for** (*especially NAmE*) a down payment on a house/home 支付／攒钱支付买房的首付金
- **apply for/arrange/take out** a mortgage/home loan 申请／商定／取得按揭／住房贷款
- (**struggle to**) **pay** the mortgage （竭力）支付按揭贷款
- **make/meet/keep up/cover** the monthly mortgage payments/(*BrE also*) repayments 支付每月的按揭贷款
- (*BrE*) **repossess**/ (*especially NAmE*) **foreclose on** sb's home/house 收回某人的房子；终止某人的房屋赎回权

Selling 出售房子

- **put your house/property** on the market/up for sale/up for auction 将房屋／房产投放市场／出售／拍卖
- **increase/lower** your price/the asking price 提高／降低价格／要价
- **have/hold/hand over** the deed/(*especially BrE*) deeds of/to the house, land, etc. 持有／移交房屋、土地等契约

SYN **household**: *Be quiet or you'll wake the whole house!* 安静点，别把全家人都吵醒！ **3** [C] (in compounds 构成复合词) a building used for a particular purpose, for example for holding meetings in or keeping animals or goods in 某种用途的建筑物: *an opera house* 歌剧院 ◇ *a henhouse* 鸡舍 ➲ SEE ALSO DOGHOUSE, DOSSHOUSE, HALFWAY HOUSE, HOTHOUSE, LIGHTHOUSE, MADHOUSE, OUTHOUSE, STOREHOUSE, WAREHOUSE **4 House** [sing.] (*BrE*) used in the names of office buildings（用于办公楼名称）大厦，大楼: *Their offices are on the second floor of Chester House.* 他们的办公室在切斯特大厦三楼。

• **COMPANY/INSTITUTION** 公司；机构 **5** [C] (in compounds 构成复合词) a company involved in a particular kind of business; an institution of a particular kind（从事某种生意的）公司，机构: ***a fashion/banking/publishing, etc. house*** 时装公司、银行、出版社等 ◇ *a religious house* (= a CONVENT or a MONASTERY) 宗教会所 ◇ *I work **in house*** (= in the offices of the company that I work for, not at home). 我在公司里上班。 ➲ SEE ALSO CLEARING HOUSE, IN-HOUSE

• **RESTAURANT** 餐馆 **6** [C] (in compounds 构成复合词) a restaurant 餐馆；餐厅: *a steakhouse* 牛排餐馆 ◇ *a coffee house* 咖啡馆 ◇ *a bottle of **house wine*** (= the cheapest wine available in a particular restaurant, sometimes not listed by name) 一瓶本店特价酒 ➲ SEE ALSO FREE HOUSE, PUBLIC HOUSE, ROADHOUSE, TIED HOUSE

• **PARLIAMENT** 议院 **7** [C] (*often* **House**) a group of people who meet to discuss and make the laws of a country 议院；议会；国会: *Legislation requires approval by both houses of parliament.* 立法须要得到议会两院的一致通过。 ➲ SEE ALSO LOWER HOUSE, UPPER HOUSE **8 the House** [sing.] the House of Commons or the House of Lords in Britain; the House of Representatives in the US（英国）下议院，上议院；（美国）众议院

• **IN DEBATE** 辩论 **9 the house** [sing.] a group of people discussing sth in a formal debate（统称）参与辩论的人: *I urge the house to vote against the motion.* 我呼吁参加辩论的诸位投票反对这项动议。

• **IN THEATRE** 剧院 **10** [C] the part of a theatre where the audience sits; the audience at a particular performance 观众席；（统称）观众: *playing to a **full/packed/empty house*** (= to a large/small audience) 演出座无虚席 / 满座 / 观众寥寥无几 ◇ *The spotlight faded and the house lights came up.* 聚光灯渐渐熄灭，观众席的灯亮了。 ➲ SEE ALSO FRONT-OF-HOUSE, FULL HOUSE (1)

• **IN SCHOOL** 学校 **11** [C] (in some British schools) an organized group of students of different ages who compete against other groups in sports competitions, etc. and who may, in BOARDING SCHOOLS, live together in one building（英国某些学校为进行体育比赛或按宿舍将学生分成的）社，舍

• **FAMILY** 家庭 **12** [C] (*usually* **the House of...**) an old and famous family 名门世家；望族: *the House of Windsor* (= the British royal family) 温莎王室

• **MUSIC** 音乐 **13** [U] = HOUSE MUSIC ➲ SEE ALSO ACID HOUSE, ART-HOUSE, OPEN HOUSE, POWERHOUSE

HELP There are many other compounds ending in **house**. You will find them at their place in the alphabet. 以 house 结尾的复合词还有很多，可在各字母中的适当位置查到。

IDM **bring the 'house down** to make everyone laugh or CHEER, especially at a performance in the theatre（尤指剧院的演出）博得满堂大笑（或喝彩） **get on like a 'house on fire** (*BrE*) (*NAmE* **get along like a 'house on fire**) (*informal*) (of people 人) to become friends quickly and have a very friendly relationship 很快就打得火热；一见如故；一拍即合 **go all round the 'houses** (*BrE, informal*) to do sth or ask a question in a very complicated way instead of in a simple, direct way 绕圈子；拐弯抹角；不直截了当 **keep 'house** to cook, clean and do all the other jobs around the house 操持家务 **on the 'house** drinks or meals that are **on the house** are provided free by the pub/bar or restaurant and you do not have to pay（酒吧或饭店）免费提供的 **put/set your (own) 'house in order** to organize your own business or improve your own behaviour before you try to criticize sb else 先管好自己的事；律人先律己 **set up 'house** to make a place your home（在某处）建立家庭: *They set up house together in a small flat in Brighton.* 他们一同在布赖顿的一个小公寓里建立了家庭。 ➲ MORE AT CLEAN *v.*, DRY *adj.*, EAT, PEOPLE *n.*, SAFE *adj.*

■ *verb* /haʊz/

• **PROVIDE HOME** 提供住所 **1 ~ sb** to provide a place for sb to live 给（某人）提供住处: *The government is committed to housing the refugees.* 政府承诺收容难民。

• **KEEP STH** 保存 **2 ~ sth** to be the place where sth is kept or where sth operates from 是（某物）的贮藏处（或安置处）；收藏；安置: *The gallery houses 2 000 works of modern art.* 美术馆收藏了 2 000 件现代艺术作品。 ◇ *The museum is housed in the Old Court House.* 博物馆设在旧法院大楼里。

'house arrest *noun* [U] the state of being a prisoner in your own house rather than in a prison 软禁: ***to be under house arrest*** 遭到软禁 ◇ *She was **placed under house arrest**.* 她遭到了软禁。

house·boat /'haʊsbəʊt; *NAmE* -boʊt/ *noun* a boat that people can live in, usually kept at a particular place on a river or CANAL 供居住的船；水上住宅 ➲ VISUAL VOCAB PAGE V16

house·bound /'haʊsbaʊnd/ *adj.* **1** unable to leave your house because you cannot walk very far as a result of being ill/sick or old（因病或年迈）不能离家的，出不了门的 **2 the housebound** *noun* [pl.] people who are housebound 出不了门的人

house·boy /'haʊsbɔɪ/ *noun* a young male servant in a house 年轻男仆

house·break·ing /'haʊsbreɪkɪŋ/ *noun* [U] (*especially BrE*) the crime of entering a house illegally by using force, in order to steal things from it 入室行窃 SYN **burglary** ▸ **house·break·er** /'haʊsbreɪkə(r)/ *noun*

'house-broken (*NAmE*) (*BrE* **'house-trained**) *adj.* (of pet cats or dogs 宠物猫或狗) trained to DEFECATE and URINATE outside the house or in a special box 经训练在户外（或专用盒子里）便溺的

house·coat /'haʊskəʊt; *NAmE* -koʊt/ *noun* a long loose piece of clothing, worn in the house by women（女式）家居袍

'house dust mite *noun* = DUST MITE

house·fly /'haʊsflaɪ/ *noun* (*pl.* **-ies**) a common fly that lives in houses 家蝇

house·ful /'haʊsfʊl/ *noun* [sing.] a large number of people in a house 一大家人；满屋子人: *He grew up in a houseful of women.* 他在一个满是女人的家庭里长大。 ◇ *They had a houseful so we didn't stay.* 他们满屋子都是人，所以我们没有留下来。

'house guest *noun* a person who is staying in your house for a short time 在家小住的客人

house·hold /'haʊshəʊld; *NAmE* -hoʊld/ *noun* all the people living together in a house or flat/apartment 一家人；家庭；同住一所（或一套）房子的人: *Most households now own at least one car.* 大多数家庭现在至少有一辆汽车。 ◇ ***low-income/one-parent, etc. households*** 低收入、单亲等家庭 ◇ *the **head of the household*** 户主 ▸ **house·hold** *adj.* [only before noun]: ***household bills/chores/goods*** (= connected with looking after a house and the people living in it) 家庭账单 / 杂务 / 用品

house·hold·er /'haʊshəʊldə(r); *NAmE* -hoʊld-/ *noun* (*formal*) a person who owns or rents the house that they live in 房主；住户

household 'name (*also less frequent* **household 'word**) *noun* a name that has become very well known 家喻户晓的名字: *She became a household name in the 1960s.* 她在 20 世纪 60 年代成为家喻户晓的人物。

'house-hunting *noun* [U] the activity of looking for a house to buy 找房子，看房子（以便购买） ▸ **'house-hunter** *noun*

H

ˈ**house husband** *noun* a man who stays at home to cook, clean, take care of the children, etc. while his wife or partner goes out to work 操持家务的丈夫；"家庭主夫" ➲ COMPARE HOUSEWIFE

house·keep·er /ˈhaʊskiːpə(r)/ *noun* **1** a person, usually a woman, whose job is to manage the shopping, cooking, cleaning, etc. in a house or an institution 管家，杂务主管（通常为女性） **2** a person whose job is to manage the cleaning of rooms in a hotel （旅馆的）房间清洁工

house·keep·ing /ˈhaʊskiːpɪŋ/ *noun* [U] **1** the work involved in taking care of a house, especially shopping and managing money 家务（尤指采购和管理开支） **2** the department in a hotel, a hospital, an office building, etc. that is responsible for cleaning the rooms, etc. （旅馆、医院、写字楼等的）总务处，后勤部： *Call housekeeping and ask them to bring us some clean towels.* 给总务处打电话，让他们给我们送些干净的毛巾来。 **3** (*also* ˈ**house-keeping money** *especially in BrE*) the money used to buy food, cleaning materials and other things needed for taking care of a house 家务开支 **4** jobs that are done to enable an organization or computer system to work well 内务处理： *Most large companies now use computers for accounting and housekeeping operations.* 多数大公司现在用计算机进行会计运算和内务操作。

house·maid /ˈhaʊsmeɪd/ *noun* (*old-fashioned*) a female servant in a large house who cleans the rooms, etc. and often lives there （家庭的）女仆，女佣

house·man /ˈhaʊsmən/ *noun* (*pl.* **-men** /-mən/) **1** (*old-fashioned, BrE*) = HOUSE OFFICER **2** (*NAmE*) a man employed to do general jobs in a house, hotel, etc. （家庭或旅馆等的）男勤杂工，男仆

ˈ**house martin** *noun* a small black and white European bird like a SWALLOW 毛脚燕（欧洲燕子）

house·mas·ter /ˈhaʊsmɑːstə(r); *NAmE* -mæs-/, **house·mis·tress** /ˈhaʊsmɪstrəs/ *noun* (*especially BrE*) a teacher in charge of a group of children (called a HOUSE) in a school, especially a private school （尤指私立学校的）舍监

house·mate /ˈhaʊsmeɪt/ *noun* a person that you share a house with, but who is not one of your family 同屋（指同住一所房子但非家庭成员的人）

ˈ**house music** (*also* **house**) *noun* [U] a type of electronic dance music with a fast beat 货仓音乐，浩室音乐（一种快节奏电子舞曲）

ˌ**house of ˈcards** *noun* [sing.] **1** a plan, an organization, etc. that is so badly arranged that it could easily fail 不可靠的计划；摇摇欲坠的组织 **2** a structure built out of PLAYING CARDS 用纸牌搭成的房子

the ˌHouse of ˈCommons (*also* **the Com·mons**) *noun* **1** [sing.+sing./pl. v.] (in Britain and Canada) the part of Parliament whose members are elected by the people of the country （英国）下议院；（加拿大）众议院 **2** [sing.] the building where the members of the House of Commons meet 下议院大楼 ➲ COMPARE HOUSE OF LORDS

ˈ**house officer** *noun* (in Britain) a doctor who has finished medical school and who is working at a hospital to get further practical experience （英国的）见习医生；实习医生 ➲ COMPARE INTERN *n.* (1)

ˌ**house of ˈGod** *noun* [usually sing.] (*pl.* **houses of God**) (*literary*) a church or other religious building 教堂；宗教建筑

the ˌHouse of ˈLords (*also* **the Lords**) *noun* **1** [sing.+sing./pl. v.] (in Britain) the part of Parliament whose members are not elected by the people of the country （英国）上议院，贵族院 **2** [sing.] the building where members of the House of Lords meet 上议院大楼 ➲ COMPARE HOUSE OF COMMONS

the ˌHouse of Repreˈsentatives *noun* [sing.] the larger part of Congress in the US, or of the Parliament in Australia, whose members are elected by the people of the country （美国国会或澳大利亚议会的）众议院 ➲ COMPARE SENATE (1) ➲ **WORDFINDER NOTE** AT CONGRESS

ˈ**house party** *noun* a party held at a large house in the country where guests stay for a few days; the guests at this party 乡村府邸聚会，乡村府邸聚会的全体宾客（常留宿几天）

house·plant /ˈhaʊsplɑːnt; *NAmE* -plænt/ (*BrE also* ˈ**pot plant**) *noun* a plant that you grow in a pot and keep indoors 室内盆栽植物 ➲ **VISUAL VOCAB** PAGE V22

ˈ**house-proud** *adj.* spending a lot of time making your house look clean and attractive, and thinking that this is important 热衷于收拾家的

house·room /ˈhaʊsruːm; -rʊm/ *noun* [U] space in a house for sb/sth 家里的容纳空间；家里放东西的地方

IDM **not give sth ˈhouseroom** (*BrE*) to not like sth and not want it in your house 不喜欢把某物放在家里

ˈ**house-sit** *verb* (**house-sitting**, **house-sat**, **house-sat**) [I] to live in sb's house while they are away in order to take care of it for them （屋主外出时）代为照看房子

the ˌHouses of ˈParliament *noun* [pl.] (in Britain 英国) the Parliament that consists of both the HOUSE OF COMMONS and the HOUSE OF LORDS; the buildings in London where the British Parliament meets （包括上、下议院的）议会；（伦敦）议会大厦

ˌ**house ˈstyle** *noun* [U, C] the way a company such as a PUBLISHER prefers its written materials to be expressed and arranged （出版社等书面材料的）特有样式，特有风格

ˌ**house-to-ˈhouse** *adj.* [only before noun] visiting every house in a particular area 挨家挨户的： ***a house-to-house** collection/search* 挨家收集 / 搜查 ◇ *The police are making house-to-house enquiries.* 警察正在逐户调查。

ˈ**house-trained** (*BrE*) (*NAmE* ˈ**house-broken**) *adj.* (of pet cats or dogs 宠物猫或狗) trained to DEFECATE and URINATE outside the house or in a special box 经训练在户外（或专用盒子里）便溺的

house·wares /ˈhaʊsweəz; *NAmE* -werz/ *noun* [pl.] (*NAmE*) (in shops/stores 商店) small items used in the house, especially kitchen equipment 家用器皿；（尤指）厨房用具

ˈ**house-warming** *noun* a party given by sb who has just moved into a new house 乔迁聚会

house·wife /ˈhaʊswaɪf/ *noun* (*pl.* **-wives** /-waɪvz/) a woman who stays at home to cook, clean, take care of the children, etc. while her husband or partner goes out to work 主妇；家庭妇女 ➲ COMPARE HOUSE HUSBAND ▸ **house·wife·ly** *adj.*

house·work /ˈhaʊswɜːk; *NAmE* -wɜːrk/ *noun* [U] the work involved in taking care of a home and family, for example cleaning and cooking 家务劳动；家务事： *to do the housework* 做家务

hous·ing /ˈhaʊzɪŋ/ *noun* **1** [U] houses, flats/apartments, etc. that people live in, especially when referring to their type, price or condition （统称，尤指住房类型、价格、条件）住房，住宅： ***public/private housing*** 公共 / 私人住房 ◇ *poor housing conditions* 恶劣的居住条件 ◇ *the housing shortage* 住房短缺 ◇ ***the housing market*** (= the activity of buying and selling houses, etc.) 住房市场 **2** [U] the job of providing houses, flats/apartments, etc. for people to live in 住房供给： *the housing department* 住房建设部门 ◇ *the council's housing policy* 市政住房政策 **3** [C] a hard cover that protects part of a machine （机器的）外壳，套： *a car's rear axle housing* 汽车的后轴套

ˈ**housing association** *noun* (in Britain) an organization that owns houses, flats/apartments, etc. and helps people to rent or buy them at a low price （英国）房屋协会（以低价出租或出售房屋）

ˈhousing benefit *noun* [U, C] (in Britain) money given by the government to people who do not earn much, to help them pay for a place to live in （英国）住房补贴

ˈhousing estate (*BrE*) (*also* **ˈhousing development** *NAmE, BrE*) *noun* an area in which a large number of houses or flats/apartments are planned and built together at the same time （统建的）住宅区，住宅群：*They live on a housing estate.* 他们住在一个住宅区里。 ➲ MORE LIKE THIS 9, page R26

ˈhousing project (*also* **pro·ject**) (*both NAmE*) *noun* a group of houses or flats/apartments built for poor families, usually with government money 公房项目；公房区（常由政府为贫困家庭建造）

hove PAST TENSE, PAST PART. OF HEAVE

hovel /ˈhɒvl; *NAmE* ˈhʌvl/ *noun* (*disapproving*) a house or room that is not fit to live in because it is dirty or in very bad condition （不适于居住的）肮脏简陋的住所

hover /ˈhɒvə(r); *NAmE* ˈhʌvər/ *verb* **1** [I] (+ **adv./prep.**) (of birds, HELICOPTERS, etc. 鸟、直升机等) to stay in the air in one place 翱翔；盘旋：*A hawk hovered over the hill.* 一只鹰在小山的上空翱翔。 **2** [I] (+ **adv./prep.**) (of a person 人) to wait somewhere, especially near sb, in a shy or uncertain manner 踌躇，彷徨（尤指在某人身边）：*He hovered nervously in the doorway.* 他在门口紧张地来回踱步。 **3** [I] + **adv./prep.** to stay close to sth, or to stay in an uncertain state 靠近（某事物）；处于不稳定状态：*Temperatures hovered around freezing.* 气温在冰点上下徘徊。◇ *He hovered on the edge of consciousness.* 他似醒非醒。◇ *A smile hovered on her lips.* 她的嘴上挂着一丝笑容。

hov·er·craft /ˈhɒvəkrɑːft; *NAmE* ˈhʌvərkræft/ *noun* a vehicle that travels just above the surface of water or land, held up by air being forced downwards 气垫船；气垫运载工具 ➲ VISUAL VOCAB PAGE V59 ➲ COMPARE HYDROFOIL

ˌHOˈV lane /ˌeɪtʃ əʊ ˈviː leɪn; *NAmE* oʊ/ *noun* (*especially NAmE*) high-occupancy vehicle lane (a part of the road that may only be used by vehicles that are carrying two or more people) 多乘员车辆车道（仅供搭载两人及以上的车辆通行）

how 🔑 /haʊ/ *adv.* **1** 🔑 in what way or manner 怎样；如何：*How does it work?* 它是如何运作的？◇ *He did not know how he ought to behave.* 他不知道自己应该怎样表现。◇ *I'll show you how to load the software.* 我给你演示一下如何安装这套软件。◇ *'Her behaviour was very odd.' 'How so?'* "她的举止非常奇怪。" "怎么会这样呢？" ◇ *It's funny how (= that) people always remember him.* 有趣的是人们总是忘不了他。◇ *Do you* ***remember how*** *(= that) the kids always loved going there?* 你记得孩子们总喜欢去那里吗？◇ ***How ever*** *did you get here so quickly?* 你这么快来到这儿，究竟是怎么办到的？ ➲ COMPARE HOWEVER **2** 🔑 used to ask about sb's health （询问健康状况）：*How are you?* 你（身体）好吗？◇ *How are you feeling now?* 你现在感觉怎么样？ **3** 🔑 used to ask whether sth is successful or enjoyable （询问是否成功或愉快）：*How was your trip?* 你旅行愉快吗？◇ *How did they play?* 他们的比赛表现怎样？ **4** 🔑 used before an adjective or adverb to ask about the amount, degree, etc. of sth, or about sb's age （后接形容词或副词）多少，多么，多大：***How often*** *do you go swimming?* 你多久去游一次泳？◇ *I didn't know how much to bring.* 我不知道该带多少。◇ ***How much*** *are those earrings (= What do they cost)?* 那对耳环多少钱？◇ ***How many*** *people were there?* 有多少人？◇ *How old is she?* 她有多大了？ **5** 🔑 used to express surprise, pleasure, etc. （表示惊奇、高兴等）：*How kind of you to help!* 你来帮忙，真是太好了！◇ *How he wished he had been there!* 他多么希望当时自己也在场！ **6** 🔑 in any way in which 以任何方式；无论用什么方法 SYN **however**：*I'll dress how I like in my own house!* 我在自己家里爱怎么穿就怎么穿！

IDM **how about...?** **1** 🔑 used when asking for information about sb/sth （询问信息）…怎么样？，…情况如何？：*I'm not going. How about you?* 我不打算去。你呢？ **2** 🔑 used to make a suggestion （提出建议）…怎么样，…行不行，…好吗：*How about a break?* 休息一下好吗？◇ *How about going for a meal?* 去吃饭好不好？◇ (*especially NAmE*) *How about we go for a meal?* 我们去吃饭好不好？ **how ˈcan/ˈcould you!** (*informal*) used to show that you strongly disapprove of sb's behaviour or are very surprised by it （表示很不赞同或吃惊）你怎么能：*Ben! How could you? After all they've done for us!* 本！他们为我们做了这么多，你怎么能这样！◇ *Ugh! How can you eat that stuff?* 啊！你怎么吃得下那种东西？ **ˌhow do you ˈdo** 🔑 (*becoming old-fashioned*) used as a formal GREETING when you meet sb for the first time. The usual reply is also *How do you do?* （首次见面时的问候语。通常的回答也是 How do you do?）你好 **ˌhow's ˈthat?** (*informal*) **1** used to ask the reason for sth 为什么；怎么会：*'I left work early today.' 'How's that (= Why)?'* "我今天提前下班了。" "为什么？" **2** used when asking sb's opinion of sth （你认为）怎么样，如何：*I'll tuck your sheets in for you. How's that? Comfortable?* 我给你把被单掖好吧。怎么样？舒服吗？◇ *Two o'clock on the dot!* ***How's that for punctuality!*** 两点整！够守时吧！ ➲ MORE AT COME *v.*

how·dah /ˈhaʊdə/ *noun* a seat for riding on the back of an ELEPHANT or a CAMEL, often for more than one person 象轿，驼轿（大象或骆驼背上的鞍座，常常可坐不止一人）

howdy /ˈhaʊdi/ *exclamation* (*NAmE, informal, often humorous*) used to say hello （招呼语）你好：*Howdy, partner.* 你好，伙计。

how·ever 🔑 /haʊˈevə(r)/ *adv.* **1** 🔑 used with an adjective or adverb to mean 'to whatever degree' （与形容词或副词连用）无论到什么程度，不管多么：*He wanted to take no risks, however small.* 他再小的风险也不想冒。◇ *She has the window open, however cold it is outside.* 不管外面多冷她都开着窗户。◇ *However carefully I explained, she still didn't understand.* 无论我解释得多么仔细，她还是没弄懂。 HELP When **ever** is used to emphasize **how**, meaning 'In what way or manner?', it is usually written as a separate word. 用 ever 来强调 how（意为"以何种方式"）时 ever 通常要写作单独的一个词：***How ever*** *did you get here so quickly?* 你这么快来到这儿，究竟是怎么办到的？ **2** 🔑 in whatever way 不管怎样；无论如何：*However you look at it, it's going to cost a lot.* 不管你怎么看，它都要花很多钱。 **3** 🔑 used to introduce a statement that contrasts with sth that has just been said 然而；

▼ LANGUAGE BANK 用语库

however

Ways of saying 'but' "但是"的表达方式

- *Politicians have promised to improve road safety. So far,* ***however****, little has been achieved.* 政客们承诺要加强道路安全。但是，迄今为止成效微乎其微。
- ***Despite*** *clear evidence from road safety studies, no new measures have been introduced.* 尽管道路安全研究已得出确切依据，但仍未实施任何新措施。
- *Politicians have promised to improve road safety.* ***In spite of this*** */* ***Despite this****, little has been achieved so far.* 政客们承诺要加强道路安全。尽管如此，迄今为止成效微乎其微。
- ***Although*** *politicians have promised to improve road safety, little has been achieved so far.* 尽管政客们承诺要加强道路安全，但是迄今为止成效微乎其微。
- *Some politicians claim that the new transport policy has been a success.* ***In fact****, it has been a total disaster.* 一些政客宣称新的交通政策非常成功，实际上却是彻头彻尾的失败。
- *Government campaigns have had a measure of success,* ***but the fact remains that*** *large numbers of accidents are still caused by careless drivers.* 政府的宣传活动取得了一定的成功，但实际情况是大量的交通事故仍然是由于驾驶者疏忽造成的。

➲ LANGUAGE BANK AT NEVERTHELESS

不过；仍然： *He was feeling bad. He went to work, however, and tried to concentrate.* 他感觉不舒服，但他仍然去上班，并且努力集中精神工作。◇ *We thought the figures were correct. However, we have now discovered some errors.* 我们原以为这些数据正确，不过我们现在发现了一些错误。

how·itz·er /ˈhaʊɪtsə(r)/ *noun* a heavy gun that fires SHELLS high into the air for a short distance 榴弹炮

howl /haʊl/ *verb, noun*

■ *verb* **1** [I] (of a dog, WOLF, etc. 狗、狼等) to make a long, loud cry 长嚎；嗥叫 **2** [I] ~ **(in/with sth)** to make a loud cry when you are in pain, angry, amused, etc. (因疼痛、愤怒、开心等) 大声叫喊： *to howl in pain* 疼得直叫喊 ◇ *We howled with laughter.* 我们放声大笑。◇ *The baby was howling* (= crying loudly) *all the time I was there.* 我在那里时孩子一直哭得很厉害。 **3** [I] (of the wind 风) to blow hard and make a long loud noise 怒号；呼啸： *The wind was howling around the house.* 狂风在房子四周呼啸。 **4** [T] ~ **sth** | + **speech** to say sth loudly and angrily 怒吼： *The crowd howled its displeasure.* 群众不满地怒吼着。

PHR V ˌ**howl sb ↔ down** to prevent a speaker from being heard by shouting angrily 以怒吼声压倒讲演者的声音 **SYN** **shout sb ↔ down**

■ *noun* **1** a long loud cry made by a dog, WOLF, etc. (狗、狼等的) 嗥叫，长嚎 **2** a loud cry showing that you are in pain, angry, amused, etc. (因疼痛、愤怒、高兴等发出的) 喊叫声： *to let out a howl of anguish* 发出痛苦的喊叫声 ◇ *The suggestion was greeted with* ***howls of laughter***. 这个建议引起了阵阵大笑。 **3** a long loud sound made when the wind is blowing strongly (狂风的) 啸鸣，怒号： *They listened to the howl of the wind through the trees.* 他们听着风在林间呼啸的声音。

howl·er /ˈhaʊlə(r)/ *noun* (*informal, especially BrE*) a stupid mistake, especially in what sb says or writes (尤指言谈或行文中的) 愚蠢的错误 **SYN** **error**: *The report is full of howlers.* 这份报告错漏百出。 ➲ SYNONYMS AT MISTAKE

howl·ing /ˈhaʊlɪŋ/ *adj.* [only before noun] **1** (of a storm, etc. 风暴等) very violent, with strong winds 怒号的；猛烈的： *a* ***howling gale/storm/wind*** 怒吼着的大风 / 风暴 / 风 **2** (*informal*) very great or extreme 很大的；极端的： *a howling success* 轰动的成就 ◇ *She flew into a howling rage.* 她暴跳如雷。

ˈ**how-to** *adj.* [only before noun] providing detailed instructions or advice on how to do sth 指导的；指南的： *how-to books on computing* 计算机操作说明书 ▶ ˈ**how-to** *noun* (*pl.* **-os**)： *Visit our downloads page for free how-tos and tutorials.* 可到我们网页的下载区获取免费指南和教程。

how·zat /ˌhaʊˈzæt/ *exclamation* used in CRICKET to tell the UMPIRE that you think the other team's BATSMAN is out 怎么办 (告知板球裁判员对方击球手可判出局)

how·zit /ˈhaʊzɪt/ *exclamation* (*SAfrE, informal*) used to say hello when you meet sb (打招呼用语) 你好： *Howzit Mandla, how's it going?* 你好，曼德拉，怎么样啊？ ◇ *Please say howzit to Nicki for me.* 请代我向尼基问好。

h.p. /ˌeɪtʃ ˈpiː/ *abbr.* **1** HORSEPOWER 马力 **2** (*also* **HP**) (*BrE*) HIRE PURCHASE 分期付款购买

HQ /ˌeɪtʃ ˈkjuː/ *abbr.* HEADQUARTERS 总部： *See you back at HQ.* 回总部见。◇ *police HQ* 警察总局

HR /ˌeɪtʃ ˈɑː(r)/ *abbr.* HUMAN RESOURCES 人事部；人力资源部

hr /ˌeɪtʃ ˈɑː(r)/ (*also* **hr.** *especially in NAmE*) *abbr.* (*pl.* **hrs** or **hr**) (in writing 书写形式) hour 小时： *Cover and chill for 1 hr.* 盖上盖子冷却 1 小时。

HRH /ˌeɪtʃ ɑːr ˈeɪtʃ/ *abbr.* His/Her ROYAL HIGHNESS (他称) 殿下： *HRH Prince Harry* 哈里王子殿下

HRT /ˌeɪtʃ ɑː ˈtiː; *NAmE* ɑːr/ *noun* [U] the abbreviation for 'hormone replacement therapy' (medical treatment for women going through the MENOPAUSE in which HORMONES are added to the body) 激素替代治疗 (全写为 hormone replacement therapy，为更年期女性注射激素以提高体内雌激素水平)

Hsiang /ʃiːˈæŋ/ *noun* [U] = XIANG

HTH /ˌeɪtʃ tiː ˈeɪtʃ/ *abbr.* (especially in messages on Internet FORUMS, etc.) hope this helps 希望有帮助 (全写为 hope this helps，尤用于互联网论坛等的信息)： *You should be able to find information about courses on the institution's website. HTH* 你应该能在该机构的网站上找到课程信息。希望这能帮上忙。

HTML /ˌeɪtʃ tiː em ˈel/ *abbr.* (*computing* 计) Hypertext Markup Language (a system used to mark text for World Wide Web pages in order to obtain colours, style, pictures, etc.) 超文本置标语言；超文本标记语言

HTTP (*also* **http**) /ˌeɪtʃ tiː tiː ˈpiː/ *abbr.* (*computing* 计) Hypertext Transfer Protocol (the set of rules that control the way data is sent and received over the Internet) 超文本传送协议

hua·rache /wæˈrɑːtʃi; wəˈr-/ *noun* a type of SANDAL (= open shoe) made of many narrow strips of leather twisted together 皮条编织的凉鞋

hub /hʌb/ *noun* **1** [usually sing.] ~ **(of sth)** the central and most important part of a particular place or activity (某地或活动的) 中心，核心： *the commercial hub of the city* 城市的商业中心 ◇ *to be at the hub of things* (= where things happen and important decisions are made) 在核心部门 ◇ *a hub airport* (= a large important one where people often change from one plane to another) 枢纽机场 **2** the central part of a wheel 轮毂 ➲ VISUAL VOCAB PAGE V55

hub·bub /ˈhʌbʌb/ *noun* [sing., U] **1** the loud sound made by a lot of people talking at the same time 喧闹声；嘈杂声： *It was difficult to hear what he was saying over the hubbub.* 声音太嘈杂，难以听清楚他的讲话。 **2** a situation in which there is a lot of noise, excitement and activity 喧闹；骚乱；混乱： *the hubbub of city life* 闹哄哄的城市生活

hubby /ˈhʌbi/ *noun* (*pl.* **-ies**) (*informal*) = HUSBAND

hub·cap /ˈhʌbkæp/ *noun* a round metal cover that fits over the HUB of a vehicle's wheel (轮) 毂盖 ➲ VISUAL VOCAB PAGE V56

hu·bris /ˈhjuːbrɪs/ *noun* [U] (*literary*) the fact of sb being too proud. In literature, a character with this pride ignores warnings and laws and this usually results in their DOWNFALL and death. 傲慢；狂妄

huckle·berry /ˈhʌklbəri; *NAmE* -beri/ *noun* (*pl.* **-ies**) a small soft round purple N American fruit. The bush it grows on is also called a huckleberry. 美洲越橘；美洲越橘树

huck·ster /ˈhʌkstə(r)/ *noun* (*old-fashioned, NAmE*) **1** (*disapproving*) a person who uses aggressive or annoying methods to sell sth 强行推销的人 **2** a person who sells things in the street or by visiting people's houses 沿街叫卖的小贩；上门推销员

HUD /ˌeɪtʃ juː ˈdiː/ *abbr.* Department of Housing and Urban Development (the US government department in charge of financial programmes to build houses and to help people buy their own homes) (美国) 住房与城市发展部

hud·dle /ˈhʌdl/ *verb, noun*

■ *verb* **1** [I] ~ **(up/together)** (+ **adv./prep.**) (of people or animals 人或动物) to gather closely together, usually because of cold or fear (通常因寒冷或害怕) 挤在一起： *We huddled together for warmth.* 我们挤在一块取暖。◇ *They all huddled around the fire.* 他们都聚集在火堆周围。 **2** [I] ~ **(up)** (+ **adv./prep.**) to hold your arms and legs close to your body, usually because you are cold or frightened (通常因寒冷或害怕) 蜷缩，缩成一团： *I huddled under a blanket on the floor.* 我在地板上盖着毯子缩成一团。 ▶ **hud·dled** *adj.*： *People were huddled together around the fire.* 人们围着火堆。◇ *huddled figures in shop doorways* 商店门口蜷缩着的人影 ◇ *We found him huddled on the floor.* 我们发现他蜷缩在地板上。

■***noun*** **1** a small group of people, objects or buildings that are close together, especially when they are not in any particular order （尤指杂乱地）挤在一起的人（或物品、建筑）： *People stood around in huddles.* 人们三五成群地到处聚集着。◇ *The track led them to a huddle of outbuildings.* 那条小路把他们带到了一片杂乱拥挤的棚子。 **2** (in AMERICAN FOOTBALL 美式足球) a time when the players gather round to hear the plan for the next part of the game 队员靠拢（磋商战术）

IDM **get/go into a ˈhuddle (with sb)** to move close to sb so that you can talk about sth without other people hearing 凑近（某人）说悄悄话；交头接耳

hue /hjuː/ *noun* **1** (*literary* or *specialist*) a colour; a particular shade of a colour 颜色；色调；色相： *His face took on an unhealthy whitish hue.* 他的脸上透出一丝病态的苍白。◇ *Her paintings capture the subtle hues of the countryside in autumn.* 她的油画捕捉住了秋天乡村的微妙色调。 ➲ SYNONYMS AT COLOUR **2** (*formal*) a type of belief or opinion 信仰；观点： *supporters of every political hue* 各种政治信仰的拥护者

IDM **ˌhue and ˈcry** strong public protest about sth 公众的强烈抗议

huff /hʌf/ *verb, noun*

■***verb*** [T, I] **(+ speech)** to say sth or make a noise in a way that shows you are offended or annoyed 生气地说；怒气冲冲： *'Well, nobody asked you,' she huffed irritably.* "哼，谁问你了。"她怒气冲冲地说。

IDM **ˌhuff and ˈpuff** (*informal*) **1** to breathe in a noisy way because you are very tired 气喘吁吁；上气不接下气： *Jack was huffing and puffing to keep up with her.* 杰克气喘吁吁地跟着她。 **2** to make it obvious that you are annoyed about sth without doing anything to change the situation 发脾气；愤然不理；生闷气；气呼呼： *After much huffing and puffing, she finally agreed to help.* 她生了好一阵闷气之后才终于同意帮忙。 ➲ MORE LIKE THIS 12, page R26

■***noun***

IDM **in a ˈhuff** (*informal*) in a bad mood, especially because sb has annoyed or upset you 怒气冲冲；生气： *She went off in a huff.* 她怒气冲冲地走了。

huffy /ˈhʌfi/ *adj.* (*informal*) in a bad mood, especially because sb has annoyed or upset you 生气的；发怒的 ▸ **huff·ily** *adv.*

hug /hʌɡ/ *verb, noun*

■***verb*** **(-gg-)** **1** [T, I] **~ (sb)** to put your arms around sb and hold them tightly, especially to show that you like or love them 拥抱；搂抱 **SYN** **embrace**: *They hugged each other.* 他们相互拥抱。◇ *She hugged him tightly.* 她紧紧地搂住他。 ◇ *They put their arms around each other and hugged.* 他们伸出双臂彼此拥抱。 **2** [T] **~ sth** to put your arms around sth and hold it close to your body 抱紧： *She sat in the chair, hugging her knees.* 她双臂抱膝坐在椅子上。◇ *He hugged the hot-water bottle to his chest.* 他把热水袋紧捂在胸口。 **3** [T] **~ sth** (of a path, vehicle, etc. 小路、车辆等) to keep close to sth for a distance 有一段距离地挨着（某物）： *The track hugs the coast for a mile.* 那条小径离海岸只有一英里。 **4** [T] **~ sth** to fit tightly around sth, especially a person's body 缠紧，缚紧（某物，尤指人体）： *figure-hugging jeans* 紧身牛仔裤 ➲ MORE LIKE THIS 36, page R29

■***noun*** an act of putting your arms around sb and holding them tightly, especially to show that you like or love them 拥抱；搂抱： *She gave her mother a big hug.* 她热烈地拥抱了她的母亲。◇ *He stopped to receive* ***hugs and kisses*** *from the fans.* 他停下来接受追随者的拥抱亲吻。 ➲ SEE ALSO BEAR HUG

huge 🔑 /hjuːdʒ/ *adj.* **1** 🔑 extremely large in size or amount; great in degree 巨大的；极多的；程度高的 **SYN** **enormous, vast**: *a huge crowd* 庞大的人群 ◇ *He gazed up at her with huge brown eyes.* 他睁着棕色的大眼睛盯着她。◇ *huge debts* 巨债 ◇ *huge amounts of data* 超大量的数据 ◇ *The sums of money involved are potentially huge.* 涉及的金额可能很大。 ◇ *The party was a huge success.* 聚会办得非常成功。◇ *This is going to be a huge problem for us.* 这将是我们的一大难题。 **2** (*informal*) very successful 非常成功的；走红的： *I think this band is going to be huge.* 我想这个乐队要走红了。

huge·ly /ˈhjuːdʒli/ *adv.* **1** extremely 极度；极其： *hugely entertaining/important/popular/successful* 极其有趣 / 重要 / 受欢迎 / 成功 **2** very much 非常；深深地；大大地： *They intended to invest hugely in new technology.* 他们打算在新技术方面投入大量资金。 ◇ *He turned around, grinning hugely.* 他转过身来，咧着嘴乐。

huh /hʌ/ *exclamation* **1** people use **Huh?** at the end of questions, suggestions, etc., especially when they want sb to agree with them （用于问题、建议等之后，尤希望对方同意）： *So you won't be coming tonight, huh?* 那么你今晚就不来了吗，嗯？ ◇ *Let's get out of here, huh?* 我们离开这里吧，嗯？ **2** people say **Huh!** to show anger, surprise, disagreement, etc. or to show that they are not impressed by sth （表示愤怒、惊奇、异议等，或认为没有什么了不起）： *Huh! Is that all you've done?* 噢！你做的就是这么多了吗？ **3** (*NAmE*) (*BrE* **eh**) people say **Huh?** to show that they have not heard what sb has just said （表示没有听清楚）： *'Are you feeling OK?' 'Huh?'* "你感觉好吗？""啊？" ➲ MORE LIKE THIS 2, page R25

hula hoop (*US* **Hula-Hoop™**) /ˈhuːlə huːp/ *noun* a large plastic ring that you spin around your waist by moving your hips 呼啦圈

hulk /hʌlk/ *noun* **1** the main part of an old vehicle, especially a ship, that is no longer used （车、船等的）残骸： *the hulk of a wrecked ship* 遇难轮船的残骸 **2** a very large person, especially one who moves in an awkward way 高大的人；（尤指）高大粗笨的人： *a great hulk of a man* 粗笨的大汉 **3** a very large object, especially one that causes you to feel nervous or afraid （尤指令人紧张或害怕的）庞然大物

hulk·ing /ˈhʌlkɪŋ/ *adj.* [only before noun] very large or heavy, often in a way that causes you to feel nervous or afraid 很大的；很沉重的；大得吓人的： *a hulking figure crouching in the darkness* 黑暗中蹲伏着的一个庞大身影 ◇ *I don't want that hulking great computer in my office.* 我不要把那台又笨又大的计算机放在我的办公室。

hull /hʌl/ *noun, verb*

■***noun*** the main, bottom part of a ship, that goes in the water 船身；船体： ***a wooden/steel hull*** 木质 / 钢质船体 ◇ *They climbed onto the upturned hull and waited to be rescued.* 他们爬上了倾覆的船体，等候救援。 ➲ VISUAL VOCAB PAGE V59

■***verb*** **~ sth** to remove the outer covering of PEAS, BEANS, etc. or the ring of leaves attached to STRAWBERRIES 剥去（豌豆、大豆等）的外壳；摘掉（草莓）的花萼

hul·la·ba·loo /ˌhʌləbəˈluː/ *noun* [sing.] a lot of loud noise, especially made by people who are annoyed or excited about sth 嘈杂；喧闹；吵闹声 **SYN** **commotion, uproar**

hullo (*especially BrE*) = HELLO

hum /hʌm/ *verb, noun*

■***verb*** **(-mm-)** **1** [I, T] to sing a tune with your lips closed 哼（曲子）： *She was humming softly to herself.* 她在轻声哼着曲子。◇ **~ sth** *What's that tune you're humming?* 你哼的是什么曲子？ ➲ COLLOCATIONS AT MUSIC **2** [I] to make a low continuous sound 发嗡嗡声： *The computers were humming away.* 计算机在嗡嗡作响。 **3** [I] to be full of activity 活跃；繁忙： *The streets were beginning to hum with life.* 街道开始热闹起来。

IDM **ˌhum and ˈhaw** (*BrE*) (*NAmE* **ˌhem and ˈhaw**) (*informal*) to take a long time to make a decision or before you say sth 犹豫不决；支支吾吾；嗯嗯呃呃

■***noun*** [sing.] **~ (of sth)** a low continuous sound 嗡嗡声；嘈杂声： *the* ***hum of bees/traffic/voices*** 蜜蜂的嗡嗡声；车辆的鸣鸣声；人的嘈杂声 ◇ *The room filled with the hum of conversation.* 房间里充满了嘈杂的谈话声。

human 🔑 /ˈhjuːmən/ *adj., noun*

■***adj.*** **1** 🔑 [only before noun] of or connected with people rather than animals, machines or gods 人的： *the human* *body/brain* 人体；人脑 ◇ *human anatomy/activity/behaviour/experience* 人体解剖学；人的活动 / 行为 / 经历 ◇ *a terrible loss of **human life*** 生命的惨重损失 ◇ *Contact with other people is a basic **human need**.* 和他人接触是人的基本需要。◇ *This food is not fit for **human consumption**.* 这种食物不适合人食用。◇ ***human geography*** (= the study of the way different people live around the world) 人文地理学 ◇ *The hostages were used as a **human shield*** (= a person or group of people that is forced to stay in a particular place where they would be hurt or killed if their country attacked it). 人质被当成了人体盾牌。◇ *Fire-fighters formed a **human chain*** (= a line of people) *to carry the children to safety.* 消防队员组成人链把孩子们救到了安全的地方。◇ ***Human remains*** (= the body of a dead person) *were found inside the house.* 在房子里发现了尸体。 **2** showing the weaknesses that are typical of people, which means that other people should not criticize the person too much 显示人类特有弱点的；人本性的： *human weaknesses/failings* 人性的弱点 / 缺点 ◇ *We must allow for **human error**.* 我们必须考虑到人为的失误。◇ ***It's only human** to want the best for your children.* 为自己的孩子谋求最好的条件是人之常情。 **3** having the same feelings and emotions as most ordinary people 有人情味的；通人情的： *He's really very human when you get to know him.* 你若了解他，就知道他确实很有人情味。◇ *The public is always attracted to politicians who have **the human touch*** (= the ability to make ordinary people feel relaxed when they meet them). 公众总是对平易近人的政治人物有好感。 ➲ COMPARE INHUMAN, NON-HUMAN

IDM the 'human face of... a person who is involved in a subject, issue, etc. and makes it easier for ordinary people to understand and have sympathy with it （某主题、话题等的）标志性人物： *He is the human face of party politics.* 他是政党政治的标志性人物。 **with a human 'face** that considers the needs of ordinary people 考虑老百姓需要的；有人情味的；人性化的： *This was science with a human face.* 这是大众需要的科学。 ➲ MORE AT MILK *n.*

■ ***noun*** (*also* **ˌhuman 'being**) a person rather than an animal or a machine 人： *Dogs can hear much better than humans.* 狗的听觉比人灵敏得多。◇ *That is no way to treat another human being.* 那绝不是对待他人的方式。

hu·mane /hjuːˈmeɪn/ *adj.* showing kindness towards people and animals by making sure that they do not suffer more than is necessary 善良的；仁慈的；人道的： *a caring and humane society* 充满关怀和人道的社会 ◇ *the humane treatment of refugees* 人道地对待难民 ◇ *the humane killing of animals* 对动物的人道毁灭 **OPP inhumane** ▶ **hu·mane·ly** *adv.*： *to treat sb humanely* 仁慈地对待某人 ◇ *meat that has been humanely produced* 通过无痛屠宰法生产的肉 ◇ *The dog was humanely destroyed.* 那条狗被人道毁灭了。

ˌhuman 'interest *noun* [U] the part of a story in a newspaper, etc. that people find interesting because it describes the experiences, feelings, etc. of the people involved （新闻报道等中的）人情味

hu·man·ism /ˈhjuːmənɪzəm/ *noun* [U] a system of thought that considers that solving human problems with the help of reason is more important than religious beliefs. It emphasizes the fact that the basic nature of humans is good. 人文主义 ▶ **hu·man·is·tic** /ˌhjuːməˈnɪstɪk/ *adj.*： *humanistic ideals* 人文主义理想

hu·man·ist /ˈhjuːmənɪst/ *noun* a person who believes in humanism 人文主义者

hu·mani·tar·ian /hjuːˌmænɪˈteəriən; *NAmE* -ˈter-/ *adj.* [usually before noun] concerned with reducing suffering and improving the conditions that people live in 人道主义的（主张减轻人类苦难、改善人类生活）；慈善的： *to provide **humanitarian aid** to the war zone* 给战区提供人道主义援助 ◇ *humanitarian issues* 人道主义问题 ◇ *a humanitarian organization* 慈善机构 ◇ *They are calling for the release of the hostages on **humanitarian grounds**.* 他们站在人道主义立场要求释放人质。◇ *The expulsion of thousands of people represents a humanitarian catastrophe of enormous proportions.* 驱逐成千上万人意味着人道主义的巨大灾难。 ▶ **hu·mani·tar·ian** *noun* **hu·mani·tar·ian·ism** /-ɪzəm/ *noun* [U]

hu·man·ity /hjuːˈmænəti/ *noun* **1** [U] people in general （统称）人；人类： *crimes against humanity* 危害人类罪 ➲ NOTE AT GENDER **2** [U] the state of being a person rather than a god, an animal or a machine 人性： *The story was used to emphasize the humanity of Jesus.* 人们用这个故事来强调耶稣人性的一面。◇ *united by a sense of common humanity* 因一种同是人的情感而团结在一起 **3** [U] the quality of being kind to people and animals by making sure that they do not suffer more than is necessary; the quality of being HUMANE 人道；仁慈： *The judge was praised for his courage and humanity.* 法官的勇气和人道受到称赞。 **OPP inhumanity 4 (the) humanities** [pl.] the subjects of study that are concerned with the way people think and behave, for example literature, language, history and philosophy 人文学科 ➲ COMPARE SCIENCE (3)

hu·man·ize (*BrE also* **-ise**) /ˈhjuːmənaɪz/ *verb* **~ sth** to make sth more pleasant or suitable for people; to make sth more HUMANE 使更适合人；使更人道： *These measures are intended to humanize the prison system.* 这些措施的目的是使监狱体制更人性化。

hu·man·kind /ˌhjuːmənˈkaɪnd/ *noun* [U] people in general （统称）人；人类 ➲ SEE ALSO MANKIND

hu·man·ly /ˈhjuːmənli/ *adv.* within human ability; in a way that is typical of human behaviour, thoughts and feelings 在人力所能及的范围内；以人特有的方式： *The doctors did all that was **humanly possible**.* 医生们尽了人力所及的最大努力。◇ *He couldn't humanly refuse to help her.* 从人道角度，他不能拒绝帮助她。

ˌhuman 'nature *noun* [U] the ways of behaving, thinking and feeling that are shared by most people and are considered to be normal 人性： *Her kindness has restored my faith in human nature* (= the belief that people are good). 她的善良使我重新燃起了对人性的信心。◇ ***It's only human nature** to be worried about change.* 对变革有忧虑不过是人之常情。

hu·man·oid /ˈhjuːmənɔɪd/ *noun* a machine or creature that looks and behaves like a human 仿真机器人；类人动物 ▶ **hu·man·oid** *adj.*

the ˌhuman 'race *noun* [sing.] all people, considered together as a group 人类

ˌhuman re'sources *noun* **1** [pl.] people's skills and abilities, seen as sth a company, an organization, etc. can make use of 人力资源 **2** (*abbr.* **HR**) [U+sing./pl. v.] the department in a company that deals with employing and training people （公司的）人事部，人力资源部 **SYN personnel**： *the human resources director* 人事部主管

ˌhuman 'right *noun* [usually pl.] one of the basic rights that everyone has to be treated fairly and not in a cruel way, especially by their government 人权： *The country has a poor record on human rights.* 这个国家人权记录不佳。◇ *to campaign for human rights* 争取人权 ◇ ***human rights abuses/violations*** 对人权的侵犯 / 践踏 ➲ WORDFINDER NOTE AT EQUAL

hum·ble /ˈhʌmbl/ *adj., verb*

■ ***adj.*** (**hum·bler** /ˈhʌmblə(r)/, **hum·blest** /ˈhʌmblɪst/) **1** showing you do not think that you are as important as other people 谦逊的；虚心的 **SYN modest**： *Be humble enough to learn from your mistakes.* 要虚心地从自己的错误中学习。◇ *my humble tribute to this great man* 鄙人对这位伟人的敬意 ➲ SEE ALSO HUMILITY **2** (*ironic* or *humorous*) used to suggest that you are not as important as other people, but in a way that is not sincere or not very serious （表示谦逊，但不够诚挚或认真）： ***In my humble opinion**, you were in the wrong.* 依拙见，你错了。◇ ***My humble apologies**. I did not understand.* 对不起。我没有弄懂。 **3** having a low rank or social position （级别或地位）低下的，卑微的： *a man of **humble birth/origins*** 出身低微的人 ◇ *a humble occupation* 卑下的职业 ◇ *the daughter of a humble shopkeeper* 一位小店主的女儿 **4** (of a thing 事物) not large or special in any way 不大的；没有特别之处的 **SYN** **modest**: *a humble farmhouse* 小农舍 ◇ *The company has worked its way up from humble beginnings to become the market leader.* 公司已从创业期的微不足道发展成了市场的主导者。 ▶ **hum·bly** /ˈhʌmbli/ *adv.*: *I would humbly suggest that there is something wrong here.* 愚以为这里有点错误。 ◇ *'Sorry,' she said humbly.* "对不起。"她谦逊地说。 **IDM** SEE EAT

■ *verb* **1** ~ **sb** to make sb feel that they are not as good or important as they thought they were 贬低；使感到卑微： *He was humbled by her generosity.* 她的大度使他觉得自己渺小。 ◇ *a humbling experience* 一次令人惭愧的经历 **2** [usually passive] ~ **sb** to easily defeat an opponent, especially a strong or powerful one 轻松打败（尤指强大的对手）： *The world champion was humbled last night in three rounds.* 这位世界冠军昨晚三个回合就被轻松击败。 **3** ~ **yourself** to show that you are not too proud to ask for sth, admit that you have been wrong, etc. 低声下气；谦逊；虚心 ➲ SEE ALSO HUMILITY

hum·bug /ˈhʌmbʌg/ *noun* **1** [U] (*old-fashioned*) dishonest language or behaviour that is intended to trick people 谎言；骗人的把戏；欺骗行为： *political humbug* 政治骗术 **2** [C] (*old-fashioned*) a person who is not sincere or honest 虚伪的人 **3** [C] (*BrE*) a hard sweet/candy made from boiled sugar, especially one that tastes of PEPPERMINT 硬糖；（尤指）薄荷糖

hum·ding·er /ˌhʌmˈdɪŋə(r)/ *noun* [sing.] (*informal*) something that is very exciting or impressive 令人兴奋的事物；出色的事物： *It turned into a real humdinger of a game.* 那场比赛变得扣人心弦。

hum·drum /ˈhʌmdrʌm/ *adj.* boring and always the same 乏味的；单调的 **SYN** **dull, tedious**: ***a humdrum existence/job/life*** 平淡的生活；乏味的工作 / 生活

hu·mec·tant /hjuːˈmektənt; *NAmE also* juː-/ *noun* (*specialist*) **1** a substance added to foods to stop them from becoming dry （保藏食物用的）保湿剂 **2** a substance added to skin cream to stop your skin from being dry （护肤霜中的）保湿剂

hu·merus /ˈhjuːmərəs/ *noun* (*pl.* **hu·meri** /ˈhjuːməraɪ/) (*anatomy* 解) the large bone in the top part of the arm between the shoulder and the elbow 肱骨 ➲ VISUAL VOCAB PAGE V64

humid /ˈhjuːmɪd/ *adj.* (of the air or climate 空气或气候) warm and damp 温暖潮湿的；湿热的： *These ferns will grow best in a humid atmosphere.* 这些蕨类植物在湿热的环境中长得最旺。 ◇ *The island is hot and humid in the summer.* 这个岛在夏季又热又潮湿。

humi·dex /ˈhjuːmɪdeks/ *noun* [sing.] (*CanE*) a scale that measures how unpleasant hot and HUMID weather feels to people 湿热指数（测量湿热天气使人不舒服的程度）

hu·midi·fier /hjuːˈmɪdɪfaɪə(r)/ *noun* a machine used for making the air in a room less dry 增湿器；加湿器 ➲ SEE ALSO DEHUMIDIFIER

hu·mid·ity /hjuːˈmɪdəti/ *noun* [U] **1** the amount of water in the air （空气中的）湿度： ***high/low humidity*** 高 / 低湿度 ◇ *70% humidity* * 70% 的湿度 **2** conditions in which the air is very warm and damp 湿热；高温潮湿： *These plants need heat and humidity to grow well.* 这些植物在高温潮湿的环境中才能生长得旺盛。 ◇ *The humidity was becoming unbearable.* 这种潮湿使人越来越难以忍受了。 ➲ WORDFINDER NOTE AT CLIMATE

hu·mili·ate /hjuːˈmɪlieɪt/ *verb* ~ **sb/yourself/sth** to make sb feel ashamed or stupid and lose the respect of other people 羞辱；使丧失尊严： *I didn't want to humiliate her in front of her colleagues.* 我不想当着她同事们的面令她难堪。 ◇ *I've never felt so humiliated.* 我从未感到如此羞辱。 ◇ *The party was humiliated in the recent elections.* 该党在新近的选举中耻辱地失败了。 ▶ **hu·mili·at·ing** *adj.*: *a humiliating defeat* 耻辱的失败 **hu·mili·ation** /hjuːˌmɪliˈeɪʃn/ *noun* [U, C]: *She suffered the humiliation of being criticized in public.* 她当众受到指责，丢了面子。

hu·mil·ity /hjuːˈmɪləti/ *noun* [U] the quality of not thinking that you are better than other people; the quality of being humble 谦逊；谦虚： *Her first defeat was an early lesson in humility.* 她的第一次失败使她很早便懂得了谦逊。 ◇ *an act of genuine humility* 真正谦虚的举动

hum·int /ˈhjuːmɪnt/ *noun* [U] the activity or job of collecting secret information about people or governments （针对人或政府的）情报收集，谍报工作 **ORIGIN** A combination of *human* and *intelligence*. 源自 human 和 intelligence 的组合。

hum·ming·bird /ˈhʌmɪŋbɜːd; *NAmE* -bɜːrd/ *noun* a small brightly coloured bird that lives in warm countries and that can stay in one place in the air by beating its wings very fast, making a continuous low sound (= a HUMMING sound) 蜂鸟（快速扇动翅膀，发出嗡嗡声，能空中悬停）

hum·mock /ˈhʌmək/ *noun* (*BrE*) a small hill or pile of earth 小山；小丘

hum·mus (*also* **hou·mous**) /ˈhʊməs; ˈhuːməs/ *noun* [U] a type of food, originally from the Middle East, that is a soft mixture of CHICKPEAS, SESAME seeds, oil, lemon juice and GARLIC 鹰嘴豆泥（中东食品，将鹰嘴豆、芝麻、油、柠檬汁和大蒜捣碎而成）

hu·mon·gous (*also* **hu·mun·gous**) /hjuːˈmʌŋgəs/ *adj.* (*informal*) very big 巨大的；庞大的 **SYN** **enormous**

humor, hu·mor·less (*especially US*) = HUMOUR, HUMOURLESS

hu·mor·ist /ˈhjuːmərɪst/ *noun* a person who is famous for writing or telling amusing stories 幽默作家；诙谐风趣的人

hu·mor·ous /ˈhjuːmərəs/ *adj.* funny and entertaining; showing a sense of humour 滑稽有趣的；有幽默感的： *He gave a humorous account of their trip to Spain.* 他饶有风趣地讲述了他们的西班牙之行。 ◇ *He had a wide mouth and humorous grey eyes.* 他有一张大嘴巴和一双滑稽的灰眼睛。 ➲ SYNONYMS AT FUNNY ▶ **hu·mor·ous·ly** *adv.*: *The poem humorously describes local characters and traditions.* 那首诗幽默地描述了当地的人物和传统。

hu·mour (*especially US* **hu·mor**) /ˈhjuːmə(r)/ *noun, verb*

■ *noun* **1** [U] the quality in sth that makes it funny or amusing; the ability to laugh at things that are amusing 幽默；幽默感： *a story full of gentle humour* 充满轻松幽默的故事 ◇ *She ignored his feeble attempt at humour.* 她没理他想表现却又差劲的幽默。 ◇ *They failed to see the humour of the situation.* 他们没有看出这情景的滑稽之处。 ◇ *I can't stand people with no* ***sense of humour****.* 我无法忍受毫无幽默感的人。 ◇ *She smiled with a rare flash of humour.* 她以少有的一丝诙谐微笑了。 ◇ *She has her very own brand of humour.* 她的幽默很独特。 ◇ *The film is only funny if you appreciate French humour* (= things that cause French people to laugh). 只有能理解法国式的幽默才会领略这部电影的趣味。 **2** [C, U] (*formal*) the state of your feelings or mind at a particular time 感觉；心情；精神状态： *to be in the best of humours* 情绪极好 ◇ *The meeting dissolved in* ***ill humour****.* 会议不欢而散。 ◇ *to be* ***out of humour*** (= in a bad mood) 心情不好 ➲ SEE ALSO GOOD HUMOUR, GOOD-HUMOURED at GOOD HUMOUR, ILL-HUMOURED at ILL HUMOUR **3** [C] (*old use*) one of the four liquids that were thought in the past to be in a person's body and to influence health and character 体液（旧时认为存在人体内，有四种，可影响健康和性格）

■ *verb* ~ **sb** to agree with sb's wishes, even if they seem unreasonable, in order to keep the person happy 迁就；顺应： *She thought it best to humour him rather than get into an argument.* 她想最好是顺他的意，而不是和他争吵。

hu·mour·less (*especially US* **hu·mor·less**) /ˈhjuːmələs; *NAmE* -ərləs/ *adj.* not having or showing the ability to laugh at things that other people think are amusing 无幽默感的 ▶ **hu·mour·less·ly** (*especially US* **hu·mor·less·ly**) *adv.*

hump /hʌmp/ *noun, verb*

■ *noun* **1** a large lump that sticks out above the surface of sth, especially the ground （平面上的）大隆起物；（尤指）土墩，丘，冈：*the dark hump of the mountain in the distance* 远处高大的黑魆魆的山 ◇ (*BrE*) *a* ***road/speed/traffic hump*** (= a hump on a road that forces traffic to drive more slowly) 公路上的限速路墩 **2** a large lump on the back of some animals, especially CAMELS （某些动物的）峰；（尤指）驼峰 **3** a large lump on the back of a person, caused by an unusual curve in the SPINE (= the row of bones in the middle of the back) （人的）驼背

IDM **be over the 'hump** to have done the most difficult part of sth 完成最困难的部分；渡过最困难阶段 **get/take the 'hump** (*BrE, informal*) to become annoyed or upset about sth 对某事恼怒（或烦恼）：*Fans get the hump when the team loses.* 球队失利时，球迷们感到沮丧。

■ *verb* **1** ~ **sth** (+ **adv./prep.**) (*BrE*) to carry sth heavy 背负（重物）：*I've been humping furniture around all day.* 我扛了一整天的家具。 **2** ~ **sb** (*taboo, slang*) to have sex with sb 与（某人）性交

hump·back /ˈhʌmpbæk/ *noun* **1** = HUMPBACK WHALE **2** = HUNCHBACK

,humpback 'bridge (*also* **,humpbacked 'bridge**) *noun* (*BrE*) a small bridge that slopes steeply on both sides 拱桥；弓形桥 ➲ VISUAL VOCAB PAGE V14

,humpback 'whale (*also* **hump·back**) *noun* a large WHALE (= a very large sea animal) with a back shaped like a HUMP 座头鲸；驼背鲸

humped /hʌmpt/ *adj.* having a HUMP or HUMPS; shaped like a HUMP 有隆起物的；似驼峰的：*a humped back* 驼背 ◇ *He was tall and broad with humped shoulders.* 他身高体宽，双肩隆起。

humph *exclamation* the way of writing the sound /həmf/ that people use to show they do not believe sth or do not approve of it （书写中代表 /həmf/ 的音，表示怀疑或不赞成）哼

hu·mun·gous = HUMONGOUS

humus /ˈhjuːməs/ *noun* [U] a substance made from dead leaves and plants, added to soil to help plants grow 腐殖质

Hun /hʌn/ *noun* (*pl.* **Huns** or **the Hun**) (*informal*) an offensive word for a German person, used especially during the First and Second World Wars （蔑称，尤用于第一次和第二次世界大战）德国佬

hunch /hʌntʃ/ *verb, noun*

■ *verb* [I, T] to bend the top part of your body forward and raise your shoulders and back 弓身；弓背；耸肩：(+ **adv./prep.**) *She leaned forward, hunching over the desk.* 她身体前倾，伏在写字台上。 ◇ ~ **sth** *He* ***hunched his shoulders*** *and thrust his hands deep into his pockets.* 他耸着肩，双手深深地插进衣袋。 ▸ **hunched** *adj.*：*a hunched figure* 弓着背的人形 ◇ *He sat hunched over his breakfast.* 他弓着背吃早饭。

■ *noun* a feeling that sth is true even though you do not have any evidence to prove it 预感；直觉：*It seemed that the doctor's hunch had been right.* 看起来医生的直觉是对的。 ◇ *I had a hunch (that) you'd be back.* 我有预感你会回来。 ◇ *to follow/back your hunches* 凭直觉做事

hunch·back /ˈhʌntʃbæk/ (*also* **hump·back**) *noun* (*offensive*) a person who has a HUMP on their back 驼背的人 ▸ **hunch·backed** *adj.*

hun·dred 🔑 /ˈhʌndrəd/ *number* (*plural verb* 复数动词) **1** 🔑 100 一百：*One hundred (of the children) have already been placed with foster families.* 有一百名（儿童）已经获安排领养。 ◇ *There were just a hundred of them there.* 他们那里只有一百人。 ◇ *This vase is worth several hundred dollars.* 这只花瓶值几百美元。 ◇ *She must be over a hundred* (= a hundred years old). 她肯定有一百多岁了。 ◇ *Hundreds of thousands of people are at risk.* 有几十万人正处于危险中。 ◇ *a hundred-year lease* 一百年的租约 HELP You say **a, one, two, several, etc. hundred** without a final 's' on 'hundred'. **Hundreds (of...)** can be used if there is no number or quantity before it. Always use a plural verb with **hundred** or **hundreds**, except when an amount of money is mentioned. 说 a, one, two, several, etc. hundred 时，hundred 后面不加 s。若前面没有数目或数量，可用 hundreds (of...)。除指金额外，hundred 和 hundreds 均用复数动词：*Four hundred (people) are expected to attend.* 预期有四百人出席。 ◇ *Two hundred (pounds) was withdrawn from the account.* 从账户里提取了二百英镑。 **2** 🔑 **a hundred** or **hundreds** (**of...**) (*usually informal*) a large amount 许多；大量：*hundreds of miles away* 数百里之遥 ◇ *for hundreds of years* 几百年来 ◇ *If I've said it once, I've said it a hundred times.* 这事我曾经说过，而且是说过很多次了。 ◇ *I have* ***a hundred and one*** *things to do.* 我有一大堆事情要做。 ◇ (*formal*) *Men died in their hundreds.* 大批的人死亡。 **3 the hundreds** [pl.] the numbers from 100 to 999 * 100 到 999 间的数目；百位数：*We're talking about a figure in the low hundreds.* 我们谈论的是一个两三百的数字。 **4 the... hundreds** [pl.] the years of a particular century 某个世纪的年代：*the early nineteen hundreds* (= written 'early 1900s') * 20 世纪早期 **5 one, two, three, etc.** ~ **hours** used to express whole hours in the 24-hour system （表示 24 小时制的整点）一点整、两点整、三点整等：*twelve hundred hours* (= 12.00, midday) 十二点整

IDM **a/one 'hundred per cent 1** in every way 在各方面；百分之百；完全 SYN **completely**：*I'm not a hundred per cent sure.* 我不能百分之百肯定。 ◇ *My family supports me one hundred per cent.* 我的家人全力支持我。 **2** completely fit and healthy 十分健康：*I still don't feel a hundred per cent.* 我还是觉得有些不舒服。 **give a 'hundred (and ten) per cent** to put as much effort into sth as you can 全力以赴；竭尽全力：*Every player gave a hundred per cent tonight.* 今天晚上所有的运动员都尽了最大的努力。 ➲ MORE AT NINETY

,hundreds and 'thousands (*BrE*) (*NAmE* **sprin·kles**) *noun* [pl.] extremely small pieces of coloured sugar, used to decorate cakes, etc. 着色珠子糖（装饰糕点等用）

hun·dredth 🔑 /ˈhʌndrədθ; -ətθ/ *ordinal number, noun*

■ *ordinal number* 🔑 100th 第一百：*her hundredth birthday* 她的百岁诞辰

■ *noun* 🔑 each of one hundred equal parts of sth 百分之一：*a/one hundredth of a second* 百分之一秒

hun·dred·weight /ˈhʌndrədweɪt/ *noun* (*pl.* **hun·dred·weight**) (*abbr.* **cwt**) a unit for measuring weight equal to 112 pounds in the UK and 100 pounds in the US. There are 20 hundredweight in a ton. 英担（在英国等于 112 磅，在美国等于 100 磅。一吨为 20 英担）

hung /hʌŋ/ *adj.* [only before noun] **1** (of a parliament or council 上下议院或市郡议会) (*BrE*) in which no political party has more elected members than all the other parties added together 任何政党都不占多数席位的 **2** (of a JURY 陪审团) unable to agree about whether sb is guilty of a crime 不能取得一致意见的 ➲ SEE ALSO HANG *v.*

hun·ger /ˈhʌŋɡə(r)/ *noun, verb*

■ *noun* **1** [U] the state of not having enough food to eat, especially when this causes illness or death 饥饿；饥荒 SYN **starvation**：*Around fifty people die of hunger every day in the camp.* 集中营里每天大约有五十人饿死。 ◇ *The organization works to alleviate world hunger and disease.* 这个机构致力于减少世界上的饥饿和疾病。 **2** [U] the feeling caused by a need to eat 饥饿感；食欲；胃口：*hunger pangs* 饥饿引起的胃痛 ◇ *I felt faint with hunger.* 我当时饿得发昏。 **3** [sing.] ~ (**for sth**) (*formal*) a strong desire for sth （对某事物的）渴望，渴求：*a hunger for knowledge* 对知识的渴求 ◇ *Nothing seemed to satisfy their hunger for truth.* 似乎没有什么能满足他们对真理的渴求。

■ *verb*

PHR V **'hunger for/after sth/sb** (*literary*) to have a strong desire or need for sth/sb 渴望得到；渴求

ˈ**hunger strike** *noun* [C, U] the act of refusing to eat for a long period of time in order to protest about sth 绝食（抗议）： *to be on/go on hunger strike* 进行绝食抗议 ➲ WORDFINDER NOTE AT PROTEST ▶ ˈ**hunger striker** *noun*

hung·over /ˌhʌŋˈəʊvə(r); *NAmE* -ˈoʊ-/ *adj.* [not usually before noun] a person who is **hungover** is feeling ill/sick because they drank too much alcohol the night before 宿醉 ➲ SEE ALSO HANGOVER

hun·gry /ˈhʌŋɡri/ *adj.* (**hun·grier, hun·gri·est**) **1** feeling that you want to eat sth 感到饿的： *I'm really hungry.* 我真是饿了。◇ *Is anyone getting hungry?* 有人觉得饿吗？◇ *All this talk of food is making me hungry.* 老这么谈吃的勾起我的食欲了。◇ *I have a hungry family to feed.* 我得养活嗷嗷待哺的一家人。 **2** not having enough food to eat 饥饿的；挨饿的： *Thousands are* ***going hungry*** *because of the failure of this year's harvest.* 由于今年粮食歉收，成千上万的人将挨饿。 **3 the hungry** *noun* [pl.] people who do not have enough food to eat （统称）饥民 **4** [only before noun] causing you to feel that you want to eat sth 使人饥饿的；引起食欲的： *All this gardening is hungry work.* 这些园艺活儿让人干了肚子饿。 **5** ~ (**for sth**) having or showing a strong desire for sth 渴望得到；渴求： *Both parties are hungry for power.* 两党都渴望掌权。◇ *power-hungry* 渴求权力 ◇ *The child is simply hungry for affection.* 这个孩子只不过是渴望得到爱。◇ *His eyes had a wild hungry look in them.* 他的目光里有一种强烈渴望的神情。 ▶ **hun·grily** /ˈhʌŋɡrəli/ *adv.*： *They gazed hungrily at the display of food.* 他们饥肠辘辘地盯着那些摆放着的食物。◇ *He kissed her hungrily.* 他如饥似渴地亲吻她。

ˌ**hung ˈup** *adj.* [not before noun] ~ (**on/about sth/sb**) (*informal, disapproving*) very worried about sth/sb; thinking about sth/sb too much 十分担忧；想得过多： *You're not still hung up on that girl?* 你不是还在念念不忘那个女孩吧？ ◇ *He's too hung up about fitness.* 他对健康过于忧心忡忡。

hunk /hʌŋk/ *noun* **1** a large piece of sth, especially food, that has been cut or broken from a larger piece （尤指食物切下或掰下的）大块，大片： *a hunk of bread/cheese/meat* 一大块面包 / 干酪 / 肉 **2** (*informal*) a man who is big, strong and sexually attractive 魁梧性感的男子；猛男： *He's a real hunk.* 他身材真结实。

hun·ker /ˈhʌŋkə(r)/ *verb*

PHR V ˌ**hunker ˈdown** **1** (*especially NAmE*) to sit on your heels with your knees bent up in front of you 蹲；蹲坐；蹲下 SYN **squat**： *He hunkered down beside her.* 他挨着她蹲下。 **2** to prepare yourself to stay somewhere, keep an opinion, etc. for a long time 准备长期待在某处（或坚持某观点等） **3** to refuse to change an opinion, way of behaving, etc. 拒绝改变观点（或行为方式等）

hun·kers /ˈhʌŋkəz; *NAmE* -kərz/ *noun* [pl.]

IDM **on your ˈhunkers** sitting on your heels with your knees bent up in front of you 蹲着；蹲坐 SYN **haunch**

hunky /ˈhʌŋki/ *adj.* (**hunk·ier, hunk·iest**) (of a man 男子) big, strong and sexually attractive 结实性感的

hunky-dory /ˌhʌŋki ˈdɔːri/ *adj.* [not before noun] (*informal*) if you say that **everything is hunky-dory**, you mean that there are no problems and that everyone is happy 平安无事；皆大欢喜

hunt /hʌnt/ *verb, noun*

■ ***verb*** **1** [I, T] to chase wild animals or birds in order to catch or kill them for food, sport or to make money 打猎；猎取；猎杀： *Lions sometimes hunt alone.* 狮子有时单独猎食。◇ ~ **sth** *Whales are still being hunted and killed in the Arctic.* 北冰洋的鲸类仍然遭到猎杀。

WORDFINDER 联想词： chase, falconry, game, open season, pack, poach, prey, safari, trail

2 [I] to look for sth that is difficult to find 搜寻；搜索 SYN **search**： *I've hunted everywhere but I can't find it.* 我到处都搜遍了，就是找不到它。◇ ~ **for sth** *She is still hunting for a new job.* 她还在找新工作。 **3** [T, I] to look for sb in order to catch them or harm them 追踪；追捕： ~ **sb** *Police are hunting an escaped criminal.* 警察正在追捕一名逃犯。◇ ~ **for sb** *Detectives are hunting for thieves who broke into a warehouse yesterday.* 侦探正在追踪昨天侵入仓库的窃贼。 **4** [I, T] ~ (**sth**) (in Britain) to chase and kill FOXES as a sport, riding horses and using dogs. Fox HUNTING with dogs has been illegal in the UK since 2005. （英国）猎狐（作为运动，自 2005 年起用狗猎狐是违法的）

PHR V ˌ**hunt sb↔ˈdown** to search for sb until you catch or find them, especially in order to punish or harm them 追捕，缉捕（某人） ˌ**hunt sth↔ˈdown/ˈout** to search for sth until you find it 搜寻，寻找（某物）

■ ***noun*** **1** [C, usually sing.] ~ (**for sb/sth**) an act of looking for sb/sth that is difficult to find 搜寻；搜索；寻找： ***The hunt is on*** *for a suitable candidate.* 正在物色合适的人选。◇ *Hundreds have joined a police hunt for the missing teenager.* 已有几百人和警方一同搜寻那名失踪的少年。◇ *a* ***murder hunt*** (= to find the person who has killed sb) 追捕杀人犯 ➲ SEE ALSO TREASURE HUNT, WITCH-HUNT **2** [C] (often in compounds 常构成复合词) an act of chasing wild animals to kill or capture them 打猎： *a tiger hunt* 猎虎 **3** [C] (in Britain) an event at which people ride horses and hunt FOXES with dogs as a sport, illegal in the UK since 2005 （英国）猎狐（作为运动，自 2005 年起用狗猎狐是违法的）： *There will be a hunt on Boxing Day.* 节礼日将有猎狐活动。◇ *a hunt meeting* 猎狐大会 **4** [C+sing./pl. v.] (in Britain) a group of people who regularly hunt FOXES as a sport （英国经常举行猎狐运动的）猎狐队伍： *There are several different hunts in the area.* 这个地区有几支不同的猎狐队。

IDM **be in the ˈhunt** to have a chance of winning 有机会（赢）： *The team are back in the hunt for the league title.* 这支队伍又有机会赢得联赛冠军了。

hunt·ed /ˈhʌntɪd/ *adj.* (of an expression on sb's face 面部表情) showing that sb is very worried or frightened, as if they are being followed or chased 惴惴不安的；惊恐万分的： *His eyes had a hunted look.* 他双眼透露出恐慌的神态。

hunt·er /ˈhʌntə(r)/ *noun* **1** a person who hunts wild animals for food or sport; an animal that hunts its food 猎人；狩猎者；（猎食其他动物的）猎兽 **2** (usually in compounds 通常构成复合词) a person who looks for and collects a particular kind of thing 搜集某种东西的人： *a bargain hunter* 四处寻找便宜货的人 ➲ SEE ALSO HEADHUNTER **3** (*BrE*) a fast strong horse used in hunting FOXES 猎狐马 **4** (*NAmE*) a dog used in hunting 猎犬

ˌ**hunter-ˈgatherer** *noun* a member of a group of people who do not live in one place but move around and live by hunting, fishing and gathering plants 游猎采集部族成员

hunt·ing /ˈhʌntɪŋ/ *noun* [U] **1** chasing and killing wild animals and birds as a sport or for food 狩猎运动；打猎： *to go hunting* 去打猎 ◇ *Since 1977 otter hunting has been illegal.* 捕猎水獭 1977 年以后就被视为非法了。 **2** (*BrE*) = FOX HUNTING **3** (in compounds 构成复合词) the process of looking for sth 找；寻找： *We're going house-hunting at the weekend.* 周末我们去找房子。◇ *How's the job-hunting going?* 工作找得怎么样了？

ˈ**hunting ground** *noun* **1** a place where people with a particular interest can easily find what they want 可以找到所需要的东西的地方： *Crowded markets are a* ***happy hunting ground*** *for pickpockets.* 拥挤的市场是扒手大显身手的好地方。 **2** a place where wild animals are hunted 猎场

hunt·ress /ˈhʌntrəs/ *noun* (*literary*) a woman who hunts wild animals 女猎人；女狩猎者

hunts·man /ˈhʌntsmən/ *noun* (*pl.* **-men** /-mən/) a man who hunts wild animals 猎人；狩猎者

hur·dle /ˈhɜːdl; *NAmE* ˈhɜːrdl/ *noun, verb*

■ ***noun*** **1** each of a series of vertical frames that a person or horse jumps over in a race （供人或马在赛跑中跨越

的）栏架，跨栏：*His horse fell at the final hurdle.* 他骑的马在最后一个栏架倒下了。◇ *to **clear a hurdle*** (= jump over it successfully) 跨过栏架 **2 hurdles** [pl.] a race in which runners or horses have to jump over hurdles 跨栏赛：*the 300 m hurdles* * 300 米跨栏赛 ➲ VISUAL VOCAB PAGE V50 **3** a problem or difficulty that must be solved or dealt with before you can achieve sth 难关；障碍 SYN **obstacle**：*The next hurdle will be getting her parents' agreement.* 下一个难关是征得她父母的同意。

■ ***verb*** **1** [T, I] to jump over sth while you are running（奔跑中）跳越（某物）：**~ sth** *He hurdled two barriers to avoid reporters.* 他跳过了两个障碍物以躲避记者。◇ **~ over sth** *to hurdle over a fence* 跳过一道栅栏 **2** [I] to run in a hurdles race 参加跨栏赛

hurd·ler /ˈhɜːdlə(r); *NAmE* ˈhɜːrd-/ *noun* a person or horse that runs in races over hurdles 跨栏运动员；参加跨栏赛的马

H

hurd·ling /ˈhɜːdlɪŋ; *NAmE* ˈhɜːrd-/ *noun* [U] the sport of racing over HURDLES 跨栏赛 ➲ VISUAL VOCAB PAGE V50

hurdy-gurdy /ˈhɜːdi ɡɜːdi; *NAmE* ˈhɜːrdi ɡɜːrdi/ *noun* (*pl.* **-ies**) a small musical instrument that is played by turning a handle with one hand and pressing keys with the other 手摇弦琴，轮擦提琴（通过摇动琴尾曲柄，使连接的木轮旋转摩擦琴弦发声）

hurl /hɜːl; *NAmE* hɜːrl/ *verb* **1** [T] **~ sth/sb + adv./prep.** to throw sth/sb violently in a particular direction 猛扔；猛投；猛摔：*He hurled a brick through the window.* 他从窗户扔了块砖。➲ SYNONYMS AT THROW **2** [T] **~ abuse, accusations, insults, etc. (at sb)** to shout insults, etc. at sb 大声说出（辱骂或斥责等）：*Rival fans hurled abuse at each other.* 两帮对立的球迷相互高声辱骂。 **3** [I] (*NAmE, slang*) to VOMIT 呕吐

hurl·ing /ˈhɜːlɪŋ; *NAmE* ˈhɜːrlɪŋ/ *noun* [U] an Irish ball game similar to HOCKEY played by two teams of 15 boys or men 爱尔兰曲棍球（两支参赛队，各 15 人）

hurly-burly /ˈhɜːli bɜːli; *NAmE* ˈhɜːrli bɜːrli/ *noun* [U] a very noisy and busy activity or situation 骚动；喧闹：*He enjoys the hurly-burly of political debate.* 他喜欢政治辩论时的喧闹。➲ MORE LIKE THIS 11, page R26

hur·rah /həˈrɑː/ (*also* **hur·ray** /həˈreɪ/) *exclamation* = HOORAY (1)

hur·ri·cane /ˈhʌrɪkən; *NAmE* ˈhɜːrəkən; -keɪn/ *noun* a violent storm with very strong winds, especially in the western Atlantic Ocean（尤指西大西洋的）飓风：*hurricane-force winds* 飓风级大风 ◇ *Hurricane Betty is now approaching the coast of Florida.* 飓风贝蒂正在逼近佛罗里达海岸。➲ WORDFINDER NOTE AT DISASTER, WIND[1] ➲ COLLOCATIONS AT WEATHER ➲ COMPARE CYCLONE, TYPHOON

ˈ**hurricane lamp** *noun* a type of lamp with glass sides to protect the flame inside from the wind 防风灯

hur·ried /ˈhʌrid; *NAmE* ˈhɜːr-/ *adj.* [usually before noun] done too quickly because you do not have enough time 匆忙完成的；仓促而就的 SYN **rushed**：*I ate a hurried breakfast and left.* 我匆匆忙忙吃完早饭就离开了。OPP **unhurried** ▶ **hur·ried·ly** *adv.*：*I hurriedly got up and dressed.* 我急忙起床穿好衣服。

hurry 🔑 /ˈhʌri; *NAmE* ˈhɜːri/ *verb, noun*

■ ***verb*** (**hur·ries, hurry·ing, hur·ried, hur·ried**) **1** 🔑 [I] to do sth more quickly than usual because there is not much time 赶快，匆忙，急忙（做某事）SYN **rush**：*You'll have to hurry if you want to catch that train.* 如果你想赶上那趟火车就得抓紧时间了。◇ *The kids hurried to open their presents.* 孩子们急忙打开礼物。HELP In spoken English **hurry** can be used with **and** plus another verb, instead of with **to** and the infinitive, especially to tell somebody to do something quickly. 口语中 hurry 可与 and 及所连接的另一个动词连用，而不和 to 所引导的不定式连用，尤用于告诉某人快点做某事：*Hurry and open your present—I want to see what it is!* 快拆开你的礼物，我想看看是什么！ **2** 🔑 [I] **+ adv./prep.** to move quickly in a particular direction（朝某方向）迅速移动 SYN **rush**：*He picked up his bags and hurried across the courtyard.* 他拎起提包匆匆穿过院子。◇ *She hurried away without saying goodbye.* 她连声再见都没说就急忙离开了。 **3** 🔑 [T] to make sb do sth more quickly 催促（某人）SYN **rush**：**~ sb** *I don't want to hurry you but we close in twenty minutes.* 我并不想催你，但我们再过二十分钟就要关门。◇ **~ sb into doing sth** *She was hurried into making an unwise choice.* 她在催逼之下作出了不明智的选择。 **4** [T] **~ sth + adv./prep.** to deal with sth quickly 迅速处理 SYN **rush**：*Her application was hurried through.* 她的申请很快得到了处理。 **5** [T, usually passive] **~ sth** to do sth too quickly 仓促（做某事）SYN **rush**：*A good meal should never be hurried.* 美餐绝不能狼吞虎咽。

PHR V ˌ**hurry ˈon** to continue speaking without giving anyone else time to say anything 喋喋不休；啰嗦得没完没了 ˌ**hurry ˈup (with sth)** 🔑 to do sth more quickly because there is not much time 赶快，急忙（做某事）：*I wish the bus would hurry up and come.* 我希望公共汽车能快点来。◇ *Hurry up! We're going to be late.* 快点！我们要迟到了。◇ *Hurry up with the scissors. I need them.* 快点用剪刀。我需要用。 ˌ**hurry sb/sth↔ˈup** to make sb do sth more quickly; to make sth happen more quickly 催促（某人）；使早些发生：*Can you do anything to hurry my order up?* 你能不能设法让我点的东西快点送来？

■ ***noun*** 🔑 [U, sing.] the need or wish to get sth done quickly 匆忙；急忙：*Take your time—there's no hurry.* 悠着点，不用急。◇ ***In my hurry to leave, I forgot my passport.*** 我匆忙动身，忘了带护照。◇ ***What's the hurry?*** *The train doesn't leave for an hour.* 慌什么？火车还有一个小时才开呢。

IDM **in a ˈhurry 1** 🔑 very quickly or more quickly than usual 迅速；赶快：*He had to leave in a hurry.* 他不得不赶快离开了。 **2** 🔑 not having enough time to do sth 仓促；匆忙：*Sorry, I haven't got time to do it now—I'm in a hurry.* 对不起，我现在没时间做这个，我忙着呢。◇ *Alice was **in a tearing hurry** as usual.* 艾丽斯一如往常地来去匆匆。 **in a ˈhurry to do sth** impatient to do sth 急于做某事：*My daughter is in such a hurry to grow up.* 我女儿恨不得一下子就长大。◇ *Why are you in such a hurry to sell?* 你为什么如此迫不及待地要卖出？ **in no ˈhurry (to do sth)** | **not in a/any ˈhurry (to do sth) 1** having plenty of time 有足够的时间，不着急（做某事）：*I don't mind waiting—I'm not in any particular hurry.* 我可以等，我没什么特别急的事。 **2** not wanting or not willing to do sth 不想，不情愿（做某事）：*We were in no hurry to get back to work after the holiday.* 假期结束后我们不想急着回去工作。 **sb will not do sth again in a ˈhurry** (*informal*) used to say that sb does not want to do sth again because it was not enjoyable 某人再不愿做某事：*I won't be going there again in a hurry—the food was terrible.* 我再不愿去那里了，那里吃的东西糟透了。

hurt 🔑 /hɜːt; *NAmE* hɜːrt/ *verb, adj., noun*

■ ***verb*** (**hurt, hurt**) **1** 🔑 [T, I] **~ (sb/sth/yourself)** to cause physical pain to sb/yourself; to injure sb/yourself（使）疼痛，受伤：*He hurt his back playing squash.* 他打壁球时背部受伤了。◇ *Did you hurt yourself?* 你伤着自己了吗？◇ *Stop it. You're hurting me.* 住手。你弄疼我了。◇ *My back is really hurting me today.* 我今天背疼得厉害。◇ *My shoes hurt—they're too tight.* 我的鞋子太紧，穿着夹脚。➲ SYNONYMS AT INJURE ➲ COLLOCATIONS AT INJURY

WORDFINDER 联想词：bandage, bleed, bruise, fracture, **injury**, plaster, sore, swell, wound

2 🔑 [I] to feel painful 感到疼痛：*My feet hurt.* 我脚疼。◇ *Ouch! That hurt!* 哎哟！好疼！◇ ***It hurts** when I bend my knee.* 我的膝盖一弯就疼。 **3** 🔑 [I, T] to make sb unhappy or upset 使不快；使烦恼：*What really hurt was that he never answered my letter.* 真正让我伤心的是他从不给我回信。◇ **~ sb/sth** *I'm sorry, I didn't mean to hurt you.* 对不起，我不是故意伤害你的。◇ *I didn't want to **hurt his feelings**.* 我并没有想伤害他的感情。◇ **it hurts (sb) to do sth** *It hurt me to think that he would lie to me.* 一想到他竟然对我说谎，我就很伤心。 **4** [I] **be hurting** (*informal*) to feel unhappy or upset 感到不高兴（或烦恼）：*I know you're hurting and I want to help you.* 我知道你心烦，我想帮助你。 **5** [T] **~ sb/sth** to have a bad effect on sb/sth 对…有不良影响：*Many people on low incomes will be hurt* *by the government's plans.* 很多低收入的人将受到政府这些方案的打击。 ➲ SYNONYMS AT DAMAGE **6** [I] **be hurting (for sth)** (*NAmE*) to be in a difficult situation because you need sth, especially money 处于困境；手头拮据： *His campaign is already hurting for money.* 他从事的社会运动已经因缺乏经费而难以为继了。

IDM **it won't/wouldn't 'hurt (sb/sth) (to do sth)** used to say that sb should do a particular thing （做某事）不会有什么损害；（某人）应该做某事： *It wouldn't hurt you to help with the housework occasionally.* 你应该偶尔帮忙做做家务。 ➲ MORE AT FLY *n.*, HIT *v.*

▪ ***adj.*** **1** injured physically （身体上）受伤的： *None of the passengers were **badly hurt**.* 乘客中没有人严重受伤。 OPP **unhurt** **2** upset and offended by sth that sb has said or done （感情上）受伤的： *a **hurt look/expression*** 伤心的眼神 / 表情 ◇ *She was **deeply hurt** that she had not been invited.* 她未被邀请，感到十分难过。 ◇ *Martha's hurt pride showed in her eyes.* 从玛莎的眼神可以看出她的自尊受到了伤害。

▪ ***noun*** [U, sing.] (*rather informal*) a feeling of unhappiness because sb has been unkind or unfair to you 心灵创伤；委屈： *There was hurt and real anger in her voice.* 她的声音里有难过，也有真正的愤怒。 ◇ *It was a hurt that would take a long time to heal.* 那是需要很长时间才能愈合的创伤。

▼ **SYNONYMS 同义词辨析**

hurt

ache · burn · sting · tingle · itch · throb

These are all words that can be used when part of your body feels painful. 以上各词均可指身体部位感到疼痛。

hurt (of part of your body) to feel painful; (of an action) to cause pain 指（身体部位）感到疼痛、（某一动作）引起疼痛： *My feet hurt.* 我脚疼。 ◇ *Ouch! That hurt!* 哎哟！好疼！

ache to feel a continuous dull pain 指疼痛、隐痛： *I'm aching all over.* 我周身疼痛。

burn (of part of your body) to feel very hot and painful 指（身体部位）火辣辣地痛、发烫： *Our eyes were burning from the chemicals in the air.* 空气中弥漫的化学物质熏得我们的眼睛火辣辣地痛。

sting to make sb feel a sharp burning pain or uncomfortable feeling in part of their body; (of part of your body) to feel this pain 指（使）身体部位感觉刺痛、灼痛： *My eyes were stinging from the smoke.* 烟熏得我眼睛痛。

tingle (of part of your body) to feel as if a lot of small sharp points are pushing into the skin there 指（身体部位）感到刺痛： *The cold air made her face tingle.* 冷空气冻得她的脸发痛。

itch to have an uncomfortable feeling on your skin that makes you want to scratch; to make your skin feel like this 指（使）皮肤发痒： *I itch all over.* 我浑身痒。 ◇ *Does the rash itch?* 皮疹痒吗？

throb (of part of your body) to feel pain as a series of regular beats 指（身体部位）有规律地抽动、抽痛： *His head throbbed painfully.* 他的头一抽一跳地痛。

PATTERNS
- your **eyes** hurt/ache/burn/sting/itch
- your **skin** hurts/burns/stings/tingles/itches
- your **flesh** hurts/burns/stings/tingles
- your **head** hurts/aches/throbs
- your **stomach** hurts/aches
- to **really** hurt/ache/burn/sting/tingle/itch/throb
- to hurt/ache/sting/itch **badly**/**a lot**
- **It** hurts/stings/tingles/itches.

hurt·ful /ˈhɜːtfl; *NAmE* ˈhɜːrtfl/ *adj.* (of comments 评论) making you feel upset and offended 伤感情的；伤害自尊的 SYN **unkind**： *I cannot forget the hurtful things he said.* 我无法忘记他说的那些伤感情的话。 ◇ **~ to sb** *The bad reviews of her new book were very hurtful to her.* 对她的新书的负面评论使她很难过。 ▸ **hurt·ful·ly** /-fəli/ *adv.*： *He said, rather hurtfully, that he had better things to do than come and see me.* 他相当刻薄地说来看我还不如去干别的事。

hur·tle /ˈhɜːtl; *NAmE* ˈhɜːrtl/ *verb* [I] **+ adv./prep.** to move very fast in a particular direction （向某个方向）飞驰，猛冲： *A runaway car **came hurtling** towards us.* 一辆失控的汽车朝我们飞驰而来。

hus·band /ˈhʌzbənd/ *noun, verb*

▪ ***noun*** (*also informal* **hubby**) the man that sb is married to; a married man 丈夫： *This is my husband, Steve.* 这位是我的丈夫，史蒂夫。 ➲ COLLOCATIONS AT MARRIAGE

IDM **ˌhusband and ˈwife** a man and woman who are married to each other 夫妇： *They lived together as husband and wife* (= as if they were married) *for years.* 他们像夫妻一样共同生活了很多年。 ◇ *a husband-and-wife team* 夫妻队

▪ ***verb*** **~ sth** (*formal*) to use sth very carefully and make sure that you do not waste it 节俭使用

hus·band·ry /ˈhʌzbəndri/ *noun* **1** farming, especially when done carefully and well （尤指精心经营的）农牧业： ***animal/crop husbandry*** 畜牧业；种植业 **2** (*old-fashioned*) the careful use of food, money and supplies 节俭使用；精打细算

hush /hʌʃ/ *verb, noun*

▪ ***verb*** **1** [I] (used especially in orders 尤用于命令) to be quiet; to stop talking or crying 安静；别说话；别叫喊： *Hush now and try to sleep.* 别出声了，睡吧。 **2** [T] **~ sb/sth** to make sb/sth become quieter; to make sb stop talking, crying, etc. 使安静下来；使停止说话（或叫喊等）

PHR V **ˌhush sth↔ˈup** to hide information about a situation because you do not want people to know about it 掩盖，蒙蔽（事实）： *He claimed that the whole affair had been hushed up by the council.* 他声称整个事件都被市政会一手捂住了。

▪ ***noun*** [sing., U] a period of silence, especially following a lot of noise, or when people are expecting sth to happen 寂静；鸦雀无声： *There was **a deathly hush** in the theatre.* 戏院里一片寂静。 ◇ ***A hush descended** over the waiting crowd.* 等候的人群变得鸦雀无声。 ◇ (*BrE, informal*) ***Can we have a bit of hush?*** (= please be quiet) 大家能安静一点吗？

hushed /hʌʃt/ *adj.* **1** (of a place 地方) quiet because nobody is talking; much quieter than usual 寂静的；宁静的： *A hushed courtroom listened as the boy gave evidence.* 那个男孩作证时法庭里的人都屏息倾听。 **2** [usually before noun] (of voices 嗓音) speaking very quietly 轻的；低声的： *a hushed whisper* 低声耳语

ˌhush-ˈhush *adj.* (*informal*) secret and not known about by many people 秘密的；不公开的： *Their wedding was very hush-hush.* 他们的婚礼非常秘密。

ˈhush money *noun* [U] money that is paid to sb to prevent them from giving other people information that could be embarrassing or damaging 封口费（用于防止某人透露令人尴尬或有损害的消息）

ˈhush puppies *noun* [pl.] small fried cakes made of CORNMEAL, eaten especially in the southern US 黄金玉米球（尤见于美国南部的一种糕点，用玉米粉炸成小球状）

husk /hʌsk/ *noun, verb*

▪ ***noun*** the dry outer covering of nuts, fruits and seeds, especially of grain （尤指谷类、果实和种子的）外壳，外皮

▪ ***verb*** **~ sth** to remove the husks from grain, seeds, nuts, etc. 去皮；去壳；去荚

husky /ˈhʌski/ *adj., noun*

▪ ***adj.*** (**husk·ier**, **husk·iest**) **1** (of a person or their voice 人或嗓音) sounding deep, quiet and rough, sometimes in an attractive way 深沉沙哑的： *She spoke in a husky whisper.* 她低沉沙哑地轻声说话。 **2** (*NAmE*) (of a man 男子) big, strong and sexually attractive 魁梧的；高大威猛的 ▸ **husk·ily** *adv.* **huski·ness** *noun* [U]

H

■ ***noun*** (*NAmE also* **huskie**) (*pl.* **-ies**) a large strong dog with thick hair, used for pulling SLEDGES across snow 哈士奇狗（高大强壮，毛厚，用来拉雪橇）

hus·sar /həˈzɑː(r)/ *noun* (in the past) a CAVALRY soldier who carried light weapons （旧时的）轻骑兵

hussy /ˈhʌsi/ *noun* (*pl.* **-ies**) (*old-fashioned, disapproving*) a girl or woman who behaves in a way that is considered shocking or morally wrong 粗野女子；淫荡女子；荡妇

hust·ings /ˈhʌstɪŋz/ *noun* **the hustings** [pl.] (*especially BrE*) the political meetings, speeches, etc. that take place in the period before an election 竞选活动（竞选前进行的政治集会、演讲等）: *Most candidates will be out* ***on the hustings*** *this week.* 大多数候选人本星期将进行竞选活动。

hus·tle /ˈhʌsl/ *verb, noun*

■ ***verb*** **1** [T] **~ sb + adv./prep.** to make sb move quickly by pushing them in a rough aggressive way 推搡；猛推: *He grabbed her arm and hustled her out of the room.* 他抓住她的胳膊把她推出房间。 **2** [T] **~ sb (into sth)** to force sb to make a decision before they are ready or sure 催促（某人作决定） **3** [T, I] **~ (sth)** (*informal, especially NAmE*) to sell or obtain sth, often illegally （常指非法地）兜售，取得: *to hustle dope* 兜售麻醉品 ◇ *They survive by hustling on the streets.* 他们靠沿街兜售为生。 **4** [I] (*NAmE, informal*) to act in an aggressive way or with a lot of energy 强行；强迫；硬干 **5** [I] (*NAmE*) to work as a PROSTITUTE 当妓女

■ ***noun*** [U] busy noisy activity of a lot of people in one place 忙碌喧嚣: *We escaped from the* ***hustle and bustle*** *of the city for the weekend.* 我们周末时躲开了城市的拥挤喧嚣。

hust·ler /ˈhʌslə(r)/ *noun* (*informal*) **1** (*especially NAmE*) a person who tries to trick sb into giving them money 要诡计骗钱的人 **2** (*NAmE*) a PROSTITUTE 妓女

hut /hʌt/ *noun* a small, simply built house or shelter 简陋的小房子（或棚、舍）: *a beach hut* 海滩棚屋 ◇ *a wooden hut* 小木屋 ➲ VISUAL VOCAB PAGE V15

hutch /hʌtʃ/ *noun* **1** a wooden box with a front made of wire, used for keeping RABBITS or other small animals in （养兔子等小动物的）笼子 **2** (*NAmE*) a large piece of wooden furniture with shelves in the top part and cupboards below, used for displaying and storing cups, plates, etc. 厨柜，餐具柜（上部为搁架，下部为柜子）

hwyl /ˈhɔɪl/ *noun* [U] (*WelshE*) a strong feeling of emotion and enthusiasm 强烈感情；激情

hya·cinth /ˈhaɪəsɪnθ/ *noun* a plant with a mass of small blue, white or pink flowers with a sweet smell that grow closely together around a thick STEM 风信子

hy·aena = HYENA

hy·brid /ˈhaɪbrɪd/ *noun* **1** an animal or plant that has parents of different SPECIES or varieties 杂种动物；杂交植物；杂种: *A mule is a hybrid of a male donkey and a female horse.* 骡子是公驴和母马交配而生的杂种动物。 ➲ COMPARE CROSS-BREED *n.* ➲ WORDFINDER NOTE AT BREED **2 ~ (between/of A and B)** something that is the product of mixing two or more different things （不同事物的）混合物，合成物 SYN **mixture**: *The music was a hybrid of Western pop and traditional folk song.* 这种音乐融合了西方流行音乐和传统民歌。 **3** a vehicle that uses two different types of power, especially petrol/gas or DIESEL and electricity 混合动力车（使用两种不同能源，尤指汽油或柴油与电混合使用） ▶ **hy·brid** *adj.* [usually before noun]: *a hybrid car/vehicle* 混合动力车

hy·brid·ize (*BrE also* **-ise**) /ˈhaɪbrɪdaɪz/ *verb* [I, T] **~ (sth)** (*specialist*) if an animal or a plant **hybridizes** or **is hybridized** with an animal or a plant of another SPECIES, they join together to produce a hybrid （使）产生杂交品种，杂交 ▶ **hy·brid·iza·tion, -isa·tion** /ˌhaɪbrɪdaɪˈzeɪʃn; *NAmE* -dəˈz-/ *noun* [U]

hydel /ˈhaɪdel/ *abbr.* (*IndE*) HYDROELECTRIC 水力发电的

hydra /ˈhaɪdrə/ *noun* **1 Hydra** (in ancient Greek stories 古希腊神话) a snake with several heads. As one head was cut off, another one grew. In the end it was killed by Hercules. 许德拉，多头蛇（砍去一个头即长出新头，后为大力神赫拉克勒斯所杀） **2** (*formal*) a thing that is very difficult to deal with, because it continues for a long time or because it has many different aspects 棘手的复杂事物；难以根绝的祸患 **3** (*biology* 生) an extremely small water creature with a tube-shaped body and TENTACLES around its mouth 水螅

hy·dran·gea /haɪˈdreɪndʒə/ *noun* a bush with white, pink or blue flowers that grow closely together in the shape of a large ball 绣球花

hy·drant /ˈhaɪdrənt/ *noun* = FIRE HYDRANT

hy·drate /ˈhaɪdreɪt; haɪˈdreɪt/ *verb* **~ sth** (*specialist*) to make sth absorb water 使水合；使吸入水分；使成水合物；使水化 ▶ **hy·dra·tion** /haɪˈdreɪʃn/ *noun* [U] ➲ COMPARE DEHYDRATE

hy·draul·ic /haɪˈdrɔːlɪk; *BrE also* -ˈdrɒl-/ *adj.* [usually before noun] **1** (of water, oil, etc. 水、油等) moved through pipes, etc. under pressure （通过水管等）液压的，水力的: *hydraulic fluid* 液压液体 **2** (of a piece of machinery 机器) operated by liquid moving under pressure 液压驱动的: *hydraulic brakes* 液压制动器 **3** connected with hydraulic systems 与水利（或液压）系统有关的: *hydraulic engineering* 水利工程 ▶ **hy·draul·ic·al·ly** /-kli/ *adv.*: *hydraulically operated doors* 液压传动门

hyˌdraulic ˈfracturing *noun* [U] (*formal* or *specialist*) = FRACKING

hy·draul·ics /haɪˈdrɔːlɪks; *BrE also* -ˈdrɒl-/ *noun* **1** [pl.] machinery that works by the use of liquid moving under pressure 液压装置 **2** [U] the science of the use of liquids moving under pressure 水力学

hydr(o)- /ˈhaɪdrəʊ; *NAmE* -droʊ/ *combining form* (in nouns, adjectives and adverbs 构成名词、形容词和副词) **1** connected with water 与水有关的；水的 **2** (*chemistry* 化) combined with HYDROGEN 含氢的；氢化的

hydro /ˈhaɪdrəʊ; *NAmE* -droʊ/ *noun* [U] (*CanE*) electricity 电: *to pay your hydro bill* 付电费

hydro·car·bon /ˌhaɪdrəˈkɑːbən; *NAmE* -ˈkɑːrb-/ *noun* (*chemistry* 化) a chemical made up of HYDROGEN and CARBON only. There are many different hydrocarbons found in petrol/gas, coal and natural gas. 烃；碳氢化合物

hydro·chlor·ic acid /ˌhaɪdrəˌklɒrɪk ˈæsɪd; *NAmE* -ˌklɔːr-/ *noun* [U] (*symb.* **HCl**) (*chemistry* 化) an acid containing HYDROGEN and CHLORINE 盐酸

hydro·chloro·fluoro·carbon /ˌhaɪdrəʊklɒrəʊˈflʊərəkɑːbən; *NAmE* ˌhaɪdroʊklɔːroʊˈflʊrəkɑːrbən/ *noun* (*chemistry* 化) = HCFC

hydro·cor·ti·sone /ˌhaɪdrəˈkɔːtɪzəʊn; *NAmE* -ˈkɔːrtɪzoʊn/ *noun* [U] a HORMONE produced in the body that is used in drugs to help with diseases of the skin and muscles 氢化可的松，皮质醇（体内分泌的激素，用于治疗皮肤和肌肉疾病）

hydro·elec·tric /ˌhaɪdrəʊɪˈlektrɪk; *NAmE* ˌhaɪdroʊ-/ *adj.* using the power of water to produce electricity; produced by the power of water 使用水力发电的；水力产生的: *a hydroelectric plant* 水力发电站 ◇ *hydroelectric power* 水力发出的电 ➲ WORDFINDER NOTE AT ENERGY ➲ VISUAL VOCAB PAGE V9 ▶ **hydro·elec·tri·city** /-ɪˌlekˈtrɪsəti/ *noun* [U]

hydro·fluoro·car·bon /ˌhaɪdrəʊˈflʊərəʊkɑːbən; *NAmE* ˌhaɪdroʊˈflʊroʊkɑːrbən/ *noun* (*chemistry* 化) = HFC

hydro·foil /ˈhaɪdrəfɔɪl/ *noun* a boat which rises above the surface of the water when it is travelling fast 水翼船 ➲ VISUAL VOCAB PAGE V59 ➲ COMPARE HOVERCRAFT

hydro·gen /ˈhaɪdrədʒən/ *noun* [U] (*symb.* **H**) a chemical element. Hydrogen is a gas that is the lightest of all the elements. It combines with OXYGEN to form water. 氢；氢气

hy·dro·gen·ated /haɪˈdrɒdʒəneɪtɪd; *NAmE* -ˈdrɑːdʒ-/ *adj.* (*chemistry* 化) **hydrogenated** oils have had hydrogen added to them （油类）氢化的，加氢的

ˈ**hydrogen bomb** (*also* ˈ**H-bomb**) *noun* a very powerful nuclear bomb 氢弹

ˌ**hydrogen peˈroxide** *noun* [U] (*symb.* H_2O_2) (*chemistry* 化) = PEROXIDE

hy·drol·ogy /haɪˈdrɒlədʒi; *NAmE* -ˈdrɑːl-/ *noun* [U] (*specialist*) the scientific study of the earth's water, especially its movement in relation to land 水文学

hy·droly·sis /haɪˈdrɒlɪsɪs; *NAmE* -ˈdrɑːl-/ *noun* [U] (*chemistry* 化) a reaction with water which causes a COMPOUND to separate into its parts 水解（化合物的加水分解）

hydro·pho·bia /ˌhaɪdrəˈfəʊbiə; *NAmE* -ˈfoʊbiə/ *noun* [U] extreme fear of water, which happens with RABIES infection in humans （狂犬病患者的）恐水，畏水 ▸ **hydro·pho·bic** /ˌhaɪdrəˈfəʊbɪk; *NAmE* -ˈfoʊ-/ *adj.*

hydro·plane /ˈhaɪdrəpleɪn/ *noun, verb*

■ ***noun*** **1** a light boat with an engine and a flat bottom, designed to travel fast over the surface of water 水上滑行艇 **2** (*NAmE*) = SEAPLANE

■ ***verb*** **1** (*NAmE*) (*BrE* **aqua·plane**) (of a motor vehicle 机动车辆) to slide out of control on a wet road 在潮湿路面上打滑失控 **2** (of a boat 船) to travel fast over the surface of the water 飞掠过水面

hydro·plan·ing /ˈhaɪdrəpleɪnɪŋ/ (*NAmE*) (*BrE* **aqua·plan·ing**) *noun* [U] the fact of a vehicle sliding on a wet surface, so that it is out of control （汽车在潮湿路面上的）打滑

hydro·pon·ics /ˌhaɪdrəˈpɒnɪks; *NAmE* -ˈpɑːn-/ *noun* [U] the process of growing plants in water or sand, rather than in soil 水培；溶液栽培

hydro·speed /ˈhaɪdrəʊspiːd; *NAmE* -droʊ-/ (*also* **hydro·speed·ing**) (*BrE*) *noun* [U] the sport of jumping into a river that is flowing fast, wearing equipment that allows you to float 急流跳水漂流

hydro·ther·apy /ˌhaɪdrəʊˈθerəpi; *NAmE* ˌhaɪdroʊ-/ *noun* [U] the treatment of disease or injury by doing physical exercises in water 水疗法

hy·drox·ide /haɪˈdrɒksaɪd; *NAmE* -ˈdrɑːks-/ *noun* (*chemistry* 化) a chemical consisting of a metal and a combination of OXYGEN and HYDROGEN 氢氧化物

hyena (*also* **hy·aena**) /haɪˈiːnə/ *noun* a wild animal like a dog, that eats the meat of animals that are already dead and has a cry like a human laugh. Hyenas live in Africa and Asia. 鬣狗（分布于非洲和亚洲，以动物尸体为食）

hy·giene /ˈhaɪdʒiːn/ *noun* [U] the practice of keeping yourself and your living and working areas clean in order to prevent illness and disease 卫生：*food hygiene* 食物卫生 ◇ *personal hygiene* 个人卫生 ◇ *In the interests of hygiene, please wash your hands.* 为了卫生，请洗手。

hy·gien·ic /haɪˈdʒiːnɪk; *NAmE usually* -ˈdʒen-/ *adj.* clean and free of bacteria and therefore unlikely to spread disease 卫生的：*Food must be prepared in hygienic conditions.* 食物必须在卫生的环境中制作。 OPP **unhygienic** ▸ **hy·gien·ic·al·ly** /-kli/ *adv.*：*Medical supplies are disposed of hygienically.* 医疗用品经卫生方法处理掉。

hy·gien·ist /haɪˈdʒiːnɪst/ (*also* ˈ**dental hygienist** *especially in NAmE*) *noun* a person who works with a dentist and whose job is to clean people's teeth and give them advice about keeping them clean 牙科保健员；牙科洁治员 ➲ WORDFINDER NOTE AT DENTIST

hymen /ˈhaɪmən/ *noun* (*anatomy* 解) a piece of skin that partly covers the opening of the VAGINA in women who have never had sex 处女膜

hymn /hɪm/ *noun* **1** a song of praise, especially one praising God and sung by Christians 赞美诗，圣歌（尤指基督徒唱的颂扬上帝的歌） **2** [usually sing.] if a film/movie, book, etc. is a **hymn to sth**, it praises it very strongly 歌颂某事物的电影（或书等） IDM SEE SING ➲ MORE LIKE THIS 20, page R27

ˈ**hymn book** (*also old-fashioned* **hym·nal** /ˈhɪmnəl/) *noun* a book of hymns 赞美诗集

hype /haɪp/ *noun, verb*

■ ***noun*** [U] (*informal, disapproving*) advertisements and discussion on television, radio, etc. telling the public about a product and about how good or important it is （电视、广播等中言过其实的）促销广告，促销讨论：*marketing/media hype* 夸张的促销 / 媒体广告 ◇ *Don't believe all the hype—the book isn't that good.* 别相信那些天花乱坠的宣传，那本书没那么好。

■ ***verb*** (*informal, disapproving*) to advertise sth a lot and exaggerate its good qualities, in order to get a lot of public attention for it 夸张地宣传（某事物）：**~ sth** *This week his much hyped new movie opens in London.* 本周他那部被大肆炒作的新电影在伦敦上映。 ◇ **~ sth up** *The meeting was hyped up in the media as an important event.* 这次会议被媒体吹成一件大事。

ˌ**hyped ˈup** *adj.* (*informal*) (of a person 人) very worried or excited about sth that is going to happen 十分担忧的；很激动的；十分兴奋的

hyper /ˈhaɪpə(r)/ *adj.* (*informal*) excited and nervous; having too much nervous energy 既兴奋又紧张的；精力过旺的

hyper- /ˈhaɪpə(r)/ *prefix* (in adjectives and nouns 构成形容词和名词) more than normal; too much 过度；过多：*hypercritical* 批评苛刻的 ◇ *hypertension* 高血压 ➲ COMPARE HYPO- ➲ MORE LIKE THIS 6, page R25

hyper·active /ˌhaɪpərˈæktɪv/ *adj.* (especially of children and their behaviour 尤指儿童及其行为) too active and only able to keep quiet and still for short periods 过分活跃的；多动的 ▸ **hyper·activ·ity** /ˌhaɪpərækˈtɪvəti/ *noun* [U]

hyper·bar·ic /ˌhaɪpəˈbærɪk; *NAmE* ˌhaɪpər-/ *adj.* (*physics* 物) (of gas 气体) at a higher pressure than normal 高气压的；高压的

hyper·bola /haɪˈpɜːbələ; *NAmE* -ˈpɜːr-/ *noun* (*pl.* **hyper·bolas** or **hyper·bolae** /-liː/) a SYMMETRICAL open curve 双曲线 ➲ PICTURE AT CONIC SECTION

hyper·bole /haɪˈpɜːbəli; *NAmE* -ˈpɜːrb-/ *noun* [U, C, usually sing.] a way of speaking or writing that makes sth sound better, more exciting, more dangerous, etc. than it really is 夸张 SYN **exaggeration** ➲ WORDFINDER NOTE AT IMAGE

hyper·bol·ic /ˌhaɪpəˈbɒlɪk; *NAmE* -pərˈbɑːl-/ *adj.* **1** (*mathematics* 数) of or related to a hyperbola 双曲线的 **2** (of language 言语) deliberately exaggerated; using hyperbole 夸张的；夸张法的

hyper·cor·rec·tion /ˌhaɪpəkəˈrekʃn; *NAmE* -pərk-/ *noun* [U, C] (*linguistics* 语言) the use of a wrong form or pronunciation of a word by sb who is trying to show that they can use language correctly. For example, the use of *I* instead of *me* in the sentence 'They invited my husband and I to dinner'. 矫枉过正；改正过头

hyper·gly·caemia (*BrE*) (*NAmE* **hyper·gly·cemia**) /ˌhaɪpəglaɪˈsiːmiə; *NAmE* -pərg-/ *noun* [U] (*medical* 医) the condition of having too high a level of blood sugar 高血糖

hyper·in·fla·tion /ˌhaɪpərɪnˈfleɪʃn/ *noun* [U] a situation in which prices rise very fast, causing damage to a country's economy 恶性通货膨胀；超通货膨胀；过度通货膨胀

hyper·link /ˈhaɪpəlɪŋk; *NAmE* -pərl-/ *noun* = LINK (4)：*Click on the hyperlink.* 点击链接。 ➲ WORDFINDER NOTE AT WEBSITE

hyper·mar·ket /ˈhaɪpəmɑːkɪt; *NAmE* -pərmɑːrk-/ *noun* (*BrE*) a very large shop located outside a town, that sells a wide range of goods 特大型商店（坐落在城外，商品种类繁多）

hyper·media /ˌhaɪpəˈmiːdiə; *NAmE* -pərˈm-/ *noun* [U] (*computing* 计) a system that links text to files containing images, sound or video 超媒体（连接文本与图像、声音或影像文件的系统）

hyper·nym /ˈhaɪpənɪm; *NAmE* -pərn-/ *noun* (*linguistics* 语言) = SUPERORDINATE ➲ COMPARE HYPONYM

hyper·sen·si·tive /ˌhaɪpəˈsensətɪv; *NAmE* -pərˈs-/ *adj.* ~ (**to sth**) **1** very easily offended 非常敏感的；很容易生气的：*He's hypersensitive to any kind of criticism.* 他对任何批评都受不了。 **2** extremely physically sensitive to particular substances, medicines, light, etc.（对某些物质、药物、光等）过敏的：*Her skin is hypersensitive.* 她的皮肤过敏。 ▸ **hyper·sen·si·tiv·ity** /ˌhaɪpəˌsensəˈtɪvəti; *NAmE* -pərˌs-/ *noun* [U]

hyper·space /ˈhaɪpəspeɪs; *NAmE* -pərs-/ *noun* [U] **1** (*specialist*) space which consists of more than three DIMENSIONS 超空间 **2** (in stories 小说) a situation in which it is possible to travel faster than light 超光速状态

hyper·ten·sion /ˌhaɪpəˈtenʃn; *NAmE* -pərˈt-/ *noun* [U] (*medical* 医) blood pressure that is higher than is normal 高血压

hyper·text /ˈhaɪpətekst; *NAmE* -pərt-/ *noun* [U] text stored in a computer system that contains links that allow the user to move from one piece of text or document to another 超文本 ➲ SEE ALSO HTML

hyper·thy·roid·ism /ˌhaɪpəˈθaɪrɔɪdɪzəm; *NAmE* -pərˈθ-/ *noun* [U] (*medical* 医) a condition in which the THYROID is too active, making the heart and other body systems function too quickly 甲状腺功能亢进

hyper·trophy /haɪˈpɜːtrəfi; *NAmE* -ˈpɜːrt-/ *noun* [U] (*biology* 生) an increase in the size of an organ or TISSUE because its cells grow in size （器官或组织的）肥大，过度生长

hyper·ven·ti·late /ˌhaɪpəˈventɪleɪt; *NAmE* -pərˈv-/ *verb* [I] (*specialist*) to breathe too quickly because you are very frightened or excited 通气过度 ▸ **hyper·ven·ti·la·tion** /ˌhaɪpəˌventɪˈleɪʃn; *NAmE* -pərˌven-/ *noun* [U]

hy·phen /ˈhaɪfn/ *noun* the mark (-) used to join two words together to make a new one, as in *back-up*, or to show that a word has been divided between the end of one line and the beginning of the next 连字符 ➲ COMPARE DASH *n.* (4)

hy·phen·ate /ˈhaɪfəneɪt/ *verb* ~ **sth** to join two words together using a hyphen; to divide a word between two lines of text using a hyphen 用连字符连接；用连字符分割（词语）：*Is your name hyphenated?* 你的名字有用连字符吗？ ▸ **hy·phen·ation** /ˌhaɪfəˈneɪʃn/ *noun* [U]: *hyphenation rules* 连字符使用规则

hyp·no·sis /hɪpˈnəʊsɪs; *NAmE* -ˈnoʊ-/ *noun* [U] **1** an unconscious state in which sb can still see and hear and can be influenced to follow commands or answer questions 催眠状态：*She only remembered details of the accident **under hypnosis**.* 她只有在催眠状态下才能记起那次事故的细节。 **2** = HYPNOTISM：*He uses hypnosis as part of the treatment.* 他用催眠术作为治疗的一部分。◇ *Hypnosis helped me give up smoking.* 催眠帮助我戒了烟。

hypno·ther·apy /ˌhɪpnəʊˈθerəpi; *NAmE* ˌhɪpnoʊ-/ *noun* [U] a kind of treatment that uses HYPNOSIS to help with physical or emotional problems 催眠疗法

hyp·not·ic /hɪpˈnɒtɪk; *NAmE* -ˈnɑːt-/ *adj.*, *noun*

■ *adj.* **1** making you feel as if you are going to fall asleep, especially because of a regular, repeated noise or movement 有催眠作用的；使人昏昏欲睡的 SYN **soporific**：*hypnotic music* 引人昏昏欲睡的音乐 ◇ *His voice had an almost hypnotic effect.* 他的声音有一种近乎催眠的作用。 **2** [only before noun] connected with or produced by hypnosis 催眠状态的；催眠状态引起的：***a hypnotic trance/state*** 催眠迷睡 / 状态 **3** (of a drug 药物) making you sleep 安眠的

■ *noun* (*specialist*) a drug that makes you sleep; a SLEEPING PILL 催眠药

hyp·no·tism /ˈhɪpnətɪzəm/ (*also* **hyp·no·sis**) *noun* [U] the practice of HYPNOTIZING a person (= putting them into an unconscious state) 催眠术；催眠

hyp·no·tist /ˈhɪpnətɪst/ *noun* a person who hypnotizes people 催眠术专家 ➲ WORDFINDER NOTE AT TREATMENT

hyp·no·tize (*BrE also* **-ise**) /ˈhɪpnətaɪz/ *verb* **1** ~ **sb** to produce a state of HYPNOSIS in sb 对（某人）施催眠术 **2** [usually passive] ~ **sb** (*formal*) to interest sb so much that they can think of nothing else 使（某人）着迷；迷住 SYN **mesmerize**

hypo- /ˈhaɪpəʊ; *NAmE* -poʊ/ (*also* **hyp-**) *prefix* (in adjectives and nouns 构成形容词和名词) under; below normal 在…下；低于；次于：*hypodermic* 皮下注射的 ◇ *hypothermia* 体温过低 ➲ COMPARE HYPER- ➲ MORE LIKE THIS 6, page R25

hypo·allergen·ic /ˌhaɪpəʊˌæləˈdʒenɪk; *NAmE* ˌhaɪpoʊˌælər-/ *adj.* (*specialist*) **hypoallergenic** substances and materials are unlikely to cause an ALLERGIC reaction in the person who uses them 不致过敏的；低变敏原的

hypo·chon·dria /ˌhaɪpəˈkɒndriə; *NAmE* -ˈkɑːn-/ *noun* [U] a state in which sb worries all the time about their health and believes that they are ill/sick when there is nothing wrong with them 疑病（症）

hypo·chon·driac /ˌhaɪpəˈkɒndriæk; *NAmE* -ˈkɑːn-/ *noun* a person who suffers from hypochondria 疑病患者：*Don't be such a hypochondriac!—there's nothing wrong with you.* 别这么忧心忡忡的了！你根本没病。 ▸ **hypo·chon·driac** (*also* **hypo·chon·driacal**) *adj.*

hyp·oc·risy /hɪˈpɒkrəsi; *NAmE* hɪˈpɑːk-/ *noun* (*pl.* **-ies**) [U, C] (*disapproving*) behaviour in which sb pretends to have moral standards or opinions that they do not actually have 伪善；虚伪：*He condemned the hypocrisy of those politicians who do one thing and say another.* 他谴责了那些说一套做一套的政客的虚伪。

hypo·crite /ˈhɪpəkrɪt/ *noun* (*disapproving*) a person who pretends to have moral standards or opinions that they do not actually have 伪君子；伪善者；虚伪的人 ▸ **hypo·crit·ical** /ˌhɪpəˈkrɪtɪkl/ *adj.*：*It would be hypocritical of me to have a church wedding when I don't believe in God.* 我不信上帝却到教堂举行婚礼，那就是我的虚伪了。 **hypo·crit·ic·al·ly** /-kli/ *adv.*

hypo·der·mic /ˌhaɪpəˈdɜːmɪk; *NAmE* -ˈdɜːrm-/ (*also* ˌ**hypodermic** ˈ**needle**, ˌ**hypodermic syˈringe**) *noun* a medical instrument with a long thin needle that is used to give sb an INJECTION under their skin 皮下注射器 ▸ **hypo·der·mic** *adj.*：*a hypodermic injection* (= one under the skin) 皮下注射

hypo·gly·caemia (*BrE*) (*NAmE* **hypo·gly·cemia**) /ˌhaɪpəʊglaɪˈsiːmiə; *NAmE* -poʊg-/ *noun* [U] (*medical* 医) the condition of having too low a level of blood sugar 低血糖

hypo·nym /ˈhaɪpənɪm/ *noun* (*linguistics* 语言) a word with a particular meaning that is included in the meaning of a more general word, for example 'dog' and 'cat' are **hyponyms** of 'animal' 下义词，下位词（如 dog 和 cat 是 animal 的下义词） ➲ COMPARE SUPERORDINATE

hypo·taxis /ˌhaɪpəʊˈtæksɪs; *NAmE* -poʊ-/ *noun* [U] (*grammar* 语法) the use of SUBORDINATE CLAUSES 从句的使用；从属关系；主从结构 ➲ COMPARE PARATAXIS

hypot·en·use /haɪˈpɒtənjuːz; *NAmE* -ˈpɑːtənuːs; -njuːz/ *noun* (*geometry* 几何) the side opposite the RIGHT ANGLE of a RIGHT-ANGLED triangle （直角三角形的）斜边，弦 ➲ PICTURE AT TRIANGLE

hypo·thal·amus /ˌhaɪpəˈθæləməs/ *noun* (*anatomy* 解) an area in the central lower part of the brain that controls body temperature, HUNGER and the release of HORMONES 下丘脑（有调节体温、摄食、内分泌等的功能）

hypo·ther·mia /ˌhaɪpəˈθɜːmiə; *NAmE* -ˈθɜːrm-/ *noun* [U] a medical condition in which the body temperature is much lower than normal 低体温；低温

hy·poth·esis AW /haɪˈpɒθəsɪs; *NAmE* -ˈpɑːθ-/ *noun* (*pl.* **hy·poth·eses** /-siːz/) **1** [C] an idea or explanation of sth that is based on a few known facts but that has not yet been proved to be true or correct（有少量事实依据但未被证实的）假说，假设 SYN **theory**: *to formulate/confirm a hypothesis* 提出 / 证实假设 ◇ *a hypothesis about the function of dreams* 关于梦的作用的假说 ➲ WORDFINDER NOTE AT SCIENCE ➲ COLLOCATIONS AT SCIENTIFIC **2** [U] guesses and ideas that are not based on certain knowledge（凭空的）猜想，猜测 SYN **speculation**: *It would be pointless to engage in hypothesis before we have the facts.* 在我们还没掌握事实之前瞎猜是毫无意义的。

hy·pothe·size AW (*BrE also* **-ise**) /haɪˈpɒθəsaɪz; *NAmE* -ˈpɑːθ-/ *verb* [T, I] ~ (**sth**) | ~ **that...** (*formal*) to suggest a way of explaining sth when you do not definitely know about it; to form a hypothesis 假设；假定: *The causes can be hypothesized but not proved.* 原因能够被假定，但不能被证实。◇ *We can only hypothesize that the cases we know about are typical.* 我们只能假设我们知道的案例是典型的。

hypo·thet·ic·al AW /ˌhaɪpəˈθetɪkl/ *adj.* based on situations or ideas which are possible and imagined rather than real and true 假设的；假定的: *a* ***hypothetical question/situation/example*** 假定的问题 / 情况 / 例子 ◇ *Let us take the hypothetical case of Sheila, a mother of two...* 我们且举关于希拉这个假定的例子，她是一位有两个孩子的母亲… ◇ *I wasn't asking about anybody in particular—it was a* ***purely hypothetical*** *question.* 我并没有问到具体某个人，那不过是个纯粹假设性的问题。▶ **hypo·thet·ic·al·ly** AW /-kli/ *adv.*

hypo·thy·roid·ism /ˌhaɪpəʊˈθaɪrɔɪdɪzəm; *NAmE* -poʊ-/ *noun* [U] (*medical* 医) a condition in which the THYROID is not active enough, making growth and mental development slower than normal 甲状腺功能减退

hyp·ox·aemia (*BrE*) (*NAmE* **hyp·ox·emia**) /ˌhaɪpɒkˈsiːmiə; *NAmE* -pɑːk-/ *noun* [U] (*medical* 医) a lower than normal amount of OXYGEN in the blood 低氧血；低氧血症

hyp·oxia /haɪˈpɒksiə; *NAmE* -ˈpɑːk-/ *noun* [U] (*medical* 医) a condition in which not enough OXYGEN reaches the body's TISSUES 缺氧；低氧

hys·ter·ec·tomy /ˌhɪstəˈrektəmi/ *noun* (*pl.* **-ies**) [C, U] a medical operation to remove a woman's WOMB 子宫切除（术）

hys·teria /hɪˈstɪəriə; *NAmE* -ˈstɪr-/ *noun* [U] **1** a state of extreme excitement, fear or anger in which a person, or a group of people, loses control of their emotions and starts to cry, laugh, etc. 歇斯底里；情绪失控: *There was* ***mass hysteria*** *when the band came on stage.* 乐队登台时观众一片疯狂。◇ *A note of hysteria crept into her voice.* 她的声音听来有点歇斯底里。 **2** (*disapproving*) an extremely excited and exaggerated way of behaving or reacting to an event 大肆鼓吹；狂热夸张；大惊小怪: *the usual media hysteria that surrounds royal visits* 媒体对于王室成员访问的惯常的大肆渲染 ◇ *public hysteria about AIDS* 公众对艾滋病谈虎色变 **3** (*medical* 医) a condition in which sb experiences violent or extreme emotions that they cannot control, especially as a result of shock 癔症；歇斯底里

hys·ter·ic·al /hɪˈsterɪkl/ *adj.* **1** in a state of extreme excitement, and crying, laughing, etc. in an uncontrolled way 歇斯底里的；情绪狂暴不可抑止的: *hysterical screams* 歇斯底里的尖叫 ◇ *a hysterical giggle* 无法控制的傻笑 ◇ *He became almost hysterical when I told him.* 我告诉他时，他几乎要发疯了。◇ *Let's not get hysterical.* 咱们别太激动。◇ (*disapproving*) *He thought I was being a hysterical female.* 他觉得我当时像个歇斯底里的女人。 **2** (*informal*) extremely funny 极其可笑的 SYN **hilarious**: *She seemed to find my situation absolutely hysterical.* 她好像觉得我的处境极端可笑。 HELP Some speakers do not pronounce the 'h' at the beginning of **hysterical** and use 'an' instead of 'a' before it. This now sounds old-fashioned. 有人说 hysterical 时不发 h 音，前面用 an 而不用 a，现在听起来过时了。▶ **hys·ter·ic·al·ly** /-kli/ *adv.*: *to laugh/cry/scream/sob hysterically* 歇斯底里地大笑 / 大哭 / 尖叫 / 哭泣 ◇ *hysterically funny* 极其可笑

hys·ter·ics /hɪˈsterɪks/ *noun* [pl.] **1** an expression of extreme fear, excitement or anger that makes sb lose control of their emotions and cry, laugh, etc. 歇斯底里的表现: *He went into hysterics when he heard the news.* 他听到这个消息时变得歇斯底里。 **2** (*informal*) wild LAUGHTER 狂笑: *She had the audience* ***in hysterics***. 她令观众捧腹大笑。

IDM **have hysterics** (*informal*) to be extremely upset and angry 极其愤怒: *My mum'll have hysterics when she sees the colour of my hair.* 我妈妈看到我的头发的颜色会火冒三丈的。

Hz *abbr.* (in writing 书写形式) HERTZ 赫；赫兹

Ii

I 🔑 /aɪ/ *noun, pron., symbol, abbr.*

■ ***noun*** (*also* **i**) [C, U] (*pl.* **Is, I's, i's** /aɪz/) the 9th letter of the English alphabet 英语字母表的第 9 个字母：*'Island' begins with (an) I/'I'.* * island 一词以字母 i 开头。IDM SEE DOT *v.*

■ ***pron.*** 🔑 used as the subject of a verb when the speaker or writer is referring to himself/herself （指称自己，作动词的主语）我：*I think I'd better go now.* 我想我最好现在就走。◇ *He and I are old friends.* 他和我是老朋友。◇ *When they asked me if I wanted the job, I said yes.* 他们问我是否想要那份工作，我说想。◇ *I'm not going to fall, am I?* 我不会摔倒的，对吧？◇ *I'm taller than her, aren't I?* 我比她高，是吧？➲ SEE ALSO ME *pron.*

■ ***symbol*** (*also* **i**) the number 1 in ROMAN NUMERALS （罗马数字）1

■ ***abbr.*** (*also* **I.**) (especially on maps) Island(s); ISLE （尤用于地图）岛，群岛

i- /aɪ/ *combining form* (in the names of products 构成产品名称) (*computing* 计) INTERACTIVE (= allowing information to be passed continuously and in both directions between a computer and the person who uses it) （人与计算机）交互的，互动的：*The i-writer teaches you how to plan and write essays.* 交互式写作程序教你如何构思与撰写文章。

I-9 form /ˌaɪ ˈnaɪn fɔːm; *NAmE* fɔːrm/ *noun* (*US*) an official document that an employer must have which shows that an employee has the right to work in the US * I-9 表，雇员雇佣资格证明（雇主必须持有，证明雇员有权在美国工作）

-ial *suffix* (in adjectives 构成形容词) typical of 有…特性的：*dictatorial* 独裁的 ▸ **-ially** (in adverbs 构成副词)：*officially* 正式地

iam·bic /aɪˈæmbɪk/ *adj.* (*specialist*) (of rhythm in poetry 诗的韵步) in which one weak or short syllable is followed by one strong or long syllable 抑扬格的（每一短或弱音节后接一长或强音节）：*a poem written in* ***iambic pentameters*** (= in lines of ten syllables, five short and five long) 抑扬格五音步诗

iam·bus /aɪˈæmbəs/ *noun* (*pl.* **iambi** /-baɪ/, **iam·buses**) (*also* **iamb** /ˈaɪæm; ˈaɪæmb/) (*specialist*) a unit of sound in poetry consisting of one weak or short syllable followed by one strong or long syllable （诗歌的）抑扬格

-ian, -an *suffix* **1** (in nouns and adjectives 构成名词和形容词) from; typical of 来自；有…特征的：*Bostonian* 波士顿人 ◇ *Brazilian* 巴西人 ◇ *Shakespearian* 莎士比亚的 ◇ *Libran* 属天秤座的 **2** (in nouns 构成名词) a specialist in 专长于…的人；…专家：*mathematician* 数学家

-iana, -ana *suffix* (in nouns 构成名词) a collection of objects, facts, stories, etc. connected with the person, place, period, etc. mentioned 集；汇编；收藏品：*Mozartiana* 莫扎特作品集 ◇ *Americana* 美国资料汇编 ◇ *Victoriana* 维多利亚时代的收藏品

IB /ˌaɪ ˈbiː/ *abbr.* INTERNATIONAL BACCALAUREATE™ 国际中学毕业会考：*to do the IB* 参加国际中学毕业会考

IBAN /ˈaɪbæn/ *noun* the abbreviation for 'International Bank Account Number' (= a bank account number that enables banks in other countries to identify your account so that money can be transferred between your account and accounts in those countries) 国际银行账号（全写为 International Bank Account Number，确认全球的银行账户的国际标准代码）

Iber·ian /aɪˈbɪəriən; *NAmE* -ˈbɪr-/ *adj.* relating to Spain and Portugal 伊比利亚的；西班牙和葡萄牙的：*the Iberian peninsula* 伊比利亚半岛

ibex /ˈaɪbeks/ *noun* (*pl.* **ibex**) a mountain GOAT with long curved horns 北山羊，羱羊（角长而弯曲）

ibid. (*also* **ib.**) *abbr.* (in writing 书写形式) in the same book or piece of writing as the one that has just been mentioned (from Latin 'ibidem') （源自拉丁语 ibidem，指在同一书或作品中）同前，同上

-ibility ➲ -ABLE

ibis /ˈaɪbɪs/ *noun* (*pl.* **ibises**) a bird with a long neck, long legs and a long beak that curves downwards, that lives near water 鹮（涉禽，长颈长腿，喙长而向下弯曲）

-ible, -ibly ➲ -ABLE

Ibo /ˈiːbəʊ; *NAmE* ˈiːboʊ/ *noun* = IGBO

ibu·profen /ˌaɪbjuːˈprəʊfen; *NAmE* -ˈproʊ-/ *noun* [U] a drug used to reduce pain and INFLAMMATION 布洛芬，异丁苯丙酸（镇痛消炎药）

-ic *suffix* **1** (in adjectives and nouns 构成形容词和名词) connected with 与…有关；…的：*scenic* 风景优美的 ◇ *economic* 经济的 ◇ *Arabic* 阿拉伯语 **2** (in adjectives 构成形容词) that performs the action mentioned 动作（或行为）…的：*horrific* 令人惊恐的 ◇ *specific* 独特的 ▸ **-ical** (in adjectives 构成形容词)：*comical* 滑稽的 **-ically** (in adverbs 构成副词)：*physically* 身体上

ICE /ˌaɪ siː ˈiː/ *abbr.* (in a mobile/cell phone contact list) the abbreviation for 'in case of emergency' (= the name and number of a person to contact if you are ill, you have an accident, etc.) （手机通讯录上的）紧急联系人（全写为 in case of emergency）：*You should make sure that you have an ICE number stored in your phone.* 务必确保手机里存储一个紧急联系人的号码。

ice 🔑 /aɪs/ *noun, verb*

■ ***noun*** **1** 🔑 [U] water that has frozen and become solid 冰：*There was ice on the windows.* 窗户上有冰花。◇ *The lake was covered with a* ***sheet of ice***. 湖面上覆盖着一层冰。◇ *My hands are as cold as ice.* 我的双手冰冷。➲ VISUAL VOCAB PAGE V5 ➲ SEE ALSO ICY, BLACK ICE, DRY ICE **2** [sing.] (*usually* **the ice**) a frozen surface that people SKATE on 冰场；溜冰场：*The dancers came out onto the ice.* 舞蹈表演者出场来到滑冰场上。◇ *Both teams are on the ice, waiting for the whistle.* 两支参赛队伍都在冰场上等待着哨音。 **3** 🔑 [U] a piece of ice used to keep food and drinks cold 冰块：*I'll have lemonade please—no ice.* 请给我来杯柠檬汽水，不要加冰块。 **4** [C] (*old-fashioned, especially BrE*) an ice cream 一份冰淇淋 **5** [U] (*NAmE*) a type of sweet food that consists of ice that has been crushed and flavoured 冰冻甜食

IDM **break the ˈice** to say or do sth that makes people feel more relaxed, especially at the beginning of a meeting, party, etc. （尤指聚会等开始时，用言语或行动）打破隔阂；打头说话 ➲ SEE ALSO ICEBREAKER (2) **cut no ˈice (with sb)** to have no influence or effect on sb （对某人）无影响，不起作用：*His excuses cut no ice with me.* 他的申辩丝毫不能说服我。 **on ˈice 1** (of wine, etc. 果酒等) kept cold by being surrounded by ice 冰镇 **2** (of a plan, etc. 计划等) not being dealt with now; waiting to be dealt with at a later time 被搁置；留待考虑：*We've had to* ***put*** *our plans* ***on ice*** *for the time being.* 我们不得不把计划暂时搁置。 **3** (of entertainment, etc. 娱乐等) performed by SKATERS on an ICE RINK 冰上表演的：*Cinderella on ice* 《灰姑娘》冰上演出 ➲ MORE AT THIN *adj.*

■ ***verb*** **~ sth** to cover a cake with ICING 在（糕饼上）加糖霜

PHR V **ˌice ˈover/ˈup** | **ˌice sth↔ˈover/ˈup** to become covered with ice; to cover sth with ice （使）结上一层冰，覆盖着冰

ˈice age (*often* **the Ice Age**) *noun* one of the long periods of time, thousands of years ago, when much of the earth's surface was covered in ice 冰期；冰川期；冰河时代

ˈice axe (*BrE*) (*US usually* **ˈice ax**) *noun* a tool used by people climbing mountains for cutting steps into ice 冰镐（登山用）➲ PICTURE AT AXE

ice·berg /ˈaɪsbɜːɡ; *NAmE* -bɜːrɡ/ *noun* an extremely large mass of ice floating in the sea 冰山（浮在海上的巨大冰块） IDM SEE TIP *n.*

ˌiceberg ˈlettuce *noun* a type of LETTUCE (= a salad vegetable) with crisp pale green leaves that form a tight ball 卷心莴苣

ice·block /ˈaɪsblɒk; *NAmE* -blɑːk/ *noun* (*AustralE, NZE*) a piece of flavoured ice on a stick 冰糕；冰棍；冰棒

ˌice-ˈblue *adj.* (especially of eyes 尤指眼睛) very pale blue in colour 淡蓝色的 ➲ **MORE LIKE THIS** 15, page R26

ˈice-bound *adj.* surrounded by or covered in ice 被冰围封的；冰封的

ice·box /ˈaɪsbɒks; *NAmE* -bɑːks/ *noun* (*old-fashioned, especially US*) = FRIDGE

ice·break·er /ˈaɪsbreɪkə(r)/ *noun* **1** a strong ship designed to break a way through ice, for example in the Arctic or Antarctic 破冰船 **2** a thing that you do or say, like a game or a joke, to make people feel more relaxed, especially at the beginning of a meeting, party, etc.（会议或聚会等场合，尤其在开始的时候）活跃气氛的游戏（或笑话等）

ˈice bucket *noun* a container filled with ice and used for keeping bottles of wine, etc. cold 冰桶（冰镇用）

ˈice cap *noun* a layer of ice permanently covering parts of the earth, especially around the North and South Poles（尤指北极和南极的）冰冠

ˌice-ˈcold *adj.* **1** as cold as ice; very cold 冰冻的；冰凉的: *ice-cold beer* 冰镇啤酒 ◇ *My hands were ice-cold.* 我双手冰冷。 **2** not having or showing any emotion 冷漠无情的；冷淡的: *His eyes had grown ice-cold.* 他的目光变得冷酷无情。

ˌice ˈcream 🔑 (*also* **ˈice cream** *especially in NAmE*) *noun* [U, C] a type of sweet frozen food made from milk fat, flavoured with fruit, chocolate, etc. and often eaten as a DESSERT; a small amount of this food intended for one person, often served in a container made of biscuit that is shaped like a CONE（一份）冰淇淋，冰激凌: *Desserts are served with cream or ice cream.* 甜点上加奶油或冰淇淋。◇ *Who wants an ice cream?* 谁要冰淇淋？

ˈice cube *noun* a small, usually square, piece of ice used for making drinks cold 小冰块（用于冷饮）

iced /aɪst/ *adj.* **1** (of drinks 饮料) made very cold; containing ice 冰镇的；加冰块的: *iced coffee/tea* 冰咖啡；冰茶 **2** (of a cake, etc. 糕饼等) covered with ICING 加糖霜的: *an iced cake* 加糖霜的蛋糕

ˈice dancing (*also* **ˈice dance**) *noun* [U] the sport of dancing on ice 冰上舞蹈；冰舞 ▶ **ˈice dancer** *noun*

ˌiced ˈwater (*BrE*) (*NAmE* **ˈice water**) *noun* water with ice in it for drinking 冰水（饮料）

ˈice field *noun* a large area of ice, especially one near the North or South Pole 冰原（尤指南、北极附近）

ˈice floe (*also* **floe**) *noun* a large area of ice, floating in the sea（海上的）大片浮冰

ˈice hockey (*BrE*) (*NAmE* **hockey**) *noun* [U] a game played on ice, in which players use long sticks to hit a hard rubber disc (called a PUCK) into the other team's goal 冰球运动；冰上曲棍球 ➲ **VISUAL VOCAB** PAGE V48

ice·house /ˈaɪshaʊs/ *noun* a building for storing ice in, especially in the past, usually underground or partly underground（尤指旧时的）藏冰窖，藏冰库

ˌice ˈlolly (*also informal* **lolly**) (*both BrE*) (*NAmE* **Pop·sicle™**) *noun* a piece of ice flavoured with fruit, served on a stick 冰棍；冰棒

ˈice pack *noun* a plastic container filled with ice that is used to cool parts of the body that are injured, etc. 冰袋（用于受伤等部位降温）

ˈice pick *noun* a tool with a very sharp point for breaking ice with 碎冰锥

ˈice rink (*also* **ˈskating rink, rink**) *noun* a specially prepared flat surface of ice, where you can ice-skate; a building where there is an ice rink 溜冰场；冰球场；溜冰馆 ➲ **VISUAL VOCAB** PAGES V44, V48

ˈice sheet *noun* (*specialist*) a layer of ice that covers a large area of land for a long period of time 冰原；冰盖

ˈice shelf *noun* (*specialist*) a layer of ice that is attached to land and covers a large area of sea 冰架（与陆地相接的厚层浮动冰体）

ˈice skate (*also* **skate**) *noun* a boot with a thin metal blade on the bottom, that is used for SKATING on ice 冰鞋；溜冰鞋 ➲ **VISUAL VOCAB** PAGE V48

ˈice-skate *verb* [I] to SKATE on ice 滑冰；溜冰 ▶ **ˈice skater** *noun*

ˈice skating *noun* [U] = SKATING: *to go ice skating* 去溜冰 ➲ **VISUAL VOCAB** PAGE V44

ˈice water (*NAmE*) (*BrE* **ˌiced ˈwater**) *noun* water with ice in it for drinking 冰水（饮料）

icicle /ˈaɪsɪkl/ *noun* a pointed piece of ice that is formed when water freezes as it falls down from sth such as a roof（屋檐等处滴水形成的）冰锥，冰柱 ➲ **WORDFINDER NOTE** AT SNOW

icily /ˈaɪsɪli/ *adv.* said or done in a very unfriendly way 冷冰冰地: *'I have nothing to say to you,' she said icily.* "我对你没什么可说的。"她冷冷地说。

icing /ˈaɪsɪŋ/ (*especially BrE*) (*NAmE usually* **frost·ing**) *noun* [U] a sweet mixture of sugar and water, milk, butter or egg white that is used to cover and decorate cakes 糖霜（用以装饰糕饼等） ➲ SEE ALSO ROYAL ICING

IDM **the icing on the ˈcake** (*US also* **the frosting on the ˈcake**) something extra and not essential that is added to an already good situation or experience and that makes it even better 锦上添花

ˈicing sugar (*BrE*) (*US* **conˈfectioner's sugar, ˈpowdered sugar**) *noun* [U] fine white powder made from sugar, that is mixed with water to make icing（制糖霜用的）糖粉 ➲ **MORE LIKE THIS** 9, page R26

icky /ˈɪki/ *adj.* (**ick·ier, icki·est**) (*informal*) unpleasant (used especially about sth that is wet and sticky) 黏糊糊（令人不舒服）的

icon /ˈaɪkɒn; *NAmE* -kɑːn/ *noun* **1** (*computing* 计) a small symbol on a computer or SMARTPHONE screen that represents a program or a file 图标；图符: *Click on the printer icon with the mouse.* 用鼠标点击打印机图标。◇ *Tap the app icon on your phone to open it.* 轻触手机上的应用程序图标将其打开。 ➲ **WORDFINDER NOTE** AT FILE ➲ **VISUAL VOCAB** PAGE V74 **2** a famous person or thing that people admire and see as a symbol of a particular idea, way of life, etc. 崇拜对象；偶像: *Madonna and other pop icons of the 1980s* 麦当娜以及其他 20 世纪 80 年代的流行音乐偶像 ◇ *a **feminist/gay icon*** (= sb that feminists/gay people admire) 女权主义者的 / 同性恋者的偶像 **3** (*also* **ikon**) (in the Orthodox Church 东正教) a painting or statue of a holy person that is also thought of as a holy object 圣像

icon·ic /aɪˈkɒnɪk; *NAmE* -ˈkɑːnɪk/ *adj.* acting as a sign or symbol of sth 符号的；图标的；图符的；偶像的

icono·clast /aɪˈkɒnəklæst; *NAmE* -ˈkɑːnə-/ *noun* (*formal*) a person who criticizes popular beliefs or established customs and ideas 批评传统信仰（或习俗、思想）的人；反传统者

icono·clas·tic /aɪˌkɒnəˈklæstɪk; *NAmE* -ˌkɑːnə-/ *adj.* (*formal*) criticizing popular beliefs or established customs and ideas 批评传统信仰（或习俗思想）的 ▶ **icono·clasm** /aɪˈkɒnəklæzəm; *NAmE* -ˈkɑːnə-/ *noun* [U]: *the iconoclasm of the early Christians* 早期基督徒废除圣像的主张

I

icon·og·raphy /ˌaɪkəˈnɒɡrəfi; NAmE -ˈnɑːɡ-/ *noun* [U] the use or study of images or symbols in art 图示法；象征手法；图像学

icon·ology /ˌaɪkəˈnɒlədʒi; NAmE -ˈnɑːl-/ *noun* [U] the fact of a work of art being an image or symbol of sth（艺术上的）象征手法

-ics *suffix* (in nouns 构成名词) the science, art or activity of …的科学（或艺术、活动）: *physics* 物理学 ◇ *poetics* 诗学 ◇ *athletics* 田径运动

ICT /ˌaɪ siː ˈtiː/ *noun* [U] (*BrE*) the abbreviation for 'information and communications technology' (the study of the use of computers, the Internet, video, and other technology as a subject at school) 信息与通信技术（全写为 information and communications technology，学科）

ICU /ˌaɪ siː ˈjuː/ *noun* intensive care unit (in a hospital) 特别护理病房；重症监护室；加护病房 ➲ WORDFINDER NOTE AT HOSPITAL

I

icy /ˈaɪsi/ *adj.* (**icier**, **ici·est**) **1** very cold 冰冷的；冰冻的 SYN **freezing**: *icy winds/water* 凛冽的风；冰冷的水 ◇ *My feet were **icy cold**.* 我双脚冰冷。 **2** covered with ice 覆盖着冰的；结满冰的：*icy roads* 结满冰的路 **3** (of a person's voice, manner, etc. 嗓音、态度等) not friendly or kind; showing feelings of dislike or anger 冷冰冰的；冷峻的：*My eyes met his icy gaze.* 我的双眼迎视他冰冷的目光。 ➲ SEE ALSO ICILY ▸ **ici·ness** *noun* [U]

ID /ˌaɪ ˈdiː/ *noun, verb*

■ ***noun*** **1** [U, C] the abbreviation for 'identity' or 'identification' (an official way of showing who you are, for example a document with your name, date of birth and often a photograph on it) 身份证明（全写为 identity 或 identification）: *You must carry ID at all times.* 你必须随身携带身份证。 ◇ *The police checked IDs at the gate.* 警察在大门口查看身份证。 ◇ *an ID card* 身份证 **2** [C] IDENTIFICATION 身份鉴定；身份证明：*The police need a witness to make a positive ID.* 警方需要有目击者加以确认。 ➲ SEE ALSO CALLER ID

■ ***verb*** (**ID's**, **ID'ing**, **ID'd**, **ID'd**) (*informal*) **1** **~ sb** to identify sb, usually a criminal or a dead body 确认，鉴定（罪犯或尸体等的身份）: *The police haven't yet managed to ID the suspect.* 警方还未能确认嫌疑人的身份。 **2** **~ sb** to ask sb to show a document that shows proof of their name, age, etc. 使出示证件；检查…的身份：*The security guards ID'd everyone at the entrance to the festival.* 保安人员在庆典入口处检查每个人的证件。

Id = EID

id /ɪd/ *noun* (*psychology* 心) the part of the unconscious mind where many of a person's basic needs, feelings and desires are supposed to exist 本我，伊德（指人的潜意识中其基本需求、感情和欲望假定存在的部分）➲ COMPARE EGO (2), SUPEREGO

I'd *short form* **1** I had **2** I would

I'D card *noun* = IDENTITY CARD

-ide *suffix* (*chemistry* 化) (in nouns 构成名词) a COMPOUND of …化合物：*chloride* 氯化物

idea /aɪˈdɪə; NAmE -ˈdiːə/ *noun*

• **PLAN/THOUGHT** 计划；思想 **1** [C] a plan, thought or suggestion, especially about what to do in a particular situation 想法；构思；主意：*It would be **a good idea** to call before we leave.* 我们离开之前打个电话是个好主意。 ◇ **~ (of sth/of doing sth)** *I like the idea of living on a boat.* 我喜欢在船上居住的主意。 ◇ **~ (for sth)** *He already had an idea for his next novel.* 他已经构思好了下一部小说。 ◇ *Her family expected her to go to college, but she had **other ideas**.* 她的家人希望她上大学，但她另有打算。 ◇ *The surprise party was Jane's idea.* 那次惊喜聚会是简的主意。 ◇ ***It might be an idea*** (= it would be sensible) *to try again later.* 稍后再试或许是明智的。 ◇ *We've been toying with the idea of* (= thinking about) *getting a dog.* 我们一直有意无意地想着养条狗。 ◇ ***It seemed like a good idea at the time**, and then it all went horribly wrong.* 那在当时似乎是个好主意，但后来却铸成大错。 ◇ *The latest **big idea** is to make women more interested in sport.* 最近的流行思想是促进妇女对体育的兴趣。

• **IMPRESSION** 印象 **2** [U, sing.] **~ (of sth)** a picture or an impression in your mind of what sb/sth is like 印象；概念：*The brochure should give you **a good idea of** the hotel.* 这本小册子详细介绍这家旅馆。 ◇ *I had **some idea of** what the job would be like.* 我对于这份工作有了一些了解。 ◇ *She doesn't seem to have any idea of what I'm talking about.* 她对我所说的似乎一点也不懂。 ◇ *I don't want anyone **getting the wrong idea*** (= getting the wrong impression about sth). 我不希望任何人有所误会。 ◇ *An evening at home watching TV is not my idea of a good time.* 晚上待在家里看电视，我不认为是什么赏心乐事。

• **OPINION** 意见 **3** [C] **~ (about sth)** an opinion or a belief about sth 意见；看法；信念：*He has some very strange ideas about education.* 他对教育有些非常奇怪的看法。

• **FEELING** 感觉 **4** [sing.] **~ (that…)** a feeling that sth is possible （认为某事可能发生的）感觉：*What gave you the idea that he'd be here?* 是什么让你想到他会来这里？ ◇ *I have a pretty good idea where I left it—I hope I'm right.* 我记得很清楚把它落在哪儿了，但愿我是对的。

• **AIM** 目标 **5** **the idea** [sing.] **~ of sth/of doing sth** the aim or purpose of sth 目标；意图：*You'll soon **get the idea*** (= understand). 你很快就会明白的。 ◇ ***What's the idea** of the game?* 这个游戏的目的是什么？ ➲ SYNONYMS AT PURPOSE

IDM **give sb i'deas | put i'deas into sb's head** to give sb hopes about sth that may not be possible or likely; to make sb act or think in an unreasonable way 使某人抱有空想（或做不切实际的事）: *Who's been putting ideas into his head?* 是谁一直在让他想入非非的？ **have no i'dea | not have the faintest, first, etc. idea** (*informal*) used to emphasize that you do not know sth 丝毫不知道：*'What's she talking about?' 'I've no idea.'* "她在讲什么？" "我一点也不了解。" ◇ *He hasn't the faintest idea how to manage people.* 他根本不懂得人事管理。 **have the right i'dea** to have found a very good or successful way of living, doing sth, etc. 找到好的（或成功的）方式；找对路：*He's certainly got the right idea—retiring at 55.* 他真的想通了，打算在 55 岁时退休。 **'that's an idea!** (*informal*) used to reply in a positive way to a suggestion that sb has made 好主意！：*Hey, that's an idea! And we could get a band, as well.* 嘿，好主意！而且我们还可以找支乐队。 **'that's the idea!** (*informal*) used to encourage people and to tell them that they are doing sth right 干得好；做得对：*That's the idea! You're doing fine.* 对啦！你做得不错。 **you have no i'dea…** (*informal*) used to show that sth is hard for sb else to imagine 你难以想象…：*You've no idea how much traffic there was tonight.* 你难以想象今晚的交通有多拥挤。 ➲ MORE AT BUCK *v.*

ideal /aɪˈdiːəl/ *adj., noun*

■ ***adj.*** **1** **~ (for sth)** perfect; most suitable 完美的；理想的；最合适的：*This beach is ideal for children.* 这个海滩是孩子的理想去处。 ◇ *She's the ideal candidate for the job.* 她是这项工作最合适的人选。 ◇ *The trip to Paris will be an **ideal opportunity** to practise my French.* 去巴黎旅行将是我练习法语的绝好机会。 **2** [only before noun] existing only in your imagination or as an idea; not likely to be real 想象的；不切实际的：*the search for ideal love* 对理想中的爱的寻求 ◇ ***In an ideal world** there would be no poverty and disease.* 在理想的世界里没有贫穷和疾病。 IDM SEE WORLD ▸ **ideal·ly** /aɪˈdiːəli/ *adv.*: *She's **ideally suited** for this job.* 她最适合这项工作。 ◇ *Ideally, I'd like to live in New York, but that's not possible.* 按理想来说，我希望住在纽约，但那是不可能的。

■ ***noun*** **1** [C] an idea or standard that seems perfect, and worth trying to achieve or obtain 理想；看似完美的思想（或标准）：*political ideals* 政治理想 ◇ *She found it hard to live up to his high ideals.* 她觉得很难达到他的高标准要求。 **2** [C, usually sing.] **~ (of sth)** a person or thing that you think is perfect 完美的人（或事物）：*It's my ideal of what a family home should be.* 这是我心目中完美的家庭住宅。

ideal·ism /aɪˈdiːəlɪzəm/ *noun* [U] **1** the belief that a perfect life, situation, etc. can be achieved, even when this is not very likely 理想主义： *He was full of youthful idealism.* 他满脑子都是年轻人的理想主义。**2** (*philosophy* 哲) the belief that our ideas are the only things that are real and that we can know about 唯心主义；唯心论；观念论；理念论 ➲ COMPARE MATERIALISM (2), REALISM ▶ **ideal·ist** *noun*： *He's too much of an idealist for this government.* 在现政府的眼中，他是一个过度的理想主义者。

ideal·is·tic /ˌaɪdiəˈlɪstɪk/ *adj.* having a strong belief in perfect standards and trying to achieve them, even when this is not realistic 理想主义的；空想的： *She's still young and idealistic.* 她还年轻并且耽于空想。 ▶ **ideal·is·tic·al·ly** /ˌaɪdiəˈlɪstɪkli/ *adv.*

ideal·ize (*BrE also* **-ise**) /aɪˈdiːəlaɪz/ *verb* ~ **sb/sth** to consider or represent sb/sth as being perfect or better than they really are 将…视为理想；将…理想化： *It is tempting to idealize the past.* 人都爱把过去的日子说得很美好。◇ *an idealized view of married life* 对于婚姻生活的理想化的看法 ▶ **ideal·iza·tion, -isa·tion** /aɪˌdiːəlaɪˈzeɪʃn; *NAmE* -ləˈz-/ *noun* [U, C]

ide·ate /ˈaɪdieɪt/ *verb* (*formal*) **1** [T] ~ **sth** to form an idea of sth; to imagine sth 对…形成概念；想象 **2** [I] to form ideas; to think 形成概念；想 ▶ **idea·tion** /ˌaɪdiˈeɪʃn/ *noun* [U]

idée fixe /ˌiːdeɪ ˈfiːks/ *noun* (*pl.* **idées fixes** /ˌiːdeɪ ˈfiːks/) (*from French*) an idea or a desire which is so strong that you cannot think about anything else 执着的想法（或欲望）；固有观念

idem /ˈɪdem/ *adv.* (*from Latin*) from the same book, article, author, etc. as the one that has just been mentioned （指出自同一书、文章、作者等）同前，同上

ident /ˈaɪdent/ *noun* (*BrE*) a piece of music or a short film that is broadcast between programmes so that people can recognize a radio station or television channel （电台或电视节目之间插播的）标志曲，标志短片

iden·ti·cal AW /aɪˈdentɪkl/ *adj.* **1** similar in every detail 完全同样的；相同的： *a row of identical houses* 完全一样的一排房子 ◇ *The two pictures are similar, although not identical.* 这两幅画很相似，虽然不完全相同。◇ ~ **to sb/sth** *Her dress is almost identical to mine.* 她的连衣裙和我的几乎一模一样。◇ ~ **with sb/sth** *The number on the card should be identical with the one on the chequebook.* 卡上的号码应该和支票簿上的相同。 ➲ LANGUAGE BANK AT SIMILARLY **2** **the identical** [only before noun] the same 同一的： *This is the identical room we stayed in last year.* 这就是我们去年住的那个房间。 ▶ **iden·ti·cal·ly** AW /-kli/ *adv.*： *The children were dressed identically.* 孩子们的穿着完全一样。

iˌdentical ˈtwin (*also specialist* **monozyˌgotic ˈtwin**) *noun* either of two children or animals born from the same mother at the same time who have developed from a single egg. Identical twins are of the same sex and look very similar. 单卵性双胞胎之一（性别相同，外貌相似） ➲ COMPARE DIZYGOTIC TWIN, FRATERNAL TWIN

iden·ti·fi·able AW /aɪˌdentɪˈfaɪəbl/ *adj.* that can be recognized 可识别的；可辨认的： *identifiable characteristics* 可识别的特征 ◇ *The house is easily identifiable by the large tree outside.* 这房子很容易从外面的这棵大树辨认出来。 OPP **unidentifiable**

iden·ti·fi·ca·tion AW /aɪˌdentɪfɪˈkeɪʃn/ *noun* **1** (*abbr.* **ID**) [U, C] the process of showing, proving or recognizing who or what sb/sth is 鉴定；辨认： *The identification of the crash victims was a long and difficult task.* 坠机事故中伤亡者的辨认工作费时而且困难重重。 ◇ *Each product has a number for easy identification.* 每件产品都有号码以便于识别。 ◇ *an identification number* 识别号码 ◇ *Only one witness could make a positive identification.* 只有一位目击者能够明确指认。 **2** [U] the process of recognizing that sth exists, or is important 确认；确定： *The early identification of children with special educational needs is very important.* 早期确认儿童有特殊教育需求很重要。 **3** (*abbr.* **ID**) [U] official papers or a document that can prove who you are 身份证明： *Can I see some identification, please?* 请出示某种身份证件好吗？ **4** [U, C] ~ (**with sb/sth**) a strong feeling of sympathy, understanding or support for sb/sth 强烈的同情感（或谅解、支持）： *her emotional identification with the play's heroine* 她与剧中女主人公在情感上的共鸣 ◇ *their increasing identification with the struggle for independence* 他们对争取独立的斗争越来越大的支持 **5** [U, C] ~ (**of sb**) (**with sb/sth**) the process of making a close connection between one person or thing and another 密切关联；紧密联系： *the voters' identification of the Democrats with high taxes* 选民把民主党和高税收画上等号

iˌdentifiˈcation parade *noun* (*also informal* **iˈdentity parade**) (*both BrE*) (*also* **ˈline-up** *NAmE, BrE*) a row of people, including one person who is suspected of a crime, who are shown to a witness to see if he or she can recognize the criminal 辨认行列，列队认人（把嫌疑犯同其他人排在一起，让目击者辨认）

iden·ti·fier /aɪˈdentɪfaɪə(r)/ *noun* (*computing* 计) a series of characters used to refer to a program or set of data within a program 标识符（可用以进入程序或其中的数据集）

iden·tify 🔑 AW /aɪˈdentɪfaɪ/ *verb* (**iden·ti·fies, iden·ti·fy·ing, iden·ti·fied, iden·ti·fied**) **1** 🔑 (*also informal* **ID**) to recognize sb/sth and be able to say who or what they are 确认；认出；鉴定： ~ **sb/sth as sb/sth** *The bodies were identified as those of two suspected drug dealers.* 那两具尸体被辨认出原是两名贩毒嫌疑犯。 ◇ ~ **sb/sth** *She was able to identify her attacker.* 她认出了袭击她的人。◇ *Passengers were asked to identify their own suitcases*

▼ **SYNONYMS** 同义词辨析

identify

know • recognize • name • make sb/sth out

These words all mean to be able to see or hear sb/sth and especially to be able to say who or what they are. 以上各词均含认出、辨别出之义。

identify to be able to say who or what sb/sth is 指确认、认出、鉴定： *She was able to identify her attacker.* 她认出了袭击她的人。

know to be able to say who or what sth is when you see or hear it because you have seen or heard it before 指能认出、能辨认出 NOTE **Know** is used especially to talk about sounds that seem familiar and when sb recognizes the quality or opportunity that sb/sth represents. * know 尤指认出熟悉的声音、辨别出人或事物所表现出的特质以及发现机会： *I couldn't see who was speaking, but I knew the voice.* 我看不到谁在讲话，但我能辨别出声音。◇ *She knows a bargain when she sees one.* 她一看就知道有没有便宜可捡。

recognize to know who sb is or what sth is when you see or hear them/it, because you have seen or heard them/it before 指认识、认出、辨别出： *I recognized him as soon as he came in the room.* 他一进屋我就认出了他。

name to say the name of sb/sth in order to show that you know who/what they are 指能说出…的名称、叫出…的名字： *The victim has not yet been named.* 受害人的姓名仍未得知。

make sb/sth out to manage to see or hear sb/sth that is not very clear 指看清、听清、分清、辨认清楚： *I could just make out a figure in the darkness.* 黑暗中我只看出了一个人的轮廓。

PATTERNS

- to identify/know/recognize sb/sth **by** sth
- to identify/recognize/name sb/sth **as** sb/sth
- to identify/know/recognize/make out **who/what/how...**
- to **easily/barely/just** identify/recognize/make out sb/sth

I

before they were put on the plane. 乘客被要求先确认自己的旅行箱再送上飞机。◇ *Many of those arrested refused to* ***identify themselves*** (= would not say who they were). 很多被逮捕的人拒不透露身份。◇ *First of all we must identify the problem areas.* 首先我们必须找出问题所在。 **2** to find or discover sb/sth 找到；发现： **~ sth** *Scientists have identified a link between diet and cancer.* 科学家发现了饮食与癌症之间的关联。◇ *As yet they have not identified a buyer for the company.* 迄今为止他们还没有为公司找到买主。◇ **~ what, which, etc....** *They are trying to identify what is wrong with the present system.* 他们正试图弄清现行制度的弊端所在。 **3 ~ sb/sth (as sb/sth)** to make it possible to recognize who or what sb/sth is 显示；说明身份： *In many cases, the clothes people wear identify them as belonging to a particular social class.* 很多情况下，人们的穿着显示出他们的社会阶层。

PHR V **i'dentify with sb** to feel that you can understand and share the feelings of sb else 与某人产生共鸣；谅解；同情 SYN **sympathize**: *I didn't enjoy the book because I couldn't identify with any of the main characters.* 我不喜欢这本书，因为我无法与其中的任何主要角色产生共鸣。 **i'dentify sb with sth** to consider sb to be sth 把某人视为： *He was not the 'tough guy' the public identified him with.* 他并不是公众所认定的那种硬汉。 **i'dentify sth with sth** to consider sth to be the same as sth else 认为某事物等同于 SYN **equate**: *You should not identify wealth with happiness.* 你不应该认为财富就等于幸福。 **be i'dentified with sb/sth | i'dentify yourself with sb/sth** to support sb/sth; to be closely connected with sb/sth 支持；与…有密切关联： *The Church became increasingly identified with opposition to the regime.* 教会日益和反对政权的势力走到一起。

Iden·ti·kit™ /aɪ'dentɪkɪt/ (*BrE*) (*US* **com·pos·ite, com'pos·ite sketch**) *noun* a set of drawings of different features that can be put together to form the face of a person, especially sb wanted by the police, using descriptions given by people who saw the person; a picture made in this way 容貌拼图（根据目击者描述拼制出人的面部像，尤指警方要捉拿的人） ➲ COMPARE E-FIT™, PHOTOFIT

iden·tity AW /aɪ'dentəti/ *noun* (*pl.* **-ies**) **1** [C, U] (*abbr.* **ID**) who or what sb/sth is 身份；本身；本体： *The police are trying to discover the identity of the killer.* 警方正努力调查杀人凶手的身份。◇ *Their identities were kept secret.* 他们的身份保密。◇ *She is innocent; it was a case of* ***mistaken identity***. 她是无辜的；那是身份判断错误。◇ *Do you have any proof of identity?* 你有身份证明吗？◇ *The thief used a false identity.* 窃贼使用的是假身份。◇ *She went through an* ***identity crisis*** *in her teens* (= was not sure of who she was or of her place in society). 她在十多岁时经历了一次身份危机。 **2** [C, U] the characteristics, feelings or beliefs that distinguish people from others 特征；特有的感觉（或信仰）： *a sense of* ***national/cultural/personal/group identity*** 民族/文化/个人/群体特性的认同感 ◇ *a plan to strengthen the* ***corporate identity*** *of the company* 加强公司的企业形象的计划 **3** [U] **~ (with sb/sth) | ~ (between A and B)** the state or feeling of being very similar to and able to understand sb/sth 同一性；相同；一致： *an identity of interests* 利益一致 ◇ *There's a close identity between fans and their team.* 球迷和他们的球队之间有密切的同一性。

i'dentity card (*also* **I'D card**) *noun* a card with a person's name, date of birth, photograph, etc. on it that proves who they are 身份证；身份卡

i'dentity parade *noun* (*BrE, informal*) = IDENTIFICATION PARADE

i'dentity theft *noun* [U] using sb else's name and personal information in order to obtain credit cards and other goods or to take money out of the person's bank accounts 身份盗窃（利用别人的名字、个人信息等获得信用卡、其他物品或从别人的账户中提取现金等）

ideo·gram /'ɪdiəgræm/ (*also* **ideo·graph** /'ɪdiəgrɑːf; *NAmE* -græf/) *noun* **1** a symbol that is used in a writing system, for example Chinese, to represent the idea of a thing, rather than the sounds of a word 表意文字（或符号） **2** (*specialist*) a sign or a symbol for sth 表意标志；表意符号

ideograms 表意文字；表意符号

Chinese character for soil
汉字的土

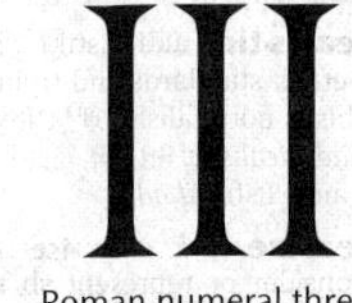

Roman numeral three
罗马数字 3

wheelchair access sign
轮椅通道标志

biohazard sign
有害生物物质标志

ideo·logue /'aɪdiəlɒg; 'ɪd-; *NAmE* -lɔːg; -lɑːg/ (*also* **ideolo·gist** /ˌaɪdi'ɒlədʒɪst; *NAmE* -'ɑːl-/) *noun* (*formal, sometimes disapproving*) a person whose actions are influenced by belief in a set of principles (= by an ideology) 理论家；思想家；空想家

ideol·ogy AW /ˌaɪdi'ɒlədʒi; *NAmE* -'ɑːl-/ *noun* [C, U] (*pl.* **-ies**) (*sometimes disapproving*) **1** a set of ideas that an economic or political system is based on 思想（体系）；思想意识： ***Marxist/capitalist ideology*** 马克思主义/资本主义思想体系 **2** a set of beliefs, especially one held by a particular group, that influences the way people behave 意识形态；观念形态： *the ideology of gender roles* 性别角色的观念形态 ◇ *alternative ideologies* 非传统的意识形态 ▸ **ideo·logic·al** AW /ˌaɪdiə'lɒdʒɪkl; *NAmE* -'lɑːdʒ-/ *adj.*: *ideological differences* 意识形态上的差别 **ideo·logic·al·ly** AW /kli/ *adv.*: *ideologically correct* 意识上正确

ides /aɪdz/ *noun* [pl.] the middle day of the month in the ancient Roman system, from which other days were calculated 月中日（古罗马历每月居中的一天）： *the ides of March* * 3 月 15 日

idi·ocy /'ɪdiəsi/ *noun* (*pl.* **-ies**) (*formal*) **1** [U] very stupid behaviour; the state of being very stupid 愚蠢行为；愚昧 SYN **stupidity** **2** [C] a very stupid act, remark, etc. 愚蠢的行动（或言论等）： *the idiocies of bureaucracy* 官僚体系所做的蠢事

idio·lect /'ɪdiəlekt/ *noun* [C, U] (*linguistics* 语言) the way that a particular person uses language 个人语型；个人言语方式 ➲ COMPARE DIALECT

idiom /'ɪdiəm/ *noun* **1** [C] a group of words whose meaning is different from the meanings of the individual words 习语；成语；惯用语： *'Let the cat out of the bag' is an idiom meaning to tell a secret by mistake.* "让猫从袋子里跑出来"是惯用语，意思是无意中泄露秘密。 ➲ SYNONYMS AT WORD **2** [U, C] (*formal*) the kind of language and grammar used by particular people at a particular time or place （某时期或某地区的人的）语言和语法 **3** [U, C] (*formal*) the style of writing, music, art, etc. that is typical of a particular person, group, period or place （写作、音乐、艺术等的）典型风格： ***the classical/contemporary/popular idiom*** 古典/当代/通俗风格

idiom·at·ic /ˌɪdiəˈmætɪk/ *adj.* **1** containing expressions that are natural to a NATIVE SPEAKER of a language 表达方式地道的；符合（某一）语言习惯的：*She speaks fluent and idiomatic English.* 她讲一口流利地道的英语。 **2** containing an idiom 包含习语的：*an idiomatic expression* 惯用语 ▸ **idiom·at·ic·al·ly** /-kli/ *adv.*

idio·syn·crasy /ˌɪdiəˈsɪŋkrəsi/ *noun* [C, U] (*pl.* **-ies**) a person's particular way of behaving, thinking, etc., especially when it is unusual; an unusual feature （个人特有的）习性；特征；癖好 SYN **eccentricity**：*The car has its little idiosyncrasies.* 这辆车有它的一些小小脾气。 ▸ **idio·syn·crat·ic** /ˌɪdiəsɪŋˈkrætɪk/ *adj.*：*His teaching methods are idiosyncratic but successful.* 他的教学方法很奇特，但很成功。

idiot /ˈɪdiət/ *noun* **1** (*informal*) a very stupid person 蠢人；笨蛋 SYN **fool**：*When I lost my passport, I felt such an idiot.* 我丢了护照时觉得自己像个大傻瓜。◊ *Not that switch, you idiot!* 不是那个开关，你这个蠢货！ **2** (*old-fashioned, offensive*) a person with very low intelligence who cannot think or behave normally 白痴

idi·ot·ic /ˌɪdiˈɒtɪk; *NAmE* -ˈɑːtɪk/ *adj.* very stupid 十分愚蠢的；白痴般的 SYN **ridiculous**：*an idiotic question* 很愚蠢的问题 ◊ *Don't be so idiotic!* 别这么傻了！ ▸ **idi·ot·ic·al·ly** /-kli/ *adv.*

idiot sav·ant /ˌiːdjəʊ sæˈvɒ̃; *NAmE* ˌiːdjoʊ sæˈvɑ̃ː/ *noun* (*pl.* **idiot sav·ants** or **idiots sav·ants** /ˌiːdjəʊ sæˈvɒ̃; *NAmE* ˌiːdjoʊ sæˈvɑ̃ː/) (*from French*) a person who has severe LEARNING DIFFICULTIES, but who has an unusually high level of ability in a particular skill, for example in art or music, or in remembering things 弱能特才，低能特才（有严重的学习障碍，但在艺术、音乐或记忆等方面有超常能力）

IDK /ˌaɪ diː ˈkeɪ/ *abbr.* (*informal*) (especially in TEXT MESSAGES, emails, etc.) I don't know 我不知道（全写为 I don't know，尤用于短信、电邮等）：*IDK what to do about it.* 我不知道这事该怎么办。

idle /ˈaɪdl/ *adj., verb*

■ ***adj.*** **1** (of people 人) not working hard 懈怠的；懒惰的 SYN **lazy**：*an idle student* 懒散的学生 **2** (of machines, factories, etc. 机器、工厂等) not in use 闲置的：*to lie/stand/remain idle* 闲置着 **3** (of people 人) without work 没有工作的；闲散的 SYN **unemployed**：*Over ten per cent of the workforce is now idle.* 现在有超过百分之十的劳动力闲置。 **4** [usually before noun] with no particular purpose or effect; useless 漫无目的的；无效的；无用的：*idle chatter/curiosity* 无聊的唠叨 / 好奇 ◊ *It was just an idle threat* (= not serious). 那只不过是吓唬吓唬而已。◊ *It is idle to pretend that their marriage is a success.* 佯装他们的婚姻有多美满是无意义的。 **5** [usually before noun] (of time 时间) not spent doing work or sth particular 空闲的：*In idle moments, he carved wooden figures.* 他空闲时就刻木雕。 IDM SEE DEVIL ▸ **idle·ness** *noun* [U]：*After a period of enforced idleness, she found a new job.* 她在被迫闲散了一段时间之后找到了份新工作。

■ ***verb*** **1** [T, I] to spend time doing nothing important 混时间；闲荡；无所事事：**~ sth** (+ **adv./prep.**) *They idled the days away, talking and watching television.* 他们天天在闲聊和看电视中消磨时光。◊ (+ **adv./prep.**) *They idled along by the river* (= walked slowly and with no particular purpose). 他们沿着河边闲逛。 **2** [I] (of an engine 发动机) to run slowly while the vehicle is not moving 空转；挂空挡；未熄火 SYN **tick over**：*She left the car idling at the roadside.* 她把汽车挂空挡停在路边。 **3** [T] **~ sb/sth** (*NAmE*) to close a factory, etc. or stop providing work for the workers, especially temporarily （尤指暂时地）关闭工厂，使（工人）闲着：*The strikes have idled nearly 4 000 workers.* 罢工使近 4 000 名工人闲着没事干。

idler /ˈaɪdlə(r)/ *noun* a person who is lazy and does not work 懒汉；无所事事的人 SYN **loafer**

idli /ˈɪdliː/ *noun* an Indian rice cake cooked using steam 印度蒸米糕

idly /ˈaɪdli/ *adv.* without any particular reason, purpose or effort; doing nothing 毫无目的地；漫不经心地；闲散地：*She sat in the sun, idly sipping a cool drink.* 她坐在阳光下懒洋洋地抿着冷饮。◊ *He wondered idly what would happen.* 他漫不经心地幻想着会发生什么事。◊ *We can't* ***stand idly by*** (= do nothing) *and let people starve.* 我们不能袖手旁观，任由人们挨饿。

idol /ˈaɪdl/ *noun* **1** a person or thing that is loved and admired very much 受到热爱和崇拜的人（或物）；偶像：***a pop/football/teen, etc. idol*** 流行音乐偶像、足球明星、青少年的偶像等 ◊ *the idol of countless teenagers* 无数青少年崇拜的偶像 ◊ ***a fallen idol*** (= sb who is no longer popular) 陨落的明星 **2** a statue that is worshipped as a god 神像

idol·atry /aɪˈdɒlətri; *NAmE* -ˈdɑːl-/ *noun* [U] **1** the practice of worshipping statues as gods 神像崇拜；偶像崇拜 **2** (*formal*) too much love or admiration for sb/sth 盲目崇拜：*football fans whose support for their team borders on idolatry* 对球队几乎到了盲目崇拜地步的足球迷 ▸ **idol·atrous** /aɪˈdɒlətrəs; *NAmE* -ˈdɑːl-/ *adj.*

idol·ize (*BrE also* **-ise**) /ˈaɪdəlaɪz/ *verb* **~ sb** to admire or love sb very much 崇拜；热爱 SYN **worship**：*a pop star idolized by millions of fans* 受数百万歌迷崇拜的流行音乐歌星 ◊ *They idolize their kids.* 他们溺爱自己的孩子。 ▸ **idol·iza·tion, -isa·tion** /ˌaɪdəlaɪˈzeɪʃn; *NAmE* -ləˈz-/ *noun* [U]

idyll /ˈɪdɪl; *NAmE* ˈaɪdl/ *noun* **1** (*literary*) a happy and peaceful place, event or experience, especially one connected with the countryside （尤指乡下的）愉快恬静的地方（或事情、经历） **2** a short poem or other piece of writing that describes a peaceful and happy scene 描述恬静愉快情景的短诗（或短文）；田园诗

idyl·lic /ɪˈdɪlɪk; *NAmE* aɪˈd-/ *adj.* peaceful and beautiful; perfect, without problems 平和美丽的；完美无瑕的：*a house set in idyllic surroundings* 在田园风光的环境中的房子 ◊ *to lead an idyllic existence* 过着诗情画意的生活 ◊ *The cottage sounds idyllic.* 小屋看来恬静宜人。 ▸ **idyl·lic·al·ly** /-kli/ *adv.*：*a house idyllically set in wooded grounds* 诗情画意般的林荫中的房子

i.e. 🔑 /ˌaɪ ˈiː/ *abbr.* used to explain exactly what the previous thing that you have mentioned means (from Latin 'id est') 也就是，亦即（源自拉丁文 id est）：

▼ **LANGUAGE BANK 用语库**

i.e.

Explaining what you mean 解释意思

- *Some poems are mnemonics,* ***i.e.*** *they are designed to help you remember something.* 有些诗歌是记忆代码，即是说，其目的是帮助人们记起某事。
- *Some poems are mnemonics,* ***that is to say,*** *they are designed to help you remember something.* 有些诗歌是记忆代码，就是说，其目的是帮助人们记起某事。
- *Mnemonic poems,* ***that is*** *poems designed to help you remember something, are an excellent way to learn lists.* 记事诗，即帮助人记起事情的诗歌，是记住一系列事物的极佳方式。
- *A limerick's rhyme scheme is A–A–B–B–A.* ***In other words,*** *the first, second, and fifth lines all rhyme with one another, while the third and fourth lines have their own rhyme.* 五行打油诗的韵律是 A-A-B-B-A。就是说，第一行、第二行和第五行押一个韵，而第三行和第四行押另一个韵。
- *In this exercise the reader is encouraged to work out the meaning,* ***or rather*** *the range of meanings, of the poem.* 这个练习鼓励读者弄清这首诗的意思，更确切地说是弄清其几种含意。
- *This is a poem about death,* ***or, more precisely,*** *dying.* 这是一首关于死亡的诗，更确切地说是关于临终的诗。
- *He says his poems deal with 'the big issues',* ***by which he means*** *love, loss, grief and death.* 他说他的诗涉及一些"重大问题"，这些问题是指爱、失去、痛苦和死亡。

➲ LANGUAGE BANK AT ABOUT

the basic essentials of life, i.e. housing, food and water 生活的基本需要，即住房、食物和水

-ie ➲ -Y

IED /ˌaɪ iː ˈdiː/ *abbr.* improvised explosive device (a bomb made and used by people who are not members of the military forces of a country) 临时爆炸装置

IELTS /ˈaɪelts/ *noun* [U] the abbreviation for 'International English Language Testing System' (a test that measures a person's ability to speak and write English at the level that is necessary to go to university in the UK, Ireland, Australia, Canada, South Africa and New Zealand) 国际英语测试系统考试，雅思考试（全写为 International English Language Testing System，英国、爱尔兰、澳大利亚、加拿大、南非和新西兰大学入学水平的英语应用能力考试）

I

if /ɪf/ *conj., noun*

■ ***conj.*** **1** used to say that one thing can, will or might happen or be true, depending on another thing happening or being true 如果；假若；倘若： *If you see him, give him this note.* 你要是见到他，就把这个便条给他。◇ *I'll only stay if you offer me more money.* 你给我更多的钱我才会留下。◇ *If necessary I can come at once.* 如果有必要，我可以马上来。◇ *You can stay for the weekend if you like.* 你如果愿意就留在这里过周末吧。◇ *If anyone calls, tell them I'm not at home.* 要是有人打电话来，就说我不在家。◇ *If he improved his IT skills, he'd* (= he would) *easily get a job.* 他如果提高了自己的信息技术技能，就会容易找到工作。◇ *You would know what was going on if you'd* (= you had) *listened.* 你若是注意听了就会知道发生什么事了。◇ *They would have been here by now if they'd caught the early train.* 假若他们赶上了早班火车，现在就该到这里了。◇ *If I was in charge, I'd do things differently.* 假若由我负责，我不会这样办事的。◇ (*rather formal*) *If I were in charge...* 假若由我负责…◇ ***Even if*** (= although) *you did see someone, you can't be sure it was him.* 即使你确实看见有个人，也不能保证那就是他。**2** when; whenever; every time 当；无论何时；每次： *If metal gets hot it expands.* 金属受热就膨胀。◇ *She glares at me if I go near her desk.* 我一走近她的办公桌，她就对我瞪眼。**3** (*formal*) used with *will* or *would* to ask sb politely to do sth （与 will 或 would 连用，表示客气地请求）： *If you will sit down for a few moments, I'll tell the manager you're here.* 请稍坐，我这就告诉经理说您来了。◇ *If you would care to leave your name, we'll contact you as soon as possible.* 麻烦您留下姓名，我们会尽快与您联系的。**4** used after *ask, know, find out, wonder,* etc. to introduce one of two or more possibilities （用于 ask、know、find out、wonder 等之后，引出两个或以上的可能性之一）是否 SYN **whether**: *Do you know if he's married?* 你知道他是否结婚了？◇ *I wonder if I should wear a coat or not.* 我不知道该不该穿外套。◇ *He couldn't tell if she was laughing or crying.* 他弄不清楚她是在笑还是在哭。◇ *Listen to the tune and see if you can remember the words.* 听听曲调，看你能否记起歌词。**5** used after verbs or adjectives expressing feelings （用于表示情感的动词或形容词之后）： *I am sorry if I disturbed you.* 很抱歉，打搅您了。◇ *I'd be grateful if you would keep it a secret.* 你如果能对此保密，我将不胜感激。◇ *Do you mind if I turn the TV off?* 我关上电视可以吗？**6** used to admit that sth is possible, but to say that it is not very important （承认某事可能，但不很重要）即使，虽然： *If she has any weakness, it is her Italian.* 如果要说她有什么缺点，那就是她的意大利语不大行。◇ ***So what if** he was late. Who cares?* 他就是迟到了又怎么样。谁在乎？**7** used before an adjective to introduce a contrast （置于形容词之前，引出对比）虽然，尽管： *He's a good driver, if a little over-confident.* 他是个好司机，虽然有点过于自信。◇ *We'll only do it once—**if at all**.* 我们就是干也只会干一次。**8** used to ask sb to listen to your opinion （请对方听自己的意见）： *If you ask me, she's too scared to do it.* 依我看，她被吓得不敢做了。◇ *If you think about it, those children must be at school by now.* 想想吧，那些孩子现在一定在学校了。◇ *If you remember, Mary was always fond of animals.* 记得吧，玛丽总是喜欢动物。**9** used before *could, may* or *might* to suggest sth or to interrupt sb politely （置于 could、may 或 might 之前，提出建议或客气地打断别人的话）： *If I may make a suggestion, perhaps we could begin a little earlier next week.* 我来提个建议吧，或许我们下个星期可以早一点开始。

IDM **ˌif and ˈwhen** used to say sth about an event that may or may not happen （谈及可能发生或不发生的事时说）： *If and when we ever meet again I hope he remembers what I did for him.* 倘若我们再次见面，我希望他还记得我为他做的事。 **if ˈanything** used to express an opinion about sth, or after a negative statement to suggest that the opposite is true （表达看法，或用在否定句之后表示反面意见才对）： *I'd say he was more like his father, if anything.* 依我看，如果一定要说他像谁的话，他比较像他的父亲。◇ *She's not thin—if anything she's on the plump side.* 她并不瘦，其实她还有点胖呢。 **if ˌI were ˈyou** used to give sb advice （提出劝告时说）： *If I were you I'd start looking for another job.* 我要是你，就会去另找工作了。 **if ˈnot 1** used to introduce a different suggestion, after a sentence with *if* （用在 if 引导的句子之后）不然，要不： *I'll go if you're going. If not* (= if you are not) *I'd rather stay at home.* 你去我就去。不然的话，我宁愿待在家里。**2** used after a *yes/no* question to say what will or should happen if the answer is 'no' （用于 yes / no 疑问句之后，表示如果答案是 no，将会或应该发生什么）： *Are you ready? If not, I'm going without you.* 你准备好了吗？否则我就自己去了。◇ *Do you want that cake? If not, I'll have it.* 你要那块蛋糕吗？不然我就要了。**3** used to suggest that sth may be even larger, more important, etc. than was first stated （表示可能更大或更重要等）： *They cost thousands if not millions of pounds to build.* 建设要耗费数千英镑，甚至可能是数百万英镑。 **if ˈonly** used to say that you wish sth was true or that sth had happened 但愿： *If only I were rich.* 但愿我很富有。◇ *If only I knew her name.* 我要是知道她的名字就好了。◇ *If only he'd remembered to send that letter.* 要是他没忘记发那封信就好了。◇ *If only I had gone by taxi.* 我要是乘出租车去就好了。 **it's not as if** used to say that sth that is happening is surprising （表示所发生的事情令人惊讶）： *I'm surprised they've invited me to their wedding—it's not as if I know them well.* 我很惊讶他们居然请我参加他们的婚礼，我跟他们似乎并不熟。 **ˈonly if** (*rather formal*) used to state the only situation in which sth can happen 只有： *Only if a teacher has given permission is a student allowed to leave the room.* 学生只有得到老师的许可才能离开教室。◇ *Only if the red light comes on is there any danger to employees.* 只有红灯闪亮时才有危及职工的险情。

▼ **GRAMMAR POINT 语法说明**

if / whether

- Both **if** and **whether** are used in reporting questions which expect 'yes' or 'no' as the answer * if 和 whether 均用于要求以 yes 或 no 作答的转述疑问句中： *She asked if/whether I wanted a drink.* 她问我要不要喝点什么。 although **whether** sounds more natural with particular verbs such as **discuss**, **consider** and **decide**. When a choice is offered between alternatives, **if** or **whether** can be used. 不过 whether 与 discuss、consider 和 decide 等动词连用听起来更自然。提供选择时用 if 或 whether 均可： *We didn't know if/whether we should write or phone.* 我们不知道是写信好还是打电话好。 In this last type of sentence, **whether** is usually considered more formal and more suitable for written English. 在最后这一句型中，一般认为 whether 较正式，更适用于书面语。

■ ***noun*** (*informal*) a situation that is not certain 不确定的情况： *If he wins—and **it's a big if**—he'll be the first Englishman to win for fifty years.* 假设他赢了，不过这还是个很大的疑问，他将成为五十年以来第一个获胜的英格兰人。◇ *There are still a lot of **ifs and buts** before everything's settled.* 在一切得以解决之前还有很多不确定因素。

iff /ɪf/ *conj.* (*mathematics* 数) an expression used in mathematics to mean 'if and only if' 当且仅当；在而且只有在…时

iffy /ˈɪfi/ *adj.* (*informal*) **1** (*especially BrE*) not in perfect condition; bad in some way 不完美的；有点坏的： *That meat smells a bit iffy to me.* 那块肉闻起来有点变质了。 **2** not certain 未确定的： *The weather looks slightly iffy.* 看来天气有些不稳定。

-ify, **-fy** *suffix* (in verbs 构成动词) to make or become 使得；变成： *purify* 净化 ◇ *solidify* 使凝固 ➲ MORE LIKE THIS 7, page R25

Igbo (*also* **Ibo**) /ˈiːbəʊ; *NAmE* ˈiːboʊ/ *noun* [U] a language spoken by the Igbo people of W Africa, especially in SE Nigeria 伊格博语，伊博语（西非伊格博族语言，尤指尼日利亚东南部方言）

igloo /ˈɪgluː/ *noun* (*pl.* **-oos**) a small round house or shelter built from blocks of hard snow by the Inuit people of northern N America （北美北部因纽特人的拱形圆顶）冰屋

ig·ne·ous /ˈɪgniəs/ *adj.* (*geology* 地) (of rocks 岩石) formed when MAGMA (= melted or liquid material lying below the earth's surface) becomes solid, especially after it has poured out of a VOLCANO 火成的（尤指火山喷出的）

ig·nite /ɪgˈnaɪt/ *verb* [I, T] (*formal*) to start to burn; to make sth start to burn （使）燃烧，着火；点燃： *Gas ignites very easily.* 汽油易燃。 ◇ (*figurative*) *Tempers ignited when the whole family spent Christmas together.* 全家凑到一起过圣诞节，大家心里都十分激动。 ◇ **~ sth** *Flames melted a lead pipe and ignited leaking gas.* 火焰熔化了一段铅管，燃着了漏出来的煤气。 ◇ (*figurative*) *His words ignited their anger.* 他的话引发了他们的怒火。

ig·ni·tion /ɪgˈnɪʃn/ *noun* **1** [C, usually sing.] the electrical system of a vehicle that makes the fuel begin to burn to start the engine; the place in a vehicle where you start this system 点火装置；点火开关： *to* ***turn the ignition on/off*** 打开／关上点火开关 ◇ *to put the key* ***in the ignition*** 把钥匙插进点火开关 ➲ COLLOCATIONS AT DRIVING ➲ VISUAL VOCAB PAGE V56 **2** [U] (*specialist*) the action of starting to burn or of making sth burn 着火；点火；点燃： *The flames spread to all parts of the house within minutes of ignition.* 着火后只有几分钟火焰就蔓延到房子的各个部分。

ig·noble /ɪgˈnəʊbl; *NAmE* -ˈnoʊ-/ *adj.* (*formal*) not good or honest; that should make you feel shame 卑劣的；不诚实的；不光彩的 **SYN** **base**： *ignoble thoughts* 可耻的想法 ◇ *an ignoble person* 卑鄙的人 **OPP** **noble**

ig·no·mini·ous /ˌɪgnəˈmɪniəs/ *adj.* (*formal*) that makes, or should make, you feel ashamed 耻辱的；可耻的；不光彩的 **SYN** **disgraceful**, **humiliating**： *an ignominious defeat* 可耻的失败 ◇ *He made one mistake and his career came to an ignominious end.* 他犯了一个错误，他的事业就很不体面地结束了。 ▸ **ig·no·mini·ous·ly** *adv.*

ig·no·miny /ˈɪgnəmɪni/ *noun* [U] (*formal*) public shame and loss of honour 公开的耻辱；不名誉 **SYN** **disgrace**： *They suffered the ignominy of defeat.* 他们蒙受了失败的耻辱。

ig·nor·amus /ˌɪgnəˈreɪməs/ *noun* (*usually humorous*) a person who does not have much knowledge 无知识的人： *When it comes to music, I'm a complete ignoramus.* 说到音乐，我完全是个门外汉。

ig·nor·ance **AW** /ˈɪgnərəns/ *noun* [U] **~ (of/about sth)** a lack of knowledge or information about sth 无知： *widespread* ***ignorance of/about*** *the disease* 对这种疾病的普遍不了解 ◇ *They fought a long battle against prejudice and ignorance.* 他们同偏见与无知进行了长期的斗争。 ◇ *She was kept* ***in ignorance of*** *her husband's activities.* 关于丈夫的活动，她一直蒙在鼓里。 ◇ *Children often behave badly* ***out of/through ignorance.*** 儿童往往出于无知而不守规矩。 ➲ EXPRESS YOURSELF AT KNOW

IDM **ˌignorance is ˈbliss** (*saying*) if you do not know about sth, you cannot worry about it 无知是福；不知道心不烦： *Some doctors believe ignorance is bliss and don't give their patients all the facts.* 有些医生认为无知是福，因此不向病人透露全部病情。

ig·nor·ant **AW** /ˈɪgnərənt/ *adj.* **1** lacking knowledge or information about sth; not educated （对某事物）不了解的；无知的；愚昧的；无学识的： *an ignorant person/question* 无知的人／提问 ◇ *Never make your students feel ignorant.* 千万别让你的学生感到无知。 ◇ **~ about sth** *He's ignorant about modern technology.* 他对现代科技一无所知。 ◇ **~ of sth** *At that time I was ignorant of events going on elsewhere.* 那时我并不了解其他地方发生的事情。 **2** (*informal*) with very bad manners 很无礼的；十分不懂规矩的 **SYN** **uncouth**： *a rude, ignorant person* 粗鲁无礼的人 ▸ **ig·nor·ant·ly** *adv.*

ig·nore 🔑 **AW** /ɪgˈnɔː(r)/ *verb* **1** 🔑 **~ sth** to pay no attention to sth 忽视；对…不予理会 **SYN** **disregard**： *He ignored all the 'No Smoking' signs and lit up a cigarette.* 他无视所有"禁止吸烟"的警示，点了香烟。 ◇ *I made a suggestion but they chose to ignore it.* 我提了个建议，但他们不予理会。 ◇ *We cannot afford to ignore their advice.* 我们不能不考虑他们的劝告。 **2** 🔑 **~ sb** to pretend that you have not seen sb or that sb is not there 佯装未见；不予理睬： *She ignored him and carried on with her work.* 她没理他，继续干她的活儿。 **OPP** **notice**

igu·ana /ɪˈgwɑːnə/ *noun* a large tropical American LIZARD (= a type of REPTILE) 美洲鬣蜥（美洲热带大蜥蜴）

iguan·odon /ɪˈgwɑːnədɒn; *NAmE* -dɑːn/ *noun* a large DINOSAUR 禽龙

ike·bana /ˌɪkɪˈbɑːnə; ˌɪkeɪ-/ *noun* [U] (*from Japanese*) Japanese flower arranging, that has strict formal rules （日本）插花艺术，花道

ikon = ICON (3)

il- *prefix* ➲ IN-

ileum /ˈɪliəm/ *noun* (*pl.* **ilea** /ˈɪliə/) (*anatomy* 解) the third part of the small INTESTINE 回肠 ➲ COMPARE DUODENUM, JEJUNUM ▸ **ileal** /ˈɪliəl/ *adj.*

ilk /ɪlk/ *noun* [usually sing.] (*sometimes disapproving*) type; kind 类型；种类： *the world of media people* ***and their ilk*** 新闻媒体一类人等 ◇ *I can't stand him, or any others* ***of that ilk.*** 我无法忍受他或他这类的人。

ill 🔑 /ɪl/ *adj., adv., noun*

■ ***adj.*** **1** 🔑 (*especially BrE*) (*NAmE usually* **sick**) [not usually before noun] suffering from an illness or disease; not feeling well 有病；不舒服： *Her father is* ***seriously ill*** *in St Luke's hospital.* 她父亲住在圣路加医院，病情很重。 ◇ *She* ***was taken ill*** *suddenly.* 她突然病倒了。 ◇ *We both started to* ***feel ill*** *shortly after the meal.* 我们俩饭后不久就都开始感到不适。 ◇ *Uncle Harry is* ***terminally ill*** *with cancer* (= he will die from his illness). 哈里叔叔癌症已到了晚期。 ◇ *the* ***mentally ill*** (= people with a mental illness) 精神病患者 ◇ (*formal*) *He* ***fell ill*** *and died soon after.* 他病倒不久便去世了。 ➲ SEE ALSO ILLNESS ➲ WORDFINDER NOTE AT MEDICINE **2** 🔑 [usually before noun] bad or harmful 坏的；不良的；有害的： *He resigned because of* ***ill health*** (= he was often ill). 他因健康状况不佳而辞职。 ◇ *She suffered no* ***ill effects*** *from the experience.* 这次经历没有使她受到不良影响。 ◇ *a woman of* ***ill repute*** (= considered to be immoral) 名声不好的女人 **3** (*formal*) that brings, or is thought to bring, bad luck 不吉利的；不祥的： *a bird of ill omen* 不祥之鸟

IDM **ˌill at ˈease** feeling uncomfortable and embarrassed 局促不安的： *I felt* ***ill at ease*** *in such formal clothes.* 我穿着这样正式的衣服觉得很拘谨。 **it's an ˌill ˈwind (that blows nobody any good)** (*saying*) no problem is so bad that it does not bring some advantage to sb 没有绝对的坏事；任何坏事都会有利于某些人 ➲ MORE AT FEELING

■ ***adv.*** **1** (especially in compounds 尤用于构成复合词) badly or in an unpleasant way 恶劣地；讨厌地： *The animals had been grossly ill-treated.* 那些动物受到了恣意虐待。 **2** (*formal*) badly; not in an acceptable way 差劲；不足： *They live in an area ill served by public transport.* 他们住在公共交通条件很差的地区。 **3** (*formal*) only with difficulty 困难地： *We're wasting valuable time, time we can ill afford.* 我们是在浪费宝贵的时间，我们浪费不起的时间。

IDM **speak/think 'ill of sb** (*formal*) to say or think bad things about sb 说…的坏话；把…往坏处想： *Don't speak ill of the dead.* 勿议已故者之短。

■ ***noun*** **1** [usually pl.] (*formal*) a problem or harmful thing; an illness 问题；弊端；疾病： *social/economic ills* 社会 / 经济弊病 ◇ *the ills of the modern world* 现代世界的弊端 **2** [U] (*literary*) harm; bad luck 伤害；厄运： *I may not like him, but I wish him no ill.* 我虽然不喜欢他，但我并不希望他倒运。

I'll /aɪl/ *short form* **1** I shall **2** I will

ˌill-adˈvised *adj.* not sensible; likely to cause difficulties in the future 不明智的；考虑不全面的；会造成困难的： *Her remarks were ill-advised, to say the least.* 她的话不够谨慎，至少可以这么说。 ◇ *You* **would be ill-advised to** *travel on your own.* 你要独自旅行是不明智的。 ➲ COMPARE WELL ADVISED ▶ **ˌill-adˈvised·ly** *adv.*

I

ˌill-asˈsort·ed *adj.* (of a group of people or things 人或事物) not seeming suited to each other 不相配的；不相称的： *They seem an ill-assorted couple.* 他俩似乎不般配。

ˌill-ˈbred *adj.* rude or badly behaved, especially because you have not been taught how to behave well 粗鲁的；没礼貌的；（尤指）没教养的 **OPP** **well bred**

ˌill-conˈcealed *adj.* (*formal*) (of feelings or expressions of feeling 感情或感情的流露) not hidden well from other people 不加掩饰的；外露的

ˌill-conˈceived *adj.* badly planned or designed 考虑不周的；构想拙劣的

ˌill-conˈsid·ered *adj.* not carefully thought about or planned 考虑欠周的；计划不严密的

ˌill-deˈfined *adj.* **1** not clearly described 不清楚的；含混的： *an ill-defined role* 不明确的角色 **2** not clearly marked or easy to see 轮廓不清的；不明显的： *an ill-defined path* 若隐若现的小径 **OPP** **well defined**

ˌill-disˈposed *adj.* ~ (**towards sb**) (*formal*) not feeling friendly towards sb 不友好的；无好感的 **OPP** **well disposed**

il·legal **AW** /ɪˈliːɡl/ *adj., noun*

■ ***adj.*** not allowed by the law 不合法的；非法的；违法的： *illegal immigrants/aliens* 非法移民 / 外侨 ◇ *It's illegal to drive through a red light.* 开车闯红灯是违章行为。 **OPP** **legal** ▶ **il·legal·ly** **AW** /-ɡəli/ *adv.*： *an illegally parked car* 违章停放的汽车 ◇ *He entered the country illegally.* 他通过非法途径进入了这个国家。

■ ***noun*** (*NAmE*) a person who lives or works in a country illegally 非法移民；非法劳工

il·legal·ity **AW** /ˌɪliˈɡæləti/ *noun* (*pl.* **-ies**) **1** [U] the state of being illegal 不合法；违法： *No illegality is suspected.* 未怀疑有违法之事。 **2** [C] an illegal act 非法行为 ➲ COMPARE LEGALITY

il·legible /ɪˈledʒəbl/ (*also* **un·read·able**) *adj.* difficult or impossible to read 难以辨认的；无法辨识的；字迹模糊的： *an illegible signature* 难以辨认的签名 **OPP** **legible** ▶ **il·legibly** /-əbli/ *adv.*

il·legit·im·ate /ˌɪləˈdʒɪtəmət/ *adj.* **1** born to parents who are not married to each other 私生的；非婚生的 **2** (*formal*) not allowed by a particular set of rules or by law 不符合规定的；非法的 **SYN** **unauthorized**： *illegitimate use of company property* 不正当使用公司财产 **OPP** **legitimate** ▶ **il·legit·im·acy** /ˌɪləˈdʒɪtəməsi/ *noun* [U] **il·legit·im·ate·ly** *adv.*

ˌill-eˈquipped *adj.* ~ (**for sth**) | ~ (**to do sth**) not having the necessary equipment or skills 装备不完善的；技术不够的

ˌill-ˈfated (*also* **fated**) *adj.* (*formal*) not lucky and ending sadly, especially in death or failure 注定要倒霉的；时运不济的；（尤指）结局悲惨的： *an ill-fated expedition* 注定不会成功的探险

ˌill-ˈfitting *adj.* not the right size or shape （大小或形状）不合适的： *ill-fitting clothes* 不合身的衣服

▼ **COLLOCATIONS** 词语搭配

Illnesses 疾病

Becoming ill 生病

- **catch** a cold/an infectious disease/the flu/(*BrE*) flu/pneumonia/a virus/(*informal*) a bug 染上感冒 / 传染病 / 流感 / 肺炎 / 病毒 / 小毛病
- **get** (*BrE*) ill/(*NAmE*) sick/a disease/AIDS/breast cancer/a cold/the flu/(*BrE*) flu/a migraine 患病 / 艾滋病 / 乳腺癌 / 感冒 / 流感 / 偏头痛
- **come down with** a cold/the flu/(*BrE*) flu 得了感冒 / 流感
- **contract** a deadly disease/a serious illness/HIV/AIDS 感染致命疾病 / 严重疾病 / 艾滋病病毒 / 艾滋病
- **be infected with** a virus/a parasite/HIV 受病毒 / 寄生虫 / 艾滋病病毒感染
- **develop** cancer/diabetes/a rash/an ulcer/symptoms of hepatitis 患上癌症 / 糖尿病 / 皮疹 / 溃疡；出现肝炎症状
- **have** a heart attack/a stroke 心脏病 / 中风发作
- **provoke**/**trigger**/**produce** an allergic reaction 引起 / 产生过敏反应
- **block**/**burst**/**rupture** a blood vessel 使血管阻塞 / 破裂
- **damage**/**sever** a nerve/an artery/a tendon 损伤 / 切断神经 / 动脉 / 肌腱

Being ill 病了

- **feel** (*BrE*) ill/sick/nauseous/queasy 感到不适 / 想吐 / 恶心
- **be running** (*BrE*) a temperature/(*NAmE*) a fever 发烧
- **have** a head cold/diabetes/heart disease/lung cancer/a headache/(*BrE*) a high temperature/(*NAmE*) a fever 患伤风感冒 / 糖尿病 / 心脏病 / 肺癌；头痛；发烧
- **suffer from** asthma/malnutrition/frequent headaches/bouts of depression/a mental disorder 患哮喘 / 营养不良症 / 经常性头痛 / 多发性抑郁症 / 精神错乱
- **be laid up with**/(*BrE*) **be in bed with** a cold/the flu/(*BrE*) flu/a migraine 因感冒 / 流感 / 偏头痛而卧床休息
- **nurse** a cold/a headache/a hangover 调治感冒 / 头痛 / 宿醉
- **battle**/**fight** cancer/depression/addiction/alcoholism 与癌症 / 抑郁症作斗争；戒瘾；戒酒

Treatments 治疗

- **examine** a patient 给病人做检查
- **diagnose** a condition/disease/disorder 诊断疾病
- **be diagnosed with** cancer/diabetes/schizophrenia 诊断为癌症 / 糖尿病 / 精神分裂症
- **prescribe**/**be given**/**be on**/**take** drugs/medicine/medication/pills/painkillers/antibiotics 开 / 得到 / 服用药 / 药片 / 止痛药 / 抗生素
- **treat sb for** cancer/depression/shock 治疗某人的癌症 / 抑郁症 / 休克
- **have**/**undergo** an examination/an operation/surgery/a kidney transplant/therapy/chemotherapy/treatment for cancer 接受检查 / 手术 / 外科手术 / 肾移植手术 / 治疗 / 化疗 / 癌症治疗
- **have**/**be given** an injection/(*BrE*) a flu jab/(*NAmE*) a flu shot/a blood transfusion/a scan/an X-ray 打针；接种流感疫苗；接受输血；做扫描检查；照 X 光
- **cure** a disease/an ailment/cancer/a headache/a patient 治疗疾病 / 病痛 / 癌症 / 头痛 / 病人
- **prevent** the spread of disease/further outbreaks/damage to the lungs 防止疾病扩散 / 疾病进一步爆发 / 对肺部造成伤害
- **be vaccinated against** the flu/(*BrE*) flu/the measles/(*BrE*) measles/polio/smallpox 接种流感 / 麻疹 / 小儿麻痹症 / 天花疫苗
- **enhance**/**boost**/**confer**/**build** immunity to a disease 增加对疾病的免疫力

ˌill-ˈfounded *adj.* (*formal*) not based on fact or truth 凭空的；无根据的；毫无理由的： *All our fears proved ill-founded.* 我们所有的担心结果都证明是杞人忧天。 OPP **well founded**

ˌill-ˈgotten *adj.* (*old-fashioned* or *humorous*) obtained dishonestly or unfairly 非法得到的；来路不正的： ***ill-gotten gains*** (= money that was not obtained fairly) 不义之财

ˌill ˈhealth *noun* [U] the poor condition of a person's body or mind（身心）健康状况差；生病： *He retired early **on grounds of ill health.*** 他由于身体不好而提早退休。 ➲ SYNONYMS AT ILLNESS

ˌill ˈhumour (*especially US* **ˌill ˈhumor**) *noun* [U, C] (*literary*) a bad mood 坏心情；坏脾气 OPP **good humour** ▸ **ˌill-ˈhumoured** (*especially US* **ˌill-ˈhumored**) *adj.*

il·lib·eral /ɪˈlɪbərəl/ *adj.* (*formal*) not allowing much freedom of opinion or action 不容言论（或行动）自由的；不开明的 SYN **intolerant**： *illiberal policies* 限制言行自由的政策

il·licit /ɪˈlɪsɪt/ *adj.* **1** not allowed by the law 非法的；违法的 SYN **illegal**： *illicit drugs* 违禁药物 **2** not approved of by the normal rules of society 违背社会常规的；不正当的： *an illicit love affair* 不正当的风流韵事 ▸ **il·licit·ly** *adv.*

ˌill-inˈformed *adj.* having or showing little knowledge of sth 了解不够的；信息不足的 OPP **well informed**

il·lit·er·ate /ɪˈlɪtərət/ *adj.*, *noun*

■ *adj.* **1** (of a person 人) not knowing how to read or write 不会读写的；不识字的；文盲的 OPP **literate** **2** (of a document or letter 文件或信函) badly written, as if by sb without much education 行文拙劣的；不通顺的 **3** (usually after a noun or adverb 通常在名词或副词之后) not knowing very much about a particular subject area（对某学科）了解不多的，外行的： *computer illiterate* 计算机盲 ◇ *musically illiterate* 音乐盲 ▸ **il·lit·er·acy** /ɪˈlɪtərəsi/ *noun* [U]

■ *noun* a person who is illiterate 文盲；无知识的人

il·li·ter·ati /ˌɪlɪtəˈrɑːti/ *noun* [pl.] people who have not had a high standard of education or who lack knowledge or information about a particular subject or area of activity 教育程度低的人；无知者；外行

ˌill-ˈjudged *adj.* (*formal*) that has not been carefully thought about; not appropriate in a particular situation 考虑不周的；判断不当的；不合实际情况的

ˌill-ˈmannered *adj.* (*formal*) not behaving well or politely in social situations 举止粗鲁的；不礼貌的 SYN **rude** OPP **well mannered**

ill·ness 🔑 /ˈɪlnəs/ *noun* **1** 🔑 [U] the state of being physically or mentally ill（身体或精神上的）疾病，病： *mental illness* 精神病 ◇ *I missed a lot of school through illness last year.* 我去年因病耽误了很多功课。 **2** 🔑 [C] a type or period of illness（某种）病；患病期： ***minor/serious illnesses*** 小病；重病 ◇ *childhood illnesses* 儿童患的各种病 ◇ *He died after a long illness.* 他久病不愈而亡。 ➲ SYNONYMS AT DISEASE ➲ WORDFINDER NOTE AT DISEASE ➲ COLLOCATIONS AT ILL

il·logic·al AW /ɪˈlɒdʒɪkl; *NAmE* -ˈlɑːdʒ-/ *adj.* not sensible or thought out in a logical way 悖理的；不合逻辑的；乖戾的： *illogical behaviour/arguments* 乖戾的行为；不合逻辑的论点 ◇ *She has an illogical fear of insects.* 她毫无道理地害怕昆虫。 OPP **logical** ▸ **il·logic·al·ity** /ɪˌlɒdʒɪˈkæləti; *NAmE* -ˌlɑːdʒ-/ *noun* [U, C] **il·logic·al·ly** AW /-kli/ *adv.*

ˌill-ˈomened *adj.* (*formal*) (of an event or activity 事情或活动) seeming likely to be unlucky or unsuccessful because there are a lot of unlucky signs relating to it 凶多吉少的；不吉利的

ˌill-preˈpared *adj.* **1** ~ (for sth) not ready, especially because you were not expecting sth to happen 未准备好的；（尤指）想不到的，猝不及防的： *The team was ill-prepared for a disaster on that scale.* 这样的惨败全队根本就没有料到。 **2** badly planned or organized 规划不周的；组织不严密的： *an ill-prepared speech* 准备不周全的讲话

ˌill-ˈstarred *adj.* (*formal*) not lucky and likely to bring unhappiness or to end in failure 注定要倒霉（或失败）的；时运不济的： *an ill-starred marriage* 注定要失败的婚姻

ˌill-ˈtempered *adj.* (*formal*) angry and rude or irritated, especially when this seems unreasonable 脾气暴躁的；动辄发怒的

ˌill-ˈtimed *adj.* done or happening at the wrong time 不适时的；不合时宜的： *an ill-timed visit* 不适时的来访 OPP **well timed**

ˌill-ˈtreat *verb* ~ sb to treat sb in a cruel or unkind way 虐待 ▸ **ˌill-ˈtreatment** *noun* [U]: *the ill-treatment of prisoners* 对犯人的虐待

il·lu·min·ate /ɪˈluːmɪneɪt/ (*also less frequent* **il·lu·mine**) *verb* **1** ~ sth (*formal*) to shine light on sth 照明；照亮；照射： *Floodlights illuminated the stadium.* 泛光灯照亮了体育场。 ◇ *The earth is illuminated by the sun.* 太阳照亮地球。 **2** ~ sth (*formal*) to make sth clearer or easier to understand 阐明；解释 SYN **clarify**： *This text illuminates the philosopher's early thinking.* 这篇文章解释了这位哲学家的早期思想。 **3** ~ sth to decorate a street, building, etc. with bright lights for a special occasion 用彩灯装饰 **4** ~ sth (*literary*) to make a person's face, etc. seem bright and excited 使容光焕发 SYN **light up**： *Her smile illuminated her entire being.* 微笑使她整个人神采奕奕。

il·lu·min·ated /ɪˈluːmɪneɪtɪd/ *adj.* [usually before noun] **1** lit with bright lights 被照明的；被照亮的： *the illuminated city at night* 夜幕中万家灯火的城市 **2** (of books, etc. 书等) decorated with gold, silver and bright colours in a way that was done in the past, by hand 用鲜明色彩手工装饰的；装饰古朴华美的： *illuminated manuscripts* 装饰华丽的手稿

▼ **SYNONYMS** 同义词辨析

illness

sickness • ill health • trouble

These are all words for the state of being physically or mentally ill. 以上各词均指身体或精神上的不适、疾病。

illness the state of being physically or mentally ill 指身体或精神上的疾病

sickness illness; bad health 指疾病、不健康： *I recommend you get insurance against sickness and unemployment.* 我建议你办个疾病和失业保险。

ILLNESS OR SICKNESS? 用 illness 还是 sickness?

Sickness is used especially in contexts concerning work and insurance. It is commonly found with words such as *pay*, *leave*, *absence* and *insurance*. **Illness** has a wider range of uses and is found in more general contexts.
* sickness 尤用于与工作和保险有关的语境中，通常与 pay、leave、absence 和 insurance 等词连用。illness 的用法较广，用于较一般的语境中。

ill health (*rather formal*) the state of being physically ill or having lots of health problems 指健康状况不佳： *She resigned because of ill health.* 她因健康状况不佳而辞职。
NOTE **Ill health** often lasts a long period of time. * ill health 常持续较长时间。

trouble illness or pain 指疾病、疼痛： *heart trouble* 心脏病 NOTE When **trouble** is used with this meaning, it is necessary to say which part of the body is affected.
* trouble 用于此义时须说明疾病或疼痛所在的身体部位。

PATTERNS

- **chronic** illness/sickness/ill health
- **to suffer from** illness/sickness/ill health/heart, etc. trouble

il·lu·min·at·ing /ɪˈluːmɪneɪtɪŋ/ *adj.* helping to make sth clear or easier to understand 富于启发性的： *We didn't find the examples he used particularly illuminating.* 我们觉得他采用的那些例证启发性不是特别大。

il·lu·min·ation /ɪˌluːmɪˈneɪʃn/ *noun* **1** [U, C] light or a place that light comes from 照明；光源： *The only illumination in the room came from the fire.* 屋子里唯一的光亮来自炉火。 **2 illuminations** [pl.] (*BrE*) bright coloured lights used to decorate a town or building for a special occasion 彩灯；灯饰： *Christmas illuminations* 圣诞节的彩灯 **3** [C, usually pl.] a coloured decoration, usually painted by hand, in an old book （旧时书上通常用手工绘制的）彩饰，彩图 **4** [U] (*formal*) understanding or explanation of sth 启示；启迪；阐明： *spiritual illumination* 精神上的启发

il·lu·mine /ɪˈluːmɪn/ *verb* (*formal*) = ILLUMINATE

ˌill-ˈused *adj.* (*old-fashioned* or *formal*) badly treated 受虐待的；被糟蹋的

I

il·lu·sion /ɪˈluːʒn/ *noun* **1** [C, U] a false idea or belief, especially about sb or about a situation 错误的观念；幻想： *She's* ***under the illusion that*** (= believes wrongly that) *she'll get the job.* 她存有幻想，认为会得到那份工作。 ◇ *The new president* ***has no illusions about*** *the difficulties facing her country* (= she knows that the country has serious problems). 新任总统清楚地知道她的国家面临的困难。 ◇ *He could no longer distinguish between illusion and reality.* 他再也分不清幻想与现实之间的区别了。 **2** [C] something that seems to exist but in fact does not, or seems to be sth that it is not 幻想的事物；错觉： *Mirrors in a room often give an illusion of space.* 房间里的镜子常给人一种空间增大的错觉。 ◇ *The idea of absolute personal freedom is an illusion.* 绝对个人自由的观念是一种幻想。 ➲ PICTURE AT OPTICAL ILLUSION

il·lu·sion·ist /ɪˈluːʒənɪst/ *noun* an entertainer who performs tricks that seem strange or impossible to believe 幻术师；魔术师

il·lu·sive /ɪˈluːsɪv/ *adj.* (*literary*) not real although seeming to be 虚幻的；虚假的；迷惑人的 **SYN illusory**： *There is an illusive sense of depth.* 有一种迷惑人的纵深感。 **HELP** *Illusive* is sometimes confused with *elusive* which has a different meaning. * illusive 有时与 elusive 混淆，两者词义不同。

il·lu·sory /ɪˈluːsəri/ *adj.* (*formal*) not real, although seeming to be 虚假的；幻觉的；迷惑人的： *an illusory sense of freedom* 虚幻的自由感

il·lus·trate 🔑 **AW** /ˈɪləstreɪt/ *verb* **1** 🔑 [usually passive] to use pictures, photographs, diagrams, etc. in a book, etc. 加插图于；给（书等）做图表： **~ sth** *an illustrated textbook* 有插图的课本 ◇ **~ sth with sth** *His lecture was illustrated with photos taken during the expedition.* 他在演讲中使用了探险时拍摄的照片。 **2** 🔑 to make the meaning of sth clearer by using examples, pictures, etc. （用示例、图画等）说明，解释： **~ sth** ***To illustrate my point,*** *let me tell you a little story.* 为了说明我的观点，让我来给你们讲个小故事。 ◇ *Last year's sales figures are illustrated in Figure 2.* 图 2 显示了去年的销售数字。 ◇ **~ how, what, etc....** *Here's an example to illustrate what I mean.* 这儿有个例子可以说明我的意思。 ➲ LANGUAGE BANK AT PROCESS[1] **3 ~ sth | ~ how, what, etc.... | ~ that...** to show that sth is true or that a situation exists 表明…真实；显示…存在 **SYN demonstrate**： *The incident illustrates the need for better security measures.* 这次事件说明了加强安全措施的必要。

il·lus·tra·tion **AW** /ˌɪləˈstreɪʃn/ *noun* **1** [C] a drawing or picture in a book, magazine, etc. especially one that explains sth （书、杂志等中的）图表，插图： *50 full-colour illustrations* * 50 张全彩色插图 **2** [U] the process of illustrating sth 图解；图示；例释： *the art of book illustration* 书籍插图的艺术 **3** [C, U] a story, an event or an example that clearly shows the truth about sth （说明事实的）故事，实例，示例： *The statistics are a clear illustration of the point I am trying to make.* 这些统计数字清楚地阐明了我要陈述的要点。 ◇ *Let me,* ***by way of illustration,*** *quote from one of her poems.* 作为说明，让我援引她的一首诗。 ➲ SYNONYMS AT EXAMPLE

il·lus·tra·tive **AW** /ˈɪləstrətɪv; *NAmE* ɪˈlʌs-/ *adj.* (*formal*) helping to explain sth or show it more clearly 说明的；解释性的 **SYN explanatory**： *an illustrative example* 示例

il·lus·tra·tor /ˈɪləstreɪtə(r)/ *noun* a person who draws or paints pictures for books, etc. （书等的）插图画家

il·lus·tri·ous /ɪˈlʌstriəs/ *adj.* (*formal*) very famous and much admired, especially because of what you have achieved 著名的；杰出的；卓越的 **SYN distinguished**： *The composer was one of many illustrious visitors to the town.* 那位作曲家是许多造访过这个城市的杰出人物之一。 ◇ *a long and illustrious career* 长期卓越的事业

ˌill ˈwill *noun* [U] bad and unkind feelings towards sb 恶意；憎恨；敌意： *I bear Sue no ill will.* 我对休没有敌意。

il·ly·whack·er /ˈɪliwækə(r)/ *noun* (*AustralE, informal*) a person who tricks others into giving him or her money, etc. 骗子（诈骗钱财等） **SYN confidence trickster**

ILO /ˌaɪ el ˈəʊ; *NAmE* ˈoʊ/ *abbr.* International Labour Organization (an organization within the United Nations concerned with work and working conditions) 国际劳工组织（全写为 International Labour Organization，联合国组织）

IM /ˌaɪ ˈem/ *noun, verb*

■ ***noun*** = INSTANT MESSAGE

■ ***verb*** (**IMs, IMing, IMd, IMd**) [T, I] **~ (sb) | ~ sb sth** = INSTANT-MESSAGE

I'm /aɪm/ *short form* I am

im- ➲ IN-

image 🔑 **AW** /ˈɪmɪdʒ/ *noun* **1** 🔑 [C, U] the impression that a person, an organization or a product, etc. gives to the public 形象；印象；声誉： *His public image is very different from the real person.* 他在公众心目中的形象与他真实的本人截然不同。 ◇ *The advertisements are intended to improve the company's image.* 这些广告旨在提高公司的形象。 ◇ *Image is very important in the music world.* 在音乐界，个人形象很重要。 ◇ *stereotyped images of women in children's books* 儿童图书中模式化的女性形象 **2** 🔑 [C] a mental picture that you have of what sb/sth is like

▼ **LANGUAGE BANK 用语库**

illustrate

Referring to a chart, graph or table 描述图或表

- *This bar chart* ***illustrates*** *how many journeys people made on public transport over a three-month period.* 这个柱状图显示三个月期间人们乘坐公共交通往来的次数。
- *This table* ***compares*** *bus, train, and taxi use between April and June.* 这个表比较了四月至六月公交车、火车和出租车的使用情况。
- *The results* ***are shown*** *in the chart below.* 结果显示在下面的图表中。
- *In this pie chart, the survey results* ***are broken down*** *by age.* 在这个饼分图中，调查结果按年龄划分。
- *This pie chart* ***breaks down*** *the survey results by age.* 这个饼分图按年龄对调查结果进行分类。
- ***As can be seen from*** *these results, younger people use buses more than older people.* 从结果可以看出，年轻人比老年人乘坐公交车的频率更高。
- ***According to*** *these figures, bus travel accounts for 60% of public transport use.* 从这些数字看，乘坐公交车出行占公共交通使用率的 60%。
- ***From the data in the above graph, it is apparent that*** *buses are the most widely used form of public transport.* 从上图的数据明显看出：公交车是公共交通中使用最广泛的类型。

➲ LANGUAGE BANK AT EVIDENCE, FALL, INCREASE, PROPORTION, SURPRISING or looks like （心目中的）形象，印象： *images of the past* 对过去的印象 ◇ *I had a **mental image** of what she would look like.* 我能想象出她的样貌如何。 **3** [C] (*formal*) a copy of sb/sth in the form of a picture or statue 画像；雕像；塑像： *Images of deer and hunters decorate the cave walls.* 洞穴壁上装饰着鹿和猎人的画像。 ◇ *a wooden image of the Hindu god Ganesh* 印度教神灵象头神的木雕像 **4** [C] a picture of sb/sth seen in a mirror, through a camera, or on a television or computer 镜像；影像；映像；图像： *He stared at his own image reflected in the water.* 他凝视着自己在水中的倒影。 ◇ *Slowly, an image began to appear on the screen.* 屏幕上慢慢地出现了一幅图像。 ➲ SEE ALSO MIRROR IMAGE **5** [C] a word or phrase used with a different meaning from its normal one, in order to describe sth in a way that produces a strong picture in the mind 比喻；意象： *poetic images of the countryside* 与乡野有关的诗歌意象 ➲ WORDFINDER NOTE AT POETRY

WORDFINDER 联想词： alliteration, euphemism, figure of speech, hyperbole, litotes, metaphor, metonymy, onomatopoeia, paradox

IDM **be the image of sb/sth** to look very like sb/sth else 酷似；和…非常相像： *He's the image of his father.* 他酷似他的父亲。 ➲ SEE ALSO SPITTING IMAGE

im·agery AW /ˈɪmɪdʒəri/ *noun* [U] **1** language that produces pictures in the minds of people reading or listening 形象的描述；意象： *poetic imagery* 诗的意象 ➲ COLLOCATIONS AT LITERATURE ➲ SEE ALSO METAPHOR **2** (*formal*) pictures, photographs, etc. 像；画像；照片： *satellite imagery* (= for example, photographs of the earth taken from space) 卫星影像（如从太空拍摄地球的照片）

im·agin·able /ɪˈmædʒɪnəbl/ *adj.* **1** used with superlatives, and with *all* and *every*, to emphasize that sth is the best, worst, etc. that you can imagine, or includes every possible example （与形容词最高级或与 all、every 连用，表示强调或概括）想象得到的： *The house has the most spectacular views imaginable.* 从这所房子可以看到所能想象的最壮丽的景色。 ◇ *They stock every imaginable type of pasta.* 他们备有各种能想到的意大利面食。 **2** possible to imagine 可想象的： *These technological developments were hardly imaginable 30 years ago.* 这些科技新产品在30年前几乎是不可想象的。

im·agin·ary /ɪˈmædʒɪnəri; NAmE -neri/ *adj.* existing only in your mind or imagination 想象中的；幻想的；虚构的： *imaginary fears* 想象中的恐惧 ◇ *The equator is an imaginary line around the middle of the earth.* 赤道是一条假想的环绕地球腰部的线。

iˌmaginary ˈnumber *noun* (*mathematics* 数) a number expressed as the SQUARE ROOT of a negative number, especially the square root of -1 虚数 ➲ COMPARE COMPLEX NUMBER, REAL NUMBER

im·agin·ation /ɪˌmædʒɪˈneɪʃn/ *noun* **1** [U, C] the ability to create pictures in your mind; the part of your mind that does this 想象力；想象： *a **vivid/fertile imagination*** 生动的 / 丰富的想象 ◇ *He's got no imagination.* 他缺乏想象力。 ◇ *It doesn't **take much imagination** to guess what she meant.* 不难猜出她的意思。 ◇ *I won't tell you his reaction—**I'll leave that to your imagination**.* 我不告诉你他的反应，你自己去想好了。 ◇ *Don't let your imagination run away with you* (= don't use too much imagination). 不要一味凭空想象。 ◇*The new policies appear to have **caught the imagination** of the public* (= they find them interesting and exciting). 新出台的政策似乎恰恰投合了公众的喜好。 ◇ *Nobody hates you—it's all **in your imagination**.* 没人讨厌你，都是你在胡思乱想。 ◇ (*informal*) ***Use your imagination!*** (= used to tell sb that they will have to guess the answer to the question they have asked you, usually because it is obvious or embarrassing) 你自己动动脑筋嘛！ **2** [U] something that you have imagined rather than sth that exists 想象的事物；幻想物： *She was no longer able to distinguish between imagination and reality.* 她再也分不清幻想和现实了。 ◇ *Is it my imagination or have you lost a lot of weight?* 是我的错觉，还是你确实瘦了许多？ **3** [U] the ability to have new and exciting ideas 创造力；创作力： *His writing lacks imagination.* 他写的东西缺乏想象。 ◇ ***With a little imagination,** you could turn this place into a palace.* 稍微动点脑筋，就能把这个地方变得富丽堂皇。

IDM **leave nothing/little to the imagiˈnation** (of clothes 衣服) to allow more of sb's body to be seen than usual （暴露身体）没有想象的余地： *Her tight-fitting dress left nothing to the imagination.* 她的紧身连衣裙令身材显露无遗。 ➲ MORE AT FIGMENT, STRETCH *n.*

im·agina·tive /ɪˈmædʒɪnətɪv/ *adj.* having or showing new and exciting ideas 富于想象力的；创新的 SYN **inventive**: *an imaginative approach/idea/child* 有创意的方法 / 思想 / 孩子 ◇ *recipes that make **imaginative use** of seasonal vegetables* 妙用时令蔬菜的菜谱 OPP **unimaginative** ▸ **imagina·tive·ly** *adv.*: *The stables have been imaginatively converted into offices.* 马房被别出心裁地改成了办公室。

im·agine /ɪˈmædʒɪn/ *verb* **1** [T, I] to form a picture in your mind of what sth might be like 想象；设想： **~ sth** *The house was just as she had imagined it.* 这房子正如她所想象的。 ◇ *I can't imagine life without the children now.* 我现在无法设想没有了孩子们的生活。 ◇ **~ (that)...** *Close your eyes and imagine (that) you are in a forest.* 闭上眼睛，设想自己在森林里。 ◇ **~ what, how, etc....** *Can you imagine what it must be like to lose your job after 20 years?* 你能想象得出干了20年之后被辞退会是什么样的滋味吗？ ◇ **~ doing sth** *She imagined walking into the office and handing in her resignation.* 她想象着自己走进办公室，递上辞呈。 ◇ *Imagine earning that much money!*

▼ **SYNONYMS** 同义词辨析

imagine

think • see • envisage • envision

These words all mean to form an idea in your mind of what sb/sth might be like. 以上各词均含想象、设想之义。

imagine to form an idea in your mind of what sb/sth might be like 指想象、设想： *The house was just as she had imagined it.* 这房子正如她所想象的。

think to imagine sth that might happen or might have happened 指猜想、想象、试想： *We couldn't think where you'd gone.* 我们猜想不出来你到哪里去了。 ◇ ***Just think**—this time tomorrow we'll be lying on a beach.* 想想看，明天这个时候我们就躺在海滩上了。

see to consider sth as a future possibility; to imagine sb as sth 指设想、想象： *I can't see her changing her mind.* 我无法想象她会改变主意。 ◇ *His colleagues see him as a future director.* 他的同事认为他很可能是未来的负责人。

envisage (*especially BrE*) to imagine what will happen in the future 指想象、设想、展望： *I don't envisage working with him again.* 我想象不出再与他一起工作的可能。 NOTE The usual word for this in American English is **envision** (see below). 在美式英语中，这一意义常用 envision（见下文）。

envision to imagine what a situation will be like in the future, especially a situation that you intend to work towards 指展望、想象： *They envision an equal society, free from poverty and disease.* 他们向往一个没有贫穷和疾病的平等社会。 NOTE **Envision** is used especially in business and political contexts. In North American English it is also used as another form of the word **envisage**.
* envision 尤用于商业和政治语境，在美式英语中亦作 envisage 的另一种形式： *I don't envision working with him again.* 我想象不出再与他一起工作的可能。

PATTERNS

- to imagine/see/envisage/envision sb/sth **as** sth
- to imagine/see/envisage/envision (sb) **doing sth**
- to imagine/think/see/envisage/envision **who/what/how...**
- to imagine/think/envisage/envision **that...**

I

想想看，竟赚那么多的钱！ ◇ ~ **sb/sth doing sth** *I can just imagine him saying that!* 我确实能想到他那么说！ ◇ ~ **sb/sth to be/do sth** *I had imagined her to be older than that.* 我本来以为她的年龄还要大一些。◇ ~ **(sb + adj./noun)** *I can imagine him really angry.* 我可以想象得出他怒气冲冲的样子。◇ (*informal*) *'He was furious.' 'I can imagine.'* "他气疯了。" "我想象得出。" ➲ MORE LIKE THIS 27, page R28 **2** [T] to believe sth that is not true 误以为；胡乱猜想；猜测： ~ **(that)**... *He's always imagining (that) we're talking about him behind his back.* 他总是胡乱猜想我们在背后说他的闲话。◇ ~ **sth** *There's nobody there. You're* ***imagining things.*** 那里根本没有人。你在胡思乱想。 **3** [I, T] to think that sth is probably true 料想；认为 SYN **suppose, assume**: *'Can we still buy tickets for the concert?' 'I imagine so.'* "我们还能买到音乐会的票吗？" "我想可以吧。" ◇ ~ **(that)**... *I don't imagine (that) they'll refuse.* 我认为他们不会拒绝。 ➲ EXPRESS YOURSELF AT SPECULATE

im·agin·eer /ɪˌmædʒɪˈnɪə(r); *NAmE* -ˈnɪr/ *noun, verb*
■ ***noun*** a person who invents sth exciting, especially a machine for people to ride on in a THEME PARK 构想工程师（发明主题公园中的机动游戏等）
■ ***verb*** ~ **sth** to invent sth exciting, especially a machine for people to ride on in a THEME PARK 构想，发明（刺激好玩的东西，如主题公园的机动游戏等） ▶ **im·agin·eer·ing** *noun* [U]

im·aging /ˈɪmɪdʒɪŋ/ *noun* [U] (*computing* 计) the process of capturing, storing and showing an image on a computer screen 成像： *imaging software* 成像软件

im·agin·ings /ɪˈmædʒɪnɪŋz/ *noun* [pl.] things that you imagine, that exist only in your mind 想象出的事物；幻想物

imago /ɪˈmeɪɡəʊ; ɪˈmɑːɡ-; *NAmE* -ɡoʊ/ *noun* **1** (*psychology* 心) a mental image of sb as being perfect that you do not realize you have and that influences your behaviour 无意识意象（无意识地对他人形成的理想形象） **2** (*pl.* **im·agos** or **im·agi·nes** /ɪˈmeɪdʒɪniːz; ɪˈmɑːdʒ-/) the final and fully developed adult stage of an insect, especially one with wings （尤指有翅昆虫的）成虫

imam /ɪˈmɑːm/ *noun* (in Islam 伊斯兰教) **1** a religious man who leads the prayers in a MOSQUE 伊玛目（在清真寺内领拜的人） **2 Imam** the title of a religious leader 伊玛目（伊斯兰教领袖头衔）

IMAX™ /ˈaɪmæks/ *noun* **1** [U] technology which allows films/movies to be shown on extremely large screens 艾麦克斯宽银幕技术；IMAX 超大银幕技术 **2** [C] a cinema/movie theater or screen that uses IMAX * IMAX 影院；艾麦克斯影院；艾麦克斯宽银幕；超大银幕

im·bal·ance /ɪmˈbæləns/ *noun* [C, U] a situation in which two or more things are not the same size or are not treated the same, in a way that is unfair or causes problems 失衡；不平衡；不公平： ~ **(in/of sth)** *a global imbalance of/in power* 全球权力的不平衡 ◇ ~ **(between A and B)** *Attempts are being made to* ***redress*** (= put right) ***the imbalance*** *between our import and export figures.* 我们正努力纠正进出口的不平衡。

im·be·cile /ˈɪmbəsiːl; *NAmE* -sl/ *noun* **1** a rude way to describe a person that you think is very stupid 笨蛋；蠢货 SYN **idiot**: *They behaved like imbeciles.* 他们表现得像傻瓜。 **2** (*old-fashioned, offensive*) a person who has a very low level of intelligence 低能者；弱智者 ▶ **im·be·cile** (*also* **im·be·cil·ic**) *adj.* [usually before noun]: *imbecile remarks* 蠢话 **im·be·cil·ity** /ˌɪmbəˈsɪləti/ *noun* [U, C]

imbed = EMBED

im·bibe /ɪmˈbaɪb/ *verb* **1** [I, T] ~ **(sth)** (*formal* or *humorous*) to drink sth, especially alcohol 喝，饮（酒等） **2** [T] ~ **sth** (*formal*) to absorb sth, especially information 吸收，接受（信息等）

im·bizo /ɪmˈbiːzəʊ; *NAmE* -zoʊ/ *noun* (*pl.* **-os**) (*SAfrE*) a meeting, especially one between politicians and members of the public, that is held in order to discuss general issues or a particular problem 讨论会；（尤指政界人士和公众的）对话会： *a government imbizo on poverty* 政府关于贫困问题的讨论会 ◇ *The minister of labour will be holding an imbizo with farmers in the area.* 劳工部长将与这一地区的农民举行对话会。

im·bro·glio /ɪmˈbrəʊliəʊ; *NAmE* ɪmˈbroʊlioʊ/ *noun* (*pl.* **-os**) (*formal*) a complicated situation that causes confusion or embarrassment, especially one that is political （尤指政治上的）乱局，尴尬处境

imbue /ɪmˈbjuː/ *verb* [often passive] ~ **sb/sth (with sth)** (*formal*) to fill sb/sth with strong feelings, opinions or values 使充满，灌输，激发（强烈感情、想法或价值） SYN **infuse**: *Her voice was imbued with an unusual seriousness.* 她的声音里充满着一种不寻常的严肃语气。◇ *He was imbued with a desire for social justice.* 他满怀着寻求社会正义的愿望。

IMF /ˌaɪ em ˈef/ *abbr.* International Monetary Fund (the organization within the United Nations which is concerned with trade and economic development) 国际货币基金组织（联合国专门机构，关注贸易和经济的发展）

IMHO /ˌaɪ em eɪtʃ ˈəʊ; *NAmE* ˈoʊ/ *abbr.* = IMO

imi·tate /ˈɪmɪteɪt/ *verb* **1** ~ **sb/sth** to copy sb/sth 模仿；仿效： *Her style of painting has been imitated by other artists.* 她的绘画风格为其他画家所模仿。◇ *Art imitates Nature.* 艺术是对大自然的仿制。 ◇ *Teachers provide a model for children to imitate.* 教师是孩子仿效的典范。◇ *No computer can imitate the complex functions of the human brain.* 任何计算机都无法模拟人脑的复杂功能。 **2** ~ **sb** to copy the way a person speaks or behaves, in order to amuse people 模仿（某人的讲话、举止）；作滑稽模仿 SYN **mimic**: *She knew that the girls used to imitate her and laugh at her behind her back.* 她知道那些女孩子过去常在背地里模仿她、嘲笑她。

imi·ta·tion /ˌɪmɪˈteɪʃn/ *noun* **1** [C] a copy of sth, especially sth expensive 仿制品；赝品： *a* ***poor/cheap imitation*** *of the real thing* 低劣的仿制品 ◇ *This latest production is a* ***pale imitation*** *of the original* (= it is not nearly as good). 最新推出的制作远不如它所依据的原著精彩。◇ *imitation leather/pearls* 人造革；假珍珠 ➲ SYNONYMS AT ARTIFICIAL **2** [U] the act of copying sb/sth 模仿；效仿： *A child learns to talk by imitation.* 小孩子通过模仿学会说话。◇ *Many corporate methods have been adopted by American managers* ***in imitation of*** *Japanese practice.* 美国的管理人员采用了很多取法日本的公司经营之道。 **3** [C] an act of copying the way sb talks and behaves, especially to make people laugh 模仿（某人）的言谈举止；（尤指）滑稽模仿 SYN **impersonation, impression**: *He does* ***an imitation of*** *Barack Obama.* 他滑稽地模仿巴拉克·奥巴马。

imi·ta·tive /ˈɪmɪtətɪv; *NAmE* -teɪtɪv/ *adj.* (*formal, sometimes disapproving*) that copies sb/sth 模仿的；仿制的；仿效的： *movies that encourage imitative crime* 助长模拟犯罪行为的电影 ◇ *His work has been criticized for being imitative and shallow.* 他的作品被批抄袭而且肤浅。

imi·ta·tor /ˈɪmɪteɪtə(r)/ *noun* a person or thing that copies sb/sth else 模仿者；模拟…的人（或事物）： *The band's success has inspired hundreds of would-be imitators.* 乐队的成功激励了数以百计未来的追随者。

im·macu·late /ɪˈmækjələt/ *adj.* **1** extremely clean and tidy 特别整洁的 SYN **spotless**: *She always looks immaculate.* 她总是打扮得干净利落。◇ *an immaculate uniform/room* 整洁的制服 / 房间 **2** containing no mistakes 无误的；无过失的 SYN **perfect**: *an immaculate performance* 完美的演出 ▶ **im·macu·late·ly** *adv.*: *immaculately dressed* 衣着整洁

the Im,maculate Con'ception *noun* [sing.] (*religion* 宗) the Christian belief that the Virgin Mary's soul was free from ORIGINAL SIN from the moment of her CONCEPTION 圣母无原罪始胎（基督教信条，认为马利亚自其母胎就无染原罪）

im·man·ent /ˈɪmənənt/ *adj.* (*formal*) present as a natural part of sth; present everywhere 内在的；固有的；无所不在的

im·ma·ter·ial /ˌɪməˈtɪəriəl; *NAmE* -ˈtɪr-/ *adj.* **1** [not usually before noun] not important in a particular situation 不重要；无关紧要 **SYN** **irrelevant**: *The cost is immaterial.* 费用并不重要。◇ **~ to sb/sth** *It is immaterial to me whether he stays or goes.* 他的去留与我无关。 **2** (*formal*) not having a physical form 无形体的；非物质的： *an immaterial God* 无形的上帝 **OPP** **material**

im·ma·ture **AW** /ˌɪməˈtjʊə(r); *NAmE* -ˈtʃʊr; -ˈtʊr/ *adj.* **1** behaving in a way that is not sensible and is typical of people who are much younger （行为）不成熟的，不够老练的，幼稚的： *immature behaviour* 不成熟的行为 **2** not fully developed or grown 未长成的；发育未全的： *immature plants* 未长成的植物 **OPP** **mature** ➲ WORDFINDER NOTE AT YOUNG ▶ **im·ma·tur·ity** **AW** /ˌɪməˈtjʊərəti; *NAmE* -ˈtʃʊr-; -ˈtʊr-/ *noun* [U]

im·meas·ur·able /ɪˈmeʒərəbl/ *adj.* (*formal*) too large, great, etc. to be measured 不可估量的；无限的；无穷的： *to cause immeasurable harm* 造成不可估量的损害 ▶ **im·meas·ur·ably** /-bli/ *adv.*: *Housing standards improved immeasurably after the war.* 战后住房水平大大提高。◇ *Stress has an immeasurably more serious effect on our lives than we realize.* 压力对我们的生活造成的影响比我们意识到的要严重得多。

im·me·di·acy /ɪˈmiːdiəsi/ *noun* [U] (*formal*) **1** the quality in sth that makes it seem as if it is happening now, close to you, and is therefore important, urgent, etc. 直接性；即时性；直观性；迫切性： *the* ***immediacy of*** *threat* 威胁的迫切性 ◇ *Email lacks the immediacy of online chat.* 电子邮件缺乏在线交谈的即时性。 **2** lack of delay; speed 立即；迅速： *Our aim is immediacy of response to emergency calls.* 我们的目标是对紧急求救电话立刻作出回应。

im·me·di·ate 🔑 /ɪˈmiːdiət/ *adj.* **1** 🔑 happening or done without delay 立即的；立刻的 **SYN** **instant**: *an* ***immediate reaction/response*** 即时的反应 / 回应 ◇ *to take* ***immediate action*** 立刻采取行动 **2** 🔑 [usually before noun] existing now and needing urgent attention 目前的；当前的；迫切的： *Our immediate concern is to help the families of those who died.* 我们的当务之急是帮助那些死者的亲属。◇ *The effects of global warming, while not immediate, are potentially catastrophic.* 全球气温上升的后果虽然并非即时发生，但可能潜伏着大灾难。◇ *The hospital says she's out of* ***immediate danger***. 医院说她眼下已脱离危险。 **3** 🔑 [only before noun] next to or very close to a particular place or time 接近的；附近的；紧接的： *in the* ***immediate vicinity*** 近在咫尺 ◇ *The prospects for the* ***immediate future*** *are good.* 短期内前景乐观。◇ *The director is standing on her immediate right.* 主管就挨在她的右边站着。◇ *my immediate predecessor in the job* (= the person who had the job just before me) 我的职位的前一任 **4** [only before noun] nearest in relationship or rank （关系或级别）最接近的，直系的，直接的： *The funeral was attended by her* ***immediate family*** (= her parents, children, brothers and sisters) *only.* 只有她的直系亲属参加了葬礼。◇ *He is my* ***immediate superior*** (= the person directly above me) *in the company.* 他在公司里是我的顶头上司。 **5** [only before noun] having a direct effect （作用）直接的： *The immediate cause of death is unknown.* 造成死亡的直接原因不明。 **IDM** SEE EFFECT *n.*

im·me·di·ate·ly 🔑 /ɪˈmiːdiətli/ *adv., conj.*

■ *adv.* **1** 🔑 without delay 立即；马上；即刻 **SYN** **at once**: *She answered almost immediately.* 她几乎立刻就回答了。◇ *The point of my question may not be immediately apparent.* 我的问题的要点可能不是一下子就能看出来的。 **2** 🔑 (usually with prepositions 通常与介词连用) next to or very close to a particular place or time 接近；紧接；附近： *Turn right immediately after the church.* 一过教堂就向右拐。◇ *the years immediately before the war* 战前的最后几年 **3** 🔑 (usually with past participles 通常与过去分词连用) closely and directly 紧接地；直接地： *Counselling is being given to those most immediately affected by the tragedy.* 目前正在向惨剧的最直接受害者提供辅导服务。

■ *conj.* (*especially BrE*) as soon as 一…就；即刻： *Immediately she'd gone, I remembered her name.* 她刚走开我就想起了她的名字。

im·me·mor·ial /ˌɪməˈmɔːriəl/ *adj.* (*formal* or *literary*) that has existed for longer than people can remember 古老的；远古的；无法追忆的： *an immemorial tradition* 古老的传统 ◇ *My family has lived in this area* ***from time immemorial*** (= for hundreds of years). 我的家族在这个地区已经生活了不知有多少年了。

im·mense /ɪˈmens/ *adj.* extremely large or great 极大的；巨大的 **SYN** **enormous**: *There is still an immense amount of work to be done.* 还有非常非常多的工作要做。◇ *The benefits are immense.* 效益是极大的。◇ *a project of immense importance* 极其重要的工程

im·mense·ly /ɪˈmensli/ *adv.* extremely; very much 极端地；非常；极大地 **SYN** **enormously**: *immensely popular/difficult/grateful* 非常受欢迎 / 艰难 / 感激 ◇ *We enjoyed ourselves immensely.* 我们玩得好极了。

im·mens·ity /ɪˈmensəti/ *noun* [U] the large size of sth 巨大；广大： *the immensity of the universe* 宇宙的浩瀚无垠 ◇ *We were overwhelmed by the sheer immensity of the task.* 任务太重，把我们都吓倒了。

im·merse /ɪˈmɜːs; *NAmE* ɪˈmɜːrs/ *verb* **1** **~ sb/sth (in sth)** to put sb/sth into a liquid so that they or it are completely covered 使浸没于 ➲ WORDFINDER NOTE AT LIQUID **2** **~ yourself/sb in sth** to become or make sb completely involved in sth （使）深陷于，沉浸在： *She immersed herself in her work.* 她埋头工作。◇ *Clare and Phil were immersed in conversation in the corner.* 克莱尔和菲尔在角落里深谈。

im·mer·sion /ɪˈmɜːʃn; *NAmE* ɪˈmɜːrʃn; -ʒn/ *noun* [U] **1** **~ (in sth)** the act of putting sb/sth into a liquid so that they or it are completely covered; the state of being completely covered by a liquid 浸没；浸： *Immersion in cold water resulted in rapid loss of heat.* 浸泡在冷水中导致热量迅速散失。◇ *baptism by total immersion* (= putting the whole body underwater) 浸水式洗礼 **2** **~ (in sth)** the state of being completely involved in sth 沉浸；专心；陷入： *his long immersion in politics* 他长期潜心从政 ◇ *a two-week immersion course in French* (= in which the student will hear and use only French) 两周的沉浸式法语课程（学生身处完全的法语环境中）

imˈmersion heater *noun* (*BrE*) a device that provides hot water for a house by heating water in a tank （家用）浸没式加热器

im·mer·sive /ɪˈmɜːsɪv; *NAmE* ɪˈmɜːrs-/ *adj.* (*specialist*) used to describe a computer system or image that seems to surround the user （计算机系统或图像）沉浸式虚拟现实的： *Immersive games can be used for training and education.* 沉浸式虚拟现实的游戏可用于培训和教育。

im·mi·grant **AW** /ˈɪmɪɡrənt/ *noun* a person who has come to live permanently in a country that is not their own （外来）移民；外侨： ***immigrant communities/families/workers*** 侨民团体 / 家庭 / 劳工 ◇ *illegal immigrants* 非法移民 ➲ COLLOCATIONS AT RACE ➲ COMPARE EMIGRANT, MIGRANT *n.* (1)

im·mi·grate **AW** /ˈɪmɪɡreɪt/ *verb* [I] **~ (to…) (from…)** (*especially NAmE*) to come and live permanently in a country after leaving your own country （从外地）移居；移民 ➲ COMPARE EMIGRATE

im·mi·gra·tion **AW** /ˌɪmɪˈɡreɪʃn/ *noun* [U] **1** the process of coming to live permanently in a country that is not your own; the number of people who do this 移居（入境）；移民人数： *laws restricting immigration into the US* 美国限制外来移民的法律 ◇ *a rise/fall in immigration* 移民人数的增加 / 减少 ◇ *immigration officers* 移民局官员 ➲ COLLOCATIONS AT RACE ➲ COMPARE EMIGRATION at EMIGRATE **2** (*also* **immiˈgration control**) the place at a port, an airport, etc. where the passports and other documents of people coming into a country are checked

I

移民局检查站： *to go through immigration* 通过移民局检查 ➲ WORDFINDER NOTE AT AIRPORT

im·mi·nent /ˈɪmɪnənt/ *adj.* (especially of sth unpleasant 尤指不愉快的事) likely to happen very soon 即将发生的；临近的： *the imminent threat of invasion* 迫在眉睫的入侵威胁 ◊ *The system is **in imminent danger of** collapse.* 这个体制面临着崩溃的危险。◊ *An announcement about his resignation is imminent.* 马上就要宣布他的辞职。 ▸ **im·mi·nence** /-əns/ *noun* [U]: *the imminence of death* 死亡的逼近 **im·mi·nent·ly** *adv.*

im·mis·cible /ɪˈmɪsəbl/ *adj.* (*specialist*) (of liquids 液体) that cannot be mixed together 不互溶的；非混相的 **OPP** **miscible**

im·mo·bile /ɪˈməʊbaɪl; *NAmE* ɪˈmoʊbl/ *adj.* **1** not moving 不动的；静止的 **SYN** **motionless**: *She stood immobile by the window.* 她一动不动地靠窗站着。**2** unable to move 不能移动的；不能活动的： *His illness has left him completely immobile.* 他的病使他完全丧失了活动能力。 **OPP** **mobile** ▸ **im·mo·bil·ity** /ˌɪməˈbɪləti/ *noun* [U]

im·mo·bil·ize (*BrE also* **-ise**) /ɪˈməʊbəlaɪz; *NAmE* ɪˈmoʊ-/ *verb* **~ sth/sb** to prevent sth/sb from moving or from working normally 使不动；使不能正常运作： *a device to immobilize the car engine in case of theft* 遇到有人盗车时使汽车引擎发动不了的装置 ◊ *Always immobilize a broken leg immediately.* 腿断了应立即加以固定。 ▸ **im·mo·bil·iza·tion, -isa·tion** /ɪˌməʊbəlaɪˈzeɪʃn; *NAmE* ɪˌmoʊbələˈz-/ *noun* [U]

im·mo·bil·izer (*also* **-iser**) /ɪˈməʊbəlaɪzə(r); *NAmE* ɪˈmoʊ-/ *noun* a device that is fitted to a car to stop it moving if sb tries to steal it 汽车防盗器（遇到有人盗车时使汽车开不动的装置）

im·mod·er·ate /ɪˈmɒdərət; *NAmE* ɪˈmɑːd-/ *adj.* [usually before noun] (*formal, disapproving*) extreme; not reasonable 极端的；不适度的；不合理的；过度的 **SYN** **excessive**: *immoderate drinking* 无节制的饮酒 **OPP** **moderate** ▸ **im·mod·er·ate·ly** *adv.*

im·mod·est /ɪˈmɒdɪst; *NAmE* ɪˈmɑːd-/ *adj.* **1** (*disapproving*) having or showing a very high opinion of yourself and your abilities 自负的；傲慢的 **SYN** **conceited** **2** not considered to be socially acceptable by most people, especially concerning sexual behaviour 不正派的；不合礼仪的；猥亵的： *an immodest dress* 有伤风化的连衣裙 **OPP** **modest**

im·mol·ate /ˈɪməleɪt/ *verb* **~ sb** (*formal*) to kill sb by burning them 烧死 ▸ **im·mol·ation** /ˌɪməˈleɪʃn/ *noun* [U]

im·moral 🔑 /ɪˈmɒrəl; *NAmE* ɪˈmɔːr-; ɪˈmɑːr-/ *adj.* **1** 🔑 (of people and their behaviour 人及其行为) not considered to be good or honest by most people 不道德的；邪恶的： *It's immoral to steal.* 偷盗是不道德的。◊ *There's nothing immoral about wanting to earn more money.* 想多赚点钱没什么不道德。 **2** 🔑 not following accepted standards of sexual behaviour 放荡的；淫荡的： *an immoral act/life/person* 淫荡的举动 / 生活 / 人 ◊ *They were charged with living off **immoral earnings*** (= money earned by working as a PROSTITUTE). 她们被控靠卖淫为生。 ➲ COMPARE AMORAL, MORAL *adj.* (3) ▸ **im·mor·al·ity** /ˌɪməˈræləti/ *noun* [U, C] (*pl.* **-ies**): *the immorality of war* 战争的邪恶 ◊ *a life of immorality* 淫荡的生活 **im·mor·al·ly** /-əli/ *adv.*

im·mor·tal /ɪˈmɔːtl; *NAmE* ɪˈmɔːrtl/ *adj., noun*

▪ *adj.* **1** that lives or lasts for ever 长生的；永世的；不朽的： *The soul is immortal.* 灵魂不灭。 **OPP** **mortal** **2** famous and likely to be remembered for ever 流芳百世的；名垂千古的： *the immortal Goethe* 名垂千古的歌德 ◊ *In the immortal words of Henry Ford, 'If it ain't broke, don't fix it.'* 按照亨利 · 福特的不朽名言："如果东西没坏掉，就不要去修理它。"

▪ *noun* **1** a person who is so famous that they will be remembered for ever 不朽的人物；名垂千古的人物： *She is one of the Hollywood immortals.* 她是一位千古流芳的好莱坞名人。 **2** a god or other BEING who is believed to live for ever 神；永生不灭者

im·mor·tal·ity /ˌɪmɔːˈtæləti; *NAmE* ˌɪmɔːrˈt-/ *noun* [U] the state of being immortal 永生；不朽；不灭： *belief in the immortality of the soul* 灵魂不灭的信念 ◊ *He is well on his way to showbusiness immortality.* 他很快就会成为娱乐界永世流芳的人物。

im·mor·tal·ize (*BrE also* **-ise**) /ɪˈmɔːtəlaɪz; *NAmE* ɪˈmɔːrt-/ *verb* **~ sb/sth** (**in sth**) to prevent sb/sth from being forgotten in the future, especially by mentioning them in literature, making films/movies about them, painting them, etc. 使不朽，使名垂千古（尤指通过文学艺术作品等）： *The poet fell in love with her and immortalized her in his verse.* 诗人爱上了她，并以诗歌使她名传后世。

im·mov·able /ɪˈmuːvəbl/ *adj.* **1** [usually before noun] that cannot be moved 不能移动的；固定的： *an immovable object* 固定的物体 **2** (of a person or an opinion, etc. 人、主张等) impossible to change or persuade 不动摇的；无法说服的： *On this issue he is completely immovable.* 他在这个问题上坚定不移。

im·mune /ɪˈmjuːn/ *adj.* [not usually before noun] **1** **~ (to sth)** that cannot catch or be affected by a particular disease or illness 有免疫力： *Adults are often immune to German measles.* 成人往往对风疹有免疫力。 **2** **~ (to sth)** not affected by sth 不受影响： *You'll eventually become immune to criticism.* 你终究会变得不在乎批评了。 **3** **~ (from sth)** protected from sth and therefore able to avoid it 受保护；免除；豁免 **SYN** **exempt**: *No one should be immune from prosecution.* 任何人都不应免于被起诉。

imˌmune resˈponse *noun* (*biology* 生) the reaction of the body to the presence of an ANTIGEN (= a substance that can cause disease) 免疫应答（机体对抗原的应答）

imˈmune system *noun* the system in your body that produces substances to help it fight against infection and disease 免疫系统

im·mun·ity /ɪˈmjuːnəti/ *noun* [U, C] (*pl.* **-ies**) **1** the body's ability to avoid or not be affected by infection and disease 免疫力： **~ (to sth)** *immunity to infection* 对传染病的免疫力 ◊ **~ (against sth)** *The vaccine provides longer immunity against flu.* 这种疫苗对流感的免疫效力时间较长。 ➲ WORDFINDER NOTE AT DISEASE ➲ COLLOCATIONS AT ILL **2** **~ (from sth)** the state of being protected from sth 受保护；豁免；免除： *The spies were all granted immunity from prosecution.* 这些间谍都获得免予公诉。 ◊ ***parliamentary/congressional immunity*** (= protection against particular laws that is given to politicians) 议会 / 国会豁免权 ◊ *Officials of all member states receive certain privileges and immunities.* 各成员国的官员均享有某些特权和豁免权。 ➲ SEE ALSO DIPLOMATIC IMMUNITY

im·mun·ize (*BrE also* **-ise**) /ˈɪmjunaɪz/ *verb* **~ sb/sth** (**against sth**) to protect a person or an animal from a disease, especially by giving them an INJECTION of a VACCINE （尤指通过注射疫苗）使免疫 ➲ COMPARE INOCULATE, VACCINATE ▸ **im·mun·iza·tion, -isa·tion** /ˌɪmjunaɪˈzeɪʃn; *NAmE* -nəˈz-/ *noun* [U, C]: *an immunization programme to prevent epidemics* 防止流行病的免疫接种方案

im·muno·defi·ciency /ˌɪˌmjuːnəʊdɪˈfɪʃnsi; *NAmE* -noʊd-/ (*also* **imˈmune deficiency**) *noun* [U] a medical condition in which your body does not have the normal ability to resist infection 免疫缺陷： *human immunodeficiency virus or HIV* 人体免疫缺陷病毒，即 HIV

im·mun·ology /ˌɪmjuˈnɒlədʒi; *NAmE* -ˈnɑːl-/ *noun* [U] the scientific study of protection against disease 免疫学 ▸ **im·muno·logic·al** /ˌɪmjunəˈlɒdʒɪkl; *NAmE* -ˈlɑːdʒɪkl/ *adj.*

im·muno·sup·pres·sion /ˌɪmjunəʊsəˈpreʃn; *NAmE* -noʊ-/ *noun* [U] (*medical* 医) the act of stopping the body from reacting against ANTIGENS, for example in order to prevent the body from rejecting a new organ 免疫抑制 ▸ **im·muno·sup·pres·sant** /ˌɪmjunəʊsəˈpresənt; *NAmE* -noʊ-/ *noun*

im·mure /ɪ'mjʊə(r); *NAmE* ɪ'mjʊr/ *verb* ~ **sb** (*literary*) to shut sb in a place so that they cannot get out 禁闭；监禁 **SYN** **imprison**

im·mut·able /ɪ'mju:təbl/ *adj.* (*formal*) that cannot be changed; that will never change 不可改变的；永恒不变的 **SYN** **unchangeable** ▸ **im·mut·abil·ity** /ɪˌmju:tə'bɪləti/ *noun* [U]

IMO /ˌaɪ em 'əʊ; *NAmE* 'oʊ/ (*also* **IMHO**) *abbr.* (used especially in TEXT MESSAGES, emails, etc. to introduce your opinion about sth) in my (humble) opinion 依我看，依拙见（全写为 in my (humble) opinion，尤用于短信、电邮等）：*It's a nice performance, not among his best, IMO.* 依愚见，这是个不错的演出，但不算他的最佳表现。

imp /ɪmp/ *noun* **1** (in stories) a small creature like a little man, that has magic powers and behaves badly （故事中的）小恶魔，小魔鬼 **2** a child who behaves badly, but not in a serious way 小淘气；顽童

im·pact 🔑 **AW** *noun, verb*

■ ***noun*** /'ɪmpækt/ [C, usually sing., U] **1** 🔑 ~ (**of sth**) (**on sb/sth**) the powerful effect that sth has on sb/sth 巨大影响；强大作用：*the environmental impact of tourism* 旅游事业对环境的巨大影响 ◇ *The report assesses the impact of AIDS on the gay community.* 这个报告评估了艾滋病对同性恋群体的影响。◇ *Her speech made a profound impact on everyone.* 她的讲话对每个人都有深远的影响。◇ *Businesses are beginning to feel the full impact of the recession.* 工商企业开始感受到了经济衰退的全面冲击。**2** 🔑 the act of one object hitting another; the force with which this happens 撞击；冲撞；冲击力：*craters made by meteorite impacts* 陨石撞击而成的陨石坑 ◇ *The impact of the blow knocked Jack off balance.* 这一记猛击把杰克打了个趔趄。◇ *The bomb explodes **on impact*** (= when it hits something). 炸弹受到撞击就爆炸。◇ *The car is fitted with **side impact** bars* (= to protect it from a blow from the side). 这辆车的两侧都安装了保险杠。

■ ***verb*** /ɪm'pækt/ **1** [I, T] to have an effect on sth （对某事物）有影响，有作用 **SYN** **affect**：~ **on/upon sth** *Her father's death impacted greatly on her childhood years.* 父亲去世对她的童年造成巨大影响。◇ ~ **sth** (*business* 商) *The company's performance was impacted by the high value of the pound.* 公司的业绩受到了英镑高值的冲击。**2** [I, T] ~ (**on/upon/with**) **sth** (*formal*) to hit sth with great force 冲击；撞击

im·pact·ed /ɪm'pæktɪd/ *adj.* (of a tooth 牙齿) that cannot grow correctly because it is under another tooth 阻生的

im·pair /ɪm'peə(r); *NAmE* ɪm'per/ *verb* ~ **sth** (*formal*) to damage sth or make sth worse 损害；削弱 ➲ SYNONYMS AT DAMAGE

im·paired /ɪm'peəd; *NAmE* ɪm'perd/ *adj.* **1** damaged or not functioning normally 受损的；损坏的；出毛病的：*impaired vision/memory* 受损的视力 / 记忆力 **2** **-impaired** having the type of physical or mental problem mentioned 有（身体或智力）缺陷的；有…障碍的：*hearing-impaired children* 听力受损的儿童 ◇ *Nowadays we say someone is 'speech-impaired', not dumb.* 现在我们说某个人"有语言障碍"，而不说是哑巴。➲ NOTE AT DISABLED

im·pair·ment /ɪm'peəmənt; *NAmE* -'perm-/ *noun* [U, C] (*specialist*) the state of having a physical or mental condition which means that part of your body or brain does not work correctly; a particular condition of this sort （身体或智力方面的）缺陷，障碍，损伤；某种缺陷：*impairment of the functions of the kidney* 肾功能障碍 ◇ *visual impairments* 视力受损

im·pala /ɪm'pɑ:lə/ *noun* (*pl.* **im·pala** or **im·palas**) an African ANTELOPE with curled horns 黑斑羚（栖息在非洲，角弯曲）

im·pale /ɪm'peɪl/ *verb* **1** ~ **sth** (**on sth**) to push a sharp pointed object through sth （用尖物）刺穿 **SYN** **spear**：*She impaled a lump of meat on her fork.* 她用叉子叉起一块肉。**2** ~ **sb/yourself on sth** if you **impale** yourself on sth, or **are impaled** on it, you have a sharp pointed object pushed into you and you may be caught somewhere by it （被）刺中，穿透：*He had fallen and been impaled on some iron railings.* 他摔下去，穿在了铁栏杆上。

im·palp·able /ɪm'pælpəbl/ *adj.* (*formal*) **1** that cannot be felt physically 触摸不到的；感觉不着的 **2** very difficult to understand 难以理解的；难懂的 **OPP** **palpable**

im·panel (*also* **em·panel**) /ɪm'pænl/ *verb* (**-ll-**, *US* **-l-**) ~ **sb/sth** (*especially US*) to choose the members of a JURY in a court case; to choose sb as a member of a JURY 选任（陪审员）；选任…为陪审员

im·part /ɪm'pɑ:t; *NAmE* ɪm'pɑ:rt/ *verb* (*formal*) **1** ~ **sth** (**to sb**) to pass information, knowledge, etc. to other people 通知；透露；传授 **SYN** **convey** **2** ~ **sth** (**to sth**) to give a particular quality to sth 把（某性质）赋予；将…给予 **SYN** **lend**：*The spice imparts an Eastern flavour to the dish.* 这种调味品给菜肴添加了一种东方风味。

im·par·tial /ɪm'pɑ:ʃl; *NAmE* ɪm'pɑ:rʃl/ *adj.* not supporting one person or group more than another 公正的；不偏不倚的；中立的 **SYN** **neutral, unbiased**：*an **impartial inquiry/observer*** 公正的调查 / 观察者 ◇ *to give **impartial advice*** 提出不偏不倚的建议 ◇ *As chairman, I must remain impartial.* 作为主席，我必须保持中立。**OPP** **partial** ▸ **im·par·ti·al·ity** /ˌɪmˌpɑ:ʃi'æləti; *NAmE* -ˌpɑ:rʃi-/ *noun* [U] **im·par·tial·ly** /-ʃəli/ *adv.*

im·pass·able /ɪm'pɑ:səbl; *NAmE* -'pæs-/ *adj.* (of a road, an area, etc. 道路、地区等) impossible to travel on or through, especially because it is in bad condition or it has been blocked by sth 不能通行的（尤指因路况恶劣或被阻断）**OPP** **passable**

im·passe /'æmpɑ:s; *NAmE* 'ɪmpæs/ *noun* [usually sing.] a difficult situation in which no progress can be made because the people involved cannot agree what to do 僵局；绝境 **SYN** **deadlock**：*to **break/end the impasse*** 打破 / 结束僵局 ◇ *Negotiations have **reached an impasse**.* 谈判已陷入僵局。

im·pas·sioned /ɪm'pæʃnd/ *adj.* [usually before noun] (usually of speech 通常指讲话) showing strong feelings about sth 充满激情的；热烈的 **SYN** **fervent**：*an **impassioned plea/speech/defence*** 热切的恳求；充满激情的讲话 / 辩护

im·pas·sive /ɪm'pæsɪv/ *adj.* not showing any feeling or emotion 无表情的；无动于衷的；不动声色的 **SYN** **emotionless**：*her **impassive expression/face*** 她冷漠的表情 / 面容 ▸ **im·pas·sive·ly** *adv.*

im·pa·tient 🔑 /ɪm'peɪʃnt/ *adj.* **1** 🔑 annoyed or irritated by sb/sth, especially because you have to wait for a long time 不耐烦的；没有耐心的：*I'd been waiting for twenty minutes and I was getting impatient.* 我等了二十分钟，有点不耐烦了。◇ ~ (**with sb/sth**) *Try not to be too impatient with her.* 尽量别对她太没耐心。◇ ~ (**at sth**) *Sarah was becoming increasingly impatient at their lack of interest.* 他们缺乏兴趣，萨拉对此越来越不能忍耐了。◇ *He waved them away with an impatient gesture.* 他厌烦地挥手把他们打发走了。**2** 🔑 wanting to do sth soon; wanting sth to happen soon 急于；热切期待：~ **to do sth** *She was clearly impatient to leave.* 她显然是迫不及待地想离开。◇ ~ **for sth** *impatient for change* 急于求变 **3** ~ **of sb/sth** (*formal*) unable or unwilling to accept sth unpleasant （对不愉快的事）不能容忍，不愿接受：*impatient of criticism* 不愿接受批评 ▸ **im·pa·tience** /ɪm'peɪʃns/ *noun* [U]：*She was bursting with impatience to tell me the news.* 她迫不及待地要告诉我这个消息。**im·pa·tient·ly** *adv.*：*We sat waiting impatiently for the movie to start.* 我们坐着，焦急地等待开演。

im·peach /ɪm'pi:tʃ/ *verb* **1** ~ **sb** (**for sth**) (of a court or other official body, especially in the US 尤指美国的法庭或其他官方机构) to charge an important public figure with a serious crime 控告（显要公职人员）犯重大罪行；弹劾 **2** ~ **sth** (*formal*) to raise doubts about sth 怀疑 **SYN** **question**：*to impeach sb's motives* 怀疑某人的动机 ▸ **im·peach·ment** *noun* [U, C]

im·peach·able /ɪm'piːtʃəbl/ *adj.* (*especially US*) (of a crime 罪行) for which a politician or a person who works for the government can be impeached 会招致控告（或弹劾）的：*an impeachable offense* 可弹劾的罪行

im·pec·cable /ɪm'pekəbl/ *adj.* without mistakes or faults 无错误的；无瑕疵的；完美的 **SYN** **perfect**：*impeccable manners/taste* 无可挑剔的举止 / 品味 ◇ *Her written English is impeccable.* 她写的英语无可挑剔。◇ *He was dressed in a suit and an impeccable white shirt.* 他身穿一套礼服和一件洁白的衬衣。▶ **im·pec·cably** /-bli/ *adv.*：*to behave impeccably* 举止无可挑剔 ◇ *impeccably dressed* 穿着十分得体

im·pe·cu·ni·ous /ˌɪmpɪ'kjuːniəs/ *adj.* (*formal* or *humorous*) having little or no money 贫穷的；不名一文的 **SYN** **penniless, poor**

im·ped·ance /ɪm'piːdns/ *noun* [U] (*physics* 物) a measurement of the total RESISTANCE of a piece of electrical equipment, etc. to the flow of an ALTERNATING CURRENT 阻抗

im·pede /ɪm'piːd/ *verb* [often passive] ~ **sth** (*formal*) to delay or stop the progress of sth 阻碍；阻止 **SYN** **hinder, hamper**：*Work on the building was impeded by severe weather.* 楼房的施工因天气恶劣而停了下来。

im·pedi·ment /ɪm'pedɪmənt/ *noun* **1** ~ (**to sth**) (*formal*) something that delays or stops the progress of sth 妨碍；阻碍；障碍 **SYN** **obstacle**：*The level of inflation is a serious impediment to economic recovery.* 通货膨胀是影响经济复苏的严重障碍。**2** a physical problem that makes it difficult to speak normally 口吃；结巴：*a speech impediment* 言语障碍

im·pedi·menta /ɪmˌpedɪ'mentə/ *noun* [pl.] (*formal* or *humorous*) the bags and other equipment that you take with you, especially when travelling, and that are difficult to carry 行囊；妨碍行进的重负（行李）；辎重

impel /ɪm'pel/ *verb* (**-ll-**) (*formal*) if an idea or feeling **impels** you to do sth, you feel as if you are forced to do it 促使；驱策；迫使：**~ sb to do sth** *He felt impelled to investigate further.* 他觉得有必要作进一步调查。◇ **~ sb** (**to sth**) *There are various reasons that impel me to that conclusion.* 有各种原因促使我作出那个结论。

im·pend·ing /ɪm'pendɪŋ/ *adj.* [only before noun] (usually of an unpleasant event 通常指不愉快的事) that is going to happen very soon 即将发生的；迫在眉睫的 **SYN** **imminent**：*his impending retirement* 他即将到来的退休 ◇ *warnings of **impending danger/disaster*** 对马上到来的危险 / 灾难的预警

im·pene·trable /ɪm'penɪtrəbl/ *adj.* **1** that cannot be entered, passed through or seen through 不可进入的；穿不过的；无法透视的：*an impenetrable jungle* 无法穿越的丛林 ◇ *impenetrable darkness* 漆黑 **OPP** **penetrable** **2** impossible to understand 不可理解的；高深莫测的 **SYN** **incomprehensible**：*an impenetrable mystery* 不解之谜 ◇ **~ to sb** *Their jargon is impenetrable to an outsider.* 他们的行话外人听不懂。▶ **im·pene·tra·bil·ity** /ɪmˌpenɪtrə'bɪləti/ *noun* [U] **im·pene·trably** /-bli/ *adv.*

im·peni·tent /ɪm'penɪtənt/ *adj.* (*formal*) not feeling ashamed or sorry about sth bad you have done 不知羞愧的；无悔意的

im·pera·tive /ɪm'perətɪv/ *adj., noun*

■ ***adj.*** **1** [not usually before noun] (*formal*) very important and needing immediate attention or action 重要紧急的；迫切的；急需处理的 **SYN** **vital**：~ (**that…**) *It is absolutely imperative that we finish by next week.* 我们的当务之急是必须于下周完成。◇ ~ (**to do sth**) *It is imperative to continue the treatment for at least two months.* 必须继续治疗至少两个月。➲ LANGUAGE BANK AT VITAL **2** (*formal*) expressing authority 表示权威的：*an imperative tone* 命令的语调 **3** [only before noun] (*grammar* 语法) expressing an order 表示命令的；祈使的：*an imperative sentence* 祈使句

■ ***noun*** **1** (*formal*) a thing that is very important and needs immediate attention or action 重要紧急的事；必要的事：*the economic imperative of quality education for all* 向全民提供高质量教育对经济发展的重要性 **2** (*grammar* 语法) the form of a verb that expresses an order; a verb in this form 祈使语气；祈使语气动词：*In 'Go away!' the verb is **in the imperative**.* * Go away! 中的动词是祈使语气动词。◇ *'Go away!' is an imperative.* * Go away! 是祈使句。

im·per·cept·ible /ˌɪmpə'septəbl; *NAmE* -pər's-/ *adj.* (*formal*) very small and therefore unable to be seen or felt（小得）无法察觉的，感觉不到的：*imperceptible changes in temperature* 难以觉察的气温变化 **OPP** **perceptible** ▶ **im·per·cept·ibly** /-əbli/ *adv.*

im·per·fect /ɪm'pɜːfɪkt; *NAmE* -'pɜːrf-/ *adj., noun*

■ ***adj.*** containing faults or mistakes; not complete or perfect 有缺点的；有缺陷的；不完全的；不完美的 **SYN** **flawed**：*an imperfect world* 不完美的世界 ◇ *an imperfect understanding of English* 对英语的不透彻理解 ◇ *All our sale items are slightly imperfect.* 我们所有的特价商品都略有瑕疵。▶ **im·per·fect·ly** *adv.*

■ ***noun*** **the imperfect** (*also* **the imˌperfect 'tense**) [sing.] (*grammar* 语法) the verb tense that expresses action in the past that is not complete. It is often called the **past progressive** or **past continuous**. 过去未完成时（常称为过去进行时）：*In 'while I was washing my hair', the verb is in the imperfect.* * while I was washing my hair 中的动词是过去未完成时。

im·per·fec·tion /ˌɪmpə'fekʃn; *NAmE* -pər'f-/ *noun* [C, U] a fault or weakness in sb/sth 缺点；瑕疵：*They learned to live with each other's imperfections.* 他们学会了容忍对方的缺点。

im·per·ial /ɪm'pɪəriəl; *NAmE* -'pɪr-/ *adj.* [only before noun] **1** connected with an empire 帝国的；皇帝的：*the imperial family/palace/army* 皇室家族；皇宫；皇家陆军 ◇ *imperial power/expansion* 皇权；帝国的扩张 **2** connected with the system for measuring length, weight and volume using pounds, inches, etc.（度量衡）英制的 ➲ COMPARE METRIC (2)

im·peri·al·ism /ɪm'pɪəriəlɪzəm; *NAmE* -'pɪr-/ *noun* [U] (*usually disapproving*) **1** a system in which one country controls other countries, often after defeating them in a war 帝国统治；帝国主义：*Roman imperialism* 罗马帝国统治 ➲ WORDFINDER NOTE AT SYSTEM **2** the fact of a powerful country increasing its influence over other countries through business, culture, etc.（商业、文化等向外国的）扩张；扩张主义：***cultural/economic imperialism*** 文化 / 经济扩张 ▶ **im·peri·al·is·t** (*also* **im·peri·al·is·tic** /ɪmˌpɪəriə'lɪstɪk; *NAmE* -ˌpɪr-/) *adj.*：*an imperialist power* 帝国主义国家 ◇ *imperialist ambitions* 帝国主义野心

im·peri·al·ist /ɪm'pɪəriəlɪst; *NAmE* -'pɪr-/ *noun* (*usually disapproving*) a person, such as a politician, who supports imperialism 帝国主义者；帝国统治拥护者

im·peril /ɪm'perəl/ *verb* (**-ll-**, *US* **-l-**) **~ sth/sb** (*formal*) to put sth/sb in danger 使陷于危险；危及 **SYN** **endanger**

im·peri·ous /ɪm'pɪəriəs; *NAmE* -'pɪr-/ *adj.* (*formal*) expecting people to obey you and treating them as if they are not as important as you 专横的；蛮横的；盛气凌人的：*an **imperious gesture/voice/command*** 盛气凌人的姿势 / 语调 / 命令 ▶ **im·peri·ous·ly** *adv.*：*'Get it now,' she demanded imperiously.* “现在就给我拿来。”她蛮横地要求。

im·per·ish·able /ɪm'perɪʃəbl/ *adj.* (*formal* or *literary*) that will last for a long time or forever 不会腐烂的；不坏的；不朽的 **SYN** **enduring**

im·per·man·ent /ɪm'pɜːmənənt; *NAmE* -'pɜːrm-/ *adj.* (*formal*) that will not last or stay the same forever 非永久的；短暂的；暂时的 **OPP** **permanent** ▶ **im·per·man·ence** /-əns/ *noun* [U]

im·per·me·able /ɪm'pɜːmiəbl; *NAmE* -'pɜːrm-/ *adj.* ~ (**to sth**) (*specialist*) not allowing a liquid or gas to pass through 不可渗透的；不透气的；不透水的 **OPP** **permeable**

im·per·mis·sible /ɪmpɜːˈmɪsəbl; *NAmE* -pɜːrˈm-/ *adj.* that cannot be allowed 不允许的；不许可的： *an impermissible invasion of privacy* 对个人隐私的非法侵犯 OPP **permissible**

im·per·son·al /ɪmˈpɜːsənl; *NAmE* -ˈpɜːrs-/ *adj.* **1** (*usually disapproving*) lacking friendly human feelings or atmosphere; making you feel unimportant 缺乏人情味的；冷淡的： *a vast impersonal organization* 庞大而不讲人情的组织 ◇ *an impersonal hotel room* 冷冰冰的旅馆房间 ◇ *Business letters need not be formal and impersonal.* 商业信函不一定就得刻板而缺乏人情味。 ◇ *a cold impersonal stare* 冷漠的凝视 **2** not referring to any particular person 非指个人的；客观的： *Let's keep the criticism general and impersonal.* 我们批评时应有普遍性，不要针对个人。 **3** (*grammar* 语法) an **impersonal** verb or sentence has 'it' or 'there' as the subject （动词或句子）无人称的，非人称的 ▶ **im·per·son·al·ity** /ɪmˌpɜːsəˈnæləti; *NAmE* -ˌpɜːrs-/ *noun* [U]: *the cold impersonality of some modern cities* 某些现代城市的冷漠无情 **im·per·son·ally** /ɪmˈpɜːsənəli; *NAmE* -ˈpɜːrs-/ *adv.*

▼ **LANGUAGE BANK** 用语库

impersonal

Giving opinions using impersonal language 用客观的语言发表意见

- ***It is vital that** more is done to prevent the illegal trade in wild animals.* 应进一步阻止非法买卖野生动物的行为，这一点至关重要。 ◇ (Compare 比较： *We have to do more to stop people trading wild animals illegally.* 我们必须进一步阻止人们非法买卖野生动物。)
- ***It is clear that** more needs to be done to protect biodiversity.* 显然，应进一步保护生物多样性。 ◇ (Compare 比较： *We clearly need to do more to protect biodiversity.* 很明显，我们需要进一步保护生物多样性。)
- ***It is unfortunate that** the practice of keeping monkeys as pets still continues.* 不幸的是，将猴子当宠物饲养的做法仍在持续。 ◇ (Compare 比较： *It's absolutely terrible that people still keep monkeys as pets.* 非常糟糕的是有人仍将猴子当宠物饲养。)
- ***It is difficult** for many people to understand the reasons why certain individuals choose to hunt animals for sport.* 许多人都难以理解为什么有些人选择捕猎作为消遣。 ◇ (Compare 比较： *I can't understand why anyone would want to kill animals for fun.* 我不明白为什么有人会以猎杀动物为乐。)
- *Unfortunately, **it would seem that** not enough is being done to support tiger conservation.* 遗憾的是，在保护老虎方面给予的支持似乎还不够。 ◇ (Compare 比较： *Governments aren't doing enough to help tiger conservation.* 政府没有采取足够措施促进对老虎的保护。)
- ***There is no doubt that** the greatest threat to polar bears comes from global warming.* 毫无疑问，对北极熊的最大威胁是全球变暖。 ◇ (Compare 比较： *I believe that the greatest threat...* 我认为最大的威胁…)

➲ **LANGUAGE BANK** AT OPINION, PERHAPS, VITAL

imˌpersonal ˈpronoun *noun* (*grammar* 语法) a pronoun (in English, the pronoun 'it') that does not refer to a person or thing or to any other part of the sentence, for example in 'it was raining' 非人称代词（如 it was raining 中的 it）

im·per·son·ate /ɪmˈpɜːsəneɪt; *NAmE* -ˈpɜːrs-/ *verb* ~ **sb** to pretend to be sb in order to trick people or to entertain them 冒充；假扮；扮演： *He was caught trying to impersonate a security guard.* 他企图假扮警卫被抓获。 ◇ *They do a pretty good job of impersonating Laurel and Hardy.* 他们扮演劳莱和哈代很成功。 ▶ **im·per·son·ation** /ɪmˌpɜːsəˈneɪʃn; *NAmE* -ˌpɜːrs-/ *noun* [C, U] SYN **impression**: *He did an extremely convincing impersonation of the singer.* 他模仿那位歌手惟妙惟肖。

im·per·son·ator /ɪmˈpɜːsəneɪtə(r); *NAmE* -ˈpɜːrs-/ *noun* a person who copies the way another person talks or behaves in order to entertain people 模仿他人的滑稽演员；扮演他人的人： *The show included a **female impersonator*** (= a man dressed as a woman). 演出中有一位男扮女装的滑稽演员。

im·per·tin·ent /ɪmˈpɜːtɪnənt; *NAmE* -ˈpɜːrtn-/ *adj.* rude and not showing respect for sb who is older or more important 粗鲁无礼的；不敬的 SYN **impolite**: *an impertinent question/child* 没有礼貌的提问 / 孩子 ◇ *Would it be impertinent to ask why you're leaving?* 问一下你为什么要离开不知是否唐突？ ➲ **SYNONYMS AT RUDE** ▶ **im·per·tin·ence** /-əns/ *noun* [U, C, usually sing.]: *She had the impertinence to ask my age!* 她居然探问我的年龄，真没礼貌！ **im·per·tin·ent·ly** *adv.*

im·per·turb·able /ˌɪmpəˈtɜːbəbl; *NAmE* -pərˈtɜːrb-/ *adj.* (*formal*) not easily upset or worried by a difficult situation; calm 冷静的；不易生气的；沉着的 ▶ **im·per·turb·ability** /ˌɪmpəˌtɜːbəˈbɪləti; *NAmE* -pərˌtɜːrb-/ *noun* [U] **im·per·turb·ably** /-əbli/ *adv.*

im·per·vi·ous /ɪmˈpɜːviəs; *NAmE* -ˈpɜːrv-/ *adj.* **1** ~ **to sth** not affected or influenced by sth 不受影响的： *impervious to criticism/pain* 能忍受批评 / 疼痛的 **2** (*specialist*) not allowing a liquid or gas to pass through 不能渗透的；不透气的；不透水的： *an **impervious rock/layer*** 不透水的岩石 / 地层 ◇ ~ **to sth** *impervious to moisture* 防潮的

im·pe·tigo /ˌɪmpɪˈtaɪɡəʊ; *NAmE* -ɡoʊ/ *noun* [U] an infectious disease that causes sore areas on the skin 脓疱病

im·petu·ous /ɪmˈpetʃuəs/ *adj.* acting or done quickly and without thinking carefully about the results 鲁莽的；冲动的；轻率的 SYN **rash, impulsive**: *an impetuous young woman* 莽撞的年轻女子 ◇ *an impetuous decision* 草率的决定 ▶ **im·petu·os·ity** /ɪmˌpetʃuˈɒsəti; *NAmE* -ˈɑːsəti/ *noun* [U] **im·petu·ous·ly** *adv.*

im·petus /ˈɪmpɪtəs/ *noun* **1** [U, sing.] something that encourages a process or activity to develop more quickly 动力；推动；促进；刺激 SYN **stimulus**: *The debate seems to have lost much of its initial impetus.* 辩论会似乎没有开始时那么大的冲劲了。 ◇ ~ **to sth/to do sth** *to give (a) **new/fresh impetus** to sth* 给某事物以新的推进力 ◇ ~ **for sth** *His articles provided the main impetus for change.* 他的那些文章是促进变革的主要推动力。 **2** [U] (*specialist*) the force or energy with which sth moves 动量；动力；惯性

im·pinge /ɪmˈpɪndʒ/ *verb* [I] ~ (**on/upon sth/sb**) (*formal*) to have a noticeable effect on sth/sb, especially a bad one 对…有明显作用（或影响）；妨碍；侵犯 SYN **encroach**: *He never allowed his work to impinge on his private life.* 他从不让他的工作妨碍私生活。

im·pious /ˈɪmpiəs; ɪmˈpaɪəs/ *adj.* (*formal*) showing a lack of respect for God and religion （对上帝或宗教）不敬的，不恭的 OPP **pious** ▶ **im·pi·ety** /ɪmˈpaɪəti/ *noun* [U]

imp·ish /ˈɪmpɪʃ/ *adj.* showing a lack of respect for sb/sth in a way that is amusing rather than serious 顽童似的；顽皮的；淘气的 SYN **mischievous**: *an impish grin/look* 顽皮的笑脸 / 表情 ➲ SEE ALSO IMP (2) ▶ **imp·ish·ly** *adv.*

im·plac·able /ɪmˈplækəbl/ *adj.* **1** (of strong negative opinions or feelings 强烈的消极看法或感情) that cannot be changed 不能改变的： *implacable hatred* 难以化解的仇恨 **2** (of a person 人) unwilling to stop opposing sb/sth 不愿和解的；不饶人的： *an implacable enemy* 死敌 ▶ **im·plac·ably** /ɪmˈplækəbli/ *adv.*: *to be implacably opposed to the plan* 坚决反对这个计划

im·plant *verb, noun*

■ *verb* /ɪmˈplɑːnt; *NAmE* -ˈplænt/ **1** [T] ~ **sth** (**in/into sth**) to fix an idea, attitude, etc. firmly in sb's mind 灌输，注入（观念、看法等）；（在思想上）生根： *Prejudices can easily become implanted in the mind.* 偏见容易在头脑中扎根。 **2** [T] ~ **sth** (**in/into sth**) to put sth (usually sth

I

artificial) into a part of the body for medical purposes, usually by means of an operation 将（人造器官等）置入；（通常指通过手术）将…植入： *an electrode implanted into the brain* 植入大脑中的电极 ➲ COMPARE TRANSPLANT *v.* (1) **3** [I] ~ (in/into sth) (of an egg or an EMBRYO 卵子或胚胎) to become fixed inside the body of a person or an animal so that it can start to develop 被移植到（人或动物体内发育） ▶ **im·plant·ation** /ˌɪmplɑːnˈteɪʃn; *NAmE* -plæn-/ *noun* [U]

■ ***noun*** /ˈɪmplɑːnt; *NAmE* -plænt/ something that is put into a person's body in a medical operation （植入人体中的）移植物，植入物： *silicone breast implants* 硅酮乳房植入体 ➲ COMPARE TRANSPLANT *n.* (2)

im·plaus·ible /ɪmˈplɔːzəbl/ *adj.* not seeming reasonable or likely to be true 似乎不合情理的；不像真实的： *an* ***implausible claim/idea/theory*** 悖于情理的要求/思想/理论 ◇ *It was all* ***highly implausible.*** 这毫无道理。 OPP **plausible** ▶ **im·plaus·ibility** *noun* [U] **im·plaus·ibly** *adv.*

I

im·ple·ment AW *verb, noun*

■ ***verb*** /ˈɪmplɪment/ ~ **sth** (*formal*) to make sth that has been officially decided start to happen or be used 使生效；贯彻；执行；实施 SYN **carry sth↔out**: *to* ***implement changes/decisions/policies/reforms*** 实行变革；执行决议/政策；实施改革 ▶ **im·ple·men·ta·tion** AW /ˌɪmplɪmenˈteɪʃn/ *noun* [U]: *the implementation of the new system* 新体制的实施

■ ***noun*** /ˈɪmplɪmənt/ (*formal*) a tool or an instrument, often one that is quite simple and that is used outdoors 工具，器具（常指简单的户外用具）： *agricultural implements* 农具

im·pli·cate AW /ˈɪmplɪkeɪt/ *verb* **1** ~ **sb (in sth)** to show or suggest that sb is involved in sth bad or criminal 牵涉，涉及（某人） SYN **incriminate**: *He tried to avoid saying anything that would implicate him further.* 他尽力避免说出任何会进一步牵连他的事情。 **2** ~ **sth (in/as sth)** to show or suggest that sth is the cause of sth bad 表明（或意指）…是起因： *The results implicate poor hygiene as one cause of the outbreak.* 这些结果说明卫生条件差是疾病爆发的一个原因。

IDM **be implicated in sth** to be involved in a crime; to be responsible for sth bad 与某罪行有牵连；对某坏事有责任： *Senior officials were implicated in the scandal.* 一些高级官员受到这一丑闻的牵连。

im·pli·ca·tion 🔑 AW /ˌɪmplɪˈkeɪʃn/ *noun* **1** 🔑 [C, usually pl.] ~ **(of sth)** (**for sth**) a possible effect or result of an action or a decision 可能的影响（或作用、结果）： *They failed to consider the wider implications of their actions.* 他们没有考虑到他们的行动会产生更广泛的影响。 ◇ *The development of the site will* ***have implications for*** *the surrounding countryside.* 这个地点的开发将会影响周围的乡村。 **2** 🔑 [C, U] something that is suggested or indirectly stated (= sth that is implied) 含意；暗指： *The implication in his article is that being a housewife is greatly inferior to every other occupation.* 他那篇文章的含意是，当家庭主妇远远不如所有其他职业。 ◇ *He criticized the Director and,* ***by implication,*** *the whole of the organization.* 他抨击主管，其实是间接批评了整个机构。 **3** [U] ~ **(of sb) (in sth)** the fact of being involved, or of involving sb, in sth, especially a crime （被）牵连，牵涉 SYN **involvement**: *He resigned after his implication in a sex scandal.* 他在涉及一件性丑闻之后辞职了。

im·pli·ca·ture /ˈɪmplɪkətʃə(r)/ *noun* (*specialist*) **1** [U] the act of suggesting that you feel or think sth is true, without saying so directly 含蓄行为；含蓄表达 **2** [C] something that you can understand from what is said, but which is not stated directly 隐含意；言外之意： *An implicature of 'Some of my friends came' is 'Some of my friends did not come'.* "我的一些朋友来了"这句话的言外之意是"我的一些朋友没有来"。

im·pli·cit AW /ɪmˈplɪsɪt/ *adj.* **1** ~ **(in sth)** suggested without being directly expressed 含蓄的；不直接言明的： *Implicit in his speech was the assumption that they were guilty.* 他话语中的言外之意是设定他们有罪。 ◇ *implicit criticism* 含蓄的批评 **2** ~ **(in sth)** forming part of sth (although perhaps not directly expressed) 成为一部分的；内含的： *The ability to listen is implicit in the teacher's role.* 作为教师自然懂得倾听。 **3** complete and not doubted 完全的；无疑问的 SYN **absolute**: *She had the implicit trust of her staff.* 她得到了全体职员的绝对信任。 ➲ COMPARE EXPLICIT ▶ **im·pli·cit·ly** AW *adv.*: *It reinforces, implicitly or explicitly, the idea that money is all-important.* 这或隐或显地强化了金钱至上这一观念。 ◇ *I trust John implicitly.* 我完全相信约翰。

im·plode /ɪmˈpləʊd; *NAmE* ɪmˈploʊd/ *verb* **1** [I] to burst or explode and collapse into the centre 向心聚爆；内爆；向内坍塌 **2** [I] (of an organization, a system, etc. 组织、体制等) to fail suddenly and completely 突然崩溃 ▶ **im·plo·sion** /ɪmˈpləʊʒn; *NAmE* -ˈploʊ-/ *noun* [C, U]

im·plore /ɪmˈplɔː(r)/ *verb* (*formal* or *literary*) to ask sb to do sth in an anxious way because you want or need it very much 恳求；哀求 SYN **beseech, beg**: **~ sb to do sth** *She implored him to stay.* 她恳求他留下。 ◇ **~ (sb) + speech** *'Help me,' he implored.* "救救我吧。"他哀求道。 ◇ **~ sb** *Tell me it's true. I implore you.* 告诉我那是真的。求求你。 ▶ **im·plor·ing** *adj.*: *She gave him an imploring look.* 她对他露出哀求的神情。

imply 🔑 AW /ɪmˈplaɪ/ *verb* (**im·plies, im·ply·ing, im·plied, im·plied**) **1** 🔑 to suggest that sth is true or that you feel or think sth, without saying so directly 含有…的意思；暗示；暗指： **~ (that)…** *Are you implying (that) I am wrong?* 你的意思是不是说我错了？ ◇ **~ sth** *I disliked the implied criticism in his voice.* 我讨厌他暗中批评的口吻。 ◇ **it is implied that…** *It was implied that we were at fault.* 这意味着我们错了。 ➲ NOTE AT INFER **2** 🔑 to make it seem likely that sth is true or exists 说明；表明 SYN **suggest**: **~ (that)…** *The survey implies (that) more people are moving house than was thought.* 调查显示，准备搬家的人口比想象的要多。 ◇ **it is implied that…** *It was implied in the survey that…* 这次调查表明… ◇ **~ sth** *The fact that she was here implies a degree of interest.* 她到场就说明了她有一定程度的兴趣。 **3** **~ sth** (of an idea, action, etc. 思想、行为等) to make sth necessary in order to be successful 必然包含；使有必要 SYN **mean**: *The project implies an enormous investment in training.* 这个项目需要在培训方面做巨大的投资。 ➲ SEE ALSO IMPLICATION

im·pol·ite /ˌɪmpəˈlaɪt/ *adj.* not polite 不礼貌的；粗鲁的 SYN **rude**: *Some people think it is impolite to ask someone's age.* 有些人认为询问别人的年龄是不礼貌的。 ➲ SYNONYMS AT RUDE ▶ **im·pol·ite·ly** *adv.* **im·pol·ite·ness** *noun* [U]

im·pol·it·ic /ɪmˈpɒlətɪk; *NAmE* -ˈpɑːl-/ *adj.* (*formal*) not wise 不明智的；不策略的 SYN **unwise**: *It would have been impolitic to refuse his offer.* 当时若拒绝了他的好意就太不明智了。

im·pon·der·able /ɪmˈpɒndərəbl; *NAmE* -ˈpɑːn-/ *noun* [usually pl.] (*formal*) something that is difficult to measure or estimate 难以衡量（或估量）的事物： *We can't predict the outcome. There are too many imponderables.* 我们无法预测结果。难以逆料的情况太多了。 ▶ **im·pon·der·able** *adj.*

im·port 🔑 *noun, verb*

■ ***noun*** /ˈɪmpɔːt; *NAmE* ˈɪmpɔːrt/ **1** 🔑 [C, usually pl.] a product or service that is brought into one country from another 进口；输入的产品（或劳务）： *food imports from abroad* 从外国进口的食物 OPP **export** ➲ COLLOCATIONS AT ECONOMY **2** 🔑 [U, pl.] the act of bringing a product or service into one country from another （产品、劳务的）进口，输入，引进： *The report calls for a ban on the import of hazardous waste.* 这篇报道呼吁禁止危险废弃物的进口。 ◇ *import controls* 进口管制 ◇ *an import licence* 进口许可证 ◇ *imports of oil* 石油的进口 OPP **export** ➲ WORDFINDER NOTE AT TRADE **3** [U] (*formal*) importance 重要性： *matters of great import* 非常重要的事情 **4 the ~ (of sth)** [sing.] (*formal*) the meaning of sth, especially when it is not immediately clear 意思；含意： *It is difficult to understand the full import of this statement.* 很难理解这份声明的全部含意。

■ ***verb*** /ɪmˈpɔːt; *NAmE* ɪmˈpɔːrt/ **1** to bring a product, a service, an idea, etc. into one country from another 进口；输入；引进： **~ sth** *The country has to import most of its raw materials.* 这个国家大多数原料依赖进口。◇ **~ sth (from…) (into…)** *goods imported from Japan into the US* 从日本输入到美国的货品 ◇ *customs imported from the West* 从西方传入的风俗习惯 **2 ~ sth (from…) (into…)** (*computing* 计) to get data from another program, changing its form so that the program you are using can read it 导入；输入；移入 OPP **export** ⊃ MORE LIKE THIS 21, page R27 ▶ **im·port·ation** /ˌɪmpɔːˈteɪʃn; *NAmE* -pɔːrˈt-/ *noun* [U, C] SYN **import**: *a ban on the importation of ivory* 禁止象牙进口的法令

im·port·ance /ɪmˈpɔːtns; *NAmE* -ˈpɔːrt-/ *noun* [U] the quality of being important 重要性；重要；重大： *She **stressed the importance of** careful preparation.* 她强调了认真准备的重要性。◇ *It's **a matter of the greatest importance to** me.* 这对我来说是最重要的事情。◇ *They **attach** great **importance** to the project.* 他们高度重视这个项目。◇ *the relative importance of the two ideas* 这两种想法的相对重要性 ◇ *State your reasons **in order of importance**.* 按重要性顺序陈述你的理由。◇ *He was very aware of his own importance* (= of his status). 他十分清楚自己的重要地位。

im·port·ant /ɪmˈpɔːtnt; *NAmE* -ˈpɔːrt-/ *adj.* **1** having a great effect on people or things; of great value 重要的；有重大影响的；有巨大价值的： *an important decision/factor* 重要决定 / 因素 ◇ *I have an important announcement to make.* 我要宣布一件重要的事情。◇ *Money played an important role in his life.* 金钱在他的生活中扮演了重要的角色。◇ *Listening is an important part of the job.* 倾听是这项工作的一个重要部分。◇ *one of the most important collections of American art* 美国艺术的最有价值的收藏品之一 ◇ ***It is important to** follow the manufacturer's instructions.* 遵照厂家的说明很重要。◇ ***It is important that** he attend every day.* 他每天都要出席，这很重要。◇ (*BrE*) ***It is important that** he should attend every day.* 他每天都要出席，这很重要。◇ ***It is important for** him to attend every day.* 他每天都要出席，这很重要。◇ **~ (to sb)** *It's very important to me that you should be there.* 你应该到场，这对我很重要。◇ ***The important thing** is to keep trying.* 重要的是要不断尝试。 ⊃ LANGUAGE BANK AT EMPHASIS **2** (of a person 人) having great influence or authority 影响很大的；权威的： *an important member of the team* 举足轻重的一位队员 ◇ *He likes to feel important.* 他喜欢感到自己很重要。 ▶ **im·port·ant·ly** *adv.*： *More importantly, can he be trusted?* 更重要的是，他值得信任吗？◇ *She was sitting importantly behind a big desk.* 她神气十足地坐在一张大写字台后面。 ⊃ LANGUAGE BANK AT EMPHASIS

im·port·er /ɪmˈpɔːtə(r); *NAmE* -ˈpɔːrt-/ *noun* a person, company, etc. that buys goods from another country in order to sell them in their own country 从事进口的人（或公司等）；进口商： *a London-based importer of Italian food* 总部设在伦敦的意大利食品进口商 ⊃ COMPARE EXPORTER

im·por·tun·ate /ɪmˈpɔːtʃənət; *NAmE* -ˈpɔːrt-/ *adj.* (*formal*) asking for things many times in a way that is annoying 再三要求的；纠缠不休的

im·por·tune /ˌɪmpɔːˈtjuːn; *NAmE* -pɔːrˈtuːn/ *verb* **~ sb (for sth) | ~ sb to do sth** (*formal*) to ask sb for sth many times and in a way that is annoying 再三要求；纠缠 SYN **pester**

im·pose AW /ɪmˈpəʊz; *NAmE* ɪmˈpoʊz/ *verb* **1** [T] **~ sth (on/upon sth/sb)** to introduce a new law, rule, tax, etc.; to order that a rule, punishment, etc. be used 推行，采用（规章制度）；强制实行： *A new tax was imposed on fuel.* 当局开始对燃油征收一项新税。 **2** [T] **~ sth (on/upon sb/sth)** to force sb/sth to have to deal with sth that is difficult or unpleasant 迫使；把…强加于： *to **impose limitations/restrictions/constraints** on sth* 强行限制 / 管制 / 约束某事物 ◇ *This system imposes additional financial burdens on many people.* 这个制度给很多人增加了额外的经济负担。 **3** [T] **~ sth (on/upon sb)** to make sb accept the same opinions, wishes, etc. as your own 使（别人）接受自己的意见： *She didn't want to impose her values on her family.* 她并不想勉强家人接受自己的价值观。◇ *It was noticeable how a few people managed to **impose their will on** the others.* 显而易见，有少数几个人设法把自己的意志强加于别人。 **4** [I] to expect sb to do sth for you or to spend time with you, when it may not be convenient for them 勉强（某人做某事）；硬要…和…在一起： *'You must stay for lunch.' 'Well, thanks, but I don't want to impose…'* "你一定得留下吃午饭。" "唔，谢谢，但我不想添麻烦…" ◇ **~ on/upon sb/sth** *Everyone imposes on Dave's good nature.* 大家都欺负戴夫脾气好。 **5** [T] **~ yourself (on/upon sb/sth)** to make sb/sth accept or be aware of your presence or ideas 使接受，使意识到（自己的在场或想法）： *European civilization was the first to impose itself across the whole world.* 欧洲文明是最先传播到全世界的。

im·pos·ing /ɪmˈpəʊzɪŋ; *NAmE* -ˈpoʊz-/ *adj.* impressive to look at; making a strong impression 壮观的；使人印象深刻的： *a grand and imposing building* 雄伟壮观的建筑物 ◇ *a tall imposing woman* 高大壮硕的女人

im·pos·ition AW /ˌɪmpəˈzɪʃn/ *noun* **1** [U] the act of introducing sth such as a new law or rule, or a new tax （新法律或规则等的）颁布，实施；（新税的）征收： *the imposition of martial law* 戒严令的实施 ◇ *the imposition of tax on domestic fuel* 家用燃料税的征收 **2** [C] an unfair or unreasonable thing that sb expects or asks you to do 不公平（或不合理）的要求： *I'd like to stay if it's not too much of an imposition.* 如果不会给您增添太多麻烦，我倒愿意留下。

im·pos·sible /ɪmˈpɒsəbl; *NAmE* -ˈpɑːs-/ *adj.* **1** that cannot exist or be done; not possible 不可能存在（或做到）的；不可能的： ***almost/virtually impossible*** 几乎不可能 ◇ ***It's impossible for** me to be there before eight.* 我在八点之前不可能赶到那里。◇ *It's impossible to prove.* 这件事无法证实。◇ ***I find it impossible** to lie to her.* 我觉得无法对她撒谎。◇ *an **impossible dream/goal*** 无法实现的梦想 / 目标 OPP **possible** **2** very difficult to deal with 难处理的；很难对付的： *I've been placed in an **impossible position**.* 我陷入了进退维谷的境地。◇ *Honestly, you're impossible at times!* 说实话，你有时真令人难以忍受。 **3 the impossible** *noun* [sing.] a thing that is or seems impossible （似乎）不可能的事： *to attempt the impossible* 明知不可为而为之 ▶ **im·pos·si·bil·ity** /ɪmˌpɒsəˈbɪləti; *NAmE* -ˌpɑːsə-/ *noun* [U, C, usually sing.] (*pl.* **-ies**): *the sheer impossibility of providing enough food for everyone* 完全无法给每个人提供足够的食物 ◇ *a virtual impossibility* 几乎不可能的事 **im·pos·sibly** /ɪmˈpɒsəbli; *NAmE* -ˈpɑːs-/ *adv.*： *an impossibly difficult problem* (= impossible to solve) 无法解决的难题 ◇ *He was impossibly handsome* (= it was difficult to believe that he could be so handsome). 简直难以相信他有这么英俊。

im·pos·tor (*BrE also* **im·pos·ter**) /ɪmˈpɒstə(r); *NAmE* -ˈpɑːs-/ *noun* a person who pretends to be sb else in order to trick people 冒名顶替者；冒名行骗者

im·pos·ture /ɪmˈpɒstʃə(r); *NAmE* -ˈpɑːs-/ *noun* [U, C] (*formal*) an act of tricking people deliberately by pretending to be sb else 冒名行骗

im·po·tent /ˈɪmpətənt/ *adj.* **1** having no power to change things or to influence a situation 无能为力的；不起作用的 SYN **powerless**: *Without the chairman's support, the committee is impotent.* 没有主席的支持，委员会是无能为力的。◇ *She blazed with impotent rage.* 她勃然大怒，但于事无补。 **2** (of a man 男子) unable to achieve an ERECTION and therefore unable to have full sex 性无能的；阳痿的 ▶ **im·po·tence** /ˈɪmpətəns/ *noun* [U]: *a feeling of impotence in the face of an apparently insoluble problem* 面对显然无法解决的问题的无力感 ◇ *male impotence* 阳痿 **im·po·tent·ly** *adv.*

im·pound /ɪmˈpaʊnd/ *verb* (*law* 律) **1 ~ sth** (of the police, courts of law, etc. 警察、法庭等) to take sth away from sb, so that they cannot use it 没收；扣押 SYN confiscate: *The car was impounded by the police after the accident.* 那辆车在发生车祸之后被警察扣留了。 **2 ~ sth** to shut up dogs, cats, etc. found on the streets in a POUND, until their owners collect them 收押（待领的狗、猫等）

im·pov·er·ish /ɪmˈpɒvərɪʃ; *NAmE* -ˈpɑːv-/ *verb* **1 ~ sb** to make sb poor 使贫穷: *These changes are likely to impoverish single-parent families even further.* 这些变革很可能使单亲家庭更加贫困。 **2 ~ sth** to make sth worse in quality 使贫瘠；使枯竭: *Intensive cultivation has impoverished the soil.* 集约耕作使土壤变得贫瘠。 ▶ **im·pov·er·ish·ment** *noun* [U]

im·pov·er·ished /ɪmˈpɒvərɪʃt; *NAmE* -ˈpɑːv-/ *adj.* **1** very poor; without money 赤贫的；不名一文的: *impoverished peasants* 贫困的农民 ◇ *the impoverished areas of the city* 这个城市的贫民区 ➲ SYNONYMS AT POOR **2** poor in quality, because sth is missing 贫乏的；贫瘠的；枯竭的

I

im·prac·tic·able /ɪmˈpræktɪkəbl/ *adj.* impossible or very difficult to do; not practical in a particular situation 不可行的；不切实际的: *It would be impracticable for each member to be consulted on every occasion.* 不可能每一次都征求每个成员的意见。 OPP **practicable** ➲ COMPARE IMPRACTICAL ▶ **im·prac·tic·abil·ity** /ɪmˌpræktɪkəˈbɪləti/ *noun* [U]

im·prac·ti·cal /ɪmˈpræktɪkl/ *adj.* **1** not sensible or realistic 不明智的；不现实的: *It was totally impractical to think that we could finish the job in two months.* 认为我们能在两个月之内完成这项工作，这完全是不切实际的。 **2** (of people 人) not good at doing things that involve using the hands; not good at planning or organizing things 手不灵巧的；不善于规划（或组织）的 OPP **practical** ➲ COMPARE IMPRACTICABLE ▶ **im·prac·ti·cal·ity** /ɪmˌpræktɪˈkæləti/ *noun* [U]

im·pre·ca·tion /ˌɪmprɪˈkeɪʃn/ *noun* (*formal*) a CURSE (= an offensive word that is used to express extreme anger) 咒骂；诅咒

im·pre·cise AW /ˌɪmprɪˈsaɪs/ *adj.* not giving exact details or making sth clear 不确切的；不精确的；不明确的 SYN **inaccurate**: *an imprecise definition* 不确切的定义 ◇ *imprecise information* 不准确的信息 ◇ *The witness's descriptions were too imprecise to be of any real value.* 证人的描述太不明确，没有任何实际价值。 OPP **precise** ▶ **im·pre·cise·ly** *adv.*: *These terms are often used imprecisely and interchangeably.* 这些词语的使用常常不够精确，而且常常交互使用。 **im·pre·ci·sion** /ˌɪmprɪˈsɪʒn/ *noun* [U]: *There is considerable imprecision in the terminology used.* 所用的术语相当不准确。

im·preg·nable /ɪmˈpreɡnəbl/ *adj.* **1** an **impregnable** building is so strongly built that it cannot be entered by force 坚不可摧的；牢不可破的: *an impregnable fortress* 坚不可摧的要塞 **2** strong and impossible to defeat or change 不可战胜的；难以改变的 SYN **invincible**: *The team built up an impregnable 5–1 lead.* 这个队以 5:1 的绝对优势领先。

im·preg·nate /ˈɪmpreɡneɪt; *NAmE* ɪmˈpreɡ-/ *verb* **1** [usually passive] **~ sth** (**with sth**) to make a substance spread through an area so that the area is full of the substance 使充满；使遍布: *The pad is impregnated with insecticide.* 垫子上满是杀虫剂。 **2 ~ sb/sth** (*formal*) to make a woman or female animal pregnant 使怀孕；使妊娠 ▶ **im·preg·na·tion** /ˌɪmpreɡˈneɪʃn/ *noun* [U]

im·pres·ario /ˌɪmprəˈsɑːriəʊ; *NAmE* -rioʊ/ *noun* (*pl.* **-os**) a person who arranges plays in the theatre, etc., especially a person who manages a theatre, OPERA or BALLET company （剧院、歌剧或芭蕾舞团的）经理

im·press 🔑 /ɪmˈpres/ *verb* **1** 🔑 [T, I] if a person or thing impresses you, you feel admiration for them or it 使钦佩；使敬仰；给…留下深刻的好印象: **~ (sb)** *We interviewed a number of candidates but none of them impressed us.* 我们和数名申请人进行了面谈，但都没有给我们留下什么印象。 ◇ *The Grand Canyon never fails to impress.* 大峡谷永远让人叹为观止。 ◇ *His sincerity impressed her.* 他的真诚打动了她。 ◇ **~ sb with sth/sb** *He impressed her with his sincerity.* 他的真诚打动了她。 ◇ **it impresses sb that…** *It impressed me that she remembered my name.* 令我佩服的是她记得我的名字。 ◇ **sb is impressed that…** *I was impressed that she remembered my name.* 令我佩服的是她记得我的名字。 ➲ SEE ALSO IMPRESSED, IMPRESSIVE **2** [T] **~ sth on/upon sb** (*formal*) to make sb understand how important, serious, etc. sth is by emphasizing it 使意识到（重要性或严肃性等）: *He impressed on us the need for immediate action.* 他让我们认识到立刻采取行动的必要。 **3** [T] **~ sth/itself on/upon sth** (*formal*) to have a great effect on sth, especially sb's mind, imagination, etc. 使铭记；给…留下深刻印象: *Her words impressed themselves on my memory.* 她的话语我铭记在心里。

im·pressed 🔑 /ɪmˈprest/ *adj.* feeling admiration for sb/sth because you think they are particularly good, interesting, etc. （对…）钦佩，敬仰，有深刻的好印象: *I must admit I am impressed.* 我得承认我很佩服。 ◇ **~ by/with sb/sth** *We were all impressed by her enthusiasm.* 我们都被她的热情打动了。 ◇ *She was* **suitably impressed** (= as impressed as sb had hoped) *with the painting.* 果然不出所料，她对那幅油画产生了兴趣。 ➲ SEE ALSO UNIMPRESSED

im·pres·sion 🔑 /ɪmˈpreʃn/ *noun*
- **IDEA/OPINION** 想法；看法 **1** 🔑 an idea, a feeling or an opinion that you get about sb/sth, or that sb/sth gives you 印象；感想: ***a general/an overall impression*** 总的 / 整体印象 ◇ ***an initial/a lasting impression*** 初次 / 持久的印象 ◇ **~ (of sb/sth)** *to get* ***a good/bad impression*** *of sb/sth* 对某人 / 某事物的印象好 / 不好 ◇ ***My first impression*** *of him was favourable.* 他给我的第一印象不错。 ◇ *She* ***gives the impression*** *of being very busy.* 她给人的印象是特别忙。 ◇ **~ (that…)** *I did not* ***get the impression*** *that they were unhappy about the situation.* 我并不觉得他们不满于当时的状况。 ◇ ***My impression is*** *that there are still a lot of problems.* 依我看问题还是挺多的。 ◇ *Try and smile. You don't want to* ***give people the wrong impression*** (= that you are not friendly). 尽量微笑。不要让人误以为你很冷漠。
- **EFFECT** 作用 **2** 🔑 the effect that an experience or a person has on sb/sth 影响；效果: ***a big impression*** 大的影响 ◇ **~ (on sb)** *His trip to India* ***made a strong impression*** *on him.* 他的印度之行对他的触动很大。 ◇ *My words* ***made no impression*** *on her.* 我的话丝毫没有对她起作用。 ◇ *You'll have to play better than that if you really want to* ***make an impression*** (= to make people admire you). 你如果真的想给人留下好印象，就得表现得更好。
- **DRAWING** 图画 **3** a drawing showing what a person looks like or what a place or a building will look like in the future 印象画: *This is an* ***artist's impression*** *of the new stadium.* 这是一位艺术家对未来新运动场作的印象画。
- **AMUSING COPY OF SB** 滑稽模仿 **4 ~ (of sb)** an amusing copy of the way a person acts or speaks （对某人举止言谈的）滑稽模仿 SYN **impersonation**: *He did an impression of Tom Hanks.* 他滑稽地模仿了汤姆·汉克斯。
- **FALSE APPEARANCE** 假象 **5** an appearance that may be false （虚假的）外观；假象: *Clever lighting creates an impression of space in a room.* 巧妙的照明会让人有屋子空间增大的感觉。
- **MARK** 痕迹 **6** a mark that is left when an object is pressed hard into a surface 压痕
- **BOOK** 书籍 **7** all the copies of a book that are printed at one time, with few or no changes to the contents since the last time the book was printed 重印本；印次 ➲ COMPARE EDITION (3)

IDM **(be) under the imˈpression that…** believing, usually wrongly, that sth is true or is happening 以为…；（通常指）误认为…: *I was under the impression that the work had already been completed.* 我还以为已经完工了呢。 ➲ SYNONYMS AT THINK

im·pres·sion·able /ɪmˈpreʃənəbl/ *adj.* (of a person, especially a young one 人，尤指年轻人) easily influenced or affected by sb/sth 易受影响的: *children at an impressionable age* 处于易受外界影响的年龄的儿童

im·pres·sion·ism /ɪmˈpreʃənɪzəm/ *noun* [U] a style in painting developed in France in the late 19th century that uses colour to show the effects of light on things and to suggest atmosphere rather than showing exact details 印象主义，印象派（19 世纪下半叶兴起于法国的绘画风格，主要表现光与色的效果，不着眼于准确的细节）▶ **im·pres·sion·ist** *adj.* [usually before noun]: *Impressionist landscapes* 印象派风景画

im·pres·sion·ist /ɪmˈpreʃənɪst/ *noun* **1** (*usually* **Impressionist**) an artist who paints in the style of Impressionism 印象派画家： *Impressionists such as Monet and Pissarro* 莫奈和毕沙罗等的印象派画家 **2** a person who entertains people by copying the way a famous person speaks or behaves 模仿演员（常模仿名人言行）

im·pres·sion·is·tic /ˌɪmpreʃəˈnɪstɪk/ *adj.* giving a general idea rather than particular facts or details 给人以大致印象的；不精确的；凭印象的

im·pres·sive 🔑 /ɪmˈpresɪv/ *adj.* (of things or people 事物或人) making you feel admiration, because they are very large, good, skilful, etc. 令人赞叹的；令人敬佩的： *an impressive building with a huge tower* 有高塔的壮观建筑 ◇ *an impressive performance* 令人难忘的演出 ◇ *one of the most impressive novels of recent years* 近年来给人印象最深的小说之一 ◇ *She was very impressive in the interview.* 她在面试中表现得十分出色。 OPP **unimpressive** ▶ **im·pres·sive·ly** *adv.*： *impressively high* 异常高 ◇ *impressively organized* 组织得有条不紊

im·pri·ma·tur /ˌɪmprɪˈmɑːtə(r)/ *noun* [sing.] (*formal*) official approval of sth, given by a person in a position of authority 正式批准；认可；同意

im·print *verb, noun*

■ ***verb*** /ɪmˈprɪnt/ **1** **~ A in/on B | ~ B with A** to have a great effect on sth so that it cannot be forgotten, changed, etc. 产生重大影响；铭刻；使铭记： *The terrible scenes were indelibly imprinted on his mind.* 那些恐怖场面深深地铭刻在他的心中。 **2** **~ A in/on B | ~ B with A** to print or press a mark or design onto a surface 印；压印： *clothes imprinted with the logos of sports teams* 印着运动队标志的衣服

■ ***noun*** /ˈɪmprɪnt/ **1** **~ (of sth) (in/on sth)** a mark made by pressing or stamping sth onto a surface 印记；压印；痕迹： *the imprint of a foot in the sand* 沙滩上的足迹 **2** [usually sing.] **~ (of sth) (on sb/sth)** (*formal*) the lasting effect that a person or an experience has on a place or a situation 持久影响 **3** (*specialist*) the name of the PUBLISHER of a book, usually printed below the title on the first page 出版商名称（通常印在第一页的书名下面）

im·prison /ɪmˈprɪzn/ *verb* [often passive] **~ sb** to put sb in a prison or another place from which they cannot escape 监禁；关押 SYN **jail**： *They were imprisoned for possession of drugs.* 他们因持有毒品而被监禁。 ◇ (*figurative*) *Some young mothers feel imprisoned in their own homes.* 有些年轻的母亲感到待在家里如同坐牢。 ➲ COLLOCATIONS AT JUSTICE ▶ **im·pris·on·ment** /-mənt/ *noun* [U]： *to be sentenced to* ***life imprisonment*** *for murder* 因犯谋杀罪被判终身监禁

im·prob·able /ɪmˈprɒbəbl; *NAmE* -ˈprɑːb-/ *adj.* **1** not likely to be true or to happen 不大可能真实的（或发生的）；不大可能的 SYN **unlikely**： *an improbable story* 大概不是真实的故事 ◇ *It all sounded* ***highly improbable****.* 一切听上去很荒唐。 ◇ **~ that...** *It seems improbable that the current situation will continue.* 当前的局势似乎不大可能继续下去。 OPP **probable** **2** seeming strange because it is not what you would expect 奇异的；荒谬的 SYN **unexpected**： *Her hair was an improbable shade of yellow.* 她的头发带有怪怪的黄色。 ▶ **im·prob·abil·ity** /ɪmˌprɒbəˈbɪləti; *NAmE* -ˌprɑːbə-/ *noun* [U, C]： *the improbability of finding them alive* 找到他们存活的可能性不大 ◇ *statistical improbability* 统计学上来说不太可能的事 **im·prob·ably** /-əbli/ *adv.*： *He claimed, improbably, that he had never been there.* 他声称从未去过那里，令人觉得不可信。 ◇ *an improbably happy ending* 看似不大可能的圆满结局

im·promptu /ɪmˈprɒmptjuː; *NAmE* -ˈprɑːmptuː/ *adj.* done without preparation or planning 无准备的；即兴的；即席的 SYN **improvise**： *an impromptu speech* 即兴讲演

im·proper /ɪmˈprɒpə(r); *NAmE* -ˈprɑːp-/ *adj.* (*formal*) **1** dishonest, or morally wrong 不诚实的；不正当的；不道德的： *improper business practices* 不正当的商业手法 ◇ *improper conduct* 不道德的行为 ◇ *There was nothing improper about our relationship* (= it did not involve sex). 我们的关系没有什么不正当的。 OPP **proper** **2** not suited or appropriate to the situation 不合适的；不适当的；不得体的 SYN **inappropriate**： *It would be improper to comment at this stage.* 在这个阶段发表评论并不恰当。 OPP **proper 3** wrong; not correct 错误的；不正确的： *improper use of the drug* 药物的误用 ▶ **im·prop·er·ly** *adv.*： *to behave improperly* 表现得没有分寸 ◇ *He was improperly dressed for the occasion.* 他的衣着不大适合这个场合。 ◇ *improperly cooked meat* 烹调不当的肉

imˌproper ˈfraction *noun* (*mathematics* 数) a FRACTION in which the top number is greater than the bottom number, for example 7/6 假分数

im·pro·pri·ety /ˌɪmprəˈpraɪəti/ *noun* [U, C] (*pl.* **-ies**) (*formal*) behaviour or actions that are dishonest, morally wrong or not appropriate for a person in a position of responsibility （身居要职者）不诚实（或不正当、不合适）的行为举止 OPP **propriety**

im·prove 🔑 /ɪmˈpruːv/ *verb* [I, T] to become better than before; to make sth/sb better than before 改进；改善： *His quality of life has improved dramatically since the operation.* 手术后他的生活质量大大改善了。 ◇ *The doctor says she should continue to improve* (= after an illness). 医生说她还会继续康复。 ◇ **~ sth** *to improve standards* 提高水平 ◇ *The company needs to improve performance in all these areas.* 公司需要在所有这些方面改善业绩。 ◇ *I need to improve my French.* 我得提高我的法语水平。

PHR V **imˈprove on/upon sth** to achieve or produce sth that is of a better quality than sth else 改进；做出比…更好的成绩： *We've certainly improved on last year's figures.* 我们的业绩的确超过了去年的数字。

im·prove·ment 🔑 /ɪmˈpruːvmənt/ *noun* **1** [U] the act of making sth better; the process of sth becoming better 改善；改进： *Sales figures continue to show signs of improvement.* 销售额持续显示出增加的迹象。 ◇ *We expect to see* ***further improvement*** *over the coming year.* 我们期望来年会有更进一步的改善。 ◇ **~ in/on/to sth** *There is still* ***room for improvement*** *in your work.* 你的工作尚有改进的余地。 **2** [C] a change in sth that makes it better; sth that is better than it was before 改进处；改善的事物： *a* ***significant/substantial/dramatic improvement*** 重要的 / 重大的 / 巨大的改进 ◇ *a* ***slight/steady improvement*** 轻微的 / 稳定的提升 ◇ **~ in/on/to sth** *an improvement in Anglo-German relations* 英德关系的改善 ◇ *This is a great improvement on your previous work.* 你的工作比先前有很大进步。 ◇ *improvements to the bus service* 公共汽车服务的改善

im·provi·dent /ɪmˈprɒvɪdənt; *NAmE* -ˈprɑːv-/ *adj.* (*formal*) not thinking about or planning for the future; spending money in a careless way 不顾将来的；没有长远打算的；挥霍的；不节俭的 OPP **provident** ▶ **im·provi·dence** /-əns/ *noun* [U]

im·pro·vise /ˈɪmprəvaɪz/ *verb* **1** [I, T] to make or do sth using whatever is available, usually because you do not have what you really need 临时拼凑；临时做： *There isn't much equipment. We're going to have to improvise.* 设备不多，我们只能将就着用。 ◇ **~ sth** *We improvised some shelves out of planks of wood and bricks.* 我们用木板和砖头临时搭了些架子。 **2** [I, T] to invent music, the words in a play, a statement, etc. while you are playing or speaking, instead of planning it in advance 即兴创作（音乐、台词、演讲词等）： *'It'll be ready some time next week, I expect,' she said, improvising.* "我估计下个星期内会准备好的。"她随口说道。 ◇ **~ on sth** *He improvised on the*

I

melody. 他即兴演奏了那首曲子。◇ ~ sth *an improvised speech* 即席讲演 ▸ **im·pro·visa·tion** /ˌɪmprəvaɪˈzeɪʃn; *NAmE* ɪmˌprɑːvəˈzeɪʃn/ *noun* [U, C]

im·pru·dent /ɪmˈpruːdnt/ *adj.* (*formal*) not wise or sensible 不明智的；不谨慎的 **SYN** **unwise**: *It would be imprudent to invest all your money in one company.* 把所有的钱都投资在一家公司是不明智的。 **OPP** **prudent** ▸ **im·pru·dence** /-ns/ *noun* [U] **im·pru·dent·ly** *adv.*

im·pu·dent /ˈɪmpjədənt/ *adj.* (*formal*) rude; not showing respect for other people 粗鲁的；不恭的 **SYN** **impertinent**: *an impudent young fellow* 莽撞的年轻人 ◇ *an impudent remark* 粗鲁的话 ▸ **im·pu·dence** /-əns/ *noun* [U]

im·pugn /ɪmˈpjuːn/ *verb* ~ **sth** (*formal*) to express doubts about whether sth is right, honest, etc. 对…表示怀疑；质疑 **SYN** **challenge**

im·pulse /ˈɪmpʌls/ *noun* **1** [C, usually sing., U] ~ **(to do sth)** a sudden strong wish or need to do sth, without stopping to think about the results 冲动；心血来潮；一时的念头：*He had a sudden impulse to stand up and sing.* 他突然心血来潮，想站起来唱歌。◇ *I resisted the impulse to laugh.* 我强忍着没有笑出来。◇ *Her first impulse was to run away.* 她的第一个念头就是逃走。◇ *The door was open and* **on (an) impulse** *she went inside.* 门开着，她一时心血来潮就走了进去。◇ *He tends to act* **on impulse**. 他往往凭一时冲动行事。 **2** [C] (*specialist*) a force or movement of energy that causes sth else to react 动力；冲力；冲量：***nerve/electrical impulses*** 神经冲动；电路脉冲 **3** [C, usually sing., U] (*formal*) something that causes sb/sth to do sth or to develop and make progress 推动力；刺激：*to give an impulse to the struggling car industry* 给予挣扎中的汽车工业一点刺激

ˈimpulse buying *noun* [U] buying goods without planning to do so in advance, and without thinking about it carefully 即兴购买 ▸ **ˈimpulse buy** *noun*: *It was an impulse buy.* 这是一时心血来潮买的。

im·pul·sion /ɪmˈpʌlʃn/ *noun* (*formal*) **1** [C] a strong desire to do sth 冲动；强烈欲望 **2** [U] a reason for doing sth 理由；缘由：*Lack of food and water provided much of the impulsion for their speed.* 缺少食物和水促使他们加快了速度。

im·pul·sive /ɪmˈpʌlsɪv/ *adj.* (of people or their behaviour 人或行为) acting suddenly without thinking carefully about what might happen because of what you are doing 凭冲动行事的；易冲动的 **SYN** **impetuous, rash**: *an* ***impulsive decision/gesture*** 冲动的决定 / 姿态 ◇ *You're so impulsive!* 你太冲动了！◇ *He has an impulsive nature.* 他生性冲动。 ▸ **im·pul·sive·ly** *adv.*: *Impulsively he reached out and took her hand.* 他一时冲动便伸手握住她的手。 **im·pul·sive·ness** *noun* [U]

im·pun·ity /ɪmˈpjuːnəti/ *noun* [U] (*formal, disapproving*) if a person does sth bad **with impunity**, they do not get punished for what they have done 免于惩罚；不受惩处；逃过惩罚

im·pure /ɪmˈpjʊə(r); *NAmE* ɪmˈpjʊr/ *adj.* **1** not pure or clean; not consisting of only one substance but mixed with one or more substances often of poorer quality 不纯的；不洁的；有杂质的：*impure gold* 不纯的金子 **2** (*old-fashioned* or *formal*) (of thoughts or feelings 思想或感情) morally bad, especially because they are connected with sex 道德败坏的；（尤指）淫乱的 **OPP** **pure**

im·pur·ity /ɪmˈpjʊərəti; *NAmE* -ˈpjʊr-/ *noun* (*pl.* **-ies**) **1** [C] a substance that is present in small amounts in another substance, making it dirty or of poor quality 杂质：*A filter will remove most impurities found in water.* 过滤器会滤掉水中的大部分杂质。 **2** [U] the state of being dirty or not pure 肮脏；不纯；淫秽 **OPP** **purity**

im·pute /ɪmˈpjuːt/ *verb*

PHR V **imˈpute sth to sb/sth** (*formal*) to say, often unfairly, that sb is responsible for sth or has a particular quality （常指不公正地把责任等）归咎于 **SYN** **attribute** ▸ **im·put·ation** /ˌɪmpjuˈteɪʃn/ *noun* [C, U]

in /ɪn/ *prep., adv., adj., noun*

■ ***prep.*** **HELP** For the special uses of **in** in phrasal verbs, look at the entries for the verbs. For example **deal in sth** is in the phrasal verb section at **deal**. * in 在短语动词中的特殊用法见有关动词词条。如 deal in sth 在词条 deal 的短语动词部分。 **1** at a point within an area or a space 在（某范围或空间内的）某一点：*a country in Africa* 非洲的一个国家 ◇ *The kids were playing in the street.* 孩子们在街上玩。◇ *It's in that drawer.* 它放在那个抽屉里。◇ *I read about it in the paper.* 我是在报纸上读到这事的。 **2** within the shape of sth; surrounded by sth 在（某物的形体或范围）中；在…内；在…中：*She was lying in bed.* 她躺在床上。◇ *sitting in an armchair* 坐在扶手椅里 ◇ *Leave the key in the lock.* 把钥匙留在锁孔里。◇ *Soak it in cold water.* 把这东西浸泡在冷水里。 **3** into sth 进入：*He dipped his brush in the paint.* 他把毛刷在涂料里蘸了蘸。◇ *She got in her car and drove off.* 她钻进汽车里，开走了。 **4** forming the whole or part of sth/sb; contained within sth/sb 构成…的整体（或部分）；包含在…之内：*There are 31 days in May.* 五月份有 31 天。◇ *all the paintings in the collection* 收藏品中的所有画作 ◇ *I recognize his father in him* (= his character is similar to his father's). 我在他身上看到了他父亲的气质。 **5** during a period of time 在（某段时间）内：*in 2009* 在 2009 年 ◇ *in the 18th century* 在 18 世纪 ◇ *in spring/summer/autumn/winter* 在春天 / 夏天 / 秋天 / 冬天 ◇ *in the fall* 在秋天 ◇ *in March* 在三月 ◇ *in the morning/afternoon/evening* 在上午 / 下午 / 晚上 ◇ *I'm getting forgetful in my old age.* 我现在上了年纪，变得健忘了。 **6** after a particular length of time 在（某段时间）之后：*to return in a few minutes/hours/days/months.* 几分钟 / 几小时 / 几天 / 几个月后回来 ◇ *It will be ready in a week's time* (= one week from now). 只需一周的时间就会准备好。◇ *She learnt to drive in three weeks* (= after three weeks she could drive). 她花了三个星期就学会开车。 **7** (used in negative sentences or after *first*, *last*, etc. 用于否定句或 first、last 等之后) for a particular period of time 在（某段时间）内：*I haven't seen him in years.* 我有好些年没见过他了。◇ *It's the first letter I've had in ten days.* 这是我十天来收到的第一封信。 **8** wearing sth 穿着；戴着：*dressed in their best clothes* 穿着他们最好的衣服 ◇ *the man in the hat* 戴帽子的男子 ◇ *to be in uniform* 穿着制服 ◇ *She was all in black.* 她穿着一身黑。 **9** used to describe physical surroundings （用以描述具体的环境）：*We went out in the rain.* 我们冒雨出去了。◇ *He was sitting alone in the darkness.* 他独自坐在黑暗中。 **10** used to show a state or condition （表示状态或状况）：*I'm in love!* 我恋爱了！◇ *The house is in good repair.* 这所房子保养得不错。◇ *I must put my affairs in order.* 我必须整理整理我的事务。◇ *a man in his thirties* 一名三十多岁的男子 ◇ *The daffodils were in full bloom.* 水仙花正盛开。 **11** involved in sth; taking part in sth 参与；参加：*to act in a play* 参加演戏 **12** used to show sb's job or profession （显示工作或职业）：*He is in the army.* 他在军队服役。◇ *She's in computers.* 她从事计算机业。◇ *in business* 从商 **13** used to show the form, shape, arrangement or quantity of sth （显示某物的形式、形状、安排或数量）：*a novel in three parts* 分为三部的小说 ◇ *Roll it up in a ball.* 把它卷成一个球。◇ *They sat in rows.* 他们一排一排地坐着。◇ *People flocked in their thousands to see her.* 现场聚集了数以千计的人争相一睹她的丰采。 **14** used to show the language, material, etc. used （表示使用的语言、材料等）：*Say it in English.* 用英语说吧。◇ *She wrote in pencil.* 她用铅笔写的。◇ *Put it in writing.* 把它写下来。◇ *I paid in cash.* 我用现金支付。◇ *He spoke in a loud voice.* 他大声说话。 **15** concerning sth 关于；在…方面：*She was not lacking in courage.* 她并不缺乏勇气。◇ *a country rich in minerals* 矿藏丰富的国家 ◇ *three metres in length* 三米长 **16** while doing sth; while sth is happening 做…时；…发生时；当…时：*In attempting to save the child from drowning, she nearly lost her own life.* 她在抢救落水的儿童时，自己差点丧命。◇ *In all the commotion I forgot to tell him the news.* 在一阵混乱之中我忘了告诉他那个消息。 **17** used to introduce the name of a person who has a particular quality （引出具某种品质的人的名字）：*We're losing a first-rate editor in Jen.* 我们即将失去珍这位

一流的编辑。 **18** used to show a rate or relative amount（显示比率或相对数量）： *a gradient of one in five* 五分之一的坡度 ◇ *a tax rate of 22 pence in the pound* 每英镑 22 便士的税率

IDM in that /ˈɪn ðət/ (*formal*) for the reason that; because 原因是；因为： *She was fortunate in that she had friends to help her.* 她很幸运，有一些朋友帮助她。

■ **adv.** **HELP** For the special uses of **in** in phrasal verbs, look at the entries for the verbs. For example **fill in (for sb)** is in the phrasal verb section at **fill**. * in 在短语动词中的特殊用法见有关动词词条。如 fill in (for sb) 在词条 fill 的短语动词部分。 **1** contained within an object, an area or a substance 在里面；在内： *We were locked in.* 我们被锁在里面了。◇ *I can't drink coffee with milk in.* 我不能喝加牛奶的咖啡。 **2** into an object, an area or a substance 进入： *She opened the door and went in.* 她打开门进去了。◇ *The kids were playing by the river and one of them fell in.* 孩子们在河边玩耍时，其中一个落水了。 **3** (of people 人) at home or at a place of work 在家里；在工作单位： *Nobody was in when we called.* 我们打电话过去时没有人在。 **OPP out** **4** (of trains, buses, etc. 火车、公共汽车等) at the place where people can get on or off, for example the station 在车站；在停靠站： *The bus is due in (= it should arrive) at six.* 公共汽车应该在六点钟到站。 **5** (of letters, etc. 信件等) received 收到；被投递到： *Applications must be in by April 30.* 申请务必于 4 月 30 日之前寄到。 **6** (of the TIDE 潮汐) at or towards its highest point on land 上涨；在最高点： *Is the tide coming in or going out?* 现在是涨潮还是落潮？ **7** elected 当选： *Several new councillors got in at the last election.* 几位新政务委员在最近一轮选举中当选。 **8** (in CRICKET, BASEBALL, etc. 板球、棒球等) if a team or team member is **in**, they are BATTING 轮上击球 **9** (in TENNIS, etc. 网球等) if the ball is **in**, it has landed inside the line （球）落在界内： *Her serve was just in.* 她发的球刚好落在界内。

IDM be in at sth to be present when sth happens 某事发生时在场： *They were in at the start.* 开始时他们在场。 **be ˈin for sth** (*informal*) to be going to experience sth soon, especially sth unpleasant 即将经历，即将遭受（不愉快的事）： *He's in for a shock!* 他很快就会感到震惊的！◇ *I'm afraid we're in for a storm.* 看来我们就要遇到暴风雨了。 **be/get ˈin on sth** (*informal*) to be/become involved in sth; to share or know about sth 参与；了解： *I'd like to be in on the plan.* 我很想参与这项计划。◇ *Is she in on the secret?* 她知道这个秘密吗？ **be (well) ˈin with sb** (*informal*) to be (very) friendly with sb, and likely to get an advantage from the friendship 和…（十分）友好（很可能从中得到好处） **ˌin and ˈout (of sth)** going regularly to a place 时常出入： *He was in and out of jail for most of his life.* 他大半生的时间都是监狱的常客。

■ **adj.** [usually before noun] (*informal*) popular and fashionable 流行的；时髦的： *Purple is the in colour this spring.* 紫色是今年春天的流行色。◇ *Exotic pets are the in thing right now.* 奇异的宠物眼下很时髦。◇ *Short skirts are in again.* 现在又时兴穿短裙了。 SEE ALSO IN-JOKE

■ **noun**

IDM an ˈin to sth = A WAY INTO STH **have an ˈin with sb** (*especially NAmE*) to have influence with sb 对某人有影响 **the ˌins and ˈouts (of sth)** all the details, especially the complicated or difficult ones（尤指复杂或难的）全部细节，详情： *the ins and outs of the problem* 问题的来龙去脉 ◇ *He quickly learned the ins and outs of the job.* 他很快就掌握了工作的全部诀窍。

in. *abbr.* (*pl.* **in.** or **ins.**) (in writing 书写形式) INCH 英寸： *Height: 6ft 2in.* 高：6 英尺 2 英寸。

in- *prefix* /ɪn/ **1** (*also* **il-** /ɪl/, **im-** /ɪm/, **ir-** /ɪr/) (in adjectives, adverbs and nouns 构成形容词、副词和名词) not; the opposite of 不；非；相反的： *infinite* 无限的 ◇ *illogical* 不合逻辑的 ◇ *immorally* 不道德地 ◇ *irrelevance* 不相关 **2** (*also* **im-** /ɪm/) (in verbs 构成动词) to put into the condition mentioned 使置于某状况： *inflame* 使愤怒 ◇ *imperil* 使陷于危险 MORE LIKE THIS 6, page R25

-in *combining form* (in nouns 构成名词) an activity in which many people take part 很多人参加的活动： *a sit-in* 静坐示威 ◇ *a teach-in* 研讨会

in·abil·ity /ˌɪnəˈbɪləti/ *noun* [U, sing.] ~ (**to do sth**) the fact of not being able to do sth 无能；无力；不能： *the government's inability to provide basic services* 政府在提供基本服务方面的无能 ◇ *Some families go without medical treatment because of their inability to pay.* 有些家庭因无力支付医疗费用而得不到医治。 **OPP ability**

in ab·sen·tia /ˌɪn æbˈsenʃiə/ *adv.* (*from Latin*) while not present at the event being referred to 缺席： *Two foreign suspects will be tried in absentia.* 两名外籍嫌疑犯将被缺席审判。

in·access·ible **AW** /ˌɪnækˈsesəbl/ *adj.* difficult or impossible to reach or to get 难以达到的；不可得到的： *They live in a remote area, inaccessible except by car.* 他们住在一处偏远地区，只能开车去。◇ ~ **to sb/sth** *The temple is now inaccessible to the public.* 这个寺庙现在不对公众开放了。◇ (*figurative*) *The language of teenagers is often completely inaccessible to (= not understood by) adults.* 青少年的语言成人往往听不懂。 **OPP accessible** ▸ **in·access·ibil·ity** /ˌɪnækˌsesəˈbɪləti/ *noun* [U]

in·accur·ate **AW** /ɪnˈækjərət/ *adj.* not exact or accurate; with mistakes 不精确的；不准确的；有错误的： *an inaccurate statement* 不确切的说法 ◇ *inaccurate information* 不准确的信息 ◇ *All the maps we had were wildly inaccurate.* 我们所有的地图误差都非常大。 **OPP accurate** ▸ **in·accur·acy** **AW** /ɪnˈækjərəsi/ *noun* [C, U] (*pl.* **-ies**): *The article is full of inaccuracies.* 这篇文章里的错误比比皆是。◇ *The writer is guilty of bias and inaccuracy.* 这位作者失于偏颇，且叙述不实。 SYNONYMS AT MISTAKE **in·accur·ate·ly** *adv.*

in·action /ɪnˈækʃn/ *noun* [U] (*usually disapproving*) lack of action; the state of doing nothing about a situation or a problem 无行动；不采取措施

in·acti·vate /ɪnˈæktɪveɪt/ *verb* ~ **sth** (*specialist*) to make sth stop doing sth; to make sth no longer active 使灭活；使停止活动

in·active /ɪnˈæktɪv/ *adj.* **1** not doing anything; not active 无行动的；不活动的；不活跃的： *Some animals are inactive during the daytime.* 有些动物白天不活动。◇ *politically inactive* 对政治不热衷 ◇ *The volcano has been inactive for 50 years.* 这座火山处于休眠状态 50 年了。 **2** not in use; not working 未使用的；不运转的： *an inactive oil well* 闲置的油井 **3** having no effect 无作用的；无效的： *an* ***inactive drug/disease*** 失效的药物；非活动性疾病 **OPP active** ▸ **in·activ·ity** /ˌɪnækˈtɪvəti/ *noun* [U]: *periods of enforced inactivity and boredom* 被迫无事可做、单调乏味的时期 ◇ *The inactivity of the government was deplorable.* 政府的无作为真是糟透了。

in·ad·equacy **AW** /ɪnˈædɪkwəsi/ *noun* (*pl.* **-ies**) **1** [U] ~ (**of sth**) the state of not being enough or good enough 不充分；不足；不够： *the inadequacy of our resources* 我们的资源的贫乏 **OPP adequacy** **2** [U] a state of not being able or confident to deal with a situation 不胜任；缺乏信心： *a* ***feeling/sense of inadequacy*** 不称职之感 **3** [C, usually pl.] ~ (**of/in sth**) a weakness; a lack of sth 弱点；缺陷；某事物的缺乏： *gross inadequacies in the data* 数据资料的极端匮乏 ◇ *He had to face up to his own inadequacies as a father.* 他不得不正视自身作为父亲的不足。

in·ad·equate **AW** /ɪnˈædɪkwət/ *adj.* **1** not enough; not good enough 不充分的；不足的；不够的： *inadequate supplies* 供应短缺 ◇ ~ **for sth** *The system is inadequate for the tasks it has to perform.* 这个系统要完成它的任务还不够完善。◇ ~ **to do sth** *The food supplies are inadequate to meet the needs of the hungry.* 食物供应还不足以应付饥民的需求。 **OPP adequate** **2** (of people 人) not able, or not confident enough, to deal with a situation 不胜任的；缺乏信心的 **SYN incompetent**: *I felt totally inadequate as a parent.* 我觉得我作为父亲（或母亲）完全不称职。 ▸ **in·ad·equate·ly** **AW** *adv.*: *to be inadequately prepared/insured/funded* 准备不充分；保额 / 资金不足

in·ad·mis·sible /ˌɪnədˈmɪsəbl/ *adj.* (*formal*) that cannot be allowed or accepted, especially in court （尤指法庭上）不允许的，不能采纳的：*inadmissible evidence* 不可采纳的证据 OPP **admissible**

in·ad·vert·ent·ly /ˌɪnədˈvɜːtəntli; *NAmE* -ˈvɜːrt-/ *adv.* by accident; without intending to 无意地；不经意地 SYN **unintentionally**：*We had inadvertently left without paying the bill.* 我们无意之中未付账就离开了。▶ **in·ad·vert·ent** *adj.*：*an inadvertent omission* 不经意的疏忽 **in·ad·ver·tence** *noun* [U]

in·ad·vis·able /ˌɪnədˈvaɪzəbl/ *adj.* [not usually before noun] ~ (**for sb**) (**to do sth**) (*formal*) not sensible or wise; that you would advise against 不明智；不可取：***It is inadvisable** to bring children on this trip.* 这次旅行带孩子不妥当。OPP **advisable**

in·ali·en·able /ɪnˈeɪliənəbl/ (*also less frequent* **un·ali·en·able**) *adj.* [usually before noun] (*formal*) that cannot be taken away from you 不可剥夺（或分割）的：*the **inalienable right** to decide your own future* 不可剥夺的决定自己未来的权利

in·am·or·ata /ɪnˌæməˈrɑːtə/ *noun* (*from Italian, formal or humorous*) a person's female lover 女情人

inane /ɪˈneɪn/ *adj.* stupid or silly; with no meaning 愚蠢的；无意义的：*an inane remark* 无聊的话语 ▶ **in·ane·ly** *adv.*：*to grin inanely* 咧嘴憨笑 **in·an·ity** /ɪˈnænəti/ *noun* [U, C, usually pl.] (*pl.* **-ies**)

in·ani·mate /ɪnˈænɪmət/ *adj.* **1** not alive in the way that people, animals and plants are 无生命的：*A rock is an inanimate object.* 岩石是无生命的物体。OPP **animate** **2** dead or appearing to be dead 死的；像已死的：*A man was lying inanimate on the floor.* 一个男子躺在地板上，看样子像是死了。

in·applic·able /ˌɪnəˈplɪkəbl; ɪnˈæplɪkəbl/ *adj.* [not before noun] ~ (**to sb/sth**) that cannot be used, or that does not apply, in a particular situation 不适用；不可应用：*These regulations are inapplicable to international students.* 这些规章不适用于外籍学生。OPP **applicable**

in·appro·pri·ate AW /ˌɪnəˈprəʊpriət; *NAmE* -ˈproʊ-/ *adj.* not suitable or appropriate in a particular situation 不适当的；不合适的：***inappropriate behaviour/language*** 不恰当的行为 / 语言 ◇ ~ (**for sb/sth**) (**to do sth**) *It would be inappropriate for me to comment.* 由我评论并不恰当。◇ ~ **to/for sth** *clothes inappropriate to the occasion* 不得体的衣着 OPP **appropriate** ▶ **in·appro·pri·acy** AW *noun* [U] **in·appro·pri·ate·ly** AW *adv.*：*She was inappropriately dressed for a funeral.* 她的穿着不适合参加葬礼。**in·appro·pri·ate·ness** *noun* [U]

in·articu·late /ˌɪnɑːˈtɪkjələt; *NAmE* -ɑːrˈtɪk-/ *adj.* **1** (of people 人) not able to express ideas or feelings clearly or easily 不善于表达的；不善于说话的 **2** (of speech 讲话) not using clear words; not expressed clearly 词不达意的；表达得不清楚的：*an inarticulate reply* 含混不清的回答 OPP **articulate** ▶ **in·articu·late·ly** *adv.*

in·as·much as /ˌɪnəzˈmʌtʃ əz/ *conj.* (*formal*) used to add a comment on sth that you have just said and to say in what way it is true 因为；鉴于；在…范围内：*He was a very unusual musician inasmuch as he was totally deaf.* 他是完全失聪的，从这点上来说，他是个很了不起的音乐家。

in·atten·tion /ˌɪnəˈtenʃn/ *noun* [U] (*usually disapproving*) lack of attention 不注意；不经心：*The accident was the result of a moment's inattention.* 这次事故是一时不小心造成的。

in·atten·tive /ˌɪnəˈtentɪv/ *adj.* (*disapproving*) not paying attention to sth/sb 不注意的；不经心：*an inattentive pupil* 注意力不集中的学生 ◇ ~ **to sth/sb** *inattentive to the needs of others* 漠视他人的需要 OPP **attentive** ▶ **in·atten·tive·ly** *adv.*

in·aud·ible /ɪnˈɔːdəbl/ *adj.* ~ (**to sb**) that you cannot hear 听不见的：*The whistle was inaudible to the human ear.* 这种哨声人耳听不到。OPP **audible** ▶ **in·audi·bil·ity** /ɪnˌɔːdəˈbɪləti/ *noun* [U] OPP **audibility** **in·aud·ibly** /ɪnˈɔːdəbli/ *adv.*

in·aug·ural /ɪˈnɔːgjərəl/ *adj.* [only before noun] (of an official speech, meeting, etc. 正式讲话、会议等) first, and marking the beginning of sth important, for example the time when a new leader or parliament starts work, when a new organization is formed or when sth is used for the first time 就职的；开幕的；成立的；创始的：*the President's inaugural address* 总统的就职演说 ◇ *the inaugural meeting of the geographical society* 地理学会的成立大会 ◇ *the inaugural flight of the space shuttle* 航天飞机的首次飞行 ▶ **in·aug·ural** *noun* [usually sing.] (*especially NAmE*)：*the presidential inaugural in January* 一月间的总统就职演说

in·aug·ur·ate /ɪˈnɔːgjəreɪt/ *verb* **1** ~ **sb** (**as sth**) | ~ **sb** + **noun** to introduce a new public official or leader at a special ceremony 为（某人）举行就职典礼：*He will be inaugurated (as) President in January.* 他将于一月份就任总统。**2** ~ **sth** to officially open a building or start an organization with a special ceremony 为…举行落成仪式（或创建仪式）：*The new theatre was inaugurated by the mayor.* 新落成的剧院由市长主持了开幕典礼。**3** ~ **sth** (*formal*) to introduce a new development or an important change 引进；开创；开始：*The moon landing inaugurated a new era in space exploration.* 登陆月球开创了太空探索的新纪元。▶ **in·aug·ur·ation** /ɪˌnɔːgjəˈreɪʃn/ *noun* [U, C]：*the President's inauguration* 总统就职典礼 ◇ *an inauguration speech* 就职演说

Iˌnaugu'ration Day *noun* (in the US) 20 January, officially the first day of a new President's period of office 美国总统就职日（1 月 20 日）

in·aus·pi·cious /ˌɪnɔːˈspɪʃəs/ *adj.* (*formal*) showing signs that the future will not be good or successful 预示前景黯淡的；不祥的；不吉利的：*an inauspicious start* 不吉利的开头 OPP **auspicious** ▶ **in·aus·pi·cious·ly** *adv.*

in·authen·tic /ˌɪnɔːˈθentɪk/ *adj.* not genuine; that you cannot believe or rely on 假的；不可信的；不可靠的 OPP **authentic** ▶ **in·authen·ti·city** /ˌɪnɔːθenˈtɪsəti/ *noun* [U]

in·board /ˈɪnbɔːd; *NAmE* -bɔːrd/ *adj.* (*specialist*) located on the inside of a boat, plane or car （船、飞机或汽车）内部的；舱内的：*an inboard motor* 舱内马达 OPP **outboard** ▶ **in·board** *adv.*

in·born /ˌɪnˈbɔːn; *NAmE* -ˈbɔːrn/ (*also less frequent* **in·bred**) *adj.* an **inborn** quality is one that you are born with 天生的；先天的 SYN **innate**

in·bound /ˈɪnbaʊnd/ *adj.* (*formal*) travelling towards a place rather than leaving it 到达的；归航的：*inbound flights/passengers* 到港航班 / 乘客 OPP **outbound**

in·bounds /ˈɪnbaʊndz/ *adj.* (in BASKETBALL 篮球) relating to a throw that puts the ball into play again after it has gone out of play 从界外掷入界内的：*an inbounds pass* 从界外掷入界内的传球

in·box /ˈɪnbɒks; *NAmE* -bɑːks/ *noun* **1** (*computing* 计) the place on a computer where new email messages are shown （电子邮件）收件箱：*I have a stack of emails in my inbox.* 我的收件箱里有很多电邮。➲ WORDFINDER NOTE AT MESSAGE ➲ COLLOCATIONS AT EMAIL **2** (*NAmE*) = IN TRAY

in·bred /ˌɪnˈbred/ *adj.* **1** produced by breeding among closely related members of a group of animals, people or plants 近交的；近亲繁殖的；同系交配的：*an inbred racehorse* 近交；同系交配的赛马 **2** = INBORN

in·breed·ing /ˈɪnbriːdɪŋ/ *noun* [U] breeding between closely related people or animals 近亲繁殖；同系交配

in·built /ˈɪnbɪlt/ *adj.* [only before noun] an **inbuilt** quality exists as an essential part of sth/sb 内在的；本质的；天生的：*His height gives him an inbuilt advantage over his opponent.* 他的身高成为他相对于对手的先天优势。➲ COMPARE BUILT-IN

ˌin-'built *adj.* = BUILT-IN

Inc. /ɪŋk/ (*also* **inc**) *abbr.* Incorporated (used after the name of a company in the US) 公司（美国用法，置于公司名称之后）：*Texaco Inc.* 德士古石油公司

inc. *abbr.* (*BrE*) = INCL.

in·cal·cul·able /ɪn'kælkjələbl/ *adj.* (*formal*) very large or very great; too great to calculate 极大的；不可计算的；不可估量的：*The oil spill has caused incalculable damage to the environment.* 这次石油泄漏对环境造成了难以估计的损害。 ➲ COMPARE CALCULABLE ▶ **in·cal·cul·ably** /-əbli/ *adv.*

in·can·des·cent /ˌɪnkæn'desnt/ *adj.* **1** (*specialist*) giving out light when heated 白热的；白炽的：*incandescent lamps* 白炽灯 **2** (*formal*) very bright 十分明亮的；耀眼的：*incandescent white* 刺眼的白色 **3** (*formal*) full of strong emotion 感情强烈的；激情的：*an incandescent musical performance* 充满激情的音乐演奏 ◇ *She was incandescent with rage.* 她怒不可遏。▶ **in·can·des·cence** /-sns/ *noun* [U]

in·can·ta·tion /ˌɪnkæn'teɪʃn/ *noun* [C, U] special words that are spoken or sung to have a magic effect; the act of speaking or singing these words 符咒；咒语；念咒语

in·cap·able AW /ɪn'keɪpəbl/ *adj.* **1** not able to do sth 没有能力（做某事）：**~ of sth** *incapable of speech* 不会说话 ◇ **~ of doing sth** *The children seem to be* ***totally incapable*** *of working by themselves.* 孩子们好像完全不能靠自己做功课。 **2** not able to control yourself or your affairs; not able to do anything well 不能克制自己的；不能自理的；什么事也做不好的：*He was found lying in the road, drunk and incapable.* 他被发现躺在路上，烂醉如泥。 ◇ *If people keep telling you you're incapable, you begin to lose confidence in yourself.* 如果人们不断地对你说你无能，你就开始失去自信心了。 OPP **capable**

in·cap·aci·tate AW /ˌɪnkə'pæsɪteɪt/ *verb* [usually passive] **~ sb/sth** (*formal*) to make sb/sth unable to live or work normally 使失去正常生活（或工作）能力

in·cap·acity /ˌɪnkə'pæsəti/ *noun* [U] (*formal*) **1 ~ (of sb/sth) (to do sth)** lack of ability or skill 无能力；缺乏技能 SYN **inability**: *their incapacity to govern effectively* 他们缺乏有效治理的能力 **2** the state of being too ill/sick to do your work or take care of yourself 卧病；孱弱：*She returned to work after a long period of incapacity.* 她病了很长一段时间之后回去工作了。

ˌin-'car *adj.* [only before noun] relating to sth that you have or use inside a car, for example a radio or CD player 车内安装（或使用）的；车内的：*in-car entertainment* 安装于车内的娱乐系统

in·car·cer·ate /ɪn'kɑːsəreɪt; *NAmE* -'kɑːrs-/ *verb* [usually passive] **~ sb (in sth)** (*formal*) to put sb in prison or in another place from which they cannot escape 监禁；关押；禁闭 SYN **imprison** ▶ **in·car·cer·ation** /ɪnˌkɑːsə'reɪʃn; *NAmE* -ˌkɑːrs-/ *noun* [U]

in·car·nate *adj., verb*

■ ***adj.*** /ɪn'kɑːnət; *NAmE* -'kɑːrn-/ (usually after nouns 通常在名词之后) (*formal*) in human form 人体化的；化身的；拟人化的：*The leader seemed the devil incarnate.* 那个首领犹如魔鬼的化身。

■ ***verb*** /'ɪnkɑːneɪt; *NAmE* -kɑːrn-/ **~ sth** (*formal*) to give a definite or human form to a particular idea or quality 将（概念或品质）具体化；使人格化；拟人化 SYN **embody**

in·car·na·tion /ˌɪnkɑː'neɪʃn; *NAmE* -kɑːr'n-/ *noun* **1** [C] a period of life in a particular form （某一段时间内的）化身：*one of the incarnations of Vishnu* 守护神毗湿奴的化身之一 ◇ *He believed he had been a prince in a previous incarnation.* 他相信他的前生是个王子。 ◇ (*figurative*) *I worked for her in her earlier incarnation* (= her previous job) *as a lawyer.* 她先前当律师时我曾受雇于她。 **2** [C] a person who represents a particular quality, for example, in human form 代表某种品质的人；化身 SYN **embodiment**: *the incarnation of evil* 邪恶的化身 **3** [sing., U] (*also* **the Incarnation**) (in Christianity 基督教) the act of God coming to earth in human form as Jesus 道成肉身（上帝化身为耶稣来到人间）

in·cau·tious /ɪn'kɔːʃəs/ *adj.* (*formal*) done without thinking carefully about the results; not thinking about what might happen 不慎重的；轻率的；鲁莽的 ▶ **in·cau·tious·ly** *adv.*

in·cen·di·ary /ɪn'sendiəri; *NAmE* -dieri/ *adj., noun*

■ ***adj.*** [only before noun] **1** designed to cause fires 放火的；纵火的；能引起燃烧的：*an* ***incendiary device/bomb/attack*** 喷火器；燃烧弹；火攻 **2** (*formal*) causing strong feelings or violence 煽动的 SYN **inflammatory**: *incendiary remarks* 煽动性言论

■ ***noun*** (*pl.* **-ies**) a bomb that is designed to make a fire start burning when it explodes 燃烧弹 SYN **firebomb**

in·cense *noun, verb*

■ ***noun*** /'ɪnsens/ [U] a substance that produces a pleasant smell when you burn it, used particularly in religious ceremonies 香（尤指宗教礼仪用的）

■ ***verb*** /ɪn'sens/ **~ sb** to make sb very angry 激怒；使大怒：*The decision incensed the workforce.* 这个决定激怒了全体员工。

in·censed /ɪn'senst/ *adj.* very angry 非常愤怒的；大怒的：*They were incensed at the decision.* 他们被这个决定激怒了。

in·cen·tive AW /ɪn'sentɪv/ *noun* **1** [C, U] **~ (for/to sb/sth) (to do sth)** something that encourages you to do sth 激励；刺激；鼓励：*There is no incentive for people to save fuel.* 没有鼓励人们节约燃料的措施。 OPP **disincentive** **2** a payment or CONCESSION (= a reduction in the amount of money that has to be paid) that encourages sb to do something 激励奖金；激励性减免优惠：*tax incentives to encourage savings* 鼓励储蓄的税收措施

in·cen·tiv·ize (*BrE also* **-ise**) /ɪn'sentɪvaɪz/ *verb* to encourage sb to behave in a particular way by offering them a reward 激励；奖励：**~ sth** *ways to incentivize innovation* 奖励创新的途径 ◇ **~ sb to do sth** *You need to incentivize your existing customers to stay with you.* 你得奖励并留住现有客户。

in·cep·tion /ɪn'sepʃn/ *noun* [sing.] (*formal*) the start of an institution, an organization, etc. （机构、组织等的）开端，创始：*The club has grown rapidly since its inception in 2007.* 这个俱乐部自从 2007 年成立以来发展迅速。

in·ces·sant /ɪn'sesnt/ *adj.* (*usually disapproving*) never stopping 不停的；持续不断的 SYN **constant**: *incessant noise/rain/chatter* 不间断的噪音 / 阴雨 / 絮叨 ◇ *incessant meetings* 接二连三的会议 ▶ **in·ces·sant·ly** *adv.*: *to talk incessantly* 滔滔不绝地谈话

in·cest /'ɪnsest/ *noun* [U] sexual activity between two people who are very closely related in a family, for example, a brother and sister, or a father and daughter 乱伦；血亲相奸

in·ces·tu·ous /ɪn'sestjuəs; *NAmE* -tʃuəs/ *adj.* **1** involving sex between two people in a family who are very closely related 乱伦的；血亲相奸的：*an incestuous relationship* 乱伦关系 **2** (*disapproving*) involving a group of people who have a close relationship and do not want to include anyone outside the group 小集团的；小团体的；排外的：*The music industry is an incestuous business.* 音乐界是一个封闭的行业。 ▶ **in·ces·tu·ous·ly** *adv.*

inch 🔑 /ɪntʃ/ *noun, verb*

■ ***noun*** **1** 🔑 (*abbr.* **in.**) a unit for measuring length, equal to 2.54 centimetres. There are 12 inches in a foot. 英寸（长度单位，等于 2.54 厘米，1 英尺等于 12 英寸）：*1.14 inches of rain fell last night.* 昨晚的降雨量为 1.14 英寸。 ◇ *She's a few inches taller than me.* 她比我高几英寸。 **2** 🔑 a small amount or distance 少量；短距离：*He escaped death* ***by an inch.*** 他差点儿丧了命。 ◇ *The car missed us* ***by inches.*** 那辆车险些撞到了我们。 ◇ *He was just inches away from scoring.* 他只差一点儿就得分了。

IDM **every inch** **1** the whole of sth 整体；全部：*The doctor examined every inch of his body.* 医生检查了他全身的每一部分。 ◇ (*figurative*) *If they try to fire me I'll fight* them **every inch of the way**. 他们要是想解雇我，我就和他们抗争到底。 **2** completely 完全地： *In his first game the young player already looked every inch a winner.* 那位年轻的选手在第一局比赛看上去就已经胜券在握了。 **give sb an 'inch (and they'll take a 'mile/'yard)** (*saying*) used to say that if you allow some people a small amount of freedom or power they will see you as weak and try to take a lot more 得寸进尺 **ˌinch by 'inch** very slowly and with great care or difficulty 缓慢而谨慎地；一步一步： *She crawled forward inch by inch.* 她一点一点地往前爬。 **not budge/give/move an 'inch** to refuse to change your position, decision, etc. even a little 寸步不让： *We tried to negotiate a lower price but they wouldn't budge an inch.* 我们试图把价还低一些，但他们寸步不让。 **within an 'inch of sth/of doing sth** very close to sth/doing sth 差一点；险些： *She was within an inch of being killed.* 她险些丧命。◇ *They beat him (to) within an inch of his life* (= very severely). 他们险些把他打死。 ➲ MORE AT TRUST *v.*

■ ***verb*** [I, T] to move or make sth move slowly and carefully in a particular direction（使朝某方向）谨慎移动： **+ adv./prep.** *She moved forward, inching towards the rope.* 她小心翼翼地慢慢向绳子挪过去。◇ **~ sth + adv./prep.** *I inched the car forward.* 我开着车一点一点往前挪。◇ *He* ***inched his way*** *through the narrow passage.* 他一点一点地穿过狭窄的通道。

in·charge /ˈɪntʃɑːdʒ; *NAmE* -tʃɑːrdʒ/ *noun* (*IndE*) the person who is officially responsible for a department, etc.（部门等的）负责人，主管： *the incharge of the district hospital* 区医院院长

in·cho·ate /ɪnˈkəʊət; ˈɪnkəʊeɪt; *NAmE* -ˈkoʊ-/ *adj.* (*formal*) just beginning to form and therefore not clear or developed 初期的；雏形的；不成熟的： *inchoate ideas* 初步想法

in·cho·ative /ɪnˈkəʊətɪv; *NAmE* -ˈkoʊə-/ *adj.* (*grammar* 语法) (of verbs 动词) expressing a change of state that happens on its own. *Opened* in *the door opened* is an example of an inchoative verb. 表始的（表示动作自动开始的，如 the door opened 中的 opened） ➲ COMPARE CAUSATIVE (2), ERGATIVE

in·ci·dence AW /ˈɪnsɪdəns/ *noun* **1** [C, usually sing.] **~ of sth** (*formal*) the extent to which sth happens or has an effect 发生范围；影响程度；发生率： *an area with a* ***high incidence*** *of crime* 犯罪率高的地区 **2** [U] (*physics* 物) the way in which light meets a surface 入射（角）： *the angle of incidence* 入射角

in·ci·dent 🔑 AW /ˈɪnsɪdənt/ *noun* **1** [C] something that happens, especially sth unusual or unpleasant 发生的事情（尤指不寻常的或讨厌的）： *His bad behaviour was just an isolated incident.* 他的不良行为只是个别事件。◇ *One particular incident sticks in my mind.* 有一件事我总忘不了。 **2** [C, U] a serious or violent event, such as a crime, an accident or an attack 严重事件，暴力事件（如犯罪、事故、袭击等）： *There was a shooting incident near here last night.* 昨夜这附近发生了枪击事件。◇ *The demonstration passed off* ***without incident***. 这次示威和平地结束了。 **3** [C] a disagreement between two countries, often involving military forces（两国间的）摩擦，冲突；（常指）军事冲突： *a* ***border/diplomatic incident*** 边境 / 外交冲突

in·ci·den·tal /ˌɪnsɪˈdentl/ *adj.*, *noun*

■ ***adj.*** **1 ~ (to sth)** happening in connection with sth else, but not as important as it, or not intended 附带发生的；次要的；非有意的： *The discovery was incidental to their main research.* 这一发现是他们主要研究中的附带收获。◇ ***incidental music*** (= music used with a play or a film/movie to give atmosphere) 配乐 ◇ *You may be able to get help with* ***incidental expenses*** (= small costs that you get in connection with sth). 你可以付些钱找人帮忙。 **2 ~ to sth** (*specialist*) happening as a natural result of sth 作为自然结果的；伴随而来的；免不了的： *These risks are incidental to the work of a firefighter.* 这些风险是担任消防员不可避免的。

■ ***noun*** [usually pl.] something that happens in connection with sth else, but is less important 附带的次要事情： *You'll need money for incidentals such as tips and taxis.* 你将需要准备好付小费和乘出租车之类的杂项开销。

in·ci·den·tal·ly AW /ˌɪnsɪˈdentli/ *adv.* **1** used to introduce a new topic, or some extra information, or a question that you have just thought of（引出新话题、附加信息或临时想到的问题）顺便提一句 SYN **by the way**: *Incidentally, have you heard the news about Sue?* 顺便问一句，你听说过休的事了吗？ **2** in a way that was not planned but that is connected with sth else 偶然；附带地： *The information was only discovered incidentally.* 这个信息只是偶然得到的。

'incident room *noun* (*BrE*) a room near where a serious crime has taken place where the police work to collect evidence and information（设在严重罪案现场附近的）案件调查室

in·cin·er·ate /ɪnˈsɪnəreɪt/ *verb* [often passive] **~ sth** (*formal*) to burn sth until it is completely destroyed 把…烧成灰烬；焚毁 ▶ **in·cin·er·ation** /ɪnˌsɪnəˈreɪʃn/ *noun* [U]: *high-temperature incineration plants* 高温焚化厂

in·cin·er·ator /ɪnˈsɪnəreɪtə(r)/ *noun* a container which is closed on all sides for burning waste at high temperatures（垃圾）焚化炉 ➲ WORDFINDER NOTE AT WASTE

in·cipi·ent /ɪnˈsɪpiənt/ *adj.* [usually before noun] (*formal*) just beginning 刚开始的；初始的；早期的： *signs of incipient unrest* 动乱的初期迹象

in·cise /ɪnˈsaɪz/ *verb* **~ sth (in/on/onto sth)** (*formal*) to cut words, designs, etc. into a surface（在表面）雕，刻；切入 ➲ COMPARE ENGRAVE

in·ci·sion /ɪnˈsɪʒn/ *noun* [C, U] a sharp cut made in sth, particularly during a medical operation; the act of making a cut in sth 割口；（尤指手术的）切口；切开： *Make a small incision below the ribs.* 在肋骨下方切开一个小口。

in·ci·sive /ɪnˈsaɪsɪv/ *adj.* (*approving*) **1** showing clear thought and good understanding of what is important, and the ability to express this 锐利的；透彻的： ***incisive comments/criticism/analysis*** 深刻的评论 / 批评 / 分析 ◇ *an incisive mind* 敏锐的头脑 **2** showing sb's ability to take decisions and act with force 果断的；当机立断的： *an incisive performance* 果敢的表现 ▶ **in·ci·sive·ly** *adv.* **in·ci·sive·ness** *noun* [U]

in·ci·sor /ɪnˈsaɪzə(r)/ *noun* one of the eight sharp teeth at the front of the mouth that are used for biting 切牙；门齿 ➲ COMPARE CANINE *n.* (1), MOLAR

in·cite /ɪnˈsaɪt/ *verb* to encourage sb to do sth violent, illegal or unpleasant, especially by making them angry or excited 煽动；鼓动： **~ sth** *to* ***incite crime/racial hatred/violence*** 教唆犯罪；煽动种族仇恨 / 暴力 ◇ **~ sb (to sth)** *They were accused of inciting the crowd to violence.* 他们被控煽动群众暴乱。◇ **~ sb to do sth** *He incited the workforce to come out on strike.* 他煽动工人罢工。

in·cite·ment /ɪnˈsaɪtmənt/ *noun* [U, C] **~ (to sth)** the act of encouraging sb to do sth violent, illegal or unpleasant 煽动；鼓动： *incitement to racial hatred* 种族仇恨的挑起

in·civil·ity /ˌɪnsəˈvɪləti/ *noun* [U, C] (*pl.* **-ies**) (*formal*) rude behaviour; rude remarks 粗鲁的举动；无礼的语言；不文明 ➲ SEE ALSO UNCIVIL

incl. (*BrE also* **inc.**) *abbr.* **1** (in advertisements 广告用) including; included 包括；连同…在内： *transport not incl.* 不包括运输 ◇ *£29.53 inc. tax* 连税在内共 29.53 英镑 **2** INCLUSIVE 包括提到的所有天数（或月、数目等）： *Open 1 April to 31 October incl.* 从 4 月 1 号到 10 月 31 号每天营业。

in·clem·ent /ɪnˈklemənt/ *adj.* (*formal*) (of the weather 天气) not pleasant; cold, wet, etc. 恶劣的（指寒冷的、潮湿的等） OPP **clement** ▶ **in·clem·ency** /-ənsi/ *noun* [U]

in·clin·ation AW /ˌɪnklɪˈneɪʃn/ *noun* **1** [U, C] a feeling that makes you want to do sth 倾向；意愿： **~ (to do sth)** *He did not show the* ***slightest inclination*** *to leave.* 他丝毫

没有表现出要离开的意思。◇ *My **natural inclination** is to find a compromise.* 我生性易于妥协。◇ *She had neither the time nor the inclination to help them.* 她既没有时间也不愿意帮助他们。◇ ~ (**towards/for sth**) *She lacked any inclination for housework.* 她一点都没有兴趣做家务。◇ *He was a loner by nature and **by inclination**.* 他天性不喜交际，而且也无意于此。◇ *You must follow your own inclinations when choosing a career.* 你必须按照自己的意愿选择职业。 **2** [C] ~ **to do sth** a tendency to do sth 趋向；趋势：*There is an inclination to treat geography as a less important subject.* 有一种趋向认为地理是一门次要的学科。 **3** [C, usually sing., U] (*specialist*) a degree of sloping 倾斜度：*an inclination of 45°* * 45° 的倾斜度 ◇ *the angle of inclination* 倾角 **4** [C] a small downward movement, usually of the head 向下的轻微动作；（通常指）点头

in·cline AW *verb, noun*

■ **verb** /ɪnˈklaɪn/ (*formal*) **1** [I, T] to tend to think or behave in a particular way; to make sb do this （使）倾向于，有…的趋势：~ **to/towards sth** *I incline to the view that we should take no action at this stage.* 我倾向于认为我们在这个阶段不应采取行动。◇ ~ **to do sth** *The government is more effective than we incline to think.* 政府比我们惯常料想的更有成效。◇ ~ **sb to/towards sth** *Lack of money inclines many young people towards crime.* 缺钱使很多年轻人产生了犯罪倾向。◇ ~ **sb to do sth** *His obvious sincerity inclined me to trust him.* 他满脸的真诚，让我愿意相信他。 **2** [T] ~ **your head** to bend your head forward, especially as a sign of agreement, welcome, etc. 点头（尤指以示同意、欢迎等） **3** [I, T] ~ (**sth**) (**to/towards sth**) to lean or slope in a particular direction; to make sth lean or slope （使）倾斜：*The land inclined gently towards the shore.* 地面缓缓向海岸倾斜。

■ **noun** /ˈɪnklaɪn/ (*formal*) a slope 斜坡；倾斜；斜度：*a **steep/slight incline*** 陡坡；缓坡

in·clined AW /ɪnˈklaɪnd/ *adj.* **1** [not before noun] ~ (**to do sth**) wanting to do sth 想（做某事）：*She was inclined to trust him.* 她愿意相信他。◇ *He writes only when he feels inclined to.* 他只在想写作的时候才动笔写。◇ *There'll be time for a swim if you **feel so inclined**.* 你要是想游泳的话，还有时间呢。 **2** ~ **to do sth** tending to do sth; likely to do sth 有…倾向；很可能：*He's inclined to be lazy.* 他喜欢偷懒。◇ *They'll be more inclined to listen if you don't shout.* 你要是不大声嚷，他们会更愿意倾听。 **3** ~ **to agree, believe, think, etc.** used when you are expressing an opinion but do not want to express it very strongly （温和地表达意见）倾向于同意（或相信、认为等）：*I'm inclined to agree with you.* 我倾向于同意你的观点。 **4** (used with particular adverbs 与某些副词连用) having a natural ability for sth; preferring to do sth 有（某种）天赋的；宁愿（做某事）的：***musically/academically inclined** children* 有音乐天赋的 / 喜欢读书的儿童 **5** sloping; at an angle 倾斜的；成某角度的

in·clude 🔑 /ɪnˈkluːd/ *verb* **1** 🔑 (not used in the progressive tenses 不用于进行时) if one thing **includes** another, it has the second thing as one of its parts 包括；包含：~ **sth** *The tour included a visit to the Science Museum.* 这次游览包括参观科学博物馆。◇ *Does the price include tax?* 这个价钱是否包括税款？◇ ~ **doing sth** *Your duties include typing letters and answering the telephone.* 你的职责包括打信件和接电话。 **2** 🔑 to make sb/sth part of sth 使成为…的一部分：~ **sb/sth** (**as/in/on sth**) *You should include some examples in your essay.* 你应该在文章里举一些例子。◇ *We all went, **me included**.* 我们都去了，连我在内。◇ ~ **sb/sth as sth** *Representatives from the country were included as observers at the conference.* 这个国家的代表都被列为会议的观察员。 OPP **exclude**

in·clud·ing 🔑 /ɪnˈkluːdɪŋ/ *prep.* (*abbr.* **incl.**) having sth as part of a group or set 包括…在内：*I've got three days' holiday including New Year's Day.* 包括元旦在内我有三天假。◇ *Six people were killed in the riot, including a policeman.* 暴乱中有六人死亡，包括一名警察。◇ *It's £7.50, **not including** tax.* 共计 7.50 英镑，不含税款。 OPP **excluding**
➲ LANGUAGE BANK AT E.G.

in·clu·sion /ɪnˈkluːʒn/ *noun* **1** [U] the fact of including sb/sth; the fact of being included （被）包括，包含：*His inclusion in the team is in doubt.* 他是否能被选入这个队还未确定。 **2** [C] a person or thing that is included 被包括的人（或事物）：*There were some surprising inclusions in the list.* 名单中包括一些意想不到的人。 OPP **exclusion**

in·clu·sive /ɪnˈkluːsɪv/ *adj.* **1** having the total cost, or the cost of sth that is mentioned, contained in the price 包含全部费用的；包括所提到的费用在内的：*The **fully inclusive** fare for the trip is £52.* 这次旅行的全部费用是 52 英镑。◇ ~ **of sth** *The rent is inclusive of water and heating.* 租金包括水费和暖气费。 OPP **exclusive** **2** (**from**)... **to**... **inclusive** (*BrE*) including all the days, months, numbers, etc. mentioned 包括提到的所有的天数（或月、数目等）在内：*We are offering free holidays for children aged two to eleven inclusive.* 我们提供的度假活动，两岁至十一岁的儿童免费。◇ *The castle is open daily from May to October inclusive.* 这个古堡从五月起每天开放，直至十月底。 **3** including a wide range of people, things, ideas, etc. 包容广阔的；范围广泛的：*The party must adopt more inclusive strategies and a broader vision.* 这个党必须采取更广泛的策略和更远大的视野。 OPP **exclusive** ▸ **in·clu·sive·ly** *adv.*：*The word 'men' can be understood inclusively* (= including men and women). * men 这个词可以作概括性的解释（包括男人和女人）。 **in·clu·sive·ness** *noun* [U]

▼ **BRITISH/AMERICAN** 英式 / 美式英语

inclusive / through

- In *BrE*, **inclusive** is used to emphasize that you are including the days, months, numbers, etc. mentioned, especially in formal or official situations. 在英式英语中，inclusive 用以强调所提到的日子、月份、数字等均包括在内，尤用于正式或官方场合：*Answer questions 8 to 12 inclusive.* 回答第 8 到第 12 题。◇ *The amusement park is open daily from May to October inclusive.* 游乐园从五月到十月底每天都开放。
- In *NAmE*, **through** is used. 美式英语用 through：*Answer questions 8 through 12.* 回答第 8 到第 12 题。◇ *The amusement park is open (from) May through October.* 游乐园从五月到十月底每天都开放。
- **To** can also be used with this meaning in *BrE* and *NAmE*. 英式英语和美式英语都可用 to：*The park is open from 1 May to 31 October.* 公园从 5 月 1 日到 10 月 31 日开放。

in·cog·nito /ˌɪnkɒɡˈniːtəʊ; *NAmE* ˌɪnkɑːɡˈniːtoʊ/ *adv.* in a way that prevents other people from finding out who you are 伪装；隐姓埋名：*Movie stars often prefer to travel incognito.* 电影明星旅行时常喜欢隐瞒身份。 ▸ **in·cog·nito** *adj.*：*an incognito visit* 化名出访

in·co·her·ent AW /ˌɪnkəʊˈhɪərənt; *NAmE* ˌɪnkoʊˈhɪr-/ *adj.* **1** (of people 人) unable to express yourself clearly, often because of emotion （常因强烈情感而）言语不清的，语无伦次的：*She broke off, incoherent with anger.* 她气得话都说不清了，便住口了。 OPP **coherent** **2** (of sounds 声音) not clear and hard to understand 不清楚的；难以分辨的；难懂的 SYN **unintelligible**：*Rachel whispered something incoherent.* 雷切尔低声说了些什么，听不清楚。 **3** not logical or well organized 逻辑不清的；不连贯的：*an incoherent policy* 前后不一致的政策 OPP **coherent** ▸ **in·co·her·ence** /-əns/ *noun* [U] **in·co·her·ent·ly** AW *adv.*

in·come 🔑 AW /ˈɪnkʌm; -kəm/ *noun* [C, U] the money that a person, a region, a country, etc. earns from work, from investing money, from business, etc. 收入；收益；所得：*people **on high/low incomes*** 高 / 低收入的人 ◇ *a weekly **disposable income*** (= the money that you have left to spend after tax, etc.) *of £200* * 200 英镑的税后实得周薪 ◇ *a rise in **national income*** 国民收入的增长 ◇ *They receive a proportion of their income from the sale of goods and services.* 他们一部分的收入来自出售货品和各种服务所

得。◇ *Tourism is a major* ***source of income*** *for the area.* 旅游业是这个地区的主要收入来源。 ◇ ***higher/middle/lower income*** *groups* 较高 / 中等 / 较低收入阶层 ➲ COLLOCATIONS AT FINANCE ➲ COMPARE EXPENDITURE

▼ SYNONYMS 同义词辨析

income

wage/wages • pay • salary • earnings

These are all words for money that a person earns or receives for their work. 以上各词均指收入、工资、薪水。

income money that a person receives for their work, or from investments or business 指收入、收益、所得： *people on low incomes* 低收入的人

wage/wages money that employees get for doing their job, usually paid every week 通常指按周领取的工资、工钱： *a weekly wage of £200* 周薪 200 英镑

pay money that employees earn for doing their job 指工资、薪水： *The job offers good rates of pay.* 这工作报酬高。

salary money that employees earn for doing their job, usually paid every month 通常指按月发放的薪水、薪金

WAGE, PAY OR SALARY? 用 wage、pay 还是 salary?

Pay is the most general of these three words. Employees who work in factories, etc. get their **wages** each week. Employees who work in offices or professional people such as teachers or doctors receive a **salary** that is paid each month, but is usually expressed as an annual figure. * pay 在这组词中含义最广。在工厂等工作的雇员按周领取的工钱用 wages。办公室工作人员、教师、医生等专业人员按月领取的薪金用 salary，但通常以年薪表示。

earnings money that a person earns from their work 指薪水、工资、收入： *a rise in average earnings for factory workers* 工厂工人平均收入的增加

PATTERNS

- (a) **high/low/basic** income/wage/pay/salary/earnings
- to **earn** an income/a wage/your pay/a salary
- to **be on** a(n) income/wage/salary of...

in·comer /ˈɪnkʌmə(r)/ *noun* (*BrE*) a person who comes to live in a particular place 新来的人；移民

ˌincome supˈport *noun* [U] (in Britain) the money that the government pays to people who have no income or a very low income （英国为无收入或收入很低者提供的）收入补贴

ˈincome tax *noun* [U, C] the amount of money that you pay to the government according to how much you earn （个人）所得税： *The standard rate of income tax was cut to 23p in the pound.* 所得税的标准税率削减到了每英镑 23 便士。

in·com·ing /ˈɪnkʌmɪŋ/ *adj.* [only before noun] **1** recently elected or chosen 新当选的；新任的： *the* ***incoming government/president/administration*** 新一届政府 / 总统 / 行政当局 OPP **outgoing** **2** arriving somewhere, or being received 正到达某地的；刚收到的： ***incoming flights*** 进港航班 ◇ *the* ***incoming tide*** 涨潮 ◇ ***incoming calls/mail*** 打进来的电话；寄来的邮件 OPP **outgoing**

in·com·men·sur·able /ˌɪnkəˈmenʃərəbl/ *adj.* ~ (**with sth**) (*formal*) if two things are **incommensurable**, they are so completely different from each other that they cannot be compared 不能相比的；大相径庭的

in·com·men·sur·ate /ˌɪnkəˈmenʃərət/ *adj.* ~ (**with sth**) (*formal*) not matching sth in size, importance, quality, etc. 不相称的；不适当的；不匹配的 OPP **commensurate**

in·com·mode /ˌɪnkəˈməʊd; *NAmE* -ˈmoʊd/ *verb* ~ **sb** (*formal*) to cause sb difficulties or problems 对…造成困难；打扰；妨碍： *We are very sorry to have incommoded you.* 很抱歉给您添麻烦了。

in·com·mu·ni·cado /ˌɪnkəˌmjuːnɪˈkɑːdəʊ; *NAmE* -ˈkɑːdoʊ/ *adj.* without communicating with other people, because you are not allowed to or because you do not want to 不允许与他人接触；不愿与他人接触： *The prisoner has been* ***held incommunicado*** *for more than a week.* 这名囚犯已被单独囚禁了一个多星期。

in·com·par·able /ɪnˈkɒmprəbl; *NAmE* -ˈkɑːm-/ *adj.* so good or impressive that nothing can be compared to it 不可比拟的；无比的；无双的 SYN **matchless**: *the incomparable beauty of Lake Garda* 加尔达湖的绝妙美景 ▶ **in·com·par·abil·ity** /ɪnˌkɒmpərəˈbɪləti; *NAmE* -ˌkɑːm-/ *noun* [U] **in·com·par·ably** *adv.*

in·com·pat·ible AW /ˌɪnkəmˈpætəbl/ *adj.* **1** ~ (**with sth**) two actions, ideas, etc. that are **incompatible** are not acceptable or possible together because of basic differences （与某事物）不一致，不相配： *The hours of the job are incompatible with family life.* 这份工作的上班时间和家庭生活有冲突。 ◇ *These two objectives are* ***mutually incompatible.*** 这两个目标相互矛盾。 **2** two people who are **incompatible** are very different from each other and so are not able to live or work happily together （与某人）合不来，不能和睦相处 **3** ~ (**with sth**) two things that are **incompatible** are of different types so that they cannot be used or mixed together （与某物）不匹配；配伍禁忌的；不兼容；互斥： *New computer software is often incompatible with older computers.* 新的计算机软件往往和旧式计算机不兼容。 ◇ *Those two blood groups are incompatible.* 那两种血型不相容。 OPP **compatible** ▶ **in·com·pati·bil·ity** AW /ˌɪnkəmˌpætəˈbɪləti/ *noun* [U, C] (*pl.* **-ies**)

in·com·pe·tence /ɪnˈkɒmpɪtəns; *NAmE* -ˈkɑːm-/ *noun* [U] the lack of skill or ability to do your job or a task as it should be done 无能力；不胜任；不称职： *professional incompetence* 专业方面不称职 ◇ *police incompetence* 警方的无能 ◇ *He was dismissed for incompetence.* 他因不称职而被解雇。

in·com·pe·tent /ɪnˈkɒmpɪtənt; *NAmE* -ˈkɑːm-/ *adj., noun*

■ ***adj.*** not having the skill or ability to do your job or a task as it should be done 无能力的；不胜任的；不称职的： *an incompetent teacher* 不称职的教师 ◇ *his incompetent handling of the affair* 他在处理这件事上的无能表现 ◇ *The Prime Minister was attacked as incompetent to lead.* 首相被抨击缺乏领导能力。 OPP **competent** ▶ **in·com·pe·tent·ly** *adv.*

■ ***noun*** a person who does not have the skill or ability to do their job or a task as it should be done 不称职（或不能胜任、无能）的人

in·com·plete /ˌɪnkəmˈpliːt/ *adj., noun*

■ ***adj.*** not having everything that it should have; not finished or complete 不完整的；不完全的；不完善的： *an incomplete set of figures* 一组不完整的数字 ◇ *Spoken language contains many incomplete sentences.* 口语中有很多不完整的句子。 OPP **complete** ▶ **in·com·plete·ly** *adv.* : *The causes of the phenomenon are still incompletely understood.* 造成这种现象的原因尚未彻底弄清。 **in·com·plete·ness** *noun* [U]

■ ***noun*** (*NAmE*) the grade that a student gets for a course of education when they have not completed all the work for that course （学业成绩评分）未修毕，未完成

in·com·pre·hen·sible /ɪnˌkɒmprɪˈhensəbl; *NAmE* -ˌkɑːm-/ *adj.* ~ (**to sb**) impossible to understand 无法理解的；难懂的 SYN **unintelligible**: *Some application forms can be incomprehensible to ordinary people.* 有些申请表格一般人可能看不懂。 ◇ *He found his son's actions totally incomprehensible.* 他感觉他儿子的行为完全理解不了。 OPP **comprehensible** ▶ **in·com·pre·hen·si·bil·ity** /ɪnˌkɒmprɪˌhensəˈbɪləti; *NAmE* -ˌkɑːm-/ *noun* [U] **in·com·pre·hen·sibly** /-səbli/ *adv.*

in·com·pre·hen·sion /ɪnˌkɒmprɪˈhenʃn; *NAmE* -ˌkɑːm-/ *noun* [U] the state of not being able to understand sb/sth 不理解；不懂： *Anna read the letter with incomprehension.* 安娜茫然不解地读了那封信。

in·con·ceiv·able AW /ˌɪnkənˈsiːvəbl/ *adj.* impossible to imagine or believe 难以想象的；无法相信的 SYN **unthinkable**: *It is inconceivable that the minister was not aware of the problem.* 令人难以置信的是那位大臣竟然没有意识到这个问题。OPP **conceivable** ▶ **in·con·ceiv·ably** AW *adv.*

in·con·clu·sive AW /ˌɪnkənˈkluːsɪv/ *adj.* not leading to a definite decision or result 非决定性的；无定论的；不确定的：*inconclusive evidence/results/tests* 没有说服力的证据；无定论的结果 / 试验 ◇ *inconclusive discussions* 无结果的讨论 OPP **conclusive** ▶ **in·con·clu·sive·ly** AW *adv.*：*The last meeting had ended inconclusively.* 上一次会议没有结果。

in·con·gru·ous /ɪnˈkɒŋgruəs; *NAmE* -ˈkɑːŋ-/ *adj.* strange, and not suitable in a particular situation 不合适的；不相称的；不协调的 SYN **inappropriate**: *Such traditional methods seem incongruous in our technical age.* 此类传统方法似乎同我们今天的科技时代格格不入。▶ **in·con·gru·ity** /ˌɪnkɒnˈgruːəti; *NAmE* ˌɪnkɑːn-/ *noun* [U, C] (*pl.* **-ies**): *She was struck by the incongruity of the situation.* 这一局面煞是怪异，让她惊愕不已。**in·con·gru·ous·ly** *adv.*：*incongruously dressed* 穿着不协调

in·con·se·quen·tial /ɪnˌkɒnsɪˈkwenʃl; *NAmE* -ˌkɑːn-/ *adj.* not important or worth considering 不重要的；微不足道的；细琐的 SYN **trivial**: *inconsequential details* 无关紧要的细节 ◇ *inconsequential chatter* 无谓的唠叨 OPP **consequential** ▶ **in·con·se·quen·tial·ly** /-ʃəli/ *adv.*

in·con·sid·er·able /ˌɪnkənˈsɪdrəbl/ *adj.*

IDM **not incon'siderable** (*formal*) large; large enough to be considered important 巨大的；值得重视的：*We have spent a not inconsiderable amount of money on the project already.* 我们已经在这一项目上投入了一笔相当可观的资金。

in·con·sid·er·ate /ˌɪnkənˈsɪdərət/ *adj.* (*disapproving*) not giving enough thought to other people's feelings or needs 不为别人着想的；不体谅别人的；考虑不周的 SYN **thoughtless**: *inconsiderate behaviour* 考虑不周的行为 ◇ *It was inconsiderate of you not to call.* 你连个电话也不打，不够体谅人。OPP **considerate** ▶ **in·con·sid·er·ate·ly** *adv.*

in·con·sist·ent AW /ˌɪnkənˈsɪstənt/ *adj.* **1** [not usually before noun] ~ (**with sth**) if two statements, etc. are **inconsistent**, or one is **inconsistent with** the other, they cannot both be true because they give the facts in a different way 不一致；相矛盾：*The report is inconsistent with the financial statements.* 这个报告与财务报表内容不一致。◇ *The witnesses' statements were inconsistent.* 各证人的证词相互抵触。**2** ~ **with sth** not matching a set of standards, ideas, etc. 不符合（某套标准、思想等）：*Her behaviour was clearly inconsistent with her beliefs.* 她的行为显然违背了她的信仰。**3** (*disapproving*) tending to change too often; not staying the same 反复无常的；没有常性的：*inconsistent results* 变幻无常的结果 ◇ *Children find it difficult if a parent is inconsistent.* 如果做父母的不始终如一，孩子会觉得无所适从。OPP **consistent** ▶ **in·con·sist·ency** AW /-ənsi/ *noun* [U, C] (*pl.* **-ies**): *There is some inconsistency between the witnesses' evidence and their earlier statements.* 证人的证词与他们先前的陈述有些出入。◇ *I noticed a few minor inconsistencies in her argument.* 我注意到她的论证中有几处小矛盾。**in·con·sist·ent·ly** *adv.*

in·con·sol·able /ˌɪnkənˈsəʊləbl; *NAmE* -ˈsoʊl-/ (*also* **un·con·sol·able**) *adj.* very sad and unable to accept help or comfort 悲痛欲绝的；无法慰藉的：*They were inconsolable when their only child died.* 他们唯一的孩子去世时，他们简直痛不欲生。▶ **in·con·sol·ably** /-əbli/ (*also* **un·con·sol·ably**) *adv.*：*to weep inconsolably* 悲痛欲绝地哭泣

in·con·spicu·ous /ˌɪnkənˈspɪkjuəs/ *adj.* not attracting attention; not easy to notice 不引人注目的；不起眼的 OPP **conspicuous** ▶ **in·con·spicu·ous·ly** *adv.*

in·con·stant /ɪnˈkɒnstənt; *NAmE* -ˈkɑːn-/ *adj.* (*formal*) **1** not faithful in love or friendship（对爱情或友情）不忠的，不专一的 SYN **fickle** **2** that frequently changes 不稳定的；经常变换的 OPP **constant** ▶ **in·con·stancy** AW /-ənsi/ *noun* [U]

in·con·test·able /ˌɪnkənˈtestəbl/ *adj.* (*formal*) that is true and cannot be disagreed with or denied 无可辩驳的；不可否认的；无可置疑的 SYN **indisputable**: *an incontestable right/fact* 无可争辩的权利；无可置疑的事实 ▶ **in·con·test·ably** /-əbli/ *adv.*

in·con·tin·ence /ɪnˈkɒntɪnəns; *NAmE* -ˈkɑːn-/ *noun* [U] the lack of ability to control the BLADDER and BOWELS 失禁 OPP **continence** ▶ **in·con·tin·ent** /-ənt; *NAmE* -ˈkɑːntɪnənt/ *adj.*：*Many of our patients are incontinent.* 我们很多病人都有失禁现象。

in·con·tro·vert·ible /ˌɪnkɒntrəˈvɜːtəbl; *NAmE* ˌɪnkɑːntrəˈvɜːrt-/ *adj.* (*formal*) that is true and cannot be disagreed with or denied 无可争辩的；不能否认的；无可置疑的 SYN **indisputable**: *incontrovertible evidence/proof* 无可置疑的证据 ▶ **in·con·tro·vert·ibly** /ˌɪnkɒntrəˈvɜːtəbli; *NAmE* ˌɪnkɑːntrəˈvɜːrt-/ *adv.*

in·con·veni·ence /ˌɪnkənˈviːniəns/ *noun, verb*

■ ***noun*** **1** [U] trouble or problems, especially concerning what you need or would like yourself 不便；麻烦；困难：*We apologize for the delay and regret any inconvenience it may have caused.* 我们对此次延误以及因此有可能造成的所有不便表示道歉。◇ *I have already been put to considerable inconvenience.* 我已经遇到了相当大的麻烦了。**2** [C] a person or thing that causes problems or difficulties 带来不便者；麻烦的人（或事物）SYN **nuisance**: *I can put up with minor inconveniences.* 我能忍受些小的不便。

■ ***verb*** ~ **sb** (*formal*) to cause trouble or difficulty for sb 给（某人）造成不便（或带来麻烦）：*I hope that we haven't inconvenienced you.* 我希望我们没有给你添麻烦。

in·con·veni·ent /ˌɪnkənˈviːniənt/ *adj.* causing trouble or problems, especially concerning what you need or would like yourself 不方便的；引起麻烦的；造成困难的：*an inconvenient time/place* 不方便的时间 / 地点 OPP **convenient** ▶ **in·con·veni·ent·ly** *adv.*

in·corp·or·ate AW /ɪnˈkɔːpəreɪt; *NAmE* -ˈkɔːrp-/ *verb* **1** to include sth so that it forms a part of sth 将…包括在内；包含；吸收；使并入：~ **sth** *The new car design incorporates all the latest safety features.* 新的汽车设计包括了所有最新的安全配备。◇ ~ **sth in/into/within sth** *We have incorporated all the latest safety features into the design.* 我们在设计中纳入了所有最新的安全装置。◇ *Many of your suggestions have been incorporated in the plan.* 你的很多建议已纳入计划中。**2** [often passive] ~ **sth** (*business* 商) to create a legally recognized company 注册成立：*The company was incorporated in 2008.* 这家公司成立于 2008 年。▶ **in·corp·or·ation** AW /ɪnˌkɔːpəˈreɪʃn; *NAmE* -ˌkɔːrp-/ *noun* [U]：*the incorporation of foreign words into the language* 这一语言对外来词汇的吸收 ◇ *the articles of incorporation of the company* 有关创建公司的条款

in·corp·or·ated /ɪnˈkɔːpəreɪtɪd; *NAmE* -ˈkɔːrp-/ *adj.* (*abbr.* **Inc.**) (*business* 商) formed into a business company with legal status 组成有法人地位的营业公司的；组成公司的

in·cor·por·eal /ˌɪnkɔːˈpɔːriəl; *NAmE* -kɔːrˈp-/ *adj.* (*formal*) without a body or form 无形体的；无形的

in·cor·rect /ˌɪnkəˈrekt/ *adj.* **1** not accurate or true 不准确的；不正确的；不真实的：*incorrect information/spelling* 失实的信息；错误的拼写 ◇ *His version of what happened is incorrect.* 他对所发生的事情的说法不准确。**2** speaking or behaving in a way that does not follow the accepted standards or rules（说话或举止）不合规矩的，不当的，不端的 OPP **correct** ➲ SEE ALSO POLITICALLY CORRECT ▶ **in·cor·rect·ly** *adv.*：*an incorrectly addressed letter* 地址有误的信件 **in·cor·rect·ness** *noun* [U]

in·cor·ri·gible /ɪnˈkɒrɪdʒəbl; *NAmE* -ˈkɔːr-; -ˈkɑːr-/ *adj.* (*disapproving* or *humorous*) having bad habits which cannot be changed or improved 无法改正的；屡教不改的 SYN **incurable**: *Her husband is an incorrigible flirt.* 她的丈夫是个积习难改的调情老手。◇ *You're incorrigible!* 你简直不可救药！▶ **in·cor·ri·gibly** /ɪnˈkɒrɪdʒəbli; *NAmE* -ˈkɔːr-; -ˈkɑːr-/ *adv.*

I

in·cor·rupt·ible /ˌɪnkəˈrʌptəbl/ *adj.* **1** (of people 人) not able to be persuaded to do sth wrong or dishonest, even if sb offers them money 廉洁的；不接受贿赂的 **2** that cannot decay or be destroyed 不会腐蚀的；不可摧毁的 OPP **corruptible** ▸ **in·cor·rupt·ibil·ity** /ˌɪnkəˌrʌptəˈbɪləti/ *noun* [U]

in·crease *verb, noun*

■ ***verb*** /ɪnˈkriːs/ [I, T] to become or to make sth greater in amount, number, value, etc. （使）增长，增多；增加：~ **(from A) (to B)** *The population has increased from 1.2 million to 1.8 million.* 人口已从 120 万增加到了 180 万。◇ *increasing levels of carbon dioxide in the earth's atmosphere* 地球大气层中日益增多的二氧化碳含量 ◇ *The price of oil increased.* 石油价格上涨了。◇ ~ **in sth** *Oil increased in price.* 石油价格上涨了。◇ ~ **by sth** *The rate of inflation increased by 2%.* 通货膨胀率增长了 2%。◇ ~ **with sth** *Disability increases with age* (= the older sb is, the more likely they are to be disabled). 身体机能随着年龄退化。◇ ~ **sth (from A) (to B)** *We need to increase productivity.* 我们需要提高生产力。◇ ~ **sth (by sth)** *They've increased the price by 50%.* 他们已经把价格提高了 50%。OPP **decrease** ▸ **in·creased** *adj.* [only before noun]: *increased demand* 增加的需求

■ ***noun*** /ˈɪŋkriːs/ [C, U] ~ **(in sth)** a rise in the amount, number or value of sth 增长；增多；增加：*an increase in spending* 开支的增长 ◇ *an increase of 2p in the pound on income tax* 所得税每英镑增加 2 便士 ◇ *an increase of nearly 20%* 近 20% 的增长 ◇ *a **significant/substantial increase** in sales* 销售量的显著/可观增长 ◇ ***price/tax/wage increases*** 价格/税额/工资的上涨 ◇ *Homelessness is **on the increase*** (= increasing). 无家可归者越来越多。OPP **decrease** ➲ MORE LIKE THIS 21, page R27

▼ **LANGUAGE BANK 用语库**

increase

Describing an increase 描述增长

- *Student numbers in English language schools in this country **increased** from 66 000 in 2008 to just over 84 000 in 2009.* 这个国家英语语言学校的学生人数从 2008 年的 66 000 增长到 2009 年的 84 000 多一点。
- *The number of students **increased** by almost 30% compared with the previous year.* 学生人数与去年相比增长了近 30%。
- *Student numbers **shot up/increased dramatically** in 2009.* 学生人数在 2009 年急剧增长。
- *The proportion of Spanish students **rose sharply** from 5% in 2008 to 14% in 2009.* 西班牙学生所占比例从 2008 年的 5% 猛增到 2009 年的 14%。
- *There was a significant **rise** in student numbers in 2009.* 学生人数在 2009 年大幅上升。
- *The 2009 figure was 84 000, **an increase of** 28% on the previous year.* * 2009 年的数据是 84 000，比前一年增长了 28%。
- *The 2009 figure was 84 000, 28 per cent **up** on the previous year.* * 2009 年的数据是 84 000，比前一年上升了 28%。
- *As the chart shows, this can partly be explained by **a dramatic increase** in students from Spain.* 如图所示，这种情况的部分原因是西班牙学生人数的急剧上升。

➲ LANGUAGE BANK AT EXPECT, FALL, ILLUSTRATE, PROPORTION

in·creas·ing·ly /ɪnˈkriːsɪŋli/ *adv.* more and more all the time 越来越多地；不断增加地：*increasingly difficult/important/popular* 越来越困难/重要/普及 ◇ *It is becoming increasingly clear that this problem will not be easily solved.* 越来越明显的是，这个问题不会轻易解决。◇ *Increasingly, training is taking place in the office rather than outside it.* 越来越多的职场培训在工作场所举行，而不是出外培训。

in·cred·ible /ɪnˈkredəbl/ *adj.* **1** impossible or very difficult to believe 不能相信的；难以置信的 SYN **unbelievable**: *an incredible story* 不可思议的故事 ◇ *It seemed incredible that she had been there a week already.* 真让人难以置信，她已经在那里待了一个星期了。**2** (*informal*) extremely good or extremely large 极好的；极大的：*The hotel was incredible.* 这家旅馆棒极了。◇ *an incredible amount of work* 极大量的工作

in·cred·ibly /ɪnˈkredəbli/ *adv.* **1** extremely 极端地；极其 SYN **unbelievably**: *incredibly lucky/stupid/difficult/beautiful* 极其幸运/愚蠢/困难/美丽 **2** in a way that is very difficult to believe 令人难以置信：*Incredibly, she had no idea what was going on.* 令人难以置信的是，她当时对发生的事一无所知。

in·credu·lous /ɪnˈkredjələs; *NAmE* -dʒəl-/ *adj.* not willing or not able to believe sth; showing an inability to believe sth 不肯相信的；不能相信的；表示怀疑的：*'Here?' said Kate, incredulous.* "这儿？"凯特表示怀疑地说。◇ *an incredulous look* 怀疑的神色 ➲ COMPARE CREDULOUS ▸ **in·credu·lity** /ˌɪnkrəˈdjuːləti; *NAmE* -ˈduː-/ *noun* [U] SYN **disbelief**: *a look of surprise and incredulity* 惊疑的神色 **in·credu·lous·ly** *adv.*: *He laughed incredulously.* 他满腹狐疑地大笑起来。

in·cre·ment /ˈɪŋkrəmənt/ *noun* **1** a regular increase in the amount of money that sb is paid for their job 定期的加薪：*a salary of £25 K with annual increments* 薪酬 25 000 英镑，并逐年增加 **2** (*formal*) an increase in a number or an amount 增量；增加 ▸ **in·cre·men·tal** /ˌɪŋkrəˈmentl/ *adj.*: *incremental costs* 增长的费用 **in·cre·men·tal·ly** /-təli/ *adv.*

in·crim·in·ate /ɪnˈkrɪmɪneɪt/ *verb* ~ **sb** to make it seem as if sb has done sth wrong or illegal 使负罪；连累：*They were afraid of answering the questions and incriminating themselves.* 他们担心因回答这些问题而受到牵连。▸ **in·crim·in·at·ing** *adj.* [usually before noun]: *incriminating evidence* 显示有罪的证据 **in·crim·in·ation** /ɪnˌkrɪmɪˈneɪʃn/ *noun* [U]

ˈin-crowd *noun* [sing.] a small group of people within a larger group who seem to be the most popular or fashionable 最受欢迎（或最时髦）的小团体；时髦一族

in·crust·ation (*also* **en·crust·ation**) /ˌɪnkrʌˈsteɪʃn/ *noun* [U, C] the process of forming a hard outer covering or layer; the covering or layer that is formed 结壳；形成硬外层；硬壳；硬外层

in·cu·bate /ˈɪŋkjubeɪt/ *verb* **1** [T] ~ **sth** (of a bird 鸟) to sit on its eggs in order to keep them warm until they HATCH 孵（卵）；孵化 **2** [T] ~ **sth** (*biology* 生) to keep cells, bacteria, etc. at a suitable temperature so that they develop 培养（细胞、细菌等） **3** [T] **be incubating sth** (*medical* 医) to have an infectious disease developing inside you before SYMPTOMS (= signs of illness) appear 有（传染病在体内）潜伏 **4** [I] (*medical* 医) (of a disease 疾病) to develop slowly without showing any signs 潜伏

in·cu·ba·tion /ˌɪŋkjuˈbeɪʃn/ *noun* **1** [U] the HATCHING of eggs 孵（卵）；孵化 **2** [C] (*also* **incuˈbation period**) (*medical* 医 or *biology* 生) the time between sb being infected with a disease and the appearance of the first SYMPTOMS (= signs) （传染病的）潜伏期 **3** [U] (*biology* 生) the development and growth of bacteria, etc. （细菌等的）繁殖

in·cu·ba·tor /ˈɪŋkjubeɪtə(r)/ *noun* **1** a piece of equipment in a hospital which new babies are placed in when they are weak or born too early, in order to help them survive （体弱或早产婴儿）恒温箱 ➲ WORDFINDER NOTE AT BABY **2** a machine like a box where eggs are kept warm until the young birds are born 孵化器

in·cu·bus /ˈɪŋkjʊbəs/ *noun* (*pl.* **in·cu·buses** or **in·cubi** /-baɪ/) **1** (*literary*) a problem that makes you worry a lot 沉重的压力；巨大的精神负担 **2** a male evil spirit, supposed in the past to have sex with a sleeping woman 梦淫妖（旧时传说中与熟睡女子交合的妖魔） ➲ COMPARE SUCCUBUS

in·cul·cate /ˈɪnkʌlkeɪt; *NAmE* ɪnˈkʌl-/ *verb* (*formal*) to cause sb to learn and remember ideas, moral principles, etc., especially by repeating them often 反复灌输；谆谆教诲： **~ sth (in/into sb)** *to inculcate a sense of responsibility in sb* 谆谆教导某人要有责任感 ◇ **~ sb with sth** *to inculcate sb with a sense of responsibility* 谆谆教导某人要有责任感 ▶ **in·cul·ca·tion** /ˌɪnkʌlˈkeɪʃn/ *noun* [U]

in·cum·bency /ɪnˈkʌmbənsi/ *noun* (*pl.* **-ies**) (*formal*) an official position or the time during which sb holds it 现任职位；任期

in·cum·bent /ɪnˈkʌmbənt/ *noun, adj.*

■ ***noun*** a person who has an official position 在职者；现任者： *the* ***present incumbent*** *of the White House* 现任美国总统

■ ***adj.*** **1** [only before noun] having an official position 在职的；现任的： *the incumbent president* 现任总统 **2** [not before noun] **~ upon/on sb** (*formal*) necessary as part of sb's duties 有责任；必须履行： *It was incumbent on them to attend.* 他们必须出席。

incur /ɪnˈkɜː(r)/ *verb* (**-rr-**) (*formal*) **1 ~ sth** if you **incur** sth unpleasant, you are in a situation in which you have to deal with it 招致；遭受；引起： *She had incurred the wrath of her father by marrying without his consent.* 她未经父亲同意就结婚，使父亲震怒。 **2 ~ sth** if you **incur** costs, you have to pay them 引致，带来（成本、花费等）： *You risk incurring bank charges if you exceed your overdraft limit.* 如果超出了透支限额，就有被银行加收费用的风险。

in·cur·able /ɪnˈkjʊərəbl; *NAmE* -ˈkjʊr-/ *adj.* **1** that cannot be cured 不能治愈的： *an* ***incurable disease/illness*** 不治之症 **OPP** **curable** **2** that cannot be changed 不能改变的；无法矫正的 **SYN** **incorrigible**： *She's an incurable optimist.* 她是个不可救药的乐天派。 ▶ **in·cur·ably** /-əbli/ *adv.*： *incurably ill/romantic* 病入膏肓；浪漫至极

in·curi·ous /ɪnˈkjʊəriəs; *NAmE* -ˈkjʊr-/ *adj.* (*formal*) having no interest in knowing or discovering things 不感兴趣的；不好奇的；漫不经心的 ▶ **in·curi·ous·ly** *adv.*

in·cur·sion /ɪnˈkɜːʃn; *NAmE* ɪnˈkɜːrʒn/ *noun* **~ (into sth)** (*formal*) **1** a sudden attack on a place by foreign armies, etc. 突然入侵；突然侵犯；袭击 **2** the sudden appearance of sth in a particular area of activity that is either not expected or not wanted （意外的）搅扰，介入

Ind. *abbr.* (*BrE, politics* 政) INDEPENDENT *adj.* (7) （从政者）无党派的，独立的： *G Green (Ind.)* * G. 格林（独立候选人）

in·daba /ɪnˈdɑːbə/ *noun* (*SAfrE*) **1** a large meeting at which politicians, professional people, etc. have discussions about an important subject （重要问题）大会，研讨会： *a national indaba on land reform* 全国土地改革大会 **2** (*informal*) a difficulty or matter that concerns you 所关心的困难（或事情）；担心；忧虑： *I don't care what he does. That's his indaba!* 我不在乎他的所作所为。那是他自己的事！

in·debt·ed /ɪnˈdetɪd/ *adj.* **1 ~ (to sb) (for sth)** (*formal*) grateful to sb for helping you 感激的；蒙恩的： *I am* ***deeply indebted*** *to my family for all their help.* 我深深感激我的家人给我的所有帮助。 **2** (of countries, governments, etc. 国家、政府等) owing money to other countries or organizations 负债的： *a list of the fifteen most* ***heavily indebted*** *nations* 十五个负债最重的国家的名单 ▶ **in·debt·ed·ness** *noun* [U]

in·decency /ɪnˈdiːsnsi/ *noun* (*pl.* **-ies**) **1** [U] behaviour that is thought to be morally or sexually offensive 下流的行为；猥亵： *an act of* ***gross indecency*** (= a sexual act that is a criminal offence) 严重猥亵（罪） **2** [C, usually sing.] an indecent act, expression, etc. 下流的动作（或表情等）

in·decent /ɪnˈdiːsnt/ *adj.* **1** (of behaviour, talk, etc. 行为、讲话等) thought to be morally offensive, especially because it involves sex or being naked 下流的；有伤风化的；猥亵的： *indecent conduct/photos* 下流的行为；淫秽的照片 ➲ COMPARE DECENT **2** (of clothes 衣服) showing parts of the body that are usually covered 过分暴露的： *That skirt of hers is positively indecent.* 她的那条裙子太暴露了。 **3** not done in the appropriate or usual amount of time 不合时宜的；不适当的： *They left the funeral with almost* ***indecent haste*** (= too quickly). 他们离开葬礼时仓促得近乎失礼。 ▶ **in·decent·ly** *adv.*： *He was charged with indecently assaulting five women.* 他被控猥亵五名妇女。

inˌdecent asˈsault *noun* [C, U] (*law* 律) a sexual attack on sb but one that does not include RAPE 猥亵（罪）；猥亵侵犯他人身体

inˌdecent exˈposure *noun* [U] (*law* 律) the crime of showing your sexual organs to other people in a public place 有伤风化罪；有伤风化的露体

in·de·cipher·able /ˌɪndɪˈsaɪfrəbl/ *adj.* (of writing or speech 文字或言语) impossible to read or understand 难以辨认（或弄懂）的

in·deci·sion /ˌɪndɪˈsɪʒn/ (*also less frequent* **in·deci·sive·ness**) *noun* [U] the state of being unable to decide 无决断力；优柔寡断： *After a moment's indecision, he said yes.* 他犹豫片刻之后答应了。 ➲ COMPARE DECISION

in·deci·sive /ˌɪndɪˈsaɪsɪv/ *adj.* **1** (of a person 人) unable to make decisions 无决断力的；优柔寡断的： *a weak and indecisive man* 软弱而且不果断的人 **2** not providing a clear and definite answer or result 模糊不清的；不明确的；无决定性的： *an indecisive battle* 非决定性的一战 **OPP** **decisive** ▶ **in·deci·sive·ly** *adv.* **in·deci·sive·ness** *noun* [U] = INDECISION

in·dec·or·ous /ɪnˈdekərəs/ *adj.* (*formal*) (of behaviour 举止) embarrassing or not socially acceptable 令人难堪的；不得体的；不适当的

in·deed /ɪnˈdiːd/ *adv.* **1** used to emphasize a positive statement or answer （强调肯定的陈述或答复）： *'Was he very angry?' 'Indeed he was.'* "他很生气吗？" "的确很生气。" ◇ *'Do you agree?' 'Indeed I do/Yes, indeed.'* "你同意吗？" "当然同意了。" ◇ *'You said you'd help?' 'I did indeed—yes.'* "你说过你要帮忙？" "是的，我的确说过。" ◇ *It is indeed a remarkable achievement.* 这的确是非凡的成就。 **2** (*especially BrE*) used after *very* and an adjective or adverb to emphasize a statement, description, etc. （用于 very 和形容词或副词之后，强调叙述、描写等）真正地： *Thank you very much indeed!* 真的很感谢您！ ◇ *I was very sad indeed to hear of your father's death.* 听到令尊大人去世，我感到非常难过。 **3** (*formal, especially BrE*) used to add information to a statement 其实；实际上： *I don't mind at all. Indeed, I would be delighted to help.* 我根本不介意。其实，我倒很乐意帮上一把。 **4** (*informal, especially BrE*) used to show that you are surprised at sth or that you find sth ridiculous （表示惊讶或觉得某事物荒谬）： *A ghost indeed! I've never heard anything so silly.* 真是见鬼！我可从没听说过这样无聊的事。 **5** (*informal*) used when you are repeating a question that sb has just asked and showing that you do not know the answer （重复对方的问题，表示不知道答案）： *'Why did he do it?' 'Why indeed?'* "他为什么那样做？" "是呀，为什么呢？"
IDM ➲ SEE FRIEND

in·defat·ig·able /ˌɪndɪˈfætɪgəbl/ *adj.* (*formal, approving*) never giving up or getting tired of doing sth 不屈不挠的；不知疲倦的： *an indefatigable defender of human rights* 不屈不挠的人权捍卫者 ▶ **in·defat·ig·ably** /ˌɪndɪˈfætɪgəbli/ *adv.*

in·defens·ible /ˌɪndɪˈfensəbl/ *adj.* **1** that cannot be defended or excused because it is morally unacceptable （道德上）无可辩解的，不能原谅的： *indefensible behaviour* 不可原谅的行为 ◇ *The Prime Minister was accused of defending the indefensible.* 首相被指责庇护不可原谅的行为。 **2** (of a place or building 地方或建筑) impossible to defend from military attack 无法防守的

in·defin·able /ˌɪndɪˈfaɪnəbl/ *adj.* difficult or impossible to define or explain 难以定义的；无法解释的： *She has that indefinable something that makes an actress a star.* 她具备了那种使演员成为明星的说不出的特质。 ▶ **in·defin·ably** /-əbli/ *adv.*

I

in·def·in·ite AW /ɪnˈdefɪnət/ *adj.* **1** lasting for a period of time that has no fixed end 无限期的；期限不定的：*She will be away for the indefinite future.* 她将离开一段时间，期限不定。**2** not clearly defined 模糊不清的；不明确的 SYN **imprecise**: *an indefinite science* 界定不明的科学

in,definite 'article *noun* (*grammar* 语法) the word *a* or *an* in English, or a similar word in another language 不定冠词（如英语中的 a 或 an）➲ COMPARE DEFINITE ARTICLE

in·def·in·ite·ly AW /ɪnˈdefɪnətli/ *adv.* for a period of time with no fixed limit 无限期地：*The trial was postponed indefinitely.* 审讯无限期延迟。

in,definite 'pronoun *noun* (*grammar* 语法) a pronoun that does not refer to any person or thing in particular, for example 'anything' and 'everyone' 不定代词（如 anything 和 everyone）

I

in·del·ible /ɪnˈdeləbl/ *adj.* **1** impossible to forget or remove 无法忘记的；不可磨灭的 SYN **permanent**: *The experience made an indelible impression on me.* 那次经历使我难以忘怀。◇ *Her unhappy childhood left an indelible mark.* 她不幸的童年留下了不可磨灭的痕迹。**2** (of ink, pens, etc. 墨水、钢笔等) leaving a mark that cannot be removed（笔迹）无法消除的，擦不掉的 SYN **permanent**: *an indelible marker* 笔迹擦不掉的记号笔 ▶ **in·del·ibly** /-əbli/ *adv.*: *That day is stamped indelibly on my memory.* 那一天在我的脑海中留下了不可磨灭的回忆。

in·deli·cate /ɪnˈdelɪkət/ *adj.* (*formal*) likely to be thought rude or embarrassing 不文雅的；颇粗鲁的；令人尴尬的：*an indelicate question* 无礼的提问 ▶ **in·deli·cacy** /-kəsi/ *noun* [U]

in·dem·nify /ɪnˈdemnɪfaɪ/ *verb* (**in·dem·ni·fies, in·dem·ni·fy·ing, in·dem·ni·fied, in·dem·ni·fied**) (*law* 律) **1** ~ sb (against sth) to promise to pay sb an amount of money if they suffer any damage or loss 保证赔偿 **2** ~ sb (for sth) to pay sb an amount of money because of the damage or loss that they have suffered 赔偿；补偿 ▶ **in·dem·ni·fi·ca·tion** /ɪnˌdemnɪfɪˈkeɪʃn/ *noun* [U]

in·dem·nity /ɪnˈdemnəti/ *noun* (*pl.* **-ies**) (*formal* or *law* 律) **1** [U] ~ (against sth) protection against damage or loss, especially in the form of a promise to pay for any damage or loss that happens 保障；赔偿；补偿：*an indemnity clause/fund/policy* 赔偿条款 / 基金 / 保险单 ◇ *indemnity insurance* 赔偿保险 **2** [C] a sum of money that is given as payment for damage or loss 赔款；补偿金

in·dent *verb, noun*
■ *verb* /ɪnˈdent/ ~ sth to start a line of print or writing further away from the edge of the page than the other lines 将（印刷或书写的行）缩进，缩格，缩排：*The first line of each paragraph should be indented.* 每段的第一行应缩格。
■ *noun* /ˈɪndent/ **1** ~ (for sth) (*business* 商, *especially BrE*) an official order for goods or equipment 订单；订购 **2** = INDENTATION (2)

in·den·ta·tion /ˌɪndenˈteɪʃn/ *noun* **1** [C] a cut or mark on the edge or surface of sth 缺口；凹陷；凹痕：*The horse's hooves left deep indentations in the mud.* 马蹄在泥地里留下了深深的蹄印。**2** (*also* **in·dent**) [C] a space left at the beginning of a line of print or writing 行首缩进；行首空格 **3** [U] the action of indenting sth or the process of being indented 造成凹陷（或缺口）；将行首缩进

in·dented /ɪnˈdentɪd/ *adj.* (of an edge or a surface 边缘或表面) an **indented** edge is not even, because parts of it are missing or have been cut away 锯齿状的；参差不齐的：*an indented coastline* 犬牙交错的海岸线

in·den·ture /ɪnˈdentʃə(r)/ *noun* a type of contract in the past that forced a servant or APPRENTICE to work for their employer for a particular period of time（旧时的）师徒契约 ▶ **in·den·tured** *adj.*

in·de·pend·ence 🔑 /ˌɪndɪˈpendəns/ *noun* [U] **1** 🔑 ~ (from sb/sth) (of a country 国家) freedom from political control by other countries 独立：*a colonial crisis which brought about independence* 引发独立的一次殖民危机 **2** 🔑 the time when a country gains freedom from political control by another country 独立（之日）：*independence celebrations* 独立纪念庆典 ◇ *the first elections since independence* 独立之后的第一次选举 **3** 🔑 the freedom to organize your own life, make your own decisions, etc. without needing help from other people 自主；自立：*He values his independence.* 他珍惜他的独立自主。◇ *a woman's financial independence* 妇女在经济上的自立 OPP **dependence** ➲ WORDFINDER NOTE AT FREEDOM

Inde'pendence Day *noun* 4 July, celebrated in the US as the anniversary of the day in 1776 when the Americans declared themselves independent of Britain 美国独立纪念日（7 月 4 日，美国国庆日，纪念 1776 年美国宣布脱离英国）➲ SEE ALSO FOURTH OF JULY

in·de·pend·ent 🔑 /ˌɪndɪˈpendənt/ *adj., noun*
■ *adj.*
• COUNTRY 国家 **1** 🔑 ~ (from/of sth) (of countries 国家) having their own government 独立的；自主的；自治的 SYN **self-governing**: *Mozambique became independent in 1975.* 莫桑比克于 1975 年获得独立。
• SEPARATE 分开 **2** 🔑 done or given by sb who is not involved in a situation and so is able to judge it fairly 不相干的人所做的（或提供的）；公正的；无偏见的：*an **independent** inquiry/witness* 独立的调查；无偏见的证人 ◇ *She went to a lawyer for some **independent advice**.* 她去找了一位律师寻求独立意见。 **3** 🔑 ~ (of sb/sth) not connected with or influenced by sth; not connected with each other 不相关的；不受影响的；无关联的：*The police force should be independent of direct government control.* 警方应该不受政府的直接控制。◇ *Two independent research bodies reached the same conclusions.* 两个彼此不相关的研究机构得出了同样的结论。
• ORGANIZATION 机构 **4** 🔑 supported by private money rather than government money 私营的：***independent television/schools*** 私营电视台；私立学校 ◇ *the independent sector* 私营部门
• PERSON 人 **5** 🔑 ~ (of sb/sth) confident and free to do things without needing help from other people 自主的；有主见的：*Going away to college has made me much more independent.* 离家上大学使我变得独立自主得多。◇ *She's a very independent-minded young woman.* 她是个很有主见的年轻女子。◇ *Students should aim to become more independent of their teachers.* 学生应该努力逐渐减少对老师的依赖。 OPP **dependent** **6** 🔑 ~ (of sb/sth) having or earning enough money so that you do not have to rely on sb else for help 自立的；自食其力的：*It was important to me to be financially independent of my parents.* 在经济上不依赖父母，这对我很重要。◇ *a man **of independent means*** (= with an income that he does not earn by working) 无须工作便可衣食无忧的人 OPP **dependent**
• POLITICIAN 从政者 **7** not representing or belonging to a particular political party 无党派的；独立的：*an independent candidate* 独立候选人
▶ **in·de·pend·ent·ly** 🔑 *adv.*: ~ (of sb/sth) *The two departments work independently of each other.* 这两个部门独立运作。◇ *It was the first time that she had lived independently.* 那是她第一次独立生活。
■ *noun* (*abbr.* **Ind.**) a member of parliament, candidate, etc. who does not belong to a particular political party 无党派议员（或候选人等）

inde,pendent 'school *noun* = PRIVATE SCHOOL

inde,pendent 'variable *noun* (*mathematics* 数) a VARIABLE whose value does not depend on another variable 自变量

,in-'depth *adj.* [usually before noun] very thorough and detailed 彻底的；深入详尽的：*an **in-depth** discussion/study* 深入彻底的讨论 / 研究 ➲ SEE ALSO DEPTH

in·des·crib·able /ˌɪndɪˈskraɪbəbl/ *adj.* so extreme or unusual it is almost impossible to describe 难以形容的；无法言传的：*The pain was indescribable.* 疼痛得无法形容。

▸ **in·des·crib·ably** /-əbli/ *adv.* : *indescribably beautiful/boring* 无法形容地美丽 / 乏味

in·des·truct·ible /ˌɪndɪˈstrʌktəbl/ *adj.* that is very strong and cannot easily be destroyed 不可摧毁的；破坏不了的： *plastic containers that are virtually indestructible* 几乎不可毁坏的塑料容器 ◇ *an indestructible bond of friendship* 坚不可摧的友谊纽带

in·de·ter·min·ate /ˌɪndɪˈtɜːmɪnət; *NAmE* -ˈtɜːrm-/ *adj.* that cannot be identified easily or exactly 模糊的；不确定的；难以识别的： *She was a tall woman of indeterminate age.* 她是个看不出年龄的高个女子。 ▸ **in·de·ter·min·acy** /-nəsi/ *noun* [U]

index 🔑 AW /ˈɪndeks/ *noun, verb*
■ *noun* **1** 🔑 (*pl.* **in·dexes**) a list of names or topics that are referred to in a book, etc., usually arranged at the end of a book in alphabetical order or listed in a separate file or book 索引： *Look it up in the index.* 在索引中查找。◇ *Author and subject indexes are available on a library database.* 作者索引和学科索引可在图书馆的数据库中找到。 **2** (*BrE*) = CARD INDEX ➲ VISUAL VOCAB PAGE V71 **3** 🔑 (*pl.* **in·dexes** or **in·dices** /ˈɪndɪsiːz/) a system that shows the level of prices and wages, etc. so that they can be compared with those of a previous date （物价和工资等的）指数： *the cost-of-living index* 生活费用指数 ◇ *The Dow Jones index fell 15 points this morning.* 道琼斯指数今天上午下跌了 15 点。◇ *stock-market indices* 股市指数 ◇ *house price indexes* 房价指数 **4** (*pl.* **in·dices** /ˈɪndɪsiːz/) a sign or measure that sth else can be judged by 标志；指标；表征；量度： *The number of new houses being built is a good index of a country's prosperity.* 在建新房屋的数量是国家繁荣程度的一个可靠指标。 **5** (*usually* **in·dices** [pl.]) (*mathematics* 数) the small number written above a larger number to show how many times that number must be multiplied by itself. In the EQUATION $4^2 = 16$, the number 2 is an index. 指数（如在等式 $4^2 = 16$ 中，2 是指数）
■ *verb* **1** ~ **sth** to make an index of documents, the contents of a book, etc.; to add sth to a list of this type 为…编索引；将…编入索引： *All publications are indexed by subject and title.* 所有出版物都按学科和名称编索引。 **2** [usually passive] ~ **sth** (**to sth**) to link wages, etc. to the level of prices of food, clothing, etc. so that they both increase at the same rate 将（工资等）与（物价水平等）挂钩；使指数化

in·dex·ation /ˌɪndekˈseɪʃn/ *noun* [U] the linking of increases in wages, etc. to increases in prices （工资等相对于物价的）指数化

ˈindex card *noun* a small card that you can write information on and keep with other cards in a box or file 索引卡 ➲ SEE ALSO CARD INDEX ➲ VISUAL VOCAB PAGE V71

ˈindex finger (*also* ˌ**first ˈfinger**) *noun* the finger next to the thumb 食指 SYN **forefinger** ➲ VISUAL VOCAB PAGE V64 ➲ COMPARE POINTER FINGER

ˌ**index-ˈlinked** *adj.* (*BrE*) (of wages, etc. 工资等) rising in value according to increases in the cost of living 按生活指数调整的 ▸ ˌ**index-ˈlinking** *noun* [U]

In·dian /ˈɪndiən/ *noun* **1** a person from India 印度人 **2** (*old-fashioned, offensive*) = NATIVE AMERICAN **3** (*CanE*) a Native Canadian who is not Inuit or Metis （非因纽特人或米提人的）加拿大土著；加拿大印第安人 ▸ **In·dian** *adj.* IDM SEE CHIEF *n.*, FILE *n.*

ˌ**Indian ˈcorn** *noun* [U] (*especially NAmE*) a type of CORN (MAIZE) with large brown and yellow grains, not usually eaten but sometimes used to make decorations, for example at Thanksgiving 印第安玉米（通常不食用，用于感恩节等装饰）

ˌ**Indian ˈink** (*also* ˌ**India ˈink**) *noun* [U] a very black ink used in drawing and technical drawing 墨；墨汁

ˌ**Indian ˈsummer** *noun* **1** a period of dry warm weather in the autumn/fall 印第安夏（秋季干燥温暖） **2** a pleasant period of success or improvement, especially later in sb's life 兴旺时期，进步时期（尤指在一生中较晚的时期）

India rub·ber /ˌɪndiə ˈrʌbə(r)/ *noun* [U] (*old-fashioned*) natural rubber 天然橡胶

in·di·cate 🔑 AW /ˈɪndɪkeɪt/ *verb*
• **SHOW** 表明 **1** 🔑 [T, I] to show that sth is true or exists 表明；标示；显示： ~ **sth** *Record profits in the retail market indicate a boom in the economy.* 零售市场上有史以来的最高利润显示出经济的突飞猛进。 ◇ ~ (**that…**) *Research indicates that eating habits are changing fast.* 研究显示，饮食习惯正迅速改变。◇ *Kingston-upon-Thames, as the name indicates, is situated on the banks of the Thames.* 泰晤士河畔金斯顿区，正如其名称所示，位于泰晤士河畔。◇ ~ **how, what etc.…** *Our results indicate how misleading it could be to rely on this method.* 我们的结果表明，依赖这种方法可能产生多么严重的误导。
• **SUGGEST** 暗示 **2** 🔑 [T] to be a sign of sth; to show that sth is possible or likely 象征；暗示： ~ **sth** *A red sky at night often indicates fine weather the next day.* 夜空呈红色往往预兆第二天天气晴朗。◇ ~ **that…** *Early results indicate that the government will be returned to power.* 早期的结果预示这个政府将重新执政。
• **MENTION** 提及 **3** 🔑 [T] to mention sth, especially in an indirect way 暗示；间接提及；示意： ~ (**to sb**) (**that**)… *In his letter he indicated to us (that) he was willing to cooperate.* 他在信中向我们透露他愿意合作。◇ ~ **sth** (**to sb**) *He indicated his willingness to cooperate.* 他暗示愿意合作。◇ ~ **whether, when, etc.…** *Has she indicated yet whether she would like to be involved?* 她表明了她是否愿意参加吗？ ➲ SYNONYMS AT DECLARE
• **POINT TO** 指向 **4** 🔑 [T] (*formal*) to make sb notice sb/sth, especially by pointing or moving your head 指示；指出： ~ **sb/sth** (**to sb**) *She took out a map and indicated the quickest route to us.* 她拿出一张地图，给我们指出最快捷的路线。◇ ~ **where, which, etc.…** *He indicated where the furniture was to go.* 他指示了家具要如何摆放。◇ ~ **that…** *She indicated that I was to sit down.* 她示意我坐下。
• **GIVE INFORMATION** 提供信息 **5** [T] ~ **sth** (*formal*) to represent information without using words 显示（信息）；标示： *The results are indicated in Table 2.* 结果列在表 2 中。 **6** [T] (*formal*) to give information in writing 写明；注出： ~ **sth** *You are allowed 20kgs of baggage unless indicated otherwise on your ticket.* 除非票上另有注明，否则可携带行李为 20 公斤。◇ ~ **which, where, etc.…** *Please indicate clearly which colour you require.* 请标明您要求的颜色。
• **SHOW MEASUREMENT** 显示量度 **7** [T] ~ **sth** | ~ **how much, how many, etc.…** (of an instrument for measuring things 测量器具) to show a particular measurement 显示（量度）： *When the temperature gauge indicates 90°F or more, turn off the engine.* 当温度计显示 90 华氏度或以上时，关闭发动机。
• **IN VEHICLE** 车辆等 **8** [I, T] (*BrE*) to show that your vehicle is going to change direction, by using lights or your arm （用灯光或手臂）打行车转向信号 SYN **signal**： *Always indicate before moving into another lane.* 开入其他车道前一定要打转向灯。◇ ~ **sth** *He indicated left and then turned right.* 他打出的是左转信号，然后却向右转了。◇ ~ (**that**)… *She indicated that she was turning right.* 她打开了右转向灯。
• **BE RECOMMENDED** 建议 **9** [T, usually passive] ~ **sth** (*formal*) to be necessary or recommended 有必要；被建议： *A course of chemotherapy was indicated.* 建议进行化疗。

in·di·ca·tion 🔑 AW /ˌɪndɪˈkeɪʃn/ *noun* [C, U] a remark or sign that shows that sth is happening or what sb is thinking or feeling 表明；标示；显示；象征： ~ (**of sth**) *They gave no indication of how the work should be done.* 他们根本没说明这项工作该怎样做。◇ ~ (**of doing sth**) *He shows every indication (= clear signs) of wanting to accept the post.* 他显然想接受这个职位。◇ ~ (**that…**) *There are clear indications that the economy is improving.* 有明显的迹象显示经济开始好转。◇ *All the indications are that the deal will go ahead as planned.* 从所有的迹象看，交易将按计划进行。 ➲ SYNONYMS AT SIGN

in·di·ca·tive AW /ɪnˈdɪkətɪv/ *adj., noun*

■ *adj.* **1** [not usually before noun] ~ (**of sth**) (*formal*) showing or suggesting sth 表明；标示；显示；暗示：*Their failure to act is indicative of their lack of interest.* 他们未采取行动，这表示他们没有兴趣。 **2** [only before noun] (*grammar* 语法) stating a fact 陈述的；指示的

■ *noun* **the indicative** [sing.] (*grammar* 语法) the form of a verb that states a fact （动词形式）陈述语气：*In 'Ben likes school', the verb 'like' is in the indicative.* 在 Ben likes school 中，动词 like 是陈述语气。

in·di·ca·tor AW /ˈɪndɪkeɪtə(r)/ *noun* **1** a sign that shows you what sth is like or how a situation is changing 指示信号；标志；迹象：*The economic indicators are better than expected.* 经济指标比预期的好。 ➲ SYNONYMS AT SIGN **2** a device on a machine that shows speed, pressure, etc. 指示器；指针：*a depth indicator* 深度指示器 **3** (*BrE*) (*NAmE* **ˈturn signal**) (*also informal* **blink·er** *NAmE, BrE*) a light on a vehicle that flashes to show that the vehicle is going to turn left or right 转向灯；方向灯 ➲ VISUAL VOCAB PAGE V56

in·dices PL. OF INDEX

in·dict /ɪnˈdaɪt/ *verb* [usually passive] ~ **sb** (**for sth**) | ~ **sb** (**on charges/on a charge of sth**) (*especially NAmE, law* 律) to officially charge sb with a crime 控告；起诉：*The senator was indicted for murder.* 那位参议员被控犯谋杀罪。◇ *She was indicted on charges of corruption.* 她被控贪腐，受到起诉。 ➲ COLLOCATIONS AT JUSTICE

in·dict·able /ɪnˈdaɪtəbl/ *adj.* (*law* 律) **1** (of a crime 罪行) for which you can be indicted 可提起公诉的：*an indictable offense* 可诉罪 **2** (of a person 人) able to be indicted 可被控告的；可被起诉的

in·dict·ment /ɪnˈdaɪtmənt/ *noun* **1** [C, usually sing.] ~ (**of/on sb/sth**) a sign that a system, society, etc. is very bad or very wrong （制度、社会等的）衰败迹象，腐败迹象：*The poverty in our cities is a damning indictment of modern society.* 我们的城市中贫民的苦况是现代社会的一大败象。 **2** [C] (*especially NAmE*) a written statement accusing sb of a crime 刑事起诉书；公诉书 **3** [U] (*especially NAmE*) the act of officially accusing sb of a crime 控告；起诉：*This led to his indictment on allegations of conspiracy.* 这件事最终使他被控犯有共谋罪。

indie /ˈɪndi/ *adj., noun*

■ *adj.* (of a company, person or product 公司、人或产品) not belonging to, working for or produced by a large organization; independent 不属于大公司的；不是大公司生产的；独立的：*an indie publisher/newspaper* 独立出版人；独立发行的报纸 ◇ *indie music* 独立音乐 ◇ *an indie band/record label* 不知名的小乐队 / 唱片公司

■ *noun* a small independent company, or sth produced by such a company 独立小公司；独立小公司的产品

in·dif·fer·ence /ɪnˈdɪfrəns/ *noun* [U, sing.] ~ (**to sb/sth**) a lack of interest, feeling or reaction towards sb/sth 漠不关心；冷淡；不感兴趣；无动于衷：*his total indifference to what people thought of him* 他对别人怎么看他丝毫不在乎的态度 ◇ *What she said is **a matter of complete indifference** to me.* 她的话对于我来说完全无关紧要。 ◇ *Their father treated them with indifference.* 他们的父亲对他们漠不关心。 ◇ *an indifference to the needs of others* 对于他人的需要置若罔闻

in·dif·fer·ent /ɪnˈdɪfrənt/ *adj.* **1** [not usually before noun] ~ (**to sb/sth**) having or showing no interest in sb/sth 漠不关心；不感兴趣：*The government cannot afford to be indifferent to public opinion.* 政府不可不关注舆论。 **2** not very good 不很好的；一般的 SYN **mediocre**：*an indifferent meal* 一般的饭食 ◇ *The festival has the usual mixture of movies—**good, bad and indifferent**.* 电影节的影片一如既往的良莠不齐，有优秀的、低劣的和一般的。 ➲ MORE LIKE THIS 23, page R27 ▶ **in·dif·fer·ent·ly** *adv.*：*He shrugged indifferently.* 他满不在乎地耸了耸肩。

in·di·gen·ous /ɪnˈdɪdʒənəs/ *adj.* (*formal*) belonging to a particular place rather than coming to it from somewhere else 本地的；当地的；土生土长的 SYN **native**：*the indigenous peoples/languages of the area* 该地区的本地人 / 语言 ◇ ~ **to...** *The kangaroo is indigenous to Australia.* 袋鼠原产于澳大利亚。

in·di·gent /ˈɪndɪdʒənt/ *adj.* [usually before noun] (*formal*) very poor 十分贫穷的

in·di·gest·ible /ˌɪndɪˈdʒestəbl/ *adj.* **1** (of food 食物) that cannot easily be DIGESTED in the stomach 不易消化的：*an indigestible meal* 难消化的一餐 **2** (of facts, information, etc. 事实、信息等) difficult to understand, and presented in a complicated way 难解的；复杂难懂的 OPP **digestible**

in·di·ges·tion /ˌɪndɪˈdʒestʃən/ *noun* [U] pain caused by difficulty in DIGESTING food 消化不良（症） SYN **dyspepsia**

in·dig·nant /ɪnˈdɪɡnənt/ *adj.* feeling or showing anger and surprise because you think that you have been treated unfairly 愤慨的；愤怒的；义愤的：*an indignant letter/look* 愤慨的信 / 神情 ◇ ~ **at/about sth** *She was very indignant at the way she had been treated.* 她对于自己受到的待遇大为光火。◇ ~ **that...** *They were indignant that they hadn't been invited.* 他们因没有受到邀请而愤愤不平。 ➲ SYNONYMS AT ANGRY ▶ **in·dig·nant·ly** *adv.*：*'I'm certainly not asking him!' she retorted indignantly.* "我当然不是在问他！"她愤然反驳说。

in·dig·na·tion /ˌɪndɪɡˈneɪʃn/ *noun* [U] ~ (**at/about sth**) | ~ (**that...**) a feeling of anger and surprise caused by sth that you think is unfair or unreasonable 愤慨；愤怒；义愤：*The rise in train fares has aroused public indignation.* 火车票提价激起了公愤。 ◇ *Joe quivered **with indignation** that Paul should speak to him like that.* 乔认为保罗竟然那样对他说话，气得直发抖。 ◇ *Some benefits apply only to men, much **to the indignation of** working women.* 让职业女性大为愤慨的是有些福利只提供给男性。 ◇ *to be full **of righteous indignation*** (= the belief that you are right to be angry even though other people do not agree) 义愤填膺

in·dig·nity /ɪnˈdɪɡnəti/ *noun* [U, C] (*pl.* **-ies**) ~ (**of sth/of doing sth**) a situation that makes you feel embarrassed or ashamed because you are not treated with respect; an act that causes these feelings 侮辱；轻蔑；侮辱性的行为 SYN **humiliation**：*The chairman **suffered the indignity of** being refused admission to the meeting.* 主席蒙受了被拒于会议之外的侮辱。 ◇ *the daily indignities of imprisonment* 身陷囹圄每日所遭受的侮辱

in·digo /ˈɪndɪɡəʊ; *NAmE* -ɡoʊ/ *adj.* very dark blue in colour 靛蓝；靛青：*an indigo sky* 靛蓝色的天空 ▶ **in·digo** *noun* [U]

in·dir·ect 🔑 /ˌɪndəˈrekt; -daɪˈr-/ *adj.* [usually before noun] **1** 🔑 happening not as the main aim, cause or result of a particular action, but in addition to it 间接的；附带的：*the **indirect effects** of the war* 战争的间接后果 ◇ *to find something out by **indirect methods*** 间接地查明某事 ◇ *The building collapsed as an **indirect result** of the heavy rain.* 暴雨间接造成了那座楼房的倒塌。 ◇ *There would be some benefit, however indirect, to the state.* 国家会得到一些利益，不管有多少。 ◇ ***indirect costs*** (= costs that are not directly connected with making a product, for example training, heating, rent, etc.) 间接成本 **2** 🔑 avoiding saying sth in a clear and obvious way 闪烁其词的；拐弯抹角的：*an indirect attack* 影射攻击 **3** 🔑 not going in a straight line 迂回的；弯曲的：*an indirect route* 迂回的路线 OPP **direct** ▶ **in·dir·ect·ly** 🔑 *adv.*：*The new law will affect us all, directly or indirectly.* 新的法规将直接或间接地影响我们所有的人。 **in·dir·ect·ness** *noun* [U]

ˌindirect ˈobject *noun* (*grammar* 语法) a noun, noun phrase or pronoun in a sentence, used after some verbs, that refers to the person or thing that an action is done to or for 间接宾语：*In 'Give him the money', 'him' is the indirect object and 'money' is the direct object.* 在 give him the money 中，him 是间接宾语，money 是直接宾语。

ˌindirect ˈquestion (*also* **reˌported ˈquestion**) *noun* (*grammar* 语法) a question in REPORTED SPEECH, for example *She asked where I was going.* 间接疑问句 **HELP** Do not put a question mark after an indirect question. 间接疑问句不加问号。

ˌindirect ˈspeech *noun* [U] (*grammar* 语法) = REPORTED SPEECH ➲COMPARE DIRECT SPEECH

ˌindirect ˈtax *noun* [C, U] a tax that is paid as an amount added to the price of goods and services and not paid directly to the government 间接税 ➲ COMPARE DIRECT TAX ▸ **ˌindirect taˈxation** *noun* [U]

in·dis·cern·ible /ˌɪndɪˈsɜːnəbl; *NAmE* -ˈsɜːrn-/ *adj.* that cannot be seen, heard or understood 隐约的；依稀的；不明显的

in·dis·cip·line /ɪnˈdɪsɪplɪn/ *noun* [U] (*formal*) a lack of control in the behaviour of a group of people 无纪律；无秩序；缺乏管理

in·dis·creet **AW** /ˌɪndɪˈskriːt/ *adj.* not careful about what you say or do, especially when this embarrasses or offends sb 不慎重的；不审慎的；鲁莽的 **OPP** **discreet** ▸ **in·dis·creet·ly** *adv.*

in·dis·cre·tion **AW** /ˌɪndɪˈskreʃn/ *noun* **1** [C] an act or remark that is indiscreet, especially one that is not morally acceptable 不慎的言行；（尤指道德上）不检点的言行： *youthful indiscretions* 年轻人的不检点行为 **2** [U] the act of saying or doing sth without thinking about the effect it may have, especially when this embarrasses or offends sb 轻率；鲁莽： *He talked to the press in a moment of indiscretion.* 他一时冲动对新闻界发表了讲话。 ➲COMPARE DISCRETION

in·dis·crim·in·ate /ˌɪndɪˈskrɪmɪnət/ *adj.* **1** an **indiscriminate** action is done without thought about what the result may be, especially when it causes people to be harmed 随意的；恣意的；不加选择的： *indiscriminate attacks on motorists by youths throwing stones* 年轻人乱扔石头袭击驾车的人 ◇ *Doctors have been criticized for their indiscriminate use of antibiotics.* 医生被指责滥用抗生素。 **2** acting without careful judgement 不加分析的；不加判断的： *She's always been indiscriminate in her choice of friends.* 她一向择友不慎。 ▸ **in·dis·crim·in·ate·ly** *adv.* : *The soldiers fired indiscriminately into the crowd.* 士兵对着人群胡乱开枪。

in·dis·pens·able /ˌɪndɪˈspensəbl/ *adj.* too important to be without 不可或缺的；必不可少的 **SYN** **essential**: *Cars have become an indispensable part of our lives.* 汽车已成了我们生活中必不可少的一部分。 ◇ **~ to sb/sth** *She made herself indispensable to the department.* 她成为这个部门不可缺少的一分子。 ◇ **~ for sth/for doing sth** *A good dictionary is indispensable for learning a foreign language.* 一本好词典是学习外语必备的。 **OPP** **dispensable** ➲SYNONYMS AT ESSENTIAL ➲LANGUAGE BANK AT VITAL

in·dis·posed /ˌɪndɪˈspəʊzd; *NAmE* -ˈspoʊzd/ *adj.* (*formal*) **1** [not usually before noun] unable to do sth because you are ill/sick, or for a reason you do not want to give（因病或不愿透露的原因）不能做某事 **SYN** **unwell** **2** [not before noun] **~ to do sth** not willing to do sth 不愿（做某事）

in·dis·pos·ition /ˌɪndɪspəˈzɪʃn/ *noun* [C, U] (*formal*) a slight illness that makes you unable to do sth 小病；微恙

in·dis·put·able /ˌɪndɪˈspjuːtəbl/ *adj.* that is true and cannot be disagreed with or denied 不容置疑的；无可争辩的；不容否认的 **SYN** **undeniable**: *indisputable evidence* 不可否认的证据 ◇ *an indisputable fact* 不容置疑的事实 ◇ *It is indisputable that the crime rate has been rising.* 毫无疑问，犯罪率一直在上升。 ➲ COMPARE DISPUTABLE ▸ **in·dis·put·ably** *adv.* : *This painting is indisputably one of his finest works.* 这幅画无疑是他最好的作品之一。

in·dis·sol·uble /ˌɪndɪˈsɒljəbl; *NAmE* -ˈsɑːl-/ *adj.* (*formal*) (of a relationship 关系) that cannot be ended 牢不可破的；稳定持久的： *an indissoluble friendship* 稳固持久的友谊 ▸ **in·dis·sol·ubly** /ˌɪndɪˈsɒljəbli; *NAmE* -ˈsɑːl-/ *adv.* : *indissolubly linked* 关系牢固

in·dis·tinct **AW** /ˌɪndɪˈstɪŋkt/ *adj.* that cannot be seen, heard or remembered clearly 模糊不清的；不清楚的 **SYN** **vague, hazy** ▸ **in·dis·tinct·ly** **AW** *adv.*

in·dis·tin·guish·able /ˌɪndɪˈstɪŋgwɪʃəbl/ *adj.* **1 ~ (from sth)** if two things are **indistinguishable**, or one is **indistinguishable from** the other, it is impossible to see any differences between them 无法分辨的；无法区分的： *The male of the species is almost indistinguishable from the female.* 这个物种的雄性和雌性几乎分辨不出。 **2** not clear; not able to be clearly identified 不清楚的；无法识别的： *His words were indistinguishable.* 他说的话听不清楚。

in·dium /ˈɪndiəm/ *noun* [U] (*symb.* **In**) a chemical element. Indium is a soft silver-white metal. 铟

in·di·vid·ual 🔑 **AW** /ˌɪndɪˈvɪdʒuəl/ *adj., noun*

■***adj.*** **1** 🔑 [only before noun] (often used after *each* 常用于 each 之后) considered separately rather than as part of a group 单独的；个别的： *We interviewed **each individual** member of the community.* 我们采访了社区中的每个成员。 ◇ *The minister refused to comment on individual cases.* 那位部长拒绝对具体方案发表评论。 **2** 🔑 [only before noun] connected with one person; designed for one person 一个人的；供一人用的： *respect for individual freedom* 对个人自由的尊重 ◇ *an individual pizza* 供一人食用的比萨饼 **3** (*usually approving*) typical of one particular person or thing in a way that is different from others 独特的；与众不同的 **SYN** **distinctive**: *a highly individual style of dress* 十分有个性的衣着风格

■***noun*** **1** 🔑 a person considered separately rather than as part of a group 个人： *The competition is open to both teams and individuals.* 团队和个人均可参加比赛。 ◇ *Treatment depends on the individual involved.* 治疗方式因人而异。 ◇ *donations from private individuals* (= ordinary people rather than companies, etc.) 私人捐赠 **2** a person who is original and very different from others 与众不同的人；有个性的人： *She's grown into quite an individual.* 她已经长成了一个相当有个性的人。 **3** (*informal, usually disapproving*) a person of a particular type, especially a strange one 某种类型的人；（尤指）古怪的人： *an odd-looking individual* 模样怪异的人 ◇ *So this individual came up and demanded money.* 于是这个怪人就走上前来要钱。

in·di·vidu·al·ism **AW** /ˌɪndɪˈvɪdʒuəlɪzəm/ *noun* [U] **1** the quality of being different from other people and doing things in your own way 个性；独特的气质 **2** the belief that individual people in society should have the right to make their own decisions, etc., rather than be controlled by the government 个人主义；个人至上： *Capitalism stresses innovation, competition and individualism.* 资本主义强调的是创新、竞争和个人至上。 ▸ **in·di·vidu·al·ist** **AW** /-əlɪst/ *noun* : *She's a complete individualist in her art.* 她在艺术创作上完全是个自行其是的人。 **in·di·vidu·al·is·tic** **AW** /ˌɪndɪˌvɪdʒuəˈlɪstɪk/ (*also* **in·di·vidu·al·ist**) *adj.* : *an individualistic culture* 有特色的文化 ◇ *His music is highly individualistic and may not appeal to everyone.* 他的音乐很独特，可能不是人人都喜欢的。

in·di·vidu·al·ity **AW** /ˌɪndɪˌvɪdʒuˈæləti/ *noun* [U] the qualities that make sb/sth different from other people or things 个性；个人（或个体）特征： *She expresses her individuality through her clothes.* 她通过穿着表现个性。

in·di·vidu·al·ize (*BrE also* **-ise**) /ˌɪndɪˈvɪdʒuəlaɪz/ *verb* **~ sth** to make sth different to suit the needs of a particular person, place, etc. 使个性化；使因人（或因地等）而异： *to individualize children's learning* 对儿童因材施教 ▸ **in·di·vidu·al·iza·tion, -isa·tion** /ˌɪndɪvɪdʒuəlaɪˈzeɪʃn; *NAmE* -ləˈz-/ *noun* [U]

in·di·vidu·al·ized (*BrE also* **-ised**) /ˌɪndɪˈvɪdʒuəlaɪzd/ *adj.* designed for a particular person or thing; connected with a particular person or thing 个性化的；与个人（或个体）有关的： *individualized teaching* 因材施教 ◇ *a highly individualized approach to management* 很有针对性的管理方法

in·di·vidu·al·ly AW /ˌɪndɪˈvɪdʒuəli/ *adv.* separately, rather than as a group 分别地；单独地；各别地：*individually wrapped chocolates* 独立包装的巧克力 ◇ *The manager spoke to them all individually.* 经理和他们逐一谈话。◇ *The hotel has 100 individually designed bedrooms.* 这家旅馆有 100 个设计各不相同的房间。

in·di·vidu·ate /ˌɪndɪˈvɪdʒueɪt/ *verb* ~ **sb/sth** (*formal*) to make sb/sth clearly different from other people or things of the same type 使个性化；使有明显特色

in·di·vis·ible /ˌɪndɪˈvɪzəbl/ *adj.* that cannot be divided into separate parts 分不开的；不可分割的 OPP **divisible** ▸ **in·di·vis·ibil·ity** /ˌɪndɪˌvɪzəˈbɪləti/ *noun* [U] **in·di·vis·ibly** /ˌɪndɪˈvɪzəbli/ *adv.*

Indo- /ˈɪndəʊ; *NAmE* ˈɪndoʊ/ *combining form* (in nouns and adjectives 构成名词和形容词) Indian 印度的；印度人：*the Indo-Pakistan border* 印巴边境

ˌIndo-Caˈnadian *noun* [C] (*CanE*) a Canadian who was born in S Asia, especially India, or whose family originally came from S Asia 生于南亚（或南亚裔）的加拿大人；（尤指）生于印度（或印度裔）的加拿大人

in·doc·trin·ate /ɪnˈdɒktrɪneɪt; *NAmE* ɪnˈdɑːk-/ *verb* ~ **sb** (**with sth**) | ~ **sb** (**to do sth**) (*disapproving*) to force sb to accept a particular belief or set of beliefs and not allow them to consider any others 强行灌输（信仰或学说）：*They had been indoctrinated from an early age with their parents' beliefs.* 他们从小就被满脑子灌入了他们父母的信仰。▸ **in·doc·trin·ation** /ɪnˌdɒktrɪˈneɪʃn; *NAmE* -ˌdɑːk-/ *noun* [U]: ***political/religious indoctrination*** 政治思想 / 宗教教义的灌输

ˌIndo-ˌEuroˈpean *adj.* of or connected with the family of languages spoken in most of Europe and parts of western Asia (including English, French, Latin, Greek, Swedish, Russian and Hindi) 印欧语系的（指欧洲大部分地区和西亚的部分地区的语言谱系，包括英语、法语、拉丁语、希腊语、瑞典语、俄语和印地语）

in·do·lent /ˈɪndələnt/ *adj.* (*formal*) not wanting to work 懒惰的；懒散的；好逸恶劳的 SYN **lazy** ▸ **in·do·lence** /-əns/ *noun* [U]

in·dom·it·able /ɪnˈdɒmɪtəbl; *NAmE* ɪnˈdɑːm-/ *adj.* (*formal, approving*) not willing to accept defeat, even in a difficult situation; very brave and determined 不屈不挠的；勇敢坚定的

in·door /ˈɪndɔː(r)/ *adj.* [only before noun] located, done or used inside a building （在）室内的；在户内进行的；在室内用的：*an indoor swimming pool* 室内游泳池 ◇ *indoor games* 室内游戏 ◇ *the world indoor 200 metres champion* 室内 200 米赛世界冠军 OPP **outdoor**

in·doors /ˌɪnˈdɔːz; *NAmE* ˌɪnˈdɔːrz/ *adv.* inside or into a building 在室内；进入户内：*to go/stay indoors* 进入 / 留在屋里 ◇ *Many herbs can be grown indoors.* 很多香草植物能在室内种植。OPP **outdoors**

in·drawn /ˌɪnˈdrɔːn/ *adj.* (*literary*) **indrawn breath** is air that sb breathes in suddenly and quickly, expressing surprise or shock （惊慌时）吸入的，倒吸的（一口气）

in·dub·it·ably /ɪnˈdjuːbɪtəbli; *NAmE* -ˈduː-/ *adv.* (*formal*) in a way that cannot be doubted; without question 不容置疑地；毫无疑问地 SYN **undoubtedly**: *He was, indubitably, the most suitable candidate.* 他无疑是最合适的人选。▸ **in·dub·it·able** *adj.*：*indubitable proof* 确证

in·duce AW /ɪnˈdjuːs; *NAmE* -ˈduːs/ *verb* **1** ~ **sb to do sth** (*formal*) to persuade or influence sb to do sth 劝说；诱使：*Nothing would induce me to take the job.* 没有什么能诱使我接受这份工作。**2** ~ **sth** (*formal*) to cause sth 引起；导致：*drugs which induce sleep* 使人昏昏欲睡的药物 ◇ *a drug-induced coma* 药物引起的昏迷状态 **3** ~ **sb/sth** (*medical* 医) to make a woman start giving birth to her baby by giving her special drugs 催产；催生：*an induced labour* 催生 ◇ *We'll have to induce her.* 我们得给她催产。➲ WORDFINDER NOTE AT BIRTH

in·duce·ment /ɪnˈdjuːsmənt; *NAmE* -ˈduːs-/ *noun* [C, U] ~ (**to/for sb**) (**to do sth**) something that is given to sb to persuade them to do sth 引诱；刺激；诱因 SYN **incentive**: *financial inducements to mothers to stay at home* 促使母亲守在家里的经济诱因 ◇ *There is little inducement for them to work harder.* 没有什么动力能促使他们加把劲工作。◇ *Government officials have been accused of accepting inducements* (= BRIBES) *from local businessmen.* 政府官员被指控接受了当地商人的贿赂。

in·duct /ɪnˈdʌkt/ *verb* [often passive] ~ **sb** (**into sth**) (**as sth**) (*formal*) **1** to formally give sb a job or position of authority, especially as part of a ceremony （尤指在典礼上）使正式就职 **2** to officially introduce sb into a group or an organization, especially the army 正式吸收（为成员）；（尤指）征召入伍 **3** to introduce sb to a particular area of knowledge 使了解；传授：*They were inducted into the skills of magic.* 他们获得传授魔术。

in·duct·ee /ˌɪndʌkˈtiː/ *noun* (*especially NAmE*) a person who is being, or who has just been, introduced into a special group of people, especially sb who has just joined the army 新成员；（尤指）新入伍者

in·duc·tion AW /ɪnˈdʌkʃn/ *noun* **1** [U, C] ~ (**into sth**) the process of introducing sb to a new job, skill, organization, etc.; a ceremony at which this takes place 就职；入门；接纳会员；就职仪式 **2** [U, C] the act of making a pregnant woman start to give birth, using artificial means such as a special drug 催产；催生 **3** [U] (*specialist*) a method of discovering general rules and principles from particular facts and examples 归纳法 ➲ COMPARE DEDUCTION (1) **4** [U] (*physics* 物) the process by which electricity or MAGNETISM passes from one object to another without them touching 电磁感应

inˈduction course *noun* (*BrE*) a training course for new employees, students, etc. that is designed to give them a general introduction to the business, school, etc. 培训课程；入门课程

inˈduction loop *noun* a system in theatres, etc., which helps people who cannot hear well. A ring of wire around the room produces a signal that can be received directly by HEARING AIDS. （剧院等的）感应环路助听系统

in·duct·ive /ɪnˈdʌktɪv/ *adj.* **1** (*specialist*) using particular facts and examples to form general rules and principles 归纳法的；归纳的：*an inductive argument* 归纳论证 ◇ *inductive reasoning* 归纳推理 ➲ COMPARE DEDUCTIVE **2** (*physics* 物) connected with the INDUCTION of electricity 电感应的 ▸ **in·duct·ive·ly** *adv.*：*a theory derived inductively from the data* 从数据中归纳出的理论

in·dulge /ɪnˈdʌldʒ/ *verb* **1** [I, T] to allow yourself to have or do sth that you like, especially sth that is considered bad for you 沉湎，沉迷，沉溺（于…）：~ **in sth** *They went into town to indulge in some serious shopping.* 他们进城去大肆购物。◇ ~ **yourself** (**with sth**) *I indulged myself with a long hot bath.* 我尽情享受了一次长时间的热水浴。**2** [T] ~ **sth** to satisfy a particular desire, interest, etc. 满足（欲望、兴趣等）：*The inheritance enabled him to indulge his passion for art.* 这笔遗产使他能够尽情投入他热爱的艺术。**3** [T] to be too generous in allowing sb to have or do whatever they like 放纵；听任：~ **sb** (**with sth**) *She did not believe in indulging the children with presents.* 她认为不能惯着孩子们要什么就给什么。◇ ~ **sth** *Her father had always **indulged her every whim**.* 她的父亲总是对她有求必应。**4** [I] ~ **in sth** to take part in an activity, especially one that is illegal 参加，参与（尤指违法活动）

in·dul·gence /ɪnˈdʌldʒəns/ *noun* **1** [U] (*usually disapproving*) the state or act of having or doing whatever you want; the state of allowing sb to have or do whatever they want 沉溺；放纵；纵容：*to lead a life of indulgence* 过着放纵的生活 ◇ *Avoid excessive indulgence in sweets and canned drinks.* 避免食用过多的甜食和罐装饮料。◇ *There is no limit to the indulgence he shows to his grandchildren.* 他无度地溺爱娇惯孙子孙女。**2** [C] something that you allow yourself to have even though it is not essential 嗜好；爱好；享受： *The holiday was an extravagant indulgence.* 那个假期是一次奢华的享受。➲ SEE ALSO SELF-INDULGENCE at SELF-INDULGENT **3** [U] (*formal*) willingness to ignore the weaknesses in sb/sth 宽容；包涵 SYN **patience**: *They begged the audience's indulgence.* 他们恳求观众包涵。

in·dul·gent /ɪnˈdʌldʒənt/ *adj.* **1** (*usually disapproving*) tending to allow sb to have or do whatever they want 纵容的；放纵的： *indulgent parents* 纵容子女的父母 ◇ *an indulgent smile* 迁就的微笑 ➲ SEE ALSO SELF-INDULGENT **2** willing or too willing to ignore the weaknesses in sb/sth 宽容的；过于宽厚的 SYN **patient**: *to take an indulgent view of sth* 宽宏大量地看待某事 ▸ **in·dul·gent·ly** *adv.*: *to laugh indulgently* 宽容地笑

in·duna /ɪnˈduːnə/ *noun* (*SAfrE*) a senior leader of a TRIBE 族长；酋长

in·dus·trial /ɪnˈdʌstriəl/ *adj.* [usually before noun] **1** connected with industry 工业的；产业的： *industrial unrest* 产业工人骚乱 ◇ *industrial output* 工业产量 ◇ *an industrial accident* 工伤事故 ◇ *They had made **industrial quantities** of food* (= a lot). 他们生产了大量的食品。 **2** used by industries 用于工业的： *industrial chemicals* 工业用化学品 **3** having many industries 有很多产业的；工业发达的： *an industrial town* 工业城市 ◇ *an industrial society* 工业发达的社会 ◇ *the world's leading **industrial nations*** 全球主要工业国 ▸ **in·dus·tri·al·ly** /-əli/ *adv.*: *industrially advanced countries* 工业发达的国家

in,dustrial 'action *noun* [U] (*especially BrE*) action that workers take, especially stopping work, to protest to their employers about sth 劳工行动；（尤指）罢工，怠工 ➲ WORDFINDER NOTE AT UNION

in,dustrial archae'ology *noun* [U] the study of machines, factories, bridges, etc. used in the past in industry 工业考古学

in,dustrial 'arts (*also* **shop, 'shop class**) *noun* [U] (*NAmE*) a school subject in which students learn to make things from wood and metal using tools and machines 工艺课

in,dustrial e'state (*BrE*) (*NAmE* **in,dustrial 'park**) *noun* an area especially for factories, on the edge of a town （位于市郊的）工业区 ➲ COMPARE TRADING ESTATE

in·dus·tri·al·ism /ɪnˈdʌstriəlɪzəm/ *noun* [U] (*specialist*) an economic and social system based on industry 工业主义；产业主义

in·dus·tri·al·ist /ɪnˈdʌstriəlɪst/ *noun* a person who owns or runs a large factory or industrial company 工业家；实业家；工厂主

in·dus·tri·al·ize (*BrE also* **-ise**) /ɪnˈdʌstriəlaɪz/ *verb* [T, I] **~ (sth)** if a country or an area **is industrialized** or if it **industrializes**, industries are developed there （使国家或地区）工业化： *The southern part of the country was slow to industrialize.* 这个国家的南部工业化进程缓慢。 ▸ **in·dus·tri·al·iza·tion, -isa·tion** /ɪn,dʌstriəlaɪˈzeɪʃn; *NAmE* -ləˈz-/ *noun* [U]: *the rapid industrialization of Japan* 日本的迅速工业化 **in·dus·tri·al·ized, -ised** *adj.*: *an industrialized country* 工业化国家

in,dustrial 'park (*NAmE*) (*BrE* **in,dustrial e'state**) *noun* an area especially for factories, on the edge of a town （位于市郊的）工业园区

in,dustrial re'lations *noun* [pl.] relations between employers and employees 劳资关系

the In,dustrial Revo'lution *noun* [sing.] the period in the 18th and 19th centuries in Europe and the US when machines began to be used to do work, and industry grew rapidly 工业革命，产业革命（指 18 及 19 世纪欧美使用机器、工业迅速发展的阶段）

in'dustrial-strength *adj.* (*often humorous*) very strong or powerful 强劲的；强效的；强大的： *industrial-strength coffee* 特别提神的咖啡

in,dustrial tri'bunal *noun* (*BrE*) = EMPLOYMENT TRIBUNAL

in·dus·tri·ous /ɪnˈdʌstriəs/ *adj.* (*approving*) working hard; busy 勤奋的；勤劳的；忙碌的 SYN **hard-working**: *an industrious student* 勤勉的学生 ▸ **in·dus·tri·ous·ly** *adv.*

in·dus·try /ˈɪndəstri/ *noun* (*pl.* **-ies**) **1** [U] the production of goods from raw materials, especially in factories 工业；生产制造： ***heavy/light industry*** 重工业；轻工业 ◇ *the needs of British industry* 英国工业的需求 ◇ *She got a job **in industry**.* 她找了份工厂里的工作。➲ COLLOCATIONS AT ECONOMY

> **WORDFINDER** 联想词： capacity, just-in-time, labour, lead time, output, raw material, shipping, supply chain, warehouse

2 [C] the people and activities involved in producing a particular thing, or in providing a particular service 行业： *the steel industry* 钢铁业 ◇ *the **catering/tourist, etc. industry*** 餐饮、旅游等行业 ◇ *We need to develop local industries.* 我们需要发展地方工业。 ◇ (*figurative*) *the Madonna industry* (= the large number of people involved in making Madonna successful) 麦当娜策划集团 ➲ SEE ALSO CAPTAIN OF INDUSTRY, COTTAGE INDUSTRY, HEAVY INDUSTRY, SUNRISE INDUSTRY, SUNSET INDUSTRY **3** [U] (*formal*) the quality of working hard 勤奋；勤劳： *We were impressed by their industry.* 他们的勤奋给我们留下深刻印象。

Indy /ˈɪndi/ (*also* **'Indy racing, Indy·Car, 'Indy·car racing**) *noun* [U] motor racing around a track which is raised at both sides 印第安那波利斯式赛车，印第车赛（跑道中间低而两侧高）

Indy·Car /ˈɪndikɑː(r)/ *noun* **1** [U] = INDY **2** [C] a car used in Indy racing 印第车赛赛车

in·ebri·ated /ɪˈniːbrieɪtɪd/ *adj.* (*formal* or *humorous*) drunk 喝醉的 ▸ **in·ebri·ation** /ɪ,niːbriˈeɪʃn/ *noun* [U]

in·ed·ible /ɪnˈedəbl/ *adj.* that you cannot eat because it is of poor quality, or poisonous 不能吃的；不宜食用的 OPP **edible**

in·effable /ɪnˈefəbl/ *adj.* (*formal*) too great or beautiful to describe in words （美好得）难以形容的，不可言喻的： *ineffable joy* 难以形容的喜悦

in·ef·fect·ive /,ɪnɪˈfektɪv/ *adj.* not achieving what you want to achieve; not having any effect 无效果的；不起作用的；不奏效的： *The new drug was ineffective.* 新药不起作用。 ◇ *ineffective management* 管理不善 ◇ **~ in doing sth** *The law proved ineffective in dealing with the problem.* 事实证明这条法规未能真正解决问题。 OPP **effective** ▸ **in·ef·fect·ive·ness** *noun* [U] **in·ef·fect·ive·ly** *adv.*

in·ef·fec·tual /,ɪnɪˈfektʃuəl/ *adj.* (*formal*) without the ability to achieve much; weak; not achieving what you want to 无能的；软弱的；达不到目的的： *an ineffectual teacher* 不称职的教师 ◇ *an ineffectual attempt to reform the law* 改革法律的徒劳无益的尝试 ▸ **in·ef·fec·tu·al·ly** /-tʃuəli/ *adv.*

in·ef·fi·cient /,ɪnɪˈfɪʃnt/ *adj.* not doing a job well and not making the best use of time, money, energy, etc. 效率低的；能力差的；浪费的： *an inefficient heating system* 效率不佳的暖气系统 ◇ *inefficient government* 无能的政府 ◇ *an extremely inefficient secretary* 极不称职的秘书 ◇ *inefficient use of time and energy* 时间和精力的浪费 OPP **efficient** ▸ **in·ef·fi·ciency** /-ənsi/ *noun* [U, C] (*pl.* **-ies**): *waste and inefficiency in government* 政府中的浪费与低效能 ◇ *inefficiencies in the system* 这个系统中的低效率现象 **in·ef·fi·cient·ly** *adv.*

in·ele·gant /ɪnˈelɪɡənt/ *adj.* not attractive or elegant 不优美的；不优雅的 OPP **elegant** ▸ **in·ele·gant·ly** *adv.*

in·eli·gible /ɪnˈelɪdʒəbl/ *adj.* not having the necessary qualifications to have or to do sth 不合格的；不符合资格的： **~ (for sth)** *ineligible for financial assistance* 无资格得到财政援助 ◇ **~ (to do sth)** *ineligible to vote* 无投票资格 OPP **eligible** ▸ **in·eli·gi·bil·ity** /ɪn,elɪdʒəˈbɪləti/ *noun* [U]

in·eluct·able /ˌɪnɪˈlʌktəbl/ *adj.* (*formal*) that you cannot avoid 无可避免的 SYN **unavoidable** ▶ **in·eluct·ably** /-əbli/ *adv.*

inept /ɪˈnept/ *adj.* acting or done with no skill 缺乏技巧的；无能的；笨拙的：*She was left feeling inept and inadequate.* 她被弄得感到笨拙无能。◇ *an inept remark* 笨拙的发言 ▶ **in·ept·ly** *adv.*

in·epti·tude /ɪˈneptɪtjuːd; *NAmE* -tuːd/ *noun* [U] lack of skill 缺乏技巧；无能；笨拙：*the ineptitude of the police in handling the situation* 警方在处理这个局面时的无能

in·equal·ity /ˌɪnɪˈkwɒləti; *NAmE* -ˈkwɑːl-/ *noun* [U, C] (*pl.* **-ies**) the unfair difference between groups of people in society, when some have more wealth, status or opportunities than others 不平等；不平衡；不平均：*inequality of opportunity* 机会的不均 ◇ *economic inequalities between different areas* 不同地区间的经济不平衡 ◇ *racial inequality* 种族不平等 OPP **equality** ⮊ COLLOCATIONS AT RACE ⮊ SEE ALSO UNEQUAL

in·equit·able /ɪnˈekwɪtəbl/ *adj.* (*formal*) not fair; not the same for everyone 不公正的；不公平的 SYN **unfair**：*inequitable distribution of wealth* 财富的不公平分配 OPP **equitable**

in·equity /ɪnˈekwəti/ *noun* [C, U] (*pl.* **-ies**) (*formal*) something that is unfair; the state of being unfair 不公正的事；不公正；不公平 SYN **injustice**

in·erad·ic·able /ˌɪnɪˈrædɪkəbl/ *adj.* (*formal*) (of a quality or situation 品质或状况) that cannot be removed or changed 不可除去的；无法改变的

inert /ɪˈnɜːt; *NAmE* ɪˈnɜːrt/ *adj.* **1** (*formal*) without power to move or act 无活动能力的；无行动力的：*He lay inert with half-closed eyes.* 他半睁着双眼一动不动地躺着。**2** (*chemistry* 化) without active chemical or other properties (= characteristics) 惰性的；不活泼的

iˌnert ˈgas *noun* (*chemistry* 化) = NOBLE GAS

in·er·tia /ɪˈnɜːʃə; *NAmE* ɪˈnɜːrʃə/ *noun* [U] **1** (*usually disapproving*) lack of energy; lack of desire or ability to move or change 缺乏活力；惰性；保守：*I can't seem to throw off this feeling of inertia.* 我好像无法摆脱这种无力的感觉。◇ *the forces of institutional inertia in the school system* 学校体制内的惰性 **2** (*physics* 物) a property (= characteristic) of MATTER (= a substance) by which it stays still or, if moving, continues moving in a straight line unless it is acted on by a force outside itself 惯性

in·er·tial /ɪˈnɜːʃl; *NAmE* ɪˈnɜːrʃl/ *adj.* (*specialist*) connected with or caused by inertia 惯性的

iˈnertia reel *noun* a round device that one end of a car SEAT BELT is wound around so that it will move freely unless it is pulled suddenly, for example in an accident （汽车安全带的）惯性卷筒

in·escap·able /ˌɪnɪˈskeɪpəbl/ *adj.* (of a fact or a situation 现实或状况) that you cannot avoid or ignore 不可避免的；逃避不了的；不能忽视的 SYN **unavoidable**：*an inescapable fact* 不可逃避的现实 ◇ *This leads to the inescapable conclusion that the two things are connected.* 这就必然得出一个结论：这两件事互有关联。▶ **in·escap·ably** /-əbli/ *adv.*

in·es·sen·tial /ˌɪnɪˈsenʃl/ *adj.* not necessary 非必需的；无关紧要的：*inessential luxuries* 不必要的奢侈 ▶ **in·es·sen·tial** *noun*：*Few people had spare cash for inessentials.* 很少人有闲钱买那些可有可无的东西。⮊ COMPARE ESSENTIAL *adj.*, NON-ESSENTIAL

in·estim·able /ɪnˈestɪməbl/ *adj.* (*formal*) too great to calculate （大得）难以估量的，无法估计的：*The information he provided was* ***of inestimable value.*** 他提供的信息价值难以估量。

in·ev·it·able 🔑 AW /ɪnˈevɪtəbl/ *adj.* **1** 🔑 that you cannot avoid or prevent 不可避免的；不能防止的 SYN **unavoidable**：*It was an inevitable consequence of the decision.* 那是这个决定的必然后果。◇ ***It was inevitable*** *that there would be job losses.* 裁员已是不可避免的事。◇ *A rise in the interest rates seems inevitable.* 提高利率似乎是不可避免的。**2** [only before noun] (*often humorous*) so frequent that you always expect it 总会发生的；照例必有的；惯常的：*the English and their inevitable cups of tea* 英国人和他们例行的饮茶 **3** **the inevitable** *noun* [sing.] something that is certain to happen 必然发生的事；不可避免的事：*You have to accept the inevitable.* 你得接受必然发生的事。◇ *The inevitable happened—I forgot my passport.* 逃不掉的事情发生了，我忘了带护照。▶ **in·ev·it·abil·ity** AW /ɪnˌevɪtəˈbɪləti/ *noun* [U, sing.]：*the inevitability of death* 死亡的必然性 ◇ *There was an inevitability about their defeat.* 他们的失败自有其必然。

in·ev·it·ably 🔑 AW /ɪnˈevɪtəbli/ *adv.* **1** 🔑 as is certain to happen 不可避免地；必然地：*Inevitably, the press exaggerated the story.* 新闻界照例又夸大了这件事。**2** (*often humorous*) as you would expect 意料之中：*Inevitably, it rained on the day of the wedding.* 果然不出所料，婚礼的那天下起了雨。

in·exact /ˌɪnɪɡˈzækt/ *adj.* not accurate or exact 不准确的；不精确的：*an inexact description* 不准确的描述 ◇ *Economics is an inexact science.* 经济学是一门不精确的科学。

in·exac·ti·tude /ˌɪnɪɡˈzæktɪtjuːd; *NAmE* -tuːd/ *noun* [U] (*formal*) the quality of being not accurate or exact 不精确；不准确

in·ex·cus·able /ˌɪnɪkˈskjuːzəbl/ *adj.* too bad to accept or forgive 不可宽恕的；无法原谅的 SYN **unjustifiable**：*inexcusable rudeness* 不可原谅的粗鲁无礼 OPP **excusable** ▶ **in·ex·cus·ably** /-əbli/ *adv.*

in·ex·haust·ible /ˌɪnɪɡˈzɔːstəbl/ *adj.* that cannot be EXHAUSTED (= finished); very great 用之不竭的；无穷无尽的：*an inexhaustible supply of good jokes* 讲不完的精彩笑话 ◇ *Her energy is inexhaustible.* 她有无穷的精力。

in·ex·or·able /ɪnˈeksərəbl/ *adj.* (*formal*) (of a process 过程) that cannot be stopped or changed 不可阻挡的；无法改变的 SYN **relentless**：*the inexorable rise of crime* 阻遏不了的犯罪上升趋势 ▶ **in·ex·or·abil·ity** /ɪnˌeksərəˈbɪləti/ *noun* [U]：*the inexorability of progress* 阻挡不了的进展趋势 **in·ex·or·ably** /ɪnˈeksərəbli/ *adv.*：*events leading inexorably towards a crisis* 不可避免地导致危机的一些事件

in·ex·pe·di·ent /ˌɪnɪkˈspiːdiənt/ *adj.* [not usually before noun] (*formal*) (of an action 行为) not fair or right 不公正；不正确；不恰当：*It would be inexpedient to raise taxes further.* 进一步加税就是不合理。OPP **expedient**

in·ex·pen·sive /ˌɪnɪkˈspensɪv/ *adj.* not costing a lot of money 不昂贵的：*a relatively inexpensive hotel* 相对廉价的旅馆 OPP **expensive** ⮊ SYNONYMS AT CHEAP ▶ **in·ex·pen·sive·ly** *adv.*

in·ex·peri·ence /ˌɪnɪkˈspɪəriəns; *NAmE* -ˈspɪr-/ *noun* [U] lack of knowledge and experience 缺乏经验；经验不足：*His mistake was due to youth and inexperience.* 他失误的原因是年轻没有经验。

in·ex·peri·enced /ˌɪnɪkˈspɪəriənst; *NAmE* -ˈspɪr-/ *adj.* having little knowledge or experience of sth 缺乏认识（或经验）的：*inexperienced drivers/staff* 没有经验的司机 / 职员 ◇ *inexperienced in modern methods* 不熟悉现代方法 ◇ *a child too young and inexperienced to recognize danger* 因太年幼无知而意识不到危险的孩子 OPP **experienced**

in·ex·pert /ɪnˈekspɜːt; *NAmE* -pɜːrt/ *adj.* without much skill 不熟练的；缺乏技巧的 ⮊ COMPARE EXPERT *adj.* ▶ **in·ex·pert·ly** *adv.*

in·ex·plic·able /ˌɪnɪkˈsplɪkəbl/ *adj.* that cannot be understood or explained 费解的；无法解释的 SYN **incomprehensible**：*inexplicable behaviour* 令人费解的行为 ◇ ***For some inexplicable reason*** *he gave up a fantastic job.* 由于某种莫名其妙的原因，他放弃了一份很不错的工作。OPP **explicable** ▶ **in·ex·plic·ably** *adv.*：*inexplicably delayed/absent* 令人不解地耽搁 / 缺席 ◇ *She inexplicably withdrew the offer.* 她不可思议地撤回了提议。

in·ex·press·ible /ˌɪnɪk'spresəbl/ *adj.* (of feelings 感情) too strong to be put into words （强烈得）难以言传的，无法形容的： *inexpressible joy* 无法形容的喜悦

in ex·tre·mis /ˌɪn ɪk'striːmɪs/ *adv.* (*from Latin, formal*) **1** in a very difficult situation when very strong action is needed 在危急关头；在紧急情况下；在绝境 **2** at the moment of death 临终；弥留之际

in·ex·tric·able /ˌɪnɪk'strɪkəbl; ɪn'ekstrɪkəbl/ *adj.* (*formal*) too closely linked to be separated 无法分开的；分不开的： *an inextricable connection between the past and the present* 过去和现在之间密不可分的关系

in·ex·tric·ably /ˌɪnɪk'strɪkəbli; ɪn'ekstrɪkəbli/ *adv.* if two things are **inextricably linked**, etc., it is impossible to separate them 不可分开地；密不可分地： *Europe's foreign policy is inextricably linked with that of the US.* 欧洲的对外政策和美国的紧密相扣。◇ *She had become inextricably involved in the campaign.* 她已陷入这场运动之中，以致无法脱身。

in·fal·lible /ɪn'fæləbl/ *adj.* **1** never wrong; never making mistakes 永无过失的；一贯正确的： *infallible advice* 绝对正确的忠告 ◇ *Doctors are not infallible.* 医生并非永不犯错。 OPP **fallible** **2** that never fails; always doing what it is supposed to do 绝对可靠的；万无一失的： *an infallible method of memorizing things* 百试百灵的记忆方法 ▶ **in·fal·li·bil·ity** /ɪnˌfælə'bɪləti/ *noun* [U]: *papal infallibility* 教皇无错 **in·fal·libly** /-əbli/ *adv.*

in·fam·ous /'ɪnfəməs/ *adj.* (*formal*) well known for being bad or evil 臭名远扬的；声名狼藉的 SYN **notorious**: *a general who was infamous for his brutality* 因残忍而恶名昭彰的将军 ◇ *the most infamous concentration camp* 最恶名远扬的集中营 ◇ (*humorous*) *the infamous British sandwich* 以难吃著名的英国三明治 ➲ COMPARE FAMOUS ➲ MORE LIKE THIS 23, page R27

in·famy /'ɪnfəmi/ *noun* (*pl.* **-ies**) (*formal*) **1** [U] the state of being well known for sth bad or evil 臭名昭著；声名狼藉： *a day that will live in infamy* 遗臭万年的一天 **2** [U, C] evil behaviour; an evil act 恶行；罪恶： *scenes of horror and infamy* 恐怖与罪恶的场面

in·fancy /'ɪnfənsi/ *noun* [U] **1** the time when a child is a baby or very young 婴儿期；幼儿期： *to die* ***in infancy*** 婴儿夭折 **2** the early development of sth 初期；初创期： *a time when the cinema was still* ***in its infancy*** 电影业尚处于初创的时期

in·fant /'ɪnfənt/ *noun, adj.*

■ ***noun*** **1** (*formal* or *specialist*) a baby or very young child 婴儿；幼儿： *a nursery for infants under two* 两岁以下婴幼儿的托儿所 ◇ *their infant son* 他们幼小的儿子 ◇ *She was seriously ill as an infant.* 她年幼时曾患重病。◇ *the infant mortality rate* 婴幼儿死亡率 ◇ *Mozart was an* ***infant prodigy*** (= a child with unusual ability). 莫扎特是个神童。 HELP In *NAmE* **infant** is only used for a baby, especially a very young one. 美式英语中 infant 仅指婴儿，尤指新生儿。 **2** (in British and Australian education 英国和澳大利亚的教育) a child at school between the ages of four and seven 四岁到七岁之间的学童： *an infant school* 幼儿学校 ◇ *infant teachers* 幼儿教师 ◇ *I've known her since we were in the infants* (= at infant school). 从幼儿学校时我就认识她了。 ➲ WORDFINDER NOTE AT AGE

■ ***adj.*** [only before noun] **1** designed to be used by infants 供婴幼儿用的： *infant formula* (= milk for babies) 婴儿配方奶粉 **2** new and not yet developed 初期的；初创期的： *infant industries* 新兴工业

in·fanti·cide /ɪn'fæntɪsaɪd/ *noun* (*formal*) **1** [U, C] the crime of killing a baby; a person who is guilty of this crime 杀婴（罪）；杀婴犯 **2** [U] (in some cultures) the practice of killing babies that are not wanted, for example because they are girls and not boys 杀婴（某些文化中杀女婴等的做法）

in·fant·ile /'ɪnfəntaɪl/ *adj.* **1** (*disapproving*) typical of a small child (and therefore not suitable for adults or older children) 婴幼儿特有的；孩子气的 SYN **childish** **2** [only before noun] (*formal* or *specialist*) connected with babies or very young children 婴儿的；幼儿的

in·fant·il·ism /ɪn'fæntɪlɪzəm/ *noun* [U] (*psychology* 心) the fact of adults continuing to behave like children, in a way that is not normal （成人的）幼稚病

in·fanti·lize (*BrE also* **-ise**) /ɪn'fæntɪlaɪz/ *verb* **~ sb** (*formal*) to treat sb as though they are a child 当作幼儿对待

in·fan·try /'ɪnfəntri/ *noun* [C+sing./pl. v.] soldiers who fight on foot （统称）步兵： *infantry units* 步兵分队 ◇ *The infantry was/were guarding the bridge.* 步兵守卫着桥梁。

in·fan·try·man /'ɪnfəntrimən/ *noun* (*pl.* **-men** /-mən/) a soldier who fights on foot （一名）步兵

in·farc·tion /ɪn'fɑːkʃn; *NAmE* -'fɑːrk-/ *noun* (*medical* 医) a condition in which the blood supply to an area of TISSUE is blocked and the TISSUE dies 梗死形成

in·fatu·ated /ɪn'fætʃueɪtɪd/ *adj.* **~ (with sb/sth)** having a very strong feeling of love or attraction for sb/sth so that you cannot think clearly and in a sensible way 热恋的；痴情的 SYN **besotted**: *She was completely infatuated with him.* 她完全迷恋上了他。

in·fatu·ation /ɪnˌfætʃu'eɪʃn/ *noun* [C, U] **~ (with/for sb/sth)** very strong feelings of love or attraction for sb/sth, especially when these are unreasonable and do not last long （尤指一时的）热恋，痴迷： *It isn't love, it's just a passing infatuation.* 那不是爱情，只不过是一时的痴迷。

in·fect 🔑 /ɪn'fekt/ *verb* **1** 🔑 to make a disease or an illness spread to a person, an animal or a plant 传染；使感染： **~ sb/sth** *It is not possible to infect another person through kissing.* 接吻不可能把这种病传染给他人。◇ **~ sb/sth with sth** *people infected with HIV* 染上艾滋病病毒的人 **2** 🔑 **~ sth (with sth)** [usually passive] to make a substance contain harmful bacteria that can spread disease 使携带病菌 SYN **contaminate**: *eggs infected with salmonella* 带沙门氏菌的鸡蛋 **3 ~ sth (with sth)** to make a computer virus spread to another computer or program 传染，使感染（计算机病毒） **4 ~ sb (with sth)** to make sb share a particular feeling 使感染（某种感情）；影响： *She infected the children with her enthusiasm for music.* 她对音乐的热爱感染了孩子们。

in·fected 🔑 /ɪn'fektɪd/ *adj.* **1** 🔑 containing harmful bacteria 带菌的；感染病菌的： *The wound from the dog bite had become infected.* 狗咬的伤口感染了。◇ *an infected water supply* 受污染的供水系统 **2** (*computing* 计) affected by a computer virus 感染电脑病毒的： *an infected PC* 中了病毒的个人电脑

in·fec·tion 🔑 /ɪn'fekʃn/ *noun* **1** 🔑 [U] the act or process of causing or getting a disease 传染；感染： *to be exposed to infection* 暴露于易受感染的环境 ◇ *to increase the* ***risk of infection*** 增加传染的危险 ➲ SEE ALSO CROSS-INFECTION ➲ COMPARE CONTAGION **2** 🔑 [C] an illness that is caused by bacteria or a virus and that affects one part of the body （身体某部位的）感染；传染病： *an ear/throat, etc. infection* 耳部、喉部等感染 ◇ *to spread an infection* 传染疾病 ➲ SYNONYMS AT DISEASE ➲ WORDFINDER NOTE AT DISEASE

in·fec·tious 🔑 /ɪn'fekʃəs/ *adj.* **1** 🔑 an infectious disease can be passed easily from one person to another, especially through the air they breathe 传染性的，感染的（尤指通过呼吸）： *Flu is highly infectious.* 流感的传染性很高。◇ (*figurative*) *infectious laughter* 富有感染力的笑声 **2** 🔑 [not usually before noun] if a person or an animal is **infectious**, they have a disease that can be spread to others 患有传染病；有传染力： *I'm still infectious.* 我还处在传染期。 ➲ COMPARE CONTAGIOUS ▶ **in·fec·tious·ly** *adv.*: *to laugh infectiously* 笑得有感染力 **in·fec·tious·ness** *noun* [U]

in·fect·ive /ɪn'fektɪv/ *adj.* (*medical* 医) able to cause infection 会传染的；传染性的

infer AW /ɪn'fɜː(r)/ *verb* (-rr-) **1** to reach an opinion or decide that sth is true on the basis of information that is available 推断；推论；推理 SYN **deduce**: ~ **sth (from sth)** *Much of the meaning must be inferred from the context.* 大部分含义必须从上下文中推断。◇ ~ **that**… *It is reasonable to infer that the government knew about these deals.* 有理由推想政府知悉这些交易。 **2** ~ **(that)**… | ~ **sth** (*non-standard*) to suggest indirectly that sth is true 间接地提出；暗示；意指：*Are you inferring (that) I'm not capable of doing the job?* 你的言外之意是不是我不能胜任这份工作？ ➲ MORE LIKE THIS 36, page R29

▼ **WHICH WORD? 词语辨析**

infer / imply

- **Infer** and **imply** have opposite meanings. The two words can describe the same event, but from different points of view. If a speaker or writer **implies** something, they suggest it without saying it directly. * infer 和 imply 意义相反，两词可能描述同一事情，但角度不同。imply 意为暗示、暗指、意味着：*The article implied that the pilot was responsible for the accident.* 文章暗指飞行员应对事故负责。 If you **infer** something from what a speaker or writer says, you come to the conclusion that this is what he or she means. * infer 意为从…中推断、推论、推定：*I inferred from the article that the pilot was responsible for the accident.* 我从这篇文章推断，飞行员应对事故负责。
- **Infer** is now often used with the same meaning as **imply**. However, many people consider that a sentence such as: *Are you inferring that I'm a liar?* is incorrect, although it is fairly common in speech. 现在 infer 常用以表达与 imply 相同的含义，不过许多人认为 Are you inferring that I'm a liar?（你意思是说我撒谎吗？）这样的句子不正确，虽然此用法在口语中相当普遍。

in·fer·ence AW /'ɪnfərəns/ *noun* **1** [C] something that you can find out indirectly from what you already know 推断的结果；结论 SYN **deduction**: *to draw/make inferences from the data* 根据资料推论出结果 ◇ *The clear inference is that the universe is expanding.* 显然结论是宇宙在扩大。 ➲ COLLOCATIONS AT SCIENTIFIC **2** [U] the act or process of forming an opinion, based on what you already know 推断；推理；推论：*If he is guilty then, by inference, so is his wife* (= it is logical to think so, from the same evidence). 如果他有罪，那么由此可以推断他的妻子也同样有罪。

in·fer·ior /ɪn'fɪəriə(r); *NAmE* -'fɪr-/ *adj., noun*

■ *adj.* **1** not good or not as good as sb/sth else 较差的；次的；比不上…的：*of inferior quality* 劣质的 ◇ *inferior goods* 劣质商品 ◇ *to make sb feel inferior* 使某人自惭形秽 ◇ ~ **to sb/sth** *Modern music is often considered inferior to that of the past.* 现代音乐常被认为不如过去的。 **2** [usually before noun] (*formal*) of lower rank; lower 级别低的；较低的：*an inferior officer* 下级军官 OPP **superior**

■ *noun* a person who is not as good as sb else; a person who is lower in rank or status 不如别人的人；级别（或地位）低的人

in·fer·ior·ity /ɪn,fɪəri'ɒrəti; *NAmE* -,fɪri'ɔːr-; -'ɑːr-/ *noun* [U] the state of not being as good as sb/sth else 低等；劣等；劣势：*a sense of inferiority* 自卑感 ◇ *social inferiority* 社会地位低下 OPP **superiority**

in,feri'ority complex *noun* a feeling that you are not as good, as important or as intelligent as other people 自卑感；自卑情结

in·fer·nal /ɪn'fɜːnl; *NAmE* ɪn'fɜːrnl/ *adj.* **1** [only before noun] (*old-fashioned*) extremely annoying 极讨厌的；可恶的：*Stop that infernal noise!* 别那么死命嚷嚷了！ **2** (*literary*) connected with hell 地狱的；阴间的 ▶ **in·fer·nal·ly** /-nəli/ *adv.*

in·ferno /ɪn'fɜːnəʊ; *NAmE* ɪn'fɜːrnoʊ/ *noun* [usually sing.] (*pl.* **-os**) a very large dangerous fire that is out of control 无法控制的大火：*a* **blazing/raging inferno** 熊熊的／烈焰冲天的火海

in·fer·tile /ɪn'fɜːtaɪl; *NAmE* ɪn'fɜːrtl/ *adj.* **1** (of people, animals and plants 人或动植物) not able to have babies or produce young 不育的；不结果实的：*an infertile couple* 一对不能生育的夫妇 **2** (of land 土地) not able to produce good crops 贫瘠的 OPP **fertile** ▶ **in·fer·til·ity** /,ɪnfɜː'tɪləti; *NAmE* -fɜːr't-/ *noun* [U]: *an infertility clinic* 医治不育症的诊所 ◇ *infertility treatment for couples* 对不育症夫妇的治疗

in·fest /ɪn'fest/ *verb* [usually passive] ~ **sth** (especially of insects or animals such as RATS 尤指昆虫或老鼠之类的动物) to exist in large numbers in a particular place, often causing damage or disease 大量滋生；大批出没于：*shark-infested waters* 鲨鱼成群的水域 ◇ *The kitchen was infested with ants.* 厨房里到处是蚂蚁。 ▶ **in·festa·tion** /,ɪnfe'steɪʃn/ *noun* [C, U]: *an infestation of lice* 长满虱子

in·fi·del /'ɪnfɪdəl/ *noun* (*old use*) an offensive way of referring to sb who does not believe in what the speaker considers to be the true religion 异教徒

in·fi·del·ity /,ɪnfɪ'deləti/ *noun* [U, C] (*pl.* **-ies**) the act of not being faithful to your wife, husband or partner, by having sex with sb else（夫妻或伴侣间的）不忠行为；通奸 SYN **unfaithfulness**: *marital infidelity* 对婚姻的不忠诚 ◇ *She could not forgive his infidelities.* 她无法原谅他的不忠行为。 OPP **fidelity**

in·field /'ɪnfiːld/ *noun, adv.*

■ *noun* [sing.] the inner part of the field in BASEBALL, CRICKET and some other sports（棒球、板球等场地的）内场 ➲ COMPARE OUTFIELD *n.*

■ *adv.* in or to the infield 在（或向）场中心：*Ronaldo came infield from the right to score.* 罗纳尔多从右侧切入场中破门。

in·fight·ing /'ɪnfaɪtɪŋ/ *noun* [U] arguments and disagreements between people in the same group who are competing for power 团体内部的争权夺利；内讧：*political infighting within the party* 党内的政治斗争

in·fill /'ɪnfɪl/ *noun* [U] **1** the filling in of a space with sth, especially the building of new houses in spaces between existing ones 填补空间；（尤指）在旧房间隙处建新房：*infill development* 市区空隙处新房的添建 **2** the material used to fill in a space or a hole 填充物；空隙填料：*gravel infill* 沙砾填料 ▶ **in·fill** *verb* [I, T] ~ (sth)

in·fil·trate /'ɪnfɪltreɪt/ *verb* **1** [T, I] to enter or make sb enter a place or an organization secretly, especially in order to get information that can be used against it（使）悄悄进入，潜入：~ **sth** *The headquarters had been infiltrated by enemy spies.* 总部混入了敌方特务。◇ ~ **sb into sth** *Rebel forces were infiltrated into the country.* 反叛力量潜入了这个国家。 ◇ ~ **into sth** *The CIA agents successfully infiltrated into the terrorist organizations.* 中央情报局的特工人员成功地渗入了恐怖分子组织。 **2** [I, T] ~ **(into) sth** (*specialist*) (especially of liquids or gases 尤指液体或气体) to pass slowly into sth 渗入；渗透：*Only a small amount of the rainwater actually infiltrates into the soil.* 实际上只有少量雨水渗进了土壤。 ▶ **in·fil·tra·tion** /,ɪnfɪl'treɪʃn/ *noun* [U]: *the infiltration of terrorists from across the border* 恐怖分子的越境渗透 ◇ *the infiltration of rain into the soil* 雨水渗透土壤

in·fil·tra·tor /'ɪnfɪltreɪtə(r)/ *noun* a person who secretly becomes a member of a group or goes to a place, to get information or to influence the group 潜入者；渗入者

in·fin·ite AW /'ɪnfɪnət/ *adj., noun*

■ *adj.* **1** very great; impossible to measure 极大的；无法衡量的 SYN **boundless**: *an infinite variety of plants* 数不清的植物种类 ◇ *a teacher with infinite patience* 有无比耐心的教师 ◇ (*ironic*) *The company* **in its infinite wisdom** *decided to close the staff restaurant* (= they thought it was a good thing to do, but nobody else agreed). 公司以

无比的智慧决定关掉职工食堂。 **2** without limits; without end 无限的；无穷尽的： *an infinite universe* 无垠的宇宙 **OPP** **finite**

■ *noun* [sing.] **1 the infinite** something that has no end 无限的事物；无穷尽的事物 **2 the Infinite** God 上帝

in·fin·ite·ly **AW** /ˈɪnfɪnətli/ *adv.* **1** (used especially in comparisons 尤用于比较) very much 非常： *Your English is infinitely better than my German.* 你的英语比我的德语好太多了。 **2** extremely; with no limit 极其；无限地： *Human beings are infinitely adaptable.* 人类的适应力是无限的。

in·fini·tesi·mal /ˌɪnfɪnɪˈtesɪml/ *adj.* (*formal*) extremely small 极小的；微量的 **SYN** **tiny**： *infinitesimal traces of poison* 微量毒素 ◇ *an infinitesimal risk* 微乎其微的风险 ▸ **in·fini·tesi·mal·ly** /-məli/ *adv.*

in·fini·tive /ɪnˈfɪnətɪv/ *noun* (*grammar* 语法) the basic form of a verb such as *be* or *run*. In English, an infinitive is used by itself, for example *swim* in *She can swim* (this use is sometimes called the **bare infinitive**), or with *to* (the **to-infinitive**) as in *She likes to swim*. （动词的）不定式（英语中的动词不定式可单独使用，如 She can swim 中的 swim，或带 to，如 She likes to swim） **IDM** SEE SPLIT *v.*

in·fin·ity /ɪnˈfɪnəti/ *noun* (*pl.* **-ies**) **1** [U] (*also* **in·fin·it·ies** [pl.]) the state of having no end or limit 无限；无穷： *the infinity/infinities of space* 太空的无垠 **2** [U] a point far away that can never be reached 无限远的点；无穷远： *The landscape seemed to stretch into infinity.* 风景似乎延伸到了无穷远处。 **3** (*symb.* ∞) [U, C] (*mathematics* 数) a number larger than any other 无穷大（的数） **4** [sing.] a large amount that is impossible to count 无法计算的量；无限大的量： *an infinity of stars* 数不清的星星

inˈfinity pool *noun* a swimming pool that is specially designed so that, when you are in it, the pool seems to stretch to the HORIZON (= where the sky seems to meet the land or sea) 无边际游泳池（经特别设计使游泳者产生水天相连之感）

in·firm /ɪnˈfɜːm; *NAmE* ɪnˈfɜːrm/ *adj.* **1** ill/sick and weak, especially over a long period or as a result of being old （长期）病弱的；年老体弱的 **2 the infirm** *noun* [pl.] people who are weak and ill/sick for a long period 病弱的人；体弱的人： *care for the elderly and infirm* 对年老体弱者的照顾

in·firm·ary /ɪnˈfɜːməri; *NAmE* -ˈfɜːrm-/ *noun* (*pl.* **-ies**) **1** (often used in names) a hospital （常用于名称）医院 **2** a special room in a school, prison, etc. for people who are ill/sick （学校、监狱等的）医务室

in·firm·ity /ɪnˈfɜːməti; *NAmE* -ˈfɜːrm-/ *noun* [U, C] (*pl.* **-ies**) weakness or illness over a long period （长期的）体弱，生病： *We all fear disability or infirmity.* 我们都害怕伤残或体弱。◇ *the infirmities of old age* 老年体弱

infix /ˈɪnfɪks/ *noun* (*grammar* 语法) a letter or group of letters added to the middle of a word to change its meaning 中缀；中加成分

in fla·grante /ˌɪn fləˈɡrænti/ *adv.* (*from Latin, literary* or *humorous*) if sb is found or caught **in flagrante**, they are discovered doing sth that they should not be doing, especially having sex 当场（尤指被捉奸）；在作案现场

in·flame /ɪnˈfleɪm/ *verb* (*formal*) **1 ~ sb/sth** to cause very strong feelings, especially anger or excitement, in a person or in a group of people 激起…的强烈感情；（尤指）使愤怒，使激动： *His comments have inflamed teachers all over the country.* 他的评论激怒了全国教师。 **2 ~ sth** to make a situation worse or more difficult to deal with 使（局势）恶化；使更棘手： *The situation was further inflamed by the arrival of the security forces.* 安全部队的到达使局势更加难以控制。

in·flamed /ɪnˈfleɪmd/ *adj.* **1** (of a part of the body 身体部位) red, sore and hot because of infection or injury 发炎的；红肿的 ➲ SYNONYMS AT PAINFUL **2** (of people, feelings, etc. 人、感情等) very angry or excited 愤怒的；非常激动的

in·flam·mable /ɪnˈflæməbl/ *adj.* **1** (*especially BrE*) = FLAMMABLE： *inflammable material* 易燃物 ➲ MORE LIKE THIS 23, page R27 **2** full of strong emotions or violence 易激动的；易激怒的

in·flam·ma·tion /ˌɪnfləˈmeɪʃn/ *noun* [U, C] a condition in which a part of the body becomes red, sore and swollen because of infection or injury 炎症；发炎

in·flam·ma·tory /ɪnˈflæmətri; *NAmE* -tɔːri/ *adj.* **1** (*disapproving*) intended to cause very strong feelings of anger 煽动性的；使人发怒的： *inflammatory remarks* 煽动的言语 **2** (*medical* 医) causing or involving inflammation 炎性的；发炎的

in·flat·able /ɪnˈfleɪtəbl/ *adj.*, *noun*

■ *adj.* needing to be filled with air or gas before you use it 需充气的： *an inflatable mattress* 充气垫

■ *noun* **1** an inflatable boat 充气小艇 **2** a large object made of plastic or rubber and filled with air or gas, used for children to play on, or as an advertisement for sth 充气玩具；大型充气宣传品

in·flate /ɪnˈfleɪt/ *verb* **1** [T, I] **~ (sth)** to fill sth or become filled with gas or air 使充气；膨胀： *Inflate your life jacket by pulling sharply on the cord.* 猛拽绳扣使你的救生衣充气。 ◇ *The life jacket failed to inflate.* 救生衣未能充气。 **2** [T] **~ sth** to make sth appear to be more important or impressive than it really is 鼓吹；吹捧 **3** [T, I] **~ (sth)** to increase the price of sth; to increase in price （使）涨价： *The principal effect of the demand for new houses was to inflate prices.* 对新住宅需求的主要结果是促使价格上涨。 ◇ *Food prices are no longer inflating at the same rate as last year.* 食物价格的上涨率已不再像去年那样高了。 ➲ COMPARE DEFLATE, REFLATE

in·flated /ɪnˈfleɪtɪd/ *adj.* **1** (especially of prices 尤指价格) higher than is acceptable or reasonable 过高的；高得不合理的： *inflated prices/salaries* 过高的价格 / 薪金 **2** (of ideas, claims, etc. 思想、主张等) believing or claiming that sb/sth is more important or impressive than they really are 夸张的；言过其实的： *He has an inflated sense of his own importance.* 他自视过高。

in·fla·tion /ɪnˈfleɪʃn/ *noun* [U] **1** a general rise in the prices of services and goods in a particular country, resulting in a fall in the value of money; the rate at which this happens 通货膨胀；通胀率： *the fight against **rising inflation*** 对抗不断升高的通货膨胀 ◇ *to **control/curb inflation*** 控制 / 抑制通货膨胀 ◇ *to **reduce/bring down** inflation* 减少 / 降低通货膨胀 ◇ *a **high/low rate of inflation*** 高 / 低通胀率 ◇ *an **inflation rate** of 3%* 通胀率 3% ◇ *Wage increases must be **in line with inflation**.* 工资的增长必须与通货膨胀率一致。 ◇ *Inflation is currently running at 3%.* 当前的通货膨胀率为 3%。 ➲ COLLOCATIONS AT ECONOMY **2** the act or process of filling sth with air or gas 充气： *life jackets with an automatic inflation device* 有自动充气装置的救生衣 **OPP** **deflation**

in·fla·tion·ary /ɪnˈfleɪʃənri; *NAmE* -neri/ *adj.* [usually before noun] causing or connected with a general rise in the prices of services and goods 通货膨胀的；引起通胀的： *the inflationary effects of price rises* 物价上涨引起的通货膨胀 ◇ *Our economy is in an **inflationary spiral** of wage and price increases* (= a continuing situation in which an increase in one causes an increase in the other). 我们的经济处于工资和物价交替上涨的循环中。

in·flect /ɪnˈflekt/ *verb* [I] (*grammar* 语法) if a word **inflects**, its ending or spelling changes according to its GRAMMATICAL function in a sentence; if a language **inflects**, it has words that do this 屈折变化；词尾变化 ➲ WORDFINDER NOTE AT GRAMMAR ▸ **in·flect·ed** *adj.* [usually before noun]: *an **inflected** language/form/verb* 有屈折变化的语言；屈折变化形式 / 动词

in·flec·tion (*also* **in·flex·ion** *especially in BrE*) /ɪnˈflekʃn/ *noun* [C, U] **1** a change in the form of a word, especially the ending, according to its GRAMMATICAL function in

I

a sentence （尤指词尾的）屈折变化 **2** a change in how high or low your voice is as you are speaking 语调的抑扬变化

in·flex·ible AW /ɪnˈfleksəbl/ *adj.* **1** (*disapproving*) that cannot be changed or made more suitable for a particular situation 缺乏弹性的；僵化的 SYN **rigid**: *an inflexible attitude/routine/system* 死硬的态度；僵化的常规 / 体制 **2** (*disapproving*) (of people or organizations 人或机构) unwilling to change their opinions, decisions, etc., or the way they do things 固守己见的；死板的；顽固的: *He's completely inflexible on the subject.* 他在这个问题上寸步不让。 **3** (of a material 材料) difficult or impossible to bend 不能弯曲的；硬的 SYN **stiff** OPP **flexible** ▶ **in·flex·ibil·ity** AW /ɪnˌfleksəˈbɪləti/ *noun* [U] **in·flex·ibly** /-əbli/ *adv.*

in·flict /ɪnˈflɪkt/ *verb* to make sb/sth suffer sth unpleasant 使遭受（不好的事情）；施加（打击、痛苦等）: **~ sth on/upon sb/sth** *They inflicted a humiliating defeat on the home team.* 他们使主队吃了一场很没面子的败仗。◇ *Heavy casualties were inflicted on the enemy.* 敌人遭受了惨重伤亡。◇ (*humorous*) *Do you have to inflict that music on us?* 你非得逼我们听那种音乐吗？ ◇ **~ sth** *They surveyed the damage inflicted by the storm.* 他们查看了暴风雨造成的损失。 ▶ **in·flic·tion** /ɪnˈflɪkʃn/ *noun* [U]: *the infliction of pain* 痛苦的施加

PHR V **inˈflict yourself/sb on sb** (*often humorous*) to force sb to spend time with you/sb, when they do not want to 不请自来；打扰: *Sorry to inflict myself on you again like this!* 对不起，又这么打扰你了！◇ *She inflicted her nephew on them for the weekend.* 她把侄儿打发到他们那儿去度周末，真是添乱。

ˌin-ˈflight *adj.* [only before noun] provided or happening during a journey on a plane 飞行中供应（或发生）的: *an in-flight meal/movie* 飞行中提供的餐食 / 电影 ◇ *in-flight refuelling* 空中加油 ➲ WORDFINDER NOTE AT PLANE

in·flow /ˈɪnfləʊ; *NAmE* -floʊ/ *noun* **1** [C, U] the movement of a lot of money, people or things into a place from somewhere else （资金、人或事物的）流入，涌入 SYN **influx** **2** [sing., U] the movement of a liquid or of air into a place from somewhere else （液体、空气的）流入，渗入: *an inflow pipe* 注入管道 OPP **outflow**

in·flu·ence 🔑 /ˈɪnfluəns/ *noun, verb*

■ *noun* **1** 🔑 [U, C] **~ (on/upon sb/sth)** the effect that sb/sth has on the way a person thinks or behaves or on the way that sth works or develops 影响；作用: *to **have/exert** a strong **influence** on sb* 对某人产生强大的影响 ◇ *the influence of the climate on agricultural production* 气候对农业生产的影响 ◇ *What exactly is the influence of television on children?* 电视对儿童究竟有什么影响？ **2** 🔑 [U] the power that sb/sth has to make sb/sth behave in a particular way 支配力；控制力；影响力: **~ (over sb/sth)** *Her parents no longer have any real influence over her.* 她的父母对她不再有任何真正的影响了。◇ **~ (with sb)** *She could probably **exert her influence** with the manager and get you a job.* 她很有可能对经理施展她的影响力，给你弄份工作。◇ *He committed the crime **under the influence of** drugs.* 他是在吸毒后犯罪的。 **3** 🔑 [C] a person or thing that affects the way a person behaves and thinks （对…）有影响的人（或事物）: *cultural influences* 文化影响 ◇ **~ (on sb/sth)** *Those friends are **a bad influence** on her.* 那些朋友对她有负面的影响。 ◇ *His first music teacher was a major influence in his life.* 他的第一位音乐老师是他一生中对他影响非常大的人。

IDM **under the ˈinfluence** having had too much alcohol to drink 喝酒过多；醉酒: *She was charged with driving under the influence.* 她被控酒后驾驶。

■ *verb* **1** 🔑 to have an effect on the way that sb behaves or thinks, especially by giving them an example to follow 影响；对…起作用: **~ sb/sth** *His writings have influenced the lives of millions.* 他的作品影响了千百万人的一生。◇ *to be **strongly influenced** by sth* 受到某事物的强烈影响 ◇ *Don't let me influence you either way.* 何去何从都别受我的影响。◇ **~ how, whether, etc....** *The wording of questions can influence how people answer.* 问题的措辞会影响人们的回答。◇ **~ sb to do sth** *She was influenced to take up voluntary work by her teacher.* 受她老师的影响，她当起义工来了。 **2** 🔑 **~ sth | ~ how, where, etc....** to have an effect on a particular situation and the way that it develops 支配；左右: *A number of social factors influence life expectancy.* 诸多社会因素左右着人的预期寿命。

ˈinfluence peddling *noun* [U] the illegal activity of a politician doing sth for sb in return for payment （从政者的）以权谋利，索贿 SYN **corruption**

in·flu·en·tial /ˌɪnfluˈenʃl/ *adj.* having a lot of influence on sb/sth 有很大影响的；有支配力的: *a highly influential book* 十分有影响力的书 ◇ **~ in sth** *She is one of the most influential figures in local politics.* 她是本地政坛举足轻重的人物。◇ **~ in doing sth** *The committee was influential in formulating government policy on employment.* 委员会左右着政府就业政策的制订。

in·flu·enza /ˌɪnfluˈenzə/ *noun* [U] (*formal*) = FLU

in·flux /ˈɪnflʌks/ *noun* [usually sing.] **~ (of sb/sth) (into...)** the fact of a lot of people, money or things arriving somewhere （人、资金或事物的）涌入，流入: *a **massive/sudden influx** of visitors* 游客的大量 / 突然涌入 ◇ *the influx of wealth into the region* 财富往这个地区的大量涌入

info /ˈɪnfəʊ; *NAmE* ˈɪnfoʊ/ *noun* **1** [U] (*informal*) information 信息；消息；资讯: *Have you had any more info about the job yet?* 关于这份工作你有进一步的消息吗？ **2 info-** (in nouns 构成名词) connected with information 信息的；消息的；资讯的: *an infosheet* 一页信息资料 ◇ *We send all potential clients an infopack.* 我们给所有潜在的客户都发了信息包。

info·graph·ic /ˌɪnfəʊˈgræfɪk; *NAmE* ˌɪnfoʊ-/ *noun* information or data that is shown in a chart, diagram, etc. so that it is easy to understand 信息图；数据表；资讯图表: *The article contained some useful infographics.* 文中有一些有用的信息图表。

info·mer·cial /ˌɪnfəʊˈmɜːʃl; *NAmE* ˌɪnfoʊˈmɜːrʃl/ *noun* (*especially NAmE*) a long advertisement on television that tries to give a lot of information about a subject, so that it does not appear to be an advertisement （电视上的）商业信息片，资讯广告节目 ➲ MORE LIKE THIS 1, page R25

in·form 🔑 /ɪnˈfɔːm; *NAmE* ɪnˈfɔːrm/ *verb* **1** 🔑 to tell sb about sth, especially in an official way 知会；通知；通告: **~ sb (of/about sth)** *Please inform us of any changes of address.* 地址若有变动请通知我们。◇ **~ sb that...** *I have been **reliably informed** (= somebody I trust has told me) that the couple will marry next year.* 我得到可靠消息说他们俩明年结婚。 ◇ **~ sb + speech** *'He's already left,' she informed us.* "他已经走了。"她告诉我们说。 ◇ **~ sb when, where, etc....** *I have not been informed when the ceremony will take place.* 没人通知我典礼何时举行。 **2 ~ yourself (of/about sth)** to find out information about sth 了解；熟悉: *We need time to inform ourselves thoroughly of the problem.* 我们需要时间对这个问题有个透彻的了解。 **3 ~ sth** (*formal*) to have an influence on sth 对…有影响: *Religion informs every aspect of their lives.* 宗教影响着他们生活的各个方面。

PHR V **inˈform on sb** to give information to the police or sb in authority about the illegal activities of sb 告发；检举: *He informed on his own brother.* 他告发了他的亲弟弟。

in·for·mal 🔑 /ɪnˈfɔːml; *NAmE* ɪnˈfɔːrml/ *adj.* **1** 🔑 relaxed and friendly; not following strict rules of how to behave or do sth 不拘礼节的；友好随便的；非正规的: *an informal atmosphere* 友好轻松的气氛 ◇ *an informal arrangement/meeting/visit* 非正式的安排 / 会议 / 访问 ◇ *Discussions are held on an informal basis within the department.* 讨论限于在本部门内非正式地进行。 **2** 🔑 (of clothes 衣服) suitable for wearing at home or when relaxing rather than for a special or an official occasion 日常的；随便的 SYN **casual** OPP **formal** **3** 🔑 (of language 语言) suitable for normal conversation and writing to friends rather than for serious speech and letters 非正式的；口语体的: *an informal expression* 非正式用语 ➲ COMPARE FORMAL,

SLANG ▸ **in·for·mal·ity** /ˌɪnfɔːˈmæləti; *NAmE* -fɔːrˈm-/ *noun* [U] **in·for·mal·ly** /ɪnˈfɔːməli; *NAmE* -ˈfɔːrm-/ *adv.*: *They told me informally* (= not officially) *that I had got the job.* 他们非正式地告诉我说，我得到了那份工作。◇ *to dress informally* 穿着便服

inˌformal ˈsettlement *noun* (*SAfrE*) a place where people decide to live and build temporary shelters, often followed by more permanent houses. Sometimes informal settlements are supplied with water, electricity, etc. and people can become owners of individual pieces of land. 非正式居所区；临时棚屋区

in·form·ant /ɪnˈfɔːmənt; *NAmE* -ˈfɔːrm-/ *noun* **1** a person who gives secret information about sb/sth to the police or a newspaper （向警方或报纸）提供消息的人，告密者，线民 SYN **informer 2** (*specialist*) a person who gives sb information about sth, for example to help them with their research （为研究等）提供资料的人；合作者：*His informants were middle-class professional women.* 他的合作者是中产阶级职业妇女。

in·form·at·ics /ˌɪnfəˈmætɪks; *NAmE* ˌɪnfər-/ *noun* [U] = INFORMATION SCIENCE

in·for·ma·tion /ˌɪnfəˈmeɪʃn; *NAmE* ˌɪnfərˈm-/ (*also informal* **info**) *noun* [U] **1** ~ (**on/about sb/sth**) facts or details about sb/sth 信息；消息；情报；资料：*a* ***piece of information*** 一则消息 ◇ *a source of information* 消息来源 ◇ *to* ***collect/gather/obtain/receive information*** 收集／搜集／获取／接收信息 ◇ *to* ***provide/give/pass on information*** 提供／给予／传递信息 ◇ ***For further information*** *on the diet, write to us at this address.* 欲知规定饮食的详情，请按这个地址给我们写信。◇ ***Our information is that*** *the police will shortly make an arrest.* 我们得到的情报是，警察不久就要逮捕人了。◇ *This leaflet is produced* ***for the information of*** (= to inform) *our customers.* 这张传单是为向我们的顾客提供信息而印制的。◇ *an information desk* 问询处 ◇ *He refused to comment before he had seen all the* ***relevant information.*** 在看到全部相关资料之前他拒绝评论。 **2** (*NAmE, informal*) = DIRECTORY ENQUIRIES ➲ MORE LIKE THIS 28, page R28 ▸ **in·for·ma·tion·al** /-ʃənl/ *adj.* [only before noun]: *the informational content of a book* 书的信息内容 ◇ *the informational role of the media* 新闻媒体的信息功能

IDM **for information ˈonly** written on documents that are sent to sb who needs to know the information in them but does not need to deal with them （文件）仅供参考 **for your inforˈmation 1** (*abbr.* **FYI**) = FOR INFORMATION ONLY **2** (*informal*) used to tell sb that they are wrong about sth （指出对方弄错）需要提醒你的是，需要说明的是：*For your information, I don't even have a car.* 你要知道，我连汽车都没有。➲ MORE AT MINE *n.*

▼ **EXPRESS YOURSELF** 情景表达

Asking for information 询问信息

When you want to find something out, it sounds more polite if you can phrase your questions in an indirect way. 用间接的方式询问所需的信息听起来更礼貌：

- ***Could you tell me*** *the best way to get to Paddington station, please?* 您能告诉我去帕丁顿车站的最佳路线吗？
- ***Do you happen to know*** *whether Amy Brown works here?* 你可知道艾米·布朗是否在这里工作？
- ***I wonder whether/if you can help me. I'm trying to find out*** *which number to call for reservations.* 不知道您能否帮帮我，我想知道打哪个号码可以预订。

inforˌmation ˈscience (*also* **in·form·at·ics**) *noun* [U] (*computing* 计) the study of processes for storing and obtaining information 信息科学

inforˌmation techˈnology *noun* [U] (*abbr.* **IT**) the study or use of electronic equipment, especially computers, for storing, accessing, analysing and sending information 信息技术

inforˈmation theory *noun* [U] (*mathematics* 数) a theory that is used to calculate the most efficient way to send information over distances in the form of signals or symbols 信息论

in·forma·tive /ɪnˈfɔːmətɪv; *NAmE* -ˈfɔːrm-/ *adj.* giving useful information 提供有用信息的；给予知识的：*The talk was both informative and entertaining.* 这次谈话既长见识又饶有趣味。OPP **uninformative**

in·formed /ɪnˈfɔːmd; *NAmE* ɪnˈfɔːrmd/ *adj.* having or showing a lot of knowledge about a particular subject or situation 有学问的；有见识的：*an informed critic* 有见地的批评家 ◇ *an* ***informed choice/decision/guess/opinion*** 有依据的选择／决定／猜测／看法 ◇ *They are not* ***fully informed*** *about the changes.* 他们不完全了解这些改变。◇ ***Keep me informed*** *of any developments.* 随时通知我进展情况。OPP **uninformed** ➲ SEE ALSO ILL-INFORMED, WELL INFORMED

in·form·er /ɪnˈfɔːmə(r); *NAmE* -ˈfɔːrm-/ *noun* a person who gives information to the police or other authority （向警方或其他当局的）告密者；线人

info·tain·ment /ˌɪnfəʊˈteɪnmənt; *NAmE* ˌɪnfoʊ-/ *noun* [U] television programmes, etc. that present news and serious subjects in an entertaining way 资讯娱乐节目

infra- *prefix* (in adjectives 构成形容词) below or beyond a particular limit 低于（或超出）某限度的：*infrared* 红外线的 ➲ COMPARE ULTRA- ➲ MORE LIKE THIS 6, page R25

in·frac·tion /ɪnˈfrækʃn/ *noun* [C, U] (*formal*) an act of breaking a rule or law 犯规；违法 SYN **infringement**: *minor infractions of EU regulations* 对欧盟规定的轻微触犯

infra dig /ˌɪnfrə ˈdɪɡ/ *adj.* [not before noun] (*old-fashioned, informal*) considered to be below the standard of behaviour appropriate in a particular situation or to sb's social position 有失身份；有失体面

in·fra·red /ˌɪnfrəˈred/ *adj.* (*physics* 物) having or using ELECTROMAGNETIC waves which are longer than those of red light in the SPECTRUM, and which cannot be seen 红外线的；使用红外线的：*infrared radiation* 红外辐射 ◇ *an infrared lamp* 红外线灯 ➲ COMPARE ULTRAVIOLET

in·fra·struc·ture AW /ˈɪnfrəstrʌktʃə(r)/ *noun* [C, U] the basic systems and services that are necessary for a country or an organization to run smoothly, for example buildings, transport and water and power supplies （国家或机构的）基础设施，基础建设 ▸ **in·fra·struc·tural** /ˌɪnfrəˈstrʌktʃərəl/ *adj.* [usually before noun]: *infrastructural development* 基础建设的发展

in·fre·quent /ɪnˈfriːkwənt/ *adj.* not happening often 不常发生的；罕见的 SYN **rare**: *her infrequent visits home* 她少有的探望家人 ◇ *Muggings are relatively infrequent in this area.* 在这个地区行凶抢劫事件相对少见。OPP **frequent** ▸ **in·fre·quent·ly** *adv.*: *This happens not infrequently* (= often). 这种事常常发生。

in·fringe /ɪnˈfrɪndʒ/ *verb* (*formal*) **1** [T] ~ **sth** (of an action, a plan, etc. 行动、计划等) to break a law or rule 违背，触犯（法规）：*The material can be copied without infringing copyright.* 这份材料可以复制，不会侵犯版权。 **2** [T, I] to limit sb's legal rights 侵犯，侵害（合法权益）：~ **sth** *They said that compulsory identity cards would infringe civil liberties.* 他们说强制办理身份证会侵犯公民的自由。◇ ~ **on/upon sth** *She refused to answer questions that infringed on her private affairs.* 她拒绝回答侵犯她隐私的问题。▸ **in·fringe·ment** /-mənt/ *noun* [U, C]: *copyright infringement* 对版权的侵犯 ◇ *an infringement of liberty* 对自由的侵犯

in·furi·ate /ɪnˈfjʊərieɪt; *NAmE* -ˈfjʊr-/ *verb* to make sb extremely angry 使极为生气；使大怒；激怒 SYN **enrage**: ~ **sb** *Her silence infuriated him even more.* 她的沉默使他更加愤怒了。◇ **it infuriates sb that.../to do sth** *It infuriates me that she was not found guilty.* 令我大怒的是她获判无罪。

in·furi·at·ing /ɪnˈfjʊərieɪtɪŋ; NAmE -ˈfjʊr-/ *adj.* making you extremely angry 使人极为生气（或愤怒）的：*an infuriating child/delay* 令人极为生气的孩子；使人愤怒的延误 ◇ *It is infuriating to talk to someone who just looks out of the window.* 和眼睛只看着窗外的人讲话很让人窝火。 ▸ **in·furi·at·ing·ly** *adv.*：*to smile infuriatingly* 笑得使人恼火 ◇ *Infuriatingly, the shop had just closed.* 真让人生气，商店刚刚关门。

in·fuse /ɪnˈfjuːz/ *verb* **1** [T] ~ **A into B** | ~ **B with A** (*formal*) to make sb/sth have a particular quality 使具有，注入（某特性）：*Her novels are infused with sadness.* 她的小说充满哀伤。 **2** [T] ~ **sth** (*formal*) to have an effect on all parts of sth 全面影响：*Politics infuses all aspects of our lives.* 政治影响着我们生活的各个方面。 **3** [T, I] ~ (**sth**) if you **infuse** HERBS, etc. or they **infuse**, you put them in hot water until the flavour has passed into the water 泡制（草药等）；泡；沏 **4** [T] ~ **sth** (**into sth**) (*medical* 医) to slowly put a drug or other substance into a person's VEIN 输注（药物等）

in·fu·sion /ɪnˈfjuːʒn/ *noun* **1** [C, U] ~ **of sth** (**into sth**) (*formal*) the act of adding sth to sth else in order to make it stronger or more successful 注入；灌输：*a cash infusion into the business* 对企业的现金注入 ◇ *an infusion of new talent into science education* 理科教育中新人才的注入 ◇ *The company needs an infusion of new blood* (= new employees with new ideas). 公司需要吸收新人。 **2** [C] a drink or medicine made by leaving HERBS, etc. in hot water 沏成的饮料；泡制的草药 **3** [C, U] (*medical* 医) an act of slowly putting a drug or other substance into a person's VEIN; the drug that is used in this way （药物等的）输注；输液用药物

-ing *suffix* used to make the present participle of regular verbs （用以构成规则动词的现在分词）：*hating* 憎恨 ◇ *walking* 步行 ◇ *loving* 爱

in·geni·ous /ɪnˈdʒiːniəs/ *adj.* **1** (of an object, a plan, an idea, etc. 物体、计划、思想等) very suitable for a particular purpose and resulting from clever new ideas 精巧的；新颖独特的；巧妙的：*an ingenious device* 精巧的装置 ◇ *ingenious ways of saving energy* 节约能源的巧妙方法 **2** (of a person 人) having a lot of clever new ideas and good at inventing things 心灵手巧的；机敏的；善于创造发明的：*an ingenious cook* 心灵手巧的厨师 ◇ *She's very ingenious when it comes to finding excuses.* 她很善于找借口。 ▸ **in·geni·ous·ly** *adv.*：*ingeniously designed* 设计巧妙

in·génue /ˈænʒemjuː; NAmE ˈændʒənuː/ *noun* (*from French*) an innocent young woman, especially in a film/movie or play （尤指电影或戏剧中的）天真少女

in·genu·ity /ˌɪndʒəˈnjuːəti; NAmE -ˈnuː-/ *noun* [U] the ability to invent things or solve problems in clever new ways 独创力；聪明才智；心灵手巧 SYN **inventiveness**

in·genu·ous /ɪnˈdʒenjuəs/ *adj.* (*formal, sometimes disapproving*) honest, innocent and willing to trust people 单纯的；天真的 SYN **naive**：*You're too ingenuous.* 你太老实了。 ◇ *an ingenuous smile* 纯真的微笑 ◇ *It is ingenuous to suppose that money did not play a part in his decision.* 如果以为他的决定没有金钱的因素，那就太天真了。 ⊃ COMPARE DISINGENUOUS ▸ **in·genu·ous·ly** *adv.*

Inger·land /ˈɪŋɡəːlænd/ *noun* (*BrE, informal, non-standard, humorous*) a way of writing and saying England used by football fans as a name for the English national football (SOCCER) team 英格兰（足球迷对 England 的书面或口头表达方式，用以称呼英格兰国家足球队）

in·gest /ɪnˈdʒest/ *verb* ~ **sth** (*specialist*) to take food, drugs, etc. into your body, usually by swallowing 摄入；食入；咽下 ▸ **in·gest·ion** *noun* [U]

ingle·nook /ˈɪŋɡlnʊk/ *noun* a space at either side of a large FIREPLACE where you can sit 壁炉边（壁炉两侧供人坐的地方）

in·glori·ous /ɪnˈɡlɔːriəs/ *adj.* [usually before noun] (*literary*) causing feelings of shame 令人羞愧的；可耻的；不光彩的 SYN **shameful**：*an inglorious chapter in the nation's history* 这个民族历史上可耻的一页 ⊃ COMPARE GLORIOUS (1) ▸ **in·glori·ous·ly** *adv.*

ˈ**in-goal area** *noun* [sing.] (in RUGBY 橄榄球) the area between the GOAL LINE and the line at the end of the field, inside which a player must put the ball in order to score a TRY 得分区

ingot /ˈɪŋɡət/ *noun* a solid piece of metal, especially gold or silver, usually shaped like a brick （尤指金、银的）铸块，锭

in·grained /ɪnˈɡreɪnd/ *adj.* **1** ~ (**in sb/sth**) (of a habit, an attitude, etc. 习惯、态度等) that has existed for a long time and is therefore difficult to change 根深蒂固的；日久难改的 SYN **deep-rooted**：*ingrained prejudices* 很深的成见 **2** (of dirt 灰尘) under the surface of sth and therefore difficult to get rid of 深嵌并难以清除的

in·grati·ate /ɪnˈɡreɪʃieɪt/ *verb* [no passive] ~ **yourself** (**with sb**) (*disapproving*) to do things in order to make sb like you, especially sb who will be useful to you 讨好；巴结；迎合：*The first part of his plan was to ingratiate himself with the members of the committee.* 他的计划的第一步是拉拢委员会的成员。

in·grati·at·ing /ɪnˈɡreɪʃieɪtɪŋ/ *adj.* (*disapproving*) trying too hard to please sb 竭力讨好的；巴结的：*an ingratiating smile* 谄媚的微笑 ▸ **in·grati·at·ing·ly** *adv.*

in·grati·tude /ɪnˈɡrætɪtjuːd; NAmE -tuːd/ *noun* [U] the state of not feeling or showing that you are grateful for sth 忘恩负义 OPP **gratitude**

in·gre·di·ent 🔑 /ɪnˈɡriːdiənt/ *noun* ~ (**of/in/for sth**) **1** 🔑 one of the things from which sth is made, especially one of the foods that are used together to make a particular dish 成分；（尤指烹饪）材料：*Coconut is a basic ingredient for many curries.* 椰子是多种咖喱菜的基本成分。 ◇ *Our skin cream contains only natural ingredients.* 我们的护肤霜只含天然成分。 **2** 🔑 one of the things or qualities that are necessary to make sth successful （成功的）因素，要素：*the essential ingredients for success* 成功的基本要素 ◇ *It has* ***all the ingredients*** *of a good mystery story.* 它具备一个好的悬疑小说的所有要素。

in·gress /ˈɪnɡres/ *noun* [U] (*formal*) the act of entering a place; the right to enter a place 进入；进入权；入境权 ⊃ COMPARE EGRESS

ˈ**in-group** *noun* (*usually disapproving*) a small group of people in an organization or a society whose members share the same interests, language, etc. and try to keep other people out 小集团；小圈子 SYN **clique**

in·grow·ing /ˈɪnɡrəʊɪŋ; NAmE -ɡroʊ-/ (*BrE*) (*also* **in·grown** /ˈɪnɡrəʊn; NAmE -ɡroʊn/ NAmE, BrE) *adj.* [only before noun] (of the nail of a toe 脚指甲) growing into the skin 长进肉里的；向内生长的

> **WORD FAMILY**
> **inhabit** *verb*
> **habitable** *adj.* (≠ uninhabitable)
> **inhabited** *adj.* (≠ uninhabited)
> **inhabitant** *noun*
> **habitation** *noun*

in·habit /ɪnˈhæbɪt/ *verb* ~ **sth** (*formal*) to live in a particular place 居住在；栖居于：*some of the rare species that inhabit the area* 生活在这个地区的一些罕见物种

in·hab·it·ant /ɪnˈhæbɪtənt/ *noun* a person or an animal that lives in a particular place （某地的）居民，栖息动物：*the oldest inhabitant of the village* 这个村最老的居民 ◇ *a town of 11 000 inhabitants* 有 11 000 名居民的城镇

in·habited /ɪnˈhæbɪtɪd/ *adj.* with people or animals living there 有人居住的；有动物栖居的：*The island is no longer inhabited.* 这个岛已经没有人居住了。 ◇ *The building is now inhabited by birds.* 这所建筑物现在有鸟儿栖息。 OPP **uninhabited**

in·hal·ant /ɪnˈheɪlənt/ *noun* a drug or medicine that you breathe in 吸入药；吸入剂

in·hale /ɪnˈheɪl/ *verb* [I, T] (*rather formal*) to take air, smoke, gas, etc. into your lungs as you breathe 吸入；吸气 SYN **breathe in**: *She closed her eyes and inhaled deeply.* 她合上双眼，深深吸了一口气。◇ *He inhaled deeply on another cigarette.* 他又点了一根烟，深深地吸了一口。◇ **~ sth** *Local residents needed hospital treatment after inhaling fumes from the fire.* 当地居民吸入了大火的浓烟，需要入院治疗。OPP **exhale** ▶ **in·hal·ation** /ˌɪnhəˈleɪʃn/ *noun* [U, C]: *Hundreds of children were treated for smoke inhalation.* 数以百计的儿童因吸入浓烟而接受了治疗。

in·haler /ɪnˈheɪlə(r)/ (*also informal* **puff·er**) *noun* a small device containing medicine that you breathe in through your mouth, used by people who have problems with breathing 吸入器（吸药用）➲ WORDFINDER NOTE AT MEDICINE

in·har·mo·ni·ous /ˌɪnhɑːˈməʊniəs; *NAmE* -hɑːrˈmoʊ-/ *adj.* (*formal*) not combining well together or with sth else 不和谐的；不协调的

in·here /ɪnˈhɪə(r); *NAmE* ɪnˈhɪr/ *verb*

PHR V **inˈhere in sth** (*formal*) to be a natural part of sth 是…的内在部分；自然存在于：*the meaning which inheres in words* 词语中的内在含义

in·her·ent AW /ɪnˈhɪərənt; -ˈher-; *NAmE* -ˈhɪr-/ *adj.* **~ (in sb/sth)** that is a basic or permanent part of sb/sth and that cannot be removed 固有的；内在的 SYN **intrinsic**: *the difficulties inherent in a study of this type* 这类研究本身的困难 ◇ *Violence is inherent in our society.* 在我们的社会中暴力是难免的。◇ *an inherent weakness in the design of the machine* 机器设计中的内在缺陷 ▶ **in·her·ent·ly** AW /ɪnˈhɪərəntli; -ˈher-; *NAmE* -ˈhɪr-/ *adv.*: *an inherently unworkable system* 根本行不通的体制

in·herit /ɪnˈherɪt/ *verb* **1** [T, I] **~ (sth) (from sb)** to receive money, property, etc. from sb when they die 继承（金钱、财产等）：*She inherited a fortune from her father.* 她从她父亲那里继承了一大笔财富。➲ COMPARE DISINHERIT ➲ WORDFINDER NOTE AT RELATION **2** [T] **~ sth (from sb)** to have qualities, physical features, etc. that are similar to those of your parents, grandparents, etc. 经遗传获得（品质、身体特征等）：*He has inherited his mother's patience.* 这种耐心是母亲遗传给他的。◇ *an inherited disease* 遗传病 **3** [T] **~ sth (from sb)** if you **inherit** a particular situation from sb, you are now responsible for dealing with it, especially because you have replaced that person in their job 接替（责任等）；继任：*policies inherited from the previous administration* 因袭上届政府的政策

in·herit·able /ɪnˈherɪtəbl/ *adj.* (*biology* 生) (of a feature or disease 特征或疾病) capable of being passed from a parent to a child in the GENES 可遗传的；有遗传性的：*inheritable characteristics* 可遗传的特性

in·her·it·ance /ɪnˈherɪtəns/ *noun* **1** [C, U] the money, property, etc. that you receive from sb when they die; the fact of receiving sth when sb dies 继承物（如金钱、财产等）；遗产；继承：*She spent all her inheritance in a year.* 她在一年之内花光了所有继承的遗产。◇ *The title passes by inheritance to the eldest son.* 这一头衔按世袭传给长子。➲ COLLOCATIONS AT FINANCE **2** [U, C, usually sing.] something from the past or from your family that affects the way you behave, look, etc. 遗传特征；遗产：*our cultural inheritance* 我们的文化遗产 ◇ *Physical characteristics are determined by genetic inheritance.* 身体的特征取决于基因遗传。

inˈheritance tax (*NAmE also* **eˈstate tax**) *noun* [U] tax that you must pay on the money or property that you receive from sb when they die 遗产税

in·heri·tor /ɪnˈherɪtə(r)/ *noun* **1** [usually pl.] **~ of sth** a person who is affected by the work, ideas, etc. of people who lived before them 后继者；继承人 SYN **heir**: *We are the inheritors of a great cultural tradition.* 我们是一个伟大文化传统的继承者。**2** a person who receives money, property, etc. from sb when they die 遗产继承人 SYN **heir**

in·hibit AW /ɪnˈhɪbɪt/ *verb* **1 ~ sth** (*formal*) to prevent sth from happening or make it happen more slowly or less frequently than normal 阻止；阻碍；抑制：*A lack of oxygen may inhibit brain development in the unborn child.* 缺氧可能阻碍胎儿的大脑发育。**2 ~ sb (from sth/from doing sth)** to make sb nervous or embarrassed so that they are unable to do sth 使拘束；使尴尬：*The managing director's presence inhibited them from airing their problems.* 总经理的在场使他们不便畅谈他们的问题。

in·hibit·ed /ɪnˈhɪbɪtɪd/ *adj.* unable to relax or express your feelings in a natural way 拘束的；拘谨的：*Boys are often more inhibited than girls about discussing their problems.* 男孩子往往不如女孩子敢于谈论自己的问题。

in·hib·ition AW /ˌɪnhɪˈbɪʃn; ˌɪnɪˈb-/ *noun* **1** [C, U] a shy or nervous feeling that stops you from expressing your real thoughts or feelings 拘谨；拘束感：*The children were shy at first, but soon lost their inhibitions.* 孩子们起初很羞涩，但很快就放开了。◇ *She had no inhibitions about making her opinions known.* 她敢于公开地谈论自己的想法。**2** [U] (*formal*) the act of restricting or preventing a process or an action 阻止；抑制；禁止：*the inhibition of growth* 对生长的抑制

in·hibi·tor /ɪnˈhɪbɪtə(r)/ *noun* **1** (*chemistry* 化) a substance which delays or prevents a chemical reaction 抑制剂；阻聚剂 **2** (*biology* 生) a GENE which prevents another gene from being effective 抑制基因

in·hos·pit·able /ˌɪnhɒˈspɪtəbl; *NAmE* ˌɪnhɑːˈs-/ *adj.* **1** (of a place 地方) difficult to stay or live in, especially because there is no shelter from the weather 不适于居住的；（尤指）无遮蔽处的，荒凉的 SYN **unwelcoming**: *inhospitable terrain* 荒凉地带 ◇ *an inhospitable climate* 不宜人的气候 **2** (of people 人) not giving a friendly or polite welcome to guests 不殷勤待客的；不好客的 OPP **hospitable**

ˌin-ˈhouse *adj.* [only before noun] existing or happening within a company or an organization （公司或机构）内部存在的，内部进行的：*an in-house magazine* 内刊 ◇ *in-house language training* 公司内的语言培训 ▶ **ˌin-ˈhouse** *adv.*: *This engine has been designed and produced in-house.* 这款发动机是公司自行设计制造的。◇ *I prefer working in-house than being at an agency.* 我喜欢在公司内部而不是代理机构工作。

in·human /ɪnˈhjuːmən/ *adj.* **1** lacking the qualities of kindness and pity; very cruel 无同情心的；冷酷无情的：*inhuman and degrading treatment* 不人道的羞辱性对待 **2** not human; not seeming to be produced by a human and therefore frightening 非人的；（似非人所为而）恐怖的：*There was a strange inhuman sound.* 有一种不像人发出的奇怪声音。➲ COMPARE HUMAN *adj.*, NON-HUMAN, SUBHUMAN

in·hu·mane /ˌɪnhjuːˈmeɪn/ *adj.* not caring about the suffering of other people or animals; very cruel （对待人或动物）残忍的，不人道的 SYN **callous**: *inhumane treatment of animals/prisoners* 对动物的残忍行为；对囚犯的非人对待 OPP **humane** ▶ **in·hu·mane·ly** *adv.*

in·human·ity /ˌɪnhjuːˈmænəti/ *noun* [U] cruel behaviour or treatment; the fact of not having the usual human qualities of kindness and pity 残酷的行为（或待遇）；无人性；不人道：*man's inhumanity to man* 人类相残 ◇ *the inhumanity of the system* 这个体制的不人道 OPP **humanity**

in·huma·tion /ˌɪnhjuːˈmeɪʃn/ *noun* [U] (*specialist*) the act of burying dead people, used especially in relation to ancient times （尤指古代）埋葬，土葬

in·imi·cal /ɪˈnɪmɪkl/ *adj.* (*formal*) **1 ~ to sth** harmful to sth; not helping sth 对…有害的；不利于…的：*These policies are inimical to the interests of society.* 这些政策有损于社会的利益。**2** unfriendly 不友好的；敌意的：*an inimical stare* 敌意的注视

I

in·im·it·able /ɪˈnɪmɪtəbl/ *adj.* too good or individual for anyone else to copy with the same effect 无与伦比的；无法仿效的：*John related in his own **inimitable way** the story of his trip to Tibet.* 约翰以他自己特有的方式讲述了他的西藏之行。

ini·qui·tous /ɪˈnɪkwɪtəs/ *adj.* (*formal*) very unfair or wrong 很不公正的；十分错误的；很不正当的 SYN **wicked**：*an iniquitous system/practice* 很不公正的制度 / 做法

ini·quity /ɪˈnɪkwəti/ *noun* [U, C] (*pl.* **-ies**) (*formal*) the fact of being very unfair or wrong; sth that is very unfair or wrong 很不公正，十分错误，很不正当（的事）：*the iniquity of racial prejudice* 种族偏见的罪恶 ◇ *the iniquities of the criminal justice system* 刑事司法系统的不公正之处

ini·tial 🔑 AW /ɪˈnɪʃl/ *adj., noun, verb*

▪ ***adj.*** 🔑 [only before noun] happening at the beginning; first 最初的；开始的；第一的：*an initial payment of £60 and ten instalments of £25* * 60 英镑的首期付款加十次 25 英镑的分期付款 ◇ *in the **initial stages*** (= at the beginning) *of the campaign* 运动的最初阶段 ◇ *My **initial reaction** was to decline the offer.* 我最初的反应是婉言谢绝这个提议。

▪ ***noun*** **1** 🔑 [C] the first letter of a person's first name （名字的）首字母：*'What initial is it, Mrs Owen?' 'It's J, J for Jane.'* "首字母是什么，欧文太太？" "是 J，Jane 的 J。" **2** 🔑 **initials** [pl.] the first letters of all of a person's names （全名的）首字母：*John Fitzgerald Kennedy was often known by his initials JFK.* 人们常以姓名的首字母 JFK 称约翰・菲茨杰拉德・肯尼迪。◇ *Just write your initials.* 写下你的姓名首字母即可。

▪ ***verb*** (**-ll-**, *especially US* **-l-**) **~ sth** to mark or sign sth with your initials 用姓名的首字母作标记（或签名）于：*Please initial each page and sign in the space provided.* 请在每一页写上姓名首字母并在规定的空白处签字。

ini·tial·ize (*BrE also* **-ise**) /ɪˈnɪʃəlaɪz/ *verb* **~ sth** (*computing* 计) to make a computer program or system ready for use or FORMAT a disk 初始化（计算机程序或系统）；预置；格式化（磁盘） ▸ **ini·tial·iza·tion, -isa·tion** /ɪˌnɪʃəlaɪˈzeɪʃn; *NAmE* -ləˈz-/ *noun* [U]

ini·tial·ly 🔑 AW /ɪˈnɪʃəli/ *adv.* at the beginning 开始；最初；起初：*Initially, the system worked well.* 开始时系统运转良好。◇ *The death toll was initially reported at around 250, but was later revised to 300.* 最初报道死亡人数约 250，后改为 300。

ini·ti·ate AW *verb, noun*

▪ ***verb*** /ɪˈnɪʃieɪt/ **1 ~ sth** (*formal*) to make sth begin 开始；发起；创始 SYN **set in motion**：*to initiate legal proceedings against sb* 对某人提起诉讼 ◇ *The government has initiated a programme of economic reform.* 政府已开始实施经济改革方案。 **2 ~ sb (into sth)** to explain sth to sb and/or make them experience it for the first time 使了解；传授；教…开始尝试：*Many of them had been initiated into drug use at an early age.* 他们中有很多人在早年就被教会了吸毒。 **3 ~ sb (into sth)** to make sb a member of a particular group, especially as part of a secret ceremony （尤指在秘密仪式上）使加入，接纳，吸收：*Hundreds are initiated into the sect each year.* 每年有好几百人被接纳到这个教派中。

▪ ***noun*** /ɪˈnɪʃiət/ a person who has been allowed to join a particular group, organization, or religion and is learning its rules and secrets 新加入某组织（或机构、宗教）的人；新入会的人

ini·ti·ation AW /ɪˌnɪʃiˈeɪʃn/ *noun* [U] **1** the act of sb becoming a member of a group, often with a special ceremony; the act of introducing sb to an activity or skill （常指通过特别仪式的）入会；介绍某人初试某活动（或技艺）：*an initiation ceremony* 入会仪式 ◇ **~ into sth** *her initiation into the world of marketing* 她初次涉足营销界 **2** (*formal*) the act of starting sth 开始；创始；发起：*the initiation of criminal proceedings* 提起刑事诉讼

ini·tia·tive 🔑 AW /ɪˈnɪʃətɪv/ *noun* **1** 🔑 [C] a new plan for dealing with a particular problem or for achieving a particular purpose 倡议；新方案：*a United Nations peace initiative* 联合国的和平倡议 ◇ *a government initiative to combat unemployment* 政府应付失业问题的新方案 **2** 🔑 [U] the ability to decide and act on your own without waiting for sb to tell you what to do 主动性；积极性；自发性：*You won't get much help. You'll have to **use your initiative**.* 你不会得到多少帮助的。你得自己想办法。◇ *She did it **on her own initiative*** (= without anyone telling her to do it). 她是主动这么做的。 **3** 🔑 **the initiative** [sing.] the power or opportunity to act and gain an advantage before other people do 掌握有利条件的能力（或机会）；主动权：*to **seize/lose the initiative*** 掌握 / 丧失先机 ◇ *It was up to the US to **take the initiative** in repairing relations.* 在修复关系方面应由美国采取主动。 **4** [C] (*NAmE, law* 律) (in some states of the US) a process by which ordinary people can suggest a new law by signing a PETITION （美国某些州的）公民立法提案程序

ini·ti·ator AW /ɪˈnɪʃieɪtə(r)/ *noun* (*formal*) the person who starts sth 发起人；创始人

in·ject /ɪnˈdʒekt/ *verb* **1** to put a drug or other substance into a person's or an animal's body using a SYRINGE （给…）注射（药物等）：**~ sth (into yourself/sb/sth)** *Adrenaline was injected into the muscle.* 往肌肉里注射了肾上腺素。◇ **~ yourself/sb/sth (with sth)** *She has been injecting herself with insulin since the age of 16.* 她从 16 岁起就开始自行注射胰岛素。 **2** to put a liquid into sth using a SYRINGE or similar instrument （给…）注射（液体）：**~ A (with B)** *The fruit is injected with chemicals to reduce decay.* 水果注入了化学药品以防腐坏。◇ **~ B (into A)** *Chemicals are injected into the fruit to reduce decay.* 水果注入了化学药品以防腐坏。 **3 ~ sth (into sth)** to add a particular quality to sth （给…）添加，增加（某品质）：*His comments injected a note of humour into the proceedings.* 他的发言给整个活动增添了一丝幽默的气氛。 **4 ~ sth (into sth)** to give money to an organization, a project, etc. so that it can function （给…）投入（资金）：*They are refusing to inject any more capital into the industry.* 他们拒绝对这一产业投入更多的资金。

in·jec·tion /ɪnˈdʒekʃn/ *noun* **1** [C, U] an act of injecting sb with a drug or other substance 注射：*to **give sb an injection*** 给某人打针 ◇ *He was treated with penicillin injections.* 他接受了青霉素注射。◇ *An anaesthetic was administered **by injection**.* 麻醉剂已注射入体内。◇ *daily injections of insulin* 每天的胰岛素注射 ➲ WORDFINDER NOTE AT CURE ➲ COLLOCATIONS AT ILL **2** [C] a large sum of money that is spent to help improve a situation, business, etc. 大量资金的投入：*The theatre faces closure unless it gets an urgent cash injection.* 剧院面临着倒闭，除非有大笔救急现金投入。 **3** [U, C] an act of forcing liquid into sth （液体的）注入，喷入：*a fuel injection system* 燃油注入装置

inˌjection ˈmoulding (*BrE*) (*NAmE* **inˌjection ˈmolding**) *noun* [U] (*specialist*) a way of shaping plastic or rubber by heating it and pouring it into a MOULD 注塑；热压铸；注射成形 ▸ **inˌjection-ˈmoulded** (*NAmE* **inˌjection-ˈmolded**) *adj.*

ˈin-joke *noun* a joke that is only understood by a particular group of people 圈子里的笑话；行内笑话

in·ju·di·cious /ˌɪndʒuˈdɪʃəs/ *adj.* (*formal*) not sensible or wise; not appropriate in a particular situation 不明智的；不当的 SYN **unwise**：*an injudicious remark* 不当的言语 OPP **judicious** ▸ **in·ju·di·cious·ly** *adv.*

Injun /ˈɪndʒən/ *noun* (*US, taboo, slang*) an offensive word for a Native American （含侮慢意）美洲土著

in·junc·tion /ɪnˈdʒʌŋkʃn/ *noun* **1** an official order given by a court which demands that sth must or must not be done （法院的）强制令，禁制令：*to **seek/obtain an injunction*** 请求 / 得到强制令 ◇ **~ against sb** *The court **granted an injunction against** the defendants.* 法庭对被告发出了禁制令。 ➲ COMPARE RESTRAINING ORDER **2** (*formal*) a warning or an order from sb in authority 警告；指令；命令

in·jure 🔑 **AW** /ˈɪndʒə(r)/ *verb* **1** 🔑 **~ sb/sth/yourself** to harm yourself or sb else physically, especially in an accident （尤指在事故中）伤害，使受伤：*He injured his knee playing hockey.* 他打曲棍球时膝盖受伤。◇ *Three people were killed and five injured in the crash.* 撞车事故中有三人死亡，五人受伤。➲ WORDFINDER NOTE AT ACCIDENT ➲ COLLOCATIONS AT INJURY **2** 🔑 **~ sth** to damage sb's reputation, pride, etc. 损害，伤害（名誉、自尊等）：*This could seriously injure the company's reputation.* 这会严重损害公司的声誉。

▼**SYNONYMS** 同义词辨析

injure

wound • hurt • bruise • sprain • pull • strain

These words all mean to harm yourself or sb else physically, especially in an accident. 以上各词主要指在事故中伤害、使受伤。

injure to harm yourself or sb else physically, especially in an accident 尤指在事故中伤害、使受伤：*He injured his knee playing hockey.* 他打曲棍球时膝盖受了伤。◇ *Three people were injured in the crash.* 撞车事故中有三人受伤。

wound [often passive] (*rather formal*) to injure part of the body, especially by making a hole in the skin using a weapon 指使身体受伤，尤指用武器伤害：*50 people were seriously wounded in the attack.* 这次攻击中有 50 人受重伤。**NOTE** **Wound** is often used to talk about people being hurt in war or in other attacks which affect a lot of people. * wound 常指在战争中或在波及许多人的其他攻击中受伤。

hurt to cause physical pain to sb/yourself; to injure sb/yourself 指（使）疼痛、受伤：*Did you hurt yourself?* 你伤着自己了吗？

INJURE OR HURT? 用 injure 还是 hurt?

You can **hurt** or **injure** a part of the body in an accident. **Hurt** emphasizes the physical pain caused; **injure** emphasizes that the part of the body has been damaged in some way. 在事故中身体受伤可用 hurt 或 injure，hurt 强调引起的身体疼痛，injure 强调身体部位受到某种程度的损伤。

bruise to make a blue, brown or purple mark (= a bruise) appear on the skin after sb has fallen or been hit; to develop a bruise 指摔伤、撞伤、（使）出现瘀伤

sprain to injure part of your body, especially your ankle, wrist or knee, by suddenly bending it in an awkward way, causing pain and swelling 指扭伤（踝、腕、膝）

pull to damage a muscle, etc., by using too much force 指拉伤、扭伤（肌肉等）

strain to injure yourself or part of your body by making it work too hard 指损伤、拉伤、扭伤：*Don't strain your eyes by reading in poor light.* 别在光线不足的地方看书把眼睛给伤了。

PATTERNS

- to injure/hurt/strain **yourself**
- to injure/hurt/sprain/pull/strain a **muscle**
- to injure/hurt/sprain your **ankle**/**foot**/**knee**/**wrist**/**hand**
- to injure/hurt/strain your **back**/**shoulder**/**eyes**
- to injure/hurt your **spine**/**neck**
- to be **badly**/**severely**/**slightly** injured/wounded/hurt/bruised/sprained

in·jured 🔑 **AW** /ˈɪndʒəd; *NAmE* -dʒərd/ *adj.* **1** 🔑 physically hurt; having an injury 受伤的；有伤的：*an injured leg* 受伤的腿 ◇ *Luckily, she isn't injured.* 幸运的是，她没受伤。◇ *Carter is playing in place of the injured O'Reilly.* 卡特替代受伤的奥赖利上场比赛。**OPP** **uninjured** **2** **the injured** *noun* [pl.] the people injured in an accident, a battle, etc. 受伤的人；伤员；伤兵：*Ambulances took the injured to a nearby hospital.* 救护车把伤者送到了附近的一所医院。➲ MORE LIKE THIS 24, page R28 **3** 🔑 (of a person or their feelings 人或感情) upset or offended because sth unfair has been done 委屈的；受到伤害的：*an* ***injured look/tone*** 委屈的样子 / 语调 ◇ ***injured pride*** 受伤的自尊心

the ˌinjured ˈparty *noun* [sing.] (*law* 律) the person who has been treated unfairly, or the person who claims in court to have been treated unfairly 受害人；受害一方

in·juri·ous /ɪnˈdʒʊəriəs; *NAmE* -ˈdʒʊr-/ *adj.* **~ (to sb/sth)** (*formal*) causing or likely to cause harm or damage 造成伤害的；有害的 **SYN** **damaging**

in·jury 🔑 **AW** /ˈɪndʒəri/ *noun* (*pl.* **-ies**) **1** 🔑 [C, U] harm done to a person's or an animal's body, for example in an accident （对躯体的）伤害，损伤：***serious injury/injuries*** 重伤 ◇ ***minor injuries*** 轻伤 ◇ *to* ***sustain injuries/an injury*** 受伤 ◇ *to* ***escape injury*** 险受伤害 ◇ **~ (to sb/sth)** *injury to the head* 头部受伤 ◇ *a head injury* 头部受伤 ◇ *Two players are out of the team* ***because of injury***. 两名队员因伤退出了比赛。◇ *There were* ***no injuries*** *in the crash* (= no people injured). 撞车事故中无人受伤。◇ (*BrE, informal*) *Don't do that. You'll* ***do yourself an injury*** (= hurt yourself). 别那样做。你会把自己弄伤的。➲ WORDFINDER NOTE AT HURT **2** [U] (*law* 律) damage to a person's feelings （对感情的）伤害，挫伤：*Damages may be awarded for emotional injury.* 可能会判处精神伤害赔偿。**IDM** ➤ SEE ADD

▼**COLLOCATIONS** 词语搭配

Injuries 身体损伤

Being injured 受伤

- **have** a fall/an injury 跌了一跤；受伤
- **receive**/**suffer**/**sustain** a serious injury/a hairline fracture/(*especially BrE*) whiplash/a gunshot wound 受重伤 / 轻微骨裂 / 鞭伤 / 枪伤
- **hurt**/**injure** your ankle/back/leg 伤到脚踝 / 背 / 大腿
- **damage** the brain/an ankle ligament/your liver/the optic nerve/the skin 损伤大脑 / 脚踝韧带 / 肝脏 / 视神经 / 皮肤
- **pull**/**strain**/**tear** a hamstring/ligament/muscle/tendon 拉伤腘绳肌腱 / 韧带 / 肌肉 / 肌腱
- **sprain**/**twist** your ankle/wrist 扭伤脚踝 / 手腕
- **break** a bone/your collarbone/your leg/three ribs 骨折；锁骨 / 大腿 / 三根肋骨骨折
- **fracture**/**crack** your skull 头盖骨破裂
- **break**/**chip**/**knock out**/**lose** a tooth 碰断了一颗牙；使牙齿崩缺了一块；磕掉 / 掉了一颗牙
- **burst**/**perforate** your eardrum 使耳膜破裂；鼓膜穿孔
- **dislocate** your finger/hip/jaw/shoulder 使手指 / 臀部 / 下巴 / 肩膀脱臼
- **bruise**/**cut**/**graze** your arm/knee/shoulder 擦伤 / 割破 / 擦破手臂 / 膝盖 / 肩膀
- **burn**/**scald** yourself/your tongue 烧伤 / 烫伤自己 / 舌头
- **bang**/**bump**/**hit**/ (*informal*) **bash** your elbow/head/knee (on/against sth) （在某物上）撞到肘部 / 头 / 膝盖

Treating injuries 治疗伤病

- **treat sb for** burns/a head injury/a stab wound 给某人治疗烧伤 / 头部伤 / 刺伤
- **examine**/**clean**/**dress**/**bandage**/**treat** a bullet wound 检查 / 清洗 / 包扎 / 用绷带包扎 / 治疗枪伤
- **repair** a damaged/torn ligament/tendon/cartilage 修复损伤的 / 拉伤的韧带 / 肌腱 / 软骨
- **amputate**/**cut off** an arm/a finger/a foot/a leg/a limb 截去一只胳膊 / 一根手指 / 一只脚 / 一条腿；截肢
- **put on**/ (*formal*) **apply**/**take off** (*especially NAmE*) a Band-Aid™/(*BrE*) a plaster/a bandage 贴上 / 使用 / 撕掉创可贴；缠上 / 使用 / 解掉绷带
- **need**/**require**/**put in**/ (*especially BrE*) **have** (**out**)/(*NAmE*) **get** (**out**) stitches 需要缝针；缝针；拆线
- **put on**/**rub on**/ (*formal*) **apply** cream/ointment/lotion 涂抹护肤霜 / 药膏 / 护肤液
- **have**/**receive**/**undergo** (*BrE*) physiotherapy/(*NAmE*) physical therapy 接受物理疗法

I

ˈinjury time *noun* [U] (*BrE*) time added at the end of a game of football (SOCCER), HOCKEY, etc. because the game has been interrupted by injured players needing treatment 伤停补时（足球、曲棍球等比赛为弥补因队员受伤处理而延迟结束的时间）

in·just·ice /ɪnˈdʒʌstɪs/ *noun* [U, C] the fact of a situation being unfair and of people not being treated equally; an unfair act or an example of unfair treatment 不公正，不公平（的对待或行为）: *fighting against poverty and injustice* 与贫困和不公平斗争 ◇ *a burning **sense** of injustice* 强烈感觉到遭受不公正待遇 ◇ *social injustice* 社会的不公平 ◇ *She was enraged at the injustice of the remark.* 她被那句话的不公激怒了。◇ *The report exposes the injustices of the system.* 报告揭露了这个制度的种种不公正。 OPP **justice**

IDM **do yourself/sb an inˈjustice** to judge yourself/sb unfairly 待…不公正；冤枉: *We may have been doing him an injustice. This work is good.* 我们可能冤枉他了。这工作干得不错。

I

ink 🔑 /ɪŋk/ *noun, verb*

■ ***noun*** 🔑 [U, C] coloured liquid for writing, drawing and printing 墨水；墨汁；油墨: *written **in ink*** 用墨水写的 ◇ *a pen and ink drawing* 钢笔画 ◇ *different coloured inks* 各种颜色的墨水 ➲ SEE ALSO INKY

■ ***verb*** **1** ~ **sth** to cover sth with ink so that it can be used for printing 给…上油墨（以供印刷） **2** ~ **sth** (*NAmE, informal*) to sign a document, especially a contract 签署，签订（合同等）: *The group has just inked a $10 million deal.* 这个集团刚刚签订了一份 1 000 万美元的协议。

PHR V **ˌink sth↔ˈin** to write or draw in ink over sth that has already been written or drawn in pencil 给（铅笔画或底线）上墨；用墨水加描: (*figurative*) *The date for the presentation should have been inked in* (= made definite) *by now.* 演出的日期现在应该敲定了。

ˈink-blot test *noun* (*psychology* 心) = RORSCHACH TEST

ink·jet printer /ˈɪŋkdʒet prɪntə(r)/ *noun* a printer that uses very small JETS to blow ink onto paper in order to form letters, numbers, etc. 喷墨打印机

ink·ling /ˈɪŋklɪŋ/ *noun* [usually sing.] a slight knowledge of sth that is happening or about to happen （对正在或即将发生的事的）略知 SYN **suspicion**: ~ **(of sth)** *He had no inkling of what was going on.* 他对正在发生的事情一无所知。◇ ~ **(that...)** *The first inkling I had that something was wrong was when I found the front door wide open.* 我发现前门大开着时就隐约感觉到出了事。

ˈink pad *noun* a thick piece of soft material full of ink, used with a rubber stamp 印台；打印台 ➲ VISUAL VOCAB PAGE V71

ink·well /ˈɪŋkwel/ *noun* a pot for holding ink that fits into a hole in a desk (used in the past) （旧时嵌入写字台的）墨水池

inky /ˈɪŋki/ *adj.* **1** black like ink 墨黑的；漆黑的: *the inky blackness of the cellar* 地窖里的一片漆黑 **2** made dirty with ink 沾有墨水的；被墨水弄脏的: *inky fingers* 沾满墨水的手指

in·laid /ˌɪnˈleɪd/ *adj.* (of furniture, floors, etc. 家具、地板等) decorated with designs of wood, metal, etc. that are set into the surface 镶嵌着（木质、金属等）图案的；嵌饰的: *an inlaid wooden box* 嵌花木盒子 ◇ ~ **with sth** *a box inlaid with gold* 镶金盒子

in·land *adv., adj.*

■ ***adv.*** /ˌɪnˈlænd/ in a direction towards the middle of a country; away from the coast 向（或在）内陆；向（或在）内地: *The town lies a few kilometres inland.* 这个城镇位于内陆几公里处。◇ *We travelled further inland the next day.* 我们第二天继续向内陆行进。

■ ***adj.*** /ˈɪnlænd/ [usually before noun] located in or near the middle of a country, not near the edge or on the coast （在）内陆的；（在）内地的: *inland areas* 内陆地区 ◇ *inland lakes* 内陆湖 ➲ COMPARE COASTAL

the ˌInland ˈRevenue *noun* [sing.] the government department in Britain that was responsible for collecting taxes until 2005 when it was replaced by HM REVENUE AND CUSTOMS （英国）国内税收署，税务局（2005 年被英国税务海关总署 (HM Revenue and Customs) 所取代） ➲ COMPARE INTERNAL REVENUE SERVICE

ˈin-law apartment (*also* **ˈmother-in-law apartment**, **ˈin-law suite**) (*all NAmE*) (*BrE* **ˈgranny flat**) *noun* (*informal*) a set of rooms for an old person, especially in a relative's house （尤指亲人家中的）老人套间

ˈin-laws *noun* [pl.] (*informal*) your relatives by marriage, especially the parents of your husband or wife 姻亲；（尤指）公婆，岳父母: *We're visiting my in-laws on Sunday.* 我们星期天要去拜访我的姻亲。 ➲ WORDFINDER NOTE AT FAMILY

inlay *verb, noun*

■ ***verb*** /ˌɪnˈleɪ/ (**in·lay·ing, in·laid, in·laid** /ˌɪnˈleɪd/) [often passive] ~ **A (with B)** | ~ **B (in/into A)** to decorate the surface of sth by putting pieces of wood or metal into it in such a way that the surface remains smooth 镶嵌；把（图案等）嵌入: *The lid of the box had been inlaid with silver.* 盒盖上镶嵌着银饰。

■ ***noun*** /ˈɪnleɪ/ [C, U] a design or pattern on a surface made by setting wood or metal into it; the material that this design is made of 镶嵌艺术；镶嵌装饰（或图案）；镶嵌材料: *The table was decorated with gold inlay.* 桌子装饰着黄金镶嵌的图案。

inlet /ˈɪnlet/ *noun* **1** a narrow strip of water that stretches into the land from the sea or a lake, or between islands （海、湖伸向陆地或岛屿间的）小湾，水湾 ➲ WORDFINDER NOTE AT COAST **2** (*specialist*) an opening through which liquid, air or gas can enter a machine （液体、空气或气体进入机器的）入口，进口: *a fuel inlet* 燃料进口 OPP **outlet**

ˌin-line ˈskate (*BrE also* **Roll·er·blade™**) *noun* a type of boot with a line of small wheels attached to the bottom 直排滚轴旱冰鞋；直排轮滑鞋 ➲ VISUAL VOCAB PAGE V44 ▶ **ˌin-line ˈskating** *noun* [U]

in loco par·en·tis /ɪn ˌləʊkəʊ pəˈrentɪs; *NAmE* ˌloʊkoʊ/ *adv.* (*from Latin, formal*) having the same responsibility for a child as a parent has 代人尽父母责任；代替家长责任

in·mate /ˈɪnmeɪt/ *noun* one of the people living in an institution such as a prison or a PSYCHIATRIC hospital （监狱或精神病院等的）同住者；同狱犯人；同病房者

in med·ias res /ɪn ˌmiːdiæs ˈreɪz/ *adv.* (*formal, from Latin*) straight into the main part of a story or account without giving any introduction 直接切入本题；单刀直入: *He began his story in medias res.* 他开门见山地讲了起来。

in me·mor·iam /ˌɪn məˈmɔːriəm/ *prep.* (*from Latin*) used to mean 'in memory of', for example on the stone over a grave （用于墓碑等）为纪念

in·most /ˈɪnməʊst; *NAmE* ˈɪnmoʊst/ *adj.* [only before noun] = INNERMOST (1)

inn /ɪn/ *noun* **1** (*old-fashioned, BrE*) a pub, usually in the country and often one where people can stay the night （通常指乡村的，常可夜宿的）小酒店 **2** (*NAmE*) a small hotel, usually in the country （通常指乡村的）小旅馆，客栈 **3 Inn** used in the names of many pubs, hotels and restaurants （用于客栈、旅馆和饭店的名称中）: *Holiday Inn* 假日酒店

in·nards /ˈɪnədz; *NAmE* ˈɪnərdz/ *noun* [pl.] (*informal*) **1** the organs inside the body of a person or an animal, especially the stomach 内脏；（尤指）胃 SYN **entrails, guts** **2** the parts inside a machine （机器的）内部结构

in·nate /ɪˈneɪt/ *adj.* (of a quality, feeling, etc. 品质、感情等) that you have when you are born 天生的；先天的；与生俱来的 SYN **inborn**: *the innate ability to learn* 天生的学习能力 ▶ **in·nate·ly** *adv.*: *He believes that humans are innately violent.* 他相信人性本恶。

inner /ˈɪnə(r)/ *adj.* [only before noun] **1** inside; towards or close to the centre of a place 里面的；向内的；内部的；接近中心的：*an inner courtyard* 内院 ◇ *inner London* 伦敦市中心区 ◇ *the inner ear* 内耳 OPP **outer** **2** (of feelings, etc. 感情等) private and secret; not expressed or shown to other people 内心的；未表达出来的；隐藏的：*She doesn't reveal much of her inner self.* 她不大流露她的内心自我。

ˌinner ˈcircle *noun* the small group of people who have a lot of power in an organization, or who control it 核心集团

ˌinner ˈcity *noun* the part near the centre of a large city, which often has social problems 内城区（常有社会问题）：*There are huge problems in our inner cities.* 我们各个内城区存在着许多大的问题。◇ *an inner-city area/school* 内城区的地区 / 学校

ˌinner ˈear *noun* (*anatomy* 解) the parts of the ear which form the organs of balance and hearing, including the COCHLEA 内耳，迷路（包括听觉器官和平衡器官）

in·ner·most /ˈɪnəməʊst; *NAmE* ˈɪnərmoʊst/ *adj.* [only before noun] **1** (*also less frequent* **in·most**) most private, personal and secret 内心深处的：*I could not express my innermost feelings to anyone.* 我不能向任何人表达我内心深处的感情。**2** nearest to the centre or inside of sth 最靠近中心的；最深处的：*the innermost shrine of the temple* 神殿最深处的圣坛 OPP **outermost**

ˈinner tube *noun* a rubber tube filled with air inside a tyre （轮胎的）内胎

in·ning /ˈɪnɪŋ/ *noun* (in BASEBALL 棒球) one of the nine periods of a game in which each team has a turn at BATTING 局；回合

in·nings /ˈɪnɪŋz/ *noun* (*pl.* **in·nings**) (in CRICKET 板球) a period of time in a game during which a team or a single player is BATTING 局；回合

IDM **sb had a good ˈinnings** (*BrE, informal*) used about sb who has died to say that they had a long life （用以指死者）…够长寿了，终其天年

innit /ˈɪnɪt/ *exclamation* (*BrE, non-standard*) **1** a way of saying 'isn't it' (即 isn't it) 是否，是不是：*Cold, innit?* 很冷，是不是？ **2** a way of saying any QUESTION TAG, such as 'don't you?' or 'haven't you?' 是吗；是不是：*You got it, innit?* 你明白了，是吗？ ➲ MORE LIKE THIS 5, page R25

inn·keep·er /ˈɪnkiːpə(r)/ *noun* (*old-fashioned*) a person who owns or manages an INN 客栈老板；（乡村）酒铺掌柜

in·no·cence /ˈɪnəsns/ *noun* [U] **1** the fact of not being guilty of a crime, etc. 清白；无辜；无罪：*She **protested her innocence*** (= said repeatedly that she was innocent). 她一再申明自己是无辜的。◇ *This new evidence will prove their innocence.* 这一新的证据将证明他们的清白。◇ *I asked if she was married **in all innocence*** (= without knowing it was likely to offend or upset her). 我问她结婚了没有，完全没有恶意。 OPP **guilt** **2** lack of knowledge and experience of the world, especially of evil or unpleasant things 天真；纯真；单纯：*Children lose their innocence as they grow older.* 儿童随着年龄的增长而失去其天真。

in·no·cent /ˈɪnəsnt/ *adj., noun*

■ *adj.* **1** not guilty of a crime, etc.; not having done sth wrong 无辜的；清白的；无罪的：*They have imprisoned an innocent man.* 他们监禁了一名无辜的男子。◇ ~ (**of sth**) *She was found innocent of any crime.* 她获判无罪。◇ *He was the **innocent party*** (= person) *in the breakdown of the marriage.* 他们的婚姻破裂，他是无过错的一方。OPP **guilty** **2** [only before noun] suffering harm or being killed because of a crime, war, etc. although not directly involved in it 无辜受害的；成为牺牲品的：*an innocent bystander* 无辜受害的旁观者 ◇ *innocent victims of a bomb blast* 炸弹爆炸中的无辜受害者 **3** having little experience of the world, especially of sexual matters, or of evil or unpleasant things 天真无邪的；纯真的 SYN **naive**：*an innocent young child* 天真无邪的小孩子 **4** not intended to cause harm or upset sb 无恶意的；无冒犯之意的 SYN **harmless**：*It was all innocent fun.* 那不过是些无恶意的玩笑。◇ *It was a perfectly innocent remark.* 那是一句毫无冒犯之意的话。 ▶ **in·no·cent·ly** *adv.*：*'Oh, Sue went too, did she?' I asked innocently* (= pretending I did not know that this was important). "噢，休也去了，是吗？"我装作若无其事地问。

■ *noun* an innocent person, especially a young child 无辜者，单纯的人（尤指天真无邪的孩子）

in·nocu·ous /ɪˈnɒkjuəs; *NAmE* ɪˈnɑːk-/ *adj.* (*formal*) **1** not intended or likely to offend or upset anyone 无恶意的；无意冒犯的 SYN **harmless**：*It seemed a perfectly innocuous remark.* 那像是一句毫无恶意的话。 **2** not harmful or dangerous 无害的；无危险的 SYN **harmless**：*an innocuous substance* 无害物质 ▶ **in·nocu·ous·ly** *adv.*

in·nov·ate AW /ˈɪnəveɪt/ *verb* [I, T] to introduce new things, ideas or ways of doing sth 引入（新事物、思想或方法）；创新；改革：*We must constantly adapt and innovate to ensure success in a growing market.* 我们必须不时地适应并创新，以确保在不断扩大的市场中取得成功。◇ ~ *sth to innovate new products* 创造新产品 ▶ **in·nov·ator** AW /ˈɪnəveɪtə(r)/ *noun*

in·nov·ation AW /ˌɪnəˈveɪʃn/ *noun* **1** [U] ~ (**in sth**) the introduction of new things, ideas or ways of doing sth （新事物、思想或方法的）创造；创新；改革：*an age of technological innovation* 技术革新的时代 **2** [C] ~ (**in sth**) a new idea, way of doing sth, etc. that has been introduced or discovered 新思想；新方法：*recent innovations in steel-making technology* 新近的炼钢技术革新

in·nova·tive AW /ˈɪnəveɪtɪv; *BrE also* ˈɪnəvətɪv/ (*also less frequent* **in·nov·atory** /ˌɪnəˈveɪtəri; *NAmE* ˈɪnəvətɔːri/) *adj.* (*approving*) introducing or using new ideas, ways of doing sth, etc. 引进新思想的；采用新方法的；革新的；创新的：*There will be a prize for the most innovative design.* 将设立一项最具创意设计奖。

in·nu·endo /ˌɪnjuˈendəʊ; *NAmE* -doʊ/ *noun* [C, U] (*pl.* **-oes** or **-os**) (*disapproving*) an indirect remark about sb/sth, usually suggesting sth bad or rude; the use of remarks like this 暗指；影射：*innuendoes about her private life* 对她私生活含沙射影的指责 ◇ *The song is full of sexual innuendo.* 那首歌充满了性的暗示。

in·nu·mer·able /ɪˈnjuːmərəbl; *NAmE* ɪˈnuː-/ *adj.* too many to be counted; very many 多得数不清的；很多的 SYN **countless**：*Innumerable books have been written on the subject.* 已经有无数书籍写过这个主题。

in·nu·mer·ate /ɪˈnjuːmərət; *NAmE* ɪˈnuː-/ *adj.* unable to count or do simple mathematics 不会数数的；不会计算的；不懂算术的 OPP **numerate**

in·ocu·late /ɪˈnɒkjuleɪt; *NAmE* ɪˈnɑːk-/ *verb* ~ **sb** (**against sth**) to protect a person or an animal from catching a particular disease by INJECTING them with a mild form of the disease （给…）接种，打预防针 ➲ COMPARE IMMUNIZE, VACCINATE ▶ **in·ocu·la·tion** /ɪˌnɒkjuˈleɪʃn; *NAmE* ɪˌnɑːk-/ *noun* [C, U]

in·offen·sive /ˌɪnəˈfensɪv/ *adj.* not likely to offend or upset anyone 不会冒犯人的；不讨人嫌的：*a shy, inoffensive young man* 腼腆温和的青年男子 OPP **offensive**

in·op·er·able /ɪnˈɒpərəbl; *NAmE* ɪnˈɑːp-/ *adj.* **1** (of an illness, especially cancer 疾病，尤指癌) not able to be cured by a medical operation 手术无法治愈的：*an inoperable brain tumour* 不能手术治疗的脑瘤 **2** (*formal*) that cannot be used or made to work; not practical 无法使用的；不能实行的；不实用的：*The policy was thought to be inoperable.* 这项政策被认为行不通。OPP **operable**

in·op·era·tive /ɪnˈɒpərətɪv; *NAmE* ɪnˈɑːp-/ *adj.* (*formal*) **1** (of a rule, system, etc. 规则、体系等) not valid or able to be used 无效的；不能实行的 **2** (of a machine 机器) not working; not functioning correctly 不运转的；运行不正常的 OPP **operative**

in·op·por·tune /ɪnˈɒpətjuːn; *NAmE* ɪnˌɑːpərˈtuːn/ *adj.* (*formal*) happening at a bad time 不合时宜的；不是时候的 SYN **inappropriate, inconvenient**: *They arrived at an inopportune moment.* 他们到的不是时候。 OPP **opportune**

in·or·din·ate /ɪnˈɔːdɪnət; *NAmE* -ˈɔːrd-/ *adj.* (*formal*) far more than is usual or expected 过度的；过分的；超乎预料的 SYN **excessive** ▶ **in·or·din·ate·ly** *adv.*: *inordinately high prices* 高得离谱的价格

in·or·gan·ic /ˌɪnɔːˈɡænɪk; *NAmE* ˌɪnɔːrˈɡ-/ *adj.* not consisting of or coming from any living substances 无生物的；无机的：*inorganic fertilizers* 无机肥料 OPP **organic**

ˌinorganic ˈchemistry *noun* [U] the branch of chemistry that deals with substances that do not contain CARBON 无机化学 ➲ COMPARE ORGANIC CHEMISTRY

in·pa·tient /ˈɪnpeɪʃnt/ *noun* a person who stays in a hospital while receiving treatment 住院病人 ➲ COMPARE OUTPATIENT ➲ WORDFINDER NOTE AT HOSPITAL

I

input AW /ˈɪnpʊt/ *noun, verb*

■ *noun* **1** [C, U] time, knowledge, ideas, etc. that you put into work, a project, etc. in order to make it succeed; the act of putting sth in 投入资源（指时间、知识、思想等）；投入；输入：~ **(into/to sth)** *Her specialist input to the discussions has been very useful.* 她在这些讨论中提供的专家建议很有助益。◇ *I'd appreciate your input on this.* 我将感激你在这方面的投入。◇ ~ **(of sth)** *There has been a big input of resources into the project from industry.* 工业界对这个项目投入了大量资源。**2** [U] (*computing* 计) the act of putting information into a computer; the information that you put in 输入；输入的信息：*data input* 数据输入 ◇ *This program accepts input from most word processors.* 这个程序可接受大多数文字处理系统输入的信息。➲ WORDFINDER NOTE AT PROGRAM **3** [C] (*specialist*) a place or means for electricity, data, etc. to enter a machine or system （电、数据等的）输入端 ➲ COMPARE OUTPUT *n.* (2)

■ *verb* (**in·put·ting, input, input** or **in·put·ting, in·put·ted, in·put·ted**) ~ **sth** to put information into a computer 输入（信息）：*to* ***input text/data/figures*** 把文本/数据/数字输入计算机 ➲ COMPARE OUTPUT *v.*

in·quest /ˈɪŋkwest/ *noun* **1** an official investigation to find out the cause of sb's death, especially when it has not happened naturally 死因审理；验尸；勘验：*An inquest was held to discover the cause of death.* 对死亡原因进行了调查。◇ ~ **(on/into sth)** *a coroner's inquest into his death* 进行验尸以探究他的死因 **2** ~ **(on/into sth)** a discussion about sth that has failed （对失败的事进行的）讨论：*An inquest was held on the team's poor performance.* 对该队在比赛中的差劲表现进行了检讨。

in·quire, in·quir·er, in·quir·ing, in·quiry = ENQUIRE, ENQUIRER, ENQUIRING, ENQUIRY

in·qui·si·tion /ˌɪŋkwɪˈzɪʃn/ *noun* **1 the Inquisition** [sing.] the organization set up by the Roman Catholic Church to punish people who opposed its beliefs, especially from the 15th to the 17th century （尤指 15 到 17 世纪天主教的）宗教裁判所，异端裁判所 **2** [C] (*formal* or *humorous*) a series of questions that sb asks you, especially when they ask them in an unpleasant way 一连串的提问；（尤指）盘问，责难 ➲ SEE ALSO SPANISH INQUISITION

in·quisi·tive /ɪnˈkwɪzətɪv/ *adj.* **1** (*disapproving*) asking too many questions and trying to find out about what other people are doing, etc. 过分打听他人私事的 SYN **curious**: *Don't be so inquisitive. It's none of your business!* 别这么追根问底的。这与你无关！ **2** very interested in learning about many different things 好学的；好奇的；兴趣广泛的 SYN **enquiring**: *an inquisitive mind* 勤学好问的精神 ▶ **in·quisi·tive·ly** *adv.* **in·quisi·tive·ness** *noun* [U]

in·quisi·tor /ɪnˈkwɪzɪtə(r)/ *noun* **1** a person who asks a lot of difficult questions, especially in a way that makes you feel threatened 连续不断地发问的人；（尤指）盘问者 **2** an officer of the Inquisition of the Roman Catholic Church （天主教异端审问的）裁判人 ▶ **in·quisi·tor·ial** /ɪnˌkwɪzəˈtɔːriəl/ *adj.*: *He questioned her in a cold inquisitorial voice.* 他像个审判官似的冷冷质问她。

in·quor·ate /ɪnˈkwɔːreɪt; -ət/ *adj.* (*BrE, specialist*) a meeting that is **inquorate** does not have enough people present for them to make official decisions by voting （会议）不构成法定人数的 OPP **quorate**

in·road /ˈɪnrəʊd; *NAmE* -roʊd/ *noun* ~ **(into sth)** something that is achieved, especially by reducing the power or success of sth else （尤指通过消耗或削弱其他事物取得的）进展：*This deal is their first major inroad into the American market.* 这交易是他们进军美国市场的首次重大收获。

IDM **make inroads into/on sth** if one thing **makes inroads into** another, it has a noticeable effect on the second thing, especially by reducing it, or influencing it 消耗，削弱，影响（某事物）：*Tax rises have made some inroads into the country's national debt.* 增加税收已使国债有所减少。

in·rush /ˈɪnrʌʃ/ *noun* [usually sing.] a sudden flow towards the inside （突然的）流入，涌入，进入：*an inrush of air/water* 空气/水的涌入

in·salu·bri·ous /ˌɪnsəˈluːbriəs/ *adj.* (of a place 地方) dirty and with many things that need to be repaired, cleaned or replaced 肮脏破旧的 OPP **salubrious**

in·sane /ɪnˈseɪn/ *adj.* **1** seriously mentally ill and unable to live in normal society 精神失常的；精神错乱的：*Doctors certified him as insane.* 医生证明他精神失常。◇ *The prisoners were slowly* ***going insane.*** 囚犯正慢慢地变得精神错乱起来。OPP **sane** ➲ SYNONYMS AT MENTALLY **2 the insane** *noun* [pl.] people who are insane 精神失常的人；精神错乱的人：*a hospital for the insane* 精神病院 ➲ MORE LIKE THIS 24, page R28 **3** (*informal*) very stupid, crazy or dangerous 十分愚蠢的；疯狂的；危险的：*I must have been insane to agree to the idea.* 我肯定是犯傻了，居然同意了这个想法。◇ *This job is* ***driving me insane*** (= making me feel very angry). 这份工作快要把我逼疯了。➲ SEE ALSO INSANITY ▶ **in·sane·ly** *adv.*: *He is insanely jealous.* 他嫉妒得发疯。

in·sani·tary /ɪnˈsænətri; *NAmE* -teri/ (*also* **un·sani·tary** *especially in NAmE*) *adj.* dirty and likely to spread disease 不卫生的；不洁的 OPP **sanitary**

in·san·ity /ɪnˈsænəti/ *noun* [U] **1** the state of being INSANE 精神失常；精神错乱；精神病 SYN **madness**: *He was found not guilty, by reason of insanity.* 他因精神失常而获判无罪。OPP **sanity** **2** actions that are very stupid and possibly dangerous 十分愚蠢的行为；荒唐的行为 SYN **madness, lunacy**: *It would be sheer insanity to attempt the trip in such bad weather.* 天气这么糟糕还要去旅行，太荒唐了。

in·sati·able /ɪnˈseɪʃəbl/ *adj.* always wanting more of sth; not able to be satisfied 不知足的；无法满足的：*an* ***insatiable appetite/curiosity/thirst*** 永不满足的食欲/好奇心/渴望 ◇ *There seems to be an* ***insatiable demand*** *for more powerful computers.* 人们对计算机性能的要求似乎永无止境。▶ **in·sati·ably** /-ʃəbli/ *adv.*

in·scribe /ɪnˈskraɪb/ *verb* to write or cut words, your name, etc. onto sth 在…上写（词语、名字等）；题；刻：~ **A (on/in B)** *His name was inscribed on the trophy.* 他的名字刻在奖杯上。◇ ~ **B (with A)** *The trophy was inscribed with his name.* 奖杯上刻着他的名字。◇ *She signed the book and inscribed the words 'with grateful thanks' on it.* 她在书上签了名，并在上面写道"谨致由衷感谢"。

in·scrip·tion /ɪnˈskrɪpʃn/ *noun* words written in the front of a book or cut in stone or metal （书首页的）题词；（石头或金属上）刻写的文字，铭刻，碑文

in·scrut·able /ɪnˈskruːtəbl/ *adj.* if a person or their expression is **inscrutable**, it is hard to know what they are thinking or feeling, because they do not show any emotion 难以捉摸的；难以理解的；神秘莫测的 ▶ **in·scrut·abil·ity** /ɪnˌskruːtəˈbɪləti/ *noun* [U] **in·scrut·ably** /ɪnˈskruːtəbli/ *adv.*

in·seam /ˈɪnsiːm/ (*NAmE*) (*BrE* ˌ**inside ˈleg**) *noun* [sing.] a measurement of the length of the inside of sb's leg, used for making or choosing trousers of the correct size 下落裆（裤腿内侧长度）

in·sect /ˈɪnsekt/ *noun* any small creature with six legs and a body divided into three parts. Insects usually also have wings. ANTS, BEES and flies are all insects. 昆虫： *insect species* 昆虫种类 ◇ ***insect repellent*** (= a chemical that keeps insects away) 驱虫剂 ◇ *an* ***insect bite*** 昆虫咬伤 ➲ COLLOCATIONS AT LIFE ➲ VISUAL VOCAB PAGE V13 ➲ SEE ALSO STICK INSECT **HELP** **Insect** is often used to refer to other small creatures, for example spiders, although this is not correct scientific language. * insect 常用以指蜘蛛等其他小动物，但从科学术语来说并不准确。

in·secti·cide /ɪnˈsektɪsaɪd/ *noun* [C, U] a chemical used for killing insects 杀虫剂；杀虫药 ➲ SEE ALSO HERBICIDE, PESTICIDE ▶ **in·secti·cidal** /ɪnˌsektɪˈsaɪdl/ *adj.*

in·sect·ivore /ɪnˈsektɪvɔː(r)/ *noun* any animal that eats insects 食虫动物 ➲ COMPARE CARNIVORE, HERBIVORE, OMNIVORE ▶ **in·sect·iv·or·ous** /ˌɪnsekˈtɪvərəs/ *adj.*

in·se·cure AW /ˌɪnsɪˈkjʊə(r); *NAmE* -ˈkjʊr/ *adj.* **1** not confident about yourself or your relationships with other people 缺乏信心的；无把握的： *He's very insecure about his appearance.* 他对自己的长相很没信心。◇ *She felt nervous and insecure.* 她感到局促不安。 **2** not safe or protected 不安全的；无保障的；不牢靠的： *Jobs nowadays are much more insecure than they were ten years ago.* 当今的工作比十年前要不安稳得多了。◇ *As an artist he was always financially insecure.* 作为一名艺术家，他在经济上总是没有保障。 ◇ *Insecure doors and windows* (= for example, without good locks) *make life easy for burglars.* 门窗不牢靠方便了窃贼。 OPP **secure** ▶ **in·se·cure·ly** *adv.* **in·secur·ity** AW /ˌɪnsɪˈkjʊərəti; *NAmE* -ˈkjʊr-/ *noun* [U, C] (*pl.* **-ies**): *feelings of insecurity* 不安全感 ◇ *job insecurity* 工作无保障 ◇ *We all have our fears and insecurities.* 我们大家都有各自的恐惧和不安全感。

in·sem·in·ate /ɪnˈsemɪneɪt/ *verb* **~ sb/sth** (*specialist*) to put SPERM into a woman or female animal in order to make her pregnant 使受精；授精： *The cows are* ***artificially inseminated.*** 这些母牛是人工授精的。 ▶ **in·sem·in·ation** /ɪnˌsemɪˈneɪʃn/ *noun* [U] ➲ SEE ALSO ARTIFICIAL INSEMINATION

in·sens·ibil·ity /ɪnˌsensəˈbɪləti/ *noun* [U] **1** (*formal*) the state of being unconscious 无知觉；不省人事 **2** the fact of not being able to react to a particular thing （对某事物的）麻木，无反应能力： *insensibility to pain* 对疼痛无感觉

in·sens·ible /ɪnˈsensəbl/ *adj.* (*formal*) **1** [not before noun] **~ (to sth)** unable to feel sth or react to it （对某事物）无感觉，无反应能力，麻木： *insensible to pain/cold* 感觉不到疼痛 / 冷 **2** [not before noun] **~ (of sth)** not aware of a situation or of sth that might happen 未察觉；意识不到 SYN **unaware**: *They were not insensible of the risks.* 他们对这些危险并非没有意识。 OPP **sensible 3** unconscious as the result of injury, illness, etc. 失去知觉；昏迷： *He drank himself insensible.* 他喝酒醉得不省人事。 ➲ MORE LIKE THIS 23, page R27 ▶ **in·sens·ibly** /-əbli/ *adv.*

in·sensi·tive /ɪnˈsensətɪv/ *adj.* **1** not realizing or caring how other people feel, and therefore likely to hurt or offend them （对他人的感受）未意识到的，漠不关心的 SYN **unsympathetic**: *an insensitive remark* 冷漠的言论 ◇ **~ to sth** *She's completely insensitive to my feelings.* 她全然不顾我的感情。 **2 ~ (to sth)** not aware of changing situations, and therefore of the need to react to them （对变化）懵然不知的，麻木不仁的： *The government seems totally insensitive to the mood of the country.* 政府似乎对全国民众的心情完全懵然不知。 **3 ~ (to sth)** not able to feel or react to sth （对某事物）无感觉，无反应： *insensitive to pain/cold* 感觉不到疼痛 / 寒冷 ◇ *He seems completely insensitive to criticism.* 他似乎对批评麻木不仁。 OPP **sensitive** ▶ **in·sensi·tive·ly** *adv.* **in·sensi·tiv·ity** /ɪnˌsensəˈtɪvəti/ *noun* [U]

in·sep·ar·able /ɪnˈseprəbl/ *adj.* **1 ~ (from sth)** not able to be separated （与某事物）不可分离的，分不开的： *Our economic fortunes are inseparable from those of Europe.* 我们的经济命运和欧洲的息息相关。 **2** if people are **inseparable**, they spend most of their time together and are very good friends 形影不离的 ▶ **in·sep·ar·ab·il·ity** /ɪnˌseprəˈbɪləti/ *noun* [U] **in·sep·ar·ably** /ɪnˈseprəbli/ *adv.*: *Our lives were inseparably linked.* 我们的生活息息相通。

in·sert AW *verb, noun*

■ ***verb*** /ɪnˈsɜːt; *NAmE* ɪnˈsɜːrt/ **1** **~ sth (in/into/between sth)** to put sth into sth else or between two things 插入；嵌入： *Insert coins into the slot and press for a ticket.* 把硬币放进投币口，按钮取票。 ◇ *They inserted a tube in his mouth to help him breathe.* 他们在他嘴里插了根导管帮助他呼吸。 **2** to add sth to a piece of writing （在文章中）添加，加插： **~ sth** *Position the cursor where you want to insert a word.* 把光标移到你想插入字词的地方。 ◇ **~ sth into sth** *Later, he inserted another paragraph into his will.* 后来他在他的遗嘱中又加了一段。 ➲ WORDFINDER NOTE AT COMMAND

■ ***noun*** /ˈɪnsɜːt; *NAmE* ˈɪnsɜːrt/ **~ (in sth) 1** an extra section added to a book, newspaper or magazine, especially to advertise sth （书报的）插页，广告附加页： *an 8-page insert on the new car models* 附加的 8 页新型汽车广告 **2** something that is put inside sth else, or added to sth else 插入物；添加物： *These inserts fit inside any style of shoe.* 这些鞋垫适合任何式样的鞋。

in·ser·tion AW /ɪnˈsɜːʃn; *NAmE* ɪnˈsɜːrʃn/ *noun* **1** [U, C] **~ (in/into sth)** the act of putting sth inside sth else; a thing that is put inside sth else 插入；嵌入；插入物： *An examination is carried out before the insertion of the tube.* 插入导管前先要进行检查。 **2** [C, U] a thing that is added to a book, piece of writing, etc.; the act of adding sth （书、文章等中）添加的东西；添加；插入： *the insertion of an extra paragraph* 插入一个附加段落

ˌ**in-ˈservice** *adj.* [only before noun] (of training, courses of study, etc. 训练、课程等) done while sb is working in a job, in order to learn new skills 在职进行的；不脱产的： *in-service training* 在职培训

inset /ˈɪnset/ *noun, verb*

■ ***noun*** **1** a small picture, map, etc. inside a larger one （套印在大图片、地图等中的）小图，小地图： *For the Shetland Islands, see inset.* 关于设得兰群岛，见小地图。 **2** something that is added on to sth else, or put inside sth else 嵌入物；附加物： *The windows have beautiful stained glass insets.* 窗户上镶着漂亮的彩色玻璃。

■ ***verb*** (**in·set·ting, inset, inset**) **1** [usually passive] to fix sth into the surface of sth else, especially as a decoration 嵌入，插入（作为装饰等）： **~ A (with B)** *The tables were inset with ceramic tiles.* 桌子上镶嵌着瓷砖。 ◇ **~ B (into A)** *Ceramic tiles were inset into the tables.* 桌子上镶嵌着瓷砖。 **2 ~ sth (into sth)** to put a small picture, map, etc. inside the borders of a bigger one （在大图片、地图等中）套印小图

in·shore /ˈɪnʃɔː(r)/ *adj.* [usually before noun] in the sea but close to the SHORE 近岸的；近海的： *an inshore breeze* 海岸边的微风 ◇ *an inshore lifeboat* (= that stays close to the land) 近海救生艇 ▶ ˌ**inˈshore** *adv.*: *The boat came inshore* (= towards the land). 船驶近海岸。 ➲ COMPARE OFFSHORE

in·side /ˌɪnˈsaɪd/ *prep., adv., noun, adj.*

■ ***prep.*** (*also* **in·side of** *especially in NAmE*) **1** on or to the inner part of sth/sb; within sth/sb 在（或向）…内；在（或向）…里： *Go inside the house.* 进屋里吧。 ◇ *Inside the box was a gold watch.* 盒子里装着一只金表。 ◇ *For years we had little knowledge of what life was like inside China.* 以往很多年我们对于中国国内的生活情况所知甚少。 ◇ *You'll feel better with a good meal inside you.* 你肚子饱了感觉就会好些的。 ◇ (*figurative*) *Inside most of us is a small child screaming for attention.* 我们大多数人的内心都藏着一个呼求关注的小孩。 OPP **outside 2** in less than the amount of time mentioned 少于（某时间）： *The job is unlikely to be finished inside (of) a year* 这项工作不大可能在一年之内完成。

I

■ *adv.* **1** 🔑 on or to the inside 在（或向）里面：*She shook it to make sure there was nothing inside.* 她把它晃了晃，以确定里面没有东西。◇ *We had to move inside* (= indoors) *when it started to rain.* 开始下雨了，我们只好躲进屋里。◇ (*figurative*) *I pretended not to care but I was screaming inside.* 表面上我佯装不在乎，但内心却在高声喊叫。**OPP** **outside** **2** (*informal*) in prison 在监狱里；被监禁：*He was sentenced to three years inside.* 他被判三年监禁。

■ *noun* **1** 🔑 [C, usually sing.] (*usually* **the inside**) the inner part, side or surface of sth 里面；内部；内侧：*The inside of the box was blue.* 盒子的内面呈蓝色。◇ *The door was locked from the inside.* 门从里面锁上了。◇ *The shell is smooth on the inside.* 贝壳内壁光滑。◇ *the insides of the windows* 窗户的内侧 **OPP** **outside** **2** **the inside** [sing.] the part of a road nearest the edge, that is used by slower vehicles （靠近路边的）慢车道：*He tried to overtake* **on the inside**. 他试图从慢车道超车。**OPP** **outside** **3** **the inside** [sing.] the part of a curved road or track nearest to the middle or shortest side of the curve （道路或跑道拐弯处的）内侧，里道，内圈：*The French runner is coming up fast on the inside.* 法国的赛跑选手正从内圈迅速赶上来。**OPP** **outside** **4** **insides** [pl.] (*informal*) a person's stomach and BOWELS （人的）肠胃，内脏：*She was so nervous, her insides were like jelly.* 她紧张得六神无主。

IDM **ˌinside ˈout** 🔑 with the part that is usually inside facing out 里面朝外：*You've got your sweater on inside out.* 你把毛线衫里外穿反了。◇ *Turn the bag inside out and let it dry.* 把包翻过来晾干。➲ COMPARE BACK TO FRONT at BACK *n.* **on the inˈside** belonging to a group or an organization and therefore able to get information that is not available to other people 属于某团伙（或组织）的；知情的：*The thieves must have had someone on the inside helping them.* 这些窃贼肯定有内应。**turn sth ˌinside ˈout** **1** to make a place very untidy when you are searching for sth 把某处翻得乱七八糟：*The burglars had turned the house inside out.* 窃贼把房子翻了个底朝天。**2** to cause large changes 引起巨大变化：*The new manager turned the old systems inside out.* 新任经理对旧体制进行了彻底的改革。➲ MORE AT KNOW *v.*

■ *adj.* [only before noun] **1** 🔑 forming the inner part of sth; not on the outside 内部的；里面的：*the inside pages of a newspaper* 报纸的内页 ◇ *an inside pocket* 里袋 ◇ (*BrE*) *I was driving in the* **inside lane** (= the part nearest the edge, not the middle of the road). 我当时驾车在慢车道上行驶。**2** known or done by sb in a group or an organization 从内部了解到的；内线干的：*inside information* 内部情报 ◇ *Any newspaper would pay big money to get* **the inside story** *on her marriage.* 任何一家报纸都愿出高价购买她婚姻的内幕消息。◇ *The robbery appeared to have been an* **inside job**. 这次抢劫像是内部人干的。

ˌinside ˈleg (*BrE*) (*NAmE* **in·seam**) *noun* [sing.] a measurement of the length of the inside of sb's leg, used for making or choosing trousers of the correct size 下落裆（裤腿内侧长度）

in·sider /ɪnˈsaɪdə(r)/ *noun* a person who knows a lot about a group or an organization, because they are part of it 知内情者；内部的人：*The situation was described by one insider as 'absolute chaos'.* 据一名内部人士说，实情是乱作一团。➲ COMPARE OUTSIDER

inˌsider ˈtrading (*also* **inˌsider ˈdealing**) *noun* [U] the crime of buying or selling shares in a company with the help of information known only by those connected with the business, before this information is available to everybody 内线交易，内幕交易（根据内线消息买卖股票的违法行为）

ˌinside ˈtrack *noun* [sing.] a position in which you have an advantage over sb else 有利位置

in·sidi·ous /ɪnˈsɪdiəs/ *adj.* (*formal, disapproving*) spreading gradually or without being noticed, but causing serious harm 潜伏的；隐袭的；隐伏的：*the insidious effects of polluted water supplies* 供水系统污染的潜在恶果 ▸ **in·sidi·ous·ly** *adv.*

in·sight **AW** /ˈɪnsaɪt/ *noun* **1** [U] (*approving*) the ability to see and understand the truth about people or situations 洞察力；领悟：*a writer of great insight* 有深刻洞察力的作家 ◇ *With a flash of insight I realized what the dream meant.* 我突然明白了这个梦意味着什么。**2** [C, U] ~ (**into sth**) an understanding of what sth is like 洞悉；了解：*The book gives us fascinating insights into life in Mexico.* 这本书生动地表现了墨西哥的生活。

in·sight·ful **AW** /ˈɪnsaɪtfʊl/ *adj.* (*approving*) showing a clear understanding of a person or situation 有深刻了解的；富有洞察力的 **SYN** **perceptive**

in·sig·nia /ɪnˈsɪɡniə/ *noun* [U+sing./pl. v.] the symbol, BADGE or sign that shows sb's rank or that they are a member of a group or an organization （级别或成员的）标记，象征；徽章；证章：*the royal insignia* 皇家徽章 ◇ *His uniform bore the insignia of a captain.* 他的制服上有上尉徽章。

in·sig·nifi·cant **AW** /ˌɪnsɪɡˈnɪfɪkənt/ *adj.* not big or valuable enough to be considered important 微不足道的；无足轻重的：*an insignificant difference* 微不足道的差别 ◇ *The levels of chemicals in the river are not insignificant.* 河水中的化学物质含量不容忽视。◇ *He made her feel insignificant and stupid.* 他使她感到卑微愚蠢。**OPP** **significant** ▸ **in·sig·nifi·cance** /-kəns/ *noun* [U]: *Her own problems* **paled into insignificance** *beside this terrible news.* 跟这个可怕的消息相比，她自己的问题显得无关紧要了。**in·sig·nifi·cant·ly** **AW** *adv.*

in·sin·cere /ˌɪnsɪnˈsɪə(r); *NAmE* -ˈsɪr/ *adj.* (*disapproving*) saying or doing sth that you do not really mean or believe 不诚恳的；不真心的：*an insincere smile* 虚情假意的微笑 **OPP** **sincere** ▸ **in·sin·cere·ly** *adv.* **in·sin·cer·ity** /ˌɪnsɪnˈserəti/ *noun* [U]: *She accused him of insincerity.* 她指责他缺乏诚意。

in·sinu·ate /ɪnˈsɪnjueɪt/ *verb* **1** to suggest indirectly that sth unpleasant is true 暗示，旁敲侧击地指出（不快的事） **SYN** **imply**: ~ **that**… *The article insinuated that he was having an affair with his friend's wife.* 文章含沙射影地点出他和朋友的妻子有染。◇ ~ **sth** *What are you trying to insinuate?* 你拐弯抹角想说什么？◇ *an insinuating smile* 暗示的微笑 **2** ~ **yourself into sth** (*formal, disapproving*) to succeed in gaining sb's respect, affection, etc. so that you can use the situation to your own advantage 钻营；活动：*In the first act, the villain insinuates himself into the household of the man he intends to kill.* 在第一幕中，恶棍混进了他企图谋杀的男子的家庭。**3** ~ **yourself/sth + adv./prep.** (*formal*) to slowly move yourself or a part of your body into a particular position or place （使）缓慢进入；慢慢伸入：*She insinuated her right hand under his arm.* 她悄悄把右手插到他胳膊底下。

in·sinu·ation /ɪnˌsɪnjuˈeɪʃn/ *noun* **1** [C] something that sb insinuates 旁敲侧击的话；影射；暗示：*She resented the insinuation that she was too old for the job.* 她憎恶暗示她太老不适合这项工作的话。**2** [U] the act of insinuating sth 旁敲侧击；含沙射影；巧妙进入

in·sipid /ɪnˈsɪpɪd/ *adj.* (*disapproving*) **1** having almost no taste or flavour 无味道的；淡而无味的 **SYN** **flavourless**: *a cup of insipid coffee* 一杯淡而无味的咖啡 **2** not interesting or exciting 没有趣味的；枯燥乏味的 **SYN** **dull**: *After an hour of insipid conversation, I left.* 经过一个小时乏味的谈话之后，我离开了。

in·sist 🔑 /ɪnˈsɪst/ *verb* **1** 🔑 [I, T] to demand that sth happens or that sb agrees to do sth 坚决要求；坚持：*I didn't really want to go but he insisted.* 我并不真的想去，但他硬要我去。◇ *'Please come with us.' 'Very well then,* **if you insist**.' "请和我们一起来吧。" "好吧，你一定要我来，我就来。" ◇ ~ **on sth/sb doing sth** (*formal*) *She insisted on his/him wearing a suit.* 她坚持要他穿西装。◇ ~ **that**… *He insists that she come.* 他执意要她来。◇ (*BrE also*) *He insists that she should come.* 他执意要她来。➲ SYNONYMS AT DEMAND **2** 🔑 [I, T] to say firmly that sth is true, especially when other people do not believe you 坚持说；固执己见：~ **on sth** *He insisted on his innocence.* 他坚持说他是

无辜的。◇ ~ (**that**)... *He insisted (that) he was innocent.* 他坚持说他是无辜的。◇ + **speech** *'It's true,' she insisted.* "那是真的。"她坚持道。

PHR V **in'sist on/upon sth** to demand sth and refuse to be persuaded to accept anything else 坚决要求：*We insisted on a refund of the full amount.* 我们坚决要求全额退款。◇ **insist on/upon doing sth** *They insisted upon being given every detail of the case.* 他们坚持要求说明事情的来龙去脉。 **in'sist on doing sth** to continue doing sth even though other people think it is annoying 执意继续做：*They insist on playing their music late at night.* 已是深夜，他们却依然在放音乐。

in·sist·ence /ɪn'sɪstəns/ *noun* [U] ~ (**on sth/on doing sth**) | ~ (**that...**) an act of demanding or saying sth firmly and refusing to accept any opposition or excuses 坚决要求；坚持；固执：*their insistence on strict standards of behaviour* 他们对严格行为规范的坚决主张 ◇ ***At her insistence,*** *the matter was dropped.* 在她的坚持下，这件事被搁置了。

in·sist·ent /ɪn'sɪstənt/ *adj.* **1** demanding sth firmly and refusing to accept any opposition or excuses 坚决要求的；坚持的；固执的：~ (**on sth/on doing sth**) *They were insistent on having a contract for the work.* 他们坚持要就这项工作立一份合同。◇ ~ (**that...**) *Why are you so insistent that we leave tonight?* 你为什么一定要我们今晚离开？◇ *She didn't want to go but her brother was insistent.* 她不想去，但她哥哥非得要她去。 **2** continuing for a long period of time in a way that cannot be ignored 持续不断的；再三的；反复的：*insistent demands* 再三的要求 ◇ *the insistent ringing of the telephone* 没完没了的电话铃声 ▸ **in·sist·ent·ly** *adv.*

in situ /ˌɪn 'sɪtjuː; 'saɪt-; NAmE 'saɪtuː/ *adv.* (*from Latin*) in the original or correct place 在原位；在原地；在合适地方

in·so·bri·ety /ˌɪnsə'braɪəti/ *noun* [U] (*formal*) the state of being drunk; wild and noisy behaviour which is typical of this state 醉酒；（酒后）撒野，无节制 OPP **sobriety**

in·so·far as /ˌɪnsə'fɑːr əz/ = IN SO/AS FAR AS

in·sole /'ɪnsəʊl; NAmE 'ɪnsoʊl/ *noun* a piece of material shaped like your foot that is placed inside a shoe to make it more comfortable 鞋垫

in·so·lent /'ɪnsələnt/ *adj.* extremely rude and showing a lack of respect 粗野的；无礼的；侮慢的：*an insolent child/smile* 粗野的孩子；侮慢的微笑 ➲ SYNONYMS AT RUDE ▸ **in·so·lence** /-əns/ *noun* [U]：*Her insolence cost her her job.* 她的蛮横态度使她丢了工作。 **in·so·lent·ly** *adv.*

in·sol·uble /ɪn'sɒljəbl; NAmE -'sɑːl-/ *adj.* **1** (*especially BrE*) (*US usually* **in·sol·vable** /ɪn'sɒlvəbl; NAmE -'sɑːl-/) (of a problem, mystery, etc. 问题、谜团等) that cannot be solved or explained 无法解决的；不能解释的 **2** ~ (**in sth**) (of a substance 物质) that does not dissolve in a liquid 不能溶解的；不溶的 OPP **soluble**

in·solv·ent /ɪn'sɒlvənt; NAmE -'sɑːl-/ *adj.* not having enough money to pay what you owe 无力偿付债务的；破产的 SYN **bankrupt**：*The company has been declared insolvent.* 这家公司被宣布破产了。 OPP **solvent** ▸ **in·solv·ency** /-ənsi/ *noun* [U, C] (*pl.* **-ies**)

in·som·nia /ɪn'sɒmniə; NAmE -'sɑːm-/ *noun* [U] the condition of being unable to sleep 失眠（症）：*to suffer from insomnia* 失眠 ➲ SEE ALSO SLEEPLESSNESS at SLEEPLESS ➲ WORDFINDER NOTE AT SLEEP

in·som·niac /ɪn'sɒmniæk; NAmE -'sɑːm-/ *noun* a person who finds it difficult to sleep 失眠患者

in·sou·ci·ance /ɪn'suːsiəns/ *noun* [U] (*formal*) the state of not being worried about anything 无忧无虑；漫不经心 SYN **nonchalance**：*She hid her worries behind an air of insouciance.* 她掩饰着自己的烦恼，表现得无忧无虑。 ▸ **in·sou·ci·ant** /-siənt/ *adj.*

Insp *abbr.* INSPECTOR (especially in the British police force)（尤指英国警察）巡官：*Chief Insp (Paul) King* 总巡官（保罗•）金

in·spect AW /ɪn'spekt/ *verb* **1** to look closely at sth/sb, especially to check that everything is as it should be 检查；查看；审视 SYN **examine**：~ **sth/sb** *The teacher walked around inspecting their work.* 老师走来走去检查他们的作业。◇ *Make sure you inspect the goods before signing for them.* 要确保在签收货物之前进行检验。◇ ~ **sth/sb for sth** *The plants are regularly inspected for disease.* 这些植物定期检查是否有病害。 ➲ SYNONYMS AT CHECK **2** ~ **sth** to officially visit a school, factory, etc. in order to check that rules are being obeyed and that standards are acceptable 视察：*Public health officials were called in to inspect the premises.* 公共卫生官员奉召来视察了建筑物。 ➲ SYNONYMS AT CHECK

in·spec·tion AW /ɪn'spekʃn/ *noun* [U, C] **1** an official visit to a school, factory, etc. in order to check that rules are being obeyed and that standards are acceptable 视察：*Regular **inspections are carried out** at the prison.* 经常有人来视察这座监狱。◇ *The head went on a **tour of inspection** of all the classrooms.* 校长巡视了所有教室。 **2** the act of looking closely at sth/sb, especially to check that everything is as it should be 检查；查看；审视 SYN **examination**：*The documents are available **for inspection**.* 这些文件可供查阅。◇ ***On closer inspection,*** *the notes proved to be forgeries.* 经进一步检查发现钞票都是伪造的。◇ *Engineers **carried out a** thorough **inspection** of the track.* 工程师对轨道进行了彻底检查。

in·spect·or AW /ɪn'spektə(r)/ *noun* **1** a person whose job is to visit schools, factories, etc. to check that rules are being obeyed and that standards are acceptable 检查员；视察员；巡视员：*a **school/health/safety, etc. inspector*** 督学；卫生、安全等检查员 ➲ SEE ALSO TAX INSPECTOR **2** (*abbr.* **Insp**) an officer of middle rank in the POLICE FORCE（警察）巡官：*Inspector Maggie Forbes* 玛吉•福布斯巡官 ➲ SEE ALSO CHIEF INSPECTOR **3** (in Britain) a person whose job is to check tickets on a bus or train to make sure that they are valid（英国公共汽车或火车上的）查票员

in·spect·or·ate /ɪn'spektərət/ *noun* [C+sing./pl. v.] (*especially BrE*) an official group of inspectors who work together on the same subject or at the same kind of institution 视察团；检查团：*The schools inspectorate has/have published a report on science teaching.* 督学团发表了关于科学教学的报告。

inˌspector of 'taxes (*also* **'tax inspector**) *noun* (in Britain) a person who is responsible for collecting the tax that people must pay on the money they earn（英国）税务员，税务稽查员 ➲ SEE ALSO TAX COLLECTOR, TAXMAN

in·spir·ation /ˌɪnspə'reɪʃn/ *noun* **1** [U] ~ (**to do sth**) | ~ (**for sth**) the process that takes place when sb sees or hears sth that causes them to have exciting new ideas or makes them want to create sth, especially in art, music or literature 灵感：*Dreams can be a rich source of inspiration for an artist.* 梦境有可能是艺术家灵感的丰富源泉。◇ *Both poets **drew their inspiration from** the countryside.* 两位诗人都从乡村得到他们的灵感。◇ *Looking for inspiration for a new dessert? Try this recipe.* 正在寻找制作新式甜食的灵感吗？试试这份食谱吧。 **2** [C, usually sing.] ~ (**for sth**) a person or thing that is the reason why sb creates or does sth 启发灵感的人（或事物）；使人产生动机的人（或事物）：*He says my sister was the inspiration for his heroine.* 他说我姐姐是他的女主人公的原型。◇ *Clark was the inspiration behind Saturday's victory.* 克拉克是星期六的胜利的灵魂。 **3** [C, usually sing.] ~ (**to/for sb**) a person or thing that makes you want to be better, more successful, etc. 鼓舞人心的人（或事物）：*Her charity work is an inspiration to us all.* 她的慈善工作激励着我们所有人。 **4** [C, usually sing., U] a sudden good idea（突然想到的）好主意，妙计：*He had an inspiration: he'd give her a dog for her birthday.* 他突然想到一个好主意，他要送她一条狗作为生日礼物。◇ *It came to me in a **flash of inspiration**.* 那是我灵机一动想到的。

I

in·spir·ation·al /ˌɪnspəˈreɪʃənl/ *adj.* providing inspiration 启发灵感的；鼓舞人心的：*an inspirational leader* 有感召力的领袖

in·spire /ɪnˈspaɪə(r)/ *verb* **1** to give sb the desire, confidence or enthusiasm to do sth well 激励；鼓舞：**~ sb (with sth)** *The actors inspired the kids with their enthusiasm.* 演员以热情鼓舞着孩子们。◇ *The actors' enthusiasm inspired the kids.* 演员们的热情鼓舞着孩子们。◇ **~ sb to sth** *His superb play inspired the team to a thrilling 5–0 win.* 他的出色表现使球队士气大振，以 5:0 大获全胜。◇ **~ sb to do sth** *By visiting schools, the actors hope to inspire children to put on their own productions.* 演员希望通过访问学校鼓励孩子们演出自己的作品。**2** [usually passive] **~ sth** to give sb the idea for sth, especially sth artistic or that shows imagination 赋予灵感；引起联想；启发思考：*The choice of decor was inspired by a trip to India.* 选用这种装饰格调是从一次印度之行中得到的启发。**3** to make sb have a particular feeling or emotion 使产生（感觉或情感）：**~ sb (with sth)** *Her work didn't exactly* ***inspire me with confidence.*** 她的工作并没有真正地使我产生信心。◇ **~ sth (in sb)** *As a general, he inspired great loyalty in his troops.* 作为一位将军，他得到了部队的精诚效忠。

in·spired /ɪnˈspaɪəd; *NAmE* ɪnˈspaɪərd/ *adj.* **1** having excellent qualities or abilities; produced with the help of INSPIRATION 品质优秀的；能力卓越的；借助于灵感创作的：*an inspired performance* 精彩的演出 ◇ *an* ***inspired choice/guess*** (= one that is right but based on feelings rather than knowledge) 得自灵感的选择 / 猜测 **OPP uninspired** **2 -inspired** used with nouns, adjectives and adverbs to form adjectives that show how sth has been influenced （与名词、形容词以及副词构成形容词）受…影响的：*politically-inspired killings* 政治性的谋杀事件

in·spir·ing /ɪnˈspaɪərɪŋ/ *adj.* exciting and encouraging you to do or feel sth 鼓舞人心的；激励的；启发灵感的：*an inspiring teacher* 启发能力强的教师 ◇ (*informal*) *The book is less than inspiring.* 那本书不大吸引人。**OPP uninspiring** ➲ SEE ALSO AWE-INSPIRING

in·stabil·ity **AW** /ˌɪnstəˈbɪləti/ *noun* [U, C, usually pl.] (*pl.* **-ies**) **1** the quality of a situation in which things are likely to change or fail suddenly 不稳定；不稳固：*political and economic instability* 政治和经济的不稳定 **2** a mental condition in which sb's behaviour is likely to change suddenly （精神的）不稳定状态，变化无常：***mental/emotional instability*** 精神 / 情绪的不稳定 **OPP stability** ➲ SEE ALSO UNSTABLE

in·stall /ɪnˈstɔːl/ *verb* **1** **~ sth** to fix equipment or furniture into position so that it can be used 安装；设置：*He's getting a phone installed tomorrow.* 他明天要装电话。◇ *The hotel chain has recently installed a new booking system.* 这家连锁旅馆最近安装了新的预订系统。**2** **~ sth** to put a new program onto a computer 安装（程序）：*I'll need some help installing the software.* 我得找人帮忙安装这个软件。◇ *Have you got Word installed on your computer?* 你的计算机安装了 Word 程序吗？➲ WORDFINDER NOTE AT SOFTWARE **3** **~ sb (as sth)** to put sb in a new position of authority, often with an official ceremony （常以正式仪式）使就职，任命：*He was installed as President last May.* 他于去年五月份正式就任总统。**4** **~ sb/yourself (+ adv./prep.)** to make sb/yourself comfortable in a particular place or position 安顿；安置：*We installed ourselves in the front row.* 我们舒舒服服地坐进了前排。

in·stal·la·tion /ˌɪnstəˈleɪʃn/ *noun* **1** [U, C] the act of fixing equipment or furniture in position so that it can be used 安装；设置：*installation costs* 安装费 ◇ *Installation of the new system will take several days.* 新系统的安装需要几天时间。**2** [C] a piece of equipment or machinery that has been fixed in position so that it can be used 安装的设备（或机器）：*a heating installation* 供暖装置 **3** [C] a place where specialist equipment is kept and used 设施：*a military installation* 军事设施 **4** [U] the act of placing sb in a new position of authority, often with a ceremony 就职；就职仪式：*the installation of the new vice chancellor* 新任校长的就职 **5** [C] (*art* 美术) a piece of modern SCULPTURE that is made using sound, light, etc. as well as objects 现代雕塑装置（除物体外用声、光等元素）

in'stallment plan (*NAmE*) (*BrE* ˌ**hire 'purchase**) *noun* [U, C] a method of buying an article by making regular payments for it over several months or years. The article only belongs to the person who is buying it when all the payments have been made. 分期付款购买 ➲ COMPARE CREDIT *n.* (1)

in·stal·ment (*especially BrE*) (*NAmE usually* **in·stall·ment**) /ɪnˈstɔːlmənt/ *noun* **1** one of a number of payments that are made regularly over a period of time until sth has been paid for （分期付款的）一期付款：*We paid for the car* ***by/in instalments.*** 我们以分期付款买了这辆车。◇ *The final instalment on the loan is due next week.* 贷款的最后一期付款下个星期到期。◇ *They were unable to keep up* (= continue to pay regularly) *the instalments.* 他们未能继续按时交付这笔分期付款。➲ SYNONYMS AT PAYMENT ➲ COLLOCATIONS AT FINANCE **2** one of the parts of a story that appears regularly over a period of time in a newspaper, on television, etc. （报章连载小说的）一节；（电视连续剧的）一集 **SYN episode**

in·stance **AW** /ˈɪnstəns/ *noun, verb*

■ ***noun*** a particular example or case of sth 例子；事例；实例：*The report highlights a number of instances of injustice.* 这篇报道重点列举了一些不公正的实例。◇ *In most instances, there will be no need for further treatment.* 多数情况下，不必继续治疗。◇ *I would normally suggest taking time off work, but* ***in this instance*** *I'm not sure that would do any good.* 我通常会建议休假，但就这个情况而言，我不敢保证休假会有什么好处。➲ SYNONYMS AT EXAMPLE

IDM **for 'instance** for example 例如；比如：*What would you do, for instance, if you found a member of staff stealing?* 比如说，如果你发现有职员偷东西，你会怎么办？➲ LANGUAGE BANK AT E.G. **in the 'first instance** (*formal*) as the first part of a series of actions 第一；首先：*In the first instance, notify the police and then contact your insurance company.* 首先是报警，然后与你的保险公司联系。

■ ***verb*** **~ sth** (*formal*) to give sth as an example 举…为例

in·stant /ˈɪnstənt/ *adj., noun*

■ ***adj.*** **1** [usually before noun] happening immediately 立即的；立刻的 **SYN immediate**：*She took an instant dislike to me.* 她立刻对我产生了反感。◇ *This account gives you instant access to your money.* 这个账户让你随时调动款项。◇ *The show was an instant success.* 演出一炮打响。**2** [only before noun] (of food 食物) that can be made quickly and easily, usually by adding hot water 速食的；即食的；速溶的；方便的：*instant coffee* 速溶咖啡

■ ***noun*** [usually sing.] **1** a very short period of time 瞬间；片刻 **SYN moment**：*I'll be back in an instant.* 我马上就回来。◇ *Just for an instant I thought he was going to refuse.* 刹那间我以为他会拒绝。**2** a particular point in time 某一时刻：*At that* (*very*) *instant, the door opened.* 就在那时，门开了。◇ *I recognized her* ***the instant*** (***that***) (= as soon as) *I saw her.* 我一眼就认出她了。◇ *Come here* ***this instant!*** (= immediately) 马上过来！

in·stant·an·eous /ˌɪnstənˈteɪniəs/ *adj.* happening immediately 立即的；立刻的；瞬间的：*an instantaneous response* 即时的反应 ◇ *Death was almost instantaneous.* 当时生命垂危。▶ **in·stant·an·eous·ly** *adv.*

in·stant·ly /ˈɪnstəntli/ *adv.* immediately 立刻；立即；马上：*Her voice is instantly recognizable.* 她的声音一下子就听出来了。◇ *The driver was killed instantly.* 司机当场死亡。

ˌ**instant 'messaging** *noun* [U] a system on the Internet that allows people to exchange written messages with each other very quickly 即时通信（互联网的快捷信息传递系统）▶ ˌ**instant 'message** (*also* **IM**) *noun* [C, U]：*to send an instant message* 发送即时消息 ◇ *Word spreads by email and instant message.* 消息通过电子邮件和即时通信广为传播。ˌ**instant-'message** (*also* **IM**) *verb* [T, I]：*She* *spent the most of the evening instant-messaging.* 她把晚上的大部分时间都花在了即时通信上。◇ **~ sb** *He instant-messaged me last night.* 他昨晚给我发了即时消息。◇ **~ sb sth** *Can you instant-message me the news?* 你把那条消息即时发送给我好吗？

ˌinstant ˈreplay (*NAmE*) (*BrE* **ˌaction ˈreplay**) *noun* part of sth, for example a sports game on television, that is immediately repeated, often more slowly, so that you can see a goal or another exciting or important moment again （体育比赛等电视画面的）即时重放，慢镜头回放

in·stead /ɪnˈsted/ *adv.* in the place of sb/sth 代替；顶替；反而；却： *Lee was ill so I went instead.* 李病了，所以我代他去了。◇ *He didn't reply. Instead, he turned on his heel and left the room.* 他没有回答，反而转身离开了房间。◇ *She said nothing, preferring instead to save her comments till later.* 她什么也没说，而是想稍后再作评论。

inˈstead of *prep.* in the place of sb/sth 代替；作为…的替换： *We just had soup instead of a full meal.* 我们没有吃全餐，只喝了汤。◇ *Now I can walk to work instead of going by car.* 现在我可以步行去上班，而不必开车了。

in·step /ˈɪnstep/ *noun* **1** the top part of the foot between the ankle and toes 足背 ➲ VISUAL VOCAB PAGE V64 **2** the part of a shoe that covers the instep 鞋面

in·sti·gate /ˈɪnstɪɡeɪt/ *verb* (*formal*) **1 ~ sth** (*especially BrE*) to make sth start or happen, usually sth official 使（正式）开始；使发生 SYN **bring sth↔about**: *The government has instigated a programme of economic reform.* 政府已实施了经济改革方案。 **2 ~ sth** to cause sth bad to happen 煽动；唆使；鼓动： *They were accused of instigating racial violence.* 他们被控煽动种族暴力。

in·sti·ga·tion /ˌɪnstɪˈɡeɪʃn/ *noun* [U] the act of causing sth to begin or happen 发起；唆使；煽动： *An appeal fund was launched **at the instigation of** the President.* 总统授意发起了一项救援基金。◇ *It was done **at his instigation**.* 那件事是在他的鼓动下干的。

in·sti·ga·tor /ˈɪnstɪɡeɪtə(r)/ *noun* **~ (of sth)** a person who causes sth to happen, especially sth bad 发起人；（尤指）唆使者，煽动者，怂恿者： *the instigators of the riots* 煽动骚乱的人

in·stil (*BrE*) (*NAmE* **in·still**) /ɪnˈstɪl/ *verb* (**-ll-**) **~ sth (in/into sb)** to gradually make sb feel, think or behave in a particular way over a period of time 逐渐灌输，逐步培养（感受、思想或行为）： *to **instil confidence/discipline/fear into sb*** 逐步使某人树立信心 / 守纪律 / 产生恐惧

in·stinct /ˈɪnstɪŋkt/ *noun* [U, C] **1 ~ (for sth/for doing sth)** | **~ (to do sth)** a natural tendency for people and animals to behave in a particular way using the knowledge and abilities that they were born with rather than thought or training 本能；天性： *maternal instincts* 母性 ◇ *Children do not know **by instinct** the difference between right and wrong.* 儿童并非生来就会分辨是非。◇ *His first instinct was to run away.* 他的本能反应就是逃跑。◇ *Horses have a well-developed instinct for fear.* 马天性易受惊吓。◇ *Even at school, he showed he **had an instinct for*** (= was naturally good at) *business.* 他早在求学时期就表现出经商的天赋。 **2 ~ (that…)** a feeling that makes you do sth or believe that sth is true, even though it is not based on facts or reason 直觉 SYN **intuition**: *Her instincts had been right.* 她当时的直觉是对的。

in·stinct·ive /ɪnˈstɪŋktɪv/ *adj.* based on instinct, not thought or training 本能的；直觉的；天生的： *instinctive knowledge* 本能的知识 ◇ *She's an instinctive player.* 她是个天生的运动员。◇ *My instinctive reaction was to deny everything.* 我的本能反应是否认一切。 ▶ **in·stinct·ive·ly** *adv.*: *He knew instinctively that something was wrong.* 他凭直觉知道出事了。

in·stinct·ual /ɪnˈstɪŋktʃuəl/ *adj.* (*psychology* 心) based on natural instinct; not learned 本能（而非习得）的

in·sti·tute AW /ˈɪnstɪtjuːt; *NAmE* -tuːt/ *noun, verb*

■ ***noun*** an organization that has a particular purpose, especially one that is connected with education or a particular profession; the building used by this organization（教育、专业等）机构，机构建筑： *a research institute* 研究所 ◇ *the Institute of Chartered Accountants* （英国皇家）特许会计师协会 ◇ *institutes of higher education* 高等学校

■ ***verb* ~ sth** (*formal*) to introduce a system, policy, etc. or start a process 建立，制定（体系、政策等）；开始；实行： *to institute criminal proceedings against sb* 对某人提起刑事诉讼 ◇ *The new management intends to institute a number of changes.* 新任管理层打算实行一些改革。

in·sti·tu·tion AW /ˌɪnstɪˈtjuːʃn; *NAmE* -ˈtuːʃn/ *noun* **1** [C] a large important organization that has a particular purpose, for example, a university or bank （大学、银行等规模大的）机构： *an **educational/financial, etc. institution*** 教育、金融等机构 ◇ *the Smithsonian Institution* 史密森学会 **2** [C] (*usually disapproving*) a building where people with special needs are taken care of, for example because they are old or mentally ill 慈善机构；社会福利机构： *a mental institution* 精神病院 ◇ *We want this to be like a home, not an institution.* 我们希望这里像个家，而不像收容所。 **3** [C] a custom or system that has existed for a long time among a particular group of people （由来已久的）风俗习惯，制度： *the institution of marriage* 婚姻制度 **4** [U] the act of starting or introducing sth such as a system or a law 建立；设立；制定： *the institution of new safety procedures* 新安全规程的制定 **5** [C] (*informal, humorous*) a person who is well known because they have been in a particular place or job for a long time （某地或某工作领域）出名的人： *You must know him—he's an institution around here!* 你一定认识他，他是这一带的知名人物！

in·sti·tu·tion·al AW /ˌɪnstɪˈtjuːʃənl; *NAmE* -ˈtuː-/ *adj.* [usually before noun] connected with an institution 机构的；慈善机构的： *institutional investors* 机构投资者 ◇ *institutional care* 慈善机构的照顾 ▶ **in·sti·tu·tion·ally** AW /-ʃənəli/ *adv.*

in·sti·tu·tion·al·ize AW (*BrE also* **-ise**) /ˌɪnstɪˈtjuːʃənəlaɪz; *NAmE* -ˈtuː-/ *verb* **1 ~ sb** to send sb who is not capable of living independently to live in a special building (= an institution) especially when it is for a long period of time 将（生活不能自理的人）送到收容机构（或社会福利机构） **2 ~ sth** to make sth become part of an organized system, society or culture, so that it is considered normal 使成惯例；使制度化 ▶ **in·sti·tu·tion·al·iza·tion, -isa·tion** /ˌɪnstɪˌtjuːʃənəlaɪˈzeɪʃn; *NAmE* -ˌtuːʃənələˈz-/ *noun* [U]

in·sti·tu·tion·al·ized AW (*BrE also* **-ised**) /ˌɪnstɪˈtjuːʃənəlaɪzd; *NAmE* -ˈtuː-/ *adj.* **1** (*usually disapproving*) that has happened or been done for so long that it is considered normal 约定俗成的；成惯例的： *institutionalized racism* 由来已久的种族偏见 **2** (of people 人) lacking the ability to live and think independently because they have spent so long in an institution （因长期生活在福利机构）缺乏自理能力的： *institutionalized patients* 失去自理能力的病人

ˌin-ˈstore *adj.* [only before noun] within a large shop/store 大商店内的；大商店所属的： *an in-store bakery* 设在大商店里的面包店

in·struct AW /ɪnˈstrʌkt/ *verb* **1** (*formal*) to tell sb to do sth, especially in a formal or official way 指示；命令；吩咐 SYN **direct, order**: **~ sb to do sth** *The letter instructed him to report to headquarters immediately.* 那封信指示他立即向总部汇报。◇ **~ sb where, what, etc.…** *You will be instructed where to go as soon as the plane is ready.* 飞机一准备好就会通知你去何处。◇ **~ sb** *She arrived at 10 o'clock **as instructed**.* 她依照指示于 10 点钟到达。◇ **~ that…** *He instructed that a wall be built around the city.* 他下令在城的周围筑一道城墙。◇ (*BrE also*) *He instructed*

I

that a wall should be built around the city. 他下令在城的周围筑一道城墙。◇ ~ (sb) + speech 'Put it there,' she instructed (them). "把它放在那儿。"她吩咐（他们）道。➲ SYNONYMS AT ORDER **2** ~ sb (in sth) (formal) to teach sb sth, especially a practical skill 教授，传授（技能等）: All our staff have been instructed in sign language. 我们的员工都接受过手语训练。**3** [usually passive] ~ sb that... (formal) to give sb information about sth 告知；通知: We have been instructed that a decision will not be made before the end of the week. 我们已获悉周末前不会作出决定。**4** ~ sb (to do sth) (law 律) to employ sb to represent you in a legal situation, especially as a lawyer 委托（律师）；托办

in·struc·tion 🔑 AW /ɪnˈstrʌkʃn/ noun, adj.
■ **noun 1** 🔑 **instructions** [pl.] detailed information on how to do or use sth 用法说明；操作指南 SYN **direction**: *Follow the instructions on the packet carefully.* 仔细按照包装上的说明操作。◇ *Always read the instructions before you start.* 使用前务请阅读操作说明。◇ ~ **on how to do sth** *The plant comes with full instructions on how to care for it.* 这棵植物附有详尽的护养说明。**2** 🔑 [C, usually pl.] ~ (to do sth) | ~ (that...) something that sb tells you to do 指示；命令；吩咐 SYN **order**: *to ignore/carry out sb's instructions* 忽视 / 执行某人的命令 ◇ *I'm under instructions to keep my speech short.* 我接到指示讲话要简短。**3** [C] a piece of information that tells a computer to perform a particular operation. （计算机的）指令 **4** [U] ~ (in sth) (formal) the act of teaching sth to sb 教授；教导；传授: *religious instruction* 教义讲授
■ **adj.** [only before noun] giving detailed information on how to do or use sth (= giving instructions) 说明用法的；操作指南的: *an instruction book/manual* 说明书；用法指南

in·struc·tion·al /ɪnˈstrʌkʃənl/ adj. [usually before noun] (formal) that teaches people sth 教学的；教育的: *instructional materials* 教材

in·struct·ive AW /ɪnˈstrʌktɪv/ adj. giving a lot of useful information 富有教益的；增长知识的: *a most instructive experience* 获益良多的经历 ◇ *It is instructive to see how other countries are tackling the problem.* 了解别的国家如何处理这个问题是具有启发性的。▶ **in·struct·ive·ly** adv.

in·struct·or AW /ɪnˈstrʌktə(r)/ noun **1** a person whose job is to teach sb a practical skill or sport 教练；导师: *a driving instructor* 驾驶教练 **2** (NAmE) a teacher below the rank of ASSISTANT PROFESSOR at a college or university （大学）讲师

in·stru·ment 🔑 /ˈɪnstrəmənt/ noun **1** 🔑 a tool or device used for a particular task, especially for delicate or scientific work 器械；仪器；器具: *surgical/optical/precision, etc. instruments* 外科器械；光学、精密等仪器 ◇ *instruments of torture* 刑具 **2** 🔑 = MUSICAL INSTRUMENT: *Is he learning an instrument?* 他在学习演奏乐器吗？◇ *brass/stringed, etc. instruments* 铜管乐器、弦乐器等 **3** 🔑 a device used for measuring speed, distance, temperature, etc. in a vehicle or on a piece of machinery （车辆、机器的）仪器，仪表: *the flight instruments* 飞行仪表 ◇ *the instrument panel* 仪表盘 **4** (formal) something that is used by sb in order to achieve sth; a person or thing that makes sth happen 促成某事的人（或事物）；手段: ~ **for sth/for doing sth** *The law is not the best instrument for dealing with family matters.* 法律并不是处理家庭问题的最佳方法。◇ ~ **of sth** *an instrument of change* 促成变革的措施 **5** ~ of sb/sth (formal) a person who is used and controlled by sb/sth that is more powerful 受利用（或控制）的人；工具: *an instrument of fate* 受命运摆布的人 **6** (law 律) a formal legal document 文据；正式法律文件

in·stru·men·tal /ˌɪnstrəˈmentl/ adj., noun
■ **adj. 1** ~ (in sth/in doing sth) important in making sth happen 起重要作用: *He was instrumental in bringing about an end to the conflict.* 他在终止冲突的过程中起了重要作用。**2** made by or for musical instruments 用乐器演奏的；为乐器谱写的: *instrumental music* 器乐曲 ▶ **in·stru·men·tal·ly** adv.
■ **noun 1** a piece of music (usually popular music) in which only musical instruments are used with no singing 器乐曲 **2** (grammar 语法) (in some languages 用于某些语言) the form of a noun, pronoun or adjective when it refers to a thing that is used to do sth 工具格；工具词

in·stru·men·tal·ist /ˌɪnstrəˈmentəlɪst/ noun a person who plays a musical instrument 乐器演奏者 ➲ COMPARE VOCALIST

in·stru·men·ta·tion /ˌɪnstrəmenˈteɪʃn/ noun [U] **1** a set of instruments used in operating a vehicle or a piece of machinery （一套）仪器，仪表 **2** the way in which a piece of music is written for a particular group of instruments 器乐谱写

in·sub·or·din·ation /ˌɪnsəˌbɔːdɪˈneɪʃn; NAmE -ˌbɔːrd-/ noun [U] (formal) the refusal to obey orders or show respect for sb who has a higher rank 不服从命令；抗命；犯上 SYN **disobedience** ▶ **in·sub·or·din·ate** /ˌɪnsəˈbɔːdɪnət; NAmE -ˈbɔːrd-/ adj.

in·sub·stan·tial /ˌɪnsəbˈstænʃl/ adj. **1** not very large, strong or important 不大的；不坚固的；不重要的: *an insubstantial construction of wood and glue* 用木头和胶黏合的简单构造 ◇ *an insubstantial argument* 不充实的论据 **2** (literary) not real or solid 非真实的；非实体的；虚幻的: *as insubstantial as a shadow* 虚无缥缈

in·suf·fer·able /ɪnˈsʌfrəbl/ adj. extremely annoying, unpleasant and difficult to bear 难以忍受的；难以容忍的 SYN **unbearable** ▶ **in·suf·fer·ably** /-əbli/ adv.: *insufferably hot* 酷热难当

in·suf·fi·cient AW /ˌɪnsəˈfɪʃnt/ adj. ~ (to do sth) | ~ (for sth) (formal) not large, strong or important enough for a particular purpose 不充分的；不足的；不够重要的 SYN **inadequate**: *insufficient time* 时间不够 ◇ *His salary is insufficient to meet his needs.* 他的薪水不够应付需要。OPP **sufficient** ▶ **in·suf·fi·cient·ly** AW adv. **in·suf·fi·ciency** /-ʃənsi/ noun [U, sing.] (specialist): *cardiac insufficiency* 心功能不全

in·su·lar /ˈɪnsjələ(r); NAmE ˈɪnsələr/ adj. **1** (disapproving) only interested in your own country, ideas, etc. and not in those from outside 只关心本国利益的；思想褊狭的；保守的: *The British are often accused of being insular.* 英国人常被指责为思想褊狭。**2** (specialist) connected with an island or islands 海岛的；岛屿的: *the coastal and insular areas* 沿海和岛屿区域 ▶ **in·su·lar·ity** /ˌɪnsjuˈlærəti; NAmE -səˈl-/ noun [U]

in·su·late /ˈɪnsjuleɪt; NAmE -səl-/ verb **1** ~ sth (from/against sth) to protect sth with a material that prevents heat, sound, electricity, etc. from passing through 使隔热；使隔音；使绝缘: *Home owners are being encouraged to insulate their homes to save energy.* 当局鼓励房主在住房加隔热装置以节约能源。➲ WORDFINDER NOTE AT ELECTRICITY ➲ COLLOCATIONS AT DECORATE **2** ~ sb/sth from/against sth to protect sb/sth from unpleasant experiences or influences 使免除（不愉快的经历）；使免受（不良影响）；隔离 SYN **shield**

in·su·lated /ˈɪnsjuleɪtɪd; NAmE -səl-/ adj. protected with a material that prevents heat, sound, electricity, etc. from passing through 有隔热（或隔音、绝缘）保护的: *insulated wires* 绝缘线 ◇ *a well-insulated house* 隔热性能好的房子

in·su·lat·ing /ˈɪnsjuleɪtɪŋ; NAmE ˈɪnsəleɪtɪŋ/ adj. [only before noun] preventing heat, sound, electricity, etc. from passing through 起隔热（或隔音、绝缘）作用的: *insulating materials* 绝缘材料

ˈ**insulating tape** (US also ˈ**friction tape**) noun [U] a strip of sticky material used for covering the ends of electrical wires to prevent the possibility of an electric shock 绝缘胶带；电线胶布

in·su·la·tion /ˌɪnsjuˈleɪʃn; NAmE -səˈl-/ noun [U] the act of protecting sth with a material that prevents heat, sound, electricity, etc. from passing through; the materials used for this 隔热；隔音；绝缘；隔热（或隔音、绝缘）材料：*Better insulation of your home will help to reduce heating bills.* 加强房子的隔热性能有助于减少供暖费用。◇ *foam insulation* 泡沫绝缘材料 ➲ COLLOCATIONS AT DECORATE

in·su·la·tor /ˈɪnsjuleɪtə(r); *NAmE* -səl-/ *noun* a material or device used to prevent heat, electricity, or sound from escaping from sth 隔热（或绝缘、隔音等的）材料（或装置）

in·su·lin /ˈɪnsjəlɪn; *NAmE* -səl-/ *noun* [U] a chemical substance produced in the body that controls the amount of sugar in the blood (by influencing the rate at which it is removed); a similar artificial substance given to people whose bodies do not produce enough naturally 胰岛素：*insulin-dependent diabetes* 胰岛素依赖型糖尿病

in·sult *verb, noun*

■ ***verb*** /ɪnˈsʌlt/ **~ sb/sth** to say or do sth that offends sb 辱骂；侮辱；冒犯：*I have never been so insulted in my life!* 我一生中从未被如此侮辱过！◇ *She felt insulted by the low offer.* 那么低的出价使她觉得受到了侮辱。

■ ***noun*** /ˈɪnsʌlt/ a remark or an action that is said or done in order to offend sb 辱骂；侮辱；冒犯：*The crowd were shouting insults at the police.* 人群大声辱骂着警察。◇ **~ to sb/sth** *His comments were seen as an insult to the president.* 他的评论被看成是对主席的冒犯。◇ *The questions were an* ***insult to our intelligence*** (= too easy). 那些问题（简单得）有辱我们的智慧。IDM SEE ADD

in·sult·ing /ɪnˈsʌltɪŋ/ *adj.* causing or intending to cause sb to feel offended 侮辱的；有冒犯性的；无礼的：*insulting remarks* 侮辱性的话语 ◇ **~ to sb/sth** *She was really insulting to me.* 她对我实在粗鲁无礼。

in·super·able /ɪnˈsuːpərəbl; *BrE also* -ˈsjuː-/ *adj.* (*formal*) (of difficulties, problems, etc. 困难、问题等) that cannot be dealt with successfully 无法克服的；难以解决的；不可逾越的 SYN **insurmountable**

in·sup·port·able /ˌɪnsəˈpɔːtəbl; *NAmE* -ˈpɔːrt-/ *adj.* so bad or difficult that you cannot accept it or deal with it 难以接受的；棘手的 SYN **intolerable**

in·sur·ance /ɪnˈʃʊərəns; -ˈʃɔːr-; *NAmE* -ˈʃʊr-/ *noun* **1** [U, C] an arrangement with a company in which you pay them regular amounts of money and they agree to pay the costs, for example, if you die or are ill/sick, or if you lose or damage sth 保险：***life/car/travel/household, etc. insurance*** 人寿、汽车、旅行平安、家庭财产等保险 ◇ *to have adequate* ***insurance cover*** 有足够的保险保障 ◇ **~ (against sth)** *to* ***take out insurance*** *against fire and theft* 办理火险和盗窃保险 ◇ ***insurance premiums*** (= the regular payments made for insurance) 保险费 ◇ *Can you claim for the loss* ***on your insurance****?* 你能向你投保的公司要求赔偿这一损失吗？➲ SEE ALSO NATIONAL INSURANCE **2** [U] the business of providing people with insurance 保险业：*an* ***insurance broker/company*** 保险经纪 / 公司 ◇ *He works in insurance.* 他在保险业工作。**3** [U] money paid by or to an insurance company 保险费；保费：*to pay insurance on your house* 交住房保险金 ◇ *When her husband died, she received £50 000 in insurance.* 她丈夫去世，她得到了一笔 5 万英镑的保险金。**4** [U, C] **~ (against sth)** something you do to protect yourself against sth bad happening in the future（防备不测的）保障措施，安全保证：*At that time people had large families as an insurance against some children dying.* 那时人们养的子女很多，以防有孩子夭折。

> **WORDFINDER** 联想词：actuary, annuity, cover, excess, no-claims bonus, policy, premium, risk, underwrite

inˈsurance adjuster (*NAmE*) (*BrE* **ˈloss adjuster**) *noun* a person who works for an insurance company and whose job is to calculate how much money sb should receive after they have lost sth or had sth damaged（保险公司的）险损估价师，损失理算人，理赔员

inˈsurance policy *noun* a written contract between a person and an insurance company 保险单：*a travel insurance policy* 旅行保险单 ◇ (*figurative*) *Always make a backup disk as an insurance policy.* 为保险起见，每次都要做备份磁盘。

in·sure /ɪnˈʃʊə(r); ɪnˈʃɔː(r); *NAmE* -ˈʃʊr/ *verb* **1** [T, I] to buy insurance so that you will receive money if your property, car, etc. gets damaged or stolen, or if you get ill/sick or die 投保；给…保险：**~ sth/yourself (for sth)** *The painting is insured for $1 million.* 这幅油画投了100万美元的保险。◇ **~ sth/yourself (against sth)** *Luckily he had insured himself against long-term illness.* 幸运的是，他为自己投保了长期病险。◇ (*figurative*) *Having a lot of children is a way of insuring themselves against loneliness in old age.* 养很多孩子是他们预防老年孤寂的一种办法。◇ **~ against sth** *We strongly recommend insuring against sickness or injury.* 我们强烈建议投伤病保险。**2** [T] **~ sb/sth** to sell insurance to sb for sth 接受投保；承保：*The company can refuse to insure a property that does not have window locks.* 保险公司可以拒绝为没有窗锁的房产提供保险。**3** (*especially NAmE*) = ENSURE

in·sured /ɪnˈʃʊəd; -ˈʃɔːd; *NAmE* -ˈʃʊrd/ *adj.* **1** having insurance 被保险的：*Was the vehicle insured?* 那辆车上保险了吗？◇ **~ to do sth** *You're not insured to drive our car.* 你开我们的车不在保险范围内。◇ **~ against sth** *It isn't insured against theft.* 它没有买盗窃险。**2 the insured** *noun* (*pl.* **the insured**) (*law* 律) the person who has made an agreement with an insurance company and who receives money if, for example, they are ill/sick or if they lose or damage sth 被保险人

in·surer /ɪnˈʃʊərə(r); -ˈʃɔːr-; *NAmE* -ˈʃʊr-/ *noun* a person or company that provides people with insurance 承保人；保险公司

in·sur·gency /ɪnˈsɜːdʒənsi; *NAmE* -ˈsɜːrdʒ-/ *noun* [U, C] (*pl.* **-ies**) an attempt to take control of a country by force 起义；叛乱；造反 SYN **rebellion** ➲ COLLOCATIONS AT WAR ➲ SEE ALSO COUNTER-INSURGENCY

in·sur·gent /ɪnˈsɜːdʒənt; *NAmE* -ˈsɜːrdʒ-/ *noun* [usually pl.] (*formal*) a person fighting against the government or armed forces of their own country 起义者；叛乱者；造反者 SYN **rebel** ▸ **in·sur·gent** *adj.* SYN **rebellious**

in·sur·mount·able /ˌɪnsəˈmaʊntəbl; *NAmE* -sərˈm-/ *adj.* (*formal*) (of difficulties, problems, etc. 困难、问题等) that cannot be dealt with successfully 无法克服的；难以解决的；不可逾越的 SYN **insuperable**

in·sur·rec·tion /ˌɪnsəˈrekʃn/ *noun* [C, U] a situation in which a large group of people try to take political control of their own country with violence 起义；叛乱；暴动 SYN **uprising** ▸ **in·sur·rec·tion·ary** /ˌɪnsəˈrekʃənri; *NAmE* -neri/ *adj.*

in·tact /ɪnˈtækt/ *adj.* [not usually before noun] complete and not damaged 完好无损；完整 SYN **undamaged**：*Most of the house* ***remains intact*** *even after two hundred years.* 即使过了两百年，这房子的大部分还保持完好。◇ *He emerged from the trial with his reputation intact.* 他受审获释，名誉丝毫未受损害。

in·take /ˈɪnteɪk/ *noun* **1** [U, C] the amount of food, drink, etc. that you take into your body（食物、饮料等的）摄取量，吸入量：*high fluid intake* 高流质摄取量 ◇ *to reduce your daily intake of salt* 减少每天的食盐量 **2** [C, U] the number of people who are allowed to enter a school, college, profession, etc. during a particular period（一定时期内）纳入的人数：*the annual student intake* 每年招收的新生人数 **3** [C] a place where liquid, air, etc. enters a machine（机器上的液体、空气等的）进口：***the air/fuel intake*** 进气口；加燃料口 **4** [C, usually sing.] an act of taking sth in, especially breath 吸收；吸入；（尤指）吸气：*a sharp intake of breath* 猛吸一口气

in·tan·gible /ɪnˈtændʒəbl/ *adj.* **1** that exists but that is difficult to describe, understand or measure 难以形容（或理解）的；不易度量的：*The old building had an intangible air of sadness about it.* 那座旧建筑笼罩着一种说不出的悲凉气氛。◇ *The benefits are intangible.* 好处是难以计算的。**2** (*business* 商) that does not exist as a physical thing but is still valuable to a company

无形的（指不以实体存在的公司资产）：*intangible assets/property* 无形资产 / 财产 OPP **tangible** ▶ **in·tan·gible** *noun* [usually pl.]: *intangibles such as staff morale and goodwill* 员工士气和商誉之类的无形资产

in·te·ger /ˈɪntɪdʒə(r)/ *noun* (*mathematics* 数) a whole number, such as 3 or 4 but not 3.5 整数 ➲ COMPARE FRACTION (2)

in·te·gral AW /ˈɪntɪɡrəl; ɪnˈteɡ-/ *adj.* **1** being an essential part of sth 必需的；不可或缺的：*Music is an integral part of the school's curriculum.* 音乐是这所学校的课程中基本的一环。◇ **~ to sth** *Practical experience is integral to the course.* 实践经验是这门课程不可缺少的部分。 **2** [usually before noun] included as part of sth, rather than supplied separately 作为组成部分的：*All models have an integral CD player.* 所有型号都有内置的激光唱片机。 **3** [usually before noun] having all the parts that are necessary for sth to be complete 完整的；完备的：*an integral system* 完整的系统 ▶ **in·te·gral·ly** /ˈɪntɪɡrəli; ɪnˈteɡ-/ *adv.*

I

ˌintegral ˈcalculus *noun* [U] (*mathematics* 数) a type of mathematics that deals with quantities that change in time. It is used to calculate a quantity between two particular moments. 积分学 ➲ COMPARE DIFFERENTIAL CALCULUS

in·te·grate AW /ˈɪntɪɡreɪt/ *verb* **1** [I, T] to combine two or more things so that they work together; to combine with sth else in this way （使）合并，成为一体：**~ into/with sth** *These programs will integrate with your existing software.* 这些程序会和你原有的软件整合起来。◇ **~ A (into/with B) | ~ A and B** *These programs can be integrated with your existing software.* 这些程序能和你原有的软件整合起来。 **2** [I, T] to become or make sb become accepted as a member of a social group, especially when they come from a different culture （使）加入，融入群体：**~ (into/with sth)** *They have not made any effort to integrate with the local community.* 他们完全没有尝试融入本地社区。◇ **~ sb (into/with sth)** *The policy is to integrate children with special needs into ordinary schools.* 这项政策旨在使有特殊需要的儿童融入普通学校。 ➲ COMPARE SEGREGATE

in·te·grated AW /ˈɪntɪɡreɪtɪd/ *adj.* [usually before noun] in which many different parts are closely connected and work successfully together 各部分密切协调的；综合的；完整统一的：*an integrated transport system* (= including buses, trains, taxis, etc.) 综合联运体系 ◇ *an integrated school* (= attended by students of all races and religions) 混合学校（招收不同种族和宗教信仰的学生）

ˌintegrated ˈcircuit *noun* (*physics* 物) a small MICROCHIP that contains a large number of electrical connections and performs the same function as a larger CIRCUIT made from separate parts 集成电路

in·te·gra·tion AW /ˌɪntɪˈɡreɪʃn/ *noun* **1** [U, C] the act or process of combining two or more things so that they work together 结合；整合；一体化：*The aim is to promote closer economic integration.* 目的是进一步促进经济一体化。◇ *His music is an integration of tradition and new technology.* 他的音乐结合了传统和新技术。 **2** [U] the act or process of mixing people who have previously been separated, usually because of colour, race, religion, etc. （不同肤色、种族、宗教信仰等的人的）混合，融合：*racial integration in schools* 学校招收不同种族的学生 ➲ COLLOCATIONS AT RACE

in·teg·rity AW /ɪnˈteɡrəti/ *noun* [U] **1** the quality of being honest and having strong moral principles 诚实正直：***personal/professional/artistic integrity*** 个人的 / 职业上的 / 艺术家的诚实正直 ◇ *to behave with integrity* 行为表现诚实正直 **2** (*formal*) the state of being whole and not divided 完整；完好 SYN **unity**：*to respect the territorial integrity of the nation* 尊重该国的领土完整

in·tel·lect /ˈɪntəlekt/ *noun* **1** [U, C] the ability to think in a logical way and understand things, especially at an advanced level; your mind （尤指高等的）智力，逻辑思维领悟力：*a man of considerable intellect* 相当有才智的人 **2** [C] a very intelligent person 智力高的人；才智超群的人：*She was one of the most formidable intellects of her time.* 她是当时的一名盖世英才。

in·tel·lec·tual /ˌɪntəˈlektʃuəl/ *adj., noun*

■ ***adj.*** **1** [usually before noun] connected with or using a person's ability to think in a logical way and understand things 智力的；脑力的；理智的 SYN **mental**：*intellectual curiosity* 求知欲 ◇ *an intellectual novel* 推理小说 **2** (of a person 人) well educated and enjoying activities in which you have to think seriously about things 有才智的；智力发达的：*She's very intellectual.* 她很聪慧。 ▶ **in·tel·lec·tual·ism** /ˌɪntəˈlektʃuəlɪzəm/ *noun* [U] (*usually disapproving*) **in·tel·lec·tu·al·ly** *adv.*：*intellectually challenging* 考验智慧的

■ ***noun*** a person who is well educated and enjoys activities in which they have to think seriously about things 知识分子；脑力劳动者

inˌtellectual ˈproperty *noun* [U] (*law* 律) an idea, a design, etc. that sb has created and that the law prevents other people from copying 知识财产：*intellectual property rights* 知识产权

in·tel·li·gence 🔑 AW /ɪnˈtelɪdʒəns/ *noun* [U] **1** 🔑 the ability to learn, understand and think in a logical way about things; the ability to do this well 智力；才智；智慧：*a person of* ***high/average/low intelligence*** 智力高的 / 一般的 / 低下的人 ◇ *He didn't even have the intelligence to call for an ambulance.* 他连呼叫救护车的头脑都没有。

▼ **SYNONYMS** 同义词辨析

intelligent

smart • clever • brilliant • bright

These words all describe people who are good at learning, understanding and thinking about things, and the actions that show this ability. 以上各词均形容人有才智、悟性强、聪明。

intelligent good at learning, understanding and thinking in a logical way about things; showing this ability 指有才智的、悟性强的、聪明的：*He's a* ***highly intelligent*** *man.* 他是一个很有才智的人。◇ *She asked a lot of intelligent questions.* 她问了许多机智的问题。

smart (*especially NAmE*) quick at learning and understanding things; showing the ability to make good business or personal decisions 指聪明的、机敏的、精明的：*She's smarter than her brother.* 她比她哥哥聪明。◇ *That was a smart career move.* 那是个人事业发展上的明智之举。

clever (*sometimes disapproving, especially BrE*) quick at learning and understanding things; showing this ability 指聪明的、聪颖的：*How clever of you to work it out!* 你解决了这个问题真是太聪明了。◇ *He's* ***too clever by half****, if you ask me.* 恕我直言，他未免聪明过头了。 **NOTE** People use **clever** in the phrase *Clever boy/girl!* to tell a young child that they have learnt or done sth well. When used to or about an adult **clever** can be disapproving. * clever 用于短语 Clever boy/girl!（多么聪颖的男孩 / 女孩！）表示孩子学习悟性强、做事聪明伶俐。clever 用于成年人可能含贬义。

brilliant extremely intelligent or skilful 指聪颖的、技艺高的：*He's a brilliant young scientist.* 他是一个才华横溢的青年科学家。

bright intelligent; quick to learn 指聪明的、悟性强的：*She's probably the brightest student in the class.* 她大概是班里最聪明的学生。 **NOTE** **Bright** is used especially to talk about young people. Common collocations of **bright** include *girl, boy, kid, student, pupil.* * bright 主要用于年轻人，常与之搭配的词有 girl、boy、kid、student、pupil 等。

PATTERNS

- clever/brilliant **at** sth
- a(n) intelligent/smart/clever/brilliant/bright **child/boy/girl/man/woman**
- a(n) intelligent/smart/clever/brilliant **thing to do**

➲ SEE ALSO ARTIFICIAL INTELLIGENCE, EMOTIONAL INTELLIGENCE **2** 🔑 secret information that is collected, for example about a foreign country, especially one that is an enemy; the people that collect this information（尤指关于敌国的）情报；情报人员： *intelligence reports* 情报人员的报告 ◇ *the US Central Intelligence Agency* 美国中央情报局

in'telligence quotient *noun* = IQ

in'telligence test *noun* a test to measure how well a person is able to understand and think in a logical way about things 智力测验

in·tel·li·gent 🔑 AW /ɪn'telɪdʒənt/ *adj.* **1** 🔑 good at learning, understanding and thinking in a logical way about things; showing this ability 有才智的；悟性强的；聪明的： *a* ***highly intelligent*** *child* 非常聪明的孩子 ◇ *to ask an intelligent question* 问一个机智的问题 OPP **unintelligent** **2** 🔑 (of an animal, a being, etc. 动物、生物等) able to understand and learn things 有智力的；有理解和学习能力的： *a search for intelligent life on other planets* 在其他行星上探索有智力的生命 **3** (*computing* 计) (of a computer, program, etc. 计算机、程序等) able to store information and use it in new situations 智能的： ***intelligent software/systems*** 智能软件 / 系统 ▶ **in·tel·li·gent·ly** AW *adv.*

in,telligent de'sign *noun* [U] the belief that the universe and living things were created by an intelligent being 智创论，智能设计论，智慧设计论（相信宇宙及生物是智能创造的结果）： *the legal battle about the teaching of intelligent design as science* 围绕将智创论作为科学进行教授的法律战 ➲ COMPARE CREATIONISM

in·tel·li·gent·sia /ɪn,telɪ'dʒentsiə/ (*usually* **the intelligentsia**) *noun* [sing.+sing./pl. v.] the people in a country or society who are well educated and are interested in culture, politics, literature, etc. 知识界；知识阶层

in·tel·li·gible /ɪn'telɪdʒəbl/ *adj.* ~ **(to sb)** that can be easily understood 易懂的；容易理解的 SYN **understandable**: *His lecture was readily intelligible to all the students.* 他的讲课学生们都能轻松地听懂。 OPP **unintelligible** ▶ **in·tel·li·gi·bil·ity** /ɪn,telɪdʒə'bɪləti/ *noun* [U] **in·tel·li·gibly** *adv.*

in·tem·per·ate /ɪn'tempərət/ *adj.* (*formal*) **1** showing a lack of control over yourself 放纵的；无节制的： *intemperate language* 过激的言语 OPP **temperate** **2** (*especially NAmE*) regularly drinking too much alcohol 酗酒的 ▶ **in·tem·per·ance** /-pərəns/ *noun* [U]

in·tend 🔑 /ɪn'tend/ *verb* **1** 🔑 [I, T] to have a plan, result or purpose in your mind when you do sth 打算；计划；想要： *We finished later than we had intended.* 我们完成时已超出原定时间。 ◇ ~ **to do sth** *I fully intended* (= definitely intended) *to pay for the damage.* 我确实诚心想赔偿损失。 ◇ ~ **sb/sth to do sth** *The writer clearly intends his readers to identify with the main character.* 作者显然想使读者能与主人公产生共鸣。 ◇ ~ **doing sth** (*BrE*) *I don't intend staying long.* 我不打算长期逗留。 ◇ ~ **sth** *The company intends a slow-down in expansion.* 公司准备放慢扩展速度。 ◇ ~ **sb sth** *He intended her no harm* (= it was not his plan to harm her). 他无意伤害她。 ◇ **it is intended that**… *It is intended that production will start next month.* 计划在下个月开始生产。 ◇ ~ **that**… *We intend that production will start next month.* 我们计划下个月开始生产。 ➲ **MORE LIKE THIS** 26, page R28 **2** 🔑 [T] (*rather formal*) to plan that sth should have a particular meaning 意指 SYN **mean**: ~ **sth (by sth)** *What exactly did you intend by that remark?* 你那句话到底想说什么？ ◇ ~ **sth (as sth)** *He intended it as a joke.* 他只想开个玩笑。

> **WORD FAMILY**
> **intend** *verb*
> **intended** *adj.*
> (≠ unintended)
> **intention** *noun*
> **intentional** *adj.*
> (≠ unintentional)
> **intentionally** *adv.*
> (≠ unintentionally)

in·tend·ed 🔑 /ɪn'tendɪd/ *adj.* **1** 🔑 [only before noun] that you are trying to achieve or reach 意欲达到的；打算的；计划的： *the intended purpose* 原来的目的 ◇ *the intended audience* 预期的观众 ◇ *The bullet missed its intended target.* 子弹未击中预定的目标。 **2** 🔑 planned or designed for sb/sth 为…打算（或设计）的： ~ **for sb/sth** *The book is intended for children.* 这本书是为儿童写的。 ◇ ~ **as sth** *The notes are intended as an introduction to the course.* 这些笔记的目的是作为对这门课程的介绍。 ◇ ~ **to be/do sth** *This list is not intended to be a complete catalogue.* 这张清单并非要做成一张完整的目录。 ➲ SEE ALSO UNINTENDED

in·tense AW /ɪn'tens/ *adj.* **1** very great; very strong 很大的；十分强烈的 SYN **extreme**: *intense heat/cold/pain* 酷热；严寒；剧痛 ◇ *The President is under intense pressure to resign.* 总统承受着沉重的辞职压力。 ◇ *the intense blue of her eyes* 她眼睛的深蓝色 ◇ *intense interest/pleasure/desire/anger* 浓厚的兴趣；十分快乐；强烈的欲望；极端愤怒 **2** serious and often involving a lot of action in a short period of time 严肃紧张的；激烈的： *intense competition* 激烈的竞争 ◇ *It was a period of intense activity.* 那是活动激烈的时期。 **3** (of a person 人) having or showing very strong feelings, opinions or thoughts about sb/sth 有强烈感情（或意见、想法）的；尖锐的；热切的： *an intense look* 热切的神情 ◇ *He's very intense about everything.* 他对一切都很热心。 ➲ COMPARE INTENSIVE ▶ **in·tense·ly** AW *adv.*: *She disliked him intensely.* 她非常讨厌他。

in·ten·si·fier /ɪn'tensɪfaɪə(r)/ *noun* (*grammar* 语法) a word, especially an adjective or an adverb, for example *so* or *very*, that makes the meaning of another word stronger 强调成分，强化词（尤指形容词或副词，如 so 或 very）

in·ten·sify AW /ɪn'tensɪfaɪ/ *verb* (**in·ten·si·fies**, **in·ten·si·fy·ing**, **in·ten·si·fied**, **in·ten·si·fied**) [I, T] to increase in degree or strength; to make sth increase in degree or strength（使）加强，增强，加剧 SYN **heighten**: *Violence intensified during the night.* 在夜间暴力活动加剧了。 ◇ ~ **sth** *The opposition leader has intensified his attacks on the government.* 反对派领袖加强了对政府的攻击。 ▶ **in·tensi·fi·ca·tion** AW /ɪn,tensɪfɪ'keɪʃn/ *noun* [U, sing.]

in·ten·sity AW /ɪn'tensəti/ *noun* (*pl.* **-ies**) **1** [U, sing.] the state or quality of being intense 强烈；紧张；剧烈： *intensity of light/sound/colour* 光 / 声音 / 色彩的强度 ◇ *intensity of feeling/concentration/relief* 感情的强烈；高度精神集中；大为宽慰 ◇ *He was watching her with an intensity that was unnerving.* 他用一种令她心慌的专注神情看着她。 ◇ *The storm resumed with even greater intensity.* 风暴更猛烈地再度肆虐。 **2** [U, C] (*specialist*) the strength of sth, for example light, that can be measured 强度；烈度： *varying intensities of natural light* 自然光不断变化的强度

in·ten·sive AW /ɪn'tensɪv/ *adj.* **1** involving a lot of work or activity done in a short time 短时间内集中紧张进行的；密集的： *an intensive language course* 速成语言课程 ◇ *two weeks of intensive training* 两周的强化训练 ◇ *intensive diplomatic negotiations* 紧张的外交谈判 **2** extremely thorough; done with a lot of care 彻底的；十分细致的： *His disappearance has been the subject of intensive investigation.* 他的失踪一直是大力调查的重点。 **3** (of methods of farming 农业方法) aimed at producing as much food as possible using as little land or as little money as possible 集约的： *Traditionally reared animals grow more slowly than those reared under intensive farming conditions.* 按传统方式饲养的家畜比集约饲养的长得慢。 ◇*intensive agriculture* 集约农业 ➲ SEE ALSO CAPITAL-INTENSIVE, LABOUR-INTENSIVE ▶ **in·ten·sive·ly** AW *adv.*: *This case has been intensively studied.* 这一案件已经过深入研究。 ◇ *intensively farmed land* 集约耕作的农田

in,tensive 'care *noun* [U] **1** continuous care and attention, often using special equipment, for people in hospital who are very seriously ill or injured（医院里的）特别护理；重症监护： *She needed intensive care for several days.* 她需要几天的特别护理。 ◇ *intensive care patients/beds* 特别护理病房的病人 / 床位 **2** (*also* **in,tensive 'care unit** [C]) (*abbr.* **ICU**) the part of a hospital that provides intensive care 重症监护治疗病房；特别护理病房；重症监护室： *The baby was* ***in intensive care*** *for 48 hours.* 婴儿在加护病房看护了 48 小时。

I

in·tent /ɪn'tent/ *adj., noun*

■ ***adj.*** **1** showing strong interest and attention 热切的；专注的： *an* ***intent gaze/look*** 专注的目光 / 神情 ◇ *His eyes were suddenly intent.* 他的目光突然专注起来。 **2** (*formal*) determined to do sth, especially sth that will harm other people 决心做（尤指伤害他人的事）： **~ on/upon sth** *They were intent on murder.* 他们存心谋杀。◇ **~ on/upon doing sth** *Are you intent upon destroying my reputation?* 你是不是存心要败坏我的名誉？ **3 ~ on/upon sth** giving all your attention to sth 专心；专注： *I was so intent on my work that I didn't notice the time.* 我专心工作，以致忘了时间。 ▶ **in·tent·ly** *adv.*： *She looked at him intently.* 她目不转睛地看着他。

■ ***noun*** [U] **~ (to do sth)** (*formal* or *law* 律) what you intend to do 意图；意向；目的 SYN **intention**： *She denies possessing the drug with intent to supply.* 她否认拥有毒品是为了提供给别人。◇ *a* ***letter/statement of intent*** 意向书 ◇ *His intent is clearly not to placate his critics.* 他的目的显然不是要安抚批评他的人。

IDM **to all intents and 'purposes** (*BrE*) (*NAmE* **for all intents and 'purposes**) in the effects that sth has, if not in reality; almost completely 几乎完全；差不多等于： *By 1981 the docks had, to all intents and purposes, closed.* 到 1981 年，这些码头几乎等于关闭了。◇ *The two items are, to all intents and purposes, identical.* 这两件物品几乎完全一样。

in·ten·tion 🔑 /ɪn'tenʃn/ *noun* [C, U] what you intend or plan to do; your aim 打算；计划；意图；目的： **~ (of doing sth)** *I* ***have no intention*** *of going to the wedding.* 我无意去参加婚礼。◇ *He left England* ***with the intention*** *of travelling in Africa.* 他离开英格兰，打算去非洲旅行。◇ *I* ***have every intention*** *of paying her back what I owe her.* 我一心想把我欠她的还给她。◇ **~ (to do sth)** *He has announced his intention to retire.* 他已经宣布他打算退休。◇ **~ (that…)** *It was not my intention that she should suffer.* 我没有要她吃苦头的意思。◇ *The original intention was to devote three months to the project.* 最初的计划是在这个项目上投入三个月的时间。◇ *She's full of* ***good intentions*** *but they rarely work out.* 她虽然处处出于善意，却往往事与愿违。◇ *I did it* ***with the best*** *(****of****)* ***intentions*** (= meaning to help), *but I only succeeded in annoying them.* 我的原意是要帮忙，却惹得他们生气了。 ➲ SYNONYMS AT PURPOSE ➲ SEE ALSO WELL INTENTIONED IDM SEE ROAD

in·ten·tion·al /ɪn'tenʃənl/ *adj.* done deliberately 故意的；有意的；存心的 SYN **deliberate, intended**： *I'm sorry I left you off the list—it wasn't intentional.* 很抱歉没把你列入名单，我不是有意的。 OPP **unintentional** ▶ **in·ten·tion·al·ly** /-ʃənəli/ *adv.*： *She would never intentionally hurt anyone.* 她从来不会故意伤害任何人。◇ *I kept my statement intentionally vague.* 我故意含糊其词。

inter /ɪn'tɜː(r)/ *verb* (**-rr-**) [usually passive] **~ sb** (*formal*) to bury a dead person 埋葬（遗体） OPP **disinter** ➲ SEE ALSO INTERMENT

inter- /'ɪntə(r)/ *prefix* (in verbs, nouns, adjectives and adverbs 构成动词、名词、形容词和副词) between; from one to another 在…之间；从此到彼；相互： *interface* 界面 ◇ *interaction* 相互作用 ◇ *international* 国际的 ➲ COMPARE INTRA- ➲ MORE LIKE THIS 6, page R25

inter·act AW /ˌɪntər'ækt/ *verb* **1** [I] **~ (with sb)** to communicate with sb, especially while you work, play or spend time with them 交流；沟通；合作： *Teachers have a limited amount of time to interact with each child.* 教师和每个孩子沟通的时间有限。 **2** [I] **~ (with sth)** if one thing **interacts** with another, or if two things **interact**, the two things have an effect on each other 相互影响；相互作用： *Perfume interacts with the skin's natural chemicals.* 香水和皮肤的天然化学物质相互作用。 ▶ **inter·action** AW /-'ækʃn/ *noun* [U, C]： **~ (between A and B)** *the interaction between performers and their audience* 演员和观众之间的互动 ◇ **~ (of A) (with B)** *the interaction of bacteria with the body's natural chemistry* 细菌和身体的天然化学变化的相互作用

inter·active AW /ˌɪntər'æktɪv/ *adj.* **1** that involves people working together and having an influence on each other 合作的；相互影响的；互相配合的： *The school believes in interactive teaching methods.* 这所学校推崇互动教学法。 **2** (*computing* 计) that allows information to be passed continuously and in both directions between a computer and the person who uses it 交互式的；人机对话的；互动的： ***interactive systems/video*** 交互式系统 / 视频 ➲ WORDFINDER NOTE AT SOFTWARE ▶ **inter·active·ly** AW *adv.* **inter·activ·ity** /ˌɪntəræk'tɪvəti/ *noun* [U]

interactive 'whiteboard (*abbr.* **IWB**) *noun* a piece of classroom equipment using a computer connected to a large screen that you can write on or use to control the computer by touching it with your finger or a pen 交互式电子白板： *Nearly every classroom has an interactive whiteboard.* 几乎每间教室都有一个交互式电子白板。 ➲ VISUAL VOCAB PAGE V72

inter alia /ˌɪntər 'eɪliə/ *adv.* (*from Latin, formal*) among other things 除了其他事物之外

inter·breed /ˌɪntə'briːd; *NAmE* -tər'b-/ *verb* [I, T] **~ (sth) (with sth)** if animals from different SPECIES **interbreed**, or sb **interbreeds** them, they produce young together （使）杂交繁殖

inter·cede /ˌɪntə'siːd; *NAmE* -tər's-/ *verb* [I] **~ (with sb) (for/on behalf of sb)** (*formal*) to speak to sb in order to persuade them to have pity on sb else or to help settle an argument （为某人）说情；（向某人）求情 SYN **intervene**： *They interceded with the authorities on behalf of the detainees.* 他们为被拘留者向当局求情。 ▶ **inter·ces·sion** /ˌɪntə'seʃn; *NAmE* -tər's-/ *noun* [U]： *the intercession of a priest* 神父的代祷

inter·cept /ˌɪntə'sept; *NAmE* -tər's-/ *verb* **~ sb/sth** to stop sb/sth that is going from one place to another from arriving 拦截；拦阻；截住： *Reporters intercepted him as he tried to leave the hotel.* 他正要离开旅馆，记者们把他拦截住了。◇ *The letter was intercepted.* 信被截查了。 ▶ **inter·cep·tion** /ˌɪntə'sepʃn; *NAmE* -tər's-/ *noun* [U, C]： *the interception of enemy radio signals* 侦听敌方无线电信号

inter·cept·or /ˌɪntə'septə(r); *NAmE* -tər's-/ *noun* a fast military plane that attacks enemy planes that are carrying bombs 截击机

inter·change *noun, verb*

■ ***noun*** /'ɪntətʃeɪndʒ; *NAmE* -tərtʃ-/ **1** [C, U] the act of sharing or exchanging sth, especially ideas or information （思想、信息等的）交换，互换： *a continuous interchange of ideas* 不断的思想交流 ◇ *electronic data interchange* 电子数据交换 **2** [C] a place where a road joins a major road such as a MOTORWAY or INTERSTATE, designed so that vehicles leaving or joining the road do not have to cross other lines of traffic （进出高速公路的）互通式立交，立体交叉道

■ ***verb*** /ˌɪntə'tʃeɪndʒ; *NAmE* -tər'tʃ-/ **1** [T] **~ sth** to share or exchange ideas, information, etc. 交换，互换（思想、信息等） **2** [T, I] to put each of two things or people in the other's place; to move or be moved from one place to another in this way 将…交换；（使）互换位置： **~ A and B** *to interchange the front and rear tyres of a car* 将汽车的前后轮胎对调 ◇ **~ (A) (with B)** *to interchange the front tyres with the rear ones* 将前后轮胎对调 ◇ *The front and rear tyres interchange* (= can be exchanged). 前后轮胎可互换。

inter·change·able /ˌɪntə'tʃeɪndʒəbl; *NAmE* -tər'tʃ-/ *adj.* that can be exchanged, especially without affecting the way in which sth works 可交换的；可互换的；可交替的： *The two words are virtually interchangeable* (= have almost the same meaning). 这两个词大体上可以通用。◇ **~ with sth** *The V8 engines are all interchangeable with each other.* * V8 型的发动机都可以相互替换。 ▶ **inter·change·abil·ity** /ˌɪntəˌtʃeɪndʒə'bɪləti; *NAmE* -tərˌtʃ-/ *noun* [U] **inter·change·ably** *adv.*： *These terms are used interchangeably.* 这些词语可通用。

inter·city /ˌɪntə'sɪti; *NAmE* -tər's-/ *adj.* [usually before noun] (of transport 交通运输) travelling between cities, usually with not many stops on the way 城市间的，城际的（通

常中途停站不多）： *an intercity rail service* 城际铁路运输服务 ◇ *intercity travel* 城际旅行

inter·col·le·gi·ate /ˌɪntəkəˈliːdʒiət; *NAmE* ˌɪntərkə-/ *adj.* (*especially NAmE*) involving competition between colleges 学院之间（竞赛）的；（大学）校际的： *intercollegiate football* 大学校际足球赛

inter·com /ˈɪntəkɒm; *NAmE* ˈɪntərkɑːm/ *noun* a system of communication by telephone or radio inside an office, plane, etc.; the device you press or switch on to start using this system 内部通话系统（或设备）： *to announce sth* ***over the intercom*** 通过内部通话系统宣布 ◇ *They called him on the intercom.* 他们用内部通话系统呼叫他。

inter·com·mu·ni·ca·tion /ˌɪntəkəˌmjuːnɪˈkeɪʃn; *NAmE* -tərkə-/ *noun* [U] the process of communicating between people or groups 相互交流；相互通信；相互沟通

inter·con·nect /ˌɪntəkəˈnekt; *NAmE* -tərkə-/ *verb* [T, I] to connect similar things; to be connected to or with similar things（使类似的事物）相联系，相互联系，相互连接： **~ A with B** *Bad housing is interconnected with debt and poverty.* 住房条件差与负债以及贫困相关联。◇ **~ A and B** *Bad housing, debt and poverty are interconnected.* 恶劣的住房条件、负债以及贫困是相互关联的。◇ **~ (with sth)** *separate bedrooms that interconnect* 相通的独立卧室 ▸ **inter·con·nec·tion** /-ˈnekʃn/ *noun* [C, U]: *interconnections between different parts of the brain* 大脑各部分间的相互联系

inter·con·tin·en·tal /ˌɪntəˌkɒntɪˈnentl; *NAmE* ˌɪntərˌkɑːn-/ *adj.* [usually before noun] between continents 洲际的；洲与洲之间的： ***intercontinental flights/missiles/travel/trade*** 洲际航班/导弹/旅行/贸易

inter·cos·tal /ˌɪntəˈkɒstl; *NAmE* ˌɪntərˈkɑːstl/ *adj.* (*anatomy* 解) located between the RIBS (= the curved bones that go around the chest) 肋间的： *intercostal muscles* 肋间肌

inter·course /ˈɪntəkɔːs; *NAmE* ˈɪntərkɔːrs/ *noun* [U] **1** = SEXUAL INTERCOURSE： *The prosecution stated that intercourse had occurred on several occasions.* 控方称发生过数次性交。◇ *anal intercourse* 肛交 **2** (*old-fashioned*) communication between people, countries, etc.（人、国家等之间的）往来，交往，交际： *the importance of social intercourse between different age groups* 不同年龄段的人之间社交的重要性

inter·cul·tural /ˌɪntəˈkʌltʃərəl; *NAmE* ˌɪntər-/ *adj.* existing or happening between different cultures 跨文化的；各文化之间的

inter·cut /ˌɪntəˈkʌt; *NAmE* ˌɪntər-/ *verb* (**inter·cut·ting, inter·cut, inter·cut**) **~ sth (with sth)** (*specialist*) to put a film/movie scene between two parts of a different scene 使（镜头）交切： *Scenes of city life were intercut with interviews with local people.* 城市生活的镜头与访问当地人的画面相互交切。

inter·de·nom·in·ation·al /ˌɪntədɪˌnɒmɪˈneɪʃənl; *NAmE* ˌɪntərdɪˌnɑːm-/ *adj.* shared by different religious groups (= different DENOMINATIONS) 各教派间共有的

inter·de·part·men·tal /ˌɪntəˌdiːpɑːtˈmentl; *NAmE* ˌɪntərˌdiːpɑːrt-/ *adj.* between departments; involving more than one department 各部门（或系）间的；多个部门（或系）的

inter·de·pend·ent /ˌɪntədɪˈpendənt; *NAmE* -tərdɪ-/ *adj.* that depend on each other; consisting of parts that depend on each other（各部分）相互依存的，相互依赖的： *interdependent economies/organizations/relationships* 相互依赖的经济体系/机构/关系 ◇ *The world is becoming increasingly interdependent.* 世界正变得越来越需要相互依存。 ▸ **inter·de·pend·ence** /-əns/ (*also less frequent* **inter·de·pend·ency** *pl.* **-ies**) *noun* [U, C]

inter·dict /ˈɪntədɪkt; *NAmE* ˈɪntərd-/ *noun* **1** (*law* 律) an official order from a court that orders you not to do sth （法庭的）禁令 **2** (*specialist*) (in the Roman Catholic Church 天主教) an order banning sb from taking part in church services, etc. 禁罚；禁行圣事令

inter·dic·tion /ˌɪntəˈdɪkʃn; *NAmE* -tərˈd-/ *noun* [U] (*formal, especially NAmE*) the act of stopping sth that is being transported from one place from reaching another place, especially by using force （强制）禁运，封锁，阻断： *the Customs Service's drug interdiction programs* 海关的毒品查禁方案

inter·dis·cip·lin·ary /ˌɪntədɪsəˈplɪnəri; *NAmE* ˌɪntərˈdɪsəplɪneri/ *adj.* involving different areas of knowledge or study 多学科的；跨学科的： *interdisciplinary research* 跨学科研究 ◇ *an interdisciplinary approach* 跨学科方法

inter·est 🔑 /ˈɪntrəst; -trest/ *noun, verb*

■ ***noun***

• **WANTING TO KNOW MORE** 求知 **1** 🔑 [sing., U] **~ (in sb/sth)** the feeling that you have when you want to know or learn more about sb/sth 兴趣；关注： *to* ***feel/have/show/express*** *(an)* ***interest*** *in sth* 对…感到/表现出/表示关注 ◇ *Do your parents* ***take an interest in*** *your friends?* 你的父母有兴趣了解你的朋友吗？ ◇ *By that time I had* ***lost*** *(****all****)* ***interest*** *in the idea.* 那时我已经对此想法（完全）失去兴趣了。◇ *I watched* ***with interest.*** 我兴致勃勃地看着。◇ ***As a matter of interest*** (= I'd like to know), *what time did the party finish?* 我想知道，晚会是什么时间结束的？◇ ***Just out of interest,*** *how much did it cost?* 我只是好奇问问，这个花了多少钱？ ➲ COMPARE DISINTEREST

• **ATTRACTION** 吸引力 **2** 🔑 [U] the quality that sth has when it attracts sb's attention or makes them want to know more about it 引人关注的性质；吸引力；趣味： *There are many* ***places of interest*** *near the city.* 这座城市附近有许多有意思的地方。◇ *The subject* ***is of no interest*** *to me at all.* 我对此课题一点也不感兴趣。◇ *These plants will add*

▼ **SYNONYMS** 同义词辨析

interest

hobby • game • pastime

These are all words for activities that you do for pleasure in your spare time. 以上各词均指业余消遣、闲暇活动。

interest an activity or a subject that you do or study for pleasure in your spare time 指业余爱好（活动或科目）： *Her main interests are music and gardening.* 她的主要爱好是音乐和园艺。

hobby an activity that you do for pleasure in your spare time 指业余爱好（活动）： *His hobbies include swimming and cooking.* 他爱好游泳和烹饪。

game a children's activity when they play with toys, pretend to be sb else, etc.; an activity that you do to have fun 指儿童游戏、玩耍、娱乐： *a game of cops and robbers* 警察抓强盗的游戏 ◇ *He was playing games with the dog.* 他在逗狗玩。

pastime an activity that people do for pleasure in their spare time 指消遣、休闲活动： *Eating out is the national pastime in France.* 在法国，下馆子是全国性的消遣活动。

INTEREST, HOBBY OR PASTIME? 用 interest、hobby 还是 pastime?

A **hobby** is often more active than an **interest**. * hobby 常较 interest 主动、积极： *His main hobby is football* (= he plays football). 他的主要业余爱好是踢足球（他踢足球）。◇ *His main interest is football* (= he watches and reads about football, and may or may not play it). 他的主要业余爱好是足球（他看足球赛和阅读有关足球的消息，但不一定踢足球）。 **Pastime** is used when talking about people in general; when you are talking about yourself or an individual person it is more usual to use **interest** or **hobby**. * pastime 泛指一般人的消遣活动，指自己或个人的业余爱好较常用 interest 或 hobby： ~~*Eating out is the national interest/hobby in France.*~~ ◇ ~~*Do you have any pastimes?*~~

PATTERNS

- a **popular** interest/hobby/pastime
- to **have**/**share** interests/hobbies
- to **take up**/**pursue** a(n) interest/hobby

I

interest to your garden in winter. 这些植物在冬季会给你的花园增添胜景。◇ *These documents are of great historical interest.* 这些文件具有重要的历史价值。◇ *to be of cultural/scientific interest* 具有文化 / 科学价值 ➲ SEE ALSO HUMAN INTEREST, LOVE INTEREST

• **HOBBY** 业余爱好 **3** 🔑 [C] an activity or a subject that you enjoy and that you spend your free time doing or studying 业余爱好: *Her main interests are music and tennis.* 她的主要爱好是音乐和网球。◇ *He was a man of wide interests outside his work.* 他是个有广泛业余爱好的人。➲ COMPARE HOBBY

• **MONEY** 钱 **4** 🔑 [U] ~ (**on sth**) (*finance* 财) the extra money that you pay back when you borrow money or that you receive when you invest money 利息: *to **pay interest** on a loan* 付贷款利息 ◇ *The money was repaid **with interest**.* 这笔钱是带息偿还的。◇ ***interest charges/payments*** 利息；利息的支付 ◇ ***Interest rates** have risen by 1%.* 利率上升了1%。◇ ***high rates of interest*** 高利率 ➲ SEE ALSO COMPOUND INTEREST, SIMPLE INTEREST ➲ **WORDFINDER NOTE** AT BANK, INVEST, LOAN

I

• **ADVANTAGE** 利益 **5** [C, usually pl., U] a good result or an advantage for sb/sth 好处；利益: *to **promote/protect/safeguard** sb's **interests*** 提高 / 保护 / 维护某人的利益 ◇ *She was acting entirely **in her own interests**.* 她所做的完全是为了自己的利益。◇ *These reforms were **in the best interests** of local government.* 这些改革对地方政府最有利。◇ *It is **in the public interest** that these facts are made known.* 公开这些真相是为了公众的利益。➲ SEE ALSO SELF-INTEREST

• **SHARE IN BUSINESS** 企业股份 **6** [C, usually pl.] ~ (**in sth**) a share in a business or company and its profits (企业或公司的) 股份；权益；股权: *She has business interests in France.* 她在法国拥有企业权益。◇ *American interests in Europe* (= money invested in European countries) 在欧洲的美国权益 ➲ SEE ALSO CONTROLLING INTEREST

• **CONNECTION** 关系 **7** [C, U] ~ (**in sth**) a connection with sth which affects your attitude to it, especially because you may benefit from it in some way 利害关系；利益关系: *I should, at this point, **declare my interest**.* 到了这个时候，我应该申明我的利益关系。◇ *Organizations **have an interest in** ensuring that employee motivation is high.* 各机构皆知获利之道在于确保员工士气高昂。➲ COMPARE DISINTEREST ➲ SEE ALSO VESTED INTEREST

• **GROUP OF PEOPLE** 团体 **8** [C, usually pl.] a group of people who are in the same business or who share the same aims which they want to protect 同行；同业；利害与共者；利益团体: *powerful farming interests* 强大的农民团体 ◇ *relationships between local government and business interests* 地方政府和企业团体之间的关系

IDM **do sth (back) with interest** to do the same thing to sb as they have done to you, but with more force, enthusiasm, etc. 加倍回报（或回击等） **have sb's interests at 'heart** to want sb to be happy and successful even though your actions may not show this 关心…的幸福成功；暗暗地替…着想 **in the interest(s) of sth** in order to help or achieve sth 为了；为帮助（或取得）: *In the interest(s) of safety, smoking is forbidden.* 禁止吸烟，以策安全。➲ MORE AT CONFLICT *n.*

■ *verb* 🔑 to attract your attention and make you feel interested; to make yourself give your attention to sth 使感兴趣；使关注: **~ sb** *Politics doesn't interest me.* 我对政治不感兴趣。◇ **~ sb/yourself in sth** *She has always interested herself in charity work.* 她始终关注慈善工作。◇ **it interests sb to do sth** *It may interest you to know that Andy didn't accept the job.* 或许你有兴趣知道，安迪没有接受这份工作。

PHR V **'interest sb in sth** to persuade sb to buy, do or eat sth 劝说某人买（或做、吃）: *Could I interest you in this model, Sir?* 先生，请你瞧瞧这个型号好吗？

inter·est·ed 🔑 /ˈɪntrəstɪd; -trest-/ *adj.* **1** 🔑 giving your attention to sth because you enjoy finding out about it or doing it; showing interest in sth and finding it exciting 感兴趣的；关心的；表现出兴趣的: **~ (in sth/sb)** *I'm very interested in history.* 我很喜欢历史。◇ **~ (in doing sth)** *Anyone interested in joining the club should contact us at the address below.* 有意加入俱乐部者请按下面的地址和我们联系。◇ **~ (to do sth)** *We would be interested to hear your views on this subject.* 我们很想听听你对这个话题的看法。◇ *an interested audience* 兴致勃勃的观众 ◇ *There's a talk on Italian art—are you interested* (= would you like to go)? 有个关于意大利艺术的演讲，你想去听吗？◇ *He sounded genuinely interested.* 听他的口气，他真的感兴趣。**2** in a position to gain from a situation or be affected by it 有利害关系的；当事人的: *As an **interested party**, I was not allowed to vote.* 作为有利害关系的一方，我不得投票。◇ *Interested groups will be given three months to give their views on the new development.* 有关团体将有三个月的时间提出他们对新开发项目的看法。➲ **MORE LIKE THIS** 23, page R27

▼ **WHICH WORD?** 词语辨析

interested / interesting / uninterested / disinterested / uninteresting

• The opposite of **interested** is **uninterested** or **not interested**. * interested 的反义词为 uninterested 或 not interested: *He is completely uninterested in politics.* 他对政治毫无兴趣。◇ *I am not really interested in politics.* 我并不真正热衷于政治。
• **Disinterested** means that you can be fair in judging a situation because you do not feel personally involved in it. * disinterested 意为不涉及个人利害关系、公正无私、不偏不倚: *A solicitor can give you disinterested advice.* 律师可给你公正的忠告。However, in speech it is sometimes used instead of **uninterested**, although this is thought to be incorrect. 不过，在口语中有时用此词代替 uninterested，但一般认为此用法不正确。
• The opposite of **interesting** can be **uninteresting**. * interesting 的反义词可以是 uninteresting: *The food was dull and uninteresting.* 食物单调无味。It is more common to use a different word such as **dull** or **boring**. 用其他词如 dull 或 boring 则更普遍。

ˌinterest-ˈfree *adj.* with no interest charged on money borrowed 免息的；不收取利息的: *an interest-free loan* 无息贷款 ◇ *interest-free credit* 免息信贷

ˈinterest group *noun* a group of people who work together to achieve sth that they are particularly interested in, especially by putting pressure on the government, etc. (尤指给政府施加压力等的) 利益集团，利益团体: *a special interest group of US lumber producers* 美国木材生产商特殊利益集团 ➲ COMPARE ADVOCACY GROUP, PRESSURE GROUP

inter·est·ing 🔑 /ˈɪntrəstɪŋ; -trest-/ *adj.* attracting your attention because it is special, exciting or unusual 有趣的；有吸引力的: *an interesting question/point/example* 耐人寻味的问题 / 论点 / 例子 ◇ *interesting people/places/work* 有趣的人 / 地方 / 工作 ◇ **~ (to do sth)** *It would be interesting to know what he really believed.* 了解他的真实信仰会很有意思。◇ *It is particularly interesting to compare the two versions.* 把两个版本加以比较特别耐人寻味。◇ **~ (that...)** *I find it interesting that she claims not to know him.* 她声称不认识他，我觉得真是耐人寻味。◇ *Can't we do something more interesting?* 我们就不能做点更有意思的事情吗？◇ *Her account makes interesting reading.* 她的叙述读起来趣味横生。➲ NOTE AT INTERESTED ▸ **inter·est·ing·ly** *adv.*: *Interestingly, there are very few recorded cases of such attacks.* 有意思的是，记录在案的此类袭击事件很少。➲ **LANGUAGE BANK** AT SURPRISING

inter·face /ˈɪntəfeɪs; *NAmE* -tərf-/ *noun, verb*

■ *noun* **1** (*computing* 计) the way a computer program presents information to a user or receives information from a user, in particular the LAYOUT of the screen and the menus (人机) 界面（尤指屏幕布局和选单）: *the user interface* 用户界面 ➲ **WORDFINDER NOTE** AT PROGRAM **2** (*computing* 计) an electrical CIRCUIT, connection or program that joins one device or system to another 接口；接口程序；连接电路: *the interface between computer* *and printer* 计算机和打印机之间的接口 **3 ~ (between A and B)** the point where two subjects, systems, etc. meet and affect each other （两学科、体系等的）接合点，边缘区域： *the interface between manufacturing and sales* 制造和销售之间的衔接

■ ***verb*** [I, T] **~ (sth) (with sth) | ~ A and B** (*computing* 计) to be connected with sth using an interface; to connect sth in this way （使通过界面或接口）接合，连接： *The new system interfaces with existing telephone equipment.* 新系统与现有的电话设备相连接。

inter·faith /ˈɪntəfeɪθ; *NAmE* -tərf-/ *adj.* [only before noun] between or connected with people of different religions 不同宗教信仰者（间）的；不同宗教团体（间）的： *an interfaith memorial service* 不同宗教团体参加的追悼仪式

inter·fere /ˌɪntəˈfɪə(r); *NAmE* ˌɪntərˈfɪr/ *verb* [I] to get involved in and try to influence a situation that does not concern you, in a way that annoys other people 干涉；干预；介入： *I wish my mother would stop interfering and let me make my own decisions.* 我希望我母亲不再干预，让我自己拿主意。 ◇ **~ in sth** *The police are very unwilling to interfere in family problems.* 警方很不情愿插手家庭问题。

PHR V **interˈfere with sb 1** to illegally try to influence sb who is going to give evidence in court, for example by threatening them or offering them money 干扰证人（企图威胁或贿赂等） **2** (*BrE*) to touch a child in a sexual way （触摸儿童）意图性侵犯 **interˈfere with sth 1** to prevent sth from succeeding or from being done or happening as planned 妨碍；干扰： *She never allows her personal feelings to interfere with her work.* 她从不让她的个人感情妨碍工作。 **2** to touch, use or change sth, especially a piece of equipment, so that it is damaged or no longer works correctly 弄坏（器材等）： *I'd get fired if he found out I'd been interfering with his records.* 要是他发现我把他的唱片捣鼓坏了，我就得被解雇了。

▼ **SYNONYMS 同义词辨析**

interesting

fascinating • compelling • stimulating • gripping • absorbing

These words all describe sb/sth that attracts or holds your attention because they are exciting, unusual or full of good ideas. 以上各词均形容人或事物有吸引力、有趣味。

interesting attracting your attention because it is exciting, unusual or full of good ideas 指有趣的、有吸引力的： *That's an interesting question, Daniel.* 那是个有趣的问题，丹尼尔。

fascinating extremely interesting or attractive 指极有吸引力的、迷人的： *The exhibition tells the fascinating story of the steam age.* 展览讲述了蒸汽时代引人入胜的故事。

compelling (*rather formal*) so interesting or exciting that it holds your attention 指引人入胜的、扣人心弦的： *Her latest book makes compelling reading.* 她新出的书读起来扣人心弦。

stimulating full of interesting or exciting ideas; making people feel enthusiastic 指趣味盎然的、激励人的、振奋人心的： *Thank you for a most stimulating discussion.* 感谢你们妙趣横生的讨论。

gripping so exciting or interesting that it holds your attention completely 指激动人心的、吸引人的、扣人心弦的： *His books are always so gripping.* 他的书总是那么扣人心弦。

absorbing so interesting or enjoyable that it holds your attention 指十分吸引人的、引人入胜的、精彩的： *Chess can be an extremely absorbing game.* 国际象棋有时就是一场引人入胜的游戏。

PATTERNS

- interesting/fascinating/stimulating **for** sb
- interesting/fascinating **to** sb
- interesting/fascinating **that…**
- interesting/fascinating **to see/hear/find/learn/know…**
- a(n) interesting/fascinating/compelling/gripping **story/read/book**
- a(n) interesting/fascinating/stimulating **experience/discussion/idea**
- **to find sth** interesting/fascinating/compelling/stimulating/gripping/absorbing

inter·fer·ence /ˌɪntəˈfɪərəns; *NAmE* -tərˈfɪr-/ *noun* [U] **1 ~ (in sth)** the act of interfering 干涉；干预；介入： *They resent foreign interference in the internal affairs of their country.* 他们憎恶对他们国家内政的外来干涉。 **2** interruption of a radio signal by another signal on a similar WAVELENGTH, causing extra noise that is not wanted （无线电信号的）干扰

IDM **run interference** (*NAmE*) **1** (in AMERICAN FOOTBALL 美式足球) to clear the way for the player with the ball by blocking players from the opposing team 掩护阻挡（为己方持球队员让出道路） **2** (*informal*) to help sb by dealing with problems for them so that they do not need to deal with them （为帮助某人）积极介入

inter·fer·ing /ˌɪntəˈfɪərɪŋ; *NAmE* -tərˈfɪr-/ *adj.* [usually before noun] (*disapproving*) involving yourself in an annoying way in other people's private lives 干涉他人私生活的；管闲事的： *She's an interfering busybody!* 她是个好管闲事的人！

inter·feron /ˌɪntəˈfɪərɒn; *NAmE* ˌɪntərˈfɪrɑːn/ *noun* [U] (*biology* 生) a substance produced by the body to prevent harmful viruses from causing disease 干扰素

inter·gal·act·ic /ˌɪntəɡəˈlæktɪk; *NAmE* -tərɡə-/ *adj.* [only before noun] existing or happening between GALAXIES of stars 星系际的： *intergalactic space/travel* 星系际空间 / 航行

inter·gov·ern·men·tal /ˌɪntəˌɡʌvənˈmentl; *NAmE* ˌɪntərˌɡʌvərn-/ *adj.* [only before noun] concerning the governments of two or more countries 政府间的： *an intergovernmental conference* 政府对政府的会议

in·terim /ˈɪntərɪm/ *adj., noun*

■ ***adj.*** [only before noun] **1** intended to last for only a short time until sb/sth more permanent is found 暂时的；过渡的： *an interim government/measure/report* 过渡政府；临时措施 / 报告 ◇ *The vice-president took power in **the interim period** before the election.* 在大选之前的过渡阶段由副总统执政。 **2** (*finance* 财) calculated before the final results of sth are known 期中的 SYN **provisional**: ***interim figures/profits/results*** 期中数字 / 利润 / 结果

■ ***noun***

IDM **in the interim** during the period of time between two events; until a particular event happens 在其间；在其前： *Despite everything that had happened in the interim, they had remained good friends.* 不管在此期间发生了什么，他们还是好朋友。 ◇ *Her new job does not start until May and she will continue in the old job in the interim.* 她的新工作要到五月份才开始，在这期间她将继续原有的工作。

in·ter·ior 🔑 /ɪnˈtɪəriə(r); *NAmE* -ˈtɪr-/ *noun, adj.*

■ ***noun*** **1** 🔑 [C, usually sing.] the inside part of sth 内部；里面： *the interior of a building/a car* 楼房 / 汽车的内部 OPP **exterior** **2 the interior** [sing.] the central part of a country or continent that is a long way from the coast 内陆；内地；腹地： *an expedition into the interior of Australia* 深入澳大利亚腹地的探险 **3 the Interior** [sing.] a country's own affairs rather than those that involve other countries （国家的）内政，内务： ***the Department/Minister of the Interior*** 内政部；内政大臣

■ ***adj.*** 🔑 [only before noun] connected with the inside part of sth 内部的；里面的： *interior walls* 内墙 OPP **exterior**

inˌterior ˈdecorator *noun* a person whose job is to design and/or decorate a room or the inside of a house, etc. with paint, paper, carpets, etc. 室内（装饰）设计师；室内设计装潢商（或装潢工） ▶ **inˌterior decoˈration** *noun* [U]: *an interior decoration scheme* 室内装饰设计方案

I

in,terior de'sign *noun* [U] the art or job of choosing the paint, carpets, furniture, etc. to decorate the inside of a house 室内设计 ▸ **in,terior de'signer** *noun*

in,terior 'monologue *noun* (in literature 文学) a piece of writing that expresses a character's inner thoughts and feelings 内心独白

inter·ject /ˌɪntəˈdʒekt; *NAmE* -tərˈdʒ-/ *verb* [T, I] + **speech** | ~ (**sth**) (*formal*) to interrupt what sb is saying with your opinion or a remark 打断（别人的讲话）；插话：*'You're wrong,' interjected Susan.* "你错了。"苏珊插嘴说。

inter·jec·tion /ˌɪntəˈdʒekʃn; *NAmE* -tərˈdʒ-/ *noun* (*grammar* 语法) a short sound, word or phrase spoken suddenly to express an emotion. *Oh!*, *Look out!* and *Ow!* are interjections. 感叹词；感叹语 **SYN** **exclamation**

inter·lace /ˌɪntəˈleɪs; *NAmE* -tərˈl-/ *verb* [T, I] ~ (**sth**) (**with sth**) (*formal*) to twist things together over and under each other; to be twisted together in this way （使）编结，交错：*Her hair was interlaced with ribbons and flowers.* 她的头发上编扎着缎带和花。◇ *interlacing branches* 交错的枝条

inter·lan·guage /ˈɪntəlæŋgwɪdʒ; *NAmE* -tərl-/ *noun* [U, C] (*linguistics* 语言) a language system produced by sb who is learning a language, which has features of the language which they are learning and also of their first language 中间语言，中介语言（第二语言学习者在学习过程中形成的语言，具有所学语言和其母语的特征）

inter·leave /ˌɪntəˈliːv; *NAmE* -tərˈl-/ *verb* ~ **sth** (**with sth**) to put sth, especially thin layers of sth, between things （尤指将片状物）插入，夹进

inter·lin·ear /ˌɪntəˈlɪniə(r); *NAmE* -tərˈl-/ *adj.* (*specialist*) written or printed between the lines of a text 行间书写（或印刷）的

inter·lin·gual /ˌɪntəˈlɪŋgwəl; *NAmE* -tərˈl-/ *adj.* **1** (*linguistics* 语言) using, between, or relating to two different languages 使用两种语言的；介于两种语言间的；语际的：*interlingual communication* 语际交流 **2** relating to an INTERLANGUAGE 中间语言的；中介语言的

inter·link /ˌɪntəˈlɪŋk; *NAmE* -tərˈl-/ *verb* [T, usually passive, I] ~ (**sth**) (**with sth**) to connect things; to be connected with other things （使）连接：*The two processes are interlinked.* 这两个过程是相互连接的。◇ *a series of short interlinking stories* 一系列相互衔接的短篇故事

inter·lock /ˌɪntəˈlɒk; *NAmE* ˌɪntərˈlɑːk/ *verb* [I, T] ~ (**sth**) (**with sth**) to fit or be fastened firmly together （使）连锁，紧密连接，扣紧：*Once the parts are interlocked, the structure stands firm.* 一旦各个部件紧密相扣，结构就会牢固。◇ *interlocking shapes/systems/pieces* 紧密相扣的形状/系统/部件

inter·locu·tor /ˌɪntəˈlɒkjətə(r); *NAmE* ˌɪntərˈlɑːk-/ *noun* (*formal*) **1** a person taking part in a conversation with you 参加谈话者；对话者 **2** a person or an organization that talks to another person or organization on behalf of sb else （代表他人的）中间对话者

inter·loper /ˈɪntələʊpə(r); *NAmE* ˈɪntərloʊpər/ *noun* a person who is present in a place or a situation where they do not belong 闯入者；干涉者 **SYN** **intruder**

inter·lude /ˈɪntəluːd; *NAmE* -tərl-/ *noun* **1** a period of time between two events during which sth different happens （两事件之间的）间歇；插入事件：*a romantic interlude* (= a short romantic relationship) 短暂的恋爱 ◇ *Apart from a brief interlude of peace, the war lasted nine years.* 除了一段短暂的和平，那场战争持续了九年。 **2** a short period of time between the parts of a play, film/movie, etc. （戏剧、电影等的）幕间休息：*There will now be a short interlude.* 现在有一段短时间的幕间休息。 **3** a short piece of music or a talk, etc. that fills this period of time 幕间乐曲（或节目、表演）：*a musical interlude* 幕间音乐插曲

inter·marry /ˌɪntəˈmæri; *NAmE* -tərˈm-/ *verb* (**inter·mar·ries**, **inter·marry·ing**, **inter·mar·ried**, **inter·mar·ried**) **1** [I] to marry sb of a different race or from a different country or a different religious group 不同种族（或国家、教派）间通婚：*Blacks and whites often intermarried* (= married each other). 黑人和白人时有通婚。◇ ~ **with sb** *They were not forbidden to intermarry with the local people.* 他们未被禁止与当地人通婚。 **2** [I] to marry sb within your own family or group 近族通婚；近亲结婚：*cousins who intermarry* 近亲结婚的堂表兄弟姐妹 ▸ **inter·mar·riage** /ˌɪntəˈmærɪdʒ/ *noun* [U, C]: *intermarriage between blacks and whites* 黑人和白人之间的通婚

inter·medi·ary /ˌɪntəˈmiːdiəri; *NAmE* ˌɪntərˈmiːdieri/ *noun* (*pl.* **-ies**) ~ (**between A and B**) a person or an organization that helps other people or organizations to make an agreement by being a means of communication between them 中间人；调解人 **SYN** **mediator, go-between**: *Financial institutions act as intermediaries between lenders and borrowers.* 金融机构充当贷方和借方的中间人。◇ *All talks have so far been conducted through an intermediary.* 到目前为止所有的谈判都是通过调停人进行的。▸ **inter·medi·ary** *adj.* [only before noun]: *to play an intermediary role in the dispute* 担任纠纷中的调解人

inter·medi·ate **AW** /ˌɪntəˈmiːdiət; *NAmE* -tərˈm-/ *adj.*, *noun*
■ *adj.* **1** [usually before noun] located between two places, things, states, etc. （两地、两物、两种状态等）之间的，中间的：*an* ***intermediate stage/step*** *in a process* 中间阶段/步骤 ◇ ~ **between A and B** *Liquid crystals are considered to be intermediate between liquid and solid.* 液晶被认为介于液态和固态之间。 **2** having more than a basic knowledge of sth but not yet advanced; suitable for sb who is at this level 中级的；中等的；适合中等程度者的：*an* ***intermediate skier/student, etc.*** 中等程度的滑雪者、学生等 ◇ *an intermediate coursebook* 中级课本 ◇ ***pre-/upper-intermediate*** *classes* 初等/高等中级班
■ *noun* a person who is learning sth and who has more than a basic knowledge of it but is not yet advanced 中级学生

,intermediate tech'nology *noun* [U] technology that is suitable for use in developing countries as it is cheap and simple and can use local materials 中间技术（因成本低廉、简便以及可使用当地原料而适用于发展中国家）

in·ter·ment /ɪnˈtɜːmənt; *NAmE* -ˈtɜːrm-/ *noun* [C, U] (*formal*) the act of burying a dead person 埋葬；安葬 **SYN** **burial** ➲ SEE ALSO INTER

inter·mesh /ˌɪntəˈmeʃ; *NAmE* -tərˈm-/ *verb* [I] (of two objects or parts 两个物体或部分) to fit closely together 互相啮合；紧密相接：*intermeshing cogs* 相互咬合的轮齿

inter·mezzo /ˌɪntəˈmetsəʊ; *NAmE* ˌɪntərˈmetsoʊ/ *noun* (*pl.* **inter·mezzi** /-ˈmetsiː/ or **inter·mezzos** /-ˈmetsəʊz; *NAmE* -ˈmetsoʊz/) (*music* 音, *from Italian*) a short piece of music for the ORCHESTRA that is played between two parts in an OPERA or other musical performance 间奏曲，幕间曲（歌剧或其他音乐表演中幕与幕之间的过场音乐）

in·ter·min·able /ɪnˈtɜːmɪnəbl; *NAmE* -ˈtɜːrm-/ *adj.* lasting a very long time and therefore boring or annoying 冗长的；没完没了的 **SYN** **endless**: *an interminable speech/wait/discussion* 无休止的讲话/等待/讨论 ◇ *The drive seemed interminable.* 这次开车好像没有尽头。▸ **in·ter·min·ably** /-əbli/ *adv.*: *The meeting dragged on interminably.* 会议没完没了地拖延着。

inter·min·gle /ˌɪntəˈmɪŋgl; *NAmE* -tərˈm-/ *verb* [T, I] (*formal*) to mix people, ideas, colours, etc. together; to be mixed in this way 使（人、思想、色彩等）混合：~ **A with B** *The book intermingles fact with fiction.* 这本书事实和虚构并存。◇ ~ **A and B** *The book intermingles fact and fiction.* 这本书事实和虚构并存。◇ ~ (**with sb/sth**) *tourists and local people intermingling in the market square* 聚集在市场广场上的观光客和当地人

inter·mis·sion /ˌɪntəˈmɪʃn; *NAmE* -tərˈm-/ *noun* [C, U] **1** (*especially NAmE*) a short period of time between the parts of a play, film/movie, etc. （戏剧、电影等的）幕间休息，中间休息：*Coffee was served during the intermission.* 幕间休息时有咖啡供应。◇ (*NAmE*) *After intermission, the second* *band played.* 幕间休息后第二支乐队开始演奏。 HELP This meaning is only [U] in *NAmE*. 作此义时在美式英语中是不可数的。 **2** a period of time during which sth stops before continuing again 间歇；暂停： *This state of affairs lasted without intermission for a hundred years.* 这种局面从未间断地持续了一百年。

inter·mit·tent /ˌɪntəˈmɪtənt; *NAmE* -tərˈm-/ *adj.* stopping and starting often over a period of time, but not regularly 断断续续的；间歇的 SYN **sporadic**: *intermittent bursts of applause* 一阵阵的掌声 ◇ *intermittent showers* 阵雨 ▶ **inter·mit·tent·ly** *adv.*: *Protests continued intermittently throughout November.* 整个十一月份抗议活动此起彼落。

inter·mix /ˌɪntəˈmɪks; *NAmE* -tərˈm-/ *verb* [T, I] ~ (sth) (with sth) to mix things together; to be mixed together （使）混合；（使）混杂： *Grass fields were intermixed with areas of woodland.* 草地和林地相互交错。

in·tern *verb, noun*

■ *verb* /ɪnˈtɜːn; *NAmE* ɪnˈtɜːrn/ [often passive] ~ **sb** (**in sth**) to put sb in prison during a war or for political reasons, although they have not been charged with a crime （战争期间或由于政治原因未经审讯）拘留，禁闭，关押 ➲ SEE ALSO INTERNEE ▶ **in·tern·ment** /ɪnˈtɜːnmənt; *NAmE* ɪnˈtɜːrnmənt/ *noun* [U]: *the internment of suspected terrorists* 拘留可疑恐怖分子 ◇ *internment camps* 拘留营

■ *noun* (*also* **in·terne**) /ˈɪntɜːn; *NAmE* ˈɪntɜːrn/ (*NAmE*) **1** an advanced student of medicine, whose training is nearly finished and who is working in a hospital to get further practical experience 实习医生 ➲ COMPARE HOUSE OFFICER **2** a student or new GRADUATE who is getting practical experience in a job, for example during the summer holiday/vacation 实习学生；毕业实习生： *a summer intern at a law firm* 暑假在法律事务所实习的学生 ➲ WORDFINDER NOTE AT TRAINING ➲ SEE ALSO INTERNSHIP

in·tern·al 🔑 AW /ɪnˈtɜːnl; *NAmE* ɪnˈtɜːrnl/ *adj.* **1** 🔑 [only before noun] connected with the inside of sth 内部的；里面的： *the internal structure of a building* 大楼的内部结构 ◇ *internal doors* 内门 OPP **external** **2** 🔑 [only before noun] connected with the inside of your body 体内的： ***internal organs/injuries*** 内脏；内伤 ◇ *The medicine is not for **internal use**.* 这种药不可内服。 OPP **external** **3** 🔑 [usually before noun] involving or concerning only the people who are part of a particular organization rather than people from outside it （机构）内部的： *an internal inquiry* 内部调查 ◇ *the internal workings of government* 政府内部的运作 ◇ *internal divisions within the company* 公司内部的各部门 OPP **external** **4** 🔑 [only before noun] connected with a country's own affairs rather than those that involve other countries 内政的；国内的 SYN **domestic**: ***internal affairs/trade/markets*** 内政；国内贸易 / 市场 ◇ *an **internal flight*** (= within a country) 国内航班 OPP **external** **5** coming from within a thing itself rather than from outside it 本身的；自身的： *a theory which lacks **internal consistency*** (= whose parts are not in agreement with each other) 自相矛盾的理论 ◇ *Some photos contain **internal evidence*** (= fashions, transport, etc.) *that may help to date them.* 有些照片自身就含有确定拍摄日期的佐证。 **6** happening or existing in your mind 内心的；头脑中的 SYN **inner**: *internal rage* 内心的愤怒 ▶ **in·tern·al·ly** AW /-nəli/ *adv.*: *internally connected rooms* 内部连通的房间 ◇ *The new posts were only advertised internally.* 新职位仅限于内部招聘。

inˌternal-comˈbustion engine *noun* a type of engine used in most cars that produces power by burning petrol/gas or other fuel inside 内燃机

in·tern·al·ize AW (*BrE also* **-ise**) /ɪnˈtɜːnəlaɪz; *NAmE* -ˈtɜːrn-/ *verb* ~ **sth** (*specialist*) to make a feeling, an attitude, or a belief part of the way you think and behave 使（感情、态度或信仰）成为思想行为的一部分；使内在化 ➲ COMPARE EXTERNALIZE ▶ **in·tern·al·iza·tion, -isa·tion** /ɪnˌtɜːnəlaɪˈzeɪʃn; *NAmE* -tɜːrnələˈz-/ *noun* [U]

inˌternal ˈmarket *noun* (*business* 商) a situation in which different departments, countries, etc. in the same organization buy goods and services from each other 内部市场；内部贸易

the Inˌternal ˈRevenue Service *noun* [sing.] (*abbr.* **IRS**) (in the US) the government department that is responsible for collecting most national taxes, for example income tax （美国）国税局 ➲ COMPARE HM REVENUE AND CUSTOMS

inter·nation·al 🔑 /ˌɪntəˈnæʃnəl; *NAmE* -tərˈn-/ *adj., noun*

■ *adj.* 🔑 [usually before noun] connected with or involving two or more countries 国际的： *international trade/law/sport* 国际贸易；国际法；国际体育运动 ◇ *an international airport/school/company* 国际机场 / 学校 / 公司 ◇ *international relations* 国际关系 ◇ *a pianist with an international reputation* 饮誉国际的钢琴家 ➲ COLLOCATIONS ON NEXT PAGE ➲ WORDFINDER NOTE AT ALLY ▶ **inter·nation·al·ly** /-nəli/ *adv.*: *internationally famous* 国际知名的

■ *noun* **1** (*BrE*) a sports competition involving teams from two countries 国际体育比赛： *the France-Scotland rugby international* 法国对苏格兰的国际橄榄球赛 **2** (*BrE*) a player who takes part in a sports competition against another country 国际体育比赛选手： *a former swimming international* 前国际游泳选手 **3** (*NAmE*) a person from a foreign country 外国人： *an English course for internationals* 为外国人开设的英语课程

the ˌInterˌnational Baccaˈlaureate™ *noun* [sing.] (*abbr.* **IB**) an exam which is taken by students in many different countries in the world around the age of 18 or 19, and which includes up to six subjects 国际中学毕业会考（考生年龄约为 18 或 19 岁，最多考六个科目）

the Interˌnational ˈDate Line (*also* **ˈDate Line**) *noun* [sing.] the imaginary line that goes from north to south through the Pacific Ocean. The date on the west side is different by one day from that on the east side. 日界线（联结地球南北极的假想线。向东航行越过此线须减去一天，向西须增加一天） ➲ WORDFINDER NOTE AT EARTH

the Inter·nation·ale /ˌɪntənæʃəˈnɑːl; *NAmE* -tərn-/ *noun* [sing.] an international SOCIALIST song written in France that was the official ANTHEM of the USSR until 1944 《国际歌》（创作于法国，1944 年之前为苏联国歌）

inter·nation·al·ism /ˌɪntəˈnæʃnəlɪzəm; *NAmE* -tərˈn-/ *noun* [U] the belief that countries should work together in a friendly way 国际主义

inter·nation·al·ist /ˌɪntəˈnæʃnəlɪst; *NAmE* -tərˈn-/ *noun* **1** a person who believes that countries should work together in a friendly way 国际主义者 **2** (*ScotE*) a player who takes part in a sports competition against another country 参加国际比赛的国家队选手： *a Scottish rugby internationalist* 参加国际比赛的苏格兰橄榄球队队员 ▶ **inter·nation·al·ist** *adj.*

inter·nation·al·ize (*BrE also* **-ise**) /ˌɪntəˈnæʃnəlaɪz; *NAmE* -tərˈn-/ *verb* ~ **sth** to bring sth under the control or protection of many nations; to make sth international 使国际共管；使国际化 ▶ **inter·nation·al·iza·tion, -isa·tion** /ˌɪntəˌnæʃnəlaɪˈzeɪʃn; *NAmE* -tərˌnæʃnələˈz-/ *noun* [U]

the Interˌnational Phoˌnetic ˈAlphabet *noun* [sing.] (*abbr.* **IPA**) an alphabet that is used to show the pronunciation of words in any language 国际音标

in·terne *noun* = INTERN

inter·necine /ˌɪntəˈniːsaɪn; *NAmE* -tərˈn-/ *adj.* [only before noun] (*formal*) happening between members of the same group, country or organization （团体、国家、组织）内部发生的，内讧的： ***internecine struggles/warfare/feuds*** 内部斗争；内战；内部世仇

in·tern·ee /ˌɪntɜːˈniː; *NAmE* ˌɪntɜːrˈniː/ *noun* a person who is put in prison for political reasons, usually without a trial （通常指未经审讯而关押的）政治犯

Inter·net (*also* **inter·net**) /ˈɪntənet; *NAmE* -tərn-/ *noun* (*usually* **the Internet**) (*also informal* **the Net**) [sing.] an international computer network connecting other networks and computers from companies, universities, etc. （国际）互联网；因特网：*I looked it up on the Internet.* 我在互联网上查过此事。◇ *You can buy our goods over the Internet.* 可以通过互联网购买我们的货品。◇ *All the rooms have access to the Internet/Internet access.* 所有的房间都可以接入互联网。◇ *an Internet service provider* (= a company that provides you with an Internet connection and services such as email, etc.) 互联网服务供应商 ➲ COLLOCATIONS AT EMAIL ➲ SEE ALSO INTRANET, WWW

ˈInternet dating = ONLINE DATING

in·tern·ist /ɪnˈtɜːnɪst; *NAmE* -ˈtɜːrn-/ *noun* (*NAmE*) a doctor who is a specialist in the treatment of diseases of the organs inside the body and who does not usually do medical operations 内科医生

in·tern·ment ➲ INTERN *v.*

in·tern·ship /ˈɪntɜːnʃɪp; *NAmE* -tɜːrn-/ *noun* (*NAmE*) **1** a period of time during which a student or new GRADUATE gets practical experience in a job, for example during the summer holiday/vacation （学生或毕业生的）实习期：*an internship at a television station* 在电视台的实习期 ➲ COMPARE PLACEMENT (2), WORK EXPERIENCE (2) **2** a job that an advanced student of medicine, whose training is nearly finished, does in a hospital to get further practical experience （医科学生的）实习工作

inter·oper·able /ˌɪntərˈɒpərəbl; *NAmE* -ˈɑːp-/ *adj.* (*specialist*) (of computer systems or programs 计算机系统或程序) able to exchange information 可互相操作的；配合动作的；互用的

inter·pene·trate /ˌɪntəˈpenɪtreɪt; *NAmE* -tərˈp-/ *verb* [I, T] ~ (**sth**) (*formal*) to spread completely through sth or from one thing to another in each direction （互相）贯穿，渗透 ▶ **inter·pene·tra·tion** /ˌɪntəˌpenɪˈtreɪʃn; *NAmE* -tərˌp-/ *noun* [U, C]

inter·per·son·al /ˌɪntəˈpɜːsənl; *NAmE* -tərˈpɜːrs-/ *adj.* [only before noun] connected with relationships between people 人际关系的；人际的：*interpersonal skills* 人际交往技巧

inter·plan·et·ary /ˌɪntəˈplænɪtri; *NAmE* ˌɪntərˈplænəteri/ *adj.* [only before noun] between planets 行星间的：*interplanetary travel* 星际旅行

▼ **COLLOCATIONS** 词语搭配

International relations 国际关系

Trade 贸易

- **facilitate/regulate** trade (with other countries) 促进 / 规范（与其他国家的）贸易
- **form/join** a trading bloc 建立 / 加入贸易同盟
- **live in/compete in** a global/the world economy 生存于全球 / 世界经济中；参与全球 / 世界经济竞争
- **support/promote** free trade 支持 / 促进自由贸易
- **adopt/call for/oppose** protectionist measures 采取 / 呼吁 / 反对保护主义措施
- **erect/impose/reduce/remove** trade barriers 设置 / 推行 / 减少 / 消除贸易壁垒
- **impose/lift/raise/eliminate** import tariffs (on sth) 征收 / 取消 / 提高 / 废除（某物的）进口关税
- **have/run** a huge/large/growing trade surplus/deficit 有巨额 / 持续增长的贸易顺差 / 逆差
- **embrace/resist/drive** globalization 接受 / 抵制 / 推进全球化

Politics and law 政治与法律

- **conduct/handle/talk about/discuss** foreign policy 执行 / 掌控 / 谈论 / 讨论外交政策
- **pursue** an aggressive/a hawkish foreign policy 执行强硬的外交政策
- **require/use/conduct** diplomacy 需要 / 使用 / 实施外交手段
- **establish/break off/sever/restore** diplomatic relations 建立 / 中断 / 断绝 / 恢复外交关系
- **foster/promote/strengthen** regional cooperation 促进地区间合作
- **facilitate/achieve** economic/political integration 促进 / 实现经济 / 政治一体化
- **exercise/defend/protect/transfer/restore/regain** national/state/full/limited sovereignty 行使 / 维护 / 保护 / 移交 / 恢复 / 重获民族 / 国家 / 全部 / 部分主权
- **consolidate/extend/lose/retain** your power (in the region) 巩固 / 扩张 / 丧失 / 保持（区域内的）势力
- **hold/maintain/change/alter/shift/be a shift in** the balance of power (in the region) 维持 / 改变（区域内的）势力均衡
- **cause/create/open/expose/heal/repair** a deep/growing/major/serious rift between X and Y 导致 / 造成 / 引发 / 暴露出 / 弥合 / 修复 X 与 Y 之间深层次的 / 不断扩大的 / 主要的 / 严重的分歧

Meetings and agreements 会议与协议

- **have/hold/host/attend** an international conference/an economic forum/a G20 summit 召开 / 举行 / 主办 / 出席国际会议 / 经济论坛 / 二十国集团峰会
- **launch** a new round of global/multilateral/world trade negotiations 发起新一轮的全球 / 多边 / 世界贸易谈判
- **send/head/lead/meet** a high-level/an official/a trade delegation 派遣 / 领导 / 带领 / 会见高层 / 官方 / 贸易代表团
- **begin/start/continue/resume** peace talks 开始 / 继续 / 重启和平谈判
- **be committed to/be opposed to/disrupt/undermine/derail/sabotage** the peace process 致力于 / 反对 / 扰乱 / 损害 / 干扰 / 破坏和平进程
- **negotiate/achieve** a lasting political settlement 达成 / 取得长期的政治协议
- **broker/sign** a peace deal/agreement/treaty 协商 / 签署和平协议

Conflict 冲突

- **be/constitute/pose** a threat to global security 构成对全球安全的一大威胁
- **compromise/endanger/protect** national security 损害 / 危及 / 保护国家安全
- **justify/be in favour of/** (*especially US*) **be in favor of/be against** military intervention 证明军事干预合理；支持 / 反对军事干预
- **threaten/authorize/launch/take/support/oppose** unilateral/pre-emptive military action 扬言采取 / 授权使用 / 发起 / 采取 / 支持 / 反对单边的 / 先发制人的军事行动
- **impose/enforce/lift/end** economic sanctions/an arms embargo/a naval blockade 强制实行 / 解除经济制裁 / 武器禁运 / 海上封锁
- **close/protect/secure/patrol** the border 封锁 / 保卫边境；在边境地区巡逻
- **lead/be involved in** a peacekeeping operation 领导 / 参与维和行动

Aid 援助

- **negotiate/announce** a $15 billion aid package/an economic stimulus package 达成 / 宣布 150 亿美元的一套援助计划 / 刺激经济的一揽子计划
- **send/provide/request/cut off** military aid 派遣 / 提供 / 请求 / 中断军事援助
- **bring/provide** emergency/humanitarian relief 带来 / 提供紧急 / 人道主义救助
- **deliver/distribute** medical supplies/(*BrE*) food parcels 运送 / 分发医疗用品 / 食品包
- **fund/run** a foreign/a local/an international NGO 资助 / 管理外国 / 当地 / 国际非政府组织
- **reduce/eradicate** child/global/world poverty 减少 / 根除儿童 / 全球性 / 世界性贫困

inter·play /ˈɪntəpleɪ; *NAmE* -tərp-/ *noun* [U, sing.] ~ (**of/between A and B**) (*formal*) the way in which two or more things or people affect each other 相互影响（或作用） **SYN** **interaction**: *the interplay between politics and the environment* 政治与环境的相互影响 ◇ *the subtle interplay of colours* 色彩的相互掩映

Inter·pol /ˈɪntəpɒl; *NAmE* ˈɪntərpoːl; ˈɪntərpɑːl/ *noun* [sing.+ sing./pl. v.] an international organization that enables the police forces of different countries to help each other to solve crimes 国际刑警组织

in·ter·pol·ate /ɪnˈtɜːpəleɪt; *NAmE* -ˈtɜːrp-/ *verb* (*formal*) **1** + **speech** | ~ **sth** to make a remark that interrupts a conversation 插话；插嘴 **SYN** **interject**: *'But why?' he interpolated.* "但为什么？"他插嘴问。 **2** ~ **sth** (**into sth**) to add sth to a piece of writing （在文章中）插入，添加内容 **SYN** **insert**: *The lines were interpolated into the manuscript at a later date.* 这几行文字是后来加到稿子中的。 **3** ~ **sth** (*mathematics* 数) to add a value into a series by calculating it from surrounding known values 插值；内插 ▶ **in·ter·pol·ation** /ɪnˌtɜːpəˈleɪʃn; *NAmE* -ˌtɜːrp-/ *noun* [U, C]

inter·pose /ˌɪntəˈpəʊz; *NAmE* ˌɪntərˈpoʊz/ *verb* (*formal*) **1** + **speech** | ~ **sth** to add a question or remark into a conversation 插入，插进（问题或话语）: *'Just a minute,' Charles interposed. 'How do you know?'* "且慢，"查尔斯插话说，"你是怎么知道的？" **2** ~ **sb/sth** (**between A and B**) to place sb/sth between two people or things 将…置于（二者）之间；插入；夹进: *He quickly interposed himself between Mel and the doorway.* 他迅速挡在梅尔和门口之间。

in·ter·pret 🔑 **AW** /ɪnˈtɜːprɪt; *NAmE* -ˈtɜːrp-/ *verb* **1** 🔑 [T] ~ **sth** to explain the meaning of sth 诠释；说明: *The students were asked to interpret the poem.* 学生们被要求诠释那首诗的意义。 **2** 🔑 [T] to decide that sth has a particular meaning and to understand it in this way 把…理解为；领会: ~ **sth as sth** *I didn't know whether to interpret her silence as acceptance or refusal.* 我不知该把她的沉默看作接受还是拒绝。 ◇ ~ **sth** *The data can be interpreted in many different ways.* 这份资料可以从多方面解读。 ➲ COMPARE MISINTERPRET **3** 🔑 [I] ~ (**for sb**) to translate one language into another as you hear it 口译；传译: *She couldn't speak much English so her children had to interpret for her.* 她讲不了几句英语，所以她的孩子们得给她翻译。 **4** [T] ~ **sth** to perform a piece of music, a role in a play, etc. in a way that shows your feelings about its meaning 演绎（按自己的感觉演奏音乐或表现角色）: *He interpreted the role with a lot of humour.* 他把这个角色演得十分幽默。 ▶ **in·ter·pret·able** /ɪnˈtɜːprɪtəbl; *NAmE* -ˈtɜːrp-/ *adj.*: *interpretable data* 可解释的资料

in·ter·pret·ation 🔑 **AW** /ɪnˌtɜːprɪˈteɪʃn; *NAmE* -ˌtɜːrp-/ *noun* [C, U] **1** 🔑 the particular way in which sth is understood or explained 理解；解释；说明: *Her evidence suggests a different interpretation of the events.* 她的证据显示这些事件可能有另外一种解释。 ◇ *It is not possible for everyone to put their own interpretation on the law.* 不可能让每个人自行阐释法律。 ◇ *Dreams are* **open to interpretation** (= they can be explained in different ways). 梦可以作各种诠释。 **2** the particular way in which sb chooses to perform a piece of music, a role in a play, etc. 演绎；演奏方式；表演方式: *a modern interpretation of 'King Lear'* 《李尔王》的现代演绎

in·ter·pret·ative **AW** /ɪnˈtɜːprɪtətɪv; *NAmE* ɪnˈtɜːrprəteɪtɪv/ (*also* **in·ter·pret·ive** /ɪnˈtɜːprɪtɪv; *NAmE* -ˈtɜːrp-/ *especially in NAmE*) *adj.* [usually before noun] (*formal*) connected with the particular way in which sth is understood, explained or performed; providing an interpretation 理解的；解释的；表演的；演绎的: *an interpretative problem* 理解方面的问题 ◇ *an interpretative exhibition* 演示

in·ter·pret·er /ɪnˈtɜːprɪtə(r); *NAmE* -ˈtɜːrp-/ *noun* **1** a person whose job is to translate what sb is saying into another language 口译工作者；口译员；传译员: *Speaking* **through an interpreter**, *the President said that the talks were going well.* 总统通过口译员说会谈进展良好。 ◇ *a sign language interpreter* (= a person who translates what sb is saying into sign language for deaf people) 手语翻译员 ➲ COMPARE TRANSLATOR **2** a person who performs a piece of music or a role in a play in a way that clearly shows their ideas about its meaning 演绎（音乐、戏剧中人物等）的人: *She is one of the finest interpreters of Debussy's music.* 她是将德彪西的音乐演绎得最出色的演奏者之一。 **3** (*computing* 计) a computer program that changes the instructions of another program into a form that the computer can understand and use 解释程序；解释器

inter·racial /ˌɪntəˈreɪʃl/ *adj.* [only before noun] involving people of different races 不同种族的人的；种族间的: *interracial marriage* 种族间的通婚

inter·reg·num /ˌɪntəˈregnəm/ *noun* [usually sing.] (*pl.* **inter·reg·nums**) (*formal*) a period of time during which a country, an organization, etc. does not have a leader and is waiting for a new one （政府改组期间的）政权空白；（机构的）权力空白

inter·relate /ˌɪntərɪˈleɪt/ *verb* [I, T, usually passive] if two or more things **interrelate**, or if they are **interrelated**, they are closely connected and they affect each other 相互关联（或影响）: *a discussion of how the mind and body interrelate* 关于精神和肉体相互联系的讨论 ◇ ~ **with sth** *a discussion of how the mind interrelates with the body* 关于精神和肉体相互联系的讨论 ◇ **be interrelated** *a discussion of how the mind and body are interrelated* 关于精神和肉体如何相互联系的讨论 ▶ **inter·related** *adj.*: *a number of interrelated problems* 一些相互关联的问题

inter·rela·tion·ship /ˌɪntərɪˈleɪʃnʃɪp/ (*also* **inter·rela·tion** /ˌɪntərɪˈleɪʃn/) *noun* [C, U] ~ (**of/between A and B**) the way in which two or more things or people are connected and affect each other 相互关联；相互影响

in·ter·ro·gate /ɪnˈterəgeɪt/ *verb* **1** ~ **sb** to ask sb a lot of questions over a long period of time, especially in an aggressive way 讯问；审问；盘问: *He was interrogated by the police for over 12 hours.* 他被警察审问了 12 个多小时。 ➲ WORDFINDER NOTE AT POLICE **2** ~ **sth** (*specialist*) to obtain information from a computer or other machine （在计算机或其他机器上）查询，询问 ▶ **in·ter·ro·ga·tion** /ɪnˌterəˈgeɪʃn/ *noun* [U, C]: *He confessed after four days* **under interrogation**. 他在受讯问四天之后招认了。 ◇ *She hated her parents' endless interrogations about where she'd been.* 她讨厌父母没完没了地盘问她去哪里了。 ➲ SYNONYMS AT INTERVIEW **in·ter·ro·ga·tor** *noun*

inter·roga·tive /ˌɪntəˈrɒgətɪv; *NAmE* -ˈrɑːg-/ *adj.*, *noun*

■ *adj.* **1** (*formal*) asking a question; in the form of a question 询问的；提问的；疑问式的: *an interrogative gesture/remark/sentence* 疑问的手势 / 言语；疑问句 **2** (*grammar* 语法) used in questions 用于疑问句的: *interrogative pronouns/determiners/adverbs* (= for example, *who, which* and *why*) 疑问代词 / 限定词 / 副词 ▶ **inter·roga·tive·ly** *adv.*

■ *noun* (*grammar* 语法) a question word, especially a pronoun or a determiner such as *who* or *which* 疑问词；（尤指）疑问代词，疑问限定词

inter·roga·tory /ˌɪntəˈrɒgətri; *NAmE* -ˈrɑːg-/ *adj.*, *noun*

■ *adj.* seeming to be asking a question or demanding an answer to sth 疑问的；质问的: *an interrogatory stare* 带着疑问的注视

■ *noun* (*pl.* **-ies**) (*law* 律) a written question, asked by one party in a legal case, which must be answered by the other party （诉讼中一方向另一方提出的）书面质询

inter·rupt 🔑 /ˌɪntəˈrʌpt/ *verb* **1** 🔑 [I, T] to say or do sth that makes sb stop what they are saying or doing 插嘴；打扰；打岔: *Sorry to interrupt, but there's someone to see you.* 对不起打扰一下，有人要见你。 ◇ ~ **with sth** *Would you mind not interrupting with questions all the time?* 请你别老是插嘴问问题好吗？ ◇ ~ **sb/sth** (**with sth**) *I hope I'm not interrupting you.* 我希望我没有打搅你。 ◇ *They were interrupted by a knock at the door.* 他们被敲门声打断了。 ◇ ~ (**sb**) + **speech** *'I have a question,' she*

I

interrupted. "我有一个问题。"她插嘴道。 **2** 🔑 [T] **~ sth** to stop sth for a short time 使暂停；使中断：*The game was interrupted several times by rain.* 比赛因下雨中断了几次。◇ *We interrupt this programme to bring you an important news bulletin.* 我们暂停本节目，插播重要新闻。 **3** [T] **~ sth** to stop a line, surface, view, etc. from being even or continuous 阻断，遮挡（连续线条、平面、景色等）

▼ **EXPRESS YOURSELF 情景表达**

Interrupting 打断别人

You may need to say something when somebody else is speaking, or you may be chairing a discussion where you have to stop one person talking too much. If you start talking at the same time as someone else, this will seem rude. To interrupt politely, you can say, for example
在别人说话时需要插话或主持讨论时某人讲话过多需要打断，直接插话或打断会显得粗鲁，可用一些礼貌的方式，比如：

- ***Sorry to interrupt**, but I have to disagree with that.* 不好意思打断一下，但那一点我得表示异议。
- ***Could I just say something here?*** 我可以插句话吗？
- ***If I could, let me stop you there for a moment and go** back to your previous point.* 请容我打断您一下，回到您先前讲到的一点。
- ***Actually, we seem to have strayed a bit from the topic. Can we go back to** the first point?* 实际上，我们似乎有点偏离了主题。我们可以回到第一点吗？
- ***Just a moment**, Sue. Can we hear what Jack has to say on this?* 稍等一下，休。我们能听听杰克对此怎么说吗？
- ***May I interrupt you there?** I don't think that's true.* (*formal*) 可以打断你一下吗？我认为那不是事实。
- ***I'm sorry, but we're running short on time.** Can you please summarize very quickly so we can finish up?* (*formal*) 抱歉，我们的时间不多了。请您快速总结一下我们就结束好吗？
- ***I appreciate your enthusiasm on this topic, but I'm afraid we have a couple more people to hear from.*** (*formal*) 感谢您对这个话题的热情，但我们还得听听另外几个人的发言。
- ***Could you two please discuss that issue privately after the meeting? We have several more items to cover and need to move on at this point.*** (*formal*) 请你们两位会后私下讨论那个问题好吗？我们还有几项内容要谈，现在该进入下一项内容了。
- ***I'm sorry, I really have to stop you there.** We've run out of time.* (*formal*) 抱歉，我必须在此打断你。我们没有时间了。
- ***Let's save that conversation for another time.*** 那事我们下次再谈吧。

inter·rup·tion 🔑 /ˌɪntəˈrʌpʃn/ *noun* [C, U] **1** 🔑 something that temporarily stops an activity or a situation; a time when an activity is stopped 阻断物；中断时间：*The birth of her son was a minor interruption to her career.* 她儿子的出生对她的事业造成一个小小的中断。◇ *an interruption to the power supply* 停电 ◇ *I managed to work for two hours **without interruption**.* 我总算连续工作了两小时。 **2** 🔑 the act of interrupting sb/sth and of stopping them from speaking 打扰；插嘴；打岔：*He ignored her interruptions.* 他没有理会她的打岔。◇ *She spoke for 20 minutes **without interruption**.* 她连续讲了 20 分钟。

inter·sect /ˌɪntəˈsekt; *NAmE* -tərˈs-/ *verb* **1** [I, T] (of lines, roads, etc. 线、道路等) to meet or cross each other 相交；交叉：**~ (sth)** *a pattern of intersecting streets* 纵横交错的街道图 ◇ *The lines intersect at right angles.* 线条垂直相交。◇ **~ with sth** *The path intersected with a busy road.* 小路与一条繁忙的大路相交。 **2** [T, usually passive] **~ sth (with sth)** to divide an area by crossing it 横穿；贯穿；横断：*The landscape is intersected with spectacular gorges.* 在大地景色中点缀着壮观的峡谷。

inter·sec·tion /ˌɪntəˈsekʃn; *NAmE* -tərˈs-/ *noun* **1** [C] (*NAmE* or *formal*, *BrE*) a place where two or more roads, lines, etc. meet or cross each other 十字路口；交叉路口；交点：*Traffic lights have been placed at all major intersections.* 所有主要的交叉路口都安装了交通信号灯。 **2** [U] the act of intersecting sth 横断；交叉；相交

inter·sex /ˈɪntəseks; *NAmE* -tərs-/ *noun* [U] (*medical* 医) the physical condition of being partly male and partly female 雌雄间性；雌雄间体

inter·sperse /ˌɪntəˈspɜːs; *NAmE* -tərˈspɜːrs/ *verb* **be interspersed with/in sth** to put sth in sth else or among or between other things 散布；散置；点缀：*Lectures will be interspersed with practical demonstrations.* 讲课中将不时插入实际示范。

inter·state /ˈɪntəsteɪt; *NAmE* -tərs-/ *adj.*, *noun*
■ ***adj.*** [only before noun] between states, especially in the US （尤指美国）州与州之间的，州际的：*interstate commerce* 州际贸易
■ ***noun*** (*also* ˌ**interstate** ˈ**highway**) (in the US) a wide road, with at least two lanes in each direction, where traffic can travel fast for long distances across many states. You can only enter and leave interstates at special RAMPS. （美国）州际公路 ➲ COMPARE MOTORWAY

inter·stel·lar /ˌɪntəˈstelə(r); *NAmE* -tərˈst-/ *adj.* [only before noun] between the stars in the sky 星际的 ➲ COMPARE STELLAR (1)

in·ter·stice /ɪnˈtɜːstɪs; *NAmE* -ˈtɜːrs-/ *noun* [usually pl.] (*formal*) a small crack or space in sth 裂缝；空隙

inter·sti·tial /ˌɪntəˈstɪʃl; *NAmE* -tərˈs-/ *adj.* (*medical* 医) in or related to small spaces between the parts of an organ or between groups of cells or TISSUES 间质的；组织间隙的：*interstitial cells* 间质细胞

inter·text·ual·ity /ˌɪntətekstʃuˈæləti; *NAmE* ˌɪntər-/ *noun* [U] (*specialist*) the relationship between texts, especially literary texts （尤指文学文本之间的）互文性

inter·twine /ˌɪntəˈtwaɪn; *NAmE* -tərˈtw-/ *verb* [usually passive] **1** [I, T] if two or more things **intertwine** or are **intertwined**, they are twisted together so that they are very difficult to separate （使）缠结，缠绕在一起：*intertwining branches* 缠绕在一起的树枝 ◇ **~ sth (with sth)** *a necklace of rubies intertwined with pearls* 缠着珍珠的红宝石项链 **2** [T, usually passive, I] **~ (sth)** to be or become very closely connected with sth/sb else 紧密相联：*Their political careers had become **closely intertwined**.* 他们的政治生涯已经紧密地结合在一起了。

inter·val 🔑 AW /ˈɪntəvl; *NAmE* ˈɪntərvl/ *noun* **1** 🔑 a period of time between two events （时间上的）间隔，间隙，间歇：*The interval between major earthquakes might be 200 years.* 大地震之间的间隔时间可能有 200 年。 **2** (*BrE*) (*also* **inter·mis·sion** *NAmE*, *BrE*) a short period of time separating parts of a play, film/movie or concert （戏剧、电影或音乐会的）幕间休息，休息时间：*There will be an interval of 20 minutes after the second act.* 第二幕结束后将休息 20 分钟。 ➲ WORDFINDER NOTE AT CONCERT **3** 🔑 [usually pl.] a short period during which sth different happens from what is happening the rest of the time （其他事情）穿插出现的间隙：*She's delirious, but has lucid intervals.* 她神志昏乱，但有时清醒。◇ (*BrE*) *The day should be mainly dry with sunny intervals.* 白天大部分时间干燥无雨，间有阳光。 **4** (*music* 音) a difference in PITCH (= how high or low a note sounds) between two notes 音程：*an interval of one octave* 一个八度音程

IDM **at (...) intervals 1** 🔑 with time between 每隔…时间；间或；不时：*Buses to the city leave **at regular intervals**.* 开往城里的公共汽车每隔一定时间发出一班。◇ *The runners started at 5-minute intervals.* 赛跑的人每隔 5 分钟出发一批。 **2** 🔑 with spaces between 每隔…距离；间隔：*Flaming torches were positioned at intervals along the terrace.* 沿排房每隔一段距离插着燃烧着的火炬。

ˈ**interval training** *noun* [U] sports training consisting of different activities which require different speeds or amounts of effort 间歇训练（包括不同速度或强度的活动）

inter·vene AW /ˌɪntəˈviːn; *NAmE* -tərˈv-/ *verb* **1** [I] to become involved in a situation in order to improve or help it 出面；介入： *She might have been killed if the neighbours hadn't intervened.* 要不是邻居介入，她可能会没命了。◇ **~ in sth** *The President intervened personally in the crisis.* 总统亲自出面处理这场危机。 **2** [T, I] (**+ speech**) to interrupt sb when they are speaking in order to say sth 插嘴；打断（别人的话）：*'But,' she intervened, 'what about the others?'* "但是，"她插嘴说，"其他的怎么办呢？" **3** [I] to happen in a way that delays sth or prevents it from happening 阻碍；阻挠；干扰： *They were planning to get married and then the war intervened.* 他们正准备结婚，不巧却因爆发战事而受阻。 **4** [I] (*formal*) to exist between two events or places 介于…之间： *I saw nothing of her during the years that intervened.* 这期间的几年中我根本没有见过她。

inter·ven·ing /ˌɪntəˈviːnɪŋ; *NAmE* -tərˈv-/ *adj.* [only before noun] coming or existing between two events, dates, objects, etc. 发生于其间的；介于中间的： *Little had changed in the intervening years.* 这些年间没有发生什么变化。

inter·ven·tion AW /ˌɪntəˈvenʃn; *NAmE* -tərˈv-/ *noun* [U, C] **1** action taken to improve or help a situation 出面；介入： *calls for government intervention to save the steel industry* 呼吁政府出面挽救钢铁业 ◇ **~ in sth** *In the second group of states, direct intervention in the economy was limited.* 对于第二组别的国家，对经济的直接干预是有限的。 **2** action by a country to become involved in the affairs of another country when they have not been asked to do so （对他国事务的）介入，干预，干涉行为： ***armed/military intervention*** 武装/军事干涉 ◇ **~ in sth** *NATO intervention in the troubled region* 北约对这一动荡地区的干预行动 ➲ COLLOCATIONS AT INTERNATIONAL **3** action taken to improve a medical condition or illness 介入治疗；医疗干预： ***a medical/surgical intervention*** 医疗/手术干预 **4 ~** (**in sth**) the act of interrupting sb when they are speaking in order to say sth 插嘴；打断（别人的话） **5** an occasion when a group of people confront a friend or family member who has an ADDICTION to drugs or alcohol, in order to help them recover （对有毒瘾或酒瘾的朋友或家人的）帮助戒毒，帮助戒酒： *Her daughters staged an intervention.* 她的女儿们开始介入，帮助戒除瘾症。

inter·ven·tion·ism /ˌɪntəˈvenʃənɪzəm; *NAmE* -tərˈv-/ *noun* [U] the policy or practice of a government influencing the economy of its own country, or of becoming involved in the affairs of other countries 政府干预（政策） ▸ **inter·ven·tion·ist** /-ʃənɪst/ *adj., noun*： *interventionist policies* 干预政策

inter·view 🔑 /ˈɪntəvjuː; *NAmE* -tərv-/ *noun, verb*

■ ***noun*** **1** 🔑 a formal meeting at which sb is asked questions to see if they are suitable for a particular job, or for a course of study at a college, university, etc. 面试；面谈： *a **job interview*** 求职面试 ◇ *to **be called for** (**an**) **interview*** 获通知约见 ◇ **~ for a job, etc.** *He **has an interview** next week for the manager's job.* 他下周要接受一个经理职位的面试。 ➲ WORDFINDER NOTE AT APPLY ➲ COLLOCATIONS AT JOB **2** 🔑 a meeting (often a public one) at which a journalist asks sb questions in order to find out their opinions （常指公开的）记者采访，访谈： *a **television/radio/newspaper interview*** 电视/电台/报纸采访 ◇ **~** (**with sb**) *an interview with the new Governor* 对新任州长的采访 ◇ *to **give an interview*** (= to agree to answer questions) 接受采访 ◇ *Yesterday, **in an interview** on German television, the minister denied the reports.* 昨天，在德国电视台的采访中，部长否认了那些报道。 ◇ *to **conduct an interview*** (= to ask sb questions in public) 进行采访 ◇ *The interview was published in all the papers.* 各家报纸都刊载了这次访谈。 **3** 🔑 **~** (**with sb**) a private meeting between people when questions are asked and answered （私下的）面谈，会谈，晤谈： *an interview with the careers adviser* 和就业顾问的面谈

■ ***verb*** **1** 🔑 [T, I] **~** (**sb**) (**for a job, etc.**) to talk to sb and ask them questions at a formal meeting to find out if they are suitable for a job, course of study, etc. 对（某人）进行面试（或面谈）： *Which post are you being interviewed for?* 你参加哪个职位的面试？ ◇ *We interviewed ten people for the job.* 我们为这份工作面试了十人。 **2** [I] (*especially NAmE*) **~** (**for a job, etc.**) to talk to sb and answer questions at a formal meeting to get a job, a place on a course of study, etc. 接受面试： *The website gives you tips on interviewing for colleges.* 这个网站为你提供大学面试的窍门。 ◇ (*BrE, NAmE*) *If you don't interview well you are unlikely to get the job.* 如果面试时表现不好，你很可能不会得到这份工作。 **3** 🔑 [T] to ask sb questions about their life, opinions, etc., especially on the radio or television or for a newspaper or magazine （媒体）采访，访问： **~ sb about sth** *Next week, I will be interviewing Spielberg about his latest movie.* 下周我将访问斯皮尔伯格，谈论他的最新电影。 ◇ **~ sb** *The Prime Minister declined to be interviewed.* 首相婉拒了采访。 **4** 🔑 [T] **~ sb** (**about sth**) to ask sb questions at a private meeting （私下）提问，面谈： *The police are waiting to interview the injured man.* 警察正等待着向受伤的男子问话。 ▸ **inter·view·ing** *noun* [U]： *The research involves in-depth interviewing.* 这一调查包括深入的采访。 ◇ *interviewing techniques* 面谈技巧

▼ **SYNONYMS 同义词辨析**

interview

interrogation • audience • consultation

These are all words for a meeting or occasion when sb is asked for information, opinions or advice. 以上各词均表示会见、询问、咨询。

interview a formal meeting at which sb is asked questions, for example, to see if they are suitable for a particular job or course of study, or in order to find out their opinions about sth 指面试、面谈： *a job interview* 求职面试

interrogation the process of asking sb a lot of questions, especially in an aggressive way, in order to get information; an occasion on which this is done 指讯问、审问、盘问： *He confessed after four days under interrogation.* 他在受讯问四天之后招认了。

audience a formal meeting with an important person 指与要人的会见、觐见： *The Pope granted her a private audience.* 教皇同意私下接见她。

consultation a meeting with an expert, especially a doctor, to get advice or treatment 指向专家请教的咨询，尤指就诊

PATTERNS

- an **in-depth** interview/consultation
- a **police** interview/interrogation
- to **have/request** a(n) interview/audience/consultation with sb
- to **give/grant** sb a(n) interview/audience/consultation
- to **carry out/conduct** an interview/interrogation

inter·view·ee /ˌɪntəvjuːˈiː; *NAmE* -tərv-/ *noun* the person who answers the questions in an interview 参加面试者；接受采访者

inter·view·er /ˈɪntəvjuːə(r); *NAmE* -tərv-/ *noun* the person who asks the questions in an interview 主持面试者；采访者

inter·war /ˌɪntəˈwɔː(r); *NAmE* -tərˈw-/ *adj.* [only before noun] happening or existing between the First and the Second World Wars 两次世界大战之间的： *the **interwar years/period*** 两次世界大战之间的时期

inter·weave /ˌɪntəˈwiːv; *NAmE* -tərˈw-/ *verb* (**inter·wove** /-ˈwəʊv/; *NAmE* -ˈwoʊv/, **inter·woven** /-ˈwəʊvn/; *NAmE* -ˈwoʊvn/) [T, usually passive, I] **~** (**sth**) (**with sth**) to twist together two or more pieces of thread, wool, etc. 交织；交错编织： *The blue fabric was interwoven with red and* gold thread. 蓝布中交织着红色和金色的线。◇ (*figurative*) *The problems are inextricably interwoven* (= very closely connected). 问题盘根错节。

in·tes·tate /ɪnˈtesteɪt/ *adj.* (*law* 律) not having made a WILL (= a legal document that says what is to happen to a person's property when they die) 未留遗嘱的 ▶ **in·tes·tacy** /ɪnˈtestəsi/ *noun* [U]

in,testinal ˈfortitude *noun* (*NAmE, formal* or *humorous*) the courage and determination necessary to do sth difficult or unpleasant (used when you want to avoid using the word *guts*) 勇气，决心，毅力（避免说 guts 时用）：*He did not have the intestinal fortitude to implement the changes.* 他没有胆量实行变革。

in·tes·tine /ɪnˈtestɪn/ *noun* [usually pl.] a long tube in the body between the stomach and the ANUS. Food passes from the stomach to the **small intestine** and from there to the **large intestine**. 肠 ➲ VISUAL VOCAB PAGE V64 ▶ **in·tes·tinal** /ɪnˈtestɪnl; ˌɪnteˈstaɪnl/ *adj.* [usually before noun]

in·tim·acy /ˈɪntɪməsi/ *noun* (*pl.* **-ies**) **1** [U] the state of having a close personal relationship with sb 亲密；密切；关系密切 **2** [C, usually pl.] a thing that a person says or does to sb that they know very well 亲密的言语（或行为） **3** [U] (*formal* or *law* 律) sexual activity, especially an act of SEXUAL INTERCOURSE 性行为；（尤指）性交

in·tim·ate *adj., verb, noun*

■ ***adj.*** /ˈɪntɪmət/ **1** (of people 人) having a close and friendly relationship 亲密的；密切的：*intimate friends* 密友 ◇ *We're not* ***on intimate terms with*** *our neighbours.* 我们和邻居来往不多。 **2** private and personal, often in a sexual way 个人隐私的（常指性方面的）：*The article revealed* ***intimate details*** *about his family life.* 文章披露了他的家庭生活中的隐私。◇ *the most intimate parts of her body* 她的身体的最隐私部位 **3** (of a place or situation 地方或情形) encouraging close, friendly relationships, sometimes of a sexual nature 宜于密切关系的；温馨的；便于有性关系的：*an intimate restaurant* 幽静温馨的餐厅 ◇ *He knew an intimate little bar where they would not be disturbed.* 他知道一处适合幽会的小酒吧，他们在那里不会受到打扰。 **4** (of knowledge 知识) very detailed and thorough 详尽的；精通的：*an intimate knowledge of the English countryside* 对英格兰乡村的透彻了解 **5** (of a link between things 事物间的联系) very close 密切的；紧密的：*an* ***intimate connection*** *between class and educational success* 社会阶层和优良教育之间的密切联系 **6** ~ (**with sb**) (*formal* or *law* 律) having a sexual relationship with sb 有性关系的；暧昧的 ▶ **in·tim·ate·ly** *adv.*：***intimately connected/linked/related*** 密切相关 ◇ *an area of the country that he knew intimately* 他十分熟悉的本国的一个地区 ◇ *She was* ***intimately involved*** *in the project.* 她已投到这个项目中去。◇ *They touched each other intimately* (= in a sexual way). 他们相互爱抚。

■ ***verb*** /ˈɪntɪmeɪt/ (*formal*) to let sb know what you think or mean in an indirect way 透露；（间接）表示；暗示 SYN **make known**：~ **sth** (**to sb**) *He has already intimated to us his intention to retire.* 他已经向我们透露了他要退休的打算。◇ ~ (**that**)... *He has already intimated (that) he intends to retire.* 他已经暗示他打算退休。

■ ***noun*** /ˈɪntɪmət/ (*formal*) a close personal friend 密友；至交；知己 ➲ MORE LIKE THIS 21, page R27

in·tim·ation /ˌɪntɪˈmeɪʃn/ *noun* [C, U] (*formal*) the act of stating sth or of making it known, especially in an indirect way 透露；间接表示；暗示：*There was no intimation from his doctor that his condition was serious.* 他的医生没有透露他的病情很严重。

in·timi·date /ɪnˈtɪmɪdeɪt/ *verb* ~ **sb** (**into sth/into doing sth**) to frighten or threaten sb so that they will do what you want 恐吓；威胁：*They were accused of intimidating people into voting for them.* 他们被控胁迫选民投他们的票。◇ *She refused to be intimidated by their threats.* 她没有被他们的威胁吓倒。▶ **in·timi·da·tion** /ɪnˌtɪmɪˈdeɪʃn/ *noun* [U]：*the intimidation of witnesses* 对目击证人的恐吓

in·timi·dated /ɪnˈtɪmɪdeɪtɪd/ *adj.* [not usually before noun] feeling frightened and not confident in a particular situation 胆怯；怯场：*We try to make sure children don't feel intimidated on their first day at school.* 我们努力确保孩子们在上学的第一天不胆怯。

in·timi·dat·ing /ɪnˈtɪmɪdeɪtɪŋ/ *adj.* frightening in a way which makes a person feel less confident 吓人的；令人胆怯的：*an intimidating manner* 使人望而生畏的态度 ◇ ~ **for/to sb** *This kind of questioning can be very intimidating to children.* 这种问话的方式可能让孩子们非常害怕。

in·timi·da·tory /ɪnˌtɪmɪˈdeɪtəri/ *adj.* (*formal*) intended to frighten or threaten sb 恐吓的；威胁的

into /ˈɪntə; *before vowels* ˈɪntu; *strong form* ˈɪntuː/ *prep.* HELP For the special uses of **into** in phrasal verbs, look at the entries for the verbs. For example **lay into sb/sth** is in the phrasal verb section at **lay**. * into 在短语动词中的特殊用法见有关动词词条。如 lay into sb/sth 在词条 lay 的短语动词部分。 **1** to a position in or inside sth 到…里面；进入：*Come into the house.* 进屋里来吧。◇ *She dived into the water.* 她潜入水中。◇ *He threw the letter into the fire.* 他把信扔进了火中。◇ (*figurative*) *She turned and walked off into the night.* 她转过身去，走进黑夜里。 **2** in the direction of sth 朝；向；对着：*Speak clearly into the microphone.* 清楚地对着麦克风讲话。◇ *Driving into the sun, we had to shade our eyes.* 面向太阳开车，我们只好遮挡着眼睛。 **3** to a point at which you hit sb/sth 撞上；碰上：*The truck crashed into a parked car.* 卡车撞上了一辆停放着的汽车。 **4** to a point during a period of time 到（一段时间的某一点）：*She carried on working late into the night.* 她一直工作到了深夜。◇ *He didn't get married until he was well into his forties.* 他到四十好几才结婚。 **5** used to show a change in state（表示状态的变化）：*The fruit can be made into jam.* 这种水果可以制成果酱。◇ *Can you translate this passage into German?* 你能把这一段文字译成德语吗？◇ *They came into power in 2008.* 他们于 2008 年上台掌权。◇ *She was sliding into depression.* 她逐渐消沉下去。 **6** used to show the result of an action（表示行动的结果）：*He was shocked into a confession of guilt.* 他被吓得认罪了。 **7** about or concerning sth 关于；有关：*an inquiry into safety procedures* 关于安全程序的调查 **8** used when you are dividing numbers（用于除数）除：*3 into 24 is 8.* * 24 除以 3 等于 8。

IDM **be ˈinto sb for sth** (*US, informal*) to owe sb money or be owed money by sb 欠某人（钱）；某人欠（钱）：*By the time he'd fixed the leak, I was into him for $500.* 他补好漏洞时，我就该付给他 500 美元。◇ *The bank was into her for $100 000.* 她欠了银行 10 万美元。 **be ˈinto sth** (*informal*) to be interested in sth in an active way 对…十分感兴趣；很喜欢：*He's into surfing in a big way.* 他迷上了冲浪运动。

in·toler·able /ɪnˈtɒlərəbl; *NAmE* -ˈtɑːl-/ *adj.* so bad or difficult that you cannot TOLERATE it; completely unacceptable 无法忍受的；不能容忍的；完全不可接受的 SYN **unbearable**：*an intolerable burden/situation* 无法承受的负担；不能容忍的情况 ◇ *The heat was intolerable.* 炎热让人受不了。▶ **in·toler·ably** /-əbli/ *adv.*：*intolerably hot* 热得无法忍受

in·toler·ant /ɪnˈtɒlərənt; *NAmE* -ˈtɑːl-/ *adj.* **1** ~ (**of sb/sth**) (*disapproving*) not willing to accept ideas or ways of behaving that are different from your own 不容忍的；偏狭的；不容异说的；偏执的 OPP **tolerant** **2** (*specialist*) not able to eat particular foods, use particular medicines, etc. without becoming ill/sick（对食物、药物等）不耐受的，不耐的：*recipes for people who are gluten intolerant* 对谷蛋白不耐受人士的食谱 ▶ **in·toler·ance** /-əns/ *noun* [U, C]：*religious intolerance* 宗教上的不宽容 ◇ *an intolerance to dairy products* 乳制品不耐受

in·ton·ation /ˌɪntəˈneɪʃn/ *noun* **1** [U, C] (*phonetics* 语音) the rise and fall of the voice in speaking, especially as this affects the meaning of what is being said 语调：*intonation patterns* 语调类型 ◇ *In English, some questions have a rising intonation.* 英语中有些疑问句使用升调。➲ COMPARE STRESS *n.* (4) ➲ WORDFINDER NOTE AT

PRONUNCIATION **2** [U] (*music* 音) the quality of playing or singing exactly in tune（演奏或唱歌中的）音准

in·tone /ɪn'təʊn; *NAmE* ɪn'toʊn/ *verb* **~ sth | + speech** (*formal*) to say sth in a slow and serious voice without much expression 缓慢庄重地说： *The priest intoned the final prayer.* 神父庄重地念了最后的祷文。

in toto /ˌɪn 'təʊtəʊ; *NAmE* 'toʊtoʊ/ *adv.* (*from Latin, formal*) completely; including all parts 完全地；完整地；全部地

in·toxi·cant /ɪn'tɒksɪkənt; *NAmE* -'tɑːk-/ *noun* (*specialist*) a substance such as alcohol that produces false feelings of pleasure and a lack of control 麻醉剂；毒品；酒类饮料

in·toxi·cated /ɪn'tɒksɪkeɪtɪd; *NAmE* -'tɑːk-/ *adj.* (*formal*) **1** under the influence of alcohol or drugs 喝醉的；（吸毒后）迷醉的： (*NAmE*) *He was arrested for DWI* (= driving while intoxicated). 他因醉酒驾驶而被拘捕。 **2 ~ (by/with sth)** very excited by sth, so that you cannot think clearly 陶醉的；忘乎所以的；极度兴奋的： *intoxicated with success* 被成功冲昏了头脑 ▸ **in·toxi·cate** *verb* **~ sb**

in·toxi·cat·ing /ɪn'tɒksɪkeɪtɪŋ; *NAmE* -'tɑːk-/ *adj.* (*formal*) **1** (of drink 饮料) containing alcohol 含酒精的；醉人的 **2** making you feel excited so that you cannot think clearly 令人陶醉的；令人头脑迷糊的： *Power can be intoxicating.* 权力能让人得意忘形。 ▸ **in·toxi·ca·tion** /ɪnˌtɒksɪ'keɪʃn; *NAmE* -ˌtɑːk-/ *noun* [U]

intra- *prefix* (in adjectives and adverbs 构成形容词和副词) inside; within 在（…）里；在（…）内： *intravenous* 静脉内的 ◇ *intra-departmental* (= within a department) 部门内的 ➲ COMPARE INTER- ➲ MORE LIKE THIS 6, page R25

in·tract·able /ɪn'træktəbl/ *adj.* (*formal*) (of a problem or a person 问题或人) very difficult to deal with 很难对付（或处理）的 **OPP tractable** ▸ **in·tract·abil·ity** /ɪnˌtræktə'bɪləti/ *noun* [U]

intra·mural /ˌɪntrə'mjʊərəl; *NAmE* -'mjʊrəl/ *adj.* (*especially NAmE*) taking place within a single institution, especially a school or college 机构内部的；（尤指）学校内的，大学内的： *Jeff played intramural basketball in high school.* 杰夫在中学时参加了校内篮球赛。

intra·mus·cu·lar /ˌɪntrə'mʌskjələ(r)/ *adj.* (*medical* 医) happening inside a muscle or put into a muscle 肌肉内的；注入肌内的： *intramuscular pain* 肌疼痛 ◇ *an intramuscular injection* 肌内注射

intra·net /'ɪntrənet/ *noun* (*computing* 计) a computer network that is private to a company, university, etc. often using the same software as the World Wide Web 内联网（公司、大学等的内部网络）

in·transi·gent /ɪn'trænsɪdʒənt; *NAmE* -'trænz-/ *adj.* (*formal, disapproving*) (of people 人) unwilling to change their opinions or behaviour in a way that would be helpful to others 不妥协的；不愿合作的；不肯让步的 **SYN stubborn** ▸ **in·transi·gence** /-əns/ *noun* [U]

in·transi·tive /ɪn'trænsətɪv/ *adj.* (*grammar* 语法) (of verbs 动词) used without a DIRECT OBJECT 不及物的 **OPP transitive**: *The verb 'die' as in 'He died suddenly', is intransitive.* * He died suddenly 中的动词 die 是不及物的。 ▸ **in·transi·tive·ly** *adv.*: *The verb is being used intransitively.* 这个动词此处作为不及物动词使用。

intra·uter·ine /ˌɪntrə'juːtəraɪn/ *adj.* (*medical* 医) within the UTERUS 子宫内的

ˌ**intrauterine de'vice** *noun* = IUD

intra·ven·ous /ˌɪntrə'viːnəs/ *adj.* (*abbr.* **IV**) (*medical* 医) (of drugs or food 药物或食物) going into a VEIN 注入静脉的；静脉内的： *intravenous fluids* 静脉供给液 ◇ *an intravenous injection* 静脉注射 ◇ *an intravenous drug user* 使用静脉注射的吸毒者 ▸ **intra·ven·ous·ly** *adv.*

'**in tray** (*NAmE also* **in·box**) *noun* (in an office) a container on your desk for letters that are waiting to be read or answered （办公室中的）收件盘 ➲ COMPARE OUT TRAY ➲ VISUAL VOCAB PAGE V71

in·trench = ENTRENCH

in·trepid /ɪn'trepɪd/ *adj.* (*formal, often humorous*) very brave; not afraid of danger or difficulties 勇敢的；无畏的 **SYN fearless**: *an intrepid explorer* 勇敢的探险家

in·tri·cacy /'ɪntrɪkəsi/ *noun* **1 in·tri·ca·cies** [pl.] **the ~ of sth** the complicated parts or details of sth 错综复杂的事物（或细节）： *the intricacies of economic policy* 经济政策的错综复杂 **2** [U] the fact of having complicated parts, details or patterns 错综复杂： *the intricacy of the design* 设计的复杂性

in·tri·cate /'ɪntrɪkət/ *adj.* having a lot of different parts and small details that fit together 错综复杂的： *intricate patterns* 复杂的图案 ◇ *an intricate network of loyalties and relationships* 忠诚与义气的复杂网络 ▸ **in·tri·cate·ly** *adv.*: *intricately carved* 精雕细刻的

in·trigue *verb, noun*

■ ***verb*** /ɪn'triːg/ **1** [T, often passive] **~ sb | it intrigues sb that...** to make sb very interested and want to know more about sth 激起…的兴趣；引发…的好奇心： *You've really intrigued me—tell me more!* 你说的真有意思，再给我讲一些吧！ **2** [I] **~ (with sb) (against sb)** (*formal*) to secretly plan with other people to harm sb 秘密策划（加害他人）；密谋

■ ***noun*** /'ɪntriːg; ɪn'triːg/ **1** [U] the activity of making secret plans in order to achieve an aim, often by tricking people 密谋策划；阴谋： *political intrigue* 政治阴谋 ◇ *The young heroine steps into a web of intrigue in the academic world.* 年轻的女主人公陷入了学术界钩心斗角的罗网。 **2** [C] a secret plan or relationship, especially one which involves sb else being tricked 密谋；秘密关系；阴谋诡计： *I soon learnt about all the intrigues and scandals that went on in the little town.* 我很快便知道了小镇上流传的种种阴谋与丑闻。 **3** [U] the atmosphere of interest and excitement that surrounds sth secret or important 神秘气氛；引人入胜的复杂情节

in·trigued /ɪn'triːgd/ *adj.* [not usually before noun] very interested in sth/sb and wanting to know more about it/them 着迷；很感兴趣；好奇： *He was intrigued by her story.* 他被她的故事迷住了。 ◇ **~ to do sth** *I'm intrigued to know what you thought of the movie.* 我很想知道你对这部电影的看法。

in·tri·guing /ɪn'triːgɪŋ/ *adj.* very interesting because of being unusual or not having an obvious answer 非常有趣的；引人入胜的；神秘的： *These discoveries raise intriguing questions.* 这些发现带来了非常有趣的问题。 ◇ *an intriguing possibility* 令人不解的可能性 ◇ *He found her intriguing.* 他觉得她很迷人。 ▸ **in·tri·guing·ly** *adv.*

in·trin·sic **AW** /ɪn'trɪnsɪk; -zɪk/ *adj.* belonging to or part of the real nature of sth/sb 固有的；内在的；本身的： *the intrinsic value of education* 教育的固有价值 ◇ *These tasks were repetitive, lengthy and lacking any intrinsic interest.* 这些作业重复冗长，没什么意义。 ◇ **~ to sth** *Small local shops are intrinsic to the town's character.* 本地的一些小店铺是这个镇的基本特点。 ➲ COMPARE EXTRINSIC ▸ **in·trin·sic·al·ly** **AW** /-kli/ *adv.*: *There is nothing intrinsically wrong with the idea* (= it is good in itself but there may be outside circumstances which mean it is not suitable). 这种想法本身并没有错。

intro /'ɪntrəʊ; *NAmE* 'ɪntroʊ/ *noun* (*pl.* **-os**) (*informal*) an introduction to sth, especially to a piece of music or writing 介绍；（尤指）前奏，前言，导言

intro·duce 🔑 /ˌɪntrə'djuːs; *NAmE* -'duːs/ *verb*

• **PEOPLE** 人 **1** 🔑 to tell two or more people who have not met before what each other's names are; to tell sb what your name is 把…介绍（给）；引见；（自我）介绍： **~ sb** *Can I introduce my wife?* 我来介绍一下我的妻子。 ◇ **~ A to B (as sth)** *He introduced me to a Greek girl at the party.* 他在聚会上介绍我认识了一位希腊姑娘。 ◇ **~ A and B** *We've already been introduced.* 我们已经介绍认识了。 ◇ **~ yourself (to sb)** *Can I introduce myself? I'm Helen Robins.* 让我来自我介绍一下吧。我叫海伦·罗宾斯。 ◇ *'Kay, this is Steve.' 'Yes, I know—we've already introduced* *ourselves.*'"凯，这是史蒂夫。""是的，我知道，我们已经自己相互介绍了。"

• **TV/RADIO SHOW** 电视 / 电台节目 **2** ~ **sb/sth** to be the main speaker in a television or radio show, who gives details about the show and who presents the people who are in it; to tell the audience the name of the person who is going to speak or perform 主持（节目）；介绍（讲演者或演员）：*The next programme will be introduced by Mary David.* 下一个节目由玛丽·戴维主持。◇ *May I introduce my first guest on the show tonight…* 请让我介绍今晚节目的第一位嘉宾…

• **NEW EXPERIENCE** 新经历 **3** to make sb learn about sth or do sth for the first time 使初次了解；使尝试：~ **sb to sth** *The first lecture introduces students to the main topics of the course.* 第一堂课是让学生了解这门课的主要内容。◇ ~ **sth (to sb)** *It was she who first introduced the pleasures of sailing to me.* 是她最先使我体会到了帆船运动的乐趣。

• **NEW PRODUCT/LAW** 新产品；新法律 **4** to make sth available for use, discussion, etc. for the first time 推行；实施；采用 SYN **bring sb/sth↔in**: ~ **sth** *The company is introducing a new range of products this year.* 公司今年将推出一系列新产品。◇ *The new law was introduced in 2007.* 这项新法律是于 2007 年开始实施的。◇ ~ **sth into/to sth** *We want to introduce the latest technology into schools.* 我们想向各学校推介最新的技术。

• **PLANT/ANIMAL/DISEASE** 动植物；疾病 **5** ~ **sth (to/into sth)** to bring a plant, an animal or a disease to a place for the first time 引进（动物或植物）；传入（疾病）：*Vegetation patterns changed when goats were introduced to the island.* 自从引进山羊之后，这个岛上的植被模式改变了。

• **START** 开始 **6** ~ **sth** to be the start of sth new 作为（新事物）的开头；使开始；创始：*Bands from London introduced the craze for this kind of music.* 伦敦的乐队引发了对这种音乐的狂热。◇ *A slow theme introduces the first movement.* 缓慢的主旋律引出了第一乐章。

• **IN PARLIAMENT** 议会 **7** ~ **sth** to formally present a new law so that it can be discussed 将（法案）提交讨论：*to introduce a bill (before Parliament)*（向议会）提交议案

• **ADD** 增加 **8** ~ **sth (into sth)** (*formal*) to put sth into sth 将…放进；添入：*Particles of glass had been introduced into the baby food.* 这种婴儿食品中被掺进了玻璃碎屑。

▼ **EXPRESS YOURSELF** 情景表达

Making introductions 作介绍

There are different ways of introducing people to one another, depending on how formal the situation is. 介绍人们彼此认识有几种不同的方式，这要取决于场合的正式程度：

- *Amy,* ***do you know my friend*** *Simon?* 艾米，你认识我的朋友西蒙吗？
- ***Have you two met?*** *Jane,* ***this is*** *Matt.* 你们两位见过面吗？简，这是马特。
- *Ted, this is Gwen—she's Porter's mother.* 泰德，这是格温，她是波特的母亲。
- ***Can I introduce you to*** *my colleague Professor Welsh?* (*formal*) 让我来介绍你认识我的同事韦尔什教授。

Responses 回应：

- ***No, I don't think we've met.*** *I'm Harry.* 不，我想我们没见过面。我是哈里。
- ***Hello. Nice to meet you.*** 你好，很高兴认识你。
- ***Hi. I'm*** *Norman Miller.* 你好，我是诺曼·米勒。

intro·duc·tion /ˌɪntrəˈdʌkʃn/ *noun*

• **BRINGING INTO USE/TO A PLACE** 采用；引进 **1** [U] the act of bringing sth into use or existence for the first time, or of bringing sth to a place for the first time 初次投入使用；采用；引进；推行：*the introduction of new manufacturing methods* 新制造方法的采用 ◇ *the introduction of compulsory military service* 义务兵役制的实行 ◇ *the 1 000th anniversary of the introduction of Christianity to Russia* 基督教传入俄罗斯 1 000 周年的纪念 **2** [C] a thing that is brought into use or introduced to a place for the first time 新采用（或新引进）的事物：*The book lists plants suitable for the British flower garden, among them many new introductions.* 这本书列出了适合英国花园种植的花草，其中有很多新引进的品种。

• **OF PEOPLE** 人 **3** [C] ~ **(to sb)** the act of making one person formally known to another, in which you tell each the other's name （正式的）介绍，引见：*Introductions were made and the conversation started to flow.* 大家相互介绍之后交谈就开始了。◇ *Our speaker today* ***needs no introduction*** (= is already well known). 我们今天的发言人就不必介绍了。◇ ***a letter of introduction*** (= a letter which tells sb who you are, written by sb who knows both you and the person reading the letter) 介绍信

• **FIRST EXPERIENCE** 初次经历 **4** [sing.] ~ **(to sth)** a person's first experience of sth 初次经历；首次体验：*This album was my first introduction to modern jazz.* 这张专辑让我初次接触了现代爵士乐。

• **OF BOOK/SPEECH** 书；讲话 **5** [C, U] ~ **(to sth)** the first part of a book or speech that gives a general idea of what is to follow 序言；引言；导论：*a brief introduction* 简短的序言 ◇ *a book with an excellent introduction and notes* 有精彩前言和注释的书 ◇ ***By way of introduction****, let me give you the background to the story.* 作为引言，我先来介绍一下故事的背景。➲ COMPARE PREFACE *n.*

• **TO SUBJECT** 学科 **6** [C] ~ **(to sth)** a book or course for people beginning to study a subject 初级读物；入门课程：*'An Introduction to Astronomy'*《天文学入门》◇ *It's a useful introduction to an extremely complex subject.* 这是对一门极为复杂的学科的有益入门教程。

• **IN MUSIC** 音乐 **7** [C] (*music* 音) a short section at the beginning of a piece of music 前奏：*an eight-bar introduction* 有八个小节的前奏

intro·duc·tory /ˌɪntrəˈdʌktəri/ *adj.* **1** written or said at the beginning of sth as an introduction to what follows 序言的；引导的；介绍的 SYN **opening**: ***introductory*** *chapters/paragraphs/remarks* 序篇；引言段；开场白 **2** intended as an introduction to a subject or an activity for people who have never done it before 入门的；初步的：***introductory*** *courses/lectures* 基础课程 / 讲座 **3** offered for a short time only, when a product is first on sale （新产品）试销的：*a special* ***introductory*** *price of just $10* 仅 10 美元的优惠上市价 ◇ *This* ***introductory*** *offer is for three days only.* 本试销优惠只为期三天。

intro·spec·tion /ˌɪntrəˈspekʃn/ *noun* [U] the careful examination of your own thoughts, feelings and reasons for behaving in a particular way 内省；反省

intro·spect·ive /ˌɪntrəˈspektɪv/ *adj.* tending to think a lot about your own thoughts, feelings, etc. 好内省的；好反省的

intro·vert /ˈɪntrəvɜːt; *NAmE* -vɜːrt/ *noun* a quiet person who is more interested in their own thoughts and feelings than in spending time with other people 内向的人；不喜欢与人交往的人 OPP **extrovert** ▸ **intro·ver·sion** /ˌɪntrəˈvɜːʃn; *NAmE* -ˈvɜːrʒn/ *noun* [U]

intro·vert·ed /ˈɪntrəvɜːtɪd; *NAmE* -vɜːrt-/ (*also* **intro·vert**) *adj.* more interested in your own thoughts and feelings than in spending time with other people 内向的；不喜欢交往的 OPP **extrovert**

in·trude /ɪnˈtruːd/ *verb* (*formal*) **1** [I] to go or be somewhere where you are not wanted or are not supposed to be 闯入；侵入；打扰：*I'm sorry to intrude, but I need to talk to someone.* 对不起打扰了，不过我有话要找人谈。◇ ~ **into/on/upon sb/sth** *legislation to stop newspapers from intruding on people's private lives* 禁止报章侵犯他人私生活的立法 **2** [I] ~ **(on/into/upon sth)** to disturb sth or have an unpleasant effect on it 扰乱；侵扰：*The sound of the telephone intruded into his dreams.* 电话铃声把他从梦中扰醒了。

in·truder /ɪnˈtruːdə(r)/ *noun* **1** a person who enters a building or an area illegally 闯入者；侵入者 **2** a person who is somewhere where they are not wanted 不受欢迎的人；不速之客：*The people in the room seemed to* *regard her as an unwelcome intruder.* 屋子里的人似乎把她当成不受欢迎的外人。

in·tru·sion /ɪn'truːʒn/ *noun* [U, C] **1** something that affects a situation or people's lives in a way that they do not want 侵扰性的事物；扰乱；侵犯：~ **(on/upon sth)** *They claim the noise from the new airport is an intrusion on their lives.* 他们声称新机场的噪音侵扰了他们的生活。◇ ~ **(into sth)** *This was another example of press intrusion into the affairs of the royals.* 这是新闻界侵扰王室成员私事的又一实例。 **2** ~ **(into/on/upon sth)** (*formal*) the act of entering a place which is private or where you may not be wanted 闯入；侵入：*She apologized for the intrusion but said she had an urgent message.* 她为径自闯进来道歉，但说她有紧急消息。

in·tru·sive /ɪn'truːsɪv/ *adj.* **1** too noticeable, direct, etc. in a way that is disturbing or annoying 侵入的；闯入的；侵扰的；烦扰的：*intrusive questions* 唐突的问题 ◇ *The constant presence of the media was very intrusive.* 媒体一直在场十分令人讨厌。 **2** (*phonetics* 语音) (of a speech sound 语音) produced in order to link two words together when speaking, for example the /r/ sound produced at the end of *law* by some English speakers in the phrase 'law and order'. Intrusive 'r' is not considered part of standard English. 添加的；插入的

in·tub·ate /'ɪntjubeɪt; *NAmE* -tu-/ *verb* [T, I] ~ **(sb/sth)** to put a tube into a hollow space in the body, for example to allow a person to breathe （给…）插管；插入喉管：*They managed to intubate the victim inside the wrecked car.* 他们设法为失事汽车里的受害者插了管。◇ *to intubate the trachea* 给气管插管 ◇ *We made the decision not to intubate.* 我们决定不插管。

in·tuit /ɪn'tjuːɪt; *NAmE* -'tuː-/ *verb* ~ **that…** | ~ **sth** | ~ **what, why, etc.…** (*formal*) to know that sth is true based on your feelings rather than on facts, what sb tells you, etc. 凭直觉知道：*She intuited that something was badly wrong.* 她凭直觉感到出了大问题。

in·tu·ition /ˌɪntju'ɪʃn; *NAmE* -tu-/ *noun* **1** [U] the ability to know sth by using your feelings rather than considering the facts 直觉力 **2** [C] ~ **(that…)** an idea or a strong feeling that sth is true although you cannot explain why （一种）直觉：*I had an intuition that something awful was about to happen.* 我直觉感到要出乱子了。

in·tui·tive /ɪn'tjuːɪtɪv; *NAmE* -'tuː-/ *adj.* **1** (of ideas 思想) obtained by using your feelings rather than by considering the facts 凭直觉得到的；直觉的：*He had an intuitive sense of what the reader wanted.* 他能直觉地感到读者需要什么。 **2** (of people 人) able to understand sth by using feelings rather than by considering the facts 有直觉力的 **3** (of computer software, etc. 计算机软件等) easy to understand and to use 易懂的；使用简便的 ▶ **in·tui·tive·ly** *adv.*：*Intuitively, she knew that he was lying.* 她凭直觉知道他在说谎。

Inuit /'ɪnjuɪt; 'ɪnuɪt/ *noun* [pl.] (*sing.* **Inuk** /'ɪnʊk/) a race of people from northern Canada and parts of Greenland and Alaska. The name is sometimes also wrongly used to refer to people from Siberia and S and W Alaska. 因纽特人（加拿大北部以及格陵兰和阿拉斯加部分地区的一个种族的人，有时误指西伯利亚及阿拉斯加南部和西部的人）➲ COMPARE ESKIMO

Inuk·ti·tut /ɪ'nʊktɪtʊt/ *noun* [U] the language of the Inuit people 因纽特语

in·un·date /'ɪnʌndeɪt/ *verb* [usually passive] **1** ~ **sb (with sth)** to give or send sb so many things that they cannot deal with them all 使不胜负荷；使应接不暇 SYN **overwhelm, swamp**：*We have been inundated with offers of help.* 主动援助多得使我们应接不暇。 **2** ~ **sth** (*formal*) to cover an area of land with a large amount of water 淹没；泛滥 SYN **flood** ▶ **in·un·da·tion** /ˌɪnʌn'deɪʃn/ *noun* [U, C]

inure /ɪ'njʊə(r); *NAmE* ɪ'njʊr/ *verb*

PHR V **i'nure sb/yourself to sth** (*formal*) to make sb/yourself get used to sth unpleasant so that they/you are no longer strongly affected by it 使习惯于，使适应（不愉快的事物）

in·vade /ɪn'veɪd/ *verb* **1** [I, T] to enter a country, town, etc. using military force in order to take control of it 武装入侵；侵略；侵犯：*Troops invaded on August 9th that year.* 军队是在那年的 8 月 9 日入侵的。◇ ~ **sth** *When did the Romans invade Britain?* 古罗马人是何时侵略不列颠的？ ➲ WORDFINDER NOTE AT ARMY **2** [T] ~ **sth** to enter a place in large numbers, especially in a way that causes damage or confusion （尤指造成损害或混乱地）涌入；侵袭：*Demonstrators invaded the government buildings.* 大批示威者闯进了政府办公大楼。◇ *As the final whistle blew, fans began invading the field.* 比赛结束的哨声一响，球迷便开始冲入球场。◇ *The cancer cells may invade other parts of the body.* 癌细胞可能扩散到身体的其他部位。 **3** [T] ~ **sth** to affect sth in an unpleasant or annoying way 侵扰；干扰：*Do the press have the right to* ***invade her privacy*** *in this way?* 新闻界有权以这种方式干扰她的私生活吗？ ➲ SEE ALSO INVASION, INVASIVE

in·vader /ɪn'veɪdə(r)/ *noun* an army or a country that enters another country by force in order to take control of it; a soldier fighting in such an army 武装入侵的军队（或国家）；侵略者：*a foreign invader* 外国侵略者 ◇ *They prepared to repel the invaders.* 他们准备赶走侵略军。◇ (*figurative*) *The white blood cells attack cells infected with an invader.* 白细胞攻击受到感染的细胞。

in·valid *adj., noun, verb*

▪ ***adj.*** /ɪn'vælɪd/ **1** not legally or officially acceptable （法律上或官方）不承认的；无效的：*The treaty was declared invalid because it had not been ratified.* 条约没有得到批准，因此被宣布无效。◇ *People with invalid papers are deported to another country.* 持无效证件的人被驱逐到别国。 **2** not based on all the facts, and therefore not correct 无充分事实的；站不住脚的：*an invalid argument* 站不住脚的论点 **3** (*computing* 计) of a type that the computer cannot recognize 不能识别的；无效的：*An error code will be displayed if any invalid information has been entered.* 输入了无效信息将显示错误代码。◇ *invalid characters* 无效字符 OPP **valid**

▪ ***noun*** /'ɪnvəlɪd; 'ɪnvəliːd/ a person who needs other people to take care of them, because of illness that they have had for a long time 病弱者；久病衰弱者：*She had been a delicate child and her parents had treated her as an invalid.* 她小时候很虚弱，父母就把她当个病人照料。◇ *his invalid wife* 他的体弱多病的妻子

▪ ***verb*** /'ɪnvəlɪd/ ~ **sb (out)** | ~ **sb (out of sth)** (*BrE*) to force sb to leave the armed forces because of an illness or injury （因伤病）令…退役：*He was invalided out of the army in 1943.* 他于 1943 年因伤病退役。

in·vali·date AW /ɪn'vælɪdeɪt/ *verb* **1** ~ **sth** to prove that an idea, a story, an argument, etc. is wrong 证明…错误；使站不住脚：*This new piece of evidence invalidates his version of events.* 这条新证据推翻了他对事件经过的说法。 **2** ~ **sth** if you **invalidate** a document, a contract, an election, etc., you make it no longer legally or officially valid or acceptable 使无效；使作废 OPP **validate** ▶ **in·vali·da·tion** /ɪnˌvælɪ'deɪʃn/ *noun* [U]

in·val·id·ity AW /ˌɪnvə'lɪdəti/ *noun* [U] **1** (*BrE, specialist*) the state of being unable to take care of yourself because of illness or injury 病弱；伤残；不能自理 **2** (*formal*) the state of not being legally or officially acceptable 无效；失效 ➲ COMPARE VALIDITY

in·valu·able /ɪn'væljuəbl/ *adj.* extremely useful 极有用的；极宝贵的 SYN **valuable**：*invaluable information* 宝贵的信息 ◇ ~ **to/for sb/sth** *The book will be invaluable for students in higher education.* 这本书对于高校学生将有重大价值。◇ ~ **in sth** *The research should* ***prove invaluable*** *in the study of children's language.* 这项调查对于儿童语言的研究应极有价值。 ➲ COMPARE VALUABLE HELP **Invaluable** means 'very valuable or useful'. The opposite of **valuable** is **valueless** or **worthless**. * invaluable 表示十分宝贵或有用，反义词是 valueless 或 worthless。 ➲ MORE LIKE THIS 23, page R27

I

in·vari·able AW /ɪnˈveəriəbl; NAmE -ˈver-/ *adj.* always the same; never changing 始终如一的；永无变化的 SYN **unchanging**: *Her routine was invariable.* 她的日常生活总是千篇一律。◇ *his invariable courtesy and charm* 他那一贯的彬彬有礼和魅力 ◇ *an invariable principle* 一贯原则 ➲ COMPARE VARIABLE *adj.* (1)

in·vari·ably AW /ɪnˈveəriəbli; NAmE -ˈver-/ *adv.* always 始终如一地；一贯地 SYN **without fail**: *This acute infection of the brain is almost invariably fatal.* 这种急性大脑传染病几乎总是导致死亡。◇ *This is not invariably the case.* 事情并非总是如此。◇ *Invariably the reply came back, 'Not now!'* 答复无例外地又是："现在不行！"

in·vari·ant /ɪnˈveəriənt; NAmE -ˈver-/ *adj.* (*specialist*) always the same; never changing 不变的；恒定的 SYN **invariable**

in·va·sion /ɪnˈveɪʒn/ *noun* [C, U] **1** the act of an army entering another country by force in order to take control of it 武装入侵；侵略；侵犯：*the German invasion of Poland in 1939* 德国于 1939 年对波兰的侵略 ◇ *the threat of invasion* 入侵的威胁 ◇ *an* ***invasion force/fleet*** 侵略军；入侵舰队 ➲ COLLOCATIONS AT WAR **2** the fact of a large number of people or things arriving somewhere, especially people or things that are disturbing or unpleasant （尤指烦扰的）涌入：*the annual tourist invasion* 一年一度游客的涌入 ◇ *Farmers are struggling to cope with an invasion of slugs.* 农民正在努力对付蛞蝓的大肆侵害。**3** an act or a process that affects sb/sth in a way that is not welcome 侵犯；干预：*The actress described the photographs of her as an* ***invasion of privacy****.* 那位女演员认为她的这些照片是对隐私权的侵犯。➲ SEE ALSO INVADE

in·va·sive /ɪnˈveɪsɪv/ *adj.* (*formal*) **1** (especially of diseases within the body 尤指体内疾病) spreading very quickly and difficult to stop 侵入的；侵袭的：*invasive cancer* 扩散性肿瘤 **2** (of medical treatment 医疗) involving cutting into the body 有创的；切入的；开刀的：*invasive surgery* 开刀手术 OPP **non-invasive** ➲ SEE ALSO INVADE

in·vec·tive /ɪnˈvektɪv/ *noun* [U] (*formal*) rude language and unpleasant remarks that sb shouts when they are very angry 辱骂；咒骂

in·veigh /ɪnˈveɪ/ *verb*
PHR V **inˈveigh against sb/sth** (*formal*) to criticize sb/sth strongly 猛烈抨击；痛骂

in·vei·gle /ɪnˈveɪgl/ *verb* **~ sb/yourself (into sth/into doing sth)** (*formal*) to achieve control over sb in a clever and dishonest way, especially so that they will do what you want 引诱；哄骗；骗取：*He* ***inveigled himself into her affections*** (= dishonestly made her love him). 他骗取了她的爱。

in·vent /ɪnˈvent/ *verb* **1** **~ sth** to produce or design sth that has not existed before 发明；创造：*Who invented the steam engine?* 谁发明了蒸汽机？ **2** **~ sth** to say or describe sth that is not true, especially in order to trick people 编造；捏造；虚构：*What excuse did he invent this time?* 他这次编了什么借口？ ◇ *Many children invent an imaginary friend.* 很多儿童都有一个假想朋友。

in·ven·tion /ɪnˈvenʃn/ *noun* **1** [C] a thing or an idea that has been invented 发明；创造：*Fax machines were a wonderful invention at the time.* 传真机在当时是一项了不起的发明。**2** [U] the act of inventing sth 发明；创造：*Such changes have not been seen since the invention of the printing press.* 自从发明了印刷机，这种变革还没有出现过。**3** [C, U] the act of inventing a story or an idea and pretending that it is true; a story invented in this way 虚构；编造；虚构的故事：*This story is apparently a complete invention.* 这个故事显然完全是虚构的。**4** [U] the ability to have new and interesting ideas 创造力；创意：*John was full of invention—always making up new dance steps and sequences.* 约翰有丰富的创造力，总能编出新的舞步和连续舞步。IDM SEE NECESSITY

in·vent·ive /ɪnˈventɪv/ *adj.* **1** (especially of people 尤指人) able to think of new and interesting ideas 善于创新的；有创意的 SYN **imaginative**: *She has a highly inventive mind.* 她的头脑非常善于创新。 **2** (of ideas 思想) new and interesting 有新意的；有创意的 ▶ **in·vent·ive·ly** *adv.* **in·vent·ive·ness** *noun* [U]

in·vent·or /ɪnˈventə(r)/ *noun* a person who has invented sth or whose job is inventing things 发明者；发明家；创造者

in·ven·tory /ˈɪnvəntri; NAmE -tɔːri/ *noun, verb*
■ *noun* (*pl.* **-ies**) **1** [C] a written list of all the objects, furniture, etc. in a particular building （建筑物里的物品、家具等的）清单；财产清单：*an inventory of the museum's contents* 博物馆馆藏清单 **2** [U] (*NAmE*) all the goods in a shop （商店的）存货，库存 SYN **stock**: *The inventory will be disposed of over the next twelve weeks.* 在未来的十二个星期中将进行清仓处理。◇ *inventory control* 库存管理 ➲ COMPARE STOCKTAKING
■ *verb* (**in·ven·tor·ies, in·ven·tory·ing, in·ven·tor·ied, in·ven·tor·ied**) **~ sth** (*formal*) to make a complete list of sth 开列清单：*I've inventoried my father's collection of prints.* 我把父亲收藏的版画列成了清单。

in·verse /ˌɪnˈvɜːs; NAmE ˌɪnˈvɜːrs/ *adj.* **1** [only before noun] opposite in amount or position to sth else （数量、位置）相反的，反向的：*A person's wealth is often* ***in inverse proportion to*** *their happiness* (= the more money they have, the less happy they are). 一个人的财富常常与他的幸福成反比。◇ *There is often an* ***inverse relationship*** *between the power of the tool and how easy it is to use.* 工具的功能越强大，操作起来往往越费事。**2 the ˈinverse** *noun* [sing.] (*specialist*) the exact opposite of sth 反面；相反的事物 ▶ **in·verse·ly** /ˌɪnˈvɜːsli; NAmE -ˈvɜːrs-/ *adv.*: *We regard health as inversely related to social class.* 我们认为健康状况与社会地位成相反关系。

in·ver·sion /ɪnˈvɜːʃn; NAmE ɪnˈvɜːrʃn; -ʒn/ *noun* [U, C] (*specialist*) the act of changing the position or order of sth to its opposite, or of turning sth upside down 倒置；颠倒；倒转：*the inversion of normal word order* 正常词序的倒装 ◇ *an inversion of the truth* 颠倒是非

in·vert /ɪnˈvɜːt; NAmE ɪnˈvɜːrt/ *verb* **~ sth** (*formal*) to change the normal position of sth, especially by turning it upside down or by arranging it in the opposite order （使）倒转，颠倒，倒置：*Place a plate over the cake tin and invert it.* 在蛋糕烤模上盖一个盘子，然后将其翻过来。

in·ver·te·brate /ɪnˈvɜːtɪbrət; NAmE -ˈvɜːrt-/ *noun* (*specialist*) any animal with no BACKBONE, for example a WORM 无脊椎动物 ➲ COMPARE VERTEBRATE ▶ **in·ver·te·brate** *adj.*: *invertebrate pests* 无脊椎害虫

inˌverted ˈcommas *noun* [pl.] (*BrE*) = QUOTATION MARKS
IDM **in inverted commas** (*informal*) used to show that you think a particular word, description, etc. is not true or appropriate （对正确性或适合性表示质疑）所谓的，加引号的：*The manager showed us to our 'luxury apartment', in inverted commas.* 经理带我们去看了我们所谓的"豪华单元房"。

inˌverted ˈsnobbery *noun* [U] (*BrE, disapproving*) the attitude that disapproves of everything connected with high social status and that is proud of low social status 倒转势利眼（反对一切与社会高层有关的事物，而为社会底层感到自豪）

in·vest AW /ɪnˈvest/ *verb* **1** [I, T] to buy property, shares in a company, etc. in the hope of making a profit 投资：**~ (in sth)** *Now is a good time to invest in the property market.* 现在是对房地产市场投资的好时机。◇ **~ sth (in sth)** *He invested his life savings in his daughter's business.* 他把一生的积蓄投资到了女儿的企业。➲ WORDFINDER NOTE AT MONEY

> **WORDFINDER** 联想词：asset, bond, capital, dividend, equity, fund, interest, portfolio, share

2 [I, T] (of an organization or government, etc. 机构、政府等) to spend money on sth in order to make it better or more successful （把资金）投入：**~ (in/on sth)** *The* *government has **invested heavily** in public transport.* 政府已对公共交通投入了大量资金。◇ **~ sth (in/on sth)** *The college is to invest $2 million in a new conference hall.* 这所学院计划投入 200 万美元建造新的会议大厅。◇ *In his time managing the club he has invested millions on new players.* 他在管理俱乐部期间投入了几百万培养新运动员。 **3** [T] **~ sth (in sth) | ~ sth (in) doing sth** to spend time, energy, effort, etc. on sth that you think is good or useful 投入（时间、精力等）: *She had invested all her adult life in the relationship.* 她把成年后的时间全用于维护那一关系。 **4** [T] (*formal*) to give sb power or authority, especially as part of their job 授予，给予（权力等）: **~ sb (with sth)** *The new position invested her with a good deal of responsibility.* 新职位赋予她重大的责任。◇ **~ sb (as sth)** *The interview was broadcast on the same day he was invested as President.* 这次采访是在他成为总统的当天播放的。 ➲ SEE ALSO INVESTITURE

PHR V **in'vest in sth** (*informal, often humorous*) to buy sth that is expensive but useful 购买昂贵有用的东西: *Don't you think it's about time you invested in a new coat?* 你不觉得该花点钱买件新外套了吗？ **in'vest sb/sth with sth** (*formal*) to make sb/sth seem to have a particular quality 使似乎具备某性质: *Being a model invests her with a certain glamour.* 当模特儿似乎给她增添了一定的魅力。

in·ves·ti·gate 🔑 AW /ɪnˈvestɪɡeɪt/ *verb* **1** 🔑 [I, T] to carefully examine the facts of a situation, an event, a crime, etc. to find out the truth about it or how it happened 调查，侦查（某事）: *The FBI has been called in to investigate.* 联邦调查局奉命进行调查。◇ (*informal*) *'What was that noise?' 'I'll go and investigate.'* "那是什么声音？" "我去看一下。" ◇ **~ sth** *Police are investigating possible links between the murders.* 警察正在调查这些谋杀案之间可能存在的关联。◇ **~ what, how, etc....** *Police are investigating what happened.* 警察正在调查事情发生的经过。 ➲ COLLOCATIONS AT CRIME **2** 🔑 [T] **~ sb (for sth)** to try to find out information about sb's character, activities, etc. 调查（某人）: *This is not the first time he has been investigated by the police for fraud.* 这不是警方第一次调查他是否有欺诈行为。 **3** 🔑 [T, I] to find out information and facts about a subject or problem by study or research 研究；调查: **~ (sth)** *Scientists are investigating the effects of diet on fighting cancer.* 科学家正在研究饮食的抗癌作用。◇ **~ how, what, etc....** *The research investigates how foreign speakers gain fluency.* 这项研究旨在调查讲外语的人如何增加流利程度。

in·ves·ti·ga·tion 🔑 AW /ɪnˌvestɪˈɡeɪʃn/ *noun* [C, U] **1** 🔑 an official examination of the facts about a situation, crime, etc. （正式的）调查，侦查: ***a criminal/murder/police investigation*** 刑事 / 凶案 / 警方调查 ◇ *She is still **under investigation**.* 她仍在接受调查。◇ **~ into sth** *The police have completed their investigations into the accident.* 警察已完成对这次事故的调查。 ➲ COLLOCATIONS AT CRIME **2** 🔑 **~ (into sth)** a scientific or academic examination of the facts of a subject or problem 科学研究；学术研究 SYN **enquiry**: *an investigation into the spending habits of teenagers* 对十几岁青少年的消费习惯进行的调查研究

in·ves·ti·ga·tive AW /ɪnˈvestɪɡətɪv; *NAmE* -ɡeɪtɪv/ (*also less frequent* **in·ves·ti·ga·tory** /ɪnˈvestɪɡətəri; *NAmE* -ɡətɔːri/) *adj.* [usually before noun] involving examining an event or a situation to find out the truth 调查研究的；侦查的: *The article was an excellent piece of **investigative journalism**.* 这是一篇优秀的调查研究报道。◇ *The police have full investigatory powers.* 警察拥有调查全权。

in·ves·ti·ga·tor AW /ɪnˈvestɪɡeɪtə(r)/ *noun* a person who examines a situation such as an accident or a crime to find out the truth 调查者；侦查员: *air safety investigators* 飞行安全调查人员 ◇ *a **private investigator*** (= a DETECTIVE) 私人侦探

in·ves·ti·ture /ɪnˈvestɪtʃə(r)/ *noun* [U, C] a ceremony at which sb formally receives an official title or special powers 授衔仪式；授权仪式

in·vest·ment 🔑 AW /ɪnˈvestmənt/ *noun* **1** 🔑 [U] the act of investing money in sth 投资: *to **encourage foreign investment*** 鼓励外国投资 ◇ *investment income* 投资收益 ◇ **~ in sth** *This country needs investment in education.* 这个国家需要对教育进行投资。 ➲ COLLOCATIONS AT ECONOMY **2** 🔑 [C] the money that you invest, or the thing that you invest in 投资额；投资物: *a minimum investment of $10 000* * 1 万美元的最低投资额 ◇ *a high **return on my investments*** 我的投资的高收益 ◇ *Our investments are not doing well.* 我们的投资境况不佳。◇ *We bought the house **as an investment*** (= to make money). 我们买这所房子作为投资。 ➲ COLLOCATIONS AT BUSINESS **3** 🔑 [C] a thing that is worth buying because it will be useful or helpful 值得买的东西；有用的投资物: *A microwave is a **good investment**.* 微波炉值得买。 **4** [U, C] the act of giving time or effort to a particular task in order to make it successful （时间、精力的）投入: *The project has demanded considerable investment of time and effort.* 该项目已让我们投入了相当多的时间和精力。

in'vestment bank (*BrE also* ˌ**merchant 'bank**) *noun* a bank that deals with large businesses 投资银行；商业银行 ▶ **inˌvestment 'banker** *noun* **inˌvestment 'banking** *noun* [U]

in·vest·or AW /ɪnˈvestə(r)/ *noun* a person or an organization that invests money in sth 投资者；投资机构: *small investors* (= private people) 小额投资者 ◇ *institutional investors* 机构投资者

in·vet·er·ate /ɪnˈvetərət/ *adj.* [usually before noun] (*formal, often disapproving*) **1** (of a person 人) always doing sth or enjoying sth, and unlikely to stop 积习难改的；有…瘾的: *an inveterate liar* 积习难改的说谎者 **2** (of a bad feeling or habit 恶感或陋习) done or felt for a long time and unlikely to change 长期形成的；根深蒂固的: *inveterate hostility* 根深蒂固的敌意

in·vidi·ous /ɪnˈvɪdiəs/ *adj.* (*formal*) unpleasant and unfair; likely to offend sb or make them jealous 讨厌而不公正的；易引起反感的；招人嫉妒的: *We were **in the invidious position** of having to choose whether to break the law or risk lives.* 我们处于左右为难的窘境，不知是要违法还是要拿生命冒险。◇ *It would be invidious to single out any one person to thank.* 单独感谢任何一个人都易引起反感。

in·vigi·late /ɪnˈvɪdʒɪleɪt/ *verb* (*BrE*) (*NAmE* **proc·tor**) [T, I] **~ (sth)** to watch people while they are taking an exam to make sure that they have everything they need, that they keep to the rules, etc. 监（考）: *to invigilate an exam* 监考 ➲ WORDFINDER NOTE AT EXAM ▶ **in·vigi·la·tion** /ɪnˌvɪdʒɪˈleɪʃn/ *noun* [U] **in·vigi·la·tor** /ɪnˈvɪdʒɪleɪtə(r)/ (*BrE*) (*NAmE* **proc·tor**) *noun*: *If you have a problem, ask the invigilator.* 有问题就问监考人。

in·vig·or·ate /ɪnˈvɪɡəreɪt/ *verb* **1** [often passive] **~ sb** to make sb feel healthy and full of energy 使生气勃勃；使精神焕发: *The cold water invigorated him.* 冷水让他打起了精神。◇ *They felt refreshed and invigorated after the walk.* 散步之后他们感到精神焕发。 **2** **~ sth** to make a situation, an organization, etc. efficient and successful 使蒸蒸日上；使兴旺发达: *They are looking into ways of invigorating the department.* 他们正在寻找激发这个部门活力的方法。 ▶ **in·vig·or·at·ing** *adj.*: *an invigorating walk/shower* 令人精神振作的散步 / 淋浴

in·vin·cible /ɪnˈvɪnsəbl/ *adj.* too strong to be defeated or changed 不可战胜的；不能改变的 SYN **unconquerable**: *The team seemed invincible.* 这个队伍似乎战无不胜。◇ *an invincible belief in his own ability* 对他自己的能力坚定不移的信念 ▶ **in·vin·ci·bil·ity** /ɪnˌvɪnsəˈbɪləti/ *noun* [U]

in·viol·able /ɪnˈvaɪələbl/ *adj.* (*formal*) that must be respected and not attacked or destroyed 不容亵渎的；不可侵犯的；不容破坏的: *the inviolable right to life* 不可侵犯的生命权 ◇ *inviolable territory* 不可侵犯的领土 ◇ *an inviolable rule* 不容违背的规则 ▶ **in·viol·abil·ity** /ɪnˌvaɪələˈbɪləti/ *noun* [U]

in·viol·ate /ɪnˈvaɪələt/ *adj.* (*formal*) that has been, or must be, respected and cannot be attacked or destroyed 未受（或不容）侵犯的；未受（或不容）亵渎的；不容破坏的

in·vis·ible AW /ɪnˈvɪzəbl/ *adj.* **1** that cannot be seen 看不见的；隐形的：*a wizard who could make himself invisible* 能隐身的术士 ◇ *She felt invisible in the crowd.* 她觉得自己淹没在人群中。◇ **~ to sb/sth** *stars invisible to the naked eye* 肉眼看不见的星球 OPP **visible** **2** (*economics* 经) connected with a service that a country provides, such as banks or TOURISM, rather than goods 无形的（与服务而非商品有关）：*invisible earnings* 无形收益 ▶ **in·visi·bil·ity** AW /ɪnˌvɪzəˈbɪləti/ *noun* [U]: *The ink had faded to invisibility.* 墨水已退色看不见了。**in·vis·ibly** /ɪnˈvɪzəbli/ *adv.*：*He looked at me and nodded, almost invisibly.* 他看着我点了点头，几乎让人看不出来。

in·vi·ta·tion /ˌɪnvɪˈteɪʃn/ *noun* **1** [C] a spoken or written request to sb to do sth or to go somewhere（口头或书面的）邀请：*to issue/extend an invitation* 发出/致送邀请 ◇ *to accept/turn down/decline an invitation* 接受/拒绝/婉拒邀请 ◇ **~ to sth** *an invitation to the party* 参加晚会的请柬 ◇ **~ to do sth** *I have an open invitation* (= not restricted to a particular date) *to visit my friend in Japan.* 我在日本的朋友邀请我随时去看他。**2** [U] the act of inviting sb or of being invited 邀请；获得邀请：*A concert was held at the invitation of the mayor.* 在市长的邀请下举办了一场音乐会。◇ *Admission is by invitation only.* 获邀者方可参加。**3** [C] a card or piece of paper that you use to invite sb to sth 请柬；请帖：*Have you ordered the wedding invitations yet?* 你定制婚礼请帖了吗？**4** [C, usually sing.] **~ to sb (to do sth)** | **~ to sth** something that encourages sb to do sth, usually sth bad 鼓励；（尤指）怂恿，招致：*Leaving the doors unlocked is an open invitation to burglars.* 出门不上锁无异于开门揖盗。

in·vi·ta·tion·al /ˌɪnvɪˈteɪʃənl/ *noun* (*especially NAmE*) (often used in names 常用于名称) a sports event that you can take part in only if you are invited 邀请赛 ▶ **in·vi·ta·tion·al** *adj.*

in·vite *verb, noun*

■ *verb* /ɪnˈvaɪt/ **1** to ask sb to come to a social event 邀请：**~ sb to sth** *Have you been invited to their party?* 你接到参加他们的聚会的邀请了吗？◇ **~ sb** *I'd have liked to have gone but I wasn't invited.* 我倒是想去，但我没接到邀请。◇ **~ sb to do sth** *They have invited me to go to Paris with them.* 他们邀请我和他们一同去巴黎。**2** (*formal*) to ask sb formally to go somewhere or do sth（正式）邀请，请求，要求：**~ sb (to/for sth)** *Successful candidates will be invited for interview next week.* 通过甄别的候选人将获邀于下周参加面试。◇ **~ sth (from sb)** *He invited questions from the audience.* 他请听众提问。◇ **~ sb to do sth** *Readers are invited to email their comments to us.* 欢迎读者通过电子邮件向我们反馈意见。**3 ~ sth** | **~ sb/sth to do sth** to make sth, especially sth bad or unpleasant, likely to happen 招致（尤指坏事）SYN **ask for**: *Such comments are just inviting trouble.* 这种评论简直是在自找麻烦。➲ SEE ALSO UNINVITED

PHR V **inˌvite sb aˈlong** to ask sb to go somewhere with you and other people 邀请某人一道去；请某人同行：*I got myself invited along.* 我争得受邀一同前往。**inˌvite sb ˈback** **1** to ask sb to come to your home after you have been somewhere together（一起相处后）邀请某人回自己家：*After the movie, she invited me back for a drink.* 看完电影后，她请我到她家去喝了一杯。**2** to ask sb to come to your home a second time, or to ask sb to come to your home after you have been to theirs 邀请再访（或回访）**inˌvite sb ˈin** to ask sb to come into your home, especially after you have been somewhere together（尤指一起到某处之后）邀请某人到自己家中 **inˌvite sb ˈover/ˈround/aˈround** to ask sb to come to your home 邀请某人到家中

■ *noun* /ˈɪnvaɪt/ (*informal*) an invitation 邀请；请柬：*Thanks for your invite.* 感谢你的邀请。

in·vit·ing /ɪnˈvaɪtɪŋ/ *adj.* making you want to do, try, taste, etc. sth 诱人的；吸引人的 SYN **attractive**: *an inviting smell* 诱人的气味 ◇ *The water looks really inviting.* 水面看上去真诱人。▶ **in·vit·ing·ly** *adv.*

in vitro /ɪn ˈviːtrəʊ; *NAmE* ˈviːtroʊ/ *adj.* (*from Latin, biology* 生) (of processes 过程) taking place outside a living body, in scientific APPARATUS 在生物体外进行的；在科学仪器中进行的：*in vitro experiments* 在仪器中进行的实验 ◇ *the development of* ***in vitro fertilization*** 体外受精的研究发展 ➲ SEE ALSO IVF ▶ **in vitro** *adv.*：*an egg fertilized in vitro* 体外受精卵

in vivo /ɪn ˈviːvəʊ; *NAmE* ˈviːvoʊ/ *adj.* (*from Latin, biology* 生) (of processes 过程) taking place in a living body 在生物体内进行的 ▶ **in vivo** *adv.*

in·vo·ca·tion /ˌɪnvəˈkeɪʃn/ *noun* [U, C] **1** (*formal*) the act of asking for help, from a god or from a person in authority; the act of referring to sth or of calling for sth to appear（向神或权威人士的）求助；祈祷 **2** (*computing* 计) the act of making a particular function start 调用；启用

in·voice /ˈɪnvɔɪs/ *noun, verb*

■ *noun* a list of goods that have been sold, work that has been done, etc., showing what you must pay 发票；（发货或服务）费用清单 SYN **bill**: *to send/issue/settle* ***an invoice*** *for the goods* 送出/开具/结清费用清单 ◇ *an invoice for £250* 一张 250 英镑的发票 ➲ SYNONYMS AT BILL

■ *verb* (*business* 商) to write or send sb a bill for work you have done or goods you have provided 开发票（或清单）；发出发票（或清单）：**~ sb (for sth)** *You will be invoiced for these items at the end of the month.* 你将于月底收到这些项目的费用清单。◇ **~ sth (to sb/sth)** *Invoice the goods to my account.* 请把货品的发票开到我的账上。

in·voke AW /ɪnˈvəʊk; *NAmE* ɪnˈvoʊk/ *verb* **1 ~ sth (against sb)** to mention or use a law, rule, etc. as a reason for doing sth 援引，援用（法律、规则等作为行动理由）：*It is unlikely that libel laws will be invoked.* 不大可能诉诸诽谤法。**2 ~ sb/sth** to mention a person, a theory, an example, etc. to support your opinions or ideas, or as a reason for sth 提及，援引（某人、某理论、实例等作为支持）：*She invoked several eminent scholars to back up her argument.* 她援引了几位赫赫有名的学者来支持她的论点。**3 ~ sth** to mention sb's name to make people feel a particular thing or act in a particular way 提出（某人的名字，以激发某种感觉或行动）：*His name was invoked as a symbol of the revolution.* 他的名字被提出作为那次革命的象征。**4 ~ sb** to make a request (for help) to sb, especially a god 向（某人）请求帮助；（尤指）祈求神助

▼ **EXPRESS YOURSELF 情景表达**

Inviting somebody to something 发出邀请

Here are some ways of making and responding to invitations. 以下是一些发出邀请及回应的方式：

- ***Would you like to come for a meal on Saturday?*** 你星期六愿意来吃顿饭吗？
- *There's a presentation of our new product at the conference on Tuesday.* ***Would you be interested in coming along?*** 星期二的会议上我们会展示新产品。你有兴趣过来看看吗？
- *I'm going to the game on Saturday—****how about joining me?*** 我星期六要去看比赛，跟我一起去怎么样？
- *We're going to Boston—****do you want to come with us?*** (*informal* or *NAmE*) 我们要去波士顿，你想跟我们一起去吗？

Responses 回应：

- ***That would be very nice, thank you.*** 那真是太好了，谢谢你。
- ***I'd love to, thanks very much.*** 我很乐意，非常感谢。
- ***I'm sorry. I've already got something on*** *at the weekend.* 抱歉，我周末已经有安排了。
- ***I'm sorry. I already have plans*** *on Saturday.* 很遗憾，我星期六已经有计划了。
- ***Thank you, I'll check*** *my diary* ***and let you know.*** (*BrE*) 谢谢，我查一下行事历再告诉你。
- ***Thank you, I'll check*** *my calendar* ***and let you know.*** (*NAmE*) 谢谢，我查一下行事历再告诉你。

5 ~ **sth** to make sb have a particular feeling or imagine a particular scene 使产生，唤起，引起（感情或想象） SYN **evoke**: *The opening paragraph invokes a vision of England in the early Middle Ages.* 头一段的引言描绘出中世纪前期的英格兰景象。 HELP Some people think this use is not correct. 有些人认为此用法不正确。 **6** ~ **sth** (*computing* 计) to begin to run a program, etc. 调用；激活： *This command will invoke the HELP system.* 这条指令将启用"帮助"系统。 **7** ~ **sb/sth** to make evil appear by using magic 用法术召唤（魔鬼）

in·vol·un·tary /ɪnˈvɒləntri; *NAmE* ɪnˈvɑːlənteri/ *adj.* **1** an **involuntary** movement, etc. is made suddenly, without you intending it or being able to control it 无意识的；不自觉的： *an involuntary cry of pain* 不由自主的痛苦的喊叫 OPP **voluntary** **2** happening without the person concerned wanting it to 非自愿的；非本意的： *the involuntary repatriation of immigrants* 对移民的强制性遣返 ◇ *involuntary childlessness* 出于无奈的无子女状况 ▶ **in·vol·un·tar·ily** /ɪnˈvɒləntrəli; *NAmE* ɪnˌvɑːlənˈterəli/ *adv.*

in·volve AW /ɪnˈvɒlv; *NAmE* ɪnˈvɑːlv/ *verb* **1** if a situation, an event or an activity **involves** sth, that thing is an important or necessary part or result of it 包含；需要；使成为必然部分（或结果） SYN **entail**: ~ **sth** *Any investment involves an element of risk.* 任何投资都有一定的风险。 ◇ *Many of the crimes involved drugs.* 许多罪案都与毒品有关。 ◇ ~ **doing sth** *The test will involve answering questions about a photograph.* 考试将包括回答一些关于一张照片的问题。 ◇ ~ **sb/sth doing sth** *The job involves me travelling all over the country.* 这份工作需要我在全国各地跑。 ◇ (*formal*) *The job involves my travelling all over the country.* 这份工作需要我在全国各地跑。 ➲ MORE LIKE THIS 27, page R28 **2** ~ **sb/sth** if a situation, an event or an activity **involves** sb/sth, they take part in it or are affected by it 牵涉；牵连；影响： *There was a serious incident involving a group of youths.* 有一起涉及一群年轻人的严重事件。 ◇ *How many vehicles were involved in the crash?* 这次撞车事故涉及多少辆汽车？ **3** to make sb take part in sth （使）参加，加入： ~ **sb** (**in sth/in doing sth**) *We want to involve as many people as possible in the celebrations.* 我们希望参加庆典的人越多越好。 ◇ ~ **yourself** (**in sth**) *Parents should involve themselves in their child's education.* 父母应当参与孩子的教育。 **4** ~ **sb** (**in sth**) to say or do sth to show that sb took part in sth, especially a crime 表明（某人参与了犯罪等） SYN **implicate**: *His confession involved a number of other politicians in the affair.* 他的自白供出其他一些政治人物也涉及此事。

PHR V **inˈvolve sb in sth** to make sb experience sth, especially sth unpleasant 把某人牵涉（或牵扯）到某事里： *You have involved me in a great deal of extra work.* 你害得我添了一大堆额外的工作。

in·volved AW /ɪnˈvɒlvd; *NAmE* ɪnˈvɑːlvd/ *adj.* **1** [not before noun] ~ (**in sth**) taking part in sth; being part of sth or connected with sth 参与；作为一部分；有关联： *to be/become/get involved in politics* 参与政治 ◇ *We need to examine all the costs involved in the project first.* 我们首先应该仔细考虑所有与这一项目有关的费用。 ◇ *We'll make our decision and contact the people involved.* 我们将作出决定，再与有关人员联系。 ◇ *Some people tried to stop the fight but I didn't want to get involved.* 有人设法阻止打斗，但我不想牵涉进去。 HELP In this meaning, **involved** is often used after a noun. * involved 作此义时常用于名词之后。 OPP **uninvolved** **2** [not usually before noun] giving a lot of time or attention to sb/sth 耗费很多时间；关注： ~ (**with sth/sb**) *She was deeply involved with the local hospital.* 她曾全心投入当地医院。 ◇ ~ (**in sth/sb**) *I was so involved in my book I didn't hear you knock.* 我全神贯注在看书，没听到你敲门。 ◇ *He's a very involved father* (= he spends a lot of time with his children). 他是个很投入的父亲。 OPP **uninvolved** **3** [not usually before noun] having a close personal relationship with sb 关系密切： *They're not romantically involved.* 他们并没有坠入情网。 ◇ ~ **with sb/sth** *You're too emotionally involved with the situation.* 你在这件事上投入太多感情了。 OPP **uninvolved** **4** complicated and difficult to understand 复杂难解的 SYN **complex**: *an involved plot* 复杂的情节

in·volve·ment AW /ɪnˈvɒlvmənt; *NAmE* -ˈvɑːlv-/ *noun* **1** [U] ~ (**in/with sth**) the act of taking part in sth 参与；加入；插手 SYN **participation**: *US involvement in European wars* 美国对欧洲战争的干预 **2** [U, C] ~ (**in/with sth**) the act of giving a lot of time and attention to sth you care about 耗费时间；投入；沉迷： *her growing involvement with contemporary music* 她对现代音乐的日益投入 **3** [C, U] ~ (**with sb**) a romantic or sexual relationship with sb that you are not married to 恋爱；性爱： *He spoke openly about his involvement with the singer.* 他公开讲述了他和那个歌手的私情。

in·vul·ner·able /ɪnˈvʌlnərəbl/ *adj.* that cannot be harmed or defeated; safe 不会受伤害的；打不败的；安全的： *to be in an invulnerable position* 立于不败之地 ◇ ~ **to sth** *The submarine is invulnerable to attack while at sea.* 潜艇在海上是不会受到攻击的。 OPP **vulnerable** ▶ **in·vul·ner·abil·ity** /ɪnˌvʌlnərəˈbɪləti/ *noun* [U]

in·ward /ˈɪnwəd; *NAmE* -wərd/ *adj.*, *adv.*

■ *adj.* **1** [only before noun] inside your mind and not shown to other people 内心的；精神的： *an inward smile* 内心的微笑 ◇ *Her calm expression hid her inward panic.* 她平静的外表掩盖了内心的恐慌。 **2** towards the inside or centre of sth 向内的；向中心的： *an inward flow* 朝里的流动 ◇ *an inward curve* 内弯 OPP **outward**

■ *adv.* (*also* **in·wards** *especially in BrE*) **1** towards the inside or centre 向内；向中心： *The door opens inwards.* 门向里开。 **2** towards yourself and your interests 向自己；向内心： *Her thoughts turned inwards.* 她的思想转向了内省。 ◇ (*disapproving*) *an inward-looking person* (= one who is not interested in other people) 对他人不感兴趣的人 OPP **outwards**

inward inˈvestment *noun* [U, C] (*business* 商) money that is invested in a particular country from outside it 对内投资

in·ward·ly /ˈɪnwədli; *NAmE* -wərd-/ *adv.* in your mind; secretly 在内心；秘密地： *She groaned inwardly.* 她在心里呻吟。 ◇ *I was inwardly furious.* 我当时怒火中烧。 OPP **outwardly**

in·ward·ness /ˈɪnwədnəs; *NAmE* -wərd-/ *noun* [U] (*formal* or *literary*) interest in feelings and emotions rather than in the world around 心性；灵性；精神性

inwards /ˈɪnwədz; *NAmE* -wərdz/ *adv.* = INWARD

in·yanga /ɪnˈjɑːŋə/ *noun* (*pl.* **in·yangas** or **izin·yanga** /ˌɪzɪnˈjɑːŋə/) (*SAfrE*) a person who treats people who are ill/sick using natural materials such as plants, etc. 草药医生；郎中 ➲ COMPARE SANGOMA

in-your-ˈface *adj.* (*informal*) used to describe an attitude, a performance, etc. that is aggressive in style and deliberately designed to make people react strongly for or against it （态度、表演等）赤裸裸的，富有刺激性的，有意惹人发怒的： *in-your-face action thrillers* 刺激的惊险动作片

iod·ide /ˈaɪədaɪd/ *noun* [C] (*chemistry* 化) a chemical which contains iodine 碘化物

iod·ine /ˈaɪədiːn; *NAmE* -daɪn/ *noun* [U] (*symb.* **I**) a chemical element. Iodine is a substance found in sea water. A liquid containing iodine is sometimes used as an ANTISEPTIC (= a substance used on wounds to prevent infection). 碘

ion /ˈaɪən; *BrE also* ˈaɪɒn; *NAmE also* ˈaɪɑːn/ *noun* (*physics* 物 or *chemistry* 化) an atom or a MOLECULE with a positive or negative electric charge caused by its losing or gaining one or more ELECTRONS 离子 ➲ WORDFINDER NOTE AT ATOM

-ion (*also* **-ation**, **-ition**, **-sion**, **-tion**, **-xion**) *suffix* (in nouns 构成名词) the action or state of …行为；…状态： *hesitation* 犹豫 ◇ *competition* 竞争 ◇ *confession* 供认 ➲ MORE LIKE THIS 7, page R25

ionic /aɪˈɒnɪk; *NAmE* -ˈɑːn-/ *adj.* **1** (*chemistry* 化) of or related to ions 离子的 **2** (*chemistry* 化) (of a chemical BOND 化学键) using the electrical pull between positive and negative ions 离子的；电价的 ➲ COMPARE COVALENT **3 Ionic** (*architecture* 建) used to describe a style of ARCHITECTURE in ancient Greece that uses a curved decoration in the shape of a SCROLL 爱奥尼亚柱式的（古希腊建筑风格，有涡卷饰）

ion·ize (*BrE also* **-ise**) /ˈaɪənaɪz/ *verb* [T, I] ~ (**sth**) (*specialist*) to change sth or be changed into ions （使）电离，离子化 ▸ **ion·iza·tion, -isa·tion** /ˌaɪənaɪˈzeɪʃn; *NAmE* -nəˈz-/ *noun* [U]

ion·izer (*BrE also* **-iser**) /ˈaɪənaɪzə(r)/ *noun* a device that is used to make air in a room fresh and healthy by producing negative IONS 负离子发生器；离子化装置

iono·sphere /aɪˈɒnəsfɪə(r); *NAmE* aɪˈɑːnəsfɪr/ *noun* **the ionosphere** [sing.] a layer of the earth's atmosphere between about 80 and 1 000 kilometres above the surface of the earth, that reflects radio waves around the earth 电离层 ➲ COMPARE STRATOSPHERE

iota /aɪˈəʊtə; *NAmE* aɪˈoʊtə/ *noun* **1** [sing.] (usually used in negative sentences 通常用于否定句) an extremely small amount 微量；极少量：*There is not one iota of truth* (= no truth at all) *in the story.* 这种说法没有丝毫真实性。◇ *I don't think that would help one iota.* 我认为那样毫无帮助。 **2** the 9th letter of the Greek alphabet (Ι, ι) 希腊字母表的第 9 个字母

IOU /ˌaɪ əʊ ˈjuː; *NAmE* oʊ/ *noun* (*informal*) a written promise that you will pay sb the money you owe them (a way of writing 'I owe you') 借据，欠条（表示 I owe you）：*an IOU for £100* * 100 英镑的借据

IPA /ˌaɪ piː ˈeɪ/ *abbr.* International Phonetic Alphabet (an alphabet that is used to show the pronunciation of words in any language) 国际音标

iPad™ /ˈaɪpæd/ *noun* a type of small thin computer with a large TOUCH SCREEN and without a physical keyboard, that is easy to carry and on which you can DOWNLOAD APPLICATIONS (= copy programs or pieces of software designed to do particular jobs from other computer systems) 苹果平板电脑：*I've downloaded a new camera app to my iPad.* 我下载了一个新的照相机应用程序到我的苹果平板电脑上。

IP address /ˌaɪ ˈpiː ədres/ *noun* (*computing* 计) a series of numbers separated by dots that identifies a particular computer connected to the Internet （计算机的）网际协议地址，IP 地址

iPhone™ /ˈaɪfəʊn; *NAmE* ˈaɪfoʊn/ *noun* a type of mobile/cell phone that also has some of the functions of a computer and on which you can DOWNLOAD APPLICATIONS (= copy programs or pieces of software designed to do particular jobs from other computer systems) 苹果手机：*I use a dictionary app on my iPhone whenever I need to know a word in Spanish.* 每当我需要知道某个西班牙语单词的意思时，就用我苹果手机上的词典应用程序。

IPO /ˌaɪ piː ˈəʊ; *NAmE* ˈoʊ/ *abbr.* (*business* 商) initial public offering (the act of selling shares in a company for the first time) （公司股票的）首次公开发行，上市

iPod™ /ˈaɪpɒd; *NAmE* -pɑːd/ *noun* a small piece of equipment (a type of MP3 PLAYER) that can store information taken from the Internet and that you carry with you, for example so that you can listen to music （便携式）苹果播放器

ipso facto /ˌɪpsəʊ ˈfæktəʊ; *NAmE* ˌɪpsoʊ ˈfæktoʊ/ *adv.* (*from Latin, formal*) because of the fact that has been mentioned 根据该事实；根据事实本身：*You cannot assume that a speaker of English is ipso facto qualified to teach English.* 你不能假定会说英语的人就有资格教英语。

IQ /ˌaɪ ˈkjuː/ *noun* the abbreviation for 'intelligence quotient' (a measurement of a person's intelligence that is calculated from the results of special tests) 智商（全写为 intelligence quotient）：*an IQ of 120* 智商 120 ◇ *to have a* ***high/low IQ*** 智商高 / 低 ◇ *IQ tests* 智商测验

ir- ➲ IN-

IRA /ˌaɪ ɑːr ˈeɪ/ *abbr.* the abbreviation for 'Irish Republican Army' (an organization which has fought for Northern Ireland to be united with the Republic of Ireland) 爱尔兰共和军（全写为 Irish Republican Army，争取北爱尔兰与爱尔兰共和国统一的组织）

iras·cible /ɪˈræsəbl/ *adj.* (*formal*) becoming angry very easily 易怒的；暴躁的 SYN **irritable** ▸ **iras·ci·bil·ity** /ɪˌræsəˈbɪləti/ *noun* [U]

irate /aɪˈreɪt/ *adj.* very angry 极其愤怒的；暴怒的：*irate customers* 愤怒的顾客 ◇ *an irate phone call* 怒气冲冲的电话 ➲ SYNONYMS AT ANGRY

IRC /ˌaɪ ɑː ˈsiː; *NAmE* ɑːr/ *abbr.* Internet Relay Chat (an area of the Internet where users can communicate directly with each other) 互联网中继聊天室，互联网接力闲谈（用户可实时聊天）

ire /ˈaɪə(r)/ *noun* [U] (*formal* or *literary*) anger 愤怒 SYN **wrath**：*to* ***arouse/raise/provoke the ire*** *of local residents* 激怒当地居民 ◇ (*US*) *to* ***draw the ire*** *of local residents* 激怒当地居民

iri·des·cent /ˌɪrɪˈdesnt/ *adj.* (*formal*) showing many bright colours that seem to change in different lights 色彩斑斓闪耀的：*a bird with iridescent blue feathers* 蓝色羽毛闪烁的鸟 ▸ **iri·des·cence** /-ˈdesns/ *noun* [U]

irid·ium /ɪˈrɪdiəm/ *noun* [U] (*symb.* **Ir**) a chemical element. Iridium is a very hard yellow-white metal, used especially in making ALLOYS. 铱

irio /ˈɪrɪɒ; *NAmE* ˈɪrɪɑː/ *noun* [U] (*EAfrE*) a type of food made from a mixture of some or all of the following: MAIZE (CORN), BEANS, green vegetables and PEAS 依丽什锦菜（用玉米、豆子、青菜和豌豆等拌和而成）

iris /ˈaɪrɪs/ *noun* **1** the round coloured part that surrounds the PUPIL of your eye 虹膜 ➲ VISUAL VOCAB PAGE V64 **2** a tall plant with long pointed leaves and large purple or yellow flowers 鸢尾属植物 ➲ VISUAL VOCAB PAGE V11

Irish /ˈaɪrɪʃ/ *noun, adj.*

■ *noun* **1** (*also* **ˌIrish ˈGaelic, Gaelic**) the Celtic language of Ireland 爱尔兰语；爱尔兰盖尔语 ➲ COMPARE ERSE **2 the Irish** [pl.] the people of Ireland 爱尔兰人

■ *adj.* of or connected with Ireland, its people or its language 爱尔兰的；爱尔兰人的；爱尔兰语的

ˌIrish ˈcoffee *noun* **1** [U] hot coffee mixed with WHISKY and sugar, with thick cream on top 爱尔兰咖啡（掺威士忌和糖及加奶油的热饮料） **2** [C] a cup or glass of Irish coffee 一杯爱尔兰咖啡

ˌIrish ˈstew *noun* [U, C] a hot dish of meat and vegetables boiled together 爱尔兰炖菜；蔬菜炖肉

irk /ɜːk; *NAmE* ɜːrk/ *verb* ~ **sb** (**to do sth**) | **it irks sb that...** (*formal* or *literary*) to annoy or irritate sb 使烦恼；激怒：*Her flippant tone irked him.* 她轻佻的语调使他很生气。

irk·some /ˈɜːksəm; *NAmE* ˈɜːrk-/ *adj.* (*formal*) annoying or irritating 使人烦恼的；令人生气的 SYN **tiresome**：*I found the restrictions irksome.* 我对那些限制感到很烦。

IRL /ˌaɪ ɑːr ˈel/ *abbr.* in real life; not on the Internet (used in chat on the Internet) 在现实生活中，不在网络上（互联网聊天用语）：*If he did that IRL he'd have a bullet in his head.* 他如果在现实生活中那么干，脑袋就会挨枪子。

iroko /ɪˈrəʊkəʊ; *NAmE* ɪˈroʊkoʊ/ *noun* (*pl.* **-os**) **1** [C, U] a tall tree found in tropical W Africa that lives for many years. Some people believe that creatures with magic powers live in irokos. 伊罗科树（西非热带的多年生高大树木，有人认为树中居住着精灵） **2** [U] the wood from this tree, which is hard and used especially for outdoor building work 伊罗科木（木质坚硬，尤用作户外建筑材料）

iron /ˈaɪən; *NAmE* ˈaɪərn/ *noun, verb, adj.*

■ ***noun***

• **METAL** 金属 **1** [U] (*symb.* **Fe**) a chemical element. Iron is a hard strong metal that is used to make steel and is also found in small quantities in blood and food. 铁：***cast/wrought/corrugated iron*** 铸铁；熟铁；波纹铁 ◇ ***iron gates/bars/railings*** 铁门；铁栅；铁栏杆 ◇ *an **iron and steel works*** 钢铁厂 ◇ ***iron ore*** (= rock containing iron) 铁矿石 ◇ *patients with **iron deficiency*** (= not enough iron in their blood) 缺铁型病人 ◇ ***iron tablets*** (= containing iron prepared as a medicine) 含铁的药片 ◇ (*figurative*) *She had a **will of iron*** (= it was very strong). 她有钢铁般的意志。

• **TOOL** 工具 **2** [C] a tool with a flat metal base that can be heated and used to make clothes smooth 熨斗：*a steam iron* 蒸汽熨斗 ➲ VISUAL VOCAB PAGE V21 **3** [C] (usually in compounds 通常构成复合词) a tool made of iron or another metal 铁器；金属工具 ➲ SEE ALSO BRANDING IRON, SOLDERING IRON, TIRE IRON

• **FOR PRISONERS** 囚犯 **4** **irons** [pl.] chains or other heavy objects made of iron, attached to the arms and legs of prisoners, especially in the past （尤指旧时的）镣铐

• **IN GOLF** 高尔夫球 **5** [C] one of the set of CLUBS (= sticks for hitting the ball with) that have a metal head 铁头球杆 ➲ COMPARE WOOD (4)

IDM **have several, etc. irons in the ˈfire** to be involved in several activities or areas of business at the same time, hoping that at least one will be successful 分散活动（或经营）；广泛撒网 ➲ MORE AT PUMP *v.*, RULE *v.*, STRIKE *v.*

■ ***verb*** [T, I] ~ (**sth**) to make clothes, etc. smooth by using an iron （用熨斗）熨，烫平：*I'll need to iron that dress before I can wear it.* 我得先把那件连衣裙烫平再穿。◇ *He was ironing when I arrived.* 我到的时候他正在熨衣服。➲ SEE ALSO IRONING

PHR V **ˌiron sth↔ˈout** **1** to remove the CREASES (= folds that you do not want) from clothes, etc. by using an iron 熨平（衣服等的）皱褶 **2** to get rid of any problems or difficulties that are affecting sth 解决影响…的问题（或困难）：*There are still a few details that need ironing out.* 还有几处细节问题需要解决。

■ ***adj.*** [only before noun] very strong and determined 坚强的；强硬坚定的：*She was known as the 'Iron Lady'.* 大家都称她为"铁娘子"。◇ *a man of **iron will*** 意志坚强的男子

IDM **an iron ˈfist/ˈhand (in a velvet ˈglove)** if you use the words **an iron fist/hand** when describing the way that sb behaves, you mean that they treat people severely. This treatment may be hidden behind a kind appearance (the **velvet glove**). （温和背后的）铁拳

the ˈIron Age *noun* [sing.] the historical period about 3 000 years ago when people first used iron tools 铁器时代

iron·clad /ˈaɪənklæd; *NAmE* ˈaɪərn-/ *adj.* so strong that it cannot be challenged or changed 铁定的；不容置疑的：*an ironclad alibi/contract/excuse/guarantee* 无懈可击的不在犯罪现场证明；铁定的合同；滴水不漏的理由；斩钉截铁的保证 ◇ *His memo is ironclad proof he was involved.* 他的备忘录是他参与其中的铁证。➲ COMPARE CAST-IRON (2)

the ˌIron ˈCurtain *noun* [sing.] the name that people used for the border that used to exist between Western Europe and the COMMUNIST countries of Central and Eastern Europe 铁幕（指昔日西欧与中东欧共产党执政国家之间想象的屏障）

ˌiron-ˈgrey (*especially BrE*) (*also* **ˌiron-ˈgray** *especially in NAmE*) *adj.* dark grey in colour 铁灰色的：*iron-grey hair* 铁灰色的毛发 ➲ MORE LIKE THIS 15, page R26

iron·ic /aɪˈrɒnɪk; *NAmE* -ˈrɑːn-/ (*also less frequent* **iron·ic·al** /aɪˈrɒnɪkl; *NAmE* -ˈrɑːn-/) *adj.* **1** showing that you really mean the opposite of what you are saying; expressing IRONY 反语的；讽刺的：*an ironic comment* 讥讽的话 **2** (of a situation 情形) strange or amusing because it is very different from what you expect （因出乎意料而）奇怪的，好笑的：***It's ironic that** she became a teacher—she used to hate school.* 令人啼笑皆非的是她成了教师——她过去一向厌恶学校。➲ SEE ALSO IRONY ▸ **iron·ic·al·ly** /aɪˈrɒnɪkli; *NAmE* -ˈrɑːn-/ *adv.*：*Ironically, the book she felt was her worst sold more copies than any of her others.* 具有讽刺意味的是，那本书她觉得最糟糕，却比她的其他任何一本书卖得都好。◇ *He smiled ironically.* 他讥讽地微微一笑。

iron·ing /ˈaɪənɪŋ; *NAmE* ˈaɪərnɪŋ/ *noun* [U] **1** the task of pressing clothes, etc. with an iron to make them smooth 熨烫：*to **do the ironing*** 熨衣服 **2** the clothes, etc. that you have just ironed or that need to be ironed 刚熨好的衣物；待熨烫的衣物：*a pile of ironing* 一堆待熨烫的衣服

ˈironing board *noun* a long narrow board covered with cloth, and usually with folding legs, that you iron clothes on 烫衣板 ➲ VISUAL VOCAB PAGE V21

iron·mon·ger /ˈaɪənmʌŋɡə(r); *NAmE* ˈaɪərn-/ (*BrE, becoming old-fashioned*) (*NAmE* **ˈhardware dealer**) *noun* **1** a person who owns or works in a shop/store selling tools and equipment for the house and garden/yard 五金商人 **2** **ironmonger's** (*pl.* **iron·mon·gers**) a shop that sells tools and equipment for the house and garden/yard 五金商店 ➲ MORE LIKE THIS 34, page R29 ▸ **iron·mon·gery** /-mʌŋɡəri/ *noun* [U] (*BrE*) = HARDWARE (2)

ˌiron ˈrations *noun* [pl.] (*often humorous*) a small amount of food that soldiers and people walking or climbing carry to use in an emergency （战士、步行者或登山者随身携带的）应急口粮

iron·stone /ˈaɪənstəʊn; *NAmE* ˈaɪərnstoʊn/ *noun* [U] a type of rock that contains iron 铁矿石

iron·work /ˈaɪənwɜːk; *NAmE* ˈaɪərnwɜːrk/ *noun* [U] things made of iron, such as gates, parts of buildings, etc. 铁制品；（建筑物的）铁结构

iron·works /ˈaɪənwɜːks; *NAmE* ˈaɪərnwɜːrks/ *noun* (*pl.* **iron·works**) [C+sing./pl. v.] a factory where iron is obtained from ORE (= rock containing metal), or where heavy iron goods are made 钢铁厂

irony /ˈaɪrəni/ *noun* (*pl.* **-ies**) **1** [U, C] the amusing or strange aspect of a situation that is very different from what you expect; a situation like this （出乎意料的）奇异可笑之处；有讽刺意味的情况：***The irony is that** when he finally got the job, he discovered he didn't like it.* 讽刺的是，当他最终得到那份工作时，他发现自己并不喜欢它。◇ *It was one of life's little ironies.* 那是生活中的一个小小的嘲弄。**2** [U] the use of words that say the opposite of what you really mean, often as a joke and with a tone of voice that shows this 反语；反话：*'England is famous for its food,' she said with **heavy irony**.* "英格兰的食物很有名哪。"她极其讽刺地说道。◇ *There was a note of irony in his voice.* 他的声音里有一丝挖苦的味道。◇ *She said it without a **hint/trace of irony**.* 她说此话没有一点嘲讽之意。

ir·radi·ance /ɪˈreɪdiəns/ *noun* [U] (*physics* 物) a measurement of the amount of light that comes from sth 辐照度

ir·radi·ate /ɪˈreɪdieɪt/ *verb* **1** ~ **sth** (*specialist*) to treat food with GAMMA RADIATION in order to preserve it 辐照（食物以放射线处理，以便贮存）**2** ~ **sth** (**with sth**) (*literary*) to make sth look brighter and happier 使生辉；使焕发：*faces irradiated with joy* 一张张高兴得神采奕奕的面孔 ▸ **ir·radi·ation** /ɪˌreɪdiˈeɪʃn/ *noun* [U]

ir·ration·al AW /ɪˈræʃənl/ *adj.* not based on, or not using, clear logical thought 不合逻辑的；没有道理的 SYN **unreasonable**：*an irrational fear* 无端的恐惧 ◇ *You're being irrational.* 你不可理喻。OPP **rational** ▸ **ir·ration·al·ity** /ɪˌræʃəˈnæləti/ *noun* [U, C, usually sing.] **ir·ration·al·ly** /ɪˈræʃnəli/ *adv.*：*to behave irrationally* 表现得没有理性

irˌrational ˈnumber (*also* **surd**) *noun* (*mathematics* 数) a number, for example π or the SQUARE ROOT of 2, that cannot be expressed as the RATIO of two whole numbers 无理数

ir·re·con·cil·able /ɪˈrekənsaɪləbl; ɪˌrekənˈsaɪləbl/ *adj.* (*formal*) **1** if differences or disagreements are **irreconcilable**, they are so great that it is not possible to settle them 不能调和的；无法化解的 **2** if an idea or opinion is **irreconcilable** with another, it is impossible for sb to have both of them together （思想、观点）相对立的，相反的，矛盾的： *This view is irreconcilable with common sense.* 这个观点有悖于常识。 **3** people who are **irreconcilable** cannot be made to agree 势不两立的： *irreconcilable enemies* 势不两立的仇敌

ir·re·cov·er·able /ˌɪrɪˈkʌvərəbl/ *adj.* (*formal*) that you cannot get back; lost 无法挽回的；丢失的；逝去的： *irrecoverable costs* 无法收回的成本 ◇ *irrecoverable loss of sight* 永久的失明 OPP **recoverable** ▸ **ir·re·cov·er·ably** /-əbli/ *adv.*

ir·re·deem·able /ˌɪrɪˈdiːməbl/ *adj.* (*formal*) too bad to be corrected, improved or saved 不能改正的；无法改进的；不能挽救的 SYN **hopeless** ▸ **ir·re·deem·ably** /-əbli/ *adv.*： *irredeemably spoilt* 娇惯得不可救药

ir·re·du·cible /ˌɪrɪˈdjuːsəbl; *NAmE* -ˈduːs-/ *adj.* (*formal*) that cannot be made smaller or simpler 不能再分的；无法简化的： *to cut staff to an irreducible minimum* 把员工人数削减到最低限度 ◇ *an irreducible fact* 不可化简的事实 ▸ **ir·re·du·cibly** /-əbli/ *adv.*

ir·re·fut·able /ˌɪrɪˈfjuːtəbl; ɪˈrefjətəbl/ *adj.* (*formal*) that cannot be proved wrong and that must therefore be accepted 无可辩驳的；不能否认的： *irrefutable evidence* 无法推翻的证据 ▸ **ir·re·fut·ably** /-əbli/ *adv.*

ir·regu·lar /ɪˈregjələ(r)/ *adj., noun*

■ *adj.* **1** not arranged in an even way; not having an even, smooth pattern or shape 不整齐的；不平整的；参差不齐的 SYN **uneven**： *irregular teeth* 不整齐的牙齿 ◇ *an irregular outline* 不平整的外形 **2** not happening at times that are at an equal distance from each other; not happening regularly 不规则的；无规律的；紊乱的： *irregular meals* 不定时的进食 ◇ *an irregular heartbeat* 心律不齐 ◇ *irregular attendance at school* 断断续续的上学 ◇ *He visited his parents **at irregular intervals**.* 他不定期地看望父母。 **3** not normal; not according to the usual rules 不正常的；不合乎常规的 SYN **abnormal**： *an irregular practice* 不合常规的做法 ◇ *His behaviour is highly irregular.* 他的行为很不正常。 **4** (*grammar* 语法) not formed in the normal way （形式）不规则的： *an irregular verb* 不规则动词 **5** (of a soldier, etc. 士兵等) not part of a country's official army 非正规军的 OPP **regular** ▸ **ir·regu·lar·ly** *adv.*

■ *noun* a soldier who is not a member of a country's official army 非正规军军人

ir·regu·lar·ity /ɪˌregjəˈlærəti/ *noun* (*pl.* **-ies**) **1** [C, U] an activity or a practice which is not according to the usual rules, or not normal 不合乎常规的行为；不正常的做法： *alleged irregularities in the election campaign* 被指称竞选运动中的不正当行为 ◇ *suspicion of financial irregularity* 对财政违规行为的怀疑 **2** [C, U] something that does not happen at regular intervals 不规则（或无规律）的事物： *a slight irregularity in his heartbeat* 他略微的心跳不齐 **3** [U, C] something that is not smooth or regular in shape or arrangement 不整齐的事物；不平整的事物： *The paint will cover any irregularity in the surface of the walls.* 油漆会遮盖住墙壁上任何不平整的地方。 ⇒ COMPARE REGULARITY

ir·rele·vance AW /ɪˈreləvəns/ (*also less frequent* **ir·rele·vancy** /-ənsi/ *pl.* **-ies**) *noun* **1** [U] lack of importance to or connection with a situation 无关紧要；不相关： *the irrelevance of the curriculum to children's daily life* 课程与孩子们日常生活的脱节 OPP **relevance** **2** [C, usually sing.] something that is not important to or connected with a situation 无关紧要的事物；不相关的事物： *His idea was rejected as an irrelevance.* 他的想法被认为离题而遭否定。

ir·rele·vant AW /ɪˈreləvənt/ *adj.* not important to or connected with a situation 无关紧要的；不相关的： ***totally/completely/largely irrelevant*** 完全/绝对/基本上无关紧要 ◇ *irrelevant remarks* 不相关的言论 ◇ *Whether I believe you or not is irrelevant now.* 我是否相信你，现在已无关紧要了。 ◇ **~ to sth/sb** *That evidence is irrelevant to the case.* 那条证据与本案无关。 ◇ *Many people consider politics irrelevant to their lives.* 许多人认为政治与他们的生活不相干。 OPP **relevant** ▸ **ir·rele·vant·ly** *adv.*

ir·re·li·gious /ˌɪrɪˈlɪdʒəs/ *adj.* (*formal*) without any religious belief; showing no respect for religion 无宗教信仰的；漠视宗教的

ir·re·me·di·able /ˌɪrɪˈmiːdiəbl/ *adj.* (*formal*) too bad to be corrected or cured 无法纠正的；不可治愈的： *an irremediable situation* 无法补救的局面 OPP **remediable** ▸ **ir·re·me·di·ably** /-əbli/ *adv.*

ir·rep·ar·able /ɪˈrepərəbl/ *adj.* (of a loss, injury, etc. 损失、伤害等) too bad or too serious to repair or put right 无法弥补的；不能修复的；不可恢复的： *to cause **irreparable damage/harm** to your health* 对健康造成不可弥补的损害 ◇ *Her death is an irreparable loss.* 她的死是无法挽回的损失。 OPP **repairable** ▸ **ir·rep·ar·ably** /-əbli/ *adv.*： *irreparably damaged* 受到无法修复的损坏

ir·re·place·able /ˌɪrɪˈpleɪsəbl/ *adj.* too valuable or special to be replaced （因贵重或独特）不能替代的 ⇒ SYNONYMS AT VALUABLE OPP **replaceable**

ir·re·press·ible /ˌɪrɪˈpresəbl/ *adj.* **1** (of a person 人) lively, happy and full of energy 情绪高涨的；劲头十足的 SYN **ebullient** **2** (of feelings, etc. 感情等) very strong; impossible to control or stop 十分强烈的；无法控制的；难以遏制的： *irrepressible confidence* 十足的信心 ▸ **ir·re·press·ibly** /-əbli/ *adv.*

ir·re·proach·able /ˌɪrɪˈprəʊtʃəbl; *NAmE* -ˈproʊ-/ *adj.* (of a person or their behaviour 人或行为) free from fault and impossible to criticize 无可指责的；无懈可击的 SYN **blameless**

ir·re·sist·ible /ˌɪrɪˈzɪstəbl/ *adj.* **1** so strong that it cannot be stopped or resisted 不可遏止的；无法抵制的： *I felt an irresistible urge to laugh.* 我禁不住想笑出来。 ◇ *His arguments were irresistible.* 他的论点无可反驳。 OPP **resistible** **2** so attractive that you feel you must have it 极诱人的；忍不住想要的： *an irresistible bargain* 忍不住想买的便宜货 ◇ *On such a hot day, the water was irresistible* (= it made you want to swim in it). 这么一个大热天，我们见了水便禁不住要下去。 ◇ **~ to sb** *The bright colours were irresistible to the baby.* 那些鲜艳的色彩逗得婴儿直想去抓。 ▸ **ir·re·sist·ibly** /-əbli/ *adv.*： *They were irresistibly drawn to each other.* 他们相互倾心。

ir·reso·lute /ɪˈrezəluːt/ *adj.* (*formal*) not able to decide what to do 踌躇的；犹豫不决的 OPP **resolute** ▸ **ir·reso·lute·ly** *adv.* **ir·reso·lu·tion** /ɪˌrezəˈluːʃn/ *noun* [U]

ir·re·spect·ive of /ˌɪrɪˈspektɪv əv/ *prep.* without considering sth or being influenced by it 不考虑；不管；不受…影响 SYN **regardless of**： *Everyone is treated equally, irrespective of race.* 不分种族，每个人都受到公平对待。 ◇ *The weekly rent is the same irrespective of whether there are three or four occupants.* 无论三个还是四个人住，周租金不变。

ir·re·spon·sible /ˌɪrɪˈspɒnsəbl; *NAmE* -ˈspɑːn-/ *adj.* (*disapproving*) (of a person 人) not thinking enough about the effects of what they do; not showing a feeling of responsibility 不负责任的；无责任感的： *an irresponsible teenager* 没有责任感的少年 ◇ *an irresponsible attitude* 不负责任的态度 ◇ ***It would be irresponsible** to ignore the situation.* 对这一状况不闻不问是不负责任。 OPP **responsible** ▸ **ir·re·spon·si·bil·ity** /ˌɪrɪˌspɒnsəˈbɪləti; *NAmE* -ˌspɑːnsə-/ *noun* [U] **ir·re·spon·sibly** /-əbli/ *adv.*

ir·re·triev·able /ˌɪrɪˈtriːvəbl/ *adj.* (*formal*) that you can never make right or get back 不可纠正的；无法挽回的： *an irretrievable situation* 无法挽回的局面 ◇ *the irretrievable breakdown of the marriage* 无法挽救的婚姻破裂 ◇ *The money already paid is irretrievable.* 已经支付的钱是无法收回的。 OPP **retrievable** ▸ **ir·re·triev·ably** /-əbli/ *adv.*： *Some of our old traditions are irretrievably lost.* 我们的一些老传统已经失传，无法追溯。

ir·rev·er·ent /ɪˈrevərənt/ *adj.* (*usually approving*) not showing respect to sb/sth that other people usually respect 不敬的；不恭的： *irreverent wit* 失礼的俏皮话 ◇ *an irreverent attitude to tradition* 不把传统放在眼里的态度 ▶ **ir·rev·er·ence** /-əns/ *noun* [U] **ir·rev·er·ent·ly** *adv.*

ir·re·vers·ible AW /ˌɪrɪˈvɜːsəbl; *NAmE* -ˈvɜːrs-/ *adj.* that cannot be changed back to what it was before 无法复原（或挽回）的；不能倒转的： *an irreversible change/decline/decision* 不可逆转的变化；不能挽救的衰落；不可撤回的决定 ◇ *irreversible brain damage* (= that will not improve) 无法治愈的脑损伤 OPP **reversible** ▶ **ir·re·vers·ibly** /-əbli/ *adv.*

ir·rev·oc·able /ɪˈrevəkəbl/ *adj.* (*formal*) that cannot be changed 无法改变的；不可更改的 SYN **final**: *an irrevocable decision/step* 最后的决定／一步 ▶ **ir·rev·oc·ably** /-əbli/ *adv.*： *irrevocably committed* 义无反顾地献身

ir·ri·gate /ˈɪrɪɡeɪt/ *verb* **1** ~ **sth** to supply water to an area of land through pipes or channels so that crops will grow 灌溉： *irrigated land/crops* 经过灌溉的土地／农作物 **2** ~ **sth** (*medical* 医) to wash out a wound or part of the body with a flow of water or liquid 冲洗（伤口或身体部位） ▶ **ir·ri·ga·tion** /ˌɪrɪˈɡeɪʃn/ *noun* [U]: *irrigation channels* 灌溉渠

ir·rit·able /ˈɪrɪtəbl/ *adj.* getting annoyed easily; showing your anger 易怒的；暴躁的 SYN **bad-tempered**: *to be tired and irritable* 劳累烦躁 ◇ *an irritable gesture* 急躁的姿势 ▶ **ir·rit·abil·ity** /ˌɪrɪtəˈbɪləti/ *noun* [U] **ir·rit·ably** /-əbli/ *adv.*

ˌ**irritable** ˈ**bowel syndrome** *noun* [U] a condition of the BOWELS that causes pain and DIARRHOEA or CONSTIPATION, often caused by stress or anxiety 肠易激综合征（常由紧张或焦虑引起，表现为腹痛、腹泻或便秘）

ir·ri·tant /ˈɪrɪtənt/ *noun* **1** (*specialist*) a substance that makes part of your body sore 刺激物 **2** something that makes you annoyed or causes trouble 令人烦恼的事物；造成麻烦的事物 ▶ **ir·ri·tant** *adj.* [usually before noun]: *irritant substances* 刺激性物质

ir·ri·tate 🔑 /ˈɪrɪteɪt/ *verb* **1** 🔑 ~ **sb** to annoy sb, especially by sth you continuously do or by sth that continuously happens 使烦恼（尤指不断重复的事情）： *The way she puts on that accent really irritates me.* 她故意操那种口音的样子实在令我恼火。 **2** 🔑 ~ **sth** to make your skin or a part of your body sore or painful 刺激（皮肤或身体部位）： *Some drugs can irritate the lining of the stomach.* 有些药物可能刺激胃内壁。 ▶ **ir·ri·tat·ing** 🔑 *adj.*： *I found her extremely irritating.* 我觉得她极其令人恼火。 ◇ *an irritating habit* 恼人的习惯 ◇ *an irritating cough/rash* 令人痛苦的咳嗽／皮疹 **ir·ri·tat·ing·ly** *adv.* **ir·ri·ta·tion** /ˌɪrɪˈteɪʃn/ *noun* [U, C]: *He noted, with some irritation, that the letter had not been sent.* 他注意到那封信还没有发出去，有点生气。 ◇ *a skin irritation* 皮肤发炎

ir·ri·tated 🔑 /ˈɪrɪteɪtɪd/ *adj.* ~ (**at/by/with sth**) annoyed or angry 烦恼；恼怒： *She was getting more and more irritated at his comments.* 她对他的评论越来越感到恼火。

ir·rupt /ɪˈrʌpt/ *verb* [I] + **adv./prep.** (*formal*) to enter or appear somewhere suddenly and with a lot of force 闯入；突然冲进；爆发： *Violence once again irrupted into their peaceful lives.* 他们平静的生活中再度爆发了暴力冲突。 ▶ **ir·rup·tion** /ɪˈrʌpʃn/ *noun* [U, C]

IRS /ˌaɪ ɑːr ˈes/ *abbr.* Internal Revenue Service （美国）国税局

Is. *abbr.* (especially on maps) Island(s); ISLE （尤用于地图）岛，群岛

is /ɪz/ ➲ BE

ISA¹ /ˈaɪsə/ *noun* Individual Savings Account (a special account in Britain in which you can invest a limited amount each year without paying tax on the income) 个人储蓄账户（全写为 Individual Savings Account，英国一种免付利息税的储蓄账户）

ISA² /ˌaɪ es ˈeɪ/ *abbr.* Industry Standard Architecture (the usual international system used for connecting computers and other devices) 工业标准体系结构（计算机等设备的国际接口系统）

-isation, **-isationally** ➲ -IZE

ISBN /ˌaɪ es biː ˈen/ *noun* the abbreviation for 'International Standard Book Number' (a number that identifies an individual book and its PUBLISHER) 国际标准图书编号（全写为 International Standard Book Number，用于识别图书及其出版商）

is·chae·mia (*NAmE* **is·che·mia**) /ɪˈskiːmiə/ *noun* [U] (*medical* 医) the situation when the supply of blood to an organ or part of the body, especially the heart muscles, is less than is needed 缺血（尤指心肌缺血）

ISDN /ˌaɪ es diː ˈen/ *abbr.* integrated services digital network (a system for carrying sound signals, images, etc. along wires at high speed) 综合业务数字网，ISDN 网（高速传送声音信号、图像等的系统）： *an ISDN Internet connection* * ISDN 互联网连接

-ise ➲ -IZE

ish /ɪʃ/ *adv.* (*BrE*, *informal*) used after a statement to make it less definite （用于陈述句之后，以缓和语气）： *I've finished. Ish. I still need to make the sauce.* 我做好了。还有，我得调些酱料。

-ish 🔑 *suffix* (in adjectives 构成形容词) **1** 🔑 from the country mentioned …国家的： *Turkish* 土耳其的 ◇ *Irish* 爱尔兰的 **2** 🔑 (*sometimes disapproving*) having the nature of; like 有…性质的；像…似的： *childish* 孩子气的 **3** 🔑 fairly; approximately 有点…的；近乎…的： *reddish* 略呈红色的 ◇ *thirtyish* 三十左右 ➲ **MORE LIKE THIS** 7, page R25 ▶ **-ishly** (in adverbs 构成副词)： *foolishly* 傻里傻气地

Islam /ˈɪzlɑːm; ɪzˈlɑːm/ *noun* [U] **1** the Muslim religion, based on belief in one God and REVEALED through Muhammad as the Prophet of Allah 伊斯兰教 **2** all Muslims and Muslim countries in the world （统称）伊斯兰教徒，伊斯兰教国家 ▶ **Is·lam·ic** /ɪzˈlæmɪk; -ˈlɑːm-/ *adj.*： *Islamic law* 伊斯兰教教法

Is·lam·ist /ˈɪzləmɪst/ *noun* a person who believes strongly in the teachings of Islam 伊斯兰主义者 ▶ **Is·lam·ism** /ˈɪzləmɪzəm/ *noun* [U] **Is·lam·ist** *adj.*

is·land 🔑 /ˈaɪlənd/ *noun* **1** 🔑 (*abbr.* **I**, **I.**, **Is.**) a piece of land that is completely surrounded by water 岛： *We spent a week on the Greek island of Kos.* 我们在希腊的科斯岛上待了一个星期。 ◇ *a remote island off the coast of Scotland* 一个远离苏格兰海岸的岛 ➲ VISUAL VOCAB PAGE V5 ➲ SEE ALSO DESERT ISLAND **2** (*BrE*) = TRAFFIC ISLAND

is·land·er /ˈaɪləndə(r)/ *noun* a person who lives on an island, especially a small one 岛上居民，岛民（尤指小岛上的）

ˈ**island-hopping** *noun* [U] the activity of travelling from one island to another in an area that has lots of islands, especially as a tourist 逐岛旅行；逐岛旅游

isle /aɪl/ *noun* (*abbr.* **I**, **I.**, **Is.**) used especially in poetry and names to mean 'island' （常用于诗歌和名称中）岛： *the Isle of Skye* 斯凯岛 ◇ *the British Isles* 英伦列岛

islet /ˈaɪlət/ *noun* a very small island 很小的岛；小岛

ism /ˈɪzəm/ *noun* (*usually disapproving*) used to refer to a set of ideas or system of beliefs or behaviour 主义；学说；体系；制度： *You're always talking in isms—sexism, ageism, racism.* 你张口闭口就是各种歧视，性别歧视、年龄歧视、种族歧视。

-ism *suffix* (in nouns 构成名词) **1** the action or result of …的行为（或结果）： *criticism* 批评 **2** the state or quality of …的状态（或品质）： *heroism* 英勇 **3** the teaching, system or movement of …的教义（或体系、运动）： *Buddhism* 佛教 **4** unfair treatment or hatred for the reason mentioned 因…的不公平对待（或敌意）： *racism* 种族偏见 **5** a feature of language of the type mentioned …语言

I

特点： *an Americanism* 美式英语的特点 ◇ *a colloquialism* 口语体 **6** a medical condition or disease 健康状况；疾病： *alcoholism* 酒精中毒 ➲ **MORE LIKE THIS** 7, page R25

isn't /ˈɪznt/ *short form* is not

ISO /ˌaɪ es ˈəʊ; *NAmE* ˈoʊ/ *abbr.* International Organization for Standardization (an organization established in 1946 to make the measurements used in science, industry and business standard throughout the world) 国际标准化组织（成立于 1946 年，制定世界通用的科学、工业及商业计算标准）

iso- /ˈaɪsəʊ; *NAmE* ˈaɪsoʊ/ *combining form* (in nouns, adjectives and adverbs 构成名词、形容词和副词) equal 相等；相同： *isotope* 同位素 ◇ *isometric* 等距的

iso·bar /ˈaɪsəbɑː(r)/ *noun* (*specialist*) a line on a weather map that joins places that have the same air pressure at a particular time （天气图上的）等压线

I

isol·ate AW /ˈaɪsəleɪt/ *verb* **1** to separate sb/sth physically or socially from other people or things （使）隔离，孤立，脱离： **~ sb/yourself/sth** *Patients with the disease should be isolated.* 这种病的患者应予以隔离。 ◇ **~ sb/yourself/sth from sb/sth** *He was immediately isolated from the other prisoners.* 他被立刻与其他囚犯隔离开来。 ◇ *This decision will isolate the country from the rest of Europe.* 这一决定会使国家孤立于欧洲其他国家。 **2 ~ sth (from sth)** (*formal*) to separate a part of a situation, problem, idea, etc. so that you can see what it is and deal with it separately 将…剔出（以便看清和单独处理）： *It is possible to isolate a number of factors that contributed to her downfall.* 可以找出造成她垮台的一些因素。 **3 ~ sth (from sth)** (*specialist*) to separate a single substance, cell, etc. from others so that you can study it 使（某物质、细胞等）分离；使离析： *Researchers are still trying to isolate the gene that causes this abnormality.* 研究人员仍然在试图分离导致这种畸形的基因。

isol·ated AW /ˈaɪsəleɪtɪd/ *adj.* **1** (of buildings and places 建筑物或地方) far away from any others 偏远的；孤零零的 SYN **remote**: *isolated rural areas* 偏僻的农村地区 ➲ **WORDFINDER NOTE AT LOCATION** **2** without much contact with other people or other countries 孤独的；孤立的： *I felt very isolated in my new job.* 我在新的工作岗位上觉得很孤独。 ◇ *Elderly people easily become socially isolated.* 上了年纪的人很容易变得与社会隔绝。 ◇ *The decision left the country isolated from its allies.* 这个决定使这个国家在盟国中受到孤立。 **3** single; happening once 单独的；只出现一次的： *The police said the attack was an isolated incident.* 警方称这次袭击只是个别事件。

isol·at·ing /ˈaɪsəleɪtɪŋ/ *adj.* (*linguistics* 语言) = ANALYTIC (2)

isol·ation AW /ˌaɪsəˈleɪʃn/ *noun* [U] **1** the act of separating sb/sth; the state of being separate 隔离；隔离状态： *geographical isolation* 地理上的隔离 ◇ *an* **isolation hospital/ward** (= for people with infectious diseases) 隔离医院 / 病房 ◇ **~ (from sb/sth)** *The country has been threatened with complete isolation from the international community unless the atrocities stop.* 这个国家受到了被国际社会完全孤立的威胁，除非其暴行得以制止。 ◇ *He lives in* **splendid isolation** (= far from, or in a superior position to, everyone else). 他过着远离尘世的生活。 **2 ~ (from sb/sth)** the state of being alone or lonely 孤独；孤立状态： *Many unemployed people experience feelings of isolation and depression.* 很多失业者有孤独沮丧的感觉。

IDM **in isolation (from sb/sth)** separately; alone 单独地；孤立地： *To make sense, these figures should not be looked at in isolation.* 这些数据不应孤立起来看，否则就没有意义。

isol·ation·ism AW /ˌaɪsəˈleɪʃənɪzəm/ *noun* [U] the policy of not becoming involved in the affairs of other countries or groups 孤立主义 ▸ **isol·ation·ist** /-ʃənɪst/ *adj.*, *noun*: *an isolationist foreign policy* 孤立主义外交政策

iso·mer /ˈaɪsəmə(r)/ *noun* **1** (*chemistry* 化) one of two or more COMPOUNDS which have the same atoms, but in different arrangements 异构体；同分异构体 **2** (*physics* 物) one of two or more NUCLEI that have the same ATOMIC NUMBER, but different energy states 同核异能素；同质异能素 ▸ **iso·mer·ic** /ˌaɪsəˈmerɪk/ *adj.* **iso·mer·ism** /ˈaɪsəmərɪzəm/ *noun* [U]

iso·met·ric /ˌaɪsəˈmetrɪk/ *adj.* **1** (*specialist*) connected with a type of physical exercise in which muscles are made to work without the whole body moving 提高肌张力的，静力锻炼的（指肌肉工作但整个身体不动） **2** (*geometry* 几何) connected with a style of drawing in three DIMENSIONS without PERSPECTIVE 等距的；等角的

iso·met·rics /ˌaɪsəˈmetrɪks/ *noun* [pl.] physical exercises in which the muscles work against each other or against a fixed object 静力锻炼；肌肉锻炼

iso·prene /ˈaɪsəpriːn/ *noun* [U] a liquid HYDROCARBON obtained from PETROLEUM that is used to make artificial rubber. Isoprene is also found in natural rubber. 异戊二烯（用于制造合成橡胶）

isos·celes tri·angle /aɪˌsɒsəliːz ˈtraɪæŋgl; *NAmE* -ˌsɑːs-/ *noun* (*geometry* 几何) a triangle with two of its three sides the same length 等腰三角形 ➲ **PICTURE AT TRIANGLE**

iso·therm /ˈaɪsəθɜːm; *NAmE* -θɜːrm/ *noun* (*specialist*) a line on a weather map that joins places that have the same temperature at a particular time （天气图上的）等温线

iso·ton·ic /ˌaɪsəʊˈtɒnɪk; *NAmE* ˌaɪsoʊˈtɑːn-/ *adj.* (of a drink 饮料) with added minerals and salts, intended to replace those lost during exercise 含矿物质和盐分的；等渗的

iso·tope /ˈaɪsətəʊp; *NAmE* -toʊp/ *noun* (*physics* 物, *chemistry* 化) one of two or more forms of a chemical element which have the same number of PROTONS but a different number of NEUTRONS in their atoms. They have different physical PROPERTIES (= characteristics) but the same chemical ones. 同位素： *radioactive isotopes* 放射性同位素 ◇ *the many isotopes of carbon* 碳的诸多同位素

ISP /ˌaɪ es ˈpiː/ *abbr.* Internet Service Provider (a company that provides you with an Internet connection and services such as email, etc.) 互联网服务供应商

I-spy /ˌaɪ ˈspaɪ/ *noun* [U] a children's game in which one player gives the first letter of a thing that they can see and the others have to guess what it is 我来猜（儿童游戏，一人说出所见物名称的第一个字母，其他人猜所指之物）

Is·rael·ite /ˈɪzrəlaɪt; ˈɪzriə-/ *noun* a member of the ancient Hebrew nation described in the Bible （《圣经》中的）希伯来人，以色列人

issue 🔑 AW /ˈɪʃuː; *BrE also* ˈɪsjuː/ *noun, verb*

■ ***noun***

• **TOPIC OF DISCUSSION** 议题 **1** 🔑 [C] an important topic that people are discussing or arguing about 重要议题；争论的问题： *a* ***key/sensitive/controversial issue*** 关键的 / 敏感的 / 有争议的问题 ◇ *This is a* ***big issue;*** *we need more time to think about it.* 这是个重大问题，我们需要花较多的时间考虑。 ◇ *She usually writes about environmental issues.* 她通常写环境方面的题材。 ◇ *The union plans to* ***raise the issue*** *of overtime.* 工会打算提出加班的问题。 ◇ *The party was divided on this issue.* 该党在这一问题上存在分歧。 ◇ *You're just* ***avoiding the issue.*** 你只不过是在回避问题。 ◇ *Don't* ***confuse the issue.*** 不要把问题弄复杂。

• **PROBLEM/WORRY** 问题；忧虑 **2** 🔑 [C] a problem or worry that sb has with sth （有关某事的）问题，担忧： *Money* ***is not an issue.*** 钱不是问题。 ◇ *I don't think my private life is the issue here.* 我认为问题并非我的私生活。 ◇ *I'm not bothered about the cost—you're the one who's* ***making an issue*** *of it.* 我不在乎花钱，是你一直在拿钱大做文章。 ◇ *Because I grew up in a dysfunctional family, anger is a big issue for me.* 我是在一个不正常的家庭里长大的，所以乱发脾气是我的一大问题。 ◇ *She's always on a diet—she* ***has issues about*** *food.* 她经常节食，她担心吃得太多。 ◇ *He still* ***has some issues with*** *women* (= has problems dealing with them). 他在与女性打交道方面仍有些问题。◇ *If you have any issues, please call this number.* 如有问题，请拨打这个电话号码。

- **MAGAZINE/NEWSPAPER** 报刊 **3** [C] one of a regular series of magazines or newspapers 一期；期号：*the July issue of 'What Car?'* 《汽车指南》的七月号 ◇ *The article appeared in issue 25.* 该文发表在第 25 期。
- **OF STAMPS/COINS/SHARES** 邮票；钱币；股份 **4** [C] a number or set of things that are supplied and made available at the same time 一次发行额（或一套）：*The company is planning a new **share issue**.* 公司正计划发行新股。◇ *a special issue of stamps* 特别发行的一套邮票
- **MAKING AVAILABLE/KNOWN** 发出；发布 **5** [U] the act of supplying or making available things for people to buy or use 发行；分发：*I bought a set of the new stamps on the date of issue.* 我在新邮票发行的当天就买了一套。◇ *the issue of blankets to the refugees* 给难民分发毯子 ◇ *the issue of a joint statement by the French and German foreign ministers* 法德两国外交部长联合声明的发布
- **CHILDREN** 孩子 **6** [U] (*law* 律) children of your own 子女；后嗣：*He died without issue.* 他死时无子嗣。

IDM **be at 'issue** to be the most important part of the subject that is being discussed 是讨论的焦点：*What is at issue is whether she was responsible for her actions.* 议论的焦点是她是否对自己的行为负有责任。 **take 'issue with sb (about/on/over sth)** (*formal*) to start disagreeing or arguing with sb about sth 向某人提出异议；开始与某人争论：*I must take issue with you on that point.* 我必须就那一点向你提出异议。 ➲ MORE AT FORCE *v.*

■ *verb*

- **MAKE KNOWN** 公布 **1** **~ sth (to sb)** to make sth known formally 宣布；公布；发出：*They issued a joint statement denying the charges.* 他们发表联合声明否认指控。◇ *The police have issued an appeal for witnesses.* 警方发出了寻找目击证人的呼吁。
- **GIVE** 给 **2** [often passive] to give sth to sb, especially officially （正式）发给，供给：**~ sth** *to **issue passports/visas/tickets*** 发护照 / 签证 / 票 ◇ **~ sb with sth** *New members will be issued with a temporary identity card.* 新成员将获发临时身份卡。◇ **~ sth to sb** *Work permits were issued to only 5% of those who applied for them.* 工作许可证只发给了 5% 的申请人。
- **LAW** 法律 **3** **~ sth** to start a legal process against sb, especially by means of an official document （尤指通过正式文件）将…诉诸法律：*to issue a writ against sb* 传讯某人 ◇ *A warrant has been issued for his arrest.* 已对他发出逮捕令。
- **MAGAZINE** 刊物 **4** **~ sth** to produce sth such as a magazine, article, etc. 出版；发表：*We issue a monthly newsletter.* 我们出版一份通讯月刊。
- **STAMPS/COINS/SHARES** 邮票；钱币；股票 **5** **~ sth** to produce new stamps, coins, shares, etc. for sale to the public 发行（新的一批）：*They issued a special set of stamps to mark the occasion.* 他们特别发行了一套纪念邮票。

PHR V **'issue from sth** (*formal*) to come out of sth 从…中出来：*A weak trembling sound issued from his lips.* 他嘴里发出了微弱颤抖的声音。

▸ **is·suer** *noun*：*credit-card issuers* 信用卡发行机构

-ist *suffix* (in nouns and some related adjectives 构成名词和某些相关的形容词) **1** a person who believes or practises sth …的信仰者；…的实行者：*atheist* 无神论者 **2** a member of a profession or business activity 专业人员；…专家；从事…的人：*dentist* 牙医 **3** a person who uses a thing …使用者：*violinist* 小提琴手 **4** a person who does sth 干…的人：*plagiarist* 剽窃者 ➲ MORE LIKE THIS 7, page R25

-ista /ˈɪstə/ *suffix* (in nouns 构成名词) a person who is very enthusiastic about sth 非常热衷于…的人：*fashionistas who are slaves to the latest trends* 被潮流牵着鼻子走的赶时髦者 ➲ MORE LIKE THIS 7, page R25

isth·mus /ˈɪsməs/ *noun* a narrow strip of land, with water on each side, that joins two larger pieces of land 地峡

IT /ˌaɪ ˈtiː/ *noun* [U] the abbreviation for 'information technology' (the study and use of electronic processes and equipment to store and send information of all kinds, including words, pictures and numbers) 信息技术（全写为 information technology）

it /ɪt/ *pron.* (used as the subject or object of a verb or after a preposition 用作动词主语或宾语，或置于介词之后) **1** used to refer to an animal or a thing that has already been mentioned or that is being talked about now （指提到过的或正在谈论的动物或事物）它：*'Where's your car?' 'It's in the garage.'* "你的汽车在哪儿？" "在车库里。" ◇ *Did you see it?* 你看见它了吗？◇ *Start a new file and put this letter in it.* 建立一个新档案，把这封信放进去。◇ *Look! It's going up that tree.* 瞧！它正在往那棵树上爬呢。◇ *We have $500. Will it be enough for a deposit?* 我们有 500 美元。够不够作押金？ **2** used to refer to a baby, especially one whose sex is not known （指婴儿，尤指性别不详者）：*Her baby's due next month. She hopes it will be a boy.* 她的孩子该下个月出生。她希望会是个男孩。 **3** used to refer to a fact or situation that is already known or happening （指已知或正在发生的事实或情况）：*When the factory closes, it will mean 500 people losing their jobs.* 工厂如果关闭，就意味着 500 人要失业。◇ *Yes, I was at home on Sunday. What about it?* (= Why do you ask?) 是的，我星期天待在家里。怎么了？◇ *Stop it, you're hurting me!* 住手，你把我弄疼了！ **4** used to identify a person （用以明确身份）：*It's your mother on the phone.* 是你母亲来的电话。◇ *Hello, Peter, it's Mike here.* 喂，彼得，我是迈克。◇ *Hi, it's me!* 嗨，是我！◇ *Was it you who put these books on my desk?* 是你把这些书放在我桌子上的吗？ **5** used in the position of the subject or object of a verb when the real subject or object is at the end of the sentence （用作形式主语或形式宾语，而真正的主语或宾语在句末）：*Does it matter what colour it is?* 它是什么颜色重要吗？◇ *It's impossible to get there in time.* 不可能及时到达那里。◇ *It's no use shouting.* 喊也没有用。◇ *She finds it boring at home.* 她觉得待在家里无聊。◇ *It appears that the two leaders are holding secret talks.* 看来两位领导人正在密谈。◇ *I find it strange that she doesn't want to go.* 她居然不想去，我觉得奇怪。 ➲ LANGUAGE BANK AT IMPERSONAL **6** used in the position of the subject of a verb when you are talking about time, the date, distance, the weather, etc. （谈论时间、日期、距离、天气等时用作主语）：*It's ten past twelve.* 现在十二点十分。◇ *It's our anniversary.* 今天是我们的周年纪念日。◇ *It's two miles to the beach.* 距离海滩两英里远。◇ *It's a long time since they left.* 他们已经离开很久了。◇ *It was raining this morning.* 今天上午在下雨。◇ *It's quite warm at the moment.* 现在天气相当暖和。 **7** used when you are talking about a situation （谈论情况时用）：*If it's convenient I can come tomorrow.* 方便的话，我可以明天过来。◇ *It's good to talk.* 谈一谈很好。◇ *I like it here.* 我喜欢这里。 **8** used to emphasize any part of a sentence （强调句子的某部分）：*It's Jim who's the clever one.* 就数吉姆聪明。◇ *It's Spain that they're going to, not Portugal.* 他们要去的是西班牙，不是葡萄牙。◇ *It was three weeks later that he heard the news.* 三个星期之后他才听到这个消息。 **9** exactly what is needed 正好是所需的；恰好：*In this business, either you've got it or you haven't.* 在这件事上，你不是成功了就是失败了。 ➲ SEE ALSO ITS

IDM **that is 'it** **1** this/that is the important point, reason, etc. 这（或那）是要点（或重要原因等）；正是这样：*That's just it—I can't work when you're making so much noise.* 问题是，你那么吵，我没法工作。 **2** this/that is the end 这（或那）就是终结：*I'm afraid that's it—we've lost.* 我看就这样了，我们输了。 **this is 'it** **1** the expected event is just going to happen （期待的事）就要发生了：*Well, this is it! Wish me luck.* 好了，要来的已经来了！祝我走运吧。 **2** this is the main point 这就是要点：*'You're doing too much.' 'Well, this is it. I can't cope with any more work.'* "你太劳累了。" "哎，你说到点子上了。我什么事都再也干不了了。"

Ital·ian·ate /ɪˈtæljəneɪt/ *adj.* in an Italian style 意大利风格的：*an Italianate villa* 意大利式别墅

Ital·ic /ɪ'tælɪk/ *adj.* [only before noun] of or connected with the branch of Indo-European languages that includes Latin and some other ancient languages of Italy, and the Romance languages 意大利语族的（包括拉丁语和其他一些古代意大利语以及罗曼诸语言）

ital·ic /ɪ'tælɪk/ *adj.* (of printed or written letters 印刷或书写字母) leaning to the right 斜体的：*The example sentences in this dictionary are printed in italic type.* 本词典中的例句都是用斜体排印的。◇ *Use an italic font.* 用斜体字。➲ COMPARE ROMAN *adj.* (4)

itali·cize (*BrE also* **-ise**) /ɪ'tælɪsaɪz/ *verb* [often passive] **~ sth** to write or print sth in italics 用斜体书写（或印刷）

ital·ics /ɪ'tælɪks/ *noun* [pl.] (*also* **italic** [sing.]) printed letters that lean to the right 斜体字：*Examples in this dictionary are in italics.* 本词典中的例子用斜体显示。◇ *Use italics for the names of books or plays.* 书名或剧名用斜体。➲ COMPARE ROMAN *n.* (3)

Italo- /'ɪtələʊ; ɪ'tæləʊ; *NAmE* 'ɪtəloʊ; ɪ'tæloʊ/ *combining form* (with nouns and adjectives 与名词和形容词结合) Italian; Italian and something else 意大利（人）的；意大利和…的：*Italo-Americans* 意裔美国人 ◇ *Italophiles* 亲意大利的人

itch /ɪtʃ/ *verb, noun*

■ ***verb*** **1** [I] to have an uncomfortable feeling on your skin that makes you want to scratch; to make your skin feel like this （使）发痒：*I itch all over.* 我浑身痒。◇ *Does the rash itch?* 皮疹痒吗？◇ *This sweater really itches.* 这件毛衣真刺痒。➲ SYNONYMS AT HURT **2** [I] (*informal*) (often used in the progressive tenses 常用于进行时) to want to do sth very much 渴望；热望：**~ for sth** *The crowd was itching for a fight.* 那群人摩拳擦掌地想打架。◇ **~ to do sth** *He's itching to get back to work.* 他巴不得马上回去工作。

■ ***noun*** **1** [C, usually sing.] an uncomfortable feeling on your skin that makes you want to scratch yourself 痒：*to get/have an itch* 觉得痒 **2** [sing.] **~ (to do sth)** (*informal*) a strong desire to do sth 渴望；热望：*She has an itch to travel.* 她渴望旅行。◇ *the creative itch* 创作欲 IDM SEE SEVEN

itchy /'ɪtʃi/ *adj.* having or producing an itch on the skin 发痒的：*an itchy nose/rash* 发痒的鼻子 / 皮疹 ◇ *I feel itchy all over.* 我觉得浑身痒。➲ SYNONYMS AT PAINFUL ▶ **itchi·ness** *noun* [U]

IDM **get/have itchy 'feet** (*informal*) to want to travel or move to a different place; to want to do sth different 渴望旅行（或换个地方、做别的事）

it'd /'ɪtəd/ *short form* **1** it had **2** it would

-ite *suffix* (in nouns 构成名词) (*often disapproving*) a person who follows or supports sb/sth 追随者；支持者：*Blairite* 布莱尔的支持者 ◇ *Trotskyite* 托洛茨基分子 ➲ MORE LIKE THIS 7, page R25

item 🔑 AW /'aɪtəm/ *noun* **1** 🔑 one thing on a list of things to buy, do, talk about, etc. 项目：*What's the next item on the agenda?* 议程的下一项是什么？ **2** 🔑 a single article or object 一件商品（或物品）：*Can I pay for each item separately?* 我能否一件一件地分别付钱？◇ *The computer was my largest single item of expenditure.* 电脑是我花钱最多的一件东西。◇ *This clock is a **collector's item*** (= because it is rare and valuable). 这座钟是一件珍藏。 **3** 🔑 a single piece of news in a newspaper, on television, etc. 一则，一条（新闻）：*an item of news/a news item* 一条新闻

IDM **be an item** (*informal*) to be involved in a romantic or sexual relationship 恋爱；有性关系：*Are they an item?* 他们在恋爱吗？

item·ize AW (*BrE also* **-ise**) /'aɪtəmaɪz/ *verb* **~ sth** to produce a detailed list of things 列出清单：*The report itemizes 23 different faults.* 报告列举了 23 处错误。◇ *an itemized phone bill* (= each call is shown separately) 电话明细账单

it·er·ate /'ɪtəreɪt/ *verb* [I] to repeat a MATHEMATICAL or COMPUTING process or set of instructions again and again, each time applying it to the result of the previous stage 迭代（数学或计算过程，或一系列指令）

it·er·ation /ˌɪtə'reɪʃn/ *noun* **1** [U, C] the process of repeating a MATHEMATICAL or COMPUTING process or set of instructions again and again, each time applying it to the result of the previous stage 迭代 **2** [C] a new version of a piece of computer software （计算机）新版软件

it·in·er·ant /aɪ'tɪnərənt/ *adj.* [usually before noun] (*formal*) travelling from place to place, especially to find work 巡回的；流动的；（尤指为找工作）四处奔波的：*itinerant workers/musicians* 流动工人；巡回乐师 ◇ *to lead an itinerant life* 过漂泊不定的生活 ▶ **it·in·er·ant** *noun*：*homeless itinerants* 无家可归的流浪者

it·in·er·ary /aɪ'tɪnərəri; *NAmE* aɪ'tɪnəreri/ *noun* (*pl.* **-ies**) a plan of a journey, including the route and the places that you visit 行程；旅行日程 ➲ WORDFINDER NOTE AT JOURNEY ➲ COLLOCATIONS AT TRAVEL

-ition ➲ -ION

-itis *suffix* (in nouns 构成名词) **1** (*medical* 医) a disease of …病：*tonsillitis* 扁桃体炎 **2** (*informal, especially humorous*) too much of; too much interest in 过度的；沉迷于：*World Cup-itis* 世界杯狂 ➲ MORE LIKE THIS 7, page R25

it'll /'ɪtl/ *short form* it will

its 🔑 /ɪts/ *det.* belonging to or connected with a thing, an animal or a baby （指事物、动物或婴儿）它的，他的，她的：*Turn the box on its side.* 把箱子侧着立起来。◇ *Have you any idea of its value?* 你知道它的价值吗？◇ *The dog had hurt its paw.* 狗弄伤了爪子。◇ *The baby threw its food on the floor.* 婴儿把食物扔到地板上了。

it's /ɪts/ *short form* **1** it is **2** it has

it·self 🔑 /ɪt'self/ *pron.* **1** 🔑 (the reflexive form of *it* * it 的反身形式) used when the animal or thing that does an action is also affected by it （指施动并受其影响的动物或事物）：*The cat was washing itself.* 猫在清洁自己。◇ *Does the computer turn itself off?* 电脑会自动关机吗？◇ *The company has got itself into difficulties.* 公司本身陷入了困境。◇ *There's no need for the team to feel proud of itself.* 那支队伍无须自鸣得意。 **2** 🔑 used to emphasize an animal, a thing, etc. （用以强调某动物、某事物等）：*The village itself is pretty, but the surrounding countryside is rather dull.* 村子本身很美，但周围的田野相当单调。

IDM **be ˌpatience, ˌhonesty, simˌplicity, etc. it'self** to be an example of complete patience, etc. 十分有耐心（或诚实、朴素等）：*The manager of the hotel was courtesy itself.* 旅馆经理彬彬有礼。 **(all) by it'self** **1** automatically; without anyone doing anything （完全）自动，无人操作：*The machine will start by itself in a few seconds.* 机器将在几秒钟后自动启动。 **2** alone 独自；单独：*The house stands by itself in an acre of land.* 房子孤零零地坐落在一大片田野间。 **in it'self** considered separately from other things; in its true nature 本身；本质上：*In itself, it's not a difficult problem to solve.* 这本身并不是个难解决的问题。 **to it'self** not shared with others 独自拥有；独占：*It doesn't have the market to itself.* 它未能独占市场。

itty-bitty /ˌɪti 'bɪti/ (*also* **itsy-bitsy** /ˌɪtsi 'bɪtsi/) *adj.* [only before noun] (*informal, especially NAmE*) very small 很小的；微小的 ➲ MORE LIKE THIS 11, page R26

ITV /ˌaɪ tiː 'viː/ *abbr.* Independent Television (a group of British companies that produce programmes that are paid for by advertising) 独立电视公司（英国集团，播放节目费用由广告支付）

-ity *suffix* (in nouns 构成名词) the quality or state of …性质；…状态：*purity* 纯净 ◇ *oddity* 古怪

IUD /ˌaɪ juː 'diː/ (*also* **coil**) *noun* the abbreviation for 'intrauterine device' (a small plastic or metal object placed inside a woman's UTERUS (= where a baby grows before it is born) to stop her becoming pregnant) 宫内避孕器（全写为 intrauterine device）

IV /ˌaɪ ˈviː/ *abbr., noun*
■ ***abbr.*** INTRAVENOUS, INTRAVENOUSLY 注入静脉的；静脉内
■ ***noun*** (*NAmE*) = DRIP (3)

I've /aɪv/ *short form* I have

-ive *suffix* (in nouns and adjectives 构成名词和形容词) tending to; having the nature of …倾向（的）；…性质（的）：*explosive* 炸药 ◇ *descriptive* 描述的

IVF /ˌaɪ viː ˈef/ *noun* [U] (*specialist*) the abbreviation for 'in vitro fertilization' (a process which FERTILIZES an egg from a woman outside her body. The egg is then put inside her UTERUS to develop.) 体外受精（全写为 in vitro fertilization，使卵子在母体外受精后再放回子宫内发育）➲ SEE ALSO TEST-TUBE BABY

ivory /ˈaɪvəri/ (*pl.* **-ies**) *noun* **1** [U] a hard yellowish-white substance like bone that forms the TUSKS (= long teeth) of ELEPHANTS and some other animals 象牙；（某些其他动物的）长牙：*a ban on the ivory trade* 象牙贸易禁令 ◇ *an ivory chess set* 一副象牙国际象棋 **2** [C] an object made of ivory 象牙制品 **3** [U] a yellowish-white colour 象牙色；乳白色

ˌivory ˈtower *noun* (*disapproving*) a place or situation where you are separated from the problems and practical aspects of normal life and therefore do not have to worry about or understand them 象牙塔（指远离问题、脱离现实的小天地）：*academics living in ivory towers* 生活在象牙塔中的学者

ivy /ˈaɪvi/ *noun* [U, C] (*pl.* **-ies**) a climbing plant, especially one with dark green shiny leaves with five points 常春藤：*stone walls covered in ivy* 爬满常春藤的石墙 ➲ VISUAL VOCAB PAGE V11 ➲ SEE ALSO POISON IVY

the ˌIvy ˈLeague *noun* [sing.] a group of eight traditional universities in the eastern US with high academic standards and a high social status 常春藤联盟（指美国东部八所学术和社会地位高的大学）➲ COMPARE OXBRIDGE ▶ **ˌIvy ˈLeague** *adj.*：*Ivy League colleges* 常春藤大学

IWB /ˌaɪ ˌdʌbljuː ˈbiː/ *abbr.* = INTERACTIVE WHITEBOARD

iwi /ˈiːwi/ *noun* (*pl.* **iwi**) (*NZE*) a Maori community or people 毛利部落；毛利部族；毛利人

-ize (*BrE also* **-ise**) *suffix* (in verbs 构成动词) **1** to become, make or make like 成为；使；使像：*privatize* 私有化 ◇ *fossilize* 变成化石 ◇ *Americanize* 美国化 **2** to speak, think, act, treat, etc. in the way mentioned 以…方式说（或想、行动、对待等）：*criticize* 批评 ◇ *theorize* 理论化 ◇ *deputize* 代表 ◇ *pasteurize* 用巴氏杀菌法消毒 **3** to place in 放在…里；置于…中：*hospitalize* 送医院治疗 ➲ MORE LIKE THIS 7, page R25 ▶ **-ization, -isation** (in nouns 构成名词)：*immunization* 免疫接种 **-izationally, -isationally** (in adverbs 构成副词)：*organizationally* 有组织地

I

J

J (*also* **j**) /dʒeɪ/ *noun* [C, U] (*pl.* **Js, J's, j's** /dʒeɪz/) the 10th letter of the English alphabet 英语字母表的第 10 个字母：*'Jelly' begins with (a) J/'J'.* * jelly 一词以字母 j 开头。

ja /jɑː/ *exclamation* (*SAfrE, informal*) yes 是；对

jab /dʒæb/ *verb, noun*
■ ***verb*** (**-bb-**) [T, I] to push a pointed object into sb/sth, or in the direction of sb/sth, with a sudden strong movement 戳；刺；捅；猛击 **SYN** **prod**：**~ sb/sth (in sth) (with sth)** *She jabbed him in the ribs with her finger.* 她用手指捅了捅他的腰。◇ **~ sth in sth** *She jabbed her finger in his ribs.* 她用手指捅了捅他的腰。◇ **~ (at sb/sth) (with sth)** *He jabbed at the picture with his finger.* 他用手指戳戳那幅画。◇ *The boxer jabbed at his opponent.* 拳击手向对手猛击。
■ ***noun*** **1** a sudden strong hit with sth pointed or with a FIST (= a tightly closed hand) 戳；刺；捅；用拳猛击：*She gave him a jab in the stomach with her elbow.* 她用胳膊肘猛顶他的肚子。◇ *a boxer's left jab* 拳击手的左刺拳 **2** (*BrE, informal*) an INJECTION to help prevent you from catching a disease 注射；接种；预防针：*a flu jab* 流感预防针

jab·ber /ˈdʒæbə(r)/ *verb* [I, T] **~ (about sth) | + speech** (*disapproving*) to talk quickly and in an excited way so that it is difficult to understand what you are saying 急促（或激动）而含混不清地说 **SYN** **gabble**：*What is he jabbering about now?* 他在叽里咕噜地说什么呢？ ▶ **jab·ber** *noun* [U]

jaca·randa /ˌdʒækəˈrændə/ *noun* [C, U] a tropical tree with blue flowers and pleasant-smelling wood; the wood of this tree 蓝花楹（热带树，木质芳香）；蓝花楹木

jack /dʒæk/ *noun, verb, adj.*
■ ***noun*** **1** [C] a device for raising heavy objects off the ground, especially vehicles so that a wheel can be changed 千斤顶，起重器（换车轮时常用） **2** [C] an electronic connection between two pieces of electrical equipment （电）插孔，插座，插口；塞孔 **3** [C] (in a PACK/DECK of cards 纸牌) a card with a picture of a young man on it, worth more than a ten and less than a queen * J 牌；杰克：*the jack of clubs* 梅花 J ➲ WORDFINDER NOTE AT CARD ➲ VISUAL VOCAB PAGE V42 **4** [C] (in the game of BOWLS 滚木球游戏) a small white ball towards which players roll larger balls 靶子球（白色，较其他球小） **5 jacks** [pl.] a children's game in which players BOUNCE a small ball and pick up small metal objects, also called jacks, before catching the ball 抛接子游戏（儿童游戏） **6** (*also* **jack ˈshit** *taboo*) [U] (*NAmE, slang*) (usually used in negative sentences 通常用于否定句) anything or nothing at all 丝毫，根本，一点儿（不）：*You don't know jack.* 你什么都不知道。➲ SEE ALSO BLACKJACK, FLAPJACK, UNION JACK
IDM **a jack of ˈall trades** a person who can do many different types of work, but who perhaps does not do them very well 博而不精的人；万金油 ➲ MORE AT ALL RIGHT *adj., adv.*, WORK *n.*
■ ***verb*** **~ sth | ~ sb (for sth)** (*NAmE, informal*) to steal sth from sb, especially sth small or of low value 偷，悄悄拿走，窃取（尤指小的或不值钱的东西）：*Someone jacked my seat.* 有人偷偷占了我的座位。
PHR V **ˌjack sb aˈround** (*NAmE, informal*) to treat sb in a way that is deliberately not helpful to them or wastes their time 把某人摆弄来摆弄去；故意不合作（或浪费某人的时间）：*Let's go. We're being jacked around here.* 咱们走吧。别在这儿浪费时间了。**ˌjack ˈin/ˈinto sth** (*informal*) to connect to a computer system 登录；联网；接入（计算机系统）：*I'm jacking into the Internet now.* 我正要接入互联网。**ˌjack sth↔ˈin** (*BrE, informal*) to decide to stop doing sth, especially your job 决定结束，决定放弃（工作等）：*After five years, he decided to jack it all in.* 五年后，他就决定完全放弃了。**ˌjack ˈoff** (*taboo, slang*) (of a man 男人) to MASTURBATE 手淫 **ˌjack ˈup** (*informal*) to INJECT an illegal drug directly into your blood 注射毒品：*Drug users were jacking up in the stairwells.* 当时瘾君子正在楼梯井注射毒品。**ˌjack sth↔ˈup** **1** to lift sth, especially a vehicle, off the ground using a jack 用千斤顶托起（汽车等） **2** (*informal*) to increase sth, especially prices, by a large amount 大幅度增加（或提高、抬高）（价格等）
■ ***adj.*** [not before noun] **~ of sb/sth** (*AustralE*) tired of or bored with sb/sth （对…）厌倦，厌烦

jackal /ˈdʒækl; -kɔːl/ *noun* a wild animal like a dog, that eats the meat of animals that are already dead and lives in Africa and Asia 豺；胡狼

jacka·napes /ˈdʒækəneɪps/ *noun* (*old use*) a person who is rude in an annoying way 粗鲁无礼的人；蛮横的人

jacka·roo /ˌdʒækəˈruː/ *noun* (*pl.* **-oos**) (*AustralE, NZE, informal*) a young man who is working on a farm in Australia/New Zealand to get experience （澳大利亚或新西兰的）农场见习青年工人，农场新手 ➲ COMPARE JILLAROO

jack·ass /ˈdʒækæs/ *noun* (*informal, especially NAmE*) a stupid person 蠢人；笨蛋；傻瓜：*Careful, you jackass!* 小心点，你这笨蛋！

jack·boot /ˈdʒækbuːt/ *noun* **1** [C] a tall boot that reaches up to the knee, worn by soldiers, especially in the past 长筒靴；（尤指旧时的）长筒军靴 **2 the jackboot** [sing.] used to refer to cruel military rule （用以指残酷的军事统治）军事压迫，暴政：*to be* ***under the jackboot of*** *a dictatorial regime* 处在专制制度的铁蹄之下

ˈJack cheese *noun* [U] (*NAmE*) = MONTEREY JACK

jack·daw /ˈdʒækdɔː/ *noun* a black and grey bird of the CROW family 寒鸦

jacked /ˈdʒækt/ (*also* **ˌjacked ˈup**) *adj.* (*especially NAmE, informal*) **1** feeling more awake or having more energy because of the effects of a drug or a similar substance （因药物等作用而）亢奋的：*I think she was jacked on caffeine because she wouldn't stop talking.* 我想是咖啡因让她精神亢奋，因为她一直说个不停。 **2** (of a person) having big muscles （人）肌肉发达的

jacket 🔑 /ˈdʒækɪt/ *noun* **1** 🔑 a piece of clothing worn on the top half of the body over a shirt, etc. that has sleeves and fastens down the front; a short, light coat 夹克衫；短上衣：*a denim/tweed jacket* 牛仔布 / 花呢夹克衫 ◇ *I have to wear a jacket and tie to work.* 我上班得穿短上衣打领带。➲ VISUAL VOCAB PAGE V66 ➲ SEE ALSO BOMBER JACKET, DINNER JACKET, DONKEY JACKET, FLAK JACKET, LIFE JACKET, SMOKING JACKET, SPORTS JACKET, STRAITJACKET (1) **2** (*also* **ˈdust jacket**) a loose paper cover for a book, usually with a design or picture on it（书籍通常带有图案或画面的）护封，书套 **3** an outer cover around a hot water pipe, etc., for example to reduce loss of heat（热水管的）保温套，绝热罩 **4** (*BrE*) the skin of a baked potato 烤过的土豆的皮：*potatoes baked in their jackets* 带皮烤的土豆 **5** (*especially NAmE*) = SLEEVE (3)

ˌjacket poˈtato *noun* = BAKED POTATO

ˌJack ˈFrost *noun* [sing.] FROST, considered as a person （拟人用法）霜：*Jack Frost was threatening to kill the new plants.* 霜降危及新作物的存活。

jack·fruit /ˈdʒækfruːt/ *noun* **1** [C, U] a large tropical fruit 木波罗，波罗蜜（热带大水果） **2** [C] the tree that jackfruits grow on 木波罗树；波罗蜜树

jack·ham·mer /ˈdʒækhæmə(r)/ (*NAmE*) (*BrE* **pneuˌmatic ˈdrill**) *noun* a large powerful tool, worked by air pressure, used especially for breaking up road surfaces 风钻；气动凿岩机

ˈjack-in-the-box *noun* a toy in the shape of a box with a figure inside on a spring that jumps up when you open the lid 玩偶匣（揭开匣盖即有玩偶跳出）

jack·knife /ˈdʒæknaɪf/ *noun, verb*
■ ***noun*** (*pl.* **jack·knives** /-naɪvz/) a large knife with a folding blade 大折刀
■ ***verb*** [I] to form a V-shape. For example if a lorry/truck that is in two parts **jackknifes**, the driver loses control and the back part moves towards the front part. 弯成 V 字形（如铰接货车失控时的弯折）

jack-o'-lantern /ˌdʒæk ə ˈlæntən; *NAmE* ˈdʒæk ə læntərn/ *noun* a PUMPKIN (= a large orange vegetable) with a face cut into it and a CANDLE put inside to shine through the holes 南瓜灯

ˈjack plug *noun* a type of plug used to make a connection between the parts of a SOUND SYSTEM, etc.（音响系统等的）插头，接头

jack·pot /ˈdʒækpɒt; *NAmE* -pɑːt/ *noun* a large amount of money that is the most valuable prize in a game of chance（在碰运气游戏中的）头奖，最高奖：*to win the jackpot* 得头奖 ◇ *jackpot winners* 头奖得主 ◇ (*figurative*) *United* ***hit the jackpot*** (= were successful) *with a 5–0 win over Liverpool.* 联队以 5:0 狂胜利物浦队。

jack·rab·bit /ˈdʒækræbɪt/ *noun* a large N American HARE (= an animal like a large RABBIT) with very long ears 杰克兔（北美野兔）

Jack Robinson /ˌdʒæk ˈrɒbɪnsn; *NAmE* ˈrɑːb-/ *noun*
IDM **before you can say Jack ˈRobinson** (*old-fashioned*) very quickly; very soon 一刹那；一眨眼工夫；突然间 ➲ MORE LIKE THIS 18, page R27

ˌjack ˈshit *noun* [U] (*NAmE, taboo, slang*) = JACK (6)

jack·sie (*also* **jack·sy**) /ˈdʒæksi/ *noun* (*BrE, informal*) your bottom (= the part of your body that you sit on) 屁股

jack·straws /ˈdʒækstrɔːz/ (*NAmE*) (*BrE* **spilli·kins**) *noun* [U] a game in which you remove a small stick from a pile, without moving any of the other sticks 挑棒游戏（挑出一堆小棒中的一根而不触动其他的小棒）

ˌJack ˈTar *noun* (*BrE, old-fashioned, informal*) a sailor 水手；船员

ˌJack the ˈLad *noun* [sing.] (*BrE, informal*) a young man who is very confident in a rude and noisy way, and enjoys going out with male friends, drinking alcohol and trying to attract women 浪荡少年 ➲ MORE LIKE THIS 18, page R27

Jaco·bean /ˌdʒækəˈbiːən/ *adj.* connected with the time when James I (1603–25) was King of England 英王詹姆斯一世时期的；具有詹姆斯一世时期风格的：*Jacobean drama* 具有詹姆斯一世时期风格的戏剧

Jaco·bite /ˈdʒækəbaɪt/ *noun* a supporter of King James II of England, Scotland and Ireland, or his son or grandson, after he was removed from power in 1688 詹姆斯党人（拥护 1688 年被废的英王詹姆斯二世及其后嗣为帝）

Ja·cuzzi™ /dʒəˈkuːzi/ (*also* **spa** *especially in NAmE*) *noun* a large bath/BATHTUB with a PUMP that moves the water around, giving a pleasant feeling to your body 极可意涡流式浴缸；按摩浴缸

jade /dʒeɪd/ *noun* [U] **1** a hard stone that is usually green and is used in making jewellery and decorative objects 玉；翡翠；碧玉：*a jade necklace* 翡翠项链 **2** objects made of jade 玉制品；玉器：*a collection of Chinese jade* 一批中国玉器 **3** (*also* **ˌjade ˈgreen**) a bright green colour 翡翠色；绿玉色 ➲ MORE LIKE THIS 15, page R26

jaded /ˈdʒeɪdɪd/ *adj.* tired and bored, usually because you have had too much of sth 精疲力竭的；厌倦的；腻烦的：*I felt terribly jaded after working all weekend.* 整个周末工作之后我感到疲惫不堪。◇ *It was a meal to tempt even the most jaded palate.* 这顿饭能使最没胃口的人产生食欲。

jag /dʒæg/ *noun* (*informal, especially NAmE*) a short period of doing sth or of behaving in a particular way, especially in a way that you cannot control（难以控制的）一阵：*a crying jag* 一阵哭泣

jagged /ˈdʒægɪd/ *adj.* with rough, pointed, often sharp edges 凹凸不平的；有尖突的；锯齿状的：*jagged rocks/peaks/edges* 高高低低的岩石；嶙峋的山峰；参差不齐的边缘

jag·uar /ˈdʒægjuə(r)/ *noun* a large animal of the cat family, that has yellowish-brown fur with black rings and spots. Jaguars live in parts of Central and S America. 美洲豹；美洲虎

Jai /dʒaɪ/ *exclamation* (*IndE*) used to show that you support or admire a leader, a nation, etc., or that you are pleased that they have been successful; an expression of worship to a god 荣耀，胜利，万岁（表示支持或崇敬、庆贺成功，或对神的崇拜）：*The whole crowd shouted 'Jai Mahatma!'* 人群全体高呼"荣耀归于圣雄！"

jail (*BrE also, old-fashioned* **gaol**) /dʒeɪl/ *noun, verb*
■ ***noun*** [U, C] a prison 监狱：*She spent a year in jail.* 她坐了一年牢。◇ *He has been released from jail.* 他已从监狱里放出来了。◇ *a ten-year jail sentence* 十年监禁的判刑 ◇ *Britain's overcrowded jails* 英国过度拥挤的监狱 ➲ COLLOCATIONS AT JUSTICE ➲ NOTE AT SCHOOL
■ ***verb*** [usually passive] **~ sb (for sth)** to put sb in prison 监禁 SYN **imprison**: *He* ***was jailed for life*** *for murder.* 他因谋杀罪被终身监禁。

jail·bait /ˈdʒeɪlbeɪt/ *noun* [U] (*informal*) a girl or boy who is too young to have sex with legally 祸水妞，祸水郎（指与之发生性关系即构成犯罪的未成年人）

jail·bird /ˈdʒeɪlbɜːd; *NAmE* -bɜːrd/ *noun* (*old-fashioned, informal*) a person who has spent a lot of time in prison 长期坐牢的囚犯

jail·break /ˈdʒeɪlbreɪk/ *noun* (*especially NAmE*) an escape from prison, usually by several people（数人）越狱

jail·er (*BrE also* **gaol·er**) /ˈdʒeɪlə(r)/ *noun* (*old-fashioned*) a person in charge of a prison and the prisoners in it 监狱看守；狱卒

jail·house /ˈdʒeɪlhaʊs/ *noun* (*NAmE*) a prison 监狱

Jain /dʒeɪn/ *noun* a member of an Indian religion whose principles include not harming any living creature and a belief in REINCARNATION 印度耆那教教徒（反对伤害众生、主张轮回说）▶ **Jain** *adj.* [only before noun] **Jain·ist** *adj.* **Jain·ism** /ˈdʒeɪnɪzəm/ *noun* [U]

jala·peño /ˌhæləˈpeɪnjəʊ; *NAmE* ˌhɑːləˈpeɪnjoʊ/ (*also* **ˌjala·ˌpeño ˈpepper**) *noun* (*from Spanish*) the small green fruit of a type of pepper plant, that has a very hot taste and is used in Mexican cooking 青辣椒（墨西哥烹饪常用）

jal·opy /dʒəˈlɒpi; *NAmE* -ˈlɑːpi/ *noun* (*pl.* **-ies**) (*old-fashioned, informal*) an old car that is in bad condition 破旧的汽车

jam /dʒæm/ *noun, verb*
■ ***noun***
• **SWEET FOOD** 甜食 **1** [U, C] a thick sweet substance made by boiling fruit with sugar, often sold in JARS and spread on bread 果酱：*strawberry jam* 草莓酱 ◇ *recipes for jams and preserves* 果酱和蜜饯的制作方法 ◇ (*BrE*) *a jam doughnut* 果酱炸面圈 ➲ COMPARE JELLY (3), MARMALADE
• **MANY PEOPLE/VEHICLES** 人多；车多 **2** [C] a situation in which it is difficult or impossible to move because there are so many people or vehicles in one particular place 拥挤；堵塞：*The bus was delayed in a five-mile jam.* 公共汽车因长达五英里的交通堵塞而延误。◇ *As fans rushed to leave, jams formed at all the exits.* 因球迷都急于离开，所有出口都给阻塞了。➲ SEE ALSO TRAFFIC JAM
• **MACHINE** 机器 **3** [C] a situation in which a machine does not work because sth is stuck in one position 卡住（因而发生故障）：*There's a paper jam in the photocopier.* 复印机卡纸了。
IDM **be in a ˈjam** (*informal*) to be in a difficult situation 陷入困境 **jam toˈmorrow** (*BrE, informal*) good things that are promised for the future but never happen 可望而不可即的美好未来；许而不予的好东西：*They refused to settle for a promise of jam tomorrow.* 他们并不满足于那些美好未来的空话。➲ MORE AT MONEY
■ ***verb*** (**-mm-**)

J

• **PUSH WITH FORCE** 用力推 **1** [T] **~ sth + adv./prep.** to push sth somewhere with a lot of force 使劲（往某处）挤（或压、塞）：*He jammed his fingers in his ears.* 他用手指使劲堵住耳朵。◇ *A stool had been jammed against the door.* 门被一把凳子顶住了。
• **STOP MOVING/WORKING** 停止移动／运转 **2** [I, T] to become unable to move or work; to make sth do this（使）卡住，不能动弹，不能运转：**~ (up)** *The photocopier keeps jamming up.* 这台复印机总是卡纸。◇ **~ sth (up)** *There's a loose part that keeps jamming the mechanism.* 有个零件松了经常卡住机器。◇ **+ adj.** *The valve has jammed shut.* 阀门给卡住了打不开。◇ **~ sth + adj.** *He jammed the door open with a piece of wood.* 他用一块木头卡住门让它开着。
• **PUT INTO SMALL SPACE** 塞进 **3** [T, I] to put sb/sth into a small space where there is very little room to move 塞入；塞进；挤进 SYN **squash, squeeze**：**~ sb/sth + adv./prep.** *Six of us were jammed into one small car.* 我们六个人被塞进一辆小汽车里。◇ *We were jammed together like sardines in a can.* 我们像罐头里的沙丁鱼一般紧紧挤在一起。◇ *The cupboards were **jammed full** of old newspapers.* 橱柜里塞满了旧报纸。◇ **+ adv./prep.** *Nearly 1 000 students jammed into the hall.* 近 1 000 名学生挤到礼堂里。➲ SEE ALSO JAM-PACKED
• **FILL WITH PEOPLE/THINGS** 挤满人／物 **4** [T] **~ sth (up) (with sb/sth)** to fill sth with a large number of people or things so that it is unable to function as it should 挤满；塞紧 SYN **block**：*Viewers jammed the switchboard with complaints.* 打电话投诉的观众使总机应接不暇。
• **RADIO BROADCAST** 无线电广播 **5** [T] **~ sth** (*specialist*) to send out radio signals to prevent another radio broadcast from being heard （发射无线电波）干扰
• **PLAY MUSIC** 演奏音乐 **6** [I, T] **~ (sth)** to play music with other musicians in an informal way without preparing or practising first 即兴演奏

IDM **jam on the brake(s) | jam the brake(s) on** to operate the BRAKES on a vehicle suddenly and with force 猛踩刹车：*The car skidded as he jammed on the brakes.* 他紧急刹车时汽车向前滑了一段路。

jamb /dʒæm/ *noun* a vertical post at the side of a door or window 门窗边框

jam·ba·laya /ˌdʒæmbəˈlaɪə/ *noun* [U] a spicy dish of rice, SEAFOOD, chicken, etc. from the southern US（美国南部的）什锦饭（用米饭、海鲜、鸡肉等加香料制作而成）

jam·bo·ree /ˌdʒæmbəˈriː/ *noun* **1** a large party or celebration 大型聚会；庆祝会：*the movie industry's annual jamboree at Cannes* 在戛纳举行的一年一度的影展 **2** a large meeting of SCOUTS or GUIDES 童子军大会；女童子军大会

ˈjam jar *noun* (*BrE*) a glass container for jam, etc. 果酱瓶；果酱罐

jammed /dʒæmd/ *adj.* **1** [not before noun] not able to move 动弹不得；卡住了 SYN **stuck**：*I can't get the door open—it's completely jammed.* 我打不开门，它卡死了。**2** (*especially NAmE*) very full; crowded 挤满的；塞满的；拥挤不堪的 SYN **jam-packed**：*Hundreds more people were waiting outside the jammed stadium.* 还有数百人在拥挤不堪的体育场外等候。

jammy /ˈdʒæmi/ *adj.* **1** covered with jam 涂有果酱的；满是果酱的：*jammy fingers* 满是果酱的手指 **2** (*BrE, informal*) lucky, especially because sth good has happened to you without you making any effort 幸运的；运气好的

ˌjam-ˈpacked *adj.* [not usually before noun] **~ (with sb/sth)** (*informal*) very full or crowded 挤满；拥挤：*The train was jam-packed with commuters.* 火车上挤满了上下班的乘客。

ˈjam session *noun* an occasion when musicians perform in an informal way without practising first 即兴演奏会

Jane Doe /ˌdʒeɪn ˈdəʊ; *NAmE* ˈdoʊ/ *noun* [sing.] (*NAmE*) **1** used to refer to a woman whose name is not known or is kept secret, especially in a court of law 无名女士，某女（不知姓名或在法庭等上隐匿真名的女当事人）**2** an average woman 普通女子 ➲ COMPARE JOHN DOE ➲ **MORE LIKE THIS** 18, page R27

jan·gle /ˈdʒæŋɡl/ *verb, noun*
▪ ***verb*** **1** [I, T] to make an unpleasant sound, like two pieces of metal hitting each other; to make sth do this（使）发出金属撞击声，发出丁零当啷的刺耳声：*The shop bell jangled loudly.* 商店的钟发出丁零当啷的巨大响声。◇ **~ sth** *He jangled the keys in his pocket.* 他把兜里的钥匙弄得丁零当啷乱响。**2** [I, T] **~ (sth)** if your nerves **jangle**, or if sb/sth **jangles** them, you feel anxious or upset 刺激，烦扰（神经）；（使）烦躁不安：*She was suddenly wide awake, her nerves jangling.* 她突然间清醒过来，神经焦躁不安。
▪ ***noun*** [usually sing.] a hard noise like that of metal hitting metal 金属撞击声；丁零当啷的刺耳声

jani·tor /ˈdʒænɪtə(r)/ *noun* (*NAmE, ScotE*) = CUSTODIAN (2)

Janu·ary 🔑 /ˈdʒænjuəri; *NAmE* -jueri/ *noun* [U, C] (*abbr.* **Jan.**) the 1st month of the year, between December and February 一月 HELP To see how **January** is used, look at the examples at **April**. * January 的用法见词条 April 下的示例。

Jap /dʒæp/ *noun* (*taboo, slang*) an offensive word for a Japanese person 日本佬；日本鬼子

jape /dʒeɪp/ *noun* (*old-fashioned, BrE*) a trick or joke that is played on sb 戏弄；恶作剧；玩笑

ja·pon·ica /dʒəˈpɒnɪkə; *NAmE* -ˈpɑːn-/ *noun* a Japanese bush that is often grown in gardens/yards, and that has red flowers and pale yellow fruit（日本）贴梗海棠

jar /dʒɑː(r)/ *noun, verb*
▪ ***noun*** **1** [C] a round glass container, with a lid, used for storing food, especially jam, HONEY, etc.（玻璃）罐子；广口瓶：*a storage jar* 广口贮藏瓶 ➲ VISUAL VOCAB PAGE V36 ➲ SEE ALSO JAM JAR **2** [C] a jar and what it contains 一罐，一瓶（的量）：*a jar of coffee* 一罐咖啡 **3** [C] a tall container with a wide mouth, with or without handles, used in the past for carrying water, etc. 缸；坛子：*a water jar* 水缸 ➲ SEE ALSO BELL JAR **4** [C] (*BrE, informal*) a glass of beer 一杯啤酒：*Do you fancy a jar after work?* 下班后去喝一杯怎么样？ **5** [sing.] an unpleasant shock, especially from two things being suddenly shaken or hit 猛然震动；撞击：*The fall gave him a nasty jar.* 这一跤把他摔得好厉害。
▪ ***verb*** **(-rr-)** **1** [T, I] to give or receive a sudden sharp painful knock（使）撞击，受震动而疼痛：**~ sth** *The jolt seemed to jar every bone in her body.* 这震动似乎把她浑身上下每根骨头都弄疼了。◇ **~ (sth) (on sth)** *The spade jarred on something metal.* 铁锹撞在什么金属物件上发出刺耳的声音。**2** [I, T] **~ (on sth) | ~ (sth)** to have an unpleasant or annoying effect（对…）产生不快的影响；使烦躁 SYN **grate**：*His constant moaning was beginning to jar on her nerves.* 他不停的呻吟使她焦躁不安起来。◇ *There was a jarring note of triumph in his voice.* 他声音里含有一种烦人的扬扬得意的口气。**3** [I] **~ (with sth)** to be different from sth in a strange or unpleasant way（与…）不协调，不和谐，相冲突 SYN **clash**：*Her brown shoes jarred with the rest of the outfit.* 她那双棕色的鞋与她的衣着不协调。

jar·gon /ˈdʒɑːɡən; *NAmE* ˈdʒɑːr-/ *noun* [U] (*often disapproving*) words or expressions that are used by a particular profession or group of people, and are difficult for others to understand 行话；行业术语；切口：***medical/legal/computer, etc. jargon*** 医学、法律、计算机等术语 ◇ *Try to avoid using too much technical jargon.* 尽量避免使用太多的技术用语。

jar·head /ˈdʒɑːhed; *NAmE* ˈdʒɑːr-/ *noun* (*NAmE, informal*) a member of the US Marine Corps (= American soldiers trained to serve on land or at sea) 钢盖头（指美国海军陆战队士兵）

jas·mine /ˈdʒæzmɪn/ *noun* [U, C] a plant with white or yellow flowers with a sweet smell, sometimes used to make PERFUME and to flavour tea 茉莉；素馨

jaun·dice /ˈdʒɔːndɪs/ *noun* [U] a medical condition in which the skin and the white parts of the eyes become yellow 黄疸；黄疸病

jaun·diced /ˈdʒɔːndɪst/ *adj.* **1** not expecting sb/sth to be good or useful, especially because of experiences that you have had in the past（尤指因以前的经历）有偏见的，狭隘的：*He had a jaundiced view of life.* 他具有狭隘的人生观。◇ *She looked on politicians **with a jaundiced eye**.* 她对政治人物有偏见。 **2** suffering from jaundice 患黄疸病的：*a **jaundiced patient/liver*** 黄疸病人；肝内胆红素过多

jaunt /dʒɔːnt/ *noun* (*old-fashioned* or *humorous*) a short journey that you make for pleasure（短途）游览，旅行 **SYN** **excursion**

jaunty /ˈdʒɔːnti/ *adj.* **1** showing that you are feeling confident and pleased with yourself 得意扬扬的；无忧无虑的；神气活现的 **SYN** **cheerful**：*a jaunty smile* 得意扬扬的微笑 **2** lively 轻松活泼的：*a jaunty tune* 轻松活泼的曲子 ▸ **jaunt·ily** *adv.*：*He set off jauntily, whistling to himself.* 他吹着口哨神气活现地出发了。 **jaunti·ness** *noun* [U]

jav·elin /ˈdʒævlɪn/ *noun* **1** [C] a light SPEAR (= a long stick with a pointed end) which is thrown in a sporting event 标枪 **2 the javelin** [sing.] the event or sport of throwing a javelin as far as possible 投掷标枪项目（或运动）➲ **VISUAL VOCAB PAGE V50**

jaw /dʒɔː/ *noun, verb*

■ ***noun*** **1** [C] either of the two bones at the bottom of the face that contain the teeth and move when you talk or eat 颌：*the **top/upper jaw*** 上颌 ◇ *the **bottom/lower jaw*** 下颌 **2** [sing.] the lower part of the face; the lower jaw 下巴；下颌：*He has a strong square jaw.* 他长着结实的方下巴。◇ *The punch broke my jaw.* 这一拳打坏了我的下巴。➲ **VISUAL VOCAB PAGE V64** **3 jaws** [pl.] the mouth and teeth of a person or an animal 口部；嘴：*The alligator's jaws snapped shut.* 钝吻鳄的嘴吧嗒一声闭上了。 **4 jaws** [pl.] the parts of a tool or machine that are used to hold things tightly（工具或机器的）钳夹部分，钳口：*the jaws of a vice* 虎钳口

IDM **sb's ˈjaw dropped/fell/sagged** used to say that sb suddenly looked surprised, shocked or disappointed（突然吃惊或失望得）张口结舌，目瞪口呆，垂头丧气 **the jaws of ˈdeath, deˈfeat, etc.** (*literary*) used to describe an unpleasant situation that almost happens 鬼门关；失败的险境：*The team snatched victory from the jaws of defeat.* 这个队翻盘而得险胜。 **the jaws of a tunnel, etc.** the narrow entrance to a tunnel, etc., especially one that looks dangerous（隧道等处尤指看起来危险的）狭窄入口

■ ***verb*** [I] (*informal, often disapproving*) to talk, especially to talk a lot or for a long time 唠唠叨叨；喋喋不休

jawan /dʒəˈwɑːn/ *noun* (*IndE*) a soldier of low rank 士兵；步兵

jaw·bone /ˈdʒɔːbəʊn; *NAmE* -boʊn/ *noun* the bone that forms the lower jaw 下颌骨 **SYN** **mandible** ➲ **VISUAL VOCAB PAGE V64**

jaw·break·er /ˈdʒɔːbreɪkə(r)/ (*NAmE*) (*BrE* **gob·stop·per**) *noun* a very large hard round sweet/candy 大块圆硬糖

ˈjaw-dropping *adj.* (*informal*) so large or good that it amazes you（巨大或好而）令人大惊失色的，令人咂舌的：*a jaw-dropping 5 million dollars* 令人吃惊的 500 万美元巨款 ◇ *The production is absolutely **jaw-dropping**.* 这部作品真是令人叫绝。 ➲ **MORE LIKE THIS** 10, page R26 ▸ **ˈjaw-droppingly** *adv.*：*jaw-droppingly beautiful* 美得让人合不拢嘴

jaw·line /ˈdʒɔːlaɪn/ *noun* the outline of the lower jaw 下颌的轮廓；下巴的外形

jay /dʒeɪ/ *noun* a European bird of the CROW family, with bright feathers and a noisy call 松鸦（见于欧洲，羽毛鲜艳，喜大声鸣叫）➲ SEE ALSO BLUEJAY

Jay·cee /ˈdʒeɪsiː/ *noun* (*NAmE, informal*) a member of the United States Junior Chamber, an organization for people between the ages of 18 and 40 that provides help in local communities in the US and other countries 美国青年商会会员（年龄在 18 至 40 岁之间，为美国和其他国家的当地社区提供援助）

jay·walk /ˈdʒeɪwɔːk/ *verb* [I] to walk along or across a street illegally or without paying attention to the traffic（无视交通规则）乱穿马路 ▸ **jay·walk·er** *noun* **jay·walk·ing** *noun* [U]

jazz /dʒæz/ *noun, verb*

■ ***noun*** [U] a type of music with strong rhythms, in which the players often IMPROVISE (= make up the music as they are playing), originally created by African American musicians 爵士乐：*a **jazz band/club*** 爵士乐队 / 夜总会 ◇ ***traditional/modern jazz*** 传统 / 现代爵士乐 ◇ *jazz musicians* 爵士乐师 ➲ **COLLOCATIONS AT MUSIC** ➲ SEE ALSO ACID JAZZ

IDM **and all that ˈjazz** (*informal*) and things like that 以及诸如此类的东西（或事情）：*How's it going? You know—love, life and all that jazz.* 怎么样啊？你知道，说的就是爱情、生活以及诸如此类的事情嘛。

■ ***verb***

PHR V **ˌjazz sth↔ˈup** (*informal*) **1** to make sth more interesting, exciting or attractive 使某事更有趣；使某事更令人兴奋；使某事更有吸引力 **2** to make a piece of music sound more modern, or more like popular music or jazz 使一段音乐听起来更现代化；使更具有流行音乐（或爵士乐）的风格：*It's a jazzed up version of an old tune.* 这是把一段古老的曲调翻新了。

jazzed /dʒæzd/ *adj.* [not before noun] (*informal*) excited 兴奋；激动：*I was jazzed to meet someone so famous.* 和这么有名的人见面我很激动。

jazzy /ˈdʒæzi/ *adj.* (*informal*) **1** in the style of jazz 爵士乐风格的：*a **jazzy melody/tune*** 爵士乐风格的曲调 **2** (*sometimes disapproving*) brightly coloured and likely to attract attention 绚丽的；花哨的 **SYN** **snazzy**：*That's a jazzy tie you're wearing.* 你系的那条领带太艳丽了。

JCB™ /ˌdʒeɪ siː ˈbiː/ *noun* (*BrE*) a powerful vehicle with a long arm for digging and moving earth * JCB 挖掘装载机

ˈJ-cloth™ *noun* a type of light cloth used for cleaning * J 清洁布；轻软抹布

JCR /ˌdʒeɪ siː ˈɑː(r)/ *noun* JUNIOR COMMON ROOM（大学的）本科生活动室

jeal·ous 🔑 /ˈdʒeləs/ *adj.* **1** 🔑 feeling angry or unhappy because sb you like or love is showing interest in sb else 吃醋的；妒忌的：*a **jealous wife/husband*** 好吃醋的妻子 / 丈夫 ◇ *He's only talking to her to make you jealous.* 他跟她讲话只是让你妒忌。 ➲ **WORDFINDER NOTE AT LOVE** **2** 🔑 ~ (**of sb/sth**) feeling angry or unhappy because you wish you had sth that sb else has 妒羡的；忌妒的 **SYN** **envious**：*She's jealous of my success.* 她忌妒我的成功。◇ *Children often feel jealous when a new baby arrives.* 新生婴儿出世时孩子常常感到忌妒。 **3** ~ (**of sth**) wanting to keep or protect sth that you have because it makes you feel proud 珍惜的；爱惜的；精心守护的：*They are very jealous of their good reputation* (= they do not want to lose it). 他们极为珍惜自己的声誉。 ▸ **jeal·ous·ly** *adv.*：*She eyed Natalia jealously.* 她妒忌地看着纳塔莉亚。◇ *a **jealously guarded** secret* 严守的秘密

jeal·ousy /ˈdʒeləsi/ *noun* (*pl.* **-ies**) **1** [U] a feeling of being jealous 忌妒；妒羡；羡慕：*I felt sick with jealousy.* 我羡慕得要死。◇ *sexual jealousy* 性妒忌 **2** [C] an action or a remark that shows that a person is jealous 忌妒，妒羡，羡慕（的言行）：*I'm tired of her petty jealousies.* 我厌烦她那小肚鸡肠的忌妒。

jeans 🔑 /dʒiːnz/ *noun* [pl.] trousers/pants made of strong cotton, especially DENIM 牛仔裤；粗斜纹棉布裤：*a faded pair of blue jeans* 一条退了色的蓝色牛仔裤 ➲ **VISUAL VOCAB PAGE V68** ➲ SEE ALSO DENIM **ORIGIN** From **Janne**, the Old French name for Genoa, where the heavy cotton now used for jeans was first made. 源自古法语 Janne，即 Genoa（热那亚），牛仔裤用的粗棉布始产于此地。

Jeep™ /dʒiːp/ *noun* a small strong vehicle used, especially by the army, for driving over rough ground 吉普车；越野车 ➲ **VISUAL VOCAB PAGE V62**

jee·pers /ˈdʒiːpəz; *NAmE* -pərz/ (*also* **ˌjeepers ˈcreepers**) *exclamation* (*especially NAmE, informal*) used to express surprise or shock（表示惊奇或震惊）天哪，哎呀：*Jeepers! That car nearly hit us!* 天哪！那辆车差点撞了我们！

jeer /dʒɪə(r); *NAmE* dʒɪr/ *verb, noun*
■ ***verb*** [I, T] to laugh at sb or shout rude remarks at them to show that you do not respect them 嘲笑；嘲弄；讥讽；奚落 **SYN taunt**: *a jeering crowd* 起哄的一群人 ◇ **~ at sb** *The police were jeered at by the waiting crowd.* 警方受到在等待的人群的嘲弄。◇ **~ sb** *The players were jeered by disappointed fans.* 球员受到大失所望的球迷奚落。◇ **+ speech** *'Coward!' he jeered.* "懦夫！"他嘲笑道。
■ ***noun*** [usually pl.] a rude remark that sb shouts at sb else to show that they do not respect or like them 嘲笑，嘲弄，讥讽，奚落（的言语） **SYN taunt**: *He walked on to the stage to be greeted with jeers and whistles.* 他登上舞台，结果迎来阵阵嘲笑和口哨嘘声。

Jeez /dʒiːz/ *exclamation* (*informal, especially NAmE*) used to express anger, surprise, etc. （表示愤怒、惊讶等）天哪，哎呀

jeg·gings /ˈdʒegɪŋz/ *noun* [pl.] trousers/pants for women, made of cloth that stretches easily, that fit tightly over the legs and look like jeans （女式）牛仔式打底裤，牛仔式紧身裤

jehad = JIHAD

Je·ho·vah /dʒɪˈhəʊvə; *NAmE* -ˈhoʊ-/ (*also* **Yah·weh**) *noun* the name of God that is used in the Old Testament of the Bible 耶和华（《〈圣经〉旧约》中对上帝的称呼）

Je,hovah's 'Witness *noun* a member of a religious organization based on Christianity, which believes that the end of the world is near and that only good people will come back to life and live peacefully forever 耶和华见证人（相信世界末日在即，只有其信徒才能免受惩罚）

je·june /dʒɪˈdʒuːn/ *adj.* (*formal*) **1** too simple 太幼稚的；不成熟的；头脑简单的 **SYN naive** **2** (of a speech, etc. 演讲等) not interesting 枯燥无味的；单调的；空洞的

je·junum /dʒɪˈdʒuːnəm/ *noun* (*anatomy* 解) the second part of the small INTESTINE 空肠 ➲ COMPARE DUODENUM, ILEUM ▸ **je·junal** /-ˈdʒuːnl/ *adj.*

Jek·yll and Hyde /ˌdʒekl ən ˈhaɪd/ *noun* [sing.] a person who is sometimes very pleasant (*Jekyll*) and sometimes very unpleasant (*Hyde*) or who leads two very separate lives 两重性格交替出现的人；具有善恶双重人格的人 ➲ MORE LIKE THIS 17, page R27 **ORIGIN** From the story by Robert Louis Stevenson, *Dr Jekyll and Mr Hyde*, in which Dr Jekyll takes a drug which separates the good and bad sides of his personality into two characters. All the negative aspects go into the character of Mr Hyde. 源自罗伯特·路易斯·史蒂文森的小说《化身博士》，小说中哲基尔医生服用了一种药，把他性格中的善与恶分在两个人物身上，所有的恶念都分给了海德先生。

jell (*especially NAmE*) (*BrE usually* **gel**) /dʒel/ *verb* **1** [I] (of two or more people 两个或更多的人) to work well together; to form a successful group 联手共事；结为一体: *We just didn't jell as a group.* 我们就是不能成为一个集体。 **2** [I] (of an idea, a thought, a plan, etc. 主意、想法、计划等) to become clearer and more definite; to work well 变得更清楚；显得更明确；有效；起作用: *Ideas were beginning to jell in my mind.* 各种想法在我头脑里逐渐明朗起来。◇ *That day, everything jelled.* 那天，一切都很顺利。 **3** [I] (*specialist*) (of a liquid 液体) to become thicker and more solid; to form a GEL 胶凝；胶化；形成胶体

jel·lied /ˈdʒelid/ *adj.* [only before noun] (*especially BrE*) prepared or cooked in jelly 做成胶冻状的: *jellied eels* 鳗鱼冻

jelly 🔑 /ˈdʒeli/ (*pl.* **-ies**) *noun* **1** 🔑 [U, C] (*BrE*) (*NAmE* **jello, Jell-O™** [U]) a cold sweet transparent food made from GELATIN, sugar and fruit juice, that shakes when it is moved 果冻: *jelly and ice cream* 果冻冰淇淋 ◇ *a raspberry jelly* 山莓冻 **2** [U] a substance like jelly made from GELATIN and meat juices, served around meat, fish, etc. 肉冻 **SYN aspic**: *chicken in jelly* 鸡肉冻 **3** 🔑 [U, C] a type of jam that does not contain any pieces of fruit（不含水果块的）果酱: *blackcurrant jelly* 黑加仑果酱 ➲ COMPARE JAM *n.* (1) **4** 🔑 [U] any thick sticky substance, especially a type of cream used on the skin 胶状物，胶凝物（尤指护肤霜） ➲ SEE ALSO PETROLEUM JELLY, ROYAL JELLY **5** (*also* **'jelly shoe**) [C] a light plastic shoe designed for wearing on the beach and in the sea（海滩和海上穿的）轻便塑料鞋 ➲ VISUAL VOCAB PAGE V69
IDM be/feel like 'jelly | turn to 'jelly (of legs or knees 双腿或双膝) to feel weak because you are nervous 紧张得发软

'jelly baby *noun* (*BrE*) a small soft sweet/candy in the shape of a baby, made from GELATIN and flavoured with fruit 娃娃胶糖（果味凝胶软糖）

'jelly bean *noun* a small sweet/candy shaped like a BEAN, with a hard outside and a centre like jelly 软心豆粒糖

jel·ly·fish /ˈdʒelifɪʃ/ *noun* (*pl.* **jel·ly·fish**) a sea creature with a body like jelly and long thin parts called TENTACLES that can give a sharp sting 水母；海蜇

'jelly roll (*NAmE*) (*BrE* **,Swiss 'roll**) *noun* a thin flat cake that is spread with jam, etc. and rolled up 卷筒蛋糕（夹有果酱等）

jembe /ˈdʒembe/ *noun* **1** [C] (*EAfrE*) a farming tool with a long handle and a blade at one end, used for digging, breaking up soil or removing WEEDS (= plants growing where they are not wanted) （长柄）锄头 **2** [C] a traditional W African drum 金贝鼓（西非的一种传统鼓） **3** [U] a type of W African music 西非打击乐

jemmy /ˈdʒemi/ (*BrE*) (*NAmE* **jimmy**) *noun* (*pl.* **-ies**) a short heavy metal bar used by thieves to force open doors and windows 短撬棍，铁撬棍（窃贼撬门窗用）

je ne sais quoi /ˌʒə nə seɪ ˈkwɑː/ *noun* [U] (*from French, often humorous*) a good quality that is difficult to describe 难以描述的好品质；妙不可言的特性: *He has that je ne sais quoi that distinguishes a professional from an amateur.* 他有那种难以言表的特质，体现出他是专业而非业余的。

jenny /ˈdʒeni/ *noun* (*pl.* **-ies**) a female DONKEY or ASS 母驴

jeop·ard·ize (*BrE also* **-ise**) /ˈdʒepədaɪz; *NAmE* -pərd-/ *verb* **~ sth/sb** (*formal*) to risk harming or destroying sth/sb 冒…的危险；危及；危害；损害 **SYN endanger**: *He would never do anything to jeopardize his career.* 他决不会做任何有损于他事业的事。

jeop·ardy /ˈdʒepədi; *NAmE* -pərdi/ *noun*
IDM in 'jeopardy in a dangerous position or situation and likely to be lost or harmed 处于危险境地；受到威胁 ➲ SEE ALSO DOUBLE JEOPARDY

jere·miad /ˌdʒerɪˈmaɪæd/ *noun* (*formal*) a very long sad complaint or list of complaints 哀诉；诉求清单

jerk /dʒɜːk; *NAmE* dʒɜːrk/ *verb, noun*
■ ***verb*** [T, I] to move or to make sth move with a sudden short sharp movement 急拉；猛推；猝然一动: **~ sth (+ adv./prep.)** *He jerked the phone away from her.* 他猛然一下从她那儿把电话抢走。◇ *She jerked her head up.* 她猛然抬起头来。◇ **+ adv./prep.** *The bus jerked to a halt.* 那辆公共汽车猛地一颠停下了。◇ *He grabbed a handful of hair and jerked at it.* 他抓住一把头发猛拉。◇ **~ sth + adj.** *She got to the door and jerked it open.* 她走到门口，猛然一把将门拉开。
PHRV ,jerk sb a'round (*informal, especially NAmE*) to make things difficult for sb, especially by not being honest with them （尤指通过不诚实的手段）给某人出难题，为某人设置障碍，为难某人: *Consumers are often jerked around by big companies.* 消费者经常受大公司的捉弄。 **,jerk 'off** (*taboo, slang*) (of a man 男子) to MASTURBATE 手淫 **,jerk 'out | ,jerk sth↔'out** to say sth in a quick and awkward way because you are nervous（紧张得）急促而断续地说出，结结巴巴地说
■ ***noun*** **1** [C] a sudden quick sharp movement 急拉；猛推；猝然一动 **SYN jolt**: *She sat up with a jerk.* 她猛地坐了起来。 **2** [C] (*informal*) a stupid person who often says or does the wrong thing 蠢人；傻瓜；笨蛋 **3** [U] meat that is MARINATED (= left in a mixture of oil and spices before being cooked) to give it a strong flavour and then

cooked over a wood fire 腌制后放在木火上烤的肉：*jerk chicken* 烤鸡

jer·kin /ˈdʒɜːkɪn; *NAmE* ˈdʒɜːrkɪn/ *noun* a short jacket without sleeves, especially one worn by men in the past（尤指旧时男子穿的）坎肩

jerky /ˈdʒɜːki; *NAmE* ˈdʒɜːrki/ *adj.*, *noun*
■ ***adj.*** making sudden starts and stops and not moving smoothly 忽动忽停的；颠簸的 ▶ **jerk·ily** /-ɪli/ *adv.*：*The car moved off jerkily.* 汽车颠簸着开走了。
■ ***noun*** [U] (*NAmE*) meat that has been cut into long strips and smoked or dried 干肉条；熏肉条：*beef jerky* 牛肉干条

jero·boam /ˌdʒerəˈbəʊəm; *NAmE* -ˈboʊ-/ *noun* a wine bottle which holds four or six times as much wine as an ordinary bottle（容量相当于普通酒瓶四倍或六倍的）大酒瓶

Jerry /ˈdʒeri/ *noun* (*pl.* **-ies**) (*taboo, BrE, slang*) an offensive word for a person from Germany, used especially during the First and Second World Wars 德国佬，德国鬼子（尤用于第一、二次世界大战期间）

ˈ**jerry-built** *adj.* (*old-fashioned, disapproving*) built quickly and cheaply without caring about quality or safety 草率建成的；粗制滥造的

jer·ry·can /ˈdʒerikæn/ *noun* (*old-fashioned*) a large metal or plastic container with flat sides, used for carrying petrol/gas or water（运送汽油或水的）大扁平容器

jer·ry·man·der, **jer·ry·man·der·ing** = GERRYMANDER, GERRYMANDERING

jer·sey /ˈdʒɜːzi; *NAmE* ˈdʒɜːrzi/ *noun* **1** [C] a shirt worn by sb playing a sports game 运动衫 ➲ **VISUAL VOCAB** PAGE V48 **2** [C] a knitted piece of clothing made of wool or cotton for the upper part of the body, with long sleeves and no buttons; a type of sweater（毛或棉的）针织套头衫 **3** [U] a type of soft fine knitted cloth used for making clothes 平针织物：*made from 100% cotton jersey* 用 100% 的棉织品做成 **4 Jersey** [C] a type of light brown cow that produces high quality milk 泽西牛（一种产优质奶的浅棕色乳牛）

Je·ru·sa·lem ar·ti·choke /dʒəˌruːsələm ˈɑːtɪtʃəʊk; *NAmE* ˈɑːrtətʃoʊk/ *noun* (*BrE also* **ar·ti·choke**) a light brown root vegetable that looks like a potato 洋姜；菊芋

jes·sie /ˈdʒesi/ (*also* **jessy**) *noun* (*pl.* **-ies**) (*BrE, old-fashioned, offensive*) a man or boy who is weak or who seems to behave too much like a woman 软弱的男子（或男孩）；娘娘腔

jest /dʒest/ *noun, verb*
■ ***noun*** (*old-fashioned* or *formal*) something said or done to amuse people 笑话；俏皮话；打趣；玩笑 **SYN joke**
IDM in ˈjest as a joke 开玩笑地；闹着玩：*The remark was made half in jest.* 这话是半开玩笑说出的。◇ *'Many a true word is spoken in jest,' thought Rosie* (= people often say things as a joke that are actually true). "许多真话都是在玩笑中说出的。" 罗西想。
■ ***verb*** [I, T] ~ (**about sth**) | + **speech** (*formal* or *humorous*) to say things that are not serious or true, especially in order to make sb laugh 开玩笑；说笑话 **SYN joke**：*Would I jest about such a thing?* 这种事我会说着玩吗？

jest·er /ˈdʒestə(r)/ *noun* a man employed in the past at the COURT of a king or queen to amuse people by telling jokes and funny stories（旧时宫廷中的）逗乐小丑，弄臣：*the court jester* 宫廷弄臣

Jes·uit /ˈdʒezjuɪt; *NAmE* ˈdʒeʒəwət/ *noun* a member of the Society of Jesus, a Roman Catholic religious group（天主教）耶稣会会士：*a Jesuit priest* 耶稣会神父

Jesus /ˈdʒiːzəs/ (*also* ˌ**Jesus ˈChrist**) *noun* = CHRIST

jet /dʒet/ *noun, verb*
■ ***noun*** **1** [C] a plane driven by JET ENGINES 喷气式飞机：*a jet aircraft/fighter/airliner* 喷气式飞机 / 战斗机 / 客机 ◇ *The accident happened as the jet was about to take off.* 事故是在喷气式飞机正要起飞时发生的。➲ SEE ALSO JUMBO *n.*, JUMP JET ➲ **WORDFINDER NOTE** AT AIRCRAFT **2** [C] a strong narrow stream of gas, liquid, steam or flame that comes very quickly out of a small opening. The opening is also called a jet. 喷射流；喷射口；喷嘴：*The pipe burst and jets of water shot across the room.* 管子爆裂，一股股水从屋子这头喷到那头。◇ *to clean the gas jets on the cooker* 把煤气灶的气嘴擦干净 **3** [U] a hard black mineral that can be polished and is used in jewellery 煤玉；黑玉；黑色大理石；贝褐碳
■ ***verb*** (-tt-) [I] + **adv./prep.** (*informal*) to fly somewhere in a plane 乘坐飞机旅行

ˌ**jet ˈblack** *adj.* deep shiny black in colour 乌黑发亮的 ➲ **WORDFINDER NOTE** AT BLONDE ➲ **MORE LIKE THIS** 15, page R26

ˌ**jet ˈengine** *noun* an engine that drives an aircraft forwards by pushing out a stream of gases behind it 喷气式发动机 ➲ **VISUAL VOCAB** PAGE V57

jet·foil /ˈdʒetfɔɪl/ *noun* a passenger boat which rises above the surface of the water when it is travelling fast and has JET ENGINES 水翼喷射船；飞翼船

ˈ**jet lag** *noun* [U] the feeling of being tired and slightly confused after a long plane journey, especially when there is a big difference in the time at the place you leave and that at the place you arrive in 飞行时差综合症；时差反应 ➲ **COLLOCATIONS** AT TRAVEL ▶ ˈ**jet-lagged** *adj.*

jet·liner /ˈdʒetlaɪnə(r)/ *noun* a large plane with a jet engine, that carries passengers（大型）喷气式客机

ˌ**jet-proˈpelled** *adj.* driven by JET ENGINES 喷气发动机推进的

ˌ**jet proˈpulsion** *noun* [U] the use of JET ENGINES for power 喷气推进

jet·sam /ˈdʒetsəm/ *noun* things that are thrown away, especially from a ship at sea and that float towards land（尤指冲到岸边的）船上投弃物 ➲ COMPARE FLOTSAM (1)

the ˈjet set *noun* [sing.+sing./pl. v.] rich and fashionable people who travel a lot 常乘飞机旅行的时尚富人族

ˈ**jet-setter** *noun* a rich, fashionable person who travels a lot 常乘飞机旅行的富豪 ▶ ˈ**jet-setting** *adj.* [usually before noun]: *her jet-setting millionaire boyfriend* 她那位常乘飞机旅行的阔男朋友

ˈ**Jet Ski™** *noun* a vehicle with an engine, like a motorcycle, for riding across water 喷气式滑艇；吉斯基水上摩托艇 ▶ ˈ**jet-skiing** *noun* [U] ➲ **VISUAL VOCAB** PAGE V54

ˈ**jet stream** *noun* **1** (*usually* **the jet stream**) [sing.] a strong wind that blows high above the earth and that has an effect on the weather（地球高空的）急流 **2** [C] the flow of gases from a plane's engine（飞机发动机的）喷气流

jet·ti·son /ˈdʒetɪsn/ *verb* **1** ~ **sth** to throw sth out of a moving plane or ship to make it lighter（为减轻重量而从行驶的飞机或船上）扔弃，丢弃，投弃：*to jettison fuel* 投弃燃料 **2** ~ **sth/sb** to get rid of sth/sb that you no longer need or want 摆脱；除掉；处理掉 **SYN discard**：*He was jettisoned as team coach after the defeat.* 他因这次失利被撤销了运动队教练职务。 **3** ~ **sth** to reject an idea, a belief, a plan, etc. that you no longer think is useful or likely to be successful 放弃，拒绝接受（想法、信念、计划等）**SYN abandon**

jetty /ˈdʒeti/ *noun* (*pl.* **-ies**) (*NAmE also* **dock**) a wall or platform built out into the sea, a river, etc., where boats can be tied and where people can get on and off boats 突堤；栈桥；登岸码头 ➲ **VISUAL VOCAB** PAGE V5

Jet·way™ /ˈdʒetweɪ/ (*NAmE*) (*BrE* ˈ**air bridge**) *noun* a bridge that can be moved and put against the door of an aircraft, so people can get on and off 旅客登机（活动）桥

Jew /dʒuː/ *noun* a member of the people and cultural community whose traditional religion is Judaism and who come from the ancient Hebrew people of Israel; a person who believes in and practises Judaism 犹太人；犹太教徒

jewel /ˈdʒuːəl/ *noun* **1** a PRECIOUS STONE such as a diamond, RUBY, etc. 宝石 SYN **gem** **2** [usually pl.] pieces of jewellery or decorative objects that contain PRECIOUS STONES 珠宝首饰：*The family jewels are locked away in a safe.* 家里的珠宝首饰都锁在保险柜里。➲ SEE ALSO CROWN JEWELS **3** a small PRECIOUS STONE or piece of special glass that is used in the machinery of a watch（手表的）宝石轴承 **4** (*informal*) a person or thing that is very important or valuable 宝贝；难能可贵的人；珍贵的东西 ➲ COMPARE GEM

IDM **the jewel in the ˈcrown** the most attractive or valuable part of sth 王冠上的宝石；最有吸引力（或珍贵、有价值）的东西

ˈjewel case *noun* a plastic box for holding a CD（塑料）光盘盒

jew·elled (*especially US* **jew·eled**) /ˈdʒuːəld/ *adj.* decorated with jewels 饰以宝石的；镶有宝石的

jew·el·ler (*especially US* **jew·el·er**) /ˈdʒuːələ(r)/ *noun* **1** a person who makes, repairs or sells jewellery and watches 宝石钟表匠；宝石钟表商 **2 jeweller's** (*pl.* **jew·el·lers**) a shop/store that sells jewellery and watches 珠宝钟表店：*I bought it at the jeweller's near my office.* 我在办公室附近的珠宝店买的。➲ MORE LIKE THIS 34, page R29

jew·el·lery 🔑 (*especially US* **jew·el·ry**) /ˈdʒuːəlri/ *noun* [U] objects such as rings and NECKLACES that people wear as decoration 珠宝；首饰：*silver/gold jewellery* 银首饰；金首饰 ◇ *She has some lovely pieces of jewellery.* 她有几件漂亮的首饰。➲ COLLOCATIONS AT FASHION ➲ VISUAL VOCAB PAGE V70 ➲ SEE ALSO COSTUME JEWELLERY

Jew·ess /ˈdʒuːəs/ *noun* (*often offensive*) an old-fashioned word for a Jewish woman 犹太女人（旧时用语）

Jew·ish /ˈdʒuːɪʃ/ *adj.* connected with Jews or Judaism; believing in and practising Judaism 犹太人的；有关犹太人的；犹太教的；信犹太教的：*We're Jewish.* 我们是犹太人。◇ *the local Jewish community* 当地的犹太人群体 ▶ **Jew·ish·ness** *noun* [U]

Jewry /ˈdʒʊəri; NAmE ˈdʒʊri; ˈdʒuː-/ *noun* [U] (*formal*) Jewish people as a group（统称）犹太人：*British Jewry* 英国犹太人

ˌJew's ˈharp *noun* a small musical instrument which is held between the teeth and played with a finger 口弦，口簧（演奏者含在齿间用指拨奏的小型乐器）

Jez·ebel /ˈdʒezəbel/ *noun* (*old-fashioned*) a woman who is thought to be sexually immoral 荡妇 ORIGIN From the name of the wife of a king of Israel in the Bible, who wore make-up and was criticized by Elijah for worshipping the god Baal. 源自《圣经》中以色列王之妻耶洗别的名字。她浓妆艳抹，因崇拜神祇巴力而受到以利亚的指责。

-ji /dʒi/ *combining form* (*IndE*) used with people's names and titles to show respect 吉（加在人名和头衔后表示尊敬）：*Lalitaji* 拉丽塔吉 ◇ *guruji* 古鲁吉

jib /dʒɪb/ *noun, verb*

■ *noun* **1** a small sail in front of the large sail on a boat 艏三角帆；主帆前的小帆 ➲ VISUAL VOCAB PAGE V61 **2** the arm of a CRANE that lifts things（起重机的）动臂，悬臂，挺杆

■ *verb* (**-bb-**) [I] ~ (**at sth/at doing sth**) (*old-fashioned, informal*) to be unwilling to do or accept sth 不愿做；不肯接受：*She agreed to attend but jibbed at making a speech.* 她同意出席但不愿发言。

jibba (*also* **jib·bah, djibba, djib·bah**) /ˈdʒɪbə/ *noun* a long coat worn by Muslim men（穆斯林男子穿的）罩袍

jibe (*also* **gibe**) /dʒaɪb/ *noun, verb*

■ *noun* **1** ~ (**at sb/sth**) an unkind or insulting remark about sb 嘲讽；嘲弄；讥讽：*He made several cheap jibes at his opponent during the interview.* 在采访中他好几次粗俗地嘲讽对手。**2** (*NAmE*) = GYBE

■ *verb* **1** [I, T] ~ (**at sth**) | ~ **that...** | + **speech** to say sth that is intended to embarrass sb or make them look silly 嘲讽；嘲弄；挖苦：*He jibed repeatedly at the errors they had made.* 他一而再、再而三地嘲弄他们所犯的错误。**2** [I] ~ (**with sth**) (*NAmE, informal*) to be the same as sth or to match it（与…）一致，相符，相匹配：*Your statement doesn't jibe with the facts.* 你的说法与事实不符。**3** (*NAmE*) = GYBE

jiffy /ˈdʒɪfi/ *noun* [usually sing.] (*informal*) (*pl.* **-ies**) a moment 一会儿；瞬间：*I'll be with you* **in a jiffy** (= very soon). 我一会儿就来。

ˈJiffy bag™ *noun* **1** (*BrE*) a thick soft envelope for sending things that might break or tear easily 有衬垫的信封（用于邮寄易碎或易受损物品）**2** (*SAfrE*) a clear plastic bag used for storing things in, especially food 透明塑料袋（贮存物品，尤用于盛装食物）

jig /dʒɪg/ *noun, verb*

■ *noun* **1** a quick lively dance; the music for this dance 吉格舞；吉格舞曲：*an Irish jig* 爱尔兰吉格舞曲 **2** a device that holds sth in position and guides the tools that are working on it 夹具

■ *verb* (**-gg-**) [I, T] ~ (**sb/sth**) (+ **adv./prep.**) to move or to make sb/sth move up and down with short quick movements（使）上下急动，蹦跳：*He jigged up and down with excitement.* 他激动得又蹦又跳。

jig·ger /ˈdʒɪgə(r)/ *noun* = CHIGGER

jig·gered /ˈdʒɪgəd; NAmE -gərd/ *adj.* [not before noun]

IDM **I'll be jiggered!** (*old-fashioned, BrE, informal*) used to show surprise（表示惊讶）天哪

jiggery-pokery /ˌdʒɪgəri ˈpəʊkəri; NAmE ˈpoʊk-/ *noun* [U] (*informal, especially BrE*) dishonest behaviour 欺骗行为；骗局；捣鬼

jig·gle /ˈdʒɪgl/ *verb* [I, T] (*informal*) to move or make sth move up and down or from side to side with short quick movements（使）上下急动，左右摇摆，抖动：(+ **adv./prep.**) *Stop jiggling around!* 别晃来晃去的！◇ *She jiggled with the lock.* 她摆弄着锁。◇ ~ **sth** (+ **adv./prep.**) *He stood jiggling his car keys in his hand.* 他站在那儿手里摆弄着汽车钥匙。

jig·saw /ˈdʒɪgsɔː/ *noun* **1** (*also* **ˈjigsaw puzzle**) (*also* **puz·zle** *especially in NAmE*) a picture printed on cardboard or wood, that has been cut up into a lot of small pieces of different shapes that you have to fit together again 拼图；拼板玩具：*to do a jigsaw* 玩拼图 ➲ VISUAL VOCAB PAGE V43 **2** a mysterious situation in which it is not easy to understand all the causes of what is happening; a complicated problem 神秘莫测的事物；谜团 **3** a SAW (= a type of tool) with a fine blade for cutting designs in thin pieces of wood or metal 线锯；镂花锯；钢丝锯

jihad (*also* **jehad**) /dʒɪˈhɑːd/ *noun* **1** (in Islam 伊斯兰教) a spiritual struggle within yourself to stop yourself breaking religious or moral laws（同自己的私欲的）斗争 **2** a holy war fought by Muslims to defend Islam（为保卫伊斯兰教进行的）抵抗战争

jiko /ˈdʒiːkɒ; NAmE -koː/ *noun* (*pl.* **-os**) (*EAfrE*) a container made of metal or CLAY and used for burning CHARCOAL or small pieces of wood. It is used for cooking or to give heat. 绩高炉（用金属或黏土制作，烧煤炭或小木块）

jil·bab /ˈdʒɪlbæb/ *noun* a full-length piece of clothing worn over other clothes by Muslim women 吉尔巴布（穆斯林女子穿的罩袍）

jill·aroo /ˌdʒɪləˈruː/ *noun* (*pl.* **-oos**) (*AustralE, informal*) a young woman who is working on a farm in Australia/New Zealand to get experience（澳大利亚或新西兰的）农场见习青年女工 ➲ COMPARE JACKAROO

jilt /dʒɪlt/ *verb* [often passive] ~ **sb** to end a romantic relationship with sb in a sudden and unkind way 抛弃，遗弃（情人）：*He was jilted by his fiancée.* 他被未婚妻抛弃了。◇ *a jilted bride/lover* 被抛弃的新娘/情人

Jim Crow /ˌdʒɪm ˈkrəʊ; NAmE ˈkroʊ/ *noun* [U] the former practice in the US of using laws that allowed black people to be treated unfairly and kept separate from white people, for example in schools（美国社会过去对黑人的）种族歧视，种族隔离 ORIGIN From the title of a song that was sung by white entertainers who tried to look and sound like African Americans. 源自一首由白人艺人演唱的歌曲名称，他们演唱时试图在外表和声音上模仿美国黑人。

jim-jams /ˈdʒɪm dʒæmz/ *noun* [pl.] (*BrE, informal*) = PYJAMAS

jimmy /ˈdʒɪmi/ (*NAmE*) (*BrE* **jemmy**) *noun* (*pl.* **-ies**) a short heavy metal bar used by thieves to force open doors and windows 短撬棍，铁撬棍（窃贼撬门窗用）

jin·gle /ˈdʒɪŋgl/ *noun, verb*

■ *noun* **1** [sing.] a sound like small bells ringing that is made when metal objects are shaken together（金属撞击发出的）叮当声：*the jingle of coins in his pocket* 他兜里硬币的叮当声 **2** [C] a short song or tune that is easy to remember and is used in advertising on radio or television（收音机或电视广告中易记的）短歌，短曲 ⊃ WORDFINDER NOTE AT RADIO

■ *verb* [I, T] ~ (**sth**) to make a pleasant gentle sound like small bells ringing; to make sth do this（使）发出叮当声：*The chimes jingled in the breeze.* 风铃在微风中叮当作响。◇ *She jingled the coins in her pocket.* 她把兜里的硬币弄得叮当响。

jingo /ˈdʒɪŋgəʊ; *NAmE* -goʊ/ *noun*

IDM **by jingo** (*old-fashioned*) used to show surprise or determination（表示惊讶或决心）天哪，嘿，加油啊

jin·go·ism /ˈdʒɪŋgəʊɪzəm; *NAmE* -goʊ-/ *noun* [U] (*disapproving*) a strong belief that your own country is best, especially when this is expressed in support of war with another country 极端爱国主义；沙文主义 ▶ **jin·go·is·tic** /ˌdʒɪŋgəʊˈɪstɪk; *NAmE* -goʊ-/ *adj.*

jink /dʒɪŋk/ *verb* [I] (**+ adv./prep.**) (*BrE, informal*) to move quickly while changing direction suddenly and often, especially in order to avoid sb/sth 急转；（尤指）躲闪，闪开

jinks /dʒɪŋks/ *noun* ⊃ HIGH JINKS

jinx /dʒɪŋks/ *noun* [sing.] ~ (**on sb/sth**) bad luck; sb/sth that is thought to bring bad luck in a mysterious way 厄运；霉运；不祥之人（或物）：*I'm convinced there's a jinx on this car.* 我深信这辆汽车沾上晦气了。⊃ WORDFINDER NOTE AT LUCK ▶ **jinx** *verb* ~ **sb/sth**

jinxed /dʒɪŋkst/ *adj.* (*informal*) having or bringing more bad luck than is normal 倒霉的；不走运的：*The whole family seemed to be jinxed.* 全家人似乎都走背字。

jism /ˈdʒɪzəm/ (*also* **jis·som** /ˈdʒɪsəm/) *noun* [U] (*slang*) a man's SEMEN 精液

JIT /ˌdʒeɪ aɪ ˈtiː/ *abbr.* JUST-IN-TIME 适时制（只有在需要时才将零部件或原材料送货到厂）

jit·ter·bug /ˈdʒɪtəbʌg; *NAmE* -tər-/ *noun* a fast dance that was popular in the 1940s 吉特巴舞（流行于 20 世纪 40 年代的快节奏舞）

jit·ters /ˈdʒɪtəz; *NAmE* -tərz/ (*often* **the jitters**) *noun* [pl.] (*informal*) feelings of being anxious and nervous, especially before an important event or before having to do sth difficult（事前的）紧张不安：*I always **get the jitters** before exams.* 我考试前总是很紧张。

jit·tery /ˈdʒɪtəri/ *adj.* (*informal*) anxious and nervous 紧张不安的；心神不宁的 ⊃ SYNONYMS AT NERVOUS

jiu-jitsu = JU-JITSU

jive /dʒaɪv/ *noun, verb*

■ *noun* **1** [U, sing.] a fast dance to music with a strong beat, especially popular in the 1950s 牛仔舞，捷舞（节奏快而强劲，20 世纪 50 年代尤为流行） **2** [U] (*NAmE, old-fashioned, informal*) nonsense 胡说；废话；蠢话：*to talk jive* 胡说八道

■ *verb* **1** [I] to dance to JAZZ or ROCK AND ROLL music 跳牛仔舞 **2** [I, T] ~ (**sb**) (*NAmE, old-fashioned, informal*) to try to make sb believe sth that is not true 欺骗；欺瞒 SYN **kid**

Jnr *abbr.* = JR

Job /dʒəʊb; *NAmE* dʒoʊb/ *noun*

IDM **the patience of ˈJob** the quality of being extremely patient and not complaining 极其耐心；心平气和：*You need the patience of Job to deal with some of our customers.* 和我们的一些顾客打交道需要有极大的耐心。 ORIGIN From **Job**, a man in the Bible who experienced much suffering, including losing his family, his home and his possessions, but continued to believe in and trust God. 源自《圣经》人物约伯（Job），虽历经失去家人、家园和财产等磨难，依然坚持信奉上帝。

job 🔑 AW /dʒɒb; *NAmE* dʒɑːb/ *noun*

• **PAID WORK** 有酬工作 **1** 🔑 work for which you receive regular payment 工作；职业；职位：*He's trying to get a job.* 他正在找工作。◇ *She **took a job** as a waitress.* 她找了个工作，当服务员。◇ *His brother's just **lost his job**.* 他的弟弟刚丢了工作。◇ *a **summer/holiday/Saturday/vacation job*** 暑期 / 假日 / 周末 / 假期工作 ◇ *a **temporary/permanent job*** 临时 / 固定工作 ◇ *I'm thinking of **applying for a new job**.* 我在考虑申请一份新工作。◇ *The takeover of the company is bound to mean more **job losses**.* 公司被接管必然意味着更多人要失业。◇ *Many women are in **part-time jobs**.* 许多妇女都做的是兼职工作。◇ *Did they **offer you the job**?* 他们给你这个职位了吗？◇ *He certainly **knows his job*** (= is very good at his job). 他对自己的工作很在行。◇ *I'm only **doing my job*** (= I'm doing what I am paid to do). 我不过在做我分内的事。◇ *He's been **out of a job*** (= unemployed) *for six months now.* 他已经失业六个月了。◇ *She's never had a **steady job*** (= a job that is not going to

▼ **SYNONYMS** 同义词辨析

job

position • **post** • **vacancy** • **appointment**

These are all words for a position doing work for which you receive regular payment. 以上各词均表示工作、职位。

job a position doing work for which you receive regular payment 指工作、职业、职位： *He's trying to get a job in a bank.* 他正设法在银行找一个工作。

position (*rather formal*) a job 指职位、职务： *a senior position in a large corporation* 在一家大公司的高级职务

JOB OR POSITION? 用 job 还是 position?

Position usually refers to a particular job within an organization, especially at a high level, and is not usually used about jobs generally. It is also often used in job applications, descriptions and advertisements. * position 通常指机构中的职位，尤指高级职位，通常不用以指一般的工作。该词亦常用于工作申请、职位描述和招聘广告中。

post a job, especially an important one in a large organization 指职位，尤指大机构的要职： *a key post in the new government* 在新政府中的要职

vacancy a job that is available for sb to do 指空缺的职位、空职： *We have several vacancies for casual workers.* 我们有几个临时工的空缺。

appointment (*rather formal, especially BrE*) a job or position of responsibility 指承担一定责任的职务、职位： *This is a permanent appointment, requiring commitment and hard work.* 这是一个固定职位，需要专心致志和勤奋工作。

PATTERNS

- a **permanent/temporary** job/position/post/vacancy/appointment
- a **full-time/part-time** job/position/post/vacancy/appointment
- to **have/have got** a(n) job/position/post/vacancy/appointment
- to **apply for/fill** a job/position/post/vacancy
- to **resign from/leave/quit** a job/position/post

end suddenly). 她从未有过稳定的工作。 ➲ WORDFINDER NOTE AT EMPLOY ➲ COLLOCATIONS AT UNEMPLOYMENT

- TASK 任务 **2** 🔑 a particular task or piece of work that you have to do（一项）任务；（一件）工作，活儿，事情：*I've got various jobs around the house to do.* 我在家里有各种各样的活儿要干。◇ *Sorting these papers out is going to be a long job.* 整理这些文件是很费工夫的事。◇ *The builder has a couple of jobs on at the moment.* 目前这家建筑商有几项工程在进行。➲ SEE ALSO BLOW JOB, NOSE JOB
- DUTY 职责 **3** 🔑 [usually sing.] (*rather informal*) a responsibility or duty 责任；职责：*It's not my job to lock up!* 上锁不是我的事儿！
- CRIME 罪行 **4** (*informal*) a crime, especially stealing 犯罪行为（尤指偷窃）：*a bank job* 银行抢劫案 ◇ *an* ***inside job*** (= done by sb in the organization where the crime happens) 内部人员作的案
- OBJECT 物体 **5** (*informal*) a particular kind of thing 东西；物件：*It's real wood—not one of those plastic jobs.* 这是实木的，不是那种塑料产品。
- COMPUTING 计算机技术 **6** an item of work which is done by a computer as a single unit（作为一个单元处理的）作业，工作

IDM **do the 'job** (*informal*) to be effective or successful in doing what you want 起作用；有效：*This extra strong glue should do the job.* 这种超黏度胶应该管用。 **do a good, bad, etc. 'job (on sth) | make a good, bad, etc. job of sth** to do sth well, badly, etc. 干得好（或差等）；将…办好（或坏等）：*They did a very professional job.* 他们干得非常内行。◇ *You've certainly made an excellent job of the kitchen* (= for example, painting it). 你们把厨房弄得好极了。 **give sb/sth up as a bad 'job** (*informal*) to decide to stop trying to help sb or to do sth because there is no hope of success 对…不再抱有希望；因没有希望而决定放弃 **good 'job!** (*especially NAmE, informal*) used to tell sb that they have done well at sth 干得不错；办得好；好呀 **a good 'job** (*informal*) used to say that you are pleased about a situation or that sb is lucky that sth happened 令人满意的状况；幸运的事；好事：*It's a good job you were there to help.* 幸亏你来帮忙。 **have a (hard/difficult) job doing/to do sth** to have difficulty doing sth 干某事很困难（或很吃力、很费力）：*You'll have a job convincing them that you're right.* 要让他们信服你是对的还要费点劲。◇ *He had a hard job to make himself heard.* 他好不容易才使别人听见他的声音。 **a job of 'work** (*BrE, old-fashioned* or *formal*) work that you are paid to do or that must be done 分内的事；必须干的工作：*There was a job of work waiting for him that he was not looking forward to.* 有一件他不想干但又必须完成的工作在等待着他。 **jobs for the 'boys** (*BrE, informal, disapproving*) people use the expression **jobs for the boys** when they are criticizing the fact that sb in power has given work to friends or relatives 为亲信安排的工作（或职位）；任人唯亲 **just the 'job** (*BrE*) (*also* **just the 'ticket** *NAmE, BrE*) (*informal, approving*) exactly what is needed in a particular situation 正需要的东西；求之不得的东西 **more than your 'job's worth (to do sth)** (*BrE, informal*) not worth doing because it is against the rules or because it might cause you to lose your job 工作所不允许的事；违反原则的事；可能会丢饭碗的事：*It's more than my job's worth to let you in without a ticket.* 没有票就让你进去，我可能会丢饭碗的。➲ SEE ALSO JOBSWORTH **on the 'job 1** while doing a particular job 在上班时；在干活时；在工作岗位上：*No sleeping on the job!* 上班时严禁睡觉！◇ *on-the-job training* 在职培训 **2** (*BrE, slang*) having sex 在交媾；在性交；在干那事 ➲ MORE AT BEST *n.*, DEVIL, WALK *v.*

job·ber /ˈdʒɒbə(r); *NAmE* ˈdʒɑːb-/ (*also* **stock·job·ber**) *noun* (*finance* 财) (in Britain in the past) a person who worked on the STOCK EXCHANGE, buying shares, etc. from BROKERS and selling them to other brokers（英国旧时的）股票经纪人，证券交易商 ➲ COMPARE BROKER-DEALER

job·bie /ˈdʒɒbi; *NAmE* ˈdʒɑːbi/ *noun* (*informal*) used to refer to an object of a particular kind（特定一类的）物品，产品：*Her bikini was one of those expensive designer jobbies.* 她的比基尼泳装是那种价格昂贵的名牌产品。

job·bing /ˈdʒɒbɪŋ; *NAmE* ˈdʒɑːb-/ *adj.* [only before noun] (*BrE*) doing pieces of work for different people rather than a regular job 打零工的；做散工的：*a jobbing actor/builder* 临时演员；打零工的建筑工人

job·centre /ˈdʒɒbsentə(r); *NAmE* ˈdʒɑːb-/ *noun* (*BrE*) a government office where people can get advice in finding work and where jobs are advertised（政府的）就业服务中心，职业介绍所

▼ COLLOCATIONS 词语搭配

Jobs 工作

Getting a job 找工作

- **look for** work 找工作
- **look for/apply for/go for** a job 找工作；申请一个职位；努力争取工作
- **get/pick up/complete/fill out/**(*BrE*) **fill in** an application (form) 得到 / 拿到 / 完成 / 填写申请（表）
- **send/email** your (*BrE*) CV/(*NAmE*) résumé/application/application form/covering letter 寄 / 通过电邮发送简历 / 申请 / 申请表 / 附函
- **be called for/have/attend** an interview 被要求参加 / 有 / 参加面试
- **offer sb** a job/work/employment/promotion 给某人提供一份工作；雇用某人；提拔某人
- **find/get/land** a job 找到工作
- **employ/**(*especially NAmE*) **hire/recruit/**(*especially BrE*) **take on** staff/workers/trainees 雇用员工 / 工人 / 实习生
- **recruit/appoint** a manager 招聘 / 任命经理

Doing a job 做工作

- **arrive at/get to/leave** work/the office/the factory 上 / 下班；到办公室 / 工厂上班；从办公室 / 工厂下班
- **start/finish** work/your shift 开始 / 结束工作 / 轮班工作时间
- **do/put in/work** overtime 加班
- **have/gain/get/lack/need** experience/qualifications 拥有 / 获得 / 缺乏 / 需要经验 / 资格
- **do/get/have/receive** training 做 / 得到 / 接受培训
- **learn/pick up/improve/develop** (your) skills 学习 / 偶然学会 / 提高 / 发展技能
- **cope with/manage/share/spread** the workload 应付 / 勉力完成 / 分担 / 分摊工作量
- **improve your/achieve a better** work-life balance 达到更好的工作与生活的平衡
- **have** (**no**) job satisfaction/job security 有 / 没有工作满足感 / 职业保障

Building a career 建立职业生涯

- **have** a job/work/a career/a vocation 有工作 / 事业 / 职业
- **find/follow/pursue/**(*especially NAmE*) **live** (**out**) your vocation 找到 / 从事 / 致力于 / 实践适合自己的职业
- **enter/go into/join** a profession 加入一个行业
- **choose/embark on/start/begin/pursue** a career 选择 / 从事 / 开始 / 致力于一种职业
- **change** jobs/profession/career 换工作 / 行业 / 职业
- **be/**(*both especially BrE*) **work/go** freelance 做自由职业
- **do/take on** temp work/freelance work 做 / 开始从事临时工作 / 特约工作
- **do/be engaged in/be involved in** voluntary work 做 / 从事 / 参与义务性工作

Leaving your job 离职

- **leave/**(*especially NAmE*) **quit/resign from** your job 离职；辞职
- **give up** work/your job/your career 放弃工作 / 事业
- **hand in** your notice/resignation 递交辞呈
- **plan to/be due to** retire in June/next year, etc. 计划 / 预计六月 / 明年等退休
- **take** early retirement 提前退休

ˈjob creation *noun* [U] the process of providing opportunities for paid work, especially for people who are unemployed（尤指为失业者）提供就业机会

ˈjob description *noun* a written description of the exact work and responsibilities of a job 工作职责说明；岗位责任说明 ➲ WORDFINDER NOTE AT APPLY

ˈjob-hunt *verb* [I] (usually used in the progressive tenses 通常用于进行时) to try to find a job 找工作；求职：*At that time I had been job-hunting for six months.* 那时我找工作已经找了六个月了。

job·less /ˈdʒɒbləs; *NAmE* ˈdʒɑːb-/ *adj.* **1** without a job 无工作的；失业的 SYN **unemployed**: *The closure left 500 people jobless.* 这次倒闭使 500 人失业。 **2 the jobless** *noun* [pl.] people who are unemployed 失业者 ➲ MORE LIKE THIS 24, page R28 ▸ **job·less·ness** *noun* [U]

ˌjob ˈlot *noun* (*informal*) a collection of different things, especially of poor quality, that are sold together 搭配成批出售的杂货（尤指质量低劣的物品）

ˌjob satisˈfaction *noun* [U] the good feeling that you get when you have a job that you enjoy 工作满足感

ˈjob seeker *noun* often used in official language in Britain to describe a person without a job who is trying to find one 求职者（英国常见的官方用语）

ˌJobseeker's Alˈlowance *noun* [U] (in Britain) money paid by the state to unemployed people who are looking for work（英国）求职津贴 ➲ SEE ALSO UNEMPLOYMENT BENEFIT

ˈjob-sharing *noun* [U] an arrangement for two people to share the hours of work and the pay of one job 工作分担制（两人分担一份全职工作，报酬一起分） ▸ **ˈjob-share** *noun*：*The company encourages job-shares and part-time working.* 这家公司鼓励工作分担和兼职工作。 **ˈjob-share** *verb* [I] ~ (**with sb**)

jobs·worth /ˈdʒɒbzwɜːθ; *NAmE* ˈdʒɑːbzwɜːrθ/ *noun* (*BrE, informal, disapproving*) a person who follows the rules of a job exactly, even when this causes problems for other people, or when the rules are not sensible 刻板的监工；工作特别机械的人

Jock /dʒɒk; *NAmE* dʒɑːk/ *noun* (*informal*) a way of describing a person from Scotland, that can be offensive 苏格兰佬；苏格兰鬼子

jock /dʒɒk; *NAmE* dʒɑːk/ *noun* **1** (*NAmE*) a man or boy who plays a lot of sport 男运动员；爱好体育的男子（或男孩） **2** (*NAmE*) a person who likes a particular activity 热衷于…的人；爱好者：*a computer jock* 电脑迷 **3** = DISC JOCKEY ➲ COMPARE SHOCK JOCK

jockey /ˈdʒɒki; *NAmE* ˈdʒɑːki/ *noun, verb*

■ ***noun*** a person who rides horses in races, especially as a job（尤指职业的）赛马骑师 ➲ VISUAL VOCAB PAGE V51

■ ***verb*** [I] ~ (**with sb**) (**for sth**) | ~ (**with sb**) (**to do sth**) to try all possible ways of gaining an advantage over other people 要各种手腕获取；运用手段谋取：*The runners **jockeyed for position** at the start.* 赛跑选手一开始就力求抢占有利位置。◇ *The bands are constantly jockeying with each other for the number one spot.* 这些乐队经常相互要手段以谋取榜首位置。

ˈjock itch *noun* (*NAmE, informal*) an infectious skin disease that affects the GROIN 股癣

jock·strap /ˈdʒɒkstræp; *NAmE* ˈdʒɑːk-/ (*also* **athˌletic supˈporter** *especially in NAmE*) *noun* a piece of men's underwear worn to support or protect the sexual organs while playing sports（男子运动时穿的）下体护身

jo·cose /dʒəˈkəʊs; *NAmE* -ˈkoʊs/ *adj.* (*formal*) humorous 幽默的；滑稽的；诙谐的

jocu·lar /ˈdʒɒkjələ(r); *NAmE* ˈdʒɑːk-/ *adj.* (*formal*) **1** humorous 幽默的；滑稽的；诙谐的：*a jocular comment* 诙谐的评论 **2** (of a person 人) enjoying making people laugh 爱开玩笑的；逗乐的；打趣的 SYN **jolly** ➲ SEE ALSO JOKE ▸ **jocu·lar·ity** /ˌdʒɒkjəˈlærəti; *NAmE* ˌdʒɑːk-/ *noun* [U] **jocu·lar·ly** *adv.*

joc·und /ˈdʒɒkənd; ˈdʒəʊk-; *NAmE* ˈdʒɑːk-; ˈdʒoʊk-/ *adj.* (*formal*) cheerful 高兴的；欢乐的；愉快的

jodh·purs /ˈdʒɒdpəz; *NAmE* ˈdʒɑːdpərz/ *noun* [pl.] trousers/pants that are loose above the knee and tight from the knee to the ankle, worn when riding a horse 马裤：*a pair of jodhpurs* 一条马裤

Joe Bloggs /ˌdʒəʊ ˈblɒgz; *NAmE* ˌdʒoʊ ˈblɑːgz/ (*BrE*) (*NAmE* **ˌJoe ˈBlow**, **ˌJohn ˈDoe**) *noun* [sing.] (*informal*) a way of referring to a typical ordinary person 普通人；平常人 ➲ MORE LIKE THIS 18, page R27

ˌJoe ˈPublic (*BrE*) (*NAmE* **ˌJohn ˌQ. ˈPublic**) *noun* [U] (*informal*) people in general; the public 老百姓；平民百姓；公众 ➲ MORE LIKE THIS 18, page R27

Joe Six·pack /ˌdʒəʊ ˈsɪkspæk; *NAmE* ˌdʒoʊ/ *noun* (*US, informal*) a man who is considered typical of a person who does MANUAL work 普通工人：*Joe Sixpack doesn't care about that.* 普通工人不在意那事。 ➲ MORE LIKE THIS 18, page R27

joey /ˈdʒəʊi; *NAmE* ˈdʒoʊi/ *noun* a young KANGAROO, WALLABY or POSSUM 幼袋鼠；幼沙袋鼠；幼负鼠 ➲ VISUAL VOCAB PAGE V12

J

jog /dʒɒg; *NAmE* dʒɑːg/ *verb, noun*

■ ***verb*** (**-gg-**) **1** (*also* **go jogging**) [I] to run slowly and steadily for a long time, especially for exercise 慢跑，慢步长跑（尤指锻炼）：*I go jogging every evening.* 我每天晚上都慢跑锻炼。 **2** [T] ~ **sth/sb** to hit sth lightly and by accident（偶然地）轻击，轻撞，轻碰 SYN **nudge**: *Someone jogged her elbow, making her spill her coffee.* 有人不小心轻轻碰了一下她的胳膊肘儿，把咖啡弄洒了。 ➲ MORE LIKE THIS 36, page R29

IDM **jog sb's ˈmemory** to say or do sth that makes sb remember sth 唤起某人的记忆；提醒某人

PHR V **ˌjog aˈlong** (*BrE, informal*) to continue as usual with little or no excitement, change or progress（同往常一样）缓慢而平稳地进行 **jog aˈlong | jog ˈon** (*BrE, informal*) used to tell sb rudely to go away or that you are not interested（粗鲁地让人走开，或表示自己没兴趣）走开，一边去

■ ***noun*** [sing.] **1** a slow run, especially one done for physical exercise 慢跑（尤指锻炼）：*I like to go for a jog after work.* 我喜欢在下班后慢跑锻炼。 **2** a light push or knock 轻推；轻碰；轻击 SYN **nudge**

jog·ger /ˈdʒɒgə(r); *NAmE* ˈdʒɑːg-/ *noun* **1** [C] a person who jogs regularly for exercise 慢跑锻炼者 **2 joggers** [pl.] (*BrE*) soft loose trousers/pants, with ELASTIC at the waist, that you wear for doing exercise in（柔软宽松、腰间有松紧带的）运动裤，运动短裤

jog·ging /ˈdʒɒgɪŋ; *NAmE* ˈdʒɑːg-/ *noun* [U] the activity of running slowly and steadily as a form of exercise 慢跑锻炼：*to go jogging* 慢跑锻炼 ➲ COLLOCATIONS AT DIET ➲ VISUAL VOCAB PAGE V46

ˈjogging suit *noun* = TRACKSUIT

jog·gle /ˈdʒɒgl; *NAmE* ˈdʒɑːgl/ *verb* [I, T] ~ (**sb/sth**) (*informal*) to move or to make sb/sth move quickly up and down or from one side to another（使）快速颠动，快速摇摆

jog·trot /ˈdʒɒgtrɒt; *NAmE* ˈdʒɑːgtrɑːt/ *noun* [sing.] a slow steady run 匀速慢跑

john /dʒɒn; *NAmE* dʒɑːn/ *noun* (*informal, especially NAmE*) a toilet 厕所；茅房

ˌJohn ˈBull *noun* [U, C] (*old-fashioned*) a word that is used to refer to England or the English people, or to a typical Englishman 约翰牛（指英格兰或典型的英格兰人） ➲ MORE LIKE THIS 18, page R27

ˌJohn ˈDoe *noun* [usually sing.] (*NAmE*) **1** a name used for a person whose name is not known or is kept secret, especially in a court of law 无名氏，某甲（不知姓名或在法庭等上隐匿真名的当事人） **2** an average man 普通男人 ➲ COMPARE JANE DOE ➲ MORE LIKE THIS 18, page R27

John Han·cock /ˌdʒɒn ˈhæŋkɒk; *NAmE* ˌdʒɑːn ˈhæŋkɑːk/ *noun* (*NAmE, informal*) a person's signature 亲笔签名 ➲ MORE LIKE THIS 18, page R27

Johnny-come-lately /ˌdʒɒni kʌm ˈleɪtli; *NAmE* ˌdʒɑːni/ *noun* [sing.] (*disapproving* or *humorous*) a person who has only recently arrived in a place or started an activity, especially sb who is more confident than they should be （尤指自负的）新人，新手

Johnny Reb /ˌdʒɒni ˈreb; *NAmE* ˌdʒɑːni/ *noun* (*NAmE, informal*) a name for a soldier who fought for the Confederate States in the American Civil War（美国内战时期的）南方联盟士兵 ➲ MORE LIKE THIS 18, page R27

John o'Groats /ˌdʒɒn əˈɡrəʊts; *NAmE* ˌdʒɑːn əˈɡroʊts/ *noun* a village in Scotland that is further north than any other place on the island of Great Britain 约翰奥格罗茨（位于大不列颠岛最北端的苏格兰小村庄） ➲ COMPARE LAND'S END

ˌJohn ˌQ. ˈPublic (*NAmE*) (*BrE* **ˌJoe ˈPublic**) *noun* [U] (*informal*) people in general; the public 老百姓；平民百姓；公众

J

joie de vivre /ˌʒwʌ də ˈviːvrə/ *noun* [U] (*from French*) a feeling of great happiness and enjoyment of life 人生的极大乐趣；生活之乐

join /dʒɔɪn/ *verb, noun*

■ *verb*

• CONNECT 连接 **1** [T, I] to fix or connect two or more things together 连接；接合；联结： **~ A to B** *Join one section of pipe to the next.* 将一段管子与相邻的管子连接起来。◇ *The island is joined to the mainland by a bridge.* 这个岛有一座桥与大陆相连。◇ **~ (A and B) (together/up)** *Join the two sections of pipe together.* 将这两段管子连接在一起。◇ *Draw a line joining (up) all the crosses.* 画条线将所有的十字连接起来。◇ *How do these two pieces join?* 这两件东西怎样接合呢？

• BECOME ONE 合二为一 **2** [I, T] if two things or groups **join**, or if one thing or group **joins** another, they come together to form one thing or group 结合；联合；汇合：*the place where the two paths join* 两条小路汇合的地方 ◇ **~ sth** *The path joins the road near the trees.* 这条小路在树林旁与公路汇合。

• CLUB/COMPANY 俱乐部；公司 **3** [T, I] **~ (sth)** to become a member of an organization, a company, a club, etc. 成为…的一员；参加；加入： *I've joined an aerobics class.* 我参加了有氧健身班。◇ *She joined the company three months ago.* 她三个月前进了这家公司。◇ (*figurative*) *to join the ranks of the unemployed* 加入失业大军 ◇ *It costs £20 to join.* 需交 20 英镑才可参加。

• DO STH WITH SB ELSE 参与 **4** [T] to take part in sth that sb else is doing or to go somewhere with them 参与；加入到…之中；与…一道去： **~ sb (for sth)** *Will you join us for lunch?* 和我们一起吃午饭好吗？◇ *Do you mind if I join you?* 我和你们在一起，可以吗？◇ **~ sth** *Over 200 members of staff joined the strike.* * 200 多名雇员参加了罢工。◇ *Members of the public joined the search for the missing boy.* 许多民众加入了搜寻失踪男孩的行动。◇ **~ sb in doing sth** *I'm sure you'll all join me in wishing Ted and Laura a very happy marriage.* 我相信大家会愿意与我一起共祝特德和劳拉喜结良缘。

• TRAIN/PLANE 火车；飞机 **5** [T] **~ sth** (*BrE*) if you **join** a train, plane, etc. you get on it 上（火车、飞机等）

• ROAD/PATH/LINE 道路；小径；行列 **6** [T] **~ sth** if you **join** a road or a line of people, you start to travel along it, or move into it 上（路）；加入（行列）

IDM **join ˈbattle (with sb)** (*formal*) to begin fighting sb 开始（与某人）交战： (*figurative*) *Local residents have joined battle with the council over the lack of parking facilities.* 当地居民就缺少停车设施一事与政务委员会展开了斗争。 **join the ˈclub** (*informal*) used when sth bad that has happened to sb else has also happened to you 同样倒霉；别人也一样倒运；彼此彼此： *So you didn't get a job either? Join the club!* 那么你也没找到工作？咱们彼此彼此！ **join ˈhands (with sb)** **1** if two people **join hands**, they hold each other's hands（与某人）拉起手，挽手 **2** to work together in doing sth 携手合作；联合；合伙： *Education has been reluctant to join hands with business.* 教育界一向不肯与商界联手。 ➲ MORE AT BEAT *v.*, FORCE *n.*

PHR V **ˌjoin ˈin (sth/doing sth) | ˌjoin ˈin (with sb/sth)** to take part in an activity with other people 参加，加入（活动）： *She listens but she never joins in.* 她只是听，但从来不发表意见。◇ *I wish he would join in with the other children.* 但愿他能跟别的孩子一块儿玩。 **ˌjoin ˈup** to become a member of the armed forces 入伍；参军 SYN **enlist** **ˌjoin ˈup (with sb)** to combine with sb else to do sth（与某人）联合，会合： *We'll join up with the other groups later.* 我们以后再与其他小组会合。

■ *noun* CONNECTION 连接 a place where two things are fixed together 连接处；接合点： *The two pieces were stuck together so well that you could hardly see the join.* 这两块黏合得太好了，几乎看不出接缝。

ˈjoined-up *adj.* [usually before noun] (*BrE*) **1** **joined-up** writing is writing in which the letters in a word are joined to each other（字体）连写的；草书的 ➲ COMPARE PRINTING **2** intelligent and involving good communication between different parts so that they can work together effectively 明智而协调的： *We need more* ***joined-up thinking*** *in our approach to the environment.* 在处理环境问题上我们需要更协调的思考。

join·er /ˈdʒɔɪnə(r)/ *noun* **1** a person whose job is to make the wooden parts of a building, especially window frames, doors, etc. 细木工人 ➲ COMPARE CARPENTER **2** a person who joins an organization, club, etc.（组织、俱乐部等的）参加者，入会者，会员： *All joiners will receive a welcome pack.* 每位入会者都会收到一个迎新包。

join·ery /ˈdʒɔɪnəri/ *noun* [U] the work of a joiner or things made by a joiner 细木工人的工作；细木工的制品

joint /dʒɔɪnt/ *adj., noun, verb*

■ *adj.* [only before noun] involving two or more people together 联合的；共同的： *a joint account* (= a bank account in the name of more than one person, for example a husband and wife) 联名账户 ◇ *The report was* ***a joint effort*** (= we worked on it together). 这个报告是大家共同努力的成果。◇ *They finished in joint first place.* 他们获得并列第一。◇ *They were joint owners of the house* (= they owned it together). 他们共同拥有这栋房子。 ▸ **joint·ly** *adv.* : *The event was organized jointly by students and staff.* 这项活动是由师生共同组织的。

■ *noun* **1** a place where two bones are joined together in the body in a way that enables them to bend and move 关节： *inflammation of the knee joint* 膝关节发炎 ➲ SEE ALSO BALL-AND-SOCKET JOINT **2** a place where two or more parts of an object are joined together, especially to form a corner（尤指构成拐角的）接头，接合处，接点 **3** (*BrE*) a piece of ROAST meat 一块烤肉： *a joint of beef* 一块烤牛肉 ◇ *the Sunday joint* (= one traditionally eaten on a Sunday) 礼拜天吃的大块烤肉 **4** (*informal*) a place where people meet to eat, drink, dance, etc., especially one that is cheap 公共场所（尤指价格低廉的饮食和娱乐场所）： *a fast-food joint* 快餐店 **5** (*informal*) a cigarette containing MARIJUANA (= an illegal drug) 大麻烟卷

IDM **out of ˈjoint** **1** (of a bone 骨头) pushed out of its correct position 脱臼；脱位 **2** not working or behaving in the normal way 混乱；无秩序；不正常 ➲ MORE AT CASE *v.*, NOSE *n.*

■ *verb* **~ sth** to cut meat into large pieces, usually each containing a bone 把…切成带骨的大块肉

ˌJoint ˌChiefs of ˈStaff *noun* [pl.] (in the US) the leaders of the ARMED FORCES who advise the President on military matters（美国）参谋长联席会议

ˌjoint deˈgree *noun* (in Britain and some other countries) a university course in which you study two subjects to the same standard（英国和其他一些国家的）双学位

joint·ed /ˈdʒɔɪntɪd/ *adj.* [usually before noun] having parts that fit together and can move 有关节的；有接缝的；活动接头的： *a doll with* ***jointed arms/legs*** 手臂 / 腿关节活动的洋娃娃

ˈjoint family *noun* (*IndE*) a family structure in which grandparents, uncles, aunts and cousins are considered as a single unit living in one house 同堂家庭，联合家庭（包括祖父母和旁系亲属同居一户的家庭）

ˌjoint resoˈlution *noun* (in the US) a decision that has been approved by the Senate and the House of Representatives（美国）国会两院的共同决议

ˌjoint-ˈstock company *noun* (*business* 商) a company that is owned by all the people who have shares in it 合股公司

ˌjoint ˈventure *noun* (*business* 商) a business project or activity that is begun by two or more companies, etc., which remain separate organizations 合营企业；合资企业

joist /dʒɔɪst/ *noun* a long thick piece of wood or metal that is used to support a floor or ceiling in a building 搁栅；托梁 ➲ WORDFINDER NOTE AT CONSTRUCTION

jo·joba /həˈhəʊbə; həʊ-; *NAmE* hoʊˈhoʊbə/ *noun* **1** [U] oil from the seeds of an American plant, often used in COSMETICS 希蒙得木油（用美洲植物霍霍巴树的蒴果制成，常用于化妆品） **2** [U, C] the plant that produces these seeds 希蒙得木；霍霍巴树

joke 🔑 /dʒəʊk; *NAmE* dʒoʊk/ *noun, verb*

■ ***noun*** **1** 🔑 something that you say or do to make people laugh, for example a funny story that you tell 笑话；玩笑：*I can't **tell jokes**.* 我不会讲笑话。◇ *She's always **cracking jokes**.* 她总爱说笑话。◇ *They often **make jokes** at each other's expense.* 他们经常相互取笑。◇ *I didn't **get the joke*** (= understand it). 我不明白这有什么好笑的。◇ *I wish he wouldn't tell **dirty jokes*** (= about sex). 但愿他别开下流的玩笑。◇ *I only did it **as a joke*** (= it was not meant seriously). 我只是开个玩笑而已。 ➲ SEE ALSO IN-JOKE, PRACTICAL JOKE ➲ WORDFINDER NOTE AT COMEDY **2** [sing.] (*informal*) a person, thing or situation that is ridiculous or annoying and cannot be taken seriously 荒唐可笑的人（或事物、局面）；笑料；笑柄：*This latest pay offer is a joke.* 最近这次提出的报酬简直是开玩笑。 ➲ SEE ALSO JOCULAR

IDM **be/get beyond a ˈjoke** to become annoying and no longer acceptable 超出开玩笑的限度（令人恼火或无法接受） **be no ˈjoke** to be difficult or unpleasant 不是轻而易举的事；不是好玩的：*It's no joke trying to find a job these days.* 这些日子想找工作可不是件容易事。 **the joke's on ˈsb** (*informal*) used to say that sb who tried to make another person look ridiculous now looks ridiculous instead 开玩笑开到自己身上了；捉弄别人反而捉弄到自己头上 **make a ˈjoke of sth** to laugh about sth that is serious or should be taken seriously 拿某事开玩笑；以某事为笑柄 **take a ˈjoke** to be able to laugh at a joke against yourself 经得起玩笑话；开得起玩笑：*The trouble with her is she can't take a joke.* 她的问题在于开不起玩笑。

■ ***verb*** ~ (**with sb**) (**about sth**) **1** 🔑 [I, T] to say sth to make people laugh; to tell a funny story 说笑话；开玩笑：*She was laughing and joking with the children.* 她同孩子们一起嘻嘻哈哈地说笑话。◇ ~ **about sth** *They often joked about all the things that could go wrong.* 凡是可能出错的事他们都常拿来开玩笑。◇ + **speech** *'I cooked it myself, so be careful!' he joked.* "我亲自下厨做的，所以要小心点哟！"他开玩笑说。 **2** 🔑 [I, T] to say sth that is not true because you think it is funny 闹着玩；说着玩：*I didn't mean that—I was only joking.* 我并没有那个意思，我只是说着玩儿的。◇ ~ **that...** *She joked that she only loved him for his money.* 她开玩笑说她只爱他的钱。

IDM **ˌjoking aˈpart** (*BrE*) | **ˌjoking aˈside** (*BrE, NAmE*) used to show that you are now being serious after you have said sth funny 言归正传；说正经的 **you're ˈjoking | you must be ˈjoking** 🔑 (*informal*) used to show that you are very surprised at what sb has just said（对某人所说的话表示吃惊）你一定是在开玩笑吧：*No way am I doing that. You must be joking!* 我决不可能做那样的事。你一定是在开玩笑吧！◇ *She's going out with Dan? You're joking!* 她在同丹谈恋爱？你是在开玩笑吧！

joker /ˈdʒəʊkə(r); *NAmE* ˈdʒoʊk-/ *noun* **1** a person who likes making jokes or doing silly things to make people laugh 爱开玩笑的人；爱说笑话的人 **2** (*informal*) a person that you think is stupid because they annoy you 蠢货；废人 **3** an extra PLAYING CARD that is used in some card games, usually as a WILD CARD（某些纸牌游戏中的）百搭，（大、小）王牌 ➲ VISUAL VOCAB PAGE V42

IDM **the ˌjoker in the ˈpack** a person or thing who could change the way that things will happen in a way that cannot be predicted 能以意想不到的方式改变形势的人（或事）

jokey (*also* **joky**) /ˈdʒəʊki; *NAmE* ˈdʒoʊki/ *adj.* (*informal*) amusing; making people laugh 逗乐的；可笑的；滑稽的

jok·ing·ly /ˈdʒəʊkɪŋli; *NAmE* ˈdʒoʊk-/ *adv.* in a way that is intended to be amusing and not serious 开玩笑地；闹着玩地；戏谑地

jol /dʒɔːl/ *noun, verb* (*SAfrE, informal*)

■ ***noun*** a time of having fun; a party 娱乐（或快活）时光；聚会：*Have a jol!* 尽情地玩吧！◇ *a New Year's Eve jol* 除夕晚会

■ ***verb*** (**-ll-**) [I] to have fun 开心地玩：*We jolled all night.* 我们尽情玩了一晚上。

jol·lof rice /ˈdʒɒləf raɪs; *NAmE* ˈdʒɑːləf/ *noun* [U] a type of STEW eaten in W Africa made from rice, CHILLIES and meat or fish（西非）辣椒炖肉（或鱼）饭

jolly /ˈdʒɒli; *NAmE* ˈdʒɑːli/ *adj., adv., verb, noun*

■ ***adj.*** (**jol·lier, jol·li·est**) **1** happy and cheerful 愉快的；快乐的；高兴的：*a jolly crowd/face/mood* 快乐的一群人；快乐的笑脸；愉快的心情 **2** (*old-fashioned*) enjoyable 令人愉快的；令人快乐的；惬意的：*a jolly evening/party/time* 令人愉快的夜晚 / 聚会 / 时光 ▶ **jol·lity** /ˈdʒɒləti; *NAmE* ˈdʒɑːl-/ *noun* [U] (*old-fashioned*)：*scenes of high-spirits and jollity* 兴高采烈的欢乐景象

■ ***adv.*** (*old-fashioned, BrE, informal*) very 非常；很：*That's a jolly good idea.* 那是个绝妙的主意。

IDM **jolly ˈgood!** (*old-fashioned, BrE, informal*) used to show that you approve of sth that sb has just said（赞同别人说的话）非常好，太好了 **ˈjolly well** (*old-fashioned, BrE*) used to emphasize a statement when you are annoyed about sth（生气时用以加强语气）当然，无疑，必然：*If you don't come now, you can jolly well walk home!* 你要是还不来，那就步行回家吧！

■ ***verb*** (**jol·lies, jolly·ing, jol·lied, jol·lied**)

PHR V **ˌjolly sb aˈlong** to encourage sb in a cheerful way（用愉快的方式）鼓励某人 **ˌjolly sb ˈinto sth/into ˈdoing sth** to persuade or encourage sb to do sth by making them feel happy about it 哄着某人做某事 **ˌjolly sb/sth ˈup** to make sb/sth more cheerful 使更有生气；使更快活

■ ***noun*** (*BrE*) a trip that you make for enjoyment 旅游；游玩

IDM **get your ˈjollies** (*informal*) to get pleasure or have fun 玩个痛快；作乐；尽情享乐

the ˌJolly ˈRoger *noun* [sing.] a black flag with a white SKULL AND CROSSBONES on it, used in the past by PIRATES（旧时的）海盗旗，骷髅旗（饰有白色骷髅和交叉股骨的黑旗）

jolt /dʒəʊlt; *NAmE* dʒoʊlt/ *verb, noun*

■ ***verb*** **1** [I, T] to move or to make sb/sth move suddenly and roughly（使）震动，摇动，颠簸 SYN **jerk**：(+ **adv./prep.**) *The truck jolted and rattled over the rough ground.* 卡车嘎吱嘎吱地在凹凸不平的地面上颠簸而行。◇ *The bus jolted to a halt.* 公共汽车猛地一颠停了下来。◇ (*figurative*) *Her heart jolted when she saw him.* 她看到他时心里咯噔一下子。◇ ~ **sb/sth** (+ **adv./prep.**) *He was jolted forwards as the bus moved off.* 公共汽车开动时他猛然向前晃了一下。 **2** [T] to give sb a sudden shock, especially so that they start to take action or deal with a situation 使受到震惊（而采取行动）；唤醒；使觉醒：~ **sb/sth** (**into sth**) *His remark jolted her into action.* 他的话使她猛然醒悟而行动起来。◇ ~ **sb/sth** (**out of sth**) *a method of jolting the economy out of recession* 使经济从衰退中复苏的方法 ◇ ~ **sb/sth + adj.** *I was suddenly jolted awake.* 我猛地一下被惊醒。

■ ***noun*** [usually sing.] **1** a sudden rough movement 颠簸；震动；摇晃 SYN **jerk**：*The plane landed with a jolt.* 飞机着

陆时颠了一下。 **2** a sudden strong feeling, especially of shock or surprise 一阵强烈的感情（尤指震惊或惊讶）：*a jolt of dismay* 一阵惊诧

Joneses /ˈdʒəʊnzɪz; NAmE ˈdʒoʊn-/ *noun* [pl.]
IDM **ˌkeep up with the ˈJoneses** (*informal, often disapproving*) to try to have all the possessions and social achievements that your friends and neighbours have（与朋友和邻居在物质和社会成就方面）攀比，比富有，比排场，比阔气

josh /dʒɒʃ; NAmE dʒɑːʃ/ *verb* [I, T] ~ (**sb**) | + **speech** (*informal*) to gently make fun of sb or talk to them in a joking way 开玩笑；戏弄 **SYN** **tease**

joss stick /ˈdʒɒstɪk; NAmE ˈdʒɑːs-/ *noun* a thin wooden stick covered with a substance that burns slowly and produces a sweet smell（烧的）香

jos·tle /ˈdʒɒsl; NAmE ˈdʒɑːsl/ *verb* [T, I] ~ (**sb**) to push roughly against sb in a crowd（在人群中）挤，推，撞，搡：*The visiting president was jostled by angry demonstrators.* 到访的总统受到愤怒的示威者的推搡。◇ *People were jostling, arguing and complaining.* 人们推推搡搡，争吵着抱怨着。
PHR V **ˈjostle for sth** to compete strongly and with force with other people for sth 争夺；争抢：*People in the crowd were jostling for the best positions.* 这群人在竞相抢占最好的位置。

jot /dʒɒt; NAmE dʒɑːt/ *verb, noun*
■ ***verb*** (**-tt-**)
PHR V **ˌjot sth↔ˈdown** to write sth quickly 草草记下；匆匆记下：*I'll just jot down the address for you.* 我这就把地址给你写下来。
■ ***noun***
IDM **not a/one ˈjot** used to mean 'not even a small amount' when you are emphasizing a negative statement 一点不；丝毫不：*There's not a jot of truth in what he says* (= none at all). 他没有一句实话。

jot·ter /ˈdʒɒtə(r); NAmE ˈdʒɑːt-/ *noun* (*BrE*) **1** a small book used for writing notes in 便笺簿；便条簿；记事簿 **2** (*ScotE*) an exercise book 练习簿；练习本

jot·tings /ˈdʒɒtɪŋz; NAmE ˈdʒɑːt-/ *noun* [pl.] short notes that are written down quickly 便条；简短的笔记

joule /dʒuːl/ *noun* (*abbr.* **J**) (*physics* 物) a unit of energy or work 焦耳（能量或功的单位）

jour·nal **AW** /ˈdʒɜːnl; NAmE ˈdʒɜːrnl/ *noun* **1** a newspaper or magazine that deals with a particular subject or profession（某学科或行业的）报纸，刊物，杂志：*a scientific/trade journal* 科学 / 行业杂志 ◇ *the British Medical Journal*《英国医学杂志》 **2** used in the title of some newspapers（用于报纸名）…报：*the Wall Street Journal*《华尔街日报》 **3** a written record of the things you do, see, etc. every day 日志；日记：*He **kept a journal** of his travels across Asia.* 他把自己的亚洲之行记录下来了。➲ COMPARE DIARY

jour·nal·ese /ˌdʒɜːnəˈliːz; NAmE ˌdʒɜːrn-/ *noun* [U] (*usually disapproving*) a style of language that is thought to be typical of that used in newspapers 新闻文体；新闻笔调

jour·nal·ism /ˈdʒɜːnəlɪzəm; NAmE ˈdʒɜːrn-/ *noun* [U] the work of collecting and writing news stories for newspapers, magazines, radio or television 新闻业；新闻工作

jour·nal·ist 🔑 /ˈdʒɜːnəlɪst; NAmE ˈdʒɜːrn-/ *noun* a person whose job is to collect and write news stories for newspapers, magazines, radio or television 新闻记者；新闻工作者 ➲ COMPARE REPORTER ➲ **WORDFINDER NOTE** AT NEWSPAPER

> **WORDFINDER** 联想词：censorship, correspondent, coverage, editor, exclusive, news agency, **newspaper**, report, stringer

jour·nal·is·tic /ˌdʒɜːnəˈlɪstɪk; NAmE ˌdʒɜːrn-/ *adj.* [usually before noun] connected with the work of a journalist 新闻业的；新闻工作（者）的：*journalistic skills* 新闻工作技巧 ◇ *his journalistic background* 他的新闻工作背景

jour·ney 🔑 /ˈdʒɜːni; NAmE ˈdʒɜːrni/ *noun, verb*
■ ***noun*** 🔑 an act of travelling from one place to another, especially when they are far apart（尤指长途）旅行，行程：*They went on a long train journey across India.* 他们乘火车作了一次横跨印度的长途旅行。◇ *Did you have a good journey?* 你一路顺利吗？◇ *on the **outward/return journey*** 在外出 / 返回途中 ◇ *We **broke our journey*** (= stopped for a short time) *in Madrid.* 我们途中在马德里作了短暂的停留。◇ (*BrE*) *Don't use the car for short journeys.* 短途旅行就别开车。◇ *It's a day's journey by car.* 开车的话要走一天。◇ (*BrE*) *I'm afraid you've had a wasted journey* (= you cannot do what you have come to do). 对不起，你白跑一趟了。◇ (*informal*) *Bye! **Safe journey!*** (= used when sb is beginning a journey) 再见！一路平安！◇ (*figurative*) *The book describes a spiritual journey from despair to happiness.* 这本书描述了从绝望到高兴的心理变化过程。➲ SYNONYMS AT TRIP

> **WORDFINDER** 联想词：commute, departure, destination, excursion, expedition, itinerary, pilgrimage, safari, **travel**

■ ***verb*** [I] (+ **adv./prep.**) (*formal* or *literary*) to travel, especially a long distance（尤指长途）旅行：*They journeyed for seven long months.* 他们旅行了七个月之久。

jour·ney·man /ˈdʒɜːnimən; NAmE ˈdʒɜːrn-/ *noun* (*pl.* **-men** /-mən/) **1** (in the past) a person who was trained to do a particular job and who then worked for sb else（旧时）学徒期满的工匠，出师的学徒工 **2** a person who has training and experience in a job but who is only average at it 熟练工；熟手

journo /ˈdʒɜːnəʊ; NAmE ˈdʒɜːrnoʊ/ (*pl.* **-os**) *noun* (*BrE, slang*) a journalist 新闻记者；新闻工作者

joust /dʒaʊst/ *verb* **1** [I] to fight on horses using a long stick (= a LANCE) to try to knock the other person off their horse, especially as part of a formal contest in the past（尤指旧时作为正式比赛一部分的）马上长矛打斗，骑马比武 **2** [I] (*formal*) to argue with sb, especially as part of a formal or public debate（尤指作为正式或公开辩论一部分的）辩论，讨论，争论 ▸ **joust** *noun*

Jove /dʒəʊv; NAmE dʒoʊv/ *noun*
IDM **by ˈJove** (*old-fashioned, informal, especially BrE*) used to express surprise or to emphasize a statement（表示惊奇或加强语气）啊，哎呀

jo·vial /ˈdʒəʊviəl; NAmE ˈdʒoʊ-/ *adj.* very cheerful and friendly 快乐的；愉快的；友好的 ▸ **jovi·al·ity** /ˌdʒəʊviˈæləti; NAmE ˌdʒoʊ-/ *noun* [U] **jo·vial·ly** /-iəli/ *adv.*

jowl /dʒaʊl/ *noun* [usually pl.] the lower part of sb's cheek when it is fat and hangs down below their chin 双下巴；下颌垂肉：*a man with heavy jowls* 下巴底下一堆肉的男人
IDM SEE CHEEK *n.*

joy 🔑 /dʒɔɪ/ *noun* **1** 🔑 [U] a feeling of great happiness 高兴；愉快；喜悦 **SYN** **delight**：*the sheer joy of being with her again* 与她重逢的无比喜悦之情 ◇ *to dance **for/with joy*** 高兴得跳起舞来 ◇ *I didn't expect them to **jump for joy** at the news* (= to be very pleased). 没想到他们听到这消息高兴得跳了起来。◇ *To his great joy, she accepted.* 使他感到非常高兴的是她接受了。➲ SYNONYMS AT PLEASURE **2** [C] a person or thing that causes you to feel very happy 令人高兴的人（或事）；乐事；乐趣：*the joys of fatherhood* 做父亲的乐趣 ◇ *The game was a joy to watch.* 这比赛看起来真开心。 **3** [U] (*BrE, informal*) (in questions and negative sentences 用于疑问句和否定句) success or satisfaction 成功；满意；满足：*We complained about our rooms but got no joy from the manager.* 我们抱怨房间不好，经理却不理会。◇ *'Any joy at the shops?' 'No, they didn't have what I wanted.'* "逛商店有收获吗？""没有，哪里都没有我想要的。"
IDM **full of the joys of ˈspring** very cheerful 快活极了；非常愉快；活泼愉快 ➲ MORE AT PRIDE *n.*

joy·ful /ˈdʒɔɪfl/ *adj.* very happy; causing people to be happy 高兴的；快乐的；令人愉快的 ➲ SYNONYMS AT HAPPY ▸ **joy·ful·ly** /-fəli/ *adv.* **joy·ful·ness** *noun* [U]

joy·less /ˈdʒɔɪləs/ *adj.* (*formal*) bringing no happiness; without joy 没有欢乐的；不快活的：*a joyless childhood* 没有欢乐的童年

joy·ous /ˈdʒɔɪəs/ *adj.* (*literary*) very happy; causing people to be happy 高兴的；快乐的；令人愉快的 SYN **joyful**: *joyous laughter* 快乐的笑声 ▶**joy·ous·ly** *adv.*

joy·rid·ing /ˈdʒɔɪraɪdɪŋ/ *noun* [U] the crime of stealing a car and driving it for pleasure, usually in a fast and dangerous way 用偷来的车兜风（常指开快车或危险驾驶）；偷开车（罪） ▶**joy·ride** *noun* **joy·rider** *noun*

joy·stick /ˈdʒɔɪstɪk/ *noun* **1** a stick with a handle used with some computer games to move images on the screen（电脑游戏的）游戏杆，操纵杆，控制杆 **2** (*informal*) a stick with a handle in an aircraft that is used to control direction or height（飞机的）操纵杆

JP /ˌdʒeɪ ˈpiː/ *noun* JUSTICE OF THE PEACE 基层法院法官；治安法官；太平绅士：*Helen Alvey JP* 海伦·阿尔维治安法官

JPEG /ˈdʒeɪpeg/ *noun* (*computing* 计) **1** [U] the abbreviation for 'Joint Photographic Experts Group' (technology which reduces the size of files that contain images) * JPEG（静止图像压缩）标准，联合图像专家组（全写为 Joint Photographic Experts Group）：*JPEG files* * JPEG 文件 **2** [C] an image created using this technology * JPEG 图像：*You can download the pictures as JPEGs.* 你可以用 JPEG 格式下载这些图像。

Jr (*also* **Jnr**) (*both BrE*) (*also* **Jr.** *NAmE, BrE*) *abbr.* JUNIOR 年少者；年资较低者 ⊃COMPARE SR

jua kali /ˌdʒʊə ˈkæli/ *noun* [U] (in Kenya) the informal jobs that people do to earn money, for example making useful things from old metal and wood（肯尼亚）家庭手工，小手工：*the **jua kali** sector* 小手工业

ju·bi·lant /ˈdʒuːbɪlənt/ *adj.* feeling or showing great happiness because of a success 喜气洋洋的；欢欣鼓舞的；欢呼雀跃的 ▶**ju·bi·lant·ly** *adv.*

jubi·la·tion /ˌdʒuːbɪˈleɪʃn/ *noun* [U] a feeling of great happiness because of a success 欢欣鼓舞；欢腾；欢庆

ju·bi·lee /ˈdʒuːbɪliː/ *noun* a special anniversary of an event, especially one that took place 25 or 50 years ago; the celebrations connected with it（尤指 25 周年或 50 周年的）周年纪念，周年大庆，周年庆祝 ⊃SEE ALSO DIAMOND JUBILEE, GOLDEN JUBILEE, SILVER JUBILEE ⊃WORDFINDER NOTE AT CELEBRATE

Ju·da·ism /ˈdʒuːdeɪɪzəm; *NAmE* -dəɪzəm/ *noun* [U] the religion of the Jewish people, based mainly on the first five books of the Bible and the Talmud 犹太教 ▶**Ju·da·ic** /dʒuːˈdeɪɪk/ *adj.* [only before noun]: *Judaic tradition* 犹太教传统

Judas /ˈdʒuːdəs/ *noun* a person who treats a friend badly by not being loyal 犹大；出卖朋友的人；叛徒 SYN **traitor**

jud·der /ˈdʒʌdə(r)/ *verb* [I] to shake violently（剧烈地）震动，震颤：*He slammed on the brakes and the car juddered to a halt.* 他猛踩刹车，汽车在剧烈震动中停下来。

judge /dʒʌdʒ/ *noun, verb*

■*noun*

• IN COURT 法庭 **1** a person in a court who has the authority to decide how criminals should be punished or to make legal decisions 法官；审判员：*a High Court judge* 高等法院的法官 ◇ *a federal judge* 联邦法院法官 ◇ *The case comes before Judge Cooper next week.* 本案下周交库珀法官审理。◇ *The judge sentenced him to five years in prison.* 法官判他五年监禁。⊃COMPARE JUSTICE OF THE PEACE, MAGISTRATE

• IN COMPETITION 竞赛 **2** a person who decides who has won a competition 裁判员；评判员：*the panel of judges at the flower show* 花展评判小组 ◇ *The judges' decision is final.* 裁判的决定为最终决定。⊃WORDFINDER NOTE AT COMPETITION

• SB WHO GIVES OPINION 鉴定人 **3** [usually sing.] a person who has the necessary knowledge or skills to give their opinion about the value or quality of sb/sth 鉴定人；鉴赏家：*She's a **good judge** of character.* 她很善于判断人的性格。◇ *'I'm not sure that's a good way to do it.' '**Let me be the judge of that.**'* "我拿不准这样做好不好。" "就让我来判断吧。"

■*verb*

• FORM OPINION 判断 **1** [I, T] to form an opinion about sb/sth, based on the information you have 判断；断定；认为：*As far as I can judge, all of them are to blame.* 依我看，他们都应承担责任。◇ ***Judging by** her last letter, they are having a wonderful time.* 从她上封信看，他们过得非常愉快。◇ ***To judge from** what he said, he was very disappointed.* 从他的话判断，他非常失望。◇ **~ sb/sth (on sth)** *Schools should not be judged only on exam results.* 学校的好坏不能仅凭考试结果来评判。◇ *Each painting must be judged on its own merits.* 任何一幅画都必须根据其本身的价值来评判。◇ **~ sb/sth + noun** *The tour was judged a great success.* 这次巡回演出被认为是大获成功。◇ **~ sb/sth to be/do sth** *The concert was judged to have been a great success.* 这场音乐会被认为是大获成功。◇ **~ sb/sth + adj.** *They judged it wise to say nothing.* 他们认为不说为妙。◇ **~ that...** *He judged that the risk was too great.* 他认为风险太大。◇ **it is judged that...** *It was judged that the risk was too great.* 据估计风险太大。◇ **~ how, what, etc....** *It was hard to judge how great the risk was.* 很难判断风险有多大。

• ESTIMATE 估计 **2** [T] to guess the size, amount, etc. of sth 估计，猜测（大小、数量等）：**~ how, what, etc....** *It's difficult to judge how long the journey will take.* 很难估计这次旅行要花多长时间。◇ **~ sb/sth to be/do sth** *I judged him to be about 50.* 我估计他年纪在 50 左右。

• IN COMPETITION 竞赛 **3** [T, I] **~ (sth)** to decide the result of a competition; to be the judge in a competition 裁判；评判；担任裁判：*She was asked to judge the essay competition.* 她被邀请担任作文比赛的评委。

• GIVE OPINION 评价 **4** [T, I] **~ (sb)** to give your opinion about sb, especially when you disapprove of them 评价；鉴定；（尤指）批评，指责：*What gives you the right to judge other people?* 你有什么权利对别人评头论足？

• IN COURT 法庭 **5** [T] to decide whether sb is guilty or innocent in a court 审判；审理；判决：**~ sth** *to judge a case* 审理案件 ◇ **~ sb + adj.** *to judge sb guilty/not guilty* 判某人有罪 / 无罪

IDM **don't judge a ˌbook by its ˈcover** (*saying*) used to say that you should not form an opinion about sb/sth from their appearance only 勿以貌取人；勿只凭外表判断

judge·ment (*also* **judg·ment** *especially in NAmE*) /ˈdʒʌdʒmənt/ *noun* **1** [U] the ability to make sensible decisions after carefully considering the best thing to do 判断力；识别力：***good/poor/sound judgement*** 判断力强 / 弱；正确的判断力 ◇ *She showed a lack of judgement when she gave Mark the job.* 她把这工作交给马克表明她缺乏判断力。◇ *It's not something I can give you rules for; you'll have to use your judgement.* 不是我把规则告诉你就行了，你得运用自己的判断力。◇ *He achieved his aim **more by luck than judgement**.* 他达到目的主要是靠运气而不是靠判断力。◇ *The accident was caused by an **error of judgement** on the part of the pilot.* 此次事故是飞行员判断失误所致。**2** [C, U] **~ (of/about/on sth)** an opinion that you form about sth after thinking about it carefully; the act of making this opinion known to others 看法；意见；评价：*He refused to **make a judgement** about the situation.* 他拒绝对形势作出评价。◇ *Who am I to **pass judgement** on her behaviour?* (= to criticize it) 我有什么资格对她的行为说三道四呢？◇ *I'd like to **reserve judgement** until I see the report.* 我还是想看到报告后再发表意见。◇ *It was, **in her judgement**, the wrong thing to do.* 在她看来，那样做是错误的。◇ *I did it **against my better judgement*** (= although I thought it was perhaps the wrong thing to do). 我这样做是违心的。**3** (*usually* **judgment**) [C, U] the decision of a court or a judge 判决；裁决：*a judgment from the European Court of Justice* 欧洲法院的判决 ◇ *The judgment will be given tomorrow.* 此案将于明日宣判。◇ *The court has yet to **pass judgment*** (= say what its decision is) *in this case.* 此案还有待法庭判决。**4** [C, usually sing.] **~ (on sth)** (*formal*) something bad that happens to sb that is thought to be a punishment from God 报应；天谴；（上帝对人的）审判 IDM SEE SIT

judge·men·tal (*BrE*) (*also* **judg·men·tal** *NAmE, BrE*) /dʒʌdʒˈmentl/ *adj.* **1** (*disapproving*) judging people and criticizing them too quickly 动辄评头论足的；动辄指责人的 **2** (*formal*) connected with the process of judging things 判断的；裁决的；判决的：*the judgemental process* 判断过程

ˈjudgement call *noun* (*informal*) a decision you have to make where there is no clear rule about what the right thing to do is, so that you have to use your own judgement 需凭判断力作出的决定

ˈJudgement Day (*also* **the ˌDay of ˈJudgement**, **the ˌLast ˈJudgement**) *noun* the day at the end of the world when, according to some religions, God will judge everyone who has ever lived（某些宗教指上帝对人类的）最后审判日，世界末日

ju·di·ca·ture /ˈdʒuːdɪkətʃə(r)/ *noun* (*law* 律) **1** [U] the system by which courts, trials, etc. are organized in a country 司法系统；审判制度 **2 the judicature** [sing.+sing./pl. v.] judges when they are considered as a group（统称）审判人员

ju·di·cial /dʒuˈdɪʃl/ *adj.* [usually before noun] connected with a court, a judge or legal judgement 法庭的；法官的；审判的；司法的：*judicial powers* 司法权 ◇ *the judicial process/system* 司法程序 / 系统 ▶ **ju·di·cial·ly** /-ʃəli/ *adv.*

juˌdicial ˈactivism *noun* [U] (*law* 律) (in the US) the idea that it is not necessary to follow the exact words of the Constitution when new laws are made（美国）司法能动主义（主张制定新法律时在用词上不必完全按照宪法）

juˌdicial reˈstraint *noun* [U] (*law* 律) (in the US) the idea that judges of the Supreme Court or other courts should not try to change a law that is allowed by the Constitution（美国）司法节制（最高法院或其他法院不应试图更改符合宪法的法律）

juˌdicial reˈview *noun* (*law* 律) **1** [U] (in the US) the power of the Supreme Court to decide if sth is allowed by the Constitution（美国）司法审查（最高法院审查某事是否符合宪法的权力） **2** [C, U] (in Britain) a procedure in which a court examines an action or decision of a public body and decides whether it was right（英国）司法审查（法院审查公共机构的行动或决定是否正确的程序）：*There is to be a judicial review of the visa changes.* 对签证程序变更将进行司法审查。

ju·di·ciary /dʒuˈdɪʃəri; *NAmE* -ʃieri/ *noun* (*usually* **the judiciary**) [C+sing./pl. v.] (*pl.* **-ies**) the judges of a country or a state, when they are considered as a group（统称）审判人员；司法部；司法系统：*an independent judiciary* 独立的司法系统 ➲ COMPARE EXECUTIVE *n.*, LEGISLATURE

ju·di·cious /dʒuˈdɪʃəs/ *adj.* (*formal, approving*) careful and sensible; showing good judgement 审慎而明智的；明断的；有见地的 OPP **injudicious** ▶ **ju·di·cious·ly** *adv.*：*a judiciously worded letter* 一封措辞审慎的信

judo /ˈdʒuːdəʊ; *NAmE* -doʊ/ *noun* [U] (*from Japanese*) a sport in which two people fight and try to throw each other to the ground 柔道：*He* **does judo**. 他是练柔道的。◇ *She's a* **black belt in judo**. 她是柔道黑带高手。

jug /dʒʌg/ *noun* **1** (*BrE*) (*NAmE* **pitch·er**) a container with a handle and a LIP, for holding and pouring liquids（有把有嘴的）壶，罐：*a milk/water jug* 奶杯；水罐 **2** (*NAmE*) (*BrE* **pitch·er**) a large round container with a small opening and a handle, for holding liquids（细口带把的）大罐：*a five-gallon jug of beer* 五加仑装的啤酒罐 **3** the amount of liquid contained in a jug 一壶，一罐（的量）：*She spilled a jug of water.* 她把一罐子水弄洒了。 **4 jugs** [pl.] (*taboo, slang*) an offensive word for a woman's breasts（含冒犯意）奶子

ju·gaad /dʒuˈgɑːd/ *noun* (*IndE*) **1** [U] the use of skill and imagination to find an easy solution to a problem or to fix or make sth using cheap, basic items 创新的变通方法；因陋就简的解决之道 **2** [C] a vehicle made from different parts of other vehicles and used for carrying people, goods, etc., that is usually open at the front and the back and often not very safe to drive 简易拼装车（用不同车辆的不同部件拼装而成，客货两用，前后敞开，安全性较差）▶ **ju·gaad** *adj.*：*jugaad innovation* 因陋就简的创新

jug·ful /ˈdʒʌgfʊl/ *noun* the amount of liquid contained in a jug 一罐的量；一壶的量

jugged hare /ˌdʒʌgd ˈheə(r); *NAmE* ˈher/ *noun* [U] a hot dish made from HARE that has been cooked slowly in liquid in a container with a lid 罐炖野兔肉；焖炖野兔肉

jug·ger·naut /ˈdʒʌgənɔːt; *NAmE* -gərn-/ *noun* **1** (*BrE, often disapproving*) a very large lorry/truck 重型卡车：*juggernauts roaring through country villages* 隆隆驶过村庄的重型卡车 **2** (*formal*) a large and powerful force or institution that cannot be controlled 不可抗拒的强大力量；无法控制的强大机构：*a bureaucratic juggernaut* 庞大的官僚机构

jug·gle /ˈdʒʌgl/ *verb* **1** [I, T] to throw a set of three or more objects such as balls into the air and catch and throw them again quickly, one at a time 玩杂耍（连续向空中抛接多个物体）：*My uncle taught me to juggle.* 我叔叔教我玩杂耍。◇ **~ with sth** *to juggle with balls* 抛接球 ◇ **~ sth** (*figurative*) *I was juggling books, shopping bags and the baby* (= I was trying to hold them all without dropping them). 我手里又是书，又是购物袋，还抱着孩子，跟演杂技一样。 **2** [T, I] **~ (sth) (with sth)** to try to deal with two or more important jobs or activities at the same time so that you can fit all of them into your life 尽力同时应付（两个或更多的重要工作或活动）：*Working mothers are used to juggling their jobs, their children's needs and their housework.* 为人母的职业女性已经习惯了既要工作，又要照顾孩子，还得做家务。 **3** [T] **~ sth** to organize information, figures, the money you spend, etc. in the most useful or effective way 有效地组织，有效利用（信息、数字、开支等）

jug·gler /ˈdʒʌglə(r)/ *noun* a person who juggles, especially an entertainer 玩杂耍的人；耍把戏的人；变戏法的人

jugu·lar /ˈdʒʌgjələ(r)/ (*also* **ˌjugular ˈvein**) *noun* any of the three large VEINS in the neck that carry blood from the head towards the heart 颈静脉
IDM **go for the ˈjugular** (*informal*) to attack sb's weakest point during a discussion, in an aggressive way（讨论中咄咄逼人地）抨击对方的致命弱点，攻其要害

juice 🔑 /dʒuːs/ *noun, verb*

■ *noun* **1** 🔑 [U, C] the liquid that comes from fruit or vegetables; a drink made from this 果汁；菜汁；果汁（或菜汁）饮料：*Add the juice of two lemons.* 加两个柠檬的汁。◇ *a carton of apple juice* 一盒苹果汁 ◇ *Two orange juices, please.* 请来两份橙汁。 **2** [C, usually pl., U] the liquid that comes out of a piece of meat when it is cooked 肉汁 **3** [C, usually pl.] the liquid in the stomach that helps you to DIGEST food 胃液；消化液：***digestive/gastric juices*** 消化液；胃液 **4** [U] (*informal, especially BrE*) petrol/gas 汽油 **5** [U] (*NAmE, informal*) electricity 电 IDM SEE STEW *v.*

■ *verb* **~ sth** to get the juice out of fruit or vegetables 榨出（水果或蔬菜的）汁液；将…榨汁：*Juice two oranges.* 将两个橙子榨汁。

jug (*BrE*)
pitcher (*NAmE*)
带把大口壶

pitcher (*BrE*)
jug (*NAmE*)
带把大陶罐

PHR V **juice sth↔up** (*informal, especially NAmE*) to make sth more exciting or interesting 使更精彩；给…增趣生色

ˈ**juice bar** *noun* a cafe serving drinks made from freshly squeezed fruit（鲜榨）果汁吧；水吧

juicer /ˈdʒuːsə(r)/ *noun* **1** a piece of electrical equipment for getting the juice out of fruit or vegetables 榨汁机 **2** (*NAmE*) (*BrE* ˈ**lemon-squeezer**) a kitchen UTENSIL (= a tool) for squeezing juice out of a fruit 榨汁器 ➲ VISUAL VOCAB PAGE V27

juicy /ˈdʒuːsi/ *adj.* (**juici·er**, **juici·est**) **1** (*approving*) containing a lot of juice and good to eat 多汁的；汁液丰富的：*soft juicy pears* 脆生多汁的梨 ◇ *The meat was tender and juicy.* 这肉又嫩汁又多。➲ WORDFINDER NOTE AT CRISP **2** (*informal*) interesting because you find it shocking or exciting 生动有趣的；妙趣横生的；刺激的：*juicy gossip* 使人感兴趣的流言 **3** (*informal*) attractive because it will bring you a lot of money or satisfaction 有吸引力的；报酬丰厚的；令人满足的：*a juicy prize* 丰厚的奖品

ju-jitsu (*also* **jiu-jitsu**) /dʒuː ˈdʒɪtsuː/ *noun* [U] a Japanese system of fighting from which the sport of JUDO was developed 柔术（日本柔道由此发展而来）

juju /ˈdʒuːdʒuː/ *noun* **1** [C] an object used in W African magic（西非土著魔法中使用的）护符，物神 **2** [U] a type of magic in W Africa（西非土著的）魔法，法术 **3** [U] a type of Nigerian music that uses GUITARS and drums 祖祖音乐（尼日利亚音乐，用吉他和鼓演奏）

juke·box /ˈdʒuːkbɒks; *NAmE* -bɑːks/ *noun* a machine in a pub, bar, etc. that plays music when you put coins into it（酒吧等的投币式）自动点唱机

julep /ˈdʒuːlep/ *noun* [U, C] **1** a sweet drink which may contain alcohol or medicine 甜药酒；草药饮料 **2** = MINT JULEP

Ju·lian cal·en·dar /ˌdʒuːliən ˈkælɪndə(r)/ *noun* [sing.] the system of arranging days and months in the year introduced by Julius Caesar, and used in Western countries until the GREGORIAN CALENDAR replaced it 儒略历（凯撒大帝制订的历法，在西方国家一直使用至以格里历取代为止）

July 🔑 /dʒuˈlaɪ/ *noun* [U, C] (*abbr.* **Jul.**) the 7th month of the year, between June and August 七月 HELP To see how **July** is used, look at the examples at **April**. * July 的用法见词条 April 下的示例。

jum·ble /ˈdʒʌmbl/ *verb, noun*

■ *verb* [usually passive] ~ **sth** (**together/up**) to mix things together in a confused or untidy way 使乱堆；使混乱；使杂乱：*Books, shoes and clothes were* ***jumbled together*** *on the floor.* 书、鞋子和衣服胡乱堆放在地上。▶ **jum·bled** *adj.*：*a jumbled collection of objects* 乱七八糟的一堆东西 ◇ *jumbled thoughts* 纷乱的思绪

■ *noun* **1** [sing.] ~ (**of sth**) an untidy or confused mixture of things 杂乱的一堆；混乱的一团：*a jumble of books and paper* 一堆杂乱的书和纸 ◇ *The essay was a meaningless jumble of ideas.* 这篇文章思路混乱，使人不知所云。 **2** [U] (*BrE*) a collection of old or used clothes, etc. that are no longer wanted and are going to be taken to a jumble sale 待义卖的一堆旧杂物

ˈ**jumble sale** (*BrE*) (*also* ˈ**rummage sale** *NAmE, BrE*) *noun* a sale of old or used clothes, etc. to make money for a church, school or other organization 旧杂物义卖（为教堂、学校或其他机构筹款）

jumbo /ˈdʒʌmbəʊ; *NAmE* -boʊ/ *noun, adj.*

■ *noun* (*pl.* **-os**) (*also* ˌ**jumbo** ˈ**jet**) a large plane that can carry several hundred passengers, especially a Boeing 747 大型客机（尤指波音 747）

■ *adj.* [only before noun] (*informal*) very large; larger than usual 巨型的；巨大的；特大的：*a jumbo pack of cornflakes* 一盒特大包装的玉米片

jump 🔑 /dʒʌmp/ *verb, noun*

■ *verb*

• **MOVE OFF/TO GROUND** 跳 **1** 🔑 [I] to move quickly off the ground or away from a surface by pushing yourself with your legs and feet 跳；跃；跳跃：*'Quick, jump!' he shouted.* "赶快，跳！"他大声叫道。◇ **+ adv./prep.** *to jump into the air/over a wall/into the water* 跳起来；跃过墙；跳进水里 ◇ *The children were jumping up and down with excitement.* 孩子们兴奋得跳来跳去。◇ *She jumped down from the chair.* 她从椅子上跳了下来。◇ *The pilot jumped from the burning plane* (= with a PARACHUTE). 飞行员从着火的飞机跳伞了。◇ **+ noun** *She has jumped 2.2 metres.* 她跳了 2.2 米。

• **PASS OVER STH** 跨跃 **2** 🔑 [T] to pass over sth by jumping 跳过；跃过；跨越 SYN **leap**：~ **sth** *Can you jump that gate?* 你能跳过那篱笆门吗？◇ *His horse fell as it jumped the last hurdle.* 他的马在跨越最后一个栏时跌倒了。◇ ~ **sth + adv./prep.** *I jumped my horse over all the fences.* 我纵马跃过了所有的障碍物。

• **MOVE QUICKLY** 快速移动 **3** 🔑 [I] **+ adv./prep.** to move quickly and suddenly 突然快速移动：*He* ***jumped to his feet*** *when they called his name.* 他们叫到他的名字时他一下子就站了起来。◇ *She jumped up and ran out of the room.* 她蓦地跳起来跑出房间。◇ *Do you want a ride? Jump in.* 你想搭车吗？快上来吧。 **4** 🔑 [I] to make a sudden movement because of surprise, fear or excitement（因吃惊、害怕或激动而）猛地一动，突然一跳：*A loud bang made me jump.* 砰的一声巨响吓我一跳。◇ *Her heart jumped when she heard the news.* 听到那消息她的心猛地一跳。

• **INCREASE** 增加 **5** 🔑 [I] to rise suddenly by a large amount 突升；猛涨；激增 SYN **leap**：~ **by…** *Prices jumped by 60% last year.* 去年，物价暴涨 60%。◇ ~ (**from…**) (**to…**) *Sales jumped from $2.7 billion to $3.5 billion.* 销售额从 27 亿美元猛增到 35 亿美元。

• **CHANGE SUDDENLY** 突然改变 **6** 🔑 [I] ~ (**about/around**) (**from sth to sth**) to change suddenly from one subject to another 突然改变，突然转换（话题、题目）：*I couldn't follow the talk because he kept jumping about from one topic to another.* 我听不明白他的讲话，因为他老是转换话题。◇ *The story then jumps from her childhood in New York to her first visit to London.* 故事接着从她在纽约的童年一下子转到她第一次去伦敦。

• **LEAVE OUT** 略去 **7** [T] ~ **sth** to leave out sth and pass to a further point or stage 略去；略过；跳过：*You seem to have jumped several steps in the argument.* 你在论证中似乎略去了好几个步骤。

• **OF MACHINE/DEVICE** 机器；器具 **8** [I] (**+ adv./prep.**) to move suddenly and unexpectedly, especially out of the correct position 突然跳出正常位置；意外地离开正常位置：*The needle jumped across the dial.* 指针突然从刻度盘的一端跳到另一端。◇ *The film jumped during projection.* 电影放映时跳了片。

• **ATTACK** 袭击 **9** [T, I] ~ (**on**) **sb** (*informal*) to attack sb suddenly 突然袭击（某人）；猛地扑向（某人）：*The thieves jumped him in a dark alleyway.* 一伙盗贼在一条漆黑的小巷里突然扑向他。

• **VEHICLE** 车辆 **10** [T] ~ **sth** (*NAmE*) to get on a vehicle very quickly 跳上（车辆等）：*to jump a bus* 跳上公共汽车 **11** (*NAmE*) = JUMP-START

• **BE LIVELY** 活泼 **12 be jumping** [I] (*informal*) to be very lively 欢跃；雀跃：*The bar's jumping tonight.* 今晚酒吧里气氛活跃。

IDM **be ˈjumping up and down** (*informal*) to be very angry or excited about sth 暴跳如雷；欢欣雀跃 **jump down sb's ˈthroat** (*informal*) to react very angrily to sb 愤怒地反驳；猛烈回击某人 **jump the ˈgun** to do sth too soon, before the right time 抢跑；过早行动 **jump the ˈlights** (*BrE*) (*also* **run a** (**red**) ˈ**light**, **run the ˈlights** *NAmE, BrE*) (*informal*) to fail to stop at a red traffic light 闯红灯 **jump out of your ˈskin** (*informal*) to move violently because of a sudden shock 大吃一惊；吓一大跳 **jump the ˈqueue** (*BrE*) (*US* **jump the ˈline**) to go to the front of a line of people without waiting for your turn 插队；加塞儿；不按次序排队 **jump the ˈrails** (of a train 火车) to leave the rails suddenly 出轨；脱轨 **jump the ˈshark** (used especially about a television series, etc.) to include something that is very hard to believe as an attempt to keep people watching（尤指电视剧等）为抓人眼球而加入荒诞的内容：*Has the show finally jumped the shark?* 这档节目为刺激收视，最终加入荒诞不经的内容了吗？ **jump** 'ship **1** to leave the ship on which you are serving, without permission 擅自弃职离船 **2** to leave an organization that you belong to, suddenly and unexpectedly 擅自离队；擅离职守 **jump through 'hoops** to do sth difficult or complicated in order to achieve sth（为达到目的而）经受磨难 **jump 'to it** (*NAmE also* **hop 'to it**) (*informal*) used to tell sb to hurry and do something quickly 赶快；加油；快点干 ➲ MORE AT BANDWAGON, CONCLUSION, DEEP *adj.*

PHR V **'jump at sb** (*NAmE*) = JUMP ON SB **'jump at sth** to accept an opportunity, offer, etc. with enthusiasm 迫不及待地接受，欣然接受（机会、建议等） SYN **leap at** **,jump 'in 1** to interrupt a conversation 打断谈话：*Before she could reply Peter jumped in with an objection.* 她还没来得及回答，彼得就迫不及待地表示反对。 **2** to start to do sth very quickly without spending a long time thinking first 匆忙行动；急于从事 **'jump on sb** (*NAmE also* **'jump at sb**) (*informal*) to criticize sb 批评，责备（某人） **,jump 'out at sb** to be very obvious and easily noticed 极易引起某人的注意 SYN **leap**: *The mistake in the figures jumped out at me.* 我一眼就看出数字上有错误。

■ *noun*

• **MOVEMENT** 运动 **1** an act of jumping 跳；跃；跳跃：*a jump of over six metres* 六米多的一跳 ◊ *The story takes a jump back in time.* 这故事一转又回到以前发生的事情。◊ *Somehow he survived the jump from the third floor of the building.* 不知怎么的，他从四楼跳下来竟然没摔死。◊ *to do a parachute jump* 跳伞 ◊ *a ski jump champion* 跳台滑雪冠军 ◊ *I sat up* ***with a jump*** (= quickly and suddenly). 我霍地坐起身来。◊ *The negotiations took a jump forward yesterday* (= they made progress). 谈判昨天取得进展。➲ SEE ALSO HIGH JUMP, LONG JUMP, SKI JUMP, TRIPLE JUMP

• **BARRIER** 障碍物 **2** a barrier like a narrow fence that a horse or a runner has to jump over in a race or competition（比赛中需跳过的）障碍物：*The horse fell at the last jump.* 那匹马在跨越最后一个障碍物时跌倒了。➲ VISUAL VOCAB PAGE V51

• **INCREASE** 增加 **3** ~ (**in sth**) a sudden increase in amount, price or value 突升；猛涨；激增：*a 20 per cent jump in pre-tax profits* 税前利润 20% 的大幅增长 ◊ *unusually large price jumps* 非同寻常的大幅度涨价

IDM **to keep, etc. one jump ahead (of sb)** to keep your advantage over sb, especially your COMPETITORS, by taking action before they do or by making sure you know more than they do（尤指竞争中比某人）有优势的地位，优先一步，略胜一筹 ➲ MORE AT HIGH JUMP, RUNNING *adj.*

'jump ball *noun* (in BASKETBALL 篮球) a ball that the REFEREE throws up between two opposing players to begin play 跳球；争球

'jump cut *noun* (*specialist*) (in films/movies 电影) a sudden change from one scene to another 跳格剪辑；跳切

'jumped-up *adj.* [only before noun] (*BrE, informal, disapproving*) thinking you are more important than you really are, particularly because you have risen in social status（尤因社会地位提高）妄自尊大的，自视甚高的

jump·er /ˈdʒʌmpə(r)/ *noun* **1** (*BrE*) a knitted piece of clothing made of wool or cotton for the upper part of the body, with long sleeves and no buttons（毛或棉的）针织套衫：*a woolly jumper* 套头毛衣 ➲ VISUAL VOCAB PAGE V68 **2** (*NAmE*) = PINAFORE (1) **3** a person, an animal or an insect that jumps 跳跃者；跳跃动物；跳虫：*He's a good jumper.* 他的弹跳力特别好。

'jumper cable (*NAmE*) (*BrE* **'jump lead**) *noun* [usually pl.] one of two cables that are used to start a car when it has no power in its battery. The jump cables connect the battery to the battery of another car. 跨接引线（用以将汽车上无电的电池连接到另一汽车的电池上以发动汽车）

,jumping-'off point (*also* **,jumping-'off place**) *noun* a place from which to start a journey or new activity 出发点；起点

'jump jet *noun* an aircraft that can take off and land by going straight up or down, without needing a RUNWAY 垂直起降喷气机 ➲ WORDFINDER NOTE AT AIRCRAFT

jump lead /ˈdʒʌmp liːd/ (*BrE*) (*NAmE* **'jumper cable**) *noun* [usually pl.] one of two cables that are used to start a car when it has no power in its battery. The jump leads connect the battery to the battery of another car. 跨接引线（用以将汽车上无电的电池连接到另一汽车的电池上以发动汽车）

'jump-off (*NAmE also* **'ride-off**) *noun* (in the sport of SHOWJUMPING 超越障碍赛马运动) an extra part of a competition in which horses that have the same score jump again to decide the winner 加赛决胜负

'jump rope *noun*, **,jump 'rope** *verb* (*NAmE*) ➲ SKIPPING ROPE, SKIP *v.* (2) ➲ VISUAL VOCAB PAGE V41

'jump shot *noun* (in BASKETBALL 篮球) a shot made while jumping 跳投

'jump-start (*NAmE also* **jump**) *verb* **1** ~ **sth** to start the engine of a car by connecting the battery to the battery of another car with JUMP LEADS 用跨接引线启动（汽车发动机） **2** ~ **sth** to put a lot of energy into starting a process or an activity or into making it start more quickly 全力启动；加快开展

jump·suit /ˈdʒʌmpsuːt; *BrE also* -sjuːt/ *noun* a piece of clothing that consists of trousers/pants and a jacket or shirt sewn together in one piece, worn especially by women（尤指女式）连体裤

jumpy /ˈdʒʌmpi/ *adj.* (*informal*) nervous and anxious, especially because you think that sth bad is going to happen 胆战心惊的；提心吊胆的；紧张不安的

junc·tion /ˈdʒʌŋkʃn/ *noun* **1** (*especially BrE*) (*NAmE usually* **inter·sec·tion**) the place where two or more roads or railway/railroad lines meet（公路或铁路的）交叉路口，汇合处，枢纽站：*It was near the junction of City Road and Old Street.* 那是在城市路与老街的交叉路口附近。◊ *Come off the motorway at junction 6.* 在 6 号交叉路口驶离高速公路。 **2** a place where two or more cables, rivers or other things meet or are joined（电缆的）主接点；（河流的）汇合处；接合点：*a telephone junction box* 电话分线盒

junc·ture /ˈdʒʌŋktʃə(r)/ *noun* (*formal*) a particular point or stage in an activity or a series of events 特定时刻；关头：*The battle had reached a crucial juncture.* 战斗已到了关键时刻。◊ ***At this juncture,*** *I would like to make an important announcement.* 此时此刻我要宣布一项重要的事情。

June /dʒuːn/ *noun* [U, C] (*abbr.* **Jun.**) the 6th month of the year, between May and July 六月 HELP To see how **June** is used, look at the examples at **April**. * June 的用法见词条 April 下的示例。

jun·gle /ˈdʒʌŋɡl/ *noun* **1** [U, C] an area of tropical forest where trees and plants grow very thickly（热带）丛林，密林：*The area was covered in dense jungle.* 这个地区丛林密布。◊ *the jungles of South-East Asia* 东南亚热带丛林 ◊ *jungle warfare* 丛林战 ◊ *Our garden is a complete jungle.* 我们的花园杂草丛生。 **2** [sing.] an unfriendly or dangerous place or situation, especially one where it is very difficult to be successful or to trust anyone 尔虞我诈的环境；危险地带：*It's a jungle out there—you've got to be strong to succeed.* 那是个弱肉强食的地方，要成功就得是强者。➲ SEE ALSO CONCRETE JUNGLE **3** (*also* **'jungle music**) [U] a type of electronic dance music developed in Britain in the early 1990s, which has a fast drum beat and a strong slower BASS[1] (1) beat 丛林音乐（20 世纪 90 年代初兴起于英国的一种电子舞曲，以快速的鼓点节拍和稍缓慢的重低音节奏为特点） IDM SEE LAW

'jungle gym (*NAmE*) (*BrE* **'climbing frame**) *noun* a structure made of metal bars joined together for children to climb and play on（儿童游乐设施）攀爬架 ➲ PICTURE AT FRAME ➲ VISUAL VOCAB PAGE V41

jun·gli /ˈdʒʌŋɡli/ *adj.* (*IndE*) wild; not educated 粗野的；未开化的；没教养的

jun·ior /ˈdʒuːniə(r)/ *adj., noun*

■ *adj.*

- **OF LOW RANK** 低层 **1** [usually before noun] having a low rank in an organization or a profession 地位（或职位、级别）低下的：*junior employees* 低层雇员 ◇ **~ to sb** *She is junior to me.* 她职位比我低。
- **IN SPORT** 体育运动 **2** [only before noun] connected with young people below a particular age, rather than with adults, especially in sports 青少年的：*the world junior tennis championships* 世界青少年网球锦标赛
- **SON** 儿子 **3 Junior** (*abbr.* **Jnr, Jr**) (especially in US) used after the name of a man who has the same name as his father, to avoid confusion （尤用于美国，置于同名父子中儿子的姓名之后）小 ➲ COMPARE THE YOUNGER at YOUNG *adj.* (6)
- **SCHOOL/COLLEGE** 学校；学院 **4** [only before noun] (*BrE*) (of a school or part of a school 学校或学校的一部分) for children under the age of 11 or 13 为 11 或 13 岁以下儿童设立的 **5** [only before noun] (*NAmE*) connected with the year before the last year in a HIGH SCHOOL or college （四年制高中或大学中）三年级生的，三年级的：*I spent my junior year in France.* 我三年级是在法国念的。➲ COMPARE SENIOR *adj.*

■ *noun*

- **LOW LEVEL JOB** 职位低的工作 **1** [C] (*especially BrE*) a person who has a job at a low level within an organization 职位较低者；低层次工作人员：*office juniors* 办公室的低级职员
- **IN SPORT** 体育运动 **2** [C] a young person below a particular age, rather than an adult 青少年；青少年运动员：*She has coached many of our leading juniors.* 她训练过我们许多名列前茅的青少年运动员。
- **IN SCHOOL/COLLEGE** 学校；学院 **3** [C] (*BrE*) a child who goes to JUNIOR SCHOOL 小学生 **4** [C] (*NAmE*) a student in the year before the last year at HIGH SCHOOL or college （四年制高中或大学的）三年级学生 ➲ COMPARE SOPHOMORE
- **SON** 儿子 **5** [sing.] (*NAmE, informal*) a person's young son 男孩子；年幼的儿子：*I leave junior with Mom when I'm at work.* 我工作时就把儿子留给母亲照看。

IDM **be...years sb's 'junior | be sb's junior (by...)** to be younger than sb, by the number of years mentioned 小某人…岁；比某人小…岁：*She's four years his junior.* 她比他小四岁。◇ *She's his junior by four years.* 她比他小四岁。

ˌjunior ˈcollege *noun* (in the US) a college that offers programmes that are two years long. Some students go to a university or a college offering four-year programmes after they have finished studying at a junior college. （美国）两年制专科学校，大专

ˌjunior ˈcommon room *noun* (*abbr.* **JCR**) (*BrE*) a room in a college, used for social purposes by students who have not yet taken their first degree （大学的）本科生活动室

ˈjunior doctor *noun* (in Britain) a doctor who has finished medical school and who is working at a hospital to get further practical experience （英国）实习医生 ➲ COMPARE HOUSE OFFICER, INTERN *n.*

ˌjunior ˈhigh school (*also* **ˌjunior ˈhigh**) *noun* [C, U] (in the US) a school for young people between the ages of 12 and 14 （美国）初级中学 ➲ COMPARE SENIOR HIGH SCHOOL

ˈjunior school *noun* [C, U] (in Britain) a school for children between the ages of 7 and 11 （英国）小学

ju·ni·per /ˈdʒuːnɪpə(r)/ *noun* [U, C] a bush with purple BERRIES that are used in medicine and to flavour GIN 刺柏，桧柏（有些种的果可供药用和杜松子酒调味之用）

junk /dʒʌŋk/ *noun, verb*

■ *noun* **1** [U] things that are considered useless or of little value 无用的东西；无价值的东西 SYN **rubbish**：*I've cleared out all that old junk in the attic.* 我把阁楼里所有的废旧杂物都清除干净了。◇ *There's nothing but junk on the TV.* 电视上全是些无聊的东西。◇ (*informal, disapproving*) *Is this all your junk (= are these all your things)?* 这是你所有的家当吗？ ➲ SYNONYMS AT THING **2** [U] = JUNK FOOD **3** [C] a Chinese boat with a square sail and a flat bottom 中国式帆船；戎克船

■ *verb* **~ sth** (*informal*) to get rid of sth because it is no longer valuable or useful 把…当作废物扔弃；丢弃；废弃

ˈjunk bond *noun* (*business* 商) a type of BOND that pays a high rate of interest because there is a lot of risk involved, often used to raise money quickly in order to buy the shares of another company 风险债券，垃圾债券（利息高、风险大，常用于迅速集资进行收购）

jun·ket /ˈdʒʌŋkɪt/ *noun* (*informal, disapproving*) a trip that is made for pleasure by sb who works for the government, etc. and that is paid for using public money （政府官员的）公费旅游

ˈjunk food (*also* **junk**) *noun* [U] (*also* **junk foods** [pl.]) (*informal, disapproving*) food that is quick and easy to prepare and eat but that is thought to be bad for your health 垃圾食品（制作、食用方便却有害健康）

junkie /ˈdʒʌŋki/ *noun* (*informal*) a drug ADDICT (= a person who is unable to stop taking dangerous drugs) 有毒瘾者；吸毒成瘾者

ˈjunk mail *noun* [U] (*disapproving*) advertising material that is sent to people who have not asked for it （未经索要寄来的）邮寄广告宣传品，垃圾广告邮件 ➲ COMPARE SPAM *n.* (2)

ˌjunk ˈscience *noun* [U] (*disapproving*) used to refer to ideas and theories that seem to be well researched and scientific but in fact have little evidence to support them 垃圾科学（貌似严谨实则缺乏证据的思想和理论）

ˈjunk shop *noun* (*especially BrE*) a shop that buys and sells old furniture and other objects, at cheap prices 旧货店；二手店

junky /ˈdʒʌŋki/ *adj.* (*informal, especially NAmE*) of poor quality or of little value 质量低劣的；无价值的

junk·yard /ˈdʒʌŋkjɑːd; *NAmE* -jɑːrd/ (*especially NAmE*) (*especially BrE* **scrap·yard**) *noun* a place where old cars, machines, etc. are collected, so that parts of them, or the metal they are made of, can be sold to be used again （堆放旧汽车、旧机器等的）废品场

junta /ˈdʒʌntə; *NAmE* ˈhʊntə/ *noun* a military government that has taken power by force （武力夺取政权的）军人集团，军政府

Ju·pi·ter /ˈdʒuːpɪtə(r)/ *noun* the largest planet of the SOLAR SYSTEM, fifth in order of distance from the sun 木星（太阳系中最大的行星）

Jur·as·sic /dʒʊˈræsɪk/ *adj.* (*geology* 地) of the PERIOD between around 208 to 146 million years ago, when the largest known dinosaurs lived; of the rocks formed during this time 侏罗纪的；侏罗纪岩系的 ▸ **the Jur·as·sic** *noun* [sing.]

jur·id·ic·al /dʒʊəˈrɪdɪkl; *NAmE* dʒʊˈr-/ *adj.* [usually before noun] (*formal*) connected with the law, judges or legal matters 法律的；司法的

jur·is·dic·tion /ˌdʒʊərɪsˈdɪkʃn; *NAmE* ˌdʒʊr-/ *noun* (*formal*) **1** [U, C] **~ (over sb/sth) | ~ (of sb/sth) (to do sth)** the authority that an official organization has to make legal decisions about sb/sth 司法权；审判权；管辖权 **2** [C] an area or a country in which a particular system of laws has authority 管辖区域；管辖范围 ▸ **jur·is·dic·tion·al** *adj.*

jur·is·pru·dence /ˌdʒʊərɪsˈpruːdns; *NAmE* ˌdʒʊr-/ *noun* [U] (*specialist*) the scientific study of law 法学；法律学：*a professor of jurisprudence* 法学教授

jur·ist /ˈdʒʊərɪst; *NAmE* ˈdʒʊr-/ *noun* (*formal*) a person who is an expert in law 法学家；法律学专家

juror /ˈdʒʊərə(r); *NAmE* ˈdʒʊr-/ *noun* a member of a jury 陪审团成员；陪审员

jury /ˈdʒʊəri; *NAmE* ˈdʒʊri/ *noun* [C+sing./pl. v.] (*pl.* **-ies**) **1** (*also* **panel**, **ˈjury panel** *especially in NAmE*) a group of members of the public who listen to the facts of a case in a court and decide whether or not sb is guilty of a crime 陪审团：***members of the jury*** 陪审团成员 ◇ *to* ***be/sit/serve on a jury*** 担任陪审员 ◇ *The jury has/have returned a verdict of guilty.* 陪审团已作出有罪裁定。◇ *the* ***right to trial by jury*** 由陪审团审判的权利 ➲ COLLOCATIONS AT JUSTICE ➲ SEE ALSO GRAND JURY **2** a group of people who decide who is the winner of a competition（比赛的）评判委员会，裁判委员会，仲裁委员会

IDM **the jury is (still) ˈout on sth** used when you are saying that sth is still not certain（某事）仍未定夺，悬而未决

ˈjury duty (*BrE usually* **ˈjury service**) *noun* [U] a period of time spent as a member of a jury in court 担任陪审员；参与陪审期

jus /ʒuː; *NAmE also* dʒuːs/ *noun* [U] (*from French*) a thin sauce, especially one made from meat juices 调味（肉）汁

just /dʒʌst/ *adv., adj.*

■ ***adv.*** **1** exactly 正好；恰好：*This jacket is just my size.* 这件夹克正合我的尺码。◇ *This gadget is* ***just the thing*** *for getting those nails out.* 这小玩意儿用来起那些钉子正合适。◇ ***Just my luck*** (= the sort of bad luck I usually have). *The phone's not working.* 我就是这么倒霉。电话又坏了。◇ *You're* ***just in time.*** 你来得正是时候。◇ **~ like…** *She looks just like her mother.* 她看上去就像她母亲。◇ **~ what…** *It's just what I wanted!* 这正是我想要的！◇ **~ as…** *It's just as I thought.* 我正是这样想的。◇ (*BrE*) *It's* ***just on six*** (= exactly six o'clock). 现在六点整。 **2** **~ as…** at the same moment as 正当…时：*The clock struck six just as I arrived.* 我到达时，时钟正敲六点。 **3** **~ as good, nice, easily, etc.** no less than; equally 不亚于；同样：*She's just as smart as her sister.* 她与她姐姐一样聪明。◇ *You can get there just as cheaply by plane.* 你坐飞机到那儿同样便宜。 **4** **(only) ~ | ~ after, before, under, etc. sth** by a small amount 刚好；差一点就不；勉强：*I got here just after nine.* 我到达这里时刚过九点。◇ *I only just caught the train.* 我差一点没赶上火车。◇ *Inflation fell to just over 4 per cent.* 通货膨胀降至4% 多一点。 **5** used to say that you/sb did sth very recently 刚才；方才：*I've just heard the news.* 我刚听到这个消息。◇ *When you arrived he had only just left.* 你到时他刚走。◇ *She has just been telling us about her trip to Rome.* 她刚才一直在给我们讲她的罗马之行。◇ (*especially NAmE*) *I just saw him a moment ago.* 我刚才还见到过他。➲ NOTE AT ALREADY **6** at this/that moment; now 此时；那时；眼下；现在：*I'm just finishing my book.* 眼下我正在完成我的一本书。◇ *I was just beginning to enjoy myself when we had to leave.* 我刚开始玩得起劲我们就得离开了。◇ *I'm just off* (= I am leaving now). 我要走了。 **7** **~ about/going to do sth** going to do sth only a few moments from now or then 正要；正准备；马上就要：*The water's just about to boil.* 水马上就要开了。◇ *I was just going to tell you when you interrupted.* 我正准备告诉你，你突然把话打断了。 **8** simply 只是；仅仅是：*It was just an ordinary day.* 那只是普普通通的一天。◇ ***I can't just*** *drop all my commitments.* 我答应要干的事不能甩手不管。◇ *This essay is* ***just not good enough.*** 这篇文章实在是不够好。◇ *I didn't mean to upset you.* ***It's just that*** *I had to tell somebody.* 我本不想烦你，只是我非得找个人说说。◇ *This is not* ***just another*** *disaster movie—it's a masterpiece.* 不能说它只是又一部灾难片，它是一部杰作。◇ ***Just because*** *you're older than me* ***doesn't mean*** *you know everything.* 你比我年长并不意味着你什么都知道。 **9** only 仅仅；只不过：**~ (for sth)** *I decided to learn Japanese* ***just for fun.*** 我决定学日语只是为了好玩。◇ **~ (to do sth)** *I waited an hour just to see you.* 我等了一个小时只是为了见你。◇ *There is just one method that might work.* 只有一个方法可能起作用。◇ *'Can I help you?' 'No thanks,* ***I'm just looking.'*** (= in a shop/store) "我能为你做点什么吗？" "不用，谢谢，我只是看看。" **10** (*informal*) really; completely 真正地；确实；完全：*The food was just wonderful!* 那吃的实在是好极了！◇ *I can just imagine his reaction.* 我完全可以想象出他的反应。 **11** used in orders to get sb's attention, give permission, etc.（引起注意、表示允许等）请，就：*Just listen to what I'm saying, will you!* 你就听我说好吗？◇ *Just help yourselves.* 请大家随便吃。 **12** used to make a polite request, excuse, etc.（提出请求、表示歉意等）请：*Could you just help me with this box, please?* 请帮我搬一搬这箱子好吗？◇ *I've just got a few things to do first.* 对不起，我正好有点事要先做。 **13** **could/might/may ~** used to show a slight possibility that sth is true or will happen（表示稍有可能）可能，也许：*Try his home number—he might just be there.* 试试他家的电话号码，他也许在那儿。 **14** used to agree with sb（表示赞同）：*'He's very pompous.' 'Isn't he just?'* "他很自负。" "可不是吗？"

IDM **could/might just as well…** used to say that you/sb would have been in the same position if you had done sth else, because you got little benefit or enjoyment from what you did do 不如；还是…的好：*The weather was so bad we might just as well have stayed at home.* 天气糟糕透了，还不如待在家里好。 **it is just as ˈwell (that…)** it is a good thing (…) 还好，倒也不错，还可以：*It is just as well that we didn't leave any later or we'd have missed him.* 还好，我们没有晚些离开，要不然我们就见不到他了。 **just about** (*informal*) **1** almost; very nearly 几乎；近乎；差不多：*I've met just about everyone.* 我几乎每个人都见到了。◇ *'Did you reach your sales target?' 'Just about.'* "你的销售目标达到了吗？" "差不多了。" **2** approximately 大概；大约：*She should be arriving just about now.* 她现在该到了。 **just a ˈminute/ˈmoment/ˈsecond** (*informal*) used to ask sb to wait for a short time 稍等一会儿；请稍候：*'Is Mr Burns available?' 'Just a second, please, I'll check.'* "我可以见伯恩斯先生吗？" "请稍等一会儿，我来查一下。" **just like ˈthat** suddenly, without warning or explanation（就是那样）突如其来，冷不防，不加解释 **just ˈnow** **1** at this moment 此时；此刻；眼下：*Come and see me later—I'm busy just now.* 过些时候再来，我这会儿正忙着呢。 **2** during this present period 目前；现阶段：*Business is good just now.* 目前生意很红火。 **3** only a short time ago 刚才；刚刚；一会儿前：*I saw her just now.* 我刚刚见到过她。 **4** (*SAfrE, informal*) later; in a short period of time 以后；一会儿后 **just ˈso** done or arranged very accurately or carefully（做或安排得）井井有条，有条不紊：*He liked polishing the furniture and making everything just so.* 他喜欢把家具擦得亮亮的，一切都安排得井井有条。 **just ˈthen** at that moment 那时；就在那时：*Just then, someone knocked at the front door.* 就在那时，大门口有人敲门。 **not just ˈyet** not now but probably quite soon 这会儿还不；尚未但可能很快：*I can't give you the money just yet.* 我这会儿还不能给你钱。 **I, etc. would just as soon do sth** used to say that you would equally well like to do sth as do sth else that has been suggested 乐意做某事（同时也乐意做所建议的事）：*I'd just as soon stay at home as go out tonight.* 今晚待在家里或出去我都乐意。 ➲ MORE AT CASE *n.*, TICKET *n.*

■ ***adj.*** [usually before noun] **1** that most people consider to be morally fair and reasonable 公正的；正义的；正当的；合理的 SYN **fair**: *a* ***just decision/law/society*** 公正的判决 / 法律 / 社会 **2** **the just** *noun* [pl.] people who are just 正直的人；公正的人 **3** appropriate in a particular situation 合适的；恰当的：*a* ***just reward/punishment*** 应有的报偿 / 惩罚 ◇ *I think she got her* ***just deserts*** (= what she deserved). 我认为她罪有应得。 OPP **unjust** ▸ **just·ly** *adv.*：*to be treated justly* 受到公平待遇 ◇ *to be justly proud of sth* 有理由为某事而骄傲

just·ice /ˈdʒʌstɪs/ *noun* **1** [U] the fair treatment of people 公平；公正：*laws based on the principles of justice* 以公正为原则的法律 ◇ *They are demanding equal rights and justice.* 他们要求平等的权利和公正的待遇。 OPP **injustice** ➲ SEE ALSO POETIC JUSTICE, ROUGH JUSTICE **2** [U] the quality of being fair or reasonable 公道；合理；公平合理：*Who can deny the justice of their cause?* 谁能否认他们的追求是合理的呢？ OPP **injustice** **3** [U] the legal system used to punish people who have committed crimes 司法制度；法律制裁；审判：*the criminal justice system* 刑事司法系统 ◇ *The European Court of Justice* 欧洲法庭 ◇ (*BrE*) *They were accused of attempting to* ***pervert the course of justice.*** 他们因企图妨碍司法公正而被控。◇ (*NAmE*) *They were accused of attempting to* ***obstruct justice.***

他们被控企图妨碍司法公正。➲ SEE ALSO MISCARRIAGE OF JUSTICE **4** (*also* **Just·ice**) [C] (*NAmE*) a judge in a court (also used before the name of a judge) 法官（亦作称谓） ➲ SEE ALSO CHIEF JUSTICE **5 Just·ice** [C] (*BrE*, *CanE*) used before the name of a judge in a COURT OF APPEAL（称谓）上诉法院法官：*Mr Justice Davies* 上诉法院法官戴维斯先生 ➲ WORDFINDER NOTE AT LAW, PRISON, TRIAL

IDM **bring sb to 'justice** to arrest sb for a crime and put them on trial in court（将某人）绳之以法，缉拿归案 **do justice to 'sb/'sth | do sb/sth 'justice 1** to treat or represent sb/sth fairly, especially in a way that shows how good, attractive, etc. they are 公平对待某人（或某事）；给予公正的评价：*That photo doesn't do you justice.* 那张照片把你给照走样了。 **2** to deal with sb/sth correctly and completely 恰当处理某人（或某事）：*You cannot do justice to such a complex situation in just a few pages.* 你不可能仅仅几页就将这么复杂的形势恰如其分地描述出来。 **do yourself 'justice** to do sth as well as you can in order to show other people how good you are 充分发挥自己的能力：*She didn't do herself justice in the exam.* 她在考试中没有充分发挥出自己的水平。➲ MORE AT PERVERT *v.*

,Justice of the 'Peace *noun* (*pl.* **Justices of the Peace**) (*abbr.* **JP**) (*formal*) an official who acts as a judge in the lowest courts of law 基层法院法官；治安法官；太平绅士 SYN **magistrate**

jus·ti·ciary /dʒʌˈstɪʃəri; *NAmE* dʒəˈstɪʃieri/ *noun* (*pl.* **-ies**) **1** (*ScotE*) [C] a judge or similar officer 司法官 **2** [U] the process by which justice is done 司法程序

jus·ti·fi·able AW /ˈdʒʌstɪfaɪəbl; ˌdʒʌstɪˈfaɪəbl/ *adj.* existing or done for a good reason, and therefore acceptable 有理由的；可证明是正当的；情有可原的 SYN **legitimate**: *justifiable pride* 无可非议的自豪感 ▶ **jus·ti·fi·ably** AW /-əbli/ *adv.*: *The university can be justifiably proud of its record.* 这所大学有理由为自己的纪录而自豪。

,justifiable 'homicide *noun* [U] (*law* 律) in some countries, a killing which is not a criminal act, for example because you were trying to defend yourself 正当杀人（在一些国家中不构成犯罪，如因自卫） ➲ COMPARE CULPABLE HOMICIDE

jus·ti·fi·ca·tion AW /ˌdʒʌstɪfɪˈkeɪʃn/ *noun* [U, C] **~ (for sth/doing sth)** a good reason why sth exists or is done 正当理由：*I can see no possible justification for any further tax increases.* 我看不出还能提出什么理由再加税。◇ *He was getting angry—and* **with some justification**. 他生气了，而这并不是没有道理的。➲ SYNONYMS AT REASON

IDM **in justifi'cation (of sb/sth)** as an explanation of why sth exists or why sb has done sth 作为（对…）的解释（或辩护）：*All I can say in justification of her actions is that she was under a lot of pressure at work.* 我唯一能为她的行为辩解的理由是她工作压力很大。

jus·ti·fied 🔑 AW /ˈdʒʌstɪfaɪd/ *adj.* **1** 🔑 **~ (in doing sth)** having a good reason for doing sth（做某事）有正当理由的：*She felt fully justified in asking for her money back.* 她认为有充分的理由要求退款。 **2** 🔑 existing or done for a good reason 事出有因的；合乎情理的：*His fears proved justified.* 他的恐惧后来证明是有原因的。 OPP **unjustified**

jus·tify 🔑 AW /ˈdʒʌstɪfaɪ/ *verb* (**jus·ti·fies**, **jus·ti·fy·ing**, **jus·ti·fied**, **jus·ti·fied**) **1** 🔑 to show that sb/sth is right or reasonable 证明…正确（或正当、有理）：**~ (sb/sth) doing sth** *How can they justify paying such huge salaries?* 他们

▼ **COLLOCATIONS** 词语搭配

Criminal justice 刑事审判

Breaking the law 犯法

- **break/violate/obey/uphold** the law 违反/违背/遵守/维护法律
- **be investigated/arrested/tried for** a crime/a robbery/fraud 因犯罪/抢劫/诈骗而被调查/逮捕/审判
- **be arrested**/(*especially NAmE*) **indicted/convicted** on charges of rape/fraud/(*especially US*) felony charges 因被控犯强奸罪/诈骗罪/重型罪遭逮捕/起诉/定罪
- **be arrested** on suspicion of arson/robbery/shoplifting 因涉嫌纵火/抢劫/在商店行窃而被逮捕
- **be accused of/be charged with** murder/(*especially NAmE*) homicide/four counts of fraud 被指控犯有谋杀罪/杀人罪/四项诈骗罪
- **face** two charges of indecent assault 面临两项猥亵罪的指控
- **admit** your guilt/liability/responsibility (for sth) 承认（对某事的）罪责/责任
- **deny** the allegations/claims/charges 否认指控
- **confess to** a crime 坦白罪行
- **grant/be refused/be released on/skip/jump** bail 准许/不准保释；交保释金获释；弃保潜逃

The legal process 法律程序

- **stand/await/bring sb to/come to/be on** trial 受审；候审；把某人送交法院审判；开庭审理；受到审判
- **take sb to/come to/settle sth out of** court 把某人告上法庭；被法庭受理；庭外和解某事
- **face/avoid/escape** prosecution 面临/免于/逃脱起诉
- **seek/retain/have the right to/be denied access to** legal counsel 寻求/聘请/有权聘用/无权聘用律师
- **hold/conduct/attend/adjourn** a hearing/trial 开庭；出庭；休庭
- **sit on/influence/persuade/convince** the jury 担任/影响/说服陪审团
- **sit/stand/appear/be put/place sb** in the dock 坐在/站在/出现在/被送上/将某人送上被告席
- **plead** guilty/not guilty to a crime 认罪；不认罪
- **be called to/enter** (*BrE*) the witness box 被召唤进入/进入证人席
- **take/put sb on** the stand/(*NAmE*) the witness stand 出庭作证；让某人出庭作证
- **call/subpoena/question/cross-examine** a witness 传唤/以传票传唤/讯问/盘问证人
- **give/hear** the evidence against/on behalf of sb 提供/听取对某人不利/有利的证据
- **raise/withdraw/overrule** an objection 提出/撤销/否决异议
- **reach** a unanimous/majority verdict 作出一致的/多数人赞同的裁决
- **return/deliver/record** a verdict of not guilty/unlawful killing/accidental death 作出/宣布无罪/非法杀人/意外死亡的裁决
- **convict/acquit** the defendant of the crime 宣判被告有罪/无罪
- **secure** a conviction/your acquittal 获得有罪/无罪判决
- **lodge/file** an appeal 提出上诉
- **appeal (against)/challenge/uphold/overturn** a conviction/verdict 对判决/裁决提出上诉/质疑；维持/撤销判决/裁决

Sentencing and punishment 判刑与惩罚

- **pass** sentence on sb 宣布对某人的判决
- **carry/face/serve** a seven-year/life sentence 会被判处/面临/服七年徒刑/无期徒刑
- **receive/be given** the death penalty 被判死刑
- **be sentenced to** ten years (in prison/jail) 被判十年（监禁）
- **carry/impose/pay** a fine (of $3 000)/a penalty (of 14 years imprisonment) 会被判处/处以/缴纳（3 000 美元的）罚金/（14 年的）监禁
- **be imprisoned/jailed for** drug possession/fraud/murder 因持有毒品罪/诈骗罪/谋杀罪被监禁
- **do/serve** time/ten years 服刑；服十年徒刑
- **be sent to/put sb in/be released from** jail/prison 被送进监狱；把某人送进监狱；被释放出狱
- **be/put sb/spend X years** on death row 在/把某人关在死囚牢房；在死囚牢房度过…年
- **be granted/be denied/break (your)** parole 获准假释；假释遭拒；违反假释规定

➲ COLLOCATIONS AT CRIME

怎能证明付这么大笔薪金是正当的呢？ ◇ ~ sth *Her success had justified the faith her teachers had put in her.* 她的成功证明了老师对她的信任是正确的。 **2** ~ **sth/yourself** (**to sb**) | ~ (**sb/sth**) **doing sth** to give an explanation or excuse for sth or for doing sth 对…作出解释；为…辩解（或辩护） SYN **defend**: *The Prime Minister has been asked to justify the decision to Parliament.* 首相被要求就这一决定向议会解释。 ◇ *You don't need to justify yourself to me.* 你不必向我解释你的理由。 **3** ~ **sth** (*specialist*) to arrange lines of printed text so that one or both edges are straight 将（打印的字行）调整为边缘对齐 IDM SEE END *n.*

ˌjust-ˌin-ˈtime *adj.* (*abbr.* **JIT**) (*business* 商) used to describe a system in which parts or materials are only delivered to a factory just before they are needed 适时制（只有在需要时才将零部件或原材料送货到厂） ➲ WORDFINDER NOTE AT INDUSTRY

jut /dʒʌt/ *verb* (**-tt-**) [I, T] to stick out further than the surrounding surface, objects, etc.; to make sth stick out （使）突出，伸出 SYN **protrude, project**: ~ (**out**) (**from, into, over, etc. sth**) *A row of small windows jutted out from the roof.* 有一排小窗户从房顶上突出来。 ◇ *A rocky headland jutted into the sea.* 嶙峋的岬角突入海中。 ◇ *a jutting chin* 突出的下巴 ◇ ~ **sth** (**out**) *She jutted her chin out stubbornly.* 她倔强地把下巴翘得高高的。 ➲ MORE LIKE THIS 36, page R29

jute /dʒuːt/ *noun* [U] FIBRES (= thin threads) from a plant, also called jute, used for making rope and rough cloth 黄麻纤维

ju·ven·ile /ˈdʒuːvənaɪl; *NAmE* -vənl/ *adj.*, *noun*

■ ***adj.*** **1** [only before noun] (*formal* or *law* 律) connected with young people who are not yet adults 少年的；未成年的：*juvenile crime/employment* 少年犯罪；童工的雇用 ◇ *juvenile offenders* 少年罪犯 ➲ WORDFINDER NOTE AT AGE **2** (*disapproving*) silly and more typical of a child than an adult 幼稚的；不成熟的；孩子气的 SYN **childish**: *juvenile behaviour* 幼稚的行为 ◇ *Don't be so juvenile!* 别那么孩子气！

■ ***noun*** (*formal* or *law* 律) a young person who is not yet an adult 少年

ˌjuvenile ˈcourt *noun* a court that deals with young people who are not yet adults 少年法院；少年法庭

ˌjuvenile deˈlinquent *noun* a young person who is not yet an adult and who is guilty of committing a crime 少年犯 ▶ **ˌjuvenile deˈlinquency** *noun* [U]

ju·ven·ilia /ˌdʒuːvəˈnɪliə/ *noun* [pl.] (*formal*) writing, poetry, works of art, etc. produced by a writer or an artist when he/she was still young（统称某作家或艺术家的）少年时代作品

juxta·pose /ˌdʒʌkstəˈpəʊz; *NAmE* -ˈpoʊz/ *verb* [usually passive] ~ **A and/with B** (*formal*) to put people or things together, especially in order to show a contrast or a new relationship between them（尤指为对比或表明其新关系而）把…并置，把…并列：*In the exhibition, abstract paintings are juxtaposed with shocking photographs.* 展览会上抽象画与令人震惊的照片并列展出。 ▶ **juxta·pos·ition** /ˌdʒʌkstəpəˈzɪʃn/ *noun* [U, C]: *the juxtaposition of realistic and surreal situations in the novel* 小说中现实主义与超现实主义情节的并置

K /keɪ/ *noun, abbr., symbol*
■ ***noun*** (*also* **k**) [C, U] (*pl.* **Ks, K's, k's** /keɪz/) the 11th letter of the English alphabet 英语字母表的第 11 个字母：*'King' begins with (a) K/'K'.* * king 一词以字母 k 开头。
■ ***abbr.*** (*pl.* **K**) **1** (*informal*) one thousand 一千：*She earns 40K (= £40 000) a year.* 她一年挣 4 万英镑。 **2** kilometre(s) 千米；公里：*a 10K race* 万米赛跑 **3** (*computing* 计) kilobyte(s) 千字节 **4** KELVIN 开（温度单位）
■ ***symbol*** the symbol for the chemical element potassium（化学元素）钾

K-12 /ˌkeɪ ˈtwelv/ *adj.* (in the US) relating to education from KINDERGARTEN (= the class that prepares children for school) to 12th GRADE（美国）从幼儿园到 12 年级教育的，中小学及学前教育的

ka·baddi /ˈkʌbədi/ *noun* [U] a S Asian sport played by teams of seven players on a RECTANGULAR sand court. A player from one team tries to capture a player from the other team and must hold his/her breath while running. 卡巴迪（南亚运动比赛，每队各有七人参加，在长方形沙地上举行，运动员需屏气追逐对手）

Kab·ba·lah (*also* **Ca·bala**, **Qa·ba·lah**) /kəˈbɑːlə; ˈkæbələ/ *noun* (in Judaism 犹太教) the ancient tradition of explaining holy texts through MYSTICAL means 喀巴拉（犹太教神秘主义体系）

ka·buki /kəˈbuːki/ *noun* [U] (*from Japanese*) traditional Japanese theatre, in which songs, dance and MIME are performed by men 歌舞伎（日本传统剧种，由男子表演）

ka-ching (*BrE also* **ker-ching**) /kəˈtʃɪŋ/ (*NAmE also* **cha-ching**) *exclamation* (*informal*) used to say that sb is getting a lot of money 哗啦（表示赚大钱）：*The money was rolling in, ka-ching, ka-ching!* 财富哗啦啦地滚滚而来！◇ *Ka-ching! I just got my first cheque.* 哗啦！我刚得到第一张支票。 **ORIGIN** A way of representing the noise made by a CASH REGISTER. 源自对收银机声响的模仿。

kaffee·klatsch /ˈkæfeɪklætʃ/ *noun* (*NAmE, from German*) a social event at which people drink coffee 咖啡派对；咖啡叙谈会

Kaf·fir /ˈkæfə(r)/ *noun* (*taboo, slang*) a very offensive word for a black African 卡菲尔人（对非洲黑人的一种蔑称）

kaf·fi·yeh = KEFFIYEH

kafir /ˈkæfɪə(r); *NAmE* ˈkæfər/ *noun* a word used by Muslims to refer to a person who is not a Muslim, that can be considered offensive 卡菲尔（穆斯林对非伊斯兰教教徒的称呼，含侮慢意）

Kaf·ka·esque /ˌkæfkəˈesk/ *adj.* used to describe a situation that is confusing and frightening, especially one involving complicated official rules and systems that do not seem to make any sense 卡夫卡式的；恐怖而怪诞的：*My attempt to get a new passport turned into a Kafkaesque nightmare.* 我试图申请新护照的过程变成了一场官样文章的噩梦。 **ORIGIN** From the name of the Czech writer Franz Kafka, whose novels often describe situations like this. 源自捷克作家弗朗兹・卡夫卡（Kafka）的名字，他的小说经常描写此类情景。

kaf·tan (*also* **caf·tan**) /ˈkæftæn/ *noun* **1** a long loose piece of clothing, usually with a belt at the waist, worn by men in Arab countries（男式束腰带）阿拉伯长袍 **2** a woman's long loose dress with long wide sleeves 宽大长袖女袍

ka·goul = CAGOULE

ka·huna /kəˈhuːnə/ *noun* (*NAmE, informal*) an important person; the person in charge 要人；负责人

kai /kaɪ/ *noun* (*NZE, informal*) food 食物

kai·ser /ˈkaɪzə(r)/ *noun* (*from German*) **1 Kaiser** (in the past) a ruler of Germany, of Austria, or of the Holy Roman Empire （旧时德国、奥地利或神圣罗马帝国的）皇帝：*Kaiser Wilhelm* 威廉皇帝 **2** (*also* **ˈkaiser roll**) (*NAmE*) a crisp bread roll 王冠松脆小面包

kai·zen /ˌkaɪˈzen/ *noun* [U] (*business* 商, *from Japanese*) the practice of continuously improving the way in which a company operates （公司经营模式的）持续改进

kajal /ˈkʌdʒəl/ *noun* [U] a type of black make-up used by S Asian women, that is put around the edge of the eyes to make them more noticeable and attractive（南亚女子用的）黑色眼影，灯黑

ka·kuro /ˌkɑːˈkʊərəʊ; *NAmE* -ˈkʊroʊ/ *noun* (*pl.* **-os**) [C, U] (*from Japanese*) a number puzzle in which you have to put numbers into white spaces in a diagram so that their total is the number given in a black space 数谜游戏，数和（图表中的白格所填数字之和等于黑格所给数字）：*She loves doing kakuros.* 她喜欢玩数谜。 ➲ COMPARE SUDOKU

Ka·lash·ni·kov /kəˈlæʃnɪkɒf; *NAmE* -kɔːf/ *noun* a type of RIFLE (= a long gun) that can fire bullets very quickly 卡拉什尼科夫步枪（或冲锋枪）

kale /keɪl/ *noun* [U] a dark green vegetable like a CABBAGE 羽衣甘蓝

kal·eido·scope /kəˈlaɪdəskəʊp; *NAmE* -skoʊp/ *noun* **1** [C] a toy consisting of a tube that you look through with loose pieces of coloured glass and mirrors at the end. When the tube is turned, the pieces of glass move and form different patterns 万花筒 **2** [sing.] a situation, pattern, etc. containing a lot of different parts that are always changing （形势、图案等的）千变万化，瞬息万变 ▸ **kal·eido·scop·ic** /kəˌlaɪdəˈskɒpɪk; *NAmE* -ˈskɑːpɪk/ *adj.*

K

ka·meez /kəˈmiːz/ *noun* (*pl.* **ka·meez** or **ka·meezes**) a piece of clothing like a long shirt worn by many people from S Asia 克米兹（许多南亚人穿的及膝长袍）

kami·kaze /ˌkæmɪˈkɑːzi/ *adj.* [only before noun] (*from Japanese*) used to describe the way soldiers attack the enemy, knowing that they too will be killed （向敌人进攻的方式）神风队的，自杀性的 **SYN** **suicidal**：*a kamikaze pilot/attack* 神风队飞行员；自杀性攻击 ◇ (*figurative*) *He made a kamikaze run across three lanes of traffic.* 他不要命地冲过了三条车道。

kanga = KHANGA

kan·ga·roo /ˌkæŋɡəˈruː/ (*also informal* **roo**) *noun* (*pl.* **-oos**) a large Australian animal with a strong tail and back legs, that moves by jumping. The female carries its young in a pocket of skin (called a POUCH) on the front of its body. 袋鼠（产于澳大利亚） ➲ VISUAL VOCAB PAGE V12

ˌkangaroo ˈcourt *noun* (*disapproving*) an illegal court that punishes people unfairly 袋鼠法庭（不公正的非法法庭）；私设的公堂

kanji /ˈkændʒi; ˈkɑːn-/ *noun* [U, C] (*pl.* **kanji**) (*from Japanese*) a Japanese system of writing based on Chinese symbols, called CHARACTERS; a symbol in this system（日语中的）汉字体系；日本汉字

Kan·nada /ˈkænədə/ (*also* **Kan·ar·ese** /ˌkænəˈriːz/) *noun* [U] a language spoken in Karnataka in SW India 坎纳达语，建那陀语，卡纳拉语（印度西南部卡纳塔克邦语言）

kanzu /ˈkænzuː/ *noun* (in E Africa) a long loose piece of outer clothing made from white cloth and worn by men 康祖长袍（东非男子穿的白色宽大长外套）

kao·lin /ˈkeɪəlɪn/ (*also* ˌ**china** ˈ**clay**) *noun* [U] a type of fine white CLAY used in some medicines and in making PORCELAIN for cups, plates, etc. 高岭土；瓷土

kapok /ˈkeɪpɒk; *NAmE* -pɑːk/ *noun* [U] a soft white material used for filling CUSHIONS, soft toys, etc. 木棉

kappa /ˈkæpə/ *noun* the 10th letter of the Greek alphabet (Κ, κ) 希腊字母表的第 10 个字母

kaput /kəˈpʊt/ *adj.* [not before noun] (*informal*) not working correctly; broken 运转不正常；坏了：*The truck's kaput.* 卡车坏了。

kara·bin·er /ˌkærəˈbiːnə(r)/ *noun* a metal ring that can open to allow a rope to pass through, used by rock CLIMBERS to attach themselves safely to things（登山者使用的）穿索铁锁，岩钉钢环

kara·oke /ˌkæriˈəʊki; *NAmE* -ˈoʊki/ *noun* [U] (*from Japanese*) a type of entertainment in which a machine plays only the music of popular songs so that people can sing the words themselves 卡拉 OK：*a karaoke machine/night/bar* 卡拉 OK 机 / 之夜 / 酒吧

karat (*NAmE*) = CARAT (2)

kar·ate /kəˈrɑːti/ *noun* [U] a Japanese system of fighting in which you use your hands and feet as weapons 空手道：*a karate chop* (= a blow with the side of the hand) 空手道的掌侧劈

karma /ˈkɑːmə; *NAmE* ˈkɑːrmə/ *noun* [U] **1** (in Buddhism and Hinduism 佛教和印度教) the sum of sb's good and bad actions in one of their lives, believed to decide what will happen to them in the next life 羯磨，业（据信为可决定来生的个人善恶行为） **2 good/bad ~** (*informal*) the good/bad effect of doing a particular thing, being in a particular place, etc. 善报；恶报；因果报应：*Vegetarians believe that eating meat is bad karma.* 素食者认为吃肉食是造恶业。

K

kart /kɑːt; *NAmE* kɑːrt/ *noun* a small motor vehicle used for racing 小型赛车；卡丁赛车

kart·ing /ˈkɑːtɪŋ; *NAmE* ˈkɑːrt-/ *noun* [U] the sport of racing in karts 卡丁车比赛；卡丁车运动

kas·bah (*also* **cas·bah**) /ˈkæzbɑː/ *noun* a castle on high ground in a N African city or the area around it（北非城市高地的）城堡，城堡周围地区

ka·tab·ol·ism = CATABOLISM

kata·kana /ˌkætəˈkɑːnə/ *noun* [U] (*from Japanese*) a set of symbols used in Japanese writing, used especially to write foreign words or to represent noises（日语中的）片假名 ➲ COMPARE HIRAGANA

kayak /ˈkaɪæk/ *noun* a light CANOE in which the part where you sit is covered over（坐的部分遮盖起来的）皮艇，皮划艇 ➲ VISUAL VOCAB PAGE V60 ▸ **kayak·ing** *noun* [U]: *to go kayaking* 去划皮艇

kayo /keɪˈəʊ; *NAmE* -ˈoʊ/ *noun* (*pl.* **-os**) = KO

kazoo /kəˈzuː/ *noun* (*pl.* **-oos**) a small simple musical instrument consisting of a hollow pipe with a hole in it, that makes a BUZZING sound when you sing into it 卡佐膜管，卡祖笛（两端点有薄膜的短管，通过对着一个侧孔哼鸣或吟唱）

KB (*also* **K**) *abbr.* (in writing 书写形式) KILOBYTE 千字节（计算机内存或数据单位）

Kb (*also* **Kbit**) *abbr.* (in writing 书写形式) KILOBIT 千比特（计算机内存或数据单位）

Kbps *abbr.* (in writing 书写形式) kilobits per second (a unit for measuring the speed of a MODEM) 千位每秒，每秒千比特（调制解调器传输速度单位）

KC /ˌkeɪ ˈsiː/ *noun* the highest level of BARRISTER, who can speak for the government in court in Britain. KC is the abbreviation for 'King's Counsel' and is used when there is a king in Britain. 英国王室法律顾问，英国御用大律师（全写为 King's Counsel）➲ COMPARE QC

kebab /kɪˈbæb/ (*also* **ˈshish kebab** *especially in NAmE*) *noun* small pieces of meat and vegetables cooked on a wooden or metal stick 烤肉串 ➲ SEE ALSO DONER KEBAB

kedg·eree /ˈkedʒəriː/ *noun* [U] a hot dish of rice, fish and eggs cooked together 鱼蛋烩饭

keel /kiːl/ *noun, verb*

■ ***noun*** the long piece of wood or steel along the bottom of a ship, on which the frame is built, and which sometimes sticks out below the bottom and helps to keep it in a vertical position in the water（船的）龙骨 IDM SEE EVEN *adj.*

■ ***verb*** [I, T] **~ (sth) (over)** (of a ship or boat 船只) to fall over sideways; to make sth fall over sideways（使）倾覆，翻倒 SYN **capsize**

PHR V **ˌkeel ˈover** to fall over unexpectedly, especially because you feel ill/sick（尤因病或感到不适）突然倒下，晕倒：*Several of them keeled over in the heat.* 他们中有好几个人在酷暑中倒下。

keel·haul /ˈkiːlhɔːl/ *verb* **1 ~ sb** (*old use*) to punish a sailor by pulling him under a ship, from one side to the other or from one end to the other（把水手）拖曳过船底（作为惩罚） **2 ~ sb** (*humorous*) to punish sb very severely or speak very angrily to sb 重罚；怒斥

keema /ˈkiːmə/ *noun* [U] (*IndE*) meat that has been finely chopped; a spicy dish made using this ingredient 碎肉；肉末；咖喱肉末

keen 🔑 /kiːn/ *adj., verb*

■ ***adj.*** (**keen·er, keen·est**)

• **EAGER/ENTHUSIASTIC** 热切；热情 **1** 🔑 (*especially BrE*) wanting to do sth or wanting sth to happen very much 渴望；热切；热衷于 SYN **eager**: **~ (to do sth)** *John was very keen to help.* 约翰很热心，愿意帮忙。◇ **~ (that…)** *We are keen that our school should get involved too.* 我们盼着自己学校也参与其中。◇ **~ (on doing sth)** *I wasn't too keen on going to the party.* 我不太想去参加这次聚会。 **2** 🔑 [usually before noun] (*especially BrE*) enthusiastic about an activity or idea, etc. 热情的；热心的：*a keen sportsman* 热心运动的人 ◇ *one of the keenest supporters of the team* 这个队最热情的支持者之一

• **LIKING SB/STH** 喜爱 **3** 🔑 (*BrE, informal*) liking sb/sth very much; very interested in sb/sth 喜爱；（对…）着迷，有兴趣： **~ on sb/sth** *Tom's very keen on Anna.* 汤姆迷上了安娜。◇ **~ on doing sth** *She's not keen on being told what to do.* 她不喜欢别人向她发号施令。 ➲ SYNONYMS AT LIKE

• **CLEVER** 聪明 **4** [only before noun] quick to understand 思维敏捷的；机灵的；机智的 SYN **sharp, acute**: *a keen mind/intellect* 敏捷的思考 / 头脑

• **IDEAS/FEELINGS** 思想；感情 **5** [usually before noun] strong or deep 强烈的；浓厚的；深厚的：*a keen sense of tradition* 强烈的传统意识 ◇ *He took a* ***keen interest*** *in his grandson's education.* 他对孙子的教育很感兴趣。

• **SENSES** 感官 **6** [only before noun] highly developed 灵敏的；敏锐的 SYN **sharp**: *Dogs have a keen sense of smell.* 狗的嗅觉很灵敏。◇ *My friend has* ***a keen eye*** *for* (= is good at noticing) *a bargain.* 我的朋友最会发现便宜货。

• **COMPETITION** 竞争 **7** involving people competing very hard with each other for sth 激烈的；紧张的： *There is keen competition for places at the college.* 要在这所学院就读，竞争是非常激烈的。

• **PRICES** 价格 **8** (*especially BrE*) kept low in order to compete with other prices 低廉的；有竞争力的 SYN **competitive**

• **WIND** 风 **9** (*literary*) extremely cold 寒冷刺骨的

• **KNIFE** 刀 **10** [usually before noun] (*literary*) having a sharp edge or point 锋利的；锐利的 SYN **sharp**

▸ **keen·ly** *adv.* : *a keenly fought contest* 争夺激烈的比赛 ◇ *We were keenly aware of the danger.* 我们深知其危险。 **keen·ness** *noun* [U]

IDM **(as) ˌkeen as ˈmustard** (*BrE, informal*) wanting very much to do well at sth; enthusiastic 极其渴望；极为热心；非常热情 ➲ MORE AT MAD

■ ***verb*** [I] (usually used in the progressive tenses 通常用于进行时) (*old-fashioned*) to make a loud high sad sound, when sb has died（为死者）恸哭，哀号

keep 🔑 /kiːp/ *verb, noun*

■ ***verb*** (**kept, kept** /kept/)

• **STAY** 保持 **1** 🔑 [I, T] to stay in a particular condition or position; to make sb/sth do this（使）保持，处于： **+ adj.** *We huddled together to keep warm.* 我们挤在一起来保暖。◇ **+ adv./prep.** *The notice said 'Keep off* (= Do not walk on) *the grass'.* 牌子上写着"勿践踏草地"。◇ *Keep left along* *the wall.* 沿着墙靠左边走。◇ **~ sb/sth + adj.** *She kept the children amused for hours.* 她陪孩子们玩了好几个小时。◇ **~ sb/sth (+ adv./prep.)** *He kept his coat on.* 他一直穿着大衣。◇ *Don't* ***keep us in suspense****—what happened next?* 别跟我们卖关子了，接下来发生了什么事？◇ *She had trouble* ***keeping her balance.*** 她保持平衡有困难。◇ **~ sb/sth doing sth** *I'm very sorry to* ***keep you waiting.*** 对不起，让你久等了。

- **CONTINUE** 继续 **2** 🔑 [I] to continue doing sth; to do sth repeatedly 继续，重复（做某事）：**~ doing sth** *Keep smiling!* 要保持笑容！◇ **~ on doing sth** *Don't keep on interrupting me!* 别老是跟我打岔！
- **DELAY** 耽搁 **3** [T] **~ sb** to delay sb 使耽搁；使延误 **SYN** **hold sb/sth↔up**: *You're an hour late—what kept you?* 你晚了一小时，什么事把你给耽误了？
- **NOT GIVE BACK** 不退还 **4** 🔑 [T] **~ sth** to continue to have sth and not give it back or throw it away 保有；留着；不退还：*Here's a five dollar bill—please* ***keep the change.*** 给你一张五美元的钞票，零钱就不用找了。◇ *I keep all her letters.* 我把她所有的信都保留着。
- **SAVE FOR SB** 为某人保留 **5** 🔑 [T] (*especially BrE*) to save sth for sb（为某人）保留，留下：**~ sth for sb** *Please keep a seat for me.* 请给我留个座位。◇ **~ sb sth** *Please keep me a seat.* 请给我留个座位。
- **PUT/STORE** 放；存放 **6** 🔑 [T] **~ sth + adv./prep.** to put or store sth in a particular place 放，存放，贮存（在某处）：*Keep your passport in a safe place.* 把你的护照放在安全的地方。
- **SHOP/RESTAURANT** 商店；餐馆 **7** [T] **~ sth** (*especially BrE*) to own and manage a shop/store or restaurant 开设，经营，管理（商店或餐馆）：*Her father kept a grocer's shop.* 她父亲开了个杂货店。
- **ANIMALS** 动物 **8** [T] **~ sth** to own and care for animals 养；饲养：*to* ***keep*** *bees/goats/hens* 养蜜蜂 / 山羊 / 母鸡
- **ABOUT HEALTH** 健康 **9** [I] **+ adv./prep.** (*informal*) used to ask or talk about sb's health（询问或谈论某人的健康）：*How is your mother* ***keeping****?* 你母亲身体好吗？◇ *We're all keeping well.* 我们都很健康。
- **OF FOOD** 食物 **10** [I] to remain in good condition 保持不坏：*Finish off the pie—it won't keep.* 把馅饼都吃了吧，这东西不耐放。◇ (*informal, figurative*) *'I'd love to hear about it, but I'm late already.' 'That's OK—****it'll keep*** (= I can tell you about it later).' "我很想听听，不过我已经迟到了。" "好吧，我以后再告诉你。"
- **SECRET** 秘密 **11** 🔑 [T] **~ a secret | ~ sth secret (from sb)** to know sth and not tell it to anyone 保守（秘密）：*Can you keep a secret?* 你能保守秘密吗？◇ *She kept her past secret from us all.* 她对我们所有人都避而不谈她的过去。
- **PROMISE/APPOINTMENT** 承诺；约会 **12** 🔑 [T] **~ your promise/word | ~ an appointment** to do what you have promised to do; to go where you have agreed to go 遵守；笃守；恪守：*She kept her promise to visit them.* 她遵守诺言去看望了他们。◇ *He failed to keep his appointment at the clinic.* 他未能按预约的时间去诊所。
- **DIARY/RECORD** 日记；记录 **13** 🔑 [T] **~ a diary, an account, a record, etc.** to write down sth as a record 记下，记录，记载（日记、账目、记录等）：*She kept a diary for over twenty years.* 她记了二十多年的日记。◇ *Keep a note of where each item can be found.* 把每样物品的位置记录下来。
- **SUPPORT SB** 供养 **14** 🔑 [T] **~ sb/yourself** to provide what is necessary for sb to live; to support sb by paying for food, etc. 供养；养活：*He scarcely earns enough to keep himself and his family.* 他挣的钱几乎不够养活他自己和家人。
- **PROTECT** 保护 **15** [T] (*formal*) to protect sb from sth 保护；使免受：**~ sb** *May the Lord bless you and keep you* (= used in prayers in the Christian Church). 愿上帝祝福你、保佑你（用于基督教的祈祷）。◇ **~ sb from sth** *His only thought was to keep the boy from harm.* 他一心想的就是不要让这男孩受到伤害。
- **IN SPORT** 体育运动 **16** [T] **~ goal** (*BrE, NAmE*) **| ~ wicket** (*BrE*) (in football (SOCCER), HOCKEY, CRICKET, etc. 足球、曲棍球、板球等) to guard or protect the goal or WICKET 守门；把守球门 ➲ SEE ALSO GOALKEEPER, WICKETKEEPER

IDM **HELP** Most idioms containing **keep** are at the entries for the nouns and adjectives in the idioms, for example **keep house** is at **house**. 大多数含 keep 的习语，都可在该等习语中的名词及形容词相关词条找到，如 keep house 在词条 house 下。 **ˌkeep ˈgoing 1** 🔑 to make an effort to live normally when you are in a difficult situation or when you have experienced great suffering（在身处困境或遭难时）尽力维持下去，坚持活下去：*You just have to keep yourself busy and keep going.* 你必须让自己忙起来并坚持下去。 **2** 🔑 (*informal*) used to encourage sb to continue doing sth（用于鼓励）继续下去，坚持下去：*Keep going, Sarah, you're nearly there.* 坚持下去，萨拉，你已经快到了。 **ˌkeep sb ˈgoing** (*informal*) to be enough for sb until they get what they are waiting for 足以使某人维持（或支撑）：*Have an apple to keep you going till dinner time.* 吃个苹果就能挨到吃晚饭了。

PHR V **ˌkeep sb ˈafter** (*NAmE*) (*BrE* **ˌkeep sb↔ˈback**) to make a student stay at school after normal hours as a punishment 罚（学生）课后留校

ˌkeep ˈat sth to continue working at sth 继续做某事（或坚持干）：*Come on, keep at it, you've nearly finished!* 快，要坚持，你马上就要完成了！ **ˌkeep sb ˈat sth** to make sb continue working at sth 使某人继续做（或坚持干）某事：*He kept us at it all day.* 他让我们不停地干了一天。

ˌkeep aˈway (from sb/sth) to avoid going near sb/sth 避免接近；远离；勿靠近：*Keep away from the edge of the cliff.* 切莫靠近悬崖边。 **ˌkeep sb/sth aˈway (from sb/sth)** to prevent sb/sth from going somewhere 不让接近某人（或某事物）；使离开：*Her illness kept her away from work for several weeks.* 她病得好几周都上不了班。

ˌkeep ˈback (from sb/sth) to stay at a distance from sb/sth（与…）保持距离：*Keep well back from the road.* 离公路远些。 **ˌkeep sb↔ˈback 1** (*BrE*) (*NAmE* **ˌkeep sb ˈafter**) to make a student stay at school after normal hours as a punishment 罚（学生）课后留校 **2** (*NAmE*) to make a student repeat a year at school because of poor marks/grades 使（学生）留级 **ˌkeep sb↔ˈback (from sb/sth)** to make sb stay at a distance from sb/sth 使某人（与…）保持距离：*Barricades were erected to keep back the crowds.* 设置了障碍，使人群无法靠近。 **ˌkeep sth↔ˈback 1** to prevent a feeling, etc. from being expressed 抑制（或阻止）感情等的流露 **SYN** **restrain**: *She was unable to keep back her tears.* 她无法忍住泪水。 **2** to continue to have a part of sth 保留（或扣留）某物的一部分：*He kept back half the money for himself.* 他把那笔钱留了一半给自己。 **ˌkeep sth↔ˈback (from sb)** to refuse to tell sb sth 拒绝告知某事；隐瞒：*I'm sure she's keeping something back from us.* 我肯定她有什么事瞒着我们。

ˌkeep ˈdown to hide yourself by not standing up straight 隐蔽；隐伏；卧倒；蹲下：*Keep down! You mustn't let anyone see you.* 蹲下！千万不要让人看见你。 **ˌkeep sb↔ˈdown** to prevent a person, group, etc. from expressing themselves freely 压制（或限制、控制）某人 **SYN** **oppress**: *The people have been kept down for years by a brutal regime.* 多年来人们一直受到残暴统治的压制。 **ˌkeep sth↔ˈdown 1** to make sth stay at a low level; to avoid increasing sth 使保持在低水平；抑制某事物的增长：*to keep down wages/prices/the cost of living* 保持低工资 / 物价 / 生活费用 ◇ *Keep your voice down—I don't want anyone else to hear.* 小声点儿，别让人听见。◇ *Keep the noise down* (= be quiet). 小声点儿。 **2** to not bring sth back through the mouth from the stomach; to not VOMIT 不使（胃中食物）吐出；不呕吐：*She's had some water but she can't keep any food down.* 她喝了点儿水，但一吃东西就吐。

ˈkeep from sth | ˈkeep yourself from sth to prevent yourself from doing sth 忍住（或克制自己）不做某事：**keep from doing sth** *She could hardly keep from laughing.* 她差一点儿笑了出来。◇ *I just managed to keep myself from falling.* 我差一点儿没摔倒。 **ˈkeep sb from sth** to prevent sb from doing sth 阻止（或防止、阻碍）某人做某事：*I hope I'm not keeping you from your work.* 希望我没有妨碍你工作。◇ **keep sb from doing sth** *The church bells keep me from sleeping.* 教堂的钟声使我不能入睡。 **ˈkeep sth from sb** to avoid telling sb sth 不将某事告诉某人；瞒着某人：*I think we ought to keep the truth from him until he's better.* 我想我们应该等他身体好些再告诉他实情。 **ˈkeep sth from sth** to make sth stay out of sth 使置于

K

某物之外；使与某物分开：*She could not keep the dismay from her voice.* 她无法使自己沉重的心情不流露在话音之中。

ˌ**keep ˈin with sb** (*BrE, informal*) to make sure that you stay friendly with sb, because you will get an advantage from doing so（为得到好处而）与某人友好相处，不得罪某人 ˌ**keep sth↔ˈin** to avoid expressing an emotion 控制（或抑制）感情 **SYN** **restrain**：*He could scarcely keep in his indignation.* 他几乎控制不住自己的愤怒。ˌ**keep sb ˈin** to make sb stay indoors or in a particular place 使某人留在室内（或某地）；使不外出 ˈ**keep sb/yourself in sth** to provide sb/yourself with a regular supply of sth 向某人持续供应某物

ˌ**keep ˈoff** if rain, snow, etc. **keeps off**, it does not fall（雨、雪等）未下 ˌ**keep ˈoff sth** **1** to avoid eating, drinking or smoking sth 避免吃（或喝、吸）某物：*I'm trying to keep off fatty foods.* 我尽量不吃高脂肪食物。**2** to avoid mentioning a particular subject 回避某话题：*It's best to keep off politics when my father's around.* 我父亲在场时最好不要谈论政治。ˌ**keep sb/sth↔ˈoff** | ˌ**keep sb/sth ˈoff sb/sth** to prevent sb/sth from coming near, touching, etc. sb/sth 使…不接近（或不接触、远离）某人/事物：*They lit a fire to keep off wild animals.* 他们点燃篝火防止野兽靠近。◇ *Keep your hands off* (= do not touch) *me!* 别碰我！

ˌ**keep ˈon** to continue 继续：*Keep on until you get to the church.* 一直往前走到教堂。ˌ**keep sb↔ˈon** to continue to employ sb 继续雇用某人 ˌ**keep sth ˈon** to continue to rent a house, flat/apartment, etc. 继续租用房子（或套房等）ˌ**keep ˈon (at sb) (about sb/sth)** (*especially BrE*) to speak to sb often and in an annoying way about sb/sth（对…）纠缠不休；老是困扰；老是唠叨 **SYN** **go on, nag**：*He does keep on so!* 他就是这样纠缠不休！◇ *I'll do it—just don't keep on at me about it!* 我会做的，就别再对我唠叨了！

ˌ**keep ˈout (of sth)** 🔑 to not enter a place; to stay outside 不进入；留在外面：*The sign said 'Private Property—Keep Out!'* 告示牌上写着"私人产业，不得入内！" ˌ**keep sb/sth↔ˈout (of sth)** to prevent sb/sth from entering a place 使不进入；防止进入；把…关在外面：*Keep that dog out of my study!* 别让那狗进我的书房！ ˌ**keep ˈout of sth** | ˌ**keep sb ˈout of sth** 🔑 to avoid sth; to prevent sb from being involved in sth or affected by sth 避免某事；使不卷入某事；使置身于…之外；使不受…的影响：*That child can't keep out of mischief.* 那孩子总是胡闹。◇ *Keep the baby out of the sun.* 别让孩子晒着。

ˈ**keep to sth** **1** to avoid leaving a path, road, etc. 不偏离（或不离开）道路等 **SYN** **stick to sth**：*Keep to the track—the land is very boggy around here.* 顺着道儿走，这一带到处是沼泽地。**2** to talk or write only about the subject that you are supposed to talk or write about 不偏离主题；不跑题：*Nothing is more irritating than people who do not **keep to the point**.* 最烦人的就是那些谈话不着边际的人。**3** to do what you have promised or agreed to do 遵守（或信守、履行）诺言：*to keep to an agreement/an undertaking/a plan* 遵守协议；信守承诺；执行计划 **4** to stay in and not leave a particular place or position 坚守，不离开（某地或某个位置）：*She's nearly 90 and mostly keeps to her room.* 她快 90 岁了，大部分时间都待在房间里。ˌ**keep (yourself) to yourˈself** to avoid meeting people socially or becoming involved in their affairs 离群索居；不与人往来；不管别人的事：*Nobody knows much about him; he keeps himself very much to himself.* 谁对他都不太了解，因为他很少和人交往。ˌ**keep sth to yourˈself** to not tell other people about sth 对…秘而不宣（或保守秘密）；不将…说出去：*I'd be grateful if you kept this information to yourself.* 你要是不把这消息传出去，我会不胜感激的。

ˌ**keep sb ˈunder** to control or OPPRESS sb 控制，压制（人）：*The local people are kept under by the army.* 当地居民受军队管制。

ˌ**keep ˈup** if particular weather **keeps up**, it continues without stopping（天气）持续不变：*The rain kept up all afternoon.* 雨下了整整一个下午。ˌ**keep ˈup (with sb/sth)** 🔑 to move, make progress or increase at the same rate as sb/sth（与…）齐步前进，并驾齐驱；跟上：*Slow down—I can't keep up!* 慢点，我跟不上了！◇ *I can't keep up with all the changes.* 我并非所有的变化都能跟得上。◇ *Wages are not keeping up with inflation.* 工资赶不上通货膨胀。 ˌ**keep ˈup with sb** to continue to be in contact with sb 与（某人）保持联系：*How many of your old school friends do you keep up with?* 你与多少老同学保持着联系？ ˌ**keep ˈup with sth** **1** 🔑 to learn about or be aware of the news, current events, etc. 熟悉，了解（消息、形势等）：*She likes to keep up with the latest fashions.* 她喜欢赶时髦。**2** 🔑 to continue to pay or do sth regularly 继续支付；继续做：*If you do not keep up with the payments you could lose your home.* 如果你不继续付款，你的住房就可能保不住了。ˌ**keep sb ˈup** to prevent sb from going to bed 使某人熬夜（或开夜车、不睡觉）：*I hope we're not keeping you up.* 希望我们没有耽误你睡觉。 ˌ**keep sth↔ˈup** **1** 🔑 to make sth stay at a high level 使某事物保持在高水平：*The high cost of raw materials is keeping prices up.* 昂贵的原料费用使价格居高不下。**2** 🔑 to continue sth at the same, usually high, level 使某事物保持（在同一水平，通常指高水平）：*The enemy kept up the bombardment day and night.* 敌人昼夜轰炸不停。◇ *We're having difficulty keeping up our mortgage payments.* 我们难以继续偿还按揭贷款。◇ *Well done! **Keep up the good work/Keep it up!*** 干得好！继续好好干吧！**3** to make sth remain at a high level 使处于高水平；使不低落：*They sang songs to keep their spirits up.* 他们唱歌以保持高昂的情绪。**4** to continue to use or practise sth 沿用（或沿袭、保持）某事物：*to keep up old traditions* 保持老传统 ◇ *Do you still keep up your Spanish?* 你还坚持说西班牙语吗？ **5** to take care of a house, garden/yard, etc. so that it stays in good condition 保养，维护（房屋、花园等）**SYN** **maintain** ➲ RELATED NOUN UPKEEP

■ *noun* **1** [U] food, clothes and all the other things that a person needs to live; the cost of these things 生活必需品；生活费用：*It's about time you got a job to **earn your keep**.* 你该找个工作挣自己的生活费了。**2** [C] a large strong tower, built as part of an old castle 城堡主楼

IDM **for ˈkeeps** (*informal*) for ever 永远；永久：*Is it yours for keeps or does he want it back?* 这东西是永远属于你了，还是要还给他？ ➲ MORE AT EARN

keep·er /ˈkiːpə(r)/ *noun* **1** (especially in compounds 尤用于构成复合词) a person whose job is to take care of a building, its contents or sth valuable 看守人；保管人：*the keeper of geology at the museum* 博物馆地质资料的保管人 ➲ SEE ALSO SHOPKEEPER **2** a person whose job is to take care of animals, especially in a zoo（尤指动物园的）饲养员 ➲ SEE ALSO GAMEKEEPER, ZOOKEEPER **3** (*BrE, informal*) = GOALKEEPER, WICKETKEEPER **4** (*informal*) something that is worth keeping 值得保留的东西 **IDM** SEE FINDER

ˌ**keep-ˈfit** *noun* [U] (*BrE*) physical exercises that you do, usually in a class with other people, in order to improve your strength and to stay healthy（集体）健身锻炼，健身操：*a keep-fit class* 健身班

keep·ing /ˈkiːpɪŋ/ *noun*

IDM **in sb's ˈkeeping** being taken care of by sb 由某人照料（或供养、饲养）➲ SEE ALSO SAFE KEEPING **in ˈkeeping (with sth)** appropriate or expected in a particular situation; in agreement with sth（与…）协调，一致：*The latest results are in keeping with our earlier findings.* 最新结果与我们先前的发现一致。 **out of ˈkeeping (with sth)** not appropriate or expected in a particular situation; not in agreement with sth（与…）不协调，不一致：*The painting is out of keeping with the rest of the room.* 这幅画和这屋子的其他陈设不协调。

keep·sake /ˈkiːpseɪk/ *noun* a small object that sb gives you so that you will remember them 纪念品 **SYN** **memento**

kef·fi·yeh (*also* **kaf·fi·yeh**) /kəˈfiːjə/ *noun* a square of cloth worn on the head by Arab men and fastened by a band（阿拉伯男子戴的）方头巾

keg /keg/ *noun* **1** [C] a round wooden or metal container with a flat top and bottom, used especially for storing beer, like a BARREL but smaller（尤指盛啤酒的）小桶 **2** [U] (*BrE*) = KEG BEER

ˈkeg beer (*BrE also* **keg**) *noun* [U, C] (in Britain) beer served from metal containers, using gas pressure（英国，用气压出的）桶装啤酒

kei·rin /keɪˈrɪn; *BrE also* ˈkɪərɪn/ *noun* [U] a racing event in which people cycle a number of times around an indoor track, initially following a small bicycle with a motor and then competing against each other to complete the race 自行车凯林赛（参赛者先是跟在一辆小型摩托车后在室内赛道上完成一定圈数，然后彼此竞速争取最先通过终点）

keis·ter /ˈkiːstə(r)/ *noun* (*NAmE, informal*) the part of the body that you sit on 屁股 SYN **bottom**

Kejia /keɪˈdʒjɑː/ *noun* = HAKKA

kelim /kəˈliːm; ˈkelɪm; *NAmE* kiːˈliːm; ˈkeləm/ *noun* = KILIM

kelp /kelp/ *noun* [U] a type of brown SEAWEED, sometimes used as a FERTILIZER to help plants grow 海带；巨型海藻

kel·pie /ˈkelpi/ *noun* **1** (in Scottish stories 苏格兰传说) a water spirit 水妖 **2** an Australian SHEEPDOG（澳大利亚）卡尔比犬

kel·vin /ˈkelvɪn/ *noun* (*abbr.* **K**) (*pl.* **kel·vin** or **kel·vins**) a unit for measuring temperature. One kelvin is equal to one degree Celsius, but the **Kelvin scale** starts at ABSOLUTE ZERO and water freezes at 273.15 kelvin. 开（开尔文温标的计量单位，1 开相当于 1 摄氏度，但以绝对零度为计算起点，水的冰点为 273.15 开）

the ˌKelvin ˈscale *noun* [sing.] a scale of temperature in which water freezes at 273.15 degrees 绝对温标；热力学温标；开尔文温标；开氏温标

ken /ken/ *noun, verb*

■ ***noun***

IDM **beyond your ken** (*old-fashioned*) if sth is **beyond your ken**, you do not know enough about it to be able to understand it 为某人所不理解；在某人的知识范围之外

■ ***verb*** **(-nn-)** [I, T] **~ (sth) | ~ (that)... | ~ what, where, etc....** (*ScotE, NEngE*) to know 知道；懂得 HELP **Kent** is the usual form of the past tense used in Scotland. 在苏格兰过去时常用 kent。

kendo /ˈkendəʊ; *NAmE* -doʊ/ *noun* [U] (*from Japanese*) a Japanese form of the sport of FENCING, using light wooden weapons 剑道（日本剑术，用轻木质剑）

ken·nel /ˈkenl/ *noun* **1** (*NAmE* **dog·house**) a small shelter for a dog to sleep in 狗窝；犬舍 **2** (*usually* **kennels**) [C+sing./pl. v.] a place where people can leave their dogs to be taken care of when they go on holiday/vacation; a place where dogs are bred（寄养狗的）养狗场；狗繁殖场：*We put the dog **in kennels** when we go away.* 我们外出时把狗寄养在养狗场。➲ SEE ALSO BOARDING KENNEL

kept PAST TENSE, PAST PART. OF KEEP

ˌkept ˈwoman *noun* (*old-fashioned, usually humorous*) a woman who is given money and a home by a man who visits her regularly to have sex（被包养的）姘妇，情妇

kera·tin /ˈkerətɪn/ *noun* [U] (*biology* 生) a PROTEIN that forms hair, feathers, horns, HOOFS, etc.（发、羽、角、蹄等的）角蛋白

kerb (*BrE*) (*NAmE* **curb**) /kɜːb; *NAmE* kɜːrb/ *noun* the edge of the raised path at the side of a road, usually made of long pieces of stone（由条石砌成的）路缘；道牙；马路牙子：*The bus mounted the kerb* (= went onto the PAVEMENT/SIDEWALK) *and hit a tree.* 那辆公共汽车开上路缘撞到了一棵树。➲ VISUAL VOCAB PAGE V3

ˈkerb-crawling *noun* [U] (*BrE*) the crime of driving slowly along a road in order to find a PROSTITUTE 路边慢驶招妓（的罪行） ▶ **ˈkerb-crawler** *noun*

kerb·side (*BrE*) (*NAmE* **curb·side**) /ˈkɜːbsaɪd; *NAmE* ˈkɜːrb-/ *noun* [U] the side of the street or path near the kerb 人行道靠近路缘的部分：*to stand at the kerbside* 站在马路牙子上

kerb·stone (*BrE*) (*NAmE* **curb·stone**) /ˈkɜːbstəʊn; *NAmE* ˈkɜːrbstoʊn/ *noun* a block of stone or concrete in a KERB/CURB 路缘石

ker·chief /ˈkɜːtʃɪf; *NAmE* ˈkɜːrtʃɪf/ *noun* (*old-fashioned*) a square piece of cloth worn on the head or around the neck 方头巾；方围巾

ker-ching *exclamation* (*BrE, informal*) = KA-CHING

ker·fuf·fle /kəˈfʌfl; *NAmE* kərˈf-/ *noun* [sing.] (*BrE, informal*) unnecessary excitement or activity（不必要的）骚动，混乱，喧闹 SYN **commotion, fuss**

ker·nel /ˈkɜːnl; *NAmE* ˈkɜːrnl/ *noun* **1** the inner part of a nut or seed（坚果或籽粒的）仁，核 **2** the central, most important part of an idea or a subject（思想或主题的）核心，中心，要点

kero·sene (*also* **kero·sine**) /ˈkerəsiːn/ *noun* [U] a type of fuel oil that is made from PETROLEUM and that is used in the engines of planes and for heat and light. In British English it is usually called PARAFFIN when it is used for heat and light. 煤油：*a kerosene lamp* 煤油灯

kes·trel /ˈkestrəl/ *noun* a small BIRD OF PREY (= a bird that kills other creatures for food) of the FALCON family 红隼（小猛禽）

KET /ket/ *noun* [U] the abbreviation for 'Key English Test' (a British test, now called 'Cambridge English: Key', set by the University of Cambridge, that measures a person's ability to speak and write English as a foreign language at a basic level) 英语入门考试，剑桥英语第一级认证（全写为 Key English Test，现称 Cambridge English: Key，英国考试，检测英语作为外语者的初级口语和写作能力）

keta·mine /ˈkiːtəmiːn/ (*also informal* **ket** /kiːt/) *noun* [U] a substance that is used as an ANAESTHETIC, and also as a drug that is taken illegally for pleasure 氯胺酮，K 粉（用作麻醉剂，也用作毒品）

ketch /ketʃ/ *noun* a sailing boat with two MASTS (= posts to support the sails) 双桅帆船

ketchup /ˈketʃəp/ *noun* [U] a thick cold sauce made from tomatoes, usually sold in bottles 番茄酱

ket·tle /ˈketl/ *noun, verb*

■ ***noun*** a container with a lid, handle and a SPOUT, used for boiling water（烧水用的）壶，水壶：*an electric kettle* 电水壶 ◇ (*BrE*) *I'll **put the kettle on*** (= start boiling some water) *and make some tea.* 我要烧壶水沏茶。➲ VISUAL VOCAB PAGE V26 IDM SEE DIFFERENT, POT *n.*

■ ***verb*** [T, I] (of the police 警方) to keep a group of people who are taking part in a DEMONSTRATION or protest confined in an area with only one exit or no immediate way out, in order to help restore order 围堵，圈围（将游行示威者限制在只有一个出口或无直接出口的区域）：*Hundreds of protesters were kettled at the start of the demonstration.* 数百名抗议者在游行开始时就被警方围堵在只有一个出口的区域。 ▶ **kettling** *noun* [U]: *Police used tactics such as kettling in an attempt to bring an end to the protest.* 警方使用了将抗议者圈围在单一出口区域等手段，以图结束抗议。

kettle·drum /ˈketldrʌm/ *noun* a large metal drum with a round bottom and a thin plastic top that can be made looser or tighter to produce different musical notes. A set of kettledrums is usually called TIMPANI. 定音鼓；锅鼓 ➲ VISUAL VOCAB PAGE V37

Kev·lar™ /ˈkevlɑː(r)/ *noun* [U] an artificial substance used to give strength to tyres and other rubber products 凯夫拉尔纤维（用于强化轮胎等橡胶制品）

key /kiː/ *noun, verb, adj.*

■ ***noun***

• **TOOL FOR LOCK** 开锁工具 **1** a specially shaped piece of metal used for locking a door, starting a car, etc. 钥匙：*to insert/turn the key in the lock* 把钥匙插入锁孔；转动锁孔中的钥匙 ◇ *the car keys* 汽车钥匙 ◇ *a bunch of keys* 一串

K

钥匙 ◇ *the spare key to the front door* 前门备用钥匙 ◇ *We'll have a duplicate key cut* (= made). 我们会配一把钥匙。

• **MOST IMPORTANT THING** 最重要的事 **2** [usually sing.] a thing that makes you able to understand or achieve sth 关键；要诀 SYN **secret**: ~ (**to sth**) *The key to success is preparation.* 成功的关键是准备。 ◇ ~ (**to doing sth**) *The driver of the car probably holds the key to solving the crime.* 这位汽车司机很可能掌握侦破这一罪案的关键证据。 ◇ (*especially NAmE*) ***The key is**, how long can the federal government control the inflation rate?* 关键在于联邦政府对通货膨胀率的控制能维持多久？

• **ON COMPUTER** 计算机 **3** any of the buttons that you press to operate a computer or TYPEWRITER（计算机或打字机的）键：*Press the return key to enter the information.* 按回车键录入信息。

• **ON MUSICAL INSTRUMENT** 乐器 **4** any of the wooden or metal parts that you press to play a piano and some other musical instruments（钢琴或其他乐器的）键 ➲ VISUAL VOCAB PAGE V38

• **MUSIC** 音乐 **5** a set of related notes, based on a particular note. Pieces of music are usually written mainly using a particular key. 调：*a sonata in the key of E flat major* 一首降 E 大调奏鸣曲 ➲ COMPARE SCALE *n.* (7)

• **ANSWERS** 答案 **6** a set of answers to exercises or problems 答案；题解：*Check your answers in the key at the back of the book.* 用书后的解答核对答案。

• **ON MAP** 地图 **7** an explanation of the symbols used on a map or plan（地图或平面图的）符号说明，图例 ➲ WORDFINDER NOTE AT MAP ➲ SEE ALSO LOW-KEY IDM SEE LOCK *n.*

■ ***verb* 1** ~ **sth (in)** | ~ **sth (into sth)** to put information into a computer using a keyboard 用键盘输入；键入 SYN **enter**: *Key (in) your password.* 用键盘输入密码。 **2** to deliberately damage a car by scratching it with a key 用钥匙划坏（汽车）

PHR V **'key sb/sth to sth** [usually passive] (*especially NAmE*) to make sb/sth suitable or appropriate for a particular purpose 使某人（或某事）适合于某事 SYN **gear**: *The classes are keyed to the needs of advanced students.* 这些课是针对高年级学生的需要开设的。

■ ***adj.*** [usually before noun] most important; essential 最重要的；主要的；关键的 SYN **critical, vital**: *the **key** issue/factor/point* 关键问题 / 因素；要点 ◇ *He was a **key figure** in the campaign.* 他是这场运动的关键人物。 ◇ *She played a **key role** in the dispute.* 她在争论中起着举足轻重的作用。 ◇ *'Caution' is the **key word** in this situation.* 在此情形之下，caution 为关键词。 ◇ *Good communication is key to our success.* 良好的沟通是我们成功的关键。 ◇ *His contribution could be key.* 他的贡献可能是最重要的。 ➲ SYNONYMS AT MAIN

keys 钥匙；键；图例

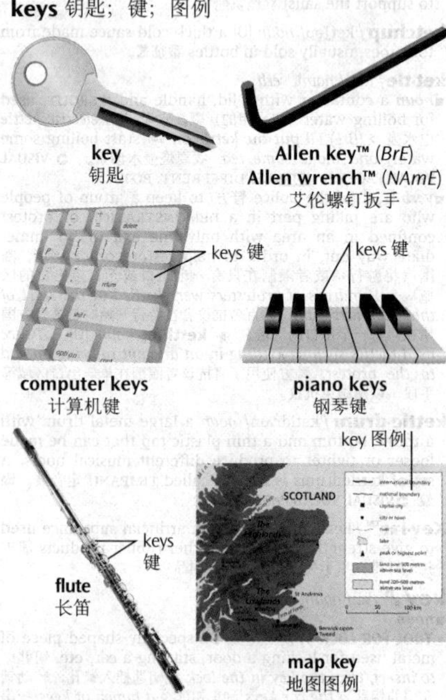

key 钥匙

Allen key™ (*BrE*) Allen wrench™ (*NAmE*) 艾伦螺钉扳手

computer keys 计算机键

piano keys 钢琴键

flute 长笛

map key 地图图例

key·board /'kiːbɔːd; *NAmE* -bɔːrd/ *noun, verb*

■ ***noun* 1** the set of keys for operating a computer or TYPEWRITER, or the set of letters that you can click on to write on a SMARTPHONE or TABLET (4)（计算机或打字机的）键盘；（智能手机或平板电脑的）虚拟键盘 ➲ WORDFINDER NOTE AT COMPUTER ➲ VISUAL VOCAB PAGE V73

WORDFINDER 联想词：backspace, click, control, cursor, escape, return, shift, slash, space bar

2 the set of black and white keys on a piano or other musical instrument（钢琴或其他乐器的）琴键，键盘 ➲ VISUAL VOCAB PAGE V40 **3** an electronic musical instrument that has keys like a piano and can be made to play in different styles or to sound like different instruments 键盘式电子乐器 ➲ COMPARE SYNTHESIZER

■ ***verb*** [T, I] ~ (**sth**) to type information into a computer 用键盘输入；将（信息）键入计算机 ▶ **key·board·ing** *noun* [U]

key·board·er /'kiːbɔːdə(r); *NAmE* -bɔːrd-/ *noun* a person whose job is to type data into a computer 操作键盘的人；键盘输入员

key·board·ist /'kiːbɔːdɪst; *NAmE* -bɔːrd-/ *noun* a person who plays an electronic musical instrument with a keyboard 键盘（乐器）手

'key card *noun* (*especially NAmE*) a special plastic card with information recorded on it which can be read by an electronic device that can be used instead of a door key 门禁卡；门卡 ➲ SEE ALSO SWIPE CARD

ˌkeyed 'up *adj.* [not before noun] nervous and excited, especially before an important event（尤指重要事件前）紧张不安，激动万分

key·hole /'kiːhəʊl; *NAmE* -hoʊl/ *noun* the hole in a lock that you put a key in 锁眼；钥匙孔

ˌkeyhole 'surgery *noun* [U] (*especially BrE*) medical operations which involve only a very small cut being made in the patient's body 微创手术

key·log·ger /'kiːlɒɡə(r); *NAmE* -lɔːɡ-; -lɑːɡ-/ *noun* (*computing* 计) a computer program that records all the keys that a user hits so that it is possible to discover secret information such as code words 按键记录程序；键盘监听程序

key·note /'kiːnəʊt; *NAmE* -noʊt/ *noun* **1** [usually sing.] the central idea of a book, a speech, etc.（书、演说等的）要旨，主题，基调：*Choice is the keynote of the new education policy.* 新教育政策的主导原则是容许选择。 ◇ *a **keynote speech/speaker*** (= a very important one, introducing a meeting or its subject) 主题发言；主要发言人 **2** (*music* 音) the note on which the KEY is based 主音 ▶ **key·noter** *noun* : *For the first time, a woman will be the keynoter at the convention this year.* 在今年的大会上将首次由一位女士当主要发言人。

key·pad /'kiːpæd/ *noun* a small set of buttons with numbers on used to operate a telephone, a television or an electronic device 数字键盘；辅助键盘；按键

key·pal /'kiːpæl/ *noun* (*informal*) a person that you regularly send emails to, often sb you have never met 键友（经常用电子邮件联系，往往不曾谋面）

'key ring *noun* a small ring that you put keys on to keep them together 钥匙圈；钥匙环 ➲ PICTURE AT RING[1]

ˈ**key signature** *noun* (*music* 音) the set of marks at the beginning of a printed piece of music to show what KEY the piece is in 调号 ➲ PICTURE AT MUSIC

key·stone /ˈkiːstəʊn; *NAmE* -stoʊn/ *noun* **1** (*architecture* 建) the central stone at the top of an ARCH that keeps all the other stones in position 拱顶石 ➲ VISUAL VOCAB PAGE V14 **2** [usually sing.] the most important part of a plan or argument that the other parts depend on（计划、论据的）主旨，基础

key·stroke /ˈkiːstrəʊk; *NAmE* -stroʊk/ *noun* a single action of pressing a key on a computer or TYPEWRITER keyboard 击键；按键

key·word /ˈkiːwɜːd; *NAmE* -wɜːrd/ *noun* **1** a word that tells you about the main idea or subject of sth 主题词：*When you're studying a language, the keyword is patience.* 学习一门语言，最重要的是有耐心。 **2** a word or phrase that you type on a computer keyboard to give an instruction or to search for information about sth 关键词，关键字（用于指令或检索）：*Enter the keyword 'restaurants' and click on Search.* 键入关键词 restaurants，点击 Search 按钮。 ➲ WORDFINDER NOTE AT PROGRAM

ˌ**key ˈworker** *noun* (*BrE*) a worker in one of the essential services such as health, education or the police 关键工作人员（指医疗保健、教育或警察等重要服务行业的工作人员）：*The city council helps key workers find affordable housing.* 市政厅帮助关键工作人员寻找可负担的住房。

kg *abbr.* (*pl.* **kg** or **kgs**) (in writing 书写形式) kilogram(s) 千克；公斤：*10kg* * 10 公斤

the KGB /ˌkeɪ dʒiː ˈbiː/ *noun* [sing.] the state security police of the former USSR 克格勃（前苏联国家安全委员会，为政治警察及安全机构）

khaki /ˈkɑːki/ *noun* **1** [U] a strong greenish or yellowish brown cloth, used especially for making military uniforms 卡其布（尤用以做军装） **2** [U] a dull greenish or yellowish brown colour 暗绿色；黄褐色 **3 khakis** [pl.] (*NAmE*) trousers/pants made from khaki cloth 卡其布长裤；卡其裤：*He wore a pair of baggy khakis.* 他穿了一条宽松的卡其裤。 ▸ **khaki** *adj.*：*khaki uniforms* 黄褐色卡其军装

khan /kɑːn/ *noun* a title given to rulers or officials in some countries of central Asia 可汗，汗（一些中亚国家统治者或高官的称号）

khan·ate /ˈkɑːneɪt/ *noun* **1** the area which is ruled by a khan 可汗的领土 **2** the position of a khan 可汗之位

khanga (*also* **kanga**) /ˈkæŋɡə/ (*also* **lesso**) *noun* (*EAfrE*) a large piece of light cloth with designs printed on it and worn by women around the waist and legs or over the head and shoulders 肯加围巾布（东非女子用作围腰布或围巾的印花薄布）

khazi /ˈkɑːzi/ (*also* **kharzy** /ˈkɑːzi; *NAmE* ˈkɑːrzi/) *noun* (*pl.* **-ies**) (*old-fashioned, BrE, slang*) a toilet 厕所；茅坑

khi·mar /kiˈmɑː(r)/ *noun* a head covering worn in public by some Muslim women, that usually covers the head and the upper part of the body 喜玛尔（穆斯林妇女使用的一种盖头，在公共场所穿戴，通常遮住头部和上身）

kHz *abbr.* (in writing 书写形式) KILOHERTZ 千赫（兹）

kia ora /ˌkiə ˈɔːrə/ *exclamation* (*NZE*) a GREETING wishing good health 你好；祝你健康

KiB *abbr.* (in writing 书写形式) KIBIBYTE 千字节（二进制计算机内存或数据单位）

Kib (*also* **Kibit**) *abbr.* (in writing 书写形式) KIBIBIT 千比特（二进制计算机内存或数据单位）

kib·bled /ˈkɪbld/ *adj.* [usually before noun] (of grain 谷粒) crushed into rough pieces 磨成粗粒的；粗磨的

kib·butz /kɪˈbʊts/ *noun* (*pl.* **kib·butz·im** /ˌkɪbʊtˈsiːm/) (in Israel) a type of farm or factory where a group of people live together and share all the work, decisions and income 基布兹，集体农场（以色列的共同生活、工作、决策和分配收入的合作农场或工厂）

kibi·bit /ˈkɪbibɪt/ *noun* (*abbr.* **Kib, Kibit**) (*computing* 计) = KILOBIT (2)

kibi·byte /ˈkɪbibaɪt/ *noun* (*abbr.* **KiB**) (*computing* 计) = KILOBYTE (2)

kib·itz /ˈkɪbɪts/ *verb* (*NAmE, informal*) **1** [I, T] (*usually disapproving*) to watch other people doing sth and make comments or give advice about it, often in an annoying way（旁观者）指手画脚，多嘴多舌：*It is rude to kibitz during a serious game.* 观看重要比赛时在一旁指手画脚很不礼貌。◇ **~ sth** *I paused to kibitz a poker game.* 我停下来去指点别人玩纸牌。 **2** [I] to talk in a friendly informal way 闲聊：*We sat around and kibitzed until about eleven.* 我们围坐着，一直聊到大约 11 点。 ▸ **kib·itz·er** *noun*

kiblah (*also* **kibla**) *noun* = QIBLAH

ki·bosh /ˈkaɪbɒʃ; *NAmE* -bɑːʃ/ *noun* [sing.]
IDM ▸ **put the ˈkibosh on sth** (*informal*) to stop sth from happening; to spoil sb's plans 阻止某事发生；挫败计划

kick 🔑 /kɪk/ *verb, noun*
■ *verb* **1** 🔑 [T, I] to hit sb/sth with your foot 踢；踹：**~ (sb/sth)** *She was punched and kicked by her attackers.* 她遭到袭击者的拳打脚踢。◇ *Stop kicking—it hurts!* 别踢了，好痛！◇ **~ sb/sth + adv./prep./adj.** *The boys were kicking a ball around in the yard.* 男孩们在院子里踢球。◇ *Vandals had kicked the door down.* 破坏公物者把门踹倒了。 **2** 🔑 [T, I] **~ (sth)** to move your legs as if you were kicking sth 踢蹬；踢（腿）：*The dancers kicked their legs in the air.* 舞者做了空中踢腿的动作。◇ *The child was dragged away,* ***kicking and screaming.*** 这孩子又踢又叫地被拖走了。 **3** [T] **~ yourself** (*informal*) to be annoyed with yourself because you have done sth stupid, missed an opportunity, etc.（因干了蠢事、失去良机等）对（自己）生气：*He'll kick himself when he finds out he could have had the job.* 一旦发现他本可以得到这个工作，他会感到懊恼的。 **4** [T] **~ sth** (in sports such as football (SOCCER) and RUGBY 体育运动，如足球和橄榄球) to score points by kicking the ball 踢球得分；射门得分：*to kick a penalty/goal* 罚点球得分；射门得分

IDM ▸ **kick (some) ˈass/ˈbutt** (*slang, especially NAmE*) **1** to act in a way that is aggressive or full of energy 干劲十足；激情高涨 **2** to succeed or win in an impressive way 大获全胜；赢得漂亮 **kick (some/sb's) ˈass** to punish or defeat sb 惩罚，击败（某人） **kick the ˈbucket** (*informal* or *humorous*) to die 死；翘辫子；蹬腿儿 **kick the can ˈdown the road** (*NAmE, informal*) to put off dealing with a problem 拖延处理问题；把难题往后推迟：*This is another attempt to kick the can down the road and leave it to the next generation.* 这又是试图把问题拖延，留给下一代人面对。 **kick the ˈhabit, ˈdrug, ˈbooze, etc.** to stop doing sth harmful that you have done for a long time 戒除恶习；戒毒；戒酒 **kick your ˈheels** (*BrE*) to have nothing to do while you are waiting for sb/sth 无聊地等待：*We were kicking our heels, waiting for some customers.* 我们百无聊赖地等待顾客光临。 **kick sb in the ˈteeth** to treat sb badly or fail to give them help when they need it 粗暴对待某人；使极度失望 **kick sth into the long ˈgrass/into ˈtouch** (*BrE*) to reject, remove or stop dealing with a problem 搁置；置之不理：*He tends to deal with disputes by kicking them into the long grass.* 他处理争议的方法往往是置之不理。 **kick over the ˈtraces** (*old-fashioned, BrE*) to start to behave badly and refuse to accept any discipline or control（开始）不听话，不守规矩，不受管束 **kick the ˈtyres** (*NAmE* **kick the ˈtires**) to test the quality of sth to see whether it is suitable for you before you buy it（购买商品前）测试质量 **kick up a ˈfuss, ˈstink, etc.** (*informal*) to complain loudly about sth 吵闹；闹事；起哄 **kick up your ˈheels** (*informal, especially NAmE*) to be relaxed and enjoy yourself 轻轻松松；尽情享乐 **kick sb upˈstairs** (*informal*) to move sb to a job that seems to be more important but which actually has less power or influence 使某人明升暗降；以升迁为名排斥某人 **kick sb when they're ˈdown** to continue to hurt sb when they are already defeated, etc. 落井下石 ➲ MORE AT ALIVE,

HELL

PHR V **ˌkick aˈbout/aˈround** (*informal*) **1** (usually used in the progressive tenses 通常用于进行时) to be lying somewhere not being used 被闲置；闲置不用：*There's a pen kicking around on my desk somewhere.* 我书桌上什么地方闲放着一支钢笔。**2** to go from one place to another with no particular purpose（无目的地）四处游荡，闲逛，到处走：*They spent the summer kicking around Europe.* 他们在欧洲各地晃悠了一夏天。**ˌkick sb aˈround** (*informal*) to treat sb in a rough or unfair way 粗暴地对待某人；虐待；凌辱 **ˌkick sth aˈbout/aˈround** (*informal*) to discuss an idea, a plan, etc. in an informal way 非正式谈论（或讨论）某事；随便谈谈 **ˈkick against sth** to protest about or resist sth 反对，反抗，抵抗（某事）：*Young people often kick against the rules.* 年轻人常常违反规定。**ˌkick ˈback** (*especially NAmE*) to relax 放松：*Kick back and enjoy the summer.* 轻松愉快地享受这夏日的时光吧。**ˌkick ˈin** (*informal*) **1** to begin to take effect 开始生效（或见效）：*Reforms will kick in later this year.* 改革将于今年下半年开始见效。**2** (*also* **ˌkick ˈin sth**) (*both NAmE*) to give your share of money or help 捐献；捐助；缴付 **ˌkick ˈoff 1** when a football (SOCCER) game or a team, etc. **kicks off**, the game starts（足球比赛等）开球，开始 ➲ RELATED NOUN KICK-OFF ➲ SYNONYMS AT START **2** to suddenly become angry or violent 发怒；动怒 **ˌkick ˈoff (with sth)** (*informal*) to start 开始：*What time shall we kick off?* 我们什么时候开始？◇ *Tom will kick off with a few comments.* 汤姆讲话时要先发表几点意见。➲ RELATED NOUN KICK-OFF **ˌkick sth↔ˈoff** to remove sth by kicking 踢开，踢掉（某物）：*to kick off your shoes* 把鞋踢掉 **ˌkick ˈoff sth** to start a discussion, a meeting, an event, etc. 开始进行讨论（或会议、项目等）SYN **open** **ˌkick ˈout (at sb/sth) 1** to try to hit sb/sth with your legs because you are angry or upset（因气愤或心烦意乱）用脚踢（人或物）**2** to react violently to sb/sth that makes you angry or upset（对令人气愤或烦恼的人或事）作出强烈反应 **ˌkick sb ˈout (of sth)** (*informal*) to make sb leave or go away (from somewhere) 使某人离开；开除；逐出 **ˌkick ˈup** (*especially NAmE*) (of wind or a storm 风或风暴) to become stronger 越来越强；逐渐加强 **ˌkick sth↔ˈup** to make sth, especially dust, rise from the ground 扬起（尤指）尘埃

■ ***noun* 1** ⚷ a movement with the foot or the leg, usually to hit sth with the foot 踢；踢脚；踢腿：*the first kick of the game* 比赛的开球 ◇ *She gave him a kick on the shin.* 她朝他的小腿踢了一脚。◇ *He aimed a kick at the dog.* 他对准狗踢了一脚。◇ *If the door won't open, give it a kick.* 门要是打不开就踹一下。◇ (*slang*) *She needs a **kick up the backside*** (= she needs to be strongly encouraged to do sth or to behave better). 她需要敲打敲打。➲ SEE ALSO FREE KICK, PENALTY KICK, SPOT KICK **2** (*informal*) a strong feeling of excitement and pleasure 极度刺激；极度兴奋；极大的乐趣 SYN **thrill**：*I **get a kick out of** driving fast cars.* 开快车给我带来极大的乐趣。◇ *He **gets his kicks** from hurting other people.* 他以伤害他人为乐。◇ *What do you do **for kicks**?* 你以什么来寻求刺激呢？➲ WORDFINDER NOTE AT ADVENTURE **3** [usually sing.] (*informal*) the strong effect that a drug or an alcoholic drink has（毒品或酒精的）效力，刺激性：*This drink has quite a kick.* 这酒的劲相当大。

IDM **a kick in the ˈteeth** (*informal*) a great disappointment; sth that hurts sb/sth emotionally 极度的失望；沉重的打击；重大的挫折

ˈkick-ass (*also* **ˈass-kicking**) *adj.* (*slang, especially NAmE*) **1** powerful and aggressive 强横的；粗暴的：*the film's kick-ass heroine* 这部影片泼辣的女主角 ◇ *his reputation as a kick-ass coach* 他那魔鬼教练的名声 **2** extremely good and successful 棒极了的；绝妙的：*a kick-ass visual feast* 视觉大餐 ◇ *truly kick-ass quality* 超棒的质量

kick·back /ˈkɪkbæk/ *noun* (*informal*) money paid illegally to sb in return for work or help（不合法的）回扣，酬金，佣金 SYN **bribe**

kick·ball /ˈkɪkbɔːl/ *noun* [U] a game that is based on BASEBALL in which players kick the ball instead of hitting it with a BAT 踢球运动（类似棒球运动，但不用球棒击球，而是用脚踢球）

ˈkick-boxing *noun* [U] a form of BOXING in which the people fighting each other can kick as well as punch (= hit with their hands) 踢拳；自由搏击

ˈkick drum *noun* (*informal*) a large drum played using a PEDAL 踏板鼓

kick·er /ˈkɪkə(r)/ *noun* **1** a person who kicks, especially the player in a sports team who kicks the ball to try to score points, for example in RUGBY 踢的人；（尤指）踢球射门的运动员 **2** (*NAmE, informal*) a surprising end to a series of events （一连串事情的）意外结局

kick·ing /ˈkɪkɪŋ/ *adj., noun*

■ ***adj.*** (*informal*) full of life and excitement 充满活力的；充满刺激的；令人兴奋的：*The club was really kicking last night.* 昨晚俱乐部真是热闹非凡。

■ ***noun*** [sing.] an act of kicking sb hard and repeatedly, especially when they are lying on the ground（尤指对躺在地上的人连续的）狠踢，猛踹：*They gave him a good kicking.* 他们狠狠地踢了他一顿。

ˈkick-off *noun* **1** [C, U] the start of a game of football (SOCCER)（足球赛的）开球，开赛：*The kick-off is at 3.* 足球比赛 3 点开球。**2** [sing.] (*informal*) the start of an activity（活动的）开始，开幕

kick·stand /ˈkɪkstænd/ *noun* a long straight piece of metal fixed to a bicycle or a motorcycle, which is kept horizontal while the bicycle is being ridden but which can be moved to a vertical position when you need to stand the bicycle somewhere（自行车或摩托车的）撑脚架，支架 ➲ VISUAL VOCAB PAGE V55

ˈkick-start *verb, noun*

■ ***verb* 1 ~ sth** to start a motorcycle by pushing down a LEVER with your foot 用脚踏启动（摩托车）**2 ~ sth** to do sth to help a process or project start more quickly 促使…开始；使（项目）尽快启动：*The government's attempt to kick-start the economy has failed.* 政府刺激经济的努力失败了。

■ ***noun* 1** (*also* **ˈkick-starter**) the part of a motorcycle that you push down with your foot in order to start it（摩托车的）脚踏启动器 **2** a quick start that you give to sth by taking some action 迅速开始（采取行动）；快速启动

ˈkick-turn *noun* **1** (in SKIING 滑雪) a turn made by lifting and turning each SKI separately so that you face the opposite direction 踢转（分别将两块滑雪板翘起转向所作的调头）**2** a turn made with the front wheels of a SKATEBOARD off the ground 前轮离地转弯，倒板（使滑板前轮抬起所作的调头）

kid ⚷ /kɪd/ *noun, verb, adj.*

■ ***noun* 1** ⚷ [C] (*informal*) a child or young person 小孩；年轻人：*A bunch of kids were hanging around outside.* 一群年轻人在外面到处游逛。◇ *a kid of 15* * 15 岁的年轻人 ◇ *She's a bright kid.* 她是个聪明孩子。◇ *How are the kids* (= your children)? 孩子们好吗？◇ *Do you have any kids?* 你有孩子吗？HELP **Kid** is much more common than **child** in informal and spoken *NAmE*. 在非正式场合和美式英语口语中 kid 远比 child 常见。➲ COLLOCATIONS AT CHILD **2** [C] a young GOAT 小山羊 **3** [U] soft leather made from the skin of a young GOAT 小山羊皮革

IDM **handle/treat, etc. sb with kid ˈgloves** to deal with sb in a very careful way so that you do not offend or upset them 小心应付某人 **ˈkids' stuff** (*BrE*) (*NAmE* **ˈkid stuff**) something that is so easy to do or understand that it is thought to be not very serious or only suitable for children 极容易的事；"小儿科"；小孩子都懂得的道理 ➲ MORE AT NEW

■ ***verb* (-dd-)** (*informal*) **1** [I, T] (usually used in the progressive tenses 通常用于进行时) to tell sb sth that is not true, especially as a joke 戏弄；开玩笑 SYN **joke**：*I thought he was kidding when he said he was going out with a rock star.* 他说他在与一个摇滚乐歌星谈恋爱，我还以为他在开玩笑呢。◇ *I didn't mean it. I was **only kidding**.* 我并没有这个意思，我只是开开玩笑而已。◇ **~ sb** *I'm not kidding you.*

It does work. 我不是戏弄你，那的确有效。 **2** [T] to allow sb/yourself to believe sth that is not true 欺骗；哄骗 **SYN** **deceive**: **~ sb/yourself** *They're kidding themselves if they think it's going to be easy.* 如果他们认为这会很容易，那是自己欺骗自己。◇ **~ sb/yourself (that)**... *I tried to kid myself (that) everything was normal.* 我试图让自己相信一切都正常。 ➲ MORE LIKE THIS 36, page R29

IDM **ˌno ˈkidding** (*informal*) **1** used to emphasize that sth is true or that you agree with sth that sb has just said（强调是真实的或同意别人刚说过的话）真的，可不是：*'It's cold!' 'No kidding!'* "天气真冷！""可不是！" **2** used to show that you mean what you are saying（表示认真）不是开玩笑，我说的是真的：*I want the money back tomorrow. No kidding.* 我希望明天钱就能退回来。这可不是开玩笑。 **you're ˈkidding | you must be ˈkidding** (*informal*) used to show that you are very surprised at sth that sb has just said（对对方刚说过的话感到非常惊奇）你是在开玩笑吧

PHR V **ˌkid aˈround** (*especially NAmE*) to behave in a silly way 做傻事；装傻相

■ ***adj.*** **~ sister/brother** (*informal, especially NAmE*) a person's younger sister/brother 妹妹；弟弟

kid·die (*also* **kiddy**) /ˈkɪdi/ (*pl.* **-ies**) *noun* (*informal*) a young child 小孩子；小家伙：*a kiddies' party* 孩子们的聚会

kid·nap /ˈkɪdnæp/ *verb* (**-pp-**, *US also* **-p-**) **~ sb** to take sb away illegally and keep them as a prisoner, especially in order to get money or sth else for returning them 劫持；绑架 **SYN** **abduct**, **seize**: *Two businessmen have been kidnapped by terrorists.* 两名商人遭恐怖分子绑架。 ➲ WORDFINDER NOTE AT ATTACK ▶ **kid·napper** *noun*: *The kidnappers are demanding a ransom of $1 million.* 劫持者索要 100 万美元赎金。 **kid·nap·ping** (*also* **kid·nap**) *noun* [U, C]: *He admitted the charge of kidnap.* 他对绑架的指控供认不讳。◇ *the kidnapping of 12 US citizens* 对 12 名美国公民的劫持

kid·ney /ˈkɪdni/ *noun* **1** [C] either of the two organs in the body that remove waste products from the blood and produce URINE 肾；肾脏：*a kidney infection* 肾感染 ➲ VISUAL VOCAB PAGE V64 **2** [U, C] the kidneys of some animals that are cooked and eaten（食用的）动物腰子：*steak and kidney pie* 牛肉腰花馅饼

ˈkidney bean *noun* a type of reddish-brown BEAN shaped like a kidney that is usually dried before it is sold and then left in water before cooking 菜豆；红腰豆；芸豆 ➲ VISUAL VOCAB PAGE V34

ˈkidney machine *noun* a machine that does the work of a KIDNEY for sb whose kidneys are damaged or have been removed 透析器；人工肾

kid·ol·ogy /kɪˈdɒlədʒi; *NAmE* -ˈdɑːl-/ *noun* [U] (*especially BrE, humorous*) the art or practice of making people believe sth which is not true 哄骗（术）；糊弄

kid·ult /ˈkɪdʌlt/ *noun* (*informal*) an adult who likes doing or buying things that are usually thought more suitable for children 童心未泯的成人，大小孩（喜欢做适合儿童做的事或购买适合儿童的物品）

kike /kaɪk/ *noun* (*taboo, slang, especially NAmE*) a very offensive word for a Jew 犹太佬；犹太鬼子

kikoi /kɪˈkɔɪ/ *noun* (*EAfrE*) a large piece of strong coloured cloth used mainly as an item of clothing around the waist and legs or over the shoulders 基科伊厚花布（主要用作围腰布或披肩）

kilim /kɪˈliːm; ˈkiːlɪm; *NAmE* kiːˈliːm; ˈkɪləm/ (*also* **kelim**) *noun* a type of Turkish carpet or RUG（土耳其）基里姆地毯

kill 🔑 /kɪl/ *verb, noun*

■ ***verb*** **1** 🔑 [T, I] **~ (sb/sth/yourself)** to make sb/sth die 杀死；弄死；导致死亡：*Cancer kills thousands of people every year.* 每年数以千计的人死于癌症。◇ *Three people were killed in the crash.* 三人在此次撞车事故中丧生。◇ *He tried to kill himself with sleeping pills.* 他试图服安眠药自杀。◇ *I bought a spray to kill the weeds.* 我买了一种喷剂来除草。◇ (*informal*) *My mother will kill me* (= be very angry with me) *when she finds out.* 我妈要是发现了会宰了我的。◇ *Don't kill yourself trying to get the work done by tomorrow. It can wait.* 别为了赶着明天把事情干完而累坏身体。这事可以等一等嘛。◇ *Tiredness while driving can kill.* 疲劳驾驶会出人命的。 **2** [T] **~ sth** to destroy or spoil sth or make it stop 毁灭；破坏；扼杀；使停止：*to kill a rumour* 平息谣言 ◇ *Do you agree that television kills conversation?* 电视扼杀人与人之间的交谈，你同意这种说法吗？◇ *The defeat last night killed the team's chances of qualifying.* 昨晚的失败使这个队失去了获得资格的机会。 **3** [T] **~ sb | it kills sb to do sth** (*informal*) (usually used in the progressive tenses and not used in the passive 通常用于进行时，不用于被动语态) to cause sb pain or suffering 使痛苦；使疼痛；使受折磨：*My feet are killing me.* 我的双脚痛死了。 **4** [T] **~ sb** (*NAmE*) to make sb laugh a lot 使笑得前仰后合；使笑死了：*Stop it! You're killing me!* 别说了！你都把我笑死了！

IDM **kill the goose that lays the golden ˈegg/ˈeggs** (*saying*) to destroy sth that would make you rich, successful, etc. 杀鸡取卵；竭泽而渔；自绝财源 **ˌkill or ˈcure** (*BrE*) used to say that what you are going to do will either be very successful or fail completely 要么医好要么治死；不是成功便是失败；成败在此一举 **kill ˈtime | kill an ˈhour, a couple of ˈhours, etc.** to spend time doing sth that is not important while you are waiting for sth else to happen（等待时）消磨时间，打发时光：*We killed time playing cards.* 我们打纸牌消磨时间。 **kill two birds with one ˈstone** to achieve two things at the same time with one action 一石二鸟；一箭双雕；一举两得 **ˌkill sb/sth with ˈkindness** to be so kind to sb/sth that you in fact harm them 宠坏 **ˌkill yourself ˈlaughing** (*BrE*) to laugh a lot 笑得前仰后合；笑破肚皮：*He was killing himself laughing.* 他笑得前仰后合。 ➲ MORE AT CURIOSITY, DRESSED, LOOK *n.*, TIME *n.*

PHR V **ˌkill sb/sth↔ˈoff** **1** to make a lot of plants, animals, etc. die 大量杀死，大量消灭（动植物等）：*Some drugs kill off useful bacteria in the user's body.* 某些药物会杀死服用者体内的有益细菌。 **2** to stop or get rid of sth 使某事物停止；除掉；排除：*He has effectively killed off any political opposition.* 他实际上已消灭了一切对立的政见。

■ ***noun*** [usually sing.] **1** an act of killing, especially when an animal is hunted or killed 杀死，捕杀（尤指动物）：*A cat often plays with a mouse before the kill.* 猫在咬死老鼠之前常常要耍弄它一番。◇ *The plane prepared to* ***move in for the kill.*** 飞机已做好击落敌机的准备。◇ *I was* ***in at the kill*** *when she finally lost her job* (= present at the end of an unpleasant process). 我亲眼目睹了她最后失去工作的情景。 **2** an animal that has been hunted and killed 被捕杀的动物；猎物：*lions feeding on their kill* 正在吃猎物的狮子

kill·er /ˈkɪlə(r)/ *noun* **1** a person, an animal or a thing that kills 杀人者；杀手；导致死亡的人（或动物、事物）：*Police are hunting his killer.* 警方正在追捕杀害他的凶手。◇ *Heart disease is the biggest killer in Scotland.* 心脏病是苏格兰的头号杀手。◇ *an electric insect killer* 电杀虫器 ◇ *The players lacked* ***the killer instinct.*** 这些运动员缺乏拼杀本能。 ➲ SEE ALSO LADYKILLER, SERIAL KILLER **2** (*informal*) something that is very difficult, very exciting or very skilful 棘手的事；令人激动的事物；精彩的事物：*The exam was a real killer.* 这考试可真费劲。◇ *The new movie is a killer.* 这部新影片精彩极了。

ˌkiller appliˈcation (*also* **ˌkiller ˈapp**) *noun* (*computing* 计) a computer program that is so popular that it encourages people to buy or use the OPERATING SYSTEM, etc. that it runs on 杀手级应用程序（促使人们购买或使用其操作系统等的受欢迎计算机程序）

ˌkiller ˈbee *noun* a type of BEE that is very aggressive 非洲蜜蜂（攻击性强）；非洲杀人蜂

ˈkiller cell *noun* (*biology* 生) a white blood cell which destroys infected cells or cancer cells 杀伤细胞

ˈkiller whale (*also* **orca**) *noun* a black and white WHALE that eats meat 逆戟鲸；虎鲸；恶鲸；杀人鲸

K

kill·ing /ˈkɪlɪŋ/ *noun, adj.*

■ ***noun*** an act of killing sb deliberately 故意杀人；谋杀 SYN **murder**: *brutal killings* 残杀 ➲ COLLOCATIONS AT CRIME ➲ SEE ALSO MERCY KILLING

IDM ˌ**make a ˈkilling** (*informal*) to make a lot of money quickly 发大财；获取暴利；财运亨通

■ ***adj.*** making you very tired 使人筋疲力尽的 SYN **exhausting**: *a killing schedule* 排得满满当当的时间表

ˈ**killing fields** *noun* [pl.] a place where very many people were killed, for example during a war 大屠杀之地；杀戮战场

kill·joy /ˈkɪldʒɔɪ/ *noun* (*disapproving*) a person who likes to spoil other people's enjoyment 使人扫兴的人；大煞风景的人

kiln /kɪln/ *noun* a large oven for baking CLAY and bricks, drying wood and grain, etc. 窑

kilo /ˈkiːləʊ; *NAmE* ˈkiːloʊ/ *noun* (*pl.* **-os**) = KILOGRAM

kilo- /ˈkɪləʊ; *NAmE* ˈkɪloʊ/ *combining form* (in nouns; used in units of measurement 构成名词，用于计量单位) **1** one thousand 千: *kilojoule* 千焦耳 **2** 2^{10}, or 1 024 千（二进制，等于 1 024）

kilo·bit /ˈkɪləbɪt/ *noun* (*abbr.* **Kb**, **Kbit**) (*computing* 计) **1** a unit for measuring computer memory or data, equal to 10^3, or 1 000 BITS 千比特（十进制计算机内存或数据的单位，等于 1 000 比特）➲ SEE ALSO KBPS **2** (*also* **kibi·bit**) a unit for measuring computer memory or data, equal to 2^{10}, or 1 024 BITS 千比特（二进制计算机内存或数据的单位，等于 1 024 比特）

kilo·byte /ˈkɪləbaɪt/ *noun* (*abbr.* **K**, **KB**) (*computing* 计) **1** a unit for measuring computer memory or data, equal to 10^3, or 1 000 BYTES 千字节（十进制计算机内存或数据单位，等于 1 000 字节）**2** (*also* **kibi·byte**) a unit for measuring computer memory or data, equal to 2^{10}, or 1 024 BYTES 千字节（二进制计算机内存或数据单位，等于 1 024 字节）

kilo·gram (*BrE also* **kilo·gramme**) /ˈkɪləgræm/ (*also* **kilo**) *noun* (*abbr.* **kg**) a unit for measuring weight; 1 000 grams 千克；公斤: *2 kilograms of rice* * 2 公斤大米 ◇ *Flour is sold by the kilogram.* 面粉按公斤出售。

kilo·hertz /ˈkɪləhɜːts; *NAmE* -hɜːrts/ *noun* (*abbr.* **kHz**) (*pl.* **kilo·hertz**) a unit for measuring radio waves 千赫（兹）

kilo·joule /ˈkɪlədʒuːl/ *noun* (*abbr.* **kJ**) a measurement of the energy that you get from food; 1 000 JOULES 千焦（耳）（食物能量单位）

kilo·metre (*especially US* **kilo·meter**) /ˈkɪləmiːtə(r); kɪˈlɒmɪtə(r); *NAmE also* kɪˈlɑːm-/ *noun* (*abbr.* **k**, **km**) a unit for measuring distance; 1 000 metres 千米；公里

kilo·watt /ˈkɪləwɒt; *NAmE* -wɑːt/ *noun* (*abbr.* **kW**) a unit for measuring electrical power; 1 000 WATTS 千瓦（电的功率计量单位，等于 1 000 瓦特）

ˌ**kilowatt-ˈhour** *noun* (*abbr.* **kWh**) a unit for measuring electrical energy equal to the power provided by one kilowatt in one hour 千瓦时；一度（电）

kilt /kɪlt/ *noun* a skirt made of TARTAN cloth that reaches to the knees and is traditionally worn by Scottish men; a similar skirt worn by women（苏格兰传统男式）短褶裙；女式苏格兰格呢短褶裙

kilt·ed /ˈkɪltɪd/ *adj.* wearing a kilt 身着苏格兰格呢褶裙的

kil·ter /ˈkɪltə(r)/ *noun* [U]

IDM **out of ˈkilter 1** not agreeing with or the same as sth else（与…）不一致，不同: *His views are out of kilter with world opinion.* 他的观点与世人的看法不一样。**2** no longer continuing or working in the normal way 不正常；失常: *Long flights throw my sleeping pattern out of kilter for days.* 长途飞行把我的睡眠习惯打乱了好几天。

ki·mono /kɪˈməʊnəʊ; *NAmE* kɪˈmoʊnoʊ/ *noun* (*pl.* **-os**) (*from Japanese*) a traditional Japanese piece of clothing like a long loose dress with wide sleeves, worn on formal occasions; a DRESSING GOWN or ROBE in this style（日本的）和服；和服式晨衣

kin /kɪn/ *noun* [pl.] (*old-fashioned* or *formal*) your family or your relatives（统称）家属，亲属，亲戚 ➲ COMPARE KINDRED *n.* (1) ➲ SEE ALSO NEXT OF KIN IDM SEE KITH

kind /kaɪnd/ *noun, adj.*

■ ***noun*** [C, U] a group of people or things that are the same in some way; a particular variety or type 同类的人（或事物）；种类: *three kinds of cakes/cake* 三种蛋糕 ◇ *music of **all/various/different kinds*** 各种类型的 / 不同种类的音乐 ◇ *Exercises of this kind are very popular.* 这种体育活动非常流行。◇ *What kind of house do you live in?* 你住的房子是哪一种？◇ *They sell **all kinds of things**.* 他们出售各种各样的东西。◇ *The school is **the first of its kind** in Britain.* 这是英国同类学校中最早的一所。◇ *She isn't **that kind of girl**.* 她不是那种类型的女孩。◇ *The regions differ in size, but not **in kind**.* 这些地区大小各异，但类型相同。◇ *I need to buy paper and pencils, that **kind of thing**.* 我需要买纸和铅笔之类的东西。◇ *I'll never have **that kind of money*** (= as much money as that). 我永远不会有那么多的钱。◇ (*formal*) *Would you like a drink **of some kind**?* 您想喝点什么吗？

IDM **in ˈkind 1** (of a payment 支付) consisting of goods or services, not money 以实物支付；以货代款；以服务偿付 **2** (*formal*) with the same thing 以同样的方法（或手段）: *She insulted him and he responded in kind.* 她侮辱了他，他也以其人之道还治其人之身。 **a ˈkind of** (*informal*) used to show that sth you are saying is not exact（表示不确切）某种，几分，隐约: *I had a kind of feeling this might happen.* 我当时就隐约地感到会出这样的事。 **ˈkind of** (*informal*) (*also* **ˈkinda** /ˈkaɪndə/) slightly; in some ways 稍微；有几分；有点儿: *That made me feel kind of stupid.* 那使我感到有点儿愚蠢。◇ *I like him, kind of.* 我有点儿喜欢他。 **nothing of the ˈkind/ˈsort** used to emphasize that the situation is very different from what has been said

▼ **GRAMMAR POINT 语法说明**

kind / sort

- Use the singular (**kind/sort**) or plural (**kinds/sorts**) depending on the word you use before them. 用单数（kind/sort）还是复数（kinds/sorts）取决于之前的用词： *each/one/every kind of animal* 每一种 / 一种 / 每一种动物 ◇ *all/many/other sorts of animals* 所有 / 许多 / 其他种类的动物
- **Kind/sort of** is followed by a singular or uncountable noun. * kind/sort of 后接单数名词或不可数名词： ***This kind of question** often appears in the exam.* 这类问题在考试中经常出现。◇ ***That sort of behaviour** is not acceptable.* 那样的行为是不允许的。
- **Kinds/sorts of** is followed by a plural or uncountable noun. * kinds/sorts of 后接复数名词或不可数名词： ***These kinds of questions** often appear in the exam.* 这几类问题在考试中经常出现。◇ ***These sorts of behaviour** are not acceptable.* 这种行为是不允许的。
- Other variations are possible but less common. 亦可能有其他结构，只是较少见： ***These kinds of question** often appear in the exam.* 此类问题在考试中经常出现。◇ ***These sort of things** don't happen in real life.* 这类事情在现实生活中不会发生。(This example is very informal and is considered incorrect by some people. 此例很不正式，有些人认为不正确。)
- Note also that these examples are possible, especially in spoken English. 另注意下列例句，尤其在口语中可能出现： *The shelf was full of **the sort of books** I like to read.* 书架上摆满了我喜欢读的那种书。◇ *He faced **the same kind of problems** as his predecessor.* 他面临着与他的前任同样的问题。◇ *There are many **different sorts of animal** on the island.* 岛上有许多不同种类的动物。◇ ***What kind of camera** is this?* 这是哪种型号的照相机？◇ ***What kind/kinds of cameras** do you sell?* 你们卖哪种 / 哪些型号的照相机？◇ *There were **three kinds of cakes/cake** on the plate.* 盘子里有三种蛋糕。

（强调情况与所说的大不相同）决不是那么回事，一点也不，才不哩；没有的事：*'I was terrible!' 'You were nothing of the kind.'* "我那时糟透了！""你才不哩。" **of a 'kind 1** (*disapproving*) not as good as it could be 不怎么样，徒有其名（指不如本应有的那么好）：*You're making progress of a kind.* 你也算是有点进步的。 **2** very similar 同一类的；类似的：*They're two of a kind—both workaholics!* 他们俩一个样，都是工作狂！ **one of a 'kind** the only one like this 独一无二；独特 SYN **unique**：*My father was one of a kind—I'll never be like him.* 我的父亲很独特，我决不会像他的。 **something of the/that 'kind** something like what has been said（与所言）类似的事物：*'He's resigning.' 'I'd suspected something of the kind.'* "他要辞职了。""我料到会有这样的事。"

■ ***adj.*** (**kind·er**, **kind·est**) **1** caring about others; gentle, friendly and generous 体贴的；慈祥的；友好的；宽容的：*a very kind and helpful person* 肯帮忙的好人 ◇ *a kind heart/face* 仁慈的心；友好的面容 ◇ *a kind action/gesture/comment* 友好的行为 / 姿态 / 评论 ◇ *You've been very kind.* 你真是体贴入微。◇ ~ **(to sb/sth)** *kind to animals* 爱护动物 ◇ (*figurative*) *Soft water is kinder to your hair.* 软性水质不易损伤头发。◇ (*figurative*) *The weather was very kind to us.* 天气非常宜人。◇ ~ **(of sb) (to do sth)** *It was really kind of you to help me.* 你帮我的忙，我太感激了。◇ (*formal*) *Thank you for your kind invitation.* 感谢你的盛情邀请。◇ (*formal*) *'Do have another.' 'That's very kind of you* (= thank you).' "一定要再来一份。""太谢谢你了。" OPP **unkind 2** (*formal*) used to make a polite request or give an order（客气请求或命令）：*Would you be kind enough to close the window?* 请把窗子关上好吗？ ➲ SEE ALSO KINDLY *adj.*, KINDNESS

kin·der /ˈkɪndə(r)/ *noun* (*AustralE, informal*) = KINDERGARTEN

kin·der·gar·ten /ˈkɪndəɡɑːtn; *NAmE* -dərɡɑːrtn/ *noun* (*from German*) **1** (*especially NAmE*) a school or class to prepare children aged five for school 学前班 **2** (*BrE, AustralE, NZE*) = NURSERY SCHOOL

ˌkind-ˈhearted *adj.* kind and generous 仁慈的；善良的；宽容的；好心的

kin·dle /ˈkɪndl/ *verb* **1** [I, T] to start burning; to make a fire start burning 开始燃烧；点燃：*We watched as the fire slowly kindled.* 我们看着火慢慢地燃烧起来。◇ ~ **sth** *to* ***kindle a fire/flame*** 点火 **2** [T, I] ~ **(sth)** to make sth such as an interest, emotion, etc. start to grow in sb; to start to be felt by sb 激起（兴趣、感情等）；发展起来；被感受到：*It was her teacher who kindled her interest in music.* 是她的老师激发了她对音乐的兴趣。 ◇ *Suspicion kindled within her.* 她渐渐产生了怀疑。

kind·ling /ˈkɪndlɪŋ/ *noun* [U] small dry pieces of wood, etc. used to start a fire 引火柴；引火物

kind·ly /ˈkaɪndli/ *adv., adj.*

■ ***adv.*** **1** in a kind way 体贴地；慈祥地；友好地；宽容地：*She spoke kindly to them.* 她与他们亲切交谈。 ◇ *He has kindly agreed to help.* 他友好地答应帮忙。 **2** (*old-fashioned, formal*) used to ask or tell sb to do sth, especially when you are annoyed（尤用于烦恼时请人或让人做某事）劳驾，请：*Kindly leave me alone!* 请不要打扰我！ ◇ *Visitors are kindly requested to sign the book.* 敬请参观者在这本册子上签名。

IDM **look 'kindly on/upon sth/sb** (*formal*) to approve of sth/sb 赞同，接受，认可（某事或人）：*He hoped they would look kindly on his request.* 他希望他们接受他的请求。 **not take 'kindly to sth/sb** to not like sth/sb 不喜欢某事物 / 人：*She doesn't take kindly to sudden change.* 她不喜欢突然的改变。

■ ***adj.*** [only before noun] (*old-fashioned* or *literary*) kind and caring 和善的；亲切的；关怀的；体贴的 ▸ **kind·li·ness** *noun* [U]

kind·ness /ˈkaɪndnəs/ *noun* **1** [U] the quality of being kind 仁慈；善良；体贴；宽容：*to treat sb with kindness and consideration* 待人体贴周到 **2** [C] a kind act 友好（或仁慈、体贴）的举动：*I can never repay your many kindnesses to me.* 我无法报答你对我无微不至的关怀。 IDM SEE KILL *v.*, MILK *n.*

kin·dred /ˈkɪndrəd/ *noun, adj.*

■ ***noun*** (*old-fashioned* or *formal*) **1** [pl.] your family and relatives（统称）家人，亲属 ➲ COMPARE KIN **2** [U] the fact of being related to another person 亲属关系；血缘关系：*ties of kindred* 亲属关系

■ ***adj.*** [only before noun] (*formal*) very similar; related 类似的；相似的；相关的；有血缘关系的：*food and kindred products* 食物及类似产品 ◇ *I knew I'd found* ***a kindred spirit*** (= a person with similar ideas, opinions, etc.). 我知道我找到了志同道合的人。

kindy /ˈkɪndi/ *noun* (*pl.* **-ies**) (*AustralE, NZE, informal*) = KINDERGARTEN

kin·esis /kɪˈniːsɪs; kaɪ-/ *noun* [U] (*specialist*) movement 运动；动作

kin·et·ic /kɪˈnetɪk; *BrE also* kaɪ-/ *adj.* [usually before noun] (*specialist*) of or produced by movement 运动的；运动引起的：*kinetic energy* 动能

kiˌnetic ˈart *noun* [U] (*art* 美术) art, especially SCULPTURE, with parts that move 动态艺术（尤指雕刻）

king /kɪŋ/ *noun* **1** the male ruler of an independent state that has a royal family 君主；国王：*the kings and queens of England* 英国国王和女王 ◇ *to* ***be crowned king*** 接受加冕为国王 ◇ *King George V* 国王乔治五世

> **WORDFINDER** 联想词：abdicate, accede, crown, **government**, monarch, throne, reign, royal, succession

2 ~ **(of sth)** a person, an animal or a thing that is thought to be the best or most important of a particular type（人、动物、事物中的）首屈一指者，最重要者，大王：*the king of comedy* 喜剧之王 ◇ *The lion is the king of the jungle.* 狮子是丛林之王。 **3** used in compounds with the names of animals or plants to describe a very large type of the thing mentioned（与动植物名称连用构成复合词，表示巨型）…之最，…之王，巨型…：*a king penguin* 王企鹅 **4** the most important piece used in the game of CHESS, that can move one square in any direction（国际象棋中的）王 ➲ VISUAL VOCAB PAGE V42 **5** a PLAYING CARD with the picture of a king on it（纸牌中的）老 K ➲ VISUAL VOCAB PAGE V42

IDM **a ˌking's ˈransom** (*literary*) a very large amount of money 一笔巨款 SYN **fortune** ➲ MORE AT EVIDENCE *n.*, UNCROWNED

king·dom /ˈkɪŋdəm/ *noun* **1** a country ruled by a king or queen 王国：*the United Kingdom* 联合王国 ◇ *the kingdom of God* (= heaven) 天国 **2** an area controlled by a particular person or where a particular thing or idea is important 管辖范围；领域 **3** one of the three traditional divisions of the natural world 自然三界之一：*the animal, vegetable and mineral kingdoms* 动物界、植物界及矿物界 **4** (*biology* 生) one of the five major groups into which all living things are organized 界（生物的五大类别之一） ➲ WORDFINDER NOTE AT BREED

IDM **blow sb/sth to kingdom 'come** (*informal*) to completely destroy sb/sth with an explosion 送…上西天；彻底炸毁 **till/until kingdom 'come** (*old-fashioned*) for ever 永远；永久

king·fish·er /ˈkɪŋfɪʃə(r)/ *noun* a bird with a long beak, that catches fish in rivers. The European kingfisher is small and brightly coloured and the American kingfisher is larger and blue-grey in colour. 翠鸟

ˈking-hit *noun* (*AustralE, NZE, informal*) a hard KNOCKOUT blow 制胜重击；打倒对手而获胜的重击 ▸ **ˈking-hit** *verb* (**king-hitting, king-hit, king-hit**) ~ **sb**

king·ly /ˈkɪŋli/ *adj.* (*literary*) like a king; connected with or good enough for a king 国王似的；国王的；君主的；适合于君主身份的 SYN **regal**

king·maker /ˈkɪŋmeɪkə(r)/ *noun* a person who has a very strong political influence and is able to bring sb else to power as a leader 能扶植领导人的有影响人物；政界元老

king·pin /ˈkɪŋpɪn/ *noun* the most important person in an organization or activity（组织或活动中的）主要人物，领袖

ˌKing's 'Bench *noun* the word for QUEEN'S BENCH when the UK has a king 王座法庭，王座法院（英国高等法院的一部分，女王在位时称 Queen's Bench）

ˌKing's 'Counsel *noun* = KC

ˌKing's 'English *noun* [U] the word for QUEEN'S ENGLISH when the UK has a king 标准英语，规范英语（女王在位时称 Queen's English）

ˌKing's 'evidence *noun* [U] the word for QUEEN'S EVIDENCE when the UK has a king（刑事被告向法庭提供的）对同案犯不利的证据（女王在位时称 Queen's evidence）

king·ship /ˈkɪŋʃɪp/ *noun* [U] the state of being a king; the official position of a king 国王身份；王位

'king-size (*also* **'king-sized**) *adj.* [usually before noun] very large; larger than normal when compared with a range of sizes 特大的；大于正常尺寸的：*a king-size bed* 特大号床 ◇ *a king-sized headache* 特别厉害的头痛

the ˌKing's 'speech *noun* the word for the QUEEN'S SPEECH when the UK has a king 英王施政演说（议会期间开始时发表，女王在位时称 the Queen's speech）

K

kink /kɪŋk/ *noun, verb*

■ ***noun*** **1** a bend or twist in sth that is usually straight（直线物体上的）弯，结：*a dog with a kink in its tail* 尾巴上有个结的狗 ◇ (*figurative*) *We need to iron out the kinks in the new system.* 我们需要理顺新制度中的一些问题。 **2** (*informal, disapproving*) an unusual feature in a person's character or mind, especially one that does not seem normal 怪癖；怪念头；奇想 **3** (*NAmE*) = CRICK

■ ***verb*** [I, T] ~ **(sth)** to develop or make sth develop a bend or twist（使）弯曲，扭结，绞缠

kinky /ˈkɪŋki/ *adj.* (*informal, usually disapproving*) used to describe sexual behaviour that most people would consider strange or unusual 性行为变态的；性行为反常的

kins·folk /ˈkɪnzfəʊk; *NAmE* -foʊk/ *noun* [pl.] (*formal* or *old-fashioned*) a person's relatives（统称个人的）亲戚，亲属

kin·ship /ˈkɪnʃɪp/ *noun* (*formal*) **1** [U] the fact of being related in a family 亲属关系：*the ties of kinship* 亲属关系 **2** [U, sing.] a feeling of being close to sb because you have similar origins or attitudes（因出身或态度相似而产生的）亲切感 **SYN affinity**

kins·man /ˈkɪnzmən/, **kins·woman** /ˈkɪnzwʊmən/ *noun* (*pl.* **-men** /-mən/, **-women** /-wɪmɪn/) (*old-fashioned* or *literary*) a relative 亲属；亲戚

kiondo /ˈkjɒndɒ; *NAmE* ˈkjɑːndɑː/ *noun* (*pl.* **-os**) (*EAfrE*) a bag with one or two long handles and made from SISAL (= dried grass twisted together) or other materials（用剑麻绳等编的）长带挎包，长带提包

kiosk /ˈkiːɒsk; *NAmE* -ɑːsk/ *noun* **1** a small shop/store, open at the front, where newspapers, drinks, etc. are sold. In some countries kiosks also sell food and things used in the home.（出售报纸、饮料等的）小亭；售货亭；报刊亭 **SYN stand** **2** (*old-fashioned, BrE*) a public telephone box 公用电话亭 **SYN booth**

kip /kɪp/ *noun, verb*

■ ***noun*** [U, C, usually sing.] (*BrE, informal*) sleep 睡觉：*I must get some kip.* 我得睡会儿觉。◇ *Why don't you have a quick kip?* 你为什么不小睡一会儿呢？

■ ***verb*** (**-pp-**) [I] (*BrE, informal*) to sleep 睡觉：*You can kip on the sofa, if you like.* 你想睡可以睡在沙发上。

kip·pa (*also* **kipa**, **kipah**, **kip·pah**) /kɪˈpɑː/ *noun* = YARMULKE

kip·per /ˈkɪpə(r)/ *noun* a HERRING (= a type of fish) that has been preserved using salt, then smoked 腌熏鲱鱼

ˌkipper 'tie *noun* (*BrE*) a brightly coloured tie that is very wide 鲜艳宽大的领带

kirby grip /ˈkɜːbi ɡrɪp; *NAmE* ˈkɜːrbi/ *noun* (*BrE*) = HAIRGRIP

kirk /kɜːk; *NAmE* kɜːrk/ *noun* **1** [C] (*ScotE*) church 教堂：*the parish kirk* 堂区教堂 **2 the Kirk** [sing.] a name often used for the official Church of Scotland 苏格兰教会

kir·pan /kɪəˈpɑːn; *NAmE* kɪr-/ *noun* a pointed knife that is worn by SIKH men as a sign of their religion（锡克族男子佩带的）圣刀

kirsch /kɪəʃ; *NAmE* kɪrʃ/ *noun* [U, C] a strong alcoholic drink made from CHERRIES 樱桃白兰地；樱桃酒

kis·met /ˈkɪzmet/ *noun* [U] (*literary*) the idea that everything that happens to you in your life is already decided and that you cannot do anything to change or control it 命运；天命 **SYN destiny, fate**

kiss /kɪs/ *verb, noun*

■ ***verb*** **1** [I, T] to touch sb with your lips as a sign of love, affection, sexual desire, etc., or when saying hello or goodbye 亲吻；接吻：*They stood in a doorway kissing* (= kissing each other). 他们站在门口亲吻。◇ *Do people in Britain kiss when they meet?* 英国人见面时亲吻吗？◇ ~ **sb** *Go and kiss your mother goodnight.* 去亲亲你母亲祝她晚安。◇ *She kissed him on both cheeks.* 她吻了吻他的双颊。◇ *He lifted the trophy up and kissed it.* 他举起奖杯吻了一下。➲ SEE ALSO AIR KISS **2** [T] ~ **sth** (*literary*) to gently move or touch sth 轻拂；轻触：*The sunlight kissed the warm stones.* 阳光洒落在温暖的石块上。

IDM ˌkiss and 'tell a way of referring to sb talking publicly, usually for money, about a past sexual relationship with sb famous（通常为了获利）泄露与名人的私情 **kiss sb's 'arse** (*BrE*) (*NAmE* **kiss sb's 'ass, kiss 'ass**) (*taboo, slang*) to be very nice to sb in order to persuade them to help you or to give you sth 谄媚巴结某人；拍某人马屁；奉承某人 **HELP** A more polite way to express this is **lick sb's boots.** 较礼貌的表达法是 lick sb's boots。 **ˌkiss sth 'better** (*informal*) to take away the pain of an injury by kissing it 以吻消除疼痛；亲一亲就不痛了：*Come here and let me kiss it better.* 过来让我亲一亲就不疼了。 **kiss sth good'bye | kiss good'bye to sth** (*informal*) to accept that you will lose sth or be unable to do sth 任其失去；放弃某事物；承认对某事无能为力：*Well, you can kiss goodbye to your chances of promotion.* 嗳，你就甭想晋升了。

PHR V ˌkiss sth↔a'way to stop sb feeling sad or angry by kissing them 以吻消除（某人的悲伤或怒气）：*He kissed away her tears.* 他吻了吻她，她就不哭了。

■ ***noun*** the act of kissing sb/sth 吻：*Come here and give me a kiss!* 过来亲亲我吧！◇ *a kiss on the cheek* 在面颊上的一吻 ◇ *We were greeted with hugs and kisses.* 我们受到欢迎，又是拥抱，又是亲吻。

IDM the kiss of 'death (*informal, especially humorous*) an event that seems good, but is certain to make sth else fail 貌似有利却肯定会在别处导致失利的事物；表面有利实则有害的事物 **the kiss of 'life** (*BrE*) a method of helping sb who has stopped breathing to breathe again by placing your mouth on theirs and forcing air into their lungs 人工呼吸（口对口） **SYN mouth-to-mouth resuscitation** ➲ MORE AT STEAL *v.*

kis·ser /ˈkɪsə(r)/ *noun* **1 good, bad, etc. ~** a person who is very good, bad, etc. at kissing 善于（或不善于等）接吻的人 **2** (*informal*) a person's mouth 嘴巴

'kiss-off *noun* [usually sing.] (*NAmE, informal*) an occasion when sb is suddenly told they are no longer wanted, especially by a lover or by a company（关系等的）突然终止；解雇：*She gave her husband the kiss-off.* 她突然向丈夫提出了离婚。◇ *He got the kiss-off from his job.* 他突然被解雇了。

kisso·gram /ˈkɪsəɡræm/ *noun* a humorous message on your birthday, etc., delivered by sb dressed in a special COSTUME who kisses you, arranged as a surprise by your friends 贺吻（为带来惊喜，由穿着特别服装者亲吻致贺生日等）

the 'KISS principle *noun* [sing.] (*especially US*) the idea that products and advertising should be as simple as possible（产品与广告的）最简原则，单纯原则 ORIGIN Formed from the first letters of the expression 'Keep it simple, stupid'. 以 Keep it simple, stupid 的首字母组合而成。

kist /kɪst/ *noun* (*SAfrE*) a large strong box, often made of wood, typically used for storing clothes, sheets, TABLECLOTHS, etc. 大木箱；衣物柜

Ki·swa·hili /ˌkiːswəˈhiːli; ˌkɪswɑːˈh-/ *noun* [U] = SWAHILI

kit /kɪt/ *noun, verb*

■ ***noun*** **1** [C] a set of parts ready to be made into sth 配套元件：*a kit for a model plane* 一套飞机模型元件 **2** [C, U] a set of tools or equipment that you use for a particular purpose 成套工具；成套设备：*a first-aid kit* 一套急救用品 ◇ *a drum kit* 一套击鼓用具 ➲ SYNONYMS AT EQUIPMENT ➲ SEE ALSO TOOLKIT **3** [U] (*BrE*) a set of clothes and equipment that you use for a particular activity 全套衣服及装备：*sports kit* 运动用品

IDM **get your 'kit off** (*BrE, slang*) to take your clothes off 把你的衣服都脱掉 ➲ MORE AT CABOODLE

■ ***verb*** **(-tt-)**

PHR V **ˌkit sb 'out/'up (in/with sth)** [usually passive] (*BrE*) to give sb the correct clothes and/or equipment for a particular activity（为特定活动而）使某人装备起来：*They were all kitted out in brand-new ski outfits.* 他们都一身全新的滑雪装备。

kit·bag /ˈkɪtbæg/ *noun* (*especially BrE*) a long narrow bag, usually made of CANVAS in which soldiers, etc. carry their clothes and other possessions（士兵等的）行囊，背包

kit·chen 🔑 /ˈkɪtʃɪn/ *noun* a room in which meals are cooked or prepared 厨房：*She's in the kitchen.* 她在厨房里。◇ *We ate at the kitchen table.* 我们在厨房里的桌子上吃饭。➲ VISUAL VOCAB PAGE V26 ➲ SEE ALSO SOUP KITCHEN

IDM **everything but the kitchen 'sink** (*informal, humorous*) a very large number of things, probably more than is necessary 过多的东西；大量的东西 ➲ MORE AT HEAT *n.*

kit·chen·ette /ˌkɪtʃɪˈnet/ *noun* a small room or part of a room used as a kitchen, for example in a flat/apartment 小厨房；套房里用作厨房的一角

ˌkitchen 'garden *noun* (*BrE*) a part of a garden/yard where you grow vegetables and fruit for your own use 家庭菜园；庭园中用作种蔬菜水果的部分

'kitchen paper (*also* **'kitchen roll, 'kitchen towel**) (*all BrE*) (*NAmE* **ˌpaper 'towel**) *noun* [U] thick paper on a roll, used for cleaning up liquid, food, etc. 厨房用卷纸 ➲ VISUAL VOCAB PAGE V26

ˌkitchen 'porter *noun* (*BrE*) a person who works in the kitchen of a restaurant, hotel, etc., washing plates and doing other simple jobs（饭店、旅馆等的）厨房杂务工

ˌkitchen-'sink *adj.* [only before noun] (of plays, films, novels, etc. 戏剧、电影、小说等) dealing with ordinary life and ordinary people, especially when this involves describing the boring or difficult side of their lives 生活化的；描写普通人的生活的；揭示现实灰暗面的：*a kitchen-sink drama* 生活化戏剧

kit·chen·ware /ˈkɪtʃɪnweə(r); *NAmE* -wer/ *noun* [U] used in shops/stores to describe objects that you use in a kitchen, such as pans, bowls, etc.（商店用语）厨房用具

kite /kaɪt/ *noun, verb*

■ ***noun*** **1** a toy made of a light frame covered with paper, cloth, etc., that you fly in the air at the end of one or more long strings 风筝：*to fly a kite* 放风筝 ➲ VISUAL VOCAB PAGE V41 **2** a BIRD OF PREY (= a bird that kills other creatures for food) of the HAWK family 鸢（猛禽）

IDM SEE FLY *v.*, HIGH *adj.*

■ ***verb*** **~ sth** (*NAmE, informal*) to use an illegal cheque to obtain money or to dishonestly change the amount written on a cheque 使用（非法支票）骗钱；涂改（支票）：*to kite checks* 用支票诈骗 ◇ *check kiting* 支票作弊

kite·surf·ing /ˈkaɪtsɜːfɪŋ; *NAmE* -sɜːrf-/ (*also* **kite·board·ing** /ˈkaɪtbɔːdɪŋ; *NAmE* -bɔːrd-/) *noun* [U] the sport of riding on water while standing on a short wide board and being pulled along by wind power, using a large kite 风筝冲浪（运动）➲ VISUAL VOCAB PAGE V54

kith /kɪθ/ *noun*

IDM **kith and kin** (*old-fashioned*) friends and relatives 亲戚朋友 ➲ MORE LIKE THIS 13, page R26

kitsch /kɪtʃ/ *noun* [U] (*disapproving*) works of art or objects that are popular but that are considered to have no real artistic value and to be lacking in good taste, for example because they are SENTIMENTAL 庸俗的艺术作品；无真正艺术价值的作品；品位不高的伤感作品 ▸ **kitsch** (*also* **kitschy**) *adj.*

kit·ten /ˈkɪtn/ *noun* a young cat 小猫

IDM **have 'kittens** (*BrE, informal*) to be very anxious, angry or upset about sth 焦虑；烦躁；心慌意乱

'kitten heels *noun* [pl.] small thin curved heels on women's shoes（女鞋的）弧状细矮跟；弧状细矮跟鞋 ➲ VISUAL VOCAB PAGE V69

kit·ten·ish /ˈkɪtnɪʃ/ *adj.* (*old-fashioned*) (of a woman 女人) lively, and trying to attract men's attention 搔首弄姿的；卖弄风情的

kit·ti·wake /ˈkɪtiweɪk/ *noun* a bird that lives in groups on sea CLIFFS 三趾鸥（海洋鸥类，营巢于悬崖）

kitty /ˈkɪti/ *noun* (*pl.* **-ies**) **1** (*informal*) if money is put in **a kitty**, a group of people all give an amount and the money is spent on sth they all agree on 共同凑集的一笔钱：*We each put £50 in the kitty to cover the bills.* 我们每人凑 50 英镑支付账单。**2** (in card games, etc. 纸牌游戏等) the sum of money that all the players bet, which is given to the winner 全部赌注 **3** (*informal*) a way of referring to a cat 猫咪；小猫

ˌkitty-'corner(ed) *adj., adv.* (*NAmE, informal*) = CATTY-CORNER(ED)

'kitty party *noun* (*especially IndE*) a regular social meeting of a group of women, held at either a member's house or a restaurant, where each person gives an amount of money and one is chosen to receive the whole sum 集资聚会（若干名妇女定期聚会，每人出一份钱，交予其中一人）

kiwi /ˈkiːwiː/ *noun* **1 Kiwi** (*informal*) a person from New Zealand 新西兰人 **2** a New Zealand bird with a long beak, short wings and no tail, that cannot fly 几维（新西兰鸟，喙长、翼短、无尾、不能飞）**3** = KIWI FRUIT

'kiwi fruit *noun* (*pl.* **kiwi fruit**) (*also* **kiwi**) a small fruit with thin brown skin covered with small hairs, soft green flesh and black seeds 猕猴桃；奇异果 ➲ VISUAL VOCAB PAGE V32

kJ *abbr.* KILOJOULE 千焦（耳）（食物能量单位）

KKK /ˌkeɪ keɪ ˈkeɪ/ *abbr.* KU KLUX KLAN 三 K 党

klap /klʌp/ *verb* (-pp-) **~ sb/sth** (*SAfrE, informal*) to hit sb/sth 打，击（某人或某物）：*I'll klap you!* 我要揍你！▸ **klap** *noun*：*to give sb a klap* 打某人

Klaxon™ /ˈklæksn/ *noun* (*BrE*) a horn, originally on a vehicle, that makes a loud sound as a warning 克莱克森高音喇叭（原为汽车喇叭）

Klee·nex™ /ˈkliːneks/ *noun* [U, C] (*pl.* **Klee·nex**) a paper HANDKERCHIEF; a TISSUE 舒洁纸巾；纸巾：*a box of Kleenex* 一盒纸巾 ◇ *Here, have a Kleenex to dry your eyes.* 来，拿一张纸巾把眼睛擦干。

klep·to·mania /ˌkleptəˈmeɪniə/ *noun* [U] a mental illness in which sb has a strong desire, which they cannot control, to steal things 偷窃狂；偷窃癖 ▸ **klep·to·maniac** /ˌkleptəˈmeɪniæk/ *noun*：*She's a kleptomaniac.* 她是个偷窃狂。

klick (*also* **click**) /klɪk/ *noun* (*NAmE, informal*) a kilometre 千米；公里：*We're twenty klicks south of your position.* 我们在你南面 20 公里处。

kludge /kluːdʒ/ *noun* (*computing* 计) a solution to a computer problem that has been quickly and badly put together 不成熟产品；蹩脚系统 ▶ **kludge** *verb* [I, T] ~ (**sth**)

klutz /klʌts/ *noun* (*informal, especially NAmE*) a person who often drops things, is not good at sport(s), etc. 木头人；不灵巧的人；笨手笨脚的人 ▶ **klutzy** /ˈklʌtsi/ *adj.*

km *abbr.* (*pl.* **km** or **kms**) (in writing 书写形式) kilometre(s) 千米；公里

knack /næk/ *noun* [sing.] (*informal*) **1** a special skill or ability that you have naturally or can learn 技能；本领：*It's easy, once you've got the knack.* 你一旦掌握这个技能就容易了。◇ ~ **of/for** (**doing**) **sth** *He's got a real knack for making money.* 他有赚钱的真本领。 **2** ~ **of doing sth** a habit of doing sth 习惯；癖好：*She has the unfortunate knack of always saying the wrong thing.* 不幸的是，她总是说错话。 ➲ MORE LIKE THIS 20, page R27

knacker /ˈnækə(r)/ *verb* (*BrE, slang*) **1** ~ **sb** to make sb very tired 使筋疲力尽；使疲惫不堪 **SYN** **exhaust** **2** ~ **sb/sth** to injure sb or damage sth 使受伤；破坏；损害 ▶ **knackering** *adj.* [not usually before noun] (*BrE, informal*)：*I don't do aerobics any more—it's too knackering.* 我再不做有氧健身操了，太累人了。

knack·ered /ˈnækəd; *NAmE* -kərd/ *adj.* (*BrE, slang*) **1** [not usually before noun] extremely tired 筋疲力尽；疲惫不堪 **SYN** **exhausted, worn out** **2** too old or broken to use 旧（或破）得不能用了

ˈ**knacker's yard** (*also* **the knackers**) *noun* [usually sing.] (*old-fashioned, BrE*) a place where old and injured horses are taken to be killed 老残马匹屠宰场

knap·sack /ˈnæpsæk/ *noun* (*old-fashioned* or *NAmE*) a small RUCKSACK 小背包

knave /neɪv/ *noun* **1** (*old-fashioned*) = JACK (3)：*the knave of clubs* 梅花 J **2** (*old use*) a dishonest man or boy 不诚实的男人（或男孩）；无赖；恶棍

knead /niːd/ *verb* **1** ~ **sth** to press and stretch DOUGH, wet CLAY, etc. with your hands to make it ready to use 揉，捏（面团、湿黏土等） ➲ VISUAL VOCAB PAGE V30 **2** ~ **sth** to rub and squeeze muscles, etc. especially to relax them or to make them less painful 揉捏，按摩，推拿（肌肉等）

knee 🔑 /niː/ *noun, verb*

■ *noun* **1** 🔑 the joint between the top and bottom parts of the leg where it bends in the middle 膝；膝盖；膝关节：*a knee injury* 膝关节受伤 ◇ *I grazed my knee when I fell.* 我摔了一跤，把膝盖擦破了。◇ *He* ***went down on one knee*** *and asked her to marry him.* 他单膝跪下向她求婚。◇ *She was* ***on her knees*** *scrubbing the kitchen floor.* 她在厨房里跪着刷洗地板。 ➲ VISUAL VOCAB PAGE V64 **2** 🔑 the part of a piece of clothing that covers the knee（裤子的）膝部：*These jeans are torn at the knee.* 这牛仔裤膝盖那儿破了。◇ *a knee patch* 膝部的补丁 **3** 🔑 the top surface of the upper part of the legs when you are sitting down（坐下时）大腿朝上的面 **SYN** **lap**：*Come and sit on Daddy's knee.* 来坐在爸爸腿上。 ➲ MORE LIKE THIS 20, page R27

IDM **bring sb to their 'knees** to defeat sb, especially in a war（尤指战争中）打败某人，使某人屈膝投降 **bring sth to its 'knees** to badly affect an organization, etc. so that it can no longer function 摧毁某物；使（组织等）瘫痪（或崩溃）：*The strikes brought the industry to its knees.* 罢工使得这个行业陷入瘫痪。 **put sb over your 'knee** to punish sb by making them lie on top of your knee and hitting their bottom 把某人放在膝上打屁股 ➲ MORE AT BEE, BEND *v.*, MOTHER *n.*, WEAK

■ *verb* (**kneed, kneed**) ~ **sb/sth** to hit or push sb/sth with your knee 用膝盖顶（或撞）：*He kneed his attacker in the groin.* 他用膝盖猛撞攻击者的下身。

knee·cap /ˈniːkæp/ *noun, verb*

■ *noun* the small bone that covers the front of the knee 膝盖骨；髌骨 **SYN** **patella**

■ *verb* (**-pp-**) ~ **sb** to shoot or break sb's kneecaps as a form of punishment that is not official and is illegal 用枪击穿膝盖骨，击碎膝盖骨（非法刑罚） ▶ **knee·cap·ping** *noun* [C, U]

ˌ**knee-ˈdeep** *adj.* up to your knees 没膝的；齐膝深的：*The snow was knee-deep in places.* 有些地方的雪已齐膝深了。◇ (*figurative*) *I was knee-deep in work.* 我当时工作缠身。 ▶ ˌ**knee-ˈdeep** *adv.*：*I waded in knee-deep.* 我在齐膝深的水中跋涉。

ˌ**knee-ˈhigh** *adj.* high enough to reach your knees 齐膝高的

IDM **knee-high to a 'grasshopper** (*informal, humorous*) very small; very young 矮小；幼小

ˈ**knee-jerk** *adj.* [only before noun] (*disapproving*) produced automatically, without any serious thought 本能地做出的；未经思考做出的：*It was* ***a knee-jerk reaction*** *on her part.* 这是她未加思索做出的反应。

kneel /niːl/ *verb* (**knelt, knelt** /nelt/) (*NAmE also* **kneeled, kneeled**) [I] to be in or move into a position where your body is supported on your knee or knees 跪；跪着；跪下：*a kneeling figure* 跪着的人影 ◇ ~ (**down**) *We knelt (down) on the ground to examine the tracks.* 我们跪在地上察看踪迹。 ➲ MORE LIKE THIS 20, page R27

ˈ**knee-length** *adj.* long enough to reach your knees 长及膝部的：*knee-length shorts/socks* 长及膝部的短裤 / 袜子

ˈ**knees-up** *noun* [usually sing.] (*BrE, informal*) a noisy party, with dancing 喧闹的社交集会；欢快的舞会

ˈ**knee trembler** *noun* (*informal*) an act of sex that is done standing up 站立性交

knell /nel/ *noun* [sing.] = DEATH KNELL

knelt PAST TENSE, PAST PART. OF KNEEL

knew PAST TENSE OF KNOW

knick·er·bockers /ˈnɪkəbɒkəz; *NAmE* ˈnɪkərbɑːkərz/ (*NAmE also* **knick·ers**) *noun* [pl.] short loose trousers/pants that fit tightly just below the knee, worn especially in the past（尤指旧时穿的膝下扎紧的）灯笼裤

knick·ers /ˈnɪkəz; *NAmE* -kərz/ *noun* [pl.] **1** (*BrE*) (*also* **pan·ties** *NAmE, BrE*) a piece of women's underwear that covers the body from the waist to the tops of the legs 女式短衬裤：*a pair of knickers* 一条女式短衬裤 **2** (*NAmE*) = KNICKERBOCKERS ▶ **knick·er** *adj.* [only before noun]: *knicker elastic*（女用）短衬裤松紧带

IDM **get your 'knickers in a twist** (*BrE, slang*) to become angry, confused or upset 恼火；困惑；烦闷 ➲ MORE AT WET *v.*

knick-knack /ˈnɪk næk/ *noun* [usually pl.] (*sometimes disapproving*) a small decorative object in a house（房子里的）小装饰物，小摆设 **SYN** **ornament**

knife 🔑 /naɪf/ *noun, verb*

■ *noun* 🔑 (*pl.* **knives** /naɪvz/) a sharp blade with a handle, used for cutting or as a weapon 刀：*knives and forks* 刀叉 ◇ *a sharp knife* 锋利的刀 ◇ *a bread knife* (= one for cutting bread) 切面包刀 ◇ *She was murdered in a frenzied knife attack.* 她被乱刀残杀。 ➲ VISUAL VOCAB PAGES V23, V27 ➲ SEE ALSO FLICK KNIFE, JACKKNIFE *n.*, PALETTE KNIFE, PAPERKNIFE, PENKNIFE, STANLEY KNIFE™ ➲ MORE LIKE THIS 20, page R27

IDM **the 'knives are out (for sb)** the situation has become so bad that people are preparing to make one person take the blame, for example by taking away their job（对某人）磨刀霍霍，兴师问罪 **like a knife through 'butter** (*informal*) easily; without meeting any difficulty 轻而易举；毫无困难 **put/stick the 'knife in | put/stick the 'knife into sb** (*informal*) to be very unfriendly to sb and try to harm them 对某人怀恨在心；加害于某人 **turn/twist the 'knife (in the wound)** to say or do sth unkind deliberately; to make sb who is unhappy feel even more unhappy 恶意地说（或做）；落井下石；往伤口上撒

盐 **under the 'knife** (*informal*) having a medical operation 接受手术；动手术

■ *verb* **~ sb** to injure or kill sb with a knife 用刀伤害（或杀害） SYN **stab**

'knife-edge *noun* [usually sing.] the sharp edge of a knife 刀刃

IDM **on a 'knife-edge 1** (of a situation, etc. 形势等) finely balanced between success and failure 胜负难料；成败未定：*The economy is balanced on a knife-edge.* 经济形势尚不明朗。**2** (of a person 人) very worried or anxious about the result of sth 十分焦虑；急于知道结果

knife·point /ˈnaɪfpɔɪnt/ *noun*

IDM **at 'knifepoint** while being threatened, or threatening sb, with a knife 在刀子威胁下：*She was raped at knifepoint.* 她遭持刀强奸。

knight /naɪt/ *noun, verb*

■ *noun* **1** (in the Middle Ages) a man of high social rank who had a duty to fight for his king. Knights are often shown in pictures riding horses and wearing ARMOUR.（中世纪的）骑士 ➲ SEE ALSO WHITE KNIGHT **2** (in Britain) a man who has been given a special honour by the king or queen and has the title *Sir* before his name（英国）爵士（其名前冠以 Sir） ➲ COMPARE BARONET **3** a piece used in the game of CHESS that is shaped like a horse's head（国际象棋中的）马 ➲ VISUAL VOCAB PAGE V42 ➲ MORE LIKE THIS 20, page R27

IDM **a knight in shining 'armour** (*usually humorous*) a man who saves sb, especially a woman, from a dangerous situation 救人（尤指女子）于危难之中的男子；（拯救美人的）英雄

■ *verb* [usually passive] **~ sb** to give sb the rank and title of a knight 封（某人）为爵士：*He was knighted by the Queen for his services to industry.* 他因对工业界的贡献获女王封为爵士。

knight 'errant *noun* (*pl.* **knights errant**) (in the Middle Ages 中世纪) a KNIGHT who travelled around, looking for adventure 游侠骑士

knight·hood /ˈnaɪthʊd/ *noun* (in Britain) the rank or title of a KNIGHT（英国）爵士头衔，骑士头衔，爵士称号，骑士称号：*He received a knighthood in the New Year's Honours list.* 他是新年受勋者之一，荣获爵士称号。

knight·ly /ˈnaɪtli/ *adj.* [usually before noun] (*literary*) consisting of knights; typical of a knight 由爵士（或骑士）组成的；爵士（或骑士）的；侠义的 SYN **chivalrous**

knit 🔑 /nɪt/ *verb, noun*

■ *verb* (**knit·ted, knit·ted**) HELP In senses 3 and 4 **knit** is usually used for the past tense and past participle. 作第 3 及第 4 义时，过去时和过去分词常用 knit。**1** 🔑 [T, I] to make clothes, etc. from wool or cotton thread using two long thin knitting needles or a machine 编织；针织；机织：**~ (sth)** *I knitted this cardigan myself.* 我自己织的这件开襟毛衣。◇ *Lucy was sitting on the sofa, knitting.* 露西坐在沙发上织毛线活儿。◇ **~ sb sth** *She's knitting the baby a shawl.* 她在给宝宝织一床小被子。**2** [T, I] **~ (sth)** to use a basic STITCH in knitting 织平针：*Knit one row, purl one row.* 织一趟平针，织一趟反针。**3** [T, I] **~ (sb/sth) (together)** to join people or things closely together or to be joined closely together（使）紧密结合，严密，紧凑：*a closely/tightly knit community* (= one in which relationships are very close) 紧密团结的群体 ◇ *Society is knit together by certain commonly held beliefs.* 社会是靠某些共同的信念来维系的。**4** [I, T] **~ (sth)** (of broken bones 断骨) to grow together again to form one piece; to make broken bones grow together again（使）愈合，接合 SYN **mend**：*The bone failed to knit correctly.* 骨头愈合得不好。➲ MORE LIKE THIS 20, page R27, 36, page R29

IDM **knit your 'brow(s)** to move your EYEBROWS together, to show that you are thinking hard, feeling angry, etc. 皱眉（表示沉思、恼怒等） SYN **frown**

■ *noun* [usually pl.] a piece of clothing that has been knitted 编织的衣服；针织衫：*winter knits* 编织的冬衣

knit·ted 🔑 /ˈnɪtɪd/ (*also* **knit**) *adj.* made by knitting wool or thread 编织的；针织的：*knitted gloves* 编织手套 ◇ *a white knit dress* 白色针织连衣裙 ◇ *a hand-knitted sweater* 手工编织的毛衣 ◇ *a cotton-knit shirt* 针织棉衬衫

knit·ter /ˈnɪtə(r)/ *noun* a person who knits 编织者；针织工

knit·ting 🔑 /ˈnɪtɪŋ/ *noun* [U] **1** 🔑 an item that is being knitted 编织物；针织品：*Where's my knitting?* 我织的东西上哪儿去了？**2** 🔑 the activity of knitting 编织；针织

'knitting needle *noun* a long thin stick with a round end that you use for knitting by hand 编织针；毛衣针 ➲ VISUAL VOCAB PAGE V45

knit·wear /ˈnɪtweə(r); *NAmE* -wer/ *noun* [U] items of clothing that have been knitted 针织衫；针织衣物

knives PL. OF KNIFE

knob /nɒb; *NAmE* nɑːb/ *noun* **1** a round switch on a machine such as a television that you use to turn it on and off, etc.（用以开关电视机等的）旋钮：*the volume control knob* 音量控制旋钮 **2** a round handle on a door or a drawer（门或抽屉的）球形把手 **3** a round lump on the surface or end of sth 疙瘩；节 ➲ PICTURE AT HANDLE **4** (*especially BrE*) a small lump of sth such as butter 小块（黄油等） **5** (*BrE, taboo, slang*) a PENIS 阴茎 ➲ MORE LIKE THIS 20, page R27

IDM **with 'knobs on** (*BrE, slang*) used to say that sth is a more complicated version of what you mention 有过之而无不及；更是如此；尤其突出：*It isn't art—it's just a horror movie with knobs on!* 那不是艺术，只是更加惊悚的恐怖片而已！

knob·bly /ˈnɒbli; *NAmE* ˈnɑːbli/ (*especially NAmE* **knobby** /ˈnɒbi; *NAmE* ˈnɑːbi/) *adj.* having small hard lumps 有节的；多疙瘩的：*knobbly knees* 骨节突出的膝盖

knock 🔑 /nɒk; *NAmE* nɑːk/ *verb, noun*

■ *verb*

• **AT DOOR/WINDOW** 门窗 **1** 🔑 [I] to hit a door, etc. firmly in order to attract attention 敲；击 SYN **rap**：*He knocked three times and waited.* 他敲了三下门就等着。◇ **~ at/on sth** *Somebody was knocking on the window.* 有人在敲窗户。

• **HIT** 击 **2** 🔑 [T, I] to hit sth, often by accident, with a short, hard blow（常为无意地）碰，撞：**~ sth (against/on sth)** *Be careful you don't knock your head on this low beam.* 小心，别把头撞在这矮梁上。◇ **~ against/on sth** *Her hand knocked against the glass.* 她的手碰了玻璃杯。**3** [T] to put sb/sth into a particular state by hitting them/it 把…撞击成（某种状态）：**~ sb/sth + adj.** *The blow knocked me flat.* 那一拳把我打倒在地。◇ *He was knocked senseless by the blow.* 他被一拳打得不省人事。◇ **~ sb/sth doing sth** *She knocked my drink flying.* 她把我的饮料打翻了。◇ **~ sb/sth + adv./prep.** *The two rooms had been knocked into one* (= the wall between them had been knocked down). 那两个房间打通了，成了一个房间。➲ SYNONYMS AT HIT **4** 🔑 [T] to hit sth so that it moves or breaks 打掉；敲动；打破：**~ sth + adv./prep.** *He'd knocked over a glass of water.* 他打翻了一杯水。◇ *I knocked the nail into the wall.* 我把钉子钉进墙里。◇ *They had to knock the door down to get in.* 他们不得不破门而入。◇ *The boys were knocking* (= kicking) *a ball around in the back yard.* 男孩们在后院踢球玩儿。◇ **~ sth** (*figurative*) *The criticism had knocked* (= damaged) *her self-esteem.* 这一批评伤了她的自尊心。➲ SYNONYMS AT HIT **5** [T] **~ sth + adv./prep.** to make a hole in sth by hitting it hard 打，凿（洞）：*They managed to knock a hole in the wall.* 他们设法在墙上凿了个洞。

• **OF HEART/KNEES** 心；膝盖 **6** [I] if your heart **knocks**, it beats hard; if your knees **knock**, they shake, for example from fear（心）怦怦跳；（膝盖）打哆嗦：*My heart was knocking wildly.* 我的心怦怦直跳。

• **OF ENGINE/PIPES** 发动机；管子 **7** [I] to make a regular sound of metal hitting metal, especially because there is sth wrong（尤指因故障）发碰撞声，嘭嘭作响

• **CRITICIZE** 批评 **8** [T] **~ sb/sth** (*informal*) to criticize sb/sth, especially when it happens unfairly（不公平地）批评；贬责；挑剔；非难：*The newspapers are always knocking the England team.* 报纸总是攻击英格兰队。◇ *'E-books?' 'Don't*

K

knock it—there's a great future in e-books.' "电子书？" "别贬损它，电子书的前景大着呢。" ➲ MORE LIKE THIS 20, page R27

IDM **I'll knock your 'block/'head off!** (*informal*) used to threaten sb that you will hit them（威胁要打人）我非揍你不可，我要揍扁你 **knock sb 'dead** (*informal*) to impress sb very much 使某人倾倒：*You look fabulous—you'll knock 'em dead tonight.* 你看上去漂亮极了，今晚肯定把他们迷倒。 **knock sb/sth into a cocked 'hat** (*old-fashioned, BrE*) to be very much better than sb/sth 远远胜过某人（或事物）；大大超过；使相形见绌 **knock it 'off!** (*informal*) used to tell sb to stop making a noise, annoying you, etc. 别吵了；别烦人了 **knock sb off their 'pedestal/'perch** to make sb lose their position as sb/sth successful or admired 使某人丧失名位 **knock sth on the 'head** (*BrE, informal*) to stop sth from happening; to stop doing sth 阻止某事发生；停止做某事：*The recession knocked on the head any idea of expanding the company.* 经济衰退使扩展公司的任何想法都化为泡影。 **ˌknock on 'wood** (*NAmE, saying*) (*BrE* **ˌtouch 'wood**) used when you have just mentioned some way in which you have been lucky in the past, to avoid bringing bad luck（表示希望继续走好运） **knock sb 'sideways** (*informal*) to surprise or shock sb so much that they are unable to react immediately 使某人惊讶得不知所措（或目瞪口呆） **knock 'spots off sb/sth** (*BrE, informal*) to be very much better than sb/sth 远远胜过；大大超过；使相形见绌 **knock the 'stuffing out of sb** (*informal*) to make sb lose their confidence and enthusiasm 使某人丧失信心（或委靡不振） **you could have knocked me down with a 'feather** (*informal*) used to express surprise（表示惊奇） ➲ MORE AT DAYLIGHTS, HEAD *n.*, HELL, SENSE *n.*, SHAPE *n.*, SIX, SOCK *n.*

PHR V **ˌknock a'round...** (*BrE also* **ˌknock a'bout...**) (*informal*) **1** to travel and live in various places 漫游：*He spent a few years knocking around Europe.* 他花了几年时间漫游欧洲。 **2** used to say that sth is in a place but you do not know exactly where（表示某物在一个地方但不知确切位置）：*It must be knocking around here somewhere.* 它肯定在这儿某个地方。 **ˌknock a'round with sb/together** (*BrE also* **ˌknock a'bout with sb/together**) (*informal*) to spend a lot of time with sb/together 常与某人交往（或做伴） **ˌknock sb/sth a'round** (*BrE also* **ˌknock sb/sth a'bout**) (*informal*) to hit sb/sth repeatedly; to treat sb/sth roughly 接连敲击某人（或某物）；粗暴对待

ˌknock sb 'back 1 (*BrE*) to prevent sb from achieving sth or making progress, especially by rejecting them or sth that they suggest or ask 阻碍，妨碍（某人取得成果或进步，尤指以回绝方式） ➲ RELATED NOUN KNOCK-BACK **2** (*BrE*) to surprise or shock sb 使某人大吃一惊（或感到惊讶）：*Hearing the news really knocked me back.* 听到这消息着实让我大吃一惊。 **ˌknock sb 'back sth** (*BrE, informal*) to cost sb a lot of money 用掉某人一大笔钱：*That house must have knocked them back a bit.* 那房子一定花了他们不少钱。 **ˌknock sth↔'back** (*informal*) to drink sth quickly, especially an alcoholic drink 很快喝掉（酒等）

ˌknock sb 'down (from sth) (to sth) (*informal*) to persuade sb to reduce the price of sth 说服…降价；使降价；杀价：*I managed to knock him down to $400.* 我设法让他把价格降到了 400 美元。 **ˌknock sb↔'down/'over** 🔑 to hit sb and make them fall to the ground 打倒（或击倒、撞倒）某人：*She was knocked down by a bus.* 她被一辆公共汽车撞倒在地。 ◇ *He knocked his opponent down three times in the first round.* 他第一局就将对手击倒三次。 **ˌknock sth↔'down** 🔑 to destroy a building by breaking its walls 推倒（或拆掉、拆毁）建筑物 SYN **demolish**: *These old houses are going to be knocked down.* 这些旧房子要拆了。 **ˌknock sth↔'down (from sth) (to sth)** (*informal*) to reduce the price of sth 减价；降价：*He knocked down the price from $80 to $50.* 他把价格从 80 美元降到了 50 美元。 ➲ SEE ALSO KNOCK-DOWN

ˌknock 'off | ˌknock 'off sth (*informal*) to stop doing sth, especially work 停止某事；中断某事；（尤指）下班，收工：*Do you want to knock off early today?* 你今天想早点儿歇工吗？ ◇ *What time do you knock off work?* 你什么时候下班？ ◇ *Let's knock off for lunch.* 咱们收工吃午饭吧。 **ˌknock sb↔'off** (*slang*) to murder sb 杀死（或干掉、除掉、结果）某人 **ˌknock sth↔'off 1** (*informal*) to complete sth quickly and without much effort 迅速而轻松地完成：*He knocks off three novels a year.* 他一年轻松完成三部小说。 **2** (*BrE, slang*) to steal sth; to steal from a place 偷（东西）；抢劫（某处）：*to knock off a DVD player* 偷 DVD 影碟机 ◇ *to knock off a bank* 抢劫银行 **ˌknock sth↔'off | ˌknock sth↔'off sth** (*informal*) to reduce the price or value of sth 降价；减价；使贬值：*They knocked off $60 because of a scratch.* 因为有擦痕，他们将价格减了 60 美元。 ◇ *The news knocked 13% off the company's shares.* 这消息使公司股价下跌 13%。

ˌknock sb↔'out 1 🔑 to make sb fall asleep or become unconscious 使入睡；使昏睡；使不省人事：*The blow knocked her out.* 这一击把她打昏了。 **2** (in boxing 拳击运动) to hit an opponent so that they cannot get up within a limited time and therefore lose the fight 击倒（获胜） ➲ RELATED NOUN KNOCKOUT **3** (*informal*) to surprise and impress sb very much 使大吃一惊；使倾倒；给某人留下深刻印象：*The movie just knocked me out.* 这电影着实令我赞叹不已。 ➲ RELATED NOUN KNOCKOUT **ˌknock sb/yourself 'out** to make sb/yourself very tired 使筋疲力尽；使疲惫不堪 SYN **wear out** **ˌknock sb↔'out (of sth)** to defeat sb so that they cannot continue competing 把…淘汰出（比赛） SYN **eliminate**: *England had been knocked out of the World Cup.* 英格兰队已被淘汰出世界杯足球赛。 ➲ SEE ALSO KNOCKOUT **ˌknock sth↔'out** (*informal*) to produce sth, especially quickly and easily 完成；快速而轻易地做成：*He knocks out five books a year.* 他一年轻松写出五本书。

ˌknock sb↔'over = KNOCK SB↔DOWN/OVER

ˌknock sth↔to'gether 1 (*informal*) to make or complete sth quickly and often not very well 草草做成；匆匆拼凑成：*I knocked some bookshelves together from old planks.* 我用旧木板拼拼凑凑做了些书架。 **2** (*BrE*) to make two rooms or buildings into one by removing the wall between them 把两间屋（或两座建筑物）打通：*The house consists of two cottages knocked together.* 这房子是将两栋小屋的隔墙打通合二为一的。

ˌknock 'up (in TENNIS, etc. 网球等) to practise for a short time before the start of a game 赛前练习 **ˌknock sb↔'up 1** (*BrE, informal*) to wake sb by knocking on their door 敲门唤醒某人 **2** (*informal*) to make a woman pregnant 使怀孕 **ˌknock sth↔'up** to prepare or make sth quickly and without much effort 迅速准备好；快速并轻易地做成：*She knocked up a meal in ten minutes.* 她十分钟就做好了一顿饭。

■ ***noun***

• **AT DOOR/WINDOW** 门窗 **1** 🔑 the sound of sb hitting a door, window, etc. with their hand or with sth hard to attract attention 敲击声；敲门（或窗等）声：*There was a knock on/at the door.* 有敲门声。

• **HIT** 击 **2** 🔑 a sharp blow from sth hard 捶击；敲击；撞击 SYN **bang**: *He got a nasty knock on the head.* 他头部遭到重重一击。

IDM **take a (hard, nasty, etc.) 'knock** to have an experience that makes sb/sth less confident or successful; to be damaged 遭受（重大等）挫折；受到（沉重等）打击；受到（严重等）破坏

knock·about /ˈnɒkəbaʊt; *NAmE* ˈnɑːk-/ *adj.* [usually before noun] (*BrE*) **knockabout** entertainment involves people acting in a deliberately silly way, for example falling over or hitting other people, in order to make the audience laugh 闹剧的；喧闹喜剧的 SYN **slapstick**

'knock-back *noun* (*informal*) a difficulty or problem that makes you feel less confident that you will be successful in sth that you are doing, especially when sb rejects you or sth you suggest or ask（尤指被人拒绝时受到的）挫折，挫伤，打击

'knock-down *adj., noun*

■ ***adj.*** [only before noun] (*informal*) **1** (of prices, etc. 价格等) much lower than usual 低廉的 SYN **rock-bottom** **2** using a lot of force 强有力的；用力的：*a knock-down punch* 强有力的一拳

■ ***noun*** **1** (in boxing 拳击运动) an act of falling to the ground after being hit 击倒 **2** (in football (SOCCER) 足球) an act of hitting a high ball down to the ground or to another player 将高球顶到地上或传给另一球员

ˌknock-down-ˈdrag-out *adj.* [only before noun] (*NAmE, informal*) (of a fight or an argument) very aggressive and unpleasant（打架或争吵）激烈的，猛烈的

knock·er /ˈnɒkə(r); *NAmE* ˈnɑːk-/ *noun* **1** (*also* **ˈdoor knocker**) [C] a metal object attached to the outside of the door of a house, etc. which you hit against the door to attract attention（固定在门上供敲门用的）门环 ➲ VISUAL VOCAB PAGE V18 **2** [C] (*informal*) a person who is always criticizing sb/sth 吹毛求疵的人；一味批评的人 **3 knockers** [pl.] (*taboo, slang*) an offensive word for a woman's breasts（冒犯语）乳房，奶子

ˈknocking copy *noun* [U] (*BrE, informal*) advertising in which an opponent's product is criticized 诋毁性广告（针对竞争对手）

ˈknocking shop *noun* (*BrE, informal*) a BROTHEL (= place where people can pay for sex) 妓院

ˌknock-ˈkneed *adj.* having legs that turn towards each other at the knees 膝外翻的

ˌknock ˈknees *noun* [pl.] legs that turn towards each other at the knees 膝外翻；X 形腿

ˌknock-ˈon *adj.* (*especially BrE*) causing other events to happen one after another in a series 使产生连锁反应的：*The increase in the price of oil had* ***a knock-on effect*** *on the cost of many other goods.* 石油价格上涨对其他许多商品的价格引起了连锁反应。

knock·out /ˈnɒkaʊt; *NAmE* ˈnɑːk-/ *noun, adj.*

■ ***noun*** **1** (*abbr.* **KO**) (in boxing 拳击运动) a blow that makes an opponent fall to the ground and be unable to get up, so that he or she loses the fight 击败对手的一击；击倒对手获胜 **2** (*informal*) a person or thing that is very attractive or impressive 引人注目（或给人留下深刻印象的）的人（或物）

■ ***adj.*** [only before noun] **1** (*especially BrE*) a **knockout** competition is one in which the winning player/team at each stage competes in the next stage and the losing one no longer takes part in the competition 淘汰赛的；淘汰的：*the knockout stages of the tournament* 锦标赛的淘汰赛阶段 **2** a **knockout** blow is one that hits sb so hard that they can no longer get up 击败对手的

ˈknock-up *noun* (*BrE*) a short practice before a game, especially of TENNIS（尤指网球的）赛前练习

knoll /nəʊl; *NAmE* noʊl/ *noun* a small round hill 圆丘；土墩 SYN **mound**

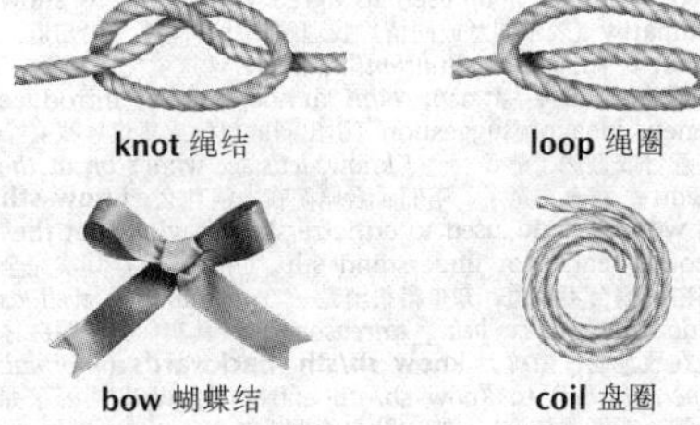

knot 🔑 /nɒt; *NAmE* nɑːt/ *noun, verb*

■ ***noun***

• **IN STRING/ROPE** 绳索 **1** 🔑 a join made by tying together two pieces or ends of string, rope, etc.（用绳索等打的）结：*to tie a knot* 打结 ◇ *Tie the two ropes together with a knot.* 将这两根绳子打结系在一起。◇ (*figurative*) *hair full of knots and tangles* (= twisted in a way that is difficult to COMB) 缠结在一起乱糟糟的头发

• **OF HAIR** 头发 **2** a way of twisting hair into a small round shape at the back of the head 发髻：*She had her hair in a knot.* 她把头发打了个髻。

• **IN WOOD** 木头 **3** a hard round spot in a piece of wood where there was once a branch 节子；节疤

• **GROUP OF PEOPLE** 一群人 **4** a small group of people standing close together 一小群人

• **OF MUSCLES** 肌肉 **5** a tight, hard feeling in the stomach, throat, etc. caused by nerves, anger, etc.（由紧张、恼怒等引起的胃、喉等的）痉挛，郁结，哽咽，哽塞：*My stomach was in knots.* 我的心揪得紧紧的。◇ *I could feel a knot of fear in my throat.* 我很害怕，感到喉咙发紧。

• **SPEED OF BOAT/PLANE** 船 / 飞机的速度 **6** a unit for measuring the speed of boats and aircraft; one NAUTICAL MILE per hour 节（船和航空器的速度计量单位，每小时一海里）IDM SEE RATE *n.*, TIE *v.*

■ ***verb*** (**-tt-**)

• **TIE WITH KNOT** 打结 **1** [T] ~ **sth** to fasten sth with a knot or knots 把…打成结（或扎牢）：*He carefully knotted his tie.* 他仔细地打着领带。

• **TWIST** 缠绕 **2** [I] to become twisted into a knot 缠结 SYN **tangle** **3** [T] ~ **sth** to twist hair into a particular shape 打发髻：*She wore her hair loosely knotted on top of her head.* 她在头顶上打了个松松的发髻。

• **MUSCLES** 肌肉 **4** [I, T] ~ (**sth**) if muscles, etc. **knot** or sth **knots** them, they become hard and painful because of fear, excitement, etc.（因害怕、激动等而）痉挛，紧缩，使痉挛：*She felt her stomach knot with fear.* 她感到害怕，心都揪紧了。➲ MORE LIKE THIS 20, page R27

IDM **get ˈknotted** (*BrE, informal, slang*) a rude way of telling sb to go away or of telling them that you are annoyed with them 滚蛋；见鬼去；别烦人

knotty /ˈnɒti; *NAmE* ˈnɑːti/ *adj.* (**knot·tier**, **knot·ti·est**) **1** complicated and difficult to solve 复杂的；难以解决的；棘手的 SYN **thorny**: *a knotty problem* 棘手的问题 **2** having parts that are hard and twisted together 有节的；缠绕在一起的：*the knotty roots of the old oak tree* 盘根错节的老橡树根

know 🔑 /nəʊ; *NAmE* noʊ/ *verb, noun*

■ ***verb*** (**knew** /njuː; *NAmE* nuː/, **known** /nəʊn; *NAmE* noʊn/) (not used in the progressive tenses 不用于进行时)

• **HAVE INFORMATION** 知悉 **1** 🔑 [T, I] to have information in your mind as a result of experience or because you have learned or been told it 知道；知悉；了解：~ **sth** *Do you know his address?* 你知道他的地址吗？◇ *The cause of the fire is not yet known.* 火灾的原因尚不清楚。◇ ***All I know*** *is that she used to work in a bank* (= I have no other information about her). 我只知道她曾在银行工作过。◇ ~ (**that**)... *I know (that) people's handwriting changes as they get older.* 我知道人们的笔迹随着年龄的增长而变化。◇ **it is known that...** *It is widely known that CFCs can damage the ozone layer.* 众所周知氯氟烃会破坏臭氧层。◇ ~ **where, what, etc....** *I knew where he was hiding.* 我知道他藏在哪里。◇ *I didn't know what he was talking about.* 我不知道他在谈什么。◇ ~ (**of/about sth**) *'You've got a flat tyre.' 'I*

▼ **EXPRESS YOURSELF** 情景表达

Saying that you don't know something or giving yourself time to think 表示不知道或需要想一想

There are various ways of telling people that you haven't got the information they are asking for. 告诉别人你不知道他们想要了解的信息，有多种方式：

- ***I really don't know.*** 我确实不知道。
- ***I'm afraid I don't have the faintest idea.*** 很抱歉，我一点都不知道。
- ***Sorry, I have absolutely no idea.*** 对不起，我完全不知道。
- *Has anyone left a message?* ***No, not to my knowledge/not as far as I know.*** 有谁留过言吗？没有，据我所知没有。
- ***Well, that's a good question.*** 嗯，这是一个很好的问题。
- ***Yes, that's an interesting point/idea.*** 是的，这观点很有意思。
- ***Well, let me see...*** 好吧，让我想一想…
- ***Let me think about that for a moment.*** 让我想一下。

K

know.' "你的车胎瘪了。" "我知道。" ◇ *'What's the answer?' 'I don't know.'* "答案是什么？" "我不知道。" ◇ *'There's no one in.' **'How do you know?'*** "一个人都没有。" "你怎么知道呢？" ◇ *You know about Amanda's baby, don't you?* 你知道阿曼达的小宝宝吧？ ◇ ***I don't know about you, but*** *I'm ready for something to eat.* 不管你怎么样，反正我要吃点东西。 ◇ ***I know of*** *at least two people who did the same thing.* 我知道至少有两人干过同样的事。 ◇ *'Is anyone else coming?' **'Not that I know of.'*** "还有别的人要来吗？" "据我所知没有了。" ◇ *'Isn't that his car?' **'I wouldn't know./How should I know?'*** (= I don't know and I am not the person you should ask.) "那不是他的汽车吗？" "我怎么会知道呢？" ◇ (*informal*) *'What are you two whispering about?' **'You don't want to know'*** (= because you would be shocked or wouldn't approve). "你们俩在说什么悄悄话？" "你还是不知道的好。" ◇ **~ to do sth** *Does he know to come here* (= that he should come here) *first?* 他知道要先到这儿来吗？ ◇ **~ sb/sth to be/do sth** *We know her to be honest.* 我们知道她很诚实。 ◇ *Two women are known to have died.* 据悉两名妇女死了。 ➲ SEE ALSO NEED-TO-KNOW ➲ EXPRESS YOURSELF AT INFORMATION

- **REALIZE** 意识到 **2** 🔑 [T, I] to realize, understand or be aware of sth 认识到；懂得；意识到： **~ (that)...** *As soon as I walked in the room I knew (that) something was wrong.* 我刚走进屋就意识到出了事。 ◇ *She knew she was dying.* 她知道自己快死了。 ◇ **~ what, how, etc....** *I knew perfectly well what she meant.* 我完全懂她的意思。 ◇ *I know exactly how you feel.* 我非常清楚你的感受。 ◇ **~ (sth)** *This case is hopeless **and he knows it*** (= although he will not admit it). 这个案子毫无希望，这一点他是清楚的。 ◇ *'Martin was lying all the time.' **'I should have known.'*** "马丁一直在撒谎。" "我本该察觉到的。"
- **FEEL CERTAIN** 确信 **3** 🔑 [T, I] to feel certain about sth 确信；确知；肯定： **~ (that)...** *He knew (that) he could trust her.* 他确信她是可以信赖的。 ◇ *I know it's here somewhere!* 我肯定它在这儿某个地方！ ◇ *I don't know that I can finish it by next week.* 我没有把握能在下周完成。 ◇ **~ (sth)** *'You were right—someone's been spreading rumours about you.' 'I knew it!'* "你说得对，有人一直在散布你的谣言。" "我早就知道！" ◇ *'She's the worst player in the team.' 'Oh, **I don't know*** (= I am not sure that I agree)*—she played well yesterday.'* "她是最糟的队员。" "哦，是吗？她昨天表现可不错。" ➲ SEE ALSO DON'T-KNOW
- **BE FAMILIAR** 熟悉 **4** 🔑 [T] **~ sb/sth** to be familiar with a person, place, thing, etc. 熟悉；认识；了解： *I've known David for 20 years.* 我认识戴维已有 20 年了。 ◇ *Do you two know each other* (= have you met before)? 你们俩认识吗？ ◇ *She's very nice when you **get to know** her.* 你了解她以后就会觉得她非常可爱。 ◇ ***Knowing Ben,*** *we could be waiting a long time* (= it is typical of him to be late). 本这个人我们了解，能叫我们等很长时间。 ◇ *This man **is known to the police*** (= as a criminal). 这男人是在警方挂了号的。 ◇ *I know Paris well.* 我很熟悉巴黎。 ◇ *Do you know the play* (= have you seen or read it before)? 你知道这出戏吗？ ◇ *The new rules could mean the end of football **as we know it*** (= in the form that we are familiar with). 这些新规则可能意味着我们熟悉的足球终结了。
- **REPUTATION** 名声 **5** 🔑 [T, usually passive] to think that sb/sth is a particular type of person or thing or has particular characteristics 把…看作是；认为…是： **~ sb/sth as sth** *It's known as the most dangerous part of the city.* 人们都认为那是市内最危险的地段。 ◇ **~ sb/sth for sth** *She is best known for her work on the human brain.* 她在对人脑的研究方面最为知名。 ◇ **~ sb/sth to be/do sth** *He's known to be an outstanding physicist.* 他被公认为杰出的物理学家。
- **GIVE NAME** 命名 **6** 🔑 [T] **~ sb/sth as sth** [usually passive] to give sb/sth a particular name or title 将…称为；把…叫做： *The drug is commonly known as Ecstasy.* 这种致幻药通常称作摇头丸。 ◇ *Peter Wilson, also known as 'the Tiger'* 彼得•威尔逊，也称"老虎"
- **RECOGNIZE** 认出 **7** 🔑 [T] **~ sb/sth** to be able to recognize sb/sth 能认出；能辨认出： *I couldn't see who was speaking, but I knew the voice.* 我看不到谁在讲话，但我能辨认出声音。 ◇ *She knows a bargain when she sees one.* 她一看就知道有没有便宜可捡。 ➲ SYNONYMS AT IDENTIFY
- **DISTINGUISH** 区分 **8** [T] **~ sb/sth from sb/sth** to be able to distinguish one person or thing from another 能区分；能分辨 SYN **differentiate**: *I hope we have taught our children to know right from wrong.* 我希望我们教给了孩子分辨是非的能力。
- **SKILL/LANGUAGE** 技能；语言 **9** 🔑 [T] to have learned a skill or language and be able to use it 学会；掌握： **~ sth** *Do you know any Japanese?* 你会日语吗？ ◇ **~ how, what, etc....** *Do you know how to use spreadsheets?* 你知道电子数据表的使用方法吗？
- **EXPERIENCE** 经历 **10** [T] (only used in the perfect tenses 仅用于完成时) to have seen, heard or experienced sth 看到过；听到过；经历过： **~ sb/sth (to) do sth** *I've never known it (to) snow in July before.* 我以前从未见到过七月份下雪。 ◇ **be known to do sth** *He has been known to spend all morning in the bathroom.* 听说他整个上午都待在盥洗室里。 **11** [T] **~ sth** to have personal experience of sth 亲身体验；亲身经历： *He has known both poverty and wealth.* 他贫富生活都亲身经历过。 ◇ *She may be successful now, but she has **known what it is like to be** poor.* 她现在算是成功了，但她尝过贫穷的滋味。 ➲ MORE LIKE THIS 20, page R27

IDM **before you know where you 'are** very quickly or suddenly 瞬息之间；转眼间；一下子： *We were whisked off in a taxi before we knew where we were.* 还没等我们弄清怎么回事，出租车就一阵风似的把我们带走了。 **be not to 'know** to have no way of realizing or being aware that you have done sth wrong 无从知道，并不知道（做错了事）： *'I'm sorry, I called when you were in bed.' 'Don't worry—you weren't to know.'* "对不起，你睡觉时打电话打扰你了。" "别在意，你不是故意的嘛。" **for all you, I, they, etc. know** (*informal*) used to emphasize that you do not know sth and that it is not important to you（强调不知道对自己无关紧要的事）不知道，说不定，亦未可知： *She could be dead for all I know.* 她说不定已经死了。 **God/goodness/Heaven knows** (*informal*) **1** 🔑 used to emphasize that you do not know sth （强调不知道）谁知道，天晓得： *God knows what else they might find.* 谁知道他们还可能找到什么。 ◇ *'Where are they?' 'Goodness knows.'* "他们在哪儿？" "天晓得。" HELP Some people may find the use of **God knows** offensive. 有人可能认为用 God knows 含冒犯意。 **2** used to emphasize the truth of what you are saying（强调所言属实）老天作证，确实，的确： *She ought to pass the exam—goodness knows she's been working hard enough.* 她应该考试合格，她已经够努力了。 **I don't know how, why, etc....** (*informal*) used to criticize sb's behaviour（批评某人的行为）真想不到，真不知道： *I don't know how you can say things like that.* 真想不到你怎么会说出这种话来。 **I know** (*informal*) **1** 🔑 /aɪ 'nəʊ; *NAmE* aɪ 'noʊ/ used to agree with sb or to show sympathy（表示同意或同情）我理解，我有同感，我知道： *'What a ridiculous situation!' 'I know.'* "这境况真荒唐！" "的确是。" **2** 🔑 /'aɪ nəʊ; *NAmE* 'aɪ noʊ/ used to introduce a new idea or suggestion（引出新的想法或建议）我有个主意（或办法、建议）： *I know, let's see what's on at the theatre.* 我有主意了，咱们看看剧院在上演什么。 **know sth as well as 'I do** used to criticize sb by saying that they should realize or understand sth （用以批评）其实完全明白，哪会不知道，知道得很清楚： *You know as well as I do that you're being unreasonable.* 其实你完全明白你是在故意胡搅蛮缠。 **know sb/sth 'backwards** (*informal, especially BrE*) to know sb/sth extremely well 对…了如指掌（或倒背如流）；把…背得滚瓜烂熟： *She must know the play backwards by now.* 她现在对这个剧本肯定是倒背如流。 **know 'best** to know what should be done, etc. better than other people 最懂得，最知道，比谁都明白（该怎么做等）： *The doctor told you to stay in bed, and she knows best.* 医生叫你卧床休息，她最清楚你该怎么做。 **know better (than that/than to do sth)** to be sensible enough not to do sth 明白事理（而不至于）；不至于糊涂到： *He knows better than to judge by appearances.* 他明白得很，决不会凭表面现象来判断。 **know sb by 'sight** to recognize sb without knowing them well 与某人面熟 **know 'different/'otherwise** (*informal*) to have information or evidence that the opposite is true 所知道的不是那么回事；所掌握的情况大不一样（或大相径庭）： *He says he doesn't care about what the critics write, but I know different.* 他说他并不在乎批评家的评论，可我知道不是那么

回事。 **know full 'well** to be very aware of a fact and unable to deny or ignore it 非常清楚；不可否认；不可忽视： *He knew full well what she thought of it.* 他非常清楚她对此事的看法。 **know sb/sth inside 'out | know sb/sth like the back of your 'hand** (*informal*) to be very familiar with sb/sth（对…）极为熟悉，了如指掌： *This is where I grew up. I know this area like the back of my hand.* 我在这儿长大的，我对这地方再熟悉不过了。 **know your own 'mind** to have very firm ideas about what you want to do 知道自己想做什么；有主见 **know your 'stuff** (*informal*) to know a lot about a particular subject or job 精通业务；对工作很内行 **know your way a'round** to be familiar with a place, subject, etc. 熟悉周围情况（或话题等） **know what you're 'talking about** (*informal*) to have knowledge about sth from your own experience 亲身经历过；作经验之谈 **know which side your 'bread is buttered** (*informal*) to know where you can get an advantage for yourself 知道自己的利益所在 **let it be known/make it known that...** (*formal*) to make sure that people are informed about sth, especially by getting sb else to tell them（尤指通过他人传达而）使人知晓，让人知道： *The President has let it be known that he does not intend to run for election again.* 总统已经公开表示他不打算再次参加竞选。 **let sb 'know** 🔑 to tell sb about sth 让某人知道；告诉（或通知）某人： *Let me know how I can help.* 我能帮什么忙，只管说。 **make yourself 'known to sb** to introduce yourself to sb 向某人作自我介绍： *I made myself known to the hotel manager.* 我向旅馆老板作了自我介绍。 **not know any 'better** to behave badly, usually because you have not been taught the correct way to behave（因缺乏教养而）表现不好；（因无人指教而）举止不良 **not know your ˌarse from your 'elbow** (*BrE, taboo, slang*) to be very stupid or completely lacking in skill 愚蠢之至；屁都不懂 **not know 'beans about sth** (*NAmE, informal*) to know nothing about a subject 完全不懂行；对…一窍不通 **not know the first thing a'bout sb/sth** to know nothing at all about sb/sth 对…一无所知；对…一窍不通 **not know sb from 'Adam** (*informal*) to not know at all who sb is 根本不认识某人；与某人素不相识 **not know what 'hit you** (*informal*) to be so surprised by sth that you do not know how to react 因吃惊而不知所措；惊呆了 **not know where to 'look** (*informal*) to feel great embarrassment and not know how to react 尴尬得不知如何是好；狼狈不堪；感到很难堪 **not know whether you're 'coming or 'going** (*informal*) to be so excited or confused that you cannot behave or think in a sensible way（激动得）不知如何是好；糊里糊涂；不知所措 **not know you are 'born** (*BrE, informal*) to have an easy life without realizing how easy it is 身在福中不知福： *You people without kids don't know you're born.* 你们没孩子，真是身在福中不知福啊。 **there's no 'knowing** used to say that it is impossible to say what might happen 难以预料；无从知道；没法说： *There's no knowing how he'll react.* 很难预料他会有什么样的反应。 **what does... know?** used to say that sb knows nothing about the subject you are talking about （某人）知道什么，懂什么： *What does he know about football, anyway?* 不管怎么说，他懂什么足球？ **what do you 'know?** (*informal*) used to express surprise（表示惊奇）你看怪不怪，真没想到： *Well, what do you know? Look who's here!* 哟，真想不到！你看谁来啦！ **ˌyou 'know** (*informal*) **1** 🔑 used when you are thinking of what to say next（说话人考虑接着说什么时用）： *Well, you know, it's difficult to explain.* 唉，你知道，这很难解释。 **2** 🔑 used to show that what you are referring to is known or understood by the person you are speaking to （表示对方知道或了解所言）你知道的： *Guess who I've just seen? Maggie! You know—Jim's wife.* 你猜我刚才看见谁了，玛吉！你知道的，就是吉姆的妻子。 ◇ *You know that restaurant round the corner? It's closed down.* 拐角那家餐馆，你知道吧？已经倒闭了。 **3** 🔑 used to emphasize sth that you are saying （加强语气）你要知道： *I'm not stupid, you know.* 你要知道，我不是傻子。 **you 'know something/'what?** (*informal*) used to introduce an interesting or surprising opinion, piece of news, etc.（引出令人感兴趣或吃惊的看法、消息等）要我告诉你吗，你听说了吗： *You know something? I've never really enjoyed Christmas.* 要我告诉你吗？圣诞节我从未真正快乐过。 **you know 'who/'what** (*informal*) used to refer to sb/sth without mentioning a name（不说出名称）你知道是谁（或什么） **you never know** 🔑 (*informal*) used to say that you can never be certain about what will happen in the future, especially when you are suggesting that sth good might happen（尤指可能会发生好事）很难说，很难预料 ➲ MORE AT ANSWER *n.*, COST *n.*, DAY, DEVIL, FAR *adv.*, LORD *n.*, OLD, PAT *adv.*, ROPE *n.*, THING, TRUTH

■ *noun*

IDM **in the 'know** (*informal*) having more information about sth than most people 知情；熟悉内幕；掌握内情： *Somebody in the know told me he's going to resign.* 有知情者告诉我他要辞职了。

'know-all (*BrE*) (*also* **'know-it-all** *NAmE, BrE*) *noun* (*informal, disapproving*) a person who behaves as if they know everything 自以为无所不知的人；百事通

Know·bot™ /'nəʊbɒt; *NAmE* 'noʊbɑːt/ *noun* (*computing* 计) a program that is designed to search for data in a large number of DATABASES when a user of a network has asked for information 知识机器人程序（用于网络数据库搜索）

'know-how *noun* [U] (*informal*) knowledge of how to do sth and experience in doing it 专门知识；技能；实际经验： *We need skilled workers and technical know-how.* 我们需要熟练工人和专业技术知识。

know·ing /'nəʊɪŋ; *NAmE* 'noʊ-/ *adj.* [usually before noun] showing that you know or understand about sth that is supposed to be secret 会意的；心照不宣的；知情的： *a knowing smile* 会意的微笑 ➲ COMPARE UNKNOWING

know·ing·ly /'nəʊɪŋli; *NAmE* 'noʊ-/ *adv.* **1** while knowing the truth or likely result of what you are doing 故意地；蓄意地 **SYN** **deliberately**: *She was accused of knowingly making a false statement to the police.* 她被指控故意向警方提供虚假供词。 **2** in a way that shows that you know or understand about sth that is supposed to be secret 会意地；心照不宣地；知情地： *He glanced at her knowingly.* 他会意地看了她一眼。

'know-it-all (*especially NAmE*) (*BrE also* **'know-all**) *noun* (*informal, disapproving*) a person who behaves as if they know everything 自以为无所不知的人；百事通

know·ledge 🔑 /'nɒlɪdʒ; *NAmE* 'nɑːl-/ *noun* **1** 🔑 [U, sing.] the information, understanding and skills that you gain through education or experience 知识；学问；学识： *practical/medical/scientific knowledge* 实际／医学／科学知识 ◇ **~ of/about sth** *He has a wide knowledge of painting and music.* 他在绘画和音乐方面知识渊博。 ◇ *There is a lack of knowledge about the tax system.* 大家对税制缺乏了解。 **2** 🔑 [U] the state of knowing about a particular fact or situation 知晓；知悉；了解： *She sent the letter **without my knowledge**.* 她背着我把信寄了出去。 ◇ *The film was made with the Prince's **full knowledge** and approval.* 这部影片是在王子充分了解和认可的情况下拍摄的。 ◇ *She was impatient **in the knowledge that** time was limited.* 她知道时间有限，所以很着急。 ◇ *I went to sleep **secure in the knowledge** that I was not alone in the house.* 我知道当时不是只有我一人在房子里，就放心地睡觉了。 ◇ *They could relax **safe in the knowledge** that they had the funding for the project.* 他们得知工程资金已有着落时就感到踏实轻松了。 ◇ *He **denied all knowledge of** the affair.* 他否认知道此事。 **3** **~ economy/industry/worker** working with information rather than producing goods 信息，知识（与产品制造相对）

IDM **be common/public 'knowledge** to be sth that everyone knows, especially in a particular community or group 常识；众所周知 **come to sb's 'knowledge** (*formal*) to become known by sb 被某人知道；被某人获悉： *It has come to our knowledge that you have been taking time off without permission.* 我们了解到你们时常未经允许就不上班。 **to your 'knowledge** from the information you have, although you may not know everything 据某人所知： *'Are they divorced?' 'Not to my knowledge.'* "他们离婚了吗？" "据我所知没有。" ➲ MORE AT BEST *n.*

K

know·ledge·able /ˈnɒlɪdʒəbl; *NAmE* ˈnɑːl-/ *adj.* ~ (**about sth**) knowing a lot 博学的；有见识的；知识渊博的 SYN **well informed**: *She is very knowledgeable about plants.* 她对植物很在行。▶ **know·ledge·ably** /-əbli/ *adv.*

known /nəʊn; *NAmE* noʊn/ *adj.* [only before noun] known about, especially by a lot of people 知名的；出了名的；已知的: *He's a known thief.* 他是个出了名的小偷。◇ *The disease has no known cure.* 这种病目前还是不治之症。➲ SEE ALSO KNOW *v.*

knuckle /ˈnʌkl/ *noun, verb*

■ *noun* **1** [C] any of the joints in the fingers, especially those connecting the fingers to the rest of the hand 指节；指关节 ➲ VISUAL VOCAB PAGE V64 **2** (*also* **hock** *especially in NAmE*) [U, C] a piece of meat from the lower part of an animal's leg, especially a pig（猪等动物的）肘，蹄 ➲ MORE LIKE THIS 20, page R27

IDM **near the ˈknuckle** (*BrE, informal*) (of a remark, joke, etc. 言语、玩笑等) concerned with sex in a way that is likely to offend people or make them feel embarrassed 近乎下流；近乎猥亵 ➲ MORE AT RAP *n.*, RAP *v.*

■ *verb*

PHR V **ˌknuckle ˈdown** (**to sth**) (*informal*) to begin to work hard at sth 开始努力做 SYN **get down to**: *I'm going to have to knuckle down to some serious study.* 我得开始认认真真地学习了。**ˌknuckle ˈunder** (**to sb/sth**) (*informal*) to accept sb else's authority 屈服；认输

ˈknuckle-dragger *noun* (*informal*) a stupid man who thinks and behaves in simple, basic ways（缺心眼儿的）莽汉，笨蛋

knuckle·dust·er /ˈnʌkldʌstə(r)/ *noun* (*NAmE also* **ˌbrass ˈknuckles**) a metal cover that is put on the fingers and used as a weapon 指节金属套（用作武器）

knuckle·head /ˈnʌklhed/ *noun* (*NAmE, informal*) a person who behaves in a stupid way 笨蛋；傻瓜

ˌknuckle ˈsandwich *noun* (*slang*) a punch in the mouth 对准嘴巴的一拳

KO (*also* **kayo**) /ˌkeɪ ˈəʊ; *NAmE* ˈoʊ/ *abbr.* KNOCKOUT 击倒

koala /kəʊˈɑːlə; *NAmE* koʊ-/ (*also* **koˌala ˈbear**) *noun* an Australian animal with thick grey fur, large ears and no tail. Koalas live in trees and eat leaves. 树袋熊；考拉；无尾熊 ➲ VISUAL VOCAB PAGE V12

koek·sister /ˈkʊksɪstə(r)/ *noun* (*SAfrE*) a South African sweet dish consisting of shaped pieces of DOUGH that are fried in oil and then covered in a sweet liquid, often eaten at the end of a meal 双姐妹麻花，糖浆麻花（南非的一种甜点，常餐后吃）: *The meal finishes with koeksisters, plaits of deep-fried dough dipped in syrup.* 最后一道餐点是双姐妹麻花，即蘸糖浆的炸麻花。

kofta /ˈkɒftə; *NAmE* ˈkɔːf-/ *noun* [U, C] a S Asian dish of meat, fish or cheese mixed with spices, crushed and shaped into balls; one of these balls 柯夫塔（用肉、鱼或干酪加香料压碎调制成丸子的南亚菜肴）；柯夫塔丸子

kohl /kəʊl; *NAmE* koʊl/ *noun* [U] a black powder that is used especially in Eastern countries. It is put around the eyes to make them more attractive. 黑色眼影粉（尤指东方人用的）

kohl·rabi /ˌkəʊlˈrɑːbi; *NAmE* ˌkoʊl-/ *noun* [U] a vegetable of the CABBAGE family whose thick round white STEM is eaten 球茎甘蓝；苤蓝

koi /kɔɪ/ *noun* (*pl.* **koi**) a large fish originally from Japan, often kept in fish PONDS 锦鲤（观赏鱼，源自日本）

ˈkola nut *noun* = COLA NUT

kombi (*also* **combi**) /ˈkɒmbi; *NAmE* ˈkɑːm-/ *noun* (*SAfrE*) a vehicle that looks like a van, has windows at the sides and carries about ten people 康比小客车（可乘坐约十人）

Ko·modo dragon /kəˌməʊdəʊ ˈdræɡən; *NAmE* kəˌmoʊdoʊ/ *noun* a very large LIZARD from Indonesia 科莫多龙，科莫多巨蜥（产于印度尼西亚）

kook /kuːk/ *noun* (*informal, especially NAmE*) a person who acts in a strange or crazy way 怪人；狂人 ▶ **kooky** *adj.*

kooka·burra /ˈkʊkəbʌrə; *NAmE* -bɜːrə/ *noun* an Australian bird that makes a strange laughing cry 笑翠鸟（产于澳大利亚）

Koori /ˈkʊəri; *NAmE* ˈkʊri/ *noun* (*AustralE*) an Aboriginal person from the south-east of Australia（澳大利亚东南部的）土著

kop /kɒp; *NAmE* kɑːp/ *noun* **1** (*SAfrE, informal*) a head 头；脑袋 **2** (*SAfrE*) (especially in place names 尤用于地名) a hill 小山 **3** (*usually* **the Kop**) (*BrE*) (especially in the past) an area of steps at a football (SOCCER) team's ground where that team's supporters stand to watch the game（尤指旧时足球队主场的）主队球迷看台

kop·pie /ˈkɒpi; *NAmE* ˈkɑːpi/ *noun* (*SAfrE*) a small hill 小山；小丘: *They went for a walk up the koppie.* 他们去小山上散步了。

kora /ˈkɔːrə/ *noun* a W African musical instrument with 21 strings that pass over a bowl-shaped body and are attached to a long wooden part 科拉琴（西非 21 弦乐器，状似竖琴）

Koran (*also* **Qur'an**) /kəˈrɑːn/ *noun* **the Koran** [sing.] the holy book of the Islamic religion, written in Arabic, containing the word of Allah as REVEALED to the Prophet Muhammad《古兰经》；《可兰经》▶ **Kor·an·ic** /kəˈrænɪk/ *adj.*

korf·ball /ˈkɔːfbɔːl; *NAmE* ˈkɔːrf-/ *noun* [U] a game similar to BASKETBALL, played by two teams of eight players, four men and four women 合球，荷兰式篮球运动，科尔夫球（比赛双方各由四男四女组队）

korma /ˈkɔːmə; *NAmE* ˈkɔːrmə/ *noun* [U, C] a S Asian dish or sauce made with cream or YOGURT, and often ALMONDS 奶油（或酸奶）浸肉（常加有杏仁的南亚菜肴或酱汁）: *chicken korma* 奶油浸鸡肉

ko·sher /ˈkəʊʃə(r); *NAmE* ˈkoʊ-/ *adj.* **1** (of food 食物) prepared according to the rules of Jewish law 合礼的（合乎犹太教教规及礼仪要求的） **2** (*informal*) honest or legal 诚实的；合法的: *Their business deals are not always completely kosher.* 他们的商业活动并不总是光明正大的。

kow·tow /ˌkaʊˈtaʊ/ *verb* [I] ~ (**to sb/sth**) (*informal, disapproving*) to show sb in authority too much respect and be too willing to obey them 叩头；磕头；卑躬屈膝；唯命是从

KP /ˌkeɪ ˈpiː/ *noun* [U] (*NAmE*) work done by soldiers in the kitchen, usually as a punishment（常作为士兵惩罚的）伙房帮厨: *The sergeant assigned him to KP.* 中士派他下伙房去帮厨。ORIGIN From 'kitchen police', a name for the soldiers. 源自 kitchen police（帮厨兵）一词。

kph /ˌkeɪ piː ˈeɪtʃ/ *abbr.* kilometres per hour 每小时所行千米（或公里）数；千米每小时

kraal /krɑːl/ *noun* (*SAfrE*) **1** a traditional African village of HUTS surrounded by a fence 栅栏村庄（传统的非洲茅屋村庄） **2** an area surrounded by a fence in which animals are kept 牲畜栏: *a cattle kraal* 牛栏

kra·ken /ˈkrɑːkən/ *noun* an extremely large imaginary creature which is said to appear in the sea near Norway（虚构的出没于挪威附近的）北海巨妖

Kraut /kraʊt/ *noun* (*taboo, slang*) an offensive word for a person from Germany 德国佬；德国鬼子

krill /krɪl/ *noun* [pl.] very small SHELLFISH that live in the sea around the Antarctic and are eaten by WHALES 南极磷虾；磷虾

kris /kriːs/ *noun* a Malay or Indonesian knife with a blade with little curves on its edge（马来或印度尼西亚的）波状刃短剑，波形刀

Kris Kringle /ˌkrɪs ˈkrɪŋɡl/ *noun* (*NAmE*) = SANTA CLAUS **ORIGIN** From *Christkindl*, the German for 'Christ child'. 源自德文 Christkindl，意为"幼年基督"。

krona /ˈkrəʊnə; *NAmE* ˈkroʊnə/ *noun* (*pl.* **kro·nor** /-nɔː(r); -nə(r)/) the unit of money in Sweden and Iceland 克朗（瑞典和冰岛货币单位）

krone /ˈkrəʊnə; *NAmE* ˈkroʊnə/ *noun* (*pl.* **kro·ner** /ˈkrəʊnə(r); *NAmE* ˈkroʊnər/) the unit of money in Denmark and Norway 克朗（丹麦和挪威货币单位）

kryp·ton /ˈkrɪptɒn; *NAmE* -tɑːn/ *noun* [U] (*symb.* **Kr**) a chemical element. Krypton is a gas that does not react with anything, used in FLUORESCENT lights and LASERS. 氪；氪气

kryp·ton·ite /ˈkrɪptənaɪt/ *noun* [U] a chemical element that exists only in stories, especially in stories about Superman, a character with special powers which he loses when he is near to kryptonite 氪（仅存在于超人等故事中的化学元素，超人若接近此元素即丧失超常能力）

kudos /ˈkjuːdɒs; *NAmE* ˈkuːdɑːs/ *noun* [U] the admiration and respect that goes with a particular achievement or position （随某成就或地位而来的）荣誉，威信，光荣，名声 **SYN** **prestige**: *the kudos of playing for such a famous team* 能为这样的名队效力的荣誉

kudu /ˈkuːduː/ *noun* (*pl.* **kudu** or **kudus**) a large greyish or brownish African ANTELOPE with white stripes on its sides. The male kudu has long twisted horns. 捻角羚（见于非洲）

kudzu /ˈkʊdzuː/ *noun* [U] a climbing plant with purple flowers that grows very fast and is used as a food and in medicines 葛

Ku Klux Klan /ˌkuː klʌks ˈklæn/ *noun* [sing.+sing./pl. v.] (*abbr.* **KKK**) a secret organization of white men in the southern states of the US who use violence to oppose social change and equal rights for black people 三 K 党（美国南部的白人秘密组织，通过暴力反对社会变革，反对黑人争取平等权利）

kulfi /ˈkʊlfi/ *noun* [C, U] a type of S Asian ice cream, usually served in the shape of a CONE （南亚）考非冰淇淋（通常为圆锥形）

kum·quat /ˈkʌmkwɒt; *NAmE* -kwɑːt/ *noun* a fruit like a very small orange with sweet skin that is eaten, and sour flesh 金柑；金橘

kung fu /ˌkʌŋ ˈfuː/ *noun* [U] (*from Chinese*) a Chinese system of fighting without weapons, similar to KARATE 功夫（中国武术）

kurta /ˈkɜːtə; *NAmE* ˈkɜːrtə/ *noun* a loose shirt, worn by men or women in S Asia 库尔塔衫，柯泰衫（南亚的宽松衬衫，男女皆宜）

kvetch /kvetʃ/ *verb* [I] (*NAmE, informal*) to complain about sth all the time 老是抱怨；总是发牢骚 **SYN** **moan, whine**

kW *abbr.* (*pl.* **kW**) (in writing 书写形式) KILOWATT 千瓦（电功率单位）: *a 2kW electric fire* 两千瓦的电炉

kwaai /kwaɪ/ *adj.* (*superlative* **kwaai·est**, *no comparative*) (*SAfrE*) (*informal*) **1** very good 极好的；很棒的: *a kwaai song* 很棒的歌 **2** angry or aggressive 生气的；好斗的: *a kwaai dog* 好斗的狗

kwaito /ˈkwaɪtəʊ; *NAmE* -toʊ/ *noun* [U] a type of South African dance music, often with words that are spoken or shouted rather than sung 库威多舞曲（南非舞曲，常伴以说唱）

Kwan·zaa /ˈkwænzɑː/ *noun* [U] a cultural festival that is celebrated in the US by some African Americans from December 26 to January 1 匡扎节（一些非裔美国人于 12 月 26 日至次年 1 月 1 日举行的节日） **ORIGIN** From a phrase in Swahili that means 'first fruits'. 源自斯瓦希里语，意为"首批收获的水果"。

kwashi·or·kor /ˌkwɒʃiˈɔːkɔː(r); ˌkwæʃ-; *NAmE* ˌkwɑːʃiˈɔːrkər/ *noun* [U] a dangerous form of MALNUTRITION that is caused by not eating enough PROTEIN 夸希奥科病；蛋白质营养不良

kwela /ˈkwelə/ *noun* [U] a type of South African JAZZ music in which the main part is usually played on a PENNY WHISTLE (= a type of long whistle with holes in it that you can cover with your fingers to produce different notes) 基维拉（南非爵士乐，主要部分由六孔小笛吹奏）

kWh *abbr.* (*pl.* **kWh**) (in writing 书写形式) KILOWATT-HOUR 千瓦时；一度（电）

kylie /ˈkaɪli/ *noun* (*AustralE*) a BOOMERANG 回力镖；飞去来器

K

Ll

L /el/ *noun, abbr., symbol*

■ ***noun*** (*also* **l**) [C, U] (*pl.* **Ls**, **L's**, **l's** /elz/) the 12th letter of the English alphabet 英语字母表的第 12 个字母：*'Lion' begins with (an) L/'L'.* * lion 一词以字母 l 开头。➲ SEE ALSO L-PLATE

■ ***abbr.*** **1 L.** (especially on maps) Lake（尤标于地图上）湖：*L. Windermere* 温德米尔湖 **2** (especially for sizes of clothes) large（尤指服装的尺码）大号：*S, M and L* (= small, medium and large) 小号、中号和大号

■ ***symbol*** (*also* **l**) the number 50 in ROMAN NUMERALS（罗马数字）50

l /el/ *abbr.* **1** (*pl.* **l**) (in writing 书写形式) litre(s) 升 **2** (*also* **l.**) (*pl.* **ll**) (in writing 书写形式) line (on a page in a book)（书页上的）行

LA (*also* **L.A.**) /ˌel ˈeɪ/ *abbr.* the city of Los Angeles 洛杉矶市

la = LAH ➲ SEE ALSO À LA

laa·ger /ˈlɑːɡə(r)/ *noun* (*SAfrE*) (in the past) a group of WAGONS that were put into a circle in order to protect people in the middle（旧时用马车围成的）临时防御阵地；车阵：*They drew their wagons into a laager and set up camp.* 他们把马车围成一圈扎起营地。◇ ***a laager mentality*** (= one that is not willing to accept new ideas) 守旧心态

Lab. *abbr.* (in British politics 英国政治) Labour 工党

lab 🔑 /læb/ *noun* (*informal*) = LABORATORY：*science labs* 实验室 ◇ *a lab technician* 实验室技术员 ◇ *a lab coat* (= a white coat worn by scientists, etc. working in a laboratory) 实验室白大褂

label
标签

price tag
价格标签

ticket
票

label 🔑 AW /ˈleɪbl/ *noun, verb*

■ ***noun*** **1** 🔑 a piece of paper, etc. that is attached to sth and that gives information about it 标签；签条；标记 SYN **tag**, **ticket**：*The washing instructions are on the label.* 洗涤说明在标签上。◇ *price/address labels* 价格标签；地址签条 ◇ *We tested various supermarkets' **own label** pasta sauces* (= those marked with the name of the shop/store where they are sold). 我们检查了各大超市的自有品牌意大利面调味汁。◇ *He'll only wear clothes with a **designer label**.* 他只穿名牌服装。➲ VISUAL VOCAB PAGE V36 **2** (*disapproving*) a word or phrase that is used to describe sb/sth in a way that seems too general, unfair or not correct（不恰当的）称谓，绰号，叫法：*I hated the label 'housewife'.* 我不喜欢"家庭主妇"这个称谓。 **3** a company that produces and sells music, CDs, etc. 唱片公司：*the Virgin record label* 维京唱片公司 ◇ *It's his first release for a major label.* 这是他在大唱片公司发行的第一张唱片。

■ ***verb*** (**-ll-**, *especially US* **-l-**) [often passive] **1** 🔑 **~ sth** to fix a label on sth or write information on sth 贴标签于；用标签标明：*We carefully labelled each item with the contents and the date.* 我们仔细地把每件物品用标签标明成分和日期。◇ *The file was labelled 'Private'.* 那档案上标明"私人"。 **2** to describe sb/sth in a particular way, especially unfairly（尤指不公正地）把…称为：**~ sb/sth as sth** | **~ sb/sth + noun** *He was labelled (as) a traitor by his former colleagues.* 他被以前的同事称为叛徒。◇ **~ sb/sth + adj.** *It is unfair to label a small baby naughty.* 硬说一个小婴儿淘气是不公平的。➲ MORE LIKE THIS 36, page R29

▼ **SYNONYMS 同义词辨析**

label

tag • sticker

These are all words for a piece of paper, fabric or plastic that is attached to sth and gives information about it. 以上各词均指标签、标记。

label a small piece of paper, fabric or plastic that is attached to sth in order to show what it is or give information about it 指标签、签条、标记：*The washing instructions are on the label.* 洗涤说明在标签上。◇ *address labels* 地址签条 ◇ *He'll only wear clothes with a **designer label**.* 他只穿名牌服装。

tag (often used in compounds) a small piece of paper, fabric or plastic that is attached to sth, or that sb wears, in order to give information about it/them（常构成复合词）指标签、标牌：*Everyone at the conference had to wear a name tag.* 所有与会者必须佩戴名牌。

LABEL OR TAG? 用 label 还是 tag?

Labels in clothes are usually made of fabric and sewn in. **Tags** on clothes are usually made of cardboard and cut off before you wear the clothes. A *name tag* can be stuck or tied onto sb to show who they are. 用于服装时，label 通常指由织物做成并缝在衣服上的标签，tag 通常指挂在衣服上的硬纸板标签，穿衣服前要将其剪下。name tag 指可贴或系在身上表明佩戴者身份的名牌：*All babies in the hospital have name tags tied round their ankles.* 医院里所有婴儿的脚踝上都系有姓名标签。

Price tag is much more frequent than *price label* and is used for both literal and figurative meanings. * price tag 指价格标签，远较 price label 常用，既可用作字面意义也可用作比喻意义：*What does the price tag say?* 标价是多少？◇ *There is a £20 million price tag on the team's star player.* 这名球队主力身价为 2 000 万英镑。 A **label** can also be a **sticker** that you put on an envelope. * label 亦可指贴在信封上的粘贴标签。

sticker a sticky label with a picture or message on it, that you stick on to sth 指粘贴标签、贴纸

PATTERNS

- a **price** label/tag/sticker
- to **have** a label/tag/sticker
- to **attach**/**put on**/**stick on** a label/tag/sticker
- The label/tag/sticker **says**...

labia /ˈleɪbiə/ *noun* [pl.] the four folds of skin at the entrance to a woman's VAGINA 阴唇

la·bial /ˈleɪbiəl/ *noun* (*phonetics* 语音) a speech sound made with the lips, for example /m/, /p/ and /v/ in *me*, *pea* and *very* 唇音 ▶ **la·bial** *adj.*

la·bio·den·tal /ˌleɪbiəʊˈdentl; *NAmE* -bioʊ-/ *noun* (*phonetics* 语音) a speech sound made by placing the top teeth against the bottom lip, for example /f/ and /v/ in *fan* and *van* 唇齿音 ▶ **la·bio·den·tal** *adj.*

la·bio·velar /ˌleɪbiəʊˈviːlə(r); *NAmE* -bioʊ-/ *noun* (*phonetics* 语音) a speech sound made using the lips and soft PALATE, for example /w/ in *we* 圆唇软腭音 ▶ **la·bio·velar** *adj.*

labor AW (*especially US*) = LABOUR

la·bora·tory 🔑 /ləˈbɒrətri; *NAmE* ˈlæbrətɔːri/ *noun* (*pl.* **-ies**) (*also informal* **lab**) a room or building used for scientific research, experiments, testing, etc. 实验室；实验大楼：*a research laboratory* 研究实验室 ◇ ***laboratory experiments/tests*** 实验室的实验 / 测试 ➲ WORDFINDER NOTE AT SCIENCE ➲ SEE ALSO LANGUAGE LABORATORY

ˈ**Labor Day** *noun* a public holiday in the US and Canada on the first Monday of September, in honour of working people 劳工节（在美国和加拿大为九月的第一个星期一）➲ COMPARE MAY DAY

la·bored, **la·bor·er**, **la·bor·ing** (*especially US*) = LABOURED, LABOURER, LABOURING

la·bori·ous /ləˈbɔːriəs/ *adj.* taking a lot of time and effort 耗时费力的；辛苦的 SYN **onerous, taxing**: *a laborious task/process* 艰巨的任务；艰难的过程 ◇ *Checking all the information will be slow and laborious.* 查看所有的信息既费时又费力。▶ **la·bori·ous·ly** *adv.*

ˈ**labor union** *noun* (*NAmE*) = UNION (1)

la·bour AW (*especially US* **labor**) /ˈleɪbə(r)/ *noun, verb*

■ ***noun***

• **WORK** 劳动 **1** [U] work, especially physical work 劳动；（尤指）体力劳动：***manual labour*** (= work using your hands) 体力劳动 ◇ *The price will include the labour and materials.* 此价格中包含人工费和材料费。◇ *The company wants to keep down* ***labour costs***. 公司想保持低劳动成本。◇ *The workers voted to* ***withdraw their labour*** (= to stop work as a means of protest). 工人投票决定罢工以示抗议。◇ *He was sentenced to two years in a* ***labour camp*** (= a type of prison where people have to do hard physical work). 他被判处两年劳改。**2** [C, usually pl.] (*formal*) a task or period of work 任务；（一段时间的）工作：*He was so exhausted from the day's labours that he went straight to bed.* 他工作了一天疲惫不堪，便直接上床休息了。

• **PEOPLE WHO WORK** 劳动者 **3** [U] the people who work or are available for work in a country or company（统称）劳工，工人；劳动力：*a shortage of labour* 劳动力的短缺 ◇ *Employers are using immigrants as* ***cheap labour***. 雇主正在把移民当作廉价劳动力使用。◇ *Repairs involve* ***skilled labour***, *which can be expensive.* 修理需要熟练技工，人工费会很昂贵。◇ *good* ***labour relations*** (= the relationship between workers and employers) 良好的劳资关系 ➲ WORDFINDER NOTE AT INDUSTRY, UNION

• **HAVING BABY** 分娩 **4** [U, C, usually sing.] the period of time or the process of giving birth to a baby 分娩期；分娩；生产：*Jane was* ***in labour*** *for ten hours.* 简分娩花了十个小时。◇ *She* ***went into labour*** *early.* 她早产了。◇ ***labour pains*** 分娩时的阵痛 ◇ *It was a difficult labour.* 那次是难产。➲ WORDFINDER NOTE AT BIRTH

• **POLITICS** 政治 **5 Labour** [sing.+sing./pl. v.] (*abbr.* **Lab.**) the British Labour Party 英国工党：*He always votes Labour.* 他老是投工党的票。◇ *Labour was/were in power for many years.* 工党曾执政多年。

IDM **a ˌlabour of ˈlove** a hard task that you do because you want to, not because it is necessary 为爱好而做的困难工作

■ ***verb***

• **STRUGGLE** 奋斗 **1** [I] to try very hard to do sth difficult 努力做（困难的事）：~ (**away**) *He was in his study labouring away over some old papers.* 他在书房里潜心研究一些旧材料。◇ ~ **to do sth** *They laboured for years to clear their son's name.* 他们为洗刷儿子的罪名努力争取了许多年。

• **WORK HARD** 努力工作 **2** [I] to do hard physical work 干苦力活：*We laboured all day in the fields.* 我们在田地里辛勤劳动了一整天。◇ (*old-fashioned*) *the labouring classes* (= the working class) 工人阶级

• **MOVE WITH DIFFICULTY** 吃力地行进 **3** [I] (+ **adv./prep.**) to move with difficulty and effort 困难吃力地行进 SYN **struggle**: *The horses laboured up the steep slope.* 那些马费力地爬上了陡坡。

IDM **labour the ˈpoint** to continue to repeat or explain sth that has already been said and understood 一再重复，反复解释（已说明的事）

PHR V ˈ**labour under sth** (*formal*) to believe sth that is not true 为…所蒙蔽：*to* ***labour under a misapprehension/delusion, etc.*** 有误解、错觉等 ◇ *He's still labouring under the impression that he's written a great book.* 他仍然有这样的错觉，以为自己撰写了一部巨著。

la·boured (*especially US* **la·bored**) /ˈleɪbəd; *NAmE* -bərd/ *adj.* **1** (of breathing 呼吸) slow and taking a lot of effort 缓慢而困难的 **2** (of writing, speaking, etc. 写作、说话等) not natural and seeming to take a lot of effort 不自然的；费力的；矫揉造作的

la·bour·er (*especially US* **la·bor·er**) /ˈleɪbərə(r)/ *noun* a person whose job involves hard physical work that is not skilled, especially work that is done outdoors（尤指户外的）体力劳动者，劳工，工人

ˈ**labour force** (*especially US* ˈ**labor force**) *noun* [C+sing./pl. v.] all the people who work for a company or in a country（全公司或全国的）劳动力 SYN **workforce**: *a skilled/an unskilled labour force* 熟练 / 非熟练工人

la·bour·ing (*especially US* **la·bor·ing**) /ˈleɪbərɪŋ/ *noun* [U] hard physical work that is not skilled 体力劳动：*a labouring job* 体力劳动工作

ˌ**labour-inˈtensive** (*especially US* ˌ**labor-inˈtensive**) *adj.* (of work 工作) needing a lot of people to do it 劳动密集型的：*labour-intensive methods* 劳动密集型方法 ➲ COMPARE CAPITAL-INTENSIVE

ˈ**labour market** (*especially US* ˈ**labor market**) *noun* the number of people who are available for work in relation to the number of jobs available 劳动力市场：*young people about to enter the labour market* 即将进入劳动力市场的年轻人

the ˈLabour Party (*also* **Labour**) *noun* [sing.+sing./pl. v.] one of the main British political parties, on the political left, that has traditionally represented the interests of working people 工党（英国主要政党之一，传统上代表劳动人民的利益）：*the Labour Party leader* 工党领袖

ˈ**labour-saving** (*especially US* ˈ**labor-saving**) *adj.* [usually before noun] designed to reduce the amount of work or effort needed to do sth 省力的；节省劳力的；降低劳动强度的：*modern labour-saving devices such as washing machines and dishwashers* 诸如洗衣机和洗碗机之类的现代化省力设备

Lab·ra·dor /ˈlæbrədɔː(r)/ *noun* a large dog that can be yellow, black or brown in colour, often used by blind people as a guide 拉布拉多猎犬（常用于导盲）：***a golden/black/chocolate Labrador*** 金黄色 / 黑色 / 深褐色拉布拉多犬

la·bur·num /ləˈbɜːnəm; *NAmE* -ˈbɜːrn-/ *noun* [C, U] a small tree with hanging bunches of yellow flowers 毒豆花（开悬垂黄花）

laby·rinth /ˈlæbərɪnθ/ *noun* (*formal*) a complicated series of paths, which it is difficult to find your way through 迷宫；曲径：*We lost our way in the labyrinth of streets.* 我们在迷宫式的街道上迷了路。◇ (*figurative*) *a labyrinth of rules and regulations* 错综复杂的规章制度 ➲ COMPARE MAZE (1) ▶ **laby·rin·thine** /ˌlæbəˈrɪnθaɪn; *NAmE also* -θɪn/ *adj.*: (*formal*) *labyrinthine corridors* 迷宫式的走廊 ◇ *labyrinthine legislation* 错综复杂的立法程序

lace /leɪs/ *noun, verb*

■ ***noun*** **1** [U] a delicate material made from threads of cotton, silk, etc. that are twisted into a pattern of holes 网眼织物；花边；蕾丝：*a lace handkerchief* 蕾丝手帕 ◇ *a tablecloth edged with lace* 镶有花边的桌布 ◇ *lace curtains* 蕾丝窗帘 ➲ SEE ALSO LACY **2** [C] = SHOELACE：*Your laces are undone.* 你的鞋带松开了。➲ VISUAL VOCAB PAGE V68

■ ***verb*** **1** [I, T] to be fastened with laces; to fasten sth with laces 由带子系紧；把…用带子系牢：~ (**up**) *She was wearing a dress that laced up at the side.* 她穿着一件在侧面系带子的连衣裙。◇ ~ **sth** (**up**) *He was sitting on the bed lacing up his shoes.* 他正坐在床边系鞋带。➲ SEE ALSO LACE-UP **2** [T] ~ **sth** to put a lace through the holes in a shoe, a boot, etc. 给（鞋、靴等）穿鞋带 ➲ RELATED NOUN LACE-UP **3** [T] ~ **sth** (**with sth**) to add a small amount of alcohol, a drug, poison, etc. to a drink 给（饮料）掺（少量的酒、药、毒药等）SYN **spike**: *He had laced her milk with rum.* 他在她的牛奶里加了少量朗姆酒。**4** [T] ~ **sth** (**with sth**) to add a particular quality to a book, speech, etc.（以…）润色（书、讲话等）：*Her conversation was laced with witty asides.* 她交谈中穿插了一些俏皮的题外话。

5 [T] ~ **sth** to twist sth together with another thing 使编织（或交织、缠绕）在一起：*They sat with their fingers laced.* 他们手指交叉着坐在那里。

la·cer·ate /ˈlæsəreɪt/ *verb* (*formal*) **1** ~ **sth** to cut skin or flesh with sth sharp 划破，割裂（皮或肉）：*His hand had been badly lacerated.* 他的一只手被严重划伤了。 **2** ~ **sb** to criticize sb very severely 严厉抨击；斥责 ▸ **la·cer·ation** /ˌlæsəˈreɪʃn/ *noun* [C, U]: *She suffered multiple lacerations to the face.* 她的面部多处被划伤。

ˈ**lace-up** *noun* [usually pl.] (*especially BrE*) a shoe that is fastened with laces 系带鞋：*a pair of lace-ups* 一双系带鞋 ◇ *lace-up boots* 系带靴子 ➲ COMPARE OXFORD (1) ➲ VISUAL VOCAB PAGE V69

lace·wing /ˈleɪswɪŋ/ *noun* an insect that has large transparent wings with lines on 草蛉（翅有网状脉）

lach·ry·mose /ˈlækrɪməʊs; *NAmE* -moʊs/ *adj.* (*formal*) having a tendency to cry easily 爱哭的；爱流泪的 SYN **tearful**

lack /læk/ *noun, verb*

■ ***noun*** [U, sing.] ~ (**of sth**) the state of not having sth or not having enough of sth 缺乏；匮乏；短缺 SYN **dearth, shortage**: *a lack of food/money/skills* 缺乏食物 / 金钱 / 技能 ◇ *The trip was cancelled* ***through lack of*** (= because there was not enough) *interest.* 因为缺乏兴趣这次旅行被取消了。◇ *There was* ***no lack of*** *volunteers.* 志愿者不乏其人。IDM SEE TRY *v.*

■ ***verb*** [no passive] ~ **sth** to have none or not enough of sth 没有；缺乏；不足；短缺：*Some houses still lack basic amenities such as bathrooms.* 有些住宅仍没有像卫生间这样的基本设施。◇ *He lacks confidence.* 他缺乏信心。◇ *She has the determination that her brother lacks.* 她有决心，而她弟弟却没有。➲ SEE ALSO LACKING (1)

IDM ˌ**lack** (**for**) ˈ**nothing** (*formal*) to have everything that you need 没有欠缺 ➲ MORE AT COURAGE

lacka·dai·si·cal /ˌlækəˈdeɪzɪkl/ *adj.* not showing enough care or enthusiasm 无精打采的；委靡不振的；懒洋洋的；不热心的

lackey /ˈlæki/ *noun* **1** (*old-fashioned*) a servant 仆人；佣人；听差；跟班 **2** (*disapproving*) a person who is treated like a servant or who behaves like one 被当作仆人看待者；卑躬屈膝的人；狗腿子；走狗

lack·ing /ˈlækɪŋ/ *adj.* [not before noun] **1** ~ (**in sth**) having none or not enough of sth 没有；匮乏；缺乏；不足：*She's not usually lacking in confidence.* 她平时并不缺乏自信心。◇ *The book is completely lacking in originality.* 这部书完全没有创意。◇ *He was taken on as a teacher but was* ***found lacking*** (= was thought not to be good enough). 他获聘为教师，能力却显得一般。 **2** not present or not available 不在场；得不到 SYN **missing**: *I feel there is something lacking in my life.* 我觉得我的生活中缺少点什么。

lack·lustre (*especially US* **lack·lus·ter**) /ˈlæklʌstə(r)/ *adj.* not interesting or exciting; dull 无趣味的；单调的；枯燥乏味的：*a lacklustre performance* 枯燥乏味的表演 ◇ *lacklustre hair* 无光泽的头发

la·con·ic /ləˈkɒnɪk; *NAmE* -ˈkɑːn-/ *adj.* using only a few words to say sth 简洁的；简明扼要的；凝练的 ▸ **la·con·ic·al·ly** /-kli/ *adv.*

lac·quer /ˈlækə(r)/ *noun, verb*

■ ***noun*** [U] **1** a liquid that is used on wood or metal to give it a hard shiny surface 漆 **2** (*old-fashioned*) a liquid that is sprayed on the hair so that it stays in place 头发定型剂；喷发胶 SYN **hairspray**

■ ***verb*** **1** ~ **sth** to cover sth such as wood or metal with lacquer 给（木制品或金属）涂漆 **2** ~ **sth** (*old-fashioned, BrE*) to put lacquer on your hair 给（头发）喷发胶

la·crosse /ləˈkrɒs; *NAmE* -ˈkrɔːs; -ˈkrɑːs/ *noun* [U] a game played on a field by two teams of ten players who use sticks with curved nets on them to catch, carry, and throw the ball 长曲棍球，袋棍球，兜网球（两队各十名队员，用带网兜的球棒接球、带球和传球）

lac·tate /lækˈteɪt/ *verb* [I] (*specialist*) (of a woman or female animal 妇女或雌性动物) to produce milk from the breasts to feed a baby or young animal 泌乳 ▸ **lac·ta·tion** /lækˈteɪʃn/ *noun* [U]: *the period of lactation* 哺乳期

lac·tic acid /ˌlæktɪk ˈæsɪd/ *noun* [U] an acid that forms in sour milk and is also produced in the muscles during hard exercise 乳酸

lacto·ba·cil·lus /ˌlæktəʊbəˈsɪləs; *NAmE* -toʊ-/ *noun* (*biology* 生) a type of bacteria that produces lactic acid 乳杆菌

lac·tose /ˈlæktəʊs; -təʊz; *NAmE* -toʊs; -toʊz/ *noun* [U] (*chemistry* 化) a type of sugar found in milk and used in some baby foods 乳糖

la·cuna /ləˈkjuːnə; *NAmE also* -ˈkuː-/ *noun* (*pl.* **-nae** /-niː/ or **la·cu·nas**) (*formal*) a place where sth is missing in a piece of writing or in an idea, a theory, etc.（文章、思想、理论等中的）缺漏，脱漏，空白，阙如 SYN **gap**

lacy /ˈleɪsi/ *adj.* made of or looking like LACE 网眼状的；蕾丝的；似蕾丝的：*lacy underwear* 蕾丝内衣

lad /læd/ *noun* **1** [C] (*old-fashioned* or *informal*) a boy or young man 男孩儿；少年；男青年；小伙子：*Things have changed since I was a lad.* 从我幼时至今，一切都发生了变化。◇ *He's a nice lad.* 他是个好小伙子。 ➲ COMPARE LASS **2 the lads** [pl.] (*BrE, informal*) a group of friends that a man works with or spends free time with 伙伴；哥们儿：*to go to the pub with the lads* 与伙伴一起去酒吧 **3** [C, usually sing.] (*BrE, informal*) a lively young man, especially one who is very interested in women and having sex, drinks a lot of alcohol and enjoys sport（精力旺盛的）放荡小伙子：*Tony was* ***a bit of a lad****—always had an eye for the women.* 托尼这小子真是个花花公子，对女人总是很有眼光。 ➲ SEE ALSO LADDISH **4** [C] (*BrE*) a person who works in a stable 马夫；马倌 ➲ SEE ALSO STABLE BOY

lad·der /ˈlædə(r)/ *noun, verb*

■ ***noun*** **1** a piece of equipment for climbing up and down a wall, the side of a building, etc., consisting of two lengths of wood or metal that are joined together by steps or RUNGS 梯子：*to* ***climb up/fall off a ladder*** 爬上 / 跌下梯子 ➲ VISUAL VOCAB PAGE V21 ➲ SEE ALSO STEPLADDER **2** [usually sing.] a series of stages by which you can make progress in your life or career（生活上进步或事业上晋升的）阶梯，途径：*to move up or down the* ***social ladder*** 爬上或跌下社会阶梯 ◇ *the* ***career ladder*** 事业上的阶梯 ◇ (*BrE*) *to get onto the* ***property ladder*** (= buy your first home) 首次购房 **3** (*BrE*) (*NAmE* **run**) a long thin hole in TIGHTS or STOCKINGS where some threads have broken（紧身裤袜或长筒袜的）滑丝，抽丝 **4** (*also* ˈ**ladder tournament**) a competition in a particular sport or game in which teams or players are arranged in a list and they can move up the list by defeating one of the teams or players above 升级比赛，升级游戏（将参赛者排名，胜者名次前提）

■ ***verb*** [I, T] ~ (**sth**) (*BrE*) if TIGHTS or STOCKINGS **ladder** or you **ladder** them, a long thin hole appears in them（紧身裤袜或长筒袜）出现滑丝，抽丝

lad·die /ˈlædi/ *noun* (*informal, especially ScotE*) a boy 男孩；小伙子 ➲ COMPARE LASS

lad·dish /ˈlædɪʃ/ *adj.* (*informal*) behaving in a way that is supposed to be typical of a young man 小伙子的；有小伙子特征的

laden /ˈleɪdn/ *adj.* ~ (**with sth**) **1** heavily loaded with sth 载满的；装满的：*passengers laden with luggage* 携带大批行李的旅客 ◇ *The trees were laden with apples.* 树上都挂满了苹果。◇ *a* ***heavily/fully laden*** *truck* 满载的卡车 ➲ COMPARE UNLADEN **2** (*literary*) full of sth, especially sth unpleasant 充满的（尤指充满令人不快的东西）：*His voice was soft, yet laden with threat.* 他说话的声音很柔和，但充满了恐吓的语气。 **3 -laden** used to form adjectives showing that sth is full of, or loaded with, the thing mentioned（用于构成形容词）充满…的，装载…的：*calorie-laden cream cakes* 高热量的奶油蛋糕

lad·ette /læˈdet/ *noun* (*BrE, informal*) a young woman who enjoys drinking alcohol, sport or other activities usually considered to be typical of young men 男性化的年轻女子，假小子（喜欢做年轻男子常做的事，如喝酒、参加体育运动等）

la-di-da (*also* **lah-di-dah**) /ˌlɑː di ˈdɑː/ *adj., exclamation*
■ ***adj.*** (*informal, especially BrE*) used to describe a way of speaking or behaving that is typical of upper-class people but that is not natural or sincere（描述像上层人的说话或举止）装腔作势的，装模作样的，做作的 **SYN affected**
■ ***exclamation*** used when sb is irritating you, because they seem to think they are more important than they really are 真可笑（用于讥讽自视过高惹人讨厌的人）

ˌladies' ˈfingers *noun* [pl.] (*BrE*) = OKRA

ˈladies' man (*also* **ˈlady's man**) *noun* a man who enjoys spending time with women and thinks he is attractive to them 喜欢与女人厮混的男人；自以为讨女人喜欢的男子

ladle /ˈleɪdl/ *noun, verb*
■ ***noun*** a large deep spoon with a long handle, used especially for serving soup 长柄勺；汤勺 ➲ VISUAL VOCAB PAGE V27
■ ***verb*** ~ **sth** to place food on a plate with a large spoon or in large quantities （用大勺）舀，盛
PHR V **ˌladle sth↔ˈout** (*sometimes disapproving*) to give sb a lot of sth, especially money or advice 大量给予（尤指金钱或建议） **SYN dole sth out**

la dolce vita /lɑː ˌdɒltʃeɪ ˈviːtə; *NAmE* ˌdoʊl-/ *noun* [sing.] (*from Italian*) a life of pleasure and expensive things, without any worries 奢华无忧的生活

lady 🔑 /ˈleɪdi/ (*pl.* **-ies**) *noun* **1** 🔑 [C] a word used to mean 'woman' that some people, especially older people, consider is more polite 女士，女子（指成年女子，有些人尤其是长者认为这样说比较礼貌）: *There's a lady waiting to see you.* 有位女士等着要见你。◇ *He was with an attractive young lady.* 他与一位漂亮的年轻女子在一起。◇ *the ladies' golf championship* 女子高尔夫球锦标赛 ◇ (*BrE*) *a tea lady* (= a woman who serves tea in an office)（办公室的）上茶女侍 ◇ (*NAmE, approving*) *She's a tough lady.* 她是个能吃苦耐劳的女士。◇ *a lady doctor/golfer* 女医生；女高尔夫球手 **HELP** Some women object to the way **lady** is used in some of these examples and prefer it to be avoided if possible. 一些妇女反对上述某些例句中的用法，喜欢尽可能避免用 lady 一词：*a doctor/a woman doctor* 一名医生；一名女医生 ◇ *There's someone waiting to see you.* 有人等着要见你。➲ SEE ALSO BAG LADY, CLEANING LADY, DINNER LADY, FIRST LADY, LEADING LADY, LUNCH LADY, OLD LADY **2** 🔑 [C] a woman who is polite and well educated, has excellent manners and always behaves well 举止文雅且有教养的女子；淑女：*His wife was a real lady.* 他的妻子真是个娴雅的淑女。➲ COMPARE GENTLEMAN (1) **3** 🔑 [C, usually pl.] (*formal*) used when speaking to or about a girl or woman, especially sb you do not know（尤用于称呼或谈及不认识的女子）女士，小姐：*Can I take your coats, ladies?* 女士们，我可以替你们拿大衣吗？◇ *Could I have your attention, **ladies and gentlemen**?* 女士们，先生们，请注意！**HELP** Some women do not like **ladies** used on its own, as in the first example, and prefer it to be left out. 在第一个例子的情况下，一些妇女不喜欢单独使用 ladies，而更喜欢省去不用。 **4** [sing.] (*especially NAmE*) an informal way to talk to a woman, showing a lack of respect（不尊重的非正式称呼）女人，女士：*Listen, lady, don't shout at me.* 听着，女士，别对我大喊大叫的。 **5** [C] (*old-fashioned*) (in Britain) a woman belonging to a high social class （英国）贵妇人，夫人，小姐：*the lords and ladies of the court* 宫廷的贵族及夫人 ◇ *a lady's maid* 贵妇人的贴身女侍 **6 Lady** [C] (in Britain) a title used by a woman who is a member of the NOBILITY, or by sb who has been given the title 'lady' as an honour. The wives and daughters of some members of the NOBILITY and the wives of KNIGHTS are also called 'Lady'.（在英国对女贵族、女爵士、贵族成员的妻女或爵士妻子的称呼）夫人，女士，小姐：*Lady Howe* 豪夫人 ◇ *Lady Jane Grey* 简·格雷小姐 ➲ COMPARE LORD *n.* (1), (4), SIR (3) **7 a/the ladies** [U] (*BrE*) (*NAmE* **ˈladies' room** [C]) a toilet/bathroom for women in a public building or place 女厕所；女卫生间；女洗手间；女盥洗室：*Could you tell me where the ladies is?* 请告诉我女卫生间在哪里好吗？ **8 Our Lady** a title used to refer to Mary, the mother of Christ, especially in the Roman Catholic Church（天主教常用）圣母：*Our Lady of Lourdes* 露德圣母 **IDM** SEE FAT *adj.*, LEISURE

lady·bird /ˈleɪdibɜːd; *NAmE* -bɜːrd/ (*BrE*) (*NAmE* **lady·bug** /ˈleɪdibʌɡ/) *noun* a small flying insect, usually red with black spots 瓢虫 ➲ VISUAL VOCAB PAGE V13

lady·boy /ˈleɪdibɔɪ/ *noun* (*informal*) a TRANSVESTITE or TRANSSEXUAL 易装癖者；易性癖者

lady·finger /ˈleɪdifɪŋɡə(r)/ *noun* (*NAmE*) a small long thin cake made with eggs, sugar and flour 手指松饼

ˌlady-in-ˈwaiting *noun* (*pl.* **ladies-in-waiting**) a woman who goes to places with, and helps, a queen or princess （女王或公主的）宫廷女侍，宫女，女侍臣

lady·kill·er /ˈleɪdikɪlə(r)/ *noun* (*old-fashioned* or *informal*) a man who is sexually attractive and successful with women, but who does not stay in a relationship with anyone for long 勾引女子的老手；使女子倾心的花心男人

lady·like /ˈleɪdilaɪk/ *adj.* (*old-fashioned*) polite and quiet; typical of what is supposed to be socially acceptable for a woman 文静的；温文尔雅的；淑女似的 **SYN refined**: *ladylike behaviour* 文静娴雅的举止 ◇ *Her language was not very ladylike.* 她的用语不怎么文雅。

ˌlady ˈmayor *noun* = MAYORESS (1)

lady·ship /ˈleɪdiʃɪp/ *noun* **1 Her/Your Ladyship** a title used when talking to or about a woman who is a member of the NOBILITY（对女贵族的称呼）夫人，小姐：*Does Your Ladyship require anything?* 夫人您需要点什么？ **2** (*BrE, informal*) a way of talking to or about a girl or woman that you think is trying to be too important（对佯装高贵的女子的用语）小姐，夫人：*Perhaps her ladyship would like to hang up her own clothes today!* 尊贵的夫人今天也许愿意自己动手把衣服挂起来吧！ ➲ COMPARE LORDSHIP (1)

ˈlady's man *noun* = LADIES' MAN

lag /læɡ/ *verb, noun*
■ ***verb*** **(-gg-)** **1** [I] **~ (behind sb/sth) | ~ (behind)** to move or develop slowly or more slowly than other people, organizations, etc. 缓慢移动；发展缓慢；滞后；落后于 **SYN trail**: *The little boy lagged behind his parents.* 那小男孩落在了父母的后面。◇ *We still lag far behind many of our competitors in using modern technology.* 我们在运用现代技术方面仍然远远落后于我们的许多竞争对手。 **2** [T] **~ sth (with sth)** (*BrE*) to cover pipes, etc. with a special material to stop the water in them from freezing, or to save heat 给（管道等）加防冻保暖层 **SYN insulate**
■ ***noun*** = TIME LAG ➲ SEE ALSO JET LAG, OLD LAG

lager /ˈlɑːɡə(r)/ *noun* **1** [U, C] a type of light pale beer that usually has a lot of bubbles 拉格啤酒，贮陈啤酒，贮藏啤酒（味淡，通常多泡沫）: *a pint of lager* 一品脱拉格啤酒 ◇ *German lagers* 德国拉格啤酒 **2** [C] a glass, can or bottle of this 一杯（或一罐、一瓶）拉格啤酒（或贮藏啤酒）

ˈlager lout *noun* (*BrE*) a young man who drinks too much alcohol and then behaves in a noisy and unpleasant way 喝酒后行为不端的年轻人；耍酒疯的青年

lag·gard /ˈlæɡəd; *NAmE* -ɡərd/ *noun* (*old-fashioned*) a slow and lazy person, organization, etc. 迟钝懒散者；迟缓者；涣散的机构

la·goon /ləˈɡuːn/ *noun* **1** a lake of salt water that is separated from the sea by a REEF or an area of rock or sand 潟湖；环礁湖；濒海湖 **2** (*NAmE*) a small area of fresh water near a lake or river（湖泊或江河附近的）小片淡水域，小淡水湖 **3** (*specialist*) an artificial area built to hold waste water before it is treated at a SEWAGE WORKS 氧化塘

lah (*also* **la**) /lɑː/ *noun* (*music* 音) the 6th note of a MAJOR SCALE 大调音阶的第 6 音

lah-di-dah = LA-DI-DA

laid PAST TENSE, PAST PART. OF LAY

ˌlaid-ˈback *adj.* (*informal*) calm and relaxed; seeming not to worry about anything 安详放松的；松弛的；仿佛无忧无虑的 **SYN** **easy-going**: *a laid-back attitude to life* 悠然自得的生活态度

lain PAST PART. OF LIE[1]

lair /leə(r); *NAmE* ler/ *noun* [usually sing.] **1** a place where a wild animal sleeps or hides 兽穴；兽窝 **2** a place where sb goes to hide or to be alone（人的）藏身处，躲藏处，独居处 **SYN** **den, hideout**

laird /leəd; *NAmE* lerd/ *noun* (in Scotland) a person who owns a large area of land（苏格兰）地主

lairy /ˈleəri; *NAmE* ˈleri/ *adj.* (*BrE, informal*) behaving in a way that seems too loud and confident 张扬的；旁若无人的

laissez-faire /ˌleseɪ ˈfeə(r); *NAmE* ˈfer/ *noun* [U] (*from French*) the policy of allowing private businesses to develop without government control（政府对私有企业的）自由放任政策 ▸ **laissez-faire** *adj.*: *a laissez-faire economy* 自由放任的经济体 ◇ *They have a laissez-faire approach to bringing up their children* (= they give them a lot of freedom). 他们采用放任自由的方法来养育子女。

laity /ˈleɪəti/ *noun* **the laity** [sing.+sing./pl. v.] all the members of a Church who are not CLERGY（统称）平信徒 ➲ SEE ALSO LAYMAN (2)

lake /leɪk/ *noun* (*abbr.* **L.**) a large area of water that is surrounded by land 湖；湖泊：*We swam in the lake.* 我们在湖里游泳。◇ *Lake Ontario* 安大略湖 ◇ (*figurative*) *a wine lake* (= a large supply of wine that is not being used) 葡萄酒池 ➲ VISUAL VOCAB PAGE V5

lake·side /ˈleɪksaɪd/ *noun* [sing.] the area around the edge of a lake 湖边；湖岸；湖畔：*We went for a walk by the lakeside.* 我们沿湖边散步。◇ *a lakeside hotel* 湖边旅馆

lakh /læk/ *number* (*plural verb*) (*pl.* **lakh** or **lakhs**) (*IndE*) a hundred thousand 十万

la-la land /ˈlɑː lɑː lænd/ (*NAmE*) (*BrE* ˌ**cloud** ˈ**cuckoo land**) *noun* [U] (*informal, disapproving*) if you say that sb is living **in la-la land**, you mean that they do not understand what a situation is really like, but think it is much better than it is 幻想世界；脱离现实的幻境

lam /læm/ *noun, verb*

■ *noun*

IDM **on the ˈlam** (*NAmE, informal*) escaping from sb, especially from the police 在逃，逃匿（尤指逃避警方追缉）

■ *verb* (**-mm-**)

PHR V ˌ**lam ˈinto sb** (*BrE, informal*) to attack sb violently with blows or words 痛打某人；猛烈抨击某人：*She really lammed into her opponent during the debate.* 在辩论中她着实给对手以猛烈的攻击。

Lama·ism /ˈlɑːməɪzəm/ *noun* [U] Tibetan Buddhism 藏传佛教

lamb /læm/ *noun, verb*

■ *noun* **1** [C] a young sheep 羔羊；小羊 **2** [U] meat from a young sheep 羊羔肉：*a leg of lamb* 羔羊腿肉 ◇ *lamb chops* 羔羊排 ➲ COMPARE MUTTON **3** [C] (*informal*) used to describe or address sb with affection or pity（慈爱或怜悯地描述或称呼某人）宝贝，乖乖：*You poor lamb!* 可怜的宝贝！ ➲ MORE LIKE THIS 20, page R27

IDM **(like) a lamb/lambs to the ˈslaughter** used to describe people who are going to do sth dangerous without realizing it（如同）羔羊被牵往屠宰场（指将遇危险而不自觉的人） ➲ MORE AT MUTTON, WELL *adv.*

■ *verb* [I] (of a sheep 羊) to give birth to a lamb 产羊羔

lam·bada /læmˈbɑːdə/ *noun* a fast Brazilian dance performed by couples who hold each other closely 兰巴达（源自巴西的快步舞，二人紧拥对方舞蹈）

lam·baste (*also* **lam·bast**) /læmˈbeɪst/ *verb* **~ sb/sth** (*formal*) to attack or criticize sb/sth very severely, especially in public（尤指公开地）猛烈抨击，狠狠批评 **SYN** **lay into sb/sth**

lambda /ˈlæmdə/ *noun* the 11th letter of the Greek alphabet (Λ, λ) 希腊字母表的第 11 个字母

lambs·wool /ˈlæmzwʊl/ *noun* [U] soft fine wool from lambs, used for knitting clothes 羔羊毛（用以编织衣服）：*a lambswool sweater* 羔羊毛套衫

lame /leɪm/ *adj.* **1** (of people or animals 人或动物) unable to walk well because of an injury to the leg or foot 瘸的；跛的 **2** (of an excuse, explanation, etc. 借口、解释等) weak and difficult to believe 站不住脚的；无说服力的 **SYN** **feeble, unconvincing** **3** not interesting or entertaining 无趣的；无聊的：*The humour is more lame than funny.* 这种幽默并不好笑，无趣得很。 ▸ **lame·ness** *noun* [U]: *The disease has left her with permanent lameness.* 那场病使她永远瘸了。

lamé /ˈlɑːmeɪ; *NAmE* lɑːˈmeɪ/ *noun* [U] a type of cloth into which gold or silver thread has been twisted 金银锦缎

lame·brain /ˈleɪmbreɪn/ *noun* (*informal, especially NAmE*) a stupid person 呆子；笨蛋 ▸ **lame·brain** (*also* **lame·brained**) *adj.*: *They invented some lamebrain scheme to get rich quick.* 为发横财，他们想出了个蠢办法。

ˌ**lame ˈduck** *noun* **1** a person or an organization that is not very successful and that needs help 不太成功而需要帮助的人（或机构）；"跛脚鸭" **2** (*US, informal*) a politician or government whose period of office will soon end and who will not be elected again（不能继续连任的）即将届满卸任的从政者（或政府）；"跛脚鸭"：***a lame-duck president/administration*** 跛脚鸭总统 / 政府

lame·ly /ˈleɪmli/ *adv.* in a way that does not sound very confident, or that does not persuade other people（听起来）信心不足地，不具说服力地，站不住脚地 **SYN** **feebly**: *'I must have made a mistake,' she said lamely.* "我一定是弄错了。" 她胆怯地说。

lam·ent /ləˈment/ *verb, noun*

■ *verb* **~ sth | ~ that... | + speech** (*formal*) to feel or express great sadness or disappointment about sb/sth 对…感到悲痛；痛惜；对…表示失望 **SYN** **bemoan, bewail**: *In the poem he laments the destruction of the countryside.* 在那首诗里他对乡村遭到的破坏流露出悲哀。

■ *noun* (*formal*) a song, poem or other expression of great sadness for sb who has died or for sth that has ended 挽歌；哀诗；悼辞

lam·ent·able /ˈlæməntəbl; ləˈment-/ *adj.* (*formal*) very disappointing 十分令人失望的；令人遗憾的；使人惋惜的 **SYN** **deplorable, regrettable**: *She shows a lamentable lack of understanding.* 她显得缺乏体谅，实在令人遗憾。 ▸ **lam·ent·ably** /-əbli/ *adv.*

lam·en·ta·tion /ˌlæmənˈteɪʃn/ *noun* [C, U] (*formal*) an expression of great sadness or disappointment 悲伤；悲痛；悲哀；十分失望

lam·ented /ləˈmentɪd/ *adj.* (*formal* or *humorous*) (of sb/sth that has died or disappeared 已死亡的人或已消失的事物) missed very much 令人悼念（或怀念）的；使人思念的：*her late lamented husband* 她那令人怀念的亡夫 ◇ *the last edition of the much lamented newspaper* 那非常令人怀念的报纸的最后一期

lamin·ate /ˈlæmɪnət/ *noun* [U, C] a material that is laminated 薄片制成的材料；层压（或黏合）材料

lamin·ated /ˈlæmɪneɪtɪd/ *adj.* **1** (of wood, plastic, etc. 木材、塑料等) made by sticking several thin layers together 由薄层粘制成的；层压的；黏合的 **2** covered with thin transparent plastic for protection 用透明塑料薄膜覆盖的：*laminated membership cards* 压膜会员卡

lam·ing·ton /ˈlæmɪŋtən/ *noun* (*AustralE, NZE*) a square piece of SPONGE cake that has been put in liquid chocolate and covered with small pieces of COCONUT 拉明顿蛋糕；椰丝巧克力方形海绵蛋糕

lamp /læmp/ *noun, verb*

■ ***noun*** **1** a device that uses electricity, oil or gas to produce light 灯：*a* ***table/desk/bicycle, etc. lamp*** 台灯、书桌灯、自行车灯等 ◇ *to* ***switch on/turn off a lamp*** 开灯；关灯 ◇ *a* ***street lamp*** 路灯 ➲ VISUAL VOCAB PAGES V22, V71 ➲ SEE ALSO FOG LAMP, HURRICANE LAMP, LAVA LAMP, STANDARD LAMP **2** an electrical device that produces RAYS of heat and that is used for medical or scientific purposes（理疗用的）发热灯；（科学上用的）射线照射器：*an* ***infrared/ultraviolet lamp*** 红外线灯；紫外线灯 ➲ SEE ALSO BLOWLAMP, SUNLAMP

■ ***verb*** (*BrE, informal*) to hit sb very hard 重击；狂殴：**~ sb** *The guy lamped me.* 那家伙打得我不轻。◇ **~ sb sth** *I'd have lamped her one!* 我本想狠狠地揍她一顿！

lamp·light /ˈlæmplaɪt/ *noun* [U] light from a lamp 灯光

lamp·lit /ˈlæmplɪt/ *adj.* [usually before noun] given light by lamps; seen by the light from lamps 用灯光照明的；在灯光下可见的：*a lamplit room* 亮着灯的房间 ◇ *a lamplit figure in the chair* 灯光下坐在椅子上的人

lam·poon /læmˈpuːn/ *verb, noun*

■ ***verb*** **~ sb/sth** to criticize sb/sth publicly in an amusing way that makes them or it look ridiculous 嘲讽；讥讽 **SYN satirize**：*His cartoons mercilessly lampooned the politicians of his time.* 他的漫画毫不留情地嘲讽了他那个年代的政治人物。

■ ***noun*** a piece of writing that criticizes sb/sth and makes them or it look ridiculous 讽刺文章；幽默讽刺作品

ˈ**lamp post** *noun* (*especially BrE*) a tall post in the street with a lamp at the top 路灯柱；灯杆：*The car skidded and hit a lamp post.* 那辆汽车打滑撞上了路灯杆。➲ COMPARE STREET LIGHT ➲ VISUAL VOCAB PAGE V3

lam·prey /ˈlæmpri/ *noun* a FRESHWATER fish with a round mouth that attaches itself to other fish and sucks their blood 七鳃鳗（以口吸附于其他鱼体，吸食宿主血液）

lamp·shade /ˈlæmpʃeɪd/ *noun* a decorative cover for a lamp that is used to make the light softer or to direct it 灯罩 ➲ VISUAL VOCAB PAGE V22

LAN /læn/ *noun* (*computing* 计) the abbreviation for 'local area network' (a system for communicating by computer within a large building or group of buildings) 局部区域网，局域网，本地网（全写为 local area network） ➲ COMPARE WAN

lance /lɑːns; *NAmE* læns/ *noun, verb*

■ ***noun*** a weapon with a long wooden handle and a pointed metal end that was used by people fighting on horses in the past（旧时骑兵的）长矛

■ ***verb*** **1** [T] **~ sth** to cut open an infected place on sb's body with a sharp knife in order to let out the PUS (= a yellow substance produced by infection) 用刀切开（感染处放脓）：*to lance an abscess* 切开脓肿 **2** [I] **+ adv./prep.** (of a pain 疼痛) to move suddenly and quickly and be very sharp 突然迅速传导；突然剧烈起来：*Pain lanced through his body.* 疼痛传到他的全身。

ˌ**lance ˈcorporal** *noun* a member of one of the lower ranks in the British army（英国陆军的）一等兵：*Lance Corporal Alan Smith* 一等兵艾伦•史密斯

lan·cer /ˈlɑːnsə(r); *NAmE* ˈlæn-/ *noun* in the past, a member of a REGIMENT that used LANCES（旧时的）长矛轻骑兵

lan·cet /ˈlɑːnsɪt; *NAmE* ˈlæn-/ *noun* a knife with a sharp point and two sharp edges, used by doctors for cutting skin and flesh（医生手术用的）柳叶刀，小刀

land /lænd/ *noun, verb*

■ ***noun***

• SURFACE OF EARTH 地球表面 **1** [U] the surface of the earth that is not sea 陆地；大地：*It was good to be back* ***on land***. 回到陆地上真好。◇ *We made the journey* ***by land***, *though flying would have been cheaper.* 虽然乘飞机会便宜些，我们还是走了陆路。◇ *In the distance the crew sighted land.* 船员在远处发现了陆地。◇ *The elephant is the largest living land animal.* 象是现今陆地上最大的动物。➲ SYNONYMS AT FLOOR, SOIL ➲ SEE ALSO DRY LAND

• AREA OF GROUND 土地 **2** [U] (*also* **lands** [pl.]) an area of ground, especially of a particular type or used for a particular purpose（尤指某类型或作某种用途的）地带，土地 **SYN terrain**：***fertile/arid/stony, etc. land*** 肥沃、贫瘠、多石等的土地 ◇ ***flat/undulating/hilly, etc. land*** 平坦、波状、丘陵等地带 ◇ ***agricultural/arable/industrial, etc. land*** 农业用地、可耕地、工业用地等 ◇ *The land was very dry and hard after the long, hot summer.* 经过漫长的炎夏这块土地又干又硬。◇ *The land rose to the east.* 那地向东隆起。◇ *a piece of* ***waste/derelict land*** 一块荒地 / 弃置的荒地 ◇ *Some of the country's richest grazing lands are in these valleys.* 全国最肥沃的一些牧场位于这些峡谷中。 **3** [U] (*also formal* **lands** [pl.]) the area of ground that sb owns, especially when you think of it as property that can be bought or sold 地产；地皮：*The price of land is rising rapidly.* 地价正在迅速上涨。◇ *During the war their lands were occupied by the enemy.* 战争期间他们的土地被敌人占据了。➲ SEE ALSO NO-MAN'S-LAND

• COUNTRYSIDE 农村 **4 the land** [U] used to refer to the countryside and the way people live in the country as opposed to in cities（与城市相对的）农村，农村生活方式：*At the beginning of the 20th century almost a third of the population* ***lived off the land*** (= grew or produced their own food). * 20 世纪初几乎有三分之一的人口依靠种

▼ SYNONYMS 同义词辨析

land

lot • ground • space • plot

These words all mean an area of land that is used for a particular purpose. 以上各词均指作特定用途的土地。

land an area of ground, especially one that is used for a particular purpose 尤指作特定用途的土地、地带：*agricultural land* 农业用地

lot (*NAmE*) a piece of land that is used or intended for a particular purpose 指作某种用途的一块地、场地：*building lots* 建筑用地 ◇ *a parking lot* 停车场

ground an area of land that is used for a particular purpose 指作特定用途的场地：*The kids were playing on waste ground near the school.* 孩子们在学校附近的荒地玩耍。◇ *the site of an ancient burial ground* 古代墓地遗址

LAND, LOT OR GROUND? 用 land、lot 还是 ground?

Land is used for large areas of open land in the country, especially when it is used for farming. A **lot** is often a smaller piece of land in a town or city, especially one intended for building or parking on. **Ground** is any area of open land; a **ground** is an area of land designed or used for a particular purpose or activity. * land 指乡间广阔的土地，尤指农业用地；lot 常指城镇或城市中的一小块地，尤指专用的建筑或停车场地；ground 作不可数名词指任何开阔地、空旷地，作可数名词指特定用途或活动的场地。

space a large area of land that has no buildings on it 指无建筑物的大片空地、开阔地：*The city has plenty of open space.* 这座城市有很多开阔的空地。◇ *the* ***wide open spaces*** *of the Canadian prairies* 加拿大一片片广袤的草原

plot a small piece of land used or intended for a particular purpose 指专用的小块土地：*She bought a small* ***plot of land*** *to build a house.* 她买了一小块地盖房子。◇ *a vegetable plot* 一块菜圃

LOT OR PLOT? 用 lot 还是 plot?

Either a **lot** or a **plot** can be used for building on. Only a **plot** can also be used for growing vegetables or burying people. * lot 和 plot 均可作建筑用地。plot 亦可作菜地或墓地。

PATTERNS

• an **open** space
• **open/empty/vacant/waste/derelict** land/ground
• a(n) **empty/vacant** lot/plot

L

地为生。◇ *Many people leave the land to find work in towns and cities.* 许多人离开农村到城镇里找工作。➲ SYNONYMS AT COUNTRY

• **COUNTRY/REGION** 国家；地区 **5** [C] (*literary*) used to refer to a country or region in a way which appeals to the emotions or the imagination（涉及感情或想象）国家，地区：*She longed to return to her **native land**.* 她渴望回到她的祖国。◇ *They dreamed of travelling to **foreign lands**.* 他们梦想去外国旅游。◇ *America is the land of freedom and opportunity.* 美国是一个拥有自由与机遇的国度。➲ SEE ALSO CLOUD CUCKOO LAND, CLUBLAND, DOCKLAND, DREAMLAND, FAIRYLAND, NEVER-NEVER LAND, PROMISED LAND, WONDERLAND **HELP** There are many other compounds ending in **land**. You will find them at their place in the alphabet. 以 land 结尾的复合词还有很多，可在各字母中的适当位置查到。

IDM **in the land of the 'living** (*often humorous*) awake or alive or no longer ill/sick 醒着；活着；在人世；康复 **the land of ˌmilk and 'honey** a place where life is pleasant and easy and people are very happy 富饶的乐土；丰裕之地 **in the ˌland of 'Nod** (*old-fashioned, humorous*) asleep 睡着；在梦乡：*Pete and Jo were still in the land of Nod, so I went out for a walk in the morning sunshine.* 皮特和乔仍沉睡未醒，于是我就在晨光中出门散步去了。 **see, etc. how the 'land lies** (*BrE*) to find out about a situation 弄清情况；摸清形势：*Let's wait and see how the land lies before we do anything.* 咱们等弄清情况以后再行动吧。➲ MORE AT LIE[1] *n.*, LIVE[1], SPY *v.*

■ ***verb***

• **OF BIRD/PLANE/INSECT** 鸟；飞机；昆虫 **1** [I] to come down through the air onto the ground or another surface 落；降落；着陆：*The plane landed safely.* 飞机安全着陆了。◇ *A fly landed on his nose.* 一只苍蝇落在他的鼻子上。**OPP** **take off** ➲ WORDFINDER NOTE AT PLANE

• **OF PILOT** 飞行员 **2** [T] **~ sth** to bring a plane down to the ground in a controlled way 使（飞机）平稳着陆：*The pilot landed the plane safely.* 飞行员驾驶飞机安全着陆。

• **ARRIVE IN PLANE/BOAT** 乘飞机/船到达 **3** [I] to arrive somewhere in a plane or a boat（乘飞机或船）着陆，登陆：*We shall be landing shortly. Please fasten your seat belts.* 我们很快就要着陆，请您系好安全带。◇ *The troops landed at dawn.* 部队已在黎明登陆。◇ *They were the first men to land on the moon.* 他们是首批登上月球的人。◇ *The ferry is due to land at 3 o'clock.* 渡轮预定 3 点钟到岸。 **4** [T] **~ sb/sth** to put sb/sth on land from an aircraft, a boat, etc.（使）着陆，降落，靠岸，登陆：*The troops were landed by helicopter.* 部队乘直升机降落。

• **FALL TO GROUND** 跌落地面 **5** [I] to come down to the ground after jumping, falling or being thrown 跳落，跌落，被抛落（地面）：*I fell and landed heavily at the bottom of the stairs.* 我从楼梯上摔了下去，重重地摔在下面。◇ *A large stone landed right beside him.* 一大块石头正好落在他身旁。

• **DIFFICULTIES** 困难 **6** [I] **+ adv./prep.** to arrive somewhere and cause difficulties that have to be dealt with 降临；使陷于（困境）；使不得不应付：*Why do complaints always **land on my desk*** (= why do I always have to deal with them)? 为什么投诉总得要我来处理？

• **JOB** 工作 **7** [T] (*informal*) to succeed in getting a job, etc., especially one that a lot of other people want 成功得到，赢得，捞到（尤指许多人想得到的工作）：**~ sth** *He's just landed a starring role in Spielberg's next movie.* 他刚得到一个机会，在斯皮尔伯格执导的下一部电影里担任主角。◇ **~ sb/yourself sth** *She's just landed herself a company directorship.* 她刚在一家公司谋到一个主管的职位。

• **FISH** 鱼 **8** [T] **~ sth** to catch a fish and bring it out of the water on to the land 捕到，钓到（鱼）

IDM **land a 'blow, 'punch, etc.** to succeed in hitting sb/sth 打中；击中：*She landed a punch on his chin.* 她对着他的下巴揍了一拳。➲ MORE AT FOOT *n.*

PHR V **'land in sth | 'land sb/yourself in sth** (*informal*) to get sb/yourself into a difficult situation 使陷入（困境）：*She was arrested and landed in court.* 她被逮捕并送上了法庭。◇ *His hot temper has landed him in trouble before.* 他脾气急躁，以前就惹过麻烦。◇ *Now you've really landed me in it!* (= got me into trouble) 你这可把我坑苦了！ **ˌland 'up in/at/on/with...** (*informal*) to reach a final position or situation, sometimes after other things have happened 终于到达（某位置）；最终落到（某种处境）**SYN** **end up**: *We travelled around for a while and landed up in Seattle.* 我们到处旅游了一段时间，最后抵达西雅图。◇ *He landed up in a ditch after he lost control of his car.* 他开车失控，栽进了沟里。 **'land sb/yourself with sth/sb** (*informal*) to give sb/yourself sth unpleasant to do, especially because nobody else wants to do it 把（苦差事）推给（某人）；主动承担（苦差事）：*As usual, I got landed with all the boring jobs.* 所有枯燥乏味的工作都照例落在了我的头上。

'land agent *noun* (*especially BrE*) a person whose job is to manage land, farms, etc. for sb else 地产管理人

lan·dau /'lændɔː; -aʊ/ *noun* a CARRIAGE with four wheels and a roof that folds down in two sections, that is pulled by horses 双排座活顶四轮马车

'land-based *adj.* [usually before noun] located on or living on the land 位于陆地上的；栖息于陆地的：*land-based missiles* 陆基导弹 ◇ *land-based animals* 陆生动物

land·ed /'lændɪd/ *adj.* [only before noun] **1** owning a lot of land 拥有大量土地的：*the landed gentry* 拥有大量土地的乡绅 **2** including a large amount of land 包括大量土地的：*landed estates* 地产

ˌlanded 'immigrant *noun* (*CanE*) a person from another country who has permission to live permanently in Canada 落地移民（在加拿大获准永久居留的外国移民）

land·fall /'lændfɔːl/ *noun* **1** [U, C] (*literary*) the act of arriving on land after a long journey by sea or by air, or the land that you first see or arrive at（航海或飞行后）踏上陆地；初见的陆地；初次踏足的陆地：*After three weeks they **made landfall** on the coast of Ireland.* 三个星期之后，他们登上了爱尔兰的海岸。 **2** [C] = LANDSLIDE (1)

land·fill /'lændfɪl/ *noun* **1** [C, U] an area of land where large amounts of waste material are buried under the earth 垃圾填埋地（或场）：*The map shows the position of the new landfills.* 这张地图上标有新的垃圾填埋场的位置。◇ *a landfill site* 垃圾填埋场地 ➲ VISUAL VOCAB PAGE V7 **2** [U] the process of burying large amounts of waste material 垃圾填埋：*the choice of landfill or incineration* 垃圾填埋还是焚烧的选择 **3** [U] waste material that will be buried 填埋的垃圾 ➲ WORDFINDER NOTE AT WASTE

land·form /'lændfɔːm; *NAmE* -fɔːrm/ *noun* (*geology* 地) a natural feature of the earth's surface 地形；地貌

land·hold·ing /'lændhəʊldɪŋ; *NAmE* -hoʊld-/ *noun* [C, U] (*specialist*) a piece of land that sb owns or rents; the fact of owning or renting land 拥有（或租用）的一块土地；拥有（或租用）土地 ▶ **land·hold·er** *noun*：*farmers and landholders* 农场主与土地所有者

land·ing /'lændɪŋ/ *noun* **1** [C] the area at the top of a set of stairs where you arrive before you go into an upstairs room or move onto another set of stairs 楼梯平台；（两段楼梯间的）过渡平台 ➲ PICTURE AT STAIRCASE **2** [C, U] an act of bringing an aircraft or a SPACECRAFT down to the ground after a journey 降落；着陆：*a perfect/smooth/safe landing* 准确/顺利/安全着陆 ◇ *the first Apollo **moon landing*** 阿波罗航天飞船首次登月着陆 ◇ *The pilot was forced to make **an emergency landing**.* 飞行员被迫紧急着陆。◇ *a landing site* 降落场 **OPP** **take-off** ➲ SEE ALSO CRASH LANDING at CRASH-LAND **3** [C] an act of bringing soldiers to land in an area that is controlled by the enemy 登陆 **4** (*BrE also* **'landing stage**) [C] a flat wooden platform on the water where boats let people get on and off, and load and unload goods 码头；浮动码头；栈桥 **SYN** **jetty**

'landing craft *noun* (*pl.* **landing craft**) a boat with a flat bottom, carried on a ship. Landing craft open at one end so soldiers and equipment can be brought to land. 登陆艇

'landing gear *noun* [U] = UNDERCARRIAGE

ˈ**landing lights** *noun* [pl.] **1** bright lamps on a plane that are switched on before it lands（飞机上的）着陆灯 **2** lights that are arranged along the sides of a RUNWAY to guide a pilot when he or she is landing a plane（飞机跑道两边的）着陆指示灯

ˈ**landing page** *noun* (*computing* 计) the part of a website that you reach first when you click on a link on the Internet（网站）登陆页：*Have a different landing page for each advertising campaign.* 为每个广告宣传活动设置不同的登陆页。 ➲ **WORDFINDER NOTE** AT WEBSITE

ˈ**landing stage** (*BrE*) (*also* **landing** *NAmE, BrE*) *noun* a flat wooden platform on the water where boats let people get on and off, and load and unload goods 码头；浮动码头；栈桥 SYN **jetty**

ˈ**landing strip** *noun* = AIRSTRIP

land·lady /ˈlændleɪdi/ *noun* (*pl.* **-ies**) **1** a woman from whom you rent a room, a house, etc. 女房东；女地主 **2** (*BrE*) a woman who owns or manages a pub or a GUEST HOUSE（酒吧或招待所的）女店主，女老板 SYN **proprietor** ➲ COMPARE LANDLORD

land·less /ˈlændləs/ *adj.* [usually before noun] not owning land for farming; not allowed to own land 无土地的；不准拥有土地的

land·line /ˈlændlaɪn/ *noun* a telephone connection that uses wires carried on poles or under the ground, in contrast to a mobile/cell phone（电话的）陆地线路，陆线，固网：*I'll call you later on the landline.* 晚些时候我会用固定线路给你打电话。 ➲ **COLLOCATIONS** AT PHONE

land·locked /ˈlændlɒkt; *NAmE* -lɑːkt/ *adj.* almost or completely surrounded by land 几乎（或完全）被陆地包围的；陆围的；内陆的：*Switzerland is completely landlocked.* 瑞士完全是个内陆国。

land·lord /ˈlændlɔːd; *NAmE* -lɔːrd/ *noun* **1** a person or company from whom you rent a room, a house, an office, etc. 业主；地主；房东 **2** (*BrE*) a man who owns or manages a pub or a GUEST HOUSE（酒吧或招待所的）店主，老板 SYN **proprietor** ➲ COMPARE LANDLADY

land·lub·ber /ˈlændlʌbə(r)/ *noun* (*informal*) a person with not much knowledge or experience of the sea or sailing 不谙航海的人

land·mark /ˈlændmɑːk; *NAmE* -mɑːrk/ *noun* **1** something, such as a large building, that you can see clearly from a distance and that will help you to know where you are 陆标，地标（有助于识别所处地点的大建筑物等）：*The Empire State Building is a familiar landmark on the New York skyline.* 帝国大厦是人们熟悉的纽约高楼大厦中的地标。 **2** ~ (**in sth**) an event, a discovery, an invention, etc. that marks an important stage in sth（标志重要阶段的）里程碑 SYN **milestone**：*The ceasefire was seen as a major landmark in the fight against terrorism.* 停火协定被看作是与恐怖主义斗争的重要里程碑。 ◇ *a **landmark decision/ruling** in the courts* 具有里程碑意义的决策 / 法庭裁决 **3** (*especially NAmE*) a building or a place that is very important because of its history, and that should be preserved 有历史意义的建筑物（或遗址） SYN **monument**

ˈ**land mass** *noun* (*specialist*) a large area of land, for example a continent 陆块；地块

land·mine /ˈlændmaɪn/ *noun* a bomb placed on or under the ground, which explodes when vehicles or people move over it 地雷

ˈ**land office** (*NAmE*) (*BrE* ˈ**land registry**) *noun* a government office that keeps a record of areas of land and who owns them 地政局；地籍局；土地登记处

land·owner /ˈlændəʊnə(r); *NAmE* -oʊn-/ *noun* a person who owns land, especially a large area of land 土地拥有者；地主 ▸ **land·owner·ship** (*also* **land·owning**) *noun* [U]: *private landownership* 土地私有制 **land·owning** *adj.* [only before noun]: *the great landowning families* 拥有大量土地的家族

ˈ**land reform** *noun* [U, C] the principle of dividing land for farming into smaller pieces so that more people can own some 土地改革

ˈ**land registry** (*BrE*) (*NAmE* ˈ**land office**) *noun* a government office that keeps a record of areas of land and who owns them 地政局；地籍局；土地登记处

ˈ**Land Rover™** (*also* ˈ**Land-Rover™**) *noun* a strong vehicle used for travelling over rough ground 路虎（越野车）

land·scape 🔑 /ˈlændskeɪp/ *noun, verb*

■ ***noun*** **1** 🔑 [C, usually sing.] everything you can see when you look across a large area of land, especially in the country（陆上，尤指乡村的）风景，景色：*the **bleak/rugged/dramatic, etc. landscape** of the area* 那个地区荒芜的景观、崎岖的地貌、引人入胜的风光等 ◇ *the woods and fields that are typical features of the English landscape* 具有典型英格兰风景特征的森林与田野 ◇ *an **urban/industrial landscape*** 都市 / 工业景观 ◇ (*figurative*) *We can expect changes in the **political landscape**.* 我们等着看政治舞台上的变化吧。

WORDFINDER 联想词： barren, fertile, lush, mountainous, rolling, rugged, undulate, volcanic, wooded

➲ **SYNONYMS** AT COUNTRY **2** 🔑 [C, U] a painting of a view of the countryside; this style of painting 乡村风景画；乡村风景画的风格：*an artist famous for his landscapes* 以风景画闻名的画家 ➲ **COLLOCATIONS** AT ART ➲ COMPARE TOWNSCAPE (2) **3** [U] (*specialist*) the way of printing a document in which the top of the page is one of the longer sides（文件的）横向打印格式：*Select the landscape option when printing the file.* 打印文件时选择横向打印格式选项。 ➲ COMPARE PORTRAIT *n.* IDM SEE BLOT *n.*

■ ***verb*** ~ **sth** to improve the appearance of an area of land by changing the design and planting trees, flowers, etc. 对…做景观美化；给…做园林美化；美化…的环境

ˌ**landscape** ˈ**architect** *noun* a person whose job is planning and designing the environment, especially so that roads, buildings, etc. combine with the landscape in an attractive way 园林建筑师；景观设计师 ▸ ˌ**landscape** ˈ**architecture** *noun* [U]

ˌ**landscape** ˈ**gardener** *noun* a person whose job is designing and creating attractive parks and gardens 园林学家；造园师；园林设计师 ▸ ˌ**landscape** ˈ**gardening** *noun* [U]

ˌ**Land's** ˈ**End** *noun* a place in Cornwall that is further west than any other place in England 兰兹角（属康沃尔郡，位于英格兰最西边） ➲ COMPARE JOHN O'GROATS

land·slide /ˈlændslaɪd/ *noun* **1** (*also* **land·fall**) a mass of earth, rock, etc. that falls down the slope of a mountain or a CLIFF（山坡或悬崖的）崩塌，塌方，滑坡，地滑 ➲ SEE ALSO LANDSLIP ➲ **WORDFINDER NOTE** AT DISASTER **2** an election in which one person or party gets very many more votes than the other people or parties 一方选票占压倒多数的选举；一方占绝对优势的选举：*She was expected to win **by a landslide**.* 预计她会以压倒多数的选票获胜。◇ *a landslide victory* 压倒性优势的选举胜利 ➲ **COLLOCATIONS** AT VOTE

land·slip /ˈlændslɪp/ *noun* a mass of rock and earth that falls down a slope, usually smaller than a landslide（通常为小规模的）崩塌，塌方，滑坡，地滑

land·ward /ˈlændwəd; *NAmE* -wərd/ *adj.* [only before noun] facing the land; away from the sea 朝陆地的；向岸的 ▸ **land·ward** (*also* **land·wards**) *adv.*：*After an hour, the ship turned landward.* 一小时后，那艘船转而驶向岸边。

ˈ**land yacht** *noun* **1** a small vehicle with a sail and no engine, that is used on land（带风帆、无发动机的）快艇车，沙滩艇 **2** (*NAmE, informal*) a large car 大型汽车

lane 🔑 /leɪn/ *noun* **1** 🔑 a narrow road in the country（乡间）小路：*winding country lanes* 蜿蜒的乡间小路 ◇ *We drove along a muddy lane to reach the farmhouse.*

我们驾车沿泥泞的小路到达农舍。 ➲ VISUAL VOCAB PAGE V3 ➲ SEE ALSO MEMORY LANE **2** (especially in place names 尤用于地名) a street, often a narrow one with buildings on both sides 小巷；胡同；里弄：*The quickest way is through the back lanes behind the bus station.* 最近的路是穿过公共汽车站后面的小巷。◇ *Park Lane* 帕克巷 **3** a section of a wide road, that is marked by painted white lines, to keep lines of traffic separate 车道：*the **inside/middle lane*** 内车道；中车道 ◇ *the **northbound/southbound lane*** 北行 / 南行车道 ◇ *to change lanes* 变换车道 ◇ *She signalled and pulled over into the slow lane.* 她给信号后把车开进了慢车道。◇ *a four-lane highway* 四车道公路 ➲ SEE ALSO BUS LANE, CYCLE LANE, FAST LANE, OUTSIDE LANE, PASSING LANE ➲ WORDFINDER NOTE AT ROAD **4** a narrow marked section of a track or a swimming pool that is used by one person taking part in a race（比赛的）跑道，泳道，球道：*The Australian in lane four is coming up fast from behind.* 第四道的澳大利亚选手正从后面快速追赶上来。 ➲ VISUAL VOCAB PAGE V50 **5** (in TENPIN BOWLING) a narrow section of floor along which the ball is BOWLED（十柱保龄球）球道：*a 20-lane bowling alley* 有 20 条球道的保龄球馆 ➲ VISUAL VOCAB PAGE V44 **6** a route used by ships or aircraft on regular journeys 航道；航线：*one of the world's busiest **shipping/sea lanes*** 世界上最繁忙的海运航线之一 IDM SEE FAST LANE

lan·gous·tine /ˈlɒŋɡustiːn; NAmE ˈlɑːŋ-/ (*also* ˌ**Norway ˈlobster**, ˌ**Dublin Bay ˈprawn**) *noun* a type of SHELLFISH like a small LOBSTER 挪威海螯虾

lan·guage /ˈlæŋɡwɪdʒ/ *noun*

• **OF A COUNTRY** 国家 **1** [C] the system of communication in speech and writing that is used by people of a particular country or area 语言：*the Japanese language* 日语 ◇ *It takes a long time to learn to **speak a language** well.* 学会说好一种语言需要花很长的时间。◇ *Italian is my **first language**.* 意大利语是我的母语。◇ *All the children must learn a **foreign language**.* 所有的儿童必须学一门外语。◇ *She **has a good command of the** Spanish **language**.* 她精通西班牙语。◇ *a qualification in **language teaching*** 语言教学的资格 ◇ *They fell in love in spite of **the language barrier*** (= the difficulty of communicating when people speak different languages). 尽管有语言障碍，他们还是相爱了。◇ *Why study Latin? It's a **dead language*** (= no longer spoken by anyone). 为什么学拉丁语？它是死语言，没人说了。◇ *Is English an **official language** in your country?* 英语在你们国家是官方语言吗？ ➲ SEE ALSO MODERN LANGUAGE

> **WORDFINDER** 联想词： accent, alphabet, dialect, **grammar**, literacy, **literature**, **pronunciation**, translate, **word**

• **COMMUNICATION** 沟通 **2** [U] the use by humans of a system of sounds and words to communicate 言语；说话；语言：*theories about the origins of language* 有关语言起源的理论 ◇ *a study of **language acquisition** in two-year-olds* 对两岁儿童语言习得的研究

• **STYLE OF SPEAKING/WRITING** 口语 / 书面语的风格 **3** [U] a particular style of speaking or writing 某种类型的言语（或语言）：***bad/foul/strong language*** (= words that people may consider offensive) 脏骂；粗骂；骂人话 ◇ ***literary/poetic language*** 文学 / 诗歌语言 ◇ *the language of the legal profession* 法律专业用语 ◇ *Give your instructions in everyday language.* 用通俗的语言发布指令。 ➲ SEE ALSO BAD LANGUAGE

• **MOVEMENTS/SYMBOLS/SOUND** 动作；符号；声音 **4** [C, U] a way of expressing ideas and feelings using movements, symbols and sound （用动作、符号和语音来表达思想感情的）表达方式，交际方式：*the language of mime* 哑剧的手势语 ◇ *the **language of dolphins/bees*** 海豚 / 蜜蜂的交流方式 ➲ SEE ALSO BODY LANGUAGE, SIGN LANGUAGE

• **COMPUTING** 计算机技术 **5** [C, U] a system of symbols and rules that is used to operate a computer 计算机语言：*a programming language* 程序设计语言

IDM **mind/watch your ˈlanguage** to be careful about what you say in order not to upset or offend sb 谨慎措辞；留神言辞：*Watch your language, young man!* 年轻人，注意你的措辞！ **speak/talk the same ˈlanguage** to be able to communicate easily with another person because you share similar opinions and experience（因意见和经历相似）能容易地沟通，说得来，有共同语言

> ▼ **SYNONYMS** 同义词辨析
>
> **language**
>
> **vocabulary • terms • wording • terminology**
>
> These are all terms for the words and expressions people use when they speak or write, or for a particular style of speaking or writing. 以上各词均指措辞、用词或某种类型的言语。
>
> **language** a particular style of speaking or writing 指某种类型的言语或语言：*Give your instructions in everyday language.* 用通俗的语言发布指令。◇ *the language of the legal profession* 法律专业用语
>
> **vocabulary** all the words that a person knows or uses, or all the words in a particular language; the words that people use when they are talking about a particular subject 指一个人掌握或使用的词汇、某种语言的词汇、某一学科的词汇：*to have a wide/limited vocabulary* 词汇丰富 / 有限 ◇ *The word has become part of advertising vocabulary.* 这个词已经成了广告用语。
>
> **terms** a way of expressing yourself or of saying sth 指表达方式、措辞、说法：*I'll try to explain in simple terms.* 我会尽量讲得通俗易懂。
>
> **wording** [usually sing.] the words that are used in a piece of writing or speech, especially when they have been carefully chosen 指措辞、用词：*It was the standard form of wording for a consent letter.* 这是同意书的标准用词。
>
> **terminology** (*rather formal*) the set of technical words or expressions used in a particular subject; words used with particular meanings 指某学科的术语、有特别含义的用语、专门用语：*medical terminology* 医学术语 ◇ *Scientists are constantly developing new terminologies.* 科学家不断发展新的专门用语。 NOTE *Literary/poetic terminology* is used for talking about literature or poetry. *Literary/poetic language* is used for writing in a literary or poetic style. * literary/poetic terminology 用于谈论文学或诗歌，literary/poetic language 用于文学或诗歌创作。
>
> **PATTERNS**
>
> • **formal/informal/everyday** language/vocabulary/terms
> • **business/scientific/technical/specialized** language/vocabulary/terminology
> • A word **enters** the language/the vocabulary.

ˌ**language engiˈneering** *noun* [U] (*computing* 计) the use of computers to process languages for industrial purposes 语言工程

ˈ**language laboratory** *noun* a room in a school or college that contains special equipment to help students learn foreign languages by listening to tapes or CDs, watching videos or DVDs, recording themselves, etc. 语言实验室；语音室

ˈ**language transfer** *noun* [U] (*linguistics* 语言) the process of using your knowledge of your first language or another language that you know when speaking or writing a language that you are learning 语言迁移，语言介入（学习者在使用目标语时用第一语言或其他语言的知识）

langue /lɒ̃ɡ; NAmE lɑːŋɡ/ *noun* (*linguistics* 语言, *from French*) a language considered as a communication system of a particular community, rather than the way individual people speak（作为特定群体内交际系统的）语言 ➲ COMPARE PAROLE *n.* (2)

lan·guid /ˈlæŋɡwɪd/ *adj.* moving slowly in an elegant manner, not needing energy or effort 慢悠悠的；慵懒的：*a languid wave of the hand* 懒洋洋一挥手 ◇ *a languid* *afternoon in the sun* 阳光下一个懒洋洋的下午 ▸ **lan·guid·ly** *adv.*：*He moved languidly across the room.* 他慢悠悠地穿过房间。

lan·guish /ˈlæŋɡwɪʃ/ *verb* (*formal*) **1** [I] ~ (**in sth**) to be forced to stay somewhere or suffer sth unpleasant for a long time 被迫滞留；长期受苦；受煎熬：*She continues to languish in a foreign prison.* 她继续被囚禁在一所外国的监狱里。 **2** [I] to become weaker or fail to make progress 变得衰弱；未能取得进展：*The share price languished at 102p.* 股票价格停滞在 102 便士上。

lan·guor /ˈlæŋɡə(r)/ *noun* [U, sing.] (*literary*) the pleasant state of feeling lazy and without energy 懒洋洋；慵懒：*A delicious languor was stealing over him.* 一种美滋滋懒洋洋的感觉悄悄传遍他的全身。 ▸ **lan·guor·ous** /ˈlæŋɡərəs/ *adj.*：*a languorous pace of life* 慢悠悠的生活节奏 **lan·guor·ous·ly** *adv.*

La Niña /lɑː ˈniːnjə/ *noun* [U] the cooling of the water in the central and eastern Pacific Ocean that happens every few years and that affects the weather in many parts of the world 拉尼娜，反厄尔尼诺（指赤道附近太平洋中部和东部水温每隔几年异常降低并影响世界很多地区的气候）➲ COMPARE EL NIÑO

lank /læŋk/ *adj.* **1** (of hair 毛发) straight, dull and not attractive 平直而无光泽的 **2** (*SAfrE*, *informal*) large in number or amount 大量的；很多的：*I've got lank work to do.* 我有很多工作要做。

lanky /ˈlæŋki/ *adj.* (**lank·ier**, **lank·iest**) (of a person 人) having long thin arms and legs and moving in an awkward way 瘦长（或胳膊、腿细长）而行动笨拙的 SYN **gangling**：*a tall, lanky teenager* 身材瘦长的少年

lano·lin /ˈlænəlɪn/ *noun* [U] an oil that comes from sheep's wool and is used to make skin creams 绵羊油（用以制作护肤霜）

lan·tern /ˈlæntən; *NAmE* -tərn/ *noun* a lamp in a transparent case, often a metal case with glass sides, that has a handle, so that you can carry it outside 灯笼；提灯 ➲ SEE ALSO CHINESE LANTERN

ˌlantern ˈjaw *noun* a long thin JAW with a large chin 瘦长突出的下巴 ▸ **ˌlantern-ˈjawed** *adj.*

lanth·anum /ˈlænθənəm/ *noun* [U] (*symb.* **La**) a chemical element. Lanthanum is a silver-white metal. 镧

lan·yard /ˈlænjɑːd; ˈlænjəd; *NAmE* -jərd/ *noun* **1** a string that you wear around your neck or wrist for holding sth 颈带；腕带：*A lanyard is useful for carrying your ID card.* 颈带适合用来挂身份证。 ◇ *a whistle lanyard* 口哨带 **2** a piece of equipment that you wear around your neck to hold the wire of an MP3 PLAYER（MP3 播放器的）挂绳，颈绳：*lanyard headphones for use with your iPod* 配合苹果播放器使用的挂绳耳机 **3** a rope used to fasten sth, for example the sail of a ship 牵索；（系船帆的）收紧索，帆牵

lap /læp/ *noun*, *verb*

■ ***noun*** [C] **1** [usually sing.] the top part of your legs that forms a flat surface when you are sitting down（坐着时的）大腿部：*There's only one seat so you'll have to sit* ***on my lap****.* 只有一个座位，你只好坐在我腿上了。 ◇ *She sat with her hands* ***in her lap****.* 她双手放在大腿上坐着。 **2** one journey from the beginning to the end of a track used for running, etc.（跑道等的）一圈：*the fastest lap on record* 创纪录的最快的一圈 ◇ *She has completed six laps.* 她跑完六圈了。 ◇ *He was overtaken on the final lap.* 他在最后一圈被超过。 ◇ *to do a* ***lap of honour*** (= go around the track again to celebrate winning) 绕场一周庆祝胜利 ◇ (*NAmE*) *to do a* ***victory lap*** 绕场一周庆祝胜利 **3** a section of a journey, or of a piece of work, etc.（行程或工作等中的）一段，环节：*They're off on the first lap of their round-the-world tour.* 他们踏上环游世界的第一段行程。 ◇ *We've nearly finished. We're* ***on the last lap****.* 我们接近完工了，正在处理最后的一部分工作。

IDM **drop/dump sth in sb's ˈlap** (*informal*) to make sth the responsibility of another person 把（某事）推给他人负责：*They dropped the problem firmly back in my lap.* 他们把问题断然给我推了回来。 **sth drops/falls into sb's lap** somebody has the opportunity to do sth pleasant without having made any effort（美事、好运等）被某人轻松得到：*My dream job just fell into my lap.* 我没费劲就找到了梦寐以求的工作。 **in the lap of the ˈgods** if the result of sth is **in the lap of the gods**, you do not know what will happen because it depends on luck or things you cannot control 由神掌管；结果难以预料；非人力所能左右 **in the lap of ˈluxury** in easy, comfortable conditions, and enjoying the advantages of being rich 生活优裕；养尊处优

■ ***verb*** (**-pp-**) **1** [I] (of water 水) to touch sth gently and regularly, often making a soft sound（轻柔而有规律地）拍打：*The waves lapped around our feet.* 波浪轻轻地拍打着我们的脚。 ◇ *the sound of water lapping against the boat* 水轻轻拍打船帮的声音 **2** [T] ~ **sth** (of animals 动物) to drink sth with quick movements of the tongue 舔食；舔着喝 **3** [T] ~ **sb** (in a race 赛跑) to pass another runner on a track who is one or more laps behind you 领先…一圈（或数圈）

PHR V **ˌlap sth↔ˈup 1** (*informal*) to accept or receive sth with great enjoyment, without thinking about whether it is good, true or sincere（不加考虑地）乐于接受：*It's a terrible movie but audiences everywhere are lapping it up.* 这部电影很差劲，可各地的观众却趋之若鹜。 ◇ *She simply lapped up all the compliments.* 什么恭维话她都照单全收。 **2** to drink all of sth with great enjoyment 开怀畅饮：*The calf lapped up the bucket of milk.* 小牛津津有味地喝光了那桶牛奶。

lapa /ˈlɑːpə/ *noun* (*SAfrE*) a shelter without walls on all sides, usually made of wooden poles and covered with THATCH (= dry grass), especially used as a place for relaxing and eating meals 草亭（尤用于休息和用餐）

lapar·os·copy /ˌlæpəˈrɒskəpi; *NAmE* -ˈrɑːs-/ *noun* (*pl.* **-ies**) (*medical* 医) an examination of the inside of the body using a tube-shaped instrument that can be put through the wall of the ABDOMEN 腹腔镜检查

lapar·ot·omy /ˌlæpəˈrɒtəmi; *NAmE* -ˈrɑːt-/ *noun* (*pl.* **-ies**) (*medical* 医) a cut in the ABDOMEN in order to perform an operation or an examination 剖腹术

ˈlap belt *noun* a type of SEAT BELT that goes across your waist 安全腰带

ˈlap dancing *noun* [U] sexually exciting dancing or STRIPTEASE which is performed close to, or sitting on, a customer in a bar or club（酒吧或夜总会中在顾客面前或坐在顾客腿上表演的）性感舞，脱衣舞

lap·dog /ˈlæpdɒɡ; *NAmE* -dɔːɡ; -dɑːɡ/ *noun* **1** a pet dog that is small enough to be carried（可携带的）宠物狗，叭儿狗 **2** (*disapproving*) a person who is under the control of another person or group 走狗 SYN **poodle**

lapel /ləˈpel/ *noun* one of the two front parts of the top of a coat or jacket that are joined to the COLLAR and are folded back（西服外衣或夹克上部胸前的）翻领 ➲ VISUAL VOCAB PAGE V66

lapi·dary /ˈlæpɪdəri; *NAmE* -deri/ *adj.* **1** (*formal*) (especially of written language 尤指书面用语) elegant and exact 优雅精确的 SYN **concise**：*in lapidary style* 以优雅严谨的文体 **2** (*specialist*) connected with stones and the work of cutting and polishing them 镌刻在石上的；宝石加工的

lapis laz·uli /ˌlæpɪs ˈlæzjʊli; *NAmE* ˈlæzəli/ *noun* [U] a bright blue stone, used in making jewellery 杂青金石（用于制作珠宝饰物）

lap·sang sou·chong /ˌlæpsæŋ ˈsuːʃɒŋ; *NAmE* -ʃɑːŋ/ *noun* [U] a type of tea that has a taste like smoke 正山小种红茶（有烟熏味）

lapse /læps/ *noun*, *verb*

■ ***noun*** **1** a small mistake, especially one that is caused by forgetting sth or by being careless 小错；（尤指）记错，过失，疏忽：*a* ***lapse of concentration/memory*** 心不在焉；记错 ◇ *A momentary lapse in the final set cost her* *the match.* 她最后一盘一时不慎，输掉了整场比赛。 **2** a period of time between two things that happen（两件事发生的）间隔时间 SYN **interval**: *After a lapse of six months we met up again.* 相隔六个月之后我们又相遇了。 **3** an example or period of bad behaviour from sb who normally behaves well 行为失检；（平时表现不错的人一时的）失足

■ *verb* **1** [I] (of a contract, an agreement, etc. 合同、协议等) to be no longer valid because the period of time that it lasts has come to an end 失效；期满终止：*She had allowed her membership to lapse.* 她的会员资格期满终止，没有再续。 **2** [I] to gradually become weaker or come to an end 衰退；衰弱；（逐渐）消失，结束 SYN **expire**: *His concentration lapsed after a few minutes.* 几分钟后他的注意力就下降了。 **3** [I] ~ (**from sth**) to stop believing in or practising your religion 背弃，放弃（宗教信仰）：*He lapsed from Judaism when he was a student.* 他当学生时就放弃了犹太教。 ▶ **lapsed** *adj.* [only before noun]: *a lapsed subscription* 失效的订购 ◇ *lapsed faith* 背弃的信仰 ◇ *a lapsed Catholic* 丧失信仰的天主教徒

PHR V **'lapse into sth 1** to gradually pass into a worse or less active state or condition（逐渐）陷入，进入：*to lapse into unconsciousness/a coma* 逐渐失去知觉 / 陷入昏迷状态 ◇ *She* ***lapsed into silence*** *again.* 她又陷入了沉默。 **2** to start speaking or behaving in a different way, often one that is less acceptable 说话或举止显得异常（常令人难以接受）：*He soon lapsed back into his old ways.* 他很快又犯老毛病了。

L

lap·top /ˈlæptɒp; *NAmE* -tɑːp/ *noun* a small computer that can work with a battery and be easily carried 笔记本电脑；便携式电脑 SYN **notebook** ➲ VISUAL VOCAB PAGES V73, V71 ➲ COMPARE DESKTOP COMPUTER, NETBOOK

lap·wing /ˈlæpwɪŋ/ (*also* **pee·wit**) *noun* a black and white bird with a row of feathers (called a CREST) standing up on its head 凤头麦鸡

lar·ceny /ˈlɑːsəni; *NAmE* ˈlɑːrs-/ *noun* [U, C] (*pl.* **-ies**) (*law* 律, *NAmE* or *old-fashioned, BrE*) the crime of stealing sth from sb; an occasion when this takes place 盗窃罪；偷盗；盗窃 SYN **theft**: *The couple were charged with* ***grand/petty larceny*** (= stealing things that are valuable/not very valuable). 那对夫妇被指控犯有重大 / 轻微盗窃罪。

larch /lɑːtʃ; *NAmE* lɑːrtʃ/ *noun* [C, U] a tree with sharp pointed leaves that fall in winter and hard dry fruit called CONES 落叶松

lard /lɑːd; *NAmE* lɑːrd/ *noun, verb*

■ *noun* [U] a firm white substance made from the melted fat of pigs that is used in cooking（烹调用的）猪油

■ *verb* ~ **sth** to put small pieces of fat on or into sth before cooking it（烹饪前）涂猪油，放入猪油

PHR V **'lard sth with sth** [usually passive] (*often disapproving*) to include a lot of a particular kind of word or expressions in a speech or in a piece of writing（在讲话或文章中）夹杂大量，大量穿插（某类词语）：*His conversation was larded with Russian proverbs.* 他的谈话夹杂了很多俄国谚语。

lard·ass /ˈlɑːdɑːs; *NAmE* ˈlɑːrdæs/ *noun* (*informal, especially NAmE, offensive*) a fat person, especially sb who is thought of as lazy（尤指被认为懒惰的）胖子

lar·der /ˈlɑːdə(r); *NAmE* ˈlɑːrd-/ *noun* (*especially BrE*) a cupboard/closet or small room in a house, used for storing food, especially in the past（尤指旧时的）食物橱柜，食物贮藏室 SYN **pantry**

lar·don /ˈlɑːdn; *NAmE* ˈlɑːr-/ *noun* [usually pl.] a small thick piece of BACON, often used to add fat to other meat in cooked dishes 咸肉丁；熏肉丁

large 🔑 /lɑːdʒ; *NAmE* lɑːrdʒ/ *adj., verb*

■ *adj.* (**larger, larg·est**) **1** 🔑 big in size or quantity 大的；大规模的；大量的：*a large area/family/house/car/appetite* 大面积；大家庭；大房子；大汽车；大胃口 ◇ *a large number of people* 很多人 ◇ *very large sums of money* 几笔巨款 ◇ *He's a very large child for his age.* 就其年龄来说，这孩子个头很大。 ◇ *A large proportion of old people live alone.* 一大部分老人都是独居。 ◇ *Women usually do the larger share of the housework.* 妇女通常承担大部分家务。 ◇ *Brazil is the world's largest producer of coffee.* 巴西是世界上最大的咖啡生产国。 ◇ *Who's the rather large* (= fat) *lady in the hat?* 那位戴帽子的丰满女士是谁？ **2** 🔑 (*abbr.* **L**) used to describe one size in a range of sizes of clothes, food, products used in the house, etc.（服装、食物、日用品等）大型号的：*small, medium, large* 小号、中号、大号 **3** 🔑 wide in range and involving many things 广泛的；众多的：*a large and complex issue* 重大而复杂的问题 ◇ *Some drugs are being used on a much larger scale than previously.* 与以前相比，某些药物的使用范围更广了。 ◇ *If we look at the larger picture of the situation, the differences seem slight.* 倘若我们对情况看得全面些，这些分歧就显得微不足道了。 ➲ NOTE AT BIG ▶ **large·ness** *noun* [U]

IDM **at 'large 1** (used after a noun 用于名词后) as a whole; in general 整个；全部；总地；一般地：*the opinion of the public at large* 普通大众的意见 **2** (of a dangerous person or animal 危险的人或动物) not captured; free 未被捕获的；自由的：*Her killer is still at large.* 杀害她的凶手仍然逍遥法外。 **give/have it 'large** (*BrE, slang*) to enjoy yourself, especially by dancing and drinking alcohol 玩个痛快；（尤指跳舞和饮酒）作乐 **in 'large part | in large 'measure** (*formal*) to a great extent 在很大程度上：*Their success is due in large part to their determination.* 他们的成功在很大程度上应归功于他们的决心。 **(as) large as 'life** (*humorous*) used to show surprise at seeing sb/sth（表示惊讶地见到）本人，本身：*I hadn't seen her for fifteen years and then there she was, (as) large as life.* 我有十五年未见过她，却在那里遇见她了，没错，就是她。 **ˌlarger than 'life** looking or behaving in a way that is more interesting or exciting than other people, and so is likely to attract attention 外表或行为惹人注目 SYN **flamboyant**: *He's a larger than life character.* 他这个人不是一般的有趣，很招眼。 ➲ MORE AT BY *adv.*, LOOM *v.*, WRIT *v.*

■ *verb*

IDM **'large it | large it 'up** (*BrE, slang*) to enjoy yourself, especially by dancing and drinking alcohol 玩个痛快；（尤指跳舞和饮酒）作乐

large·ly 🔑 /ˈlɑːdʒli; *NAmE* ˈlɑːrdʒli/ *adv.* to a great extent; mostly or mainly 在很大程度上；多半；主要地：*the manager who is largely responsible for the team's victory* 对该队获胜起主要作用的主教练 ◇ *It was* ***largely a matter of*** *trial and error.* 这主要是个反复试验的问题。 ◇ *He resigned largely because of the stories in the press.* 他的辞职多半是因为新闻界的一些报道。

ˌlarge-'scale *adj.* [usually before noun] **1** involving many people or things, especially over a wide area 大规模的；大批的；大范围的：*large-scale development* 大规模的开发 ◇ *the large-scale employment of women* 对女性大批的雇用 **2** (of a map, model, etc. 地图、模型等) drawn or made to a scale that shows a small area of land or a building in great detail 按大比例绘制（或制作）的；大比例尺的 OPP **small-scale**

lar·gesse (*also* **lar·gess**) /lɑːˈdʒes; *NAmE* lɑːrˈdʒes/ *noun* [U] (*formal* or *humorous*) the act or quality of being generous with money; money that you give to people who have less than you 慷慨解囊；施舍；（给穷人的）钱，赠款：*She is not noted for her largesse* (= she is not generous). 她不以出手大方出名。 ◇ *to dispense largesse to the poor* 把钱施舍给穷人

lar·gish /ˈlɑːdʒɪʃ; *NAmE* ˈlɑːrdʒɪʃ/ *adj.* fairly large 相当大的

largo /ˈlɑːɡəʊ; *NAmE* ˈlɑːrɡoʊ/ *adv., adj., noun* (*music* 音, *from Italian*)

■ *adv., adj.* (used as an instruction 指示语) in a slow, serious way 缓慢而庄严地（的）

■ *noun* (*pl.* **-os**) a piece of music to be performed in a slow, serious way 广板（风格缓慢、庄严）

lark /lɑːk; *NAmE* lɑːrk/ *noun, verb*

■ *noun* **1** a small brown bird with a pleasant song 百灵鸟；云雀 ➲ SEE ALSO SKYLARK **2** [usually sing.] (*informal*) a thing that you do for fun or as a joke 嬉戏；玩乐；玩笑：*The boys didn't mean any harm—they just did it for* *a lark.* 那些男孩并无恶意，他们只是闹着玩罢了。 **3** (*BrE, informal*) (used after another noun 用于另一名词后) an activity that you think is a waste of time or that you do not take seriously（认为）浪费时间的活动；不受重视的活动：*Perhaps this riding lark would be more fun than she'd thought.* 也许这次骑马的无聊活动比她所想象的要好玩一些。

IDM **be/get up with the 'lark** (*old-fashioned, BrE*) to get out of bed very early in the morning 清晨早起；鸡鸣即起 **blow/sod that for a lark** (*BrE, slang*) used by sb who does not want to do sth because it involves too much effort（因太费力而不想干时说）：*Sod that for a lark! I'm not doing any more tonight.* 拉倒吧！我今晚再也不做了。

■ *verb*

PHR V **,lark a'bout/a'round** (*old-fashioned, informal, especially BrE*) to enjoy yourself by behaving in a silly way 傻玩；胡闹；嬉戏 SYN **mess around**

lark·spur /ˈlɑːkspɜː(r); *NAmE* ˈlɑːrk-/ *noun* [C, U] a tall garden plant with blue, pink or white flowers growing up its STEM 飞燕草（高株园艺植物，开蓝色、粉红或白色花）

lar·ney (*also* **lar·nie**) /ˈlɑːni; *NAmE* ˈlɑːr-/ *adj.* (*SAfrE*) very smart; expensive 高档的；昂贵的：*We were invited to a larney function.* 我们获邀参加一个盛大的庆典。◇ *a larney hotel* 高档酒店

LARP /lɑːp; *NAmE* lɑːrp/ *noun* the abbreviation for 'live action role-playing game' (= a type of game in which players pretend to be imaginary characters in a story, usually using special clothes and objects to make the story appear more real) 真人角色扮演游戏（全写为 live action role-playing game） ▶ **LARPer** *noun* **LARPing** *noun* [U]

lar·ri·kin /ˈlærɪkɪn/ *noun* (*AustralE, NZE*) a person who ignores the normal rules of society or of an organization 不守规矩的人；无视规章制度的人

larva /ˈlɑːvə; *NAmE* ˈlɑːrvə/ *noun* (*pl.* **lar·vae** /ˈlɑːviː; *NAmE* ˈlɑːrviː/) an insect at the stage when it has just come out of an egg and looks like a short fat WORM 幼虫；幼体 ▶ **lar·val** /ˈlɑːvl; *NAmE* ˈlɑːrvl/ *adj.* [only before noun]: *an insect in its larval stage* 处于幼体阶段的昆虫 ➲ VISUAL VOCAB PAGE V13

la·ryn·geal /ləˈrɪndʒiəl/ *adj.* (*biology* 生, *phonetics* 语音) related to or produced by the larynx 喉的；喉音的

laryn·gi·tis /ˌlærɪnˈdʒaɪtɪs/ *noun* [U] an infection of the larynx that makes speaking painful 喉炎

lar·ynx /ˈlærɪŋks/ *noun* (*pl.* **la·ryn·ges** /ləˈrɪndʒiːz/) (*anatomy* 解) the area at the top of the throat that contains the VOCAL CORDS 喉 SYN **voice box** ➲ VISUAL VOCAB PAGE V64

la·sagne (*also* **la·sagna**) /ləˈzænjə/ *noun* **1** [U] large flat pieces of PASTA 宽面条 **2** [U, C] an Italian dish made from layers of lasagne, finely chopped meat and/or vegetables and white sauce 意大利千层面（以多层宽面条夹肉末、蔬菜和白汁制成）

la·scivi·ous /ləˈsɪviəs/ *adj.* (*formal, disapproving*) feeling or showing strong sexual desire 好色的；淫荡的；淫欲的；猥亵的：*a lascivious person* 淫荡的人 ◇ *lascivious thoughts* 淫猥的念头 ▶ **la·scivi·ous·ly** *adv.* **la·scivi·ous·ness** *noun* [U]

laser /ˈleɪzə(r)/ *noun* a device that gives out light in which all the waves OSCILLATE (= change direction and strength) together, typically producing a powerful beam of light that can be used for cutting metal, in medical operations, etc. 激光器：*a laser beam* 激光束 ◇ *a laser navigation device* 激光导航装置 ◇ *The barcodes on the products are read by lasers.* 产品上的条码是用激光读取的。◇ *a* ***laser show*** (= lasers used as entertainment) 激光表演 ◇ *She's had* ***laser surgery*** *on her eye.* 她做了眼部激光手术。

laser·disc (*also* **laser·disk**) /ˈleɪzədɪsk; *NAmE* ˈleɪzər-/ *noun* a plastic disc like a large CD on which large amounts of information, such as video or music, can be stored, and which can be read by a laser 激光光盘；激光影碟

'laser gun *noun* a piece of equipment which uses a laser to read a BARCODE or to find out how fast a vehicle or other object is moving 激光条码扫描仪；激光测速仪

'laser printer *noun* a printer that produces good quality printed material by means of a laser 激光打印机

lash /læʃ/ *verb, noun*

■ *verb* **1** [I, T] to hit sb/sth with great force 猛击；狠打 SYN **pound**: **+ adv./prep.** *The rain lashed at the windows.* 雨点猛烈地打在窗户上。◇ **~ sth** *Huge waves lashed the shore.* 巨浪拍打着海岸。➲ SYNONYMS AT BEAT **2** [T] **~ sb/sth** to hit a person or an animal with a WHIP, rope, stick, etc. 鞭打；抽打 SYN **beat** **3** [T] **~ sb/sth** to criticize sb/sth in a very angry way 怒斥 SYN **attack** **4** [T] **~ sth + adv./prep.** to fasten sth tightly to sth else with ropes 捆绑；捆扎：*Several logs had been lashed together to make a raft.* 几根原木捆扎在一起做成了木筏。◇ *During the storm everything on deck had to be lashed down.* 暴风雨中甲板上所有的东西都必须系牢。 **5** [I, T] **~ (sth)** to move or to move sth quickly and violently from side to side（使）迅猛摆动，甩动：*The crocodile's tail was lashing furiously from side to side.* 鳄鱼的尾巴在急速地左右甩动。

PHR V **,lash 'out (at sb/sth)** **1** to suddenly try to hit sb/sth（突然）狠打，痛打：*She suddenly lashed out at the boy.* 她突然狠狠地打那个男孩。 **2** to criticize sb in an angry way 怒斥；严厉斥责：*In a bitter article he lashed out at his critics.* 他写了一篇尖刻的文章，猛烈驳斥批评他的人。 **,lash 'out on sth** (*BrE, informal*) to spend a lot of money on sth 在…上大量花费

L

■ *noun* **1** = EYELASH： *her long dark lashes* 她那长长的黑睫毛 **2** a hit with a WHIP, given as a form of punishment（作为惩罚的）鞭打，抽打：*They each received 20 lashes for stealing.* 他们因盗窃每人挨了 20 鞭。◇ (*figurative*) *to feel the lash of sb's tongue* (= to be spoken to in an angry and critical way) 领教某人言语如鞭的厉害 **3** the thin leather part at the end of a WHIP 鞭端皮条；鞭梢

lash·ing /ˈlæʃɪŋ/ *noun* **1** **lashings** [pl.] (*BrE, informal*) a large amount of sth, especially of food and drink 大量，许多（尤指食物和饮料）：*a bowl of strawberries with lashings of cream* 一碗浇了大量奶油的草莓 **2** [C] an act of hitting sb with a WHIP as a punishment（作为惩罚的）鞭打；笞刑：(*figurative*) *He was given a severe tongue-lashing* (= angry criticism). 他受到了严厉的斥责。 **3** [C, usually pl.] a rope used to fasten sth tightly to sth else 捆绑用的绳索

lass /læs/ (*also* **las·sie** /ˈlæsi/) *noun* (*ScotE, NEngE*) a girl; a young woman 女孩；少女；年轻女子 ➲ COMPARE LAD (1), LADDIE

lassa fever /ˈlæsə fiːvə(r)/ *noun* [U] a serious disease, usually caught from RATS and found especially in W Africa 拉沙热（常由鼠类传染，尤见于西非）

lassi /ˈlæsi/ *noun* [U, C] a S Asian drink made from YOGURT （南亚）拉西酸奶奶昔

las·si·tude /ˈlæsɪtjuːd; *NAmE* -tuːd/ *noun* [U] (*formal*) a state of feeling very tired in mind or body; lack of energy 倦怠；疲乏；无精打采

lasso /læˈsuː, ˈlæsəʊ; *NAmE* ˈlæsoʊ/ *noun, verb*

■ *noun* (*pl.* **-os** or **-oes**) a long rope with one end tied into a LOOP that is used for catching horses, cows, etc.（捕马、套牛等用的）套索

■ *verb* **~ sth** to catch an animal using a lasso 用套索套捕（动物）

last¹ /lɑːst; *NAmE* læst/ *det., adv., noun, verb* ➲ SEE ALSO LAST²

■ *det.* **1** happening or coming after all other similar things or people 最后的；最末的；末尾的：*We caught the last bus home.* 我们赶上了回家的末班公共汽车。◇ *It's the last house on the left.* 是左边尽头那栋房子。◇ *She was last to arrive.* 她是最后到的。 **2** [only before noun] most recent 最近的；上一个的： *last night/Tuesday/month/summer/year* 昨晚；上个星期二；上个月；去年夏季；去年 ◇ *her last book* 她最近出版的书 ◇ *This last point is crucial.*

刚讲的这一点是关键的。◇ *The **last time** I saw him was in May.* 我上次见到他是在五月份。 **3** [only before noun] only remaining 仅剩下的；最终的 SYN **final**: *This is our last bottle of water.* 这是我们最后的一瓶水了。◇ *He knew this was his last hope of winning.* 他知道这是他取胜的最后希望。 **4** used to emphasize that sb/sth is the least likely or suitable （强调）最不可能的，最不适当的： ***The last thing she needed** was more work.* 她最不需要的就是更多的工作。◇ *He's the **last person** I'd trust with a secret.* 我要是有什么秘密，告诉谁也不能告诉他。

IDM **be on your/its last 'legs** to be going to die or stop functioning very soon; to be very weak or in bad condition 濒临死亡；奄奄一息；行将就木；快不能用了 **the day, week, month, etc. before 'last** the day, week, etc. just before the most recent one; two days, weeks, etc. ago 前天；上上星期；上上月；两天（或两周等）以前： *I haven't seen him since the summer before last.* 我已有两个夏天没见过他了。 **every last...** every person or thing in a group （某群体中的）每一个，全部： *We spent every last penny we had on the house.* 我们把所有的钱都花在房子上了。 **have the last 'laugh** to be successful when you were not expected to be, making your opponents look stupid （在本未指望时）笑在最后，取得最后胜利 **in the last re'sort** when there are no other possible courses of action 作为最后的一招 SYN **at a pinch**: *In the last resort we can always walk home.* 顶多我们走回家就是了。 **your/the last 'gasp** the point at which you/sth can no longer continue living, fighting, existing, etc. 奄奄一息；苟延残喘；临终；垂死 ➲ SEE ALSO LAST-GASP **the ˌlast 'minute/'moment** the latest possible time before an important event （重大事情前的）最后一刻，紧要关头： *They changed the plans at the last minute.* 事到临头他们却改变了计划。◇ *Don't leave your decision to the last moment.* 别等到最后一刻才来作决定。 **a/your last re'sort** the person or thing you rely on when everything else has failed 最后可依赖的人（或事物）： *I've tried everyone else and now you're my last resort.* 其他人我都试过了，现在就靠你了。 **the ˌlast 'word (in sth)** the most recent, fashionable, advanced, etc. thing 最新（或时髦、先进等）的事物： *These apartments are the last word in luxury.* 这些公寓最为豪华。 ➲ MORE AT ANALYSIS, BREATH, FAMOUS, LONG *adj.*, MAN *n.*, STRAW, THING, WEEK, WORD *n.*

■ ***adv.*** **1** after anyone or anything else; at the end 最后；最终；终结： *He came last in the race.* 这次赛跑他得了最后一名。◇ *They arrived last of all.* 他们来得比谁都晚。 **2** most recently 最新；最近；上一次： *When did you see him last?* 你最后一次是什么时候见过他？◇ *I saw him last/I last saw him in New York two years ago.* 我上一次是两年前在纽约见到他的。◇ *They last won the cup in 2006.* 他们上一次获得奖杯是在 2006 年。

IDM **ˌlast but not 'least** used when mentioning the last person or thing of a group, in order to say that they are not less important than the others （提及最后的人或事物时说）最后但同样重要的： *Last but not least, I'd like to thank all the catering staff.* 最后但同样重要的是，我要感谢所有的餐饮工作人员。 **ˌlast 'in, ˌfirst 'out** used, for example in a situation when people are losing their jobs, to say that the last people to be employed will be the first to go （形容裁员等情况）最后雇用的人最先被解雇，后来者先走 ➲ MORE AT FIRST *adv.*, LAUGH *v.*

■ ***noun*** **the last** (*pl.* **the last**) **1** the person or thing that comes or happens after all other similar people or things 最后来的人（或发生的事）： *Sorry I'm late—am I the last?* 对不起，我来晚了。我是最后到的人吗？◇ *They were the last to arrive.* 他们是最后到达的人。 **2 the last** [sing.] the latest 最新事物；最新消息： *That was the last I heard of him.* 那是我最后一次听到他的消息。 **3** ~ **of sth** the only remaining part or items of sth 仅剩下的部分（或事项）： *These are the last of our apples.* 这是我们最后剩下的几个苹果。 **4 the last** (*pl.* **the last**) the least likely 最不可能的： *'I'll be **the last to admit** that I know anything about cars!', she said.* "我完全不敢说对汽车有多少认识！"她说。◇ *Known for their self-sufficiency, fishermen would be **the last to admit** to mental strain.* 渔民以自给自足著称，最不可能承认有精神压力。

IDM **at (long) 'last** after much delay, effort, etc.; in the end （经过长时间的延误或努力等之后）终于，最终 SYN **finally**: *At last we're home!* 我们终于到家了！◇ *At long last the cheque arrived.* 支票终于到了。 ➲ NOTE AT LASTLY **hear/see the 'last of sb/sth** to hear/see sb/sth for the last time 最后一次听见（或看见）： *That was the last I ever saw of her.* 那是我最后一次见到她。◇ *Unfortunately, I don't think we've heard the last of this affair.* 遗憾的是，我认为这件事还没有了结。 **the last I 'heard** used to give the most recent news you have about sb/sth （提供最新消息时说）我最近听到的消息： *The last I heard he was still working at the garage.* 我最近听到的消息是他还在汽车修理厂工作。 **next/second to 'last** (*BrE also* **ˌlast but 'one**) the one before the last one 倒数第二： *She finished second to last.* 她得了倒数第二。 **to/till the 'last** until the last possible moment, especially until death 直到最后一刻；（尤指）直至死亡： *He died protesting his innocence to the last.* 他至死都坚决辩称自己无罪。 ➲ MORE AT BREATHE, FIRST *n.*

■ ***verb*** **1** [I] (not used in the progressive tenses 不用于进行时) to continue for a particular period of time 持续；继续；延续： *The meeting only lasted (for) a few minutes.* 会议只开了几分钟。◇ *Each game lasts about an hour.* 每场比赛约一小时。◇ *How long does the play last?* 那出戏要演多长时间？ **2** [I, T] to continue to exist or to function well 继续存在；持续起作用；持久： *This weather won't last.* 这种天气持续不了多久。◇ *He's making a big effort now, and I hope it lasts.* 现在他正加紧努力，我希望他能坚持下去。◇ ~ **sb** *These shoes should last you till next year.* 你这双鞋应该能穿到明年。 **3** [I, T] to survive sth or manage to stay in the same situation, despite difficulties （在困境等中）坚持下去；熬过（困境等）： *She won't last long in that job.* 她那份工作干不了多久。◇ ~ **(out)** *Can you last (out) until I can get help?* 你能支撑到我找来帮手吗？◇ ~ **(out) sth** *Doctors say that she probably won't last out the night* (= she will probably die before the morning). 医生都说她很可能活不过今晚。◇ *He was injured early on and didn't last the match.* 他开赛后不久就受了伤，没法坚持到底。 **4** [I, T] to be enough for sb to use, especially for a particular period of time 够用，足够维持（尤指某段时间）： ~ **(out)** *Will the coffee last out till next week?* 咖啡够喝到下周吗？◇ ~ **sb (out)** *We've got enough food to last us (for) three days.* 我们的食物足够维持三天。

▼ WHICH WORD? 词语辨析

last / take

Last and **take** are both used to talk about the length of time that something continues. * last 和 take 均表示某事持续的时间。

- **Last** is used to talk about the length of time that an event continues. * last 表示某事持续的时间： *How long do you think this storm will last?* 你看这暴风雨会持续多久？◇ *The movie lasted over two hours.* 这部电影长两个多小时。 **Last** does not always need an expression of time. * last 并非总需要与表示时间的词语连用： *His annoyance won't last.* 他的烦恼不会持续多久。 **Last** is also used to say that you have enough of something. * last 亦可表示够用、足够维持： *We don't have enough money to last until next month.* 我们的钱不足以维持到下个月。
- **Take** is used to talk about the amount of time you need in order to go somewhere or do something. It must be used with an expression of time. * take 表示到某地或做某事需要的时间，必须与表示时间的词语连用： *It takes (me) at least an hour to get home from work.* （我）下班回家至少得花一个小时。◇ *How long will the flight take?* 此次航程将需要多长时间？◇ *The water took ages to boil.* 好半天水才开了。

last² /lɑːst; *NAmE* læst/ *noun* a block of wood or metal shaped like a foot, used in making and repairing shoes 鞋楦 ➲ SEE ALSO LAST¹ *n.*

ˌlast 'call *noun* **1** (*especially NAmE*) (*BrE also* **ˌlast 'orders**) the last opportunity for people to buy drinks in a pub or a bar before it closes（酒吧打烊前）买饮料的最后机会 **2** the final request at an airport for passengers to get on their plane（机场对旅客的）最后一次登机通知

ˌlast-ˈditch *adj.* [only before noun] used to describe a final attempt to achieve sth, when there is not much hope of succeeding 作最后努力（或尝试）的；孤注一掷的：*She underwent a heart transplant in a* ***last-ditch attempt*** *to save her.* 她动了心脏移植手术，这是为挽救她的生命而作的最后一次努力。

ˌlast-ˈgasp *adj.* [only before noun] done or achieved at the last possible moment 最后时刻做成（或取得）的；最后关头的：*a last-gasp 2–1 victory* 最后一刻取得的 2:1 的胜利

last·ing /ˈlɑːstɪŋ; *NAmE* ˈlæstɪŋ/ *adj.* [usually before noun] continuing to exist or to have an effect for a long time 继续存在的；持久的；耐久的 SYN **durable**：*Her words left* ***a lasting impression*** *on me.* 她的话给我留下了难忘的印象。◇ *I formed several lasting friendships at college.* 我在大学与几个同学建立了牢固的友谊。◇ *The training was of no lasting value.* 这种训练不会有长久的效果。➲ SEE ALSO LONG-LASTING ▸ **last·ing·ly** *adv.*

the ˌLast ˈJudgement *noun* [sing.] = JUDGEMENT DAY

last·ly /ˈlɑːstli; *NAmE* ˈlæstli/ *adv.* **1** used to introduce the final point that you want to make 最后一点；最后 SYN **finally**：*Lastly, I'd like to ask you about your plans.* 最后，我想问一下你们的计划。➲ LANGUAGE BANK AT FIRST **2** at the end; after all the other things that you have mentioned 最后；最后要说的是…：*Lastly, add the lemon juice.* 最后，加上柠檬汁。

▼ **WHICH WORD?** 词语辨析

lastly / at last

- **Lastly** is used to introduce the last in a list of things or the final point you are making. * lastly 用以引出所列事情中的最后一项或最后一点：*Lastly, I would like to thank my parents for all their support.* 最后，我想感谢父母对我的全力支持。
- **At last** is used when something happens after a long time, especially when there has been some difficulty or delay. * at last 表示经过很长一段时间，尤其是经过困难或耽搁之后的事：*At last, after twenty hours on the boat, they arrived at their destination.* 乘船二十小时之后，他们终于到达了目的地。You can also use **finally**, **eventually** or **in the end** with this meaning, but not *lastly*. 此义亦可用 finally、eventually 或 in the end，但不能用 lastly。

ˌlast-ˈminute *adj.* [usually before noun] done, decided or organized just before sth happens or before it is too late 最后一分钟才完成（或决定、安排好）的；紧急关头的：*a last-minute holiday* 最后一分钟定下来的休假

ˈlast name *noun* your family name 姓 ➲ COMPARE SURNAME

ˌlast ˈorders *noun* [pl.] (*BrE*) (*also* **ˌlast ˈcall** *NAmE, BrE*) the last opportunity for people to buy drinks in a pub or a bar before it closes（酒吧打烊前）买饮料的最后机会：*'Last orders, please!'* "要酒的，请抓住最后机会！"

the ˌlast ˈpost *noun* [sing.] (*BrE*) a tune played on a BUGLE at military funerals and at the end of the day in military camps 军人葬礼号；军营熄灯号

the ˌlast ˈrites *noun* [pl.] a Christian religious ceremony that a priest performs for, and in the presence of, a dying person（基督教的）临终礼仪，临终圣事：*to administer the last rites to sb* 给某人举行临终圣事 ◇ *to receive the last rites* 领受临终圣事

lat. *abbr.* (in writing 书写形式) LATITUDE 纬度

latch /lætʃ/ *noun, verb*

■ ***noun*** **1** a small metal bar that is used to fasten a door or a gate. You raise it to open the door, and drop it into a metal hook to fasten it. 门闩；插销：*He lifted the latch and opened the door.* 他拉起门闩开了门。 **2** (*especially BrE*) a type of lock on a door that needs a key to open it from the outside 碰锁；弹簧锁：*She listened for his key in the latch.* 她留神听着他把钥匙插入门锁。

IDM **on the ˈlatch** (*BrE*) closed but not locked 关着但未锁上：*Can you leave the door on the latch so I can get in?* 你别锁门好不好？我好进来。

■ ***verb*** **~ sth** to fasten sth with a latch 用插销插上；用碰锁锁上

PHR V **ˌlatch ˈon (to sth)** | **ˌlatch ˈonto sth** (*informal*) to understand an idea or what sb is saying 理解，懂得，领会（想法或某人的话）：*It was a difficult concept to grasp, but I soon latched on.* 那是个难以弄明白的概念，但我很快就理解了。 **ˌlatch ˈon (to sb/sth)** | **ˌlatch ˈonto sb/sth** (*informal*) **1** to become attached to sb/sth 变得依附于：*antibodies that latch onto germs* 依附于细菌的抗体 **2** to join sb and stay in their company, especially when they would prefer you not to be with them 纠缠，缠住（某人） **3** to develop a strong interest in sth 对…产生浓厚的兴趣：*She always latches on to the latest craze.* 她总是对最新时尚有浓厚的兴趣。

latch·key /ˈlætʃkiː/ *noun* a key for the front or the outer door of a house, etc.（房屋等前门或大门的）碰锁钥匙

ˈlatchkey child (*also* **ˈlatchkey kid**) *noun* (*usually disapproving*) a child who is at home alone after school because both parents are at work（因父母双双上班放学后独自在家的）挂钥匙儿童

late /leɪt/ *adj., adv.*

■ ***adj.*** **(later, lat·est) 1** [only before noun] near the end of a period of time, a person's life, etc. 接近末期的；晚年的：*in the late afternoon* 傍晚 ◇ *in late summer* 夏末 ◇ *She married in her late twenties* (= when she was 28 or 29). 她快三十岁时才结婚。◇ *In later life he started playing golf.* 他晚年开始打高尔夫球。◇ *The school was built in the late 1970s.* 这所学校建于 20 世纪 70 年代末。OPP **early** **2** [not usually before noun] arriving, happening or done after the expected, arranged or usual time 迟到；迟发生；迟做：*I'm sorry I'm late.* 对不起，我迟到了。◇ *She's late for work every day.* 她每天上班都迟到。◇ *My flight was an hour late.* 我那趟航班晚点了一小时。◇ *We apologize for the late arrival of this train.* 我们对本趟列车的晚点表示歉意。◇ *Because of the cold weather the crops are later this year.* 因天气寒冷，农作物今年成熟得较晚。◇ *Interest will be charged for late payment.* 逾期付款需支付利息。◇ *Here is a late newsflash.* 现在插播刚刚收到的简讯。OPP **early** **3** near the end of the day 近日暮的；近深夜的：*Let's go home—it's getting late.* 咱们回家吧，时间不早了。◇ *Look at the time—it's much later than I thought.* 看看时间吧，比我想象的要晚多了。◇ *What are you doing up at this* ***late hour****?* 深更半夜的，你还没睡，在做什么？◇ *What is the latest time I can have an appointment?* 最晚的预约时间是几点钟？◇ *I've had too many* ***late nights*** *recently* (= when I've gone to bed very late). 我最近熬夜太多。OPP **early** **4** [only before noun] (*formal*) (of a person 人) no longer alive 已故的：*her late husband* 她已故的丈夫 ◇ *the late Paul Newman* 已故的保罗・纽曼 ▸ **late·ness** *noun* [U]：*They apologized for the lateness of the train.* 他们对火车晚点表示了歉意。◇ *Despite the lateness of the hour, the children were not in bed.* 尽管已是深夜，孩子们仍未就寝。➲ SEE ALSO LATER *adj.*, LATEST *adj.*

IDM **be too ˈlate** happening after the time when it is possible to do sth 为时已晚；已失时机：*It's too late to save her now.* 现在来拯救她的生命已为时太晚。◇ *Buy now before it's too late.* 欲购从速，勿失良机。

■ ***adv.*** (*comparative* **later**, *no superlative*) **1** after the expected, arranged or usual time 迟；晚：*I got up late.* 我起晚了。◇ *Can I stay up late tonight?* 我今晚可以晚点儿睡吗？◇ *She has to work late tomorrow.* 她明天得熬夜工作。◇ *The big stores are open later on Thursdays.* 每逢星期四大商店营业时间延长。◇ *She married late.* 她结婚晚。◇ *The birthday card arrived three days late.* 生日贺卡晚到了三天。 **2** near the end of a period of time, a person's life, etc. 接近末期；在晚年：*late in March/the afternoon*

三月下旬；傍晚 ◇ *It happened late last year.* 那事发生在去年年底。◇ ***As late as*** (= as recently as) *the 1950s, tuberculosis was still a fatal illness.* 直到 20 世纪 50 年代，结核病仍然是一种致命的疾病。◇ *He became an author* ***late in life.*** 他到晚年成为作家。 **3** near the end of the day 临近日暮；接近午夜：*There's a good film on late.* 深夜有一场好电影。◇ *Late that evening, there was a knock at the door.* 那天深夜，有人敲门。◇ *Share prices fell early on but rose again late in the day.* 那天股票价格起先跌了，临近收盘时又涨了。 OPP **early** ➲ SEE ALSO LATER *adv.*

IDM ˌ**better** ˌ**late than** ˈ**never** (*saying*) used especially when you, or sb else, arrive/arrives late, or when sth such as success happens late, to say that this is better than not coming or happening at all 迟到总比不到好；迟发生总比不发生强 ˌ**late in the** ˈ**day** (*disapproving*) after the time when an action could be successful 为时已晚；已失时机：*He started working hard much too late in the day—he couldn't possibly catch up.* 他太晚才开始努力工作，不可能赶上了。 **late of...** (*formal*) until recently working or living in the place mentioned 直至最近工作（或居住）的地方：*Professor Jones, late of Oxford University* 直到不久前还在牛津大学任教的琼斯教授 **of** ˈ**late** (*formal*) recently 最近；新近；近来：*I haven't seen him of late.* 我最近没见过他。 **too** ˈ**late** after the time when it is possible to do sth successfully 过迟；太晚：*She's left it too late to apply for the job.* 她申请那份工作已为时太晚。◇ *I realized the truth too late.* 我太晚才知道真相。 ➲ MORE AT NIGHT, SOON

L

▼ **GRAMMAR POINT** 语法说明

late / lately

- **Late** and **lately** are both adverbs, but **late** is used with similar meanings to the adjective **late**, whereas **lately** can only mean 'recently'. * late 和 lately 均为副词，但 late 与作形容词的 late 意义相似，而 lately 只含近来之义：*We arrived two hours late.* 我们迟到了两小时。◇ *I haven't heard from him lately.* 我最近没听过他的消息。 **Lately** is usually used with a perfect tense of the verb. * lately 常与动词的完成时连用。
- Look also at the idioms **be too late** (at the adjective) and **too late** (at the adverb). 另见习语 be too late（形容词部分）和 too late（副词部分）。

late·comer /ˈleɪtkʌmə(r)/ *noun* a person who arrives late 迟到者；来迟者

late·ly /ˈleɪtli/ *adv.* recently; in the recent past 最近；新近；近来；不久前：*Have you seen her lately?* 你最近见过她吗？◇ *It's only lately that she's been well enough to go out.* 她只是最近才康复，可出去走一走了。◇ (*BrE*) *I haven't been sleeping well just lately.* 我就是在最近才一直睡不好觉。◇ *She had lately returned from India.* 不久前她从印度回来了。

ˌ**late-**ˈ**night** *adj.* [only before noun] happening late at night; available after other things finish 深夜的；午夜的；（其他事情完成后）可得到的：*a late-night movie* 午夜电影 ◇ *late-night shopping* 深夜购物

la·tent /ˈleɪtnt/ *adj.* [usually before noun] existing, but not yet very noticeable, active or well developed 潜在的；潜伏的；隐藏的：*latent disease* 隐匿性疾病 ◇ *These children have a huge reserve of latent talent.* 这些孩子蕴藏着极大的潜在天赋。 ▸ **la·tency** /ˈleɪtənsi/ *noun* [U]

later /ˈleɪtə(r)/ *adv., adj.*

■ *adv.* **1** at a time in the future; after the time you are talking about 后来；以后；其后；随后：*See you later.* 回头见。◇ *I met her again three years later.* 三年后我又遇见她了。◇ *His father died later that year.* 那年晚些时候他的父亲去世了。◇ *We're going to Rome later in the year.* 我们年内晚些时候要到罗马去。◇ *She later became a doctor.* 她后来当了医生。 OPP **early** **2 Later!** (*informal*) a way of saying goodbye, used by young people（年轻人告别时说）再见：*Later, guys!* 伙计们，再见！

IDM **later** ˈ**on** (*informal*) at a time in the future; after the time you are talking about 后来；以后；其后；随后：*I'm going out later on.* 我过一会儿要外出。◇ *Much later on, she realized what he had meant.* 过了好长时间，她才明白他的意思。 **not/no later than...** by a particular time and not after it 不晚于…；不迟于…：*Please arrive no later than 8 o'clock.* 请 8 点之前到达。

■ *adj.* [only before noun] **1** coming after sth else or at a time in the future 后来的；以后的：*This is discussed in more detail in a later chapter.* 在后面的一章中对这一点有更详细的讨论。◇ *The match has been postponed to a later date.* 比赛已被推迟举行。 **2** near the end of a period of time, life, etc. 接近末期的；晚年的：*the later part of the seventeenth century* * 17 世纪末叶 ◇ *She found happiness in her later years.* 她在晚年才寻得幸福。 OPP **early** IDM SEE SOON

lat·eral /ˈlætərəl/ *adj., noun*

■ *adj.* [usually before noun] (*specialist*) connected with the side of sth or with movement to the side 侧面的；横向的；向侧面移动的：*the lateral branches of a tree* 树的侧枝 ◇ *lateral eye movements* 眼睛的两侧运动 ▸ **lat·eral·ly** /ˈlætərəli/ *adv.*

■ *noun* (*also* ˌ**lateral** ˈ**consonant**) (*phonetics* 语音) a consonant sound which is produced by placing a part of the tongue against the PALATE so that air flows around it on both sides, for example /l/ in *lie* 边音（如 lie 一词中 /l/ 的发音）

ˌ**lateral** ˈ**thinking** *noun* [U] (*especially BrE*) a way of solving problems by using your imagination to find new ways of looking at the problem 水平思考，横向思维（即用想象力寻求解决问题的新方法）

lat·est /ˈleɪtɪst/ *adj., noun*

■ *adj.* [only before noun] the most recent or newest 最近的；最新的：*the latest unemployment figures* 最新失业数字 ◇ *the latest craze/fashion/trend* 最新时尚 / 款式 / 动向 ◇ *her latest novel* 她最近出版的小说 ◇ *Have you heard the latest news?* 你听到最新消息了吗？

■ *noun* [U] **the latest** (*informal*) the most recent or the newest thing or piece of news 最新事物；最新消息：*This is the latest in robot technology.* 这是最新的机器人技术。◇ *Have you heard the latest?* 你听到最新消息了吗？

IDM **at the** ˈ**latest** no later than the time or the date mentioned 最迟；最晚；至迟：*Applications should be in by next Monday at the latest.* 最迟须于下星期一递交申请书。

latex /ˈleɪteks/ *noun* [U] **1** a thick white liquid that is produced by some plants and trees, especially rubber trees. Latex becomes solid when exposed to air, and is used to make medical products.（天然）胶乳；（尤指橡胶树的）橡浆：*latex gloves* 合成胶手套 **2** an artificial substance similar to this that is used to make paints, glues, etc. 人工合成胶乳（用于制作油漆、黏合剂等）

lath /lɑːθ; *NAmE* læθ/ *noun* (*pl.* **laths** /lɑːθs; *NAmE* læðz/) a thin narrow strip of wood that is used to support PLASTER (= material used for covering walls) on the inside walls and the ceilings of buildings 灰板条；板条；板筋

lathe /leɪð/ *noun* a machine that shapes pieces of wood or metal by holding and turning them against a fixed cutting tool 车床

la·ther /ˈlɑːðə(r); *NAmE* ˈlæð-/ *noun, verb*

■ *noun* [U, sing.] a white mass of small bubbles that is produced by mixing soap with water （皂液的）泡沫；皂沫

IDM **get into a** ˈ**lather** | **work yourself into a** ˈ**lather** (*informal*) to get anxious or angry about sth, especially when it is not necessary（尤指不必要地）焦躁不安，发怒 **in a** ˈ**lather** (*BrE, informal*) in a nervous, angry or excited state 紧张；愤怒；激动 SYN **worked up**

■ *verb* **1** [T] **~ sth** to cover sth with lather 给…涂上皂沫；用皂沫覆盖：*I lathered my face and started to shave.* 我往脸上涂了皂沫，然后开始刮胡子。 **2** [I] to produce lather 产生泡沫；起泡沫：*Soap does not lather well in hard water.* 肥皂在硬水中起不了多少泡沫。

lathi /ˈlɑːtiː/ *noun* (*IndE*) a long thick stick, especially one used as a weapon or by the police 长而粗的棍子；（尤指）警棍

Latin /ˈlætɪn; *NAmE* ˈlætn/ *noun, adj.*
■ ***noun* 1** [U] the language of ancient Rome and the official language of its empire 拉丁语 **2** [C] a person from countries where languages that have developed from Latin, such as Spanish, Portuguese, Italian or French, are spoken 拉丁人（来自拉丁语系国家如西班牙、葡萄牙、意大利或法国） **3** [U] music of a kind that came originally from Latin America, typically with strong dance rhythms 拉丁音乐（源自拉丁美洲，节奏感强，适于跳舞）
■ ***adj.* 1** of or in the Latin language 拉丁语的；用拉丁语写成的：*Latin poetry* 拉丁语诗歌 **2** connected with or typical of the countries or peoples using languages developed from Latin, such as Spanish, Portuguese, Italian or French 拉丁语系国家（或民族）的（如西班牙、葡萄牙、意大利或法国）；拉丁人的：*a Latin temperament* 拉丁人的气质

La·tina /læˈtiːnə/ *noun* a woman or girl, especially one who is living in the US, who comes from Latin America, or whose family came from there（尤指居住在美国的）拉丁美洲（裔）女子 ➲ COMPARE LATINO ▶ **La·tina** *adj.* [usually before noun]

ˌLatin Aˈmerica *noun* [U] the parts of the Americas in which Spanish or Portuguese is the main language 拉丁美洲（以西班牙语或葡萄牙语为主要语言的美洲地区） ➲ NOTE AT AMERICAN ➲ COMPARE SOUTH AMERICA

Lat·in·ate /ˈlætɪneɪt/ *adj.* (of words or language 词或语言) from Latin, or relating to Latin 从拉丁语派生（或演化）的；与拉丁语有关的：*formal Latinate terms* 正式拉丁术语

ˌLatin ˈlover *noun* (*informal*) a man from the Mediterranean region or from Latin America who is considered a good lover 拉丁情人（地中海地区或拉丁美洲男子，被视为有魅力的情人）

La·tino /læˈtiːnəʊ; *NAmE* -noʊ/ *noun* (*pl.* **-os**) a person, especially one who is living in the US, who comes from Latin America, or whose family came from there（尤指居住在美国的）拉丁美洲人，拉丁美洲人后裔 ➲ COMPARE CHICANO ▶ **La·tino** *adj.* [usually before noun]

lati·tude /ˈlætɪtjuːd; *NAmE* -tuːd/ *noun* **1** (*abbr.* **lat.**) [U] the distance of a place north or south of the EQUATOR (= the line around the world dividing north and south), measured in degrees 纬度 ➲ COMPARE LONGITUDE ➲ WORDFINDER NOTE AT EARTH, MAP **2 latitudes** [pl.] a region of the world that is a particular distance from the EQUATOR 纬度地区：*the northern latitudes* 北纬地区 **3** [U] (*formal*) freedom to choose what you do or the way that you do it 选择（做什么事或做事方式）的自由 SYN **liberty** ➲ SEE ALSO LEEWAY

la·trine /ləˈtriːn/ *noun* a toilet in a camp, etc., especially one made by digging a hole in the ground（营地等的）厕所；（尤指）茅坑，便坑

latte /ˈlɑːteɪ/ *noun* = CAFFÈ LATTE

lat·ter /ˈlætə(r)/ *adj., noun*
■ ***adj.*** [only before noun] **1** used to refer to the second of two things or people mentioned（提及的两者中）后者的：*He chose the latter option.* 他选择了后者。◇ *The latter point is the most important.* 后面提及的那一点是最重要的。 **2** nearer to the end of a period of time than the beginning 后半期的；后面的：*the latter half of the year* 下半年 **3** recent 最近的：*In latter years, the population has grown a lot here.* 这里的人口最近几年增长了很多。➲ COMPARE FORMER
■ ***noun*** **the latter** (*pl.* **the latter**) the second of two things or people mentioned（提及的两者中）后者：*He presented two solutions. The latter seems much better.* 他提出了两个解决方案，后一个看起来要好得多。◇ *The town has a concert hall and two theatres. The latter were both built in the 1950s.* 这座城镇有一个音乐厅和两个剧院。这两个剧院都是在 20 世纪 50 年代建成的。

ˈlatter-day *adj.* [only before noun] being a modern version of a person or thing in the past（旧时的人或物的）现代翻版的：*a latter-day Robin Hood* 当代的罗宾汉

lat·ter·ly /ˈlætəli; *NAmE* -tərli/ *adv.* (*formal*) **1** most recently 最近；新近：*Latterly his painting has shown a new freedom of expression.* 最近，他的绘画展示出一种新的自由表现形式。 **2** towards the end of a period of time 在最后一段时间：*Her health declined rapidly and latterly she never left the house.* 她的健康状况急剧衰退，此后她再未离开过家。

lat·tice /ˈlætɪs/ *noun* [U, C] (*also* **ˈlat·tice·work** [U]) a structure that is made of strips of wood or metal that cross over each other with spaces shaped like a diamond between them, used, for example, as a fence; any structure or pattern like this 格子木架，格子金属架，格栅（用作篱笆等）；斜条结构；斜格图案：*a low wall of stone latticework* 石砌格构的矮墙 ◇ *a lattice of branches* 树枝篱笆 ▶ **lat·ticed** /ˈlætɪst/ *adj.*

ˌlattice ˈwindow (*also* **ˌlat·ticed ˈwindow**) *noun* a window with small pieces of glass shaped like diamonds in a FRAMEWORK of metal strips 花格窗；斜条格构窗

laud /lɔːd/ *verb* **~ sb/sth** (*formal*) to praise sb/sth 赞扬；赞美；称赞

laud·able /ˈlɔːdəbl/ *adj.* (*formal*) deserving to be praised or admired, even if not really successful 应受赞扬的；值得赞美的 SYN **commendable**：*a laudable aim/attempt* 值得称赞的志向 / 尝试 ▶ **laud·ably** /-əbli/ *adv.*

laud·anum /ˈlɔːdənəm/ *noun* [U] a drug made from OPIUM. In the past, people used to take laudanum to reduce pain and anxiety, and to help them sleep. 阿片酊（旧时用以镇痛、镇静及安眠）

laud·atory /ˈlɔːdətəri; *NAmE* -tɔːri/ *adj.* (*formal*) expressing praise or admiration 称赞的；赞美的；颂扬的

laugh /lɑːf; *NAmE* læf/ *verb, noun*
■ ***verb* 1** [I, T] to make the sounds and movements of your face that show you are happy or think sth is funny 笑；发笑：*to* ***laugh loudly/aloud/out loud*** 大声 / 高声 / 出声地笑 ◇ **~ (at/about sth)** *You never laugh at my jokes!* 你听了我的笑话从不发笑！ ◇ *The show was hilarious—I couldn't stop laughing.* 表演十分滑稽，弄得我笑个不停。◇ *She always* ***makes me laugh.*** 她老是引得我发笑。 ◇ *He* ***burst out laughing*** (= suddenly started laughing). 他突然大笑起来。◇ *She laughed to cover her nervousness.* 她笑了，想以此来掩饰自己紧张的心情。◇ *I told him I was worried but he laughed scornfully.* 我告诉他我很担忧，可他却轻蔑地一笑。◇ **+ speech** *'You're crazy!' she laughed.* "你疯啦！" 她哈哈大笑起来。 **2** [I] **be laughing** (*informal*) used to say that you are in a very good position, especially because you have done sth successfully（尤因成功而）处于有利地位：*If we win the next game we'll be laughing.* 要是赢了下一场比赛，我们就占优势了。

IDM **don't make me ˈlaugh** (*informal*) used to show that you think what sb has just said is impossible or stupid（认为不可能或愚蠢）别让我笑掉大牙了，别开玩笑了：*'Will your dad lend you the money?' 'Don't make me laugh!'* "你父亲会借给你钱吗？" "别开玩笑了！" **he who laughs ˌlast laughs ˈlongest** (*saying*) used to tell sb not to be too proud of their present success; in the end another person may be more successful 别高兴得太早；笑到最后才笑得最好 **laugh all the way to the ˈbank** (*informal*) to make a lot of money easily and feel very pleased about it 发大财而喜笑颜开 **laugh in sb's ˈface** to show in a very obvious way that you have no respect for sb 当面嘲笑；公然蔑视 **laugh like a ˈdrain** (*BrE*) to laugh very loudly 哈哈大笑；放声大笑 **laugh on the other side of your ˈface** (*BrE, informal*) to be forced to change from feeling pleased or satisfied to feeling disappointed or annoyed 转喜为忧；得意变成失意；笑脸变为苦脸 **laugh sb/sth out of ˈcourt** (*BrE, informal*) to completely reject an idea, a story, etc. that you think is not worth taking seriously at all 对（某主意、说法等）一笑

置之；置之不理；不屑一顾 **laugh till/until you 'cry** to laugh so long and hard that there are tears in your eyes 笑得流泪；笑出眼泪 **laugh up your 'sleeve (at sb/sth)** (*informal*) to be secretly amused about sth 暗自发笑；窃笑 **laugh your 'head off** to laugh very loudly and for a long time 大笑不止；狂笑不已 **not know whether to ˌlaugh or 'cry** (*informal*) to be unable to decide how to react to a bad or unfortunate situation（面对恶劣或不幸情况）不知所措，哭笑不得 **you ˌhave/you've ˌgot to 'laugh** (*informal*) used to say that you think there is a funny side to a situation 还是值得一笑；还有可笑之处：*Well, I'm sorry you've lost your shoes, but you've got to laugh, haven't you?* 啊，真糟糕，你的鞋子丢了，可是这也挺逗的，是不是？ ➲ MORE AT KILL *v.*, PISS *v.*

PHR V **'laugh at sb/sth** 🔑 to make sb/sth seem stupid or not serious by making jokes about them/it 嘲笑；讥笑 SYN **ridicule**: *Everybody laughs at my accent.* 大家都拿我的口音取笑。◇ *She is not afraid to laugh at herself* (= is not too serious about herself). 她勇于自嘲。**ˌlaugh sth↔'off** (*informal*) to try to make people think that sth is not serious or important, especially by making a joke about it 一笑置之，付之一笑（尤指用笑话摆脱）：*He laughed off suggestions that he was going to resign.* 传言他要辞职，他一笑置之。

■ *noun* **1** 🔑 [C] the sound you make when you are amused or happy 笑声：*to* ***give a laugh*** 大笑一声 ◇ *a short/nervous/hearty laugh* 短促的／紧张的／开心的笑声 ◇ *His first joke* ***got the biggest laugh*** *of the night.* 他讲的第一个笑话博得了当晚最开怀的笑声。 ➲ SEE ALSO BELLY LAUGH **2 a laugh** [sing.] (*informal*) an enjoyable and amusing occasion or thing that happens 令人开心的时刻；引人发笑的事；笑料：*Come to the karaoke night—it should be a good laugh.* 来参加卡拉 OK 晚会吧，一定会很开心的。◇ *And he didn't realize it was you? What a laugh!* 他竟没认出是你？真有意思！ **3 a laugh** [sing.] a person who is amusing and fun to be with 引人发笑的人；逗笑好玩的人：*Paula's a good laugh, isn't she?* 葆拉是个活宝，是不是？

IDM **do sth for a 'laugh/for 'laughs** to do sth for fun or as a joke 逗趣；开玩笑：*I just did it for a laugh, but it got out of hand.* 我只是开开玩笑，然而却一发不可收拾。 **have a (good) 'laugh (about sth)** to find sth amusing 觉得可笑（或有趣）：*I was angry at the time but we had a good laugh about it afterwards.* 我当时很生气，可后来我们却又觉得十分可笑。 ➲ MORE AT BARREL *n.*, LAST[1] *det.*

▼ **VOCABULARY BUILDING 词汇扩充**

Different ways of laughing 笑的不同方式

- **cackle** to laugh in a loud, unpleasant way, especially in a high voice * cackle 指令人讨厌地嘎嘎大笑，尤指高声笑。
- **chuckle** to laugh quietly, especially because you are thinking about something funny * chuckle 指轻声笑，尤指想到滑稽事时发笑。
- **giggle** to laugh in a silly way because you are amused, embarrassed or nervous * giggle 指因开心、尴尬或紧张而傻笑。
- **guffaw** to laugh noisily * guffaw 指哄笑、狂笑、大笑。
- **roar** to laugh very loudly * roar 指放声大笑。
- **snigger/snicker** to laugh in a quiet unpleasant way, especially at something rude or at someone's problems or mistakes * snigger/snicker 指窃笑、暗笑，尤指对无礼行为或因他人的问题或错误发笑。
- **titter** to laugh quietly, especially in a nervous or embarrassed way * titter 指窃笑，尤指紧张或尴尬地笑。

You can also **be convulsed with laughter** or **dissolve into laughter** when you find something very funny. In *BrE* people also **shriek with laughter** or **howl with laughter**. 认为某事非常滑稽可笑亦可用 be convulsed with laughter（笑得前仰后合）或 dissolve into laughter（不禁大笑）。在英式英语中亦用 shriek with laughter（尖声大笑）或 howl with laughter（狂笑）。

laugh·able /ˈlɑːfəbl; *NAmE* ˈlæf-/ *adj.* silly or ridiculous, and not worth taking seriously 荒唐可笑的；荒谬的；不值得当真的 SYN **absurd** ▶ **laugh·ably** /-əbli/ *adv.*

laugh·ing /ˈlɑːfɪŋ; *NAmE* ˈlæfɪŋ/ *adj.* showing AMUSEMENT or happiness 笑的；带笑意的：*his laughing blue eyes* 他带着笑意的蓝眼睛 ◇ *laughing faces* 笑脸

IDM **be no laughing 'matter** to be sth serious that you should not joke about 不是开玩笑的事；严肃的事 ➲ MORE AT DIE *v.*, SPLIT *v.*

'laughing gas *noun* [U] (*informal*) = NITROUS OXIDE

laugh·ing·ly /ˈlɑːfɪŋli; *NAmE* ˈlæf-/ *adv.* **1** in an amused way 带笑地；笑着：*He laughingly agreed.* 他笑着同意了。 **2** used to show that you think a particular word is not at all a suitable way of describing something and therefore seems ridiculous（表示用词）荒唐可笑：*I finally reached what we laughingly call civilization.* 我终于到了我们戏称为文明之地的地方。

'laughing stock *noun* [usually sing.] a person that everyone laughs at because they have done sth stupid 笑柄；笑料：*I can't wear that! I'd be a laughing stock.* 我可不能戴那个东西！否则会成为笑柄的。

ˌlaugh-out-'loud *adj.* (*abbr.* **LOL**) [only before noun] (*informal*) extremely funny 非常滑稽的：*a laugh-out-loud moment* 十分逗乐的时刻 ◇ *The best scenes in the movie are laugh-out-loud funny.* 这部影片中最棒的几个镜头简直笑死人。 HELP The abbreviation **LOL** is also used in text messages, emails or Internet chat to show that you think sth is funny or do not mean it seriously. 缩写形式 LOL 也用于短信、电邮或互联网聊天，表示认为某事滑稽，或随便一说而已。

laugh·ter /ˈlɑːftə(r); *NAmE* ˈlæf-/ *noun* [U] the act or sound of laughing 笑；笑声：*to* ***roar with laughter*** 放声大笑 ◇ ***tears/gales/peals/shrieks of laughter*** 笑得流眼泪；阵阵笑声；哈哈大笑；阵阵尖声大笑 ◇ *to* ***burst/dissolve into laughter*** 突然／情不自禁大笑起来 ◇ *a house full of laughter* (= with a happy atmosphere) 充满欢声笑语的房子 IDM SEE SPLIT *v.*

launch 🔑 /lɔːntʃ/ *verb, noun*

■ *verb* **1** 🔑 **~ sth** to start an activity, especially an organized one 开始从事，发起，发动（尤指有组织的活动）：*to* ***launch an appeal/an inquiry/an investigation/a campaign*** 开始上诉／质询／调查／一场运动 ◇ *to* ***launch an attack/invasion*** 发起攻击；发动侵略 **2** 🔑 **~ sth** to make a product available to the public for the first time（首次）上市，发行：*a party to launch his latest novel* 他最新小说的首发式 ◇ *The new model will be launched in July.* 新型号产品将在七月推出。 **3** 🔑 **~ sth** to put a ship or boat into the water, especially one that has just been built 使（船，尤指新船）下水：*The Navy is to launch a new warship today.* 海军今天有一艘新军舰要下水。◇ *The lifeboat was launched immediately.* 那艘救生艇被立刻放下了水。 **4** 🔑 **~ sth** to send sth such as a SPACECRAFT, weapon, etc. into space, into the sky or through water 发射；把（航天器、武器等）发射上天；水中发射：*to launch a communications satellite* 发射通信卫星 ◇ *to* ***launch a missile/rocket/torpedo*** 发射导弹／火箭／鱼雷 ➲ WORDFINDER NOTE AT SPACE **5 ~ yourself at, from, etc. sth | ~ yourself forwards, etc.** to jump forwards with a lot of force 猛扑向前：*Without warning he launched himself at me.* 他突然向我猛扑过来。 **6 ~ sth** (*computing* 计) to start a computer program 启动（计算机程序）：*You can launch programs and documents from your keyboard.* 你可以从键盘启动程序和文件。

PHR V **'launch into sth | 'launch yourself into sth** to begin sth in an enthusiastic way, especially sth that will take a long time（热情地）开始做，投入：*He launched into a lengthy account of his career.* 他开始啰啰嗦嗦地讲述自己的工作经历。 **ˌlaunch 'out** to do sth new in your career, especially sth more exciting 开始从事，投身于（新的、尤指更令人兴奋的事业）：*It's time I launched out on my own.* 该是我自己创业的时候了。

■ *noun* **1** 🔑 [usually sing.] the action of launching sth; an event at which sth is launched（航天器的）发射；（船的）下水；（产品的）上市；（事件的）发起：*the successful launch of the Ariane rocket* 阿里亚娜火箭的成功发射 ◇ *a product launch* 产品的投放市场 ◇ *The official launch date is in May.* 正式的发行日期是在五月。 **2** a large boat with a motor 大型汽艇；机动大舢板；交通艇

launch·er /ˈlɔːntʃə(r)/ *noun* (often in compounds 常构成复合词) a device that is used to send a ROCKET, a MISSILE, etc. into the sky（火箭、导弹等的）发射装置，发射器：*a rocket launcher* 火箭发射装置

ˈlaunch pad (*also* **ˈlaunching pad**) *noun* a platform from which a SPACECRAFT, etc. is sent into the sky（航天器等的）发射平台：(*figurative*) *She regards the job as a launch pad for her career in the media.* 她把这份工作当作她从事媒体职业的跳板。

laun·der /ˈlɔːndə(r)/ *verb* **1** ~ **sth** (*formal*) to wash, dry and iron clothes, etc. 洗熨（衣物）：*freshly laundered sheets* 刚洗的被单 **2** ~ **sth** to move money that has been obtained illegally into foreign bank accounts or legal businesses so that it is difficult for people to know where the money came from 洗（钱）

laun·der·ette (*also* **laun·drette**) /lɔːnˈdret/ (*both BrE*) (*NAmE* **Laun·dro·mat™** /ˈlɔːndrəmæt/) *noun* a place where you can wash and dry your clothes in machines that you operate by putting in coins 投币式自助洗衣店

laun·dry /ˈlɔːndri/ *noun* (*pl.* **-ies**) **1** [U] clothes, sheets, etc. that need washing, that are being washed, or that have been washed recently 要（或正在）洗的衣物；刚洗好的衣物 SYN **washing**：*a pile of* ***clean/dirty laundry*** 一摞干净的 / 脏的衣物 ◇ *a* ***laundry basket/room*** 洗衣筐；洗衣间 **2** [U, sing.] the process or the job of washing clothes, sheets, etc. 洗衣物；洗衣物的活：*to do the laundry* 干洗衣活 ◇ *The hotel has a laundry service.* 旅馆提供洗衣服务。 **3** [C] a business or place where you send sheets, clothes, etc. to be washed 洗衣店；洗衣房

ˈlaundry list *noun* a long list of people or things 一长串名单；清单：*a laundry list of problems* 一长串问题

Laur·asia /lɔːˈreɪʃə; -ʒə/ *noun* [sing.] (*geology* 地) a very large area of land that existed in the northern HEMISPHERE millions of years ago. It was made up of the present N America, Greenland, Europe and most of Asia. 劳亚古大陆（几百万年前存在于北半球的大片陆地，由如今的北美洲、格陵兰、欧洲和亚洲大部分组成）

laure·ate /ˈlɒriət; *NAmE* ˈlɔːr-; ˈlɑːr-/ *noun* **1** a person who has been given an official honour or prize for sth important they have achieved 荣誉获得者；获奖者：*a Nobel laureate* 诺贝尔奖获得者 **2** = POET LAUREATE

laurel /ˈlɒrəl; *NAmE* ˈlɔːr-; ˈlɑːr-/ *noun* **1** [U, C] a bush with dark smooth shiny leaves that remain on the bush and stay green through the year 月桂灌木；月桂树 **2 laurels** [pl.] honour and praise given to sb because of sth that they have achieved 荣誉；赞誉；荣耀

IDM **look to your ˈlaurels** to be careful that you do not lose the success or advantage that you have over other people 小心翼翼地保持成就（或优势） **rest/sit on your ˈlaurels** (*usually disapproving*) to feel so satisfied with what you have already achieved that you do not try to do any more 满足于既得成就；不思进取

ˈlaurel wreath *noun* a ring of laurel leaves that was worn on the head in the past as a sign of victory 桂冠（旧时作为胜利的象征）

lav /læv/ *noun* (*BrE, informal*) a toilet 厕所

lava /ˈlɑːvə/ *noun* [U] **1** hot liquid rock that comes out of a VOLCANO（火山喷出的）熔岩，岩浆：*molten lava* 熔化的火山岩浆 **2** this type of rock when it has cooled and become hard 火山岩

lav·age /ˈlævɪdʒ; læˈvɑːʒ/ *noun* (*medical* 医) the process of washing a space inside the body such as the stomach or COLON 灌洗（胃、肠等）

ˈlava lamp *noun* an electric lamp that contains a liquid in which a coloured substance like oil moves up and down in shapes that keep changing 熔岩灯（装有可上下流动和变形的彩色油状物）

lava·tor·ial /ˌlævəˈtɔːriəl/ *adj.* (*especially BrE*) **lavatorial** humour refers in a rude way to parts of the body, going to the toilet, etc. 粗俗的，下流的（指粗俗地谈论身体部位或上厕所等）

lav·atory /ˈlævətri; *NAmE* -tɔːri/ *noun* (*pl.* **-ies**) (*old-fashioned* or *formal*) **1** (*especially BrE*) a toilet, or a room with a toilet in it 抽水马桶；厕所；卫生间；洗手间；盥洗室：*There's a bathroom and a lavatory upstairs.* 楼上有浴室和卫生间。 **2** (*BrE*) a public building or part of a building, with toilets in it 公共厕所（或卫生间、洗手间、盥洗室）：*The nearest public lavatory is at the station.* 最近的公共厕所在车站。

lav·en·der /ˈlævəndə(r)/ *noun* [U] **1** a garden plant or bush with bunches of purple flowers with a sweet smell 薰衣草（园林植物或灌木，开紫花，有香味） **2** the flowers of the lavender plant that have been dried, used for making sheets, clothes, etc. smell nice 干薰衣草花（用以熏香床单、衣物等）：*lavender oil* 薰衣草油 **3** a pale purple colour 淡紫色

lav·ish /ˈlævɪʃ/ *adj., verb*

▪ ***adj.*** **1** large in amount, or impressive, and usually costing a lot of money 大量的；给人印象深刻的；耗资巨大的 SYN **extravagant, luxurious**：*lavish gifts/costumes/celebrations* 丰厚的礼品；昂贵的服装；规模盛大的庆典 ◇ *They lived a very* ***lavish lifestyle.*** 他们过着挥霍无度的生活。◇ *They rebuilt the house on an even more* ***lavish scale*** *than before.* 他们重建了房子，规模甚至比以前更大。 **2** ~ (**with/in sth**) giving or doing sth generously 慷慨的；大方的：*He was lavish in his praise for her paintings.* 他大力称赞她的绘画。 ▶ **lav·ish·ly** *adv.*：*lavishly illustrated* 有大量插图

▪ ***verb***

PHR V **ˈlavish sth on/upon sb/sth** to give a lot of sth, often too much, to sb/sth 过分给予；滥施：*She lavishes most of her attention on her youngest son.* 她对她小儿子过分关爱。

law /lɔː/ *noun*

• **SYSTEM OF RULES** 规则体系 **1** (*also* **the law**) [U] the whole system of rules that everyone in a country or society must obey 法律（体系）：*If they entered the building they would be* ***breaking the law.*** 如果进入那栋大楼，他们就会触犯法律。◇ *In Sweden it is* ***against the law*** *to hit a child.* 在瑞典打小孩是违法的。◇ *Defence attorneys can use any means* ***within the law*** *to get their client off.* 辩护律师可在法律许可的范围内利用任何手段为当事人脱罪。◇ *British schools are now required* ***by law*** *to publish their exam results.* 现在英国的学校得按法律规定公布考试结果。◇ *The reforms have recently* ***become law.*** 这些改革措施最近已成为法律。◇ *Do not think you are* ***above the law*** (= think that you cannot be punished by the law). 别以为你能凌驾于法律之上。◇ *the need for better* ***law enforcement*** 加强执法力度的必要 ◇ (*humorous*) *Kate's word was law in the Brown household.* 凯特的话在布朗家就是金科玉律。 ➲ COLLOCATIONS AT JUSTICE

WORDFINDER 联想词：abide by sth, court, **crime**, **justice**, legal, **police**, prosecute, punish, **trial**

2 [U] a particular branch of the law 法规：***company/international/tax, etc. law*** 公司法、国际法、税法等 ➲ SEE ALSO CANON LAW, CASE LAW, CIVIL LAW, COMMON LAW, PRIVATE LAW, STATUTE LAW

• **ONE RULE** 一条法规 **3** [C] a rule that deals with a particular crime, agreement, etc.（针对某项罪行、协议等的一条）法律，法规：~ (**against sth**) *the 1996 law against the hiring of illegal immigrants* 禁止雇用非法移民的 1996 法规 ◇ ~ (**on sth**) *The government has introduced some tough new laws on food hygiene.* 政府对食品卫生出台了一些强硬的新法规。◇ ***strict*** *gun* ***laws*** 严格的枪支法 ◇ *a* ***federal/state law*** 联邦法律；州法律 ◇ ***to pass a law*** (= officially make it part of the system of laws) 通过一项

L

法律 ◇ (*informal*) *There ought to be a law against it!* 应该立法加以禁止！ ➲ SEE ALSO BY-LAW, LICENSING LAWS ➲ WORDFINDER NOTE AT PARLIAMENT

• **SUBJECT/PROFESSION** 学科；职业 **4** [U] the study of the law as a subject at university, etc.; the profession of being a lawyer 法学；法律学；律师业：*Jane is studying law.* 简正在学习法律。◇ (*NAmE*) *He's in* ***law school.*** 他在读法学院。◇ (*BrE*) *He's at law school.* 他在读法学院。◇ *What made you go into law?* 是什么促使你从事法律行业的呢？◇ *a law firm* 律师事务所

• **POLICE** 警察 **5** **the law** [sing.] used to refer to the police and the legal system 警方；法律机构：*Jim is always getting into trouble with the law.* 吉姆总是因惹事落到警察手里。

• **OF ORGANIZATION/ACTIVITY** 机构；活动 **6** [C] one of the rules which controls an organization or activity 规则；规章；条例：*the laws of the Church* 教会的戒律 ◇ *The first law of kung fu is to defend yourself.* 功夫的首要原则是自卫。◇ *the laws of cricket* 板球规则

• **OF GOOD BEHAVIOUR** 良好的品行 **7** [C] a rule for good behaviour or how you should behave in a particular place or situation 良好行为的准则；（某地或某场合下的）行为规范：*moral laws* 道德准则 ◇ *the unspoken laws of the street* 不言而喻的街头规矩

• **IN BUSINESS/NATURE/SCIENCE** 商业；自然；科学 **8** [C] the fact that sth always happens in the same way in an activity or in nature 规律；法则；原理 SYN **principle**: *the laws of supply and demand* 供求规律 ◇ *the law of gravity* 万有引力定律 **9** [C] a scientific rule that sb has stated to explain a natural process 定律：*the first law of thermodynamics* 热力学第一定律 ➲ SEE ALSO MURPHY'S LAW, PARKINSON'S LAW, SOD'S LAW, LEGAL, LEGALIZE, LEGISLATE

IDM **be a law unto your'self** to behave in an independent way and ignore rules or what other people want you to do 自行其是；我行我素 **go to 'law** (*BrE*) to ask a court to settle a problem or disagreement 诉诸法律；提起诉讼；打官司 **ˌlaw and 'order** a situation in which people obey the law and behave in a peaceful way 法治；治安；遵纪守法：*The government struggled to maintain law and order.* 政府努力维持治安。◇ *After the riots, the military was brought in to restore law and order.* 暴乱以后，军队出动来恢复治安。◇ *They claim to be the party of law and order.* 他们声称自己是重视治安问题的政党。 **the ˌlaw of 'averages** the principle that one thing will happen as often as another if you try enough times 平均定律：*Keep applying and by the law of averages you'll get a job sooner or later.* 继续申请吧，根据平均定律你迟早会找到工作的。 **the ˌlaw of the 'jungle** a situation in which people are prepared to harm other people in order to succeed 丛林法则；弱肉强食 **lay down the 'law** to tell sb with force what they should or should not do 发号施令；严格规定 **take the law into your own 'hands** to do sth illegal in order to punish sb for doing sth wrong, instead of letting the police deal with them 不通过法律擅自处理 **there's no 'law against sth** (*informal*) used to tell sb who is criticizing you that you are not doing anything wrong（对批评自己的人说）谁也管不着：*I'll sing if I want to—there's no law against it.* 我想唱就唱，谁也管不着。 ➲ MORE AT LETTER *n.*, POSSESSION, RULE *n.*, WRONG *adj.*

'law-abiding *adj.* obeying and respecting the law 遵纪守法的；安分守己的：*law-abiding citizens* 遵纪守法的公民

law·break·er /'lɔːbreɪkə(r)/ *noun* a person who does not obey the law 不守法者；违法者；不法分子 ▸ **law·break·ing** *noun* [U]

'law court *noun* = COURT OF LAW ➲ NOTE AT COURT

law·ful /'lɔːfl/ *adj.* (*formal*) allowed or recognized by law; legal 法定的；法律承认的；合法的：*his lawful heir* 他的合法继承人 OPP **unlawful** ▸ **law·ful·ly** /-fəli/ *adv.*：*a lawfully elected government* 合法选举产生的政府 **law·ful·ness** *noun* [U]

▼ **MORE ABOUT ...** 补充说明

lawyers

- **Lawyer** is a general term for a person who is qualified to advise people about the law, to prepare legal documents for them and/or to represent them in a court of law. * lawyer 泛指律师，有资格提供法律咨询、为当事人准备法律文件、在法庭上代表当事人。
- In England and Wales, a **lawyer** who is qualified to speak in the higher courts of law is called a **barrister**. In Scotland a **barrister** is called an **advocate**. 在英格兰和威尔士，有资格在高等法院出庭辩护的律师叫 barrister；在苏格兰 barrister 称作 advocate。
- In *NAmE* **attorney** is a more formal word used for a **lawyer** and is used especially in job titles. 在美式英语中，attorney 较 lawyer 正式，尤用于职务头衔：*district attorney* 地方检察官
- **Counsel** is the formal legal word used for a lawyer who is representing someone in court. * counsel 为正式的法律用语，指代表当事人出庭的律师：*counsel for the prosecution* 控方律师
- **Solicitor** is the *BrE* term for a lawyer who gives legal advice and prepares documents, for example when you are buying a house, and sometimes has the right to speak in a court of law. * solicitor 为英式英语，指提供法律咨询、准备法律文件（如购买房屋时）、有时有权出庭辩护的律师。
- In *NAmE* **solicitor** is only used in the titles of some lawyers who work for the government. 在美式英语中，solicitor 只用于政府某些法务官员的头衔：*Solicitor General* 司法部副部长

lawks /lɔːks/ *exclamation* (*old-fashioned, BrE*) used to show that you are surprised, angry or impatient（表示惊讶、生气或不耐烦）天哪，啊呀

law·less /'lɔːləs/ *adj.* **1** (of a country or an area 国家或地区) where laws do not exist or are not obeyed 无法律的；不遵守法律的：*lawless streets* 没有法纪的街区 ◇ *the lawless days of the revolution* 那场革命期间无法无天的日子 **2** (of people or their actions 人或行为) without respect for the law 不遵守法律的；目无法纪的；不法的 SYN **anarchic, wild**: *lawless gangs* 目无法纪的团伙 ▸ **law·less·ness** *noun* [U]

'law lord *noun* (*BrE*) a member of the British House of Lords who was qualified to perform its legal work. In 2009 the law lords' role was taken over by the judges of the new Supreme Court.（英国上议院的）司法议员（2009 年其职责由新的最高法院的法官接管）

law·maker /'lɔːmeɪkə(r)/ *noun* a person in government who makes the laws of a country 立法者 SYN **legislator**

law·man /'lɔːmæn/ *noun* (*pl.* **-men** /-men/) (*especially US*) an officer responsible for keeping law and order, especially a SHERIFF 执法官；（尤指）县（或城镇）治安官

lawn /lɔːn/ *noun* **1** [C] an area of ground covered in short grass in a garden/yard or park, or used for playing a game on 草坪；草地：*In summer we have to mow the lawn twice a week.* 夏天我们每周得修剪草坪两次。◇ *a croquet lawn* 槌球场 ➲ VISUAL VOCAB PAGE V20 **2** [U] a type of fine cotton or LINEN cloth used for making clothes 上等细棉布（或麻布）

'lawn bowling *noun* [U] (*NAmE*) = BOWL (6)

'lawn chair *noun* (*especially NAmE*) a chair that can be folded and that people use when sitting outside 草坪椅；户外折叠椅

lawn·mow·er /'lɔːnməʊə(r); *NAmE* -moʊ-/ (*also* **mower**) *noun* a machine for cutting the grass on LAWNS 割草机；剪草机 ➲ VISUAL VOCAB PAGE V20

'lawn sign *noun* (*NAmE*) a board that people put outside their house in order to advertise sth or to show that they support a particular politician or political party 草坪插

牌，户外告示牌（置于宅前，用于广告或表明户主支持某政治人物或政党）

ˌlawn ˈtennis *noun* [U] (*formal*) = TENNIS

law·ren·cium /lɒˈrensiəm; *NAmE* lɔːˈr-/ *noun* [U] (*symb.* **Lr**) a chemical element. Lawrencium is a RADIOACTIVE metal. 铹（放射性化学元素）

law·suit /ˈlɔːsuːt; *BrE also* -sjuːt/ (*also* **suit**) *noun* a claim or complaint against sb that a person or an organization can make in court 诉讼；起诉：*He **filed a lawsuit against** his record company.* 他对给他录制唱片的公司提起了诉讼。

law·yer /ˈlɔːjə(r)/ *noun* a person who is trained and qualified to advise people about the law and to represent them in court, and to write legal documents 律师

lax /læks/ *adj.* **1** (*disapproving*) not strict, severe or careful enough about work, rules or standards of behaviour 不严格的；不严厉的；马虎的 SYN **slack, careless**: *lax security/discipline* 不严格的保安措施 / 纪律 ◇ *a lax attitude to health and safety regulations* 对卫生与安全条例的马虎态度 **2** (*phonetics* 语音) (of a speech sound 语音) produced with the muscles of the speech organs relaxed 松弛的；松音的 OPP **tense** ▶ **lax·ity** /ˈlæksəti/ *noun* [U]

laxa·tive /ˈlæksətɪv/ *noun* a medicine, food or drink that makes sb empty their BOWELS easily 轻泻药；通便剂；有通便作用的饮食 ▶ **laxa·tive** *adj.*

lay /leɪ/ *verb, adj., noun* ➲ SEE ALSO LIE[1] *v.*

■ *verb* (**laid, laid** /leɪd/)

• **PUT DOWN/SPREAD** 放下；展开 **1** [T] to put sb/sth in a particular position, especially when it is done gently or carefully（尤指轻轻地或小心地）放置，安放，搁：**~ sb/sth (+ adv./prep.)** *She laid the baby down gently on the bed.* 她把婴儿轻轻地放在床上。◇ *He laid a hand on my arm.* 他把手搭在我的胳膊上。◇ *The horse laid back its ears.* 那匹马把耳朵往后竖着。◇ *Relatives laid wreaths on the grave.* 死者亲属在墓前献了花圈。◇ **~ sb/sth + adj.** *The cloth should be laid flat.* 布应展开平放。HELP Some speakers confuse this sense of **lay** with **lie**, especially in the present and progressive tenses. However, **lay** has an object and **lie** does not. 有些人把 lay 这一义项与 lie 混淆了，尤其是在现在时和进行时中。然而，lay 后可接宾语，lie 后则不接宾语：*She was lying on the beach.* 她躺在沙滩上。◇ ~~*She was laying on the beach.*~~ ◇ *Why don't you lie on the bed?* 你为什么不到床上躺着？◇ ~~*Why don't you lay on the bed?*~~ In the past tenses **laid** (from: *lay*) is often wrongly used for **lay** or **lain** (from: *lie*). 在过去式中，laid（原形是 lay）常被误作 lay 或 lain（原形是 lie）：*She had lain there all night.* 她在那儿躺了一整晚。◇ ~~*She had laid there all night.*~~ **2** [T] **~ sth (down)** to put sth down, especially on the floor, ready to be used 铺，铺放，铺设（尤指在地板上）：*to **lay** a carpet/cable/pipe* 铺地毯；铺设电缆；铺管道 ◇ *The foundations of the house are being laid today.* 今天正在给房子打地基。◇ (*figurative*) *They had laid the groundwork for future development.* 他们为此后的发展奠定了基础。**3** [T] to spread sth on sth; to cover sth with a layer of sth（在某物上）摊开，涂，敷；用一层…覆盖：**~ A (on/over B)** *Before they started they laid newspaper on the floor.* 他们开始前在地板上铺了报纸。◇ *The grapes were laid to dry on racks.* 葡萄被摊放在架子上晾干。◇ **~ B with A** *The floor was laid with newspaper.* 地板上铺了报纸。

• **EGGS** 卵 **4** [T, I] **~ (sth)** if a bird, an insect, a fish, etc. **lays** eggs, it produces them from its body（鸟、昆虫、鱼等）下（蛋），产（卵）：*The cuckoo lays its eggs in other birds' nests.* 杜鹃在其他鸟的巢中下蛋。◇ *new-laid eggs* 鲜蛋 ◇ *The hens are not laying well* (= not producing many eggs). 母鸡现在不爱下蛋。

• **TABLE** 桌子 **5** [T] **~ sth** (*BrE*) to arrange knives, forks, plates, etc. on a table ready for a meal 摆放餐具于（准备就餐）SYN **set**: *to lay the table* 摆好餐具准备用餐

• **PRESENT PROPOSAL** 提出建议 **6** [T] **~ sth + adv./prep.** to present a proposal, some information, etc. to sb for them to think about and decide on 提出，提交（建议、信息等）：*The bill was laid before Parliament.* 议案已提交议会审议。

• **DIFFICULT SITUATION** 困境 **7** [T] **~ sb/sth + adv./prep.** (*formal*) to put sb/sth in a particular position or state, especially a difficult or unpleasant one 使处于特定状态（尤指困境）SYN **place**: *to lay a responsibility/burden on sb* 把责任 / 重担加于某人身上 ◇ *to lay sb under an obligation to do sth* 使某人承担做某事的义务

• **WITH NOUNS** 与名词连用 **8** [T] **~ sth + adv./prep.** used with a noun to form a phrase that has the same meaning as the verb related to the noun（与名词连用构成短语，其含义与该名词的相关动词相同）：*to lay the blame on sb* (= to blame sb) 归咎于某人 ◇ *Our teacher lays great stress on good spelling* (= stresses it strongly). 我们老师着力强调要拼写正确。

• **PLAN/TRAP** 计划；圈套 **9** [T] **~ sth** to prepare sth in detail 周密准备；筹划；设置：*to lay a trap for sb* 给某人设下圈套 ◇ *She began to **lay her plans** for her escape.* 她开始周密策划准备逃走。◇ *Bad weather can upset even the **best-laid plans**.* 天气不好，再好的计划也会打乱。

• **HAVE SEX** 性交 **10** [T, often passive] **~ sb** (*slang*) to have sex with sb 与（某人）性交：*He went out hoping to **get laid** that night.* 他那天晚上外出希望找个女人睡一宿。

• **FIRE** 火 **11** [T] **~ sth** to prepare a fire by arranging wood, sticks or coal（摆好木、柴或煤）生火

• **BET** 打赌 **12** [T] to bet money on sth; to place a bet 对…下赌金；下赌注：**~ sth** *to lay a bet* 下赌注 ◇ **~ sth on sth** *She had laid $100 on the favourite.* 她在那匹夺标呼声最高的马上下注 100 美元。◇ **~ (sb) sth (that)...** *I'll lay you any money you like (that) he won't come.* 我看他不来了，你愿意赌多少钱我都奉陪。HELP This pattern is not used in the passive. 此句型不用于被动语态。

IDM HELP Idioms containing **lay** are at the entries for the nouns and adjectives in the idioms, for example **lay sth bare** is at **bare**. 含 lay 的习语，都可在该等习语中的名词及形容词相关词条找到，如 lay sth bare 在词条 bare 下。

PHR V **ˌlay aˈbout sb (with sth)** (*BrE*) to attack sb violently 袭击（或猛打）某人：*The gang laid about him with sticks.* 那伙人用棍棒狠狠揍他。**ˌlay aˈbout you/yourself (with sth)** (*BrE*) to hit sb/sth without control or move your arms or legs violently in all directions 乱打；（向四面）拳打脚踢，猛打：*She laid about herself with her stick to keep the dogs off.* 她挥棒乱打以赶走那几条狗。**ˌlay sth↔aˈside** (*formal*) **1** to put sth on one side and not use it or think about it 把…放在一边（或搁置一旁）SYN **set sth↔aside**: *He laid aside his book and stood up.* 他把书放在一边，站了起来。◇ (*figurative*) *Doctors have to lay their personal feelings aside.* 医生不得不把个人的情感置之度外。**2** (*also* **ˌlay sth ˈby**) to keep sth to use, or deal with later 留存备用；留待以后处理 SYN **put sth↔aside**: *They had laid money aside for their old age.* 他们存钱防老。**ˌlay sth↔ˈdown 1** to put sth down or stop using it 放下；停止使用 SYN **put down**: *She laid the book down on the table.* 她把书放在桌上。◇ *Both sides were urged to lay down their arms* (= stop fighting). 双方都被敦促放下武器。**2** (*formal*) to stop doing a job, etc. 中断（工作）；辞（职）；放弃：*to lay down your duties* 停止履行职责 **3** if you **lay down** a rule or a principle, you state officially that people must obey it or use it 规定，制定（条例或原则）：*You can't lay down hard and fast rules.* 规则不能定得太死。◇ **it is laid down that...** *It is laid down that all candidates must submit three copies of their dissertation.* 根据规定，所有学位答辩人均须提交论文一式三份。**4** [usually passive] to produce sth that is stored and gradually increases 积存：*If you eat too much, the surplus is laid down as fat.* 要是吃得太多，过剩的营养就会积聚成为脂肪。**ˌlay sth↔ˈin/ˈup** to collect and store sth to use in the future 贮备；贮存：*to lay in food supplies* 贮存食物 **ˌlay ˈinto sb/sth** (*informal*) to attack sb violently with blows or words 猛打；痛打；责骂；抨击：*His parents really laid into him for wasting so much money.* 他因挥霍这么多钱财被父母狠狠地责骂了一顿。**ˌlay ˈoff | ˌlay ˈoff sb/sth** (*informal*) used to tell sb to stop doing sth（让人停止做某事）停止，别再打扰：*Lay off me will you—it's nothing to do with me.* 别找我好不好，这事与我无关。◇ **lay off doing sth** *Lay off bullying Jack.* 别再欺负杰克。**ˌlay ˈoff sth** (*informal*) to stop using sth 停止使用：*I think you'd better lay off fatty foods for a while.* 我认为你最好暂时别吃油腻的食物。**ˌlay sb↔ˈoff** to stop employing sb because there is not enough work for them to do（因工作不多而）解雇 SYN redundant ➲ RELATED NOUN LAY-OFF ˌ**lay sth↔'on** (*BrE, informal*) to provide sth for sb, especially food or entertainment 提供（尤指食物或娱乐）： *to lay on food and drink* 提供饮食 ◇ *A bus has been laid on to take guests to the airport.* 已安排公共汽车运送客人去机场。ˌ**lay sth 'on sb** (*informal*) to make sb have to deal with sth unpleasant or difficult 使不得不处理（讨厌或困难的事）： *Stop laying a guilt trip on me* (= making me feel guilty). 别再让我感到内疚了。ˌ**lay sb↔'out 1** to knock sb unconscious 把…打昏 **2** to prepare a dead body to be buried（给死者）作殡葬准备 ˌ**lay sth↔'out 1** to spread sth out so that it can be seen easily or is ready to use 铺开；摆开；展开： *He laid the map out on the table.* 他把地图在桌子上展开。◇ **+ adj.** *Lay the material out flat.* 把布料摊开放平。 **2** [often passive] to plan how sth should look and arrange it in this way 布置；策划；安排；设计： *The gardens were laid out with lawns and flower beds.* 花园里设置了草坪和花坛。◇ *a well-laid-out magazine* 设计精美的杂志 ➲ RELATED NOUN LAYOUT **3** to present a plan, an argument, etc. clearly and carefully 清晰谨慎地提出，策划（计划、论点等） SYN **set out**: *All the terms and conditions are laid out in the contract.* 所有的条款与条件在合同中均已清楚地列明。 **4** (*informal*) to spend money 花钱 SYN **fork out**: *I had to lay out a fortune on a new car.* 我只好花一大笔钱买了辆新车。➲ RELATED NOUN OUTLAY ˌ**lay 'over (at/in...)** (*NAmE*) to stay somewhere for a short time during a long journey（长途旅行期间）作短暂停留 ➲ RELATED NOUN LAYOVER ➲ SEE ALSO STOP OVER (AT/IN...) at STOP ˌ**lay sb 'up** [usually passive] if sb is **laid up**, they are unable to work, etc. because of an illness or injury（因病或受伤而）卧床歇工： *She's laid up with a broken leg.* 她因腿部骨折卧床养病。ˌ**lay sth↔'up 1** = LAY STH↔IN/UP **2** if you **lay up** problems or trouble for yourself, you do sth that will cause you problems later 自找（麻烦）；自讨（苦吃） **3** to stop using a ship or other vehicle while it is being repaired（船或其他交通工具维修时）停止使用，搁置不用

■ ***adj.*** [only before noun] **1** not having expert knowledge or professional qualifications in a particular subject 外行的；非专业的；缺少专门知识的： *His book explains the theory for the lay public.* 他的书为普通大众阐明了这个理论。 **2** not in an official position in the Church 平信徒的；在俗的： *a lay preacher* 在俗传道员 ➲ SEE ALSO LAYMAN, LAYPERSON, LAYWOMAN

■ ***noun* 1** (*taboo, informal*) a partner in sex, especially a woman 性伙伴；（尤指）性交的女人： ***an easy lay*** (= a person who is ready and willing to have sex) 淫妇 ◇ *to be a great lay* 为荒淫无度的荡妇 **2** (*old use*) a poem that was written to be sung, usually telling a story（供吟唱的）叙事诗

IDM **the ˌlay of the 'land** (*NAmE*) (*BrE* **the ˌlie of the 'land**) **1** the way the land in an area is formed and what physical characteristics it has 地貌；地势；地形 **2** the way a situation is now and how it is likely to develop 目前的形势及发展趋势

lay·about /'leɪəbaʊt/ *noun* (*old-fashioned, BrE, informal*) a lazy person who does not do much work 游手好闲的人；懒汉；二流子

lay·away /'leɪəweɪ/ *noun* [U] (*NAmE*) a system of buying goods in a store, where the customer pays a small amount of the price for an article and the store keeps the goods until the full price has been paid 预付订金购货法（余额结清后取货）

'lay-by *noun* **1** [C] (*BrE*) an area at the side of a road where vehicles may stop for a short time 路边临时停车处；路侧停车带 ➲ COMPARE REST AREA ➲ **WORDFINDER NOTE** AT ROAD **2** [U] (*AustralE, NZE, SAfrE*) a system of paying some money for an article so that it is kept for you and you can pay the rest of the money later 预付订金购买： *You could secure it on lay-by.* 你可以预付订金方式购买此货。

layer AW /'leɪə(r); 'leə(r); *NAmE* 'ler/ *noun, verb*

■ ***noun* 1** a quantity or thickness of sth that lies over a surface or between surfaces 层；表层： *A thin layer of dust covered everything.* 所有的物品上都积了薄薄的一层灰尘。◇ *How many layers of clothing are you wearing?* 你穿了几层衣服？ **2** a level or part within a system or set of ideas 层次；阶层： *There were too many layers of management in the company.* 这家公司管理层级太多。◇ *the layers of meaning in the poem* 这首诗不同层次的含义

■ ***verb*** [often passive] **~ sth** to arrange sth in layers 把…分层堆放： *Layer the potatoes and onions in a dish.* 把土豆和洋葱叠放在盘子里。◇ *Her hair had been layered* (= cut to several different lengths). 她的头发被剪出层次。 ➲ **VISUAL VOCAB PAGE V65**

lay·ette /leɪ'et/ *noun* a set of clothes and other things for a new baby 新生儿的全套用品

lay·man /'leɪmən/ *noun* (*pl.* **-men** /-mən/) (*also* **lay·per·son**) **1** a person who does not have expert knowledge of a particular subject 非专业人员；外行；门外汉： *a book written for professionals and laymen alike* 一本内行外行都可以读的书 ◇ *to explain sth* ***in layman's terms*** (= in simple language) 用通俗易懂的语言解释某事 **2** a person who is a member of a Church but is not a priest or member of the CLERGY 平信徒，在俗教徒（非神职人员） ➲ SEE ALSO LAYWOMAN ➲ NOTE AT GENDER

'lay-off *noun* **1** an act of making people unemployed because there is no more work left for them to do（因工作不多的）解雇，裁员 **2** a period of time when sb is not working or not doing sth that they normally do regularly 歇工期；停工期： *an eight-week lay-off with a broken leg* 因腿部骨折歇工休养八周

lay·out /'leɪaʊt/ *noun* [usually sing.] the way in which the parts of sth such as the page of a book, a garden or a building are arranged 布局；布置；设计；安排： *the layout of streets* 街道的布局 ◇ *the magazine's attractive new page layout* 杂志漂亮的新版面设计

lay·over /'leɪəʊvə(r); *NAmE* -oʊ-/ (*NAmE*) (*BrE, NAmE* **stop·over**) *noun* a short stay somewhere between two parts of a journey 中途停留

lay·per·son /'leɪpɜːsn; *NAmE* -pɜːrsn/ *noun* (*also* **'lay person**) (*pl.* **lay people** or **lay·persons**) = LAYMAN： *The layperson cannot really understand mental illness.* 外行人无法完全了解精神疾病。

'lay-up *noun* **1** (in BASKETBALL 篮球) a shot made with one hand from under or beside the BASKET 单手上篮 **2** (in GOLF 高尔夫球) a shot made from a difficult position to a position that will allow an easier next shot 打点（将球送到较容易击打的位置的一击）

lay·woman /'leɪwʊmən/ *noun* (*pl.* **-women** /-wɪmɪn/) a woman who is a member of a Church but is not a priest or a member of the CLERGY 女平信徒，在俗女教徒（非神职人员） ➲ SEE ALSO LAYMAN (2), LAYPERSON ➲ NOTE AT GENDER

Laz·a·rus /'læzərəs/ *noun* used to refer to sb who improves or starts to be successful again after a period of failure 东山再起者（失败后重新振作或再取得成功的人）

ORIGIN From the story of **Lazarus** in the Bible. He was a man who died but was then brought back to life by Jesus Christ. 源自《圣经》中耶稣让已死去的拉撒路（Lazarus）复活的故事。

laze /leɪz/ *verb* [I] to relax and do very little 懒散；懒惰；偷懒： *We lazed by the pool all day.* 我们整天都在池塘边消磨。◇ **~ about/around** *I've spent the afternoon just lazing around.* 我一下午就那样懒洋洋地打发了。

PHR V **'laze sth↔away** to spend time relaxing and doing very little 懒散地打发时间；混日子；消磨时光 SYN **lounge**: *They lazed away the long summer days.* 他们懒懒散散地混过了漫长的夏天。

lazy /'leɪzi/ *adj.* (**lazi·er**, **lazi·est**) **1** (*disapproving*) unwilling to work or be active; doing as little as possible 不愿工作的；懒散的；懒惰的 SYN **idle**: *He was not stupid, just lazy.* 他不笨，只是懒。◇ *I was feeling too lazy to go out.* 我当时懒得动，不愿意外出。 **2** not involving much energy or activity; slow and relaxed 无精打采的；懒洋洋的： *We spent a lazy day on the beach.* 我们在海滩上懒洋洋地度过了一天。 **3** (*disapproving*) showing a lack of effort or care 没下功夫的；粗枝大叶的；马虎的：*a lazy piece of work* 粗制滥造的作品 **4** (*literary*) moving slowly 行进缓慢的；慢吞吞的 SYN **torpid**：*the lazy river* 缓缓流淌的河水 ▶ **lazi·ly** *adv.*：*She woke up and stretched lazily.* 她醒来伸了个懒腰。**lazi·ness** *noun* [U]

lazy·bones /ˈleɪzibəʊnz; *NAmE* -boʊnz/ *noun* [sing.] (*old-fashioned, informal*) used to refer to a lazy person 懒汉；懒虫；懒骨头：*Come on, lazybones, get up!* 赶快，你这懒骨头，起床了！

ˌ**lazy ˈeye** *noun* an eye that does not see well because it is not used enough （因少用而致的）弱视眼

ˌ**lazy ˈSusan** *noun* a round plate or TRAY on a base, which can be spun around so that the objects on it can be easily reached 餐桌转盘（方便取食）

lb (*BrE*) (*NAmE* **lb.**) *abbr.* (*pl.* **lb** or **lbs**) a pound in weight, equal to about 454 grams (from Latin 'libra') 磅（源自拉丁语 libra，约等于 454 克）

lbw /ˌel biː ˈdʌbljuː/ *abbr.* (in CRICKET 板球) leg before wicket (When the ball hits a player's leg instead of hitting his or her BAT, and would have hit the WICKET if the leg had not stopped it, then that player is **out lbw** and has to stop BATTING.) 腿碰球（击球手用腿截球犯规出局）

l.c. /ˌel ˈsiː/ *abbr.* **1** in the piece of text that has been quoted (from Latin 'loco citato') 在引文中 **2** (in writing 书写形式) LETTER OF CREDIT 信用证；信用状 **3** (in writing 书写形式) LOWER CASE 小写字体

LCD /ˌel siː ˈdiː/ *noun* **1** liquid crystal display (a way of showing information in electronic equipment. An electric current is passed through a special liquid and numbers and letters can be seen on a small screen.) 液晶显示；液晶显示器：*a pocket calculator with LCD* 液晶显示袖珍计算器 ◇ *an LCD screen* 液晶显示屏 **2** LOWEST COMMON DENOMINATOR 最小公分母

lea /liː/ *noun* (*literary*) an open area of land covered in grass 草原；草地

leach /liːtʃ/ *verb* (*specialist*) **1** [I] ~ (**from sth**) (**into sth**) | ~ **out/away** (of chemicals, minerals, etc. 化学物质、矿物质等) to be removed from soil, etc. by water passing through it 淋洗；淋失：*Nitrates leach from the soil into rivers.* 硝酸盐由土壤淋洗入江河。**2** [T] ~ **sth** (**from sth**) (**into sth**) | ~ **sth out/away** (of a liquid 液体) to remove chemicals, minerals, etc. from soil 过滤；滤去：*The nutrient is quickly leached away.* 养分很快就被滤掉了。

lead¹ /liːd/ *verb, noun* ➲ SEE ALSO LEAD²

■ *verb* (**led**, **led** /led/)

• **SHOW THE WAY** 带路 **1** [I, T] to go with or in front of a person or an animal to show the way or to make them go in the right direction 带路；领路；引领 SYN **guide**：*If you lead, I'll follow.* 你领头，我跟着。◇ ~ **sb/sth + adv./prep.** *He led us out into the grounds.* 他领我们进了庭院。◇ *The receptionist* **led the way** *to the boardroom.* 接待员领路到董事会会议室。◇ *She led the horse back into the stable.* 她把那匹马牵回了马厩。◇ (*figurative*) *I tried to lead the discussion back to the main issue.* 我试图把讨论引回到主要问题上。➲ SYNONYMS AT TAKE

• **CONNECT TWO THINGS** 连接两事物 **2** [I] ~ **from/to sth** (**to/from sth**) to connect one object or place to another （与…）相连，相通：*the pipe leading from the top of the water tank* 与水箱顶部相通的管道 ◇ *The wire led to a speaker.* 这电线连接着扬声器。

• **OF ROAD/PATH/DOOR** 道路；小路；门 **3** [I, T] to go in a particular direction or to a particular place 通向；通往：**+ adv./prep.** *A path led up the hill.* 有一条小路通往山上。◇ *Which door leads to the yard?* 哪扇门通向庭院？◇ ~ **sb + adv./prep.** *The track led us through a wood.* 我们沿着那条小道穿过了树林。

• **CAUSE** 原因 **4** [I] ~ **to sth** to have sth as a result 导致，造成（后果）SYN **result in**：*Eating too much sugar can lead to health problems.* 食用过多的糖会引起健康问题。➲ LANGUAGE BANK AT CAUSE **5** [T] to be the reason why sb does or thinks sth 使得出（观点）；引导（某人）：~ **sb** (**to sth**) *What led you to this conclusion?* 你是如何得出这个结论的？◇ *He's too* **easily led** (= easily persuaded to do or think sth). 他太容易受人左右了。◇ ~ **sb to do sth** *This has led scientists to speculate on the existence of other galaxies.* 这就使得科学家推测还有其他星系存在。◇ *The situation is far worse than we had been* **led to believe**. 情况比我们听信的要糟糕得多。

• **LIFE** 生活 **6** [T] ~ **sth** to have a particular type of life 过（某种生活）：*to lead a quiet life/a life of luxury/a miserable existence* 过宁静 / 奢侈 / 悲惨的生活

• **BE BEST/FIRST** 属最佳 / 第一 **7** [T, I] to be the best at sth; to be in first place 最擅长于；处于首位；处于领先地位：~ (**sb/sth**) (**in sth**) *The department led the world in cancer research.* 这个系在癌症研究方面走在了世界前列。◇ *We* **lead the way** *in space technology.* 我们在航天技术方面处于领先地位。◇ ~ (**sb/sth**) **by sth** *The champion is leading (her nearest rival) by 18 seconds.* 冠军领先了（紧随其后的对手）18 秒钟。

• **BE IN CONTROL** 控制 **8** [T, I] ~ (**sth**) to be in control of sth; to be the leader of sth 控制；掌管；领导；率领：*to lead an expedition* 率领探险队 ◇ *to lead a discussion* 主持讨论 ◇ *Who will lead the party in the next election?* 下一届选举谁来领导这个党？

• **IN CARD GAMES** 纸牌游戏 **9** [I, T] to play first; to play sth as your first card 开牌；率先出牌：*It's your turn to lead.* 轮到你开牌了。◇ ~ **sth** *to lead the ten of clubs* 先出梅花十

IDM **lead sb by the ˈnose** to make sb do everything you want; to control sb completely 牵着某人的鼻子走；完全操纵（或控制）某人 **lead sb a** (**merry**) **ˈdance** (*BrE*) to cause sb a lot of trouble or worry 给某人造成许多麻烦（或忧虑）**lead from the ˈfront** to take an active part in what you are telling or persuading others to do 带头；带动；引导 **lead** (**sb**) **nowhere** to have no successful result for sb 毫无成果：*This discussion is leading us nowhere.* 我们这场讨论将毫无结果。**lead sb up/down the garden ˈpath** to make sb believe sth which is not true 给某人误导的信息（或提示）；误导某人 SYN **mislead** ➲ MORE AT BLIND *adj.*, HORSE *n.*, LIFE, THING

PHR V ˌ**lead ˈoff** (**from**) **sth** to start at a place and go away from it 起始于（某地）：*narrow streets leading off from the main square* 起始于大广场的狭窄街道 ˌ**lead ˈoff** | ˌ**lead sth↔ˈoff** to start sth 开始（某事）：*Who would like to lead off the debate?* 谁愿带头发言开始辩论？ˌ**lead sb ˈon** (*informal*) to make sb believe sth which is not true, especially that you love them or find them attractive 使误信，误导某人（尤指谎称自己喜爱对方或认为对方有魅力）ˌ**lead ˈup to sth** to be an introduction to or the cause of sth 是…的先导；是导致…的原因：*the weeks leading up to the exam* 临近考试的几个星期 ◇ *the events leading up to the strike* 导致罢工的事件 ˈ**lead with sth 1** (of a newspaper 报纸) to have sth as the main item of news 把…作为头条新闻 **2** (in boxing 拳击运动) to use a particular hand to begin an attack （用…手）率先出击，开始进攻：**to lead with your right/left** 用右拳 / 左拳率先出击

■ *noun*

• **FIRST PLACE** 首位 **1 the lead** [sing.] the position ahead of everyone else in a race or competition （竞赛中的）领先地位：*She* **took the lead** *in the second lap.* 她在第二圈时取得领先。◇ *He has gone* **into the lead**. 他已处于领先地位。◇ *The Democrats now appear to be* **in the lead**. 现在看来好像民主党人占优势。◇ *to* **hold/lose the lead** 保持 / 失去领先地位 ◇ *The lead car is now three minutes ahead of the rest of the field.* 现在跑在最前面的汽车较赛场上其余的赛车领先三分钟。**2** [sing.] ~ (**over sb/sth**) the amount or distance that sb/sth is in front of sb/sth else 超前量；领先的距离 SYN **advantage**：*He managed to* **hold a lead** *of two seconds over his closest rival.* 他比跟得最紧的对手领先两秒钟。◇ *The polls have given Labour a five-point lead.* 投票选举中工党领先五个百分点。◇ *a* **commanding/comfortable lead** 遥遥 / 轻松领先 ◇ *to* **increase/widen your lead** 加大 / 扩大领先优势 ◇ *Manchester lost their early two-goal lead.* 曼彻斯特队失去了他们开场不久领先两球的优势。

• **EXAMPLE** 实例 **3** [sing.] an example or action for people to copy 实例；范例；榜样：*If one bank raises interest rates, all the others will* **follow their lead**. 要是有一家银行提高利

率，所有其他银行都会效法。◇ *If we **take the lead** in this* (= start to act), *others may follow.* 如果我们在这方面带头行动，其余的人就会跟着来。◇ *You go first, I'll take my lead from you.* 你领头，我来照样做。

• **INFORMATION** 信息 **4** [C] a piece of information that may help to find out the truth or facts about a situation, especially a crime（尤指有关犯罪的）线索 **SYN** **clue**: *The police will **follow up** all possible **leads**.* 警方将追踪所有可能有用的线索。

• **ACTOR/MUSICIAN** 演员；音乐家 **5** [C] the main part in a play, film/movie, etc.; the person who plays this part（戏剧、电影等中的）主角；扮演主角的演员：*Who is **playing the lead**?* 谁是主演？◇ *the **male/female lead*** 男主角；女主角 ◇ *a lead role* 主角的角色 ◇ *the lead singer in a band* 乐队的主唱歌手

• **FOR DOG** 狗 **6** (*BrE*) (*also* **leash** *NAmE*, *BrE*) [C] a long piece of leather, chain or rope used for holding and controlling a dog（牵狗用的）皮带，链条，绳索：*Dogs must be kept on a lead in the park.* 狗在公园里必须系着牵狗带。

• **FOR ELECTRICITY** 电 **7** [C] (*BrE*) a long piece of wire, usually covered in plastic, that is used to connect a piece of electrical equipment to a source of electricity 电线；导线 ➲ SEE ALSO EXTENSION LEAD, JUMP LEAD

lead² /led/ *noun* ➲ SEE ALSO LEAD¹ *n.* **1** [U] (*symb.* **Pb**) a chemical element. Lead is a heavy soft grey metal, used especially in the past for water pipes or to cover roofs. 铅 **2** [C, U] the thin black part of a pencil that marks paper 铅笔芯 ➲ VISUAL VOCAB PAGE V71

IDM **go ˌdown like a lead balˈloon** (*informal*) to be very unsuccessful; to not be accepted by people 非常失败；不被接受 ➲ MORE AT SWING *v.*

lead·ed /ˈledɪd/ *adj.* [usually before noun] **1** (of petrol, metal, etc. 汽油、金属等) with lead² (1) added to it 加铅的；含铅的 **OPP** **unleaded** **2** with a cover or a frame of lead² (1) 铅皮覆盖的；铅框的：*a leaded roof* 铅屋顶

ˌleaded ˈlight (*also* **ˌleaded ˈwindow**) *noun* [usually pl.] (*BrE*) a window made from small pieces of glass that are arranged in diamond shapes and are separated by strips of LEAD² (1) 菱形铅条玻璃窗

lead·en /ˈledn/ *adj.* (*literary*) **1** dull grey in colour, like LEAD² (1) 铅灰色的：*leaden skies* 铅灰色的天空 **2** dull, heavy or slow 沉闷的；阴郁的；迟钝的；呆滞的：*a leaden heart* (= because you are sad) 沉重的心情

lead·er /ˈliːdə(r)/ *noun* **1** a person who leads a group of people, especially the head of a country, an organization, etc. 领导者；领袖；首领：*a **political/spiritual, etc. leader*** 政治、精神等领袖 ◇ *the leader of the party* 该党的领导人 ◇ *union leaders* 工会领导人 ◇ *He was not a **natural leader**.* 他并非天生的领袖。◇ *She's a **born leader**.* 她是个天生的领袖。 **2** a person or thing that is the best, or in first place in a race, business, etc. 最佳的人（或物）；（在赛跑、商业等活动中）处于领先地位的人（或物）：*She was among the leaders of the race from the start.* 比赛一开始她就与领先的几位选手并驾齐驱。◇ *The company is a **world leader** in electrical goods.* 这家公司的电器产品在全世界首屈一指。 ➲ SEE ALSO MARKET LEADER **3** (*BrE*) (*also* **con·cert·master** *NAmE*, *BrE*) the most important VIOLIN player in an ORCHESTRA（管弦乐队的）首席小提琴手 **4** (*BrE*) = EDITORIAL

ˈleader board *noun* a sign showing the names and scores of the top players, especially in a GOLF competition（尤指高尔夫球比赛中的）领先选手积分牌；选手积分榜

lead·er·less /ˈliːdələs; *NAmE* -dərl-/ *adj.* without a leader 无领导的：*Her sudden death left the party leaderless.* 她的猝然去世使该党陷入群龙无首的境地。

the ˌLeader of the ˈHouse *noun* [sing.] (in Britain) a member of the government who is responsible for deciding what is discussed in Parliament（英国）国会领袖，上（或下）议院议长

lead·er·ship /ˈliːdəʃɪp; *NAmE* -dərʃ-/ *noun* **1** [U] the state or position of being a leader 领导；领导地位：*a leadership contest* 领导地位的角逐 ◇ *The party thrived **under his leadership**.* 该党在他的领导下壮大起来。 **2** [U] the ability to be a leader or the qualities a good leader should have 领导才能；领导应有的品质：***leadership qualities/skills*** 领导的素质 / 技巧 ◇ *Strong leadership is needed to captain the team.* 担任这个队的队长需要强有力的领导才能。 **3** [C+sing./pl. v.] a group of leaders of a particular organization, etc. 领导班子；领导层：*The party leadership is/are divided.* 这个党的领导阶层意见不合。

lead-free /ˌled ˈfriː/ *adj.* (of petrol, paint, etc. 汽油、涂料等) without any of the metal LEAD² (1) added to it 无铅的

lead guitar /ˌliːd ɡɪˈtɑː(r)/ *noun* [U] a GUITAR style that consists mainly of SOLOS and tunes rather than only CHORDS 主音吉他，独奏吉他，主奏吉他（主要为独奏和奏出曲调而非只有和弦的吉他演奏风格）➲ COMPARE RHYTHM GUITAR

lead-in /ˈliːd ɪn/ *noun* an introduction to a subject, story, show, etc.（主题、故事、表演等的）引子，介绍，开场白

lead·ing¹ /ˈliːdɪŋ/ *adj.* [only before noun] **1** most important or most successful 最重要的；一流的：*leading experts* 最杰出的专家 ◇ *She was offered the **leading role** in the new TV series.* 她获得主演那部新的电视连续剧的机会。◇ *He **played a leading part** in the negotiations.* 他在谈判中起到了至关重要的作用。 **2** ahead of others in a race or contest（赛跑或比赛中）领先的，最前的：*She started the last lap just behind the leading group.* 她开始跑最后一圈时紧跟在领先的一组人后面。◇ *These are the leading first-round scores.* 这些是第一轮比赛的领先成绩。

lead·ing² /ˈledɪŋ/ *noun* [U] (*specialist*) the amount of white space between lines of printed text 行距（印刷文本两行之间的距离）

ˌleading ˈarticle (*also* **lead·er**) *noun* (*both BrE*) = EDITORIAL

ˌleading ˈedge *noun* **1** [sing.] the most important and advanced position in an area of activity, especially technology（某活动领域的）最重要位置，领先地位；（尤指技术上的）前沿，尖端：*at the leading edge of scientific research* 在科学研究的前沿 **2** [C] (*specialist*) the front or forward edge of sth moving, especially an aircraft wing 前缘；（尤指飞机的）机翼前缘 ➲ VISUAL VOCAB PAGE V57 ▶ **ˌleading-ˈedge** *adj.* [only before noun] **SYN** **cutting edge**: *leading-edge technology* 尖端技术

ˌleading ˈlady, **ˌleading ˈman** *noun* the actor with the main female or male part in a play or film/movie 饰主角的演员

ˌleading ˈlight *noun* an important, active or respected person in a particular area of activity（某活动范围内）重要的活跃人物，受敬重的人物：*She's one of the leading lights in the opera world.* 她是歌剧界的一位大腕。

ˌleading ˈquestion *noun* a question that you ask in a particular way in order to get the answer you want 诱导性（或暗示性）问题

lead-off /ˈliːd ɒf; *NAmE* ɔːf/ *adj.* (*NAmE*) being the first of a series（系列中）开头的，起始的：*the lead-off track on the album* 专辑的第一首歌

lead shot /ˌled ˈʃɒt; *NAmE* ˈʃɑːt/ *noun* = SHOT (3)

lead story /ˈliːd stɔːri/ *noun* the main or first item of news in a newspaper, magazine or news broadcast 重要新闻；头条新闻

lead time /ˈliːd taɪm/ *noun* the time between starting and completing a production process 从投产至完成生产间相隔的时间；订货交付时间 ➲ WORDFINDER NOTE AT INDUSTRY

leaf /liːf/ *noun, verb*

■ ***noun*** (*pl.* **leaves** /liːvz/) **1** [C] a flat green part of a plant, growing from a STEM or branch or from the root 叶；叶片；叶子：*lettuce/cabbage/oak leaves* 莴苣叶；卷心菜叶；橡树叶 ◇ *The trees are just **coming into leaf**.* 树木正好在长叶子。◇ *the dead leaves of autumn/the fall* 秋天

的枯叶 ➲ COLLOCATIONS AT LIFE ➲ VISUAL VOCAB PAGE V10 ➲ SEE ALSO BAY LEAF, FIG LEAF **2 -leaf, -leafed, -leaved** (in adjectives 构成形容词) having leaves of the type or number mentioned 有…状叶的；有…片叶的：*a four-leaf clover* 四叶车轴草 ◇ *a broad-leaved plant* 阔叶植物 **3** [C] a sheet of paper, especially a page in a book（纸）页，张；（尤指书的）页 ➲ SEE ALSO FLYLEAF, LOOSE-LEAF, OVERLEAF **4** [U] metal, especially gold or silver, in the form of very thin sheets 薄金属片；（尤指金或银）箔：*gold leaf* 金箔 **5** [C] a part of a table that can be lifted up or pulled into position in order to make the table bigger 活动桌板；折叠桌板

IDM **take a leaf from/out of sb's 'book** to copy sb's behaviour and do things in the same way that they do, because they are successful 效仿，模仿（成功之人的举止和行为） SYN **emulate** ➲ MORE AT NEW

■ *verb*

PHR V **'leaf through sth** to quickly turn over the pages of a book, etc. without reading them or looking at them carefully 匆匆翻阅；浏览

leaf·less /ˈliːfləs/ *adj.* having no leaves 无叶的 SYN **bare**

leaf·let /ˈliːflət/ *noun, verb*

■ *noun* a printed sheet of paper or a few printed pages that are given free to advertise or give information about sth 散页印刷品；传单；（宣传或广告）小册子 SYN **booklet, pamphlet**：*a leaflet on local places of interest* 介绍当地名胜的小册子 ➲ WORDFINDER NOTE AT ADVERTISE

■ *verb* [I, T] ~ (**sb/sth**) to give out leaflets to people 散发传单（或小册子）：*We did a lot of leafleting in the area.* 我们在此地散发了许多传单。

'leaf mould (*BrE*) (*NAmE* **'leaf mold**) *noun* [U] soil consisting mostly of dead, decayed leaves 腐叶土

leafy /ˈliːfi/ *adj.* (**leaf·ier, leafi·est**) **1** having a lot of leaves 多叶的；叶茂的：*Eat plenty of leafy green vegetables.* 多吃绿叶蔬菜。 **2** (*approving*) (of a place 地方) having a lot of trees and plants 多树木的；多植物的：*leafy suburbs* 树木茂密的郊区 **3** made by a lot of leaves or trees 叶制的；由树木构成的：*We sat in the leafy shade of an oak tree.* 我们坐在一棵枝繁叶茂的栎树树荫下。

league /liːɡ/ *noun* **1** a group of sports teams who all play each other to earn points and find which team is best（体育运动队的）联合会，联赛：*major league baseball* 棒球大联赛 ◇ *United were league champions last season.* 联队是上个赛季的联赛冠军。 ➲ SEE ALSO MINOR-LEAGUE **2** (*informal*) a level of quality, ability, etc.（质量、能力等的）等级，级别，水平：*As a painter, he is **in a league of his own*** (= much better than others). 作为画家，他独领风骚。 ◇ *They're **in a different league** from us.* 他们与我们不属同一个级别。 ◇ *When it comes to cooking, I'm **not in her league*** (= she is much better than me). 提到烹饪，我的水平远比不上她。 ◇ *A house like that is **out of our league*** (= too expensive for us). 那样的房子不是我们买得起的。 **3** a group of people or nations who have combined for a particular purpose 联盟；同盟 SYN **alliance**：*the League of Nations* 国际联盟 ◇ *a meeting of the Women's League for Peace* 妇女和平联盟会议 ➲ SEE ALSO IVY LEAGUE **4** (*old use*) a unit for measuring distance, equal to about 3 miles or 4 000 metres 里格（长度单位，约等于 3 英里或 4 000 米） ➲ MORE LIKE THIS 20, page R27

IDM **in 'league (with sb)** making secret plans with sb（与…）秘密串通，勾结

'league table *noun* (*BrE*) **1** a table that shows the position of sports teams and how successfully they are performing in a competition（运动队的）积分排名表 **2** a table that shows how well institutions such as schools or hospitals are performing in comparison with each other（学校、医院等的）排名表

leak /liːk/ *verb, noun*

■ *verb* **1** [I, T] to allow liquid or gas to get in or out through a small hole or crack 漏；渗漏；泄漏：*a leaking pipe* 渗漏的管道 ◇ *The roof was leaking.* 屋顶在漏水。 ◇ **~ sth** *The tank had leaked a small amount of water.* 水箱渗漏出少量的水。 **2** [I] (of a liquid or gas 液体或气体) to get in or out through a small hole or crack in sth 渗入；漏出：*Water had started to leak into the cellar.* 水已开始渗入地下室。 **3** [T] **~ sth (to sb)** to give secret information to the public, for example by telling a newspaper 泄露，透露（秘密信息）；走漏 SYN **disclose**：*The contents of the report were leaked to the press.* 报告的内容泄露到新闻界了。 ◇ *a leaked document* 已外泄的文件

PHR V **,leak 'out** (of secret information 秘密信息) to become known to the public 泄露；走漏；透露：*Details of the plan soon leaked out.* 计划的细节很快就泄露出去了。

■ *noun* **1** a small hole or crack that lets liquid or gas flow in or out of sth by accident 漏洞；裂缝；缝隙：*a leak in the roof* 屋顶的漏洞 ◇ *a leak in the gas pipe* 煤气管道的裂缝 ➲ COLLOCATIONS AT DECORATE **2** liquid or gas that escapes through a hole in sth 泄漏出的液体（或气体）：*a gas leak* 煤气泄漏 ◇ *oil leaks/leaks of oil* 漏油 **3** a deliberate act of giving secret information to the newspapers, etc.（秘密信息的）透露：*a leak to the press about the government plans on tax* 有关政府税收计划的消息对新闻界的泄露 **4** (*slang*) an act of passing URINE from the body 撒尿：*to **have/take a leak*** 撒尿 IDM SEE SPRING *v.*

leak·age /ˈliːkɪdʒ/ *noun* [C, U] an amount of liquid or gas escaping through a hole in sth; an occasion when there is a leak 泄漏量；漏损量；泄漏；渗漏：*a leakage of toxic waste into the sea* 有毒废物的泄漏入海 ◇ *Check bottles for leakage before use.* 使用前应检查瓶子是否渗漏。

leaky /ˈliːki/ *adj.* having holes or cracks that allow liquid or gas to escape 有漏洞的；有漏隙的；渗漏的：*a leaky roof* 漏水的屋顶

lean /liːn/ *verb, adj., noun*

■ *verb* (**leaned, leaned**) (*BrE also* **leant, leant** /lent/) **1** [I] (**+ adv./prep.**) to bend or move from a vertical position 前俯（或后仰）；倾斜：*I leaned back in my chair.* 我仰靠在椅背上。 ◇ *The tower is leaning dangerously.* 那座塔倾斜了，很危险。 ◇ *A man was leaning out of the window.* 一个人正探身窗外。 **2** [I] to rest on or against sth for support 倚靠；靠在；靠置： **~ against sth** *A shovel was leaning against the wall.* 一把铁铲靠墙放着。 ◇ **~ on sth** *She walked slowly, leaning on her son's arm.* 她倚靠着她儿子的手臂缓慢行走。 **3** [T] **~ sth against/on sth** to make sth rest against sth in a sloping position 使斜靠：*Can I lean my bike against the wall?* 我能把自行车靠在这墙上吗？ IDM SEE BACKWARDS

PHR V **'lean on sb/sth 1** to depend on sb/sth for help and support 依靠，依赖（…的帮助和支持） SYN **rely**：*He leans heavily on his family.* 他在很大程度上依赖他的家庭。 **2** to try to influence sb by threatening them 对…施加压力；威胁；恐吓：*The government has been leaning on the TV company not to broadcast the show.* 政府一直给电视公司施加压力，不准播放此节目。 **'lean to/towards/toward sth** to have a tendency to prefer sth, especially a particular opinion or interest 倾向，偏向（尤指某意见或利益）：*The UK leant towards the US proposal.* 英国倾向于美国的提案。

■ *adj.* (**lean·er, lean·est**) **1** (*usually approving*) (of people, especially men, or animals 人，尤指男人或动物) without much flesh; thin and fit 肉少的；瘦且健康的：*a lean, muscular body* 清瘦而肌肉发达的身体 ◇ *He was tall, lean and handsome.* 他长得瘦高而英俊。 **2** (of meat 肉) containing little or no fat 脂肪少的；无脂肪的 **3** [usually before noun] (of a period of time 一段时间) difficult and not producing much money, food, etc. 难以赚钱的；生产不出（食物等）的；贫乏的：*a **lean period/spell*** 不景气时期 ◇ *The company recovered well after going through several **lean years**.* 经历了几年的萧条后，这家公司的业务完全恢复了正常。 **4** (of organizations, etc. 机构等) strong and efficient because the number of employees has been reduced 精干的；效率高的：*The changes made the company leaner and more competitive.* 改革使公司更精干，更有竞争力。 ▶ **lean·ness** /ˈliːnnəs/ *noun* [U]

■ *noun* [U] the part of meat that has little or no fat 瘦肉

lean·ing /ˈliːnɪŋ/ *noun* [usually pl.] **~ (toward(s) sth)** a tendency to prefer sth or to believe in particular ideas, opinions, etc. 倾向；偏向；爱好 SYN **inclination, tendency**: *a leaning towards comedy rather than tragedy* 偏爱喜剧而不是悲剧 ◇ *a person with socialist leanings* 具有社会主义倾向的人

ˈlean-to *noun* (*pl.* **-tos** /-tuːz/) a small building with its roof leaning against the side of a large building, wall or fence（搭在高大建筑物、墙壁或栅栏上建的）单坡屋顶小房，披屋，披棚: *a lean-to garage* 单坡屋顶车库

leap /liːp/ *verb, noun*

■ *verb* (**leapt, leapt** /lept/ or **leaped, leaped**) **1** [I, T] to jump high or a long way 跳；跳跃；跳越: **+ adv./prep.** *A dolphin leapt out of the water.* 海豚跃出水面。◇ *We leapt over the stream.* 我们跳过了那条小溪。◇ **~ sth** *The horse leapt a five-foot wall.* 那匹马跃过了一道五英尺高的墙。**2** [I] **+ adv./prep.** to move or do sth suddenly and quickly 猛冲；突然做（某事）: *She leapt out of bed.* 她突然翻身下了床。◇ *He leapt across the room to answer the door.* 他冲过房间去应门。◇ *I **leapt to my feet*** (= stood up quickly). 我赶紧站了起来。◇ *They **leapt into action** immediately.* 他们立即断然采取了行动。◇ (*figurative*) *She was quick to **leap to my defence*** (= speak in support of me). 她马上挺身而出为我辩护。◇ *The photo seemed to **leap off the page*** (= it got your attention immediately). 那张照片跃然纸上，引人注目。◇ *His name **leapt out at me*** (= I saw it immediately). 他的名字立刻映入了我的眼帘。**3** [I] **~ (in sth) (from…) (to…)** to increase suddenly and by a large amount 骤增；剧增；猛涨 SYN **shoot up**: *The shares leapt in value from 476p to close at 536p.* 股价从 476 便士猛涨到收盘时的 536 便士。

IDM ˌ**look before you ˈleap** (*saying*) used to advise sb to think about the possible results or dangers of sth before doing it 三思而后行 ➲ MORE AT CONCLUSION, HEART

PHR V ˈ**leap at sth** to accept a chance or an opportunity quickly and with enthusiasm 赶紧抓住，急不可待地接受（机会） SYN **jump at**: *I leapt at the chance to go to France.* 我立刻抓住了去法国的机会。

■ *noun* **1** a long or high jump 跳越；跳跃；跳高: *a leap of six metres* 一跳跳了六米 ◇ *She took a **flying leap** and landed on the other side of the stream.* 她助跑后一个飞跃跳到小溪的对面。◇ (*figurative*) *His heart gave a sudden leap when he saw her.* 他看见她时，心猛地一跳。◇ (*figurative*) *Few people successfully make the leap from television to the movies.* 从电视业转向电影业很少有人成功。**2** **~ (in sth)** a sudden large change or increase in sth 骤变；剧增；激增: *a leap in profits* 利润跃升 ➲ SEE ALSO QUANTUM LEAP

IDM **by/in ˌleaps and ˈbounds** very quickly; in large amounts 非常迅速；飞跃地；突飞猛进；大量地: *Her health has improved in leaps and bounds.* 她的健康已迅速好转。**a leap in the ˈdark** an action or a risk that you take without knowing anything about the activity or what the result will be 冒险举动

leap·frog /ˈliːpfrɒɡ; *NAmE* -frɔːɡ; -frɑːɡ/ *noun, verb*

■ *noun* [U] a children's game in which players take turns to jump over the backs of other players who are bending down 跳背游戏（游戏者轮流从其他弯背站立者身上跳过）

■ *verb* (**-gg-**) [T, I] **~ (sb/sth)** to get to a higher position or rank by going past sb else or by missing out some stages 越级提升: *The win allowed them to leapfrog three teams to gain second place.* 这场胜利使他们连超三个队，跃居第二位。

ˈleap year *noun* one year in every four years when February has 29 days instead of 28 闰年

learn 🔑 /lɜːn; *NAmE* lɜːrn/ *verb* (**learnt, learnt** /lɜːnt; *NAmE* lɜːrnt/ or **learned, learned**) **1** 🔑 [T, I] to gain knowledge or skill by studying, from experience, from being taught, etc. 学；学习；学到；学会: **~ sth** *to learn a language/a musical instrument/a skill* 学一种语言 / 乐器 / 技能 ◇ **~ sth from sb/sth** *I learned a lot from my father.* 我从父亲那里学到了许多东西。◇ **~ sth from doing sth** *You can learn a great deal just from watching other players.* 你只要注意看其他运动员怎么做就能学到许多东西。◇ **~ (about sth)** *She's very keen to learn about Japanese culture.* 她热衷于学习日本文化。◇ *The book is about how children learn.* 这本书是有关小孩怎样学习的。◇ **~ to do sth** *He's learning to dance.* 他在学跳舞。◇ **~ how, what, etc.…** *Today we learnt how to use the new software.* 今天我们学习了怎样使用这个新软件。 ➲ MORE LIKE THIS 26, page R28 **2** 🔑 [I, T] to become aware of sth by hearing about it from sb else 听到；得知；获悉 SYN **discover**: **~ of/about sth** *I learnt of her arrival from a close friend.* 我从一位好友那里听说她到了。◇ **~ (that)…** *We were very surprised to learn (that) she had got married again.* 我们听说她又结婚了，感到很惊讶。◇ **~ who, what, etc.…** *We only learned who the new teacher was a few days ago.* 我们几天前才得知新教师是谁。◇ **~ sth** *How did they react when they learned the news?* 他们听到这个消息有什么反应？◇ **it is learned that…** *It has been learned that 500 jobs are to be lost at the factory.* 据悉工厂将要裁减 500 个工作岗位。**3** 🔑 [T] **~ sth** to study and repeat sth in order to be able to remember it 记住；背熟；熟记 SYN **memorize**: *We have to learn one of Hamlet's speeches for school tomorrow.* 我们明天上学得背诵一段哈姆雷特的台词。 **4** 🔑 [I, T] to gradually change your attitudes about sth so that you behave in a different way 认识到；意识到；（从…）吸取教训: **~ (from sth)** *I'm sure she'll learn from her mistakes.* 我肯定她会从错误中吸取教训。◇ **~ (that)…** *He'll just have to learn (that) he can't always have his own way.* 他一定要明白不能老是随心所欲。◇ **~ to do sth** *I soon learned not to ask too many questions.* 我很快就意识到不能问太多的问题。

IDM ˌ**learn (sth) the ˈhard way** to find out how to behave by learning from your mistakes or from unpleasant experiences, rather than from being told 历经挫折才懂得 **learn your ˈlesson** to learn what to do or not to do in the future because you have had a bad experience in the past 吸取教训 ➲ MORE AT COST *n.*, LIVE[1], ROPE *n.*

▼ **VOCABULARY BUILDING 词汇扩充**

Learning 表示学习、练习的词

- **learn** 学；学习： *He's learning Spanish/to swim.* 他在学西班牙语 / 游泳。
- **study** 学习；研究： *She studied chemistry for three years.* 她学了三年化学。
- **revise** (*BrE*) (*NAmE* **review**) 复习；温习： *In this class we'll revise/review what we did last week.* 本节课我们将复习上周所学的内容。
- **practise** (*BrE*) (*NAmE* **practice**) 练习；实习： *If you practise speaking English, you'll soon improve.* 只要你练习说英语，很快就会进步。
- **rehearse** 排练： *We only had two weeks to rehearse the play.* 我们只有两周时间排练此剧。

learn·ed /ˈlɜːnɪd; *NAmE* ˈlɜːrnɪd/ *adj.* [usually before noun] **1** (*formal*) having a lot of knowledge because you have studied and read a lot 有学问的；知识渊博的；博学的: *a learned professor* 学识渊博的教授 ➲ SEE ALSO FRIEND (5) **2** (*formal*) connected with or for learned people; showing and expressing deep knowledge（为）学者的；学术性的；学问精深的 SYN **scholarly**: *a learned journal* 学术性刊物 ➲ MORE LIKE THIS 22, page R27 **3** /lɜːnd; *NAmE* lɜːrnd/ developed by training or experience; not existing at birth 通过训练（或经历）形成的；学到的；非天生的: *a learned skill* 学来的技能

learn·er /ˈlɜːnə(r); *NAmE* ˈlɜːrn-/ *noun* **1** a person who is finding out about a subject or how to do sth 学习者: *a **slow/quick learner*** 迟钝的 / 聪明的学生 ◇ *a dictionary for learners of English* 英语学习词典 ◇ *learner-centred teaching methods* 以学生为中心的教学方法 **2** (*also* ˌ**learner ˈdriver**) a person who is learning to drive a car 学习驾车者；学习驾驶员

ˈlearner's permit (*NAmE*) (*BrE* **proˌvisional ˈlicence**) *noun* an official document that you must have when you start to learn to drive 实习驾驶执照；学员驾照

learn·ing /ˈlɜːnɪŋ; *NAmE* ˈlɜːrnɪŋ/ *noun* [U] **1** the process of learning sth 学习: *computer-assisted learning* 计算机辅助学习 ◇ *Last season was a learning experience for me.* 上个

季度对我来说是一次学习。➲ SEE ALSO DISTANCE LEARNING **2** knowledge that you get from reading and studying 知识；学问；学识：*a woman of great learning* 学识渊博的女子

'learning curve *noun* the rate at which you learn a new subject or a new skill; the process of learning from the mistakes you make 学习曲线；吸取教训过程曲线

'learning difficulties *noun* [pl.] mental problems that people may have from birth, or that may be caused by illness or injury, that affect their ability to learn things 学习障碍（先天性或由疾病、受伤引起）

'learning disability *noun* [usually pl.] a mental problem that people may have from birth, or that may be caused by illness or injury, that affects their ability to learn things 学习无能（先天性或由疾病、受伤引起）

lease /liːs/ *noun, verb*

■ ***noun*** a legal agreement that allows you to use a building, a piece of equipment or some land for a period of time, usually in return for rent（房屋、设备或土地的）租约，租契：*to **take out a lease** on a house* 办理房屋租约 ◇ *The **lease expires/runs out** next year.* 这份租约明年到期。◇ *Under **the terms of the lease**, you have to pay maintenance charges.* 按租约的条款，你得支付维修费。➲ WORDFINDER NOTE AT HOME ➲ COLLOCATIONS AT HOUSE

IDM **a (ˌnew) lease of 'life** (*BrE*) (*NAmE* **a (ˌnew) lease on 'life**) the chance to live or last longer, or with a better quality of life 延年益寿；生活质量更好：*Since her hip operation she's had a new lease of life.* 她自髋关节手术以后活得更有劲了。

■ ***verb*** to use or let sb use sth, especially property or equipment, in exchange for rent or a regular payment 租用，租借，出租（尤指房地产或设备）SYN **rent**: **~ sth** *We lease all our computer equipment.* 我们所有的计算机设备都是租来的。◇ **~ sth from sb** *They lease the land from a local farmer.* 他们从当地一位农场主手中租得这块土地。◇ **~ sb sth** *A local farmer leased them the land.* 这块地是当地的一个农场主租给他们的。◇ **~ sth (out) (to sb)** *Parts of the building are leased out to tenants.* 这栋大楼有一部分租出去了。▶ **leas·ing** *noun* [U]: *car leasing* 汽车租赁 ◇ *a leasing company* 租赁公司

lease·back /ˈliːsbæk/ *noun* [U] (*law* 律) the process of allowing the former owner of a property to continue to use it if they pay rent to the new owner; a legal agreement where this happens 售后回租（将地产出售后再租回）；售后回租契约

lease·hold /ˈliːshəʊld; *NAmE* -hoʊld/ *adj., noun*

■ ***adj.*** (*especially BrE*) (of property or land 房产或土地) that can be used for a limited period of time, according to the arrangements in a LEASE 租赁的；租用的：*a leasehold property* 租赁的房地产 ▶ **lease·hold** *adv.*: *to purchase land leasehold* 购买有租约的土地 ➲ COMPARE FREEHOLD

■ ***noun*** [U] (*especially BrE*) the right to use a building or a piece of land according to the arrangements in a LEASE（按租约使用房屋或土地的）租赁权：*to obtain/own the leasehold of a house* 获得 / 拥有一所房子的租赁权 ➲ COMPARE FREEHOLD

lease·hold·er /ˈliːshəʊldə(r); *NAmE* -hoʊld-/ *noun* (*especially BrE*) a person who is allowed to use a building or a piece of land according to the arrangements in a LEASE 租赁人；承租人；租借人 ➲ COMPARE FREEHOLDER

leash /liːʃ/ *noun, verb*

■ ***noun*** (*especially NAmE*) (*BrE also* **lead**) a long piece of leather, chain or rope used for holding and controlling a dog（牵狗用的）皮带，链条，绳索：*All dogs must be kept **on a leash** in public places.* 在公共场所所有的狗必须用皮带牵住。IDM SEE STRAIN *v.*

■ ***verb*** **~ sth** to control an animal, especially a dog, with a LEAD[1] (6)/LEASH 用皮带系住，拴住，缚住（尤指狗）

least 🔑 /liːst/ *det., pron., adv.*

■ ***det., pron.*** 🔑 (*usually* **the least**) smallest in size, amount, degree, etc. 最小的；最少的；程度最轻的：*He's the best teacher, even though he has the least experience.* 他虽然经验最少，却是最出色的老师。◇ *She never had the least idea what to do about it.* 这事怎么办，她一点主意都没有。◇ *He gave (the) least of all towards the wedding present.* 买结婚礼物，他出的钱最少。◇ *How others see me is **the least of** my worries* (= I have more important things to worry about). 别人怎么看我，我一点都不在乎。◇ ***It's the least I can do** to help* (= I feel I should do more). 这是我所能帮忙做的最起码的事。

IDM **at the (very) 'least** used after amounts to show that the amount is the lowest possible（用于数量之后）至少，最少：*It'll take a year, at the very least.* 这至少需要一年时间。**ˌnot in the 'least** not at all 一点也不；丝毫不：*Really, I'm not in the least tired.* 说真的，我一点也不累。◇ *'Do you mind if I put the television on?' 'No, not in the least.'*"我开电视机你介意吗？""不，一点也不介意。"➲ MORE AT SAY *v.*

■ ***adv.*** 🔑 to the smallest degree 最小；最少；微不足道：*He always turns up just when you least expect him.* 他总是在你最意料不到的时候出现。◇ *She chose the least expensive of the hotels.* 她挑了一家最便宜的旅馆。◇ *I never hid the truth, **least of all** from you.* 我从不隐瞒事实，尤其是对你。

IDM **at 'least** **1** 🔑 not less than 至少；不少于：*It'll cost at least 500 dollars.* 这东西至少要花 500 美元。◇ *She must be at least 40.* 她至少应该有 40 岁了。◇ *Cut the grass at least once a week in summer.* 夏天至少每周割一次草。◇ *I've known her at least as long as you have.* 我认识她至少和你认识她的时间一样久了。**2** 🔑 used to add a positive comment about a negative situation（用于对否定情况补充肯定的评论）起码：*She may be slow but at least she's reliable.* 她虽然迟钝，但起码还很可靠。**3** 🔑 even if nothing else is true or you do nothing else 无论如何；反正：*You could at least listen to what he says.* 你至少可以听一听他说些什么。◇ *Well, at least they weren't bored.* 唔，反正他们没有厌烦。**4** 🔑 used to limit or make what you have just said less definite（用以减轻前面所说的话的肯定性）至少 SYN **anyway**: *They seldom complained—officially at least.* 他们很少抱怨，至少不在正式场合这样做。◇ *It works, at least I think it does.* 它行，反正我认为它行。**not 'least** especially 特别；尤其：*The documentary caused a lot of bad feeling, not least among the workers whose lives it described.* 那部纪录片引起了许多人的反感，片中描写到其生活的工人尤其如此。➲ MORE AT LAST[1] *adv.*, LINE *n.*, SAY *v.*

ˌleast ˌcommon de'nominator *noun* (*NAmE*) = LOWEST COMMON DENOMINATOR

ˌleast ˌcommon 'multiple *noun* (*NAmE*) = LOWEST COMMON MULTIPLE

least·ways /ˈliːstweɪz/ *adv.* (*NAmE, informal*) at least 至少；起码：*It isn't cheap to get there, leastways not at this time of year.* 去那里费用可不低，至少在一年中的这个时节是这样。

lea·ther 🔑 /ˈleðə(r)/ *noun* **1** 🔑 [U, C] material made by removing the hair or fur from animal skins and preserving the skins using special processes 皮革：*a leather jacket* 皮夹克 ◇ *The soles are made of leather.* 鞋底是皮革做的。◇ *a leather-bound book* 皮面装帧的书 ➲ VISUAL VOCAB PAGE V66 **2** **leathers** [pl.] clothes made from leather, especially those worn by people riding motorcycles（尤指骑摩托车人穿的）皮衣，皮外套 ➲ SEE ALSO CHAMOIS (2), PATENT LEATHER IDM SEE HELL

lea·ther·back /ˈleðəbæk; *NAmE* -ðərb-/ (*also* **ˌleatherback 'turtle**, **ˌleathery 'turtle**) *noun* a very large sea TURTLE with a shell that looks like leather 棱皮龟；革龟

lea·ther·ette /ˌleðəˈret/ *noun* [U] an artificial material that looks and feels like leather 人造革；人造皮

lea·thery /ˈleðəri/ *adj.* that looks or feels hard and tough like leather 坚韧粗糙的；似皮革的：*leathery skin* 粗糙的皮肤

leave 🔑 /liːv/ *verb, noun*

■ ***verb*** (**left**, **left** /left/)

• **PLACE/PERSON** 地方；人 **1** 🔑 [I, T] to go away from a person or a place 离开（某人或某处）：*Come on, it's time we left.* 快点，我们该走了。◇ **~ for...** *The plane leaves for*

L

Dallas at 12.35. 飞机于 12:35 起飞前往达拉斯。◇ **~ sth** *I hate leaving home.* 我讨厌离开家。◇ *The plane leaves Heathrow at 12.35.* 飞机于 12:35 在希思罗机场起飞。

• **HOME/JOB/SCHOOL** 家；工作；学校 **2** [I, T] to stop living at a place, belonging to a group, working for an employer, etc. 离开居住地点（或群体、工作单位等）：*My secretary has threatened to leave.* 我的秘书以辞职相要挟。◇ **~ sth** (*BrE*) *Some children leave school at 16.* 有些学生 16 岁毕业。

• **WIFE/HUSBAND** 妻子；丈夫 **3** [T] **~ sb** (**for sb**) to leave your wife, husband or partner permanently 遗弃；丢弃：*She's leaving him for another man.* 她要抛弃他去跟另一个男人。

• **STH TO DO LATER** 以后要做的事 **4** [T] to not do sth or deal with sth immediately 不立刻做；不马上处理：**~ sth** *Leave the dishes—I'll do them later.* 盘子先搁着吧，我等会儿再洗。◇ **~ sth until...** *Why do you always leave everything until the last moment?* 你怎么什么事都留到最后一刻才处理？

• **SB/STH IN CONDITION/PLACE** 处于某种状态；在某地方 **5** [T] to make or allow sb/sth to remain in a particular condition, place, etc. 使保留，让…处于（某种状态、某地等）：**~ sb/sth (+ adj.)** *Leave the door open, please.* 请把门开着吧。◇ *The bomb blast left 25 people dead.* 那颗炸弹炸死了 25 个人。◇ **~ sb/sth doing sth** *Don't leave her waiting outside in the rain.* 别让她在外边雨里等着。◇ **~ sb/sth to do sth** *Leave the rice to cook for 20 minutes.* 把大米煮 20 分钟。 **6** [T] to make sth happen or remain as a result 使发生；造成，使留下为（某种结果）：**~ sth** *Red wine leaves a stain.* 红葡萄酒会留下污渍。◇ **~ sb with sth** *She left me with the impression that she was unhappy with her job.* 她给我的印象是她不满意自己的工作。◇ **~ sb sth** *I'm afraid you leave me no choice.* 恐怕你没有给我选择的余地。 **7** **be left** [T] to remain to be used, sold, etc. 留下备用（或销售等）：*Is there any coffee left?* 还有咖啡剩下吗？◇ *How many tickets do you have left?* 你还剩下多少张票？◇ **be left of sth** (*figurative*) *They are fighting to save what is left of their business.* 他们在拼命抢救他们仅余的业务。◇ **be left to sb** *The only course of action left to me was to notify her employer.* 我可以采取的唯一措施就是通知她的雇主。 **8** [T] to go away from a place without taking sth/sb with you 忘了带；丢下：**~ sth/sb (+ adv./prep.)** *I've left my bag on the bus.* 我把包忘在公共汽车上了。◇ **~ sth/sb behind** *Don't leave any of your belongings behind.* 别忘了带上自己的随身物品。◇ *He wasn't well, so we had to leave him behind.* 他身体不适，因此我们只好把他留下。

• **MATHEMATICS** 数学 **9** [T] **~ sth** to have a particular amount remaining 剩余；余下：*Seven from ten leaves three.* * 10 减 7 得 3。

• **AFTER DEATH** 死后 **10** [T] **~ sb** to have family remaining after your death 遗下（家人）：*He leaves a wife and two children.* 他遗下妻子和两个孩子。 **11** [T] to give sth to sb when you die（去世时）遗赠，遗留 **SYN** **bequeath**：**~ sth** (**to sb**) *She left £1 million to her daughter.* 她遗留给女儿 100 万英镑。◇ **~ sb sth** *She left her daughter £1 million.* 她遗留给女儿 100 万英镑。

• **RESPONSIBILITY TO SB** 留给某人的责任 **12** [T] to allow sb to take care of sth 把…留交；交托；委托：**~ sb/sth + adv./prep.** *You can leave the cooking to me.* 你可以把做饭的事交给我。◇ *She left her assistant in charge.* 她委托助手来负责。◇ ***Leave it with me****—I'm sure I can sort it out.* 把这事交给我吧，我一定会解决的。◇ *'Where shall we eat?' 'I'll leave it entirely (up) to you* (= you can decide).' "我们上哪儿吃去？""我全交给你来决定好了。" ◇ *They left me with all the clearing up.* 他们把什么都留给我来收拾。◇ **~ sb/sth to do sth** *I was left to cope on my own.* 就剩下我一个人来单独对付。

• **DELIVER** 递送 **13** [T] to deliver sth and then go away 递送；递交；投递：**~ sth** (**for sb**) *Someone left this note for you.* 有人给你送来了这张便条。◇ **~ sb sth** *Someone left you this note.* 有人给你送来了这张便条。 ➲ MORE LIKE THIS 33, page R28

IDM HELP Most idioms containing **leave** are at the entries for the nouns and adjectives in the idioms, for example **leave sb in the lurch** is at **lurch**. 大多数含 leave 的习语，都可在该等习语中的名词及形容词相关词条找到，如 leave sb in the lurch 在词条 lurch 下。 **ˌleave ˈgo** (**of sth**) (*BrE, informal*) to stop holding on to sth 松手；撒手；放开 **SYN** **let go**: *Leave go of my arm—you're hurting me!* 放开我的手臂，你弄痛我了！ **leave it at ˈthat** (*informal*) to say or do nothing more about sth 别再说了；到此为止；就这样算了：*We'll never agree, so let's just leave it at that.* 咱们不可能意见一致，所以这事就这样吧。 **ˌleave it ˈout** (*BrE, informal*) used to tell sb to stop doing sth（让人停止做某事）行啦，就这样吧 ➲ MORE AT TAKE *v.*

PHR V **ˌleave sth↔aˈside** to not consider sth 不予考虑；搁置一边：*Leaving the expense aside, do we actually need a second car?* 且不说费用多少，我们真的还需要一辆汽车吗？ **ˌleave sb/sth beˈhind 1** [usually passive] to make much better progress than sb 比…取得好得多的进展；把…抛在后面；超过：*Britain is being left behind in the race for new markets.* 英国在开拓新市场方面正被甩在后面。 **2** to leave a person, place or state permanently 永久离开（某人或某地）；永久脱离（某状态）：*She knew that she had left childhood behind.* 她知道童年已一去不复返了。 ➲ SEE ALSO LEAVE *v.* (8) **ˌleave ˈoff** (*informal*) to stop doing sth 停止（做某事）；中断：*Start reading from where you left off last time.* 从上次停下来的地方接着读吧。◇ **leave off doing sth** *He left off playing the piano to answer the door.* 他停止弹钢琴，应门去了。 **ˌleave sb/sth↔ˈoff** (**sth**) to not include sb/sth on a list, etc. 不把…列入；不包括；不含：*You've left off a zero.* 你漏掉了一个零。◇ *We left him off the list.* 我们未把他列入名单。 **ˌleave sb/sth ˈout** (**of sth**) to not include or mention sb/sth in sth 不包括；不提及：*Leave me out of this quarrel, please.* 请别把我牵扯进这场争吵。◇ *He hadn't been asked to the party and was feeling very left out.* 他未被邀请参加聚会，感到颇受冷落。◇ *She left out an 'm' in 'accommodation'.* 她在 accommodation 一词中漏掉了一个字母 m。 **be ˌleft ˈover** (**from sth**) to remain when all that is needed has been used 剩下；残留：*There was lots of food left over.* 饭菜剩下了不少。 ➲ RELATED NOUN LEFTOVER

■ ***noun*** [U] **1** a period of time when you are allowed to be away from work for a holiday/vacation or for a special reason 假期；休假：*to take a month's **paid/unpaid leave*** 带薪 / 不带薪休假一个月 ◇ *soldiers home **on leave*** 回家休假的士兵 ◇ *to be on **maternity/study leave*** 休产假；脱产进修 ◇ *How much **annual leave** do you get?* 你们的年假有多长？ ➲ SEE ALSO COMPASSIONATE LEAVE, SICK LEAVE **2** (*formal*) official permission to do sth 准许；许可：*to be absent **without leave*** 未经许可擅自离开 ◇ **~ to do sth** *The court granted him leave to appeal against the sentence.* 法庭准许他对判决提出上诉。◇ *She asked for **leave of absence*** (= permission to be away from work) *to attend a funeral.* 她请了假去参加葬礼。

IDM **ˌby/ˌwith your ˈleave** (*formal*) with your permission 如蒙您允许的话；承蒙俯允 **take ˌleave of your ˈsenses** (*old-fashioned*) to start behaving as if you are crazy 丧失理智；发疯 **take** (**your**) **ˈleave** (**of sb**) (*formal*) to say goodbye 告辞；辞别：*With a nod and a smile, she took leave of her friends.* 她点头微笑着向朋友告辞。 **without a ˌby your ˈleave; without so much as a ˌby your ˈleave** (*old-fashioned*) without asking permission; rudely 擅自；未经许可；粗鲁地；无礼地 ➲ MORE AT BEG, FRENCH *adj.*

-leaved /liːvd/ ➲ LEAF *n.* (2)

leaven /ˈlevn/ *noun, verb*

■ ***noun*** [U] a substance, especially YEAST, that is added to bread before it is cooked to make it rise 发酵剂；（尤指）酵母，面肥：(*figurative*) *A few jokes add leaven to a boring speech.* 几句笑话可给枯燥无味的演讲增添活跃的气氛。

■ ***verb*** [often passive] **~ sth** (**with sth**) (*formal*) to make sth more interesting or cheerful by adding sth to it（添加…）使较有趣，使更令人愉快：*Her speech was leavened with a touch of humour.* 几分幽默使她的讲话更为有趣。

leav·er /ˈliːvə(r)/ *noun* (often in compounds 常构成复合词) a person who is leaving a place 离去者：*school-leavers* 中学毕业生

leaves PL. OF LEAF

ˈleave-taking *noun* [U, C, usually sing.] (*formal*) the act of saying goodbye 告别；告辞 **SYN** **farewell**

leav·ings /ˈliːvɪŋz/ *noun* [pl.] something that you leave because you do not want it, especially food（不要的）剩余物（尤指剩余饭菜）

lech /letʃ/ *noun, verb* (*BrE, informal, disapproving*)
■ ***noun*** a man who shows an unpleasant sexual interest in sb 好色之徒；色鬼
■ ***verb***
PHR V **ˈlech after sb** to show an unpleasant sexual interest in sb 对某人生邪念；对某人起色心

lech·er /ˈletʃə(r)/ *noun* (*disapproving*) a man who is always thinking about sex and looking for sexual pleasure 好色之徒；色鬼；淫棍 ▶ **lech·ery** *noun* [U]

lech·er·ous /ˈletʃərəs/ *adj.* (*disapproving*) having too much interest in sexual pleasure 好色的；淫荡的 **SYN** **lustful, lascivious**

leci·thin /ˈlesɪθɪn/ *noun* [U] a natural substance found in animals, plants and in egg YOLKS. Lecithin is used as an ingredient in some foods. 卵磷脂，磷脂酰胆碱（用作食物添加剂）

lec·tern /ˈlektən; *NAmE* -tərn/ (*NAmE also* **po·dium**) *noun* a stand for holding a book, notes, etc. when you are reading in church, giving a talk, etc.（教堂中的）诵经台；（演讲的）讲台

lec·tor /ˈlektɔː(r)/ *noun* a person who teaches in a university, especially sb who teaches their own language in a foreign country（尤指在国外教授其母语的）大学讲师，大学教师 ➲ COMPARE LECTRICE

lec·trice /lekˈtriːs; *NAmE* ˈlektrɪs/ *noun* a female LECTOR in a university（尤指在国外教授其母语的）大学女讲师，大学女教师

lec·ture 🔑 **AW** /ˈlektʃə(r)/ *noun, verb*
■ ***noun*** ~ (**to sb**) (**on/about sth**) **1** 🔑 a talk that is given to a group of people to teach them about a particular subject, often as part of a university or college course（通常指大学里的）讲座，讲课，演讲：*to* ***deliver/give a lecture*** *to first-year students* 给一年级学生讲课 ◇ *to attend* ***a series of lectures*** *on Jane Austen* 听关于简·奥斯汀的系列讲座 ◇ ***a lecture room/hall*** 演讲室；演讲厅 ➲ **SYNONYMS** AT SPEECH ➲ **WORDFINDER NOTE** AT UNIVERSITY ➲ **COLLOCATIONS** AT EDUCATION **2** a long angry talk that sb gives to one person or a group of people because they have done sth wrong（冗长的）教训，训斥，谴责：*I know I should stop smoking—don't give me a lecture about it.* 我知道我该戒烟，别再教训我了。
■ ***verb*** **1** [I] ~ (**in/on sth**) to give a talk or a series of talks to a group of people on a subject, especially as a way of teaching in a university or college（尤指在大学里）开讲座，讲授，讲课：*She lectures in Russian literature.* 她讲授俄罗斯文学。 **2** [T] ~ **sb** (**about/on sth**) | ~ **sb** (**about doing sth**) to criticize sb or tell them how you think they should behave, especially when it is done in an annoying way（尤指恼人地）指责，训斥，告诫：*He's always lecturing me about the way I dress.* 他对我的衣着总是指手画脚的。

lec·tur·er **AW** /ˈlektʃərə(r)/ *noun* **1** a person who gives a lecture 讲课者；讲授者；讲演者：*She's a superb lecturer.* 她是一个出色的演讲者。 **2** (especially in Britain) a person who teaches at a university or college（尤指英国大学的）讲师：*He's a lecturer in French at Oxford.* 他是牛津大学的法语讲师。

lec·ture·ship /ˈlektʃəʃɪp; *NAmE* -tʃərʃ-/ *noun* the position of lecturer at a British university or college（英国大学的）讲师职位：*a lectureship in media studies* 大众传播学讲师职位

ˈlecture theatre (*BrE*) (*NAmE* **ˈlecture theater**) *noun* a large room with rows of seats on a slope, where lectures are given 阶梯教室

LED /ˌel iː ˈdiː/ *noun* light emitting diode (a device that produces a light on electrical and electronic equipment) 发光二极管：*A single red LED shows that the power is switched on.* 单支红色发光二极管表示电源已接通。

led /led/ **1** PAST TENSE, PAST PART. OF LEAD[1] **2 -led** (in adjectives 构成形容词) influenced or organized by 起主导作用的：*a consumer-led society* 以消费者主导的社会 ◇ *student-led activities* 学生领导的活动

ledge /ledʒ/ *noun* **1** a narrow flat piece of rock that sticks out from a CLIFF 悬崖岩石突出部；岩架：*seabirds nesting on rocky ledges* 在岩架上筑巢的海鸟 **2** a narrow flat shelf fixed to a wall, especially one below a window（平窄的）壁架，横档；（尤指）窗台：*She put the vase of flowers on the window ledge.* 她把那瓶花放在窗台上。 ➲ SEE ALSO SILL

ledger /ˈledʒə(r)/ *noun* a book in which a bank, a business, etc. records the money it has paid and received 收支总账；分类账簿；分户账簿：*to enter figures in the* ***purchase/sales ledger*** 把金额录入购货 / 销售分类账

lee /liː/ *noun* **1** [sing.] the side or part of sth that provides shelter from the wind 背风处；避风处 ➲ COMPARE LEEWARD *n.*, WINDWARD *n.* **2 lees** [pl.] the substance that is left at the bottom of a bottle of wine, a container of beer, etc.（酒瓶等容器中的）沉淀物，残渣 **SYN** **dregs**

leech /liːtʃ/ *noun* **1** a small WORM that usually lives in water and that attaches itself to other creatures and sucks their blood. Leeches were used in the past by doctors to remove blood from sick people. 水蛭；蚂蟥 **2** (*disapproving*) a person who depends on sb else for money, or takes the profit from sb else's work 依赖他人钱财者；攫取他人收益者；寄生虫

leek /liːk/ *noun* a vegetable like a long onion with many layers of wide flat leaves that are white at the bottom and green at the top. Leeks are eaten cooked. The leek is a national symbol of Wales. 韭葱（威尔士民族的象征） ➲ **VISUAL VOCAB PAGE V33**

leer /lɪə(r); *NAmE* lɪr/ *verb, noun*
■ ***verb*** [I] ~ (**at sb**) to look or smile at sb in an unpleasant way that shows an evil or sexual interest in them 邪恶地（或色迷迷地）看；奸笑；淫笑 ➲ **WORDFINDER NOTE** AT EXPRESSION
■ ***noun*** an unpleasant look or smile that shows sb is interested in a person in an evil or sexual way 邪恶的（或色迷迷的）目光；奸笑；淫笑：*He looked at her with an evil leer.* 他用不怀好意的目光看着她。

leery /ˈlɪəri; *NAmE* ˈlɪri/ *adj.* (*informal*) ~ (**of sth/sb**) | ~ (**of doing sth**) suspicious or careful about sth/sb, and trying to avoid doing it or dealing with them 猜疑的；谨防的；极力躲避的 **SYN** **wary**：*The government is leery of changing the current law.* 政府对是否修改现行法律存有疑虑。

leet /liːt/ (*also* **leetspeak** /ˈliːtspiːk/) *noun* [U] an informal language or a code used on the Internet, often in online GAMING, in which some letters are replaced by numbers, special symbols, etc. 火星文，黑客文（在互联网上使用的一种非正式语言或代码，常用于线上游戏，用数字、特殊符号等代替某些字母）

lee·ward /ˈliːwəd; ˈluːəd; *NAmE* -wərd; -ərd/ *adj., noun*
■ ***adj.*** on the side of sth that is sheltered from the wind 在背风面的；背风的；下风的：*a harbour on the leeward side of the island* 位于岛的背风面的海港 ▶ **lee·ward** *adv.* ➲ COMPARE WINDWARD *adj.*
■ ***noun*** [U] the side or direction that is sheltered from the wind 背风面；下风 ➲ COMPARE WINDWARD *n.*

lee·way /ˈliːweɪ/ *noun* [U] the amount of freedom that you have to change sth or to do sth in the way you want to 自由活动的空间 **SYN** **latitude**：*How much leeway should parents give their children?* 父母应该给孩子多少自由的空间？
IDM **make up ˈleeway** (*BrE*) to get out of a bad position that you are in, especially because you have lost a lot of time 摆脱逆境；（尤指）弥补损失的时间

left 🔑 /left/ *adj., adv., noun* ➲ SEE ALSO LEAVE *v.*
■ ***adj.*** 🔑 [only before noun] on the side of your body which is

towards the west when you are facing north 左边的：*Fewer people write with their left hand than with their right.* 用左手写字的人比用右手的人少。◇ *I broke my left leg.* 我的左腿骨折了。◇ *the left side of the field* 田地的左边 ◇ *The university is on the left bank of the river.* 大学在河的左岸。◇ *Take a left turn at the intersection.* 在十字路口向左转。◇ (*sport* 体育) *a left back/wing* 左后卫；左边锋 ◇ *a left hook* 左钩拳 **OPP right**

IDM **have two left 'feet** (*informal*) to be very awkward in your movements, especially when you are dancing or playing a sport（尤指跳舞或体育运动时）非常笨拙，笨手笨脚

■ ***adv.*** on or to the left side 朝左边；向左侧：*Turn left at the intersection.* 在十字路口向左拐。◇ *Look left and right before you cross the road.* 左右看一看，然后再过马路。

IDM **ˌleft, right and 'centre** (*also* **ˌright, left and 'centre**) (*informal*) in all directions; everywhere 四面八方；到处；处处：*He's giving away money left, right and centre.* 他到处赠款。➲ MORE AT RIGHT *adv.*

■ ***noun*** **1** **the/sb's left** [sing.] the left side or direction 左边；左方；左：*She was sitting* ***on my left.*** 她坐在我的左边。◇ *Twist your body to the left, then to the right.* 向左转体，然后向右转体。◇ *Take the next road* ***on the left.*** 在下一个路口向左拐。◇ ***To the left of*** *the library is the bank.* 图书馆的左边是银行。 **2** [sing.] **the first, second, etc. left** the first, second, etc. road on the left side 左边的第一（或第二等）条路：*Take the first left.* 在下一个路口向左转。 **3** **a left** [sing.] a turn to the left 左转弯：(*BrE*) *to* ***take a left*** 往左拐 ◇ (*NAmE*) *to* ***hang/make a left*** 向左拐弯 **4** **the left, the Left** [sing.+sing./pl. v.] political groups who support the ideas and beliefs of SOCIALISM（拥护社会主义思想和信念的）左派政治团体，左派：*The Left only has/have a small chance of winning power.* 左派取得政权的机会渺茫。◇ *a left-leaning newspaper* 思想左倾的报纸 **5** **the left** [sing.+sing./pl. v.] the part of a political party whose members are most in favour of social change（政党内的）激进派，激进分子：*She is on the far left of the party.* 她是这个党的极左分子。 **6** [C] (in boxing 拳击运动) a blow that is made with your left hand 左手拳：*He hit him with two sharp lefts.* 他给了他两记猛烈的左手拳。**OPP right**

ˌleft 'brain *noun* [U, sing.] the left side of the human brain, that is thought to be used for analysing and for processing language 左脑 ➲ COMPARE RIGHT BRAIN

ˌleft 'field *noun* [sing.] **1** (in BASEBALL 棒球) the left part of the field, or the position played by the person who is there 左外场；左场手位置 **2** (*informal*) an opinion or a position that is strange or unusual and a long way from the normal position 离奇古怪的看法（或意见）；怪诞的态度（或立场）：*The governor is* ***way out/over in left field.*** 州长的看法怪得出了格。

'left-field *adj.* (*informal*) not following what is usually done; different, surprising and interesting 出乎意料的；怪诞有趣的：*a left-field comedy drama* 怪诞喜剧

'left-hand *adj.* [only before noun] **1** on the left side of sth 左手的；左边的；左面的：*the left-hand side of the street* 街的左侧 ◇ *the top left-hand corner of the page* 页面左上角 **2** connected with a person's left hand 左手的：*a tennis player with a left-hand grip* 左手握拍的网球运动员 ◇ *a left-hand glove* 左手用的手套 **OPP right-hand**

ˌleft-hand 'drive *adj.* (of a vehicle 车辆) with the STEERING WHEEL on the left side 左舵的 **OPP right-hand drive**

ˌleft-'handed *adj.* **1** (of a person 人) finding it easier to use the left hand to write, hit a ball, etc. than the right 惯用左手的；左撇子的：*a left-handed golfer* 左手握杆的高尔夫球手 ◇ *I'm left-handed.* 我是左撇子。 **2** (of tools, etc. 工具等) designed to be used by sb who finds it easier to use their left hand 供惯用左手者使用的：*left-handed scissors* 左手用的剪刀 **3** (of actions, etc. 动作等) done with your left hand 用左手做的：*a left-handed serve* 用左手发球 **OPP right-handed** ▶ **ˌleft-'handed** *adv.*：*She writes left-handed.* 她用左手写字。 **ˌleft-'handed·ness** *noun* [U]

IDM **ˌleft-handed 'compliment** (*NAmE*) = A BACKHANDED COMPLIMENT

ˌleft-'hander *noun* a person who finds it easier to use their left hand to write, etc. with than their right 惯用左手的人；左撇子 **OPP right-hander**

leftie = LEFTY

left·ist /ˈleftɪst/ *noun* a person who supports LEFT-WING political parties and their ideas 左派人士；左翼分子 **OPP rightist** ▶ **left·ism** *noun* [U] **left·ist** *adj.*：*leftist groups* 左派团体

ˌleft-'luggage office (*also* **left 'luggage**) *noun* (*both BrE*) a place where you can pay to leave bags or suitcases for a short time, for example at a station（火车站等的）行李寄存处

left·most /ˈleftməʊst; *NAmE* -moʊst/ *adj.* [only before noun] furthest to the left 最左边的；最左面的；最左的

ˌleft-of-'centre *adj.* = CENTRE-LEFT

left·over /ˈleftəʊvə(r); *NAmE* -oʊv-/ *noun* **1** [usually pl.] food that has not been eaten at the end of a meal 吃剩的食物；残羹剩饭 **2** an object, a custom or a way of behaving that remains from an earlier time 遗留物；残存物；遗留下来的风俗习惯 **SYN relic**：*He's a leftover from the hippies in the 1960s.* 他是 20 世纪 60 年代嬉皮士的残余分子。▶ **left·over** *adj.* [only before noun] **SYN surplus**：*Use any leftover meat to make a curry.* 要是有剩肉就做咖喱菜。

left·ward /ˈleftwəd; *NAmE* -wərd/ (*BrE also* **left·wards**) *adj.* [only before noun] **1** towards the left 向左的；向左侧的：*to move your eyes in a leftward direction* 目光向左移动 **2** towards more LEFT-WING political ideas（政治上）左倾的：*a leftward swing in public opinion* 舆论向左转变 **OPP rightward** ▶ **left·ward** (*BrE also* **left·wards**) *adv.*

ˌleft 'wing *noun* **1** [sing.+sing./pl. v.] the part of a political party whose members are most in favour of social change（政党中的）左翼，左派：*on the left wing of the party* 属于这个政党的左翼 **2** [C, U] an attacking player or position on the left side of the field in a sports game（体育比赛的）左边锋，左翼

ˌleft-'wing *adj.* strongly supporting the ideas of SOCIALISM 左翼的；左派的：*left-wing groups* 左翼团体

ˌleft-'winger *noun* **1** a person on the LEFT WING of a political party 左翼人士；左派成员：*a Labour left-winger* 工党的左翼成员 **2** a person who plays on the left side of the field in a sports game（体育比赛的）左边锋，左翼 **OPP right-winger**

lefty (*also* **leftie**) /ˈlefti/ *noun* (*pl.* **-ies**) (*informal*) **1** (*disapproving, especially BrE*) a person who has SOCIALIST views 左派分子 **2** (*especially NAmE*) a person who uses their left hand to write, hit a ball, etc. 左撇子 ▶ **lefty** *adj.*：*a lefty feminist lecturer* 激进的女权主义演讲者

leg /leg/ *noun, verb*

■ ***noun***

• **PART OF BODY** 身体部位 **1** [C] one of the long parts that connect the feet to the rest of the body 腿：*I broke my leg playing football.* 我的腿踢足球时骨折了。◇ *How many legs does a centipede have?* 蜈蚣有多少条腿？◇ ***front/back legs*** 前腿；后腿 ◇ ***forelegs/hind legs*** 前腿；后腿 ◇ *a wooden leg* 木假腿 ➲ COLLOCATIONS AT PHYSICAL ➲ VISUAL VOCAB PAGE V64 ➲ SEE ALSO BOW LEGS, DADDY-LONG-LEGS, INSIDE LEG, LEGGY, LEGROOM, PEG LEG, SEA LEGS

• **MEAT** 食用肉 **2** [C, U] the leg of an animal, especially the top part, cooked and eaten（尤指供食用的）动物的腿，腿肉：*frogs' legs* 青蛙腿 ◇ *chicken legs* 鸡腿 ◇ *~ of sth roast leg of lamb* 烤羊腿

• **OF TROUSERS/PANTS** 裤子 **3** [C] the part of a pair of trousers/pants that covers the leg 裤腿：*a trouser/pant leg* 一只裤腿 ◇ *These jeans are too long* ***in the leg.*** 这条牛仔裤的裤腿太长。

• **OF TABLE/CHAIR** 桌椅 **4** [C] one of the long thin parts on the bottom of a table, chair, etc. that support it（桌椅等的）腿：*a chair leg* 椅子腿

• **-LEGGED** 有…腿 **5** /ˈlegɪd; legd/ (in adjectives 构成形容词) having the number or type of legs mentioned 有…腿的：

a three-legged stool 三条腿的凳子 ◇ *a long-legged insect* 长腿昆虫 **HELP** When **-legged** is used with numbers, it is nearly always pronounced /'legɪd/; in other adjectives it can be pronounced /'legɪd/ or /legd/. * -legged 与数字连用几乎总是读作 /'legɪd/；构成其他形容词时可读作 /'legɪd/ 或 /legd/。 ➲ SEE ALSO CROSS-LEGGED

• **OF JOURNEY/RACE** 行程；赛跑 **6** [C] ~ (**of sth**) one part of a journey or race 一段路程（或赛程） **SYN** **section, stage**

• **SPORTS GAME** 体育比赛 **7** [C] (*BrE*) one of a pair of matches played between the same opponents in a sports competition, which together form a single ROUND (= stage) of the competition（相同对手间同一回合两场比赛中的）一场

IDM **break a 'leg!** (*informal*) used to wish sb good luck（表示良好祝愿）祝你好运！ **get your 'leg over** (*BrE, informal*) to have sex 性交 **have 'legs** (*informal*) if you say that a news story, etc. **has legs**, you mean that people will continue to be interested in it for a long time（新闻报道等）会长期受到关注 **not have a ˌleg to 'stand on** (*informal*) to be in a position where you are unable to prove sth or explain why sth is reasonable 无法证实；无法解释（理由）；站不住脚： *Without written evidence, we don't have a leg to stand on.* 我们没有书面证据就站不住脚。 ➲ MORE AT ARM *n.*, FAST *adv.*, LAST[1] *det.*, PULL *v.*, SHAKE *v.*, STRETCH *v.*, TAIL *n.*, TALK *v.* ➲ SEE ALSO LEG-UP

■ ***verb*** (**-gg-**)

IDM **'leg it** (*informal, especially BrE*) to run, especially in order to escape from sb 跑；（尤指）逃跑： *We saw the police coming and legged it down the road.* 我们看见警察来了就顺着马路逃跑了。

leg·acy /'legəsi/ *noun, adj.*

■ ***noun*** (*pl.* **-ies**) **1** money or property that is given to you by sb when they die 遗产；遗赠财物 **SYN** **inheritance**: *They each received a legacy of $5 000.* 他们每人得到了 5 000 美元的遗产。 **2** a situation that exists now because of events, actions, etc. that took place in the past 遗留问题；后遗症： *Future generations will be left with a legacy of pollution and destruction.* 留给子孙后代的将是环境的污染与破坏。

■ ***adj.*** [only before noun] used to describe a computer system or product that is no longer available to buy but is still used because it would be too difficult or expensive to replace it（计算机系统或产品）已停产的，老化的，老式的： *How can we integrate new technology with our legacy systems?* 我们该如何将新技术整合到我们老化的系统上？ ◇ *legacy hardware/software* 老式硬件 / 软件

legal 🔑 **AW** /'liːɡl/ *adj.* **1** 🔑 [only before noun] connected with the law 与法律有关的；法律的： *the **legal profession/system*** 法律行业 / 体系 ◇ *to take/seek **legal advice*** 听取 / 寻求法律咨询 ◇ *a legal adviser* 法律顾问 ◇ *legal costs* 律师费用 **2** 🔑 allowed or required by law 法律允许的；合法的；法律要求的： *The driver was more than three times over the **legal limit*** (= the amount of alcohol you are allowed to have in your body when you are driving). 那名司机体内的酒精含量是法律允许限度的三倍多。 ◇ *Should euthanasia be made legal?* 安乐死是否应定为合法？ **OPP** **illegal** ➲ WORDFINDER NOTE AT LAW ▸ **le·gal·ly** 🔑 **AW** /'liːɡəli/ *adv.* : *a **legally binding** agreement* 具有法律约束力的协议 ◇ *to be **legally responsible** for sb/sth* 对某人 / 某事负有法律责任

ˌlegal 'action *noun* [U] (*also* **ˌlegal pro'ceedings**) the act of using the legal system to settle a disagreement, etc. 法律诉讼： *to **take/begin legal action** against sb* 起诉某人 ◇ *They have threatened us with legal action.* 他们用起诉来要挟我们。

ˌlegal 'aid *noun* [U] money that is given by the government or another organization to sb who needs help to pay for legal advice or a lawyer 法律援助（政府或某机构向需要帮助的人提供费用，使其能够寻求法律咨询或聘请律师）

ˌlegal 'eagle (*also* **ˌlegal 'beagle**) *noun* (*humorous*) a lawyer, especially one who is very clever（尤指精明的）律师

le·gal·ese /ˌliːɡə'liːz/ *noun* [U] (*informal*) the sort of language used in legal documents that is difficult to understand（深奥难懂的）法律术语，法律用语

ˌlegal 'high *noun* a substance that people smoke, INJECT (1), etc. for the physical and mental effects it has, and that is not banned by the law 合法兴奋剂

ˌlegal 'holiday *noun* (in the US) a public holiday that is fixed by law（美国）法定假日 ➲ COMPARE BANK HOLIDAY

le·gal·is·tic /ˌliːɡə'lɪstɪk/ *adj.* (*disapproving*) obeying the law too strictly 墨守法规的；条文主义的；死抠法律条文的： *a legalistic approach to family disputes* 死抠法律条文解决家庭纠纷的方法

le·gal·ity **AW** /liː'ɡæləti/ *noun* (*pl.* **-ies**) **1** [U] the fact of being legal 合法（性）： *They intended to challenge the legality of his claim in the courts.* 他们打算在法庭上对他索赔的合法性提出质疑。 ◇ *The arrangement is of doubtful legality.* 这项约定是否合法值得怀疑。 ◇ *The government does not recognize the legality of this court.* 政府不承认这个法庭的合法性。 **2** [C, usually pl.] the legal aspect of an action or a situation（某行为或情况的）法律方面： *You need a lawyer to explain all the legalities of the contracts.* 你需要律师来解释这些合同在法律上的各项细节。 ➲ COMPARE ILLEGALITY

le·gal·ize (*BrE also* **-ise**) /'liːɡəlaɪz/ *verb* ~ **sth** to make sth legal 使合法化；使得到法律认可 ▸ **le·gal·iza·tion, -isa·tion** *noun* [U]

'legal pad *noun* (*NAmE*) a number of sheets of paper with lines on them, fastened together at one end 信笺簿；横线簿

ˌlegal pro'ceedings *noun* [pl.] = LEGAL ACTION

'legal-size (*also* **legal**) *adj.* (*NAmE*) (of paper 纸张) 8½ inches (215.9 mm) wide and 14 inches (355.6 mm) long 法律文件尺寸的（宽 8½ 英寸或 215.9 毫米，长 14 英寸或 355.6 毫米）

ˌlegal 'tender *noun* [U] money that can be legally used to pay for things in a particular country 法定货币

leg·ate /'leɡət/ *noun* the official representative of the Pope in a foreign country 教廷使节： *a papal legate* 教廷使节

lega·tee /ˌleɡə'tiː/ *noun* (*law* 律) a person who receives money or property (= a LEGACY) when sb dies 遗产继承人；受遗赠人

le·ga·tion /lɪ'ɡeɪʃn/ *noun* **1** a group of DIPLOMATS representing their government in a foreign country in an office that is below the rank of an EMBASSY 公使馆全体人员 **2** the building where these people work 公使馆

legato /lɪ'ɡɑːtəʊ; *NAmE* -toʊ/ *adj.* (*music* 音, *from Italian*) to be played or sung in a smooth, even manner 连音的 ▸ **le·gato** *adv.* **OPP** **staccato**

le·gend /'ledʒənd/ *noun* **1** [C, U] a story from ancient times about people and events, that may or may not be true; this type of story 传说；传奇故事 **SYN** **myth**: *the legend of Robin Hood* 罗宾汉的传奇故事 ◇ *the heroes of Greek legend* 希腊传说中的英雄 ◇ ***Legend has it*** *that the lake was formed by the tears of a god.* 据传说这个湖是一位神仙的眼泪积聚而成的。 ➲ COMPARE URBAN MYTH **2** [C] a very famous person, especially in a particular field, who is admired by other people（尤指某领域中的）传奇人物： *a **jazz/tennis, etc. legend*** 爵士乐、网球等的传奇人物 ◇ *She **was a legend in her own lifetime**.* 她在世的时候就是一个传奇人物。 ◇ *Many of golf's **living legends** were playing.* 当时有许多当世高尔夫球传奇选手在打球。 **3** [C] (*specialist*) the explanation of a map or a diagram in a book（地图或书中图表的）图例，说明，解释 **SYN** **key** **4** [C] (*formal*) a piece of writing on a sign, a label, a coin, etc.（标志、徽记、硬币等物品上的）刻印文字，铭文

le·gend·ary /'ledʒəndri; *NAmE* -deri/ *adj.* **1** very famous and talked about a lot by people, especially in a way that shows admiration 非常著名的；享有盛名的： *a legendary figure* 大名鼎鼎的人物 ◇ *the legendary Bob Dylan* 名扬四海的鲍勃•迪伦 ◇ *Her patience and tact are legendary.* 她

的耐心与老练是出了名的。 **2** [only before noun] mentioned in stories from ancient times 传奇的；传说的：*legendary heroes* 传奇故事中的英雄 ➲ COMPARE FABLED

le·ger·de·main /ˌledʒədəˈmeɪn; *NAmE* -dʒərd-/ *noun* [U] (*from French, formal*) = SLEIGHT OF HAND (1)

leg·gings /ˈlegɪŋz/ *noun* [pl.] **1** trousers/pants for women that fit tightly over the legs, made of cloth that stretches easily 女式紧身裤：*a pair of leggings* 一条女式紧身裤 **2** outer coverings for the legs, worn as protection 护腿；绑腿；裹腿

leggy /ˈlegi/ *adj.* (*informal*) (especially of girls and women 尤指女孩或妇女) having long legs 腿长的：*a tall leggy schoolgirl* 个高腿长的女学生

le·gible /ˈledʒəbl/ *adj.* (of written or printed words 手写或印刷文字) clear enough to read 清晰可读的；清楚的：*legible handwriting* 清楚易读的笔迹 ◇ *The signature was still legible.* 签名仍清晰可辨。 **OPP illegible** ▸ **le·gi·bil·ity** /ˌledʒəˈbɪləti/ *noun* [U] **le·gibly** /-əbli/ *adv.*

le·gion /ˈliːdʒən/ *noun, adj.*

■ ***noun*** **1** a large group of soldiers that forms part of an army, especially the one that existed in ancient Rome （尤指古罗马的）军团：*the French Foreign Legion* 法国外籍军团 ◇ *Caesar's legions* 恺撒军团 **2** (*formal*) a large number of people of one particular type 大量，大批（某类型的人）：*legions of photographers* 众多的摄影师

■ ***adj.*** [not before noun] (*formal*) very many 很多；极多 **SYN numerous**：*The medical uses of herbs are legion.* 草本植物的医药效用数不胜数。

le·gion·ary /ˈliːdʒənəri; *NAmE* -neri/ *noun* (*pl.* **-ies**) a soldier who is part of a legion 军团士兵 ▸ **le·gion·ary** *adj.* [only before noun]

le·gion·naire /ˌliːdʒəˈneə(r); *NAmE* -ˈner/ *noun* a member of a LEGION, especially the French Foreign Legion 军团成员；（尤指法国军队中的）外籍军团成员

ˌlegionˈnaires' disease *noun* [U] a serious lung disease caused by bacteria, especially spread by AIR CONDITIONING and similar systems 军团病（由细菌引起的严重肺部疾病，尤通过空调及类似系统传播）

le·gis·late **AW** /ˈledʒɪsleɪt/ *verb* [I] **~ (for/against/on sth)** (*formal*) to make a law affecting sth 制定法律；立法：*The government will legislate against discrimination in the workplace.* 政府将制定法规，在工作场所禁止歧视。 ◇ (*figurative*) *You can't legislate against bad luck!* 坏运气总是难免的！ ◇ *They promised to legislate to protect people's right to privacy.* 他们承诺立法保护公民的隐私权。

le·gis·la·tion **AW** /ˌledʒɪsˈleɪʃn/ *noun* [U] **1** a law or a set of laws passed by a parliament 法规；法律：*an important **piece of legislation*** 一条重要的法规 ◇ *New legislation on the sale of drugs will be introduced next year.* 有关药品销售的新法规将于明年实施。 ➲ COLLOCATIONS AT POLITICS **2** the process of making and passing laws 立法；制定法律：*Legislation will be difficult and will take time.* 立法既费力又耗时。 ➲ WORDFINDER NOTE AT PARLIAMENT

le·gis·la·tive **AW** /ˈledʒɪslətɪv; *NAmE* -leɪtɪv/ *adj.* [only before noun] (*formal*) connected with the act of making and passing laws 立法的；制定法律的：***a legislative assembly/body/council*** 立法议会 / 机构 / 委员会 ◇ *legislative powers* 立法权

le·gis·la·tor **AW** /ˈledʒɪsleɪtə(r)/ *noun* (*formal*) a member of a group of people that has the power to make laws 立法委员

le·gis·la·ture **AW** /ˈledʒɪsleɪtʃə(r)/ *noun* (*formal*) a group of people who have the power to make and change laws 立法机关：*a democratically elected legislature* 民主选举产生的立法机关 ◇ *the **national/state legislature*** 国家 / 州立法机构 ➲ COMPARE EXECUTIVE *n.* (3), JUDICIARY

legit /lɪˈdʒɪt/ *adj.* (*informal*) legal, or acting according to the law or the rules 合法的；守法的；按法律（或法规）行事的：*The business seems legit.* 这笔生意看起来是合法的。

le·git·im·ate /lɪˈdʒɪtɪmət/ *adj.* **1** for which there is a fair and acceptable reason 正当合理的；合情合理的 **SYN valid, justifiable**：*a legitimate grievance* 合乎情理的抱怨 ◇ *It seemed a **perfectly legitimate** question.* 这似乎是完全合乎情理的问题。 ◇ *Politicians are legitimate targets for satire.* 政客理所当然成为讽刺的对象。 **2** allowed and acceptable according to the law 合法的；法律认可的；法定的 **SYN legal**：*the legitimate government of the country* 这个国家的合法政府 ◇ *Is his business strictly legitimate?* 他的生意是否绝对合法？ **OPP illegitimate** **3** (of a child 小孩) born when its parents are legally married to each other 合法婚姻所生的 **OPP illegitimate** ▸ **le·git·im·acy** /lɪˈdʒɪtɪməsi/ *noun* [U]：*the dubious legitimacy of her argument* 她的论点不一定站得住脚 ◇ *I intend to challenge the legitimacy of his claim.* 我打算对他的声明是否正确提出质疑。 **le·git·im·ate·ly** *adv.*：*She can now legitimately claim to be the best in the world.* 现在她可以理所当然地声称自己是世界上最优秀的。

le·git·im·ize (*BrE also* **-ise**) /lɪˈdʒɪtəmaɪz/ *verb* (*formal*) **1 ~ sth** to make sth that is wrong or unfair seem acceptable 使（坏事或不正当的事）看起来可以接受：*The movie has been criticized for apparently legitimizing violence.* 这部电影因明显地美化暴力而受到了指责。 **2 ~ sth** to make sth legal 使合法 **SYN legalize** **3 ~ sb** to give a child whose parents are not married to each other the same rights as those whose parents are 赋予（非婚生子）合法权利

leg·less /ˈlegləs/ *adj.* **1** without legs 无腿的 **2** (*BrE, informal*) very drunk 醉醺醺的；烂醉如泥的

Lego™ /ˈlegəʊ; *NAmE* -goʊ/ *noun* [U] a children's toy that consists of small coloured bricks that fit together 乐高（儿童积木玩具）

ˈleg-pull *noun* a joke played on sb, usually by making them believe sth that is not true 愚弄

leg·room /ˈleguːm; ˈlegrʊm/ *noun* [U] the amount of space available for your legs when you are sitting in a car, plane, theatre, etc. (汽车、飞机、剧院等座位前的）供伸腿的空间，放腿处

leg·ume /ˈlegjuːm; lɪˈgjuːm/ *noun* (*specialist*) any plant that has seeds in long PODS. PEAS and BEANS are legumes. 豆科作物

le·gum·in·ous /lɪˈgjuːmɪnəs/ *adj.* [usually before noun] (*specialist*) relating to plants of the legume family 豆科（植物）的

ˈleg-up *noun*

IDM **give sb a ˈleg-up** (*BrE, informal*) **1** to help sb to get on a horse, over a wall, etc. by allowing them to put their foot in your hands and lifting them up 用双手托脚帮助（某人上马、翻墙等） **2** to help sb to improve their situation 帮助，援助（改善处境）

ˈleg warmer *noun* [usually pl.] a kind of sock without a foot that covers the leg from the ankle to the knee, often worn when doing exercise 腿套；护腿

leg·work /ˈlegwɜːk; *NAmE* -wɜːrk/ *noun* [U] (*informal*) difficult or boring work that takes a lot of time and effort, but that is thought to be less important 跑腿活儿；吃力不讨好的活儿

leis·ure /ˈleʒə(r); *NAmE* ˈliːʒər/ *noun* [U] time that is spent doing what you enjoy when you are not working or studying 闲暇；空闲；休闲：*These days we have more money and more leisure to enjoy it.* 如今我们钱多了，也有更多时间来花钱享受了。 ◇ ***leisure activities/interests/pursuits*** 业余活动 / 爱好 / 嗜好

IDM **at ˈleisure** **1** with no particular activities; free 闲散；悠闲：*Spend the afternoon at leisure in the town centre.* 下午到城中心区玩儿去吧。 **2** without hurrying 不慌不忙；从容：*Let's have lunch so we can talk at leisure.* 咱们吃午饭吧，边吃边谈。 **at your ˈleisure** (*formal*) when you have the time to do sth without hurrying 有空时；空闲时：*I suggest you take the forms away and read them at your* *leisure.* 我建议你把表格带回去有空慢慢看。 **a ˌgentleman/ˌlady of ˈleisure** (*humorous*) a man/woman who does not have to work 不必工作的男人（或女人）

ˈleisure centre *noun* (*BrE*) a public building where people can go to do sports and other activities in their free time 休闲（或业余）活动中心

leis·ured /ˈleʒəd; *NAmE* ˈliːʒərd/ *adj.* **1** [only before noun] not having to work and therefore having a lot of time to do what you enjoy 有空的；悠闲自在的：*the leisured classes* 有闲阶级 **2** = LEISURELY

leis·ure·ly /ˈleʒəli; *NAmE* ˈliːʒərli/ (*also* **leis·ured**) *adj.* [usually before noun] done without hurrying 不慌不忙的；慢悠悠的：*a leisurely meal* 悠闲的一餐 ◇ *They set off at a leisurely pace.* 他们步态悠闲地出发了。 ▶ **leis·ure·ly** *adv.*：*Couples strolled leisurely along the beach.* 成双成对的情侣沿着海滩悠然漫步。

ˈleisure suit *noun* (*NAmE*) an informal suit consisting of a shirt and trousers/pants made of the same cloth, popular in the 1970s 休闲套装（流行于 20 世纪 70 年代，包括相同布料的衬衣和裤子）

leis·ure·wear /ˈleʒəweə(r); *NAmE* ˈliːʒərwer/ *noun* [U] (used especially by shops/stores and clothes companies 尤用于商店和服装公司) informal clothes worn for relaxing or playing sports in 休闲服；便装；休闲运动服

leit·motif (*also* **leit·motiv**) /ˈlaɪtməʊtiːf; *NAmE* -moʊ-/ *noun* (*from German*) **1** (*music* 音) a short tune in a piece of music that is often repeated and is connected with a particular person, thing or idea（音乐的）主旋律，主导主题 **2** an idea or a phrase that is repeated often in a book or work of art, or is typical of a particular person or group （书、艺术品等的）中心思想，主题，主旨

lek·got·la /leˈxɒtlə; *NAmE* -ˈxɑːt-/ *noun* (*SAfrE*) an important meeting of politicians or government officials（政界人士或政府官员的）重要会议

lek·ker /ˈlekə(r)/ *adj., adv.* (*SAfrE, informal*)
■ ***adj.*** good or nice; tasting good 好的；不错的；味道好的：*It was lekker to see you again.* 很高兴再次见到你。◇ *a lekker meal* 美味的一餐
■ ***adv.*** very 很；非常：*I'm lekker full.* 我吃得很饱。

lemma /ˈlemə/ *noun* (*pl.* **lem·mas** or **lem·mata** /-mətə/) **1** (*specialist*) a statement that is assumed to be true in order to test the truth of another statement 引理；辅助定理 **2** (*linguistics* 语言) the basic form of a word, for example the singular form of a noun or the infinitive form of a verb, as it is shown at the beginning of a dictionary entry 词根，词元（词的基本形式，如名词单数或动词的不定式形式）

lem·ming /ˈlemɪŋ/ *noun* a small animal like a mouse, that lives in cold northern countries. Sometimes large groups of lemmings MIGRATE (= move from one place to another) in search of food. Many of them die on these journeys and there is a popular belief that lemmings kill themselves by jumping off CLIFFS. 旅鼠（许多人认为旅鼠会从悬崖上跳下自杀）：*Lemming-like we rushed into certain disaster.* 我们像旅鼠一样忙不迭地冲进灾难。

lemon 🔑 /ˈlemən/ *noun, adj.*
■ ***noun*** **1** 🔑 [C, U] a yellow CITRUS fruit with a lot of sour juice. Slices of lemon and lemon juice are used in cooking and drinks. 柠檬：*lemon tea* 柠檬茶 ◇ *a gin and tonic with ice and lemon* 一杯加冰和柠檬的杜松子酒奎宁水 ◇ *Squeeze the juice of half a lemon over the fish.* 把半个柠檬的汁挤在鱼上。◇ *a lemon tree* 柠檬树 ➲ VISUAL VOCAB PAGE V33 **2** 🔑 [U, C] lemon juice or a drink made from lemon 柠檬汁；柠檬饮料 ➲ SEE ALSO BITTER LEMON **3** 🔑 (*also* **ˌlemon ˈyellow**) [U] a pale yellow colour 浅黄色；柠檬色 ➲ MORE LIKE THIS 15, page R26 **4** [C] (*informal, especially NAmE*) a thing that is useless because it does not work as it should 无用的东西；蹩脚货；废物 SYN **dud** **5** [C] (*BrE*) a stupid person 蠢人；无用的人 SYN **idiot**
■ ***adj.*** (*also* **ˌlemon ˈyellow**) pale yellow in colour 浅黄色的；柠檬色的

lem·on·ade /ˌleməˈneɪd/ *noun* **1** [U, C] (*BrE*) a sweet FIZZY drink (= with bubbles) with a lemon flavour 柠檬味汽水 **2** [U, C] a drink made from lemon juice, sugar and water 柠檬饮料 **3** [C] a glass or bottle of lemonade 一杯（或一瓶）柠檬饮料 ➲ COMPARE ORANGEADE

ˈlemon balm *noun* [U] a HERB with leaves that taste of lemon 柠檬薄荷（草本植物，叶子有柠檬香味）

ˌlemon ˈcurd *noun* [U] a thick sweet yellow substance made from lemon, sugar, eggs and butter, spread on bread, etc. or used to fill cakes 柠檬酪（用柠檬、糖、鸡蛋及黄油制作的果酱）

ˈlemon grass *noun* [U] a type of grass with a lemon flavour that grows in hot countries and is used especially in SE Asian cooking 柠檬草（生长在热带国家，尤用于东南亚烹饪）

ˌlemon ˈsole *noun* a common European FLATFISH, often eaten as food 小头油鲽（常见的欧洲比目鱼）

ˈlemon-squeezer (*BrE*) (*NAmE* **juicer**) *noun* a kitchen UTENSIL (= a tool) for squeezing juice out of a fruit 榨汁器 ➲ VISUAL VOCAB PAGE V27

lem·ony /ˈleməni/ *adj.* tasting or smelling of lemon 柠檬味的；柠檬香的：*a lemony flavour* 柠檬味

lemur /ˈliːmə(r)/ *noun* an animal like a MONKEY, with thick fur and a long tail, that lives in trees in Madagascar 狐猴（栖居于马达加斯加岛）

lend 🔑 /lend/ *verb* (**lent, lent** /lent/) **1** 🔑 [T] to give sth to sb or allow them to use sth that belongs to you, which they have to return to you later 借给；借出 SYN **loan**：~ **(out) sth (to sb)** *I've lent the car to a friend.* 我把车借给一位朋友了。◇ ~ **sb sth** *Can you lend me your car this evening?* 你今晚能把汽车借给我用一下吗？◇ *Has he returned that book you lent him?* 你借给他的那本书还你了吗？ ➲ NOTE AT BORROW **2** 🔑 [T, I] (of a bank or financial institution 银行或金融机构) to give money to sb on condition that they pay it back over a period of time and pay interest on it （向…）贷（款） SYN **loan**：~ **(sth) (to sb)** *The bank refused to lend the money to us.* 银行拒绝向我们贷款。◇ ~ **sb sth** *They refused to lend us the money.* 他们拒绝向我们贷款。 ➲ COMPARE BORROW (2) ➲ WORDFINDER NOTE AT LOAN **3** [T] (*formal*) to give a particular quality to a person or a situation 给…增加，增添（特色）：~ **sth (to sb/sth)** *The setting sun lent an air of melancholy to the scene.* 落日给景色增添了伤感的气氛。◇ ~ **sb/sth sth** *Her presence lent the occasion a certain dignity.* 她的出席使那场面增添了几分光彩。 **4** [T] to give or provide help, support, etc. 给予，提供（帮助、支持等）：~ **sth (to sb/sth)** *I was more than happy to lend my support to such a good cause.* 我非常乐意给这样崇高的事业提供援助。◇ ~ **sb/sth sth** *He came along to lend me moral support.* 他来给予我精神上的支持。 ➲ MORE LIKE THIS 33, page R28

IDM **lend ˈcolour to sth** (*BrE*) to make sth seem true or probable 使显得真实（或可能）：*Most of the available evidence lends colour to this view.* 现有的大部分证据支持这个观点。 **lend an ˈear (to sb/sth)** to listen in a patient and sympathetic way to sb 聆听；倾听 **lend (sb) a (helping) ˈhand (with sth)** (*informal*) to help sb with sth 帮助；援助；搭把手：*I went over to see if I could lend a hand.* 我走过去看我能不能帮上忙。 **lend your name to sth** (*formal*) **1** to let it be known in public that you support or agree with sth 公开表示支持：*I am more than happy to lend my name to this campaign.* 我非常愿意公开表示支持这个运动。 **2** to have a place named after you 以…的名字命名（某地方） **lend supˈport, ˈweight, ˈcredence, etc. to sth** to make sth seem more likely to be true or genuine 对…提供支持（或强有力的证据、可靠性等来增加可信度）：*This latest evidence lends support to her theory.* 这一最新的证据印证了她的理论。 ➲ MORE AT HELP *v.*

PHR V **ˈlend itself to sth** to be suitable for sth 适合于：*Her voice doesn't really lend itself well to blues singing.* 她的嗓子不是很适于唱布鲁斯歌曲。

lend·er /ˈlendə(r)/ *noun* (*finance* 财) a person or an organization that lends money 放款人 ➲ COMPARE BORROWER ➲ SEE ALSO MONEYLENDER

lend·ing /ˈlendɪŋ/ *noun* [U] (*finance* 财) the act of lending money 放款；贷放：*Lending by banks rose to $10 billion last year.* 去年银行发放的贷款增至 100 亿美元。

ˈlending library *noun* a public library from which you can borrow books and take them away to read at home（书籍可外借的）公共图书馆 ➲ COMPARE REFERENCE LIBRARY

ˈlending rate *noun* (*finance* 财) the rate of interest that you must pay when you borrow money from a bank or another financial organization 贷款利率；放款利率

length /leŋθ/ *noun*
- **SIZE/MEASUREMENT** 大小；度量 **1** [U, C] the size or measurement of sth from one end to the other 长；长度：*This room is twice the length of the kitchen.* 这个房间的长度是厨房的两倍。◇ *The river is 300 miles* ***in length***. 这条河长 300 英里。◇ *The snake usually reaches a length of 100 cm.* 蛇一般长达 100 厘米。◇ *He ran the entire length of the beach* (= from one end to the other). 他从海滩一头跑到另一头。◇ *Did you see the length of his hair?* 你看见他头发有多长吗？ ➲ COMPARE BREADTH (1), WIDTH (1)
- **TIME** 时间 **2** [U, C] the amount of time that sth lasts（持续）时间的长短：*We discussed shortening the length of the course.* 我们就缩短这门课程的时间进行了讨论。◇ *He was disgusted at* ***the length of time*** *he had to wait.* 他非常讨厌要等那么长时间。◇ *She got a headache if she had to read* ***for any length of time*** (= for a long time). 她读书时间长了就头疼。◇ *Size of pension depends partly on length of service with the company.* 退休金的多少部分取决于为公司服务时间的长短。◇ *Each class is 45 minutes* ***in length***. 每一节课为 45 分钟。
- **OF BOOK/MOVIE** 书；电影 **3** [U, C] the amount of writing in a book, or a document, etc.; the amount of time that a film/movie lasts（书或文件等的）篇幅；（电影的）片长：*Her novels vary in length.* 她的小说篇幅长短不一。
- **-LENGTH** …长度 **4** (in adjectives 构成形容词) having the length mentioned 有…长度的：*shoulder-length hair* 长及肩的头发 ➲ SEE ALSO FULL-LENGTH, KNEE-LENGTH
- **OF SWIMMING POOL** 游泳池 **5** [C] the distance from one end of a swimming pool to the other 游泳池长度（一端至另一端的距离）：*He swims 50 lengths a day.* 他每天游 50 个游泳池那么长的距离。 ➲ COMPARE WIDTH (3) ➲ WORDFINDER NOTE AT SWIM
- **IN RACE** 比赛 **6** [C] the size of a horse or boat from one end to the other, when it is used to measure the distance between two horses or boats taking part in a race（马或船的）自身长度：*The horse won by two clear lengths.* 那匹马以整整领先两个马身的优势获胜。
- **LONG THIN PIECE** 细长的段 **7** [C] a long thin piece of sth 细长的一段（或一节、一根等）：*a length of rope/string/wire* 一根绳子 / 细线 / 金属线 ➲ SEE ALSO LONG *adj.*

IDM **at ˈlength | at... length** **1** for a long time and in detail 长时间；详尽地：*He quoted at length from the report.* 他大段大段地引用报告中的话。◇ *We have already discussed this matter at great length.* 我们已经十分详尽地讨论了这个问题。 **2** (*literary*) after a long time 经过一段长时间以后；最后：*'I'm still not sure,' he said at length.* "我还是没把握。"他最后说道。 **go to any, some, great, etc. ˈlengths (to do sth)** to put a lot of effort into doing sth, especially when this seems extreme 竭尽全力；不遗余力：*She goes to extraordinary lengths to keep her private life private.* 她竭尽全力让自己的私生活不受干扰。 **the length and ˈbreadth of...** in or to all parts of a place 到处；处处；各地：*They have travelled the length and breadth of Europe giving concerts.* 他们为举行音乐会走遍了欧洲各地。 ➲ MORE AT ARM *n.*

length·en /ˈleŋθən/ *verb* [I, T] to become longer; to make sth longer（使）变长：*The afternoon shadows lengthened.* 下午影子渐渐变长了。◇ **~ sth** *I need to lengthen this skirt.* 我需要把这条裙子放长。 OPP shorten

length·ways /ˈleŋθweɪz/ (*also* **length·wise** /ˈleŋθwaɪz/) *adv.* in the same direction as the longest side of sth 纵向；纵长：*Cut the banana in half lengthways.* 把香蕉竖着切成两半。 ➲ COMPARE WIDTHWAYS

lengthy /ˈleŋθi/ *adj.* (**length·ier**, **lengthi·est**) very long, and often too long, in time or size 很长的；漫长的；冗长的：*lengthy delays* 多次长时间拖延 ◇ *the lengthy process of obtaining a visa* 取得签证的漫长过程 ◇ *a lengthy explanation* 冗长的解释

le·ni·ent /ˈliːniənt/ *adj.* not as strict as expected when punishing sb or when making sure that rules are obeyed（惩罚或执法时）宽大的，宽容的，仁慈的：*a lenient sentence/fine* 从宽的判刑 / 罚款 ◇ *The judge was far too lenient with him.* 法官对他太宽容了。 ▶ **le·ni·ency** /-ənsi/ (*also less frequent* **le·ni·ence**) *noun* [U]: *She appealed to the judge for leniency.* 她向法官请求宽大处理。 **le·ni·ent·ly** *adv.*：*to treat sb leniently* 宽待某人

Lenin·ism /ˈlenɪnɪzəm/ *noun* [U] the political and economic policies of Lenin, the first leader of the Soviet Union, which were based on Marxism 列宁主义 ▶ **Lenin·ist** /ˈlenɪnɪst/ *noun, adj.*

lens /lenz/ *noun* **1** a curved piece of glass or plastic that makes things look larger, smaller or clearer when you look through it 透镜；镜片：*a pair of glasses with tinted lenses* 一副有色镜片眼镜 ◇ *a camera with an adjustable lens* 带有可调镜头的照相机 ◇ ***a lens cap/cover*** 镜头帽；镜头盖 ➲ PICTURE AT BINOCULARS, FRAME ➲ VISUAL VOCAB PAGE V72 ➲ SEE ALSO FISHEYE LENS, TELEPHOTO LENS, WIDE-ANGLE LENS, ZOOM LENS **2** (*informal*) = CONTACT LENS：*Have you got your lenses in?* 你戴了隐形眼镜吗？ **3** (*anatomy* 解) the transparent part of the eye, behind the PUPIL, that focuses light so that you can see clearly（眼球的）晶状体 ➲ VISUAL VOCAB PAGE V64

lens·man /ˈlenzmən/ *noun* (*pl.* **-men** /-mən/) a professional photographer or CAMERAMAN（专职）摄影师

Lent /lent/ *noun* [U] in the Christian Church, the period of 40 days from Ash Wednesday to the day before Easter, during which some Christians give up some type of food or activity that they enjoy in memory of Christ's suffering 大斋期，四旬期（从圣灰日至复活节前一日，共 40 天）

lent PAST TENSE, PAST PART. OF LEND

len·tigo /lenˈtaɪɡəʊ; *NAmE* -ɡoʊ/ *noun* [U] (*medical* 医) a condition in which small brown areas appear on the skin, usually in old people 雀斑痣；（尤指）老人斑 ➲ SEE ALSO LIVER SPOT

len·til /ˈlentl/ *noun* a small green, orange or brown seed that is usually dried and used in cooking, for example in soup or STEW 兵豆

Leo /ˈliːəʊ; *NAmE* ˈliːoʊ/ *noun* **1** [U] the fifth sign of the ZODIAC, the Lion 黄道第五宫；狮子宫；狮子（星）座 **2** [C] (*pl.* **-os**) a person born when the sun is in this sign, that is between 23 July and 22 August, approximately 属狮子座的人（约出生于 7 月 23 日至 8 月 22 日）

leo·nine /ˈliːənaɪn/ *adj.* (*literary*) like a LION 像狮子一样的；狮子般的

leop·ard /ˈlepəd; *NAmE* -ərd/ *noun* a large animal of the cat family, that has yellowish-brown fur with black spots. Leopards live in Africa and southern Asia. 豹 ➲ COMPARE LEOPARDESS

IDM **a leopard cannot change its ˈspots** (*saying*) people cannot change their character, especially if they have a bad character 本性难改；禀性难移

ˈleopard-crawl *verb* [I] **+ adv./prep.** (*SAfrE*) (often used about soldiers) to move with your body as close to the ground as possible, using your elbows and knees to push you forward（常用于士兵）匍匐前进

leop·ard·ess /ˈlepədes; *NAmE* -ərd-/ *noun* a female leopard 母豹

leo·tard /ˈliːətɑːd; *NAmE* -tɑːrd/ *noun* a piece of clothing that fits tightly over the body from the neck down to the tops of the legs, usually covering the arms, worn by dancers, women doing physical exercises, etc. (舞蹈演员、女性体育锻炼者等穿的通常有袖的) 紧身连衣裤

LEP /ˌel iː ˈpiː/ *abbr.* [only before noun] (*NAmE, specialist*) Limited English Proficient (used to describe students who cannot speak English very well) 英语水平有限的(用于描述英语口语不够流利的学生): *schools with large numbers of LEP children* 有很多英语水平有限的学童的学校

leper /ˈlepə(r)/ *noun* **1** a person suffering from LEPROSY 麻风病患者 **2** a person that other people avoid because they have done sth that these people do not approve of (因其所为而) 被大家躲避的人; 别人避之唯恐不及的人

lep·re·chaun /ˈleprəkɔːn/ *noun* (in Irish stories) a creature like a little man, with magic powers (爱尔兰传说中像小矮人的) 魔法精灵, 矮妖

lep·rosy /ˈleprəsi/ *noun* [U] an infectious disease that causes painful white areas on the skin and can destroy nerves and flesh 麻风 ➲ SEE ALSO LEPER (1)

lep·rous /ˈleprəs/ *adj.* affected by LEPROSY 麻风病的

les·bian /ˈlezbiən/ (*also informal, offensive* **lezzy, lezzie**) *noun* a woman who is sexually attracted to other women 女同性恋者: *lesbians and gays* 女同性恋者与男同性恋者 ➲ COMPARE GAY *n.*, HOMOSEXUAL ▸ **les·bian** *adj.*: *the lesbian and gay community* 男女同性恋群体 ◇ *a lesbian relationship* 女性同性恋关系 **les·bian·ism** *noun* [U]

lese-majesty /ˌliːz ˈmædʒəsti; *NAmE* ˌleɪz/ *noun* [U] (*from French, formal*) the act or crime of insulting the king, queen or other ruler (对君主、元首等的) 不敬罪, 叛逆罪

le·sion /ˈliːʒn/ *noun* (*medical* 医) damage to the skin or part of the body caused by injury or by illness (因伤病导致皮肤或器官的) 损伤, 损害: *skin/brain lesions* 皮肤 / 大脑损伤

less 🔑 /les/ *det., pron., adv., prep.*

■ ***det., pron.*** 🔑 used with uncountable nouns to mean 'a smaller amount of' (与不可数名词连用) 较少的, 更少的: *less butter/time/importance* 较少的黄油 / 时间; 次要 ◇ *He was advised to smoke fewer cigarettes and drink less beer.* 有人劝他少抽烟、少喝啤酒。◇ *We have less to worry about now.* 现在我们要担忧的事少一些了。◇ *It is* ***less*** *of a problem* ***than*** *I'd expected.* 问题不像我预料的那么大。◇ *We'll be there in* ***less than no time*** (= very soon). 我们马上就到。◇ *The victory was* ***nothing less than*** *a miracle.* 这场胜利是个不折不扣的奇迹。 HELP People often use **less** with countable nouns. * less 与可数名词连用颇常见: *There were less cars on the road then.* 那时候路上车流量较少。This is not considered correct by some people, and **fewer** should be used instead. 有人认为这不正确, 应用 fewer。

IDM **ˌless and ˈless** 🔑 smaller and smaller amounts 越来越少: *As time passed, she saw less and less of all her old friends at home.* 随着时间的消逝, 她越来越见不到家乡那些老朋友了。 **ˌless is ˈmore** (*saying*) include only what is essential in order to create an effective product or result 少即是多; 以少见多; 简单就是美: *His simple, elegant paintings reflect his principle that less is more.* 他简洁典雅的绘画体现出他简约就是美的原则。 **no ˈless** (*often ironic*) used to suggest that sth is surprising or impressive (表示惊讶或钦佩) 竟, 居然: *She's having lunch with the Director, no less.* 她居然正在与主管一起进午餐。 **no less than…** used to emphasize a large amount (强调大数量) 不少于, 多达: *The guide contains details of no less than 115 hiking routes.* 这本旅游指南包括多达 115 条徒步旅行路线的详细介绍。

■ ***adv.*** 🔑 to a smaller degree; not so much 较少; 较小; 更少; 更小; 没那么多; 少: *less expensive/likely/intelligent* 价钱较便宜; 可能性较小; 智力较差 ◇ *less often/enthusiastically* 不那么经常 / 热情 ◇ *I read much less now than I used to.* 我现在看的书比过去少得多。◇ *The receptionist was* ***less than*** (= not at all) *helpful.* 那接待员一点忙都不愿帮。◇ *She wasn't* ***any the less*** *happy for* (= she was perfectly happy) *being on her own.* 她并不因独自一人而有一丁点儿不快活。◇ *That this is a positive stereotype makes it* ***no less a*** *stereotype, and therefore unacceptable.* 这种成见即使是积极的也依然是成见, 因而是不可取的。

IDM **even/much/still ˈless** and certainly not 更不用说; 更何况: *No explanation was offered, still less an apology.* 连个解释都不给, 就更不用说道歉了。 **ˌless and ˈless** 🔑 continuing to become smaller in amount 越来越少; 越来越小: *She found the job less and less attractive.* 她发觉那工作越来越没意思。 ➲ MORE AT MORE *adv.*

■ ***prep.*** used before a particular amount that must be taken away from the amount just mentioned 减去; 扣除 SYN **minus**: *a monthly salary of $2 000 less tax and insurance* 月薪 2 000 美元, 从中扣除税款和保险费

-less /ləs/ *suffix* (in adjectives 构成形容词) **1** without 没有; 无: *treeless* 没有树木的 ◇ *meaningless* 无意义的 **2** not doing; not affected by 不做; 不受影响: *tireless* 孜孜不倦的 ◇ *selfless* 无私的 ▸ **-less·ly** (in adverbs 构成副词): *hopelessly* 绝望地 **-less·ness** (in nouns 构成名词): *helplessness* 无助 ➲ MORE LIKE THIS 7, page R25

les·see /leˈsiː/ *noun* (*law* 律) a person who has use of a building, an area of land, etc. on a LEASE 承租人; 租户 ➲ COMPARE LESSOR

less·en /ˈlesn/ *verb* [I, T] to become or make sth become smaller, weaker, less important, etc. (使) 变小, 变少, 减弱, 减轻 SYN **diminish**: *The noise began to lessen.* 噪音开始减弱。◇ **~ sth** *to lessen the risk/impact/effect of sth* 减少某事物的风险 / 影响 / 效果 ▸ **less·en·ing** *noun* [sing., U]: *a lessening of tension* 紧张状态的减缓

less·er /ˈlesə(r)/ *adj.* [only before noun] **1** not as great in size, amount or importance as sth/sb else 较小的; 较少的; 次要的: *people of lesser importance* 次要人物 ◇ *They were all involved* ***to a greater or lesser degree*** (= some were more involved than others). 他们或多或少都受到了牵连。◇ *The law was designed to protect wives, and, to a lesser extent, children.* 这条法律是为了保护妻子, 其次是保护子女。◇ *He was encouraged to plead guilty to the lesser offence.* 有人怂恿他认那个较轻的罪。 **2** used in the names of some types of animals, birds and plants which are smaller than similar kinds (用于比同类小的动植物名称) 小 OPP **great** ▸ **less·er** *adv.*: *one of the lesser-known Caribbean islands* 加勒比海不甚知名的岛屿之一

IDM **the ˌlesser of two ˈevils | the ˌlesser ˈevil** the less unpleasant of two unpleasant choices 两害相权之轻者

lesso /ˈlesəʊ; *NAmE* ˈlesoʊ/ *noun* (*pl.* **-os**) = KHANGA

les·son 🔑 /ˈlesn/ *noun* **1** 🔑 a period of time in which sb is taught sth 一节课; 一课时: *She gives piano lessons.* 她教授钢琴课。◇ *All new students are given* ***lessons in/on*** *how to use the library.* 所有新生都要上如何利用图书馆的课。◇ *I'm* ***having/taking*** *driving lessons.* 我在学开车。◇ (*especially BrE*) *Our first lesson on Tuesdays is French.* 我们星期二的第一节课是法语。◇ (*especially BrE*) *What did we do last lesson?* 我们上节课学了什么内容? ➲ COLLOCATIONS AT EDUCATION ➲ COMPARE CLASS *n.* (2) **2** 🔑 something that is intended to be learned 课; 教学单元: *The course book is divided into 30 lessons.* 这本教科书分为 30 课。◇ *Other countries can* ***teach us a lesson*** *or two on industrial policy.* 其他国家的工业政策, 我们可以借鉴一二。 **3** 🔑 an experience, especially an unpleasant one, that sb can learn from so that it does not happen again in the future 经验; 教训: *a salutary lesson* 有益的经验 ◇ *The accident* ***taught me a lesson*** *I'll never forget.* 那事故给我的教训永远也不会忘记。◇ **~ to sb** ***Let that be a lesson to you*** (= so that you do not make the same mistake again). 你要以此为鉴。 ➲ SEE ALSO OBJECT LESSON **4** a passage from the Bible that is read to people during a church service (教堂礼拜中的) 《圣经》选读 IDM SEE LEARN

les·sor /leˈsɔː(r)/ *noun* (*law* 律) a person who gives sb the use of a building, an area of land, etc. on a LEASE 出租人 ➲ COMPARE LESSEE

lest /lest/ *conj.* (*formal* or *literary*) **1** in order to prevent sth from happening 免得; 以免: *He gripped his brother's arm lest he be trampled by the mob.* 他紧抓着他弟弟的胳膊, 怕他让暴民踩着。 **2** used to introduce the reason for the particular emotion mentioned (引出产生某种情感的

L

原因）唯恐，担心： *She was afraid lest she had revealed too much.* 她担心她泄露得太多了。

let 🔑 /let/ *verb, noun*

■ ***verb*** **(let·ting, let, let)**

• **ALLOW** 允许 **1** 🔑 [no passive] to allow sb to do sth or sth to happen without trying to stop it 允许；让： **~ sb/sth do sth** *Let them splash around in the pool for a while.* 让他们在水池里扑腾一会儿吧。◇ *Don't let her upset you.* 别让她搅得你心烦。◇ *Let your body relax.* 让你的身体放松。◇ **~ sb/sth** *He'd eat chocolate all day long if I let him.* 我要是不拦着，他会整天不停地吃巧克力。 **2** 🔑 to give sb permission to do sth 准许；许可；同意： **~ sb/sth do sth** *They won't let him leave the country.* 他们不许他离开这个国家。◇ **~ sb/sth** *She wanted to lend me some money but I wouldn't let her.* 她想借给我一些钱，可我不同意。 **3** 🔑 **~ sb/sth + adv./prep.** to allow sb/sth to go somewhere 允许（去某处）：*to let sb into the house* 允许某人进屋 ◇ *I'll give you a key so that you can let yourself in.* 我把钥匙给你，你可以自己开门进去。◇ *Please let me past.* 请让我过去。◇ *The cat wants to be let out.* 那只猫想要出去。

• **MAKING SUGGESTIONS** 提出建议 **4** 🔑 **let's** [no passive] **~ (do sth)** used for making suggestions（提出建议时说）：*Let's go to the beach.* 咱们去海滩吧。◇ *Let's not tell her what we did.* 咱们干的事可别告诉她。◇ (*BrE*) *Don't let's tell her what we did.* 咱们干的事可别告诉她。◇ *I don't think we'll make it, but let's try anyway.* 我不认为我们会成功，但不管怎样还是试一试吧。◇ *'Shall we check it again?' 'Yes, let's.'* "我们再检查一下好吗？""好的。"

• **OFFERING HELP** 提供帮助 **5** 🔑 [no passive] **~ sb/sth do sth** used for offering help to sb（提出帮助时说）让，由： *Here, let me do it.* 喂，让我来吧。◇ *Let us get those boxes down for you.* 让我们帮你把那些箱子搬下来吧。

• **MAKING REQUESTS** 提出要求 **6** [no passive] **~ sb/sth do sth** used for making requests or giving instructions（提出请求或给予指示时说）要： *Let me have your report by Friday.* 星期五以前要把你的报告交给我。

• **CHALLENGING** 挑战 **7** [no passive] **~ sb/sth do sth** used to show that you are not afraid or worried about sb doing sth（表示不害怕或担忧某人做某事）让： *If he thinks he can cheat me, just let him try!* 要是他以为能够骗过我，就让他来试一下吧！

• **WISHING** 祝愿 **8** [no passive] **~ sb/sth do sth** (*literary*) used to express a strong wish for sth to happen（表达强烈的愿望）让： *Let her come home safely!* 让她平平安安回家吧！

• **INTRODUCING STH** 引出某事 **9** [no passive] **~ sb/sth do sth** used to introduce what you are going to say or do（引出要讲或要做的事）让： *Let me give you an example.* 让我来举一个例子吧。◇ *Let me just finish this and then I'll come.* 让我把这个弄完，随后就来。

• **IN CALCULATING** 计算 **10** [no passive] **~ sb/sth do sth** (*specialist*) used to say that you are supposing sth to be true when you calculate sth（计算时说）假设，设： *Let line AB be equal to line CD.* 设 AB 线与 CD 线等长。

• **HOUSE/ROOM** 房屋；房间 **11** 🔑 **~ sth (out) (to sb)** (*especially BrE*) to allow sb to use a house, room, etc. in return for regular payments 出租（房屋、房间等）： *I let the spare room.* 我把那间空房出租了。◇ *They decided to let out the smaller offices at low rents.* 他们决定以低租金把那些较小的办公室租出去。 ➲ WORDFINDER NOTE AT HOME ➲ COLLOCATIONS AT HOUSE ➲ NOTE AT RENT

IDM **HELP** Most idioms containing **let** are at the entries for the nouns and adjectives in the idioms, for example **let alone** is at **alone**. 大多数含 let 的习语，都可在该等习语中的名词及形容词相关词条找到，如 let alone 在词条 alone 下。 **ˌlet ˈfall sth** to mention sth in a conversation, by accident or as if by accident（好像）无意中提及；脱口说出 **SYN** **drop**: *She let fall a further heavy hint.* 她似乎无意中又说出了一个明显的提示。 **ˌlet sb ˈgo 1** 🔑 to allow sb to be free 放，释放（某人） **SYN** **free**: *Will they let the hostages go?* 他们是否会释放人质？ **2** to make sb have to leave their job 解雇；开除： *They're having to let 100 employees go because of falling profits.* 由于利润下降，他们将不得不解雇 100 名员工。 **ˌlet sb/sth ˈgo | ˌlet ˈgo (of sb/sth) 1** 🔑 to stop holding sb/sth 放开；松手： *Don't let the rope go.* 别松开绳子。◇ *Don't let go of the rope.* 别松开绳子。◇ *Let go! You're hurting me!* 放手！你把我弄疼了！ **2** to give up an idea or an attitude, or control of sth 放弃，摒弃（想法、态度或控制）： *It's time to let the past go.* 该忘掉过去了。◇ *It's time to let go of the past.* 该忘掉过去了。 **ˌlet sth ˈgo** to stop taking care of a house, garden, etc. 不再照管，撒手不管（房屋、花园等）： *I'm afraid I've let the garden go this year.* 恐怕我今年没有照看好园子。 **ˌlet yourself ˈgo 1** to behave in a relaxed way without worrying about what people think of your behaviour 放松；随心所欲： *Come on, enjoy yourself, let yourself go!* 来吧，尽情地玩，玩个痛快吧！ **2** to stop being careful about how you look and dress, etc. 不注重仪表；不修边幅： *He has let himself go since he lost his job.* 他失业后就不修边幅了。 **let sb ˈhave it** (*informal*) to attack sb physically or with words 打，揍，用言语攻击（某人） **let it ˈgo (at ˈthat)** to say or do no more about sth 不再多说（或多做）；就到此为止： *I don't entirely agree, but I'll let it go at that.* 我不完全同意，但也就这样吧。◇ *I thought she was hinting at something, but I let it go.* 我想她在暗示什么，然而我也没有再多问。 **ˌlet me ˈsee/ˈthink** 🔑 used when you are thinking or trying to remember sth 让我想一想；让我思考一下： *Now let me see—where did he say he lived?* 嗯，让我想想，他说他住在哪里呢？ **let us ˈsay** used when making a suggestion or giving an example（提议或举例时）譬如说，比方说，例如： *I can let you have it for, well let's say £100.* 我可以把这东西卖给你，嗯，比如说作价 100 英镑吧。

PHR V **ˌlet sb↔ˈdown** 🔑 to fail to help or support sb as they had hoped or expected 不能帮助，不能支持（某人）；使失望： *I'm afraid she let us down badly.* 很遗憾，她让我们大失所望。◇ *This machine won't let you down.* 你尽管放心，这台机器不会出毛病。◇ *He trudged home feeling lonely and let down.* 他步履艰难地往家走，感到孤独而沮丧。 ➲ RELATED NOUN LET-DOWN **ˌlet sb/sth↔ˈdown** to make sb/sth less successful than they/it should be（使）略逊一筹，美中不足： *She speaks French very fluently, but her pronunciation lets her down.* 她法语讲得很流利，但美中不足的是发音不大好。 **ˌlet sth↔ˈdown 1** to let or make sth go down 放下；降低；降下： *We let the bucket down by a rope.* 我们用绳子把吊桶放下去。 **2** to make a dress, skirt, coat, etc. longer, by reducing the amount of material that is folded over at the bottom（把连衣裙、裙子、外套等）放长；放出（褶边） **OPP** **take sth↔up 3** (*BrE*) to allow the air to escape from sth deliberately（故意地）放气： *Some kids had let my tyres down.* 几个小孩子故意把我的轮胎放了气。 **ˌlet sb/yourself ˈin for sth** (*informal*) to involve sb/yourself in sth that is likely to be unpleasant or difficult 使陷入；使卷入；牵涉： *I volunteered to help, and then I thought 'Oh no, what have I let myself in for!'* 我自告奋勇要帮忙，然后又一想："啊，不好，我干吗把自己卷进去呢！" **ˌlet sb ˈin on sth | ˌlet sb ˈinto sth** (*informal*) to allow sb to share a secret 告知，透露（秘密）： *Are you going to let them in on your plans?* 你是不是打算让他们知道你的计划呀？ **ˌlet sth ˈinto sth** to put sth into the surface of sth so that it does not stick out from it 把…置入，把…嵌进（某物的表层）： *a window let into a wall* 嵌进墙壁的窗户 **ˌlet sb ˈoff (with sth)** 🔑 to not punish sb for sth they have done wrong, or to give them only a light punishment 不惩罚；放过；宽恕；从轻处罚： *They let us off lightly.* 他们对我们从轻发落了。◇ *She was let off with a warning.* 她没被处罚，只是受了个警告。 **ˌlet sb ˈoff sth** (*BrE*) to allow sb not to do sth or not to go somewhere 允许（某人）不做；准许（某人）不去（某处）： *He let us off homework today.* 他今天免了我们的家庭作业。 **ˌlet sth ˈoff** to fire a gun or make a bomb, etc. explode 放（枪等）；使爆炸： *The boys were letting off fireworks.* 那些男孩在放花炮。 **ˌlet ˈon (to sb)** (*informal*) to tell a secret （对某人）说出秘密，泄密： *I'm getting married next week, but please don't let on to anyone.* 我下周就要结婚了，但这事请对谁都不要说。◇ **let on (to sb) that…** *She let on that she was leaving.* 她透露说她要离开。 **ˌlet ˈout** (*NAmE*) (of school classes, films/movies, meetings, etc. 课堂、电影、会议等) to come to an end, so that it is time for people to leave 结束；下课；散场；散会： *The movie has just let out.* 电影刚刚散场。 **ˌlet sb ˈout** to make sb stop feeling that they are involved in sth or have to do sth 使某人解脱： *They think the attacker* *was very tall—so that lets you out.* 他们认为歹徒是个高个子，这样就没你什么事儿了。 ➲ RELATED NOUN LET-OUT ˌ**let sth ˈout 1** to give a cry, etc. 发出（叫声等）：*to let out a scream of terror* 发出恐怖的尖叫 ◇ *to let out a gasp of delight* 满意地松一口气 OPP **hold in 2** to make a shirt, coat, etc. looser or larger（把衬衣、外套等）放大，放长，加宽 OPP **take in** ˌ**let ˈup** (*informal*) **1** to become less strong 减弱；减轻：*The pain finally let up.* 疼痛终于减轻了。 **2** to make less effort 放松（努力）；松劲：*We mustn't let up now.* 我们现在决不能放松。 ➲ RELATED NOUN LET-UP

■ ***noun***

• **IN TENNIS** 网球 **1** a SERVE that lands in the correct part of the COURT but must be taken again because it has touched the top of the net （发球时的）擦网球

• **HOUSE/ROOM** 房屋；房间 **2** (*BrE*) an act of renting a home, etc. 出租；租借：*a* ***long-term/short-term let*** 长期 / 短期出租

IDM **without ˌlet or ˈhindrance** (*formal* or *law* 律) without being prevented from doing sth; freely 毫无阻碍；顺畅地；自由地

-let *suffix* (in nouns 构成名词) small; not very important 小的；不很重要的：*booklet* 小册子 ◇ *piglet* 猪崽 ◇ *starlet* 渴望出名的年轻女演员 ➲ MORE LIKE THIS 7, page R25

ˈlet-down *noun* [C, usually sing., U] (*informal*) something that is disappointing because it is not as good as you expected it to be 令人失望的事；失望；沮丧 SYN **disappointment, anticlimax**

le·thal /ˈliːθl/ *adj.* **1** causing or able to cause death 致命的；可致死的 SYN **deadly, fatal**：*a lethal dose of poison* 毒药的致死剂量 ◇ *a lethal weapon* 致命的武器 ◇ (*figurative*) *The closure of the factory dealt a lethal blow to the town.* 那家工厂的关闭对这座城镇是致命的打击。 **2** (*informal*) causing or able to cause a lot of harm or damage 危害极大的；破坏性极大的：*You and that car—it's a lethal combination!* 你和那辆车真是致命的组合！ ▶ **le·thal·ly** /ˈliːθəli/ *adv.*

leth·argy /ˈleθədʒi; *NAmE* ˈleθərdʒi/ *noun* [U] the state of not having any energy or enthusiasm for doing things 无精打采；没有热情；冷漠 SYN **listlessness, inertia** ▶ **leth·ar·gic** /ləˈθɑːdʒɪk; *NAmE* -ˈθɑːrdʒ-/ *adj.*：*The weather made her lethargic.* 那天气使得她无精打采。

Lethe /ˈliːθi/ *noun* [U] (in ancient Greek stories 古希腊故事) an imaginary river whose water, when drunk, was thought to make the dead forget their life on Earth 勒忒，忘川（假想的河流，死者饮此河的水即忘记尘世一生）

ˈlet-out *noun* [sing.] (*BrE*) an event or a statement that allows sb to avoid having to do sth 逃脱的机会；漏洞：*Good—we have a let-out now.* 好！我们现在有机可乘。◇ *a let-out clause* (= in a contract) 免责条款

let's /lets/ *short form* let us 让我们：*Let's break for lunch.* 咱们停下来吃午饭吧。

let·ter 🔑 /ˈletə(r)/ *noun, verb*

■ ***noun* 1** 🔑 a message that is written down or printed on paper and usually put in an envelope and sent to sb 信；函：*a* ***business/thank-you, etc. letter*** 商业信函、感谢信等 ◇ ***a letter of*** *complaint* 投诉信 ◇ (*BrE*) *to* ***post a letter*** 寄信 ◇ (*NAmE*) *to* ***mail a letter*** 寄信 ◇ *There's a letter for you from your mother.* 有你母亲的一封来信。 ◇ *You will be notified* ***by letter.*** 将用信函通知你。 HELP You will find compounds ending in **letter** at their place in the alphabet. 以 letter 结尾的复合词可在各字母中适当的位置查到。 **2** 🔑 a written or printed sign representing a sound used in speech 字母：*'B' is the second letter of the alphabet.* * b 是字母表的第二个字母。◇ *Write your name* ***in capital/block letters.*** 用大写字母书写姓名。 **3** (*NAmE*) a sign in the shape of a letter that is sewn onto clothes to show that a person plays in a school or college sports team（缝制在运动服上的）校运动队字母标志

IDM **the ˌletter of the ˈlaw** (*often disapproving*) the exact words of a law or rule rather than its general meaning 法律（或法规）的准确字面意义：*They insist on sticking to the letter of the law.* 他们坚持严守法律的字面意义。 **to the ˈletter** doing/following exactly what sb/sth says, paying attention to every detail 丝毫不差；不折不扣；精确地：*I followed your instructions to the letter.* 我是严格遵照你的指示办的。

■ ***verb* 1** [T, usually passive] **~ sth (+ noun)** to give a letter to sth as part of a series or list 用字母标明（于清单等上）：*the stars lettered Alpha and Beta* 以 α 和 β 命名的星 **2** [T, usually passive] **~ sth (in sth)** to print, paint, sew, etc. letters onto sth 把字母印刷（或缝制等）于：*a black banner lettered in white* 印有白色字母的黑色横幅 **3** [I] (*NAmE*) to receive a letter made of cloth that you sew onto your clothes for playing in a school or college sports team 领取到学校运动队布制字母标志

ˈletter bomb *noun* a small bomb that is sent to sb hidden in a letter that explodes when the envelope is opened 书信炸弹（匿藏在书信中，开封即爆炸） ➲ SEE ALSO PARCEL BOMB

letter boxes 邮箱；信箱

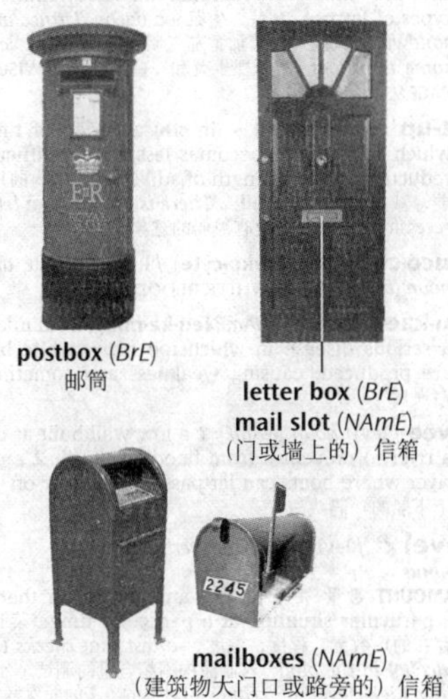

postbox (*BrE*) 邮筒

letter box (*BrE*)
mail slot (*NAmE*)
（门或墙上的）信箱

mailboxes (*NAmE*)
（建筑物大门口或路旁的）信箱

ˈletter box *noun* (*BrE*) **1** (*NAmE* **ˈmail slot**) a narrow opening in a door or wall through which mail is delivered（门或墙上的）信箱 ➲ VISUAL VOCAB PAGE V18 **2** (*NAmE* **ˈmail·box**) a small box near the main door of a building or by the road, which mail is delivered to（建筑物大门口或路旁的）信箱 **3** = POSTBOX ➲ COMPARE PILLAR BOX

let·ter·box /ˈletəbɒks; *NAmE* ˈletərbɑːks/ *noun, verb*

■ ***noun*** [U] = WIDESCREEN

■ ***verb* ~ sth** to present a film/movie on television with the width a lot greater than the height, and with a black band at the top and bottom 宽银幕模式播放：*a letterboxed edition* 宽银幕模式的版本

ˈletter carrier *noun* (*NAmE*) = MAIL CARRIER

let·ter·head /ˈletəhed; *NAmE* -tərh-/ *noun* the name and address of a person, a company or an organization printed at the top of their writing paper 信头（印于信笺上端的个人、公司或组织的名称和地址）

let·ter·ing /ˈletərɪŋ/ *noun* [U] **1** letters or words that are written or printed in a particular style（用某种字体书写或印刷的）字母，字：*Gothic lettering* 哥特体黑体字 **2** the process of writing, drawing or printing letters or words 写字；描字；印字

L

ˌ**letter of ˈcredit** *noun* (*pl.* **letters of credit**) (*finance* 财) a letter from a bank that allows you to get a particular amount of money from another bank 信用证；信用状

ˈ**letter opener** *noun* (*especially NAmE*) = PAPERKNIFE

ˌ**letter-ˈperfect** *adj.* (*NAmE*) **1** correct in all details 准确无误的；一字不差的；无讹的 **2** (*BrE* ˌ**word-ˈperfect**) able to remember and repeat sth exactly without making any mistakes 能背得一字不差的；能背得滚瓜烂熟的

ˈ**letter-size** (*also* **letter**) *adj.* (*NAmE*) (of paper 纸张) 8½ inches (215.9 mm) wide and 11 inches (279.4 mm) long 信纸尺寸的（宽 8½ 英寸或 215.9 毫米，长 11 英寸或 279.4 毫米）

let·ting /ˈletɪŋ/ *noun* (*BrE*) a period of time when you let a house or other property to sb else（房屋或其他财产的）出租期限：*holiday lettings* 假日出租

let·tuce /ˈletɪs/ *noun* [U, C] a plant with large green leaves that are eaten raw, especially in salad. There are many types of lettuce. 莴苣；生菜：*a bacon, lettuce and tomato sandwich* 咸肉、生菜加番茄三明治 ◇ *Buy a lettuce and some tomatoes.* 买一棵生菜和一些番茄。➲ VISUAL VOCAB PAGE V34

ˈ**let-up** *noun* [U, sing.] ~ (**in sth**) a period of time during which sth stops or becomes less strong, difficult, etc.; a reduction in the strength of sth（一段时间内的）停止，减弱，减少强度 SYN **lull**：*There is no sign of a let-up in the recession.* 经济衰退没有减弱的迹象。

L

leuco·cyte (*also* **leuko·cyte**) /ˈluːkəsaɪt; *BrE also* -kəʊs-/ *noun* (*biology* 生) = WHITE BLOOD CELL

leu·kae·mia (*BrE*) (*NAmE* **leu·ke·mia**) /luːˈkiːmiə/ *noun* [U] a serious disease in which too many white blood cells are produced, causing weakness and sometimes death 白血病

levee /ˈlevi/ *noun* (*NAmE*) **1** a low wall built at the side of a river to prevent it from flooding 防洪堤 **2** a place on a river where boats can let passengers on or off（河边乘客上下船的）码头

level /ˈlevl/ *noun, adj., verb*

■ *noun*

• **AMOUNT** 数量 **1** [C] the amount of sth that exists in a particular situation at a particular time（某时某情况下存在的）数量，程度，浓度：*a test that checks the level of alcohol in the blood* 对血液中酒精含量的测试 ◇ *a relatively* ***low/high level*** *of crime* 相对低的／高的罪案数字 ◇ ***low/high*** *pollution* ***levels*** 轻度／重度污染 ◇ *Profits were* ***at the same level*** *as the year before.* 利润和前一年持平。

• **STANDARD** 标准 **2** [C, U] a particular standard or quality 标准；水平；质量；品级：*a* ***high level of*** *achievement* 高水平的成就 ◇ *a computer game with 15 levels* * 15 级的电脑游戏 ◇ *What is the level of this course?* 这门课程是什么程度？◇ *He studied French to* ***degree level****.* 他的法语学到了拿学位的水平。◇ *Both players are* ***on a level*** (= of the same standard). 两位选手的水平不相上下。◇ *I refuse to* ***sink to their level*** (= behave as badly as them). 我不愿堕落到他们那种地步。➲ SEE ALSO A LEVEL, ENTRY-LEVEL

• **RANK IN SCALE** 级别 **3** [U, C] a position or rank in a scale of size or importance 层次；级别：*a decision taken at board level* 由董事会作出的决定 ◇ *Discussions are currently being held at national level.* 目前讨论正在全国进行。

• **POINT OF VIEW** 观察的角度 **4** [C] a particular way of looking at, reacting to or understanding sth 看待（或应对、理解）事物的方式：*On a more personal level, I would like to thank Jean for all the help she has given me.* 从较为个人的角度我要感谢琼所给予我的一切帮助。◇ *Fables can be understood on various levels.* 寓言可从不同的角度去理解。

• **HEIGHT** 高度 **5** [C, U] the height of sth in relation to the ground or to what it used to be（与地面或过去位置相对的）高度：*the level of water in the bottle* 瓶中的水位 ◇ *The cables are buried one metre below* ***ground level****.* 电缆埋在地平面下一米深的地方。◇ *The floodwater nearly reached roof level.* 洪水几乎涨到屋顶。◇ *The tables are not* ***on a level*** (= the same height). 这些桌子高矮不一。➲ SEE ALSO EYE LEVEL, SEA LEVEL

• **FLOOR/LAYER** 楼层；层面 **6** [C] a floor of a building; a layer of ground 楼层；地层：*The library is all on one level.* 图书馆全部在同一层楼上。◇ *Archaeologists found pottery in the lowest level of the site.* 考古学家在挖掘现场的最下层发现了陶器。◇ *a multi-level parking lot* 多层停车场 ➲ SEE ALSO SPLIT-LEVEL

• **TOOL** 工具 **7** [C] = SPIRIT LEVEL

IDM **on the ˈlevel** (*NAmE also* **on the ˌup and ˈup**) (*informal*) honest; legal 诚实；诚恳；合法；正当 SYN **above board**：*I'm not convinced he's on the level.* 我不相信他是真诚的。◇ *Are you sure this deal is on the level?* 你确信这笔交易合法吗？

■ *adj.*

• **FLAT** 平坦 **1** having a flat surface that does not slope 平的；平坦的：*Pitch the tent on level ground.* 把帐篷搭建在平地上。◇ *Add a* ***level tablespoon*** *of flour* (= enough to fill the spoon but not so much that it goes above the level of the edge of the spoon). 加一平匙面粉。➲ COMPARE HEAPED

• **EQUAL** 相等 **2** having the same height, position, value, etc. as sth 等高的；地位相同的；价值相等的：*Are these pictures level?* 这些画挂得一样高吗？◇ **~ with sth** *This latest rise is intended to keep wages level with inflation.* 最近这次加薪目的是使工资与通货膨胀保持相同的水平。◇ *She* ***drew level with*** (= came beside) *the police car.* 她开车赶上来和警车并排行驶。 **3** ~ (**with sb**) (*especially BrE, sport* 体育) having the same score as sb 得分相同：*A good second round brought him level with the tournament leader.* 他第二轮发挥良好，与锦标赛领先选手得分持平。◇ *France took an early lead but Wales soon* ***drew level*** (= scored the same number of points). 法国队开始领先，但很快就被威尔士队把比分扳平。

• **VOICE/LOOK** 声音；目光 **4** not showing any emotion; steady 平静的；冷静的；平稳的 SYN **even**：*a level gaze* 目光平静的凝视 ➲ SEE ALSO LEVELLY

IDM **be ˌlevel ˈpegging** (*BrE*) having the same score 势均力敌；不分胜负：*The contestants were level pegging after round 3.* 参赛选手在第 3 轮以后成绩不相上下。 **do/try your level ˈbest (to do sth)** to do as much as you can to try to achieve sth 尽自己最大的努力；竭尽全力；全力以赴 **a ˌlevel ˈplaying field** a situation in which everyone has the same opportunities 人人机会均等

■ *verb* (**-ll-**, *especially US* **-l-**)

• **MAKE FLAT** 使平坦 **1** [T] ~ **sth** (**off/out**) to make sth flat or smooth 使平坦；使平整：*If you're laying tiles, the floor will need to be levelled first.* 你如果要铺瓷砖，得先整平地面。

• **DESTROY** 摧毁 **2** [T] ~ **sth** to destroy a building or a group of trees completely by knocking it down 摧毁，夷平（建筑物或树林） SYN **raze**：*The blast levelled several buildings in the area.* 那次爆炸把当地几座建筑物夷为平地。

• **MAKE EQUAL** 使相等 **3** [T, I] ~ (**sth**) to make sth equal or similar 使相等；使平等；使相似：*Davies levelled the score at 2 all.* 戴维斯把比分拉成 2:2 平。

• **POINT** 瞄准 **4** [T] ~ **sth** (**at sb**) to point sth, especially a gun, at sb（尤指用枪）瞄准，对准：*I had a gun levelled at my head.* 有一支枪对准了我的头。➲ MORE LIKE THIS 36, page R29

IDM ˌ**level the ˈplaying field** to create a situation where everyone has the same opportunities 创造人人机会均等的局面

PHR V ˈ**level sth against/at sb** to say publicly that sb is to blame for sth, especially a crime or a mistake（尤指对犯罪或犯错的人）公开指责，谴责：*The speech was intended to answer the charges levelled against him by his opponents.* 他演讲的目的在于回应对手对他的公开指责。

ˌ**level sth↔ˈdown** to make standards, amounts, etc. be of the same low or lower level 使（标准、数量等）降至同等水平；使降至更低水平：*Teachers are accused of levelling standards down to suit the needs of less able students.* 有人指责教师降低标准以适应学习较差的学生的需要。

ˌ**level ˈoff/ˈout 1** to stop rising or falling and remain horizontal（停止升降而）保持水平：*The plane levelled off at 1 500 feet.* 飞机在 1 500 英尺的高空保持水平飞行。◇ *After the long hill, the road levelled out.* 过了漫长的山路

后，道路就变得平坦了。 **2** to stay at a steady level of development or progress after a period of sharp rises or falls（经过急剧的涨落后）保持平稳发展：*Sales have levelled off after a period of rapid growth.* 销售经过一段时间的快速增长后呈稳定状态。 ➲ WORDFINDER NOTE AT TREND

ˌlevel sth↔ˈup to make standards, amounts, etc. be of the same high or higher level 把（标准、数量等）拉平；使达到更高水平 **ˈlevel with sb** (*informal*) to tell sb the truth and not hide any unpleasant facts from them 对某人说实话；直言相告

ˌlevel ˈcrossing (*BrE*) (*NAmE* **ˈrailroad crossing**) *noun* a place where a road crosses a railway/railroad line（公路与铁路交会的）道口，平面交叉

ˌlevel-ˈheaded *adj.* calm and sensible; able to make good decisions even in difficult situations 冷静明智的；头脑清醒的；（在困境中）能作出正确决策的

lev·el·ler (*especially US* **lev·el·er**) /ˈlevələ(r)/ *noun* [usually sing.] an event or a situation that makes everyone equal whatever their age, importance, etc. 使人人平等的事（或局面）：*death, the great leveller* 凡人皆要面对的死亡

lev·el·ly /ˈlevəli/ *adv.* in a calm and steady way 冷静地；平静地；沉稳地：*She looked at him levelly.* 她平静地看着他。

lever /ˈliːvə(r); *NAmE* ˈlevər/ *noun, verb*

■ ***noun*** **1** a handle used to operate a vehicle or piece of machinery（车辆或机器的）操纵杆，控制杆：*Pull the lever towards you to adjust the speed.* 把操纵杆往你身前拉动以调节速度。 ➲ SEE ALSO GEAR LEVER **2** a long piece of wood, metal, etc. used for lifting or opening sth by sb placing one end of it under an object and pushing down on the other end 杠杆 **3** ~ **(for/against sth)** an action that is used to put pressure on sb to do sth they do not want to do 施压的行为：*The threat of sanctions is our most powerful lever for peace.* 实施制裁的威胁是我们争取和平最有力的施压手段。

■ ***verb*** to move sth with a lever（用杠杆）撬动 **SYN** **prise**：**~ sth + adv./prep.** *I levered the lid off the pot with a knife.* 我用刀撬掉了罐盖。◇ **~ sth + adj.** *They managed to lever the door open.* 他们设法撬开了门。

le·ver·age /ˈliːvərɪdʒ; *NAmE* ˈlev-/ *noun, verb*

■ ***noun*** [U] **1** (*formal*) the ability to influence what people do 影响力：*diplomatic leverage* 外交影响力 **2** (*specialist*) the act of using a lever to open or lift sth; the force used to do this 杠杆作用；杠杆效力 **3** (*NAmE*) (*BrE* **gear·ing**) (*finance* 财) the relationship between the amount of money that a company owes and the value of its shares 杠杆比率；资本与负债比率

■ ***verb*** **~ sth** (*business* 商) to get as much advantage or profit as possible from sth that you have 充分利用：*The company needs to leverage its resources.* 该公司需要充分利用其资源。

ˌleveraged ˈbuyout *noun* (*business* 商, *especially NAmE*) the act of a small company buying a larger company using money that is borrowed based on the value of this larger company 杠杆式贷款收购，衡平收购（小公司以大公司的价值抵押贷款来收购这家大公司的方法）

lev·eret /ˈlevərət/ *noun* a young HARE 小野兔；野兔幼崽

le·via·than /ləˈvaɪəθən/ *noun* **1** (in the Bible) a very large sea MONSTER 利维坦（《圣经》中的怪兽） **2** (*literary*) a very large and powerful thing 庞然大物：*the leviathan of government bureaucracy* 政府庞大的官僚机构

Levi's™ /ˈliːvaɪz/ *noun* [pl.] a US make of jeans (= trousers/pants made of DENIM)（美国）李维斯牛仔裤

levi·tate /ˈlevɪteɪt/ *verb* [I, T] ~ **(sth)** to rise and float in the air with no physical support, especially by means of magic or by using special mental powers; to make sth rise in this way（尤指用魔力或特别的精神力量）升空，空中飘浮，使升空，使飘浮 ▸ **levi·ta·tion** /ˌlevɪˈteɪʃn/ *noun* [U]

lev·ity /ˈlevəti/ *noun* [U] (*formal*) behaviour that shows a lack of respect for sth serious and that treats it in an amusing way 轻率的举止；轻浮；轻佻 **SYN** **frivolity**

levy **AW** /ˈlevi/ *noun, verb*

■ ***noun*** (*pl.* **-ies**) ~ **(on sth)** an extra amount of money that has to be paid, especially as a tax to the government 征收额；（尤指）税款：*to put/impose a levy on oil imports* 对进口石油征税

■ ***verb*** (**lev·ies**, **levy·ing**, **lev·ied**, **lev·ied**) ~ **sth (on sb/sth)** to use official authority to demand and collect a payment, tax, etc. 征收；征（税）：*a tax levied by the government on excess company profits* 政府对公司超额利润征收的税

lewd /luːd; *BrE also* ljuːd/ *adj.* referring to sex in a rude and offensive way 粗野下流的；淫荡的；猥亵的 **SYN** **obscene**：*lewd behaviour/jokes/suggestions* 粗俗下流的行为 / 玩笑 / 暗示 ▸ **lewd·ly** *adv.* **lewd·ness** *noun* [U]

lex·eme /ˈleksiːm/ (*also* **ˌlexical ˈunit**) *noun* (*linguistics* 语言) a word or several words that have a meaning that is not expressed by any of its separate parts 词位，词素（最小的意义单位）

lex·ic·al /ˈleksɪkl/ *adj.* [usually before noun] (*linguistics* 语言) connected with the words of a language 词汇的：*lexical items* (= words and phrases) 词项 ▸ **lex·ic·al·ly** /-kli/ *adv.*

ˈlexical meaning *noun* [U, C] the meaning of a word, without paying attention to the way that it is used or to the words that occur with it（不考虑用法或搭配的）词汇意义，词义

ˌlexical ˈunit *noun* = LEXEME

lexi·cog·raph·er /ˌleksɪˈkɒɡrəfə(r); *NAmE* -ˈkɑːɡ-/ *noun* a person who writes and EDITS dictionaries 词典编纂者

lexi·cog·raphy /ˌleksɪˈkɒɡrəfi; *NAmE* -ˈkɑːɡ-/ *noun* [U] the theory and practice of writing dictionaries 词典编纂学；词典编纂

lexi·col·ogy /ˌleksɪˈkɒlədʒi; *NAmE* -ˈkɑːl-/ *noun* [U] the study of the form, meaning and behaviour of words 词汇学

lexi·con /ˈleksɪkən; *NAmE also* -kɑːn/ *noun* **1** (*also* **the lexicon**) [sing.] (*linguistics* 语言) all the words and phrases used in a particular language or subject; all the words and phrases used and known by a particular person or group of people（某语言或学科、某人或群体使用的）全部词汇：*the lexicon of finance and economics* 财经词汇 **2** [C] a list of words on a particular subject or in a language in alphabetical order（某学科或语言的）词汇表：*a lexicon of technical scientific terms* 科技术语词汇表 **3** [C] a dictionary, especially one of an ancient language, such as Greek or Hebrew（尤指希腊语或希伯来语等古代语言的）词典，字典

lexis /ˈleksɪs/ *noun* [U] (*linguistics* 语言) all the words and phrases of a particular language（某语言的）全部词汇 **SYN** **vocabulary**

ley /leɪ/ *noun* **1** (*also* **ˈley line**) an imaginary line that is believed to follow the route of an ancient track and to have special powers（被认为与古代路径重合并具有超常力量的）假想线 **2** (*specialist*) an area of land where grass is grown temporarily instead of crops 暂作草地的可耕地；轮作的草地

Ley·land cy·press /ˌleɪlənd ˈsaɪprəs/ (*also* **ley·landii** /leɪˈlændiaɪ/) *noun* a tree (a type of CONIFER) that grows very quickly, often used to divide gardens 莱兰柏（生长迅速，常用以分隔花园）

lezzy (*also* **lezzie**) /ˈlezi/ *noun, adj.* (*pl.* **-ies**) (*informal, offensive, especially BrE*) = LESBIAN

LGBT /ˌel dʒiː biː ˈtiː/ *abbr.* lesbian, gay, bisexual and transgendered 非异性恋者族群（全写为 lesbian, gay, bisexual and transgendered，即女同性恋者、男同性恋者、双性恋者与易性癖者）

l.h. *abbr.* (in writing 书写形式) LEFT HAND 左手

L

li·abil·ity /ˌlaɪəˈbɪləti/ *noun* (*pl.* **-ies**) **1** [U] ~ (**for sth**) | ~ (**to do sth**) the state of being legally responsible for sth（法律上对某事物的）责任，义务：*The company cannot accept liability for any damage caused by natural disasters.* 该公司对自然灾害造成的任何损失概不承担责任。 **2** [C, usually sing.] (*informal*) a person or thing that causes you a lot of problems 惹麻烦的人（或事）：*Since his injury, Jones has become more of a liability than an asset to the team.* 琼斯负伤以来，与其说他是全队的骨干倒不如说他已成为队里的累赘。 **3** [C, usually pl.] the amount of money that a person or company owes 欠债；负债；债务：*The company is reported to have liabilities of nearly $90 000.* 据说公司负债近 9 万美元。 ➲ COMPARE ASSET (2)

li·able /ˈlaɪəbl/ *adj.* [not before noun] **1** ~ (**for sth**) legally responsible for paying the cost of sth（法律上）负有偿付责任：*You will be liable for any damage caused.* 你必须对造成的任何损失负赔偿责任。◇ *The court ruled he could not be held personally liable for his wife's debts.* 法庭裁定他个人不负有偿付妻子债务的责任。 **2** ~ **to do sth** likely to do sth 可能（做某事）：*We're all liable to make mistakes when we're tired.* 人在疲劳时都可能出差错。◇ *The bridge is liable to collapse at any moment.* 那座桥可能随时坍塌。 **3** ~ **to sth** likely to be affected by sth 可能受…影响 **SYN** **prone**: *You are more liable to injury if you exercise infrequently.* 不经常运动就更容易受伤。 **4** ~ **to sth** likely to be punished by law for sth 可能受法律惩处：*Offenders are liable to fines of up to $500.* 违者可能被处以最多 500 美元的罚款。 **5** ~ **for/to sth** | ~ **to do sth** having to do sth by law 必须按法律做（某事）；负有…责任：*People who earn under a certain amount are not liable to pay tax.* 收入低于一定数额者不必纳税。

li·aise /liˈeɪz/ *verb* **1** [I] ~ (**with sb**) (*especially BrE*) to work closely with sb and exchange information with them（与某人）联络，联系：*He had to liaise directly with the police while writing the report.* 写报告的时候他不得不直接与警方取得联系。 **2** [I] ~ (**between A and B**) to act as a link between two or more people or groups 做联系人；担当联络员：*Her job is to liaise between students and teachers.* 她的工作是做师生间的联系人。

li·aison /liˈeɪzn; *NAmE* liˈeɪzɑːn; ˈliəzɑːn/ *noun* **1** [U, sing.] ~ (**between A and B**) a relationship between two organizations or different departments in an organization, involving the exchange of information or ideas 联络；联系：*Our role is to ensure liaison between schools and parents.* 我们的职责是确保学校与家长间的联系。◇ *We work in close liaison with the police.* 我们与警方密切配合。 **2** [C] ~ (**to/with sb/sth**) a person whose job is to make sure there is a good relationship between two groups or organizations 联络员；联系人：*the White House liaison to organized labor* 白宫与工人组织的联络人 **3** [C] ~ (**with sb**) a secret sexual relationship, especially if one or both partners are married （尤指一方或双方已婚的）私通，通奸 **SYN** **affair**

liˈaison officer *noun* a person whose job is to make sure that there is a good relationship between two groups of people, organizations, etc. 联络人 ➲ SEE ALSO LIAISON (2)

liar /ˈlaɪə(r)/ *noun* a person who tells lies 说谎者；撒谎者

lib /lɪb/ *noun* (*informal*) the abbreviation for 'liberation' (used in the names of organizations demanding greater freedom, equal rights, etc.) 解放（全写为 liberation，用于组织名称）：*women's lib* 妇女解放运动

li·ba·tion /laɪˈbeɪʃn/ *noun* (*formal*) (in the past) a gift of wine to a god（旧时供奉神的）奠酒，祭酒

Lib Dem /ˌlɪb ˈdem/ *abbr.* (in British Politics 英国政治) LIBERAL DEMOCRAT 自由民主党成员（或支持者）：*I voted Lib Dem.* 我投了自由民主党的票。

libel /ˈlaɪbl/ *noun, verb*

■ ***noun*** [U, C] the act of printing a statement about sb that is not true and that gives people a bad opinion of them（文字）诽谤，中伤：*He sued the newspaper for libel.* 他控告那家报社犯有诽谤罪。◇ *a libel action* (= a case in a court of law) 诽谤诉讼 ➲ COMPARE SLANDER *n.*

■ ***verb*** (**-ll-**, *especially US* **-l-**) ~ **sb** to publish a written statement about sb that is not true 发表文字诽谤（某人）：*He claimed he had been libelled in an article the magazine had published.* 他声称他遭到了那家杂志发表的一篇文章的诽谤。 ➲ COMPARE SLANDER *v.*

li·bel·lous (*especially US* **li·bel·ous**) /ˈlaɪbələs/ *adj.* containing a LIBEL about sb 含有诽谤性文字的：*a libellous statement* 诽谤性的声明

lib·eral **AW** /ˈlɪbərəl/ *adj., noun*

■ ***adj.***

• **RESPECTING OTHER OPINIONS** 尊重他人意见 **1** willing to understand and respect other people's behaviour, opinions, etc., especially when they are different from your own; believing people should be able to choose how they behave 宽宏大度的；心胸宽阔的；开明的：*liberal attitudes/views/opinions* 开明的态度 / 观点 / 意见

• **POLITICS** 政治 **2** wanting or allowing a lot of political and economic freedom and supporting gradual social, political or religious change（政治经济上）自由的，开明的；支持（社会、政治或宗教）变革的：*Some politicians want more liberal trade relations with Europe.* 有些政治家想与欧洲大陆建立更加自由的贸易关系。◇ *liberal democracy* 自由民主 ◇ *liberal theories* 自由主义的理论 ◇ *a liberal politician* 支持改革的政治家 **3** **Liberal** connected with the British Liberal Party in the past, or of a Liberal Party in another country（旧时）英国自由党的；（英国以外国家）自由党的 ➲ WORDFINDER NOTE AT SYSTEM

• **GENEROUS** 慷慨 **4** ~ (**with sth**) generous; given in large amounts 慷慨的；大方的；大量给予的 **SYN** **lavish**: *She is very liberal with her money.* 她用钱很大方。◇ *I think Sam is too liberal with his criticism* (= he criticizes people too much). 我认为萨姆太爱批评人。

• **EDUCATION** 教育 **5** concerned with increasing sb's general knowledge and experience rather than particular skills 通识（教育）的：*a liberal education* 通识教育

• **NOT EXACT** 不精确 **6** not completely accurate or exact 不完全准确的；不精确的；不严格的 **SYN** **free**: *a liberal translation of the text* 不拘泥于原文的翻译 ◇ ***a liberal interpretation** of the law* 对法律的灵活解释

▸ **lib·er·al·ly** **AW** /-rəli/ *adv.*：*Apply the cream liberally.* 抹上大量的奶油。◇ *The word 'original' is liberally interpreted in copyright law.* * original 一词在版权法中解释很灵活。

■ ***noun***

• **SB WHO RESPECTS OTHERS** 尊重他人者 **1** a person who understands and respects other people's opinions and behaviour, especially when they are different from their own 理解且尊重他人意见的人；宽容的人；开明的人

• **POLITICS** 政治 **2** a person who supports political, social and religious change 支持（社会、政治或宗教）变革的人：*Reform is popular with middle-class liberals.* 改革受到了中产阶级支持变革者的普遍欢迎。 **3** **Liberal** (*politics* 政) a member of the British Liberal Party in the past, or of a Liberal Party in another country（旧时）英国自由党成员；（英国以外国家的）自由党成员

ˌliberal ˈarts *noun* [pl.] (*especially NAmE*) subjects of study that develop students' general knowledge and ability to think, rather than their technical skills 文科

ˌLiberal ˈDemocrat *noun* (*abbr.* **Lib Dem**) a member or supporter of the Liberal Democrats 自由民主党成员（或支持者）

the ˌLiberal ˈDemocrats *noun* [pl.] (*abbr.* **Lib Dems**) one of the main British political parties, in favour of some political and social change, but not extreme（英国）自由民主党 ➲ COMPARE CONSERVATIVE PARTY, LABOUR PARTY

lib·er·al·ism **AW** /ˈlɪbərəlɪzəm/ *noun* [U] liberal opinions and beliefs, especially in politics 自由主义

lib·er·al·ity /ˌlɪbəˈræləti/ *noun* [U] (*formal*) **1** respect for political, religious or moral views, even if you do not agree with them（对政治、宗教或道德观点的）尊重，宽容，宽宏大度 **2** the quality of being generous 慷慨；大方

lib·er·al·ize AW (*BrE also* **-ise**) /ˈlɪbrəlaɪz/ *verb* **~ sth** to make sth such as a law or a political or religious system less strict 使自由化；放宽对…的限制 ▸ **lib·er·al·iza·tion, -isa·tion** AW /ˌlɪbrəlaɪˈzeɪʃn; *NAmE* -ləˈz-/ *noun* [U]

lib·er·ate AW /ˈlɪbəreɪt/ *verb* **1 ~ sb/sth (from sb/sth)** to free a country or a person from the control of sb else 解放：*The city was liberated by the advancing army.* 军队向前挺进，解放了那座城市。 **2 ~ sb (from sth)** to free sb from sth that restricts their control over and enjoyment of their own life 使自由；使摆脱约束（或限制）：*Writing poetry liberated her from the routine of everyday life.* 写诗使她从日常生活的例行公事中解脱出来。 ▸ **lib·er·ation** AW /ˌlɪbəˈreɪʃn/ *noun* [U, sing.]: *a war of liberation* 解放战争 ◇ *liberation from poverty* 摆脱贫困 ◇ *women's liberation* 妇女解放运动 **lib·er·ator** AW *noun*

lib·er·ated AW /ˈlɪbəreɪtɪd/ *adj.* free from the restrictions of traditional ideas about social and sexual behaviour（社会及性行为）不受传统思想束缚的，解放的，开放的

libeˌration theˈology *noun* [U] a Christian movement, developed mainly by Latin American Catholics, which deals with social justice and the problems of people who are poor, as well as with spiritual matters 解放神学（拉丁美洲天主教徒倡导社会正义，针对穷人以及神学问题）

lib·er·tar·ian /ˌlɪbəˈteəriən; *NAmE* -bərˈter-/ *noun* a person who strongly believes that people should have the freedom to do and think as they like 自由论者

lib·er·tine /ˈlɪbətiːn; *NAmE* -bərt-/ *noun* (*formal, disapproving*) a person, usually a man, who leads an immoral life and is interested in pleasure, especially sexual pleasure 放荡的男人；放荡不羁的人；浪荡公子

lib·erty /ˈlɪbəti; *NAmE* -bərti/ *noun* (*pl.* **-ies**) **1** [U] freedom to live as you choose without too many restrictions from government or authority 自由（自己选择生活方式而不受政府或权威的过多限制）：*the fight for justice and liberty* 争取正义和自由的斗争 **2** [U] the state of not being a prisoner or a SLAVE 自由（不受关押或奴役的状态）：*He had to endure six months' loss of liberty.* 他得忍受六个月失去自由之苦。 **3** [C] the legal right and freedom to do sth 自由（做某事的合法权利及行动自由）：*The right to vote should be a liberty enjoyed by all.* 投票权应当是人人享有的合法权利。 ◇ *People fear that security cameras could infringe personal liberties.* 人们担心保安摄像机会侵犯人身自由。 ➲ SEE ALSO CIVIL LIBERTY **4** [sing.] an act or a statement that may offend or annoy sb, especially because it is done without permission or does not show respect 冒犯行为（或言语）；放肆；失礼：*He* ***took the liberty of*** *reading my files while I was away.* 他趁我不在时擅自看我的文件。 ◇ *They've got a liberty, not even sending me a reply.* 他们真无礼，连个答复也不给我。 ➲ WORDFINDER NOTE AT FREEDOM

IDM **at liberty** (*formal*) (of a prisoner or an animal 囚犯或动物) no longer in prison or in a CAGE 不再受监禁；自由 SYN **free** **at liberty to do sth** (*formal*) having the right or freedom to do sth 有权做…；有…自由 SYN **free**: *You are at liberty to say what you like.* 你尽可畅所欲言。 **take ˈliberties with sb/sth** **1** to make important and unreasonable changes to sth, especially a book（尤指对书）任意窜改：*The movie takes considerable liberties with the novel that it is based on.* 影片对小说原著作了相当大的改动。 **2** (*old-fashioned*) to be too friendly with sb, especially in a sexual way 过分亲昵；放肆；狎昵；调戏

li·bid·in·ous /lɪˈbɪdɪnəs/ *adj.* (*formal*) having or expressing strong sexual feelings 性欲强的；好色的；淫荡的

li·bido /lɪˈbiːdəʊ; ˈlɪbɪdəʊ; *NAmE* -doʊ/ *noun* (*pl.* **-os**) [U, C, usually sing.] (*specialist*) sexual desire 力比多；性欲；性冲动：*loss of libido* 性欲的丧失

Libra /ˈliːbrə/ *noun* **1** [U] the 7th sign of the ZODIAC, the SCALES 黄道第七宫；天秤宫；天秤（星）座 **2** [C] a person born when the sun is in this sign, that is between 23 September and 22 October, approximately 属天秤座的人（约出生于 9 月 23 日至 10 月 22 日） ▸ **Li·bran** *noun, adj.*

li·brar·ian /laɪˈbreəriən; *NAmE* -ˈbrer-/ *noun* a person who is in charge of or works in a library 图书馆馆长；图书管理员 ▸ **li·brar·ian·ship** *noun* [U]: *a degree in librarianship* 图书管理学学位

li·brary /ˈlaɪbrəri; ˈlaɪbri; *NAmE* -breri/ *noun* (*pl.* **-ies**) **1** a building in which collections of books, CDs, newspapers, etc. are kept for people to read, study or borrow 图书馆；藏书楼：***a public/reference/university, etc. library*** 公共图书馆、参考书阅览室、大学图书馆等 ◇ ***a library book*** 图书馆藏书 ◇ ***a toy library*** (= for borrowing toys from) 玩具出借馆 **2** a room in a large house where most of the books are kept 图书室；资料室 **3** (*formal*) a personal collection of books, CDs, etc.（书、激光唱片等的）个人收藏：*a new edition to add to your library* 可收藏的新版本 **4** a series of books, recordings, etc. produced by the same company and similar in appearance 系列丛书（或录制的音像等）；文库：*a library of children's classics* 儿童文学名著系列丛书

the ˌLibrary of ˈCongress *noun* [sing.] the US national library（美国）国会图书馆

li·bret·tist /lɪˈbretɪst/ *noun* a person who writes the words for an OPERA or a musical play（歌剧或音乐剧的）剧本作者，歌词作者

li·bretto /lɪˈbretəʊ; *NAmE* -toʊ/ *noun* (*pl.* **-os** or **li·bretti** /-tiː/) (*music* 音, *from Italian*) the words that are sung or spoken in an OPERA or a musical play（歌剧或音乐剧的）唱词，歌词 ➲ WORDFINDER NOTE AT OPERA

lice PL. OF LOUSE

li·cence AW (*especially US* **li·cense**) /ˈlaɪsns/ *noun* **1** [C] an official document that shows that permission has been given to do, own or use sth 许可证；执照：*a driving licence* 驾驶执照 ◇ *James lost his licence for six months* (= had his licence taken away by the police as a punishment). 詹姆斯的执照被警方扣了六个月。 ◇ **~ (for sth)** *a licence for the software* 软件许可证 ◇ *Is there a licence fee?* 要交许可证费吗？ ◇ **~ (to do sth)** *You need a licence to fish in this river.* 你在这条河里钓鱼要有许可证。 ◇ *a licence holder* (= a person who has been given a licence) 许可证持有人 ➲ WORDFINDER NOTE AT CAR **2** [U, sing.] **~ (to do sth)** (*formal*) freedom to do or say whatever you want, often sth bad or unacceptable 放肆；放纵：*Lack of punishment seems to give youngsters licence to break the law.* 由于缺少惩罚，年轻人似乎便恣意违法。 **3** [U] (*formal*) freedom to behave in a way that is considered sexually immoral 放荡；纵欲；淫乱

IDM **artistic/poetic ˈlicence** the freedom of artists or writers to change facts in order to make a story, painting, etc. more interesting or beautiful 艺术上自由发挥的权利；诗的破格 **a licence to print ˈmoney** (*disapproving*) used to describe a business which makes a lot of money with little effort 不费劲挣大钱；一本万利；摇钱树 **under ˈlicence** (of a product 产品) made with the permission of a company or an organization 获得生产许可

li·cense AW /ˈlaɪsns/ *verb, noun*

■ ***verb*** (*BrE also, less frequent* **li·cence**) to give sb official permission to do, own, or use sth 批准；许可：**~ sth** *The new drug has not yet been licensed in the US.* 这种新药尚未在美国获得许可。 ◇ (*BrE*) *licensing hours* (= the times when alcohol can be sold at a pub, etc.) 限定的售酒时间 ◇ **~ sb/sth to do sth** *They had licensed the firm to produce the drug.* 他们批准了那家公司生产这种药物。

■ ***noun*** (*NAmE*) = LICENCE：*a driver's license* 驾驶执照 ◇ *a license for the software* 软件许可证 ◇ *a license holder* (= a person who has been given a license) 许可证持有人

li·censed AW /ˈlaɪsnst/ *adj.* **1** (*BrE*) having official permission to sell alcoholic drinks 有售酒许可的；获准售酒的：*a licensed restaurant* 有售酒许可的餐馆 **2** that you have official permission to own 获准拥有的：*Is that gun licensed?* 那支枪有持枪执照吗？ **3** having official

L

permission to do sth 得到正式许可的：*She is licensed to fly solo.* 她已获准单飞。

ˌlicensed ˈvictualler *noun* = VICTUALLER

li·cen·see /ˌlaɪsənˈsiː/ *noun* **1** (*BrE*) a person who has a licence to sell alcoholic drinks 售酒执照持有者 **2** a person or company that has a licence to make sth or to use sth 特许制作（或使用）…的人（或公司）

ˈlicense number (*NAmE*) (*BrE* **regiˈstration number**, **regis·tra·tion**) *noun* the series of letters and numbers that are shown on a LICENSE PLATE at the front and back of a vehicle to identify it（车辆的）登记号码，牌照号码

ˈlicense plate (*NAmE*) (*BrE* **ˈnumber plate**) *noun* a metal or plastic plate on the front and back of a vehicle that shows its LICENSE NUMBER（车辆的）牌照，号码牌

ˈlicensing laws *noun* [pl.] British laws that state where and when alcoholic drinks can be sold（英国的）售酒法

li·cen·ti·ate /laɪˈsenʃiət/ *noun* (*specialist*) a person with official permission to work in a particular profession 持职业执照者

li·cen·tious /laɪˈsenʃəs/ *adj.* (*formal, disapproving*) behaving in a way that is considered sexually immoral 放荡的；淫荡的；淫乱的 ▶ **li·cen·tious·ness** *noun* [U]

li·chee = LYCHEE

li·chen /ˈlaɪkən; ˈlɪtʃən/ *noun* [U, C] a very small grey or yellow plant that spreads over the surface of rocks, walls and trees and does not have any flowers 地衣 ➲ VISUAL VOCAB PAGE V11 ➲ COMPARE MOSS

lich·gate ➲ LYCHGATE

licit /ˈlɪsɪt/ *adj.* (*formal*) allowed or legal 准许的；合法的 OPP **illicit** ▶ **licit·ly** *adv.*

lick /lɪk/ *verb, noun*

■ *verb* **1** [T] to move your tongue over the surface of sth in order to eat it, make it wet or clean it 舔：**~ sth** *He licked his fingers.* 他舔了一下自己的手指。◇ *I'm tired of licking envelopes.* 我舔信封都舔烦了。◇ *The cat sat licking its paws.* 那只猫坐着舔爪子。◇ **~ sth + adj.** *She licked the spoon clean.* 她把调羹舔得干干净净。 **2** [T] **~ sth + adv./prep.** to eat or drink sth by licking it 舔吃；舔着喝：*The cat licked up the milk.* 猫把牛奶舔光了。◇ *She licked the honey off the spoon.* 她舔光了调羹上的蜂蜜。 **3** [T, I] (of flames 火焰) to touch sth lightly 掠过；（火舌）舔食：**~ sth** *Flames were soon licking the curtains.* 火焰很快就烧着了窗帘。◇ **~ at sth** *The flames were now licking at their feet.* 火焰现正在他们脚下蔓延。 **4** [T] **~ sb/sth** (*informal*) to easily defeat sb or deal with sth 轻松战胜；轻易对付：*We thought we **had them licked**.* 我们以为已经轻易地把他们对付过去了。◇ *It was a tricky problem but I think we've licked it.* 这是一个棘手的问题，但我认为我们轻而易举地把它解决了。

IDM **lick sb's ˈboots** (*also taboo, slang* **lick sb's ˈarse**) (*disapproving*) to show too much respect for sb in authority because you want to please them 阿谀奉承；谄媚；拍马屁 SYN **crawl** **lick your ˈwounds** to spend time trying to get your strength or confidence back after a defeat or disappointment（失败或失望后）恢复元气，重整旗鼓 ➲ MORE AT LIP, SHAPE *n.*

■ *noun* **1** [C] an act of licking sth with the tongue 舔：*Can I have a lick of your ice cream?* 我能尝一口你的冰淇淋吗？ **2** [sing.] **a ~ of paint** (*informal*) a small amount of paint, used to make a place look better 一点儿（涂料）：*What this room needs is a lick of paint.* 这房间所需要的是刷点儿涂料。 **3** [C] (*informal*) a short piece of music which is part of a song and is played on a GUITAR（吉他演奏的歌曲）小过门：*a **guitar/blues lick*** 用吉他演奏的/布鲁斯乐的小过门

IDM **a lick and a ˈpromise** (*informal*) the act of performing a task quickly and carelessly, especially of washing or cleaning sth quickly 草草了事，敷衍塞责（尤指快速地洗刷东西） **at a (fair) ˈlick** (*informal*) fast; at a high speed 迅速；高速地

lickety-split /ˌlɪkəti ˈsplɪt/ *adv.* (*NAmE, old-fashioned, informal*) very quickly; immediately 急速地；立即

lick·ing /ˈlɪkɪŋ/ *noun* [sing.] (*informal*) a severe defeat in a battle, game, etc.（在战争、比赛等中的）惨败，一败涂地 SYN **thrashing**

lick·spit·tle /ˈlɪkspɪtl/ *noun* (*old-fashioned, disapproving*) a person who tries to gain the approval of an important person 谄媚者；阿谀奉承者

lic·orice *noun* [U] (*especially NAmE*) = LIQUORICE

lid /lɪd/ *noun* **1** a cover over a container that can be removed or opened by turning or lifting it（容器的）盖，盖子：*a dustbin lid* 垃圾箱盖 ◇ *I can't get the lid off this jar.* 我打不开这广口瓶的盖子。 ➲ VISUAL VOCAB PAGES V23, V28, V36, V40 **2** = EYELID

IDM **keep a/the ˈlid on sth** **1** to keep sth secret or hidden 保守秘密；守口如瓶；遮掩；隐瞒 **2** to keep sth under control 把…控制住；抑制住：*The government is keeping the lid on inflation.* 政府正在控制通货膨胀。 **lift the ˈlid on sth | take/blow the ˈlid off sth** to tell people unpleasant or shocking facts about sth 揭露…的真相：*Her article lifts the lid on child prostitution.* 她的文章揭露了儿童卖淫的丑闻。 **put the (tin) ˈlid on sth/things** (*BrE, informal*) to be the final act or event that spoils your plans or hopes 对…是最后的一击；最后使计划（或希望）落空 ➲ MORE AT FLIP *v.*

▼ **SYNONYMS** 同义词辨析

lid

top • cork • cap • plug

These are all words for a cover for a container. 以上各词均指容器的盖、盖子。

lid a cover over a container that can be removed or opened by turning or lifting it 指容器的盖、盖子：*a jar with a tight-fitting lid* 盖子很紧的广口瓶

top a thing that you put over the end of sth such as a pen or bottle in order to close it 指笔帽、瓶盖、瓶塞

cork a small round object made of cork or plastic that is used for closing bottles, especially wine bottles 指尤用于酒瓶的软木塞、塑料瓶塞

cap (often in compounds) a top for a pen or a protective cover for sth such as the lens of a camera（常构成复合词）指钢笔、照相机镜头等的盖、帽

plug a round piece of material that you put into a hole in order to block it; a flat round rubber or plastic thing that you put into the hole of a sink in order to stop the water from flowing out 指栓塞、堵塞物、水池的塞子：*a bath plug* 浴缸塞子

PATTERNS

- a **tight-fitting** lid/top/cap
- a **screw** top/cap
- a **pen** lid/top
- to **put on/screw on/take off/unscrew** the lid/top/cap
- to **pull out** the cork/plug

lid·ded /ˈlɪdɪd/ *adj.* [usually before noun] **1** (of containers 容器) having a lid 有盖的 **2** (*literary*) used to describe a person's expression when their EYELIDS appear large or their eyes are almost closed 眼睑低垂的；眯缝着眼的：*heavily-lidded eyes* 耷拉着眼皮的眼睛 ◇ *his lidded gaze* 他眯缝着眼凝视 ➲ MORE LIKE THIS 8, page R25

lido /ˈliːdəʊ; *NAmE* -doʊ/ *noun* (*pl.* **-os**) (*BrE*) a public outdoor swimming pool or part of a beach used by the public for swimming, water sports, etc. 公共露天游泳池；海滨浴场；海滨水上运动场

lido·caine /ˈlɪdəkeɪn; *BrE also* -dəʊk-/ (*also* **lig·no·caine**) *noun* [U] a substance used as a LOCAL ANAESTHETIC, for example to stop people feeling pain when teeth are removed 利多卡因（局部麻醉药）

lie[1] /laɪ/ *verb, noun* ➲ SEE ALSO LIE[2]

■ ***verb*** (**lies, lying, lay** /leɪ/, **lain** /leɪn/) **1** [I] (of a person or an animal 人或动物) to be or put yourself in a flat or horizontal position so that you are not standing or sitting 躺；平躺；平卧：**+ adv./prep.** *to lie on your back/side/front* 仰卧；侧卧；俯卧 ◇ **+ adj.** *The cat was lying fast asleep by the fire.* 猫卧在炉火旁睡得很熟。 **2** [I] (of a thing 物品) to be or remain in a flat position on a surface 平放：**+ adv./prep.** *Clothes were lying all over the floor.* 地板上到处都堆放着衣服。 ◇ **+ adj.** *The book lay open on his desk.* 那本书摊开放在他的书桌上。 **3** [I] to be, remain or be kept in a particular state 处于，保留，保持（某种状态）：**+ adj.** *Snow was lying thick on the ground.* 厚厚的积雪覆盖着大地。 ◇ *These machines have lain idle since the factory closed.* 工厂关闭以来，这些机器就一直闲置着。 ◇ **+ adv./prep.** *a ship lying at anchor* 锚泊的船 ◇ *I'd rather use my money than leave it lying in the bank.* 我宁愿把钱花掉也不愿搁在银行里不用。 **4** [I] **+ adv./prep.** (of a town, natural feature, etc. 城镇、自然特征等) to be located in a particular place 位于；坐落在：*The town lies on the coast.* 这个小镇位于海滨。 **5** [I] **+ adv./prep.** to be spread out in a particular place 伸展；铺展；展开：*The valley lay below us.* 峡谷展现在我们的脚下。 **6** [I] ~ (**in sth**) (of ideas, qualities, problems, etc. 思想、特征、问题等) to exist or be found 存在；在于：*The problem lies in deciding when to intervene.* 问题在于决定何时介入。 **7** [I] (*BrE*) to be in a particular position during a competition（比赛时）名列，排名：**+ adv./prep.** *Thompson is lying in fourth place.* 汤姆森名列第四。 ◇ **+ adj.** *After five games the German team are lying second.* 经过五场比赛后，德国队排名第二。 ➲ COMPARE LAY *v.*

IDM **lie a'head/in 'store** to be going to happen to sb in the future 将来要发生：*You are young and your whole life lies ahead of you.* 你年纪轻，今后的日子还长着呢。 **lie in 'state** (of the dead body of an important person 重要人物的遗体) to be placed on view in a public place before being buried （安葬前停放在公共场所）供人瞻仰 **lie in 'wait (for sb)** to hide, waiting to surprise, attack or catch sb 隐蔽待机以出其不意；伏击；埋伏以待：*He was surrounded by reporters who had been lying in wait for him.* 他被暗中守候他的记者团团围住。 **lie 'low** (*informal*) to try not to attract attention to yourself 尽量不引起注意；不露面；不露声色 **take sth lying 'down** to accept an insult or offensive act without protesting or reacting 甘受屈辱；逆来顺受 ➲ MORE AT BED *n.*, BOTTOM *n.*, HEAVY *adv.*, LAND *n.*, SLEEP *v.*

PHR V **lie a'round** (*BrE also* **lie a'bout**) **1** to be left somewhere in an untidy or careless way, not put away in the correct place 到处乱放；乱搁：*Don't leave toys lying around—someone might trip over them.* 别弄得到处是玩具，说不定会绊倒谁。 **2** (of a person 人) to spend time doing nothing and being lazy 无所事事地混日子；懒散度日；游手好闲 ➲ RELATED NOUN LAYABOUT **,lie 'back** to do nothing except relax 悠闲；休息；放松：*You don't have to do anything—just lie back and enjoy the ride.* 你什么事也不必做，只管悠闲享受这次旅程的乐趣吧。 **,lie be'hind sth** to be the real reason for sth, often hidden 是…的真实原因（或理由）：*What lay behind this strange outburst?* 这反常的情绪激动的真正原因是什么？ **,lie 'down** to be or get into a flat position, especially in bed, in order to sleep or rest 躺下，平卧（尤指在床上睡觉或休息）：*Go and lie down for a while.* 去躺一会儿吧。 ◇ *He lay down on the sofa and soon fell asleep.* 他在沙发上躺下，很快就睡着了。 ➲ RELATED NOUN LIE-DOWN **,lie 'in** (*BrE*) (*also* **,sleep 'in** *NAmE, BrE*) to stay in bed after the time you usually get up 睡懒觉；起得晚：*It's a holiday tomorrow, so you can lie in.* 明天放假，你可以睡懒觉了。 ➲ RELATED NOUN LIE-IN **'lie with sb (to do sth)** (*formal*) to be sb's duty or responsibility 是…的职责（或责任）：*It lies with you to accept or reject the proposals.* 接受或是拒绝这些建议由你决定。

■ ***noun***

IDM **the ,lie of the 'land** (*BrE*) (*NAmE* **the ,lay of the 'land**) **1** the way the land in an area is formed and what physical characteristics it has 地貌；地势；地形 **2** the way a situation is now and how it is likely to develop 目前的形势及发展趋势：*Check out the lie of the land before you make a decision.* 要摸清情况后再作决定。

lie[2] /laɪ/ *verb, noun* ➲ SEE ALSO LIE[1]

■ ***verb*** (**lies, lying, lied, lied**) [I] to say or write sth that you know is not true 说谎；撒谎；编造谎言：*You could see from his face that he was lying.* 从他的表情你可以看出他在说谎。 ◇ ~ (**to sb**) (**about sth**) *Don't lie to me!* 别对我撒谎！ ◇ *She lies about her age.* 她谎报自己的年龄。 ◇ *The camera cannot lie* (= give a false impression). 照相机不会作假。 ➲ SEE ALSO LIAR

IDM **lie through your 'teeth** (*informal*) to say sth that is not true at all 满口谎言；撒弥天大谎；睁着眼说瞎话：*The witness was clearly lying through his teeth.* 那证人分明是在睁着眼睛说瞎话。 **lie your way into/out of sth** to get yourself into or out of a situation by lying 由于撒谎而处于某种境地（或摆脱某种处境）

■ ***noun*** a statement made by sb knowing that it is not true 谎言；谎话：*to tell a lie* 说谎 ◇ *The whole story is nothing but* ***a pack of lies.*** 整个叙述只不过是一派谎言。 ◇ *a* ***barefaced lie*** (= a lie that is deliberate and shocking) 厚颜无耻的谎话 ➲ SEE ALSO WHITE LIE

IDM **give the lie to sth** (*formal*) to show that sth is not true 证实…是虚假的；证明不实；揭穿谎言 **I tell a 'lie** (*BrE, informal*) used to say that sth you have just said is not true or correct（表示刚说的话不真实或不正确）我说错了，我说的不对：*We first met in 2006, no, I tell a lie, it was 2007.* 我们第一次见面是在 2006 年，不，我说错了，是 2007 年。 ➲ MORE AT LIVE[1], TISSUE

lied /liːd/ *noun* (*pl.* **lieder** /ˈliːdə(r)/) (*from German*) a German song for one singer and piano 利德（钢琴伴奏的德国独唱歌曲）

'lie detector (*also specialist, formal* **poly·graph**) *noun* a piece of equipment that is used, for example by the police, to find out if sb is telling the truth 测谎器

,lie-'down *noun* [sing.] (*BrE, informal*) a short rest, especially on a bed （尤指在床上）小睡，小憩

lief /liːf/ *adv.* (*old use*) willingly; happily 乐意地；情愿地；高兴地：*I would as lief kill myself as betray my master.* 我宁愿自杀也不会出卖我的主人。

liege /liːdʒ/ (*also* **,liege 'lord**) *noun* (*old use*) a king or lord 君主；领主

,lie-'in *noun* (*BrE*) a time when you stay in bed longer than normal in the morning 睡懒觉

lien /ˈliːən/ *noun* [U] ~ (**in/over sth**) (*law* 律) the right to keep sb's property until a debt is paid 扣押权，留置权（扣押某人财产直至其偿清债务）

lieu /luː; *BrE also* ljuː/ *noun* (*formal*)

IDM **in lieu (of sth)** instead of 替代：*They took cash in lieu of the prize they had won.* 他们没有领奖品而是领了现金。 ◇ *We work on Saturdays and have a day off in lieu during the week.* 我们每周星期六上班，用其他的日子补休一天。

Lieut. (*also* **Lt**) (*both BrE*) (*NAmE* **Lt.**) *abbr.* (in writing 书写形式) LIEUTENANT （陆军）中尉；（海军或空军）上尉

lieu·ten·ant /lefˈtenənt; *NAmE* luːˈt-/ *noun* (*abbr.* **Lieut.**, **Lt**) **1** an officer of middle rank in the army, navy, or AIR FORCE （陆军）中尉；（海军或空军）上尉：*Lieutenant Paul Fisher* 保罗・费希尔陆军中尉 ➲ SEE ALSO FLIGHT LIEUTENANT, SECOND LIEUTENANT, SUB LIEUTENANT **2** (in compounds 构成复合词) an officer just below the rank mentioned 仅低于…官阶的官员：*a lieutenant colonel* 中校 **3** (in the US) a police officer of fairly high rank （美国警察的）一定级别的警官 **4** a person who helps sb who is above them in rank or who performs their duties when that person is unable to 副职官员；助理官员；代理官员

lieu,tenant 'colonel *noun* an officer of middle rank in the US army, US AIR FORCE or British army （美国）陆军中校，空军中校；（英国）陆军中校

L

lieu,tenant com'mander *noun* an officer of middle rank in the navy 海军少校

lieu,tenant 'general *noun* an officer of very high rank in the army 陆军中将

Lieu,tenant-'Governor *noun* (in Canada) the representative of THE CROWN in a PROVINCE （加拿大）省督

life /laɪf/ *noun* (*pl.* **lives** /laɪvz/)

• **STATE OF LIVING** 生存状态 **1** [U] the ability to breathe, grow, reproduce, etc. which people, animals and plants have before they die and which objects do not have 生命：*life and death* 生与死 ◇ *The body was cold and showed* ***no signs of life.*** 那躯体冰凉，显现不出有生命的迹象。◇ *My father died last year—I wish I could bring him* ***back to life.*** 去年我父亲逝世了，我要是能使他起死回生该多好啊。 ◇ *In spring the countryside bursts into life.* 乡村在春天生机盎然。 **2** [U, C] the state of being alive as a human; an individual person's existence 人命；性命；人的存活：*The floods caused a massive* ***loss of life*** (= many people were killed). 洪水造成许多人丧生。◇ *He* ***risked his life*** *to save his daughter from the fire.* 他冒着生命危险从火中救出他的女儿。 ◇ *Hundreds of lives were threatened when the building collapsed.* 数百条性命在大楼垮塌时受到了威胁。◇ *The operation* ***saved her life.*** 手术挽救了她的生命。◇ *My grandfather* ***lost his life*** (= was killed) *in the war.* 我的祖父在战争中丧生。 ◇ *Several attempts have been made on the President's life* (= several people have tried to kill him). 已有数人试图谋杀总统。

• **LIVING THINGS** 生物 **3** [U] living things 生物；活物：***plant/animal life*** 植物；动物 ◇ ***marine/pond life*** 海洋 / 池塘生物 ◇ *Is there intelligent life on other planets?* 在其他星球上存在具有智力的生命吗？

• **PERIOD OF TIME** 时期 **4** [C, U] the period between sb's birth and their death; a part of this period 一生；终身；寿命；一生中的部分时间： *He's lived here* ***all his life.*** 他在这里住了一辈子了。◇ *I've lived in England for most of my life.* 我大半生都住在英格兰。◇ *to have a* ***long/short life*** 寿命长；寿命短 ◇ *He became very weak towards the end of his life.* 他临终时很虚弱。◇ *Brenda took up tennis* ***late in life.*** 布伦达在晚年打起网球来了。◇ *He will spend* ***the rest of his life*** (= until he dies) *in a wheelchair.* 他将在轮椅上度过他的余生。◇ *There's no such thing as a job* ***for life*** *any longer.* 不会再有像终身职位这样的事了。 ◇ *She is a* ***life member*** *of the club.* 她是这个俱乐部的终身会员。◇ *in* ***early/adult life*** 幼年；成年 ➲ SEE ALSO CHANGE OF LIFE **5** [C] (used with an adjective 与形容词连用) a period of sb's life when they are in a particular situation or job（某情景或工作的）一段生活经历： *She has been an accountant all her* ***working life.*** 她在整个职业生涯中一直是会计师。◇ *He met a lot of interesting people during his life as a student.* 他在学生时代接触过许多有趣的人。◇ *They were very happy throughout their* ***married life.*** 他们婚后生活一直很幸福。 **6** [C] the period of time when sth exists or functions 存在期；（某物的）寿命；有效期：*The International Stock Exchange* ***started life as*** *a London coffee shop.* 国际证券交易所起初就是伦敦的一家咖啡馆。◇ *They could see that the company had a limited life* (= it was going to close). 他们意识到公司的寿命不长了。◇ *In Italy the average life of a government is eleven months.* 意大利每届政府的平均寿命是十一个月。 ➲ SEE ALSO SHELF LIFE

• **PUNISHMENT** 惩罚 **7** [U] the punishment of being sent to prison for life; life IMPRISONMENT 无期徒刑；终身监禁：*The judge* ***gave him life.*** 法官判他无期徒刑。

• **EXPERIENCE/ACTIVITIES** 经历；活动 **8** [U] the experience and activities that are typical of all people's existences 生活经历：*the worries of everyday life* 日常生活中的操心事 ◇ *He is young and has little* ***experience of life.*** 他年轻，不谙世事。◇ *Commuting is a part of* ***daily life*** *for many people.* 乘车上下班是许多人日常生活的一部分。 ◇ *Jill wants to travel and see life for herself.* 吉尔想出去旅行，亲身体验一下生活。 ◇ *We bought a dishwasher* ***to make life easier.*** 为使生活轻松些我们买了一台洗碗机。◇ *In London life can be hard.* 在伦敦生活会很艰苦。◇ *In* ***real life*** (= when she met him) *he wasn't how she had imagined him at all.* 一见面才发现他完全不是她所想象的那样。◇ *Life isn't like in the movies, you know.* 你知道，生活不像在电影里那样。 **9**

▼ **COLLOCATIONS** 词语搭配

The living world 生物界

Animals 动物

- animals **mate/breed/reproduce/feed (on sth)** 动物交配 / 繁育 / 繁殖 / 以…为食
- fish/amphibians **swim/spawn** (= lay eggs) 鱼 / 两栖动物游动 / 产卵
- birds **fly/migrate/nest/sing** 鸟飞翔 / 迁徙 / 筑巢 / 啼叫
- insects **crawl/fly/bite/sting** 昆虫爬 / 飞 / 咬 / 叮
- insects/bees/locusts **swarm** 昆虫 / 蜜蜂 / 蝗虫成群地飞来飞去
- bees **collect/gather** nectar/pollen 蜜蜂采蜜 / 花粉
- spiders **spin/weave** a web 蜘蛛结网 / 织网
- snakes/lizards **shed their skins** 蛇 / 蜥蜴蜕皮
- bears/hedgehogs/frogs **hibernate** 熊 / 刺猬 / 青蛙冬眠
- insect larvae **grow/develop/pupate** 昆虫的幼虫生长 / 发育 / 化蛹
- an egg/a chick/a larva **hatches** 卵孵化；小鸡出壳；幼虫孵出
- **attract/find/choose** a mate 吸引 / 找到 / 选择配偶
- **produce/release** eggs/sperm 产卵；排卵；产生 / 释放精子
- **lay/fertilize/incubate/hatch** eggs 产卵；使卵受精；孵卵
- **inhabit** a forest/a reef/the coast 栖居于森林 / 礁石 / 海岸
- **mark/enter/defend** (a) territory 标出 / 进入 / 保卫领地
- **stalk/hunt/capture/catch/kill** prey 悄悄接近 / 猎杀 / 捕获 / 杀死猎物

Plants and fungi 植物和真菌

- trees/plants **grow/bloom/blossom/flower** 树木 / 植物生长 / 开花
- a seed **germinates/sprouts** 种子发芽
- leaves/buds/roots/shoots **appear/develop/form** 叶子 / 花蕾 / 根茎 / 幼苗长出来 / 长大 / 成形
- flower buds **swell/open** 花蕾含苞欲放 / 绽放
- a fungus **grows/spreads/colonizes sth** 菌类生长 / 扩散 / 长满…
- **pollinate/fertilize** a flower/plant 给花 / 植物授粉
- **produce/release/spread/disperse** pollen/seeds/spores 长出 / 传播花粉 / 种子 / 孢子
- **produce/bear** fruit 结果
- **develop/grow/form** roots/shoots/leaves 长出根茎 / 嫩芽 / 叶子
- **provide/supply/absorb/extract/release** nutrients 提供 / 吸收 / 提取 / 释放营养物
- **perform/increase/reduce** photosynthesis 进行 / 增加 / 减少光合作用

Bacteria and viruses 细菌和病毒

- bacteria/microbes/viruses **grow/spread/multiply** 细菌 / 微生物 / 病毒生长 / 扩散 / 繁殖
- bacteria/microbes **live/thrive** in/on sth 细菌 / 微生物在…中存活 / 大量生长
- bacteria/microbes/viruses **evolve/colonize sth/cause disease** 细菌 / 微生物 / 病毒进化 / 长满… / 引发疾病
- bacteria **break sth down/convert sth (into sth)** 细菌（将某物）分解 / 转化（成某物）
- a virus **enters/invades** sth/the body 病毒进入 / 侵入某物 / 身体
- a virus **mutates/evolves/replicates (itself)** 病毒变异 / 演化 / （自我）复制
- be **infected with/contaminated with/exposed to** a new strain of a virus/drug-resistant bacteria 感染上 / 接触到一种新病毒 / 抗药性细菌
- **contain/carry/harbour**/(*especially US*) **harbor** bacteria/a virus 带有细菌 / 病毒
- **kill/destroy/eliminate** harmful/deadly bacteria 杀灭有害的 / 致命的细菌

🔑 [U, C] the activities and experiences that are typical of a particular way of living (某种方式的) 生活: ***country/city life*** 乡村 / 城市生活 ◇ *She enjoyed political life.* 她喜欢政治生活。 ◇ ***family/married life*** 家庭 / 婚姻生活 ◇ *How do you find life in Japan?* 你觉得日本的生活如何? **10** 🔑 [C] a person's experiences during their life; the activities that form a particular part of a person's life 个人生活; 个人经历; 个人生活某一方面的活动: *He has had **a good life**.* 他一直过着优裕的生活。 ◇ ***a hard/an easy life*** 艰难 / 安逸舒适的生活 ◇ *My **day-to-day life** is not very exciting.* 我的日常生活很平淡。 ◇ ***a life of** luxury* 奢侈的生活 ◇ *Her **daily life** involved meeting lots of people.* 她在日常生活中要接触很多人。 ◇ *Many of these children have led very **sheltered lives*** (= they have not had many different experiences). 这些儿童中很多人都是温室里的花朵。 ◇ *They emigrated to **start a new life** in Canada.* 他们移居加拿大, 开始了新的生活。 ◇ *He doesn't like to talk about his **private life**.* 他不愿谈及他的私生活。 ◇ *She has a full **social life**.* 她的社交活动非常频繁。 ◇ *articles about the **love lives** of the stars* 有关明星爱情生活的文章 ➲ SEE ALSO SEX LIFE

- **ENERGY/EXCITEMENT** 活力; 兴奋 **11** 🔑 [U] the quality of being active and exciting 活力; 生命力; 生气 SYN **vitality**: *This is a great holiday resort that is **full of life**.* 这里生气勃勃, 是一个绝妙的度假胜地。
- **IN ART** 艺术 **12** [U] a living model or a real object or scene that people draw or paint (绘画的) 模特儿, 实物, 实景: *She had lessons in drawing from life.* 她学了实物写生课程。 ◇ ***a life class*** (= one in which art students draw a naked man or woman) 人体写生课 ➲ SEE ALSO STILL LIFE
- **STORY OF LIFE** 传记 **13** [C] a story of sb's life 生平事迹; 传记 SYN **biography**: *She wrote a life of Mozart.* 她写了一部莫扎特的传记。
- **IN CHILDREN'S GAMES** 儿童游戏 **14** [C] one of a set number of chances before a player is out of a game (玩游戏者出局前几次机会中的) 一次机会: *He's lost two lives, so he's only got one left.* 他失去了两次机会, 所以只剩下一次了。

IDM **be sb's 'life** be the most important person or thing to sb 对某人至关重要的人 (或事物): *My children are my life.* 我这几个孩子就是我的命根子。 ◇ *Writing is his life.* 写作是他的生命。 **bring sb/sth to 'life** to make sb/sth more interesting or exciting 使更有趣; 使更生动: *The new teacher really brought French to life for us.* 新来的老师给我们把法语教得生动活泼。 ◇ *Flowers can bring a dull room back to life.* 鲜花可使沉闷的房间恢复生气。 **come to 'life** **1** to become more interesting, exciting or full of activity 变得更有趣 (或使人兴奋); 变得活跃: *The match finally came to life in the second half.* 比赛在下半场终于精彩起来。 **2** to start to act or move as if alive (仿佛活着) 开始动起来: *In my dream all my toys came to life.* 在我的梦里, 玩具都活过来了。 **for dear 'life | for your 'life** as hard or as fast as possible 尽最大努力; 拼命; 尽快: *She was holding on to the rope for dear life.* 她死命抓着那根绳子。 ◇ *Run for your life!* 快跑啊! **for the 'life of you** (*informal*) however hard you try 无论怎样努力: *I cannot for the life of me imagine why they want to leave.* 我怎么也想象不出他们为什么要走。 **frighten/scare the 'life out of sb** to frighten sb very much 把某人吓得魂不附体; 使魂飞魄散 **full of 'beans/'life** having a lot of energy 充满活力; 精力充沛; 生气勃勃 **get a 'life** (*informal*) used to tell sb to stop being boring and to do sth more interesting (让人别再令人厌烦, 要做更有趣的事) 来点儿有意思的 **lay down your 'life (for sb/sth)** (*literary*) to die in order to save sb/sth (为…) 牺牲生命, 献身 SYN **sacrifice** **lead/live the life of 'Riley** (*old-fashioned, often disapproving*) to live an enjoyable and comfortable life with no problems or responsibilities 无忧无虑地生活; 安逸地生活; 舒适愉快地生活 **life after 'death** the possibility or belief that people continue to exist in some form after they die 来世; 来生 **the life and 'soul of the party, etc.** (*BrE*) the most amusing and interesting person at a party, etc. (聚会等场合) 最活跃风趣的人 **life is 'cheap** (*disapproving*) used to say that there is a situation in which it is not thought to be important if people somewhere die or are treated badly 把他人生死视同儿戏; 视人性命如草芥; 人命不值钱 **(have) a life of its 'own** (of an object 物体) seeming to move or function by itself without a person touching or working it (具有) 自身生命力, 原动力 **life's too 'short** (*informal*) used to say that it is not worth wasting time doing sth that you dislike or that is not important 人生苦短; 不可枉费此生 **make life 'difficult (for sb)** to cause problems for sb (给某人) 惹麻烦, 造成困难, 出难题 **the 'man/'woman in your life** (*informal*) the man or woman that you are having a sexual or romantic relationship with 闯进你生活中的男人 (或女人) **not on your 'life** (*informal*) used to refuse very firmly to do sth (断然拒绝) 决不会 **take sb's 'life** to kill sb 杀死 (某人); 取某人的性命 **take your (own) 'life** to kill yourself 自杀 **take your life in your 'hands** to risk being killed 冒生命危险; 豁出性命; 把脑袋别在裤腰带上: *You take your life in your hands just crossing the road here.* 你在这里过马路简直是冒险玩命。 **that's 'life** (*informal*) used when you are disappointed about sth but know that you must accept it (表示失望但无可奈何) 这就是生活, 生活就是这样 **where there's 'life (, there's 'hope)** (*saying*) in a bad situation you must not give up hope because there is always a chance that it will improve 活着 (就有希望); 留得青山在 (, 不怕没柴烧) ➲ MORE AT BET *v.*, BREATH, BREATHE, DEPART, DOG *n.*, END *v.*, FACT, FEAR *n.*, FIGHT *v.*, KISS *n.*, LARGE *adj.*, LEASE *n.*, LIGHT *n.*, MATTER *n.*, MISERY, NINE, RISK *v.*, SAVE *v.*, SLICE *n.*, SPRING *v.*, STAFF *n.*, STORY, TIME *n.*, TRUE *adj.*, VARIETY, WALK *n.*, WAY *n.*

ˌlife-and-'death (*also* **ˌlife-or-'death**) *adj.* [only before noun] extremely serious, especially when there is a situation in which people might die 生死攸关的; 关系重大的: *a life-and-death decision/struggle* 生死攸关的决定; 生死存亡的斗争

'life assurance *noun* [U] (*BrE*) = LIFE INSURANCE

life·belt /ˈlaɪfbelt/ *noun* **1** (*BrE*) a large ring made of material that floats well, that is used to rescue sb who has fallen into water, to prevent them from DROWNING 救生圈 **2** (*NAmE*) a special belt worn to help sb float in water (使人不下沉的) 救生带 ➲ SEE ALSO LIFE JACKET, LIFE PRESERVER

life·blood /ˈlaɪfblʌd/ *noun* [U] **1** ~ **(of sth)** the thing that keeps sth strong and healthy and is necessary for successful development (事物的) 命脉; 生命线; 命根子: *Tourism is the lifeblood of the city.* 旅游业是这座城市的命脉。 **2** (*literary*) a person's blood, when it is thought of as the thing that is necessary for life (人的) 命脉; 生命必需的血液

life·boat /ˈlaɪfbəʊt; *NAmE* -boʊt/ *noun* **1** a special boat that is sent out to rescue people who are in danger at sea (派往海上救助的) 救生艇, 救生船: ***a lifeboat crew/station*** 救生船全体船员 / 停泊港 ➲ VISUAL VOCAB PAGE V59 **2** a small boat carried on a ship in order to save the people on board if the ship sinks (船上备用的) 救生艇

life·buoy /ˈlaɪfbɔɪ; *NAmE also* -buːi/ *noun* a piece of material that floats well, used to rescue sb who has fallen into water, by keeping them above water 救生带; 救生圈

'life coach (*also* **coach**) *noun* a person who is employed by sb to give them advice about how to achieve the things they want in their life and work 人生教练, 生涯顾问 (受雇帮助他人实现人生和工作目标) ▸ **'life coaching** (*also* **coaching**) *noun* [U]

'life cycle *noun* **1** (*biology* 生) the series of forms into which a living thing changes as it develops 生命周期, 生活周期 (生物发展过程的系列变形): *the life cycle of the butterfly* 蝴蝶的生命周期 **2** the period of time during which sth, for example a product, is developed and used 生命周期, 寿命 (产品等从开发到使用完毕的一段时间)

'life-enhancing *adj.* making you feel happier and making life more enjoyable 增加生活乐趣的

'life expectancy (*also* **ˌexpectation of 'life**) *noun* [U, C] the number of years that a person is likely to live; the length of time that sth is likely to exist or continue for 预期寿命; 预计存在 (或持续) 的期限

L

'life force *noun* [U] **1** the force that gives sb/sth their strength or energy 生命力；活力：*He looked very ill—his life force seemed to have drained away.* 他看上去病得很厉害，他的生命力似乎枯竭了。 **2** the force that keeps all life in existence 生命气息；生命的能量：*In Hindi philosophy the life force is known as prana.* 在印度哲学中生命气息称为 prana（息）。

'life form *noun* (*specialist*) a living thing such as a plant or an animal 生物；活物

'life-giving *adj.* [usually before noun] (*literary*) that gives life or keeps sth alive 赋予生命的；维持生命的

life·guard /'laɪfɡɑːd; *NAmE* -ɡɑːrd/ (*AustralE, NZE* **life-saver, 'surf lifesaver**) *noun* a person who is employed at a beach or a swimming pool to rescue people who are in danger in the water（海滩或游泳池的）救生员

ˌlife 'history *noun* all the events that happen in the life of a person, an animal or a plant 生平；（生物的）生活史

'life insurance (*BrE also* **'life assurance**) *noun* [U] a type of insurance in which you make regular payments so that you receive a sum of money when you are a particular age, or so that your family will receive a sum of money when you die 人寿保险：*a life insurance policy* 人寿保险单

'life jacket (*NAmE also* **'life vest**) *noun* a jacket without sleeves, that can be filled with air, designed to help you float if you fall in water 救生衣 ➲ VISUAL VOCAB PAGE V60

life·less /'laɪfləs/ *adj.* **1** (*formal*) dead or appearing to be dead 死的；像是死的 SYN **inanimate** **2** not living; not having living things growing on or in it 无生命的；无生物生长的：*lifeless machines* 无生命的机器 ◇ *a lifeless planet* 没有生命存在的行星 **3** dull; lacking the qualities that make sth/sb interesting and full of life 枯燥的；单调的；缺乏生气的 SYN **lacklustre**：*his lifeless performance on stage* 他在舞台上死气沉沉的表演

life·like /'laɪflaɪk/ *adj.* exactly like a real person or thing 逼真的；生动的；栩栩如生的 SYN **realistic**： *a lifelike statue/drawing/toy* 栩栩如生的雕塑 / 绘画；逼真的玩具

life·line /'laɪflaɪn/ *noun* **1** a line or rope thrown to rescue sb who is in difficulty in the water（水上救援的）救生索 **2** a line attached to sb who goes deep under the sea（深海潜水员的）信号绳 **3** something that is very important for sb and that they depend on 命脉；生命线：*The extra payments are a lifeline for most single mothers.* 额外补助对大多数单身母亲来说都是赖以生存的生命线。

life·long /'laɪflɒŋ; *NAmE* -lɔːŋ; -lɑːŋ/ *adj.* [only before noun] lasting or existing all through your life 终身的；毕生的

ˌlife-or-'death *adj.* = LIFE-AND-DEATH

ˌlife 'peer *noun* (in Britain) a person who is given the title of PEER (= 'Lord' or 'Lady') but who cannot pass it on to their son or daughter（英国爵位不能世袭的）终身贵族

'life preserver *noun* (*NAmE*) a piece of material that floats well, or a jacket made of such material, used to rescue a person who has fallen into water, by keeping them above water 救生用具

lifer /'laɪfə(r)/ *noun* (*informal*) a person who has been sent to prison for their whole life 终身囚犯；无期徒刑犯

'life raft *noun* an open rubber boat filled with air, used for rescuing people from sinking ships or planes 充气救生船；橡皮救生筏

life·saver /'laɪfseɪvə(r)/ *noun* **1** a thing that helps sb in a difficult situation; sth that saves sb's life 救助物；救命物：*The new drug is a potential lifesaver.* 这种新药有可能成为一种救命药。 **2** (*also* **'surf lifesaver**) (*AustralE, NZE*) = LIFEGUARD

'life-saving *adj., noun*

■ ***adj.*** [usually before noun] that is going to save sb's life 救命的；救生的：*a life-saving heart operation* 挽救生命的心脏手术

■ ***noun*** [U] the skills needed to save sb who is in water and is DROWNING（对溺水者的）救生术：*a life-saving qualification* 救生资格

'life sciences *noun* [pl.] the sciences concerned with studying humans, animals or plants 生命科学 ➲ COMPARE EARTH SCIENCE, NATURAL SCIENCE, PHYSICAL SCIENCE

'life sentence *noun* the punishment by which sb spends the rest of their life in prison 无期徒刑；终身监禁

'life-size (*also* **'life-sized**) *adj.* the same size as a person or thing really is 与真人（或实物）一样大小的：*a life-size statue* 与真人一样大的雕像

life·span /'laɪfspæn/ *noun* the length of time that sth is likely to live, continue or function 寿命；可持续年限；有效期：*Worms have a lifespan of a few months.* 蠕虫的寿命为几个月。

'life story *noun* the story that sb tells you about their whole life 生平事迹

life·style /'laɪfstaɪl/ *noun* [C, U] the way in which a person or a group of people lives and works 生活方式；工作方式：*a **comfortable/healthy/lavish, etc. lifestyle*** 舒适、健康、挥霍无度等的生活方式 ◇ *It was a big change in lifestyle when we moved to the country.* 我们迁居到乡下，这在生活方式上是个巨大的变化。◇ *the lifestyle section of the newspaper* (= the part which deals with clothes, furniture, hobbies, etc.) 报纸的生活栏目

ˌlife sup'port *noun* [U] the fact of sb being on a life-support machine（用机器设备）维持生命：*Families want the right to refuse life support.* 病人亲属要求有权拒绝使用机器维持生命。◇ *She's critically ill, **on life support**.* 她病情危急，靠机器来维持生命。

ˌlife-sup'port machine (*also* **ˌlife-sup'port system**) *noun* a piece of equipment that keeps sb alive when they are extremely ill/sick and cannot breathe without help 生命维持设备；用以维持生命的机器：*He was put on a life-support machine in intensive care.* 在特护期间给他使用了生命维持设备。

ˌlife's 'work (*BrE*) (*NAmE* **life·work** /ˌlaɪf'wɜːk; *NAmE* -'wɜːrk/) *noun* [sing.] the main purpose or activity in a person's life, or their greatest achievement 毕生的主要目的（或活动）；终生最大的成就

'life-threatening *adj.* that is likely to kill sb 可能致命的；威胁着生命的： *His heart condition is not life-threatening.* 他的心脏病不会危及生命。

life·time /'laɪftaɪm/ *noun* the length of time that sb lives or that sth lasts 一生；终身；有生之年；（某物的）存在期，寿命，使用期限：*His diary was not published during his lifetime.* 他的日记在他生前未曾发表过。◇ *a lifetime of experience* 毕生的经验 ◇ *in the lifetime of the present government* 在本届政府的任期内

IDM **the chance, etc. of a 'lifetime** a wonderful opportunity, etc. that you are not likely to get again 终身难得的机遇；千载难逢的机会 **once in a 'lifetime** used to describe sth special that is not likely to happen to you again（可能）一生只有一次：*An opportunity like this comes once in a lifetime.* 像这样的机会一生也许只会遇到一次。◇ *a once-in-a-lifetime experience* 一生只会拥有一次的经历

'life vest *noun* (*NAmE*) = LIFE JACKET

lift 🔑 /lɪft/ *verb, noun*

■ ***verb***

• **RAISE** 提升 **1** 🔑 [T, I] to raise sb/sth or be raised to a higher position or level（被）提起，举起，抬高，吊起：**~ sb/sth (up) (+ adv./prep.)** *He stood there with his arms lifted above his head.* 他站在那里，胳臂举过了头顶。◇ *I lifted the lid of the box and peered in.* 我掀起箱盖往里看。◇ (*figurative*) *John lifted his eyes* (= looked up) *from his book.* 约翰从书本上抬起眼睛。◇ **~ (up)** *Her eyebrows lifted. 'Apologize? Why?'* 她的眉毛竖了起来："道歉？为什么？"

• **MOVE SB/STH** 挪动某人 / 某物 **2** 🔑 [T] **~ sb/sth (+ adv./prep.)** to take hold of sb/sth and move them/it to a different position 移开；移动：*I lifted the baby out of the chair.* 我

把婴儿从椅子上抱起来。◇ *He lifted the suitcase down from the rack.* 他把手提箱从行李架上搬下来。 **3** [T] ~ **sb/sth** (+ **adv./prep.**) to transport people or things by air 空运: *The survivors were lifted to safety by helicopter.* 幸存者由直升机运往安全的地方。 ➲ SEE ALSO AIRLIFT *v.*

• **REMOVE LAW/RULE** 撤销法律 / 规则 **4** [T] ~ **sth** to remove or end restrictions 解除，撤销，停止（限制）: *to **lift a ban/curfew/blockade*** 解除禁令 / 宵禁 / 封锁 ◇ *Martial law has now been lifted.* 戒严令现已解除。

• **HEART/SPIRITS** 心情; 情绪 **5** [I, T] to become or make sb more cheerful 高兴起来; 使更愉快: *His heart lifted at the sight of her.* 他一看见她心里就高兴起来了。◇ ~ **sth** *The news lifted our spirits.* 这消息使我们群情振奋。

• **OF MIST/CLOUDS** 雾; 云 **6** [I] to rise and disappear 消散; 消失 SYN **disperse**: *The fog began to lift.* 雾开始散了。◇ (*figurative*) *Gradually my depression started to lift.* 我的沮丧情绪开始逐渐消失。

• **STEAL** 偷盗 **7** [T] ~ **sth** (**from sb/sth**) (*informal*) to steal sth 偷盗; 盗窃: *He had been lifting electrical goods from the store where he worked.* 他一直从他工作的商店里偷窃电器商品。 ➲ SEE ALSO SHOPLIFTING

• **COPY IDEAS/WORDS** 剽窃观点 / 言语 **8** [T] ~ **sth** (**from sth**) to use sb's ideas or words without asking permission or without saying where they come from 剽窃; 盗用; 抄袭 SYN **plagiarize**: *She lifted most of the ideas from a book she had been reading.* 大部分观点都是她从一直在看的一本书里抄来的。

• **VEGETABLES** 蔬菜 **9** [T] ~ **sth** to dig up vegetables or plants from the ground 挖出，刨出，拔起（蔬菜或植物）: *to lift potatoes* 刨土豆

• **INCREASE** 增加 **10** [T, I] ~ (**sth**) to make the amount or level of sth greater; to become greater in amount or level 提高; 增加; （使）增长: *Interest rates were lifted yesterday.* 昨天利率提高了。

IDM **not lift/raise a finger/hand** (**to do sth**) (*informal*) to do nothing to help sb 一点忙也不帮; 油瓶倒了都不扶: *The children never lift a finger to help around the house.* 孩子们从不帮着做家务。

PHR V **ˌlift ˈoff** (of a ROCKET or, less frequently, an aircraft 火箭，有时也指飞行器) to leave the ground and rise into the air 发射; 起飞; 升空 ➲ RELATED NOUN LIFT-OFF

■ ***noun***

• **MACHINE** 机器 **1** (*BrE*) (*NAmE* **ele·va·tor**) [C] a machine that carries people or goods up and down to different levels in a building or a mine 电梯; 升降机: *It's on the sixth floor—let's **take the lift**.* 在七楼，咱们乘电梯吧。 ➲ SEE ALSO CHAIRLIFT, SKI LIFT

• **FREE RIDE** 免费搭车 **2** (*NAmE also* **ride**) [C] a free ride in a car, etc. to a place you want to get to 免费搭车; 搭便车: *I'll **give you a lift** to the station.* 我用车顺便送你去车站。◇ *She **hitched a lift** on a truck.* 她免费搭乘了一辆卡车。

• **HAPPIER FEELING** 更好的心情 **3** [sing.] a feeling of being happier or more confident than before 较好的心情; 更大的信心 SYN **boost**: *Passing the exam gave him a real lift.* 他通过了考试，情绪好多了。

• **RISING MOVEMENT** 上升运动 **4** [sing.] a movement in which sth rises or is lifted up 提; 抬; 举; 上升; 吊: *the puzzled lift of his eyebrows* 他迷惑不解地皱起眉头

• **ON AIRCRAFT** 飞行器 **5** [U] the upward pressure of air on an aircraft when flying（飞行时的）提升力，升力 ➲ COMPARE DRAG *n.* (5)

ˈlift-off *noun* [C, U] the act of a SPACECRAFT leaving the ground and rising into the air（航天器的）发射，起飞，升空 SYN **blast-off**: *Ten minutes to lift-off.* 离发射还有十分钟。

liga·ment /ˈlɪɡəmənt/ *noun* a strong band of TISSUE in the body that connects bones and supports organs and keeps them in position 韧带: *I've torn a ligament.* 我的韧带撕裂了。 ➲ COLLOCATIONS AT INJURY

li·gate /lɪˈɡeɪt; *NAmE* ˈlaɪɡ-/ *verb* ~ **sth** (*medical* 医) to tie up an ARTERY or other BLOOD VESSEL or tube in the body, with a LIGATURE 结扎（动脉或血管等） ▶ **li·ga·tion** *noun* [U]

liga·ture /ˈlɪɡətʃə(r)/ *noun* (*specialist*) something that is used for tying sth very tightly, for example to stop the loss of blood from a wound（用于紧缚的）带子，绳索，绷带;（用于止血等的）结扎丝，缚线

lig·ger /ˈlɪɡə(r)/ *noun* (*BrE, informal*) a person who always takes the opportunity to go to a free party or event that is arranged by a company to advertise its products 免费广告活动常客

light /laɪt/ *noun, adj., verb, adv.*

■ ***noun***

• **FROM SUN/LAMPS** 太阳; 灯 **1** [U] the energy from the sun, a lamp, etc. that makes it possible to see things 光; 光线; 光亮: ***bright/dim light*** 明亮 / 暗淡的光线 ◇ *a room with good **natural light*** 采光好的房间 ◇ *in the fading light of a summer's evening* 在夏天渐渐暗淡的暮色中 ◇ *The light was beginning to fail* (= it was beginning to get dark). 天色渐暗。◇ *She could just see **by the light of** the candle.* 她借着烛光勉强能看见。◇ *Bring it **into the light** so I can see it.* 把它拿到亮的地方，好让我看见。◇ *a **beam/ray of light*** 一束 / 一缕光线 ◇ *The knife gleamed as it **caught the light*** (= as the light shone on it). 刀子被光线一照闪闪发亮。 ➲ SEE ALSO FIRST LIGHT **2** [C] a particular type of light with its own colour and qualities（具有某种颜色和特性的）光: *A cold grey light crept under the curtains.* 一丝幽暗阴冷的光从窗帘下面透过来。 ➲ SEE ALSO NORTHERN LIGHTS

• **LAMP** 灯 **3** [C] a thing that produces light, especially an electric light 发光体; 光源;（尤指）电灯: *to **turn/switch the lights on/off*** 开灯; 关灯 ◇ *to **turn out the light(s)*** 把灯关掉 ◇ *Suddenly all the **lights went out**.* 突然间所有的灯都灭了。◇ *It was an hour before the **lights came on again**.* 一个小时后灯才再亮了。◇ *to **turn down/dim the lights*** 把灯光调暗 ◇ *A light was still burning in the bedroom.* 卧室里依然亮着灯。◇ ***ceiling/wall lights*** 顶灯; 壁灯 ◇ *Keep going—the lights* (= traffic lights) *are green.* 不用停车，是绿灯。◇ *Check your car before you drive to make sure that your lights are working.* 开车前要检查一下，灯一定都要运作正常。 ➲ VISUAL VOCAB PAGE V55 ➲ SEE ALSO BRAKE LIGHT, GREEN LIGHT, HEADLIGHT, LEADING LIGHT, RED LIGHT

• **FOR CIGARETTE** 香烟 **4** [sing.] a match or device with which you can light a cigarette 火柴; 打火机; 点火器: (*BrE*) *Have you got a light?* 你有火儿吗? ◇ (*NAmE, BrE*) *Do you have a light?* 你有火儿吗?

• **EXPRESSION IN EYES** 眼神 **5** [sing.] an expression in sb's eyes which shows what they are thinking or feeling 眼神: *There was a soft light in her eyes as she looked at him.* 她望着他，眼神很温柔。

• **IN PICTURE** 图画 **6** [U] light colours in a picture, which contrast with darker ones（图画中和暗色对比的）亮色，浅色: *the artist's use of light and shade* 画家对明暗对比手法的运用

• **WINDOW** 窗户 **7** [C] (*architecture* 建) a window or an opening to allow light in 窗; 窗户; 光线进口; 采光孔: *leaded lights* 花饰铅条窗 ➲ SEE ALSO SKYLIGHT

IDM **according to sb's/sth's ˈlights** (*formal*) according to the standards which sb sets for himself or herself 根据自己设定的标准 **be/go out like a ˈlight** (*informal*) to go to sleep very quickly 很快入睡 **be in sb's ˈlight** to be between sb and a source of light 挡住某人的光线: *Could you move—you're in my light.* 挪动一下好吗? 你挡住我的光线了。 **bring sth to ˈlight** to make new information known to people 揭露; 披露; 暴露; 揭发: *These facts have only just been brought to light.* 这些事实刚刚才被披露出来。 **cast/shed/throw ˈlight on sth** to make a problem, etc. easier to understand 使（问题等）较容易理解: *Recent research has thrown new light on the causes of the disease.* 最近的研究让人们进一步了解了导致这种疾病的原因。 **come to ˈlight** to become known to people 为人所知; 变得众所周知; 暴露: *New evidence has recently come to light.* 新的证据最近已披露出来。 **in ˌa good, bad, favourable, etc. ˈlight** if you see sth or put sth **in a good, bad, etc. light**, it seems good, bad, etc. 从好（或坏、有利等）的角度: *You must not view what happened in a negative light.* 你切切不要从负面的角度来看待发生的事。◇ *They want to present their policies in the best* *possible light.* 他们想尽可能从好的方面来介绍他们的政策。 **in the light of sth** (*BrE*) (*NAmE* **in light of sth**) after considering sth 考虑到；鉴于： *He rewrote the book in the light of further research.* 他根据进一步的研究重写了那部书。 **the lights are 'on but nobody's 'home** (*saying, humorous*) used to describe sb who is stupid, not thinking clearly or not paying attention 稀里糊涂；没头脑；心不在焉 **light at the end of the 'tunnel** something that shows you are nearly at the end of a long and difficult time or situation 快要熬出头了；曙光在即 **(the) light 'dawned (on sb)** somebody suddenly understood or began to understand sth 豁然开朗；恍然大悟： *I puzzled over the problem for ages before the light suddenly dawned.* 我对这个问题冥思苦想了很久才豁然开朗。 **the light of sb's 'life** the person sb loves more than any other 心爱的人；心肝宝贝 **run a (red) 'light | run the 'lights** (*both especially NAmE*) (*BrE also* **jump the 'lights**) (*informal*) to fail to stop at a red traffic light 闯红灯 **see the 'light 1** to finally understand or accept sth, especially sth obvious 终于领悟，最终明白，最后接受（尤指显而易见的事） **2** to begin to believe in a religion 开始信教；皈依宗教 **see the 'light (of 'day)** to begin to exist or to become publicly known about 开始存在；问世；开始为人所知： *He's written a lot of good material that has never seen the light of day.* 他写了许多鲜为人知的好材料。 **set 'light to sth** (*especially BrE*) to make sth start burning 点燃；引火烧 **SYN** **ignite**: *A spark from the fire had set light to a rug.* 从火炉迸出的火星点燃了地毯。 ➲ MORE AT BRIGHT *adj.*, COLD *adj.*, HIDE *v.*, SWEETNESS

▼ **WHICH WORD? 词语辨析**

light / lighting

- The noun **light** has several different meanings and is used in many phrases. **Lighting** can only be used to talk about the type of light in a place or how lights are used to achieve a particular effect. 名词 light 有几个不同的含义，可用于许多短语中。lighting 只用以指照明或照明技术： *the lighting system* 照明系统 ◇ *the movie's interesting lighting effects* 这部电影精彩的灯光效果 ◇ *The lighting at the disco was fantastic.* 迪斯科舞厅里灯光奇幻。

■ ***adj.*** (**light·er, light·est**)

- **WITH NATURAL LIGHT** 自然光 **1** 🔑 full of light; having the natural light of day 充满亮光的；明亮的；有自然光的： *We'll leave in the morning as soon as **it's light**.* 明天早晨天一亮我们就出发。 ◇ *It **gets light** at about 5 o'clock.* 大约 5 点钟天就亮了。 ◇ *It was a light spacious apartment at the top of the building.* 是大楼顶层一套宽敞明亮的房子。 **OPP** **dark**
- **COLOURS** 颜色 **2** 🔑 pale in colour 浅色的；淡色的： *light blue eyes* 浅蓝色的眼睛 ◇ *Lighter shades suit you best.* 较浅色的衣服对你最合适。 ◇ *People with pale complexions should avoid wearing light colours.* 面色苍白的人应当避免穿浅色衣服。 **OPP** **dark**
- **WEIGHT** 重量 **3** 🔑 easy to lift or move; not weighing very much 轻的；轻便的；不太重的： *Modern phones are light and easy to carry.* 现在的手机轻巧易携带。 ◇ *Carry this bag—it's the lightest.* 你拿这个包，它最轻。 ◇ *He's lost a lot of weight—he's three kilos lighter than he was.* 他的体重减了许多，比以前轻了三公斤。 ◇ *The little girl was **as light as a feather**.* 那小女孩轻得很。 ◇ *The aluminium body is 12% lighter than if built with steel.* 主体部分用铝比用钢制作重量要轻 12%。 **OPP** **heavy** **4** 🔑 [usually before noun] of less than average or usual weight （比平均或平常重量）轻的： *light summer clothes* 轻薄的夏装 ◇ *Only light vehicles are allowed over the old bridge.* 只有轻型车辆才准许通过那座旧桥。 **OPP** **heavy** **5** used with a unit of weight to say that sth weighs less than it should do （与重量单位连用）分量不足的： *The delivery of potatoes was several kilos light.* 送货送来的土豆少了好几公斤。
- **GENTLE** 轻柔 **6** 🔑 [usually before noun] gentle or delicate; not using much force 轻柔的；柔和的；不太用力的： *She felt a light tap on her shoulder.* 她感到有人在她肩上轻轻地拍了一下。 ◇ *the sound of quick light footsteps* 轻快的脚步声 ◇ *You only need to apply light pressure.* 你只要轻轻地一压就行了。 ◇ *As a boxer, he was always **light on his feet*** (= quick and elegant in the way he moved). 身为拳击手，他的脚步总是十分轻盈。 **OPP** **heavy**
- **WORK/EXERCISE** 工作；锻炼 **7** 🔑 [usually before noun] easy to do; not making you tired 容易做的；轻松的；不使人疲劳的： *After his accident he was moved to lighter work.* 他出事故以后就改做轻活儿了。 ◇ *some light housework* 一些轻松的家务活 ◇ *You are probably well enough to take a little light exercise.* 你恢复得不错，大概可以做些轻微的运动了。
- **NOT GREAT** 不大 **8** 🔑 not great in amount, degree, etc. 少量的；程度低的： *light traffic* 来往车辆稀少 ◇ *The forecast is for light showers.* 天气预报有小阵雨。 ◇ *light winds* 微风 ◇ *Trading on the stock exchange was light today.* 证券交易今日交易量很少。 **OPP** **heavy**
- **NOT SEVERE/SERIOUS** 不严厉；不严肃 **9** not severe 不严厉的；轻的： *He was convicted of assaulting a police officer but he got off with a **light sentence**.* 他被定了袭警罪，不过得到从轻判处。 **10** 🔑 entertaining rather than serious and not needing much mental effort 娱乐性的；消遣性的；轻松的： ***light reading** for the beach* 海滩消遣读物 ◇ *a concert of light classical music* 古典轻音乐会 **11** 🔑 not serious 不严肃的： *She kept her tone light.* 她一直用温和的语气说话。 ◇ *This programme looks at the **lighter side** of politics.* 这个节目着眼于政治较轻松的方面。 ◇ *We all needed a little **light relief** at the end of a long day* (= something amusing or entertaining that comes after sth serious or boring). 在漫长的一天结束时我们都需要一点轻松的调剂。 ◇ ***On a lighter note**, we end the news today with a story about a duck called Quackers.* 为了轻松一下，我们最后讲一个名叫"嘎嘎"的鸭子的故事来结束今天的新闻报道。
- **CHEERFUL** 愉快 **12** [usually before noun] free from worry; cheerful 无忧无虑的；愉快的；快活的： *I left the island with a light heart.* 我怀着愉快的心情离开了那个小岛。
- **FOOD** 食物 **13** (of a meal 一餐饭) small in quantity 少量的： *a **light supper/snack*** 简单的晚餐；小吃 ◇ *I just want something light for lunch.* 我午饭稍微吃点就够了。 **OPP** **heavy** **14** not containing much fat or not having a strong flavour and therefore easy for the stomach to DIGEST 不腻的；清淡的；易消化的： *Stick to a light diet.* 饮食要清淡。 ➲ SEE ALSO LITE **15** containing a lot of air 含有许多空气的；松软的： *This pastry is so light.* 这种酥皮糕点可真松软啊。
- **DRINK** 饮料 **16** low in alcohol 酒精含量低的；低度酒的： *a light beer* 低度啤酒 **17** (*IndE*) (of tea or coffee 茶或咖啡) containing a lot of water 淡的 **SYN** **weak**: *I don't like my coffee too light.* 我不喜欢喝太淡的咖啡。 **OPP** **strong**
- **SLEEP** 睡眠 **18** [only before noun] a person in a **light** sleep is easy to wake 睡得不沉的；易醒的： *She drifted into a light sleep.* 她迷迷糊糊地进入浅睡。 ◇ *I've always been a light sleeper.* 我睡觉总是容易醒。 **OPP** **deep**

▸ **light·ness** *noun* [U] ➲ SEE ALSO LIGHTLY

IDM **be light on sth** (*BrE*) to not have enough of sth 不足；缺乏： *We seem to be light on fuel.* 我们好像燃料不多了。 **a light touch** the ability to deal with sth in a delicate and relaxed way 灵巧的处事能力： *She handles this difficult subject with a light touch.* 她处理起这个难题来得心应手。 **make 'light of sth** to treat sth as not being important and not serious 轻视；对…等闲视之 **make light 'work of sth** to do sth quickly and with little effort 轻而易举地做（某事） ➲ MORE AT HAND *n.*

■ ***verb*** (**lit, lit** /lɪt/) **HELP** **Lighted** is also used for the past tense and past participle, especially in front of nouns. 过去式和过去分词也用 lighted，尤置于名词前。

- **START TO BURN** 开始燃烧 **1** 🔑 [T] **~ sth** to make sth start to burn 点燃；点火： *She lit a candle.* 她点着了蜡烛。 ◇ *The candles were lit.* 蜡烛都点着了。 ◇ *I put a lighted match to the letter and watched it burn.* 我划了根火柴点着了那封信，然后看着它燃烧。 **2** 🔑 [I] to start to burn 开始燃烧；燃起来： *The fire wouldn't light.* 这火炉点不着。
- **GIVE LIGHT** 照亮 **3** 🔑 [T, usually passive] **~ sth** to give light to sth or to a place 照亮；使明亮： *The stage was lit by*

bright spotlights. 舞台上有明亮的聚光灯照亮着。 ◇ ***well/ badly lit** streets* 灯光明亮的 / 昏暗的街道 **4** [T] **~ sth** (*literary*) to guide sb with a light 用光指引： *Our way was lit by a full moon.* 一轮满月照亮了我们的路。

PHR V **ˈlight on/upon sth** (*literary*) to see or find sth by accident 偶然遇见；偶尔发现： *His eye lit upon a small boat on the horizon.* 他无意中看见地平线上有一条小船。 **ˌlight ˈup | ˌlight sth↔ˈup 1** (*informal*) to begin to smoke a cigarette 开始抽烟： *They all lit up as soon as he left the room.* 他一离开房间他们就都抽起烟来。 ◇ *He sat back and lit up a cigarette.* 他往椅背上一靠，点上烟吸了起来。 **2** to become or to make sth become bright with light or colour（使）光亮，放光彩： *There was an explosion and the whole sky lit up.* 一声爆炸照亮了整个天空。 **3** if sb's eyes or face **light up**, or sth **lights them up**, they show happiness or excitement 喜形于色；喜气洋洋： *His eyes lit up when she walked into the room.* 看见她走进房间，他两眼一亮。 ◇ *A smile lit up her face.* 她微微一笑，脸上露出了喜色。

■***adv.*** **IDM** SEE TRAVEL *v.*

ˌlight ˈaircraft *noun* (*pl.* **light aircraft**) a small plane with seats for no more than about six passengers（最多载六名乘客的）轻型飞机 ➲VISUAL VOCAB PAGE V57

ˈlight bulb *noun* = BULB (1)

ˌlight-ˈcoloured (*especially US* **ˌlight-ˈcolored**) *adj.* pale in colour; not dark 浅色的；淡色的

light·ed /ˈlaɪtɪd/ *adj.* **1** a **lighted** CANDLE, cigarette, match, etc. is burning 点燃的；燃烧的 **2** a **lighted** window is bright because there are lights on inside the room 灯火通明的；灯光照亮的 **OPP** **unlit**

light·en /ˈlaɪtn/ *verb* **1** [T] **~ sth** to reduce the amount of work, debt, worry, etc. that sb has 减轻，减少（工作量、债务、担忧等） **SYN** **lessen**: *equipment to **lighten the load** of domestic work* 减轻家务负担的设备 ◇ *The measures will lighten the tax burden on small businesses.* 这些措施将减轻小型企业的纳税负担。 **2** [I, T] to become or make sth become brighter or lighter in colour （使）变明亮，变成淡色： *The sky began to lighten in the east.* 东方开始透亮了。 ◇ **~ sth** *Use bleach to lighten the wood.* 用漂白剂把木材颜色漂浅。 **3** [I, T] to feel or make sb feel less sad, worried or serious （使）感到不那么悲伤（或担忧、严肃）；缓和 **SYN** **cheer**: **~ (up)** *My mood gradually lightened.* 我的心情渐渐好起来。 ◇ **~ sth (up)** *She told a joke to lighten the atmosphere.* 她讲了个笑话以缓和气氛。 **4** [T] **~ sth** to make sth lighter in weight 减轻…的重量

PHR V **ˌlighten ˈup** (*informal*) used to tell sb to become less serious or worried about sth 别那么严肃；别担忧： *Come on, John. Lighten up!* 约翰，加油，别紧张！

light·er /ˈlaɪtə(r)/ *noun* **1** (*also* **cigaˈrette lighter**) a small device that produces a flame for lighting cigarettes, etc. 打火机 **2** a boat with a flat bottom used for carrying goods to and from ships in HARBOUR 驳船

ˌlight-ˈfingered *adj.* (*informal*) likely to steal things 惯扒窃的；惯偷的

ˌlight-ˈfooted *adj.* moving quickly and easily, in an elegant way 脚步轻松的；步履轻盈的

ˌlight-ˈheaded *adj.* not completely in control of your thoughts or movements; slightly faint 头晕的；眩晕的： *After four glasses of wine he began to feel light-headed.* 他四杯酒下肚后开始感到头晕目眩起来。

ˌlight-ˈhearted *adj.* **1** intended to be amusing or easily enjoyable rather than too serious 轻松的；愉快的： *a light-hearted speech* 轻松愉快的讲话 **2** cheerful and without problems 无忧无虑的： *She felt light-hearted and optimistic.* 她感到无忧无虑，很乐观。 ▸ **ˌlight-ˈhearted·ly** *adv.*

light·house /ˈlaɪthaʊs/ *noun* a tower or other building that contains a strong light to warn and guide ships near the coast 灯塔 ➲VISUAL VOCAB PAGES V5, V15

ˌlight ˈindustry *noun* [U, C] industry that produces small or light objects such as things used in the house 轻工业 ➲COMPARE HEAVY INDUSTRY

light·ing /ˈlaɪtɪŋ/ *noun* [U] **1** the arrangement or type of light in a place 照明；灯光；布光： ***electric/natural lighting*** 电力 / 自然照明 ◇ ***good/poor lighting*** 照明好 / 差 ◇ *The play had excellent sound and lighting effects.* 这出戏剧的音响和灯光效果极佳。 **2** the use of electric lights in a place 照明： *the cost of heating and lighting* 供暖和照明费用 ◇ *street lighting* 街道照明 ➲NOTE AT LIGHT *n.*

ˈlighting engineer *noun* a person who works in television, the theatre, etc. and whose job is to control and take care of the lights 照明工程师；灯光师

light·ly /ˈlaɪtli/ *adv.* **1** gently; with very little force or effort 轻柔地；轻微地；轻轻地： *He kissed her lightly on the cheek.* 他轻轻吻了一下她的脸颊。 **2** to a small degree; not much 少许；不多： *It began to snow lightly.* 开始下小雪了。 ◇ *She tended to sleep lightly nowadays* (= it was easy to disturb her). 她如今睡觉容易惊醒。 ◇ *I try to eat lightly* (= not to eat heavy or GREASY food). 我尽量饮食清淡。 **3** in a way that sounds as though you are not particularly worried or interested 漫不经心地；满不在乎地 **SYN** **nonchalantly**: *'I'll be all right,' he said lightly.* "我会好的。"他满不在乎地说道。 **4** without being seriously considered 不慎重地；草率地；轻率地： *This is not a problem we should **take lightly**.* 这个问题我们可不能掉以轻心。

IDM **get off/be let off ˈlightly** (*informal*) to be punished or treated in a way that is less severe than you deserve or may have expected 只受轻罚；获从轻发落

ˈlight meter *noun* a device used to measure how bright the light is before taking a photograph （摄影）曝光表

light·ning /ˈlaɪtnɪŋ/ *noun, adj.*

■***noun*** [U] a flash, or several flashes, of very bright light in the sky caused by electricity 闪电： *a **flash of lightning*** 一道闪电 ◇ *a violent storm with **thunder and lightning*** 夹着雷鸣电闪的暴风雨 ◇ *He was **struck by lightning** and killed.* 他被闪电击中而死。 ◇ ***Lightning strikes** caused scores of fires across the state.* 雷击给整个州造成了多起火灾。 ➲COLLOCATIONS AT WEATHER

IDM **lightning never strikes (in the same place) twice** (*saying*) an unusual or unpleasant event is not likely to happen in the same place or to the same people twice 倒霉的事不可能在同一场所（或同一人身上）重复发生；一事不过二 **like (greased) ˈlightning** very fast 闪电般；飞快地；一溜烟地

■***adj.*** [only before noun] very fast or sudden 闪电般的；飞快的；突然的

ˈlightning bug *noun* (*NAmE*) = FIREFLY

ˈlightning conductor (*BrE*) (*NAmE* **ˈlightning rod**) *noun* a long straight piece of metal or wire leading from the highest part of a building to the ground, put there to prevent lightning damaging the building 避雷针

ˈlightning rod *noun* **1** (*NAmE*) = LIGHTNING CONDUCTOR **2** (*especially NAmE*) a person or thing that attracts criticism, especially if the criticism is then not directed at sb/sth else 引火烧身的人（或事）

ˌlightning ˈstrike *noun* **1** an incident in which LIGHTNING hits sb/sth 雷击 **2** (*BrE*) a strike by a group of workers that is sudden and without warning 闪电式罢工

ˈlight pen *noun* **1** a piece of equipment, shaped like a pen, that is sensitive to light and that can be used to pass information to a computer when it touches the screen（用于向计算机输入信息的）光笔 **2** a similar piece of equipment that is used for reading BARCODES 光笔；条码识读器

ˈlight pollution *noun* [U] the existence of too much artificial light in the environment, for example from street lights, which makes it difficult to see the stars 光污染（人工照明造成）

L

light·ship /ˈlaɪtʃɪp/ *noun* a small ship that stays at a particular place at sea and that has a powerful light on it to warn and guide other ships（海上导航用的）灯船

ˈlight show *noun* a display of changing coloured lights, for example at a pop concert（流行音乐会等的）灯光变幻表演

ˈlight stick *noun* = GLOWSTICK

ˈlight water *noun* [U] **1** (*chemistry* 化) water that contains the normal amount of DEUTERIUM 轻水（即普通水，水中氘含量不超过正常值） ➲ COMPARE HEAVY WATER **2** (*specialist*) a type of FOAM (= mass of bubbles) used to put out fires 泡沫灭火剂

light·weight /ˈlaɪtweɪt/ *adj., noun*

■ ***adj.*** **1** made of thinner material and less heavy than usual（布料）薄且轻的：*a lightweight jacket* 轻便的短上衣 **2** (*disapproving*) not very serious or impressive 不严肃的；给人印象不深的：*a lightweight book* 内容平庸的书 ◇ *He was considered too lightweight for the job.* 有人认为他资历太浅，不适合做这工作。

■ ***noun*** **1** a BOXER weighing between 57 and 61 kilograms, heavier than a FEATHERWEIGHT 轻量级拳击手（体重在 57 至 61 公斤之间）：*a lightweight champion* 轻量级拳击冠军 **2** a person or thing that weighs less than is usual 体重低于通常重量的人；比通常重量轻的东西 **3** (*informal, disapproving*) a person or thing of little importance or influence 无足轻重的人（或事）；没有影响力的人（或事）：*a political lightweight* 政治上的无名之辈 ◇ *He's an intellectual lightweight* (= he does not think very deeply or seriously). 他是个智力平庸的人。

ˈlight year *noun* **1** (*astronomy* 天) the distance that light travels in one year, 9.4607×10^{12} kilometres 光年（指光在一年中走过的距离，为 9.4607×10^{12} 公里）：*The nearest star to earth is about 4 light years away.* 地球离最近的恒星大约为 4 光年。 **2 light years** [pl.] a very long time 很长时间；很久：*Full employment still seems light years away.* 充分就业好像依然遥遥无期。

lig·nite /ˈlɪgnaɪt/ *noun* [U] a soft brown type of coal 褐煤

lig·no·caine /ˈlɪgnəkeɪn; *BrE also* -nəʊk-/ *noun* [U] = LIDOCAINE

lik·able (*especially NAmE*) = LIKEABLE

like 🔑 /laɪk/ *prep., verb, conj., noun, adj., adv.*

■ ***prep.*** **1** 🔑 similar to sb/sth 相似；类似；像：*She's wearing a dress like mine.* 她穿的连衣裙和我的相似。◇ *He's very like his father.* 他很像他的父亲。◇ *She looks* ***nothing like*** (= not at all like) *her mother.* 她长得一点也不像她母亲。◇ *That sounds like* (= I think I can hear) *him coming now.* 听声音像是他来了。 **2** 🔑 used to ask sb's opinion of sb/sth（询问意见）…怎么样：*What's it like studying in Spain?* 在西班牙念书怎么样？◇ *This new girlfriend of his—what's she like?* 他这个新的女朋友是个什么样的人？ **3** 🔑 used to show what is usual or typical for sb（指某人常做的事）符合…的特点，像…才会：*It's just like her to tell everyone about it.* 她就是那样，会把这事见谁就告诉谁。 **4** 🔑 in the same way as sb/sth 像…一样：*Students were angry at being treated like children.* 学生对于把他们当小孩子对待感到气愤。◇ *He ran like the wind* (= very fast). 他跑得飞快。◇ *You do it like this.* 你照这样做。◇ *I, like everyone else, had read these stories in the press.* 我像大家一样，也已经从报纸上看过这些报道。 ◇ *Don't look at me like that.* 别那样看着我。◇ (*informal*) *The candles are arranged* ***like so*** (= in this way). 蜡烛都是像这样排列的。 ➲ LANGUAGE BANK AT SIMILARLY **5** 🔑 for example 例如；譬如；比方：*anti-utopian novels like 'Animal Farm' and '1984'* 诸如《动物庄园》和《1984》之类的反乌托邦小说 ➲ NOTE AT AS

IDM **more like...** used to give a number or an amount that is more accurate than one previously mentioned（提供比以前更准确的数量）差不多，更接近：*He believes the figure should be more like $10 million.* 他认为数额若是 1 000 万美元就差不多了。 **more ˈlike (it)** (*informal*) **1** better; more acceptable 比较好；还差不多；才像话：*This is more like it! Real food—not that canned muck.* 这才像样嘛！是真正的食物，而不是那种罐装的垃圾食品。 **2** used to give what you think is a better description of sth（更恰当地描述）倒更像是，说…还差不多：*Just talking? Arguing more like it.* 仅仅是谈论？说是争论还差不多。 **what is sb ˈlike?** (*BrE, informal*) used to say that sb has done sth annoying, silly, etc.（表示某人做了令人讨厌、愚蠢之类的事）某人怎么回事，某人怎么会是这个样子：*Oh, what am I like? I just completely forgot it.* 啊，我这是怎么啦？我竟把这事忘得一干二净了。

■ ***verb*** (not usually used in the progressive tenses 通常不用于进行时) **1** 🔑 [T] to find sb/sth pleasant, attractive or of a good enough standard; to enjoy sth 喜欢；喜爱：**~ sb/sth** *She's nice. I like her.* 她人很好，我喜欢她。◇ *Do you like their new house?* 你喜欢他们的新房子吗？◇ *Which tie do you like best?* 你最喜欢哪条领带？ ◇ *How did you like Japan* (= did you find it pleasant)? 你觉得日本怎么样？◇ *I don't like the way he's looking at me.* 我讨厌他看着我的样子。◇ *You've got to go to school, whether you like it or not.* 不管你喜欢不喜欢，你得上学。 ◇ **~ doing sth** *She's never liked swimming.* 她从不喜欢游泳。◇ **~ sb/sth doing sth** *I didn't like him taking all the credit.* 我讨厌他把所有的功劳归于自己。◇ (*formal*) *I didn't like his taking all the credit.* 我讨厌他把所有的功劳归于自己。◇ **~ to do sth** *I like to see them enjoying themselves.* 我就愿意看着他们玩得高兴。◇ **~ it when...** *I like it when you do that.* 我喜欢你那样做。➲ SYNONYMS AT LOVE **2** 🔑 [T, no passive] to prefer to do sth; to prefer sth to be made or to happen in a particular way 喜欢做；喜欢（以某种方式制作或产生的东西）：**~ to do sth** *At weekends I like to sleep late.* 周末我爱睡懒觉。◇ **~ sth + adj.** *I like my coffee strong.* 咖啡我爱喝浓的。 **3** 🔑 [T, no passive] **what/whatever sb ~** to want 想；要；希望：*Do what you like—I don't care.* 你想做什么就做什么，我不在乎。◇ *You can dye your hair whatever colour you like.*

▼ **SYNONYMS 同义词辨析**

like

love • be fond of • be keen on sth • adore

These words all mean to find sth pleasant, attractive or satisfactory, or to enjoy sth. 以上各词均含喜欢、喜爱某事物之义。

like to find sth pleasant, attractive or satisfactory; to enjoy sth 指喜欢、喜爱：*Do you like their new house?* 你喜欢他们的新房子吗？◇ *I like to see them enjoying themselves.* 我就愿意看着他们玩得高兴。

love to like or enjoy sth very much 指非常喜欢、喜爱：*He loved the way she smiled.* 他喜欢她微笑的样子。

be fond of sth to like or enjoy sth, especially sth you have liked or enjoyed for a long time 指喜爱（尤指已爱上很长时间的事物）：*We were fond of the house and didn't want to leave.* 我们喜欢上了这座房子，不想搬家。

be keen on sth (*BrE, informal*) (often used in negative statements) to like or enjoy sth（常用于否定句）指喜欢、喜爱：*I'm not keen on spicy food.* 我不喜欢加有香料的食物。◇ *She's not keen on being told what to do.* 她不喜欢别人向她发号施令。

adore (*informal*) to like or enjoy sth very much 指非常喜爱、热爱：*She adores working with children.* 她热爱参与儿童工作。

LOVE OR ADORE? 用 love 还是 adore?

Adore is more informal than **love**, and is used to express a stronger feeling. * adore 较 love 非正式，用以表达更强烈的感情。

PATTERNS

- to like/love/be fond of/be keen on/adore **doing sth**
- to like/love **to do sth**
- to like/love sth **very much**
- **I** like/love/adore **it** here/there/when...
- to like/love/adore **the way** sb does sth
- to **really** like/love/adore sb/sth
- to be **really** fond of/keen on sth

你的头发你想怎么染就怎么染。 **4** 🔑 [T] used in negative sentences to mean 'to be unwilling to do sth'（用于否定句）愿做：**~ to do sth** *I didn't like to disturb you.* 我本不愿打搅你。◊ **~ doing sth** *He doesn't like asking his parents for help.* 他不愿向父母求助。 **5** 🔑 [T, I] used with *would* or *should* as a polite way to say what you want or to ask what sb wants（与 would 或 should 连用表示客气）想，想要，希望：**~ sth** *Would you like a drink?* 你想喝一杯吗？◊ **~ to do sth** *I'd like to think it over.* 我想考虑一下这个问题。◊ *Would you like to come with us?* 你想不想和我们一块儿去？◊ (*formal*) *We would like to apologize for the delay.* 我们对延迟表示歉意。◊ *How can they afford it? That's what I'd like to know.* 他们怎么买得起这东西？这倒是我所想知道的。◊ **~ sb/sth to do sth** *We'd like you to come and visit us.* 我们想请你来我们这儿做客。◊ **~ for sb to do sth** (*NAmE*) *I'd like for us to work together.* 我希望我们在一起工作。 ➲ NOTE AT WANT ➲ EXPRESS YOURSELF AT PLEASE **6 ~ sth** if you like sth on a SOCIAL NETWORKING service, news website, BLOG, etc. you show that you agree with it or that you think it is good by clicking a special button（在社交网络、新闻网站、博客等上）给…点赞：*By the next morning, over twenty of my friends had liked my new profile picture.* 到第二天早上，我的二十多个朋友对我的新用户头像点了赞。

IDM **how would 'you like it?** used to emphasize that sth bad has happened to you and you want some sympathy（强调遭遇不佳并想得到同情）你会感觉怎么样呢：*How would you like it if someone called you a liar?* 如果有人说你撒谎，你会怎么想呢？ **if you 'like** (*informal*) **1** 🔑 used to politely agree to sth or to suggest sth（礼貌地同意或建议）如果你要这样做，你要是愿意的话：*'Shall we stop now?' 'If you like.'* "我们现在停下来好吗？" "听你的。" ◊ *If you like, we could go out this evening.* 你如果愿意的话，咱们今晚可以出去。 **2** used when you express sth in a new way or when you are not confident about sth（用新方式表达或不确定时说）换句话说，可以说：*It was, if you like, the dawn of a new era.* 换句话说，那就是新时代的黎明。 **I like 'that!** (*old-fashioned, informal*) used to protest that sth that has been said is not true or fair（抗议所言不实或不公）亏你说得出口：*'She called you a cheat.' 'Well, I like that!'* "她说你是骗子。" "哦，说得好哇！" **I/I'd like to think** used to say that you hope or believe that sth is true（表示希望或相信某事属实）我倒想…：*I like to think I'm broad-minded.* 我倒想心胸开阔。 **ˌwhat's ˌnot to 'like?** (*informal, humorous*) used to say that sth is very good or enjoyable（用以表示非常好或令人愉快）：*You get paid to eat chocolate. So what's not to like?* 你吃巧克力还能得到报酬，这不很好吗？

■ ***conj.*** (*informal*) **1** 🔑 in the same way as 像…一样；如同：*No one sings the blues like she did.* 没人像她那样唱蓝调歌曲。◊ *It didn't turn out like I intended.* 这结果与我的本意相悖。◊ ***Like I said*** (= as I said before), *you're always welcome to stay.* 正如我以前所说的一样，我永远都欢迎你留下来。 **2** 🔑 as if 好像；仿佛；似乎：*She acts like she owns the place.* 她的举动就像那地方是她的一样。 HELP You will find more information about this use of **like** at the entries for the verbs **act**, **behave**, **feel**, **look** and **sound** and in the note at **as**. 在动词 act、behave、feel、look 和 sound 词条下，以及在 as 用法说明中有 like 此种用法的更多说明。

■ ***noun*** **1 likes** [pl.] the things that you like 喜好；爱好：*We all have different* ***likes and dislikes***. 我们各有不同的好恶。 **2** [sing.] a person or thing that is similar to another 类似的人（或物）：*jazz, rock* ***and the like*** (= similar types of music) 爵士乐、摇滚乐以及诸如此类的音乐 ◊ *a man whose like we shall not see again* 我们再也不会见到的那种男人 ◊ *You're not comparing* ***like with like***. 你比较的不是同类的东西。 **3 the likes of sb/sth** (*informal*) used to refer to sb/sth that is considered as a type, especially one that is considered as good as sb/sth else（尤指被视为和某人或某事物一样好的）种类，类型：*She didn't want to associate with the likes of me.* 她不想与我这种类型的人交往。 **4** if something on a SOCIAL NETWORKING service, news website, BLOG, etc. receives a like, it means that somebody has shown that they agree with it or think it is good by clicking a special button（对社交网络、新闻网站、博客等的内容的）点赞：*The band now has thousands of likes.* 该乐队现在得到了成千上万个点赞。

■ ***adj.*** [only before noun] (*formal*) having similar qualities to another person or thing 类似的；相似的：*a chance to meet people of like mind* (= with similar interests and opinions) 结识志趣相投的人的机会 ◊ *She responded in like manner.* 她以类似的方式作出了反应。

■ ***adv.*** **1** used in very informal speech, for example when you are thinking what to say next, explaining sth, or giving an example of sth（非正式口语，思考该说什么、解释或举例时用）：*It was, like, weird.* 这事儿，就是说，有点怪。◊ *It was kind of scary, like.* 这还挺可怕的。◊ *It's really hard. Like I have no time for my own work.* 这事真费劲，弄得我没时间做自己的工作了。 **2** used in very informal speech to show that what you are saying may not be exactly right but is nearly so（非正式口语）大概，可能：*I'm leaving in like twenty minutes.* 我大概 20 分钟后离开。◊ *It's going to cost like a hundred dollars.* 这可能要花 100 美元。 **3 I'm, he's, she's, etc. ~** used in very informal speech, to mean 'I say', 'he/she says', etc.（非正式口语）我说，他说，她说：*And then I'm like 'No Way!'* 接着我说"没门儿！" **4** used in informal speech instead of *as* to say that sth happens in the same way（非正式口语，代替 as）和…一样，如，像：*There was silence, but not like before.* 没有声音，但与以前不一样。 ➲ NOTE AT AS

IDM **(as) like as 'not | like e'nough | most/very 'like** (*old-fashioned*) quite probably 很可能；大概：*She would be in bed by now, as like as not.* 这时候她很可能睡了。

-like *combining form* (in adjectives 构成形容词) similar to; typical of 类似…的；有…特征的：*childlike* 孩子般的 ◊ *shell-like* 似壳的

like·able (*especially BrE*) (*also* **lik·able** *NAmE, BrE*) /ˈlaɪkəbl/ *adj.* pleasant and easy to like 可爱的；讨人喜欢的：*a very likeable man* 十分讨人喜爱的人

like·li·hood /ˈlaɪklihʊd/ *noun* [U, sing.] the chance of sth happening; how likely sth is to happen 可能；可能性 SYN **probability**：*There is very little likelihood of that happening.* 几乎没有发生那种事情的可能。◊ ***In all likelihood*** (= very probably) *the meeting will be cancelled.* 这次会议十有八九要被取消。◊ ***The likelihood is that*** (= it is likely that) *unemployment figures will continue to fall.* 很有可能失业人数会继续下降。

like·ly 🔑 /ˈlaɪkli/ *adj., adv.*

■ ***adj.*** (**like·lier**, **like·li·est**) HELP **more likely** and **most likely** are the usual forms 常用 more likely 和 most likely。 **1** 🔑 probable or expected 可能的；预料的；有希望的：*the most likely outcome* 最可能的结果 ◊ **~ (to do sth)** *Tickets are likely to be expensive.* 入场券可能很贵。◊ **~ (that...)** *It's* ***more than likely that*** *the thieves don't know how much it is worth.* 盗贼很可能不知道此物的价值。◊ *They might*

▼ **EXPRESS YOURSELF** 情景表达

Expressing likelihood 表达可能性

When you are talking about possible situations, you can express how likely you think they are. 表达可能性有多大可用以下方式：

- ***It's pretty much inevitable*** *that prices will go up this year.* 今年价格上涨几乎是不可避免的了。
- ***I think it's likely*** *to rain this afternoon.* 我觉得今天下午有可能下雨。
- *I'm* ***probably*** *going to be away then.* 到那时候我可能就要离开了。
- ***I guess there's a fifty per cent chance that*** *they'll say no.* 我估计他们不同意的几率有百分之五十。
- ***It's unlikely, but not totally impossible, I suppose.*** 我想这不大可能，但并非完全没有可能。
- ***They can't possibly/really be*** *serious about buying a boat!* 他们不可能真要买一条船吧！
- *Let's start without them.* ***They're bound to be*** *late.* 咱们不等他们了，先开始吧。他们肯定会迟到。

refuse to let us do it, but it's ***hardly likely****.* 他们也许不会让我们做这工作，但这可能性太小。 ➲ LANGUAGE BANK AT EXPECT **2** seeming suitable for a purpose 似乎合适的；仿佛恰当的 SYN **promising**: *She seems the most likely candidate for the job.* 这项工作，她似乎是最适宜的人选了。

IDM **a 'likely story** (*informal, ironic*) used to show that you do not believe what sb has said（表示不相信某人的话）说得好像真有这回事似的，煞有介事

■ *adv.*

IDM **as ˌlikely as 'not | most/very 'likely** very probably 很可能：*As likely as not she's forgotten all about it.* 她很可能把这事忘得一干二净了。 **not 'likely!** (*informal, especially BrE*) used to disagree strongly with a statement or suggestion （表示坚决不同意）决不可能，绝对不会：*Me? Join the army? Not likely!* 我？参军入伍？不可能！

▼ **GRAMMAR POINT 语法说明**

likely

- In standard *BrE* the adverb **likely** is often used with a word such as *most, more* or *very.* 在标准的英式英语中，副词 likely 常与 most、more 或 very 等词连用：*We will most likely see him later.* 我们很可能晚些时候会见到他。 In journalism and less formal language, however, **likely** is used on its own. 但在新闻和不太正式的用语中，likely 则单独使用：*The deal will likely result in more cuts to services.* 这项协议可能会导致对服务行业的进一步削减。 In informal *NAmE* **likely** is often used on its own, and this is not considered incorrect. 在非正式的美式英语中，likely 常单独使用，且不被视为有误：*We will likely see him later.* 我们可能晚些时候会见到他。◇ *He said that he would likely run for President.* 他说他可能竞选总统。

ˌlike-'minded *adj.* having similar ideas and interests 想法相同的；志趣相投的

liken /ˈlaɪkən/ *verb*

PHR V **'liken sth/sb to sth/sb** (*formal*) to compare one thing or person to another and say they are similar 把…比作…：*Life is often likened to a journey.* 人们常把人生比作旅程。

like·ness /ˈlaɪknəs/ *noun* **1** [C, U] the fact of being similar to another person or thing, especially in appearance; an example of this 相像；相似；相似之处 SYN **resemblance**: *Joanna bears a strong likeness to her father.* 乔安娜长得酷似她父亲。◇ *Do you notice any family likeness between them?* 你看没看出他们长得像是一家人？ **2** [C, usually sing.] a painting, drawing, etc. of a person, especially one that looks very like them（尤指画得像的）肖像，画像：*The drawing is said to be* ***a good likeness*** *of the girl's attacker.* 据说那幅嫌犯的画像画得很像袭击女孩的歹徒本人。

likes *noun* ➲ LIKE *n.* (1)

like·wise AW /ˈlaɪkwaɪz/ *adv.* **1** (*formal*) the same; in a similar way 同样地；类似地：*He voted for the change and he expected his colleagues to* ***do likewise****.* 他投票赞成变革并期望他的同事投同样的票。 **2** (*formal*) also 也；还；亦；而且：*Her second marriage was likewise unhappy.* 她的第二次婚姻也不幸福。 **3** (*informal*) used to show that you feel the same towards sb or about sth（表示感觉相同）我也是，我有同感：*'Let me know if you ever need any help.' 'Likewise.'* "你要是需要帮助就告诉我。""你也一样。"

lik·ing /ˈlaɪkɪŋ/ *noun* [sing.] ~ (**for sb/sth**) the feeling that you like sb/sth; the enjoyment of sth 喜欢；喜好；嗜好；乐趣 SYN **fondness**: *He* ***had a liking for*** *fast cars.* 他喜欢快车。◇ *She had* ***taken a liking to him*** *on their first meeting.* 她对他一见钟情。

IDM **for your 'liking** if you say, for example, that sth is too hot **for your liking**, you mean that you would prefer it to be less hot 适合…的口味（或愿望）：*The town was too crowded for my liking.* 这座城镇太拥挤了，我不喜欢。 **to sb's 'liking** (*formal*) suitable, and how sb likes sth 适合某人的胃口；中某人的意：*The coffee was just to his liking.* 这咖啡正合他的口味。

lilac /ˈlaɪlək/ *noun* **1** [U, C] a bush or small tree with purple or white flowers with a sweet smell that grow closely together in the shape of a CONE 丁香 **2** [U] a pale purple colour 淡紫色；丁香紫 ▶ **lilac** *adj.*：*a lilac dress* 一件淡紫色的连衣裙

Lil·li·pu·tian /ˌlɪlɪˈpjuːʃn/ *adj.* (*formal*) extremely small 极小的；微小的 SYN **diminutive, tiny** ➲ MORE LIKE THIS 17, page R27 ORIGIN From the land of **Lilliput**, in Jonathan Swift's *Gulliver's Travels*, where the people are only 15 cm high. 源自乔纳森 • 斯威夫特的《格利佛游记》中的小人国（Lilliput），那里的居民仅有 15 厘米高。

lilo /ˈlaɪləʊ; *NAmE* -loʊ/ (*also* **Li-Lo™**) *noun* (*pl.* **-os**) (*BrE*) a plastic or rubber bed that is filled with air and used when camping or for floating on water 充气垫（用于露营或水上漂浮）

lilt /lɪlt/ *noun* [sing.] **1** the pleasant way in which a person's voice rises and falls（说话声的）抑扬顿挫：*Her voice had a soft Welsh lilt to it.* 她讲话的声音柔和而抑扬顿挫，有些威尔士口音。 **2** a regular rising and falling pattern in music, with a strong rhythm 节奏欢快的旋律；轻快活泼的曲调 ▶ **lilt·ing** *adj.*

lily /ˈlɪli/ *noun* (*pl.* **-ies**) a large white or brightly coloured flower with PETALS that curl back from the centre. There are many types of lily. 百合花 ➲ VISUAL VOCAB PAGE V11 ➲ SEE ALSO WATER LILY IDM SEE GILD

lily-livered /ˈlɪli lɪvəd; *NAmE* -vərd/ *adj.* (*old-fashioned*) lacking courage 胆怯的；懦弱的 SYN **cowardly**

ˌlily of the 'valley *noun* [C, U] (*pl.* **lilies of the valley**) a plant with small white flowers shaped like bells 铃兰

'lily pad *noun* a round floating leaf of a WATER LILY 睡莲的漂浮叶

ˌlily-'white *adj.* **1** almost pure white in colour 近纯白的：*lily-white skin* 白皙的皮肤 **2** morally perfect 纯洁的；完美无瑕的：*They want me to conform, to be lily-white.* 他们要我循规蹈矩，要我清白无瑕。 ➲ MORE LIKE THIS 15, page R26

lima bean /ˈliːmə biːn/ *noun* (*NAmE*) a type of round, pale green BEAN. Several lima beans grow together inside a flat POD. 利马豆

limb /lɪm/ *noun* **1** an arm or a leg; a similar part of an animal, such as a wing 肢；臂；腿；翼；翅膀：*an artificial limb* 假肢 ◇ *For a while, she lost the use of her limbs.* 好一会儿她四肢都动弹不得。 **2 -limbed** (in adjectives 构成形容词) having the type of limbs mentioned 有…肢（或翼、翅膀）的：*long-limbed* 四肢细长的 ◇ *loose-limbed* 四肢柔软灵活的 ➲ MORE LIKE THIS 8, page R25 **3** a large branch of a tree（树的）大枝，主枝 ➲ VISUAL VOCAB PAGE V10 ➲ MORE LIKE THIS 20, page R27

IDM **out on a 'limb** (*informal*) not supported by other people 无人支持；孤立无援：*Are you prepared to* ***go out on a limb*** (= risk doing sth that other people are not prepared to do) *and make your suspicions public?* 你愿意冒险把你怀疑的事公开吗？ **tear/rip sb ˌlimb from 'limb** (*often humorous*) to attack sb very violently 猛烈攻击某人 ➲ MORE AT RISK *v.*

limba /ˈlɪmbə/ *noun* = AFARA

lim·ber /ˈlɪmbə(r)/ *verb*

PHR V **ˌlimber 'up** to do physical exercises in order to stretch and prepare your muscles before taking part in a race, sporting activity, etc.（赛跑、体育运动等前）做准备活动，做热身运动 SYN **warm up**

lim·bic sys·tem /ˈlɪmbɪk sɪstəm/ *noun* (*biology* 生) a system of nerves in the brain involving several different areas, concerned with basic emotions such as fear and anger and basic needs such as the need to eat and to have sex（大脑）边缘系，边缘系统

limbo /ˈlɪmbəʊ; *NAmE* -boʊ/ *noun* (*pl.* **-os**) **1** [C] a West Indian dance in which you lean backwards and go under a bar which is made lower each time you go under it 林波舞（西印度群岛舞蹈，舞者向后弯腰钻过一次比一次降低的横杆） **2** [U, sing.] a situation in which you are not certain what to do next, cannot take action, etc., especially because you are waiting for sb else to make a decision （尤指因等待他人作决定）处于不定状态：*the limbo of the stateless person* 无国籍人的不安定状态 ◇ *His life seemed stuck* ***in limbo****; he could not go forward and he could not go back.* 他的生活好像陷入了不知所措的境地，进退两难。

lime /laɪm/ *noun, verb*

■ ***noun*** **1** (*also* **quick·lime**) [U] a white substance obtained by heating LIMESTONE, used in building materials and to help plants grow 石灰 **2** [C, U] a small green fruit, like a lemon, with a lot of sour juice, used in cooking and in drinks; the juice of this fruit 来檬；来檬汁：*lime juice* 来檬汁 ◇ *slices of lime* 来檬片 ➲ VISUAL VOCAB PAGE V33 **3** (*also* **ˈlime tree**) [C] a tree on which limes grow 来檬树 **4** (*also* **ˈlime tree, ˈlinden tree, linden**) [C] a large tree with light green heart-shaped leaves and yellow flowers 欧椴树：*an avenue of limes* 两边栽有欧椴树的林荫道 **5** [U] = LIME GREEN

■ ***verb*** **~ sth** to add the substance lime to soil, especially in order to control the acid in it（尤指为控制酸度而给土壤）掺加石灰，撒石灰

lime·ade /ˌlaɪmˈeɪd/ *noun* [U, C] **1** a sweet FIZZY drink (= with bubbles) with a LIME flavour 来檬汽水 **2** a drink made from LIME juice, sugar and water 来檬汁饮料

ˌlime ˈgreen *adj.* (*also* **lime**) bright yellowish green in colour 来檬绿的；淡绿色的 ▸ **ˌlime ˈgreen** (*also* **lime**) *noun* [U] ➲ MORE LIKE THIS 15, page R26

lime·light /ˈlaɪmlaɪt/ (*usually* **the limelight**) *noun* [U] the centre of public attention 公众注意的中心：*to be* ***in the limelight*** 成为公众注目的中心 ◇ *to stay* ***out of the limelight*** 避免引人注目 ◇ *to* ***steal/hog the limelight*** (= take attention away from other people) 把公众的注意力吸引过来

lim·er·ick /ˈlɪmərɪk/ *noun* a humorous short poem, with two long lines that RHYME with each other, followed by two short lines that rhyme with each other and ending with a long line that rhymes with the first two 五行打油诗（幽默短诗，起始两长句押韵，中间两短句押韵，最后一长句与开头两句押韵）

lime·scale /ˈlaɪmskeɪl/ *noun* [U] (*BrE*) the hard white substance that is left by water on the inside of pipes, etc.（管道等内的）水垢

lime·stone /ˈlaɪmstəʊn; *NAmE* -stoʊn/ *noun* [U] a type of white stone that contains CALCIUM, used in building and in making CEMENT 石灰岩

ˈlime water *noun* [U] (*chemistry* 化) a liquid containing CALCIUM HYDROXIDE which shows the presence of CARBON DIOXIDE by turning white 石灰水

Limey /ˈlaɪmi/ *noun* (*old-fashioned, NAmE*) a slightly insulting word for a British person 英国佬

limit 🔑 /ˈlɪmɪt/ *noun, verb*

■ ***noun*** **1** 🔑 **~ (to sth)** a point at which sth stops being possible or existing 限度；限制：*There is a limit to the amount of pain we can bear.* 我们能忍受的疼痛是有限度的。◇ *The team performed* ***to the limit*** *of its capabilities.* 这个队已竭尽全力。◇ *She knew the limits of her power.* 她知道自己的权限。◇ *to push/stretch/test sb/sth* ***to the limit*** 最大限度地推 / 拉 / 考查某人（或某物） ◇ *His arrogance* ***knew*** (= had) ***no limits***. 他极其傲慢。 **2** 🔑 **~ (on sth)** the greatest or smallest amount of sth that is allowed 极限；限量；限额 SYN **restriction**：*a time/speed/age limit* 时间 / 速度 / 年龄限制 ◇ *The EU has* ***set*** *strict* ***limits*** *on levels of pollution.* 欧盟对污染程度作了严格的限定。◇ *They were travelling at a speed that was double the* ***legal limit***. 他们正以两倍于法定限速的速度行驶。◇ *You can't drive—you're* ***over the limit*** (= you have drunk more alcohol than is legal when driving). 你饮酒过量，不能驾车。 **3** the furthest edge of an area or a place （地区或地方的）境界，界限，范围：*We were reaching the limits of civilization.* 我们快到蛮荒地界了。◇ *the* ***city limits*** (= the imaginary line which officially divides the city from the area outside) 城市境界 ➲ SEE ALSO OFF-LIMITS

▼ **SYNONYMS 同义词辨析**

limit

restriction • control • constraint • restraint • limitation

These are all words for sth that limits what you can do or what can happen. 以上各词均表示限制或限定。

limit the greatest or smallest amount of sth that is allowed 指极限、限量、限额：*The EU has set strict limits on pollution levels.* 欧盟对污染程度作了严格的限定。◇ *the speed limit* 速度限制

restriction (*rather formal*) a rule or law that limits what you can do 指限制规定、限制法规：*There are no restrictions on the amount of money you can withdraw.* 取款没有限额。

control (often in compounds) the act of limiting or managing sth; a method of doing this （常构成复合词）指限制、约束、管理、管制：*arms control* 军备控制

constraint (*rather formal*) a fact or decision that limits what you can do 指限制、限定、约束：*We have to work within severe constraints of time and money.* 我们必须在时间紧迫、资金紧张的限制下工作。

restraint (*rather formal*) a decision, a rule, an idea, etc. that limits what you can do; the act of limiting sth because it is necessary or sensible to do so 指约束力、管制措施、制约因素、控制、限制：*The government has imposed export restraints on some products.* 政府对一些产品实行了出口控制。◇ *The unions are unlikely to accept any sort of wage restraint.* 工会不大可能接受任何形式的工资限制。

limitation the act or process of limiting sth; a rule, fact or condition that limits sth 指限制、控制、起限制作用的规则、事实或条件：*They would resist any limitation of their powers.* 他们会抵制对他们权力的任何限制。

RESTRICTION, CONSTRAINT, RESTRAINT OR LIMITATION?
用 restriction、constraint、restraint 还是 limitation?

These are all things that limit what you can do. A **restriction** is rule or law that is made by sb in authority. A **constraint** is sth that exists rather than sth that is made, although it may exist as a result of sb's decision. A **restraint** is also sth that exists: it can exist outside yourself, as the result of sb else's decision; but it can also exist inside you, as a fear of what other people may think or as your own feeling about what is acceptable. 以上各词均表示限制规定。restriction 指掌权者所作的规定或法规。constraint 指现存的限制或约束而非作出的决定，尽管这种约束也可能是因他人的决定而存在。restraint 亦指现存的限制或制约因素，既可能指自身以外的因素，如他人的决定；也可能指自身因素，如担心别人的想法或顾虑自己的做法能否被接受：*moral/social/cultural restraints* 道德 / 社会 / 文化制约因素 A **limitation** is more general and can be a rule that sb makes or a fact or condition that exists. * limitation 较通用，可指人为的规定，也可指客观存在的构成限制的事实或条件。

PATTERNS

- limits/restrictions/controls/constraints/restraints/limitations **on** sth
- limits/limitations **to** sth
- **severe** limits/restrictions/controls/constraints/restraints/limitations
- **tight** limits/restrictions/controls/constraints
- to **impose**/**remove** limits/restrictions/controls/constraints/restraints/limitations
- to **lift** restrictions/controls/constraints/restraints

L

IDM **be the 'limit** (*old-fashioned, informal*) to be extremely annoying 极其令人讨厌 **within 'limits** to some extent; with some restrictions 在某种程度上；有一定限制：*I'm willing to help, within limits.* 我愿意帮忙，可有一定的限度。➲ MORE AT SKY *n.*

■ *verb* **1** ~ **sth (to sth)** to stop sth from increasing beyond a particular amount or level 限制；限定 **SYN** **restrict**: *measures to limit carbon dioxide emissions from cars* 限制汽车二氧化碳排放的措施 ◇ *The amount of money you have to spend will limit your choice.* 你要消费的金额会限制你的选择。 **2** ~ **yourself/sb (to sth)** to restrict or reduce the amount of sth that you or sb can have or use 限量；减量：*Families are limited to four free tickets each.* 每户限发四张免费票。◇ *I've limited myself to 1 000 calories a day to try and lose weight.* 我为了减肥，限定自己每天摄入 1 000 大卡的热量。

PHR V **'limit sth to sb/sth** [usually passive] to make sth exist or happen only in a particular place or within a particular group 使（某事只在某地或某群体内）存在（或发生）：*Violent crime is not limited to big cities.* 暴力犯罪并不局限于大城市。◇ *The teaching of history should not be limited to dates and figures.* 教授历史不应该局限于讲年代和人物。

limi·ta·tion /ˌlɪmɪˈteɪʃn/ *noun* **1** [U] the act or process of limiting or controlling sb/sth 限制；控制 **SYN** **restriction**: *They would resist any limitation of their powers.* 他们会抵制对他们权力的任何限制。➲ SYNONYMS AT LIMIT ➲ SEE ALSO DAMAGE LIMITATION **2** [C] ~ **(on sth)** a rule, fact or condition that limits sth 起限制作用的规则（或事实、条件） **SYN** **curb, restraint**: *to impose limitations on imports* 对进口加以限制 ◇ *Disability is a physical limitation on your life.* 残疾会给生活带来身体方面的限制。➲ SEE ALSO STATUTE OF LIMITATIONS **3** [C, usually pl.] a limit on what sb/sth can do or how good they or it can be 局限；限度：*This technique is useful but it **has its limitations**.* 这种技巧实用，但也有局限性。

limit·ed /ˈlɪmɪtɪd/ *adj.* **1** not very great in amount or extent 有限的：*We are doing our best with the limited resources available.* 我们利用可获得的有限资源，尽最大的努力。 **2** ~ **(to sth)** restricted to a particular limit of time, numbers, etc. 受（…的）限制：*This offer is for a limited period only.* 此次减价时间有限。➲ SEE ALSO LTD

ˌlimited 'company (*also* **ˌlimited liaˈbility company**) *noun* (in Britain) a company whose owners only have to pay a limited amount of its debts（英国的）有限责任公司，股份有限公司 ➲ SEE ALSO LTD

ˌlimited eˈdition *noun* a fixed, usually small, number of copies of a book, picture, etc. produced at one time（书、画等的）限定版，限数本

ˌlimited liaˈbility *noun* [U] (*law* 律) the legal position of having to pay only a limited amount of your or your company's debts 有限责任

limit·ing /ˈlɪmɪtɪŋ/ *adj.* putting limits on what is possible 限制性的：*Lack of cash is a limiting factor.* 现金短缺是一个制约因素。

limit·less /ˈlɪmɪtləs/ *adj.* without a limit; very great 无限制的；无界限的；无限度的；无止境的 **SYN** **infinite**: *the limitless variety of consumer products* 种类繁多的消费产品 ◇ *The possibilities were almost limitless.* 可能性几乎是无穷无尽的。

limo /ˈlɪməʊ; *NAmE* ˈlɪmoʊ/ *noun* (*pl.* **-os**) (*informal*) = LIMOUSINE

lim·ou·sine /ˈlɪməziːn; ˌlɪməˈziːn/ (*also informal* **limo**) *noun* **1** a large expensive comfortable car 大型高级轿车；豪华轿车：*a long black chauffeur-driven limousine* 由专职司机驾驶的黑色豪华加长轿车 ➲ SEE ALSO STRETCH LIMO **2** (*especially NAmE*) a van or small bus that takes people to and from an airport（往返机场接送旅客的）中型客车，小型公共汽车

limp /lɪmp/ *adj., verb, noun*

■ *adj.* **1** lacking strength or energy 无力的；无生气的；无精神的：*His hand went limp and the knife clattered to the ground.* 他的手一软，刀子当啷一声掉到地上。◇ *She felt limp and exhausted.* 她感到浑身无力，累极了。 **2** not stiff or firm 柔软的；不直挺的：*The hat had become limp and shapeless.* 这帽子软得不成样子了。▶ **limp·ly** *adv.*: *Her hair **hung limply** over her forehead.* 她的头发蓬松地垂在前额上。

■ *verb* **1** [I] to walk slowly or with difficulty because one leg is injured 瘸着走；跛行；蹒跚：*She had twisted her ankle and was limping.* 她把脚踝扭伤了，一瘸一拐地走着。◇ **+ adv./prep.** *Matt limped painfully off the field.* 马特忍着痛歪歪斜斜地走出了运动场。 **2** [I] **+ adv./prep.** to move slowly or with difficulty after being damaged（受损后）缓慢行进，艰难地移动：*The plane limped back to the airport.* 受损的飞机艰难地返回了机场。◇ (*figurative*) *The government was limping along in its usual way.* 政府按老一套挣扎着应付。

■ *noun* [usually sing.] a way of walking in which one leg is used less than normal because it is injured or stiff 跛行：*to walk with a **slight/pronounced limp*** 有点 / 明显地一瘸一拐地走

lim·pet /ˈlɪmpɪt/ *noun* a small SHELLFISH that sticks very tightly to rocks 帽贝，钥孔蝛（依附在岩石上）：*The Prime Minister clung to his job like a limpet, despite calls for him to resign.* 首相不顾众人要求他辞职的呼声，死赖着不下台。

lim·pid /ˈlɪmpɪd/ *adj.* (*literary*) (of liquids, etc. 液体等) clear 清澈的；清晰的；透明的 **SYN** **transparent**: ***limpid eyes/water*** 明亮的眼睛；清澈的水

ˌlimp-ˈwristed *adj.* (*informal*) an offensive word for HOMOSEXUAL 娘娘腔的（含冒犯意，形容男同性恋者）

LINC /lɪŋk/ *abbr.* Language Instruction for Newcomers to Canada (free language classes provided by the government to people from other countries who come to live in Canada) 加拿大新移民语言培训（加拿大政府提供的免费课程）

linch·pin (*also* **lynch·pin**) /ˈlɪntʃpɪn/ *noun* a person or thing that is the most important part of an organization, a plan, etc., because everything else depends on them or it（组织、计划等的）关键人物，关键事物

Lin·coln's Birth·day /ˌlɪŋkənz ˈbɜːθdeɪ; *NAmE* ˈbɜːrθ-/ *noun* [U] (in some US states) a legal holiday on 12 February in memory of the birthday of Abraham Lincoln 林肯诞辰纪念日（2 月 12 日，美国某些州的法定假日）

linc·tus /ˈlɪŋktəs/ *noun* [U] (*BrE*) thick liquid medicine that you take for a sore throat or a cough 润喉止咳糖浆；药糖剂：*cough linctus* 止咳糖浆

lin·den /ˈlɪndən/ (*also* **'linden tree**) *noun* = LIME (4)

line /laɪn/ *noun, verb*

■ *noun*

• **LONG THIN MARK** 线 **1** [C] a long thin mark on a surface 线；线条：*a **straight/wavy/dotted/diagonal line*** 直线；波状线；虚线；对角线 ◇ *a **vertical/horizontal line*** 垂直线；水平线 ◇ ***parallel lines*** 平行线 ◇ *Draw a thick black line across the page.* 在此页上横画一条粗黑线。 **2** [C] a long thin mark on the ground to show the limit or border of sth, especially of a playing area in some sports 界线；（尤指运动场地的）场地线，场界：*The ball **went over the line**.* 球越线出界了。◇ *Be careful not to **cross the line*** (= the broken line painted down the middle of the road). 小心别越过道路的中界线。◇ *Your feet must be behind the line when you serve* (= in TENNIS). 发球时你的脚必须站在底线的外面。◇ *They were all waiting on the **starting line**.* 他们全都在起跑线上等待着。➲ SEE ALSO FINISHING LINE, GOAL LINE, SIDELINE *n.*, TOUCHLINE **3** [C] a mark like a line on sb's skin that people usually get as they get older 皱纹；褶子 **SYN** **wrinkle**: *He has **fine lines** around his eyes.* 他的眼睛周围有细细的皱纹。

• **DIVISION** 分界线 **4** [C] an imaginary limit or border between one place or thing and another 分界线；边界线：*He was convicted of illegally importing weapons across **state lines**.* 他被判犯有非法越州偷运武器罪。◇ *a district/*

county line 行政区界；郡界 ◇ ***lines of longitude and latitude*** 经线和纬线 ➲ SEE ALSO COASTLINE, DATE LINE, DIVIDING LINE, PICKET LINE, TREELINE, WATERLINE **5** [C] the division between one area of thought or behaviour and another （思想或行为的）界限，界线： *We want to cut across lines of race, sex and religion.* 我们要超越种族、性别和宗教的界限。 ◇ *There is **a fine line between** showing interest in what someone is doing and interfering in it.* 关心别人正在做的事情和进行干预之间存在着细微的差别。 ➲ SEE ALSO RED LINE

• **SHAPE** 形状 **6** [C] the edge, outline or shape of sb/sth 边线；轮廓线；形体；形状： *He traced the line of her jaw with his finger.* 他用手指顺着她的下巴外缘抚摸。 ◇ *a beautiful sports car with sleek lines* 线条流畅、美观的跑车 ➲ SEE ALSO BIKINI LINE

• **ROW OF PEOPLE/THINGS** 人或物的行列 **7** [C] a row of people or things next to each other or behind each other 排；行；列： *a long line of trees* 一长排树 ◇ *The children all stood **in a line**.* 孩子们全都站成一排。 ◇ *They were stuck in a line of traffic.* 他们塞在汽车长龙里面了。 **8** [C] (*NAmE*) a QUEUE of people （人）队伍，行列： *to **stand/wait in line** for sth* 排队等候某事物 ◇ *A line formed at each teller window.* 银行每个出纳员的窗口前都排起了队。

• **IN FACTORY** 工厂 **9** [C] a system of making sth, in which the product moves from one worker to the next until it is finished 生产线；流水线 ➲ SEE ALSO ASSEMBLY LINE, PRODUCTION LINE

• **SERIES** 系列 **10** [C, usually sing.] a series of people, things or events that follow one another in time 按时间顺序排列的人（或物、事件）；家系；家族： *She came from **a long line of** doctors.* 她来自一个医生世家。 ◇ *to pass sth down through the **male/female line*** 通过父系 / 母系代代相传某物 ◇ *This novel is the latest in a long line of thrillers that he has written.* 这部小说是他写的系列惊险小说中最近出版的一部。 **11** [C, usually sing.] a series of people in order of importance 一系列按重要性排列的人： *Orders came down the line from the very top.* 命令从最高领导人逐级传达下来。 ◇ *a line of command* 一系列按职务排序的指挥人员 ◇ *He is second **in line** to the chairman.* 他的地位仅次于主席。 ◇ *to be **next in line** to the throne* 为王位第一顺位继承人 ➲ SEE ALSO LINE MANAGER at LINE MANAGEMENT

• **WORDS** 文字 **12** [C] (*abbr.* **l**) a row of words on a page or the empty space where they can be written; the words of a song or poem 字行；便条；留言条；歌词；诗行： *Look at line 5 of the text.* 看正文第 5 行。 ◇ *Write the title of your essay on the top line.* 把文章的标题写在首行。 ◇ *I can only remember the first two lines of that song.* 我只记得那首歌的头两句歌词。 ➲ WORDFINDER NOTE AT PLAY ➲ SEE ALSO BOTTOM LINE **13** [C] the words spoken by an actor in a play or film/movie （戏剧或电影的）台词，对白： *to learn your lines* 背台词 ◇ *a line from the film 'Casablanca'* 电影《卡萨布兰卡》里的一句话 **14 lines** [pl.] (*BrE*) (in some schools) a punishment in which a child has to write out a particular sentence a number of times （某些学校）重复抄写句子的惩罚 **15** [C] (*informal*) a remark, especially when sb says it to achieve a particular purpose （尤指为达到某种目的说的）话，言语： *Don't give me that line about having to work late again.* 别再跟我说不得不工作到很晚这样的话。 ◇ (*BrE*) *That's the worst **chat-up line** I've ever heard.* 我听过的调情的话里没有比这更差劲的了。

• **ROPE/WIRE/PIPE** 绳索；金属线；管子 **16** [C] a long piece of rope, thread, etc., especially when it is used for a particular purpose 一段绳（或索、线等）： *a **fishing line*** 钓鱼线 ◇ *He hung the towels out **on the line*** (= clothes line). 他把那些毛巾挂在晒衣绳上。 ◇ *They dropped the sails and threw a line to a man on the dock.* 他们放下风帆，把船缆抛给码头上的人。 ➲ WORDFINDER NOTE AT FISHING ➲ SEE ALSO LIFELINE **17** [C] a pipe or thick wire that carries water, gas or electricity from one place to another 管道；线路 ➲ SEE ALSO POWER LINE

• **TELEPHONE** 电话 **18** [C] a telephone connection; a particular telephone number 电话线路；电话号码： *Your bill includes line rental.* 你的账单包括电话线路的租用费。 ◇ *The company's lines have been jammed* (= busy) *all day with people making complaints.* 公司的电话整天都因人们打投诉电话而占线。 ◇ *I was talking to John when the **line** suddenly **went dead**.* 我正和约翰谈话，突然电话断了。 ◇ *If you **hold the line*** (= stay on the telephone and wait), *I'll see if she is available.* 请你不要挂断电话，我去看看她能不能接电话。 ➲ SEE ALSO HELPLINE, HOTLINE, LANDLINE, OFFLINE, ONLINE ➲ WORDFINDER NOTE AT CALL

• **RAILWAY/RAILROAD** 铁道 **19** [C] a railway/railroad track; a section of a railway/railroad system 轨道；铁道；（铁路的）段，线路： *The train was delayed because a tree had fallen across the line.* 火车晚点是因为有一棵树横倒在铁轨上。 ◇ *a branch line* 铁路支线 ◇ *the East Coast line* 东海岸铁路线 ➲ SEE ALSO MAIN LINE

• **ROUTE/DIRECTION** 路线；方向 **20** [C, usually sing.] the direction that sb/sth is moving or located in （行进的）方向，路线；方位： *Just keep going **in a straight line**; you can't miss it.* 只管照直走，你不会找不到那地方的。 ◇ *The town is in a direct line between London and the coast.* 这个镇在伦敦与海岸之间的直线上。 ◇ *Please move; you're right in my **line of vision*** (= the direction I am looking in). 请挪动一下，你正好挡住了我的视线。 ◇ *They followed the line of the river for three miles.* 他们沿着那条河走了三英里。 ◇ *Be careful to stay out of the **line of fire*** (= the direction sb is shooting in). 注意待在射击路线以外。 **21** [C] a route from one place to another especially when it is used for a particular purpose 路线；路径；渠道： *Their aim was to block guerrilla **supply lines**.* 他们的目的是封锁游击队的供给线。

• **ATTITUDE/ARGUMENT** 态度；论点 **22** [C, usually sing.] an attitude or a belief, especially one that sb states publicly （尤指公开表明的）态度，看法： *The government is **taking a firm line on** terrorism.* 政府现在对恐怖主义采取强硬的态度。 ◇ *He supported the **official line** on education.* 他支持官方的教育理念。 ➲ SEE ALSO HARD LINE, PARTY LINE **23** [C] a method or way of doing or thinking about sth 方法；方式： *I don't follow your **line of reasoning**.* 我不理解你的推理方法。 ◇ *She decided to try a different **line of argument*** (= way of persuading sb of sth). 她决定换一种说理方式。 ◇ *sb's first **line of attack/defence*** 某人进行抨击 / 辩护的第一着 ◇ *The police are pursuing a new **line of enquiry/inquiry*** (= way of finding out information). 警方正在实施一种新的调查方法。

• **ACTIVITY** 活动 **24** [sing.] a type or area of business, activity or interest 行业；活动的范围： *My **line of work** pays pretty well.* 我的职业报酬颇丰厚。 ◇ *You can't do much in the art line without training.* 没经过训练，你在艺术行业是不会有多大作为的。 ➲ SEE ALSO SIDELINE *n.* (1)

• **PRODUCT** 产品 **25** [C] a type of product 种类；类型： *We are starting a new line in casual clothes.* 我们将着手经营一组新的休闲服系列。 ◇ *Some lines sell better than others.* 有些品种的货物销售得好些，有些则较差。

• **TRANSPORT** 运输 **26** [C] (often used in names 常用于名称) a company that provides transport for people or goods 运输公司；航运公司： *a **shipping/bus line*** 航运 / 公共汽车公司 ➲ SEE ALSO AIRLINE

• **SOLDIERS** 士兵 **27** [C] a row or series of military defences where the soldiers are fighting during a war 防线；前线；战线： *The regiment was sent to fight in **the front line*** (= the position nearest the enemy). 这个团被派到前线作战。 ◇ *They were trapped **behind enemy lines*** (= in the area controlled by the enemy). 他们在敌人后方遭到围困。

• **DRUGS** 毒品 **28** [C] (*slang*) an amount of COCAINE that is spread out in a thin line, ready to take （准备吸用的）散放成一条细线的可卡因

IDM **along/down the 'line** (*informal*) at some point during an activity or a process 在某一环节；在某一时刻： *Somewhere along the line a large amount of money went missing.* 有一笔巨款在某一环节上不翼而飞。 ◇ *We'll make a decision on that further down the line.* 我们将在以后的阶段对此问题作出决策。 **along/on (the)... 'lines 1** (*informal*) in the way that is mentioned 按…方式： *The new system will operate **along the same lines** as the old one.* 新系统的运作方式将与旧系统一样。 ◇ *They voted along class lines.* 他们按各社会等级进行投票。 **2** (*informal*) similar to the way or thing that is mentioned 类似于（提及的方式或东西）： *Those aren't his exact words, but he said something along those lines.* 那些不是他的原话，但他说的大致就是这个意思。 **be, come, etc. on 'line 1** to be

L

working or functioning 正运转；在运行：*The new working methods will come on line in June.* 新的操作方法将在六月实行。 **2** using or connected to a computer or the Internet; communicating with other people by computer 联机；在线：*All the new homes are on line.* 所有的新建住宅都已联机。 ➲ SEE ALSO ONLINE **bring sb/sth, come, get, fall, etc. into 'line (with sb/sth)** to behave or make sb/sth behave in the same way as other people or how they should behave 使一致；使规范；使符合；（和…）一致：*Britain must be brought into line with the rest of Europe on taxes.* 英国必须在税收上与其他欧洲国家达成一致。 **in (a) 'line (with sth)** in a position that forms a straight line with sth （与…）成一排，成一直线：*An eclipse happens when the earth and moon are in line with the sun.* 地球和月亮与太阳处在一条直线上就会发生日食或月食。 **in 'line for sth** likely to get sth 有可能获得某物：*She is in line for promotion.* 她有可能得到提升。 **in the ˌline of 'duty** while doing a job 在执行任务时；在履行职责时：*A policeman was injured in the line of duty yesterday.* 昨天有一名警察在执行公务时受伤。 **in 'line with sth** similar to sth or so that one thing is closely connected with another 与…相似（或紧密相连）：*Annual pay increases will be in line with inflation.* 每年加薪幅度将与通货膨胀挂钩。 **ˌlay it on the 'line** (*informal*) to tell sb clearly what you think, especially when they will not like what you say 坦率地说；实话实说：*The manager laid it on the line—some people would have to lose their jobs.* 经理开门见山地说，有些人将要失去工作。 **(choose, follow, take, etc.) the line of least re'sistance** (to choose, etc.) the easiest way of doing sth （采取）最省事的方法 **(put sth) on the 'line** (*informal*) at risk 冒风险：*If we don't make a profit, my job is on the line.* 我们要是赚不了钱，我就有失业的危险。 **out of 'line (with sb/sth) 1** not forming a straight line 不成直线 **2** different from sth 与…不同（或不一致）；不符合：*London prices are way out of line with the rest of the country.* 伦敦的物价与英国其他地方的有很大的差异。 **3** (*NAmE*) (*BrE* **ˌout of 'order**) (*informal*) behaving in a way that is not acceptable or right 行为不当；举止让人难以接受 **walk/tread a fine/thin line** to be in a difficult or dangerous situation where you could easily make a mistake 处于困境（或险境）；如履薄冰；走钢丝：*He was walking a fine line between being funny and being rude.* 他想滑稽而不粗鲁，难以把握分寸。 ➲ MORE AT BATTLE *n.*, DRAW *v.*, END *n.*, FIRING LINE, FIRM *adj.*, FRONT LINE, HARD *adj.*, HOOK *n.*, JUMP *v.*, OVERSTEP, PITCH *v.*, READ *v.*, SIGN *v.*, STEP *v.*, TOE *v.*

■ *verb*

• **COVER INSIDE** 做衬里 **1** [often passive] **~ sth (with sth)** to cover the inside of sth with a layer of another material to keep it clean, make it stronger, etc. （用…）做衬里：*Line the pan with greaseproof paper.* 在烤盘里垫一层防油纸。 **2 ~ sth** to form a layer on the inside of sth （在某物的内部）形成一层：*the membranes that line the nose* 在鼻腔里形成的一层内膜

• **FORM ROWS** 形成行 **3** [often passive] to form lines or rows along sth 沿…形成行（或列、排）：**~ sth** *Crowds of people lined the streets to watch the race.* 人群站在街道两旁观看比赛。 ◇ **~ sth with sth** *The walls were lined with books.* 靠墙是一排排的图书。 ➲ SEE ALSO LINED

IDM **line your (own)/sb's 'pockets** to get richer or make sb richer, especially by taking unfair advantage of a situation or by being dishonest （尤指通过占便宜或欺诈而）中饱私囊，（使）发财

PHR V **ˌline 'up** to stand in a line or row; to form a QUEUE/LINE 排成一行；站队；排队（等候）：*Line up, children!* 孩子们，站成一排！ ◇ *Cars lined up waiting to board the ship.* 汽车排队等候上船。 **ˌline sb/sth↔'up 1** to arrange people or things in a straight line or row 使站成一队；使排列成一行：*The suspects were lined up against the wall.* 嫌疑犯靠墙站成了一排。 ◇ *He lined the bottles up along the shelf.* 他把瓶子排列在架子上。 **2** to arrange for an event or activity to happen, or arrange for sb to be available to do sth 组织，安排（活动）；邀集（人做某事）：*Mark had a job lined up when he left college.* 马克大学毕业时，工作已经安排好了。 ◇ *I've got a lot lined up this week* (= I'm very busy). 我这周有许多事要做。 ◇ *She's lined up a live band for the party.* 她为聚会安排了一个乐队来现场演奏。 **ˌline sth↔'up (with sth)** to move one thing into a correct position in relation to another thing 使…（与相关的另一物）排齐；使…对齐

lin·eage /ˈlɪniɪdʒ/ *noun* [U, C] (*formal*) the series of families that sb comes from originally 世系；宗系；家系；血统 **SYN** **ancestry**

lin·eal /ˈlɪniəl/ *adj.* [only before noun] (*formal*) coming in a direct line from an earlier or later generation of the same family as sb 直系的；嫡系的：*a lineal descendant of the company's founder* 公司创始人的直系后裔

lin·ea·ments /ˈlɪniəmənts/ *noun* [pl.] (*formal*) the typical features of sth （某事物的）典型特征

lin·ear /ˈlɪniə(r)/ *adj.* **1** of or in lines 线的；直线的；线状的：*In his art he broke the laws of scientific linear perspective.* 他在自己的绘画艺术中打破了科学的直线透视法规律。 **2** going from one thing to another in a single series of stages （进展）直线式的：*Students do not always progress in a linear fashion.* 学生的进步不会总是直线式的。 **OPP** **non-linear 3** of length 长度的：*linear measurement* (= for example metres, feet, etc.) 长度测量 **4** (*mathematics* 数) able to be represented by a straight line on a GRAPH 线性的：*linear equations* 线性方程 ▸ **lin·ear·ity** /ˌlɪniˈærəti/ *noun* [U]: *She abandoned the linearity of the conventional novel.* 她摒弃了写小说惯用的线性叙事的写法。 **lin·ear·ly** *adv.*

line·back·er /ˈlaɪnbækə(r)/ *noun* (in AMERICAN FOOTBALL 美式足球) a DEFENSIVE player who tries to TACKLE members of the other team 线卫

'line-caught *adj.* (of fish 鱼) caught with a hook, not in a net 被钓到的：*We sell only line-caught wild fish.* 我们只卖钓来的野生鱼。

lined /laɪnd/ *adj.* **1** (of skin, especially on the face 尤指面部皮肤) having folds or lines because of age, worry, etc. 有皱纹的 **SYN** **wrinkled**: *a deeply lined face* 布满深深皱纹的脸 **2** (of paper 纸) having lines printed or drawn across it 画有横线的；印有格的：*Lined paper helps keep handwriting neat.* 印有横线的纸有助于书写工整。 **3** (of clothes 衣服) having a LINING inside them 有衬里的；有内衬的：*a lined skirt* 带衬里的裙子 **4 -lined** having the object mentioned along an edge or edges, or as a LINING 沿边缘有…的；有…做衬里的：*a tree-lined road* 两旁栽着树的马路

'line dancing *noun* [U] a type of dancing originally from the US, in which people dance in lines, all doing a complicated series of steps at the same time 队列舞（源于美国）

'line drawing *noun* a drawing that consists only of lines 线条画；白描

'line drive *noun* (in BASEBALL 棒球) a powerful hit in a straight line near to the ground 平直球，平飞球（贴近地面猛力击打的直线球）

line·man /ˈlaɪnmən/ *noun* (*pl.* **-men** /-mən/) (*NAmE*) **1** a player in the front line of an AMERICAN FOOTBALL team （美式足球的）前锋，线上的队员 **2** = LINESMAN (2)

'line management *noun* [U] (*BrE*) the system of organizing a company, etc. in which information and instructions are passed from each employee and manager to the person one rank above or below them （公司等的）分级管理制 ▸ **'line manager** *noun*: *Review your training needs with your line manager.* 和你的部门经理探讨一下你需要哪些方面的培训。

linen /ˈlɪnɪn/ *noun* [U] **1** a type of cloth made from FLAX, used to make high-quality clothes, sheets, etc. 亚麻布：*a linen tablecloth* 亚麻桌布 **2** sheets, TABLECLOTHS, PILLOWCASES, etc. 日用织品：(*BrE*) *a linen cupboard* 家庭日用织品壁橱 ◇ (*NAmE*) *a linen closet* 家庭日用织品壁橱 ➲ SEE ALSO BED LINEN ➲ **WORDFINDER NOTE** AT STORE **IDM** SEE WASH *v.*

ˌline of 'sight (*also* **ˌline of 'vision**, **'sight-line**) *noun* an imaginary line that goes from sb's eye to sth that they are looking at 视线： *There was a column directly in my line of sight, so I could only see half the stage.* 有一根柱子正挡着我的视线，所以我只能看见舞台的一半。

ˈline-out *noun* (in RUGBY 橄榄球) a situation that happens when the ball goes out of play, when players from opposing teams stand in lines and jump to try to catch the ball when it is thrown back in（球出界后再抛球入场时的）争边球

ˈline printer *noun* a machine that prints very quickly, producing a complete line of print at a time 行式打印机

liner /ˈlaɪnə(r)/ *noun* **1** a large ship that carries passengers 邮轮： *an ocean liner* 远洋客轮 ◇ *a luxury cruise liner* 豪华游轮 ➲ VISUAL VOCAB PAGE V59 **2** (especially in compounds 尤用于构成复合词) a piece of material used to cover the inside surface of sth 衬里；内衬： *bin/nappy liners* 衬在垃圾桶内的塑料袋；尿布衬垫 **3** = EYELINER

ˈliner note (*BrE also* **ˈsleeve note**) *noun* [usually pl.] information about the music or the performers that comes with a CD or is printed on the cover of a record（激光唱片或唱片的）封套内容简介

lines·man /ˈlaɪnzmən/ *noun* (*pl.* **-men** /-mən/) **1** an official who helps the REFEREE in some games that are played on a field or court, especially in deciding whether or where a ball crosses one of the lines. Linesmen are now officially called **referee's assistants** in football (SOCCER).（足球等比赛中的）边线裁判员，巡边员，司线员 **2** (*BrE*) (*NAmE* **line·man**) a person whose job is to repair telephone or electricity power lines 架线工；线务员

ˈline-up *noun* [usually sing.] **1** the people who are going to take part in a particular event 阵容；阵式： *an impressive line-up of speakers* 给人印象深刻的演讲者阵容 ◇ *the starting line-up* (= the players who will begin the game) 比赛首发队员阵容 **2** a set of items, events etc. arranged to follow one another 节目安排；项目安排 SYN **programme**： *A horror movie completes this evening's TV line-up.* 今晚电视节目最后安排了一部恐怖影片。 **3** (*especially NAmE*) (*BrE also* **iˌdentifiˈcation parade**, *informal* **iˈdentity parade**) a row of people, including one person who is suspected of a crime, who are shown to a witness to see if he or she can recognize the criminal 辨认行列，列队认人（把嫌疑犯同其他人排在一起，让目击者辨认）

ling /lɪŋ/ *noun* [U] a low plant that is a type of HEATHER and that grows on areas of wild open land (= MOORLAND) 欧石楠（低矮灌木，生长在荒野里）

-ling /lɪŋ/ *suffix* (in nouns 构成名词) (*sometimes disapproving*) small; not important 幼小；不重要： *duckling* 小鸭 ◇ *princeling* 小国的国君 ➲ MORE LIKE THIS 7, page R25

lin·ger /ˈlɪŋɡə(r)/ *verb* **1** [I] to continue to exist for longer than expected 继续存留；缓慢消失： *The faint smell of her perfume lingered in the room.* 房间里仍飘溢着她那淡淡的香水味。 ◇ **~ on** *The civil war lingered on well into the 1930s.* 这次内战到 20 世纪 30 年代还拖了好几年。 **2** [I] (+ **adv./prep.**) to stay somewhere for longer because you do not want to leave; to spend a long time doing sth 流连；逗留；徘徊；花很长时间做（某事）；磨蹭： *She lingered for a few minutes to talk to Nick.* 她多待了几分钟，想跟尼克谈一谈。 ◇ *We lingered over breakfast on the terrace.* 我们在平台上慢条斯理地吃着早餐。 **3** [I] **~ (on sb/sth)** to continue to look at sb/sth or think about sth for longer than usual 持续看（或思考）： *His eyes lingered on the diamond ring on her finger.* 他一直注视着她手指上的钻戒。 **4** [I] **~ (on)** to stay alive but become weaker 苟延残喘；奄奄一息： *He lingered on for several months after the heart attack.* 他心脏病发作后又拖了几个月才去世。

lin·ge·rie /ˈlænʒəri; *NAmE* ˌlɑːndʒəˈreɪ/ *noun* [U] (used especially by shops/stores 尤用于商店) women's underwear 女内衣 ➲ WORDFINDER NOTE AT STORE

lin·ger·ing /ˈlɪŋɡərɪŋ/ *adj.* slow to end or disappear 拖延的；缠绵的；缓慢消失的；迟迟不去的： *a painful and lingering death* 痛苦而拖延时日的死亡 ◇ *a last lingering look* 依依不舍的最后一瞥 ◇ *lingering doubts* 挥之不去的疑虑 ◇ *a lingering smell of machine oil* 飘浮不散的机油味 ▶ **lin·ger·ing·ly** *adv.*

lingo /ˈlɪŋɡəʊ; *NAmE* -ɡoʊ/ *noun* [sing.] (*informal*) **1** a language, especially a foreign language 语言；（尤指）外国语，外国话： *He doesn't speak the lingo.* 他不会讲这种外国话。 **2** (*especially NAmE*) expressions used by a particular group of people 行话；术语 SYN **jargon**： *baseball lingo* 棒球术语

lin·gua franca /ˌlɪŋɡwə ˈfræŋkə/ *noun* [usually sing.] (*linguistics* 语言) a shared language of communication used between people whose main languages are different（母语不同的人共用的）通用语： *English has become a lingua franca in many parts of the world.* 英语在世界上许多地方都成了通用语。

lin·gual /ˈlɪŋɡwəl/ *adj.* **1** (*anatomy* 解) related to the tongue 舌的 **2** related to speech or language 话语的；语言的 **3** (*phonetics* 语音) (of a speech sound 语音) produced using the tongue 舌的；舌音的 ▶ **lin·gual·ly** /ˈlɪŋɡwəli/ *adv.*

lin·guist /ˈlɪŋɡwɪst/ *noun* **1** a person who knows several foreign languages well 通晓数国语言的人： *She's an excellent linguist.* 她精通数国语言。 ◇ *I'm afraid I'm no linguist* (= I find foreign languages difficult). 对不起，我不懂外语。 **2** a person who studies languages or LINGUISTICS 语言学家

lin·guis·tic /lɪŋˈɡwɪstɪk/ *adj.* connected with language or the scientific study of language 语言的；语言学的： *linguistic and cultural barriers* 语言和文化上的障碍 ◇ *a child's innate linguistic ability* 儿童的先天语言能力 ◇ *new developments in linguistic theory* 语言学理论的新发展 ▶ **lin·guis·tic·al·ly** /-kli/ *adv.*

lin·guis·tics /lɪŋˈɡwɪstɪks/ *noun* [U] the scientific study of language or of particular languages 语言学： *a course in applied linguistics* 应用语言学课程 ➲ MORE LIKE THIS 29, page R28

lini·ment /ˈlɪnəmənt/ *noun* [C, U] a liquid, especially one made with oil, that you rub on a painful part of your body to reduce the pain（尤指油质、镇痛的）搽剂，擦剂；镇痛油

lin·ing /ˈlaɪnɪŋ/ *noun* **1** [C] a layer of material used to cover the inside surface of sth 衬层；内衬；衬里： *a pair of leather gloves with fur linings* 一双毛皮衬里的皮手套 ➲ WORDFINDER NOTE AT SEW ➲ VISUAL VOCAB PAGE V66 **2** [U] the covering of the inner surface of a part of the body（身体器官内壁的）膜： *the stomach lining* 胃黏膜 IDM SEE CLOUD *n.*

link AW /lɪŋk/ *noun, verb*

■ *noun* **1** **~ (between A and B)** a connection between two or more people or things 联系；连接： *Police suspect there may be a link between the two murders.* 警方怀疑那两桩凶杀案可能有关联。 ◇ *evidence for a strong causal link between exposure to sun and skin cancer* 太阳暴晒与皮肤癌之间有紧密因果关系的证据 ➲ SEE ALSO MISSING LINK **2** a relationship between two or more people, countries or organizations 关系；纽带： **~ (with sth)** *to establish* ***trade links*** *with Asia* 与亚洲建立贸易关系 ◇ **~ (between A and B)** *Social customs provide a vital link between generations.* 社会风俗在不同世代之间起到了极其重要的纽带作用。 **3** a means of travelling or communicating between two places 交通路线；通讯手段： *a high-speed* ***rail link*** 高速的铁路交通 ◇ *a link road* 连接道路 ◇ *a video link* 视频线路 ◇ *The speech was broadcast via a* ***satellite link***. 这次演讲是通过卫星播放的。 **4** (*also* **hot·link**, **hyper·link**) (*computing* 计) a place in an electronic document that is connected to another electronic document or to another part of the same document 链接： *To visit similar websites to this one, click on the links at the bottom of the page.* 要访问与这个网站类似的网站，点击网页底部的链接。 ➲ VISUAL VOCAB PAGE V74 **5** each ring of a chain（链状物的）环，节，圈 ➲ PICTURE AT ROPE ➲ SEE ALSO CUFFLINK

IDM **a link in the ˈchain** one of the stages in a process or a line of argument 链条中的一个环节；整个过程中的一个阶段 ➲ MORE AT WEAK

■ *verb* [often passive] **1** 🔑 to make a physical or electronic connection between one object, machine, place, etc. and another 把（物体、机器、地方等）连接起来 SYN **connect**: **~ A to B** *The video cameras are linked to a powerful computer.* 这些摄像机是与一台功能强大的计算机相连接的。◇ **~ A with B** *The Channel Tunnel links Britain with the rest of Europe.* 英吉利海峡隧道把英国和欧洲其他国家连接起来了。◇ **~ A and B (together)** *When computers are networked, they are linked together so that information can be transferred between them.* 计算机联网连接，即彼此可互传信息。 **2** 🔑 if sth **links** two things, facts or situations, or they **are linked**, they are connected in some way 联系；相关联： **~ A to/with B** *Exposure to ultraviolet light is* ***closely linked*** *to skin cancer.* 受紫外线照射与皮肤癌紧密相关。◇ **~ A and B** *The two factors are* ***directly linked.*** 这两个因素直接联系在一起。◇ *The personal and social development of the child are* ***inextricably linked*** (= they depend on each other). 儿童在自身和与人交往两方面的成长是相辅相成的。 **3 ~ A to/with B | ~ A and B** to state that there is a connection or relationship between two things or people 说明（两件东西或两人之间）有联系（或关系）SYN **associate**: *Detectives have linked the break-in to a similar crime in the area last year.* 侦探认为这起入室盗窃案与去年此地区一类似案件有关。◇ *Newspapers have linked his name with the singer.* 报章报道把他的名字与那名歌手连在一起。 **4 ~ A and B** to join two things by putting one through the other 挽住；钩住；套在一起： *The two girls* ***linked arms*** *as they strolled down the street.* 两个女孩挽着胳臂沿街漫步而行。

PHR V **,link 'up (with sb/sth)** to join or become joined with sb/sth （与…）连接，结合；使连接；使结合： *The two spacecraft will link up in orbit.* 两艘宇宙飞船将在轨道上对接。◇ *The bands have linked up for a charity concert.* 这些乐队已联合起来，准备办一场慈善音乐会。 ➲ RELATED NOUN LINK-UP

link·age AW /ˈlɪŋkɪdʒ/ *noun* **1** [U, C] **~ (between A and B)** the act of linking things; a link or system of links 连接；联系；链环；连锁 SYN **connection**: *This chapter explores the linkage between economic development and the environment.* 本章探讨的是经济发展与环境之间的关系。 **2** [C] a device that links two or more things 联动装置

'linking verb (*also* **cop·ula**) *noun* (*grammar* 语法) a verb such as *be* or *become* that connects a subject with the adjective or noun (called the COMPLEMENT) that describes it 系词；连系动词： *In 'She became angry', the verb 'became' is a linking verb.* 在 She became angry 一句中，动词 became 为连系动词。

link·man /ˈlɪŋkmæn/ *noun* (*pl.* **-men** /-men/) (*BrE*) **1** a person who helps two people or groups of people to communicate with each other 联系人；中间人；居间人 **2** a person who works on the radio or television introducing the programmes or telling people about future programmes （广播或电视的）节目主持人

links /lɪŋks/ *noun* = GOLF LINKS

'link-up *noun* a connection formed between two things, for example two companies or two broadcasting systems 连接，联系（指两事物如两家公司或两个广播系统的结合）： *a live satellite link-up with the conference* 对会议的卫星实况转播

Lin·naean (*also* **Lin·nean**) /lɪˈneɪən; -ˈniːən/ *adj.* (*biology* 生) relating to the system of naming and arranging living things into scientific groups which was invented by Carolus Linnaeus (Carl von Linné) 林奈氏命名法的，林奈氏分类系统的（统一生物命名，定义生物属种）

lin·net /ˈlɪnɪt/ *noun* a small brown and grey bird of the FINCH family 赤胸朱顶雀

lino /ˈlaɪnəʊ; *NAmE* -noʊ/ *noun* [U] (*BrE, informal*) = LINOLEUM

lino·cut /ˈlaɪnəʊkʌt; *NAmE* -noʊ-/ *noun* a design or shape cut in a piece of LINO, used to make a print; a print made in this way 油毡浮雕图案；油毡浮雕版印染品

li·no·leum /lɪˈnəʊliəm; *NAmE* -ˈnoʊ-/ (*also BrE, informal* **lino**) *noun* [U] a type of strong material with a hard shiny surface, used for covering floors 油地毡

Lino·type™ /ˈlaɪnəʊtaɪp; *NAmE* -noʊ-/ *noun* a machine used in the past for printing newspapers, that produces a line of words as one strip of metal 莱诺铸排机（旧时用于报纸印刷）

lin·seed oil /ˌlɪnsiːd ˈɔɪl/ (*also* **flax·seed oil**) *noun* [U] an oil made from FLAX seeds, used in paint or to protect wood, etc. 亚麻籽油

lint /lɪnt/ *noun* [U] **1** (*especially BrE*) a type of soft cotton cloth used for covering and protecting wounds（敷伤口用的）纱布 **2** (*specialist*) short fine FIBRES that come off the surface of cloth when it is being made（织物在制作过程中从表面掉落的）纤维屑，飞花 **3** (*especially NAmE*) (*BrE usually* **fluff**) small soft pieces of wool, cotton, etc. that stick on the surface of cloth （毛料、棉布等的）绒毛

lin·tel /ˈlɪntl/ *noun* (*architecture* 建) a piece of wood or stone over a door or window, that forms part of the frame （门窗的）过梁；门楣

Linux™ /ˈlɪnəks/ *noun* [U] (*computing* 计) an OPERATING SYSTEM based on UNIX that is available free in the basic version * Linux 操作系统，Linux 作业系统（基于 Unix 操作系统，基本版本可免费取得）

lion /ˈlaɪən/ *noun* a large powerful animal of the cat family, that hunts in groups and lives in parts of Africa and southern Asia. Lions have yellowish-brown fur and the male has a MANE (= long thick hair round its neck). 狮；狮子 ➲ VISUAL VOCAB PAGE V12 ➲ COMPARE LIONESS ➲ SEE ALSO MOUNTAIN LION

IDM **the 'lion's den** a difficult situation in which you have to face a person or people who are unfriendly or aggressive towards you 龙潭虎穴 **the 'lion's share (of sth)** the largest or best part of sth when it is divided 最大（或最好）的一份 ➲ MORE AT BEARD *v.* ➲ SEE ALSO BRITISH LIONS

lion·ess /ˈlaɪənes/ *noun* a female lion 母狮

lion·ize (*BrE also* **-ise**) /ˈlaɪənaɪz/ *verb* **~ sb** (*formal*) to treat sb as a famous or important person 把（某人）当成名人（或要人）对待

lip 🔑 /lɪp/ *noun* **1** 🔑 [C] either of the two soft edges at the opening to the mouth 嘴唇： *The assistant pursed her lips.* 那女助手噘起了嘴。◇ *your* ***upper/lower/top/bottom lip*** 你的上/下嘴唇 ◇ *She kissed him* ***on the lips.*** 她吻了他的嘴唇。◇ *Not a drop of alcohol* ***passed my lips*** (= I didn't drink any). 我滴酒未沾。 ➲ COLLOCATIONS AT PHYSICAL ➲ VISUAL VOCAB PAGE V64 **2 -lipped** (in adjectives 构成形容词) having the type of lips mentioned 嘴唇…的： *thin-lipped* 嘴唇薄的 ◇ *thick-lipped* 嘴唇厚的 ➲ SEE ALSO TIGHT-LIPPED **3** [C] **~ (of sth)** the edge of a container or a hollow place in the ground（容器或凹陷地方的）边，边沿 SYN **rim**: *He ran his finger around the lip of the cup.* 他用手指沿杯口抹了一下。◇ *Lava bubbled a few feet below the lip of the crater.* 熔岩在火山口下几英尺处沸腾。 ➲ PICTURE AT JUG **4** [U] (*informal*) words spoken to sb that are rude and show a lack of respect for that person 粗鲁无礼的话 SYN **cheek**: *Don't let him* ***give you*** *any* ***lip!*** 不要让他对你说粗鲁无礼的话！

IDM **lick/smack your 'lips** **1** to move your tongue over your lips, especially before eating sth good（尤指在吃好东西前）舔嘴唇 **2** (*informal*) to show that you are excited about sth and want it to happen soon 迫不及待；渴望： *They were licking their lips at the thought of clinching the deal.* 他们一想到马上要做成这笔交易就显得急不可待了。 **my lips are 'sealed** used to say that you will not repeat sb's secret to other people（表示不会说出某人的秘密）我把嘴封住，我绝口不提 **on everyone's 'lips** if sth is on everyone's lips, they are all talking about it 大家都在谈论 ➲ MORE AT BITE *v.*, PASS *v.*, READ *v.*, SLIP *n.*, STIFF *adj.*

lip·ase /ˈlaɪpeɪz/ *noun* [U] (*chemistry* 化) an ENZYME (= a chemical substance in the body) that makes fats change into acids and alcohol 脂（肪）酶

ˈlip gloss /ˈlɪp glɒs; *NAmE* ˈlɪp glɑːs; ˈlɪp glɔːs/ *noun* [U, C] a substance that is put on the lips to make them look shiny 唇彩；唇蜜 ➲ VISUAL VOCAB PAGE V65

lipid /ˈlɪpɪd/ *noun* (*chemistry* 化) any of a group of natural substances which do not dissolve in water, including plant oils and STEROIDS 脂质；类脂

ˈlip liner *noun* [U] a substance that is put on the outline of the lips, to prevent LIPSTICK from spreading 唇线笔 ➲ VISUAL VOCAB PAGE V65

lipo·pro·tein /ˈlɪpəprəʊtiːn; ˈlaɪ-; *NAmE* -proʊ-/ *noun* (*biology* 生) a PROTEIN that combines with a lipid and carries it to another part of the body in the blood 脂蛋白

lipo·some /ˈlɪpəsəʊm; ˈlaɪ-; *NAmE* -soʊm/ *noun* a very small bag formed of lipid MOLECULES, used to carry a drug to a particular part of the body 脂质体

lipo·suc·tion /ˈlɪpəʊsʌkʃn; ˈlaɪ-; *NAmE* ˈlɪ-; ˈlaɪpoʊ-/ *noun* [U] a way of removing fat from sb's body by using SUCTION 吸脂术；脂肪抽吸（术）

lippy /ˈlɪpi/ *adj.*, *noun*
■ *adj.* (*BrE, informal*) showing a lack of respect in the way that you speak to sb 出言不逊的；冒犯顶撞的 SYN **cheeky**
■ *noun* [U] (*BrE, informal*) = LIPSTICK

ˈlip-read *verb* [I, T] ~ (**sb**) to understand what sb is saying by watching the way their lips move 观唇辨意；唇读 ▸ **ˈlip-reading** *noun* [U]

lip·salve /ˈlɪpsælv/ *noun* [U] (*BrE*) a substance in the form of a stick, like a LIPSTICK, that you put on your lips to stop them becoming sore 护唇膏；润唇膏

ˈlip service *noun* [U] if sb pays **lip service** to sth, they say that they approve of it or support it, without proving their support by what they actually do 空口的应酬话；口惠：*All the parties pay lip service to environmental issues.* 对环境问题各方都是口惠而实不至。

lip·stick /ˈlɪpstɪk/ *noun* [U, C] a substance made into a small stick, used for colouring the lips; a small stick of this substance 口红；唇膏：*She was wearing bright red lipstick.* 她搽着鲜红色的口红。 ➲ WORDFINDER NOTE AT MAKE-UP ➲ PICTURE AT STICK ➲ VISUAL VOCAB PAGE V65

ˌlipstick ˈlesbian *noun* (*informal*) a LESBIAN who is a fashionable and attractive woman 口红女同性恋者（指时髦有魅力的女同性恋者）：*the lipstick lesbian stereotype* 口红女同性恋者的模式化形象

lip-sync (*also* **lip-synch**) /ˈlɪp sɪŋk/ *verb* [I, T] to move your mouth, without speaking or singing, so that its movements match the sound on a recorded song, etc. 对口型；假唱：~ (**to sth**) *She lip-synced to a Beatles song.* 她对口型假唱一首披头士乐队的歌曲。 ◇ ~ **sth** *He lip-synced 'Return to Sender'.* 他对口型假唱了《退回寄信人》。

li·quefy /ˈlɪkwɪfaɪ/ *verb* (**li·que·fies**, **li·que·fy·ing**, **li·que·fied**, **li·que·fied**) [I, T] ~ (**sth**) (*formal*) to become liquid; to make sth liquid （使）液化

li·queur /lɪˈkjʊə(r); *NAmE* -ˈkɜːr/ (*NAmE also* **cor·dial**) *noun* **1** [U, C] a strong sweet alcoholic drink, sometimes flavoured with fruit. It is usually drunk in very small glasses after a meal. （通常餐后少量饮用的）烈性甜酒 **2** [C] a glass of liqueur 一杯烈性甜酒

li·quid 🔑 /ˈlɪkwɪd/ *noun, adj.*
■ *noun* 🔑 [U, C] a substance that flows freely and is not a solid or a gas, for example water or oil 液体：*She poured the dark brown liquid down the sink.* 她把深棕色的液体倒进了洗碗槽。 ◇ *the transition from liquid to vapour* 从液体到蒸气的转化 ➲ SEE ALSO WASHING-UP LIQUID

> **WORDFINDER** 联想词：absorb, condense, dilute, dissolve, evaporate, filter, immerse, rinse, saturated

■ *adj.* **1** 🔑 in the form of a liquid; not a solid or a gas 液体的；液态的：*liquid soap* 肥皂液 ◇ *liquid nitrogen* 液态氮 ◇ *The detergent comes in powder or* ***liquid form***. 这种洗涤剂有粉状或液态两种。 ◇ *a bar selling snacks and* ***liquid refreshment*** (= drinks) 售卖小吃和饮料的柜台 **2** (*finance* 财) in cash, or that can easily be changed into cash 流动性好的；易变现的：*liquid assets* 流动资产 **3** (*literary*) clear, like water 清澈的；明亮的；晶莹的 SYN **limpid**：*liquid blue eyes* 晶莹的蓝眼睛 **4** (*literary*) (of sounds 声音) clear, pure and flowing 清脆流畅的；清澈圆润的：*the liquid song of a blackbird* 乌鸫清脆的鸣啭

li·quid·ate /ˈlɪkwɪdeɪt/ *verb* **1** [I, T] ~ (**sth**) to close a business and sell everything it owns in order to pay debts 清算，清盘（停业后将资产出售，偿还债务） **2** [T] ~ **sth** (*finance* 财) to sell sth in order to get money 变卖；变现：*to liquidate assets* 变卖资产 **3** [T] ~ **sth** (*finance* 财) to pay a debt 偿还，清偿（债务） **4** [T] ~ **sb/sth** to destroy or remove sb/sth that causes problems 消灭；摧毁；清除 SYN **annihilate**：*The government tried to liquidate the rebel movement and failed.* 政府试图肃清反叛运动，结果失败了。

li·quid·ation /ˌlɪkwɪˈdeɪʃn/ *noun* [U] **1** (*BrE, AustralE, law* 律) the process of closing a company, selling what it owns and paying its debts （公司的）清盘，清算；（债务的）清偿：*The company has* ***gone into liquidation***. 这家公司已破产清算。 ➲ COLLOCATIONS AT BUSINESS ➲ COMPARE CHAPTER 11 **2** (*finance* 财) the action of selling sth to get money or to avoid losing money （资产的）变现，变卖：*Falling prices may lead to further liquidation of stocks.* 股价下跌可能导致股票的进一步变现。

li·quid·ator /ˈlɪkwɪdeɪtə(r)/ *noun* a person responsible for closing down a business and using any profits from the sale to pay its debts 清算人；清盘人

ˌliquid ˌcrystal disˈplay *noun* = LCD (1)

li·quid·ity /lɪˈkwɪdəti/ *noun* [U] (*finance* 财) the state of owning things of value that can easily be exchanged for cash 资产流动性；资产变现能力

li·quid·ize (*BrE also* **-ise**) /ˈlɪkwɪdaɪz/ *verb* ~ **sth** (*especially BrE*) to crush fruit, vegetables, etc. into a thick liquid 把（水果、蔬菜等）榨成汁 SYN **purée**

li·quid·izer (*BrE also* **-iser**) /ˈlɪkwɪdaɪzə(r)/ *noun* (*BrE*) = BLENDER

ˌliquid ˈparaffin (*BrE*) (*NAmE* **ˈmineral oil**) *noun* [U] a liquid with no colour and no smell that comes from PETROLEUM and is used in medicines and COSMETICS 液体石蜡（用于制造药品和化妆品）

li·quor /ˈlɪkə(r)/ *noun* [U] **1** (*especially NAmE*) strong alcoholic drink 烈性酒 SYN **spirit**：*hard liquor* 烈性酒 ◇ *She drinks wine and beer but no liquor.* 她喝葡萄酒和啤酒，但不沾烈性酒。 **2** (*BrE, specialist*) any alcoholic drink 含酒精饮料：*intoxicating liquor* 烈酒

li·quor·ice (*especially BrE*) (*NAmE usually* **lic·orice**) /ˈlɪkərɪʃ; -rɪs/ *noun* [U, C] a firm black substance with a strong flavour, obtained from the root of a plant, used in medicine and to make sweets/candy; a sweet/candy made from this substance 甘草（用于制药或糖果）；甘草糖

li·quor·ice all·sorts /ˌlɪkərɪʃ ˈɔːlsɔːts; -rɪs; *NAmE* -sɔːrts/ *noun* [pl.] (*BrE*) brightly coloured sweets/candy made with liquorice 什锦甘草糖果

ˈliquor store (*also* **ˈpackage store**) (*both US*) (*BrE* **ˈoff-licence**) *noun* a shop that sells alcoholic drinks in bottles and cans to take away 外卖酒店

lira /ˈlɪərə; *NAmE* ˈlɪrə/ *noun* (*pl.* **lire** /ˈlɪərə; *NAmE* ˈlɪreɪ/) (*abbr.* **l.**) the unit of money in Malta, Syria and Turkey, and formerly in Italy (replaced there in 2002 by the euro) 里拉（马耳他、叙利亚、土耳其和意大利货币单位，在意大利于 2002 年为欧元所取代）

lisle /laɪl/ *noun* [U] a fine smooth cotton thread used especially for making TIGHTS and STOCKINGS 莱尔线（尤用于织连裤袜和长袜）

lisp /lɪsp/ *noun, verb*
■ *noun* [usually sing.] a speech fault in which the sound 's' is pronounced 'th' 咬舌（语言缺陷，把 s 说成 th）：*She spoke with a slight lisp.* 她说话有点咬舌。

■ ***verb*** [I, T] (+ **speech**) to speak with a lisp 说话口齿不清；咬舌

lis·som (*also* **lis·some**) /ˈlɪsəm/ *adj.* (*literary*) (of sb's body 人体) thin and attractive 轻盈优美的；苗条的；袅娜的 **SYN** **lithe**

list /lɪst/ *noun, verb*

■ ***noun*** **1** [C] a series of names, items, figures, etc., especially when they are written or printed 一览表；名单；目录；清单：*a **shopping/wine/price list*** 购物单；酒类表；价目表 ◇ *to **make a list** of things to do* 把要做的事列成清单 ◇ (*formal*) *to **draw up a list*** 拟订清单 ◇ *Is your name **on the list**?* 表上有你的名字吗？◇ *Having to wait hours came **high on the list** of complaints.* 在投诉当中，最多的是抱怨等候时间太长。➲ SEE ALSO A-LIST, HIT LIST, LAUNDRY LIST, MAILING LIST, SHORTLIST *n.*, WAITING LIST, WAIT LIST **2** [sing.] the fact of a ship leaning to one side（船的）倾斜 **IDM** SEE DANGER

■ ***verb*** **1** [T] **~ sth** to write a list of things in a particular order（按某次序）把…列表，列清单，拟订清单：*We were asked to list our ten favourite songs.* 我们应要求列出自己最喜爱的十首歌曲。◇ *Towns in the guide are listed alphabetically.* 旅游指南里的城镇是按字母顺序排列的。 **2** [T] **~ sb/sth** to mention or include sb/sth in a list 列举；把…列入一览表：*The koala is listed among Australia's endangered animals.* 树袋熊已列为澳大利亚濒临绝种的动物之一。◇ *soldiers listed as missing* 列入失踪名单的士兵 **3** [I, T] **~ (at sth)** | **~ sth** (*NAmE*) to be put or put sth in a list of things for sale（被）列入销售清单，列入价目表：*This CD player lists at $200.* 这台激光唱片播放机在价目单上定为 200 美元。 **4** [I] (of a ship 船) to lean to one side（向一侧）倾斜

ˌlisted ˈbuilding *noun* (*BrE*) a building that is officially protected because it has artistic or historical value 正式列入文物保护范围的建筑物 ➲ SEE ALSO LANDMARK

lis·ten /ˈlɪsn/ *verb, noun*

■ ***verb*** **1** [I] to pay attention to sb/sth that you can hear（注意地）听；倾听：*Listen! What's that noise? Can you hear it?* 听！那是什么响声？你能听见吗？◇ *Sorry, I wasn't really listening.* 对不起，我刚才没注意听。◇ **~ to sb/sth** *to listen to music* 听音乐 ◇ *I listened carefully to her story.* 我认真听了她说的情况。 **HELP** You cannot 'listen sth' (without 'to'). 不能说 listen sth（不带介词 to）：*I'm fond of listening to classical music.* 我喜欢听古典音乐。◇ ~~*I'm fond of listening classical music.*~~ **2** [I] **~ (to sb/sth)** to take notice of what sb says to you so that you follow their advice or believe them 听信；听从：*None of this would have happened if you'd listened to me.* 你要是听了我的话，这一切就不会发生了。◇ *Why won't you **listen to reason**?* 你怎么就不听劝呢？ **3** [I] (*informal*) used to tell sb to take notice of what you are going to say（让对方注意）听着，注意听：*Listen, there's something I have to tell you.* 听着，我有事要告诉你。➲ MORE LIKE THIS 20, page R27

PHR V **ˈlisten for sth** | **ˈlisten ˈout for sth** to be prepared to hear a particular sound 留心听（某种声音）：*Can you listen out for the doorbell?* 你能留心听着门铃吗？ **ˌlisten ˈin (on/to sth)** **1** to listen to a conversation that you are not supposed to hear 窃听；偷听；监听：*You shouldn't listen in on other people's conversations.* 你不应该偷听别人的谈话。 **2** to listen to a radio broadcast 收听（无线电广播） **ˌlisten ˈup** (*informal, especially NAmE*) used to tell people to listen carefully because you are going to say sth important 注意听，留心听（因有要事要讲而要人注意听）

■ ***noun*** [usually sing.] an act of listening 听：*Have a listen to this.* 听一听这个。

lis·ten·able /ˈlɪsnəbl/ *adj.* (*informal*) pleasant to listen to 悦耳的；好听的

lis·ten·er /ˈlɪsənə(r)/ *noun* **1** a person who listens 听者：*a good listener* (= sb who you can rely on to listen with attention or sympathy) 认真倾听的人 **2** a person listening to a radio programme 收听广播节目的人

ˈlistening post *noun* a place where people who are part of an army listen to enemy communications to try to get information that will give them an advantage（军队的）潜听哨

lis·teria /lɪˈstɪəriə; *NAmE* -ˈstɪr-/ *noun* [U] a type of bacteria that makes people sick if they eat infected food 利斯特菌

list·ing /ˈlɪstɪŋ/ *noun* **1** [C] a list, especially an official or published list of people or things, often arranged in alphabetical order（常按字母顺序排列的）表册，目录，列表：*a comprehensive listing of all airlines* 所有航线的总目录 **2 listings** [pl.] information in a newspaper or magazine about what films/movies, plays, etc. are being shown in a particular town or city（报章或杂志有关某城市电影、戏剧等的）上映信息，演出信息：*a listings magazine* 演出信息杂志 **3** [C] a position or an item on a list（表册上的）位置，项目：(*business* 商) *The company is seeking a stock exchange listing* (= for trading shares). 这家公司正在争取上市。

list·less /ˈlɪstləs/ *adj.* having no energy or enthusiasm 没有活力的；无精打采的；不热情的 **SYN** **lethargic**：*The illness left her feeling listless and depressed.* 那场病使她感到虚弱消沉。 ▶ **list·less·ly** *adv.* **list·less·ness** *noun* [U]

ˈlist price *noun* [usually sing.] (*business* 商) the price at which goods are advertised for sale, for example in a CATALOGUE（商品目录等中的）价目表价格，定价

lit PAST TENSE, PAST PART. OF LIGHT

lit·any /ˈlɪtəni/ *noun* (*pl.* **-ies**) **1** a series of prayers to God for use in church services, spoken by a priest, etc., with set responses by the people 连祷文，总祷文（连祷启应的祷文） **2** **~ (of sth)** (*formal*) a long boring account of a series of events, reasons, etc.（对一系列事件、原因等）枯燥冗长的陈述：*a litany of complaints* 喋喋不休的抱怨

lit·chi (*especially US*) = LYCHEE

lite /laɪt/ *adj.* (*informal*) **1** (of food or drink 食物或饮料) containing fewer CALORIES than other types of food, and therefore less likely to make you fat (a way of spelling 'light') 低热量的，清淡的（light 的一种拼写方法）：*lite ice cream* 低热量冰淇淋 **2** (used after a noun 用于名词后) (*disapproving*) used to say that a thing is similar to sth else but lacks many of its serious or important qualities 类似…的劣质品：*I would describe this movie as 'Hitchcock lite'.* 我把这部电影称为"模仿希区柯克导演手法的平庸之作"。

liter (*NAmE*) = LITRE

lit·er·acy /ˈlɪtərəsi/ *noun* [U] the ability to read and write 读写能力：*a campaign to promote adult literacy* 提高成人文化水平的运动 ◇ *basic literacy skills* 基本的读写技巧 **OPP** **illiteracy** ➲ WORDFINDER NOTE AT LANGUAGE ➲ SEE ALSO COMPUTER LITERACY at COMPUTER-LITERATE

lit·eral /ˈlɪtərəl/ *adj.* **1** [usually before noun] being the most basic meaning of a word or phrase, rather than an extended or POETIC meaning 字面意义的：*I am not referring to 'small' people in the literal sense of the word.* 我指的不是字面意义上的"小"人。◇ *The literal meaning of 'petrify' is 'turn to stone'.* * petrify 的字面意思是 turn to stone（变成石头）。➲ COMPARE FIGURATIVE (1), METAPHORICAL **2** [usually before noun] that follows the original words exactly 完全按原文的：*a literal translation* 直译 ➲ COMPARE FREE *adj.* (13) **3** (*disapproving*) lacking imagination 缺乏想象力的：*Her interpretation of the music was too literal.* 她演奏的音乐太平淡乏味。 ▶ **lit·er·al·ness** *noun* [U]

lit·er·al·ly /ˈlɪtərəli/ *adv.* **1** in a literal way 按字面；字面上 **SYN** **exactly**：*The word 'planet' literally means 'wandering body'.* * planet 一词字面上的意思是 wandering body（游荡的天体）。◇ *When I told you to 'get lost' I didn't expect **to be taken literally**.* 我叫你"滚开"，并没让你按字面意思来理解呀。 **2** used to emphasize the truth of sth that may seem surprising（强调事实可能令人惊讶）真正地，确实地：*There are literally hundreds of prizes to win.* 可赢取的奖品真的有好几百份。 **3** (*informal*) used to emphasize a word or phrase, even if it is not actually true in a literal sense （用于加强语气，虽然并非词语的字面意义）简直：*I literally jumped out of my skin.* 我简直给吓了一大跳。

lit·er·ary /ˈlɪtərəri; *NAmE* -reri/ *adj.* **1** connected with literature 文学的；文学上的：***literary criticism/theory*** 文学批评/理论 **2** (of a language or style of writing 语言或写作文体) suitable for or typical of a work of literature 适于文学作品的；有典型文学作品特征的：*It was Chaucer who really turned English into a literary language.* 是乔叟使英语真正变成了文学语言。 **3** liking literature very much; studying or writing literature 爱好文学的；从事文学研究（或写作）的：*a literary man* 文人

ˈ**literary agent** *noun* a person whose job is to represent authors and persuade companies to publish their work 作品经纪人，作家代理人（说服出版社出版作品）

lit·er·ate /ˈlɪtərət/ *adj.* able to read and write 有读写能力的；有文化的 OPP **illiterate** ⊃ SEE ALSO NUMERATE at NUMERACY, COMPUTER-LITERATE

lit·er·ati /ˌlɪtəˈrɑːti/ **the literati** *noun* [pl.] (*formal*) educated and intelligent people who enjoy literature 文人学士

lit·era·ture 🔑 /ˈlɪtrətʃə(r); *NAmE also* -tʃʊr/ *noun* [U] **1** 🔑 pieces of writing that are valued as works of art, especially novels, plays and poems (in contrast to technical books and newspapers, magazines, etc.) 文学；文学作品：*French literature* 法国文学 ◇ ***great works of literature*** 文学巨著 ⊃ WORDFINDER NOTE AT WRITE **2** ~ (**on sth**) pieces of writing or printed information on a particular subject （某学科的）文献，著作，资料：*I've read all the available literature on keeping rabbits.* 我阅读了我能找到的关于养兔的全部资料。 ◇ *sales literature* 推销商品的宣传资料 ⊃ WORDFINDER NOTE AT LANGUAGE

lithe /laɪð/ *adj.* (of a person or their body 人或人体) moving or bending easily, in a way that is elegant 优美柔软的；易弯曲的；柔韧性好 ▸ **lithe·ly** *adv.*

lith·ium /ˈlɪθiəm/ *noun* [U] (*symb.* **Li**) a chemical element. Lithium is a soft, very light, silver-white metal used in batteries and ALLOYS. 锂

litho·graph /ˈlɪθəɡrɑːf; *NAmE* -ɡræf/ *noun* a picture printed by lithography 平版印刷画

lith·og·raphy /lɪˈθɒɡrəfi; *NAmE* -ˈθɑːɡ-/ *noun* (*also informal* **litho** /ˈlaɪθəʊ; *NAmE* -θoʊ/) [U] the process of printing from a smooth surface, for example a metal plate, that has been specially prepared so that ink only sticks to the design to be printed 平版印刷术 ▸ **litho·graph·ic** /ˌlɪθəˈɡræfɪk/ *adj.*

lith·ology /lɪˈθɒlədʒi; *NAmE* lɪˈθɑːl-/ *noun* [U] the study of the general physical characteristics of rocks 岩性学；岩石学

litho·sphere /ˈlɪθəsfɪə(r); *NAmE* -sfɪr/ *noun* [sing.] (*geology* 地) the layer of rock that forms the outer part of the earth 岩石圈；岩石层

liti·gant /ˈlɪtɪɡənt/ *noun* (*law* 律) a person who is making or defending a claim in court 诉讼当事人

liti·gate /ˈlɪtɪɡeɪt/ *verb* [I, T] ~ (**sth**) (*law* 律) to take a claim or disagreement to court （就…）提起诉讼，打官司 ▸ **liti·ga·tor** *noun*

liti·ga·tion /ˌlɪtɪˈɡeɪʃn/ *noun* [U] (*law* 律) the process of making or defending a claim in court 诉讼；打官司：*The company has been in litigation with its previous auditors*

▼ COLLOCATIONS 词语搭配

Literature 文学

Being a writer 当作家

- **write/publish** literature/poetry/fiction/a book/a story/a poem/a novel/a review/an autobiography 写/发表文学作品/诗集/小说/书/故事/诗歌/长篇小说/评论/自传
- **become** a writer/novelist/playwright 成为作家/小说家/剧作家
- **find/have** a publisher/an agent 找到/有出版商/代理人
- **have** a new book out 出版一部新书
- **edit/revise/proofread** a book/text/manuscript 编辑/修订/校对书/文章/原稿
- **dedicate** a book/poem to… 把一本书/一首诗献给…

Plot, character and atmosphere 情节、人物和氛围

- **construct/create/weave/weave sth into** a complex narrative 构思/创作/编写/把某事编成一部复杂的叙事小说
- **advance/drive** the plot 推进故事情节的发展
- **introduce/present** the protagonist/a character 介绍主人公/一个人物
- **describe/depict/portray** a character (as…)/(sb as) a hero/villain 描述人物/英雄/坏蛋；把一个人物描绘成…；把某人描绘成英雄/坏蛋
- **create** an exciting/a tense atmosphere 营造一种令人兴奋/紧张的气氛
- **build/heighten** the suspense/tension 制造/增加悬念/紧张气氛
- **evoke/capture** the pathos of the situation 唤起对这种状况的同情
- **convey** emotion/an idea/an impression/a sense of… 传达…情感/思想；给人…印象/感觉
- **engage** the reader 吸引读者
- **seize/capture/grip** the (reader's) imagination 抓住（读者的）想象力
- **arouse/elicit** emotion/sympathy (in the reader) 唤起（读者的）情感/同情
- **lack** imagination/emotion/structure/rhythm 缺乏想象力/情感/精心组织/节奏感

Language, style and imagery 语言、风格和形象语言

- **use/employ** language/imagery/humour/(*especially US*) humor/an image/a symbol/a metaphor/a device 使用语言/形象语言/幽默/意象/象征/暗喻/手段
- **use/adopt/develop** a style/technique 使用/采用/形成一种风格/技巧
- **be rich in/be full of** symbolism 富含象征意义
- **evoke** images of…/a sense of…/a feeling of… 唤起…的形象/感觉
- **create/achieve** an effect 创造/取得效果
- **maintain/lighten** the tone 维持/缓和基调
- **introduce/develop** an idea/a theme 引入/发展一种思想/一个主题
- **inspire** a novel/a poet/sb's work/sb's imagination 促成小说的创作；给诗人以灵感；促成某人作品的诞生；激发某人的想象力

Reading and criticism 阅读与评论

- **read** an author/sb's work/fiction/poetry/a text/a poem/a novel/a chapter/a passage 读一个作家的作品/某人的著作/小说/诗集/一篇文章/一首诗/一部小说/一个章节/一段文章
- **review** a book/a novel/sb's work 评论一本书/一部小说/某人的作品
- **give sth/get/have/receive** a good/bad review 给予/得到好评/恶评
- **be hailed** (as)/**be recognized as** a masterpiece 被誉为一部杰作
- **quote** a phrase/line/stanza/passage/author 引用一个短语/一行诗/一节诗/一段文章/作者的话
- **provoke/spark** discussion/criticism 引发讨论/评论
- **study/interpret/understand** a text/passage 研读/解读/理解一篇文章/一段文章
- **translate** sb's work/a text/a passage/a novel/a poem 翻译某人的作品/一篇文章/一段文章/一部小说/一首诗

for a full year. 那家公司与前任审计员已打了整整一年的官司。

li·ti·gious /lɪˈtɪdʒəs/ *adj.* (*formal, disapproving*) too ready to take disagreements to court 好诉讼的；爱打官司的 ▶ **li·ti·gious·ness** *noun* [U]

lit·mus /ˈlɪtməs/ *noun* [U] a substance that turns red when it touches an acid and blue when it touches an ALKALI 石蕊（一种遇酸变红而遇碱则变蓝的物质）：*litmus paper* 石蕊试纸

ˈ**litmus test** *noun* **1** (*especially NAmE*) = ACID TEST：*The outcome will be seen as a litmus test of government concern for conservation issues.* 这结果将被视为检验政府是否关注自然资源保护问题的试金石。 **2** a test using litmus 石蕊试验

li·to·tes /laɪˈtəʊtiːz; *NAmE* -ˈtoʊ-/ *noun* [U] (*specialist*) the use of a negative or weak statement to emphasize a positive meaning, for example *he wasn't slow to accept the offer* (= he was quick to accept the offer) 反叙法，曲言（用否定或较弱的语气加强表示肯定） ➲ COMPARE UNDERSTATEMENT ➲ WORDFINDER NOTE AT IMAGE

litre 🔑 (*especially US* **liter**) /ˈliːtə(r)/ *noun* (*abbr.* **l**) a unit for measuring volume, equal to 1.76 British pints or 2.11 American pints 升（容量单位，等于英国的 1.76 品脱或美国的 2.11 品脱）：*3 litres of water* * 3 升水 ◇ *a litre bottle of wine* 一升容量的瓶装酒 ◇ *a car with a 3.5 litre engine* 配有 3.5 升发动机的汽车

lit·ter /ˈlɪtə(r)/ *noun, verb*

■ ***noun*** **1** [U] small pieces of rubbish/garbage such as paper, cans and bottles, that people have left lying in a public place（在公共场所乱扔的）垃圾，废弃物，杂物：*There will be fines for people who* **drop litter**. 乱扔垃圾的人将被罚款。 **2** [sing.] **~ of sth** a number of things that are lying in an untidy way 乱七八糟的东西；乱放的杂物：*The floor was covered with a litter of newspapers, clothes and empty cups.* 地板上到处都是乱七八糟的报纸、衣服和空杯子。 **3** [U] a dry substance that is put in a shallow open box for pets, especially cats, to use as a toilet when they are indoors（供宠物，尤指猫，在室内便溺的）猫砂，便溺垫物：*cat litter* 猫砂 ◇ (*BrE*) *a litter tray* 猫砂盘 ◇ (*NAmE*) *a litter box* 铺了便溺垫物的箱子 **4** [C] a number of baby animals that one mother gives birth to at the same time（动物一胎所生的）一窝幼崽：*a litter of puppies* 一窝小狗 ◇ *the runt* (= the smallest and weakest baby) *of the litter* 一窝中最弱小的幼畜 **5** [U] the substance, especially STRAW, that is used for farm animals to sleep on（供牲畜睡卧用的）垫草，褥草，铺栏草 **6** [C] a kind of chair or bed that was used in the past for carrying important people（旧时抬要人的）轿，舆

■ ***verb*** **1** [T] **~ sth** to be spread around a place, making it look untidy 使乱七八糟；使凌乱：*Piles of books and newspapers littered the floor.* 地板上乱七八糟地堆了许多书和报纸。 ◇ *Broken glass littered the streets.* 街上到处是玻璃碎片。 **2** [T, usually passive, I] **~ (sth) (with sth)** to leave things in a place, making it look untidy 乱扔：*The floor was littered with papers.* 地板上乱七八糟扔了许多文件。 ◇ (*NAmE*) *He was arrested for littering.* 他因乱扔垃圾被拘捕。 **3** [T] **be littered with sth** to contain or involve a lot of a particular type of thing, usually sth bad 使饱含，使遍布（一般指不好的东西）：*Your essay is littered with spelling mistakes.* 你的文章里到处是拼写错误。

ˈ**litter bin** (*BrE*) (*NAmE* ˈ**trash can**) *noun* a container for people to put rubbish/garbage in, in the street or in a public building（街道上或公共建筑物里的）垃圾箱，废物箱 ➲ VISUAL VOCAB PAGE V3

ˈ**litter lout** (*BrE*) (*also* ˈ**lit·ter·bug** *NAmE, BrE*) *noun* (*informal, disapproving*) a person who leaves LITTER in public places（在公共场所）乱扔垃圾的人；垃圾虫

lit·tle 🔑 /ˈlɪtl/ *adj., det., pron., adv.*

■ ***adj.*** [usually before noun] **HELP** The forms **littler** /ˈlɪtlə(r)/ and **littlest** /ˈlɪtlɪst/ are rare. It is more common to use **smaller** and **smallest**. * littler 和 littlest 都很少见，常用的是 smaller 和 smallest。 **1** 🔑 not big; small; smaller than others 小的；比较小的：*a little house* 小房子 ◇ *a little group of tourists* 一小群游客 ◇ *a little old lady* 一位小老太太 ◇ *the classic little black dress* 典雅的黑色小连衣裙 ◇ *'Which do you want?' 'I'll take the little one.'* "你要哪一个？" "我要那个小的。" ◇ *She gave a little laugh.* 她笑了一笑。 ◇ (*BrE*) *We should manage, with* **a little bit** *of luck.* 我们只要有一点点运气就能应付过去。 ◇ *Here's* **a little something** (= a small present) *for your birthday.* 这是送给你的生日小礼物。 **2** 🔑 used after an adjective to show affection or dislike, especially in a PATRONIZING way (= one that suggests that you think you are better than sb)（用在形容词的后面表示喜爱或厌恶，尤指屈尊俯就地）可爱的，可怜的，讨厌的：*The* **poor little thing**! *It's lost its mother.* 这可怜的小家伙！没有了妈妈。 ◇ *What a nasty little man!* 多么令人讨厌的家伙！ ◇ *She's a good little worker.* 她是个讨人喜欢的工人。 ◇ *He'd become* **quite the little** *gentleman.* 他成了颇有风度的绅士了。 **3** 🔑 young 年幼的；幼小的：*a* **little boy/girl** 小男孩；小女孩 ◇ *my* **little brother/sister** (= younger brother/sister) 我的弟弟 / 妹妹 ◇ *I lived in America when I was little.* 我小时候生活在美国。 **4** 🔑 (of distance or time 距离或时间) short 短的；近的；短暂的：*A* **little while** *later the phone rang.* 过了一小会儿电话响了起来。 ◇ *Shall we walk a little way?* 我们走一小段路好吗？ **5** 🔑 not important; not serious 微不足道的；不严重的：*I can't remember every little detail.* 我记不住每一个微小的细节。 ◇ *You soon get used to the little difficulties.* 你很快就会习惯这些小小的不便了。 ▶ **little·ness** *noun* [U]

IDM **a little ˈbird told me** (*informal*) used to say that sb told you sth but you do not want to say who it was（不想说出是谁告诉的）有人告诉我的，不告诉你我是怎么知道的 ➲ MORE AT OAK, WONDER *n.*

■ ***det., pron.*** **1** 🔑 used with uncountable nouns to mean 'not much'（与不可数名词连用）不多的：*There was little doubt in my mind.* 我心里几乎没有疑问。 ◇ *Students have* **little or no** *choice in the matter.* 学生在这个问题上很少有或没有选择余地。 ◇ *I understood little of what he said.* 我几乎听不懂他讲的。 ◇ *She said* **little or nothing** (= hardly anything) *about her experience.* 她对自己的经历几乎只字不提。 ◇ *Tell him* **as little as possible**. 尽量少告诉他。 **2** 🔑 **a little** used with uncountable nouns to mean 'a small amount', 'some'（与不可数名词连用）少量的，一些：*a little milk/sugar/tea* 少许牛奶 / 糖 / 茶 ◇ *If you have any spare milk, could you give me a little?* 你要是有多余的牛奶，给我一些好吗？ ◇ *I've only read a little of the book so far.* 这本书我才读了一小部分。 ◇ (*formal*) *It caused* **not a little/no little** (= a lot of) *confusion.* 这事引起了不小的混乱。 ◇ *After a little* (= a short time) *he got up and left.* 过了一会儿他站起来走了。

IDM ˌ**little by ˈlittle** 🔑 slowly; gradually 缓慢地；逐渐地；一点一点地：*Little by little the snow disappeared.* 雪渐渐融化了。 ◇ *His English is improving little by little.* 他的英语正在逐步提高。

■ ***adv.*** (**less, least**) **1** 🔑 not much; only slightly 不多；稍许；略微：*He is little known as an artist.* 几乎没人知道他是个艺术家。 ◇ *I slept very little last night.* 昨晚我几乎没怎么睡。 ◇ ***Little did I know*** *that this spelled the end of my career.* 我一点也没想到这会断送了我的职业生涯。 **2** 🔑 **a little (bit)** to a small degree 少许；少量；一点：*She seemed a little afraid of going inside.* 她好像有点害怕进去。 ◇ *These shoes are a little (bit) too big for me.* 我穿这双鞋太大了一点。 ◇ (*informal*) *Everything has become* ***just that little bit*** *harder.* 一切都变得有点更艰难了。 ◇ (*formal*) *She felt tired and* ***more than a little*** *worried.* 她感到既疲劳又非常担忧。 ➲ NOTE AT BIT

the ˌLittle ˈBear *noun* = URSA MINOR

ˌ**Little ˈEnglander** *noun* (*usually disapproving*) an English person who believes England (or, in practice, Britain) should not get involved in international affairs 英格兰本土主义者（主张英国不参与国际事务）

ˌ**little ˈfinger** *noun* the smallest finger of the hand 小指 **SYN** pinky ➲ VISUAL VOCAB PAGE V64

IDM **twist/wrap/wind sb around your little ˈfinger** (*informal*) to persuade sb to do anything that you want 任意摆布某人；左右某人

ˈ**Little League** *noun* [sing., U] (in the US 美国) a BASEBALL league for children 少年棒球联盟

ˈ**little people** *noun* [pl.] **1** all the people in a country who have no power（统称）平民，百姓，小老百姓 **2** extremely small people, who will never grow to a normal size because of a physical problem 异常矮小的人；侏儒；"袖珍"人 **3 the little people** small imaginary people with magic powers 小精灵；小仙子 **SYN** fairies

lit·toral /ˈlɪtərəl/ *noun* (*specialist*) the part of a country that is near the coast 沿海地区 ▶ **lit·toral** *adj.* [only before noun]: *littoral states* 沿海各州

lit·urgy /ˈlɪtədʒi; NAmE ˈlɪtərdʒi/ *noun* [C, U] (*pl.* **-ies**) a fixed form of public worship used in churches 礼拜仪式 ▶ **li·tur·gic·al** /lɪˈtɜːdʒɪkl; NAmE -ˈtɜːrdʒ-/ *adj.* **li·tur·gic·al·ly** /-kli/ *adv.*

liv·able *adj.* = LIVEABLE

live¹ /lɪv/ *verb* ➲ SEE ALSO LIVE²

• **IN A PLACE** 在某地 **1** [I] **+ adv./prep.** to have your home in a particular place 住；居住：*to live in a house* 住在一座房子里 ◇ *Where do you live?* 你住在什么地方？◇ *She needs to find **somewhere to live**.* 她需要找个住的地方。◇ *We used to live in London.* 我们过去住在伦敦。◇ *Both her children still live at home.* 她的两个孩子仍住在家里。◇ (*informal*) *Where do these plates live* (= where are they usually kept)? 这些盘子通常放哪儿？

• **BE ALIVE** 活着 **2** [I] to remain alive 生存；活着：*The doctors said he only had six months to live.* 医生说他只能活六个月了。◇ *Spiders can live for several days without food.* 蜘蛛几天不吃食依然可存活。◇ **~ to do sth** *She lived to see her first grandchild.* 她一直活到抱上第一个孙子。 **3** [I] to be alive, especially at a particular time（尤指在某时期）活着：*When did Handel live?* 亨德尔是什么时期的人？◇ *He's the greatest player who ever lived.* 他是史上最出色的运动员。

• **TYPE OF LIFE** 生活方式 **4** [I, T] to spend your life in a particular way（以某种方式）生活，过日子：*He lived in poverty most of his life.* 他大半辈子过的都是穷日子。◇ **~ sth** *She lived a very peaceful life.* 她过着十分宁静的生活。◇ **+ noun** *She lived and died a single woman.* 她过了一辈子的独身生活。

• **BE REMEMBERED** 被记住 **5** [I] to continue to exist or be remembered 继续存在；留存；被铭记 **SYN** **remain**：*This moment will live in our memory for many years to come.* 这一时刻将在我们的记忆中留存许多年。◇ *Her words have lived with me all my life.* 她的话我一辈子都铭记着。

• **HAVE EXCITEMENT** 兴奋 **6** [I] to have a full and exciting life 享受充实而令人兴奋的生活：*I don't want to be stuck in an office all my life—I want to live!* 我不想一辈子都憋在办公室里，我要享受人生乐趣！

IDM ˌ**live and ˈbreathe sth** to be very enthusiastic about sth 热衷于（某事）：*He just lives and breathes football.* 他非常热衷于足球。 **live and ˈlet live** (*saying*) used to say that you should accept other people's opinions and behaviour even though they are different from your own 自己活也让别人活；宽以待人；互相宽容 **live by your ˈwits** to earn money by clever or sometimes dishonest means 靠要小聪明赚钱；（有时）靠玩花招捞钱 **live (from)** ˌ**hand to ˈmouth** to spend all the money you earn on basic needs such as food without being able to save any money 仅够糊口度日 **live in the ˈpast** to behave as though society, etc. has not changed, when in fact it has 仿佛生活在过去；落伍 **live in ˈsin** (*old-fashioned* or *humorous*) to live together and have a sexual relationship without being married 未婚同居；姘居 **live it ˈup** (*informal*) to enjoy yourself in an exciting way, usually spending a lot of money 尽情欢乐；狂欢；纵情挥霍享乐 **live a ˈlie** to keep sth important about yourself a secret from other people, so that they do not know what you really think, what you are really like, etc. 过两面人的生活；过骗人的生活；为人虚伪 **live off the fat of the ˈland** to have enough money to be able to afford expensive things, food, drink, etc. 过奢侈的生活；锦衣玉食 **live off the ˈland** to eat whatever food you can grow, kill or find yourself 靠耕种（或狩猎）为生 ˌ**live to fight another ˈday** (*saying*) used to say that although you have failed or had a bad experience, you will continue（虽已失败或经历很糟但仍要）改日再战，卷土重来 **you haven't ˈlived** used to tell sb that if they have not had a particular experience their life is not complete（表示若没有某种经历生活便不完整）你白活了：*You've never been to New York? You haven't lived!* 你从未去过纽约？你真是白活了！ **you live and ˈlearn** used to express surprise at sth new or unexpected you have been told（对得知的事物感到惊讶或意外）真是得活到老学到老，真想不到 ➲ MORE AT BORROW, CLOVER, HALF *n.*, LIFE, LONG *adv.*, PEOPLE *n.*, POCKET *n.*, ROUGH *adv.*

PHR V ˈ**live by sth** to follow a particular belief or set of principles 按照（某信念或原则）生活：*That's a philosophy I could live by.* 那就是我所信奉的人生哲学。 ˈ**live by doing sth** to earn money or to get the things you need by doing a particular thing 靠做某事赚钱为生（或获取所需）：*a community that lives by fishing* 靠捕鱼为生的群体 ˌ**live sth↔ˈdown** to be able to make people forget about sth embarrassing you have done 能使人忘却（做过的令人尴尬的事）：*She felt so stupid. She'd never be able to live it down.* 她觉得自己做了傻事，恐怕永远无法挽回自己的面子了。 ˈ**live for sb/sth** to think that sb/sth is the main purpose of or the most important thing in your life 以…为主要生活目的；为…而活着：*She lives for her work.* 她活着是为了工作。◇ *After his wife died, he had nothing to live for.* 妻子去世后，他便没有了生活目标。 ˌ**live ˈin** to live at the place where you work or study 住在工作（或学习）的地方：*They have an au pair living in.* 他们有个互惠女生住在家里。 ➲ SEE ALSO LIVE-IN ˈ**live off sb/sth** (*often disapproving*) to receive the money you need to live from sb/sth because you do not have any yourself 靠…过活；依赖…生活：*She's still living off her parents.* 她还在靠父母养活。◇ *to live off welfare* 靠救济过活 ˈ**live off sth** to have one particular type of food as the main thing you eat in order to live 以吃…为生：*He seems to live off junk food.* 他好像靠吃垃圾食品为生。 ˌ**live ˈon** to continue to live or exist 继续活着；继续存在：*She died ten years ago but her memory lives on.* 她十年前就去世了，但她还留在人们的记忆中。 ˈ**live on sth 1** to eat a particular type of food to live 以吃…为生：*Small birds live mainly on insects.* 小鸟主要靠吃昆虫为生。 **2** (*often disapproving*) to eat only or a lot of a particular type of food 仅以（一种食物）为主要食物：*She lives on burgers.* 她只喜欢吃汉堡包。 **3** to have enough money for the basic things you need to live 靠（…钱）生活：*You can't live on forty pounds a week.* 你靠每周四十英镑没法过活。 ˌ**live ˈout** to live away from the place where you work or study 不住在工作（或学习）的地方：*Some college students will have to live out.* 有些大学生将不得不住在校外。 ˌ**live ˈout sth 1** to actually do what you have only thought about doing before 实践（以前想要做的事）：*to live out your fantasies* 实现梦想 **2** to spend the rest of your life in a particular way （以某种方式）度过余生：*He lived out his days alone.* 他独自度过余生。 ˌ**live ˈthrough sth** to experience a disaster or other unpleasant situation and survive it 经历（灾难或其他困境）而幸存：*He has lived through two world wars.* 他经历了两次世界大战。 ˈ**live together** (*also* ˈ**live with sb**) **1** to live in the same house 在一起生活 **2** to share a home and have a sexual relationship without being married 未婚同居；姘居 **SYN** **cohabit** ˌ**live ˈup to sth** to do as well as or be as good as other people expect you to 达到，符合，不辜负（他人的期望）：*He failed to live up to his parents' expectations.* 他辜负了父母的期望。◇ *The team called 'The No-Hopers' certainly lived up to its name.* 叫做"无望者"的球队果真名副其实。 ˈ**live with sb** = LIVE TOGETHER ˈ**live with sth** to accept sth unpleasant 忍受，容忍（不快的事）：*I just had to learn to live with the pain.* 我不得不学会忍受痛苦。

live² /laɪv/ *adj., adv.* ➲ SEE ALSO LIVE¹

■ *adj.* [usually before noun]

• **NOT DEAD** 活的 **1** living; not dead 活的：*live animals* 活动物 ◇ *the number of live births* (= babies born alive) 活产婴儿数 ◇ *We saw a **real live** rattlesnake!* 我们看见了一条活生生的响尾蛇！ ➲ MORE LIKE THIS 32, page R28

L

• NOT RECORDED 非录制 **2** (of a broadcast 广播) sent out while the event is actually happening, not recorded first and broadcast later 现场直播的；实况转播的：*live coverage of the World Cup* 世界杯赛的实况转播 **3** (of a performance 表演) given or made when people are watching, not recorded 现场演出的：*The club has live music most nights.* 该俱乐部大多数晚上有现场演奏的音乐。◇ *a live recording made at Wembley Arena* 温布利运动场的现场录音 ◇ *the band's new live album* 这个乐队新出的演唱会专辑 ◇ *It was the first interview I'd done in front of a* **live audience** (= with people watching). 那是我首次在观众面前做现场采访。
• ELECTRICITY 电 **4** (of a wire or device 电线或装置) connected to a source of electrical power 连着电源的；通电的：*That terminal is live.* 那个端子有电。
• BULLETS/MATCHES 子弹；火柴 **5** still able to explode or light; ready for use 仍可爆炸的；仍可点燃的；随时可用的：*live ammunition* 实弹
• COALS 煤块 **6 live** coals are burning or are still hot and red 燃烧着的；仍灼热发红的
• YOGURT 酸奶 **7 live** YOGURT still contains the bacteria needed to turn milk into yogurt 含乳酸菌的
• QUESTION/SUBJECT 问题；话题 **8** of interest or importance at the present time 当前所关心的；时下重大的：*Pollution is still very much a live issue.* 污染仍然是目前让人非常关注的问题。
• INTERNET 互联网 **9** (of an electronic link 电子链接) functioning correctly, so that it is connected to another document or page on the Internet 有效的；功能正常的；活的：*Here are some live links to other aviation-related web pages.* 这是另外一些航空相关网页的有效链接。
IDM **a live 'wire** a person who is lively and full of energy 活跃而精力充沛的人；生龙活虎的人
■ ***adv.*** broadcast at the time of an actual event; played or recorded at an actual performance 在现场直播；在现场表演（或录制）：*The show is going out live.* 这场演出正在实况直播。
IDM **go 'live** (*computing* 计) (of a computer system, website, etc. 计算机系统、网站等) to become OPERATIONAL (= ready to be used) 正式投入运行；正式上线

live·able (*also* **liv·able**) /ˈlɪvəbl/ *adj.* **1** (*BrE also* **live·able in** [not before noun]) (of a house, etc. 房屋等) fit to live in 适于居住的 SYN **habitable**: *safer and more liveable residential areas* 更安全和更适于居住的住宅区 ◇ *The place looks liveable in.* 这地方看起来适于居住。 **2** (of life 生活) worth living 值得一过的 SYN **endurable 3** [not before noun] **~ with** that can be dealt with 能对付；可处理：*The problem is paying the mortgage—everything else is liveable with.* 问题在于偿还按揭贷款，别的一切事情都能对付。 **4** [only before noun] (of a wage, etc. 工资等) enough to live on 足够维持生活的：*a liveable salary* 足以维持生活的薪水

live action /ˌlaɪv ˈækʃn/ *noun* [U] part of a film/movie that is made using real people or animals, rather than using drawings, models or computers（电影中的）真人实拍片段 ▶ **ˌlive-'action** *adj.* [only before noun]: *a live-action movie* 一部真人实物影片

ˌlive 'blog /ˌlaɪv ˈblɒɡ; *NAmE* ˈblɑːɡ/ *noun* a BLOG or a MICROBLOG on which a description of an event is given as it takes place 直播博客；实时博客（或微博客） ▶ **'live-blog** *verb* [T, I]: *He live-blogged from the top of the mountain.* 他从山顶进行博客直播。◇ **~ sth** *to live-blog an event/an election/a debate* 以博客直播事件 / 选举 / 辩论

ˈlived-in *adj.* (of a place 地方) that has been used so continuously for so long that it does not look new 长期有人居住（而不再簇新）的；长期使用中的：(*approving*) *The room had a comfortable, lived-in feel about it.* 这房间里有一种一直有人居住的温馨感觉。

live-in /ˈlɪv ɪn/ *adj.* **1** (of an employee 雇员) living in the house where they work 住在工作场所的：*a live-in nanny* 住家保姆 **2 ~ lover, boyfriend, girlfriend, etc.** a person who lives with their sexual partner but is not married to them 未婚同居者

live·li·hood /ˈlaɪvlihʊd/ *noun* [C, usually sing., U] a means of earning money in order to live 赚钱谋生的手段；生计 SYN **living**: *Communities on the island depended on whaling for their livelihood.* 岛上的居民靠捕鲸为生。◇ ***a means/source of livelihood*** 生计；生活来源

live·long /ˈlɪvlɒŋ; *NAmE* -lɔːŋ; -lɑːŋ/ *adj.*
IDM **the livelong 'day** (*literary*) the whole length of the day 一整天

live·ly /ˈlaɪvli/ *adj.* (**live·lier, live·li·est**) **1** full of life and energy; active and enthusiastic 精力充沛的；生气勃勃的；活跃热情的 SYN **animated, vivacious**: *an intelligent and lively young woman* 聪慧而充满活力的年轻女士 ◇ *a lively and enquiring mind* 思维活跃、善于探索的头脑 ◇ *He showed a lively interest in politics.* 他对政治表现出浓厚的兴趣。 **2** (of a place, an event, etc. 地方、事件等) full of interest or excitement 充满趣味的；令人兴奋的：*a lively bar* 气氛热闹的酒吧 ◇ *a lively debate* 热烈的辩论 **3** (of colours 颜色) strong and definite 浓的；鲜艳的：*a lively shade of pink* 鲜艳的粉红色调 **4** (*especially BrE*) busy and active 繁忙活跃的；兴旺的：*They do a lively trade in souvenirs and gifts.* 他们做纪念品和礼品生意，做得有声有色。▶ **live·li·ness** *noun* [U]

liven /ˈlaɪvn/ *verb*
PHR V **ˌliven 'up | ˌliven sb/sth 'up** to become or to make sb/sth more interesting or exciting（使）更有趣，更令人兴奋：*The game didn't liven up till the second half.* 那场比赛直到下半场才精彩起来。◇ *Let's put some music on to liven things up.* 咱们放些音乐活跃一下气氛吧。

liver /ˈlɪvə(r)/ *noun* **1** [C] a large organ in the body that cleans the blood and produces BILE 肝 ➲ VISUAL VOCAB PAGE V64 **2** [U, C] the liver of some animals that is cooked and eaten（动物供食用的）肝：*liver and onions* 洋葱炒肝尖 ◇ *chicken livers* 鸡肝

ˈliver fluke *noun* a small WORM which, in an adult form, lives in the LIVER of people or animals, often causing disease 肝吸虫（侵害宿主肝脏）

liv·er·ied /ˈlɪvərid/ *adj.* **1** (*BrE*) painted in a LIVERY 涂成专用颜色的：*liveried aircraft* 涂着航空公司专用颜色的飞机 **2** wearing LIVERY 穿制服的；穿号衣的：*liveried servants* 穿制服的仆人

Liv·er·pud·lian /ˌlɪvəˈpʌdliən; *NAmE* ˌlɪvərˈp-/ *noun* a person from Liverpool in NW England 利物浦人 ▶ **Liv·er·pud·lian** *adj.*

ˈliver sausage (*BrE*) (*NAmE* **liv·er·wurst** /ˈlɪvəwɜːst; *NAmE* ˈlɪvərwɜːrst/) *noun* [U] a type of soft SAUSAGE made from finely chopped LIVER, usually spread cold on bread 肝泥香肠

ˈliver spot *noun* a small brown spot on the skin, especially found in older people 雀斑；黄褐斑；（尤指）老人斑

liv·ery /ˈlɪvəri/ *noun* [U, C] (*pl.* **-ies**) **1** (*BrE*) the colours in which the vehicles, aircraft, etc. of a particular company are painted（车辆、飞机等涂的）公司专用色彩 **2** a special uniform worn by servants or officials, especially in the past（尤指旧时仆人或官员的）制服

ˈlivery stable *noun* a place where people can pay to keep their horses or can hire a horse（代客饲养马或租马的）马房

lives PL. OF LIFE

live·stock /ˈlaɪvstɒk; *NAmE* -stɑːk/ *noun* [U, pl.] the animals kept on a farm, for example cows or sheep 牲畜；家畜 ➲ WORDFINDER NOTE AT FARM ➲ VISUAL VOCAB PAGE V3

live-stream /ˈlaɪv striːm/ *verb, noun*
■ ***verb*** [T] to broadcast or receive live video and sound of an event over the Internet 实时流播，网络直播（通过互联网实时播放或接收声像）
■ ***noun*** (*usually* **livestream**) a live broadcast of an event over the Internet 网络直播；实况流播

live·ware /ˈlaɪvweə(r); *NAmE* -wer/ *noun* [U] (*informal*) people who work with computers, rather than the programs or computers with which they work 人件，活件（用计算机工作的人）

livid /ˈlɪvɪd/ *adj.* **1** extremely angry 暴怒的；狂怒的 SYN **furious** **2** dark bluish-grey in colour 乌青色的；青灰色的：*a livid bruise* 青瘀

liv·ing /ˈlɪvɪŋ/ *adj., noun*

■ ***adj.*** **1** alive now 活着的；活的：*all* ***living things*** 所有生物 ◇ *living organisms* 活的机体 ◇ *the finest living pianist* 健在的最杰出的钢琴家 **2** [only before noun] used or practised now 在使用的；在实施的：*living languages* (= those still spoken) 现用语言 ◇ *a living faith* 现今有人信奉的信仰

IDM **be living 'proof of sth/that...** to show by your actions or qualities that a particular fact is true（用行动或品格）证明…属实：*He is living proof that not all engineers are boring.* 并非所有工程师都缺乏情趣，他就是活生生的例子。 **within/in ˌliving 'memory** at a time, or during the time, that is remembered by people still alive 在仍活着的人们的记忆中；记忆犹新：*the coldest winter in living memory* 人们记忆中最寒冷的冬天 ⊃ MORE AT DAYLIGHTS

■ ***noun*** **1** [C, usually sing.] money to buy the things that you need in life 生计；谋生；收入：*She* ***earns her living*** *as a freelance journalist.* 她靠做自由撰稿记者来维持生计。◇ *to* ***make a good/decent/meagre living*** 过优裕的 / 体面的 / 贫困的生活 ◇ *What do you* ***do for a living?*** 你靠什么谋生？◇ *to* ***scrape/scratch a living*** *from part-time tutoring* 靠做兼职家庭教师勉强维持生活 **2** [U] a way or style of life 生活方式：*everyday living* 日常生活 ◇ *communal living* 集体生活 ◇ *plain living* 简朴的生活 ◇ *Their* ***standard of living*** *is very low.* 他们的生活水平很低。◇ *The* ***cost of living*** *has risen sharply.* 生活费用已急剧上涨。◇ *poor* ***living conditions/standards*** 恶劣的生活条件；低下的生活水准 **3 the living** [pl.] people who are alive now 活着的人：*the living and the dead* 生者与死者 IDM SEE LAND *n.* **4** [C] (*BrE*) (especially in the past) a position in the Church as a priest and the income and house that go with this（尤指旧时）有俸金住房的牧师职位 SYN **benefice**

ˌliving 'death *noun* [sing.] a life that is worse than being dead 活受罪；生不如死

ˌliving 'hell *noun* [sing.] a very unpleasant situation that causes a lot of suffering and lasts a long time 活受煎熬；活地狱；活受罪；人间地狱

ˌliving 'roof *noun* = GREEN ROOF

'living room (*BrE also* **'sitting room**) *noun* a room in a house where people sit together, watch television, etc. 客厅；起居室 SYN **lounge** ⊃ MORE LIKE THIS 9, page R26

ˌliving 'wage *noun* [sing.] a wage that is high enough for sb to buy the things they need in order to live 基本生活工资；仅能维持生活的工资

ˌliving 'will *noun* a document stating your wishes concerning medical treatment in the case that you become so ill/sick that you can no longer make decisions about it, in particular asking doctors to stop treating you and let you die（尤指要求在病弱以致无法做决定时不再医治的）生前预嘱

liz·ard /ˈlɪzəd; *NAmE* -ərd/ *noun* a small REPTILE with a rough skin, four short legs and a long tail 蜥蜴

ll *abbr.* (in writing 书写形式) lines (the plural form of 'l') 行（l 的复数形式）

llama /ˈlɑːmə/ *noun* a S American animal kept for its soft wool or for carrying loads 羊驼（产于南美）

LLB (*BrE*) (*NAmE* **LL.B.**) /ˌel el ˈbiː/ *noun* the abbreviation for 'Bachelor of Laws' (a first university degree in law) 法学学士（全写为 Bachelor of Laws，大学法学的初级学位）

LLD (*BrE*) (*NAmE* **LL.D.**) /ˌel el ˈdiː/ *noun* the abbreviation for 'Doctor of Laws' (the highest university degree in law) 法学博士（全写为 Doctor of Laws，大学法学的最高学位）

LLM (*BrE*) (*NAmE* **LL.M.**) /ˌel el ˈem/ *noun* the abbreviation for 'Master of Laws' (a second university degree in law) 法学硕士（全写为 Master of Laws，大学法学的中级学位）

lm *abbr.* LUMEN 流（明）（光通量单位）

LMS /ˌel em ˈes/ *noun* the abbreviation for 'learning management system' (a software system for managing training and education using the Internet) 学习管理系统（全写为 learning management system，利用互联网管理培训与教育的软件系统）

lo /ləʊ; *NAmE* loʊ/ *exclamation* (*old use* or *humorous*) used for calling attention to a surprising thing（引起对令人惊讶的事的注意）瞧，看哪

IDM **ˌlo and be'hold** (*humorous*) used for calling attention to a surprising or annoying thing（用于引起对令人惊讶或讨厌之事的注意）哎哟，你瞧，嗨，真想不到

load /ləʊd; *NAmE* loʊd/ *noun, verb*

■ ***noun***

• **STH CARRIED** 负载物 **1** [C] something that is being carried (usually in large amounts) by a person, vehicle, etc. 负载；负荷 SYN **cargo**：*The trucks waited at the warehouse to pick up their loads.* 货车在仓库等着装载货物。◇ *The women came down the hill with their loads of firewood.* 妇女们背着柴火下了山。◇ *These backpacks are designed to* ***carry a heavy load.*** 这些背包是为携带重物设计的。◇ *A lorry* ***shed its load*** (= accidentally dropped its load) *on the motorway.* 一辆卡车意外地把运载的货物掉落在高速公路上。 **2** [C] (often in compounds 常构成复合词) the total amount of sth that sth can carry or contain 装载量；容纳量：*a busload of tourists* 一公共汽车游客 ◇ *They ordered three truckloads of sand.* 他们订购了三卡车沙子。◇ *He put half a load of washing in the machine.* 他把要洗的衣物放进洗衣机，洗衣机装了个半满。◇ *The plane took off with a* ***full load.*** 飞机满载起飞。

• **WEIGHT** 重量 **3** [C, usually sing.] the amount of weight that is pressing down on sth 承载量：*a load-bearing wall* 承重墙 ◇ *Modern backpacks spread the load over a wider area.* 新式背包把承重分散在更大的面积上。

• **LARGE AMOUNT** 大量 **4** [sing.] (*also* **loads** [pl.]) ~ (**of sth**) (*informal*) a large number or amount of sb/sth; plenty 大量；许多：*She's got loads of friends.* 她有很多朋友。◇ *There's loads to do today.* 今天有好多的事要做。◇ *He wrote loads and loads of letters to people.* 他给人们写了很多很多的信。◇ *Uncle Jim brought a whole load of presents for the kids.* 吉姆大叔给孩子们带来了一大堆礼物。

• **RUBBISH/NONSENSE** 胡说八道；废话 **5** [sing.] **~ of rubbish, garbage, nonsense, etc.** (*informal, especially BrE*) used to emphasize that sth is wrong, stupid, bad, etc.（强调错误、愚蠢、糟糕等）胡说八道，废话：*You're talking a load of rubbish.* 你说的都是一派胡言。

• **WORK** 工作 **6** [C] an amount of work that a person or machine has to do 工作量；负荷：*Teaching loads have increased in all types of school.* 各种学校的教学工作量都增加了。⊃ SEE ALSO CASELOAD, WORKLOAD

• **RESPONSIBILITY/WORRY** 责任；忧虑 **7** [C, usually sing.] a feeling of responsibility or worry that is difficult to deal with（责任或忧虑的）沉重感 SYN **burden**：*She thought she would not be able to* ***bear the load*** *of bringing up her family alone.* 她认为她无法独自一人担负起养家的重任。◇ *Knowing that they had arrived safely* ***took a load off my mind.*** 得知他们平安到达后我如释重负。

• **ELECTRICAL POWER** 电力 **8** [C] the amount of electrical power that is being supplied at a particular time 供电量

IDM **get a load of sb/sth** (*informal*) used to tell sb to look at or listen to sb/sth（用以让人）看，听：*Get a load of that dress!* 你瞧那件衣服！

■ ***verb***

• **GIVE/RECEIVE LOAD** 装载；承载 **1** [T, I] to put a large quantity of things or people onto or into sth（把大量…）装上，装入：**~ sth** *We loaded the car in ten minutes.* 我们十分钟就装好了车。◇ *Can you help me load the dishwasher?* 你帮我把碗碟放进洗碗机里好吗？◇ **~ sth (up) (with sth)** *Men were loading up a truck with timber.* 工人正在把木料装上卡车。◇ **~ sth/sb (into/onto sth)** *Sacks were being loaded onto the truck.* 人们正在把麻袋装上卡车。◇ **~ (up) | ~ (up with sth)** *We finished loading and set off.* 我们装完货物就出发了。 OPP **unload** **2** [I] to receive a load 承载；装载：*The ship was still loading.* 那条船还在装货。

OPP **unload** **3** [T] ~ **sb with sth** to give sb a lot of things, especially things they have to carry 大量给予（尤指得携带的东西）：*They loaded her with gifts.* 他们送了她很多礼物。

- **GUN/CAMERA** 枪支；照相机 **4** [T, I] to put sth into a weapon, camera or other piece of equipment so that it can be used 把…装入（武器、照相机或其他设备）：**~ sth (into sth)** *She loaded film into the camera.* 她把胶卷装到照相机里。◇ **~ sth (with sth)** *She loaded the camera with film.* 她在照相机里装了胶卷。◇ **~ (sth)** *Is the gun loaded?* 那支枪子弹上膛了吗？ **OPP** **unload**
- **COMPUTING** 计算机技术 **5** [T, I] ~ **(sth)** to put data or a program into the memory of a computer 载入，加载（数据或程序）：*Have you loaded the software?* 你载入这种软件了吗？◇ *Wait for the game to load.* 等着游戏软件载入完成。➲ COMPARE DOWNLOAD *v.*

IDM **load the 'dice (against sb)** [usually passive] to put sb at a disadvantage 使（某人）处于不利地位：*He has always felt that the dice were loaded against him in life.* 他总觉得自己一辈子都背运。

PHR V **,load sb/sth 'down (with sth)** [usually passive] to give sb/sth a lot of heavy things to carry 给…加以重负 **SYN** **weigh sb/sth↔down**: *She was loaded down with bags of groceries.* 她提着很多装着食品杂货的袋子。

load·ed /ˈləʊdɪd; *NAmE* ˈloʊd-/ *adj.*

- **FULL** 满 **1** carrying a load; full and heavy 装载的；满载而沉重的 **SYN** **laden**: *a fully loaded truck* 满载货物的卡车 ◇ **~ (with sth)** *a truck loaded with supplies* 装满供给品的卡车 ◇ *She came into the room carrying a loaded tray.* 她端着装满食物的托盘走进了房间。 **2** **~ with sth** (*informal*) full of a particular thing, quality or meaning 充满…的：*cakes loaded with calories* 含高卡路里的糕点
- **RICH** 富有 **3** [not before noun] (*informal*) very rich 非常富有：*Let her pay—she's loaded.* 让她付钱吧，她钱多得很。
- **ADVANTAGE/DISADVANTAGE** 有利；不利 **4** **~ in favour of sb/sth** | **~ against sb/sth** acting either as an advantage or a disadvantage to sb/sth in a way that is unfair（不公平地）对…有利，对…不利：*a system that is loaded in favour of the young* (= gives them an advantage) 对年轻人有利的体制
- **WORD/STATEMENT** 言语；陈述 **5** having more meaning than you realize at first and intended to make you think in a particular way 意味深长的；含蓄的：*It was a **loaded question** and I preferred not to comment.* 这是个带有圈套的问题，我还是不作评论为好。
- **GUN/CAMERA** 枪支；照相机 **6** containing bullets, film, etc. 装有（子弹、胶卷等）的：*a loaded shotgun* 装有子弹的猎枪
- **DRUNK** 喝醉 **7** (*informal, especially NAmE*) very drunk 烂醉的；大醉的

load·ing /ˈləʊdɪŋ; *NAmE* ˈloʊd-/ *noun* [U, C] **1** (*AustralE, NZE*) extra money that sb is paid for their job because they have special skills or qualifications 附加工资（因有特别技能或资格） **2** an extra amount of money that you must pay in addition to the usual price 附加费用：*The 2% loading for using the card abroad has been removed.* 在国外使用此卡的 2% 附加费已经取消。

'load line *noun* = PLIMSOLL LINE

'load-shedding *noun* [U] the practice of stopping the supply of electricity for a period of time because the demand is greater than the supply 切负荷，减负荷，减（负）载（用电超过配电量时暂时切断电力的做法）

load·star *noun* = LODESTAR

load·stone *noun* = LODESTONE

loaf /ləʊf; *NAmE* loʊf/ *noun, verb*

■ *noun* (*pl.* **loaves** /ləʊvz; *NAmE* loʊvz/) an amount of bread that has been shaped and baked in one piece 一条（面包）：*a loaf of bread* 一条面包 ◇ *Two white loaves, please.* 请给我两条白面包。◇ *a sliced loaf* 一条切片面包 ➲ SEE ALSO COTTAGE LOAF, FRENCH LOAF, MEAT LOAF **IDM** SEE HALF *det., pron.*, USE *v.*

■ *verb* [I] ~ **(about/around)** (*informal*) to spend your time not doing anything, especially when you should be working 游手好闲；无所事事；闲荡 **SYN** **hang about**: *A group of kids were loafing around outside.* 一群小孩在外面四处游荡。

loaf·er /ˈləʊfə(r); *NAmE* ˈloʊf-/ *noun* **1** a person who wastes their time rather than working 虚度光阴者；游手好闲者；浪子；二流子 **2** a flat leather shoe that you can put on your foot without fastening it 平底便鞋 ➲ VISUAL VOCAB PAGE V69

loam /ləʊm; *NAmE* loʊm/ *noun* [U] (*specialist*) good quality soil containing sand, CLAY and decayed vegetable matter 壤土；肥土；沃土 ▶ **loamy** *adj.*

loan /ləʊn; *NAmE* loʊn/ *noun, verb*

■ *noun* **1** [C] money that an organization such as a bank lends and sb borrows 贷款；借款：*to **take out/repay a loan*** (= to borrow money/pay it back) 取得 / 偿还贷款 ◇ ***bank loans** with low interest rates* 银行低息贷款 ◇ *It took three years to repay my **student loan*** (= money lent to a student). 我花了三年的时间才还清我的学生贷款。◇ *a car loan* (= a loan to buy a car) 购车贷款 ➲ WORDFINDER NOTE AT BANK ➲ COLLOCATIONS AT FINANCE

> **WORDFINDER** 联想词：credit, debt, deposit, interest, lend, **money**, mortgage, overdraft, risk

2 [sing.] ~ **(of sth)** the act of lending sth; the state of being lent 借出；贷给；被借出：*I even **gave her the loan of** my car.* 我甚至把车也借给了她。◇ *an exhibition of paintings **on loan*** (= borrowed) *from private collections* 借用私人收藏品举办的画展

■ *verb* **1** (*especially NAmE*) to lend sth to sb, especially money 借出，贷与（尤指钱）：**~ sth (to sb)** *The bank is happy to loan money to small businesses.* 银行乐于贷款给小型企业。◇ **~ sb sth** *A friend loaned me $1 000.* 有一位朋友借给我 1 000 美元。 **2** (*especially BrE*) to lend a valuable object to a museum, etc. 出借（贵重物品给博物馆等）：**~ sth (out) (to sb/sth)** *This exhibit was kindly loaned by the artist's family.* 这件展品是艺术家的家人惠借而展出的。◇ **~ sb sth** *He loaned the museum his entire collection.* 他把自己的全部收藏品都借给了博物馆。

'loan shark *noun* (*disapproving*) a person who lends money at very high rates of interest 放高利贷者；放印子钱者

'loan translation *noun* (*linguistics* 语言) = CALQUE

loan·word /ˈləʊnwɜːd; *NAmE* ˈloʊnwɜːrd/ *noun* (*linguistics* 语言) a word from another language used in its original form 借词；外来词：*'Latte' is a loanword from Italian.* * latte 是借自意大利语的外来词。

loath (*also less frequent* **loth**) /ləʊθ; *NAmE* loʊθ/ *adj.* **~ to do sth** (*formal*) not willing to do sth 不情愿；不乐意；勉强：*He was loath to admit his mistake.* 他不愿承认自己的错误。

loathe /ləʊð; *NAmE* loʊð/ *verb* (not used in the progressive tenses 不用于进行时) **~ sb/sth** | **~ doing sth** to dislike sb/sth very much 极不喜欢；厌恶 **SYN** **detest**: *I loathe modern art.* 我很不喜欢现代艺术。◇ *They loathe each other.* 他们相互讨厌对方。➲ SYNONYMS AT HATE

loath·ing /ˈləʊðɪŋ; *NAmE* ˈloʊð-/ *noun* [sing., U] ~ **(for/of sb/sth)** (*formal*) a strong feeling of hatred 憎恨；憎恶；仇恨：*She looked at her attacker with **fear and loathing**.* 她盯着袭击她的歹徒，既害怕又憎恨。◇ *Many soldiers returned with a **deep loathing** of war.* 许多士兵回来时对战争都深恶痛绝。

loath·some /ˈləʊðsəm; *NAmE* ˈloʊð-/ *adj.* (*formal*) extremely unpleasant; disgusting 令人憎恶的；令人厌恶的；令人反感的 **SYN** **repulsive**

loaves PL. OF LOAF

lob /lɒb; *NAmE* lɑːb/ *verb* (-bb-) **1** **~ sth + adv./prep.** (*informal*) to throw sth so that it goes quite high through the air（往空中）高扔，高抛，高掷：*Stones were lobbed over the wall.* 有人把石块扔过了围墙。➲ SYNONYMS AT THROW **2** **~ sth (+ adv./prep.)** (*sport* 体育) to hit or kick a ball in a high curve through the air, especially so that it lands behind the person you are playing against 吊高球，挑高球（尤指把球击或踢到对方的身后）: *He lobbed the ball over the defender's head.* 他把球高挑过防守队员的头顶。 ▶ **lob** *noun* : *to play a lob* 放高球

lobby /ˈlɒbi; *NAmE* ˈlɑːbi/ *noun, verb*

■ ***noun*** (*pl.* **-ies**) **1** [C] a large area inside the entrance of a public building where people can meet and wait（公共建筑物进口处的）门厅，前厅，大厅 SYN **foyer**: *a hotel lobby* 旅馆大厅 **2** [C] (in the British Parliament) a large hall that is open to the public and used for people to meet and talk to Members of Parliament（英国议会的）民众接待厅 **3** [C+sing./pl. v.] a group of people who try to influence politicians on a particular issue（就某议题企图影响从政者的）游说团体 SYN **pressure group**: *The gun lobby is/are against any change in the law.* 赞同拥有枪支的团体反对作任何法律上的修改。 **4** [C, sing.] (*BrE*) an organized attempt by a group of people to influence politicians on a particular issue（就某议题企图影响从政者的）游说: *a recent lobby of Parliament by pensioners* 领养老金者近来在议会的游说

■ ***verb*** (**lob·bies**, **lobby·ing**, **lob·bied**, **lob·bied**) [T, I] ~ (**sb**) (**for/against sth**) to try to influence a politician or the government and, for example, persuade them to support or oppose a change in the law 游说（从政者或政府）: *Farmers will lobby Congress for higher subsidies.* 农民将游说国会提高对农业的补贴。 ◇ *Women's groups are lobbying to get more public money for children.* 妇女组织在游说政府，要求增加对儿童的拨款。 ▶ **lobby·ist** /-ɪst/ *noun* : *political lobbyists* 政治说客

lobe /ləʊb; *NAmE* loʊb/ *noun* **1** = EARLOBE **2** a part of an organ in the body, especially the lungs or brain（身体器官的）叶；（尤指）肺叶，脑叶

lo·belia /ləʊˈbiːliə; *NAmE* loʊ-/ *noun* [C, U] a small garden plant with small blue, red or white flowers 半边莲（园圃植物，花小，呈蓝、红或白色）

lob·ola /ləˈbəʊlə; lɒˈbɔːlə; *NAmE* loʊˈb-/ *noun* [U] (*SAfrE*) in traditional African culture, a sum of money or number of CATTLE that a man's family pays to a woman's family in order that he can marry her（非洲传统文化中男方为娶亲送给女方的）彩礼，彩牛礼: *to pay lobola* 出彩礼

lob·ot·om·ize (*BrE also* **-ise**) /ləˈbɒtəmaɪz; *NAmE* -ˈbɑːt-/ *verb* **1** ~ **sb** to perform a LOBOTOMY on sb 为…施行脑叶切断术 **2** ~ **sb** to make sb less intelligent or less mentally active 使迟钝；使愚笨

lob·ot·omy /ləʊˈbɒtəmi; ləˈb-; *NAmE* loʊˈbɑːt-/ *noun* (*pl.* **-ies**) a rare medical operation that cuts into part of a person's brain in order to treat mental illness 脑叶切断术

lob·ster /ˈlɒbstə(r); *NAmE* ˈlɑːb-/ *noun* **1** [C] a sea creature with a hard shell, a long body divided into sections, eight legs and two large CLAWS (= curved and pointed arms for catching and holding things). Its shell is black but turns bright red when it is boiled. 龙虾 ➲ PICTURE AT SHELLFISH **2** [U] meat from a lobster, used for food（供食用的）龙虾肉

ˈlobster pot *noun* a trap for lobsters that is shaped like a BASKET 诱捕龙虾的笼

local 🔑 /ˈləʊkl; *NAmE* ˈloʊkl/ *adj., noun*

■ ***adj.*** [usually before noun] **1** 🔑 belonging to or connected with the particular place or area that you are talking about or with the place where you live 地方的；当地的；本地的: *a local farmer* 当地的农民 ◇ *A local man was accused of the murder.* 有一本地男子被指控为这起谋杀案的凶手。 ◇ *Our children go to the local school.* 我们的小孩在本地学校就读。 ◇ *a* ***local newspaper*** (= one that gives local news) 地方报纸 ◇ ***local radio*** (= a radio station that broadcasts to one area only) 地方广播电台 ◇ *decisions made at local rather than national level* 地方性而非全国性的决策 ◇ *It was difficult to understand the local dialect.* 当地的方言很难懂。 **2** affecting only one part of the body（身体）局部的: *Her tooth was extracted under* ***local anaesthetic.*** 她的牙齿是局部麻醉下拔出的。 ▶ **lo·cal·ly** 🔑 /-kəli/ *adv.* : *to work locally* 在本地工作 ◇ *Do you live* ***locally*** (= in this area)? 你住在这个地区吗？ ◇ *locally grown fruit* 当地产的水果

■ ***noun*** **1** [usually pl.] a person who lives in a particular place or district 当地人；本地人: *The locals are very friendly.* 当地人很友好。 **2** (*BrE, informal*) a pub near where you live 住处附近的酒吧: *I called in at my local on the way home.* 我回家途中去了我住处附近的酒吧。 **3** (*NAmE*) a branch of a trade/labor union（工会的）地方分会 **4** (*NAmE*) a bus or train that stops at all places on the route（沿线每站都停的）公共汽车，火车

lo·cal /ˌləʊ ˈkæl; *NAmE* ˌloʊ/ *adj.* (*informal*) = LOW-CAL

ˌlocal ˌarea ˈnetwork *noun* = LAN

ˌlocal auˈthority *noun* (*BrE*) the organization which is responsible for the government of an area in Britain（英国的）地方当局，地方政府

ˈlocal call *noun* a telephone call to a place that is near 本地电话；市内电话

ˌlocal ˈcolour (*especially US* **ˌlocal ˈcolor**) *noun* [U] the typical things, customs, etc. in a place that make it interesting, and that are used in a picture, story or film/movie to make it seem real（文艺作品的）地方特色，乡土色彩

lo·cale /ləʊˈkɑːl; *NAmE* loʊˈkæl/ *noun* (*specialist* or *formal*) a place where sth happens 发生地点；现场

ˌlocal ˈgovernment *noun* **1** [U] (*especially BrE*) the system of government of a town or an area by elected representatives of the people who live there 地方自治 **2** [C] (*NAmE*) the organization that is responsible for the government of a local area and for providing services, etc. 地方政府（机构）: *state and local governments* 州和地方政府

lo·cal·ity /ləʊˈkæləti; *NAmE* loʊ-/ *noun* (*pl.* **-ies**) (*formal*) **1** the area that surrounds the place you are in or are talking about（围绕所处或提及的）地区 SYN **vicinity**: *people living in the locality of the power station* 居住在发电站周围地区的人 ◇ *There is no airport* ***in the locality.*** 这个地区没有机场。 **2** the place where sb/sth exists（某人或某物存在的）地方，地点: *We talk of the brain as the locality of thought.* 我们把进行思维的地方叫做大脑。 ◇ *The birds are found in over 70 different localities.* 现已发现这种鸟栖息在 70 多个不同的地区。

lo·cal·ize (*BrE also* **-ise**) /ˈləʊkəlaɪz; *NAmE* ˈloʊ-/ *verb* **1** ~ **sth** to limit sth or its effects to a particular area 使局限（于某地区）；使局部化 SYN **confine** **2** ~ **sth** (*formal*) to find out where sth is 找出…的地点；发现…的位置: *animals' ability to localize sounds* 动物确定声音发自某地点的能力 **3** to make sth suitable for a particular place, area or market 使适合特定地区（或市场）；使本土化: *We will localize the app into French, Japanese, and two written forms of Chinese.* 我们会将该应用程序本地化，使其支持法语、日语和两种书写形式的中文。 ▶ **lo·cal·iza·tion**, **-isa·tion** /ˌləʊkəlaɪˈzeɪʃn; *NAmE* ˌloʊkələˈz-/ *noun* [U]

lo·cal·ized (*BrE also* **-ised**) /ˈləʊkəlaɪzd; *NAmE* ˈloʊ-/ *adj.* (*formal*) happening within one small area 在小范围内的；局部的: *a localized infection* (= in one part of the body) 局部感染 ◇ *localized fighting* 局部战斗

ˈlocal time *noun* [U] the time of day in the particular part of the world that you are talking about 地方时；当地时间: *We reach Delhi at 2 o'clock local time.* 我们在当地时间 2 时到达德里。

lo·cate 🔑 AW /ləʊˈkeɪt; *NAmE* ˈloʊkeɪt/ *verb* **1** 🔑 [T] ~ **sb/sth** to find the exact position of sb/sth 找出…的准确位置；确定…的准确地点: *The mechanic located the fault immediately.* 机修工立即找到了出故障的地方。 ◇ *Rescue planes are trying to locate the missing sailors.* 救援飞机正在努力查明失踪水手的下落。 **2** 🔑 [T] ~ **sth + adv./prep.** to put or build sth in a particular place 把…安置在（或建造于） SYN **site**: *They located their headquarters in Swindon.* 他们把总部设在了斯温登。 ➲ COMPARE RELOCATE **3** [I] + **adv./prep.** (*especially NAmE*) to start a business in a particular place 创办于（某地）: *There are tax breaks* for businesses that locate in rural areas. 在农村地区创办企业享有税收减免。

lo·cated AW /ləʊˈkeɪtɪd; *NAmE* ˈloʊkeɪ-/ *adj.* [not before noun] if sth is **located** in a particular place, it exists there or has been put there 位于；坐落在 SYN **situated**: *a small town located 30 miles south of Chicago* 位于芝加哥以南 30 英里的一个小镇 ◇ *The offices are conveniently located just a few minutes from the main station.* 办事处所处的位置很方便，离总站仅有几分钟的路。

lo·ca·tion AW /ləʊˈkeɪʃn; *NAmE* loʊ-/ *noun* **1** [C] a place where sth happens or exists; the position of sth 地方；地点；位置：*a honeymoon in a secret location* 在一个秘密地点度的蜜月 ◇ *What is the exact location of the ship?* 那条船的确切位置在哪里？ ➲ **SYNONYMS** AT PLACE ➲ **WORDFINDER NOTE** AT HOME

WORDFINDER 联想词: isolated, neighbourhood, outskirts, provincial, residential, rough, rural, suburban, urban

2 [C, U] a place outside a film studio where scenes of a film/movie are made （电影的）外景拍摄地：*The village was used as the location for a popular TV series.* 这个村庄被用作一部热门电视剧集的外景地。◇ *The movie was shot entirely* ***on location*** *in Italy.* 这部影片的外景全是在意大利拍摄的。 ➲ **WORDFINDER NOTE** AT FILM **3** [U] the act of finding the position of sb/sth 定位

L

loca·tive /ˈlɒkətɪv; *NAmE* ˈlɑːk-/ *adj.* (*grammar* 语法) (in some languages 用于某些语言) the form of a noun, pronoun or adjective when it expresses the idea of place （名词、代词或形容词）表示位置的 ➲ SEE ALSO ACCUSATIVE, DATIVE, GENITIVE, NOMINATIVE, VOCATIVE

lo·ca·tor /ləʊˈkeɪtə(r); *NAmE* loʊˈkeɪtər; ˈloʊkeɪtər/ *noun* a device or system for finding sth 定位器；定位系统：*The company lists 5 000 stores on the store locator part of its website.* 这家公司在其网站的商店定位系统部分列出了 5 000 家商店。

loc. cit. /ˌlɒk ˈsɪt; *NAmE* ˌlɑːk/ *abbr.* in the piece of text quoted (from Latin 'loco citato') 在上述引文中（源自拉丁语 loco citato）

loch /lɒk; lɒx; *NAmE* lɑːk; lɑːx/ *noun* (in Scotland 苏格兰) a lake or a narrow strip of sea almost surrounded by land 湖；狭长的海湾 ➲ SEE ALSO LOUGH

loci PL. OF LOCUS

lock /lɒk; *NAmE* lɑːk/ *verb, noun*

■ ***verb*** **1** [T, I] ~ **(sth)** to fasten sth with a lock; to be fastened with a lock （用锁）锁上；被锁住：*Did you lock the door?* 你锁门了吗？ ◇ *This suitcase doesn't lock.* 这手提箱锁不上。 **2** [T] **~ sth + adv./prep.** to put sth in a safe place and lock it 把…锁起来：*She locked her passport and money in the safe.* 她把自己的护照和钱锁在了保险柜里。 **3** [I, T] ~ **(sth) (in/into/around, etc. sth)** | ~ **(sth) (together)** to become or make sth become fixed in one position and unable to move （使）固定，卡住，塞住：*The brakes locked and the car skidded.* 汽车刹车抱死，车打滑了。 ◇ *He locked his helmet into position with a click.* 他咔哒一声把头盔扣好。 **4** [T] **be locked in/into sth** to be involved in a difficult situation, an argument, a disagreement, etc. 陷入，卷入（困境、争论、争执等）：*The two sides are locked into a bitter dispute.* 双方陷入了激烈的争论。 ◇ *She felt locked in a loveless marriage.* 她觉得自己陷入了一桩没有爱情的婚姻。 **5** [T] **be locked together/in sth** to be held very tightly by sb 被紧紧抓住（或抱住）：*They were locked in a passionate embrace.* 他们热烈地拥抱在一起。 **6** [T] **~ sth** (*computing* 计) to prevent computer data from being changed or looked at by sb without permission 加锁；锁（定、紧）：*These files are locked to protect confidentiality.* 为了保密，这些文件都加了锁。

IDM **lock 'horns (with sb) (over sth)** to get involved in an argument or a disagreement with sb 涉及（与某人的）争论（或争端、纠纷）：*The company has locked horns with the unions over proposed pay cuts.* 公司与工会就减薪计划争论不休。

PHR V **ˌlock sb aˈway** = LOCK SB↔UP/AWAY **ˌlock sth aˈway** = LOCK STH↔UP/AWAY **ˌlock sb/yourself ˈin (...)** to prevent sb from leaving a place by locking the door 把…锁在屋里；把…关押起来：*At 9 p.m. the prisoners are locked in for the night.* 晚上 9 点犯人被关进牢房里过夜。 **ˌlock ˈonto sth** (of a MISSILE, etc. 导弹等) to find the thing that is being attacked and follow it 跟踪，锁定（攻击目标） **ˌlock sb/yourself ˈout (of sth)** to prevent sb from entering a place by locking the door 把…锁在门外：*I'd locked myself out of the house and had to break a window to get in.* 我把自己锁在了门外，不得不破窗而入。 **ˌlock sb ˈout** (of an employer 雇主) to refuse to allow workers into their place of work until they agree to particular conditions （在工人答应某些条件前）不准进入工作场地 ➲ RELATED NOUN LOCKOUT **ˌlock ˈup** | **ˌlock sth↔ˈup** to make a building safe by locking the doors and windows 锁好门窗：*Don't forget to lock up at night.* 晚上别忘了锁好门窗。◇ *He locked up the shop and went home.* 他锁好商店的门窗后回家了。 **ˌlock sb↔ˈup/aˈway** (*informal*) to put sb in prison 把某人关进监狱 ➲ RELATED NOUN LOCK-UP **ˌlock sth↔ˈup/aˈway** **1** to put sth in a safe place that can be locked 把…收好并锁起来 **2** to put money into an investment that you cannot easily turn into cash 把（钱）搁死（成为不易兑现的资本）：*Their capital is all locked up in property.* 他们把所有资金都搁死在地产上了。

■ ***noun*** **1** [C] a device that keeps a door, window, lid, etc. shut, usually needing a key to open it 锁：*She turned the key in the lock.* 她转动锁眼里的钥匙。 ➲ SEE ALSO COMBINATION LOCK **2** [C] a device with a key that prevents a vehicle or machine from being used 车锁；制动器；锁定器；制轮楔：*a bicycle lock* 自行车的车锁 ◇ *a steering lock* 转向锁 **3** [U] a state in which the parts of a machine, etc. do not move （机器部件等的）锁定 **4** [U, sing.] (*BrE*) (on a car, etc. 汽车等) the amount that the front wheels can be turned in one direction or the other in order to turn the vehicle 前轮转向角度：*I had the steering wheel* ***on full lock*** (= I had turned it as far as it would turn). 我把方向盘转到了底。 **5** [C] a section of CANAL or river with a gate at either end, in which the water level can be changed so that boats can move from one level of the canal or river to another （运河或河流的）闸，船闸 **6** [C] a few hairs that hang or lie together on your head 一绺（或一缕）头发：*John brushed a* ***lock of hair*** *from his eyes.* 约翰撩开眼前的一绺头发。 **7 locks** [pl.] (*literary*) a person's hair 头发：*She shook her long, flowing locks.* 她甩了甩她那飘逸的长发。 **8** [C] (in RUGBY 橄榄球) a player in the second row of the SCRUM （并列争球的）第二排前锋，锁球队员 **9** [sing.] **a ~ (on sth)** (*NAmE*) total control of sth （对某事物的）完全控制：*One company* ***had a virtual lock on*** *all orange juice sales in the state.* 有一家公司实际上垄断了整个州的橙汁销售。 ➲ SEE ALSO ARMLOCK, HEADLOCK

IDM **ˌlock, stock and ˈbarrel** including everything 全部；所有：*He sold the business lock, stock and barrel.* 他把生意全盘卖掉了。 **(keep sth/put sth/be) under ˌlock and ˈkey** locked up safely somewhere; in prison 把…安全地锁起来；在押；被囚禁：*We keep our valuables under lock and key.* 我们把贵重物品锁起来收好了。 ◇ *I will not rest until the murderer is under lock and key.* 杀人凶手一天不关起来我一天不罢休。 ➲ MORE AT PICK *v.*

lock·able /ˈlɒkəbl; *NAmE* ˈlɑːk-/ *adj.* that you can lock with a key 可锁定的；能锁的

lock·down /ˈlɒkdaʊn; *NAmE* ˈlɑːk-/ *noun* [C, U] (*especially NAmE*) an official order to control the movement of people or vehicles because of a dangerous situation （对人或交通工具的）活动限制，行动限制：*a three-day lockdown of American airspace* 美国为期三天的领空关闭 ◇ *Prisoners have been placed on lockdown to prevent further violence at the jail.* 已对囚犯实行活动限制，以免狱中再出现暴力行为。

ˌlocked-ˈin syndrome *noun* [U] a medical condition, usually resulting from a STROKE, in which the person is conscious but unable to feel or move the body and most of the muscles in the face 闭锁综合征（患者意识清

醒，但身体和脸部肌肉失去知觉且难以动弹，通常为脑卒中后遗症）

lock·er /ˈlɒkə(r); *NAmE* ˈlɑːk-/ *noun* a small cupboard that can be locked, where you can leave your clothes, bags, etc. while you play a sport or go somewhere（体育馆等的）有锁存物柜，寄存柜 ➲ VISUAL VOCAB PAGE V72

ˈlocker room *noun* a room with lockers in it, at a school, GYM, etc., where people can change their clothes（学校、体育馆等设有锁柜的）更衣室，衣物间 ➲ COMPARE CHANGING ROOM

locket /ˈlɒkɪt; *NAmE* ˈlɑːk-/ *noun* a piece of jewellery in the form of a small case that you wear on a chain around your neck and in which you can put a picture, piece of hair, etc. 盒式项链坠（可放照片、头发等）➲ VISUAL VOCAB PAGE V70

ˈlock-in *noun* (*BrE*) an occasion when customers are locked in a bar or club after it has closed so that they can continue drinking privately（酒吧或夜总会打烊后）留置顾客续饮

lock·jaw /ˈlɒkdʒɔː; *NAmE* ˈlɑːk-/ *noun* [U] (*old-fashioned, informal*) a form of the disease TETANUS in which the JAWS become stiff and closed 牙关紧闭；口噤

ˈlock-keeper *noun* a person who is in charge of a LOCK on a CANAL or river, and opens and closes the gates（运河或河流上的）船闸管理员

lock·out /ˈlɒkaʊt; *NAmE* ˈlɑːk-/ *noun* a situation when an employer refuses to allow workers into their place of work until they agree to various conditions 闭厂，停工（雇主在工人答应各种条件前不准其进入工作场地）

lock·smith /ˈlɒksmɪθ; *NAmE* ˈlɑːk-/ *noun* a person whose job is making, fitting and repairing locks 锁匠；修锁工

lock·step /ˈlɒkstep; *NAmE* ˈlɑːk-/ *noun* [U] (*especially NAmE*) **1** a way of walking together where people move their feet at the same time 齐步走（步伐）：*The coffin was carried by six soldiers walking* ***in lockstep***. 灵柩由齐步行进的六名士兵抬着。◇ (*figurative*) *Politicians and the media are* ***marching in lockstep*** *on this issue* (= they agree). 政界和媒体在这一问题上保持一致。 **2** a situation where things happen at the same time or change at the same rate 同生同变：*a lockstep approach to teaching* 使学生齐头并进的教学方法 ◇ *Cases of breathing difficulties increase* ***in lockstep with*** *air pollution.* 呼吸困难的病例随空气污染的加剧而增加。

ˈlock-up *noun* **1** a small prison where prisoners are kept for a short time 拘留所；（短期关押犯人的）监狱 **2** (*BrE*) a small shop that the owner does not live in; a garage that is usually separate from other buildings and that is rented to sb（店主不住在内的）小商店；（不和其他建筑物相连供出租的）车库 ▶ **ˈlock-up** *adj.* [only before noun]: *a lock-up garage* 出租的独立车库

loco /ˈləʊkəʊ; *NAmE* ˈloʊkoʊ/ *noun, adj.*
▪ ***noun*** (*pl.* **-os**) (*informal*) = LOCOMOTIVE ➲ SEE ALSO IN LOCO PARENTIS
▪ ***adj.*** [not before noun] (*slang, especially NAmE*) crazy 发疯；发狂

loco·mo·tion /ˌləʊkəˈməʊʃn; *NAmE* ˌloʊkəˈmoʊʃn/ *noun* [U] (*formal*) movement or the ability to move 移动（力）；运动（力）

loco·mo·tive /ˌləʊkəˈməʊtɪv; *NAmE* ˌloʊkəˈmoʊ-/ (*also informal* **loco**) *noun, adj.*
▪ ***noun*** a railway engine that pulls a train 机车；火车头：***steam/diesel/electric locomotives*** 蒸汽 / 内燃 / 电力机车 ➲ WORDFINDER NOTE AT TRAIN ➲ VISUAL VOCAB PAGE V63
▪ ***adj.*** (*formal*) connected with movement 移动的；运动的

locum /ˈləʊkəm; *NAmE* ˈloʊ-/ *noun* (*BrE*) a doctor or priest who does the work of another doctor or priest while they are sick, on holiday, etc. 代班医生；代理牧师

locus /ˈləʊkəs; *NAmE* ˈloʊ-/ *noun* (*pl.* **loci** /ˈləʊsaɪ; *NAmE* ˈloʊsaɪ/) (*specialist or formal*) the exact place where sth happens or which is thought to be the centre of sth（某事发生的）确切地点；（被视为某物的）中心，核心

lo·cust /ˈləʊkəst; *NAmE* ˈloʊ-/ *noun* a large insect that lives in hot countries and flies in large groups, destroying all the plants and crops of an area 蝗虫：*a swarm of locusts* 一大群蝗虫

lo·cu·tion /ləˈkjuːʃn/ *noun* (*specialist*) **1** [U] a style of speaking 语言风格；语言表达方式 **2** [C] a particular phrase, especially one used by a particular group of people（尤指某类人的）惯用语，习语

lode /ləʊd; *NAmE* loʊd/ *noun* a line of ORE (= metal in the ground or in rocks) 矿脉

lode·star (*also* **load·star**) /ˈləʊdstɑː(r); *NAmE* ˈloʊd-/ *noun* **1** the POLE STAR (= a star that is used by sailors to guide a ship) 北极星（海员借以导航） **2** (*formal*) a principle that guides sb's behaviour or actions（某人行为或行动的）指导原则

lode·stone (*also* **load·stone**) /ˈləʊdstəʊn; *NAmE* ˈloʊdstoʊn/ *noun* a piece of iron that acts as a MAGNET 磁铁矿

lodge /lɒdʒ; *NAmE* lɑːdʒ/ *noun, verb*
▪ ***noun*** **1** [C] a small house in the country where people stay when they want to take part in some types of outdoor sport（供参加户外运动者暂住的）乡间小屋，小舍：*a hunting lodge* 供打猎者居住的小屋 **2** [C] a small house at the gates of a park or in the land belonging to a large house（公园或宅第的）门口小屋，门房 **3** [C] a room at the main entrance to a building for the person whose job is to see who enters and leaves the building 管理员室；传达室：*All visitors should report to the porter's lodge.* 所有来访者都应先到传达室通报。 **4** [C+sing./pl. v.] the members of a branch of a society such as the Freemasons; the building where they meet（共济会等会社的）地方分会，集会处：*a masonic lodge* 共济会的地方分会 **5** [C] the home of a BEAVER or an OTTER（河狸或水獭的）穴，窝 **6** [C] a Native American's tent or home built of LOGS（美洲土著居民的）帐篷，原木住宅 **7** [C] a small house, often made from wood, where people stay on holiday/vacation, especially in a small village that has been built for this purpose（乡村）度假小屋：*a holiday lodge* 度假小屋
▪ ***verb*** **1** [T] **~ sth (with sb) (against sb/sth)** (*formal*) to make a formal statement about sth to a public organization or authority（向公共机构或当局）正式提出（声明等）SYN **register, submit**: *They lodged a compensation claim against the factory.* 他们向工厂提出了赔偿要求。◇ *Portugal has lodged a complaint with the International Court of Justice.* 葡萄牙向国际法院提出了申诉。 **2** [I] **+ adv./prep.** (*old-fashioned*) to pay to live in a room in sb's house（付款）寄住，借宿；租住 SYN **board**: *He lodged with Mrs Brown when he arrived in the city.* 他初到这座城市时租住在布朗太太的家里。 **3** [T] **~ sb (+ adv./prep.)** to provide sb with a place to sleep or live 为（某人）提供住宿 SYN **accommodate**: *The refugees are being lodged at an old army base.* 难民被安置在一座旧的军事基地里住宿。 **4** [I, T] to become fixed or stuck somewhere; to make sth become fixed or stuck somewhere（被）固定，卡住：**~ in sth** *One of the bullets lodged in his chest.* 有一颗子弹嵌在了他的胸部。◇ **~ sth in sth** *She lodged the number firmly in her mind.* 她把号码牢牢记在心中。 **5** [T] **~ sth with sb/in sth** to leave money or sth valuable in a safe place 存放，寄存（钱或贵重物品）SYN **deposit**: *Your will should be lodged with your lawyer.* 你的遗嘱应该交律师保管。

lodg·er /ˈlɒdʒə(r); *NAmE* ˈlɑːdʒ-/ *noun* (*especially BrE*) a person who pays rent to live in sb's house 租房人；房客

lodg·ing /ˈlɒdʒɪŋ; *NAmE* ˈlɑːdʒ-/ *noun* (*especially BrE*) **1** [U] temporary accommodation 暂住；寄宿；借宿：*full board and lodging* (= a room to stay in and all meals provided) 食宿全包 **2** [C, usually pl.] (*old-fashioned*) a room or rooms in sb else's house that you rent to live in 租住的房间：*It was cheaper to live in lodgings than in a hotel.* 住出租的房间比住旅馆便宜。

ˈlodging house *noun* (*old-fashioned, BrE*) a house in which lodgings can be rented 有供出租用房间的公寓（或房屋）

L

loft /lɒft; *NAmE* lɔːft; lɑːft/ *noun, verb*
■ *noun* **1** (*especially BrE*) a space just below the roof of a house, often used for storing things and sometimes made into a room 阁楼，顶楼（常用以贮物，间或作房间）：*a **loft conversion*** (= one that has been made into a room or rooms for living in) 用阁楼改装的居室 ➲ COMPARE ATTIC, GARRET **2** an upper level in a church, or a farm or factory building（教堂的）楼厢；（农场的）厩楼；（工厂的）上层楼面：*the organ loft* 教堂内的管风琴台 **3** a flat/apartment in a former factory, etc., that has been made suitable for living in（由工厂等改建的）套房，公寓：*They lived in a SoHo loft.* 他们居住在索霍区改建的公寓里。 **4** (*NAmE*) a part of a room that is on a higher level than the rest（房间的）跃层：*The children slept in a loft in the upstairs bedroom.* 孩子们睡在楼上卧室里的跃层上。
■ *verb* ~ sth (*sport* 体育) to hit, kick or throw a ball very high into the air 向高处击（或踢、掷）

lofty /ˈlɒfti; *NAmE* ˈlɔːfti; ˈlɑːfti/ *adj.* (**loft·ier**, **lofti·est**) (*formal*) **1** (of buildings, mountains, etc. 建筑物、山等) very high and impressive 巍峨的；高耸的：*lofty ceilings/rooms/towers* 高高的顶棚；屋顶高的房间；高耸的塔楼 **2** [usually before noun] (*approving*) (of a thought, an aim, etc. 思想、目标等) deserving praise because of its high moral quality 崇高的；高尚的：***lofty ambitions/ideals/principles*** 崇高的抱负 / 理想 / 原则 **3** (*disapproving*) showing a belief that you are worth more than other people 傲慢的；高傲的 SYN **haughty**：*her lofty disdain for other people* 她对别人不屑一顾的傲慢态度 ▸ **loft·ily** /-ɪli/ *adv.* **lofti·ness** *noun* [U]

log /lɒg; *NAmE* lɔːg; lɑːg/ *noun, verb*
■ *noun* **1** a thick piece of wood that is cut from or has fallen from a tree 原木：*logs for the fire* 烧火用的木材 ➲ VISUAL VOCAB PAGE V10 **2** (*also* **log·book**) an official record of events during a particular period of time, especially a journey on a ship or plane（某时期事件的）正式记录，日志；（尤指）航海日志，飞行日志：*The captain keeps a log.* 船长记航海日志。 **3** (*informal*) = LOGARITHM
IDM SEE EASY *adj.*, SLEEP *v.*
■ *verb* (-gg-) **1** ~ sth to put information in an official record or write a record of events 把…载入正式记录；记录 SYN **record**：*The police log all phone calls.* 警方对所有电话都做了记录。 **2** ~ sth to travel a particular distance or for a particular length of time 行驶，行进（若干距离或时间）SYN **clock up**：*The pilot has logged 1 000 hours in the air.* 这位飞行员有 1 000 小时的飞行记录。 **3** ~ sth to cut down trees in a forest for their wood 采伐（森林的）树木；伐木 ➲ MORE LIKE THIS 36, page R29
PHR V ˌ**log ˈin/ˈon** (*computing* 计) to perform the actions that allow you to begin using a computer system 登录，注册，进入，登入（计算机系统）：*You need a password to log on.* 登录需要密码。 ˌ**log sb ↔ˈin/ˈon** (*computing* 计) to allow sb to begin using a computer system 让某人登录，使注册，使进入（计算机系统）：*The system is unable to log you on.* 这个系统无法让你登录。 ˌ**log ˈoff/ˈout** (*computing* 计) to perform the actions that allow you to finish using a computer system 退出，注销（计算机系统） ˌ**log sb ↔ˈoff/ˈout** (*computing* 计) to cause sb to finish using a computer system 使注销，使退出（计算机系统）

-log (*NAmE*) = -LOGUE

lo·gan·berry /ˈləʊgənbəri; *NAmE* ˈloʊgənberi/ *noun* (*pl.* **-ies**) a soft dark red fruit, like a large RASPBERRY, that grows on a bush 罗甘莓

loga·rithm /ˈlɒgərɪðəm; *NAmE* ˈlɔːg-; ˈlɑːg-/ (*also informal* **log**) *noun* (*mathematics* 数) any of a series of numbers set out in lists which make it possible to work out problems by adding and SUBTRACTING instead of multiplying and dividing 对数 ➲ WORDFINDER NOTE AT MATHS ▸ **loga·rith·mic** /ˌlɒgəˈrɪðmɪk; *NAmE* ˌlɔːg-; ˌlɑːg-/ *adj.*

log·book /ˈlɒgbʊk; *NAmE* ˈlɔːg-; ˈlɑːg-/ *noun* **1** (*BrE, becoming old-fashioned*) a document that records official details about a vehicle, especially a car, and its owner（交通工具，尤指小汽车的）行驶日志 ➲ COMPARE REGISTRATION (2) **2** = LOG (2)

ˌ**log ˈcabin** *noun* a small house built of logs 原木小屋 ➲ VISUAL VOCAB PAGE V15

log·ger /ˈlɒgə(r); *NAmE* ˈlɔːg-; ˈlɑːg-/ *noun* = LUMBERJACK

log·ger·heads /ˈlɒgəhedz; *NAmE* ˈlɔːgər-; ˈlɑːgər-/ *noun*
IDM **at loggerheads (with sb) (over sth)** in strong disagreement（与某人）不和；相争；严重分歧：*The two governments are still at loggerheads over the island.* 两国政府依然对这个岛的归属问题争执不下。

log·gia /ˈləʊdʒə; ˈlɒdʒiə; *NAmE* ˈloʊdʒə; ˈlɑːdʒiə/ *noun* a room or GALLERY with one or more open sides, especially one that forms part of a house and has one side open to the garden 凉廊（敞向花园的房间或走廊）

log·ging /ˈlɒgɪŋ; *NAmE* ˈlɔːg-; ˈlɑːg-/ *noun* [U] the work of cutting down trees for their wood 伐木作业

logic 🔑 AW /ˈlɒdʒɪk; *NAmE* ˈlɑːdʒɪk/ *noun* **1** 🔑 [U] a way of thinking or explaining sth 思维方式；解释方法；逻辑：*I fail to see the logic behind his argument.* 我不明白支持他论据的是什么逻辑。 ◇ *The two parts of the plan were governed by the same logic.* 计划的两个部分基于同一思维方式。 **2** 🔑 [U, sing.] sensible reasons for doing sth（做某事的）道理，合乎情理的原因：*Linking the proposals in a single package did have a certain logic.* 把这些提议联系起来成为一揽子提议确有一定的道理。 ◇ *a strategy based on sound commercial logic* 基于合理商业考虑的策略 ◇ *There is **no logic to/in** any of their claims.* 他们的说法全都不合理。 **3** 🔑 [U] (*philosophy* 哲) the science of thinking about or explaining the reason for sth using formal methods 逻辑学：*the rules of logic* 逻辑学规则 **4** [U] (*computing* 计) a system or set of principles used in preparing a computer to perform a particular task 逻辑系统；操作规则

lo·gic·al 🔑 AW /ˈlɒdʒɪkl; *NAmE* ˈlɑːdʒ-/ *adj.* **1** 🔑 (of an action, event, etc. 行动、事件等) seeming natural, reasonable or sensible 必然的；合乎情理的；合乎常理的：*a logical thing to do in the circumstances* 在那种环境下按理应做的事 ◇ *It was a logical conclusion from the child's point of view.* 从小孩的观点来看这是个合乎情理的结论。 **2** 🔑 following or able to follow the rules of logic in which ideas or facts are based on other true ideas or facts 符合逻辑的；按照逻辑的：*a logical argument* 合乎逻辑的论证 ◇ *Computer programming needs someone with a logical mind.* 计算机编程需要擅长逻辑思维的人。 OPP **illogical** ▸ **logic·al·ly** AW /-kli/ *adv.*：*to argue logically* 合乎逻辑地辩论

-logical, **-logic** ➲ -OLOGY

ˌ**logical ˈpositivism** *noun* [U] (*philosophy* 哲) the belief that the only problems which have meaning are those that can be solved using logical thinking 逻辑实证论，逻辑实证主义，逻辑经验主义（认为只有能用逻辑思维解决的问题才有意义）

ˈ**logic circuit** *noun* (*computing* 计) a series of logic gates that performs operations on data that is put into a computer 逻辑电路（由一系列进行数据运算的逻辑门组成）

ˈ**logic gate** (*also* **gate**) *noun* (*computing* 计) an electronic switch that reacts in one of two ways to data that is put into it. A computer performs operations by passing data through a very large number of logic gates. 逻辑门，逻辑闸（以两种方式之一对所输入数据进行输出的电子开关）

lo·gi·cian AW /ləˈdʒɪʃn/ *noun* a person who studies or is skilled in logic 逻辑学研究者；逻辑学家

login /ˈlɒgɪn; *NAmE* ˈlɔːg-; ˈlɑːg-/ (*also* **logon**) *noun* **1** [U] the act of starting to use a computer system, usually by typing a name or word that you choose to use 注册，登录（通过键入名称或词进入计算机系统的操作）：*If you've forgotten your login ID, click this link.* 如果忘记了自己的注册账号就点击此链接。 **2** [C] the name that you use to enter a computer system 登录名：*Enter your login and password and press 'go'.* 键入登录名和密码，然后按下 go 按钮。

-logist ➲ -OLOGY

lo·gis·tics /lə'dʒɪstɪks/ *noun* **1** [U+sing./pl. v.] ~ (**of sth**) the practical organization that is needed to make a complicated plan successful when a lot of people and equipment are involved 后勤；组织工作：*the logistics of moving the company to a new building* 把公司搬迁到一座新大楼的过程中需要进行的组织工作 **2** [U] (*business* 商) the business of transporting and delivering goods 物流 **3** [U] the activity of moving equipment, supplies and people for military operations 军事后勤：*a revolution in military logistics* 军队后勤变革 ▶ **lo·gis·tic** (*also* **lo·gis·tic·al** /lə'dʒɪstɪkl/) *adj.*：*logistic support* 后勤支持 ◇ *Organizing famine relief presents huge logistical problems.* 组织饥荒救济工作涉及繁重的安排协调问题。**lo·gis·tic·al·ly** /-kli/ *adv.*

log·jam /'lɒgdʒæm; *NAmE* 'lɔːg-; 'lɑːg-/ *noun* **1** a difficult situation in which you cannot make progress easily because there are too many things to do（因事情太多造成的）困境，僵局 SYN **bottleneck** **2** a mass of LOGS floating on a river and blocking it（河面上）漂浮原木造成的阻塞

logo /'ləʊgəʊ; *NAmE* 'loʊgoʊ/ *noun* (*pl.* **-os**) a printed design or symbol that a company or an organization uses as its special sign（某公司或机构的）标识，标志，徽标

log·off /'lɒgɒf; *NAmE* 'lɔːgɔːf; 'lɑːg-; -ɑːf/ (*also* **log·out**) *noun* [U] the act of finishing using a computer system（从计算机系统）退出；注销

logo·gram /'lɒgəgræm; *NAmE* 'lɔːg-; 'lɑːg-/ (*also* **logo·graph** /'lɒgəgrɑːf; *NAmE* 'lɔːgəgræf; 'lɑːgəgræf/) *noun* (*specialist*) a symbol that represents a word or phrase, for example those used in ancient writing systems 词符；语符；速记符

logon /'lɒgɒn; *NAmE* 'lɔːgɑːn; 'lɑːg-; -ɔːn/ *noun* = LOGIN

log·out /'lɒgaʊt; *NAmE* 'lɔːg-; 'lɑːg-/ *noun* = LOGOFF

log·roll·ing /'lɒgrəʊlɪŋ; *NAmE* 'lɔːgroʊ-; 'lɑːg-/ *noun* [U] (*NAmE*) **1** (in US politics 美国政治) the practice of agreeing with sb that you will vote to pass a law that they support so that they will later vote to pass a law that you support 互投赞成票（促使议案通过） **2** a sport in which two people stand on a LOG floating on water and try to knock each other off by moving the log with their feet 水上滚木比赛（两人同时站在浮于水面的圆木上设法转动滚木使对方落水）

-logue (*NAmE also* **-log**) *combining form* (in nouns 构成名词) talk or speech 谈话；讲话：*a monologue* 独白

-logy ➲ -OLOGY

loin /lɔɪn/ *noun* **1** [U, C] a piece of meat from the back or sides of an animal, near the tail（动物的）腰肉：*loin of pork* 猪后腰肉 **2** **loins** [pl.] (*old-fashioned*) the part of the body around the hips between the waist and the tops of the legs 腰部；后腰 **3** **loins** [pl.] (*literary*) a person's sex organs（人的）性器官，阴部，下身 IDM SEE GIRD

loin·cloth /'lɔɪnklɒθ; *NAmE* -klɔːθ; -klɑːθ/ *noun* a piece of cloth worn around the body at the hips by men in some hot countries, sometimes as the only piece of clothing worn（某些热带国家男子的）缠腰布，遮羞布

loi·ter /'lɔɪtə(r)/ *verb* [I] to stand or wait somewhere especially with no obvious reason 闲站着；闲荡；徘徊 SYN **hang around**：*Teenagers were loitering in the street outside.* 青少年在外面街上闲荡。

LOL /ˌel əʊ 'el; *NAmE* oʊ/ *abbr.* LAUGH-OUT-LOUD 非常滑稽的

Lo·li·ta /ləʊ'liːtə; *NAmE* loʊ-/ *noun* a young girl who behaves in a more sexually developed way than is usual for her age, which makes her sexually attractive to older men（吸引年长男性的）早熟性感少女 ORIGIN From the name of the main character in Vladimir Nabokov's novel *Lolita*. 源自弗拉基米尔·纳博科夫所著小说《洛丽塔》中主人公的名字。

loll /lɒl; *NAmE* lɑːl/ *verb* **1** [I] + **adv./prep.** to lie, sit or stand in a lazy, relaxed way 懒洋洋地躺着（或坐着、站着）：*He lolled back in his chair by the fire.* 他懒洋洋地靠着椅背坐在炉火边。 **2** [I] + **adv./prep.** (of your head, tongue, etc. 头、舌等) to move or hang in a relaxed way 耷拉；下垂：*My head lolled against his shoulder.* 我把头懒懒地靠在他的肩上。

lol·li·pop /'lɒlipɒp; *NAmE* 'lɑːlipɑːp/ (*also BrE, informal* **lolly**) (*also NAmE, informal* **suck·er**) *noun* a hard round or flat sweet/candy made of boiled sugar on a small stick 棒棒糖

'lollipop man, 'lollipop lady *noun* (*BrE, informal*) a person whose job is to help children cross a busy road on their way to and from school by holding up a sign on a stick telling traffic to stop（手持车辆暂停牌以帮助学童穿越马路的）交通安全员

lol·lop /'lɒləp; *NAmE* 'lɑːləp/ *verb* [I] (+ **adv./prep.**) (*informal, especially BrE*) to walk or run with long awkward steps 跌跌撞撞地走（或跑）：*The dog came lolloping towards them.* 那条狗蹒跚地向他们跑来。

lolly /'lɒli; *NAmE* 'lɑːli/ *noun* (*pl.* **-ies**) (*informal*) **1** [C] (*BrE*) = LOLLIPOP **2** [C] (*BrE*) = ICE LOLLY **3** [U] (*old-fashioned, BrE*) money 钱 **4** [C] (*AustralE, NZE*) a sweet or a piece of candy 糖果；糖块儿

lolz (*also* **lols**) /lɒlz; *NAmE* lɑːlz/ *exclamation* (*informal*) (in emails, comments on SOCIAL NETWORKING websites, etc.) used to express fun, laughter or the feeling that sth is amusing（用于电邮、社交网站上的评论等，表示逗乐、大笑或好玩）：*The dog kept running around chasing its tail. Lolz.* 那只狗一直追着自己的尾巴转圈跑。真逗！➲ COMPARE LULZ ▶ **lolz** *noun* [pl.]：*This is no time for lolz—we're dealing with a serious matter!* 这不是玩闹的时候，我们正在处理一件严肃的事！◇ *He went to the supermarket in his pyjamas, just for lolz.* 他穿着睡衣去了超市，就为了搞笑。

Lon·don·er /'lʌndənə(r)/ *noun* a person from London in England 伦敦人

lone /ləʊn; *NAmE* loʊn/ *adj.* [only before noun] **1** without any other people or things 单独的；独自的；孤零零的 SYN **solitary**：*a lone sailor crossing the Atlantic* 独自横渡大西洋的人 **2** (*especially BrE*) without a husband, wife or partner to share the care of children 单亲的 SYN **single**：*a lone mother/parent/father* 单亲母亲 / 父亲 ➲ NOTE AT ALONE ➲ MORE LIKE THIS 32, page R28

IDM **a ˌlone 'wolf** a person who prefers to be alone 好独处的人；喜欢单干的人

lone·ly /'ləʊnli; *NAmE* 'loʊn-/ *adj.* (**lone·lier**, **lone·li·est**) **1** unhappy because you have no friends or people to talk to 孤独的；寂寞的：*She lives alone and often feels lonely.* 她孑然一身，常感到寂寞。 **2** (of a situation or period of time 情况或一段时间) sad and spent alone 在孤单中度过的：*all those lonely nights at home watching TV* 所有那些在家看电视的孤寂夜晚 **3** [only before noun] (of places 地方) where only a few people ever come or visit 偏僻的；人迹罕至的 SYN **isolated**：*a lonely beach* 人迹罕至的海滩 ➲ NOTE AT ALONE ▶ **lone·li·ness** *noun* [U]：*a period of loneliness in his life* 他一生中孤苦伶仃的一段时间

ˌlonely 'hearts *adj.* [only before noun] a **lonely hearts** column in a newspaper, etc. is where people can advertise for a new lover or friend（在报纸等征友专栏登广告）征求爱侣的，征友的：*He placed a lonely hearts ad in a magazine.* 他在一份杂志上刊登了征友广告。

ˌlone-parent 'family *noun* = ONE-PARENT FAMILY

loner /'ləʊnə(r); *NAmE* 'loʊn-/ *noun* a person who is often alone or who prefers to be alone, rather than with other people 独来独往的人；喜欢独处的人；不合群的人

lone·some /'ləʊnsəm; *NAmE* 'loʊn-/ *adj.*, *noun*

■ *adj.* (*especially NAmE*) **1** unhappy because you are alone and do not want to be or because you have no friends 孤独的；寂寞的：*I felt so lonesome after he left.* 他离开后我感到非常孤单。 **2** (of a place 地方) where not many people go; a long way from where people live 人烟稀少

的；荒凉的；偏僻的：*a lonesome road* 偏僻的路 ➲ NOTE AT ALONE

■ ***noun***

IDM **(all) by/on your lonesome** (*informal*) alone 单独；独自：*Are you here all by your lonesome?* 只有你一个人在这儿吗？

long 🔑 /lɒŋ; *NAmE* lɔːŋ; lɑːŋ/ *adj., adv., verb*

> **WORD FAMILY**
> **long** *adj., adv.*
> **length** *noun*
> **lengthy** *adj.*
> **lengthen** *verb*

■ ***adj.*** (**long·er** /ˈlɒŋɡə(r); *NAmE* ˈlɔːŋ-; ˈlɑːŋ-/, **long·est** /ˈlɒŋɡɪst; *NAmE* ˈlɔːŋ-; ˈlɑːŋ-/)

• **DISTANCE** 距离 **1** 🔑 measuring or covering a great length or distance, or a greater length or distance than usual （长度或距离）长的：*She had long dark hair.* 她留着黑黑的长发。◇ *He walked down the long corridor.* 他沿长廊走去。◇ *It was the world's longest bridge.* 那座桥当时是世界上最长的。◇ ***a long journey/walk/drive/flight*** 长途旅行 / 步行 / 驾驶 / 飞行 ◇ *We're* ***a long way*** *from anywhere here.* 我们这里离任何一个地方都很远。◇ *It's* ***a long way away.*** 那儿离这里很远。 ➲ VISUAL VOCAB PAGE V65 OPP **short** **2** 🔑 used for asking or talking about particular lengths or distances（询问或谈论长度或距离）长：***How long*** *is the River Nile?* 尼罗河有多长？◇ *The table is six feet long.* 那张桌子长六英尺。◇ *The report is only three pages long.* 这份报告仅有三页。

• **TIME** 时间 **3** 🔑 lasting or taking a great amount of time or more time than usual 长时间的；长久的；长期的：*He's been ill* ***(for) a long time.*** 他生病很久了。◇ *There was a long silence before she spoke.* 沉默了很长时间她才开口。◇ *I like it now the days are getting longer* (= it stays light for more time each day). 白天越来越长了，我很喜欢。◇ ***a long book/film/list*** (= taking a lot of time to read/watch/deal with) 篇幅长的书；放映时间长的电影；一份很长的清单 ◇ *Nurses have to work* ***long hours*** (= for more hours in the day than is usual). 护士都不得不长时间地工作。◇ (*NAmE*) *He stared at them* ***for the longest time*** (= for a very long time) *before answering.* 他盯着他们看了好长时间才回答。 OPP **short** **4** 🔑 used for asking or talking about particular periods of time（询问或谈论某段时间）：***How long*** *is the course?* 这门课程要念多久？◇ *I think it's only three weeks long.* 我想只有三个星期长。◇ *How long a stay did you have in mind?* 你原打算待多长时间？ **5** 🔑 seeming to last or take more time than it really does because, for example, you are very busy or not happy （因忙或不愉快等）似乎比实际时间长的：*I'm tired. It's been a long day.* 我累了。这一天可真够长的。◇ *We were married for ten long years.* 我们结婚有十年之久了。 OPP **short**

• **CLOTHES** 衣物 **6** 🔑 covering all or most of your legs or arms 长的（完全或大部分覆盖腿或臂的）：*She usually wears long skirts.* 她通常穿长裙。◇ *a long-sleeved shirt* 长袖衬衫 OPP **short**

• **VOWEL SOUNDS** 元音 **7** (*phonetics* 语音) taking more time to make than a short vowel sound in the same position 长音的 OPP **short**

IDM **as long as your ˈarm** (*informal*) very long 很长：*There's a list of repairs as long as your arm.* 有一份长得要命的修理单。 **at long last** after a long time 最后；终于 SYN **finally**：*At long last his prayers had been answered.* 他的祷告终于应验了。 **at the ˈlongest** not longer than the particular time given 最长，至多（不超过某特定时间）：*It will take an hour at the longest.* 这事最多花一小时。 **by a ˈlong way** by a great amount 大量地；大大地 **go back a long ˈway** (of two or more people 两个或两个以上的人) to have known each other for a long time 相识很久：*We go back a long way, he and I.* 我跟他，我们俩相识很久了。 **go a long ˈway** (of money, food, etc. 钱、食物等) to last a long time 经用；够维持很长时间：*She seems to make her money go a long way.* 看起来她用钱细水长流。◇ *A small amount of this paint goes a long way* (= covers a large area). 这种涂料用一点就可涂一大片。◇ (*ironic*) *I find that* ***a little of*** *Jerry's company can* ***go a long way*** (= I quickly get tired of being with him). 我发觉跟杰里待上一会儿就受不了啦。 **have come a long ˈway** to have made a lot of progress 取得大的进步；大有长进：*We've come a long way since the early days of the project.* 这项目开始以来我们已取得很大进展。 **have a long way to ˈgo** to need to make a lot of progress before you can achieve sth 还有很长的路要走；还有很大差距：*She still has a long way to go before she's fully fit.* 她还需要很长时间才能完全恢复健康。 **how long is a piece of ˈstring?** (*BrE, informal*) used to say that there is no definite answer to a question 一条线有多长（意指没有确切的答案）：*'How long will it take?' 'How long's a piece of string?'* "需要多长时间？" "没准儿。" **in the ˈlong run** concerning a longer period in the future 从长远来看：*This measure inevitably means higher taxes in the long run.* 从长远来看这项措施的结果免不了要多纳税。 **it's a ˌlong ˈstory** (*informal*) used to say that the reasons for sth are complicated and you would prefer not to give all the details 一言难尽；说来话长 **the long arm of sth** the power and/or authority of sth （某事物的）权力，权威：*There is no escape from the long arm of the law.* 法网恢恢，疏而不漏。 **the long and (the) ˈshort of it** used when you are telling sb the essential facts about sth or what effect it will have, without explaining all the details 总而言之；总的情况 **(pull, wear, etc.) a long ˈface** (to have) an unhappy or disappointed expression 闷闷不乐；哭丧着脸；愁眉苦脸 **ˌlong in the ˈtooth** (*humorous, especially BrE*) old or too old 年齿渐长；老朽 ORIGIN This originally referred to the fact that a horse's teeth appear to be longer as it grows older, because its gums shrink. 源自马越老因牙龈收缩而牙齿显得越长。 **ˈlong on sth** (*informal*) having a lot of a particular quality 擅长；颇具（某种特性）：*The government is long on ideas but short on performance.* 这个政府想法很多但成效太少。 **a ˈlong shot** an attempt or a guess that is not likely to be successful but is worth trying 成功希望不大的尝试；把握不大的猜测；姑妄一猜：*It's a long shot, but it just might work.* 没有什么把握，但也许行得通。 **long time no ˈsee** (*informal*) used to say hello to sb you have not seen for a long time 好久不见了 **not by a ˈlong chalk** (*BrE*) (*also* **not by a ˈlong shot** *NAmE, BrE*) not nearly; not at all 差得远；绝不；一点也不：*It's not over yet—not by a long chalk.* 这事还没有了结，还差得远呢。 **take a long (cool/hard) ˈlook at sth** to consider a problem or possibility very carefully and without hurrying 极其慎重地考虑（问题或可能性）：*We need to take a long hard look at all the options.* 我们需要十分谨慎地考虑所有的选择。 **take the ˈlong view (of sth)** to consider what is likely to happen or be important over a long period of time rather than only considering the present situation 从长远考虑 **to cut a long story ˈshort** (*BrE*) (*NAmE* **to make a long story ˈshort**) (*informal*) used when you are saying that you will get to the point of what you are saying quickly, without including all the details 长话短说；扼要地说；简而言之 ➲ MORE AT BROAD *adj.*, KICK *v.*, TERM *n.*, WAY *n.*

■ ***adv.*** (**long·er** /ˈlɒŋɡə(r); *NAmE* ˈlɔːŋ-; ˈlɑːŋ-/, **long·est** /ˈlɒŋɡɪst; *NAmE* ˈlɔːŋ-; ˈlɑːŋ-/) **1** 🔑 for a long time 长期地；长久地：*Have you been here long?* 你来这里时间长吗？◇ *Stay as long as you like.* 你愿待多久就待多久。◇ *The party went on long into the night.* 聚会持续到深夜。◇ *This may* ***take longer*** *than we thought.* 这事花的时间也许比我们预料的要多些。◇ *I won't* ***be long*** (= I'll return, be ready, etc. soon). 我一会儿就行。◇ ***How long*** *have you been waiting?* 你等了多久了？◇ *These reforms are long overdue.* 这些改革早就该进行了。 **2** 🔑 a long time before or after a particular time or event（在某一时间或事件之前或以后）很久地：*He retired long before the war.* 他在战争之前早就退休了。◇ *It wasn't long before she had persuaded him* (= it only took a short time). 她没用多久就把他说服了。◇ *We'll be home* ***before long*** (= soon). 我们很快就要到家了。◇ *The house was pulled down* ***long ago.*** 那栋房子很久以前就被拆掉了。◇ *They had* ***long since*** (= a long time before the present time) *moved away.* 他们早就搬走了。 **3** used after a noun to emphasize that sth happens for the whole of a particular period of time（用于名词后强调某事发生在某整段时间）：*We had to wait* ***all day long.*** 我们不得不整天等候着。◇ *The baby was crying* ***all night long.*** 婴儿整夜在哭。◇ *They stayed up* ***the whole night long.*** 他们彻夜未眠。

IDM **as/so 'long as 1** only if 只要：*We'll go as long as the weather is good.* 只要天气好我们就去。 **2** since; to the extent that 既然；由于；就…来说：*So long as there is a demand for these drugs, the financial incentive for drug dealers will be there.* 只要对这些毒品有需求，就存在着对贩毒者的经济诱因。 **for (so) 'long** for (such) a long time 长久地；（这么）长时间地：*Will you be away for long?* 你要离开很久吗？◇ *I'm sorry I haven't written to you for so long.* 真抱歉，我这么长时间未给你写信。 **how long have you 'got?** (*BrE*) (*NAmE* **how long do you 'have?**) (*informal*) used to say that sth is going to take a long time to explain 你有多少时间（指需要很长时间来解释）：*What do I think about it? How long have you got?* 这事我是怎么想的？说来话长，你有时间听吗？ **long live sb/sth** used to say that you hope sb/sth will live or last for a long time …万岁；…万古长青 **no/any 'longer** used to say that sth which was possible or true before, is not now 不再；不复：*I can't wait any longer.* 我不能再等了。◇ *He no longer lives here.* 他不再住这儿了。 **so 'long** (*informal*) goodbye 再见 ➲ MORE AT LAUGH *v.*

▼ WHICH WORD? 词语辨析

(for) long / (for) a long time

- Both **(for) long** and **(for) a long time** are used as expressions of time. In positive sentences **(for) a long time** is used. * (for) long 和 (for) a long time 均用以表示时间。肯定句用 (for) a long time：*We've been friends a long time.* 我们是老朋友了。 **(For) long** is not used in positive sentences unless it is used with *too, enough, as, so, seldom*, etc. * (for) long 只有与 too、enough、as、so、seldom 等词连用时才用于肯定句中：*I stayed out in the sun for too long.* 我在太阳底下待的时间太长了。◇ *You've been waiting long enough.* 你等得够久的了。 Both **(for) long** and **(for) a long time** can be used in questions, but **(for) long** is usually preferred. * (for) long 和 (for) a long time 均可用于疑问句，但 (for) long 较常用：*Have you been waiting long?* 你等了很长时间吗？
- In negative sentences **(for) a long time** sometimes has a different meaning from **(for) long**. 在否定句中 (for) a long time 和 (for) long 有时含义不同。 Compare 比较：*I haven't been here for a long time* (= It is a long time since the last time I was here). 我已很久没来这里了。 and 和：*I haven't been here long* (= I arrived here only a short time ago). 我到这里没多长时间。

■ ***verb*** [I] to want sth very much especially if it does not seem likely to happen soon（尤指对看似不会很快发生的事）渴望 **SYN** **yearn**：**~ for sb/sth** *Lucy had always longed for a brother.* 露西一直渴望有个弟弟。◇ **~ for sb to do sth** *He longed for Pat to phone.* 他期盼着帕特来电话。◇ **~ to do sth** *I'm longing to see you again.* 我渴望再次见到你。 ➲ SEE ALSO LONGED-FOR

long. *abbr.* (in writing 书写形式) LONGITUDE 经度

,long-a'waited *adj.* that people have been waiting for for a long time 等待（或期待）已久的：*her long-awaited new novel* 她的令人期待已久的一部新小说

long·board /ˈlɒŋbɔːd; *NAmE* ˈlɔːŋbɔːrd/ *noun* a long board used in SURFING 冲浪板

long·boat /ˈlɒŋbəʊt; *NAmE* ˈlɔːŋboʊt; ˈlɑːŋboʊt/ *noun* a large ROWING BOAT, used especially for travelling on the sea（尤用于航海的）大划艇

long·bow /ˈlɒŋbəʊ; *NAmE* ˈlɔːŋboʊ; ˈlɑːŋboʊ/ *noun* a large BOW[2] (1) made of a long thin curved piece of wood that was used in the past for shooting arrows（旧时用于射箭的）长弓，大弓

,long-'distance *adj.* [only before noun] **1** travelling or involving travel between places that are far apart 长途的；长距离的：*a long-distance commuter* 长途通勤者 ◇ *long-distance flights* 长途航班 **2** operating between people and places that are far apart 长途运作的：*a long-distance phone call* 长途电话 ► **,long 'distance** *adv.*：*It's a relaxing car to drive long distance.* 这辆轿车跑长途，开起来很轻松。◇ *to call long distance* 打长途电话

,long-,distance 'footpath *noun* a route that people can walk along to see the countryside or the coast（乡间或海岸的）观光步道

,long di'vision *noun* [U] (*mathematics* 数) a method of dividing one number by another in which all the stages involved are written down 长除法（把每一步骤都写下来）

,long-drawn-'out (*also less frequent* **'long-drawn, ,drawn-'out**) *adj.* lasting a very long time, often too long 持续很久的；拖长的 **SYN** **protracted**：*long-drawn-out negotiations* 旷日持久的谈判

,long 'drink *noun* a cold drink that fills a tall glass, such as LEMONADE or beer 大杯冷饮料（如柠檬汽水或啤酒）

'longed-for *adj.* [only before noun] that sb has been wanting or hoping for very much 渴望的；期待已久的：*the birth of a longed-for baby* 一个盼望已久的婴儿的出生

lon·gev·ity /lɒnˈdʒevəti; *NAmE* lɔːn-; lɑːn-/ *noun* [U] (*formal*) long life; the fact of lasting a long time 长寿；长命；持久：*We wish you both health and longevity.* 我们祝愿您二位健康长寿。◇ *He prides himself on the longevity of the company.* 他为公司悠久的历史而感到骄傲。

long·hair /ˈlɒŋheə(r); *NAmE* ˈlɔːŋher; ˈlɑːŋher/ *noun* a breed of cat with long hair 长毛猫 ➲ COMPARE SHORTHAIR

long·hand /ˈlɒŋhænd; *NAmE* ˈlɔːŋ-; ˈlɑːŋ-/ *noun* [U] ordinary writing, not typed or written in SHORTHAND 普通书写（非打字或速记）

,long 'haul *noun* [usually sing.] a difficult task that takes a long time and a lot of effort to complete 费时费力的工作：*She knows that becoming world champion is going to be a long haul.* 她知道要成为世界冠军需要长时间的艰苦努力。

IDM **be in sth for the long 'haul** to be willing to continue doing a task until it is finished 愿意坚持到底：*I promise I am in this for the long haul.* 我保证我会对这事坚持到底。 **over the long 'haul** (*especially NAmE*) over a long period of time 长时间；长久

'long-haul *adj.* [only before noun] involving the transport of goods or passengers over long distances（运送货物或旅客）长途的，远距离的：***long-haul flights/routes*** 远程航班；长途运输路线 **OPP** **short-haul** ➲ WORDFINDER NOTE AT PLANE

long·horn /ˈlɒŋhɔːn; *NAmE* -hɔːrn/ *noun* a type of cow with long horns 长角牛

long·house /ˈlɒŋhaʊs; *NAmE* ˈlɔːŋ-; ˈlɑːŋ-/ *noun* **1** (in Britain) an old type of house in which people and animals lived together（英国旧式人畜共居的）长屋 **2** (in the US) a traditional house used by some Native Americans（美国某些印第安人的传统住宅）长屋

long·ing /ˈlɒŋɪŋ; *NAmE* ˈlɔːŋ-/ *noun, adj.*

■ ***noun*** [C, U] a strong feeling of wanting sth/sb（对…的）渴望，热望：**~ (for sb/sth)** *a longing for home* 对故乡的思念 ◇ **~ (to do sth)** *She was filled with longing to hear his voice again.* 她热切希望再听到他的声音。◇ *romantic longings* 对爱情的渴望 ◇ *His voice was husky with longing* (= sexual desire). 他因欲火攻心而声音嘶哑。

■ ***adj.*** [only before noun] feeling or showing that you want sth very much 渴望的；热望的；表示渴望的：*He gave a longing look at the ice cream.* 他看了看那冰淇淋，显出很想吃的样子。 ► **long·ing·ly** *adv.*：*We looked longingly towards the hills.* 我们不胜向往地朝群山望去。

long·ish /ˈlɒŋɪʃ; *NAmE* ˈlɔːŋ-/ *adj.* [only before noun] fairly long 稍长的；较长的：*longish hair* 颇长的头发 ◇ *There was a longish pause.* 有一个略长的停顿。

lon·gi·tude /ˈlɒŋgɪtjuːd; ˈlɒndʒɪ-; *NAmE* ˈlɑːndʒətuːd; ˈlɔːndʒətuːd/ *noun* [U] (*abbr.* **long.**) the distance of a place east or west of the Greenwich MERIDIAN, measured in degrees 经度：*the longitude of the island* 那座岛的经度 ➲ COMPARE LATITUDE (1)

lon·gi·tu·din·al /ˌlɒŋɡɪˈtjuːdɪnl; ˌlɒndʒɪ-; *NAmE* ˌlɑːndʒəˈtuːdnl; ˌlɔːndʒəˈtuːdnl/ *adj.* (*specialist*) **1** going downwards rather than across 纵的；纵向的：*The plant's stem is marked with thin green longitudinal stripes.* 这种植物的茎上长有绿色的细长纵向条纹。 **2** concerning the development of sth over a period of time 纵观的：*a longitudinal study of ageing* 对衰老问题的纵向研究 **3** connected with longitude 经度的：*the town's longitudinal position* 这座城镇的经度位置 ▶ **lon·gi·tu·din·al·ly** /-nəli/ *adv.*

longiˌtudinal ˈwave *noun* (*physics* 物) a wave that VIBRATES in the direction that it is moving 纵波 ➲ COMPARE TRANSVERSE WAVE

ˈlong johns *noun* [pl.] (*informal*) warm UNDERPANTS with long legs down to the ankles（至踝部的）长内裤，衬裤：*a pair of long johns* 一条长衬裤

the ˈlong jump (*NAmE also* **the ˈbroad jump**) *noun* [sing.] a sporting event in which people try to jump as far forward as possible after running up to a line 跳远

ˌlong-ˈlasting *adj.* that can or does last for a long time（可）持久的；长期的 SYN **durable**：*long-lasting effects* 长期的影响 ◇ *a long-lasting agreement* 长期的协议

ˌlong-ˈlife *adj.* **1** made to last longer than the ordinary type 长（寿）命的；经久耐用的；使用期限特别长的：*long-life batteries* 长效电池 **2** (*BrE*) made to remain fresh longer than the ordinary type 做过保鲜处理的；保鲜期特别长的：*long-life milk* 保鲜期长的牛奶

ˌlong-ˈlived *adj.* having a long life; lasting for a long time 寿命长的；长寿的；经久耐用的；持久的 ➲ SYNONYMS AT OLD

ˈlong-lost *adj.* [only before noun] that you have not seen or received any news of for a long time 长时间没见面的；杳无音信的：*a long-lost friend* 长久没有音信的朋友

ˈlong-range *adj.* [only before noun] **1** travelling a long distance 远距离的；远程的：*long-range missiles* 远程导弹 **2** made for a period of time that will last a long way into the future 长远的；长期的：*a long-range weather forecast* 远期天气预报 ◇ *long-range plans* 长远的计划 ➲ COMPARE SHORT-RANGE

ˈlong-running *adj.* [only before noun] that has been continuing for a long time 持续时间长的：*a long-running dispute* 长期的争端 ◇ *a long-running TV series* 长期连播的电视剧

ˈlong-serving *adj.* [only before noun] having had the job or position mentioned for a long time 长期供职的：*long-serving employees* 资深雇员

long·ship /ˈlɒŋʃɪp; *NAmE* ˈlɔːŋ-; ˈlɑːŋ-/ *noun* a long narrow ship used by the Vikings 北欧海盗船；维京海盗船

long·shore drift /ˌlɒŋʃɔː ˈdrɪft; *NAmE* ˌlɔːŋʃɔːr; ˌlɑːŋ-/ *noun* [U] (*specialist*) the movement of sand, etc. along a beach caused by waves hitting the beach at an angle 沿岸泥沙流

long·shore·man /ˈlɒŋʃɔːmən; *NAmE* ˈlɔːŋʃɔːrmən; ˈlɑːŋʃɔːrmən/ *noun* (*pl.* **-men** /-mən/) (*NAmE*) a man whose job is moving goods on and off ships 码头工人；港口装卸工

ˌlong-ˈsighted (*especially BrE*) (*also* **ˌfar-ˈsighted** *especially in NAmE*) *adj.* [not usually before noun] not able to see things that are close to you clearly 远视 OPP **short-sighted** ▶ **ˌlong-ˈsighted·ness** (*also* **ˌlong ˈsight**) *noun* [U]

ˌlong-ˈstanding *adj.* [usually before noun] that has existed or lasted for a long time 存在已久的；悠久的：*a long-standing relationship* 长期的关系

ˈlong-stay *adj.* [usually before noun] **1** likely to need treatment or care for a long time 可能需要长期治疗（或护理）的：*long-stay patients* 需要长期治疗的病人 ◇ ***long-stay hospitals/institutions/wards*** (= for long-stay patients) 长期病人医院 / 机构 / 病房 **2** for people who wish to park their cars for a long period 供长期停放汽车的：*long-stay parking* 长期停放车辆的停车场

ˌlong-ˈsuffering *adj.* bearing problems or another person's unpleasant behaviour with patience 长期忍受的；忍耐的：*his long-suffering wife* 他那长期受罪的妻子

ˌlong-ˈterm *adj.* [usually before noun] **1** that will last or have an effect over a long period of time 长期的；长远的；长期有效的：*a long-term strategy* 长期的策略 ◇ *the long-term effects of fertilizers* 肥料的长远影响 ◇ *a long-term investment* 长线投资 **2** that is not likely to change or be solved quickly 近期不大可能改变的；不大可能很快解决的：*long-term unemployment* 长期失业 ➲ COMPARE SHORT-TERM

ˈlong-time *adj.* [only before noun] having been the particular thing mentioned for a long time 为时甚久的：*his long-time colleague* 他的老同事

lon·gueurs /lɒŋˈɡɜːz; *NAmE* loʊŋˈɡɜːrz/ *noun* [pl.] (*from French, literary*) very boring parts or aspects of sth 冗长乏味的部分（或方面）

ˈlong wave *noun* [U, C] (*abbr.* **LW**) a radio wave with a length of more than 1 000 metres 长波：*to broadcast **on long wave*** 用长波播送 ➲ COMPARE SHORT WAVE

long·ways /ˈlɒŋweɪz; *NAmE* ˈlɔːŋ-; ˈlɑːŋ-/ (*also* **long·wise** /ˈlɒŋwaɪz; *NAmE* ˈlɔːŋ-/) *adv.* in the same direction as the longest side of sth 纵向地；长地 SYN **lengthways**

ˌlong weekˈend *noun* a holiday/vacation of three or four days from Friday or Saturday to Sunday or Monday（三天或四天的）周末长假

ˌlong-ˈwinded *adj.* (*disapproving*) (especially of talking or writing 尤指说话或写作) continuing for too long and therefore boring 冗长枯燥的；啰嗦的；唠唠叨叨的 SYN **tedious**

loo /luː/ *noun* (*pl.* **loos**) (*BrE, informal*) a toilet/bathroom 厕所；盥洗室；洗手间：*She's gone to the loo.* 她去盥洗室了。 ◇ *Can I use your loo, please?* 我可以用一下你的厕所吗？

loo·fah /ˈluːfə/ *noun* a long rough bath SPONGE made from the dried fruit of a tropical plant（擦澡用的）丝瓜络 ➲ VISUAL VOCAB PAGE V25

look 🔑 /lʊk/ *verb, noun, exclamation*

■ ***verb***

• **USE EYES** 用眼睛 **1** 🔑 [I] to turn your eyes in a particular direction 看；瞧：*If you look carefully you can just see our house from here.* 你要是仔细看，从这里就可以看见我们的房子。 ◇ **~ (at sb/sth)** *She looked at me and smiled.* 她看了看我，笑了。 ◇ *'Has the mail come yet?' 'I'll look and see.'* "邮件来了吗？" "我看看。" ◇ *Look! I'm sure that's Brad Pitt!* 看！那一定是布拉德・皮特！ ◇ *Don't look now, but there's someone staring at you!* 你现在别看，有人正盯着你呢！ ➲ SEE ALSO FORWARD-LOOKING

• **SEARCH** 搜寻 **2** 🔑 [I] to try to find sb/sth 寻找；寻求：*I can't find my book—I've looked everywhere.* 我找不到我的书，我到处都找遍了。 ◇ **~ for sb/sth** *Where have you been? We've been looking for you.* 你上哪儿去了？我们一直在找你。 ◇ *Are you still looking for a job?* 你还在找工作吗？

• **PAY ATTENTION** 注意 **3** 🔑 [I, T] to pay attention to sth 注意；留心；留神：**~ (at sth)** *Look at the time! We're going to be late.* 注意一下时间！我们要迟到了。 ◇ **~ where, what, etc....** *Can't you look where you're going?* 你走路可不可以小心点？

• **APPEAR/SEEM** 显得；似乎 **4** 🔑 *linking verb* to seem; to appear 看来好像；似乎；显得：**+ adj.** *to look pale/happy/tired* 显得苍白 / 高兴 / 疲倦 ◇ *That book looks interesting.* 那本书好像很有趣。 ◇ **~ (to sb) like sb/sth** *That looks like an interesting book.* 那好像是本有趣的书。 ◇ **+ noun** *That looks an interesting book.* 那好像是本有趣的书。 ◇ *You made me look a complete fool!* 你把我弄得像个十足的傻瓜！ ➲ SEE ALSO GOOD-LOOKING **5** 🔑 [I] (not usually used in the progressive tenses 通常不用于进行时) to have a similar appearance to sb/sth; to have an appearance that suggests that sth is true or will happen 与…外表相似；好像；仿佛：**~ (to sb) like sb/sth** *That photograph doesn't* *look like her at all.* 那张照片看上去一点也不像她。◇ *It looks like rain* (= it looks as if it's going to rain). 像是要下雨的样子。◇ **~ (to sb) as if.../as though...** *You look as though you slept badly.* 你好像没睡好觉。HELP In spoken English people often use **like** instead of **as if** or **as though** in this meaning, especially in *NAmE*. 英语口语中，尤其是美式英语，常用 like 代替 as if 或 as though 表示此义：*You look like you slept badly.* 你好像没睡好觉。This is not considered correct in written *BrE*. 书面英式英语中，此用法被视为不正确。 **6** [I] to seem likely 看起来好像；似乎有可能：**~ (to sb) as if.../as though...** *It doesn't look as if we'll be moving after all.* 看样子我们还是不搬了。◇ **~ (to sb) like...** (*informal*) *It doesn't look like we'll be moving after all.* 看样子我们还是不搬了。HELP This use of **like** instead of **as if** or **as though** is not considered correct in written *BrE*. 用 like 代替 as if 或 as though，此用法在书面英式英语中被视为不正确。

• **FACE** 面向 **7** [I] **+ adv./prep.** to face a particular direction 面向；正对；朝向：*The house looks east.* 这房子朝东。◇ *The hotel looks out over the harbour.* 从这家旅馆朝外看可俯视港湾。

IDM HELP Most idioms containing **look** are at the entries for the nouns and adjectives in the idioms, for example **look daggers at sb** is at **dagger**. 大多数含 look 的习语，都可在该等习语中的名词及形容词相关词条找到，如 look daggers at sb 在词条 dagger 下。 **be just 'looking** used in a shop/store to say that you are not ready to buy sth（在商店中表示无意购买某物）只是看一看：*'Can I help you?' 'I'm just looking, thank you.'* "请问您要买什么？" "谢谢，我只是看看。" **be looking to do sth** to try to find ways of doing sth 试图找到做某事的方法：*The government is looking to reduce inflation.* 政府正在力求降低通货膨胀率。 **look 'bad | not look 'good** to be considered bad behaviour or bad manners 被视为举止不佳；失礼；不得体：*It looks bad not going to your own brother's wedding.* 连亲兄弟的婚礼都不参加，这太不像话了。 **look 'bad (for sb)** to show that sth bad might happen 显示不好的事可能发生；看来不利于：*He's had another heart attack; things are looking bad for him, I'm afraid.* 他又犯了一次心脏病，恐怕他情况不妙。 **look 'good** to show success or that sth good might happen 显现成功（或好事可能发生）；看来充满希望：*This year's sales figures are looking good.* 今年的销售数字情况看好。 **look 'here** (*old-fashioned*) used to protest about sth（表示抗议）喂，听着：*Now look here, it wasn't my fault.* 喂，那不是我的错！ **look how/what/who...** used to give an example that proves what you are saying or makes it clearer（用于举例证实或说明）瞧：*Look how lazy we've become.* 瞧我们变得有多懒。◇ *Be careful climbing that ladder. Look what happened last time.* 爬那梯子时小心点儿。上次不就出事了么。 **look sb ˌup and 'down** to look at sb in a careful or critical way 上下仔细打量，挑剔地审视（某人） **(not) look your'self** to not have your normal healthy appearance 气色不像往常那样好：*You're not looking yourself today* (= you look tired or ill/sick). 今天你看上去气色不太好。 **never/not look 'back** (*informal*) to become more and more successful 一帆风顺；蒸蒸日上：*Her first novel was published in 2007 and since then she hasn't looked back.* 她的第一部小说于 2007 年发表，自此她便一发而不可收。 **not much to 'look at** (*informal*) not attractive 相貌平平；不起眼 **to 'look at sb/sth** judging by the appearance of sb/sth 由外表判断：*To look at him you'd never think he was nearly fifty.* 看他的外表，谁也想不到他年近五十了。

PHR V **ˌlook 'after yourself/sb/sth** (*especially BrE*) **1** to be responsible for or to take care of sb/sth 对…负责；照料；照顾：*Who's going to look after the children while you're away?* 你不在时谁来照料小孩？◇ *I'm looking after his affairs while he's in hospital.* 他住院时由我处理他的事务。◇ *Don't worry about me—I can look after myself* (= I don't need any help). 别担心我，我能照顾好自己。 ⇨ NOTE AT CARE **2** to make sure that things happen to sb's advantage 确保有利于：*He's good at looking after his own interests.* 他善于照顾自己的利益。

ˌlook a'head (to sth) to think about what is going to happen in the future 展望未来；为将来设想

ˌlook a'round/'round to turn your head so that you can see sth 环视；环顾；四下察看：*People came out of their houses and looked around.* 人们走出家门四处察看。

ˌlook a'round/'round (sth) to visit a place or building, walking around it to see what is there 游览；参观：*Let's look round the town this afternoon.* 咱们今天下午游览市区吧。 **ˌlook a'round/'round for sth** to search for sth in a number of different places 到处寻找；搜寻：*We're looking around for a house in this area.* 我们正在这个地区四处找住房。

'look at sth 1 to examine sth closely（仔细）察看，检查：*Your ankle's swollen—I think the doctor ought to look at it.* 你的脚踝肿了，我认为得找医生检查一下。◇ *I haven't had time to look at* (= read) *the papers yet.* 我还没来得及看这些论文。 **2** to think about, consider or study sth 思考；考虑；研究：*The implications of the new law will need to be looked at.* 新法规可能造成的影响需要仔细研究一下。 **3** to view or consider sth in a particular way（用某种方式）看待，考虑：*Looked at from that point of view, his decision is easier to understand.* 从那个角度来看，他的决定比较容易理解。

ˌlook 'back (on sth) to think about sth in your past 回首（往事）；回忆；回顾 SYN **reflect**: *to look back on your childhood* 回顾自己的童年

ˌlook 'down on sb/sth to think that you are better than sb/sth 蔑视；轻视；瞧不起：*She looks down on people who haven't been to college.* 她瞧不起没上过大学的人。

'look for sth to hope for sth; to expect sth 期望；期待；盼望：*We shall be looking for an improvement in your*

▼ **SYNONYMS 同义词辨析**

look

watch • see • view • observe

These words all mean to turn your eyes in a particular direction. 以上各词均含看、观看之义。

look to turn your eyes in a particular direction 指看、瞧：*If you look carefully you can just see our house from here.* 你要是仔细看，从这里就可以看见我们的房子。◇ *She* ***looked at*** *me and smiled.* 她看了看我，笑了。

watch to look at sb/sth for a time, paying attention to what happens 指看、注视、观看、观察：*to watch television* 看电视 ◇ *Watch what I do, then you try.* 你注意看我的动作，然后试着做。

see to watch a game, television programme, performance, etc. 指观看（比赛、电视节目、演出等）：*In the evening we went to see a movie.* 晚上我们去看了一场电影。

view (*formal*) to look at sth, especially when you look carefully; to watch television, a film/movie, etc. 指看、观看（尤指仔细观察）；看（电视、电影等）：*People came from all over the world to view her work.* 观众从世界各地涌来欣赏她的作品。

WATCH, SEE OR VIEW? 用 watch、see 还是 view?

You can *see/view a film/movie/programme*, but you cannot ~~*see/view television*~~. **View** is more formal than **see** and is used especially in business contexts. 可以说 see/view a film/movie/programme，但不能说 see/view television。view 较 see 正式，尤用于商务语境。

observe (*formal*) to watch sb/sth carefully, especially to learn more about them or it 指观察、注视、监视：*The patients were observed over a period of several months.* 这些病人被观察了数月之久。

PATTERNS

- to look/watch **for** sb/sth
- to watch/observe **what/who/how...**
- to look/watch/view/observe (sb/sth) **with** amazement/surprise/disapproval, etc.
- to watch/see/view a **film/movie/show/programme**
- to watch/see a **match/game/fight**
- to look (at sb/sth)/watch (sb/sth)/observe sb/sth **carefully/closely**

work this term. 我们期待你这学期功课有进步。

ˌlook ˈforward to sth 🔑 to be thinking with pleasure about sth that is going to happen (because you expect to enjoy it)（高兴地）盼望，期待：*I'm looking forward to the weekend.* 我盼着过周末呢。◇ **look forward to doing sth** *We're really looking forward to seeing you again.* 我们非常盼望能再见到你。

ˌlook ˈin (on sb) to make a short visit to a place, especially sb's house when they are ill/sick or need help（尤指当某人生病或需要帮助时到其住处）短暂探访：*She looks in on her elderly neighbour every evening.* 她每天晚上都要看望一下年长的邻居。◇ *Why don't you look in on me next time you're in town?* 你下次进城顺便来看看我好吗？

ˌlook ˈinto sth 🔑 to examine sth 调查；审查：*A working party has been set up to look into the problem.* 已成立一个工作小组来调查这个问题。

ˌlook ˈon 🔑 to watch sth without becoming involved in it yourself 旁观：*Passers-by simply looked on as he was attacked.* 他遭人袭击，路人只在一边袖手旁观。➲ RELATED NOUN ONLOOKER **ˈlook on sb/sth as sb/sth** to consider sb/sth to be sb/sth 把…看作；把…视为：*She's looked on as the leading authority on the subject.* 她被视为这门学科的最重要的权威。 **ˈlook on sb/sth with sth** 🔑 to consider sb/sth in a particular way（以某种方式）看待 SYN **regard**: *They looked on his behaviour with contempt.* 他们对他的行为不屑一顾。

ˌlook ˈout 🔑 used to warn sb to be careful, especially when there is danger（表示警告，尤指有危险）小心，当心，留神 SYN **watch out**: *Look out! There's a car coming.* 当心！有车来了。 **ˌlook ˈout for sb** to take care of sb and make sure nothing bad happens to them 关照某人 **ˌlook ˈout for sb/sth 1** 🔑 to try to avoid sth bad happening or doing sth bad 当心；提防；留心防备 SYN **watch out**: *You should look out for pickpockets.* 你应当提防扒手。◇ *Do look out for spelling mistakes in your work.* 一定要杜绝你作业中的拼写错误。 **2** 🔑 to keep trying to find sth or meet sb 留心寻觅：*I'll look out for you at the conference.* 我会在开会时来找你。➲ RELATED NOUN LOOK-OUT **ˌlook ˈout for sb/yourself** to think only of sb's/your own advantage, without worrying about other people 只考虑某人/自己的利益：*You should look out for yourself from now on.* 从现在起你应该多为自己着想。

ˌlook sth↔ˈout (for sb/sth) (*BrE*) to search for sth from among your possessions 把…找出来：*I'll look out those old photographs you wanted to see.* 我会找出你想看的那些旧照片的。

ˌlook sth↔ˈover to examine sth to see how good, big, etc. it is 查看；检查：*We looked over the house again before we decided we would rent it.* 那房子我们再看了一次才决定租下来。

ˌlook ˈround 🔑 (*BrE*) to turn your head to see sb/sth behind you 转过头看；回头看：*She looked round when she heard the noise.* 她听到响声，就回过头去看。

ˌlook ˈthrough sb [no passive] to ignore sb by pretending not to see them 佯装没有看见而不理会某人：*She just looked straight through me.* 她竟然假装没看见我。 **ˈlook through sth** 🔑 [no passive] to examine or read sth quickly 快速查看；浏览：*She looked through her notes before the exam.* 她考试前匆匆看了一下笔记。

ˈlook to sb for sth | ˈlook to sb to do sth (*formal*) to rely on or expect sb to provide sth or do sth 依赖，期待，指望（某人提供某物或做某事）：*We are looking to you for help.* 我们指望得到你的帮助。 **ˈlook to sth** (*formal*) to consider sth and think about how to make it better 注意，考虑（改进）：*We need to look to ways of improving our marketing.* 我们得考虑改进营销方法。

ˌlook ˈup (*informal*) (of business, sb's situation, etc. 生意、某人的情况等) to become better 好转；改善 SYN **improve**: *At last things were beginning to look up.* 情况终于开始好转了。 **ˌlook ˈup (from sth)** 🔑 to raise your eyes when you are looking down at sth（在低头看某物时）抬头往上看：*She looked up from her book as I entered the room.* 我进房间时，她从书本上抬起头来看了看。 **ˌlook sb↔ˈup** [no passive] (*informal*) to visit or make contact with sb, especially when you have not seen them for a long time（尤指在久别之后）拜访，看望，联系：*Do look me up the next time you're in London.* 你下次到伦敦，一定要来看我。 **ˌlook sth↔ˈup** 🔑 to look for information in a dictionary or REFERENCE BOOK, or by using a computer（在词典、参考书中或通过电脑）查阅，查检：*Can you look up the opening times on the website?* 你可以在网站上查一下开放的时间吗？◇ *I looked it up in the dictionary.* 我在词典里查过这个词。 **ˌlook ˈup to sb** 🔑 to admire or respect sb 钦佩；仰慕；尊敬

■ ***noun***

• **USING EYES** 用眼睛 **1** 🔑 [C, usually sing.] ~ (**at sb/sth**) an act of looking at sb/sth 看；瞧：*Here, **have a look** at this.* 来，看一看这个。◇ ***Take a look** at these figures!* 看一下这些数字吧！◇ *Make sure you get a **good look** at their faces.* 你一定要仔细看清他们的面孔。◇ ***One look** at his face and Jenny stopped laughing.* 珍妮一看见他那张脸，就止住不笑了。◇ *A look passed between them* (= they looked at each other). 他们互相看了一眼。◇ *It's an interesting place. Do you want to take **a look around**?* 这个地方很好玩，你要不要到处看看？◇ *We'll be taking a **close look** at these proposals* (= examining them carefully). 我们会仔细审查这些方案。

• **SEARCH** 找寻 **2** 🔑 [C, usually sing.] ~ (**for sth/sb**) an act of trying to find sth/sb 查找：*I've **had a good look** for it, but I can't find it.* 我仔细找过了，可是找不着。

• **EXPRESSION** 表情 **3** 🔑 [C] an expression in your eyes or face 眼神；表情；神情；脸色：*a **look of** surprise* 惊讶的表情 ◇ *He didn't like the look in her eyes.* 他不喜欢她的眼神。◇ *She had a worried look on her face.* 她一脸担忧的样子。

• **APPEARANCE** 外貌 **4** 🔑 [C, usually sing.] the way sb/sth looks; the appearance of sb/sth 样子；外观；相貌；外表：*It's going to rain today **by the look of it*** (= judging by appearances). 看样子今天要下雨了。◇ *Looks can be deceptive.* 外表有时是靠不住的。◇ ***I don't like the look of** that guy* (= I don't trust him, judging by his appearance). 我不喜欢他那副样子。 **5** 🔑 **looks** [pl.] a person's appearance, especially when the person is attractive（尤指吸引人的）相貌，容貌：*She has her father's **good looks**.* 她有父亲俊秀的容貌。◇ *He **lost his looks*** (= became less attractive)

▼ SYNONYMS 同义词辨析

look

glance • gaze • stare • glimpse • glare

These are all words for an act of looking, when you turn your eyes in a particular direction. 以上各词均表示看的动作。

look an act of looking at sb/sth 指看、瞧：*Here, have a look at this.* 来，看一看这个。

glance a quick look 指匆匆一看、一瞥、扫视：*She stole a glance at her watch.* 她偷偷看了看表。

gaze a long steady look at sb/sth 指凝视、注视：*She felt embarrassed under his steady gaze.* 她在他凝视的目光下感到很尴尬。

stare a long look at sb/sth, especially in a way that is unfriendly or that shows surprise 尤指不友善或吃惊的盯、凝视、注视：*She gave the officer a blank stare and shrugged her shoulders.* 她面无表情地盯着那个军官，耸了耸肩。

glimpse a look at sb/sth for a very short time, when you do not see the person or thing completely 指一瞥、一看：*He caught a glimpse of her in the crowd.* 他在人群里一眼瞥见了她。

glare a long angry look at sb/sth 指长久的怒视、瞪眼：*She fixed her questioner with a hostile glare.* 她带着敌意瞪着向她提问的人。

PATTERNS

- a look/glance **at** sb/sth
- a **penetrating/piercing** look/glance/gaze/stare
- a **long** look/glance/stare
- a **brief** look/glance/glimpse
- to **have/get/take** a look/glance/glimpse
- to **avoid** sb's glance/gaze/stare

in later life. 他英俊的相貌在晚年已不复存在。 ➲ SEE ALSO GOOD-LOOKING

• FASHION 时尚 **6** [sing.] a fashion; a style 时尚；式样；风格：*The punk look is back in fashion.* 朋克式装扮又时兴起来了。◇ *They've given the place a completely new look.* 他们使得这地方焕然一新。 ➲ SEE ALSO WET LOOK

IDM **if looks could 'kill...** used to describe the very angry or unpleasant way sb is/was looking at you 眼神吓死人；一脸怒气；满脸不高兴：*I don't know what I've done to upset him, but if looks could kill...* 我不知道做了什么惹他生气了，但看他那吓人的样子… ➲ MORE AT DIRTY *adj.*, LONG *adj.*

■ ***exclamation*** used to make sb pay attention to what you are going to say, often when you are annoyed（常为不悦时唤起他人注意）喂，听我说：*Look, I think we should go now.* 喂，我想我们现在得走了。◇ *Look, that's not fair.* 嘿，那样不公平。

look·alike /'lʊkəlaɪk/ *noun* (often used after a person's name 常用于人名后) a person who looks very similar to the person mentioned 长得极像（某人）的人：*an Elvis lookalike* 长得很像埃尔维斯的人

ˌlook-and-'say *noun* [U] a method of teaching people to read based on the recognition of whole words, rather than on the association of letters with sounds 视读法，直呼法（一种识字教学方法，根据对整词的辨认而不是字母与发音的联系） ➲ COMPARE PHONICS

look·er /'lʊkə(r)/ *noun* (*informal*) a way of describing an attractive person, usually a woman 美人；靓女：*She's a real looker!* 她真是个美人！

'look-in *noun*

IDM **(not) get/have a 'look-in** (*BrE, informal*) (not) to get a chance to take part or succeed in sth（没）有参加的机会；（没）有成功的机会；（没）有份儿：*She talks so much that nobody else can get a look-in.* 她老是滔滔不绝，别人谁也插不上嘴。

'looking glass *noun* (*old-fashioned*) a mirror 镜子

look·out /'lʊkaʊt/ *noun* **1** a place for watching from, especially for danger or an enemy coming towards you 监视处；观察所；瞭望台：*a* ***lookout point/tower*** 瞭望哨；瞭望塔 **2** a person who has the responsibility of watching for sth, especially danger, etc. 监视员；观察员；瞭望员：*One of the men stood at the door to act as a lookout.* 有一个人站在门口望风。

IDM **be 'sb's lookout** (*BrE, informal*) used to say that you do not think sb's actions are sensible, but that it is their own problem or responsibility（认为某人的行为不明智）是某人自己的责任，是某人自己的事：*If he wants to waste his money, that's his lookout.* 他要乱花钱，那是他自己的事。 **be on the 'lookout (for sb/sth) | keep a 'lookout (for sb/sth)** (*informal*) to watch carefully for sb/sth in order to avoid danger, etc. or in order to find sth you want 注意；警戒；留心：*The public should be on the lookout for symptoms of the disease.* 公众应当留心这种疾病的症状。

ˌlook-'see *noun* [sing.] (*informal*) a quick look at sth 飞快一瞥：*Come and have a look-see.* 快来看一眼吧。

loom /luːm/ *verb, noun*

■ ***verb*** **1** [I] **(+ adv./prep.)** to appear as a large shape that is not clear, especially in a frightening or threatening way 赫然耸现；（尤指）令人惊恐地隐现：*A dark shape loomed up ahead of us.* 一个黑糊糊的影子隐隐出现在我们的前面。**2** [I] to appear important or threatening and likely to happen soon 显得突出；逼近：*There was a crisis looming.* 危机迫在眉睫。

IDM **ˌloom 'large** to be worrying or frightening and seem hard to avoid 令人忧虑，令人惊恐（并似乎难以避免）：*The prospect of war loomed large.* 战争的阴影在逼近，令人忧虑。

■ ***noun*** a machine for making cloth by twisting threads between other threads which go in a different direction 织布机

'loom bands *noun* [pl.] coloured rings of elastic which can be linked together to make BRACELETS often made by children to wear or to give to their friends 橡皮圈手环，彩色编织手环（常由儿童制作佩戴或送给朋友）

loon /luːn/ *noun* **1** a large N American bird that eats fish and has a cry like a laugh 潜鸟（北美食鱼大鸟，叫声似笑声） **2** = LOONY

loonie /'luːni/ *noun* (*CanE*) the Canadian dollar or a Canadian one-dollar coin 加拿大元；一加元硬币

loony /'luːni/ *adj., noun*

■ ***adj.*** (*informal*) crazy or strange 发狂的；疯狂的；怪异的；古怪的

■ ***noun*** (*pl.* **-ies**) (*also* **loon**) (*informal*) a person who has strange ideas or who behaves in a strange way 狂人；疯子；怪人

'loony bin *noun* (*old-fashioned, slang*) a humorous and sometimes offensive way of referring to a hospital for people who are mentally ill 疯人院（幽默用语，有时含冒犯意）

loop /luːp/ *noun, verb*

■ ***noun*** **1** a shape like a curve or circle made by a line curving right round and crossing itself 环形；环状物；圆圈：*The road went in a huge loop around the lake.* 那条路环湖绕了一个大圈。**2** a piece of rope, wire, etc. in the shape of a curve or circle（绳、电线等的）环，圈：*He tied a loop of rope around his arm.* 他在手臂上用绳子系了一个圈。◇ *Make a loop in the string.* 在绳子上打个圈。◇ *a belt loop* (= on trousers/pants, etc. for holding a belt in place) 皮带襻 ➲ PICTURE AT KNOT **3** a strip of film or tape on which the pictures and sound are repeated continuously 循环电影胶片；循环音像磁带：*The film is on a loop.* 这部电影已制成循环音像磁带。◇ (*figurative*) *His mind kept turning in an endless loop.* 他思绪万千。**4** (*computing* 计) a set of instructions that is repeated again and again until a particular condition is satisfied 循环；回路；（程序中）一套重复的指令 **5** a complete CIRCUIT for electrical current 环路；回线；回路 **6** (*BrE*) a railway line or road that leaves the main track or road and then joins it again（铁道或公路的）环线 **7 the Loop** (*US, informal*) the business centre of the US city of Chicago 大环（指美国芝加哥市的商业中心）

IDM **in the 'loop | out of the 'loop** (*informal*) part of a group of people that is dealing with sth important; not part of this group 属（处理要务的）圈内 / 圈外人士 **knock/throw sb for a 'loop** (*NAmE, informal*) to shock or surprise sb 使震惊；使惊讶

■ ***verb*** **1** [T] **~ sth + adv./prep.** to form or bend sth into a loop 使成环；使绕成圈：*He looped the strap over his shoulder.* 他把带子绕了一个圈挎在肩上。**2** [I] **+ adv./prep.** to move in a way that makes the shape of a loop 成环形移动：*The river loops around the valley.* 那条河顺着山谷绕了个大弯儿。◇ *The ball looped high up in the air.* 球高高飞起，在空中画了一条弧线。

IDM **ˌloop the 'loop** to fly or make a plane fly in a circle going up and down（使飞机）翻跟头飞行

loop·hole /'luːphəʊl; *NAmE* -hoʊl/ *noun* **~ (in sth)** a mistake in the way a law, contract, etc. has been written which enables people to legally avoid doing sth that the law, contract, etc. had intended them to do（法律、合同等的）漏洞，空子：*a legal loophole* 法律的漏洞 ◇ *to close existing loopholes* 堵住现有的漏洞

loopy /'luːpi/ *adj.* (*informal*) **1** not sensible; strange 失去理智的；疯狂的；奇怪的；怪异的 SYN **crazy** **2** (*BrE*) very angry 很生气的；十分愤怒的 SYN **furious**：*He'll go loopy when he hears!* 他听了会气坏的！

loose /luːs/ *adj., verb, noun*

■ ***adj.*** **(loos·er, loos·est)**

• NOT FIXED/TIED 不固定；未系住 **1** not firmly fixed where it should be; able to become separated from sth 未固定牢的；可分开的：*a loose button/tooth* 松动的纽扣 / 牙齿 ◇ *Check that the plug has not come loose.* 检查一下别让插头松脱了。**2** not tied together; not held in position by anything or contained in anything 未系（或捆）

L

在一起的；未固定的；零散的：*She usually wears her hair loose.* 她通常披散着头发。◇ *The potatoes were sold loose, not in bags.* 土豆是散装而不是袋装出售。 **3** [not usually before noun] free to move around without control; not tied up or shut in somewhere 不受约束；未束缚；自由：*The sheep had got out and were loose on the road.* 那些羊跑了出来在路上自由自在地走动。◇ *The horse had* **broken loose** (= escaped) *from its tether.* 那匹马挣脱缰绳跑了。◇ *During the night, somebody had cut the boat loose from its moorings.* 有人在夜间砍断了泊船的缆绳。

• **CLOTHES** 衣服 **4** not fitting closely 宽松的：*a loose shirt* 宽大的衬衣 **OPP** **tight**

• **NOT SOLID/HARD** 不结实；不坚固 **5** not tightly packed together; not solid or hard 疏松的；不结实的；不坚固的：*loose soil* 疏松的土壤 ◇ *a fabric with a loose weave* 编织稀疏的织物

• **NOT STRICT/EXACT** 不严格；不精确 **6** not strictly organized or controlled 组织不严密的；未严加控制的：*a loose alliance/coalition/federation* 松散的联盟／同盟／联邦 **7** not exact; not very careful 不精确的；不严谨的；不周密的：*a loose translation* 不准确的译文 ◇ *loose thinking* 不严密的思想

• **IMMORAL** 不道德 **8** [usually before noun] (*old-fashioned*) having or involving an attitude to sexual relationships that people consider to be immoral 放荡的；淫荡的：*a young man of loose morals* 生活放荡的年轻人

• **BALL** 球 **9** (*sport* 体育) not in any player's control 无球员控制的：*He pounced on a* **loose ball**. 他猛然扑向一个无人控制的球。

• **BODY WASTE** 人体粪便 **10** having too much liquid in it 稀的：*a baby with loose bowel movements* 患腹泻的婴儿

▸ **loose·ness** *noun* [U]

IDM **break/cut/tear (sb/sth) 'loose from sb/sth** to separate yourself or sb/sth from a group of people or their influence, etc.（使）摆脱，挣脱：*The organization broke loose from its sponsors.* 那家机构摆脱了赞助商。◇ *He cut himself loose from his family.* 他摆脱了家庭的束缚。 **hang/stay 'loose** (*informal, especially NAmE*) to remain calm; to not worry 保持镇静；不着急：*It's OK—hang loose and stay cool.* 没事的，你要镇定，冷静。 **have a loose 'tongue** to talk too much, especially about things that are private（尤指对隐私）多嘴，饶舌 **let 'loose** (*BrE*) (*NAmE* **cut 'loose**) (*informal*) to do sth or to happen in a way that is not controlled 不受控制；自在发生：*Teenagers need a place to let loose.* 青少年需要一个可纵情嬉闹的地方。 **let 'loose sth** to make a noise or remark, especially in a loud or sudden way（尤指大声或突然）发出，喊出，发表：*She let loose a stream of abuse.* 她破口大骂起来。 **let sb/sth 'loose 1** to free sb/sth from whatever holds them/it in place 让…自由；释放；放开：*She let her hair loose and it fell around her shoulders.* 她的头发一解开，便顺着肩膀垂了下来。◇ *Who's let the dog loose?* 谁把狗放出来了？ **2** to give sb complete freedom to do what they want in a place or situation 任（某人）自由行动；使随心所欲；放任：*He was at last let loose in the kitchen.* 终于放手让他干厨房里的活儿了。◇ *A team of professionals were* **let loose on** *the project.* 有一组专业人员在全权负责这个项目。 ⊃ MORE AT FAST *adv.*, HELL, SCREW *n.*

■ *verb* (*formal*)

• **RELEASE** 释放 **1 ~ sth (on/upon sb/sth)** to release sth or let it happen or be expressed in an uncontrolled way 释放；放任；不受约束地表达：*His speech loosed a tide of nationalist sentiment.* 他的讲话表露出一种强烈的民族主义情绪。

• **MAKE STH LOOSE** 松开 **2 ~ sth** to make sth loose, especially sth that is tied or held tightly 松开，放开（尤指束紧或紧握的东西） **SYN** **loosen**：*He loosed the straps that bound her arms.* 他松开了绑在她手臂上的带子。

• **FIRE BULLETS** 射子弹 **3 ~ sth (off) (at sb/sth)** to fire bullets, arrows, etc. 射出（子弹、箭等） **HELP** Do not confuse this verb with **to lose** = 'to be unable to find sth'. 不要将此动词与 to lose（遗失）混淆。

■ *noun*

IDM **on the 'loose** (of a person or an animal 人或动物) having escaped from somewhere; free 已逃出；自由 **SYN** at large：*Three prisoners are still on the loose.* 有三名囚犯仍然在逃。

'loose box *noun* (*BrE*) a small area in a building or a vehicle where a horse can move freely 单厩间，散放圈（建筑物或车辆中可供马自由活动的一小块地方）

,loose 'cannon *noun* a person, usually a public figure, who often behaves in a way that nobody can predict 大炮（指举止无法预料的知名人士）

,loose 'change *noun* [U] coins that you have in a pocket or a bag（口袋或包里随身带的）零钱

,loose 'cover (*BrE*) (*NAmE* **slipcover**) *noun* [usually pl.] a cover for a chair, etc. that you can take off, for example to wash it（椅子等的）活套，活罩

,loose 'end *noun* [usually pl.] a part of sth such as a story that has not been completely finished or explained（故事等的）悬念，未了结的部分，未交代清楚的情节：*The play has too many loose ends.* 这部剧有太多地方未交代清楚。◇ *There are still a few loose ends to tie up* (= a few things to finish). 还有几件小事需要了结。

IDM **at a loose 'end** (*BrE*) (*NAmE usually* **at loose 'ends**) having nothing to do and not knowing what you want to do 无所事事；无事可做：*Come and see us, if you're at a loose end.* 你要是闲着无事就来我们这儿坐坐吧。

,loose-'fitting *adj.* (of clothes 衣服) not fitting the body tightly 宽松的；肥大的

,loose 'forward *noun* (in RUGBY 橄榄球) a player who plays at the back of the SCRUM（并列争球时后排的）松头前锋

,loose 'head *noun* (in RUGBY 橄榄球) the player in the front row of a team in the SCRUM who is nearest to where the ball is put in 自由前锋

,loose-'leaf *adj.* [usually before noun] (of a book, file, etc. 书、档案等) having pages that can be taken out and put in separately 活页的：*a loose-leaf binder* 活页夹

,loose-'limbed *adj.* (*literary*) (of a person 人) moving in an easy, not stiff, way 四肢柔软灵活的

loose·ly /ˈluːsli/ *adv.* **1** in a way that is not firm or tight 宽松地；松散地：*She fastened the belt loosely around her waist.* 她把皮带松松地系在腰上。 **2** in a way that is not exact 不精确地：*to use a term loosely* 宽泛地使用术语 ◇ *The play is loosely based on his childhood in Russia.* 那部剧大致上是根据他在俄罗斯的童年生活写成的。

loos·en /ˈluːsn/ *verb* **1** [T, I] **~ (sth)** to make sth less tight or firmly fixed; to become less tight or firmly fixed（使）放松，变松 **SYN** **slacken**：*First loosen the nuts, then take off the wheel.* 先松开螺母，然后卸下车轮。◇ *The rope holding the boat loosened.* 系船的绳子松了。 **2** [T] **~ sth** to make a piece of clothing, hair, etc. loose, when it has been tied or fastened 解开，松开（衣服、头发等） **3** [T] **~ your hands, hold, etc.** to hold sb/sth less tightly 松开，放开（手等）：*He loosened his grip and let her go.* 他松手放开了她。◇ (*figurative*) *The military regime has not loosened its hold on power.* 军事政权尚未放松对权力的控制。 **4** [T] **~ sth** to make sth weaker or less controlled than before（使）变弱，松散，疏远 **SYN** **relax**：*The party has loosened its links with big business.* 这个政党与大企业的关系疏远了。 **OPP** **tighten**

IDM **loosen sb's 'tongue** to make sb talk more freely than usual 使无拘束地说话；使自由自在地说：*A bottle of wine had loosened Harry's tongue.* 一瓶酒下肚，哈里的话匣子便打开了。

PHR V **,loosen 'up** to relax and stop worrying 放松不再担忧：*Come on, Jo. Loosen up.* 得啦，乔，放松些，别再担忧了。 **,loosen 'up | ,loosen sb/sth↔'up** to relax your muscles or parts of the body or to make them relax, before taking exercise, etc.（在运动或其他活动前使肌肉或身体部位）放松

loot /luːt/ *verb, noun*

■ *verb* **1** [T, I] **~ (sth)** to steal things from shops/stores or buildings after a RIOT, fire, etc.（暴乱、火灾等后）打劫，抢劫，劫掠：*More than 20 shops were looted.* 有 20 多家商店遭到了抢劫。 **2** (*IndE*) **~ sth (from sb/sth)** to steal sth (from sb/sth)（从某人或某处）偷，偷走：*A gang went through the train and looted money from passengers.* 几名扒手从火车车厢中走过去，偷乘客的钱。◇ *Clothes and jewellery were looted from her house.* 她家的衣物和首饰被盗。 **3** (*IndE*) **~ sb/sth** to steal money or property from a person or a place（从某人或某处）偷钱（或财物）：(*figurative*) *The Government is looting the public.* 该国政府正在窃取老百姓的财富。◇ *He was stopped by the police while trying to loot a bank.* 他正要偷银行，警察制住了他。 ▶ **loot·er** /ˈluːtə(r)/ *noun* **loot·ing** *noun* [U]

■ *noun* [U] **1** money and valuable objects taken by soldiers from the enemy after winning a battle 战利品；掠夺品 SYN **booty** **2** (*informal*) money and valuable objects that have been stolen by thieves 赃物；被盗物 **3** (*informal*) money 钱

lop /lɒp; *NAmE* lɑːp/ *verb* (-pp-) **~ sth** to cut down a tree, or cut some large branches off it 砍伐；剪（枝）

PHR V **ˌlop sth↔ˈoff (sth)** **1** to remove part of sth by cutting it, especially to remove branches from a tree 砍掉；剪掉；修剪（树枝） SYN **chop** **2** to make sth smaller or less by a particular amount 削减；减少：*They lopped 20p off the price.* 他们把价格降了 20 便士。

lope /ləʊp; *NAmE* loʊp/ *verb* [I] **+ adv./prep.** to run taking long relaxed steps 轻松地大步跑：*The dog loped along beside her.* 那条狗在她身旁轻松地奔跑。◇ *He set off with a loping stride.* 他迈着轻快的步伐出发了。 ▶ **lope** *noun* [usually sing.]

ˈlop-ears *noun* [pl.] ears that hang down at the side of an animal's head 垂耳；耷拉耳 ▶ **ˈlop-eared** *adj.*：*a lop-eared rabbit* 垂耳兔

lop·sided /ˌlɒpˈsaɪdɪd; *NAmE* ˌlɑːp-/ *adj.* having one side lower, smaller, etc. than the other 一侧比另一侧低（或小等）的；向一侧倾斜的；不平衡的：*a lopsided grin/mouth* 撇着嘴笑；撇嘴 ◇ (*figurative*) *The article presents a somewhat lopsided view of events.* 这篇文章对事情的看法显得有些片面。 ▶ **lop·sided·ly** *adv.*

lo·qua·cious /ləˈkweɪʃəs/ *adj.* (*formal*) talking a lot 话多的；健谈的；喋喋不休的 SYN **talkative** ▶ **lo·qua·city** /ləˈkwæsəti/ *noun* [U]

lo·quat /ˈləʊkwɒt; *NAmE* ˈloʊkwɑːt/ *noun* a round pale orange fruit that grows on bushes in China, Japan and the Middle East 枇杷

lord 🔑 /lɔːd; *NAmE* lɔːrd/ *noun, verb*

■ *noun* **1** 🔑 [C] (in Britain) a man of high rank in the NOBILITY (= people of high social class), or sb who has been given the title 'lord' as an honour（英国）贵族 ➲ COMPARE LADY (6) **2** 🔑 **Lord** (in Britain) the title used by a lord 勋爵（英国贵族的称号）：*Lord Beaverbrook* 比弗布鲁克勋爵 **3 Lord** a title used for some high official positions in Britain（英国用于某些高级官员的职位前）阁下，大人，大臣：*the Lord Chancellor* 大法官 ◇ *the Lord Mayor* 市长阁下 **4 My Lord** (in Britain) a title of respect used when speaking to a judge, BISHOP or some male members of the NOBILITY (= people of high social class)（英国用以称呼法官、主教或某些男性贵族成员，表示尊敬）大人，阁下 ➲ COMPARE LADY (6) **5** a powerful man in MEDIEVAL Europe, who owned a lot of land and property（中世纪欧洲的）领主：*a feudal lord* 封建领主 ◇ *the lord of the manor* 庄园主 ➲ SEE ALSO OVERLORD, WARLORD **6** (*usually* **the Lord**) [sing.] a title used to refer to God or Christ 主；上主；上帝：*Love the Lord with all your heart.* 要全心全意地爱主。 **7 Our Lord** [sing.] a title used to refer to Christ 主耶稣；主基督 **8 the Lords** [sing.+sing./pl. v.] = HOUSE OF LORDS：*The Lords has/have not yet reached a decision.* 上议院尚未作出决定。 ➲ COMPARE COMMONS ➲ SEE ALSO LAW LORD

IDM **(good) ˈLord! | oh ˈLord!** *exclamation* used to show that you are surprised, annoyed or worried about sth（表示惊讶、烦恼或忧虑）主啊，天哪：*Good Lord, what have you done to your hair!* 天啊，你把头发弄成什么样子啦！ **ˈLord knows…** used to emphasize what you are saying（强调所说的话）众所周知，谁都知道：*Lord knows, I tried to teach her.* 谁都知道，我曾经努力想教她。 **ˈLord (ˈonly) knows (what, where, why, etc.)…** (*informal*) used to say that you do not know the answer to sth（表示不知道答案）天知道，天晓得：*'Why did she say that?' 'Lord knows!'* "她为何那样说？" "只有天知道！" HELP Some people may find the use of **Lord** in these expressions offensive. 有人可能认为这些表达法用 Lord 含冒犯意。 ➲ MORE AT DRUNK *adj.*, YEAR

■ *verb*

IDM **ˈlord it over sb** (*disapproving*) to act as if you are better or more important than sb 对某人举止霸道（或逞威风）

ˌLord Lieuˈtenant *noun* in the UK, an officer in charge of local government and local judges（英国）郡治安长官

lord·ly /ˈlɔːdli; *NAmE* ˈlɔːrd-/ *adj.* **1** behaving in a way that suggests that you think you are better than other people 傲慢的；高傲的 SYN **haughty** **2** large and impressive; suitable for a lord 宏伟的；堂皇的；贵族气派的 SYN **imposing**：*a lordly mansion* 富丽堂皇的宅第

ˌLord ˈMayor *noun* the title of the mayor of the City of London and some other large British cities 市长大人（伦敦城和其他一些英国大城市市长的称号）

lord·ship /ˈlɔːdʃɪp; *NAmE* ˈlɔːrd-/ *noun* **1 His/Your Lordship** a title of respect used when speaking to or about a judge, a BISHOP or a NOBLEMAN（对法官、主教或贵族的尊称）阁下，大人，爵爷：*His Lordship is away on business.* 爵爷有事出去了。 ➲ COMPARE LADYSHIP **2** (*BrE, informal*) a humorous way of talking to or about a boy or man that you think is trying to be too important（对自以为了不起的男孩或男子幽默的称呼）阁下：*Can his lordship manage to switch off the TV?* 请阁下设法关掉电视机好不好？ **3** [U] the power or position of a LORD 贵族的权力（或身份、地位）

the ˌLord's ˈPrayer *noun* [sing.] the prayer that Jesus Christ taught the people who followed him, that begins 'Our Father…' 主祷文；天主经

lore /lɔː(r)/ *noun* [U] knowledge and information related to a particular subject, especially when this is not written down; the stories and traditions of a particular group of people（尤指口头流传的）某一方面的学问；（某一群体的）传说，传统：*weather lore* 天气的知识 ◇ *Celtic lore* 凯尔特人的传说 ➲ SEE ALSO FOLKLORE

lo-res /ˌləʊ ˈrez; *NAmE* ˌloʊ/ *adj.* = LOW-RESOLUTION

lor·gnette /lɔːˈnjet; *NAmE* lɔːrˈnjet/ *noun* an old-fashioned pair of glasses that you hold to your eyes on a long handle 长柄眼镜

lori·keet /ˈlɒrɪkiːt; *NAmE* ˈlɔːrəkiːt; ˈlɑːr-/ *noun* a small bird found mainly in New Guinea 吸蜜鹦鹉（主要见于新几内亚）

lorry 🔑 /ˈlɒri; *NAmE* ˈlɔːri; ˈlɑːri/ (*BrE*) *noun* (*pl.* **-ies**) (*also* **truck** *NAmE, BrE*) a large vehicle for carrying heavy loads by road 卡车；货运汽车：*a lorry driver* 卡车司机 ◇ *Emergency food supplies were brought in* ***by lorry***. 应急食物是用卡车运来的。◇ *a lorry load of frozen fish* 装满一卡车的冷冻鱼 ➲ VISUAL VOCAB PAGE V62 IDM SEE BACK *n.*

lose 🔑 /luːz/ *verb* (**lost**, **lost** /lɒst; *NAmE* lɔːst; lɑːst/)

• **NOT FIND** 找不到 **1** 🔑 [T] **~ sth/sb** to be unable to find sth/sb 遗失；丢失 SYN **mislay**：*I've lost my keys.* 我把钥匙丢了。◇ *The tickets seem to have* ***got lost***. 那些票好像给弄丢了。◇ *She lost her husband in the crowd.* 她在人群中与丈夫走散了。

• **HAVE STH/SB TAKEN AWAY** 丧失 **2** 🔑 [T] **~ sth/sb** to have sth/sb taken away from you as a result of an accident, getting old, dying, etc.（因事故、年老、死亡等）损失，丧失，失去：*She lost a leg in a car crash.* 她在一次车祸中失去了一条腿。◇ *to* ***lose your hair/teeth*** (= as a result of getting old) 脱发；掉牙 ◇ *He's* ***lost his job***. 他失业了。◇ *Some families* ***lost everything*** (= all they owned) *in the flood.* 有些家庭的财产在洪水中损失得精光。◇ *They lost both their sons* (= they were killed) *in the war.* 他们的两个儿子都被战争夺去了生命。◇ *The ship was* ***lost at sea*** (= it sank). 那条船沉没了。◇ *Many people* ***lost their lives*** (=

L

were killed). 有许多人丧生。 **3** [T] ~ **sth** (**to sb/sth**) to have sth taken away by sb/sth 被…夺去: *The company has lost a lot of business to its competitors.* 公司的许多生意都被对手夺走了。 **4** [T] ~ **sth** to have to give up sth; to fail to keep sth 被迫放弃; 失去: *You will lose your deposit if you cancel the order.* 如果撤销订单，订金将不予退还。 ◇ *Sit down or you'll lose your seat.* 坐下吧，要不这个座位就没啦。

• HAVE LESS 减少 **5** [T] ~ **sth** to have less and less of sth, especially until you no longer have any of it 降低; 减少; 渐渐丧失: *He* **lost his nerve** *at the last minute.* 他在最后一刻失去了勇气。 ◇ *She seemed to have* **lost interest** *in food.* 她好像对食物不感兴趣了。 ◇ *At that moment he* **lost his balance** *and fell.* 他在那一瞬间失去平衡摔倒了。 ◇ *I've lost ten pounds since I started this diet.* 这次节食开始以来我体重减了十磅。 ◇ *The train was* **losing speed**. 火车当时正在减速。

• NOT WIN 未赢 **6** [T, I] to be defeated; to fail to win a competition, a court case, an argument, etc. 被打败; 输掉（比赛、诉讼案件、辩论等）: ~ **sth** (**to sb**) ***to lose a game/a race/an election/a battle/a war*** 输掉比赛 / 赛跑 / 选举 / 战役 / 战争 ◇ ~ **to sb** *We lost to a stronger team.* 我们输给了一支实力更强的队。 ◇ ~ (**sth**) (**by sth**) *He lost by less than 100 votes.* 他以不到 100 张选票败北。

• NOT KEEP 未保留 **7** [T, I] to fail to keep sth you want or need, especially money; to cause sb to fail to keep sth（使）失去（所需要的东西，尤指钱）: ~ **sth** *The business is losing money.* 这家公司正在亏损。 ◇ *Poetry always loses something in translation.* 诗歌一经翻译总会失去某些东西。 ◇ ~ **sth** (**on sth/by doing sth**) ***You have nothing to lose*** *by telling the truth.* 你讲真话是不会吃亏的。 ◇ ~ **on sth/by doing sth** *We lost on that deal.* 我们那笔交易做亏了。 ◇ ~ **sb sth** *His carelessness lost him the job.* 他粗枝大叶，丢了工作。

• NOT UNDERSTAND/HEAR 弄不懂; 听不见 **8** [T] ~ **sth** to fail to get, hear or understand sth 不明白; 听不见; 弄不懂: *His words were lost* (= could not be heard) *in the applause.* 他的讲话让掌声淹没了。 **9** [T] ~ **sb** (*informal*) to be no longer understood by sb 使弄不懂; 使不理解: *I'm afraid* ***you've lost me*** *there.* 很抱歉，我没听明白你的话。

• ESCAPE 逃避 **10** [T] ~ **sb/sth** to escape from sb/sth 逃避; 逃脱 SYN **evade, shake sb↔off**: *We managed to lose our pursuers in the darkness.* 我们设法在黑暗中摆脱了追赶者。

• TIME 时间 **11** [T] ~ **sth** to waste time or an opportunity 浪费（时间）; 错过（机会）: *We lost twenty minutes changing a tyre.* 我们换轮胎耽误了二十分钟。 ◇ ***Hurry—there's no time to lose!*** 快点，抓紧时间吧！ ◇ ***He lost no time in*** *setting out for London.* 他赶紧启程去了伦敦。 **12** [T, I] ~ (**sth**) if a watch or clock **loses** or **loses time**, it goes too slowly or becomes a particular amount of time behind the correct time（钟、表）走慢，慢（若干时间）: *This clock loses two minutes a day.* 这时钟每天慢两分钟。 OPP **gain**

IDM HELP Most idioms containing **lose** are at the entries for the nouns and adjectives in the idioms, for example **lose your bearings** is at **bearing**. 大多数含 lose 的习语，都可在该等习语中的名词及形容词相关词条找到，如 lose your bearings 在词条 bearing 下。 **'lose it** (*informal*) to be unable to stop yourself from crying, laughing, etc.; to become crazy 禁不住（哭、笑等）; 变得疯狂: *Then she just lost it and started screaming.* 然后她再也控制不住，尖叫起来。

PHR V **'lose yourself in sth** to become so interested in sth that it takes all your attention 沉迷于; 专心致志于 **,lose 'out (on sth)** (*informal*) to not get sth you wanted or feel you should have 得不到（想要或觉得应有的东西）: *While the stores make big profits, it's the customer who loses out.* 商店赚大钱，而吃亏的是顾客。 **,lose 'out to sb/sth** (*informal*) to not get business, etc. that you expected or used to get because sb/sth else has taken it 被…取代: *Small businesses are losing out to the large chains.* 小商店被大型的连锁店抢了生意。

loser /ˈluːzə(r)/ *noun* **1** a person who is defeated in a competition（比赛的）输者，败者: *winners and losers* 赢家与输家 ◇ *He's* ***a good/bad loser*** (= he accepts defeat well/badly). 他是个输得起 / 输不起的人。 **2** (*rather informal*) a person who is regularly unsuccessful, especially when you have a low opinion of them 屡屡失败的人（尤指评价较低者）: *She's one of life's losers.* 她是个生活的失败者。 ◇ *He's* ***a born loser***. 他生来就是个失败者。 **3** a person who suffers because of a particular action, decision, etc.（因某行为、决定等的）受损害者: *The real losers in all of this are the students.* 在这一切中真正受损害的是学生。

loss /lɒs; *NAmE* lɔːs; lɑːs/ *noun* **1** [U, C, usually sing.] the state of no longer having sth or as much of sth; the process that leads to this 丧失; 损失; 丢失: *I want to report the loss of a package.* 我要报告丢失了一个包裹。 ◇ ***loss of blood*** 失血 ◇ ***weight loss*** 体重减少 ◇ *The closure of the factory will lead to a number of* ***job losses***. 工厂倒闭会使许多人失业。 ◇ *When she died I was filled with* ***a sense of loss***. 她去世后我心里充满了失落感。 ◇ ***loss of earnings*** (= the money you do not earn because you are prevented from working) 收入损失 **2** [C] money that has been lost by a business or an organization 亏损; 亏蚀: *The company has announced* ***net losses*** *of $1.5 million.* 公司宣布净亏损 150 万美元。 ◇ *We* ***made a loss on*** (= lost money on) *the deal.* 我们做那笔交易亏了。 ◇ *We are now operating* ***at a loss***. 我们现在是亏本经营。 OPP **profit** **3** [C, U] the death of a person 去世; 逝世: *The loss of his wife was a great blow to him.* 他妻子去世对他是个巨大的打击。 ◇ *Enemy troops suffered* ***heavy losses***. 敌军伤亡惨重。 ◇ *The drought has led to widespread* ***loss of life***. 旱灾导致了许多人的死亡。 **4** [sing.] the disadvantage that is caused when sb leaves or when a useful or valuable object is taken away; a person who causes a disadvantage by leaving（某人离开或珍贵物品被取走造成的）损失; 因离去而造成损失者: *Her departure is a* ***big loss*** *to the school.* 她这一走对学校来说是一个巨大的损失。 ◇ *She will be a* ***great loss*** *to the school.* 她这一走对学校来说将是一个巨大的损失。 ◇ *If he isn't prepared to accept this money, then* ***that's his loss***. 如果他不打算接受这笔钱，那他就亏了。 ➲ SEE ALSO DEAD LOSS **5** [C] a failure to win a contest 失败; 输; 失利: *Brazil's 2–1 loss to Argentina* 巴西对阿根廷 1:2 的落败

IDM **at a 'loss** not knowing what to say or do 不知所措; 困惑: *His comments left me* ***at a loss for words***. 他的评论让我不知说什么才好。 ◇ *I'm at a loss what to do next.* 我对下一步做什么心里没谱。 **cut your 'losses** to stop doing sth that is not successful before the situation becomes even worse 不成功就住手（免得情况更糟）; 趁早罢手

'loss adjuster (*BrE*) (*NAmE* **in'surance adjuster**) *noun* a person who works for an insurance company and whose job is to calculate how much money sb should receive after they have lost sth or had sth damaged（保险公司的）理赔员

'loss-leader *noun* an item that a shop/store sells at a very low price to attract customers 为招徕顾客而低价出售的商品

loss·less /ˈlɒsləs; *NAmE* ˈlɔːs-; ˈlɑːs-/ *adj.* (*specialist*) involving no loss of data or electrical energy（数据或电能）无损的; 无损耗的 OPP **lossy**

'loss-making *adj.* (of a company or business 公司或生意) not making a profit; losing money 不赢利的; 亏损的

lossy /ˈlɒsi; *NAmE* ˈlɔːsi; ˈlɑːsi/ *adj.* (*specialist*) involving the loss of data or electrical energy（数据或电能）有损的; 有损耗的 OPP **lossless**

lost /lɒst; *NAmE* lɔːst; lɑːst/ *adj.* **1** unable to find your way; not knowing where you are 迷路的; 迷失的: *We always* ***get lost*** *in London.* 我们在伦敦老是迷路。 ◇ *We're completely lost.* 我们完全迷路了。 **2** that cannot be found or brought back 失去的; 丢失的; 丧失的; 无法恢复的: *I'm still looking for that lost file.* 我还在找那份丢失的档案。 ◇ *Your cheque must have* ***got lost*** *in the post.* 你的支票一定是邮寄中遗失的。 **3** [usually before noun] that cannot be obtained; that cannot be found or created again 得不到的; 无法再找到的; 无法再造的: *The strike cost them thousands of pounds in* ***lost business***. 罢工使他们失去了几千英镑的生意。 ◇ *She's trying to recapture her* ***lost youth***. 她在努力追回逝去的青春。 ◇ *He regretted the* ***lost*** (= wasted) ***opportunity*** *to apologize to her.* 他后悔错

过了向她道歉的机会。 **4** [not before noun] unable to deal successfully with a particular situation 不知所措；一筹莫展：*We would* **be lost without** *your help.* 我们没有你的帮助就会一筹莫展。◇ *I felt so lost after my mother died.* 我母亲去世后我觉得茫然无措。◇ *He's a* **lost soul** (= a person who does not seem to know what to do, and seems unhappy). 他是个迷惘的人。 **5** [not before noun] unable to understand sth because it is too complicated 弄不懂；困惑：*They spoke so quickly I just got lost.* 他们说得太快，我跟不上了。◇ *Hang on a minute—I'm lost.* 等一下，我没弄明白。 ➲ SEE ALSO LOSE

IDM ˌ**all is not 'lost** there is still some hope of making a bad situation better 还有一线希望 **be lost for 'words** to be so surprised, confused, etc. that you do not know what to say（非常惊讶、困惑等而）不知说什么才好 **be 'lost in sth** to be giving all your attention to sth so that you do not notice what is happening around you 全神贯注；沉浸于：*to be lost in thought* 陷入沉思 **be 'lost on sb** to be not understood or noticed by sb 未被某人理解（或注意）：*His jokes were completely lost on most of the students.* 他讲的那些笑话大多数学生一点都没能领会。 **be lost to the 'world** to be giving all your attention to sth so that you do not notice what is happening around you（全神贯注于某事而）不注意周围的事情 **get 'lost** (*informal*) a rude way of telling sb to go away, or of refusing sth（让人走开或拒绝某事的不礼貌说法）滚开，别来烦我 **give sb up for 'lost** (*formal*) to stop expecting to find sb alive 认为某人没有生还的可能；认定某人已死 **make up for lost 'time** to do sth quickly or very often because you wish you had started doing it sooner（加快或加紧做某事以）弥补失去的时间 ➲ MORE AT LOVE *n.*

ˌ**lost and 'found** (*NAmE*) (*BrE* ˌ**lost 'property**) *noun* [U] the place where items that have been found are kept until they are collected 失物招领处

ˌ**lost 'cause** *noun* something that has failed or that cannot succeed 业已失败的事情；没有希望的事情

ˌ**lost 'property** *noun* [U] (*BrE*) **1** items that have been found in public places and are waiting to be collected by the people who lost them（待招领的）失物：*a lost-property office* 失物招领处 **2** (*NAmE* ˌ**lost and 'found**) the place where items that have been found are kept until they are collected 失物招领处

lot /lɒt; *NAmE* lɑːt/ *pron., det., adv., noun*

■ ***pron.*** **a lot** (*also informal* **lots**) ~ (**to do**) a large number or amount 大量；许多：*'How many do you need?' 'A lot.'* "你需要多少？" "很多。" ◇ *Have some more cake. There's lots left.* 再吃点蛋糕吧。还剩下好多呢。◇ *She still has* **an awful lot** (= a very large amount) *to learn.* 她要学的还多着呢。◇ *He has invited nearly a hundred people but a lot aren't able to come.* 他邀请了差不多一百人，但很多人都来不了。 ➲ NOTE AT MANY, MUCH

■ ***det.*** **a lot of** (*also informal* **lots of**) a large number or amount of sb/sth 大量；许多：*What a lot of presents!* 礼品真多啊！◇ *A lot of people are coming to the meeting.* 有很多人要来参加这次会议。◇ *black coffee with lots of sugar* 不加奶多放糖的咖啡 ◇ *I saw a lot of her* (= I saw her often) *last summer.* 去年夏天我经常见到她。 ➲ NOTE AT MANY, MUCH

■ ***adv.*** (*informal*) **1** **a lot** (*also informal* **lots**) used with adjectives and adverbs to mean 'much'（与形容词和副词连用）很，非常：*I'm feeling a lot better today.* 我今天感觉好多了。◇ *I eat lots less than I used to.* 我比以前吃得少多了。 **2** **a lot** used with verbs to mean 'a great amount'（与动词连用）非常：*I care a lot about you.* 我非常在乎你。◇ *Thanks a lot for your help.* 非常感谢你的帮助。◇ *I play tennis quite a lot* (= often) *in the summer.* 我夏天常打网球。 ➲ NOTE AT MUCH

■ ***noun***

• **WHOLE AMOUNT/NUMBER** 全数 **1 the lot, the whole lot** [sing.+sing./pl. v.] (*informal*) the whole number or amount of people or things 全体；全部；整个：*He's bought a new PC, colour printer, scanner—the lot.* 他买了新的个人电脑、彩色打印机、扫描仪，样样齐备。◇ *Get out of my house, the lot of you!* 你们别待在我家里，通通给我滚出去！◇ *That's the lot!* (= that includes everything) 全都在这儿了！◇ *That's your lot!* (= that's all you're getting) 你的那份儿全在那儿了！

• **GROUP/SET** 群；套 **2** [C+sing./pl. v.] (*especially BrE*) a group or set of people or things（一）组，群，批，套：*The first lot of visitors has/have arrived.* 首批游客已经到达。◇ *I have several lots of essays to mark this weekend.* 这周末我有几批文章要批改。◇ (*informal*) *What do* **you lot** *want?* 你们这帮人想要怎么样？

• **ITEMS TO BE SOLD** 待售物品 **3** [C] an item or a number of items to be sold, especially at an AUCTION 待售商品；（尤指）拍卖品：*Lot 46: six chairs* 拍卖品 46 号：六把椅子

• **AREA OF LAND** 一块地 **4** [C] an area of land used for a particular purpose（作某种用途的）一块地，场地：*a parking lot* 停车场 ◇ *a vacant lot* (= one available to be built on or used for sth) 一块空地 ◇ (*especially NAmE*) *We're going to build a house on this lot.* 我们打算在这块地上建造一座房子。 ➲ SYNONYMS AT LAND

• **LUCK/SITUATION** 运气；境况 **5** [sing.] a person's luck or situation in life 命运；生活状况 SYN **destiny**：*She was feeling dissatisfied with her lot.* 她对自己的生活状况感到不满。

IDM **all 'over the lot** (*NAmE*) = ALL OVER THE PLACE **a bad 'lot** (*old-fashioned, BrE*) a person who is dishonest 不诚实的人；骗子 **by 'lot** using a method of choosing sb to do sth in which each person takes a piece of paper, etc. from a container and the one whose paper has a special mark is chosen 抽签；抓阄 **draw/cast 'lots (for sth/to do sth)** to choose sb/sth by lot 抽签（选定）；抓阄（决定）：*They drew lots for the right to go first.* 他们拈阄儿决定谁先走。 **fall to sb's 'lot (to do sth)** (*formal*) to become sb's task or responsibility 成为某人的任务（或责任）；落到某人肩上 **throw in your 'lot with sb** to decide to join sb and share their successes and problems 决心与某人共命运 ➲ MORE AT BEST *n.*

ˌ**lo-'tech** *adj.* = LOW-TECH

loth = LOATH

Loth·ario /ləˈθeəriəʊ; ləˈθɑːriəʊ; *NAmE* ləˈθerioʊ; ləˈθɑːrioʊ/ *noun* (*pl.* **-os**) a man who has sex with a lot of women 迷人浪子：*He has a reputation as the office Lothario.* 他在办公室泡妞乱搞是出了名的。 ➲ MORE LIKE THIS 17, page R27

ORIGIN From the name of a character in an 18th century play by Nicholas Rowe. 源自 18 世纪尼古拉斯•罗所写的戏剧人物洛萨里奥。

lo·tion /ˈləʊʃn; *NAmE* ˈloʊʃn/ *noun* [C, U] a liquid used for cleaning, protecting or treating the skin 洁肤液；护肤液；润肤乳：(*a*) ***body/hand lotion*** 护肤 / 护手乳液 ◇ *suntan lotion* 防晒露

lotta /ˈlɒtə; *NAmE* ˈlɑːtə/ (*also* **lotsa** /ˈlɒtsə; *NAmE* ˈlɑːtsə/) (*informal, non-standard*) a written form of 'lot of' or 'lots of' that shows how it sounds in informal speech 许多：*We're gonna have a lotta fun.* 我们将玩得非常开心。 HELP You should not write this form unless you are copying somebody's speech. 除非转述他人话语，否则不应写成这种形式。

lot·tery /ˈlɒtəri; *NAmE* ˈlɑːt-/ *noun* (*pl.* **-ies**) **1** [C] a way of raising money for a government, charity, etc. by selling tickets that have different numbers on them that people have chosen. Numbers are then chosen by chance and the people who have those numbers on their tickets win prizes.（用发行彩票为政府、慈善机构等集资的）抽彩给奖法：*the* ***national/state lottery*** 全国的 / 州的彩票抽奖 ◇ *a lottery ticket* 彩票 ➲ COMPARE DRAW *n.* (3), RAFFLE *n.* ➲ WORDFINDER NOTE AT GAMBLING **2** [sing.] (*often disapproving*) a situation whose success or result is based on luck rather than on effort or careful organization 碰运气的事 SYN **gamble**：*Some people think that marriage is a lottery.* 有些人认为婚姻靠的是运气。 ➲ SEE ALSO POSTCODE LOTTERY

lotto /ˈlɒtəʊ; *NAmE* ˈlɑːtoʊ/ *noun* (*pl.* **lottos**) **1** [U] a game of chance similar to BINGO but with the numbers drawn from a container by the players instead of being called out 抽号码赌博游戏 **2** [C] a lottery 彩票

lotus /ˈləʊtəs; *NAmE* ˈloʊ-/ *noun* **1** a tropical plant with white or pink flowers that grows on the surface of lakes in Africa and Asia 莲属植物：*a lotus flower* 莲花 ➲ VISUAL VOCAB PAGE V11 **2** a picture in the shape of the lotus plant, used in art and ARCHITECTURE, especially in ancient Egypt 莲花图案，荷花饰（尤用于古埃及艺术和建筑） **3** (in ancient Greek stories 古希腊神话) a fruit that is supposed to make you feel happy and relaxed when you have eaten it, as if in a dream 落拓枣，忘忧果（食后感到梦幻般的快乐轻松）

ˈlotus position *noun* [sing.] a way of sitting with your legs crossed, used especially when people MEDITATE or do YOGA（尤指冥想或做瑜伽时）跏趺坐，莲花坐

louche /luːʃ/ *adj.* (*especially BrE, formal*) not socially acceptable, but often still attractive despite this 声名不好却有吸引力的

loud /laʊd/ *adj., adv.*

■ *adj.* (**loud·er**, **loud·est**) **1** making a lot of noise 喧闹的；响亮的；大声的：*loud laughter* 响亮的笑声 ◇ *a deafeningly loud bang* 震耳欲聋的巨响 ◇ *She spoke in a very loud voice.* 她声音洪亮地讲了话。◇ *That music's too loud—please turn it down.* 那音乐太吵了，请把音量调低一点。 **2** (of a person or their behaviour 人或行为) talking very loudly, too much and in a way that is annoying 说话太大声的；吵闹的 **3** (of colours, patterns, etc. 颜色、图案等) too bright and lacking good taste 俗艳的；花哨的 SYN **gaudy, garish** ▸ **loud·ly** *adv.*：*She screamed as loudly as she could.* 她声声嘶力竭地尖叫着。 **loud·ness** *noun* [U]

■ *adv.* (**loud·er**, **loud·est**) (*informal*) in a way that makes a lot of noise or can be easily heard 喧闹地；大声地；响亮地 SYN **loudly**：*Do you have to play that music so loud?* 你非得把音乐放那么响吗？◇ *You'll have to speak louder—I can't hear you.* 你得说大声点，我听不见你的话。

IDM ˌ**loud and ˈclear** in a way that is very easy to understand 清楚明白：*The message is coming through loud and clear.* 消息传达得清楚明白。 ˌ**out ˈloud** in a voice that can be heard by other people 出声；大声地：*I laughed out loud.* 我放声大笑。◇ *Please read the letter out loud.* 请把信大声念出来。 ➲ COMPARE ALOUD ➲ MORE AT ACTION *n.*, CRY *v.*, THINK *v.*

▼ **WHICH WORD? 词语辨析**

loud / loudly / aloud

- **Loudly** is the usual adverb from the adjective **loud**. * loudly 为形容词 loud 的常用副词：*The audience laughed loudly at the joke.* 观众听到这笑话大笑起来。
- **Loud** is very common as an adverb in informal language. It is nearly always used in phrases such as **loud enough**, **as loud as** or with *too*, *very*, *so*, etc. * loud 作非正式用语常为副词，几乎总是用于 loud enough、as loud as 等短语中，或与 too、very、so 等词连用：*Don't play your music too loud.* 你播放音乐声音别太大。◇ *I shouted as loud as I could.* 我声嘶力竭地喊着。
- **Louder** is also used in informal styles to mean 'more loudly'. * louder 亦作非正式用语指以更大的声音：*Can you speak louder?* 你说话大声些行吗？
- **Out loud** is a common adverb meaning 'so that people can hear'. * out loud 为常用副词，意为出声地、大声地：*Can you read the letter out loud?* 你把信念出来行吗？◇ *He laughed out loud at his own joke.* 他对自己的笑话大笑起来。 **Aloud** has the same meaning but is fairly formal. It can also mean 'in a loud voice'. * aloud 意义相同，但相当正式，亦含大声之义。

loud·hail·er /ˌlaʊdˈheɪlə(r)/ (*BrE*) (*NAmE* **bull·horn**) *noun* an electronic device, shaped like a horn, with a MICROPHONE at one end, that you speak into in order to make your voice louder so that it can be heard at a distance 电子喇叭；扩音器 ➲ COMPARE MEGAPHONE

loud·mouth /ˈlaʊdmaʊθ/ *noun* (*informal*) a person who is annoying because they talk too loudly or too much in an offensive or stupid way 说话大声大气的人；喋喋不休的人 ▸ ˈ**loud-mouthed** *adj.*

loud·speak·er /ˌlaʊdˈspiːkə(r)/ *noun* **1** a piece of equipment that changes electrical signals into sound, used in public places for announcing things, playing music, etc. 扬声器；扩音器；喇叭：*Their names were called over the loudspeaker.* 喇叭里叫着他们的名字。 ➲ SEE ALSO PUBLIC ADDRESS SYSTEM, TANNOY™ **2** (*old-fashioned*) the part of a radio or piece of musical equipment that the sound comes out of（收音机或音响设备的）扬声器，喇叭 SYN **speaker**

lough /lɒk; lɒx; *NAmE* lɑːk; lɑːx/ *noun* (in Ireland 爱尔兰) a lake or a long strip of sea that is almost surrounded by land 湖；狭长的海湾：*Lough Corrib* 科里布湖 ➲ SEE ALSO LOCH

lounge /laʊndʒ/ *noun, verb*

■ *noun* **1** a room for waiting in at an airport, etc.（机场等的）等候室：*the departure lounge* 候机室 ➲ WORDFINDER NOTE AT AIRPORT **2** a public room in a hotel, club, etc. for waiting or relaxing in（旅馆、俱乐部等的）休息室：*the television lounge* 电视放映室 **3** (*BrE*) a room in a private house for sitting and relaxing in（私宅中的）起居室 SYN **living room, sitting room** ➲ SEE ALSO SUN LOUNGE **4** (*BrE*) = LOUNGE BAR

■ *verb* [I] (+ **adv./prep.**) to stand, sit or lie in a lazy way 懒洋洋地站（或坐、躺）着 SYN **laze**：*Several students were lounging around, reading newspapers.* 有几个学生懒洋洋地坐着看报。

ˈ**lounge bar** (*also* **sal·oon**) (*both BrE*) *noun* a bar in a pub, hotel, etc. which is more comfortable than the other bars and where the drinks are usually more expensive（酒馆、旅馆等的）高级酒吧，豪华酒吧 ➲ COMPARE PUBLIC BAR

ˈ**lounge lizard** *noun* (*old-fashioned, informal*) a person who does no work and who likes to be with rich, fashionable people（爱与时髦富人厮混的）二流子

loun·ger /ˈlaʊndʒə(r)/ *noun* (*especially BrE*) a long comfortable chair that supports your legs, used for sitting or lying on, especially outdoors 日光浴椅；日光浴床 ➲ COMPARE SUNLOUNGER

ˈ**lounge suit** *noun* (*BrE*) a man's suit of matching jacket and trousers/pants, worn especially in offices and on fairly formal occasions（尤指在办公室及较正式场合穿的）男式套装

lour *verb* = LOWER²

louse /laʊs/ *noun, verb*

■ *noun* **1** (*pl.* **lice** /laɪs/) a small insect that lives on the bodies of humans and animals 虱；虱子：*head lice* 头虱 ➲ SEE ALSO WOODLOUSE **2** (*pl.* **louses**) (*informal, disapproving*) a very unpleasant person 不受欢迎的人；讨厌鬼

■ *verb*

PHR V ˌ**louse sth↔ˈup** (*informal*) to spoil sth or do it very badly 搞坏；弄糟

lousy /ˈlaʊzi/ *adj.* (**lous·ier**, **lousi·est**) (*informal*) **1** very bad 非常糟的；很坏的；恶劣的 SYN **awful, terrible**：*What lousy weather!* 这天气真糟糕！◇ *She felt lousy* (= ill). 她觉得很不舒服。 **2** [only before noun] used to show that you feel annoyed or insulted because you do not think that sth is worth very much（认为某事物无太大价值而感到不满或受辱）讨厌的，倒霉的：*All she bought me was this lousy T-shirt.* 她给我买的就这件破 T 恤。 **3** ~ **with sth/sb** (*NAmE*) having too much of sth or too many people（某事物或人）太多的：*This place is lousy with tourists in August.* 在八月份，这个地方挤满游人。

lout /laʊt/ *noun* a man or boy who behaves in a rude and aggressive way 举止粗野的男人（或男孩） SYN **yob** ➲ SEE ALSO LAGER LOUT, LITTER LOUT ▸ **lout·ish** *adj.*：*loutish behaviour* 粗野无礼的行为

louvre (*especially US* **lou·ver**) /ˈluːvə(r)/ *noun* one of a set of narrow strips of wood, plastic, etc. in a door or a window that are designed to let air and some light in, but to keep out strong light or rain; a door or a window that has these strips across it 百叶窗板；百叶门；百叶窗 ▶ **louvred** (*especially US* **lou·vered**) *adj.*

lov·able (*also* **love·able**) /ˈlʌvəbl/ *adj.* having qualities that people find attractive and easy to love, often despite any faults 可爱的；惹人爱的；讨人喜欢的 SYN **endearing**: *a lovable child* 讨人喜欢的小孩 ◇ *a lovable rogue* 可爱的淘气鬼

love /lʌv/ *noun, verb*

■ *noun*

• **AFFECTION** 喜爱 **1** [U] a strong feeling of deep affection for sb/sth, especially a member of your family or a friend 爱；热爱；慈爱： *a mother's love for her children* 母亲对孩子的爱 ◇ *love of your country* 对祖国的热爱 ◇ *He seems incapable of love.* 他似乎没有能力去爱人。

• **ROMANTIC** 浪漫 **2** [U] a strong feeling of affection for sb that you are sexually attracted to 爱情；恋爱： *a love song/story* 爱情歌曲 / 故事 ◇ *We're* ***in love!*** 我们相爱了！◇ *She was* ***in love with*** *him.* 她与他相爱了。◇ *They* ***fell in love*** *with each other.* 他们彼此相爱了。◇ *It was* ***love at first sight*** (= they were attracted to each other the first time they met). 那是一见钟情。◇ *They're* ***madly in love.*** 他们狂热地相爱。◇ *Their love grew with the years.* 他们的爱逐年加深。

> **WORDFINDER** 联想词： affair, date, go out with sb, jealous, **marriage**, partner, passionate, relationship, romantic

• **ENJOYMENT** 乐趣 **3** [U, sing.] the strong feeling of enjoyment that sth gives you 喜好；喜爱： *a love* ***of*** *learning* 对知识的喜爱 ◇ *He's* ***in love with*** *his work.* 他热爱自己的工作。◇ *I* ***fell in love with*** *the house.* 我喜欢上了这房子。

• **SB/STH YOU LIKE** 所爱的人 / 事物 **4** [C] a person, a thing or an activity that you like very much 心爱的人；钟爱之物；爱好： *Take care, my love.* 保重，我的爱人。◇ *He was* ***the love of my life*** (= the person I loved most). 他是我一生中最爱的人。◇ *I like most sports but tennis is my* ***first love.*** 大多数运动我都喜欢，而网球是我的第一爱好。

• **FRIENDLY NAME** 友好的称呼 **5** [C] (*BrE, informal*) a word used as a friendly way of addressing sb（昵称）亲爱的： *Can I help you, love?* 亲爱的，我能帮你忙吗？ ➲ COMPARE DUCK *n.* (4)

• **IN TENNIS** 网球 **6** [U] a score of zero (points or games) 零分： *40–love!* * 40 比 0！◇ *She won the first set* ***six–love/six games to love.*** 她以六比零赢了第一盘。

IDM **(just) for ˈlove | (just) for the ˈlove of sth** without receiving payment or any other reward 出于爱好；不收报酬；无偿： *They're all volunteers, working for the love of it.* 他们都是义务工作的志愿者。 **for the love of ˈGod** (*old-fashioned, informal*) used when you are expressing anger and the fact that you are impatient（表示愤怒和不耐烦）看在上帝的分上，哎呀，求求你： *For the love of God, tell me what he said!* 看在上帝的分上，告诉我他说了些什么！ **give/send my love to sb** (*informal*) used to send good wishes to sb 向某人致意（或问候）： *Give my love to Mary when you see her.* 你见到玛丽代我向她问好。◇ *Bob sends his love.* 鲍勃向你致意。 **ˈlove from | lots of ˈlove (from)** (*informal*) used at the end of a letter to a friend or to sb you love, followed by your name（用于给朋友或所爱的人的信结尾具名前）爱你的： *Lots of love, Jenny* 非常爱你的珍妮 **love is ˈblind** (*saying*) when you love sb, you cannot see their faults 爱情是盲目的，爱让人蒙蔽双眼（指恋爱中的人看不到对方缺点） **make ˈlove (to sb)** to have sex 有性行为；性交；做爱： *It was the first time they had made love.* 那是他们第一次发生性关系。 **not for love or/nor ˈmoney** if you say you cannot do sth **for love nor money**, you mean it is completely impossible to do it 决不；无论怎样也不： *We couldn't find a taxi for love nor money.* 我们无论如何也找不到一辆出租车。 **there's little/no ˈlove lost between A and B** they do not like each other（…之间）彼此厌恶，互无好感： *There's no love lost between her and her in-laws.* 她和她的姻亲彼此嫌恶。 ➲ MORE AT CUPBOARD, FAIR *adj.*, HEAD *n.*, LABOUR *n.*

■ *verb*

• **FEEL AFFECTION** 感到爱 **1** **~ sb/sth** (not used in the progressive tenses 不用于进行时) to have very strong feelings of affection for sb 爱；热爱： *I love you.* 我爱你。◇ *If you love each other, why not get married?* 要是你们彼此相爱，干吗不结婚呢？◇ *Her much-loved brother lay dying of AIDS.* 她至爱的兄弟因艾滋病而濒临死亡。◇ *He had become a well-loved member of staff.* 他已成为受人喜爱的职员。◇ *Relatives need time to grieve over* ***loved ones*** *they have lost.* 失去所爱的人，亲人们总要悲伤一段时间。◇ *to love your country* 热爱你的祖国

• **LIKE/ENJOY** 喜欢；爱好 **2** to like or enjoy sth very much 喜欢；喜爱 SYN **adore**: **~ sth** *I really love summer evenings.* 我非常喜欢夏天的夜晚。◇ ***I just love it when*** *you bring me presents!* 我就喜欢你送我礼物！◇ *He* ***loved the way*** *she smiled.* 他喜欢她微笑的样子。◇ ***I love it*** *in Spain* (= I like the life there). 我喜欢西班牙的生活。◇ *It was one of his best-loved songs.* 这是他最受喜爱的歌曲之一。◇ (*ironic*) ***You're going to love this.*** *They've changed their minds again.* 你会喜欢的，他们又改变主意了。◇ **~ doing sth** (*especially in BrE*) *My dad loves going to football games.* 我父亲爱去看足球赛。◇ **~ to do sth** (*especially NAmE*) *I love to go out dancing.* 我喜欢出去跳舞。◇ **~ sb/sth to do sth** *He loved her to sing to him.* 他喜欢让她唱歌给他听。 ➲ SYNONYMS AT LIKE **3** **would love** used to say that you would very much like sth 很喜欢；很愿意： **~ to do sth** *Come on Rory, the kids would love to hear you sing.* 来吧，罗里，孩子们都很喜欢听你唱歌。◇ *I haven't been to Brazil, but I'd love to go.* 我没去过巴西，但很想去。◇ **~ sb/sth to do sth** *I'd love her to come and live with us.* 我很愿意让她来和我们住在一起。◇ **~ sth** *'Cigarette?' 'I'd love one, but I've just given up.'* "要抽支烟吗？" "我倒很乐意抽一支，可我刚把烟戒了。"

IDM **ˌlove you and ˈleave you** (*informal, humorous*) used

> ▼ **SYNONYMS** 同义词辨析
>
> **love**
>
> **like • be fond of sb • adore • be devoted to sb • care for sb • dote on sb**
>
> These words all mean to have feelings of love or affection for sb. 以上各词均含喜爱、爱慕某人之义。
>
> **love** to have strong feelings of affection for sb 指爱、热爱： *I love you.* 我爱你。
>
> **like** to find sb pleasant and enjoy being with them 指喜欢、喜爱： *She's nice. I like her.* 她人很好，我喜欢她。
>
> **be fond of sb** to feel affection for sb, especially sb you have known for a long time 指喜爱（尤指认识已久的人）： *I've always been very fond of your mother.* 我一直非常喜欢你的母亲。
>
> **adore** to love sb very much 指热爱、爱慕： *It's obvious that she adores him.* 她显然深深地爱着他。
>
> **be devoted to sb** to love sb very much and be loyal to them 指深爱、忠诚于某人： *They are devoted to their children.* 他们深爱着自己的孩子。
>
> **care for sb** to love sb, especially in a way that is based on strong affection or a feeling of wanting to protect them, rather than sex 指深深地爱、非常喜欢，但不指性爱： *He cared for her more than she realized.* 她不知道他是多么在乎她。 NOTE **Care for sb** is often used when sb has not told anyone about their feelings or is just starting to be aware of them. It is also used when sb wishes that sb loved them, or doubts that sb does. * care for sb 常用于未向任何人吐露感情或刚开始意识到这种感情时，亦用于希望别人爱自己或不知别人是否爱自己时： *If he really cared for you, he wouldn't behave like that.* 如果他真的在乎你，就不会干出那样的事。
>
> **dote on sb** to feel and show great love for sb, ignoring their faults 指溺爱、宠爱、过分喜爱： *He dotes on his children.* 他溺爱自己的孩子。
>
> **PATTERNS**
>
> • to **really** love/like/adore/care for/dote on sb
> • to be **really/genuinely** fond of/devoted to sb
> • to love/like/care for sb **very much**

to say that you must go, although you would like to stay longer （表示想留却必须离开）不得不走： *Well, time to love you and leave you.* 唉，我该走了，不想走也得走哇。

ˈlove affair *noun* **1** a romantic and/or sexual relationship between two people who are in love and not married to each other 风流韵事；（非夫妻间的）性关系 **2** great enthusiasm for sth （对某事）极大的热情，强烈的兴趣 **SYN** **passion**: *the English love affair with gardening* 英格兰人对园艺的热爱

love·bird /ˈlʌvbɜːd; *NAmE* -bɜːrd/ *noun* **1** [C] a small African PARROT (= a bird with brightly coloured feathers) 情侣鹦鹉，爱情鸟（产于非洲） **2 lovebirds** [pl.] (*humorous*) two people who love each other very much and show this in their behaviour 恩爱情侣；热恋的恋人

ˈlove bite (*BrE*) (*NAmE* **hickey**) *noun* a red mark on the skin that is caused by sb biting or sucking their partner's skin when they are kissing 爱痕（拥吻时在皮肤上咬或吮吸的红色痕迹）

ˈlove child *noun* (used especially in newspapers, etc. 尤用于报刊等) a child born to parents who are not married to each other 私生子

ˌloved-ˈup *adj.* (*informal*) **1** happy and excited because of the effects of the illegal drug ECSTASY （因服用违禁迷幻药而）兴奋的，激情勃发的 **2** full of romantic love for sb （对某人）充满爱恋的

ˈlove handles *noun* [pl.] (*informal, humorous*) extra fat on a person's waist 腰部赘肉

ˌlove-ˈhate relationship *noun* [usually sing.] a relationship in which your feelings for sb/sth are a mixture of love and hatred 爱恨交加的感情关系

ˈlove-in *noun* (*informal*) **1** (*old-fashioned*) a party at which people freely show their affection and sexual attraction for each other, associated with HIPPIES in the 1960s （20 世纪 60 年代嬉皮士的）爱情聚会 **2** (*disapproving*) an occasion when people are being especially pleasant to each other, in a way that you believe is not sincere 虚情假意的场合；假热情

ˈlove interest *noun* [C, usually sing.] a character in a film/movie or story who has a romantic role, often as the main character's lover （电影或小说中的）恋爱角色（常为主角的情人） ➲ WORDFINDER NOTE AT CHARACTER

love·less /ˈlʌvləs/ *adj.* without love 没有爱的；无爱情的：*a loveless marriage* 没有爱情的婚姻

ˈlove letter *noun* a letter that you write to sb telling them that you love them 情书

ˈlove life *noun* the part of your life that involves your romantic and sexual relationships 爱情生活

love·li·ness /ˈlʌvlinəs/ *noun* [U] (*formal*) the state of being very attractive 美丽动人；漂亮可爱；楚楚动人 **SYN** **beauty**

love·lorn /ˈlʌvlɔːn; *NAmE* -lɔːrn/ *adj.* (*literary*) unhappy because the person you love does not love you 单相思的；失恋的

love·ly 🔑 /ˈlʌvli/ *adj., noun*

■ *adj.* (**love·lier, love·li·est**) **HELP** You can also use **more lovely** and **most lovely**. 亦可用 more lovely 和 most lovely。 (*especially BrE*) **1** 🔑 beautiful; attractive 美丽的；优美的；有吸引力的；迷人的：*lovely countryside/eyes/flowers* 美丽的乡村 / 眼睛 / 花朵 ◇ *She* **looked** *particularly lovely that night.* 她那天晚上特别妩媚动人。◇ *He has a lovely voice.* 他说话的声音很好听。 ➲ SYNONYMS AT BEAUTIFUL **2** 🔑 (*informal*) very enjoyable and pleasant; wonderful 令人愉快的；极好的：*'Can I get you anything?' 'A cup of tea would be lovely.'* "要我给你来点什么吗？" "一杯茶就很好了。" ◇ *What a lovely surprise!* 真让人感到惊喜！◇ *How lovely to see you!* 见到你多么让人高兴！◇ *Isn't it a lovely day?* 天气真好呀！◇ *We've had a lovely time.* 我们玩得很痛快。◇ *It's a lovely old farm.* 那是个宜人的老农场。◇ *It's been lovely having you here.* 有你在这儿真是太好了。◇ (*ironic*) *You've got yourself into a lovely mess, haven't you?* 你惹的这麻烦可真够瞧的，是吧？ ➲ SYNONYMS AT WONDERFUL **3** 🔑 (*informal*) (of a person 人) very kind, generous and friendly 亲切友好的；慷慨大方的：*Her mother was a lovely woman.* 她母亲是个心地善良的女人。 **HELP** **Very lovely** is not very common and is only used about the physical appearance of a person or thing. * very lovely 不很常见，仅用于形容人的外貌或事物的外观。

IDM **lovely and ˈwarm, ˈcold, ˈquiet, etc.** (*BrE, informal*) used when you are emphasizing that sth is good because of the quality mentioned （用以强调某事物因具有所说的特质而很好）：*It's lovely and warm in here.* 这里温暖宜人。

■ *noun* (*pl.* **-ies**) (*old-fashioned*) a beautiful woman 美女；美人；佳人

love·mak·ing /ˈlʌvmeɪkɪŋ/ *noun* [U] sexual activity between two lovers, especially the act of having sex 性行为；做爱；性交

ˈlove match *noun* a marriage of two people who are in love with each other 恋爱结婚；爱情的结合

ˈlove nest *noun* [usually sing.] (*informal*) a house or an apartment where two people who are not married but are having a sexual relationship can meet 情侣幽会处；情人安乐窝

lover 🔑 /ˈlʌvə(r)/ *noun* **1** 🔑 a partner in a sexual relationship outside marriage （婚外的）情人，情侣：*He denied that he was her lover.* 他否认是她的情夫。◇ *We were lovers for several years.* 我们相爱了好几年。◇ *The park was full of young lovers holding hands.* 公园里到处是手拉着手的年轻情侣。 **2** 🔑 (often in compounds 常构成复合词) a person who likes or enjoys a particular thing 爱好者；热爱者：*a lover of music* 音乐爱好者 ◇ *an art-lover* 爱好艺术的人 ◇ *a nature-lover* 热爱大自然的人

ˈlove seat *noun* a comfortable seat with a back and arms, for two people to sit on 双人座椅；鸳鸯椅 ➲ VISUAL VOCAB PAGE V22

love·sick /ˈlʌvsɪk/ *adj.* unable to think clearly or behave in a sensible way because you are in love with sb, especially sb who is not in love with you 害相思病的（尤指单相思的）

ˈlove triangle *noun* [usually sing.] a situation that involves three people, each of whom loves at least one of the others, for example a married woman, her husband, and another man that she loves 三角恋

lovey (*also* **luvvy**) /ˈlʌvi/ *noun* (*BrE, informal*) used as a friendly way of addressing sb （昵称）亲爱的，心肝，宝贝：*Ruth, lovey, are you there?* 鲁思，宝贝，你在吗？

lovey-dovey /ˌlʌvi ˈdʌvi/ *adj.* (*informal*) expressing romantic love in a way that is slightly silly 过于情意绵绵的

lov·ing /ˈlʌvɪŋ/ *adj.* **1** feeling or showing love and affection for sb/sth 爱的；充满爱的 **SYN** **affectionate, tender**: *a warm and loving family* 温馨而充满爱的家庭 ◇ *She chose the present with loving care.* 她满怀爱意精心挑选了这件礼物。 **2 -loving** (in adjectives 构成形容词) enjoying the object or activity mentioned 爱好…的；钟爱…的：*fun-loving young people* 喜欢玩乐的年轻人 ▸ **lov·ing·ly** *adv.*: *He gazed lovingly at his children.* 他慈爱地注视着自己的孩子。◇ *The house has been lovingly restored.* 这所房子已经过精心修复。

ˈloving cup *noun* (*old use*) a large cup with two handles, which guests pass around and drink from 赞颂杯（双耳大杯，供客人轮饮）

low 🔑 /ləʊ; *NAmE* loʊ/ *adj., adv., noun, verb*

■ *adj.* (**lower, low·est**)

• NOT HIGH/TALL 低；矮 **1** 🔑 not high or tall; not far above the ground 低的；矮的；离地面近的：*a low wall/building/table* 矮墙；矮建筑物；矮桌子 ◇ *a low range of hills* 低矮的冈峦 ◇ *low clouds* 低云 ◇ *flying at low altitude* 低空飞行 ◇ *The sun was low in the sky.* 太阳低挂在天空。 **OPP** **high**

• NEAR BOTTOM 接近底部 **2** 🔑 at or near the bottom of

sth 在底部的；近底部的：*low back pain* 腰疼 ◇ *the lower slopes of the mountain* 山麓斜坡 ◇ *temperatures in the low 20s* (= no higher than 21–23°) 略高于 20 度的温度 **OPP high**

- **CLOTHING** 衣服 **3** not high at the neck 领口开得低的：*a dress with a low neckline* 领口低的连衣裙 ➲ SEE ALSO LOW-CUT
- **LEVEL/VALUE** 水平；价值 **4** (*also* **low-**) (often in compounds 常构成复合词) below the usual or average amount, level or value 低于通常（或平均）数量（或水平、价值）的：*low prices* 低价 ◇ *low-income families* 低收入家庭 ◇ *a low-cost airline* 低成本运作的航空公司 ◇ *the lowest temperature ever recorded* 有记录以来最低的温度 ◇ *a low level of unemployment* 低失业率 ◇ *Yogurt is usually very low in fat.* 酸奶的脂肪含量通常很低。◇ *low-fat yogurt* 低脂酸奶 ◇ *low-tar cigarettes* 焦油含量低的卷烟 **OPP high** **5** having a reduced amount or not enough of sth（数量）减少的，缩减的；（某物）不足的：*The reservoir was low after the long drought.* 久旱之后水库的水位下降了。◇ *Our supplies are **running low*** (= we only have a little left). 我们的供给品快用完了。◇ *They were **low on** fuel.* 他们的燃料快耗尽了。
- **SOUND** 声音 **6** not high; not loud 低声的；小声的；轻声的：*The cello is lower than the violin.* 大提琴的声音比小提琴低沉。◇ *They were speaking in low voices.* 他们在低声说话。**OPP high**
- **STANDARD** 标准 **7** below the usual or expected standard 低于通常（或预期）标准的：*students with low marks/grades in their exams* 考试得分低的学生 ◇ *a low standard of living* 生活水平低 **OPP high**
- **STATUS** 地位 **8** below other people or things in importance or status 低下的；次要的；低等的：*low forms of life* (= creatures with a very simple structure) 低等生物 ◇ *jobs with low status* 社会地位低下的职业 ◇ *Training was given a very low priority.* 培训被摆在了非常次要的位置。◇ *the **lower classes** of society* 下层社会 **OPP high**
- **OPINION** 看法 **9** [usually before noun] not very good 不好的；差的 **SYN poor**：*She has a very low opinion of her own abilities.* 她认为自己的能力很差。**OPP high**
- **DEPRESSED** 沮丧 **10** weak or depressed; with very little energy 虚弱的；沮丧的；消沉的；无精打采的 **SYN down**：*I'm feeling really low.* 我现在很消沉。◇ *They were in low spirits.* 他们精神不振。
- **NOT HONEST** 不诚实 **11** (of a person 人) not honest 不诚实的；不正直的 **SYN disreputable**：*He mixes with some pretty low types.* 他和一些不三不四的人厮混在一起。
- **LIGHT** 光线 **12** not bright 暗淡的；微弱的 **SYN dim**：*The lights were low and romance was in the air.* 灯光暗淡，弥漫着浪漫情调。
- **IN VEHICLE** 交通工具 **13** if a vehicle is in **low gear**, it travels at a slower speed in relation to the speed of the engine 低速挡的
- **PHONETICS** 语音学 **14** (*phonetics* 语音) = OPEN (19)

IDM at a low 'ebb in a poor state; worse than usual 处于低潮；状况不佳：*Morale among teachers is at a low ebb.* 教师的精神面貌不佳。 **be brought 'low** (*old-fashioned*) to lose your wealth or your high position in society 失去财富；丧失社会地位 **lay sb 'low** if sb is **laid low** by/with an injury or illness, they feel very weak and are unable to do much（伤或病）使感到衰弱 **the ˌlowest of the 'low** people who are not respected at all because they are dishonest, immoral or not at all important 卑鄙小人；道德败坏的人；无足轻重的人 ➲ MORE AT PROFILE *n.*

■ ***adv.*** **(lower, low·est)**

- **NOT HIGH** 不高 **1** in or into a low position, not far above the ground 低；向下；不高：*to crouch/bend low* 蹲下；俯身 ◇ *a plane flying low over the town* 在城镇上方低空飞行的飞机 ◇ *low-flying aircraft* 低空飞行的飞机 ◇ *The sun sank lower towards the horizon.* 太阳渐渐西沉。
- **NEAR BOTTOM** 接近底部 **2** in or into a position near the bottom of sth 在靠近…底部的位置；向…底部：*a window set low in the wall* 窗台低的窗户 ◇ *The candles were burning low.* 蜡烛快烧完了。
- **LEVEL** 水平 **3** (especially in compounds 尤用于构成复合词) at a level below what is usual or expected 低于通常（或预期）的水平：*low-priced goods* 低价商品 ◇ *a low-powered PC* 低功率的个人电脑 ◇ *a very low-scoring game* 得分很低的比赛
- **SOUND** 声音 **4** not high; not loudly 低声地；小声地：*He's singing an octave lower than the rest of us.* 他唱的比我们其他人都低八度。◇ *Can you turn the music lower—you'll wake the baby.* 能不能把音乐放小声点，别把孩子吵醒了。**IDM** SEE HIGH *adv.*, LIE[1] *v.*, SINK *v.*, STOOP *v.*

■ ***noun***

- **LEVEL/VALUE** 水平；价值 **1** a low level or point; a low figure 低水平；低点；低数目：*The yen has fallen to **an all-time low** against the dollar.* 日元对美元的比价已跌至空前的低点。◇ *The temperature reached a record low in London last night.* 昨晚伦敦的气温降到了有记录以来的最低点。◇ *The government's popularity has hit a new low.* 政府的声望降到了一个新的低点。
- **DIFFICULT TIME** 艰难时期 **2** a very difficult time in sb's life or career（一生或事业中的）艰难时期，低谷：*The break-up of her marriage marked **an all-time low** in her life.* 婚姻破裂标志着她开始了一生中最艰难的日子。
- **WEATHER** 天气 **3** an area of low pressure in the atmosphere 低气压区：*Another low is moving in from the Atlantic.* 另一个低气压区正从大西洋逼近。**OPP high**

■ ***verb*** [I] (*literary*) when a cow **lows**, it makes a deep sound（牛）哞哞叫 **SYN moo**

low·ball /ˈləʊbɔːl; *NAmE* ˈloʊ-/ *verb* ~ **sth** (*NAmE*, *informal*) to deliberately make an estimate of the cost, value, etc. of sth that is too low 有意压低（成本、价值等的）估价；虚报低价：*He lowballed the cost of the project in order to obtain federal funding.* 他为了得到联邦资助而故意压低项目的成本价格。**OPP highball**

ˌlow-ˈborn *adj.* (*old-fashioned* or *formal*) having parents who are members of a low social class 出身低微的 **OPP high-born**

low·brow /ˈləʊbraʊ; *NAmE* ˈloʊ-/ *adj.* (*usually disapproving*) having no connection with or interest in serious artistic or cultural ideas 无艺术文化修养的；对艺术文化无兴趣的 **OPP highbrow** ➲ COMPARE MIDDLEBROW

low-cal (*also* **lo-cal**) /ˌləʊ ˈkæl; *NAmE* ˌloʊ/ *adj.* (*informal*) (of food and drink 食物和饮料) containing very few CALORIES 低卡路里的；低热量的

ˌLow ˈChurch *adj.* connected with the part of the Anglican Church that considers priests and the traditional forms and ceremonies of the Anglican Church to be less important than personal faith and worship 低派教会的（圣公会的一派，认为牧师和传统宗教仪式不如个人的信仰和崇拜重要）

ˌlow-ˈclass *adj.* **1** of poor quality 低劣的；低级的 **2** connected with a low social class 社会地位低下的；下层社会的 **OPP high-class**

ˌlow-ˈcost *adj.* [usually before noun] **1** below the usual cost; cheap 低成本的；便宜的：*low-cost housing/transport/food* 低成本住房 / 交通 / 食品 **2** producing or supplying sth that is cheap or costs less than usual to buy 生产（或提供）廉价商品的；低廉的：*a low-cost airline* 廉价航空公司 ◇ *They can now successfully compete against low-cost foreign producers.* 现在他们可以成功抗衡外国低成本生产商。

the ˈLow Countries *noun* [pl.] the region of Europe which consists of the Netherlands, Belgium and Luxembourg (used especially in the past) 低地国家（包括荷兰、比利时和卢森堡，尤用于旧时）

ˌlow-ˈcut *adj.* (of dresses etc. 连衣裙等) with the top very low so that you can see the neck and the top of the chest 领口开得低的；袒胸露颈的

ˈlow-down *adj.*, *noun*

■ ***adj.*** [only before noun] (*informal*) not fair or honest 不公正的；不诚实的；欺诈的 **SYN mean**：*What a dirty, low-down trick!* 多么肮脏、卑劣的伎俩！

■ ***noun* the low-down** [sing.] ~ **on (sb/sth)** (*informal*) the true facts about sb/sth, especially those considered most important to know 真相；（尤指）重要事实：*Jane gave* *me the low-down on the other guests at the party.* 简告诉了我聚会上其他来宾的真实情况。

ˈlow-end *adj.* [usually before noun] at the cheaper end of a range of similar products （产品）低档的，低端的

lower¹ /ˈləʊə(r); *NAmE* ˈloʊ-/ *adj., verb* ➲ SEE ALSO LOWER²

■ ***adj.*** [only before noun] **1** located below sth else, especially sth of the same type, or the other of a pair （尤指位于同类物品或成对物品中另一个的）下面的，下方的：*the lower deck of a ship* 船的下甲板 ◇ *His lower lip trembled.* 他的下唇在颤抖。 **2** at or near the bottom of sth 在底部的；近底部的：*the mountain's lower slopes* 山麓斜坡 **3** (of a place 地方) located towards the coast, on low ground or towards the south of an area 朝海岸的；低洼的；向南的：*the lower reaches of the Nile* 尼罗河的下游 OPP **upper**

■ ***verb*** **1** [T] to let or make sth/sb go down 把…放低；使…降下：**~ sth** *He had to lower his head to get through the door.* 他得低头才能过这道门。 ◇ *She lowered her newspaper and looked around.* 她放低报纸往四下看了看。 ◇ **~ sth/sb + adv./prep.** *They lowered him down the cliff on a rope.* 他们用绳索把他放下悬崖。 OPP **raise** **2** [T, I] **~ (sth)** to reduce sth or to become less in value, quality, etc. 减少；缩小；降低：*He lowered his voice to a whisper.* 他压低了声音悄悄地说。 ◇ *This drug is used to lower blood pressure.* 这种药用于降血压。 ◇ *Her voice lowered as she spoke.* 她一边说一边压低了嗓音。 OPP **raise**

IDM **lower the ˈbar** to set a new, lower standard of quality or performance 降低标准：*In the current economic climate we may need to lower the bar on quotas.* 在目前的经济气候下，我们可能需要降低配额标准。 OPP **raise the bar** ➲ COMPARE SET THE BAR at BAR *n.* **ˈlower yourself (by doing sth)** (usually used in negative sentences 通常用于否定句) to behave in a way that makes other people respect you less 降低自己的身份；自贬人格 SYN **demean**：*I wouldn't lower myself by working for him.* 我不会贬低自己的身份去为他工作。 ➲ MORE AT SIGHT *n.*, TEMPERATURE

lower² (*also* **lour**) /ˈlaʊə(r)/ *verb* [I] (*literary*) (of the sky or clouds 天空或云) to be dark and threatening 变昏暗；变恶劣；变阴沉 ➲ SEE ALSO LOWER¹

ˌlower ˈcase *noun* [U] (*specialist*) (in printing and writing 印刷和书写) small letters 小写字体：*The text is all in lower case.* 正文一律用小写字体。 ◇ *lower-case letters* 小写字母 ➲ COMPARE CAPITAL *n.* (5), UPPER CASE

ˌlowerˈchamber *noun* = LOWER HOUSE

the ˌlower ˈclasses *noun* [pl.] (*also* **the ˌlower ˈclass** [sing.]) the groups of people who are considered to have the lowest social status and who have less money and/or power than other people in society 下层社会；社会地位低下的阶层 ▸ **ˌlower ˈclass** *adj.*：*The new bosses were condemned as 'too lower class'.* 这些新头头被指责为"层次太低"。 ◇ *a lower-class accent* 下层社会的口音 ➲ COMPARE UPPER CLASS

ˌlower ˈhouse (*also* **ˌlower ˈchamber**) *noun* [sing.] the larger group of people who make laws in a country, usually consisting of elected representatives, such as the House of Commons in Britain or the House of Representatives in the US （英国）下议院，平民院；（美国）众议院 ➲ COMPARE UPPER HOUSE

the ˌlower ˈorders *noun* [pl.] (*old-fashioned*) people who are considered to be less important because they belong to groups with a lower social status 下层社会

ˈlower school *noun* a school, or the classes in a school, for younger students, usually between the ages of 11 and 14 低年级学校，低年级班（学生年龄通常在 11 至 14 岁之间） ➲ COMPARE UPPER SCHOOL

lowest ˌcommon deˈnominator *noun* **1** (*NAmE usually* **ˌleast ˌcommon deˈnominator**) (*mathematics* 数) the smallest number that the bottom numbers of a group of FRACTIONS can be divided into exactly 最小公分母 **2** (*NAmE also* **ˌleast ˌcommon deˈnominator**) (*disapproving*) something that is simple enough to seem interesting to, or to be understood by, the highest number of people in a particular group; the sort of people who are least intelligent or accept sth that is of low quality 大众化的东西；最平庸的人：*The school syllabus seems aimed at the lowest common denominator.* 学校的教学大纲似乎是针对接受能力最差的学生制订的。

ˌlowest ˌcommon ˈmultiple (*NAmE usually* **ˌleast ˌcommon ˈmultiple**) *noun* (*mathematics* 数) the smallest number that a group of numbers can be divided into exactly 最小公倍数

ˌlow-ˈfat *adj.* [usually before noun] containing only a very small amount of fat 低脂肪的

ˌlow-ˈgrade *adj.* [usually before noun] **1** of low quality 质量差的；劣质的 **2** (*medical* 医) of a less serious type 不太严重的；轻度的：*a low-grade infection* 轻度感染

ˌlow-ˈimpact *adj.* [usually before noun] **1** involving movements that do not put a lot of stress on the body （动作）低力度的，低强度的：*low-impact aerobics* 低强度有氧运动 **2** not causing very many problems or changes, especially in the environment （尤指对环境）低冲击的，负面影响小的：*low-impact tourism* 对环境负面影响甚小的旅游业

ˌlow-ˈkey *adj.* not intended to attract a lot of attention 低调的；不招摇的：*Their wedding was a very low-key affair.* 他们的婚礼办得很低调。

low·land /ˈləʊlənd; *NAmE* ˈloʊ-/ *adj., noun*

■ ***adj.*** [only before noun] connected with an area of land that is fairly flat and not very high above sea level 低地的 ➲ COMPARE HIGHLAND *adj.*

■ ***noun*** [pl., U] an area of land that is fairly flat and not very high above sea level 低地：*the lowlands of Scotland* 苏格兰低地 ◇ *Much of the region is lowland.* 这地区低洼地很多。 ➲ COMPARE HIGHLAND *n.*

low·land·er /ˈləʊləndə(r); *NAmE* ˈloʊ-/ *noun* a person who comes from an area which is flat and low 低地人 ➲ COMPARE HIGHLANDER (1)

ˌlow-ˈlevel *adj.* [usually before noun] **1** close to the ground 离地面近的；低的：*low-level bombing attacks* 低空轰炸袭击 **2** of low rank; involving people of junior rank 低级别的；初级的：*a low-level job* 低级职位 ◇ *low-level negotiations* 低级别的谈判 **3** not containing much of a particular substance especially RADIOACTIVITY （尤指放射性）含量低的：*low-level radioactive waste* 放射性低的废料 **4** (*computing* 计) (of a computer language 计算机语言) similar to MACHINE CODE in form 类似机器码的；低级的 OPP **high-level**

ˈlow life *noun* [U] the life and behaviour of people who are outside normal society, especially criminals 下层社会的生活及行为；社会渣滓的生活及行为 ▸ **ˈlow-life** *adj.*：*a low-life bar* 社会渣滓聚集的酒吧

low·lights /ˈləʊlaɪts; *NAmE* ˈloʊl-/ *noun* [pl.] areas of hair that have been made darker than the rest, with the use of a chemical substance 颜色较暗的染发部位 ➲ COMPARE HIGHLIGHT *n.* (2)

lowly /ˈləʊli; *NAmE* ˈloʊli/ *adj.* (**low·lier, low·li·est**) (*often humorous*) low in status or importance 地位低的；不重要的；无足轻重的 SYN **humble, obscure**

ˌlow-ˈlying *adj.* (of land 土地) not high, and usually fairly flat 低的；低洼的

ˌlow-ˈmaintenance *adj.* not needing much attention or effort 无须费神（或费力）的；易养护的：*a low-maintenance garden* 易于养护的花园 OPP **high-maintenance**

ˌlow-ˈpaid *adj.* earning or providing very little money 挣钱少的；报酬低的：*low-paid workers* 挣钱少的工人 ◇ *It is one of the lowest-paid jobs.* 那是薪水最低的一种职业。

ˌlow-ˈpitched *adj.* (of sounds 声音) deep; low 低沉的；低声的：*a low-pitched voice* 低沉的嗓音 OPP **high-pitched**

ˈlow point *noun* the least interesting, enjoyable or worst part of sth 最无趣的部分；最差的部分 OPP **high point**

ˌlow ˈpressure *noun* [U] **1** the condition of air, gas or liquid that is kept in a container with little force（气体或液体的）低压：*Water supplies to the house are **at low pressure**.* 这房子的供水水压低。 **2** a condition of the air which affects the weather when the pressure is lower than average（影响天气的）低气压 ➲ COMPARE HIGH PRESSURE

ˌlow-ˈprofile *adj.* [only before noun] receiving or involving very little attention 不引人注目的；不显眼的；低调的；低姿态的：*a low-profile campaign* 不引人注目的运动 ➲ SEE ALSO PROFILE *n.*

ˌlow-ˈranking *adj.* junior; not very important 低级别的；地位低的：*a **low-ranking officer/official*** 下级军官 / 官员 **OPP** **high-ranking**

ˌlow-ˈrent *adj.* (*especially NAmE*) of poor quality or low social status 劣质的；社会地位低的：*her low-rent boyfriend* 她那卑微的男朋友

ˌlow-resoˈlution (*also* **lo-res**, **low-res** /ˌləʊ ˈrez; *NAmE* ˌloʊ/) *adj.* (of a photograph or an image on a computer or television screen 照片或计算机、电视屏幕影像) not showing a lot of clear detail 低分辨率的；低解析度的：*a low-resolution scan* 低分辨率扫描 **OPP** **high-resolution**

ˈlow-rise *adj.*, *noun*

■ ***adj.*** [only before noun] **1** (of a building 建筑物) low, with only a few floors 楼层少的；低层的：*low-rise housing* 低层住宅 ➲ COMPARE HIGH-RISE **2** (of a pair of jeans, etc. 牛仔裤等) cut so that the top is much lower than waist-level 低腰剪裁的

■ ***noun*** a low building with only a few floors 低层建筑

ˌlow-ˈrisk *adj.* [usually before noun] involving only a small amount of danger and little risk of injury, death, damage, etc. 低风险的 **SYN** **safe**：*a low-risk investment* 低风险投资 ◇ *low-risk patients* (= who are very unlikely to get a particular illness) 低危人群 **OPP** **high-risk**

ˈlow season (*also* **ˈoff season**) *noun* [U, sing.] (*especially BrE*) the time of year when a hotel or tourist area receives fewest visitors（旅馆或旅游地区的）淡季 **OPP** **high season**

ˌlow ˈslung *adj.* very low and close to the ground 低的；接近地面的

ˌlow-ˈtech (*also* **ˌlo-ˈtech**) *adj.* (*informal*) not involving the most modern technology or methods 低技术的；低科技的；不涉及最现代技术（或方法）的 **OPP** **high-tech**

ˌlow ˈtide (*also* **ˌlow ˈwater**) *noun* [U, C] the time when the sea is at its lowest level; the sea at this time（大海的）低潮时期，低潮：*The island can only be reached **at low tide**.* 这座岛只能在退潮时上去。 **OPP** **high tide**

ˌlow-ˈwater mark *noun* a line or mark showing the lowest point that the sea reaches at low tide 低潮线；低潮水位标记 **OPP** **high-water mark**

lox /lɒks; *NAmE* lɑːks/ *noun* [U] (*NAmE*) smoked SALMON (= a type of fish) 熏鲑鱼；熏大麻哈鱼

loyal 🔑 /ˈlɔɪəl/ *adj.* ~ **(to sb/sth)** remaining faithful to sb/sth and supporting them or it 忠诚的；忠实的 **SYN** **true**：*a loyal friend/supporter* 忠实的朋友 / 支持者 ◇ *She has always **remained loyal to** her political principles.* 她总是信守自己的政治原则。 **OPP** **disloyal** ▶ **loy·al·ly** /ˈlɔɪəli/ *adv.*

loyal·ist /ˈlɔɪəlɪst/ *noun* **1** a person who is loyal to the ruler or government, or to a political party, especially during a time of change（尤指在变动时期对统治者、政府或政党）忠诚的人 **2** **Loyalist** a person who supports the union between Great Britain and Northern Ireland 支持大不列颠和北爱尔兰联合的人 ➲ COMPARE REPUBLICAN *n.* (3)

loy·alty /ˈlɔɪəlti/ *noun* (*pl.* **-ies**) **1** [U] ~ **(to/towards sb/sth)** the quality of being faithful in your support of sb/sth 忠诚；忠实；忠心耿耿：*They swore their loyalty to the king.* 他们宣誓效忠国王。 ◇ *Can I count on your loyalty?* 我能指望你对我忠诚吗？ **2** [C, usually pl.] a strong feeling that you want to be loyal to sb/sth 要忠于…的强烈感情：*a case of **divided loyalties*** (= with strong feelings of support for two different causes, people, etc.) 两面效忠

ˈloyalty card *noun* (*BrE*) a card given to customers by a shop/store to encourage them to shop there regularly. Each time they buy sth they collect points which will allow them to have an amount of money taken off goods they buy in the future. 顾客忠诚卡，积分卡（凭消费累积的积分可优惠购物） ➲ **WORDFINDER NOTE AT BUY**

loz·enge /ˈlɒzɪndʒ; *NAmE* ˈlɑːz-/ *noun* **1** (*geometry* 几何) a figure with four sides in the shape of a diamond that has two opposite angles more than 90° and the other two less than 90° 菱形 **2** a small sweet/candy, often in a lozenge shape, especially one that contains medicine and that you dissolve in your mouth 菱形糖果；（尤指）菱形含片药物：***throat/cough lozenges*** 润喉 / 止咳糖片

LP /ˌel ˈpiː/ *noun* the abbreviation for 'long-playing record' (a record that plays for about 25 minutes each side and turns 33 times per minute) 密纹唱片（全写为 long-playing record，每面约 25 分钟、每分钟 33 转的唱片）

LPG /ˌel piː ˈdʒiː/ *noun* [U] the abbreviation for 'liquefied petroleum gas' (a fuel which is a mixture of gases kept in a liquid form by the pressure in a container) 液化石油气（全写为 liquefied petroleum gas）

ˈL-plate *noun* (in Britain and some other countries) a white sign with a large red letter L on it, that you put on a car when you are learning to drive 红 L 字牌，学车牌（在英国等地学驾驶时置于车上的白底红字标志）

LPN /ˌel piː ˈen/ *noun* (in the US) licensed practical nurse（美国）持执照职业护士

LSAT /ˌel es eɪ ˈtiː/ *noun* Law School Admission Test (a test taken by students who want to study law in the US)（美国）法学院入学考试

LSD /ˌel es ˈdiː/ (*also slang* **acid**) *noun* [U] a powerful illegal drug that affects people's minds and makes them see and hear things that are not really there 麦角酰二乙胺；迷幻药；致幻药

Lt (*BrE*) (*NAmE* **Lt.**) *abbr.* (in writing 书写形式) LIEUTENANT（陆军）中尉；（海军或空军）上尉：*Lt (Helen) Brown*（海伦·）布朗陆军中尉

Ltd *abbr.* Limited (used after the name of a British company or business) 有限责任公司，股份有限公司（用于英国公司或商行名称之后）：*Pearce and Co. Ltd* 皮尔斯有限公司

LTE /ˌel tiː ˈiː/ *noun* [U] the abbreviation for 'long-term evolution' (an international system for digital communication using mobile/cell phones on which the Internet can be accessed at high speeds) 长期演进（全写为 long-term evolution，应用于手机高速数据传输的国际标准）

lu·bri·cant /ˈluːbrɪkənt/ (*also informal* **lube** /luːb/) *noun* [U, C] a substance, for example oil, that you put on surfaces or parts of a machine so that they move easily and smoothly 润滑剂；润滑油

lu·bri·cate /ˈluːbrɪkeɪt/ *verb* ~ **sth** to put a lubricant on sth such as the parts of a machine, to help them move smoothly 给…上润滑油；上油 **SYN** **grease, oil** ▶ **lu·bri·ca·tion** /ˌluːbrɪˈkeɪʃn/ *noun* [U]

lu·bri·cious /luːˈbrɪʃəs/ *adj.* (*formal*) showing a great interest in sex in a way that is considered unpleasant or unacceptable 淫荡的；淫秽的；猥亵的 **SYN** **lewd**

lucid /ˈluːsɪd/ *adj.* **1** clearly expressed; easy to understand 表达清楚的；易懂的 **SYN** **clear**：*a lucid style/explanation* 明白易懂的风格；清楚的解释 **2** able to think clearly, especially during or after a period of illness or confusion（尤指生病期间或病愈后，糊涂状态中或过后）头脑清晰的，清醒的：*In a rare lucid moment, she looked at me and smiled.* 在难得清醒的时刻，她看看我，笑了笑。 ▶ **lu·cid·ity** /luːˈsɪdəti/ *noun* [U] **lu·cid·ly** *adv.*

L

Lu·ci·fer /ˈluːsɪfə(r)/ *noun* [sing.] the DEVIL 路济弗尔（魔王） **SYN** **Satan**

luck /lʌk/ *noun, verb*

■ *noun* [U] **1** good things that happen to you by chance, not because of your own efforts or abilities 好运；幸运；侥幸：***With*** *(any)* ***luck,*** *we'll be home before dark.* 如果一切顺利的话，我们可在天黑前回到家。◇ *(BrE)* ***With a bit of luck,*** *we'll finish on time.* 如果我们运气好，就能够准时完成。◇ *So far I have had no luck with finding a job.* 我找工作一直不走运。◇ *I* ***could hardly believe my luck*** *when he said yes.* 听他说行，我几乎不敢相信自己会这么走运。◇ *It was* ***a stroke of luck*** *that we found you.* 真巧我们找到了你。◇ ***By sheer luck*** *nobody was hurt in the explosion.* 万幸的是，没有人在爆炸中受伤。◇ *We* ***wish her luck*** *in her new career.* 我们祝愿她在新的事业中一帆风顺。◇ *You're* ***in luck*** (= lucky)*—there's one ticket left.* 你运气不错，还剩一张票。◇ *You're* ***out of luck****. She's not here.* 真不巧，她不在。◇ *What a piece of luck!* 运气真好！ ➲ SEE ALSO BEGINNER'S LUCK **2** chance; the force that causes good or bad things to happen to people 机遇；命运；运气 **SYN** **fortune**: *to have* ***good/bad luck*** 运气好；运气坏 ➲ SEE ALSO HARD-LUCK STORY

WORDFINDER 联想词：amulet, charm, coincidence, fate, fortune, jinx, mascot, superstition, talisman

IDM **any ˈluck?** *(informal)* used to ask sb if they have been successful with sth （询问是否成功）运气怎么样：*'Any luck?' 'No, they're all too busy to help.'* "运气怎么样？" "不怎么样，他们都没空帮忙。" **as luck would ˈhave it** in the way that chance decides what will happen 碰巧；偶然；幸而；不巧：*As luck would have it, the train was late.* 不巧火车晚点了。 **bad, hard, etc. luck (on sb)** used to express sympathy for sb （表示同情）运气不佳，不幸：*Bad luck, Helen, you played very well.* 海伦，你表现得非常好，只是运气欠佳。◇ *It's hard luck on him that he wasn't chosen.* 他未被选中真是不幸。 **be down on your ˈluck** *(informal)* to have no money because of a period of bad luck 因一时不走运而没有钱；穷困潦倒 **the best of ˈluck (with sth)** | **good ˈluck (with sth)** *(informal)* used to wish sb success with sth 祝成功；祝好运：*The best of luck with your exams.* 祝你考试成功！◇ *Good luck! I hope it goes well.* 祝你交好运！我希望这事进展顺利。 **ˌbetter luck ˈnext time** *(informal)* used to encourage sb who has not been successful at sth （鼓励未成功的人）祝下次好运 **for ˈluck 1** because you believe it will bring you good luck, or because this is a traditional belief 图个吉利；为了带来好运：*Take something blue. It's for luck.* 挑件蓝色的东西吧，求个吉利。 **2** *(informal)* for no particular reason 无缘无故：*I hit him once more for luck.* 我无故又打了他一下。 **good ˈluck to sb** *(informal)* used to say that you do not mind what sb does as it does not affect you, but you hope they will be successful （与己无关而不介意某人的所为）祝某人成功，祝某人走运：*It's not something I would care to try myself but if she wants to, good luck to her.* 这件事我自己是不想做的，但如果她想试一试，祝愿她成功。 **just my/sb's ˈluck** *(informal)* used to show you are not surprised sth bad has happened to you, because you are not often lucky （对自己的遭遇并不惊讶）常不走运，就这运气：*Just my luck to arrive after they had left.* 我总是这样倒霉，他们离去后我才赶到。 **your/sb's ˈluck is in** used to say that sb has been lucky or successful 交好运；走运 **the luck of the ˈdraw** the fact that chance decides sth, in a way that you cannot control 运气的结果 **no such ˈluck** used to show disappointment that sth you were hoping for did not happen （所希望的事情没有发生而失望）没那么走运 ➲ MORE AT HARD *adj.*, POT *n.*, PUSH *v.*, TOUGH *adj.*, TRY *v.*, WORSE *adj.*

▼ **EXPRESS YOURSELF** 情景表达

Wishing somebody luck 祝人好运

If someone is going to do something difficult, you can wish them luck. 别人要做困难的事，可用以下表达方式祝其好运：

- ***Good luck!*** 祝你好运！
- ***The best of luck*** *for the exam!* *(BrE)* 祝考试成功！
- ***I hope it goes well!*** *We'll be thinking about you.* 我希望一切顺利！我们会想念你的。
- ***All the best! I'll keep my fingers crossed for you.*** 祝一切顺利！我会为你祈求好运。

Responses 回应：

- ***Thanks.*** 谢谢。
- ***I'll do my best.*** 我会尽力的。

▼ **SYNONYMS** 同义词辨析

luck

chance • coincidence • accident • fate • destiny

These are all words for things that happen or the force that causes them to happen. 以上各词均指机遇、命运、运气。

luck the force that causes good or bad things to happen to people 指机遇、命运、运气：*This ring has always brought me good luck.* 这戒指总是给我带来好运。

chance the way that some things happen without any cause that you can see or understand 指偶然、碰巧、意外：*The results could simply be due to chance.* 这结果可能纯属意外。

coincidence the fact of two things happening at the same time by chance, in a surprising way 指出人意料的巧合、巧事：*They met through a series of strange coincidences.* 他们因一连串奇妙的巧合而相遇。

accident something that happens unexpectedly and is not planned in advance 指意外、偶然的事：*Their early arrival was just an accident.* 他们早到仅仅是偶然而已。

fate the power that is believed to control everything that happens and that cannot be stopped or changed 指命运、天数、定数、天意：*Fate decreed that she would never reach America.* 命中注定她永远到不了美国。

destiny the power that is believed to control events 指主宰事物的力量、命运之神：*I believe there's some force guiding us—call it God, destiny or fate.* 我认为有某种力量在指引着我们，称之为上帝也罢，天意也罢，或是命运也罢。

FATE OR DESTINY? 用 fate 还是 destiny?

Fate can be kind, but this is an unexpected gift; just as often, **fate** is cruel and makes people feel helpless. **Destiny** is more likely to give people a sense of power: people who have *a strong sense of destiny* usually believe that they are meant to be great or do great things. * fate 有时是善意的，但那只是意外的恩赐；fate 也是残酷的，使人感到无能为力；destiny 更可能给人力量的感觉，have a strong sense of destiny 指人具有强烈使命感，通常认为自己必将不同凡响或成就伟业。

PATTERNS

- **by** ...luck/chance/coincidence/accident
- **It's no** coincidence/accident **that...**
- **pure/sheer** luck/chance/coincidence/accident
- to **believe in** luck/coincidences/fate/destiny

■ *verb*

PHR V **ˌluck ˈout** *(NAmE, informal)* to be lucky 走运；交好运：*I guess I really lucked out when I met her.* 我想，我遇到她真是交了好运。

luck·less /ˈlʌkləs/ *adj.* having bad luck 运气不好的；不走运的；不幸的 **SYN** **unlucky**: *the luckless victim of the attack* 遭到袭击的不幸受害者

lucky /ˈlʌki/ *adj.* **(luck·ier, lucki·est) 1** having good luck 有好运的；运气好的；幸运的 **SYN** **fortunate**: **~ (to do sth)** *His friend was killed and he knows he is lucky to be alive.* 他的朋友丧了命，他知道自己还活着是侥幸。◇ *She was lucky enough to be chosen for the team.* 她很幸运被选中参加此队。◇ **~ (that...)** *You were lucky (that) you spotted* the danger in time. 幸好你及时发现了险情。◇ *You can* ***think yourself lucky*** *you didn't get mugged.* 你未遭暴力抢劫，可算是万幸了。◇ *She* ***counted herself lucky*** *that she still had a job.* 她认为自己很幸运，仍有一份工作。◇ *Mark* ***is one of the lucky ones*** *—he at least has somewhere to sleep.* 马克是个幸运的人，他至少还有地方睡觉。◇ *the lucky winners* 幸运的获胜者 **2** ~ (**for sb**) (**that...**) being the result of good luck 好运带来的：***It was lucky for us that*** *we were able to go.* 我们能去是我们的运气好。◇ *That was the luckiest escape of my life.* 那次逃脱是我一生中最大的幸运。◇ *a lucky guess* 侥幸猜中 **3** bringing good luck 带来好运的：*a lucky charm* 吉祥配饰 ▶ **luck·ily** /ˈlʌkɪli/ *adv.*：~ (**for sb**) *Luckily for us, the train was late.* 我们真凑巧，火车晚点了。◇ *Luckily, I am a good swimmer.* 幸好我是个游泳好手。

IDM **lucky ˈyou, ˈme, etc.** (*informal*) used to show that you think sb is lucky to have sth, be able to do sth, etc. 你（或我等）真走运：*'I'm off to Paris.' 'Lucky you!'* "我要去巴黎了。""你真幸运！" **ˌyou'll be ˈlucky** (*informal*) used to tell sb that sth that they are expecting probably will not happen（告诉某人所期盼的事很可能不会发生）但愿你会走运：*'I was hoping to get a ticket for Saturday.' 'You'll be lucky.'* "我盼望弄到一张星期六的票。""但愿你会走运。" **ˌyou, etc. should be so ˈlucky** (*informal*) used to tell sb that they will probably not get what they are hoping for, and may not deserve it（告诉某人所希望之物可能得不到，且本不该其得到）你不见得这么走运吧 ➲ MORE AT STRIKE *v.*, THANK, THIRD *ordinal number*

ˌlucky ˈdip (*BrE*) (*NAmE* **ˈgrab bag**) *noun* [usually sing.] a game in which people choose a present from a container of presents without being able to see what it is going to be 摸彩游戏

lu·cra·tive /ˈluːkrətɪv/ *adj.* producing a large amount of money; making a large profit 赚大钱的；获利多的：*a* ***lucrative business/contract/market*** 利润丰厚的生意 / 合同 / 市场 ➲ SYNONYMS AT SUCCESSFUL ▶ **lu·cra·tive·ly** *adv.*

lucre /ˈluːkə(r)/ *noun* [U] (*disapproving*) money, especially when it has been obtained in a way that is dishonest or immoral（尤指来路不正的）钱财：*the lure of* ***filthy lucre*** 不义之财的诱惑

Lud·dite /ˈlʌdaɪt/ *noun* (*disapproving*) a person who is opposed to new technology or working methods 反对新技术（或新工作方法）的人 **ORIGIN** Named after Ned **Lud**, one of the workers who destroyed machinery in factories in the early 19th century, because they believed it would take away their jobs. 源自 19 世纪初的工人内德・卢德，他同其他一些工人认为机器会夺走其工作而将工厂机器捣毁。

ludic /ˈluːdɪk/ *adj.* (*formal*) showing a tendency to play and have fun, make jokes, etc., especially when there is no particular reason for doing this 顽皮的；爱开玩笑的

ludi·crous /ˈluːdɪkrəs/ *adj.* unreasonable; that you cannot take seriously 不合理的；不能当真的 **SYN** **absurd, ridiculous**：*a ludicrous suggestion* 荒谬的建议 ◇ *It was ludicrous to think that the plan could succeed.* 认为此计划会取得成功是荒唐的。▶ **ludi·crous·ly** *adv.*：*ludicrously expensive* 贵得出奇 **ludi·crous·ness** *noun* [U]

ludo /ˈluːdəʊ; *NAmE* -doʊ/ *noun* [U] (*BrE*) a simple game played with DICE and COUNTERS on a special board, similar to the American game, PARCHEESI 卢多（一种用骰子和筹码在棋盘上玩的游戏，类似于美国的巴棋戏）

lug /lʌg/ *verb, noun*

■ ***verb*** (**-gg-**) ~ **sth + adv./prep.** (*informal*) to carry or drag sth heavy with a lot of effort 吃力地搬运；用力拖；使劲拉：*I had to lug my bags up to the fourth floor.* 我只得费劲地把我的几个包拖上五楼。

■ ***noun*** **1** (*specialist*) a part of sth that sticks out, used as a handle or support 手柄；把柄；把手 **2** (*also* **lug·hole**) (*both BrE, humorous*) an ear 耳朵

luge /luːʒ; luːdʒ/ *noun* **1** [C] a type of SLEDGE (= a vehicle for sliding over ice) for racing, used by one or two people lying on their back with their feet pointing forwards 无舵雪橇，单雪橇（比赛用的单人或双人仰卧雪橇）**2** **the luge** [sing.] the event or sport of racing down a track of ice on a luge 无舵雪橇运动；单雪橇运动 ➲ VISUAL VOCAB PAGE V52

Luger™ /ˈluːgə(r)/ *noun* a type of small gun which was made in Germany 卢格尔手枪（以前由德国制造）

lug·gage /ˈlʌgɪdʒ/ (*especially BrE*) (*also* **bag·gage** *especially in NAmE*) *noun* [U] bags, cases, etc. that contain sb's clothes and things when they are travelling 行李：*There's room for one more piece of luggage.* 还有地方再放一件行李。◇ *You stay there with the luggage while I find a cab.* 你看着行李，我去找出租车。➲ COLLOCATIONS AT TRAVEL ➲ NOTE AT BAGGAGE ➲ SEE ALSO HAND LUGGAGE, LEFT-LUGGAGE OFFICE ➲ MORE LIKE THIS 28, page R28

ˈluggage rack *noun* **1** a shelf for luggage above the seats in a train, bus, etc.（火车、公共汽车等座位上方的）行李架 ➲ WORDFINDER NOTE AT TRAIN ➲ PICTURE AT RACK **2** (*especially NAmE*) = ROOF RACK

ˈluggage van (*BrE*) (*NAmE* **ˈbaggage car**) *noun* a coach/car on a train for carrying passengers' luggage（火车的）行李车厢

lug·hole /ˈlʌghəʊl; *NAmE* -hoʊl/ *noun* (*BrE, humorous*) = LUG (2)

lu·gu·bri·ous /ləˈguːbriəs/ *adj.* sad and serious 阴郁的；悲伤的 **SYN** **doleful**：*a lugubrious expression* 悲伤的神情 ▶ **lu·gu·bri·ous·ly** *adv.*

lug·worm /ˈlʌgwɜːm; *NAmE* -wɜːrm/ *noun* a large WORM that lives in the sand by the sea. Lugworms are often used as BAIT on a hook to catch fish. 海蚯蚓，沙蠋（常用作钓饵）

luke·warm /ˌluːkˈwɔːm; *NAmE* -ˈwɔːrm/ *adj.* (*often disapproving*) **1** slightly warm 微温的；不冷不热的；温和的 **SYN** **tepid**：*Our food was only lukewarm.* 我们的食物只是温乎的。➲ SYNONYMS AT COLD **2** not interested or enthusiastic 无兴趣的；不热情的：*a lukewarm response* 冷淡的反应 ◇ ~ **about sb/sth** *She was lukewarm about the plan.* 她对这个计划不大感兴趣。

lull /lʌl/ *noun, verb*

■ ***noun*** [usually sing.] ~ (**in sth**) a quiet period between times of activity（活动间的）平静时期，间歇：*a* ***lull in the conversation/fighting*** 谈话 / 战斗中的沉寂 ◇ *Just before an attack everything would go quiet but we knew it was just* ***the lull before the storm*** (= before a time of noise or trouble). 就在攻击开始前一切都变得沉寂，我们知道这只是风暴前的平静。

■ ***verb*** **1** [T] ~ **sb** to make sb relaxed and calm 使放松；使镇静 **SYN** **soothe**：*The vibration of the engine* ***lulled*** *the children* ***to sleep***. 发动机的颤动使得孩子们睡着了。**2** [T, I] ~ (**sth**) to make sth, or to become, less strong （使）减弱；缓和：*His father's arrival lulled the boy's anxiety.* 男孩在他父亲来了后便不那么焦躁不安了。

PHR V **ˌlull sb ˈinto sth** to make sb feel confident and relaxed, especially so that they do not expect it when sb does sth bad or dishonest 麻痹；诱使：*His friendly manner* ***lulled her into a false sense of security*** (= made her feel safe with him when she should not have). 他友善的举止迷惑了她，让她以为和他在一起是安全的。

lul·laby /ˈlʌləbaɪ/ *noun* (*pl.* **-ies**) a soft gentle song sung to make a child go to sleep 摇篮曲；催眠曲

lulz (*also* **luls**) /lʌlz/ *exclamation* (*informal*) (in emails, comments on SOCIAL NETWORKING websites, etc. 用于电邮、社交网站评论等) used to express the feeling that sth is amusing, especially because sb has done sth that makes them look silly（表示觉得某事好笑，尤因别人的滑稽行为）：*She didn't realize that there was ice cream all over the back of her dress! Lulz.* 她没意识到她的连衣裙后面沾满了冰淇淋，太好笑了！➲ COMPARE LOLZ ▶ **lulz** *noun* [pl.]：*They posted embarrassing photos of him on the Internet, just for the lulz.* 他们把他的窘照贴到了网上，就为了搞笑。

L

lum·bago /lʌmˈbeɪɡəʊ; NAmE -ɡoʊ/ *noun* [U] pain in the muscles and joints of the lower back 腰痛

lum·bar /ˈlʌmbə(r)/ *adj.* [only before noun] (*medical* 医) relating to the lower part of the back 腰（部）的

ˌlumbar ˈpuncture (*NAmE also* **ˈspinal tap**) *noun* the removal of liquid from the lower part of the SPINE with a hollow needle 腰椎穿刺

lum·ber /ˈlʌmbə(r)/ *noun, verb*

■ ***noun*** [U] **1** (*especially NAmE*) = TIMBER (2) **2** (*BrE*) pieces of furniture, and other large objects that you do not use any more 废旧家具；不用的大件物品：***a lumber room*** (= for storing lumber in) 杂物贮藏室

■ ***verb*** **1** [I] **+ adv./prep.** to move in a slow, heavy and awkward way 缓慢吃力地移动；笨拙地行进：*A family of elephants lumbered by.* 一群大象迈着缓慢而沉重的步子从旁边经过。 **2** [T, usually passive] **~ sb (with sb/sth)** (*informal*) to give sb a responsibility, etc., that they do not want and that they cannot get rid of 迫使担负（职责等）：*When our parents went out, my sister got lumbered with me for the evening.* 父母外出时，晚上姐姐就得照管我。

lum·ber·ing /ˈlʌmbərɪŋ/ *adj.* moving in a slow, heavy and awkward way 缓慢吃力的；步态笨拙的：*a lumbering dinosaur* 迈着缓慢而沉重步子的恐龙

L

lum·ber·jack /ˈlʌmbədʒæk; NAmE -bərdʒ-/ (*also* **log·ger**) *noun* (especially in the US and Canada) a person whose job is cutting down trees or cutting or transporting wood （尤指美国和加拿大的）伐木工，木材采运工

lum·ber·yard /ˈlʌmbəjɑːd; NAmE ˈlʌmbərjɑːrd/ (*NAmE*) (*BrE* **ˈtim·ber yard**) *noun* a place where wood for building, etc. is stored and sold 木料场；贮木场

lu·men /ˈluːmen/ *noun* (*abbr.* **lm**) (*physics* 物) a unit for measuring the rate of flow of light 流（明）（光通量单位）

lu·mi·nance /ˈluːmɪnəns/ *noun* [U] (*physics* 物) the amount of light given out in a particular direction from a particular area 亮度

lu·mi·nary /ˈluːmɪnəri; NAmE -neri/ *noun* (*pl.* **-ies**) a person who is an expert or a great influence in a special area or activity 专家；权威；有影响的人物

lu·mi·nes·cence /ˌluːmɪˈnesns/ *noun* [U] (*specialist* or *literary*) a quality in sth that produces light 发光；光辉 ▶ **lu·mi·nes·cent** *adj.*

lu·mi·nous /ˈluːmɪnəs/ *adj.* **1** shining in the dark; giving out light 夜光的；发光的；发亮的：*luminous paint* 发光漆 ◇ *luminous hands on a clock* 钟的夜光指针 ◇ *staring with huge luminous eyes* 用亮晶晶的大眼睛盯着 ◇ (*figurative*) *the luminous quality of the music* 美妙动听的音乐 **2** very bright in colour 鲜亮的；鲜艳的：*They painted the door a luminous green.* 他们把门漆成了翠绿色。 ➲ SYNONYMS AT BRIGHT ▶ **lu·mi·nous·ly** *adv.* **lu·mi·nos·ity** /ˌluːmɪˈnɒsəti; NAmE -ˈnɑːs-/ *noun* [sing., U]

lumme /ˈlʌmi/ *exclamation* (*old-fashioned, BrE, informal*) used to show surprise or interest（表示惊讶或感兴趣）哎呀，啊

lump 🔑 /lʌmp/ *noun, verb*

■ ***noun*** **1** 🔑 a piece of sth hard or solid, usually without a particular shape（通常为无定形的）块：*a lump of coal/cheese/wood* 一块煤 / 奶酪 / 木头 ◇ *This sauce has lumps in it.* 这调味汁里有结块。 **2** (*BrE*) = SUGAR LUMP：*One lump or two?* 加一块方糖还是两块？ **3** 🔑 a swelling under the skin, sometimes a sign of serious illness 肿块；隆起：*He was unhurt apart from a lump on his head.* 除了头上起了个包，他没有别的伤。◇ *Check your breasts for lumps every month.* 每月要检查一次乳房是否有肿块。 **4** (*informal, especially BrE*) a heavy, lazy or stupid person 笨重的人；懒汉；傻大个

IDM **have, etc. a lump in your throat** to feel pressure in the throat because you are very angry or emotional（因愤怒或情绪激动而）喉咙哽住，哽咽 **take your ˈlumps** (*NAmE, informal*) to accept bad things that happen to you without complaining 毫无怨言地忍受

■ ***verb*** **~ A and B together | ~ A (in) with B** to put or consider different things together in the same group 把…归并一起（或合起来考虑）：*You can't lump all Asian languages together.* 你不能把所有的亚洲语言混为一谈。

IDM **ˈlump it** (*informal*) to accept sth unpleasant because there's no other choice（因别无选择而）勉强接受，将就，勉为其难：*I'm sorry you're not happy about it but you'll just have to lump it.* 你不满意我很抱歉，可你只好将就一点了。◇ *That's the situation—like it or lump it!* 情况就是这样，不管你高兴还是不高兴！

lump·ec·tomy /ˌlʌmˈpektəmi/ *noun* (*pl.* **-ies**) an operation to remove a TUMOUR from sb's body, especially from a woman's breast（尤指女性乳房的）肿块切除术

lump·en /ˈlʌmpən/ *adj.* (*BrE, literary*) looking heavy and awkward or stupid 看起来笨重的；样子愚蠢的

lump·ish /ˈlʌmpɪʃ/ *adj.* heavy and awkward; stupid 笨重的；笨拙的；愚蠢的 **SYN** **clumsy**

ˌlump ˈsum (*also* **ˌlump ˌsum ˈpayment**) *noun* an amount of money that is paid at one time and not on separate occasions 一次总付的钱款

lumpy /ˈlʌmpi/ *adj.* full of lumps; covered in lumps 多块状物的；为块状物覆盖的：*lumpy sauce* 有颗粒的调味汁 ◇ *a lumpy mattress* 凹凸不平的床垫

lu·nacy /ˈluːnəsi/ *noun* [U] **1** behaviour that is stupid or crazy 愚蠢的行为；疯狂 **SYN** **madness**：*It's sheer lunacy driving in such weather.* 天气这样糟糕还开车，真是疯了。 **2** (*old-fashioned*) mental illness 精神病；精神错乱；精神失常 **SYN** **madness**

lunar /ˈluːnə(r)/ *adj.* [usually before noun] connected with the moon 月球的；月亮的：*a lunar eclipse/landscape* 月食；月球的地貌

ˌlunar ˈcycle *noun* (*astronomy* 天) a period of 19 years, after which the new moon and full moon return to the same day of the year 太阴周，月运周期，默冬章（周期为19年，之后月相会在一年的同一天重现）

ˌlunar ˈmonth *noun* the average time between one new moon and the next (about 29½ days) 朔望月；太阴月；会合月 ➲ COMPARE CALENDAR MONTH (1)

ˌlunar ˈyear *noun* a period of twelve lunar months (about 354 days) 太阴年（12 个太阴月，约 354 天）

lu·na·tic /ˈluːnətɪk/ *noun, adj.*

■ ***noun*** **1** a person who does crazy things that are often dangerous 精神错乱者；狂人 **SYN** **maniac**：*This lunatic in a white van pulled out right in front of me!* 这个疯子开着一辆白色货车直接插到了我前面！ **2** (*old-fashioned*) a person who is severely mentally ill (the use of this word is now offensive) 严重精神病患者，疯子（现为冒犯语）

ORIGIN Originally from the Latin *lunaticus* (*luna* = moon), because people believed that the changes in the moon made people go mad temporarily. 源自拉丁文 lunaticus（luna 即月亮），因人们相信月的盈亏可引发暂时的神经错乱。

■ ***adj.*** crazy, ridiculous or extremely stupid 疯狂的；荒唐可笑的；极其愚蠢的：*lunatic ideas* 荒谬的想法 ◇ *a lunatic smile* 傻笑

IDM **the ˌlunatic ˈfringe** *noun* [sing.+sing./pl. v.] (*disapproving*) those members of a political or other group whose views are considered to be very extreme and crazy 极端分子；极端（或狂热）分子集团

ˈlunatic asylum *noun* (*old-fashioned, especially BrE*) an institution where mentally ill people live 精神病院；疯人院

lunch 🔑 /lʌntʃ/ *noun, verb*

■ ***noun*** 🔑 [U, C] a meal eaten in the middle of the day 午餐；午饭：*She's gone to lunch.* 她吃午饭去了。◇ *I'm ready for some lunch.* 我想吃点午饭了。◇ *What shall we have for lunch?* 我们午餐吃什么？◇ *We serve hot and cold lunches.* 我们供应冷热午餐。◇ ***a one-hour lunch break*** 一小时午餐时间 ◇ ***Let's do lunch*** (= have lunch together). 咱们共进午

餐吧。➲ COLLOCATIONS AT RESTAURANT ➲ NOTE AT MEAL ➲ SEE ALSO BAG LUNCH, BOX LUNCH, PACKED LUNCH, PLOUGHMAN'S LUNCH

IDM ˌout to ˈlunch (*informal, especially NAmE*) behaving in a strange or confused way 行为怪异；心不在焉 ➲ MORE AT FREE *adj.*

■ ***verb*** [I] (*formal*) to have lunch, especially at a restaurant（尤指在餐馆）用午餐：*He lunched with a client at the Ritz.* 他与一位客户在里茨餐馆共进了午餐。

ˈlunch box *noun* a container to hold a meal that you take away from home to eat（从家带饭的）午餐盒，饭盒

lunch·eon /ˈlʌntʃən/ *noun* [C, U] a formal lunch or a formal word for lunch 午餐，午宴（正式的午餐或正式用语）：*a charity luncheon* 慈善午餐会 ◇ *Luncheon will be served at one, Madam.* 夫人，午餐在一点钟开始。

lunch·eon·ette /ˌlʌntʃəˈnet/ *noun* (*old-fashioned, NAmE*) a small restaurant serving simple meals 快餐馆；小吃店

ˈluncheon meat *noun* [U] finely chopped cooked meat that has been pressed together in a container, usually sold in cans and served cold in slices（通常以罐装出售的）午餐肉

ˈluncheon voucher *noun* a ticket given by some employers in Britain that sb can exchange for food at some restaurants and shops/stores（英国某些雇主提供的可在餐馆用餐或在商店换取食物的）午餐券

ˈlunch home *noun* (*IndE*) a restaurant 餐馆

ˈlunch hour *noun* the time around the middle of the day when you stop work or school to eat lunch 午餐时间；午休：*I usually go to the gym during my lunch hour.* 我通常在午休时间去健身房。

ˈlunch lady (*US*) (*BrE* **ˈdinner lady**) *noun* a woman whose job is to serve meals to children in schools（学校里照顾孩子吃饭的）女膳食服务员

lunch·room /ˈlʌntʃruːm; -rʊm/ *noun* (*NAmE*) a large room in a school or office where people eat lunch（学校或办公楼的）食堂，餐厅

lunch·time /ˈlʌntʃtaɪm/ *noun* [U, C] the time around the middle of the day when people usually eat lunch 午餐时间：*The package still hadn't arrived by lunchtime.* 包裹到午餐时间都还没有送到。◇ *a lunchtime concert* 午间音乐会 ◇ *The sandwich bar is generally packed at lunchtimes.* 在午餐时间三明治柜台前通常都挤满了人。

lung 🔑 /lʌŋ/ *noun* either of the two organs in the chest that you use for breathing 肺：*lung cancer* 肺癌 ➲ VISUAL VOCAB PAGE V64

ˈlung-busting *adj.* [only before noun] needing so much effort and energy that you have difficulty breathing 要累炸肺的；令人气喘吁吁的 SYN **exhausting**：*a lung-busting climb/hill* 上气不接下气的攀登；攀爬费力的山丘 ◇ *She won a bronze medal for her lung-busting efforts in the 1 500 metres final.* 她拼尽全力，跑得上气不接下气，在1 500 米决赛中获得铜牌。➲ MORE LIKE THIS 10, page R26

lunge /lʌndʒ/ *verb, noun*

■ ***verb*** [I] ~ **(at/towards/for sb/sth)** | ~ **(forward)** to make a sudden powerful forward movement, especially in order to attack sb or take hold of sth 猛冲；猛扑

■ ***noun*** [usually sing.] **1** ~ **(at sb)** | ~ **(for sb/sth)** a sudden powerful forward movement of the body and arm that a person makes towards another person or thing, especially when attacking or trying to take hold of them 猛冲；猛扑：*He made a lunge for the phone.* 他向电话扑了过去。 **2** (in the sport of FENCING 击剑运动) a THRUST made by putting one foot forward and making the back leg straight 弓箭步刺；戳

lung·fish /ˈlʌŋfɪʃ/ *noun* (*pl.* **lung·fish**) a long fish that can breathe air and survive for a period of time out of water 肺鱼

lung·ful /ˈlʌŋfʊl/ *noun* the amount of sth such as air or smoke that is breathed in at one time 一大口（一次吸入的空气、烟等）

lungi /ˈlʊŋgiː/ *noun* a piece of clothing worn in S and SE Asia consisting of a piece of cloth, usually worn wrapped around the hips and reaching the ankles（南亚和东南亚人长及脚踝的）缠腰布，腰布

lunk·head /ˈlʌŋkhed/ *noun* (*NAmE, informal*) a stupid person 傻瓜；笨蛋

lupin (*BrE*) (*NAmE* **lu·pine**) /ˈluːpɪn/ *noun* a tall garden plant with many small flowers growing up its thick STEM 羽扇豆

lu·pine /ˈluːpaɪn/ *adj.* (*formal*) like a WOLF; connected with a wolf or wolves 狼似的；狼（群）的

lupus /ˈluːpəs/ *noun* [U] a disease that affects the skin or sometimes the joints 狼疮

lurch /lɜːtʃ; *NAmE* lɜːrtʃ/ *verb, noun*

■ ***verb*** **1** [I] **(+ adv./prep.)** to make a sudden, unsteady movement forward or sideways 突然前倾（或向一侧倾斜）SYN **stagger, sway**：*Suddenly the horse lurched to one side and the child fell off.* 马突然歪向一边，小孩就摔了下来。◇ *The man lurched drunkenly out of the pub.* 那男人醉醺醺地踉跄着走出了酒吧。◇ (*figurative*) *Their relationship seems to lurch from one crisis to the next.* 他们的关系好像坎坷不平，危机不断。 **2** [I] if your heart or stomach **lurches**, you have a sudden feeling of fear or excitement（突然感到恐怖或激动时心或胃）猛地一跳（或动）

■ ***noun*** [usually sing.] a sudden strong movement that moves you forward or sideways and nearly makes you lose your balance 突然前倾（或向一侧倾斜）：*The train gave a violent lurch.* 火车突然向前猛动了一下。◇ *His heart gave a lurch when he saw her.* 他见到她时心怦然一跳。

IDM **leave sb in the ˈlurch** (*informal*) to fail to help sb when they are relying on you to do so（在某人需要帮助时）弃之不顾

lurch·er /ˈlɜːtʃə(r); *NAmE* ˈlɜːrtʃ-/ *noun* (*BrE*) a dog that is a mixture of two different breeds of dog, one of which is usually a GREYHOUND 混种狗；杂种猎狗

lure /lʊə(r); ljʊə(r); *NAmE* lʊr/ *verb, noun*

■ ***verb*** ~ **sb (+ adv./prep.)** (*disapproving*) to persuade or trick sb to go somewhere or to do sth by promising them a reward 劝诱；引诱；诱惑 SYN **entice**：*The child was lured into a car but managed to escape.* 那小孩被诱骗上了车，但又设法逃掉了。◇ *Young people are lured to the city by the prospect of a job and money.* 年轻人希望打工赚钱，从而被吸引到城市。

■ ***noun*** **1** [usually sing.] the attractive qualities of sth 吸引力；诱惑力；魅力：*Few can resist **the lure of** adventure.* 很少有人能抵挡历险的诱惑力。 **2** a thing that is used to attract fish or animals, so that they can be caught 鱼饵；诱饵

Lurex™ /ˈlʊəreks; ˈljʊə-; *NAmE* ˈlʊr-/ *noun* [U] a type of thin metal thread; a cloth containing this thread, used for making clothes 卢勒克斯金属细丝；卢勒克斯金属丝织物

lurgy /ˈlɜːgi; *NAmE* ˈlɜːrgi/ *noun* (*pl.* **-ies**) [C, usually sing.] (*BrE, humorous*) a mild illness or disease 小恙；小病：*I've caught some kind of lurgy.* 我有点小病。◇ *It's the **dreaded** lurgy!* 就是那种吓人的小病！

lurid /ˈlʊərɪd; ˈljʊər-; *NAmE* ˈlʊr-/ *adj.* (*disapproving*) **1** too bright in colour, in a way that is not attractive 俗艳的；花哨的 **2** (especially of a story or piece of writing 尤指故事或文章) shocking and violent in a way that is deliberate（故意地）骇人听闻的，令人毛骨悚然的：*lurid headlines* 骇人的标题 ◇ *The paper gave all the lurid details of the murder.* 这份报纸对这起凶杀案骇人听闻的细节描述得淋漓尽致。 ▸ **lur·id·ly** *adv.*

lurk /lɜːk; *NAmE* lɜːrk/ *verb, noun*

■ ***verb*** **1** [I] **(+ adv./prep.)** to wait somewhere secretly, especially because you are going to do sth bad or illegal（尤指为做不正当的事而）埋伏，潜伏 SYN **skulk**：*Why are you lurking around outside my house?* 你在我房子外面鬼鬼祟祟的，想干什么？◇ *A crocodile was lurking just*

L

below the surface. 有条鳄鱼就潜伏在水面下。 **2** [I] (**+ adv./prep.**) when sth unpleasant or dangerous **lurks**, it is present but not in an obvious way（不好或危险的事）潜在，隐藏着： *At night, danger lurks in these streets.* 夜晚这些街上隐藏着危险。 **3** [I] (*computing* 计) to read a discussion in a CHAT ROOM, etc. on the Internet, without taking part in it yourself 潜水，隐身（在网上聊天室等阅读别人的讨论但不参与其中）

▪ ***noun*** (*AustralE, NZE, informal*) a clever trick that is used in order to get sth 诡计；妙计；花招

lurve /lɜːv; *NAmE* lɜːrv/ *noun* [U] (*BrE, informal, humorous*) a non-standard spelling of 'love', used especially to refer to romantic love 爱（love 的非标准拼写法，尤用于指爱情）： *It's Valentine's Day and lurve is in the air.* 今天是情人节，空气中弥漫着爱情的气息。

lus·cious /ˈlʌʃəs/ *adj.* **1** having a strong pleasant taste 美味的；甘美的；可口的 SYN **delicious**: *luscious fruit* 香甜的水果 **2** (of cloth, colours or music 织物、颜色或音乐) soft and deep or heavy in a way that is pleasing to feel, look at or hear 柔软的；柔和的；绚丽的；悦耳的 SYN **rich**: *luscious silks and velvets* 柔软光滑的丝绸和天鹅绒 **3** (especially of a woman 尤指女人) sexually attractive 肉感的；性感的： *a luscious young girl* 性感的年轻女郎

lush /lʌʃ/ *adj., noun*

▪ ***adj.*** **1** (of plants, gardens, etc. 植物、花园等) growing thickly and strongly in a way that is attractive; covered in healthy grass and plants 茂盛的；茂密的；草木繁茂的 SYN **luxuriant**: *lush vegetation* 茂盛的草木 ◇ *the lush green countryside* 郁郁葱葱的乡村 ➲ WORDFINDER NOTE AT LANDSCAPE **2** beautiful and making you feel pleasure; seeming expensive 华丽舒适的；豪华的： *a lush apartment* 豪华的公寓 **3** (*slang*) attractive or pleasant 吸引人的；令人愉悦的： *This shampoo smells lush.* 这洗发水味道真好闻。

▪ ***noun*** (*NAmE, informal*) = ALCOHOLIC

luso·phone /ˈluːsəfəʊn; *NAmE* -foʊn/ *adj.* (*linguistics* 语言) speaking Portuguese as the main language 主要讲葡萄牙语的；以葡萄牙语为主的

lust /lʌst/ *noun, verb*

▪ ***noun*** (*often disapproving*) [U, C] **1** ~ (**for sb**) very strong sexual desire, especially when love is not involved 强烈的性欲；色欲；淫欲： *Their affair was driven by pure lust.* 他们私通纯粹是受淫欲的驱使。 **2** ~ (**for sth**) very strong desire for sth or enjoyment of sth 强烈欲望；享受欲： *to satisfy his* ***lust for power*** 满足他对权力的强烈欲望 ◇ *She has a real* ***lust for life*** (= she really enjoys life). 她真懂得享受生活。 ➲ SEE ALSO BLOODLUST

▪ ***verb***

PHR V **ˈlust after/for sb/sth** (*often disapproving*) to feel an extremely strong, especially sexual, desire for sb/sth 对…有极强的欲望（尤指性欲）

lust·ful /ˈlʌstfl/ *adj.* (*often disapproving*) feeling or showing strong sexual desire 有强烈性欲的；淫荡的；好色的 SYN **lascivious**

lustre (*especially US* **lust·er**) /ˈlʌstə(r)/ *noun* [U] **1** the shining quality of a surface 光泽；光辉 SYN **sheen**: *Her hair had lost its lustre.* 她的头发失去了光泽。 **2** the quality of being special in a way that is exciting 荣光；光彩；荣耀： *The presence of the prince added lustre to the occasion.* 王子的出现给那场面增添了光彩。 ➲ COMPARE LACKLUSTRE

lus·trous /ˈlʌstrəs/ *adj.* (*formal*) soft and shining 柔软光亮的 SYN **glossy**: *thick lustrous hair* 浓密柔软的亮发

lusty /ˈlʌsti/ *adj.* healthy and strong 健壮的；强壮的 SYN **vigorous**: *a lusty young man* 健壮的年轻人 ◇ *lusty singing* 洪亮的歌声 ▶ **lust·ily** /-ɪli/ *adv.* : *singing lustily* 起劲地唱歌

lute /luːt/ *noun* an early type of musical instrument with strings, played like a GUITAR 琉特琴，诗琴（拨弦乐器）

lu·ten·ist (*also* **lu·tan·ist**) /ˈluːtənɪst/ *noun* a person who plays the lute 琉特琴（或诗琴）弹奏者

lu·te·tium /luːˈtiːʃiəm; *BrE also* -siəm/ *noun* [U] (*symb.* **Lu**) a chemical element. Lutetium is a rare silver-white metal used in the nuclear industry. 镥（用于核工业）

Lu·ther·an /ˈluːθərən/ *noun* a member of a Christian Protestant Church that follows the teaching of the 16th century German religious leader Martin Luther 信义宗信徒；路德宗信徒 ▶ **Lu·ther·an** *adj.*

luv /lʌv/ *noun* **1** (*BrE*) a way of spelling 'love', when used as an informal way of addressing sb（love 用于非正式称呼的拼写法）亲爱的，宝贝： *Never mind, luv.* 没关系，亲爱的。 **2** an informal way of spelling 'love', for example when ending a letter（love 用于书信结尾等的非正式拼写法）爱： *See you soon, lots of luv, Sue.* 盼早日见到你，非常爱你的，休。

luvvy (*also* **luv·vie**) /ˈlʌvi/ *noun* (*pl.* **-ies**) (*BrE, informal*) **1** (*disapproving*) an actor, especially when he or she behaves in a way that seems exaggerated and not sincere 演员；（尤指）表演造作的演员 **2** = LOVEY

lux·uri·ant /lʌɡˈʒʊəriənt; *NAmE* -ˈʒʊr-/ *adj.* **1** (of plants or hair 植物或头发) growing thickly and strongly in a way that is attractive 茂盛的；浓密的： *luxuriant vegetation* 茂密的草木 ◇ *thick, luxuriant hair* 浓密的头发 **2** (especially of art or the atmosphere of a place 尤指艺术或氛围) rich in sth that is pleasant or beautiful 丰富的；华丽的；富饶的： *the poet's luxuriant imagery* 诗人丰富的意象 ▶ **lux·uri·ance** /-əns/ *noun* [U]: *the luxuriance of the tropical forest* 茂密的热带森林

lux·uri·ant·ly /lʌɡˈʒʊəriəntli; *NAmE* -ˈʒʊr-/ *adv.* **1** in a way that is thick and attractive 茂盛地；浓密地： *a tall, luxuriantly bearded man* 留有浓密胡须的高个子男人 **2** (especially of a way of moving your body 尤指身体动作) in a way that is comfortable and enjoyable 舒适愉快地： *She turned luxuriantly on her side, yawning.* 她打着哈欠，舒适地转身侧向一边。

lux·uri·ate /lʌɡˈʒʊərieɪt; *NAmE* -ˈʒʊr-/ *verb*

PHR V **luˈxuriate in sth** to relax while enjoying sth very pleasant 尽情享受；纵情享乐： *She luxuriated in all the attention she received.* 她既备受关注，一路陶醉其中。

lux·uri·ous /lʌɡˈʒʊəriəs; *NAmE* -ˈʒʊr-/ *adj.* very comfortable; containing expensive and enjoyable things 十分舒适的；奢侈的 SYN **sumptuous**: *a luxurious hotel* 豪华旅馆 ◇ *luxurious surroundings* 豪华舒适的环境 OPP **spartan** ▶ **lux·uri·ous·ly** *adv.* : *luxuriously comfortable* 豪华舒适 ◇ *a luxuriously furnished apartment* 布置得富丽堂皇的公寓 ◇ *She stretched luxuriously on the bed.* 她惬意地在床上舒展着身子。

lux·ury /ˈlʌkʃəri/ *noun* (*pl.* **-ies**) **1** [U] the enjoyment of special and expensive things, particularly food and drink, clothes and surroundings 奢侈的享受；奢华： *Now we'll be able to live* ***in luxury*** *for the rest of our lives.* 如今我们可在有生之年过豪华生活了。 ◇ *to lead* ***a life of luxury*** 过奢侈的生活 ◇ *a luxury hotel* 豪华酒店 ◇ *luxury goods* 奢侈品 **2** [C] a thing that is expensive and enjoyable but not essential 奢侈品 SYN **extravagance**: *small luxuries like chocolate and flowers* 像巧克力和鲜花之类的小奢侈品 ◇ *I love having a long, hot bath—it's one of* ***life's little luxuries***. 我喜欢在热水浴缸里多泡一会儿，这是生活里一种小小的享受。 ◇ *It was a luxury if you had a washing machine in those days.* 那时候有洗衣机就算是奢侈了。 **3** [U, sing.] a pleasure or an advantage that you do not often have 不常有的乐趣（或享受、优势） SYN **indulgence**: *We had the luxury of being able to choose from four good candidates for the job.* 我们的挑选余地大，有四位出色的职位候选人可供选择。 IDM SEE LAP *n.*

LW *abbr.* (*especially BrE*) LONG WAVE 长波： *1 500m LW* 长波 1 500 米

-ly *suffix* **1** (in adverbs 构成副词) in the way mentioned 以…方式： *happily* 幸福地 ◇ *stupidly* 愚蠢地 **2** (in adjectives 构成形容词) having the qualities of 具有…性质： *cowardly* 怯懦的 ◇ *scholarly* 学者型的 **3** (in adjectives and adverbs 构成形容词和副词) at intervals of 每隔…时间: *hourly* 每小时 ◇ *daily* 每天 ➲ MORE LIKE THIS 7, page R25

ly·chee (*also* **li·chee**) (*also* **lit·chi** *especially in US*) /ˌlaɪˈtʃiː; ˈlaɪtʃiː/ *noun* a small Chinese fruit with thick rough reddish skin, white flesh and a large seed inside 荔枝 ➲ VISUAL VOCAB PAGE V32

lych·gate (*also* **lich·gate**) /ˈlɪtʃɡeɪt/ *noun* a gate with a roof at the entrance to a CHURCHYARD 停柩门，墓地大门（教堂墓地入口处有顶盖的大门）

Lycra™ /ˈlaɪkrə/ (*also* **span·dex**) *noun* [U] an artificial material that stretches, used for making clothes that fit close to the body 莱卡（有弹性的人造材料，用于制作紧身衣）

lye /laɪ/ *noun* [U] a chemical used in various industrial processes, including washing 碱液

lying PRES. PART. OF LIE[1], LIE[2]

ˌlying-ˈin *noun* [sing.] (*old-fashioned*) the period of time during which a woman in the past stayed in bed before and after giving birth to a child（旧时妇女产前产后的）卧床期

ˌlying-in-ˈstate *noun* [U] the period when the dead body of a ruler is displayed to the public before being buried; the display of the body in this way（统治者死后的）遗体瞻仰（期）

Lyme disease /ˈlaɪm dɪziːz/ *noun* [U] a serious disease that causes fever and pain in the joints of the body, caused by bacteria carried by TICKS (= small insects) 莱姆病（由蜱传播，症状为发烧和关节疼痛）

lymph /lɪmf/ *noun* [U] a clear liquid containing white blood cells that helps to clean the TISSUES of the body and helps to prevent infections from spreading 淋巴 ▸ **lymph·at·ic** /lɪmˈfætɪk/ *adj.* [only before noun]: *the lymphatic system* 淋巴系统

ˈlymph node (*also* **ˈlymph gland**) *noun* one of the small round parts of the LYMPHATIC system that stores LYMPHOCYTES and helps fight infection 淋巴结

lympho·cyte /ˈlɪmfəsaɪt/ *noun* (*biology* 生) a type of small white blood cell with one round NUCLEUS, found especially in the LYMPHATIC system 淋巴细胞

lymph·oma /lɪmˈfəʊmə; *NAmE* -ˈfoʊ-/ *noun* [U] cancer of the LYMPH NODES 淋巴瘤

lynch /lɪntʃ/ *verb* **~ sb** if a crowd of people **lynch** sb whom they consider guilty of a crime, they capture them, do not allow them to have a trial in court, and kill them illegally, usually by hanging 用私刑处死（被认为有罪的人，通常为绞刑） ▸ **lynch·ing** *noun* [C, U]

ˈlynch mob *noun* a crowd of people who gather to lynch sb 施用私刑的暴民

lynch·pin = LINCHPIN

lynx /lɪŋks/ *noun* (*pl.* **lynx** or **lynxes**) a wild animal of the cat family, with spots on its fur and a very short tail 猞猁

lyre /ˈlaɪə(r)/ *noun* an ancient musical instrument with strings fastened in a frame shaped like a U. It was played with the fingers. 里拉琴（古代 U 形拨弦乐器）

lyre·bird /ˈlaɪəbɜːd; *NAmE* ˈlaɪrbɜːrd/ *noun* a large Australian bird 琴鸟（栖于澳大利亚）

lyric /ˈlɪrɪk/ *adj., noun*

■ ***adj.*** **1** (of poetry 诗歌) expressing a person's personal feelings and thoughts 抒情的 ➲ COMPARE EPIC *adj.* (1) ➲ WORDFINDER NOTE AT POETRY **2** connected with, or written for, singing 吟唱的；为吟唱谱写的

■ ***noun*** **1** [C] a lyric poem 抒情诗 ➲ COMPARE EPIC *n.* (1) **2** **lyrics** [pl.] the words of a song 歌词: *music and lyrics by Rodgers and Hart* 由罗杰斯和哈特作词作曲

lyr·ic·al /ˈlɪrɪkl/ *adj.* expressing strong emotion in a way that is beautiful and shows imagination 抒情的 SYN **expressive**: *a lyrical melody* 抒情的旋律 ◇ *He began to* ***wax lyrical*** (= talk in an enthusiastic way) *about his new car.* 他开始兴高采烈地谈论他的新车。

lyr·ic·al·ly /ˈlɪrɪkli/ *adv.* **1** in a way that expresses strong emotion 情感强烈地；抒情地 **2** connected with the words of a song 歌词上: *Both musically and lyrically it is very effective.* 这首歌的音乐和歌词都给人留下非常深刻的印象。

lyri·cism /ˈlɪrɪsɪzəm/ *noun* [U] the expression of strong emotion in poetry, art, music, etc.（诗歌、艺术、音乐等的）抒情

lyri·cist /ˈlɪrɪsɪst/ *noun* a person who writes the words of songs 歌词作者

Mm

M /em/ *noun, abbr., symbol*
■ ***noun*** (*also* **m**) [C, U] (*pl.* **Ms, M's, m's** /emz/) the 13th letter of the English alphabet 英语字母表的第 13 个字母：*'Milk' begins with (an) M/'M'.* * milk 一词以字母 m 开头。
■ ***abbr.*** **1** (*also* **med.**) (especially for sizes of clothes) medium（尤指服装的尺码）中号：*S, M and L* (= small, medium and large) 小号、中号、大号 **2** (used with a number to show the name of a British MOTORWAY) 高速公路（英国公路代号，后接数字）：*heavy traffic on the M25* * 25 号高速公路上繁忙的交通
■ ***symbol*** (*also* **m**) the number 1 000 in ROMAN NUMERALS（罗马数字）1 000

m /em/ (*also* **m.**) *abbr.* **1** male 男性 **2** married 已婚 **3** metre(s) 米：*800m medium wave* 中波 800 米 **4** million(s) 百万：*population: 10m* 人口：1 000 万

MA (*BrE*) (*NAmE* **M.A.**) /ˌem ˈeɪ/ *noun* the abbreviation for 'Master of Arts' (a second university degree in an ARTS subject, or, in Scotland, a first university degree in an arts subject) 文科硕士（全写为 Master of Arts，大学文科中的中级学位，或苏格兰大学文科中的初级学位）：*to* ***be/have/do an MA*** 成为文科硕士；有 / 攻读文科硕士学位 ◇ (*BrE*) *Julie Bell MA* 文科硕士朱莉·贝尔

ma /mɑː/ *noun* (*informal*) mother 母亲；妈妈；妈：*I'm going now, ma.* 妈，我走啦。◇ *'I want my ma,' sobbed the little girl.* 小女孩抽泣着说："我要妈妈。"

ma'am *noun* [sing.] **1** /mæm/ (*NAmE*) used as a polite way of addressing a woman（尊称）女士，夫人：*'Can I help you, ma'am?'* "要帮忙吗，夫人？" ➲ COMPARE SIR (1) **2** /mɑːm/ (*BrE*) used when addressing the Queen or senior women officers in the police or army（对女王或高级女警官、女军官的敬称）= MADAM (1)

maas /mɑːs/ *noun* (*SAfrE*) = AMASI

Mac /mæk/ *noun* [sing.] (*NAmE, informal*) used to address a man whose name you do not know（用于称呼不知姓名的男子）老兄，老弟，伙计，哥们儿

mac (*also* **mack**) /mæk/ (*also old-fashioned* **mack·in·tosh**) *noun* (*all BrE*) a coat made of material that keeps you dry in the rain 雨衣；雨披

ma·cabre /məˈkɑːbrə/ *adj.* unpleasant and strange because connected with death and frightening things 可怕的，恐怖的（尤指与死亡等相联系的） **SYN** **ghoulish, grisly**：*a macabre tale/joke/ritual* 令人毛骨悚然的故事 / 笑话 / 仪式

mac·adam /məˈkædəm/ *noun* [U] a road surface made of layers of broken stones, mixed with TAR 柏油碎石路面

maca·da·mia /ˌmækəˈdeɪmiə/ (*also* **maca'damia nut**) *noun* the round nut of an Australian tree 澳洲坚果 ➲ VISUAL VOCAB PAGE V35

ma·caque /məˈkæk; -ˈkɑːk/ *noun* a type of MONKEY that lives in Africa and Asia 猕猴

maca·roni /ˌmækəˈrəʊni; *NAmE* -ˈroʊni/ *noun* [U] PASTA in the shape of hollow tubes 通心粉；空心面；通心面

ˌmacaroni ˈcheese (*BrE*) (*NAmE* **ˌmacaroni and ˈcheese**) *noun* [U] a hot dish of macaroni in a cheese sauce 干酪酱通心面

maca·roon /ˌmækəˈruːn/ *noun* a soft round sweet biscuit/cookie made with ALMONDS or COCONUT 蛋白杏仁饼干（或曲奇）；蛋白椰子饼干（或曲奇）

macaw /məˈkɔː/ *noun* a large Central and S American tropical bird of the PARROT family, with bright feathers and a long tail 金刚鹦鹉（热带美洲鹦鹉，尾长而毛色艳丽）

Mace™ /meɪs/ *noun* [U] a chemical that makes your eyes and skin sting, that some people, including police officers, carry in spray cans so that they can defend themselves against people attacking them 梅斯催泪气体

mace /meɪs/ *noun* **1** [C] a decorative stick, carried as a sign of authority by an official such as a mayor 权杖 ➲ COMPARE SCEPTRE **2** [C] a large heavy stick that has a head with metal points on it, used in the past as a weapon 钉头锤；狼牙棒（古代兵器） **3** [U] the dried outer covering of NUTMEGS (= the hard nuts of a tropical tree), used in cooking as a spice 肉豆蔻干皮，肉豆蔻种衣（烹调香料）

ma·cer·ate /ˈmæsəreɪt/ *verb* [T, I] ~ (**sth**) (*specialist*) to make sth (especially food) soft by leaving it in a liquid; to become soft in this way 把（食物等）浸软；被浸软

Mach /mɑːk; mæk/ *noun* [U] (often followed by a number 常后接数字) a measurement of speed, used especially for aircraft. Mach 1 is the speed of sound. 马赫，马赫数（速度单位，尤用于计算飞行速度，1 马赫等于音速）：*a fighter plane with a top speed of Mach 3* (= 3 times the speed of sound) 最高速度为 3 马赫的歼击机

ma·chete /məˈʃeti/ *noun* a broad heavy knife used as a cutting tool and as a weapon 大刀；大砍刀

Ma·chia·vel·lian /ˌmækiəˈveliən/ *adj.* (*formal, disapproving*) using clever plans to achieve what you want, without people realizing what you are doing 马基雅弗利主义的；不择手段的；阴险狡诈的 **SYN** **cunning, unscrupulous**
ORIGIN From the name of **Niccolò Machiavelli**, an Italian politician (1469–1527), who explained in his book *The Prince*, that it was often necessary for rulers to use immoral methods in order to achieve power and success. 源自意大利政治家尼科洛·马基雅弗利（1469–1527），他在其《君主论》一书中声称，统治者为谋取权力和成功常需要采取一些不道德的手段。

ma·chin·ation /ˌmæʃɪˈneɪʃn/ *noun* [usually pl.] (*disapproving*) a secret and complicated plan 阴谋；诡计 **SYN** **plot, intrigue**

ma·chine 🔑 /məˈʃiːn/ *noun, verb*
■ ***noun*** **1** 🔑 (often in compounds 常构成复合词) a piece of equipment with moving parts that is designed to do a particular job. The power used to work a machine may be electricity, steam, gas, etc. or human power. 机器；机械装置：*Machines have replaced human labour in many industries.* 在许多行业中，机器已经替代了人力。◇ *to* ***operate/run a machine*** 操作机器 ◇ *How does this machine work?* 这部机器是如何工作的？ ◇ *a* ***washing/sewing machine*** 洗衣机；缝纫机 ◇ *a machine for making plastic toys* 生产塑料玩具的机器 ◇ *I left a message on her answering machine.* 我在她的电话答录机上留了言。 ◇ *The potatoes are planted* ***by machine***. 这些土豆是用机器种植的。➲ SEE ALSO VOTING MACHINE **2** 🔑 (*informal*) a particular machine, for example in the home, when you do not refer to it by its full name（不提全称时的简略说法）机器：*Just put those clothes in the machine* (= the washing machine). 把那些衣服放到洗衣机里就行了。 ◇ *The new machines* (= computers) *will be shipped next month.* 新计算机下个月推向市场。**3** a group of people that control an organization or part of an organization（组织的）核心机构：*the president's propaganda machine* 总统的宣传团队 **4** (*often disapproving*) a person who acts automatically, without allowing their feelings to show or to affect their work 机械化的人（做事呆板、感情不外露）➲ SEE ALSO MECHANICAL, FRUIT MACHINE, SLOT MACHINE, TIME MACHINE
HELP You will find other compounds ending in **machine** at their place in the alphabet. 其他以 machine 结尾的复合词可在各字母中的适当位置查到。 **IDM** SEE COG
■ ***verb*** [T, I] ~ (**sth**) (*specialist*) to make or shape sth with a machine（用机器）制造，加工成型：*This material can be cut and machined easily.* 这种材料很容易用机器切割并加工成型。

ma'chine code (*also* **ma'chine language**) *noun* [C, U] (*computing* 计) a code in which instructions are written in the form of numbers so that a computer can understand and act on them 机器码

ma'chine gun *noun* a gun that automatically fires many bullets one after the other very quickly 机关枪；机枪：*a burst/hail of machine-gun fire* 一阵猛烈的机关枪扫射

ma'chine-gun *verb* (-nn-) ~ **sb/sth** to shoot at sb/sth with a machine gun 用机关枪射击

ma,chine-'made *adj.* made by a machine 机器制造的；机制的 ➲ COMPARE HANDMADE

ma,chine-'readable *adj.* (of data 数据或资料) in a form that a computer can understand 机器可读的

ma·chin·ery /mə'ʃiːnəri/ *noun* **1** [U] machines as a group, especially large ones（统称）机器；（尤指）大型机器：*agricultural/industrial machinery* 农业 / 工业机械 ◇ *a piece of machinery* 一部机器 **2** [U] the parts of a machine that make it work 机器的运转部分；机械装置 **3** [U, sing.] the organization or structure of sth; the system for doing sth 组织；机构；系统；体制：~ (**of sth**) *the machinery of government* 政府机构 ◇ ~ (**for doing sth**) *There is no machinery for resolving disputes.* 根本没有解决纷争的机制。

ma'chine tool *noun* a tool for cutting or shaping metal, wood, etc., driven by a machine 机床；工具机

ma,chine trans'lation *noun* [U] the process of translating language by computer 机器翻译；计算机翻译

ma·chin·ist /mə'ʃiːnɪst/ *noun* **1** a person whose job is operating a machine, especially machines used in industry for cutting and shaping things, or a sewing machine 机工；（尤指）车工，缝纫机工 **2** a person whose job is to make or repair machines 机械师；机械安装修理工

mach·ismo /mə'tʃɪzməʊ; *NAmE* mɑː'tʃiːzmoʊ/ *noun* [U] (*from Spanish, usually disapproving*) aggressive male behaviour that emphasizes the importance of being strong rather than being intelligent and sensitive 大男子气概；大男子主义行为

macho /'mætʃəʊ; *NAmE* 'mɑːtʃoʊ/ *adj.* (*usually disapproving*) male in an aggressive way 大男子气的；男子汉的：*He's too macho to ever admit he was wrong.* 他太大男子主义了，从不认错。◇ *macho pride/posturing* 大男子汉的高傲 / 姿态

mack = MAC

mack·erel /'mækrəl/ *noun* [C, U] (*pl.* **mack·erel**) a sea fish with greenish-blue bands on its body, that is used for food 鲭（鱼）：*smoked mackerel* 熏鲭鱼

mack·in·tosh /'mækɪntɒʃ; *NAmE* -tɑːʃ/ *noun* (*old-fashioned*) = MAC

mac·ramé /mə'krɑːmi/ *noun* [U] the art of tying knots in string in a decorative way, to make things 装饰编结艺术；编结艺术

macro /'mækrəʊ; *NAmE* 'mækroʊ/ *noun* (*pl.* **-os**) (*computing* 计) a single instruction in a computer program that automatically causes a complete series of instructions to be put into effect, in order to perform a particular task 宏指令

macro- /'mækrəʊ; *NAmE* 'mækroʊ/ *combining form* (in nouns, adjectives and adverbs 构成名词、形容词和副词) large; on a large scale 大的；宏观的；大规模的：*macroeconomics* 宏观经济学 OPP **micro-**

macro·bi·ot·ic /,mækrəʊbaɪ'ɒtɪk; *NAmE* -kroʊbaɪ'ɑːt-/ *adj.* consisting of whole grains and vegetables grown without chemical treatment 延年益寿的，养生饮食的（吃未经化学品助长的全谷和蔬菜）：*a macrobiotic diet* 长寿饮食

macro·cosm /'mækrəʊkɒzəm; *NAmE* -kroʊkɑːz-/ *noun* any large complete structure that contains smaller structures, for example the universe 大而完整的结构；宇宙；宏观世界 ➲ COMPARE MICROCOSM

macro·eco·nom·ics /,mækrəʊ,iːkə'nɒmɪks; *NAmE* -kroʊ,ekə'nɑːm-/ *noun* [U] the study of large economic systems, such as those of whole countries or areas of the world 宏观经济学 ▸ **macro·eco·nom·ic** *adj.*：*macroeconomic policy* 宏观经济政策

mac·ron /'mækrɒn; *NAmE* 'meɪkrɑːn/ *noun* (*linguistics* 语言) the mark (¯) which is placed over a vowel in some languages and in the International Phonetic Alphabet to show that the vowel is stressed or long 长音符；平调符

macro·phage /'mækrəfeɪdʒ/ *noun* (*biology* 生) a large cell that is able to remove harmful substances from the body, and is found in blood and TISSUE 巨噬细胞

mad /mæd/ *adj.* (**mad·der**, **mad·dest**) **1** (*especially BrE*) having a mind that does not work normally; mentally ill 疯的；神经错乱的；有精神病的：*They realized that he had* **gone mad**. 他们意识到他疯了。◇ *Inventors are not mad scientists.* 发明家不是精神不正常的科学家。◇ *I'll* **go mad** *if I have to wait much longer.* 如果还要等更久的话，我会发疯的。◇ *She seemed to have gone* **stark raving mad**. 她好像是完全疯了。➲ SEE ALSO BARKING MAD **2** (*informal, especially BrE*) very stupid; not at all sensible 极愚蠢的；很不明智的：*You* **must be mad** *to risk it.* 你去冒这种风险，简直是疯了。◇ *It was a mad idea.* 那是个愚蠢透顶的想法。◇ *'I'm going to buy some new clothes.' 'Well, don't go mad* (= spend more than is sensible).' "我要去买几件新衣服。""去吧，可别乱花钱。" **3** [not before noun]

▼ **SYNONYMS 同义词辨析**

mad

crazy • nuts • batty • out of your mind • (not) in your right mind

These are all informal words that describe sb who has a mind that does not work normally. 以上各词均为非正式用语，指人神经错乱、精神失常。

mad (*informal, especially BrE*) having a mind that does not work normally 指疯的、神经错乱的、有精神病的：*I thought I'd go mad if I stayed any longer.* 我觉得再待久一点我就会发疯。NOTE **Mad** is an informal word used to suggest that sb's behaviour is very strange, often because of extreme emotional pressure. It is offensive if used to describe sb suffering from a real mental illness; use **mentally ill** instead. **Mad** is not usually used in this meaning in North American English; use **crazy** instead. * mad 为非正式用语，暗指由于极度的精神压力而行为怪异，用于真正的精神病患者意含冒犯，故用 mentally ill 代之。在美式英语中，通常不用 mad 表示此义，而用 crazy。

crazy (*informal*) having a mind that does not work normally 指疯的、神经错乱的、有精神病的：*A crazy old woman rented the upstairs room.* 一个疯老太婆租了楼上那个房间。NOTE Like **mad**, **crazy** is offensive if used to describe sb suffering from a real mental illness. 与 mad 一样，crazy 用于真正的精神病患者具冒犯意。

nuts [not before noun] (*informal*) mad 指发疯、神经错乱：*That noise is driving me nuts!* 那噪音吵得我要疯了！◇ *You guys are nuts!* 你们这些家伙全疯了！

batty (*informal, especially BrE*) slightly mad, in a harmless way 指疯疯癫癫的、古怪的：*Her mum's completely batty.* 她妈妈完全是疯疯癫癫的。

out of your mind (*informal*) unable to think or behave normally, especially because of extreme shock or anxiety 尤指因极度震惊或焦虑而心智失常、发疯：*She was out of her mind with grief.* 她悲痛得精神失常了。

(not) in your right mind (*informal*) (not) mentally normal 指精神（不）正常：***No one in their right mind*** *would choose to work there.* 任何一个精神正常的人都不会选择去那里工作。

PATTERNS

- to be mad/crazy/nuts/out of your mind/not in your right mind **to do sth**
- to **go** mad/crazy/nuts/batty
- to **drive sb** mad/crazy/nuts/batty/out of their mind
- **completely** mad/crazy/nuts/batty/out of your mind

M

~ (at/with sb) | ~ (about sth) (*informal, especially NAmE*) very angry 很生气；气愤：*He got mad and walked out.* 他大动肝火，愤然离去。◇ *She's* **mad at me** *for being late.* 我迟到了，她非常气愤。◇ (*BrE*) *That noise is* **driving me mad.** 那噪声真让我受不了。◇ (*BrE*) *He'll* **go mad** *when he sees the damage.* 他看到这样的破坏准会气疯的。➲ **SYNONYMS** AT ANGRY **4** [not usually before noun] **~ (about/on sth/sb)** (*BrE, informal*) liking sth/sb very much; very interested in sth 特别喜欢；痴迷；迷恋：*to be mad on tennis* 对网球着迷 ◇ *He's always been mad about kids.* 他一向特别喜欢孩子。◇ *football-mad boys* 迷恋足球的男孩儿 ◇ *She's completely power-mad.* 她权迷心窍。 **5** done without thought or control; wild and excited 不理智的；疯狂的；激动的：*The crowd made a* **mad rush** *for the exit.* 人群疯狂地冲向出口处。◇ *Only a* **mad dash** *got them to the meeting on time.* 他们一阵狂奔，总算准时到达会场。◇ (*BrE*) *The team won and the fans* **went mad**. 球队获胜了，球迷欣喜若狂。◇ **~ with sth** (*BrE*) *to be mad with anger/excitement/grief/love* 因气愤 / 兴奋 / 悲伤 / 爱而丧失理智 ➲ COMPARE CRAZY *adj.* ➲ **MORE LIKE THIS** 35, page R29

IDM **be mad for sb/sth** (*BrE, informal*) to like or want sb/sth very much 非常喜欢；极为需要；对…想得发狂：*Scott's mad for peanuts.* 斯科特疯狂地喜欢花生。 **like 'crazy/'mad** (*informal*) very fast, hard, much, etc. 非常快（或拼命、厉害等）：*I had to run like mad to catch the bus.* 为了赶上公共汽车，我不得不拼命跑。 **(as) mad as a 'hatter/a March 'hare** (*informal*) (of a person 人) mentally ill; very silly 发狂的；非常愚蠢的 **ORIGIN** Because of the chemicals used in hat-making, workers often suffered from mercury poisoning, which can cause loss of memory and damage to the nervous system. Lewis Carroll was probably thinking of this when he created the eccentric character of the Hatter in *Alice's Adventures in Wonderland*. A **March hare** was called mad because of the strange behaviour of hares during the mating season. 在过去，做帽子用的化学药品经常使工人汞中毒，令他们丧失记忆，神经系统受损。刘易斯·卡罗尔在创作《艾丽丝漫游奇境记》中帽商 (Hatter) 这个怪人时，很可能想到了这些。三月的兔子 (March hare) 正处在交配期，行为怪异，因而被称为疯狂的兔子。➲ **MORE LIKE THIS** 14, page R26 **mad 'keen (on sth/sb)** (*BrE, informal*) liking sth/sb very much; very interested in sth（对…）痴迷，迷恋；特别喜欢：*He's mad keen on planes.* 他对飞机十分着迷。 ➲ MORE AT HOPPING *adv.*, RAVING *adv.*

madam /ˈmædəm/ *noun* **1** [sing.] (*formal*) used when speaking or writing to a woman in a formal or business situation 夫人；女士：*Can I help you, madam?* 要帮忙吗，夫人？◇ *Dear Madam* (= used like *Dear Sir* in a letter) 尊敬的女士 / 夫人（用于书信开头，同 Dear Sir）➲ SEE ALSO MA'AM (2) **2** [C] (*informal, disapproving, especially BrE*) a girl or young woman who expects other people to do what she wants 喜欢支使别人的年轻女子；任性妄为的年轻女子：*She's a proper little madam.* 她真是个说一不二的小姑奶奶。**3** [C] a woman who is in charge of the PROSTITUTES in a BROTHEL 老鸨；鸨母；妓院女老板

mad·cap /ˈmædkæp/ *adj.* [usually before noun] (*informal*) (of people, plans, etc. 人、计划等) crazy and not caring about danger; not sensible 鲁莽的；狂妄的；不明智的 **SYN** reckless: *madcap schemes/escapades* 冒险的计划；鲁莽的冒险行动

mad 'cow disease *noun* [U] (*informal*) = BSE

mad·den /ˈmædn/ *verb* [usually passive] **~ sb/sth** to make a person or an animal very angry or crazy 使非常生气；使发疯 **SYN** **infuriate** ▶ **mad·den·ing** /ˈmædnɪŋ/ *adj.*: *maddening delays* 令人非常气恼的延误 **mad·den·ing·ly** *adv.*: *Progress is maddeningly slow.* 进展慢得令人心烦。

mad·ding /ˈmædɪŋ/ *adj.* (*literary*) behaving in a crazy way; making you feel angry or crazy 疯狂的；使人愤怒（或疯狂）的

IDM **,far from the madding 'crowd** in a quiet and private place 远离尘嚣

made /meɪd/ **1** PAST TENSE, PAST PART. OF MAKE **2 -made** (in adjectives 构成形容词) made in the way, place, etc. mentioned …制造的；制作…的：*well-made* 制作精良的 ◇ *home-made* 家庭自制的 ➲ SEE ALSO SELF-MADE

IDM **have (got) it 'made** (*informal*) to be sure of success; to have everything that you want 胸有成竹；具备所需的一切 **(be) 'made for sb/each other** to be completely suited to sb/each other 完全适合；非常般配：*Peter and Judy seem made for each other, don't they?* 彼得和朱迪像是天生的一对，不是吗？ **what sb is 'made of** (*informal*) how sb reacts in a difficult situation 某人有多厉害（在困境中表现出来的应对能力）

Ma·deira /məˈdɪərə; *NAmE* məˈdɪrə/ (*also* **Ma,deira 'wine**) *noun* **1** [U, C] a strong wine, often sweet, from the island of Madeira 马德拉白葡萄酒（产于大西洋马德拉岛，味甜，度数高）**2** [C] a glass of Madeira 一杯马德拉白葡萄酒

Ma'deira cake (*BrE*) (*NAmE* **'pound cake**) *noun* [U, C] a plain yellow cake made with eggs, fat, flour and sugar 马德拉蛋糕

mad·eleine /ˈmædleɪn; ˈmædlen/ *noun* a type of small cake 奶油茶糕；玛德琳小蛋糕

,made to 'measure *adj.* (of clothes, curtains, etc. 衣服、窗帘等) made specially to fit a particular person, window, etc. 量身定制的；按尺寸制作的

,made to 'order *adj.* (*especially NAmE*) (of clothes, furniture, etc. 衣服、家具等) made specially for a particular customer 定制的；定做的

'made-up *adj.* **1** wearing make-up 化妆的：*a heavily* **made-up** *face/woman* 浓妆的脸 / 女人 **2** not true or real; invented 不真实的；编造的：*a* **made-up** *story/word/name* 虚构的故事；谎话；假名

mad·house /ˈmædhaʊs/ *noun* **1** [usually sing.] (*informal*) a place where there is confusion and noise 混乱吵闹的地方：*Don't work in that department; it's a madhouse.* 别在那个部门工作，那里太乱。**2** (*old use*) a hospital for people who are mentally ill 疯人院；精神病院

Madi·son Av·enue /ˌmædɪsn ˈævənjuː/ *noun* [U] the US advertising industry 美国广告业 ➲ **MORE LIKE THIS** 19, page R27 **ORIGIN** From the name of the street in New York where many advertising companies have their offices. 源自纽约市美国广告公司集中的麦迪逊大街街名。

madly /ˈmædli/ *adv.* **1** (only used *after* a verb 仅用于动词后) in a way that shows a lack of control 发狂地；无法控制地：*She was rushing around madly trying to put out the fire.* 她疯了似的跑来跑去，试图把火扑灭。◇ *His heart thudded madly against his ribs.* 他的心都要跳出来了。**2** (*informal*) very, extremely 极端地；非常地：*madly excited/jealous* 非常激动 / 嫉妒 ◇ *She's* **madly in love** *with him.* 她疯狂地爱着他。

mad·man /ˈmædmən/ *noun* (*pl.* **-men** /-mən/) a man who has a serious mental illness 疯子；精神病患者：*The killing was the act of a madman.* 这起凶杀案是一个疯子所为。◇ *He drove* **like a madman**. 他像疯了似的开着车。◇ *Some madman* (= stupid person) *deleted all the files.* 不知哪个笨蛋把所有的文件都删掉了。➲ SEE ALSO MADWOMAN

mad·ness /ˈmædnəs/ *noun* [U] **1** (*old-fashioned*) the state of having a serious mental illness 精神失常；疯狂 **SYN** **insanity**: *There may be a link between madness and creativity.* 在疯狂和创造力之间也许有着某种联系。**2** crazy or stupid behaviour that could be dangerous（会带来危险的）癫狂，疯狂，愚蠢行为：*It would be sheer madness to trust a man like that.* 信任他这样的人简直是愚蠢至极。◇ *In a* **moment of madness** *she had agreed to go out with him.* 由于一时糊涂，她同意和他约会。 **IDM** SEE METHOD

ma·donna /məˈdɒnə; *NAmE* məˈdɑːnə/ *noun* **1 the Madonna** [sing.] the Virgin Mary, mother of Jesus Christ 圣母马利亚 **2** [C] a statue or picture of the Virgin Mary 圣母马利亚的雕像（或画像等）

ma·dras /məˈdræs; -ˈdrɑːs; *NAmE also* ˈmædrəs/ *noun* [U, C] a spicy Indian dish, usually containing meat 马德拉斯咖喱菜（通常含肉）：*chicken madras* 马德拉斯咖喱鸡

ma·dra·sa (*also* **ma·dra·sah**) /mə'dræsə/ *noun* a college where the Islamic faith is taught 马德拉塞；伊斯兰学校；宗教院校

mad·ri·gal /'mædrɪɡl/ *noun* a song for several singers, usually without musical instruments, popular in the 16th century（流行于 16 世纪的）牧歌

mad·woman /'mædwʊmən/ *noun* (*pl.* **-women** /-wɪmɪn/) a woman who has a serious mental illness 疯女人；女精神病患者 ➲ SEE ALSO MADMAN

mael·strom /'meɪlstrɒm; *NAmE* -strɑːm/ *noun* [usually sing.] **1** (*literary*) a situation full of strong emotions or confusing events, that is hard to control and makes you feel frightened（思想、感情、事态的）混乱，骚乱，动乱 **2** a very strong current of water that moves in circles 大旋涡 **SYN** **whirlpool**

maes·tro /'maɪstrəʊ; *NAmE* -stroʊ/ *noun* (*pl.* **-os**) (often used as a way of addressing sb, showing respect 常作呼语，表尊敬) a great performer, especially a musician 大师；音乐大师：*Maestro Giulini* 音乐大师朱利尼 ◇ *The winning goal was scored by the maestro himself.* 制胜的一球是大师自己拿下的。

Mafia /'mæfiə; *NAmE* 'mɑːf-/ *noun* **1 the Mafia** [sing.+sing./pl. v.] a secret organization of criminals, that is active especially in Sicily, Italy and the US 黑手党（尤活跃于意大利西西里和美国）**2 mafia** [C+sing./pl. v.] a group of people within an organization or a community who use their power to get advantages for themselves 小集团；小帮派；团伙；社会黑帮：*a member of the local mafia* 当地黑社会中的一名成员 ◇ *Politics is still dominated by the middle-class mafia.* 政治仍然操纵在中产阶级帮派手中。

Mafi·oso /ˌmæfi'əʊsəʊ; *NAmE* ˌmɑːfi'oʊsoʊ/ *noun* (*pl.* **Mafi·osi** /-siː/) a member of the Mafia 黑手党成员

maga·zine /ˌmæɡə'ziːn; *NAmE* 'mæɡəziːn/ *noun* **1** (*also informal* **mag** /mæɡ/) a type of large thin book with a paper cover that you can buy every week or month, containing articles, photographs, etc., often on a particular topic 杂志；期刊：*a* ***weekly/monthly magazine*** 周刊；月刊 ◇ *a* ***magazine article/interview*** 杂志文章 / 访谈 ◇ *an* ***online magazine*** 在线期刊 ◇ *Her designer clothes were from the pages of a glossy fashion magazine.* 她的名师设计的服装取材于一份精美的时装杂志。**2** a radio or television programme that is about a particular topic（电视、广播）专题节目：*a regional news magazine on TV* 以地区新闻为主题的电视节目 ◇ *a* ***magazine programme/program*** 专题节目 **3** the part of a gun that holds the bullets before they are fired 弹仓；弹盒；弹盘 **4** a room or building where weapons, EXPLOSIVES and bullets are stored 弹药库；军火库；军械库

ma·genta /mə'dʒentə/ *adj.* reddish-purple in colour 紫红色的；洋红色的 ▸ **ma·genta** *noun* [U]

mag·got /'mæɡət/ *noun* a creature like a small short WORM, that is the young form of a fly and is found in decaying meat and other food. Maggots are often used as BAIT on a hook to catch fish. 蛆

Magi /'meɪdʒaɪ/ **the Magi** *noun* [pl.] (in the Bible《圣经》) the three wise men from the East who are said to have brought presents to the baby Jesus（带礼物朝拜耶稣圣婴的）东方三博士，东方三王

magic /'mædʒɪk/ *noun, adj., verb*

■ ***noun*** [U] **1** the secret power of appearing to make impossible things happen by saying special words or doing special things 魔法；法术；巫术：*Do you believe in magic?* 你相信巫术吗？ ◇ *He suddenly appeared* ***as if by magic.*** 他突然神奇地出现了。◇ *A passage was cleared through the crowd* ***like magic.*** 好像有一股神奇的力量在人群中间开出了一条通道。➲ SEE ALSO BLACK MAGIC **2** the art of doing tricks that seem impossible in order to entertain people 戏法；魔术 **SYN** **conjuring** **3** a special quality or ability that sb/sth has, that seems too wonderful to be real 魔力；魅力；神奇 **SYN** **enchantment**：*dance and music which capture the magic of India* 具有印度独特魅力的舞蹈和音乐 ◇ *Like all truly charismatic people, he can* ***work his magic on*** *both men and women.* 像所有真正富有魅力的人一样，他让男人和女人都很着迷。◇ *Our year in Italy was* ***pure/sheer*** *magic.* 我们在意大利的那一年真是太神奇了。 **IDM** SEE WEAVE *v.*

■ ***adj.*** **1** having or using special powers to make impossible things happen or seem to happen 有魔力的；（施）巫术的；有神奇力量的：*a* ***magic spell/charm/potion/trick*** 魔咒；魔药；魔法 ◇ *There is no magic formula for passing exams—only hard work.* 根本没有通过考试的魔法，唯一的方法就是勤奋学习。 **2** (*informal*) having a special quality that makes sth seem wonderful 神奇的；有魔力的；美好的：*It was a magic moment when the two sisters were reunited after 30 years.* * 30 年后姐妹俩重逢，就像做梦一样。◇ *She has a* ***magic touch*** *with the children and they do everything she asks.* 她对孩子们很有两下子，说什么是什么。◇ *Trust is the magic ingredient in our relationship.* 信任是维系我们相互关系的神奇力量。 **3** [not before noun] (*BrE, informal*) very good or enjoyable 好极了；棒极了：*'What was the trip like?' 'Magic!'* "旅行感觉如何？""棒极了！"

■ ***verb*** **(-ck-)** **~ sb/sth + adv./prep.** to make sb/sth appear somewhere, disappear or turn into sth, by magic, or as if by magic（像）用魔法变出（或使消失、使变成…等）

magic·al /'mædʒɪkl/ *adj.* **1** containing magic; used in magic 有魔力的；用于巫术的：*magical powers* 魔力 ◇ *Her words had a magical effect on us.* 她的话对我们有一种魔力般的作用。**2** (*informal*) wonderful; very enjoyable 奇妙的；令人愉快的 **SYN** **enchanting**：*a truly magical feeling* 真正奇妙的感觉 ◇ *We spent a magical week in Paris.* 我们在巴黎度过了十分愉快的一周。 ▸ **ma·gic·al·ly** /-kli/ *adv.*

ˌmagical 'realism *noun* [U] = MAGIC REALISM

ˌmagic 'bullet *noun* **1** (*medical* 医) a medical treatment which works very quickly and effectively against a particular illness （针对某种疾病的）灵丹妙药，神奇疗法 **2** a fast and effective solution to a serious problem（解决某一问题的）灵丹妙药

ˌmagic 'carpet *noun* (in stories 故事中) a carpet that can fly and carry people（可载人飞行的）魔毯

ma·gi·cian /mə'dʒɪʃn/ *noun* **1** a person who can do magic tricks 魔术师；变戏法的人 **SYN** **conjuror** **2** (in stories 故事中) a person who has magic powers 巫师；术士；施妖术的人 **SYN** **sorcerer**

ˌmagic 'lantern *noun* a piece of equipment used in the past to make pictures appear on a white wall or screen 幻灯；幻灯机

ˌmagic 'mushroom (*BrE* or *becoming old-fashioned, NAmE*) (*NAmE usually, informal* **shroom**) *noun* a type of MUSHROOM that has an effect like some drugs and that may make people who eat it HALLUCINATE (= see things that are not there) 致幻蘑菇

ˌmagic 'realism (*also* **ˌmagical 'realism**) *noun* [U] a style of writing that mixes realistic events with FANTASY 魔幻现实主义

ˌmagic 'wand *noun* = WAND (1)： *I wish I could* ***wave a magic wand*** *and make everything all right again.* 真希望我能魔杖一挥使一切又都好起来。

magis·ter·ial /ˌmædʒɪ'stɪəriəl; *NAmE* -'stɪr-/ *adj.* (*formal*) **1** (especially of a person or their behaviour 尤指人或行为) having or showing power or authority 权威的；威严的；傲慢的：*He talked with the magisterial authority of the head of the family.* 他说起话来俨然一副一家之主的口吻。**2** (of a book or piece of writing 书或文章) showing great knowledge or understanding 睿智的；有洞察力的；知识丰富的 **SYN** **authoritative**：*his magisterial work 'The Roman Wall in Scotland'* 他的睿智之作《苏格兰的罗马墙》 **3** [only before noun] connected with a magistrate 治安法官的；基层司法官员的 ▸ **magis·teri·al·ly** /-iəli/ *adv.*

the magis·tracy /'mædʒɪstrəsi/ *noun* [sing.+sing./pl. v.] magistrates as a group（统称）治安法官，基层司法官员

M

magis·trate /ˈmædʒɪstreɪt/ *noun* an official who acts as a judge in the lowest courts of law 治安法官；基层司法官员 **SYN** **Justice of the Peace**: *a magistrates' court* 治安法院◇ *to come up before the magistrates* 在地方法院出庭

magma /ˈmæɡmə/ *noun* [U] (*specialist*) very hot liquid rock found below the earth's surface 岩浆

Magna Carta /ˌmæɡnə ˈkɑːtə; *NAmE* ˈkɑːrtə/ *noun* a document officially stating the political and legal rights of the English people, that King John was forced to sign in 1215 (often referred to as the basis for modern English law)《大宪章》，《英格兰大宪章》（1215 年英王约翰被迫签署，保障英格兰公民的政治和法律权利，常被视作现代英格兰法律的基础）

magna cum laude /ˌmæɡnə kʊm ˈlɔːdi; ˈlaʊdeɪ/ *adv.*, *adj.* (*from Latin*) (in the US) at the second of the three highest levels of achievement that students can reach when they finish their studies at college 以优秀成绩（美国大学毕业的成绩等级，为三等优异成绩的第二等）: *She graduated magna cum laude from UCLA.* 她以优秀成绩毕业于加州大学洛杉矶分校。 ➲ COMPARE CUM LAUDE, SUMMA CUM LAUDE

mag·nani·mous /mæɡˈnænɪməs/ *adj.* (*formal*) kind, generous and forgiving, especially towards an enemy or a rival 宽宏的，大度的（尤指对敌人或对手）: *a magnanimous gesture* 大度的姿态◇ *He was magnanimous in defeat and praised his opponent's skill.* 他对失败表现得很洒脱，并且赞扬了对手的才能。 ▸ **mag·na·nim·ity** /ˌmæɡnəˈnɪməti/ *noun* [U]: *She accepted the criticism with magnanimity.* 她很大度地接受了批评。 **mag·nani·mous·ly** *adv.*

M

mag·nate /ˈmæɡneɪt/ *noun* a person who is rich, powerful and successful, especially in business 权贵；要人；富豪；（尤指）产业大亨: *a* ***media/property/shipping magnate*** 媒体 / 房地产 / 航运业大亨

mag·ne·sia /mæɡˈniːʒə; *BrE also* -ziə; *NAmE* -ʃə/ *noun* [U] a white substance containing MAGNESIUM, used to help with INDIGESTION 氧化镁，镁砂（用于治疗消化不良）

mag·ne·sium /mæɡˈniːziəm/ *noun* [U] (*symb.* **Mg**) a chemical element. Magnesium is a light, silver-white metal that burns with a bright white flame. 镁

mag·net /ˈmæɡnət/ *noun* **1** a piece of iron that attracts objects made of iron towards it, either naturally or because of an electric current that is passed through it 磁铁；磁石；吸铁石 ➲ **VISUAL VOCAB** PAGE V72 **2** [usually sing.] **~ (for sb/sth)** a person, place or thing that sb/sth is attracted to 有吸引力的人（或地方、事物）: *In the 1990s the area became a magnet for new investment.* 这个地区在 20 世纪 90 年代成了新的投资热点。 **3** an object with a magnetic surface that you can stick onto a metal surface 磁体；磁性物体: *fridge magnets of your favourite cartoon characters* 你最喜欢的动画人物冰箱贴

mag·net·ic /mæɡˈnetɪk/ *adj.* [usually before noun] **1** behaving like a magnet (1) 像磁铁的；有磁性的: *magnetic materials* 磁性材料◇ *The block becomes magnetic when the current is switched on.* 一通上电流，这块板就会有磁性。 **2** connected with or produced by magnetism 磁的；磁性的: ***magnetic properties/forces*** 磁性；磁力◇ *a* ***magnetic disk*** (= one containing magnetic tape that stores information to be used by a computer) 磁盘 **3** that people find very powerful and attractive 富有吸引力的；有魅力的: *a magnetic personality* 富有魅力的个性 ▸ **mag·net·ic·al·ly** /-kli/ *adv.*

magˌnetic ˈcompass *noun* = COMPASS (1)

magˌnetic ˈfield *noun* an area around a MAGNET or MAGNETIC object, where there is a force that will attract some metals towards it 磁场

magˌnetic ˈmedia *noun* [pl., U] the different methods, for example MAGNETIC TAPE, that are used to store information for computers 磁体媒介（计算机存储信息的方法）

magˌnetic ˈnorth *noun* [U] the direction that is approximately north as it is shown on a magnetic compass 磁北 ➲ COMPARE TRUE NORTH

magˌnetic ˈstorm *noun* a situation in which the magnetic field of the earth or of another planet, star, etc. is disturbed 磁暴（地球或其他星球等磁场的扰动）

magˌnetic ˈstrip *noun* a line of MAGNETIC material on a plastic card, containing information（塑料卡上附有信息的）磁条

magˌnetic ˈtape *noun* [U] a type of plastic tape that is used for recording sound, pictures or computer information 磁带

mag·net·ism /ˈmæɡnətɪzəm/ *noun* [U] **1** a physical property (= characteristic) of some metals such as iron, produced by electric currents, that causes forces between objects, either pulling them towards each other or pushing them apart 磁性；磁力 **2** the qualities of sth, especially a person's character, that people find powerful and attractive 吸引力；魅力: *She exudes sexual magnetism.* 她洋溢着性感的魅力。

mag·net·ize (*BrE also* **-ise**) /ˈmæɡnətaɪz/ *verb* **1** [usually passive] **~ sth** (*specialist*) to make sth metal behave like a MAGNET 磁化；使有磁性 **2 ~ sb** to strongly attract sb 吸引；迷住: *Cities have a powerful magnetizing effect on young people.* 城市对青年人有着强大的吸引力。

mag·neto /mæɡˈniːtəʊ; *NAmE* -ˈniːtoʊ/ *noun* (*pl.* **-os**) a small piece of equipment that uses MAGNETS to produce the electricity that lights the fuel in the engine of a car, etc. 磁石发电机；永磁打火装置

ˈmagnet school *noun* (*NAmE*) a school in a large city that offers extra courses in some subjects in order to attract students from other areas of the city（大城市中提供额外课程招收其他地区学生的）有吸引力的学校，磁力学校

mag·ni·fi·ca·tion /ˌmæɡnɪfɪˈkeɪʃn/ *noun* **1** [U] the act of making sth look larger 放大: *The insects were examined under magnification.* 这些昆虫是放大后加以观察的。 **2** [C, U] the degree to which sth is made to look larger; the degree to which sth is able to make things look larger 放大率；放大倍数: *a magnification of 10 times the actual size* * 10 倍于实物的放大率◇ ***high/low magnification*** 高 / 低放大率◇ *The telescope has a magnification of 50.* 这个望远镜可以放大 50 倍。

mag·nifi·cent /mæɡˈnɪfɪsnt/ *adj.* extremely attractive and impressive; deserving praise 壮丽的；宏伟的；值得赞扬的 **SYN** **splendid**: *The Taj Mahal is a magnificent building.* 泰姬陵是一座宏伟的建筑。◇ *She looked magnificent in her wedding dress.* 她穿着婚纱，看上去漂亮极了。◇ *You've all done a magnificent job.* 你们活儿干得都很出色。 ▸ **mag·nifi·cence** /-sns/ *noun* [U]: *the magnificence of the scenery* 景色壮观 **mag·nifi·cent·ly** *adv.*: *The public have responded magnificently to our appeal.* 对于我们的呼吁，公众的反响极为热烈。

mag·ni·fier /ˈmæɡnɪfaɪə(r)/ *noun* a piece of equipment that is used to make things look larger 放大器；放大镜

mag·nify /ˈmæɡnɪfaɪ/ *verb* (**mag·ni·fies**, **mag·ni·fy·ing**, **mag·ni·fied**, **mag·ni·fied**) **1 ~ sth (to/by sth)** to make sth look bigger than it really is, for example by using a LENS or MICROSCOPE 放大 **SYN** **enlarge**: *bacteria magnified to 1 000 times their actual size* 放大了 1 000 倍的细菌◇ *an image magnified by a factor of 4* 放大了 4 倍的图像 **2 ~ sth** to make sth bigger, louder or stronger 扩大；增强: *The sound was magnified by the high roof.* 高高的屋顶使声音更响亮。◇ *The dry summer has magnified the problem of water shortages.* 干燥的夏季加剧了缺水的问题。 **3 ~ sth** to make sth seem more important or serious than it really is 夸大（重要性或严重性）；夸张 **SYN** **exaggerate**

ˈmagnifying glass *noun* a round piece of glass, usually with a handle, that you look through and that makes things look bigger than they really are 放大镜 ➲ **VISUAL VOCAB** PAGE V45

mag·ni·tude /ˈmæɡnɪtjuːd; *NAmE* -tuːd/ *noun* ~ **(of sth)** **1** [U] (*formal*) the great size or importance of sth; the degree to which sth is large or important 巨大；重大；重要性：*We did not realize the magnitude of the problem.* 我们没有意识到这个问题的重要性。◇ *a discovery of the first magnitude* 一项极重要的发现 **2** [C, U] (*astronomy* 天) the degree to which a star is bright 星等；星的亮度：*The star varies in brightness by about three magnitudes.* 这颗星的亮度大约在三个星等之间变化。**3** [C, U] (*geology* 地) the size of an EARTHQUAKE 震级

mag·no·lia /mæɡˈnəʊliə; *NAmE* -ˈnoʊ-/ *noun* **1** [C] a tree with large white, pink or purple flowers that smell sweet 木兰；木兰树 **2** [U] (*BrE*) a very pale cream colour 浅乳白色

mag·num /ˈmæɡnəm/ *noun* a bottle containing 1.5 litres of wine, etc.（容量为 1.5 升的）大酒瓶，大瓶

ˌmagnum ˈopus *noun* [sing.] (*from Latin*) a large and important work of art, literature or music, especially one that people think is the best work ever produced by that artist, writer, etc. 代表作；杰作

mag·pie /ˈmæɡpaɪ/ *noun* a black and white bird with a long tail and a noisy cry. There is a popular belief that magpies like to steal small bright objects. 鹊；喜鹊

magus /ˈmeɪɡəs/ *noun* (*pl.* **magi** /ˈmeɪdʒaɪ/) **1** a member of the group to which priests in ancient Persia belonged 古波斯祭司 **2** a man with magic powers 术士

ma·hala /məˈhɑːlʌ/ *adj.*, *adv.* (*SAfrE*) (*informal*) free of charge 免费的；不用钱

maha·raja (*also* **maha·ra·jah**) /ˌmɑːhəˈrɑːdʒə/ *noun* an Indian prince, especially one who ruled over one of the states of India in the past（印度的）大王，王公；（尤指过去的）土邦主

maha·rani (*also* **maha·ra·nee**) /ˌmɑːhəˈrɑːniː/ *noun* the wife of a maharaja（印度的）王公妃；土邦主妃

Maha·rishi /ˌmɑːhəˈrɪʃi; -ˈriː-/ *noun* a Hindu spiritual leader or wise man（印度教）精神领袖；（印度教）哲人

ma·hatma /məˈhætmə; -ˈhɑːt-/ *noun* **1** a holy person in S Asia who is respected by many people（南亚的）圣人 **2 the Ma·hatma** Mahatma Gandhi, the Indian spiritual leader who opposed British rule in India 圣雄甘地

Maha·yana /ˌmɑːhəˈjɑːnə/ (*also* **ˌMahaˌyana ˈBuddhism**) *noun* [U] one of the two major forms of Buddhism 大乘佛教（佛教两个主要派别之一）➲ COMPARE THERAVADA

mah·jong (*also* **mah·jongg** *especially in NAmE*) /mɑːˈdʒɒŋ; *NAmE* -ˈʒɑːŋ; -ˈʒɔːŋ/ *noun* [U] (*from Chinese*) a Chinese game played with small pieces of wood with symbols on them 麻将

ma·hog·any /məˈhɒɡəni; *NAmE* -ˈhɑːɡ-/ *noun* [U] **1** the hard reddish-brown wood of a tropical tree, used for making furniture 红木；桃花心木：*a mahogany table* 红木桌子 **2** a reddish-brown colour 红褐色：*skin tanned to a deep mahogany* 晒成深红褐色的皮肤

ma·hout /məˈhaʊt/ *noun* a person who works with, rides and cares for an ELEPHANT 象夫；驭象人；驯象人

maid /meɪd/ *noun* **1** (often in compounds 常构成复合词) a female servant in a house or hotel 女仆；侍女；（旅馆的）女服务员：*There is a maid to do the housework.* 有个女仆做家务事。➲ SEE ALSO BARMAID, CHAMBERMAID, DAIRYMAID, HOUSEMAID, MILKMAID, NURSEMAID **2** (*old use*) a young woman who is not married 少女；年轻姑娘；未婚年轻女子 ➲ SEE ALSO OLD MAID

mai·dan /maɪˈdɑːn/ *noun* an open space in or near a town in S Asia, usually covered with grass（南亚城镇中或近郊的）草地，广场，空地

maid·en /ˈmeɪdn/ *noun*, *adj.*

■ ***noun*** **1** (*literary*) a young girl or woman who is not married 少女；处女；未婚女子：*stories of knights and fair maidens* 关于骑士和美女的故事 **2** (*also* **ˌmaiden ˈover**) (in CRICKET 板球) an OVER in which no points are scored 未得分的一轮投球

■ ***adj.*** [only before noun] being the first of its kind 首次的；初次的：*a **maiden flight/voyage*** (= the first journey made by a plane/ship) 初次飞行；首航 ◇ ***a maiden speech*** (= the first speech made by an MP in the parliaments of some countries) 议员在议会的初次演讲

ˌmaiden ˈaunt *noun* (*old-fashioned*) an aunt who has not married（未婚的）姑，姨

maid·en·hair /ˈmeɪdnheə(r); *NAmE* -her/ (*also* **ˌmaiden-hair ˈfern**) *noun* [U, C] a type of FERN with long thin STEMS and delicate pale green leaves that are shaped like fans 铁线蕨

ˈmaidenhair tree *noun* = GINKGO

maid·en·head /ˈmeɪdnhed/ *noun* (*old use*) **1** the state of being a VIRGIN 处女身份；童贞 **2** = HYMEN

ˈmaiden name *noun* a woman's family name before marriage（女子的）娘家姓：*Kate kept her maiden name when she got married* (= did not change her surname to that of her husband). 凯特结婚后仍用她娘家的姓。

ˌmaid of ˈhonour (*especially US* **ˌmaid of ˈhonor**) *noun* (*pl.* **maids of honour/honor**) (especially in the US) a young woman or girl who is not married and who is the main BRIDESMAID at a wedding（尤用于美国，指未婚的）首席女傧相，伴娘 ➲ COMPARE MATRON OF HONOUR

maid·ser·vant /ˈmeɪdsɜːvənt; *NAmE* -sɜːrv-/ *noun* (*old-fashioned*) a female servant in a house 女仆；女佣；侍女

mail 🔑 /meɪl/ *noun*, *verb*

■ ***noun*** [U] **1** 🔑 (*BrE also* **post**) the official system used for sending and delivering letters, packages, etc. 邮政；邮递系统：*a **mail service/train/van*** 邮政服务 / 列车 / 汽车 ◇ *the Royal Mail* 皇家邮政 ◇ *Your cheque is in the mail.* 你的支票在邮递途中。◇ *We do our business **by mail**.* 我们通过邮递做生意。➲ SEE ALSO AIRMAIL, SNAIL MAIL, VOICEMAIL **2** 🔑 (*BrE also* **post**) letters, packages, etc. that are sent and delivered 邮件；信件；邮包：*There isn't much mail today.* 今天邮件不多。◇ *I sat down to open **the mail**.* 我坐下来打开信件。◇ *Is there a letter from them **in the mail**?* 邮件里有他们来的信吗？◇ ***hate mail*** (= letters containing insults and threats) 恐吓侮辱信 ➲ SEE ALSO JUNK MAIL, SURFACE MAIL ➲ NOTE AT POST **3** 🔑 messages that are sent or received on a computer 电子邮件；电邮：*Check regularly for new mail.* 定期查看新邮件。➲ SEE ALSO ELECTRONIC MAIL, EMAIL *n.* **4** used in the title of some newspapers（用作报纸名称）邮报：*the Mail on Sunday*《星期日邮报》**5** = CHAIN MAIL：*a coat of mail* 一副锁子甲

■ ***verb*** **1** 🔑 (*especially NAmE*) to send sth to sb using the POSTAL system 邮寄：**~ sth (to sb/sth)** *Don't forget to mail that letter to your mother.* 别忘了把那封信给你妈寄去。◇ **~ sb sth** *Don't forget to mail your mother that letter.* 别忘了把那封信给你妈寄去。◇ **~ sb/sth** *The company intends to mail 50 000 households in the area.* 公司计划给当地的 5 万个家庭寄信。➲ NOTE AT POST **2** 🔑 to send a message to sb by email 用电子邮件传送；发电邮给：**~ sb** *Please mail us at the following email address.* 请按下面的电邮地址发电邮给我们。◇ **~ sth (to sb/sth)** *The virus mails itself forward to everyone in your address book.* 这种病毒通过电子邮件自动转发给通讯录中的所有人。◇ **~ sb sth** *Can you mail me that document you mentioned?* 你能把你提及的那份文件发给我吗？

PHR V **ˌmail sth↔ˈout** to send out a large number of letters, etc. at the same time 批量邮寄：*The brochures were mailed out last week.* 小册子已于上周批寄出去了。

mail·bag /ˈmeɪlbæɡ/ (*BrE also* **post·bag**) *noun* **1** a large strong bag that is used for carrying letters and packages 邮袋 **2** [usually sing.] all the letters, emails, etc. received by a newspaper, a TV station, a website, or an important person at a particular time or about a particular subject（寄给报纸、电视台、网站、要人等的）公众来信

ˈmail bomb *noun*, *verb*

■ ***noun*** **1** (*NAmE*) = LETTER BOMB **2** an extremely large number of email messages that are sent to sb 电邮轰炸（指发给某人的超大量电子邮件）

■ *verb* ˈ**mail-bomb** ~ **sb/sth** to send sb an extremely large number of email messages 发动电邮轰炸（指向某人发送超大量电子邮件）：*The newspaper was mail-bombed by angry readers after the article was published.* 文章发表后，这家报纸受到了愤怒读者的电邮轰炸。

mail·box /ˈmeɪlbɒks; *NAmE* -bɑːks/ *noun* **1** (*NAmE*) (*BrE* ˈ**letter box**) a small box near the main door of a building or by the road, which mail is delivered to（建筑物大门口或路旁的）信箱 **2** (*NAmE*) (*BrE* **post·box**, ˈ**letter box**) a public box, for example in the street, that you put letters into when you send them 邮筒；邮箱 ➲ VISUAL VOCAB PAGE V3 ➲ PICTURE AT LETTER BOX **3** the area of a computer's memory where email messages are stored 电子邮箱，信箱区（计算机的电邮存储区）

ˈ**mail carrier** (*also* ˈ**letter carrier**) (*both NAmE*) *noun* ➲ MAILMAN

ˈ**mail drop** *noun* **1** (*especially NAmE*) an address where sb's mail is delivered, which is not where they live or work 中转通信地址；只作收邮件用的地址 **2** (*NAmE*) a box in a building where sb's mail is kept for them to collect（大楼内的）私人信箱 **3** (*BrE*) an occasion when mail is delivered 邮件的递送

mail·er /ˈmeɪlə(r)/ *noun* (*NAmE*) **1** = MAILING (2) **2** an envelope, box, etc. for sending small things by mail 邮件封套（或小箱、盒等）

mail·ing /ˈmeɪlɪŋ/ *noun* **1** [U] the act of sending items by mail 邮递；邮寄：*The strike has delayed the mailing of tax reminders.* 罢工耽搁了催税单的投寄。◇ *a mailing address* 邮寄地址 **2** (*NAmE also* **mailer**) [C] a letter or package that is sent by mail, especially one that is sent to a large number of people 邮件（尤指成批寄发的）：*An order form is included in the mailing.* 随信寄上订单一份。 ➲ WORDFINDER NOTE AT ADVERTISE

ˈ**mailing list** *noun* **1** a list of the names and addresses of people who are regularly sent information, advertising material, etc. by an organization 邮寄名单；邮寄名址录：*I am already on your mailing list.* 我已经列在你的邮寄名单上了。**2** a list of names and email addresses kept on a computer so that you can send a message to a number of people at the same time（计算机中存储的）邮件发送清单

mail·man /ˈmeɪlmæn/ *noun* (*pl.* **-men** /-men/) (*also* ˈ**mail carrier**, ˈ**letter carrier**) (*all NAmE*) a person whose job is to collect and deliver letters, etc. 邮递员 ➲ SEE ALSO POSTMAN ➲ NOTE AT GENDER

ˈ**mail merge** *noun* [U] a computer program that allows names and addresses to be automatically added to letters and envelopes, so that letters with the same contents can be sent to many different people 邮件合并程序（可自动给内容相同的信件和信封添加姓名和地址以发给多人）

ˌ**mail** ˈ**order** *noun* [U] a system of buying and selling goods through the mail 邮购（制度）：*All our products are available by mail order.* 我们的商品都可以邮购。◇ *a mail-order company* 邮购公司 ◇ *a mail-order catalogue* 邮购商品目录

mail·shot /ˈmeɪlʃɒt; *NAmE* -ʃɑːt/ *noun* advertising or information that is sent to a large number of people at the same time by mail 邮寄广告材料；广告邮件 ➲ WORDFINDER NOTE AT ADVERTISE

ˈ**mail slot** (*NAmE*) (*BrE* ˈ**letter box**) *noun* a narrow opening in a door or wall through which mail is delivered（门或墙上的）信箱 ➲ PICTURE AT LETTER BOX

maim /meɪm/ *verb* ~ **sb** to injure sb seriously, causing permanent damage to their body 使残废；使受重伤 SYN **incapacitate**：*Hundreds of people are killed or maimed in car accidents every week.* 每周都有数百人因车祸而丧命或致残。

main 🔑 /meɪn/ *adj., noun*

■ *adj.* 🔑 [only before noun] being the largest or most important of its kind 主要的；最重要的：*Be careful crossing the **main road**.* 过大马路时小心点儿。◇ *the **main course*** (= of a meal) 主菜 ◇ *We have our main meal at lunchtime.* 我们的正餐是午饭。◇ *Reception is in the main building.* 接待处在主楼。◇ *Poor housing and unemployment are the main problems.* 住房条件差和失业是主要问题。◇ ***The main thing** is to stay calm.* 最重要的是要保持冷静。 IDM ➲ SEE EYE *n.*

■ *noun* **1** [C] a large pipe that carries water or gas to a building; a large cable that carries electricity to a building（通往建筑物的）主管道，总管，输电干线：*a leaking gas main* 漏气的煤气总管 ➲ SEE ALSO WATER MAIN **2** a large pipe that carries waste water and SEWAGE (= human waste, etc.) away from a building（建筑物的）污水总管道 **3 the mains** [U, pl.] (*BrE*) the place where the supply of water, gas or electricity to a building or an area starts; the system of providing gas, water and electricity to a building or of carrying it away from a building 水源；煤气源；电源；（水、煤气、电等的）供应系统；下水道系统：*The house is not yet connected to the mains.* 这房子还没有通水电。◇ *The electricity supply has been cut off **at the mains**.* 电的供应在电源处被切断了。◇ *Plug the transformer into the mains* (= the place on a wall where electricity is brought into a room). 将变压器插入电源。◇ ***mains gas/water/electricity*** 煤气 / 水 / 电供应系统 ◇ *The shaver will run off batteries or mains.* 这个剃须刀可用电池或电源驱动。◇ *mains drainage* 排水系统

IDM **in the** ˈ**main** used to say that a statement is true in most cases 大体上；基本上：*The service here is, in the main, reliable.* 这里的服务基本上是可靠的。

ˌ**main** ˈ**clause** *noun* (*grammar* 语法) a group of words that includes a subject and a verb and can form a sentence 主句 ➲ COMPARE SUBORDINATE CLAUSE

the ˌ**main** ˈ**drag** *noun* [sing.] (*NAmE, informal*) the most important or the busiest street in a town（城镇的）大街，主要街道，最繁华的街道

the main·land /ˈmeɪnlænd/ *noun* [sing.] the main area of land of a country, not including any islands near to it 大陆；（不包括附近岛屿的）国土的主体：*a boat **to/from the mainland*** 驶往大陆的船；由大陆来的船 ◇ *The Hebrides are to the west of the Scottish mainland.* 赫布里底群岛位于苏格兰本土的西面。▶ **main·land** *adj.* [only before noun]: *mainland Greece* 希腊大陆

ˌ**main** ˈ**line** *noun* an important railway/railroad line between two cities（城际）铁路主干线 ▶ ˌ**main-**ˈ**line** *adj.*: *a main-line station* 干线车站

main·line /ˈmeɪnlaɪn/ *adj., verb*

■ *adj.* (*especially NAmE*) belonging to the system, or connected with the ideas that most people accept or believe in 传统的；主流的 SYN **mainstream**: ***mainline churches/faiths*** 主流教会 / 宗教

■ *verb* [T, I] ~ (**sth**) (*slang*) to take an illegal drug by INJECTING it into a VEIN 静脉注射（毒品）：*At 18 he was mainlining heroin.* 他 18 岁时就注射海洛因。

main·ly 🔑 /ˈmeɪnli/ *adv.* **1** 🔑 more than anything else; also used to talk about the most important reason for sth 主要地；首要地 SYN **chiefly, primarily**: *They eat mainly fruit and nuts.* 他们主要吃水果和坚果。◇ *'Where do you export to?' 'France, mainly.'* "你们出口到哪里？" "主要是法国。" ◇ *The population almost doubles in summer, **mainly because of** the jazz festival.* 主要是爵士音乐节的缘故，在夏季这里的人口几乎比平时多一倍。**2** 🔑 in most cases; used to talk about the largest part of a group of people or things 大部分；大多：*Anorexia is an illness that occurs mainly in adolescents.* 厌食症是一种多发于青少年的疾病。◇ *The people in the hotel were mainly foreign tourists.* 酒店里住的大多是外国游客。 ➲ LANGUAGE BANK AT GENERALLY

ˌ**main** ˈ**man** *noun* [sing.] (*informal*) a man who is important to you because he is a trusted friend or employee 重要的人；密友；心腹雇员：*Of course I trust you—you're my main man!* 我当然信任你，你是我的左膀右臂！

main·sail /ˈmeɪnseɪl; ˈmeɪnsl/ *noun* the largest and most important sail on a boat or ship 主帆 ➲ VISUAL VOCAB PAGE V61

main·spring /ˈmeɪnsprɪŋ/ *noun* **1** [usually sing.] ~ (**of sth**) (*formal*) the most important part of sth; the most important influence on sth 主体部分；主要影响 **2** the most important spring in a watch, clock, etc.（钟表等的）主发条

main·stay /ˈmeɪnsteɪ/ *noun* [usually sing.] ~ (**of sth**) a person or thing that is the most important part of sth and enables it to exist or be successful 支柱；中流砥柱：*Cocoa is the country's economic mainstay.* 可可是这个国家的经济支柱。

main·stream /ˈmeɪnstriːm/ *noun, adj., verb*

■ ***noun* the mainstream** [sing.] the ideas and opinions that are thought to be normal because they are shared by most people; the people whose ideas and opinions are most accepted 主流思想；主流群体：*His radical views place him outside the mainstream of American politics.* 他的激进观点使他脱离了美国政治的主流。▶ **main·stream** *adj.* [usually before noun]：*mainstream education* 主流教育

■ ***verb*** **1** ~ **sth** to make a particular idea or opinion accepted by most people 使为大多数人所接受：*Vegetarianism has been mainstreamed.* 素食主义已为大多数人所接受。 **2** ~ **sb** (*especially NAmE*) to include children with mental or physical problems in ordinary school classes 让（身心有缺陷的儿童）融入主流教育

ˌmainstream ˈmedia (*abbr.* **MSM**) *noun* [U+sing./pl. v.] traditional media such as newspapers and broadcasting 主流媒体（报纸、广播等）：*The mainstream media was/were not covering the story.* 主流媒体没有报道此事。

ˈmain street *noun* (*NAmE*) **1** (*BrE* **ˈhigh street**) [C] (especially in names 尤用于名称) the main street of a town, where most shops/stores, banks, etc. are 大街（城镇的主要商业街道） ➲ VISUAL VOCAB PAGE V3 **2 Main Street** [U] typical middle-class Americans 典型的美国中产阶级：*Main Street won't be happy with this new program.* 中产阶级不会对这个新计划感到高兴的。➲ MORE LIKE THIS 19, page R27

main·tain 🔑 AW /meɪnˈteɪn/ *verb* **1** 🔑 ~ **sth** to make sth continue at the same level, standard, etc. 维持；保持 SYN **preserve**：***to maintain law and order/standards/a balance*** 维持治安；保持水平/平衡 ◇ *The two countries have always maintained close relations.* 这两个国家一直保持着密切关系。◇ (*formal*) *She maintained a dignified silence.* 她一言不发，面容威严。◇ *to maintain prices* (= prevent them falling or rising) 维持价格的稳定 **2** 🔑 ~ **sth** to keep a building, a machine, etc. in good condition by checking or repairing it regularly 维修；保养：*The house is large and difficult to maintain.* 房子很大，难以养护。 **3** 🔑 to keep stating that sth is true, even though other people do not agree or do not believe it 坚持（意见）；固执己见 SYN **insist**：~ (**that**)... *The men maintained (that) they were out of the country when the crime was committed.* 这几个男人坚持说案发时他们在国外。◇ ~ **sth** *She has always **maintained her innocence**.* 她一直坚持说她是无辜的。◇ **+ speech** *'But I'm innocent!' she maintained.* "但是我是无辜的！"她坚持道。➲ LANGUAGE BANK AT ARGUE **4** 🔑 ~ **sb/sth** to support sb/sth over a long period of time by giving money, paying for food, etc. 供养；扶养 SYN **keep**：*Her income was barely enough to maintain one child, let alone three.* 她的收入养活一个孩子几乎都不够，更不用说三个了。

main·ten·ance AW /ˈmeɪntənəns/ *noun* [U] **1** ~ (**of sth**) the act of keeping sth in good condition by checking or repairing it regularly 维护；保养：*The school pays for heating and the maintenance of the buildings.* 学校负担这些大楼的供热和维修费用。◇ *car maintenance* 汽车保养 **2** ~ (**of sth**) the act of making a state or situation continue 维持；保持：*the maintenance of international peace* 维护世界和平 **3** (*law* 律, *BrE*) money that sb must pay regularly to their former wife, husband or partner, especially

▼ SYNONYMS 同义词辨析

main

major • key • central • principal • chief • prime

These words all describe sb/sth that is the largest or most important of its kind. 以上各词均用以形容主要的、最重要的人或事物。

main [only before noun] largest or most important 指主要的、最重要的：*Be careful crossing the main road.* 过大马路时小心点。◇ *The main thing is to remain calm.* 最重要的是要保持冷静。

major [usually before noun] very large or important 指主要的、重要的、大的：*He played a major role in setting up the system.* 他在建立这个系统的过程中起了主要的作用。
NOTE **Major** is most often used after *a* with a singular noun, or no article with a plural noun. When it is used with *the* or *my/your/his/her/our/their* it means 'the largest or most important'. * major 最常用于不定冠词 a 之后，与单数名词连用；或不用冠词，与复数名词连用。major 与 the 或 my/your/his/her/our/their 连用时意为最主要的、最重要的：*Our major concern here is combatting poverty.* 在这里我们最关心的是解决贫穷问题。 In this meaning it is only used to talk about ideas or worries that people have, not physical things, and it is also more formal than **main**. 在该含义中 major 只用以指人的想法或担忧，而非物质的东西，且较 main 正式：~~*Be careful crossing the major road.*~~ ◇ ~~*The major thing is to remain calm.*~~

key [usually before noun] most important; essential 指最重要的、主要的、关键的：*He was a key figure in the campaign.* 他是这场运动的关键人物。 NOTE **Key** is used most frequently in business and political contexts. It can be used to talk about ideas, or the part that sb plays in a situation, but not physical things. It is slightly more informal than **major**, especially when used after a noun and linking verb. * key 最常用于商务和政治语境，可用来形容想法或某人在某情势下起的作用，而非物质的东西。key 较 major 稍非正式，用于名词加连系动词后尤其如此：*Speed is key at this point.* 在这个时候速度是关键。

central (*rather formal*) most important 指最重要的、首要的、主要的：*The central issue is that of widespread racism.* 最重要的问题是种族主义泛滥。 NOTE **Central** is used in a similar way to **key**, but is more formal. It is most frequently used in the phrase *sth is central to sth else*. * central 与 key 用法相似，但更正式，最常用于 be central to 短语中。

principal [only before noun] (*rather formal*) most important 指最重要的、主要的：*The principal reason for this omission is lack of time.* 跳过它的主要原因是时间不足。
NOTE **Principal** is mostly used for statements of fact about which there can be no argument. To state an opinion, or to try to persuade sb of the facts as you see them, it is more usual to use **key** or **central**. * principal 主要用于陈述无可争辩的事实。表明意见或说服别人相信你所见到的事实，较常用 key 或 central：*The key/central issue here is...* 这里的关键问题是…

chief [only before noun] (*rather formal*) most important 指最重要的、首要的、主要的：*Unemployment was the chief cause of poverty.* 失业是贫穷的主要原因。

prime [only before noun] (*rather formal*) most important; to be considered first 指主要的、首要的：*My prime concern is to protect my property.* 我最关心的是保护自己的财产。

PATTERNS

- a/the main/major/key/central/principal/chief/prime **aim/concern**
- a/the main/major/principal **road/town/city**
- the main/key **thing** is to...
- to be **of** major/key/central/prime **importance**

M

when they have had children together（依法应负担的）生活费；抚养费：*He has to pay maintenance to his ex-wife.* 他必须付给前妻生活费。◇ *child maintenance* 儿童抚养费 ◇ *a maintenance order* (= given by a court of law)（法院下达的）生活费支付令 ➲ SEE ALSO ALIMONY

ˌmain ˈverb *noun* [usually sing.] (*grammar* 语法) the verb in a MAIN CLAUSE 主要动词（主句中的动词）

mai·son·ette /ˌmeɪzəˈnet/ *noun* (*BrE*) a flat/apartment with rooms on two floors within a building, usually with a separate entrance 两层独立公寓

maître d' /ˌmeɪtrə ˈdiː; *NAmE also* ˌmeɪtər/ *noun* (*pl.* **maître d's** /ˌmeɪtrə ˈdiːz; *NAmE also* ˌmeɪtər) (*also formal* **maître d'hôtel** /ˌmeɪtrə dəʊˈtel; *NAmE also* doʊˈtel; *also* ˌmeɪtər/ *pl.* **maîtres d'hôtel** /ˌmeɪtrə dəʊˈtel; *NAmE also* doʊˈtel; *also* ˌmeɪtər/) (*from French, informal*) **1** a head waiter 侍者总管；领班 **2** a man who manages a hotel 旅馆经理；旅馆老板

maize /meɪz/ *noun* [U] **1** (*BrE*) (*NAmE* **corn**) a tall plant grown for its large yellow grains that are used for making flour or eaten as a vegetable; the grains of this plant 玉蜀黍；玉米 ➲ VISUAL VOCAB PAGE V35 ➲ SEE ALSO CORN ON THE COB, SWEETCORN **2** (*especially NAmE*) = INDIAN CORN

Maj. *abbr.* (in writing 书写形式) MAJOR (1) 少校：*Maj. (Tony) Davies*（托尼•）戴维斯少校 ◇ *Maj. Gen.* (= Major General) 少将

M

ma·jes·tic /məˈdʒestɪk/ *adj.* impressive because of size or beauty 雄伟的；威严的；壮观的 SYN **awe-inspiring, splendid**：*a majestic castle/river/view* 雄伟的城堡；壮丽的河流 / 景色 ▸ **ma·jes·tic·al·ly** /-kli/ *adv.*

maj·esty /ˈmædʒəsti/ *noun* (*pl.* **-ies**) **1** [U] the impressive and attractive quality that sth has 雄伟壮观；庄严；威严：*the sheer majesty of St Peter's in Rome* 罗马圣彼得大教堂的雄伟庄严 ◇ *the majesty of the music* 那音乐的庄严气氛 **2** [C] **His/Her Majesty, Your Majesty** a title of respect used when speaking about or to a king or queen（对国王或女王的尊称）陛下 **3** [U] royal power 王权

major AW /ˈmeɪdʒə(r)/ *adj., noun, verb*

■ *adj.* **1** [usually before noun] very large or important 主要的；重要的；大的：*a major road* 一条大马路 ◇ *major international companies* 大跨国公司 ◇ *to play a major role in sth* 在某事中起重要作用 ◇ *We have encountered major problems.* 我们遇上了大问题。◇ *There were calls for major changes to the welfare system.* 有人要求对福利制度进行重大改革。OPP **minor** ➲ SYNONYMS AT MAIN ➲ SEE ALSO MINOR-LEAGUE (2) **2** [not before noun] (*NAmE*) serious 严重：*Never mind—it's not major.* 别担心，这不严重。**3** (*music* 音) based on a SCALE (= a series of eight notes) in which the third note is two whole TONES/STEPS higher than the first note 大调的：*the key of D major* * D 大调 ➲ COMPARE MINOR *adj.* (2) **4** (*NAmE*) related to sb's main subject of study in college（课程）主修的

■ *noun* **1** [C] (*abbr.* **Maj.**) an officer of fairly high rank in the army or the US AIR FORCE 少校：*Major Smith* 史密斯少校 ◇ *He's a major in the US army.* 他是美国陆军少校。➲ SEE ALSO DRUM MAJOR, SERGEANT MAJOR **2** [C] (*NAmE*) the main subject or course of a student at college or university 主修课程；专业课：*Her major is French.* 她的专业课是法语。➲ COMPARE MINOR *n.* (2) ➲ WORDFINDER NOTE AT UNIVERSITY **3** [C] (*NAmE*) a student studying a particular subject as the main part of their course 主修学生；主修生：*She's a French major.* 她是法语专业的学生。**4 the majors** [pl.] (*sport* 体育, *NAmE*) the MAJOR LEAGUES 大联盟

■ *verb*

PHR V **ˈmajor in sth** (*NAmE*) to study sth as your main subject at a university or college 主修：*She majored in History at Stanford.* 她在斯坦福主修历史。**ˈmajor on sth** (*BrE*) to pay particular attention to one subject, issue, etc. 专门研究（课题、问题等）

major-domo /ˌmeɪdʒə ˈdəʊməʊ; *NAmE* ˌmeɪdʒər ˈdoʊmoʊ/ *noun* (*pl.* **-os**) a senior servant who manages a large house（大宅的）总管家，大管家

ma·jor·ette /ˌmeɪdʒəˈret/ *noun* (*especially NAmE*) = DRUM MAJORETTE

ˌmajor ˈgeneral *noun* an officer of very high rank in the army or the US AIR FORCE 陆军少将；（美）空军少将：*Major General William Hunt* 陆军少将威廉•亨特

ma·jor·ity AW /məˈdʒɒrəti; *NAmE* -ˈdʒɔːr-; -ˈdʒɑːr-/ *noun* (*pl.* **-ies**) **1** [sing.+sing./pl. v.] **~ (of sb/sth)** the largest part of a group of people or things 大部分；大多数：*The majority of people interviewed prefer TV to radio.* 大多数接受采访的人都喜欢看电视多于听收音机。◇ *The majority was/were in favour of banning smoking.* 大多数人支持禁烟。◇ *This treatment is not available in the* ***vast majority*** *of hospitals.* 绝大部分医院都不提供这种治疗。◇ *a majority decision* (= one that is decided by what most people want) 根据大多数人的意见作出的决定 ◇ *In the nursing profession, women are* ***in a/the majority.*** 女性在护理行业中占大多数。OPP **minority** ➲ SEE ALSO MORAL MAJORITY, SILENT MAJORITY **2** [C] the number of votes by which one political party wins an election; the number of votes by which one side in a discussion, etc. wins（获胜的）票数；多数票：*She was elected* ***by/with a majority*** *of 749.* 她以 749 票的多数票当选。◇ *a clear* (= large) *majority* 明显多数票 ◇ **~ (over sb)** *They had a large majority over their nearest rivals.* 他们所得的票数远远超出名次仅次于他们的对手。◇ *The government does not have an* ***overall majority*** (= more members than all the other parties added together). 政府没有获得绝对多数票。◇ *The resolution was carried by a huge majority.* 这项决议以绝大多数票赞成而获得通过。➲ WORDFINDER NOTE AT DEMOCRACY ➲ COLLOCATIONS AT VOTE ➲ SEE ALSO ABSOLUTE MAJORITY **3** [C] (*NAmE*) the difference between the number of votes given to the candidate who wins the election and the total number of votes of all the other candidates 超出其余各方票数总和的票数 ➲ SEE ALSO PLURALITY **4** [U] (*law* 律) the age at which you are legally considered to be an adult 成年的法定年龄

maˈjority leader *noun* the leader of the political party that has the majority in either the House of Representatives or the Senate in the US（美国众议院或参议院的）多数派政党领袖

maˌjority ˈrule *noun* [U] a system in which power is held by the group that has the largest number of members 多数裁定原则

maˌjority ˈverdict *noun* (*law* 律) a decision made by a JURY in a court case that most members, but not all, agree with 多数裁决（陪审团根据多数票作出）

ˈmajor league (*also* **ˈMajor league**) *noun* (*NAmE*) a league of professional sports teams, especially in BASEBALL, that play at the highest level（尤指棒球）第一流的职业队伍联盟；大联盟

ˈmajor-league *adj.* [only before noun] (*NAmE*) **1** (*sport* 体育) connected with teams that play in the major leagues, especially in BASEBALL（尤指棒球）职业球队联盟的，大联盟的：*a major-league team* 大联盟球队 **2** very important and having a lot of influence 非常重要的；颇有影响力的：*a major-league business* 举足轻重的企业

major·ly /ˈmeɪdʒəli; *NAmE* -dʒərli/ *adv.* (used before an adjective 用于形容词前) (*informal, especially NAmE*) very; extremely 非常地；极端地：*majorly disappointed* 无比失望

make /meɪk/ *verb, noun* ➲ SEE ALSO MADE

■ *verb* (**made, made** /meɪd/)

• CREATE 制造 **1** to create or prepare sth by combining materials or putting parts together 制造；做；组装：**~ sth** *to make a table/dress/cake* 做桌子 / 连衣裙 / 蛋糕 ◇ *to make bread/cement/paper* 制作面包；生产水泥 / 纸张 ◇ *She makes her own clothes.* 她自己做衣服。◇ *made in France* (= on a label) 法国制造 ◇ **~ sth (out) of sth** *What's your shirt made of?* 你的衬衣是用什么做的？◇ **~ sth from sth** *Wine is made from grapes.* 葡萄酒是用葡萄做的。◇ **~ sth into sth** *The grapes are made into wine.* 这些葡萄用来

做酒。◇ **~ sth for sb** *She made coffee for us all.* 她给我们大家冲了咖啡。◇ **~ sb sth** *She made us all coffee.* 她给我们大家冲了咖啡。 ➲ NOTE AT DO[1] **2** ⚷ **~ sth** to write, create or prepare sth 写；出产；制定：*These regulations were made to protect children.* 这些规章制度是为了保护儿童而制定的。◇ *My lawyer has been urging me to make a will.* 我的律师一直在催促我立遗嘱。◇ *She has made* (= directed or acted in) *several movies.* 她已经出了好几部电影。

• **A BED** 床 **3** ⚷ **~ a bed** to arrange a bed so that it is neat and ready for use 铺床

• **CAUSE TO APPEAR/HAPPEN/BECOME/DO** 使出现 / 发生 / 成为 / 做 **4** ⚷ **~ sth (+ adv./prep.)** to cause sth to appear as a result of breaking, tearing, hitting or removing material 造成（破坏、破损等）：*The stone made a dent in the roof of the car.* 石头把车顶砸了个坑。◇ *The holes in the cloth were made by moths.* 布上的窟窿是虫子蛀的。 **5** ⚷ **~ sth** to cause sth to exist, happen or be done 使出现；引发；使产生：*to* ***make a noise/mess/fuss*** 产生噪音；弄得一团糟；小题大做 ◇ *She tried to* ***make a good impression*** *on the interviewer.* 她努力给主持面试者留个好印象。◇ *I keep* ***making*** *the same* ***mistakes***. 我总是犯同样的错误。 **6** ⚷ **~ sb/sth/yourself + adj.** to cause sb/sth to be or become sth 使变得；使成为：*The news made him very happy.* 这则消息使他非常高兴。◇ *She made her objections clear.* 她明确表示反对。◇ *He* ***made it clear that*** *he objected.* 他明确表示反对。◇ *The full story was never* ***made public***. 全部情况从未公之于世。◇ *Can you* ***make yourself understood*** *in Russian?* 你能用俄语表达你的意思吗？◇ *She couldn't* ***make herself heard*** *above the noise of the traffic.* 车辆噪音很大，她无法让人听到她的声音。◇ *The terrorists* ***made it known that*** *tourists would be targeted.* 恐怖分子宣称游客将成为他们袭击的目标。 **7** ⚷ **~ sb/sth do sth** to cause sb/sth to do sth 促使；使得：*She always makes me laugh.* 她总是让我发笑。◇ *This dress makes me look fat.* 这衣服我穿着显胖。◇ *What makes you say that* (= why do you think so)? 你为什么这么说？ ◇ *Nothing will make me change my mind.* 什么也改变不了我的主意。 **8** ⚷ to cause sb/sth to be or become sth 使变得；使成为： **~ sth of sb/sth** *This isn't very important—I don't want to* ***make an issue of it***. 这不太重要，我不想把它当回事儿。 ◇ *Don't* ***make a habit of it***. 别养成习惯。◇ *You've* ***made a*** *terrible* ***mess of*** *this job.* 你把这件事儿搞得一团糟。◇ *It's important to try and* ***make something of*** (= achieve sth in) *your life.* 在一生中有所成就是很重要的。 ◇ *We'll make a tennis player of you yet.* 早晚有一天，我们会让你成为一名网球选手的。◇ **~ sth + noun** *I made painting the house my project for the summer.* 把房子粉刷了一遍，这就是我的夏季工程。 ◇ *She* ***made it her business*** *to find out who was responsible.* 她一定要查清楚到底是谁干的。

• **A DECISION/GUESS/COMMENT, ETC.** 决定、猜测、评论等 **9** ⚷ **~ a decision, guess, comment, etc.** to decide, guess, etc. sth 做，作出（决定、估计等）：*Come on! It's time we made a start.* 快点！我们该开始了。 **HELP** **Make** can be used in this way with a number of different nouns. These expressions are included at the entry for each noun. * make 可以和许多名词这样搭配使用，表达方式列在各有关名词词条下。

• **FORCE** 迫使 **10** ⚷ to force sb to do sth 迫使；强迫： **~ sb do sth** *They made me repeat the whole story.* 他们非让我把整个事件再说一遍。◇ **be made to do sth** *She must be made to comply with the rules.* 必须让她遵守规则。◇ **~ sb** *He never cleans his room and his mother never tries to make him.* 他从不收拾自己的房间，而他妈也从不要求他收拾。

• **REPRESENT** 表现 **11** ⚷ to represent sb/sth as being or doing sth 表现；表示；描绘： **~ sb/sth + adj.** *You've made my nose too big* (= for example in a drawing). 你把我的鼻子画得太大了。◇ **~ sb/sth + noun** *He makes King Lear a truly tragic figure.* 他把李尔王刻画成一个真正的悲剧人物。

• **APPOINT** 任命 **12** ⚷ **~ sb + noun** to elect or choose sb as sth 选举；挑选；任命：*She made him her assistant.* 她挑选他做她的助手。

• **BE SUITABLE** 适合 **13** ⚷ *linking verb* **~ sb/sth + noun** to become or develop into sth; to be suitable for sth 成为；适合：*She would have made an excellent teacher.* 她本可以成为一位出色的教师。◇ *This room would make a nice office.* 这间屋子做办公室挺不错。

• **EQUAL** 等于 **14** ⚷ *linking verb* **+ noun** to add up to or equal sth 合计；等于：*5 and 7 make 12.* * 5 加 7 等于 12。◇ *A hundred cents make one euro.* 一百分等于一欧元。 **15** *linking verb* **+ noun** to be a total of sth 成为总数；是…的总和：*That makes the third time he's failed his driving test!* 他这已经是第三次驾驶考试不及格了！

• **MONEY** 钱 **16** ⚷ **~ sth** to earn or gain money 挣钱；赚钱：*She makes $100 000 a year.* 她一年赚 10 万美元。◇ *to* ***make a profit/loss*** 获利；赔钱 ◇ *We need to think of ways to* ***make money***. 我们需要想办法挣钱。◇ *He* ***made a fortune*** *on the stock market.* 他在股票市场发了大财。◇ *He* ***makes a living*** *as a stand-up comic.* 他靠说单口相声为生。

• **CALCULATE** 计算 **17** [no passive] **~ sth + noun** to think or calculate sth to be sth 估计；计算：*What time do you* ***make it***? 你估计现在几点了？◇ *I make that exactly $50.* 我算出正好是 50 元。

• **REACH** 达到 **18** [no passive] **~ sth** to manage to reach or go to a place or position （尽力）赶往，到达，达到：*Do you think we'll make Dover by 12?* 你觉得我们 12 点前能到多佛吗？ ◇ *I'm sorry I couldn't make your party last night.* 很抱歉，昨晚没能参加你们的聚会。 ◇ *He'll never make* (= get a place in) *the team.* 他绝不可能成为该队的队员。◇ *The story made* (= appeared on) *the front pages of the national newspapers.* 这件事登在了全国性报纸的头版。◇ *We just managed to* ***make the deadline*** (= to finish sth in time). 我们总算勉强按期完成。

• **STH SUCCESSFUL** 成功 **19** **~ sth** to cause sth to be a success 使成功；使圆满：*Good wine can make a meal.* 酒美饭亦香。◇ *The news really* ***made my day***. 这消息确实使我一天都很愉快。 ➲ MORE LIKE THIS 33, page R28

IDM **HELP** Most idioms containing **make** are at the entries for the nouns and adjectives in the idioms, for example **make merry** is at **merry**. 大多数含 make 的习语，都可在该等习语中的名词及形容词相关词条找到，如 make merry 在词条 merry 下。 **make as if to do sth** to make a movement that makes it seem as if you are just going to do sth 似乎；假装：*He made as if to speak.* 他似乎要说点什么。 **make 'do (with sth)** to manage with sth that is not really good enough 凑合；将就：*We were in a hurry so we had to make do with a quick snack.* 我们很匆忙，只好将就着来了点小吃。 **make 'good** to become rich and successful 变得富有；获得成功 **make sth 'good 1** to pay for, replace or repair sth that has been lost or damaged 赔偿；替换；修理：*She promised to make good the damage.* 她答应赔偿损失。 **2** to do sth that you have promised, threatened, etc. to do 履行，执行（曾承诺、威胁等的事） **SYN** **fulfil** **'make it 1** ⚷ to be successful in your career 获得成功：*He never really made it as an actor.* 他从来就不是一个成功的演员。 **2** ⚷ to succeed in reaching a place in time, especially when this is difficult （尤指在困难情况下）准时到达：*The flight leaves in twenty minutes—we'll never make it.* 再过二十分钟飞机就起飞了，咱们无论如何也赶不上了。 **3** ⚷ to be able to be present at a place 能够出席（或到场）：*I'm sorry I won't be able to make it* (= for example, to a party) *on Saturday.* 很抱歉，星期六我出席不了。 **4** ⚷ to survive after a serious illness or accident; to deal successfully with a difficult experience 幸免于难；渡过难关：*The doctors think he's going to make it.* 医生认为他能挺过去。◇ *I don't know how I* ***made it through*** *the week.* 我不知道自己是怎么熬过那个星期的。 **'make it with sb** (*NAmE, slang*) to have sex with sb （与某人）发生性关系 **make like...** (*NAmE, informal*) to pretend to be, know or have sth in order to impress people （为给别人留下印象）假装，装出…样子：*He makes like he's the greatest actor of all time.* 他装模作样，仿佛自己是有史以来最棒的演员。 **make the 'most of sth/sb/yourself** to gain as much advantage, enjoyment, etc. as you can from sb/sth 充分利用；尽情享受：*It's my first trip abroad so I'm going to make the most of it.* 这是我第一次出国，我要充分利用这个机会。◇ *She doesn't know how to make the most of herself* (= make herself appear in the best possible way). 她不知道如何充分表现自己。 **make 'much of sth/sb** to treat sth/sb as very important 重视；认为很重要：*He always makes much of his humble origins.* 他总是非常在意他卑微的出身。 **ˌmake or 'break sb/sth** to be the thing that makes sb/sth either a success or a failure 为…成败的关

M

键: *This movie will make or break him as a director.* 这部电影将要决定他当导演是行还是不行。◇ *It's make-or-break time for the company.* 这是公司盛衰的关键时刻。**'make something of yourself** to be successful in your life 获得成功; 事业有成

PHR V **'make for sth 1** to move towards sth 向…移动 **2** to help to make sth possible 促成: *Constant arguing doesn't make for a happy marriage.* 不断争吵不可能使婚姻幸福。➲ SEE ALSO (BE) MADE FOR SB/EACH OTHER at MADE

'make sb/sth into sb/sth 🔑 to change sb/sth into sb/sth 把…变成 **SYN** **turn into**: *We're making our attic into an extra bedroom.* 我们要把阁楼改装一下，增加一间卧室。

'make sth of sb/sth to understand the meaning or character of sb/sth 领会; 理解; 懂得: ***What do you make of it all?*** 你明白那都是什么意思吗? ◇ *I can't make anything of this note.* 我根本不懂这封短信的意思。◇ *I don't know **what to make of** (= think of) the new manager.* 这位新经理，我不知道怎么说他才好。

ˌmake 'off to hurry away, especially in order to escape 匆忙离开; （尤指）仓惶逃跑 **ˌmake 'off with sth** to steal sth and hurry away with it 偷走某物; 顺手牵羊

ˌmake 'out 1 (*informal*) used to ask if sb managed well or was successful in a particular situation（询问是否处理得当）应付，过: *How did he make out while his wife was away?* 他妻子不在家时他是怎么过的? **2 make out (with sb)** (*NAmE, informal*) to kiss and touch sb in a sexual way; to have sex with sb 亲吻抚摸（某人）;（与某人）性交 **ˌmake sb 'out** to understand sb's character 看透，弄懂（某人）**ˌmake sb/sth↔'out 1** to manage to see sb/sth or read or hear sth 看清; 听清; 分清; 辨认清楚 **SYN** **distinguish**: *I could just make out a figure in the darkness.* 黑暗中我只看出了一个人的轮廓。◇ **make out what, who, etc....** *I could hear voices but I couldn't make out what they were saying.* 我能听到说话的声音，却听不清他们在说什么。➲ SYNONYMS AT IDENTIFY **2** to say that sth is true when it may not be 声称; 把…说成 **SYN** **claim**: *She's not as rich as people make out.* 她并不像人们说的那样富有。◇ **make out that...** *He made out that he had been robbed.* 他说他被人抢劫了。◇ **make sb/sth out to be/do sth** *She makes herself out to be smarter than she really is.* 她说自己多么聪明，未免言过其实。**ˌmake sth↔'out 1** to write out or complete a form or document 开具，填写（表格或文件）: *He made out a cheque for €100.* 他开了一张 100 欧元的支票。◇ *The doctor made out a prescription for me.* 医生给我开了一张处方。**2** (used in negative sentences and questions 用于否定句和疑问句) to understand sth; to see the reasons for sth 理解; 明白（事理）: *How do you make that out* (= what are your reasons for thinking that)? 你为什么这么想? ◇ **make out what, why, etc....** *I can't make out what she wants.* 我不明白她想要什么。

ˌmake sth↔'over (to sb/sth) 1 to legally give sth to sb（合法地）给予，转让: *He made over the property to his eldest son.* 他把财产传给了他的长子。**2** to change sth in order to make it look different or use it for a different purpose; to give sb a different appearance by changing their clothes, hair, etc. 改造; 修饰; 彻底改变形象 **SYN** **transform** ➲ RELATED NOUN MAKEOVER

'make towards sth to start moving towards sth 向…移动; 朝…走去: *He made towards the door.* 他向门口走去。

ˌmake 'up | ˌmake yourself/sb↔'up to put powder, LIPSTICK, etc. on your/sb's face to make it more attractive or to prepare for an appearance in the theatre, on television, etc. 化妆; 上妆 ➲ RELATED NOUN MAKE-UP (1) **ˌmake sth↔'up 1** 🔑 to form sth 形成; 构成 **SYN** **constitute**: *Women make up 56% of the student numbers.* 女生占学生人数的 56%。➲ RELATED NOUN MAKE-UP (3) ➲ SYNONYMS AT CONSIST ➲ **LANGUAGE BANK** AT PROPORTION **2** to put sth together from several different things 拼装; 组成 ➲ RELATED NOUN MAKE-UP (3) **3** 🔑 to invent a story, etc., especially in order to trick or entertain sb 编造（故事、谎言等）: *He made up some excuse about his daughter being sick.* 他编了个借口，说他的女儿病了。◇ *I told the kids a story, making it up as I went along.* 我给孩子们讲了个故事，是现编的。◇ *You made that up!* 你瞎编! **4** to complete a number or an amount required 凑数: *We need one more person to make up a team.* 我们还需要一个人才能组成一个队。 **5** to replace sth that has been lost; to COMPENSATE for sth 补上（失去的东西）; 作出补偿: *Can I leave early this afternoon and make up the time tomorrow?* 我今天下午早点儿走，明天补上这段时间，可以吗? **6** to prepare a medicine by mixing different things together 配药 **7** to prepare a bed for use; to create a temporary bed 铺床; 临时搭床: *We made up the bed in the spare room.* 我们在空着没用的房间里搭了张床。◇ *They made up a bed for me on the sofa.* 他们给我在沙发上铺了个床。**8** (*especially NAmE*) to clean a hotel room and make the bed 打扫（酒店房间）: *The maid asked if she could make up the room.* 清洁女工问她是不是可以整理房间。 **ˌmake 'up for sth** 🔑 to do sth that corrects a bad situation 弥补; 补偿 **SYN** **compensate**: *Nothing can make up for the loss of a child.* 失去一个孩子是任何东西都

▼ SYNONYMS 同义词辨析

make

do • create • develop • produce • generate • form

These words all mean to make sth from parts or materials, or to cause sth to exist or happen. 以上各词均含制造、使产生之义。

make to create or prepare sth by combining materials or putting parts together; to cause sth to exist or happen 指制造、做、组装、使产生: *She makes her own clothes.* 她自己做衣服。◇ *She **made a good impression** on the interviewer.* 她给主持面试者留下了很好的印象。

do (*rather informal*) to make or prepare sth, especially sth artistic or sth to eat 指制作、准备（尤指艺术品或食品）: *He did a beautiful drawing of a house.* 他画了一栋漂亮的房子。◇ *Who's doing the food for the party?* 谁准备聚会的食物?

create to make sth exist or happen, especially sth new that did not exist before 指创造、创作、创建: *Scientists disagree about how the universe was created.* 科学家对宇宙是怎样形成的有分歧。

MAKE OR CREATE? 用 make 还是 create?

Make is a more general word and is more often used for physical things: you would usually *make a table/dress/cake* but *create jobs/wealth*. You can use **create** for sth physical in order to emphasize how original or unusual the object is. * make 较通用，较常用以指物质的东西，如制造桌子、做衣服、做蛋糕通常用 make，但创造就业机会 / 财富用 create。要强调某物品或实体事物是原创的或不同寻常，也可用 create: *Try this new dish, created by our head chef.* 品尝一下这道新菜吧，是我们厨师长首创的。

develop (used especially in business contexts) to think of and produce a new product（尤用于商务语境）指开发、研制（产品）: *to develop new software* 开发新软件

produce to make things to be sold; to create sth using skill 指生产、制造（商品），（运用技巧）制作、造出: *a factory that produces microchips* 微芯片制造厂

generate to produce or create sth, especially power, money or ideas 指创造、产生（电、财富或主意）: *to generate electricity* 发电 ◇ *Brainstorming is a good way of generating ideas.* 集思广益是出主意的好办法。

form [often passive] to make sth from sth else; to make sth into sth else 指制作、组成、制成: *Rearrange the letters to form a new word.* 重新排列字母，组成另一单词。◇ *The chain is formed from 136 links.* 这根链条由 136 个链节组成。

PATTERNS

- to make/create/develop/produce/generate/form sth **from/out of** sth
- to make/form sth **into** sth
- to make/produce **wine**
- to create/develop a **new product**
- to create/produce/generate **income/profits/wealth**
- to produce/generate **electricity/heat/power**

无法弥补的。◇ *After all the delays, we were anxious to* ***make up for lost time.*** 耽搁了这么久，我们急着想弥补失去的时间。◇ *Her enthusiasm makes up for her lack of experience.* 她的热情弥补了她经验的不足。**,make 'up (to sb) for sth** to do sth for sb or give them sth because you have caused them trouble, suffering or disappointment and wish to show that you are sorry（对某人）表示歉意，给以补偿 SYN **compensate**: *How can I make up for the way I've treated you?* 我这样对你，该怎么向你表示歉意呢？◇ (*informal*) *I'll* ***make it up to you,*** *I promise.* 我保证我一定会补偿你的。**,make 'up to sb** (*BrE, informal, disapproving*) to be pleasant to sb, praise them, etc., especially in order to get an advantage for yourself 献媚；奉承；讨好 **,make 'up (with sb)** (*BrE also* **,make it 'up**) to end a disagreement with sb and become friends again（与某人）言归于好：*Why don't you two* ***kiss and make up****?* 你们两个干吗不和好算了？◇ *Has he made it up with her yet?* 他跟她和好了吗？◇ *Have they made it up yet?* 他们和解了吗？

■ ***noun*** ~ (**of sth**) the name or type of a machine, piece of equipment, etc. that is made by a particular company（机器、设备等的）品牌，型号：*What make of car does he drive?* 他开的是什么品牌的车？◇ *There are so many different makes to choose from.* 有很多不同的型号可供选择。◇ *a Swiss make of watch* 一块瑞士表

IDM **on the 'make** (*informal, disapproving*) trying to get money or an advantage for yourself 谋取利益

'make-believe *noun* [U] **1** (*disapproving*) imagining or pretending things to be different or more exciting than they really are 虚构；想象；编造 SYN **fantasy**: *They live in a world of make-believe.* 他们生活在虚幻的世界里。**2** imagining that sth is real, or that you are sb else, for example in a child's game 假扮；假装：*'Let's play make-believe,' said Sam.* 萨姆说："咱们来玩假装的游戏吧。"

make·over /ˈmeɪkəʊvə(r); *NAmE* -oʊ-/ *noun* [C, U] the process of improving the appearance of a person or a place, or of changing the impression that sth gives（外观的）改进，改善；修饰；翻新

maker /ˈmeɪkə(r)/ *noun* **1** [C] ~ (**of sth**) (often in compounds 常构成复合词) a person, company or piece of equipment that makes or produces sth 生产者；制造者；制定者：*a* ***decision/law/policy maker*** 作出决定 / 制定法律 / 制定政策的人 ◇ *programme makers* 方案制定者 ◇ *a new film/movie from the makers of 'Terminator'* 由《终结者》的制作班子制作的一部新电影 ◇ *If it doesn't work, send it back to the maker.* 如果不管用，就把它退还给制造厂家。◇ *an electric coffee-maker* 电咖啡壶 ◇ *one of the best winemakers in France* 法国最好的葡萄酒酿造厂之一 ➲ VISUAL VOCAB PAGE V26 ➲ SEE ALSO HOLIDAYMAKER, PEACEMAKER, TROUBLEMAKER **2 the, his, your, etc. Maker** [sing.] God 上帝 IDM SEE MEET *v.*

make·shift /ˈmeɪkʃɪft/ *adj.* [usually before noun] used temporarily for a particular purpose because the real thing is not available 临时替代的；权宜的 SYN **provisional, improvised**: *A few cushions formed a makeshift bed.* 临时用几个垫子拼了一张床。

'make-up *noun* **1** [U] substances used especially by women to make their faces look more attractive, or used by actors to change their appearance 化妆品：*eye make-up* 眼妆 ◇ *to* ***put on your make-up*** 上妆 ◇ *She never* ***wears make-up.*** 她从来不化妆。◇ *a make-up artist* (= a person whose job is to put make-up on the faces of actors and models) 化妆师 ➲ COLLOCATIONS AT FASHION ➲ VISUAL VOCAB PAGE V65

> **WORDFINDER 联想词**：blusher, cleanser, eyeliner, eyeshadow, foundation, lipstick, mascara, moisturizer, nail polish

2 [sing.] the different qualities that combine to form sb's character or being 性格；气质：*Jealousy is not part of his make-up.* 嫉妒不是他的本质。◇ *a person's genetic make-up* 一个人的遗传性格 **3** [sing.] ~ (**of sth**) the different things, people, etc. that combine to form sth; the way in which they combine 组成成分；构成方式：*the make-up of a TV audience* 电视观众的构成 ◇ (*specialist*) *the page make-up of a text* (= the way in which the words and pictures are arranged on a page) 文本的版面设计 **4** [C] (*NAmE*) a special exam taken by students who missed or failed an earlier one 补考

make·weight /ˈmeɪkweɪt/ *noun* an unimportant person or thing that is only added or included in sth in order to make it the correct number, quantity, size, etc. 充数的人（或物）

'make-work *noun* [U] (*NAmE*) work that has little value but is given to people to keep them busy（占用人手的）无价值的工作；帮闲工作：*In some departments there is too much make-work.* 有些部门的无聊琐事太多。◇ *These are simply make-work schemes for accountants.* 这些方案只不过是让会计师继续忙碌而已。

mak·ing /ˈmeɪkɪŋ/ *noun* [U] ~ (**of sth**) (often in compounds 常构成复合词) the act or process of making or producing sth 生产；制造：*strategic decision making* 战略决策 ◇ *filmmaking* 制片 ◇ *dressmaking* 制衣 ◇ *tea and coffee making facilities* 沏茶煮咖啡的用具 ◇ *the making of social policy* 社会政策的制定 ➲ SEE ALSO HAYMAKING, NON-PROFIT

IDM **be the 'making of sb** to make sb become a better or more successful person 使成为更好（或更有作为）的人：*University was the making of Joe.* 大学造就了乔。**have the 'makings of sth** to have the qualities that are necessary to become sth 具备了成为…的必要条件：*Her first novel has all the makings of a classic.* 她的第一部小说堪称经典之作。**in the 'making** in the process of becoming sth or of being made 在生产（或形成）过程中：*This model was two years in the making.* 这种型号是用两年时间制成的。◇ *These events are* ***history in the making.*** 这些事件将载入史册。**of your own 'making** (of a problem, difficulty, etc. 问题、困难等) created by you rather than by sb/sth else 自己造成的

ma·kuti /mæˈkuːti/ *noun* [pl.] the leaves of a PALM tree, used as a material to make fences, BASKETS, etc. and roofs, especially on the coast of E Africa 马库提（尤指东非海滨的一种棕榈树叶，用于篱笆、篮筐、屋顶等）：*a makuti roof* 马库提屋顶

mal- /mæl/ *combining form* (in nouns, verbs and adjectives 构成名词、动词和形容词) bad or badly; not correct or correctly 糟糕；坏；错误：*malpractice* 玩忽职守 ◇ *malodorous* 有恶臭的 ◇ *malfunction* 故障

mal·ach·ite /ˈmæləkaɪt/ *noun* [U] a green mineral that can be polished, used to make decorative objects 孔雀石

mal·adjust·ed /ˌmæləˈdʒʌstɪd/ *adj.* (especially of children 尤指儿童) having mental and emotional problems that lead to unacceptable behaviour 适应不良的；心理失调的 ➲ COMPARE WELL ADJUSTED ▸ **mal·adjust·ment** /ˌmæləˈdʒʌstmənt/ *noun* [U]

mal·admin·is·tra·tion /ˌmælədˌmɪnɪˈstreɪʃn/ *noun* [U] (*formal*) the fact of managing a business or an organization in a bad or dishonest way 管理不善；腐败

mal·adroit /ˌmæləˈdrɔɪt/ *adj.* (*formal*) done without skill, especially in a way that annoys or offends people 不灵巧的；笨拙的 SYN **clumsy**

mal·ady /ˈmælədi/ *noun* (*pl.* **-ies**) **1** (*formal*) a serious problem 严重问题；痼疾 SYN **ill**: *Violent crime is only one of the maladies afflicting modern society.* 暴力犯罪仅仅是困扰现代社会的严重问题之一。**2** (*old use*) an illness 疾病

mal·aise /məˈleɪz/ *noun* [U, sing.] (*formal*) **1** the problems affecting a particular situation or group of people that are difficult to explain or identify（影响某个情况或某群人的）难以捉摸的问题，无法描述的问题：***economic/financial/social malaise*** 揣摩不透的经济 / 金融 / 社会问题 **2** a general feeling of being ill/sick, unhappy or not satisfied, without signs of any particular problem 莫名的不适（或不快、不满等）SYN **unease**: *a serious malaise among the staff* 员工极为不满的情绪

M

mala·prop·ism /ˈmæləprɒpɪzəm; *NAmE* -prɑːp-/ *noun* an amusing mistake sb makes when they use a word which sounds similar to the word they wanted to use, but means sth different 近音词误用（常产生滑稽效果） **ORIGIN** From Mrs Malaprop, a character in Richard Brinsley Sheridan's play *The Rivals*, who confuses words like this all the time. 源自理查德·布林斯利·谢里丹的戏剧《情敌》中的人物马拉普洛普太太，她总是误用词语。

mal·aria /məˈleəriə; *NAmE* -ˈler-/ *noun* [U] a disease that causes fever and SHIVERING (= shaking of the body) caused by the bite of some types of MOSQUITO 疟疾 ▶ **mal·ar·ial** /-iəl/ *adj.*: *malarial insects/patients/regions* 传播疟疾的昆虫；疟疾病人 / 流行区域

ma·lar·key /məˈlɑːki; *NAmE* məˈlɑːrki/ *noun* [U] (*informal, disapproving*) behaviour or an idea that you think is nonsense or has no meaning 无聊的话语（或行为）；废话

Ma·lay·alam /ˌmʌləˈjɑːləm; ˌmɑːlə-/ *noun* [U] a language spoken in Kerala in SW India 马拉雅拉姆语，马拉亚兰语（印度西南部喀拉拉邦的语言）

mal·con·tent /ˈmælkəntent; *NAmE* ˌmælkənˈtent/ *noun* [usually pl.] (*formal, disapproving*) a person who is not satisfied with a situation and who complains about it, or causes trouble in order to change it 不满者；牢骚满腹的人；反叛者

male /meɪl/ *adj., noun*
■ *adj.* **1** (*abbr.* **m**) belonging to the sex that does not give birth to babies; connected with this sex 男性的；雄性的；男的：*a male bird* 雄鸟 ◇ *All the attackers were male, aged between 25 and 30.* 所有的袭击者都是男性，年龄在 25 到 30 岁之间。◇ ***a male nurse/model/colleague*** 男护士；男模特儿；男同事 ◇ *male attitudes to women* 男人对女人的看法 ◇ ***male bonding*** (= the act of forming close friendships between men) 男性间的亲密友谊 ◇ ***the male menopause*** (= emotional and physical problems that affect some men at about the age of 50) 男性更年期 ➲ COMPARE MASCULINE *adj.* (1) **2** (*biology* 生) (of most plants 大多数植物) producing POLLEN 雄性的：*a male flower* 雄花 **3** (*specialist*) (of electrical PLUGS, parts of tools, etc. 电器插头、工具部件等) having a part that sticks out which is designed to fit into a hole, SOCKET, etc. 阳的；凸形的 ➲ COMPARE FEMALE *adj.* (5) ▶ **male·ness** *noun* [U]: *the chromosome that determines maleness* 决定男性性别的染色体
■ *noun* a male person, animal or plant 男性；雄性；雄株：*The male of the species has a white tail.* 这一物种的雄性有一条白色的尾巴。◇ *a male-dominated profession* 男性主宰的职业 ◇ (*formal*) *The body is that of a white male aged about 40.* 尸体是一名 40 岁上下的白人男子。 ➲ COMPARE FEMALE *n.* ➲ SEE ALSO ALPHA MALE

ˌmale ˈchauvinism (*also* **chauvinism**) *noun* [U] (*disapproving*) the belief held by some men that men are more important, intelligent, etc. than women 大男子主义

ˌmale ˈchauvinist (*also* **chauvinist**) *noun* (*disapproving*) a man who believes men are more important, intelligent, etc. than women 大男子主义者：*I hate working for that **male chauvinist pig** Steve.* 我讨厌给史蒂夫这个可恶的大男子主义者干活儿。

mal·efac·tor /ˈmælɪfæktə(r)/ *noun* (*formal*) a person who does wrong, illegal or immoral things 犯罪分子；作恶的人；道德败坏的人

ma·levo·lent /məˈlevələnt/ *adj.* [usually before noun] (*formal*) having or showing a desire to harm other people 有恶意的；有坏心肠的 **SYN** **malicious, wicked** **OPP** **benevolent** ▶ **ma·levo·lence** /-əns/ *noun* [U]: *an act of pure malevolence* 纯粹恶意的举动 **ma·levo·lent·ly** *adv.*

mal·for·ma·tion /ˌmælfɔːˈmeɪʃn; *NAmE* -fɔːrˈm-/ *noun* **1** [C] a part of the body that is not formed correctly（身体的）畸形：*Some fetal malformations cannot be diagnosed until late in pregnancy.* 有些胎儿畸形要到妊娠后期才能诊断出来。 **2** [U] the state of not being correctly formed 畸形

mal·formed /ˌmælˈfɔːmd; *NAmE* -ˈfɔːrmd/ *adj.* (*specialist*) badly formed or shaped 畸形的

mal·func·tion /ˌmælˈfʌŋkʃn/ *verb* [I] (of a machine, etc. 机器等) to fail to work correctly 运转失常；失灵；出现故障 ▶ **mal·func·tion** *noun* [C, U]

mal·ice /ˈmælɪs/ *noun* [U] a feeling of hatred for sb that causes a desire to harm them 恶意；怨恨：*He sent the letter **out of malice**.* 他出于恶意寄出了这封信。◇ *She is entirely without malice.* 她完全没有恶意。◇ *He certainly **bears you no malice*** (= does not want to harm you). 他对你一定不会有什么恶意。
IDM **with ˌmalice aˈforethought** (*law* 律) with the deliberate intention of committing a crime or harming sb（谋杀罪）有恶意预谋

ma·li·cious /məˈlɪʃəs/ *adj.* having or showing hatred and a desire to harm sb or hurt their feelings 怀有恶意的；恶毒的 **SYN** **malevolent, spiteful**: *malicious gossip/lies/rumours* 恶毒的流言蜚语 / 谎言 / 谣言 ◇ *He took malicious pleasure in telling me what she had said.* 他幸灾乐祸地告诉我她说的那些话。 ▶ **ma·li·cious·ly** *adv.*

ma·lign /məˈlaɪn/ *verb, adj.*
■ *verb* **~ sb/sth** (*formal*) to say bad things about sb/sth publicly（公开地）诽谤，毁谤，中伤 **SYN** **slander**: *She feels she has been **much maligned** by the press.* 她觉得她遭到了新闻界的恣意诽谤。➲ MORE LIKE THIS 20, page R27
■ *adj.* [usually before noun] (*formal*) causing harm 有害的；引起伤害的：***a malign force/influence/effect*** 有害的势力 / 影响 / 作用 ➲ COMPARE BENIGN (2)

ma·lig·nancy /məˈlɪgnənsi/ *noun* (*pl.* **-ies**) (*formal*) **1** [C] a malignant mass of TISSUE in the body 恶性肿瘤 **SYN** **tumour** **2** [U] the state of being malignant 恶性；恶毒

ma·lig·nant /məˈlɪgnənt/ *adj.* **1** (of a TUMOUR or disease 肿瘤或疾病) that cannot be controlled and is likely to cause death 恶性的：*malignant cells* 恶性癌细胞 **OPP** **non-malignant** ➲ COMPARE BENIGN (3) **2** (*formal*) having or showing a strong desire to harm sb 恶意的；恶毒的 **SYN** **malevolent**

ma·lin·ger /məˈlɪŋgə(r)/ *verb* (*usually* **be malingering**) [I] (*disapproving*) to pretend to be ill/sick, especially in order to avoid work 装病（尤指为逃避工作） ▶ **ma·lin·ger·er** *noun*

mall /mɔːl; *BrE also* mæl/ *noun* (*also* **shopping mall**) (*both especially NAmE*) a large building or covered area that has many shops/stores, restaurants, etc. inside it 购物商场；购物广场：*Let's go to the mall.* 我们去商场吧。◇ *Some teenagers were hanging out at the mall.* 有些青少年在购物广场里闲逛。➲ COLLOCATIONS AT SHOPPING ➲ COMPARE ARCADE (3)

mal·lam (*also* **Mallam**) /ˈmæləm/ *noun* (*WAfrE*) a Muslim religious teacher; sometimes used as a title of respect for anybody who is seen as wise or highly educated, for example a university teacher 穆斯林宗教老师；马拉姆（有时用作尊称，指智者或学者，如大学教师）

mal·lard /ˈmælɑːd; *NAmE* ˈmælərd/ *noun* (*pl.* **mal·lards** or **mal·lard**) a common wild DUCK 绿头鸭

mal·le·able /ˈmæliəbl/ *adj.* **1** (*specialist*) (of metal, etc. 金属等) that can be hit or pressed into different shapes easily without breaking or cracking 可锻造的；可轧压的；易成型的 **2** (of people, ideas, etc. 人、思想等) easily influenced or changed 可塑的；易受影响（或改变）的 ▶ **mal·le·abil·ity** /ˌmæliəˈbɪləti/ *noun* [U]

mal·let /ˈmælɪt/ *noun* **1** a hammer with a large wooden head 木槌 ➲ VISUAL VOCAB PAGE V21 **2** a hammer with a long handle and a wooden head, used for hitting the ball in the games of CROQUET and POLO（槌球和马球运动的）球棍，球棒 ➲ VISUAL VOCAB PAGE V51

mal·low /ˈmæləʊ; *NAmE* -loʊ/ *noun* [C, U] a plant with STEMS covered with small hairs and pink, purple or white flowers 锦葵

mall·rat /ˈmɔːlræt/ *noun* (*NAmE, informal*) a young person who spends a lot of time in SHOPPING MALLS, often in a large group of friends 爱（成群）逛大型商场的年轻人

mal·nour·ished /ˌmælˈnʌrɪʃt; *NAmE* -ˈnɜːr-/ *adj.* in bad health because of a lack of food or a lack of the right type of food 营养不良的

mal·nu·tri·tion /ˌmælnjuːˈtrɪʃn; *NAmE* -nuː-/ *noun* [U] a poor condition of health caused by a lack of food or a lack of the right type of food 营养不良 ➲ COMPARE NUTRITION

mal·odor·ous /ˌmælˈəʊdərəs; *NAmE* -ˈoʊdərəs/ *adj.* (*formal* or *literary*) having an unpleasant smell 恶臭的

mal·prac·tice /ˌmælˈpræktɪs/ *noun* [U, C] (*law* 律) careless, wrong or illegal behaviour while in a professional job 渎职；玩忽职守：*medical malpractice* 医疗失误 ◇ *a malpractice suit* 渎职诉讼 ◇ *He is currently standing trial for alleged malpractices.* 他被控营私舞弊，正在受审。

malt /mɔːlt; *BrE also* mɒlt/ *noun* **1** [U] grain, usually BARLEY, that has been left in water for a period of time and then dried, used for making beer, WHISKY, etc. 麦芽 **2** [U, C] = MALT WHISKY **3** [U, C] (*NAmE*) = MALTED MILK

malt·ed /ˈmɔːltɪd/ *adj.* [only before noun] **1** having been made into malt 成为麦芽的：*malted barley* 大麦芽 **2** having had malt added to it 加入麦芽的

ˌ**malted** ˈ**milk** (*NAmE also* **malt**) *noun* [U, C] a hot or cold drink made from malt and dried milk mixed with water or milk and usually sugar, sometimes with ice cream and/or chocolate added 麦乳精；麦芽奶

Mal·tese /ˈmɔːltiːz/ *adj., noun* (*pl.* **Mal·tese**)
■ ***adj.*** from or connected with Malta 马耳他的
■ ***noun*** **1** [C] a person from Malta 马耳他人 **2** [U] the language of Malta 马耳他语

ˌ**Maltese** ˈ**cross** *noun* a cross whose arms are equal in length and have wide ends with V-shapes cut out of them 马耳他十字（四臂长度均等、末端宽大呈 V 字形）

malt·house /ˈmɔːlthaʊs/ (*also* **malt·ings** /ˈmɔːltɪŋz/ *BrE*) *noun* a building in which MALT is prepared and stored 麦芽作坊

Mal·thusian /mælˈθjuːziən/ *adj.* related to the theory of Thomas Malthus that, since populations naturally grow faster than the supply of food, failure to control their growth leads to disaster 马尔萨斯人口论的（认为由于人口增长快于粮食供给，因此人口增长失控会导致灾难）

mal·tose /ˈmɔːltəʊz; -təʊs; *NAmE* -toʊz; -toʊs/ *noun* [U] (*biology* 生) a sugar that substances in the body make from STARCH (= a food substance found in flour, rice, potatoes, etc.) 麦芽糖

mal·treat /ˌmælˈtriːt/ *verb* ~ **sb/sth** to be very cruel to a person or an animal 虐待 **SYN** **ill-treat** ▸ **mal·treat·ment** *noun* [U]

ˌ**malt** ˈ**vinegar** *noun* [U] VINEGAR which is made from grain rather than from wine 麦芽醋（用谷物而非果酒酿制）

ˌ**malt** ˈ**whisky** (*also* **malt**) *noun* [U, C] high quality WHISKY from Scotland; a glass of this（一杯）麦芽威士忌

mal·ware /ˈmælweə(r); *NAmE* -wer/ *noun* [U] software such as a virus on a computer or computer network that the user does not know about or want 恶意软件（指电脑病毒等） **ORIGIN** A combination of *malicious* and *software*. 该词由 malicious 与 software 结合而成。

mam /mæm/ *noun* (*BrE, dialect, informal*) mother 妈妈

mama (*also* **mamma**) /ˈmæmə/ *noun* **1** /ˈmæmə; *BrE also* məˈmɑː/ (*NAmE* or *BrE, old-fashioned*) mother 妈妈 ➲ SEE ALSO MUMMY (1) **2** in some places in Africa, a mother or older woman (often used as a title that shows respect) 妈妈，大妈（非洲某些地方对母亲的称呼或对年长妇女的尊称）：*Leave this work to us, mama.* 这活儿留给我们干吧，妈妈。◇ *Miriam Makeba became known as Mama Africa.* 米丽亚姆・马凯巴被称为非洲之母。◇ *Mama Ngina Kenyatta* 恩金纳・肯雅塔夫人

ˈ**mama's boy** (*NAmE*) (*BrE* ˈ**mummy's boy**) *noun* (*disapproving*) a boy or man who depends too much on his mother 离不开妈妈的男孩（或男子）；妈宝男

mamba /ˈmæmbə/ *noun* a black or green poisonous African snake 树眼镜蛇，曼巴蛇（黑色或绿色，分布于非洲，有剧毒）

mambo /ˈmæmbəʊ; *NAmE* -boʊ/ *noun* (*pl.* **-os**) **1** a lively Latin American dance 曼波舞（拉丁美洲轻快舞蹈）**2** a female VOODOO priest 伏都教女祭司

mam·mal /ˈmæml/ *noun* any animal that gives birth to live babies, not eggs, and feeds its young on milk. Cows, humans and WHALES are all mammals. 哺乳动物 ➲ VISUAL VOCAB PAGE V12 ▸ **mam·ma·lian** /mæˈmeɪliən/ *adj.*

mam·mary /ˈmæməri/ *adj.* [only before noun] (*biology* 生) connected with the breasts 乳房的：*mammary glands* (= parts of the breast that produce milk) 乳腺

mam·mo·gram /ˈmæməgræm/ *noun* an examination of a breast using X-RAYS to check for cancer 乳房 X 光检查

mam·mog·raphy /mæˈmɒgrəfi; *NAmE* -ˈmɑːg-/ *noun* [U] the use of X-RAYS to check for cancer in a breast 乳房 X 线照相术

Mam·mon /ˈmæmən/ *noun* [U] (*formal, disapproving*) a way of talking about money and wealth when it has become the most important thing in sb's life and as important as a god 玛门（指财富、金钱）；财神

mam·moth /ˈmæməθ/ *noun, adj.*
■ ***noun*** an animal like a large ELEPHANT covered with hair, that lived thousands of years ago and is now EXTINCT 猛犸（象）
■ ***adj.*** [usually before noun] extremely large 极其巨大的；庞大的 **SYN** **huge**：*a mammoth task* 巨大的任务 ◇ *a financial crisis of mammoth proportions* 极其严重的金融危机

mammy /ˈmæmi/ *noun* (*pl.* **-ies**) **1** (*dialect, informal*) mother 妈；妈妈 **2** an offensive word used in the past in the southern states of the US for a black woman who cared for a white family's children 黑人保姆（旧时美国南方各州对照看白人孩子的黑人女子的贬称）

ˈ**mammy-wagon** *noun* (*old-fashioned, WAfrE*) a lorry/truck with a roof and seats for people to travel in（带顶棚的）小卡车，小客车

mam·para /mʌmˈpɑːrə/ *noun* (*SAfrE*) = MOMPARA

man 🔑 /mæn/ *noun, verb, exclamation*
■ ***noun*** (*pl.* **men** /men/)
• **MALE PERSON** 男人 **1** 🔑 [C] an adult male human 成年男子；男人：*a good-looking young man* 英俊的年轻男子 ◇ *the relationships between men and women* 男女间的关系 ➲ SEE ALSO DIRTY OLD MAN, LADIES' MAN, MEN'S ROOM
• **HUMANS** 人 **2** 🔑 [U] humans as a group or from a particular period of history 人类；（特定历史时期的）人：*the damage caused by man to the environment* 人类给环境带来的破坏 ◇ ***early/modern/prehistoric man*** 早期人；现代人；史前人 ➲ NOTE AT GENDER **3** [C] (*literary* or *old-fashioned*) a person, either male or female（不论性别的）人：*All men must die.* 所有的人都会死。
• **PARTICULAR TYPE OF MAN** 某类人 **4** [C] (in compounds 构成复合词) a man who comes from the place mentioned or whose job or interest is connected with the thing mentioned（来自某地、从事某种工作或有某种兴趣等的）人：*a Frenchman* 法国人 ◇ *a businessman* 生意人 ◇ *a medical man* 医务工作者 ◇ *a sportsman* 运动员 ➲ NOTE AT GENDER **5** [C] a man who likes or who does the thing mentioned（喜欢或做某事的）人：*a **betting/drinking/fighting man*** 赌博 / 喝酒 / 打架的人 ➲ SEE ALSO FAMILY MAN **6** [C] a man who works for or supports a particular organization, comes from a particular town, etc.（来自某处、支持某组织或为其工作的）人：*the BBC's man in Moscow* (= the man who reports on news from Moscow) 英国广播公司驻莫斯科的新闻记者 ◇ *a loyal Republican Party man* 一名忠诚的共和党人 ➲ SEE ALSO RIGHT-HAND MAN, YES-MAN

M

- **SOLDIER/WORKER** 战士；工人 **7** [C, usually pl.] a soldier or a male worker who obeys the instructions of a person of higher rank 士兵；（男性）工人：*The officer refused to let his men take part in the operation.* 这军官拒绝让他的士兵参加这项军事行动。**8** [C] a man who comes to your house to do a job 上门服务的人：*the gas man* 煤气工人 ◇ *The man's coming to repair the TV today.* 修理工今天来修电视。
- **FORM OF ADDRESS** 称呼 **9** [sing.] (*informal, especially NAmE*) used for addressing a male person 伙计；哥儿们：*Nice shirt, man!* 好漂亮的衬衣啊，哥儿们！◇ *Hey man. Back off!* 喂，伙计，退后！**10** [sing.] (*old-fashioned*) used for addressing a male person in an angry or impatient way （不耐烦或生气时对男人的称呼）你这家伙：*Don't just stand there, man—get a doctor!* 你这家伙，别只是站着，赶紧去找医生呀！
- **HUSBAND/BOYFRIEND** 丈夫；男友 **11** [C] (*sometimes disapproving*) a husband or sexual partner 丈夫；性伴侣：*What's her new man like?* 她的新男友怎么样？◇ *I now pronounce you man and wife* (= you are now officially married). 我现在正式宣布你们结为夫妇。➲ SEE ALSO OLD MAN
- **STRONG/BRAVE PERSON** 强壮的 / 勇敢的人 **12** [C] a person who is strong and brave or has other qualities that some people think are particularly male 勇敢强壮的人；男子汉：*Come on, now—be a man.* 加油，像个男子汉的样子。◇ *She's more of a man than he is.* 她比他更有男子气。➲ SEE ALSO HE-MAN, MUSCLEMAN, SUPERMAN
- **SERVANT** 仆人 **13** [sing.] (*old-fashioned, formal*) a male servant 男仆：*My man will drive you home.* 我的仆人会开车送你回家。
- **IN CHESS** 国际象棋 **14** [C] one of the figures or objects that you play with in a game such as CHESS 棋子 ➲ SEE ALSO CHESSMAN

IDM **as one ˈman** with everyone doing or thinking the same thing at the same time; in agreement 同心协力；协调一致 **be sb's ˈman** to be the best or most suitable person to do a particular job, etc. 最合适的人；最佳人选：*For a superb haircut, David's your man.* 要想理个好发型，你最好是去找戴维。**be ˈman enough (to do sth/for sth)** to be strong or brave enough 有足够的勇气或意志：*He was not man enough to face up to his responsibility.* 他没有足够的勇气去承担责任。 **every man for himˈself** (*saying*) people must take care of themselves and not give or expect any help 人各为己；自己顾自己：*In business, it's every man for himself.* 生意场上都是人各为己。**make a ˈman (out) of sb** to make a young man develop and become more adult 使成为男子汉；使长大成人 **a/the ˌman about ˈtown** a man who frequently goes to fashionable parties, clubs, theatres, etc. 喜欢社交者；社交界名人 **ˌman and ˈboy** from when sb was young to when they were old or older 从小到大；一辈子：*He's been doing the same job for 50 years—man and boy.* 他从小就干着同一份工作，有 50 年了。**the ˌman (and/or ˌwoman) in the ˈstreet** an average or ordinary person, either male or female 平民；老百姓：*Politicians often don't understand the views of the man in the street.* 从政者通常不理解平民百姓的观点。**a ˌman of ˈGod/the ˈcloth** (*old-fashioned, formal*) a religious man, especially a priest or a CLERGYMAN 神职人员；（尤指）牧师，司铎 **the ˌman of the ˈmatch** (*BrE, sport* 体育) the member of a team who plays the best in a particular game（某场比赛的）最佳运动员 **a ˌman of the ˈpeople** (especially of a politician 尤指从政者) a man who understands and is sympathetic to ordinary people 体恤民情者；体察民意者 **man's best ˈfriend** a way of describing a dog 人类的好朋友（指狗） **a ˌman's ˌhome is his ˈcastle** (*US*) (*BrE* **an ˌEnglishman's ˌhome is his ˈcastle**) (*saying*) a person's home is a place where they can be private and safe and do as they like 人之住宅即其城堡；人在家中，自成一统 **a ˈman's man** a man who is more popular with men than with women 更受男人欢迎的男人 **be your own ˈman/ˈwoman** to act or think independently, not following others or being ordered 独立自主 **ˌman to ˈman** between two men who are treating each other honestly and equally（男人间）诚实相待，坦率：*I'm telling you all this man to man.* 我要把这一切都坦率地告诉你。◇ *a man-to-man talk* 坦率的谈话 **one man's ˌmeat is another man's ˈpoison** (*saying*) used to say that different people like different things; what one person likes very much, another person does not like at all 兴趣爱好因人而异；一人手中宝，他人脚下草 **separate/sort out the ˌmen from the ˈboys** to show or prove who is brave, skilful, etc. and who is not 表明 / 证明谁有技能（或更勇敢等） **to a ˈman | to the last ˈman** used to emphasize that sth is true of all the people being described 一致；毫无例外：*They answered 'Yes,' to a man.* 他们异口同声地回答："是。" ◇ *They were all destroyed, to the last man.* 他们无一例外全部被歼。**you can't keep a good man ˈdown** (*saying*) a person who is determined or wants sth very much will succeed 有志者事竟成；决心大的人终有出头之日 ➲ MORE AT GRAND *adj.*, HEART, MARKED, NEXT *adj.*, ODD, PART *n.*, POOR, POSSESSED, SUBSTANCE, THING, WORD *n.*, WORLD

- ▪ ***verb*** (**-nn-**) **~ sth** to work at a place or be in charge of a place or a machine; to supply people to work somewhere 在…岗位上工作；操纵（机器等）；配备（人员） SYN **crew, staff**: *Soldiers manned barricades around the city.* 士兵把守着城市周围的路障。◇ *The telephones are manned 24 hours a day by volunteers.* 每天 24 小时都有志愿者接听电话。

PHR V **ˌman ˈup** (*informal*) to start being brave or strong in order to deal with a difficult situation 拿出男人气概；勇对难境：*He should man up and tell his boss what he really thinks.* 他应该勇敢一点，告诉老板他真正的想法。

- ▪ ***exclamation*** (*informal, especially NAmE*) used to express surprise, anger, etc.（表示惊奇、气愤等）嘿，天哪：*Man, that was great!* 哇，太棒了！

man·acle /ˈmænəkl/ *noun, verb*

- ▪ ***noun*** [usually pl.] one of two metal bands joined by a chain, used for fastening a prisoner's ankles or wrists together 手铐；脚镣；镣铐
- ▪ ***verb*** [usually passive] **~ sb/sth** to put manacles on sb's wrists or ankles, to stop them from escaping 给…戴上镣铐

man·age /ˈmænɪdʒ/ *verb*

- **DO STH DIFFICULT** 做难做的事 **1** [T, I] to succeed in doing sth, especially sth difficult 完成（困难的事）；勉力完成：**~ sth** *In spite of his disappointment, he managed a weak smile.* 尽管他很失望，他还是勉强露出一丝微笑。◇ *I don't know exactly how we'll* ***manage it****, but we will, somehow.* 我说不准我们如何去完成这件事，但不管怎样我们一定会完成的。◇ *Can you manage another piece of cake?* (= eat one) 你还能再吃块蛋糕吗？◇ **~ (to do sth)** *We managed to get to the airport in time.* 我们设法及时赶到了机场。◇ *How did you manage to persuade him?* 你是怎么说服他的？◇ (*humorous*) *He always manages to say the wrong thing.* 他总是哪壶不开提哪壶。◇ *We couldn't have managed without you.* 没有你，我们就办不成了。◇ *'Need any help?' 'No, thanks. I can manage.'* "要帮忙吗？" "不了，谢谢。我应付得了。" ➲ NOTE AT CAN[1] ➲ MORE LIKE THIS 26, page R28
- **DEAL WITH PROBLEMS** 处理问题 **2** [I] to be able to solve your problems, deal with a difficult situation, etc. 能解决（问题）；应付（困难局面等） SYN **cope**: *She's 82 and can't manage on her own any more.* 她 82 岁了，照顾不了自己的生活了。◇ **~ with/without sb/sth** *How do you manage without a car?* 没有车你怎么应付的？
- **MONEY/TIME/INFORMATION** 金钱；时间；信息 **3** [I] **~ (on sth)** to be able to live without having much money 凑合着活下去；支撑：*He has to manage on less than £100 a week.* 他就靠每周不到 100 英镑来维持生活。**4** [T] **~ sth** to use money, time, information, etc. in a sensible way 明智地使用（金钱、时间、信息等）：*Don't tell me how to manage my affairs.* 用不着你来告诉我怎样管我自己的事。◇ *a computer program that helps you manage data efficiently* 帮助你有效地处理数据的电脑程序 **5** [T] **~ sth** to be able to do sth at a particular time（在某一时间）能办到，能做成：*Let's meet up again—can you manage next week sometime?* 我们再见一次面吧。下周找个时间，行吗？
- **BUSINESS/TEAM** 公司；队伍 **6** [T, I] **~ (sth)** to control or be in charge of a business, a team, an organization, etc. 管理，负责（公司、队伍、组织等）：*to* ***manage a factory/bank/hotel/soccer team*** 管理工厂 / 银行 / 酒店 / 足球队 ◇ *to* ***manage a department/project*** 负责一个部门 /

项目 ◇ *We need people who are good at managing.* 我们需要擅长管理的人。

• CONTROL 控制 **7** [T] ~ **sb/sth** to keep sb/sth under control; to be able to deal with sb/sth 控制住；操纵；能对付：*It's like trying to manage an unruly child.* 这就像试图管住一个任性的孩子。◇ *Can you manage that suitcase?* 你弄得动那个箱子吗？

man·age·able /ˈmænɪdʒəbl/ *adj.* possible to deal with or control 可操纵的；可处理的：*Use conditioner regularly to make your hair soft and manageable.* 经常使用护发剂来使你的头发柔软而且易于梳理。◇ *The debt has been reduced to a more manageable level.* 债务减到了比较能够应付的程度。 OPP **unmanageable**

man·aged /ˈmænɪdʒd/ *adj.* [only before noun] carefully taken care of and controlled 妥善照看的；受监管的；受监督的：*The money will be invested in managed funds.* 这笔钱将投资于管理基金。◇ *Only wood from managed forests is used in our furniture.* 我们的家具完全是用监管林中的木材做的。➲ WORDFINDER NOTE AT GREEN

man·age·ment /ˈmænɪdʒmənt/ *noun* **1** [U] the act of running and controlling a business or similar organization 经营；管理：*a career in management* 管理方面的职业 ◇ ***hotel/project management*** 酒店 / 项目管理 ◇ *a management training course* 管理培训课程 ◇ *The report blames bad management.* 报告归咎于管理不善。**2** [C+sing./pl. v., U] the people who run and control a business or similar organization 经营者；管理部门；资方：*The management is/are considering closing the factory.* 经营者在考虑关闭这家工厂。◇ *The shop is now **under new management**.* 这家商店现由新的经营者管理。◇ ***junior/middle/senior management*** 初级 / 中级 / 高级管理人员 ◇ *a **management decision/job*** 资方的决定 / 工作 ◇ *My role is to act as a mediator between employees and management.* 我的角色就是协调雇员与管理者之间的关系。◇ *Most managements are keen to avoid strikes.* 大多数经营者都很希望避免罢工的发生。**3** [U] the act or skill of dealing with people or situations in a successful way（成功的）处理手段；（有效的）处理能力：***classroom management*** 课堂组织能力 ◇ ***time management*** (= the way in which you organize how you spend your time) 时间管理 ◇ *management of staff* 管理员工的能力 ◇ *Diet plays an important role in the management of heart disease.* 饮食对于心脏病的治疗有重要作用。

ˌmanagement ˈsummary *noun* = EXECUTIVE SUMMARY

man·ager /ˈmænɪdʒə(r)/ *noun* **1** a person who is in charge of running a business, a shop/store or a similar organization or part of one（企业、店铺等的）经理，经营者，老板：*a **bank/hotel manager*** 银行 / 酒店经理 ◇ *the **sales/marketing/personnel manager*** 销售部 / 市场部 / 人事部经理 ◇ *a meeting of area managers* 地区经理会议 ➲ SEE ALSO MIDDLE MANAGER at MIDDLE MANAGEMENT ➲ WORDFINDER NOTE AT BUSINESSMAN, COMPANY **2** a person who deals with the business affairs of an actor, a musician, etc.（演员、音乐家等的）经理人，经纪人，个人经理 **3** a person who trains and organizes a sports team（运动队的）主教练：*the new manager of Italy* 意大利队的新主教练

man·ager·ess /ˌmænɪdʒəˈres/ *noun* (*BrE, becoming old-fashioned*) a woman who is in charge of a small business, for example, a shop/store, restaurant or hotel 女经理；女老板 ➲ NOTE AT GENDER

man·ager·ial /ˌmænəˈdʒɪəriəl; *NAmE* -ˈdʒɪr-/ *adj.* [usually before noun] connected with the work of a manager 经理的；管理的：*Does she have any managerial experience?* 她有没有什么管理经验？➲ WORDFINDER NOTE AT WORK

ˌmanaging diˈrector *noun* (*abbr.* **MD**) (*especially BrE*) the person who is in charge of a business 总裁；总经理；常务董事

ma·ñana /mænˈjɑːnə/ *adv.* (*from Spanish*) at some time in the future (used when a person cannot or will not say exactly when) 在将来某时；在以后的不确定时间

mana·tee /ˈmænətiː/ *noun* a large water animal with front legs and a strong tail but no back legs, that lives in America and Africa 海牛（水生哺乳动物，栖息于美洲和非洲）

ˈman bag *noun* a bag designed for men to carry money, keys, small pieces of equipment, etc. 男士包

ˈman boob *noun* [usually pl.] (*informal*) a man's breast that is large and fat 肥大的男性乳房；男波波

Man·cu·nian /mænˈkjuːniən/ *noun* a person from Manchester in NW England（英格兰西北部的）曼彻斯特人 ▶ **Man·cu·nian** *adj.*

man·dala /ˈmændələ/ *noun* a round picture that represents the universe in some Eastern religions 曼荼罗（某些东方宗教用以代表宇宙的圆形图）

man·da·rin /ˈmændərɪn/ *noun* **1** [C] a powerful official of high rank, especially in the CIVIL SERVICE 政界要员；（尤指）内务官员 SYN **bureaucrat** **2** [C] a government official of high rank in China in the past（旧时）中国政府高级官吏 **3** **Mandarin** [U] the standard form of Chinese, which is the official language of China（中文）普通话 **4** (*also* **ˌmandarin ˈorange**) [C] a type of small orange with loose skin that comes off easily 柑橘

ˌmandarin ˈcollar *noun* a small COLLAR that stands up and fits closely around the neck 中式领；紧口立领

man·date *noun, verb*

■ ***noun*** /ˈmændeɪt/ **1** the authority to do sth, given to a government or other organization by the people who vote for it in an election（政府或组织等经选举而获得的）授权：~ (**to do sth**) *The election victory gave the party a clear mandate to continue its programme of reform.* 选举获胜使得这个政党拥有了明确的继续推行改革的权力。◇ ~ (**for sth**) *a mandate for an end to the civil war* 停止内战的权力 **2** the period of time for which a government is given power（政府的）任期：*The presidential mandate is limited to two terms of four years each.* 总统的任期不得超过两届，每届四年。**3** ~ (**to do sth**) (*formal*) an official order given to sb to perform a particular task 委托书；授权令：*The bank had no mandate to honour the cheque.* 银行没有得到指令来承兑这张支票。**4** the power given to a country to govern another country or region, especially in the past（尤指旧时授予某国对别国或地区的）委任统治权

■ ***verb*** /ˈmændeɪt; ˌmænˈdeɪt/ [often passive] (*formal*) **1** ~ **that ...** | ~ **sb** (**to do sth**) (*especially NAmE*) to order sb to behave, do sth or vote in a particular way 强制执行；委托办理：*The law mandates that imported goods be identified as such.* 法律规定进口货物必须如实标明。**2** ~ **sb/sth to do sth** to give sb, especially a government or a committee, the authority to do sth 授权：*The assembly was mandated to draft a constitution.* 大会获授权起草一份章程。

man·dated /ˈmændeɪtɪd/ *adj.* [only before noun] (*formal*) **1** (of a country or state 国家) placed under the rule of another country 委托别国管辖的；托管的：*mandated territories* 托管地区 **2** required by law 依法的；按法律要求的：*a mandated curriculum* 法定课程 **3** having a mandate to do sth 获得授权的：*a mandated government* 获授权的政府

man·da·tory /ˈmændətəri; *BrE also* mænˈdeɪtəri; *NAmE* ˈmændətɔːri/ *adj.* (*formal*) required by law 强制的；法定的；义务的 SYN **compulsory**：*The offence carries a mandatory life sentence.* 这种罪行依照法律要判无期徒刑。◇ ~ (**for sb**) (**to do sth**) *It is mandatory for blood banks to test all donated blood for the virus.* 血库必须检查所有捐献的血是否含有这种病毒。

man·dazi /mænˈdɑːzi/ *noun* (*pl.* **man·dazi**) (*EAfrE*) a small cake made of fried DOUGH 油炸小面饼

man·dible /ˈmændɪbl/ *noun* (*anatomy* 解) **1** the JAWBONE 下颌骨 ➲ VISUAL VOCAB PAGE V64 **2** the upper or lower part of a bird's beak 鸟的上喙（或下喙）**3** either of the two parts that are at the front and on either side of an insect's mouth, used especially for biting and crushing food（昆虫的）上颚 ➲ VISUAL VOCAB PAGE V13

man·dir /ˈmændɪə(r); *NAmE* -dɪr/ *noun* (*IndE*) a TEMPLE（印度教）寺庙

man·do·lin /ˈmændəlɪn; ˌmændəˈlɪn/ *noun* a musical instrument with metal strings (usually eight) arranged in pairs, and a curved back, played with a PLECTRUM 曼陀林（拨弦乐器）➲ VISUAL VOCAB PAGE V40

man·drake /ˈmændreɪk/ *noun* [C, U] a poisonous plant used to make drugs, especially ones to make people sleep, thought in the past to have magic powers 茄参（可制药，旧时认为具有魔力）

man·drill /ˈmændrɪl/ *noun* a large W African MONKEY with a red and blue face 山魈（面部有蓝色和红色的西非大猴）

mane /meɪn/ *noun* **1** the long hair on the neck of a horse or a LION（马）鬃；（狮）鬣毛 ➲ VISUAL VOCAB PAGE V12 **2** (*informal* or *literary*) a person's long or thick hair 长发；浓密的头发

ˈman-eater *noun* **1** a wild animal that attacks and eats humans 食人兽 **2** (*humorous*) a woman who has many sexual partners 男人杀手（指有多个性伴侣的女子）▸ **ˈman-eating** *adj.* [only before noun]: *a man-eating tiger* 噬人的老虎

man·eu·ver, **man·eu·ver·able**, **man·eu·ver·ing** (*especially US*) = MANOEUVRE, MANOEUVRABLE, MANOEUVRING

ˌman ˈFriday *noun* a male assistant who does many different kinds of work 得力的男助手；男仆 ➲ COMPARE GIRL FRIDAY **ORIGIN** From a character in Daniel Defoe's novel *Robinson Crusoe* who is rescued by Crusoe and works for him. 源自丹尼尔・笛福所著的小说《鲁宾逊漂流记》中的人物。他为鲁宾逊所救，后成为鲁宾逊的仆人。

man·ful·ly /ˈmænfəli/ *adv.* using a lot of effort in a brave and determined way 有男子气概地；勇敢坚定地 ▸ **man·ful** *adj.* [only before noun]

manga /ˈmæŋgə/ *noun* [C, U] (*pl.* **manga**) (*from Japanese*) a Japanese form of COMIC STRIP, often one with violent or sexual contents 日本漫画（常有暴力或色情内容）

man·ga·nese /ˈmæŋgəniːz/ *noun* [U] (*symb.* **Mn**) a chemical element. Manganese is a grey-white metal that breaks easily, used in making glass and steel. 锰

mange /meɪndʒ/ *noun* [U] a skin disease which affects MAMMALS, caused by a PARASITE（兽）疥癣 ➲ SEE ALSO MANGY (1)

man·ger /ˈmeɪndʒə(r)/ *noun* a long open box that horses and cows can eat from 马槽；牛槽；饲料槽 **IDM** SEE DOG *n.*

mange·tout /ˌmɑːnʒˈtuː/ (*BrE*) (*NAmE* **ˈsnow pea**) *noun* [usually pl.] a type of very small PEA that grows in long, flat green PODS that are cooked and eaten whole 荷兰豆

man·gle /ˈmæŋgl/ *verb, noun*

■ *verb* [usually passive] **1** ~ **sth** to crush or twist sth so that it is badly damaged 压碎；撕烂；严重损坏：*His hand was mangled in the machine.* 他的手卷到机器里轧烂了。**2** ~ **sth** to spoil sth, for example a poem or a piece of music, by saying it wrongly or playing it badly 糟蹋（如蹩脚的诗朗诵或拙劣的演奏）**SYN** **ruin** ▸ **man·gled** *adj.*: *mangled bodies/remains* 面目全非的尸体 / 遗迹

■ *noun* (*also* **wring·er**) a machine with two ROLLERS used especially in the past for squeezing the water out of clothes that had been washed（尤指旧时的）衣物轧干机

mango /ˈmæŋgəʊ; *NAmE* -goʊ/ *noun* [C, U] (*pl.* **-oes** or **-os**) a tropical fruit with smooth yellow or red skin, soft orange flesh and a large seed inside 芒果 ➲ VISUAL VOCAB PAGE V33

man·go·steen /ˈmæŋgəstiːn/ *noun* a tropical fruit with a thick reddish-brown skin and sweet white flesh with a lot of juice 山竹，莽吉柿，倒捻子（热带水果，肉白，多汁）➲ VISUAL VOCAB PAGE V33

man·grove /ˈmæŋgrəʊv; *NAmE* -groʊv/ *noun* a tropical tree that grows in mud or at the edge of rivers and has roots that are above ground 红树林植物（生长在淤泥或河边的热带树木，有支柱根暴露在空气中）：*mangrove swamps* 红树林沼泽地

mangy /ˈmeɪndʒi/ *adj.* [usually before noun] **1** (of an animal 动物) suffering from MANGE 患疥癣的：*a mangy dog* 患疥癣的狗 **2** (*informal*) dirty and in bad condition 污秽的；糟糕的 **SYN** **moth-eaten**: *a mangy old coat* 破烂不堪的旧外套

man·handle /ˈmænhændl/ *verb* **1** ~ **sb** to push, pull or handle sb roughly（粗暴地）推搡，拉扯，对待：*Bystanders claim they were manhandled by security guards.* 旁观者声称他们遭到了保安人员的粗暴推搡。**2** ~ **sth** + **adv./prep.** to move or lift a heavy object using a lot of effort 用力移动；用力举起 **SYN** **haul**: *They were trying to manhandle an old sofa across the road.* 他们正努力要把一张旧沙发搬到马路对面去。

man·hat·tan /ˌmænˈhætn/ *noun* an alcoholic drink made by mixing WHISKY or another strong alcoholic drink with VERMOUTH 曼哈顿鸡尾酒（用威士忌或其他烈酒与苦艾酒调制而成）

man·hole /ˈmænhəʊl; *NAmE* -hoʊl/ *noun* a hole in the street that is covered with a lid, used when sb needs to go down to examine the pipes or SEWERS below the street（检查地下管道用的）人孔，检查井

man·hood /ˈmænhʊd/ *noun* **1** [U] the state or time of being an adult man rather than a boy 成年；成年时期 **2** [U] the qualities that a man is supposed to have, for example courage, strength and sexual power 男儿气质：*Her new-found power was a threat to his manhood.* 她最近具有的能力对他的男子汉气概是个威胁。**3** [sing.] (*literary* or *humorous*) a man's PENIS. People use 'manhood' to avoid saying 'penis'.（与 penis 同义，即阴茎）**4** [U] (*literary*) all the men of a country 一国的男子：*The nation's manhood died on the battlefields of World War I.* 这个国家的男子都在第一次世界大战的战场上牺牲了。➲ COMPARE WOMANHOOD

ˈman-hour *noun* [usually pl.] the amount of work done by one person in one hour 工时（每人每小时的工作量）

man·hunt /ˈmænhʌnt/ *noun* an organized search by a lot of people for a criminal or a prisoner who has escaped（对罪犯或逃犯的）搜捕，追捕

mania /ˈmeɪniə/ *noun* **1** [C, usually sing., U] ~ (**for sth/for doing sth**) an extremely strong desire or enthusiasm for sth, often shared by a lot of people at the same time（通常指许多人共有的）强烈的欲望，狂热，极大的热情 **SYN** **craze**: *He had a mania for fast cars.* 他是个飞车狂。◇ *Football mania is sweeping the country.* 足球热正风靡全国。**2** [U] (*psychology* 心) a mental illness in which sb has an OBSESSION about sth that makes them extremely anxious, violent or confused 躁狂症

-mania *combining form* (in nouns 构成名词) mental illness of a particular type …狂；…癖：*kleptomania* 偷窃癖 ▸ **-maniac** (in nouns 构成名词): *a pyromaniac* 纵火狂

ma·niac /ˈmeɪniæk/ *noun* **1** (*informal*) a person who behaves in an extremely dangerous, wild or stupid way 行为极其危险（或狂暴、愚蠢）的人；疯子；狂人 **SYN** **madman**: *He was driving like a maniac.* 他发了疯似的开车。**2** a person who has an extremely strong desire or enthusiasm for sth, to an extent that other people think is not normal 狂热分子；过激分子 **SYN** **fanatic** **3** (*psychology* 心) a person suffering from mania 躁狂症患者；疯子：*a homicidal maniac* 杀人狂 ▸ **ma·niac** *adj.* [only before noun]: *a maniac driver/killer* 疯狂的司机 / 杀手

ma·ni·acal /məˈnaɪəkl/ *adj.* wild or violent 狂野的；粗暴的：*maniacal laughter* 狂野的笑声 ▸ **ma·ni·acal·ly** /-kli/ *adv.*

manic /ˈmænɪk/ *adj.* **1** (*informal*) full of activity, excitement and anxiety; behaving in a busy, excited, anxious way 狂热的；兴奋的；忙乱的 SYN **hectic**: *Things are manic in the office at the moment.* 这会儿办公室里一片忙乱。◇ *The performers had a manic energy and enthusiasm.* 表演者有一种疯狂的劲头和激情。 **2** (*psychology* 心) connected with MANIA (2) 躁狂的：*manic mood swings* 喜怒无常的情绪变化 ▶ **man·ic·al·ly** /-kli/ *adv.*: *I rushed around manically, trying to finish the housework.* 我手忙脚乱地跑来跑去，想把家务活干完。

ˌmanic deˈpression *noun* [U] (*old-fashioned*) = BIPOLAR DISORDER

ˌmanic-deˈpressive *adj., noun* (*old-fashioned*) = BIPOLAR

Mani·chae·an (*also* **Mani·che·an**) /ˌmænɪˈkiːən/ *adj.* (*religion* 宗, *philosophy* 哲) based on the belief that there are two opposites in everything, for example good and evil or light and dark 二元对立论的

mani·cure /ˈmænɪkjʊə(r); *NAmE* -kjʊr/ *noun, verb*
- *noun* [C, U] the care and treatment of a person's hands and nails 修剪指甲；指甲护理：*to have a manicure* 修指甲 ➲ COMPARE PEDICURE
- *verb* **~ sth** to care for and treat your hands and nails 修剪（指甲）；护理（手）

mani·cured /ˈmænɪkjʊəd; *NAmE* -kjʊrd/ *adj.* **1** (of hands or fingers 手或手指) with nails that are neatly cut and polished 精心护理的；修剪整齐的 **2** (of gardens, a LAWN, etc. 花园、草坪等) very neat and well cared for 整齐的；护理得很好的

mani·cur·ist /ˈmænɪkjʊərɪst; *NAmE* -kjʊr-/ *noun* a person whose job is the care and treatment of the hands and nails 指甲美容师；指甲修理师；护手师

mani·fest /ˈmænɪfest/ *verb, adj., noun*
- *verb* (*formal*) **1 ~ sth (in sth)** to show sth clearly, especially a feeling, an attitude or a quality 表明，清楚显示（尤指情感、态度或品质） SYN **demonstrate**: *Social tensions were manifested in the recent political crisis.* 最近的政治危机显示了社会关系的紧张。 **2 ~ itself (in sth)** to appear or become noticeable 显现；使人注意到 SYN **appear**: *The symptoms of the disease manifested themselves ten days later.* 十天后，这种病的症状显现出来。
- *adj.* **~ (to sb) (in sth)** (*formal*) easy to see or understand 明显的；显而易见的 SYN **clear**: *His nervousness was manifest to all those present.* 所有在场的人都看出了他很紧张。◇ *The anger he felt is manifest in his paintings.* 他的愤怒明显地表现在他的绘画之中。 ▶ **mani·fest·ly** *adv.*: *manifestly unfair* 明显不公平 ◇ *The party has manifestly failed to achieve its goal.* 这一政党显然没有达到自己的目标。
- *noun* (*specialist*) a list of goods or passengers on a ship or an aircraft（船或飞机的）货单，旅客名单

mani·fest·ation /ˌmænɪfeˈsteɪʃn/ *noun* (*formal*) **1** [C, U] **~ (of sth)** an event, action or thing that is a sign that sth exists or is happening; the act of appearing as a sign that sth exists or is happening 显示；表明；表示：*The riots are a clear manifestation of the people's discontent.* 骚乱清楚地表明了人民的不满情绪。◇ *Some manifestation of your concern would have been appreciated.* 你当时要是表现出一些关心就好了。 **2** [C] an appearance of a GHOST or spirit（幽灵的）显现，显灵：*The church is the site of a number of supernatural manifestations.* 这座教堂是个鬼魂屡次出没的地方。

mani·festo /ˌmænɪˈfestəʊ; *NAmE* -ˈfestoʊ/ *noun* (*pl.* **-os**) a written statement in which a group of people, especially a political party, explain their beliefs and say what they will do if they win an election 宣言：*an election manifesto* 竞选宣言 ◇ *the party manifesto* 政党宣言 ➲ WORDFINDER NOTE AT DEMOCRACY

mani·fold /ˈmænɪfəʊld; *NAmE* -foʊld/ *adj., noun*
- *adj.* (*formal*) many; of many different types 多的；多种多样的；许多种类的：*The possibilities were manifold.* 有很多种可能性。
- *noun* (*specialist*) a pipe or chamber with several openings for taking gases in and out of a car engine 歧管（汽车引擎用以进气和排气）：*the exhaust manifold* 排气歧管

mani·kin (*also* **man·ni·kin**) /ˈmænɪkɪn/ *noun* **1** a model of the human body that is used for teaching art or medicine（医疗或艺术教学用的）人体模型 ➲ COMPARE MANNEQUIN (1) **2** (*old-fashioned*) a very small man 侏儒；小矮人 SYN **dwarf**

Ma·nila (*also* **Ma·nilla**) /məˈnɪlə/ *noun* [U] strong brown paper, used especially for making envelopes 马尼拉纸

man·ioc /ˈmæniɒk; *NAmE* -ɑːk/ *noun* [U] = CASSAVA

ma·nipu·late AW /məˈnɪpjuleɪt/ *verb* **1** (*disapproving*) to control or influence sb/sth, often in a dishonest way so that they do not realize it（暗中）控制，操纵，影响：**~ sb/sth** *She uses her charm to manipulate people.* 她利用自身的魅力来摆布别人。◇ *As a politician, he knows how to manipulate public opinion.* 身为政客，他知道如何左右公众舆论。◇ **~ sb into sth/into doing sth** *They managed to manipulate us into agreeing to help.* 他们总算促使我们答应提供帮助了。 **2 ~ sth** (*formal*) to control or use sth in a skilful way（熟练地）操作，使用：*to manipulate the gears and levers of a machine* 熟练地操纵机器的排挡和变速杆 ◇ *Computers are very efficient at manipulating information.* 计算机在处理信息方面效率极高。 **3 ~ sth** (*specialist*) to move a person's bones or joints into the correct position 正骨；治疗脱臼 ▶ **ma·nipu·la·tion** AW /məˌnɪpjuˈleɪʃn/ *noun* [U, C]: *Advertising like this is a cynical manipulation of the elderly.* 作这样的广告宣传就是要弄老年人。◇ *data manipulation* 数据处理 ◇ *manipulation of the bones of the back* 对脊椎骨的推拿治疗

ma·nipu·la·tive AW /məˈnɪpjələtɪv; *NAmE* -leɪtɪv/ *adj.* **1** (*disapproving*) skilful at influencing sb or forcing sb to do what you want, often in an unfair way 善于操纵的；会控制的；会摆布人的 **2** (*formal*) connected with the ability to handle objects skilfully 熟练操作的；有操作能力的：*manipulative skills such as typing and knitting* 诸如打字、编织这样的技能

ma·nipu·la·tor /məˈnɪpjuleɪtə(r)/ *noun* (*often disapproving*) a person who is skilful at influencing people or situations in order to get what they want 操纵者；控制者

man·kind /mænˈkaɪnd/ *noun* [U] all humans, thought about as one large group; the human race 人类：*the history of mankind* 人类的历史 ◇ *an invention for the good of all mankind* 造福全人类的一项发明 ➲ NOTE AT GENDER ➲ COMPARE WOMANKIND ➲ SEE ALSO HUMANKIND

manky /ˈmæŋki/ *adj.* (*BrE, informal*) dirty and unpleasant 肮脏的；污秽的

manly /ˈmænli/ *adj.* (*often approving*) (**man·lier**, **man·li·est**) having the qualities or physical features that are admired or expected in a man 有男子汉气概的；强壮的 ▶ **man·li·ness** *noun* [U]

ˌman-ˈmade *adj.* made by people; not natural 人造的；非天然的 SYN **artificial**: *a man-made lake* 人工湖 ◇ *man-made fibres such as nylon and polyester* 尼龙和涤纶之类的人造纤维 ➲ SYNONYMS AT ARTIFICIAL

manna /ˈmænə/ *noun* [U] (in the Bible《圣经》) the food that God provided for the people of Israel during their 40 years in the desert 吗哪，玛纳（以色列人在荒野 40 年中神赐的食粮）：(*figurative*) *To the refugees, the food shipments were* ***manna from heaven*** (= an unexpected and very welcome gift). 对于难民来说，运来的食物有如天降吗哪。

manned /mænd/ *adj.* if a machine, a vehicle, a place or an activity is **manned**, it has or needs a person to control or operate it（机器、车辆、地方或活动）有人控制的，需人操纵的：*manned space flight* 载人航天飞行 OPP **unmanned**

man·ne·quin /ˈmænɪkɪn/ *noun* **1** a model of a human body, used for displaying clothes in shops/stores（商店中用于陈列服装的）人体模型 ➲ COMPARE MANIKIN (1) **2** (*old-fashioned*) a person whose job is to wear and display new styles of clothes 时装模特儿 SYN **model**

man·ner /ˈmænə(r)/ *noun* **1** [sing.] (*formal*) the way that sth is done or happens 方式；方法：*She answered in a businesslike manner.* 她回答时显出一副公事公办的样子。◇ *The manner in which the decision was announced was extremely regrettable.* 宣布决定的方式非常令人遗憾。**2** [sing.] the way that sb behaves towards other people 举止；行为方式：*to have an aggressive/a friendly/a relaxed manner* 带着一副咄咄逼人的／友好的／悠闲的样子 ◇ *His manner was polite but cool.* 他举止有礼但很冷漠。➲ SEE ALSO BEDSIDE MANNER **3** **manners** [pl.] behaviour that is considered to be polite in a particular society or culture 礼貌；礼仪：*to have* ***good/bad manners*** 有／没有礼貌 ◇ *It is bad manners to talk with your mouth full.* 嘴里塞满了东西跟人说话是不礼貌的。◇ *He* ***has no manners*** (= behaves very badly). 他毫无礼貌。➲ SEE ALSO TABLE MANNERS **4** **manners** [pl.] (*formal*) the habits and customs of a particular group of people 规矩；习俗：*the social morals and manners of the seventeenth century* * 17 世纪的社会道德和习俗 ➲ WORDFINDER NOTE AT BEHAVIOUR

IDM **all ˈmanner of sb/sth** many different types of people or things 各种各样的人（或事）；形形色色的人（或事）：*The problem can be solved in all manner of ways.* 这个问题可以用各种方法加以解决。**in a manner of ˈspeaking** if you think about it in a particular way; true in some but not all ways 可以说；不妨说；从某种意义上说：*All these points of view are related, in a manner of speaking.* 所有这些观点都在某方面相互关联。**in the manner of sb/sth** (*formal*) in a style that is typical of sb/sth 以某人（或某物）的典型风格：*a painting in the manner of Raphael* 拉斐尔风格的绘画 **(as/as if) to the manner ˈborn** (*formal*) as if sth is natural for you and you have done it many times in the past 仿佛天生的；生来就习惯的 **what manner of…** (*formal* or *literary*) what kind of… 什么样的…：*What manner of man could do such a terrible thing?* 究竟什么人能做出这样可怕的事呢?

man·nered /ˈmænəd; *NAmE* -nərd/ *adj.* **1** (*disapproving*) (of behaviour, art, writing, etc. 行为、艺术、写作等) trying to impress people by being formal and not natural 矫揉造作的；不自然的 SYN **affected** ➲ WORDFINDER NOTE AT STORY **2** **-mannered** (in compounds 构成复合词) having the type of manners mentioned 态度…的；举止…的：*a bad-mannered child* 没有礼貌的孩子 ➲ SEE ALSO ILL-MANNERED, MILD-MANNERED, WELL MANNERED

man·ner·ism /ˈmænərɪzəm/ *noun* **1** [C] a particular habit or way of speaking or behaving that sb has but is not aware of 习性；言谈举止：***nervous/odd/irritating mannerisms*** 紧张的／古怪的／令人不快的习惯 **2** [U] too much use of a particular style in painting or writing（绘画、写作中）过分的独特风格 **3** **Mannerism** [U] a style in 16th century Italian art that did not show things in a natural way but made them look strange or out of their usual shape 风格主义，矫饰主义（16 世纪意大利的一种艺术风格，以怪诞、变形的方式表现事物）

man·ner·ist /ˈmænərɪst/ (*usually* **Man·ner·ist**) *adj.* (of painting or writing 绘画或写作) in the style of Mannerism 风格主义的；矫饰主义的

man·ni·kin = MANIKIN

man·nish /ˈmænɪʃ/ *adj.* (*usually disapproving*) (of a woman or of sth belonging to a woman 妇女或其所有物) having qualities that are thought of as typical of or suitable for a man 像男人的；男子气的；男性化的

mano-a-mano /ˌmɑːnəʊ æ ˈmɑːnəʊ; *NAmE* ˌmɑːnoʊ ɑː ˈmɑːnoʊ/ *adv.*, *noun* (*informal, especially NAmE, from Spanish*)

■ *adv.* with two people facing each other directly in order to decide an argument or a competition（较量时）面对面：*It's time to settle this mano-a-mano.* 现在是当面解决这个问题的时候了。

■ *noun* (*pl.* **mano-a-manos**) a fight or contest, especially one between two people（尤指两人间的）格斗，较量，比试

man·oeuv·rable (*BrE*) (*NAmE* **man·euv·er·able**) /məˈnuːvərəbl/ *adj.* that can easily be moved into different positions 可调遣的；机动的；灵活的：*a highly manoeuvrable vehicle* 非常机动灵活的交通工具 ▶ **man·oeuv·ra·bil·ity** (*BrE*) (*NAmE* **man·eu·ver·abil·ity**) *noun* [U]

man·oeuvre (*especially US* **man·eu·ver**) /məˈnuːvə(r)/ *noun*, *verb*

■ *noun* **1** [C] a movement performed with care and skill 细致巧妙的移动；机动动作：*a* ***complicated/skilful manoeuvre*** 复杂的／熟练的移动 ◇ *You will be asked to perform some standard manoeuvres during your driving test.* 驾驶考试中会要求你做几个标准的机动动作。**2** [C, U] a clever plan, action or movement that is used to give sb an advantage 策略；手段；花招；伎俩 SYN **move**：*diplomatic manoeuvres* 外交策略 ◇ *a complex manoeuvre in a game of chess* 国际象棋中复杂的应对套路 **3** **manoeuvres** [pl.] military exercises involving a large number of soldiers, ships, etc. 军事演习；作战演习：*The army is* ***on manoeuvres*** *in the desert.* 军队在沙漠中进行军事演习。

IDM **freedom of/room for maˈnoeuvre** the chance to change the way that sth happens and influence decisions that are made 改变事态的机会；回旋余地

■ *verb* **1** [I, T] to move or turn skilfully or carefully; to move or turn sth skilfully or carefully（使谨慎或熟练地）移动，运动；转动：**~ (for sth)** *The yachts manoeuvred for position.* 那些游艇灵活地寻找位置。◇ *There was very little room to manoeuvre.* 几乎没有什么活动空间。◇ **~ sth (+ adv./prep.)** *She manoeuvred the car carefully into the garage.* 她小心翼翼地将车开进了车库。**2** [I, T] to control or influence a situation in a skilful but sometimes dishonest way 操纵；控制；使花招：*The new laws have left us little* ***room to manoeuvre*** (= not much opportunity to change or influence a situation). 新法律没给我们留下多少回旋的余地。◇ **~ sth + adv./prep.** *She manoeuvred her way to the top of the company.* 她施展手腕使自己进入了公司最高领导层。

man·oeuv·ring (*especially US* **man·eu·ver·ing**) /məˈnuːvərɪŋ/ *noun* [U, C] clever, skilful, and often dishonest ways of achieving your aims 手段；伎俩；花招

ˌman of ˈletters *noun* a man who is a writer, or who writes about literature 文人；作家

ˌman-of-ˈwar *noun* (*pl.* **men-of-war**) a sailing ship used in the past for fighting （旧时的）军舰，战舰

manor /ˈmænə(r)/ *noun* (*BrE*) **1** (*also* **ˈmanor house**) a large country house surrounded by land that belongs to it 庄园宅第 **2** an area of land with a manor house on it 庄园；庄园领地 **3** (*BrE, slang*) an area in which sb works or for which they are responsible, especially officers at a police station 工作区；（尤指警察的）管辖区

man·orial /məˈnɔːriəl/ *adj.* typical of or connected with a manor, especially in the past（尤指旧时）庄园的，采邑的

man·power /ˈmænpaʊə(r)/ *noun* [U] the number of workers needed or available to do a particular job 劳动力；人手；人力：*a need for* ***trained/skilled manpower*** 对受过培训的／熟练的劳动力的需求 ◇ *a manpower shortage* 劳动力短缺

man·qué /ˈmɒŋkeɪ; *NAmE* mɑːŋˈkeɪ/ *adj.* (following nouns 用于名词后) (*from French, formal* or *humorous*) used to describe a person who hoped to follow a particular career but who failed in it or never tried it 愿望落空的；壮志未酬的；未成功的：*He's really an artist manqué.* 他很想当艺术家，但未能如愿。

man·sard /ˈmænsɑːd; *NAmE* -sɑːrd/ (*also* **ˌmansard ˈroof**) *noun* (*specialist*) a roof with a double slope in which the upper part is less steep than the lower part 孟莎式屋顶，折面屋顶（下部比上部陡）

manse /mæns/ *noun* the house of a Christian minister, especially in Scotland（尤指苏格兰的）牧师住宅

man·ser·vant /ˈmænsɜːvənt; *NAmE* -sɜːrv-/ *noun* (*pl.* **men·ser·vants**) (*old-fashioned*) a male servant, especially a man's personal servant 男仆；家丁；（尤指）随身男侍从

man·sion /ˈmænʃn/ *noun* **1** [C] a large impressive house 公馆；宅第：*an 18th century country mansion* * 18 世纪的乡村宅第 **2 Mansions** [pl.] (*BrE*) used in the names of blocks of flats（用于公寓楼名）：*2 Moscow Mansions, Cromwell Road* 克伦威尔路莫斯科公寓 2 号

ˈman-sized *adj.* [only before noun] suitable or large enough for a man 宜于成年男人的；够一个男人用的：*a man-sized breakfast* 够一个大男人吃的早餐

man·slaugh·ter /ˈmænslɔːtə(r)/ *noun* [U] (*law* 律) the crime of killing sb illegally but not deliberately 过失杀人 ➲ COMPARE CULPABLE HOMICIDE, HOMICIDE, MURDER *n.* (1)

manta /ˈmæntə/ (*also* ˌ**manta ˈray**) *noun* a large fish that lives in tropical seas and swims by moving two parts like large flat wings 双吻前口蝠鲼（体宽大于长，见于暖水海域）

man·tel·piece /ˈmæntlpiːs/ (*also* **man·tel** /ˈmæntl/ *especially in NAmE*) *noun* a shelf above a FIREPLACE 壁炉台 ➲ VISUAL VOCAB PAGE V22

man·tis /ˈmæntɪs/ *noun* (*pl.* **man·tises** or **man·tids** /ˈmæntɪdz/) = PRAYING MANTIS

man·tle /ˈmæntl/ *noun, verb*

■ ***noun*** **1** [sing.] **the ~ of sb/sth** (*literary*) the role and responsibilities of an important person or job, especially when they are passed on from one person to another（可继承的）责任，职责，衣钵：*The vice-president must now **take on the mantle** of supreme power.* 副总统现在必须承担起最高权力的重任。**2** [C] (*literary*) a layer of sth that covers a surface 覆盖层：*hills with a mantle of snow* 白雪覆盖的山峦 **3** [C] a loose piece of clothing without sleeves, worn over other clothes, especially in the past（尤指旧时的）披风，斗篷 SYN **cloak, covering** **4** (*also* **ˈgas mantle**) [C] a cover around the flame of a gas lamp that becomes very bright when it is heated（煤气灯的）白炽罩 **5** [sing.] (*geology* 地) the part of the earth below the CRUST and surrounding the core 地幔

■ ***verb*** **~ sth** (*literary*) to cover the surface of sth 覆盖；遮盖

man·tra /ˈmæntrə/ *noun* a word, phrase or sound that is repeated again and again, especially during prayer or MEDITATION 曼怛罗（某些宗教的念咒）；咒语：*a Buddhist mantra* 佛教咒语

man·trap /ˈmæntræp/ *noun* **1** a trap used in the past for catching people, especially people who tried to steal things from sb's land（旧时私人地界防小偷等的）诱捕陷阱 **2** any electronic device that is used to catch people who are doing sth dishonest 电子诱捕系统

man·ual AW /ˈmænjuəl/ *adj., noun*

■ ***adj.*** **1** (of work, etc. 工作等) involving using the hands or physical strength 用手的；手工的；体力的：***manual labour/jobs/skills*** 体力劳动 / 活儿；手工技巧 ◇ *manual and non-manual workers* 体力劳动者和非体力劳动者 ➲ WORDFINDER NOTE AT WORK **2** operated or controlled by hand rather than automatically or using electricity, etc. 手动的；手控的；用手操作的：*a manual gearbox* 手动变速箱 ◇ *My camera has manual and automatic functions.* 我的照相机有手调和自动两种功能。**3** connected with using the hands 手工的；用手的：*manual dexterity* 手的灵巧 ▸ **manu·al·ly** AW /-juəli/ *adv.*: *manually operated* 手工操作的

■ ***noun*** a book that tells you how to do or operate sth, especially one that comes with a machine, etc. when you buy it 使用手册；说明书；指南：*a **computer/car/instruction manual*** 电脑 / 汽车说明书；用法指南 ➲ COMPARE HANDBOOK

IDM **on ˈmanual** not being operated automatically 处于非自动状态；处于手动状态：*Leave the controls on manual.* 让操纵杆处于手动状态。

manu·fac·ture /ˌmænjuˈfæktʃə(r)/ *verb, noun*

■ ***verb*** **1** **~ sth** to make goods in large quantities, using machinery（用机器）大量生产，成批制造 SYN **mass-produce**：*manufactured goods* 工业品 **2** **~ sth** to invent a story, an excuse, etc. 编造；捏造：*a news story manufactured by an unscrupulous journalist* 一个不道德的记者编造的一篇新闻报道 **3** **~ sth** (*specialist*) to produce a substance 生成，产生（一种物质）：*Vitamins cannot be manufactured by our bodies.* 维生素不能由人体来生成。

■ ***noun*** **1** [U] the process of producing goods in large quantities 大量制造；批量生产 SYN **mass production**：*the manufacture of cars* 汽车制造 **2 manufactures** [pl.] (*specialist*) manufactured goods 工业品：*a major importer of cotton manufactures* 棉花产品的主要进口商

manu·fac·tur·er /ˌmænjuˈfæktʃərə(r)/ *noun* a person or company that produces goods in large quantities 生产者；制造者；生产商 SYN **maker**：*a car/computer manufacturer* 汽车 / 计算机制造商 ◇ *Always follow the manufacturer's instructions.* 务必按厂家的用法说明使用。◇ *Faulty goods should be returned to the manufacturers.* 有问题的产品应退还生产厂家。

manu·fac·tur·ing /ˌmænjuˈfæktʃərɪŋ/ *noun* [U] the business or industry of producing goods in large quantities in factories, etc. 制造业：*Many jobs in manufacturing were lost during the recession.* 在经济衰退期，制造业有很多人失业了。

ma·nure /məˈnjʊə(r); *NAmE* məˈnʊr/ *noun, verb*

■ ***noun*** [U] the waste matter from animals that is spread over or mixed with the soil to help plants and crops grow 粪肥；肥料 SYN **dung**

■ ***verb*** **~ sth** to put manure on or in soil to help plants grow 给…施肥

manu·script /ˈmænjuskrɪpt/ *noun* (*abbr.* **MS**) **1** a copy of a book, piece of music, etc. before it has been printed 手稿；原稿：*an **unpublished/original manuscript*** 未经发表的 / 原始的手稿 ◇ *I read her poems **in manuscript**.* 我读过她的诗作的手稿。**2** a very old book or document that was written by hand before printing was invented（印刷术发明以前书籍或文献的）手写本，手抄本：*medieval illuminated manuscripts* 中世纪装饰精美的手抄本

ˈmanuscript paper *noun* [U] paper printed with STAVES for writing music on 五线谱稿纸

Manx /mæŋks/ *adj.* of or connected with the Isle of Man, its people or the language once spoken there 马恩岛的；马恩岛人的；马恩语的

ˌManx ˈcat *noun* a breed of cat with no tail 马恩岛猫（一种无尾家猫）

many /ˈmeni/ *det., pron.* **1** used with plural nouns and verbs, especially in negative sentences or in more formal English, to mean 'a large number of'. Also used in questions to ask about the size of a number, and with 'as', 'so' and 'too'. 许多（与复数名词及动词连用，尤用于否定句或正式用语，表示大量；也用于疑问句以询问数字大小，并可与 as、so 和 too 连用）：*We don't have very many copies left.* 我们所剩的册数不多。◇ *You can't have one each. We haven't got many.* 你们不能一人一个。我们没有很多。◇ *Many people feel that the law should be changed.* 许多人都觉得这项法律应该修改。◇ *Many of those present disagreed.* 许多到场的人都不同意。◇ ***How many** children do you have?* 你有几个孩子？◇ *There are **too many** mistakes in this essay.* 这篇文章错误太多。◇ *He made ten mistakes **in as many** (= in ten) lines.* 他在十行中就出了十个错。◇ *New drivers have **twice as many** accidents as experienced drivers.* 新手司机所出的事故是熟练司机的两倍。◇ *Don't take **so many**.* 别拿这么多。◇ *I've known her for **a great many** (= very many) years.* 我认识她好多好多年了。◇ *Even if one person is hurt that is **one too many**.* 即使伤一个人，都嫌太多。◇ *It was one of my many mistakes.* 这是我犯的许多错误中的一个。◇ *a many-headed monster* 一只多头怪兽 **2 the many** used with a plural verb to mean 'most people'（与复数动词连用）大多数人：*a government which improves conditions for the many* 为大多数人改善生活条件的政府 **3 many a** (*formal*) used with a singular noun and verb to mean 'a large number of'（与单数名词及动词连用）许多，大量：*Many a good man has been destroyed by drink.* 许多好人都毁在了饮酒上。

IDM **as many as…** used to show surprise that the number of people or things involved is so large（表示惊讶）多达，如此多：*There were as many as 200 people at the lecture.* 听讲的有 200 人之多。**have had ˌone too ˈmany** (*informal*) to be slightly drunk 微醉；醉意朦胧 **many's the…** (*formal*) used to show that sth happens often 许多次；常常：*Many's the time I heard her use those words.* 我不止一次听她说过那样的话。

▼ GRAMMAR POINT 语法说明

many / a lot of / lots of

- Many is used only with countable nouns. It is used mainly in questions and negative sentences. * many 只与可数名词连用，主要用于疑问句和否定句中：*Do you go to many concerts?* 你常去听音乐会吗？◇ *How many people came to the meeting?* 多少人来参加了会议？◇ *I don't go to many concerts.* 我不常去听音乐会。Although it is not common in statements, it is used after *so*, *as* and *too*. 该词在陈述句中不很常用，但用于 so、as 和 too 之后：*You made too many mistakes.* 你犯的错误太多了。
- In statements **a lot of** or **lots of** (*informal*) are much more common. 在陈述句中 a lot of 或 lots of（非正式）常用得多：*I go to a lot of concerts.* 我常去听音乐会。◇ *'How many CDs have you got?' 'Lots!'* "你有几张光盘？""多着呢！" However, they are not used with measurements of time or distance. 不过，上述词语不与表示时间和距离的量词连用：*I stayed in England for many/quite a few/ten weeks.* 我在英格兰逗留了许多周 / 好几周 / 十周。◇ ~~*I stayed in England a lot of weeks.*~~ When **a lot of/lots of** means 'many', it takes a plural verb. * a lot of / lots of 意为 many 时，谓语动词用复数：*Lots of people like Italian food.* 许多人喜欢意大利食物。You can also use **plenty of** (*informal*). 亦可用 plenty of（非正式）：*Plenty of stores stay open late.* 许多商店都营业到很晚。These phrases can also be used in questions and negative sentences. 以上短语亦可用于疑问句和否定句中。
- **A lot of/lots of** is still felt to be informal, especially in *BrE*, so in formal writing it is better to use **many** or **a large number of** in statements. * a lot of / lots of 在英式英语中尤被视为非正式，因此在正式的书面陈述句中较宜用 many 或 a large number of。

➲ NOTE AT MUCH

Mao·ism /ˈmaʊɪzəm/ *noun* [U] the ideas of the 20th century Chinese COMMUNIST leader Mao Zedong 毛（泽东）主义；毛泽东思想 ▶ **Mao·ist** /ˈmaʊɪst/ *noun, adj.*

Maori /ˈmaʊri/ *noun* **1** [C] a member of a race of people who were the original people living in New Zealand（新西兰）毛利人 **2** [U] the language of the Maori people 毛利语 ▶ **Maori** *adj.*

map /mæp/ *noun, verb*

■ *noun* a drawing or plan of the earth's surface or part of it, showing countries, towns, rivers, etc. 地图：*a map of France* 法国地图 ◇ *a street map of Miami* 迈阿密街区图 ◇ *to* ***read a/the map*** (= understand the information on a map) 查看地图 ◇ *large-scale maps* 大比例尺地图 ◇ *Can you find Black Hill* ***on the map****?* 你能在地图上找到布莱克山吗？◇ *I'll draw you a map of how to get to my house.* 我给你画一张到我家的路线图。➲ WORDFINDER NOTE AT EARTH ➲ VISUAL VOCAB PAGE V44 ➲ SEE ALSO ROAD MAP

WORDFINDER 联想词：compass, globe, GPS, grid, key, latitude, navigate, reference, scale

IDM **put sb/sth on the ˈmap** to make sb/sth famous or important 使出名；使有重要性：*The exhibition has helped put the city on the map.* 展览会使这个城市名扬四方。➲ MORE AT WIPE *v.*

■ *verb* (**-pp-**) **1** **~ sth** to make a map of an area 绘制…的地图 SYN **chart**：*an unexplored region that has not yet been mapped* 一个尚未绘制地图的未经勘察的地区 **2 ~ sth** to discover or give information about sth, especially the way it is arranged or organized 了解信息，提供信息（尤指其编排或组织方式）：*It is now possible to map the different functions of the brain.* 现在已有可能了解大脑的各种功能。▶ **map·ping** *noun* [U]：*the mapping of the Indian subcontinent* 印度次大陆地图的绘制 ◇ *gene mapping* 基因定位

PHR V **ˈmap sth on/onto sth** to link a group of qualities, items, etc. with their source, cause, position on a scale, etc. 把…与…相联系：*Grammar information enables students to map the structure of a foreign language onto their own.* 语法知识使学生能够把外语结构和母语结构联系起来。**ˌmap sth↔ˈout** to plan or arrange sth in a careful or detailed way（精心细致地）规划，安排：*He has his career path clearly mapped out.* 他精心规划了自己的事业前途。

maple /ˈmeɪpl/ *noun* **1** [C, U] (*also* **ˈmaple tree**) a tall tree with leaves that have five points and turn bright red or yellow in the autumn/fall. Maples grow in northern countries. 槭树；枫树 **2** [U] the wood of the maple tree 槭木

ˈmaple leaf *noun* **1** [C] the leaf of the maple tree, used as a symbol of Canada 枫叶（加拿大的象征） **2 the Maple Leaf** [sing.] the flag of Canada 枫叶旗（加拿大国旗）

ˌmaple ˈsyrup *noun* [U] a sweet sticky sauce made with liquid obtained from some types of maple tree, often eaten with PANCAKES 槭树汁；槭糖浆

mar /mɑː(r)/ *verb* (**-rr-**) **~ sth** to damage or spoil sth good 破坏；毁坏；损毁；损害 SYN **blight, ruin**：*The game was marred by the behaviour of drunken fans.* 喝醉了的球迷行为不轨，把比赛给搅了。

ma·racas /məˈrækəz; *NAmE* -rɑː-/ *noun* [pl.] a pair of simple musical instruments consisting of hollow balls containing BEADS or BEANS that are shaken to produce a sound 砂槌，响葫芦（成对的打击乐器，内装珠子或豆粒，摇动以发声）➲ VISUAL VOCAB PAGE V37

mar·as·chino /ˌmærəˈʃiːnəʊ; -ˈskiːnəʊ; *NAmE* -noʊ/ *noun* (*pl.* **-os**) **1** [U, C] a strong sweet alcoholic drink made from black CHERRIES 马拉斯加樱桃酒；黑樱桃酒 **2** (*also* **ˌmaraschino ˈcherry**) [C] a preserved CHERRY used to decorate alcoholic drinks 马拉斯加酒渍樱桃（用于装点酒类饮料）

Ma·ra·thi (*also* **Mah·ratti**) /məˈrɑːti; -ˈræti/ *noun* [U] a language spoken in Maharashtra in western India 马拉塔语（印度西部一种语言）

mara·thon /ˈmærəθən; *NAmE* -θɑːn/ *noun* **1** a long running race of about 42 kilometres or 26 miles 马拉松赛跑（距离约 42 公里，合 26 英里）：*the London marathon* 伦敦马拉松赛跑 ◇ *to run a marathon* 参加马拉松赛跑 **2** an activity or a piece of work that lasts a long time and requires a lot of effort and patience 马拉松式的活动（或工作）：*The interview was a real marathon.* 这次面试真是一场马拉松。ORIGIN From the story that in ancient Greece a messenger ran from Marathon to Athens (22 miles) with the news of a victory over the Persians. 源自古希腊的传说，一名信使从马拉松奔跑 22 英里到雅典报捷。▶ **mara·thon** *adj.* [only before noun]：*a marathon journey lasting 56 hours* 持续了 56 小时的马拉松式的旅程 ◇ *a marathon legal battle* 一场马拉松式的法律斗争

ma·raud·ing /məˈrɔːdɪŋ/ *adj.* [only before noun] (of people or animals 人或动物) going around a place in search of things to steal or people to attack（到处）抢劫的，打劫的，劫掠的：*marauding wolves* 到处猎食的狼群 ▶ **ma·raud·er** /məˈrɔːdə(r)/ *noun*

mar·ble /ˈmɑːbl; *NAmE* ˈmɑːrbl/ *noun* **1** [U] a type of hard stone that is usually white and often has coloured lines in it. It can be polished and is used in building and for making statues, etc. 大理石：*a* ***slab/block of marble*** 一块大理石板 ◇ *a* ***marble floor/sculpture*** 大理石地板 / 雕刻 **2** [C] a small ball of coloured glass that children roll along the ground in a game（玻璃）弹子 **3 marbles** [U] a game played with marbles 弹子游戏：*Three boys were playing marbles.* 三个男孩儿在玩弹子游戏。**4 marbles** [pl.] (*informal*) a way of referring to sb's intelligence or mental ability 理智；智力：*He's **losing his marbles*** (= he's not behaving in a sensible way). 他失去理智了。

mar·bled /ˈmɑːbld; *NAmE* ˈmɑːrbld/ *adj.* having the colours and/or patterns of marble 有大理石颜色（或花纹）的：*marbled wallpaper* 有大理石花纹的墙纸

marb·ling /ˈmɑːblɪŋ; *NAmE* ˈmɑːrb-/ *noun* [U] the method of decorating sth with a pattern that looks like marble 大理石纹饰；仿大理石（装饰）

marc /mɑːk; *NAmE* mɑːrk/ *noun* **1** [U, sing.] the substance left after GRAPES have been pressed to make wine（酿酒时将葡萄压榨后的）残渣；葡萄果渣 **2** [U, C] a strong alcoholic drink made from this substance 葡萄渣酒

March /mɑːtʃ; *NAmE* mɑːrtʃ/ *noun* [U, C] (*abbr.* **Mar.**) the 3rd month of the year, between February and April 三月 HELP To see how **March** is used, look at the examples at **April**. * March 的用法见词条 April 下的示例。IDM SEE MAD

march /mɑːtʃ; *NAmE* mɑːrtʃ/ *verb, noun*

■ *verb* **1** [I] to walk with stiff regular steps like a soldier 齐步走；行进：(+ **adv./prep.**) *Soldiers were marching up and down outside the government buildings.* 士兵在政府大楼外面来回练习队列行进。◇ *Quick march!* (= the order to start marching)（口令）齐步走！◇ + **noun** *They marched 20 miles to reach the capital.* 他们行进了 20 英里才到达首都。**2** [I] + **adv./prep.** to walk somewhere quickly in a determined way（坚定地向某地）前进，进发：*She marched over to me and demanded an apology.* 她毅然走过来，要我向她道歉。**3** [I] to walk through the streets in a large group in order to protest about sth 游行示威；游行抗议 SYN **demonstrate** ➲ WORDFINDER NOTE AT PROTEST **4** [T] **~ sb + adv./prep.** to force sb to walk somewhere with you 使同行；强迫（某人）一起走：*The guards marched the prisoner away.* 卫兵押着囚犯离开了。

IDM **get your ˈmarching orders** (*informal*) to be ordered to leave a place, a job, etc. 奉命离开；被解职 **give sb their ˈmarching orders** (*informal*) to order sb to leave a place, their job, etc. 命令某人离开；解雇 **march to (the beat of) a different ˈdrummer/ˈdrum** to behave in a different way from other people; to have different attitudes or ideas 与众不同：*She was a gifted and original artist who marched to a different drummer.* 她有天赋，具独创性，是个与众不同的艺术家。

PHR V **ˌmarch ˈon** to move on or pass quickly 继续行进；快速经过：*Time **marches on** and we still have not made a decision.* 时间过得飞快，而我们却还没有拿定主意。**ˈmarch on…** to march to a place to protest about sth or to attack it 向…行进（以示抗议或进行攻击）：*Several thousand people marched on City Hall.* 数千人涌往市政厅进行抗议。

■ *noun* **1** [C] an organized walk by many people from one place to another, in order to protest about sth, or to express their opinions 示威游行；抗议游行：*protest marches* 抗议游行 ◇ *to go on a march* 进行示威游行 ➲ COMPARE DEMONSTRATION (1) **2** [C] an act of marching; a journey made by marching 行进；行军：*The army began their long march to the coast.* 部队开始了他们开往沿海地区的长途行军。**3** [sing.] **the ~ of sth** the steady development or forward movement of sth 稳步发展；稳步前进：*the march of progress/technology/time* 平稳的进步；技术的稳步发展；时光的推移 **4** [C] a piece of music written for marching to 进行曲：*a funeral march* 葬礼进行曲

IDM **on the ˈmarch** marching somewhere 在行军中；在行进中；在进展中：*The enemy are on the march.* 敌人正在行军途中。➲ MORE AT STEAL *v.*

march·er /ˈmɑːtʃə(r); *NAmE* ˈmɑːrtʃ-/ *noun* a person who is taking part in a march as a protest 游行示威者；抗议游行者 SYN **demonstrator**

ˈmarching band *noun* [C+sing./pl. v.] a group of musicians who play while they are marching 行进乐队；边行走边演奏的乐队

ˈmarching season *noun* (in Northern Ireland) the time in July and August when PROTESTANT groups march through the streets in memory of victories over CATHOLICS in the 17th century 游行季节（北爱尔兰新教徒为纪念 17 世纪战胜天主教徒而在七、八月份上街游行）

mar·chion·ess /ˌmɑːʃəˈnes; *NAmE* ˌmɑːrʃ-/ *noun* **1** a woman who has the rank of a MARQUESS 女侯爵 **2** the wife of a MARQUESS 侯爵夫人 ➲ COMPARE MARQUISE

ˈmarch past *noun* [sing.] a ceremony in which soldiers march past an important person, etc. 分列式（军人列队通过检阅台）SYN **parade**

Mardi Gras /ˌmɑːdi ˈɡrɑː; *NAmE* ˈmɑːrdi ɡrɑː/ *noun* [U] (*from French*) the day before the beginning of Lent, celebrated as a holiday in some countries, with music and dancing in the streets 肥美的星期二，狂欢节（大斋期的前一天）➲ COMPARE SHROVE TUESDAY

mare /meə(r); *NAmE* mer/ *noun* **1** a female horse or DONKEY 母马；母驴 ➲ COMPARE BROOD MARE, FILLY, STALLION **2** (*BrE*) (*informal*) = NIGHTMARE (2)：*I had a complete mare booking tickets for the concert.* 我预订音乐会门票的经历真是糟糕透顶。

IDM **a ˈmare's nest 1** a discovery that seems interesting but is found to have no value（看似有趣但）毫无价值的发现 **2** a very complicated situation 复杂的形势；变幻莫测的局势

marg /mɑːɡ; *NAmE* mɑːrɡ/ *noun* (*IndE*) a road, street or path 路；街道；小径：*Mahatma Gandhi Marg* 圣雄甘地路 ◇ *He trekked along the lonely Badrinath paidal marg.* 他沿着人迹罕至的伯德里纳特步行小道跋涉。◇ (*figurative*) *The Bhatki marg (the path of devotion) teaches followers to forget the physical self in pursuit of the Lord.* 虔诚之路教导信徒在追随神时忘掉身体自我。

mar·gar·ine /ˌmɑːdʒəˈriːn; *NAmE* ˈmɑːrdʒərən/ (*also BrE, informal* **marge** /mɑːdʒ; *NAmE* mɑːrdʒ/) *noun* [U] a yellow substance like butter made from animal or vegetable fats, used in cooking or spread on bread, etc. 人造黄油；人造奶油

mar·ga·rita /ˌmɑːɡəˈriːtə; *NAmE* ˌmɑːrɡ-/ *noun* an alcoholic drink made by mixing fruit juice with TEQUILA 玛格丽特酒（用果汁与墨西哥龙舌兰酒调制而成）

mar·gin AW /ˈmɑːdʒɪn; *NAmE* ˈmɑːrdʒən/ *noun* [C] **1** the empty space at the side of a written or printed page 页边空白；白边：*the **left-hand/right-hand margin*** 左 / 右页边 ◇ *a **narrow/wide margin*** 窄 / 宽空白边 ◇ *notes **scribbled in the margin*** 随手写在页边上的笔记 **2** [usually sing.] the amount of time, or number of votes, etc. by which sb wins sth（获胜者在时间或票数上领先的）幅度，差额，差数：*He won by a **narrow margin**.* 他以微小的差额获胜。◇ *She beat the other runners **by a margin of** ten seconds.* 她以领先十秒的优势战胜了其他赛跑者。**3** (*business* 商) = PROFIT MARGIN：*What are your average operating margins?* 你的平均营业利润率是多少？◇ *a gross margin of 45%* * 45% 的毛利 **4** [usually sing.] an extra amount of sth such as time, space, money, etc. that you include in order to make sure that sth is successful 余地；备用的时间（或空间、金钱等）：*a safety margin* 安全距离 ◇ *The narrow gateway left me little **margin for error** as I reversed the car.* 门口狭窄，弄得我倒车时几乎不能出任何差错。➲ SEE ALSO MARGIN OF ERROR **5** (*formal*) the extreme edge or limit of a place 边缘；极限；界限：*the eastern margin of the Indian Ocean* 印度洋的东岸 **6** [usually pl.] the part that is not included in the main part of a group or situation 边缘部分；非主体部分 SYN **fringe**：*people living **on the margins** of society* 生活在社会边缘的人 **7** (*AustralE, NZE*) an amount that is added to a basic wage, paid for special skill or responsibility（基本工资以外的）技术津贴，职务补贴

mar·gin·al AW /ˈmɑːdʒɪnl; *NAmE* ˈmɑːrdʒ-/ *adj., noun*

■ *adj.* **1** small and not important 小的；微不足道的；不重要的 SYN **slight**：*a marginal improvement in weather conditions* 天气条件的略微好转 ◇ *The story will only be of marginal interest to our readers.* 我们的读者对这则故事不会很感兴趣。**2** not part of a main or important group or situation 非主体的；边缘的：*marginal groups in society* 社会

M

中的非主流群体 **3** (*politics* 政, *especially BrE*) won or lost by a very small number of votes and therefore very important or interesting as an indication of public opinion（议席或选区）边缘的（以微弱票数决定成败）：*a* ***marginal seat/constituency*** 边缘席位 / 选区 **4** [only before noun] written in the margin of a page 写在页边空白处的：***marginal notes/comments*** 页边的注解 / 评论 **5** (of land 土地) that cannot produce enough good crops to make a profit 贫瘠的（因而盈利有限）

■ ***noun*** (*BrE*) a seat in a parliament, on a local council, etc. that was won by a very small number of votes（议会或地方委员会的）边缘席位：*a Labour marginal* 工党的边缘席位

mar·gi·na·lia /ˌmɑːdʒɪˈneɪliə; *NAmE* ˌmɑːrdʒ-/ *noun* [pl.] **1** notes written in the margins of a book, etc.（书等的）旁注，边注 **2** facts or details that are not very important 无足轻重的事情；细枝末节

mar·gin·al·ize (*BrE also* **-ise**) /ˈmɑːdʒɪnəlaɪz; *NAmE* ˈmɑːrdʒ-/ *verb* **~ sb** to make sb feel as if they are not important and cannot influence decisions or events; to put sb in a position in which they have no power 使显得微不足道；使处于边缘；使无实权 ➲ WORDFINDER NOTE AT EQUAL ▶ **mar·gin·al·iza·tion**, **-isa·tion** *noun* [U]: *the marginalization of the elderly* 老年人的边缘化

mar·gin·al·ly AW /ˈmɑːdʒɪnəli; *NAmE* ˈmɑːrdʒ-/ *adv.* very slightly; not very much 轻微地；很少地；微不足道地：*They now cost marginally more than they did last year.* 现在并不比去年贵多少。

M

ˌmargin of ˈerror *noun* [usually sing.] an amount that you allow when you calculate sth, for the possibility that a number is not completely accurate 误差幅度：*The survey has a margin of error of 2.5%.* 测量的误差幅度为 2.5%。

mar·guer·ite /ˌmɑːɡəˈriːt; *NAmE* ˌmɑːrɡ-/ *noun* a small white garden flower with a yellow centre 春白菊；滨菊；法兰西菊

mari·achi /ˌmæriˈɑːtʃi/ *noun* [C, U] a musician who plays traditional Mexican music, usually as part of a small group that travels from place to place; the type of music played by these musicians 马里亚奇音乐演奏者，墨西哥传统音乐演奏者（常为街头乐队成员）；马里亚奇音乐；墨西哥街头音乐：*a mariachi band* 马里亚奇乐队

Mar·ian /ˈmeəriən; *NAmE* ˈmer-/ *adj.* (*religion* 宗) relating to the Virgin Mary in the Christian church（基督教）有关圣母马利亚的

mari·cul·ture /ˈmærɪkʌltʃə(r)/ *noun* [U] (*specialist*) a type of farming in which fish or other sea animals and plants are bred or grown for food 海水养殖

Marie Celeste /ˌmæri sɪˈlest; ˌmɑːri/ *noun* [sing.] = MARY CELESTE

mari·gold /ˈmæriɡəʊld; *NAmE* -ɡoʊld/ *noun* an orange or yellow garden flower. There are several types of marigold. 万寿菊；金盏花

ma·ri·juana (*also* **ma·ri·huana**) /ˌmærəˈwɑːnə/ (*also informal* **pot**) *noun* [U] a drug (illegal in many countries) made from the dried leaves and flowers of the HEMP plant, which gives the person smoking it a feeling of being relaxed 大麻；大麻毒品 SYN **cannabis**

ma·rimba /məˈrɪmbə/ *noun* a musical instrument like a XYLOPHONE 马林巴

mar·ina /məˈriːnə/ *noun* a specially designed HARBOUR for small boats and YACHTS 小船坞；游艇停靠区

mar·in·ade /ˌmærɪˈneɪd/ *noun* [C, U] a mixture of oil, wine, spices, etc., in which meat or fish is left before it is cooked in order to make it softer or to give it a particular flavour 腌泡汁

marin·ate /ˈmærɪneɪt/ (*also* **mar·in·ade**) *verb* [T, I] **~ (sth)** if you **marinate** food or it **marinates**, you leave it in a marinade before cooking it 腌，浸泡（食物）；（食物）腌，浸泡

mar·ine /məˈriːn/ *adj., noun*

■ ***adj.*** [only before noun] **1** connected with the sea and the creatures and plants that live there 海的；海产的；海生的：*marine life* 海洋生物 ◇ *a marine biologist* (= a scientist who studies life in the sea) 海洋生物学家 **2** connected with ships or trade at sea 海船的；货船的；海上贸易的

■ ***noun*** a soldier who is trained to serve on land or at sea, especially one in the US Marine Corps or the British Royal Marines（尤指美国或英国皇家）海军陆战队士兵

mari·ner /ˈmærɪnə(r)/ *noun* (*old-fashioned* or *literary*) a sailor 水手

mar·io·nette /ˌmæriəˈnet/ *noun* a PUPPET whose arms, legs and head are moved by strings 牵线木偶

mari·tal /ˈmærɪtl/ *adj.* [only before noun] connected with marriage or with the relationship between a husband and wife 婚姻的；夫妻关系的：***marital difficulties/breakdown*** 婚姻纠葛 / 破裂

ˌmarital ˈstatus *noun* [U] (*formal*) (used especially on official forms 尤用于正式表格) the fact of whether you are single, married, etc. 婚姻状况：*questions about age, sex and marital status* 关于年龄、性别、婚姻状况的问题

mari·time /ˈmærɪtaɪm/ *adj.* **1** connected with the sea or ships 海的；海事的；海运的；船舶的：*a maritime museum* 海洋博物馆 **2** (*formal*) near the sea 靠近海的：*maritime Antarctica* 南极近海地区

mar·joram /ˈmɑːdʒərəm; *NAmE* ˈmɑːrdʒ-/ *noun* [U] a plant with leaves that smell sweet and are used in cooking as a HERB, often when dried 牛至（叶子芳香，常在干后用作烹调辅料）

mark 🔑 /mɑːk; *NAmE* mɑːrk/ *verb, noun*

■ ***verb***

• **WRITE/DRAW** 写；画 **1** 🔑 [T] to write or draw a symbol, line, etc. on sth in order to give information about it 做记号；做标记：**~ A (with B)** *Items marked with an asterisk can be omitted.* 打星号的项目可以删去。◇ **~ B on A** *Prices are marked on the goods.* 价格标在商品上。◇ **~ sb/sth + adj.** *The teacher marked her absent* (= made a mark by her name to show that she was absent). 老师在她的名字旁做了个缺课的记号。◇ *Why have you marked this wrong?* 你为什么批这道题为错？◇ *Do not open any mail marked 'Confidential'.* 不要打开任何标有“机密”的邮件。

• **SPOIL/DAMAGE** 搞糟；损坏 **2** 🔑 [T, I] **~ (sth)** to make a mark on sth in a way that spoils or damages it; to become spoilt or damaged in this way 留下痕迹；弄污；使有污点：*A large purple scar marked his cheek.* 他的面颊上有一块大紫疤。◇ *The surfaces are made from a material that doesn't mark.* 这些台面是由不会留下污渍的材料做的。

• **SHOW POSITION** 表示方位 **3** 🔑 [T] **~ sth** to show the position of sth 标明方位；标示 SYN **indicate**: *The cross marks the spot where the body was found.* 十字记号标明了发现死尸的地点。◇ *The route has been marked in red.* 路线用红色标明了。

• **CELEBRATE** 庆贺 **4** 🔑 [T] **~ sth** to celebrate or officially remember an event that you consider to be important 纪念；庆贺：*a ceremony to mark the 50th anniversary of the end of the war* 纪念战争结束 50 周年的庆典

• **SHOW CHANGE** 标示变化 **5** [T] **~ sth** to be a sign that sth new is going to happen 是…的迹象；成为…的征兆；表明：*This speech may* ***mark a change in*** *government policy.* 这篇演讲表明政府的政策可能会有变化。◇ *The agreement marks a new phase in international relations.* 这一协议标志着国际关系新时期的到来。

• **GIVE MARK/GRADE** 打分；给成绩 **6** 🔑 [T, I] **~ (sth)** (*especially BrE*) to give marks to students' work 给（学生作业）打分，评分，评成绩：*I hate marking exam papers.* 我讨厌阅卷。◇ *I spend at least six hours a week marking.* 我每周至少要花六个小时批改作业。➲ COMPARE GRADE *v.* (2)

• **GIVE PARTICULAR QUALITY** 赋予特征 **7** [T, usually passive] (*formal*) to give sb/sth a particular quality or character 赋予特征；给…确定性质 SYN **characterize**: **~ sb/sth** *a life marked by suffering* 痛苦的一生 ◇ **~ sb/sth as sth** *He was marked as an enemy of the poor.* 他被列为穷人的敌人。

• **PAY ATTENTION** 注意 **8** [T] (*old-fashioned*) used to tell sb to pay careful attention to sth 留心；留意；注意：**~ sth** *There'll be trouble over this,* ***mark my words.*** 记住我的

话，这件事是会有麻烦的。◇ **~ what, how, etc....** *You mark what I say, John.* 约翰，注意听着。

• IN SPORT 体育运动 **9** [T] **~ sb** (in a team game 成队比赛) to stay close to an opponent in order to prevent them from getting the ball 钉人防守；钉住（对手）: *Hughes was marking Taylor.* 休斯在钉防泰勒。◇ *Our defence had him closely marked.* 我方后卫已经紧紧地钉住了他。➲ SEE ALSO MARKING (4)

IDM ˌ**mark ˈtime 1** to pass the time while you wait for sth more interesting 等待时机: *I'm just marking time in this job—I'm hoping to get into journalism.* 我干这件工作只是在等待时机，我希望能从事新闻工作。**2** (of soldiers 士兵) to make marching movements without moving forwards 原地踏步 ˌ**mark ˈyou** (*old-fashioned, informal, especially BrE*) used to remind sb of sth they should consider in a particular case 无论如何；尽管如此；反正；然而: *She hasn't had much success yet. Mark you, she tries hard.* 她还没取得什么成功，可是她非常努力。

PHR V ˌ**mark sb ˈdown** (*BrE*) to reduce the mark/grade given to sb in an exam, etc. 给低分；压低成绩: *She was marked down because of poor grammar.* 她因语法不好被扣了分。ˌ**mark sb ˈdown as sth** (*especially BrE*) to recognize sb as a particular type 将某人看作；认定某人为: *I hadn't got him marked down as a liberal.* 我当时还没有把他看作自由主义者。ˌ**mark sth↔ˈdown 1** to reduce the price of sth 减价；打折: *All goods have been marked down by 15%.* 所有商品都打八五折。OPP **mark up** ➲ RELATED NOUN MARKDOWN **2** to make a note of sth for future use or action 记下；将…记录下: *The factory is already marked down for demolition.* 这家工厂已登记在案，准备拆除。ˌ**mark sb/sth ˈoff (from sb/sth)** to make sb/sth seem different from other people or things 使与众不同；使有别于其他人（或物）: *Each of London's districts had a distinct character that marked it off from its neighbours.* 伦敦的每个区都有鲜明的特征，与邻近地区不同。ˌ**mark sth↔ˈoff** to separate sth by marking a line between it and sth else 画线分隔；划开: *The playing area was marked off with a white line.* 运动场地用白线画了出来。ˌ**mark sb ˈout as/for sth** to make people recognize sb as special in some way 选定；挑选: *She was marked out for early promotion.* 她被选定要尽早得到擢升。ˌ**mark sth↔ˈout** to draw lines to show the edges of sth 画出界限；画出边界；用线画出范围: *They marked out a tennis court on the lawn.* 他们在草坪上标出网球场。ˌ**mark sth↔ˈup 1** to increase the price of sth 提价；加价；涨价: *Share prices were marked up as soon as trading started.* 交易一开始，股票价格就涨上去了。OPP **mark down** ➲ RELATED NOUN MARKUP (1) **2** (*specialist*) to mark or correct a text, etc., for example for printing 审校；标注排版说明: *to mark up a manuscript* 审校手稿

■ ***noun***

• SPOT/DIRT 污点 **1** 🔑 a small area of dirt, a spot or a cut on a surface that spoils its appearance 污点；污渍；斑点；疤痕: *The children left dirty marks all over the kitchen floor.* 孩子们把厨房的地板弄得污渍斑斑。◇ *a burn/scratch mark* 一块灼伤的 / 抓伤的疤痕 ◇ *Detectives found no marks on the body.* 侦探没有在尸体上发现任何痕迹。**2** 🔑 a noticeable spot or area of colour on the body of a person or an animal which helps you to recognize them（人或动物身上有助于识别的）斑点，记号，色斑: *a horse with a white mark on its head* 头上有块白斑的马 ◇ *He was about six feet tall, with no* ***distinguishing marks****.* 他身高约六英尺，没什么特别的记号。➲ SYNONYMS AT PATCH ➲ SEE ALSO BIRTHMARK, MARKING (1)

• SYMBOL 记号 **3** 🔑 a written or printed symbol that is used as a sign of sth, for example the quality of sth or who made or owns it 符号；记号；（显示质量、制造者或所有者等的）标记: *punctuation marks* 标点符号 ◇ *Any piece of silver bearing his mark is extremely valuable.* 带有他的印记的每一件银器都极有价值。◇ *I put a mark in the margin to remind me to check the figure.* 我在页边做了个记号来提醒自己核对一下这个数字。➲ SEE ALSO EXCLAMATION MARK, QUESTION MARK, TRADEMARK

• SIGN 迹象 **4** a sign that a quality or feeling exists（品质或情感的）标志，迹象，表示: *On the day of the funeral businesses remained closed as* ***a mark of respect****.* 葬礼那天，商户停业以示敬意。◇ *Such coolness under pressure is the mark of a champion.* 在压力下仍能这样保持冷静，这就是冠军相。

• STANDARD/GRADE 标准；成绩 **5** 🔑 (*especially BrE*) a number or letter that is given to show the standard of sb's work or performance or is given to sb for answering sth correctly 成绩；分数；等级: *to get a* ***good/poor mark*** *in English* 英语得分高 / 低 ◇ *to give sb a* ***high/low mark*** 给某人高分 / 低分 ◇ *What's the* ***pass mark*** (= the mark you need in order to pass)? 合格分数是多少？ ◇ *I got* ***full marks*** (= the highest mark possible) *in the spelling test.* 我在拼写测验中得了个满分。◇ (*ironic*) *'You're wearing a tie!'* ***'Full marks*** *for observation.'* "你打领带啦！" "你真眼尖，我给你打满分。" ➲ SEE ALSO BLACK MARK, GRADE *n.* (3) ➲ WORDFINDER NOTE AT EXAM

• LEVEL 水平 **6** a level or point that sth reaches that is thought to be important（重要的）水平，标准点，指标: *Unemployment has passed the four million mark.* 失业人数已突破四百万大关。◇ *She was leading at the half-way mark.* 赛程到一半时是她领先。

• MACHINE/VEHICLE 机器；车辆 **7 Mark** (followed by a number 后接数字) a particular type or model of a machine or vehicle 型号: *the Mark II engine* * II 型发动机

• IN GAS OVEN 煤气烤箱 **8 Mark** (*BrE*) (followed by a number 后接数词) a particular level of temperature in a gas oven 燃气挡；温度刻度: *Preheat the oven to gas Mark 6.* 将烤箱预热到 6 挡。

• SIGNATURE 签名 **9** a cross made on a document instead of a signature by sb who is not able to write their name（文盲在文件上代替签名的）花押

• TARGET 目标 **10** (*formal*) a target 目标；靶子: *Of the blows delivered, barely half found their mark.* 仅有不到半

▼ **SYNONYMS** 同义词辨析

mark

stain • fingerprint • streak • speck • blot • smear • spot

These are all words for a small area of dirt or another substance on a surface. 以上各词均指污点、斑点、污迹。

mark a small area of dirt or other substance on the surface of sth, especially one that spoils its appearance 指污点、污迹、斑点： *The kids left dirty marks all over the kitchen floor.* 孩子们把厨房的地板弄得污迹斑斑。

stain a dirty mark on sth that is difficult to remove, especially one made by a liquid 指污点、污渍： *blood stains* 血迹

fingerprint a mark on a surface made by the pattern of lines on the end of a person's finger, often used by the police to identify criminals 指指纹、指印： *Her fingerprints were all over the gun.* 那支枪上布满了她的指纹。

streak a long thin mark or line that is a different colour from the surface it is on 指条纹、条痕： *She had streaks of grey in her hair.* 她头上已是白发绺绺。

speck a very small mark, spot or piece of a substance on sth 指小点、污点： *There isn't a speck of dust anywhere in the house.* 整间房子一尘不染。

blot a spot or dirty mark left on sth by a substance such as ink or paint being dropped on a surface 指污点、墨渍

smear a mark made by sth such as oil or paint being spread or rubbed on a surface 指污迹、油渍、污渍、污点

spot a small dirty mark on sth 指污迹、污渍、污点： *There were grease spots all over the walls.* 墙上满是油渍。

PATTERNS

- a streak/speck/blot/smear/spot **of** sth
- a **greasy** mark/stain/smear
- an **ink** mark/stain/blot/spot
- a **grease** mark/stain/spot
- to **leave** a mark/stain/fingerprint/streak/speck/blot/smear

M

数的出拳击中目标。◇ *to hit/miss the mark* 击中 / 错过目标 • GERMAN MONEY 德国货币 **11** = DEUTSCHMARK

IDM **be close to/near the 'mark** to be fairly accurate in a guess, statement, etc.（猜测、陈述等）接近准确，几乎无误 **be off the 'mark** not to be accurate in a guess, statement, etc.（猜测、陈述等）不准确，相去甚远，离题：*No, you're way off the mark.* 不行，你根本没说到重点。**be on the 'mark** to be accurate or correct 精确；准确无误：*That estimate was right on the mark.* 那个估计分毫不差。**get off the 'mark** to start scoring, especially in CRICKET（尤指板球运动）开始得分：*Stewart got off the mark with a four.* 斯图尔特以一记四分球开始得分。**,hit/,miss the 'mark** to succeed/fail in achieving or guessing sth 达到 / 没有达到目的；猜测正确 / 错误：*He blushed furiously and Robyn knew she had hit the mark.* 他满脸通红，萝宾知道自己击中了要害。**,leave your/its/a 'mark (on sth/sb)** to have an effect on sth/sb, especially a bad one, that lasts for a long time 留下久远的影响（尤指坏影响）：*Such a traumatic experience was bound to leave its mark on the children.* 这样的痛苦经历一定会长期对孩子们有影响。**,make your/a 'mark (on sth)** to become famous and successful in a particular area（在某领域）取得成功，出名 **not be/feel ,up to the 'mark** (*old-fashioned, BrE*) not to feel as well or lively as usual 感觉不舒服 **on your ,marks, get ,set, 'go!** used to tell runners in a race to get ready and then to start（径赛口令）各就各位，预备，跑！**quick/slow off the 'mark** fast/slow in reacting to a situation（对形势）反应敏捷 / 迟钝 **,up to the 'mark** (*BrE*) (*NAmE* **,up to 'snuff**) as good as it/they should be 达到要求；符合标准 SYN **up to scratch**：*Your work isn't really up to the mark.* 你的工作没有真正达到要求。➲ MORE AT OVERSTEP, TOE *v.*, WIDE *adj.*

mark·down /'mɑːkdaʊn; *NAmE* 'mɑːrk-/ *noun* [usually sing.] a reduction in price 减价；降价

marked /mɑːkt; *NAmE* mɑːrkt/ *adj.* **1** easy to see 显而易见的；明显的；显著的 SYN **noticeable, distinct**：*a marked difference/improvement* 明显的差异 / 进步 ◇ *a marked increase in profits* 利润的显著提高 ◇ *She is quiet and studious, in marked contrast to her sister.* 她沉静勤奋，与她妹妹形成了鲜明的对照。**2** (*linguistics* 语言) (of a word or form of a word 单词或词形) showing a particular feature or style, such as being formal or informal 有标记成分的（如正式或非正式用语）OPP **unmarked** ▶ **mark·ed·ly** /'mɑːkɪdli; *NAmE* 'mɑːrk-/ *adv.*：*Her background is markedly different from her husband's.* 她的背景和她丈夫的截然不同。◇ *This year's sales have risen markedly.* 今年的销售额明显提高了。

IDM **a marked 'man/'woman** a person who is in danger because their enemies want to harm them（遭计划攻击的）目标人物

mark·er /'mɑːkə(r); *NAmE* 'mɑːrk-/ *noun* **1** [C] an object or a sign that shows the position of sth（表示方位的）标记，记号：*a boundary marker* 界标 ◇ *He placed a marker where the ball had landed.* 他在球落地的地方放了个标记。**2** [sing.] **a ~ (of/for sth)** a sign that sth exists or that shows what it is like 标志；标识；表示：*Price is not always an accurate marker of quality.* 价格并不总是质量的准确标志。**3** (*BrE also* **'marker pen**) a pen with a thick FELT tip 记号笔；毡头笔 ➲ VISUAL VOCAB PAGE V71 **4** (*BrE*) (*NAmE* **grader**) a person who marks/grades students' work or exam papers 阅卷人；判作业的人 **5** (*BrE*) (in team games, especially football (SOCCER) 团队比赛，尤指足球) a player who stays close to a player on the other team in order to stop them getting the ball 紧逼防守的队员；钉人的防守队员

mar·ket 🔑 /'mɑːkɪt; *NAmE* 'mɑːrk-/ *noun, verb*

■ *noun* **1** 🔑 [C] an occasion when people buy and sell goods; the open area or building where they meet to do this 集市；市场；商场：*a fruit/flower/antiques market* 水果 / 鲜花 / 古玩市场 ◇ *an indoor/a street market* 室内 / 街头市场 ◇ *market stalls/traders* 集市货摊 / 商贩 ◇ *We buy our fruit and vegetables at the market.* 我们在市场上购买水果和蔬菜。◇ *Thursday is market day.* 星期四是赶集日。◇ *a market town* (= a town in Britain where a regular market is or was held)（英国定期举行集市贸易的）集镇 ➲ VISUAL VOCAB PAGE V3 ➲ SEE ALSO FARMERS' MARKET **2** 🔑 [sing.] business or trade, or the amount of trade in a particular type of goods 交易；买卖；交易量：*the world market in coffee* 世界咖啡交易 ◇ *They have increased their share of the market by 10%.* 他们将其所占的市场份额增加了 10%。◇ *the property/job market* (= the number and type of houses, jobs, etc. that are available) 房地产 / 就业市场 ◇ *They have cornered the market in sportswear* (= sell the most). 他们垄断了运动装的销售。➲ WORDFINDER NOTE AT TRADE ➲ COLLOCATIONS AT BUSINESS **3** 🔑 [C] a particular area, country or section of the population that might buy goods 商品的销售地；行销地区；消费群体：*the Japanese market* 日本市场 ◇ *the global/domestic market* 全球 / 国内销售市场 **4** 🔑 [sing.] **~ (for sth)** the number of people who want to buy sth（顾客对货物或服务的）需求 SYN **demand**：*a growing/declining market for second-hand cars* 不断扩大的 / 萎缩的二手车市场 **5** (*often* **the market**) [sing.] people who buy and sell goods in competition with each other（处于竞争中的）市场经营者，市场：*The market will decide if the TV station has any future.* 电视台是否有前途将取决于市场。◇ *a market-based/market-driven/market-led economy* 以市场为基础的 / 市场推动的 / 市场引导的经济 ➲ SEE ALSO BLACK MARKET, MARKET FORCES **6** [C] = STOCK MARKET：*the futures market* 期货市场 ◇ *a market crash* 股市暴跌 HELP There are many other compounds ending in **market**. You will find them at their place in the alphabet. 以 market 结尾的复合词还有很多，可在各字母中的适当位置查到。

IDM **in the 'market for sth** interested in buying sth 有意购买：*I'm not in the market for a new car at the moment.* 我现在还不想买新车。**on the 'market** available for people to buy 出售；上市；有现货供应：*to put your house on the market* 出售房屋 ◇ *The house came on the market last year.* 这栋房屋去年就上市了。◇ *There are hundreds of different brands on the market.* 有数百种不同的品牌供应。**on the open 'market** available to buy without any restrictions 敞开销售；自由买卖 **play the 'market** to buy and sell STOCKS and shares in order to make a profit 买卖证券和股票 ➲ MORE AT BUYER, PRICE *v.*, SELLER

■ *verb* **~ sth (to sb) (as sth)** to advertise and offer a product for sale; to present sth in a particular way and make people want to buy it 推销；促销 SYN **promote**：*It is marketed as a low-alcohol wine.* 它作为一种低度酒投放市场。◇ *School meals need to be marketed to children in the same way as other food.* 校餐也要以其他食品的推销方法推销给孩子。➲ SEE ALSO MARKETING

mar·ket·able /'mɑːkɪtəbl; *NAmE* 'mɑːrk-/ *adj.* easy to sell; attractive to customers or employers 容易出售的；畅销的；有销路的：*marketable products/skills/qualifications* 受欢迎的产品 / 技能 / 资历 ▶ **mar·ket·abil·ity** /,mɑːkɪtə'bɪləti; *NAmE* ,mɑːrk-/ *noun* [U]

mar·ket·eer /,mɑːkɪ'tɪə(r); *NAmE* ,mɑːrkə'tɪr/ *noun* (usually in compounds 通常构成复合词) a person who is in favour of a particular system of buying and selling 喜欢某种贸易体制的人：*a free marketeer* (= a person who believes in a FREE MARKET system of trade) 主张自由贸易者 ➲ SEE ALSO BLACK MARKETEER

,market 'forces *noun* [pl.] a free system of trade in which prices and wages rise and fall without being controlled by the government 市场调节作用；市场力量

,market 'garden (*BrE*) (*US* **'truck farm**) *noun* a type of farm where vegetables are grown for sale（种植蔬菜和水果以供出售的）商品果蔬农场 ▶ **,market 'gardener** *noun* **,market 'gardening** *noun* [U]

mar·ket·ing 🔑 /'mɑːkɪtɪŋ; *NAmE* 'mɑːrk-/ *noun* [U] the activity of presenting, advertising and selling a company's products or services in the best possible way 市场营销：*a marketing campaign* 促销活动 ◇ *She works in sales and marketing.* 她在市场营销部工作。➲ WORDFINDER NOTE AT ADVERTISE ➲ COLLOCATIONS AT BUSINESS ➲ SEE ALSO DIRECT MARKETING ▶ **mar·ket·er** *noun*：*a company that is a developer and marketer of software* 一家软件开发和销售公司

ˈmarketing mix *noun* (*business* 商) the combination of the features of a product, its price, the way it is advertised and where it is sold, each of which a company can adjust to persuade people to buy the product 营销组合（即产品特征、价格、广告宣传方式以及营销地的组合，企业可调整这些项目以实现其营销目标）

ˌmarket ˈleader *noun* **1** the company that sells the largest quantity of a particular kind of product 同类商品的销售大户；市场份额的最大占有者 **2** a product that is the most successful of its kind 最畅销产品；同类商品中的佼佼者

mar·ket·place /ˈmɑːkɪtpleɪs; *NAmE* ˈmɑːrk-/ *noun* **1 the marketplace** [sing.] the activity of competing with other companies to buy and sell goods, services, etc. 市场竞争：*Companies must be able to survive in the marketplace.* 公司必须有能力在市场竞争中生存下去。◇ *the education marketplace* 教育市场 **2** (*also* **ˌmarket ˈsquare**) [C] an open area in a town where a market is held 集市；市场

ˌmarket ˈprice *noun* the price that people are willing to pay for sth at a particular time 市场价；市价；时价

ˌmarket reˈsearch (*also* **ˌmarket ˈresearch**) *noun* [U] the work of collecting information about what people buy and why 市场调研；市场调查

ˌmarket ˈshare *noun* [U, sing.] (*business* 商) the amount that a company sells of its products or services compared with other companies selling the same things 市场占有率；市场份额：*They claim to have a 40% worldwide market share.* 他们声称占有全球 40% 的市场。➲ COLLOCATIONS AT BUSINESS

ˌmarket ˈvalue *noun* [U, sing.] what sth would be worth if it were sold 市场价值；市值

mark·ing /ˈmɑːkɪŋ; *NAmE* ˈmɑːrk-/ *noun* **1** [C, usually pl.] a pattern of colours or marks on animals, birds or wood（兽类、鸟类或树木的）斑纹，花纹，斑点 **2** [C, usually pl.] lines, colours or shapes painted on roads, vehicles, etc.（刷在道路、车辆等上的）线条，颜色，形状：*Road markings indicate where you can stop.* 道路标志告诉你哪里可以停车。**3** [U] (*especially BrE*) (*NAmE usually* **grad·ing**) the activity of checking and correcting the written work or exam papers of students 批改；打分；阅卷：*She does her marking in the evenings.* 她晚上批改作业。**4** [U] (in team games, especially football (SOCCER) 团队比赛，尤指足球) the practice of staying close to a player on the other team in order to stop them getting the ball 钉人防守

marks·man /ˈmɑːksmən; *NAmE* ˈmɑːrk-/, **marks·woman** /ˈmɑːkswʊmən; *NAmE* ˈmɑːrk-/ *noun* (*pl.* **-men** /-mən/, **-women** /-wɪmɪn/) a person who is skilled in accurate shooting 神枪手；神射手

marks·man·ship /ˈmɑːksmənʃɪp; *NAmE* ˈmɑːrk-/ *noun* [U] skill in shooting 射击术

mark·up /ˈmɑːkʌp; *NAmE* ˈmɑːrk-/ *noun* **1** [usually sing.] an increase in the price of sth based on the difference between the cost of producing it and the price it is sold at （基于成本价与销售价之间差价的）加成：*an average markup of 10%* 平均 10% 的加成 **2** [U] (*computing* 计) the symbols used in computer documents which give information about the structure of the document and tell the computer how it is to appear on the computer screen, or how it is to appear when printed 置标，标记符号（标示计算机文档结构和显示、打印形式）：*a markup language* 置标语言

marl /mɑːl; *NAmE* mɑːrl/ *noun* **1** [U, C] soil consisting of CLAY and LIME (1) 泥灰岩；泥灰 **2** [U] a type of cloth with threads in it that are not of an even colour 夹花纱线织物：*blue marl leggings* 蓝底夹花纱线绑腿

mar·lin /ˈmɑːlɪn; *NAmE* ˈmɑːrlɪn/ *noun* (*pl.* **mar·lin**) a large sea fish with a long sharp nose, that people catch for sport 枪鱼，旗鱼，马林鱼（吻长而尖）

mar·ma·lade /ˈmɑːməleɪd; *NAmE* ˈmɑːrm-/ *noun* [U] jam/jelly made from oranges, lemons, etc., eaten especially for breakfast 橘子酱；酸果酱 ➲ COMPARE JAM *n.* (1)

Mar·mite™ /ˈmɑːmaɪt; *NAmE* ˈmɑːrm-/ *noun* [U] (*BrE*) a dark substance made from YEAST and spread on bread, etc. 马麦酱（由酵母制成，呈黑色，抹在面包等食物上食用） SYN **yeast extract**：*Marmite sandwiches* 马麦酱三明治 HELP Because it is thought that people either love or hate Marmite, it is used to refer to things that create strong reactions. 由于人们对马麦酱的反应两极化，要么非常喜爱，要么非常厌恶，这个词因此被用来形容引起激烈反应的事物：*a marmite issue* 反应两极化的议题 ◇ *They're a marmite band.* 他们是一支争议性极大的乐队。

mar·mo·set /ˈmɑːməzet; *NAmE* ˈmɑːrm-/ *noun* a small MONKEY with a long thick tail, that lives in Central and S America 狨（栖于中南美洲的小长尾猴）

mar·mot /ˈmɑːmət; *NAmE* ˈmɑːrmət/ *noun* a small European or American animal that lives in holes in the ground 旱獭，土拨鼠（居于地穴，分布于欧洲及美洲）

ma·roon /məˈruːn/ *adj., noun, verb*
■ ***adj.*** dark brownish-red in colour 紫褐色的；褐红色的
■ ***noun*** **1** [U] a dark brownish-red colour 褐红色；紫褐色 **2** [C] a large FIREWORK that shoots into the air and makes a loud noise, used to attract attention, especially at sea（海上作为信号的）鞭炮
■ ***verb*** [usually passive] **~ sb** to leave sb in a place that they cannot escape from, for example an island 困住；使无法逃脱 SYN **strand**：*'Lord of the Flies' is a novel about English schoolboys marooned on a desert island.*《蝇王》是一本关于一群被困在荒岛上的英国男学童的小说。

marque /mɑːk; *NAmE* mɑːrk/ *noun* (*formal*) a well-known make of a product, especially a car, that is expensive and fashionable 知名品牌（尤指汽车）：*the Porsche marque* 保时捷的品牌

mar·quee /mɑːˈkiː; *NAmE* mɑːrˈkiː/ *noun, adj.*
■ ***noun*** **1** a large tent used at social events（大型活动用的）大帐篷 **2** (*NAmE*) a covered entrance to a theatre, hotel, etc., often with a sign on or above it（戏院、酒店等入口处，通常带有标记的）遮檐
■ ***adj.*** [only before noun] (*especially NAmE*) (especially in sport 尤用于体育运动) most important or most popular 最重要的；最受欢迎的；杰出的：*He is one of the marquee names in men's tennis.* 他是男子网球坛大名鼎鼎的人物之一。

mar·quess (*also* **mar·quis**) /ˈmɑːkwɪs; *NAmE* ˈmɑːrk-/ *noun* (in Britain) a NOBLEMAN of high rank between an EARL and a DUKE（英国）侯爵：*the Marquess of Bath* 巴斯侯爵 ➲ COMPARE MARCHIONESS

mar·quet·ry /ˈmɑːkɪtri; *NAmE* ˈmɑːrk-/ *noun* [U] patterns or pictures made of pieces of wood on the surface of furniture, etc.; the art of making these patterns（家具等的）镶嵌细工，镶嵌艺术

mar·quis /ˈmɑːkwɪs; *NAmE* ˈmɑːrk-/ *noun* **1** (in some European countries but not Britain) a NOBLEMAN of high rank between a COUNT and a DUKE（除英国外一些欧洲国家的）侯爵 **2** = MARQUESS

mar·quise /mɑːˈkiːz; *NAmE* mɑːrˈkiːz/ *noun* **1** the wife of a marquis 侯爵夫人 **2** a woman who has the rank of a marquis 女侯爵 ➲ COMPARE MARCHIONESS

mar·ram grass /ˈmærəm ɡrɑːs; *NAmE* ɡræs/ (*also* **mar·ram**) *noun* [U] a type of grass that grows in sand, often planted to prevent sand DUNES from being destroyed by the wind, rain, etc. 滩草，沙茅草（用以固沙）

mar·riage 🔑 /ˈmærɪdʒ/ *noun* **1** 🔑 [C] the legal relationship between a husband and wife 结婚；婚姻：***a happy/an unhappy marriage*** 幸福的 / 不幸福的婚姻 ◇ *All of her children's marriages ended in divorce.* 她的孩子们最终都离了婚。◇ *an* ***arranged marriage*** (= one in which the parents choose a husband or wife for their child) 一桩包办的婚姻 ◇ *She has two children by a previous marriage.* 她和前夫有两个孩子。➲ SEE ALSO MIXED **2** [C] (in some countries) a relationship similar to husband and wife between partners of the same sex（某些国家）同性婚姻

M

3 [U] the state of being married 婚姻生活；已婚状态：*They don't believe in marriage.* 他们不相信婚姻。◇ *My parents are celebrating 30 years of marriage.* 我的父母亲即将庆祝结婚 30 周年。4 [C] the ceremony in which two people become husband and wife 婚礼：*Their marriage took place in a local church.* 他们的婚礼是在当地一所教堂里举行的。HELP **Wedding** is more common in this meaning. 表示"婚礼"，wedding 更为常见。➲ WORDFINDER NOTE AT LOVE, WEDDING

IDM **by 'marriage** when sb is related to you **by marriage**, they are married to sb in your family, or you are married to sb in their family 通过姻亲关系 ➲ MORE AT HAND *n.*

mar·riage·able /ˈmærɪdʒəbl/ *adj.* (*old-fashioned*) suitable for marriage 适婚的：*She had reached marriageable age.* 当时她已经到了适婚年龄。

'marriage broker *noun* a person who is paid to arrange for two people to meet and marry（职业）婚姻介绍人，媒人

'marriage bureau *noun* (*old-fashioned, BrE*) an organization that introduces people who are looking for sb to marry 婚姻介绍所

'marriage certificate (*US* **'marriage license**) *noun* a legal document that proves two people are married 结婚证书

,marriage 'guidance *noun* [U] (*BrE*) advice that is given by specially trained people to couples with problems in their marriage 婚姻指导；婚姻咨询

'marriage licence (*BrE*) (*NAmE* **'marriage license**) *noun* **1** a document that allows two people to get married 结婚许可证 **2** (*US*) (*BrE, NAmE also* **'marriage certificate**) a legal document that proves two people are married 结婚证（书）

,marriage of con'venience *noun* a marriage that is made for practical, financial or political reasons and not because the two people love each other（出于实际需要、金钱或政治原因的）权宜婚姻

mar·ried /ˈmærid/ *adj.* **1** having a husband or wife 已婚的：*a* ***married man/woman*** 已婚男子 / 女子 ◇ *Is he married?* 他结婚了吗？◇ *a happily married couple* 一对幸福结合的伉俪 ◇ *She's* ***married to*** *John.* 她嫁给了约翰。◇ *Rachel and David are* ***getting married*** *on Saturday.* 雷切尔和戴维将在星期六结婚。◇ *How long have you been married?* 你结婚多长时间了？OPP **unmarried** ➲ COLLOCATIONS AT MARRIAGE **2** [only before noun] connected with marriage 婚姻的；结婚的：*Are you enjoying married life?* 你喜欢你的婚姻生活吗？◇ *Her married name* (= the family name of her husband) *is Jones.* 她婚后随夫姓琼斯。**3 ~ to sth** very involved in sth so that you have no time for other activities or interests 专心（于某事）；全神贯注（于某事）：*My brother is married to his job.* 我弟弟一心扑在工作上。

mar·row /ˈmærəʊ; *NAmE* -roʊ/ *noun* **1** [U] = BONE MARROW **2** (*BrE*) [U, C] a large vegetable that grows on the ground. Marrows are long and thick with dark green skin and white flesh. 西葫芦 ➲ VISUAL VOCAB PAGE V34

mar·row·bone /ˈmærəʊbəʊn; *NAmE* ˈmæroʊboʊn/ *noun* a bone which still contains the MARROW (= the substance inside) and is used in making food（烹饪用）髓骨

marry /ˈmæri/ *verb* (**mar·ries, marry·ing, mar·ried, mar·ried**) **1** [T, I] to become the husband or wife of sb; to get married to sb（和某人）结婚；嫁；娶：**~ (sb)** *She married a German.* 她嫁给了一个德国人。◇ *He never married.* 他终身未娶。◇ *I guess I'm* ***not the marrying kind*** (= the kind of person who wants to get married). 我觉得我不是那种想结婚的人。◇ **+ adj.** *They* ***married young.*** 他们很年轻时就结了婚。HELP It is more common to say: *They're* ***getting married*** *next month.* than: *They're* ***marrying*** *next month.* * They're getting married next month 比 They're marrying next month 更为常见。➲ COLLOCATIONS AT MARRIAGE **2** [T] **~ sb** to perform a ceremony in which a man and woman

> **WORD FAMILY**
> marry *verb*
> marriage *noun*
> married *adj.* (≠ unmarried)

M

▼ **COLLOCATIONS** 词语搭配

Marriage and divorce 结婚和离婚

Romance 恋爱

- **fall/be** (madly/deeply/hopelessly) **in love** (with sb)（疯狂地 / 深深地 / 无可救药地）爱上 / 爱着（某人）
- **be/believe in/fall in** love at first sight 是 / 相信一见钟情；一见钟情
- **be/find** true love/the love of your life 是 / 找到真爱 / 一生的爱
- **suffer** (**from**) (the pains/pangs of) unrequited love 受单相思之苦
- **have/feel/show/express** great/deep/genuine affection for sb/sth 对某人 / 某事有着 / 表示出强烈的 / 深深的 / 真挚的爱慕之情
- **meet/marry** your husband/wife/partner/fiancé/fiancée/boyfriend/girlfriend 与丈夫 / 妻子 / 伴侣 / 未婚夫 / 未婚妻 / 男朋友 / 女朋友结识 / 结婚
- **have/go on** a (blind) **date** 有个 / 去约会 / 相亲
- **be going out with**/ (*especially NAmE*) **dating** a guy/girl/boy/man/woman 与一个小伙子 / 女生 / 男生 / 男人 / 女人在谈恋爱
- **move in with/live with** your boyfriend/girlfriend/partner 与男朋友 / 女朋友 / 伴侣同居

Weddings 婚礼

- **get/be** engaged/married/divorced 订婚；结婚；离婚
- **arrange/plan** a wedding 安排婚礼
- **have** a big wedding/a honeymoon/a happy marriage 举行隆重的婚礼；度蜜月；婚姻幸福
- **have/enter into** an arranged marriage 有一个 / 走入包办婚姻
- **call off/cancel/postpone** your wedding 取消 / 推迟婚礼
- **invite sb to/go to/attend** a wedding/a wedding ceremony/a wedding reception 邀请某人出席 / 参加婚礼 / 结婚典礼 / 结婚喜宴
- **conduct/perform** a wedding ceremony 举行结婚典礼
- **exchange** rings/wedding vows/marriage vows 交换戒指；互致结婚誓言
- **congratulate/toast/raise a glass to** the happy couple 祝贺这对幸福的新人；为这对幸福的伉俪干杯
- **be/go on** honeymoon (with your wife/husband)（与妻子 / 丈夫）在 / 去度蜜月
- **celebrate** your first (wedding) anniversary 庆祝第一个（结婚）纪念日

Separation and divorce 分居和离婚

- **be unfaithful to**/ (*informal*) **cheat on** your husband/wife/partner/fiancé/fiancée/boyfriend/girlfriend 对丈夫 / 妻子 / 伴侣 / 未婚夫 / 未婚妻 / 男朋友 / 女朋友不忠
- **have** an affair (with sb)（和某人）有暧昧关系
- **break off/end** an engagement/a relationship 解除 / 终止婚约 / 恋爱关系
- **break up with/split up with**/ (*informal*) **dump** your boyfriend/girlfriend 与男友 / 女友分手；甩掉男友 / 女友
- **separate from/be separated from/leave/divorce** your husband/wife 和丈夫 / 妻子分居；离弃丈夫 / 妻子；与丈夫 / 妻子离婚
- **annul/dissolve** a marriage 宣布婚姻无效；解除婚姻关系
- **apply for/ask for/go through/get** a divorce 申请 / 要求 / 办理离婚；离婚
- **get/gain/be awarded/have/lose** custody of the children 获得 / 被判予 / 拥有 / 失去对孩子的监护权
- **pay** alimony/child support (to your ex-wife/husband)（向前妻 / 前夫）支付生活费 / 子女抚养费

become husband and wife 为…主持婚礼：*They were married by the local priest.* 当地牧师为他们主持了婚礼。 **3** [T] **~ sb (to sb)** to find a husband or wife for sb, especially your daughter or son 把…嫁给；为…娶亲 **4** [T] **~ sth and/to/with sth** (*formal*) to combine two different things, ideas, etc. successfully（使不同的事物、观点等）相结合，结合在一起 SYN **unite**: *The music business marries art and commerce.* 音乐行业将艺术和商业结合在一起。

IDM **marry in 'haste (, repent at 'leisure)** (*saying*) people who marry quickly, without really getting to know each other, may discover later that they have made a mistake 草草结婚后悔多 **marry 'money** to marry a rich person 和富人结婚

PHR V **ˌmarry 'into sth** to become part of a family or group because you have married sb who belongs to it 因结婚而成为（家庭或团体的）成员：*She married into the aristocracy.* 她因为婚姻关系而跻身贵族。**ˌmarry sb↔'off (to sb)** (*disapproving*) to find a husband or wife for sb, especially your daughter or son 把…嫁给；为…娶亲 **ˌmarry sth↔'up (with sth)** to combine two things, people or parts of sth successfully（将两个事物、人或部分）结合，匹配

Mars /mɑːz; *NAmE* mɑːrz/ *noun* the planet in the SOLAR SYSTEM that is fourth in order of distance from the sun, between the Earth and Jupiter 火星

Mar·sala /mɑːˈsɑːlə; *NAmE* mɑːrˈs-/ *noun* [U] a dark strong sweet wine from Sicily. It is usually drunk with the sweet course of a meal. 马尔萨拉葡萄酒（产于西西里岛的马尔萨拉，通常吃甜食时饮用）

marsh /mɑːʃ; *NAmE* mɑːrʃ/ *noun* [C, U] an area of low land that is always soft and wet because there is nowhere for the water to flow away to 湿地；沼泽；草本沼泽：*Cows were grazing on the marshes.* 牛群在湿地上吃草。 ➲ VISUAL VOCAB PAGE V3 ▸ **marshy** *adj.*：*marshy ground/land* 沼泽地

mar·shal /ˈmɑːʃl; *NAmE* ˈmɑːrʃl/ *noun, verb*
- **noun 1** (usually in compounds 通常构成复合词) an officer of the highest rank in the British army or AIR FORCE（英国）陆军元帅，空军元帅：*Field Marshal Lord Haig* 陆军元帅黑格勋爵 ◇ *Marshal of the Royal Air Force* 皇家空军元帅 ➲ SEE ALSO AIR CHIEF MARSHAL, AIR MARSHAL, AIR VICE-MARSHAL, FIELD MARSHAL **2** a person responsible for making sure that public events, especially sports events, take place without any problems, and for controlling crowds 司仪；典礼官 SYN **steward** **3** (in the US) an officer whose job is to put court orders into effect（美国法院的）执行官：*a federal marshal* 联邦法庭的执行官 **4** (in some US cities) an officer of high rank in a police or fire department（一些美国城市的）警察局长，消防局长
- **verb** (**-ll-**, *US* **-l-**) (*formal*) **1 ~ sth** to gather together and organize the people, things, ideas, etc. that you need for a particular purpose 结集；收集；安排 SYN **muster**: *They have begun **marshalling forces** to send relief to the hurricane victims.* 他们已经开始结集队伍将救济物资送给遭受飓风侵害的灾民。◇ *to **marshal your arguments/thoughts/facts*** 整理你的论点 / 想法 / 论据 **2 ~ sb** to control or organize a large group of people 控制人群；组织；维持秩序：*Police were brought in to marshal the crowd.* 警察奉命来维持秩序。

'marshalling yard *noun* (*BrE*) a place where railway WAGONS are connected, prepared, etc. to form trains（铁路的）调车场，编组站

ˌMarshal of the ˌRoyal 'Air Force *noun* the highest rank of officer in the British AIR FORCE（英国）空军元帅

'marsh gas *noun* [U] a gas that is produced in a marsh when plants decay 沼气

marsh·land /ˈmɑːʃlænd; *NAmE* ˈmɑːrʃ-/ *noun* [U, C] an area of soft wet land 沼泽地

marsh·mal·low /ˌmɑːʃˈmæləʊ; *NAmE* ˈmɑːrʃmeloʊ/ *noun* [C, U] a pink or white sweet/candy that feels soft and ELASTIC when you chew it 棉花软糖

mar·su·pial /mɑːˈsuːpiəl; *NAmE* mɑːrˈs-/ *noun* any animal that carries its young in a pocket of skin (called a POUCH) on the mother's stomach. KANGAROOS and KOALAS are marsupials. 有袋类动物（如袋鼠和树袋熊）➲ VISUAL VOCAB PAGE V12 ▸ **mar·su·pial** *adj.* [only before noun]

mart /mɑːt; *NAmE* mɑːrt/ *noun* (*especially NAmE*) a place where things are bought and sold 贸易场所；集市：*a used car mart* 旧车市场

mar·ten /ˈmɑːtɪn; *NAmE* ˈmɑːrtn/ *noun* a small wild animal with a long body, short legs and sharp teeth. Martens live in forests and eat smaller animals. 貂：*a pine marten* 松貂

mar·tial /ˈmɑːʃl; *NAmE* ˈmɑːrʃl/ *adj.* (*formal*) [only before noun] connected with fighting or war 战争的；军事的

ˌmartial 'art *noun* [usually pl.] any of the fighting sports that include JUDO and KARATE 武术

ˌmartial 'law *noun* [U] a situation where the army of a country controls an area instead of the police during a time of trouble 军事管制；戒严：*to **declare/impose/lift martial law*** 宣布 / 实行 / 取消军事管制 ◇ *The city remains firmly **under martial law**.* 这个城市仍实施严格的军事管制。

Mar·tian /ˈmɑːʃn; *NAmE* ˈmɑːrʃn/ *adj., noun*
- **adj.** (*astronomy* 天) related to or coming from the planet Mars 火星的；来自火星的
- **noun** an imaginary creature from the planet Mars（假想的）火星人，火星生物

mar·tinet /ˌmɑːtɪˈnet; *NAmE* ˌmɑːrtnˈet/ *noun* (*formal*) a very strict person who demands that other people obey orders or rules completely 严格执行纪律的人

mar·tini /mɑːˈtiːni; *NAmE* mɑːrˈt-/ *noun* **1 Martini™** [U] a type of VERMOUTH 马提尼酒（一种品牌的味美思酒）**2** [U, C] an alcoholic drink made with GIN and VERMOUTH 马提尼酒（由杜松子酒和味美思酒调配而成）**3** [C] a glass of martini 一杯马提尼酒：*a dry martini* 一杯干马提尼酒

ˌMartin ˌLuther ˌKing 'Jr. Day *noun* a national holiday in the US on the third Monday in January to celebrate the birthday of Martin Luther King, Jr., who was active in the struggle to win more rights for Black Americans 马丁・路德・金纪念日（美国假日，在一月份第三个星期一，纪念积极争取美国黑人权利的马丁・路德・金的生日）

mar·tyr /ˈmɑːtə(r); *NAmE* ˈmɑːrt-/ *noun, verb*
- **noun 1** a person who suffers very much or is killed because of their religious or political beliefs 殉道者；烈士：*the early Christian martyrs* 早期基督教殉道者 ◇ *a martyr to the cause of freedom* 为了自由事业而献身的烈士 **2** (*usually disapproving*) a person who tries to get sympathy from other people by telling them how much he or she is suffering 乞怜者（向人诉苦以博取同情）**3 ~ to sth** (*informal*) a person who suffers very much because of an illness, problem or situation（因疾病或困难局面）长期受苦者，长期受折磨者：*She's a martyr to her nerves.* 她长期忍受神经紧张之苦。
- **verb** [usually passive] **~ sb** to kill sb because of their religious or political beliefs（因宗教或政治信仰）使殉难，处死

mar·tyr·dom /ˈmɑːtədəm; *NAmE* ˈmɑːrtərdəm/ *noun* [U] the suffering or death of a martyr 殉难；殉道

mar·tyred /ˈmɑːtəd; *NAmE* ˈmɑːrtərd/ *adj.* [usually before noun] (*disapproving*) showing pain or suffering so that people will be kind and sympathetic towards you（为赢得同情）表现出痛苦的，满脸苦相的：*She wore a perpetually martyred expression.* 她总是那么一副可怜兮兮的样子。

mar·vel /ˈmɑːvl; *NAmE* ˈmɑːrvl/ *noun, verb*
- **noun 1** a wonderful and surprising person or thing 令人惊异的人（或事）；奇迹 SYN **wonder**: *the **marvels** of nature/technology* 大自然的 / 技术的奇迹 **2 marvels** [pl.] wonderful results or things that have been achieved 不平凡的成果；成就；奇迹 SYN **wonders**: *The doctors have done marvels for her.* 医生为她创造了奇迹。

M

■ *verb* (-ll-, *US* -l-) [I, T] ~ (at sth) | ~ that… | + speech to be very surprised or impressed by sth 感到惊奇；大为赞叹：*Everyone marvelled at his courage.* 人人都对他的勇气惊叹不已。➲ MORE LIKE THIS 36, page R29

mar·vel·lous (*US* **mar·vel·ous**) /ˈmɑːvələs; *NAmE* ˈmɑːrv-/ *adj.* extremely good; wonderful 极好的；非凡的 SYN **fantastic, splendid**: *This will be a marvellous opportunity for her.* 这对她可是千载难逢的机会。◇ *The weather was marvellous.* 天气棒极了。◇ ***It's marvellous** what modern technology can do.* 现代技术所能做的真是太了不起了。▸ **mar·vel·lous·ly** (*US* **mar·vel·ous·ly**) *adv.*

Marx·ism /ˈmɑːksɪzəm; *NAmE* ˈmɑːrks-/ *noun* [U] the political and economic theories of Karl Marx (1818–83) which explain the changes and developments in society as the result of opposition between the social classes 马克思主义 ▸ **Marx·ist** /ˈmɑːksɪst; *NAmE* ˈmɑːrksɪst/ *noun* **Marx·ist** /ˈmɑːksɪst; *NAmE* ˈmɑːrksɪst/ *adj.*: ***Marxist theory/doctrine/ideology*** 马克思主义理论 / 信条 / 意识形态

Mary Celeste /ˌmeəri sɪˈlest; *NAmE* ˌmeri/ (*also* **Marie Celeste**) *noun* [sing.] used to talk about a place where all the people who should be there have disappeared in a mysterious way 神秘的失踪地：*Where is everyone? It's like the Mary Celeste here today.* 人都到哪儿去了？今天这里的人都神秘失踪了。ORIGIN From the name of the US ship *Mary Celeste*, which in 1872 was found at sea with nobody on board. 源自美国玛丽·西莉斯特号轮船船名，1872 年在海上被发现时船上空无一人。

M

mar·zi·pan /ˈmɑːzɪpæn; ˌmɑːzɪˈpæn; *NAmE* ˈmɑːrtsəpæn; ˈmɑːrz-/ *noun* [U] a sweet firm substance, sometimes with yellow colour added, made from ALMONDS, sugar and eggs and used to make sweets/candy and to cover cakes 杏仁蛋白糖（用于制作糖果或装饰蛋糕）

ma·sala /məˈsɑːlə/ *noun* [U] **1** a mixture of spices used in S Asian cooking 马萨拉（用于南亚烹饪的混合调味品）**2** a dish made with masala 马萨拉菜肴：*chicken masala* 马萨拉鸡

mas·cara /mæˈskɑːrə; *NAmE* -ˈskærə/ *noun* [U] a substance that is put on EYELASHES to make them look dark and thick 睫毛膏；染睫毛油 ➲ WORDFINDER NOTE AT MAKE-UP ➲ VISUAL VOCAB PAGE V65

mas·cot /ˈmæskət; *NAmE* -skɑːt/ *noun* an animal, a toy, etc. that people believe will bring them good luck, or that represents an organization, etc. 吉祥物：*The team's mascot is a giant swan.* 这个队的吉祥物是只大天鹅。◇ *Fuleco—the official mascot of the 2014 FIFA World Cup* * 2014 年世界杯足球赛的指定吉祥物 —— 福来哥 ➲ WORDFINDER NOTE AT LUCK

mas·cu·line /ˈmæskjəlɪn/ *adj.*, *noun*

■ *adj.* **1** having the qualities or appearance considered to be typical of men; connected with or like men 男子汉的；男人的；像男人的：*He was handsome and strong, and very masculine.* 他英俊强壮，富有男子汉气概。◇ *That suit makes her look very masculine.* 她穿那套衣服看起来很男性化。➲ COMPARE FEMININE *adj.* (1), MALE *adj.* (1) **2** (*grammar* 语法) belonging to a class of words that refer to male people or animals and often have a special form 阳性的：*'He' and 'him' are masculine pronouns.* * he 和 him 都是阳性代词。**3** (*grammar* 语法) (in some languages 用于某些语言) belonging to a class of nouns, pronouns or adjectives that have masculine GENDER, not FEMININE or NEUTER 阳性的：*The French word for 'sun' is masculine.* 法语单词"太阳"是阳性的。

■ *noun* **1 the masculine** [sing.] the masculine GENDER (= form of nouns, adjectives and pronouns) （词语的）阳性 **2** [C] a masculine word or word form 阳性词；阳性词形 ➲ COMPARE FEMININE *n.*, NEUTER *adj.*

mas·cu·lin·ity /ˌmæskjuˈlɪnəti/ *noun* [U] the quality of being masculine 男子气概；男性；阳性：*He felt it was a threat to his masculinity.* 他觉得这对他的男子气概是一种威胁。

mas·cu·lin·ize (*BrE also* **-ise**) /ˈmæskjələnaɪz/ *verb* ~ **sth/sb** (*formal*) to make sth or sb more like a man 使男性化；使雄性化

mash /mæʃ/ *noun*, *verb*

■ *noun* **1** (*especially BrE*) = MASHED POTATO **2** [U] grain cooked in water until soft, used to feed farm animals （煮软的）谷物饲料 **3** [U] a mixture of MALT grains and hot water, used for making beer, etc. 麦芽浆（用于酿制啤酒）**4** [sing.] **a ~ (of sth)** any food that has been crushed into a soft mass 糊状食物：*The soup was a mash of grain and vegetables.* 那是用粮食和蔬菜做成的浓汤。➲ SEE ALSO MISHMASH

■ *verb* ~ **sth (up)** to crush food into a soft mass 捣烂，捣碎（食物）：*Mash the fruit up with a fork.* 用叉子将水果捣烂。➲ COLLOCATIONS AT COOKING ▸ **mashed** *adj.*：*mashed banana* 香蕉泥

ˌmashed poˈtato (*also* **ˌmashed poˈtatoes**, **mash** *especially in BrE*) *noun* [U] potatoes that have been boiled and crushed into a soft mass, often with butter and milk 土豆泥，马铃薯泥（常调入黄油和牛奶）

mashup /ˈmæʃʌp/ *noun* a combination of elements from different sources used to create a new song, video, computer file, program, etc. 聚合应用，跨界，混搭（集成不同资源，创建新的歌曲、视频、计算机文件、程序等）：*a video mashup* 视频混搭

masks 面具；面罩

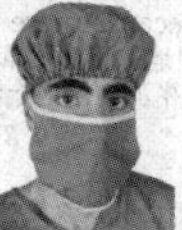

surgical mask
医用口罩

Halloween mask
万圣节面具

mask /mɑːsk; *NAmE* mæsk/ *noun*, *verb*

■ *noun* **1** a covering for part or all of the face, worn to hide or protect it 面具；面罩：*a gas/surgical mask* 防毒面具；医用口罩 ◇ *The robbers wore stocking masks.* 强盗戴着长筒袜面罩。➲ VISUAL VOCAB PAGES V44, V48, V52 ➲ SEE ALSO OXYGEN MASK **2** something that covers your face and has another face painted on it 假面具：*The kids were all wearing animal masks.* 孩子们都戴着动物面具。➲ SEE ALSO DEATH MASK **3** a thick cream made of various substances that you put on your face and neck in order to improve the quality of your skin 护肤膜；面膜：*a face mask* 面膜 **4** [usually sing.] a manner or an expression that hides your true character or feelings 伪装；掩饰：*He longed to throw off the mask of respectability.* 他渴望丢掉那副道貌岸然的伪装。◇ *Her face was a cold blank mask.* 她装出一副冷冰冰毫无表情的样子。

■ *verb* ~ **sth** to hide a feeling, smell, fact, etc. so that it cannot be easily seen or noticed 掩饰；掩藏 SYN **disguise, veil**: *She masked her anger with a smile.* 她用微笑来掩饰她的愤怒。➲ SYNONYMS AT HIDE

masked /mɑːskt; *NAmE* mæskt/ *adj.* wearing a mask 戴着面具（或面罩）的：*a masked gunman* 戴着面具的持枪歹徒

ˌmasked ˈball *noun* a formal party at which guests wear masks 假面舞会；化装舞会

ˈmasking tape *noun* [U] sticky tape that you use to keep an area clean or protected when you are painting around or near it 胶纸带，遮盖胶带（刷油漆时盖住不需油漆的部分）

maso·chism /ˈmæsəkɪzəm/ *noun* [U] **1** the practice of getting sexual pleasure from being physically hurt 性受虐狂 ➲ COMPARE SADISM (2) **2** (*informal*) the enjoyment of sth that most people would find unpleasant or painful 受虐狂：*You spent the whole weekend in a tent in the* *rain? That's masochism!* 下着雨，你就在帐篷里度过了整个周末？真是自讨苦吃！ ▶ **maso·chist** /-kɪst/ *noun* **maso·chis·tic** /ˌmæsəˈkɪstɪk/ *adj.*：*masochistic behaviour/tendencies* 受虐狂行为 / 倾向

mason /ˈmeɪsn/ *noun* **1** a person who builds using stone, or works with stone 石匠；泥瓦匠 **2 Mason** = FREEMASON

the Mason-Dixon Line /ˌmeɪsn ˈdɪksn laɪn/ *noun* [sing.] the border between the US states of Maryland and Pennsylvania that is thought of as the dividing line between the south of the US and the north. In the past it formed the northern border of the states where SLAVES were owned. 梅森－迪克森线（美国马里兰州与宾夕法尼亚州之间的分界线，为过去蓄奴州的最北边界线）

Ma·son·ic /məˈsɒnɪk; *NAmE* -ˈsɑːn-/ *adj.* connected with FREEMASONS 共济会会员的

Mason·ite™ /ˈmeɪsənaɪt/ *noun* [U] a US make of board that is used in building, made of small pieces of wood that are pressed together and stuck with glue （美国）美森耐纤维板（建筑材料）

ma·son·ry /ˈmeɪsənri/ *noun* [U] the parts of a building that are made of stone 砖石结构；砖石建筑：*She was injured by falling masonry.* 她被倒塌的石墙砸伤了。◇ *He acquired a knowledge of carpentry and masonry* (= building with stone) 他掌握了木工和石工知识。➲ WORDFINDER NOTE AT CONSTRUCTION

masque /mɑːsk; *NAmE* mæsk/ *noun* a play written in VERSE, often with music and dancing, popular in England in the 16th and 17th centuries 假面剧（16 至 17 世纪盛行于英国的一种诗剧，常伴以音乐和舞蹈）

mas·quer·ade /ˌmæskəˈreɪd; *BrE also* ˌmɑːsk-/ *noun, verb*
■ *noun* **1** (*formal*) a way of behaving that hides the truth or a person's true feelings 掩藏；掩饰 **2** (*especially NAmE*) a type of party where people wear special COSTUMES and MASKS over their faces, to hide their identities 化装舞会；假面舞会
■ *verb* [I] **~ as sth** to pretend to be sth that you are not 假扮；乔装；伪装：*commercial advertisers masquerading as private individuals* 乔装成普通百姓的商业广告商

Mass /mæs/ *noun* **1** (*sometimes* **mass**) [U, C] (especially in the Roman Catholic Church) a ceremony held in memory of the last meal that Christ had with his DISCIPLES （尤指罗马天主教的）弥撒：*to go to **Mass*** 参加弥撒 ◇ *a priest **celebrating/saying Mass*** 主持弥撒的神父 ➲ SEE ALSO EUCHARIST, COMMUNION **2** [C] a piece of music that is written for the prayers, etc. of this ceremony 弥撒曲：*Bach's Mass in B minor* 巴赫的 B 小调弥撒曲

mass 🔑 /mæs/ *noun, adj., verb*
■ *noun* **1** 🔑 [C] **~ (of sth)** a large amount of a substance that does not have a definite shape or form 团；块；堆：*a mass of snow and rocks falling down the mountain* 从山上滚下来的一堆积雪和石块 ◇ *The hill appeared as a black mass in the distance.* 远远地看去，那座山是黑魆魆一片。◇ *The sky was full of dark masses of clouds.* 天空中乌云密布。 **2** 🔑 [C, usually sing.] **~ of sth** a large amount or quantity of sth 大量；许多：*a mass of blonde hair* 一头金发 ◇ *I began sifting through the mass of evidence.* 我开始认真筛选大量的证据。 **3** 🔑 [sing.] **~ of sth** a large number of people or things grouped together, often in a confused way （常指混乱的）一群，一堆：*I struggled through the mass of people to the exit.* 我在人群里挤来挤去，挤到了出口处。◇ *The page was covered with a mass of figures.* 纸上写满了密密麻麻的数字。 **4** 🔑 **masses** [pl.] **~ (of sth)** (*informal*) a large number or amount of sth 大量的东西 SYN **lots**：*There were masses of people in the shops yesterday.* 昨天商店里人如潮涌。◇ *I've got masses of work to do.* 我有一大堆的工作要做。◇ *Don't give me any more. I've eaten masses!* 别再给我了，我已经吃了很多了！ **5 the masses** [pl.] the ordinary people in society who are not leaders or who are considered to be not very well educated 群众；平民百姓：*government attempts to suppress dissatisfaction among the masses* 政府试图压制群众不满情绪的做法 ◇ *a TV programme that brings science to the masses* 普及科学知识的电视节目 **6 the mass of sth** [sing.] the most; the majority 大多数；多数：*The reforms are unpopular with the mass of teachers and parents.* 大多数教师和家长并不赞成这些改革。 **7** [U, C] (*specialist*) the quantity of material that sth contains 质量：*calculating the mass of a planet* 计算一个行星的质量 ◇ *a mass of 46.3 kg* * 46.3 千克的质量 HELP **Weight** is used in non-technical language for this meaning. 非专业语言用 weight 表示此义。 ➲ SEE ALSO BIOMASS, CRITICAL MASS, LAND MASS
IDM **be a ˈmass of** to be full of or covered with sth 充满；布满：*The rose bushes are a mass of flowers in June.* 六月的玫瑰园花团锦簇。◇ *Her arm was a mass of bruises.* 她的胳膊上伤痕累累。
■ *adj.* 🔑 [only before noun] affecting or involving a large number of people or things 大批的；数量极多的；广泛的：***mass unemployment/production*** 大批失业；批量生产 ◇ *weapons of mass destruction* 大规模杀伤性武器 ◇ *Their latest product is aimed at the **mass market**.* 他们的最新产品瞄准了大众市场。➲ SEE ALSO MASS-MARKET
■ *verb* [I, T] to come together in large numbers; to gather people or things together in large numbers 集结；聚集：(**+ adv./prep.**) *Demonstrators had massed outside the embassy.* 示威者聚集在大使馆的外面。◇ *Dark clouds massed on the horizon.* 天边乌云密布。◇ **~ sb/sth** *The general massed his troops for a final attack.* 将军把军队都集中起来准备发动最后的进攻。 ▶ **massed** *adj.*：*the **massed ranks** of his political opponents* 他的大批政敌

mas·sacre /ˈmæsəkə(r)/ *noun, verb*
■ *noun* [C, U] **1** the killing of a large number of people especially in a cruel way 屠杀；残杀：*the bloody massacre of innocent civilians* 对无辜平民的血腥屠杀 ◇ *Nobody survived the massacre.* 这次大屠杀无人幸免。 **2** (*informal*) a very big defeat in a game or competition （运动或比赛中的）惨败：*The game was a 10–0 massacre for our team.* 这场比赛我们队以 0:10 惨败。
■ *verb* **1 ~ sb** to kill a large number of people, especially in a cruel way 屠杀；杀戮 **2 ~ sb** (*informal*) to defeat sb in a game or competition by a high score （在运动或比赛中）使惨败

mas·sage /ˈmæsɑːʒ; *NAmE* məˈsɑːʒ/ *noun, verb*
■ *noun* [U, C] the action of rubbing and pressing a person's body with the hands to reduce pain in the muscles and joints 按摩：*Massage will help the pain.* 按摩能减轻疼痛。◇ *a back massage* 背部按摩 ◇ *to give sb a massage* 给某人按摩 ◇ *massage oils* 按摩油 ➲ WORDFINDER NOTE AT TREATMENT
■ *verb* **1 ~ sth** to rub and press a person's body with the hands to reduce pain in the muscles and joints 按摩；推拿：*He massaged the aching muscles in her feet.* 他给她按摩脚上疼痛的肌肉。◇ (*figurative*) *to massage sb's ego* (= to make sb feel better, more confident, attractive, etc.) 增强某人的自信心 **2 ~ sth into sth** to rub a substance into the skin, hair, etc. 用…揉擦（皮肤、头发等）：*Massage the cream into your skin.* 将护肤霜揉擦到皮肤上。 **3 ~ sth** (*disapproving*) to change facts, figures, etc. in order to make them seem better than they really are 美化（事实）；虚报（数量）；粉饰：*The government was accused of massaging the unemployment figures.* 政府被指责谎报了失业数字。

ˈmassage parlour (*especially US* **masˈsage parlor**) *noun* **1** a place where you can pay to have a massage 按摩院；按摩房 **2** a place that is supposed to offer the service of massage, but is also where men go to pay for sex with PROSTITUTES （打着按摩院幌子的）妓院

masse ➲ EN MASSE

mas·seur /mæˈsɜː(r)/ *noun* a person whose job is giving people MASSAGE 按摩师

mas·seuse /mæˈsɜːz; *NAmE* məˈsuːs/ *noun* a woman whose job is giving people MASSAGE 女按摩师

mas·sif /mæˈsiːf/ *noun* (*specialist*) a group of mountains that form a large mass 山峦；群山

mas·sive /ˈmæsɪv/ *adj.* **1** very large, heavy and solid 巨大的；大而重的；结实的： *a massive rock* 一块巨大的岩石 ◇ *the massive walls of the castle* 厚实坚固的城堡围墙 **2** extremely large or serious 巨大的；非常严重的： *The explosion made a massive hole in the ground.* 爆炸在地面留下了一个巨大的坑。 ◇ *a massive increase in spending* 开支的大幅度增加 ◇ *He suffered a massive heart attack.* 他的心脏病严重发作了。 ◇ (*BrE, informal*) *Their house is massive.* 他们的房子大极了。 ◇ *They have a massive great house.* 他们有一座非常大的房子。 ▶ **mas·sive·ly** *adv.*

ˌmass-ˈmarket *adj.* [only before noun] (of goods etc. 商品等) produced for very large numbers of people 面向大众的

the ˌmass ˈmedia *noun* [pl.] sources of information and news such as newspapers, magazines, radio and television, that reach and influence large numbers of people 大众传媒

ˈmass noun *noun* (*grammar* 语法) **1** an uncountable noun 不可数名词 **2** a noun that is usually uncountable but can be made plural or used with *a* or *an* when you are talking about different types of sth. For example, *bread* is used as a mass noun in *the shop sells several different breads*. 物质名词（通常为不可数，但表示不同种类时可用复数或与 a 或 an 连用，例如 The shop sells several different breads 中的 bread）

ˈmass number *noun* (*chemistry* 化) the total number of PROTONS and NEUTRONS in an atom （原子）质量数

ˌmass-proˈduce *verb* **~ sth** to produce goods in large quantities, using machinery （用机器）批量生产，大量生产 ▶ **ˌmass-proˈduced** *adj.*： *mass-produced goods* 批量生产的货品 **ˌmass proˈduction** *noun* [U]： *the mass production of consumer goods* 消费品的批量生产

mast /mɑːst; *NAmE* mæst/ *noun* **1** a tall pole on a boat or ship that supports the sails 桅杆；船桅 ➲ VISUAL VOCAB PAGE V61 **2** a tall metal tower with an AERIAL that sends and receives radio or television signals 天线塔 **3** a tall pole that is used for holding a flag 旗杆 IDM SEE NAIL *v.* ➲ SEE ALSO HALF MAST

mast·ec·tomy /mæˈstektəmi/ *noun* (*pl.* **-ies**) a medical operation to remove a person's breast 乳房切除术

mas·ter /ˈmɑːstə(r); *NAmE* ˈmæs-/ *noun, verb, adj.*

■ *noun*

• OF SERVANTS 仆人 **1** (*old-fashioned*) a man who has people working for him, often as servants in his home （男）主人，雇主： *They lived in fear of their master.* 他们惧怕主人，提心吊胆地过日子。

• PERSON IN CONTROL 主宰 **2 ~ of sth** a person who is able to control sth 主宰；主人；有控制力的人： *She was no longer master of her own future.* 她已无法把握自己的未来。

• SKILLED PERSON 有技能的人 **3 ~ (of sth)** a person who is skilled at sth 能手；擅长…者： *a master of disguise* 精于伪装的人 ◇ *a master of the serve-and-volley game* 发球上网的高手 ➲ SEE ALSO PAST MASTER

• DOG OWNER 狗的主人 **4** the male owner of a dog 狗的男主人： *The dog saved its master's life.* 这条狗救了它的主人。 ➲ COMPARE MISTRESS (4)

• TEACHER 教师 **5** (*BrE, old-fashioned*) a male teacher at a school, especially a private school （尤指私立学校的）男教师： *the physics master* 物理老师 ➲ COMPARE SCHOOLMASTER, MISTRESS (2)

• UNIVERSITY DEGREE 大学学位 **6 master's** (*also* **ˈmaster's degree**) a second university degree, or, in Scotland, a first university degree, such as an MA 硕士学位（大学的中级学位；在苏格兰指初级学位）： *He has a Master's in Business Administration.* 他获得了工商管理硕士学位。 ➲ SEE ALSO MA, MB (1), MBA, MSc **7** (*usually* **Master**) a person who has a master's degree 硕士；有硕士学位的人： *a Master of Arts/Science* 文科 / 理科硕士

• CAPTAIN OF SHIP 船长 **8** the captain of a ship that transports goods （货船的）船长

• FAMOUS PAINTER 著名画家 **9** a famous painter who lived in the past （已故）著名画家，绘画大师： *an exhibition of work by the French master, Monet* 法国著名画家莫奈的作品展 ➲ SEE ALSO OLD MASTER (1)

• ORIGINAL RECORD/TAPE/MOVIE 原版录音 / 磁带 / 电影 **10** (often used as an adjective 常用作形容词) a version of a record, tape, film/movie, etc. from which copies are made 母带；母片；原始拷贝： *the master copy* 原始拷贝

• TITLE 称谓 **11 Master** (*old-fashioned*) a title used when speaking to or about a boy who is too young to be called *Mr* (also used in front of the name on an envelope, etc.) （对年龄小而不便称作"先生"的男孩的称谓；也用在信封等处的人名前）少爷，君 **12 Master** (in Britain) the title of the head of some schools and university colleges （英国）校长，院长： *the Master of Wolfson College* 沃尔夫森学院院长 **13 Master** a title used for speaking to or about some religious teachers or leaders （对宗教导师或领袖的称谓）大师，师父 HELP There are many other compounds ending in **master**. You will find them at their place in the alphabet. 以 master 结尾的复合词还有很多，可在各字母中的适当位置查到。

IDM **be your own ˈmaster/ˈmistress** to be free to make your own decisions rather than being told what to do by sb else 独立自主 ➲ MORE AT SERVE *v.*

■ *verb*

• LEARN/UNDERSTAND 学会；理解 **1 ~ sth** to learn or understand sth completely 精通；掌握： *to master new skills/techniques* 掌握新的技能 / 技术 ◇ *French was a language he had never mastered.* 法语他一直没有学好。

• CONTROL 控制 **2 ~ sth** to manage to control an emotion 控制（情绪）： *She struggled hard to master her temper.* 她竭力按住性子，不发脾气。 **3 ~ sth/sb** to gain control of an animal or a person 控制（动物或人）

■ *adj.* [only before noun]

• SKILLED 熟练 **1 ~ baker/chef/mason, etc.** used to describe a person who is very skilled at the job mentioned （描述精于某职业的人）熟练的，灵巧的，有技能的

• MOST IMPORTANT 最重要 **2** the largest and/or most important 最大的；最重要的： *the master bedroom* 主卧室 ◇ *a master file/switch* 主文件；总开关

mas·ter·class /ˈmɑːstəklɑːs; *NAmE* ˈmæstərklæs/ *noun* a lesson, especially in music, given by a famous expert to very skilled students （大师授课的）高级音乐讲习班；深造班

mas·ter·ful /ˈmɑːstəfl; *NAmE* ˈmæstərfl/ *adj.* **1** (of a person, especially a man 人，尤指男人) able to control people or situations in a way that shows confidence as a leader 有控制能力的；有驾驭能力的 **2** = MASTERLY： *a masterful performance* 技艺高超的表演 ▶ **mas·ter·ful·ly** /-fəli/ *adv.*： *He took her arm masterfully and led her away.* 他很强势地挽着她的胳膊，带着她走了。

ˈmaster key (*also* **ˈpass key**) *noun* a key that can be used to open many different locks in a building 万能钥匙

mas·ter·ly /ˈmɑːstəli; *NAmE* ˈmæstərli/ (*also* **mas·ter·ful**) *adj.* showing great skill or understanding 技艺精湛的；理解透彻的： *a masterly performance* 精湛的表演 ◇ *Her handling of the situation was masterly.* 她对情势的处理非常巧妙。

mas·ter·mind /ˈmɑːstəmaɪnd; *NAmE* ˈmæstərm-/ *noun, verb*

■ *noun* [usually sing.] an intelligent person who plans and directs a complicated project or activity (often one that involves a crime) （极具才智的）决策者；主谋；出谋划策者

■ *verb* **~ sth** to plan and direct a complicated project or activity 策划，操纵，领导（复杂的事情）

ˌmaster of ˈceremonies *noun* (*abbr.* **MC**) a person who introduces guests or entertainers at a formal occasion 司仪；仪式主持人

mas·ter·piece /ˈmɑːstəpiːs; *NAmE* ˈmæstərp-/ (*also* **mas·ter·work**) *noun* a work of art such as a painting, film/movie, book, etc. that is an excellent, or the best, example of the artist's work 代表作；杰作；名著： *The museum houses several of his Cubist masterpieces.* 博物馆收藏了他的几件立体派杰作。 ◇ *Her work is a masterpiece of* (= an excellent example of) *simplicity.* 她的作品是朴实的典范。

ˈmaster plan *noun* [sing.] a detailed plan that will make a complicated project successful 总体规划；总计划

ˈmaster's degree (*also* **master's**) *noun* a further university degree that you study for after a first degree 硕士学位

mas·ter·stroke /ˈmɑːstəstrəʊk; *NAmE* ˈmæstərstroʊk/ *noun* [usually sing.] something clever that you do that gives a successful result 绝招；高招；妙举

mas·ter·work /ˈmɑːstəwɜːk; *NAmE* ˈmæstərwɜːrk/ *noun* = MASTERPIECE

mas·tery /ˈmɑːstəri; *NAmE* ˈmæst-/ *noun* **1** [U, sing.] ~ (**of sth**) great knowledge about or understanding of a particular thing 精通；熟练掌握 SYN **command**: *She has mastery of several languages.* 她精通数门语言。 **2** [U] ~ (**of/over sb/sth**) control or power 控制；驾驭；控制力量: *human mastery of the natural world* 人类对自然界的控制

mast·head /ˈmɑːsthed; *NAmE* ˈmæs-/ *noun* **1** the top of a MAST on a ship 桅顶 **2** the name of a newspaper at the top of the front page （报纸头版顶端的）刊头 **3** (*NAmE*) the part of a newspaper or a news website which gives details of the people who work on it and other information about it （报刊或新闻网站上载有其工作人员和其他相关信息的）报头栏，刊头

mas·tic /ˈmæstɪk/ *noun* [U] **1** a substance that comes from the BARK of a tree and is used in making VARNISH 乳香树脂；乳香 **2** a substance that is used in building to fill holes and keep out water 玛琋脂；胶泥

mas·ti·cate /ˈmæstɪkeɪt/ *verb* [I] (*specialist*) to chew food 咀嚼（食物） ▸ **mas·ti·ca·tion** /ˌmæstɪˈkeɪʃn/ *noun* [U]

mas·tiff /ˈmæstɪf/ *noun* a large strong dog with short hair, often used to guard buildings 大驯犬，獒（常用作守卫）

mas·titis /mæˈstaɪtɪs/ *noun* [U] (*medical* 医) painful swelling of the breast or UDDER usually because of infection 乳腺炎

mas·tur·bate /ˈmæstəbeɪt; *NAmE* -stərb-/ *verb* **1** [I, T] ~ (**yourself**) to give yourself sexual pleasure by rubbing your sexual organs 手淫 **2** [T] ~ **sb** to give sb sexual pleasure by rubbing their sexual organs 对（某人）行手淫 ▸ **mas·tur·ba·tion** /ˌmæstəˈbeɪʃn; *NAmE* -stərˈb-/ *noun* [U] **mas·tur·ba·tory** /ˌmæstəˈbeɪtəri; *NAmE* ˈmæstərbətɔːri/ *adj.*

mat /mæt/ *noun, adj.*

■ ***noun*** **1** a small piece of thick carpet or strong material that is used to cover part of a floor 小地毯；垫子: *Wipe your feet on the mat before you come in, please.* 请在垫子上擦擦脚再进来。 ➲ SEE ALSO BATH MAT, DOORMAT (1), MOUSE MAT **2** a piece of thick material such as rubber or plastic used especially in some sports for people to lie on or fall onto （体育运动用的）厚垫子: ***a judo/an exercise mat*** 柔道垫；健身垫 **3** a small piece of plastic, wood or cloth used on a table for decoration or to protect the surface from heat or damage （装饰或保护桌面的）衬垫，小垫: *a beer mat* 啤酒杯垫 ➲ SEE ALSO TABLE MAT **4** a thick mass of sth that is stuck together 团；簇；丛: *a mat of hair* 一团毛发 ➲ SEE ALSO MATTED

IDM **go to the ˈmat (with sb) (for sb/sth)** (*NAmE, informal*) to support or defend sb/sth in an argument with sb （为支持或维护…）（与某人）争辩 **take sb/sth to the ˈmat** (*US, informal*) to get involved in an argument with sb/sth 与…进行辩论

■ ***adj.*** (*US*) = MATT

mata·dor /ˈmætədɔː(r)/ *noun* (*from Spanish*) a person who fights and kills the BULL in a BULLFIGHT 斗牛士

ma·tatu /mæˈtætuː/ *noun* (in Kenya) a small privately owned bus, often decorated with pictures, words or phrases, that carries passengers and has a driver that you pay to take you somewhere, usually along a fixed route with other stops for people to get on and off 马塔图小巴士（肯尼亚的一种私营公交车，车身上常涂有彩绘图案或文字）

match 🔑 /mætʃ/ *noun, verb*

■ ***noun***

• FOR LIGHTING FIRES 用于点火 **1** 🔑 [C] a small stick made of wood or cardboard that is used for lighting a fire, cigarette, etc. 火柴: *a box of matches* 一盒火柴 ◇ *to* ***strike a match*** (= to make it burn) 划火柴 ◇ *to* ***put a match to sth*** (= set fire to sth) 用火柴点燃某物

• IN SPORT 体育运动 **2** 🔑 [C] (*especially BrE*) a sports event where people or teams compete against each other 比赛；竞赛: (*BrE*) *a football match* 足球比赛 ◇ (*NAmE, BrE*) *a tennis match* 网球比赛 ◇ *They are playing an important match against Liverpool on Saturday.* 星期六他们和利物浦队有一场重要比赛。 ◇ *to* ***win/lose a match*** 赢得 / 输掉比赛 ➲ SEE ALSO SHOOTING MATCH, SLANGING MATCH, TEST MATCH ➲ WORDFINDER NOTE AT SPORT

• AN EQUAL 匹敌者 **3** [sing.] **a ~ for sb | sb's match** a person who is equal to sb else in strength, skill, intelligence, etc. 敌手；旗鼓相当的人: *I was* ***no match for*** *him at tennis.* 打网球我根本不是他的对手。 ◇ *I was his match at tennis.* 打网球我跟他难分伯仲。

• SB/STH THAT COMBINES WELL 相称的人 / 物 **4** 🔑 [sing.] a person or thing that combines well with sb/sth else 相配的人（或物）；般配的人（或物）: *The curtains and carpet are a* ***good match.*** 窗帘和地毯非常相配。 ◇ *Jo and Ian are a* ***perfect match*** *for each other.* 乔和伊恩真是天设的一对，地配的一双。

• STH THE SAME 相同的东西 **5** [C] a thing that looks exactly the same as or very similar to sth else 相同的东西；非常相似的东西: *I've found a vase that is an exact match of the one I broke.* 我找到了一只花瓶，和我打碎的那个一模一样。

• MARRIAGE 婚姻 **6** [C] (*old-fashioned*) a marriage or a marriage partner 婚姻；配偶 ➲ SEE ALSO LOVE MATCH

IDM **find/meet your ˈmatch (in sb)** to meet sb who is equal to or even better than you in strength, skill or intelligence 遇到对手；棋逢对手 ➲ MORE AT MAN *n.*

■ ***verb***

• COMBINE WELL 匹配 **1** 🔑 [T, I] ~ (**sth**) if two things **match**, or if one thing **matches** another, they have the same colour, pattern, or style and therefore look attractive together 般配；相配: *The doors were painted blue to match the walls.* 门漆成了蓝色，以便与墙的颜色相配。 ◇ *a scarf with gloves* ***to match*** 一条围巾还有和它相配的手套 ◇ *None of these glasses match* (= they are all different). 这些杯子没有能配对儿的。 ➲ SEE ALSO MATCHING

• BE THE SAME 相同 **2** 🔑 [T, I] ~ (**sth**) if two things **match** or if one thing **matches** another, they are the same or very similar 相同；相似；相一致: *Her fingerprints match those found at the scene of the crime.* 她的指纹与犯罪现场的指纹相吻合。 ◇ *As a couple they are not very well matched* (= they are not very suitable for each other). 作为夫妻，他们并不十分般配。 ◇ *The two sets of figures don't match.* 这两组数字不一致。

• FIND STH SIMILAR/CONNECTED 配对 **3** 🔑 [T] ~ **sb/sth (to/with sb/sth)** to find sb/sth that goes together with or is connected with another person or thing 找相称（或相关）的人（或物）；配对: *The aim of the competition is to match the quote to the person who said it.* 比赛的要求是把引文和它的作者配在一起。

• BE EQUAL/BETTER 一样；更好 **4** [T] ~ **sb/sth** to be as good, interesting, successful, etc. as sb/sth else 与…相匹敌；和…不相上下 SYN **equal**: *The profits made in the first year have never been matched.* 历年获得的利润都比不上第一年的。 ◇ *The teams were* ***evenly matched.*** 各队的水平旗鼓相当。 **5** [T] ~ **sth** to make sth the same as or better than sth else 使等同于；使优于: *The company was unable to match his current salary.* 当时公司付不起和他现在相同的工资。

• PROVIDE STH SUITABLE 提供合适的东西 **6** [T] ~ **sth** to provide sth that is suitable for or enough for a particular situation 适应；满足: *Investment in hospitals is needed now to match the future needs of the country.* 为了适应国家未来的需要，必须现在就投资医院建设。 IDM SEE MIX *v.*

PHR V **ˈmatch sth against sth** to compare sth with sth

M

else in order to find things that are the same or similar 拿…与…比较；对照：*New information is matched against existing data in the computer.* 新的资料和电脑中已有的数据作了比较。 **'match sb/sth against/with sb/sth** to arrange for sb to compete in a game or competition against sb else 让…同…较量：*We are matched against last year's champions in the first round.* 我们第一轮即遭遇了去年的冠军。 **,match 'up (to sb/sth)** (usually used in negative sentences 通常用于否定句) to be as good, interesting, successful as sb/sth 相称；相当；配得上 SYN **measure up**：*The trip failed to match up to her expectations.* 这次旅行令她很失望。 **,match 'up (with sth)** to be the same or similar （和某物）相同，相似 SYN **tally, agree**：*The suspects' stories just don't match up.* 各嫌疑犯交代的内容不一致。 **,match sth↔'up (with sth)** to find things that belong together or that look attractive together 归类；配套；搭配：*She spent the morning matching up orders with invoices.* 她花了一上午工夫把订单和发票都给对好了。

match·book /ˈmætʃbʊk/ *noun* (*NAmE*) a piece of folded card containing matches and a surface to light them on 纸板火柴

match·box /ˈmætʃbɒks; *NAmE* -bɑːks/ *noun* a small box for holding matches 火柴盒 ➲ VISUAL VOCAB PAGE V36

'match-fixing *noun* [U] (in sport) the act of deciding in a way that is not honest what the result of a particular game will be before it is played （体育运动）操纵比赛，比赛造假：*Several countries have suffered soccer match-fixing scandals.* 有几个国家陷入了足球假球丑闻。 ➲ COMPARE SPOT-FIXING

match·ing /ˈmætʃɪŋ/ *adj.* [only before noun] (of clothing, material, objects, etc. 衣服、材料、物件等) having the same colour, pattern, style, etc. and therefore looking attractive together （颜色、形状、款式等）相同的，相称的，相配的：*a pine table with four matching chairs* 一张松木桌子和四把配套的椅子

match·less /ˈmætʃləs/ *adj.* (*formal*) so good that nothing can be compared with it 无可匹敌的；无比的；无双的；无法媲美的 SYN **incomparable**：*matchless beauty/skill* 绝色；绝技

match·maker /ˈmætʃmeɪkə(r)/ *noun* a person who tries to arrange marriages or relationships between others 媒人；牵线搭桥的人；红娘 ▸ **match·mak·ing** *noun* [U]

'match play *noun* [U] a way of playing GOLF in which your score depends on the number of holes that you win rather than the number of times you hit the ball in the whole game （高尔夫球）比洞赛（与比杆赛有别） ➲ COMPARE STROKE PLAY

,match 'point *noun* [U, C] (especially in TENNIS 尤指网球) a point that, if won by a player, will also win them the match 决胜分；赛点

match·stick /ˈmætʃstɪk/ *noun* a single wooden match 火柴杆；火柴棍：*starving children with legs like matchsticks* 腿瘦得像火柴杆儿一样的饥饿儿童

'matchstick figure (*BrE*) (*NAmE* **'stick figure**) *noun* a picture of a person drawn only with thin lines for the arms and legs, a circle for the head, etc. 人物线条画；简笔人物画

match·wood /ˈmætʃwʊd/ *noun* [U] very small pieces of wood 小木条；木料碎片

mate /meɪt/ *noun, verb*

■ *noun*

• **FRIEND** 朋友 **1** [C] (*BrE, AustralE, informal*) a friend 朋友；伙伴：*They've been best mates since school.* 他们从上学时期以来就是最要好的朋友。◇ *I was with a mate.* 我和一个朋友在一起。 ➲ WORDFINDER NOTE AT FRIEND

• **FRIENDLY NAME** 友好的称呼 **2** [C] (*BrE, AustralE, informal*) used as a friendly way of addressing sb, especially between men （男人之间常用）哥儿们，伙计，老兄：*Sorry mate, you'll have to wait.* 对不起，伙计，你得等着。◇ *All right, mate?* 行吗，哥儿们？

• **SB YOU SHARE WITH** 伙伴 **3** [C] (in compounds 构成复合词) a person you share an activity or accommodation with 同伴；同事；一同居住的人：***workmates/teammates/playmates/classmates*** 工友；队友；游戏伙伴；同学 ◇ *my room-mate/flatmate* 我的室友；和我同住一套公寓的人 ➲ SEE ALSO RUNNING MATE, SOULMATE

• **BIRD/ANIMAL** 鸟；兽 **4** [C] either of a pair of birds or animals 偶；伴侣：*A male bird sings to attract a mate.* 雄鸟鸣唱以吸引雌鸟。

• **SEXUAL PARTNER** 性伴侣 **5** [C] (*informal*) a husband, wife or other sexual partner 配偶；性伴侣

• **JOB** 职业 **6** [C] (*BrE*) a person whose job is to help a skilled worker （熟练工人的）助手，下手：*a builder's/plumber's mate* 建筑工的 / 管子工的助手

• **ON SHIP** 船舶 **7** [C] an officer in a commercial ship below the rank of captain or MASTER （商船的）大副 ➲ SEE ALSO FIRST MATE

• **IN CHESS** 国际象棋 **8** [U] = CHECKMATE (1)

■ *verb*

• **ANIMALS/BIRDS** 兽；鸟 **1** [I] ~ (with sth) (of two animals or birds 一对兽或鸟) to have sex in order to produce young 交配；交尾：*Do foxes ever mate with dogs?* 狐狸会和狗交配吗？ ➲ SEE ALSO MATING **2** [T] ~ **sth (to/with sth)** to put animals or birds together so that they will have sex and produce young 使交配

• **IN CHESS** 国际象棋 **3** [T] = CHECKMATE

ma·ter·ial /məˈtɪəriəl; *NAmE* -ˈtɪr-/ *noun, adj.*

■ *noun* **1** [U, C] cloth used for making clothes, curtains, etc. 布料 SYN **fabric**：*a piece of material* 一块布料 ◇ *'What material is this dress made of?' 'Cotton.'* "这件连衣裙是用什么料子做的？" "棉布。" ➲ SYNONYMS AT FABRIC **2** [C, U] a substance that things can be made from 材料；原料：***building materials*** (= bricks, sand, glass, etc.) 建筑材料 ➲ SEE ALSO RAW MATERIAL **3** [C, usually pl., U] things that are needed in order to do a particular activity （某一活动所需的）材料：*teaching materials* 教材 ◇ *The company produces its own training material.* 公司自行编写培训教材。◇ (*figurative*) *The teacher saw her as good university material* (= good enough to go to university). 老师认为她是块上大学的料。 ➲ SYNONYMS AT EQUIPMENT **4** [U] information or ideas used in books, etc. 素材；用以创作的材料（或构想）：*She's collecting material for her latest novel.* 她在为其最新的小说收集素材。 **5** [U] items used in a performance 节目；曲目；剧目：*The band played all new material at the gig.* 在现场音乐会上，乐队演奏的都是新曲目。

■ *adj.* **1** [only before noun] connected with money, possessions, etc. rather than with the needs of the mind or spirit 物质的，实际的（非精神需求的）：*material comforts* 物质享受 ◇ *changes in your material circumstances* 物质环境的改变 OPP **spiritual** **2** [only before noun] connected with the physical world rather than with the mind or spirit 物质的；客观存在的：*the material world* 物质世界 OPP **immaterial** **3** (*formal* or *law* 律) important and needing to be considered 重要的；必要的：*material evidence* 重要的证据 ◇ ~ **to sth** *She omitted information that was material to the case.* 她遗漏了此案的重要资料。 ➲ SEE ALSO IMMATERIAL ▸ **ma·teri·ally** /-iəli/ *adv.*：*Materially they are no better off.* 他们的物质生活并没有改善。◇ *Their*

matchstick man 线条画男子 **matchstick woman** 线条画女子

comments have not materially affected our plans (= in a noticeable or important way). 他们的评价并没有对我们的计划产生多么重要的影响。

ma·teri·al·ism /məˈtɪəriəlɪzəm; *NAmE* -ˈtɪr-/ *noun* [U] **1** (*usually disapproving*) the belief that money, possessions and physical comforts are more important than spiritual values 实利主义；物质主义 **2** (*philosophy* 哲) the belief that only material things exist 唯物主义；唯物论 ➲ COMPARE IDEALISM

ma·teri·al·ist /məˈtɪəriəlɪst; *NAmE* -ˈtɪr-/ *noun* **1** a person who believes that money, possessions and physical comforts are more important than spiritual values in life 物质享乐主义者；实利主义者 **2** a person who believes in the philosophy of materialism 唯物主义者；唯物论者

ma·teri·al·is·tic /məˌtɪəriəˈlɪstɪk; *NAmE* -ˌtɪr-/ *adj.* (*disapproving*) caring more about money and possessions than anything else 物质享乐主义的；贪图享乐的

ma·teri·al·ize (*BrE also* **-ise**) /məˈtɪəriəlaɪz; *NAmE* -ˈtɪr-/ *verb* **1** [I] (usually used in negative sentences 通常用于否定句) to take place or start to exist as expected or planned 实现；发生；成为现实：*The promotion he had been promised failed to materialize.* 答应给他晋升的许诺未能实现。 **2** [I] to appear suddenly and/or in a way that cannot be explained 突然显现；奇怪地出现：*A tall figure suddenly materialized at her side.* 一个高高的身影突然出现在她的身边。◇ (*informal*) *The train failed to materialize* (= it did not come). 列车始终没有来。 ▶ **ma·teri·al·iza·tion, -isa·tion** /məˌtɪəriəlaɪˈzeɪʃn; *NAmE* -ˌtɪriələˈz-/ *noun* [U]

ma·ter·iel /məˌtɪəriˈel; *NAmE* -ˌtɪr-/ *noun* [U] (*specialist*) military weapons and equipment 军用物资；武器装备

ma·ter·nal /məˈtɜːnl; *NAmE* məˈtɜːrnl/ *adj.* **1** having feelings that are typical of a caring mother towards a child 母亲的；母亲般慈爱的：*maternal love* 母爱 ◇ *I'm not very maternal.* 我不太像个母亲。◇ *She didn't have any maternal instincts.* 她没有一点做母亲的天性。 **2** connected with being a mother 母亲的；作为母亲的：*Maternal age affects the baby's survival rate.* 母亲的年龄影响婴儿的成活率。 **3** [only before noun] related through the mother's side of the family 母系的；母亲方面的：*my maternal grandfather* (= my mother's father) 我的外祖父 ▶ **ma·ter·nal·ly** /-nəli/ *adv.*：*She behaved maternally towards her students.* 她以母亲般的慈爱对待自己的学生。 ➲ COMPARE PATERNAL

ma·ter·nity /məˈtɜːnəti; *NAmE* -ˈtɜːrn-/ *noun* [U] the state of being or becoming a mother 母亲身份；怀孕：*maternity clothes* (= clothes for women who are pregnant) 孕妇装 ◇ *a* **maternity ward/hospital** (= one where women go to give birth to their babies) 产科病房；妇产医院

maˈternity leave *noun* [U] a period of time when a woman temporarily leaves her job to have a baby 产假 ➲ WORDFINDER NOTE AT PREGNANT ➲ COLLOCATIONS AT CHILD ➲ SEE ALSO PARENTAL LEAVE, PATERNITY LEAVE

mate·ship /ˈmeɪtʃɪp/ *noun* [U] (*AustralE, NZE, informal*) friendship, especially between men （尤指男性之间的）友谊，友情，交情

matey /ˈmeɪti/ *adj., noun*

■ ***adj.*** ~ (**with sb**) (*BrE, informal*) friendly, sometimes in a way that is not completely sincere 友好；亲热；套近乎：*She started off being quite matey with everyone.* 她一上来就和每个人套近乎。

■ ***noun*** (*BrE*) used by men as an informal way of addressing another man 哥儿们；兄弟

math /mæθ/ (*NAmE*) (*BrE* **maths** /mæθs/) *noun* [U] **1** mathematics, especially as a subject in school 数学（尤作为学校课程）：*a math teacher* 数学老师 **2** the process of calculating using numbers 运算；计算：*Is your math correct?* 你的计算正确吗？

IDM **do the ˈmath** to think carefully about sth before doing it so that you know all the relevant facts or figures 周密估算；斟酌：*If only someone had done the math!* 要是有人事先合计过就好了！

math·em·at·ician /ˌmæθəməˈtɪʃn/ *noun* a person who is an expert in mathematics 数学家

math·emat·ics 🔑 /ˌmæθəˈmætɪks/ (*formal*) (*BrE also* **maths** /mæθs/) (*NAmE also* **math** /mæθ/) *noun* **1** 🔑 [U] the science of numbers and shapes. Branches of mathematics include ARITHMETIC, ALGEBRA, GEOMETRY and TRIGONOMETRY. 数学：*the school mathematics curriculum* 学校数学课程 **2** 🔑 [U+sing./pl. v.] the process of calculating using numbers运算；计算：*He worked out the very difficult mathematics in great detail.* 他十分详细地解答了那些很难的运算。 ▶ **math·emat·ic·al** /ˌmæθəˈmætɪkl/ *adj.*：*mathematical calculations/problems/models* 数学计算 / 问题 / 模型 ◇ *to assess children's mathematical ability* 评估孩子们的计算能力 **math·emat·ic·al·ly** /-kli/ *adv.*：*It's mathematically impossible.* 这在数学上是不可能的。◇ *Some people are very mathematically inclined* (= interested in and good at mathematics). 有些人特别喜欢并擅长数学。

maths /mæθs/ (*BrE*) (*NAmE* **math** /mæθ/) *noun* **1** [U] mathematics, especially as a subject in school 数学（尤作为学校课程）：*The core subjects are English, Maths and Science.* 主课是英语、数学和自然科学。◇ *a maths teacher* 数学老师 **2** [U+sing./pl. v.] the process of calculating using numbers 运算；计算：*If my maths is/are right, the answer is 142.* 如果我计算没错，答案是 142。

> **WORDFINDER** 联想词：algebra, arithmetic, calculus, equation, geometry, logarithm, numeracy, problem, trigonometry

IDM **do the ˈmaths** to think carefully about sth before doing it so that you know all the relevant facts or figures 周密估算；斟酌：*Do the maths before you take on more debt.* 再借债之前要三思。

Ma·tilda /məˈtɪldə/ *noun* (*old use, AustralE, NZE*) a pack of things tied or wrapped together and carried by a BUSHMAN （布须曼人的）行囊，背囊

mat·inee (*also* **mat·inée**) /ˈmætɪneɪ; *NAmE* ˌmætnˈeɪ/ *noun* an afternoon performance of a play, etc.; an afternoon showing of a film/movie （戏剧、电影的）午后场，日场 ➲ WORDFINDER NOTE AT PERFORMANCE

ˈmatinee idol (*also* **ˈmatinée idol**) *noun* (*old-fashioned*) an actor who is popular with women 受女性喜爱的男演员；偶像派男演员

mat·ing /ˈmeɪtɪŋ/ *noun* [U, C] sex between animals 交尾；交配：*the mating season* 交配季节

mat·ins (*also* **mat·tins**) /ˈmætɪnz; *NAmE* ˈmætnz/ *noun* [U] the service of morning prayer, especially in the Anglican Church （尤指圣公会的）晨祷 ➲ COMPARE EVENSONG, VESPERS

ma·toke /mæˈtɒkə; *NAmE* mæˈtɑːkə/ *noun* [U] a type of green BANANA grown in Uganda and other places in E Africa and used for cooking; the cooked food made from this type of banana and eaten with STEW （乌干达等东非地带用于烹调的）青香蕉（和炖菜一起食用的）

ma·tri·arch /ˈmeɪtriɑːk; *NAmE* -ɑːrk/ *noun* a woman who is the head of a family or social group 女家长；女族长 ➲ COMPARE PATRIARCH (1)

ma·tri·arch·al /ˌmeɪtriˈɑːkl; *NAmE* -ˈɑːrkl/ *adj.* (of a society or system 社会或体制) controlled by women rather than men; passing power, property, etc. from mother to daughter rather than from father to son 母系的；母权的：*The animals live in matriarchal groups.* 这些动物按母系群体生活。 ➲ COMPARE PATRIARCHAL (1)

ma·tri·archy /ˈmeɪtriɑːki; *NAmE* -ɑːrki/ *noun* (*pl.* **-ies**) a social system that gives power and authority to women rather than men 母权制；母系社会 ➲ COMPARE PATRIARCHY

ma·tric /məˈtrɪk/ *noun* [U] (*SAfrE*) **1** the final year of school （中学的）毕业学年：*We studied that book in matric.* 我们毕业那年学了那本书。 **2** the work and examinations in the final year of school 中学毕业学年的学业和考试：*He* *passed matric with four distinctions.* 他以四个优等成绩通过中学毕业考试。◇ *She's preparing to write matric.* 她正准备参加毕业考试。

matri·ces PL. OF MATRIX

maˌtric eˈxemption *noun* [U] (*SAfrE*) the fact of successfully completing the final year of school and being able to study at university or college 中学毕业；具备大学入学资格：*A senior certificate with matric exemption is required for entry to university.* 上大学需要有中学毕业的资格证书。

matri·cide /ˈmætrɪsaɪd/ *noun* [U, C] (*formal*) the crime of killing your mother; a person who is guilty of this crime 弑母；弑母者 ➲ COMPARE FRATRICIDE (1), PARRICIDE, PATRICIDE

ma·tric·ulate /məˈtrɪkjuleɪt/ *verb* **1** [I] (*formal*) to officially become a student at a university （正式）被大学录取；注册入大学：*She matriculated in 1995.* 她于 1995 年升入大学。 **2** [I] (*SAfrE*) to successfully complete the final year of school （从学校）毕业 ▸ **ma·tricu·la·tion** /məˌtrɪkjuˈleɪʃn/ *noun* [U]

matri·lin·eal /ˌmætrɪˈlɪniəl/ *adj.* (*specialist*) used to describe the relationship between mother and children that continues in a family with each generation, or sth that is based on this relationship 母系的；基于母系的：*She traced her family history by matrilineal descent* (= starting with her mother, her mother's mother, etc.). 她按母系血统追溯她的家族史。➲ COMPARE PATRILINEAL

M

matri·mo·nial /ˌmætrɪˈməʊniəl; *NAmE* -ˈmoʊ-/ *adj.* [usually before noun] (*formal* or *specialist*) connected with marriage or with being married 婚姻的：*matrimonial problems* 婚姻问题 ◇ *the matrimonial home* 婚姻住所

matri·mony /ˈmætrɪməni; *NAmE* -moʊni/ *noun* [U] (*formal* or *specialist*) marriage; the state of being married 婚配：*holy matrimony* 婚配圣事

mat·rix /ˈmeɪtrɪks/ *noun* (*pl.* **matri·ces** /ˈmeɪtrɪsiːz/) **1** (*mathematics* 数) an arrangement of numbers, symbols, etc. in rows and columns, treated as a single quantity 矩阵 **2** (*formal*) the formal social, political, etc. situation from which a society or person grows and develops （人或社会成长发展的）社会环境，政治局势：*the European cultural matrix* 欧洲文化的发源地 **3** (*formal* or *literary*) a system of lines, roads, etc. that cross each other, forming a series of squares or shapes in between 线路网；道路网 SYN **network**：*a matrix of paths* 纵横交错的小路 **4** (*specialist*) a MOULD in which sth is shaped 基体；铸模 **5** (*computing* 计) a group of electronic CIRCUIT elements arranged in rows and columns like a GRID 矩阵转接电路 ➲ SEE ALSO DOT MATRIX PRINTER **6** (*geology* 地) a mass of rock in which minerals, PRECIOUS STONES, etc. are found in the ground 杂基

ma·tron /ˈmeɪtrən/ *noun* **1** (*BrE*) a woman who works as a nurse in a school （学校的）女舍监 **2** (*old-fashioned, BrE*) a senior female nurse in charge of the other nurses in a hospital (now usually called a **senior nursing officer**) 女护士长（现常称为 senior nursing officer） **3** (*becoming old-fashioned*) an older married woman 上年纪的已婚妇女

ma·tron·ly /ˈmeɪtrənli/ *adj.* (*disapproving*) (of a woman 妇女) no longer young, and rather fat 韶华已逝而且肥胖的

ˈmatron of honour (*especially US* **ˈmatron of honor**) *noun* [sing.] a married woman who is the most important BRIDESMAID at a wedding （已婚的）首席女傧相，伴娘 ➲ COMPARE MAID OF HONOUR

matro·nym·ic /ˌmætrəˈnɪmɪk/ *noun* (*specialist*) a name formed from the name of your mother or a female ANCESTOR, especially by adding sth to the beginning or end of their name 母系姓氏；源于母名的姓 ➲ COMPARE PATRONYMIC

matt (*BrE*) (*US* **mat**) (*also* **matte** *NAmE, BrE*) /mæt/ *adj.* (of a colour, surface, or photograph 色彩、表面或照片) not shiny 不光亮的；无光泽的；亚光的：*a matt finish* 亚光罩面漆 ◇ *matt white paint* 亚光白漆 ◇ *Prints are available on matt or glossy paper.* 粗面相片或光面相片均可洗印。

mat·ted /ˈmætɪd/ *adj.* (of hair, etc. 毛发等) forming a thick mass, especially because it is wet and dirty 缠结的；湿脏蓬乱的

mat·ter 🔑 /ˈmætə(r)/ *noun, verb*

■ ***noun***

• **SUBJECT/SITUATION** 课题；情况 **1** 🔑 [C] a subject or situation that you must consider or deal with 课题；事情；问题 SYN **affair**：*It's a private matter.* 这是件私事儿。◇ *They had important matters to discuss.* 他们有些重要的问题要讨论。◇ *She may need your help with some business matters.* 她也许需要你帮助处理一些生意方面的事情。◇ *I always consulted him on matters of policy.* 我总是向他咨询一些政策问题。◇ *It's **a matter for** the police* (= for them to deal with). 这事须由警方处理。◇ *That's a matter for you to take up with your boss.* 这个问题你得去和你的老板进行交涉。◇ *Let's get on with the **matter in hand*** (= what we need to deal with now). 我们继续解决手头的问题吧。◇ *I wasn't prepared to **let the matter drop*** (= stop discussing it). 我没打算把这件事搁下不提。◇ *It was **no easy matter** getting him to change his mind.* 让他改变主意可不是件容易的事儿。◇ *It should have been a simple matter to check.* 检查核对本来应该是件简单的事情。◇ (*ironic*) *And then there's **the little matter** of the fifty pounds you owe me.* 还有件小事儿，你欠我五十英镑呢。◇ (*formal*) *It was **a matter of** some concern to most of those present* (= something they were worried about). 这是当时在场的多数人关心的问题。◇ *I did not feel that we had got to **the heart of the matter*** (= the most important part). 我认为我们还没有触及问题的关键。◇ *And that is **the crux of the matter*** (= the most important thing about the situation). 这就是问题的症结所在。 **2** 🔑 **matters** [pl.] the present situation, or the situation that you are talking about 事态；当前的状况 SYN **things**：*Unfortunately, there is nothing we can do to improve matters.* 很遗憾，我们无力改善目前的状况。◇ *I'd forgotten the keys, which didn't **help matters**.* 我忘记带钥匙了，这让我情况更糟。◇ *Matters were made worse by a fire in the warehouse.* 仓库失火使得事态更为严重。◇ *And then, **to make matters worse**, his parents turned up.* 接着，更糟糕的是，他的父母亲来了。◇ *I decided to **take matters into my own hands*** (= deal with the situation myself). 我决定亲自处理问题。◇ ***Matters came to a head*** (= the situation became very difficult) *with his resignation.* 随着他的辞职，局面恶化得难以收拾。

• **PROBLEM** 问题 **3** 🔑 **the matter** [sing.] used (to ask) if sb is upset, unhappy, etc. or if there is a problem （用于询问某人的情况）：***What's the matter?** Is there something wrong?* 怎么了？出了什么事儿吗？◇ *Is **anything the matter**?* 有什么问题吗？◇ **~ with sb/sth** *Is **something the matter** with Bob? He seems very down.* 鲍勃有什么事儿吧？他好像情绪很低落。◇ *There's something the matter with my eyes.* 我的眼睛出了点毛病。◇ *'We've bought a new TV.' 'What was the matter with the old one?'* "我们买了台新电视。" "那台旧的怎么了？" ◇ ***What's the matter with** you today* (= why are you behaving like this)? 你今天是怎么了？

• **A MATTER OF STH/OF DOING STH** 关于…的问题 **4** 🔑 [sing.] a situation that involves sth or depends on sth 关乎…的事情 SYN **question**：*Learning to drive is all a matter of coordination.* 学开车主要是靠协调。◇ *Planning a project is just a matter of working out the right order to do things in.* 规划一个项目就是要设计出正确的工作顺序。◇ *That's not a problem. It's **simply a matter of** letting people know in time.* 这没问题，不就是及时通知大家吗。◇ *Some people prefer the older version to the new one. It's **a matter of taste**.* 有些人喜欢老版本而不喜欢新版本。这只是个趣味问题。◇ *She resigned over **a matter of principle**.* 她因为原则问题而辞职。◇ *The government must deal with this **as a matter of urgency**.* 政府必须将此事当作紧急的事情来处理。◇ *Just **as a matter of interest*** (= because it is interesting, not because it is important), *how much did you pay for it?* 我只是感兴趣，你这是花多少钱买的？◇ *'I think this is the best so far.' 'Well, that's **a matter of opinion***

(= other people may think differently). "我认为这是迄今为止最好的。" "唔，仁者见仁，智者见智嘛。"

• **SUBSTANCE** 物质 **5** [U] (*physics* 物) physical substance that everything in the world is made of; not mind or spirit (统称) 物质: *to study the properties of matter* 研究物质的属性 **6** [U] (*formal*) a substance or things of a particular sort (某种) 东西，物品，材料: *Add plenty of organic matter to improve the soil.* 施用大量的有机肥料以改良土壤。◇ *elimination of **waste matter** from the body* 体内废物的排除 ◇ *She didn't approve of their choice of **reading matter**.* 她不赞同他们选用的阅读材料。➲ SEE ALSO SUBJECT MATTER

IDM **as a matter of 'fact** **1** used to add a comment on sth that you have just said, usually adding sth that you think the other person will be interested in 事实上；其实；说真的: *It's a nice place. We've stayed there ourselves, as a matter of fact.* 那个地方不错。事实上，我们在那儿待过。 **2** used to disagree with sth that sb has just said (表示不同意) 事实上，其实 **SYN** **actually**: *'I suppose you'll be leaving soon, then?' 'No, as a matter of fact I'll be staying for another two years.'* "我想你快要离开了吧？" "不。事实上，我还要再待两年呢。" **be another/a different 'matter** to be very different 另外一回事；又是一回事；另当别论: *I know which area they live in, but whether I can find their house is a different matter.* 我知道他们住在哪一地区，但能不能找到他们的房子则是另外一回事了。 **for 'that matter** used to add a comment on sth that you have just said 就此而论；在这方面: *I didn't like it much. Nor did the kids, for that matter.* 我不怎么喜欢它。孩子们也同样不喜欢。 **it's just/only a matter of 'time (before...)** used to say that sth will definitely happen, although you are not sure when 早晚的事；只是时间问题: *It's only a matter of time before they bring out their own version of the software.* 他们推出自己的软件只是个时间问题。 **(as) a matter of 'course** (as) the usual and correct thing to do (作为) 理所当然的事；(当作) 常规: *We always check people's addresses as a matter of course.* 我们总是照例检查一下人们的地址。 **a matter of 'hours, 'minutes, etc.** | **a matter of 'inches, 'metres, etc.** only a few hours, minutes, etc. 只有几个小时、几分钟 (或几英寸、几米等) 之多；不多于…: *It was all over in a matter of minutes.* 几分钟就全部结束了。◇ *The bullet missed her by a matter of inches.* 子弹几乎擦着她的身体飞过。 **a ˌmatter of ˌlife and 'death** used to describe a situation that is very important or serious 生死攸关的事；成败的关键 **a ˌmatter of 'record** (*formal*) something that has been recorded as being true 有案可查的事 **no matter** used to say that sth is not important 没关系；不要紧；不重要 **no matter who, what, where, etc.** used to say that sth is always true, whatever the situation is, or that sb should certainly do sth 不论…；无论…；不管…: *They don't last long no matter how careful you are.* 不管你如何小心，这些东西都维持不了很久。◇ *Call me when you get there, no matter what the time is.* 无论什么时间，你到了那儿就给我打电话。➲ MORE AT FACT, LAUGHING

■ ***verb*** [I, T] (not used in the progressive tenses 不用于进行时) to be important or have an important effect on sb/sth 事关紧要；要紧；有重大影响: **~ (to sb)** *The children matter more to her than anything else in the world.* 对于她来说，在这个世界上没有比孩子更重要的了。◇ *'What did you say?' 'Oh, it doesn't matter'* (= it is not important enough to repeat). "你说什么？" "噢，没什么。" ◇ *'I'm afraid I forgot that book again.' 'It doesn't matter* (= it is not important enough to worry about).*'* "很抱歉，我又忘了把那本书带来了。" "没事儿。" ◇ ***What does it matter** if I spent $100 on it—it's my money!* 我花 100 美元买这东西有什么问题，那是我的钱！◇ *As long as you're happy, that's **all that matters**.* 你幸福就行了，这才是最重要的。◇ *After his death, nothing seemed to matter any more.* 他死了以后，好像一切都无所谓了。◇ *He's been in prison, you know— **not that it matters*** (= that information does not affect my opinion of him). 你知道，他坐过牢，可那倒无关紧要。◇ **~ (to sb) who, what, etc....** *Does it really matter who did it?* 是谁干的真的很重要吗？◇ ***It doesn't matter** to me what you do.* 你做什么我无所谓。◇ **~ (to sb) that...** *It didn't matter that the weather was bad.* 天气不好并没什么影响。

ˌmatter-of-'fact *adj.* said or done without showing any emotion, especially in a situation in which you would expect sb to express their feelings 不动感情的；据实的 **SYN** **unemotional**: *She told us the news of his death in a very matter-of-fact way.* 她很平静地把他去世的消息告诉了我们。▶ **ˌmatter-of-'factly** *adv.*

mat·ting /'mætɪŋ/ *noun* rough WOVEN material for making MATS 编垫子的材料: *coconut matting* 制垫椰衣

mat·tins *noun* [U] = MATINS

mat·tock /'mætək/ *noun* a heavy garden tool with a long handle and a metal head, used for breaking up soil, cutting roots, etc. 鹤嘴锄

mat·tress /'mætrəs/ *noun* the soft part of a bed, that you lie on 床垫: *a **soft/hard mattress*** 软/硬床垫 ➲ VISUAL VOCAB PAGE V24

mat·ur·ation **AW** /ˌmætʃu'reɪʃn/ *noun* [U] (*formal*) **1** the process of becoming or being made mature (= ready to eat or drink after being left for a period of time) 成熟过程；成熟 **2** the process of becoming adult 成年过程；长大成人 ▶ **mat·ur·ation·al** **AW** *adj.*

ma·ture **AW** /mə'tʃʊə(r); mə'tjʊə(r); *NAmE* -'tʃʊr; -'tʊr/ *adj.*, *verb*

■ ***adj.*** **HELP** **maturer** is occasionally used instead of **more mature** 有时不用 more mature，而用 maturer。

• **SENSIBLE** 明智 **1** (of a child or young person 儿童或年轻人) behaving in a sensible way, like an adult 明白事理的；成熟的；像成人似的: *Jane is very mature for her age.* 简年龄不大，却很成熟。◇ *a mature and sensible attitude* 一副深谙世事的态度 **OPP** **immature**

• **FULLY GROWN** 成熟 **2** (of a person, a tree, a bird or an animal 人、树木、鸟或兽) fully grown and developed 成熟的；发育完全的: *sexually mature* 性成熟的 ◇ *a mature oak/eagle/elephant* 成熟的橡树；成年的鹰/象 **OPP** **immature** ➲ SYNONYMS AT OLD

• **WINE/CHEESE** 葡萄酒；干酪 **3** developed over a period of time to produce a strong, rich flavour 发酵成熟的；酿成的

• **NO LONGER YOUNG** 不再年轻 **4** used as a polite or humorous way of saying that sb is no longer young (礼貌或幽默的说法) 成年的，不再年轻的: *clothes for the mature woman* 成年妇女的服装 ◇ *a man of mature years* 中年男人

• **WORK OF ART** 艺术作品 **5** created late in an artist's life and showing great understanding and skill 成熟的；技艺精湛的；创作于晚年的

• **INSURANCE POLICY** 保险单 **6** (*business* 商) ready to be paid 到期 (应该支付) 的

▶ **ma·ture·ly** *adv.*

IDM **on mature re'flection/conside'ration** (*formal*) after thinking about sth carefully and for a long time 经过深思熟虑；经过审慎考虑

■ ***verb***

• **BECOME FULLY GROWN** 成熟 **1** [I] to become fully grown or developed 成熟；长成: *This particular breed of cattle matures early.* 这一品种的牛发育成熟快。◇ *Technology in this field has matured considerably over the last decade.* 这一领域的技术经过过去十年的发展已经相当完善。

• **BECOME SENSIBLE** 变得明智 **2** [I] to develop emotionally and start to behave like a sensible adult (情感和认识) 成熟；有判断力: *He has matured a great deal over the past year.* 经过过去这一年，他成熟了许多。

• **DEVELOP SKILL** 提高技能 **3** [I] **~ (into sth)** to fully develop a particular skill or quality 使 (技能或素质) 成熟；充分发展: *She has matured into one of the country's finest actresses.* 她已经成长为这个国家一位最优秀的演员。

• **WINE/CHEESE** 葡萄酒；干酪 **4** [I, T] **~ (sth)** if wine, cheese, etc. **matures** or **is matured**, it develops over a period of time to produce a strong, rich flavour 酿成；制成；发酵成熟

• **INSURANCE POLICY** 保险单 **5** [I] (*business* 商) to reach the date when it must be paid 到期 (应付款)

ma,ture 'student *noun* (*BrE*) an adult student who goes to college or university some years after leaving school 成年学生（中学毕业几年后再读大学的学生）

ma·tur·ity AW /mə'tʃʊərəti; -'tjʊə-; *NAmE* -'tʃʊr-; -'tʊr-/ *noun* [U] **1** the quality of thinking and behaving in a sensible, adult manner （思想行为、作品等）成熟：*He has maturity beyond his years.* 他过于老成。◇ *Her poems show great maturity.* 她的诗歌显得非常成熟。➲ COMPARE IMMATURITY at IMMATURE **2** (of a person, an animal, or a plant 人或动植物) the state of being fully grown or developed 成熟；成年；完全长成：*The forest will take 100 years to* ***reach maturity.*** 这片森林要花 100 年时间才能成材。➲ COMPARE IMMATURITY at IMMATURE **3** (*business* 商) (of an insurance policy, etc. 保险单等) the time when money you have invested is ready to be paid 到期（应付款）

matzo /'mætsəʊ; *NAmE* 'mɑːtsoʊ/ *noun* [U, C] (*pl.* **-os**) a type of bread in the form of a large flat biscuit, traditionally eaten by Jews during Passover; one of these biscuits 无酵饼（犹太人在逾越节时吃）

maud·lin /'mɔːdlɪn/ *adj.* **1** talking in a silly, emotional way, often full of pity for yourself, especially when drunk （尤指醉酒时）言语伤感的，感情脆弱的，自怜的 SYN **sentimental** **2** (of a book, film/movie, or song 书籍、电影或歌曲) expressing or causing exaggerated emotions, especially in way that is not sincere 渲染感情的；煽情的 SYN **sentimental**

M

maul /mɔːl/ *verb* **1** ~ **sb** (of an animal 动物) to attack and injure sb by tearing their flesh 袭击；撕咬 SYN **savage** **2** ~ **sb/sth** to touch sb/sth in an unpleasant and/or violent way 粗手粗脚地摆弄；粗暴地对待 **3** ~ **sth/sb** to criticize sth/sb severely and publicly 狠狠地批评；猛烈抨击 SYN **savage** **4** ~ **sb** (*informal*) to defeat sb easily 轻易击败 SYN **trash** ▶ **maul·ing** *noun* [sing.]: *The play received a mauling from the critics.* 这出戏受到了剧评人无情的抨击。◇ *They face a mauling by last year's winners.* 他们面临去年的优胜者的严重威胁。

maun·der /'mɔːndə(r)/ *verb* [I] ~ (**on**) (**about sth**) (*BrE*) to talk or complain about sth in a boring and/or annoying way 唠叨；咕哝；抱怨

Maundy Thurs·day /,mɔːndi 'θɜːzdeɪ; -di; *NAmE* 'θɜːrz-/ *noun* [U, C] (in the Christian Church) the Thursday before Easter （基督教）圣星期四，濯足节

mau·so·leum /,mɔːsə'liːəm/ *noun* a special building made to hold the dead body of an important person or the dead bodies of a family 陵墓：*the royal mausoleum* 王室陵墓

mauve /məʊv; *NAmE* moʊv/ *adj.* pale purple in colour 淡紫色的 ▶ **mauve** *noun* [U]

maven /'meɪvn/ *noun* (*NAmE*) an expert on sth 专家；内行

mav·er·ick /'mævərɪk/ *noun* a person who does not behave or think like everyone else, but who has independent, unusual opinions 持不同意见者；独行其是者；言行与众不同者 ▶ **mav·er·ick** *adj.* [only before noun]: *a maverick film director* 独行其是的电影导演

maw /mɔː/ *noun* **1** (*literary*) something that seems like a big mouth that swallows things up completely 无底洞；吞噬一切的深渊 **2** (*old-fashioned*) an animal's stomach or throat （动物的）胃，咽喉

mawk·ish /'mɔːkɪʃ/ *adj.* (*disapproving*) expressing or sharing emotion in a way that is exaggerated or embarrassing 无病呻吟的；自作多情的；多愁善感的 SYN **sentimental**: *a mawkish poem* 无病呻吟的诗歌 ▶ **mawk·ish·ness** *noun* [U]

max AW /mæks/ *abbr., verb*

■ ***abbr.*** **1** (*also* **max.** *especially in NAmE*) maximum 最高的；最多的；最大极限的：*max temperature 18°C* 最高气温 18 摄氏度 **2** (*informal*) at the most 至多：*It'll cost $50 max.* 这东西至多花 50 美元。OPP **min.**

IDM **to the 'max** to the highest level or greatest amount possible 最高程度地；最大数量地：*She believes in living life to the max.* 她认为人应当尽量活得充实。

■ ***verb***

PHR V **,max (sth) 'out** (*NAmE, informal*) to reach, or make sth reach, the limit at which nothing more is possible （使）达到最高极限：*The car maxed out at 150 mph.* 汽车达到了每小时 150 英里的最快速度。

maxi /'mæksi/ *noun* a long coat, dress or skirt that reaches to the ankles （长至脚踝的）大衣，连衣裙，长裙

max·illa /mæk'sɪlə/ *noun* (*pl.* **max·il·lae** /-liː/) (*anatomy* 解) the JAW 上颌骨 ▶ **max·il·lary** /mæk'sɪləri/ *adj.* [only before noun]：*a maxillary fracture* 上颌骨骨裂

maxim /'mæksɪm/ *noun* a well-known phrase that expresses sth that is usually true or that people think is a rule for sensible behaviour 格言；箴言；座右铭

max·imal /'mæksɪml/ *adj.* [usually before noun] (*specialist*) as great or as large as possible 最大的；最高的 ➲ COMPARE MINIMAL

maxi·mize AW (*BrE also* **-ise**) /'mæksɪmaɪz/ *verb* **1** ~ **sth** to increase sth as much as possible 使增加到最大限度：*to* ***maximize efficiency/fitness/profits*** 最大限度地提高效率 / 增强体质 / 增加利润 ◇ (*computing* 计) *Maximize the window to full screen.* 将窗口最大化。 **2** ~ **sth** to make the best use of sth 充分利用；最大限度地利用：*to* ***maximize opportunities/resources*** 充分利用机会 / 资源 OPP **minimize** ▶ **maxi·miza·tion**, **-isa·tion** AW /,mæksɪmaɪ'zeɪʃn; *NAmE* -mə'z-/ *noun* [U]

max·imum 🔑 AW /'mæksɪməm/ *adj., noun*

■ ***adj.*** 🔑 [only before noun] (*abbr.* **max**) as large, fast, etc. as is possible, or the most that is possible or allowed 最高的；最多的；最大极限的：*the* ***maximum speed/temperature/volume*** 最快速度；最高气温；最大体积 ◇ ***For maximum effect*** *do the exercises every day.* 每天锻炼以取得最佳效果。◇ *a maximum security prison* 最高戒备等级的监狱 ➲ COMPARE MINIMUM *adj.*

■ ***noun*** 🔑 [usually sing.] (*pl.* **max·ima** /'mæksɪmə/) (*abbr.* **max**) the greatest amount, size, speed, etc. that is possible, recorded or allowed 最大量；最大限度；最高限度：*a maximum of 30 children in a class* 每班至多 30 名学生 ◇ *The job will require you to use all your skills* ***to the maximum.*** 这项工作将要求你最大限度地发挥你的技能。◇ *The July maximum* (= the highest temperature recorded in July) *was 30°C.* 七月的最高气温是 30 摄氏度。◇ *What is the absolute maximum you can afford to pay?* 你最多能出多少钱？ OPP **minimum**

May 🔑 /meɪ/ *noun* [U, C] the fifth month of the year, between April and June 五月 HELP To see how **May** is used, look at the examples at **April**. * May 的用法见词条 April 下的示例。

may 🔑 /meɪ/ *modal verb, noun*

■ ***modal verb*** (*negative* **may not**, *rare short form* **mayn't** /'meɪənt/, **might** /maɪt/, **might not**, **mightn't** /'maɪtnt/)

1 🔑 used to say that sth is possible （有可能但不肯定）也许，可能：*That may or may not be true.* 这可能是真的，也可能不是。◇ *He may have* (= perhaps he has) *missed his train.* 他可能没赶上火车。◇ *They* ***may well*** *win.* 他们完全可能赢。◇ *There is a range of programs on the market which may be described as design aids.* 市场上有各种程序，可以称为设计辅助工具。 **2** 🔑 used when admitting that sth is true before introducing another point, argument, etc. （转折前所述情况属实）也许，可能：*He may be a good father but he's a terrible husband.* 他或许是一位好父亲，但却是个很糟糕的丈夫。 **3** 🔑 (*formal*) used to ask for or give permission （征求同意或表示允许）可以：*May I come in?* 我可以进来吗？ ◇ *You may come in if you wish.* 你想进来就进来吧。➲ NOTE AT CAN[1] **4** (*formal*) used as a polite way of making a comment, asking a question, etc. （礼貌地评价或提问等）可以：*You look lovely, if I may say so.* 我觉得你看上去很可爱。◇ *May I ask why you took that decision?* 我可否问一下你为什么要作出那样的决定？ ◇ *If I may just add one thing…* 我想再补充一点… **5** (*formal*) used to express wishes and hopes （表示愿望）但愿：*May she rest in peace.* 愿她安息。◇ *Business has been* *thriving in the past year.* ***Long may it continue*** *to do so.* 在过去的一年里生意蒸蒸日上。但愿这种情况能持续下去。 **6** (*formal*) used to say what the purpose of sth is （表明目的）可以，能够： *There is a need for more resources so that all children may have a decent education.* 需要更多的资源投入，让所有的孩子都受到良好的教育。 ➲ NOTE AT MODAL

IDM be that as it 'may (*formal*) despite that 尽管如此 **SYN nevertheless**: *I know that he has tried hard; be that as it may, his work is just not good enough.* 我知道他已经尽力了，尽管如此，他的工作仍不太理想。

▪ ***noun*** [U] the white or pink flowers of the HAWTHORN 山楂花

maybe /ˈmeɪbi/ *adv.* **1** used when you are not certain that sth will happen or that sth is true or is a correct number （不确定）大概，或许，可能 **SYN perhaps**: *Maybe he'll come, maybe he won't.* 他可能来，也可能不来。 ◇ *'Are you going to sell your house?' 'Maybe.'* "你要卖房子吗？" "也许吧。" ◇ *It will cost two, maybe three hundred pounds.* 这个要花二百英镑，或许三百英镑。 ◇ *We go there maybe once or twice a month.* 我们每月大概去那里一到两次。 **2** used when making a suggestion （提出建议）或许，也许 **SYN perhaps**: *I thought maybe we could go together.* 我觉得或许我们可以一起去。 ◇ *Maybe you should tell her.* 也许你应该告诉她。 **3** used to agree with sb, and to add more information that should be thought about （赞同并补充信息）或许，也许，可能 **SYN perhaps**: *'You should stop work when you have the baby.' 'Maybe, but I can't afford to.'* "有了孩子你就不应该工作了。" "或许是吧，可我负担不起呀。" **4** used when replying to a question or an idea, when you are not sure whether to agree or disagree （不置可否）也许，或许 **SYN perhaps**: *'I think he should resign.' 'Maybe.'* "我觉得他应该辞职。" "也许是吧。"

'May bug *noun* = COCKCHAFER

'May Day *noun* the first day of May, celebrated as a spring festival and, in some countries, as a holiday in honour of working people 五朔节；（某些国家的）五一劳动节 ➲ COMPARE LABOR DAY

May·day /ˈmeɪdeɪ/ *noun* [U] an international radio signal used by ships and aircraft needing help when they are in danger （船只或航空器遇险时用的国际无线电求救信号）
ORIGIN From the French *venez m'aider*, meaning 'come and help me'. 源自法语 venez m'aider，意为"速来救助"。

may·fly /ˈmeɪflaɪ/ *noun* (*pl.* **-ies**) a small insect that lives near water and only lives for a very short time 蜉蝣

may·hem /ˈmeɪhem/ *noun* [U] confusion and fear, usually caused by violent behaviour or by some sudden shocking event 骚乱；慌乱： *There was absolute mayhem when everyone tried to get out at once.* 众人蜂拥而出，造成了极大的混乱。

may·on·naise /ˌmeɪəˈneɪz; *NAmE* ˈmeɪəneɪz/ (*also informal* **mayo** /ˈmeɪəʊ; *NAmE* ˈmeɪoʊ/) *noun* [U] a thick cold white sauce made from eggs, oil and VINEGAR, used to add flavour to SANDWICHES, salads, etc. 蛋黄酱（用作三明治、色拉等的调味品）： *egg mayonnaise* (= a dish made with hard-boiled eggs and mayonnaise) 鸡蛋美奶滋（由煮老的鸡蛋和蛋黄酱制成）

mayor /meə(r); *NAmE* ˈmeɪər/ *noun* **1** (in England, Wales and Northern Ireland) the head of a town, BOROUGH or county council, chosen by other members of the council to represent them at official ceremonies, etc. （英格兰、威尔士和北爱尔兰由议员选举产生的）镇长，市长，郡长： *the Lord Mayor of London* 伦敦市长 ➲ COMPARE PROVOST (3) **2** the head of the government of a town or city, etc., elected by the public （民选的）市长；镇长： *the Mayor of New York* 纽约市长 ◇ *Mayor Bob Anderson* 鲍勃・安德森市长 ▸ **may·oral** /ˈmeərəl; *NAmE* ˈmeɪə-/ *adj.* [only before noun]: ***mayoral robes/duties*** 市长的礼袍 / 职责

may·or·alty /ˈmeərəlti; *NAmE* ˈmeɪər-/ *noun* (*pl.* **-ies**) (*formal*) **1** the title or position of a mayor 市长头衔；市长职位 **2** the period of time during which a person is a mayor 市长任期

may·or·ess /meəˈres; *NAmE* ˈmeɪərəs/ *noun* **1** (*also* **ˌlady 'mayor**) a woman who has been elected mayor 女市长 ➲ NOTE AT GENDER **2** (in England, Wales and Northern Ireland) the wife of a mayor or a woman who helps a mayor at official ceremonies （英格兰、威尔士和北爱尔兰）市长（或镇长、郡长）夫人，市长（或镇长、郡长）女助理

may·pole /ˈmeɪpəʊl; *NAmE* -poʊl/ *noun* a decorated pole that people dance round in celebrations on MAY DAY 五朔节花柱；五月柱

maz·door /mʌzˈdʊə(r); -ˈdɔː(r); *NAmE* mʌzˈdʊr/ *noun* (*IndE*) a person whose job involves hard physical work that is not skilled 苦力；劳工

maze /meɪz/ *noun* **1** a system of paths separated by walls or HEDGES built in a park or garden, that is designed so that it is difficult to find your way through 迷宫： *We got lost in the maze.* 我们在迷宫里迷失了方向。 ◇ (*figurative*) *The building is a maze of corridors.* 这座建筑长廊交错，简直就是一座迷宫。 ➲ COMPARE LABYRINTH **2** [usually sing.] a large number of complicated rules or details that are difficult to understand 纷繁复杂的规则；复杂难懂的细节： *a maze of regulations* 一大堆纷繁复杂的规章制度 **3** (*NAmE*) a printed PUZZLE in which you have to draw a line that shows a way through a complicated pattern of lines 迷宫图

ma·zurka /məˈzɜːkə; *NAmE* məˈzɜːrkə/ *noun* a fast Polish dance for four or eight couples, or a piece of music for this dance 马祖卡舞（节奏轻快的波兰舞，由四对或八对舞伴参加）；马祖卡舞曲

MB *abbr.* **1** /ˌem ˈbiː/ (in Britain) Bachelor of Medicine (a university degree in medicine) 医学学士（英国的大学医学学位）： *Philip Watt MB* 医学学士菲利普・瓦特 **2** (in writing 书写形式) MEGABYTE 兆字节（计算机内存或数据单位）： *512MB of memory* * 512 兆内存

Mb (*also* **Mbit**) *abbr.* (in writing 书写形式) MEGABIT 兆比特（计算机内存或数据单位）

MBA /ˌem biː ˈeɪ/ *noun* the abbreviation for 'Master of Business Administration' (a second university degree in business) 工商管理硕士（全写为 Master of Business Administration）： *to do an MBA* 攻读工商管理学硕士学位

MBE /ˌem biː ˈiː/ *noun* the abbreviation for 'Member (of the Order) of the British Empire' (an award given to some people in Britain for a special achievement) 英帝国勋位获得者，英帝国员佐勋衔获得者（全写为 Member (of the Order) of the British Empire，授予有特殊功勋者的奖章）： *She was made an MBE in 2007.* 她于 2007 年获得英帝国勋位。 ◇ *Jim Cronin MBE* 英帝国勋位获得者吉姆・克罗宁

MC /ˌem ˈsiː/ *noun* **1** the abbreviation for MASTER OF CEREMONIES 司仪，仪式主持人（全写为 master of ceremonies） **2 M.C.** the abbreviation for 'Member of Congress' 议会议员，国会议员（全写为 Member of Congress） **3** a person who provides entertainment at a club or party by instructing the DJ (1) and performing RAP (2) music 说唱歌手

MCAT /ˈemkæt/ *noun* the abbreviation for 'Medical College Admission Test' (a test that students must pass in order to study medicine in the US) （美国）医学院入学考试（全写为 Medical College Admission Test）

Mc·Carthy·ism /məˈkɑːθiɪzəm; *NAmE* -ˈkɑːrθ-/ *noun* [U] an aggressive investigation during the 1950s against people in the US government and other institutions who were thought to be COMMUNISTS, in which many people lost their jobs 麦卡锡反共审查（20 世纪 50 年代在美国政府等机构中进行，很多人因此失业）；麦卡锡主义

McCoy /məˈkɔɪ/ *noun*
IDM the real Mc'Coy (*informal*) something that is genuine and that has value, not a copy 真货；真品： *It's an*

M

American flying jacket, the real McCoy. 这是件真正的美国飞行员夹克。

ˈm-commerce *noun* [U] (*BrE, business* 商) the business of buying and selling products on the Internet by using mobile/cell phones and other similar technology 移动（电子）商务（用手机等技术手段通过互联网进行交易）：*m-tickets and other m-commerce products* 移动电子票务等移动业务产品

MD /ˌem ˈdiː/ *noun* **1** the abbreviation for 'Doctor of Medicine' 医学博士（全写为 Doctor of Medicine）：*Paul Clark MD* 医学博士保罗・克拉克 **2** (*BrE*) the abbreviation for MANAGING DIRECTOR 总裁，总经理，常务董事（全写为 managing director）：*Where's the MD's office?* 总经理办公室在哪儿?

MDF /ˌem diː ˈef/ *noun* [U] the abbreviation for 'medium density fibreboard' (a building material made of wood or other plant FIBRES pressed together to form boards) 中密度纤维板（全写为 medium density fibreboard，建筑材料）

MDT /ˌem diː ˈtiː/ *abbr.* MOUNTAIN DAYLIGHT TIME 山区夏令时间

ME /ˌem ˈiː/ *noun* **1** (*BrE*) (*also* **ˌchronic faˈtigue syndrome** *NAmE, BrE*) [U] the abbreviation for 'myalgic encephalomyelitis' (an illness that makes people feel extremely weak and tired and that can last a long time) 肌痛性脑脊髓炎（全写为 myalgic encephalomyelitis，一种慢性疲劳症） **2** (*NAmE*) MEDICAL EXAMINER 法医；验尸官

me 🔑 *pron., noun*

▪ ***pron.*** 🔑 /mi; *strong form* miː/ the form of *I* that is used when the speaker or writer is the object of a verb or preposition, or after the verb *be* （I 的宾格）我：*Don't hit me.* 别打我。◇ *Excuse me!* 劳驾！◇ *Give it to me.* 给我。◇ *You're taller than me.* 你比我高。◇ *Hello, it's me.* 喂，是我。◇ *'Who's there?' 'Only me.'* "谁在那儿？" "只有我。" **HELP** The use of **me** in the last three examples is correct in modern standard English. **I** in these sentences would be considered much too formal for almost all contexts, especially in *BrE*. 后三例中 me 的用法符合现代英语的标准。若在这些句子中使用 I，几乎在任何语境里都会显得过于正式，尤其是在英式英语中。

▪ ***noun*** (*also* **mi**) /miː/ (*music* 音) the third note of a MAJOR SCALE 大调音阶的第 3 音

mea culpa /ˌmeɪə ˈkʊlpə/ *exclamation* (*from Latin, often humorous*) used when you are admitting that sth is your fault 是我的错；是我的责任

mead /miːd/ *noun* [U] a sweet alcoholic drink made from HONEY and water, drunk especially in the past （尤指旧时的）蜜糖酒，蜂蜜酒

meadow /ˈmedəʊ; *NAmE* -doʊ/ *noun* a field covered in grass, used especially for HAY 草地；牧场：*water meadows* (= near a river) 岸边的草地 ➲ VISUAL VOCAB PAGE V3

meadow·lark /ˈmedəʊlɑːk; *NAmE* -doʊlɑːrk/ *noun* a singing bird that lives on the ground 草地鹨（鸣禽，栖于地面）

meagre (*especially US* **mea·ger**) /ˈmiːɡə(r)/ *adj.* small in quantity and poor in quality 少量且劣质的 **SYN** **paltry**：*a meagre diet of bread and water* 只有面包和水的简朴饮食 ◇ *She supplements her meagre income by cleaning at night.* 她靠做夜间清洁工来补贴其微薄的收入。

meal 🔑 /miːl/ *noun* **1** 🔑 [C] an occasion when people sit down to eat food, especially breakfast, lunch or dinner 早（或午、晚）餐；一顿饭：*Try not to eat between meals.* 两餐之间尽量别吃东西。◇ *Lunch is his main meal of the day.* 午饭是他的正餐。◇ (*especially BrE*) *to* ***go out for a meal*** (= to go to a restaurant to have a meal) 去餐馆用餐 ◇ *What time would you like your evening meal?* 你打算几点钟吃晚饭？ ➲ WORDFINDER NOTE AT EAT ➲ COLLOCATIONS AT RESTAURANT **2** 🔑 [C] the food that is eaten at a meal 一餐所吃的食物：*Enjoy your meal.* 请用餐。◇ *a three-course meal* 有三道菜的一顿饭 **3** [U] (often in compounds 常构成复合词) grain that has been crushed to produce a powder, used as food for animals and for making flour 谷物粗粉（用作饲料或加工面粉） ➲ SEE ALSO BONEMEAL, OATMEAL (1), WHOLEMEAL

IDM **make a ˈmeal of sth** (*informal*) to spend a lot of time, energy, etc. doing sth in a way that other people think is unnecessary and/or annoying 小题大做；做事过于认真 ➲ MORE AT SQUARE *adj.*

▼ **MORE ABOUT ...** 补充说明

meals

- People use the words **dinner**, **lunch**, **supper** and **tea** in different ways depending on which English-speaking country they come from. In Britain it may also depend on which part of the country or which social class a person comes from. 来自不同英语国家的人使用 dinner、lunch、supper 和 tea 的方式各不相同。在英国，这些词的用法按某人来自的地区和社会阶层而有所区别。
- A meal eaten in the middle of the day is usually called **lunch**. If it is the main meal of the day it may also be called **dinner** in *BrE*, especially in the north of the country. 午餐通常叫作 lunch，但在英式英语中，尤其在英国北部，如果是一天的主餐，亦可叫作 dinner。
- A main meal eaten in the evening is usually called **dinner**, especially if it is a formal meal. **Supper** is also an evening meal, but more informal than **dinner** and usually eaten at home. It can also be a late meal or something to eat and drink before going to bed. 晚上的主餐，尤其是正式用餐，通常叫作 dinner。supper 亦为晚餐，但不如 dinner 正式，而且一般在家里吃，亦可指较晚的晚餐或睡前夜宵。
- In *BrE*, **tea** is a light meal in the afternoon with sandwiches, cakes, etc. and a cup of tea. 在英式英语中，tea 指下午的茶点，包括三明治、糕点等和一杯茶：*a cream tea* 奶油茶点 It can also be a main meal eaten early in the evening, especially by children. * tea 亦可指傍晚主餐，尤指孩子傍晚食用的：*What time do the kids have their tea?* 孩子们什么时候用傍晚主餐？
- As a general rule, if **dinner** is the word someone uses for the meal in the middle of the day, they probably call the meal in the evening **tea** or **supper**. If they call the meal in the middle of the day **lunch**, they probably call the meal in the evening **dinner**. 一般说来，若午餐叫 dinner，晚餐则大多叫 tea 或 supper。如果午餐叫 lunch，晚餐则大多叫 dinner。
- **Brunch**, a combination of breakfast and lunch, is becoming more common, especially as a meal where your guests serve themselves. * brunch 是早餐和午餐合二为一的早午餐，如今日趋普遍，尤为自助餐形式。

meal·ie /ˈmiːli/ *noun* [C, usually pl., U] (*SAfrE*) **1** = MAIZE **2** = CORN ON THE COB

ˌmeals on ˈwheels *noun* [pl.] a service that takes meals to old or sick people in their homes （为老弱病残者提供的）上门送餐服务

ˈmeal ticket *noun* **1** (*informal*) a person or thing that you see only as a source of money and food 被视为金钱和食物来源的人（或物）：*He suspected that he was just a meal ticket for her.* 他感到对她来说自己不过是一张餐券。 **2** (*NAmE*) a card or ticket that gives you the right to have a cheap or free meal, for example at school 饭票；餐券

meal·time /ˈmiːltaɪm/ *noun* a time in the day when you eat a meal 就餐时间；进餐时间

meal·worm /ˈmiːlwɜːm; *NAmE* -wɜːrm/ *noun* a LARVA which is used to feed pet birds 大黄粉虫幼体（用作宠物鸟食）

mealy /ˈmiːli/ *adj.* (especially of vegetables or fruit 尤指蔬菜或水果) soft and dry when you eat them 干软的；面的；吃起来松软干爽的

M

ˌ**mealy-ˈmouthed** *adj.* (*disapproving*) not willing or honest enough to speak in a direct or open way about what you really think 不直爽的；说话拐弯抹角的：*mealy-mouthed politicians* 言不由衷的政客

mean /miːn/ *verb, adj., noun*

■ ***verb*** (**meant, meant** /ment/)

• **HAVE AS MEANING** 有含意 **1** (not used in the progressive tenses 不用于进行时) to have sth as a meaning 表示…的意思：**~ sth** *What does this sentence mean?* 这个句子是什么意思？ ◇ ***What is meant by** 'batch processing'?* * batch processing 是什么意思？ ◇ **~ sth to sb** *Does the name 'Jos Vos' **mean anything to you*** (= do you know who he is)? 你知道乔斯·沃斯是谁吗？ ◇ **~ (that)…** *The flashing light means (that) you must stop.* 闪烁的灯光表示你必须停下。

• **INTEND AS MEANING** 意思是 **2** (not used in the progressive tenses 不用于进行时) to intend to say sth on a particular occasion 意思是；本意是：**~ sth** *What did he mean by that remark?* 他说那话是什么意思？ ◇ *'Perhaps we should try another approach.' '**What do you mean?**'* (= I don't understand what you are suggesting.) "也许我们应该试一试别的方法。" "你指的是什么方法？" ◇ ***What do you mean**, you thought I wouldn't mind?* (= of course I mind and I am very angry) 你这是什么意思？你以为我不会在意吗？ ◇ ***What she means is** that there's no point in waiting here.* 她的意思是说在这儿等下去没什么意思。 ◇ *I always found him a little strange, **if you know what I mean*** (= if you understand what I mean by 'strange'). 我总觉得他有点儿怪，如果你明白我这话是什么意思。 ◇ ***I know what you mean*** (= I understand and feel sympathy). *I hated learning to drive too.* 我明白你的意思。我也不愿意学开车。 ◇ (*informal*) *It was like—weird. **Know what I mean?*** 它有点儿，怪异。你明白我的意思吗？ ◇ ***I see what you mean*** (= I understand although I may not agree), *but I still think it's worth trying.* 我知道你是什么意思，但我仍然认为值得一试。 ◇ ***See what I mean*** (= I was right and this proves it, doesn't it)? *She never agrees to anything I suggest.* 这下可证明我说的对了吧？我说什么她都不听。 ◇ *'But Pete doesn't know we're here!' '**That's what I mean!**'* (= that's what I have been trying to tell you.) "可是皮特不知道我们在这儿呀！" "我就是这个意思嘛！" ◇ *Do you mean Ann Smith or Mary Smith?* 你是说安·史密斯，还是说玛丽·史密斯？ ◇ **~ (that)…** *Did he mean (that) he was dissatisfied with our service?* 他是不是表示对我们的服务不满意？ ◇ ***You mean*** (= are you telling me) *we have to start all over again?* 你是不是说我们必须从头再来一遍？ ➲ LANGUAGE BANK AT I.E. ➲ EXPRESS YOURSELF AT CORRECT

• **HAVE AS PURPOSE** 有目的 **3** to have sth as a purpose or intention 打算；意欲；有…的目的 SYN **intend**：**~ sth** ***What did she mean by** leaving so early* (= why did she do it)? 她为什么这么早就走了？ ◇ *Don't laugh! **I mean it*** (= I am serious). 别笑！我是认真的。 ◇ *He **means trouble*** (= to cause trouble). 他存心捣乱。 ◇ **~ sth as sth** *Don't be upset—I'm sure she meant it as a compliment.* 别不高兴，我肯定她的原意是要称赞你的。 ◇ **~ what…** *He **means what he says*** (= is not joking, exaggerating, etc.). 他说话是当真的。 ◇ **~ sth for sb/sth** *The chair was clearly meant for a child.* 这椅子显然是专为儿童设计的。 ◇ *Don't be angry. I'm sure she **meant it for the best*** (= intended to be helpful). 别生气了。我相信她是真心想要帮忙的。 ◇ **~ to do sth** *She means to succeed.* 她一意求成。 ◇ *I'm sorry I hurt you. I **didn't mean to**.* 对不起，弄疼你了。我不是故意的。 ◇ *I'm feeling very guilty—**I've been meaning** to call my parents for days, but still haven't got around to it.* 我感到非常内疚，几天来我一直打算给父母打电话，但还是没机会打。 ◇ **~ sb/sth to do sth** *I didn't mean you to read the letter.* 我没打算让你看那封信。 ◇ ***You're meant to*** (= you are supposed to) *pay before you go in.* 你要先交钱才能进去。 ◇ **~ (that)…** (*formal*) *I never meant (that) you should come alone.* 我从来没打算让你一个人来。

• **INTEND SB TO BE/DO STH** 让某人成为 / 做 **4** [often passive] to intend sb to be or do sth 想要某人成为；想要某人去做：**~ sb for sth/sb** *I was never **meant for** the army* (= did not have the qualities needed to become a soldier). 我根本就不是块当兵的料。 ◇ *Duncan and Makiko **were meant for each other*** (= are very suitable as partners). 邓肯和真纪子真是天生的一对。 ◇ **~ sb/sth to be sth** *His father meant him to be an engineer.* 他父亲想让他当工程师。 ◇ *She did everything to get the two of them together, but I guess it just wasn't **meant to be**.* 她极力撮合他们俩，但我觉得那根本不可能。

• **HAVE AS RESULT** 有结果 **5** to have sth as a result or a likely result 产生…结果；意味着 SYN **entail**：**~ sth** *Spending too much now will mean a shortage of cash next year.* 现在花销太多就意味着明年现金短缺。 ◇ **~ to be/do sth** *Do you have any idea **what it means to** be poor?* 你知不知道贫穷意味着什么？ ◇ **~ (that)…** *We'll have to be careful with money but **that doesn't mean** (that) we can't enjoy ourselves.* 我们必须精打细算，可也并不是说我们就不能享受生活。 ◇ **~ doing sth** *This new order will mean working overtime.* 这新订单一来，我们就得加班加点。 ◇ **~ sb/sth doing sth** *The injury could mean him missing next week's game.* 这次受伤可能使他无法参加下周的比赛。 ➲ MORE LIKE THIS 26, page R28

• **BE IMPORTANT** 重要 **6** [no passive] **~ sth to sb** to be of value or importance to sb 对某人重要（或有价值）：*Your friendship means a great deal to me.* 你的友谊对我来说是很珍贵的。 ◇ ***$20 means a lot*** (= represents a lot of money) *when you live on $100 a week.* 当你每周就靠 100 美元维持生活时，20 美元可是个大数目。 ◇ *Money **means nothing to him**.* 金钱对于他来说毫无价值。 ◇ *Her children **mean the world to her**.* 她的孩子就是她的一切。

IDM **be meant to be sth** to be generally considered to be sth 被普遍认为是：*This restaurant is meant to be excellent.* 都说这家饭店很棒。 **I mean** (*informal*) used to explain or correct what you have just said（解释或更正刚说过的话）我是说，意思是说：*It was so boring—I mean, nothing happened for the first hour!* 真是无聊。我是说，一个小时都过去了，什么事儿都没发生！ ◇ *She's English—Scottish, I mean.* 她是英格兰人，不对，是苏格兰人。 **mean ˈbusiness** (*informal*) to be serious in your intentions 是认真的；说话算数：*He has the look of a man who means business.* 他看上去像是个说话算话的人。 **mean (sb) no ˈharm | not mean (sb) any ˈharm** to not have any intention of hurting sb 没有恶意；并非出于恶意 **mean to ˈsay** used to emphasize what you are saying or to ask sb if they really mean what they say（强调要说的话，或问对方是否真是这个意思）意思是说：*I mean to say, you should have known how he would react!* 我的意思是说，你本应料到他会作何反应！ ◇ *Do you mean to say you've lost it?* 你是说你把那东西给弄丢了？ **ˈmean well** (*usually disapproving*) to have good intentions, although their effect may not be good 本意是好的；出于好心

■ ***adj.*** (**mean·er, mean·est**)

• **NOT GENEROUS** 吝啬 **1** (*BrE*) (*NAmE* **cheap**) not willing to give or share things, especially money 吝啬的；小气的：*She's always been mean with money.* 她在花钱方面总是非常吝啬。 OPP **generous** ➲ SEE ALSO STINGY

• **UNKIND** 不友善 **2 ~ (to sb)** (of people or their behaviour 人或行为) unkind, for example by not letting sb have or do sth 不善良；刻薄：*Don't be so mean to your little brother!* 别对你弟弟那么刻薄！

• **ANGRY/VIOLENT** 愤怒；凶暴 **3** (*especially NAmE*) likely to become angry or violent 要发怒的；要发狂的：*That's a mean-looking dog.* 那狗看上去很凶。

• **SKILFUL** 熟练 **4** (*informal, especially NAmE*) very good and skilful 熟练的；出色的：*He's a mean tennis player.* 他是一名出色的网球选手。 ◇ *She plays a mean game of chess.* 她的国际象棋下得很棒。

• **AVERAGE** 平均 **5** [only before noun] (*specialist*) average; between the highest and the lowest, etc. 平均的；介于中间的：*the mean temperature* 平均气温

• **INTELLIGENCE** 智力 **6** (*formal*) (of a person's understanding or ability 人的理解力或能力) not very great 平庸的；一般的：*This should be clear even to the meanest intelligence.* 就是对智力最平庸的人来说，这也应当是非常明了的。

• **POOR** 穷 **7** (*literary*) poor and dirty in appearance 又穷又脏的：*mean houses/streets* 脏乱的房屋 / 街道 **8** (*old-fashioned*) born into or coming from a low social class 出身卑贱的；社会地位低下的

▶ **mean·ly** *adv.* **mean·ness** *noun* [U]

M

IDM be no mean... (*approving*) used to say that sb is very good at doing sth 了不起；很出色：*His mother was a painter, and he's no mean artist himself.* 他的母亲是画家，他本人也是很出色的艺术家。

■ ***noun*** ➲ SEE ALSO MEANS

• **MIDDLE WAY** 中间 **1** ~ (**between A and B**) a quality, condition, or way of doing sth that is in the middle of two extremes and better than either of them 中间；中庸；折中：*He needed to find a mean between frankness and rudeness.* 他需要在坦诚与唐突之间找到折中的方法。

• **AVERAGE** 平均 **2** (*also* **arith,metic 'mean**) (*mathematics* 数) the value found by adding together all the numbers in a group, and dividing the total by the number of numbers 算术平均；平均数；平均值 ➲ SEE ALSO GEOMETRIC MEAN

IDM the happy/golden 'mean (*approving*) a course of action that is not extreme 中庸之道

me·ander /mi'ændə(r)/ *verb* **1** [I] (+ **adv./prep.**) (of a river, road, etc. 河流、道路等) to curve a lot rather than being in a straight line 蜿蜒而行；迂回曲折：*The stream meanders slowly down to the sea.* 这条小河弯弯曲曲缓慢地流向大海。 **2** [I] (+ **adv./prep.**) to walk slowly and change direction often, especially without a particular aim 漫步；闲逛 SYN **wander** **3** [I] (+ **adv./prep.**) (of a conversation, discussion, etc. 谈话、讨论等) to develop slowly and change subject often, in a way that makes it boring or difficult to understand （乏味地、令人费解地）漫谈，闲聊 ▶ **me·ander** *noun* : *the meanders of a river* 河流的各处河曲 ➲ VISUAL VOCAB PAGE V5

M

me·ander·ings /mi'ændrɪŋz/ *noun* [pl.] **1** a course that does not follow a straight line 蜿蜒曲折的路程：*the meanderings of a river/path* 曲折蜿蜒的一条河 / 小路 **2** walking or talking without any particular aim 漫步；闲逛；闲聊；漫话：*his philosophical meanderings* 他的哲学漫谈

meanie (*also* **meany**) /'mi:ni/ *noun* (*pl.* **-ies**) (*informal*) used especially by children to describe an unkind person who will not give them what they want （儿童用语）小气鬼，刻薄鬼

mean·ing /'mi:nɪŋ/ *noun, adj.*

■ ***noun***

• **OF SOUND/WORD/SIGN** 声音；文字；信号 **1** [U, C] ~ (**of sth**) the thing or idea that a sound, word, sign, etc. represents （声音、文字、信号等传递的）意义，意思：*What's the meaning of this word?* 这个单词的意思是什么？◇ *Words often have several meanings.* 单词往往有若干个意思。◇ *'Honesty'? He doesn't know the meaning of the word!* "诚实"？他不明白这个词是什么意思！ ➲ WORDFINDER NOTE AT DICTIONARY, WORD

• **OF WHAT SB SAYS/DOES** 某人的言行 **2** [U, C] the things or ideas that sb wishes to communicate to you by what they say or do （想要表达的）意义，意思：*I don't quite get your meaning* (= understand what you mean to say). 我不太明白你要说的意思。◇ *What's the meaning of this? I explicitly told you not to leave the room.* 这是什么意思？我明确地告诉过你不要离开这个房间。

• **OF FEELING/EXPERIENCE** 情感；经历 **3** [U] the real importance of a feeling or experience 真正重要性；价值：*With Anna he learned the meaning of love.* 通过与安娜相处，他明白了爱意味着什么。

• **OF BOOK/PAINTING** 书籍；绘画 **4** [U, C] the ideas that a writer, artist, etc. wishes to communicate through a book, painting, etc. （作家或艺术家要表达的）意义，含意，思想：*several layers of meaning* 若干层意义 ◇ *There are, of course, deeper meanings in the poem.* 当然，这首诗里还有更深层的含意。

• **SENSE OF PURPOSE** 追求的目标 **5** [U] the quality or sense of purpose that makes you feel that your life is valuable （人生的）意义，价值，目标：*Her life seemed to have lost all meaning.* 她的生活似乎已毫无价值。◇ *Having a child gave new meaning to their lives.* 有了孩子使他们的生活有了新的方向。

■ ***adj.*** [usually before noun] = MEANINGFUL (2)

mean·ing·ful /'mi:nɪŋfl/ *adj.* **1** serious and important 严肃的；重要的；重大的：*a meaningful relationship/discussion/experience* 重要的关系 / 讨论 / 经历 **2** (*also less frequent* **mean·ing**) intended to communicate or express sth to sb, without any words being spoken 意味深长的；意在言外的：*She gave me a meaningful look.* 她意味深长地看了我一眼。 **3** having a meaning that is easy to understand 意义明显的；易于理解的：*These statistics are not very meaningful.* 这些统计数字说明不了什么问题。 ▶ **mean·ing·ful·ly** /-fəli/ *adv.* **mean·ing·ful·ness** *noun* [U]

mean·ing·less /'mi:nɪŋləs/ *adj.* **1** without any purpose or reason and therefore not worth doing or having 毫无意义的；毫无目的的；无价值的 SYN **pointless**：*a meaningless existence* 毫无意义的存在 ◇ *We fill up our lives with meaningless tasks.* 我们终日忙忙碌碌，过得毫无意义。 **2** not considered important 不重要的；无所谓的 SYN **irrelevant**：*Fines are meaningless to a huge company like that.* 对于这样一家大公司，罚金根本算不了什么。 **3** not having a meaning that is easy to understand 意思不明确的；晦涩的：*To me that painting is completely meaningless.* 对我来说，这幅油画晦涩难懂。 ▶ **mean·ing·less·ly** *adv.* **mean·ing·less·ness** *noun* [U]

means /mi:nz/ *noun* (*pl.* **means**) **1** [C] ~ (**of sth/of doing sth**) an action, an object or a system by which a result is achieved; a way of achieving or doing sth 方式；方法；途径：*Television is an effective means of communication.* 电视是一种有效的传播手段。◇ *Is there any means of contacting him?* 有没有什么办法和他取得联系？◇ *Have you any **means of identification**?* 你有没有任何身份证件？◇ *We needed to get to London but we had no **means of transport**.* 我们需要去伦敦，但却没有任何交通工具。 **2** [pl.] the money that a person has 财富；钱财：*People should pay **according to their means**.* 人们应该按照各自的负担能力来消费。◇ *He doesn't have the means to support a wife and child.* 他无钱养活妻小。◇ *Private school fees are **beyond the means of most people*** (= more than they can afford). 私立学校的费用是大多数人无力支付的。◇ *Are the monthly repayments **within your means*** (= can you afford them)? 这样按月还钱，你负担得了吗？◇ *Try to **live within your means*** (= not spend more money than you have). 要尽可能量入为出。◇ *a man of means* (= a rich man) 有钱人

IDM by 'all means used to say that you are very willing for sb to have sth or do sth 可以；当然行；没问题：*'Do you mind if I have a look?' 'By all means.'* "我看一眼行吗？""当然可以。" **by means of sth** (*formal*) with the help of sth 借助…手段；依靠…方法：*The load was lifted by means of a crane.* 重物是用起重机吊起来的。 **by 'no means | not by 'any (manner of) means** not at all 决不；一点也不：*She is by no means an inexperienced teacher.* 她绝不是个毫无经验的教师。◇ *We haven't won yet, not by any means.* 我们离成功还远着呢。 **a ,means to an 'end** a thing or action that is not interesting or important in itself but is a way of achieving sth else （本身并不重要或有趣的）达到目的的手段：*He doesn't particularly like the work but he sees it as a means to an end.* 他不怎么喜欢这项工作，只是把它看作达到目的的手段而已。 ➲ MORE AT END *n.*, FAIR *adj.*, WAY *n.*

'means test *noun* an official check of sb's wealth or income in order to decide if they are poor enough to receive money from the government, etc. for a particular purpose 收入调查，经济情况调查（以确定是否可领取政府补贴等） ▶ **'means-test** *verb* ~ **sb**

'means-tested *adj.* paid to sb according to the results of a means test 按收入调查结果支付的：*means-tested benefits* 按经济情况调查结果支付的补助

meant PAST TENSE, PAST PART. OF MEAN

mean·time /'mi:ntaɪm/ *noun, adv.*

■ ***noun***

IDM for the 'meantime (*BrE*) for a short period of time but not permanently 眼下；暂时：*I'm changing my email address but for the meantime you can use the old one.* 我要更换电邮地址，不过那个旧的暂时也还可以用。 **in the 'meantime** in the period of time between two times or two events 其间；同时 SYN **meanwhile**：*My first novel* *was rejected by six publishers. In the meantime I had written a play.* 我的第一部小说遭到六家出版商的拒绝。其间我又完成了一部戏剧。

■ **adv.** (*informal*) = MEANWHILE (1), (2)：*I'll contact them soon. Meantime don't tell them I'm back.* 我会尽快和他们联系。在此期间，不要告诉他们我回来了。

mean·while /ˈmiːnwaɪl/ *adv., noun*

■ **adv. 1** (*also informal* **mean·time**) while sth else is happening 同时；与此同时：*Bob spent fifteen months alone on his yacht. Ann, meanwhile, took care of the children on her own.* 鲍勃独自在他的游艇上待了十五个月。在这段时间，安一个人照顾孩子。 **2** (*also informal* **mean·time**) in the period of time between two times or two events 其间：*The doctor will see you again next week. Meanwhile, you must rest as much as possible.* 医生下周还会给你看病。在此期间，你一定要尽可能多休息。 **3** used to compare two aspects of a situation（比较两方面）对比之下：*Stress can be extremely damaging to your health. Exercise, meanwhile, can reduce its effects.* 压力可能严重损害你的健康，锻炼则可以减轻这些损害。

■ **noun**

IDM **for the ˈmeanwhile** (*BrE*) for a short period of time but not permanently 一会儿；暂时：*We need some new curtains, but these will do for the meanwhile.* 我们需要一些新的窗帘，但这些暂时还可以用。 **in the ˈmeanwhile** in the period of time between two times or two events 在此期间；与此同时：*I hope to go to medical school eventually. In the meanwhile, I am going to study chemistry.* 我希望最终能上医学院。这期间我打算学化学。

meany = MEANIE

mea·sles /ˈmiːzlz/ *noun* [U] an infectious disease, especially of children, that causes fever and small red spots that cover the whole body 麻疹 ➲ SEE ALSO GERMAN MEASLES

measly /ˈmiːzli/ *adj.* (*informal, disapproving*) very small in size or quantity; not enough 很小的；很少的；不足的：*I get a measly £4 an hour.* 我每小时只拿少得可怜的 4 英镑。

meas·ur·able /ˈmeʒərəbl/ *adj.* **1** that can be measured 可测量的；可度量的 **2** [usually before noun] large enough to be noticed or to have a clear and noticeable effect 显著的；有明显影响的：*measurable improvements* 显著的改进 ▶ **meas·ur·ably** /-əbli/ *adv.*：*Working conditions have changed measurably in the last ten years.* 十年来，工作环境有了明显的改变。

mea·sure /ˈmeʒə(r)/ *verb, noun*

■ **verb**

• **SIZE/QUANTITY** 大小；数量 **1** to find the size, quantity, etc. of sth in standard units 测量；度量：**~ sth (in sth)** *A ship's speed is measured in knots.* 船速以节测量。◇ *a device that measures the level of radiation in the atmosphere* 测量大气中辐射强度的仪器 ◇ ***measuring equipment/instruments*** 测量装备 / 仪器 ◇ **~ sb/sth for sth** *He's gone to be measured for a new suit.* 他去量尺寸做新套装去了。◇ **~ how much, how long, etc....** *A dipstick is used to measure how much oil is left in an engine.* 量油尺是用来探查引擎中的剩余油量的。 **2** *linking verb* (not used in the progressive tenses 不用于进行时) **+ noun** to be a particular size, length, amount, etc.（指尺寸、长短、数量等）量度为：*The main bedroom measures 12ft by 15ft.* 主卧室宽 12 英尺，长 15 英尺。◇ *The pond measures about 2 metres across.* 这个池塘宽约 2 米。

• **JUDGE** 判断 **3** **~ sth | ~ how, what, etc....** to judge the importance, value or effect of sth 估量，判定（重要性、价值或影响等）SYN **assess**：*It is difficult to measure the success of the campaign at this stage.* 在现阶段还难以估量这场运动的成败。

PHRV **ˈmeasure sb/sth against sb/sth** to compare sb/sth with sb/sth 使相比较：*The figures are not very good when measured against those of our competitors.* 和我们的竞争者相比，我们的数字并不乐观。 **ˌmeasure sth↔ˈout** to take the amount of sth that you need from a larger amount 取出（或量出）所需量：*He measured out a cup of milk and added it to the mixture.* 他倒了一杯牛奶，掺了进去。 **ˌmeasure ˈup | ˌmeasure sb/sth↔ˈup** to measure sb/sth 测量；量度：*We spent the morning measuring up and deciding where the furniture would go.* 我们花了一上午量来量去，决定家具怎么摆。 **ˌmeasure ˈup (to sth/sb)** (usually used in negative sentences and questions 通常用于否定句和疑问句) to be as good, successful, etc. as expected or needed 达到预期的要求；符合标准 SYN **match up**：*Last year's intake just didn't measure up.* 去年纳入的人数没有达到预期的要求。◇ *The job failed to measure up to her expectations.* 这项工作没有满足她的期望。

■ **noun**

• **OFFICIAL ACTION** 正式行动 **1** [C] an official action that is done in order to achieve a particular aim 措施；方法：***safety/security/austerity measures*** 安全 / 保安 / 紧缩措施 ◇ ***a temporary/an emergency measure*** 临时 / 紧急措施 ◇ **~ (to do sth)** *We must take **preventive measures** to reduce crime in the area.* 我们必须采取预防措施来减少这个地区的犯罪。◇ *The government is introducing tougher measures to combat crime.* 政府正在引入更强硬的手段来打击犯罪。◇ *measures against racism* 反种族主义措施 ◇ *Police in riot gear were in attendance as a **precautionary measure**.* 身着防暴服的警察到场戒备。 ➲ SYNONYMS AT ACTION ➲ SEE ALSO HALF MEASURES

• **UNIT OF SIZE/QUANTITY** 度量单位 **2** [C, U] a unit used for stating the size, quantity or degree of sth; a system or a scale of these units 度量单位；计量标准：***weights and measures*** 度量衡 ◇ *The Richter Scale is a measure of ground motion.* 里氏震级是测量地动的单位。◇ ***liquid/dry measure*** 液量；干量 ◇ *Which measure of weight do pharmacists use?* 药剂师使用什么剂量单位？ **3** [C] (especially of alcohol 尤指酒) a standard quantity 标准量：*a generous measure of whisky* 比标准量稍多一点的威士忌

• **AMOUNT** 程度 **4** [sing.] a particular amount of sth, especially a fairly large amount （一定的）量，程度 SYN **degree**：*A measure of technical knowledge is desirable in this job.* 做这项工作最好多懂一些技术知识。◇ *She achieved some measure of success with her first book.* 她出第一部书就获得了相当的成功。

• **INSTRUMENT FOR MEASURING** 测量仪器 **5** [C] an instrument such as a stick, a long tape or a container that is marked with standard units and is used for measuring 量器；计量工具 ➲ SEE ALSO TAPE MEASURE

• **WAY OF SHOWING/JUDGING** 展示方式；判断方法 **6** [sing.] a sign of the size or the strength of sth 尺度；标准；程度：*Sending flowers is a measure of how much you care.* 送花能表明你有多关心。 **7** [C] a way of judging or measuring sth 判断；衡量：*an accurate measure of ability* 能力的准确评判 ◇ *Is this test a good measure of reading comprehension?* 这种测试是判断阅读理解力的好方法吗？

• **SUGGESTED NEW LAW** 法案 **8** [C] (*NAmE*) a written suggestion, especially one for a new law made by the lawmakers of a state （尤指州立法者的）提案，法案，议案：*a motion to refer the measure to another committee* 将提案提交给另一个委员会的动议 ◇ *a ballot measure* (= a change in the law that voters decide on) 投票表决的法案

• **IN MUSIC** 音乐 **9** (*NAmE*) (*BrE usually* **bar**) [C] one of the short sections of equal length that a piece of music is divided into, and the notes that are in it （乐谱的）小节（音乐节拍单位） ➲ PICTURE AT MUSIC

IDM **beyond ˈmeasure** (*formal*) very much 非常；极其：*He irritated me beyond measure.* 他使我非常生气。 **for good ˈmeasure** as an extra amount of sth in addition to what has already been done or given 作为额外增添；外加的项目：*Use 50g of rice per person and an extra spoonful for good measure.* 按每人 50 克大米的分量，再额外加一勺。 **full/short ˈmeasure** the whole of sth or less of sth than you expect or should have 足量；不足量：*We experienced the full measure of their hospitality.* 我们领受了他们十足的盛情。◇ *The concert only lasted an hour, so we felt we were getting short measure.* 音乐会仅仅持续了一个小时，让我们有一种缺斤少两的感觉。 **in full ˈmeasure** (*formal*) to the greatest possible degree 最大程度地；最大限度地 **get/take/have the ˈmeasure of sb | get/have/take sb's ˈmeasure** (*formal*) to form an opinion about sb's character or abilities so that you can deal with them 摸清某人的底细：*After only one game, the chess*

M

champion had the measure of his young opponent. 仅仅一局过后，这位国际象棋冠军就摸清了年轻对手的实力。 **in no small ˈmeasure | in some, equal, etc. ˈmeasure** (*formal*) to a large extent or degree; to some, etc. extent or degree 在很大（或某种、同样等）程度上： *The introduction of a new tax accounted in no small measure for the downfall of the government.* 这届政府的垮台在很大程度上归因于征收一种新税。◇ *Our thanks are due in equal measure to every member of the team.* 我们同样感谢每一位队员。 **ˌmade to ˈmeasure** (*BrE*) made especially for one person according to particular measurements 量身定制的 **SYN** **bespoke**: *You'll need to get a suit made to measure.* 你得定做一套西装。◇ *a made-to-measure suit* 定做的套装 ➲ MORE AT LARGE *adj.*

meas·ured /ˈmeʒəd; *NAmE* -ərd/ *adj.* slow and careful; controlled 缓慢谨慎的；慎重的；克制的： *She replied in a measured tone to his threat.* 她以很有分寸的语气回应了他的威胁。◇ *He walked down the corridor with measured steps.* 他迈着缓慢而匀称的脚步沿着走廊走去。

meas·ure·less /ˈmeʒələs; *NAmE* -ʒərl-/ *adj.* (*literary*) very great or without limits 极大的；无边无际的： *the measureless oceans* 浩瀚的海洋

meas·ure·ment 🔑 /ˈmeʒəmənt; *NAmE* ˈmeʒərm-/ *noun* **1** 🔑 [U] the act or the process of finding the size, quantity or degree of sth 测量；度量： *the metric system of measurement* 公制度量衡 ◇ *Accurate measurement is very important in science.* 在科学领域，精确的测量非常重要。 ➲ COLLOCATIONS AT SCIENTIFIC **2** 🔑 [C, usually pl.] the size, length or amount of sth （某物的）尺寸，长度，数量： *to take sb's **chest/waist measurement*** 量某人的胸围 / 腰围 ◇ *Do you know your measurements* (= the size of parts of your body)? 你知道自己的尺寸吗？◇ *The exact measurements of the room are 3 metres 20 by 2 metres 84.* 这间屋子的准确尺寸是长 3.20 米，宽 2.84 米。

ˈmeasuring cup *noun* a metal or plastic container used in the US for measuring quantities when cooking （美国烹饪用的）量杯 ➲ VISUAL VOCAB PAGE V27

ˈmeasuring jug *noun* (*BrE*) a glass or plastic container for measuring liquids when cooking 量壶；量杯 ➲ VISUAL VOCAB PAGE V27

ˈmeasuring spoon *noun* a metal or plastic spoon used in the US for measuring quantities when cooking （烹调用）量匙 ➲ VISUAL VOCAB PAGE V27

ˈmeasuring tape *noun* = TAPE MEASURE

meat 🔑 /miːt/ *noun* **1** 🔑 [U, C] the flesh of an animal or a bird eaten as food; a particular type of this 肉；（某种）食用肉： *a **piece/slice of meat*** 一块 / 一片肉 ◇ *horse meat* (= from a horse) 马肉 ◇ *dog meat* (= for a dog) 喂狗的肉 ◇ *meat-eating animals* 食肉动物 ◇ *There's not much meat on this chop.* 这块肉排没什么肉。◇ (*figurative, humorous*) *There's not much meat on her* (= she is very thin). 她太骨感了。 ➲ SEE ALSO LUNCHEON MEAT, MINCEMEAT, RED MEAT, SAUSAGE MEAT, WHITE MEAT **2** [U] ~ (**of sth**) the important or interesting part of sth 重要的部分；有趣的部分 **SYN** **substance**: *This chapter contains the real meat of the writer's argument.* 这一章包含了作者的主要论点。

IDM **ˌmeat and ˈdrink to sb** something that sb enjoys very much 让某人非常开心的事 ➲ MORE AT DEAD *adj.*, MAN *n.*

ˌmeat and poˈtatoes *noun* [U] (*NAmE*) the most basic and important aspects or parts of sth 最基本的部分；最必要的部分： *Issues like this are the newspaper's meat and potatoes.* 像这样的话题是报纸赖以生存的素材。

ˌmeat-and-poˈtatoes *adj.* [only before noun] (*NAmE*) **1** dealing with the most basic and important aspects of sth 根本的；基本的；主要的： *a meat-and-potatoes argument* 基本论据 **2** liking plain, simple things 喜欢简朴的： *He's a real meat-and-potatoes guy.* 他是个十分崇尚简朴的人。

ˌmeat and two ˈveg *noun* [U] (*BrE, informal*) a dish of meat with potatoes and another vegetable, considered as typical traditional British food 双素炖肉（双素之一为土豆，典型的传统英国菜）

meat·ball /ˈmiːtbɔːl/ *noun* a small ball of finely chopped meat, usually eaten hot with a sauce 肉丸

ˈmeat grinder *noun* (*NAmE*) = MINCER

ˌmeat ˈloaf *noun* [C, U] finely chopped meat, onions, etc. that are mixed together and shaped like a LOAF of bread and then baked 肉糕

ˈmeat packing *noun* [U] (*NAmE*) the process of killing animals and preparing the meat for sale 肉类加工

meaty /ˈmiːti/ *adj.* (**meat·ier, meati·est**) **1** containing a lot of meat 含肉多的 **2** smelling, or tasting like meat 气味（或味道）像肉的： *a meaty taste* 肉香的口味 **3** (*approving*) containing a lot of important or interesting ideas 富含重要（或有趣）的观点的 **SYN** **substantial**: *a meaty discussion* 内容充实的讨论 **4** (*informal*) large and fat; with a lot of flesh 肥硕的；多肉的 **SYN** **fleshy**: *a meaty hand* 肥胖的手 ◇ *big, meaty tomatoes* 又大又多肉的西红柿

mebi·bit /ˈmebibɪt/ *noun* (*abbr.* **Mib, Mibit**) (*computing* 计) = MEGABIT (2)

mebi·byte /ˈmebibaɪt/ *noun* (*abbr.* **MiB**) (*computing* 计) = MEGABYTE (2)

Mecca /ˈmekə/ *noun* **1** a city in Saudi Arabia that is the holiest city of Islam, being the place where the Prophet Muhammad was born 麦加（沙特阿拉伯城市，伊斯兰教圣地，先知穆罕默德出生地） **2** (*usually* **mecca**) a place that many people like to visit, especially for a particular reason 热门地方： *The coast is a mecca for tourists.* 这个海岸是旅游的热门景点。

mech·an·ic /məˈkænɪk/ *noun* **1** [C] a person whose job is repairing machines, especially the engines of vehicles 机械师；机械修理工；技工： *a car mechanic* 汽车修理工 **2 mechanics** [U] the science of movement and force 力学 ➲ SEE ALSO QUANTUM MECHANICS **3 mechanics** [U] the practical study of machinery 机械学： *the school's car maintenance department where students learn basic mechanics* 该校学生可以学习基础机械学的汽车保养系 **4 the mechanics** [pl.] the way sth works or is done 方法；手段： *The exact mechanics of how payment will be made will be decided later.* 确切的付款方法以后再作决定。

mech·an·ic·al /məˈkænɪkl/ *adj.* **1** operated by power from an engine 机动的；机械驱动的；机械的： *a **mechanical device/toy/clock*** 机械装置 / 玩具 / 钟表 ◇ *mechanical parts* 机械部件 **2** connected with machines and engines 机器的；机械的；发动机的： ***mechanical problems/defects*** 机械问题 / 缺陷 ◇ *The breakdown was due to a mechanical failure.* 抛锚是机械故障造成的。 **3** (*disapproving*) (of people's behaviour and actions 人的行为或行动) done without thinking, like a machine 机械般的；呆头呆脑的；无思想的 **SYN** **routine**: *a **mechanical gesture/response*** 机械式的手势 / 回答 **4** connected with the physical laws of movement and cause and effect (= with MECHANICS) 机械的；机械学的： *mechanical processes* 机械过程 **5** (of a person 人) good at understanding how machines work 擅长于机械原理的 ▸ **mech·an·ic·al·ly** /-kli/ *adv.* : *a mechanically powered vehicle* 机械驱动的交通工具 ◇ *She spoke mechanically, as if thinking of something else.* 她机械地说着话，仿佛在想着什么别的事情。◇ *He's always been mechanically minded.* 他对机械方面一直很在行。

meˌchanical engiˈneering *noun* [U] the study of how machines are designed, built and repaired 机械工程学 ▸ **meˌchanical engiˈneer** *noun*

mech·an·ism **AW** /ˈmekənɪzəm/ *noun* **1** a set of moving parts in a machine that performs a task 机械装置；机件： *a delicate watch mechanism* 精致的手表机件 **2** a method or a system for achieving sth 方法；机制： *mechanisms for dealing with complaints from the general public* 处理公众投诉的机制 **3** a system of parts in a living thing that together perform a particular function （生物体内

的）机制，构造：*the balance mechanism in the ears* 耳内的平衡机制 ◇ *Pain acts as a natural* ***defence mechanism.*** 疼痛起着自然防护机制的作用。

mech·an·is·tic /ˌmekəˈnɪstɪk/ *adj.* (*often disapproving*) connected with the belief that all things in the universe can be explained as if they were machines 机械论的：*the mechanistic philosophy that compares the brain to a computer* 将人脑比作电脑的机械论哲学 ▶ **mech·an·is·ti·cal·ly** /-kli/ *adv.*

mech·an·ize (*BrE also* **-ise**) /ˈmekənaɪz/ *verb* [usually passive] **~ sth** to change a process, so that the work is done by machines rather than people 机械化；使机械化 **SYN** **automate**：*The production process is now highly mechanized.* 现在的生产过程高度机械化。 ▶ **mech·an·iza·tion, -isa·tion** /ˌmekənaɪˈzeɪʃn; *NAmE* -nəˈz-/ *noun* [U]: *the increasing mechanization of farm work* 越来越高的农活机械化程度

mecha·tron·ics /ˌmekəˈtrɒnɪks; *NAmE* -ˈtrɑːn-/ *noun* [U] technology that combines ELECTRONICS and MECHANICAL ENGINEERING 机电一体化；机电工程 ➲ MORE LIKE THIS 1, page R25

Med /med/ **the Med** *noun* [sing.] (*informal*) the Mediterranean Sea 地中海

med /med/ *adj.* (*informal, especially NAmE*) = MEDICAL：*a med student* 医学系的学生 ◇ *She's in med school.* 她在念医学。

medals 奖章　**shield** 盾形奖牌

trophy 奖座　**rosette** 玫瑰形饰物　**cup** 奖杯

medal /ˈmedl/ *noun, verb*

■ ***noun*** a flat piece of metal, usually shaped like a coin, that is given to the winner of a competition or to sb who has been brave, for example in war 奖章；勋章：*to win a gold medal in the Olympics* 在奥林匹克运动会上赢得一枚金牌 ◇ *to award a medal for bravery* 奖赏一枚英勇勋章 **IDM** ▶ SEE DESERVE

■ ***verb*** (**-ll-**, *especially US* **-l-**) [I] to win a medal in a competition （在比赛中）获得奖牌（或奖章）：*Evans has medalled at several international events.* 埃文斯已经多次在国际比赛中获奖。

med·al·lion /məˈdæliən/ *noun* a piece of jewellery in the shape of a large flat coin worn on a chain around the neck （状似大奖章的）项链垂饰 ➲ VISUAL VOCAB PAGE V70

med·al·list (*BrE*) (*US* **med·al·ist**) /ˈmedəlɪst/ *noun* a person who has received a medal, usually for winning a competition in a sport （通常指体育比赛的）奖牌获得者：*an Olympic medallist* 奥运会奖牌获得者 ◇ *a* ***gold/silver/bronze medallist*** 金牌 / 银牌 / 铜牌获得者

ˌMedal of ˈHonor *noun* the highest award that the US gives to a member of the armed forces who has shown very great courage in a war 荣誉勋章（美国授予英勇军人的最高奖赏）

ˈmedal play *noun* [U] = STROKE PLAY

med·dle /ˈmedl/ *verb* (*disapproving*) **1** [I] **~ (in/with sth)** to become involved in sth that does not concern you 管闲事；干涉；干预 **SYN** **interfere**：*He had no right to meddle in her affairs.* 他无权干涉她的事情。 **2** [I] **~ (with sth)** to touch sth in a careless way, especially when it is not yours or when you do not know how to use it correctly 瞎摘，乱弄（尤指不应管或不懂的事物）：*Somebody had been meddling with her computer.* 有人擅自弄过她的电脑。 ▶ **med·dling** *noun* [U]

med·dler /ˈmedlə(r)/ *noun* (*disapproving*) a person who tries to get involved in sth that does not concern them 管闲事的人 **SYN** **busybody**

meddle·some /ˈmedlsəm/ *adj.* (*disapproving*) (of people 人) enjoying getting involved in situations that do not concern them 好管闲事的；爱干预的 **SYN** **interfering**

mede·vac /ˈmedɪvæk/ *noun* [U] (*especially NAmE*) the movement of injured soldiers or other people to hospital in a HELICOPTER or other aircraft （伤员等的）空运救护，飞行送院 ➲ COMPARE AIR AMBULANCE

media 🔑 **AW** /ˈmiːdiə/ *noun* **1** 🔑 **the media** [U+sing./pl. v.] the main ways that large numbers of people receive information and entertainment, that is television, radio, newspapers and the Internet 大众传播媒介，大众传播工具（指电视、广播、报纸、互联网）：***the news/broadcasting/national media*** 新闻 / 广播 / 国家的大众传播媒介 ◇ *The trial was fully reported in the media.* 媒体对这次审判进行了全面报道。 ◇ *The media was/were accused of influencing the final decision.* 媒体受责左右了终审判决。 ◇ *Any event attended by the actor received widespread* ***media coverage.*** 这位演员参加任何一项活动，媒体都作了广泛报道。 ➲ SEE ALSO MASS MEDIA, NEW MEDIA **2** PL. OF MEDIUM ➲ MORE LIKE THIS 30, page R28

medi·aeval = MEDIEVAL

med·ial /ˈmiːdiəl/ *adj.* (*specialist*) located in the middle, especially of the body or of an organ （身体或器官等）内侧的，近中的

me·dian /ˈmiːdiən/ *adj., noun*

■ ***adj.*** [only before noun] (*specialist*) **1** having a value in the middle of a series of values 中间值的；中间的：*the* ***median age/price*** 中年；中等价位 **2** located in or passing through the middle 在中间的；通过中点的：*a* ***median point/line*** 中点；中线

■ ***noun*** **1** (*mathematics* 数) the middle value of a series of numbers arranged in order of size 中位数 **2** (*geometry* 几何) a straight line passing from a point of a triangle to the centre of the opposite side. （三角形的）中线 **3** (*also* **ˈmedian strip**) (*both NAmE*) (*BrE* **ˌcentral reserˈvation**) a narrow strip of land that separates the two sides of a major road such as a MOTORWAY or INTERSTATE （高速公路、州际公路等的）中间带

ˈmedia studies *noun* [U+sing./pl. v.] the study of newspapers, television, radio, etc. as a subject at school, etc. 大众传播学；大众传媒学

me·di·ate **AW** /ˈmiːdieɪt/ *verb* **1** [I, T] to try to end a disagreement between two or more people or groups by talking to them and trying to find things that everyone can agree on 调停；调解；斡旋：**~ (in sth)** *The Secretary-General was asked to mediate in the dispute.* 秘书长被请来调解这次纷争。 ◇ **~ between A and B** *An independent body was brought in to mediate between staff and management.* 由一个独立机构介入，在劳资之间进行调解。 ◇ **~ sth** ***to mediate differences/disputes/problems*** 调解分歧 / 争端 / 问题 **2** [T] **~ sth** to succeed in finding a solution to a disagreement between people or groups 找到（解决分

歧的）方法；促成…的解决 SYN **negotiate**: *They mediated a settlement.* 他们找到了一个解决方案。**3** [T, usually passive] **~ sth** (*formal* or *specialist*) to influence sth and/or make it possible for it to happen 影响…的发生；使…可能发生：*Educational success is mediated by economic factors.* 经济因素影响着教育的成功。▸ **me·di·ation** AW /ˌmiːdiˈeɪʃn/ *noun* [U]

me·di·ator /ˈmiːdieɪtə(r)/ *noun* a person or an organization that tries to get agreement between people or groups who disagree with each other 调停者；斡旋者；解决纷争的人（或机构）

medic /ˈmedɪk/ *noun* **1** (*informal, especially BrE*) a medical student or doctor 医科学生；医生；大夫 **2** (*NAmE*) a person who is trained to give medical treatment, especially sb in the armed forces（尤指军队中的）医护人员；军医

Me·dic·aid /ˈmedɪkeɪd/ *noun* [U] (in the US) the insurance system that provides medical care for poor people 医疗补助制度（美国政府向贫困者提供医疗保险）

med·ic·al AW /ˈmedɪkl/ *adj., noun*

■ ***adj.*** [usually before noun] **1** connected with illness and injury and their treatment 医学的；医疗的：***medical advances/care/research*** 医学上的进展；医疗；医学研究 ◇ *her* ***medical condition/history/records*** 她的疾病 / 病史 / 病历 ◇ *the* ***medical profession*** 医疗职业 ◇ *a* ***medical student/school*** 医科学生；医学院 ◇ *a medical certificate* (= a statement by a doctor that gives details of your state of health) 健康证明 ➲ SEE ALSO MED **2** connected with ways of treating illness that do not involve cutting the body 内科的：*medical or surgical treatment* 内科或外科疗法 ▸ **med·ic·al·ly** AW /-kli/ *adv.*: ***medically fit/unfit*** 体格健康 / 不佳

■ ***noun*** (*also* ˌ**medical examiˈnation**) a thorough examination of your body that a doctor does, for example before you start a particular job 体格检查 ➲ SEE ALSO EXAM (2)

ˌ**medical eˈxaminer** *noun* (*abbr.* **ME**) (*NAmE*) a doctor whose job is to examine a dead body in order to find out the cause of death 法医；验尸官 ➲ COMPARE PATHOLOGIST

ˈ**medical hall** *noun* (*IndE, informal*) a chemist's shop/drugstore 药店；药房

ˈ**medical officer** *noun* (*abbr.* **MO**) a person, usually a doctor, employed in an organization to deal with medical and health matters 卫生人员；卫生干事；（某机构的）专职医生

ˈ**medical school** (*NAmE also* ˈ**med school** *informal*) *noun* a college where students study to obtain a degree in medicine 医学院

ˌ**medical ˈtourism** *noun* [U] = HEALTH TOURISM

Medi·care /ˈmedɪkeə(r); *NAmE* -ker/ *noun* [U] **1** (in the US) the federal insurance system that provides medical care for people over 65 医疗保障制度，老年保健医疗制度（美国政府向 65 岁以上的人提供医疗保险）**2** (in Australia and Canada) the national medical care system for all people that is paid for by taxes (spelt 'medicare' in Canada) 医疗保健制度（澳大利亚和加拿大政府为所有国民而设，资源来自税收；加拿大拼写为 medicare）

medi·cate /ˈmedɪkeɪt/ *verb* **~ sb** to give sb medicine, especially a drug that affects their behaviour 给…用药（尤指影响行为的药物）；用药物治疗

medi·cated /ˈmedɪkeɪtɪd/ *adj.* containing a substance for preventing or curing infections of your skin or hair 药物的，含药的（用于防治皮肤或头发感染）：***medicated shampoo/soap*** 药物洗发液 / 肥皂

medi·ca·tion /ˌmedɪˈkeɪʃn/ *noun* [U, C] a drug or another form of medicine that you take to prevent or to treat an illness 药；药物：*to be* ***on medication*** 进行药物治疗 ◇ *Are you currently taking any medication?* 你目前在服用什么药吗？◇ *Many flu medications are available without a prescription.* 许多流感药不用处方就可以买到。➲ WORDFINDER NOTE AT CURE, MEDICINE ➲ COLLOCATIONS AT ILL

me·di·cin·al /məˈdɪsɪnl/ *adj.* helpful in the process of healing illness or infection 有疗效的；药用的；药的：***medicinal herbs/plants*** 草药；药用植物 ◇ ***medicinal properties/use*** 药性；药用 ◇ (*humorous*) *He claims he keeps a bottle of brandy only* ***for medicinal purposes.*** 他说他存放着一瓶白兰地只是为了药用。

medi·cine /ˈmedsn; -dɪsn/ *noun* **1** [U] the study and treatment of diseases and injuries 医学：*advances in modern medicine* 现代医学的发展 ◇ ***to study/practise medicine*** 学医；行医 ◇ ***traditional/conventional/orthodox medicine*** 传统 / 常规 / 正统医学 ◇ ***alternative medicine*** 替代疗法 ➲ SEE ALSO AYURVEDIC MEDICINE, DEFENSIVE MEDICINE **2** [U, C] a substance, especially a liquid that you drink or swallow in order to cure an illness 药；（尤指）药水：*Did you take your medicine?* 你吃过药了吗？◇ *cough medicine* 咳嗽药 ◇ *Chinese herbal medicines* 中国草药 ➲ WORDFINDER NOTE AT DOCTOR, HEALTH ➲ COLLOCATIONS AT ILL

> **WORDFINDER** 联想词：administer, capsule, dispense, dose, **ill**, inhaler, medication, pharmacy, placebo

IDM **the best ˈmedicine** the best way of improving a situation, especially of making you feel happier（改进状况的）最佳方法；（尤指）除去心病的良方：*Laughter is the best medicine.* 欢笑是一服良药。 **a taste/dose of your own ˈmedicine** the same bad treatment that you have given to others 自己曾给别人的苦头：*Let the bully have a taste of his own medicine.* 让那个恶棍得到报应吧。

ˈ**medicine ball** *noun* a large heavy ball which is thrown and caught as a form of exercise 健身实心球

ˈ**medicine man** *noun* a person who is believed to have special magic powers of healing, especially among Native Americans 巫医（尤指美洲土著）➲ COMPARE WITCH DOCTOR

med·ico /ˈmedɪkəʊ; *NAmE* -koʊ/ *noun* (*pl.* **-os**) (*informal*) a doctor 医生；大夫

medi·eval (*also* **medi·aeval**) /ˌmediˈiːvl; *NAmE also* ˌmiːd-/ *adj.* [usually before noun] connected with the Middle Ages (about AD 1000 to AD 1450) 中世纪的（约公元 1000 到 1450 年）：*medieval architecture/castles/manuscripts* 中世纪的建筑 / 城堡 / 手稿 ◇ *the literature of the late medieval period* 中世纪后期的文学

me·di·ocre /ˌmiːdiˈəʊkə(r); *NAmE* -ˈoʊkər/ *adj.* (*disapproving*) not very good; of only average standard 平庸的；普通的；平常的：*a mediocre musician/talent/performance* 平庸的音乐家 / 才能 / 表演 ◇ *I thought the play was only mediocre.* 我认为这部戏剧只是平庸之作。

me·di·oc·rity /ˌmiːdiˈɒkrəti; *NAmE* -ˈɑːk-/ *noun* (*pl.* **-ies**) (*disapproving*) **1** [U] the quality of being average or not very good 平庸；普通；平常：*His acting career started brilliantly, then sank into mediocrity.* 他的演艺生涯开场时轰轰烈烈，然后就变得庸庸碌碌。**2** [C] a person who is not very good at sth 平庸之人；碌碌无为者：*a brilliant leader, surrounded by mediocrities* 周围全是些庸才的杰出领导

medi·tate /ˈmedɪteɪt/ *verb* **1** [I] **~ (on/upon sth)** to think deeply, usually in silence, especially for religious reasons or in order to make your mind calm 冥想；沉思 **2** [T] **~ sth** (*formal*) to plan sth in your mind; to consider doing sth 暗自策划；考虑；谋划 SYN **contemplate**: *They were meditating revenge.* 他们在谋划进行报复。

medi·ta·tion /ˌmedɪˈteɪʃn/ *noun* **1** [U] the practice of thinking deeply in silence, especially for religious reasons or in order to make your mind calm 冥想；沉思；深思：*She found peace through yoga and meditation.* 她通过瑜伽和冥想找到了宁静。◇ *He was deep* ***in meditation*** *and didn't see me come in.* 他正在沉思，没有看见我进来。**2** [C, usually pl.] **~ (on sth)** (*formal*) serious thoughts on a particular subject that sb writes down or speaks 沉思录：*his meditations on life and art* 他对生活和艺术的沉思录

medi·ta·tive /ˈmedɪtətɪv; *NAmE* -teɪt-/ *adj.* (*formal*) thinking very deeply; involving deep thought 深思的；陷入沉思的 SYN **thoughtful**: *She found him in a meditative mood.* 她发现他正在沉思。◇ *a meditative poem* 一首冥想诗

Medi·ter·ra·nean /ˌmedɪtəˈreɪniən/ *adj.* [only before noun] connected with the Mediterranean Sea or the countries and regions that surround it; typical of this area 地中海的：*a Mediterranean country* 地中海国家 ◇ *a Mediterranean climate* 地中海气候

me·dium AW /ˈmiːdiəm/ *adj., noun*

■ ***adj.*** [usually before noun] (*abbr.* **M**) in the middle between two sizes, amounts, lengths, temperatures, etc. 中等的；中号的 SYN **average**: ***a medium-size car/business/town*** 中型汽车 / 企业；中等城镇 ◇ *a man of **medium height/build*** 中等身材的人 ◇ *There are three sizes—small, medium and large.* 有三种尺寸，分别是小号、中号和大号。◇ *Cook over a medium heat for 15 minutes.* 用中火煮 15 分钟。◇ *a **medium dry** white wine* 中度干白葡萄酒 ◇ *Choose **medium to large** tomatoes.* 挑选个头中等到大个的西红柿。

IDM SEE TERM *n.*

■ ***noun*** (*pl.* **media** /ˈmiːdiə/ or **me·diums**) **1** a way of communicating information, etc. to people （传播信息的）媒介，手段，方法：*the **medium of radio/television*** 广播 / 电视媒介 ◇ ***electronic/audiovisual media*** 电子 / 视听媒体 ◇ *Television is the modern **medium of communication**.* 电视是现代传媒。◇ *A T-shirt can be an excellent medium for getting your message across.* * T 恤衫可以成为一种极好的表达信息的媒介。HELP The plural in this meaning is usually **media**. 此义的复数形式通常为 media。➲ SEE ALSO MEDIA, MASS MEDIA **2** something that is used for a particular purpose 手段；工具；方法：*English is the **medium of instruction*** (= the language used to teach other subjects). 用英语进行教学。◇ *Video is a good medium for learning a foreign language.* 视频是学习外语的一种好方法。**3** the material or the form that an artist, a writer or a musician uses （文艺创作中使用的）材料，形式：*the **medium of paint/poetry/drama*** 绘画 / 诗歌 / 戏剧的表现手法 ◇ *Watercolour is his favourite medium.* 水彩画是他最喜欢的表现方式。**4** (*biology* 生) a substance that sth exists or grows in or that it travels through 介质；培养基；环境：*The bacteria were growing in a sugar medium.* 细菌在糖基中生长。**5** (*pl.* **me·diums**) a person who claims to be able to communicate with the spirits of dead people 通灵的人；灵媒；巫师 IDM SEE HAPPY ➲ MORE LIKE THIS 30, page R28

ˈmedium-sized *adj.* of average size 中等大小的；中型的；中号的：*a medium-sized saucepan* 中号的锅

ˈmedium-term *adj.* used to describe a period of time that is a few weeks or months into the future 中期的：*the government's medium-term financial strategy* 政府的中期金融策略

ˈmedium wave (*abbr.* **MW**) *noun* [U] (*also* **the medium wave** [sing.]) a band of radio waves with a length of between 100 and 1 000 metres 中波（波长 100 到 1 000 米）：*648 m on (the) medium wave* 中波 648 米 ➲ COMPARE SHORT WAVE

med·lar /ˈmedlə(r)/ *noun* a brownish fruit which is eaten when it has started to decay and become soft 欧楂果（开始凋萎时方能食用）

med·ley /ˈmedli/ *noun* **1** a piece of music consisting of several songs or tunes played or sung one after the other 混成曲（多首声乐曲或器乐曲串联在一起）：*a medley of Beatles hits* 披头士乐队歌曲大联唱 **2** a mixture of people or things of different kinds 混杂物；混合物；混杂的人群：*a **medley of flavours/smells*** 各种味道 / 气味混合在一起 **3** a swimming race in which each member of a team uses a different stroke 混合泳接力：*the 4 × 100 metres medley* * 4 × 100 米混合泳接力

ˈmed school *noun* (*NAmE, informal*) = MEDICAL SCHOOL

meek /miːk/ *adj.* (**meek·er, meek·est**) **1** quiet, gentle, and always ready to do what other people want without expressing your own opinion 温顺的；谦恭的；驯服的 SYN **compliant, self-effacing**: *They called her Miss Mouse because she was so **meek and mild**.* 他们称她为"鼠小姐"，因为她总是那么懦弱温和。**2 the meek** *noun* [pl.] people who are meek 温顺的人；谦恭的人 ▸ **meek·ly** *adv.*: *He meekly did as he was told.* 他温顺地听从吩咐。**meek·ness** *noun* [U]

meer·kat /ˈmɪəkæt; *NAmE* ˈmɪr-/ *noun* a small southern African animal with a long tail, which often stands up on its back legs. Meerkats are a type of MONGOOSE. 灰沼狸

meet /miːt/ *verb, noun*

■ ***verb*** (**met, met** /met/)

• **BY CHANCE** 偶然地 **1** [I, T, no passive] to be in the same place as sb by chance and talk to them 相遇；相逢；遇见：*Maybe we'll meet again some time.* 说不定我们什么时候还会再见面。◇ **~ sb** *Did you meet anyone in town?* 你在城里碰见什么人了吗？

• **BY ARRANGEMENT** 通过安排 **2** [I, T, no passive] to come together formally in order to discuss sth 开会；会晤：*The committee meets on Fridays.* 委员会每周五开会。◇ **~ sb** *The Prime Minister met other European leaders for talks.* 首相与其他欧洲首脑举行会谈。◇ **~ with sb** *The President met with senior White House aides.* 总统会见了白宫的高级幕僚。**3** [I, T, no passive] to come together socially after you have arranged it （与…）会面；集合：**~ (for sth)** *Let's meet for a drink after work.* 下班后我们一起去喝一杯吧。◇ **~ sb (for sth)** *We're meeting them outside the theatre at 7.* 我们 7 点钟在剧院外面和他们会合。**4** [T] **~ sb/sth** to go to a place and wait there for a particular person to arrive 迎接：*Will you meet me at the airport?* 你到机场接我好吗？◇ *The hotel bus meets all incoming flights.* 酒店有车在机场迎接各航班的旅客。◇ *I met him off the plane.* 他下飞机后我就接到了他。

• **FOR THE FIRST TIME** 初次 **5** [T, no passive, I] **~ (sb)** to see and know sb for the first time; to be introduced to sb 相识；结识；被引见介绍（给某人）：*Where did you first meet your husband?* 你是在哪儿和你丈夫初次相识的？◇ (*especially BrE*) ***Pleased to meet you.*** 很高兴认识你。◇ (*NAmE*) ***Nice meeting you.*** 很高兴认识你。◇ *There's someone I want you to meet.* 我想介绍你认识一个人。◇ *I don't think we've met.* 我想我们没见过面吧。

• **IN CONTEST** 比赛 **6** [I, T, no passive] to play, fight, etc. together as opponents in a competition 遭遇；交锋：*Smith and Jones met in last year's final.* 史密斯和琼斯在去年的决赛中相遇。◇ **~ sb** *Smith met Jones in last year's final.* 在去年的决赛中，史密斯与琼斯交锋。

• **EXPERIENCE STH** 经历 **7** [T] **~ sth** to experience sth, often sth unpleasant 经历（常指不愉快的事）SYN **come across, encounter**: *Others have met similar problems.* 其他人遇到过同样的问题。◇ *How she **met her death** will probably never be known.* 她的死因也许永远无人知晓。

• **TOUCH/JOIN** 接触；连接 **8** [I, T] to touch sth; to join 接触（某物）；连接：*The curtains don't meet in the middle.* 这窗帘中间合不拢。◇ **~ sth** *That's where the river meets the sea.* 这条河就在这里流入大海。◇ *His hand met hers.* 他的手碰到她的手。

• **SATISFY** 满足 **9** [T] **~ sth** to do or satisfy what is needed or what sb asks for 满足；使满意 SYN **fulfil**: *How can we best **meet the needs** of all the different groups?* 我们怎样才能最好地满足各种人的需要呢？◇ *Until these **conditions are met** we cannot proceed with the sale.* 除非这些条件得到满足，否则我们不能继续这项交易。◇ *I can't possibly meet that deadline.* 我不可能如期完成。

• **PAY** 支付 **10** [T] **~ sth** to pay sth 支付；偿付：*The cost will be met by the company.* 费用将由公司支付。

IDM **meet sb's ˈeye(s) | meet sb's ˈgaze, ˈlook, etc. | people's ˈeyes meet 1** [T, I] if you **meet sb's eye(s)**, you look directly at them as they look at you; if two people's **eyes meet**, they look directly at each other （和某人）对视，目光相遇：*She was afraid to meet my eye.* 她不敢正眼看我。◇ *Their eyes met across the crowded room.* 他们隔着拥挤的房间目光相遇了。◇ *She met his gaze without flinching.* 她毫不畏缩地与他对视。**2** [T] **~ your eyes** if a sight **meets your eyes**, you see it 呈现；显现：*A terrible sight met their eyes.* 一幅可怕的景象映入他们的眼帘。**meet sb halfˈway** to reach an agreement with sb by

M

giving them part of what they want 和某人妥协；对某人作出让步 **meet your 'Maker** (*especially humorous*) to die 死；见上帝 **there is more to sb/sth than meets the 'eye** a person or thing is more complicated or interesting than you might think at first 某人（或物）比料想的更为复杂（或有趣） ➲ MORE AT END *n.*, MATCH *n.*, RUBBER, TWAIN

PHR V **,meet 'up (with sb)** (*rather informal*) to meet sb, especially by arrangement （按照安排）见面，会面： *They met up again later for a drink.* 后来他们又在一起喝过酒。 **'meet with sb** to meet sb, especially for discussions 和某人会晤（商讨问题等）： *The President met with senior White House aides.* 总统会见了白宫的高级幕僚。 **'meet with sth** **1** to be received or treated by sb in a particular way 遭遇（某事）；受到某种对待： *Her proposal met with resistance from the Left.* 她的建议遭到了左翼的抵制。 ◇ *to meet with success/failure* 成功；失败 **2** to experience sth unpleasant 经历，体验（不愉快的事）： *She was worried that he might have met with an accident.* 她怕他出了车祸。 **'meet sth with sth** to react to sth in a particular way （对某事）作出…反应；以…作为回应 **SYN** **receive**: *His suggestion was met with howls of protest.* 他的建议引起了一阵阵的抗议声。

■ **noun** **1** (*especially NAmE*) a sports competition 体育比赛；运动会： *a track meet* 径赛运动会 **2** (*BrE*) an event at which horse riders and dogs hunt FOXES. FOX HUNTING with dogs is now illegal in the UK. 猎狐运动（现在于英国用狗猎狐属违法行为）

M

,meet-and-'greet *adj.* [only before noun] (of an event 活动) arranged so that sb, especially a famous person, can meet and talk to people （尤指名人）与公众见面的 ▸ **,meet and 'greet** *noun*

meet·ing /'miːtɪŋ/ *noun* **1** [C] an occasion when people come together to discuss or decide sth 会议；集会： *to **have/hold/call/attend a meeting*** 召开 / 举办 / 召集 / 参加会议 ◇ *a **committee/staff meeting*** 委员会 / 员工会议 ◇ *What time is the meeting?* 什么时候开会？ ◇ *Helen will **chair the meeting*** (= be in charge of it). 海伦将主持这次会议。 ◇ *I'll be **in a meeting** all morning—can you take my calls?* 我整个上午都要开会，你能不能帮我接一下电话？ ◇ *a meeting of the United Nations Security Council* 联合国安理会会议 ◇ *They rely on videoconferencing for virtual meetings.* 他们依靠视频会议系统举行虚拟会议。

WORDFINDER 联想词： agenda, AGM, apology, brainstorming, breakout, chair, committee, convene, the minutes

2 the meeting [sing.] the people at a meeting （统称）与会者： *The meeting voted to accept the pay offer.* 与会者投票接受这一工资提议。 **3** [C] a situation in which two or more people meet together, because they have arranged it or by chance 会面；集会；集合 **SYN** **encounter**: *At our first meeting I was nervous.* 我们第一次见面时我很紧张。 ◇ *It was a **chance meeting** that would change my life.* 那次偶然的会面改变了我的一生。 ◇ *He remembered their childhood meetings with nostalgia.* 他怀念地回忆起他们孩提时代的聚会。 **4** [C] (*BrE*) a sports event or set of races, especially for horses 运动会；（尤指）赛马： *an athletics meeting* 运动会 ◇ *a race meeting* 赛马大会

IDM **a meeting of 'minds** a close understanding between people with similar ideas, especially when they meet to do sth or meet for the first time 彼此间的深刻理解（尤指初会时就意见一致）

'meeting house *noun* a place where Quakers meet for worship （贵格会的）礼拜堂

'meeting place *noun* a place where people often meet 聚集的地方；会场： *The cafe is a popular meeting place for students.* 咖啡馆是学生喜欢的聚会场所。 ➲ MORE LIKE THIS 9, page R26

meg /meg/ *noun* (*informal*) = MEGABYTE： *more than 512 megs of memory* 超过 512 兆的内存 ◇ *24-meg broadband* * 24 兆的宽带

mega /'megə/ *adj.* [usually before noun] (*informal*) very large or impressive 巨大的；极佳的 **SYN** **huge, great**: *The song was a mega hit last year.* 这首歌是去年很热门的歌曲。 ▸ **mega** *adv.*： *They're mega rich.* 他们极其富有。

mega- /'megə/ *combining form* (in nouns 构成名词) **1** very large or great 巨大的；了不起的： *a megastore* 大商场 **2** (in units of measurement 用于计量单位) one million 百万： *a megawatt* 百万瓦特 **3** (in units of measurement 用于计量单位) 2^{20}, or 1 048 576 兆（二进制，等于 1 048 576）

mega·bit /'megəbɪt/ *noun* (*abbr.* **Mb**, **Mbit**) (*computing* 计) **1** a unit of computer memory or data, equal to 10^6, or $1\,000^2$, (= 1 000 000) BITS 百万比特，兆比特（十进制计算机内存或数据单位，等于 1 000 000 比特） **2** (*also* **mebi·bit**) a unit of computer memory or data, equal to 2^{20}, or $1\,024^2$, (= 1 048 576) BITS 兆比特（二进制计算机内存或数据单位，等于 1 048 576 比特）

mega·bucks /'megəbʌks/ *noun* [pl.] (*informal*) a very large amount of money 一大笔钱： *He earns megabucks.* 他大笔大笔地赚钱。

mega·byte /'megəbaɪt/ (*also informal* **meg**) *noun* (*abbr.* **MB**) (*computing* 计) **1** a unit of computer memory or data, equal to 10^6, or $1\,000^2$, (= 1 000 000) BYTES 百万字节，兆字节（十进制计算机内存或数据单位，等于 1 000 000 字节）： *a 512-megabyte flash drive* * 512 兆字节的闪存盘 **2** (*also* **mebi·byte**) a unit of computer memory or data, equal to 2^{20}, or $1\,024^2$, (= 1 048 576) BYTES 兆字节（二进制计算机内存或数据单位，等于 1 048 576 字节）

mega·city /'megəsɪti/ *noun* (*pl.* **-ies**) a very large city, usually one with a population of over 10 million people （通常人口超过一千万的）特大城市

mega·hertz /'megəhɜːts; *NAmE* -hɜːrts/ *noun* (*pl.* **mega·hertz**) (*abbr.* **MHz**) a unit for measuring radio waves and the speed at which a computer operates; 1 000 000 HERTZ 兆赫；百万赫兹

mega·lith /'megəlɪθ/ *noun* a very large stone, especially one put in a place that was used for ceremonies in ancient times （尤指古代用于祭祀的）巨石 ▸ **mega·lith·ic** /,megə'lɪθɪk/ *adj.*

meg·alo·mania /,megələ'meɪniə/ *noun* [U] **1** (*specialist*) a mental illness or condition in which sb has an exaggerated belief in their own importance or power 自大狂；夸大狂；妄自尊大 **2** a strong feeling that you want to have more and more power 渴望权力；权欲熏心

meg·alo·maniac /,megələ'meɪniæk/ *noun* a person suffering from or showing megalomania 夸大狂患者 ▸ **meg·alo·maniac** *adj.*

meg·alop·olis /,megə'lɒpəlɪs; *NAmE* -'lɑːp-/ *noun* (*formal*) a very large city or group of cities where a great number of people live 大都会（区）

megaphone 扩音器

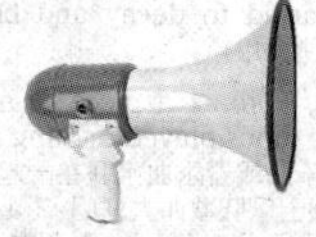

mega·phone /'megəfəʊn; *NAmE* -foʊn/ *noun* a device for making your voice sound louder, that is wider at one end, like a CONE, and is often used at outside events 扩音器；喇叭筒；传声筒 ➲ COMPARE LOUDHAILER

mega·pixel /'megəpɪksl/ *noun* a million PIXELS (= very small individual areas on a computer screen), used to measure the quality of a digital screen or image 百万像素： *a 12 megapixel digital camera* * 1 200 万像素的数码相机

mega·star /ˈmegəstɑː(r)/ *noun* (*informal*) a very famous singer, actor or entertainer 演艺巨星；娱乐界的巨星

mega·store /ˈmegəstɔː(r)/ *noun* a very large shop, especially one that sells one type of product, for example computers or furniture 大商店；（尤指）大型专卖店

mega·ton (*also* **mega·tonne**) /ˈmegətʌn/ *noun* a unit for measuring the power of an EXPLOSIVE, equal to one million tons of TNT 百万吨级（爆炸能量计量单位，相当于一百万吨黄色炸药的威力）：*a one megaton nuclear bomb* 一枚一百万吨级的核炸弹

mega·watt /ˈmegəwɒt; *NAmE* -wɑːt/ *noun* (*abbr.* **MW**) a unit for measuring electrical power; one million WATTS 兆瓦，百万瓦特（电能计量单位）

meh /me/ *exclamation, adj.* (*NAmE, informal*) used to show that you are not at all interested in or impressed by sth 哦（表示对某事根本不感兴趣或未被打动）：*'So how was the movie?' 'Meh. The action scenes aren't awful, but there's nothing great about it.'* "那么电影怎么样呢？""呃。动作镜头还不坏，不过没什么意思。" ◇ *She does an OK job on a meh song.* 那歌本来就不怎样，她唱得还可以。

mehndi (*also* **mehendi**) /ˈmendi/ *noun* (*IndE*) **1** [U] the art of applying a temporary design to a person's skin using a reddish-brown DYE (= a substance used to change the colour of sth), especially for their wedding day 曼海蒂，人体彩绘术（非永久性的身体彩绘，尤在婚礼前涂绘）**2** [U] a type of decoration that is applied to a person's skin, usually on their hands, using a reddish-brown DYE 曼海蒂纹彩（通常涂绘在手部）：*She wore traditional dress and mehndi at the event.* 她在活动中身着传统服装，手上饰有曼海蒂彩绘。 **3** [C] a temporary design applied to a person's skin using a reddish-brown DYE 曼海蒂纹饰；人体彩绘图案：*She had her hands decorated with mehndis before her wedding.* 她在婚礼前让人在她的双手饰上彩绘图案。 **4** [U] a type of reddish-brown DYE made from HENNA that is used to create temporary designs on a person's skin, usually on their hands 曼海蒂染料；散沫花染剂

mei·osis /maɪˈəʊsɪs; *NAmE* -ˈoʊs-/ *noun* [U] (*biology* 生) the division of a cell in two stages that results in four cells, each with half the number of CHROMOSOMES of the original cell（细胞的）减数分裂

-meister /ˈmaɪstə(r)/ *combining form* (in nouns 构成名词) (*informal*) a person thought of as skilled at a particular activity or important in a particular field …方面的专家；…领域的高手：*a horror-meister* 恐怖大师

meit·ner·ium /maɪtˈnɪəriəm; *NAmE* -ˈnɪr-/ *noun* [U] (*symb.* **Mt**) a RADIOACTIVE chemical element. Meitnerium is produced when atoms COLLIDE (= crash into each other). 鿏（放射性化学元素）

mela /ˈmeɪlə/ *noun* (*IndE*) a type of entertainment event, usually held outdoors, or a religious festival 集会，节（通常在户外举行的娱乐活动）；（宗教）节

mela·mine /ˈmeləmiːn/ *noun* [U] a strong hard plastic material, used especially for covering surfaces such as the tops of tables, and for making cups, etc. 三聚氰胺；密胺树脂

mel·an·cho·lia /ˌmelənˈkəʊliə; *NAmE* -ˈkoʊ-/ *noun* (*old-fashioned*) a mental illness in which the patient is depressed and worried by unnecessary fears 忧郁症

mel·an·chol·ic /ˌmelənˈkɒlɪk; *NAmE* -ˈkɑːl-/ *adj.* (*old-fashioned* or *literary*) feeling or expressing sadness, especially when the sadness is like an illness 忧郁的；忧郁症的

mel·an·choly /ˈmelənkəli; -kɒli; *NAmE* -kɑːli/ *noun, adj.*

■ ***noun*** [U] (*formal*) a deep feeling of sadness that lasts for a long time and often cannot be explained 忧郁；伤悲：*A mood of melancholy descended on us.* 一种悲伤的情绪袭上我们的心头。

■ ***adj.*** very sad or making you feel sadness （令人）悲哀的；（令人）沮丧的 **SYN** **mournful, sombre**: ***melancholy thoughts/memories*** 悲哀的想法 / 记忆 ◇ *The melancholy song died away.* 哀婉的歌声渐渐消失了。

me·lange /meɪˈlɑːnʒ/ *noun* (*from French, formal*) a mixture or variety of different things 混合物；大杂烩：*a melange of different cultures* 不同文化的融合

mel·anin /ˈmelənɪn/ *noun* [U] (*specialist*) a dark substance in the skin and hair that causes the skin to change colour in the sun's light 黑（色）素

mela·noma /ˌmeləˈnəʊmə; *NAmE* -ˈnoʊmə/ *noun* [C, U] (*medical* 医) a type of cancer that appears as a dark spot or TUMOUR on the skin 黑（色）素瘤；黑瘤

mela·to·nin /ˌmeləˈtəʊnɪn; *NAmE* -ˈtoʊn-/ *noun* [U] (*biology* 生) a HORMONE that affects skin colour and is thought to be involved in controlling the REPRODUCTIVE cycle 褪黑（激）素

meld /meld/ *verb* [I, T] ~ (**A**) **with B** | ~ (**A and B**) (**together**) (*formal*) to combine with sth else; to make sth combine with sth else （使）融合，合并，结合 **SYN** **blend**

melee /ˈmeleɪ; *NAmE* ˈmeɪleɪ/ *noun* [sing.] (*from French*) a situation in which a crowd of people are rushing or pushing each other in a confused way 混乱；混乱的人群

mel·lif·lu·ous /meˈlɪfluəs/ *adj.* (*formal*) (of music or of sb's voice 音乐或人的声音) sounding sweet and smooth; very pleasant to listen to 甜美流畅的；悦耳动听的

mel·low /ˈmeləʊ; *NAmE* -loʊ/ *adj., verb*

■ ***adj.*** (**mel·low·er**, **mel·low·est**) **1** (of colour or sound 色彩或声音) soft, rich and pleasant 柔和丰富的：*mellow autumn colours* 宜人的秋色 ◇ *Mellow music and lighting helped to create the right atmosphere.* 柔和的音乐和灯光衬托出了适宜的氛围。 **2** (of a taste or flavour 味道或香味) smooth and pleasant 醇香的；甘美的：*a mellow, fruity wine* 醇正浓香的葡萄酒 **3** (of people 人) calm, gentle and reasonable because of age or experience 老练的；成熟的：*Dad's certainly grown mellower with age.* 随着年龄的增长，父亲当然是更老练了。**4** (*informal*) (of people 人) relaxed, calm and happy, especially after drinking alcohol（尤指酒后）飘飘然的，怡然自得的：*After two glasses of wine, I was feeling mellow.* 两杯葡萄酒下肚，我就飘飘然了。

■ ***verb*** **1** [I, T] to become or make sb become less extreme in behaviour, etc., especially as a result of growing older （使）成熟，老成：*She had mellowed a great deal since their days at college.* 大学毕业以后，她成熟了许多。◇ **~ sb** *A period spent working abroad had done nothing to mellow him.* 他在海外工作了一段时间，却没有变得老练。**2** [I, T] ~ (**sth**) to become or to make a colour become less bright, especially over a period of time （尤指一段时间后颜色）变柔和；（使颜色）柔和 **3** [I, T] ~ (**sth**) to develop or make wine develop a pleasant and less bitter taste over a period of time （使酒）更加醇香

PHR V **ˌmellow ˈout** (*informal, especially NAmE*) to enjoy yourself by relaxing and not doing much 悠然自得；怡然休闲

me·lod·ic /məˈlɒdɪk; *NAmE* -ˈlɑːd-/ *adj.* **1** [only before noun] connected with the main tune in a piece of music 主旋律的；旋律的：*The melodic line is carried by the two clarinets.* 主旋律由两支单簧管奏出。 **2** = MELODIOUS

me·lod·ica /məˈlɒdɪkə; *NAmE* -ˈlɑːd-/ *noun* a musical instrument that has a keyboard and a part that you blow into 口风琴

me·lo·di·ous /məˈləʊdiəs; *NAmE* -ˈloʊ-/ (*also* **me·lod·ic**) *adj.* pleasant to listen to, like music 悦耳的；优美动听的；像音乐的：*a rich melodious voice* 圆润悦耳的嗓音 ▸ **me·lo·di·ous·ly** *adv.*

melo·dist /ˈmelədɪst/ *noun* a person who writes tunes; a person who is very good at writing tunes 作曲家；善于作曲的人

melo·drama /ˈmelədrɑːmə/ *noun* [U, C] **1** a story, play or novel that is full of exciting events and in which the characters and emotions seem too exaggerated to be real 情节剧；通俗剧；情节剧式故事（或小说）：*a*

M

gripping Victorian melodrama 动人心弦的维多利亚时代情节剧 ◇ *Instead of tragedy, we got melodrama.* 我们看的是情节剧，不是悲剧。 **2** events, behaviour, etc. which are exaggerated or extreme 戏剧性的事件（或行为等）；过于夸大的事件（或行为等）： *Her love of melodrama meant that any small problem became a crisis.* 她喜欢夸大其词，会把任何小问题说成危机。

melo·dra·mat·ic /ˌmelədrəˈmætɪk/ *adj.* (*often disapproving*) full of exciting and extreme emotions or events; behaving or reacting to sth in an exaggerated way 情节剧式的；夸大的；耸人听闻的： *a melodramatic plot full of deceit and murder* 充满欺骗和凶杀的耸人听闻的情节 ▶ **melo·dra·mat·ic·al·ly** /-kli/ *adv.*

melo·dra·mat·ics /ˌmelədrəˈmætɪks/ *noun* [pl.] behaviour or events that are melodramatic 传奇剧式行为（或事情）；夸张行为（或事情）： *Let's have no more melodramatics, if you don't mind.* 如果你不介意的话，咱们就别再夸张了。

mel·ody /ˈmelədi/ *noun* (*pl.* **-ies**) **1** [C] a tune, especially the main tune in a piece of music written for several instruments or voices 旋律；曲调；（尤指）主旋律： *a haunting melody* 萦绕心头的旋律 ◇ *The melody is then taken up by the flutes.* 接着由长笛奏主旋律。 ➲ COLLOCATIONS AT MUSIC **2** [C] a piece of music or a song with a clear or simple tune （旋律简洁的）乐曲，歌曲： *old Irish melodies* 古老的爱尔兰歌曲 **3** [U] the arrangement of musical notes in a tune 乐曲的音符编排： *a few bars of melody drifted towards us* 几小节乐曲从远处传来。 ➲ WORDFINDER NOTE AT SING

melon /ˈmelən/ *noun* [C, U] a large fruit with hard green, yellow or orange skin, sweet flesh and juice and a lot of seeds 甜瓜；瓜： *a slice of melon* 一片瓜 ➲ SEE ALSO HONEYDEW MELON, WATERMELON

melt 🔑 /melt/ *verb* **1** 🔑 [I, T] to become or make sth become liquid as a result of heating （使）熔化，融化： *The snow showed no sign of melting.* 雪没有一点融化的迹象。 ◇ *melting ice* 正在融化的冰 ◇ **~ sth** *The sun had melted the snow.* 阳光融化了积雪。 ◇ *First, melt two ounces of butter.* 先溶好两盎司黄油。 ➲ COLLOCATIONS AT COOKING ➲ COMPARE DEFROST, DE-ICE **2** [I, T] to become or to make a feeling, an emotion, etc. become gentler and less strong （使）软化，变得温柔： *The tension in the room began to melt.* 屋里的紧张气氛开始缓和。 ◇ **~ sth** *Her trusting smile melted his heart.* 她那信任的微笑使他的心变软了。

IDM **ˌmelt in your ˈmouth** (of food 食物) to be soft and very good to eat 爽滑可口；柔嫩好吃 ➲ MORE AT BUTTER *n.*

PHR V **ˌmelt aˈway | ˌmelt sth↔aˈway** to disappear or make sth disappear gradually （使）慢慢消失： *At the first sign of trouble, the crowd melted away.* 人群一看有麻烦，便作鸟兽散。 **ˌmelt sth↔ˈdown** to heat a metal or WAX object until it is liquid, especially so that the metal or wax can be used to make sth else 将（金属或蜡）熔化 ➲ RELATED NOUN MELTDOWN **ˈmelt into sth** to gradually become part of sth and therefore become difficult to see 逐渐融入；渐渐与某物成为一体

melt·down /ˈmeltdaʊn/ *noun* [U, C] **1** a serious accident in which the central part of a nuclear REACTOR melts, causing harmful RADIATION to escape 核反应堆堆芯熔化（导致核辐射泄漏） **2** (*economics* 经) a situation where sth fails or becomes weaker in a sudden or dramatic way 崩溃；垮台： *The country is in economic meltdown.* 该国的经济崩溃。 ◇ *a meltdown on the New York Stock Exchange* 纽约股票市场的崩盘

melt·ing /ˈmeltɪŋ/ *adj.* [usually before noun] persuading you to feel love, pity or sympathy 感人的；柔情似水的；令人爱怜的；可同情的： *his melting eyes* 他那双能打动人的眼睛 ▶ **melt·ing·ly** *adv.*

ˈmelting point *noun* [U, C] the temperature at which a substance will melt 熔点

ˈmelting pot *noun* [usually sing.] a place or situation in which large numbers of people, ideas, etc. are mixed together 熔炉（指多种民族、多种思想等融合混杂的地方或状况）： *the vast melting pot of American society* 美国社会这个大熔炉

IDM **in the ˈmelting pot** (*especially BrE*) likely to change; in the process of changing 要起变化；处于变化之中

mem·ber 🔑 /ˈmembə(r)/ *noun* **1** 🔑 **~ (of sth)** a person, an animal or a plant that belongs to a particular group 成员；分子： ***a member of staff/society/the family*** 职工 / 社会 / 家庭中的一员 ◇ *characteristics common to all members of the species* 这一物种中所有个体的共同特点 **2** 🔑 a person, a country or an organization that has joined a particular group, club or team 成员；会员： ***party/union members*** 党员；工会会员 ◇ ***a meeting of member countries/states*** 成员国会议 ◇ *How much does it cost to become a member?* 要成为会员得花多少钱？ ◇ **~ of sth** *an active member of the local church* 当地教会的一名积极分子 ➲ WORDFINDER NOTE AT CLUB **3** (*old use* or *literary*) a part of the body, especially an arm or a leg 身体部位（尤指胳膊或腿） **4** a PENIS. People say 'member' to avoid saying 'penis'. （委婉说法，与 penis 同义，即阴茎） **5 Member** (in Britain) a Member of Parliament （英国）下院议员： *the Hon. Member for Brent North* 布伦特北区议员阁下 ➲ SEE ALSO PRIVATE MEMBER

ˌMember of ˈParliament *noun* = MP (1)

mem·ber·ship 🔑 /ˈmembəʃɪp; *NAmE* -bərʃ-/ *noun* **1** 🔑 [U] (*BrE*) **~ (of sth)** | (*NAmE*) **~ (in sth)** the state of being a member of a group, a club, an organization, etc. 会员资格；成员资格： *Who is eligible to apply for membership of the association?* 谁有资格申请加入这个协会？ ◇ ***a membership card/fee*** 会员卡；会费 **2** 🔑 [C+sing./pl. v.] the members, or the number of members, of a group, a club, an organization, etc. （统称）会员，成员；会员人数；成员数： *The membership has/have not yet voted.* 会员还没有进行投票。 ◇ *The club has a membership of more than 500.* 俱乐部的会员人数超过了 500 名。

mem·brane /ˈmembreɪn/ *noun* [C, U] **1** a thin layer of skin or TISSUE that connects or covers parts inside the body （身体内的）膜 ➲ SEE ALSO MUCOUS MEMBRANE **2** a very thin layer found in the structure of cells in plants （植物的）细胞膜 **3** a thin layer of material used to prevent air, liquid, etc. from entering a particular part of sth （可起防水、防风等作用的）膜状物： *a waterproof membrane* 防水薄膜 ▶ **mem·bran·ous** /ˈmembrənəs/ *adj.*

meme /miːm/ *noun* **1** an idea that is passed from one member of society to another, not in the GENES but often by people copying it 模因（常指通过模仿而非遗传的方式传递的观念）： *Other cultures have similar versions of this meme.* 其他文化有与此类似的模因。 ◇ *the political and cultural memes of the 21st century* * 21 世纪的政治和文化模因 **2** an image, a video, a piece of text, etc. that is passed very quickly from one Internet user to another, often with slight changes that make it humorous 爆红的网络话题（互联网上短时间内快速传播的图像、视频、文字等）： *an Internet meme/a blog meme* 互联网 / 博客段子

me·mento /məˈmentəʊ; *NAmE* -toʊ/ *noun* (*pl.* **-oes** or **-os**) a thing that you keep or give to sb to remind you or them of a person or place 纪念品 **SYN** **souvenir**: *a memento of our trip to Italy* 我们意大利之旅的纪念品

me·mento mori /məˌmentəʊ ˈmɔːri; məˌmentəʊ ˈmɔːraɪ; *NAmE* məˌmentoʊ ˈmɔːri; məˌmentoʊ ˈmɔːraɪ/ *noun* (*pl.* **me·mento mori**) an object or symbol that reminds or warns you of death 使人想到死亡的物品（或图符）；死亡警告

memo /ˈmeməʊ; *NAmE* -moʊ/ *noun* (*pl.* **-os**) (*also formal* **memo·ran·dum**) **~ (to sb)** an official note from one person to another in the same organization 备忘录： *to **write/send/circulate a memo*** 写 / 发送 / 传阅备忘录

mem·oir /ˈmemwɑː(r)/ *noun* **1 memoirs** [pl.] an account written by sb, especially sb famous, about their life and experiences （尤指名人的）回忆录；自传 **2** [C] (*formal*) a written account of sb's life, a place, or an event, written by sb who knows it well 传说；地方志；大事记

mem·ora·bilia /ˌmemərəˈbɪliə/ *noun* [pl.] things that people collect because they once belonged to a famous person, or because they are connected with a particular interesting place, event or activity 收藏品；纪念品：*football/Beatles memorabilia* 足球 / 披头士乐队纪念品

mem·or·able /ˈmemərəbl/ *adj.* ~ (**for sth**) special, good or unusual and therefore worth remembering or easy to remember 值得纪念的；难忘的 **SYN unforgettable**：*a truly memorable occasion* 非常难忘的时刻 ▶ **mem·or·ably** /-əbli/ *adv.*

memo·ran·dum /ˌmeməˈrændəm/ *noun* (*pl.* **memo·randa** /ˌmeməˈrændə/) **1** (*formal*) = MEMO：*an internal memorandum* 内部备忘录 **2** (*law* 律) a record of a legal agreement which has not yet been formally prepared and signed 协议备忘录 **3** a proposal or report on a particular subject for a person, an organization, a committee, etc. 建议书；报告：*a detailed memorandum to the commission on employment policy* 呈交委员会的有关就业政策的详细报告

me·mor·ial /məˈmɔːriəl/ *noun, adj.*

■ ***noun*** **1** [C] a statue, stone, etc. that is built in order to remind people of an important past event or of a famous person who has died 纪念碑（或像等）：*a **war memorial*** (= in memory of soldiers who died in a war) 阵亡将士纪念碑 ◇ **~ to sb/sth** *a memorial to victims of the Holocaust* 大屠杀遇难者的纪念碑 **2** [sing.] **~ to sb/sth** a thing that will continue to remind people of sb/sth 纪念物；纪念品：*The painting will be a lasting memorial to a remarkable woman.* 这幅油画将成为对一位杰出女性的永久纪念。

■ ***adj.*** [only before noun] created or done in order to remember sb who has died 纪念的；悼念的：*a **memorial statue/plaque/prize*** 纪念像；纪念牌；纪念奖 ◇ *The **memorial service** will be held at a local church.* 悼念仪式将在当地的一所教堂举行。◇ *the John F Kennedy Memorial Hospital* 肯尼迪纪念医院

Meˈmorial Day *noun* a holiday in the US, usually the last Monday in May, in honour of members of the armed forces who have died in war 阵亡将士纪念日（美国假日，通常为五月的最后一个星期一） ➲ SEE ALSO REMEMBRANCE SUNDAY, VETERANS DAY

me·mor·ial·ize (*BrE also* **-ise**) /məˈmɔːriəlaɪz/ *verb* **~ sb/sth** (*formal*) to produce sth that will continue to exist and remind people of sb who has died or sth that has gone 纪念 **SYN commemorate**

me·mor·iam /məˈmɔːriəm/ ➲ IN MEMORIAM

mem·or·ize (*BrE also* **-ise**) /ˈmeməraɪz/ *verb* **~ sth** to learn sth carefully so that you can remember it exactly 记忆；记住：*to memorize a poem* 记住一首诗

mem·ory 🔑 /ˈmeməri/ (*pl.* **-ies**) *noun*

• **ABILITY TO REMEMBER** 记忆力 **1** 🔑 [C, U] **~ (for sth)** your ability to remember things 记忆力；记性：*I have a bad memory for names.* 我不善于记名字。◇ *People have **short memories*** (= they soon forget). 人是健忘的。◇ *He had a **long memory** for people who had disappointed him.* 谁让他失望，他总是记恨在心。◇ *She can recite the whole poem **from memory**.* 她能背诵全诗。◇ *He suffered loss of memory for weeks after the accident.* 事故之后他有几个星期失去记忆。◇ *Are you sure? Memory can play tricks on you.* 你肯定吗？记忆也会捉弄人的。 **2** 🔑 [U] the period of time that sb is able to remember events 记忆所及的时期；回忆所及的范围：*There hasn't been peace in the country **in/within my memory**.* 在我的记忆里，这个国家从没太平过。◇ *It was the worst storm in recent memory.* 最近能记得的风暴中，这是最厉害的一次。◇ *This hasn't happened **in living memory*** (= nobody alive now can remember it happening). 在世的人都不记得发生过这样的事。

• **STH YOU REMEMBER** 记住的事 **3** 🔑 [C] a thought of sth that you remember from the past 回忆；记忆 **SYN recollection**：*childhood memories* 童年的回忆 ◇ *I have vivid memories of my grandparents.* 我依然清楚地记得我的祖父母。◇ *What is your earliest memory?* 你最早能记得的是什么？◇ *The photos **bring back** lots of good **memories**.* 这些照片唤起了许多美好的回忆。 **4** [U] (*formal*) what is remembered about sb after they have died 对死者的记忆：*Her memory lives on* (= we still remember her). 我们永远怀念她。

• **COMPUTING** 计算机技术 **5** 🔑 [C, U] the part of a computer where information is stored; the amount of space in a computer for storing information 存储器；内存；记忆体 ➲ SEE ALSO RAM ➲ WORDFINDER NOTE AT COMPUTER

IDM **if (my) memory serves me well, correctly, etc.** if I remember correctly 如果我没有记错的话 **in memory of sb | to the memory of sb** 🔑 intended to show respect and remind people of sb who has died 作为对某人的纪念：*He founded the charity in memory of his late wife.* 他创办了这一慈善事业以纪念他已故的妻子。➲ MORE AT ETCH, JOG *v.*, SIEVE *n.*

ˈmemory bank *noun* the memory of a device such as a computer（计算机等的）存储体，记忆库

ˈmemory card *noun* an electronic device that can be used to store data, used especially with digital cameras, mobile/cell phones, music players, etc. 存储卡（尤用于数码相机、手机、音乐播放器等） ➲ COMPARE SD CARD, SDHC CARD

ˌmemory ˈlane *noun*

IDM **a trip/walk down ˌmemory ˈlane** time that you spend thinking about and remembering the past or going to a place again in order to remind yourself of past experiences 回忆往事；重游故地

ˈmemory stick *noun* (*especially BrE*) a small memory device that can be used to store data from a computer and to move it from one computer to another 闪存盘；闪盘；U 盘 **SYN flash drive** ➲ VISUAL VOCAB PAGE V73

mem·sahib /ˈmemsɑːb/ *noun* used in India, especially in the past, to address a married woman with high social status, often a European woman 夫人，太太（尤指旧时印度对来自欧洲等上层社会已婚妇女的称呼）

men PL. OF MAN

men·ace /ˈmenəs/ *noun, verb*

■ ***noun*** **1** [C, usually sing.] **~ (to sb/sth)** a person or thing that causes, or may cause, serious damage, harm or danger 威胁；危险的人（或物） **SYN threat**：*a new initiative aimed at beating the menace of illegal drugs* 旨在打击非法毒品威胁的新举措 **2** [U] an atmosphere that makes you feel threatened or frightened 恐怖的氛围；危险气氛：***a sense/an air/a hint of menace** in his voice* 他的话音里的威胁语气 / 腔调 / 意味 **3** [C, usually sing.] (*informal*) a person or thing that is annoying or causes trouble 烦人的人（或事物）；引起麻烦的人（或事物） **SYN nuisance** **4 menaces** [pl.] (*law* 律, *BrE*) threats that sb will cause harm if they do not get what they are asking for 恐吓；威胁：*to demand money **with menaces*** 勒索钱财

■ ***verb*** **~ sth/sb** (*formal*) to be a possible danger to sth/sb 对…构成危险；危及；威胁到 **SYN threaten**：*The forests are being menaced by major development projects.* 大型开发项目正在危及森林。

men·acing /ˈmenəsɪŋ/ *adj.* seeming likely to cause you harm or danger 威胁的；恐吓的；危险的 **SYN threatening**：*a menacing face/tone* 恶狠脸色 / 口吻 ◇ *At night, the dark streets become menacing.* 在夜晚，漆黑的街道变得阴森森的。 ▶ **men·acing·ly** *adv.*：*The thunder growled menacingly.* 雷声轰鸣，叫人害怕。

mé·nage /meɪˈnɑːʒ/ *noun* [usually sing.] (*from French, formal or humorous*) all the people who live together in one house 家庭；全体家庭成员 **SYN household**

ménage à trois /ˌmemɑːʒ ɑː ˈtrwʌ/ *noun* (*pl.* **ménages à trois** /ˌmemɑːʒ ɑː ˈtrwʌ/) [usually sing.] (*from French*) a situation where three people, especially a husband, wife and lover, live together and have sexual relationships with each other 三人同居，三角家庭（尤指夫妇和情人同居）

men·agerie /məˈnædʒəri/ *noun* a collection of wild animals （一群关起来的）野生动物

mend /mend/ *verb, noun*

■ *verb* **1** [T] ~ **sth** (*BrE*) to repair sth that has been damaged or broken so that it can be used again 修理；修补：*Could you mend my bike for me?* 你能帮我修一下自行车吗？ ➲ SEE ALSO FENCE-MENDING **2** [T] ~ **sth** to repair a hole in a piece of clothing, etc. 缝补；织补：*He mended shoes for a living.* 他靠修鞋为生。 **3** [T] ~ **sth** to find a solution to a problem or disagreement 弥合（分歧）；解决（争端）：*They tried to mend their differences.* 他们试图消除他们之间的分歧。 **4** [I] (*old-fashioned*) (of a person) to improve in health after being ill/sick 痊愈；恢复健康 SYN **recover**：*He's mending slowly after the operation.* 手术后，他正在缓慢好转。 **5** [I] (of a broken bone 骨折) to heal 愈合；痊愈

IDM **mend (your) fences (with sb)** to find a solution to a disagreement with sb 解决纷争；消除隔阂 **mend your ˈways** to stop behaving badly 改过自新；改邪归正 ➲ MORE AT SAY *v.*

■ *noun*

IDM **on the ˈmend** (*informal*) getting better after an illness or injury; improving after a difficult situation 康复；好转；改善；改进：*My leg is definitely on the mend now.* 我的腿正在明显地好转。 ◇ *Does he believe the economy's really on the mend?* 他相信经济确实在复苏吗？

men·da·cious /menˈdeɪʃəs/ *adj.* (*formal*) not telling the truth 撒谎的；不真实的；捏造的 SYN **lying**

men·da·city /menˈdæsəti/ *noun* [U] (*formal*) the act of not telling the truth 撒谎；捏造；说瞎话 SYN **lying**

men·del·evium /ˌmendəˈliːviəm; -ˈleɪv-/ *noun* [U] (*symb.* **Md**) a chemical element. Mendelevium is a RADIOACTIVE element that does not exist naturally. 钔（放射性化学元素）

mend·er /ˈmendə(r)/ *noun* (*BrE*) (usually in compounds 通常构成复合词) a person who mends sth 修理工；修补者：*road menders* 修路工

men·di·cant /ˈmendɪkənt/ *adj.* (*formal*) (especially of members of religious groups 尤指宗教成员) living by asking people for money and food 化缘的；行乞的 ▶ **men·di·cant** *noun*

men·folk /ˈmenfəʊk; *NAmE* -foʊk/ *noun* [pl.] (*old-fashioned*) men of a particular family or community （统称家庭或社群中的）男人：*a society sending its menfolk off to war* 把男人送上战场的社会 ➲ COMPARE WOMENFOLK

me·nial /ˈmiːniəl/ *adj., noun*

■ *adj.* (*usually disapproving*) (of work 工作) not skilled or important, and often boring or badly paid 不需技巧的；枯燥的；报酬低的：***menial jobs/work*** 枯燥的工作 ◇ *menial tasks like cleaning the floor* 擦地板这种琐碎的工作

■ *noun* (*old-fashioned*) a person with a menial job 仆人；佣人

men·in·ges /məˈnɪndʒiːz/ *noun* [pl.] (*anatomy* 解) the three MEMBRANES (= thin layers of material) that surround the brain and SPINAL CORD 脑脊膜

men·in·gi·tis /ˌmenɪnˈdʒaɪtɪs/ *noun* [U] a serious disease in which the TISSUES surrounding the brain and SPINAL CORD become infected and swollen, causing severe headache, fever and sometimes death 脑膜炎；脑脊膜炎

me·nis·cus /məˈnɪskəs/ *noun* (*pl.* **me·nisci** /-saɪ/) **1** (*physics* 物) the curved surface of a liquid in a tube （液柱的）弯月面 **2** (*anatomy* 解) a thin layer of CARTILAGE between the surfaces of some joints, for example the knee （膝关节等的）半月板

Men·non·ite /ˈmenənaɪt/ *noun* a member of a PROTESTANT religious group that lives in the US and Canada. Mennonites live a simple life and do not work as public officials or soldiers. 门诺派教徒（美国和加拿大一个新教教派的成员，生活简朴，不当公务员或服兵役）

meno·pause /ˈmenəpɔːz/ (*also informal* **the ˈchange (of life)**) *noun* [U] (*often* **the menopause**) [sing.] the time during which a woman gradually stops MENSTRUATING, usually at around the age of 50 绝经期；（妇女的）更年期：*to reach (the) menopause* 到更年期 ▶ **meno·pausal** /ˌmenəˈpɔːzl/ *adj.*：***menopausal women/symptoms*** 更年期的妇女 / 症状

me·norah /mɪˈnɔːrə/ *noun* a traditional Jewish object to hold seven or nine CANDLES （传统的犹太人所使用的可插七或九支蜡烛的）大烛台，多连灯烛台

mensch /menʃ/ *noun* (*NAmE, informal*) a good person, especially sb who does sth kind or helpful 好人；乐于助人的人

men·ses /ˈmensiːz/ *noun* (*often* **the menses**) [pl.] (*specialist*) the flow of blood each month from a woman's body 月经；行经

ˈmen's room *noun* (*NAmE*) a public toilet/bathroom for men 男厕所；男盥洗室

men·strual /ˈmenstruəl/ *adj.* connected with the time when a woman menstruates each month 月经的：*The average length of a woman's* ***menstrual cycle*** *is 28 days.* 妇女的平均月经周期是 28 天。 ◇ *menstrual blood* 经血 ◇ (*formal*) *a menstrual period* 月经期 ➲ COMPARE PREMENSTRUAL

men·stru·ate /ˈmenstrueɪt/ *verb* [I] (*formal*) when a woman **menstruates**, there is a flow of blood from her womb, usually once a month 行经；来月经

men·stru·ation /ˌmenstruˈeɪʃn/ *noun* [U] (*formal*) the process or time of menstruating 行经；月经来潮 ➲ COMPARE PERIOD *n.* (5)

mens·wear /ˈmenzweə(r); *NAmE* -wer/ *noun* [U] used especially in shops/stores to describe clothes for men 男服（尤用于商店中）：*the menswear department* 男装部 ➲ WORDFINDER NOTE AT STORE

-ment *suffix* (in nouns 构成名词) the action or result of … 的行为（或结果）：*bombardment* 炮击 ◇ *development* 发展 ➲ MORE LIKE THIS 7, page R25 ▶ **-mental** (in adjectives 构成形容词)：*governmental* 政府的 ◇ *judgemental* 审判的

men·tal 🔑 AW /ˈmentl/ *adj.* **1** 🔑 [usually before noun] connected with or happening in the mind; involving the process of thinking 思想的；精神的；思考的；智力的：*the mental process of remembering* 记忆的心理过程 ◇ *Do you have a* ***mental picture*** *of what it will look like?* 在你想象中它会是什么样子？ ◇ ***I made a mental note*** *to talk to her about it.* 我记着要去和她谈谈这事儿。 ◇ *He has a complete* ***mental block*** (= difficulty in understanding or remembering) *when it comes to physics.* 他对物理一窍不通。 **2** 🔑 [usually before noun] connected with the state of health of the mind or with the treatment of illnesses of the mind 精神病治疗的；精神健康的 SYN **psychological**：***mental health*** 精神健康 ◇ *a* ***mental disorder/illness/hospital*** 精神紊乱病；精神病院 ◇ *She was suffering from physical and mental exhaustion.* 她当时已经是精疲力竭。 ➲ COMPARE PSYCHIATRIC **3** [not usually before noun] (*BrE, slang*) crazy 疯狂；发疯：*Watch him. He's mental.* 看着他，他疯了。 ◇ *My dad will* ***go mental*** (= be very angry) *when he finds out.* 我父亲要是发现了，他会气疯的。

ˌmental ˈage *noun* [C, usually sing.] the level of sb's ability to think, understand, etc. that is judged by comparison with the average ability for children of a particular age 智力年龄；心理年龄：*She is sixteen but* ***has a mental age*** *of five.* 她十六岁，但智力年龄是五岁。 ➲ COMPARE CHRONOLOGICAL (2)

ˌmental aˈrithmetic *noun* [U] adding, multiplying, etc. numbers in your mind without writing anything down or using a CALCULATOR 心算

men·tal·ity AW /menˈtæləti/ *noun* [usually sing.] (*pl.* **-ies**) the particular attitude or way of thinking of a person or group 心态；思想状况；思想方法 SYN **mindset**：*I cannot understand the mentality of football hooligans.* 我无法理解足球流氓的心态。 ◇ *a* ***criminal/ghetto mentality*** 犯罪心态；种族聚居区的思想意识 ➲ SEE ALSO SIEGE MENTALITY

men·tal·ly AW /ˈmentəli/ *adv.* connected with or happening in the mind 精神上；智力上；思想上： *mentally ill* 有精神病 ◇ *The baby is very mentally alert.* 这孩子脑子很机灵。 ◇ *Mentally, I began making a list of things I had to do.* 我开始在脑子里盘算我该做哪些事情。 ➲ WORDFINDER NOTE AT CONDITION

▼ SYNONYMS 同义词辨析

mentally ill

insane • neurotic • psychotic • disturbed • unstable

These words all describe sb who is suffering from a mental illness. 以上各词均用以形容患有精神疾病的人。

mentally ill suffering from an illness of the mind, especially in a way that affects the way you think and behave 指有精神病

insane [not usually before noun] (*rather formal*) suffering from a serious mental illness and unable to live in normal society 指精神失常、神经错乱： *The question is, was the man insane when he committed the crime?* 问题在于这男人犯罪时是否处于精神失常状态？ NOTE In informal English **insane** can describe sb who is not suffering from a mental illness, but whose mind does not work normally, especially because they are under pressure. This meaning is used especially in the phrases *go insane* and *drive sb insane*. 在非正式英语中，insane 可用于未患精神病但尤因压力导致心智不正常的人。这一含义尤用于 go insane 和 drive sb insane 短语中。

neurotic (*medical*) suffering from or connected with neurosis (= a mental illness in which a person suffers strong feelings of fear and worry) 指神经机能病的、神经官能症的： *the treatment of anxiety in neurotic patients* 对神经官能症病人焦虑感的治疗 NOTE In informal English **neurotic** is also used to describe sb who is not suffering from a mental illness, but is not behaving in a calm way because they are worried about sth. 在非正式英语中，neurotic 亦用以指未患精神病、但因担忧而变得神经质的人： *She became neurotic about keeping the house clean.* 她对保持房子清洁有点神经质。

psychotic (*medical*) suffering from or connected with psychosis (= a serious mental illness in which thought and emotions lose connection with external reality) 指精神错乱的、有精神病的 NOTE In informal English **psychotic** is sometimes used to describe anyone suffering from a mental illness, but in correct medical usage it only describes people who have difficulty relating to external reality. It contrasts with **neurotic**, which describes people who are less seriously mentally ill and are still able to distinguish what is real from what is not. 在非正式英语中，psychotic 有时用以泛指患有精神疾病，但在正确的医学用语中，只用以描述难以与客观现实建立联系的人，这与 neurotic 形成对比； neurotic 用以描述患精神错乱程度较轻，仍能区分现实与虚幻的人。

disturbed mentally ill, especially because of very unhappy or shocking experiences 指有精神病的、心理不正常的、精神紊乱的，尤因不幸或受刺激所致： *He works with emotionally disturbed children.* 他从事跟精神异常儿童有关的工作。

unstable having emotions and behaviour that are likely to change suddenly and unexpectedly 指情绪、行为反复无常的、不稳定的

PATTERNS

- neurotic/psychotic/disturbed/unstable **behaviour**
- neurotic/psychotic **illnesses/disorders/symptoms/patients**
- **seriously** mentally ill/neurotic/psychotic/disturbed
- **emotionally/mentally** disturbed/unstable

ˌ**mentally ˈhandicapped** *adj.* (*old-fashioned*) (of a person 人) slow to learn or to understand things because of a problem with the brain 弱智的；智力残障的；精神残疾的 HELP It is now more usual to say that people with this kind of problem **have learning difficulties**.现在常把有此类问题的人说成 have learning difficulties（有学习障碍）。

men·tee /ˌmenˈtiː/ *noun* a person who is advised and helped by a more experienced person over a period of time 受指导者；门生： *the mentor/mentee relationship* 师徒关系 ➲ COMPARE MENTOR

men·thol /ˈmenθɒl; *NAmE* -θɔːl; -θɑːl/ *noun* [U] a substance that tastes and smells of MINT, that is used in some medicines for colds and to give a strong cool flavour to cigarettes, TOOTHPASTE, etc. 薄荷醇

men·thol·ated /ˈmenθəleɪtɪd/ *adj.* containing menthol 含薄荷醇的： *mentholated sweets* 薄荷糖

men·tion /ˈmenʃn/ *verb, noun*

■ *verb* to write or speak about sth/sb, especially without giving much information 提到；写到；说到： **~ sth/sb (to sb)** *Nobody mentioned anything to me about it.* 没人跟我提过这事儿。 ◇ *Sorry, I won't mention it again.* 对不起，我再也不提它了。 ◇ ***Now that you mention it**, she did seem to be in a strange mood.* 既然你说到这事儿，她确实好像情绪不大对。 ◇ **~ sth/sb as sth/sb** *His name has been mentioned as a future MP.* 有人提到他，认为他将来可以当下院议员。 ◇ **~ where, why, etc....** *Did she mention where she was going?* 她有没有说起她要去哪儿？ ◇ **~ that...** *You mentioned in your letter that you might be moving abroad.* 你在信中谈到你可能要移居国外。 ◇ **~ doing sth**

▼ SYNONYMS 同义词辨析

mention

refer to sb/sth • speak • cite • quote

These words all mean to write or speak about sb/sth, often in order to give an example or prove sth. 以上各词均含写到、说到、谈及或举例说明之义。

mention to write or speak about sth/sb, especially without giving much information 指提到、写到、说到，尤指未给出详细信息： *Nobody mentioned anything to me about it.* 没人跟我提过这事。

refer to sb/sth (*rather formal*) to mention or speak about sb/sth 指提到、谈及、说起： *I promised not to refer to the matter again.* 我答应过再不提这事了。

speak to mention or describe sb/sth 指提起、讲述： *Witnesses **spoke of** a great ball of flame.* 目击者都谈到有个大火球。

cite (*formal*) to mention sth as a reason or an example, or in order to support what you are saying 指提及（原因）、举出（示例）证明： *He cited his heavy workload as the reason for his breakdown.* 他提到繁重的工作负荷是导致他累垮的原因。

quote to mention an example of sth to support what you are saying 指举例说明： *Can you quote me an instance of when this happened?* 你能否给我举例说明一下发生这事的情况？

CITE OR QUOTE? 用 cite 还是 quote?

You can **cite** reasons or examples, but you can only **quote** examples. * cite 可指提及原因或举出示例，但 quote 只用于举例： ~~*He quoted his heavy workload as the reason for his breakdown.*~~ **Cite** is a more formal word than **quote** and is often used in more formal situations, for example in descriptions of legal cases.
* cite 较 quote 正式，常用于较正式的场合中，如说明法律案件。

PATTERNS

- to mention/refer to/speak of/cite/quote sb/sth **as** sb/sth
- to mention/refer to/cite/quote a(n) **example/instance/case** of sth
- **frequently/often** mentioned/referred to/spoken of/cited/quoted
- the example mentioned/referred to/cited/quoted **above/earlier/previously**

M

Did I mention going to see Vicky on Sunday? 我说过周日要去看望维基了吗? ➲ SEE ALSO ABOVE-MENTIONED, AFORE-MENTIONED ➲ MORE LIKE THIS 27, page R28

IDM **don't 'mention it** (*informal*) used as a polite answer when sb has thanked you for sth (别人道谢时回答)不客气 SYN **you're welcome**: *'Thanks for all your help.' 'Don't mention it.'* "多谢你帮忙。" "不用客气。" **not to mention** used to introduce extra information and emphasize what you are saying 更不用说; 且不说: *He has two big houses in this country, not to mention his villa in France.* 他在这个国家有两座大房子, 更别提他在法国的别墅了。

■ **noun** [U, C, usually sing.] an act of referring to sb/sth in speech or writing 提及; 说起; 写上一笔: *He made no **mention of** her work.* 他根本没提她的工作。◇ *The concert didn't even **get a mention** in the newspapers.* 报纸对这场音乐会只字未提。◇ *Phil deserves (a) **special mention** for all the help he gave us.* 菲尔对我们的帮助很大, 理应特别提一提。

men·tor /ˈmentɔː(r)/ *noun* an experienced person who advises and helps sb with less experience over a period of time 导师; 顾问 ➲ COMPARE MENTEE ▶ **men·tor·ing** *noun* [U]: *a mentoring programme* 指导计划

menu /ˈmenjuː/ *noun* **1** a list of the food that is available at a restaurant or to be served at a meal 菜单: *to ask **for/look at the menu*** 要菜单; 看菜单 ◇ *What's **on the menu*** (= for dinner) *tonight?* 今晚有什么菜? ➲ WORDFINDER NOTE AT RESTAURANT ➲ COLLOCATIONS AT RESTAURANT **2** (*computing* 计) a list of possible choices that are shown on a computer screen (功能选择) 菜单; 选单: *a pull-down menu* 下拉式菜单 ➲ SEE ALSO DROP-DOWN MENU ➲ WORDFINDER NOTE AT FILE

'menu bar *noun* (*computing* 计) a horizontal bar at the top of a computer screen that contains DROP-DOWN MENUS such as 'File', 'Edit' and 'Help' (下拉) 菜单栏, 选单栏

meow (*especially NAmE*) (*BrE usually* **miaow**) /miˈaʊ/ *noun* the crying sound made by a cat 喵 (猫叫声) ➲ SEE ALSO MEW ▶ **meow** (*especially NAmE*) (*BrE usually* **miaow**) *verb* [I] ➲ MORE LIKE THIS 4, page R25

MEP /ˌem iː ˈpiː/ *noun* the abbreviation for 'Member of the European Parliament' 欧洲议会议员 (全写为 Member of the European Parliament): *the Labour MEP for South East Wales* 东南威尔士的工党欧洲议会议员

mephe·drone /ˈmefədrəʊn; *NAmE* -droʊn/ *noun* [U] (*also* **'miaow miaow, 'meow meow**) a drug, made from chemical substances, that affects people's moods and makes them feel more awake. Use of the drug is illegal in some countries. 甲氧麻黄酮, 喵喵 (一种化学合成兴奋剂, 在有些国家属非法毒品)

Meph·is·toph·elian /ˌmefɪstəˈfiːliən; *NAmE also* ˌmefɪˌstɑːfəˈliən/ *adj.* (*formal*) very evil; like the DEVIL 十分邪恶的; 魔鬼似的 ➲ MORE LIKE THIS 16, page R27 ORIGIN From **Mephistopheles**, an evil spirit to whom, according to the German legend, Faust sold his soul. 源自魔鬼精灵墨菲斯托菲里斯 (Mephistopheles)。根据德国民间传说, 浮士德把自己的灵魂出卖给了它。

mer·can·tile /ˈmɜːkəntaɪl; *NAmE* ˈmɜːrk-; -tiːl/ *adj.* (*formal*) connected with trade and commercial affairs 商业的; 贸易的

mer·can·ti·lism /mɜːˈkæntɪlɪzəm; *NAmE* mɜːrˈk-/ *noun* [U] the economic theory that trade increases wealth 重商主义, 商业本位 (认为商业可增加财富) ▶ **mer·can·ti·list** /-lɪst/ *adj.* **mer·can·ti·list** /-lɪst/ *noun*

Mer·ca·tor projection /mɜːˈkeɪtə prədʒekʃn; *NAmE* mɜːrˈkeɪtər/ *noun* [sing.] a traditional map of the world, on which the relative size of some countries is not accurate 墨卡托投影 (一种传统的世界地图投影, 其中一些国家的面积失准) ➲ COMPARE PETERS PROJECTION

mer·cen·ary /ˈmɜːsənəri; *NAmE* ˈmɜːrsəneri/ *noun, adj.*
■ **noun** (*pl.* **-ies**) a soldier who will fight for any country or group that offers payment 雇佣兵: *foreign mercenaries* 外国雇佣兵 ◇ *mercenary soldiers* 雇佣兵
■ **adj.** (*disapproving*) only interested in making or getting money 只为金钱的: *a **mercenary society/attitude*** 唯利是图的社会 / 态度 ◇ *She's interested in him for purely mercenary reasons.* 她对他感兴趣完全是为了贪图金钱。

merch /mɜːtʃ; *NAmE* mɜːrtʃ/ *noun* [U] (*informal*) = MERCHANDISE

mer·chan·dise *noun, verb*
■ **noun** /ˈmɜːtʃəndaɪs; -daɪz; *NAmE* ˈmɜːrtʃ-/ (*also* **merch** *informal*) [U] **1** (*formal*) goods that are bought or sold; goods that are for sale in a shop/store 商品; 货品: *a wide selection of merchandise* 品种丰富的商品 ➲ SYNONYMS AT PRODUCT **2** things you can buy that are connected with or that advertise a particular event or organization 相关商品; 指定商品: *official Olympic merchandise* 奥林匹克运动会官方指定商品
■ **verb** /-daɪz; *NAmE* ˈmɜːrtʃ-/ **~ sth** to sell sth using advertising, etc. 推销; (运用广告等进行) 销售

mer·chan·dis·ing /ˈmɜːtʃəndaɪzɪŋ; *NAmE* ˈmɜːrtʃ-/ *noun* [U] **1** (*especially NAmE*) the activity of selling goods, or of trying to sell them, by advertising or displaying them 推销; 展销 **2** products connected with a popular film/movie, person or event; the process of selling these goods (根据受欢迎的电影、人物或事件而生产的) 周边产品; 相关产品的销售: *millions of pounds' worth of Batman merchandising* 价值数百万英镑的蝙蝠侠的周边产品

mer·chant /ˈmɜːtʃənt; *NAmE* ˈmɜːrtʃ-/ *noun, adj.*
■ **noun** **1** a person who buys and sells goods in large quantities, especially one who imports and exports goods 商人; 批发商; (尤指) 进出口批发商: ***builders' merchants*** (= who sell supplies to the building trade) 建材批发商 ◇ *a **coal/wine merchant*** 煤炭 / 葡萄酒批发商 ◇ *Venice was once a city of rich merchants.* 威尼斯曾是富商云集的城市。 ➲ SEE ALSO SQUEEGEE MERCHANT **2** (*BrE, informal, disapproving*) a person who likes a particular activity (某活动的) 爱好者; 热衷于…的人: *a speed merchant* (= sb who likes to drive fast) 好开快车的人 ◇ *noise merchants* (= for example, a band who make a lot of noise) 噪音迷 IDM SEE DOOM *n.*
■ **adj.** [only before noun] connected with the transport of goods by sea 海上货运的: *merchant seamen* 商船船员

mer·chant·able /ˈmɜːtʃəntəbl; *NAmE* ˈmɜːrtʃ-/ *adj.* (*law* 律) in a good enough condition to be sold 适于销售的: *of merchantable quality* 质量符合销售标准的

ˌmerchant ˈbank *noun* (*BrE*) = INVESTMENT BANK ▶ **ˌmerchant ˈbanker** *noun* **ˌmerchant ˈbanking** *noun* [U]

mer·chant·man /ˈmɜːtʃəntmən; *NAmE* ˈmɜːrtʃ-/ (*pl.* **-men** /-mən/) (*also* **'merchant ship**) *noun* a ship used for carrying goods for trade rather than a military ship 商船

ˌmerchant ˈnavy (*BrE*) (*NAmE* **ˌmerchant maˈrine**) *noun* [C+sing./pl. v.] a country's commercial ships and the people who work on them (国家的) 商船队; 全体商船船员

mer·ci·ful /ˈmɜːsɪfl; *NAmE* ˈmɜːrs-/ *adj.* **1** ready to forgive people and show them kindness 宽大的; 仁慈的; 慈悲的 SYN **humane**: *a merciful God* 仁慈的上帝 ◇ *They asked her to be merciful to the prisoners.* 他们请求她对犯人仁慈。 **2** (of an event 事件) seeming to be lucky, especially because it brings an end to sb's problems or suffering 还算幸运的, 不幸而可取的 (因能解决问题或能解除痛苦): *Death came as a merciful release.* 死神的到来算是一种幸运的解脱。 ➲ SEE ALSO MERCY

mer·ci·ful·ly /ˈmɜːsɪfəli; *NAmE* ˈmɜːrs-/ *adv.* **1** used to show that you feel sb/sth is lucky because a situation could have been much worse (不幸中) 幸运地 SYN **thankfully**: *Deaths from the disease are mercifully rare.* 这种疾病很少造成死亡, 算是不幸中之幸。 ◇ *Mercifully, everyone arrived on time.* 幸而每个人都按时赶到。 **2** in a kind way 仁慈地; 宽大地: *He was treated mercifully.* 他受到了宽大对待。

mer·ci·less /'mɜːsɪləs; *NAmE* 'mɜːrs-/ *adj.* showing no kindness or pity 毫不怜悯的；无情的；残忍的 **SYN** **cruel**: *a merciless killer/attack* 无情的杀手 / 攻击 ◇ *the merciless heat of the sun* 太阳的酷热 ▶ **mer·ci·less·ly** *adv.* ➲ SEE ALSO MERCY

mer·cur·ial /mɜː'kjʊəriəl; *NAmE* mɜːr'kjʊr-/ *adj.* **1** (*literary*) often changing or reacting in a way that is unexpected 多变的；变幻莫测的 **SYN** **volatile**: *Emily's mercurial temperament made her difficult to live with.* 埃米莉脾气反复无常，很难与她相处。 **2** (*literary*) lively and quick 活泼的；机智的: *a brilliant, mercurial mind* 敏捷而富有才智的头脑 **3** (*specialist*) containing MERCURY 含水银的；水银的

Mer·cury /'mɜːkjəri; *NAmE* 'mɜːrk-/ *noun* the smallest planet in the SOLAR SYSTEM, nearest to the sun 水星

mer·cury /'mɜːkjəri; *NAmE* 'mɜːrk-/ *noun* [U] (*symb.* **Hg**) a chemical element. Mercury is a poisonous silver liquid metal, used in THERMOMETERS. 汞；水银

mercy /'mɜːsi; *NAmE* 'mɜːrsi/ *noun* (*pl.* **-ies**) **1** [U] a kind or forgiving attitude towards sb that you have the power to harm or right to punish 仁慈；宽恕 **SYN** **humanity**: *to ask/beg/plead for mercy* 请求 / 乞求 / 祈求宽恕 ◇ *They* ***showed no mercy*** *to their hostages.* 他们对人质丝毫不讲仁慈。◇ *God* ***have mercy on us.*** 上帝怜悯我们吧。◇ *The troops are on* ***a mercy mission*** (= a journey to help people) *in the war zone.* 部队出发救助战地民众。 **2** [C, usually sing.] (*informal*) an event or a situation to be grateful for, usually because it stops sth unpleasant 幸运；恩惠: ***It's a mercy*** *she wasn't seriously hurt.* 幸运的是她伤势不重。 ➲ SEE ALSO MERCIFUL, MERCILESS

IDM **at the mercy of sb/sth** not able to stop sb/sth harming you because they have power or control over you 任…处置；对…无能为力；任由…摆布: *I'm not going to put myself at the mercy of the bank.* 我不想任由银行摆布。◇ *We were at the mercy of the weather.* 我们受制于天气。 **leave sb/sth to the mercy/mercies of sb/sth** to leave sb/sth in a situation that may cause them to suffer or to be treated badly 听任某人可能受苦或受到虐待（而无能为力） **throw yourself on sb's mercy** (*formal*) to put yourself in a situation where you must rely on sb to be kind to you and not harm or punish you 指望某人能够善待（或宽恕）自己 ➲ MORE AT SMALL *adj.*

'mercy killing *noun* [C, U] the act of killing sb out of pity, for example because they are in severe pain 安乐死；无疼痛致死术 **SYN** **euthanasia**

mere 🔑 /mɪə(r); *NAmE* mɪr/ *adj., noun*

■ ***adj.*** [only before noun] (*superlative* **mer·est**, *no comparative*) **1** 🔑 used when you want to emphasize how small, unimportant, etc. sb/sth is 仅仅的；只不过: *It took her a mere 20 minutes to win.* 她只花了 20 分钟就赢了。◇ *A mere 2% of their budget has been spent on publicity.* 他们的预算开支只有 2% 用于宣传。◇ *He seemed so young, a mere boy.* 他看来那么年轻，只是个孩子。◇ *You've got the job. The interview will be a mere formality.* 你已经得到了这份工作。面试不过是个形式。 **2** used when you are saying that the fact that a particular thing is present in a situation is enough to have an influence on that situation 只凭…就足以: *His mere presence* (= just the fact that he was there) *made her feel afraid.* 他当时在场，这就足以让她害怕了。◇ *The* ***mere fact that*** *they were prepared to talk was encouraging.* 他们愿意商谈，这就很不错了。◇ *The* ***mere thought of*** *eating made him feel sick.* 他一想到吃东西就觉得恶心。◇ *The merest* (= the slightest) *hint of smoke is enough to make her feel ill.* 最细微的一丝烟就能使她感到不舒服。 ➲ MORE LIKE THIS 32, page R28

■ ***noun*** (*BrE, literary*) (also used in names 也用于名称) a small lake 小湖；池塘

mere·ly 🔑 /'mɪəli; *NAmE* 'mɪrli/ *adv.* used meaning 'only' or 'simply' to emphasize a fact or sth that you are saying 仅仅；只不过: *It is* ***not merely*** *a job, but a way of life.* 这不仅仅是一份工作，而且是一种生活方式。◇ *He said nothing, merely smiled and watched her.* 他什么也没说，只是微笑着看着她。◇ *They agreed to go merely because they were getting paid for it.* 他们同意去只是因为他们会得到酬劳。◇ *I'm merely stating what everybody knows anyway.* 我说的不过是些常识。

mere·tri·cious /ˌmerə'trɪʃəs/ *adj.* (*formal*) seeming attractive, but in fact having no real value 华而不实的；虚有其表的；金玉其外的

merge /mɜːdʒ; *NAmE* mɜːrdʒ/ *verb* **1** [I, T] to combine or make two or more things combine to form a single thing （使）合并，结合，并入: *The banks are set to merge next year.* 这几家银行准备明年合并。◇ *The two groups have merged to form a new party.* 两大组织合并组成一个新党。◇ **~ with sth** *His department will merge with mine.* 他的部门将和我的合并。◇ **~ into sth** *The villages expanded and merged into one large town.* 这些村庄扩大了并且结合成了一个大集镇。◇ **~ (A and B) (together)** *Fact and fiction merge together in his latest thriller.* 在他最新的惊险小说中，真实和虚构交织在一起。◇ **~ A with B** *His department will be merged with mine.* 他的部门将和我的合并。◇ **~ sth** *The company was formed by merging three smaller firms.* 公司是由三家小公司合并组成的。 **2** [I] **~ (into sth)** if two things **merge**, or if one thing **merges into** another, the differences between them gradually disappear so that it is impossible to separate them 相融；融入；渐渐消失在某物中: *The hills merged into the dark sky behind them.* 山峦渐渐隐入背后漆黑的夜空之中。

IDM **merge into the 'background** (of a person 人) to behave quietly when you are with a group of people so that they do not notice you 悄悄融入整体；不求闻达

mer·ger /'mɜːdʒə(r); *NAmE* 'mɜːrdʒ-/ *noun* [C] the act of joining two or more organizations or businesses into one（机构或企业的）合并，归并: **~ (between/of A and B)** *a merger between the two banks* 两家银行的合并 ◇ **~ (with sth)** *our proposed merger with the university* 我们与这所大学提议中的合并 ➲ WORDFINDER NOTE AT DEAL ➲ COLLOCATIONS AT BUSINESS

me·rid·ian /mə'rɪdiən/ *noun* one of the lines that is drawn from the North Pole to the South Pole on a map of the world 子午线；经线

mer·ingue /mə'ræŋ/ *noun* [U, C] a sweet white mixture made from egg whites and sugar, usually baked until crisp and used to make cakes; a small cake made from this mixture 蛋白酥；蛋糖脆皮: *a lemon meringue pie* 柠檬蛋糖馅饼

me·rino /mə'riːnəʊ; *NAmE* -noʊ/ *noun* (*pl.* **-os**) **1** [C] a breed of sheep with long fine wool 美利奴羊（其绒细长） **2** [U] the wool of the merino sheep or a type of cloth made from this wool, used for making clothes 美利奴羊毛；美利奴羊毛织品

merit /'merɪt/ *noun, verb*

■ ***noun*** **1** [U] (*formal*) the quality of being good and of deserving praise, reward or admiration 优点；美德；价值 **SYN** **worth**: *a work of outstanding artistic merit* 具有杰出艺术价值的作品 ◇ *The plan is entirely without merit.* 这个计划毫无价值。◇ *I want to get the job* ***on merit.*** 我要凭才能得到这份工作。 **2** [C, usually pl.] a good feature that deserves praise, reward or admiration 值得赞扬（或奖励、钦佩）的特点；功绩；长处 **SYN** **strength**: *We will* ***consider each case on its (own) merits*** (= without considering any other issues, feelings, etc.). 我们将根据每件事情本身的情况来考虑。◇ *They weighed up the* ***relative merits*** *of the four candidates.* 他们对四名候选人各自的优点作了比较。 **3** [C] (*BrE*) a mark/grade in an exam or for a piece of work at school or university which is excellent（学校考试或作业的）良好 **4** [C] (*BrE*) a mark/grade given as a reward for good behaviour at school （在校操行好而获得的）良好

■ ***verb*** (not used in the progressive tenses 不用于进行时) **~ (doing) sth** (*formal*) to do sth to deserve praise, attention, etc. 应得；值得 **SYN** **deserve**: *He claims that their success was not merited.* 他声称他们不应该获得成功。◇ *The case does not merit further investigation.* 这个案子不值得进一步调查。

mer·it·oc·racy /ˌmerɪˈtɒkrəsi; *NAmE* -ˈtɑːk-/ *noun* (*pl.* **-ies**) **1** [C, U] a country or social system where people get power or money on the basis of their ability 精英领导体制；英才管理制度 **2 the meritocracy** [sing.] the group of people with power in this kind of social system 精英管理班子 ▶ **mer·ito·crat·ic** /ˌmerɪtəˈkrætɪk/ *adj.*

meri·tori·ous /ˌmerɪˈtɔːriəs/ *adj.* (*formal*) deserving praise 值得赞扬的 **SYN** **praiseworthy**

mer·lin /ˈmɜːlɪn; *NAmE* ˈmɜːrlɪn/ *noun* a small BIRD OF PREY (= a bird that kills other creatures for food) of the FALCON family 灰背隼

mer·maid /ˈmɜːmeɪd; *NAmE* ˈmɜːrm-/ *noun* (in stories) a creature with a woman's head and body, and a fish's tail instead of legs （传说中的）美人鱼

mer·man /ˈmɜːmæn; *NAmE* ˈmɜːr-/ *noun* (*pl.* **-men** /-men/) (in stories) a creature with a man's head and body and a fish's tail instead of legs, like a male MERMAID （传说中的）人鱼

mer·rily /ˈmerəli/ *adv.* **1** in a happy, cheerful way 高兴地；愉快地：*They chatted merrily.* 他们愉快地聊着。 **2** without thinking about the problems that your actions might cause 自顾自地；毫无顾忌地 **SYN** **gaily**: *She carried on merrily, not realizing the offence she was causing.* 她毫无顾忌地胡闹，没意识到惹人生气了。

mer·ri·ment /ˈmerimənt/ *noun* [U] (*formal*) happy talk, enjoyment and the sound of people laughing 欢乐；嬉戏；欢笑 **SYN** **jollity, mirth**

merry /ˈmeri/ *adj.* (**mer·rier**, **mer·ri·est**) **1** happy and cheerful 愉快的；高兴的 **SYN** **cheery**: *a merry grin* 愉快的笑 **2 Merry Christmas** used at Christmas to say that you hope that sb has an enjoyable holiday （圣诞节祝贺语）圣诞快乐 **3** (*informal, especially BrE*) slightly drunk 微醺 **SYN** **tipsy**

IDM **make ˈmerry** (*old-fashioned*) to enjoy yourself by singing, laughing, drinking, etc. 行乐；宴乐 **the ˌmore the ˈmerrier** (*saying*) the more people or things there are, the better the situation will be or the more fun people will have 人越多越好玩；（东西）多多益善，越多越好：*'Can I bring a friend to your party?' 'Sure—the more the merrier!'* "我能带个朋友来你的聚会吗？" "当然，人越多越好玩嘛！" ➲ MORE AT EAT, HELL, LEAD[1] *v.*

ˈmerry-go-round *noun* **1** (*also* **car·ou·sel** *especially in NAmE*) (*BrE also* **round·about**) a round platform with model horses, cars, etc. that turns around and around and that children ride on at a FAIRGROUND 旋转木马 ➲ PICTURE AT ROUNDABOUT **2** (*NAmE*) (*BrE* **round·about**) a round platform for children to play on in a park, etc. that is pushed round while the children are sitting on it （游乐设施）旋转平台 **3** continuous busy activity or a continuous series of changing events 一连串的繁忙活动；走马灯似的更迭：*He was tired of the merry-go-round of romance and longed to settle down.* 他厌倦了没完没了的风流韵事，渴望安定下来。

merry·mak·ing /ˈmerimeɪkɪŋ/ *noun* [U] (*literary*) fun and enjoyment with singing, laughing, drinking, etc. 嬉笑玩乐；行乐 **SYN** **revelry**

mesa /ˈmeɪsə/ *noun* (*pl.* **mesas**) a hill with a flat top and steep sides that is common in the south-west of the US 桌子山，方山（常见于美国西南部）

mes·cal /ˈmeskæl; meˈskæl/ *noun* = PEYOTE (1)

mes·ca·line (*also* **mes·ca·lin**) /ˈmeskəlɪn/ *noun* [U] a drug obtained from a type of CACTUS, that affects people's minds and makes them see and hear things that are not really there 墨斯卡林；仙人球毒碱（从某种仙人掌中提取的致幻剂）

mesh /meʃ/ *noun, verb*

■ *noun* **1** [U, C] material made of threads of plastic rope or wire that are twisted together like a net 网状物；网状织物：*wire mesh over the door of the cage* 罩在笼子门上的铁丝网 **2** [C, usually sing.] a complicated situation or system that it is difficult to escape from 陷阱；困境；圈套 **SYN** **web**

■ *verb* (*formal*) **1** [I, T] to fit together or match closely, especially in a way that works well; to make things fit together successfully （使）吻合，相配，匹配，适合：**~ (sth) (with sth)** *This evidence meshes with earlier reports of an organized riot.* 这一证据和先前关于一次有组织暴乱的报告相吻合。◇ **~ (sth) (together)** *His theories mesh together various political and religious beliefs.* 他的理论把各种政治和宗教信仰完美地结合起来。 **2** [I] (*specialist*) (of parts of a machine 机器零件) to fit together as they move 啮合：*If the cogs don't mesh correctly, the gears will keep slipping.* 如果嵌齿不能完好啮合，齿轮就会总是脱落。

mes·mer·ic /mezˈmerɪk/ *adj.* [usually before noun] (*formal*) having such a strong effect on people that they cannot give their attention to anything else 迷人的；不可抗拒的 **SYN** **hypnotic**

mes·mer·ize (*BrE also* **-ise**) /ˈmezməraɪz/ *verb* [usually passive] **~ sb** to have such a strong effect on you that you cannot give your attention to anything else 迷住；吸引 **SYN** **fascinate** ▶ **mes·mer·iz·ing, -is·ing** *adj.*: *Her performance was mesmerizing.* 她的表演让人入迷。

meso·phyll /ˈmezəfɪl; ˈmiːz-; *BrE also* ˈmes-; *BrE also* miːs-/ *noun* [U] (*biology* 生) the material that the inside of a leaf is made of 叶肉

meso·sphere /ˈmezəsfɪə(r); ˈmiːz-; *NAmE* -sfɪr/ *noun* [usually sing.] the part of the earth's atmosphere which is between 50 and 80 kilometres from the ground, between the STRATOSPHERE and the THERMOSPHERE （大气层的）中间层

mes·quite /meˈskiːt; ˈmeskiːt/ (*also* **meˈsquite tree**) *noun* a N American tree, often used for making CHARCOAL for GRILLING food 牧豆树（产于北美，常用以制烧烤用的木炭）：*mesquite-grilled chicken* 牧豆树炭烤鸡

mess 🔑 /mes/ *noun, verb*

■ *noun*

• **UNTIDY STATE** 不整洁 **1** 🔑 [C, usually sing.] a dirty or untidy state 肮脏；杂乱；不整洁：*The room was* ***in a mess.*** 房间杂乱不堪。◇ *The kids* ***made a mess*** *in the bathroom.* 孩子们把浴室搞得一塌糊涂。◇ *'What a mess!' she said, surveying the scene after the party.* 看着聚会后的场面，她说："真是一片狼藉！"◇ *My hair's a real mess!* 我的头发太乱了。

• **DIFFICULT SITUATION** 困境 **2** 🔑 [C, usually sing.] a situation that is full of problems, usually because of a lack of organization or because of mistakes that sb has made （组织欠佳或人为导致的）麻烦，困境，混乱：*The economy is* ***in a mess.*** 经济陷入了困境。◇ *I feel I've* ***made a mess of things.*** 我觉得我把事情搞糟了。◇ *The whole situation is a mess.* 整个情况都是一团糟。◇ *Let's try to sort out the mess.* 我们来收拾一下残局吧。◇ *The biggest question is how they got into this mess in the first place.* 关键问题是他们是怎么惹出这样的麻烦的。

• **PERSON** 人 **3** [sing.] a person who is dirty or whose clothes and hair are not tidy 不整洁（或邋遢、不修边幅）的人：*You're a mess!* 你真邋遢！ **4** [sing.] (*informal*) a person who has serious problems and is in a bad mental condition 有严重问题且精神失常的人

• **ANIMAL WASTE** 动物粪便 **5** [U, C] (*informal*) the EXCREMENT (= solid waste matter) of an animal, usually a dog or cat （狗、猫等的）粪便

• **A LOT** 许多 **6** [sing.] **a ~ of sth** (*NAmE, informal*) a lot of sth 许多；大量：*There's a mess of fish down there, so get your lines in the water.* 那底下有很多鱼，快下钩吧。

• **ARMED FORCES** 武装力量 **7** [C] (*also* **ˈmess hall** *especially in NAmE*) a building or room in which members of the armed forces have their meals （军队的）食堂，餐厅：*the officers' mess* 军官食堂

■ *verb*

• **MAKE UNTIDY** 使不整洁 **1** [T] **~ sth** (*informal, especially NAmE*) to make sth dirty or untidy 使不整洁；弄脏；弄乱：*Careful—you're messing my hair.* 小心，你弄乱我的头发了。

• **OF AN ANIMAL** 动物 **2** [I] to empty its BOWELS somewhere that it should not 随地便溺

IDM ˌ**no ˈmessing** (*informal*) used to say that sth has been done easily 毫不费力；不费吹灰之力；轻而易举：*We finished in time, no messing.* 我们不费吹灰之力，就按时完成了。 **not mess aˈround** (*BrE also* **not mess aˈbout**) (*informal*) to do sth quickly, efficiently or in the right way 不磨蹭；不拖沓；麻利地做；妥善处理：*When they decide to have a party they don't mess around.* 他们决定了要搞聚会，便会迅速操办起来。

PHR V ˌ**mess aˈround** (*BrE also* ˌ**mess aˈbout**) **1** to behave in a silly and annoying way, especially instead of doing sth useful 胡闹；瞎闹 **SYN** **fool around**：*Will you stop messing around and get on with some work?* 别瞎闹了，干点正经事儿不行吗？ **2** to spend time doing sth for pleasure in a relaxed way 逍遥自在地做事：*We spent the day messing around on the river.* 我们在河边闲逛了一整天。 ˌ**mess aˈround with sb** (*BrE also* ˌ**mess aˈbout with sb**) to have a sexual relationship with sb, especially when you should not 勾搭；与某人调情；随便与人发生性关系 ˌ**mess aˈround with sth** (*BrE also* ˌ**mess aˈbout with sth**) **1** to touch or use sth in a careless and/or annoying way 乱弄；玩弄：*Who's been messing around with my computer?* 谁瞎动过我的电脑？ **2** to spend time playing with sth, repairing sth, etc. 花时间摆弄（或修理等）；瞎忙活 ˌ**mess sb aˈbout/aˈround** (*BrE*) to treat sb in an unfair and annoying way, especially by changing your mind a lot or not doing what you said you would 粗鲁地（或轻率地）对待 ˌ**mess ˈup** | ˌ**mess sth↔ˈup** to spoil sth or do it badly 把…弄糟；胡乱地做：*I've really messed up this time.* 这次我真的把事情给弄糟了。◇ *If you cancel now you'll mess up all my arrangements.* 如果你现在取消，就会破坏我所有的安排。 ˌ**mess sb↔ˈup 1** (*informal*) to cause sb to have serious emotional or mental problems 使心情恶劣；使精神崩溃 **2** (*NAmE, informal*) to physically hurt sb, especially by hitting them 打伤；殴打：*He was messed up pretty bad by the other guy.* 他被另一个家伙打成了重伤。 ˌ**mess sth↔ˈup** to make sth dirty or untidy 使不整洁；弄脏；弄乱：*I don't want you messing up my nice clean kitchen.* 我不想让你弄脏我整洁的厨房。 ˈ**mess with sb/sth** (usually used in negative sentences 通常用于否定句) to get involved with sb/sth that may be harmful 卷入不好的事；与某人有牵连：*I wouldn't mess with him if I were you.* 我要是你就会离他远点儿。

mes·sage 🔑 /ˈmesɪdʒ/ *noun, verb*

■ ***noun*** **1** 🔑 a written or spoken piece of information, etc. that you send to sb or leave for sb when you cannot speak to them yourself （书面或口头的）信息，消息，音信：*There were no messages for me at the hotel.* 旅馆里没有给我的留言。◇ *We've had an urgent message saying that your father's ill.* 我们得到个紧急消息说你父亲病了。◇ *Jenny's not here at the moment.* ***Can I take a message?*** 珍妮这会儿不在。要我给你传个话吗？◇ *I* ***left a message*** *on her voicemail.* 我给她的语音信箱留言了。◇ *I've been trying to get you all day—don't you ever listen to your messages?* 我整天都在设法跟你联系，难道你就没有听一下电话留言？◇ **~ (from sb) (to sb)** *Messages of support have been arriving from all over the country.* 表示声援的言论从全国各地纷至沓来。◇ *a televised message from the President to the American people* 电视播出的总统告美国人民书 ➲ WORDFINDER NOTE AT CALL ➲ SEE ALSO ERROR MESSAGE **2** 🔑 a piece of information sent in electronic form, for example by email or mobile/cell phone 电邮信息；（手机）短信息：*an email message* 电邮信息 ◇ *There were four messages in my inbox.* 我的收件箱里有四封邮件。◇ *He sent me a message.* 他给我发了一条信息。

> **WORDFINDER** 联想词：address, attachment, compose, draft, **email**, emoticon, forward, inbox, re

3 🔑 [usually sing.] an important moral, social or political idea that a book, speech, etc. is trying to communicate （书、演讲等的）要旨，要点，教训：*a film with a strong religious message* 有强烈的宗教启示的电影 ◇ *The campaign is trying to* ***get the message across*** *to young people that drugs are dangerous.* 这次运动旨在让年轻人认识毒品的危害。 **4** a piece of information that is sent from the brain to a part of the body, or from a part of the body to the brain （从大脑发给身体某部位或身体某部位向大脑发送的）信息：*The message arrives in your brain in a fraction of a second.* 信息瞬间便可传递到大脑。 **5 messages** [pl.] (*ScotE*) shopping 购物；买东西：*to do the messages* 买东西 ◇ *to go for the messages* 去买东西 ◇ *You can leave your messages (= the things that you have bought) here.* 你可以把你买的东西放在这儿。

IDM **get the ˈmessage** (*informal*) to understand what sb is trying to tell you indirectly 领悟，理解，明白（别人的暗示）：*When he started looking at his watch, I got the message and left.* 他开始看表了，我明白他的意思，就走了。 **on/off ˈmessage** (of a politician 从政者) stating/not stating the official view of their political party 说明（或不说明）所属政党的官方观点

> ▼ **EXPRESS YOURSELF** 情景表达
>
> **Leaving a phone message** 电话留言
>
> If you phone someone who is not able to take your call, you may need to leave a message. 给人打电话对方不能接时，需要留言可以这么说：
>
> - ***Could I speak to Jay Black, please?*** 请让杰伊·布莱克接电话好吗？
> - ***Could you give him a message?*** 你帮我给他留个言好吗？
> - ***Is there a time that might be good for me to try him again?*** 我什么时间再给他打电话比较方便？
> - ***Can you let him know I'll call back?*** 请告诉他我会再打电话来好吗？
> - ***Could you ask him to call me back? My number is…*** 请让他给我回电话好吗？我的号码是…

■ ***verb*** to send a TEXT MESSAGE, or a message through an INSTANT MESSAGING service, etc. to sb （给某人）发短信，发即时信息：**~ sb** *Fiona just messaged me.* 菲奥纳刚给我发来电邮。◇ **~ sb sth** *Brian messaged me the news.* 布赖恩用短信告诉了我这个消息。 ▶ **mes·saging** *noun* [U]: *a multimedia messaging service* 多媒体信息服务 ◇ *picture messaging* 图像传送

ˈ**message board** *noun* a place on a website where a user can write or read messages （网站）留言板：*I posted a question on the message board.* 我在留言板上贴出了一个问题。

mes·sen·ger /ˈmesɪndʒə(r)/ *noun* a person who gives a message to sb or who delivers messages to people as a job 送信人；通信员；邮递员；信使：*He sent the order by messenger.* 他通过邮递员发出订单。◇ *a motorcycle messenger* 骑摩托车的邮递员 **IDM** SEE SHOOT *v.*

Mes·siah /məˈsaɪə/ *noun* **1 the Messiah** [sing.] (in Christianity 基督教) Jesus Christ who was sent by God into the world to save people from evil and SIN 弥赛亚；默西亚；救世主基督 **2 the Messiah** [sing.] (in Judaism 犹太教) a king who will be sent by God to save the Jewish people 弥赛亚（上帝要派去拯救犹太人民的国王） **3 messiah** a leader who people believe will solve the problems of a country or the world 人们信赖的领导者；救世主；救星 **SYN** **saviour**：*He's seen by many as a political messiah.* 许多人将他视为政治救星。

mes·si·an·ic /ˌmesiˈænɪk/ *adj.* (*formal*) **1** relating to a messiah 有关救世主的；救星的 **2** attempting to make big changes in society or to a political system in an extremely determined and enthusiastic way 有雄心壮志的；狂热的：*The reforms were carried out with an almost messianic zeal.* 改革是以极大的热情进行的。

Messrs (*BrE*) (*NAmE* **Messrs.**) /ˈmesəz; *NAmE* -sərz/ *abbr.* (used as the plural of 'Mr' before a list of names and before names of business companies) (Mr 的复数形式，用于一组人名或公司名称前)：*Messrs Smith, Brown and Jones* 史密斯、布朗和琼斯先生 ◇ *Messrs T Brown and Co* * T. 布朗公司

messy /ˈmesi/ *adj.* (**mess·ier**, **messi·est**) **1** dirty and/or untidy 肮脏的；凌乱的；不整洁的 **SYN** **chaotic**: *The house was always messy.* 这房子总是乱糟糟的。◇ (*NAmE*) *Her long black hair was messy and dirty.* 她乌黑的长发又脏又乱。 **2** making sb/sth dirty and/or untidy 使脏乱的；使不整洁的: *It was a messy job.* 这是项很脏的工作。 **3** (of a situation 状况) unpleasant, confused or difficult to deal with 混乱的；难以处理的；令人厌烦的: *The divorce was painful and messy.* 那次离婚令人痛苦而又纠葛不清。

mes·tiza /meˈstiːzə/ *noun* a female MESTIZO 梅斯蒂索女混血儿

mes·tizo /meˈstiːzəʊ; *NAmE* -zoʊ/ *noun* (*pl.* **-os**) a Latin American who has both Spanish and Native American ANCESTORS 梅斯蒂索混血儿（有西班牙和美洲土著血统的拉丁美洲人）

Met /met/ *abbr.* (*informal*) **1** METEOROLOGICAL 气象的；气象学的: *the Met Office weather forecast service* 国家气象局天气预报处 **2 the Met** the Metropolitan Opera House (in New York)（纽约）大都会歌剧院 **3 the Met** the Metropolitan Police (the police force in London) 伦敦警队

met PAST TENSE, PAST PART. OF MEET

meta- /ˈmetə/ *combining form* (in nouns, adjectives and verbs 构成名词、形容词和动词) **1** connected with a change of position or state（位置或状态）变化的: *metamorphosis* 变形 ◇ *metabolism* 新陈代谢 **2** higher; beyond 高于；在上；在外: *metaphysics* 形而上学 ◇ *metalanguage* 元语言

me·tab·ol·ism /məˈtæbəlɪzəm/ *noun* [U, sing.] (*biology* 生) the chemical processes in living things that change food, etc. into energy and materials for growth 新陈代谢: *The body's metabolism is slowed down by extreme cold.* 严寒可以使身体新陈代谢的速度下降。 ▶ **meta·bol·ic** /ˌmetəˈbɒlɪk; *NAmE* -ˈbɑːl-/ *adj.* [usually before noun]: *a metabolic process/disorder* 新陈代谢过程 / 紊乱 ◇ *a high/low metabolic rate* 高 / 低新陈代谢速度

me·tab·ol·ize (*BrE also* **-ise**) /məˈtæbəlaɪz/ *verb* ~ **sth** (*biology* 生) to turn food, minerals, etc. in the body into new cells, energy and waste products by means of chemical processes 新陈代谢（将食物、矿物质等通过化学过程转换成新细胞、能量和废料）

meta·car·pal /ˌmetəˈkɑːpl; *NAmE* -ˈkɑːrpl/ *noun* (*anatomy* 解) any of the five bones in the hand between the wrist and the fingers 掌骨（人的腕骨与指骨之间的五根小型长骨）

meta·data /ˈmetədeɪtə; -dɑːtə; *NAmE also* -dætə/ *noun* [U] information that describes other information in order to help you understand or use it 元数据: *In the metadata she found the author and location of the file.* 她从元数据中找到了文件的作者和位置。

meta·fic·tion /ˈmetəfɪkʃn/ *noun* [U] a type of play, novel, etc. in which the author deliberately reminds the audience, reader, etc. that it is FICTION and not real life 元虚构作品（叙事时有意识让观众、读者等意识到虚构性的戏剧或小说等）

metal 🔑 /ˈmetl/ *noun* [C, U] a type of solid mineral substance that is usually hard and shiny and that heat and electricity can travel through, for example tin, iron and gold 金属: *a piece of metal* 一块金属 ◇ *a* ***metal pipe/bar/box*** 金属管 / 棍 / 盒子 ◇ *The frame is made of metal.* 框子是用金属做的。 **IDM** SEE PEDAL *n.* ➲ SEE ALSO HEAVY METAL (2), PRECIOUS METAL

meta·lan·guage /ˈmetəlæŋɡwɪdʒ/ *noun* [C, U] (*linguistics* 语言) the words and phrases that people use to talk about or describe language or a particular language 元语言（用于讲述或描述语言或某种语言的词和短语）

ˈ**metal detector** *noun* **1** an electronic device that you use to look for metal objects that are buried under the ground 金属矿藏探测器 **2** an electronic machine that is used, for example at an airport, to see if people are hiding metal objects such as weapons（机场等处的）金属物品检测机

ˈ**metal fatigue** *noun* [U] weakness in metal that is frequently put under pressure that makes it likely to break 金属疲劳

meta·lin·guis·tic /ˈmetəlɪŋɡwɪstɪk/ *adj.* (*linguistics* 语言) related to METALANGUAGE 元语言的 ▶ **meta·lin·guis·tics** /ˈmetəlɪŋɡwɪstɪks/ *noun* [U]

met·alled /ˈmetld/ *adj.* (of a road or track 道路) made or repaired with small pieces of broken stone 碎石铺面的

me·tal·lic /məˈtælɪk/ *adj.* [usually before noun] **1** that looks, tastes or sounds like metal 金属般的；有金属味（或声音）的: ***metallic paint/colours/blue*** 有金属光泽的颜料 / 颜色 / 蓝色 ◇ *a metallic taste* 金属味 ◇ *a* ***metallic sound/click*** 金属声；金属碰撞的叮当声 ◇ *a metallic voice* (= that sounds unpleasant) 尖厉刺耳的声音 **2** made of or containing metal 金属制的；含金属的: *a metallic object* 金属物品 ◇ *metallic compounds* 金属合成物

met·al·loid /ˈmetlɔɪd/ (*BrE also* **semi·metal**) *noun* (*chemistry* 化) a chemical element which has properties both of metals and of other solid substances 半金属

me·tal·lur·gist /məˈtælədʒɪst; *NAmE* ˈmetlɜːrdʒɪst/ *noun* a scientist who studies metallurgy 冶金学家

me·tal·lurgy /məˈtælədʒi; *NAmE* ˈmetlɜːrdʒi/ *noun* [U] the scientific study of metals and their uses 冶金学 ▶ **me·tal·lur·gical** /ˌmetəˈlɜːdʒɪkl; *NAmE* ˌmetlˈɜːrdʒ-/ *adj.*

met·al·work /ˈmetlwɜːk; *NAmE* -wɜːrk/ *noun* [U] **1** the activity of making objects out of metal; objects that are made out of metal 金属制品的制造（或加工）；金属制品 **2** the metal parts of sth 金属配件: *cracks in the metalwork* 金属件上的裂缝 ▶ **met·al·work·er** *noun*

meta·morph·ic /ˌmetəˈmɔːfɪk; *NAmE* -ˈmɔːrf-/ *adj.* (*geology* 地) (of rocks 岩石) formed by the action of heat or pressure 变质的

meta·morph·ose /ˌmetəˈmɔːfəʊz; *NAmE* -ˈmɔːrfoʊz/ *verb* [I, T] ~ (**sth/sb**) (**from sth**) (**into sth**) (*formal*) to change or make sth/sb change into sth completely different, especially over a period of time（使）变形，变化，发生质变 **SYN** **transform**: *The caterpillar will eventually metamorphose into a butterfly.* 毛毛虫最终将蜕变成一只蝴蝶。

meta·mor·phosis /ˌmetəˈmɔːfəsɪs; *NAmE* -ˈmɔːrf-/ *noun* (*pl.* **meta·mor·phoses** /-əsiːz/) [C, U] (*formal*) a process in which sb/sth changes completely into sth different 变形；质变 **SYN** **transformation**: *the metamorphosis of a caterpillar into a butterfly* 从毛毛虫到蝴蝶的蜕变 ◇ *She had undergone an amazing metamorphosis from awkward schoolgirl to beautiful woman.* 她经历了从笨拙的女学生到大美人这一令人惊讶的变化。

meta·phor /ˈmetəfə(r); -fɔː(r)/ *noun* [C, U] a word or phrase used to describe sb/sth else, in a way that is different from its normal use, in order to show that the two things have the same qualities and to make the description more powerful, for example *She has a heart of stone*; the use of such words and phrases 暗喻；隐喻: *a game of football used as a metaphor for the competitive struggle of life* 用来喻指生活中的激烈斗争的一场足球比赛 ◇ *the writer's striking use of metaphor* 这位作家对于隐喻的独到运用 ➲ COLLOCATIONS AT LITERATURE ➲ COMPARE SIMILE ➲ WORDFINDER NOTE AT IMAGE

meta·phor·ical /ˌmetəˈfɒrɪkl; *NAmE* -ˈfɔːr-/ *adj.* connected with or containing metaphors 隐喻的；含比喻的；比喻性的: *metaphorical language* 比喻的语言 ➲ COMPARE FIGURATIVE, LITERAL ▶ **meta·phor·ic·al·ly** /-kli/ *adv.*: *I'll leave you in Robin's capable hands—****metaphorically speaking****, of course!* 我要把你放到罗宾能干的手中。当然，这只是打个比方。

metaˌphysical ˈpoets *noun* [pl.] a group of 17th century English POETS who explored the nature of the world and human life, and who used images that were surprising at that time（17 世纪英国的）玄学派诗人

meta·phys·ics /ˌmetəˈfɪzɪks/ *noun* [U] the branch of philosophy that deals with the nature of existence, truth and knowledge 形而上学；玄学 ▸ **meta·phys·ic·al** /ˌmetəˈfɪzɪkl/ *adj.*：*metaphysical problems/speculation* 形而上学的问题 / 思辨

me·tas·ta·sis /məˈtæstəsɪs/ *noun* [U] (*medical* 医) the development of TUMOURS in different parts of the body resulting from cancer that has started in another part of the body （瘤）转移 ▸ **me·tas·ta·tic** /ˌmetəˈstætɪk/ *adj.*

meta·tar·sal /ˌmetəˈtɑːsl; *NAmE* -ˈtɑːrsl/ *noun* (*anatomy* 解) any of the bones in the part of the foot between the ankle and the toes 跖骨（组成人体足底的小型长骨）

mete /miːt/ *verb*

PHR V **ˌmete sth↔ˈout** (**to sb**) (*formal*) to give sb a punishment; to make sb suffer bad treatment 给予惩罚；责罚；使受苦：*Severe penalties were meted out by the court.* 法庭判定予以严惩。◇ *the violence meted out to the prisoners* 施加在囚犯身上的暴力

me·teor /ˈmiːtiə(r); -iɔː(r)/ *noun* a piece of rock from outer space that makes a bright line across the night sky as it burns up while falling through the earth's atmosphere 流星：*a meteor shower* 流星雨 ➲ SEE ALSO SHOOTING STAR

me·teor·ic /ˌmiːtiˈɒrɪk; *NAmE* -ˈɔːr-/ *adj.* **1** achieving success very quickly 迅速成功的：*a meteoric rise to fame* 迅速成名 ◇ *a meteoric career* 迅速成功的事业 **2** connected with meteors 流星的：*meteoric craters* 流星撞击形成的坑

me·teor·ite /ˈmiːtiəraɪt/ *noun* a piece of rock from outer space that hits the earth's surface 陨石 ➲ WORDFINDER NOTE AT UNIVERSE

me·teor·olo·gist /ˌmiːtiəˈrɒlədʒɪst; *NAmE* -ˈrɑːl-/ *noun* a scientist who studies meteorology 气象学家

me·teor·ology /ˌmiːtiəˈrɒlədʒi; *NAmE* -ˈrɑːl-/ *noun* [U] the scientific study of the earth's atmosphere and its changes, used especially in forecasting the weather (= saying what it will be like) 气象学 ▸ **me·teoro·logic·al** /ˌmiːtiərəˈlɒdʒɪkl; *NAmE* -ˈlɑːdʒ-/ *adj.*

meter /ˈmiːtə(r)/ *noun, verb*

■ ***noun*** **1** (especially in compounds 尤用于构成复合词) a device that measures and records the amount of electricity, gas, water, etc. that you have used or the time and distance you have travelled, etc. （用于测量电、煤气、水等，以及时间和距离的）计量器，计量表：*A man came to read the gas meter.* 有个男子来查过煤气表。◇ *The cab driver left the meter running while he waited for us.* 在等我们的时候，出租车司机让计程表继续走字。➲ SEE ALSO LIGHT METER **2** = PARKING METER **3** **-meter** (in compounds 构成复合词) a device for measuring the thing mentioned 计；仪；表：*speedometer* 速度计 ◇ *altimeter* 高度表 ◇ *calorimeter* 热量计 **4** (*NAmE*) = METRE：*Who holds the record in the 100 meters?* * 100 米纪录是谁保持的？

■ ***verb*** **~ sth** to measure sth (for example how much gas, electricity, etc. has been used) using a meter 用仪表计量

meth /meθ/ (*also* **crystal meth**, **crystal**) *noun* [U] (*informal*) a powerful illegal drug, METHAMPHETAMINE, that looks like small pieces of glass 冰毒（即甲基苯丙胺）：*the growing meth problem in our rural communities* 我们乡村社区越来越严重的冰毒问题

metha·done /ˈmeθədəʊn; *NAmE* -doʊn/ *noun* [U] a drug that is used to treat people who are trying to stop taking the illegal drug HEROIN 美沙酮，美散痛（用于戒除海洛因毒瘾）

meth·am·pheta·mine /ˌmeθæmˈfetəmiːn/ (*also informal* **meth**, **ˈcrystal meth**) *noun* [U] a powerful illegal drug 甲基苯丙胺；脱氧麻黄碱；（俗称）冰毒

me·thane /ˈmiːθeɪn; *NAmE* ˈmeθ-/ *noun* [U] (*symb.* CH_4) a gas without colour or smell, that burns easily and is used as fuel. Natural gas consists mainly of methane. 甲烷；沼气

metha·nol /ˈmeθənɒl; *NAmE* -nɔːl; -noʊl/ *noun* [U] (*symb.* CH_3OH) a poisonous form of alcohol formed when METHANE reacts with OXYGEN 甲醇

methi·cil·lin /ˌmeθɪˈsɪlɪn/ *noun* [U] a drug that can be used against infections where PENICILLIN is not effective 甲氧西林；甲氧苯青霉素

me·thinks /mɪˈθɪŋks/ *verb* (*pt* **me·thought**) (not used in the perfect tenses 不用于完成时) [I, T] **~** (**that**)... (*old use* or *humorous*) I think 我想；我以为；据我看来

method 🔑 AW /ˈmeθəd/ *noun* **1** 🔑 [C] a particular way of doing sth 方法；办法；措施：**~** (**of sth**) ***a reliable/an effective/a scientific method*** *of data analysis* 可靠的 / 有效的 / 科学的数据分析方法 ◇ **~** (**of doing sth**) *a new method of solving the problem* 解决问题的新方法 ◇ ***traditional/alternative methods*** 传统的 / 另类的方式 ◇ **~** (**for sth/for doing sth**) *the best method for arriving at an accurate prediction of the costs* 准确预测成本的最佳方法 ➲ SEE ALSO DIRECT METHOD **2** [U] the quality of being well planned and organized 条理；有条不紊

IDM **there's** (**a**) **method in sb's madness** there is a reason for sb's behaviour and it is not as strange or as stupid as it seems 看来奇怪（或愚蠢）的行为有其道理

ˈmethod acting *noun* [U] a method of preparing for a role in which an actor tries to experience the life and feelings of the character he or she will play （深入角色生活和内心的）体验派表演，方法演技 ▸ **ˈmethod actor** *noun*

meth·od·ic·al AW /məˈθɒdɪkl; *NAmE* -ˈθɑːd-/ *adj.* **1** done in a careful and logical way 有条理的；有条不紊的：*a* ***methodical approach/study*** 条理清晰的方法 / 研究 **2** (of a person 人) doing things in a careful and logical way 办事有条不紊的 SYN **disciplined, precise**：*to have a methodical mind* 思想有条理 ▸ **meth·od·ic·al·ly** /-kli/ *adv.*：*They sorted slowly and methodically through the papers.* 他们慢慢地有条理地整理文件。

Meth·od·ist /ˈmeθədɪst/ *noun* a member of a Christian Protestant Church that broke away from the Church of England in the 18th century 循道宗信徒（18 世纪从英国国教分离出的基督教新教教徒） ▸ **Meth·od·ism** /ˈmeθədɪzəm/ *noun* [U] **Meth·od·ist** *adj.*：*a Methodist church/preacher* 循道宗教会 / 牧师

meth·od·ology AW /ˌmeθəˈdɒlədʒi; *NAmE* -ˈdɑːl-/ *noun* (*pl.* **-ies**) [C, U] (*formal*) a set of methods and principles used to perform a particular activity （从事某一活动的）方法，原则：*recent changes in the methodology of language teaching* 语言教学法最近的变化 ▸ **meth·odo·logic·al** AW /ˌmeθədəˈlɒdʒɪkl; *NAmE* -ˈlɑːdʒ-/ *adj.* [usually before noun]：*methodological problems* 方法问题 **meth·odo·logic·al·ly** /-kli/ *adv.*

methought PAST TENSE OF METHINKS

meths /meθs/ *noun* [U] (*informal, especially BrE*) = METHYLATED SPIRIT

Me·thu·selah /məˈθjuːzələ/ *noun* used to describe a very old person 玛士撒拉式的老人；老寿星：*I'm feeling older than Methuselah.* 我觉得自己老态龙钟。ORIGIN From Methuselah, a man in the Bible who is supposed to have lived for 969 years. 源自《圣经》人物玛士撒拉，据传享寿 969 岁。

meth·yl·ated spirit /ˌmeθəleɪtɪd ˈspɪrɪt/ (*also* **meth·yl·ated spirits**) (*also informal* **meths**) *noun* [U] a type of alcohol that is not fit for drinking, used as a fuel for lighting and heating and for cleaning off dirty marks 变性酒精，甲基化酒精（不适宜饮用，用作照明、加热燃料或清洗剂）

me·ticu·lous /məˈtɪkjələs/ *adj.* paying careful attention to every detail 细心的；小心翼翼的 SYN **fastidious, thorough**：***meticulous planning/records/research*** 周密的计划；详细的记录；一丝不苟的研究 ◇ **~ in sth/doing sth** *He's always meticulous in keeping the records up to date.* 他总

M

是十分细心地适时更新存档资料。◇ ~ about sth *My father was meticulous about his appearance.* 我父亲对自己的外表很讲究。▶ **me·ticu·lous·ly** *adv.*：*a meticulously planned schedule* 计划周密的日程安排 ◇ *meticulously clean* 一尘不染 **me·ticu·lous·ness** *noun* [U]

mé·tier /ˈmetieɪ; *NAmE* ˈmeɪt-/ *noun* [usually sing.] (*from French, formal*) a person's work, especially when they have a natural skill or ability for it 职业；工作；行业；（尤指）专长

ˈme-time *noun* [U] (*informal*) time when a person who is normally very busy relaxes or does sth they enjoy 私人专属时间；自我享受时间：*The spa is popular with women who want a bit of me-time.* 矿泉疗养中心受到想找点时间自我放松一下的女士的青睐。

Metis /meɪˈtiː/ *noun* (*pl.* **Metis** /meɪˈtiː; meɪˈtiːz/) (*CanE*) (especially in Canada) a person with one Aboriginal parent and one European parent, or a person whose family comes from both Aboriginal and European backgrounds 米提人；梅蒂人（尤指加拿大土著和欧洲人或有土著和欧洲血统的混血儿）

me·ton·ymy /məˈtɒnəmi; *NAmE* -ˈtɑːn-/ *noun* [U] (*specialist*) the act of referring to sth by the name of sth else that is closely connected with it, for example using *the White House* for *the US president* 转喻（用一名称来指代与之密切相关的事物，例如用 the White House 来指代 the US president） ➲ WORDFINDER NOTE AT IMAGE

ˌme-ˈtoo *adj.* [only before noun] (*informal*) done or produced because of sth successful that sb else has done 仿效别人（成功之事）的：*The magazine 'Hello!' gave rise to a number of me-too publications.* 《你好！》杂志带动了许多效仿它的刊物问世。

metre 🔑 (*especially US* **meter**) /ˈmiːtə(r)/ *noun* **1** 🔑 [C] (*abbr.* **m**) a unit for measuring length; a hundred centimetres 米；公尺 **2** [C, U] (*abbr.* **m**) used in the name of races 用于竞赛名称：*She came second in the 200 metres.* 在 200 米比赛中，她取得了第二名。◇ *the 4 × 100 metre(s) relay* * 4 × 100 米接力赛 **3** [U, C] the arrangement of strong and weak stresses in lines of poetry that produces the rhythm; a particular example of this （诗的）格律

met·ric /ˈmetrɪk/ *adj.* **1** based on the metric system 米制的；公制的：***metric units/measurements/sizes*** 公制单位 / 尺寸 / 大小 ◇ *British currency went metric in 1971.* 英国的货币于 1971 年实行公制。 **2** made or measured using the metric system 按公制制作的；用公制测量的：*These screws are metric.* 这些螺丝钉是用公制尺码制造的。➲ COMPARE IMPERIAL **3** = METRICAL

met·ric·al /ˈmetrɪkl/ (*also* **met·ric**) *adj.* connected with the rhythm of a poem, produced by the arrangement of stress on the syllables in each line 格律的

met·ri·ca·tion /ˌmetrɪˈkeɪʃn/ *noun* [U] the process of changing to using the metric system 施行公制度量衡；公制化

met·rics /ˈmetrɪks/ *noun* [pl.] **1** a set of statistics used for measuring sth, especially results that show how well a business, school, computer program, etc. is doing 度量工具，衡量指标（尤用以考评企业、学校、计算机程序等的表现）：*Companies are scored on key financial metrics.* 给公司打分的依据是关键财务指标。 **2** the use or study of METRE in poetry （诗的）用律；格律学

the ˈmetric system *noun* [sing.] the system of measurement that uses the metre, the kilogram and the litre as basic units 公制；米制

ˌmetric ˈton *noun* = TONNE

metro /ˈmetrəʊ; *NAmE* ˈmetroʊ/ *noun, adj.*
■ *noun* (*pl.* **-os**) **1** (*also* **the Metro**) [sing.] an underground train system, especially the one in Paris 地铁；（尤指）巴黎地铁：*to travel on the metro/by metro* 乘地铁旅行 ◇ *the Paris Metro* 巴黎地铁 ◇ *a metro station* 地铁站 ➲ NOTE AT UNDERGROUND **2** (*IndE*) a large or capital city, especially Delhi, Kolkata, Mumbai or Chennai 大城市，大都市（尤指德里、加尔各答、孟买或钦奈）：*Here are the temperatures recorded at the four metros at 5 o'clock this morning.* 这是今天早晨 5 点钟时四大城市的气温记录。
■ *adj.* (*NAmE, informal*) = METROPOLITAN：*the New York metro areas* 纽约市区

me·trol·ogy /məˈtrɒlədʒi; *NAmE* -ˈtrɑːl-/ *noun* [U] the scientific study of measurement 计量学 ▶ **me·tro·logic·al** /ˌmetrəˈlɒdʒɪkl; *NAmE* -ˈlɑːdʒ-/ *adj.*

metronome 节拍器

met·ro·nome /ˈmetrənəʊm; *NAmE* -noʊm/ *noun* a device that makes a regular sound like a clock and is used by musicians to help them keep the correct rhythm when playing a piece of music 节拍器 ▶ **met·ro·nom·ic** /ˌmetrəˈnɒmɪk; *NAmE* -ˈnɑːm-/ *adj.*：*His financial problems hit the headlines with almost metronomic regularity.* 他的财政问题几乎定期成为头条新闻。

me·trop·olis /məˈtrɒpəlɪs; *NAmE* məˈtrɑːp-/ *noun* a large important city (often the capital city of a country or region) 大都会；大城市；首都；首府

met·ro·pol·itan /ˌmetrəˈpɒlɪtən; *NAmE* -ˈpɑːl-/ *adj.* [only before noun] **1** (*also NAmE, informal* **metro**) connected with a large or capital city 大城市的；大都会的：*the New York metropolitan area* 纽约都市区 ◇ ***metropolitan districts/regions*** 都市区 ➲ WORDFINDER NOTE AT CITY **2** connected with a particular country rather than with the other regions of the world that the country controls 本土的：***metropolitan France/Spain*** 法国 / 西班牙本土

met·ro·sex·ual /ˌmetrəˈsekʃuəl/ *noun* (*informal*) a HETEROSEXUAL man who lives in a city and is interested in things like fashion and shopping 都市丽男，都会美男（爱好时尚和购物等的异性恋男子） ▶ **met·ro·sex·ual** *adj.* ➲ MORE LIKE THIS 1, page R25

met·tle /ˈmetl/ *noun* [U] the ability and determination to do sth successfully despite difficult conditions 奋斗精神；毅力：*The next game will be a real test of their mettle.* 下一场比赛就要看他们的拼搏精神了。

IDM **on your ˈmettle** prepared to use all your skills, knowledge, etc. because you are being tested 奋发起来；准备尽最大努力

mew /mjuː/ *noun* the soft high noise that a cat makes （猫叫声）喵 ▶ **mew** *verb* [I]：*The kitten mewed pitifully.* 小猫喵喵地叫，挺可怜的。

mewl /mjuːl/ *verb* [I] to make a weak crying sound 呜咽；啜泣 ▶ **mewl·ing** *noun* [U] **mewl·ing** *adj.*：*mewling babies* 呜呜哭的婴儿

mews /mjuːz/ *noun* (*pl.* **mews**) (*BrE*) a short, narrow street with a row of stables (= buildings used to keep horses in) that have been made into small houses 马厩街（周围排列着马厩改建的住房）

ˈmews house (*BrE*) (*US* **ˈcarriage house**) *noun* a house in a mews 马厩改建的房屋

Mex·ican /ˈmeksɪkən/ *adj., noun*
■ *adj.* from or connected with Mexico 墨西哥的
■ *noun* a person from Mexico 墨西哥人

ˌ**Mexican ˈwave** (*BrE*) (*NAmE* **the ˈwave**) *noun* a continuous movement that looks like a wave on the sea, made by a large group of people, especially people watching a sports game, when one person after another stands up, raises their arms, and then sits down again 人浪（尤指体育比赛中看台上的观众依次站起坐下而形成的波浪状场面）

mez·za·nine /ˈmezəniːn; ˈmetsə-/ *noun* **1** a floor that is built between two floors of a building and is smaller than the other floors （介于两层楼之间、比其他楼层小的）夹层： *a bedroom on the mezzanine* 夹层楼面上的卧室 ◇ *a mezzanine floor* 夹楼层 **2** (*NAmE*) the first area of seats above the ground floor in a theatre; the first few rows of these seats （戏院的）最低层楼厅（前座） ➲ SEE ALSO DRESS CIRCLE

mezzo-soprano /ˌmetsəʊ səˈprɑːnəʊ; *NAmE* ˌmetsoʊ səˈprɑːnoʊ; -ˈpræn-/ (*also* **mezzo**) *noun* (*pl.* **mezzo-sopranos**, **mezzos**) (*from Italian*) a singing voice with a range between SOPRANO and ALTO; a woman with a mezzo-soprano voice 女中音；女中音歌手

mg *abbr.* (in writing 书写形式) milligram(s) 毫克

Mgr *abbr.* (in writing 书写形式) MONSIGNOR 蒙席（天主教会圣职人员的荣衔）

MHA /ˌem eɪtʃ ˈeɪ/ *noun* (*CanE*) Member of the House of Assembly (the parliament in Newfoundland and Labrador) （纽芬兰和拉布拉多的）议会议员

mhm /əmˈhm/ *exclamation* used to say 'yes', or to show sb that you are listening to them （表示同意或在听对方说话）哦，嗯： *'Can I borrow your pen?' 'Mhm.'* "借你的钢笔用一下好吗？""可以。" ◇ *'I phoned Alan…' 'Mhm.' '…and he said he's going to come.'* "我给艾伦打电话了…""噢。""…他说他要来。"

MHz *abbr.* (in writing 书写形式) MEGAHERTZ 兆赫

mi = ME *n.*

MI5 /ˌem aɪ ˈfaɪv/ *noun* [U] the British government organization that deals with national security within Britain. Its official name is 'the Security Service'. 军情五处（英国安全局，负责英国国内安全，正式名称为 the Security Service）

MI6 /ˌem aɪ ˈsɪks/ *noun* [U] the British government organization that deals with national security from outside Britain. Its official name is 'the Secret Intelligence Service'. 军情六处（负责与英国国家安全有关的海外情报，正式名称为 the Secret Intelligence Service）

MIA /ˌem aɪ ˈeɪ/ *abbr.* (*especially NAmE*) (of a soldier 士兵) missing in action (missing after a battle) 在战斗中失踪

miaow (*BrE*) (*also* **meow** *NAmE, BrE*) /miˈaʊ/ *noun* the crying sound made by a cat （猫叫声）喵 ➲ SEE ALSO MEW ▸ **miaow** (*BrE*) (*also* **meow** *NAmE, BrE*) *verb* [I]

ˈ**miaow miaow** *noun* [U] = MEPHEDRONE

mi·asma /miˈæzmə; maɪˈæ-/ *noun* [C, usually sing., U] (*literary*) a mass of air that is dirty and smells unpleasant 污浊难闻的空气： *A miasma of stale alcohol hung around him.* 他身上常带着难闻的酒精味。◇ (*figurative*) *the miasma of depression* 压抑的气氛

MiB *abbr.* (in writing 书写形式) MEBIBYTE 兆字节（二进制计算机内存或数据单位）

Mib (*also* **Mibit**) *abbr.* (in writing 书写形式) MEBIBIT 兆比特（二进制计算机内存或数据单位）

mic /maɪk/ *noun* (*informal*) = MICROPHONE

mica /ˈmaɪkə/ *noun* [U] a clear mineral that splits easily into thin flat layers and is used to make electrical equipment 云母

mice PL. OF MOUSE

Mich·ael·mas /ˈmɪklməs/ *noun* [U] (in the Christian Church) the holy day in honour of St Michael, 29 September 米迦勒节（基督教节日，每年 9 月 29 日）

ˌ**Michaelmas ˈdaisy** *noun* a plant that has blue, white, pink or purple flowers with dark centres, that appear in the autumn/fall 荷兰紫菀

Michelin man /ˈmɪtʃəlɪn mæn; ˈmɪʃ-/ *noun*
IDM **like the/a ˈMichelin man** having a wide round body because of being very fat or wearing a lot of thick heavy clothes 身宽体圆；穿着臃肿 **ORIGIN** From the fat cartoon character made of tyres used as a symbol of the Michelin™ tyre company. 源自作为米其林轮胎公司标志的肥胖卡通人物，全身用轮胎形象勾画。

Mick /mɪk/ *noun* (*taboo, slang*) an offensive word for a person from Ireland （含侮慢意）爱尔兰佬

mickey /ˈmɪki/ *noun*
IDM **take the ˈmickey/ˈmick (out of sb)** (*BrE, informal*) to make sb look or feel silly by copying the way they talk, behave, etc. or by making them believe sth that is not true, often in a way that is not intended to be unkind （通过模仿某人或使其信以为真）取笑，戏弄 **SYN** **tease**, **mock**

Mickey Finn /ˌmɪki ˈfɪn/ *noun* a drink containing a drug or a lot of alcohol, given to sb who does not realize what is in it 蒙汗药饮料（给不防备的人喝的饮料，掺有药或酒）

ˌ**Mickey ˈMouse** *adj.* (*disapproving*) not of high quality; too easy 质量不高的；太容易的： *It's only a Mickey Mouse job.* 这活儿太容易了。

micro /ˈmaɪkrəʊ; *NAmE* -kroʊ/ *noun* (*pl.* **-os**) = MICROCOMPUTER

micro- /ˈmaɪkrəʊ; *NAmE* -kroʊ/ *combining form* **1** (in nouns, adjectives and adverbs 构成名词、形容词和副词) small; on a small scale 微小的；规模小的： *microchip* 微芯片 ◇ *microorganism* 微生物 **OPP** **macro-** **2** (in nouns; used in units of measurement 构成名词，用于计量单位) one millionth 微；百万分之一： *a microlitre* 百万分之一升

mi·crobe /ˈmaɪkrəʊb; *NAmE* -kroʊb/ *noun* an extremely small living thing that you can only see under a MICROSCOPE and that may cause disease 微生物 ➲ COLLOCATIONS AT LIFE

micro·biolo·gist /ˌmaɪkrəʊbaɪˈɒlədʒɪst; *NAmE* -kroʊbaɪˈɑːl-/ *noun* a scientist who studies microbiology 微生物学家

micro·biol·ogy /ˌmaɪkrəʊbaɪˈɒlədʒi; *NAmE* -kroʊbaɪˈɑːl-/ *noun* [U] the scientific study of very small living things, such as bacteria 微生物学 ▸ **micro·bio·logic·al** /ˌmaɪkrəʊˌbaɪəˈlɒdʒɪkl; *NAmE* -kroʊˌbaɪəˈlɑːdʒ-/ *adj.*

micro·blog·ging /ˈmaɪkrəʊblɒɡɪŋ; *NAmE* -kroʊblɑːɡ-/ *noun* [U] the activity of sending regular short messages, photos or videos over the Internet, either to a selected group of people, or so that they can be viewed by anyone, as a means of keeping people informed about your activities and thoughts 微博维护；微博更新 ▸ **micro·blog** *noun* **micro·blog** *verb* (**-gg-**) [I] ➲ COMPARE TWITTER™

micro·brew·ery /ˈmaɪkrəʊbruːəri; *NAmE* -kroʊ-/ *noun* (*pl.* **-ies**) a small BREWERY (= a factory where beer is made), that often sells its beer to visitors or only sells it locally 小啤酒厂

micro·chip /ˈmaɪkrəʊtʃɪp; *NAmE* -kroʊ-/ *noun, verb*
▪ *noun* (*also* **chip**) a very small piece of a material that is a SEMICONDUCTOR, used to carry a complicated electronic CIRCUIT 微芯片；芯片
▪ *verb* (**-pp-**) **~ sth** to put a microchip under the skin of an animal as a way of identifying it 植微芯片于（动物皮下，作识别用途）

micro·cli·mate /ˈmaɪkrəʊklaɪmət; *NAmE* -kroʊ-/ *noun* (*specialist*) the weather in a particular small area, especially when this is different from the weather in the surrounding area （尤指有别于周围地区的）小气候

M

micro·com·puter /ˈmaɪkrəʊkəmpjuːtə(r); *NAmE* -kroʊ-/ (*also* **micro**) *noun* a small computer that contains a MICROPROCESSOR 微型计算机 ➲ COMPARE PERSONAL COMPUTER

micro·cosm /ˈmaɪkrəʊkɒzəm; *NAmE* -kroʊkɑːz-/ *noun* a thing, a place or a group that has all the features and qualities of sth much larger 缩影；具体而微者：*The family is a microcosm of society.* 家庭是社会的缩影。➲ COMPARE MACROCOSM

IDM **in microcosm** on a small scale 小规模地：*The developments in this town represent in microcosm what is happening in the country as a whole.* 这座城镇的发展以小见大，体现了整个国家的发展。

micro·dot /ˈmaɪkrəʊdɒt; *NAmE* -kroʊdɑːt/ *noun* **1** a very small photograph about one millimetre in size, usually of a printed document 微点照片，缩微影印文件（约一毫米） **2** a very small round piece of a drug, especially the illegal drug LSD 超小型药丸；（尤指）小粒迷幻药

micro·elec·tron·ics /ˌmaɪkrəʊɪˌlekˈtrɒnɪks; *NAmE* -kroʊɪˌlekˈtrɑːn-/ *noun* [U] the design, production and use of very small electronic CIRCUITS 微电子学 ▶ **micro·elec·tron·ic** *adj.* [only before noun]

micro·fibre (*especially US* **micro·fiber**) /ˈmaɪkrəʊfaɪbə(r); *NAmE* -roʊf-/ *noun* [U] a very light and warm artificial material that is used especially for making coats and jackets 微纤维，超细纤维（轻柔温暖的人造纤维，尤用以做外衣）

micro·fiche /ˈmaɪkrəʊfiːʃ; *NAmE* -kroʊ-/ *noun* [U, C] a piece of film with written information on it in print of very small size. Microfiches can only be read with a special machine. 缩微胶片；缩微平片：*The directory is available* ***on microfiche.*** 名录有缩微胶片版。

micro·film /ˈmaɪkrəʊfɪlm; *NAmE* -kroʊ-/ *noun* [U, C] film used for storing written information on in print of very small size 缩微胶卷

micro·fi·nance /ˈmaɪkrəʊfaɪnæns; *NAmE* -kroʊ-/ *noun* [U] a system of providing services such as lending money and saving for people who are too poor to use banks 微金融（向无力使用银行的穷人提供贷款和储蓄服务的体系）

micro·gram /ˈmaɪkrəʊɡræm; *NAmE* -kroʊ-/ *noun* (*symb.* **µg**) a unit for measuring weight; a millionth of a gram 微克（重量单位）；百万分之一克

micro·light /ˈmaɪkrəʊlaɪt; *NAmE* -kroʊ-/ (*BrE*) (*NAmE* **ultra·light**) *noun* a very small light aircraft for one or two people 微型飞机 ➲ VISUAL VOCAB PAGE V58

micro·manage /ˈmaɪkrəʊmænɪdʒ; *NAmE* -kroʊ-/ *verb* [T, I] ~ (**sth**) (*especially NAmE, disapproving*) to control every detail of a business, especially your employees' work 微观管理，对…管头管脚（尤指雇员的工作）：*The problem may be that you are micromanaging your team.* 问题可能是你对团队的管理过于苛严而琐细。◇ *bosses who micromanage* 管头管脚的老板 ▶ **micro·man·age·ment** *noun* [U] **micro·man·ager** *noun*

micro·meter /maɪˈkrɒmɪtə(r); *NAmE* -ˈkrɑːm-/ *noun* **1** (*especially US*) = MICROMETRE **2** a device used for measuring very small distances or spaces, using a screw with a very fine THREAD 螺旋测微器；千分尺

micro·metre (*especially US* **micro·meter**) /ˈmaɪkrəʊmiːtə(r); *NAmE* -kroʊ-/ *noun* (*symb.* **µm**) a unit for measuring length, equal to one millionth of a metre 微米（= 百万分之一米）

mi·cron /ˈmaɪkrɒn; *NAmE* -krɑːn/ *noun* (*old-fashioned*) = MICROMETRE

microorganism /ˌmaɪkrəʊˈɔːɡənɪzəm; *NAmE* -kroʊˈɔːrɡ-/ *noun* (*specialist*) a very small living thing that you can only see under a MICROSCOPE 微生物

micro·pay·ment /ˈmaɪkrəʊpeɪmənt; *NAmE* -kroʊ-/ *noun* a very small payment that you make online, for example each time you use a particular page or service on the Internet 微支付（在线进行的小额资金支付）

micro·phone /ˈmaɪkrəfəʊn; *NAmE* -foʊn/ (*also informal* **mic, mike**) *noun* a device that is used for recording sounds or for making your voice louder when you are speaking or singing to an audience 麦克风；话筒；传声器：*to speak into the microphone* 对着麦克风讲话 ◇ *Their remarks were picked up by the hidden microphones.* 他们的话透过暗藏的麦克风被听到。➲ VISUAL VOCAB PAGE V73 ➲ WORDFINDER NOTE AT CONCERT

micro·pro·ces·sor /ˌmaɪkrəʊˈprəʊsesə(r); *NAmE* -kroʊˈproʊ-/ *noun* (*computing* 计) a small unit of a computer that contains all the functions of the CENTRAL PROCESSING UNIT 微处理器；微处理机

micro·scope /ˈmaɪkrəskəʊp; *NAmE* -skoʊp/ *noun* an instrument used in scientific study for making very small things look larger so that you can examine them carefully 显微镜：*a microscope slide* 显微镜载片 ◇ *The bacteria were then examined* ***under a/the microscope.*** 随后把细菌放到显微镜下进行检查。◇ (*figurative*) *In the play, love and marriage are* ***put under the microscope.*** 这部话剧对爱情和婚姻进行了细致入微的探讨。➲ VISUAL VOCAB PAGE V72 ➲ SEE ALSO ELECTRON MICROSCOPE

micro·scop·ic /ˌmaɪkrəˈskɒpɪk; *NAmE* -ˈskɑːpɪk/ *adj.* **1** [usually before noun] extremely small and difficult or impossible to see without a microscope 极小的；微小的；需用显微镜观察的：*a* ***microscopic creature/particle*** 微生物；微粒 ◇ (*humorous*) *The sandwiches were microscopic!* 这些三明治小得都快看不见了！ **2** [only before noun] using a microscope 使用显微镜的：*a* ***microscopic analysis/examination*** 显微镜分析 / 检查 ▶ **micro·scop·ic·al·ly** /-kli/ *adv.*: *microscopically small creatures* 微生物 ◇ *All samples are examined microscopically.* 所有样品都进行了精细的检查。

micro·scopy /maɪˈkrɒskəpi; *NAmE* -ˈkrɑːs-/ *noun* [U] (*specialist*) the use of MICROSCOPES to look at very small creatures, objects, etc. 显微术；显微镜观察

micro·sec·ond /ˈmaɪkrəʊsekənd; *NAmE* -kroʊ-/ *noun* (*specialist*) (*symb.* **µs**) one millionth of a second 微秒；百万分之一秒

micro·site /ˈmaɪkrəʊsaɪt; *NAmE* -kroʊ-/ *noun* a small website containing more detailed information that can be accessed from a larger website 微型网站（可从更大的网站访问，包含某方面更详细的信息）：*The museum has a microsite to accompany the exhibition.* 博物馆为配合这次展览建了一个微型网站。

micro·sur·gery /ˈmaɪkrəʊsɜːdʒəri; *NAmE* -kroʊsɜːr-/ *noun* [U] the use of extremely small instruments and MICROSCOPES in order to perform very detailed and complicated medical operations 显微外科；显微手术

micro·wave /ˈmaɪkrəweɪv/ *noun, verb*

■ *noun* **1** (*also formal* ˌ**microwave ˈoven**) a type of oven that cooks or heats food very quickly using ELECTROMAGNETIC waves rather than heat 微波炉：*Reheat the soup in the microwave.* 把汤放到微波炉里再热一热。◇ ***microwave cookery/meals*** 微波炉烹饪 / 制作的食品 ➲ VISUAL VOCAB PAGE V26 ➲ COMPARE OVEN **2** (*specialist*) an ELECTROMAGNETIC wave that is shorter than a radio wave but longer than a light wave 微波

■ *verb* ~ **sth** to cook or heat sth in a microwave 用微波炉烹调（或加热） ➲ COLLOCATIONS AT COOKING ▶ **micro·wave·able** (*also* **micro·wav·able**) *adj.*: *microwaveable meals* 可用微波炉制作的饭菜

mic·tur·ate /ˈmɪktjʊreɪt; *NAmE* ˈmɪktʃə-/ *verb* [I] (*specialist*) to URINATE 排尿；小便 ▶ **mic·tur·ition** /ˌmɪktjuˈrɪʃn; *NAmE* -tʃəˈrɪʃn/ *noun* [U]

mid /mɪd/ *prep.* (*literary*) = AMID

mid- 🔑 /mɪd/ *combining form* (in nouns and adjectives 构成名词和形容词) in the middle of 居中；在中间：*mid-morning coffee* 上午十点钟左右的咖啡 ◇ *She's in her mid-thirties.* 她三十五六岁了。

ˌ**mid-ˈair** *noun* [U] a place in the air or the sky, not on the ground 半空中；悬空： *The bird caught the insects* ***in mid-air*** 鸟在半空中捕捉了昆虫。 ▶ ˌ**mid-ˈair** *adj.* : *a mid-air collision* 在空中发生的碰撞

Midas touch /ˈmaɪdəs tʌtʃ/ *noun* (*usually* **the Midas touch**) [sing.] the ability to make a financial success of everything you do 事事都能赚大钱的本领 ➲ MORE LIKE THIS 16, page R27 ORIGIN From the Greek myth in which King Midas was given the power to turn everything he touched into gold. 源自希腊神话，其中的迈达斯国王具有点石成金的能力。

ˌ**mid-Atˈlantic** *adj.* [only before noun] **1** connected with the area on the east coast of the US, that is near New York and immediately to the south of it 美国东海岸纽约附近及其以南地区的： *the* ***mid-Atlantic states/coast*** 纽约附近各州；纽约附近的沿海地区 **2** in the middle of the Atlantic ocean 大西洋中部的；中大西洋的： (*figurative*) *a mid-Atlantic accent* (= a form of English that uses a mixture of British and American sounds) 大西洋中部地区口音（兼备英美发音特征的英语）

mid·brain /ˈmɪdbreɪn/ *noun* (*anatomy* 解) a small central part of the brain 中脑

mid·day 🔑 /ˌmɪdˈdeɪ/ *noun* [U] 12 o'clock in the middle of the day; the period around this time 中午；正午 SYN **noon**: *The train arrives at midday.* 列车正午到达。 ◇ *a midday meal* 午餐 ◇ *the heat of the midday sun* 正午骄阳的热力

mid·den /ˈmɪdn/ *noun* a pile of waste near a house, in the past 贝丘（史前废物堆）

mid·dle 🔑 /ˈmɪdl/ *noun, adj.*

■ *noun* **1** 🔑 **the middle** [sing.] the part of sth that is at an equal distance from all its edges or sides; a point or a period of time between the beginning and the end of sth 中间；中部；中央；中心： *a lake with an island* ***in the middle*** 中央有一个小岛的湖 ◇ *He was standing in the middle of the room.* 他站在屋子的中间。 ◇ *The phone rang in the middle of the night.* 半夜里响起了电话铃声。 ◇ *This chicken isn't cooked in the middle.* 这只鸡还没有熟透。 ◇ *His picture was* ***right/bang*** (= exactly) ***in the middle of*** *the front page.* 他的照片就登在头版的正中央。 ◇ *Take a sheet of paper and draw a line* ***down the middle.*** 拿出一张纸，在中间画一条线。 ◇ *I should have finished* ***by the middle of*** *the week.* 我在这周过半的时候应该就能完成。 ➲ SEE ALSO MONKEY IN THE MIDDLE, PIGGY IN THE MIDDLE **2** [C, usually sing.] (*informal*) a person's waist 腰部： *He grabbed her around the middle.* 他拦腰抱住她。

IDM **be in the middle of sth/of doing sth** to be busy doing sth 忙于做： *They were in the middle of dinner when I called.* 我打电话的时候，他们正在吃饭。 ◇ *I'm in the middle of writing a difficult letter.* 我正在写一封很难写的信。 **the middle of ˈnowhere** (*informal*) a place that is a long way from other buildings, towns, etc. 偏远的地方： *She lives on a small farm in the middle of nowhere.* 她住在一个偏远的小农场。 ˌ**split/diˌvide sth down the ˈmiddle** to divide sth into two equal parts 平分；分为相等的两半： *The country was split down the middle over the strike* (= half supported it, half did not). 国内支持和反对罢工的人势均力敌。

■ *adj.* 🔑 [only before noun] in a position in the middle of an object, group of objects, people, etc.; between the beginning and the end of sth 中间的；中央的；居中的；正中的： *Pens are kept in the middle drawer.* 钢笔在中间那个抽屉里。 ◇ *She's the middle child of three.* 三个孩子，她是老二。 ◇ *He was very successful in his middle forties.* 他在四十五六岁时很成功。 ◇ *a middle-sized room* 中等大小的房间 ◇ *the middle-income groups in society* 社会中等收入阶层

IDM **(steer, take, etc.) a middle ˈcourse | (find, etc.) a/the middle ˈway** (to take/find) an acceptable course of action that avoids two extreme positions （走）中间道路；（取）中庸之道；（采取）折中办法

ˌ**middle ˈage** *noun* [U] the period of your life when you are neither young nor old, between the ages of about 45 and 60 中年（45 岁到 60 岁左右）： *a pleasant woman in early/late middle age* 刚到中年的 / 接近老年的亲切和蔼的女人 ➲ COLLOCATIONS AT AGE

ˌ**middle-ˈaged** *adj.* **1** (of a person 人) neither young nor old 中年的 ➲ WORDFINDER NOTE AT AGE **2** **the middle aged** *noun* [pl.] people who are middle-aged 中年人 ➲ MORE LIKE THIS 24, page R28 **3** (*disapproving*) (of a person's attitudes or behaviour 人的态度或行为) rather boring and old-fashioned 烦人的；保守的；过时的

the ˌMiddle ˈAges *noun* [pl.] in European history, the period from about AD 1000 to AD 1450 中世纪（欧洲历史上从公元 1000 年到 1450 年）

ˌ**middle-age ˈspread** (*also* ˌ**middle-aged ˈspread**) *noun* [U] (*humorous*) the fat around the stomach that some people develop in middle age 中年发福（某些人中年时腹部长出的脂肪）

ˌ**Middle Aˈmerica** *noun* [U] the middle class in the US, especially those people who represent traditional social and political values, and who come from small towns and SUBURBS rather than cities 美国中产阶级（尤指那些来自小镇或郊区、代表传统社会和政治价值观的人）

middle·brow /ˈmɪdlbraʊ/ *adj.* [usually before noun] (*usually disapproving*) (of books, music, art, etc. 书籍、音乐、艺术等) of good quality but not needing a lot of thought to understand 品位一般的；平庸的 ➲ COMPARE HIGHBROW, LOWBROW

ˌ**middle ˈC** *noun* [U] the musical note C near the middle of the piano keyboard （钢琴键盘的）中央 C，中央 C 音

ˌ**middle ˈclass** *noun* [C+sing./pl. v.] the social class whose members are neither very rich nor very poor and that includes professional and business people 中产阶级；中等收入阶层： *the* ***upper/lower middle class*** 中等偏上 / 偏下收入阶层 ◇ *the growth of the middle classes* 中产阶级的壮大 ➲ COMPARE UPPER CLASS, WORKING CLASS

ˌ**middle-ˈclass** *adj.* **1** connected with the middle social class 中产阶级的；中等收入阶层的： *a* ***middle-class background/family/suburb*** 中产阶级背景 / 家庭 / 居住的郊区 **2** (*disapproving*) typical of people from the middle social class, for example having traditional views 典型中产阶级特色的；带有中产阶级传统观念的；古板的： *a middle-class attitude* 中产阶级的（保守）态度 ◇ *The magazine is very middle-class.* 这份杂志太古板了。

the ˌmiddle ˈdistance *noun* [sing.] the part of a painting or a view that is neither very close nor very far away 中景： *His eyes were fixed on a small house in the middle distance.* 他凝视着不远处的一座小房子。

ˌ**middle-ˈdistance** *adj.* [only before noun] (*sport* 体育) connected with running a race over a distance that is neither very short nor very long （赛跑）中距离的： *a middle-distance runner* (= for example, somebody who runs 800 or 1500 metre races) 中距离赛跑选手（如 800 米或 1 500 米跑选手）

ˌ**middle ˈear** *noun* [sing.] the part of the ear behind the EARDRUM, containing the little bones that transfer sound VIBRATIONS 中耳

the ˌMiddle ˈEast (*also less frequent* **the ˌNear ˈEast**) *noun* [sing.] an area that covers SW Asia and NE Africa 中东（包括亚洲西南部和非洲东北部） ➲ COMPARE FAR EAST ▶ ˌ**Middle ˈEastern** (*also less frequent* ˌ**Near ˈEastern**) *adj.*

ˌ**Middle ˈEngland** *noun* [U] the middle classes in England, especially people who have traditional social and political ideas and do not live in London （尤指持有传统社会和政治观念、不居住在伦敦的）英国中产阶级

ˌ**Middle ˈEnglish** *noun* [U] an old form of English that was used between about AD 1150 and AD 1500 中古英语（约公元 1150 至 1500 年间的英语） ➲ COMPARE OLD ENGLISH

ˌ**Middle-Euroˈpean** *adj.* of or related to central Europe or its people 欧洲中部（人）的；中欧（人）的

M

ˌ**middle ˈfinger** *noun* the longest finger in the middle of each hand 中指 ➲ VISUAL VOCAB PAGE V64

ˈ**middle ground** *noun* [U] a set of opinions, decisions, etc. that two or more groups who oppose each other can agree on; a position that is not extreme 中间立场；中间观点：*Negotiations have failed to establish any middle ground.* 谈判未能达成任何妥协。◇ *The ballet company now* ***occupies the middle ground between*** *classical ballet and modern dance.* 这个芭蕾舞团现在的风格介于古典芭蕾和现代舞之间。

middle·man /ˈmɪdlmæn/ *noun* (*pl.* **-men** /-men/) **1** a person or a company that buys goods from the company that makes them and sells them to sb else 中间商；经销商：*Buy direct from the manufacturer and* ***cut out the middleman.*** 直接从生产厂家购买，绕过中间商。**2** a person who helps to arrange things between people who do not want to talk directly to each other 经纪人；中间人；掮客 SYN **intermediary, go-between**

ˌ**middle ˈmanagement** *noun* [U+sing./pl. v.] the people who are in charge of small groups of people and departments within a business organization but who are not involved in making important decisions that will affect the whole organization 中层管理人员；中间管理层 ▶ ˌ**middle ˈmanager** *noun*

ˌ**middle ˈname** *noun* a name that comes between your first name and your family name 中名（名和姓之间的名字）

IDM **be sb's middle ˈname** (*informal*) used to say that sb has a lot of a particular quality 是某人的突出个性：*'Patience' is my middle name!* 我的最大特点就是有耐心！

ˌ**middle-of-the-ˈroad** *adj.* (of people, policies, etc. 人、政策等) not extreme; acceptable to most people 不极端的；多数人能接受的；取中间立场的 SYN **moderate**：*a middle-of-the-road newspaper* 观点中立的报纸 ◇ *Their music is very middle-of-the-road.* 他们的音乐很大众化。

ˌ**middle-ˈranking** *adj.* [only before noun] having a responsible job or position, but not one of the most important 中层的；中级的

ˈ**middle school** *noun* **1** (in Britain) a school for children between the ages of about 9 and 13（英国为 9 到 13 岁儿童所设的）中间学校 **2** (in the US) a school for children between the ages of about 11 and 14（美国为 11 到 14 岁儿童所设的）中学，初中 ➲ COMPARE UPPER SCHOOL

middle·ware /ˈmɪdlweə(r); *NAmE* -wer/ *noun* [U] (*computing* 计) software that allows different programs to work with each other 中间件（允许不同程序协同工作）

middle·weight /ˈmɪdlweɪt/ *noun* a BOXER weighing between 67 and 72.5 kilograms, heavier than a WELTERWEIGHT 中量级拳击手（体重在 67 到 72.5 公斤之间，略重于次中量级拳击手）：*a middleweight champion* 中量级拳击冠军

the ˌMiddle ˈWest *noun* [sing.] = MIDWEST

mid·dling /ˈmɪdlɪŋ/ *adj.* [usually before noun] of average size, quality, status, etc.（大小、品质、地位等）中间的，普通的，中等的 SYN **moderate, unremarkable**：*a golfer of middling talent* 能力一般的高尔夫球手 IDM SEE FAIR *adj.*

mid·field /ˈmɪdfiːld; ˌmɪdˈfiːld/ *noun* [U, C, sing.] the central part of a sports field; the group of players in this position（运动场的）中场；中场队员：*He plays* (***in***) ***midfield.*** 他是中场队员。◇ *The team's midfield looks strong.* 这个球队的中场显得很强大。◇ *a midfield player* 中场球员 ▶ **mid·field·er** /ˌmɪdˈfiːldə(r)/ *noun*

midge /mɪdʒ/ *noun* a small flying insect that lives especially in damp places and that bites humans and animals 蠓；摇蚊

midget /ˈmɪdʒɪt/ *noun, adj.*

■ *noun* **1** (*taboo, offensive*) an extremely small person, who will never grow to a normal size because of a physical problem; a person suffering from DWARFISM 侏儒；矮人 **2** (*informal*) a very small person or animal 小矮子；小东西（指人或动物）

■ *adj.* [only before noun] very small 极小的

MIDI /ˈmɪdi/ *noun* [U] a connection or program that connects electronic musical instruments and computers（连接计算机的）乐器数字接口（或程序）

ˈ**midi system** *noun* (*BrE*) a SOUND SYSTEM with several parts that fit together into a small space 迷笛音响系统；紧凑型组合音响系统

Mid·lands /ˈmɪdləndz/ *noun* **the Midlands** [sing.+sing./pl. v.] the central part of a country, especially the central counties of England（一国的）中部，中部地区；（尤指）英格兰中部地区 ▶ **Mid·land** *adj.* [only before noun]

mid·life /ˌmɪdˈlaɪf/ *noun* [U] the middle part of your life when you are neither young nor old 中年；中年生活：*It is not difficult to take up a new career in midlife.* 人到中年开始新的事业并不难。◇ *midlife stresses* 中年生活的压力

ˌ**midlife ˈcrisis** *noun* [usually sing.] the feelings of worry, disappointment or lack of confidence that a person may feel in the middle part of their life 中年危机（人在步入中年后可能产生的焦虑、失望和缺乏自信）➲ COLLOCATIONS AT AGE

mid·night /ˈmɪdnaɪt/ *noun* [U] **1** 12 o'clock at night 午夜；子夜：*They had to leave* ***at midnight.*** 他们不得不半夜离开。◇ ***on the stroke of midnight*** /*shortly after* ***midnight*** 半夜 12 点整；午夜时分 ◇ *She heard the clock strike midnight.* 她听见钟敲子夜 12 点。◇ *We have to catch the midnight train.* 我们得乘半夜 12 点的火车。**2** (*especially NAmE*) = MIDNIGHT BLUE IDM SEE BURN *v.*, FLIT *n.*

ˌ**midnight ˈblue** (*also* **mid·night** *especially in NAmE*) *noun* [U] a very dark blue colour 深蓝色 ▶ ˌ**midnight ˈblue** *adj.* ➲ MORE LIKE THIS 15, page R26

the ˌmidnight ˈsun *noun* [sing.] the sun that you can see in the middle of the summer near the North and South Poles 子夜太阳（在南北极的夏季能见到）

ˈ**mid-point** *noun* [usually sing.] the point that is at an equal distance between the beginning and the end of sth; the point that is at an equal distance between two things 中点；正中央：*the mid-point of the decade* 十年过半的时候 ◇ *At its mid-point, the race had no clear winner.* 赛跑进行到一半时尚难分胜负。◇ *the mid-point between the first number and the last* 第一个数和最后一个数的中点

ˌ**mid-ˈrange** *adj.* [only before noun] (especially of a product for sale 尤指供销售的产品) neither the best nor the worst that is available 中档的；大众型的：*a mid-range computer* 中档电脑

mid·riff /ˈmɪdrɪf/ *noun* the middle part of the body between the chest and the waist 腹部；肚子：*a bare midriff* 裸露的腹部

mid·ship·man /ˈmɪdʃɪpmən/ *noun* (*pl.* **-men** /-mən/) a person training to be an officer in the navy 海军军官候补生；海军学校学员：*Midshipman Paul Brooks* 海军学校学员保罗•布鲁克斯

ˌ**mid-ˈsized** (*also* ˌ**mid-ˈsize**) (*both especially NAmE*) *adj.* of average size, neither large nor small 中号的；中等尺寸的

midst /mɪdst/ *noun* (*formal*) (used after a preposition 用于介词后) the middle part of sth 中部；中间 SYN **middle**：*Such beauty was unexpected* ***in the midst of*** *the city.* 市中心有这样的美景真是出乎意料。

IDM **in the midst of sth/of doing sth** while sth is happening or being done; while you are doing sth 当某事发生时；在某人做某事时：*a country in the midst of a recession* 处于衰退中的国家 ◇ *She discovered it in the midst of sorting out her father's things.* 她在整理父亲的东西时发现了它。 **in their/our/its/your midst** (*formal*) among or with them/us/it/you 在（他们、我们、你们）中间；和…一起：*There is a traitor in our midst.* 我们中间有个叛徒。

mid·stream /ˌmɪdˈstriːm/ *noun* [U] the middle part of a river, stream, etc. 中流；河流中心： *We anchored in midstream.* 我们在河中心抛锚停泊。

IDM **(in) midstream** in the middle of doing sth; while sth is still happening 在进行中；在中途： *Their conversation was interrupted in midstream by the baby crying.* 他们的谈话被婴儿的啼哭打断了。 ➲ MORE AT CHANGE *v.*

mid·sum·mer /ˌmɪdˈsʌmə(r)/ *noun* [U] the middle of summer, especially the period in June in northern parts of the world, in December in southern parts 仲夏，盛夏（尤指北半球六月间，南半球十二月间）： *a midsummer evening* 仲夏之夜

ˌMidsummer's ˈDay (*BrE*) (*also* **ˌMidsummer ˈDay** *NAmE, BrE*) *noun* 24 June, in northern parts of the world 施洗约翰节（世界北方地区的 6 月 24 日）

mid·term /ˌmɪdˈtɜːm; *NAmE* -ˈtɜːrm/ *adj.* [only before noun] **1** in the middle of the period that a government, a council, etc. is elected for （任期）中期的： *midterm elections* 中期选举 **2** for or connected with a period of time that is neither long nor short; in the middle of a particular period 中期的： *a midterm solution* 中期解决方案 ◇ *midterm losses* 中期损失 ➲ SEE ALSO LONG-TERM, SHORT-TERM **3** in the middle of one of the main periods of the academic year 学期中间的；期中的： *a* ***midterm examination/break*** 期中考试 / 休假 ➲ SEE ALSO HALF-TERM

mid·town /ˈmɪdtaʊn/ *noun* [U] (*NAmE*) the part of a city that is between the central business area and the outer parts 市中心区： *a house in midtown* 市中心区的房子 ◇ *midtown Manhattan* 曼哈顿市中心区 ➲ COMPARE DOWNTOWN, UPTOWN *adv.*

mid·way /ˌmɪdˈweɪ/ *adv.* in the middle of a period of time; between two places 在（时间的）中途；在两地之间 **SYN** **halfway**: *The goal was scored midway through the first half.* 上半场中段时攻进一球。 ▶ **mid·way** *adj.* : *to reach the midway point* 到达中间点

mid·week /ˌmɪdˈwiːk/ *noun* [U] the middle of the week 一周的中间： *to play a match* ***in midweek*** 在周中进行比赛 ◇ *By midweek he was too tired to go out.* 一周才刚过半，他就累得不想外出了。 ◇ *a midweek defeat for the team* 这个队在周中比赛遭受的失败 ▶ **mid·week** *adv.* : *It's cheaper to travel midweek.* 在星期中间旅行较便宜。

the Mid·west /ˌmɪdˈwest/ (*also* **the ˌMiddle ˈWest**) *noun* [sing.] the northern central part of the US （美国）中西部，中西部地区 ▶ **Mid·west·ern** /ˌmɪdˈwestən; *NAmE* -ərn/ *adj.*

mid·wife /ˈmɪdwaɪf/ *noun* (*pl.* **mid·wives** /-waɪvz/) a person, especially a woman, who is trained to help women give birth to babies 助产士；接生员；产婆 ➲ COMPARE DOULA ➲ **WORDFINDER NOTE** AT BIRTH

mid·wif·ery /ˌmɪdˈwɪfəri; *NAmE also* -ˈwaɪf-/ *noun* [U] the profession and work of a midwife 助产；接生

mid·win·ter /ˌmɪdˈwɪntə(r)/ *noun* [U] the middle of winter, around December in northern parts of the world, June in southern parts 仲冬，隆冬（北半球约在十二月，南半球约在六月）： *midwinter weather* 仲冬时节的天气

mien /miːn/ *noun* [sing.] (*formal* or *literary*) a person's appearance or manner that shows how they are feeling 外表；样子；风度

miffed /mɪft/ *adj.* [not before noun] (*informal*) slightly angry or upset 有点恼火；有点不高兴 **SYN** **annoyed**

might 🔑 /maɪt/ *modal verb, noun*

▪ ***modal verb*** (*negative* **might not**, *short form* **mightn't** /ˈmaɪtnt/) **1** 🔑 used as the past tense of *may* when reporting what sb has said （may 的过去式，用于间接引语）可能，可以： *He said he might come tomorrow.* 他说他明天可能来。 **2** 🔑 used when showing that sth is or was possible （表示可能性）可能： *He might get there in time, but I can't be sure.* 他有可能准时到达，但我不敢肯定。 ◇ *I know Vicky doesn't like the job, but I mightn't find it too bad.* 我知道维基不喜欢这工作，但我也许并不觉得它很差。 ◇ *The pills might have helped him, if only he'd taken them regularly.* 他当时要是按时服药，也许可以对他有帮助的。 ◇ *He might say that now* (= it is true that he does), *but he can soon change his mind.* 他现在也许会那么说，但他很快就会改变主意。 **3** 🔑 used to make a polite suggestion （用于有礼貌地提出建议）可以： *You might try calling the help desk.* 你可以试着给服务台打个电话。 ◇ *I thought we might go to the zoo on Saturday.* 我觉得周六我们可以去动物园。 **4** 🔑 (*BrE*) used to ask permission politely （用于有礼貌地提出请求）可以： *Might I use your phone?* 我可以用一下你的电话吗？ ◇ *If I might just say something…* 要是叫我说… **5** (*formal*) used to ask for information （用于询问）： *How might the plans be improved upon?* 这些计划还能怎么改进呢？ ◇ *And who might she be?* 那么她会是谁呢？ **6** used to show that you are annoyed about sth that sb could do or could have done （对某人未做某事表示不满）应该： *I think you might at least offer to help!* 我认为你至少应该主动提出帮忙吧！ ◇ *Honestly, you might have told me!* 说实话，你事先应该告诉我呀！ **7** used to say that you are not surprised by sth （表示不感意外）： *I might have guessed it was you!* 我猜就是你！ **8** used to emphasize that an important point has been made （强调提出了重点）： *'And where is the money coming from?' 'You might well ask!'* "钱又从哪里来呢？" "你这就问到点子上了！" ➲ NOTE AT MODAL **IDM** SEE WELL *adv.*

▪ ***noun*** [U] (*formal* or *literary*) great strength, energy or power 强大力量；威力： *America's military might* 美国的军事力量 ◇ *I pushed the rock* ***with all my might***. 我用尽全力推这块石头。

IDM **ˌmight is ˈright** (*saying*) having the power to do sth gives you the right to do it 强权即公理： *Their foreign policy is based on the principle that 'might is right'.* 他们的外交政策遵循"强权即公理"的原则。

ˈmight-have-been *noun* [usually pl.] (*informal*) an event or situation that could have happened or that you wish had happened, but which did not 本来可能发生的事；未遂心愿的事

might·ily /ˈmaɪtɪli/ *adv.* (*old-fashioned*) **1** very; very much 很；非常： ***mightily impressed/relieved*** 印象深刻的；如释重负的 **2** (*formal*) with great strength or effort 全力以赴地；极其努力地： *We have struggled mightily to win back lost trade.* 我们已经尽了最大的努力以挽回损失的贸易额。

mighty /ˈmaɪti/ *adj., adv.*

▪ ***adj.*** (**might·ier**, **mighti·est**) **1** (*especially literary*) very strong and powerful 强而有力的： *a mighty warrior* 威猛的斗士 ◇ *He struck him with a mighty blow across his shoulder.* 他猛一下砸在他的肩膀上。 **2** large and impressive 巨大的；非凡的 **SYN** **great**: *the mighty Mississippi River* 浩荡的密西西比河 **IDM** SEE HIGH *adj.*, PEN *n.*

▪ ***adv.*** (*informal, especially NAmE*) (with adjectives and adverbs 与形容词和副词连用) very 非常；很；极其 **SYN** **really**: *mighty difficult* 极其困难 ◇ *driving mighty fast* 飞速驾驶

mi·graine /ˈmiːɡreɪn; ˈmaɪɡ-; *NAmE* ˈmaɪɡ-/ *noun* [U, C] a very severe type of headache which often makes a person feel sick and have difficulty in seeing 偏头痛： *severe migraine* 严重的偏头痛 ◇ *I'm getting a migraine.* 我得了偏头痛。 ➲ **COLLOCATIONS** AT ILL

mi·grant **AW** /ˈmaɪɡrənt/ *noun, adj.*

▪ ***noun*** **1** a person who moves from one place to another, especially in order to find work （为工作）移居者；移民 ➲ **COLLOCATIONS** AT RACE ➲ COMPARE EMIGRANT, IMMIGRANT ➲ SEE ALSO ECONOMIC MIGRANT **2** a bird or an animal that moves from one place to another according to the season 候鸟；迁徙动物

▪ ***adj.*** [only before noun] **1** moving from one place to another, especially in order to find work （为工作）迁移的： *These industries relied on migrant workers from poorer rural areas.* 这些行业依赖来自贫困农村地区的流动劳工。 **2** moving from one place to another according to the season （随季节变化）迁徙的： *Migrant birds bring new viruses when they fly into the country.* 候鸟迁徙到这个国家时带来了新病毒。

M

mi·grate AW /maɪˈɡreɪt; NAmE ˈmaɪɡreɪt/ *verb* **1** [I] (of birds, animals, etc. 鸟类、动物等) to move from one part of the world to another according to the season（随季节变化）迁徙：*Swallows migrate south in winter.* 燕子在冬天迁徙到南方。 **2** [I] (of a lot of people 许多人) to move from one town, country, etc. to go and live and/or work in another 移居；迁移 SYN **emigrate**：*Thousands were forced to migrate from rural to urban areas in search of work.* 成千上万的人为了寻找工作被迫从农村涌进城市。 **3** [I] (*specialist*) to move from one place to another 移动；转移：*The infected cells then migrate to other areas of the body.* 受感染的细胞接着转移到身体的其他部位。 **4** [I, T] ~ (**sb**) (*computing* 计) to change, or cause sb to change, from one computer system to another（使）转移（到另一计算机系统） **5** [T] ~ **sth** (*computing* 计) to move programs or HARDWARE from one computer system to another 将（程序或硬件）迁移，转移（到另一系统）

mi·gra·tion AW /maɪˈɡreɪʃn/ *noun* [U, C] **1** the movement of large numbers of people, birds or animals from one place to another 迁移；移居；迁徙：*seasonal migration* 季节性迁徙 ◇ *mass migrations* 大规模的迁移 **2** the act of moving programs, etc. from one computer system to another; the fact of changing from one computer system to another（程序或硬件的）迁移，转移；（计算机系统的）改变

mi·gra·tory AW /ˈmaɪɡrətri; maɪˈɡreɪtəri; NAmE ˈmaɪɡrətɔːri/ *adj.* (*specialist*) connected with, or having the habit of, regular migration 迁移的；迁徙的；移栖的：*migratory flights/birds* 迁徙飞行的鸟群；候鸟

M

mi·kado /mɪˈkɑːdəʊ; NAmE -doʊ/ *noun* (*pl.* **-os**) (*from Japanese*) a title given in the past to the EMPEROR of Japan（日本天皇的旧称）

mike /maɪk/ *noun* (*informal*) = MICROPHONE ➲ SEE ALSO OPEN MIKE

mi·lady /mɪˈleɪdi/ *noun* (*pl.* **-ies**) (*old use* or *humorous*) used when talking to or about a woman who is a member of the British NOBILITY or of high class 夫人，太太（对英国贵族或上流社会妇女的称呼） ➲ COMPARE MILORD

mil·age = MILEAGE

milch cow /ˈmɪltʃ kaʊ/ *noun* (*BrE*) a person, an organization or a product from which it is easy to make money 财源，摇钱树（指人、机构或产品）

mild /maɪld/ *adj., noun*

■ ***adj.*** (**mild·er, mild·est**) **1** not severe or strong 温和的；和善的；不严厉的：*a mild form of the disease* 病势不重 ◇ *a mild punishment/criticism* 轻微的责罚；和善的批评 ◇ *It's safe to take a mild sedative.* 服用药性不强的镇定剂没有危险。◇ *Use a soap that is mild on the skin.* 使用对皮肤刺激性不强的肥皂。 **2** (of weather 天气) not very cold, and therefore pleasant 温和的；和煦的：*the mildest winter since records began* 自有记载以来最温暖舒适的冬天 ◇ *a mild climate* 温和的气候 ➲ COMPARE HARD *adj.* (10) **3** (of feelings 情感) not great or extreme 温和的；不强烈的；轻微的 SYN **slight**：*mild irritation/amusement/disapproval* 几分恼怒 / 喜悦 / 不赞成 ◇ *She looked at him in mild surprise.* 她略带吃惊地看着他。 **4** (of people or their behaviour 人或行为) gentle and kind; not usually getting angry or violent 和善的；随和的 SYN **equable**：*a mild woman, who never shouted* 从不大声叫喊的随和的女人 **5** (of a flavour 味道) not strong, spicy or bitter 不浓的；淡味的：*a mild curry* 淡味咖喱 ◇ *mild cheese* 淡味奶酪 OPP **hot** ▶ **mild·ness** *noun* [U]：*the mildness of a sunny spring day* 春日阳光融融的温暖 ◇ *her mildness of manner* 她温柔随和的举止

■ ***noun*** [U] (*BrE*) a type of dark beer with a mild flavour 淡味啤酒：*Two pints of mild, please.* 请来两品脱淡啤酒。 ➲ COMPARE BITTER *n.* (1)

mil·dew /ˈmɪldjuː; NAmE -duː/ *noun* [U] a very small white FUNGUS that grows on walls, plants, food, etc. in warm wet conditions 霉；霉菌

mil·dewed /ˈmɪldjuːd; NAmE -duːd/ *adj.* with MILDEW growing on it 发霉的

mild·ly /ˈmaɪldli/ *adv.* **1** slightly; not very much 轻微地；稍微地：*mildly surprised/irritated/interested* 有点儿吃惊 / 生气 / 感兴趣 **2** in a gentle manner 和善地；温和地：*'I didn't mean to upset you,' he said mildly.* 他和颜悦色地说："我并不是想让你不高兴。"

IDM **to put it ˈmildly** used to show that what you are talking about is much more extreme, etc. than your words suggest 说得委婉些；说得好听一点：*The result was unfortunate, to put it mildly* (= it was extremely unfortunate). 说得好听一点，结果是不幸的。

ˌmild-ˈmannered *adj.* (of a person 人) gentle and not usually getting angry or violent 温和的；随和的

ˌmild ˈsteel *noun* [U] a type of steel containing very little CARBON which is very strong but not easy to shape 软钢；低碳钢

mile /maɪl/ *noun* **1** [C] a unit for measuring distance equal to 1 609 metres or 1 760 yards 英里（= 1 609 米或 1 760 码）：*a 20-mile drive to work* 开车 20 英里去上班 ◇ *an area of four square miles* 四平方英里的面积 ◇ *a mile-long procession* 一英里长的游行队伍 ◇ *The nearest bank is about half a mile down the road.* 最近的银行沿着这条路要走半英里。◇ *We did about 30 miles a day on our cycling trip.* 我们骑车旅行，每天约骑 30 英里。◇ *The car must have been doing at least 100 miles an hour.* 这车速肯定每小时至少 100 英里。◇ (*BrE*) *My car does 35 miles to the gallon.* 我的车一加仑油能跑 35 英里。◇ (*NAmE*) *My car gets 35 miles to the gallon.* 我的车一加仑油能跑 35 英里。 ➲ SEE ALSO AIR MILES™, MPH, NAUTICAL MILE **2** **miles** [pl.] a large area or a long distance 大面积；长距离：*miles and miles of desert* 广阔无垠的沙漠 ◇ *There isn't a house for miles around here.* 附近数英里以内没有一座房子。◇ *I'm not walking—it's **miles away**.* 我不会走路去的，太远了。 **3** [C, usually pl.] (*informal*) very much; far 很多；远远地：*I'm feeling miles better today, thanks.* 多谢，我今天感觉好多了。◇ *I'm miles behind with my work.* 我的工作远远地落在了后面。◇ *She's taller than you by a mile.* 她比你高多了。 **4 the mile** [sing.] a race over one mile 一英里赛跑：*He ran the mile in less than four minutes.* 他用了不到四分钟就跑完一英里。◇ *a four-minute mile* 四分钟一英里赛跑

IDM **be ˈmiles away** (*informal*) to be thinking deeply about sth and not aware of what is happening around you 想出了神 **go the ˌextra ˈmile (for sb/sth)** to make a special effort to achieve sth, help sb, etc. 孜孜以求；加倍努力；加把劲 **ˌmiles from ˈanywhere** (*informal*) in a place that is a long way from a town and surrounded only by a lot of open country, sea, etc. 在偏远的地方：*We broke down miles from anywhere.* 在一个偏远的地方，我们的车坏了。 **run a ˈmile (from sb/sth)** (*informal*) to show that you are very frightened of doing sth 尽量避开 **see, spot, tell, smell, etc. sth a ˈmile off** (*informal*) to see or realize sth very easily and quickly 轻而易举地看出（或意识到）：*He's wearing a wig—you can see it a mile off.* 他戴着假发，你一眼就能看出来。 **stand/stick out a ˈmile** to be very obvious or noticeable 显而易见 ➲ MORE AT INCH *n.*, MISS *n.*

mile·age (*also* **mil·age**) /ˈmaɪlɪdʒ/ *noun* **1** [U, C, usually sing.] the distance that a vehicle has travelled, measured in miles 英里里程：*My annual mileage is about 10 000.* 我一年的行驶里程大约为 1 万英里。◇ *a used car with one owner and a low mileage* 只经过一人之手且行驶里程少的旧汽车 ◇ *The car rental included unlimited mileage, but not fuel.* 汽车租金不限里程，但不包括燃油费。◇ *I get a **mileage allowance** if I use my car for work* (= an amount of money paid for each mile I travel). 如果我因公开自己的车，就有一笔里程补贴。 **2** [U, C] the number of miles that a vehicle can travel using a particular amount of fuel（车辆使用某定量燃料可行驶的）英里数：*If you drive carefully you can get better mileage from your car.* 你只要小心开车，你的车就能多跑很多里程。 **3** [U] (*informal*) the amount of advantage or use that you can get from a particular event or situation 好处；利益：*I don't think* *the press can get any more mileage out of that story.* 我不认为报界可以再从那件事中捞到什么好处。

mile·om·eter *noun* = MILOMETER

mile·post /ˈmaɪlpəʊst; *NAmE* -poʊst/ *noun* (*especially NAmE*) **1** a post by the side of the road that shows how far it is to the next town, and to other places 里程标 **2** = MILESTONE (1)

mile·stone /ˈmaɪlstəʊn; *NAmE* -stoʊn/ *noun* **1** (*also* **mile·post** *especially in NAmE*) a very important stage or event in the development of sth 重要事件；重要阶段；转折点；里程碑 SYN **landmark** **2** a stone by the side of a road that shows how far it is to the next town and to other places 里程碑

mi·lieu /miːˈljɜː/ *noun* [C, usually sing.] (*pl.* **mi·lieux** or **mi·lieus** /-ˈljɜːz/) (*from French, formal*) the social environment that you live or work in 社会环境；社会背景 SYN **background**

mili·tant /ˈmɪlɪtənt/ *adj.* using, or willing to use, force or strong pressure to achieve your aims, especially to achieve social or political change 动武的；好战的；有战斗性的：*militant groups/leaders* 好战团伙 / 头目 ▶ **mili·tancy** /-ənsi/ *noun* [U]：*a growing militancy amongst the unemployed* 失业者中不断增长的好斗倾向 **mili·tant** *noun*：*Student militants were fighting with the police.* 激进的学生在与警察对抗。 **mili·tant·ly** *adv.*

mili·tar·ism /ˈmɪlɪtərɪzəm/ *noun* [U] (*usually disapproving*) the belief that a country should have great military strength in order to be powerful 军国主义 ▶ **mili·tar·ist** *noun*：*Militarists ran the country.* 军国主义者把持这个国家。 **mili·tar·is·tic** /ˌmɪlɪtəˈrɪstɪk/ *adj.*：*militaristic government* 军国主义政府

mili·tar·ize (*BrE also* **-ise**) /ˈmɪlɪtəraɪz/ *verb* [usually passive] **1** ~ sth to send armed forces to an area 向（某地）派遣武装力量：*a militarized zone* 军事化地区 OPP **demilitarize** **2** ~ sth to make sth similar to an army 使具有军事性质；武装化：*a militarized police force* 武装警察部队 ▶ **mili·tar·iza·tion**, **-isa·tion** /ˌmɪlɪtəraɪˈzeɪʃn; *NAmE* -rəˈz-/ *noun* [U]

mili·tary 🔑 AW /ˈmɪlətri; *NAmE* -teri/ *adj., noun*
■ ***adj.*** 🔑 [usually before noun] connected with soldiers or the armed forces 军事的；军队的；武装的：*military training/intelligence* 军训；军事情报 ◇ *a military coup* 军事政变 ◇ *military uniform* 军服 ◇ *We may have to take military action.* 我们可能不得不采取军事行动。 ➲ COLLOCATIONS AT WAR ➲ COMPARE CIVILIAN ▶ **mili·tar·ily** *adv.*：*a militarily superior country* 军事强国 ◇ *We may have to intervene militarily in the area.* 我们可能只好对这一地区进行军事干预。
■ ***noun*** **the military** [sing.+sing./pl. v.] soldiers; the armed forces 军人；军队；军方：*The military was/were called in to deal with the riot.* 已调来军队平息暴乱。

ˌmilitary ˈband *noun* a large group of soldiers who play wind instruments and drums, sometimes while marching 军乐队 ➲ COMPARE CONCERT BAND

ˌmilitary poˈlice *noun* (*abbr.* **MP**) (*often* **the military police**) [pl.] the police force which is responsible for the army, navy, etc. 宪兵

ˌmilitary ˈservice *noun* [U] **1** a period during which young people train in the armed forces 兵役：*to be called up for military service* 被征召服兵役 ◇ *She has to do her military service.* 她必须服兵役。 **2** the time sb spends in the armed forces 服役期：*He's completed 30 years of active military service.* 他已经服完 30 年的现役。

mili·tate /ˈmɪlɪteɪt/ *verb*
PHR V **ˈmilitate against sth** (*formal*) to prevent sth; to make it difficult for sth to happen or exist 防止，阻碍（某事的发生或存在） SYN **hinder**：*The supervisor's presence militated against a relaxed atmosphere.* 主管人的出现驱散了松懈的气氛。

mili·tia /məˈlɪʃə/ *noun* [sing.+sing./pl. v.] a group of people who are not professional soldiers but who have had military training and can act as an army 民兵组织；国民卫队

mili·tia·man /məˈlɪʃəmən/ *noun* (*pl.* **-men** /-mən/) a member of a militia 民兵；国民卫队队员

milk 🔑 /mɪlk/ *noun, verb*
■ ***noun*** [U] **1** 🔑 the white liquid produced by cows, GOATS and some other animals as food for their young and used as a drink by humans（牛或羊等的）奶：***a pint/litre of milk*** 一品脱 / 一升奶 ◇ ***a bottle/carton of milk*** 一瓶 / 一纸盒奶 ◇ ***fresh/dried/powdered milk*** 鲜奶；奶粉 ◇ *Do you take milk in your tea?* 你茶里加奶吗？ ◇ *milk products* (= butter, cheese, etc.) 乳制品 ➲ SEE ALSO BUTTERMILK, CONDENSED MILK, EVAPORATED MILK, MALTED MILK, SKIMMED MILK **2** 🔑 the white liquid that is produced by women and female MAMMALS for feeding their babies（人或哺乳动物的）奶，乳汁：*breast milk* 母乳 **3** the white juice of some plants and trees, especially the COCONUT（椰子等植物的）白色汁液，乳液 ➲ VISUAL VOCAB PAGE V33 ➲ SEE ALSO SOYA MILK
IDM **the milk of human ˈkindness** (*literary*) kind behaviour, considered to be natural to humans 人的善良天性；恻隐之心 ➲ MORE AT CRY *v.*, LAND *n.*
■ ***verb*** **1** ~ sth to take milk from a cow, GOAT, etc. 挤奶 **2** (*disapproving*) to obtain as much money, advantage, etc. for yourself as you can from a particular situation, especially in a dishonest way 趁机牟利；捞一把；捞好处：~ A (**from** B) *She's milked a small fortune from the company over the years.* 许多年来她揩公司的油，发了一笔小财。 ◇ ~ B (**of** A) *She's milked the company of a small fortune.* 她揩公司的油，发了一笔小财。 ◇ *I know he's had a hard time lately, but he's certainly **milking it for all it's worth*** (= using it as an excuse to do things that people would normally object to). 我知道他最近的日子不好过，但他却以此为借口为所欲为。 IDM SEE DRY *adj.*

ˌmilk ˈchocolate *noun* [U] light brown chocolate made with milk 牛奶巧克力 ➲ COMPARE DARK CHOCOLATE

ˈmilk float *noun* (*BrE*) a small electric vehicle used for delivering milk to people's houses（电动）送奶车

milk·ing /ˈmɪlkɪŋ/ *noun* [U] the process of taking milk from a cow, etc. 挤奶：***milking machines/sheds*** 挤奶机；挤奶棚

milk·maid /ˈmɪlkmeɪd/ *noun* (in the past) a woman whose job was to take milk from cows and make butter and cheese（旧时的）挤奶女工

milk·man /ˈmɪlkmən/ *noun* (*pl.* **-men** /-mən/) (especially in Britain) a person whose job is to deliver milk to customers each morning（尤指英国的）送奶人

ˈmilk powder (*also* **ˌpowdered ˈmilk**) (*both BrE*) (*US* **ˌdry ˈmilk**) *noun* [U] dried milk in the form of a powder 奶粉

ˌmilk ˈpudding *noun* [U, C] a PUDDING (= sweet dish) made with milk and rice, or with milk and another grain 牛奶布丁

ˈmilk round *noun* **1** (in Britain) the job of going from house to house regularly, delivering milk; the route taken by sb doing this job（英国）挨家送奶的工作；送奶路线 **2** (*also* **the milk round**) (in Britain) a series of visits that large companies make each year to colleges and universities, to talk to students who are interested in working for them（英国各大公司每年对高等院校进行的）巡回招聘

ˈmilk run *noun* (*informal*) [C] (*especially BrE*) a regular journey that is easy and in which nothing unusual happens, especially one by plane 轻松的例行旅程；（尤指）无风险的例行飞行

milk·shake /ˈmɪlkʃeɪk/ (*also* **shake**) *noun* a drink made of milk, and sometimes ice cream, with an added flavour of fruit or chocolate, which is mixed or shaken until it is

M

full of bubbles 奶昔（将牛奶或冰淇淋，以及水果或巧克力味的香料混合或搅拌至起泡的饮料）： *a banana milkshake* 香蕉味奶昔

milk·sop /ˈmɪlksɒp; *NAmE* -sɑːp/ *noun* (*old-fashioned, disapproving*) a man or boy who is not brave or strong 懦弱的男子（或男孩）；弱不禁风的男子（或男孩）

ˈmilk tooth (*BrE*) (*also* **ˈbaby tooth** *NAmE, BrE*) *noun* any of the first set of teeth in young children that drop out and are replaced by others 乳齿；乳牙

milky /ˈmɪlki/ *adj.* **1** made of milk; containing a lot of milk 奶制的；含奶多的；奶的： *a hot milky drink* 热奶饮料 ◇ *milky tea/coffee* 奶茶；牛奶咖啡 **2** like milk 像奶的；如奶般的： *milky* (= not clear) *blue eyes* 浑浊不清的蓝眼睛 ◇ *milky* (= white) *skin* 乳白色的皮肤

the ˌMilky ˈWay *noun* [sing.] = GALAXY (2)

mill /mɪl/ *noun, verb*

■ ***noun* 1** a building fitted with machinery for GRINDING grain into flour 磨坊；面粉厂 ➲ SEE ALSO WATERMILL, WINDMILL (1) **2** (often in compounds 常构成复合词) a factory that produces a particular type of material 工厂；制造厂： *a cotton/cloth/steel/paper mill* 纱厂；纺织厂；钢厂；造纸厂 ◇ *mill owners/workers* 工厂主；工人 ➲ SYNONYMS AT FACTORY ➲ SEE ALSO ROLLING MILL, SAWMILL **3** (often in compounds 常构成复合词) a small machine for crushing or GRINDING a solid substance into powder 磨粉机；磨面机： *a pepper mill* 胡椒研磨器 ➲ VISUAL VOCAB PAGE V27 ➲ SEE ALSO RUN-OF-THE-MILL, TREADMILL

IDM **go through the ˈmill | put sb through the ˈmill** to have or make sb have a difficult time（使）陷于困境；于某人为难 ➲ MORE AT GRIST

■ ***verb*** [often passive] **~ sth** to crush or GRIND sth in a mill（用磨粉机）碾碎，磨成粉

PHR V **ˌmill aˈround** (*also* **ˌmill aˈbout**) (especially of a large group of people 尤指一大群人) to move around an area without seeming to be going anywhere in particular 闲逛；转悠： *Fans were milling around outside the hotel.* 追星族在酒店外徘徊。➲ SEE ALSO MILLING

mil·len·ar·ian /ˌmɪlɪˈneəriən; *NAmE* -ˈner-/ *noun* a member of a religious group which believes in a future age of happiness and peace when Christ will return to Earth 千禧年信徒（笃信未来基督再临地球时会出现太平盛世） ▸ **mil·len·ar·ian** *adj.* **mil·len·ar·ian·ism** /-ˈneəriənɪzəm; *NAmE* -ˈner-/ *noun* [U]

mil·len·nium /mɪˈleniəm/ *noun* (*pl.* **mil·len·nia** /-niə/ or **mil·len·niums**) **1** a period of 1 000 years, especially as calculated before or after the birth of Christ 一千年，千年期（尤指公元纪年）： *the second millennium AD* 公元第二个千年 **2 the millennium** the time when one period of 1 000 years ends and another begins 千周年纪念日；千禧年： *How did you celebrate the millennium?* 你们是如何欢庆千禧年的？

mille·pede ➲ MILLIPEDE

mill·er /ˈmɪlə(r)/ *noun* a person who owns or works in a MILL for making flour 磨坊主；磨坊工人

mil·let /ˈmɪlɪt/ *noun* [U] a type of plant that grows in hot countries and produces very small seeds. The seeds are used as food, mainly to make flour, and also to feed to birds and animals. 黍类；谷子；粟 ➲ VISUAL VOCAB PAGE V35

milli- /ˈmɪli/ *combining form* (in nouns; used in units of measurement 构成名词，用于计量单位) one thousandth 千分之一： *milligram* 毫克

milli·bar /ˈmɪlibɑː(r)/ a unit for measuring the pressure of the atmosphere. One thousand millibars are equal to one BAR. 毫巴（大气压强单位）

milli·gram 🔑 (*BrE also* **milli·gramme**) /ˈmɪliɡræm/ *noun* (*abbr.* **mg**) a unit for measuring weight; a 1 000th of a gram 毫克；千分之一克

milli·litre (*especially US* **milli·liter**) /ˈmɪliliːtə(r)/ *noun* (*abbr.* **ml** /mɪl/) a unit for measuring the volume of liquids and gases; a 1 000th of a litre 毫升；千分之一升

milli·metre 🔑 (*especially US* **milli·meter**) /ˈmɪlimiːtə(r)/ *noun* (*abbr.* **mm**) a unit for measuring length; a 1 000th of a metre 毫米；千分之一米

mill·iner /ˈmɪlɪnə(r)/ *noun* a person whose job is making and/or selling women's hats 女帽制造商；制造（或销售）女帽的人

mill·in·ery /ˈmɪlɪnəri; *NAmE* ˈmɪlɪneri/ *noun* [U] **1** the work of a milliner 女帽业 **2** hats sold in shops/stores（商店的）帽类

mill·ing /ˈmɪlɪŋ/ *adj.* [only before noun] (of people 人) moving around in a large mass 成群乱转的： *I had to fight my way through the* ***milling crowd.*** 我不得不在涌动的人潮中挤出一条路来。

mil·lion 🔑 /ˈmɪljən/ *number* (*plural verb* 复数动词) **1** 🔑 (*abbr.* **m**) 1 000 000 一百万： *a population of half a million* 五十万人口 ◇ *tens of millions of dollars* 数千万元 ◇ *It must be worth a million* (= pounds, dollars, etc.). 它一定值一百万。HELP You say **a, one, two, several, etc. million** without a final 's' on 'million'. **Millions (of...)** can be used if there is no number or quantity before it. Always use a plural verb with **million** or **millions**, except when an amount of money is mentioned. * million 前有 a、one、two、several 等词时，million 后面不加 s。若前面没有数目或数量，可用 millions (of...)。million 和 millions 均用复数动词，指金额时除外： *Four million* (*people*) *were affected.* 四百万人受影响。◇ *Two million* (*pounds*) *was withdrawn from the account.* 从账户中提取了两百万（英镑）。**2** 🔑 **a million** or **millions** (**of...**) (*informal*) a very large amount 大量： *I still have a million things to do.* 我还有很多很多的事情要做。◇ *There were millions of people there.* 那里人山人海。◇ *He* ***made his millions*** (= all his money) *on currency deals.* 他的万贯家财都是通过外汇交易得到的。HELP There are more examples of how to use numbers at the entry for **hundred**. 更多数词用法示例见 hundred 条。

IDM **look/feel like a million ˈdollars/ˈbucks** (*informal*) to look/feel extremely good 看上去／感觉好极了 **one, etc. in a ˈmillion** a person or thing that is very unusual or special 万里挑一的人（或物）；不同寻常的人（或物）： *He's a man in a million.* 他是个出类拔萃的人物。

mil·lion·aire /ˌmɪljəˈneə(r); *NAmE* -ˈner/ *noun* a person who has a million pounds, dollars, etc.; a very rich person 百万富翁；大富豪： *an oil millionaire* 石油行业的百万富翁 ◇ *She's a millionaire several times over.* 她是个亿万富婆。◇ *a millionaire businessman* 十分富有的商人

mil·lion·air·ess /ˌmɪljəˈneərəs; *NAmE* -ˈner-/ *noun* (*old-fashioned*) a woman who is a millionaire 女（百万）富翁

mil·lionth 🔑 /ˈmɪljənθ/ *ordinal number, noun*

■ ***ordinal number*** 🔑 1 000 000th 第一百万

■ ***noun*** 🔑 each of one million equal parts of sth 百万分之一： *a/one millionth of a second* 百万分之一秒

milli·pede (*also* **millepede**) /ˈmɪlɪpiːd/ *noun* a small creature like an insect, with a long thin body divided into many sections, each with two pairs of legs 马陆；千足虫

milli·sec·ond /ˈmɪlisekənd/ *noun* (*specialist*) a 1 000th of a second 毫秒；千分之一秒： (*figurative*) *I hesitated a millisecond too long.* 我稍稍犹豫了一下。

mil·li·volt /ˈmɪlivəʊlt; -vɒlt; *NAmE* -voːlt/ *noun* (*physics* 物) a unit for measuring the force of an electric current; a 1 000th of a VOLT 毫伏（特）；千分之一伏特

mill·pond /ˈmɪlpɒnd; *NAmE* -pɑːnd/ *noun* a small area of water used especially in the past to make the wheel of a MILL turn（尤指旧时用于推动磨坊水车的）磨坊水池： *The sea was as calm as a millpond.* 海上风平浪静。

ˌMills and ˈBoon™ *noun* a company that publishes popular romantic novels 米尔斯和布恩出版公司（出版通俗爱情小说）： *He was tall, dark and handsome, like a Mills and Boon hero.* 他身材高大、皮肤黝黑、相貌英俊，就像通俗爱情小说里的男主角。

mill·stone /ˈmɪlstəʊn; *NAmE* -stoʊn/ *noun* one of two flat round stones used, especially in the past, to crush grain to make flour 磨石；磨盘

IDM **a millstone around/round your ˈneck** a difficult problem or responsibility that it seems impossible to solve or get rid of 难以摆脱的沉重负担：*My debts are a millstone around my neck.* 债务成了我难以摆脱的负担。

mill·stream /ˈmɪlstriːm/ *noun* a stream whose water turns a wheel that provides power for machinery in a WATERMILL 水磨动力水流

ˈmill wheel *noun* a large wheel that is turned by water and that makes the machinery of a MILL work （带动磨坊机器运转的）水车轮

mil·om·eter (*also* **mile·ometer**) /maɪˈlɒmɪtə(r); *NAmE* -ˈlɑːm-/ (*both BrE*) (*NAmE* **odom·eter**) (*also informal* **the clock** *US, BrE*) *noun* an instrument in a vehicle that measures the number of miles it has travelled 里程表；计程器 ➲ VISUAL VOCAB PAGE V56

mi·lord /mɪˈlɔːd; *NAmE* -ˈlɔːrd/ *noun* (*old use* or *humorous*) used when talking to or about a man who is a member of the British NOBILITY （对英国贵族的称呼）老爷，大人 ➲ COMPARE MILADY

mime /maɪm/ *noun, verb*

■ *noun* (*also less frequent* **dumb·show**) [U, C] (especially in the theatre) the use of movements of your hands or body and the expressions on your face to tell a story or to act sth without speaking; a performance using this method of acting 哑剧表演；哑剧；默剧：*The performance consisted of dance, music and mime.* 演出包括舞蹈、音乐和哑剧。◇ *a mime artist* 哑剧表演艺术家 ◇ *She performed a brief mime.* 她表演了一小段哑剧。

■ *verb* **1** [T, I] to act, tell a story, etc. by moving your body and face but without speaking 表演哑剧；用哑剧动作表现：**~ (sth)** *Each player has to mime the title of a movie, play or book.* 每一名参加者都得用哑剧动作表现出一部电影、戏剧或一本书的标题。◇ **~ doing sth** *He mimed climbing a mountain.* 他用哑剧形式表示爬山。 **2** [I, T] **~ (to sth)** | **~ (sth)** to pretend to sing a song that is actually being sung by sb else on a tape, etc. （按照播放录音等）模拟歌唱；假唱：*The band was miming to a backing tape.* 乐队在跟着伴奏带假唱。

mi·mesis /mɪˈmiːsɪs; maɪˈm-/ *noun* [U] **1** (*specialist*) the way in which the real world and human behaviour is represented in art or literature （文学艺术创作中的）模拟，模仿 **2** (*specialist*) the fact of a particular social group changing their behaviour by copying the behaviour of another social group （社会团体之间的）行为模仿 **3** (*biology* 生) the fact of a plant or animal developing a similar appearance to another plant or animal. （生物的）拟态 **4** (*medical* 医) the fact of a set of SYMPTOMS suggesting that sb has a particular disease, when in fact that person has a different disease or none 疾病模仿

mi·met·ic /mɪˈmetɪk/ *adj.* (*specialist* or *formal*) copying the behaviour or appearance of sb/sth else 模仿的；拟态的

mimic /ˈmɪmɪk/ *verb, noun*

■ *verb* (**-ck-**) **1 ~ sb/sth** | **+ speech** to copy the way sb speaks, moves, behaves, etc., especially in order to make other people laugh 模仿（某人的言行举止）；（尤指）做滑稽模仿：*She's always mimicking the teachers.* 她总喜欢模仿老师的言谈举止。◇ *He mimicked her southern accent.* 他滑稽地模仿她的南方口音。 **2 ~ sth** (*specialist* or *formal*) to look or behave like sth else （外表或行为举止）像，似 SYN **imitate**：*The robot was programmed to mimic a series of human movements.* 机器人按程序设计可模仿人的一系列动作。

■ *noun* a person or an animal that can copy the voice, movements, etc. of others 会模仿的人（或动物）

mim·ic·ry /ˈmɪmɪkri/ *noun* [U] the action or skill of being able to copy the voice, movements, etc. of others 模仿；模仿的技巧：*a talent for mimicry* 模仿的天才

mi·mosa /mɪˈməʊzə; -ˈməʊsə; *NAmE* -ˈmoʊ-/ *noun* **1** [C, U] a tropical bush or tree with balls of yellow flowers and leaves that are sensitive to touch and light 含羞草；银荆；白粉金合欢 **2** (*NAmE*) (*BrE* ˌ**Buck's ˈFizz**) [C] an alcoholic drink made by mixing SPARKLING white wine (= with bubbles) with orange juice 巴克泡腾酒（发泡白葡萄酒与橙汁调合而成）

Min /mɪn/ *noun* [U] a form of Chinese spoken mainly in SE China 闽方言；福建话

min. *abbr.* **1** (in writing 书写形式) minute(s) 分钟：*Cook for 8–10 min. until tender.* 煮 8 到 10 分钟，至软嫩为止。 **2** (in writing 书写形式) minimum 最低的；最小的；最低限度的：*min. charge £4.50* 最低收费 4.5 英镑 OPP **max**

min·aret /ˌmɪnəˈret/ *noun* a tall thin tower, usually forming part of a MOSQUE, from which Muslims are called to prayer 宣礼塔（常为清真寺的一部分）

min·atory /ˈmɪnətəri; *NAmE* -tɔːri/ *adj.* (*formal*) threatening 威胁的；恐吓的：*minatory words* 威吓的话

mince /mɪns/ *verb, noun*

■ *verb* **1** (*NAmE also* **grind**) [T] **~ sth** to cut food, especially meat, into very small pieces using a special machine (called a MINCER) 用绞肉机绞（食物，尤指肉）：*minced beef* 绞碎的牛肉 **2** [I] **+ adv./prep.** (*disapproving*) to walk with quick short steps, in a way that is not natural 装模作样地小步快走：*He minced over to serve us.* 他迈着碎步过来招待我们。

IDM **not mince (your) ˈwords** to say sth in a direct way even though it might offend other people 毫不隐讳；直言不讳

■ *noun* (*BrE*) [U] meat, especially beef, that has been finely chopped in a special machine 绞碎的肉，肉末（尤指牛肉）：*a pound of mince* 一磅碎肉 ➲ SEE ALSO HAMBURGER (2)

mince·meat /ˈmɪnsmiːt/ *noun* [U] (*especially BrE*) a mixture of dried fruit, spices, etc. used especially for making PIES 百果馅（干水果、香料等做成，尤用于做馅饼）

IDM **make ˈmincemeat of sb** (*informal*) to defeat sb completely in a fight, an argument or a competition 彻底击败；完全驳倒

ˌ**mince ˈpie** *noun* a small round PIE filled with mincemeat, traditionally eaten at Christmas, especially in Britain （尤指英国传统上于圣诞节食用的）百果馅饼

min·cer /ˈmɪnsə(r)/ (*especially BrE*) (*NAmE usually* **ˈmeat grinder**) *noun* a machine for cutting food, especially meat, into very small pieces 食物绞碎机；（尤指）绞肉机

min·cing /ˈmɪnsɪŋ/ *adj.* (*disapproving*) (of a way of walking or speaking 言谈步态) very delicate, and not natural 故作斯文的；装模作样的；扭怩作态的：*short mincing steps* 扭怩作态的小碎步

mind 🔑 /maɪnd/ *noun, verb*

■ *noun*

• **ABILITY TO THINK** 思考能力 **1** 🔑 [C, U] the part of a person that makes them able to be aware of things, to think and to feel 头脑；大脑：***the conscious/subconscious mind*** 意识；潜意识 ◇ *There were all kinds of thoughts running through my mind.* 各种念头在我脑海中闪过。◇ *There was no doubt in his mind that he'd get the job.* 他毫不怀疑自己能得到这份工作。◇ *'Drugs' are associated in most people's minds with drug abuse.* 大多数人把 drugs 与嗜毒联想在一起。◇ *She was in a disturbed **state of mind**.* 她的脑子里一片混乱。 ◇ *I could not have complete **peace of mind** before they returned.* 他们不回来，我心里就不踏实。 ➲ SEE ALSO FRAME OF MIND, PRESENCE OF MIND **2** 🔑 [C] your ability to think and reason; your intelligence; the particular way that sb thinks 思考能力；智慧；思维方式 SYN **intellect**：*to have a **brilliant/good/keen mind*** 有非凡的智力 / 良好的思考能力 / 敏锐的头脑 ◇ *a **creative/evil/suspicious mind*** 富创意的头脑；邪恶的用心；怀疑的心态 ◇ *She had a lively and enquiring mind.* 她思想活跃，善于探索。◇ *His mind is as sharp as ever.* 他思维敏锐，一如既往。◇ *I've no idea how her mind works!* 我真不知道她是怎么想的！ ◇ *He had the body of a man and the mind of a child.* 他四肢发达，头脑简单。◇ *insights into the criminal*

M

mind 对罪犯内心世界的洞察 ➲ SEE ALSO ONE-TRACK MIND
• **INTELLIGENT PERSON** 智者 **3** [C] a person who is very intelligent 聪明人；富有才智的人 SYN **brain**: *She was one of the greatest minds of her generation.* 她是她那一代人中最聪慧的人之一。 ➲ SEE ALSO MASTERMIND *n.*
• **THOUGHTS** 思想 **4** [C] your thoughts, interest, etc. 心思：*Keep your mind on your work!* 专心干你的活吧！◇ *Her mind is completely occupied by the new baby.* 她一心扑在刚出世的宝宝身上。◇ *The lecture dragged on and my mind wandered.* 演讲没完没了，我都心不在焉。◇ *He gave his mind to the arrangements for the next day.* 他认真考虑第二天的安排。◇ *As for avoiding you, **nothing could be further from my mind*** (= I was not thinking of it at all). 至于说躲避你，我根本就没有这样的想法。
• **MEMORY** 记忆 **5** [C, usually sing.] your ability to remember things 记忆力：*When I saw the exam questions my **mind just went blank*** (= I couldn't remember anything). 我看到考题时，脑子里一下子变得一片空白。◇ *Sorry—your name has gone right out of my mind.* 对不起，我完全想不起你的名字了。

IDM **be all in sb's/the 'mind** to be sth that only exists in sb's imagination 只是凭空想象：*These problems are all in your mind, you know.* 你知道，这些问题都只是你的凭空想象而已。 **bear/keep sb/sth in 'mind | bear/keep in 'mind that...** to remember sb/sth; to remember or consider that... 将…记在心中；记住；考虑到 **be bored, frightened, pissed, stoned, etc. out of your 'mind** (*informal*) to be extremely bored, etc. 感到非常无聊（或害怕等）；烂醉如泥；晕头转向 **be/go ˌout of your 'mind** to be unable to think or behave in a normal way; to become crazy 心智失常；发疯：(*informal*) *You're lending them money? You must be out of your tiny mind!* 你要把钱借给他们？你真是疯到家了。 ➲ SYNONYMS AT MAD **be in two 'minds about sth/about doing sth** (*BrE*) (*NAmE* **be of two 'minds about sth/about doing sth**) to be unable to decide what you think about sb/sth, or whether to do sth or not 犹豫不决；拿不定主意：*I was in two minds about the book* (= I didn't know if I liked it or not). 我说不清我是否喜欢这本书。◇ *She's in two minds about accepting his invitation.* 是否接受他的邀请，她犹豫不决。 **be of one/the same 'mind (about sb/sth)** to have the same opinion about sb/sth 对…意见一致；对…看法相同 **be ˌout of your 'mind with worry, etc.** to be extremely worried, etc. 极度焦虑（或愁苦等）；忧心忡忡 **bring/call sb/sth to 'mind** (*formal*) **1** to remember sb/sth 想起；记起 SYN **recall**: *She couldn't call to mind where she had seen him before.* 她想不起来曾在哪里见过他。 **2** to remind you of sb/sth 使想起；使记起 SYN **recall**: *The painting brings to mind some of Picasso's early works.* 这幅油画使人想起了毕加索早期的一些作品。 **come/spring to 'mind** if sth **comes/springs to mind**, you suddenly remember or think of it 突然记起（或想到）：*When discussing influential modern artists, three names immediately come to mind.* 讨论现代有影响力的艺术家时，有三个名字一下子出现在脑海中。 **have a good mind to do sth | have half a mind to do sth 1** used to say that you think you will do sth, although you are not sure 想去做某事，可能会做某事（但不确定）：*I've half a mind to come with you tomorrow.* 明天我可能会和你一起去。 **2** used to say that you disapprove of what sb has done and should do sth about it, although you probably will not（表明有心做某事，但未必采取行动）：*I've a good mind to write and tell your parents about it.* 我真想写信给你父母，告诉他们这件事。 **have sb/sth in 'mind (for sth)** to be thinking of sb/sth, especially for a particular job, etc. 心中有适当人选（或想做的事等）：*Do you have anyone in mind for this job?* 你有没有想到什么人可以做这项工作？◇ *Watching TV all evening wasn't exactly what I had in mind!* 我才不愿整个晚上看电视呢！ **have it in mind to do sth** (*formal*) to intend to do sth 打算做某事 **have a mind of your 'own** to have your own opinion and make your own decisions without being influenced by other people 有主见；能自作决定：*She has a mind of her own and isn't afraid to say what she thinks.* 她有主见，并且敢于表达自己的观点。◇ (*humorous*) *My computer seems to have a mind of its own!* 我的电脑好像也有它自己的想法！ **lose your 'mind** to become mentally ill 发疯；神经错乱 **make up your 'mind | make your 'mind up** to decide sth 作出决定；下定决心：*They're both beautiful—I can't make up my mind.* 两个都很漂亮，我难以决定。◇ *Have you made up your minds where to go for your honeymoon?* 你们决定好到哪里去度蜜月了吗？◇ *You'll never persuade him to stay—**his mind's made up*** (= he has definitely decided to go). 你根本无法劝他留下来，他已经拿定主意了。◇ *Come on—**it's make your mind up time!*** 嗨，你该作出决定了！ **ˌmind over 'matter** the use of the power of your mind to deal with physical problems 精神胜过物质（用精神力量处理物质问题） **your mind's 'eye** your imagination 想象：*He pictured the scene in his mind's eye.* 他想象出了这一场面。 **on your 'mind** if sb/sth is **on your mind**, you are thinking and worrying about them/it a lot 挂在心上；惦念：*You've been on my mind all day.* 我一整天都在为你担心。◇ *Don't bother your father tonight—**he's got a lot on his mind.*** 今晚就别打扰你父亲了，他的烦心事儿已经够多了。 **put/get sth out of your 'mind** to stop thinking about sb/sth; to deliberately forget sb/sth 不再想；有意忘记：*I just can't get her out of my mind.* 我就是忘不掉她。 **put sb in mind of sb/sth** (*old-fashioned*) to make sb think of sb/sth; to remind sb of sb/sth 使某人想起 **put/set sb's 'mind at ease/rest** to do or say sth to make sb stop worrying about sth 安慰；宽解；使宽心 SYN **reassure** **put/set/turn your 'mind to sth | set your 'mind on sth** to decide you want to achieve sth and give this all your attention 集中精力做；下决心做：*She could have been a brilliant pianist if she'd put her mind to it.* 如果她专心致志，坚持到底，她本可以成为一名杰出的钢琴家。 **take your mind off sth** to make you forget about sth unpleasant for a short time 转移一下注意力；暂时将不好的事忘记 SYN **distract** **to 'my mind** in my opinion 依我看；以我之见：*It was a ridiculous thing to do, to my mind.* 依我看，这样做是很荒唐的。 ➲ MORE AT BACK *n.*, BEND *v.*, BLOW *v.*, BOGGLE, CAST *v.*, CHANGE *v.*, CHANGE *n.*, CLOSE[1] *v.*, CROSS *v.*, ETCH, GREAT *adj.*, KNOW *v.*, MEETING, OPEN *adj.*, OPEN *v.*, PIECE *n.*, PREY *v.*, PUSH *v.*, RIGHT *adj.*, SIEVE *n.*, SIGHT *n.*, SLIP *v.*, SPEAK, STICK *v.*, TURN *n.*, UNSOUND

■ *verb*
• **BE UPSET/ANNOYED** 烦恼；苦恼 **1** [T, I] (used especially in questions or with negatives; not used in the passive 尤用于疑问句或否定句，不用于被动句) to be upset, annoyed or worried by sth 对（某事）烦恼，苦恼，焦虑；介意：**~ (sth)** *I don't mind the cold—it's the rain I don't like.* 冷我不在乎，我是讨厌下雨。◇ *I hope you don't mind the noise.* 希望你不介意这声音。◇ *He wouldn't have minded so much if she'd told him the truth.* 如果她把真相告诉他，他就不会那么焦虑了。◇ **~ about sth** *Did she mind about not getting the job?* 她没得到这份工作是不是很介意？◇ **~ doing sth** *Did she mind not getting the job?* 她没得到这份工作是不是很介意？◇ **~ sb/sth doing sth** *Do your parents mind you leaving home?* 你父母舍得你离开家吗？◇ (*formal*) *Do your parents mind your leaving home?* 你父母舍得你离开家吗？◇ **~ how, what, etc....** *She never minded how hot it was.* 她从不在乎天气有多热。◇ **~ that...** *He minded that he hadn't been asked.* 没被邀请，他很是耿耿于怀。
• **ASKING PERMISSION** 请求允许 **2** [I, T] used to ask for permission to do sth, or to ask sb in a polite way to do sth（请求允许或客气地请人做事）介意：*Do you mind if I open the window?* 我开开窗户好吗？◇ **~ sb doing sth** *Are you married, if you don't mind me asking?* 如果你不介意，请问你结婚了吗？◇ (*formal*) *Are you married, if you don't mind my asking?* 如果你不介意，请问你结婚了吗？◇ **~ doing sth** *Would you mind explaining that again, please?* 请你再解释一遍行吗？◇ *Do you mind driving? I'm feeling pretty tired.* 你来开车好吗？我太累了。 ➲ EXPRESS YOURSELF AT HELP, PERMISSION
• **NOT CARE/WORRY** 不关心；不担心 **3** **not mind** [I, T, no passive] to not care or not be concerned about sth 不关心；不在意；不考虑：*'Would you like tea or coffee?' 'I don't mind—either's fine.'* "你要茶还是要咖啡？" "无所谓，什么都行。" ◇ **~ sb** *Don't mind her—she didn't mean what she said.* 别理她，她只是随便说说。◇ *Don't mind me* (= don't let me disturb you)—*I'll just sit here quietly.* 别管我，我就在这儿静静地坐坐。

• **BE WILLING** 愿意 **4** **not mind doing sth** [T] to be willing to do sth 愿意做；乐意做：*I don't mind helping if you can't find anyone else.* 如果你找不到别人，我乐意帮忙。➲ MORE LIKE THIS 27, page R28

• **WARNING** 警告 **5** (BrE) (also **watch** NAmE, BrE) [T] used to tell sb to be careful about sth or warn them about a danger 当心；注意：**~ sth** *Mind* (= Don't fall on) *that step!* 注意台阶！◇ *Mind your head!* (= for example, be careful you don't hit it on a low ceiling) 小心，别碰着头！◇ *Mind your language!* (= don't speak in a rude or offensive way) 说话注意点！◇ **~ how, where, etc....** *Mind how you go!* (= often used when you say goodbye to sb) 您走好！◇ *Mind where you're treading!* 当心脚下！◇ **~ (that)...** *Mind you don't cut yourself—that knife's very sharp.* 小心别伤着，这刀子快得很。◇ *You must be home for dinner, mind.* 记住，你一定得回来吃饭。**HELP** 'That' is nearly always left out in this pattern. 这种句型一般都把 that 略去。

• **OBEY** 服从 **6** [T] **~ sb** (NAmE, IrishE) to pay attention to what sb says, and obey them 听从：*And the moral of the story is: always mind your mother!* 这个故事的寓意是：一定要听母亲的话！

• **TAKE CARE OF** 关心 **7** (especially BrE) (NAmE usually **watch**) [T] **~ sb/sth** to take care of sb/sth 关心，照看（人或物）**SYN** **look after**：*Who's minding the children this evening?* 今天晚上谁看孩子？◇ *Could you mind my bags for a moment?* 你能不能照看一下我的袋子？

IDM **,do you 'mind?** (ironic) used to show that you are annoyed about sth that sb has just said or done 别这样好不好：*Do you mind? I was here before you.* 你别这样好不好？我比你先到。**I don't mind ad'mitting, 'telling you..., etc.** used to emphasize what you are saying, especially when you are talking about sth that may be embarrassing for you 我不在乎承认（或告诉等）：*I was scared, I don't mind telling you!* 说真的，我吓坏了。**I don't mind if I 'do** (informal) used to say politely that you would like sth you have been offered （礼貌地表示愿意接受）好的，可以：*'Cup of tea, Brian?' 'I don't mind if I do.'* "喝杯茶吧，布赖恩？""好的。" **if you ,don't 'mind | if you ,wouldn't 'mind** **1** used to check that sb does not object to sth you want to do, or to ask sb politely to do sth （想要确保对方不反对，或客气地请人做事）你不会在意吧，你若不介意的话：*I'd like to ask you a few questions, if you don't mind.* 如果你不介意的话，我想问你几个问题。◇ *Can you read that form carefully, if you wouldn't mind, and then sign it.* 请您仔细看一看那份表格，然后签个字，行吗？ **2** (often ironic) used to show that you object to sth that sb has said or done （表示反对某人所做的事或所说的话）如蒙你不在意：*I give the orders around here, if you don't mind.* 不好意思，在这里我说了算。**3** used to refuse an offer politely（表示委婉拒绝）：*'Will you come with us tonight?' 'I won't, if you don't mind—I've got a lot of work to do.'* "你今晚和我们一起去吗？""对不起，我不去了，我有好多事要做。" **if you ,don't mind me/my 'saying so...** used when you are going to criticize sb or say sth that might upset them （批评等之前说）你不会在意我这么说吧：*That colour doesn't really suit you, if you don't mind my saying so.* 这颜色并不十分适合你。我这么说，你不会介意吧。**I wouldn't mind sth/doing sth** used to say politely that you would very much like sth/to do sth 我很想要；我很乐意做：*I wouldn't mind a cup of coffee, if it's no trouble.* 要是不麻烦的话，我很想来杯咖啡。◇ *I wouldn't mind having his money!* 我愿意接受他的钱！ **,mind your ,own 'business** (informal) to think about your own affairs and not ask questions about or try to get involved in other people's lives 想自己的事；别管闲事：*'What are you reading?' 'Mind your own business!'* "你在读什么呢？""少管闲事！"◇ *I was just sitting there, minding my own business, when a man started shouting at me.* 我就坐在那儿，也没招谁惹谁，忽然有个男人对我大喊大叫。**mind the 'shop** (BrE) (NAmE **mind the 'store**) to be in charge of sth for a short time while sb is away 临时代管；帮忙关照：*Who's minding the shop while the boss is abroad?* 老板出国期间由谁代管？ **,mind 'you** (informal) used to add sth to what you have just said, especially sth that makes it less strong （对刚说过的话加以补充，尤使语气减弱）请注意，告诉你吧：*I've heard they're getting divorced. Mind you, I'm not surprised—they were always arguing.* 听说他们要离婚了。告诉你吧，我并不感到意外，因为他们总是争吵。**,mind your Ps and 'Qs** (informal) to behave in the most polite way you can 要礼貌庄重 **,never 'mind** **1** (especially BrE) used to tell sb not to worry or be upset （用于安慰）没关系：*Have you broken it? Never mind, we can buy another one.* 你把它打碎了？没关系，我们可以再买一个。**2** used to suggest that sth is not important （表示并不重要）没关系，无所谓：*This isn't where I intended to take you—but never mind, it's just as good.* 我没想带你到这里来。不过没什么，这里也不错。**3** used to emphasize that what is true about the first thing you have said is even more true about the second 更不用说 **SYN** **let alone**：*I never thought she'd win once, never mind twice!* 我还以为她一次都赢不了，更别说两次了！ **never mind (about) (doing) sth** used to tell sb they shouldn't think about sth or do sth because it is not as important as sth else, or because you will do it （因为某事是次要的，或因为你要做某事）别想它，先别管：*Never mind your car—what about the damage to my fence?* 先别管你的车，我的围栏撞坏了，怎么办？◇ *Never mind washing the dishes—I'll do them later.* 别管洗碟子的事了，等一下我会洗。 **,never you 'mind** (informal) used to tell sb not to ask about sth because you are not going to tell them （表明不会告诉对方）不要问，别管：*'Who told you about it?' 'Never you mind!'* "谁告诉你这事儿的？""别问了！"◇ *Never you mind how I found out—it's true, isn't it?* 别问我是怎么知道的。这是真的，对不对？➲ MORE AT LANGUAGE, STEP *n.*

PHR V **,mind 'out** (BrE, informal) used to tell sb to move so that you can pass 请让一下；借借光 **SYN** **watch out**：*Mind out—you're in the way there!* 请让一让，你挡着路啦！ **,mind 'out (for sb/sth)** (BrE) used to warn sb of danger 当心；注意：*Have some of my plum jam—but mind out for the stones.* 尝尝我的李子酱，但得当心有核儿。

'mind-bending *adj.* (informal) (especially of drugs 尤指麻醉品) having a strong effect on your mind 致幻的；使极度兴奋的

'mind-blowing *adj.* (informal) very exciting, impressive or surprising 非常令人兴奋的；给人印象极深的；非常令人吃惊的：*Watching your baby being born is a mind-blowing experience.* 看你的孩子出生是一次非常难忘的经历。

'mind-boggling *adj.* (informal) very difficult to imagine or to understand; extremely surprising 难以想象的；难以理解的；令人惊愕的：*a problem of mind-boggling complexity* 复杂得难以想象的问题 ➲ COMPARE BOGGLE ➲ MORE LIKE THIS 10, page R26

mind·ed /ˈmaɪndɪd/ *adj.* **1** (used with adjectives to form compound adjectives 与形容词连用，构成复合形容词) having the way of thinking, the attitude or the type of character mentioned 思维（或态度、性格）…的：*a fair-minded employer* 公正的雇主 ◇ *high-minded principles* 高尚的原则 ◇ *I appeal to all like-minded people to support me.* 我呼吁所有志同道合的人来支持我。➲ SEE ALSO ABSENT-MINDED, BLOODY-MINDED, SINGLE-MINDED **2** (used with adverbs to form compound adjectives 与副词连用，构成复合形容词) having the type of mind that is interested in or able to understand the areas mentioned 对…有兴趣（或能理解）；有…头脑：*I'm not very politically minded.* 我对政治不怎么感兴趣。**3** (used with nouns to form compound adjectives 与名词连用，构成复合形容词) interested in or enthusiastic about the thing mentioned 对…感兴趣的；对…有热情的：*a reform-minded government* 热衷于改革的政府 **4** [not before noun] **~ (to do sth)** (formal) wishing or intending to do sth 情愿；有意 **SYN** **inclined**：*She was minded to accept their offer.* 她有意接受他们的提议。

mind·er /ˈmaɪndə(r)/ *noun* (especially BrE) a person whose job is to take care of and protect another person 看护人；照顾者：*a star surrounded by her minders* 被保镖簇拥着的女明星 ➲ SEE ALSO CHILDMINDER

M

mind·ful /ˈmaɪndfl/ *adj.* **~ of sb/sth | ~ that...** (*formal*) remembering sb/sth and considering them or it when you do sth 记着；想着；考虑到 SYN **conscious**: *mindful of our responsibilities* 意识到我们的责任 ◇ *Mindful of the danger of tropical storms, I decided not to go out.* 想到热带风暴的危险，我决定不出门。

ˈ**mind game** *noun* something that you do or say in order to make sb feel less confident, especially to gain an advantage for yourself （尤指为了压倒对方而展开的）心理游戏，心理战术

mind·less /ˈmaɪndləs/ *adj.* **1** done or acting without thought and for no particular reason or purpose 没头脑的；无谓的；盲目的 SYN **senseless**: *mindless violence* 无谓的暴力 ◇ *mindless vandals* 盲目破坏公物者 **2** not needing thought or intelligence 无需动脑筋的；机械的 SYN **dull**: *a mindless and repetitive task* 机械重复的工作 **3 ~ of sb/sth** (*formal*) not remembering sb/sth and not considering them or it when you do sth 不顾虑: *We explored the whole town, mindless of the cold and rain.* 我们不顾寒冷和下雨，在整个城市到处转。 ▶ **mind·less·ly** *adv.*

ˈ**mind-numbing** *adj.* very boring 非常乏味的；令人厌烦的: *mind-numbing conversation* 很无聊的谈话 ▶ **mind-numbing·ly** *adv.*: *The lecture was mind-numbingly tedious.* 那堂课冗长乏味。

ˈ**mind reader** *noun* (*often humorous*) a person who knows what sb else is thinking without being told 洞悉他人心思的人

mind·set /ˈmaɪndset/ *noun* a set of attitudes or fixed ideas that sb has and that are often difficult to change 观念模式；思维倾向 SYN **mentality**: *a conservative mindset* 保守的思维模式 ◇ *the mindset of the computer generation* 计算机时代的思维倾向

mind·share /ˈmaɪndʃeə(r); *NAmE* -ʃer/ *noun* [U] (*business* 商) the extent of knowledge of a company or product among consumers, compared with their knowledge of others of the same type 心理份额，心理占有率（指公司或产品相对于同类为消费者所了解的程度）

mine 🔑 /maɪn/ *pron., noun, verb*

■ *pron.* (the possessive form of *I* * I 的所有格形式) **1** 🔑 of or belonging to the person writing or speaking 我的: *That's mine.* 这是我的。 ◇ *He's a friend of mine* (= one of my friends). 他是我的一个朋友。 ◇ *She wanted one like mine* (= like I have). 她想要一个和我的一样的。 **2** (*BrE, informal*) my home 我的家: *Let's go back to mine after the show.* 看完表演后我们去我家吧。

■ *noun* **1** 🔑 a deep hole or holes under the ground where minerals such as coal, gold, etc. are dug 矿井；矿: *a copper/diamond mine* 铜矿；钻石矿 ➲ COMPARE PIT *n.* (3), QUARRY *n.* (1) ➲ SEE ALSO MINING, COAL MINE, GOLD MINE **2** 🔑 a type of bomb that is hidden under the ground or in the sea and that explodes when sb/sth touches it 地雷；水雷 ➲ SEE ALSO LANDMINE

IDM **a mine of inforˈmation (about/on sb/sth)** a person, book, etc. that can give you a lot of information on a particular subject 信息源泉；知识宝库

■ *verb* **1** [T, I] to dig holes in the ground in order to find and obtain coal, diamonds, etc. （在某地）开矿，采矿: **~ sth (for sth)** *The area has been mined for slate for centuries.* 这个地区开采板岩有数百年了。 ◇ **~ (for sth)** *They were mining for gold.* 他们在开采黄金。 **2** [T] **~ sth** to place mines below the surface of an area of land or water; to destroy a vehicle with mines 埋雷于；布雷；用雷炸毁（车辆）: *The coastal route had been mined.* 沿海道路上布了地雷。 ◇ *The UN convoy was mined on its way to the border.* 联合国车队在驶往边界的途中触雷被炸。

ˈ**mine dump** *noun* (*SAfrE*) = DUMP (2)

mine·field /ˈmaɪnfiːld/ *noun* **1** an area of land or water where MINES (= bombs that explode when they are touched) have been hidden 雷区；布雷区 **2** a situation that contains hidden dangers or difficulties 危机四伏的局面；充满潜在危险的形势: *a legal minefield* 法律上有潜在危险的局面 ◇ *Tax can be a minefield for the unwary.* 粗心大意的人在纳税方面很容易出错。

mine·hunt·er /ˈmaɪnhʌntə(r)/ *noun* (*BrE*) a military ship for finding and destroying MINES (= bombs that explode when they are touched) 扫雷艇；猎雷艇

miner /ˈmaɪnə(r)/ *noun* a person who works in a mine taking out coal, gold, diamonds, etc. 矿工；采矿者 ➲ SEE ALSO COAL MINER

min·eral 🔑 /ˈmɪnərəl/ *noun* **1** 🔑 [C, U] a substance that is naturally present in the earth and is not formed from animal or vegetable matter, for example gold and salt. Some minerals are also present in food and drink and in the human body and are essential for good health. 矿物；矿物质: *mineral deposits/extraction* 矿藏；矿物开采 ◇ *the recommended intake of vitamins and minerals* 维生素和矿物质的建议摄入量 ➲ COLLOCATIONS AT DIET ➲ COMPARE VEGETABLE (1) **2** [C, usually pl.] (*BrE, formal*) (*NAmE* **soda**) a sweet drink in various flavours that has bubbles of gas in it and does not contain alcohol 汽水: *Soft drinks and minerals sold here.* 此处销售各种软饮料和汽水。

min·er·al·ogist /ˌmɪnəˈrælədʒɪst/ *noun* a scientist who studies mineralogy 矿物学家

min·er·al·ogy /ˌmɪnəˈrælədʒi/ *noun* [U] the scientific study of minerals 矿物学 ▶ **min·er·al·ogic·al** /ˌmɪnərəˈlɒdʒɪkl; *NAmE* -ˈlɑːdʒ-/ *adj.*

ˈ**mineral oil** *noun* [U] **1** (*BrE*) = PETROLEUM **2** (*NAmE*) (*BrE* ˌ**liquid** ˈ**paraffin**) a liquid with no colour and no smell that comes from PETROLEUM and is used in medicines and COSMETICS 矿物油（用于制造药品和化妆品）

ˈ**mineral water** *noun* **1** [U, C] water from a SPRING in the ground that contains mineral salts or gases 矿泉水: *A glass of mineral water, please.* 请给我来杯矿泉水。 **2** [C] a glass or bottle of mineral water 一杯（或一瓶）矿泉水

mine·shaft /ˈmaɪnʃɑːft; *NAmE* -ʃæft/ *noun* a deep narrow hole that goes down to a mine 井筒；竖井

min·es·trone /ˌmɪnəˈstrəʊni; *NAmE* -ˈstroʊ-/ *noun* [U] an Italian soup containing small pieces of vegetables and PASTA （含蔬菜和意大利面的）意大利浓菜汤

mine·sweeper /ˈmaɪnswiːpə(r)/ *noun* a ship used for finding and clearing away MINES (= bombs that explode when they are touched) 扫雷艇

mine·work·er /ˈmaɪnwɜːkə(r); *NAmE* -wɜːrk-/ *noun* a person who works in a mine 矿工

minge /mɪndʒ/ *noun* (*BrE, taboo, slang*) the female sex organs or PUBIC hair （女性）阴部，阴毛

ming·er /ˈmɪŋə(r)/ *noun* (*BrE, informal*) a person who is not attractive 毫无魅力的人

min·ging /ˈmɪŋɪŋ/ *adj.* (*BrE, informal*) very bad, unpleasant or ugly 非常糟糕的；令人不快的；丑陋的

min·gle /ˈmɪŋgl/ *verb* **1** [I, T] to combine or make one thing combine with another （使）与…结合；使混合；使联结: *The sounds of laughter and singing mingled in the evening air.* 笑声和歌声交织在夜空中。 ◇ **~ (A) (with B)** *Her tears mingled with the blood on her face.* 她的泪水和脸上的血混在了一起。 ◇ *He felt a kind of happiness mingled with regret.* 他感到既高兴又遗憾。 ◇ **~ (A and B) (together)** *The flowers mingle together to form a blaze of colour.* 鲜花锦簇，色彩绚烂。 ➲ SYNONYMS AT MIX **2** [I] to move among people and talk to them, especially at a social event （尤指在社交场所）相交往，混杂其中 SYN **circulate**: *The princess was not recognized and mingled freely with the crowds.* 公主没有人认出，随意混杂在人群之中。 ◇ *If you'll excuse me, I must go and mingle* (= talk to other guests). 对不起，我得去和其他客人聊聊。

mingy /ˈmɪndʒi/ *adj.* (*BrE, informal*) small, not generous 小的；吝啬的 SYN **stingy**

M

mini /ˈmɪni/ *noun* = MINISKIRT

mini- /ˈmɪni/ *combining form* (in nouns 构成名词) small 小的；短的：*mini-break* (= a short holiday/vacation) 短假 ◇ *minigolf* 迷你高尔夫球运动

mini·ature /ˈmɪnətʃə(r); *NAmE also* -tʃʊr/ *adj.*, *noun*
■ ***adj.*** [only before noun] very small; much smaller than usual 很小的；微型的；小型的：*miniature roses* 小玫瑰花 ◇ *a rare breed of miniature horses* 一种罕见的小矮马 ◇ *It looks like a miniature version of James Bond's car.* 它看上去像一辆小型的詹姆斯·邦德的汽车。
■ ***noun*** **1** a very small detailed painting, often of a person 微型画；小画像 **2** a very small copy or model of sth; a very small version of sth 缩微模型；微型复制品：*brandy miniatures* (= very small bottles) 小瓶白兰地
IDM **in miniature** on a very small scale 小规模的；小型的：*a doll's house with everything in miniature* 样样东西都很小的玩具小屋 ◇ *Through play, children act out in miniature the dramas of adult life.* 通过游戏，孩子们演出了成年人生活的缩影。

ˈ**miniature golf** *noun* [U] (*NAmE*) = MINIGOLF

mini·atur·ist /ˈmɪnɪtʃərɪst/ *noun* a painter who paints small works of art 细密画画家

mini·atur·ize (*BrE also* **-ise**) /ˈmɪnətʃəraɪz/ *verb* ~ **sth** to make a much smaller version of sth 使微型化；使成为缩影 ▸ **mini·atur·iza·tion**, **-isa·tion** /ˌmɪnətʃəraɪˈzeɪʃn; *NAmE* -rəˈz-/ *noun* [U] **mini·atur·ized**, **-ised** *adj.* [only before noun]: *a miniaturized listening device* 微型监听装置

mini·bar /ˈmɪnibɑː(r)/ *noun* a small fridge/refrigerator in a hotel room, with drinks in it for guests to use 迷你吧（旅馆房间里放有饮料的小冰箱）

mini·beast /ˈmɪnibiːst/ *noun* (*BrE*) (used especially in schools 尤用于学校) any small animal that does not have a BACKBONE 小型无脊椎动物：*minibeasts such as worms, snails, centipedes and spiders* 蠕虫、蜗牛、蜈蚣以及蜘蛛等小型无脊椎动物

mini·bus /ˈmɪnibʌs/ *noun* a small vehicle with seats for about twelve people 小型公共汽车；中巴 ➲ VISUAL VOCAB PAGE V62

mini·cab /ˈmɪnikæb/ *noun* (*BrE*) a taxi that you have to order by telephone and cannot stop in the street （须电话预订而不能自由揽客的）出租汽车

mini·cam /ˈmɪnikæm/ *noun* a video camera that is small enough to hold in one hand 小型摄像机；迷你摄像机

mini·disc /ˈmɪnidɪsk/ *noun* a disc like a small CD that can record and play sound or data 小型磁盘；迷你光碟

mini·dress /ˈmɪnidres/ *noun* a very short dress 迷你连衣裙；超短连衣裙

mini·golf /ˈmɪnigɒlf; *NAmE* -gɑːlf; -gɔːlf/ (*NAmE also* **ˈmini·ature golf**) (*BrE also* **ˈcrazy golf**) *noun* [U] a type of GOLF in which people go around a small course hitting a ball through or over little tunnels, hills, bridges and other objects 迷你高尔夫球运动

minim /ˈmɪnɪm/ (*BrE*) (*NAmE* **ˈhalf note**) *noun* (*music* 音) a note that lasts twice as long as a CROTCHET/QUARTER NOTE 二分音符 ➲ PICTURE AT MUSIC

min·imal **AW** /ˈmɪnɪməl/ *adj.* very small in size or amount; as small as possible 极小的；极少的；最小的：*The work was carried out at minimal cost.* 这项工作是以最少的开销完成的。◇ *There's only a minimal amount of risk involved.* 所冒的风险极小。◇ *The damage to the car was minimal.* 汽车受到的损坏很小。➲ COMPARE MAXIMAL ▸ **min·im·al·ly** **AW** *adv.*: *minimally invasive surgery* 微创手术 ◇ *The episode was reported minimally in the press.* 这段逸闻在报章杂志中鲜有报道。

min·im·al·ist **AW** /ˈmɪnɪməlɪst/ *noun* an artist, a musician, etc. who uses very simple ideas or a very small number of simple elements in their work 极简抽象派艺术家；简约主义者 ▸ **min·im·al·ism** *noun* [U] **min·im·al·ist** *adj.*

ˌ**minimal ˈpair** *noun* (*phonetics* 语音) a pair of words, sounds, etc. which are distinguished from each other by only one feature, for example *pin* and *bin* 最小对立体（只在一个特征上有区别的一对词、发音等，如 pin 和 bin）

mini·mart /ˈmɪnimɑːt; *NAmE* -mɑːrt/ *noun* (*NAmE*) a small shop/store that sells food, newspapers, etc. and stays open very late （很晚才打烊的）杂货铺

min·im·ize **AW** (*BrE also* **-ise**) /ˈmɪnɪmaɪz/ *verb* **1** ~ **sth** to reduce sth, especially sth bad, to the lowest possible level 使减少到最低限度：*Good hygiene helps to minimize the risk of infection.* 保持清洁有助于最大限度地减少感染的危险。**OPP** **maximize** **2** ~ **sth** to try to make sth seem less important than it really is 降低；贬低；使显得不重要 **SYN** **play down**: *He always tried to minimize his own faults, while exaggerating those of others.* 他总是试图对自己的错误轻描淡写，对别人的错误夸大其词。**3** ~ **sth** to make sth small, especially on a computer screen （尤指在计算机屏幕上）使最小化：*Minimize any windows you have open.* 把你打开的所有窗口最小化。**OPP** **maximize** ▸ **minim·iza·tion**, **-isa·tion** /ˌmɪnɪmaɪˈzeɪʃn; *NAmE* -məˈz-/ *noun* [U]

mini·moto (*also* **mini-moto**) /ˈmɪniməʊtəʊ; *NAmE* -moʊtoʊ/ *noun* (*pl.* **-os**) a small motorcycle about 60cm high that people ride for fun and in races, but not on public roads 迷你摩托车（用于游戏和比赛，但不上路）

min·imum 🔑 **AW** /ˈmɪnɪməm/ *adj.*, *noun*
■ ***adj.*** 🔑 [usually before noun] (*abbr.* **min.**) the smallest that is possible or allowed; extremely small 最低的；最小的；最低限度的：*a* ***minimum charge/price*** 最低收费 / 价格 ◇ *the minimum age for retirement* 退休的最低年龄 ◇ *The work was done with the minimum amount of effort.* 做这项工作没费什么劲。**OPP** **maximum** ▸ **min·imum** *adv.*: *You'll need £200 minimum for your holiday expenses.* 你至少需要 200 英镑作为你的假日开销。
■ ***noun*** (*pl.* **min·ima** /-mə/) [C, usually sing.] **1** 🔑 (*abbr.* **min.**) the smallest or lowest amount that is possible, required or recorded 最小值；最少量；最低限度：*Costs should* ***be kept to a minimum.*** 成本应保持在最低限度。◇ *The class needs a minimum of six students to continue.* 这个班最少需要六名学生才可以继续办下去。◇ *As an* ***absolute minimum,*** *you should spend two hours in the evening studying.* 你每天晚上应花两个小时学习，这绝对是最低要求。◇ *Temperatures will fall to a minimum of 10 degrees.* 气温会降到最低点 10 度。**2** 🔑 [sing.] an extremely small amount 极小量：*He passed the exams with the minimum of effort.* 他没费什么劲就通过了考试。**OPP** **maximum**

ˌ**minimum seˈcurity prison** (*NAmE*) (*BrE* ˌ**open ˈprison**) *noun* a prison in which prisoners have more freedom than in ordinary prisons 开放式监狱（对犯人的自由限制较少）

ˌ**minimum ˈwage** *noun* [sing.] the lowest wage that an employer is allowed to pay by law （法定的）最低工资

min·ing /ˈmaɪnɪŋ/ *noun* [U] the process of getting coal and other minerals from under the ground; the industry involved in this 采矿；采矿业：***coal/diamond/gold/tin mining*** 煤矿 / 钻石矿 / 金矿 / 锡矿开采 ◇ ***a mining company/community/engineer*** 采矿公司 / 界别 / 工程师 ➲ SEE ALSO MINE *n.* (1)

min·ion /ˈmɪniən/ *noun* (*disapproving* or *humorous*) an unimportant person in an organization who has to obey orders; a servant 下属；小卒；杂役

ˌ**mini-ˈroundabout** *noun* (*BrE*) a white circle painted on a road at a place where two or more roads meet, that all traffic must go around in the same direction 迷你环岛，微型环交，微型环岛交叉口（道路交会处的环形白圈）

mini·ser·ies /ˈmɪnɪsɪəriːz; *NAmE* -sɪriːz/ *noun* (*pl.* **mini·ser·ies**) a television play that is divided into a number of parts and shown on different days 小型电视系列片；电视连续剧

M

mini·skirt /ˈmɪniskɜːt; *NAmE* -skɜːrt/ (*also* **mini**) *noun* a very short skirt 超短裙；迷你裙

min·is·ter /ˈmɪnɪstə(r)/ *noun, verb*
■ *noun* **1** (*often* **Minister**) (in Britain and many other countries) a senior member of the government who is in charge of a government department or a branch of one（英国及其他许多国家的）部长，大臣：*the Minister of Education* 教育部长 ◇ *a meeting of EU Foreign Ministers* 欧盟外交部长会议 ◇ *senior ministers in the Cabinet* 内阁中的高级部长 ◇ *cabinet ministers* 内阁大臣 ➲ SEE ALSO FIRST MINISTER, PRIME MINISTER ➲ WORDFINDER NOTE AT GOVERNMENT **2** (in some Protestant Christian Churches 某些新教教会) a trained religious leader 牧师：*a Methodist minister* 循道宗牧师 ➲ COMPARE PASTOR, PRIEST, VICAR **3** a person, lower in rank than an AMBASSADOR, whose job is to represent their government in a foreign country 公使；外交使节
■ *verb*
PHR V **ˈminister to sb/sth** (*formal*) to care for sb, especially sb who is sick or old, and make sure that they have everything they need 照料，服侍（年老或体弱者等）SYN **tend**

min·is·ter·ial AW /ˌmɪnɪˈstɪəriəl; *NAmE* -ˈstɪr-/ *adj.* connected with a government minister or ministers 部长的；大臣的：*decisions taken at ministerial level* 部长级的决定 ◇ *to* ***hold ministerial office*** (= to have the job of a government minister) 担任部长职务

min·is·ter·ing /ˈmɪnɪstərɪŋ/ *adj.* [only before noun] (*formal*) caring for people 关心的；体贴的：*She could not see herself in the role of* ***ministering angel.*** 她想象不出自己成为一名救死扶伤的天使会是什么样。

ˌMinister of ˈState *noun* a British government minister but not one who is in charge of a department （英国）国务大臣

min·is·tra·tions /ˌmɪnɪˈstreɪʃnz/ *noun* [pl.] (*formal* or *humorous*) the act of helping or caring for sb especially when they are ill/sick or in trouble 照料；服侍；看护

min·is·try AW /ˈmɪnɪstri/ *noun* (*pl.* **-ies**) **1** [C] a government department that has a particular area of responsibility （政府的）部：*the Ministry of Defence* 国防部 ◇ *a ministry spokesperson* 部发言人 **2 the Ministry** [sing.+sing./pl. v.] ministers of religion, especially Protestant ministers, when they are mentioned as a group （尤指基督教新教的）全体牧师 **3** [C, usually sing.] the work and duties of a minister in the Church; the period of time spent working as a minister in the Church 神职；牧师职位；神职任期

mini·van /ˈmɪnivæn/ (*especially NAmE*) (*BrE* **ˈpeople carrier**, **ˈpeople mover**) *noun* a large car, like a van, designed to carry up to eight people 小型面包车；（八人）小客车 ➲ VISUAL VOCAB PAGE V56

mink /mɪŋk/ *noun* (*pl.* **mink** or **minks**) **1** [C] a small wild animal with thick shiny fur, a long body and short legs. Mink are often kept on farms for their fur. 水貂：*a mink farm* 水貂饲养场 **2** [U] the skin and shiny brown fur of the mink, used for making expensive coats, etc. 貂皮：*a mink jacket* 貂皮外套 **3** [C] a coat or jacket made of mink 貂皮大衣；貂皮外套

minke /ˈmɪŋki; -kə/ (*also* **ˈminke whale**) *noun* a small WHALE that is dark grey on top and white underneath 小鳁鲸；小须鲸

min·now /ˈmɪnəʊ; *NAmE* -noʊ/ *noun* **1** a very small FRESHWATER fish 米诺鱼（多种小型鱼类的总称）**2** a company or sports team that is small or unimportant 无足轻重的（小）公司；不起眼的（小型）运动队

minor AW /ˈmaɪnə(r)/ *adj., noun, verb*
■ *adj.* **1** [usually before noun] not very large, important or serious 较小的；次要的；轻微的：*a minor road* 小路 ◇ *minor injuries* 轻伤 ◇ *to undergo minor surgery* 接受小手术 ◇ *youths imprisoned for minor offences* 因犯轻罪而被关押的年轻人 ◇ *There may be some minor changes to the schedule.* 时间安排上也许会有些微的变动。◇ *Women played a relatively minor role in the organization.* 在这个组织中，妇女发挥着相对次要的作用。OPP **major** **2** (*music* 音) based on a SCALE in which the third note is a SEMITONE/HALF STEP higher than the second note 小调的；小音阶的：*the key of C minor* * C 小调 ➲ COMPARE MAJOR *adj.* (3)
■ *noun* **1** (*law* 律) a person who is under the age at which you legally become an adult and are responsible for your actions 未成年人：*It is an offence to serve alcohol to minors.* 向未成年人提供含酒精的饮料是违法的。➲ WORDFINDER NOTE AT AGE **2** (*especially NAmE*) a subject that you study at university in addition to your MAJOR 辅修科目；辅修课程
■ *verb*
PHR V **ˈminor in sth** (*NAmE*) to study sth at college, but not as your main subject 辅修 ➲ COMPARE MAJOR *v.*

mi·nor·ity AW /maɪˈnɒrəti; *NAmE* -ˈnɔːr-/ *noun* (*pl.* **-ies**) **1** [sing.+sing./pl. v.] the smaller part of a group; less than half of the people or things in a large group 少数；少数派；少数人：*Only a small minority of students is/are interested in politics these days.* 目前，只有极少数学生对政治感兴趣。◇ *minority shareholders in the bank* 银行的少数股东 OPP **majority** **2** [C] a small group within a community or country that is different because of race, religion, language, etc. 少数派；少数民族；少数群体：*the rights of* ***ethnic/racial minorities*** 少数民族/族裔的权利 ◇ *minority languages* 少数民族语言 ◇ *a large German-speaking minority in the east of the country* 在这个国家东部一个人口众多的讲德语的少数民族 ◇ (*NAmE*) *The school is 95 per cent minority* (= 95 per cent of children are not white Americans but from different groups). 这所学校里 95% 的学生来自少数族裔。◇ (*NAmE*) *minority neighborhoods* (= where no or few white people live) 有色种族聚居区 ➲ COLLOCATIONS AT RACE **3** [U] (*law* 律) the state of being under the age at which you are legally an adult 未成年
IDM **be in a/the miˈnority** to form much less than half of a large group 占少数；成为少数派 **be in a minority of ˈone** (*often humorous*) to be the only person to have a particular opinion or to vote a particular way 是唯一持不同意见者；是唯一投此票者

miˌnority ˈgovernment *noun* [C, U] a government that has fewer seats in parliament than the total number held by all the other parties 少数党政府（组成政府的政党在议会中占的席位少于其他政党所占席位的总和）

miˌnority ˈleader *noun* (in the US Senate or House of Representatives) a leader of a political party that does not have a majority （美国参议院和众议院中的）少数党领袖

ˈminor league (*also* **ˈMinor league**) *noun* (*NAmE*) a league of professional sports teams, especially in BASEBALL, that play at a lower level than the major leagues （尤指棒球）职业球队小联盟

ˈminor-league *adj.* [only before noun] (*NAmE*) **1** (*sport* 体育) connected with teams in the minor leagues in BASEBALL 职业棒球小联盟的：*a minor-league team* 职业棒球小联盟球队 **2** not very important and having little influence 次要的；无影响力的：*a minor-league business* 一家微不足道的企业

Mi·no·taur /ˈmaɪnətɔː(r); ˈmɪn-/ *noun* (in ancient Greek stories 古希腊神话) an imaginary creature who was half man and half BULL 弥诺陶洛斯（人身牛头怪物）

min·ster /ˈmɪnstə(r)/ *noun* (*BrE*) a large or important church 大教堂：*York Minster* 约克大教堂

min·strel /ˈmɪnstrəl/ *noun* a musician or singer in the Middle Ages （中世纪的）游方艺人

mint /mɪnt/ *noun, verb*
■ *noun* **1** [U] a plant with dark green leaves that have a fresh smell and taste and are added to food and drinks to give flavour, and used in cooking as a HERB and to decorate food 薄荷：*mint-flavoured toothpaste* 薄荷味的牙膏 ◇ *I decorated the fruit salad with a sprig of mint.*

我用小薄荷枝装点水果色拉。◇ *roast lamb with mint sauce* 烤小羊肉蘸薄荷沙司 ➲ VISUAL VOCAB PAGE V35 **2** [C] a sweet/candy flavoured with a type of mint called PEPPERMINT 薄荷糖：*after-dinner mints* 餐后薄荷糖 **3** [C] a place where money is made 铸币厂：*the Royal Mint* (= the one where British coins and notes are made) 皇家铸币厂 **4 a mint** [sing.] (*informal*) a large amount of money 大量的钱：*to make/cost a mint* 赚大钱；耗费大笔的钱

IDM **in mint con'dition** new or as good as new; in perfect condition 崭新；完美；完好无缺

■ *verb* ~ sth to make a coin from metal 铸（币）；铸造（硬币）

mint·ed /'mɪntɪd/ *adj.* **1 freshly/newly ~** recently produced, invented, etc. 新生产（或发明等）的：*a newly minted expression* 刚出现的词语 **2** (of food 食物) flavoured with mint 薄荷味的 **3** (*BrE, informal*) very rich 富有的；富裕的

,mint 'julep (*also* **julep**) *noun* [U, C] an alcoholic drink made by mixing BOURBON with crushed ice, sugar and MINT 薄荷冰酒（用波旁威士忌、碎冰、糖和薄荷调制而成）

minty /'mɪnti/ *adj.* tasting or smelling of MINT 薄荷味的：*a minty flavour/smell* 薄荷口味 / 气味

min·uet /,mɪnju'et/ *noun* a slow elegant dance that was popular in the 17th and 18th centuries; a piece of music for this dance 小步舞，小步舞曲（盛行于 17、18 世纪）

minus /'maɪnəs/ *prep., noun, adj.*

■ *prep.* **1** used when you SUBTRACT (= take away) one number or thing from another one 减；减去：*Seven minus three is four* (7 – 3 = 4). 七减去三等于四。◇ *the former Soviet Union, minus the Baltic republics and Georgia* 前苏联，不包括波罗的海诸共和国及格鲁吉亚 **2** used to express temperature below zero degrees 零下：*It was minus ten.* 气温为零下十度。◇ *The temperature dropped to minus 28 degrees centigrade* (–28°C). 气温降到零下 28 摄氏度。**3** (*informal*) without sth that was there before 无，欠缺（曾经有过的东西）：*We're going to be minus a car for a while.* 我们要过一段没有车的日子。OPP plus[1] IDM SEE PLUS[1] *prep.*

■ *noun* **1** (*also* **'minus sign**) The symbol (–), used in mathematics 减号；负号 **2** (*informal*) a negative quality; a disadvantage 负值；缺点：*Let's consider the pluses and minuses of changing the system.* 我们来考虑一下改变系统的利弊吧。OPP plus[1]

■ *adj.* **1** (*mathematics* 数) lower than zero 小于零的；负的：*a minus figure/number* 负数 **2** making sth seem negative and less attractive or good 负面的；使显得有欠缺的：*What are the car's **minus points*** (= the disadvantages)? 这车的缺点是什么？◇ ***On the minus side,** rented property is expensive and difficult to find.* 不利因素是租房又贵又不好找。**3** [not before noun] (used in a system of marks/grades 用于记分系统) slightly lower than the mark/grade A, B, etc. 略低于（A、B 等）：*I got (a) B minus (B–) in the test.* 我考试得了个 B–。OPP plus[1]

min·us·cule /'mɪnəskju:l/ *adj.* extremely small 极小的；微小的

min·ute[1] 🔑 /'mɪnɪt/ *noun, verb* ➲ SEE ALSO MINUTE[2]

■ *noun*

• PART OF HOUR 分钟 **1** 🔑 [C] (*abbr.* **min.**) each of the 60 parts of an hour, that are equal to 60 seconds 分钟；分：*It's four minutes to six.* 差四分六点。◇ *I'll be back in a few minutes.* 我一会儿就回来。◇ *Boil the rice for 20 minutes.* 将米煮 20 分钟。◇ *a ten-minute bus ride* 乘公共汽车十分钟的路程 ◇ *I enjoyed every minute of the party.* 我在这次聚会上从头到尾都非常开心。

• VERY SHORT TIME 短暂的时间 **2** 🔑 [sing.] (*informal*) a very short time 一会儿；一会儿的工夫：*It only takes a minute to make a salad.* 只要一会儿就能做好色拉。◇ ***Hang on a minute**—I'll just get my coat.* 等一下，我去拿外套。◇ *I just have to finish this—I won't be a minute.* 我得做完这活儿，一会儿就好。◇ *Could I see you for a minute?* 我能见你一下吗？◇ *I'll be with you **in a minute**, Jo.* 一会儿见，乔。◇ *Typical English weather—one minute it's raining and the next minute the sun is shining.* 典型的英国天气，时雨时晴。

• EXACT MOMENT 时刻 **3** 🔑 [sing.] an exact moment in time 时刻：*At that very minute, Tom walked in.* 就在这时候，汤姆走了进来。

• ANGLES 角 **4** [C] each of the 60 equal parts of a degree, used in measuring angles 分（角度单位，六十分之一度）：*37 degrees 30 minutes* (37°30′) * 37 度 30 分

• RECORD OF MEETING 会议记录 **5 the minutes** [pl.] a summary or record of what is said or decided at a formal meeting 会议记录；会议纪要：*We read through the minutes of the last meeting.* 我们认真通读了上次会议的纪要。◇ *Who is going to **take the minutes*** (= write them)? 谁来做会议记录？➲ WORDFINDER NOTE AT MEETING

• SHORT NOTE 简短记录 **6** [C] a short note on a subject, especially one that recommends a course of action 摘要；简短记录；备忘录

IDM **(at) any 'minute ('now)** 🔑 very soon 很快；马上：*Hurry up! He'll be back any minute now.* 快点！他随时都会回来。 **the minute (that)...** 🔑 as soon as... 一…就：*I want to see him the minute he arrives.* 他一到我就要见他。 **,not for a/one 'minute** certainly not; not at all 当然不；绝不：*I don't think for a minute that she'll accept but you can ask her.* 我认为她绝不会接受，但你可以问问她。 **this minute** 🔑 immediately; now 立刻；马上；现在：*Come down this minute!* 马上下来！◇ *I don't know what I'm going to do yet—I've **just this minute** found out.* 我还不知道我要怎么做，我刚刚才弄清情况。 **to the 'minute** exactly 准确地；确切地：*The train arrived at 9.05 to the minute.* 列车 9:05 准时到达。 **,up to the 'minute** (*informal*) **1** fashionable and modern 时髦；紧跟时尚；入时：*Her styles are always up to the minute.* 她的装束总是非常时髦。**2** having the latest information 包含最新信息的；时时更新的：*The traffic reports are up to the minute.* 交通信息报道是最新的。➲ SEE ALSO UP-TO-THE-MINUTE ➲ MORE AT BORN *v.*, JUST *adv.*, LAST[1] *det.*, WAIT *v.*

■ *verb* ~ sth | ~ that... to write down sth that is said at a meeting in the official record (= the minutes) 将（某事）写进会议记录：*I'd like that last remark to be minuted.* 我希望把刚才那句话记录在案。

mi·nute[2] /maɪ'nju:t; *NAmE also* -'nu:t/ *adj.* ➲ SEE ALSO MINUTE[1] (**mi·nuter, minut·est**) **1** extremely small 极小的；微小的；细微的 SYN **tiny**：*minute amounts of chemicals in the water* 水中含量极小的化学成分 ◇ *The kitchen on the boat is minute.* 小船上的厨房小极了。**2** very detailed, careful and thorough 细致入微的；详细的：*a **minute examination/inspection*** 细致的检查 / 视察 ◇ *She remembered everything **in minute detail/in the minutest detail(s)**.* 她记得每一件事的细节。 ▸ **mi·nute·ly** *adv.*：*The agreement has been examined minutely.* 协议经过了细致入微的审查。

'minute hand *noun* [usually sing.] the hand on a watch or clock that points to the minutes （钟表的）分针 ➲ PICTURE AT CLOCK

Min·ute·man /'mɪnɪtmæn/ *noun* (*pl.* **-men** /-men/) (*US*) (during the American Revolution) a member of a group of men who were not soldiers but who were ready to fight immediately when they were needed （美国革命时期的）即时应召民兵

mi·nu·tiae /maɪ'nju:ʃii:; *NAmE* mɪ'nu:ʃii:/ *noun* [pl.] very small details 微小的细节：*the minutiae of the contract* 合同细节

minx /mɪŋks/ *noun* [sing.] (*old-fashioned* or *humorous*) a girl or young woman who is clever at getting what she wants, and does not show respect 狡猾轻佻的女孩（或年轻女子）

MIPS /mɪps/ *abbr.* (*computing* 计) million instructions per second (a unit for measuring computer speed) 百万条指令每秒（计算机速度单位）

mir·acle /'mɪrəkl/ *noun* **1** [C] an act or event that does not follow the laws of nature and is believed to be caused by God 圣迹；神迹 SYN **wonder** **2** [sing.] (*informal*) a lucky thing that happens that you did not expect or think was possible 奇迹；不平凡的事 SYN **wonder**：*an*

M

economic miracle 经济方面的奇迹 ◇ *It's a miracle (that) nobody was killed in the crash.* 撞车事故中竟然没有一人丧生，这真是奇迹。◇ *It would take a miracle to make this business profitable.* 让这个公司赢利简直是天方夜谭。◇ *a miracle cure/drug* 有奇效的疗法；灵丹妙药 **3** [C] **~ of sth** a very good example or product of sth 极好的例子；精品 SYN **wonder**: *The car is a miracle of engineering.* 这辆车是汽车工程的精品。

IDM **work/perform 'miracles** to achieve very good results 创造奇迹；有奇效：*Her exercise programme has worked miracles for her.* 她的健身计划对她很有效。

mi·racu·lous /mɪˈrækjələs/ *adj.* like a miracle; completely unexpected and very lucky 奇迹般的；不可思议的；不平凡的 SYN **extraordinary, phenomenal**: *miraculous powers of healing* 神奇的治病能力 ◇ *She's made a miraculous recovery.* 她奇迹般地康复了。▶ **mi·racu·lous·ly** *adv.*: *They miraculously survived the plane crash.* 在空难中，他们奇迹般地幸免于难。

mir·age /ˈmɪrɑːʒ; mɪˈrɑːʒ; *NAmE* məˈrɑːʒ/ *noun* **1** an effect caused by hot air in deserts or on roads, that makes you think you can see sth, such as water, which is not there 蜃景；海市蜃楼 **2** a hope or wish that you cannot make happen because it is not realistic 幻想；妄想 SYN **illusion**: *His idea of love was a mirage.* 他的爱情观不现实。

Mi·randa /mɪˈrændə/ *adj.* (in the US) relating to the fact that the police must tell sb who has been arrested about their rights, including the right not to answer questions, and warn them that anything they say may be used as evidence against them （美国）米兰达原则的（即警察必须告诉被拘捕者其权利，包括有权保持缄默，以及他所说的话可能用作对他不利的证据）：*The police read him his Miranda rights.* 警察向他宣读了他的米兰达权利。ORIGIN From the decision of the Supreme Court on the case of Miranda v the State of Arizona in 1966. 源自 1966 年美国联邦最高法院有关米兰达诉亚利桑那州一案的裁决。

mire /ˈmaɪə(r)/ *noun* [U] an area of deep mud 泥潭；泥沼 SYN **bog**: *The wheels sank deeper into the mire.* 轮子在泥潭中陷得更深了。◇ (*figurative*) *My name had been dragged through the mire* (= my reputation was ruined). 我的名声受到了玷污。◇ (*figurative*) *The government was sinking deeper and deeper **into the mire*** (= getting further into a difficult situation). 政府在泥潭中越陷越深。

mired /ˈmaɪəd; *NAmE* ˈmaɪərd/ *adj.* [not before noun] **~ in sth** (*literary*) **1** in a difficult or unpleasant situation that you cannot escape from 陷入困境；处境艰难：*The country was mired in recession.* 这个国家陷入了经济衰退的困境。**2** stuck in deep mud 陷入泥沼；深陷泥潭

mir·ror /ˈmɪrə(r)/ *noun, verb*

■ ***noun*** **1** [C] a piece of special flat glass that reflects images, so that you can see yourself when you look in it 镜子：*He looked at himself **in the mirror**.* 他照了照镜子。◇ *a rear-view mirror* (= in a car, so that the driver can see what is behind) （车内的）后视镜 ◇ (*BrE*) *a wing mirror* (= on the side of a car) 装在车外侧面的后视镜 ◇ (*NAmE*) *a side-view mirror* 侧视镜 ➲ VISUAL VOCAB PAGES V24, V55, V65 **2** **a ~ of sth** [sing.] something that shows what sth else is like 写照；反映某种情况的事物：*The face is the mirror of the soul.* 相由心生。**3** = MIRROR SITE

■ ***verb*** **1** **~ sth** to have features that are similar to sth else and which show what it is like 反映 SYN **reflect**: *The music of the time mirrored the feeling of optimism in the country.* 这个时期的音乐反映出这个国家的乐观精神。**2** **~ sb/sth** to show the image of sb/sth on the surface of water, glass, etc. 映照；反射 SYN **reflect**: *She saw herself mirrored in the window.* 她看到自己在窗玻璃上照出的影像。

mir·ror·ball /ˈmɪrəbɔːl; *NAmE* ˈmɪrər-/ *noun* a decoration consisting of a large ball covered in small mirrors that hangs from the ceiling and turns to produce lighting effects （悬挂在天花板、产生灯光效果的）镜面球，反光球

mir·rored /ˈmɪrəd; *NAmE* -rərd/ *adj.* [only before noun] having a mirror or mirrors or behaving like a mirror 有镜子的；像镜子的：*mirrored doors/sunglasses* 有镜子的门；反光太阳镜

,mirror 'image *noun* an image of sth that is like a REFLECTION of it, either because it is exactly the same or because the right side of the original object appears on the left and the left side appears on the right 镜像；映像；反像

'mirror site (*also* **mir·ror**) *noun* (*computing* 计) a website which is a copy of another website but has a different address on the Internet 镜像站点；复制网络站点

mirth /mɜːθ; *NAmE* mɜːrθ/ *noun* [U] happiness, fun and the sound of people laughing 欢乐；欢笑 SYN **merriment**: *The performance produced much mirth among the audience.* 这场演出使观众笑声不断。

mirth·less /ˈmɜːθləs; *NAmE* ˈmɜːrθ-/ *adj.* (*formal*) showing no real enjoyment or AMUSEMENT 不快乐的；忧郁的：*a mirthless laugh/smile* 苦笑 ▶ **mirth·less·ly** *adv.*

MIS /ˌem aɪ ˈes/ *abbr.* (*computing* 计) management information system (a system that stores information for use by business managers) （商业）管理信息系统，管理资讯系统

mis- /mɪs/ *prefix* (in verbs and nouns 构成动词和名词) bad or wrong; badly or wrongly 坏（或错）的；糟糕（或错误）地：*misbehaviour* 行为不端 ◇ *misinterpret* 误解 ➲ MORE LIKE THIS 6, page R25

mis·ad·ven·ture /ˌmɪsədˈventʃə(r)/ *noun* **1** [U] (*BrE, law* 律) death caused by accident, rather than as a result of a crime 意外致死：*a verdict of **death by misadventure*** 意外死亡的裁决 **2** [C, U] (*formal*) bad luck or a small accident 厄运；恶运；不幸遭遇 SYN **mishap**

mis·aligned /ˌmɪsəˈlaɪnd/ *adj.* not in the correct position in relation to sth else 方向偏离的；未对准的：*a misaligned vertebra* 错位的脊椎骨 ▶ **mis·align·ment** /ˌmɪsəˈlaɪnmənt/ *noun* [U]: *The tests revealed a slight misalignment of the eyes.* 经检测发现双眼有轻度斜视。

mis·an·thrope /ˈmɪsənθrəʊp; *NAmE* -θroʊp/ *noun* (*formal*) a person who hates and avoids other people 厌恶人类的人；厌世者；不愿与人交往者

mis·an·throp·ic /ˌmɪsənˈθrɒpɪk; *NAmE* -ˈθrɑːp-/ *adj.* (*formal*) hating and avoiding other people 厌世的；不愿与别人交往的 ▶ **mis·an·thropy** /mɪˈsænθrəpi/ *noun* [U]

mis·ap·pli·ca·tion /ˌmɪsæplɪˈkeɪʃn/ *noun* [U, C] (*formal*) the use of sth for the wrong purpose or in the wrong way 误用；不正当使用

mis·ap·ply /ˌmɪsəˈplaɪ/ *verb* (**mis·ap·plies, mis·ap·ply·ing, mis·ap·plied, mis·ap·plied**) [usually passive] **~ sth** (*formal*) to use sth for the wrong purpose or in the wrong way 误用；滥用；挪用

mis·ap·pre·hen·sion /ˌmɪsæprɪˈhenʃn/ *noun* [U, C] (*formal*) a wrong idea about sth, or sth you believe to be true that is not true 误解；误会：*I was **under the misapprehension that** the course was for complete beginners.* 我误以为这门课是给零基础的初学者开的。

mis·ap·pro·pri·ate /ˌmɪsəˈprəʊprieɪt; *NAmE* -ˈproʊ-/ *verb* **~ sth** (*formal*) to take sb else's money or property for yourself, especially when they have trusted you to take care of it 私吞；挪用 SYN **embezzle** ➲ COMPARE APPROPRIATE *v.* ▶ **mis·ap·pro·pri·ation** /ˌmɪsəˌprəʊpriˈeɪʃn; *NAmE* -ˌproʊ-/ *noun* [U]

mis·be·got·ten /ˌmɪsbɪˈɡɒtn; *NAmE* -ˈɡɑːtn/ *adj.* [usually before noun] (*formal*) badly designed or planned 设计（或规划）拙劣的

mis·be·have /ˌmɪsbɪˈheɪv/ *verb* [I, T] to behave badly 行为不端：*Any child caught misbehaving was made to stand at the front of the class.* 调皮捣蛋的孩子要是被当场抓住，都要在全班人前面罚站。◇ **~ yourself** *I see the dog has been misbehaving itself again.* 我发现这条狗又不乖了。OPP **behave** ▶ **mis·be·hav·iour** (*BrE*) (*NAmE* **mis·be·hav·ior**) /ˌmɪsbɪˈheɪvjə(r)/ *noun* [U]

mis·cal·cu·late /ˌmɪsˈkælkjuleɪt/ *verb* **1** [T, I] to estimate an amount, a figure, a measurement, etc. wrongly 错误地估计；误算：**~ (sth)** *They had seriously miscalculated the effect of inflation.* 关于通货膨胀的影响，他们的判断严重失误。◇ **~ how long, how much, etc....** *He had miscalculated how long the trip would take.* 这次旅行要花多少时间，他当时估计错了。**2** [T, I] **~ (sth)** | **~ how, what, etc....** to judge a situation wrongly （对形势）判断错误 **SYN misjudge**: *She miscalculated the level of opposition to her proposals.* 她没想到她的建议会受到这样强烈的反对。▶ **mis·cal·cu·la·tion** /ˌmɪskælkjuˈleɪʃn/ *noun* [C, U]: *to make a miscalculation* 计算错误

mis·car·riage /ˈmɪskærɪdʒ; *BrE also* ˌmɪsˈk-/ *noun* [C, U] the process of giving birth to a baby before it is fully developed and able to survive; an occasion when this happens 流产：*to have a miscarriage* 流产 ◇ *The pregnancy ended in miscarriage at 11 weeks.* 怀孕到第 11 周便流产了。➲ COLLOCATIONS AT CHILD ➲ COMPARE ABORTION ➲ WORDFINDER NOTE AT PREGNANT

misˌcarriage of ˈjustice *noun* [U, C] (*law* 律) a situation in which a court makes a wrong decision, especially when sb is punished when they are innocent 误判；错判；审判不公；司法不公

mis·carry /ˌmɪsˈkæri/ *verb* (**mis·car·ries**, **mis·carry·ing**, **mis·car·ried**, **mis·car·ried**) **1** [I, T] **~ (sth)** to give birth to a baby before it is fully developed and able to live 流产：*The shock caused her to miscarry.* 她因惊吓而流产了。**2** [I] (*formal*) (of a plan 计划) to fail 失败 **SYN come to nothing**

mis·cast /ˌmɪsˈkɑːst; *NAmE* -ˈkæst/ *verb* (**mis·cast**, **mis·cast**) [usually passive] **~ sb (as sb/sth)** to choose an actor to play a role for which they are not suitable 角色选择不当；给（演员）分配不适当的角色

mis·ce·gen·ation /ˌmɪsɪdʒəˈneɪʃn/ *noun* [U] (*formal*) the fact of children being produced by parents who are of different races, especially when one parent is white （尤指白人和非白人）混种生育子女；异族通婚

mis·cel·lan·eous /ˌmɪsəˈleɪniəs/ *adj.* [usually before noun] consisting of many different kinds of things that are not connected and do not easily form a group 混杂的；各种各样的 **SYN diverse, various**: *a sale of miscellaneous household items* 各种生活用品大减价 ◇ *She gave me some money to cover any miscellaneous expenses.* 她给了我一些零花钱。

mis·cel·lany /mɪˈseləni; *NAmE* ˈmɪsəleɪni/ *noun* [sing.] (*formal*) a group or collection of different kinds of things 杂集；混合体 **SYN assortment**

mis·chance /ˌmɪsˈtʃɑːns; *NAmE* -ˈtʃæns/ *noun* [U, C] (*formal*) bad luck 不幸；厄运

mis·chief /ˈmɪstʃɪf/ *noun* [U] **1** bad behaviour (especially of children) that is annoying but does not cause any serious damage or harm 淘气；恶作剧；顽皮：*Those children are always* ***getting into mischief.*** 那些孩子总是淘气。◇ *I try to* ***keep out of mischief.*** 我尽量不胡闹。◇ *It's very quiet upstairs; they must be* ***up to some mischief!*** 楼上很安静，他们一定在搞什么恶作剧！ **2** the wish or tendency to behave or play in a way that causes trouble 恶意；使坏的念头：*Her eyes were full of mischief.* 她眼睛里满是使坏的神情。 **3** (*formal*) harm or injury that is done to sb or to their reputation 伤害；毁损：*The incident caused a great deal of political mischief.* 这一事件造成了严重的政治危害。

IDM **ˌdo yourself a ˈmischief** (*BrE, informal*) to hurt yourself physically 伤害自己的身体：*Watch how you use those scissors—you could do yourself a mischief!* 看你那是怎么用剪刀啊，你会伤着自己的！ **make ˈmischief** to do or say sth deliberately to upset other people, or cause trouble between them 搬弄是非；挑拨离间

ˈmischief-making *noun* [U] the act of deliberately causing trouble for people, such as harming their reputation 挑拨离间；搬弄是非

mis·chiev·ous /ˈmɪstʃɪvəs/ *adj.* **1** enjoying playing tricks and annoying people 顽皮的；捣蛋的 **SYN naughty**: *a mischievous boy* 淘气的男孩 ◇ *a* ***mischievous grin/smile/look*** 顽皮地咧着嘴笑；顽皮地微微一笑；显出淘气的神情 **2** (*formal*) (of an action or a statement 行为或言论) causing trouble, such as damaging sb's reputation 招惹是非的；恶意的：*mischievous lies/gossip* 招惹是非的谎言 / 闲言碎语 ▶ **mis·chiev·ous·ly** *adv.*

mis·cible /ˈmɪsəbl/ *adj.* (*specialist*) (of liquids 液体) that can be mixed together 可混合的 **OPP immiscible**

mis·com·mu·ni·ca·tion /ˌmɪskəˌmjuːnɪˈkeɪʃn/ *noun* [U, C] failure to make information or your ideas and feelings clear to sb, or to understand what sb says to you 传达（或理解）失败；交流失误

mis·con·ceive /ˌmɪskənˈsiːv/ *verb* **~ sth** (*formal*) to understand sth in the wrong way 误解；误会 **SYN misunderstand**

mis·con·ceived /ˌmɪskənˈsiːvd/ *adj.* badly planned or judged; not carefully thought about 计划不周的；判断失误的；欠考虑的：*a misconceived education policy* 考虑不周的教育政策 ◇ *their misconceived expectations of country life* 他们原先对乡村生活的错误想法

mis·con·cep·tion /ˌmɪskənˈsepʃn/ *noun* [C, U] **~ (about sth)** a belief or an idea that is not based on correct information, or that is not understood by people 错误认识；误解：*frequently held misconceptions about the disease* 对这种疾病常见的误解 ◇ *a* ***popular misconception*** (= one that a lot of people have) 普遍的错误观念 ◇ *Let me deal with some* ***common misconceptions.*** 我来谈谈一些常见的错误认识。◇ *views based on misconception and prejudice* 由误解和偏见而形成的观点 ➲ COMPARE PRECONCEPTION

mis·con·duct /ˌmɪsˈkɒndʌkt; *NAmE* -ˈkɑːn-/ *noun* [U] (*formal*) **1** unacceptable behaviour, especially by a professional person 失职；处理不当；行为不端：*a doctor accused of* ***gross misconduct*** (= very serious misconduct) 被控严重失职的医生 ◇ *professional misconduct* 玩忽职守 **2** bad management of a company, etc. 管理不善：*misconduct of the company's financial affairs* 对公司财务的管理不善

mis·con·struc·tion /ˌmɪskənˈstrʌkʃn/ *noun* [U, C] (*formal*) a completely wrong understanding of sth 完全错误的理解；误解

mis·con·strue /ˌmɪskənˈstruː/ *verb* **~ sth (as sth)** (*formal*) to understand sb's words or actions wrongly 误解（某人的言行） **SYN misinterpret**: *It is easy to misconstrue confidence as arrogance.* 很容易将自信误解为傲慢。

mis·count /ˌmɪsˈkaʊnt/ *verb* [T, I] **~ (sth)** to count sth wrongly 数错：*The votes had been miscounted.* 选票数计错了。

mis·cre·ant /ˈmɪskriənt/ *noun* (*literary*) a person who has done sth wrong or illegal 缺德的人；不法之徒

mis·deed /ˌmɪsˈdiːd/ *noun* [usually pl.] (*formal*) a bad or evil act 恶行；不义之举 **SYN wrongdoing**

mis·de·mean·our (*especially US* **mis·de·meanor**) /ˌmɪsdɪˈmiːnə(r)/ *noun* **1** (*formal*) an action that is bad or unacceptable, but not very serious 不正当的行为；不检点的行为：*youthful misdemeanours* 年轻人的越轨行为 **2** (*law* 律, *especially US*) a crime that is not considered to be very serious 轻罪 ➲ COMPARE FELONY

mis·diag·nose /mɪsˈdaɪəgnəʊz; *NAmE* -noʊz/ *verb* **~ sth (as sth)** to give an explanation of the nature of an illness or a problem that is not correct 误诊；错误判断：*Her depression was misdiagnosed as stress.* 她的抑郁症被误诊为精神紧张。 ▶ **mis·diag·nosis** /ˌmɪsdaɪəgˈnəʊsɪs; *NAmE* -ˈnoʊ-/ *noun* [C, U] (*pl.* **mis·diag·noses** /-siːz/)

mis·dial /ˌmɪsˈdaɪəl/ *verb* (**-ll-**, *NAmE* **-l-**) [I, T] **~ (sth)** to call the wrong telephone number by mistake 拨错（电话号码）

mis·dir·ect /ˌmɪsdəˈrekt; -daɪˈrekt/ *verb* **1** [usually passive] **~ sth** to use sth in a way that is not appropriate to a particular situation 误用；使用不当：*Their efforts over*

M

the past years have been largely misdirected. 他们过去几年的努力大都白费了。 **2** ~ **sb/sth** to send sb/sth in the wrong direction or to the wrong place 指错方向；引错路；误导 **3** ~ **sb/sth** (*law* 律) (of a judge 法官) to give a JURY (= the group of people who decide if sb is guilty of a crime) wrong information about the law 误导，错误指示（陪审团） ▸ **mis·dir·ec·tion** /ˌmɪsdəˈrekʃn; -daɪˈrek-/ *noun* [U]

mise en scène /ˌmiːz ɒn ˈsen; *NAmE* ɑːn/ *noun* [sing.] (*from French*) **1** the arrangement of furniture, SCENERY, LIGHTING, etc. used on the stage for a play in the theatre, or in front of the camera in a film/movie 场景；舞台调度；场面调度 **2** (*formal*) the place or scene where an event takes place 事发地点；现场：*Venice provided the mise en scène for the conference.* 威尼斯是这次会议的地点。

miser /ˈmaɪzə(r)/ *noun* (*disapproving*) a person who loves money and hates spending it 吝啬鬼；守财奴

mis·er·able /ˈmɪzrəbl/ *adj.* **1** very unhappy or uncomfortable 痛苦的；非常难受的；可怜的：*We were cold, wet and thoroughly miserable.* 我们又冷又湿，难受极了。◇ *Don't look so miserable!* 别一副闷闷不乐的样子！◇ *She knows how to* **make life miserable** *for her employees.* 她知道如何整治她的雇员。 **2** making you feel very unhappy or uncomfortable 使难受的；使不舒服的；令人不快的 SYN **depressing**：*miserable housing conditions* 恶劣的住房条件 ◇ *I spent a miserable weekend alone at home.* 我独自一人在家度过了一个惨兮兮的周末。◇ *What a miserable day!* (= cold and wet) 多么难受的天气呀！◇ *The play was* **a miserable failure**. 这部话剧是个可悲的失败。 **3** [only before noun] (*disapproving*) (of a person 人) always unhappy, bad-tempered and unfriendly 乖戾的；脾气坏的 SYN **grumpy**：*He was a miserable old devil.* 他真是个令人厌烦的老家伙。 **4** too small in quantity 太少的；少得可怜的 SYN **paltry**：*How can anyone live on such a miserable wage?* 这么少的工资让人怎么活呀？ ▸ **mis·er·ably** /-əbli/ *adv.*：*They wandered around miserably.* 他们可怜兮兮地四处游荡。◇ *a miserably cold day* 令人难受的寒冷天气 ◇ *He* **failed miserably** *as an actor.* 作为演员，他败得很惨。 IDM SEE SIN *n.*

miser·ly /ˈmaɪzəli; *NAmE* -ərli/ *adj.* (*disapproving*) **1** (of a person 人) hating to spend money 吝啬的；小气的 SYN **mean** **2** (of a quantity or amount 数量) too small 极少的；太小的 SYN **paltry**

mis·ery /ˈmɪzəri/ *noun* (*pl.* **-ies**) **1** [U] great suffering of the mind or body 痛苦；悲惨 SYN **distress**：*Fame brought her nothing but misery.* 名声只给她带来了痛苦。 **2** [U] very poor living conditions 穷困；悲惨的生活 SYN **poverty**：*The vast majority of the population lives in utter misery.* 这里的人绝大多数生活在极度贫困之中。 **3** [C] something that causes great suffering of mind or body 不幸的事；痛苦的事：*the miseries of unemployment* 失业的痛苦 **4** [C] (*BrE, informal*) a person who is always unhappy and complaining 老发牢骚的人；爱抱怨的人：*Don't be such an old misery!* 别老这么牢骚满腹了！

IDM ▸ **make sb's life a ˈmisery** to behave in a way that makes sb else feel very unhappy 使别人遭殃；让人痛苦 **put an animal, a bird, etc. out of its ˈmisery** to kill a creature because it has an illness or injury that cannot be treated 结束动物的生命以解除其痛苦 **put sb out of their ˈmisery** (*informal*) to stop sb worrying by telling them sth that they are anxious to know （告知情况以）消除某人的忧虑：*Put me out of my misery—did I pass or didn't I?* 别再让我着急了，我及不及格？

ˈmisery memoir *noun* a story of a person's life, written by that person, in which the author describes unpleasant personal experiences, usually suffered during childhood, and how they recovered from them 苦难回忆录（通常描述作者本人童年痛苦经历以及如何走出逆境）

mis·file /ˌmɪsˈfaɪl/ *verb* ~ **sth** to put away a document in the wrong place 归错（文档）：*The missing letter had been misfiled.* 找不着的那封信放错地方了。

mis·fire /ˌmɪsˈfaɪə(r)/ *verb* **1** [I] (of a plan or joke 计划或笑话) to fail to have the effect that you had intended 不奏效；不起作用 SYN **go wrong** **2** (*also* **miss**) [I] (of an engine 发动机) to not work correctly because the petrol/gas does not burn at the right time 不起动；打不着火 **3** [I] (of a gun, etc. 枪等) to fail to send out a bullet, etc. when fired 不发火；射不出子弹 ➲ COMPARE BACKFIRE

mis·fit /ˈmɪsfɪt/ *noun* a person who is not accepted by a particular group of people, especially because their behaviour or their ideas are very different 与别人合不来的人；行为（或思想）怪异的人：*a social misfit* 与社会格格不入的人

mis·for·tune /ˌmɪsˈfɔːtʃuːn; *NAmE* -ˈfɔːrtʃ-/ *noun* **1** [U] bad luck 厄运；不幸：*He has known great misfortune in his life.* 他一生中经历过巨大的不幸。◇ *We* **had the misfortune** *to run into a violent storm.* 我们不幸遭遇了猛烈的暴风雨。 **2** [C] an unfortunate accident, condition or event 不幸的事故（或情况、事件） SYN **blow, disaster**：*She bore her misfortunes bravely.* 她勇敢地承受不幸的遭遇。

mis·giv·ing /ˌmɪsˈɡɪvɪŋ/ *noun* [C, usually pl., U] ~ **about sth/about doing sth** feelings of doubt or anxiety about what might happen, or about whether or not sth is the right thing to do 疑虑；顾虑：*I had grave misgivings about making the trip.* 对于这次旅行我有过极大的顾虑。◇ *I read the letter with a sense of misgiving.* 我带着疑虑看了那封信。

mis·govern /ˌmɪsˈɡʌvn; *NAmE* -ˈɡʌvərn/ *verb* ~ **sth** to govern a country or state badly or unfairly 对（国家）治理不善（或失当） ▸ **mis·gov·ern·ment** /ˌmɪsˈɡʌvənmənt; *NAmE* -ˈɡʌvərn-/ *noun* [U]

mis·guided /ˌmɪsˈɡaɪdɪd/ *adj.* wrong because you have understood or judged a situation badly （因理解或判断失误）搞错的 SYN **inappropriate**：*She only did it in a misguided attempt to help.* 她是要帮忙，只是想法不对头。 ▸ **mis·guided·ly** *adv.*

mis·handle /ˌmɪsˈhændl/ *verb* **1** ~ **sth** to deal badly with a problem or situation 处理不当 SYN **mismanage**：*The entire campaign had been badly mishandled.* 整个活动搞得一塌糊涂。 **2** ~ **sb/sth** to touch or treat sb/sth in a rough and careless way 粗暴对待；胡乱操作：*The equipment could be dangerous if mishandled.* 这套设备如果使用不当会有危险。 ▸ **mis·hand·ling** *noun* [U]：*the government's mishandling of the economy* 政府对经济问题的不当处理

mis·hap /ˈmɪshæp/ *noun* [C, U] a small accident or piece of bad luck that does not have serious results 小事故；晦气：*a slight mishap* 小小的不幸 ◇ *a series of mishaps* 一连串的倒霉事 ◇ *I managed to get home* **without** (**further**) **mishap**. 我总算平安回到了家。

mis·hear /ˌmɪsˈhɪə(r); *NAmE* -ˈhɪr/ *verb* (**mis·heard**, **mis·heard** /-ˈhɜːd; *NAmE* -ˈhɜːrd/) [T, I] ~ (**sb**) | ~ **what…** to fail to hear correctly what sb says, so that you think they said sth else 误听；听错：*You may have misheard her—I'm sure she didn't mean that.* 你可能听错她的话了，我肯定她不是这个意思。◇ *I thought he said he was coming today, but I must have misheard.* 我以为他说他今天来，不过我一定是听错了。

mis·hit /ˌmɪsˈhɪt/ *verb* (**mis·hit·ting**, **mis·hit**, **mis·hit**) ~ **sth** (in a game 体育比赛) to hit the ball badly so that it does not go where you had intended 误击；把（球）打歪 ▸ **mis·hit** *noun*

mish·mash /ˈmɪʃmæʃ/ *noun* [sing.] (*informal, usually disapproving*) a confused mixture of different kinds of things, styles, etc. 混杂物（或样式等）；杂烩 ➲ MORE LIKE THIS 11, page R26

mis·in·form /ˌmɪsɪnˈfɔːm; *NAmE* -ˈfɔːrm/ *verb* [often passive] ~ **sb** (**about sth**) to give sb wrong information about sth 误报；误传：*They were deliberately misinformed about their rights.* 有人故意向他们错误地说明了他们的权利。◇ *a misinformed belief* (= based on wrong information) 被误导的信念 ▸ **mis·in·for·ma·tion** /ˌmɪsɪnfəˈmeɪʃn/ *noun* [U]：*a campaign of misinformation* 传播假消息的活动

M

mis·in·ter·pret AW /ˌmɪsɪnˈtɜːprɪt; NAmE -ˈtɜːrp-/ *verb* **~ sth (as sth/doing sth)** to understand sth/sb wrongly 误解；误释 SYN **misconstrue, misread**: *His comments were misinterpreted as a criticism of the project.* 他的评论被误解为对这个项目的批评。➲ COMPARE INTERPRET ▸ **mis·in·ter·pret·ation** AW /ˌmɪsɪntɜːprɪˈteɪʃn; NAmE -tɜːrp-/ *noun* [U, C]: *A number of these statements could be* ***open to misinterpretation*** (= could be understood wrongly). 这些话有许多可能被误解。

mis·judge /ˌmɪsˈdʒʌdʒ/ *verb* [T, I] **1 ~ sb/sth | ~ how, what, etc....** to form a wrong opinion about a person or situation, especially in a way that makes you deal with them or it unfairly 形成错误认识；错看：*She now realizes that she misjudged him.* 她现在意识到她错看了他。 **2 ~ sth | ~ how long, how far, etc....** to estimate sth such as time or distance wrongly 对（时间、距离等）判断错误：*He misjudged the distance and his ball landed in the lake.* 他对距离判断错误，使球落到了湖里。▸ **mis·judge·ment** (*also* **mis·judg·ment**) *noun* [C, U]

mis·lay /ˌmɪsˈleɪ/ *verb* (**mis·laid, mis·laid** /-ˈleɪd/) **~ sth** (*formal, especially BrE*) to put sth somewhere and then be unable to find it again, especially for only a short time 随意搁置，乱放（而一时找不到）SYN **lose**: *I seem to have mislaid my keys.* 我好像不知道把钥匙放在哪儿了。

mis·lead /ˌmɪsˈliːd/ *verb* (**mis·led, mis·led** /-ˈled/) **~ sb (about sth) | ~ sb (into doing sth)** to give sb the wrong idea or impression and make them believe sth that is not true 误导；引入歧途；使误信 SYN **deceive**: *He deliberately misled us about the nature of their relationship.* 关于他们究竟是什么关系，他故意给我们留下错误印象。

mis·lead·ing /ˌmɪsˈliːdɪŋ/ *adj.* giving the wrong idea or impression and making you believe sth that is not true 误导的；引入歧途的 SYN **deceptive**: ***misleading information/advertisements*** 使人产生误解的信息 / 广告 ▸ **mis·lead·ing·ly** *adv.*: *These bats are sometimes misleadingly referred to as 'flying foxes'.* 这些蝙蝠有时被误称为“飞狐”。

mis·man·age /ˌmɪsˈmænɪdʒ/ *verb* **~ sth** to deal with or manage sth badly 对…处理失当；对…管理不当 SYN **mishandle** ▸ **mis·man·age·ment** *noun* [U]: *accusations of corruption and financial mismanagement* 对于腐败和财务管理不当的指控

mis·match /ˈmɪsmætʃ/ *noun* **~ (between A and B)** a combination of things or people that do not go together well or are not suitable for each other 误配；错配；搭配不当：*a mismatch between people's real needs and the available facilities* 人民的切实需要和现有设施之间的不协调 ▸ **mis·match** *verb* [often passive]: **~ sb/sth** *They made a mismatched couple.* 他们夫妻俩不般配。

mis·name /ˌmɪsˈneɪm/ *verb* [usually passive] **~ sb/sth** to give sb/sth a name that is wrong or not appropriate 错误命名；取名不当

mis·nomer /ˌmɪsˈnəʊmə(r); NAmE -ˈnoʊ-/ *noun* a name or a word that is not appropriate or accurate 使用不恰当（或不准确）的名称；用词不当：*'Villa' was* ***something of a misnomer****—the place was no more than an old farmhouse.* “别墅”一说有点不妥，那地方只不过是座旧农舍。

miso /ˈmiːsəʊ; NAmE -soʊ/ *noun* [U] a substance made from BEANS, used in Japanese cooking 味噌；日本豆酱

mis·ogyn·ist /mɪˈsɒdʒɪnɪst; NAmE -ˈsɑːdʒ-/ *noun* (*formal*) a man who hates women 厌恶女人的男人 ▸ **mis·ogyn·is·tic** /mɪˌsɒdʒɪˈnɪstɪk; NAmE mɪˌsɑːdʒɪˈnɪstɪk/ (*also* **mis·ogyn·ist**) *adj.*: *misogynistic attitudes* 厌恶女人的态度 **mis·ogyny** *noun* [U]

mis·place /ˌmɪsˈpleɪs/ *verb* **~ sth** to put sth somewhere and then be unable to find it again, especially for a short time 随意搁置，乱放（而一时找不到）SYN **mislay**

mis·placed /ˌmɪsˈpleɪst/ *adj.* **1** not appropriate or correct in the situation 不合时宜的；不适宜的：***misplaced confidence/optimism/fear*** 不应有的信心 / 乐观精神 / 恐惧 **2** (of love, trust, etc. 爱情、信任等) given to a person who does not deserve or return those feelings 给错对象的；不该给的：*misplaced loyalty* 无谓的忠诚

mis·print /ˈmɪsprɪnt/ *noun* a mistake such as a spelling mistake that is made when a book, etc. is printed 印刷错误 ➲ SYNONYMS AT MISTAKE

mis·pro·nounce /ˌmɪsprəˈnaʊns/ *verb* **~ sth** to pronounce a word wrongly 发错音；读错字音 ▸ **mis·pro·nun·ci·ation** /ˌmɪsprənʌnsiˈeɪʃn/ *noun* [C, U]

mis·quote /ˌmɪsˈkwəʊt; NAmE -ˈkwoʊt/ *verb* **~ sb/sth** to repeat what sb has said or written in a way that is not correct 错误地引用；误引：*The senator claims to have been misquoted in the article.* 参议员声称文章错误地引用了他的话。▸ **mis·quo·ta·tion** /ˌmɪskwəʊˈteɪʃn; NAmE -kwoʊ-/ *noun* [C, U]

mis·read /ˌmɪsˈriːd/ *verb* (**mis·read, mis·read** /-ˈred/) **1** to understand sb/sth wrongly 误解 SYN **misinterpret**: **~ sth** *I'm afraid I completely misread the situation.* 恐怕我完全看错了形势。◇ **~ sth as sth** *His confidence was misread as arrogance.* 他的自信被误解为傲慢。 **2 ~ sth (as sth)** to read sth wrongly 读错；误读：*I misread the 1 as a 7.* 我把 1 错当成 7 了。

mis·re·mem·ber /ˌmɪsrɪˈmembə(r)/ *verb* [T, I] to remember sth in a way that is not accurate or true 记错：**~ sth** *People often misremember their vacations as more idyllic than they actually were.* 人们对度假的记忆常常有误，就是比实际情况更具诗情画意。

mis·re·port /ˌmɪsrɪˈpɔːt; NAmE -ˈpɔːrt/ *verb* **~ sth | ~ what, how, etc.... | it is misreported that...** to give a report of an event, etc. that is not correct 误报；错报；谎报：*The newspapers misreported the facts of the case.* 报纸对案情的报道有误。

mis·rep·re·sent /ˌmɪsˌreprɪˈzent/ *verb* [often passive] (*formal*) to give information about sb/sth that is not true or complete so that other people have the wrong impression about them/it 误传；不实报道；歪曲：**~ sb/sth** *He felt that the book misrepresented his opinions.* 他觉得这本书歪曲了他的观点。◇ **~ sb/sth as sth** *In the article she was misrepresented as an uncaring mother.* 这篇文章把她歪曲成一名缺少爱心的母亲。◇ **~ what, how, etc....** *The report misrepresented what the group believes.* 这个报告歪曲了小组成员的看法。▸ **mis·rep·re·sen·ta·tion** /ˌmɪsˌreprɪzenˈteɪʃn/ *noun* [C, U]: *a deliberate misrepresentation of the facts* 故意歪曲事实

mis·rule /ˌmɪsˈruːl/ *noun* [U] (*formal*) bad government 管治不善；暴政：*The regime finally collapsed after 25 years of misrule.* 在施行了 25 年的暴政后，这个政权最终垮台。

miss 🔑 /mɪs/ *verb, noun*

■ ***verb***

• **NOT HIT, CATCH, ETC.** 未击中；错过 **1** 🔑 [T, I] to fail to hit, catch, reach, etc. sth 未击中；未得到；未达到；错过：**~ (sb/sth)** *How many goals has he missed this season?* 这个赛季他射丢了多少个球？◇ *The bullet missed her by about six inches.* 子弹从她身边飞过，离她大约只有六英寸。◇ *She threw a plate at him and only* ***narrowly missed****.* 她朝他甩出一个盘子，差一点打中他。◇ **~ doing sth** *She narrowly missed hitting him.* 她差一点没打着他。

• **NOT HEAR/SEE** 不闻；不见 **2** 🔑 [T] **~ sth** to fail to hear, see or notice sth 未见到；未听到；未觉察：*The hotel is the only white building on the road—****you can't miss it****.* 酒店是这条路上唯一的白色建筑，你不会看不见的。◇ *Don't miss next week's issue!* 别错过下周那一期！◇ *I missed her name.* 我没听清她的名字。◇ *Your mother will know who's moved in—she* ***doesn't miss much****.* 你妈会知道谁搬进来了，很少有她注意不到的。

• **NOT UNDERSTAND** 不懂 **3** 🔑 [T] **~ sth** to fail to understand sth 不理解；不懂：*He completely missed the joke.* 这个笑话他一点也没听懂。◇ *You're* ***missing the point*** (= failing to understand the main part) *of what I'm saying.* 你没明白我的意思。

M

- **NOT BE/GO SOMEWHERE** 不在；不去 **4** [T] ~ **sth** to fail to be or go somewhere 不在；不去；错过：*She hasn't missed a game all year.* 她一年中一场比赛都没错过。◇ *You missed a good party last night* (= because you did not go). 你昨晚错过了一次愉快的聚会。◇ *'Are you coming to the school play?' '**I wouldn't miss it for the world.**'* "你来看学生演戏吗？""我说什么也不能错过呀。"
- **NOT DO STH** 不做 **5** [T] ~ **sth** to fail to do sth 不做；错过：*You can't afford to miss meals* (= not eat meals) *when you're in training.* 你在接受训练，可不能不吃饭呀。◇ *to miss a turn* (= to not play when it is your turn in a game) 错过一轮比赛 **6** [T] ~ (**doing**) **sth** to not take the opportunity to do sth 错过机会：*The sale prices were **too good to miss**.* 那次价格优惠真的不可错过。◇ *It was an opportunity **not to be missed**.* 机不可失，时不再来。
- **BE LATE** 迟到 **7** [T] ~ **sth/sb** | ~ **doing sth** to be or arrive too late for sth 迟到；赶不上；错过：*If I don't leave now I'll miss my plane.* 现在不走我就赶不上飞机了。◇ *Sorry I'm late—have I missed anything?* 对不起，我来晚了。我错过什么了吗？◇ *'Is Ann there?' 'You've just missed her* (= she has just left).*'* "安在吗？""她刚走。"
- **FEEL SAD** 伤心 **8** [T] to feel sad because you can no longer see sb or do sth that you like 怀念；思念：~ **sb/sth** *She will be greatly missed when she leaves.* 她走了以后，人们会非常思念她的。◇ *What did you miss most when you were in France?* 你在法国的时候最怀念的是什么？◇ ~ (**sb/sth**) **doing sth** *I don't miss getting up at six every morning!* 我才不想每天早上六点钟起床哩！
- **NOTICE STH NOT THERE** 发觉某物不在 **9** [T] ~ **sb/sth** to notice that sb/sth is not where they/it should be 发觉丢失；发觉…不在原处：*When did you first miss the necklace?* 你最早发觉项链不见了是什么时候？◇ *We seem to be missing some students this morning.* 今天早上我们好像有几位同学没到。
- **AVOID STH BAD** 避开坏事 **10** [T] to avoid sth unpleasant 避开（不愉快的事）**SYN** **escape**：~ **sth** *If you go now you should miss the crowds.* 你如果现在走，就可以避开人群。◇ ~ **doing sth** *He fell and just missed knocking the whole display over.* 他摔了一跤，差一点把全部展品碰翻。➲ MORE LIKE THIS 27, page R28
- **OF ENGINE** 发动机 **11** = MISFIRE (2)

IDM **he, she, etc. doesn't miss a 'trick** (*informal*) used to say that sb notices every opportunity to gain an advantage 不失时机；很机敏 **,miss the 'boat** (*informal*) to be unable to take advantage of sth because you are too late 错失良机：*If you don't buy now, you may find that you've missed the boat.* 你如果现在不买，你会错失良机的。 **,miss your 'guess** (*NAmE, informal*) to make a mistake 做错；犯错：***Unless I miss my guess,** your computer needs a new hard drive.* 我的判断没错的话，你的电脑需要更换一个新的硬盘驱动器。➲ MORE AT HEART, MARK *n.*

PHR V **,miss sb/sth↔'out** (*BrE*) to fail to include sb/sth in sth 不包括…在内；遗漏 **SYN** **omit**：*I'll just read through the form again to make sure I haven't missed anything out.* 我要再认真看一遍这份表格，免得漏掉什么。 **,miss 'out (on sth)** to fail to benefit from sth useful or enjoyable by not taking part in it 错失获利（或取乐等）的机会：*Of course I'm coming—I don't want to miss out on all the fun!* 我当然要来，我可不想错过好玩的机会。

■ ***noun***

- **TITLE/FORM OF ADDRESS** 称谓 **1** **Miss** used before the family name, or the first and family names, of a woman who is not married, in order to speak or write to her politely（用于未婚女子姓氏或姓名前，以示礼貌）小姐，女士：*That's all, thank you, Miss Lipman.* 就这些，谢谢，李普曼小姐。➲ COMPARE MRS, MS **2** **Miss** a title given to the winner of a beauty contest in a particular country, town, etc.（选美比赛优胜者的头衔）小姐：*Miss Brighton* 布赖顿小姐 ◇ *the Miss World contest* 世界小姐选美比赛 **3** **Miss** (*informal*) used especially by men to address a young woman when they do not know her name（称呼不知姓名的年轻女子）小姐：*Will that be all, Miss?* 就这些吗，小姐？ **4** **Miss** (*BrE, informal*) used as a form of address by children in some schools to a woman teacher, whether she is married or not（学生对女教师的称呼）：*Good morning, Miss!* 老师早！➲ COMPARE SIR (4) **5** (*old-fashioned*) a girl or young woman 少女；年轻女子
- **NOT HIT, CATCH, ETC.** 未击中；错过 **6** a failure to hit, catch or reach sth 未击中；未得到；未到达；错过：*He scored two goals and had another two **near misses**.* 他攻进两球，另有两球也险些破门。

IDM **give sth a 'miss** (*informal, especially BrE*) to decide not to do sth, eat sth, etc. 不予理睬；不理会；决定不做：*I think I'll give badminton a miss tonight.* 我今晚不想打羽毛球了。 **a ,miss is as ,good as a 'mile** (*saying*) there is no real difference between only just failing in sth and failing in it badly because the result is still the same 错误再小也是错；功败垂成仍为败

mis·sal /ˈmɪsl/ *noun* a book that contains the prayers etc. that are used at MASS in the Roman Catholic Church（天主教的）弥撒经书

,mis-'sell *verb* (**mis-sold, mis-sold**) to sell sb sth that is not suitable for their needs, for example by not giving them all the information they need 以误导方式推销；不当销售：~ **sth** *If the policy was mis-sold, the insurance company must be responsible.* 如果这份保险单是以不当手法销售的，保险公司必须为此负责。◇ ~**sb sth** | ~ **sth to sb** *The bank had mis-sold them a £200 000 loan.* 银行让他们错贷了 20 万英镑。▶ **,mis-'selling** *noun* [U]：*the mis-selling of financial products* 金融产品的不当销售 ◇ *mis-selling complaints* 对不当销售的投诉

mis·sel thrush = MISTLE THRUSH

mis·sha·pen /ˌmɪsˈʃeɪpən/ *adj.* with a shape that is not normal or natural 畸形的；扭曲变形的：*misshapen feet* 畸形脚

mis·sile /ˈmɪsaɪl; *NAmE* ˈmɪsl/ *noun* **1** a weapon that is sent through the air and that explodes when it hits the thing that it is aimed at 导弹：*nuclear missiles* 核导弹 ◇ *a **missile base/site*** 导弹基地 / 发射场 ➲ COLLOCATIONS AT WAR ➲ SEE ALSO BALLISTIC MISSILE, CRUISE MISSILE, GUIDED MISSILE **2** an object that is thrown at sb to hurt them 发射物；投掷物 **SYN** **projectile**

miss·ing /ˈmɪsɪŋ/ *adj.* **1** that cannot be found or that is not in its usual place, or at home 找不到的；不在的；丢失的 **SYN** **lost**：*I never found the missing piece.* 我一直没找到丢了的那件。◇ *My gloves have been missing for ages.* 我的手套已经丢了很久了。◇ *Two files have **gone missing**.* 两份档案不见了。◇ *They still hoped to find their missing son.* 他们仍然希望找到他们丢失的儿子。◇ (*especially BrE*) *Our cat's **gone missing** again.* 我们的猫又走丢了。 **2** that has been removed, lost or destroyed and has not been replaced 被去除的；丢失的；被损毁的；缺少的：*The book has two pages **missing/missing** pages.* 这本书缺了两页。◇ *He didn't notice there was anything missing from his room until later on.* 后来他才注意到他的屋里丢了东西。 **3** (of a person 人) not present after an accident, battle, etc. but not known to have been killed 失踪的：*He was reported **missing, presumed dead**.* 有报道说他失踪了，并推定已经丧生。◇ *Many soldiers were listed as **missing in action**.* 许多士兵都被列在战斗失踪人员名单上。 **4** not included, often when it should have been 缺少的；未被包括在内的：*Fill in the missing words in this text.* 填出文中空缺的单词。◇ *There were several candidates missing from the list.* 有几名候选人没有出现在名单中。

,missing 'link *noun* **1** [C] something, such as a piece of information, that is necessary for sb to be able to understand a problem or in order to make sth complete（理解问题或使事物完整的）必要的环节，不可缺少的一环 **2 the missing link** [sing.] an animal similar to humans that was once thought to exist at the time that APES were developing into humans 缺环（推想中从类人猿发展到人类之间的过渡动物）

,missing 'person *noun* (*pl.* **missing persons**) a person who has disappeared from their home and whose family are trying to find them with the help of the police 失踪的人；下落不明者

mis·sion /ˈmɪʃn/ *noun, verb*

■ ***noun***

• **OFFICIAL JOB/GROUP** 官方使命；正式组织 **1** [C] an important official job that a person or group of people is given to do, especially when they are sent to another country 官方使命；使团的使命：*a trade mission to China* 赴华贸易使命 ◇ *a fact-finding mission* 核查事实的工作 ◇ *a mercy mission to aid homeless refugees* 帮助无家可归的难民的慈善工作 **2** [C] a group of people doing such a job; the place where they work 使团；代表团；执行任务的地点：*the head of the British mission in Berlin* 在柏林的英国使团团长

• **TEACHING CHRISTIANITY** 传教 **3** [C, U] the work of teaching people about Christianity, especially in a foreign country; a group of people doing such work （尤指在海外的）传教，布道；布道团：*a Catholic mission in Africa* 在非洲的天主教传教士 ◇ *Gandhi's attitude to mission and conversion* 甘地对于布道和改变信仰的态度 **4** [C] a building or group of buildings used by a Christian mission 布道所；传教区

• **YOUR DUTY** 职责 **5** [C] particular work that you feel it is your duty to do 使命；天职 SYN **vocation**：*Her* ***mission in life*** *was to work with the homeless.* 她以帮助无家可归者为己任。

• **OF ARMED FORCES** 军队 **6** [C] an important job that is done by a soldier, group of soldiers, etc. 军事行动：*The squadron flew on a reconnaissance mission.* 这支空军中队执行一项侦察任务。➲ COLLOCATIONS AT WAR

• **SPACE FLIGHT** 太空飞行 **7** [C] a flight into space 太空飞行任务：*a US space mission* 美国的太空飞行 ◇ *mission control* (= the people on earth who control and communicate with the people on the mission) 太空飞行的地面指挥人员 ➲ WORDFINDER NOTE AT SPACE

• **TASK** 任务 **8** [C] (*BrE, informal*) a task or journey that is very difficult and takes a long time to complete （极其艰巨且需长时间才能完成的）任务，旅行：*It's a mission to get there.* 一路上要经历艰辛才能到达那里。

IDM **ˌmission acˈcomplished** used when you have successfully completed what you have had to do 任务已完成；大功告成

■ ***verb*** [I] + **adv./prep.** (*informal*) to go on a long and difficult journey, especially one that involves going to many different places 作艰苦的长途旅行（尤指去许多地方）：*We had to mission round all the bars until we found him.* 我们跑遍了所有的酒吧才找到他。

mis·sion·ary /ˈmɪʃənri; *NAmE* -neri/ *noun* (*pl.* **-ies**) a person who is sent to a foreign country to teach people about Christianity 传教士：*Baptist missionaries* 浸礼会传教士 ◇ *missionary work* 传教士的工作 ◇ (*figurative*) *She spoke about her new project with* ***missionary zeal*** (= with great enthusiasm). 她以极大的热忱谈论自己的新项目。

the ˈmissionary position *noun* [sing.] a position for having sex in which a man and a woman face each other, with the man lying on top of the woman 正常体位，传教士体位（男上女下的性交姿势）

ˌmission-ˈcritical *adj.* essential for an organization to function successfully （对于机构的成功运作）关键的，至关重要的：*mission-critical employees* 不可或缺的雇员

ˈmission statement *noun* an official statement of the aims of a company or an organization （公司或组织的）宗旨说明，任务说明

mis·sis *noun* = MISSUS (1), (3)

mis·sive /ˈmɪsɪv/ *noun* (*formal* or *humorous*) a letter, especially a long or an official one 信函；（尤指）长信，公函

mis·speak /ˌmɪsˈspiːk/ *verb* [I, T] (*especially NAmE*) (**mis·spoke** /ˌmɪsˈspəʊk; *NAmE* -ˈspoʊk/, **mis·spoken** /ˌmɪsˈspəʊkn; *NAmE* -ˈspoʊ-/) to say sth in a way that is not clear or not accurate 表达不清；词不达意：**~ (to sb)** *He was confused and may have misspoken to reporters.* 他被弄糊涂了，可能对记者没说清楚。◇ **~ yourself** *Let me rephrase, I think I misspoke myself.* 我换个说法吧，我刚才可能没说清楚。◇ **~ sth** *a misspoken word* 一处口误

mis·spell /ˌmɪsˈspel/ *verb* (**mis·spelled**, **mis·spelled** or **mis·spelt**, **mis·spelt** /ˌmɪsˈspelt/) **~ sth** to spell a word wrongly 拼错；写错 ▸ **mis·spell·ing** *noun* [C, U]

mis·spend /ˌmɪsˈspend/ *verb* (**mis·spent**, **mis·spent** /-ˈspent/) [usually passive] **~ sth** to spend time or money in a careless rather than a useful way 挥霍，浪费，滥用（时间或金钱）SYN **waste**：*He joked that being good at cards was the sign of* ***a misspent youth*** (= having wasted his time when he was young). 他开玩笑地说擅长打牌表明他虚度了青春年华。

mis·step /ˌmɪsˈstep/ *noun* (*NAmE*) a mistake; a wrong action 错误；失策

mis·sus /ˈmɪsɪz/ *noun* (*BrE*) **1** (*also* **mis·sis**) (*informal, becoming old-fashioned*) (used after 'the', 'my', 'your', 'his' 用于 the、my、your 和 his 之后) a man's wife 老婆；妻子：*How's the missus* (= your wife)? 你老婆怎么样？ **2** (*informal*) (used especially by young people 尤为年轻人使用) girlfriend 女友：*My missus doesn't like computer games.* 我女友不喜欢玩电脑游戏。◇ *my current missus* 我的现任女友 **3** (*also* **mis·sis**) (*slang, becoming old-fashioned*) used by some people as a form of address to a woman whose name they do not know （称呼不知姓名的妇女）大姐：*Is this your bag, missus?* 大姐，这是你的袋子吗？

missy /ˈmɪsi/ *noun* used when talking to a young girl, especially to express anger or affection （表示生气或喜爱）小姐，丫头：*Don't you speak to me like that, missy!* 不许那样对我讲话，小丫头！

mist /mɪst/ *noun, verb*

■ ***noun*** **1** [U, C] a cloud of very small drops of water in the air just above the ground, that make it difficult to see 薄雾；水汽：*The hills were* ***shrouded in mist.*** 这些小山笼罩在薄雾之中。◇ *Early morning mist patches will soon clear.* 清晨弥漫着的水汽很快会散尽。◇ *The origins of the story are* ***lost in the mists of time*** (= forgotten because it happened such a long time ago). 这个故事的起源由于年代久远而变得模糊不清。◇ (*figurative*) *She gazed at the scene through a mist of tears.* 她泪眼模糊，凝视着面前的景象。➲ COLLOCATIONS AT WEATHER ➲ COMPARE FOG *n.* (1) ➲ SEE ALSO MISTY **2** [sing.] a fine spray of liquid, for example from an AEROSOL can 液体喷雾

■ ***verb*** **1** [T, I] **~ (sth) (up)** | **~ (over)** when sth such as glass **mists** or **is misted**, it becomes covered with very small drops of water, so that it is impossible to see through it （使）结满雾气（模糊不清）：*The windows were misted up with condensation.* 窗户上凝满了水珠，一片模糊。◇ *As he came in from the cold, his glasses misted up.* 他从寒冷的户外进来，眼镜马上蒙上了一层雾气。 **2** [I, T] if your eyes **mist** or sth **mists** them, they fill with tears （眼）含泪水；泪水模糊：**~ (over/up)** *Her eyes misted over as she listened to the speech.* 她听着演讲，眼中噙满了泪水。◇ **~ sth (up)** *Tears misted his eyes.* 泪水模糊了他的双眼。 **3** [T] **~ sth** to spray the leaves of a plant with very small drops of water 朝（植物）喷雾

mis·take 🔑 /mɪˈsteɪk/ *noun, verb*

■ ***noun*** **1** 🔑 an action or an opinion that is not correct, or that produces a result that you did not want （言语或行为上的）错误，失误：*It's easy to* ***make a mistake.*** 犯错误很容易。◇ *This letter is addressed to someone else—there must be some mistake.* 这封信是给别人的，一定是搞错了。◇ *It would be a mistake to ignore his opinion.* 忽略他的意见是不对的。◇ *Don't worry, we all* ***make mistakes.*** 没关系，我们都会犯错。◇ *You must try to* ***learn from your mistakes.*** 你得从所犯错误中吸取教训。◇ *Leaving school so young was the biggest mistake of my life.* 我一生中最大的错误就是那么年轻就离开了学校。◇ ***I made the mistake of giving him my address.*** 我真不该把我的地址给他。◇ *It was a big mistake on my part to have trusted her.* 我相信了她，这是我的一大错误。◇ *a* ***great/serious/terrible mistake*** 大错；严重错误 ◇ *It's* ***a common mistake*** (= one that a lot of people make). 这是常犯的错误。 **2** 🔑 a word, figure, etc. that is not said or written down correctly （用词或数字等上的）错误，口误，笔误 SYN **error**：*It's a*

M

common mistake among learners of English. 这是学英语的人常犯的错误。◇ The waiter **made a mistake (in)** adding up the bill. 服务员结账时算错了账。◇ Her essay is full of **spelling mistakes.** 她的文章到处都是拼写错误。

IDM **and 'no mistake** (*old-fashioned, especially BrE*) used to show that you are sure about the truth of what you have just said 准确无误；毫无疑问： *This is a strange business and no mistake.* 这确实是件怪事。 **by mi'stake** by accident; without intending to 错误地；无意中： *I took your bag instead of mine by mistake.* 我不巧错拿了你的包。 **,make no mi'stake (about sth)** used to emphasize what you are saying, especially when you want to warn sb about sth 别搞错；注意： *Make no mistake (about it), this is one crisis that won't just go away.* 要知道，这是一场不会自行消失的危机。 **in mi'stake for sth** thinking that sth is sth else 误以为是；错看成： *Children may eat pills in mistake for sweets.* 孩子可能会把药片错当成糖果吃。

▼ SYNONYMS 同义词辨析

mistake

error • inaccuracy • slip • howler • misprint

These are all words for a word, figure or fact that is not said, written down or typed correctly. 以上各词均指用词、数字、事实等的错误、口误、笔误。

mistake a word or figure that is not said or written down correctly 指用词或数字上的错误、口误、笔误： *It's a common mistake among learners of English.* 这是学英语的人常犯的错误。◇ *spelling mistakes* 拼写错误

error (*rather formal*) a word, figure, etc. that is not said or written down correctly 指用词、数字等的错误、口误、笔误： *There are too many errors in your work.* 你的工作失误太多。 NOTE **Error** is a more formal way of saying **mistake.** * error 为 mistake 的较正式用语。

inaccuracy (*rather formal*) a piece of information that is not exactly correct 指信息不准确、有误： *The article is full of inaccuracies.* 这篇文章里不准确的地方比比皆是。

slip a small mistake, usually made by being careless or not paying attention 指常因粗心或未予以重视造成的差错、疏漏、纰漏

howler (*informal, especially BrE*) a stupid mistake, especially in what sb says or writes 尤指言谈或行文中的愚蠢错误： *The report is full of howlers.* 这份报告错漏百出。 NOTE A **howler** is usually an embarrassing mistake which shows that the person who made it does not know sth that they really should know. * howler 通常指令人难堪的错误，表明犯错误者不知道应该知道的东西。

misprint a small mistake in a printed text 指印刷文本上的错误

PATTERNS

- a(n) mistake/error/inaccuracy/slip/howler/misprint **in** sth
- to **make** a(n) mistake/error/slip/howler
- to **contain/be full of** mistakes/errors/inaccuracies/howlers/misprints

■ *verb* (**mis·took** /mɪ'stʊk/, **mis·taken** /mɪ'steɪkən/) to not understand or judge sb/sth correctly 误会；误解；看错 SYN **misconstrue**: **~ sb/sth** *I admit that I mistook his intentions.* 我承认我误解了他的意图。◇ *There was no* **mistaking** (= it was impossible to mistake) *the bitterness in her voice.* 她的声音里流露出怨恨的情绪，这是很明显的。◇ **~ sb/sth as sb/sth** *I mistook her offer as a threat.* 我把她的好心错看成威胁了。◇ **~ what...** *Sorry—I mistook what you said.* 不好意思，我误解你的话了。

PHR V **mi'stake sb/sth for sb/sth** to think wrongly that sb/sth is sb/sth else 把…错当成 SYN **confuse**: *I think you must be mistaking me for someone else.* 我看你准是认错人了。

mis·taken /mɪ'steɪkən/ *adj.* **1** [not usually before noun] **~ (about sb/sth)** wrong in your opinion or judgement 错误；不正确： *You are completely mistaken about Jane.* 你对简的看法完全错了。◇ *Unless I'm very much mistaken, that's Paul's wife over there.* 要是我没太弄错的话，那边那个就是保罗的妻子。 **2** based on a wrong opinion or bad judgement 判断错误的；被误解的 SYN **misguided**: *mistaken views/ideas* 错误的观点／想法 ◇ *I told her my secret* **in the mistaken belief** *that I could trust her.* 我误以为可以相信她，就把我的秘密告诉了她。 ▶ **mis·taken·ly** *adv.*： *He mistakenly believed that his family would stand by him.* 他误以为他的家人会支持他。

mi,staken i'dentity *noun* [U] a situation in which you think wrongly that you recognize sb or have found the person you are looking for 认错人： *He was shot in what seems to have been* **a case of mistaken identity.** 他像是被人认错了而遭到枪击的。

mis·ter /'mɪstə(r)/ *noun* **1 Mister** the full form, not often used in writing, of the abbreviation *Mr* 先生（Mr 的全写，书写时不常用） **2** (*informal*) used, especially by children, to address a man whose name they do not know （儿童常用，称呼不知姓名的男子）先生： *Please, mister, can we have our ball back?* 求求你，先生，能把球还给我们吗？

mis·time /,mɪs'taɪm/ *verb* **~ sth** to do sth at the wrong time, especially when this makes sth bad or unpleasant happen 在不适当的时机做；选错…的时机： *The horse completely mistimed the jump and threw its rider.* 这匹马起跳的时机完全不对，把骑手摔了下来。 ▶ **mis·tim·ing** *noun* [U]： *The failure of the talks was mainly due to insensitivity and mistiming.* 会谈失败主要是由于反应迟钝和时机不对。

mis·tle thrush (*also* **mis·sel thrush**) /'mɪsl θrʌʃ/ *noun* a large THRUSH (= a type of bird) with spots on its front 槲鸫（前胸有斑点）

mistle·toe /'mɪsltəʊ; 'mɪzl-; *NAmE* -toʊ/ *noun* [U] a plant with small shiny white BERRIES that grows on other trees and is often used as a decoration at Christmas 槲寄生（结白色小浆果，寄生于其他树木，常用于圣诞节装饰）： *the tradition of kissing under the mistletoe* 在槲寄生枝下亲吻的习俗

mis·took PAST TENSE OF MISTAKE

mis·tral /'mɪstrəl; mɪ'strɑːl/ *noun* [sing.] a strong cold wind that blows through southern France, mainly in winter 密史脱拉风（法国南部主要出现于冬季的寒冷强风）

mis·treat /,mɪs'triːt/ *verb* **~ sb/sth** to treat a person or an animal in a cruel, unkind or unfair way 虐待 SYN **ill-treat, maltreat** ▶ **mis·treat·ment** *noun* [U]

mis·tress /'mɪstrəs/ *noun* **1** a man's (usually a married man's) **mistress** is a woman that he is having a regular sexual relationship with and who is not his wife 情妇 **2** (*BrE, old-fashioned*) a female teacher in a school, especially a private school （尤指私立学校的）女教师： *the Biology mistress* 生物学女教师 **3** (in the past) the female head of a house, especially one who employed servants （尤指旧时雇用仆人的）女主人，主妇： *the mistress of the house* 这房子的女主人 **4** the female owner of a dog or other animal （狗或其他动物的）女主人 **5** (*formal*) a woman who is in a position of authority or control, or who is highly skilled in sth 有权势的女子；女能人；女强人；女主宰： *She wants to be mistress of her own affairs* (= to organize her own life). 她希望自己的事自己做主。 ➲ COMPARE MASTER *n.*

mis·trial /,mɪs'traɪəl/ *noun* (*law* 律) **1** a trial that is not considered valid because of a mistake in the way it has been conducted （诉讼程序错误的）无效审判 **2** (*NAmE*) a trial in which the JURY cannot reach a decision （陪审团无法作出裁决的）未决审判

mis·trust /,mɪs'trʌst/ *verb, noun*

■ *verb* **~ sb/sth** to have no confidence in sb/sth because you think they may be harmful; to not trust sb/sth 猜疑；不信任 SYN **distrust** ➲ NOTE AT DISTRUST

■ *noun* [U, sing.] a feeling that you cannot trust sb/sth 猜

疑；疑虑；不信任 SYN **suspicion**: *a climate of mistrust and fear* 充满猜疑和恐惧的氛围 ◇ *She has a deep mistrust of strangers.* 她对陌生人的猜疑极深。▶ **mis·trust·ful** /-fl/ *adj.*: ~ (**of sb/sth**) *Some people are very mistrustful of computers.* 有些人对电脑很不放心。**mis·trust·ful·ly** /-fəli/ *adv.*

misty /ˈmɪsti/ *adj.* **1** with a lot of MIST 多雾的；薄雾笼罩的：*a misty morning* 薄雾弥漫的早晨 **2** not clear or bright 模糊的；不明晰的 SYN **blurred**: *misty memories* 朦胧的记忆 ◇ (*literary*) *His eyes grew misty* (= full of tears) *as he talked.* 他说话的时候双眼模糊了。

ˌmisty-ˈeyed *adj.* feeling full of emotion, as if you are going to cry （十分激动）泪眼蒙眬的

mis·un·der·stand /ˌmɪsʌndəˈstænd; *NAmE* -dərˈs-/ *verb* (**mis·un·der·stood**, **mis·un·der·stood** /-ˈstʊd/) [T, I] ~ (**sb/sth**) | ~ **what, how, etc.…** to fail to understand sb/sth correctly 误解；误会：*I completely misunderstood her intentions.* 我完全误会了她的意图。◇ *Don't misunderstand me—I am grateful for all you've done.* 别误解我的意思，我对你所做的一切都很感激。◇ *I thought he was her husband—I must have misunderstood.* 我以为他是她丈夫，我一定是误会了。

mis·un·der·stand·ing /ˌmɪsʌndəˈstændɪŋ; *NAmE* -dərˈs-/ *noun* **1** [U, C] a situation in which a comment, an instruction, etc. is not understood correctly 误解；误会：*There must be some misunderstanding—I thought I ordered the smaller model.* 一定是搞错了，我以为我订的是更小型号的。◇ ~ **of/about sth** *There is still a fundamental misunderstanding about the real purpose of this work.* 对于这项工作的真正目的，仍然存在着严重的误解。◇ ~ **between A and B** *All contracts are translated to avoid any misunderstanding between the companies.* 所有的合同都经过翻译，以避免公司间发生任何误解。 **2** [C] a slight disagreement or argument 意见不一；不和；争执：*We had a little misunderstanding over the bill.* 我们对这个提案的看法有点分歧。

mis·un·der·stood /ˌmɪsʌndəˈstʊd; *NAmE* -dərˈs-/ *adj.* having qualities that people do not see or fully understand 遭误解的；不为人理解的：*a much misunderstood illness* 一种遭到许多人误解的疾病 ◇ *She felt very alone and misunderstood.* 她觉得非常孤独，得不到别人的理解。

mis·use *noun, verb*

■ ***noun*** /ˌmɪsˈjuːs/ [U, C, usually sing.] (*formal*) the act of using sth in a dishonest way or for the wrong purpose 误用；滥用；盗用 SYN **abuse**: ***alcohol/drug misuse*** 酗酒；滥用药物 ◇ *the* ***misuse of power/authority*** 滥用职权

■ ***verb*** /ˌmɪsˈjuːz/ (*formal*) **1** ~ **sth** to use sth in the wrong way or for the wrong purpose 误用；滥用 SYN **abuse, ill-treat**: *individuals who misuse power for their own ends* 以权谋私的人 **2** ~ **sb** to treat sb badly and/or unfairly 虐待

mite /maɪt/ *noun* **1** a very small creature like a spider that lives on plants, animals, carpets, etc. 螨（状似蜘蛛的微小动物，在动植物、地毯等上生活）：*house dust mites* 房内的粉尘螨 ➲ SEE ALSO DUST MITE **2** a small child or animal, especially one that you feel sorry for （可怜的）小孩子，小动物：*Poor little mite!* 可怜的小家伙！ **3** (*old-fashioned*) a small amount of sth 少量：*The place looked* ***a mite*** (= a little) *expensive.* 这地方看上去稍微有点儿贵。

miter (*NAmE*) = MITRE

miti·gate /ˈmɪtɪɡeɪt/ *verb* ~ **sth** (*formal*) to make sth less harmful, serious, etc. 减轻；缓和 SYN **alleviate**: *action to mitigate poverty* 减轻贫穷的行动 ◇ *Soil erosion was mitigated by the planting of trees.* 土壤侵蚀的情况在经过植树后缓和了。

miti·gat·ing /ˈmɪtɪɡeɪtɪŋ/ *adj.* [only before noun] ~ **circumstances/factors** (*law* 律 or *formal*) circumstances or factors that provide a reason that explains sb's actions or a crime, and make them easier to understand so that the punishment may be less severe 可考虑从轻处置的情节（或因素） ➲ MORE LIKE THIS 32, page R28

miti·ga·tion /ˌmɪtɪˈɡeɪʃn/ *noun* [U] (*formal*) a reduction in how unpleasant, serious, etc. sth is 减轻；缓解

IDM **in mitiˈgation** (*law* 律) with the aim of making a crime seem less serious or easier to forgive 旨在减轻罪行；意在开脱罪责：*In mitigation, the defence lawyer said his client was seriously depressed at the time of the assault.* 为了减轻罪行，辩护律师说他的当事人在袭击人的时候精神极度压抑。

mi·to·chon·drion /ˌmaɪtəʊˈkɒndriən; *NAmE* ˌmaɪtoʊˈkɑːn-/ *noun* (*pl.* **mitochondria** /ˌmaɪtəʊˈkɒndriə; *NAmE* ˌmaɪtoʊˈkɑːn-/) (*biology* 生) a small part found in most cells, in which the energy in food is released （细胞内的）线粒体，粒线体 ▶ **mito·chon·drial** /-driəl/ *adj.*: *mitochondrial DNA* 线粒体 DNA

mi·tosis /maɪˈtəʊsɪs; *NAmE* -ˈtoʊs-/ *noun* [U] (*biology* 生) the process of cell division （细胞的）有丝分裂

mitre (*especially US* **miter**) /ˈmaɪtə(r)/ *noun, verb*

■ ***noun*** **1** a tall pointed hat worn by BISHOPS at special ceremonies as a symbol of their position and authority 主教冠 **2** (*also* **ˈmitre joint**) a corner joint, formed by two pieces of wood each cut at an angle, as in a picture frame 斜接头；阳角接 ➲ PICTURE AT DOVETAIL

■ ***verb*** ~ **sth** (*specialist*) to join two pieces of wood together with a mitre joint 斜接

mitt /mɪt/ *noun* **1** = MITTEN **2** (in BASEBALL 棒球) a large thick leather glove worn for catching the ball 接球手套；棒球手套 **3** [usually pl.] (*slang*) a hand 手：*I'd love to get my mitts on one of those.* 我很想得到一个那样的东西。

mit·ten /ˈmɪtn/ (*also* **mitt**) *noun* a type of glove that covers the four fingers together and the thumb separately 连指手套 ➲ VISUAL VOCAB PAGE V70

Mitty ➲ WALTER MITTY

mix 🔑 /mɪks/ *verb, noun*

■ ***verb***

• **COMBINE** 结合 **1** 🔑 [I, T] if two or more substances **mix** or you **mix** them, they combine, usually in a way that means they cannot easily be separated （使）混合，掺和，融合：*Oil and water do not mix.* 油和水不相融。◇ ~ **with sth** *Oil does not mix with water.* 油不融于水。◇ ~ **A and B** (**together**) *Mix all the ingredients together in a bowl.* 把所有的配料放在碗里，搅和一下。◇ *If you mix blue and yellow, you get green.* 蓝色和黄色相混合就是绿色。◇ ~ **A with B** *I don't like to* ***mix business with pleasure*** (= combine social events with doing business). 我不喜欢将社交活动和做生意混在一块儿。 **2** 🔑 [T] to prepare sth by combining two or more different substances 调配；配制：~ **sth** *With this range of paints, you can mix your own colours.* 用这一组油彩可以调配出你所需要的颜色。◇ ~ **sth for sb** *Why don't you mix a cocktail for our guests?* 你给客人调制鸡尾酒好吗？◇ ~ **sb sth** *Why don't you mix our guests a cocktail?* 你给客人调制鸡尾酒好吗？ **3** 🔑 [I] if two or more things, people or activities **do not mix**, they are likely to cause problems or danger if they are combined 相容；平安相处：*Children and fireworks don't mix.* 孩子不宜玩烟火。

• **MEET PEOPLE** 与人交往 **4** 🔑 [I] ~ (**with sb**) to meet and talk to different people, especially at social events 交往；相处；交际 SYN **socialize**: *They don't mix much with the neighbours.* 他们不怎么与邻居来往。

• **MUSIC/SOUNDS** 音乐；声音 **5** [T] ~ **sth** (*specialist*) to combine different recordings of voices and/or instruments to produce a single piece of music 混合录音；混录；混音

IDM **be/get mixed ˈup in sth** 🔑 to be/become involved in sth, especially sth illegal or dishonest 卷入（不正当的事）；与某事有牵连 **be/get mixed ˈup with sb** to be/become friendly with or involved with sb that other people do not approve of 与（不适合的人）交往；和某人厮混 **ˌmix and ˈmatch** to combine things in different ways for different purposes 混合重组；混合搭配：*You can mix and match courses to suit your requirements.* 你可以根据自己的要求将课程自由组合。➲ MORE LIKE THIS 13, page R26 **ˈmix it** (**with sb**) (*BrE*) (*NAmE* **ˌmix it ˈup** (**with sb**)) (*informal*) to argue with sb or cause trouble （与某人）吵架；找（某人的）茬

PHR V **ˌmix sth↔ˈin** (**with sth**) to add one substance to others, especially in cooking （烹调时）掺入，和入： *Mix the remaining cream in with the sauce.* 把剩下的奶油掺到调味酱里。 **'mix sth into sth** to combine one substance with others, especially in cooking （烹调时）掺和，将…和入；使与…混合： *Mix the fruit into the rest of the mixture.* 把水果和别的东西拌在一起。 **'mix sth into/to sth** to produce sth by combining two or more substances, especially in cooking （烹调时）将…混合制成 SYN **blend**: *Add the milk and mix to a smooth dough.* 加入牛奶再揉成光滑的面团。 **ˌmix sth↔'up** to change the order or arrangement of a group of things, especially by mistake or in a way that you do not want 弄错；弄乱 SYN **muddle**: *Someone has mixed up all the application forms.* 有人把申请表都弄乱了。 ➲ RELATED NOUN MIX-UP **ˌmix sb/sth 'up (with sb/sth)** to think wrongly that sb/sth is sb/sth else 误以为…是；弄错；搞错 SYN **confuse**: *I think you must be mixing me up with someone else.* 我觉得你一定是把我错当成别人了。 ➲ SEE ALSO MIXED UP

▼ SYNONYMS 同义词辨析

mix

stir • mingle • blend

These words all refer to substances, qualities, ideas or feelings combining or being combined. 以上各词均指物质、品质、想法或情感的混合、掺和、融合。

mix to combine two or more substances, qualities, ideas or feelings, usually in a way that means they cannot easily be separated; to be combined in this way 指（使）两种或以上物质、品质、想法或情感等混合、掺和、融合： *Mix all the ingredients together in a bowl.* 把所有的配料放在碗里搅和一下。 ◇ *Oil and water do not mix.* 油和水不相融。

stir to move a liquid or substance around, using a spoon or sth similar, in order to mix it thoroughly 指搅动、搅和、搅拌（液体或物质）： *She stirred her tea.* 她搅了搅茶。

mingle to combine or be combined 指（使）混合、掺和、融合 NOTE **Mingle** can be used to talk about sounds, colours, feelings, ideas, qualities or substances. It is used in written English to talk about how a scene or event appears to sb or how they experience it. * mingle 可用以指声音、颜色、情感、想法、品质或物质等交织在一起，用于书面语表示对某一场景或事件的感受或经历： *The sounds of laughter and singing mingled in the evening air.* 笑声和歌声交织在夜空中。 ◇ *He felt a kind of happiness mingled with regret.* 他感到既高兴又遗憾。

blend to mix two or more substances or flavours together; to be mixed together 指（使）两种或以上物质或味道混合、掺和： *Blend the flour with the milk to make a smooth paste.* 把面粉和牛奶调成均匀的面糊。

MIX OR BLEND? 用 mix 还是 blend?

If you **blend** things when you are cooking you usually combine them more completely than if you just **mix** them. **Mix** can be used to talk about colours, feelings or qualities as well as food and substances. In this meaning **blend** is mostly used in the context of cooking. It is also used to talk about art, music, fashion, etc. with the meaning of 'combine in an attractive way'. 烹饪时用 blend 表示把各种材料完全掺和到一起，用 mix 只表示将这些东西混合在一起。mix 可指将食物、物质混合在一起，也可指颜色、情感、品质融合在一起。在这一含义中，blend 主要用于烹饪语境。blend 亦可表示艺术、音乐、时尚等元素和谐地融合在一起。

PATTERNS

- to mix/mingle/blend (sth) **with** sth
- to mix/stir/mingle/blend sth **into** sth
- to mix/stir/mingle/blend sth **together**
- to mix/stir/blend **ingredients**
- to mix/mingle/blend **flavours**
- to mix/blend **colours**
- mixed/mingled **feelings**
- to mix/stir/blend sth **thoroughly/well/gently**

■ ***noun***

• **COMBINATION** 结合 **1** [C, usually sing.] a combination of different people or things 混合；混杂；结合 SYN **blend**: *a school with a good social mix of children* 有适当比例的不同社会阶层的孩子上学的学校 ◇ *The town offers a fascinating mix of old and new.* 这个小镇新旧结合，很有魅力。◇ *a pair of wool mix socks* (= made of wool and other materials) 一双羊毛混纺袜子 **2** [C, U] a combination of things that you need to make sth, often sold as a powder to which you add water, etc. 配料，混合料（常为粉状）： *a cake mix* 蛋糕粉 ◇ *cement mix* 水泥配料

• **IN POPULAR MUSIC** 流行音乐 **3** [C] = REMIX **4** [sing.] the particular way that instruments and voices are arranged in a piece of music 混录；混音 **5** [C] an arrangement of several songs or pieces of music into one continuous piece, especially for dancing 乐曲组合；连奏；连唱

mixed /mɪkst/ *adj.* **1** having both good and bad qualities or feelings 混合的；混杂的： *The weather has been very mixed recently.* 最近天气总是阴晴不定。◇ *I still have **mixed feelings** about going to Brazil* (= I am not sure what to think). 去不去巴西，我仍然拿不定主意。◇ *The play was given a **mixed reception** by the critics* (= some liked it, some did not). 剧评人对这出戏的评价毁誉参半。◇ *British athletes had mixed fortunes in yesterday's competition.* 英国运动员在昨天的比赛中有输有赢。 **2** [only before noun] consisting of different kinds of people, for example, people from different races and cultures 人员混杂的；由不同种族的人组成的： *a mixed community* 多文化的社区 ◇ *people of mixed race* 不同种族的人 ◇ *a mixed marriage* (= between two people of different races or religions) 异族（或异教）通婚 **3** [only before noun] consisting of different types of the same thing 混合的；掺杂在一起的： *a mixed salad* 什锦色拉 **4** [usually before noun] of or for both males and females 男女混杂的；男女混合的： *a mixed school* 男女同校的学校 ◇ *I'd rather not talk about it in mixed company.* 在男女混杂的场合，我不愿意谈论这件事。

ˌmixed-a'bility *adj.* [usually before noun] with or for students who have different levels of ability 学生能力不一的；为各种水平的学生的： *a mixed-ability class* 学生能力水平不一的班级 ◇ *mixed-ability teaching* 针对能力参差不齐的学生的教学

ˌmixed 'bag *noun* [sing.] (*informal*) a collection of things or people of very different types 混合体；大杂烩

ˌmixed 'blessing *noun* [usually sing.] something that has advantages and disadvantages 利弊并存之事；祸福参半之事

ˌmixed 'doubles *noun* [U+sing./pl. v.] (in TENNIS, etc. 网球等) a game in which a man and a woman play together against another man and woman 混合双打

ˌmixed e'conomy *noun* an economic system in a country in which some companies are owned by the state and some are private 混合经济（国有与私营企业并存的经济体系）

ˌmixed 'farming *noun* [U] a system of farming in which farmers both grow crops and keep animals （耕种和畜牧的）混合农业

ˌmixed 'grill *noun* (*BrE*) a hot dish of different types of meat and vegetables that have been GRILLED 烤杂排： *a mixed grill of bacon, sausages, tomatoes and mushrooms* 由咸熏肉、香肠、番茄和蘑菇做成的烤杂排

ˌmixed 'metaphor *noun* a combination of two or more METAPHORS or idioms that produces a ridiculous effect, for example, 'He put his foot down with a firm hand.' 混合隐喻；多重隐喻

ˌmixed 'number *noun* (*mathematics* 数) a number consisting of a whole number and a PROPER FRACTION, for example 3¼ 带分数

ˌmixed-'race *adj.* (*NAmE also* **bi·racial**) concerning or containing members of two different races 混血的： *a*

mixed-race child (= with parents of different races) 混血儿 HELP You can also say *a child of mixed race.* 表示"混血儿"也可以说 a child of mixed race。 ➲ SEE ALSO RACE *n.* (4)

ˌmixed ˈup *adj.* (*informal*) confused because of mental, emotional or social problems 迷茫的： ***a mixed-up kid/teenager*** 迷茫的孩子 / 少年 ➲ WORDFINDER NOTE AT YOUNG

mixer /ˈmɪksə(r)/ *noun* **1** a machine or device used for mixing things 搅拌器；混合器： *a food mixer* 食物搅拌器 ◇ (*BrE*) *a mixer tap* (= one in which hot and cold water can be mixed together before it comes out of the pipe) 冷热水混合龙头 ➲ SEE ALSO CEMENT MIXER **2** a drink such as fruit juice that is not alcoholic and that can be mixed with alcohol 调酒用的饮料： *low-calorie mixers* 低热量调酒配料 **3** (*specialist*) a device used for mixing together different sound or picture signals in order to produce a single sound or picture; a person whose job is to operate this device 声音（或图像）混合器；声音（或图像）混合操作员

IDM **a good/bad ˈmixer** a person who finds it easy/difficult to talk to people they do not know, for example at a party 擅长 / 不擅长交际的人

mixie /ˈmɪksi/ *noun* (*IndE*) an electric machine used for mixing food or liquid 食物搅拌机

ˈmixing bowl *noun* a large bowl for mixing food in （混合食物的）大碗，海碗

ˈmixing desk *noun* a piece of electronic equipment for mixing sounds, used especially when recording music or to improve its sound after recording it 混录台；调音台

mix·ture 🔑 /ˈmɪkstʃə(r)/ *noun* **1** 🔑 [C, usually sing.] a combination of different things 混合；结合体： *The city is a mixture of old and new buildings.* 这座城市是新老建筑兼而有之。 ◇ *We listened to the news with a mixture of surprise and horror.* 我们怀着惊恐交加的心情收听了这则消息。 **2** 🔑 [C, U] a substance made by mixing other substances together 混合物： *cake mixture* 蛋糕糊 ◇ *Add the eggs to the mixture and beat well.* 将鸡蛋加进混合料中，搅拌均匀。 ➲ SEE ALSO COUGH MIXTURE **3** [C] (*specialist*) a combination of two or more substances that mix together without any chemical reaction taking place 混合物；集合体 ➲ COMPARE COMPOUND *n.* (2) **4** [U] the act of mixing different substances together 混合

ˈmix-up *noun* (*informal*) a situation that is full of confusion, especially because sb has made a mistake 混乱；杂乱 SYN **muddle**: *There has been a mix-up over the dates.* 日期完全搅乱了。

miz·zen (*also* **mizen**) /ˈmɪzn/ *noun* (*specialist*) **1** (*also* **miz·zen·mast** /ˈmɪznmɑːst; *NAmE* -mæst/) the MAST of a ship that is behind the main mast 后桅；次桅 **2** (*also* **miz·zen·sail** /ˈmɪznseɪl/) a sail on the mizzen of a ship 后桅纵帆；后帆

ml *abbr.* (*pl.* **ml** or **mls**) (in writing 书写形式) MILLILITRE 毫升： *25ml water* * 25 毫升水

MLA /ˌem el ˈeɪ/ *noun* (in Canada and Northern Ireland 加拿大和北爱尔兰) Member of the Legislative Assembly 立法会议员

ˈm-learning (*also* **ˌmobile ˈlearning**) *noun* [U] a system of learning that uses mobile devices such as mobile/cell phones, small computers that can be carried, etc. so that people can learn anywhere at any time 移动学习（利用移动电子设备随时随地学习） ➲ SEE ALSO E-LEARNING

M'lud /məˈlʌd/ *noun* (*BrE*) used when speaking to the judge in court （法庭用语）法官大人： *My client pleads guilty, M'lud.* 法官大人，我的当事人认罪。

mm *abbr., exclamation*

■ ***abbr.*** (in writing 书写形式) MILLIMETRE 毫米： *rainfall 6mm* * 6 毫米的降雨量 ◇ *a 35mm camera* * 35 毫米照相机

■ ***exclamation*** (*also* **mmm**) the way of writing the sound /m/ that people make to show that they are listening to sb or that they agree, they are thinking, they like sth, they are not sure, etc. 唔，嗯（书写中表示同意、思考中、喜欢、犹豫等发出的声音）： *Mm, I know what you mean.* 唔，我知道你的意思。 ◇ *Mm, what lovely cake!* 哇，好棒的蛋糕啊！ ◇ *Mmm, I'm not so sure that's a good idea.* 嗯，我不知道这想法行不行。 ➲ MORE LIKE THIS 2, page R25

MMR /ˌem em ˈɑː(r)/ *abbr.* MEASLES, MUMPS, RUBELLA 麻疹－腮腺炎－风疹： *an MMR jab* (= a VACCINE given to small children to prevent these three diseases) 麻风腮疫苗

MMS /ˌem em ˈes/ *noun* [U, C] the abbreviation for 'Multimedia Messaging Service' (a system for sending colour pictures and sounds as well as short written messages from one mobile/cell phone to another) （手机）多媒体消息服务，彩信业务（全写为 Multimedia Messaging Service）： *an MMS message* 多媒体短信 ◇ *He sent me an MMS.* 他给我发了条彩信。

MNA /ˌem en ˈeɪ/ *noun* (*CanE*) Member of the National Assembly 国会议员

mne·mon·ic /nɪˈmɒnɪk; *NAmE* -ˈmɑːn-/ *noun* a word, sentence, poem, etc. that helps you to remember sth 帮助记忆的词句（或诗歌等）；助记符号 ▶ **mne·mon·ic** *adj.* [only before noun]: *a mnemonic device* 记忆手段

MO /ˌem ˈəʊ; *NAmE* ˈoʊ/ *noun* **1** (*BrE*) MEDICAL OFFICER （某机构的）专职医生 **2** (*also* **M.O.**) MODUS OPERANDI 工作方法

mo /məʊ; *NAmE* moʊ/ *noun* [sing.] (*BrE, informal*) a very short period of time 顷刻；瞬间 SYN **moment**: *See you in a mo!* 一会儿见！

moa /ˈməʊə; *NAmE* ˈmoʊə/ *noun* a large bird that could not fly, that was found in New Zealand but is now EXTINCT (= no longer exists) 恐鸟（曾发现于新西兰，不能飞行，已灭绝）

moan /məʊn; *NAmE* moʊn/ *verb, noun*

■ ***verb*** **1** [I, T] (of a person 人) to make a long deep sound, usually expressing unhappiness, suffering or sexual pleasure 呻吟 SYN **groan**: *The injured man was lying on the ground, moaning.* 受伤的人躺在地上呻吟着。 ◇ **~ in/with sth** *to moan in/with pain* 痛苦地呻吟 ◇ **+ speech** *'I might never see you again,' she moaned.* 她呻吟着说："我可能再也见不到你了。" **2** [I, T] **~ (at sb)** (*informal*) to complain about sth in a way that other people find annoying 抱怨 SYN **grumble, whine**: **~ (on) (about sth) (to sb)** *What are you moaning on about now?* 你在抱怨什么呢？ ◇ **~ (at sb) (about sth)** *They're always **moaning and groaning** about how much they have to do.* 他们总是牢骚满腹，抱怨有很多事要做。 ◇ **~ that...** *Bella moaned that her feet were cold.* 贝拉抱怨说她双脚冷。 ➲ SYNONYMS AT COMPLAIN **3** [I] (*literary*) (especially of the wind 尤指风) to make a long deep sound 呼啸；发出萧萧声 ▶ **moan·er** *noun*

■ ***noun*** **1** [C] a long deep sound, usually expressing unhappiness, suffering or sexual pleasure 呻吟声 SYN **groan**: *a **low moan of despair/anguish*** 在绝望 / 痛苦中发出的低沉的呻吟声 **2** [C] (*informal*) a complaint about sth 抱怨： *We had a good moan about work.* 我们对工作大大地抱怨了一番。 ◇ *His letters are full of the usual moans and groans.* 他的来信总是满纸怨言。 **3** [sing.] (*literary*) a long deep sound, especially the sound that is made by the wind （尤指风的）呼啸声，萧萧声

moat /məʊt; *NAmE* moʊt/ *noun* a deep wide channel that was dug around a castle, etc. and filled with water to make it more difficult for enemies to attack 护城河 ➲ VISUAL VOCAB PAGE V15 ▶ **moat·ed** *adj.* [usually before noun]: *a moated manor house* 周围有壕沟的庄园宅第

mob /mɒb; *NAmE* mɑːb/ *noun, verb*

■ ***noun*** **1** [C, sing.+sing./pl. v.] a large crowd of people, especially one that may become violent or cause trouble 人群；（尤指）暴民： *an **angry/unruly mob*** 愤怒的 / 失控的暴民 ◇ *The mob was/were preparing to storm the building.* 聚集的群众准备猛攻大楼。 ◇ *an excited mob of fans* 一群激动的球迷 ◇ ***mob rule*** (= a situation in which a mob has control, rather than people in authority) 暴民统治 ➲ SEE ALSO LYNCH MOB **2** [C, usually sing.] (*informal*) a group of

M

people who are similar in some way 一群；一帮 SYN gang: *All the usual mob were there.* 所有帮派成员都在那里。 **3 the Mob** [sing.] (*informal*) the people involved in organized crime; the MAFIA 犯罪团伙；黑手党 **4** [C] (*AustralE, NZE*) a group of animals （动物的）群 SYN **flock, herd**: *a mob of cattle* 一群牛 IDM SEE HEAVY *adj.*

■ *verb* (**-bb-**) [usually passive] **1 ~ sth** if a crowd of birds or animals **mob** another bird or animal, they gather round it and attack it （鸟群或兽群）围攻，聚众袭击 **2 ~ sb** if a person is **mobbed** by a crowd of people, the crowd gathers round them in order to see them and try and get their attention （人群）围聚，围拢 SYN **besiege**

'mob cap *noun* a light cotton cap covering all the hair, worn by women in the 18th and 19th centuries （18、19 世纪的）头巾式女帽

mo·bile /ˈməʊbaɪl; *NAmE* ˈmoʊbl/ *adj., noun*

■ *adj.* **1** [usually before noun] that is not fixed in one place and can be moved easily and quickly 非固定的；可移动的：*mobile equipment* 可移动装备 ◇ *a **mobile shop/library*** (= one inside a vehicle) 流动商店 / 图书馆 ➲ COMPARE STATIONARY (1) **2** [not usually before noun] (of a person 人) able to move or travel around easily 行动方便；腿脚灵便：*a kitchen especially designed for the elderly or people who are less mobile* 专门为上了年纪或行动不便的人设计的厨房 ◇ *You really need to be mobile* (= have a car) *if you live in the country.* 如果你住在乡村，你确实要有一辆汽车。 OPP **immobile** **3** (of people 人) able to change your social class, your job or the place where you live easily 易于变换社会阶层（或工作、住处）的；流动的：*a highly mobile workforce* (= people who can move easily from place to place) 具有很强流动性的劳动力 ➲ SEE ALSO UPWARDLY MOBILE **4** (of a face or its features 脸或面部特征) changing shape or expression easily and often 多变的；易变的

■ *noun* **1** = MOBILE PHONE：*Call me on my mobile.* 打手机给我。 ◇ *What's your mobile number?* 你的手机号码是多少？ ◇ *the mobile networks* (= companies that provide mobile phone services) 移动电话网络公司 **2** a decoration made from wire, etc. that is hung from the ceiling and that has small objects hanging from it which move when the air around them moves 风铃；（可随风摆动的）悬挂饰物

,mobile de'vice *noun* any small computing device that will fit into your pocket, such as a SMARTPHONE 移动电子装置（如智能手机）

,mobile 'home *noun* **1** (*especially NAmE*) (*also* **trailer** *NAmE*) a small building for people to live in that is made in a factory and moved to a permanent place 活动住房 ➲ VISUAL VOCAB PAGE V16 **2** (*BrE*) (*NAmE* **trailer**) a large CARAVAN that can be moved, sometimes with wheels, that is usually parked in one place and used for living in 旅游房车；（拖车式）活动房屋

,mobile 'learning *noun* [U] = M-LEARNING

,mobile 'library (*BrE*) (*NAmE* **book·mobile**) *noun* a van/truck that contains a library and travels from place to place so that people in different places can borrow books 流动图书馆；图书馆车

,mobile 'phone (*also* **mo·bile**) (*both BrE*) (*also* **cell phone**, **'cellular phone**, *informal* **cell** *NAmE, BrE*) *noun* a telephone that does not have wires and works by radio, that you can carry with you and use anywhere 移动电话；手机：*Please make sure all mobile phones are switched off during the performance.* 请确保演出时所有手机关机。 ➲ COLLOCATIONS AT PHONE

mo·bil·ity /məʊˈbɪləti; *NAmE* moʊ-/ *noun* [U] **1** the ability to move easily from one place, social class, or job to another（住处、社会阶层、职业方面的）流动能力：***social/geographical/career mobility*** 社会地位 / 区域 / 职业流动性 ➲ SEE ALSO UPWARD MOBILITY at UPWARDLY MOBILE **2** the ability to move or travel around easily 移动的能力；易于行走的能力：*An electric wheelchair has given her greater mobility.* 电动轮椅让她行动起来方便多了。 ➲ WORDFINDER NOTE AT OLD

mo'bility scooter *noun* a type of light electric vehicle with a seat, a bar for steering and three or more wheels, designed for people who are unable to move easily from one place to another because they are elderly, disabled, etc. 电动代步车，电动踏板车（为老年人、残疾人等行动不便者设计）

mo·bil·ize (*BrE also* **-ise**) /ˈməʊbəlaɪz; *NAmE* ˈmoʊ-/ *verb* **1** [T, I] ~ (**sb**) to work together in order to achieve a particular aim; to organize a group of people to do this 组织；鼓动；动员 SYN **rally**: *The unions mobilized thousands of workers in a protest against the cuts.* 各级工会组织了数千名工人抗议削减工资。 **2** [T] **~ sth** to find and start to use sth that is needed for a particular purpose 调动；调用 SYN **marshal**: *They were unable to mobilize the resources they needed.* 他们无法调用他们需要的资源。 **3** [T, I] ~ (**sb/sth**) if a country **mobilizes** its army, or if a country or army **mobilizes**, it makes itself ready to fight in a war （战时）动员：*The troops were ordered to mobilize.* 部队接到了动员令。 ➲ COMPARE DEMOBILIZE ▶ **mo·bil·iza·tion, -isa·tion** /ˌməʊbəlaɪˈzeɪʃn; *NAmE* ˌmoʊbələˈz-/ *noun* [U]

Möbius strip 麦比乌斯带

Mö·bius strip (*also* **Moe·bius strip**) /ˈmɜːbiəs strɪp/ *noun* a surface with one continuous side, formed by joining the ends of a strip of material after twisting one end through 180 degrees 麦比乌斯带（只有一面的连续曲面，把一条带子的一端扭转 180 度后将两端连接起来构成）

mob·log /ˈmɒblɒg; ˈməʊ-; *NAmE* ˈmɑːblɑːg/ *noun* (*computing* 计, *BrE*) a website that belongs to a particular person who puts pictures and other material from a mobile/cell phone on it 移动博客，手机博客（通过手机将图片等上传至网站）

mob·ster /ˈmɒbstə(r); *NAmE* ˈmɑːb-/ *noun* a member of a group of people who are involved in organized crime 暴徒；犯罪分子；匪徒

moc·ca·sin /ˈmɒkəsɪn; *NAmE* ˈmɑːk-/ *noun* a flat shoe that is made from soft leather and has large STITCHES around the front, of a type originally worn by Native Americans 莫卡辛软皮鞋（原为美洲土著所穿）；软帮皮鞋 ➲ VISUAL VOCAB PAGE V69

mocha /ˈmɒkə; *NAmE* ˈmoʊkə/ *noun* **1** [U] a type of coffee of very good quality 摩卡咖啡；优等咖啡 **2** [C, U] a drink made or flavoured with this, often with chocolate added 加巧克力的摩卡咖啡饮料

mock /mɒk; *NAmE* mɑːk/ *verb, adj., noun*

■ *verb* **1** [T, I] ~ (**sb/sth**) | ~ (**sb**) + **speech** to laugh at sb/sth in an unkind way, especially by copying what they say or do 嘲笑；（模仿）嘲弄 SYN **make fun of sb/sth**: *He's always mocking my French accent.* 他总是嘲笑我的法国口音。 ◇ *The other children mocked her, laughing behind their hands.* 其他孩子学她的样子，用手捂着嘴笑。 ◇ *You can mock, but at least I'm willing to have a try!* 你可以嘲笑我，但我至少愿意试一试。 **2** [T] **~ sth** (*formal*) to show no respect for sth 不尊重；蔑视：*The new exam mocked the needs of the majority of children.* 新的考试无视大多数孩子的需求。 ▶ **mock·er** *noun*

■ *adj.* [only before noun] **1** not sincere 虚假的；不诚实的 SYN **sham**: ***mock horror/surprise*** 假装恐惧；故作惊讶 **2** that is a copy of sth; not real 模仿的；模拟的：*a mock election* 模拟选举 ◇ *a **mock interview/examination*** (= used to practise for the real one) 模拟面试 / 考试

■ *noun* (*informal*) (in Britain) a practice exam that you do before the official one （英国）模拟考试：*The mocks are* in November. 模拟考试在 11 月进行。◇ *What did you get in the mock?* 你的模拟考试得了多少分？

mock·ers /ˈmɒkəz; *NAmE* ˈmɑːkərz/ *noun* [pl.]
IDM **put the ˈmockers on sth/sb** (*BrE, informal*) to stop sth from happening; to bring bad luck to sth/sb 使（活动等）告吹；使倒霉：*We were going to have a barbecue but the rain put the mockers on that idea.* 我们打算露天烧烤，但因为下雨，计划泡汤了。

mock·ery /ˈmɒkəri; *NAmE* ˈmɑːk-/ *noun* **1** [U] comments or actions that are intended to make sb/sth seem ridiculous 嘲笑；愚弄 **SYN** **ridicule, scorn**: *She couldn't stand any more of their mockery.* 她再也无法忍受他们的愚弄了。**2** [sing.] (*disapproving*) an action, a decision, etc. that is a failure and that is not as it is supposed to be 笑柄；被嘲笑的对象 **SYN** **travesty**: *It was a mockery of a trial.* 这次审判实在可笑。
IDM **make a ˈmockery of sth** to make sth seem ridiculous or useless 取笑；愚弄；嘲笑：*The trial made a mockery of justice.* 这次审判是对正义的嘲弄。

mock·ing /ˈmɒkɪŋ; *NAmE* ˈmɑːk-/ *adj.* (of behaviour, an expression, etc. 行为、脸色等) showing that you think sb/sth is ridiculous 嘲笑的；嘲弄的；愚弄的 **SYN** **contemptuous**: *a mocking smile* 嘲弄的微笑 ◇ *Her voice was faintly mocking.* 她的声音略带一丝嘲弄。▶ **mock·ing·ly** *adv.*

mock·ing·bird /ˈmɒkɪŋbɜːd; *NAmE* ˈmɑːkɪŋbɜːrd/ *noun* a grey and white American bird that can copy the songs of other birds 嘲鸫（美洲鸣禽，能模仿别种鸟的鸣叫）

mock·ney /ˈmɒkni; *NAmE* ˈmɑːkni/ *noun* [U] (*BrE, informal, often disapproving*) a way of speaking English by educated people from London which copies the words and sounds of COCKNEY speech (= a way of speaking typical of the East End of London)（英国受过教育的人中）仿伦敦东区口音：*She speaks in this ridiculous mockney accent.* 她模仿伦敦东区人的口音拿腔拿调地说话。 ➲ MORE LIKE THIS 1, page R25

ˈmock-up *noun* a model or a copy of sth, often the same size as it, that is used for testing, or for showing people what the real thing will look like 实体模型；实尺寸模型

MOD /ˌem əʊ ˈdiː; *NAmE* oʊ/ *abbr.* Ministry of Defence (the government department in Britain that is responsible for defence)（英国）国防部

mod /mɒd; *NAmE* mɑːd/ *noun* a member of a group of young people, especially in Britain in the 1960s, who wore neat, fashionable clothes and rode MOTOR SCOOTERS 摩登派青年（尤指 20 世纪 60 年代英国的穿着时髦整洁、骑小型摩托车的青年）➲ COMPARE ROCKER (3)

modal /ˈməʊdl; *NAmE* ˈmoʊdl/ (*also* **modal ˈverb, modal auˈxiliary, modal auˈxiliary verb**) *noun* (*grammar* 语法) a verb such as *can, may* or *will* that is used with another verb (not a modal) to express possibility, permission, intention, etc. 情态动词（如 can、may 或 will 等，和实义动词连用表示可能、许可、意图等）▶ **modal** *adj.* ➲ COMPARE AUXILIARY *n.* (1)

mo·dal·ity /məʊˈdæləti; *NAmE* moʊˈd-/ *noun* (*pl.* **-ies**) **1** [C] (*formal*) the particular way in which sth exists, is experienced or is done 形式；样式；方式；形态：*They are researching a different modality of treatment for the disease.* 他们正在研究这种疾病的另一种疗法。**2** [U] (*linguistics* 语言) the idea expressed by modals 情态 **3** [C] (*biology* 生) the kind of senses that the body uses to experience things 感觉模式；感觉形式：*the visual and auditory modalities* 视觉和听觉

mod cons /ˌmɒd ˈkɒnz; *NAmE* ˌmɑːd ˈkɑːnz/ *noun* [pl.] (*BrE, informal*) (especially in advertisements 尤用于广告) the things in a house or flat/apartment that make living there easier and more comfortable 现代化的生活设备

mod·ding /ˈmɒdɪŋ; *NAmE* ˈmɑːdɪŋ/ *noun* [U] (*computing* 计, *informal*) the activity of changing a piece of computer equipment or a computer program so that it works in a way that was not intended by the producer（电脑设备的）改装；（电脑程序的）改编：*There are stiff penalties for illegal modding.* 非法改装会受到重罚。▶ **mod** /mɒd; *NAmE* mɑːd/ *verb* (**-dd-**): ~ **sth** *a specially modded system* 经特别改编的系统

mode **AW** /məʊd; *NAmE* moʊd/ *noun* **1** [C] a particular way of doing sth; a particular type of sth 方式；风格；样式：*a mode of communication* 交流方式 ◇ *a mode of behaviour* 行为模式 ◇ *environment-friendly modes of transport* 环保型的运输模式 **2** [C, U] the way in which a piece of equipment is set to perform a particular task（设备的）模式，工作状态：*Switch the camera into the automatic mode.* 将照相机调到自动拍摄模式。**3** [U] a particular way of feeling or behaving（情感或行为的）状态，状况：*to be in holiday mode* 处于假日状态 **4** [C, usually sing.] a particular style or fashion in clothes, art, etc.（衣着、艺术等的）形式，风格：*a pop video made by a director who really understands the mode* 由真正了解流行风格的导演执导的流行音乐录像带 ➲ SEE ALSO À LA MODE, MODISH **5** [sing.] (*specialist*) a set of notes in music which form a SCALE（音乐的）调式：***major/minor mode*** 大调 / 小调调式 **6** [sing.] (*mathematics* 数) the value that appears most frequently in a series of numbers 众数（一组数字中出现次数最多的数）

model 🔑 /ˈmɒdl; *NAmE* ˈmɑːdl/ *noun, verb*
■ ***noun***
• **SMALL COPY 模型** **1** 🔑 a copy of sth, usually smaller than the original object（依照实物按比例制成的）模型：*a **working model*** (= one in which the parts move) *of a fire engine* 消防车的活动模型 ◇ *a model aeroplane* 飞机模型 ◇ *The architect had produced a **scale model** of the proposed shopping complex.* 建筑师为拟建的购物中心做了一个比例模型。➲ VISUAL VOCAB PAGE V45
• **DESIGN 设计** **2** 🔑 a particular design or type of product 样式；设计；型：*The latest models will be on display at the motor show.* 最新的车型将会在这次汽车展上展出。
• **DESCRIPTION OF SYSTEM 体系描述** **3** a simple description of a system, used for explaining how sth works or calculating what might happen, etc.（用于示范运作方法等的）模型：*a mathematical model for determining the safe level*

▼ **GRAMMAR POINT 语法说明**

modal verbs

- The **modal verbs** are **can, could, may, might, must, ought to, shall, should, will** and **would. Dare, need, have to** and **used to** also share some of the features of modal verbs. * can、could、may、might、must、ought to、shall、should、will 和 would 均为情态动词。dare、need、have to 和 used to 亦具有情态动词的某些特性。
- Modal verbs have only one form. They have no *-ing* or *-ed* forms and do not add *-s* to the 3rd person singular form. 情态动词只有一种形式，没有 -ing 或 -ed 形式，第三人称单数也不加 -s：*He can speak three languages.* 他会说三种语言。◇ *She will try and visit tomorrow.* 她明天将设法去参观。
- Modal verbs are followed by the infinitive of another verb without **to**. The exceptions are **ought to, have to** and **used to**. 情态动词后跟不带 to 的动词不定式，但 ought to、have to 和 used to 例外：*You must find a job.* 你必须找到一份工作。◇ *You ought to stop smoking.* 你应当戒烟。◇ *I used to smoke but I gave up two years ago.* 我过去抽烟，但两年前就戒了。
- Questions are formed without **do/does** in the present, or **did** in the past. 疑问句现在时不用 do / does，过去时不用 did：*Can I invite Mary?* 我可以邀请玛丽吗？◇ *Should I have invited Mary?* 我本该邀请玛丽吗？
- Negative sentences are formed with **not** or the short form **-n't** and do not use **do/does** or **did**. 否定句用 not 或简约式 -n't，不用 do / does 或 did。

You will find more help with how to use modal verbs at the dictionary entries for each verb. 情态动词的不同用法可参考本词典里各情态动词词条。

M

of *pesticides in food* 测算食物中农药的安全含量的数学模型 ➲ COLLOCATIONS AT SCIENTIFIC

• EXAMPLE TO COPY 可仿效的样板 **4** something such as a system that can be copied by other people 样本；范例：*The nation's constitution provided a model that other countries followed.* 这个国家的宪法成了别国仿效的范例。**5** (*approving*) a person or thing that is considered an excellent example of sth 模范；典型：*It was a model of clarity.* 这是表达清晰的范例。◇ *a model student* 模范生 ◇ *a model farm* (= one that has been specially designed to work well) 示范农场 ➲ SEE ALSO ROLE MODEL

• FASHION 时装 **6** a person whose job is to wear and show new styles of clothes and be photographed wearing them 模特儿：*a fashion model* 时装模特儿 ◇ *a male model* 男模特儿

• FOR ARTIST 艺术家的 **7** a person who is employed to be painted, drawn, photographed, etc. by an artist or photographer 模特儿

■ *verb* (-ll-, *especially US* -l-)

• WORK AS MODEL 做模特儿 **1** [I] to work as a model for an artist or in the fashion industry 做模特儿

• CLOTHES 衣服 **2** [T] ~ **sth** to wear clothes in order to show them to people who might want to buy them（向顾客）穿戴展示：*The wedding gown is being modelled for us by the designer's daughter.* 结婚礼服正由设计者的女儿穿在身上给我们看。

• CREATE COPY 复制 **3** [T] ~ **sth** to create a copy of an activity, a situation, etc. so that you can study it before dealing with the real thing 将…做成模型；复制 SYN **simulate**: *The program can model a typical home page for you.* 这个程序可以使用模板帮你制作一个标准的主页。

• CLAY, ETC. 黏土等 **4** [T] ~ **sth** to shape CLAY, etc. in order to make sth 将（黏土等）做成模型：*a statue modelled in bronze* 青铜像 ➲ MORE LIKE THIS 36, page R29

PHR V **'model yourself on sb** to copy the behaviour, style, etc. of sb you like and respect in order to be like them 仿效；以某人为榜样：*As a politician, he modelled himself on Churchill.* 作为一名从政者，他以丘吉尔为榜样。 **'model sth on/after sth** to make sth so that it looks, works, etc. like sth else 模仿；仿照：*The country's parliament is modelled on the British system.* 这个国家的议会是模仿英国的体制建立的。

'model home (*NAmE*) (*BrE* **'show house, 'show home**) *noun* a house in a group of new houses that has been painted and filled with furniture, so that people who might want to buy one of the houses can see what they will be like 样品房，样板间（供购买房子的顾客参观）

mod·el·ler (*especially US* **mod·el·er**) /'mɒdələ(r); *NAmE* 'mɑːd-/ *noun* **1** a person who makes models of objects （实物）模型制作者 **2** a person who makes a simple description of a system or a process that can be used to explain it, etc. 系统模型制作者；系统模型设计者

mod·el·ling (*especially US* **mod·el·ing**) /'mɒdəlɪŋ; *NAmE* 'mɑːd-/ *noun* [U] **1** the work of a fashion model（时装）模特儿工作，模特儿表演：*a career in modelling* 模特儿生涯 ◇ *a modelling agency* 模特儿经纪公司 **2** the activity of making models of objects（实物）模型制造：*clay modelling* 黏土模型制造 **3** the work of making a simple description of a system or a process that can be used to explain it, etc. 系统模型化；系统模型的建立：***mathematical/statistical/computer modelling*** 数学 / 统计学 / 电脑模型的建立

ˌmodel 'village *noun* **1** a small model of a village, or a collection of small models of famous buildings arranged like a village 微缩村庄；（取材著名建筑物制作的）模型村 **2** (*old use*) a village with good-quality houses, especially one built in the past by an employer for workers to live in 模范村（尤指旧时雇主为工人修建的优质房屋）

modem /'məʊdem; *NAmE* 'moʊ-/ *noun* a device that connects one computer system to another using a telephone line so that data can be sent 调制解调器

mod·er·ate *adj., verb, noun*

■ *adj.* /'mɒdərət; *NAmE* 'mɑːd-/ **1** that is neither very good, large, hot, etc. nor very bad, small, cold, etc. 适度的；中等的：*students of moderate ability* 能力一般的学生 ◇ *Even moderate amounts of the drug can be fatal.* 这种药的用量即使不很大也会致命。◇ *The team enjoyed only moderate success last season.* 上个赛季，这个队伍只取得了中等成绩。◇ *Cook over a moderate heat.* 用文火烹调。**2** having or showing opinions, especially about politics, that are not extreme 温和的；不激烈的；不偏激的：***moderate views/policies*** 温和的见解 / 政策 ◇ *a moderate socialist* 温和的社会主义者 **3** staying within limits that are considered to be reasonable by most people 适中的；合理的：*a moderate drinker* 不过多饮酒的人 ◇ *moderate wage demands* 合理的工资要求 OPP **immoderate**

■ *verb* /'mɒdəreɪt; *NAmE* 'mɑːd-/ **1** [I, T] (*formal*) to become or make sth become less extreme, severe, etc. 缓和；使适中：*By evening the wind had moderated slightly.* 到黄昏时，风稍稍减弱了。◇ ~ **sth** *We agreed to moderate our original demands.* 我们同意降低我们原先的要求。**2** [T, I] ~ (**sth**) (*BrE*) to check that an exam has been marked fairly and in the same way by different people 审核评分（查看不同阅卷人所打分数是否公平一致）**3** [T, I] ~ (**sth**) to be in charge of a discussion or debate and make sure it is fair 主持（讨论、辩论等）：*The television debate was moderated by a law professor.* 这场电视辩论由一位法学教授主持。◇ *a moderated newsgroup* 有主持人的网络新闻组

■ *noun* /'mɒdərət; *NAmE* 'mɑːd-/ a person who has opinions, especially about politics, that are not extreme 持温和观点者（尤指政见）➲ MORE LIKE THIS 21, page R27

mod·er·ate·ly /'mɒdərətli; *NAmE* 'mɑːd-/ *adv.* **1** to an average extent; fairly but not very 一般地；勉强地 SYN **reasonably**: *a moderately successful career* 还算成功的事业 ◇ *She only did moderately well in the exam.* 她这次考试成绩还好。◇ *Cook in a moderately hot oven.* 用烤箱以中火烤制。**2** within reasonable limits 适度；适量；适中：*He only drinks (alcohol) moderately.* 他喝酒不过量。

mod·er·ation /ˌmɒdə'reɪʃn; *NAmE* ˌmɑːd-/ *noun* [U] **1** the quality of being reasonable and not being extreme 适度；适中；合理：*There was a call for moderation on the part of the trade unions.* 有人呼吁工会保持克制。◇ *Alcohol should only ever be taken* ***in moderation*** (= in small quantities). 酒只可少量饮用。**2** (*BrE*) (in education 教育) the process of making sure that the same standards are used by different people in marking exams, etc. 评分审核制

mod·er·ator /'mɒdəreɪtə(r); *NAmE* 'mɑːd-/ *noun* **1** a person whose job is to help the two sides in a disagreement to reach an agreement 调解人；调停人 ➲ SEE ALSO MEDIATOR **2** (*especially NAmE*) a person whose job is to make sure that a discussion or a debate is fair 会议主持；辩论会主席 **3** (*BrE*) a person whose job is to make sure that an exam is marked fairly 评分监督 **4** (*computing* 计) a person who is responsible for preventing offensive material from being published on a website（论坛等的）管理员，版主：*moderators of online discussion groups* 网上讨论组的管理员 **5 Moderator** a religious leader in the Presbyterian Church who is in charge of the Church council 长老会会议主席

mod·ern /'mɒdn; *NAmE* 'mɑːdərn/ *adj.* **1** [only before noun] of the present time or recent times 现代的；当代的；近代的 SYN **contemporary**: *the modern industrial world* 当今工业世界 ◇ *Modern European history* 欧洲近代史 ◇ *modern Greek* 现代希腊语 ◇ *Stress is a major problem of modern life.* 压力是现代生活中的主要问题。**2** [only before noun] (of styles in art, music, fashion, etc. 艺术、音乐、时装等的风格) new and intended to be different from traditional styles 新式的；有别于传统的 SYN **contemporary**: ***modern art/architecture/drama/jazz*** 现代艺术 / 建筑 / 戏剧 / 爵士乐 **3** (*usually approving*) using the latest technology, designs, materials, etc. 现代化的；先进的；最新的 SYN **up to date**: *a modern computer system* 最新的电脑系统 ◇ *modern methods of farming* 现代化的耕作方式 ◇ *the most modern, well-equipped hospital in London* 伦敦最先进的、设备最精良的医院 **4** (of ways of behaving, thinking, etc. 行为、思想等的方式) new and not always accepted by most members of society 新式的，超前的（大部分公众不一定接受）：*She has very modern ideas about educating her children.* 在教育子女方面，她有非常新式的观点。

ˌmodern ˈdance *noun* [U] a form of dance that was developed in the early 20th century by people who did not like the restrictions of traditional BALLET 现代舞（20世纪初发展起来的一种摆脱芭蕾舞限制的舞蹈形式）

ˌmodern-ˈday *adj.* [only before noun] **1** of the present time 现代的；当代的 **SYN contemporary**: *modern-day America* 当代美国 **2** used to describe a modern form of sb/sth, usually sb/sth bad or unpleasant, that existed in the past 现代版的，翻新的（通常用于消极事物）：*It has been called modern-day slavery.* 人们称之为现代版的奴隶制度。

ˌmodern ˈEnglish *noun* [U] the English language in the form it has been in since about 1500 现代英语（公元1500年前后至今的英语）

mod·ern·ism /ˈmɒdənɪzəm; *NAmE* ˈmɑːdərn-/ *noun* [U] **1** modern ideas or methods 现代主义；现代思想（或方法） **2** a style and movement in art, ARCHITECTURE and literature popular in the middle of the 20th century in which modern ideas, methods and materials were used rather than traditional ones 现代派，现代风格，现代主义（盛行于20世纪中期的艺术、建筑和文学风格）➲ COMPARE POSTMODERNISM ▶ **mod·ern·ist** /ˈmɒdənɪst; *NAmE* ˈmɑːdərn-/ *adj.* [only before noun]: *modernist art* 现代派艺术 **mod·ern·ist** /ˈmɒdənɪst; *NAmE* ˈmɑːdərn-/ *noun*

mod·ern·is·tic /ˌmɒdəˈnɪstɪk; *NAmE* ˌmɑːdərˈn-/ *adj.* (of a painting, building, piece of furniture, etc. 绘画、房屋、家具等) painted, designed, etc. in a very modern style 现代派的；时髦的

mod·ern·ity /məˈdɜːnəti; *NAmE* -ˈdɜːrn-/ *noun* [U] the condition of being new and modern 现代性

mod·ern·ize (*BrE also* **-ise**) /ˈmɒdənaɪz; *NAmE* ˈmɑːdərn-/ *verb* **1** [T] **~ sth** to make a system, methods, etc. more modern and more suitable for use at the present time 使（制度、方法等）现代化 **SYN update**: *The company is investing $9 million to modernize its factories.* 这家公司要投资900万美元将其工厂现代化。**2** [I] to start using modern equipment, ideas, etc. 使（设备、概念等）现代化：*Unfortunately we lack the resources to modernize.* 遗憾的是我们缺乏现代化所需的财力。▶ **mod·ern·iza·tion, -isa·tion** /ˌmɒdənaɪˈzeɪʃn; *NAmE* ˌmɑːdərnəˈz-/ *noun* [U]

ˌmodern ˈlanguage *noun* (*especially BrE*) a language that is spoken or written now, especially a European language, such as French or Spanish, that you study at school, university or college 现代语言（尤指在学校里教授的欧洲语言）：*the department of modern languages* 现代语言系 ◇ *a degree in modern languages* 现代语言专业的学位

mod·est /ˈmɒdɪst; *NAmE* ˈmɑːd-/ *adj.* **1** not very large, expensive, important, etc. 些许的；不太大（或太贵、太重要等）的：*modest improvements/reforms* 不太显著的改进/改革 ◇ *He charged a relatively modest fee.* 他收取的费用不算高。◇ *a modest little house* 简朴的小房子 ◇ *The research was carried out on a modest scale.* 这个研究项目开展的规模不算太大。**2** (*approving*) not talking much about your own abilities or possessions 谦虚的；谦逊的：*She's very modest about her success.* 她对自己的成功非常谦虚。◇ *You're too modest!* 你太谦虚了！**OPP immodest** **3** (of people, especially women, or their clothes 人，尤指妇女或其衣着) shy about showing much of the body; not intended to attract attention, especially in a sexual way 庄重的；朴素的；不性感的 **SYN demure**: *a modest dress* 端庄的连衣裙 **OPP immodest** ▶ **mod·est·ly** *adv.*

mod·esty /ˈmɒdəsti; *NAmE* ˈmɑːd-/ *noun* [U] **1** the fact of not talking much about your abilities or possessions 谦虚；谦逊：*He accepted the award with characteristic modesty.* 他以他一贯的谦逊态度接受了奖项。◇ *I hate false* (= pretended) *modesty.* 我讨厌虚伪的谦逊。**2** the action of behaving or dressing so that you do not show your body or attract sexual attention 庄重；朴素；贤淑 **3** the state of being not very large, expensive, important, etc. 不突出；有限：*They tried to disguise the modesty of their achievements.* 他们不想让人知道自己取得的那一点成绩。

modi·cum /ˈmɒdɪkəm; *NAmE* ˈmɑːd-; ˈmɔːd-/ *noun* [sing.] (*formal*) a fairly small amount, especially of sth good or pleasant 少量，一点点（好事或愉快的事）：*They should win, given a modicum of luck.* 只要有一点点运气，他们就会赢。

modi·fi·ca·tion **AW** /ˌmɒdɪfɪˈkeɪʃn; *NAmE* ˌmɑːd-/ *noun* [U, C] **~ (of/to/in sth)** the act or process of changing sth in order to improve it or make it more acceptable; a change that is made 修改；改进；改变 **SYN adaptation**: *Considerable modification of the existing system is needed.* 需要对现有的系统进行相当大的改进。◇ *It might be necessary to make a few slight modifications to the design.* 也许有必要对这个设计稍作几处修改。

modi·fier /ˈmɒdɪfaɪə(r); *NAmE* ˈmɑːd-/ *noun* (*grammar* 语法) a word or group of words that describes a noun phrase or restricts its meaning in some way 修饰语 ➲ COMPARE POSTMODIFIER, PREMODIFIER

mod·ify **AW** /ˈmɒdɪfaɪ; *NAmE* ˈmɑːd-/ *verb* (**modi·fies, modi·fy·ing, modi·fied, modi·fied**) **1 ~ sth** to change sth slightly, especially in order to make it more suitable for a particular purpose 调整；稍作修改；使更适合 **SYN adapt**: *The software we use has been modified for us.* 我们使用的软件已按我们的需要作过修改。◇ *Patients are taught how to modify their diet.* 病人获得有关如何调节自己饮食的指导。**2 ~ sth** to make sth less extreme 缓和；使温和 **SYN adjust**: *to* ***modify your behaviour/language/views*** 使你的行为/语言/观点更容易让人接受 **3 ~ sth** (*grammar* 语法) a word, such as an adjective or adverb, that **modifies** another word or group of words describes it or restricts its meaning in some way 修饰：*In 'walk slowly', the adverb 'slowly' modifies the verb 'walk'.* 在 walk slowly 中，副词 slowly 修饰动词 walk。

mod·ish /ˈməʊdɪʃ; *NAmE* ˈmoʊ-/ *adj.* (*sometimes disapproving*) fashionable 时髦的；流行的

modu·lar /ˈmɒdjələ(r); *NAmE* ˈmɑːdʒə-/ *adj.* **1** (of a course of study, especially at a British university or college 尤指英国大学里的课程) consisting of separate units from which students may choose several 分单元的（由独立单元组成，学生可选修）：*a modular course* 单元课程 **2** (of machines, buildings, etc. 机器、建筑等) consisting of separate parts or units that can be joined together 组合式的；模块化的；标准组件的

modu·late /ˈmɒdjuleɪt; *NAmE* ˈmɑːdʒə-/ *verb* **1** [T] **~ sth** (*formal*) to change the quality of your voice in order to create a particular effect by making it louder, softer, lower, etc. 调节（嗓音的大小、强弱、高低等） **2** [I] **~ (from sth) (to/into sth)** (*music* 音) to change from one musical KEY (= set of notes) to another 变调；转调 **3** [T] **~ sth** (*specialist*) to affect sth so that it becomes more regular, slower, etc. 调整；调节；控制：*drugs that effectively modulate the disease process* 可以有效控制疾病发展的药品 **4** [T] **~ sth** (*specialist*) to change the rate at which a sound wave or radio signal VIBRATES (= the FREQUENCY) so that it is clearer 调制（声波或无线电波频率）；调谐 ▶ **modu·la·tion** /ˌmɒdjuˈleɪʃn; *NAmE* ˌmɑːdʒəˈl-/ *noun* [U, C]

mod·ule /ˈmɒdjuːl; *NAmE* ˈmɑːdʒuːl/ *noun* **1** a unit that can form part of a course of study, especially at a college or university in Britain 单元（尤指英国大学课程的一部分）：*The course consists of ten core modules and five optional modules.* 这门课程包括十个必修单元和五个选修单元。**2** (*computing* 计) a unit of a computer system or program that has a particular function 模块；功能块；程序块 **3** one of a set of separate parts or units that can be joined together to make a machine, a piece of furniture, a building, etc. 组件；模块；配件 **4** a unit of a SPACECRAFT that can function independently of the main part（航天器上独立的）舱：*the lunar module* 登月舱

modus op·er·andi /ˌməʊdəs ˌɒpəˈrændiː; *NAmE* ˌmoʊdəs ˌɑːpə-/ *noun* [sing.] (*from Latin, formal*) (*abbr.* **MO**) a particular method of working 工作方法

M

modus vi·vendi /ˌməʊdəs vɪˈvendiː; *NAmE* ˌmoʊdəs/ *noun* [sing.] (*from Latin, formal*) an arrangement that is made between people, institutions or countries who have very different opinions or ideas, so that they can live or work together without arguing 妥协

Moe·bius strip *noun* = MÖBIUS STRIP

mog·gie (*also* **moggy**) /ˈmɒɡi; *NAmE* ˈmɑːɡi/ *noun* (*pl.* **-ies**) (*BrE, informal*) a cat 猫

mogul /ˈməʊɡl; *NAmE* ˈmoʊɡl/ *noun* **1** a very rich, important and powerful person 大亨；有权势的人 SYN magnate: *a movie mogul* 电影大亨 **2** **Mogul** (*also* **Mo·ghul**, **Mug·hal** /ˈmuːɡɑːl/) a member of the Muslim race that ruled much of India from the 16th to the 19th century 莫卧儿人（穆斯林的一支，16 至 19 世纪统治印度大部分地区） **3** a raised area of hard snow that you jump over when you are SKIING 雪丘，雪墩，"猫跳"（滑雪坡道上需跳越的硬雪堆）

mo·hair /ˈməʊheə(r); *NAmE* ˈmoʊher/ *noun* [U] soft wool or cloth made from the fine hair of the ANGORA GOAT, used for making clothes 安哥拉山羊毛毛线（或织物）；马海毛毛线（或织物）: *a mohair sweater* 马海毛毛衣

Mo·ham·med *noun* = MUHAMMAD

Mo·hawk /ˈməʊhɔːk; *NAmE* ˈmoʊ-/ *noun* (*pl.* **Mohawk** or **Mohawks**) a member of a Native American people, many of whom live in New York State and Canada 莫霍克人（美洲土著，多生活在美国纽约州和加拿大）

M

Mo·hi·can /məʊˈhiːkən; *NAmE* moʊ-/ (*especially BrE*) (*also* **Mo·hawk** /ˈməʊhɔːk; *NAmE* ˈmoʊ-/ *especially in NAmE*) *noun* a way of cutting the hair in which the head is shaved except for a strip of hair in the middle that is sometimes made to stick up 莫希干发型，"鸡冠头"发型（只保留头中间一道直立的头发）

moi /mwɑː/ *exclamation* (*humorous, from French*) me（宾格）我: *'Did you eat all the biscuits?' 'Who? Moi?'* "你把饼干吃光了？""谁？我？"

moire /mwɑː(r); *NAmE also* ˈmɔɪər/ (*also* **moiré** /ˈmwɑːreɪ/) *noun* [U] a type of silk cloth with a pattern on its surface like small waves 波纹丝绸

moist /mɔɪst/ *adj.* slightly wet 微湿的；湿润的: *warm moist air* 温暖潮湿的空气 ◇ *a rich moist cake* 松软味浓的蛋糕 ◇ *Water the plants regularly to keep the soil moist.* 定时浇灌植物以保持土壤湿润。◇ *Her eyes were moist* (= with tears). 她眼含泪水。➲ SYNONYMS AT WET ▶ **moist·ness** *noun* [U]

mois·ten /ˈmɔɪsn/ *verb* [T, I] ~ (**sth**) to become or make sth slightly wet （使）变得潮湿，变得湿润: *He moistened his lips before he spoke.* 他润了润嘴唇，接着就开始讲话。

mois·ture /ˈmɔɪstʃə(r)/ *noun* [U] very small drops of water that are present in the air, on a surface or in a substance 潮气；水汽；水分: *the skin's natural moisture* 皮肤的天然水分 ◇ *a material that is designed to* ***absorb/retain moisture*** 用来吸收 / 保持水分的材料

mois·tur·ize (*BrE also* **-ise**) /ˈmɔɪstʃəraɪz/ *verb* [T, I] ~ (**sth**) to put a special cream on your skin to make it less dry 使皮肤湿润；（用脂膏）滋润: *a* ***moisturizing cream/lotion*** 润肤霜；润肤液 ◇ *a product that soothes and moisturizes* 使皮肤柔软湿润的产品

mois·tur·izer (*BrE also* **-iser**) /ˈmɔɪstʃəraɪzə(r)/ *noun* [C, U] a cream that is used to make the skin less dry 润肤霜；润肤膏 ➲ WORDFINDER NOTE AT MAKE-UP

mojo /ˈməʊdʒəʊ; *NAmE* ˈmoʊdʒoʊ/ *noun* (*pl.* **mojos**) **1** [U] magic power 魔力 **2** [C] a small object, or a collection of small objects in a bag, that is believed to have magic powers 符咒（袋）；护身符 **3** [U] the power of sb's attractive personality （人的）魅力

molar /ˈməʊlə(r); *NAmE* ˈmoʊ-/ *noun* any of the twelve large teeth at the back of the mouth used for crushing and chewing food 磨牙；臼齿 ➲ COMPARE CANINE *n.* (1), INCISOR

mo·las·ses /məˈlæsɪz/ (*NAmE*) (*BrE* **trea·cle**) *noun* [U] a thick black sweet sticky liquid produced when sugar is REFINED (= made pure), used in cooking（制糖时产生的）糖浆，糖蜜

mold (*especially US*) (*BrE, CanE* **mould**) /məʊld; *NAmE* moʊld/ *noun, verb*

■ ***noun*** **1** [C] a container that you pour a liquid or soft substance into, which then becomes solid in the same shape as the container, for example when it is cooled or cooked 模具；铸模: *A clay mold is used for casting bronze statues.* 用黏土模具来浇铸青铜塑像。◇ *Pour the chocolate into a heart-shaped mold.* 将巧克力倒入心形模子。◇ *They* ***broke the mold*** *when they made you* (= there is nobody like you). 你是世界上唯一的。**2** [C, usually sing.] a particular style showing the characteristics, attitudes or behaviour that are typical of sb/sth（独特）类型，个性，风格: *a hero in the 'Superman' mold* "超人"式的英雄 ◇ *He is cast in a different mold from his predecessor.* 他和他的前任风格不一样。◇ *She doesn't fit* (*into*) *the traditional mold of an academic.* 她不像一个传统的学者。**3** [U, C] a fine soft green, grey or black substance like fur that grows on old food or on objects that are left in warm wet air 霉；霉菌: *There's mold on the cheese.* 干酪发霉了。◇ *molds and fungi* 霉菌和真菌 ◇ *mold growth* 霉的生长 ➲ SEE ALSO LEAF MOULD

IDM ▶ **break the 'mold** (**of sth**) to change what people expect from a situation, especially by acting in a dramatic and original way 改变…的模式；打破…的模式

■ ***verb*** **1** [T] to shape a soft substance into a particular form or object by pressing it or by putting it into a mold （用模具）浇铸，塑造: ~ **A** (**into B**) *First, mold the clay into the desired shape.* 首先，将陶土做成需要的形状。◇ ~ **B** (**from/out of/in A**) *The figure had been molded in clay.* 这座人像是用黏土塑造的。**2** [T] to strongly influence the way sb's character, opinions, etc. develop 对…影响重大；将…塑造成: ~ **sb/sth** *The experience had molded and coloured her whole life.* 这次经历影响了她的一生。◇ ~ **sb/sth into sb/sth** *He molded them into a superb team.* 他将他们打造成一支非凡的团队。**3** [I, T] ~ (**sth**) **to sth** to fit or make sth fit tightly around the shape of sth （使）紧贴于，吻合: *The fabric molds to the body.* 这种织物很贴身。

mol·der *verb* [I] (*especially US*) = MOULDER

mold·ing (*especially US*) (*BrE, CanE* **mould·ing**) /ˈməʊldɪŋ; *NAmE* ˈmoʊ-/ *noun* a decorative strip of plastic, stone, wood, etc. around the top edge of a wall, on a door, etc. 线脚（用于檐口、门楣等的凹凸带形装饰）

moldy (*especially US*) (*BrE, CanE* **mouldy**) /ˈməʊldi; *NAmE* ˈmoʊ-/ *adj.* **1** covered with or containing MOLD 发霉的；带霉斑的: ***moldy bread/cheese*** 发霉的面包 / 干酪 ◇ ***Strawberries go moldy*** *very quickly.* 草莓很容易发霉。**2** old and not in good condition 破旧的

mole /məʊl; *NAmE* moʊl/ *noun* **1** a small animal with dark grey fur, that is almost blind and digs tunnels under the ground to live in 鼹鼠（体小，视力极差，居住在挖掘的地道）➲ SEE ALSO MOLEHILL **2** a small dark brown mark on the skin, sometimes slightly higher than the skin around it 色素痣 ➲ COMPARE FRECKLE **3** a person who works within an organization and secretly passes important information to another organization or country 间谍；内奸 **4** (*chemistry* 化) a unit for measuring the amount of substance 摩尔（计量物质的数量单位）

mol·ecule /ˈmɒlɪkjuːl; *NAmE* ˈmɑːl-/ *noun* (*chemistry* 化) the smallest unit, consisting of a group of atoms, into which a substance can be divided without a change in its chemical nature 分子: *A molecule of water consists of two atoms of hydrogen and one atom of oxygen.* 水分子由两个氢原子和一个氧原子构成。➲ WORDFINDER NOTE AT CHEMISTRY, PHYSICS ▶ **mo·lecu·lar** /məˈlekjələ(r)/ *adj.* [only before noun]: ***molecular structure/biology*** 分子结构 / 生物学

mole·hill /ˈməʊlhɪl; *NAmE* ˈmoʊl-/ *noun* a small pile of earth that a MOLE leaves on the surface of the ground when it digs underground 鼹丘（由鼹鼠挖洞扒出的泥土堆成） IDM SEE MOUNTAIN

mole·skin /ˈməʊlskɪn; NAmE ˈmoʊl-/ *noun* [U] a type of strong cotton cloth with a soft surface, used for making clothes 厚毛头斜纹棉布

mo·lest /məˈlest/ *verb* **1** ~ sb to attack sb, especially a child, sexually 对（儿童）性骚扰 SYN **abuse** **2** ~ sb (*old-fashioned*) to attack sb physically 攻击；伤害 ▶ **mo·lest·ation** /ˌmɒleˈsteɪʃn; NAmE ˌmoʊ-/ *noun* [U] **mo·lest·er** /məˈlestə(r)/ *noun*: *a child molester* 性骚扰儿童者

moll /mɒl; NAmE mɑːl/ *noun* (*old-fashioned, slang*) the female friend of a criminal 恶棍的女友

mol·lify /ˈmɒlɪfaɪ; NAmE ˈmɑːl-/ *verb* (**mol·li·fies, mol·li·fy·ing, mol·li·fied, mol·li·fied**) ~ sb (*formal*) to make sb feel less angry or upset 使平静；抚慰 SYN **placate**

mol·lusc (*BrE*) (*US* **mol·lusk**) /ˈmɒləsk; NAmE ˈmɑːl-/ *noun* (*specialist*) any creature with a soft body that is not divided into different sections, and usually a hard outer shell. SNAILS and SLUGS are molluscs. 软体动物（门） ➲ COMPARE BIVALVE, SHELLFISH

molly·cod·dle /ˈmɒlikɒdl; NAmE ˈmɑːlikɑːdl/ *verb* (*disapproving, becoming old-fashioned*) ~ sb to protect sb too much and make their life too comfortable and safe 溺爱；宠爱 ➲ COMPARE CODDLE (1)

Molo·tov cock·tail /ˌmɒlətɒf ˈkɒkteɪl; NAmE ˌmɑːlətɔːf ˈkɑːk-; ˌmɔːl-/ (*BrE also* **ˈpetrol bomb**) *noun* a simple bomb that consists of a bottle filled with petrol/gas and a piece of cloth in the end that is made to burn just before the bomb is thrown 瓶装汽油弹；莫洛托夫燃烧瓶

molt (*especially US*) (*BrE, CanE* **moult**) /məʊlt; NAmE moʊlt/ *verb* [I] (of a bird or an animal 鸟或兽) to lose feathers or hair before new feathers or hair grow 换羽；蜕毛

mol·ten /ˈməʊltən; NAmE ˈmoʊl-/ *adj.* (of metal, rock, or glass 金属、岩石或玻璃) heated to a very high temperature so that it becomes liquid 熔化的；熔融的

mo·lyb·denum /məˈlɪbdənəm/ *noun* [U] (*symb.* **Mo**) a chemical element. Molybdenum is a silver-grey metal that breaks easily and is used in some ALLOY steels. 钼

mom 🔑 /mɒm; NAmE mɑːm/ *noun* (*NAmE*) (*BrE* **mum**) (*informal*) a mother 妈妈；妈：*Where's my mom?* 我妈在哪儿？◇ *Mom and Dad* 妈妈和爸爸 ◇ *Are you listening, Mom?* 妈，你在听吗？➲ SEE ALSO SOCCER MOM

ˌmom-and-ˈpop *adj.* [only before noun] (*NAmE*) (of a shop/store or business 商店或企业) owned and run by a husband and wife, or by a family 夫妻（或家庭）经营的

mo·ment 🔑 /ˈməʊmənt; NAmE ˈmoʊ-/ *noun* **1** a very short period of time 片刻；瞬间：*Could you **wait a moment**, please?* 请您稍等一下，好吗？◇ ***One moment, please*** (= Please wait a short time). 请稍候。◇ *He thought **for a moment** before replying.* 他想了一下才回答。◇ *I'll be **back in a moment**.* 我一会儿就回来。◇ *We arrived **not a moment too soon*** (= almost too late). 我们到得一点也不早。◇ ***Moments later*** (= a very short time later), *I heard a terrible crash.* 过了一会儿，我听到一声可怕的撞击声。➲ SEE ALSO SENIOR MOMENT **2** [sing.] an exact point in time 某个时刻；当时：*We're busy **at the moment*** (= now). 我们这会儿很忙。◇ *I agreed **in a moment of** weakness.* 我一时心软就答应了。◇ ***At that very moment**, the phone rang.* 就在那时，电话铃响了。◇ ***From that moment on**, she never felt really well again.* 从那时候开始，她就再也没真正好受过。 **3** [C] a particular occasion; a time for doing sth 时机；机遇；时光；做某事的时刻：*I'm waiting **for the right moment** to tell him the bad news.* 我得找个适当的时机告诉他这个坏消息。 ◇ *Have I caught you at a bad moment?* 我是不是来得不是时候？

IDM **(at) any ˈmoment (ˈnow)** very soon 很快；随时：*Hurry up! He'll be back any moment now.* 快点！他随时都会回来。 **at this moment in ˈtime** (*informal*) now, at the present time 现在；此时此刻：*At this moment in time, I don't know what my decision will be.* 此时此刻，我不知道自己会作出什么决定。 **for the ˈmoment/ˈpresent** for now; for a short time 目前；暂时：*This house is big enough for the moment, but we'll have to move if we have children.* 这房子现在还够大。要是有了孩子，我们还得搬。 **have its/your ˈmoments** to have short times that are better, more interesting, etc. than others 有短暂的好时候：*The job isn't exciting all the time, but it has its moments.* 这工作并不总是很带劲，但也有让人兴奋的时候。 **the ˌmoment of ˈtruth** a time when sb/sth is tested, or when important decisions are made 考验的时刻；（决策的）关键时刻 **the moment (that)**... as soon as... 一…就…：*I want to see him the moment he arrives.* 希望他一到我就见到他。 **ˌnot for a/one ˈmoment** certainly not; not at all 当然不；一点也不：*I don't think for a moment that she'll accept but you can ask her.* 我觉得她一定不会接受的，不过你可以去问问她。 **of ˈmoment** very important 非常重要：*matters of great moment* 极其重要的事 **of the ˈmoment** (of a person, a job, an issue, etc. 人、工作、议题等) famous, important and talked about a lot now 红极一时；盛行一时；广为谈论：*She's the fashion designer of the moment.* 她是当前最红的时装设计师。➲ MORE AT EVIL *adj.*, JUST *adv.*, LAST[1] *det.*, NOTICE *n.*, PSYCHOLOGICAL, SPUR *n.*, WAIT *v.*

mo·ment·ar·ily /ˈməʊməntrəli; NAmE ˌmoʊmənˈterəli/ *adv.* **1** for a very short time 短促地；片刻地 SYN **briefly**: *He paused momentarily.* 他稍作停顿。 **2** (*NAmE*) very soon; in a moment 立即；马上：*I'll be with you momentarily.* 我马上就到你这儿来。

mo·ment·ary /ˈməʊməntri; NAmE ˈmoʊmənteri/ *adj.* lasting for a very short time 短促的；短暂的；片刻的 SYN **brief**: *a momentary lapse of concentration* 走神儿 ◇ *momentary confusion* 一时糊涂

mo·men·tous /məˈmentəs; NAmE moʊˈm-/ *adj.* very important or serious, especially because there may be important results 关键的；重要的；重大的 SYN **historic**: *a **momentous decision/event/occasion*** 重大决定 / 事件；重要时刻

mo·men·tum /məˈmentəm; NAmE moʊˈm-/ *noun* [U] **1** the ability to keep increasing or developing 推进力；动力；势头：*The fight for his release **gathers momentum** each day.* 争取使他获释的斗争声势日益加强。◇ *They began to **lose momentum** in the second half of the game.* 在比赛的下半场，他们的势头就逐渐减弱。 **2** a force that is gained by movement 冲力：*The vehicle **gained momentum** as the road dipped.* 那辆车顺着坡越跑冲力越大。 **3** (*specialist*) the quantity of movement of a moving object, measured as its mass multiplied by its speed 动量

momma /ˈmɒmə; NAmE ˈmɑːmə/ *noun* (*NAmE, informal*) = MOMMY

mommy /ˈmɒmi; NAmE ˈmɑːmi/ *noun* (*pl.* **-ies**) (*also* **momma**) (*both NAmE*) (*BrE* **mummy**) (*informal*) a child's word for a mother（儿语）妈咪

mom·para /mɒmˈpʌrə; NAmE mɑːm-/ (*also* **mam·para**) *noun* (*SAfrE*) an insulting name for a person that you think is stupid（含侮慢意）傻瓜，蠢货

mon- ➲ MONO-

monad /ˈmɒnæd; ˈməʊn-; NAmE ˈmɑːn-; ˈmoʊn-/ *noun* (*philosophy* 哲) a single simple thing that cannot be divided, for example an atom or a person 单子（不可分割的实体）

mon·arch /ˈmɒnək; NAmE ˈmɑːnərk; -ɑːrk/ *noun* a person who rules a country, for example a king or a queen 君主；帝王 ➲ WORDFINDER NOTE AT KING

mo·nar·chic·al /məˈnɑːkɪkl; NAmE -ˈnɑːrk-/ *adj.* [usually before noun] (*formal*) connected with a ruler such as a king or a queen or with the system of government by a king or queen 君主的；帝王的；君主制的

mon·arch·ist /ˈmɒnəkɪst; NAmE ˈmɑːnərk-/ *noun* a person who believes that a country should be ruled by a king or queen 拥护君主制度者；君主主义者 ▶ **mon·arch·ist** *adj.*

mon·archy /ˈmɒnəki; NAmE ˈmɑːnərki/ *noun* (*pl.* **-ies**) **1** **the monarchy** [sing.] a system of government by a king

M

or a queen 君主制；君主政体：*plans to abolish the monarchy* 废除君主政体的计划 ➲ COLLOCATIONS AT POLITICS **2** [C] a country that is ruled by a king or a queen 君主国：*There are several constitutional monarchies in Europe.* 欧洲有若干个君主立宪国。➲ COMPARE REPUBLIC **3 the monarchy** [sing.] the king or queen of a country and their family 君主及其家庭成员

mon·as·tery /ˈmɒnəstri; *NAmE* ˈmɑːnəsteri/ *noun* (*pl.* **-ies**) a building in which MONKS (= members of a male religious community) live together 隐修院；修道院；寺院 ➲ COLLOCATIONS AT RELIGION

mo·nas·tic /məˈnæstɪk/ *adj.* **1** connected with MONKS or monasteries 僧侣的；隐修院的；修道院的 **2** (of a way of life 生活方式) simple and quiet and possibly CELIBATE 宁静简朴的；清修的；禁欲的 SYN **ascetic**

mo·nas·ti·cism /məˈnæstɪsɪzəm/ *noun* [U] the way of life of MONKS in monasteries 僧侣生活；隐修院生活；修道院生活

Mon·day /ˈmʌndeɪ; -di/ *noun* [C, U] (*abbr.* **Mon.**) the day of the week after Sunday and before Tuesday, the first day of the working week 星期一：*It's Monday today, isn't it?* 今天是星期一，对吧？◇ *She started work* ***last Monday.*** 她上个星期一开始工作。◇ *Are you busy* ***next Monday?*** 下周一你忙吗？◇ ***Monday morning/afternoon/evening*** 星期一上午 / 下午 / 晚上 ◇ *We'll discuss this at Monday's meeting.* 我们将在星期一的会上讨论这件事。◇ *Do we still have Monday's paper?* 我们还有周一的报纸吗？◇ *I work Monday to Friday.* 我星期一到星期五上班。◇ *I work Mondays to Fridays.* 我每周星期一到星期五工作。◇ ***On Monday(s)*** (= Every Monday) *I do yoga.* 我每个星期一做瑜伽。◇ *I always do yoga* ***on a Monday.*** 我总是在星期一做瑜伽。◇ *He was born on a Monday.* 他出生的那天是星期一。◇ *I went to Paris on Thursday, and came back the following Monday.* 我星期四去了巴黎，第二周的星期一就回来了。◇ *We'll meet* ***on Monday.*** 我们星期一见。◇ (*BrE*) *'When did the accident happen?' 'It was the Monday* (= the Monday of the week we are talking about).' "事故是什么时候发生的？" "就在那个星期一。" ◇ (*BrE*) *Come back Monday week* (= a week after next Monday). 下下星期一回来。◇ (*informal* or *NAmE*) *We'll meet Monday.* 咱们星期一见。ORIGIN From the Old English for 'day of the moon', translated from Latin *lunae dies.* 源自古英语，原意为 day of the moon (月亮日)，古英语则译自拉丁文 lunae dies.

ˌMonday morning ˈquarterback *noun* (*NAmE, informal, disapproving*) a person who criticizes or comments on an event after it has happened "星期一早上的四分卫"；事后指手画脚的人 ORIGIN The quarterback directs the play in an American football match and matches are usually played at the weekend. 源自美式橄榄球，四分卫指挥比赛，而比赛往往在周末举行。

mon·et·ar·ism /ˈmʌnɪtərɪzəm/ *noun* [U] the policy of controlling the amount of money available in a country as a way of keeping the economy strong 货币主义（控制货币量以调控经济）

mon·et·ar·ist /ˈmʌnɪtərɪst/ *noun* a person who supports monetarism 货币主义者 ▸ **mon·et·ar·ist** *adj.*: *a monetarist economic policy* 货币主义经济政策

mon·et·ary /ˈmʌnɪtri; *NAmE* -teri/ *adj.* [only before noun] connected with money, especially all the money in a country 货币的，钱的（尤指一国的货币）：***monetary policy/growth*** 货币政策 / 增长 ◇ *an item of little monetary value* 不怎么值钱的东西 ◇ *closer European political, monetary and economic union* 更为密切的欧洲政治、货币及经济联盟 ➲ SYNONYMS AT ECONOMIC

money /ˈmʌni/ *noun* **1** [U] what you earn by working or selling things, and use to buy things 钱；薪水；收入：*to* ***borrow/save/spend/earn money*** 借钱；存钱；花钱；挣钱 ◇ *How much money is there in my account?* 我的账上还有多少钱？◇ *The money is much better in my new job.* 我的新工作薪水高多了。◇ *If the item*

money 钱

is not satisfactory, you will get your money back. 东西不满意，可以退款。◇ *We'll need to raise more money* (= collect or borrow it) *next year.* 明年我们需要筹集更多的钱。◇ *Can you lend me some money until tomorrow?* 能借我点儿钱吗？明天就还。◇ *Be careful with that—it* ***cost a lot of money.*** 小心别弄坏那东西，它可值钱了。➲ WORDFINDER NOTE AT LOAN ➲ COLLOCATIONS AT FINANCE

WORDFINDER 联想词: afford, **bank**, bankrupt, capital, **economy**, expense, **finance**, **invest**, profit

2 [U] coins or paper notes 钱币；钞票：*I counted the money carefully.* 我仔细点过这笔钱。◇ *Where can I change my money into dollars?* 什么地方能把我的钱兑换成美元？➲ SEE ALSO FUNNY MONEY, PAPER MONEY, READY MONEY **3** [U] a person's wealth including their property 财产；财富：*He lost all his money.* 他失去了全部财产。◇ *The family made their money in the 18th century.* 这个家族在 18 世纪创下了家业。**4 moneys** or **monies** [pl.] (*law* or *old use*) sums of money 款项：*a statement of all monies paid into your account* 存入你的账户的所有金额的清单 HELP You will find other compounds ending in **money** at their place in the alphabet. 其他以 money 结尾的复合词可在各字母中的适当位置查到。

IDM **be in the ˈmoney** (*informal*) to have a lot of money to spend 有钱 **for ˈmy money** (*informal*) in my opinion 依我看；我觉得：*For my money, he's one of the greatest comedians of all time.* 依我看，历来的喜剧演员，他是数一数二的。**get your ˈmoney's worth** to get enough value or enjoyment out of sth, considering the amount of money, time, etc. that you are spending on it（钱或时间等）值得花 **good ˈmoney** a lot of money; money that you earn with hard work 大笔的钱；血汗钱：*Thousands of people paid good money to watch the band perform.* 成千上万的人花很多钱去观看这支乐队的演出。◇ *Don't waste good money on that!* 别把血汗钱浪费在那上头！**have money to ˈburn** to have so much money that you do not have to be careful with it 钱多得花不完；有用不完的钱 **ˈmade of money** (*informal*) very rich 极其富有 **make ˈmoney** to earn a lot of money; to make a profit 赚钱；获利：*The movie should make money.* 这部电影应该会赚大钱。◇ *There's money to be made from tourism.* 旅游业非常有利可图。**make/lose money ˌhand over ˈfist** to make/lose money very fast and in large quantities 赚大钱；破大财 **money for ˈjam/old ˈrope** (*BrE, informal*) money that is earned very easily, for sth that needs little

▼ **SYNONYMS 同义词辨析**

money

cash • change

These are all words for money in the form of coins or paper notes. 以上各词均表示金钱，包括硬币和钞票。

money money in the form of coins or paper notes 指金钱，包括硬币和钞票： *I counted the money carefully.* 我仔细点过这笔钱。◇ *Where can I change my money into dollars?* 什么地方能把我的钱兑换成美元？◇ ***paper money*** (= money that is made of paper, not coins) 纸币

cash money in the form of coins or paper notes 指现金： *How much cash do you have on you?* 你身上带着多少现金？◇ *Payments can be made by cheque or **in cash**.* 支票或现金付款均可。

MONEY OR CASH? 用 money 还是 cash?

If it is important to contrast money in the form of coins and notes and money in other forms, use **cash**. 强调现金而非其他形式的货币时用 cash： *How much money/cash do you have on you?* 你身上带着多少现金？◇ ~~*Payments can be made by cheque or in money.*~~◇ ~~*Customers are offered a discount if they pay money.*~~

change the money that you get back when you have paid for sth giving more money than the amount it costs; coins rather than paper money 指找给的零钱、硬币： *The ticket machine doesn't give change.* 自动售票机不找零。◇ *I don't have any **small change*** (= coins of low value). 我没有零钱。

PATTERNS

- to **draw out/get out/take out/withdraw** money/cash
- **ready** money/cash (= money that you have available to spend immediately)

effort 容易赚的钱财 **money is no 'object** money is not sth that needs to be considered, because there is plenty of it available 钱不成问题： *She travels around the world as if money is no object.* 她周游世界，好像钱不是问题。 **money 'talks** (*saying*) people who have a lot of money have more power and influence than others 财大气粗；有钱就有势 **on the 'money** correct; accurate 正确的；准确的： *His prediction was **right on the money**.* 他的预测准确无误。 **put 'money into sth** to invest money in a business or a particular project 投资于： *We would welcome interest from anyone prepared to put money into the club.* 任何人有意向俱乐部投资，我们都欢迎。 **put your 'money on sb/sth 1** to bet that a particular horse, dog, etc. will win a race 在（马、狗等）上下赌注 **2** to feel very sure that sth is true or that sb will succeed 确信： *He'll be there tonight. I'd put money on it.* 我十分肯定他今晚会在那儿。 **put your money where your 'mouth is** (*informal*) to support what you say by doing sth practical; to show by your actions that you really mean sth 用行动证明自己的话 **throw your 'money about/around** (*informal*) to spend money in a careless and obvious way 肆意挥霍；大手大脚 **throw good money after 'bad** (*disapproving*) to spend more money on sth, when you have wasted a lot on it already 继续花钱打水漂 **throw 'money at sth** (*disapproving*) to try to deal with a problem or improve a situation by spending money on it, when it would be better to deal with it in other ways 白（往某事上）扔钱： *It is inappropriate simply to throw money at these problems.* 只是用钱去处理这些问题是不适当的。➲ MORE AT BEST *n.*, CAREFUL, COIN *v.*, COLOUR *n.*, EASY *adj.*, FOOL *n.*, GROW, LICENCE, LOVE *n.*, MARRY, OBJECT *n.*, PAY *v.*, POT *n.*, ROLL *v.*, RUN *n.*, TIME *n.*

ˌmoney-back guaranˈtee *noun* an official promise by a shop/store, etc. to return the money you have paid for sth if it is not of an acceptable standard（商店对不合格商品的）退款保证

money·bags /ˈmʌnibæɡz/ *noun* (*pl.* **money·bags**) (*informal, humorous*) a very rich person 阔佬；大款

ˈmoney box *noun* (*especially BrE*) a small closed box with a narrow opening and sometimes with a lock and key, into which children put coins as a way of saving money 存钱罐；存钱盒 ➲ COMPARE PIGGY BANK

mon·eyed (*also* **mon·ied**) /ˈmʌnid/ *adj.* [only before noun] (*formal*) having a lot of money 极有钱的；富有的 SYN **rich**: *the moneyed classes* 富有阶层

ˈmoney-grubbing (*also* **ˈmoney-grabbing**) *adj.* [only before noun] (*informal, disapproving*) trying to get a lot of money 聚敛钱财的；试图挣大钱的 ▶ **ˈmoney-grubber** (*also* **ˈmoney-grabber**) *noun*

money·lend·er /ˈmʌnilendə(r)/ *noun* (*old-fashioned*) a person whose business is lending money, usually at a very high rate of interest 放债者；放高利贷者

money·maker /ˈmʌnimeɪkə(r)/ *noun* a product, business, etc. that produces a large profit 赚大钱的产品（或企业等） ▶ **money·mak·ing** *adj.*: *a moneymaking movie* 赢利颇丰的电影 **money·mak·ing** *noun* [U]

ˈmoney market *noun* the banks and other institutions that lend or borrow money, and buy and sell foreign money 货币市场；金融市场

ˈmoney order (*especially NAmE*) (*BrE also* **ˈpostal order**) *noun* an official document that you can buy at a bank or a post office and send to sb so that they can exchange it for money（银行或邮政）汇票

ˈmoney-saving *adj.* [only before noun] that helps you spend less money 省钱的；便宜的；廉价的： ***money-saving offers/tips*** 省钱的优惠价格 / 窍门

ˈmoney-spinner *noun* (*BrE, informal*) something that earns a lot of money 赚大钱的东西；摇钱树

ˈmoney supply *noun* [sing., U] (*economics* 经) the total amount of money that exists in the economy of a country at a particular time 货币供应量

mon·gol /ˈmɒŋɡəl; *NAmE* ˈmɑːŋ-/ (*NAmE usually* **mongol·oid** /ˈmɒŋɡəlɔɪd; *NAmE* ˈmɑːŋ-/) *noun* (*old-fashioned*) an offensive word for a person with DOWN'S SYNDROME（蔑称）唐氏综合征患者 ▶ **mon·gol·ism** *noun* [U]

mon·goose /ˈmɒŋɡuːs; *NAmE* ˈmɑːŋ-/ *noun* (*pl.* **mon·gooses** /-sɪz-/) a small tropical animal with fur, that kills snakes, RATS, etc. 獴（生活在热带地区，捕食蛇、鼠等）

mon·grel /ˈmʌŋɡrəl/ (*especially BrE*) (*also* **mutt** *especially in NAmE*) *noun* a dog that is a mixture of different breeds 杂种狗

mon·ied = MONEYED

moni·ker /ˈmɒnɪkə(r); *NAmE* ˈmɑːn-/ *noun* (*humorous*) a name 姓名；名

mon·ism /ˈmɒnɪzəm; ˈməʊn-; *NAmE* ˈmɑːn-; ˈmoʊn-/ *noun* (*religion* 宗) the belief that there is only one god 一元论

moni·tor 🔑 AW /ˈmɒnɪtə(r); *NAmE* ˈmɑːn-/ *noun, verb*

■ ***noun* 1** 🔑 a television screen used to show particular kinds of information; a screen that shows information from a computer 显示屏；监视器；（计算机）显示器： *The details of today's flights are displayed on the monitor.* 今天航班的详细情况都显示在屏幕上。◇ *a PC with a 17-inch colour monitor* 带 17 英寸彩色显示器的个人电脑 ➲ VISUAL VOCAB PAGE V73 **2** a piece of equipment used to check or record sth 监控器；监测器： *a heart monitor* 心脏监测器 **3** a student in a school who performs special duties, such as helping the teacher 班长；级长；班代表 **4** a person whose job is to check that sth is done fairly and honestly, especially in a foreign country（尤指派往国外的）监督员，核查员： *UN monitors declared the referendum fair.* 联合国核查员宣布这次全民投票是公正的。 **5** a large tropical LIZARD (= a type of REPTILE) 巨蜥

■ ***verb* 1** 🔑 **~ sth | ~ what, how, etc....** to watch and check sth over a period of time in order to see how it develops, so that you can make any necessary changes 监视；检

M

查；跟踪调查 SYN **track**: *Each student's progress is closely monitored.* 每一位同学的学习情况都受到密切的关注。 **2 ~ sth** to listen to telephone calls, foreign radio broadcasts, etc. in order to find out information that might be useful 监听（电话、外国无线电广播等）

monk /mʌŋk/ *noun* a member of a religious group of men who often live apart from other people in a MONASTERY and who do not marry or have personal possessions 僧侣；修道士: ***Benedictine/Buddhist monks*** 本笃会修士；佛教僧侣 ➲ COMPARE FRIAR, NUN ➲ SEE ALSO MONKISH

mon·key /ˈmʌŋki/ *noun* **1** an animal with a long tail, that climbs trees and lives in hot countries. There are several types of monkey and they are related to APES and humans. 猴子 **2** (*informal*) a child who is active and likes playing tricks on people 顽皮的孩子；调皮鬼；捣蛋鬼: *Come here, you cheeky little monkey!* 过来，你这没有教养的小捣蛋鬼！ **3** (*BrE, slang*) £500 * 500 英镑

IDM **get a monkey off your ˈback** to free yourself of something that causes you worry or difficulty 解除忧虑；排除困难: *The team have never beaten Germany and they'll be desperate to get that monkey off their backs.* 该队从未打败过德国队，他们太想战胜这个对手，一吐心中的郁闷了。 **I don't/couldn't give a ˈmonkey's** (*BrE, slang*) used to say, in a way that is not very polite, that you do not care about sth, or are not at all interested in it 我根本无所谓；我压根儿就不在乎 **make a ˈmonkey (out) of sb** to make sb seem stupid 捉弄；愚弄 ➲ MORE AT BRASS

ˈmonkey business *noun* [U] (*informal*) dishonest or silly behaviour 欺骗；胡闹；恶作剧

ˈmonkey chanting *noun* [U] (*BrE*) abuse of a black player by white people who are watching a contest, especially a football (SOCCER) game 猴舞般的哄骂（白人看比赛时对黑人运动员的咒骂，尤指足球比赛时）

ˌmonkey in the ˈmiddle (*NAmE*) (*BrE* **ˌpiggy in the ˈmiddle, ˌpig in the ˈmiddle**) *noun* **1** a children's game where two people throw a ball to each other over the head of another person who tries to catch it 过顶传球（儿童游戏，由两人抛传球，中间一人争抢） **2** a person who is caught between two people or groups who are fighting or arguing（被夹在中间而）左右为难的人

ˈmonkey nut *noun* (*BrE*) a PEANUT with its shell still on 落花生

ˈmonkey puzzle (*also* **ˈmonkey puzzle tree**) *noun* a CONIFER tree with leaves like scales, that are thin, tough and very sharp 猴谜树；智利南洋杉

ˌmonkey's ˈwedding *noun* (*SAfrE*) (*informal*) used to describe a period of time when it is raining while the sun is shining 晴雨天；太阳雨: *Look! It's a monkey's wedding!* 看！出着太阳还下雨！

ˈmonkey wrench (*BrE also* **ˌadjustable ˈspanner**) *noun* a tool that can be adjusted to hold and turn things of different widths 活动扳手 ➲ VISUAL VOCAB PAGE V21 ➲ COMPARE SPANNER, WRENCH *n.* (1)

IDM **throw a ˈmonkey wrench in/into sth** (*also* **throw a ˈwrench in/into sth**) (*NAmE, informal*) to do sth to spoil sb's plans 破坏，阻挠（计划）

monk·ish /ˈmʌŋkɪʃ/ *adj.* like a MONK; connected with MONKS 修士（般）的；僧侣（般）的

mono /ˈmɒnəʊ; *NAmE* ˈmɑːnoʊ/ *adj., noun*

■ *adj.* (*also* **mono·phon·ic**) (*music* 音) recording or producing sound which comes from only one direction 单声道的: *a mono recording* 单声道录音 ➲ COMPARE STEREO (2)

■ *noun* [U] **1** a system of recording or producing sound which comes from only one direction 单声道录音（或放音）系统: *recorded in mono* 用单声道录音系统录制的 ➲ COMPARE STEREO (2) **2** (*NAmE, informal*) = MONONUCLEOSIS

mono- /ˈmɒnəʊ; *NAmE* ˈmɑːnoʊ/ (*also* **mon-**) *combining form* (in nouns and adjectives 构成名词和形容词) one; single 单；单一: *monorail* 单轨铁路 ◇ *monogamy* 一夫一妻制

mono·chrome /ˈmɒnəkrəʊm; *NAmE* ˈmɑːnəkroʊm/ *adj.* **1** (of photographs, etc. 照片等) using only black, white and shades of grey 黑白的: ***monochrome illustrations/images*** 黑白插图 / 肖像 ◇ (*figurative*) *a dull monochrome life* 枯燥单调的生活 **2** using different shades of one colour 单色的 ▶ **mono·chro·mat·ic** /ˌmɒnəkrəˈmætɪk; *NAmE* ˌmɑːnəkroʊˈm-/ *adj.*: *a monochromatic colour scheme* 单一色彩的调配 **mono·chrome** *noun* [U]: *an artist who works in monochrome* 从事单色绘画的艺术家

mon·ocle /ˈmɒnəkl; *NAmE* ˈmɑːn-/ *noun* a single glass LENS for one eye, held in place by the muscles around the eye and used by people in the past to help them see clearly 单片眼镜

mono·coty·ledon /ˌmɒnəʊˌkɒtɪˈliːdn; *NAmE* ˌmɑːnoʊˌkɑːt-/ (*also* **mono·cot** /ˈmɒnəkɒt; *NAmE* ˈmɑːnəkɑːt/) *noun* (*biology* 生) a plant whose seeds form EMBRYOS that produce a single leaf 单子叶植物 ➲ COMPARE DICOTYLEDON

mono·cul·ture /ˈmɒnəkʌltʃə(r); *NAmE* ˈmɑːn-/ *noun* **1** [U] the practice of growing only one type of crop on a certain area of land 单作；单种栽培 ➲ WORDFINDER NOTE AT CROP **2** [C, U] a society consisting of people who are all the same race, all share the same beliefs, etc. 单一文化社会；单种族社会；一元化社会: *a global economic monoculture* 全球经济一元化社会

mono·cycle /ˈmɒnəsaɪkl; *NAmE* ˈmɑːn-/ *noun* = UNICYCLE

mono·cyte /ˈmɒnəsaɪt; *NAmE* ˈmɑːn-/ *noun* (*biology* 生) a type of large white blood cell with a simple round NUCLEUS that can remove harmful substances from the body 单核细胞，单核白血球（能清除对肌体有害物质的大型白细胞）

mon·og·amy /məˈnɒɡəmi; *NAmE* məˈnɑːɡ-/ *noun* [U] **1** the fact or custom of being married to only one person at a particular time 一夫一妻（制） ➲ COMPARE BIGAMY, POLYGAMY **2** the practice or custom of having a sexual relationship with only one partner at a particular time 单配偶；单配性 ▶ **mon·og·am·ous** /məˈnɒɡəməs; *NAmE* məˈnɑːɡ-/ *adj.*: *a monogamous marriage* 一夫一妻制的婚姻 ◇ *Most birds are monogamous.* 大多数飞禽都是单配性的。

mono·glot /ˈmɒnəɡlɒt; *NAmE* ˈmɑːnəɡlɑːt/ *noun* (*specialist*) a person who speaks only one language 只说一种语言的人 ➲ COMPARE POLYGLOT

mono·gram /ˈmɒnəɡræm; *NAmE* ˈmɑːn-/ *noun* two or more letters, usually the first letters of sb's names, that are combined in a design and marked on items of clothing, etc. that they own 字母组合图案，交织字母，花押字（常由姓名首字母组成，标在自己的衣服等物品上） ▶ **mono·grammed** *adj.*: *a monogrammed handkerchief* 有字母组合图案的手绢

mono·graph /ˈmɒnəɡrɑːf; *NAmE* ˈmɑːnəɡræf/ *noun* (*specialist*) a detailed written study of a single subject, usually in the form of a short book 专论；专题文章；专著

mono·lin·gual /ˌmɒnəˈlɪŋɡwəl; *NAmE* ˌmɑːn-/ *adj.* speaking or using only one language 单语的；只用一种语言的: *a monolingual dictionary* 单语词典 ➲ COMPARE BILINGUAL, MULTILINGUAL

mono·lith /ˈmɒnəlɪθ; *NAmE* ˈmɑːn-/ *noun* **1** a large single vertical block of stone, especially one that was shaped into a column by people living in ancient times, and that may have had some religious meaning（尤指古人凿成、表示某种宗教意义的）单块巨石，独石柱 **2** (*often disapproving*) a single, very large organization, etc. that is very slow to change and not interested in individual people（少有变化，不关心个人的）单一庞大的组织 ▶ **mono·lith·ic** /ˌmɒnəˈlɪθɪk; *NAmE* ˌmɑːnəˈlɪθɪk/ *adj.*: *a monolithic block* 巨大的石块 ◇ *the monolithic structure of the state* 统一庞大的国家结构

mono·logue (*NAmE also* **mono·log**) /ˈmɒnəlɒɡ; *NAmE* ˈmɑːnələːɡ; -lɑːɡ/ *noun* **1** [C] a long speech by one person during a conversation that stops other people from speaking or expressing an opinion 滔滔不绝的讲话；个人的长篇大论：*He went into a long monologue about life in America.* 他开始滔滔不绝地谈起美国的生活。**2** [U, C] a long speech in a play, film/movie, etc. spoken by one actor, especially when alone（戏剧、电影等的）独白 **3** [C, U] a dramatic story, especially in VERSE, told or performed by one person 独角戏：*a dramatic monologue* 戏剧独白 ➲ COMPARE DIALOGUE, SOLILOQUY

mono·mania /ˌmɒnəˈmeɪniə; *NAmE* ˌmɑːn-/ *noun* [U] (*psychology* 心) too much interest in or enthusiasm for just one thing so that it is not healthy 单狂，偏狂（非理性的固执）

mono·nucle·osis /ˌmɒnəʊˌnjuːkliˈəʊsɪs; *NAmE* ˌmɑːnoʊˌnuːkliˈoʊsɪs/ (*NAmE* or *BrE*, *medical* 医) (*NAmE*, *informal* **mono**) (*BrE* ˌ**glandular** ˈ**fever**) *noun* [U] an infectious disease that causes swelling of the LYMPH GLANDS and makes the person feel very weak for a long time 单核细胞增多症

mono·phon·ic /ˌmɒnəˈfɒnɪk; *NAmE* ˌmɑːnəˈfɑːnɪk/ *adj.* (*music* 音) = MONO

mono·plane /ˈmɒnəpleɪn; *NAmE* ˈmɑː-/ *noun* an early type of plane with one set of wings 单翼飞机 ➲ COMPARE BIPLANE

mon·op·ol·ist /məˈnɒpəlɪst; *NAmE* məˈnɑːp-/ *noun* (*specialist*) a person or company that has a MONOPOLY 垄断者；专卖者；专营者

mon·op·ol·is·tic /məˌnɒpəˈlɪstɪk; *NAmE* məˌnɑːpə-/ *adj.* (*formal*) controlling or trying to get complete control over sth, especially an industry or a company 垄断的；控制的；独占的

mon·op·ol·ize (*BrE also* **-ise**) /məˈnɒpəlaɪz; *NAmE* məˈnɑːp-/ *verb* **1** ~ **sth** to have or take control of the largest part of sth so that other people are prevented from sharing it 独占；垄断；包办：*Men traditionally monopolized jobs in the printing industry.* 在传统上，男人包揽了印刷行业中的所有工作。◇ *As usual, she completely monopolized the conversation.* 她和往常一样，完全垄断了这次谈话。**2** ~ **sb** to have or take a large part of sb's attention or time so that they are unable to speak to or deal with other people 占去（某人的大部分注意力或时间）；独占；霸占；使无法摆脱 ▶ **mon·op·ol·iza·tion, -isa·tion** /məˌnɒpəlaɪˈzeɪʃn; *NAmE* məˌnɑːpələˈz-/ *noun* [U]

mon·op·oly /məˈnɒpəli; *NAmE* məˈnɑːp-/ *noun* (*pl.* **-ies**) **1** ~ **(in/of/on sth)** (*business* 商) the complete control of trade in particular goods or the supply of a particular service; a type of goods or a service that is controlled in this way 垄断；专营服务；被垄断的商品（或服务）：*In the past central government had a monopoly on television broadcasting.* 过去，中央政府对电视节目播放实行垄断。◇ *Electricity, gas and water were considered to be natural monopolies.* 电、煤气和水垄断经营过去被认为是理所当然的。➲ COMPARE DUOPOLY ➲ WORDFINDER NOTE AT TRADE **2** [usually sing.] ~ **in/of/on sth** the complete control, possession or use of sth; a thing that belongs only to one person or group and that other people cannot share 独占；专利；专利品：*Managers do not have a monopoly on stress.* 并不只是经营管理者有压力。◇ *A good education should not be the monopoly of the rich.* 良好的教育不应该成为富人的专利。**3 Monopoly™** a BOARD GAME in which players have to pretend to buy and sell land and houses, using pieces of paper that look like money "大富翁"（棋类游戏，游戏者以玩具钞票买卖房地产）

Moˈnopoly money *noun* [U] money that does not really exist or has no real value 假钞票；无实际价值的钱：*Inflation was so high that the notes were like Monopoly money.* 通货膨胀严重，货币变得跟"大富翁"游戏钞票无异。**ORIGIN** From the toy money used in the board game *Monopoly*™. 源自"大富翁"游戏中使用的游戏币。

mono·rail /ˈmɒnəʊreɪl; *NAmE* ˈmɑːnoʊ-/ *noun* **1** [U] a railway/railroad system in which trains travel along a track consisting of a single rail, usually one placed high above the ground 单轨铁路（通常为高架）**2** [C] a train used in a monorail system 单轨列车

mono·so·dium glu·ta·mate /ˌmɒnəˌsəʊdiəm ˈɡluːtəmeɪt; *NAmE* ˌmɑːnəˌsoʊ-/ *noun* [U] (*abbr.* **MSG**) a chemical that is sometimes added to food to improve its flavour 谷氨酸一钠；谷氨酸钠；味精；味素

mono·syl·lab·ic /ˌmɒnəsɪˈlæbɪk; *NAmE* ˌmɑːn-/ *adj.* **1** having only one syllable 单音节的：*a monosyllabic word* 单音节词 **2** (of a person or their way of speaking 人或说话方式) saying very little, in a way that appears rude to other people 寡言少语的；说话少而无礼的

mono·syl·lable /ˈmɒnəsɪləbl; *NAmE* ˈmɑːn-/ *noun* a word with only one syllable, for example, 'it' or 'no' 单音节词

mono·the·ism /ˈmɒnəʊθiɪzəm; *NAmE* ˈmɑːnoʊ-/ *noun* [U] the belief that there is only one God 一神教；一神论 ➲ COMPARE POLYTHEISM ▶ **mono·the·ist** /ˈmɒnəʊθiɪst; *NAmE* ˈmɑːnoʊ-/ *noun* **mono·the·is·tic** /ˌmɒnəʊθiˈɪstɪk; *NAmE* ˌmɑːnoʊ-/ *adj.*

mono·tone /ˈmɒnətəʊn; *NAmE* ˈmɑːnətoʊn/ *noun, adj.*
▪ ***noun*** [sing.] a dull sound or way of speaking in which the tone and volume remain the same and therefore seem boring 单调；单调的声音：*He spoke in a flat monotone.* 他说话单调低沉。
▪ ***adj.*** [only before noun] without any changes or differences in sound or colour（声音或色彩）单调的：*He spoke in a monotone drawl.* 他用慢吞吞又单调的语气说话。◇ *monotone engravings* 单调的版画

mon·ot·on·ous /məˈnɒtənəs; *NAmE* məˈnɑːt-/ *adj.* never changing and therefore boring 单调乏味的 **SYN** **dull, repetitious**: *a* ***monotonous voice/diet/routine*** 单调乏味的声音/饮食/日常事务 ◇ *monotonous work* 单调乏味的工作 ◇ *New secretaries came and went with* ***monotonous regularity***. 秘书不停地更换，令人厌烦。▶ **mon·ot·on·ous·ly** *adv.*

mon·ot·ony /məˈnɒtəni; *NAmE* məˈnɑːt-/ *noun* [U] boring lack of variety 单调乏味；千篇一律：*She watches television to relieve the monotony of everyday life.* 她天天靠看电视来解闷儿。

mono·treme /ˈmɒnətriːm; *NAmE* ˈmɑːn-/ *noun* (*specialist*) a class of animal including the ECHIDNA and the PLATYPUS, which lays eggs, but also gives milk to its babies 单孔目动物（卵生哺乳动物）

mono·un·sat·ur·ated fat /ˌmɒnəʊʌnˌsætʃəreɪtɪd ˈfæt; *NAmE* ˌmɑːnoʊ-/ *noun* [C, U] a type of fat found, for example, in OLIVES and nuts, which does not encourage the harmful development of CHOLESTEROL 单不饱和脂肪（橄榄和坚果等中所含脂肪，不会促进胆固醇的有害增长）➲ SEE ALSO POLYUNSATURATED FAT, SATURATED FAT, TRANS-FATTY ACID, UNSATURATED FAT

mono·zyg·ot·ic twin /ˌmɒnəʊzaɪˈɡɒtɪk twɪn; *NAmE* ˌmɑːnoʊzaɪˈɡɑːtɪk/ (*also* **mono·zyg·ous twin** /ˌmɒnəʊˈzaɪɡəs twɪn; *NAmE* ˌmɑːnoʊ-/) *noun* (*specialist*) = IDENTICAL TWIN ➲ COMPARE DIZYGOTIC TWIN

Mon·si·gnor /mɒnˈsiːnjə(r); *NAmE* mɑːn-/ *noun* (*abbr.* **Mgr**) used as a title when speaking to or about a priest of high rank in the Roman Catholic Church 蒙席（罗马天主教会授予某些圣职人员的荣衔）

mon·soon /ˌmɒnˈsuːn; *NAmE* ˌmɑːn-/ *noun* **1** a period of heavy rain in summer in S Asia; the rain that falls during this period（南亚地区的）雨季，雨季的降雨 **2** a wind in S Asia that blows from the south-west in summer, bringing rain, and the north-east in winter 季风，季节风（盛行于南亚地区，夏季刮西南风，带来雨水，冬季刮东北风）➲ WORDFINDER NOTE AT RAIN

mons pubis /ˌmɒnz ˈpjuːbɪs; *NAmE* ˌmɑːnz/ (*also* **mons Ven·eris** /ˌmɒnz ˈvenərɪs; *NAmE* ˌmɑːnz/) *noun* (*formal*) the curved area of fat over the joint of the PUBIC bones, especially in women（尤指女性的）阴阜

M

mon·ster /ˈmɒnstə(r); *NAmE* ˈmɑːn-/ *noun, adj.*
■ ***noun*** **1** (in stories) an imaginary creature that is very large, ugly and frightening（传说中的）怪物，怪兽：*a monster with three heads* 三头怪兽 ◇ *prehistoric monsters* 史前怪物 **2** an animal or a thing that is very large or ugly 庞然大物；庞大的丑怪物；丑恶的东西：*Their dog's an absolute monster!* 他们的狗是一头庞然大物！ **3** a person who is very cruel and evil 恶棍；恶魔 **4** (*humorous*) a child who behaves badly 小恶魔；小坏蛋
■ ***adj.*** [only before noun] (*informal*) unusually large 巨大的；庞大的 SYN **giant**：*monster mushrooms* 巨大的蘑菇

ˌmonster ˈtruck *noun* an extremely large PICKUP TRUCK with very large wheels, often used for racing 超大型卡车，大脚车（轮子巨大的大卡车，常用于赛车）

mon·stros·ity /mɒnˈstrɒsəti; *NAmE* mɑːnˈstrɑːs-/ *noun* (*pl.* **-ies**) something that is very large and very ugly, especially a building 巨大而丑陋之物（尤指建筑） SYN **eyesore**：*a concrete monstrosity* 混凝土建成的庞大怪物

mon·strous /ˈmɒnstrəs; *NAmE* ˈmɑːn-/ *adj.* **1** considered to be shocking and unacceptable because it is morally wrong or unfair 丑恶的；道德败坏的；骇人的 SYN **outrageous**：*a **monstrous lie/injustice*** 弥天大谎；骇人听闻的不公 **2** very large 巨大的 SYN **gigantic**：*a monstrous wave* 巨浪 **3** very large, ugly and frightening 巨大丑陋的；庞大骇人的 SYN **horrifying**：*a **monstrous figure/creature*** 巨大的人影；骇人的动物 ▶ **mon·strous·ly** *adv.*：*monstrously unfair* 极不公正 ◇ *a monstrously fat man* 胖得吓人的男子

M

mont·age /ˌmɒnˈtɑːʒ; ˈmɒn-; *NAmE* ˌmɑːnˈtɑːʒ/ *noun* **1** [C] a picture, film/movie or piece of music or writing that consists of many separate items put together, especially in an interesting or unusual combination 蒙太奇；剪辑组合物：*a photographic montage* 摄影的剪辑组合作品 **2** [U] the process of making a montage 剪辑；蒙太奇手法

mon·tane /ˈmɒnteɪn; *NAmE* ˈmɑːn-/ *adj.* [only before noun] (*specialist*) connected with mountains 山地的；山的

Mon·terey Jack /ˌmɒntəreɪ ˈdʒæk; *NAmE* ˌmɑːn-/ (*NAmE also* **ˈJack cheese**) *noun* [U] a type of white American cheese with a mild flavour 蒙特里杰克干酪

month 🔑 /mʌnθ/ *noun* **1** 🔑 [C] any of the twelve periods of time into which the year is divided, for example May or June 月；月份：*the month of August* 八月份 ◇ *We're moving house **next month**.* 我们下个月搬家。◇ *She earns $1 000 **a month**.* 她每月赚 1 000 美元。◇ *The rent is £300 **per month**.* 租金是每月 300 英镑。◇ *Have you read this month's 'Physics World'?* 你看过这个月的《物理世界》吗？◇ *Prices continue to rise **month after month*** (= over a period of several months). 近几个月价格持续上升。◇ *Her anxiety mounted **month by month*** (= as each month passed). 她的焦虑之情逐月加重。➲ SEE ALSO CALENDAR MONTH **2** 🔑 [C] a period of about 30 days, for example, 3 June to 3 July 约 30 天的时间；一个月的时间：*The baby is three months old.* 这婴儿三个月大了。◇ *a three-month-old baby* 三个月大的婴儿 ◇ *They lived in Toronto during their first few months of marriage.* 他们婚后的头几个月住在多伦多。◇ *several months later* 几个月以后 ◇ *a six-month contract* 一份六个月的合约 ◇ *a month-long strike* 长达一个月的罢工 ◇ *He visits Paris once or twice a month.* 他一个月去一两次巴黎。➲ SEE ALSO LUNAR MONTH **3** 🔑 **months** [pl.] a long time, especially a period of several months 数月；很长时间：*He had to wait for months for the visas to come through.* 他不得不等好几个月才领到签证。◇ *It will be months before we get the results.* 我们要等很长时间才能得到结果。
IDM **in a ˌmonth of ˈSundays** (*informal*) used to emphasize that sth will never happen 遥遥无期；根本不会发生：*You won't find it, not in a month of Sundays.* 你找不到它的，根本不可能找到。➲ MORE AT FLAVOUR *n.*

month·ly /ˈmʌnθli/ *adj., adv., noun*
■ ***adj.*** **1** happening once a month or every month 每月的；每月一次的：*a **monthly meeting/visit/magazine*** 每月一次的会议 / 拜访；月刊 **2** paid, valid or calculated for one month 按月结算的；有效期为一个月的：*a monthly salary of £1 000* * 1 000 英镑的月薪 ◇ *a monthly season ticket* 月票 ◇ *Summers are hot, with monthly averages above 22°C.* 夏天很热，月平均温度在 22 摄氏度以上。
■ ***adv.*** every month or once a month 每个月；每月一次：*She gets paid monthly.* 她按月领薪水。
■ ***noun*** (*pl.* **-ies**) a magazine published once a month 月刊：*the fashion monthlies* 时装月刊

monty /ˈmɒnti; *NAmE* ˈmɑːnti/ *noun*
IDM **the ˌfull ˈmonty** the full amount that people expect or want 所期望的一切；全部：*They'll do the full monty* (= take off all their clothes) *if you pay them enough.* 如果你给足够的钱，她们会把所有的衣服脱光。

monu·ment /ˈmɒnjumənt; *NAmE* ˈmɑːn-/ *noun* **1** ~ **(to sb/sth)** a building, column, statue, etc. built to remind people of a famous person or event 纪念碑（或馆、堂、像等）：*A monument to him was erected in St Paul's Cathedral.* 在圣保罗大教堂为他修了一座纪念碑。**2** a building that has special historical importance 历史遗迹；有历史价值的建筑：*an ancient monument* 古迹 **3** ~ **to sth** a thing that remains as a good example of sb's qualities or of what they did 丰碑；永久的典范：*These recordings are a monument to his talent as a pianist.* 这些录音是展现他钢琴家才华的不朽之作。

monu·men·tal /ˌmɒnjuˈmentl; *NAmE* ˌmɑːn-/ *adj.* **1** [usually before noun] very important and having a great influence, especially as the result of years of work 重要的；意义深远的；不朽的 SYN **historic**：*Gibbon's monumental work 'The Decline and Fall of the Roman Empire'* 吉本的不朽著作《罗马帝国衰亡史》 **2** [only before noun] very large, good, bad, stupid, etc. 非常大（或好、坏、蠢等）的 SYN **major**：*a book of monumental significance* 一本意义非凡的书 ◇ *We have a monumental task ahead of us.* 极其繁重的工作在等着我们。◇ *It seems like an act of monumental folly.* 这似乎是一种非常愚蠢的行为。**3** [only before noun] appearing in or serving as a monument 作为纪念碑的；纪念碑上的：*a **monumental inscription/tomb*** 碑文；陵墓 ◇ *a **monumental mason*** (= a person who makes monuments) 纪念碑石工

monu·men·tal·ly /ˌmɒnjuˈmentəli; *NAmE* ˌmɑːn-/ *adv.* (used to describe negative qualities) extremely（用于表述负面性质）极端地，极度地：***monumentally difficult/stupid*** 极其困难 / 愚蠢

moo /muː/ *noun* (*pl.* **moos**) the long deep sound made by a cow（牛叫声）哞 ▶ **moo** *verb* [I] ➲ MORE LIKE THIS 4, page R25

mooch /muːtʃ/ *verb* (*informal*) **1** [I] **+ adv./prep.** (*BrE*) to walk slowly with no particular purpose; to be somewhere not doing very much 溜达；闲逛 SYN **potter**：*He's happy to mooch around the house all day.* 他就愿意在家里闲待着。**2** [I, T] ~ **(sth) (off sb)** (*NAmE*) to get money, food, etc. from sb else instead of paying for it yourself 白吃（或用等）；要别人白给（金钱、食物等） SYN **cadge**：*He's always mooching off his friends.* 他总是向朋友讨钱花。

mood 🔑 /muːd/ *noun* **1** 🔑 [C] the way you are feeling at a particular time 情绪；心情：*She's **in a good mood** today* (= happy and friendly). 她今天心情很好。◇ *He's always **in a bad mood*** (= unhappy, or angry and impatient). 他总是情绪不好。◇ *to be **in a foul/filthy mood*** 情绪很差 ◇ *Some addicts suffer violent **mood swings*** (= changes of mood) *if deprived of the drug.* 一些吸毒成瘾的人一旦没有毒品就会出现情绪的激烈波动。◇ *I'm just not **in the mood for** a party tonight.* 我今晚就是没心情参加聚会。◇ *I'm not really **in the mood to** go out tonight.* 我今晚真的没心情出门。◇ *He was **in no mood for** being polite to visitors.* 他当时没心思以礼待客。 **2** [C] a period of being angry or impatient 坏心境；坏脾气：*I wonder why he's **in such a mood** today.* 我不知道他为什么今天脾气这么坏。◇ *She was **in one of her moods*** (= one of her regular periods of being angry or impatient). 她又闹情绪了。**3** 🔑 [sing.] the way a group of people feel about sth; the atmosphere in a place or among a group of people 气氛；氛围：*The mood of the meeting was distinctly pessimistic.* 这次会议的气氛显然很悲观。◇ *The movie captures the mood of the* *interwar years perfectly.* 这部电影恰如其分地捕捉到了两次世界大战之间那些年的氛围。**4** [C] (*grammar* 语法) any of the sets of verb forms that show whether what is said or written is certain, possible, necessary, etc. 表达语气的动词屈折变化 **5** [C] (*grammar* 语法) one of the categories of verb use that expresses facts, orders, questions, wishes or conditions （动词的）语气： *the **indicative/imperative/subjunctive mood*** 陈述 / 祈使 / 虚拟语气

ˈmood-altering *adj.* (of drugs 药物) having an effect on your mood 对情绪有影响的；改变情绪的： *mood-altering substances* 改变情绪的物质

ˈmood music *noun* [U] music intended to create a particular atmosphere, especially a relaxed or romantic one 情调音乐，气氛音乐（尤为营造轻松或浪漫的气氛）

moody /ˈmuːdi/ *adj.* (**mood·ier**, **moodi·est**) **1** having moods that change quickly and often 情绪多变的；喜怒无常的： *Moody people are very difficult to deal with.* 喜怒无常的人很难打交道。**2** bad-tempered or upset, often for no particular reason 脾气坏的；郁郁寡欢的 SYN **grumpy**: *Why are you so moody today?* 你今天怎么这么闷闷不乐啊？ **3** (of a film/movie, piece of music or place 电影、音乐或场所) suggesting particular emotions, especially sad ones 表现出…情调的；感伤的；抑郁的；令人悲伤的 ▸ **mood·ily** /-ɪli/ *adv.* : *He stared moodily into the fire.* 他忧郁地盯着火光。 **moodi·ness** *noun* [U]

mooli /ˈmuːli/ (*also* **dai·kon**) *noun* [U, C] a long white root vegetable that you can eat 白萝卜（也称“大根”） ➲ VISUAL VOCAB PAGE V34

moon 🔑 /muːn/ *noun, verb*

■ ***noun*** **1** 🔑 (*usually* **the moon**) (*also* **the Moon**) [sing.] the round object that moves around the earth once every 27½ days and shines at night by light reflected from the sun 月球： *the surface of the moon* 月球表面 ◇ *a moon landing* 月球登陆 **2** 🔑 [sing.] the moon as it appears in the sky at a particular time 月亮；月相： *a crescent moon* 新月 ◇ *There's no moon tonight* (= no moon can be seen). 今晚看不见月亮。◇ *By the light of the moon I could just make out shapes and outlines.* 月光下，我只能分辨出形状和轮廓。 ➲ SEE ALSO FULL MOON, HALF-MOON, NEW MOON **3** [C] a natural SATELLITE that moves around a planet other than the earth 卫星： *How many moons does Jupiter have?* 木星有多少颗卫星？

IDM **ask, cry, etc. for the ˈmoon** (*informal*) to ask for sth that is difficult or impossible to get or achieve 想做办不到的事情；想要得不到的东西 **many ˈmoons ago** (*literary*) a very long time ago 很久以前 **over the ˈmoon** (*informal, especially BrE*) extremely happy and excited 欣喜若狂 ➲ MORE AT ONCE *adv.*, PROMISE *v.*

■ ***verb*** [I] (*informal*) to show your bottom to people in a public place as a joke or an insult 以屁股示人（在公共场所进行的恶作剧或侮辱）

PHR V **ˌmoon aˈbout/aˈround** (*BrE, informal*) to spend time doing nothing or walking around with no particular purpose, especially because you are unhappy （尤指无精打采地）闲逛，消磨时光 **ˈmoon over sb** (*informal*) to spend time thinking about sb that you love, especially when other people think this is silly or annoying 痴痴地思念（所爱的人） SYN **pine for**

moon·beam /ˈmuːnbiːm/ *noun* a stream of light from the moon （一道）月光

ˈMoon Boot™ *noun* a thick warm boot made of cloth or plastic, worn in snow or cold weather 雪地靴；棉靴

moong /muːŋ/ *noun* = MUNG

Moonie /ˈmuːni/ *noun* an offensive word for a member of the Unification Church 文鲜明信徒（含贬义，指文鲜明统一教教徒）

moonie /ˈmuːni/ *noun*

IDM **do a ˈmoonie** (*BrE, informal*) to show your naked bottom in public 当众露屁股

moon·less /ˈmuːnləs/ *adj.* without a moon that can be seen 无月亮的： *a **moonless night/sky*** 没有月亮的夜晚 / 天空

moon·light /ˈmuːnlaɪt/ *noun, verb*

■ ***noun*** [U] the light of the moon 月光： *to go for a walk **by moonlight/in the moonlight*** 在月光下散步 IDM SEE FLIT *n.*

■ ***verb*** (**moon·lighted**, **moon·lighted**) [I] (*informal*) to have a second job that you do secretly, usually without paying tax on the extra money that you earn （暗中）兼职，从事第二职业

moon·lit /ˈmuːnlɪt/ *adj.* lit by the moon 月光照耀的： *a **moonlit night/beach*** 月光照耀的夜晚 / 海滨

moon·scape /ˈmuːnskeɪp/ *noun* **1** a view of the surface of the moon 月球表面景色 **2** an area of land that is empty, with no trees, water, etc., and looks like the surface of the moon 像月球表面一样荒凉的地区

moon·shine /ˈmuːnʃaɪn/ *noun* [U] **1** (*old-fashioned, NAmE*) WHISKY or other strong alcoholic drinks made and sold illegally 非法酿制并销售的威士忌（或其他烈酒）；私酿酒 **2** (*informal*) silly talk 蠢话；胡言乱语 SYN **nonsense**

moon·stone /ˈmuːnstəʊn; *NAmE* -stoʊn/ *noun* [C, U] a smooth white shiny SEMI-PRECIOUS stone 月长石

moon·struck /ˈmuːnstrʌk/ *adj.* slightly crazy, especially because you are in love （尤指因爱）发痴的

moon·walk /ˈmuːnwɔːk/ *verb* **1** [I] to walk on the moon 在月球行走 **2** [I] to do a dance movement which consists of walking backwards, sliding the feet smoothly over the floor （舞蹈时）走太空步 ▸ **moon·walk** *noun*

Moor /mɔː(r); mʊə(r); *NAmE* mʊr/ *noun* a member of a race of Muslim people living in NW Africa who entered and took control of part of Spain in the 8th century 摩尔人（居住在非洲西北部的穆斯林，曾于 8 世纪占领西班牙部分地区） ▸ **Moor·ish** *adj.* : *the Moorish architecture of Córdoba* 科尔多瓦市的摩尔式建筑

moor /mɔː(r); mʊə(r); *NAmE* mʊr/ *noun, verb*

■ ***noun*** (*especially BrE*) **1** [C, usually pl.] a high open area of land that is not used for farming, especially an area covered with rough grass and HEATHER 旷野；荒野；高沼；漠泽： *the North York moors* 北约克郡的漠泽 ◇ *to go for a walk on the moors* 到旷野去散步 **2** [U] = MOORLAND : *moor and rough grassland* 高沼地和苍莽的草原

■ ***verb*** [I, T] to attach a boat, ship, etc. to a fixed object or to the land with a rope, or ANCHOR it （使）停泊；系泊 SYN **tie up**: *We moored off the north coast of the island.* 我们停泊在岛的北部岸边。◇ **~ sth (to sth)** *A number of fishing boats were moored to the quay.* 很多渔船系泊在码头。

moor·hen /ˈmɔːhen; ˈmʊə-; *NAmE* ˈmʊrhen/ *noun* a small black bird with a short reddish-yellow beak that lives on or near water 黑水鸡；泽鸡；雌苏格兰雷鸟；红松鸡

moor·ing /ˈmɔːrɪŋ; ˈmʊər-; *NAmE* ˈmʊr-/ *noun* **1 moorings** [pl.] the ropes, chains, etc. by which a ship or boat is MOORED 系泊用具： *The boat slipped its moorings and drifted out to sea.* 船的系泊绳索滑落，船漂向大海。 **2** [C] the place where a ship or boat is MOORED 停泊处；系泊区： *private moorings* 私人停泊区 ◇ *to find a mooring* 找一个停泊地 ◇ *mooring ropes* 停泊区的绳索

moor·land /ˈmɔːlənd; ˈmʊə-; *NAmE* ˈmʊrlənd/ (*also* **moor**) *noun* [U, C, usually pl.] (*especially BrE*) land that consists of MOORS 高沼地： *walking across open moorland* 穿越开阔的高沼地

moose /muːs/ *noun* (*pl.* **moose**) a large DEER that lives in N America. In Europe and Asia it is called an ELK. 驼鹿（产于北美，在欧洲和亚洲称为 elk） ➲ PICTURE AT ELK

ˈmoose milk *noun* (*CanE*) **1** [U, C] an alcoholic drink made by mixing RUM with milk 驼鹿奶酒（用朗姆酒和牛奶调制而成） **2** [U] any strong alcoholic drink which is made at home 家酿酒

moot /muːt/ *adj.*, *verb*

■ ***adj.*** (*NAmE*) unlikely to happen and therefore not

M

worth considering（因不大可能发生而）无考虑意义的：*He argued that the issue had become moot since the board had changed its policy.* 他争辩说这项议题已变得毫无实际意义，因为董事会已经改变了政策。

IDM **a moot 'point/'question** (*BrE, NAmE*) a matter about which there may be disagreement or confusion 悬而未决的事；有争议的问题

■ ***verb*** [usually passive] ~ sth (*formal*) to suggest an idea for people to discuss 提出…供讨论 SYN **propose, put forward**

'moot court *noun* (*especially NAmE*) a MOCK court in which law students practise trials（法学专业学生实习的）模拟法庭

mop /mɒp; *NAmE* mɑːp/ *noun, verb*

■ ***noun* 1** a tool for washing floors that has a long handle with a bunch of thick strings or soft material at the end 拖把；墩布：*a mop and bucket* 带水桶的拖把 ➲ VISUAL VOCAB PAGE V21 **2** a kitchen UTENSIL (= a tool) for washing dishes, that has a short handle with soft material at one end 洗碗刷 **3** a mass of thick, often untidy, hair 乱蓬蓬的头发：*a mop of curly red hair* 乱蓬蓬的红色鬈发

■ ***verb*** (**-pp-**) **1** ~ sth to clean sth with a mop 用拖把擦干净：*She wiped all the surfaces and mopped the floor.* 她把所有的陈设都擦干净，还拖了地板。 **2** ~ sth (from sth) to remove liquid from the surface of sth using a cloth 用布擦掉（表面）的液体：*He took out a handkerchief to* ***mop his brow*** (= to remove the sweat). 他拿出手绢来擦额头上的汗水。 IDM SEE FLOOR *n.*

PHR V **,mop sth/sb↔'up** to remove the liquid from sth using sth that absorbs it 吸干净；吸去…的水分：*Do you want some bread to mop up that sauce?* 要不要用块面包把这酱料蘸蘸吃了？ ◇ (*figurative*) *A number of smaller companies were mopped up* (= taken over) *by the American multinational.* 有若干较小的公司都被那家美国跨国集团兼并了。 ◇ (*figurative*) *New equipment mopped up* (= used up) *what was left of this year's budget.* 新设备用光了本年度的预算余额。 **,mop sb/sth↔'up 1** to complete or end sth by dealing with the final parts 完成，结束（最后部分）；收尾：*There are a few things that need mopping up before I can leave.* 我还有几件事儿，了结了才能走。 **2** to get rid of the last few people who continue to oppose you, especially by capturing or killing them 消灭（残敌）：*Troops combed the area to mop up any remaining resistance.* 部队对这一地区进行了清剿，以扫除一切残余的抵抗势力。

mope /məʊp; *NAmE* moʊp/ *verb* [I] to spend your time doing nothing and feeling sorry for yourself 闷闷不乐；自怨自艾 SYN **brood**：*Moping won't do any good!* 自怨自艾一点用处都没有！

PHR V **,mope a'bout/a'round** (...) (*disapproving*) to spend time walking around a place with no particular purpose, especially because you feel sorry for yourself（尤指闷闷不乐地）闲荡，闲逛：*Instead of moping around the house all day, you should be out there looking for a job.* 不要整天闷闷不乐地在家里晃悠，你应该出去找份工作。

moped /'məʊped; *NAmE* 'moʊ-/ *noun* a motorcycle with a small engine and also PEDALS 机器脚踏车；摩托自行车

mop·pet /'mɒpɪt; *NAmE* 'mɑːp-/ *noun* (*informal*) an attractive small child, especially a girl（可爱的）小孩，小娃娃，小女孩

mo·quette /mɒ'ket; *NAmE* moʊ-/ *noun* [U] a type of thick cloth with a soft surface made of a mass of small threads, used for making carpets and covering furniture 绒头织物，割绒织物（用于制作地毯和家具罩单）

MOR /,em əʊ 'ɑː(r); *NAmE* oʊ/ *noun* [U] music that is pleasant to listen to, but is not exciting or original (the abbreviation for 'middle-of-the-road') 中庸音乐，大众流行音乐（全写为 middle-of-the-road，不刺激，无创新性）

mo·raine /mə'reɪn; *BrE also* mɒ'reɪn/ *noun* [U, C] (*specialist*) a mass of earth, stones, etc., carried along by a GLACIER and left when it melts 冰碛

moral /'mɒrəl; *NAmE* 'mɔːr-; 'mɑːr-/ *adj., noun*

■ ***adj.* 1** [only before noun] concerned with principles of right and wrong behaviour 道德的：*a* ***moral issue/dilemma/question*** 道德方面的议题 / 困境 / 问题 ◇ *traditional moral values* 传统的道德观念 ◇ *a decline in* ***moral standards*** 道德水准的下降 ◇ *moral philosophy* 道德哲学 ◇ *a deeply religious man with a highly developed* ***moral sense*** 道德意识极强的笃信宗教的人 ◇ *The newspapers were full of* ***moral outrage*** *at the weakness of other countries.* 报纸总是道貌岸然地说别的国家不好。 **2** [only before noun] based on your own sense of what is right and fair, not on legal rights or duties 道义上的；道德上的 SYN **ethical**：***moral responsibility/duty*** 道义上的责任 / 义务 ◇ *Governments have at least a* ***moral obligation*** *to answer these questions.* 政府至少在道义上有责任回应这些问题。 ◇ *The job was to call on all her diplomatic skills and* ***moral courage*** (= the courage to do what you think is right). 这项工作需要她发挥全部的外交才能和捍卫正义的勇气。 **3** following the standards of behaviour considered acceptable and right by most people 品行端正的；有道德的 SYN **good, honourable**：*He led a very moral life.* 他这个人一向很正派。 ◇ *a very moral person* 品行非常端正的人 ➲ COMPARE AMORAL, IMMORAL **4** [only before noun] able to understand the difference between right and wrong 能辨别是非的：*Children are not naturally moral beings.* 儿童并非天生就能分辨是非。

IDM **take, claim, seize, etc. the moral 'high ground** to claim that your side of an argument is morally better than your opponents' side; to argue in a way that makes your side seem morally better 声称自己的论点在道义上占优势

■ ***noun* 1 morals** [pl.] standards or principles of good behaviour, especially in matters of sexual relationships 品行，道德（尤指性关系方面）：*Young people these days have no morals.* 现在的年轻人根本不讲道德。 ◇ *The play was considered an affront to* ***public morals.*** 人们认为这出戏侮辱了公众道德。 ◇ (*old-fashioned*) *a woman of* ***loose morals*** (= with a low standard of sexual behaviour) 放荡的女人 **2** [C] a practical lesson that a story, an event or an experience teaches you 寓意；教益：*And the moral is that crime doesn't pay.* 寓意就是犯罪得不偿失。

mor·ale /mə'rɑːl; *NAmE* -'ræl/ *noun* [U] the amount of confidence and enthusiasm, etc. that a person or a group has at a particular time 士气：*to* ***boost/raise/improve morale*** 提高士气 ◇ *Morale amongst the players is very high at the moment.* 此刻选手们士气高昂。 ◇ *Staff are suffering from low morale.* 员工士气低落。

,moral 'fibre (*BrE*) (*NAmE* **,moral 'fiber**) *noun* [U] the inner strength to do what you believe to be right in difficult situations 道德力量；道义精神

mor·al·ist /'mɒrəlɪst; *NAmE* 'mɔːr-/ *noun* **1** (*often disapproving*) a person who has strong ideas about moral principles, especially one who tries to tell other people how they should behave 道德说教者；卫道士 **2** a person who teaches or writes about moral principles 道德学家

mor·al·is·tic /,mɒrə'lɪstɪk; *NAmE* ,mɔːr-/ *adj.* (*usually disapproving*) having or showing very fixed ideas about what is right and wrong, especially when this causes you to judge other people's behaviour 是非观念坚定的；道学的；说教的

mor·al·ity /mə'ræləti/ *noun* (*pl.* **-ies**) **1** [U] principles concerning right and wrong or good and bad behaviour 道德；道德准则；道义：*matters of* ***public/private morality*** 公众 / 个人道德问题 ◇ *Standards of morality seem to be dropping.* 道德标准似乎在下降。 **2** [U] the degree to which sth is right or wrong, good or bad, etc. according to moral principles 合乎道德的程度：*a debate on the morality of abortion* 有关堕胎是否道德的辩论 **3** [U, C] a system of moral principles followed by a particular group of people 道德规范；道德体系 SYN **ethics** ➲ COMPARE IMMORALITY at IMMORAL ➲ WORDFINDER NOTE AT BEHAVIOUR

mo'rality play *noun* a type of play that was popular in the 15th and 16th centuries and was intended to teach a moral lesson, using characters to represent good and bad qualities 道德剧，寓意剧（流行于 15 和 16 世纪，剧中人物代表善与恶）

mor·al·ize (*BrE also* **-ise**) /ˈmɒrəlaɪz; *NAmE* ˈmɔːr-; ˈmɑːr-/ *verb* [I] (*usually disapproving*) to tell other people what is right and wrong especially in order to emphasize that your opinions are correct 进行道德说教 **SYN** **preach**

mor·al·ly /ˈmɒrəli; *NAmE* ˈmɔːr-/ *adv.* according to principles of good behaviour and what is considered to be right or wrong 道义上；道德上：*to act morally* 循规蹈矩 ◇ ***morally right/wrong/justified/unacceptable*** 从道义上讲是正确的 / 错误的 / 正当的 / 不可接受的 ◇ *He felt morally responsible for the accident.* 他觉得在道义上应对这次事故负责。

the ˌmoral maˈjority *noun* [sing.+sing./pl. v.] the largest group of people in a society, considered as having very traditional ideas about moral matters, religion, sexual behaviour, etc.（对道德、宗教、性行为等）持传统观念的最大群体

ˌmoral supˈport *noun* [U] the act of giving encouragement by showing your approval and interest, rather than by giving financial or practical support 道义上的支持；精神支持：*My sister came along just to give me some moral support.* 我姐姐只是过来给我一些精神上的支持。

ˌmoral ˈvictory *noun* a situation in which your ideas or principles are proved to be right and fair, even though you may not have succeeded where practical results are concerned 道义上的胜利

mor·ass /məˈræs/ *noun* [usually sing.] (*formal*) **1** an unpleasant and complicated situation that is difficult to escape from 困境；陷阱 **SYN** **web** **2** a dangerous area of low soft wet land 沼泽 **SYN** **bog, quagmire**

mora·tor·ium /ˌmɒrəˈtɔːriəm; *NAmE* ˌmɔːr-/ *noun* (*pl.* **-riums** or **-toria** /-riə/) ~ (**on sth**) a temporary stopping of an activity, especially by official agreement 暂停，中止（尤指经官方同意的）：*The convention called for a two-year moratorium on commercial whaling.* 会议呼吁两年内暂停商业捕鲸活动。

moray /ˈmɒreɪ; ˈmɒreɪ; *NAmE* ˈmɔːreɪ/ (*also* ˌ**moray ˈeel**) *noun* a type of EEL that hides among rocks in tropical waters 海鳝（栖于热带水域岩礁间的鳗类）

mor·bid /ˈmɔːbɪd; *NAmE* ˈmɔːrbɪd/ *adj.* **1** having or expressing a strong interest in sad or unpleasant things, especially disease or death 病态的；不正常的：*He had a morbid fascination with blood.* 他对血有着一种病态的喜好。◇ *'He might even die.' 'Don't be so morbid.'* "他甚至会死的。" "别胡思乱想。" **2** (*medical* 医) connected with disease 病的；与疾病有关的 ▸ **mor·bid·ity** /mɔːˈbɪdəti; *NAmE* mɔːrˈb-/ *noun* [U] **mor·bid·ly** *adv.*

morcha /ˈmɔːtʃə; *NAmE* ˈmɔːrtʃə/ *noun* (*IndE*) a march or large public meeting, organized to support a particular idea or political party 示威游行；大型公众集会：*They're planning on taking out a morcha at the minister's house.* 他们计划在部长宅邸发起集会。

mor·dant /ˈmɔːdnt; *NAmE* ˈmɔːrdnt/ *adj.* (*formal*) critical and unkind, but funny 尖刻而又风趣的；讽刺幽默的 **SYN** **caustic**: *His mordant wit appealed to students.* 他那尖刻的妙语受到学生的欢迎。▸ **mor·dant·ly** *adv.*

more /mɔː(r)/ *det., pron., adv.*

■ ***det., pron.*** (used as the comparative of 'much', 'a lot of', 'many' 用作 much、a lot of 和 many 的比较级) ~ (**sth/of sth**) (**than...**) a larger number or amount of（数、量等）更多的，更大的：*more bread/cars* 更多的面包 / 汽车 ◇ *Only two more days to go!* 仅仅剩下两天了！◇ *people with more money than sense* 金钱多于智慧的人 ◇ *I can't stand much more of this.* 我可承受不了太多这样的事了。◇ *She earns a lot more than I do.* 她赚的钱比我多多了。◇ *There is room for* ***no more than*** *three cars.* 这地方只能停放三辆车。◇ *I hope we'll see more of you* (= see you again or more often). 希望我们能经常见面。

IDM ˌ**more and ˈmore** continuing to become larger in number or amount（数量上）越来越多：*More and more people are using the Internet.* 越来越多人在使用互联网。◇ *She spends more and more time alone in her room.* 她一个人待在屋里的时间越来越多。

■ ***adv.*** ~ (**than...**) **1** used to form the comparative of adjectives and adverbs with two or more syllables（与两个或两个以上音节的形容词或副词连用，构成比较级）更：*She was far more intelligent than her sister.* 她比她姐姐聪明多了。◇ *He read the letter more carefully the second time.* 他把信又更仔细地看了一遍。**2** to a greater degree than sth else; to a greater degree than usual（程度上）更强，更多：*I like her more than her husband.* 我喜欢她多于喜欢她丈夫。◇ *a course for more advanced students* 为更高程度的学生设置的课程 ◇ *It had more the appearance of a deliberate crime than of an accident.* 这件事看来更像是故意犯罪，而不是事故。◇ *Could you repeat that* ***once more*** (= one more time)? 你能再重复一遍吗？◇ *I had no complaints and* ***no more*** (= neither) *did Tom.* 我没什么怨言，汤姆也没有。◇ *Signing the forms is* ***little more than*** (= only) *a formality.* 在那些表格上签名只是一种形式。◇ *I'm* ***more than*** *happy* (= extremely happy) *to take you there in my car.* 我非常乐意用我的车带你去那儿。◇ *She was* ***more than a little*** *shaken* (= extremely shaken) *by the experience.* 这次经历对她产生了极大的震动。◇ (*formal*) *I will torment you* ***no more*** (= no longer). 我再也不会让你痛苦了。➲ SEE ALSO ANY MORE

IDM ˌ**more and ˈmore** continuing to become larger in number or amount（数量上）越来越多 **SYN** **increasingly**: *I was becoming more and more irritated by his behaviour.* 我对他的行为越来越感到恼火。ˌ**more or ˈless** **1** almost 几乎；差不多：*I've more or less finished the book.* 我差不多已经读完这本书了。**2** approximately 大概；大约：*She could earn $200 a night, more or less.* 她一晚上大约能挣 200 美元。**the more, less, etc...., the more, less, etc....** used to show that two things change to the same degree 越…，越…；愈…，愈…：*The more she thought about it, the more depressed she became.* 这件事她越想越感到沮丧。◇ *The less said about the whole thing, the happier I'll be.* 对这整件事情谈得越少，我越高兴。**what is ˈmore** used to add a point that is even more important 更有甚者；更为重要的是：*You're wrong, and what's more you know it!* 你错了！而且你明明知道你错了！➲ LANGUAGE BANK AT ADDITION

more·ish /ˈmɔːrɪʃ/ *adj.* (*BrE, informal*) if food or drink is **moreish**, it tastes so good that you want to have more of it（食物、饮料滋味好）令人想再吃的

morel /məˈrel/ (*also* **moˌrel ˈmushroom**) *noun* a type of MUSHROOM that you can eat, with a top that is full of holes 羊肚菌

more·over /mɔːrˈəʊvə(r); *NAmE* -ˈoʊvər/ *adv.* (*formal*) used to introduce some new information that adds to or supports what you have said previously 此外；而且 **SYN** **in addition (to sb/sth)**: *A talented artist, he was, moreover, a writer of some note.* 他是一位有才华的艺术家，同时也是颇有名气的作家。➲ LANGUAGE BANK AT ADDITION

mores /ˈmɔːreɪz/ *noun* [pl.] (*formal*) the customs and behaviour that are considered typical of a particular social group or community 风俗习惯；传统 **SYN** **conventions**

morgue /mɔːg; *NAmE* mɔːrg/ *noun* **1** a building in which dead bodies are kept before they are buried or CREMATED (= burned) 停尸房；太平间 ➲ COMPARE MORTUARY ➲ WORDFINDER NOTE AT DIE **2** a place where dead bodies that have been found are kept until they can be identified（供辨认尸首的）陈尸所

mori·bund /ˈmɒrɪbʌnd; *NAmE* ˈmɔːr-; ˈmɑːr-/ *adj.* (*formal*) **1** (of an industry, an institution, a custom, etc. 企业、机构、习俗等) no longer effective and about to come to an end completely 行将灭亡的；即将倒闭的；濒于崩溃的 **2** in a very bad condition; dying 垂死的；濒临死亡的：*a* ***moribund patient/tree*** 濒临死亡的病人 / 树

Mor·mon /ˈmɔːmən; *NAmE* ˈmɔːrmən/ *noun* a member of a religion formed by Joseph Smith in the US in 1830,

M

officially called 'the Church of Jesus Christ of Latter-day Saints' 摩门教徒（摩门教正式名称为"耶稣基督末世圣徒教会"，1830 年由约瑟夫·史密斯于美国创建）：*a Mormon church/chapel* 摩门教教会 / 教堂

morn /mɔːn; *NAmE* mɔːrn/ *noun* [usually sing.] (*literary*) morning 早晨；上午

morn·ing /ˈmɔːnɪŋ; *NAmE* ˈmɔːrnɪŋ/ *noun* **1** the early part of the day from the time when people wake up until midday or before lunch 早晨；上午：*They left for Spain early this morning.* 他们今天一早就出发去西班牙了。◇ *See you **tomorrow morning**.* 明天上午见。◇ *I prefer coffee **in the morning**.* 我早晨喜欢喝咖啡。◇ *She woke every morning at the same time.* 她每天早上都在同一时间醒来。◇ *Our group meets on Friday mornings.* 我们组每周五上午碰面。◇ *I walk to work most mornings.* 我大多数早晨步行去上班。◇ *We got the news **on the morning of** the wedding.* 我们在举行婚礼的那天上午得到这个消息。◇ *He's been in a meeting all morning.* 他一上午都在开会。◇ *the morning papers* 晨报 ➲ SEE ALSO GOOD MORNING **2** the part of the day from midnight to midday 午夜至正午的时间：*I didn't get home until two in the morning!* 我凌晨两点才到家！◇ *He died in the early hours of Sunday morning.* 他于星期天凌晨去世。 **3 mornings** *adv.* in the morning of each day 在上午；在早晨；每天上午：*I only work mornings.* 我只在上午工作。

IDM **in the ˈmorning 1** during the morning of the next day; tomorrow morning 次日上午；明天上午：*I'll give you a call in the morning.* 我明天上午给你打电话。**2** between midnight and midday 午夜至正午间：*It must have happened at about five o'clock in the morning.* 这件事一定发生在凌晨五点钟左右。 **morning, noon and ˈnight** at all times of the day and night (used to emphasize that sth happens very often or that it happens continuously) 从早到晚；一天到晚：*She talks about him morning, noon and night.* 她整天把他挂在嘴边。◇ *The work continues morning, noon and night.* 这项工作从早到晚持续进行。 ➲ MORE AT OTHER

ˌmorning-ˈafter *adj.* [only before noun] **1** happening the next day, after an exciting or important event（令人兴奋或重要之事后）次日发生的：*After his election victory, the president held a morning-after news conference.* 选举获胜后，总统于次日召开了记者招待会。**2** used to describe how sb feels the next morning, after an occasion when they have drunk too much alcohol 宿醉的：*a morning-after headache* 宿醉头痛

ˌmorning-ˈafter pill *noun* a drug that a woman can take some hours after having sex in order to avoid becoming pregnant（房事后服用的）女用口服避孕丸

ˈmorning coat (*BrE*) (*NAmE* **cut·away**) *noun* a black or grey jacket for men, short at the front and very long at the back, worn as part of morning dress（男子穿的黑色或灰色）晨燕尾服，常燕尾服 ➲ COMPARE TAIL (6)

ˈmorning dress *noun* [U] clothes worn by a man on very formal occasions, for example a wedding, including a morning coat and dark trousers/pants 常礼服（男子在隆重场合穿的服装，包括常燕尾服和黑裤子）

ˌmorning ˈglory *noun* [C, U] a climbing plant with flowers shaped like TRUMPETS that open in the morning and close in late afternoon 牵牛花

ˈmorning room *noun* (*old-fashioned, especially BrE*) (in some large houses, especially in the past 尤指过去的大房子) a room that you sit in in the morning 晨用起居室

ˈmorning sickness *noun* [U] the need to VOMIT that some women feel, often only in the morning, when they are pregnant, especially in the first months 早孕反应；（孕妇）晨吐 ➲ WORDFINDER NOTE AT PREGNANT

the ˌmorning ˈstar *noun* [sing.] the planet Venus, when it shines in the east before the sun rises 晨星，启明星（黎明前在东方闪烁的金星）

ˈmorning suit *noun* (*BrE*) a suit worn by a man on very formal occasions, for example a wedding, including a MORNING COAT and dark trousers/pants 男式晨礼服，男式常礼服（在婚礼等很正式的场合穿，包括晨燕尾服和黑裤子）

mo·rocco /məˈrɒkəʊ; *NAmE* məˈrɑːkoʊ/ *noun* [U] fine soft leather made from the skin of a GOAT, used especially for making shoes and covering books 摩洛哥山羊皮革（柔软细腻，尤用于制鞋或书封皮）

moron /ˈmɔːrɒn; *NAmE* -rɑːn/ *noun* (*informal*) an offensive way of referring to sb that you think is very stupid 笨蛋；蠢货：*They're a bunch of morons.* 他们是一群蠢货。◇ *You moron—now look what you've done!* 你这个笨蛋，看你都干了些什么！ ▶ **mor·on·ic** /məˈrɒnɪk; *NAmE* -ˈrɑːn-/ *adj.*：*a moronic stare* 傻傻的凝视 ◇ *a moronic TV programme* 愚蠢的电视节目

mor·ose /məˈrəʊs; *NAmE* məˈroʊs/ *adj.* unhappy, bad-tempered and not talking very much 阴郁的；脾气不好的；闷闷不乐的 SYN **gloomy**：*She just sat there looking morose.* 她就那样阴郁地坐在那儿。 ▶ **mor·ose·ly** *adv.*

morph /mɔːf; *NAmE* mɔːrf/ *verb* **1** [I, T] ~ (**sth**) (**into sth**) to change smoothly from one image to another using computer ANIMATION; to make an image change in this way（利用电脑动画制作使图像）平稳变换 **2** [I, T] ~ (**sb/sth**) (**into sb/sth**) to change, or make sb/sth change, into sth different（使）变化；（使）改变

mor·pheme /ˈmɔːfiːm; *NAmE* ˈmɔːrf-/ *noun* (*grammar* 语法) the smallest unit of meaning that a word can be divided into 词素；语素：*The word 'like' contains one morpheme but 'un-like-ly' contains three.* * like 一词含一个词素，而 un-like-ly 则含三个。

mor·phine /ˈmɔːfiːn; *NAmE* ˈmɔːrf-/ (*also old-fashioned* **mor·phia** /ˈmɔːfiə; *NAmE* ˈmɔːrf-/) *noun* [U] a powerful drug that is made from OPIUM and used to reduce pain 吗啡

morph·ology /mɔːˈfɒlədʒi; *NAmE* mɔːrˈfɑːl-/ *noun* [U] **1** (*biology* 生) the form and structure of animals and plants, studied as a science 形态学；形态论 **2** (*linguistics* 语言) the forms of words, studied as a branch of linguistics 词法；形态学 ➲ COMPARE GRAMMAR, SYNTAX (1) ▶ **mor·pho·logic·al** /ˌmɔːfəˈlɒdʒɪkl; *NAmE* ˌmɔːrfəˈlɑːdʒ-/ *adj.*

mor·ris dance /ˈmɒrɪs dɑːns; *NAmE* ˈmɔːrɪs dæns; ˈmɑːrɪs dæns/ *noun* a traditional English dance that is performed by people wearing special clothes decorated with bells and carrying sticks that they hit together 莫里斯舞（英格兰的一种传统民间化装舞蹈） ▶ **ˈmorris dancer** *noun* **ˈmorris dancing** *noun* [U]

mor·row /ˈmɒrəʊ; *NAmE* ˈmɔːr-; ˈmɑːroʊ/ *noun* **the morrow** [sing.] (*old-fashioned, literary*) the next day; tomorrow 次日；明天：*We had to leave **on the morrow**.* 我们明天就得离去。◇ *Who knows what the morrow* (= the future) *will bring?* 谁知道明天会是什么样？

Morse code /ˌmɔːs ˈkəʊd; *NAmE* ˌmɔːrs ˈkoʊd/ *noun* [U] a system for sending messages, using combinations of long and short sounds or flashes of light to represent letters of the alphabet and numbers 莫尔斯（电）码

mor·sel /ˈmɔːsl; *NAmE* ˈmɔːrsl/ *noun* a small amount or a piece of sth, especially food 少量，一块（食物）：*a tasty morsel of food* 一点儿可口的食物 ◇ *He ate it all, down to the last morsel.* 他全吃光了，一点儿不剩。

mor·tal /ˈmɔːtl; *NAmE* ˈmɔːrtl/ *adj., noun*

■ *adj.* **1** that cannot live for ever and must die 不能永生的；终将死亡的：*We are all mortal.* 我们都总有一死。 OPP **immortal** **2** (*literary*) causing death or likely to cause death; very serious 导致死亡的；致命的；非常危急的：*a mortal blow/wound* 致命的一击 / 伤口 ◇ *to be in mortal danger* 处于极度的危险之中 ◇ (*figurative*) *Her reputation suffered a mortal blow as a result of the scandal.* 这一丑闻毁了她的名声。 ➲ COMPARE FATAL (1) **3** [only before noun] (*formal*) lasting until death 至死方休的；不共戴天的 SYN **deadly**：*mortal enemies* 不共戴天的敌人 ◇ *They were locked **in mortal combat*** (= a fight that will only end with the death of one of them). 他们陷入了一场你死我活的争斗中。**4** [only before noun] (*formal*) (of fear, etc. 恐惧等) extreme 极端的；非常厉害的：*We lived* ***in mortal dread*** *of him discovering our secret.* 因为害怕他发现我们的秘密，我们终日惶恐不安。

■ ***noun*** (*often humorous*) a human, especially an ordinary person with little power or influence 人；凡人；普通人 **SYN human being**：*old stories about gods and mortals* 关于天神和凡人的古老传说 ◇ (*humorous*) *Such things are not for* ***mere mortals*** *like ourselves.* 这种事不会落在我们这样的凡夫俗子身上。◇ (*humorous*) *She can deal with complicated numbers in her head, but we* ***lesser mortals*** *need calculators!* 她可以心算复杂的数字，而我们常人就需要计算器！

mor·tal·ity /mɔːˈtæləti; *NAmE* mɔːrˈt-/ *noun* (*pl.* **-ies**) **1** [U] the state of being human and not living for ever 生命的有限：*After her mother's death, she became acutely aware of her own mortality.* 她母亲去世后，她开始强烈意识到自己的生命是有限的。**2** [U] the number of deaths in a particular situation or period of time 死亡数量；死亡率：*the infant mortality rate* (= the number of babies that die at or just after birth) 婴儿死亡率 ◇ *Mortality from lung cancer is still increasing.* 死于肺癌的人数仍在上升。**3** [C] (*specialist*) a death 死亡：*hospital mortalities* (= deaths in hospital) 医院里的死亡数字

mor·tal·ly /ˈmɔːtəli; *NAmE* ˈmɔːrt-/ *adv.* (*literary*) **1** causing or resulting in death 致死；致命 **SYN fatally**：***mortally wounded/ill*** 受致命伤；得绝症 **2** extremely 极端；非常：***mortally afraid/offended*** 怕得要死；极为恼怒

ˌmortal ˈsin *noun* [C, U] (in the Roman Catholic Church 天主教) a very serious SIN for which you can be sent to HELL unless you CONFESS and are forgiven 死罪；大罪

mor·tar /ˈmɔːtə(r); *NAmE* ˈmɔːrt-/ *noun, verb*

■ ***noun*** **1** [U] a mixture of sand, water, LIME and CEMENT used in building for holding bricks and stones together 砂浆；灰浆 **2** [C] a heavy gun that fires bombs and SHELLS high into the air; the bombs that are fired by this gun 迫击炮；迫击炮弹：*to come under* ***mortar fire/attack*** 受到迫击炮火的袭击 **3** [C] a small hard bowl in which you can crush substances such as seeds and grains into powder with a special object (called a PESTLE) 研钵；臼 ➲ VISUAL VOCAB PAGES V27, V72 ➲ SEE ALSO BRICKS AND MORTAR

■ ***verb*** [I, T] ~ (**sb/sth**) to attack sb/sth using a mortar 用迫击炮攻击（或袭击）

ˈmortar board *noun* a black hat with a stiff square top, worn by some university teachers and students at special ceremonies 学位帽，方顶帽（大学师生在一些隆重场合戴的黑色帽）➲ VISUAL VOCAB PAGE V70 ➲ COMPARE CAP *n.* (3)

mort·gage /ˈmɔːɡɪdʒ; *NAmE* ˈmɔːrɡ-/ *noun, verb*

■ ***noun*** (*also informal* **ˌhome ˈloan**) a legal agreement by which a bank or similar organization lends you money to buy a house, etc., and you pay the money back over a particular number of years; the sum of money that you borrow 按揭（由银行等提供房产等的抵押借款）；按揭贷款：*to* ***apply for/take out/pay off a mortgage*** 申请 / 取得 / 还清抵押贷款 ◇ *mortgage rates* (= of interest) 按揭贷款利率 ◇ *a mortgage on the house* 一项房产按揭 ◇ *a mortgage of £60 000* * 6 万英镑的按揭贷款 ◇ *monthly mortgage payments* 月供 ➲ WORDFINDER NOTE AT HOME, LOAN ➲ COLLOCATIONS AT HOUSE

■ ***verb*** **~ sth** to give a bank, etc. the legal right to own your house, land, etc. if you do not pay the money back that you have borrowed from the bank to buy the house or land（向银行等）抵押（房地产）：*He had to mortgage his house to pay his legal costs.* 他不得不把房子抵押出去来付诉讼费。➲ MORE LIKE THIS 20, page R27

ˈmortgage bond *noun* (*SAfrE*) = BOND (4)

mort·ga·gee /ˌmɔːɡɪˈdʒiː; *NAmE* ˌmɔːrɡ-/ *noun* (*specialist*) a person or an organization that lends money to people to buy houses, etc. 受押人；抵押权人

mort·ga·gor /ˈmɔːɡɪdʒɔː(r); *NAmE* ˈmɔːrɡ-/ *noun* (*specialist*) a person who borrows money from a bank or a similar organization to buy a house, etc. 抵押人；出押人

mor·ti·cian /mɔːˈtɪʃn; *NAmE* mɔːrˈt-/ *noun* (*NAmE*) = UNDERTAKER

mor·tify /ˈmɔːtɪfaɪ; *NAmE* ˈmɔːrt-/ *verb* (**mor·ti·fies, mor·ti·fy·ing, mor·ti·fied, mor·ti·fied**) [usually passive] **~ sb** (**to do sth**) | **it mortifies sb that…** to make sb feel very ashamed or embarrassed 使难堪；使羞愧 **SYN humiliate**：*She was* ***mortified*** *to realize he had heard every word she said.* 她意识到自己的每句话都被他听到了，直羞得无地自容。
▸ **mor·ti·fi·ca·tion** /ˌmɔːtɪfɪˈkeɪʃn; *NAmE* ˌmɔːrt-/ *noun* [U]
mor·ti·fy·ing *adj.*：*How mortifying to have to apologize to him!* 要向他道歉，多难为情啊！

mor·tise (*also* **mor·tice**) /ˈmɔːtɪs; *NAmE* ˈmɔːrtɪs/ *noun* (*specialist*) a hole cut in a piece of wood, etc. to receive the end of another piece of wood, so that the two are held together 榫眼；卯眼 ➲ SEE ALSO TENON

ˈmortise lock *noun* a lock that is fitted inside a hole cut into the edge of a door, not one that is screwed into the surface of one side 插锁；暗锁

mor·tu·ary /ˈmɔːtʃəri; *NAmE* ˈmɔːrtʃueri/ *noun* (*pl.* **-ies**) **1** a room or building, for example part of a hospital, in which dead bodies are kept before they are buried or CREMATED (= burned) 太平间；停尸房 **2** (*NAmE*) = FUNERAL PARLOUR ➲ COMPARE MORGUE (1)

mo·saic /məʊˈzeɪɪk; *NAmE* moʊ-/ *noun* [C, U] a picture or pattern made by placing together small pieces of glass, stone, etc. of different colours 镶嵌图案；马赛克：*a Roman mosaic* 罗马镶嵌画 ◇ *a design in mosaic* 马赛克图案 ◇ *mosaic tiles* 马赛克瓷砖 ◇ (*figurative*) *A mosaic of fields, rivers and woods lay below us.* 我们下方是由田野、河流和林木交织成的图画。

Moses basket /ˈməʊzɪz bɑːskɪt; *NAmE* ˈmoʊzɪz bæskɪt/ (*BrE*) (*NAmE* **bas·sinet**) *noun* a BASKET for a small baby to sleep in 摩西筐；婴儿睡篮

mosey /ˈməʊzi; *NAmE* ˈmoʊzi/ *verb* [I] + **adv./prep.** (*informal*) to go in a particular direction slowly and with no definite purpose 漫步；溜达：*He moseyed on over to the bar.* 他溜达着朝酒吧走去。

mosh /mɒʃ; *NAmE* mɑːʃ/ *verb* [I] to dance and jump up and down violently or without control at a concert where rock music is played（在摇滚音乐会上）狂舞，劲舞

ˈmosh pit *noun* the place, just in front of the stage, where the audience at a concert of rock music dances and jumps up and down（摇滚音乐会舞台前观众的）狂舞区，摇滚区

Mos·lem /ˈmɒzləm; *NAmE* ˈmɑːz-/ *noun* = MUSLIM
▸ **Mos·lem** *adj.* = MUSLIM **HELP** The form **Moslem** is some times considered old-fashioned. Use **Muslim**. * Moslem 这一拼法有时被视为过时。用 Muslim。

mosque /mɒsk; *NAmE* mɑːsk/ *noun* a building in which Muslims worship 清真寺

mos·quito /məˈskiːtəʊ; *BrE also* mɒˈs-; *NAmE* -toʊ/ *noun* (*pl.* **-oes** or **-os**) a flying insect that bites humans and animals and sucks their blood. One type of mosquito can spread the disease MALARIA. 蚊子：*a mosquito bite* 蚊子叮伤 ➲ VISUAL VOCAB PAGE V13

moˈsquito net *noun* a net that you hang over a bed, etc. to keep mosquitoes away from you 蚊帐

moss /mɒs; *NAmE* mɔːs/ *noun* [U, C] a very small green or yellow plant without flowers that spreads over damp surfaces, rocks, trees, etc. 苔藓；地衣：*moss-covered walls* 青苔覆盖的墙壁 ➲ VISUAL VOCAB PAGE V11 ➲ COMPARE LICHEN ➲ SEE ALSO SPANISH MOSS **IDM** SEE ROLL *v.*

mossy /ˈmɒsi; *NAmE* ˈmɔːsi/ *adj.* covered with moss 苔藓覆盖的；长满苔藓的

most 🔑 /məʊst; *NAmE* moʊst/ *det., pron., adv.*

■ ***det., pron.*** (used as the superlative of 'much', 'a lot of', 'many' * much、a lot of 和 many 的最高级) **1** 🔑 the largest

M

in number or amount（数量上）最多，最大：*Who do you think will get (the) most votes?* 你认为谁会得到最多的选票？◇ *She had the most money of all of them.* 在这些人当中，她最有钱。◇ *I spent most time on the first question.* 我在第一个问题上花的时间最多。◇ *Who ate the most?* 谁吃得最多？◇ *The director has **the most to lose**.* 主任可能会损失最大。**HELP** **The** can be left out in informal *BrE*. 在非正式英式英语中，the 可以省略。**2** more than half of sb/sth; almost all of sb/sth 大多数；几乎所有：*I like most vegetables.* 几乎什么蔬菜我都喜欢。◇ *Most classical music sends me to sleep.* 大多数古典音乐都会让我睡着。◇ *As most of you know, I've decided to resign.* 你们大多数人都知道，我已经决定辞职了。◇ *Most of the people I had invited turned up.* 我邀请的人多半都来了。◇ *There are thousands of verbs in English and most (of them) are regular.* 英语有数千个动词，大多数是规则的。**HELP** **The** is not used with **most** in this meaning. 表达此义时，most 之前不加 the。

IDM **at (the) 'most** not more than 至多；不超过：*As a news item it merits a short paragraph at most.* 作为一则新闻，它至多只能占一小段。◇ *There were 50 people there, at the very most.* 那儿最多有 50 个人。

■ ***adv.*** **1** used to form the superlative of adjectives and adverbs of two or more syllables（与两个或两个以上音节的形容词或副词连用，构成最高级）最：*the most boring/beautiful part* 最烦人的／最美丽的部分 ◇ *It was the people with the least money who gave most generously.* 最没钱的人最慷慨大方。**HELP** When **most** is followed only by an adverb, **the** is not used * most 后只接副词时不用 the: *This reason is mentioned most frequently.* 这是人们最常提及的理由。but 但要说：*This is **the most** frequently mentioned reason.* 这是人们最常提及的理由。**2** to the greatest degree（程度上）最大，最多，最高：*What did you enjoy (the) most?* 你最欣赏的是什么？◇ *It was what she wanted **most of all**.* 这就是她最想得到的。**HELP** **The** is often left out in informal English. 在非正式英语中，the 常常省略。**3** (*formal*) very; extremely; completely 非常；极其；完全：*It was most kind of you to meet me.* 你来接我真是太好了。◇ *We shall most probably never meet again.* 我们极有可能再也见不到面了。◇ *This technique looks easy, but it most certainly is not.* 这项技术看上去简单，但绝不是那么回事。**4** (*NAmE, informal*) almost 几乎；差不多：*I go to the store most every day.* 我几乎每天都去商店。

-most *suffix* (in adjectives 构成形容词) the furthest 最远的；最深远的：*inmost* (= the furthest in) 最深处的 ◇ *southernmost* 最南的 ◇ *topmost* (= the furthest up/nearest to the top) 最高的 ➲ MORE LIKE THIS 7, page R25

,most favoured 'nation *noun* a country to which another country allows the most advantages in trade, because they have a good relationship（贸易）最惠国

most·ly /ˈməʊstli; *NAmE* ˈmoʊ-/ *adv.* mainly; generally 主要地；一般地；通常：*The sauce is mostly cream.* 这沙司主要是奶油。◇ *We're mostly out on Sundays.* 我们星期天一般不在家。

MOT /ˌem əʊ ˈtiː; *NAmE* oʊ/ (*also* **MOT test**) *noun* the abbreviation for 'Ministry of Transport' (a test that any vehicle in Britain over three years old must take in order to make sure that it is safe and in good condition) 车辆性能检测（英国对超过三年的机动车进行的强制性检测，全写为 Ministry of Transport）：*I've got to take the car in for its MOT.* 我得把车开去进行车检。◇ *to **pass/fail the MOT*** 车辆性能检测合格／不合格

mote /məʊt; *NAmE* moʊt/ *noun* (*old-fashioned*) a very small piece of dust 尘埃；微粒 **SYN** **speck**

motel /məʊˈtel; *NAmE* moʊ-/ (*also* **'motor lodge**) (*NAmE also* **'motor inn**) *noun* a hotel for people who are travelling by car, with space for parking cars near the rooms 汽车旅馆（附有停车设施）➲ MORE LIKE THIS 1, page R25

motet /məʊˈtet; *NAmE* moʊ-/ *noun* a short piece of church music, usually for voices only 经文歌（通常为清唱）➲ COMPARE CANTATA

moth /mɒθ; *NAmE* mɔːθ/ *noun* a flying insect with a long thin body and four large wings, like a BUTTERFLY, but less brightly coloured. Moths fly mainly at night and are attracted to bright lights. 蛾；飞蛾 ➲ VISUAL VOCAB PAGE V13

moth·ball /ˈmɒθbɔːl; *NAmE* ˈmɔːθ-/ *noun, verb*

■ ***noun*** a small white ball made of a chemical with a strong smell, used for keeping moths away from clothes 卫生球；樟脑丸

IDM **in 'mothballs** stored and not in use, often for a long time（长期）封存；（长期）搁置

■ ***verb*** [usually passive] **~ sth** to decide not to use or develop sth, for a period of time, especially a piece of equipment or a plan 封存；搁置不用 **SYN** **shelve**: *The original proposal had been mothballed years ago.* 最初的建议多年前就束之高阁了。

'moth-eaten *adj.* **1** (of clothes, etc. 衣服等) damaged or destroyed by moths 被虫蛀的；蛀坏的 **2** (*informal, disapproving*) very old and in bad condition 破旧的；过时的 **SYN** **shabby**

mother /ˈmʌðə(r)/ *noun, verb*

■ ***noun*** **1** a female parent of a child or animal; a person who is acting as a mother to a child 母亲；妈妈：*I want to buy a present for my mother and father.* 我想给爸爸妈妈买件礼物。◇ *the relationship between mother and baby* 母婴关系 ◇ *She's the mother of twins.* 她有一对双胞胎。◇ *a mother of three* (= with three children) 三个孩子的妈妈 ◇ *an expectant* (= pregnant) *mother* 孕妇 ◇ *She was a wonderful mother to both her natural and adopted children.* 她对亲生的和领养的孩子一样好。◇ *the mother chimpanzee caring for her young* 照料着幼崽的母猩猩 **2** the title of a woman who is head of a CONVENT (= a community of NUNS)（对女修道院院长的尊称）➲ SEE ALSO MOTHER SUPERIOR

IDM **at your ,mother's 'knee** when you were very young 小时候；孩提时：*I learnt these songs at my mother's knee.* 我小时候学过这些歌曲。 **the 'mother of (all) sth** (*informal*) used to emphasize that sth is very large, unpleasant, important, etc. 非常大（或讨厌、重要等）的事情：*I got stuck in the mother of all traffic jams.* 我被困在一次超级严重的大塞车之中。➲ MORE AT NECESSITY, OLD

■ ***verb*** **~ sb/sth** to care for sb/sth because you are their mother, or as if you were their mother 给以母亲的关爱；像母亲般地照顾：*He was a disturbed child who needed mothering.* 他是个心理失常的孩子，需要悉心照顾。◇ *Stop mothering me!* 我不要你的照顾！

mother·board /ˈmʌðəbɔːd; *NAmE* ˈmʌðərbɔːrd/ *noun* (*computing* 计) the main board of a computer, containing all the CIRCUITS 母板；主板

'mother country *noun* [sing.] **1** the country where you or your family were born and which you feel a strong emotional connection with 祖国 **2** the country that controls or used to control the government of another country（控制别国的）母国

'mother figure *noun* an older woman that you go to for advice, support, help, etc., as you would to a mother（能向其讨教、寻求支持或帮助等的）慈母般的人 ➲ SEE ALSO FATHER FIGURE

mother·fuck·er /ˈmʌðəfʌkə(r); *NAmE* -ðərf-/ *noun* (*taboo, slang, especially NAmE*) an offensive word used to insult sb, especially a man, and to show anger or dislike（常用于男性）浑蛋，杂种

,mother 'hen *noun* (*usually disapproving*) a woman who likes to care for and protect people and who worries about them a lot 喜欢关心人的妇女；爱操心的女人

mother·hood /ˈmʌðəhʊd; *NAmE* -ðərh-/ *noun* [U] the state of being a mother 母亲身份；母性：*Motherhood suits her.* 她很适合做母亲。

mother·ing /ˈmʌðərɪŋ/ *noun* [U] the act of caring for and protecting children or other people 呵护；照料：*an example of **good/poor mothering*** 良好呵护的范例；照顾不周的例子

ˈMother·ing Sun·day *noun* [U, C] (*BrE, becoming old-fashioned*) = MOTHER'S DAY

ˈmother-in-law *noun* (*pl.* **mothers-in-law**) the mother of your husband or wife 婆婆；岳母 ➲ COMPARE FATHER-IN-LAW

ˈmother-in-law apartment *noun* (*NAmE*) = IN-LAW APARTMENT

mother·land /ˈmʌðəlænd; *NAmE* -ðərl-/ *noun* (*formal*) the country that you were born in and that you feel a strong emotional connection with 祖国 ➲ SEE ALSO FATHERLAND

mother·less /ˈmʌðələs; *NAmE* -ðərl-/ *adj.* having no mother because she has died or does not live with you 无母亲的；没娘的

ˈmother lode *noun* [usually sing.] (*especially NAmE*) a very rich source of gold, silver, etc. in a mine 主矿脉；母脉：(*figurative*) *Her own experiences have provided her with a mother lode of material for her songs.* 她自身的经历为她的歌曲提供了取之不尽的素材。

mother·ly /ˈmʌðəli; *NAmE* -ərli/ *adj.* having the qualities of a good mother; typical of a mother 慈母般的；母亲的 **SYN** **maternal**: *motherly love* 慈母般的爱 ◇ *She was a kind, motherly woman.* 她是一位善良的充满母爱的女人。

ˌMother ˈNature *noun* [U] the natural world, when you consider it as a force that affects the world and humans 大自然；自然界

ˌmother-of-ˈpearl (*also* **pearl**) *noun* [U] the hard smooth shiny substance in various colours that forms a layer inside the shells of some types of SHELLFISH and is used in making buttons, decorative objects, etc. 珠母层；珍珠母

ˈMother's Day *noun* a day on which mothers traditionally receive cards and gifts from their children, celebrated in Britain on the fourth Sunday in Lent and in the US on the second Sunday in May 母亲节（在英国为大斋期的第四个星期日，美国为五月的第二个星期日）

ˈmother ship *noun* a large ship or SPACECRAFT that smaller ones go out from 母舰；航天运载飞船

ˌmother's ˈmilk *noun* [U] a thing that a person really needs or enjoys 真正需要（或喜爱）的事物：*Jazz is mother's milk to me.* 爵士乐对于我来说是不可或缺的。

ˌmother's ˈruin *noun* [U] (*old-fashioned, BrE, informal*) the alcoholic drink GIN 杜松子酒

ˌMother Suˈperior *noun* a woman who is the head of a female religious community, especially a CONVENT (= a community of NUNS) 女修道院院长

ˌmother-to-ˈbe *noun* (*pl.* **mothers-to-be**) a woman who is pregnant 孕妇；准妈妈

ˌmother ˈtongue *noun* the language that you first learn to speak when you are a child 母语；本国语 **SYN** **first language**

motif /məʊˈtiːf; *NAmE* moʊ-/ *noun* **1** a design or a pattern used as a decoration 装饰图案；装饰图形：*wallpaper with a flower motif* 有鲜花图案的墙纸 **2** a subject, an idea or a phrase that is repeated and developed in a work of literature or a piece of music（文学作品或音乐的）主题，主旨，动机 ➲ SEE ALSO LEITMOTIF **SYN** **theme**

mo·tion 🔑 /ˈməʊʃn; *NAmE* ˈmoʊʃn/ *noun, verb*

■ ***noun*** **1** 🔑 [U, sing.] the act or process of moving or the way sth moves 运动；移动；动：*Newton's laws of motion* 牛顿的运动定律 ◇ *The swaying motion of the ship was making me feel seasick.* 船身摇摆不定，让我觉得恶心。◇ (*formal*) *Do not alight while the train is still* ***in motion*** (= moving). 列车未停稳时不要下车。◇ *Rub the cream in with a circular motion.* 一圈一圈地揉擦乳霜。 ➲ SEE ALSO SLOW MOTION **2** [C] a particular movement made usually with your hand or your head, especially to communicate sth（为传递信息用手或头做的）动作 **SYN** **gesture**: *At a single motion of his hand, the room fell silent.* 他手一挥，屋子里便安静了下来。**3** [C] a formal proposal that is discussed and voted on at a meeting 动议；提议：*to table/put forward a motion* 提出一项动议 ◇ *to propose a motion* (= to be the main speaker in favour of a motion) 提出动议 ◇ *The* ***motion was adopted/carried*** *by six votes to one.* 这项提议以六比一的票数通过。 ➲ WORDFINDER NOTE AT DEBATE **4** [C] (*BrE, formal*) an act of emptying the BOWELS; the waste matter that is emptied from the bowels 通便；大便

IDM **go through the ˈmotions (of doing sth)** to do or say sth because you have to, not because you really want to 做姿态；走过场 **set/put sth in ˈmotion** to start sth moving 让…动起来：*They set the machinery in motion.* 他们将机器开动起来。◇ (*figurative*) *The wheels of change have been set in motion.* 变革的车轮已经开始运转。

■ ***verb*** [I, T] to make a movement, usually with your hand or head, to show sb what you want them to do（以头或手）做动作，示意：**~ to sb (to do sth)** *I motioned to the waiter.* 我向侍者打了个手势。◇ **~ (for) sb to do sth** *He motioned for us to follow him.* 他示意我们跟他走。◇ **~ sb + adv./prep.** *She motioned him into her office.* 她示意他到她办公室来。

mo·tion·less /ˈməʊʃnləs; *NAmE* ˈmoʊʃn-/ *adj.* not moving; still 静止的；一动不动的：*She stood absolutely motionless.* 她纹丝不动地站在那里。

ˌmotion ˈpicture *noun* (*especially NAmE*) a film/movie that is made for the cinema 电影

ˈmotion sickness *noun* [U] the unpleasant feeling that you are going to VOMIT, that some people have when they are moving, especially in a vehicle 运动病；晕动病（尤指晕车）

mo·tiv·ate **AW** /ˈməʊtɪveɪt; *NAmE* ˈmoʊ-/ *verb* **1** [often passive] **~ sb** to be the reason why sb does sth or behaves in a particular way 成为…的动机；是…的原因：*He is motivated entirely by self-interest.* 他做事完全出于私利。**2** to make sb want to do sth, especially sth that involves hard work and effort 推动…甘愿苦干；激励；激发：**~ sb** *She's very good at motivating her students.* 她非常擅长激励她的学生。◇ **~ sb to do sth** *The plan is designed to motivate employees to work more efficiently.* 这个计划旨在促使员工更加卓有成效地工作。**3 ~ sth** (*SAfrE, formal*) to give reasons for sth that you have stated（就所说的话）给出理由；说明…的原因：*Please motivate your answer to question 5.* 请解释你对第 5 题所作的回答。▶ **mo·tiv·ated** **AW** *adj.*：*a racially motivated attack* 种族问题引发的攻击 ◇ *a highly motivated student* (= one who is very interested and works hard) 学习积极性很高的学生 **OPP** **unmotivated** **mo·tiv·ation** **AW** /ˌməʊtɪˈveɪʃn; *NAmE* ˌmoʊ-/ *noun* [C, U]: *What is the* ***motivation behind*** *this sudden change?* 这个突然转变背后的动机是什么？ ◇ *Most people said that pay was their main motivation for working.* 大多数人说赚取报酬是他们工作的主要动机。◇ *He's intelligent enough but he lacks motivation.* 他很聪明，但缺乏积极性。◇ (*SAfrE*) *All research proposals must be accompanied by a full motivation.* 所有研究计划书均须详述研究动机。**mo·tiv·ation·al** /-ʃənl/ *adj.* (*formal*)：*an important motivational factor* 重要的促进因素 **mo·tiv·ator** /ˈməʊtɪveɪtə(r); *NAmE* ˈmoʊ-/ *noun*：*Desire for status can be a powerful motivator.* 追逐地位的欲望可以成为强大的动力。

mo·tive **AW** /ˈməʊtɪv; *NAmE* ˈmoʊ-/ *noun, adj.*

■ ***noun*** **~ (for sth)** a reason for doing sth 动机；原因；目的：*There seemed to be no motive for the murder.* 这起谋杀案看不出有什么动机。◇ *I'm suspicious of his motives.* 我怀疑他的动机。◇ *the profit motive* (= the desire to make a profit) 谋利的动机 ◇ *I have an* ***ulterior motive*** *in offering to help you.* 我主动提出要帮助你是有私心的。➲ SYNONYMS AT REASON ▶ **mo·tive·less** *adj.*：*an apparently motiveless murder/attack* 表面上没有动机的谋杀 / 袭击

■ ***adj.*** [only before noun] (*specialist*) causing movement or action 发动的；导致运动的：***motive power/force*** (= for example electricity to operate machinery) 原动力

mot juste /ˌməʊ ˈʒuːst; *NAmE* ˌmoʊ/ *noun* (*pl.* **mots justes** /ˌməʊ ˈʒuːst; *NAmE* ˌmoʊ ˈʒuːst/) (*from French*) the exact

M

word that is appropriate for the situation 恰当的用词；贴切的字眼

mot·ley /ˈmɒtli; *NAmE* ˈmɑːtli/ *adj.* (*disapproving*) consisting of many different types of people or things that do not seem to belong together 混杂的；杂七杂八的：*The room was filled with a motley collection of furniture and paintings.* 屋子里摆满了五花八门的家具和绘画。◇ *The audience was a* **motley crew** *of students and tourists.* 观众是一群混杂在一起的学生和游客。

moto·cross /ˈməʊtəʊkrɒs; *NAmE* ˈmoʊtoʊkrɔːs; ˈmoʊtoʊkrɑːs/ (*BrE also* **scram·bling**) *noun* [U] the sport of racing motorcycles over rough ground 摩托车越野赛

moto·neur·on /ˌməʊtəˈnjʊərɒn; *NAmE* ˌmoʊtəˈnjuːrɑːn; -ˈnuː-/ *noun* = MOTOR NEURON

motor /ˈməʊtə(r); *NAmE* ˈmoʊ-/ *noun, adj., verb*

■ ***noun*** **1** a device that uses electricity, petrol/gas, etc. to produce movement and makes a machine, a vehicle, a boat, etc. work 发动机；马达：*an electric motor* 电动机 ◇ *He started the motor.* 他启动了发动机。➲ SEE ALSO OUTBOARD MOTOR **2** (*BrE*, *old-fashioned* or *humorous*) a car 汽车

■ ***adj.*** [only before noun] **1** having an engine; using the power of an engine 有引擎的；由发动机推动的：*motor vehicles* 机动车辆 **2** (*especially BrE*) connected with vehicles that have engines 机动车的；汽车的：*the* ***motor industry/trade*** 汽车工业 / 贸易 ◇ *a motor accident* 机动车事故 ◇ *motor insurance* 汽车保险 ◇ *motor fuel* 汽车燃料 **3** (*specialist*) connected with movement of the body that is produced by muscles; connected with the nerves that control movement 肌肉运动的；运动神经的：*uncoordinated motor activity* 不协调的肌肉运动 ◇ *Both motor and sensory functions are affected.* 运动功能和感觉功能都受到影响。

■ ***verb*** [I] + **adv./prep.** (*old-fashioned, BrE*) to travel by car, especially for pleasure 乘车旅行；驾车旅行 ▸ **motor·ing** *noun* [U]: *They're planning a motoring holiday to France this year.* 他们计划今年驾车到法国去度假。

motor·bike /ˈməʊtəbaɪk; *NAmE* ˈmoʊtərb-/ *noun* **1** (*especially BrE*) = MOTORCYCLE：*Ben drove off on his motorbike.* 本骑着摩托车走了。 **2** (*NAmE*) a bicycle which has a small engine 助力自行车；摩托自行车

motor·boat /ˈməʊtəbəʊt; *NAmE* ˈmoʊtərboʊt/ *noun* a small fast boat driven by an engine 摩托艇；汽艇；汽船

motor·cade /ˈməʊtəkeɪd; *NAmE* ˈmoʊtərkeɪd/ *noun* a line of vehicles including one or more that famous or important people are travelling in（载着要人的）车队：*The President's motorcade glided by.* 总统的车队一溜烟开了过去。

ˈmotor car *noun* (*BrE, formal*) (*NAmE, old-fashioned*) a car 汽车

motor·cycle /ˈməʊtəsaɪkl; *NAmE* ˈmoʊtərs-/ (*also* **motor·bike** *especially in BrE*) *noun* a road vehicle with two wheels, driven by an engine, with one seat for the driver and often a seat for a passenger behind the driver 摩托车：*motorcycle racing* 摩托车赛 ◇ *a motorcycle accident* 摩托车事故 ➲ COLLOCATIONS AT DRIVING ➲ VISUAL VOCAB PAGE V55

motor·cyc·ling /ˈməʊtəsaɪklɪŋ; *NAmE* ˈmoʊtərs-/ *noun* [U] the sport of riding motorcycles 摩托车运动

motor·cyc·list /ˈməʊtəsaɪklɪst; *NAmE* ˈmoʊtərs-/ *noun* a person riding a motorcycle 骑摩托车的人：*a police motorcyclist* 驾驶摩托车的警察 ◇ *leather-clad motorcyclists* 穿着皮衣的摩托车手

motor·home /ˈməʊtəhəʊm; *NAmE* ˈmoʊtərhoʊm/ (*NAmE also* **motor home**, **RV**, **recreˌational ˈvehicle**) (*BrE also* **camp·er**, **ˈcamper van**) *noun* a large vehicle designed for people to live and sleep in when they are travelling 野营车（供旅行时居住）➲ VISUAL VOCAB PAGE V63

motor·ing /ˈməʊtərɪŋ; *NAmE* ˈmoʊ-/ *adj.* [only before noun] connected with driving a car 开汽车的：*a motoring offence* 违章汽车驾驶

motor·ist /ˈməʊtərɪst; *NAmE* ˈmoʊ-/ *noun* a person driving a car 驾车者；开汽车的人 ➲ WORDFINDER NOTE AT CAR ➲ COMPARE PEDESTRIAN *n.*

motor·ized (*BrE also* **-ised**) /ˈməʊtəraɪzd; *NAmE* ˈmoʊ-/ *adj.* [only before noun] **1** having an engine 有引擎的；机动的：*motorized vehicles* 机动车辆 ◇ *a motorized wheelchair* 机动轮椅 **2** (of groups of soldiers, etc. 部队等) using vehicles with engines 使用机动车的；摩托化的；机动化的：***motorized forces/divisions*** 摩托化部队 / 师

ˈmotor lodge (*NAmE also* **ˈmotor inn**) *noun* = MOTEL

motor·mouth /ˈməʊtəmaʊθ; *NAmE* ˈmoʊtərm-/ *noun* (*pl.* **motor·mouths** /-maʊðz/) (*informal*) a person who talks loudly and too much 说话大声且健谈者；喋喋不休的人

ˌmotor ˈneuron (*also* **moto·neur·on**) *noun* (*biology* 生) a nerve cell which sends signals to a muscle or GLAND 运动神经元

ˌmotor ˈneurone disease *noun* [U] a disease in which the nerves and muscles become gradually weaker until the person dies 运动神经元病

ˈmotor park *noun* (*WAfrE*) a station for passengers to get on or off buses or taxis 公共汽车站；出租车停靠站：*Passengers are set down at Molete Motor Park.* 乘客在莫里特站下车。

ˈmotor pool (*especially US*) (*BrE also* **ˈcar pool**) *noun* a group of cars owned by a company or an organization, that its staff can use（公司或机构的）公用车队

ˈmotor racing (*especially BrE*) (*NAmE usually* **ˈauto racing**) *noun* [U] the sport of racing fast cars on a special track 赛道汽车赛

ˈmotor scooter (*especially NAmE*) (*BrE also* **scoot·er**) *noun* a light motorcycle, usually with small wheels and a curved metal cover at the front to protect the rider's legs 小型摩托车 ➲ VISUAL VOCAB PAGE V55

motor·sport /ˈməʊtəspɔːt; *NAmE* ˈmoʊtərspɔːrt/ *noun* [U] (*especially BrE*) (*NAmE usually* **motorsports** [pl.]) the sport of racing fast cars or motorcycles on a special track 赛车运动

ˈmotor vehicle *noun* any road vehicle driven by an engine 机动车

motor·way /ˈməʊtəweɪ; *NAmE* ˈmoʊtərweɪ/ *noun* [C, U] (in Britain) a wide road, with at least two lanes in each direction, where traffic can travel fast for long distances between large towns. You can only enter and leave motorways at special JUNCTIONS.（英国）高速公路：***busy/congested motorways*** 繁忙的 / 拥挤的高速公路 ◇ *Join the motorway at Junction 19.* 在 19 号路口进入高速公路。◇ *Leave the motorway at the next exit.* 在下个出口驶出高速公路。◇ *A nine-mile stretch of motorway has been closed.* 一段九英里长的高速公路已关闭。◇ ***a motorway service area/service station*** 高速公路服务区 / 站 ➲ COMPARE INTERSTATE *n.* ➲ WORDFINDER NOTE AT ROAD

Mo·town™ /ˈməʊtaʊn; *NAmE* ˈmoʊ-/ *noun* [U] a style of music popular in the 1960s and 1970s, produced by a black music company based in Detroit 摩城音乐（流行于 20 世纪 60 和 70 年代，由本部在底特律的一家黑人唱片公司发行）**ORIGIN** From the informal name for the city of Detroit, known for its motor industry. 源自底特律城的非正式名称（汽车城）。

motte /mɒt; *NAmE* mɑːt/ *noun* the small hill on which the FORT is built in a motte-and-bailey castle 城堡丘陵（大型城堡中建有堡垒的高地或小山）

ˌmotte-and-ˌbailey ˈcastle *noun* an old type of castle that consists of a FORT on a small hill surrounded by an outer wall（旧时的）大型城堡（堡垒建在高地，带围墙）

mot·tled /ˈmɒtld; *NAmE* ˈmɑːtld/ *adj.* marked with shapes of different colours without a regular pattern 斑驳的；杂色的

motto /ˈmɒtəʊ; *NAmE* ˈmɑːtoʊ/ *noun* (*pl.* **-oes** or **-os**) a short sentence or phrase that expresses the aims and beliefs of a person, a group, an institution, etc. and is used as a rule of behaviour 座右铭；格言；箴言：*The school's motto is: 'Duty, Honour, Country'.* 这所学校的校训是：尽责、知耻、爱国。◇ *'Live and let live.' That's my motto.* "待人宽如待己"，这是我的座右铭。

mould (*especially US* **mold**) /məʊld; *NAmE* moʊld/ *noun, verb*

■ *noun* **1** [C] a container that you pour a liquid or soft substance into, which then becomes solid in the same shape as the container, for example when it is cooled or cooked 模具；铸模：*A clay mould is used for casting bronze statues.* 用黏土模具来浇铸青铜塑像。◇ *Pour the chocolate into a heart-shaped mould.* 将巧克力倒入心形模子。◇ *They* ***broke the mould*** *when they made you* (= there is nobody like you). 你是世上独一无二的。**2** [C, usually sing.] a particular style showing the characteristics, attitudes or behaviour that are typical of sb/sth（独特）类型，个性，风格：*a hero in the 'Superman' mould* "超人"式的英雄 ◇ *He is cast in a different mould from his predecessor.* 他和他的前任风格不一样。◇ *She doesn't fit* (*into*) *the traditional mould of an academic.* 她不像一个传统的学者。**3** [U, C] a fine soft green, grey or black substance like fur that grows on old food or on objects that are left in warm wet air 霉；霉菌：*There's mould on the cheese.* 干酪发霉了。◇ *moulds and fungi* 霉菌和真菌 ◇ *mould growth* 霉的生长 ➲ SEE ALSO LEAF MOULD

IDM **break the ˈmould** (**of sth**) to change what people expect from a situation, especially by acting in a dramatic and original way 改变…的模式；打破…的模式

■ *verb* **1** [T] to shape a soft substance into a particular form or object by pressing it or by putting it into a mould（用模具）浇铸，塑造：**~ A** (**into B**) *First, mould the clay into the desired shape.* 首先，将陶土做成需要的形状。◇ **~ B** (**from/out of/in A**) *The figure had been moulded in clay.* 这座人像是用黏土塑造的。**2** [T] to strongly influence the way sb's character, opinions, etc. develop 对…影响重大；将…塑造成：**~ sb/sth** *The experience had moulded and coloured her whole life.* 这次经历影响了她的一生。◇ **~ sb/sth into sb/sth** *He moulded them into a superb team.* 他将他们打造成一支非凡的队伍。**3** [I, T] **~** (**sth**) **to sth** to fit or make sth fit tightly around the shape of sth（使）紧贴于，吻合：*The fabric moulds to the body.* 这种织物很贴身。

mould·er (*US* **mol·der**) /ˈməʊldə(r); *NAmE* ˈmoʊ-/ *verb* [I] to decay slowly and steadily 腐烂；腐朽：*The room smelt of disuse and mouldering books.* 房间里有一股长期不用和书籍发霉的味道。

mould·ing (*especially US* **mold·ing**) /ˈməʊldɪŋ; *NAmE* ˈmoʊ-/ *noun* a decorative strip of plastic, stone, wood, etc. around the top edge of a wall, on a door, etc. 线脚（用于檐口、门楣等的凹凸带形装饰）

mouldy (*especially US* **moldy**) /ˈməʊldi; *NAmE* ˈmoʊ-/ *adj.* **1** covered with or containing MOULD 发霉的：*mouldy bread/cheese* 发霉的面包 / 干酪 ◇ *Strawberries go mouldy very quickly.* 草莓很容易发霉。**2** old and not in good condition 破旧的

moult (*especially US* **molt**) /məʊlt; *NAmE* moʊlt/ *verb* [I] (of a bird or an animal 鸟或兽) to lose feathers or hair before new feathers or hair grow 换羽；蜕毛

mound /maʊnd/ *noun* **1** a large pile of earth or stones; a small hill 土墩；小丘；小山岗：*a Bronze Age burial mound* 青铜时代的坟冢 ◇ *The castle was built on top of a natural grassy mound.* 这座城堡建在一个天然的绿草如茵的小丘上。**2** a pile 一堆 **SYN** **heap**：*a small mound of rice/sand* 一小堆米 / 沙子 **3 ~ of sth** (*informal*) a large amount of sth 许多；大量 **SYN** **heap**：*I've got a mound of paperwork to do.* 我有一堆文案工作要做。**4** (in BASEBALL 棒球) the small hill where the player who throws the ball (called the PITCHER) stands 投球区土墩

mount 🔑 /maʊnt/ *verb, noun*

■ *verb*

• **ORGANIZE** 组织 **1** 🔑 [T] **~ sth** to organize and begin sth 准备；安排；组织开展 **SYN** **arrange**：*to mount a protest/campaign/an exhibition* 发起抗议 / 运动；举办展览

• **INCREASE** 增加 **2** 🔑 [I] to increase gradually 逐步增加：*Pressure is mounting on the government to change the law.* 迫使政府修改法律的压力不断增加。◇ *The death toll continues to mount.* 死亡人数持续增加。➲ SEE ALSO MOUNTING *adj.*

• **GO UP STH** 攀登 **3** 🔑 [T] **~ sth** (*formal*) to go up sth, or up on to sth that is raised 登上；爬上；攀登 **SYN** **ascend**：*She slowly mounted the steps.* 她慢慢地爬上台阶。◇ *He mounted the platform and addressed the crowd.* 他登上讲台对人群发表演说。

• **BICYCLE/HORSE** 自行车；马 **4** 🔑 [T, I] **~** (**sth**) (*rather formal*) to get on a bicycle, horse, etc. in order to ride it 骑上；乘上；跨上：*He mounted his horse and rode away.* 他骑上马走了。**OPP** **dismount** ➲ SEE ALSO MOUNTED (1)

• **PICTURE/JEWEL, ETC.** 图画、宝石等 **5** [T] **~ sth** (**on/onto/in sth**) to fix sth into position on sth, so that you can use it, look at it or study it 镶嵌；安置：*The specimens were mounted on slides.* 标本安放在载片上。◇ *The diamond is mounted in gold.* 这颗钻石镶在金饰物上。

• **OF MALE ANIMAL** 雄性动物 **6** [T] **~ sth** to get onto the back of a female animal in order to have sex 爬上（雌性动物的背）交配 **IDM** SEE GUARD *n.*

PHR V ˌ**mount ˈup** to increase gradually in size and quantity（尺寸和数量上）增加，上升 **SYN** **build up**：*Meanwhile, my debts were mounting up.* 同时，我的债务在不断增加。

■ *noun*

• **MOUNTAIN** 山 **1** 🔑 **Mount** (*abbr.* **Mt**) (used in modern English only in place names 在现代英语里仅用于地名) a mountain or a hill 山；山峰：*Mt Kilimanjaro* 乞力马扎罗山 ◇ *St Michael's Mount* 圣迈克尔山

• **HORSE** 马 **2** (*formal* or *literary*) a horse that you ride on 坐骑

• **FOR DISPLAYING/SUPPORTING STH** 用以展示 / 支持某物 **3** something such as a piece of card or glass that you put sth on or attach sth to, to display it 衬纸板；载片；裱褙 **4** (*also* **mount·ing**) something that an object stands on or is attached to for support 托架；支撑架：*an engine/gun mount* 发动机架；炮架

moun·tain 🔑 /ˈmaʊntən; *NAmE* ˈmaʊntn/ *noun* **1** 🔑 a very high hill, often with rocks near the top 高山；山岳：*a chain/range of mountains* 山峦；山脉 ◇ *to climb a mountain* 爬山 ◇ *We spent a week walking* ***in the mountains.*** 我们在群山中走了一个星期。◇ *to enjoy the* ***mountain air/scenery*** 享受山上的空气；欣赏山中景色 ◇ ***mountain roads/streams/villages*** 山路；山中的溪流；山村 ◇ *a* ***mountain rescue team*** 登山营救队 ➲ VISUAL VOCAB PAGE V5

> **WORDFINDER** 联想词：altitude, foothill, peak, precipice, ridge, slope, summit, valley, **volcano**

2 ~ of sth (*informal*) a very large amount or number of sth 许多；大量：*a mountain of work* 大量的工作 ◇ *We made mountains of sandwiches.* 我们做了一大堆三明治。◇ *the problem of Europe's butter mountain* (= the large amount of butter that has to be stored because it is not needed) 欧洲的黄油过剩问题

IDM **make a ˌmountain out of a ˈmolehill** (*disapproving*) to make an unimportant matter seem important 小题大做；夸大其词

ˌ**mountain ˈash** *noun* = ROWAN

ˈ**mountain bike** *noun* a bicycle with a strong frame, wide tyres and many gears, designed for riding on rough ground 山地自行车；越野单车 ► ˈ**mountain biking** *noun* [U] ➲ VISUAL VOCAB PAGE V55

moun·tain·board /ˈmaʊntənbɔːd; *NAmE* ˈmaʊntnbɔːrd/ (*also* ˌ**all-terrain ˈboard**) *noun* a short narrow board with wheels like a SKATEBOARD that can be used for going down mountains 山地滑板；越野滑板 ► **moun·tain·board·ing** *noun* [U]

ˌMountain ˈDaylight Time *noun* [U] (*abbr.* **MDT**) the time used in summer in parts of the US and Canada near the Rocky Mountains that is six hours behind UTC 山区夏令时间（美国和加拿大落基山脉地区的夏季时间，比协调世界时晚六小时）

moun·tain·eer /ˌmaʊntəˈnɪə(r); *NAmE* ˌmaʊntnˈɪr/ *noun* a person who climbs mountains as a sport 登山者；登山运动员

moun·tain·eer·ing /ˌmaʊntəˈnɪərɪŋ; *NAmE* -tnˈɪrɪŋ/ *noun* [U] the sport or activity of climbing mountains 登山运动：*to go mountaineering* 去爬山 ◇ *a mountaineering expedition* 登山探险

ˈmountain lion *noun* (*NAmE*) = PUMA

ˈmountain man *noun* (*NAmE*) a man who lives alone in the mountains, especially one who catches and kills animals for their fur（尤指猎取毛皮的）山地人，山里人

moun·tain·ous /ˈmaʊntənəs/ *adj.* **1** having many mountains 多山的：*a* ***mountainous region/terrain*** 多山的地区 / 地形 ➲ WORDFINDER NOTE AT LANDSCAPE **2** very large in size or amount; like a mountain 巨大的；山一般的 **SYN** **huge**：*mountainous waves* 如山的巨浪

moun·tain·side /ˈmaʊntənsaɪd/ *noun* the side or slope of a mountain 山坡：*Tracks led up the mountainside.* 足迹通向山坡。

ˌMountain ˈStandard Time *noun* [U] (*abbr.* **MST**) the time used in winter in parts of the US and Canada near the Rocky Mountains that is seven hours behind UTC 山区冬季时间（美国和加拿大落基山脉地区的冬季时间，比协调世界时晚七小时）

ˈMountain time *noun* [U] the standard time in the parts of the US and Canada that are near the Rocky Mountains 山区标准时间（美国和加拿大落基山脉地区的时间）

moun·tain·top /ˈmaʊntəntɒp; *NAmE* ˈmaʊntntɑːp/ *noun* the top of a mountain 山顶 ► **moun·tain·top** *adj.* [only before noun]：*a mountaintop ranch* 山顶上的大牧场

moun·te·bank /ˈmaʊntɪbæŋk/ *noun* (*old-fashioned*) a person who tries to trick people, especially in order to get their money 江湖骗子

mount·ed /ˈmaʊntɪd/ *adj.* [only before noun] **1** (of a person, especially a soldier or a police officer 人，尤指士兵或警察) riding a horse 骑马的：*mounted policemen* 骑警 **2** placed on sth or attached to sth for display or support 装裱好的；安装好的：*a mounted photograph* 裱好的照片 **3 -mounted** (in compounds 构成复合词) attached to the thing mentioned for support 安装在…上的：*a ceiling-mounted fan* 吊扇 ➲ SEE ALSO WALL-MOUNTED

Moun·tie /ˈmaʊnti/ *noun* (*informal*) a member of the Royal Canadian Mounted Police 加拿大皇家骑警队员

mount·ing /ˈmaʊntɪŋ/ *adj., noun*

■ ***adj.*** [only before noun] increasing, often in a manner that causes or expresses anxiety 上升的；增长的 **SYN** **growing**：***mounting excitement/concern/tension*** 越来越兴奋 / 关注 / 紧张 ◇ *There is mounting evidence of serious effects on people's health.* 有越来越多的证据表明对人的健康有严重影响。

■ ***noun*** = MOUNT (4)：*The engine came loose from its mountings.* 发动机从托架上松开了。

mourn /mɔːn; *NAmE* mɔːrn/ *verb* [T, I] to feel and show sadness because sb has died; to feel sad because sth no longer exists or is no longer the same（因失去…而）哀悼，忧伤 **SYN** **grieve**：**~ sth** *He was still mourning his brother's death.* 他仍然在为哥哥的去世而悲伤。◇ *They mourn the passing of a simpler way of life.* 他们对较为淳朴的生活的消逝感到惋惜。◇ **~ (for sb/sth)** *Today we mourn for all those who died in two world wars.* 今天，我们向所有在两次世界大战中死难的人表示哀悼。◇ *She mourned for her lost childhood.* 她为失去的童年而伤感。➲ WORDFINDER NOTE AT DIE

mourn·er /ˈmɔːnə(r); *NAmE* ˈmɔːrn-/ *noun* a person who attends a funeral, especially a friend or a relative of the dead person 吊唁者；哀悼者

mourn·ful /ˈmɔːnfl; *NAmE* ˈmɔːrnfl/ *adj.* very sad 忧伤的；悲痛的 **SYN** **melancholy**：*mournful eyes* 忧伤的眼睛 ◇ *mournful music* 伤感的音乐 ◇ *I couldn't bear the mournful look on her face.* 我受不了她脸上那忧伤的神情。► **mourn·ful·ly** /-fəli/ *adv.*：*The dog looked mournfully after its owner.* 狗悲伤地目送主人离去。

mourn·ing /ˈmɔːnɪŋ; *NAmE* ˈmɔːrn-/ *noun* [U] **1** sadness that you show and feel because sb has died 伤逝；哀悼 **SYN** **grief**：*The government announced a day of national mourning for the victims.* 政府宣布全国为受害者哀悼一日。◇ *She was still* ***in mourning*** *for her husband.* 她仍在为丈夫服丧。**2** clothes that people wear to show their sadness at sb's death 丧服

mouse 🔑 /maʊs/ *noun, verb*

■ ***noun*** (*pl.* **mice** /maɪs/) **1** 🔑 a small animal that is covered in fur and has a long thin tail. Mice live in fields, in people's houses or where food is stored. 老鼠；耗子：*a field mouse* 田鼠 ◇ *a house mouse* 家鼠 ◇ *The stores were overrun with rats and mice.* 仓库里到处都是大大小小的老鼠。◇ *She crept upstairs,* ***quiet as a mouse.*** 她像耗子一样悄悄地爬上楼去。◇ (*figurative*) *He was a weak little mouse of a man.* 他是个懦弱无能的人。➲ SEE ALSO DORMOUSE **2** 🔑 (*pl.* **mice** or **mouses**) (*computing* 计) a small device that is moved by hand across a surface to control the movement of the CURSOR on a computer screen 鼠标：*Click the left mouse button twice to highlight the program.* 双击鼠标左键来加亮突出这个程序。◇ *Use the mouse to drag the icon to a new position.* 用鼠标将图标拖到一个新的位置。➲ VISUAL VOCAB PAGE V73 **IDM** SEE CAT

■ ***verb***

PHR V **ˈmouse over sth** (*computing* 计) to use the mouse to move over sth on a computer screen 使鼠标悬停于：*Mouse over the link in the original message.* 使鼠标悬停在原始信息的链接上。► **mouse·over** /ˈmaʊsəʊvə(r); *NAmE* -oʊ-/ *noun*：*the use of mouseovers in web design* 网页设计中鼠标悬停的使用

ˈmouse mat (*BrE*) (*especially NAmE* **ˈmouse pad**) *noun* a small square of plastic that is the best kind of surface on which to use a computer mouse 鼠标垫 ➲ VISUAL VOCAB PAGE V71

ˈmouse potato *noun* (*informal, disapproving*) a person who spends too much time using a computer 电脑迷

mouser /ˈmaʊsə(r)/ *noun* a cat that catches mice 捕鼠的猫

mouse·trap /ˈmaʊstræp/ *noun* a trap with a powerful spring that is used, for example in a house, for catching mice 捕鼠器；老鼠夹

mousey = MOUSY

mous·saka /muːˈsɑːkə/ *noun* [U, C] a Greek dish made from layers of AUBERGINE and finely chopped meat with cheese on top（希腊菜肴）肉末茄子饼，茄合子

mousse /muːs/ *noun* [C, U] **1** a cold DESSERT (= a sweet dish) made with cream and egg whites and flavoured with fruit, chocolate, etc.; a similar dish flavoured with fish, vegetables, etc. 奶油冻，木斯，慕斯（用奶油和蛋清加水果、巧克力等做成甜食，或加鱼肉、菜等做成凉菜）：*a* ***chocolate/strawberry mousse*** 巧克力 / 草莓奶油冻 ◇ ***salmon/mushroom mousse*** 鲑鱼 / 蘑菇奶油冻 **2** a substance that is sold in AEROSOLS, for example the light white substance that is used on hair to give it a particular style or to improve its condition 头发定型剂；摩丝

mous·tache (*especially US* **mus·tache**) /məˈstɑːʃ; *NAmE* ˈmʌstæʃ; məˈstæʃ/ *noun* **1** a line of hair that a man allows to grow on his upper lip 上唇的胡子；髭 ➲ COLLOCATIONS AT PHYSICAL ➲ VISUAL VOCAB PAGE V65 **2** **moustaches** [pl.] a very long moustache 长髭 ➲ COMPARE BEARD *n.*

mous·tached (*especially US* **mus·tached**) /məˈstɑːʃt; *NAmE* ˈmʌstæʃt; məˈstæʃt/ *adj.* [usually before noun] having a moustache 长胡子的；有胡子的 ➲ COMPARE MUSTACHIOED

mousy (*also* **mousey**) /ˈmaʊsi/ *adj.* (*disapproving*) **1** (of hair 毛发) of a dull brown colour 暗灰褐色的 ➲ WORDFINDER NOTE AT BLONDE **2** (*usually disapproving*) (of people 人) shy and quiet; without a strong personality 沉静害羞的；个性不强的

mouth *noun, verb*

■ ***noun*** /maʊθ/ (*pl.* **mouths** /maʊðz/)

• **PART OF FACE** 脸的部位 **1** the opening in the face used for speaking, eating, etc.; the area inside the head behind this opening 嘴；口：*She* ***opened her mouth*** *to say something.* 她张开嘴要说什么。◇ *His mouth twisted into a wry smile.* 他硬挤出一丝干涩的微笑。◇ *Their mouths* ***fell open*** (= they were surprised). 他们张口结舌。◇ *Don't* ***talk with your mouth full*** (= when eating). 不要一边吃一边说话。◇ *The creature was* ***foaming at the mouth.*** 这家伙在口吐白沫。➲ VISUAL VOCAB PAGE V64 ➲ SEE ALSO FOOT-AND-MOUTH DISEASE

• **PERSON NEEDING FOOD** 需要食物的人 **2** a person considered only as sb who needs to be provided with food 需要供养的人：*Now there would be another* ***mouth to feed.*** 现在又多一个要吃饭的人。◇ *The world will not be able to support all these extra* ***hungry mouths.*** 这个世界养活不起这么些额外的饥民。

• **ENTRANCE/OPENING** 入口；出口 **3** **~ (of sth)** the entrance or opening of sth 入口；开口：*the mouth of a cave/pit* 山洞口；矿井口 ➲ SEE ALSO GOALMOUTH

• **OF RIVER** 河流 **4** the place where a river joins the sea 入海口；河口

• **WAY OF SPEAKING** 讲话方式 **5** a particular way of speaking 讲话方式；言谈：*He has a foul mouth on him!* 他满嘴脏话！◇ *Watch your mouth!* (= stop saying things that are rude and/or offensive) 说话注意点儿！➲ SEE ALSO LOUDMOUTH

• **-MOUTHED** …口 **6** (in adjectives 构成形容词) having the type or shape of mouth mentioned 有…嘴的；…口的：*a wide-mouthed old woman* 大嘴的老太太 ◇ *a narrow-mouthed cave* 洞口狭窄的山洞 ➲ SEE ALSO OPEN-MOUTHED **7** (in adjectives 构成形容词) having a particular way of speaking 言谈…的；口齿…的：*a rather crude-mouthed individual* 言谈非常粗鲁的人 ➲ SEE ALSO FOUL-MOUTHED, MEALY-MOUTHED ➲ MORE LIKE THIS 8, page R25

IDM **be all ˈmouth** (*informal*) if you say sb is **all mouth**, you mean that they talk a lot about doing sth, but are, in fact, not brave enough to do it 只说不做 **down in the ˈmouth** unhappy and depressed 闷闷不乐；沮丧 **keep your ˈmouth shut** (*informal*) to not talk about sth to sb because it is a secret or because it will upset or annoy them 守口如瓶；保持缄默：*I've warned them to keep their mouths shut about this.* 我警告过他们对此事要守口如瓶。◇ *Now she's upset—why couldn't you keep your mouth shut?* 瞧她现在心烦意乱的样子，你就不能闭上嘴？ **out of the ˌmouths of ˈbabes (and ˈsucklings)** (*saying*) used when a small child has just said sth that seems very wise or clever 童言有道 **run off at the ˈmouth** (*NAmE, informal*) to talk too much, in a way that is not sensible 夸夸其谈；信口开河；喋喋不休 ➲ MORE AT BIG *adj.*, BORN *v.*, BREAD, BUTTER *n.*, FOAM *v.*, FOOT *n.*, GIFT *n.*, HEART, HORSE *n.*, LIVE[1], MELT, MONEY, SHOOT *v.*, SHUT *v.*, TASTE *n.*, WATCH *v.*, WORD *n.*

■ ***verb*** /maʊð/ **1 ~ sth | + speech** to move your lips as if you were saying sth, but without making a sound（动嘴唇）不出声地说：*He mouthed a few obscenities at us and then moved off.* 他不出声地朝我们骂了几句脏话，然后走了。**2 ~ sth | + speech** (*disapproving*) to say sth that you do not really feel, believe or understand 言不由衷地说：*They're just mouthing empty slogans.* 他们只是在空喊口号。

PHR V **ˌmouth ˈoff (at/about sth)** (*informal*) to talk or complain loudly about sth 大声地讲述；大声地抱怨

mouth·feel /ˈmaʊθfiːl/ *noun* the way an item of food or drink feels in the mouth（食物或饮料的）口感：*The drink has a creamy mouthfeel.* 这种饮料口感柔滑细腻。

mouth·ful /ˈmaʊθfʊl/ *noun* **1** [C] an amount of food or drink that you put in your mouth at one time 一口，一满口（的量）：*She took a mouthful of water.* 她喝了一大口水。**2** [sing.] (*informal*) a word or a phrase that is long and complicated or difficult to pronounce 又长又拗口的词（或短语）

IDM **give sb a ˈmouthful** (*informal, especially BrE*) to speak angrily to sb, perhaps swearing at them 对某人恶言恶语；大骂某人 **say a ˈmouthful** (*NAmE, informal*) to say sth important using only a few words 言简意赅；说到点子上

mouth·guard /ˈmaʊθɡɑːd; *NAmE* -ɡɑːrd/ (*NAmE*) (*BrE* **gum·shield**) *noun* a cover that a sports player wears in his/her mouth to protect the teeth and GUMS（运动员所含的）护齿

ˈmouth organ *noun* = HARMONICA

mouth·piece /ˈmaʊθpiːs/ *noun* **1** the part of the telephone that is next to your mouth when you speak（电话的）话筒 **2** the part of a musical instrument that you place between your lips（乐器的）吹口 ➲ VISUAL VOCAB PAGE V38 **3 ~ (of/for sb)** a person, newspaper, etc. that speaks on behalf of another person or group of people 喉舌；代言人；发言人：*The newspaper has become the official mouthpiece of the opposition party.* 这份报纸已经成为反对党的官方喉舌。◇ *The Press Secretary serves as the President's mouthpiece.* 新闻部长担任总统的代言人。

ˌmouth-to-ˌmouth reˌsusciˈtation (*also* **ˌmouth-to-ˈmouth**) *noun* [U] the act of breathing into the mouth of an unconscious person in order to fill their lungs with air 口对口人工呼吸 SYN **the kiss of life** ➲ COMPARE ARTIFICIAL RESPIRATION

ˈmouth ulcer (*BrE*) (*NAmE* **ˈcanker sore**) *noun* a small sore area in the mouth 口腔溃疡

mouth·wash /ˈmaʊθwɒʃ; *NAmE* -wɔːʃ; -wɑːʃ/ *noun* [C, U] a liquid used to make the mouth fresh and healthy 漱口剂

ˈmouth-watering *adj.* (*approving*) **mouth-watering** food looks or smells so good that you want to eat it immediately（食物）令人垂涎的，非常好吃的 SYN **tempting**：*a mouth-watering display of cakes* 令人垂涎的蛋糕展示 ◇ (*figurative*) *mouth-watering travel brochures* 诱人的旅游手册

mouthy /ˈmaʊθi; -ði/ *adj.* (*informal, disapproving*) used to describe a person who talks a lot, sometimes expressing their opinions strongly and in a rude way 夸夸其谈的

mov·able (*also* **move·able**) /ˈmuːvəbl/ *adj., noun*

■ ***adj.*** **1** that can be moved from one place or position to another 可移动的；活动的：*movable partitions* 可移动的隔板 ◇ *a doll with a movable head* 头可活动的洋娃娃 **2** (*law* 律) (of property 财产) able to be taken from one house, etc. to another 活动的；不固定的

■ ***noun*** [C, usually pl.] (*law* 律) a thing that can be moved from one house, etc. to another; a personal possession 动产；个人财物

ˌmovable ˈfeast *noun* a religious festival, such as Easter, whose date changes from year to year 因年而异的宗教节日（日期每年都可有变化）

move /muːv/ *verb, noun*

■ ***verb***

• **CHANGE POSITION** 改变位置 **1** [I, T] to change position or make sb/sth change position in a way that can be seen, heard or felt（使）改变位置，移动：*Don't move—stay perfectly still.* 别动，一点都别动。◇ *The bus was already moving when I jumped onto it.* 我跳上车的时候，公共汽车已经开动了。◇ **+ adv./prep.** *He could hear someone moving around in the room above.* 他能听到楼上屋里有人走动。◇ *Phil moved towards the window.* 菲尔朝窗户走去。◇ ***You can hardly move*** *in this pub on Saturdays* (= because it is so crowded). 这家酒吧星期六总是挤得令人无法挪动。◇ ***You can't move for*** *books in her room.* 她的屋里书多得让人挪不开步。◇ **~ sth** *I can't move my fingers.* 我的手指动不了了。◇ **~ sth + adv./prep.** *We moved our chairs a little nearer.* 我们把椅子挪近了一点。

• **CHANGE IDEAS/TIME** 改变主意 / 时间 **2** [I, T] to change; to change sth 变化；改变；转变 SYN **shift**：(+ adv./prep.)

M

The government has not moved on this issue. 政府在这个问题上立场没有转变。◇ **~ sth (+ adv./prep.)** *Let's move the meeting to Wednesday.* 我们把开会时间改到星期三吧。

- **MAKE PROGRESS** 取得进展 **3** [I] **~ (on/ahead)** to make progress in the way or direction mentioned 前进；进步；进展 SYN **progress**: *Time is moving on.* 时代在进步。◇ *Share prices moved ahead today.* 今天的股票价格上升了。◇ *Things are not moving as fast as we hoped.* 事情的进展不像我们希望的那么快。
- **TAKE ACTION** 采取行动 **4** [I] to take action; to do sth 采取行动；做（事）SYN **act**: *The police moved quickly to dispel the rumours.* 警察迅速采取行动来消除谣言。➲ SYNONYMS AT ACTION
- **CHANGE HOUSE/JOB** 搬家；换工作 **5** [I, T] to change the place where you live, have your work, etc. 搬家；搬迁：*We don't like it here so we've decided to move.* 我们不喜欢这地方，所以决定搬走。◇ **~ (from…) (to…)** *The company's moving to Scotland.* 公司准备迁往苏格兰。◇ **~ away** *She's been all on her own since her daughter moved away.* 自从她女儿搬走以后，她一直独自生活。◇ **~ house** (*BrE*) *We moved house last week.* 我们上星期搬家了。 **6** [T] **~ sb (from…) (to…)** to make sb change from one job, class, etc. to another 使变换；调动 SYN **transfer**: *I'm being moved to the New York office.* 我要调到纽约办事处去。
- **IN BOARD GAMES** 棋类游戏 **7** [I, T] (in CHESS and other board games 国际象棋和其他棋类游戏) to change the position of a piece 走棋；移动棋子：*It's your turn to move.* 该你走棋了。◇ **~ sth** *She moved her queen.* 她走了一步王后棋。
- **CAUSE STRONG FEELINGS** 使感动 **8** [T] to cause sb to have strong feelings, especially of sympathy or sadness 使感动（尤指因为同情或悲伤）；打动：**~ sb** *We were deeply* ***moved*** *by her plight.* 她的困境深深地打动了我们。◇ **~ sb to sth** *Grown men were* ***moved to tears*** *at the horrific scenes.* 这样悲惨的场面甚至让铮铮汉子潸然泪下。➲ SEE ALSO MOVING (1)
- **MAKE SB DO STH** 促使 **9** [T] (*formal*) to cause sb to do sth 促使，迫使（某人做某事）；使去做 SYN **prompt**: **~ sb to do sth** *She felt moved to address the crowd.* 她不由得想给大家讲一番话。◇ **~ sb** *He works when the spirit moves him* (= when he wants to). 他只有在想干活的时候才干活。
- **SUGGEST FORMALLY** 正式提出 **10** [T] (*formal*) to suggest sth formally so that it can be discussed and decided（正式地）提出，提议 SYN **put forward**: **~ sth** *The Opposition moved an amendment to the Bill.* 反对党对法案提出修正案。◇ **~ that…** *I move that a vote be taken on this.* 我提议就此进行投票。

IDM **get 'moving** (*informal*) to begin, leave, etc. quickly 马上行动；迅速开始（或离去等）：*It's late—we'd better get moving.* 天不早了，咱们走吧。 **get sth 'moving** (*informal*) to cause sth to make progress 使进步；推动：*The new director has really got things moving.* 新来的主任确实使事情有了进展。 **move heaven and 'earth** to do everything you possibly can in order to achieve sth 竭尽所能；竭尽全力 **move with the 'times** to change the way you think and behave according to changes in society 顺应时代；顺应潮流 ➲ MORE AT ASS, FORWARD *adv.*

PHR V **,move a'long** to go to a new position, especially in order to make room for other people 移动一下，向前移动（以腾出空间）：*The bus driver asked them to move along.* 公共汽车司机让他们往里走走。 **,move 'in | ,move 'into sth** to start to live in your new home 搬进新居：*Our new neighbours moved in yesterday.* 我们的新邻居昨天搬来了。OPP **move out** **'move in sth** to live, spend your time, etc. in a particular social group 涉足，出入，生活在（某群体）：*She only moves in the best circles.* 她只涉足那些精英圈子。 **,move 'in (on sb/sth)** to move towards sb/sth from all directions, especially in a threatening way 从四面八方逼近；进逼：*The police moved in on the terrorists.* 警察从四面八方向恐怖分子进逼。 **,move 'in with sb** to start living with sb in the house or flat/apartment where they already live 搬来和某人一起居住 **,move 'off** (especially of a vehicle 尤指交通工具) to start moving; to leave 启动；离去 **,move 'on (to sth)** to start doing or discussing sth new 开始做（别的事）；换话题：*I've been in this job long enough—it's time I moved on.* 这工作我已经干得够久了，我该干点别的了。◇ *Can we move on to the next item on the agenda?* 我们可以接着讨论下一项议程吗？ **,move sb 'on** (of police, etc. 警察等) to order sb to move away from the scene of an accident, etc. 让（某人）离开（事故现场等） **,move 'out** to leave your old home 搬出去；迁出 OPP **move in** **,move 'over** (*also* **,move 'up**) to change your position in order to make room for sb 挪开；让位：*There's room for another one if you move up a bit.* 如果你挪开一点，这里还可以再容纳一个人。

■ ***noun***

- **ACTION** 行动 **1** **~ (towards/to sth) | ~ (to do sth)** an action that you do or need to do to achieve sth 行动：*This latest move by the government has aroused fierce opposition.* 政府最近采取的行动引起了强烈的反对。◇ *The management have made no move to settle the strike.* 管理层没有采取任何措施来解决罢工问题。◇ *Getting a job in marketing was a good* ***career move***. 找份市场营销的工作是一个不错的职业选择。➲ SEE ALSO FALSE MOVE
- **CHANGE OF POSITION** 位置变换 **2** [usually sing.] a change of place or position 移动；活动：*Don't* ***make a move!*** 别动！◇ *Every move was painful.* 每动一下都很痛。◇ *She felt he was watching her* ***every move***. 她觉得他在注意她的一举一动。➲ SEE ALSO MOVEMENT (1), (2)
- **CHANGE OF IDEAS/BEHAVIOUR** 想法 / 行为的改变 **3** **~ to/away from sth** a change in ideas, attitudes or behaviour 改变；转变；动摇 SYN **shift, trend**: *There has been a move away from nuclear energy.* 人们对于原子能的看法已经转变。
- **CHANGE OF HOUSE/JOB** 搬家；调动工作 **4** an act of changing the place where you live or work 搬家；搬迁；调动：*What's the date of your move?* 你什么时候搬家？◇ *Their move from Italy to the US has not been a success.* 他们从意大利迁到美国并不成功。◇ *Her new job is just a sideways move.* 她的新工作只是平级调动。
- **IN BOARD GAMES** 棋类游戏 **5** an act of changing the position of a piece in CHESS or other games that are played on a board 走棋；（棋子的）移动：*The game was over in only six moves.* 这盘棋只走了六步就结束了。◇ *It's your move.* 该你走了。

IDM **be on the 'move** **1** to be travelling from place to place（经常）变换地点 **2** to be moving; to be going somewhere 在行进中；在移动中：*The car was already on the move.* 汽车已经开动了。◇ *The firm is on the move to larger offices.* 公司正在迁往更大的办公楼。 **3** = BE ON THE GO **get a 'move on** (*informal*) you tell sb to **get a move on** when you want them to hurry 赶快 **make the first 'move** to do sth before sb else, for example in order to end an argument or to begin sth 抢先行动；抢占先机；主动示好：*If he wants to see me, he should make the first move.* 他要是想见我，就得采取主动。 **make a 'move** (*BrE, informal*) to begin a journey or a task 动身；开始行动：*It's getting late—we'd better make a move.* 时间不早了，我们得动身了。 **make a 'move on sb** (*informal*) **1** to try to start a sexual relationship with sb 意图与某人发生性关系 **2** (*sport* 体育) to try to pass sb who is in front of you in a race（速度竞赛时）试图超越某人 **make a, your, etc. 'move** to do the action that you intend to do or need to do in order to achieve sth 采取行动；开始行动：*The rebels waited until nightfall before they made their move.* 叛乱者一直等到夜幕降临才开始行动。

move·able *adj.* = MOVABLE

move·ment /ˈmuːvmənt/ *noun*

- **CHANGING POSITION** 改变位置 **1** [C, U] an act of moving the body or part of the body（身体部位的）运动，转动，活动：***hand/eye movements*** 手 / 眼睛的活动 ◇ *She observed the gentle movement of his chest as he breathed.* 她观察着他呼吸时胸部的微微起伏。◇ *Loose clothing gives you greater freedom of movement.* 衣服宽松，可以活动自如。◇ *There was a sudden movement in the undergrowth.* 矮树丛里突然有什么东西动了一下。 **2** [C, U] an act of moving from one place to another or of moving sth from one place to another 移动；迁移；转移；活动：*enemy troop movements* 敌军的调动 ◇ *laws to allow free movement of goods and services* 允许商品和服务自由流动的法律
- **GROUP OF PEOPLE** 群体 **3** [C+sing./pl. v.] a group of

people who share the same ideas or aims（具有共同思想或目标的）运动：*the women's/peace movement* 妇女/和平运动 ◇ *the Romantic movement* (= for example in literature) 浪漫主义运动 ◇ *a mass movement for change* 要求变革的群众运动 ➲ COLLOCATIONS AT POLITICS
• PERSON'S ACTIVITIES 人的活动 **4 movements** [pl.] a person's activities over a period of time, especially as watched by sb else（尤指受监视者的）活动；行踪：*The police are keeping a close watch on the suspect's movements.* 警察正在密切监视嫌疑犯的活动。
• CHANGE OF IDEAS/BEHAVIOUR 想法/行为的改变 **5** [sing.] ~ (**away from/towards sth**) a gradual change in what people in society do or think 逐步的转变 SYN **trend**: *a movement towards greater sexual equality* 朝着更进一步的性别平等的转变
• PROGRESS 进展 **6** [U] ~ (**in sth**) progress, especially in a particular task（尤指某一工作的）进步，进展：*It needs cooperation from all the countries to get any movement in arms control.* 要在军控方面取得进展需要所有国家的合作。
• CHANGE IN AMOUNT 量的改变 **7** [U, C] ~ (**in sth**) a change in amount 量的变化；增减：*There has been no movement in oil prices.* 石油价格没有变化。
• MUSIC 音乐 **8** [C] any of the main parts that a long piece of music is divided into 乐章：*the slow movement of the First Concerto* 第一协奏曲的和缓乐章
• OF BOWELS 肠 **9** [C] (*specialist*) = BOWEL MOVEMENT

mover /ˈmuːvə(r)/ *noun* **1** a person or thing that moves in a particular way 以某方式移动的人（或物）：*a great mover on the dance floor* 舞场中舞姿优美的人 ➲ SEE ALSO PRIME MOVER **2** a machine or a person that moves things from one place to another, especially sb who moves furniture from one house to another 运送物品的机器（或人）；搬运家具的人：*an earth mover* 运土机 ◇ *professional furniture movers* 专业搬家工人 ➲ SEE ALSO REMOVER (2)
IDM ˌ**movers and ˈshakers** people with power in important organizations（重要机构中）有权势的人

movie 🔑 /ˈmuːvi/ *noun* (*especially NAmE*) **1** 🔑 [C] a series of moving pictures recorded with sound that tells a story, shown at the cinema/movie theater 电影 SYN **film**: *to make a horror movie* 制作恐怖电影 ◇ *Have you seen the latest Miyazaki movie?* 你看过宫崎骏最新的电影吗？◇ *a famous* ***movie director/star*** 著名的电影导演/明星 ➲ COLLOCATIONS AT CINEMA ➲ SEE ALSO ROAD MOVIE **2** 🔑 **the movies** [pl.] = CINEMA (2): *Let's go to the movies.* 我们去看电影吧。**3** 🔑 **the movies** [pl.] = CINEMA (3): *I've always wanted to work in the movies.* 我一直想从事电影业。

movie·goer /ˈmuːvigəʊə(r); *NAmE* -goʊ-/ *noun* (*especially NAmE*) = FILM-GOER

ˈ**movie star** *noun* (*especially NAmE*) = FILM STAR

ˈ**movie theater** 🔑 (*also* **theater**) *noun* (*NAmE*) = CINEMA (1): *The documentary opens tomorrow in movie theaters nationwide.* 这部纪录片明日起在全国各地的影院上映。

mov·ing 🔑 /ˈmuːvɪŋ/ *adj.* **1** 🔑 causing you to have deep feelings of sadness or sympathy 动人的；令人感动的：*a deeply moving experience* 非常动人的经历 ➲ WORDFINDER NOTE AT STORY **2** 🔑 [only before noun] (of things 事物) changing from one place or position to another 移动的；运动的：*the moving parts of a machine* 机器的活动部件 ◇ *fast-moving water* 快速流动的水 ◇ *a moving target* 活动靶 ▸ **mov·ing·ly** /ˈmuːvɪŋli/ *adv.*: *She described her experiences in Africa very movingly.* 她十分动人地描述了她在非洲的经历。

ˈ**moving van** (*NAmE*) (*BrE* **reˈmoval van**, ˈ**furniture van**) *noun* a large van used for moving furniture from one house to another 搬家卡车

mow /məʊ; *NAmE* moʊ/ *verb* (**mowed**, **mown** /məʊn; *NAmE* moʊn/ or **mowed**) [T, I] ~ (**sth**) to cut grass, etc. using a machine or tool with a special blade or blades 刈；割；修剪：*I mow the lawn every week in summer.* 夏天我每周都要修剪草坪。◇ *the smell of new-mown hay* 新割的草料的气味

PHR V ˌ**mow sb↔ˈdown** to kill sb using a vehicle or a gun, especially when several people are all killed at the same time（用交通工具或枪）杀死，撂倒，扫倒

mower /ˈməʊə(r); *NAmE* ˈmoʊ-/ *noun* (especially in compounds 尤用于构成复合词) a machine that cuts grass 割草机；剪草机：*a lawnmower* 剪草机 ◇ *a* ***motor/rotary mower*** 机动/滚筒割草机 ➲ VISUAL VOCAB PAGES V20

moxie /ˈmɒksi; *NAmE* ˈmɑːksi/ *noun* [U] (*NAmE, informal*) courage, energy and determination 人格力量（指勇气、精力和决心）

moz·za·rella /ˌmɒtsəˈrelə; *NAmE* ˌmɑːts-/ *noun* [U] a type of soft white Italian cheese with a mild flavour 莫泽雷勒干酪（一种色白味淡的意大利干酪）

moz·zie /ˈmɒzi; *NAmE* ˈmɑːzi; ˈmɔːzi/ *noun* (*pl.* **-ies**) (*informal*) a MOSQUITO 蚊子

MP /ˌem ˈpiː/ *noun* **1** the abbreviation for 'Member of Parliament' (a person who has been elected to represent the people of a particular area in a parliament) 议员（全写为 Member of Parliament，经选举在议会中代表某一选区者）：*Michael Phillips MP* 下院议员迈克尔•菲利普斯 ◇ *Write to your local MP to protest.* 给你们地区的议员写信抗议。◇ *Conservative/Labour MPs* 议会中的保守党/工党议员 ◇ *the MP for Oxford East* 代表牛津东区的议员 ◇ *a Euro-MP* 欧洲议会议员 **2** a member of the MILITARY POLICE 宪兵

MP3 /ˌem piː ˈθriː/ *noun* [U, C] a method of reducing the size of a computer file containing sound, or a file that is reduced in size in this way * MP3 技术（指 MPEG 第三层声音压缩技术）；MP3 文件

ˌ**MPˈ3 player** *noun* a small piece of equipment that can store information taken from the Internet and that you can carry with you, for example so that you can listen to music * MP3 播放器 ➲ VISUAL VOCAB PAGES V22, V73

MP4 /ˌem piː ˈfɔː(r)/ *noun* [U, C] a method of reducing the size of a computer file containing sound and images; a file that is reduced in size in this way * MP4 技术（一种影音压缩技术）；MP4 文件

MPEG /ˈempeg/ *noun* (*computing* 计) **1** [U] technology which reduces the size of files that contain video images or sounds * MPEG（运动图像压缩）标准：*an MPEG file* * MPEG 文件；MPEG 档 **2** [C] a file produced using this technology * MPEG 文件

mpg /ˌem piː ˈdʒiː/ *abbr.* miles per gallon (used for saying how much petrol/gas a vehicle uses) 每加仑燃料所行英里数；英里每加仑：*It does 40 mpg.* 这车每加仑跑 40 英里。◇ (*NAmE*) *It gets 40 mpg.* 这车每加仑跑 40 英里。

mph /ˌem piː ˈeɪtʃ/ *abbr.* miles per hour 每小时所行英里数；英里每小时：*a 60 mph speed limit* 每小时 60 英里的限速

MPV /ˌem piː ˈviː/ *noun* the abbreviation for 'multipurpose vehicle' (a large car like a van) 多功能车，多用途车（全写为 multipurpose vehicle）SYN **people carrier**

Mr 🔑 (*BrE*) (*also* **Mr.** *NAmE, BrE*) /ˈmɪstə(r)/ *abbr.* **1** 🔑 a title that comes before a man's family name, or before his first and family names together（用于男子的姓氏或姓名前）先生：*Mr Brown* 布朗先生 ◇ *Mr John Brown* 约翰•布朗先生 ◇ *Mr and Mrs Brown* 布朗先生和夫人 **2** a title used to address a man in some official positions（用于称呼要员）先生：*Thank you, Mr Chairman.* 谢谢你，主席先生。◇ *Mr. President* 总统先生 ➲ SEE ALSO MISTER (1)
IDM ˌ**Mr ˈNice Guy** (*informal*) a way of describing a man who is very honest and thinks about the wishes and feelings of other people 大好人；大善人：*I was tired of helping other people. From now on it was* ***no more Mr Nice Guy*** (= I would stop being pleasant and kind). 我已对帮助他人感到厌烦。从今以后我不做大善人了。**Mr ˈRight** (*informal*) the man who would be the right husband for a particular woman 如意郎君；理想夫婿：*I'm not getting married in a hurry—I'm waiting for Mr Right to come along.* 我不想匆忙结婚，我在等如意郎君出现。

M

ˌMr. ˈCharlie *noun* (*US, slang, offensive*) a name used by African Americans for a white man（非裔美国人对白人的称呼）查理先生

ˌMr. ˈClean *noun* (*US, informal*) a man, especially a politician, who is considered to be very honest and good 清廉先生，正人君子（尤指从政者）：*The scandal destroyed his image as Mr. Clean.* 这个丑闻破坏了他的清廉形象。

Mr Fixit /ˌmɪstə ˈfɪksɪt/ *noun* (*informal*) a person who organizes things and solves problems 组织协调大王；解决问题能手

MRI /ˌem ɑːr ˈaɪ/ *abbr.* (*medical* 医) magnetic resonance imaging (a method of using a strong MAGNETIC FIELD to produce an image of the inside of a person's body) 磁共振成像；磁力共振成像：*an MRI scan* 磁共振成像扫描

Mrs (*BrE*) (*also* **Mrs.** *NAmE, BrE*) /ˈmɪsɪz/ *abbr.* a title that comes before a married woman's family name or before her first and family names together（用于女子的姓氏或姓名前）太太，夫人：*Mrs Hill* 希尔太太 ◇ *Mrs Susan Hill* 苏珊·希尔太太 ◇ *Mr and Mrs Hill* 希尔先生和夫人 ➲ COMPARE MISS *n.* (1), (3), MS

MRSA /ˌem ɑːr es ˈeɪ/ *noun* [U] the abbreviation for 'methicillin-resistant Staphylococcus aureus' (a type of bacteria that cannot be killed by standard ANTIBIOTICS) 抗甲氧西林金黄色葡萄球菌，抗甲氧苯青霉素金黄葡萄球菌（全写为 methicilin-resistant Staphylococcus aureus，抗药性细菌）：*rising rates of MRSA infections in hospitals* 医院里感染抗甲氧西林金黄色葡萄球菌的病例不断上升 ➲ SEE ALSO SUPERBUG

M

MS (*NAmE also* **M.S.**) /ˌem ˈes/ *abbr.* **1** MULTIPLE SCLEROSIS 多发性硬化 **2** MANUSCRIPT 手稿；原稿；手抄本 **3** = MSc

Ms (*BrE*) (*also* **Ms.** *NAmE, BrE*) /mɪz; məz/ *abbr.* a title that comes before a woman's family name or before her first and family names together, and that can be used when you do not want to state whether she is married or not（用于女子的姓氏或姓名前，不指明婚否）女士：*Ms Murphy* 墨菲女士 ◇ *Ms Jean Murphy* 琼·墨菲女士 ➲ COMPARE MISS *n.* (1), (3), MRS

MSc /ˌem es ˈsiː/ (*BrE*) (*NAmE* **M.S., MS**) *noun* the abbreviation for 'Master of Science' (a second university degree in science) 理科硕士（全写为 Master of Science，大学理科中的中级学位）：(*BrE*) *to* ***be/have/do an MSc*** 是理科硕士；有理科硕士学位；攻读理科硕士 ◇ (*BrE*) *J Stevens MSc* 理科硕士 J. 史蒂文斯

MSG /ˌem es ˈdʒiː/ *abbr.* MONOSODIUM GLUTAMATE 谷氨酸一钠盐；谷氨酸钠；味精；味素

MSM /ˌem es ˈem/ *noun* [U+sing./pl. v.] (*computing* 计) = MAINSTREAM MEDIA: *The line is beginning to blur between influential blogs and MSM.* 有影响的博客和主流媒体之间的界限开始变得模糊。

MSP /ˌem es ˈpiː/ *noun* the abbreviation for 'Member of the Scottish Parliament' 苏格兰议会议员（全写为 Member of the Scottish Parliament）：*Alex Neil MSP* 苏格兰议会议员亚历克斯·尼尔 ◇ *Write to your local MSP to protest.* 给你们地区的苏格兰议会议员写信抗议。◇ *Labour MSPs* 苏格兰议会中的工党议员

MST /ˌem es ˈtiː/ *abbr.* MOUNTAIN STANDARD TIME 山区冬季时间

Mt (*also* **Mt.** *especially in NAmE*) *abbr.* (especially on maps) MOUNT（尤用于地图）山：*Mt Kenya* 肯尼亚山

MTV™ /ˌem tiː ˈviː/ *noun* (the abbreviation for 'music television') a television channel that shows music videos and other light entertainment programmes 音乐电视频道

mu /mjuː/ *noun* the 12th letter of the Greek alphabet (M, μ) 希腊字母表的第 12 个字母

much /mʌtʃ/ *det., pron., adv.*

■ ***det., pron.*** used with uncountable nouns, especially in negative sentences to mean 'a large amount of sth', or after 'how' to ask about the amount of sth. It is also used with 'as', 'so' and 'too'.（与不可数名词连用，尤用于否定句；或与 how 连用以询问数量；也可与 as、so 和 too 连用）许多，大量：*I don't have much money with me.* 我没带多少钱。◇ *'Got any money?' '**Not much.**'* "有钱吗？" "不太多。" ◇ ***How much*** *water do you need?* 你要多少水？◇ ***How much is it*** (= What does it cost)? 这东西多少钱？◇ *Take* ***as much*** *time* ***as*** *you like.* 你想花多少时间就花多少时间。◇ *There was* ***so much*** *traffic* ***that*** *we were an hour late.* 路上交通很拥堵，我们因此迟到了一个小时。◇ *I've got far* ***too much*** *to do.* 我要做的事情太多了。◇ (*formal*) *I lay awake for much of the night.* 我大半夜都没睡着。◇ (*formal*) *There was much discussion about the reasons for the failure.* 就失败的原因进行了大量的讨论。

IDM **as ˈmuch** the same 一样；同等：*Please help me get this job—you know I would do as much for you.* 请帮我弄到这份工作，你知道我也会为你的事同样尽力。◇ *'Roger stole the money.' 'I thought as much.'* "那钱是罗杰偷的。" "我也这么认为。" **as much as sb can do** used to say that sth is difficult to do（表示难以做到）：*No dessert for me, thanks. It was as much as I could do to finish the main course.* 谢谢，别给我甜食了。我吃完这道主菜就不错了。 **not much ˈin it** used to say that there is little difference between two things 没什么区别；差别不大：*I won, but there wasn't much in it* (= our scores were nearly the same). 我赢了，但比分相差不大。 **ˈnot much of a...** not a good... 不是很好；不怎么样：*He's not much of a tennis player.* 他算不上网球好手。 **ˈthis much** used to introduce sth positive or definite（引出正面的或肯定的话）：*I'll say this much for him—he never leaves a piece of work unfinished.* 我要为他说句公道话，他从不半途而废。

■ ***adv.*** (**more, most**) to a great degree 非常；十分；很：*Thank you* ***very much*** *for the flowers.* 非常感谢你的这些花。◇ *I would very much like to see you again.* 我很想再见到你。◇ *He isn't in the office much* (= often). 他不怎么待在办公室。◇ *You worry* ***too much.*** 你过于担心了。◇ *My new job is* ***much the same as*** *the old one.* 我的新工作和原来的差不多。◇ ***Much to her surprise*** *he came back the next day.* 让她非常吃惊的是他第二天就回来了。◇ *She's* ***much*** *better today.* 她今天好多了。◇ *The other one was* ***much too*** *expensive.* 另一个太贵了。◇ *Nikolai's English was* ***much the worst.*** 尼柯莱的英语糟糕透了。◇ *We are* ***very much aware*** *of the lack of food supplies.* 我们完全了解食物供应的缺乏。◇ *I'm* ***not much good at*** *tennis.* 我不太擅长打网球。◇ *He was much loved by all who knew him.* 认识他的人都很喜欢他。◇ *an appeal to raise much-needed cash* 筹集急需资

▼ **GRAMMAR POINT 语法说明**

much / a lot of / lots of

- **Much** is used only with uncountable nouns. It is used mainly in questions and negative sentences. * much 只与不可数名词连用，主要用于疑问句和否定句中：*Do you have much free time?* 你空闲时间多吗？◇ ***How much*** *experience have you had?* 你经验如何？◇ *I don't have much free time.* 我没有多少空闲时间。
- In statements **a lot of** or **lots of** (*informal*) is much more common. 在陈述句中 a lot of 或 lots of（非正式）常用得多： *'How much (money) does she earn?* "她挣多少（钱）？" ◇ *She earns a lot of money.* 她挣很多钱。You can also use **plenty** (**of**). These phrases can also be used in questions and negative sentences. 亦可用 plenty (of)。以上短语亦可用于疑问句和否定句中。
- **A lot of/lots of** is still felt to be informal, especially in *BrE*, so in formal writing it is better to use **much, a great deal of** or **a large amount of**. * a lot of / lots of 仍被视为非正式，尤其在英式英语中，因此在正式的书面语中宜用 much、a great deal of 或 a large amount of。
- **Very much** and **a lot** can be used as adverbs. * very much 和 a lot 可作副词：*I miss my family very much.* 我很想念我的家人。◇ ~~*I miss very much my family.*~~ ◇ *I miss my family a lot.* 我很想念我的家人。◇ *Thanks a lot.* 多谢。In negative sentences you can use **much**. 在否定句中可用 much： *I didn't enjoy the film (very) much.* 我不大喜欢这部影片。

➲ NOTE AT MANY

金的呼吁 ➲ NOTE AT MUCH

IDM **'much as** although 尽管；虽然：*Much as I would like to stay, I really must go home.* 尽管我很想留下来，但我确实必须回家。➲ MORE AT LESS *adv.*

much·ness /'mʌtʃnəs/ *noun*

IDM **ˌmuch of a 'muchness** very similar; almost the same 非常相似；几乎相同；不分伯仲：*The two candidates are much of a muchness—it's hard to choose between them.* 两位候选人不相上下，很难挑选。

muck /mʌk/ *noun, verb*

■ *noun* **1** waste matter from farm animals（牲畜的）粪便，粪肥 SYN **manure**: *to spread muck on the fields* 将粪肥撒到地里 **2** (*informal, especially BrE*) dirt or mud 脏东西；泥浆；淤泥：*Can you wipe the muck off the windows?* 你把窗户上的脏东西擦掉好吗？**3** (*informal, especially BrE*) something very unpleasant 令人厌恶的事物：*I can't eat this muck!* 我吃不下这些令人恶心的东西！

IDM **where there's ˌmuck there's 'brass** (*BrE, saying*) used to say that a business activity that is unpleasant or dirty can bring in a lot of money 哪儿有脏活哪儿有钱赚；要挣大钱就别怕脏

■ *verb*

PHR V **ˌmuck a'bout/a'round** (*BrE, informal*) to behave in a silly way, especially when you should be working or doing sth else 游手好闲；游荡；胡混 SYN **mess around** **ˌmuck a'bout/a'round with sth** (*BrE, informal, disapproving*) to do sth, especially to a machine, so that it does not work correctly 瞎弄；乱搞 SYN **mess around with sth**: *Who's mucking around with my radio?* 谁在摆弄我的收音机呀？**ˌmuck sb a'bout/a'round** (*BrE, informal*) to treat sb badly, especially by changing your mind a lot, or by not being honest 糊弄；耍弄 SYN **mess sb about/around**: *They've really mucked us about over our car insurance.* 在我们的汽车保险问题上他们确实糊弄了我们。**ˌmuck 'in** (*BrE, informal*) **1** to work with other people in order to complete a task 加入工作；合伙：*If we all muck in, we could have the job finished by the end of the week.* 如果我们大家一块儿干，到本周末就可以完成工作。**2** to share food, accommodation, etc. with other people 分享；共享：*We didn't have much money, but everyone just mucked in together.* 我们没有多少钱，只是大家都把钱拿出来一块儿花。**ˌmuck 'out | ˌmuck sth↔'out** to clean out the place where an animal lives 打扫（畜栏）**ˌmuck sth↔'up** (*informal, especially BrE*) **1** to do sth badly so that you fail to achieve what you wanted or hoped to achieve 做得很糟 SYN **mess up**: *He completely mucked up his English exam.* 他英语考得一塌糊涂。**2** to spoil a plan or an arrangement 破坏；弄糟；贻误 SYN **mess up** **3** to make sth dirty 弄脏：*I don't want you mucking up my nice clean floor.* 我这地板又漂亮，又干净，不想让你弄脏。

muck·er /'mʌkə(r)/ *noun* (*BrE, informal*) used when talking to or about a friend to refer to them（用作称呼）朋友，伙计：*It's my old mucker John!* 是我的老朋友约翰！

muck·rak·ing /'mʌkreɪkɪŋ/ *noun* [U] (*informal, disapproving*) the activity of looking for information about people's private lives that they do not wish to make public 探听揭发丑闻；揭露黑幕

mucky /'mʌki/ *adj.* (*informal, especially BrE*) **1** dirty 肮脏的；污秽的：*mucky hands* 肮脏的手 **2** sexually offensive 淫秽的；下流的 SYN **obscene**: *mucky books/jokes* 淫秽书籍；下流的笑话

ˌmucous 'membrane *noun* (*anatomy* 解) a thin layer of skin that covers the inside of the nose and mouth and the outside of other organs in the body, producing mucus to prevent these parts from becoming dry 黏膜

mucus /'mju:kəs/ *noun* [U] a thick liquid that is produced in parts of the body, such as the nose, by a mucous membrane 黏液；鼻涕 ▶ **mu·cous** /'mju:kəs/ *adj.*: *mucous glands* 分泌黏液的腺体

MUD /mʌd/ *noun* (*computing* 计) the abbreviation for 'multi-user dungeon/dimension' (a computer game played over the Internet by several players at the same time) "泥巴" 游戏，多用户网络游戏（全写为 multi-user dungeon/dimension）

mud 🔑 /mʌd/ *noun* [U] wet earth that is soft and sticky 泥；淤泥；泥浆：*The car wheels got stuck in the mud.* 汽车轮子陷到泥里去了。◇ *Your boots are covered in mud.* 你的靴子上都是泥。◇ ***mud bricks/huts*** (= made of dried mud) 泥砖；土坯屋 ➲ SYNONYMS AT SOIL

IDM **fling, sling, etc. 'mud (at sb)** to criticize sb or accuse sb of bad or shocking things in order to damage their reputation, especially in politics（尤指政治上）故意抹黑，向…泼污水，污蔑 ➲ SEE ALSO MUD-SLINGING **ˌmud 'sticks** (*saying*) people remember and believe the bad things they hear about other people, even if they are later shown to be false 恶事如泥巴，沾身洗不清；烂泥沾身洗不清 ➲ MORE AT CLEAR *adj.*, NAME *n.*

mud·bath /'mʌdbɑ:θ; *NAmE* -bæθ/ *noun* **1** a bath in hot mud that contains a lot of minerals, which is taken, for example, to help with RHEUMATISM 泥浴（用于减轻风湿症状等）**2** a place where there is a lot of mud 泥沼；泥泞地：*Heavy rain turned the campsite into a mudbath.* 大雨把露营地变成了一片泥沼。

mud·dle /'mʌdl/ *verb, noun*

■ *verb* (*especially BrE*) **1** to put things in the wrong order or mix them up 弄乱；搅混：**~ sth** *Don't do that—you're muddling my papers.* 别动，你会弄乱我的文件的。◇ **~ sth up** *Their letters were all muddled up together in a drawer.* 他们的信都乱七八糟地放在一个抽屉里。**2 ~ sb (up)** to confuse sb 使困惑；使糊涂：*Slow down a little—you're muddling me.* 说慢点儿，你都把我搞糊涂了。**3 ~ sb/sth (up) | ~ A (up) with B** to confuse one person or thing with another 混淆；搅混；分不清 SYN **mix sth↔up**: *I muddled the dates and arrived a week early.* 我搞错了日期，早到了一个星期。◇ *He **got all muddled up** about what went where.* 他对什么东西放在哪里全然记不清了。◇ *They look so alike, I always **get them muddled up**.* 他们看上去那么像，我总是把他们给搞混了。

PHR V **ˌmuddle a'long** (*especially BrE*) to continue doing sth without any clear plan or purpose 混日子；得过且过：*We can't just keep muddling along like this.* 我们不能就这样混日子。**ˌmuddle 'through** to achieve your aims even though you do not know exactly what you are doing and do not have the correct equipment, knowledge, etc. 胡乱应付过去：*We'll muddle through somehow.* 我们能想办法应付过去。

■ *noun* (*especially BrE*) **1** [C, usually sing.] a state of mental confusion 糊涂；困惑；茫然：*Can you start from the beginning again—I'm **in a muddle**.* 请你从头再来一遍吧，我还是搞不清楚。**2** [C, usually sing., U] **~ (about/over sth)** a situation in which there is confusion about arrangements, etc. and things are done wrong（局面）一团糟，混乱：*There was a muddle over the theatre tickets.* 戏票问题搞得一团糟。◇ *There followed a long period of confusion and muddle.* 接下来是很长一段时间的困惑和混乱。**3** [C, usually sing., U] a state of confusion in which things are untidy 混乱；乱七八糟 SYN **mess**: *My papers are all **in a muddle**.* 我的文件混乱不堪。

mud·dled /'mʌdld/ *adj.* (*especially BrE*) confused 糊涂的；困惑的；混乱的：*He gets muddled when the teacher starts shouting.* 老师一喊叫他就心烦意乱。◇ *muddled thinking* 混乱的思想

ˌmuddle-'headed *adj.* confused or with confused ideas 头脑混乱的；糊涂的：*muddle-headed thinkers* 思路混乱的人

mud·dling /'mʌdlɪŋ/ *adj.* (*especially BrE*) causing confusion; difficult to understand 引起困惑的；使人糊涂的；难以理解的

muddy /'mʌdi/ *adj., verb*

■ *adj.* (**mud·dier, mud·di·est**) **1** full of or covered in mud 多泥的；泥泞的：*a **muddy field/track*** 泥泞的田野 / 小径 ◇ ***muddy boots/knees*** 沾满泥浆的靴子 / 膝盖 ➲ SYNONYMS AT DIRTY **2** (of a liquid 液体) containing mud; not clear 含

M

泥的；浑浊的：*muddy water* 泥水 ◇ *a muddy pond* 浑浊的池塘 **3** (of colours 色彩) not clear or bright 灰暗的；暗淡的：*muddy green/brown* 暗绿色；暗褐色

■ *verb* (**mud·dies**, **muddy·ing**, **mud·died**, **mud·died**) ~ **sth** to make sth muddy 使变得泥泞；使浑浊

IDM **muddy the 'waters, 'issue, etc.** (*disapproving*) to make a simple situation confused and more complicated than it really is 搅浑水；添乱

mud·flap /ˈmʌdflæp/ *noun* one of a set of pieces of FLEXIBLE material that are fixed behind the wheels of a car, motorcycle, etc. to prevent them from throwing up mud, stones or water（车轮后的）挡泥帘，挡泥板

mud·flat /ˈmʌdflæt/ *noun* [usually pl.] an area of flat muddy land that is covered by the sea when it comes in at HIGH TIDE 潮泥滩

mud·guard /ˈmʌdgɑːd; *NAmE* -gɑːrd/ (*BrE*) (*NAmE* **fender**) *noun* a curved cover over a wheel of a bicycle（自行车）挡泥板

'mud pack *noun* a substance containing CLAY that you put on your face and take off after a short period of time, used to improve the condition of your skin（护肤用）泥膏，泥面膜

,mud 'pie *noun* wet earth that is made into the shape of a PIE as part of a game played by children（儿童游戏时做的）泥饼

mud·slide /ˈmʌdslaɪd/ *noun* a large amount of mud sliding down a mountain, often destroying buildings and injuring or killing people below 泥流

'mud-slinging *noun* [U] (*disapproving*) the act of criticizing sb and accusing them of sth in order to damage their reputation 故意抹黑；恶意中伤

muesli /ˈmjuːzli/ *noun* [U] a mixture of grains, nuts, dried fruit, etc. served with milk and eaten for breakfast 牛奶什锦早餐（谷物、坚果、干果加牛奶）

muez·zin /muːˈezɪn; mjuː-/ *noun* a man who calls Muslims to prayer, usually from the tower of a MOSQUE 穆安金，宣礼员（通常在清真寺宣礼塔上召唤穆斯林礼拜）

muff /mʌf/ *noun, verb*

■ *noun* a short tube of fur or other warm material that you put your hands into to keep them warm in cold weather 暖手筒；皮手筒 ➲ SEE ALSO EARMUFFS

■ *verb* ~ **sth** (*informal, disapproving*) to miss an opportunity to do sth well 错过（机会）；做错：*He muffed his lines* (= he forgot them or said them wrongly). 他忘了台词。◇ *It was a really simple shot, and I muffed it.* 这确实是一记简单的射门，而我竟然没射进。

muf·fin /ˈmʌfɪn/ *noun* **1** (*BrE*) (*NAmE* **,English 'muffin**) a type of round flat bread roll, usually TOASTED and eaten hot with butter 英格兰松饼（通常烤热加黄油吃） **2** a small cake in the shape of a cup, often containing small pieces of fruit, etc. 杯状小松糕（常含小块水果等）：*a blueberry muffin* 蓝莓松糕

'muffin top *noun* a roll of fat around a woman's waist that you can see above the top of a skirt, pair of trousers, etc. that is too tight 松糕肚（女性因裙子或裤子过紧而凸出的腰部赘肉）

muf·fle /ˈmʌfl/ *verb* **1** ~ **sth** to make a sound quieter or less clear 压抑（声音）；使（声音）降低；使听不清：*He tried to muffle the alarm clock by putting it under his pillow.* 他把闹钟塞在枕头底下，想减低声音。**2** ~ **sb/sth** (**up**) **in sth** to wrap or cover sb/sth in order to keep them/it warm 裹住，覆盖，蒙住（以保暖）：*She muffled the child up in a blanket.* 她用毯子将孩子裹得严严实实。

muf·fled /ˈmʌfld/ *adj.* (of sounds 声音) not heard clearly because sth is in the way that stops the sound from travelling easily 沉闷的；压抑的；模糊不清的：*muffled voices from the next room* 从隔壁房间里传来的沉闷声音

muf·fler /ˈmʌflə(r)/ *noun* **1** (*old-fashioned*) a thick piece of cloth worn around the neck for warmth 围巾 SYN **scarf** **2** (*NAmE*) (*BrE* **si·len·cer**) a device that is fixed to the EXHAUST of a vehicle in order to reduce the amount of noise that the engine makes（发动机的）消音器 ➲ VISUAL VOCAB PAGE V55 **3** a device that is fitted to an instrument in order to reduce the amount of noise that it makes, or to a camera, a MICROPHONE, etc. to reduce the amount of noise coming from things that you do not want to record 消声器；减声器

mufti /ˈmʌfti/ *noun* **1** [C] (*also* **Mufti**) a Muslim who is an expert in legal matters connected with Islam 穆夫提（伊斯兰教法典说明官） **2** [U] (*old-fashioned*) ordinary clothes worn by people such as soldiers who wear uniform in their job（穿制服上班的士兵等穿的）便装，便服：*officers in mufti* 身着便装的军官

mug /mʌg/ *noun, verb*

■ *noun* **1** a tall cup for drinking from, usually with straight sides and a handle, used without a SAUCER 大杯；缸子；马克杯：*a coffee mug* 咖啡缸子 ◇ *a beer mug* (= a large glass with a handle) 大啤酒杯 ➲ VISUAL VOCAB PAGE V23 **2** a mug and what it contains 一缸子（的量）：*a mug of coffee* 一大杯咖啡 **3** (*slang*) a person's face（人的）脸：*I never want to see his ugly mug again.* 我再也不想看到他那张丑恶的面孔。**4** (*informal*) a person who is stupid and easy to trick 傻瓜；笨蛋：*They made me look a complete mug.* 他们弄得我像个十足的傻瓜。◇ *He's no mug.* 他可不傻。

IDM **a 'mug's game** (*disapproving, especially BrE*) an activity that is unlikely to be successful or make a profit 徒劳无功的事；不易成功的事；不易获利的事

■ *verb* (**-gg-**) **1** [T] ~ **sb** to attack sb violently in order to steal their money, especially in a public place（公然）行凶抢劫，打劫：*She had been mugged in the street in broad daylight.* 光天化日之下，她在街上遭到抢劫。**2** [I] ~ (**for sb/sth**) (*informal, especially NAmE*) to make silly expressions with your face or behave in a silly, exaggerated way, especially on the stage or before a camera（尤指在舞台上或摄影机前）扮鬼脸，扮怪相：*to mug for the cameras* 在摄影机前扮怪相 ➲ MORE LIKE THIS 36, page R29

PHR V **,mug sth↔'up** | **,mug 'up on sth** (*BrE, informal*) to learn sth, especially in a short time for a particular purpose, for example an exam 突击式学习

mug·ger /ˈmʌgə(r)/ *noun* a person who threatens or attacks sb in order to steal their money, especially in a public place 抢劫犯；拦路抢劫者

mug·ging /ˈmʌgɪŋ/ *noun* [U, C] the crime of attacking sb violently, or threatening to do so, in order to steal their money, especially in a public place 公然行凶抢劫案；拦路抢劫罪：*Mugging is on the increase.* 抢劫犯罪呈上升趋势。◇ *There have been several muggings here recently.* 最近这里发生了几起行凶抢劫案。

mug·gins /ˈmʌgɪnz/ *noun* [sing.] (*BrE, informal, humorous*) used without 'a' or 'the' to refer to yourself when you feel stupid because you have let yourself be treated unfairly（不用 a 或 the，表示因受到不公正待遇而觉得自己很蠢）傻瓜，笨蛋：*And muggins here had to clean up all the mess.* 而我这个傻瓜现在不得不清理这个烂摊子。

muggy /ˈmʌgi/ *adj.* (of weather 天气) warm and damp in an unpleasant way 闷热潮湿的 SYN **close**[2]：*a muggy August day* 八月里闷热的一天

Mug·hal /ˈmuːgɑːl/ *noun* = MOGUL

mug·shot /ˈmʌgʃɒt; *NAmE* -ʃɑːt/ *noun* (*informal*) a photograph of sb's face kept by the police in their records to identify criminals（警方存档识别罪犯的）面部照片

mug·wump /ˈmʌgwʌmp/ *noun* (*NAmE, often disapproving*) a person who cannot decide how to vote or who refuses to support a political party 投票拿不定主意的人；（不支持任何政党的）游离者

Mu·ham·mad (*also* **Mo·ham·med**) /məˈhæmɪd/ *noun* the Arab PROPHET through whom the Koran was REVEALED and the religion of Islam established and completed 穆罕默德（阿拉伯的先知、伊斯兰教的创立人）

mu·ja·hi·deen (*also* **mu·ja·hi·din**) /ˌmuːdʒəhəˈdiːn/ *noun* [pl.] (in some Muslim countries 某些伊斯兰国家) soldiers fighting in support of their strong Muslim beliefs 穆斯林圣战者；穆斯林游击队员

mukene /muːˈkeɪneɪ/ *noun* [C, U] (*pl.* **mukene**) (*EAfrE*) small fish that are dried to preserve them, and often fried and then cooked with tomatoes and milk to make a STEW 小鱼干（常炸过后与番茄和牛奶同煮，做成炖菜）

muk·luk /ˈmʌklʌk/ *noun* (*CanE*) a high soft winter boot that is traditionally made with the skin of SEALS 高筒软靴，海豹皮靴（传统上以海豹皮制作）

mu·latto /mjuˈlætəʊ; məˈl-; *NAmE* -toʊ/ *noun* (*pl.* **-os** or **-oes**) (*offensive*) a person with one black parent and one white parent 黑白混血儿

mul·berry /ˈmʌlbəri; *NAmE* -beri/ *noun* (*pl.* **-ies**) **1** (*also* **ˈmulberry tree**) [C] a tree with broad dark green leaves and BERRIES that can be eaten. SILKWORMS (that make silk) eat the leaves of the white mulberry. 桑树 **2** [C] the small purple or white BERRY of the mulberry tree 桑葚 **3** [U] a deep reddish-purple colour 深紫红色

mulch /mʌltʃ/ *noun, verb*

■ ***noun*** [C, U] material, for example, decaying leaves, that you put around a plant to protect its base and its roots, to improve the quality of the soil or to stop WEEDS growing 覆盖物，覆盖料（用以保护植物根基、改善土质或防止杂草生长）

■ ***verb*** **~ sth** to cover the soil or the roots of a plant with a mulch 用覆盖物覆盖（土壤或根部）

mule /mjuːl/ *noun* **1** an animal that has a horse and a DONKEY as parents, used especially for carrying loads 骡子：*He's as* ***stubborn as a mule.*** 他像骡子一样倔。**2** (*slang*) a person who is paid to take drugs illegally from one country to another 越境运毒者 **3** a SLIPPER (= a soft shoe for wearing indoors) that is open around the heel（跟部敞开的）凉拖鞋 ➲ VISUAL VOCAB PAGE V69

mule·teer /ˌmjuːləˈtɪə(r); *NAmE* -ˈtɪr/ *noun* a person who controls MULES (= the animals) and makes them go in the right direction 赶骡人

mul·ish /ˈmjuːlɪʃ/ *adj.* unwilling to change your mind or attitude or to do what other people want you to do 执拗的；顽固的 SYN **stubborn**

mull /mʌl/ *verb*

PHR V **ˌmull sth↔ˈover** to spend time thinking carefully about a plan or proposal 认真琢磨，反复思考（计划、建议等） SYN **consider**: *I need some time to mull it over before making a decision.* 在作出决定之前我需要一些时间来认真琢磨一下。

mul·lah /ˈmʌlə; ˈmʊlə/ *noun* a Muslim teacher of religion and holy law 毛拉（穆斯林宗教和教法的教师）

mulled /mʌld/ *adj.* [only before noun] **mulled** wine has been mixed with sugar and spices and heated（指葡萄酒）放入糖和香料加热过的

mul·lered /ˈmʌləd; *NAmE* ˈmʌlərd/ *adj.* (*slang*) very drunk 大醉；烂醉：*to be/get mullered* 喝得烂醉

mul·let /ˈmʌlɪt/ *noun* **1** (*pl.* **mul·let**) [C, U] a sea fish that is used for food. The two main types are **red mullet** and **grey mullet**. 鲻鱼；绯鲤 **2** [C] (*informal*) a HAIRSTYLE for men in which the hair is short at the front and sides and long at the back 胭脂鱼发型（男子发型，前面和两侧的头发短，脑后的头发长）

mul·li·ga·tawny /ˌmʌlɪɡəˈtɔːni/ *noun* [U] a hot spicy soup, originally from India（源自印度的）咖喱肉汤 ORIGIN From a Tamil word meaning 'pepper water'. 源自泰米尔语中表示"胡椒水"的词。

mul·lion /ˈmʌliən/ *noun* (*architecture* 建) a solid vertical piece of stone, wood or metal between two parts of a window（窗扇间的）中竖框 ▸ **mul·lioned** /ˈmʌliənd/ *adj.* [only before noun]: *mullioned windows* 有中竖框的窗户

multi- /ˈmʌlti/ *combining form* (in nouns and adjectives 构成名词和形容词) more than one; many 多个；许多：*multicoloured* 多色的 ◇ *a multimillionaire* 拥有几百万财产的富翁 ◇ *a multimillion-dollar business* 数百万美元资金的企业 ◇ *a multi-ethnic society* 多种族社会

ˌmulti-ˈaccess *adj.* (*computing* 计) allowing several people to use the same system at the same time（系统）多路接入的，多重存取的

multi·buy /ˈmʌltibaɪ/ *adj.* (*BrE*) used for describing items in a shop/store that are cheaper if you buy several of them（商品）多买可享优惠的：*Click here to see some of our multibuy offers.* 点击此处查看我们的一些多买优惠商品。▸ **multi·buy** *noun*

multi·chan·nel /ˈmʌltitʃænl/ *adj.* having or using many different television or communication channels 多频道的；多通道的

multi·col·oured (*especially US* **multi·col·ored**) /ˌmʌltiˈkʌləd; *NAmE* -ˈkʌlərd/ (*BrE also* **multi·col·our**) (*US also* **multi·col·or**) *adj.* consisting of or decorated with many colours, especially bright ones 多色的；五彩斑斓的：*a multicoloured dress* 色彩斑斓的连衣裙

multi·cul·tural /ˌmʌltiˈkʌltʃərəl/ *adj.* for or including people of several different races, religions, languages and traditions 多元文化的；多种文化融合的：*We live in a multicultural society.* 我们生活在一个多元文化的社会中。◇ *a multicultural approach to education* 多种文化融合的教育方法 ➲ COLLOCATIONS AT RACE

multi·cul·tural·ism /ˌmʌltiˈkʌltʃərəlɪzəm/ *noun* [U] the practice of giving importance to all cultures in a society 多元文化主义（重视社会中各种文化） ➲ COLLOCATIONS AT RACE

M

multi·di·men·sion·al AW /ˌmʌltidaɪˈmenʃənl; -dɪ-/ *adj.* having several DIMENSIONS (= measurements in space) 多维的：*multidimensional space* 多维空间

multi·dis·cip·lin·ary /ˌmʌltidɪsəˈplɪnəri; *NAmE* -ˈdɪsəpləneri/ *adj.* involving several different subjects of study（涉及）多门学科的：*a multidisciplinary course* 涉及多个学科的课程

multi·fa·cet·ed /ˌmʌltiˈfæsɪtɪd/ *adj.* (*formal*) having many different aspects to be considered 多方面的；要从多方面考虑的：*a complex and multifaceted problem* 一个复杂的需从多方面考虑的问题

multi·fari·ous /ˌmʌltɪˈfeəriəs; *NAmE* -ˈfer-/ *adj.* (*formal*) of many different kinds; having great variety 多种的；各种各样的；多样的：*the multifarious life forms in the coral reef* 珊瑚礁上的多种生命形式 ◇ *a vast and multifarious organization* 一个庞大而又形式多样的机构

multi·func·tion·al /ˌmʌltiˈfʌŋkʃənl/ *adj.* having several different functions 多功能的；起多种作用的：*a multifunctional device* 多功能装置

multi·grain /ˈmʌltiɡreɪn/ *adj.* containing several different types of grain 含多种谷物的；杂粮的：*multigrain bread* 杂粮面包

multi·gym /ˈmʌltidʒɪm/ (*BrE*) *noun* a piece of equipment which can be used to exercise different parts of the body 多功能健身器

multi·lat·eral /ˌmʌltiˈlætərəl/ *adj.* **1** in which three or more groups, nations, etc. take part 多边的；多国的：*multilateral negotiations* 多边谈判 **2** having many sides or parts 有多条边的；有多个部分的 ➲ COMPARE BILATERAL, TRILATERAL, UNILATERAL

multi·lat·eral·ism /ˌmʌltiˈlætərəlɪzəm/ *noun* [U] (*politics* 政) the policy of trying to make multilateral agreements in order to achieve nuclear DISARMAMENT 多边主义，多边政策（为达成核裁军多边协议）

multi·lin·gual /ˌmʌltiˈlɪŋɡwəl/ *adj.* **1** speaking or using several different languages 说（或用）多种语言的：*multilingual translators/communities/societies* 多语翻译者 / 社群 / 社会 ◇ *a multilingual classroom* 多语课堂 **2** written or printed in several different languages 用多种

语言书写（或印刷）的：*a multilingual phrase book* 多种语言会话手册 ➲ COMPARE BILINGUAL, MONOLINGUAL

multi·media /ˌmʌltiˈmiːdiə/ *adj.* [only before noun] **1** (in computing 计算机技术) using sound, pictures and film in addition to text on a screen 多媒体的：***multimedia systems/products*** 多媒体系统 / 产品 ◇ *the multimedia industry* (= producing CD-ROMs etc.) 多媒体工业 **2** (in teaching and art 教学和艺术) using several different ways of giving information or several different materials 使用多媒体的：*a multimedia approach to learning* 运用多媒体的学习方法 ▶ **multi·media** *noun* [U]: *the use of multimedia in museums* 多媒体在博物馆中的运用

multi·mill·ion·aire /ˌmʌltimɪljəˈneə(r); *NAmE* -ˈner/ *noun* a person who has money and possessions worth several million pounds, dollars, etc. 拥有数百万资产的富翁；千万富翁

multi·nation·al /ˌmʌltiˈnæʃnəl/ *adj., noun*

■ ***adj.*** existing in or involving many countries 跨国的；涉及多国的：***multinational companies/corporations*** 跨国公司 ◇ *A multinational force is being sent to the trouble spot.* 一支多国部队正赶往多事的地区。

■ ***noun*** a company that operates in several different countries, especially a large and powerful company 跨国公司

multi·party /ˌmʌltiˈpɑːti; *NAmE* -ˈpɑːrti/ *adj.* [only before noun] involving several different political parties 多党派的；涉及多党派的

M

multi·play·er /ˈmʌltipleɪə(r)/ *adj.* [usually before noun] used to describe a computer game that can be played by more than one person at the same time（电脑游戏）多人模式的（支持多个玩家同时玩）：*The game will support up to four players in multiplayer mode.* 这款游戏在多人模式下最多支持四名玩家。

mul·tiple /ˈmʌltɪpl/ *adj., noun*

■ ***adj.*** [only before noun] many in number; involving many different people or things 数量多的；多种多样的：*multiple copies of documents* 各种文件的大量的副本 ◇ *a multiple entry visa* 多次入境签证 ◇ *to suffer multiple injuries* (= in many different places in the body) 多处受伤 ◇ *a multiple birth* (= several babies born to a mother at one time) 多胎分娩 ◇ *a multiple pile-up* (= a crash involving many vehicles) 连环车祸 ◇ *a house in **multiple ownership/occupancy*** (= owned/occupied by several different people or families) 多户所有 / 使用的房屋

■ ***noun*** **1** (*mathematics* 数) a quantity that contains another quantity an exact number of times 倍数：*14, 21 and 28 are all multiples of 7.* * 14、21 和 28 都是 7 的倍数。◇ *18 is the lowest **common multiple** of 6 and 9.* * 18 是 6 和 9 的最小公倍数。◇ *Traveller's cheques are available in multiples of €10* (= to the value of €10, €20, €30, etc.). 购买旅行支票以 10 欧元的倍数计算面值。**2** (*also* ˌ**multiple ˈstore**) (*both BrE*) = CHAIN STORE

ˌ**multiple-ˈchoice** *adj.* (of questions 问题) showing several possible answers from which you must choose the correct one 多选一的

ˌ**multiple-persoˈnality disorder** (*also less frequent* ˌ**split-persoˈnality disorder**) *noun* (*psychology* 心) a rare condition in which a person seems to have one or more different personalities 多重人格障碍

ˌ**multiple scleˈrosis** *noun* [U] (*abbr.* **MS**) a disease of the nervous system that gets worse over a period of time with loss of feeling and loss of control of movement and speech 多发性硬化

multi·plex /ˈmʌltɪpleks/ (*BrE also* ˌ**multiplex ˈcinema**) *noun* a large cinema/movie theater with several separate rooms with screens 多厅影院；多银幕电影院 ➲ MORE LIKE THIS 1, page R25

multi·pli·ca·tion /ˌmʌltɪplɪˈkeɪʃn/ *noun* [U] the act or process of multiplying 乘；相乘；增加：*the multiplication sign* (×) 乘号 ◇ *Multiplication of cells leads to rapid growth of the organism.* 细胞的繁殖导致有机体的迅速生长。➲ COMPARE DIVISION (2)

ˌ**multipliˈcation table** (*also* **table**) *noun* a list showing the results when a number is multiplied by a set of other numbers, especially 1 to 12, in turn 乘法表

multi·pli·city /ˌmʌltɪˈplɪsəti/ *noun* [sing., U] (*formal*) a great number and variety of sth 多样性；多种多样：*This situation can be influenced by a multiplicity of different factors.* 当前的形势可能受到各种不同因素的影响。

multi·plier /ˈmʌltɪplaɪə(r)/ *noun* (*mathematics* 数) a number by which another number is multiplied 乘数；倍数

multi·ply 🔑 /ˈmʌltɪplaɪ/ *verb* (**multi·plies, multi·ply·ing, multi·plied, multi·plied**) **1** 🔑 [I, T] to add a number to itself a particular number of times 乘；乘以：*The children are already learning to multiply and divide.* 孩子们已经开始学习乘法和除法了。◇ ~ **A by B** *2 multiplied by 4 is/equals/makes 8* (= 2×4 = 8) * 2 乘以 4 等于 8。◇ ~ **A and B** (**together**) *Multiply 2 and 6 together and you get 12.* * 2 和 6 相乘得 12。**2** 🔑 [I, T] to increase or make sth increase very much in number or amount 成倍增加；迅速增加：*Our problems have multiplied since last year.* 自去年以来，我们的问题成倍增加。◇ ~ **sth** *Cigarette smoking multiplies the risk of cancer.* 抽烟会大大增加得癌症的风险。**3** [I, T] (*biology* 生) to reproduce in large numbers; to make sth do this（使）繁殖，增殖：*Rabbits multiply rapidly.* 兔子繁殖迅速。◇ ~ **sth** *It is possible to multiply these bacteria in the laboratory.* 在实验室里繁殖这些细菌是可以做到的。

multi·pro·ces·sor /ˌmʌltiˈprəʊsesə(r); *NAmE* -ˈprɑːs-; -ˈproʊ-/ *noun* a computer with more than one CENTRAL PROCESSING UNIT 多处理器

multipurpose /ˌmʌltiˈpɜːpəs; *NAmE* -ˈpɜːrp-/ *adj.* able to be used for several different purposes 多用途的；多功能的：*a **multipurpose** tool/machine* 多用途的工具 / 机器 ➲ SEE ALSO MPV

multi·racial /ˌmʌltiˈreɪʃl/ *adj.* including or involving several different races of people 多种族的：*a multiracial society* 多种族的社会

ˌ**multi-ˈskilling** *noun* [U] (*business* 商) the fact of a person being trained in several different jobs which require different skills 多才多艺；（人才的）复合型技能

ˌ**multi-storey ˈcar park** (*also* ˌ**multi-ˈstorey**) (*both BrE*) (*NAmE* ˈ**parking garage**) *noun* a large building with several floors for parking cars in 多层停车场；立体停车场

multi·task /ˌmʌltiˈtɑːsk; *NAmE* -ˈtæsk/ *verb* **1** [I] (of a computer 计算机) to operate several programs at the same time 多任务 **2** [I] to do several things at the same time 同时做多件事情：*Women seem to be able to multitask better than men.* 女性似乎比男性更擅长同时做多件事情。

multi·tasking /ˌmʌltiˈtɑːskɪŋ; *NAmE* -ˈtæsk-/ *noun* [U] **1** (*computing* 计) the ability of a computer to operate several programs at the same time 多任务处理 **2** the ability to do several things at the same time 能同时处理多项事情的

multi·touch™ /ˈmʌltitʌtʃ/ *noun* [U] a range of functions that enables you to give instructions on a TOUCH SCREEN, keyboard, etc. by touching different areas or keys at the same time 多点触控；多点感应：*a multitouch screen/display/keyboard* 多点触控屏幕 / 显示 / 键盘 ◇ *multitouch capability/technology* 多点触控性能 / 技术

multi·track /ˈmʌltitræk/ *adj.* (*specialist*) relating to the mixing of several different pieces of music 多音轨混合的；多声道的

multi·tude /ˈmʌltɪtjuːd; *NAmE* -tuːd/ *noun* (*formal*) **1** [C] ~ (**of sth/sb**) an extremely large number of things or people 众多；大量：*a multitude of possibilities* 众多的可能性 ◇ *a multitude of birds* 一大群鸟 ◇ *These elements can be combined in a multitude of different ways.* 这些因素可以通过无数不同的方式进行组合。◇ *The region attracts tourists in their multitudes.* 这个地区吸引大批游人。**2 the multitude** [sing.+sing./pl. v.] (*also* **the multi·tudes** [pl.])

(*sometimes disapproving*) the mass of ordinary people 群众；大批百姓；民众：*It was an elite that believed its task was to enlighten the multitude.* 精英人物会认为自己的职责是启迪群众。◇ *to feed the starving multitudes* 使饥饿的群众有饭吃 **3** [C] (*literary*) a large crowd of people 人群 SYN **throng**: *He preached to the assembled multitude.* 他向聚集在那里的民众布道。

IDM **cover/hide a multitude of sins** (*often humorous*) to hide the real situation or facts when these are not good or pleasant 掩藏实情；掩盖真相

multi·tu·di·nous /ˌmʌltɪˈtjuːdɪnəs; *NAmE* -ˈtuːdɪnəs/ *adj.* (*formal*) extremely large in number 大量的；众多的

ˌmulti-ˈuser *adj.* (*computing* 计) able to be used by more than one person at the same time 多用户（共享）的：*a multi-user software licence* 多用户共享软件许可

multi·vita·min /ˌmʌltiˈvɪtəmɪn; *NAmE* ˌmʌltɪˈvaɪt-/ *noun* a pill or medicine containing several VITAMINS 复合维生素

ˌmulti-ˈword *adj.* [only before noun] (*linguistics* 语言) consisting of more than one word 含多个单词的；多词组合的：*multi-word units such as 'fall in love'* 如 fall in love 的多词组合单位

mum /mʌm/ *noun, adj.*

■ ***noun*** (*BrE*) (*NAmE* **mom**) (*informal*) a mother 妈妈；妈：*My mum says I can't go.* 我妈说我不能去。◇ *Happy Birthday, Mum.* 妈妈，生日快乐！◇ *A lot of* **mums and dads** *have the same worries.* 许多父母都有同样的担忧。

■ ***adj.***

IDM **keep mum** (*informal*) to say nothing about sth; to stay quiet 缄口不言；保持沉默：*He kept mum about what he'd seen.* 他对他所看到的只字不说。**ˌmum's the ˈword!** (*informal*) used to tell sb to say nothing about sth and keep it secret（提醒别人保守秘密）不要外传

mum·ble /ˈmʌmbl/ *verb, noun*

■ ***verb*** [I, T] to speak or say sth in a quiet voice in a way that is not clear 嘟哝；口齿不清地说 SYN **mutter**: **~ (to sb/yourself)** *I could hear him mumbling to himself.* 我听到他在喃喃自语。◇ **~ sth (to sb/yourself)** *She mumbled an apology and left.* 她嘟嘟囔囔地道了歉就走了。◇ **+ speech** *'Sorry,' she mumbled.* 她含含糊糊地说："对不起。" ◇ **~ that...** *She mumbled that she was sorry.* 她含含糊糊地说了声对不起。

■ ***noun*** [usually sing.] (*also* **mum·bling** [C, usually pl., U]) speech or words that are spoken in a quiet voice in a way that is not clear 喃喃自语；嘟哝：*He spoke in a low mumble, as if to himself.* 他自言自语般地嘟哝着。◇ *They tried to make sense of her mumblings.* 他们试图弄明白她在嘟哝些什么。

mumbo jumbo /ˌmʌmbəʊ ˈdʒʌmbəʊ; *NAmE* ˌmʌmboʊ ˈdʒʌmboʊ/ *noun* [U] (*informal, disapproving*) language or a ceremony that seems complicated and important but is actually without real sense or meaning; nonsense 繁琐严肃但无意义的语言（或仪式）；繁文缛节；胡言乱语 ➲ MORE LIKE THIS 11, page R26

mum·mer /ˈmʌmə(r)/ *noun* an actor in an old form of drama without words 哑剧演员

mum·mify /ˈmʌmɪfaɪ/ *verb* (**mum·mi·fies, mum·mi·fy·ing, mum·mi·fied, mum·mi·fied**) [usually passive] **~ sth** to preserve a dead body by treating it with special oils and wrapping it in cloth 把（尸体）制成木乃伊 SYN **embalm**

mummy /ˈmʌmi/ *noun* (*pl.* **-ies**) **1** (*BrE*) (*NAmE* **mommy, momma**) (*informal*) a child's word for a mother（儿语）妈咪：*'I want my mummy!' he wailed.* 他哭叫着："我要妈妈！" ◇ *It hurts, Mummy!* 妈妈，疼！◇ *Mummy and Daddy will be back soon.* 妈妈爸爸就要回来了。**2** a body of a human or an animal that has been mummified 木乃伊；经处理保存的人体或动物干尸：*an Egyptian mummy* 一具埃及木乃伊

ˈmummy's boy (*BrE*) (*NAmE* **ˈmama's boy**) *noun* (*disapproving*) a boy or man who depends too much on his mother 离不开妈妈的男孩（或男子）

mumps /mʌmps/ *noun* [U] a disease, especially of children, that causes painful swellings in the neck 腮腺炎

mumsy /ˈmʌmzi/ *adj.* (*BrE, informal*) having a comfortable, but dull and old-fashioned appearance 家常的；呆板的；不时髦的：*a mumsy dress* 式样一般的连衣裙

munch /mʌntʃ/ *verb* [I, T] to eat sth steadily and often noisily, especially sth crisp 大声咀嚼，用力咀嚼（脆的食物）SYN **chomp**: **~ on/at sth** *She munched on an apple.* 她在大口啃苹果。◇ **~ sth** *He sat in a chair munching his toast.* 他坐在椅子上大嚼烤面包片。◇ *I* **munched my way through** *a huge bowl of cereal.* 我狼吞虎咽地吃了一大碗麦片粥。

Munch·ausen's syn·drome /ˈmʊntʃaʊzənz sɪndrəʊm; *NAmE* -droʊm/ *noun* [U] a mental condition in which sb keeps pretending that they are ill/sick in order to receive hospital treatment 闵希豪生综合征（表现为幻想生病以便求医或住院的精神障碍）

munch·ies /ˈmʌntʃɪz/ *noun* [pl.] (*informal*) small pieces of food for eating with drinks at a party（聚会上提供的）小吃，点心

IDM **have the ˈmunchies** (*informal*) to feel hungry 感觉饿

mun·dane /mʌnˈdeɪn/ *adj.* (*often disapproving*) not interesting or exciting 单调的；平凡的 SYN **dull, ordinary**: *a* **mundane task/job** 平凡的任务/职业 ◇ *I lead a pretty mundane existence.* 我过着相当平淡的生活。◇ *On a more mundane level, can we talk about the timetable for next week?* 说点儿实际的吧，我们能谈谈下周的时间安排吗？

mung /mʌŋ; muːŋ/ (*also* **moong**) *noun* **1** (*also* **ˈmung bean**) a small round green BEAN 绿豆 **2** the tropical plant that produces these beans 绿豆（指植物）

mu·ni·ci·pal /mjuːˈnɪsɪpl/ *adj.* [usually before noun] connected with or belonging to a town, city or district that has its own local government 市政的；地方政府的：**municipal elections/councils** 地方政府选举；市政委员会 ◇ *municipal workers* 市政工作者 ◇ *the Los Angeles Municipal Art Gallery* 洛杉矶市立美术馆

mu·ni·ci·pal·ity /mjuːˌnɪsɪˈpæləti/ *noun* (*pl.* **-ies**) (*formal*) a town, city or district with its own local government; the group of officials who govern it 自治市；（市下的）自治区；市（或区）政当局

mu·nifi·cent /mjuːˈnɪfɪsnt/ *adj.* (*formal*) extremely generous 极慷慨的：*a* **munificent patron/gift/gesture** 慷慨的赞助人/馈赠/表示 ▸ **mu·nifi·cence** /-sns/ *noun* [U]

mu·ni·tions /mjuːˈnɪʃnz/ *noun* [pl.] military weapons, AMMUNITION and equipment 军需品；军火：*a shortage of munitions* 军需品缺乏 ◇ *a munitions factory* 兵工厂 ▸ **mu·ni·tion** *adj.* [only before noun]: *a munition store* 军需库

munt·jac (*also* **munt·jak**) /ˈmʌntdʒæk/ *noun* a type of small DEER, originally from SE Asia 麂（一种小鹿，产于东南亚）

mup·pet /ˈmʌpɪt/ *noun* (*BrE, informal*) a stupid person 笨蛋；蠢人

mural /ˈmjʊərəl; *NAmE* ˈmjʊrəl/ *noun* a painting, usually a large one, done on a wall, sometimes on an outside wall of a building 壁画 ▸ **mural** *adj.*：*mural paintings* 壁画

mur·der /ˈmɜːdə(r); *NAmE* ˈmɜːrd-/ *noun, verb*

■ ***noun*** **1** [U, C] the crime of killing sb deliberately 谋杀；凶杀 SYN **homicide**: *He was found guilty of murder.* 经裁决，他犯有谋杀罪。◇ *She has been charged with the* **attempted murder** *of her husband.* 她被指控意图谋杀丈夫。◇ *to* **commit (a) murder** 犯谋杀罪 ◇ *a* **murder case/investigation/trial** 凶杀案件/调查；谋杀案的审判 ◇ *The rebels were responsible for the* **mass murder** *of 400 civilians.* 叛乱者对屠杀 400 名平民负有责任。◇ *What was the* **murder weapon**? 用的是什么凶器？◇ *The play is a* **murder mystery**. 这出戏说的是一桩神秘的凶杀案。➲ COLLOCATIONS AT CRIME ➲ COMPARE MANSLAUGHTER **2** [U] (*informal*) used to describe sth that is difficult or unpleasant 困难的事；讨厌的事：*It's murder trying to get to the airport at*

M

this time of day. 这个时候要赶到机场简直要命。◇ It was murder (= very busy and unpleasant) in the office today. 今天办公室里忙乱得要命。

IDM **get away with 'murder** (informal, often humorous) to do whatever you want without being stopped or punished 逍遥法外；（做了错事而）安然无事 ➲ MORE AT SCREAM v.

■ *verb* **1** ~ sb to kill sb deliberately and illegally 谋杀；凶杀：*He denies murdering his wife's lover.* 他否认谋杀了妻子的情人。◇ *The murdered woman was well known in the area.* 被杀害的女人在这个地区很有名气。**2** ~ sth to spoil sth because you do not do it very well 糟蹋；毁坏；弄坏 SYN **butcher**: *Critics accused him of murdering the English language* (= writing or speaking it very badly). 批评家指责他把英语给糟蹋了。**3** ~ sb (informal) to defeat sb completely, especially in a team sport（尤指在团队运动中）彻底打败，打垮 SYN **thrash**

IDM **I could murder a...** (informal, especially BrE) used to say that you very much want to eat or drink sth 我非常想吃（或喝）：*I could murder a beer.* 我很想来杯啤酒。**sb will 'murder you** (informal) used to warn sb that another person will be very angry with them 某人会要你的命

mur·der·er /'mɜːdərə(r); NAmE 'mɜːrd-/ *noun* a person who has killed sb deliberately and illegally 杀人犯；杀人凶手 SYN **killer**: *a convicted murderer* 被判有罪的谋杀犯 ◇ *a mass murderer* (= who has killed a lot of people) 杀死很多人的凶手

mur·der·ess /'mɜːdəres; NAmE 'mɜːrd-/ *noun* (old-fashioned) a woman who has killed sb deliberately and illegally; a female murderer 女杀人犯；女杀人凶手

mur·der·ous /'mɜːdərəs; NAmE 'mɜːrd-/ *adj.* intending or likely to murder 蓄意谋杀的；凶残的；凶恶的 SYN **savage**: *a **murderous villain/tyrant*** 凶残的恶棍 / 暴君 ◇ *a murderous attack* 凶恶的进攻 ◇ *She gave him **a murderous look*** (= a very angry one). 她恶狠狠地瞪了他一眼。▶ **mur·der·ous·ly** *adv.*

murk /mɜːk; NAmE mɜːrk/ *noun* (usually **the murk**) [U] DARKNESS caused by smoke, FOG, etc. 阴暗；昏暗 SYN **gloom**

murky /'mɜːki; NAmE 'mɜːrki/ *adj.* (**murk·ier**, **murki·est**) **1** (of a liquid 液体) not clear; dark or dirty with mud or another substance 浑浊的；污浊的 SYN **cloudy**: *She gazed into the murky depths of the water.* 她注视着那幽暗的水底。**2** (of air, light, etc. 空气、光等) dark and unpleasant because of smoke, FOG, etc. 昏暗的；阴暗的；朦胧的：*a murky night* 昏暗的夜 **3** (disapproving or humorous) (of people's actions or character 人的行为或性格) not clearly known and suspected of not being honest 隐晦的；含糊的；暧昧可疑的：*He had a somewhat murky past.* 他有一段不清白的过去。◇ *the murky world of arms dealing* 黑暗的军火交易行业

mur·mur /'mɜːmə(r); NAmE 'mɜːrm-/ *verb, noun*

■ *verb* **1** [T, I] ~ (sth) | + speech | ~ that... to say sth in a soft quiet voice that is difficult to hear or understand 低语；喃喃细语：*She murmured her agreement.* 她低声表示同意。◇ *He murmured something in his sleep.* 他在睡梦里嘟囔了些什么。◇ *She was murmuring in his ear.* 她在他耳边悄声说话。**2** [I] to make a quiet continuous sound 连续发出低沉的声音：*The wind murmured in the trees.* 风在树林中沙沙作响。**3** [I] ~ (**against sb/sth**) (literary) to complain about sb/sth, but not openly（私下）发怨言，发牢骚

■ *noun* **1** [C] a quietly spoken word or words 低语；喃喃声：*She answered in a faint murmur.* 她低声应答。◇ *Murmurs of 'Praise God' went around the circle.* 周围的人群发出了"赞美主"的低语声。**2** [C] (also **mur·mur·ings** [pl.]) a quiet expression of feeling 嘟囔；咕哝：*a **murmur of agreement/approval/complaint*** 表示同意 / 赞同 / 抱怨的低语声 ◇ *He paid the extra cost **without a murmur*** (= without complaining at all). 他一声不吭地付了额外的费用。◇ *polite murmurings of gratitude* 有礼貌地连连低声道谢 **3** (also **mur·mur·ing**) [sing.] a low continuous sound in the background 接连从远处传来的低沉的声音：*the distant murmur of traffic* 远处传来的车辆的嘈杂声 **4** [C] (medical 医) a faint sound in the chest, usually a sign of damage or disease in the heart（胸部的）杂音：*a heart murmur* 心脏杂音

Murphy's Law /ˌmɜːfiz 'lɔː; NAmE ˌmɜːrfiz/ *noun* (humorous) a statement of the fact that, if anything can possibly go wrong, it will go wrong 墨菲法则（认为任何可能出错之事必将出错）

mur·ram /'mʌrəm/ *noun* [U] a type of reddish soil that is often used to make roads in Africa（非洲筑路用的）红土

mus·cat /'mʌskæt/ *noun* [U, C] **1** a type of wine, especially a strong sweet white wine 麝香葡萄酒（尤指一种白色烈性甜酒）**2** a type of GRAPE which can be eaten or used to make wine or RAISINS 麝香葡萄（用于酿酒或制葡萄干）

mus·ca·tel /ˌmʌskə'tel/ (also **mus·ca·delle**, **mus·ca·del** /-'del/) *noun* [U, C] a type of GRAPE used in sweet white wines and for drying to make RAISINS 玫瑰香葡萄

muscle /'mʌsl/ *noun, verb*

■ *noun* **1** [C, U] a piece of body TISSUE that you contract and relax in order to move a particular part of the body; the TISSUE that forms the muscles of the body 肌肉；肌：*a **calf/neck/thigh muscle*** 小腿 / 脖颈 / 大腿肌肉 ◇ *to **pull/tear/strain a muscle*** 拉伤 / 撕裂 / 扭伤肌肉 ◇ *This exercise will work the muscles of the lower back.* 这样的运动可以锻炼腰部的肌肉。◇ *He **didn't move a muscle*** (= stood completely still). 他一动不动地站着。➲ COLLOCATIONS AT INJURY **2** [U] physical strength 体力：*He's an intelligent player but lacks the muscle of older competitors.* 他是个聪明的选手，但却缺乏老选手的体力。**3** [U] the power and influence to make others do what you want 权力；威信；影响力：*to exercise **political/industrial/financial muscle*** 运用在政治 / 产业 / 金融界的影响力 ➲ MORE LIKE THIS 20, page R27 ▶ **muscled** *adj.*: *heavily muscled shoulders* 非常强壮的肩膀 IDM SEE FLEX v.

■ *verb*

PHR V **ˌmuscle 'in (on sb/sth)** (informal, disapproving) to involve yourself in a situation when you have no right to do so, in order to get sth for yourself 强行干涉；粗暴干涉

'muscle-bound *adj.* having large stiff muscles as a result of too much exercise（运动过度造成的）肌肉粗大僵硬的

muscle·man /'mʌslmæn/ *noun* (pl. **-men** /-men/) a big strong man, especially one employed to protect sb/sth 强壮男子；保镖；打手

mus·cu·lar /'mʌskjələ(r)/ *adj.* **1** connected with the muscles 肌肉的：***muscular tension/power/tissue*** 肌肉张力 / 力量 / 组织 **2** (also informal **muscly** /'mʌsli/) having large strong muscles 强壮的；肌肉发达的：*a **muscular body/build/chest*** 强壮的身体 / 体格；肌肉发达的胸部 ◇ *He was tall, lean and muscular.* 他高挑瘦削，强壮有力。

muscular dystrophy /ˌmʌskjələ 'dɪstrəfi; NAmE -lər/ *noun* [U] a medical condition that some people are born with in which the muscles gradually become weaker 肌营养不良；肌肉萎缩

mus·cu·lat·ure /'mʌskjələtʃə(r)/ *noun* [U, sing.] (biology 生) the system of muscles in the body or part of the body 肌肉系统

muse /mjuːz/ *noun, verb*

■ *noun* **1** a person or spirit that gives a writer, painter, etc. ideas and the desire to create things（作家、画家等的）灵感；创作冲动的源泉 SYN **inspiration**: *He felt that his muse had deserted him* (= that he could no longer write, paint, etc.). 他觉得他已失去了创作灵感。**2 Muse** (in ancient Greek and Roman stories) one of the nine *also* GODDESSES who encouraged poetry, music and other branches of art and literature 缪斯（古希腊和古罗马神话中执掌诗歌、音乐和其他文学艺术分支的九位女神之一）

■ *verb* (formal) **1** [I] ~ (**about/on/over/upon sth**) to think carefully about sth for a time, ignoring what is happening around you 沉思；冥想 SYN **ponder**: *I sat quietly, musing on the events of the day.* 我静静地坐着，沉思一天中所发生的事。➲ SEE ALSO MUSING **2** [T] + speech | ~ that...

to say sth to yourself in a way that shows you are thinking carefully about it 沉思地自言自语: *'I wonder why?' she mused.* "这是为什么呢?" 她若有所思地问自己。

mu·seum /mju'zi:əm/ *noun* a building in which objects of artistic, cultural, historical or scientific interest are kept and shown to the public 博物馆: *a museum of modern art* 现代艺术博物馆 ◇ *a science museum* 科学博物馆 ➲ VISUAL VOCAB PAGE V3

mu'seum piece *noun* **1** an object that is of enough historical or artistic value to have in a museum 珍藏品; 足以收入博物馆的物品 **2** (*humorous*) a thing or person that is old-fashioned, or old and no longer useful 老古董; 过时的物(或人)

mush /mʌʃ/ *noun* **1** [U, sing.] (*usually disapproving*) a soft thick mass or mixture 软稠的一摊; 糊状物: *The vegetables had turned to mush.* 蔬菜都烂成了一堆。◇ *His insides suddenly felt like mush.* 他内心突然伤感起来。**2** [U] (*NAmE*) a type of thick PORRIDGE made from CORN (MAIZE) 玉米粥

musher /'mʌʃə(r)/ *noun* (*NAmE*) a person who drives a dog SLED 赶狗拉雪橇的人

mush·room /'mʌʃrʊm; -ru:m/ *noun, verb*

■ ***noun*** a FUNGUS with a round flat head and short STEM. Many mushrooms can be eaten. 蘑菇; 蕈; 伞菌: *a field mushroom* (= the most common type that is eaten, often just called a 'mushroom', and often grown to be sold) 洋蘑菇 ◇ *fried mushrooms* 油炸蘑菇 ◇ *cream of mushroom soup* 奶油蘑菇汤 ➲ VISUAL VOCAB PAGE V33 ➲ SEE ALSO BUTTON MUSHROOM, TOADSTOOL

■ ***verb*** **1** [I] to rapidly grow or increase in number 快速生长; 迅速增长: *We expect the market to mushroom in the next two years.* 我们期望未来两年内市场会迅速发展。**2** (*usually* **go mushrooming**) [I] to gather mushrooms in a field or wood 采蘑菇

'mushroom cloud *noun* a large cloud, shaped like a mushroom, that forms in the air after a nuclear explosion (核爆炸形成的)蘑菇云

mushy /'mʌʃi/ *adj.* (**mush·ier, mushi·est**) **1** soft and thick, like mush 软而稠的; 糊状的: *Cook until the fruit is soft but not mushy.* 将水果煮至柔软, 但不要煮成糊状。➲ WORDFINDER NOTE AT CRISP **2** (*informal, disapproving*) too emotional in a way that is embarrassing 多愁善感的; 过于感伤多情的 SYN **sentimental**: *mushy romantic novels* 过于感伤的浪漫小说

,mushy 'peas *noun* [pl.] (*BrE*) cooked PEAS that are made into a soft mixture 豌豆粥; 豌豆糊

music /'mju:zɪk/ *noun* [U] **1** sounds that are arranged in a way that is pleasant or exciting to listen to. People sing music or play it on instruments. 音乐; 乐曲: ***pop/dance/classical/church music*** 流行音乐; 舞曲; 古典 / 教堂音乐 ◇ *to listen to music* 听音乐 ◇ *She could hear music playing somewhere.* 她听到某个地方在演奏音乐。◇ *It was a charming **piece of music**.* 那是一首动听的乐曲。◇ *the popularity of Mozart's music* 对莫扎特乐曲的普遍欢迎 ◇ *He wrote the music but I don't know who wrote the words.* 他创作了乐曲, 但我不知道谁填写的歌词。◇ *The poem has been **set to music**.* 这首诗被谱了曲。◇ *Every week they get together to **make music*** (= to play music or sing). 每个星期他们都聚在一起唱歌奏乐。➲ SEE ALSO CHAMBER MUSIC, COUNTRY MUSIC, ROCK MUSIC, SOUL MUSIC ➲ WORDFINDER NOTE AT DANCE, SING **2** the art of writing or playing music 音乐; 乐曲创作(或演奏)艺术: *to study music* 学习音乐 ◇ *a career in music* 音乐生涯 ◇ *music lessons* 音乐课程 ◇ *the **music business/industry*** 音乐行业 / 产业 **3** the written or printed signs that represent the sounds to be played or sung in a piece of music 乐谱: *Can you **read music*** (= understand the signs in order to play or sing a piece of music)? 你识谱吗? ◇ *I had to play it without the music.* 我只得不看乐谱演奏了。◇ *The music* (= the paper or book with the musical notes on it) *was still open on the piano.* 乐谱仍摊开在钢琴上。➲ SEE ALSO SHEET MUSIC

IDM **music to your 'ears** news or information that you are very pleased to hear 好消息; 令人满意的信息 ➲ MORE AT FACE *v.*

mu·sic·al /'mju:zɪkl/ *adj., noun*

■ ***adj.*** **1** [only before noun] connected with music; containing music 音乐的; 有音乐的: *the musical director of the show* 这场演出的音乐总监 ◇ ***musical talent/ability/skill*** 音乐天赋 / 才能 / 技巧 ◇ ***musical styles/tastes*** 音乐风格 / 品味

M

▼ COLLOCATIONS 词语搭配

Music 音乐

Listening 听

- **listen to/enjoy/love/be into** music/classical music/jazz/pop/hip-hop, etc. 听 / 欣赏 / 喜爱 / 迷上音乐 / 古典音乐 / 爵士乐 / 流行音乐 / 嘻哈音乐等
- **listen to** the radio/an MP3 player/a CD 听收音机 / MP3 播放器 / CD
- **put on/play** a CD/a song/some music 播放 CD / 歌曲 / 音乐
- **turn down/up** the music/radio/volume/bass 调小 / 调大音乐 / 收音机 / 音量 / 低音
- **go to** a concert/festival/gig/performance/recital 去听音乐会; 去看会演 / 现场演唱会 / 演出 / 音乐演奏会
- **copy/burn/rip** music/a CD/a DVD 复制 / 刻录 / 翻录音乐 / CD / DVD
- **download** music/an album/a song/a demo/a video 下载音乐 / 专辑 / 歌曲 / 录音样带 / 视频

Playing 演奏

- **play** a musical instrument/the piano/percussion/a note/a riff/the melody/a concerto/a duet/by ear 演奏乐器 / 钢琴 / 打击乐 / 音符 / 重复段 / 主旋律 / 协奏曲 / 二重奏; 凭听觉记忆演奏
- **sing** an anthem/a ballad/a solo/an aria/the blues/in a choir/soprano/alto/tenor/bass/out of tune 唱国歌 / 民歌; 独唱; 唱咏叹调 / 蓝调歌曲; 在合唱团演唱; 唱女高音 / 中音 / 男高音 / 男低音; 唱歌走调
- **hum** a tune/a theme tune/a lullaby 哼曲子 / 主题曲 / 摇篮曲
- **accompany** a singer/choir 为歌手 / 合唱团伴奏
- **strum** a chord/guitar 弹奏和弦 / 吉他

Performing 表演

- **form/start/get together/join/quit/leave** a band 组建 / 创办 / 组成 / 加入 / 退出 / 离开乐队
- **give** a performance/concert/recital 表演节目; 举办音乐会 / 音乐演奏会
- **do** a concert/recital/gig 开音乐会 / 音乐演奏会 / 现场演唱会
- **play** a concert/gig/festival/venue 在音乐会 / 现场演唱会 / 会演 / 音乐厅演出
- **perform** (*BrE*) at/in a concert/(*especially NAmE*) a concert 在音乐会上演出
- **appear** at a festival/live 现身会演; 现场表演
- **go on/embark on** a (world) tour 进行 / 开始(全球)巡演

Recording 录制

- **write/compose** music/a ballad/a melody/a tune/a song/a theme song/an opera/a symphony 写 / 创作音乐 / 民谣 / 旋律 / 曲子 / 歌曲 / 主题歌 / 歌剧 / 交响曲
- **land/get/sign** a record deal 获得 / 签署唱片合约
- **be signed to/be dropped by** a record company 与唱片公司签约; 被唱片公司解约
- **record/release/put out** an album/a single/a CD 录制 / 发行 / 出版专辑 / 单曲 / CD
- **be top of/top** the charts 高居每周流行唱片排行榜之首
- **get to/go straight to/go straight in at/enter the charts** at number one 位列 / 一举登上 / 进入排行榜首位

◇ *a musical production/entertainment* 音乐作品 / 娱乐项目 **2** 🔑 (of a person 人) with a natural skill or interest in music 有音乐天赋的；喜爱音乐的：*She's very musical.* 她极具音乐天赋。 **OPP unmusical** **3** (of a sound 声音) pleasant to listen to, like music 悦耳的；音乐般的：*a musical voice* 悦耳的声音 **OPP unmusical**

■ *noun* (*also old-fashioned* ˌ**musical ˈcomedy**) a play or a film/movie in which part or all of the story is told using songs and often dancing 音乐剧

ˈ**musical box** *noun* (*especially BrE*) = MUSIC BOX

ˌ**musical ˈchairs** *noun* [U] **1** a children's game in which players run round a row of chairs while music is playing. Each time the music stops, players try to sit down on one of the chairs, but there are always more players than chairs. 抢座位游戏（参加者随音乐绕一圈椅子走，音乐一停就抢椅子坐，但参加者总是比椅子多） **2** (*often disapproving*) a situation in which people frequently exchange jobs or positions 人员的经常更迭流动

ˌ**musical diˈrector** *noun* the person who is in charge of the music in a show in the theatre（舞台表演的）音乐总监

ˌ**musical ˈinstrument** (*also* **in·stru·ment**) *noun* an object used for producing musical sounds, for example a piano or a drum 乐器：*Most pupils learn (to play) a musical instrument.* 多数小学生都学习演奏乐器。 ◇ *the instruments of the orchestra* 管弦乐队的乐器 ➲ VISUAL VOCAB PAGES V37-40

mu·sic·al·ity /ˌmjuːzɪˈkæləti/ *noun* [U] (*formal*) skill and understanding in performing music 乐感；音乐欣赏能力；音乐才能

music·al·ly /ˈmjuːzɪkli/ *adv.* **1** in a way that is connected with music 音乐上；在音乐方面：*musically gifted* 音乐方面有天赋的 ◇ *Musically speaking, their latest album is nothing special.* 在音乐方面，他们最新的专辑没什么特别的。 **2** with musical skill 有音乐技能：*He plays really musically.* 他的演奏娴熟动听。 **3** in a way that is pleasant to listen to, like music 和谐地；悦耳地；音乐般地：*to laugh/speak musically* 笑声 / 讲话悦耳

ˈ**music box** (*also* ˈ**musical box** *especially in BrE*) *noun* a box containing a device that plays a tune when the box is opened 音乐盒；八音盒

ˈ**music hall** *noun* (*BrE*) **1** (*also* **vaude·ville** *NAmE, BrE*) [U] a type of entertainment popular in the late 19th and early 20th centuries, including singing, dancing and comedy（盛行于 19 世纪末 20 世纪初的）歌舞杂耍表演 **2** (*NAmE* ˈ**vaudeville theater**) [C] a theatre used for popular entertainment in the late 19th and early 20th centuries 歌舞杂耍戏院

mu·si·cian 🔑 /mjuˈzɪʃn/ *noun* a person who plays a musical instrument or writes music, especially as a job 音乐家；作曲家；乐师：*a jazz/rock musician* 爵士乐 / 摇滚乐乐师

mu·si·cian·ship /mjuˈzɪʃnʃɪp/ *noun* [U] skill in performing or writing music 音乐才能；音乐技能

mu·sic·ology /ˌmjuːzɪˈkɒlədʒi; *NAmE* -ˈkɑːl-/ *noun* [U] the study of the history and theory of music 音乐学 ▶ **mu·sic·olo·gist** /ˌmjuːzɪˈkɒlədʒɪst; *NAmE* -ˈkɑːl-/ *noun*

ˈ**music stand** *noun* a frame, especially one that you can fold, that is used for holding sheets of music while you play a musical instrument 乐谱架

ˈ**music video** *noun* = VIDEO (3)

mus·ing /ˈmjuːzɪŋ/ *noun* [U, C, usually pl.] a period of thinking carefully about sth or telling people your thoughts about it 沉思；冥想；诉说想法：*We had to sit and listen to his musings on life.* 我们只好坐着听他谈论人生。

musk /mʌsk/ *noun* [U] a substance with a strong smell that is used in making some PERFUMES. It is produced naturally by a type of male DEER. 麝香 ▶ **musky** *adj.*：*a musky perfume* (= smelling of or like musk) 有麝香味的香水

mus·ket /ˈmʌskɪt/ *noun* an early type of long gun that was used by soldiers in the past（旧时的）火枪，滑膛枪，毛瑟枪

mus·ket·eer /ˌmʌskəˈtɪə(r); *NAmE* -ˈtɪr/ *noun* a soldier who uses a musket 火枪手；滑膛枪手

ˈ**musk ox** *noun* a large animal of the cow family that is covered with hair and has curved horns 麝牛

musk·rat /ˈmʌskræt/ *noun* a N American water animal that has a strong smell and is hunted for its fur 麝鼠（北美洲半水栖鼠，有麝香味，毛皮可作商品）

Mus·lim /ˈmʊzlɪm; ˈmʌz-; -ləm/ *noun* a person whose religion is Islam 穆斯林；伊斯兰教信徒 ▶ **Mus·lim** *adj.* ➲ SEE ALSO MOSLEM

mus·lin /ˈmʌzlɪn/ *noun* [U] a type of fine cotton cloth that is almost transparent, used, especially in the past, for making clothes and curtains 平纹细布，细平布（旧时尤用于做衣物和窗帘）

muso /ˈmjuːzəʊ; *NAmE* -zoʊ/ *noun* (*pl.* **-os**) (*BrE, informal*) a person who plays, or is very interested in, music and knows a lot about it 乐师；乐迷；音乐通

mus·quash /ˈmʌskwɒʃ; *NAmE* -kwɑːʃ; -kwɔːʃ/ *noun* [U] the fur of the MUSKRAT 麝鼠皮

muss /mʌs/ *verb* ~ **sth** (**up**) (*NAmE*) to make sb's clothes or hair untidy 弄乱（衣服或头发）；使邋遢：*Hey, don't muss up my hair!* 嗨，别弄乱了我的头发！

mus·sel /ˈmʌsl/ *noun* a small SHELLFISH that can be eaten, with a black shell in two parts 贻贝 ➲ PICTURE AT SHELLFISH

must 🔑 *modal verb, noun*

■ ***modal verb*** /məst; *strong form* mʌst/ (*negative* **must not**, *short form* **mustn't** /ˈmʌsnt/) **1** 🔑 used to say that sth is necessary or very important (sometimes involving a rule or a law) （表示必要或很重要）必须：*All visitors must report to reception.* 所有来宾必须到接待处报到。◇ *Cars must not park in front of the entrance* (= it is not allowed). 车辆不得停在入口处。◇ (*formal*) *I must ask you not to do that again.* 我得劝你别再那样做了。◇ *You mustn't say things like that.* 你千万别说那样的话。◇ *I must go to the bank and get some money.* 我得上银行取点儿钱。◇ ***I must admit*** (= I feel that I should admit) *I was surprised it cost so little.* 我得承认，这么便宜，真让我惊讶。◇ (*especially BrE*) *Must you always question everything I say?* (= it is annoying) 我说什么你都非要提出质疑吗？◇ *'Do we have to finish this today?' 'Yes, you must.'* "我们今天一定得完成这工作吗？""对，必须完成。" **HELP** Note that the negative for the last example is: *'No, you don't have to.'* 注意最后这个示例的否定式是 No, you don't have to。➲ EXPRESS YOURSELF AT HAVE TO **2** 🔑 used to say that sth is likely or logical（表示很可能或符合逻辑）一定：*You must be hungry after all that walking.* 走了这么远的路，你一定饿了吧。◇ *He must have known* (= surely he knew) *what she wanted.* 他一定早已知道她想要什么了。◇ *I'm sorry, she's not here. She must have left already* (= that must be the explanation). 抱歉，她不在这儿。准是走了。**3** 🔑 (*especially BrE*) used to recommend that sb does sth because you think it is a good idea（提出建议）应该，得：*You simply must read this book.* 这本书你可一定要看一看。◇ *We must get together soon for lunch.* 我们得马上集合去吃午饭。➲ NOTE AT MODAL

IDM **if you 'must (do sth)** used to say that sb may do sth but you do not really want them to（表示虽不赞同但可允许）如果你一定要（那么做）：*'Can I smoke?' 'If you must.'* "我可以抽烟吗？""好吧，如果你一定要抽的话。"◇ *It's from my boyfriend,* ***if you must know.*** 倘使你一定要知道的话，这是我男朋友给的。 **must-see/must-read/must-have, etc.** used to tell people that sth is so good or interesting that they should see, read, get it, etc. 必看（或必读、必备等）：*Sydney is one of the world's must-see cities.* 悉尼是世界上的必游城市之一。◇ *The magazine is a must-read in the show business world.* 这份杂志是演艺界人士的必读刊物。➲ MORE AT NEEDS

■ ***noun*** /mʌst/ [usually sing.] (*informal*) something that you must do, see, buy, etc. 必须做（或看、买等）的事：*His new novel is a must for all lovers of crime fiction.* 他的新作是所有犯罪小说爱好者的必读书。

mus·tache (*especially US*) (*also BrE* **mous·tache**) /məˈstɑːʃ; *NAmE* ˈmʌstæʃ; məˈstæʃ/ *noun* **1** a line of hair that a man allows to grow on his upper lip 上唇的胡子；髭 ➲ VISUAL VOCAB PAGE V65 **2 mustaches** [pl.] a very long mustache 长髭 ➲ COMPARE BEARD *n.*

mus·tached (*especially US*) (*BrE* **mous·tached**) /məˈstɑːʃt; *NAmE* ˈmʌstæʃt; məˈstæʃt/ *adj.* [usually before noun] having a mustache 长胡子的；有胡子的 ➲ COMPARE MUSTACHIOED

mus·tachi·oed /məˈstæʃiəʊd; *NAmE* -ʃioʊd/ *adj.* (*literary*) having a large moustache with curls at the ends 有大鬈曲八字胡的

mus·tang /ˈmʌstæŋ/ *noun* a small American wild horse 北美野马

mus·tard /ˈmʌstəd; *NAmE* -tərd/ *noun* [U] **1** a thick cold yellow or brown sauce that tastes hot and spicy and is usually eaten with meat 芥末酱：*a jar of mustard* 一罐芥末酱 ◇ *mustard powder* 芥末粉 ◇ ***French/English mustard*** 法国/英格兰芥末 **2** a small plant with yellow flowers, grown for its seeds that are crushed to make mustard 芥；芥菜 **3** (*BrE*) the leaves of the mustard plant that are eaten raw in salads 芥菜叶：*mustard and cress* (= leaves of white mustard grown with CRESS) 芥菜叶和水芹 **4** a brownish-yellow colour 芥末黄；褐黄色 ▶ **mus·tard** *adj.*：*a mustard sweater* 芥末黄毛线衣

IDM **(not) cut the 'mustard** to (not) be as good as expected or required（不）如所期待的那么好；（不）符合要求：*I didn't cut the mustard as a hockey player.* 我不是一个合格的曲棍球手。➲ MORE AT KEEN *adj.*

'mustard gas *noun* [U] a poisonous gas that burns the skin, used in chemical weapons, for example during the First World War 芥子气（损害皮肤，用于化学武器）

'mustard greens *noun* [pl.] the dark green leaves of a type of MUSTARD plant, that are cooked or eaten raw in

▼ **GRAMMAR POINT** 语法说明

must / have (got) to / must not / don't have to

Necessity and Obligation 必要和义务

- **Must** and **have (got) to** are used in the present to say that something is necessary or should be done. **Have to** is more common in *NAmE*, especially in speech. * must 和 have (got) to 用于现在时，表示某事有必要或应该做。have to 较常用于美式英语，尤其是口语中：*You must be home by 11 o'clock.* 你必须在 11 点之前回家。◇ *I must wash the car tomorrow.* 我明天必须洗汽车。◇ *I have to collect the children from school at 3 o'clock.* 我得在 3 点钟到学校接孩子。◇ *Nurses have to wear a uniform.* 护士必须穿制服。
- In *BrE* there is a difference between them. **Must** is used to talk about what the speaker or listener wants, and **have (got) to** about rules, laws and other people's wishes. 在英式英语中，两词之间有差异。must 是基于说话者或听话者的主观意愿，have (got) to 关乎规定、法律和他人的愿望：*I must finish this essay today. I'm going out tomorrow.* 我今天一定要完成这篇论文，因为我明天要出去。◇ *I have to finish this essay today. We have to hand them in tomorrow.* 我今天得完成这篇论文，因为我们明天必须交。
- There are no past or future forms of **must**. To talk about the past you use **had to** and **has had to**. * must 无过去和将来形式。表示过去用 had to 或 has had to：*I had to wait half an hour for a bus* 我得等半小时的公共汽车。**Will have to** is used to talk about the future, or **have to** if an arrangement has already been made. 说将来的事用 will have to，如果已作好安排亦可用 have to：*We'll have to borrow the money we need.* 我们需要的这笔钱只好去借了。◇ *I have to go to the dentist tomorrow.* 我明天得去看牙医。
- Questions with **have to** are formed using **do**. 带有 have to 的疑问句由 do 构成：*Do the children have to wear a uniform?* 孩子们必须穿制服吗？ In negative sentences both **must not** and **don't have to** are used, but with different meanings. **Must not** is used to tell somebody not to do something. 在否定句中，用 must not 和 don't have to，但二者含义不同。must not 用于告诉某人不要做某事：*Passengers must not smoke until the signs have been switched off.* 指示灯未熄灭之前乘客不许抽烟。The short form **mustn't** is used especially in *BrE*. 缩略形式 mustn't 尤用于英式英语：*You mustn't leave the gate open.* 你一定不要让大门敞开着。**Don't have to** is used when it is not necessary to do something. 表示没有必要做某事用 don't have to：*You don't have to pay for the tickets in advance.* 你不必预付票款。◇ *She doesn't have to work at weekends.* 她周末不用上班。

➲ NOTE AT NEED

Certainty 肯定

- Both **must** and **have to** are used to say that you are certain about something. **Have to** is the usual verb used in *NAmE* and this is becoming more frequent in *BrE* in this meaning. 表示肯定用 must 和 have to 均可。have to 通常用于美式英语中，在英式英语中也越来越常用于此义：*He has (got) to be the worst actor on TV!* 他无疑是最糟糕的电视演员！◇ (*BrE*) *This must be the most boring party I've ever been to.* 这无疑是我参加过的最无聊的聚会。 If you are talking about the past, use **must have**. 说过去的事用 must have：*Your trip must have been fun!* 你这次旅行一定很开心吧！

M

salads, especially in the Southern US 芥菜叶（烹调或拌色拉用，尤见于美国南部）

mus·ter /ˈmʌstə(r)/ *verb, noun*
■ *verb* **1** [T] **~ sth (up)** to find as much support, courage, etc. as you can 找寻，聚集，激起（支持、勇气等） SYN **summon**: *We mustered what support we could for the plan.* 我们极尽所能为这项计划寻求支持。◇ *She left the room with all the dignity she could muster.* 她尽量庄重体面地走了出去。**2** [I, T] to come together or to bring people, especially soldiers, together, for example for military action 集合，召集，集结（尤指部队） SYN **gather**: *The troops mustered.* 部队集结起来。◇ **~ sb/sth** *to muster an army* 集合一支部队 **3** [T] **~ sth** (*AustralE, NZE*) to gather together sheep or cows 赶拢（牛、羊）
■ *noun* a group of people, especially soldiers, that have been brought together 聚集的人群；（尤指）集结的兵力：*muster stations* (= parts of a building, a ship, etc. that people must go to if there is an emergency) 集结站
IDM SEE PASS *v.*

musty /ˈmʌsti/ *adj.* (**must·ier, musti·est**) smelling damp and unpleasant because of a lack of fresh air 有霉味的；发霉的 SYN **dank**: *a musty room* 有霉味的房间

mut·able /ˈmjuːtəbl/ *adj.* (*formal*) that can change; likely to change 可变的；会变的 ▶ **mut·abil·ity** /ˌmjuːtəˈbɪləti/ *noun* [U]

mu·tant /ˈmjuːtənt/ *adj., noun*
■ *adj.* (*biology* 生) (of a living thing 生物) different in some way from others of the same kind because of a change in its GENETIC structure 因基因变异而不同的；变异的；突变的：*a mutant gene* 突变基因
■ *noun* **1** (*biology* 生) a living thing with qualities that are different from its parents' qualities because of a change in its GENETIC structure 突变型；突变体 **2** (*informal*) (in stories about space, the future, etc. 未来和太空等故事) a living thing with an unusual and frightening appearance because of a change in its GENETIC structure 突变异体怪物；异形

M

mu·tate /mjuːˈteɪt; *NAmE* ˈmjuːteɪt/ *verb* **1** [I, T] (*biology* 生) to develop or make sth develop a new form or structure, because of a GENETIC change （使）变异，突变：**~ (into sth)** *the ability of the virus to mutate into new forms* 该病毒突变成新毒株的能力 ◇ **~ sth** *mutated genes* 发生变异的基因 **2** [I] **~ (into sth)** to change into a new form 转变；转换：*Rhythm and blues mutated into rock and roll.* 节奏布鲁斯演变成为摇滚乐。➲ SEE ALSO MUTATION

mu·ta·tion /mjuːˈteɪʃn/ *noun* **1** [U, C] (*biology* 生) a process in which the GENETIC material of a person, a plant or an animal changes in structure when it is passed on to children, etc., causing different physical characteristics to develop; a change of this kind （生物物种的）突变，变异：*cells affected by mutation* 受到突变影响的细胞 ◇ *genetic mutations* 基因突变 ➲ WORDFINDER NOTE AT BIOLOGY **2** [U, C] a change in the form or structure of sth （形式或结构的）转变，改变：(*linguistics* 语言) *vowel mutation* 元音变化

mu·ta·tis mu·tan·dis /mjuːˌtɑːtɪs mjuːˈtændɪs; muːˌtɑːtɪs muːˈtændɪs/ *adv.* (*from Latin, formal*) (used when you are comparing two or more things or situations) making the small changes that are necessary for each individual case, without changing the main points （用于比较两种或以上的事物或状况）作必要的小更改：*The same contract, mutatis mutandis, will be given to each employee* (= the contract is basically the same for everybody, but the names, etc. are changed). 把姓名等细节稍作修改之后，同一份合同将发给每个员工，人手一份。

mute /mjuːt/ *adj., noun, verb*
■ *adj.* **1** not speaking 沉默的；不出声的；无声的 SYN **silent**: *a look of mute appeal* 默默请求的表情 ◇ *The child sat mute in the corner of the room.* 这孩子坐在屋子的角落里，一声不吭。**2** (*old-fashioned*) (of a person 人) unable to speak 哑的 SYN **dumb**
■ *noun* **1** (*music* 音) a device made of metal, rubber or plastic that you use to make the sound of a musical instrument softer 弱音器 **2** (*old-fashioned*) a person who is not able to speak 哑巴
■ *verb* **1 ~ sth** to make the sound of sth, especially a musical instrument, quieter or softer, sometimes using a mute 消音；减音；减弱（尤指乐器）的声音：*He muted the strings with his palm.* 他用手掌抹琴弦消音。**2 ~ sth** to make sth weaker or less severe 减弱；缓解 SYN **tone down**: *She thought it better to mute her criticism.* 她觉得还是婉转地提出批评比较好。

ˈmute button *noun* **1** a button on a telephone that you press in order to stop yourself from being heard by the person at the other end of the line (while you speak to sb else) （电话机上的）静音键 **2** a button that you press in order to switch off a television's sound （电视机的）静音按钮

muted /ˈmjuːtɪd/ *adj.* **1** (of sounds 声音) quiet; not as loud as usual 静静的；减轻的：*They spoke in muted voices.* 他们轻声说着话。**2** (of emotions, opinions, etc. 情感、意见等) not strongly expressed 含糊不清的；表达不明确的：*The proposals received only a muted response.* 这个倡议没有得到明确的回应。**3** (of colours, light, etc. 色彩、光亮等) not bright 暗淡的；不明亮的：*a dress in muted shades of blue* 暗蓝色调的连衣裙 **4** (of musical instruments 乐器) used with a mute 使用弱音器的：*muted trumpets* 装有弱音器的小号

mute·ly /ˈmjuːtli/ *adv.* without speaking 无言地；一语不发地 SYN **silently**

muti /ˈmuːti/ *noun* [U] (*SAfrE*) **1** African medicines or magic CHARMS that are prepared from plants, animals, etc. （在非洲用植物、动物等制成的）草药，土药，符咒 **2** any kind of medicine 药

mu·ti·late /ˈmjuːtɪleɪt/ *verb* **1 ~ sb/sth** to damage sb's body very severely, especially by cutting or tearing off part of it 使残废；使残缺不全；毁伤：*The body had been badly mutilated.* 尸体被严重毁伤。**2 ~ sth** to damage sth very badly 严重损毁；毁坏 SYN **vandalize**: *Intruders slashed and mutilated several paintings.* 闯进来的人毁坏了好几幅油画。▶ **mu·ti·la·tion** /ˌmjuːtɪˈleɪʃn/ *noun* [U, C]: *Thousands suffered death or mutilation in the bomb blast.* 在炸弹爆炸事件中，数千人被炸死，或成为残废。

mu·tin·eer /ˌmjuːtəˈnɪə(r); *NAmE* -ˈnɪr/ *noun* a person who takes part in a MUTINY 叛变者；暴动者；反叛者

mu·tin·ous /ˈmjuːtənəs/ *adj.* **1** refusing to obey the orders of sb in authority; wanting to do this 不驯服的；桀骜不驯的；有意反抗的 SYN **rebellious**: *mutinous workers* 桀骜不驯的工人 ◇ *a mutinous expression* 反抗的神色 **2** taking part in a mutiny 参与叛乱的；参与暴动的 ▶ **mu·tin·ous·ly** *adv.*

mu·tiny /ˈmjuːtəni/ *noun, verb*
■ *noun* (*pl.* **-ies**) [U, C] the act of refusing to obey the orders of sb in authority, especially by soldiers or sailors （尤指士兵或船员的）哗变，暴动：*Discontent among the ship's crew finally led to the outbreak of mutiny.* 船员的不满情绪最终酿成了暴乱。◇ *the famous movie 'Mutiny on the Bounty'* 著名电影《叛舰喋血记》◇ *We have a family mutiny on our hands!* 我们家出了叛逆之事，需要处理！
■ *verb* (**mu·tin·ies, mu·tiny·ing, mu·tin·ied, mu·tin·ied**) [I] (especially of soldiers or sailors 尤指士兵或船员) to refuse to obey the orders of sb in authority 不服从；反抗；反叛

mut·ism /ˈmjuːtɪzəm/ *noun* [U] (*medical* 医) a medical condition in which a person is unable to speak 缄默症；哑症

mutt /mʌt/ *noun* (*informal, especially NAmE*) a dog, especially one that is not of a particular breed 狗；杂种狗 SYN **mongrel**

mut·ter /ˈmʌtə(r)/ *verb, noun*
■ *verb* **1** [T, I] to speak or say sth in a quiet voice that is difficult to hear, especially because you are annoyed about sth 嘀咕；嘟囔：**+ speech** *'How dare she,' he muttered under his breath.* 他轻声嘀咕道："她怎么敢。"◇

~ (sth) (to sb/yourself) (about sth) *She just sat there muttering to herself.* 她坐在那儿独自唧唧咕咕的。◇ *I muttered something about needing to get back to work.* 我嘀咕着说要接着干活了。◇ ~ that... *He muttered that he was sorry.* 他轻声嘀咕了一声对不起。**2** [I, T] ~ (about sth) | ~ that... to complain about sth, without saying publicly what you think (私下)抱怨,发牢骚 SYN **grumble**: *Workers continued to mutter about the management.* 工人私下对资方还是有怨言。

■ *noun* [usually sing.] a quiet sound or words that are difficult to hear 嘀咕;嘟哝;低语声: *the soft mutter of voices* 柔和的低语声

mut·ter·ing /ˈmʌtərɪŋ/ *noun* [U] **1** (*also* **mutterings** [pl.]) complaints that you express privately rather than openly (私下的)抱怨,牢骚: *There have been mutterings about his leadership.* 底下对他的领导一直怨声不断。**2** words that you speak very quietly to yourself 喃喃自语

mut·ton /ˈmʌtn/ *noun* [U] meat from a fully grown sheep 羊肉 ➲ COMPARE LAMB *n.* (2)

IDM **mutton dressed as 'lamb** (*BrE, informal, disapproving*) used to describe a woman who is trying to look younger than she really is, especially by wearing clothes that are designed for young people 扮俏的女人;老来俏

ˌmutton 'chops (*also* **ˌmutton chop 'whiskers**) *noun* [pl.] hair at the sides of a man's face which is grown so that it is very wide and round in shape at the bottom 羊排络腮胡(长于脸颊两边,底部呈宽圆形)

mu·tual AW /ˈmjuːtʃuəl/ *adj.* **1** used to describe feelings that two or more people have for each other equally, or actions that affect two or more people equally 相互的;彼此的: ***mutual respect/understanding*** 相互的尊敬/理解 ◇ ***mutual support/aid*** 相互的支持/帮助 ◇ *I don't like her, and I think **the feeling is mutual*** (= she doesn't like me either). 我不喜欢她,我觉得她也不喜欢我。**2** [only before noun] shared by two or more people 共有的;共同的: *We met at the home of a mutual friend.* 我们在彼此都认识的朋友家中会面。◇ *They soon discovered a mutual interest in music.* 他们很快发现对音乐有着共同的兴趣。▶ **mu·tu·al·ity** /ˌmjuːtʃuˈæləti/ *noun* [U, C] (*formal*)

'mutual fund (*NAmE*) (*BrE* **ˌunit 'trust**) *noun* a company that offers a service to people by investing their money in various different businesses 共同基金,单位信托投资公司(代客户进行不同组合的投资)

mu·tu·al·ly AW /ˈmjuːtʃuəli/ *adv.* felt or done equally by two or more people 相互地;彼此;共同地: *a **mutually beneficial/supportive** relationship* 互惠/互助的关系 ◇ *Can we find a mutually convenient time to meet?* 我们可以找个双方都适当的时间会面吗? ◇ *The two views are not **mutually exclusive*** (= both can be true at the same time). 这两种观点并不互相排斥。

Muzak™ /ˈmjuːzæk/ *noun* [U] (*often disapproving*) continuous recorded music that is played in shops, restaurants, airports, etc. 米尤扎克背景音乐(常在商店、餐馆、机场等处播放) ➲ COMPARE PIPED MUSIC

muz·zle /ˈmʌzl/ *noun, verb*

■ *noun* **1** the nose and mouth of an animal, especially a dog or a horse (狗、马等动物的)口鼻 ➲ VISUAL VOCAB PAGE V12 ➲ COMPARE SNOUT (1) **2** a device made of leather or plastic that you put over the nose and mouth of an animal, especially a dog, to prevent it from biting people (防止动物咬人的)口套,鼻笼 **3** the open end of a gun, where the bullets come out 枪口;炮口

■ *verb* **1** [usually passive] ~ **sth** to put a muzzle over a dog's head to prevent it from biting people (给狗)戴口套 **2** ~ **sb/sth** to prevent sb from expressing their opinions in public as they want to 压制,钳制(言论);使缄默 SYN **gag**: *They accused the government of muzzling the press.* 他们指责政府压制新闻自由。

muzzy /ˈmʌzi/ *adj.* (*BrE, informal*) **1** unable to think in a clear way 头脑混乱的;迷糊的: *a muzzy head* 稀里糊涂的大脑 ◇ *Those drugs made me feel muzzy.* 那些药使我昏昏欲睡。**2** not clear 模模糊糊的;不清楚的: *a muzzy voice* 模糊不清的声音 ◇ *muzzy plans* 过于笼统的计划

MV /ˌem ˈviː/ *abbr.* (*BrE*) (used before the name of a ship) motor vessel (用于船名前)内燃机船: *the MV Puma* 美洲狮号机动船

MVP /ˌem viː ˈpiː/ *noun* (*especially NAmE*) most valuable player (the best player in a team) 最优秀选手;最有价值球员: *He has just earned his fourth MVP award this season.* 这个赛季他刚获得了他的第四个"最有价值球员奖"。

MW *abbr.* **1** MEDIUM WAVE 中波 **2** (*pl.* **MW**) MEGAWATT 兆瓦(特)

MWA /ˌem dʌbljuː ˈeɪ/ *noun* Member of the Welsh Assembly 威尔士议会议员

mwah (*also* **mwa**) /mwɑː/ *exclamation* used to represent the sound that some people make when they kiss sb on the cheek (亲吻脸颊的声音)吧 ➲ MORE LIKE THIS 3, page R25

mwa·limu /mwɑːˈliːmuː/ *noun* (*EAfrE*) **1** a teacher 教师;老师 **2 Mwalimu** a title or form of address for sb who is respected as a teacher (头衔或尊称)老师,导师: *Mwalimu Julius Nyerere* 朱利叶斯•尼雷尔导师

mwa·nan·chi /mwəˈnæntʃi/ *noun* [sing.] (*EAfrE*) an ordinary citizen; a member of the public 普通公民;平民;百姓: *The common mwananchi is demanding change.* 普通民众要求变革。➲ SEE ALSO WANANCHI

my 🔑 /maɪ/ *det.* (the possessive form of *I* * I 的所有格形式) **1** 🔑 of or belonging to the speaker or writer 我的: *Where's my passport?* 我的护照在哪儿? ◇ *My feet are cold.* 我的脚冷。**2** used in exclamations to express surprise, etc. (用于感叹句,表示吃惊等): *My goodness! Look at the time!* 天哪!看看几点了! **3** used when addressing sb, to show affection (称呼别人时使用,表示亲切): ***my dear/darling/love*** 亲爱的;我的宝贝儿/心肝儿 **4** used when addressing sb that you consider to have a lower status than you (对下级的称呼): *My dear girl, you're wrong.* 我亲爱的姑娘,你错了。

my·al·gia /maɪˈældʒə/ *noun* [U] (*medical* 医) pain in a muscle 肌痛 ▶ **my·al·gic** /-dʒɪk/ *adj.* ➲ SEE ALSO ME (1)

my·al·gic en·ceph·alo·my·eli·tis /maɪˌældʒɪk enˌsefələʊmaɪəˈlaɪtɪs; *NAmE* -ˌsefəlem-/ *noun* [U] = ME (1)

my·col·ogy /maɪˈkɒlədʒi; *NAmE* -ˈkɑːl-/ *noun* [U] the scientific study of FUNGI 真菌学 ➲ SEE ALSO FUNGUS

mye·lin /ˈmaɪəlɪn/ *noun* [U] (*biology* 生) a mixture of PROTEINS and fats that surrounds many nerve cells, increasing the speed at which they send signals 髓磷脂,髓鞘质(由脂质、蛋白质组成,包绕在神经细胞轴突上)

mye·loma /ˌmaɪəˈləʊmə; *NAmE* -ˈloʊmə/ (*pl.* **mye·lo·mas** or **mye·lo·mata** /-mətə/) *noun* (*medical* 医) a type of cancer found as a TUMOUR inside the bone 骨髓瘤

mynah /ˈmaɪnə/ (*also* **'mynah bird**) *noun* a SE Asian bird with dark feathers, that can copy human speech (东南亚一种能模仿人说话的)黑羽鸟

MYOB /ˌem waɪ əʊ ˈbiː; *NAmE* oʊ/ *abbr.* (*informal*) (especially in emails, comments on SOCIAL NETWORKING websites, etc.) mind your own business (think about your own affairs and do not ask questions about or try to get involved in other people's lives) 不关你的事,少管闲事(全写为 mind your own business,尤用于电邮、社交网站评论等)

my·opia /maɪˈəʊpiə; *NAmE* -ˈoʊpiə/ *noun* [U] **1** (*specialist*) the inability to see things clearly when they are far away 近视 SYN **short sight, short-sightedness** **2** (*formal, disapproving*) the inability to see what the results of a particular action or decision will be; the inability to think about anything outside your own situation 目光短浅;缺乏远见 SYN **short sight, short-sightedness** ▶ **my·opic** /maɪˈɒpɪk; *NAmE* -ˈɑːpɪk/ *adj.*: (*specialist*) *a **myopic child/eye*** 近视的孩子/眼 ◇ (*disapproving*) *a myopic strategy* 缺

M

乏远见的策略 ◇ *myopic voters* 目光短浅的投票者 ➲ SEE ALSO SHORT-SIGHTED (1) **my·opic·al·ly** /maɪˈɒpɪkli; *NAmE* -ˈɑːpɪk-/ *adv.*

myr·iad /ˈmɪriəd/ *noun* (*literary*) an extremely large number of sth 无数；大量：*Designs are available in a myriad of colours.* 各种色彩的款式应有尽有。▶ **myr·iad** *adj.*：*the myriad problems of modern life* 现代生活中的大量问题

myrrh /mɜː(r)/ *noun* [U] a sticky substance with a sweet smell that comes from trees and is used to make PERFUME and INCENSE 没药（芳香液状树脂，用于制香水等）

myr·tle /ˈmɜːtl; *NAmE* ˈmɜːrtl/ *noun* [U, C] a bush with shiny leaves, pink or white flowers and bluish-black BERRIES 香桃木；爱神木；番樱桃

my·self /maɪˈself/ *pron.* **1** (the reflexive form of *I* *I 的反身形式) used when the speaker or writer is also the person affected by an action（用于动作影响说话人或作者时）我自己：*I cut myself on a knife.* 我用刀时割伤了自己。◇ *I wrote a message to myself.* 我给自己留了个便条。◇ *I found myself unable to speak.* 我发现自己说不出话了。◇ *I haven't been feeling myself recently* (= I have not felt well). 我最近感觉不太好。◇ *I needed space to be myself* (= not influenced by other people). 我需要给自己留点儿空间。**2** used to emphasize the fact that the speaker is doing sth（强调说话者在做某事）我本人，亲自：*I'll speak to her myself.* 我要亲自去跟她说。◇ *I myself do not agree.* 我本人不同意。

IDM **(all) by my'self 1** alone; without anyone else（我）独自，单独：*I live by myself.* 我自己一个人生活。 **2** without help（我）独立地：*I painted the room all by myself.* 我独自一人粉刷了屋子。 **(all) to my'self** for the speaker or writer alone; not shared 独自享用：*I had a whole pizza to myself.* 我独自吃了一整个比萨饼。

My·space™ /ˈmaɪspeɪs/ *noun* a SOCIAL NETWORKING website 聚友网

mys·teri·ous /mɪˈstɪəriəs; *NAmE* -ˈstɪr-/ *adj.* **1** difficult to understand or explain; strange 神秘的；奇怪的；不易解释的：*He died in mysterious circumstances.* 他的死因是个谜。◇ *A mysterious illness is affecting all the animals.* 一种奇怪的疾病正在侵袭所有的动物。**2** (especially of people 尤指人) strange and interesting because you do not know much about them 神秘的；陌生的 SYN **enigmatic**：*A mysterious young woman is living next door.* 一位神秘的年轻女子住在隔壁。**3** (of people 人) not saying much about sth, especially when other people want to know more 诡秘的；故弄玄虚的：*He was being very mysterious about where he was going.* 他十分诡秘，闭口不谈他要去哪里。▶ **mys·teri·ous·ly** *adv.*：*My watch had mysteriously disappeared.* 我的手表不知怎么就不见了。◇ *Mysteriously, the streets were deserted.* 不知怎的，街上空无一人。◇ *She was silent, smiling mysteriously.* 她沉默不语，神秘地笑着。 **mys·teri·ous·ness** *noun* [U]

mys·tery /ˈmɪstri/ *noun* (*pl.* **-ies**) **1** [C] something that is difficult to understand or to explain 神秘的事物；不可理解之事；奥秘：*It is one of the great* ***unsolved mysteries*** *of this century.* 这是本世纪尚未解开的大奥秘之一。◇ *Their motives remain a mystery.* 他们的动机仍然是个谜。◇ ***It's a complete mystery*** *to me why they chose him.* 我真无法理解他们为什么会选他。**2** [C] (often used as an adjective 常用作形容词) a person or thing that is strange and interesting because you do not know much about them or it 神秘的人（或事物）；陌生而有趣的人（或事物）：*He's a bit of a mystery.* 他这个人有点儿神秘。◇ *There was a* ***mystery guest*** *on the programme.* 节目中有位神秘嘉宾。◇ *The band was financed by a mystery backer.* 这个乐队是由一个神秘人资助的。◇ (*BrE*) *a* ***mystery tour*** (= when you do not know where you are going) 神秘之旅 **3** [U] the quality of being difficult to understand or to explain, especially when this makes sb/sth seem interesting and exciting 神秘；不可思议；奥秘：*Mystery surrounds her disappearance.* 她的失踪引起了重重疑团。◇ *His past is* ***shrouded in mystery*** (= not much is known about it). 他来历不明。◇ *The dark glasses give her an* ***air of mystery***. 这墨镜使她显得有些神秘。**4** [C] a story, a film/movie or a play in which crimes and strange events are only explained at the end 悬疑小说（或电影、戏剧）：*I enjoy murder mysteries.* 我喜欢凶杀悬疑作品。**5 mysteries** [pl.] secret religious ceremonies; secret knowledge 秘密的宗教仪式；秘密知识：(*figurative*) *the teacher who initiated me into the mysteries of mathematics* 把我引进神秘的数学世界的老师 **6** [C] a religious belief that cannot be explained or proved in a scientific way（宗教信仰的）奥义，奥秘，奥迹：*the mystery of creation* 造物的奥秘

'mystery play (*also* **'miracle play**) *noun* a type of play that was popular between the 11th and 14th centuries and was based on events in the Bible or the lives of the Christian SAINTS 奥迹剧，神秘剧（11 到 14 世纪间流行的一种宗教剧，以《圣经》故事或基督教圣徒的生活为素材）

,mystery 'shopper *noun* a person whose job is to visit or telephone a shop/store or other business pretending to be a customer, in order to get information on the quality of the service, the facilities, etc. 神秘顾客（受雇假扮成顾客去了解服务质量等的人）▶ **,mystery 'shopping** *noun* [U]

mys·tic /ˈmɪstɪk/ *noun* a person who tries to become united with God through prayer and MEDITATION and so understand important things that are beyond normal human understanding 潜修者；神秘主义者

mys·tic·al /ˈmɪstɪkl/ (*also less frequent* **mys·tic** /ˈmɪstɪk/) *adj.* **1** having spiritual powers or qualities that are difficult to understand or to explain 神秘的；不可思议的；难以解释的：***mystical forces/powers*** 神秘的力量 / 能力 ◇ *mystic beauty* 不可思议的美丽 ◇ *Watching the sun rise over the mountain was an almost mystical experience.* 看着太阳爬上山冈，这几乎是一种难以言传的体验。 **2** connected with mysticism 潜修的；神秘主义的：*the mystical life* 潜修生活 ▶ **mys·tic·al·ly** /-kli/ *adv.*

mys·ti·cism /ˈmɪstɪsɪzəm/ *noun* [U] the belief that knowledge of God and of real truth can be found through prayer and MEDITATION rather than through reason and the senses 神秘主义：*Eastern mysticism* 东方神秘主义

mys·tify /ˈmɪstɪfaɪ/ *verb* (**mys·ti·fies, mys·ti·fy·ing, mys·ti·fied, mys·ti·fied**) **~ sb** to make sb confused because they do not understand sth 迷惑；使迷惑不解；使糊涂 SYN **baffle**：*They were totally mystified by the girl's disappearance.* 那女孩失踪使他们大惑不解。 ▶ **mys·ti·fi·ca·tion** /ˌmɪstɪfɪˈkeɪʃn/ *noun* [U]：*He looked at her in mystification.* 他困惑地看着她。 **mys·ti·fy·ing** *adj.*

mys·tique /mɪˈstiːk/ *noun* [U, sing.] the quality of being mysterious or secret that makes sb/sth seem interesting or attractive 神秘性：*The mystique surrounding the monarchy has gone for ever.* 王室的神秘性已不复存在了。

myth /mɪθ/ *noun* [C, U] **1** a story from ancient times, especially one that was told to explain natural events or to describe the early history of a people; this type of story 神话；神话故事 SYN **legend**：*ancient Greek myths* 古希腊神话 ◇ *a creation myth* (= that explains how the world began) 创世的神话 ◇ *the heroes of myth and legend* 神话和传说中的英雄 **2** something that many people believe but that does not exist or is false 虚构的东西；荒诞的说法；不真实的事 SYN **fallacy**：*It is time to dispel the myth of a classless society* (= to show that it does not exist). 该消除那种无阶级社会的神话了。◇ *Contrary to* ***popular myth****, women are not worse drivers than men.* 都说女人开车比男人差，其实不然。➲ SEE ALSO URBAN MYTH

myth·ic /ˈmɪθɪk/ *adj.* **1** = MYTHICAL (1), (2) **2** (*also* **myth·ic·al**) that has become very famous, like sb/sth in a myth 著名的；神话般的 SYN **legendary**：*Scott of the Antarctic was a national hero of mythic proportions.* 南极探险家斯科特是位赫赫有名的民族英雄。

myth·ic·al /ˈmɪθɪkl/ *adj.* [usually before noun] **1** (*also less frequent* **myth·ic**) existing only in ancient myths 神话

的；神话里的 **SYN** **legendary**: *mythical beasts/heroes* 神话里的野兽 / 英雄 **2** (*also less frequent* **myth·ic**) that does not exist or is not true 并不存在的；虚无的；不真实的 **SYN** **fictitious**: *the mythical 'rich uncle' that he boasts about* 他所吹嘘而并不存在的"富伯" **3** = MYTHIC (2)

mytho·logic·al /ˌmɪθəˈlɒdʒɪkl; *NAmE* -ˈlɑːdʒ-/ *adj.* [usually before noun] connected with ancient MYTHS 神话的；神话学的：*mythological subjects/figures/stories* 神话题材 / 人物 / 故事

myth·ology /mɪˈθɒlədʒi; *NAmE* -ˈθɑːl-/ *noun* (*pl.* **-ies**) [U, C] **1** ancient MYTHS in general; the ancient MYTHS of a particular culture, society, etc. （统称）神话；某文化（或社会等）的神话：*Greek mythology* 希腊神话 ◇ *a study of the religions and mythologies of ancient Rome* 关于古罗马的宗教和神话的研究 **2** ideas that many people think are true but that do not exist or are false 虚幻的想法；错误的观点：*the popular mythology that life begins at forty* 生活四十方起步这种普遍的错误观点

myxo·ma·tosis /ˌmɪksəməˈtəʊsɪs; *NAmE* -ˈtoʊ-/ *noun* [U] an infectious disease of RABBITS that usually causes death 兔黏液瘤病；多发黏液瘤病

mzee /mˈziː/ *noun* (*EAfrE*) **1** a person who is respected because of their age, experience or authority; an ELDER （因年长、阅历丰富或有权力而）受尊敬的人；老人；长者；权威人士 **2** **Mzee** a title for a man that shows respect（对男子的尊称）前辈，大人：*Mzee Kenyatta* 肯雅塔大人

mzungu /mˈzʊŋgʊ/ *noun, adj.* (*EAfrE*)

■ ***noun*** (*pl.* **wazungu** /wəˈzʊŋgʊ/) a white person with EUROPEAN family origins 欧裔白人：*He was the only mzungu there.* 他是那里唯一的欧裔白人。

■ ***adj.*** connected with white EUROPEAN family origins 欧裔白人的

N /en/ *noun, abbr., symbol*
■ ***noun*** (*also* **n**) (*pl.* **Ns, N's, n's** /enz/) **1** [C, U] the 14th letter of the English alphabet 英语字母表的第 14 个字母：*'Night' begins with (an) N/'N'.* * night 一词以字母 n 开头。 **2** [U] (*mathematics* 数) used to represent a number whose value is not mentioned （表示不定数）：*The equation is impossible for any value of n greater than 2.* 这个等式对于任何大于 2 的数值都不成立。 ➲ SEE ALSO NTH
■ ***abbr.*** **1** (*NAmE also* **No.**) north; northern 北方（的）；北部（的）：*N Ireland* 北爱尔兰 **2** NEWTON 牛（顿）（力的单位）
■ ***symbol*** the symbol for the chemical element nitrogen （化学元素）氮

n. *abbr.* noun 名词

n/a *abbr.* **1** not applicable (used on a form as an answer to a question that does not apply to you) （用于回答表格问题）不相关，不适用 **2** not available 没有；无法得到

NAACP /ˌen dʌbəl ˌeɪ siː ˈpiː/ *abbr.* National Association for the Advancement of Colored People (an organization in the US that works for the rights of African Americans) 全国有色人种协进会（美国一黑人人权组织）

NAAFI /ˈnæfi/ *noun* [sing.] the abbreviation for 'Navy, Army and Air Force Institutes' (an organization which provides shops and places to eat for British soldiers) 海陆空军协会（全写为 Navy, Army and Air Force Institutes，为英军经营商店及食堂）

naan /nɑːn/ *noun* [U] = NAN²

naar·tjie /ˈnɑːtʃi; *NAmE* ˈnɑːrtʃi/ *noun* (*SAfrE*) a type of small orange with a loose skin that you can remove easily 南非柑橘

nab /næb/ *verb* (**-bb-**) (*informal*) **1 ~ sb** to catch or arrest sb who is doing sth wrong 捉住；当场逮捕 **SYN collar**：*He was nabbed by the police for speeding.* 他超速行驶被警察逮住了。 **2 ~ sth** to take or get sth 获得；拿取：*Who's nabbed my drink?* 谁拿了我的饮料？

nabob /ˈneɪbɒb; *NAmE* -bɑːb/ *noun* **1** a Muslim ruler or officer in the Mogul empire （莫卧儿帝国时代的）穆斯林官员，地方行政长官 **2** a rich or important person 富豪；要人

nachos /ˈnætʃəʊz; *NAmE* -tʃoʊz/ *noun* [pl.] (*from Spanish*) a Mexican dish of crisp pieces of TORTILLA served with BEANS, cheese, spices, etc. 墨西哥玉米片（可用豆、干酪、辛香料等作配料食用）

nada /ˈnɑːdə/ *noun* [U] (*from Spanish, informal, especially NAmE*) nothing 无：*What is it worth? Zero, zilch, nada!* 它值多少？零，一分钱也不值！

nadir /ˈneɪdɪə(r); *NAmE* -dɪr/ *noun* [sing.] (*formal*) the worst moment of a particular situation 最糟糕的时刻；最低点：*the nadir of his career* 他事业上的低谷 ◇ *Company losses reached their nadir in 2009.* * 2009 年公司的亏损达到了最严重的程度。 **OPP zenith**

nae /neɪ/ *det.* (*ScotE*) no 无；没有：*We have nae money.* 我们没有钱。 ▶ **nae** *adv.*：*It's nae (= not) bad.* 还不坏。

naff /næf/ *adj.* (*BrE, informal*) lacking style, taste, quality, etc. 无特色的；没有品位的；蹩脚的：*There was a naff band playing.* 有一支蹩脚的乐队在演奏。

nag /næg/ *verb, noun*
■ ***verb*** (**-gg-**) **1** [I, T] to keep complaining to sb about their behaviour or keep asking them to do sth 唠叨；不停地抱怨 **SYN pester**：**~ (at sb)** *Stop nagging—I'll do it as soon as I can.* 别唠叨了，我会尽快做的。 ◇ **~ sb (to do sth)** *She had been nagging him to paint the fence.* 她一直唠叨，要他把围栏油漆一下。 **2** [I, T] to worry or irritate you continuously 不断困扰；老使人烦恼：**~ at sb** *A feeling of unease nagged at her.* 一种不安的感觉一直困扰着她。 ◇ **~ sb** *Doubts nagged me all evening.* 我一晚上都没有摆脱心中的疑虑。 ➲ MORE LIKE THIS 36, page R29
■ ***noun*** (*old-fashioned, informal*) a horse 马

na·gana /nəˈgɑːnə/ *noun* [U] (*EAfrE*) a serious illness that cows can get from a type of fly (= a TSETSE FLY) 非洲锥虫病，那加那病（由舌蝇传播，主要侵害牛）

nagar /ˈnʌgə(r)/ *noun* (*IndE*) a town, a city, an area in a city, or a SUBURB (= an area where people live that is outside the centre of a city) 镇子；城市；城区；市郊

nag·ging /ˈnægɪŋ/ *adj.* [only before noun] **1** continuing for a long time and difficult to cure or remove 纠缠不休的；难以摆脱的：*a **nagging pain/doubt*** 难以消除的疼痛 / 怀疑 **2** complaining 唠叨的；抱怨的；诉苦的：*a nagging voice* 唠唠叨叨的声音

nah /nɑː/ *exclamation* (*slang*) = NO

naiad /ˈnaɪæd/ *noun* (*pl.* **naiads** or **nai·ades** /-diːz/) (in ancient stories 神话故事) a water spirit 那伊阿得（水泽仙女）

nail 🔑 /neɪl/ *noun, verb*
■ ***noun*** **1** 🔑 thin hard layer covering the outer tip of the fingers or toes 指甲；趾甲：*Stop biting your nails!* 别咬指甲！ ◇ *nail clippers* 指甲钳 ➲ VISUAL VOCAB PAGE V64 ➲ SEE ALSO FINGERNAIL, TOENAIL **2** 🔑 a small thin pointed piece of metal with a flat head, used for hanging things on a wall or for joining pieces of wood together 钉；钉子：*She hammered the nail in.* 她把钉子敲了进去。 ➲ COLLOCATIONS AT DECORATE ➲ VISUAL VOCAB PAGE V21 ➲ COMPARE SCREW *n.* (1), TACK *n.* (3)
IDM **a nail in sb's/sth's ˈcoffin** something that makes the end or failure of an organization, sb's plans, etc. more likely to happen 导致失败的事物；导致某事终结之物 **on the ˈnail** (*BrE, informal*) (of payment 付款) without delay 立刻；马上；毫不拖延：*They're good customers who always pay on the nail.* 他们是好主顾，付账从不耽搁。 ➲ MORE AT FIGHT *v.*, HARD *adj.*, HIT *v.*, TOUGH *adj.*
■ ***verb*** **1 ~ sth (+ adv./prep./adj.)** to fasten sth to sth with a nail or nails （用钉子）钉牢，固定：*I nailed the sign to a tree.* 我将标示牌钉到了一棵树上。 **2 ~ sb** (*informal*) to catch sb and prove they are guilty of a crime or of doing sth bad 抓获并证明有罪；抓住：*The police haven't been able to nail the killer.* 警方还没有抓到杀人凶手。 **3 ~ sth** (*informal*) to prove that sth is not true 证明…不属实；揭露；揭发：*We must nail this lie.* 我们一定要戳穿这个谎言。 **4 ~ sth** (*informal*) to achieve sth or do sth right, especially in sport （尤指体育运动中）获得，赢得，击中：*He nailed a victory in the semi-finals.* 他在半决赛中获胜。 ◇ *She nailed it on her second jump.* 她在第二跳中表现出色，赢了比赛。
IDM **nail your colours to the ˈmast** (*especially BrE*) to say publicly and firmly what you believe or who you support 公开宣称；公开表态
PHR V **ˌnail sth↔ˈdown 1** to fasten sth down with a nail or nails （用钉子）将…钉牢，将…固定 **2** to reach an agreement or a decision, usually after a lot of discussion 达成一致；作出决定：*All the parties seem anxious to nail down a ceasefire.* 各方似乎都渴望将停火之事敲定。 **ˌnail sb↔ˈdown (to sth)** to force sb to give you a definite promise or tell you exactly what they intend to do 迫使明确保证（或准确说出想做之事） **SYN pin down**：*She says she'll come, but I can't nail her down to a specific time.* 她说要来，但我无法让她敲定具体什么时候来。 **ˌnail sth↔ˈup 1** to fasten sth to a wall, post, etc. with a nail or nails 用钉子将…固定到（墙上、柱子上等） **2** to put nails into a door or window so that it cannot be opened 用钉子封住，封死（门或窗）

ˈnail bar *noun* a place where you can pay to have your nails shaped, coloured and made more attractive 美甲店

ˈnail-biting *adj.* [usually before noun] making you feel very excited or anxious because you do not know what is going to happen 令人焦躁不安的；令人紧张的：*a nail-biting finish* 令人担心的结局 ◇ *It's been a nail-biting couple*

of weeks waiting for my results. 这几个星期等结果，弄得我坐立不安。 ➲ MORE LIKE THIS 10, page R26

'nail brush *noun* a small stiff brush for cleaning your nails 指甲刷 ➲ VISUAL VOCAB PAGE V25

'nail clippers *noun* [pl.] a small tool for cutting the nails on your fingers and toes 指甲钳；指甲刀 ➲ VISUAL VOCAB PAGE V25

ˌnailed 'on *adj.* (*BrE, informal*) **1** certain or definite 确定无疑；板上钉钉： *That penalty was nailed on—it should never have been denied by the referee!* 那个点球毫无疑问，裁判绝不应该拒绝判罚！ **2** (in betting) believed to be very likely to succeed （打赌）胜算很大的： *a nailed-on bet* 胜算很大的赌局

'nail file *noun* a small metal tool with a rough surface for shaping your nails 指甲锉 ➲ VISUAL VOCAB PAGE V25 ➲ SEE ALSO EMERY BOARD

'nail polish (*BrE also* **'nail varnish**) *noun* [U] clear or coloured liquid that you paint on your nails to make them look attractive 指甲油： *nail polish/varnish remover* 洗甲水 ➲ WORDFINDER NOTE AT MAKE-UP ➲ VISUAL VOCAB PAGE V65

'nail scissors *noun* [pl.] small scissors that are usually curved, used for cutting the nails on your fingers and toes 指甲剪： *a pair of nail scissors* 一把指甲剪 ➲ VISUAL VOCAB PAGE V25

naive (*also* **naïve**) /naɪ'iːv/ *adj.* **1** (*disapproving*) lacking experience of life, knowledge or good judgement and willing to believe that people always tell you the truth 缺乏经验的；幼稚的；无知的；轻信的： *to be politically naive* 对政治一无所知 ◇ *I can't believe you were so naive as to trust him!* 真是难以相信你会幼稚到信任他！ ◇ *a naive question* 无知的问题 ➲ WORDFINDER NOTE AT YOUNG **2** (*approving*) (of people and their behaviour 人及其行为) innocent and simple 天真的；率直的 SYN **artless**： *Their approach to life is refreshingly naive.* 他们对待生活的态度天真率直，令人耳目一新。 ➲ COMPARE SOPHISTICATED (1) **3** (*specialist*) (of art 艺术) in a style which is deliberately very simple, often uses bright colours and is similar to that produced by a child 稚拙派的（简单质朴，色彩明快） ▸ **naive·ly** (*also* **naïve·ly**) *adv.*： *I naively assumed that I would be paid for the work.* 我天真地以为这活儿是有报酬的。 **naiv·ety** (*also* **naïv·ety**) /naɪ'iːvəti/ *noun* [U]： *They laughed at the naivety of his suggestion.* 他们嘲笑他提的建议太幼稚。 ◇ *She has lost none of her naivety.* 她丝毫没有失去那份天真烂漫。

naked 🔑 /'neɪkɪd/ *adj.* **1** 🔑 not wearing any clothes 裸体的；裸露的；不穿衣服的 SYN **bare**： *a naked body* 赤裸的身体 ◇ *naked shoulders* 裸露的肩膀 ◇ *They often wandered around the house* ***stark naked*** (= completely naked). 他们经常赤身裸体地在房子里走来走去。 ◇ *They found him* ***half naked*** *and bleeding to death.* 他们发现他身体半裸，流着血，快不行了。 ◇ *The prisoners were* ***stripped naked.*** 囚犯被剥得赤条条的。 ➲ SEE ALSO BUCK NAKED **2** [usually before noun] without the usual covering 无遮盖的；裸露的 SYN **bare**： *a naked light* 无罩灯 ◇ *a naked sword* 出鞘之剑 ◇ *Mice are born naked* (= without fur). 老鼠出生时遍体无毛。 ◇ (*BrE*) *a naked flame* 明火 HELP In American English this is called an *open flame.* 美式英语称作 open flame。 **3** [only before noun] (of emotions, attitudes, etc. 情感、态度等) expressed strongly and not hidden 直白的；露骨的；毫不掩饰的： *naked aggression* 赤裸裸的攻击 ◇ *the naked truth* 明摆着的事实 **4** [not usually before noun] unable to protect yourself from being harmed, criticized, etc. 缺乏保护；无力自卫 SYN **helpless**： *He still felt naked and drained after his ordeal.* 经历了这场磨难之后，他仍然感到无法自卫，而且筋疲力尽。 ➲ MORE LIKE THIS 22, page R27 ▸ **naked·ly** *adv.*： *nakedly aggressive* 赤裸裸地挑衅 **naked·ness** *noun* [U]

IDM **the naked 'eye** the normal power of your eyes without the help of an instrument 肉眼： *The planet should be visible* ***with/to the naked eye.*** 这颗行星肉眼应该就能看得见。

na·mas·kar /ˌnʌmʌs'kɑː(r)/ *noun* [U] (*IndE*) a way of GREETING sb in which the hands are placed together as in prayer and the head is bent forwards 合十礼（双手合十并颔首的问候方式）

namby-pamby /ˌnæmbi 'pæmbi/ *adj.* (*informal, disapproving*) weak and too emotional 脆弱的；多愁善感的

name 🔑 /neɪm/ *noun, verb*

▪ *noun* **1** 🔑 a word or words that a particular person, animal, place or thing is known by 名字；名称： *What's your name?* 你叫什么名字？ ◇ *What is/was the name, please?* (= a polite way of asking sb's name) 请问您叫什么名字？ ◇ *Please write your full* ***name and address*** *below.* 请将您的姓名和地址写在下面。 ◇ *Do you know the name of this flower?* 你知道这是什么花吗？ ◇ *Rubella is just another name for German measles.* 风疹只是德国麻疹的另一个名称。 ◇ *Are you changing your name when you get married?* 结婚时你要改姓氏吗？ ➲ SEE ALSO ASSUMED NAME, BRAND NAME, CODE NAME, FAMILY NAME, FILENAME, FIRST NAME, FORENAME, HOUSEHOLD NAME, MAIDEN NAME, MIDDLE NAME, NICKNAME *n.*, PEN NAME, PET NAME, PLACE NAME, SURNAME, TRADE NAME, USERNAME **2** [usually sing.] a reputation that sb/sth has; the opinion that people have about sb/sth 名誉；名声；名气： *She first* ***made her name*** *as a writer of children's books.* 她最初是以儿童读物作家成名的。 ◇ *He's* ***made*** *quite* ***a name for himself*** (= become famous). 他闯出了名气。 ◇ *The college has a* ***good name for*** *languages.* 这所大学的语言教学颇有名气。 ◇ *This kind of behaviour* ***gives*** *students* ***a bad name.*** 这种行为使学生们背上骂名。 **3** (in compound adjectives 构成复合形容词) having a name or a reputation of the kind mentioned, especially one that is known by a lot of people 有…名称的；以…著名的；有…名声的： *a big-name company* 著名公司 ◇ *brand-name goods* 名牌产品 ➲ SEE ALSO HOUSEHOLD NAME **4** a famous person 名人： *Some of the biggest names in the art world were at the party.* 一些艺术界的头面人物参加了聚会。

IDM **by 'name** using the name of sb/sth 凭名字；用…的名字： *She asked for you by name.* 她点名要找你。 ◇ *The principal knows all the students by name.* 校长能叫出所有学生的姓名。 ◇ *I only know her by name* (= I have heard

▼ **WHICH WORD?** 词语辨析

naked / bare

Both these words can be used to mean 'not covered with clothes' and are frequently used with the following nouns. 以上两词均含裸露、未穿衣服之义，常与下列名词连用：

naked ~	**bare ~**
body	feet
man	arms
fear	walls
aggression	branches
flame	essentials

- **Naked** is more often used to describe a person or their body and **bare** usually describes a part of the body. * naked 较常用以表示赤身裸体，而 bare 通常指身体某部位裸露着。
- **Bare** can also describe other things with nothing on them. * bare 亦可用以描述其他没有遮盖或光秃的东西： *bare walls* 没有装饰的墙 ◇ *a bare hillside* 光秃秃的小山坡 **Naked** can mean 'without a protective covering'. * naked 含无保护性遮盖之义： *a naked sword* 出鞘的剑
- **Bare** can also mean 'just enough'. * bare 亦含仅够之义： *the bare minimum* 最低限度 **Naked** can be used to talk about strong feelings that are not hidden. * naked 可用以表示赤裸裸、无掩饰的强烈感情： *naked fear* 不加掩饰的恐惧 Note also the idiom. 另注意习语： (*visible*) *to/with* ***the naked eye*** 肉眼（可见）

N

about her but I have not met her). 我只是听说过她的名字。 **by the name of...** (*formal*) who is called 名叫…的: *a young actor by the name of Tom Rees* 名叫汤姆·里斯的年轻演员 **enter sb's/your 'name (for sth) | put sb's/your 'name down (for sth)** to apply for a place at a school, in a competition, etc. for sb or yourself 申请参加；替…报名（入学、参赛等）: *Have you entered your name for the quiz yet?* 你报名参加这次问答比赛了吗？ **give your 'name to sth** to invent sth which then becomes known by your name 用自己的名字命名所发明之物 **go by the name of...** to use a name that may not be your real one 自称为…；假称是… **have your/sb's 'name on it | with your/sb's 'name on it** (*informal*) if sth **has your name on it**, or there is sth **with your name on it**, it is intended for you 是冲…来的；是为…准备的: *He took my place and got killed. It should have been me—that bullet had my name on it.* 他代替我，结果送了命。死的本该是我，那颗子弹是冲着我来的。◊ *Are you coming for dinner this evening? I've got a steak here with your name on it!* 今晚你来吃饭吗？我为你准备了一块牛排呢！ **in ˌall but 'name** used to describe a situation which exists in reality but that is not officially recognized （表示实际存在但未得到正式认可）在只缺正式名分情况下: *He runs the company in all but name.* 他虽没有名分，却实际上在管理这家公司。 **in 'God's/'Heaven's name | in the name of 'God/'Heaven** used especially in questions to show that you are angry, surprised or shocked （尤用于疑问句，表示愤怒、惊奇或震惊）看在上帝的分上，到底，究竟: *What in God's name was that noise?* 那噪音究竟是怎么回事？ ◊ *Where in the name of Heaven have you been?* 你到底上哪儿去了？ **in the name of 'sb/'sth | in sb's/sth's 'name 1** 🔑 for sb; showing that sth officially belongs to sb 为（某人）；在…名下: *We reserved two tickets in the name of Brown.* 我们用布朗的名字预订了两张票。◊ *The car is registered in my name.* 这辆车是用我的名字登记的。 **2** using the authority of sb/sth; as a representative of sb/sth 凭…的权威；代表: *I arrest you in the name of the law.* 我依法逮捕你。 **3** used to give a reason or an excuse for doing sth, often when what you are doing is wrong 以…的名义；以…为借口: *crimes committed in the name of religion* 以宗教名义进行的犯罪活动 **in 'name only** officially recognized but not existing in reality 名义上；有名无实: *He's party leader in name only.* 他只是名义上的政党领袖。 **sb's name is 'mud** (*informal, usually humorous*) used to say that sb is not liked or popular because of sth they have done 某人臭名昭著 **the name of the 'game** (*informal*) the most important aspect of an activity; the most important quality needed for an activity 问题的实质；最为重要的方面: *Hard work is the name of the game if you want to succeed in business.* 要想生意兴旺，勤奋工作是关键。 **a name to 'conjure with** (*BrE*) **1** (*NAmE* **a name to 'reckon with**) a person or thing that is well known and respected in a particular field 大名鼎鼎的人；重量级人物；影响巨大的事物: *Miyazaki is still a name to conjure with among anime fans.* 宫崎骏在日本动漫迷中仍是一个大名鼎鼎的名字。 **2** (*humorous*) used when you mention a name that you think is difficult to remember or pronounce 难记的名字；拗口的名字: *He comes from Tighnabruaich—now there's a name to conjure with!* 他来自 Tighnabruaich，这个名字真够拗口的！ **put a 'name to sb/sth** to know or remember what sb/sth is called 知道…的名称；记住…的称呼: *I recognize the tune but I can't put a name to it.* 这曲子我听过，但想不起叫什么了。 **take sb's name in 'vain** to show a lack of respect when using sb's name 滥用…的名义；亵渎…的名字: (*humorous*) *Have you been taking my name in vain again?* 你又在对我说三道四了吧？ **(have sth) to your 'name** to have or own sth 拥有；获得；收归某人的名下: *an Olympic athlete with five gold medals to his name* 夺得五枚金牌的一名奥林匹克运动员 ◊ *She doesn't have a penny/cent to her name* (= she is very poor). 她身无分文。 **under the name (of)...** using a name that may not be your real name 用…名字；以…假名 ➲ MORE AT ANSWER *v.*, BIG *adj.*, CALL *v.*, DOG *n.*, DROP *v.*, LEND, MIDDLE NAME, NAME *v.*, REJOICE, ROSE *n.*

■ *verb* **1** 🔑 to give a name to sb/sth 命名；给…取名 **SYN** **call**: **~ sb/sth (after sb)** | (*NAmE also*) **~ sb/sth (for sb)** *He was named after his father* (= given his father's first name). 他的名字跟他父亲一样。◊ **~ sb/sth + noun** *They named their son John.* 他们给儿子起了个名字叫约翰。 **2** 🔑 to say the name of sb/sth 说出…的名称；叫出…的名字 **SYN** **identify**: **~ sb/sth** *The victim has not yet been named.* 受害人的姓名仍未得知。◊ *Can you name all the American states?* 你能说出美国所有的州名吗？◊ **~ sb/sth as sb/sth** *The missing man has been named as James Kelly.* 失踪者已被确认为詹姆斯·凯利。 ➲ SYNONYMS AT IDENTIFY **3 ~ sth** to state sth exactly 确定；说定；准确陈述 **SYN** **specify**: ***Name your price.*** 给个价吧。◊ *They're engaged, but they haven't yet **named the day*** (= chosen the date for their wedding). 他们订婚了，但还未确定结婚

▼ **MORE ABOUT ... 补充说明**

names and titles 名字和称谓

Names 名字

- Your **name** is either your whole name or one part of your name. * name 既指全名也指名字的一部分: *My name is Maria.* 我的名字叫玛丽亚。◊ *His name is Tom Smith.* 他的名字叫汤姆·史密斯。
- Your **last name** or **family name** (also called **surname** in *BrE*) is the name that all members of your family share. * last name 或 family name 指姓氏（在英式英语中亦称 surname）。
- Your **first name/names** (*formal* **forename**) is/are the name(s) your parents gave you when you were born. In *BrE* some people use the expression **Christian name(s)** to refer to a person's first name(s). * first name/names（正式用语为 forename）指出生时父母给取的名字。在英式英语中，有些人用 Christian name(s) 指 first name(s)（名字）。
- Your **middle name(s)** is/are any name your parents gave you other than the one that is placed first. The initial of this name is often used as part of your name, especially in America. * middle name(s) 指父母给取的第一个名字外的名字。此名字的首字母常用作名字的一部分，尤其在美国: *John T. Harvey* 约翰·T. 哈维
- Your **full name** is all your names, usually in the order: first + middle + last name. * full name 通常指以 first + middle + last name 为顺序的全名。
- A woman's **maiden name** is the family name she had before she got married. Some women keep this name after they are married and do not use their husband's name. In North America, married women often use their maiden name followed by their husband's family name. * maiden name 指女子婚前娘家的姓。有的妇女婚后仍保留此姓，不用丈夫的姓。在北美，已婚妇女通常在自己娘家的姓后加上丈夫的姓: *Hillary Rodham Clinton* 希拉里·罗德汉姆·克林顿

Titles 称谓

- **Mr** (for both married and unmarried men) 称已婚和未婚男子
- **Mrs** (for married women) 称已婚妇女
- **Miss** (for unmarried women) 称未婚女子
- **Ms** (a title that some women prefer to use as it does not distinguish between married and unmarried women) 有些妇女喜欢用此称谓，因为没有指明已婚或未婚
- **Doctor, Professor, President, Vice-President, Reverend** (or **Rev**), etc. 医生、教授、校长、副校长、牧师等

The correct way to talk to someone is 正确的称呼为:

- first name, if you know them well 如果相熟可直呼其名: *Hello, Maria.* 你好，玛丽亚。
- or title + surname 或称谓 + 姓: *Hello, Mr Brown.* 你好，布朗先生。
- or *Doctor* (medical), *Professor*, etc. on its own. 或单独用医生、教授等: *Thank you, Doctor.* 谢谢你，医生。This is only used for a very limited number of titles. 此说法只限于为数很少的几个称谓。

N

日期。◇ *Activities available include squash, archery and swimming, to name but a few.* 所设活动项目包括壁球、射箭、游泳等等，不一而足。◇ *Chairs, tables, cabinets—you name it, she makes it* (= she makes anything you can imagine). 椅子、桌子、橱柜，凡是你说得出的她都能做。**4** to choose sb for a job or position 任命；委任 SYN **nominate**：**~ sb (as) sth | ~ sb + noun** *I had no hesitation in naming him (as) captain.* 我毫不犹豫地任命他为队长。◇ **~ sb (to sth)** *When she resigned, he was named to the committee in her place.* 她辞职后，他被指定取代她进入委员会。

IDM ,**name and 'shame** (*BrE*) to publish the names of people or organizations who have done sth wrong or illegal 公布行为不当或违法者的名单；公布黑名单 ➲ MORE LIKE THIS 12, page R26 **name 'names** to give the names of the people involved in sth, especially sth wrong or illegal 供出，说出（犯事者等）的名字

'name-calling *noun* [U] the act of using rude or insulting words about sb 辱骂

name·check /ˈneɪmtʃek/ *noun, verb*

■ *noun* an occasion when the name of a person or thing is mentioned or included in a list 提到名字；列出名字：*She started her speech by giving a namecheck to all the people who had helped her.* 她在讲话开始时提到所有帮助过她的人的名字。

■ *verb* **~ sb/sth** to mention or include sb/sth in a list 提及，列出（某人或某事物的名字）：*The songs namecheck other artists and bands.* 这些歌提到了其他演员和乐队的名字。◇ *The book was namechecked in today's paper.* 这本书在今天的报纸上提到了。

'name day *noun* a day which is special for a Christian with a particular name because it is the day which celebrates a SAINT with the same name 命名日（基督徒庆祝与自己同名的圣徒纪念日）

'name-dropping *noun* [U] (*disapproving*) the act of mentioning the names of famous people you know or have met in order to impress other people 提到所认识的名人以引起别人的注意 ▶ **'name-drop** *verb* [I] ➲ SEE ALSO DROP NAMES at DROP *v.*

name·less /ˈneɪmləs/ *adj.* **1** [usually before noun] having no name; whose name you do not know 无名的；不知名的：*a nameless grave* 无名冢 ◇ *thousands of nameless and faceless workers* 成千上万默默无闻的工人 **2** whose name is kept secret 匿名的；隐姓埋名的 SYN **anonymous**：*a nameless source in the government* 政府中的一位匿名消息人士 ◇ *a well-known public figure **who shall remain nameless*** 一位不便透露姓名的知名人士 **3** [usually before noun] (*literary*) difficult or too unpleasant to describe 不可名状的；难以形容的：*nameless horrors* 不可名状的恐惧 ◇ *a nameless longing* 难以形容的渴望

name·ly /ˈneɪmli/ *adv.* used to introduce more exact and detailed information about sth that you have just mentioned 即；也就是：*We need to concentrate on our target audience, namely women aged between 20 and 30.* 我们须针对我们的目标观众，即年龄在 20 到 30 岁之间的妇女。

name·plate /ˈneɪmpleɪt/ *noun* **1** a sign on the door or the wall of a building showing the name of a company or the name of a person who is living or working there （标明公司名字或居住、生活在该处的人的姓名的）名牌，标示牌，名匾 **2** a piece of metal or plastic on an object showing the name of the person who owns it, made it or presented it（标示所有者、制造者或提供者姓名的）名称牌

name·sake /ˈneɪmseɪk/ *noun* a person or thing that has the same name as sb/sth else 同名的人（或物）：*Unlike his more famous namesake, this Gordon Brown has little interest in politics.* 这位戈登 · 布朗与那位同名的著名人物不同，对政治没什么兴趣。

'name tag *noun* a small piece of plastic, paper or metal that you wear, with your name on it （佩戴于胸前的）名牌；胸佩 ➲ WORDFINDER NOTE AT CONFERENCE

'name tape *noun* a small piece of cloth that is sewn or stuck onto a piece of clothing and that has the name of the owner on it （衣物上的）姓名标签

nan¹ /næn/ *noun* (*BrE*) = NANNY (2)

nan² (*also* **naan**) /nɑːn/ (*also* **'nan bread**, **'naan bread**) *noun* [U] a type of soft flat S Asian bread 南亚式面包（松软扁平）

nana¹ (*BrE also* **nanna**) /ˈnænə/ *noun* (*informal*) = NANNY (2)

nana² /ˈnɑːnə/ *noun* (*old-fashioned, BrE, informal*) a stupid person 呆子；傻瓜 SYN **idiot**：*I felt a right nana.* 我觉得自己真傻。

nancy /ˈnænsi/ *noun* (*pl.* **-ies**) (*also* **'nancy boy**, **nance** /næns/) (*taboo, slang, especially BrE*) an offensive word for a HOMOSEXUAL man, or a man who behaves in a way that is thought to be typical of women 假娘儿们（含冒犯意，指同性恋男子或举止像女性的男子）

nanny /ˈnæni/ *noun* (*pl.* **-ies**) **1** a woman whose job is to take care of young children in the children's own home （儿童家中的）保姆 **2** (*also* **nan**) (*both BrE*) (used by children, especially as a form of address 儿童用语，尤作称呼) a grandmother 奶奶；姥姥：*When is Nanny coming to stay?* 奶奶什么时候来住？◇ *my nan and grandad* 我的爷爷、奶奶 ➲ SEE ALSO GRANNY

IDM **the 'nanny state** a disapproving way of talking about the fact that government seems to get too much involved in people's lives and to protect them too much, in a way that limits their freedom 保姆式国家

'nanny goat *noun* a female GOAT 母山羊；雌山羊 ➲ COMPARE BILLY GOAT

nanny·ing /ˈnæniɪŋ/ *noun* [U] **1** the job of being a child's NANNY 保姆工作；照看小孩 **2** (*BrE, disapproving*) the fact of helping and protecting sb too much 帮忙过多；过于呵护；过分关心

nano- /ˈnænəʊ; *NAmE* ˈnænoʊ/ *combining form* (*specialist*) (in nouns and adjectives; used especially in units of measurement 构成名词和形容词，尤用于计量单位) one thousand millionth 纳（诺）；毫微；十亿分之一：*nanosecond* 毫微秒

nano·metre (*especially US* **nano·meter**) /ˈnænəʊmiːtə(r); *NAmE* ˈnænoʊ-/ *noun* (*abbr.* **nm**) one thousand millionth of a metre 纳米；毫微米；十亿分之一米

nano·par·ticle /ˈnænəʊpɑːtɪkl; *NAmE* ˈnænoʊpɑːrt-/ *noun* a piece of matter less than 100 nanometres long 纳米粒

nano·scale /ˈnænəʊskeɪl; *NAmE* ˈnænoʊ-/ *adj.* [usually before noun] of a size that can be measured in nanometres 纳米（尺度）的：*nanoscale particles/devices/electronics* 纳米粒 / 装置 / 电子学

nano·sec·ond /ˈnænəʊsekənd; *NAmE* ˈnænoʊ-/ *noun* (*abbr.* **ns**) one thousand millionth of a second 纳秒；毫微秒；十亿分之一秒

nano·tech·nol·ogy /ˌnænəʊtekˈnɒlədʒi; *NAmE* ˌnænoʊtekˈnɑːlədʒi/ *noun* [U] the branch of technology that deals with structures that are less than 100 NANOMETRES long. Scientists often build these structures using individual MOLECULES of substances. 纳米技术 ▶ **nano·tech·nolo·gist** *noun* **nano·tech·no·logic·al** /ˌnænəʊˌteknəˈlɒdʒɪkl; *NAmE* ˌnænoʊˌteknəˈlɑːdʒɪkl/ *adj.*：*nanotechnological research* 纳米技术研究

nap /næp/ *noun, verb*

■ *noun* **1** [C] a short sleep, especially during the day （日间的）小睡，打盹 SYN **snooze**：*to take/have a nap* 打个盹；小睡一会儿 ➲ SYNONYMS AT SLEEP ➲ COMPARE SIESTA ➲ SEE ALSO CATNAP, POWER NAP **2** [sing.] the short fine threads on the surface of some types of cloth, usually lying in the same direction（某些织物表面的）短绒毛 **3** [C] (*BrE*) advice given by an expert on which horse is most likely to win a race 赛马情报；赛马结果预测

■ *verb* (**-pp-**) [I] to sleep for a short time, especially during the day 打盹，小睡（尤指日间）IDM SEE CATCH *v.*

napa *noun* [U] = NAPPA

N

na·palm /ˈneɪpɑːm/ *noun* [U] a substance like jelly, made from petrol/gas, that burns and is used in making bombs 凝固汽油（用于制造炸弹）

nape /neɪp/ *noun* [sing.] ~ (**of sb's neck**) the back of the neck 颈背；脖颈：*Her hair was cut short at the nape of her neck.* 她脖子后面的头发剪得很短。➲ VISUAL VOCAB PAGE V64

naph·tha /ˈnæfθə/ *noun* [U] a type of oil that starts burning very easily, used as fuel or in making chemicals 石脑油（作燃料或用于制造化学品）

naph·tha·lene /ˈnæfθəliːn; *NAmE also* ˈnæpθə-/ *noun* [U] (*chemistry* 化) a substance used in products that keep MOTHS away from clothes, and in industrial processes 萘（用于制作卫生球等）

nap·kin /ˈnæpkɪn/ *noun* **1** (*also* **ˈtable napkin**) a piece of cloth or paper used at meals for protecting your clothes and cleaning your lips and fingers 餐巾；餐巾纸 SYN **serviette** ➲ VISUAL VOCAB PAGE V23 **2** (*NAmE*) = SANITARY NAPKIN **3** (*BrE, old-fashioned* or *formal*) = NAPPY

nappa (*also* **napa**) /ˈnæpə/ *noun* [U] a type of soft leather made from the skin of sheep or GOATS 纳帕软羊皮革

nappe /næp/ *noun* [U] (*geology* 地) a thin layer of rock that lies on top of a different type of rock 推覆体（层状岩体）

nappy /ˈnæpi/ *noun* (*pl.* **-ies**) (*BrE*) (*NAmE* **di·aper**) a piece of soft cloth or other thick material that is folded around a baby's bottom and between its legs to absorb and hold its body waste 尿布：*I'll change her nappy.* 我要给她换尿布。◇ *a disposable nappy* (= one that is made to be used once only) 一次性尿布 ◇ *nappy rash* 尿布疹 ➲ WORDFINDER NOTE AT BABY ➲ COLLOCATIONS AT CHILD

N

narc /nɑːk; *NAmE* nɑːrk/ (*also* **narco** /ˈnɑːkəʊ; *NAmE* ˈnɑːrkoʊ/) *noun* (*NAmE, informal*) a police officer whose job is to stop people selling or using drugs illegally 缉毒警察

nar·cis·sism /ˈnɑːsɪsɪzəm; *NAmE* ˈnɑːrs-/ *noun* [U] (*formal, disapproving*) the habit of admiring yourself too much, especially your appearance 自我陶醉，自赏，自恋（尤指对自己的容貌）➲ MORE LIKE THIS 16, page R27 ▶ **nar·cis·sist** *noun* **nar·cis·sis·tic** /ˌnɑːsɪˈsɪstɪk; *NAmE* ˌnɑːrs-/ *adj.*
ORIGIN From the Greek myth in which **Narcissus**, a beautiful young man, fell in love with his own reflection in a pool. He died and was changed into the flower which bears his name. 源自希腊神话，貌美青年那喀索斯 (Narcissus) 爱上了自己在水中的倒影。他死后化作水仙花，此花即因之命名。

nar·cis·sus /nɑːˈsɪsəs; *NAmE* nɑːrˈs-/ *noun* (*pl.* **nar·cissi** /nɑːˈsɪsaɪ; *NAmE* nɑːrˈs-/) a plant with white or yellow flowers that appear in spring. There are many types of narcissus, including the DAFFODIL. 水仙；水仙花

nar·co·lepsy /ˈnɑːkəʊlepsi; *NAmE* ˈnɑːrkoʊ-/ *noun* [U] (*medical* 医) a condition in which sb falls into a deep sleep when they are in relaxing surroundings 发作性睡病

nar·co·sis /nɑːˈkəʊsɪs; *NAmE* nɑːrˈkoʊsɪs/ *noun* [U] (*medical* 医) a state caused by drugs in which sb is unconscious or keeps falling asleep 麻醉

nar·cot·ic /nɑːˈkɒtɪk; *NAmE* nɑːrˈkɑː-/ *noun, adj.*
■ *noun* **1** (*formal*) a powerful illegal drug that affects the mind in a harmful way. HEROIN and COCAINE are narcotics. 致幻毒品；麻醉品：*a narcotics agent* (= a police officer investigating the illegal trade in drugs) 缉毒警察 **2** (*medical* 医) a substance that relaxes you, reduces pain or makes you sleep 麻醉性镇痛药；麻醉药；镇静剂：*a mild narcotic* 药性温和的镇静剂
■ *adj.* **1** (of a drug 药物) that affects your mind in a harmful way 致幻的；麻醉的 **2** (of a substance 物质) making you sleep 催眠的：*a mild narcotic effect* 温和的催眠作用

nark /nɑːk; *NAmE* nɑːrk/ *noun* (*BrE, slang*) a person who is friendly with criminals and who gives the police information about them 警察的线人

narked /nɑːkt; *NAmE* nɑːrkt/ *adj.* [not usually before noun] (*old-fashioned, BrE, informal*) annoyed 厌烦；苦恼；恼火

narky /ˈnɑːki; *NAmE* ˈnɑːrki/ *adj.* (**nark·ier, narki·est**) (*BrE, informal*) easily becoming angry or annoyed 易怒的；脾气坏的

nar·rate /nəˈreɪt; *NAmE also* ˈnæreɪt/ *verb* **1** ~ **sth** (*formal*) to tell a story 讲（故事）；叙述 SYN **relate**：*She entertained them by narrating her adventures in Africa.* 她讲述她在非洲的历险来逗他们开心。➲ WORDFINDER NOTE AT PLOT **2** ~ **sth** to speak the words that form the text of a DOCUMENTARY film or programme 给（纪录片或节目）解说：*The film was narrated by Andrew Sachs.* 这部电影是由安德鲁•萨克斯解说的。

nar·ra·tion /nəˈreɪʃn; næˈr-/ *noun* (*formal*) **1** [U, C] the act or process of telling a story, especially in a novel, a film/movie or a play （尤指小说、电影或戏剧中的）叙述，讲述 **2** [C] a description of events that is spoken during a film/movie, a play, etc. or with music （电影、戏剧等中对情节的）解说，旁白：*He has recorded the narration for the production.* 他录制了这部作品的解说词。

nar·ra·tive /ˈnærətɪv/ *noun* (*formal*) **1** [C] a description of events, especially in a novel （尤指小说中的）描述，叙述 SYN **story**：*a gripping narrative of their journey up the Amazon* 他们沿亚马孙河而上的扣人心弦的描述 ➲ COLLOCATIONS AT LITERATURE **2** [U] the act, process or skill of telling a story 讲故事；叙述；叙事技巧：*The novel contains too much dialogue and not enough narrative.* 这部小说对话过多，而叙述不足。▶ **nar·ra·tive** *adj.* [only before noun]：*narrative fiction* 叙事小说

nar·ra·tor /nəˈreɪtə(r)/ *noun* a person who tells a story, especially in a book, play or film/movie; the person who speaks the words in a television programme but who does not appear in it （书、戏剧或电影中的）叙述者，讲述者；（电视节目中的）幕后解说员，旁白员：*a first-person narrator* 第一人称叙述者 ➲ WORDFINDER NOTE AT BOOK, CHARACTER

nar·row 🔑 /ˈnærəʊ; *NAmE* -roʊ/ *adj., verb*
■ *adj.* (**nar·row·er, nar·row·est**) **1** 🔑 measuring a short distance from one side to the other, especially in relation to length 狭窄的；窄小的：*narrow streets* 狭窄的街道 ◇ *a narrow bed/doorway/shelf* 狭窄的床 / 门口 / 架子 ◇ *narrow shoulders/hips* 窄小的肩头 / 臀部 ◇ *There was only a narrow gap between the bed and the wall.* 床和墙之间只有

▼ **WHICH WORD?** 词语辨析

narrow / thin

These adjectives are frequently used with the following nouns. 以上形容词常与下列名词连用：

narrow ~	**thin ~**
road	man
entrance	legs
bed	ice
stairs	line
majority	layer
victory	material
range	cream

- **Narrow** describes something that is a short distance from side to side. **Thin** describes people, or something that has a short distance through it from one side to the other. * narrow 表示窄。thin 指人瘦或物细、薄。
- **Thin** is also used of things that are not as thick as you expect. **Narrow** can be used with the meanings 'only just achieved' and 'limited'. * thin 亦用以指薄。narrow 可表示勉强达到、仅仅。

一条窄缝。◇ (*figurative*) *the narrow confines of prison life* 狱中生活的狭小天地 OPP **broad, wide 2** [usually before noun] only just achieved or avoided 勉强的；刚刚好的： *a* ***narrow victory*** 险胜 ◇ *He lost the race by the* ***narrowest of margins***. 他以极小的差距在赛跑中落败。◇ *She was elected by a* ***narrow majority***. 她以微弱多数当选。◇ *He had a* ***narrow escape*** *when his car skidded on the ice.* 车在冰上打滑，他险些出事。 **3** limited in a way that ignores important issues or the opinions of other people 狭隘的；目光短浅的： *narrow interests* 目光短浅的利益 ◇ *She has a very narrow view of the world.* 她对世界的认识是非常狭隘的。 OPP **broad 4** limited in variety or numbers（种类或数目）有限的；范围小的 SYN **restricted**: *The shop sells only a narrow range of goods.* 这家商店商品的种类有限。◇ *a narrow circle of friends* 有限的交友圈子 OPP **wide 5** limited in meaning; exact 狭义的；严格的；准确的： *I am using the word 'education' in the narrower sense.* 我说的是较狭义的"教育"。 OPP **broad** ▸ **nar·row·ness** *noun* [U, sing.]: *The narrowness of the streets caused many traffic problems.* 街道狭窄，造成很多交通问题。◇ *We were surprised by the narrowness of our victory.* 我们对自己勉强获胜感到惊讶。◇ *His attitudes show a certain narrowness of mind.* 他的态度显示他的思想有些狭隘。 IDM SEE STRAIGHT *adj.*

■ *verb* [I, T] to become or make sth narrower 使窄小；变窄；缩小： *This is where the river narrows.* 这条河就是在这里变窄的。◇ *The gap between the two teams has narrowed to three points.* 两队之间的差距缩小到三分了。◇ *Her eyes* ***narrowed*** (= almost closed) *menacingly.* 她咄咄逼人地眯起眼睛。◇ ~ **sth** *He narrowed his eyes at her.* 他向她挤了挤眼睛。◇ *We need to try and narrow the health divide between rich and poor.* 我们需要设法缩小穷人和富人之间的健康差距。

PHRV **ˌnarrow sth↔ˈdown (to sth)** to reduce the number of possibilities or choices 把（可能性或选择）缩小（到）；缩小范围： *We have narrowed down the list to four candidates.* 我们把范围缩小到四位候选者。

nar·row·band /ˈnærəʊbænd; *NAmE* -roʊ-/ *noun* [U] (*specialist*) signals that use a narrow range of FREQUENCIES 窄带；窄频 ➲ COMPARE BROADBAND

nar·row·boat /ˈnærəʊbəʊt; *NAmE* ˈnæroʊboʊt/ *noun* (*BrE*) a long narrow boat, used on CANALS 运河船 ➲ VISUAL VOCAB PAGE V59

ˈnarrow gauge *noun* [U] a size of railway/railroad track that is not as wide as the standard track that is used in Britain and the US 窄轨： *a narrow-gauge railway* 窄轨铁路

nar·row·ly /ˈnærəʊli; *NAmE* -roʊ-/ *adv.* **1** only by a small amount 勉强地；以毫厘之差： *The car narrowly missed a cyclist.* 汽车差点儿撞上一位骑自行车的人。◇ *She narrowly escaped injury.* 她险些受伤。◇ *The team lost narrowly.* 该队以微弱差距败北。 **2** (*sometimes disapproving*) in a way that is limited 狭隘地；严格地： *a narrowly defined task* 严格确定的任务 ◇ *a narrowly specialized education* 严格区分专业的教育 **3** closely; carefully 小心地；仔细地： *She looked at him narrowly.* 她仔细打量着他。

ˌnarrow-ˈminded *adj.* (*disapproving*) not willing to listen to new ideas or to the opinions of others 气量小的；小心眼的；狭隘的 SYN **bigoted, intolerant**: *a narrow-minded attitude* 狭隘的态度 ◇ *a narrow-minded nationalist* 狭隘的民族主义者 OPP **broad-minded, open-minded** ▸ **ˌnarrow-ˈminded·ness** *noun* [U]

nar·rows /ˈnærəʊz; *NAmE* -roʊz/ *noun* [pl.] a narrow channel that connects two larger areas of water 海峡；（江河的）峡谷

nar·whal /ˈnɑːwəl; *NAmE* ˈnɑːrwɑːl/ *noun* a small white WHALE from the Arctic region. The male narwhal has a long TUSK (= outer tooth). 独角鲸（生活于北极地区，雄性有一长牙）

nary /ˈneəri; *NAmE* ˈneri/ *adj.* (*old use* or *dialect*) not a; no 没有一个的；没有的

NASA /ˈnæsə/ *abbr.* National Aeronautics and Space Administration (a US government organization that does research into space and organizes space travel) 美国国家航空航天局

nasal /ˈneɪzl/ *adj.* **1** connected with the nose 鼻的；与鼻子相关的： *the nasal passages* 鼻道 ◇ *a nasal spray* 鼻腔喷剂 **2** (of sb's voice 嗓音) sounding as if it is produced partly through the nose 带鼻音的： *a nasal accent* 带鼻音的口音 **3** (*phonetics* 语音) (of a speech sound 语音) produced by sending a stream of air through the nose. The nasal consonants in English are /m/, /n/ and /ŋ/, as in *sum, sun* and *sung*. 从鼻腔发出的；鼻音的

na·sal·ize (*BrE also* **-ise**) /ˈneɪzlaɪz/ *verb* ~ **sth** (*phonetics* 语音) to produce a speech sound, especially a vowel, with the air in the nose VIBRATING 使鼻音化（尤指元音） ▸ **na·sal·iza·tion, -isa·tion** /ˌneɪzlaɪˈzeɪʃn; *NAmE* -ləˈz-/ *noun* [U]

nas·cent /ˈnæsnt/ *adj.* (*formal*) beginning to exist; not yet fully developed 新生的；萌芽的；未成熟的

the NASDAQ /ˈnæzdæk/ *noun* [sing.] National Association of Securities Dealers Automated Quotations (a computer system in the US that supplies the current price of shares to the people who sell them) 纳斯达克；美国全国证券交易商协会自动报价系统

na·stur·tium /nəˈstɜːʃəm; *NAmE* -ˈstɜːrʃ-/ *noun* a garden plant with round flat leaves and red, orange or yellow flowers that are sometimes eaten in salads 旱金莲（有时用于色拉）

nasty /ˈnɑːsti; *NAmE* ˈnæsti/ *adj.* (**nas·tier, nas·ti·est**) **1** very bad or unpleasant 极差的；令人厌恶的；令人不悦的： *a nasty accident* 严重事故 ◇ *The news gave me a nasty shock.* 这消息可把我吓死了。◇ *I had a nasty feeling that he would follow me.* 我有一种极糟糕的预感：他会跟着我。◇ *He had a nasty moment when he thought he'd lost his passport.* 他一时以为护照丢了，苦恼极了。◇ *This coffee has a nasty taste.* 这咖啡真难喝。◇ *Don't buy that coat—it looks* ***cheap and nasty***. 别买那件外套，一看就是差劲的便宜货。 **2** unkind; unpleasant 不友好的；恶意的；令人不愉快的 SYN **mean**: *to make nasty remarks about sb* 说某人的坏话 ◇ *the nastier side of her character* 她个性较为恶毒的一面 ◇ *to have a nasty temper* 脾气坏 ◇ *Don't be so nasty to your brother.* 别对你弟弟那么凶。◇ *That was a nasty little trick.* 这是个可恶的小骗局。◇ *Life has a* ***nasty habit*** *of repeating itself.* 生活总是令人厌烦地重复着。 **3** dangerous or serious 危险的；严重的： *a nasty bend* (= dangerous for cars going fast) 危险的弯道 ◇ *a nasty injury* 重伤 **4** offensive; in bad taste 无礼的；污秽的；下流的： *to have a nasty mind* 思想肮脏 ◇ *nasty jokes* 下流的笑话 ▸ **nas·tily** /-ɪli/ *adv.*: *'I hate you,' she said nastily.* 她咬牙切齿地说："我恨你。" **nas·ti·ness** *noun* [U]

IDM **get/turn ˈnasty 1** to become threatening and violent 翻脸；变凶： *You'd better do what he says or he'll turn nasty.* 你最好照他说的做，否则他就不客气了。 **2** to become bad or unpleasant 变坏；变得令人讨厌： *It looks as though the weather is going to turn nasty again.* 好像又要变天了。 **a nasty piece of ˈwork** (*BrE, informal*) a person who is unpleasant, unkind or dishonest 恶棍；令人讨厌的人；靠不住的人 ➲ MORE AT TASTE *n.*

natal /ˈneɪtl/ *adj.* [only before noun] (*formal*) relating to the place where or the time when sb was born 出生地的；出生时的： *her natal home* 她出生的房子

na·tal·ity /nəˈtæləti/ *noun* [U] (*specialist*) the number of births every year for every 1 000 people in the population 出生率（每年每 1 000 人的出生人数） SYN **birth rate**

natch /nætʃ/ *adv.* (*slang*) used to say that sth is obvious or exactly as you would expect 当然；自然；毫无疑问 SYN **naturally**: *He was wearing the latest T-shirt, natch.* 当然啦，他穿着最新款式的 T 恤衫。

na·tion /ˈneɪʃn/ *noun* **1** [C] a country considered as a group of people with the same language, culture and history, who live in a particular area under one government 国家；民族： *an independent nation* 独立的

N

国家 ◇ *the African nations* 非洲各国 **2** [sing.] all the people in a country 国民 SYN **population**: *The entire nation, it seemed, was watching TV.* 好像全国的人都在看电视。 ▶ **na·tion·hood** /ˈneɪʃnhʊd/ *noun* [U]: *Citizenship is about the sense of nationhood.* 公民身份涉及国家意识。

na·tion·al /ˈnæʃnəl/ *adj., noun*
■ *adj.* [usually before noun] **1** connected with a particular nation; shared by a whole nation 国家的；民族的；全国的: *national and local newspapers* 全国性的和地方的报纸 ◇ *national and international news* 国内和国际新闻 ◇ *national and regional politics* 国家和地区政治 ◇ *a national election* 全国性选举 ◇ *These buildings are part of our national heritage.* 这些建筑是我们民族遗产的一部分。 ◇ *They are afraid of losing their national identity.* 他们担心会失去他们的民族特色。 **2** owned, controlled or paid for by the government 国有的；国立的；国营的: *a national airline/museum/theatre* 国营航空公司；国立博物馆；国家剧院
■ *noun* (*specialist*) a citizen of a particular country （某国的）公民: *Polish nationals living in Germany* 生活在德国的波兰公民

ˌnational ˈanthem *noun* the official song of a nation that is sung on special occasions 国歌

the ˌNational Asˌsembly for ˈWales *noun* = WELSH ASSEMBLY

ˌnational conˈvention *noun* a meeting held by a political party, especially in the US, to choose a candidate to take part in the election for President （尤指美国政党推选总统候选人的）全国代表大会

N

ˌnational ˈcostume *noun* [C, U] (*also* **ˌnational ˈdress** [U]) the clothes traditionally worn by people from a particular country, especially on special occasions or for formal ceremonies （某一国家的）民族服装

the ˌnational curˈriculum *noun* [sing.] (in Britain) a programme of study in all the main subjects that children aged 5 to 16 in state schools must follow （英国国立中小学）全国统一课程

ˌnational ˈdebt *noun* [usually sing.] the total amount of money that the government of a country owes 国债

the ˌNational ˈFront *noun* [sing.+sing./pl. v.] (in Britain) a small political party with extreme views, especially on issues connected with race （英国）民族阵线（一小型政党，尤在种族问题上持极端观点）

ˌnational ˈgrid *noun* [sing.] (*BrE*) the system of power lines that joins the places where electricity is produced, and takes electricity to all parts of the country 全国高压输电线网

the ˌNational ˈGuard *noun* [sing.] **1** a small army, often used to protect a political leader （保护政界领导人的）警卫队 **2** the army in each state of the US that can be used by the federal government if needed （美国）后备役军人，国民警卫队

the ˌNational ˈHealth Service *noun* [sing.] (*abbr.* **NHS**) the public health service in Britain that provides medical care and is paid for by taxes （英国）国民医疗服务体系: *I got my glasses on the National Health (Service).* 我配眼镜是国民医疗服务体系资助的。

ˌNational Inˈsurance *noun* [U] (*abbr.* **NI**) (in Britain) a system of payments that have to be made by employers and employees to provide help for people who are sick, old or unemployed （英国）国民保险制度

na·tion·al·ism /ˈnæʃnəlɪzəm/ *noun* [U] **1** the desire by a group of people who share the same race, culture, language, etc. to form an independent country 国家主义: *Scottish nationalism* 苏格兰国家主义 **2** (*sometimes disapproving*) a feeling of love for and pride in your country; a feeling that your country is better than any other 民族主义；民族自豪感；民族优越感

na·tion·al·ist /ˈnæʃnəlɪst/ *noun* **1** a person who wants their country to become independent 国家主义者: *Scottish nationalists* 苏格兰国家主义者 **2** (*sometimes disapproving*) a person who has a great love for and pride in their country; a person who has a feeling that their country is better than any other 民族主义者；怀有本民族优越感者 ▶ **na·tion·al·ist** *adj.*: *nationalist sentiments* 民族主义感情

na·tion·al·is·tic /ˌnæʃnəˈlɪstɪk/ *adj.* (*usually disapproving*) having very strong feelings of love for and pride in your country, so that you think that it is better than any other 国家主义的；民族主义的

na·tion·al·ity /ˌnæʃəˈnæləti/ *noun* (*pl.* **-ies**) **1** [U, C] the legal right of belonging to a particular nation 国籍: *to take/have/hold French* ***nationality*** 获得/持有/拥有法国国籍 ◇ *All applicants will be considered regardless of age, sex, religion or nationality.* 所有申请者，不论其年龄、性别、宗教信仰及国籍，都将被考虑。 ◇ *The college attracts students of all nationalities.* 这所大学吸引着各国的学生。 ◇ *She has* ***dual nationality*** (= is a citizen of two countries). 她具有双重国籍。 **2** [C] a group of people with the same language, culture and history who form part of a political nation （构成国家一部分的）民族: *Kazakhstan alone contains more than a hundred nationalities.* 单是哈萨克斯坦就有一百多个民族。

na·tion·al·ize (*BrE also* **-ise**) /ˈnæʃnəlaɪz/ *verb* **~ sth** to put an industry or a company under the control of the government, which becomes its owner 将…国有化: *nationalized industries* 国有化行业 OPP **denationalize, privatize** ▶ **na·tion·al·iza·tion, -isation** /ˌnæʃnəlaɪˈzeɪʃn; *NAmE* -ləˈz-/ *noun* [U, C]

the ˌNational ˈLeague *noun* (in the US) one of the two organizations for professional BASEBALL （美国）全国职业棒球联盟，国家棒球联盟 SEE ALSO AMERICAN LEAGUE

na·tion·al·ly /ˈnæʃnəli/ *adv.* relating to a country as a whole; relating to a particular country 全国性地；与某国相关地: *The programme was broadcast nationally.* 这个节目曾在全国播放过。 ◇ *Meetings were held locally and nationally.* 举行的会议有地方性的，也有全国性的。 ◇ *He's a talented athlete who competes nationally and internationally.* 他是一位有才华的运动员，既参加国内比赛，也参加国际比赛。

the ˌNational ˈMotto *noun* [sing.] the official US motto 'In God we trust' （美国）国家箴言（即"我们相信上帝"）

ˌnational ˈpark *noun* an area of land that is protected by the government for people to visit because of its natural beauty and historical or scientific interest 国家公园

ˌnational ˈservice *noun* [U] the system in some countries in which young people have to do military training for a period of time 兵役 SYN **military service**: *to do your national service* 服兵役

ˌNational ˈSocialism *noun* [U] (*politics* 政) the policies of the German Nazi party （德国纳粹党推行的）国家社会主义，纳粹主义 ▶ **ˌNational ˈSocialist** *noun, adj.*

ˌnational ˈtrail *noun* a long route through beautiful country where people can walk or ride （修于美丽乡间的）国家级步道，观光道

the ˌNational ˈTrust *noun* an organization that owns and takes care of places of historical interest or natural beauty in England, Wales and Northern Ireland, so that people can go and visit them 全国托管协会（负责管理并保护英格兰、威尔士及北爱尔兰的历史遗迹和自然景观）

ˌnation ˈstate *noun* a group of people with the same culture, language, etc. who have formed an independent country 民族国家；单一民族的独立国家

na·tion·wide /ˌneɪʃnˈwaɪd/ *adj.* happening or existing in all parts of a particular country 全国性的；遍及全国的；全国范围的: *a nationwide campaign* 全国性运动 ▶ **na·tion·wide** *adv.*: *The company has over 500 stores nationwide.* 这家公司在全国各地有 500 多家商店。

na·tive /ˈneɪtɪv/ *adj., noun*

■ ***adj.*** **1** [only before noun] connected with the place where you were born and lived for the first years of your life 出生地的；儿时居住地的：*your **native land/country/city*** 你的故乡 / 祖国 / 故里 ◇ *It is a long time since he has visited his native Chile.* 他很久没有回故乡智利了。◇ *Her native language is Korean.* 她的母语是朝鲜语。➲ SEE ALSO NATIVE SPEAKER **2** [only before noun] connected with the place where you have always lived or have lived for a long time 本地的；当地的：*native Berliners* 土生土长的柏林人 **3** [only before noun] (*sometimes offensive*) connected with the people who originally lived in a country before other people, especially white people, came there 土著的；土著人的：*native peoples* 土著民族 ◇ *native art* 土著艺术 **4 ~ (to...)** (of animals and plants 动植物) existing naturally in a place 原产于某地的；土产的；当地的 SYN **indigenous**：*the native plants of America* 美国的土生植物 ◇ *The tiger is native to India.* 这种虎原产于印度。◇ *native species* 当地的物种 **5** [only before noun] that you have naturally without having to learn it 天赋的；与生俱来的 SYN **innate**：*native cunning* 与生俱来的狡猾

IDM **go ˈnative** (*often humorous*) (of a person staying in another country 移居异国的人) to try to live and behave like the local people 入乡随俗；同化

■ ***noun*** **1** a person who was born in a particular country or area 出生于某国（或某地）的人：*a native of New York* 纽约人 **2** a person who lives in a particular place, especially sb who has lived there a long time 本地人；当地人 SYN **local**：*You can always tell the difference between the tourists and the natives.* 游客与当地人之间的区别一望即知。◇ *She speaks Italian like a native.* 她的意大利语说得和意大利人一样。**3** (*old-fashioned, offensive*) a word used in the past by Europeans to describe a person who lived in a place originally, before white people arrived there（旧时欧洲人用以称呼先于白人居住在某地的人）土著：*disputes between early settlers and natives* 早期移民和土著之间的纷争 **4** an animal or a plant that lives or grows naturally in a particular area 本地的动物（或植物）：*The kangaroo is a native of Australia.* 袋鼠是产于澳大利亚的动物。

ˌNative Aˈmerican (*also* **Aˌmerican ˈIndian**) *noun* a member of any of the races of people who were the original people living in America 美洲土著居民 ▶ **ˌNative Aˈmerican** *adj.*：*Native American languages* 美洲土著语言

ˌNative Caˈnadian *noun* (*CanE*) an Aboriginal Canadian; a Canadian Indian, Inuit or Metis 加拿大土著居民；加拿大印第安人（或因纽特人、米提人）

ˌnative ˈspeaker *noun* a person who speaks a language as their first language and has not learned it as a foreign language 说本族语的人；母语使用者

na·tiv·ity /nəˈtɪvəti/ *noun* **1 the Nativity** [sing.] the birth of Jesus Christ, celebrated by Christians at Christmas 耶稣降生；圣诞 **2** a picture or a model of the baby Jesus Christ and the place where he was born 耶稣降生图

naˈtivity play *noun* a play about the birth of Jesus Christ, usually performed by children at Christmas 圣诞剧（通常由儿童于圣诞节时演出）

NATO /ˈneɪtəʊ; *NAmE* -toʊ/ (*also* **Nato**) *abbr.* North Atlantic Treaty Organization. NATO is an organization to which many European countries and the US and Canada belong. They agree to give each other military help if necessary. 北约；北大西洋公约组织

nat·ter /ˈnætə(r)/ *verb* [I] **~ (away/on) (about sth)** (*informal*) to talk for a long time, especially about unimportant things 唠叨；闲聊 SYN **chat** ▶ **nat·ter** *noun* [sing.] (*BrE, informal*)：*to have a good natter* 好好聊聊

natty /ˈnæti/ *adj.* (*old-fashioned, informal*) **1** neat and fashionable 整洁时髦的：*a natty suit* 笔挺时新的套装 **2** well designed; clever 设计精妙的；聪明的：*a natty little briefcase* 设计精巧的小公文包 ▶ **nat·tily** *adv.*

nat·ural /ˈnætʃrəl/ *adj., noun*

■ ***adj.***

• **IN NATURE** 自然 **1** [only before noun] existing in nature; not made or caused by humans 自然的；天然的：*natural disasters* 自然灾害 ◇ ***the natural world*** (= of trees, rivers, animals and birds) 自然界 ◇ *a country's **natural resources*** (= its coal, oil, forests, etc.) 一国的自然资源 ◇ *wildlife in its natural habitat* 自然栖息地里的野生生物 ◇ *natural yogurt* (= with no flavour added) 原味酸奶 ◇ *My hair soon grew back to its natural colour* (= after being DYED). 我的头发很快又恢复了本色。◇ *The clothes are available in warm natural colours.* 这些衣服有各种自然的暖色调可供挑选。➲ COMPARE SUPERNATURAL (1)

• **EXPECTED** 意料之中 **2** normal; as you would expect 正常的；自然的；意料之中的：*to die of **natural causes*** (= not by violence, but normally, of old age) 自然死亡 ◇ *He thought social inequality was all part of the natural order of things.* 他认为社会不平等完全合乎事物的自然规律。◇ *She was the natural choice for the job.* 做那份工作，她是当然人选。➲ COMPARE UNNATURAL

• **BEHAVIOUR** 行为 **3** used to describe behaviour that is part of the character that a person or an animal was born with 天生的；本能的；与生俱来的：*the natural agility of a cat* 猫天生的敏捷灵活 ◇ *the natural processes of language learning* 学习语言的自然过程 ◇ *It's **only natural** to worry about your children.* 为孩子操心是很自然的。

• **ABILITY** 能力 **4** [only before noun] having an ability that you were born with 天赋的；天生具有某种能力的：*He's a natural leader.* 他是个天生领袖。

• **RELAXED** 放松 **5** relaxed and not pretending to be sb/sth different 不拘束的；不做作的；自然的：*It's difficult to look natural when you're feeling nervous.* 当你紧张的时候，很难显得轻松自然。

• **PARENTS/CHILDREN** 父母；孩子 **6** [only before noun] (of parents or their children 父母或其子女) related by blood 有血缘关系的；亲生的：*His natural mother was unable to care for him so he was raised by an aunt.* 他的生母不能照顾他，所以他是姑姑抚养大的。**7** [only before noun] (*old use or formal*) (of a son or daughter 儿女) born to parents who are not married 非婚生的；私生的 SYN **illegitimate**：*She was a natural daughter of King James II.* 她是国王詹姆斯二世的私生女。

• **BASED ON HUMAN REASON** 符合理性 **8** [only before noun] based on human reason alone 符合人的理性的；正常的；自然的：***natural justice/law*** 自然公道 / 规律

• **IN MUSIC** 音乐 **9** used after the name of a note to show that the note is neither SHARP nor FLAT. The written symbol is (♮). 本位音的，标有还原号的（书写符号为♮）：*B natural* * B 本位音 ➲ PICTURE AT MUSIC

■ ***noun***

• **PERSON** 人 **1 ~ (for sth)** a person who is very good at sth without having to learn how to do it, or who is perfectly suited for a particular job 有天赋的人；擅长做某事的人：*She took to flying like a natural.* 她迷上了飞行，仿佛天生就会似的。◇ *He's a natural for the role.* 他是这个角色的最佳人选。

• **IN MUSIC** 音乐 **2** a normal musical note, not its SHARP or FLAT form. The written symbol is (♮). 本位音，还原音，本位号（书写符号为♮）

ˈnatural-born *adj.* [only before noun] having a natural ability or skill that you have not had to learn 天生的；天赋的；与生俱来的

ˌnatural ˈchildbirth *noun* [U] a method of giving birth to a baby in which a woman chooses not to take drugs and does special exercises to make her relaxed 自然分娩

ˌnatural ˈgas *noun* [U] gas that is found under the ground or the sea and that is used as a fuel 天然气

ˌnatural ˈhistory *noun* [U, C] the study of plants and animals; an account of the plant and animal life of a particular place 博物学；博物志：*the Natural History Museum* 自然博物馆 ◇ *He has written a natural history of Scotland.* 他写了一本苏格兰博物志。

nat·ur·al·ism /ˈnætʃrəlɪzəm/ *noun* [U] **1** a style of art or writing that shows people, things and experiences as they really are 自然主义（文学、艺术以反映现实为宗旨）

N

2 (*philosophy* 哲) the theory that everything in the world and life is based on natural causes and laws, and not on spiritual or SUPERNATURAL ones 自然主义（认为万事万物都是受自然原因和自然规律支配，而非受精神或超自然力量支配）

nat·ur·al·ist /ˈnætʃrəlɪst/ *noun* a person who studies animals, plants, birds and other living things 博物学家

nat·ur·al·is·tic /ˌnætʃrəˈlɪstɪk/ *adj.* **1** (of artists, writers, etc. or their work 艺术家、作家等及其作品) showing things as they appear in the natural world 自然主义的；自然主义风格的 **2** copying the way things are in the natural world 写实的；模仿自然的：*to study behaviour in laboratory and naturalistic settings* 研究实验室里的以及仿自然环境中的行为

nat·ur·al·ize (*BrE also* **-ise**) /ˈnætʃrəlaɪz/ *verb* [usually passive] **1** [T] **~ sb** to make sb who was not born in a particular country a citizen of that country 使加入…国籍；使成为某国公民；归化 **2** [T] **~ sth** to introduce a plant or an animal to a country where it is not NATIVE 引进（动植物）；移植 **3** [I] (of a plant or an animal 动植物) to start growing or living naturally in a country where it is not NATIVE 适应异域生长环境 ▸ **nat·ur·al·iza·tion, -isa·tion** /ˌnætʃrəlaɪˈzeɪʃn; *NAmE* -ləˈz-/ *noun* [U]

ˌnatural ˈlanguage *noun* [C, U] a language that has developed in a natural way and is not designed by humans 自然语言（自然发展而成，并非人造）

ˌnatural ˈlanguage processing *noun* [U] (*abbr.* **NLP**) the use of computers to process natural languages, for example for translating （计算机）自然语言处理

N

ˌnatural ˈlaw *noun* [U] a set of moral principles on which human behaviour is based 自然法（人类行为所基于的道德原则）

nat·ur·al·ly 🔑 /ˈnætʃrəli/ *adv.* **1** 🔑 in a way that you would expect 自然地；当然地 SYN **of course**: *Naturally, I get upset when things go wrong.* 事情出了错，我当然就会很烦。◇ *After a while, we naturally started talking about the children.* 过了一会儿，我们自然而然地谈起了孩子。◇ *'Did you complain about the noise?' 'Naturally.'* "你投诉噪音了吗？" "那还用说。" **2** 🔑 without special help, treatment or action by sb 天然地；自然而然地：*naturally occurring chemicals* 天然存在的化学物质 ◇ *plants that grow naturally in poor soils* 贫瘠土壤中自然生长的植物 **3** 🔑 as a normal, logical result of sth 合理地；理所当然地；顺理成章地：*This leads naturally to my next point.* 这必然引出我的下一个论点。**4** 🔑 in a way that shows or uses abilities or qualities that a person or an animal is born with 天生地；本能地：*to be naturally artistic* 有艺术天赋 ◇ *a naturally gifted athlete* 有天赋的运动员 **5** in a relaxed and normal way 自然地；大方地：*Just act naturally.* 放自然点儿就行了。

IDM **come ˈnaturally (to sb/sth)** if sth **comes naturally** to you, you are able to do it very easily and very well 轻而易举：*Making money came naturally to him.* 赚钱对他来说轻而易举。

nat·ur·al·ness /ˈnætʃrəlnəs/ *noun* [U] **1** the state or quality of being like real life 自然状态；自然；逼真：*The naturalness of the dialogue made the book so true to life.* 自然逼真的对话使得这本书非常贴近生活。**2** the quality of behaving in a normal, relaxed or innocent way 自然；大方；纯真：*Teenagers lose their childhood simplicity and naturalness.* 十几岁的青少年就不像儿时那么淳朴天真了。**3** the style or quality of happening in a normal way that you would expect 当然；必然性：*the naturalness of her reaction* 她的必然反应

ˌnatural ˈnumber *noun* (*mathematics* 数) a positive whole number such as 1, 2, or 3, and sometimes also zero 正整数；自然数

ˌnatural phiˈlosophy *noun* [U] (*old use*) the study of the physical world, which developed into the natural sciences 自然哲学（对物质世界的研究，后发展为自然科学）

ˌnatural ˈscience *noun* [C, U] a science concerned with studying the physical world. Chemistry, biology and physics are all natural sciences. 自然科学 ➲ COMPARE EARTH SCIENCE, LIFE SCIENCES

ˌnatural seˈlection *noun* [U] the process by which plants, animals, etc. that can adapt to their environment survive and reproduce, while the others disappear 自然选择；物竞天择

ˌnatural ˈwastage (*BrE*) (*also* **at·tri·tion** *NAmE, BrE*) *noun* [U] the process of reducing the number of people who are employed by an organization by, for example, not replacing people who leave their jobs 自然减员

na·ture 🔑 /ˈneɪtʃə(r)/ *noun*

> **WORD FAMILY**
> **nature** *noun*
> **natural** *adj.* (≠ unnatural)
> **naturally** *adv.* (≠ unnaturally)

• **PLANTS, ANIMALS** 动植物 **1** 🔑 (*often* **Nature**) [U] all the plants, animals and things that exist in the universe that are not made by people 自然界；大自然：*the beauties of nature* 自然界中美好的东西 ◇ *man-made substances not found in nature* 自然界里找不到的人造物质 ◇ *nature conservation* 自然保护 HELP You cannot use 'the nature' in this meaning. 此义不可用 the nature: ~~*the beauties of the nature*~~ It is often better to use another appropriate word, for example **the countryside**, **the scenery** or **wildlife**. 最好用其他恰当的词，如 the countryside、the scenery 或 wildlife: *We stopped to admire the scenery.* 我们中途停下来欣赏一下风景。◇ ~~*We stopped to admire the nature.*~~ **2** 🔑 (*often* **Nature**) [U] the way that things happen in the physical world when it is not controlled by people 自然；自然方式：*the forces/laws of nature* 自然力 / 规律 ◇ *Just let nature take its course.* 就顺其自然吧。◇ *Her illness was Nature's way of telling her to do less.* 她生病了，这是身体在告诉她不要太劳累。➲ SEE ALSO MOTHER NATURE

• **CHARACTER** 性质 **3** 🔑 [C, U] the usual way that a person or an animal behaves that is part of their character 天性；本性；性格：*It's* **not in his nature** *to be unkind.* 他天生不会刻薄。◇ *She is very sensitive* **by nature**. 她生性很敏感。◇ *We appealed to his* **better nature** (= his kindness). 我们设法唤起他的善良本性。➲ SEE ALSO GOOD NATURE, HUMAN NATURE, SECOND NATURE

• **BASIC QUALITIES** 基本特征 **4** 🔑 [sing.] the basic qualities of a thing 基本特征；本质；基本性质：*the changing nature of society* 不断变化的社会性质 ◇ *It's difficult to define the exact nature of the problem.* 很难给这个问题确切定性。◇ *My work is very specialized* **in nature**. 我的工作特点是非常专业化。

• **TYPE/KIND** 种类 **5** [sing.] a type or kind of sth 种类；类型：*books of a scientific nature* 科学书籍 ◇ *Don't worry about things of that nature.* 别担心那类事情。

• **-NATURED** 本性 **6** (in adjectives 构成形容词) having the type of character or quality mentioned 有…本性的；…性情的：*a good-natured man* 脾气好的人

IDM **against ˈnature** not natural; not moral 违反自然的；有违天性的；不道德的：*Murder is a crime against nature.* 谋杀是一种有违天性的罪行。 **(get, go, etc.) back to ˈnature** (to return to) a simple kind of life in the country, away from cities 回归自然；返璞归真 **in the nature of ˈsth** similar to sth; a type of sth; in the style of sth 与…类似；…之类；以…风格：*His speech was in the nature of an apology.* 他的话也就是道歉。 **in the ˈnature of things** in the way that things usually happen 理所当然地；自然地：*In the nature of things, young people often rebel against their parents.* 年轻人常常会反抗他们的父母，这很自然。➲ MORE AT CALL *n.*, FORCE *n.*

ˈnature reserve *noun* an area of land where the animals and plants are protected 自然保护区

ˈnature strip *noun* (*AustralE*) a piece of public land between the edge of a house, or other building, and the street, usually planted with grass （房屋或建筑物前靠路边的）公共绿化带

ˈnature trail *noun* a path through countryside which you can follow in order to see the interesting plants and animals that are found there 自然游道；观景小径

na·tur·ism /ˈneɪtʃərɪzəm/ *noun* [U] (*especially BrE*) = NUDISM

na·tur·ist /ˈneɪtʃərɪst/ *noun* (*especially BrE*) = NUDIST

na·tur·op·athy /ˌneɪtʃəˈrɒpəθi; *NAmE* -ˈrɑːp-/ *noun* [U] a system for treating diseases or conditions using natural foods and herbs and various other techniques, rather than artificial drugs 自然疗法（指用天然食物、草药和其他手段治疗疾病，而不用人造药物） ▶ **na·turo·path** /ˈneɪtʃərəpæθ/ *noun*：*A medical herbalist or naturopath will be able to advise on individual treatment plans.* 草药医生或自然疗法医生能够对个体治疗方案提供咨询。 **na·turo·path·ic** /ˌneɪtʃərəˈpæθɪk/ *adj.* [only before noun]: *naturopathic medicine* 自然疗法医学 ◇ *a naturopathic physician* 自然疗法医师

naught *noun* = NOUGHT (2)

naughty /ˈnɔːti/ *adj.* (**naugh·tier**, **naugh·ti·est**) **1** (especially of children 尤指儿童) behaving badly; not willing to obey 顽皮的；淘气的；不听话的：*a naughty boy/girl* 淘气的男孩 / 女孩 ◇ (*humorous*) *I'm being very naughty—I've ordered champagne!* 我今天放肆一回，我要了香槟！ **2** (*informal, often humorous*) slightly rude; connected with sex 粗俗的；下流的 SYN **risqué**：*a naughty joke/word* 下流的笑话；粗俗的字眼 ▶ **naugh·tily** *adv.* **naugh·ti·ness** *noun* [U]

ˈ**naughty step** *noun* [sing.] (*BrE*) a quiet place, for example a step, where a child has to stay for a short period of time as a punishment for behaving badly 淘气角（孩子因顽皮受罚的地方，如楼梯处）：*He wouldn't stop shouting so she made him sit on the naughty step until he had calmed down.* 他一直大喊大叫，她就罚他坐在淘气角直到安静下来。◇ (*figurative*) *The MP is now on the naughty step for leaking confidential information to the press.* 这名议员向新闻界泄露了机密，正被罚思过呢。

nau·sea /ˈnɔːziə; ˈnɔːsiə/ *noun* [U] the feeling that you have when you want to VOMIT, for example because you are ill/sick or are disgusted by sth 恶心；作呕；反胃：*A wave of nausea swept over her.* 她觉得一阵恶心。◇ *Nausea and vomiting are common symptoms.* 恶心呕吐是常见的症状。 ➲ SEE ALSO AD NAUSEAM

nau·se·ate /ˈnɔːzieɪt; ˈnɔːsieɪt/ *verb* **1 ~ sb** to make sb feel that they want to VOMIT 使恶心；使作呕 **2 ~ sb** to make sb feel disgusted 使厌恶；使厌烦 SYN **revolt, sicken**：*I was nauseated by the violence in the movie.* 影片中的暴力场面让我感到恶心。 ▶ **nau·se·at·ing** *adj.*：*a nauseating smell* 令人作呕的气味 ◇ *his nauseating behaviour* 他那令人厌恶的行为 **nau·se·at·ing·ly** *adv.*

nau·se·ous /ˈnɔːziəs; ˈnɔːsiəs; *NAmE* ˈnɔːʃəs/ *adj.* **1** feeling as if you want to VOMIT 恶心的；想呕吐的：*She felt dizzy and nauseous.* 她觉得头晕、恶心。 **2** making you feel as if you want to VOMIT 令人作呕的；令人厌恶的：*a nauseous smell* 令人作呕的气味

naut·ical /ˈnɔːtɪkl/ *adj.* connected with ships, sailors and sailing 航海的；海员的；船舶的：*nautical terms* 航海术语

ˌ**nautical** ˈ**mile** (*also* ˈ**sea mile**) *noun* a unit for measuring distance at sea; 1 852 metres 海里（合 1 852 米）

naut·ilus /ˈnɔːtɪləs/ *noun* a creature with a shell that lives in the sea. It has TENTACLES around its mouth and its shell fills with gas to help it float. 鹦鹉螺

Nav·ajo (*also* **Nava·ho**) /ˈnævəhəʊ; *NAmE* -hoʊ/ *noun* (*pl.* **Nav·ajo** or **Nav·ajos**) a member of the largest group of Native American people, most of whom live in the US states of Arizona, New Mexico and Utah 纳瓦霍人（美洲最大的土著民族成员，多数居于美国亚利桑那州、新墨西哥州和犹他州）

naval /ˈneɪvl/ *adj.* connected with the navy of a country 海军的：*a naval base/officer/battle* 海军基地 / 军官；海战

Nava·rat·ri /ˌnævəˈrætri/ (*also* **Nava·rat·ra** /-trə/) *noun* a Hindu festival lasting for nine nights, which takes place in the autumn/fall 九夜节（印度教秋季的节日，历时九个夜晚）

nave /neɪv/ *noun* the long central part of a church where most of the seats are 教堂正厅 ➲ COMPARE TRANSEPT

navel /ˈneɪvl/ (*also informal* ˈ**belly button**) (*also informal* ˈ**tummy button**) *noun* the small hollow part or lump in the middle of the stomach where the UMBILICAL CORD was cut at birth 肚脐；脐 ➲ VISUAL VOCAB PAGE V64

ˈ**navel-gazing** *noun* [U] (*disapproving*) the fact of thinking too much about a single issue and how it could affect you, without thinking about other things that could also affect the situation 一根筋；钻牛角尖

ˌ**navel** ˈ**orange** *noun* a large orange without seeds that has a part at the top that looks like a navel 脐橙

nav·ig·able /ˈnævɪɡəbl/ *adj.* (of rivers, etc. 河流等) wide and deep enough for ships and boats to sail on 可航行的；适于通航的 ▶ **nav·ig·abil·ity** /ˌnævɪɡəˈbɪləti/ *noun* [U]

navi·gate /ˈnævɪɡeɪt/ *verb* **1** [I, T] to find your position or the position of your ship, plane, car etc. and the direction you need to go in, for example by using a map 导航；确定（船、飞机、汽车等）的位置和方向：*to navigate by the stars* 根据星辰确定航向 ◇ *I'll drive, and you can navigate.* 我开车，你引路。◇ **~ your way…** *How do you navigate your way through a forest?* 你怎么才能设法走出森林？ ➲ WORDFINDER NOTE AT MAP **2** [T] **~ sth** to sail along, over or through a sea, river etc. 航行；航海；横渡：*The river became too narrow and shallow to navigate.* 河道变得又窄又浅，无法航行。 **3** [T] **~ sth** to find the right way to deal with a difficult or complicated situation 正确处理，有效应对（困难或复杂的情况）：*We next had to navigate a complex network of committees.* 我们下一步必须设法使各级委员会予以通过。 **4** [I, T] **~ (sth)** (*computing* 计) to find your way around on the Internet or on a particular website（在互联网或网站上）导航 ➲ WORDFINDER NOTE AT WEB

navi·ga·tion /ˌnævɪˈɡeɪʃn/ *noun* [U] **1** the skill or the process of planning a route for a ship or other vehicle and taking it there 导航；领航：*navigation systems* 导航系统 ◇ *an expert in navigation* 导航专家 **2** the movement of ships or aircraft 航行：*the right of navigation through international waters* 通过国际水域的航行权 **3** the way that you move around a website or the Internet when you are looking for information（网站或互联网的）导航：*The site was redesigned to improve navigation.* 该网站为改进导航重新进行了设计。 ▶ **navi·ga·tion·al** /-ʃənl/ *adj.*：*navigational aids* 导航设备

naviˈgation bar *noun* a long narrow area near the top or side of a page on a website that contains links to other pages（网页上的）导航条，导航栏 ➲ COMPARE ADDRESS BAR

navi·ga·tor /ˈnævɪɡeɪtə(r)/ *noun* a person who navigates, for example on a ship or an aircraft（飞机、船舶等上的）领航员

navvy /ˈnævi/ *noun* (*pl.* **-ies**) (*BrE*) a person employed to do hard physical work, especially building roads, etc. 壮工；苦力；（尤指）筑路工

navy 🔑 /ˈneɪvi/ *noun* (*pl.* **-ies**) **1** [C+sing./pl. v.] the part of a country's armed forces that fights at sea, and the ships that it uses 海军；海军部队：*the British and German navies* 英国和德国的海军部队 ◇ *He's joined the navy/the Navy.* 他参加了海军。◇ *an officer in the navy/the Navy* 海军军官 ◇ *The navy is/are considering buying six new warships.* 海军正在考虑购买六艘新战舰。 ➲ COLLOCATIONS AT WAR ➲ SEE ALSO NAVAL

WORDFINDER 联想词：admiral, aircraft carrier, base, captain, command, fleet, submarine, torpedo, warship

2 [U] = NAVY BLUE

ˈ**navy bean** (*NAmE*) (*BrE* **hari·cot**, ˌ**haricot** ˈ**bean**) *noun* a type of small white BEAN that is usually dried before it is sold and then left in water before cooking 菜豆；芸豆

N

ˌ**navy ˈblue** (*also* **navy**) *adj.* very dark blue in colour 海军蓝的；深蓝的： *a navy blue suit* 一套海军蓝的套装 ▸ ˌ**navy ˈblue** (*also* **navy**) *noun* [U]: *She was dressed in navy blue.* 她穿着深蓝色的衣服。 ➲ MORE LIKE THIS 15, page R26

naw /nɔː/ *exclamation* (*informal*) no, used when answering a question （用于回答）不，不是，没有： *'Want some toast?' 'Naw.'* "要吃烤面包片吗？" "不要。"

nawab /nəˈwɑːb/ *noun* **1** an Indian ruler during the Mogul empire 纳瓦布（莫卧儿帝国时代的省级地方行政长官） **2** (*IndE*) a Muslim with high social status or rank 纳瓦布；社会地位（或等级）较高的穆斯林

Naxa·lite /ˈnæksəlaɪt/ *noun* (in India) a member of a group which believes in political revolution in order to change the system of how land is owned. It took its name from Naxalbari in West Bengal, where it started. 纳萨尔派分子（印度主张通过政治革命改变土地所有制的组织成员，因发起于西孟加拉邦的纳萨尔巴里地区而得名）

nay /neɪ/ *adv.* **1** (*old-fashioned*) used to emphasize sth you have just said by introducing a stronger word or phrase （强调刚提及之事）不仅如此，而且： *Such a policy is difficult, nay impossible.* 这一政策很难实施，甚至是不可能的。 **2** (*old use or dialect*) no 不 ➲ COMPARE YEA

Nazi /ˈnɑːtsi/ *noun* **1** a member of the National Socialist party which controlled Germany from 1933 to 1945 纳粹党人，纳粹分子（1933 至 1945 年间统治德国的国家社会主义工人党成员） **2** (*disapproving*) a person who uses their power in a cruel way; a person with extreme and unreasonable views about race 凶残的人；极端种族主义分子 ▸ **Nazi** *adj.* **Naz·ism** /ˈnɑːtsɪzəm/ *noun* [U]

N

NB (*also* **N.B.**) /ˌen ˈbiː/ *abbr.* used in writing to make sb take notice of a particular piece of information that is important (from Latin 'nota bene') 注意，留心（用于书面提示重要事项，源自拉丁语 nota bene）： *NB The office will be closed from 1 July.* 注意：办事处将从 7 月 1 日起关闭。

NBA /ˌen biː ˈeɪ/ *abbr.* National Basketball Association (the US organization responsible for professional BASKETBALL) （美国）全国篮球协会

NBC /ˌen biː ˈsiː/ *abbr.* National Broadcasting Company (a US company that produces television and radio programmes) （美国）全国广播公司： *NBC News* 全国广播公司新闻节目

NCO /ˌen siː ˈəʊ; *NAmE* ˈoʊ/ *noun* non-commissioned officer (a soldier who has a rank such as CORPORAL or SERGEANT) 军士

NCT /ˌen siː ˈtiː/ *noun* **1** (in Britain) the abbreviation for 'National Curriculum Test' (a test taken by children at the ages of 7 and 11, also called SAT) （英国）国家课程考试（全写为 National Curriculum Test，学生在 7 岁和 11 岁时参加，又称 SAT） **2** (in Ireland) the abbreviation for 'National Car Test' (a test that all cars over 4 years old must have to check whether they are safe to drive) （爱尔兰）国家汽车检测（全写为 National Car Test，行驶超过 4 年的汽车必须接受的安全性能检测）

ndugu /nˈdʊɡʊ/ *noun* (*EAfrE*) (*usually* **Ndugu**) (in Tanzania) a title for a man or woman that shows respect （坦桑尼亚敬称）大哥，大姐

NE *abbr.* north-east; north-eastern 东北方（的）；东北部（的）： *NE England* 英格兰东北部

Ne·an·der·thal /niˈændətɑːl; *NAmE* -dərt-/ (*also* **neanderthal**) *adj.* **1** used to describe a type of human being who used stone tools and lived in Europe during the early period of human history （石器时代生活于欧洲的）尼安德特人的 **2** (*disapproving*) very old-fashioned and not wanting any change 守旧的；僵化过时的： *neanderthal attitudes* 守旧的态度 **3** (*disapproving*) (of a man 男子) unpleasant, rude and not behaving in a socially acceptable way 粗鲁无礼的；野蛮的 ▸ **Ne·an·der·thal** *noun*

neap tide /ˈniːp taɪd/ (*also* **neap**) *noun* a TIDE in the sea in which there is only a very small difference between the level of the water at HIGH TIDE and that at LOW TIDE （海水的）小潮

near 🔑 /nɪə(r); *NAmE* nɪr/ *adj., adv., prep., verb*

■ *adj.* (**near·er**, **near·est**) HELP In senses 1 to 4 **near** and **nearer** do not usually go before a noun; **nearest** can go either before or after a noun. 第 1 至第 4 义中，near 和 nearer 通常不用于名词前；nearest 可用于名词之前或之后。 **1** 🔑 a short distance away 距离近；不远 SYN **close**²: *His house is very near.* 他的房子就在附近。 ◇ *Where's the nearest bank?* 最近的银行在哪儿？ ➲ NOTE AT NEXT **2** 🔑 a short time away in the future 不久以后： *The conflict is unlikely to be resolved* **in the near future** (= very soon). 冲突短期内不大可能解决。 **3** 🔑 coming next after sb/sth 随后；接近： *She has a 12-point lead over her nearest rival.* 她领先紧随其后的对手 12 分。 **4** 🔑 (*usually* **nearest**) similar; most similar 近似；相似；不分伯仲： *He was* **the nearest thing to** (= the person most like) *a father she had ever had.* 她接触过的人中，他最像个父亲。 ➲ SEE ALSO O.N.O. **5** 🔑 [only before noun] (no comparative or superlative 无比较级或最高级) close to being sb/sth 接近的；差不多的： *The election proved to be a near disaster for the party.* 这次选举对该党来说几乎是一场灾难。 ◇ *a near impossibility* 几乎不可能的事 **6** 🔑 ~ **relative/relation** used to describe a close family connection （亲属关系）近亲： *Only the nearest relatives were present at the funeral.* 只有几位近亲参加了葬礼。 ▸ **near·ness** *noun* [U]: *the nearness of death* 死亡的临近

IDM **your ˌnearest and ˈdearest** (*informal*) your close family and friends 至亲；至爱；最亲密的亲友 **a ˌnear ˈthing** a situation in which you are successful, but which could also have ended badly 侥幸做成的事： *Phew! That was a near thing! It could have been a disaster.* 哎呀！好险哪！差一点儿出事。 ◇ *We won in the end but it was a near thing.* 我们最后赢了，但是险胜。 **to the nearest...** followed by a number when counting or measuring approximately 近似于；约等于： *We calculated the cost to the nearest 50 dollars.* 我们计算费用时尽量凑成 50 美元的倍数。

▼ **WHICH WORD? 词语辨析**

near / close

- The adjectives **near** and **close** are often the same in meaning, but in some phrases only one of them may be used. 形容词 near 和 close 通常含义相同，但在某些短语中只能用其中一个： *the near future* 不久的将来 ◇ *a near neighbour* 近邻 ◇ *a near miss* 差点儿命中 ◇ *a close contest* 势均力敌的竞赛 ◇ *a close encounter* 近距离接触 ◇ *a close call* 侥幸脱险 **Close** is more often used to describe a relationship between people. * close 更常用于描述人与人之间的关系： *a close friend* 密友 ◇ *close family* 关系亲密的家庭 ◇ *close links* 紧密的联系 You do not usually use **near** in this way. * near 通常不这样用。

■ *adv.* (**near·er**, **near·est**) **1** 🔑 at a short distance away 距离不远；在附近： *A bomb exploded somewhere near.* 一颗炸弹在附近爆炸。 ◇ *She took a step nearer.* 她走近一步。 ◇ *Visitors came from* **near and far**. 游客来自四面八方。 **2** 🔑 a short time away in the future 不久以后： *The exams are* **drawing near**. 考试越来越近了。 **3** (especially in compounds 尤用于构成复合词) almost 几乎；差不多： *a near-perfect performance* 近乎完美的表演 ◇ *I'm as near certain as can be.* 我几乎完全可以确定。

IDM **as near as** as accurately as 准确到…的程度；大约： *There were about 3 000 people there, as near as I could judge.* 据我判断，大约有 3 000 人在那里。 **as ˌnear as ˈdamn it/ˈdammit** (*BrE, informal*) used to say that an amount is so nearly correct that the difference does not matter （数量）相差无几，没什么分别： *It will cost £350, or as near as dammit.* 这要花 350 英镑上下。 **near eˈnough** (*BrE, informal*) used to say that sth is so nearly true that the difference does not matter 确实；差不多： *We've been here twenty years, near enough.* 我们在这里待

了差不多二十年了。 **not anywhere near/nowhere near** far from; not at all 远非；绝不是： *The job doesn't pay anywhere near enough for me.* 这份工作付给我的报酬远远不够。 **so ˌnear and ˌyet so ˈfar** used to comment on sth that was almost successful but in fact failed 功败垂成；功亏一篑 ➲ MORE AT PRETTY *adv.*

■ ***prep.*** (*also* **near to, near·er (to), near·est (to)**) HELP **Near to** is not usually used before the name of a place, person, festival, etc. * near to 通常不用于地点、人物、节日等名称前。 **1** ⚷ at a short distance away from sb/sth 在…附近；靠近： *Do you live near here?* 你住在这附近吗？ ◇ *Go and sit nearer (to) the fire.* 坐得靠炉子近点儿。 ➲ NOTE AT NEXT **2** ⚷ a short period of time from sth 接近；临近： *My birthday is very near Christmas.* 我的生日离圣诞节很近。 ◇ *I'll think about it* ***nearer (to) the time*** (= when it is just going to happen). 到时候我会考虑的。 **3** ⚷ used before a number to mean 'approximately', 'just below or above' （用于数词前）大约，上下，接近： *Share prices are near their record high of last year.* 股票价格接近去年的最高纪录。 ◇ *Profits fell from $11 million to nearer $8 million.* 利润从 1 100 万美元下跌到大约 800 万美元。 **4** ⚷ similar to sb/sth in quality, size, etc. （质量、大小等）相仿，接近： *Nobody else comes near her in intellect.* 谁也赶不上她聪明。 ◇ *He's nearer 70 than 60.* 他 60 多岁，快 70 岁了。 ◇ *This colour is nearest (to) the original.* 这种颜色最接近原色。 **5** ⚷ **~ (doing) sth** close to a particular state 接近于（某种状态）；濒临；快要： *a state near (to) death* 濒死状态 ◇ *She was* ***near to tears*** (= almost crying). 她就要哭了。 ◇ ***We came near to*** *being killed.* 我们差点丢了性命。

IDM SEE HAND *n.*, HEART, MARK *n.*

■ ***verb*** [T, I] **~ (sth)** (*rather formal*) to come close to sth in time or space （时间或空间上）接近，靠近，临近 SYN **approach**： *The project is* ***nearing completion.*** 这项工程就要竣工了。 ◇ *She was* ***nearing the end*** *of her life.* 她已经临近生命的尽头。 ◇ *We neared the top of the hill.* 我们快到山顶了。 ◇ *As Christmas neared, the children became more and more excited.* 快过圣诞节了，孩子们越来越兴奋。

near·by ⚷ /ˌnɪəˈbaɪ; *NAmE* ˌnɪrˈbaɪ/ *adj., adv.*

■ ***adj.*** ⚷ [usually before noun] near in position; not far away 附近的；邻近的： *Her mother lived in a nearby town.* 她母亲住在附近一个小镇上。 ◇ *There were complaints from nearby residents.* 附近的居民有些怨言。

■ ***adv.*** ⚷ a short distance from sb/sth; not far away 在附近；不远： *They live nearby.* 他们住在附近。 ◇ *The car is parked nearby.* 车就停在附近。

ˌnear-ˌdeath exˈperience *noun* an occasion when you almost die, which is often remembered as leaving your body or going down a tunnel 濒死经历（常留下灵魂出窍或穿过隧道的记忆）

the ˌNear ˈEast *noun* [sing.] = MIDDLE EAST

near·ly ⚷ /ˈnɪəli; *NAmE* ˈnɪrli/ *adv.* almost; not quite; not completely 几乎；差不多；将近： *The bottle's nearly empty.* 这瓶子差不多空了。 ◇ *I've worked here for nearly two years.* 我已经在这里工作了将近两年。 ◇ *It's nearly time to leave.* 差不多该走了。 ◇ *The audience was nearly all men.* 观众几乎全都是男的。 ◇ *He's nearly as tall as you are.* 他差不多和你一样高了。 ◇ *They're nearly always late.* 他们几乎总是迟到。 ◇ *She very nearly died.* 她差点儿死了。 ➲ NOTE AT ALMOST

IDM **not ˈnearly** ⚷ much less than; not at all 远非；绝不是： *It's not nearly as hot as last year.* 天气绝没有去年那么热。 ◇ *There isn't nearly enough time to get there now.* 现在根本没有足够的时间赶到那儿。 ➲ MORE AT PRETTY *adv.*

ˌnear ˈmiss *noun* **1** a situation when a serious accident or a disaster very nearly happens 侥幸脱险 **2** a bomb or a shot that nearly hits what it is aimed at but misses it （炸弹或射击）近距脱靶： (*figurative*) *He should have won the match—it was a near miss.* 这场比赛本该是他赢的，真是功亏一篑。 ➲ SEE ALSO A NEAR THING at NEAR *adj.*

near·side /ˈnɪəsaɪd; *NAmE* ˈnɪrs-/ *adj.* [only before noun] (*BrE*) (for a driver) on the side that is nearest the edge of the road （对于驾驶员）靠近人行道的： *the car's nearside doors* 左边的车门 ◇ *Keep to the nearside lane.* 不要偏离左边的车道。 ▸ **the near·side** *noun* [sing.]: *The driver lost control and veered to the nearside.* 驾驶员失去控制，车猛地转向左侧。 OPP **offside**

near·sight·ed /ˌnɪəˈsaɪtɪd; *NAmE* ˌnɪr-/ *adj.* (*especially NAmE*) = SHORT-SIGHTED OPP **far-sighted** ▸ **near·sight·ed·ness** *noun* [U]

neat ⚷ /niːt/ *adj.* (**neat·er, neat·est**) **1** ⚷ tidy and in order; carefully done or arranged 整洁的；整齐的；有序的： *a neat desk* 整洁的课桌 ◇ *neat handwriting* 工整的笔迹 ◇ *neat rows of books* 一排排整齐的书 ◇ *She was wearing a neat black suit.* 她穿着整洁的黑色套装。 ◇ *They sat in her* ***neat and tidy*** *kitchen.* 他们坐在她那干净整齐的厨房里。 **2** ⚷ (of people 人) liking to keep things tidy and in order; looking tidy or doing things in a tidy way 有条理的；爱整洁的： *Try and be neater!* 干净利落点！ **3** small, with a pleasing shape or appearance 小巧优雅的 SYN **trim**： *her neat figure* 她那娇小玲珑的身材 **4** simple but clever 简洁的；睿智的；灵巧的： *a neat explanation* 简明的解释 ◇ *a neat solution to the problem* 解决这个问题的捷径 **5** (*NAmE, informal*) good; excellent 好的；极好的： *It's a really neat movie.* 这真是一部极好的电影。 ◇ *We had a great time—it was pretty neat.* 我们玩得很痛快，棒极了。 **6** (*BrE*) (*NAmE* **straight**) (especially of alcoholic drinks 尤指酒) not mixed with water or anything else 未掺水的；纯的： *neat whisky* 纯威士忌酒 ▸ **neat·ly** ⚷ *adv.*： *neatly folded clothes* 折叠整齐的衣服 ◇ *The box fitted neatly into the drawer.* 这盒子放在抽屉里正合适。 ◇ *She summarized her plan very neatly.* 她非常简明地总结了她的计划。 **neat·ness** *noun* [U]

neat·en /ˈniːtn/ *verb* **~ sth** to make sth tidy 使整洁

neb·bish /ˈnebɪʃ/ *noun* (*NAmE, informal*) a man who behaves in an anxious and nervous way and without confidence 怯懦的男人；胆小鬼

neb·ula /ˈnebjələ/ *noun* (*pl.* **nebu·lae** /-liː/) (*astronomy* 天) a mass of dust or gas that can be seen in the night sky, often appearing very bright; a bright area in the night sky caused by a large cloud of stars that are far away 星云；外观似星云的星系

nebu·lous /ˈnebjələs/ *adj.* (*formal*) not clear 模糊的；不清楚的 SYN **vague**： *a nebulous concept* 模糊的概念

ne·ces·sar·ies /ˈnesəsəriz; *NAmE* ˈnesəseriz/ *noun* [pl.] (*old-fashioned*) the things that you need, especially in order to live 必需品；（尤指）生活必需品

ne·ces·sar·ily ⚷ /ˌnesəˈserəli; *BrE also* ˈnesəsərəli/ *adv.* used to say that sth cannot be avoided 必然地；不可避免地： *The number of places available is necessarily limited.* 录取名额不可避免地很有限。

IDM **ˌnot necesˈsarily** ⚷ used to say that sth is possibly true but not definitely or always true 不一定；未必： *The more expensive articles are not necessarily better.* 较贵的东西不见得就较好。 ◇ *Biggest doesn't necessarily mean best.* 最大的不一定是最好的。 ◇ *'We're going to lose.' 'Not necessarily.'* "我们会输的。" "未必。"

ne·ces·sary ⚷ /ˈnesəsəri; *NAmE* -seri/ *adj.* **1** ⚷ **~ (for sb/sth) (to do sth)** that is needed for a purpose or a reason 必需的；必要的 SYN **essential**： *It may be necessary to buy a new one.* 也许有必要买个新的了。 ◇ *It doesn't seem necessary for us to meet.* 我们似乎没必要见面。 ◇ *Only use your car when absolutely necessary.* 非用不可的时候才用你的汽车。 ◇ ***If necessary,*** *you can contact me at home.* 必要的话，我在家时你也可以和我联系。 ◇ *I'll make the necessary arrangements.* 我会做一些必要的安排。 **2** ⚷ [only before noun] that must exist or happen and cannot be avoided 必然的；无法避免的 SYN **inevitable**： *This is a necessary consequence of progress.* 这是事情发展的必然后果。

IDM **a ˌnecessary ˈevil** a thing that is bad or that you do not like but which you must accept for a particular reason 无法避免的坏事；不得已的事

ne·ces·si·tate /nəˈsesɪteɪt/ *verb* (*formal*) to make sth necessary 使成为必要： **~ sth** *Recent financial scandals*

N

have necessitated changes in parliamentary procedures. 最近的金融丑闻使得议会程序必须改革。◇ **~ doing sth** *Increased traffic necessitated widening the road.* 交通量增大，这就需要拓宽道路。◇ **~ sb/sth doing sth** *His new job necessitated him/his getting up at six.* 新工作使他不得不六点钟起床。

ne·ces·sity /nəˈsesəti/ *noun* **1** [U] the fact that sth must happen or be done; the need for sth 必然；必要；需要：**~ (for sth)** *We recognize the necessity for a written agreement.* 我们认为有必要签订一份书面协议。◇ **~ (of sth/of doing sth)** *We were discussing the necessity of employing more staff.* 我们在讨论是否需要雇用更多员工。◇ **~ (for sb) to do sth** *There had never been any necessity for her to go out to work.* 她从来就没有出去工作的必要。◇ *This is, of* ***necessity****, a brief and incomplete account.* 这必然是一个简略的、不完全的描述。 **2** [C] a thing that you must have and cannot manage without 必需的事物；必需品：*Many people cannot even afford* ***basic necessities*** *such as food and clothing.* 许多人甚至买不起食物和衣服之类的基本必需品。◇ *Air-conditioning is an absolute necessity in this climate.* 这样的气候绝对需要有空调。 **3** [C, usually sing.] a situation that must happen and that cannot be avoided 必然性；不可避免的情况：*Living in London, he felt, was an unfortunate necessity.* 他觉得在伦敦生活是迫于无奈。

IDM **neˌcessity is the ˌmother of inˈvention** (*saying*) a difficult new problem forces people to think of a solution to it 需求是发明之母 ➲ MORE AT VIRTUE

N

neck 颈；衣领

neck of a bottle 瓶颈

neck of a violin 小提琴琴颈

neck /nek/ *noun, verb*

■ ***noun*** **1** [C] the part of the body between the head and the shoulders 颈；脖子：*He tied a scarf around his neck.* 他脖子上围着围巾。◇ *Giraffes have very long necks.* 长颈鹿脖子很长。◇ *She* ***craned*** (= stretched) ***her neck*** *to get a better view.* 她伸长了脖子，想看得清楚一点。◇ *He broke his neck in the fall.* 他摔断了脖子。◇ *Somebody's going to* ***break their neck*** (= injure themselves) *on these steps.* 会有人在这台阶上摔伤的。 ➲ COLLOCATIONS AT PHYSICAL ➲ VISUAL VOCAB PAGE V64 **2** [C] the part of a piece of clothing that fits around the neck 衣领；领子；领圈：*What neck size do you take?* 你的领围是多少？ ➲ SEE ALSO CREW NECK, POLO NECK, TURTLENECK, V-NECK ➲ VISUAL VOCAB PAGE V68 **3 -necked** (in adjectives 构成形容词) having the type of neck mentioned 有…衣领的；有…脖子的：*a round-necked sweater* 一件圆领毛衣 ➲ SEE ALSO OPEN-NECKED, STIFF-NECKED ➲ MORE LIKE THIS 8, page R25 **4** [C] **~ (of sth)** a long narrow part of sth （物体的）细长部分，颈部：*the neck of a bottle* 瓶颈 ◇ *a neck of land* 陆地的狭窄地带 **5** [U] **~ (of sth)** the neck of an animal, cooked and eaten （烹制食用的）动物颈肉：*neck of lamb* 小羊颈肉 ➲ SEE ALSO BOTTLENECK, REDNECK, ROUGHNECK

IDM **be up to your neck in sth** to have a lot of sth to deal with 深陷于；忙于应付：*We're up to our neck in debt.* 我们债务累累。◇ *He's in it* (= trouble) *up to his neck.* 他遇上了麻烦，难以解脱。 **by a ˈneck** if a person or an animal wins a race **by a neck**, they win it by a short distance 以微弱优势（获胜） **ˌget it in the ˈneck** (*BrE, informal*) to be shouted at or punished because of sth that you have done 受到严厉责骂；受重罚 **ˌneck and ˈneck (with sb/sth)** (*also* **ˌnip and ˈtuck (with sb)** *especially in US*) level with sb in a race or competition （比赛中）势均力敌，不分上下，平手 **ˌneck of the ˈwoods** (*informal*) a particular place or area 某地方；某地区：*He's from your neck of the woods* (= the area where you live). 他是你那一带的人。 ➲ MORE AT BLOCK *n.*, BRASS, BREATHE, MILLSTONE, PAIN *n.*, RISK *v.*, SAVE *v.*, SCRUFF, STICK *v.*, WRING

■ ***verb*** (*usually* **be necking**) [I] (*old-fashioned, informal*) when two people **are necking**, they are kissing each other in a sexual way 搂着脖子亲吻；相拥互吻

neck·er·chief /ˈnekətʃiːf; *NAmE* -kər-/ *noun* a square of cloth that you wear around your neck 围巾；领巾

neck·lace /ˈnekləs/ *noun, verb*

■ ***noun*** a piece of jewellery consisting of a chain, string of BEADS, etc. worn around the neck 项链：*a diamond necklace* 一条钻石项链 ➲ VISUAL VOCAB PAGE V70

■ ***verb*** **~ sb** to kill sb by putting a burning car tyre around their neck 给（某人）戴火项链（将燃烧的轮胎挂在脖子上将其烧死） ▸ **neck·lacing** *noun* [U]

neck·line /ˈneklaɪn/ *noun* the edge of a piece of clothing, especially a woman's, which fits around or below the neck （尤指女装的）领口，开领：*a dress with a low/round/plunging neckline* 低领 / 圆领 / 深 V 字领的连衣裙

neck·tie /ˈnektaɪ/ *noun* (*old-fashioned* or *NAmE*) = TIE (1)

necro·man·cer /ˈnekrəʊmænsə(r); *NAmE* ˈnekroʊ-/ *noun* a person who claims to communicate by magic with people who are dead 通灵者；巫师

necro·mancy /ˈnekrəʊmænsi; *NAmE* ˈnekroʊ-/ *noun* [U] **1** the practice of claiming to communicate by magic with the dead in order to learn about the future 通灵术；巫术 **2** the use of magic powers, especially evil ones 妖术；巫术

necro·philia /ˌnekrəˈfɪliə/ *noun* [U] sexual interest in dead bodies 恋尸癖 ▸ **necro·phil·iac** *noun*

ne·crop·olis /nəˈkrɒpəlɪs; *NAmE* -ˈkrɑːp-/ *noun* (*pl.* **ne·crop·olises** /-lɪsɪz/) a CEMETERY (= place where dead people are buried), especially a large one in an ancient city 墓场；（尤指古代城市的）大墓地

nec·ropsy /ˈnekrɒpsi; *NAmE* ˈnekrɑːpsi/ *noun* (*pl.* **-ies**) (*NAmE*) an official examination of a dead body (especially that of an animal) in order to discover the cause of death （尤指对动物的）尸体剖验，尸检 SYN **autopsy**

ne·cro·sis /neˈkrəʊsɪs; *NAmE* -ˈkroʊ-/ *noun* [U] (*medical* 医) the death of most or all of the cells in an organ or TISSUE caused by injury, disease, or a loss of blood supply （器官或组织细胞的）坏死

nec·tar /ˈnektə(r)/ *noun* [U] **1** a sweet liquid that is produced by flowers and collected by BEES for making HONEY 花蜜：(*figurative*) *On such a hot day, even water was nectar* (= very good). 这么热的天，清水都是甘露。 **2** the thick juice of some fruits as a drink 果汁（饮料）：*peach nectar* 桃汁

nec·tar·ine /ˈnektəriːn/ *noun* a round red and yellow fruit, like a PEACH with smooth skin 油桃（桃的变种，果皮光滑）

née /neɪ/ *adj.* (*from French*) a word used after a married woman's name to introduce the family name that she had when she was born （用于已婚妇女姓名后，其娘家姓前）原姓的，娘家姓的：*Jane Smith, née Brown* 简·史密斯，原姓布朗

need /niːd/ *verb, modal verb, noun*

■ ***verb*** **1** to require sth/sb because they are essential or very important, not just because you would like to have them 需要；必需：**~ sth/sb** *Do you need any help?* 你需要帮忙吗？◇ *It's here if you need it.* 你需要的话就拿去吧。◇ *Don't go—I might need you.* 别走，我可能要你帮忙。◇ *They **badly needed** a change.* 他们迫切需要变革。◇ *Food aid is urgently needed.* 迫切需要食物援助。◇ *What do you need your own computer for? You can use ours.* 你干吗还要自己买电脑？你可以用我们的。◇ *I don't need your comments, thank you.* 谢谢，我不需要你来评头论足。◇ **~ to do sth** *I need to get some sleep.* 我需要睡会儿觉。◇ *He needs to win this game to stay in the match.* 他得赢下这场比赛以免被淘汰出局。◇ *You don't need to leave yet, do you?* 你不必现在就走吧？◇ *This shirt needs to be washed.* 这件衬衣该洗了。◇ **~ doing sth** *This shirt needs washing.* 这件衬衣该洗了。**2** **~ to do sth** used to show what you should or have to do （表示应该或不得不做）有必要：*All you need to do is complete this form.* 你要做的就是填好这个表格。◇ *I didn't need to go to the bank after all—Mary lent me the money.* 我最终还是不必去银行了，玛丽借我钱了。

IDM **need (to have) your 'head examined** (*informal*) to be crazy 发疯

■ ***modal verb*** (*negative* **need not**, *short form* **needn't** /ˈniːdnt/) used to state that sth is/was not necessary or that only very little is/was necessary; used to ask if sth is/was necessary （表示没有必要或询问是否有必要）需要：**~ (not) do sth** *You needn't bother asking Rick—I know he's too busy.* 你不必费神去问里克，我知道他太忙了。◇ *I **need hardly** tell you* (= you must already know) *that the work is dangerous.* 这工作很危险，这就不用我说了。◇ *If she wants anything, she **need only** ask.* 她想要什么东西，只要开一下口就行了。◇ ***All you need** bring are sheets.* 你需要带的就是床单。◇ **~ (not) have done sth** *You needn't have worried* (= it was not necessary for you to worry, but you did)—*it all turned out fine.* 你本不必担心，一切都很顺利。◇ ***Need you** have paid so much?* 你用得着花那么多钱吗？➲ NOTE AT MODAL

■ ***noun*** **1** [sing., U] a situation when sth is necessary or must be done 需要；必须：*to **satisfy/meet/identify a need*** 满足/迎合/看出某种需要 ◇ **~ (for sth)** *There is an urgent need for qualified teachers.* 迫切需要合格教师。◇ *We will contact you again if the need arises.* 如果有必要，我们会再次和你联系。◇ *The house is **in need of** a thorough clean.* 这房子需要来个大扫除。◇ **~ (for sb/sth) to do sth** *There is **no need** for you to get up early tomorrow.* 你明天不必早起。◇ *I **had no need to** open the letter—I knew what it would say.* 我没必要拆开那封信，我知道里面会说些什么。◇ *There's no need to cry* (= stop crying). 不要哭了。**2** [C, U] a strong feeling that you want sb/sth or must have sth 特别需要；迫切要求：*to fulfil an emotional need* 满足感情的迫切需要 ◇ *She felt the need to talk to someone.* 她特别想和人聊聊。◇ *I'm **in need of** some fresh air.* 我很想呼吸一点新鲜空气。◇ *She **had no** more **need of** me.* 她再也不需要我了。**3** [C, usually pl.] the things that sb requires in order to live in a comfortable way or achieve what they want 需要的事物；欲望：*financial needs* 经济上的需要 ◇ *a programme to **suit** your individual **needs*** 满足个人需要的计划 ◇ *to **meet** children's special educational **needs*** 满足儿童的特殊教育需求 **4** [U] the state of not having enough food, money or support （食物、钱或生活来源的）短缺，缺乏 SYN **hardship**：*The charity aims to provide assistance to people **in need**.* 这个慈善机构的宗旨是向贫困者提供帮助。◇ *He helped me in my **hour of need**.* 在我生活困难的时候他帮助了我。➲ SEE ALSO NEEDY

IDM **if need 'be** if necessary 如果需要的话；有必要的话：*There's always food in the freezer if need be.* 如果需要，冰箱里总有食物。➲ MORE AT CRYING *adj.*, FRIEND

> ▼ **GRAMMAR POINT** 语法说明
>
> **need**
>
> - There are two separate verbs **need**. 有两个各不相同的动词 need。
> - **Need** as a main verb has the question form **do you need?**, the negative **you don't need** and the past forms **needed, did you need?** and **didn't need**. It has two meanings. * need 作主要动词时，疑问式为 do you need?，否定式为 you don't need，过去时为 needed、did you need? 和 didn't need。其含义有二：1. to require something or to think that something is necessary 需要或认为有必要：*Do you need any help?* 你需要帮助吗？◇ *I needed to get some sleep.* 我需要睡一会儿。2. to have to or to be obliged to do sth 必须或一定要：*Will we need to show our passports?* 我们要出示护照吗？
> - **Need** as a modal verb has **need** for all forms of the present tense, **need you?** as the question form and **need not (needn't)** as the negative. The past is **need have, needn't have**. It is used to say that something is or is not necessary. * need 作情态动词时，现在时均作 need，疑问式为 need you?，否定式为 need not (needn't)，过去时为 need have、needn't have，用以表示某事有必要或没有必要：*Need I pay the whole amount now?* 我必须现在全部付清吗？

'need-blind *adj.* (*US*) (of a university's or college's policy of choosing which people to offer places on a course of study 大学招生政策) depending only on sb's academic ability, without considering their ability to pay for it 不考虑经济能力的（仅依据学生能力）：*a need-blind admissions policy* 不考虑经济能力的录取政策

need·ful /ˈniːdfl/ *adj.* (*old-fashioned*) necessary 必要的；必需的；必然的

nee·dle /ˈniːdl/ *noun, verb*

■ ***noun*** [C]

- **FOR SEWING** 缝纫 **1** a small thin piece of steel that you use for sewing, with a point at one end and a hole for the thread at the other 针；缝衣针：*a **needle and thread*** 针线 ◇ *the eye* (= hole) *of a needle* 针眼 ➲ VISUAL VOCAB PAGE V45 ➲ SEE ALSO PINS AND NEEDLES
- **FOR KNITTING** 编织 **2** a long thin piece of plastic or metal with a point at one end that you use for knitting. You usually use two together. 编织针：*knitting needles* 编织针 ➲ VISUAL VOCAB PAGE V45
- **FOR DRUGS** 药品 **3** a very thin, pointed piece of steel used on the end of a SYRINGE for putting a drug into sb's body, or for taking blood out of it 注射针；针头：*a hypodermic needle* 皮下注射器针头
- **ON INSTRUMENT** 仪器 **4** a thin piece of metal on a scientific instrument that moves to point to the correct measurement or direction 指针：*The compass needle was pointing north.* 罗盘指针指向北方。
- **ON PINE TREE** 松树 **5** [usually pl.] the thin, hard, pointed leaf of a PINE tree 针叶；松针 ➲ VISUAL VOCAB PAGE V10
- **ON RECORD PLAYER** 唱机 **6** the very small pointed piece of metal that touches a record that is being played in order to produce the sound 唱针；磁针 SYN **stylus**

IDM **a needle in a 'haystack** a thing that is almost impossible to find 草垛里的针；几乎不可能找到的东西：*Searching for one man in this city is like looking for a needle in a haystack.* 在这个城市里找一个人无异于大海捞针。

■ ***verb*** **~ sb** (*informal*) to deliberately annoy sb, especially by criticizing them continuously 刺激；故意招惹；（尤指）不断地数落 SYN **antagonize**：*Don't let her needle you.* 别让她数落你。

needle·cord /ˈniːdlkɔːd; *NAmE* -kɔːrd/ *noun* [U] (*BrE*) a type of fine CORDUROY 细条灯芯绒；细条绒

needle·point /ˈniːdlpɔɪnt/ *noun* [U] a type of decorative sewing in which you use very small STITCHES to make a picture on strong cloth 针绣；帆布刺绣

need·less /ˈniːdləs/ *adj.* **needless** death or suffering is not necessary because it could have been avoided 不必要的；可以避免的 SYN **unnecessary**：*needless suffering* 不

N

必要的痛苦 ◇ *Banning smoking would save needless deaths.* 禁止吸烟会避免不必要的死亡。 ▶ **need·less·ly** *adv.*: *Many soldiers died needlessly.* 许多战士白白地牺牲了。 ◇ *The process was needlessly slow.* 进程本无需这么慢。

IDM ˌ**needless to ˈsay** used to emphasize that the information you are giving is obvious 不必说；不用说： *The problem, needless to say, is the cost involved.* 不用说，问题是所涉及的费用。

needle·woman /ˈniːdlwʊmən/ *noun* (*pl.* **-women** /-wɪmɪn/) a woman who sews well 缝纫女工；女裁缝；擅做针线活的女子

needle·work /ˈniːdlwɜːk; *NAmE* -wɜːrk/ *noun* [U] things that are sewn by hand, especially for decoration; the activity of making things by sewing 缝制品；刺绣品；女红；针线活

needn't /ˈniːdnt/ *short form* need not 不用；不必

needs /niːdz/ *adv.* (*old use*) in a way that cannot be avoided 必定；必须： *We must needs depart.* 我们必须离开。

IDM **needs ˈmust (when the Devil drives)** (*saying*) in certain situations it is necessary for you to do sth that you do not like or enjoy（情势所迫）只好如此；不得已而为之

need-to-ˈknow *adj.*

IDM **on a ˌneed-to-ˈknow basis** with people being told only the things they need to know when they need to know them, and no more than that 仅限于人们需要知道的范围： *Information will be released strictly on a need-to-know basis.* 资讯发布将严格限制在人们需要知道的范围之内。

needy /ˈniːdi/ *adj.* (**need·ier**, **needi·est**) **1** (of people 人) not having enough money, food, clothes, etc. 缺乏生活必需品的；贫困的 ➲ SYNONYMS AT POOR **2 the needy** *noun* [pl.] people who do not have enough money, food, etc. 穷困的人 **3** (of people 人) not confident, and needing a lot of love and emotional support from other people 缺乏自信的；需要精神支持的

neep /niːp/ *noun* (*ScotE, informal*) a SWEDE (= a large round yellow root vegetable) 芜菁甘蓝；大头菜： *neeps and tatties* 芜菁甘蓝泥和土豆泥

ne'er /neə(r); *NAmE* ner/ *adv.* (*literary*) = NEVER

ˈ**ne'er-do-well** *noun* (*old-fashioned*) a useless or lazy person 无用的人；懒汉

NEET /niːt/ *noun* (*BrE*) the abbreviation for 'not in education, employment or training' (a young person who is no longer in the education system and who is not working or being trained for work) 尼特族，待业青年（全写为 not in education, employment or training，指不上学、没工作、不在接受职业培训的年轻人）

ne·fari·ous /nɪˈfeəriəs; *NAmE* -ˈfer-/ *adj.* (*formal*) criminal; immoral 罪恶的；不道德的： *nefarious activities* 罪恶活动

neg. *abbr.* NEGATIVE 结果为阴性（或否定）的

neg·ate AW /nɪˈɡeɪt/ *verb* (*formal*) **1 ~ sth** to stop sth from having any effect 取消；使无效 SYN **nullify**: *Alcohol negates the effects of the drug.* 酒精能使这种药物失效。 **2 ~ sth** to state that sth does not exist 否定；否认

neg·ation /nɪˈɡeɪʃn/ *noun* (*formal*) **1** [C, usually sing., U] the exact opposite of sth; the act of causing sth not to exist or to become its opposite 反面；对立面；否定： *This political system was the negation of democracy.* 这种政治制度是对民主的否定。 **2** [U] disagreement or refusal 否定；拒绝： *She shook her head in negation.* 她摇头表示拒绝。

nega·tive 🔑 AW /ˈneɡətɪv/ *adj., noun, verb*

■ *adj.*

• **BAD** 坏 **1** 🔑 bad or harmful 坏的；有害的： *The crisis had **a negative effect on** trade.* 这次危机对贸易产生了很坏的影响。 ◇ *The whole experience was definitely more positive than negative.* 整个经历当然是利多于弊。 OPP **positive**

• **NOT HOPEFUL** 不乐观 **2** 🔑 considering only the bad side of sth/sb; lacking enthusiasm or hope 消极的；负面的；缺乏热情的： *Scientists have a fairly **negative attitude** to the theory.* 科学家对这个理论的态度是相当消极的。 ◇ *'He probably won't show up.' 'Don't be so negative.'* "他很可能不会露面。" "别那么悲观嘛。" OPP **positive**

• **NO** 不 **3** 🔑 expressing the answer 'no' 否定的： *His response was negative.* 他的回答是否定的。 ◇ *They received a negative reply.* 他们得到一个否定的答复。 OPP **affirmative**

• **GRAMMAR** 语法 **4** 🔑 containing a word such as 'no', 'not', 'never', etc. 含有否定词的；否定的： *a **negative form/sentence*** 否定形式/句

• **SCIENTIFIC TEST** 化验 **5** 🔑 (*abbr.* **neg.**) not showing any evidence of a particular substance or medical condition 结果为阴性的（或否定的）： *Her pregnancy test was negative.* 她的孕检呈阴性。 OPP **positive**

• **ELECTRICITY** 电 **6** (*specialist*) containing or producing the type of electricity that is carried by an ELECTRON 负极的；阴极的： *a **negative charge/current*** 负电荷；负电流 ◇ *the negative terminal of a battery* 电池的负极柱 OPP **positive**

• **NUMBER/QUANTITY** 数量 **7** less than zero 负的；小于零的： *a negative trade balance* 贸易逆差 OPP **positive**

▶ **nega·tive·ly** AW *adv.*: *to react negatively to stress* 对压力反应消极 ◇ *to respond negatively* 作出否定的回应 ◇ *negatively charged electrons* 带负电荷的电子

■ *noun*

• **NO** 不 **1** a word or statement that means 'no'; a refusal or DENIAL 否定词；否定；拒绝 (*formal*)： *She answered in the negative* (= said 'no'). 她作了否定的回答。 OPP **affirmative**

• **IN PHOTOGRAPHY** 摄影 **2** a developed film showing the dark areas of an actual scene as light and the light areas as dark 负片；底片 ➲ COMPARE POSITIVE *n.* (2)

• **IN SCIENTIFIC TEST** 化验 **3** the result of a test or an experiment that shows that a substance or condition is not present 属阴性（或否定）的结果： *The percentage of **false negatives** generated by the cancer test is of great concern.* 癌症检查的结果中，假阴性占一定比例的现象受到极大关注。 OPP **positive**

■ *verb* (*formal*) **1 ~ sth** to refuse to agree to a proposal or a request 拒绝；否定 **2 ~ sth** to prove that sth is not true 否定…的真实性；证伪

ˌ**negative ˈequity** *noun* [U] the situation in which the value of sb's house is less than the amount of money that is still owed to a MORTGAGE company, such as a bank 资产负值，负资产（资产值低于抵押款）

nega·tiv·ity /ˌneɡəˈtɪvəti/ (*also* **nega·tiv·ism** /ˈneɡətɪvɪzəm/) *noun* [U] (*formal*) a tendency to consider only the bad side of sth/sb; a lack of enthusiasm or hope 否定性；消极性

neg·lect /nɪˈɡlekt/ *verb, noun*

■ *verb* **1 ~ sb/sth** to fail to take care of sb/sth 疏于照顾；未予看管： *She denies neglecting her baby.* 她不承认没有照看好她的孩子。 ◇ *The buildings had been neglected for years.* 这些大楼多年来一直无人看管。 **2 ~ sth** to not give enough attention to sth 忽略；忽视；不予重视： *Dance has been neglected by television.* 电视节目一向不重视舞蹈。 ◇ *She has neglected her studies.* 她忽视了她的学习。 **3 ~ to do sth** (*formal*) to fail or forget to do sth that you ought to do 疏忽；疏漏 SYN **omit**: *You neglected to mention the name of your previous employer.* 你遗漏了你前雇主的名字。 ➲ SEE ALSO NEGLIGENCE ➲ MORE LIKE THIS 26, page R28

■ *noun* [U] **~ (of sth/sb)** the fact of not giving enough care or attention to sth/sb; the state of not receiving enough care or attention 忽略；忽视；未被重视： *The law imposes penalties for the neglect of children.* 法律对疏于照管儿童有处罚措施。 ◇ *The buildings are crumbling from **years of neglect**.* 由于多年无人维修，这些建筑物行将倒塌。 ◇ *The place smelled of decay and neglect.* 这地方有一股污浊腐朽的气味。

neg·lect·ed /nɪˈɡlektɪd/ *adj.* not receiving enough care or attention 被忽略的；被忽视的；未被重视的： *neglected* *children* 无人照看的孩子 ◇ *a neglected area of research* 被人忽略了的研究领域

neg·lect·ful /nɪˈglektfl/ *adj.* (*formal*) not giving enough care or attention to sb/sth 马虎的；不重视的；忽视的：*neglectful parents* 漫不经心的父母 ◇ **~ of sth/sb** *She became neglectful of her appearance.* 她变得不修边幅起来。

neg·ligee (*also* **neg·ligée**) /ˈneglɪʒeɪ; *NAmE* ˌneglɪˈʒeɪ/ *noun* a woman's DRESSING GOWN made of very thin cloth （质地轻薄的）女式晨衣

neg·li·gence /ˈneglɪdʒəns/ *noun* [U] (*law* 律 or *formal*) the failure to give sb/sth enough care or attention 疏忽；失职；失误；过失：*The accident was caused by negligence on the part of the driver.* 事故是由于司机的过失造成的。◇ *The doctor was sued for medical negligence.* 这名医生因玩忽职守被起诉。

neg·li·gent /ˈneglɪdʒənt/ *adj.* **1** (*law* 律 or *formal*) failing to give sb/sth enough care or attention, especially when this has serious results 疏忽的；造成过失的：*The school had been negligent in not informing the child's parents about the incident.* 校方疏忽了，没有向这孩子的父母通报这件事。◇ *grossly negligent* 严重失职 **2** (*literary*) (of a person or their manner 人或行为方式、态度) relaxed; not formal or awkward 放松的；随便的；不拘谨的 SYN **nonchalant**: *He waved his hand in a negligent gesture.* 他漫不经心地挥了挥手。▶ **neg·li·gent·ly** *adv.*: *The defendant drove negligently and hit a lamp post.* 被告不小心驾驶，撞到一根路灯柱上了。◇ *She was leaning negligently against the wall.* 她很随便地靠着墙。

neg·li·gible /ˈneglɪdʒəbl/ *adj.* of very little importance or size and not worth considering 微不足道的；不重要的；不值一提的 SYN **insignificant**: *The cost was negligible.* 费用不大，无关紧要。◇ *a negligible amount* 很小的量

ne·go·ti·able /nɪˈgəʊʃiəbl; *NAmE* -ˈgoʊ-/ *adj.* **1** that you can discuss or change before you make an agreement or a decision 可协商的；可讨论的：*The terms of employment are negotiable.* 雇用的条件可以协商。◇ *The price was not negotiable.* 价格没有商量的余地。**2** (*business* 商) that you can exchange for money or give to another person in exchange for money 流通的；可兑现的；可转让的 OPP **non-negotiable**

ne·go·ti·ate /nɪˈgəʊʃieɪt; *NAmE* -ˈgoʊ-/ *verb* **1** [I] **~ (with sb) (for/about sth)** to try to reach an agreement by formal discussion 谈判；磋商；协商：*The government will not negotiate with terrorists.* 政府不会和恐怖分子谈判。◇ *We have been negotiating for more pay.* 我们一直在为增加工资进行协商。◇ *a strong negotiating position* 强硬的谈判立场 ◇ *negotiating skills* 谈判技巧 ➲ WORDFINDER NOTE AT PEACE **2** [T] **~ sth** to arrange or agree sth by formal discussion 商定，达成（协议）：*to **negotiate a deal/contract/treaty/settlement*** 达成交易；确立合同；商定条约内容 / 解决措施 ◇ *We successfully negotiated the release of the hostages.* 我们成功地达成了释放人质的协议。**3** [T] **~ sth** (*formal*) to successfully get over or past a difficult part on a path or route 通过，越过（险要路段）：*The climbers had to negotiate a steep rock face.* 攀登者必须攀越陡峭的岩壁。

the neˈgotiating table *noun* [sing.] (used mainly in newspapers 主要用于报章) a formal discussion to try and reach an agreement 谈判桌（指正式的谈判会议）：*We want to get all the parties back to the negotiating table.* 我们想把有关各方拉回到谈判桌上来。

ne·go·ti·ation /nɪˌgəʊʃiˈeɪʃn; *NAmE* -ˌgoʊʃi-/ *noun* [C, usually pl., U] formal discussion between people who are trying to reach an agreement 谈判；磋商；协商：***peace/trade/wage, etc. negotiations*** 和谈、贸易洽谈、工资谈判等 ◇ *They begin another **round of negotiations** today.* 他们今天开始另一轮的谈判。◇ ***to enter into/open/conduct negotiations with sb*** 和某人开始 / 展开 / 进行谈判 ◇ *The rent is a **matter for negotiation** between the landlord and the tenant.* 租金可以由房东和租户协商确定。◇ *A contract is prepared **in negotiation with** our clients.* 我们和客户协商起草了一份合同。◇ *The issue is still **under negotiation**.* 这个问题还在商讨之中。◇ *The price is generally **open to negotiation**.* 一般来讲，价格可以商量。➲ WORDFINDER NOTE AT DEAL ➲ COLLOCATIONS AT INTERNATIONAL

ne·go·ti·ator /nɪˈgəʊʃieɪtə(r); *NAmE* -ˈgoʊʃi-/ *noun* a person who is involved in formal political or financial discussions, especially because it is their job 谈判代表；协商者

Ne·gress /ˈniːgres/ *noun* (*old-fashioned, often offensive*) a Negro woman or girl 黑人女子

neg·ri·tude /ˈnegrɪtjuːd; *NAmE* -tuːd; *also* ˈniː-/ *noun* [U] (*formal*) the quality or fact of being of black African origin 非裔黑人特征；非裔黑人血统

Negro /ˈniːgrəʊ; *NAmE* -groʊ/ *noun* (*pl.* **-oes**) (*old-fashioned, often offensive*) a member of a race of people with dark skin who originally came from Africa 黑人

ˌNegro ˈspiritual *noun* = SPIRITUAL

neigh /neɪ/ *verb* [I] when a horse **neighs** it makes a long high sound （马）嘶鸣 ▶ **neigh** *noun* ➲ MORE LIKE THIS 4, page R25

neigh·bour (*especially US* **neigh·bor**) /ˈneɪbə(r)/ *noun, verb*

■ ***noun*** **1** a person who lives next to you or near you 邻居；邻人：*We've had a lot of support from all our **friends and neighbours**.* 我们得到了朋友和邻里的很多照顾。◇ *Our **next-door neighbours** are very noisy.* 我们隔壁的邻居非常吵。➲ WORDFINDER NOTE AT FRIEND **2** a country that is next to or near another country 邻国：*What is Britain's nearest neighbour?* 英国最近的邻国是哪个国家？ **3** a person or thing that is standing or located next to another person or thing 身边的人；靠近的东西；邻近的人（或物）：*Stand quietly, children, and try not to talk to your neighbour.* 孩子们，站好，保持安静，不要交头接耳。◇ *The tree fell slowly, its branches caught in those of its neighbours.* 这棵树慢慢地倒下，枝杈和旁边的树交错在一起了。 **4** (*literary*) any other human 他人；世人：*We should all love our neighbours.* 我们都要爱邻人。

■ ***verb*** [T] **~ sth** to be situated next to or near to 与…相邻；邻近：*The farm neighbours the holiday village.* 农场邻近度假村。

neigh·bour·hood (*especially US* **neigh·bor·hood**) /ˈneɪbəhʊd; *NAmE* ˈneɪbər-/ *noun* **1** a district or an area of a town; the people who live there 街区；城区；（统称）某街区（或城区）的居民：*We grew up in the same neighbourhood.* 我们小时候同在一个街区。◇ *a poor/quiet/residential neighbourhood* 贫困的街区；安静的城区；居民区 ◇ *Manhattan is divided into distinct neighborhoods.* 曼哈顿分为几个区，风格各异。◇ *the neighbourhood police* 社区警察 ◇ *He shouted so loudly that the whole neighbourhood could hear him.* 他叫得那么大声，整条街的人都能听到。**2** the area that you are in or the area near a particular place 所在地；邻近的地方 SYN **vicinity**: *We searched the surrounding neighbourhood for the missing boy.* 我们在附近寻找失踪的男孩儿。◇ *Houses **in the neighbourhood of** Paris are extremely expensive.* 巴黎附近一带的住房极其昂贵。➲ WORDFINDER NOTE AT LOCATION

IDM **in the neighbourhood of** (of a number or an amount 数量) approximately; not exactly 大约；上下：*It cost in the neighbourhood of $500.* 这大约花费了 500 美元。

ˌneighbourhood ˈwatch (*especially US* **ˌneighborhood ˈwatch**) *noun* [U] an arrangement by which a group of people in an area watch each other's houses regularly as a way of preventing crime 邻里守望（邻居定期相互照看住宅，防止犯罪）

neigh·bour·ing (*especially US* **neigh·bor·ing**) /ˈneɪbərɪŋ/ *adj.* [only before noun] located or living near or next to a place or person 邻近的；附近的；毗邻的：*a neighbouring house* 附近的房子 ◇ *neighbouring towns* 毗邻的城镇 ◇ *a neighbouring farmer* 邻近的农场主

N

neigh·bour·ly (*especially US* **neigh·bor·ly**) /ˈneɪbəli; *NAmE* -bərli/ *adj.* **1** involving people, countries, etc. that live or are located near each other 邻近的；接壤的；住在附近的：*the importance of good neighbourly relations between the two states* 这两国间睦邻友好关系的重要性 ◇ *neighbourly help* 邻里间的帮助 ◇ *a neighbourly dispute* 邻居间的纷争 **2** friendly and helpful 热心肠的；乐于助人的 SYN **kind**: *It was a neighbourly gesture of theirs.* 这是他们友好的表示。▶ **neigh·bour·li·ness** (*especially US* **neighbor·li·ness**) *noun* [U]: *good neighbourliness* 睦邻关系 ◇ *a sense of community and neighbourliness* 社区互助意识

nei·ther /ˈnaɪðə(r); ˈniːðə(r)/ *det., pron., adv.*

■ ***det., pron.*** not one nor the other of two things or people 两者都不：*Neither answer is correct.* 两个答案都不对。◇ ***Neither of them*** *has/have a car.* 他们两个都没有汽车。◇ *They produced two reports,* ***neither of which*** *contained any useful suggestions.* 他们提交了两个报告，都没有任何有用的建议。◇ *'Which do you like?' 'Neither. I think they're both ugly.'* "你喜欢哪一个？" "两个都不喜欢。我觉得两个都很难看。"

■ ***adv.*** **1** used to show that a negative statement is also true of sb/sth else（否定的陈述同样适用于其他人或物）也不：*He didn't remember and* ***neither did I.*** 他没记住，我也忘了。◇ *I hadn't been to New York before and* ***neither had Jane.*** 我以前没有去过纽约，简也没去过。◇ *'I can't understand a word of it.'* ***'Neither can I.'*** "我一个字都弄不懂。" "我也是。" ◇ (*informal*) *'I don't know.'* ***'Me neither.'*** "我不知道。" "我也不知道。" **2** **neither… nor…** used to show that a negative statement is true of two things（否定的陈述适用于两方面）既不…也不…：*I neither knew nor cared what had happened to him.* 我既不知道也不关心他出了什么事。◇ *Their house is neither big nor small.* 他们的房子不大也不小。◇ *Neither the TV nor the DVD player actually work/works.* 电视机和数字影碟机都坏了。

▼ **GRAMMAR POINT 语法说明**

neither / either

- After **neither** and **either** you use a singular verb. * neither 和 either 后用单数动词：*Neither candidate was selected for the job.* 申请这个工作的两个候选人都未获选。
- **Neither of** and **either of** are followed by a plural noun or pronoun and a singular or plural verb. A plural verb is more informal. * neither of 和 either of 后接复数名词或代词加单数或复数动词，用复数动词较非正式：*Neither of my parents speaks/speak a foreign language.* 我的父母都不会说外语。
- When **neither… nor…** or **either… or…** are used with two singular nouns, the verb can be singular or plural. A plural verb is more informal. * neither ... nor ... 或 either ... or ... 与两个单数名词连用时，谓语动词可用单数或复数；用复数动词较非正式。

nel·son /ˈnelsn/ *noun* a move in which a WRESTLER stands behind his/her opponent, puts one or both arms underneath the opponent's arm(s) and holds the back of the opponent's neck. When done with one arm it is called a **half nelson**, and with both arms a **full nelson**. 肩下握颈（从背后通过对手腋下钩住其后颈的摔跤动作，分单臂握颈和双臂握颈）

nema·tode /ˈnemətəʊd; *NAmE* -toʊd/ (*also* ˌ**nematode ˈworm**) *noun* a WORM with a thin, tube-shaped body that is not divided into sections 线虫（身体不分节）

nem·esis /ˈneməsɪs/ *noun* (*pl.* **nem·eses** /ˈneməsiːz/) (*formal*) **1** [C] the person or thing that causes somebody to lose their power, position, etc. and that cannot be avoided 给以报应的人（或事物）；报复者；天谴：*Has she finally met her nemesis?* 她最终遭报应了吗？ **2** [C] a person or thing that has competed with somebody or been an enemy for a long time 宿敌；宿仇：*He strode out to face his old nemesis.* 他大步向前去面对他的老对手。 **3** [U, sing.] punishment or defeat that is deserved and cannot be avoided 报应；应得的惩罚；不可避免的失败

neo- /ˈniːəʊ; *NAmE* ˈniːoʊ/ *combining form* (in adjectives and nouns 构成形容词和名词) new; in a later form 新的；新式的：*neo-Georgian* 新乔治王朝时期风格的 ◇ *neo-fascist* 新法西斯主义者

neo·clas·sic·al /ˌniːəʊˈklæsɪkl; *NAmE* ˌniːoʊ-/ *adj.* [usually before noun] used to describe art and ARCHITECTURE that is based on the style of ancient Greece or Rome, or music, literature, etc. that uses traditional ideas or styles 新古典主义的

neo·co·lo·nial·ism /ˌniːəʊkəˈləʊniəlɪzəm; *NAmE* ˌniːoʊkəˈloʊ-/ *noun* [U] (*disapproving*) the use of economic or political pressure by powerful countries to control or influence other countries 新殖民主义（强国通过施加经济或政治压力来控制或影响其他国家）

neo·con·ser·va·tive /ˌniːəʊkənˈsɜːvətɪv; *NAmE* ˌniːoʊkənˈsɜːrvətɪv/ *adj.* (*politics* 政) relating to political, economic, religious, etc. beliefs that return to traditional conservative views in a slightly changed form 新保守主义者的，新保守派的（在政治、经济、宗教等信仰方面转向传统保守主义但形式稍有区别）▶ **neo·con·ser·va·tive** (*also* **neo·con** /ˈniːəʊkɒn; *NAmE* ˈniːoʊkɑːn/) *noun*

neo·cor·tex /ˌniːəʊˈkɔːteks; *NAmE* ˌniːoʊˈkɔːrteks/ *noun* (*anatomy* 解) part of the brain that controls sight and hearing （大脑）新皮质

neo·dym·ium /ˌniːəʊˈdɪmiəm; *NAmE* ˌniːoʊ-/ *noun* [U] (*symb.* **Nd**) a chemical element. Neodymium is a silver-white metal. 钕

neo·liberal /ˌniːəʊˈlɪbərəl; *NAmE* ˌniːoʊ-/ *adj.* [usually before noun] (*politics* 政) relating to a type of LIBERALISM that believes in a global free market, without government regulation, with businesses and industry controlled and run for profit by private owners 新自由主义的（主张不受政府调控的全球自由市场，工商企业由私有者经营以获利）

Neo·lith·ic /ˌniːəˈlɪθɪk/ *adj.* of the later part of the STONE AGE 新石器时代的：*Neolithic stone axes* 新石器时代的石斧 ◇ *Neolithic settlements* 新石器时代的聚落

neolo·gism /niˈɒlədʒɪzəm; *NAmE* -ˈɑːl-/ *noun* (*formal*) a new word or expression or a new meaning of a word 新词；新语汇；新义

neon /ˈniːɒn; *NAmE* ˈniːɑːn/ *noun* [U] (*symb.* **Ne**) a chemical element. Neon is a gas that does not react with anything and that shines with a bright light when electricity is passed through it. 氖；氖气：***neon lights/signs*** 霓虹灯；霓虹灯标牌

neo·natal /ˌniːəʊˈneɪtl; *NAmE* ˌniːoʊ-/ *adj.* (*specialist*) connected with a child that has just been born 新生儿的：*the hospital's neonatal unit* 医院的新生儿科 ◇ *neonatal care* 新生儿的护理

neo·nate /ˈniːəʊneɪt; *NAmE* ˈniːoʊ-/ *noun* (*medical* 医) a baby that has recently been born, especially within the last four weeks （尤指出生不足四周的）新生儿

neo·phyte /ˈniːəfaɪt/ *noun* (*formal*) **1** a person who has recently started an activity 初学者；新手；生手：*The site gives neophytes the chance to learn from experts.* 这个网站给新手提供了向专家学习的机会。 **2** a person who has recently changed to a new religion 刚接受新宗教信仰的人；新皈依者 **3** a person who has recently become a priest or recently entered a religious order 新受圣职的司铎；修会初学生

neo·prene /ˈniːəpriːn/ *noun* [U] an artificial material which looks like rubber, used for making WETSUITS 氯丁橡胶（用于制作潜水衣等的合成橡胶）

NEPAD /ˈniːpæd/ *abbr.* (*SAfrE*) New Partnership for Africa's Development (= a plan decided by governments in Africa to help the continent's economy) 非洲发展新伙伴计划（非洲各国政府制订的促进非洲大陆经济发展的计划）

N

nephew /ˈnefjuː; ˈnevjuː/ *noun* the son of your brother or sister; the son of your husband's or wife's brother or sister 侄子；外甥 ➲ COMPARE NIECE

ne plus ultra /ˌneɪ plʊs ˈʊltrɑː; *NAmE* ˈʊltrə/ *noun* (*from Latin, formal*) the perfect example of sth 完美的范例；典范；典型

nepo·tism /ˈnepətɪzəm/ *noun* [U] (*disapproving*) giving unfair advantages to your own family if you are in a position of power, especially by giving them jobs 裙带关系；任人唯亲

Nep·tune /ˈneptjuːn; *NAmE also* -tuːn/ *noun* a planet in the SOLAR SYSTEM that is 8th in order of distance from the sun 海王星

nep·tun·ium /nepˈtjuːniəm; *NAmE also* -ˈtuːn-/ *noun* [U] (*symb.* **Np**) a chemical element. Neptunium is a RADIO-ACTIVE metal. 镎（放射性化学元素）

nerd /nɜːd; *NAmE* nɜːrd/ *noun* (*informal, disapproving*) **1** a person who is boring, stupid and not fashionable 呆笨无趣的人；呆子；土包子 **2** a person who is very interested in computers 电脑迷 SYN **geek** ▶ **nerdy** *adj.*

nerve /nɜːv; *NAmE* nɜːrv/ *noun, verb*

■ *noun* **1** [C] any of the long threads that carry messages between the brain and parts of the body, enabling you to move, feel pain, etc. 神经：*the optic nerve* 视神经 ◇ *nerve cells* 神经细胞 ◇ *nerve endings* 神经末梢 ◇ *Every nerve in her body was tense.* 她的每一根神经都绷得紧紧的。 ➲ VISUAL VOCAB PAGE V64 **2** **nerves** [pl.] feelings of worry or anxiety 神经质；神经紧张：*Even after years as a singer, he still suffers from nerves before a performance.* 尽管已做歌手多年，他在演出前仍然神经紧张。 ◇ *I need something to* ***calm/steady my nerves.*** 我需要点东西来稳定一下我的情绪。 ◇ *Everyone's* ***nerves were on edge*** (= everyone felt TENSE). 人人都觉得紧张。 ◇ *He* ***lives on his nerves*** (= is always worried). 他总是神经紧张。 **3** [U] the courage to do sth difficult or dangerous 勇气；气魄 SYN **guts**：*It took a lot of nerve to take the company to court.* 将这个公司告上法庭需要极大的勇气。 ◇ *I was going to have a go at parachuting but* ***lost my nerve*** *at the last minute.* 我想尝试一下跳伞，可在最后关头却失去了勇气。 ◇ *He* ***kept his nerve*** *to win the final set 6–4.* 他鼓足斗志以 6 比 4 赢了最后一盘。 **4** [sing., U] (*informal*) a way of behaving that other people think is rude or not appropriate 鲁莽；冒失；厚颜 SYN **cheek**：*I don't know how you* ***have the nerve*** *to show your face after what you said!* 真不知道你说了那些话以后怎么还有脸露面！ ◇ *He's* ***got a nerve*** *asking us for money!* 他还觍着脸跟我们借钱！ ◇ *'Then she demanded to see the manager!' '****What a nerve!****'* "她还要求见经理！" "真不要脸！"

IDM **be a bag/bundle of ˈnerves** (*informal*) to be very nervous 非常紧张 **get on sb's ˈnerves** (*informal*) to annoy sb 烦扰；使心神不定 **have nerves of steel** to be able to remain calm in a difficult or dangerous situation 意志坚强；沉着冷静 **hit/touch a (raw/sensitive) ˈnerve** to mention a subject that makes sb feel angry, upset, embarrassed, etc. 触及要害；触动痛处：*You touched a raw nerve when you mentioned his first wife.* 你谈起他的第一任妻子，这就触到了他的痛处。 ➲ MORE AT BRASS, STRAIN *v.*, WAR

■ *verb* **~ yourself for sth/to do sth** to give yourself the courage or strength to do sth 鼓足勇气；振作精神：*He nerved himself to ask her out.* 他鼓足勇气去约她出来。

ˈnerve centre (*BrE*) (*especially US* **ˈnerve center**) *noun* the place from which an activity or organization is controlled and instructions are sent out 神经中枢；控制中心

ˈnerve gas *noun* a poisonous gas used in war that attacks your CENTRAL NERVOUS SYSTEM 神经性毒气，神经瓦斯（能损害神经系统正常功能）

nerve·less /ˈnɜːvləs; *NAmE* ˈnɜːrv-/ *adj.* **1** having no strength or feeling 无力的；麻木的：*The knife fell from her nerveless fingers.* 刀从她无力的手指间落下。 **2** having no fear 无畏的；镇定从容的；勇敢的：*She is a nerveless rider.* 她是一位勇敢的骑手。 OPP **nervous**

ˈnerve-racking (*also* **ˈnerve-wracking**) *adj.* making you feel very nervous and worried 令人十分紧张的；令人焦虑不安的

ner·vous /ˈnɜːvəs; *NAmE* ˈnɜːrvəs/ *adj.* **1** anxious about sth or afraid of sth 焦虑的；担忧的；惶恐的：**~ (about/of sth)** *Consumers are very nervous about the future.* 消费者对未来非常忧虑。 ◇ *The horse may be nervous of cars.* 这匹马可能害怕汽车。 ◇ **~ (about/of doing sth)** *He had been nervous about inviting us.* 他过去一直不敢邀请我们。 ◇ *I felt really nervous before the interview.* 面试前我感到惶恐不安。 ◇ *a* ***nervous glance/smile/voice*** (= one that shows that you feel anxious) 胆怯的一瞥/微笑/声音 ◇ *By the time the police arrived, I was a* ***nervous wreck.*** 警察到达时，我已经紧张得不行了。 OPP **confident** ➲ SYNONYMS AT WORRIED **2** easily worried or frightened 神经质的；易紧张焦虑的；胆怯的：*She was a thin, nervous girl.* 她是个瘦削而又胆怯的女孩儿。 ◇ *He's not the nervous type.* 他不是那种好紧张的人。 ◇ *She was* ***of a nervous disposition.*** 她生性容易紧张。 **3** connected with the body's nerves and often affecting you mentally or emotionally 神经系统的：*a* ***nervous condition/disorder/disease*** 神经系统疾病；神经紊乱；神经症 ◇ *She was in a state of* ***nervous exhaustion.*** 她的神经处于极度疲劳状态。 IDM SEE SHADOW *n.* ▶ **ner·vous·ly** *adv.*：*She smiled nervously.* 她露出不安的微笑。 **ner·vous·ness** *noun* [U]：*He tried to hide his nervousness.* 他试图掩饰他的惶恐不安。

SYNONYMS 同义词辨析

nervous

neurotic • on edge • jittery

These words all describe people who are easily frightened or are behaving in a frightened way. 以上各词均形容人神经质、易紧张焦虑、胆怯。

nervous easily worried or frightened 指神经质的、易紧张焦虑的、胆怯的：*She was* ***of a nervous disposition.*** 她生性容易紧张。 NOTE See also the entry for **worried**. 另见 worried 词条。

neurotic not behaving in a reasonable, calm way, because you are worried about sth 指神经质的、神经过敏的：*She became neurotic about keeping the house clean.* 她变得对保持房屋清洁有点神经质。

on edge nervous or bad-tempered 指紧张不安的、烦躁的、易怒的：*She was always on edge before an interview.* 她在面试前总是紧张不安。

jittery (*informal*) anxious and nervous 指紧张不安的、心神不宁的：*All this talk of job losses was making him jittery.* 所有这些关于失业的话题使他心神不宁。

PATTERNS

- a nervous/neurotic **man/woman/girl**
- **to feel** nervous/on edge/jittery
- **a bit** nervous/on edge/jittery

ˌnervous ˈbreakdown (*also* **break·down**) *noun* a period of mental illness in which sb becomes very depressed, anxious and tired, and cannot deal with normal life 精神崩溃：*to have a nervous breakdown* 精神崩溃

ˈnervous system *noun* the system of all the nerves in the body 神经系统 ➲ SEE ALSO CENTRAL NERVOUS SYSTEM

nervy /ˈnɜːvi; *NAmE* ˈnɜːrvi/ *adj.* (*informal*) **1** (*BrE*) anxious and nervous 焦虑的；紧张的 **2** (*NAmE*) brave and confident in a way that might offend other people, or show a lack of respect 莽撞的；冒失的

N

-ness *suffix* (in nouns 构成名词) the quality, state or character of …的性质（或状态、特点）： *dryness* 干燥 ◇ *blindness* 失明 ◇ *silliness* 愚蠢 ➲ MORE LIKE THIS 7, page R25

nest /nest/ *noun, verb*

■ ***noun*** **1** [C] a hollow place or structure that a bird makes or chooses for laying its eggs in and sheltering its young 鸟巢；鸟窝 ➲ VISUAL VOCAB PAGE V12 **2** [C] a place where insects or other small creatures live and produce their young 巢穴；窝 **3** [sing.] a secret place which is full of bad people and their activities 藏匿处；秘密窝点： *a nest of thieves* 贼窝 **4** [sing.] the home, thought of as the safe place where parents bring up their children 家；安乐窝： *to* ***leave the nest*** (= leave your parents' home) 离开父母过独立生活 ➲ SEE ALSO EMPTY NEST **5** [C, usually sing.] a group or set of similar things that are made to fit inside each other（套叠在一起的）一套物件： *a nest of tables* 一套桌子 IDM SEE FEATHER *v.*, FLY *v.*, HORNET, MARE

■ ***verb*** **1** [I] to make and use a nest 筑巢；巢居： *Thousands of seabirds are nesting on the cliffs.* 成千上万的海鸟在悬崖上筑巢。 **2** [T] **~ sth** (*specialist*) to put types of information together, or inside each other, so that they form a single unit 嵌套（信息）

'nest box (*also* **'nesting box**) *noun* a box provided for a bird to make its nest in 鸟巢箱；鸟舍箱

'nest egg *noun* (*informal*) a sum of money that you save to use in the future 备用的钱；储备金

nes·tle /'nesl/ *verb* **1** [I] **+ adv./prep.** to sit or lie down in a warm or soft place 依偎；舒适地坐（或卧）： *He hugged her and she nestled against his chest.* 他拥抱着她，她则依偎在他的怀里。 **2** [T] **~ sb/sth + adv./prep.** to put or hold sb/sth in a comfortable position in a warm or soft place 抱；安置： *He nestled the baby in his arms.* 他怀里抱着孩子。 **3** [I] **+ adv./prep.** to be located in a position that is protected, sheltered or partly hidden 位处，坐落（于安全、隐蔽之处）： *The little town nestles snugly at the foot of the hill.* 这个小镇偎依在小山脚下。

nest·ling /'nestlɪŋ/ *noun* a bird that is too young to leave the nest 留巢雏

net /net/ *noun, adj., verb*

■ ***noun*** **1** [U] a type of material that is made of string, thread or wire twisted or tied together, with small spaces in between 网；网状物： *net curtains* 网眼窗帘 ➲ SEE ALSO FISHNET, NETTING **2** [C] (especially in compounds 尤用于构成复合词) a piece of net used for a particular purpose, such as catching fish or covering sth 有专门用途的网： *fishing nets* 渔网 ◇ *a mosquito net* (= used to protect you from MOSQUITOES) 蚊帐 ➲ WORDFINDER NOTE AT FISHING ➲ SEE ALSO HAIRNET, SAFETY NET **3 the net** [sing.] (in sports 体育运动) the frame covered in net that forms the goal 球门网： *to kick the ball* ***into the back of the net*** 把球踢进网窝 **4 the net** [sing.] (in TENNIS, etc. 网球等) the piece of net between the two players that the ball goes over 球网 ➲ VISUAL VOCAB PAGE V48 **5** **the Net** (*also* **the net**) (*informal*) = INTERNET IDM SEE CAST *v.*, SLIP *v.*, SPREAD *v.*

■ ***adj.*** (*BrE also* **nett**) **1** [usually before noun] a **net** amount of money is the amount that remains when nothing more is to be taken away 净得的；纯的： *a* ***net profit*** *of £500* * 500 英镑的纯利润 ◇ ***net income/earnings*** (= after tax has been paid) 纯收入 ➲ COMPARE GROSS *adj.* (1) **2** [only before noun] the **net** weight of sth is the weight without its container or the material it is wrapped in 净的： *450 gms net weight* 净重 450 克 ➲ COMPARE GROSS *adj.* (1) **3** [only before noun] final, after all the important facts have been included 最后的；最终的： *The* ***net result*** *is that small shopkeepers are being forced out of business.* 最终结果是小店主被迫停业。 ◇ *Canada is now a substantial net importer of medicines* (= it imports more than it exports). 加拿大现在是一个药物净进口大国。 ◇ *a net gain* 最终收益 ▶ **net** *adv.*： *a salary of $50 000 net* * 5 万美元的税后薪水 ◇ *Interest on the investment will be paid net* (= tax will already have been taken away). 投资的利息将按税后的数额支付。 ➲ COMPARE GROSS *adv.*

■ ***verb*** **(-tt-)** **1 ~ sth** to earn an amount of money as a profit after you have paid tax on it 净赚；净得： *The sale of paintings netted £17 000.* 卖画净得 17 000 英镑。 **2 ~ sth** to catch sth, especially fish, in a net （尤指）用网捕捉（鱼等） **3 ~ sb/sth** to catch sb or obtain sth in a skilful way （巧妙地）捕获，得到： *A swoop by customs officers netted a large quantity of drugs.* 海关人员突击搜查，缉获大量毒品。 **4 ~ sth** (*especially BrE*) to kick or hit a ball into the goal （将球）踢入球门，射入球门 SYN **score**： *He has netted 21 goals so far this season.* 这个赛季至今他已射入 21 球。 **5 ~ sth** to cover sth with a net or nets 用网覆盖

net·ball /'netbɔːl/ *noun* [U] a game played by two teams of seven players, especially women or girls. Players score by throwing a ball through a high net hanging from a ring on a post. （女子）无挡板篮球

net·book /'netbʊk/ *noun* a small LAPTOP computer, designed especially for using the Internet and email 上网本（尤用于上网和处理电子邮件的小型笔记本电脑） ➲ COMPARE NOTEBOOK (3)

,net 'curtain (*BrE*) (*NAmE* **cur·tain**) *noun* a very thin curtain that you hang at a window, which allows light to enter but stops people outside from being able to see inside 网眼窗帘

nether /'neðə(r)/ *adj.* [only before noun] (*literary or humorous*) lower 较低的；下方的： *a person's nether regions* (= their GENITALS) 人的下身

the neth·er·world /'neðəwɜːld; *NAmE* 'neðərwɜːrld/ *noun* [sing.] (*literary*) the world of the dead 阴间；冥府；地狱 SYN **hell**

neti·quette /'netɪket/ *noun* [U] (*informal, humorous*) the rules of correct or polite behaviour among people using the Internet 网络礼仪

neti·zen /'netɪzn/ *noun* (*informal, humorous*) a person who uses the Internet a lot 网民；网虫；网迷

'Net surfer *noun* = SURFER (2)

nett *adj.* (*BrE*) = NET

net·ting /'netɪŋ/ *noun* [U] material that is made of string, thread or wire twisted or tied together, with spaces in between 网；网状材料： *wire netting* 金属丝网

net·tle /'netl/ *noun, verb*

■ ***noun*** (*also* **'stinging nettle**) a wild plant with leaves that have pointed edges, are covered in fine hairs and sting if you touch them 荨麻 ➲ VISUAL VOCAB PAGE V11 IDM SEE GRASP *v.*

■ ***verb*** [usually passive] **~ sb | it nettles sb that…** (*informal, especially BrE*) to make sb slightly angry 使烦恼；使生气 SYN **annoy**： *My remarks clearly nettled her.* 我的话显然惹恼了她。

nettle·rash /'netlræʃ/ *noun* [U] = URTICARIA

net·tle·some /'netlsəm/ *adj.* (*especially NAmE*) causing trouble or difficulty 引起麻烦（或困难）的；棘手的；恼人的

net·work AW /'netwɜːk; *NAmE* -wɜːrk/ *noun, verb*

■ ***noun*** **1** a complicated system of roads, lines, tubes, nerves, etc. that cross each other and are connected to each other 网络；网状系统： *a* ***rail/road/canal network*** 铁路网；公路网；运河网 ◇ *a network of veins* 脉络 **2** a closely connected group of people, companies, etc. that exchange information, etc. 关系网；人际网；相互关系（或配合）的系统： *a* ***communications/distribution network*** 通信网；分销网 ◇ *a network of friends* 朋友网 **3** (*computing* 计) a number of computers and other devices that are connected together so that equipment and information can be shared （互联）网络： *The office network allows users to share files and software, and to use a central printer.* 办公室网络让用户共享文件和软件，并使用中央打印机。 ➲ SEE ALSO LAN, WAN **4** a group of radio or television stations in different places that are connected and that broadcast the same programmes at the same time 广播网；电视网：*the four big US television networks* 美国四大电视网 IDM SEE OLD BOY

■ ***verb*** **1** [T] **~ sth** (*computing* 计) to connect a number of computers and other devices together so that equipment and information can be shared 将…连接成网络 **2** [T] **~ sth** to broadcast a television or radio programme on stations in several different areas at the same time 联播 **3** [I] to try to meet and talk to people who may be useful to you in your work 建立工作关系：*Conferences are a good place to network.* 各种会议是建立联系的好地方。

net·work·ing /ˈnetwɜːkɪŋ; *NAmE* -wɜːrk-/ *noun* [U] a system of trying to meet and talk to other people who may be useful to you in your work 人际关系网

neur·al /ˈnjʊərəl; *NAmE* ˈnʊrəl/ *adj.* (*specialist*) connected with a nerve or the NERVOUS SYSTEM 神经的；神经系统的：*neural processes* 神经系统的作用

neur·al·gia /njʊəˈrældʒə; *NAmE* nʊˈr-/ *noun* [U] (*medical* 医) a sharp pain felt along a nerve, especially in the head or face（尤指头部或面部）神经痛 ▶ **neur·al·gic** /njʊəˈrældʒɪk; *NAmE* nʊˈr-/ *adj.*

ˌ**neural** ˈ**network** (*also* ˌ**neural** ˈ**net**) *noun* (*computing* 计) a system which is designed to work in a similar way to the human brain and nervous system 神经网络

neur·as·the·nia /ˌnjʊərəsˈθiːniə; *NAmE* ˌnʊrəs-/ *noun* [U] (*old-fashioned*) a condition in which sb feels tired and depressed over a long period of time 神经衰弱

neuro- /ˈnjʊərəʊ; *NAmE* ˈnʊroʊ/ *combining form* (in nouns, adjectives and adverbs 构成名词、形容词和副词) connected with the nerves 神经系统有关的：*neuroscience* 神经科学 ◇ *a neurosurgeon* 神经外科医生

neuro·lin·guis·tic pro·gram·ming /ˌnjʊərəʊlɪŋˌgwɪstɪk ˈprəʊgræmɪŋ; *NAmE* ˌnʊroʊlɪŋˌgwɪstɪk ˈproʊgræmɪŋ/ (*abbr.* **NLP**) *noun* [U] (*psychology* 心) a technique that people use to help themselves or others think in a more positive way, and which uses neurolinguistics as its basis 神经语言程序技术

neuro·lin·guis·tics /ˌnjʊərəʊlɪŋˈgwɪstɪks; *NAmE* ˌnʊroʊ-/ *noun* [U] (*psychology* 心) the study of the way the human brain processes language 神经语言学

neuro·logic·al /ˌnjʊərəˈlɒdʒɪkl; *NAmE* ˌnʊrəˈlɑːdʒ-/ *adj.* relating to nerves or to the science of NEUROLOGY 神经系统的；神经（病）学的：*neurological damage* 神经损伤

neurolo·gist /njʊəˈrɒlədʒɪst; *NAmE* nʊˈrɑːl-/ *noun* a doctor who studies and treats diseases of the nerves 神经病学家；神经科医生 ➲ WORDFINDER NOTE AT SPECIALIST

neurol·ogy /njʊəˈrɒlədʒi; *NAmE* nʊˈrɑːl-/ *noun* [U] the scientific study of nerves and their diseases 神经病学；神经学

neuron /ˈnjʊərɒn; *NAmE* ˈnʊrɑːn/ (*also* **neur·one** /ˈnjʊərəʊn; *NAmE* ˈnʊroʊn/ *especially in BrE*) *noun* (*biology* 生) a cell that carries information within the brain and between the brain and other parts of the body; a nerve cell 神经元 ➲ SEE ALSO MOTOR NEURONE DISEASE

neuro·physi·ology /ˌnjʊərəʊfɪziˈɒlədʒi; *NAmE* ˌnʊroʊfɪziˈɑːlədʒi/ *noun* [U] the scientific study of the normal functions of the NERVOUS SYSTEM 神经生理学

neuro·science /ˈnjʊərəʊsaɪəns; *NAmE* ˈnʊroʊ-/ *noun* [U] the science that deals with the structure and function of the brain and the NERVOUS SYSTEM 神经科学 ▶ **neuro·scientist** /-saɪəntɪst/ *noun*

neur·osis /njʊəˈrəʊsɪs; *NAmE* nʊˈroʊ-/ *noun* [C, U] (*pl.* **neur·oses** /-əʊsiːz; *NAmE* -oʊ-/) **1** (*medical* 医) a mental illness in which a person suffers strong feelings of fear and worry 神经症；神经官能症 **2** any strong fear or worry 过分的恐惧（或焦虑） SYN **anxiety**

neuro·sur·gery /ˈnjʊərəʊsɜːdʒəri; *NAmE* ˈnʊroʊsɜːrdʒəri/ *noun* [U] medical operations performed on the nervous system, especially the brain 神经外科（学）

neur·ot·ic /njʊəˈrɒtɪk; *NAmE* nʊˈrɑː-/ *adj., noun*

■ ***adj.*** **1** caused by or suffering from neurosis 神经症的；神经官能症的：*neurotic obsessions* 神经症引起的强迫观念 ➲ SYNONYMS AT MENTALLY **2** not behaving in a reasonable, calm way, because you are worried about sth 神经质的；神经过敏的：*She became neurotic about keeping the house clean.* 她变得对保持房屋清洁有点神经质。◇ *a brilliant but neurotic actor* 杰出但有些神经质的男演员 ➲ SYNONYMS AT NERVOUS ▶ **neur·ot·ic·al·ly** /-kli/ *adv.*

■ ***noun*** a neurotic person 神经症患者；神经质者

neuro·toxin /ˌnjʊərəʊˈtɒksɪn; *NAmE* ˌnʊroʊˈtɑːksɪn/ *noun* (*specialist*) a poison that affects the NERVOUS SYSTEM 神经毒素

neuro·trans·mit·ter /ˈnjʊərəʊtrænzmɪtə(r); *NAmE* ˈnʊroʊ-/ *noun* (*biology* 生) a chemical that carries messages from nerve cells to other nerve cells or muscles 神经递质（在神经细胞间或向肌肉传递信息）

neu·ter /ˈnjuːtə(r); *NAmE* ˈnuːtər/ *adj., verb*

■ ***adj.*** (*grammar* 语法) (in some languages 用于某些语言) belonging to a class of nouns, pronouns, adjectives or verbs whose GENDER is not FEMININE or MASCULINE 中性的：*The Polish word for 'window' is neuter.* 波兰语里"窗户"一词是中性的。

■ ***verb*** **1** **~ sth** to remove part of the sex organs of an animal so that it cannot produce young 阉割（动物）：*Has your cat been neutered?* 你家的猫阉过了吗？ **2** **~ sth** (*disapproving*) to prevent sth from having the effect that it ought to have 使失去作用

neu·tral AW /ˈnjuːtrəl; *NAmE* ˈnuː-/ *adj., noun*

■ ***adj.***

• **IN DISAGREEMENT/CONTEST** 分歧；争执 **1** not supporting or helping either side in a disagreement, competition, etc. 中立的；持平的；无倾向性的 SYN **impartial, unbiased**: *Journalists are supposed to be politically neutral.* 新闻工作者在政治上应持中立态度。◇ *I didn't take my father's or my mother's side; I tried to* ***remain neutral.*** 我既不支持父亲也不袒护母亲，尽力做到不偏不倚。

• **IN WAR** 战争 **2** not belonging to any of the countries that are involved in a war; not supporting any of the countries involved in a war 中立国的；中立的：***neutral territory/waters*** 中立国的领土 / 领海 ◇ *Switzerland was neutral during the war.* 瑞士在战争期间保持了中立。

• **WITHOUT STRONG FEELING/INFLUENCE** 无强烈的感情 / 影响 **3** deliberately not expressing any strong feeling 中性的；不含褒贬义的：*'So you told her?' he said in a neutral tone of voice.* "那么你告诉她了？"他平静地说。 **4** not affected by sth 不受影响的；没有倾向的：*He believes that technology is morally neutral until it is applied.* 他认为技术在投入应用以前是无关乎道德的。

• **COLOUR** 色彩 **5** not very bright or strong, such as grey or light brown 素净的；淡素的；不鲜艳的：*a neutral colour scheme* 中性色的色彩搭配 ◇ *neutral tones* 中性色调

• **CHEMISTRY** 化学 **6** neither acid nor ALKALINE 中性的；非酸性又非碱性的

• **ELECTRICAL** 与电有关 **7** (*abbr.* **N**) having neither a positive nor a negative electrical charge 中性的；不带电的：*the neutral wire in a plug* 插头里的零线

▶ **neu·tral·ly** /-rəli/ *adv.*

IDM **on neutral ground/territory** in a place that has no connection with either of the people or sides who are meeting and so does not give an advantage to either of them 在中立地区；在第三方地区：*We decided to meet on neutral ground.* 我们决定在第三方领土上会晤。

■ ***noun***

• **IN VEHICLE** 车辆 **1** [U] the position of the gears of a vehicle in which no power is carried from the engine to the wheels（汽车排挡）空挡：*to leave the car* ***in neutral*** 将车的排挡置于空挡位

• **IN DISAGREEMENT/WAR** 分歧；战争 **2** [C] a person or country that does not support either side in a disagreement, competition or war 中立者；中立国

N

• COLOUR 色彩 **3** [C] a colour that is not bright or strong, such as grey or light brown 中性色；无彩色；素净色：*The room was decorated in neutrals.* 房间用了中性色来装饰。

neu·tral·ist /ˈnjuːtrəlɪst; *NAmE* ˈnuː-/ *noun* (*especially NAmE*) a person who does not support either side in a war 中立主义者 ▶ **neu·tral·ist** *adj.*：*a neutralist state* 中立国家

neu·tral·ity AW /njuːˈtræləti; *NAmE* nuː-/ *noun* [U] the state of not supporting either side in a disagreement, competition or war 中立；中立状态

neu·tral·ize AW (*BrE also* **-ise**) /ˈnjuːtrəlaɪz; *NAmE* ˈnuː-/ *verb* **1** ~ **sth** to stop sth from having any effect 使无效：*The latest figures should neutralize the fears of inflation.* 最新的数据应该可以消除对通货膨胀的担忧。 **2** ~ **sth** (*chemistry* 化) to make a substance NEUTRAL (6) 中和；使成为中性 **3** ~ **sth** to make a country or an area NEUTRAL (2) 使中立 ▶ **neu·tral·iza·tion**, **-isa·tion** AW /ˌnjuːtrəlaɪˈzeɪʃn; *NAmE* ˌnuːtrələˈz-/ *noun* [U]

ˈ**neutral zone** *noun* **1** (in ICE HOCKEY 冰球) an area that covers the central part of the RINK, between two blue lines 中区 **2** (in AMERICAN FOOTBALL 美式足球) an imaginary area between the teams where no player except the CENTRE is allowed to step until play has started 中立区（比赛开始前对阵双方之间除中锋外的球员不准进入的区域）

neu·trino /njuːˈtriːnəʊ; *NAmE* nuːˈtriːnoʊ/ *noun* (*pl.* **-os**) (*physics* 物) an extremely small PARTICLE that has no electrical charge, and which rarely reacts with other matter 中微子

N

neu·tron /ˈnjuːtrɒn; *NAmE* ˈnuːtrɑːn/ *noun* (*physics* 物) a very small piece of matter (= a substance) that carries no electric charge and that forms part of the NUCLEUS (= central part) of an atom 中子 ➲ SEE ALSO ELECTRON, PROTON ➲ WORDFINDER NOTE AT ATOM

ˈ**neutron bomb** *noun* a bomb that can kill people by giving out neutrons, but does not cause a lot of damage to buildings 中子弹（可杀人，但对建筑物损坏不大）

never 🔑 /ˈnevə(r)/ *adv., exclamation*

■ *adv.* **1** 🔑 not at any time; not on any occasion 从不；绝不；从未；未曾：*You never help me.* 你从不帮我。◇ *He has never been abroad.* 他从未出过国。◇ *'Would you vote for him?' 'Never.'* "你会投他一票吗？""决不。"◇ *'I work for a company called Orion Technology.' 'Never heard of them.'* "我在一家名为奥里昂科技的公司工作。""从来没听说过。" ◇ ***Never in all my life*** *have I seen such a horrible thing.* 我一辈子也没见过这么恐怖的事。◇ ***Never ever*** *tell anyone your password.* 不要把你的密码告诉任何人。 **2** 🔑 used to emphasize a negative statement instead of 'not'（与 not 同义，语气较强）一点都不，从未：***I never knew*** (= didn't know until now) *you had a twin sister.* 我从来不知道你还有个双胞胎姐姐。◇ (*especially BrE*) *Someone might find out, and that* ***would never do*** (= that is not acceptable). 也许有人会发现，那是绝对不行的。◇ *He* ***never so much as*** *smiled* (= did not smile even once). 他从未笑过。◇ (*especially BrE*) *'I told my boss exactly what I thought of her.' 'You never did!'* (= 'Surely you didn't!') "我对老板说了我对她的真实看法。""不可能！"◇ (*BrE, slang*) *'You took my bike.' 'No, I never.'* "你把我的车骑走了吧。""没有，我没骑。"◇ (*old-fashioned* or *humorous*) ***Never fear*** (= Do not worry), *everything will be all right.* 别担心，一切都会好的。

IDM **on the ˌnever-ˈnever** (*BrE, informal*) on HIRE PURCHASE (= by making payments over a long period) 以分期付款的方式：*to buy a new car on the never-never* 以分期付款的方式购买一辆新车 **Well, I never (did)!** (*old-fashioned*) used to express surprise or disapproval（表示惊奇或不赞同）不会吧，不行的

■ *exclamation* (*informal*) used to show that you are very surprised about sth because you do not believe it is possible（表示惊讶，因为觉得不可能）不会吧：*'I got the job.' 'Never!'* "我得到那份工作了。""不可能吧！" IDM SEE MIND *v.*

ˌ**never-ˈending** *adj.* seeming to last for ever 永无止境的；没完没了的 SYN **endless, interminable**：*Housework is a never-ending task.* 家务活做起来真是没完没了。

never·more /ˌnevəˈmɔː(r); *NAmE* ˌnevərˈm-/ *adv.* (*old use*) never again 不再

ˌ**never-ˈnever land** *noun* [sing.] an imaginary place where everything is wonderful 虚幻的乐土；世外桃源

never·the·less 🔑 AW /ˌnevəðəˈles; *NAmE* -vərðə-/ *adv.* despite sth that you have just mentioned 尽管如此；不过；然而 SYN **nonetheless**：*There is little chance that we will succeed in changing the law. Nevertheless, it is important that we try.* 我们几乎没有可能改变法律。不过，重要的是我们要努力争取。◇ *Our defeat was expected but it is disappointing nevertheless.* 我们的失败是意料中的事，尽管如此，还是令人失望。

▼ LANGUAGE BANK 用语库

nevertheless

Conceding a point and making a counter-argument 承认一个观点的正确性，并提出一个对立的观点

- ***While*** *the film is undoubtedly too long, it is* ***nevertheless*** *an intriguing piece of cinema.* 虽然这部电影的确太长了，但它不失为一部有趣的影片。
- ***It can be argued that*** *the movie is too long. It is* ***nonetheless*** *an intriguing piece of cinema.* 可以认为这部电影太长了，但它不失为一部有趣的影片。
- *The film is undoubtedly too long.* ***Still,*** *it is an intriguing piece of cinema.* 这部电影的确太长了，但它仍不失为一部有趣的影片。
- ***Of course,*** *huge chunks of the book have been sacrificed in order to make a two-hour movie,* ***but it is nevertheless*** *a successful piece of storytelling.* 当然，为了制作一部两小时的电影，该书中的大部分内容都被舍弃了，不过它仍不失为一部成功的故事片。
- *Critics are wrong to argue that the film's plot is too complicated.* ***Certainly*** *there are a couple of major twists,* ***but*** *audiences will have no difficulty following them.* 批评家认为这部电影的情节过于复杂，这种观点是不恰当的。影片中确实有几次大的情节变化，但观众还是不难看懂的。
- ***It is true that*** *you cannot make a good movie without a good script,* ***but it is equally true*** *that a talented director can make a good script into an excellent film.* 的确，没有好的剧本不可能拍出好的电影，但有天赋的导演能将较好的剧本制作成非常好的电影，这一点也是没有疑问的。
- ***It remains to be seen whether*** *these two movies herald a new era of westerns,* ***but there is no doubt that*** *they represent welcome additions to the genre.* 这两部电影是否预示着西部片新时代的来临还有待观察。但是毫无疑问，它们作为这一电影类型的新作而受到欢迎。

➲ LANGUAGE BANK AT ARGUE, HOWEVER, IMPERSONAL, OPINION

new 🔑 /njuː; *NAmE* nuː/ *adj.* (**newer**, **new·est**)

• NOT EXISTING BEFORE 从前没有 **1** 🔑 not existing before; recently made, invented, introduced, etc. 刚出现的；新的；新近推出的：*Have you read her new novel?* 你看过她新出的小说了吗？◇ *new ways of doing things* 做事的新方法 ◇ *This idea isn't new.* 这主意不新鲜。◇ *The latest model has over 100 new features.* 最新的款式有 100 多种新特色。 OPP **old** ➲ SEE ALSO BRAND NEW **2 the new** *noun* [U] something that is new 新东西；新事物：*It was a good mix of the old and the new.* 这是新旧的完美结合。

• RECENTLY BOUGHT 新买的 **3** 🔑 recently bought 新买的：*Let me show you my new dress.* 给你看看我新买的连衣裙。

• NOT USED BEFORE 从未用过 **4** 🔑 not used or owned by anyone before 没被用过的；未曾被人占有过的；崭新的：*A second-hand car costs a fraction of a new one.* 二手车的花费只是新车的零头。

- **DIFFERENT** 不同 **5** different from the previous one 有别于从前的；新颖的：*I like your new hairstyle.* 我喜欢你的新发型。◇ *When do you start your new job?* 你什么时候开始你的新工作？◇ *He's made a lot of new friends.* 他交了许多新朋友。**OPP** **old**
- **NOT FAMILIAR** 不熟悉 **6** already existing but not seen, experienced, etc. before; not familiar 刚体验到的；初见的；不熟悉的：*This is a new experience for me.* 对于我来说，这是一次从未有过的经历。◇ *I'd like to learn a new language.* 我想学习一门新的语言。◇ *the discovery of a new star* 一颗新星的发现 ◇ **~ to sb** *Our system is probably new to you.* 你也许不熟悉我们的系统。
- **RECENTLY ARRIVED** 新到 **7** **~ (to sth)** not yet familiar with sth because you have only just started, arrived, etc. 初来乍到的；初学乍练的；新鲜的：*I should tell you, I'm completely new to this kind of work.* 我得告诉你，我干这活完全是个新手。◇ *I am new to the town.* 我刚刚来到这座小镇。◇ *a* **new arrival/recruit** 刚刚到达的人；新兵 ◇ *You're new here, aren't you?* 你是新来的，是吗？
- **NEW-** 新… **8** used in compounds to describe sth that has recently happened （用于构成复合词）新的，新近的：*He was enjoying his new-found freedom.* 他享受着刚刚获得的自由。
- **MODERN** 现代 **9** (usually with *the* 通常与 the 连用) modern; of the latest type 现代的；最新型的：*the new morality* 现代的道德 ◇ *They called themselves the New Romantics.* 他们自称新浪漫主义者。
- **JUST BEGINNING** 初始 **10** [usually before noun] just beginning or beginning again 刚开始的；初始的；重新开始的：*a new day* 新的一天 ◇ *It was a new era in the history of our country.* 这是我国历史上的一个新纪元。◇ *She went to Australia to start a new life.* 她去澳大利亚开始新的生活。
- **WITH FRESH ENERGY** 有新鲜活力 **11** having fresh energy, courage or health 富有朝气的；生气勃勃的：*Since he changed jobs he's looked like a new man.* 他跳槽之后像换了一个人似的。
- **RECENTLY PRODUCED** 新近产生 **12** only recently produced or developed 新近产生的；新开发的；时鲜的：*The new buds are appearing on the trees now.* 树上现在露出了新芽。◇ *new potatoes* (= ones dug from the soil early in the season) 早土豆

▶ **new·ness** *noun* [U] ➲ SEE ALSO NEWLY

IDM ˌ**break new 'ground** to make a new discovery or do sth that has not been done before 有所发现；开拓创新 ➲ SEE ALSO GROUNDBREAKING **(as)** ˌ**good as 'new | like 'new** in very good condition, as it was when it was new 完好如新：*I've had your coat cleaned—it's as good as new now.* 你的外套洗好了，像新的一样。**... is the new...** (*informal*) used to say that sth has become very fashionable and can be thought of as replacing sth else （表示某事物已非常时髦，被视为可替代其他事物）：*Brown is the new black.* 棕色取代了黑色变得时髦起来。◇ *Comedy is the new rock and roll.* 喜剧的风头直追摇滚乐。◇ *Fifty is the new forty.* 四十尚未老，五十正当年。**a new 'broom** (*BrE, often disapproving*) a person who has just started to work for an organization, department, etc., especially in a senior job, and who is likely to make a lot of changes 新就职者；（尤指）刚上任的新官：*Well, you know what they say—a new broom sweeps clean.* 唉，你知道他们说什么，新官上任三把火。**a/the** ˌ**new kid on the 'block** (*informal*) a person who is new to a place, an organization, etc. （地方、机构等的）新来者，新手：*Despite his six years in politics, he was still regarded by many as the new kid on the block.* 尽管他已经从政六年，但很多人仍把他视为初出茅庐的新手。**a new one on 'me** (*informal*) used to say that you have not heard a particular idea, piece of information, joke, etc. before 未听说过（或接触过）的；很生疏的：*'Have you come across this before?' 'No, it's a new one on me.'* "你以前碰到过这样的事吗？" "没有，从来没听说过。" **turn over a new 'leaf** to change your way of life to become a better, more responsible person 改恶从善；重新做人 **what's 'new?** (*informal*) used as a friendly GREETING （友好的问候）你好吗，怎么样：*Hi! What's new?* 嗨！你好吗？ ➲ MORE AT BLOOD *n.*, BRAVE *adj.*, BREATHE, COMPLEXION, TEACH

ˌ**New 'Age** *adj.* connected with a way of life that rejects modern Western values and is based on spiritual ideas and beliefs, ASTROLOGY, etc. 新潮生活的，新时代生活方式的（摒弃西方现代价值观，注重精神性、占星术等）：*a New Age festival* 新潮生活节 ◇ ***New Age travellers*** (= people in Britain who reject the values of modern society and travel from place to place, living in their vehicles) 新时代迁移者（摒弃现代社会价值，住在车内四处旅行的人） ▶ ˌ**New 'Age** *noun* [U]

new·bie /ˈnjuːbi; *NAmE* ˈnuːbi/ (*also* **newb** /njuːb; *NAmE* nuːb/ *especially NAmE*) *noun* (*informal*) a person who is new and has little experience in doing sth, especially in using computers （尤指使用电脑的）新手 **SYN** **novice** ➲ SEE ALSO NOOB

new·born /ˈnjuːbɔːn; *NAmE* ˈnuːbɔːrn/ *adj.* [only before noun] recently born 新生的；初生的：*a newborn baby* 新生儿

ˈ**new-build** *noun* [C, U] (*BrE*) a building, ship or aircraft that has been built very recently or that is to be built soon; buildings, etc. of this type 新建物（指建筑、船舶或飞机；亦指拟建的）：*new-build properties/apartments* 新建楼房 / 公寓

New·cas·tle /ˈnjuːkɑːsl; *NAmE* ˈnuːkæsl/ *noun* [U] **IDM** SEE COAL

new·comer /ˈnjuːkʌmə(r); *NAmE* ˈnuː-/ *noun* **~ (to sth)** a person who has only recently arrived in a place or started an activity 新来者；新手

newel post /ˈnjuːəl pəʊst; *NAmE* ˈnuːəl poʊst/ (*also* **newel**) *noun* a post at the top or bottom of a set of stairs 中柱；楼梯望柱

ˌ**New 'England** *noun* an area in the north-eastern US that includes the states of Maine, New Hampshire, Vermont, Massachusetts, Rhode Island and Connecticut 新英格兰（包括缅因、新罕布什尔、佛蒙特、马萨诸塞、罗得岛、康涅狄格诸州的美国东北部地区）

new·fan·gled /ˌnjuːˈfæŋɡld; *NAmE* ˌnuːˈf-/ *adj.* [usually before noun] (*disapproving*) used to describe sth that has recently been invented or introduced, but that you do not like because it is not what you are used to, or is too complicated 新奇怪异的；时髦复杂的

new·fie /ˈnjuːfi; *NAmE* ˈnuːfi/ *noun* (*CanE, informal*) a person from Newfoundland in Canada （加拿大）纽芬兰人

ˌ**new-'found** *adj.* [only before noun] recently discovered or achieved 新发现的；新取得的：*How is she handling her new-found fame?* 对于自己最近成名一事，她是如何应付的？◇ *his new-found freedom/confidence/enthusiasm* 他刚获得的自由 / 找到的信心 / 产生的热情

New·found·land Time /njuːˈfaʊndlənd taɪm; *NAmE* nuːˈf-/ *noun* [U] (*CanE*) the standard time system that is used in an area which includes the island of Newfoundland 纽芬兰时间（纽芬兰岛地区标准时间）

ˌ**New 'Labour** *noun* [sing.+sing./pl. v.] (in Britain) the modern Labour Party which moved away from the political left in the 1990s in order to appeal to more people （英国）新工党（对现今工党的称呼，因其于 20 世纪 90 年代脱离左派传统以求获得更多人的支持）

newly /ˈnjuːli; *NAmE* ˈnuːli/ *adv.* (usually before a past participle 通常用于过去分词前) recently 最近；新近：*a newly qualified doctor* 新近获得行医许可的医生 ◇ *a newly created job* 新设置的岗位 ◇ *a newly independent republic* 刚独立的共和国

ˈ**newly-wed** *noun* [usually pl.] a person who has recently got married 新婚者 ▶ ˈ**newly-wed** *adj.*

ˌ**new 'man** *noun* (*BrE*) a man who shares the work in the home that is traditionally done by women, such as cleaning, cooking and taking care of children. New men are considered sensitive and not aggressive. 新派男子（分担家务及照顾子女的工作）

N

ˌnew ˈmedia *noun* [pl.] new information and entertainment technologies, such as the Internet, CD-ROMs and digital television 新媒体（像互联网、光盘和数字电视等新的信息和娱乐技术）

ˌnew ˈmoon *noun* **1** the moon when it looks like a thin curved shape (= a CRESCENT) 新月 **2** the time of the month when the moon has this shape 新月期 ➲ COMPARE FULL MOON, HALF-MOON (1)

the ˌNew ˈRight *noun* [sing.] (in the US) politicians and political groups who support conservative social and political policies and religious ideas based on Christian FUNDAMENTALISM （美国）新右派（支持保守的社会和政治政策和基于基督教基要主义的宗教思想）

news /njuːz; *NAmE* nuːz/ *noun* [U] **1** new information about sth that has happened recently 消息；音信：*What's the latest news?* 有什么最新消息吗？ ◇ *Have you heard the news? Pat's leaving!* 你听说了吗？帕特要走了！ ◇ *That's great news.* 这真是好消息。 ◇ *Tell me all your news.* 把你最近的情况全都告诉我。 ◇ *Have you had any **news of** Patrick?* 你有没有帕特里克的消息？ ◇ *Any news on the deal?* 这笔交易有消息吗？ ◇ *Messengers brought **news that** the battle had been lost.* 通信员送来消息说这场战斗失败了。 ◇ *Do you want the **good news** or the **bad news** first?* 你是想先听好消息还是坏消息？ ◇ *a **piece/bit of news*** 一条 / 一则新闻 ◇ (*informal*) *It's news to me* (= I haven't heard it before). 这事我第一次听说。 **2** reports of recent events that appear in newspapers or on television or radio 媒体对重要事情的报道；新闻：*national/international news* 国内 / 国际新闻 ◇ *a **news story/item/report*** 一则新闻；新闻报道 ◇ *News of a serious road accident is just coming in.* 刚收到一则重大交通事故的消息。 ◇ ***breaking news*** (= news that is arriving about events that have just happened) 突发新闻 ◇ *She is always **in the news**.* 她老在媒体露面。 ◇ *The wedding was **front-page news**.* 这次婚礼成了头版新闻。 **3** **the news** a regular television or radio broadcast of the latest news （电视或广播中的）新闻报道：*to **listen to/watch the news*** 收听 / 收看新闻节目 ◇ *Can you put the news on?* 请你打开新闻好吗？ ◇ *I saw it **on the news**.* 我是在新闻节目中看到的。 ◇ *the nine o'clock news* 九点的新闻报道 ➲ WORDFINDER NOTE AT PROGRAMME **4** a person, thing or event that is considered to be interesting enough to be reported as news 新闻人物；新闻事件：*Pop stars are always news.* 流行音乐明星总是新闻人物。 ➲ SEE ALSO NEWSY ➲ MORE LIKE THIS 28, page R28

IDM **be bad ˈnews (for sb/sth)** to be likely to cause problems 对…不利：*Central heating is bad news for indoor plants.* 中央供暖系统不利于室内植物。 **break the ˈnews (to sb)** to be the first to tell sb some bad news 最先（向…）透露坏消息；说出实情 **be good news (for sb/sth)** to be likely to be helpful or give an advantage 对…有利（或有益处）：*The cut in interest rates is good news for homeowners.* 降低利率对于私房买主来说是个福音。 **ˌno news is ˈgood news** (*saying*) if there were bad news we would hear it, so as we have heard nothing, it is likely that nothing bad has happened 没有消息就是好消息

ˈnews agency (*also* **ˈpress agency**) *noun* an organization that collects news and supplies it to newspapers and television and radio companies 通讯社 ➲ WORDFINDER NOTE AT JOURNALIST

news·agent /ˈnjuːzeɪdʒənt; *NAmE* ˈnuːz-/ (*BrE*) (*US* **news·deal·er**) *noun* **1** a person who owns or works in a shop selling newspapers and magazines, and often sweets/candy and cigarettes 报刊经销人；报刊经销商 **2** **news·agent's** (*pl.* **news·agents**) (*BrE also* **ˈpaper shop**) a shop/store that sells newspapers, magazines, sweets/candy, etc. 报刊经销店；书报亭：*I'll go to the newsagent's on my way home.* 回家时我要去趟报刊店。 ➲ MORE LIKE THIS 34, page R29

news·cast /ˈnjuːzkɑːst; *NAmE* ˈnuːzkæst/ *noun* (*especially NAmE*) a news programme on radio or television 新闻节目；新闻广播

news·cast·er /ˈnjuːzkɑːstə(r); *NAmE* ˈnuːzkæstər/ (*BrE also* **news·read·er**) *noun* a person who reads the news on television or radio 新闻播音员

ˈnews conference *noun* (*especially NAmE*) = PRESS CONFERENCE

news·deal·er /ˈnjuːzdiːlə(r); *NAmE* ˈnuːz-/ (*US*) (*BrE* **news·agent**) *noun* **1** a person who owns or works in a shop selling newspapers and magazines, and often sweets/candy and cigarettes 报刊经销人；报刊经销商 **2** (*BrE also* **ˈpaper shop**) a shop/store that sells newspapers, magazines, sweets/candy, etc. 报刊经销店；书报亭 ➲ SEE ALSO NEWS STAND

ˈnews desk *noun* the department of a newspaper office or a radio or television station where news is received and prepared for printing or broadcasting （报社、电台或电视台的）新闻编辑部，新闻采编部：*She works on the news desk.* 她在新闻采编部工作。

news·flash /ˈnjuːzflæʃ; *NAmE* ˈnuːz-/ (*also* **flash**) *noun* (*especially BrE*) a short item of important news that is broadcast on radio or television, often interrupting a programme （插播的）简明新闻，快讯

news·gather·ing /ˈnjuːzgæðərɪŋ; *NAmE* ˈnuːz-/ *noun* [U] the process of doing research on news items, especially ones that will be broadcast on television or printed in a newspaper （尤指电视或报纸的）新闻采集 ▶ **news·gather·er** /ˈnjuːzgæðərə(r); *NAmE* ˈnuːz-/ *noun*

news·group /ˈnjuːzgruːp; *NAmE* ˈnuːz-/ *noun* a place in a computer network, especially the Internet, where people can discuss a particular subject and exchange information about it （网络）新闻组

news·let·ter /ˈnjuːzletə(r); *NAmE* ˈnuːz-/ *noun* a printed report containing news of the activities of a club or organization that is sent regularly to all its members （某组织的）内部通讯，简讯 ➲ WORDFINDER NOTE AT CLUB

news·man /ˈnjuːzmæn; *NAmE* ˈnuːz-/, **news·woman** /ˈnjuːzwʊmən; *NAmE* ˈnuːz-/ *noun* (*pl.* **-men** /-men/, **-women** /-wɪmɪn/) a journalist who works for a newspaper or a television or radio station 新闻记者：*a crowd of reporters and TV newsmen* 一群记者和电视新闻采编人员

news·paper /ˈnjuːzpeɪpə(r); *NAmE* ˈnuːz-/ *noun* **1** [C] a set of large printed sheets of paper containing news, articles, advertisements, etc. and published every day or every week 报纸；报：*a **daily/weekly newspaper*** 日报；周报 ◇ *a **local/national newspaper*** 地方性 / 全国性报纸 ◇ *an **online newspaper*** 在线报纸 ◇ *a **newspaper article*** 报纸上发表的文章 ◇ *I read about it **in the newspaper**.* 我在报上看到了这件事。 ◇ *a **newspaper cutting*** 剪报 ◇ *She works for the local newspaper* (= the company that produces it). 她在那家地方报社工作。 ◇ *newspaper proprietors* 报业老板 ➲ SEE ALSO PAPER *n.* (2) ➲ WORDFINDER NOTE AT JOURNALIST

> WORDFINDER 联想词：article, columnist, editorial, feature, headline, **journalist**, obituary, review, supplement

2 [U] paper taken from old newspapers 旧报纸：*Wrap all your glasses in newspaper.* 把你的玻璃杯全用旧报纸包起来。

news·paper·man /ˈnjuːzpeɪpəmæn; *NAmE* ˈnuːzpeɪpər-mæn/, **news·paper·woman** /ˈnjuːzpeɪpəwʊmən; *NAmE* ˈnuːzpeɪpər-/ *noun* (*pl.* **-men** /-men/, **-women** /-wɪmɪn/) a journalist who works for a newspaper 报社记者

new·speak /ˈnjuːspiːk; *NAmE* ˈnuː-/ *noun* [U] language that is not clear or honest, for example the language that is used in political PROPAGANDA 新话（模棱两可的政治宣传语言）

news·print /ˈnjuːzprɪnt; *NAmE* ˈnuːz-/ *noun* [U] the cheap paper that newspapers are printed on 新闻纸；白报纸

news·read·er /ˈnjuːzriːdə(r); *NAmE* ˈnuːz-/ *noun* (*BrE*) = NEWSCASTER

news·reel /ˈnjuːzriːl; *NAmE* ˈnuːz-/ *noun* a short film of news that was shown in the past in cinemas/movie theaters （旧时在电影院播放的）新闻短片

news·room /ˈnjuːzruːm; -rʊm; *NAmE* ˈnuːz-/ *noun* the room at a newspaper office or a radio or television station where news is received and prepared for printing or broadcasting （报社、电台或电视台的）新闻编辑室

ˈnews-sheet *noun* a small newspaper with only a few pages （只有几页的）小报

ˈnews stand (*NAmE* **news·stand** /ˈnjuːzstænd; *NAmE* ˈnuːz-/) *noun* a place on the street, at a station, etc. where you can buy newspapers and magazines 报摊；书报亭

ˈnews ticker (*also* **ticker**) *noun* a line of text containing news which passes across the screen of a computer or television （计算机或电视屏幕上的）滚动新闻条

news·wire /ˈnjuːzwaɪə(r); *NAmE* ˈnuːz-/ *noun* a service that provides the latest news, for example using the Internet 新闻专线（通过互联网等提供最新新闻的服务）

news·worthy /ˈnjuːzwɜːði; *NAmE* ˈnuːzwɜːrði/ *adj.* interesting and important enough to be reported as news 有新闻价值的；值得报道的

newsy /ˈnjuːzi; *NAmE* ˈnuːzi/ *adj.* (*informal*) full of interesting and entertaining news 新闻多的；充满有趣信息的： *a newsy letter* 一封有很多消息的信

newt /njuːt; *NAmE* nuːt/ *noun* a small animal with short legs, a long tail and cold blood, that lives both in water and on land (= is an AMPHIBIAN) 蝾螈（水陆两栖） IDM SEE PISSED

the ˌNew ˈTestament *noun* [sing.] the second part of the Bible, that describes the life and teachings of Jesus Christ 《〈圣经〉新约》 ➲ COMPARE OLD TESTAMENT

new·ton /ˈnjuːtən; *NAmE* ˈnuː-/ *noun* (*abbr.* **N**) (*physics* 物) a unit of force. One newton is equal to the force that would give a mass of one kilogram an ACCELERATION (= an increase in speed) of one metre per second per second. 牛（顿）（力的单位，1 牛顿等于使 1 千克质量的物体产生 1 米每平方秒的加速度所需要的力）

ˈnew town *noun* one of the complete towns that were planned and built in Britain after 1946 （英国于 1946 年后规划建设的）新市镇

ˌnew ˈwave *noun* [U, sing.] **1** a group of people who together introduce new styles and ideas in art, music, cinema, etc. 新浪潮（统称艺术、音乐、电影等领域的共同开拓创新者）： *one of the most exciting directors of the Australian new wave* 澳大利亚新浪潮派中最为振奋人心的导演之一 ◇ *new wave films* 新浪潮电影 **2** a style of rock music popular in the 1970s 新浪潮音乐（流行于 20 世纪 70 年代的一种摇滚乐）

the ˌNew ˈWorld *noun* [sing.] a way of referring to N, Central and S America, used especially in the past 新大陆；美洲大陆 ➲ COMPARE OLD WORLD

ˌnew ˈyear (*also* **ˌNew ˈYear**) *noun* [U, sing.] the beginning of the year 新年： *Happy New Year!* 新年快乐！ ◇ *We're going to Germany for Christmas and New Year.* 我们要去德国过圣诞和新年。 ◇ *I'll see you in the new year.* 新的一年里再见。 ➲ SEE ALSO RESOLUTION (4)

ˌNew Year's ˈDay (*NAmE also* **ˈNew Year's**) *noun* [U] 1 January 元旦；1 月 1 日

ˌNew Year's ˈEve (*NAmE also* **ˈNew Year's**) *noun* [U] 31 December, especially the evening of that day 除夕；12 月 31 日；（尤指）除夕夜

next 🔑 /nekst/ *adj., adv., noun*

■ *adj.* [only before noun] **1** 🔑 (usually with *the* 通常与 the 连用) coming straight after sb/sth in time, order or space 下一个的；紧接着的；接下来的： *The next train to Baltimore is at ten.* 下一趟去巴尔的摩的列车十点钟开。 ◇ *The next six months will be the hardest.* 接下来的六个月将是最难熬的。 ◇ *the next chapter* 下一章 ◇ *Who's next?* 下一位是谁？ ◇ *the woman in the next room* 隔壁房间里的女子 ◇ *I fainted and **the next thing I knew** I was in the hospital.* 我昏迷了，醒来时只知道自己在医院里。 ◇ (*informal*) *Round here, you leave school at sixteen and **next thing you know**, you're married with three kids.* 这一带的人十六岁中学毕业，接着就结婚，生三个孩子。 **2** 🔑 (used without *the* 不与 the 连用) **~ Monday, week, summer, year, etc.** the Monday, week, etc. immediately following 紧随其后的；下一个的： *Next Thursday is 12 April.* 下个星期四是 4 月 12 日。 ◇ ***Next time** I'll bring a book.* 下次我带本书来。

IDM **the ˈnext man, woman, person, etc.** the average person 平常人；一般的人： *I can enjoy a joke **as well as the next man**, but this is going too far.* 我和平常人一样喜欢开玩笑，可这太过分了。 ➲ MORE AT DAY, LUCK *n.*

▼ **WHICH WORD?** 词语辨析

next / nearest

- **(The) next** means 'after this/that one' in time or in a series of events, places or people. * (the) next 指下一个时间、事情、地点或人： *When is your next appointment?* 你下一次预约时间是什么时候？ ◇ *Turn left at the next traffic lights.* 在下一个红绿灯处向左拐。 ◇ *Who's next?* 下一个是谁？ **(The) nearest** means 'closest' in space. * (the) nearest 指空间上最近： *Where's the nearest supermarket?* 最近的超市在哪儿？
- Notice the difference between the prepositions **nearest to** and **next to**. 注意介词 nearest to 和 next to 的区别： *Janet's sitting nearest to the window* (= of all the people in the room). 珍妮特坐在（屋里所有人中）离窗户最近的地方。 ◇ *Sarah's sitting next to the window* (= right beside it). 萨拉坐在窗户旁边。 In informal *BrE* **nearest** can be used instead of **nearest to**. 在非正式的英式英语中，nearest 可用以代替 nearest to： *Who's sitting nearest the door?* 谁坐在离门最近的地方？

■ *adv.* **1** 🔑 after sth else; then; afterwards 紧接着；随后： *What happened next?* 随后发生了什么？ ◇ *Next, I heard the sound of voices.* 接着，我听到了说话的声音。 ➲ LANGUAGE BANK AT FIRST, PROCESS[1] **2** 🔑 **~ best, biggest, most important, etc....** (**after/to sb/sth**) following in the order mentioned 其次的；依次的；仅次于…的： *Jo was the next oldest after Martin.* 马丁下面年龄最大的就是乔了。 ◇ ***The next best thing** to flying is gliding.* 好玩程度仅次于飞行的就是滑翔。 **3** used in questions to express surprise or confusion （用于询问，表示吃惊或困惑）： *You're going bungee jumping? **Whatever next?*** 你要去蹦极？还想干什么？

■ *noun* 🔑 (*usually* **the next**) [sing.] a person or thing that is next 下一位；下一个；下一件： *One moment he wasn't there, the next he was.* 他前一刻还不在那里，一会儿又在了。 ◇ *the week **after next*** 下下周

ˌnext ˈdoor *adv., adj., noun*

■ *adv.* in the next room, house or building 在隔壁： *The cat is from the house next door.* 这只猫是隔壁家的。 ◇ *The manager's office is just next door.* 经理办公室就在隔壁。 ◇ *We live **next door to** the bank.* 我们住在银行的隔壁。

▶ **ˌnext-ˈdoor** *adj.* [only before noun]: *our next-door neighbours* 我们的隔壁邻居 ◇ *the next-door house* 相邻的房子

■ *noun* [U+sing./pl. v.] (*BrE, informal*) the people who live in the house or flat/apartment next to yours 隔壁邻居；住在隔壁的人： *Is that next door's dog?* 那是邻居家的狗吗？

ˌnext of ˈkin *noun* [C, U] (*pl.* **next of kin**) your closest living relative or relatives 直系亲属；最近亲： *I'm her next of kin.* 我是她的直系亲属。 ◇ *Her next of kin have been informed.* 她最近的亲属已得到通知了。 ◇ *The form must be signed by next of kin.* 这表格必须有直系亲属签字。

ˈnext to 🔑 *prep.* **1** 🔑 in or into a position right beside sb/sth 紧邻；在…近旁： *We sat next to each other.* 我们

N

紧挨着坐在一起。 ➲ NOTE AT NEXT **2** following in order or importance after sb/sth 仅次于；紧接：*Next to skiing my favourite sport is skating.* 我最喜欢的运动除了滑雪就是溜冰。 **3** almost 几乎：*Charles knew **next to nothing** about farming.* 查尔斯对耕作几乎一无所知。◇ *The horse came **next to last*** (= the one before the last one) *in the race.* 这匹马在比赛中跑了个倒数第二。 **4** in comparison with sb/sth 与…相比：*Next to her I felt like a fraud.* 和她相比，我觉得自己是滥竽充数。

nexus /ˈneksəs/ *noun* [sing.] (*formal*) a complicated series of connections between different things （错综复杂的）关系，联结，联系

Nez Percé /ˌnez ˈpɜːs; *NAmE* ˈpɜːrs/ *noun* (*pl.* **Nez Percé** or **Nez Percés**) a member of a Native American people, many of whom now live in the US state of Idaho 内兹佩尔塞人（美洲土著居民，其中许多居于美国爱达荷州） ORIGIN From the French for 'pierced nose'. 源自法语词"穿鼻"。

NFC /ˌen ef ˈsiː/ *abbr.* **1 the NFC** (in the US) the National Football Conference (one of the two groups of teams in the National Football League) （美国）国家橄榄球联合会（国家橄榄球联盟的两个联合会之一） **2** near field communication (a type of technology that allows communication over short distances between mobile/cell phones and other electronic devices in order to make payments, etc.) 近场通信（全写为 near field communication，使手机与其他电子设备在短距离内进行数据传输的技术，可用于移动支付等）：*an NFC device/payment* 近场通信设备 / 支付

NFL /ˌen ef ˈel/ *abbr.* (in the US) National Football League (the US organization for professional AMERICAN FOOTBALL with two groups of teams, the National Football Conference and the American Football Conference) 国家橄榄球联盟（美国职业橄榄球组织，包括两组球队：国家橄榄球联合会和美国橄榄球联合会）

NGO /ˌen dʒiː ˈəʊ; *NAmE* ˈoʊ/ *noun* non-governmental organization (a charity, association, etc. that is independent of government and business) 非政府组织（独立于政府或商界的慈善机构、协会等）

ngoma /əŋˈɡəʊmə; *NAmE* -ˈɡoʊ-/ *noun* **1** [C] a traditional drum from southern or eastern Africa 恩格玛鼓（非洲南部或东部的一种传统鼓） **2** [C, U] (*EAfrE*) a celebration or performance that involves dancing, singing and playing drums （伴有歌舞鼓乐的）狂欢庆典，盛大表演

NHS /ˌen eɪtʃ ˈes/ *abbr.* National Health Service (the public health service in Britain that provides medical treatment and is paid for by taxes) 国民医疗服务体系（全写为 National Health Service，英国靠税收维持的公众医疗服务）：*an NHS hospital* 国民医疗服务体系所辖的医院 ◇ *I had the operation done **on the NHS*** (= paid for by the NHS). 我做这次手术是国民医疗服务体系资助的。

NI /ˌen ˈaɪ/ *abbr.* (in Britain) NATIONAL INSURANCE （英国）国民保险制度

nia·cin /ˈnaɪəsɪn/ (*also* ˌ**nico·tin·ic ˈacid**) *noun* [U] a VITAMIN of the B group that is found in foods such as milk and meat 烟酸，尼克酸，烟碱酸（B 类维生素，存在于牛奶、肉类等食物中）

nib /nɪb/ *noun* the metal point of a pen 钢笔尖 ➲ VISUAL VOCAB PAGE V71

nib·ble /ˈnɪbl/ *verb, noun*

■ *verb* **1** [T, I] to take small bites of sth, especially food 小口咬，一点点地咬（食物）：**~ sth** *We sat drinking wine and nibbling olives.* 我们坐在那儿，喝着葡萄酒嚼着橄榄。◇ *He nibbled her ear playfully.* 他开玩笑地轻咬着她的耳朵。◇ **~ (at/on sth)** *She took some cake from the tray and nibbled at it.* 她从盘子里拿了块蛋糕小口地吃着。 **2** [I] **~ (at sth)** to show a slight interest in an offer, idea, etc. （对…）略微表现出兴趣：*He nibbled at the idea, but would not make a definite decision.* 他对这个主意略感兴趣，但还不愿意作出明确决定。

PHR V ˌ**nibble aˈway at sth** to take away small amounts of sth, so that the total amount is gradually reduced 慢慢地削弱；蚕食 SYN **erode**：*Inflation is nibbling away at spending power.* 通货膨胀正在慢慢地减弱消费能力。

■ *noun* **1** [C] a small bite of sth 一小口 **2 nibbles** [pl.] small things to eat with a drink before a meal or at a party （餐前或聚会中的）点心，小吃

nibs /nɪbz/ *noun*

IDM **his nibs** (*old-fashioned, BrE, informal*) used to refer to a man who is, or thinks he is, more important than other people （用以称自命不凡的人）

nice /naɪs/ *adj.* (**nicer, nicest**)

• **PLEASANT/ATTRACTIVE** 令人愉快；吸引人 **1** pleasant, enjoyable or attractive 令人愉快的；宜人的；吸引人的：*a nice day/smile/place* 舒适的一天；舒心的微笑；宜人的地方 ◇ *nice weather* 好天气 ◇ *Did you **have a nice time**?* 你玩得痛快吗？◇ *You look very nice.* 你很好看。◇ *'Do you want to come, too?' 'Yes, **that would be nice**.'* "你也想来吗？""是啊，很高兴来。"◇ *The nicest thing about her is that she never criticizes us.* 她最大的好处就是从不批评我们。◇ **~ (to do sth)** ***Nice to meet you!*** (= a friendly GREETING when you meet sb for the first time) 很高兴见到你！◇ **~ (doing sth)** ***It's been nice meeting you.*** 这次见到你真高兴。◇ **~ (that…)** ***It's nice that** you can come with us.* 你能和我们一起去真是太好了。◇ ***It would be nice if** he moved to London.* 他要是搬到伦敦就好了。◇ *We all had the flu last week—it wasn't very nice.* 真不走运，上周我们都得了流感。◇ ***It's nice to know that** somebody appreciates what I do.* 知道有人欣赏我所做的事真让人开心。 **2** used before adjectives or adverbs to emphasize how pleasant sth is （用于形容词或副词前以加强语气）：*a nice hot bath* 舒舒服服的热水浴 ◇ *a nice long walk* 长时间很愉快的散步 ◇ *It was nice and warm yesterday.* 昨天的天气暖洋洋的。◇ *Everyone arrived nice and early.* 大家都早早地到了。 HELP **Nice and** with another adjective cannot be used before a noun. * nice and 加另一个形容词不可用于名词前：~~*a nice and quiet place*~~

• **KIND/FRIENDLY** 好心；友好 **3** kind; friendly 好心的；和蔼的；友好的：*Our new neighbours are very nice.* 我们的新邻居很和气。◇ *He's a really nice guy.* 他真是个好人。◇ **~ to sb** *Be nice to me. I'm not feeling well.* 我有点不舒服，对我好点。◇ **~ of sb (to do sth)** *It was nice of them to invite us.* 他们真好，邀请了我们。◇ **~ about sth** *I complained to the manager and he was very nice about it.* 我向经理投诉，他态度很好。◇ *I asked him **in the nicest possible way** to put his cigarette out.* 我尽量客气地请他把香烟掐了。 OPP nasty

• **NOT NICE** 不好 **4** (*ironic*) bad or unpleasant 坏的；令人不愉快的：*That's a nice thing to say!* 这种话也说得出口！◇

▼ **VOCABULARY BUILDING** 词汇扩充

Nice and very nice

Instead of saying that something is **nice** or **very nice**, try to use more precise and interesting adjectives to describe things. 指某事物好或非常好，除了用 nice 或 very nice 外，尽量用更贴切更有意思的形容词。

- **pleasant**/**perfect**/ **beautiful** weather 宜人的 / 理想的 / 风和日丽的天气
- a **cosy**/a **comfortable**/an **attractive** room 暖融融的 / 舒适的 / 招人喜爱的房间
- a **pleasant**/an **interesting**/an **enjoyable** experience 令人愉快的 / 有趣的 / 愉快的经历
- **expensive**/ **fashionable**/ **smart** clothes 昂贵的 / 时尚的 / 漂亮的衣服
- a **kind**/a **charming**/an **interesting** man 和蔼的 / 有魅力的 / 有趣的男子
- The party was **fun**. 这聚会真有意思。

In conversation you can also use **great**, **wonderful**, **lovely** and (in *BrE*) **brilliant**. 口语中亦可用 great、wonderful 和（英式英语）brilliant：*The party was great.* 这聚会真棒。◇ *We had a brilliant weekend.* 我们周末过得非常开心。

➲ NOTE AT GOOD

N

That's a nice way to speak to your mother! 你竟然对你母亲这么说话！

• SMALL DETAILS 细节 **5** (*formal*) involving a very small detail or difference 细微的；精细的 SYN **subtle**: *a nice point of law* (= one that is difficult to decide) 法律上难以决断之处

▸ **nice·ness** *noun* [U]: *In some professions, niceness does not get you very far.* 在某些行业，做老好人成不了大事。

IDM **as ˌnice as ˈpie** (*informal*) very kind and friendly, especially when you are not expecting it 非常友好的，很善良的（尤指出乎意料） **have a nice ˈday!** (*informal, especially NAmE*) a friendly way of saying goodbye, especially to customers （与顾客道别时常用）再见 **ˈnice one!** (*BrE, informal*) used to show you are pleased when sth good has happened or sb has said sth amusing 太好了；好极了：*You got the job? Nice one!* 你得到那份工作了？太好了！ **nice ˈwork!** (*informal, especially BrE*) used to show you are pleased when sb has done sth well 干得好：*You did a good job today. Nice work, James!* 你今天干得不错。好样的，詹姆斯！ **nice work if you can ˈget it** (*informal*) used when you wish that you had sb's success or good luck and think they have achieved it with little effort（认为对方耕耘少，收获多）能有这样的好事儿就好了 ➲ MORE AT MR

ˌnice-ˈlooking *adj.* attractive 好看的；有吸引力的：*What a nice-looking young man!* 多帅的小伙子啊！

nice·ly 🔑 /ˈnaɪsli/ *adv.* **1** 🔑 in an attractive or acceptable way; well 有吸引力；令人满意；令人愉快；很好地：*The room was nicely furnished.* 这房间布置得很舒适。◇ *The plants are **coming along nicely*** (= growing well). 植物长势良好。 **2** 🔑 in a kind, friendly or polite way 和善地；温和地；友好地；有礼貌地：*If you ask her nicely she might say yes.* 好好地跟她说，她也许会同意的。 **3** (*formal*) carefully; exactly 细致地；精确地：*His novels nicely describe life in Britain between the wars.* 他的小说细致地描述了两次大战之间英国的生活状况。

IDM **do ˈnicely 1** to be making good progress 进展良好：*Her new business is doing very nicely.* 她的新事业一帆风顺。 **2** to be acceptable 令人满意：*Tomorrow at ten will do nicely* (= will be a good time). 明天上午十点挺合适。

ni·cety /ˈnaɪsəti/ *noun* (*pl.* **-ies**) (*formal*) **1** [C, usually pl.] the small details or points of difference, especially concerning the correct way of behaving or of doing things 细节；细微的差别 **2** [U] (*formal*) the quality of being very detailed or careful about sth 精确；准确；严密；仔细 SYN **precision**: *the nicety of his argument* 他那论点的精确严密

niche /niːʃ; nɪtʃ/ *noun* **1** a comfortable or suitable role, job, way of life, etc. 舒适或称心的工作（或生活等）：*He eventually found his niche in sports journalism.* 最后他在体育新闻界找到了理想的工作。 **2** (*business* 商) an opportunity to sell a particular product to a particular group of people "利基"，商机，市场补缺（针对特定消费者群体的市场需求）：*They spotted a niche in the market, with no serious competition.* 他们在市场上发现了一个竞争不大的商机。◇ *a niche market* 利基市场 ◇ *the development of **niche marketing*** (= aiming products at particular groups) 利基市场营销的开发 **3** a small hollow place, especially in a wall to contain a statue, etc., or in the side of a hill 壁龛；（山体）凹进的地方 SYN **nook 4** (*biology* 生) a position or role taken by a kind of living thing within its community. Different living things may occupy the same niche in different places, for example ANTELOPES in Africa and KANGAROOS in Australia. 生态位（一种生物在群落中的地位或作用）

nick /nɪk/ *noun, verb*

■ *noun* **1 the nick** [sing.] (*BrE, slang*) a prison or a police station 监狱；警察局：*He'll end up in the nick.* 他早晚得进局子。 **2** a small cut in the edge or surface of sth 裂口；刻痕

IDM **in good, etc. ˈnick** (*BrE, informal*) in good, etc. condition or health 身体健康（等）；状况良好（等） **in the ˌnick of ˈtime** (*informal*) at the very last moment; just in time before sth bad happens 在最后一刻；紧要关头；恰是时候

■ *verb* **1** [T] ~ **sth/yourself** to make a small cut in sth 在…上划刻痕；使有缺口；使有破损：*He nicked himself while shaving.* 他刮胡子刮了个口子。 **2** [T] ~ **sth** (**from sb/sth**) (*BrE, informal*) to steal sth 扒窃；偷窃 SYN **pinch**: *Who nicked my pen?* 谁偷走了我的钢笔？ **3** [T] ~ **sb** (**for sth**) (*BrE, informal*) to arrest sb for committing a crime 逮捕：*You're nicked!* 你被捕了！ **4** [I] + **adv./prep.** (*AustralE, NZE, informal*) to go somewhere quickly 迅速去（某地）

nickel /ˈnɪkl/ *noun* **1** [U] (*symb.* **Ni**) a chemical element. Nickel is a hard silver-white metal used in making some types of steel and other ALLOYS. 镍 **2** [C] a coin of the US and Canada worth 5 cents （美国和加拿大的）5 分镍币

ˌnickel-and-ˈdime *adj., verb*

■ *adj.* (*NAmE, informal*) involving only a small amount of money; not important 只涉小钱的；微不足道的

■ *verb* ~ **sth/sb** (*NAmE*) to spend or save very small amounts of money; to charge small amounts of money for lots of extra items 一点一点地花钱；一分分地节省；只收一点小钱：*Set the money aside so you don't nickel-and-dime it away.* 把钱存起来，这样你就不会一点一点地花掉了。◇ *She's careful not to nickel-and-dime clients for extra charges.* 她尽量不向客户收取一点儿额外费用。

nicker /ˈnɪkə(r)/ *noun* (*pl.* **nicker**) (*BrE, slang*) a pound (in money) （一）英镑

nick·name /ˈnɪkneɪm/ *noun, verb*

■ *noun* an informal, often humorous, name for a person that is connected with their real name, their personality or appearance, or with sth they have done 绰号；诨名；外号

■ *verb* [often passive] ~ **sb/sth** + **noun** to give a nickname to sb/sth 给…起绰号：*She was nicknamed 'The Ice Queen'.* 她外号叫"冰上王后"。

nico·tine /ˈnɪkətiːn/ *noun* [U] a poisonous substance in TOBACCO that people become ADDICTED to, so that it is difficult to stop smoking 尼古丁；烟碱

nico·tin·ic acid /ˌnɪkətɪnɪk ˈæsɪd/ *noun* [U] = NIACIN

niece 🔑 /niːs/ *noun* the daughter of your brother or sister; the daughter of your husband's or wife's brother or sister 侄女；外甥女 ➲ COMPARE NEPHEW

nifty /ˈnɪfti/ *adj.* (*informal*) **1** skilful and accurate 有技巧的；精确的：*There's some nifty guitar work on his latest CD.* 他最新的激光唱片里有一些吉他曲弹得非常精彩。 **2** practical; working well 实用的；灵便的 SYN **handy**: *a nifty little gadget for slicing cucumbers* 片黄瓜的小巧工具

nig·gard·ly /ˈnɪɡədli; *NAmE* -ɡərd-/ *adj.* (*formal, disapproving*) **1** unwilling to be generous with money, time, etc. 吝啬的；小气的；不大度的 SYN **mean 2** (of a gift or an amount of money 礼品或钱数) not worth much and given unwillingly 不值钱的；抠门儿的；小气的 SYN **miserly**

nig·ger /ˈnɪɡə(r)/ *noun* (*taboo, slang*) a very offensive word for a black person （对黑人的冒犯称呼）黑鬼

nig·gle /ˈnɪɡl/ *noun, verb*

■ *noun* **1** (*BrE*) a small criticism or complaint 轻微的批评；小牢骚 **2** a slight feeling, such as worry, doubt, etc. that does not go away 一丝挥不去的烦恼（或疑虑等）：*a niggle of doubt* 一丝挥之不去的疑虑 **3** a slight pain 轻微疼痛：*He gets the occasional niggle in his right shoulder.* 他的右肩有时隐隐作痛。

■ *verb* **1** [I, T] to irritate or annoy sb slightly; to make sb slightly worried 使烦恼；使焦虑 SYN **bother**: ~ (**at sb**) *A doubt niggled at her.* 一丝疑惑困扰着她。◇ **it niggles sb that...** (*BrE*) *It niggled him that she had not phoned back.* 她没给他回电话，这使他有些不安。◇ ~ **sb** (*BrE*) *Something was niggling her.* 她有点烦心的事儿。 **2** [I] ~ (**about/over sth**) | ~ (**at sb**) (**for sth**) to argue about sth unimportant; to criticize sb for sth that is not important 吹毛求疵；挑剔 SYN **quibble**

nig·gling /ˈnɪɡlɪŋ/ (*also less frequent* **nig·gly** /-li/) *adj.* **1** used to describe a slight feeling of worry or pain that does not go away （不严重却不断）烦人的，疼痛的： *She had niggling doubts about their relationship.* 她时常对他们的关系有一丝疑虑。◇ *a series of niggling injuries* 接连不断的小伤痛 **2** not important 不重要的；微不足道的 **SYN** **petty**: *niggling details* 琐碎的细节

nigh /naɪ/ *adv.* **1** ~ **on** (*old-fashioned*) almost; nearly 几乎；差不多： *They've lived in that house for nigh on 30 years.* 他们在那所房子里住了差不多 30 年了。➲ SEE ALSO WELL-NIGH **2** (*old use* or *literary*) near 靠近；近： *Winter was drawing nigh.* 冬天快到了。

night 🔑 /naɪt/ *noun* [U, C] **1** 🔑 the time between one day and the next when it is dark, when people usually sleep 夜；夜晚： *These animals only come out **at night**.* 这些动物只在夜晚出来。◇ *They sleep by day and hunt **by night**.* 他们白天睡觉，夜晚捕猎。◇ *The accident happened on Friday night.* 事故发生在星期五夜里。◇ ***on the night of** 10 January/January 10* 在 1 月 10 日夜里 ◇ *Did you hear the storm **last night**?* 昨天夜里下大雨，你听见了吗？◇ *I lay awake **all night**.* 我一夜没睡着。◇ *Where did you **spend the night**?* 你是在哪里过夜的？◇ *You're welcome to **stay the night** here.* 欢迎你在这里留宿。◇ *What is he doing calling **at this time of night**?* 他干吗这么晚了还打电话？◇ *You'll feel better after you've had **a good night's sleep**.* 你好好睡一夜就会觉得好些了。◇ *The trip was for ten nights.* 这次旅行要住十个晚上。◇ *The hotel costs €65 per person **per night**.* 住这家酒店，每人每天要 65 欧元。◇ *the **night train/boat/flight*** 夜间列车 / 轮船 / 飞机班次 ◇ ***Night fell*** (= it became dark). 夜幕降临。 **2** 🔑 the evening until you go to bed 晚上，夜晚（夜里就寝前的一段时间）： *Let's go out **on Saturday night**.* 我们星期六晚上出去吧。◇ *Bill's parents came for dinner **last night**.* 昨天晚上，比尔的父母来吃晚饭了。◇ *She doesn't like to walk home **late at night**.* 她不喜欢深夜步行回家。◇ *I saw her in town **the other night*** (= a few nights ago). 前两天晚上我在城里见过她。◇ *I'm working late **tomorrow night**.* 明晚我要工作到很晚。➲ SEE ALSO GOODNIGHT **3** an evening when a special event happens （举行盛事的）夜晚；…之夜： *the **first/opening night*** (= of a play, film/movie, etc.) 首映 / 首演之夜 ◇ *a karaoke night* 卡拉 OK 之夜 ◇ ***an Irish/a Scottish, etc. night*** (= with Irish/Scottish music, entertainment, etc.) 一场爱尔兰、苏格兰等歌舞晚会 ➲ SEE ALSO STAG NIGHT ▶ **nights** *adv.* (*especially NAmE*): *He can't get used to working nights* (= at night). 他不能适应上夜班。

IDM **have an early/a late ˈnight** to go to bed earlier or later than usual 比平时睡得早 / 晚： *I've had a lot of late nights recently.* 最近我常常睡得很晚。 **have a good/bad ˈnight** to sleep well/badly during the night 夜里睡得很好 / 很糟 **have a night on the ˈtiles** (*BrE, informal*) to stay out late enjoying yourself 深夜在外玩乐 **ˌnight and ˈday** | **ˌday and ˈnight** all the time; continuously 日日夜夜；夜以继日；连续不断： *The machines are kept running night and day.* 这些机器夜以继日地运转着。 **night ˈnight** used by children or to children, to mean 'Good night' （儿童用语或对儿童使用的语言）晚安： *'Night night, sleep tight!'* "宝宝睡觉觉，睡个好觉觉！" **a night ˈout** an evening that you spend enjoying yourself away from home 在外玩乐的夜晚： *They enjoy a night out occasionally.* 他们偶尔出去玩上一个晚上。 ➲ MORE AT ALL RIGHT *adj.*, DANCE *v.*, DEAD *n.*, MORNING, SPEND *v.*, STILL *adj.*, THING

night·cap /ˈnaɪtkæp/ *noun* **1** a drink, usually containing alcohol, taken before going to bed 睡前饮料；（常指）夜酒 **2** (in the past) a soft cap worn in bed （旧时的）睡帽

night·clothes /ˈnaɪtkləʊðz; *NAmE* -kloʊðz/ *noun* [pl.] clothes that you wear in bed 睡衣

night·club /ˈnaɪtklʌb/ *noun* a place that is open late in the evening where people can go to dance, drink, etc. 夜总会

ˈnight depository (*US*) (*BrE* **ˈnight safe**) *noun* a SAFE in the outside wall of a bank where money, etc. can be left when the bank is closed 夜间保险箱，夜间保险柜（装于银行外墙，银行关门后供客户存放现金等）

night·dress /ˈnaɪtdres/ (*BrE*) (*NAmE* or *old-fashioned* **night·gown**) (*also informal* **nightie** *BrE, NAmE*) *noun* a long loose piece of clothing like a thin dress, worn by a woman or girl in bed 睡裙；女式睡袍 ➲ VISUAL VOCAB PAGE V68

ˈnight duty *noun* [U] work that people have to do at night, for example in a hospital 夜班；夜岗： *to be on night duty* 值夜班

night·fall /ˈnaɪtfɔːl/ *noun* [U] (*formal* or *literary*) the time in the evening when it becomes dark 黄昏；傍晚 **SYN** **dusk**

night·gown /ˈnaɪtɡaʊn/ *noun* (*NAmE* or *old-fashioned*) = NIGHTDRESS

nightie /ˈnaɪti/ *noun* (*informal*) = NIGHTDRESS

night·in·gale /ˈnaɪtɪŋɡeɪl/ *noun* a small brown bird, the male of which has a beautiful song 夜莺

night·jar /ˈnaɪtdʒɑː(r)/ *noun* a brown bird with a long tail and a rough unpleasant cry, that is active mainly at night 夜鹰

night·life /ˈnaɪtlaɪf/ *noun* [U] entertainment that is available in the evening and at night 夜生活 ➲ COLLOCATIONS AT TOWN

ˈnight light *noun* a light or CANDLE that is left on at night 夜间照明灯（或烛光）；夜灯

ˈnight-long *adj.* [only before noun] lasting all night 通宵的；彻夜的

night·ly /ˈnaɪtli/ *adj.* happening every night 每夜的；每晚的： *a nightly news bulletin* 每晚的新闻简报 ▶ **night·ly** *adv.*

night·mare /ˈnaɪtmeə(r); *NAmE* -mer/ *noun* **1** a dream that is very frightening or unpleasant 噩梦；梦魇： *He still has nightmares about the accident.* 他仍然做噩梦梦见这场事故。 **2** ~ **(for sb)** an experience that is very frightening and unpleasant, or very difficult to deal with 可怕的经历；难以处理之事；噩梦： *The trip turned into a nightmare when they both got sick.* 这次旅行成了一场噩梦，他们俩都病了。◇ (*informal*) *Nobody knows what's going on—**it's a nightmare!*** 谁也不知道是怎么回事，真是糟透了！◇ (*informal*) *Filling in all those forms was a nightmare.* 填写了那么多的表格，真是太可怕了。◇ *Losing a child is most people's **worst nightmare**.* 对于大多数人来说，丧子之痛是最可怕的噩梦。◇ *If it goes ahead, it will be the **nightmare scenario*** (= the worst thing that could happen). 这件事如果继续下去就糟透了。◇ *a nightmare situation* 恶劣的形势 ▶ **night·mar·ish** /ˈnaɪtmeərɪʃ; *NAmE* -mer-/ *adj.*: *nightmarish living conditions* 噩梦般的生活条件

ˈnight owl *noun* (*informal*) a person who enjoys staying up late at night 喜欢熬夜的人；夜猫子

ˈnight safe (*BrE*) (*US* **ˈnight depository**) *noun* a SAFE in the outside wall of a bank where money, etc. can be left when the bank is closed 夜间保险箱，夜间保险柜（装于银行外墙，银行关门后供客户存放现金等）

ˈnight school *noun* [U, C] (*old-fashioned*) classes for adults, held in the evening （成人）夜校

night·shirt /ˈnaɪtʃɜːt; *NAmE* -ʃɜːrt/ *noun* a long loose shirt worn in bed 睡衣

night·spot /ˈnaɪtspɒt; *NAmE* -spɑːt/ *noun* (*informal*) a place people go to for entertainment at night 夜总会；夜间娱乐场所 **SYN** **nightclub**

night·stand /ˈnaɪtstænd/ (*also* **ˈnight table**) (*both NAmE*) *noun* = BEDSIDE TABLE

night·stick /ˈnaɪtstɪk/ *noun* (*NAmE*) = BATON (1)

ˈnight-time *noun* [U] the time when it is dark 夜间；黑夜；夜晚： *This area can be very noisy **at night-time**.* 这个地方夜间有时会非常吵。

night·watch·man /naɪt'wɒtʃmən; *NAmE* -'wɑːtʃ-/ *noun* (*pl.* **-men** /-mən/) a man whose job is to guard a building such as a factory at night 守夜人

night·wear /'naɪtweə(r); *NAmE* -wer/ *noun* [U] a word used by shops/stores for clothes that are worn in bed （商店用语）睡衣

ni·hil·ism /'naɪɪlɪzəm/ *noun* [U] (*philosophy* 哲) the belief that nothing has any value, especially that religious and moral principles have no value 虚无主义 ▶ **ni·hil·is·tic** /ˌnaɪɪ'lɪstɪk/ *adj.*: *Her latest play is a nihilistic vision of the world of the future.* 她最近出的这个剧本对未来世界作了虚无主义的诠释。

ni·hil·ist /'naɪɪlɪst/ *noun* a person who believes in nihilism 虚无主义者

the Nikkei index /'nɪkeɪ ɪndeks/ (*also* **the 'Nikkei aver·age**) *noun* [sing.] a figure that shows the relative price of shares on the Tokyo Stock Exchange 日经（平均）指数（日本东京证券交易所股票交易指数）

nil /nɪl/ *noun* [U] **1** (*especially BrE*) the number 0, especially as the score in some games （数字）零；（体育比赛中的）0 分 **SYN** **zero**: *Newcastle beat Leeds four nil/by four goals to nil.* 纽卡斯尔队以四比零战胜利兹队。 **2** nothing 无；零: *The doctors rated her chances as nil* (= there was no chance). 医生认为她没有希望了。

nim·ble /'nɪmbl/ *adj.* (**nim·bler** /'nɪmblə(r)/, **nim·blest** /'nɪmblɪst/) **1** able to move quickly and easily 灵活的；敏捷的 **SYN** **agile**: *You need nimble fingers for that job.* 干这活需要手指灵巧。◇ *She was extremely nimble on her feet.* 她的双脚特别灵活。 **2** (of the mind 头脑) able to think and understand quickly 思路敏捷的；机敏的 ▶ **nim·bly** /'nɪmbli/ *adv.*

nim·bus /'nɪmbəs/ *noun* (*specialist*) **1** [C, usually sing., U] a large grey rain cloud （大片的）雨云 **2** [C, usually sing.] a circle of light 光环

nimby /'nɪmbi/ *noun* (*pl.* **-ies**) (*disapproving, humorous*) a person who claims to be in favour of a new development or project, but objects if it is too near their home and will disturb them in some way 不得在我后院论者（声称支持某个项目但却反对在自家附近施工者） **ORIGIN** Formed from the first letters of 'not in my back yard'. 由 not in my back yard 的首字母构成。

nin·com·poop /'nɪŋkəmpuːp/ *noun* (*old-fashioned, informal*) a stupid person 头脑简单的人；幼稚的人；傻子

nine /naɪn/ *number* 9 九 **HELP** There are examples of how to use numbers at the entry for **five**. 数词用法示例见 five 条。

IDM **have nine 'lives** (especially of a cat 尤指猫) to be very lucky in dangerous situations 有九条命；命大 **a ˌnine days' 'wonder** a person or thing that makes people excited for a short time but does not last very long 昙花一现；轰动一时的人（或事物） **ˌnine times out of 'ten** almost every time 十之八九；几乎总是；差不多每次: *I'm always emailing her, but nine times out of ten she doesn't reply.* 我常常给她发电邮，但十之八九她都不回复。 **ˌnine to 'five** the normal working hours in an office 九点至五点；正常办公时间: *I work nine to five.* 我九点至五点上班。◇ *a nine-to-five job* 一份朝九晚五的工作 **the ˌwhole ˌnine 'yards** (*informal, especially NAmE*) everything, or a situation which includes everything 一切；全部: *When Dan cooks dinner he always goes the whole nine yards, with three courses and a choice of dessert.* 丹做饭总是做全份的：三道菜，还可选一种甜食。➲ MORE AT DRESSED, POSSESSION

nine·pins /'naɪnpɪnz/ *noun*

IDM **ˌgo down, ˌdrop, etc. like 'ninepins** (*BrE, informal*) to fall down or become ill/sick in great numbers 大量倒下；大批病倒

nine·teen /ˌnaɪn'tiːn/ *number* 19 十九 ▶ **nine·teenth** /ˌnaɪn'tiːnθ/ *ordinal number, noun* **HELP** There are examples of how to use ordinal numbers at the entry for **fifth**. 序数词用法示例见 fifth 条。

IDM **talk, etc. nineteen to the 'dozen** (*BrE, informal*) to talk, etc. without stopping 喋喋不休: *She was chatting away, nineteen to the dozen.* 她没完没了地聊着。

ninety /'naɪnti/ **1** *number* 90 九十 **2** *noun* **the nineties** [pl.] numbers, years or temperatures from 90 to 99 九十几；九十年代: *The temperature must be in the nineties today.* 今天的气温肯定有九十多度。▶ **nine·ti·eth** /'naɪntiəθ/ *ordinal number, noun* **HELP** There are examples of how to use ordinal numbers at the entry for **fifth**. 序数词用法示例见 fifth 条。

IDM **in your nineties** between the ages of 90 and 99 * 90 多岁 **ˌninety-nine ˌtimes out of a 'hundred** almost always 几乎没有例外；几乎总是

ning-nong /'nɪŋ nɒŋ; *NAmE* nɑːŋ/ (*also* **nong**) *noun* (*AustralE, NZE, informal*) a stupid person 呆子；傻瓜

ninja /'nɪndʒə/ *noun* (*pl.* **ninjas** or **ninja**) (*from Japanese*) a person trained in traditional Japanese skills of fighting and moving quietly 忍者（受过日本传统打斗和轻功训练的人）

ninny /'nɪni/ *noun* (*pl.* **-ies**) (*old-fashioned, informal*) a stupid person 笨蛋；傻子

ninth /naɪnθ/ *ordinal number, noun*
- *ordinal number* 9th 第九 **HELP** There are examples of how to use ordinal numbers at the entry for **fifth**. 序数词用法示例见 fifth 条。
- *noun* each of nine equal parts of sth 九分之一

nio·bium /naɪ'əʊbiəm; *NAmE* -'oʊ-/ *noun* [U] (*symb.* **Nb**) a chemical element. Niobium is a silver-grey metal used in steel ALLOYS. 铌

nip /nɪp/ *verb, noun*
- *verb* (**-pp-**) **1** [T, I] to give sb/sth a quick painful bite or PINCH 啃咬；掐；咬住；夹住: **~ sth** *He winced as the dog nipped his ankle.* 狗咬了他的脚腕子，疼得他龇牙咧嘴。◇ **~ (at sth)** *She nipped at my arm.* 她掐了一下我的胳膊。 **2** [I, T] (of cold, wind, etc. 寒气、风等) to harm or damage sth 伤害；损害: **~ (at sth)** *The icy wind nipped at our faces.* 寒风刺疼了我们的脸。◇ **~ sth** *growing shoots nipped by frost* 遭受霜冻的幼芽 **3** [I] **+ adv./prep.** (*BrE, informal*) to go somewhere quickly and/or for only a short time 快速去（某处）；急忙赶往 **SYN** **pop**: *He's just nipped out to the bank.* 他急匆匆去银行了。◇ *A car nipped in* (= got in quickly) *ahead of me.* 一辆车突然插到我前面。

IDM **nip sth in the 'bud** to stop sth when it has just begun because you can see that problems will come from it 将…扼杀在萌芽状态；防患于未然

PHR V **ˌnip sth↔'off** to remove a part of sth with your finger or with a tool 掐去；剪掉

- *noun* **1** the act of giving sb a small bite or PINCH (= squeezing their skin between your finger and thumb) 啃咬；掐 **2** (*informal*) a feeling of cold 寒冷；寒意: *There was a real nip in the air.* 空中有一股刺骨的寒气。➲ SEE ALSO NIPPY (2) **3** (*informal*) a small drink of strong alcohol 少量的烈酒

ˌnip and 'tuck *adj., adv., noun*
- *adj., adv.* (*especially NAmE*) = NECK AND NECK (WITH SB/STH): *The presidential contest is nip and tuck.* 总统竞选势均力敌。
- *noun* (*informal*) a medical operation in which skin is removed or made tighter to make sb look younger or more attractive, especially a FACELIFT 拉皮（或去皱）整形手术；（尤指）去皱整容手术，面部拉皮手术

nip·per /'nɪpə(r)/ *noun* (*informal*) a small child 小孩子

nip·ple /'nɪpl/ *noun* **1** either of the two small round dark parts on a person's chest. Babies can suck milk from their mother's breasts through the nipples. 乳头 ➲ VISUAL VOCAB PAGE V64 **2** (*NAmE*) (*BrE* **teat**) the rubber part at the end of a baby's bottle that the baby sucks in order to get milk, etc. from the bottle 奶嘴；橡胶乳头 **3** a small metal, plastic or rubber object that is shaped like a nipple with a small hole in the end, especially one that is used as part of a machine to direct oil, etc. into a particular place 乳头状物品；（机器的）喷嘴：*a grease nipple* 油脂枪喷嘴

nippy /ˈnɪpi/ *adj.* **1** (*BrE*) able to move quickly and easily 灵巧的；敏捷的：*a nippy little sports car* 小巧灵便的跑车 **2** (*informal*) (of the weather 天气) cold 冷的；寒冷的

niqab /nɪˈkɑːb/ *noun* a piece of cloth that covers the face but not usually the eyes, worn in public by some Muslim women 尼卡布（一些穆斯林妇女在公共场合戴的面纱，通常露出眼睛）

nir·vana /nɪəˈvɑːnə; *NAmE* nɪrˈv-/ *noun* [U] (in the religion of Buddhism 佛教) the state of peace and happiness that a person achieves after giving up all personal desires 涅槃（超脱一切烦恼的境界）

Nis·sen hut /ˈnɪsn hʌt/ (*BrE*) (*NAmE* **Quonset hut™**) *noun* a shelter made of metal with curved walls and roof 尼森式半筒形铁皮屋

nit /nɪt/ *noun* **1** the egg or young form of a LOUSE (= a small insect that lives in human hair) 虱子卵；小虱子 **2** (*BrE, informal*) a stupid person 傻瓜；笨蛋

nit·pick·ing /ˈnɪtpɪkɪŋ/ *noun* [U] (*informal, disapproving*) the habit of finding small mistakes in sb's work or paying too much attention to small details that are not important 吹毛求疵；挑刺儿 ▶ **nit·pick·er** *noun* **nit·pick·ing** *adj.*

ni·trate /ˈnaɪtreɪt/ *noun* [U, C] (*chemistry* 化) a COMPOUND containing NITROGEN and OXYGEN. There are several different nitrates and they are used especially to make soil better for growing crops. 硝酸盐；硝态氮肥：*We need to cut nitrate levels in water.* 我们需要降低水中的硝酸盐含量。

ni·tric acid /ˌnaɪtrɪk ˈæsɪd/ *noun* [U] (*chemistry* 化) (*symb.* **HNO_3**) a powerful clear acid that can destroy most substances and is used to make EXPLOSIVES and other chemical products 硝酸

ni·trify /ˈnaɪtrɪfaɪ/ *verb* (**ni·tri·fies, ni·tri·fying, ni·tri·fied, ni·tri·fied**) **~ sth** (*chemistry* 化) to change a substance into a COMPOUND that contains NITROGEN （使）硝化 ➲ SEE ALSO NITRATE

ni·trite /ˈnaɪtraɪt/ *noun* [U, C] (*chemistry* 化) a COMPOUND containing NITROGEN and OXYGEN. There are several different nitrites. 亚硝酸盐；亚硝酸酯

ni·tro·gen /ˈnaɪtrədʒən/ *noun* [U] (*symb.* **N**) a chemical element. Nitrogen is a gas that is found in large quantities in the earth's atmosphere. 氮；氮气 ▶ **ni·tro·gen·ous** /naɪˈtrɒdʒənəs; *NAmE* -ˈtrɑːdʒ-/ *adj.*

ˈnitrogen cycle *noun* [C, U] the processes by which nitrogen is passed from one part of the environment to another, for example when plants decay 氮循环（各种形式的氮在自然界的循环）

ˌnitrogen diˈoxide *noun* [U] (*chemistry* 化) a brown poisonous gas. Nitrogen dioxide is formed when some metals are dissolved in NITRIC ACID. 二氧化氮

nitro·gly·cer·ine /ˌnaɪtrəʊˈɡlɪsəriːn; -rɪn; *NAmE* ˌnaɪtroʊˈɡlɪsərən/ (*especially BrE*) (*US usually* **nitro·gly·cerin** /-rɪn; *NAmE* -rən/) *noun* [U] a powerful liquid EXPLOSIVE 硝化甘油

ni·trous oxide /ˌnaɪtrəs ˈɒksaɪd; *NAmE* ˈɑːk-/ (*also informal* **ˈlaughing gas**) *noun* [U] a gas used especially in the past by dentists to prevent you from feeling pain 氧化亚氮，笑气（旧时牙医用作麻醉剂）

the nitty-gritty /ˌnɪti ˈɡrɪti/ *noun* [sing.] (*informal*) the basic or most important details of an issue or a situation 基本事实；重要细节：*Time ran out before we could get down to the real nitty-gritty.* 我们还没来得及探讨真正的重要细节，时间就过去了。 ➲ MORE LIKE THIS 11, page R26

nit·wit /ˈnɪtwɪt/ *noun* (*informal*) a stupid person 笨蛋；傻瓜

nivas /ˈnɪvæs/ *noun* (*pl.* **nivases**) (*IndE*) a building where people live or stay, such as a house, a block of flats/apartment building, a hotel, etc. 房屋；公寓楼；旅馆

nix /nɪks/ *verb, noun*
▪ *verb* **~ sth** (*NAmE, informal*) to prevent sth from happening by saying 'no' to it 阻止；拒绝
▪ *noun* [U] (*NAmE, informal*) nothing 无；没有什么；没有东西

NLP /ˌen el ˈpiː/ *abbr.* **1** NEUROLINGUISTIC PROGRAMMING（心理学）神经语言程序技术 **2** NATURAL LANGUAGE PROCESSING（计算机）自然语言处理

No. *abbr.* **1** (*also* **no.**) (*pl.* **Nos, nos**) number 号码：*Room No. 145* * 145 号房间 **2** (*NAmE*) north; northern 北方（的）；北部（的）

no 🔑 /nəʊ; *NAmE* noʊ/ *exclamation, det., adv., noun*
▪ *exclamation* **1** 🔑 used to give a negative reply or statement （用于否定的回答或陈述）不；没有；不是：*Just say yes or no.* 只要说"是"或"不是"。◇ *'Are you ready?' 'No, I'm not.'* "准备好了吗？""没有，我没准备好。"◇ *Sorry, the answer's no.* 对不起，回答是不。◇ *'Another drink?' 'No, thanks.'* "再来一杯？""不要了，谢谢。"◇ *It's about 70—no, I'm wrong—80 kilometres from Rome.* 距离罗马大约是 70，不，不对，是 80 公里。◇ *No! Don't touch it! It's hot.* 别！别碰它！很烫。◇ *'It was Tony.' 'No, you're wrong. It was Ted.'* "是托尼。""不对，你错了。是特德。"◇ *'It's not very good, is it?' 'No, you're right, it isn't* (= I agree).' "这不太好，是吧？""你说得对，这不太好。" **2** 🔑 used to express shock or surprise at what sb has said （对某人所说的话感到惊讶）不，不要：*'She's had an accident.' 'Oh, no!'* "她发生了意外。""怎么会呢！"◇ *'I'm leaving!' 'No!'* "我要走了！""别走！"
IDM **not take no for an answer** to refuse to accept that sb does not want sth, will not do sth, etc. 非让人接受（或听从）：*You're coming and I won't take no for an answer!* 你一定要来，不来可不行！ ➲ MORE AT YES *exclamation*
▪ *det.* **1** 🔑 not one; not any; not a 没有；无：*No student is to leave the room.* 学生一律不许离开这房间。◇ *There were no letters this morning.* 今天早上一封信也没有。◇ *There's no bread left.* 一片面包都没有了。◇ *No two days are the same.* 一天一个样。 ➲ SEE ALSO NO ONE **2** 🔑 used, for example on notices, to say that sth is not allowed 不准；禁止：*No smoking!* 禁止吸烟！ **3** 🔑 **there's ~ doing sth** used to say that it is impossible to do sth 没有可能（做某事）：*There's no telling what will happen next.* 下一步还不定会发生什么事。 **4** 🔑 used to express the opposite of what is mentioned （表示情况的反面）不是，并不：*She's no fool* (= she's intelligent). 她并不傻。◇ *It was no easy matter* (= it was difficult). 这件事不容易。
▪ *adv.* used before adjectives and adverbs to mean 'not' （与 not 同义，用于形容词和副词前）不：*She's feeling no better this morning.* 她今天早晨还是不见好转。◇ *Reply by no later than 21 July.* 请于 7 月 21 日前答复。
▪ *noun* (*pl.* **noes** /nəʊz; *NAmE* noʊz/) **1** an answer that shows you do not agree with an idea, a statement, etc.; a person who says 'no' 否定的回答；作否定回答的人：*Can't you give me a straight yes or no?* "是"还是"否"，你就不能给我个直截了当的回答吗？◇ *When we took a vote there were nine yesses and three noes.* 我们投票表决，有九人赞同，三人反对。◇ *I'll put you down as a no.* 我就当你是反对了。 **2 the noes** [pl.] the total number of people voting 'no' in a formal debate, for example in a parliament （统称）投反对票者：*The noes have it* (= more people have voted against sth than for it). 投反对票者占多数。 **OPP** **ayes**

No. 10 = NUMBER TEN

Noah's ark /ˌnəʊəz ˈɑːk; *NAmE* ˌnoʊəz ˈɑːrk/ *noun* = ARK

nob /nɒb; *NAmE* nɑːb/ *noun* (*old-fashioned, BrE, informal*) a person who has a high social position; a member of the upper class 社会地位高的人；上层人士；大人物

ˌno-ˈball *noun* (in CRICKET 板球) a ball that is BOWLED (= thrown) in a way that is not allowed and which means that a RUN (= a point) is given to the other team 投球犯规

nob·ble /ˈnɒbl; NAmE ˈnɑːbl/ *verb* (*BrE, informal*) **1 ~ sth** to prevent a horse from winning a race, for example by giving it drugs 阻止（赛马）取胜 **2 ~ sb** to persuade sb to do what you want, especially illegally, by offering them money 买通：*his attempts to nobble the jury* 他想收买陪审团的种种企图 **3 ~ sb** to prevent sb from achieving what they want 阻挠；使遭受挫折 SYN **thwart** **4 ~ sb** to catch sb or get their attention, especially when they are unwilling（尤指有违其意愿）抓住，引起注意：*He was nobbled by the press who wanted details of the affair.* 新闻界紧盯住他不放，要了解事件的详情。▶ **nob·bling** *noun* [U]

no·bel·ium /nəʊˈbiːliəm; -ˈbel-; NAmE noʊ-/ *noun* [U] (*symb.* **No**) a chemical element. Nobelium is a RADIOACTIVE metal that does not exist naturally and is produced from CURIUM. 锘（放射性化学元素）

Nobel Prize /nəʊˌbel ˈpraɪz; NAmE noʊ-/ *noun* one of six international prizes given each year for excellent work in physics, chemistry, medicine, literature, ECONOMICS and work towards world peace 诺贝尔奖

no·bil·ity /nəʊˈbɪləti; NAmE noʊ-/ *noun* **1 the nobility** [sing.+sing./pl. v.] people of high social position who have titles such as that of DUKE or DUCHESS 贵族 SYN **aristocracy** **2** [U] (*formal*) the quality of being noble in character 高贵的品质

noble /ˈnəʊbl; NAmE ˈnoʊbl/ *adj., noun*

■ *adj.* (**no·bler** /ˈnəʊblə(r); NAmE ˈnoʊ-/, **nob·lest** /ˈnəʊblɪst; NAmE ˈnoʊ-/) **1** having fine personal qualities that people admire, such as courage, HONESTY and care for others 崇高的；品质高尚的：*a noble leader* 伟大的领袖 ◇ *noble ideals* 崇高的理想 ◇ *He died for a noble cause.* 他为了高尚的事业而牺牲。➲ COMPARE IGNOBLE **2** very impressive in size or quality 宏伟的；壮丽的 SYN **splendid**：*a noble building* 雄伟的大楼 **3** belonging to a family of high social rank (= belonging to the nobility) 贵族的；高贵的 SYN **aristocratic**：*a man of noble birth* 出身高贵的人 ▶ **nobly** /ˈnəʊbli; NAmE ˈnoʊ-/ *adv.*：*She bore the disappointment nobly.* 她很失望，但表现得很大度。◇ *to be nobly born* 出身贵族

■ *noun* a person who comes from a family of high social rank; a member of the nobility 出身高贵的人；贵族成员 SYN **aristocrat**

ˌnoble ˈgas (*also* **iˌnert ˈgas, ˈrare gas**) *noun* (*chemistry* 化) any of a group of gases that do not react with other chemicals. ARGON, HELIUM, KRYPTON and NEON are noble gases. 惰性气体；稀有气体

noble·man /ˈnəʊblmən; NAmE ˈnoʊbl-/, **noble·woman** /ˈnəʊblwʊmən; NAmE ˈnoʊbl-/ *noun* (*pl.* **-men** /-mən/, **-women** /-wɪmɪn/) a person from a family of high social rank; a member of the NOBILITY 出身高贵的人；贵族成员 SYN **aristocrat** ➲ MORE LIKE THIS 25, page R28

ˌnoble ˈsavage *noun* a word used in the past to refer in a positive way to a person or people who did not live in an advanced human society 高尚的野蛮人（指未开化原始人的善良、天真、不受文明罪恶玷污）：*The book contrasts modern civilization with the ideal of the noble savage who lived in harmony with nature.* 这本书将现代文明同与自然界和谐相处的高尚野蛮人的理想放在一起对比。

no·blesse ob·lige /nəʊˌbles əˈbliːʒ; NAmE noʊ-/ *noun* [U] (*from French*) the idea that people who have special advantages of wealth, etc. should help other people who do not have these advantages 位高则任重；显贵者应有高尚品德；贵族义务

no·body 🔑 /ˈnəʊbədi; NAmE ˈnoʊ-/ *pron., noun*

■ *pron.* 🔑 = NO ONE：*Nobody knew what to say.* 谁也不知道该说什么。HELP **Nobody** is more common than **no one** in spoken English. 在英语口语中，nobody 比 no one 更常用。OPP **somebody**

■ *noun* (*pl.* **-ies**) a person who has no importance or influence 小人物；无足轻重的人 SYN **nonentity**：*She rose from being a nobody to become a superstar.* 她从无名小辈一跃成为超级明星。➲ COMPARE SOMEONE

no-brainer /ˌnəʊ ˈbreɪnə(r); NAmE ˌnoʊ ˈbreɪnər/ *noun* (*informal*) a decision or a problem that you do not need to think about much because it is obvious what you should do 无需用脑的事；容易的决定

ˌno-ˈclaims bonus (*also* **ˌno-ˈclaim bonus, ˌno-ˈclaim(s) discount**) *noun* (*all BrE*) a reduction in the cost of your insurance because you made no claims in the previous year 无索赔赠金（因前一年未申报保险赔偿而获得）➲ WORDFINDER NOTE AT INSURANCE

noc·tur·nal /nɒkˈtɜːnl; NAmE nɑːkˈtɜːrnl/ *adj.* **1** (of animals 动物) active at night 夜行的；夜出的 OPP **diurnal** **2** (*formal*) happening during the night 夜间发生的：*a nocturnal visit* 夜访

noc·turne /ˈnɒktɜːn; NAmE ˈnɑːktɜːrn/ *noun* a short piece of music in a romantic style, especially for the piano 夜曲（主要为钢琴曲）

Nod /nɒd; NAmE nɑːd/ *noun* [U] IDM SEE LAND *n.*

nod /nɒd; NAmE nɑːd/ *verb, noun*

■ *verb* (**-dd-**) **1** [I, T] if you **nod**, **nod** your head or your head **nods**, you move your head up and down to show agreement, understanding, etc. 点头：*I asked him if he would help me and he nodded.* 我问他能不能帮我一下，他点了点头。◇ *Her head nodded in agreement.* 她点头表示同意。◇ **~ sth** *He nodded his head sympathetically.* 他同情地点点头。◇ *She nodded approval.* 她点头表示赞同。**2** [I, T] to move your head down and up once to say hello to sb or to give them a sign to do sth 点头致意；点头示意：**~ (to/at sb)** *The president nodded to the crowd as he passed in the motorcade.* 当总统的车队经过时，他向人群点头致意。◇ **~ to/at sb to do sth** *She nodded at him to begin speaking.* 她点头示意他开始讲话。◇ **~ sth (to/at sb)** *to nod a greeting* 点头问候 **3** [I] **+ adv./prep.** to move your head in the direction of sb/sth to show that you are talking about them/it（朝…方向）点头（表示所谈论的人或物）：*I asked where Steve was and she nodded in the direction of the kitchen.* 我问史蒂夫在哪儿，她朝厨房点了点头。**4** [I] to let your head fall forward when you are sleeping in a chair 打盹；打瞌睡：*He sat nodding in front of the fire.* 他坐在炉火前打盹儿。➲ MORE LIKE THIS 36, page R29

IDM **have a nodding acˈquaintance with sb/sth** to only know sb/sth slightly 与…有点头之交；对…略知一二

PHR V **ˌnod ˈoff** (*informal*) to fall asleep for a short time while you are sitting in a chair 打盹；打瞌睡

■ *noun* a small quick movement of the head down and up again 点头：*to give a nod of approval/agreement/encouragement* 点头表示赞同 / 同意 / 鼓励

IDM **get the ˈnod** (*informal*) to be chosen for sth; to be given permission or approval to do sth 被选中；得到许可：*He got the nod from the team manager* (= he was chosen for the team). 他被球队主教练看中了。**give sb/sth the ˈnod** (*informal*) **1** to give permission for sth; to agree to sth 允许；对…表示同意：*We've been given the nod to expand the business.* 我们得到允许扩大企业规模。◇ *I hope he'll give the nod to the plan.* 我希望他会同意这个计划。**2** to choose sb for sth 挑选 **a ˌnod and a ˈwink | a ˌnod is as good as a ˈwink** used to say that a suggestion or a HINT will be understood, without anything more being said 一点就懂；（心有灵犀）一点通：*Everything could be done by a nod and a wink.* 每件事只靠点拨一下就能办妥了。**on the ˈnod** (*BrE, informal*) if a proposal is accepted **on the nod**, it is accepted without any discussion（未经讨论）一致同意

nod·dle /ˈnɒdl; NAmE ˈnɑːdl/ (*NAmE usually* **noo·dle**) *noun* (*old-fashioned, slang*) your head; your brain 头；脑袋

node /nəʊd; NAmE noʊd/ *noun* **1** (*biology* 生) a place on the STEM of a plant from which a branch or leaf grows 茎节 **2** (*biology* 生) a small swelling on a root or branch（根或枝上的）节 **3** a point at which two lines or systems meet or cross 结点；节点：*a network node* 网络节点 **4** (*computing* 计) a piece of equipment such as a

N

computer, that is attached to a network 连接到网络的设备（如计算机） **5** (*anatomy* 解) a small hard mass of TISSUE, especially near a joint in the human body （尤指人体关节附近的）硬结： *a lymph node* 淋巴结 ▶ **nodal** *adj.*

nod·ule /ˈnɒdjuːl; *NAmE* ˈnɑːdʒuːl/ *noun* a small round lump or swelling, especially on a plant （尤指植物上的）节，节结

Noel /nəʊˈel; *NAmE* noʊ-/ *noun* [C, U] a word for 'Christmas' used especially in songs or on cards 圣诞节（尤用于歌曲和贺卡）： *Joyful Noel* 快乐的圣诞节

noes PL. OF NO

ˌ**no-ˈfault** *adj.* [only before noun] (*law* 律, *especially NAmE*) not involving a decision as to who is to blame for sth 不追究责任的；无过失的： *no-fault insurance* (= in which the insurance company pays for damage, etc. without asking whose fault it was) 不追究责任的保险

ˌ**no-ˈfly zone** *noun* an area above a country where planes from other countries are not allowed to fly 禁飞区（禁止别国飞机飞行的地区）

ˌ**no-ˈfrills** *adj.* [only before noun] (especially of a service or product 尤指服务或产品) including only the basic features, without anything that is unnecessary, especially things added to make sth more attractive or comfortable 只包括基本元素的；无装饰的： *a no-frills airline* 只提供基本服务的航空公司

ˌ**no-ˈgo area** *noun* (*especially BrE*) an area, especially in a city, which is dangerous for people to enter, or that the police or army do not enter, often because it is controlled by a violent group 禁区（常因被暴力团伙控制）： (*figurative*) *Some clubs are no-go areas for people over 30.* 对于 30 岁以上的人来说，有些俱乐部是禁区。◇ (*figurative*) *This subject is definitely a no-go area* (= we must not discuss it). 这个话题绝对禁止谈论。

N

ˈ**no-good** *adj.* [only before noun] (*slang*) (of a person 人) bad or useless 坏的；无用的

Noh (*also* **No**) /nəʊ; *NAmE* noʊ/ *noun* [U] traditional Japanese theatre in which songs, dance, and MIME are performed by people wearing MASKS 能剧（日本传统戏剧）

ˌ**no-ˈhoper** *noun* (*informal*) a person or an animal that is considered useless or very unlikely to be successful 无望取胜的人（或动物）；无用之辈；无能之人

noise 🔑 /nɔɪz/ *noun* **1** 🔑 [C, U] a sound, especially when it is loud, unpleasant or disturbing 声音；响声；噪音；吵闹声： *a rattling noise* 咔嗒咔嗒的声音 ◇ *What's that noise?* 哪来的响声？ ◇ *Don't make a noise.* 别出声。◇ *They were making too much noise.* 他们太吵了。◇ *I was woken by the noise of a car starting up.* 我被汽车的启动声吵醒了。◇ *We had to shout above the noise of the traffic.* 车辆噪声太大，我们不得不扯着嗓子说话。◇ *to reduce* ***noise levels*** 减少噪音量 **2** [U] (*specialist*) extra electrical or electronic signals that are not part of the signal that is being broadcast or TRANSMITTED and which may damage it 噪声；干扰；电子干扰信号 **3** [U] information that is not wanted and that can make it difficult for the important or useful information to be seen clearly 干扰信息；垃圾信息： *There is some noise in the data which needs to be reduced.* 资料里有一些需要删除的不适用信息。

IDM **make a ˈnoise (about sth)** (*informal*) to complain loudly 大声诉苦；大声抱怨 **make ˈnoises (about sth)** (*informal*) **1** to talk in an indirect way about sth that you think you might do 放出…的风声： *The company has been making noises about closing several factories.* 公司放出风声说要关闭几家工厂。 **2** to complain about sth 抱怨；埋怨 **make soothing, encouraging, reassuring, etc. noises** to make remarks of the kind mentioned, even when that is not what you really think 说安慰（或鼓励、使人放心等）的话（有时言不由衷地）： *He made all the right noises at the meeting yesterday* (= said what people wanted to hear). 在昨天的会上，他的话句句都合大家的胃口。 ➲ MORE AT BIG *adj.*

> ▼ **WHICH WORD?** 词语辨析
>
> **noise / sound**
>
> - **Noise** is usually loud and unpleasant. It can be countable or uncountable. * noise 通常指噪音，既可作可数名词，也可作不可数名词： *Try not to make so much noise.* 别那么吵吵闹闹的。◇ *What a terrible noise!* 多么令人讨厌的噪音啊！
> - **Sound** is a countable noun and means something that you hear. * sound 为可数名词，意为听到的声音或响声： *All she could hear was the sound of the waves.* 她听得到的只有海浪声。 You do not use words like *much* or *a lot of* with **sound**. * sound 不与 much 或 a lot of 等词语连用。

noise·less /ˈnɔɪzləs/ *adj.* (*formal*) making little or no noise 没有噪音的；寂静的；不出声的 SYN **silent**: *He moved with noiseless steps.* 他脚下无声地走动。 ▶ **noise·less·ly** *adv.*

ˌ**noises ˈoff** *noun* [pl.] **1** (in theatre 剧院) sounds made off the stage, intended to be heard by the audience 音响效果（为演出需要在后台发出的各种声响） **2** (*humorous*) noise in the background which interrupts you 背景噪音

noi·some /ˈnɔɪsəm/ *adj.* (*formal*) extremely unpleasant or offensive 恶心的；极令人厌烦的；使人很不快的： *noisome smells* 令人厌恶的气味

noisy 🔑 /ˈnɔɪzi/ *adj.* (**nois·ier**, **noisi·est**) **1** 🔑 making a lot of noise 吵闹的；聒噪的；嘈杂的： *noisy children/traffic/crowds* 吵闹的孩子；喧闹的交通；嘈杂的人群 ◇ *a noisy protest* (= when people shout) 吵吵嚷嚷的抗议声 ◇ *The engine is very noisy at high speed.* 这个发动机转速高时噪音非常大。 **2** 🔑 full of noise 充满噪音的；吵吵闹闹的： *a noisy classroom* 吵闹的教室 ▶ **nois·ily** 🔑 /-ɪli/ *adv.*: *The children were playing noisily upstairs.* 孩子们在楼上吵闹地玩耍。

nol·lie /ˈnɒli; *NAmE* ˈnɑːli/ *noun* (in SKATEBOARDING and SNOWBOARDING 滑板和滑雪板运动) a jump that is done by pushing one foot down hard on the front of the board 板鼻翱骊，反脚豚跳（一脚猛踩滑板前部的带板起跳动作） ➲ COMPARE OLLIE

Nolly·wood /ˈnɒliwʊd; *NAmE* ˈnɑːli-/ *noun* [U] (*informal*) used to refer to the Nigerian film/movie industry, mainly based in Lagos 瑙莱坞（指以拉各斯为主要基地的尼日利亚电影业） ➲ COMPARE BOLLYWOOD, HOLLYWOOD

nomad /ˈnəʊmæd; *NAmE* ˈnoʊ-/ *noun* a member of a community that moves with its animals from place to place 游牧部落的人 ▶ **no·mad·ic** /nəʊˈmædɪk; *NAmE* noʊ-/ *adj.*: *nomadic tribes* 游牧部落 ◇ *the nomadic life of a foreign correspondent* 驻国外记者的流浪生活

ˈ**no-man's-land** *noun* [U, sing.] an area of land between the borders of two countries or between two armies, that is not controlled by either （边境的）无人区域；（两军之间的）无人地带

nom de guerre /ˌnɒm də ˈgeə(r); *NAmE* ˌnɑːm də ˈger/ *noun* (*pl.* **noms de guerre** /ˌnɒm də ˈgeə(r); *NAmE* ˌnɑːm də ˈger/) (*from French, formal*) a false name that is used, for example, by sb who belongs to a military organization that is not official 假名；化名

nom de plume /ˌnɒm də ˈpluːm; *NAmE* ˌnɑːm/ *noun* (*pl.* **noms de plume** /ˌnɒm də ˈpluːm; *NAmE* ˌnɑːm/) (*from French*) a name used by a writer instead of their real name 笔名 SYN **pen name, pseudonym**

no·men·cla·ture /nəˈmenklətʃə(r); *NAmE* ˈnoʊmənkleɪtʃər/ *noun* [U, C] (*formal*) a system of naming things, especially in a branch of science （尤指某学科的）命名（法）

nom·in·al /ˈnɒmɪnl; *NAmE* ˈnɑːm-/ *adj.* **1** being sth in name only, and not in reality 名义上的；有名无实的：*the nominal leader of the party* 这个政党的名义领袖 ◇ *He remained in nominal control of the business for another ten years.* 他名义上又掌管了这家公司十年。**2** (of a sum of money 款额) very small and much less than the normal cost or charge 很小的；象征性的 **SYN** **token**：*We only pay a nominal rent.* 我们只象征性地付一点租金。**3** (*grammar* 语法) connected with a noun or nouns 名词性的；名词的 ▸ **nom·in·al·ly** /-nəli/ *adv.*：*He was nominally in charge of the company.* 他名义上管理着这家公司。

nom·in·al·ize /ˈnɒmɪnəlaɪz; *NAmE* ˈnɑːm-/ *verb* ~ **sth** (*grammar* 语法) to form a noun from a verb or adjective, for example 'truth' from 'true' 使（动词或形容词）转变为名词；使名词化

nom·in·ate /ˈnɒmɪneɪt; *NAmE* ˈnɑːm-/ *verb* **1** to formally suggest that sb should be chosen for an important role, prize, position, etc. 提名；推荐 **SYN** **propose**：**~ sb (for sth)** *She has been nominated for the presidency.* 她已经获得了董事长职位的提名。◇ **~ sb (as) sth | ~ sb + noun** *He was nominated (as) best actor.* 他获得了最佳男演员的提名。◇ **~ sb to do sth** *I nominated Paul to take on the role of treasurer.* 我推荐保罗担任司库。**2** to choose sb to do a particular job 任命；指派 **SYN** **appoint**：**~ sb (to/as sth)** *I have been nominated to the committee.* 我被任命为委员会委员。◇ **~ sb to do sth** *She was nominated to speak on our behalf.* 她被指派代表我们发言。**3** ~ **sth (as sth)** to choose a time, date or title for sth 挑选，指定（时间、日期、名称等）**SYN** **select**：*1 December has been nominated as the day of the election.* * 12 月 1 日被指定为选举日。

nom·in·ation /ˌnɒmɪˈneɪʃn; *NAmE* ˌnɑːm-/ *noun* [U, C] the act of suggesting or choosing sb as a candidate in an election, or for a job or an award; the fact of being suggested for this 提名；推荐；任命；指派：*Membership of the club is by nomination only.* 俱乐部的会员资格仅可通过推荐获得。◇ *He won the nomination as Democratic candidate for the presidency.* 他赢得了民主党总统候选人的提名。◇ *They opposed her nomination to the post of Deputy Director.* 他们反对任命她为副主任。◇ *He has had nine Oscar nominations.* 他已经获得九次奥斯卡提名。➲ WORDFINDER NOTE AT CONGRESS

nom·ina·tive /ˈnɒmɪnətɪv; *NAmE* ˈnɑːm-/ (*also* **sub·ject·ive**) *noun* (*grammar* 语法) (in some languages 用于某些语言) the form of a noun, a pronoun or an adjective when it is the subject of a verb 主格；主格词 ➲ COMPARE ABLATIVE, ACCUSATIVE, DATIVE, GENITIVE, VOCATIVE ▸ **nom·ina·tive** *adj.*：*nominative pronouns* 主格代词

nom·inee /ˌnɒmɪˈniː; *NAmE* ˌnɑːm-/ *noun* **1** a person who has been formally suggested for a job, a prize, etc. 被提名人；被任命者：*a presidential nominee* 被提名为总统候选人的人 ◇ *an Oscar nominee* 获得奥斯卡提名的人 **2** (*business* 商) a person in whose name money is invested in a company, etc. （投资等的）名义持有人

non- 🔑 /nɒn; *NAmE* nɑːn/ *prefix* (in nouns, adjectives and adverbs 构成名词、形容词和副词) not 无；没有：*nonsense* 废话 ◇ *non-fiction* 纪实文学 ◇ *non-alcoholic* 不含酒精的 ◇ *non-profit-making* 非营利性的 ◇ *non-committally* 含糊其词 **HELP** Most compounds with **non** are written with a hyphen in *BrE* but are written as one word with no hyphen in *NAmE*. 大多数含 non 的复合词在英式英语里要加连字符，而在美式英语里则写成一个词。➲ MORE LIKE THIS 6, page R25

nona·gen·ar·ian /ˌnɒnədʒəˈneəriən; ˌnəʊn-; *NAmE* ˌnɑːnədʒəˈner-; ˌnoʊn-/ *noun* a person who is between 90 and 99 years old * 90 多岁的人 ▸ **nona·gen·ar·ian** *adj.*

ˌnon-agˈgres·sion *noun* [U] (often used as an adjective 常用作形容词) a relationship between two countries that have agreed not to attack each other （两国间的）不侵犯，不侵略：*a policy of non-aggression* 互不侵犯政策 ◇ *a non-aggression pact/treaty* 互不侵犯协定 / 条约

ˌnon-alcoˈhol·ic *adj.* (of a drink 饮料) not containing any alcohol 不含酒精的：*a non-alcoholic drink* 软饮料 ◇ *Can I have something non-alcoholic?* 给我来杯软饮料好吗？

ˌnon-aˈligned *adj.* not providing support for or receiving support from any of the powerful countries in the world 不结盟的 ▸ **ˌnon-aˈlignment** *noun* [U]：*a policy of non-alignment* 不结盟政策

ˌnon-alphaˈbet·ic (*also* **ˌnon-alphaˈbetical**) *adj.* not being one of the letters of the alphabet 不属于字母表的；非字母的 ➲ COMPARE ALPHABETIC

ˌnon-apˈpear·ance *noun* [U] (*formal*) failure to be in a place where people expect to see you 不露面；不到场

ˌnon-atˈtend·ance *noun* [U] failure to go to a place at a time or for an event where you are expected 缺席；不出席；不到场

ˌnon-biodeˈgrad·able *adj.* a substance or chemical that is **non-biodegradable** cannot be changed to a harmless natural state by the action of bacteria, and may therefore damage the environment （物质或化学品）不可生物降解的，非生物降解的 **OPP** **biodegradable**

nonce /nɒns; *NAmE* nɑːns/ *adj.* a **nonce** word or expression is one that is invented for one particular occasion （词语）临时造的，偶用的，只使用一次的

non·cha·lant /ˈnɒnʃələnt; *NAmE* ˌnɑːnʃəˈlɑːnt/ *adj.* behaving in a calm and relaxed way; giving the impression that you are not feeling any anxiety 若无其事的；冷静的；漠不关心的 **SYN** **casual**：*to* ***appear/look/sound nonchalant*** 显得 / 看上去 / 听起来满不在乎的样子 ◇ *'It'll be fine,' she replied, with a nonchalant shrug.* 她若无其事地耸耸肩答道："会没事的。" ▸ **non·cha·lance** /-ləns; *NAmE* -ˈlɑːns/ *noun* [U]：*an air of nonchalance* 一副满不在乎的样子 **non·cha·lant·ly** *adv.*：*He was leaning nonchalantly against the wall.* 他漫不经心地斜倚着墙。

ˌnon-ˈcitizen *noun* (*NAmE*) = ALIEN (1)

ˌnon-ˈcombat·ant *noun* **1** a member of the armed forces who does not actually fight in a war, for example an army doctor （军队中的）非战斗人员 **2** in a war, a person who is not a member of the armed forces （战争时期的）平民，非军事人员 **SYN** **civilian** ➲ COMPARE COMBATANT

ˌnon-commis·sioned ˈofficer *noun* (*abbr.* **NCO**) a soldier in the army, etc. who has a rank such as SERGEANT or CORPORAL, but not a high rank 军士 ➲ COMPARE COMMISSIONED OFFICER

ˌnon-coˈmmit·tal *adj.* not giving an opinion; not showing which side of an argument you agree with 态度不明朗的；不表态的；含糊的：*a* ***non-committal reply/tone*** 含糊其词的回答 / 语调 ◇ *The doctor was non-committal about when I could drive again.* 关于我何时可以再开车的问题，医生没有表态。➲ SEE ALSO COMMIT (4) ▸ **non-com·mit·tal·ly** *adv.*

ˌnon-comˈpli·ance *noun* [U] ~ **(with sth)** the fact of failing or refusing to obey a rule 不服从；不顺从；违反：*There are penalties for non-compliance with the fire regulations.* 不遵守消防规章的行为要受到处罚。**OPP** **compliance**

ˌnon ˌcompos ˈmentis (*also* **ˌnon ˈcompos**) *adj.* (*formal*) not in a normal mental state 精神不健全的 **OPP** **compos mentis**

non·con·form·ist **AW** /ˌnɒnkənˈfɔːmɪst; *NAmE* ˌnɑːnkənˈfɔːrm-/ *noun* **1** **Nonconformist** (in England and Wales) a member of a Protestant Church that does not follow the beliefs and practices of the Church of England （英格兰和威尔士）不从国教者，不遵奉圣公会的新教教徒 **2** a person who does not follow normal ways of thinking or behaving 不遵循传统规范的人；不认同主流思想的人 ▸ **non·con·form·ist, Non·con·form·ist** *adj.*

non·con·form·ity **AW** /ˌnɒnkənˈfɔːməti; *NAmE* ˌnɑːnkənˈfɔːrm-/ (*also* **non·con·form·ism** /ˌnɒnkənˈfɔːmɪzəm; *NAmE* ˌnɑːnkənˈfɔːrm-/) *noun* [U] **1** the fact of not following normal ways of thinking and behaving

N

不遵从传统规范；不认同主流思想 **2 Nonconformity** the beliefs and practices of Nonconformist Churches 非国教教义；不信奉英国国教

ˌnon-ˈcontact sport *noun* a sport in which players do not have physical contact with each other 无身体接触的体育运动；非接触性体育运动 **OPP contact sport**

ˌnon-conˈtribu·tory *adj.* (of an insurance or pension plan 保险或养老金计划) paid for by the employer and not the employee 全部由雇主承担的；非分摊制的 **OPP contributory**

ˌnon-contro·ˈver·sial *adj.* not causing, or not likely to cause, any disagreement 不会引起争议的；一致的 **OPP controversial** **HELP** This is not as strong as **uncontroversial**, which is more common. 语气没有 uncontroversial 强，也较为少用。

ˌnon-coˌopeˈr·ation *noun* [U] refusal to help a person in authority by doing what they have asked you to do, especially as a form of protest 不合作（作为一种反抗的手段）：*A strike is unlikely, but some forms of non-cooperation are being considered.* 罢工不太可能，但是某种形式的不合作正在酝酿之中。

ˌnon-ˈcount *adj.* (*grammar* 语法) = UNCOUNTABLE

ˌnon-cuˈstod·ial *adj.* [only before noun] (*law* 律) **1** (of a punishment 惩罚) that does not involve a period of time in prison 监外执行的：*a* ***non-custodial sentence/penalty*** 监外执行的判决 / 惩罚 **2** (of a parent 父或母) not having CUSTODY of a child 无监护权的 **OPP custodial**

ˌnon-ˈdairy *adj.* [only before noun] not made with milk or cream 非奶制的；非乳制的：*a non-dairy whipped topping* 打好的非奶制糕点配料

ˌnon-deˈfining *adj.* = NON-RESTRICTIVE

non·de·script /ˈnɒndɪskrɪpt; *NAmE* ˈnɑːn-/ *adj.* (*disapproving*) having no interesting or unusual features or qualities 无特征的；平庸的；毫无个性的 **SYN dull**

non-dom /ˌnɒn ˈdɒm; *NAmE* ˌnɑːn ˈdɑːm/ *noun* (*BrE*) a person who lives in a country but says officially that they do not intend to live there permanently, which sometimes means that they pay less tax in that country 长期客居者，非永久居民（生活在某国但表明不以该国为永久居住地的人，有时这意味着可以少缴税）：*He admits that he's a non-dom for tax purposes.* 他承认他是为避税而做非永久居民。

none 🔑 /nʌn/ *pron., adv.*

■ ***pron.*** 🔑 ~ (of sb/sth) not one of a group of people or things; not any 没有一个；毫无：*None of these pens works/work.* 这些钢笔没有一支能用。◇ *We have three sons but none of them lives/live nearby.* 我们有三个儿子，但他们都不住在附近。◇ *We saw several houses but none we really liked.* 我们看了几所房子，但都不怎么喜欢。◇ *Tickets for Friday? Sorry we've got none left.* 星期五的票？对不起，一张也没有了。◇ *He told me all the news but none of it was very exciting.* 他告诉了我所有的新闻，但没有一件激动人心的。◇ *'Is there any more milk?' 'No, none at all.'* "还有牛奶吗？""没了，一点都没了。"◇ (*formal*) *Everybody liked him but none* (= nobody) *more than I.* 大家都喜欢他，但谁也比不过我。

> **▼ GRAMMAR POINT 语法说明**
>
> **none of**
>
> - When you use **none of** with an uncountable noun, the verb is in the singular. * none of 与不可数名词连用时，动词用单数：*None of the work was done.* 那些工作全都未干。
> - When you use **none of** with a plural noun or pronoun, or a singular noun referring to a group of people or things, you can use either a singular or a plural verb. The singular form is used in a formal style in *BrE*. * none of 与复数名词、代词或单数集合名词连用时，动词用单数或复数均可。英式英语的正式文体用单数形式：*None of the trains is/are going to London.* 这些列车都不去伦敦。◇ *None of her family has/have been to college.* 她的一家谁都没上过大学。

IDM **ˈnone but** (*literary*) only 仅仅；只有：*None but he knew the truth.* 只有他知道真相。 **none ˈother than** used to emphasize who or what sb/sth is, when this is surprising （强调出人意料的人或事）竟然：*Her first customer was none other than Mrs Obama.* 她的第一位顾客竟然是奥巴马夫人。 **have/want none of sth** to refuse to accept sth 拒绝接受；什么也不要：*I offered to pay but he was having none of it.* 我提出付账，但他坚决不让我付。 **ˌnone the ˈless** = NONETHELESS

■ ***adv.*** **1** used with *the* and a comparative to mean 'not at all' （与 the 加比较级连用）一点都不，绝无：*She told me what it meant at great length but I'm afraid I'm* ***none the wiser.*** 她费尽口舌给我解释它的意思，可我恐怕还是不明白。◇ *He seems* ***none the worse*** *for the experience.* 这次经历似乎没有给他造成丝毫伤害。 **2** used with *too* and an adjective or adverb to mean 'not at all' or 'not very' （与 too 加形容词或副词连用）绝不，不怎么：*She was looking none too pleased.* 她看上去一点也不高兴。

non·en·tity /nɒˈnentəti; *NAmE* nɑːˈn-/ *noun* (*pl.* **-ies**) (*disapproving*) a person without any special qualities, who has not achieved anything important 无专长的人；无成就的人 **SYN nobody**

ˌnon-esˈsential *adj.* [usually before noun] not completely necessary 非必需的；不重要的 ➲ COMPARE ESSENTIAL *adj.* (1) **HELP** This is not as strong as **inessential** and is more common. **Inessential** can suggest disapproval. 不如 inessential 语气强，但较常用。inessential 有不赞成的意思。▸ **ˌnon-esˈsential** *noun* [usually pl.]: *I have no money for non-essentials.* 我没有钱应付那些非必要的花费。

nonet /nəʊˈnet; nɒˈnet; *NAmE* noʊˈnet/ *noun* **1** [C+sing./pl. v.] a group of nine people or things, especially nine musicians 九人组；九个一组；（尤指）九重奏乐团，九重唱组合 **2** [C] a piece of music for nine singers or musicians 九重奏（曲）；九重唱（曲）

none·the·less **AW** /ˌnʌnðəˈles/ (*also* **ˌnone the ˈless**) *adv.* (*formal*) despite this fact 尽管如此 **SYN nevertheless**: *The book is too long but, nonetheless, informative and entertaining.* 这本书篇幅太长，但是很有知识性和趣味性。◇ *The problems are not serious. Nonetheless, we shall need to tackle them soon.* 问题不严重。不过我们还是需要尽快处理。➲ LANGUAGE BANK AT NEVERTHELESS

ˌnon-eˈvent *noun* (*informal*) an event that was expected to be interesting, exciting and popular but is in fact very disappointing 令人失望的事；扫兴的事 **SYN anticlimax**

ˌnon-exˈecutive *adj.* [only before noun] (*BrE, business* 商) a **non-executive** director of a company can give advice at a high level but does not have the power to make decisions about the company 非执行的；非主管的；无决策权的

ˌnon-eˈxistent *adj.* not existing; not real 不存在的；不真实的：*a non-existent problem* 不存在的问题 ◇ *'How's your social life?' 'Non-existent, I'm afraid.'* "你的社交生活如何？""我恐怕没有社交生活。"◇ *Hospital beds were scarce and medicines were* ***practically non-existent.*** 当时医院病床紧缺，药物几乎没有。➲ COMPARE EXISTENT *adj.* ▸ **ˌnon-eˈxistence** *noun* [U]

ˌnon-ˈfiction *noun* [U] books, articles or texts about real facts, people and events 非虚构作品：*I prefer reading non-fiction.* 我喜欢看非虚构作品。◇ *the non-fiction section of the library* 图书馆的非虚构作品区 **OPP fiction**

ˌnon-ˈfinite *adj.* (*grammar* 语法) a **non-finite** verb form or clause does not show a particular tense, PERSON or NUMBER 非限定的 **OPP finite**

ˌnon-ˈflammable *adj.* not likely to burn easily 不易燃的：*non-flammable nightwear* 不易燃的睡衣 **OPP flammable**

nong /nɒŋ; *NAmE* nɑːŋ; nɔːŋ/ *noun* (*AustralE, NZE, informal*) = NING-NONG

ˌnon-ˈgradable *adj.* (*grammar* 语法) (of an adjective 形容词) that cannot be used in the comparative and superlative forms, or be used with words like 'very' and 'less' 非级差的；不与程度副词连用的 **OPP gradable**

ˌnon-ˈhuman *adj.* not human 非人类的：*similarities between human and non-human animals* 人和其他动物之间的相似之处 ➲ COMPARE HUMAN *adj.*, INHUMAN

ˌnon-iˌdentical ˈtwin *noun* = FRATERNAL TWIN

ˌnon-interˈven·tion (*also* **ˌnon-interˈfer·ence**) *noun* [U] the policy or practice of not becoming involved in other people's disagreements, especially those of foreign countries (尤指对外国事务的) 不干涉 ▶ **ˌnon-interˈven·tion·ism** *noun* [U] **ˌnon-interˈven·tion·ist** *adj.*

ˌnon-inˈvasive *adj.* (of medical treatment 治疗) not involving cutting into the body 非侵入的；非创伤的；无创的

ˌnon-ˈissue *noun* a subject of little or no importance 无足轻重的事；不重要的事

ˌnon-ˈlinear *adj.* (*specialist*) that does not develop from one thing to another in a single smooth series of stages 非线性的 **OPP linear**

ˌnon-maˈlignant *adj.* (of a TUMOUR 肿瘤) not caused by cancer and not likely to be dangerous 非恶性的；良性的 **SYN benign OPP malignant**

ˌnon-ˈnative *adj.* **1** (of animals, plants, etc. 动物、植物等) not existing naturally in a place but coming from somewhere else 非本地的；引进的；移植的 **2** a **non-native** speaker of a language is one who has not spoken it from the time they first learnt to talk 非母语的 **OPP native**

ˌnon-neˈgoti·able *adj.* **1** that cannot be discussed or changed 不可谈判解决的；无法改变的 **2** (of a cheque, etc. 支票等) that cannot be changed for money by anyone except the person whose name is on it 只限本人使用的；禁止转让的 **OPP negotiable**

ˈno-no *noun* [sing.] (*informal*) a thing or a way of behaving that is not acceptable in a particular situation 不可做的事；不可接受的行为

ˌnon-obˈservance *noun* [U] (*formal*) the failure to keep or to obey a rule, custom, etc. 违反，不遵从（规章、习俗等） **OPP observance**

ˌno-ˈnonsense *adj.* [only before noun] simple and direct; only paying attention to important and necessary things 简单直接的；言简意赅的；不说废话的

non·par·eil /ˌnɒnpəˈreɪl; *NAmE* ˌnɑːnpəˈrel/ *noun* [sing.] (*formal*) a person or thing that is better than others in a particular area 无与伦比的人（或事物）

ˌnon-partiˈsan *adj.* [usually before noun] not supporting the ideas of one particular political party or group of people strongly 无党派之见的；中立的 **OPP partisan**

ˌnon-ˈpayment *noun* [U] (*formal*) failure to pay a debt, a tax, rent, etc. 未支付，不支付（欠债、税款、租金等）

ˌnon-ˈperson *noun* (*pl.* **non-persons**) a person who is thought not to be important, or who is ignored 不受重视（或被忽视）的人；小人物

ˌnon-ˈplayer character *noun* (*abbr.* **NPC**) a video game character that is not controlled by a player of the game （电子游戏中的）非玩家角色

non·plussed (*US also* **non·plused**) /ˌnɒnˈplʌst; *NAmE* ˌnɑːn-/ *adj.* so surprised and confused that you do not know what to do or say 惊呆的；非常困惑的 **SYN dumbfounded**

ˌnon-preˈscrip·tion *adj.* (of drugs 药品) that you can buy directly without a special form from a doctor 非处方类的；不用医生处方可以买的

ˌnon-proˈfes·sion·al *adj.* **1** having a job that does not need a high level of education or special training; connected with a job of this kind 非专业的；未经专门训练的；非专业性工作的：*training for non-professional staff* 对非专业员工的培训 **2** doing sth as a hobby rather than as a paid job 非职业的；业余的：*non-professional actors* 非职业演员 ➲ COMPARE PROFESSIONAL *adj.*, UNPROFESSIONAL ➲ SEE ALSO AMATEUR *adj.*

ˌnon-ˈprofit (*BrE also* **ˌnon-ˈprofit-making**) *adj.* (of an organization 机构) without the aim of making a profit 不以营利为目的的；非营利的：*an independent non-profit organization* 独立的非营利机构 ◇ *The centre is run on a non-profit basis.* 这个中心的运作不以营利为目的。◇ *The charity is non-profit-making.* 这个慈善团体不以营利为目的。

non·profit /ˌnɒnˈprɒfɪt; *NAmE* ˌnɑːnˈprɑːfɪt/ *adj.*, *noun* = NOT-FOR-PROFIT

ˌnon-proˌlifeˈr·ation *noun* [U] a limit to the increase in the number of nuclear and chemical weapons that are produced 限制核武器和化学武器的增加；防止核扩散

ˌnon-proˈpri·etary *adj.* not made by or belonging to a particular company 无产权的；非专属的；非专利的：*non-proprietary medicines* 非专利药物 **OPP proprietary**

ˌnon-reˈfund·able (*also* **ˌnon-reˈturnable**) *adj.* (of a sum of money 款额) that cannot be returned 不可偿还的；不能退款的：*a non-refundable deposit* 不能退回的订金 ◇ *a non-refundable ticket* (= you cannot return it and get your money back) 不可退的票

ˌnon-reˈnewable *adj.* **1** (of natural resources such as gas or oil 天然气、石油等自然资源) that cannot be replaced after use 非再生的；非可再生的 **2** that cannot be continued or repeated for a further period of time after it has ended 非延续性的；不可重复有效的：*a non-renewable contract* 不可延续的合同 **OPP renewable**

ˌnon-ˈresident *adj.*, *noun*

▪ ***adj.*** (*formal*) **1** (of a person or company 人或公司) not living or located permanently in a particular place or country 非当地居住的；非常设的；非常驻的 **2** not living in the place where you work or in a house that you own 不在（工作地点等）居住的；不寄宿的；非居民的 **3** not staying at a particular hotel 不在（某旅馆）住宿的：*Non-resident guests are welcome to use the hotel swimming pool.* 欢迎非旅馆住客使用本旅馆的游泳池。

▪ ***noun*** **1** a person who does not live permanently in a particular country 非永久居民 **2** a person not staying at a particular hotel 不在某旅馆住的人；非旅馆住客

ˌnon-resiˈdent·ial *adj.* **1** that is not used for people to live in 不用于居住的；非住宅的 **2** that does not require you to live in the place where you work or study 通勤的；走读的：*a non-residential course* 走读课程

ˌnon-reˈstric·tive (*also* **ˌnon-deˈfining**) *adj.* (*grammar* 语法) (of RELATIVE CLAUSES 关系从句) giving extra information about a noun phrase, inside commas in writing or in a particular INTONATION in speech. In 'My brother, who lives in France, is coming to Rome with us', the part between the commas is a non-restrictive relative clause. 非限制性的；非限定的 ➲ COMPARE RESTRICTIVE

ˌnon-reˈturn·able *adj.* **1** = NON-REFUNDABLE **2** that you cannot give back, for example to a shop/store, to be used again; that will not be given back to you 不可退回的；不回收的：*non-returnable bottles* 不回收的瓶子 **OPP returnable**

ˌnon-scienˈti·fic *adj.* not involving or connected with science or scientific methods 不涉及科学的；与科学无关的 ➲ COMPARE SCIENTIFIC, UNSCIENTIFIC

non·sense 🔑 /ˈnɒnsns; *NAmE* ˈnɑːnsens; -sns/ *noun* **1** 🔑 [U, C] ideas, statements or beliefs that you think are ridiculous or not true 谬论；胡扯；胡言乱语 **SYN rubbish**：*Reports that he has resigned are nonsense.* 有关他已经辞职的报道是无稽之谈。◇ *You're **talking nonsense**!* 你在胡说八道！◇ *'I won't go.' 'Nonsense! You must go!'* "我不想去。""胡扯！你一定得去！"◇ ***It's nonsense to** say they don't care.* 说他们不在意那是瞎扯。◇ *The idea is*

N

an economic nonsense. 这种观点是经济学上的谬论。 **2** [U] silly or unacceptable behaviour 愚蠢的行为；冒失；不可接受的行为：*The new teacher won't stand for any nonsense.* 这位新教师不会容忍任何无礼行为。 ➲ SEE ALSO NO-NONSENSE **3** [U] spoken or written words that have no meaning or make no sense 毫无意义的话；没有意义的文章：*a book of children's nonsense poems* 一本儿童胡话诗集 ◇ *Most of the translation he did for me was complete nonsense.* 他给我做的大多数译文完全不知所云。

IDM **make (a) 'nonsense of sth** to reduce the value of sth by a lot; to make sth seem ridiculous 使…的价值大打折扣；使…显得荒诞：*If people can bribe police officers, it makes a complete nonsense of the legal system.* 如果人们可以收买警察，法律体系就会变得一文不值。 ➲ MORE AT STUFF *n.*

'nonsense word *noun* a word with no meaning 无意义的词

non·sens·ical /nɒn'sensɪkl; *NAmE* nɑːn-/ *adj.* ridiculous; with no meaning 荒谬的；无意义的 SYN **absurd**

non sequi·tur /ˌnɒn 'sekwɪtə(r); *NAmE* ˌnɑːn/ *noun* (*from Latin, formal*) a statement that does not seem to follow what has just been said in any natural or logical way 不合逻辑的推论；未根据前提的推理

ˌnon-'slip *adj.* that helps to prevent sb/sth from slipping; that does not slip 防滑的；不滑的：*a non-slip bath mat* 浴室防滑垫

ˌnon-'smoker *noun* a person who does not smoke 不吸烟的人 OPP **smoker**

N

ˌnon-'smoking (*also* **ˌno-'smoking**) *adj.* [usually before noun] **1** (of a place 地方) where people are not allowed to smoke 禁烟的；不允许吸烟的：*This is a non-smoking area.* 这是非吸烟区。 **2** (of a person 人) who does not smoke 不吸烟的：*She's a non-smoking, non-drinking fitness fanatic.* 她不吸烟、不喝酒、热衷健身。 ▶ **ˌnon-'smoking** (*also* **ˌno-'smoking**) *noun* [U]: *Non-smoking is now the norm in most workplaces.* 大多数工作场所现在都已禁止吸烟。

ˌnon-spe'cif·ic *adj.* [usually before noun] **1** not definite or clearly defined; general 不明确的；非特定的；泛泛的：*The candidate's speech was non-specific.* 这位候选人的讲话只是泛泛之谈。 **2** (*medical* 医) (of pain, a disease, etc. 疼痛、疾病等) with more than one possible cause 非特异性的；不止一种病因的；有多种致病可能的

ˌnon-speˌcific ure'thritis *noun* [U] (*abbr.* **NSU**) (*medical* 医) a condition in which the URETHRA becomes sore and swollen. It is often caused by an infection caught by having sex. 非特异性尿道炎（多因性交感染）

ˌnon-'standard *adj.* **1** (of language 语言) not considered correct by most educated people 非标准的；不规范的：*non-standard dialects* 不规范的方言 ◇ *non-standard English* 非标准英语 ➲ COMPARE STANDARD *adj.* (4) **2** not the usual size, type, etc.（尺寸、型号等）不标准的，非常用的：*The paper was of non-standard size.* 这种纸的大小不标准。

ˌnon-'starter *noun* (*informal*) a thing or a person that has no chance of success 无望取得成功的人（或事）：*As a business proposition, it's a non-starter.* 作为一份商业建议，它不可能取得成功。

ˌnon-'stick *adj.* [usually before noun] (of a pan or a surface 锅或物体表面) covered with a substance that prevents food from sticking to it 不粘食物的；不粘的

ˌnon-'stop *adj.* **1** (of a train, a journey, etc. 列车、旅程等) without any stops 直达的；不在途中停留的 SYN **direct**: *a non-stop flight to Tokyo* 到东京的直达航班 ◇ *a non-stop train/service* 直达列车 / 服务 **2** without any pauses or stops 不间断的；不停的 SYN **continuous**: *non-stop entertainment/work* 连续不断的娱乐 / 工作 ▶ **ˌnon-'stop** *adv.*: *We flew non-stop from Paris to Chicago.* 我们从巴黎直飞芝加哥。◇ *It rained non-stop all week.* 雨连续下了整整一个星期。

ˌnon-tra'ditional AW *adj.* not following the usual methods, practices, etc. in a particular area of activity 非传统的；不符合传统的：*students from non-traditional backgrounds* 非传统出身的学生 OPP **traditional**

ˌnon-'U *adj.* (*old-fashioned, informal*) (of language or social behaviour 语言或社交行为) not considered socially acceptable among the upper classes 不为上层阶级所接受的 ORIGIN From the abbreviation **U** for 'upper class'. 源自 upper class 的缩写字母 U。

ˌnon-'union (*also less frequent* **ˌnon-'unionized, -ised**) *adj.* [usually before noun] **1** not belonging to a trade/labor union 不属于工会的：*non-union labour/workers* 未加入工会的劳工 / 工人 **2** (of a business, company, etc. 企业、公司等) not accepting trade/labor unions or employing trade/labor union members 不接受工会的；不雇用工会会员的

ˌnon-vege'tar·ian (*also informal* **ˌnon-'veg**) *noun* (*IndE*) a person who eats meat, fish, eggs, etc. 非素食者；荤食者：*They ordered a non-veg meal.* 他们要了一餐荤菜。

ˌnon-'verbal *adj.* [usually before noun] not involving words or speech 不涉及言语的；非言语的：*non-verbal communication* 非语言交际

ˌnon-'vintage *adj.* (of wine 葡萄酒) not made only from GRAPES grown in a particular place in a particular year 非特定地区特定年份酿造的 OPP **vintage**

ˌnon-'violence *noun* [U] the policy of using peaceful methods, not force, to bring about political or social change 非暴力政策

ˌnon-'violent *adj.* **1** using peaceful methods, not force, to bring about political or social change（政策）非暴力的，不诉诸武力的：*non-violent resistance* 非暴力抵抗 ◇ *a non-violent protest* 非暴力抗议 **2** not involving force, or injury to sb（行为）非暴力的：*non-violent crimes* 非暴力犯罪

ˌnon-'white *noun* a person who is not a member of a race of people who have white skin 非白种人 ▶ **ˌnon-'white** *adj.*

noob /nuːb/ *noun* (*informal*) a person who takes part in an activity, usually an online video game, but lacks relevant knowledge and therefore performs badly（通常指网络游戏的）新手，菜鸟

noo·dle /'nuːdl/ *noun* **1** [usually pl.] a long thin strip of PASTA, used especially in Chinese and Italian cooking 面条：*chicken noodle soup* 鸡汤面 ◇ *Would you prefer rice or noodles?* 你喜欢吃米饭还是面条？ **2** [C] (*old-fashioned, NAmE, slang*) = NODDLE

nook /nʊk/ *noun* a small quiet place or corner that is sheltered or hidden from other people 僻静处；幽静的角落：*a shady nook in the garden* 花园里阴凉的一角 ◇ *dark woods full of secret* ***nooks and crannies*** 充满了神秘色彩的幽暗的树林

IDM **every ˌnook and 'cranny** (*also IndE* **every ˌnook and 'corner**) (*informal*) every part of a place; every aspect of a situation 到处；各个方面

nooky (*also* **nookie**) /'nʊki/ *noun* [U] (*slang*) sexual activity 性行为；性交

noon /nuːn/ *noun* [U] 12 o'clock in the middle of the day 正午；中午 SYN **midday**: *We should be there by noon.* 我们应该最晚中午到达。◇ *The conference opens at 12 noon on Saturday.* 这次会议在星期六中午 12 点开幕。 ◇ *the noon deadline for the end of hostilities* 中午结束敌对状态这一最后期限 ◇ *I'm leaving on the noon train.* 我坐中午的火车走。◇ *the glaring light of* ***high noon*** 正午眩目的阳光

IDM SEE MORNING

noon·day /'nuːndeɪ/ *adj.* [only before noun] (*old-fashioned* or *literary*) happening or appearing at noon 正午发生的；中午出现的：*the noonday sun* 正午的太阳

'no one (*also* **no·body**) *pron.* not anyone; no person 没有人；没有任何人：*No one was at home.* 没有人在家。

◇ *There was no one else around.* 周围没有其他人。◇ *We were told to speak to no one.* 要求我们不要和任何人说话。HELP **No one** is much more common than **nobody** in written English. 在书面英语中，no one 比 nobody 更为常用。

noon·tide /ˈnuːntaɪd/ *noun* [U] (*literary*) around 12 o'clock in the middle of the day 正午；亭午

noose /nuːs/ *noun* a circle that is tied in one end of a rope with a knot that allows the circle to get smaller as the other end of the rope is pulled 绳套；套索；活扣：*a hangman's noose* 绞索 ◇ (*figurative*) *His debts were a noose around his neck.* 债务就像套在他脖子上的一条套索。

nope /nəʊp; *NAmE* noʊp/ *exclamation* (*informal*) used to say 'no' 不；不行；没有：*'Have you seen my pen?' 'Nope.'* "你看见我的笔了吗？""没有。"

ˈno place *adv.* (*informal, especially NAmE*) = NOWHERE：*I have no place else to go.* 我没有其他地方可去。

nor /nɔː(r)/ *conj., adv.* **1** **neither… nor… | not… nor…** and not 也不：*She seemed neither surprised nor worried.* 她似乎既不惊讶也不担心。◇ *He wasn't there on Monday. Nor on Tuesday, for that matter.* 他星期一没在那儿。星期二也一样，也不在。◇ (*formal*) *Not a building nor a tree was left standing.* 房屋树木无一幸存。 **2** used before a positive verb to agree with sth negative that has just been said（用于肯定动词前，表示同意刚提及的否定命题）也不：*She doesn't like them and nor does Jeff.* 她不喜欢他们，杰夫也不喜欢。◇ *'I'm not going.' 'Nor am I.'* "我不想去。""我也不去。"

Nor·dic /ˈnɔːdɪk; *NAmE* ˈnɔːrdɪk/ *adj.* **1** of or connected with the countries of Scandinavia, Finland and Iceland 斯堪的纳维亚的；北欧国家的 **2** typical of a member of a European race of people who are tall and have blue eyes and blonde hair 北欧人的；有北欧民族特征的

ˌNordic ˈwalking *noun* [U] the sport of walking with special poles attached to your wrists 越野行走，北欧式健走（使用特殊手杖快速行走的一种运动）

norm AW /nɔːm; *NAmE* nɔːrm/ *noun, verb*

■ ***noun*** **1** (*often* **the norm**) [sing.] a situation or a pattern of behaviour that is usual or expected 常态；正常行为 SYN **rule**：*a departure from the norm* 一反常态 ◇ *Older parents seem to be the norm rather than the exception nowadays.* 人们在年龄较大时才生育子女在今天似乎成了常事，而不是个例。 **2 norms** [pl.] standards of behaviour that are typical of or accepted within a particular group or society 规范；行为标准：***social/cultural norms*** 社会 / 文化规范 ➲ COLLOCATIONS AT RACE **3** [C] a required or agreed standard, amount, etc. 标准；定额；定量：*detailed education norms for children of particular ages* 针对具体年龄儿童的详细教育标准

■ ***verb*** **~ sth** to adjust sth so that it is of the required standard; to establish a required or agreed standard for sth 规范；规定：*You can use the information to norm the test.* 你可以用这些资料去规范测试。

nor·mal AW /ˈnɔːml; *NAmE* ˈnɔːrml/ *adj., noun*

■ ***adj.*** **1** typical, usual or ordinary; what you would expect 典型的；正常的；一般的：***quite/perfectly*** (= completely) ***normal*** 相当 / 完全正常 ◇ *Her temperature is normal.* 她的体温正常。◇ ***It's normal to*** *feel tired after such a long trip.* 这样长途旅行之后感到疲劳是正常的。◇ *Divorce is complicated enough* ***in normal circumstances***, *but this situation is even worse.* 在一般情况下，离婚已经够复杂了，但这一次情况更糟。◇ ***Under normal circumstances***, *I would say 'yes'.* 一般情况下，我会说"行"。◇ *He should be able to* ***lead a*** *perfectly* ***normal life***. 他应该能够过上完全正常的生活。◇ ***In the normal course of events*** *I wouldn't go to that part of town.* 通常我是不会到那个城区去的。◇ *We are open during normal office hours.* 我们在正常的办公时间内开放。 **2** not suffering from any mental DISORDER 精神正常的；意识健全的：*People who commit such crimes aren't normal.* 犯这种罪的人心理不正常。OPP **abnormal** IDM SEE PER

■ ***noun*** [U] the usual or average state, level or standard 常态；通常标准；一般水平：***above/below normal*** 通常标准之上 / 之下 ◇ *Things soon* ***returned to normal***. 情况很快恢复了正常。

ˌnormal distriˈbution *noun* (*statistics* 统计) the usual way in which a particular feature varies among a large number of things or people, represented on a GRAPH by a line that rises to a high SYMMETRICAL curve in the middle 正态分布 ➲ COMPARE BELL CURVE

nor·mal·ity AW /nɔːˈmæləti; *NAmE* nɔːrˈm-/ (*also* **nor·malcy** /ˈnɔːmlsi; *NAmE* ˈnɔːrm-/ *especially in NAmE*) *noun* [U] a situation where everything is normal or as you would expect it to be 常态；正常的形势：*They are hoping for a* ***return to normality*** *now that the war is over.* 既然战争结束了，他们希望一切都恢复常态。

nor·mal·ize AW (*BrE also* **-ise**) /ˈnɔːməlaɪz; *NAmE* ˈnɔːrm-/ *verb* [T, I] **~ (sth)** (*formal*) to fit or make sth fit a normal pattern or condition（使）正常化，标准化，常规化：*a lotion to normalize oily skin* 使油性皮肤恢复正常的护肤液 ◇ *The two countries agreed to* ***normalize relations*** (= return to a normal, friendly relationship, for example after a disagreement or war). 两国同意恢复正常关系。◇ *It took time until the political situation had normalized.* 政治局势过了很长时间才恢复正常。 ▶ **nor·mal·iza·tion, -isa·tion** AW /ˌnɔːməlaɪˈzeɪʃn; *NAmE* ˌnɔːrmələˈz-/ *noun* [U]：*the normalization of relations* 关系的正常化

nor·mal·ly AW /ˈnɔːməli; *NAmE* ˈnɔːrm-/ *adv.* **1** usually; in normal circumstances 通常；正常情况下：*I'm not normally allowed to stay out late.* 通常情况下，我不能在外很晚不归。◇ *It's normally much warmer than this in July.* 通常七月要比现在热得多。◇ *It normally takes 20 minutes to get there.* 去那儿一般要花 20 分钟。 **2** in the usual or ordinary way 正常地；平常地：*Her heart is beating normally.* 她心跳正常。◇ *Just try to behave normally.* 尽量表现得若无其事。

Nor·man /ˈnɔːmən; *NAmE* ˈnɔːrm-/ *adj.* **1** used to describe the style of ARCHITECTURE in Britain in the 11th and 12th centuries that developed from the ROMANESQUE style 诺曼式的；诺曼式建筑风格的：*a Norman church/castle* 诺曼式的教堂 / 城堡 **2** connected with the Normans (= the people from northern Europe who defeated the English in 1066 and then ruled the country) 诺曼人的：*the Norman Conquest* 诺曼征服

nor·ma·tive /ˈnɔːmətɪv; *NAmE* ˈnɔːrm-/ *adj.* (*formal*) describing or setting standards or rules of behaviour 规范的；标准的：*a normative approach* 规范的方法

noro·virus /ˈnɒrəʊvaɪrəs; *NAmE* ˈnɔːroʊ-/ *noun* [U, sing.] (*BrE* **ˌwinter ˈvomiting bug/virus** [C]) a very infectious disease that makes people VOMIT and have DIARRHOEA very badly for a few days 诺如病毒，冬季呕吐症（传染性强，患者连续几天严重呕吐和腹泻）

Norse /nɔːs; *NAmE* nɔːrs/ *noun* [U] the Norwegian language, especially in an ancient form, or the Scandinavian language group 诺尔斯语；（古）挪威语；古斯堪的纳维亚语

north /nɔːθ; *NAmE* nɔːrθ/ *noun, adj., adv.*

■ ***noun*** [U, sing.] (*abbr.* **N**, **No.**) **1** (*usually* **the north**) the direction that is on your left when you watch the sun rise; one of the four main points of the COMPASS 北；北方：*Which way is north?* 哪边是北？◇ *cold winds coming from the north* 从北方袭来的寒风 ◇ *Mount Kenya* ***is to the north of*** (= further north than) *Nairobi.* 肯尼亚山在内罗毕以北。➲ PICTURE AT COMPASS ➲ COMPARE EAST *n.* (1), SOUTH *n.* (1), WEST *n.* (1) ➲ SEE ALSO MAGNETIC NORTH, TRUE NORTH **2** **the north, the North** the northern part of a country, a region or the world 北部；北部地区：*birds migrating from the north* 从北方迁徙来的鸟 ◇ *Houses are less expensive in the North* (= of England) *than in the South.* 北方的房子比南方便宜。 **3 the North** the NE states of the US which fought against the South in the American Civil War（美国南北战争时与南方作战的）北部各州，北方 **4 the North** the

N

richer and more developed countries of the world, especially in Europe and N America 北方发达国家（尤指欧洲和北美各国）

■ ***adj.*** [only before noun] **1** (*abbr.* **N**, **No.**) in or towards the north 北方的；向北的；北部的：*North London* 伦敦北区 ◇ *the north bank of the river* 这条河的北岸 **2** a **north wind** blows from the north 北风的；北方吹来的 ➲ COMPARE NORTHERLY *adj.*

■ ***adv.*** **1** towards the north 向北；朝北：*The house faces north.* 这房子朝北。 **2** **~ of sth** nearer to the north than sth 某物以北：*They live ten miles north of Boston.* 他们居住在波士顿以北 10 英里处。 **3** **~ of sth** (*finance* 财 or *NAmE*, *informal*) more or higher than sth 超过：*The estimated value is north of $5.4 billion.* 估价高于 54 亿美元。 OPP **south**

IDM **up 'north** (*informal*) to or in the north of a country, especially England 在北方，到北方（尤指英格兰北部）：*They've gone to live up north.* 他们已经搬到北方去住了。

ˌNorth A'merica *noun* [U] the continent consisting of Canada, the United States, Mexico, the countries of Central America and Greenland 北美洲，北美大陆（包括加拿大、美国、墨西哥、中美各国和格陵兰）

the ˌNorth Atˌlantic 'Drift *noun* [sing.] (*specialist*) a current of warm water in the Atlantic Ocean, that has the effect of making the climate of NW Europe warmer 北大西洋暖流（能使欧洲西北部气候变暖）

north·bound /'nɔːθbaʊnd; *NAmE* 'nɔːrθ-/ *adj.* travelling or leading towards the north 北行的；向北的：*northbound traffic* 北上的交通运输 ◇ *the northbound carriageway of the motorway* 高速公路的北行车道

'north-country *adj.* [only before noun] connected with the northern part of a country or region 北国的；（国家或地区）北部的：*a north-country accent* 北部地区的口音

ˌnorth-'east *noun* (*usually* **the north-east**) [sing.] (*abbr.* **NE**) the direction or region at an equal distance between north and east 东北；东北方；东北地区 ➲ PICTURE AT COMPASS ▸ **ˌnorth-'east** *adv.*, *adj.*

ˌnorth-'easter·ly *adj.* **1** [only before noun] in or towards the north-east 东北方的；向东北的；东北部的：*travelling in a north-easterly direction* 向东北行驶 **2** [usually before noun] (of winds 风) blowing from the north-east 从东北吹来的

ˌnorth-'eastern *adj.* [only before noun] (*abbr.* **NE**) connected with the north-east 东北的；东北方向的

ˌnorth-'eastwards (*also* **ˌnorth-'eastward**) *adv.* towards the north-east 向东北；朝东北 ▸ **ˌnorth-'eastward** *adj.*

north·er·ly /'nɔːðəli; *NAmE* 'nɔːrðərli/ *adj.*, *noun*

■ ***adj.*** **1** [only before noun] in or towards the north 北方的；向北的；北部的：*travelling in a northerly direction* 向北行驶 **2** [usually before noun] (of winds 风) blowing from the north 从北方吹来的：*a northerly breeze* 微微的北风 ➲ COMPARE NORTH *adj.*

■ ***noun*** (*pl.* **-ies**) a wind that blows from the north 北风

north·ern /'nɔːðən; *NAmE* 'nɔːrðərn/ (*also* **Northern**) *adj.* [usually before noun] (*abbr.* **N**, **No.**) located in the north or facing north; connected with or typical of the north part of the world or a region 北方的；向北的；北部的：*the northern slopes of the mountains* 山脉的北坡 ◇ *northern Scotland* 苏格兰北部 ◇ *a northern accent* 北方口音

north·ern·er /'nɔːðənə(r); *NAmE* 'nɔːrðən-/ *noun* a person who comes from or lives in the northern part of a country 北方人

the ˌNorthern ˌIreland As'sembly *noun* [sing.] **1** the regional government of Northern Ireland from 1973 to 1986（1973 至 1986 年间的）北爱尔兰地方政府 **2** the parliament of Northern Ireland that was first elected in 1998（1998 年首次通过选举产生的）北爱尔兰议会

the ˌNorthern 'Lights *noun* [pl.] (*also* **aur·ora bor·ealis**) bands of coloured light, mainly green and red, that are sometimes seen in the sky at night in the most northern countries of the world 北极光

north·ern·most /'nɔːðənməʊst; *NAmE* 'nɔːrðərnmoʊst/ *adj.* [usually before noun] furthest north 最北的；最北端的；最北部的：*the northernmost city in the world* 世界最靠北的城市

ˌnorth-north-'east *noun* [sing.] (*abbr.* **NNE**) the direction at an equal distance between north and north-east 北东北；北北东 ▸ **ˌnorth-north-'east** *adv.*

ˌnorth-north-'west *noun* [sing.] (*abbr.* **NNW**) the direction at an equal distance between north and north-west 北西北；北北西 ▸ **ˌnorth-north-'west** *adv.*

the ˌNorth 'Pole *noun* [sing.] the point on the surface of the earth that is furthest north 北极

the ˌNorth 'Sea *noun* [sing.] the part of the Atlantic Ocean that is next to the east coast of Britain 北海（英国东海岸附近的大西洋海域）

the ˌNorth-South Di'vide *noun* [sing.] (*BrE*) the economic and social differences between the north of England and the richer south 南北鸿沟（指英格兰北部和较富裕的南部之间的经济与社会差别）

north·wards /'nɔːθwədz; *NAmE* 'nɔːrθwərdz/ (*also* **north·ward**) *adv.* towards the north 向北；朝北：*to go/look/turn northwards* 向北走 / 看 / 掉转 ▸ **north·ward** *adj.*：*in a northward direction* 向北方

ˌnorth-'west *noun* (*usually* **the north-west**) [sing.] (*abbr.* **NW**) the direction or region at an equal distance between north and west 西北；西北方；西北地区 ➲ PICTURE AT COMPASS ▸ **ˌnorth-'west** *adv.*, *adj.*

ˌnorth-'wester·ly *adj.* **1** [only before noun] in or towards the north-west 西北方的；向西北的；西北部的 **2** (of winds 风) blowing from the north-west 从西北吹来的

ˌnorth-'western *adj.* [only before noun] (*abbr.* **NW**) connected with the north-west 西北的；西北方向的

ˌnorth-'westwards (*also* **ˌnorth-'westward**) *adv.* towards the north-west 向西北；朝西北 ▸ **ˌnorth-'westward** *adj.*

ˌNorway 'lobster *noun* = LANGOUSTINE

ˌNorway 'rat *noun* = BROWN RAT

nose /nəʊz; *NAmE* noʊz/ *noun*, *verb*

■ ***noun*** **1** [C] the part of the face that sticks out above the mouth, used for breathing and smelling things 鼻；鼻子：*He broke his nose in the fight.* 他打架时打断了鼻梁。◇ *She wrinkled her nose in disgust.* 她厌恶地皱起鼻子。◇ *He* ***blew his nose*** (= cleared it by blowing strongly into a HANDKERCHIEF). 他擤了擤鼻子。◇ *a* ***blocked/runny nose*** 堵塞的 / 流鼻涕的鼻子 ◇ *Stop* ***picking your nose!*** (= removing dirt from it with your finger) 别抠鼻孔了！ ➲ COLLOCATIONS AT PHYSICAL ➲ VISUAL VOCAB PAGE V64 ➲ SEE ALSO NASAL, PARSON'S NOSE, ROMAN NOSE **2** **-nosed** (in adjectives 构成形容词) having the type of nose mentioned 有…鼻子的：*red-nosed* 红鼻子的 ◇ *large-nosed* 大鼻子的 ➲ SEE ALSO HARD-NOSED, TOFFEE-NOSED ➲ MORE LIKE THIS 8, page R25 **3** [C] the front part of a plane, SPACECRAFT, etc.（飞机、太空船等的）头部，头锥；机头 ➲ VISUAL VOCAB PAGE V57 **4** [sing.] **a ~ for sth** a special ability for finding or recognizing sth 发现（或辨别）事物的能力；嗅觉 SYN **instinct**：*As a journalist, she has always had a nose for a good story.* 作为一名记者，她总是能够捕捉到好新闻。 **5** [sing.] a sense of smell 嗅觉：*a dog with a good nose* 嗅觉灵敏的狗 **6** [sing.] (of wine 葡萄酒) a characteristic smell 特有的气味 SYN **bouquet**

IDM **cut off your nose to spite your 'face** (*informal*) to do sth when you are angry that is meant to harm sb else but which also harms you（恼怒之下）伤人害己，损人不利己 **get up sb's 'nose** (*BrE*, *informal*) to annoy sb 烦扰 **have your nose in 'sth** (*informal*) to be reading sth and giving it all your attention 专心致志地阅读 **have a nose 'round** (*BrE*, *informal*) to look around a place; to look for sth in a place 环视（某地）；在（某地）寻找 **keep your**

ˈ**nose clean** (*informal*) to avoid doing anything wrong or illegal 循规蹈矩；不做违法的事： *Since leaving prison, he's managed to keep his nose clean.* 自从出狱以来，他已做到规规矩矩。 **keep your nose out of sth** to try not to become involved in things that do not concern you 避免插手（他人的事）；尽力不卷入（或介入） **keep your nose to the ˈgrindstone** (*informal*) to work hard for a long period of time without stopping 连续辛勤地工作 **look down your ˈnose at sb/sth** (*informal, especially BrE*) to behave in a way that suggests that you think that you are better than sb or that sth is not good enough for you 对…不屑一顾；蔑视 SYN **look down on sb/sth** ˌ**nose to ˈtail** (*BrE*) if cars, etc. are **nose to tail**, they are moving slowly in a long line with little space between them （汽车等）首尾相连（缓缓行进） **on the ˈnose** (*informal, especially NAmE*) exactly 准确地；确切地： *The budget should hit the $136 billion target on the nose.* 预算应该正好达到 1 360 亿美元的目标。 **poke/stick your nose into ˈsth** (*informal*) to try to become involved in sth that does not concern you 多管闲事；插手（与己无关的事） **put sb's ˈnose out of joint** (*informal*) to upset or annoy sb, especially by not giving them enough attention （冷落）使难堪；惹恼 **turn your ˈnose up at sth** (*informal*) to refuse sth, especially because you do not think that it is good enough for you 拒绝；看不上；看不起 **under sb's ˈnose** (*informal*) **1** if sth is **under sb's nose**, it is very close to them but they cannot see it 就在某人面前（却看不见）： *I searched everywhere for the letter and it was under my nose all the time!* 我到处找这封信，可它一直就在我面前。 **2** if sth happens **under sb's nose**, they do not notice it even though it is not being done secretly 当着某人的面，就在某人眼皮底下（却没有被察觉）： *The police didn't know the drugs ring was operating right under their noses.* 警方不知道贩毒集团就在他们的眼皮底下运作。 **with your nose in the air** (*informal*) in a way that is unfriendly and suggests that you think that you are better than other people 傲慢；看不起人；鼻孔朝天，自高自大 ➲ MORE AT FOLLOW, LEAD[1] *v.*, PAY *v.*, PLAIN *adj.*, POWDER *v.*, RUB *v.*, SKIN *n.*, THUMB *v.*

■ ***verb*** **1** [I, T] to move forward slowly and carefully 小心翼翼地向前移动： **+ adv./prep.** *The plane nosed down through the thick clouds.* 飞机穿过厚厚的云层慢慢向下降落。 ◇ **~ your way + adv./prep.** *The taxi nosed its way back into the traffic.* 出租车慢慢地又汇入车流。 **2** [I] **+ adv./prep.** (of an animal 动物) to search for sth or push sth with its nose （用鼻子）嗅，拱，顶： *Dogs nosed around in piles of refuse.* 一群狗在垃圾堆上嗅来嗅去。

PHR V ˌ**nose aˈbout/aˈround (for sth)** to look for sth, especially information about sb 探查；打探；搜寻 SYN **poke about/around**： *We found a man nosing around in our backyard.* 我们发现有个人在我们后院里找什么东西。 ˌ**nose sth↔ˈout** (*informal*) to discover information about sb/sth by searching for it 侦察出；打探出；查出： *Reporters nosed out all the details of the affair.* 记者们打探出了这件事情的所有细节。

nose·bag /ˈnəʊzbæɡ; *NAmE* ˈnoʊz-/ (*BrE*) (*NAmE* **feed·bag**) *noun* a bag containing food for a horse, that you hang from its head （挂在马头上的）饲料袋

nose·band /ˈnəʊzbænd; *NAmE* ˈnoʊz-/ *noun* a leather band that passes over a horse's nose and under its chin and is part of its BRIDLE （马的）鼻羁

nose·bleed /ˈnəʊzbliːd; *NAmE* ˈnoʊz-/ *noun* a flow of blood that comes from the nose 鼻出血

ˈ**nose cone** *noun* the pointed front end of a ROCKET, an aircraft, etc. （火箭、飞机等的）前锥体，鼻锥体，头锥

nose·dive /ˈnəʊzdaɪv; *NAmE* ˈnoʊz-/ *noun, verb*

■ ***noun*** [sing.] **1** a sudden steep fall or drop; a situation where sth suddenly becomes worse or begins to fail 急剧下降；急转直下；暴跌： *Oil prices **took a nosedive** in the crisis.* 危机期间，石油价格暴跌。 ◇ *These policies have sent the construction industry into an abrupt nosedive.* 这些政策使得建筑业的形势急转直下。 **2** the sudden sharp fall of an aircraft towards the ground with its front part pointing down （飞行器的）俯冲

■ ***verb*** **1** [I] (of prices, costs, etc. 价格、费用等) to fall suddenly 骤降；急剧下跌；暴跌 SYN **plummet**： *Building costs have nosedived.* 建筑费用猛跌下来。 **2** [I] (of an aircraft 飞行器) to fall suddenly with the front part pointing towards the ground 俯冲

nose·gay /ˈnəʊzɡeɪ; *NAmE* ˈnoʊz-/ *noun* (*old-fashioned*) a small bunch of flowers 小花束

ˈ**nose job** *noun* (*informal*) a medical operation on the nose to improve its shape 鼻部整形手术

ˈ**nose ring** *noun* **1** a ring that is put in an animal's nose for leading it （用于牵引动物的）鼻环，鼻圈 **2** a ring worn in the nose as a piece of jewellery 环形鼻饰；鼻环

nosey = NOSY

nosh /nɒʃ; *NAmE* nɑːʃ/ *noun, verb*

■ ***noun*** **1** [U, sing.] (*old-fashioned, BrE, slang*) food; a meal 食物；一餐： *She likes her nosh.* 她喜欢她的饭菜。 ◇ *Did you have a good nosh?* 你吃得好吗？ **2** [C] (*especially NAmE*) a small meal that you eat quickly between main meals 小吃；点心

■ ***verb*** [I, T] **~ (sth)** (*informal*) to eat 吃

ˌ**no-ˈshow** *noun* (*informal*) a person who is expected to be somewhere and does not come; a situation where this happens 没有如期出现的人；失约；放弃预订

ˈ**nosh-up** *noun* (*slang, especially BrE*) a large meal 丰盛的一餐；大餐： *We went for a nosh-up at that new restaurant in town.* 我们到城里那家新餐馆大吃了一顿。

ˌ**no-ˈsmoking** *adj.* = NON-SMOKING

nos·tal·gia /nɒˈstældʒə; *NAmE* nəˈs-; nɑːˈs-/ *noun* [U] a feeling of sadness mixed with pleasure and affection when you think of happy times in the past 怀旧；念旧： *a **sense/wave/pang of nostalgia*** 怀旧感；一阵强烈的怀旧之情 ◇ *She is filled with nostalgia for her own college days.* 她对自己的大学时代充满了怀念之情。 ▸ **nos·tal·gic** /nɒˈstældʒɪk; *NAmE* nəˈs-; nɑːˈs-/ *adj.*： *nostalgic memories* 引起怀旧之情的回忆 ◇ *I feel quite nostalgic for the place where I grew up.* 我很怀念我成长的地方。 **nos·tal·gic·al·ly** /-kli/ *adv.*： *to look back nostalgically to your childhood* 缅怀童年时光

nos·tril /ˈnɒstrəl; *NAmE* ˈnɑːs-/ *noun* either of the two openings at the end of the nose that you breathe through 鼻孔 ➲ VISUAL VOCAB PAGE V64

nos·trum /ˈnɒstrəm; *NAmE* ˈnɑːs-/ *noun* **1** (*formal, disapproving*) an idea that is intended to solve a problem but that will probably not succeed 并非灵验的招数；不会奏效的计策 **2** (*old-fashioned*) a medicine that is not made in a scientific way, and that is not effective 江湖药

nosy (*also* **nosey**) /ˈnəʊzi; *NAmE* ˈnoʊzi/ *adj.* (*informal, disapproving*) too interested in things that do not concern you, especially other people's affairs 好管闲事的；爱打听的 SYN **inquisitive**： *nosy neighbours* 好管闲事的邻居 ◇ *Don't be so nosy—it's none of your business.* 别管那么多闲事，这与你无关。 ▸ **nosi·ly** *adv.* **nosi·ness** *noun* [U]

ˌ**nosy ˈparker** *noun* (*BrE, informal, becoming old-fashioned*) a person who is too interested in other people's affairs 爱管闲事的人；好事者

not /nɒt; *NAmE* nɑːt/ *adv.* **1** used to form the negative of the verbs *be*, *do* and *have* and modal verbs like *can* or *must* and often reduced to *n't* （构成动词 be、do 和 have 及情态动词 can 或 must 等的否定形式，常缩略为 n't）不，没有： *She did not/didn't see him.* 她没看见他。 ◇ *It's not/It isn't raining.* 没下雨。 ◇ *I can't see from here.* 我从这儿看不见。 ◇ *He must not go.* 他绝不能走。 ◇ *Don't you eat meat?* 你不吃肉吗？ ◇ *It's cold, isn't it?* 很冷，是吧？ **2** used to give the following word or phrase a negative meaning, or to reply in the negative （否定后面的词或短语，或作否定的回答）不，没有： *He warned me not to be late.* 他提醒我不要迟到。 ◇ *I was sorry not to have seen them.* 我很遗憾没有见到他们。 ◇ *Not everybody agrees.* 不是每一个人都同意。 ◇ *'Who's next?' 'Not me.'* "下一位是谁？" "不是我。" ◇ *'What did you do at*

N

school?' 'Not a lot.' "你在学校干什么了？" "没做多少事。" ◇ It's not easy being a parent (= it's difficult). 为人父母真不容易啊。 3 🔑 used after hope, expect, believe, etc. to give a negative reply (用于 hope、expect、believe 等动词后，作为否定的回答）不，没有： 'Will she be there?' 'I hope not.' "她会在那儿吗？" "但愿不会。" ◇ 'Is it ready?' 'I'm afraid not.' "准备好了吗？" "恐怕还没呢。" ◇ (formal) 'Does he know?' 'I believe not.' "他知道吗？" "我想他不知道。" 4 🔑 or ~ used to show a negative possibility（表示否定的可能性）否，或许不： I don't know if he's telling the truth or not. 我不知道他是否说了真话。 5 🔑 used to say that you do not want sth or will not allow sth （拒绝或不允许）不： 'Some more?' 'Not for me, thanks.' "再来点儿吗？" "我不要了，谢谢。" ◇ 'Can I throw this out?' 'Certainly not.' "我把这个扔了，行吗？" "当然不行。"

IDM **not a... | not one...** 🔑 used for emphasis to mean 'no thing or person'（用于强调）一个也不，一件也没： He didn't speak to me—not one word. 他没跟我说话，一个字也没说。 **ˌnot at ˈall** 🔑 used to politely accept thanks or to agree to sth（礼貌地答谢或同意）别客气，没关系，没什么： 'Thanks a lot.' 'Not at all.' "非常感谢。" "不客气。" ◇ 'Will it bother you if I smoke?' 'Not at all.' "我抽烟你介意吗？" "没关系。" **not only... (but) also...** 🔑 used to emphasize that sth else is also true 不仅…而且…： She not only wrote the text but also selected the illustrations. 她不仅写了正文，而且还挑选了插图。 **ˈnot that** used to state that you are not suggesting sth 倒不是；并不是说： She hasn't written—not that she said she would. 她还没写信来——倒不是她说过她要写。

not·able /ˈnəʊtəbl; NAmE ˈnoʊ-/ adj., noun

■ **adj.** (rather formal) deserving to be noticed or to receive attention; important 值得注意的；显著的；重要的 SYN **striking**: a **notable success/achievement/example** 显著的成功 / 成就；明显的事例 ◇ His eyes are his most **notable feature**. 他的双眼是他最明显的特征。 ◇ ~ (**for sth**) The town is notable for its ancient harbour. 这座小镇因其古老的港口而出名。 ◇ **With a few notable exceptions**, everyone gave something. 人人都给了些东西，只有几个人例外，很是显眼。

■ **noun** [usually pl.] (formal) a famous or important person 名人；重要人物： All the usual local notables were there. 经常露面的地方名流都在那里。

not·ably /ˈnəʊtəbli; NAmE ˈnoʊ-/ adv. 1 used for giving a good or the most important example of sth 尤其；特别 SYN **especially**: The house had many drawbacks, most notably its price. 这房子有很多缺陷，尤其是它的价格。 2 to a great degree 极大程度上；非常 SYN **remarkably**: This has not been a notably successful project. 这个项目没有取得很大的成功。

no·tar·ize (BrE also **-ise**) /ˈnəʊtəraɪz; NAmE ˈnoʊ-/ verb ~ **sth** (law 律) if a document is **notarized**, it is given legal status by a NOTARY 公证；由公证人证实

no·tary /ˈnəʊtəri; NAmE ˈnoʊ-/ noun (pl. **-ies**) (also specialist **ˌnotary ˈpublic** pl. **notaries public**) a person, especially a lawyer, with official authority to be a witness when sb signs a document and to make this document valid in law 公证人

no·ta·tion /nəʊˈteɪʃn; NAmE noʊ-/ noun [U, C] a system of signs or symbols used to represent information, especially in mathematics, science and music 记谱法；标记法 ➲ PICTURE AT MUSIC

notch /nɒtʃ; NAmE nɑːtʃ/ noun, verb

■ **noun** 1 a level on a scale, often marking quality or achievement 等级；档次；位阶： The quality of the food here has dropped a notch recently. 这里的饭菜质量最近下降了一级。 ➲ SEE ALSO TOP-NOTCH 2 a V-shape or a circle cut in an edge or a surface, sometimes used to keep a record of sth（表面或边缘的）V 形刻痕，圆形切口： For each day he spent on the island, he cut a new notch in his stick. 他在岛上每过一天，就在手杖上刻一个新的记号。 ◇ She tightened her belt an extra notch. 她将腰带又束紧了一格。

■ **verb** 1 ~ **sth** (**up**) (informal) to achieve sth such as a win or a high score 赢取；获得： The team has notched up 20 goals already this season. 这支球队本赛季已经攻进 20 个球。 2 ~ **sth** to make a small V-shaped cut in an edge or a surface（在表面或边缘）刻 V 形痕，刻下切口

note 🔑 /nəʊt; NAmE noʊt/ noun, verb

■ **noun**

• **TO REMIND YOU** 提醒自己 1 🔑 [C] a short piece of writing to help you remember sth 笔记；记录： Please **make a note of** the dates. 请记下日期。 ◇ She **made a mental note** (= decided that she must remember) to ask Alan about it. 她提醒自己要记住向艾伦问问这事。

• **SHORT LETTER** 短信 2 🔑 [C] a short informal letter 短笺；便条： Just a quick note to say thank you for a wonderful evening. 仅以此短笺感谢您安排的美好夜晚。 ◇ She left a note for Ben on the kitchen table. 她在厨房的餐桌上给本留了个便条。 ◇ a suicide note 绝命书

• **IN BOOK** 书籍 3 🔑 [C] a short comment on a word or passage in a book 注释；按语；批注： a new edition of 'Hamlet', with explanatory notes 附注释的新版《哈姆雷特》 ◇ See note 3, page 259. 见第 259 页注释 3。 ➲ SEE ALSO FOOTNOTE (1)

• **INFORMATION** 资料 4 🔑 **notes** [pl.] information that you write down when sb is speaking, or when you are reading a book, etc.（听讲或读书等时的）记录，笔记： He sat **taking notes** of everything that was said. 他坐在那儿记下了所说的每一件事。 ◇ Can I borrow your **lecture notes**? 我可以借你的课堂笔记看看吗？ ◇ Patients' **medical notes** have gone missing. 患者的病历丢失了。 5 🔑 [C, usually pl.] information about a performance, an actor's career, a piece of music, etc. printed in a special book or on a CD case, record cover, etc.（有关演出、演员经历、音乐等的）图书资料，录音或唱片等封套介绍： The sleeve notes include a short biography of the performers on this recording. 封套上的介绍包括本唱片中的演奏者生平简介。

• **MONEY** 钱币 6 🔑 (BrE) (also **bank·note** especially in BrE) (NAmE usually **bill**) [C] a piece of paper money 纸币： a £5 note 一张面值为 5 英镑的纸币 ◇ We only exchange notes and traveller's cheques. 我们只兑换纸币和旅行支票。 ➲ PICTURE AT MONEY

• **IN MUSIC** 音乐 7 🔑 [C] a single sound of a particular length and PITCH (= how high or low a sound is), made by the voice or a musical instrument; the written or printed sign for a musical note 单音；音调；音符： He played the first few notes of the tune. 他演奏了这支曲子开始的几个音。 ◇ **high/low notes** 高音；低音 ➲ WORDFINDER NOTE AT SING ➲ PICTURE AT MUSIC

• **QUALITY** 性质 8 [sing.] ~ (**of sth**) a particular quality in sth, for example in sb's voice or the atmosphere at an event 特征；口气；调子；气氛 SYN **air**: There was a note of amusement in his voice. 听他的口气，是觉得很有意思。 ◇ **On a more serious note** (= speaking more seriously)... 说点严肃的… ◇ **On a slightly different note** (= changing the subject slightly), let's talk about... 咱们略微换一下话题，谈谈…

• **OFFICIAL DOCUMENT** 正式文件 9 [C] an official document with a particular purpose 正式文件；票据；证明书： a sick note from your doctor 医生开具的病假证明 ◇ The buyer has to sign a delivery note as proof of receipt. 购买者必须签收送货单表明货已收到。 ➲ SEE ALSO CREDIT NOTE, PROMISSORY NOTE 10 [C] (specialist) an official letter from the representative of one government to another（外交文书）照会；通牒： an exchange of diplomatic notes 外交照会的互换

IDM **of ˈnote** of importance or of great interest 重要的；引人注目的： a scientist of note 著名的科学家 ◇ The museum contains nothing of great note. 这家博物馆没有什么很有价值的东西。 **hit/strike the right/wrong ˈnote** (especially BrE) to do, say or write sth that is suitable/not suitable for a particular occasion 做（或说、写）得得体 / 不得体 **sound/strike a ˈnote (of ˈsth)** to express feelings or opinions of a particular kind 表达某种情感（或观点）： She sounded a note of warning in her speech. 她在讲话中透出了警告的意味。 **take ˈnote (of sth)** to pay attention to sth and be sure to remember it 注意到；将…铭记在心： Take note of what he says. 牢记他说的话。 ➲ MORE AT COMPARE v.

■ ***verb*** (*rather formal*) **1** 🔑 to notice or pay careful attention to sth 注意；留意： **~ sth** *Note the fine early Baroque altar inside the chapel.* 注意小教堂里精致的早期巴罗克风格的祭坛。◇ **~ (that)...** *Please note (that) the office will be closed on Monday.* 请注意办事处星期一将关闭。◇ **~ how, where, etc....** *Note how these animals sometimes walk with their tails up in the air.* 注意观察这些动物如何有时翘起尾巴走路。◇ **it is noted that...** *It should be noted that dissertations submitted late will not be accepted.* 应该注意的是迟交的论文将不予接受。➲ SYNONYMS AT NOTICE ➲ LANGUAGE BANK AT EMPHASIS **2 ~ sth | ~ that... | ~ how, where, etc.... | it is noted that...** to mention sth because it is important or interesting 指出；特别提到： *It is worth noting that the most successful companies had the lowest prices.* 值得指出的是最成功的公司价格最低。➲ SYNONYMS AT COMMENT ➲ LANGUAGE BANK AT ARGUE

PHR V **ˌnote sth↔ˈdown** 🔑 to write down sth important so that you will not forget it 记录；记下 SYN **jot**

note·book /ˈnəʊtbʊk; *NAmE* ˈnoʊt-/ *noun* **1** a small book of plain paper for writing notes in 笔记本 ➲ VISUAL VOCAB PAGE V71 **2** (*NAmE*) (*BrE* **ˈexercise book**) a small book for students to write their work in 练习本 ➲ VISUAL VOCAB PAGE V72 **3** (*also* **ˌnotebook comˈputer**) a small computer that can work with a battery and be easily carried 笔记本式计算机；笔记本电脑 SYN **laptop** ➲ COMPARE DESKTOP COMPUTER, NETBOOK

note·card /ˈnəʊtkɑːd; *NAmE* ˈnoʊtkɑːrd/ *noun* **1** a small folded card, sometimes with a picture on the front, that you use for writing a short letter on （正面有图而折叠的）便笺卡，万用卡 ➲ SEE ALSO NOTELET **2** (*especially NAmE*) a card on which notes are written, for example by sb to use when making a speech 摘记卡片；纲要卡片

noted /ˈnəʊtɪd; *NAmE* ˈnoʊt-/ *adj.* well known because of a special skill or feature （以…）见称，闻名，著名 SYN **famous**: *a noted dancer* 著名的舞蹈演员 ◇ **~ for sth** *He is not noted for his sense of humour.* 他没什么幽默感。◇ **~ as sth** *The lake is noted as a home to many birds.* 这个湖作为许多鸟类的栖息地而闻名。

note·let /ˈnəʊtlət; *NAmE* ˈnoʊt-/ *noun* (*BrE*) a small folded sheet of paper or card with a picture on the front that you use for writing a short letter on （正面有图而折叠的）便笺；短柬

note·pad /ˈnəʊtpæd; *NAmE* ˈnoʊt-/ *noun* sheets of paper that are held together at the top and used for writing notes on 记事本；便条本： *a notepad by the phone for messages* 电话机旁用于记录信息的记事本 ➲ VISUAL VOCAB PAGE V71

note·paper /ˈnəʊtpeɪpə(r); *NAmE* ˈnoʊt-/ (*also* **ˈwriting paper**) *noun* [U] paper for writing letters on 信纸；便笺

note·worthy /ˈnəʊtwɜːði; *NAmE* ˈnoʊtwɜːrði/ *adj.* deserving to be noticed or to receive attention because it is unusual, important or interesting 值得注意的；显著的；重要的 SYN **significant**

ˌnot-for-ˈprofit (*also* **non·profit**) *adj., noun*

■ ***adj.*** without the aim of making a profit 非营利的： *a not-for-profit organization* 非营利组织

■ ***noun*** an organization that does not aim to make a profit 非营利组织

ˈnother /ˈnʌðə(r)/ *adj.* (*non-standard*) = ANOTHER： *Now that's a whole 'nother question.* 但那完全是另一个问题。➲ MORE LIKE THIS 5, page R25

noth·ing 🔑 /ˈnʌθɪŋ/ *pron.* **1** 🔑 not anything; no single thing 没有什么；没有一件东西： *There was nothing in her bag.* 她的包里什么都没有。◇ *There's nothing you can do to help.* 你什么忙也帮不上。◇ *The doctor said there was nothing wrong with me.* 医生说我什么毛病也没有。◇ ***Nothing else** matters to him apart from his job.* 对他来说，除了工作以外，什么事都无关紧要。◇ *It cost us nothing to go in.* 我们没花钱就进去了。◇ (*BrE*) *He's five foot nothing* (= exactly five feet tall). 他正好五英尺高。 **2** 🔑 something that is not at all important or interesting 无关紧要的东西；毫无趣味的事： *'What's that in your pocket?' 'Oh, nothing.'* "你口袋里装的是什么？" "哦，没什么重要的。" ◇ *We did nothing at the weekend.* 我们周末什么也没干。

IDM **be ˈnothing to sb** to be a person for whom sb has no feelings 对（某人）来说是无所谓的人： *I used to love her but she's nothing to me any more.* 我爱过她，但现在对她再也没什么感情了。 **be/have nothing to do with sb/sth** 🔑 to have no connection with sb/sth 与…毫不相干；与…无关： *Get out! It's nothing to do with you* (= you have no right to know about it). 出去！这根本就不关你的事。◇ *That has nothing to do with what we're discussing.* 那与我们所讨论的问题毫不相干。 **for ˈnothing 1** 🔑 without payment 不花钱；免费 SYN **free**: *She's always trying to get **something for nothing**.* 她总想不劳而获。 **2** 🔑 with no reward or result 无酬劳；毫无结果；白白地： *All that preparation was for nothing because the visit was cancelled.* 访问被取消，所有的准备工作都白费了。 **have nothing on sb** (*informal*) **1** to have much less of a particular quality than sb/sth 远比不上某人；比某人差得多： *I'm quite a fast worker, but I've got nothing on her!* 我做事已经很麻利了，但比她还差得远。 **2** (of the police, etc. 警察等) to have no information that could show sb to be guilty of sth 没有某人的罪证 **not for ˈnothing** for a very good reason 有充分理由；有正当理由： *Not for nothing was he called the king of rock and roll.* 他被称作摇滚之王不是没有道理的。 **ˈnothing but** 🔑 only; no more/less than 只；只有；只是；仅仅： *Nothing but a miracle can save her now.* 现在只有出现奇迹才能救活她。◇ *I want nothing but the best for my children.* 我只想给我的孩子最好的一切。 **ˈnothing if not** extremely; very 极其；非常： *The trip was nothing if not varied.* 这次旅行极其丰富多彩。 **ˈnothing less than** used to emphasize how great or extreme sth is 简直是；极其；不亚于： *It was nothing less than a disaster.* 这简直就是一场灾难。 **nothing ˈlike** (*informal*) **1** 🔑 not at all like 完全不像；根本不像： *It looks nothing like a horse.* 它看上去根本不像一匹马。 **2** 🔑 not nearly; not at all 完全不；根本没有： *I had nothing like enough time to answer all the questions.* 我根本来不及回答所有的问题。 **ˌnothing ˈmuch** not a great amount of sth; nothing of great value or importance 不很多；不太重要；价值不太大： *There's nothing much in the fridge.* 冰箱里没什么东西了。◇ *I got up late and did nothing much all day.* 我起来晚了，一天没怎么做事。 **(there's) ˌnothing ˈto it** (it's) very easy （这事）轻而易举，非常简单： *You'll soon learn. There's nothing to it really.* 你很快就能学会。真的很简单。 **there is/was nothing (else) ˈfor it (but to do sth)** there is no other action to take except the one mentioned （除了做某事）别无办法： *There was nothing else for it but to resign.* 除了辞职，没有别的办法。 **there is/was nothing in sth** something is/was not true （某事）不可信，不真实： *There was a rumour she was going to resign, but there was nothing in it.* 有传言说她要辞职，不过这靠不住。 **there's nothing like sth** used to say that you enjoy sth very much …非常好；…太棒了： *There's nothing like a brisk walk on a cold day!* 冷天出来快步走走，简直太舒服了。➲ MORE AT STOP *v.*, SWEET *adj.*

noth·ing·ness /ˈnʌθɪŋnəs/ *noun* [U] a situation where nothing exists; the state of not existing 不存在；虚无

no·tice 🔑 /ˈnəʊtɪs; *NAmE* ˈnoʊ-/ *noun, verb*

■ ***noun***

• PAYING ATTENTION 注意 **1** 🔑 [U] the fact of sb paying attention to sb/sth or knowing about sth 注意；理会；察觉： ***Don't take any notice of** what you read in the papers.* 别在意你在报上看到的东西。◇ ***Take no notice of** what he says.* 别理会他说的话。◇ *These protests have really made the government **sit up and take notice*** (= realize the importance of the situation). 这些抗议活动确实引起了政府的警觉和注意。◇ *It was Susan who **brought** the problem **to my notice*** (= told me about it). 是苏珊使我注意到这个问题的。◇ *Normally, the letter would not have **come to my notice*** (= I would not have known about it). 通常情况下，我是不会看到这封信的。◇ (*formal*) *It will not have **escaped your notice** that there have been some major changes in the company.* 你肯定会注意到公司已经发生了一些重大的变化。

N

• GIVING INFORMATION 通报信息 **2** [C] a sheet of paper giving written or printed information, usually put in a public place 通告；布告；通知：*There was a notice on the board saying the class had been cancelled.* 布告牌上有一则通知说这堂课取消了。 **3** [C] a board or sign giving information, an instruction or a warning 公告牌；警示牌：*a notice saying 'Keep off the Grass'* 写着"勿踏草地"的公告牌

• ANNOUNCING STH 宣布 **4** [C] a small advertisement or ANNOUNCEMENT in a newspaper or magazine 启事；声明：*notices of births, marriages and deaths* 出生喜报、结婚启事和讣告 **5** [C] a short ANNOUNCEMENT made at the beginning or end of a meeting, a church service, etc.（会议、宗教活动等开头或结尾时的）通知：*There are just two notices this week.* 本周只有两项通知。

• WARNING 警告 **6** [U] information or a warning given in advance of sth that is going to happen 预告；警告：*You must give* ***one month's notice.*** 你必须提前一个月发出通知。◇ *Prices may be altered without notice.* 价格变动不另行通知。◇ *The bar is closed* ***until further notice*** (= until you are told that it is open again). 酒吧停止营业，直到另行通知。◇ *You are welcome to come and stay as long as you give us plenty of notice.* 只要你及早通知，我们都欢迎你来住宿。

• WHEN LEAVING JOB/HOUSE 辞职；搬迁 **7** [U] a formal letter or statement saying that you will or must leave your job or house at the end of a particular period of time 辞职信；搬迁通知：*He has* ***handed in his notice.*** 他递交了辞呈。◇ *They* ***gave*** *her* ***two weeks' notice.*** 他们通知她两周后搬走。

• REVIEW OF BOOK/PLAY 书评；剧评 **8** [C] a short article in a newspaper or magazine, giving an opinion about a book, play, etc.（报刊上对书籍、戏剧等的）评论，短评

IDM **at short 'notice | at a moment's 'notice** not long in advance; without warning or time for preparation 随时；一经通知立即；没有准备时间：*This was the best room we could get at such short notice.* 这是我们临时能弄到的最好的房间了。◇ *You must be ready to leave at a moment's notice.* 你必须随时准备出发。 **on short 'notice** (*NAmE*) = AT SHORT NOTICE

■ ***verb*** (not usually used in the progressive tenses 通常不用于进行时)

• SEE/HEAR 看到；听到 **1** [I, T] to see or hear sb/sth; to become aware of sb/sth 看（或听）到；注意到；意识到：*People were making fun of him but he didn't seem to notice.* 人们在拿他开玩笑，但他好像没有意识到。◇ **~ sb/sth** *The first thing I noticed about the room was the smell.* 我首先注意到的是这屋子里的气味。◇ **~ (that)...** *I couldn't help noticing (that) she was wearing a wig.* 我一眼就看出她戴着假发。◇ **~ how, what, etc....** *Did you notice how Rachel kept looking at her watch?* 你有没有注意到雷切尔在不停地看她的手表？◇ **~ sb/sth do sth** *I noticed them come in.* 我注意到他们进来了。◇ **~ sb/sth doing sth** *I didn't notice him leaving.* 我没看到他离开。

• PAY ATTENTION 注意 **2** [T] **~ sb/sth** to pay attention to sb/sth 注意；留意：*She wears those strange clothes just to get herself noticed.* 她穿那些奇装异服不过是想引人注意而已。

> **▼ SYNONYMS 同义词辨析**
>
> **notice**
>
> **note • detect • observe • witness**
>
> These words all mean to see sth, especially when you pay careful attention to it. 以上各词均含看到、注意到之义。
>
> **notice** to see, hear or become aware of sb/sth; to pay attention to sb/sth 指看（或听）到、注意到、意识到、注意、留意：*The first thing I noticed about the room was the smell.* 我首先注意到的是这屋子里的气味。
>
> **note** (*rather formal*) to notice or pay careful attention to sth 指注意、留意：*Please note (that) the office will be closed on Monday.* 请注意办事处星期一将关闭。 NOTE This word is very common in business English. 该词在商务英语中非常通用：*Note that the prices are inclusive of VAT.* 注意这些价格含增值税。
>
> **detect** to discover or notice sth, especially sth that is not easy to see, hear, etc. 指发现、查明、侦察出：*The tests are designed to detect the disease early.* 这些检查旨在及早查出疾病。
>
> **observe** (*formal*) to see or notice sb/sth 指看到、注意、观察到：*Have you observed any changes lately?* 最近你注意到什么变化没有？◇ *The police observed a man enter the bank.* 警察注意到一个男人走进了银行。
>
> **witness** (*rather formal*) to see sth happen 指当场看到、目击：*Police have appealed for anyone who witnessed the incident to contact them.* 警方呼吁目击这一事件的人与他们联系。
>
> **PATTERNS**
>
> • to notice/note/detect/observe **that/how/what/where/who...**
> • to notice/observe/witness **sth happen/sb do sth**

no·tice·able /ˈnəʊtɪsəbl; *NAmE* ˈnoʊ-/ *adj.* easy to see or notice; clear or definite 显著的；显而易见的：*a noticeable improvement* 显而易见的改进 ◇ **~ in sb/sth** *This effect is particularly noticeable in younger patients.* 这种作用在年轻一些的病人身上尤为明显。◇ **~ that...** ***It was noticeable that*** *none of the family were present.* 很明显这一家没有人在场。▶ **no·tice·ably** /-əbli/ *adv.*：*Her hand was shaking noticeably.* 很明显她的手在颤抖。◇ *Marks were noticeably higher for girls than for boys.* 女孩子的分数明显地高于男孩子。

no·tice·board /ˈnəʊtɪsbɔːd; *NAmE* ˈnoʊtɪsbɔːrd/ (*BrE*) (*NAmE* **'bulletin board**) (*also* **board** *BrE, NAmE*) *noun* a board for putting notices on 告示牌；布告板 ➲ VISUAL VOCAB PAGE V71

no·ti·fi·able /ˈnəʊtɪfaɪəbl; *NAmE* ˈnoʊ-/ *adj.* [usually before noun] (*formal*) (of a disease or a crime 疾病或罪行) so dangerous or serious that it must by law be reported officially to the authorities 依法须报告当局的；依法须向官方汇报的

no·ti·fi·ca·tion /ˌnəʊtɪfɪˈkeɪʃn; *NAmE* ˌnoʊ-/ *noun* [U, C] (*formal*) the act of giving or receiving official information about sth 通知；通告；告示：***advance/prior notification*** (= telling sb in advance about sth) 预先通告 ◇ *written notification* 书面通知 ◇ *You should receive (a) notification of our decision in the next week.* 关于我们的决定，下周你会接到通知。

no·tify /ˈnəʊtɪfaɪ; *NAmE* ˈnoʊ-/ *verb* (**no·ti·fies, no·ti·fy·ing, no·ti·fied, no·ti·fied**) (*formal*) to formally or officially tell sb about sth（正式）通报，通知 SYN **inform**：**~ sb** *Competition winners will be notified by post.* 将发信通知竞赛的优胜者。◇ **~ sb of sth** *The police must be notified of the date of the demonstration.* 必须向警方报告游行示威的日期。◇ **~ sth to sb** *The date of the demonstration must be notified to the police.* 游行示威的日期必须报告警方。◇ **~ sb that...** *Members have been notified that there will be a small increase in the fee.* 会员已经得到通知，费用将有小幅上调。

no·tion AW /ˈnəʊʃn; *NAmE* ˈnoʊʃn/ *noun* an idea, a belief or an understanding of sth 观念；信念；理解：**~ (of sth)** *a political system based on the notions of equality and liberty* 建立在自由平等观念基础上的政治体系 ◇ *She had only a vague notion of what might happen.* 对于可能发生的事她只有一个模糊的概念。◇ **~ (that...)** *I have to reject the notion that greed can be a good thing.* 我不能接受那种认为贪欲也可以是件好事的想法。

no·tion·al /ˈnəʊʃənl; *NAmE* ˈnoʊ-/ *adj.* (*formal*) based on a guess, estimate or theory; not existing in reality 猜测的；估计的；理论上的；想象的 ▶ **no·tion·al·ly** /ˈnəʊʃənəli; *NAmE* ˈnoʊ-/ *adv.*

no·tori·ety /ˌnəʊtəˈraɪəti; *NAmE* ˌnoʊ-/ *noun* [U, sing.] fame for being bad in some way 恶名；坏名声：**~ (for sth)** *She achieved notoriety for her affair with the senator.* 她因为和参议员的风流韵事而声名狼藉。◇ **~ (as sth)** *He gained a certain notoriety as a gambler.* 他落了个赌徒的恶名。

no·tori·ous /nəʊˈtɔːriəs; *NAmE* noʊ-/ *adj.* well known for being bad 声名狼藉的；臭名昭著的： *a notorious criminal* 恶名昭彰的罪犯 ◊ **~ for sth/for doing sth** *The country is notorious for its appalling prison conditions.* 这个国家因监狱状况恶劣而臭名远扬。◊ **~ as sth** *The bar has become notorious as a meeting-place for drug dealers.* 这家酒吧因作为毒品贩子接头的场所而声名狼藉。 ▸ **no·tori·ous·ly** *adv.*： *Mountain weather is notoriously difficult to predict.* 山地气候难以预料是人所共知的。

not·with·stand·ing AW /ˌnɒtwɪθˈstændɪŋ; -wɪð-; *NAmE* ˌnɑːt-/ *prep., adv.*

■ ***prep.*** (*formal*) (also used following the noun it refers to 亦用于其所指名词之后) without being affected by sth; despite sth 虽然；尽管： *Notwithstanding some major financial problems, the school has had a successful year.* 虽然有些重大的经费问题，这所学校一年来还是很成功。◊ *The bad weather notwithstanding, the event was a great success.* 尽管天气恶劣，活动还是取得了巨大的成功。

■ ***adv.*** (*formal*) despite this 尽管如此 SYN **however, nevertheless**： *Notwithstanding, the problem is a significant one.* 然而，这个问题仍很重要。

nou·gat /ˈnuːɡɑː; *NAmE* ˈnuːɡət/ *noun* [U] a hard sweet/candy that has to be chewed a lot, often containing nuts, CHERRIES, etc. and pink or white in colour 牛轧糖（含果仁、樱桃等，呈粉红色或白色）

nought /nɔːt/ *noun* **1** [C, U] (*BrE*) (*also* **zero** *NAmE, BrE*) the figure 0（数字）零： *A million is written with six noughts.* 一百万写出来有六个零。◊ *nought point one* (= written 0.1) 零点一 ◊ *I give the programme nought out of ten for humour.* 我给这个节目的幽默打零分。 **2** (*also* **naught**) [U] (*literary*) used in particular phrases to mean 'nothing'（用于某些短语）无，零： *All our efforts have* ***come to nought*** (= have not been successful). 我们所付出的努力都已付诸东流。

the Nought·ies /ˈnɔːtiz/ *noun* [pl.] (*BrE*) the years from 2000 to 2009 * 21 世纪头十年（即从 2000 年到 2009 年）

ˌnoughts and ˈcrosses (*BrE*) (*NAmE* **ˌtic-tac-ˈtoe**) *noun* [U] a simple game in which two players take turns to write Os or Xs in a set of nine squares. The first player to complete a row of three Os or three Xs is the winner. 圈叉游戏（二人轮流在井字形九格中画 O 或 X，先将三个 O 或 X 连成一线者获胜） ➲ VISUAL VOCAB PAGE V42

noun /naʊn/ *noun* (*grammar* 语法) (*abbr.* **n.**) a word that refers to a person (such as *Ann* or *doctor*), a place (such as *Paris* or *city*) or a thing, a quality or an activity (such as *plant*, *sorrow* or *tennis*) 名词 ➲ SEE ALSO ABSTRACT NOUN, COMMON NOUN, PROPER NOUN ➲ WORDFINDER NOTE AT GRAMMAR

ˈnoun phrase *noun* (*grammar* 语法) a word or group of words in a sentence that behaves in the same way as a noun, that is as a subject, an object, a COMPLEMENT, or as the object of a preposition 名词短语；名词词组： *In the sentence 'I spoke to the driver of the car', 'the driver of the car' is a noun phrase.* 在句子 I spoke to the driver of the car 中，the driver of the car 是名词短语。

nour·ish /ˈnʌrɪʃ; *NAmE* ˈnɜːrɪʃ/ *verb* **1 ~ sb/sth** to keep a person, an animal or a plant alive and healthy with food, etc. 抚养；滋养；养育： *All the children were well nourished and in good physical condition.* 所有这些孩子都营养良好，身体健康。 **2 ~ sth** (*formal*) to allow a feeling, an idea, etc. to develop or grow stronger 培养，促进（情绪、观点等）： *By investing in education, we nourish the talents of our children.* 我们通过教育投资，培养孩子们的才能。 ▸ **nour·ish·ing** *adj.*： *nourishing food* 滋补食品

nour·ish·ment /ˈnʌrɪʃmənt; *NAmE* ˈnɜːr-/ *noun* [U] (*formal* or *specialist*) food that is needed to stay alive, grow and stay healthy 营养；营养品： *Can plants obtain adequate nourishment from such poor soil?* 土壤这样贫瘠，植物能获得足够的养分吗？ ◊ (*figurative*) *As a child, she was starved of intellectual nourishment.* 她小时候缺乏汲取知识的机会。

nous /naʊs/ *noun* [U] (*BrE, informal*) intelligence and the ability to think and act in a practical way 智力；理性；常识 SYN **common sense**

nou·veau riche /ˌnuːvəʊ ˈriːʃ; *NAmE* ˌnuːvoʊ/ *noun* (*pl.* **nou·veaux riches** /ˌnuːvəʊ ˈriːʃ; *NAmE* ˌnuːvoʊ/ or **the nou·veau riche**) (*from French, disapproving*) a person who has recently become rich and likes to show how rich they are in a very obvious way 暴发户 ▸ **nou·veau riche** *adj.*

nou·velle cuis·ine /ˌnuːvel kwɪˈziːn/ *noun* [U] (*from French*) a modern style of cooking that avoids heavy foods and serves small amounts of different dishes arranged in an attractive way on the plate 新式烹饪（讲求食物清淡，量少而精美）

nova /ˈnəʊvə; *NAmE* ˈnoʊvə/ *noun* (*pl.* **novae** /-viː/ or **novas**) (*astronomy* 天) a star that suddenly becomes much brighter for a short period 新星（短期内突然变得很亮） ➲ COMPARE SUPERNOVA

novel /ˈnɒvl; *NAmE* ˈnɑːvl/ *noun, adj.*

■ ***noun*** a story long enough to fill a complete book, in which the characters and events are usually imaginary（长篇）小说： *to write/publish/read a novel* 创作 / 发表 / 阅读长篇小说 ◊ ***detective/historical/romantic novels*** 侦探 / 历史 / 言情小说 ◊ *the novels of Jane Austen* 简•奥斯汀的小说 ➲ WORDFINDER NOTE AT BOOK ➲ COLLOCATIONS AT LITERATURE

■ ***adj.*** (*often approving*) different from anything known before; new, interesting and often seeming slightly strange 新颖的；与众不同的；珍奇的： *a novel feature* 新特征

nov·el·ette /ˌnɒvəˈlet; *NAmE* ˌnɑːv-/ *noun* a short novel, especially a romantic novel that is considered to be badly written 中篇小说（尤指被认为很蹩脚的言情小说）

nov·el·ist /ˈnɒvəlɪst; *NAmE* ˈnɑːv-/ *noun* a person who writes novels 小说家： *a romantic/historical novelist* 言情 / 历史小说家 ➲ COLLOCATIONS AT LITERATURE

nov·el·is·tic /ˌnɒvəˈlɪstɪk; *NAmE* ˌnɑːv-/ *adj.* (*formal*) typical of or used in novels 小说的；小说中使用的

nov·ella /nəˈvelə/ *noun* a short novel 中篇小说

nov·elty /ˈnɒvlti; *NAmE* ˈnɑːv-/ *noun, adj.*

■ ***noun*** (*pl.* **-ies**) **1** [U] the quality of being new, different and interesting 新奇；新颖；新鲜： *It was fun working there at first but* ***the novelty soon wore off*** (= it became boring). 开始的时候在那里工作很有趣，但这股新鲜劲很快就过去了。◊ *There's a certain* ***novelty value*** *in this approach.* 这种方法有一定的新意。 **2** [C] a thing, person or situation that is interesting because it is new, unusual or has not been known before 新奇的事物（或人、环境）： *Electric cars are still something of a novelty.* 电动汽车仍然是一种新鲜玩意儿。 **3** [C] a small cheap object sold as a toy or a decorative object 廉价小饰物；小玩意儿

■ ***adj.*** [only before noun] different and unusual; intended to be amusing and to catch people's attention 新奇的；风格独特的： *a novelty teapot* 新颖独特的茶壶

No·vem·ber /nəʊˈvembə(r); *NAmE* noʊ-/ *noun* [U, C] (*abbr.* **Nov.**) the 11th month of the year, between October and December 十一月 HELP To see how **November** is used, look at the examples at **April**. * November 的用法见词条 April 下的示例。

nov·ice /ˈnɒvɪs; *NAmE* ˈnɑːv-/ *noun* **1** a person who is new and has little experience in a skill, job or situation 新手；初学者： *I'm a complete novice at skiing.* 滑雪我完全是个新手。◊ *computer software for novices/the novice user* 给初学者设计的电脑软件 **2** a person who has joined a religious group and is preparing to become a MONK or a NUN 初学修士（或修女）；（修会等的）初学生 **3** a horse that has not yet won an important race 尚未赢过大赛的赛马

novi·ti·ate (*also* **novi·ci·ate**) /nəʊˈvɪʃiət; *NAmE* noʊ-/ *noun* (*formal*) a period of being a novice (2) (修士或修女的)初学期

novo·caine /ˈnəʊvəkeɪn; *NAmE* ˈnoʊ-/ *noun* [U] (*medical* 医) = PROCAINE

now /naʊ/ *adv., conj.*

■ *adv.* **1** (at) the present time 现在；目前；此刻： *Where are you living now?* 你现在住在哪里？◇ *It's been two weeks now since she called.* 她上次来电距今已经有两个星期了。◇ *It's too late now.* 现在太晚了。◇ ***From now on** I'll be more careful.* 从今以后，我会更加细心。◇ *He'll be home **by now**.* 他现在该到家了。◇ *I've lived at home **up till now**.* 我至今一直住在家里。◇ *That's all **for now**.* 暂时就这些。 **2** at or from this moment, but not before 现在；从现在开始： *Start writing now.* 现在开始写吧。◇ *I am now ready to answer your questions.* 我现在可以回答你们的问题了。 **3** (*informal*) used to show that you are annoyed about sth (表示厌烦)： *Now they want to tax food!* 他们竟然要对食品收税！◇ *What do you want now?* 你又想要什么？◇ *It's broken. Now I'll have to get a new one.* 这东西坏了，我只好去买个新的了。 **4** used to get sb's attention before changing the subject or asking them to do sth (改变话题或要对方做某事前，引起对方注意)喂，哎，嗨： *Now, listen to what she's saying.* 嗨，听听她在讲什么。◇ *Now, the next point is quite complex.* 请注意，下一点非常复杂。◇ *Now come and sit down.* 喂，过来坐下。◇ *Now let me think…* 嗯，让我想想…

IDM **(every) now and aˈgain/ˈthen** from time to time; occasionally 有时；偶尔；时常： *Every now and again she checked to see if he was still asleep.* 她隔一会儿就看看他是否还在睡觉。 **now for ˈsb/ˈsth** used when turning to a fresh activity or subject (转向新的活动或话题)下面，接下来： *And now for some travel news.* 下面播报几条旅游新闻。 **ˌnow, ˈnow** (*also* **ˌnow ˈthen**) used to show in a mild way that you do not approve of sth (温和地表示不赞同)可是，好啦： *Now then, that's enough noise.* 好啦，这够吵了。 **now… now…** at one time… at another time… 时而…时而…： *Her moods kept changing—now happy, now sad.* 她的情绪总是变幻不定，时而欢喜，时而忧伤。 **(it's) ˌnow or ˈnever** this is the only opportunity sb will have to do sth 机不可失；勿失良机 **ˈnow then** **1** = NOW, NOW **2** used when making a suggestion or an offer (提出建议或提供帮助)喂，听我说： *Now then, who wants to come for a walk?* 喂，谁想出去走走？ **ˈnow what?** (*informal*) **1** (*also* **what is it ˈnow?**) used when you are annoyed because sb is always asking questions or interrupting you (对某人的不断提问或打扰感到厌烦)又怎么了： *'Yes, but Dad…' 'Now what?'* "是的，可是爸爸…" "又怎么了？" **2** used to say that you do not know what to do next in a particular situation (不知道下一步该做什么)现在该怎么办

■ *conj.* ~ (that)… because the thing mentioned is happening or has just happened 既然；由于： *Now that the kids have left home we've got a lot of extra space.* 孩子们都离开家了，我们住着就更宽绰了。

now·adays /ˈnaʊədeɪz/ *adv.* at the present time, in contrast with the past 现今；现在；目前： *Nowadays most kids prefer watching TV to reading.* 现在大多数孩子都喜欢看电视而不喜欢阅读。

no·where /ˈnəʊweə(r); *NAmE* ˈnoʊwer/ (*also* **ˈno place** *especially in NAmE*) *adv.* not in or to any place 无处；哪里都不： *This animal is found in Australia, and nowhere else.* 这种动物生长在澳大利亚，别处没有。◇ *There was nowhere for me to sit.* 我无处可坐。◇ *'Where are you going this weekend?' 'Nowhere special.'* "这个周末你打算去哪儿？" "没什么地方可去。" ◇ *Nowhere is the effect of government policy more apparent than in agriculture.* 政府的政策对农业的影响最为显著。

IDM **get/go ˈnowhere | get sb ˈnowhere** to make no progress or have no success; to not enable sb to make progress or have success (让某人)毫无进展： *We discussed it all morning but got nowhere.* 我们就此事讨论了一上午，可是毫无进展。◇ *Talking to him will get you nowhere.* 和他谈话你会一无所获。 **nowhere to be ˈfound/ˈseen | nowhere in ˈsight** impossible for anyone to find or see 不可能找到(或看见)： *The children were nowhere to be seen.* 根本看不到孩子们在哪儿。◇ *A peace settlement is nowhere in sight* (= is not likely in the near future). 近期内无望和平解决。 ➲ MORE AT LEAD[1] *v.*, MIDDLE *n.*, NEAR *adv.*

ˌno-ˈwin *adj.* [only before noun] (of a situation, policy, etc. 情形、政策等) that will end badly whatever you decide to do 终将失败的；无望取胜的： *We are considering the options available to us in this no-win situation.* 在这种取胜无望的情形下，我们在细想还有什么选择。

ˈnow-now *adv.* (*SAfrE, informal*) **1** within a short period of time 一会儿；立刻： *I'll be with you now-now.* 我马上就来。 **2** a short time ago 刚刚；刚才： *She left now-now.* 她刚走。

nowt /naʊt/ *pron.* (*BrE, dialect, informal*) nothing 无；没有什么： *There's nowt wrong with it.* 这没什么错。

nox·ious /ˈnɒkʃəs; *NAmE* ˈnɑːk-/ *adj.* (*formal*) poisonous or harmful 有毒的；有害的： *noxious fumes* 有毒烟雾

noz·zle /ˈnɒzl; *NAmE* ˈnɑːzl/ *noun* a narrow piece that is attached to the end of a pipe or tube to direct the stream of liquid, air or gas passing through 管口；喷嘴

NPC /ˌen piː ˈsiː/ *noun* = NON-PLAYER CHARACTER

NQ /ˌen ˈkjuː/ *noun* (in Scotland) the abbreviation for 'National Qualification', one of a range of courses and exams that are taken in a number of different subjects and at different levels between the ages of approximately 15 and 18. These include National 3, 4 and 5 (replacing STANDARD GRADE and HIGHER exams). (苏格兰)国家资格(全写为 National Qualification，众多学科不同等级的一系列课程和考试之一，学生在约 15 至 18 岁时参加，包括国家 3 级、4 级和 5 级，取代标准级别和高级证书考试)

nr *abbr.* (*BrE*) near (used, for example, in the address of a small village) 靠近(用于小村庄等的地址中)： *Howden, nr Goole* 靠近古尔的豪顿村

NRA /ˌen ɑːr ˈeɪ/ *abbr.* National Rifle Association (a US organization that supports the right of citizens to own a gun) (美国)全国步枪协会(支持公民拥有枪支的权利)

NRI /ˌen ɑːr ˈaɪ/ *noun* (*IndE*) Non-Resident Indian (a person of Indian origin who is working somewhere else but who keeps links with India) 非常住印度人(不居住在印度但与印度保持联系的国外印度裔人)

ns *abbr.* (in writing 书写形式) NANOSECOND 毫微秒；十亿分之一秒

NSFW *abbr.* not safe (or suitable) for work (used in emails, on Internet FORUMS, etc. to show a link to a website or WEB PAGE that contains images, text or video that people may find offensive) 工作时不宜，不适合上班时观看(全写为 not safe / suitable for work，用于电邮、互联网论坛等，表示链接的网站或网页中包含可能令人反感的图文或视频)

NST /ˌen es ˈtiː/ *abbr.* (*CanE*) Newfoundland Standard Time 纽芬兰标准时间

NSU /ˌen es ˈjuː/ *abbr.* NON-SPECIFIC URETHRITIS 非特异性尿道炎

nth /enθ/ *adj.* [only before noun] (*informal*) used when you are stating that sth is the last in a long series and emphasizing how often sth has happened (某事已发生多次，并强调其频繁性)第 n 个的，第 n 次的： *It's the nth time I've explained it to you.* 这件事我已经向你解释过无数遍了。

IDM **to the nth ˈdegree** extremely; to an extreme degree 极端地；非常地；极大程度上

NTSC /ˌen tiː es ˈsiː/ *noun* [U] (*specialist*) a television broadcasting system that is used in N America and Japan * NTSC 制(北美和日本使用的电视广播系统) ➲ COMPARE PAL

nu /njuː/ *noun* the 13th letter of the Greek alphabet (Ν, ν) 希腊字母表的第 13 个字母

nu·ance /ˈnjuːɑːns; *NAmE* ˈnuː-/ *noun* [C, U] a very slight difference in meaning, sound, colour or sb's feelings that is not usually very obvious （意义、声音、颜色、感情等方面的）细微差别： *He watched her face intently to catch every nuance of expression.* 他认真地注视着她的脸，捕捉每一丝细微的表情变化。

nub /nʌb/ *noun* [sing.] **the ~ (of sth)** the central or essential point of a situation, problem, etc. 中心；要点；实质： ***The nub of the matter*** *is that business is declining.* 问题的核心是营业额在萎缩。

nu·bile /ˈnjuːbaɪl; *NAmE* ˈnuː-; ˈnuːbl/ *adj.* (of a girl or young woman 女孩或年轻女子) sexually attractive 性感的；迷人的

nu·buck /ˈnjuːbʌk; *NAmE* ˈnuː-/ *noun* [U] a type of leather that has been rubbed on one side to make it feel soft like SUEDE 正绒面革（单面打磨的软皮革）

nu·clear 🔑 AW /ˈnjuːkliə(r); *NAmE* ˈnuː-/ *adj.* [usually before noun] **1** 🔑 using, producing or resulting from nuclear energy 原子能的；核能的： *a nuclear power station* 核电站 ◇ *the nuclear industry* 原子能工业 ◇ *nuclear-powered submarines* 核动力潜艇 ➲ WORDFINDER NOTE AT ENERGY **2** 🔑 connected with weapons that use nuclear energy 核武器的： *a **nuclear weapon/bomb/missile*** 核武器；核弹；核导弹 ◇ *a **nuclear explosion/attack/war*** 核爆炸 / 攻击 / 战争 ◇ *the country's **nuclear capability*** (= the fact that it has nuclear weapons) 这个国家的核力量 ◇ ***nuclear capacity*** (= the number of nuclear weapons a country has) 核能力 **3** (*physics* 物) of the NUCLEUS (= central part) of an atom 核子的；原子核的： *nuclear particles* 核粒子 ◇ *a nuclear reaction* 核反应 ➲ WORDFINDER NOTE AT PHYSICS

ˌnuclear ˈenergy (*also* **ˌnuclear ˈpower**) *noun* [U] a powerful form of energy produced by converting matter into energy by splitting the NUCLEI (= central parts) of atoms. It is used to produce electricity. 核能；原子能

ˌnuclear ˈfamily *noun* (*specialist*) a family that consists of father, mother and children, when it is thought of as a unit in society 核心家庭，小家庭（只包括父母和子女） ➲ COMPARE EXTENDED FAMILY

ˌnuclear ˈfission *noun* [U] = FISSION (1)

ˌnuclear-ˈfree *adj.* [usually before noun] (of a country or a region 国家或地区) not having or allowing nuclear energy, weapons or materials 无核的： *a nuclear-free zone* 无核区

ˌnuclear ˈfuel *noun* [U] a substance that can be used as a source of NUCLEAR ENERGY because it is capable of NUCLEAR FISSION 核燃料

ˌnuclear ˈfusion *noun* [U] = FUSION (2)

ˈnuclear option *noun* (*politics* 政) the most extreme possible response to a particular situation 核选择（指可能做出的最极端反应）： *Currency controls would be the nuclear option.* 货币管制将是最极端的选择。

ˌnuclear ˈphysics *noun* [U] the area of physics which deals with the NUCLEUS of atoms and with nuclear energy （原子）核物理学 ▶ **ˌnuclear ˈphysicist** *noun*

ˌnuclear ˈpower *noun* [U] = NUCLEAR ENERGY

ˌnuclear reˈactor *noun* = REACTOR

ˌnuclear ˈwaste *noun* [U] waste material which is RADIOACTIVE, especially used fuel from nuclear power stations 核废料

ˌnuclear ˈwinter *noun* a period without light, heat or growth which scientists believe would follow a nuclear war 核冬天（科学家认为核战争之后会出现的一段昏暗、寒冷、荒芜的时期）

nu·cle·ic acid /njuːˌkliːɪk ˈæsɪd; -ˌkleɪɪk; *NAmE* nuː-/ *noun* [U] (*chemistry* 化) either of two acids, DNA and RNA, that are present in all living cells 核酸

nu·cleus /ˈnjuːkliəs; *NAmE* ˈnuː-/ *noun* (*pl.* **nu·clei** /-kliaɪ/) **1** (*physics* 物) the part of an atom that contains most of its mass and that carries a positive electric charge 核；原子核 ➲ SEE ALSO NEUTRON, PROTON **2** (*biology* 生) the central part of some cells, containing the GENETIC material 细胞核 **3** the central part of sth around which other parts are located or collected 核心；中心： *These paintings will form the nucleus of a new collection.* 这些画将构成新的收藏系列的基础。

nude /njuːd; *NAmE* nuːd/ *adj.*, *noun*

■ ***adj.*** **1** (especially of a human figure in art 尤指艺术人像) not wearing any clothes 裸体的 SYN **naked**: *a nude model* 裸体模特儿 ◇ *He asked me to pose nude for him.* 他请我给他摆裸体造型。 **2** involving people who are naked 裸体者的： *a nude photograph* 裸体照片 ◇ *Are there any nude scenes in the movie?* 电影里有裸体镜头吗？ **3** (*NAmE*) (of TIGHTS/PANTYHOSE, etc. 裤袜等) skin-coloured 肉色的

■ ***noun*** a work of art consisting of a naked human figure; a naked human figure in art 裸体画；人物裸体作品；裸体人像： *a bronze nude by Rodin* 罗丹创作的青铜裸体像 ◇ *a reclining nude* 一个斜倚着的裸体人像

IDM **in the ˈnude** not wearing any clothes 裸体的 SYN **naked**: *She refuses to be photographed in the nude.* 她拒绝拍裸体照片。

nudge /nʌdʒ/ *verb*, *noun*

■ ***verb*** **1** [T] **~ sb/sth** to push sb gently, especially with your elbow, in order to get their attention （用肘）轻推，轻触： *He nudged me and whispered, 'Look who's just come in.'* 他用胳膊肘碰了我一下，低声说："瞧谁进来了。" **2** [T] **~ sb/sth + adv./prep.** to push sb/sth gently or gradually in a particular direction （朝某方向）轻推，渐渐推动： *He nudged the ball past the goalie and into the net.* 他轻松地将球推过守门员，送入网中。 ◇ *She nudged me out of the way.* 她将我轻轻地推开了。 ◇ (*figurative*) *He nudged the conversation towards the subject of money.* 他将谈话逐步引到钱这个话题上。 ◇ (*figurative*) *She tried to nudge him into changing his mind* (= persuade him to do it). 她试图慢慢说服他改变主意。 **3** [T, I] **~ (sth) + adv./prep.** to move forward by pushing with your elbow 用胳膊肘挤开往前走： ***He nudged his way*** *through the crowd.* 他用胳膊肘开路穿过人群。 **4** [T] **~ sth (+ adv./prep.)** to reach or make sth reach a particular level （使）达到，接近： *Inflation is nudging 20%.* 通货膨胀即将达到 20%。 ◇ *This afternoon's sunshine could nudge the temperature above freezing.* 今天下午的阳光可使温度达到冰点以上。

■ ***noun*** a slight push, usually with the elbow （肘部的）轻推，碰： *She gave me a gentle nudge in the ribs to tell me to shut up.* 她用胳膊肘轻轻捅了一下我的腰，让我住口。 ◇ (*figurative*) *He can work hard but he needs a nudge now and then.* 他能够努力工作，但偶尔需要督促一下。

IDM **ˌnudge ˈnudge, ˌwink ˈwink | a ˌnudge and a ˈwink** used to suggest sth to do with sex without actually saying it （暗指与性行为有关的事）你懂的： *They've been spending a lot of time together, nudge nudge, wink wink.* 他们花很多时间厮混在一起，你懂我的意思吧。

nudie /ˈnjuːdi; *NAmE* ˈnuː-/ *adj.* (*informal*) showing or including people wearing no clothes 展示裸体的；有裸体的： *nudie photographs* 裸体照片

nud·ism /ˈnjuːdɪzəm; *NAmE* ˈnuː-/ (*also* **na·tur·ism** *especially in BrE*) *noun* [U] the practice of not wearing any clothes because you believe this is more natural and healthy 裸体主义（认为裸体更自然更有益健康）

nud·ist /ˈnjuːdɪst; *NAmE* ˈnuː-/ (*also* **na·tur·ist** *especially in BrE*) *noun* a person who does not wear any clothes because they believe this is more natural and healthy 裸体主义者： *a **nudist beach/camp*** 裸泳海滩；裸体营

nud·ity /ˈnjuːdəti; *NAmE* ˈnuː-/ *noun* [U] the state of being naked 裸体；赤裸： *The committee claimed that there was too much nudity on television.* 委员会指出电视里的裸体镜头太多。

N

nuf·fin /ˈnʌfɪn/ (*also* **nuf·fink** /ˈnʌfɪŋk/) *pron.* (*BrE, informal*) nothing 没有东西；没有什么

nu·ga·tory /ˈnjuːɡətəri; *NAmE* ˈnuːɡətɔːri/ *adj.* (*formal*) having no purpose or value 无目的的；无价值的 SYN **worthless**

nug·get /ˈnʌɡɪt/ *noun* **1** a small lump of a valuable metal or mineral, especially gold, that is found in the earth 天然贵重金属块；（尤指）天然金块 **2** a small round piece of some types of food （某些食品的）小圆块：*chicken nuggets* 鸡肉块 **3** a small thing such as an idea or a fact that people think of as valuable 有价值的小东西；有用的想法（或事实） SYN **snippet**：*a useful nugget of information* 一条有用的信息

nuis·ance /ˈnjuːsns; *NAmE* ˈnuː-/ *noun* **1** [C, usually sing.] a thing, person or situation that is annoying or causes trouble or problems 麻烦事；讨厌的人（或东西）：*I don't want to **be a nuisance** so tell me if you want to be alone.* 我不想讨人嫌，你要是想一个人待着就说一声。◇ *I hope you're not **making a nuisance of yourself**.* 我希望你没有讨人嫌。◇ ***It's a nuisance** having to go back tomorrow.* 明天不得不回去，真烦人。◇ *What a nuisance!* 真麻烦！ **2** [C, U] (*law* 律) behaviour by sb that annoys other people and that a court can order the person to stop 妨害行为：*He was charged with causing a public nuisance.* 他被控妨害公共利益罪。

ˈ**nuisance call** *noun* a telephone call made by a person who wants to annoy sb, sometimes by making comments about sex, or to threaten them 骚扰电话

ˈ**nuisance value** *noun* [U] (*BrE*) a quality that makes sth useful because it causes problems for your opponents 阻碍价值

nuke /njuːk; *NAmE usually* nuːk/ *verb, noun* (*informal*)
■ *verb* **~ sth** to attack a place with nuclear weapons 用核武器攻击
■ *noun* a nuclear weapon 核武器

null /nʌl/ *adj.* (*specialist*) having the value zero 零值的；等于零的：*a null result* 毫无结果

IDM ˌ**null and** ˈ**void** (*law* 律) (of an election, agreement, etc. 选举、协议等) having no legal force; not valid 无法律效力的；无效的：*The contract was declared null and void.* 合同被宣布无效。

ˈ**null hypothesis** *noun* (*statistics* 统计) the idea that an experiment that is done using two groups of people will show the same results for each group 零假设，原假设，虚无假设（即用两组人分别实验而结果相同）

nul·lify /ˈnʌlɪfaɪ/ *verb* (**nul·li·fies**, **nul·li·fy·ing**, **nul·li·fied**, **nul·li·fied**) (*formal*) **1 ~ sth** to make sth such as an agreement or order lose its legal force 使失去法律效力；废止 SYN **invalidate**：*Judges were unwilling to nullify government decisions.* 法官们不愿废止政府决定。 **2 ~ sth** to make sth lose its effect or power 使无效；抵消 SYN **negate**：*An unhealthy diet will nullify the effects of training.* 不健康的饮食会抵消锻炼的效果。

nul·lity /ˈnʌləti/ *noun* [sing.] (*formal* or *law* 律) the fact of sth, for example a marriage, having no legal force or no longer being valid; something which is no longer valid 无法律约束力；无效；无法律效力的事物

numb /nʌm/ *adj., verb*
■ *adj.* **1** if a part of your body is **numb**, you cannot feel anything in it, for example because of cold 麻木的；失去知觉的：*to **be/go numb*** 麻木；失去知觉 ◇ *numb with cold* 冻僵 ◇ *I've just been to the dentist and my face is still numb.* 我刚刚去看了牙医，脸上现在还没知觉呢。 **2** unable to feel, think or react in the normal way 麻木的；迟钝的；呆滞的：*He felt numb with shock.* 他惊呆了。➲ SEE ALSO NUMBING ▶ **numb·ly** *adv.*：*Her life would never be the same again, she realized numbly.* 她模模糊糊地意识到她再也回不到过去的生活了。 **numb·ness** *noun* [U]：*pain and numbness in my fingers* 我的手指又疼又麻 ◇ *He was still in a state of numbness and shock from the accident.* 由于这事故，他还处于麻木与震惊状态之中。
■ *verb* **1 ~ sth** to make a part of your body unable to feel anything, for example because of cold 使失去知觉；使麻木：*His fingers were numbed with the cold.* 他的手指冻僵了。 **2 ~ sb** to make sb unable to feel, think or react in a normal way, for example because of an emotional shock 使麻木；使迟钝 SYN **stun**：*We sat there in silence, numbed by the shock of her death.* 我们默默地坐在那里发愣，因为她的死使我们感到震惊。

num·ber 🔑 /ˈnʌmbə(r)/ *noun, verb*
■ *noun*
• WORD/SYMBOL 单词；符号 **1** 🔑 [C] a word or symbol that represents an amount or a quantity 数字；数；数量 SYN **figure**：*Think of a number and multiply it by two.* 想出一个数，然后乘以二。◇ *a **high/low number*** 高位 / 低位数 ◇ ***even numbers*** (= 2, 4, 6, etc.) 偶数 ◇ ***odd numbers*** (= 1, 3, 5, etc.) 奇数 ◇ *You owe me 27 dollars? Make it 30, that's a good **round number**.* 你欠我 27 美元？凑到 30 吧，讨个整数好记。➲ SEE ALSO CARDINAL *n.* (2), ORDINAL, PRIME NUMBER, WHOLE NUMBER
• POSITION IN SERIES 序列中的位置 **2** 🔑 [C] (*abbr.* **No.**) (*symb.* **#**) used before a figure to show the position of sth in a series 编号；序数：*They live at number 26.* 他们住在 26 号。◇ *The song reached number 5 in the charts.* 这首歌在排行榜中位列第 5。
• TELEPHONE, ETC. 电话等 **3** 🔑 [C] (often in compounds 常构成复合词) a number used to identify sth or communicate by telephone, etc. （电话等的）号码：*My phone number is 266998.* 我的电话号码是 266998。◇ *I'm sorry, I think you have the **wrong number*** (= wrong telephone number). 对不起，我想你打错了。◇ *What is your account number, please?* 请问你的账号是多少？ ➲ SEE ALSO BOX NUMBER, E-NUMBER, PIN, REGISTRATION NUMBER, SERIAL NUMBER
• QUANTITY 量 **4** 🔑 [C] **~ (of sb/sth)** a quantity of people or things 数量；数额：*A large number of people have applied for the job.* 许多人申请了这工作。◇ *The number of homeless people has increased dramatically.* 无家可归者的人数急剧增加了。◇ *Huge numbers of* (= very many) *animals have died.* 有大量的动物死去。◇ ***A number of*** (= some) *problems have arisen.* 已经出现了一些问题。◇ *I could give you **any number of*** (= a lot of) *reasons for not going.* 我可以给你许多不去的理由。◇ *We were eight **in number*** (= there were eight of us). 我们有八个人。◇ *Nurses are leaving the profession in increasing numbers.* 越来越多的护士退出这一职业。◇ ***Sheer weight of numbers*** (= the large number of soldiers) *secured them the victory.* 他们只是靠重兵取胜。◇ *staff/student numbers* 员工 / 学生数量 HELP A plural verb is needed after **a/an (large, small, etc.) number of...** 在 a / an (large、small 等) number of ... 之后用复数动词。
• GROUP OF PEOPLE 人群 **5** [sing.] (*formal*) a group or quantity of people 一群人；许多人：*one of our number* (= one of us) 我们中的一人 ◇ *The prime minister is elected by MPs from among their number.* 首相是下院议员从他们当中选出的。
• MAGAZINE 杂志 **6** [C] (*BrE*) the version of a magazine, etc. published on a particular day, in a particular month, etc. 期；号 SYN **issue**：*the October number of 'Vogue'* 《时尚》十月号 ➲ SEE ALSO BACK NUMBER
• SONG/DANCE 歌；舞蹈 **7** [C] a song or dance, especially one of several in a performance 一首歌，一段舞蹈（尤指演出的节目）：*They sang a slow romantic number.* 他们演唱了一首舒缓的浪漫歌曲。
• THING ADMIRED 令人羡慕的东西 **8** [sing.] (*informal*) (following one or more adjectives 接在一个或多个形容词后) a thing, such as a dress or a car, that is admired 令人羡慕的东西：*She was wearing a black velvet number.* 她穿着一件时髦的黑天鹅绒礼服。
• GRAMMAR 语法 **9** [U] the form of a word, showing whether one or more than one person or thing is being talked about 数（表示所叙述的人或事物是一个或多个）：*The word 'men' is plural in number.* * men 一词是复数形式。◇ *The subject of a sentence and its verb must agree in number.* 句子的主语和动词的数必须一致。

IDM **by** ˈ**numbers** following a set of simple instructions identified by numbers 按数字指令：*painting by numbers*

按数字顺序着色 **by the 'numbers** (*NAmE*) following closely the accepted rules for doing sth 严格遵循规则；一板一眼 **have (got) sb's 'number** (*informal*) to know what sb is really like and what they plan to do 了解某人的底细；对某人知根知底：*He thinks he can fool me but I've got his number.* 他以为他能糊弄我，但我清楚他的真面目。 **your 'number is up** (*informal*) the time has come when you will die or lose everything 劫数已到；死期已至 **'numbers game** a way of considering an activity, etc. that is concerned only with the number of people doing sth, things achieved, etc., not with who or what they are 数字游戏（即只注重参与的人数、达成了几项结果等，而不考虑参与者是谁、结果是什么）：*MPs were playing the numbers game as the crucial vote drew closer.* 在至关重要的表决临近时，下院议员们玩起了数字游戏。 ➲ MORE AT CUSHY, OPPOSITE *adj.*, SAFETY, WEIGHT *n.*

■ *verb*

• **MAKE A SERIES** 排序 **1** [T] to give a number to sth as part of a series or list 标号；给…编号：**~ sth** *All the seats in the stadium are numbered.* 运动场里所有的座位都编了号。◇ *I couldn't work out the numbering system for the hotel rooms.* 我搞不清楚酒店房间的编号系统。◇ **~ sth from... to...** *Number the car's features from 1 to 10 according to importance.* 将车的特征按重要性从 1 到 10 编号。◇ **~ sth + noun** *The doors were numbered 2, 4, 6 and 8.* 门上的编号为 2、4、6 和 8。

• **MAKE STH AS TOTAL** 总计 **2** [I] **+ noun** to make a particular number when added together 总计；共计；数以…计 SYN **add up to**：*The crowd numbered more than a thousand.* 聚集的人群共计一千多人。◇ *We numbered 20* (= there were 20 of us in the group). 我们总共 20 人。

• **INCLUDE** 包括 **3** [T, I] (*formal*) to include sb/sth in a particular group; to be included in a particular group 把…算作；（被）归入：**~ sb/sth among sth** *I number her among my closest friends.* 我把她算作我最好的朋友之一。◇ **~ among sth** *He numbers among the best classical actors in Britain.* 他被看作是英国最好的古典剧目演员之一。 IDM SEE DAY

'number crunching *noun* [U] (*informal*) the process of calculating numbers, especially when a large amount of data is involved and the data is processed in a short space of time 数字密集运算

numbered *adj.* having a number to show that it is part of a series or list 编号的：*The players all wear numbered shirts.* 队员都穿着有编号的运动衫。 IDM SEE DAY

num·ber·less /ˈnʌmbələs; *NAmE* -bərl-/ *adj.* (*literary*) too many to be counted 无数的；难以计数的 SYN **innumerable**

ˌnumber 'one *noun, adj.* (*informal*)

■ *noun* **1** [U] the most important or best person or thing 头号人物（或事物）；最重要的人（或事物）；最好的人（或事物）：*We're number one in the used car business.* 在二手车交易中我们是老大。 **2** [U, C] the pop song or record that has sold the most copies in a particular week 周销售量最高的流行歌曲（或唱片）：*The new album went straight to number one.* 这张新专辑一举登上了周销售量榜首。◇ *She's had three number ones.* 她已有三张唱片曾经名列周销售量排行榜榜首。**3** [U] yourself 自己：*Looking after number one is all she thinks about.* 她一心只顾着自己。 **4** [sing.] (*informal*) an expression used especially by children or when speaking to children to talk about passing liquid waste from the body（尤作为儿童用语）撒尿：*It's only a number one.* 只撒了尿。 ➲ COMPARE NUMBER TWO

■ *adj.* most important or best 头号的；最重要的；最好的：*the world's number one athlete* 世界头号运动员 ◇ *the number one priority* 要最先处理的事

'number plate (*BrE*) (*NAmE* **'license plate**) *noun* a metal or plastic plate on the front and back of a vehicle that shows its REGISTRATION NUMBER （车辆的）牌照，号码牌

ˌNumber 'Ten (*also* **No. 10**) *noun* [U+sing./pl. v.] 10 Downing Street, London, the official home of the British prime minister, often used to refer to the government 唐宁街十号（英国首相的伦敦官邸，常指英国政府）：*Number Ten had nothing to say on the matter.* 唐宁街十号对此不作评论。 ➲ MORE LIKE THIS 19, page R27

ˌnumber 'two *noun* [sing.] (*informal*) an expression used especially by children or when speaking to children to talk about passing solid waste from the body （尤作为儿童用语）拉屁屁，拉屎：*Mum, I need a number two.* 妈妈，我要拉屁屁。 ➲ COMPARE NUMBER ONE *n.*

numb·ing /ˈnʌmɪŋ/ *adj.* (of an experience or a situation 经历或情形) making you unable to feel anything 令人麻木的；使人失去知觉的：*numbing cold/fear* 令人麻木的严寒；使人发懵的恐惧 ◇ *Watching television had a numbing effect on his mind.* 看电视使他头脑麻木。

numb·skull (*also* **num·skull**) /ˈnʌmskʌl/ *noun* (*informal*) a stupid person 蠢人；笨蛋

nu·mer·acy /ˈnjuːmərəsi; *NAmE* ˈnuː-/ *noun* [U] a good basic knowledge of mathematics; the ability to understand and work with numbers 数学基础知识；识数；计算能力：*standards of literacy and numeracy* 读写和计算的水平 ➲ WORDFINDER NOTE AT MATHS ▶ **nu·mer·ate** /ˈnjuːmərət; *NAmE* ˈnuː-/ *adj.*：*All students should be numerate and literate when they leave school.* 所有的学生毕业时都应具备计算和读写的能力。 OPP **innumerate**

nu·meral /ˈnjuːmərəl; *NAmE* ˈnuː-/ *noun* a sign or symbol that represents a number 数字；数码 ➲ SEE ALSO ARABIC NUMERAL, ROMAN NUMERAL

nu·mer·ator /ˈnjuːməreɪtə(r); *NAmE* ˈnuː-/ *noun* (*mathematics* 数) the number above the line in a FRACTION, for example 3 in the FRACTION ¾（分数中的）分子 ➲ COMPARE DENOMINATOR

nu·mer·ic·al /njuːˈmerɪkl; *NAmE* nuː-/ (*also less frequent* **nu·mer·ic** /-ɪk/) *adj.* relating to numbers; expressed in numbers 数字的；用数字表示的：*numerical data* 数字数据 ◇ *The results are expressed in descending* ***numerical order****.* 结果按数字降序列出。 ▶ **nu·mer·ic·al·ly** /-kli/ *adv.*：*to express the results numerically* 以数字形式显示结果

nu·mer·ology /ˌnjuːməˈrɒlədʒi; *NAmE* ˌnuːməˈrɑːlədʒi/ *noun* [U] the use of numbers to try to tell sb what will happen in the future 数字命理学（用数字预测未来）；数字占卜术 ▶ **nu·mero·logic·al** /ˌnjuːmərəˈlɒdʒɪkl; *NAmE* ˌnuːmərəˈlɑːdʒɪkl/ *adj.*

nu·mer·ous /ˈnjuːmərəs; *NAmE* ˈnuː-/ *adj.* (*formal*) existing in large numbers 众多的；许多的 SYN **many**：*He has been late on numerous occasions.* 他已经迟到过无数次了。◇ *The advantages of this system are too numerous to mention.* 这套系统的好处不胜枚举。

nu·min·ous /ˈnjuːmɪnəs; *NAmE* ˈnuː-/ *adj.* (*formal*) having a strong religious and spiritual quality that makes you feel that God is present 超自然的；精神上的；神圣的

nu·mis·mat·ics /ˌnjuːmɪzˈmætɪks; *NAmE* ˌnuː-/ *noun* [U] the study of coins and MEDALS 钱币学；奖章的研究 ▶ **nu·mis·mat·ic** *adj.*

nu·mis·ma·tist /njuːˈmɪzmətɪst; *NAmE* nuː-/ *noun* a person who collects or studies coins or MEDALS 钱币（或奖章）收藏家；钱币学家；奖章研究者

numpty /ˈnʌmpti/ (*pl.* **-ies**) *noun* (*ScotE, informal*) a stupid person 傻瓜；笨蛋

num·skull = NUMBSKULL

nun /nʌn/ *noun* a member of a religious community of women who promise to serve God all their lives and often live together in a CONVENT 修女；尼姑 ➲ COMPARE MONK

nun·cio /ˈnʌnsiəʊ; *NAmE* -sioʊ/ *noun* (*pl.* **-os**) a representative of the POPE (= the leader of the Roman Catholic Church) in a foreign country 罗马教廷大使：*a papal nuncio* 教廷大使

nun·nery /ˈnʌnəri/ *noun* (*pl.* **-ies**) (*old-fashioned* or *literary*) = CONVENT

N

nup·tial /ˈnʌpʃl/ *adj.* [only before noun] (*formal*) connected with marriage or a wedding 婚姻的；婚礼的：*nuptial bliss* 婚姻美满 ◇ *a nuptial mass* 婚礼弥撒

nup·tials /ˈnʌpʃlz/ *noun* [pl.] (*old-fashioned*) a wedding 婚礼

nurse /nɜːs; *NAmE* nɜːrs/ *noun, verb*

■ ***noun*** **1** a person whose job is to take care of sick or injured people, usually in a hospital 护士：*a qualified/registered nurse* 合格的 / 注册护士 ◇ *student nurses* 实习护士 ◇ *a male nurse* 男护士 ◇ *a dental nurse* (= one who helps a dentist) 牙科护士 ◇ *a psychiatric nurse* (= one who works in a hospital for people with mental illnesses) 精神病医院的护士 ◇ *Nurse Bennett* 贝内特护士 ◇ *Nurse, come quickly!* 护士，快过来！ ➲ SEE ALSO CHARGE NURSE, DISTRICT NURSE, PRACTICAL NURSE, REGISTERED NURSE, STAFF NURSE ➲ **WORDFINDER NOTE** AT HOSPITAL ➲ **NOTE** AT GENDER **2** (*also* **nurse·maid**) (*old-fashioned*) (in the past) a woman or girl whose job was to take care of babies or small children in their own homes （旧时雇主家中的）女保育员，保姆，女仆 ➲ SEE ALSO NURSERY NURSE, WET NURSE

■ ***verb*** **1** [T] ~ **sb** to care for sb who is ill/sick or injured 看护，照料（病人或伤者）：*He worked in a hospital for ten years nursing cancer patients.* 他在一所医院里工作了十年，护理癌症病人。 ◇ *She* ***nursed*** *her daughter* ***back to health.*** 她照料女儿，使她康复。 **2** [T] ~ **sth** to take care of an injury or illness 调治，调养（伤病）：*Several weeks after the match, he was still nursing a shoulder injury.* 比赛过去几个星期了，他仍在疗养肩伤。 ◇ *You'd better go to bed and nurse that cold.* 你最好上床睡觉，把感冒治好。 ◇ (*figurative*) *She was nursing her hurt pride.* 她的自尊受挫，正在慢慢恢复。 ➲ **COLLOCATIONS** AT ILL **3** [T] ~ **sth** (*formal*) to have a strong feeling or idea in your mind for a long time 怀抱；怀有；心藏 SYN **harbour**：*to nurse an* ***ambition/a grievance/a grudge*** 心怀壮志 / 不满 / 怨恨 ◇ *She had been nursing a secret desire to see him again.* 她一直暗暗渴望再次见到他。 **4** [T] ~ **sth** to give special care or attention to sb/sth 培育；培养；悉心照料：*to nurse tender young plants* 悉心照料嫩苗 **5** [T] ~ **sb/sth** to hold sb/sth carefully in your arms or close to your body 搂抱；小心抱着：*He sat nursing his cup of coffee.* 他坐在那里小心翼翼地捧着他那杯咖啡。 **6** [I, T] (of a woman or female animal 妇女或雌性动物) to feed a baby with milk from the breast 喂奶；哺育 SYN **suckle**：*a* ***nursing mother*** 正在喂奶的母亲 ◇ ~ **sb/sth** *The lioness is still nursing her cubs.* 这只母狮还在给它的幼崽喂奶。 ➲ COMPARE BREASTFEED **7** [I] (of a baby 婴儿) to suck milk from its mother's breast 吃奶；吸奶 SYN **suckle**

nurse·maid /ˈnɜːsmeɪd; *NAmE* ˈnɜːrs-/ *noun* (*old-fashioned*) = NURSE

ˌ**nurse pracˈtitioner** *noun* a nurse who is trained to do many of the tasks usually done by a doctor 从业护士

nur·sery /ˈnɜːsəri; *NAmE* ˈnɜːrs-/ *noun, adj.*

■ ***noun*** (*pl.* **-ies**) **1** = DAY NURSERY **2** = NURSERY SCHOOL：*Her youngest child is* ***at nursery*** *now.* 她最小的孩子现在上幼儿园。 **3** (*NAmE* or *old-fashioned*) a room in a house where a baby sleeps 婴儿室 **4** (*old-fashioned*) a room in a house where young children can play （供游戏的）儿童室 **5** a place where young plants and trees are grown for sale or for planting somewhere else 苗圃

■ ***adj.*** [only before noun] (*BrE*) connected with the education of children from 2 to 5 years old 幼儿教育的：*nursery education* 幼儿教育 ◇ *a nursery teacher* 幼儿教师

nur·sery·man /ˈnɜːsərimən; *NAmE* ˈnɜːrs-/ *noun* (*pl.* **-men** /-mən/) a person who owns or works in a nursery (5) 苗圃主；苗圃工人；园丁

ˈ**nursery nurse** *noun* (*BrE*) a person whose job involves taking care of small children in a DAY NURSERY （日托）托儿所保育员

ˈ**nursery rhyme** *noun* a simple traditional poem or song for children 童谣；儿歌

ˈ**nursery school** *noun* a school for children between the ages of about two and five 幼儿园 SYN **preschool** ➲ COMPARE KINDERGARTEN, PLAYGROUP

ˈ**nursery slope** (*BrE*) (*NAmE* ˈ**bunny slope**) *noun* [usually pl.] a slope that is not very steep and is used by people who are learning to SKI （初学滑雪者的）平缓坡地

nurs·ing /ˈnɜːsɪŋ; *NAmE* ˈnɜːrs-/ *noun* [U] the job or skill of caring for people who are sick or injured 护理；看护：*a career in nursing* 护理生涯 ◇ *nursing care* 看护 ◇ *the nursing profession* 护理职业

ˈ**nursing home** *noun* a small private hospital, especially one where old people live and are cared for 小型私立疗养院；（尤指）私立养老院 ➲ **MORE LIKE THIS** 9, page R26

nur·ture /ˈnɜːtʃə(r); *NAmE* ˈnɜːrtʃ-/ *verb, noun*

■ ***verb*** (*formal*) **1** ~ **sb/sth** to care for and protect sb/sth while they are growing and developing 养育；养护；培养：*These delicate plants need careful nurturing.* 这些幼嫩的植物需要精心培育。 ◇ *children nurtured by loving parents* 受到慈爱的父母养育的孩子 **2** ~ **sth** to help sb/sth to develop and be successful 扶持；帮助；支持 SYN **foster**：*It's important to nurture a good working relationship.* 维持良好的工作关系非常重要。 **3** ~ **sth** to have a feeling, an idea, a plan, etc. for a long time and encourage it to develop 滋长；助长：*She secretly nurtured a hope of becoming famous.* 她暗暗滋生出成名的愿望。

■ ***noun*** [U] (*formal*) care, encouragement and support given to sb/sth while they are growing 养育；培养

nut /nʌt/ *noun, verb*

■ ***noun*** **1** (often in compounds 常构成复合词) a small hard fruit with a very hard shell that grows on some trees 坚果：*to* ***crack a nut*** (= open it) 破开坚果 ◇ *a Brazil nut* 巴西果 ◇ *a hazelnut* 榛子 ◇ *nuts and raisins* 果仁和葡萄干 ➲ **VISUAL VOCAB** PAGES V10, V35 ➲ SEE ALSO MONKEY NUT **2** a small piece of metal with a hole through the centre that is screwed onto a BOLT to hold pieces of wood, machinery, etc. together 螺母；螺帽：*to tighten a nut* 拧紧螺母 ◇ *a wheel nut* 车轮螺母 ➲ **VISUAL VOCAB** PAGE V21 **3** (*BrE, slang*) a person's head or brain 人的头（或大脑） **4** (*BrE also* **nut·ter**) (*informal*) a strange or crazy person 怪人；疯子：*He's a complete nut, if you ask me.* 要我说，他是个十足的疯子。 ➲ SEE ALSO NUTS, NUTTY (2) **5** (*informal*) (in compounds 构成复合词) a person who is extremely interested in a particular subject, activity, etc. 着迷的人；专注于某事的人；…迷：*a* ***fitness/tennis/computer, etc. nut*** 健美迷、网球迷、电脑迷等 **6 nuts** [pl.] (*slang*) a man's TESTICLES 睾丸

IDM **do your ˈnut** (*BrE, informal*) to become very angry 暴跳如雷；气炸 **a hard/tough ˈnut** (*informal*) a person who is difficult to deal with or to influence 难对付的人；难说服的人 **a hard/tough ˈnut (to ˈcrack)** a difficult problem or situation to deal with 棘手的问题；不好对付的情形 **the ˌnuts and ˈbolts (of sth)** (*informal*) the basic practical details of a subject or an activity 基本要点 ˌ**off your ˈnut** (*BrE, informal*) crazy 疯狂 ➲ MORE AT SLEDGEHAMMER

■ ***verb*** (**-tt-**) ~ **sb** (*BrE, informal*) to deliberately hit sb hard with your head （故意）以头撞击

PHR V ˌ**nut sth ˈout** (*AustralE, NZE, informal*) to calculate sth or find the answer to sth 计算；找…的答案：*I'm going to have to nut it out on a piece of paper.* 我得在纸上计算一下。

ˌ**nut-ˈbrown** *adj.* dark brown in colour 栗色的；深棕色的：*nut-brown hair* 深棕色的头发 ➲ **MORE LIKE THIS** 15, page R26

nut·case /ˈnʌtkeɪs/ *noun* (*informal*) a crazy person 疯子

nut·crack·er /ˈnʌtkrækə(r)/ *noun* (*BrE also* **nut·crack·ers** [pl.]) a tool for cracking open the shells of nuts 坚果钳 ➲ **VISUAL VOCAB** PAGE V27

ˌ**nut ˈcutlet** *noun* nuts, bread and HERBS mixed together and cooked in a shape like a piece of meat 坚果炸饼（用坚果、面包和草本香料烤成）

nut·meg /ˈnʌtmeg/ *noun* [U, C] the hard seed of a tropical tree originally from SE Asia, used in cooking as a spice, especially to give flavour to cakes and sauces 肉豆蔻（尤用作调味料）：*freshly grated nutmeg* 新磨碎的肉豆蔻末 ➲ VISUAL VOCAB PAGE V35

nutra·ceut·ical /ˌnjuːtrəˈsuːtɪkl/ *noun* = FUNCTIONAL FOOD

nu·tri·ent /ˈnjuːtriənt; *NAmE* ˈnuː-/ *noun* (*specialist*) a substance that is needed to keep a living thing alive and to help it to grow 营养素；营养物：*a lack of **essential nutrients*** 基本营养的缺乏 ◇ *Plants draw minerals and other nutrients from the soil.* 植物从土壤中吸取矿物质和其他养分。◇ *children suffering from a serious **nutrient deficiency*** 严重缺乏营养的儿童 ➲ COLLOCATIONS AT DIET, LIFE

nu·tri·tion /njuˈtrɪʃn; *NAmE* nu-/ *noun* [U] the process by which living things receive the food necessary for them to grow and be healthy 营养；滋养；营养的补给：*advice on diet and nutrition* 有关饮食和营养的建议 ◇ *to study food science and nutrition* 研究食物科学和营养 ➲ WORDFINDER NOTE AT FIT ➲ COLLOCATIONS AT DIET ➲ COMPARE MALNUTRITION ▶ **nu·tri·tion·al** /-ʃənl/ (*also less frequent* **nu·tri·tive** /ˈnjuːtrətɪv; *NAmE* ˈnuː-/) *adj.*：*the nutritional value of milk* 牛奶的营养价值 **nu·tri·tion·al·ly** /-ʃənəli/ *adv.*：*a nutritionally balanced menu* 营养均衡的菜谱

nu·tri·tion·ist /njuˈtrɪʃənɪst; *NAmE* nu-/ *noun* a person who is an expert on the relationship between food and health 营养学家 ➲ SEE ALSO DIETITIAN

nu·tri·tious /njuˈtrɪʃəs; *NAmE* nu-/ *adj.* (*approving*) (of food 食物) very good for you; containing many of the substances which help the body to grow 有营养的；营养丰富的 SYN **nourishing**：*tasty and nutritious meals* 既可口又有营养的饭菜

nuts /nʌts/ *adj.* [not before noun] (*informal*) **1** crazy 疯狂：*My friends think I'm nuts for saying yes.* 朋友们认为我答应是疯了。◇ *That phone ringing all the time is **driving me nuts**!* 那电话铃一直响个不停，吵得我快要发疯了。➲ SYNONYMS AT MAD **2** **~ about sb/sth** very much in love with sb; very enthusiastic about sth 执着；迷恋；狂热：*He's absolutely nuts about her.* 他绝对迷恋上她了。IDM SEE SOUP *n.*

nut·shell /ˈnʌtʃel/ *noun*

IDM **(put sth) in a nutshell** (to say or express sth) in a very clear way, using few words 简而言之；用简明的话：*To put it in a nutshell, we're bankrupt.* 简单地说，我们破产了。

nut·ter /ˈnʌtə(r)/ *noun* (*BrE, informal*) = NUT (4)

nutty /ˈnʌti/ *adj.* (**nut·tier**, **nut·ti·est**) **1** tasting of or containing nuts 坚果味的；含果仁的：*a nutty taste* 坚果口味 **2** (*informal*) slightly crazy 疯疯癫癫的：*She's got some nutty friends.* 她有几个疯疯癫癫的朋友。◇ *He's **as nutty as a fruitcake*** (= completely crazy). 他疯狂到了极点。

nuz·zle /ˈnʌzl/ *verb* [T, I] to touch or rub sb/sth with the nose or mouth, especially to show affection（用鼻子或嘴）摩擦，触（尤指表达爱意）：**~ sb/sth** *She nuzzled his ear.* 她用嘴磨蹭他的耳朵。◇ **+ adv./prep.** *The child nuzzled up against his mother.* 这孩子依偎着他妈妈。

NVQ /ˌen viː ˈkjuː/ *noun* the abbreviation for 'National Vocational Qualification' (a British qualification that shows that you have reached a particular standard in the work that you do) 国家职业资格证书，国家职业资格认证（全写为 National Vocational Qualification，英国证明从业者职业水平的证书）：*NVQ Level 3 in Catering* 国家职业资格认证饮食业三级

NW *abbr.* north-west; north-western 西北方（的）；西北部（的）：*NW Australia* 澳大利亚西北部

NY *abbr.* New York 纽约

NYC *abbr.* New York City 纽约市

nylon /ˈnaɪlɒn; *NAmE* -lɑːn/ *noun* **1** [U] a very strong artificial material, used for making clothes, rope, brushes, etc. 尼龙：*a nylon fishing line* 尼龙钓线 ◇ *This material is 45% nylon.* 这种材料含 45% 的尼龙。**2 nylons** [pl.] (*old-fashioned*) women's STOCKINGS or TIGHTS/PANTYHOSE made of nylon（女用）尼龙长袜，尼龙连袜裤

nymph /nɪmf/ *noun* **1** (in ancient Greek and Roman stories) a spirit of nature in the form of a young woman, that lives in rivers, woods, etc.（古希腊、罗马神话中居于山林水泽的）仙女 **2** (*biology* 生) a young insect that has a body form which compares with that of the adult 若虫（与成虫相似的昆虫幼体）：*a dragonfly nymph* 蜻蜓若虫

nymph·et /ˈnɪmfet; nɪmˈfet/ *noun* a young girl who is very sexually attractive 性感少女；美丽的少女

nym·pho·maniac /ˌnɪmfəˈmeɪniæk/ (*also informal* **nym·pho** /ˈnɪmfəʊ; *NAmE* -foʊ/ *pl.* **-os**) *noun* (*disapproving*) a woman who has, or wants to have, sex very often 女色情狂 ▶ **nym·pho·mania** *noun* [U]

NZ (*also* **N.Z.**) *abbr.* New Zealand 新西兰

Oo

O /əʊ; *NAmE* oʊ/ *noun, exclamation, symbol*
- *noun* (*also* **o**) (*pl.* **Os, O's, o's** /əʊz; *NAmE* oʊz/) **1** [C, U] the 15th letter of the English alphabet 英语字母表的第 15 个字母: *'Orange' begins with (an) O/'O'.* * orange 一词以字母 o 开头。 **2** used to mean 'zero' when saying telephone numbers, etc.（说电话号码等时表示）零: *My number is six o double three* (= 6033). 我的号码是六零三三。 ➲ SEE ALSO O GRADE, O LEVEL
- *exclamation* (*especially literary*) = OH
- *symbol* the symbol for the chemical element Oxygen（化学元素）氧

o' /ə/ *prep.* used in written English to represent an informal way of saying *of*（用于书面英语中，代替 of 的非正式说法）: *a couple o' times* 几次

oaf /əʊf; *NAmE* oʊf/ *noun* a stupid, unpleasant or awkward person, especially a man 傻瓜，蠢材，笨蛋（尤指男人）: *Mind that cup, you clumsy oaf!* 当心那个杯子，你这笨手笨脚的家伙！ ▸ **oaf·ish** *adj.*

oak /əʊk; *NAmE* oʊk/ *noun* **1** [C, U] (*also* **'oak tree** [C]) a large tree that produces small nuts called ACORNS. Oaks are common in northern countries and can live to be hundreds of years old. 栎树；橡树: *a gnarled old oak tree* 多节瘤的老栎树 ◇ *forests of oak and pine* 长有松树和栎树的森林 ➲ VISUAL VOCAB PAGE V10 ➲ SEE ALSO POISON OAK **2** [U] the hard wood of the oak tree 栎木；橡木: *oak beams* 栎木梁 ◇ *This table is made of solid oak.* 这张桌子是用实心栎木制作的。

IDM **great/tall ˌoaks from little acorns 'grow** (*saying*) something large and successful often begins in a very small way 参天橡树长自小橡实；合抱之树，生于毫末

oaken /'əʊkən; *NAmE* 'oʊkən/ *adj.* [only before noun] (*literary*) made of oak 橡木的；橡木制作的

oakum /'əʊkəm; *NAmE* 'oʊkəm/ *noun* [U] a material obtained by pulling old rope to pieces, a job done in the past by prisoners 麻刀，麻絮（旧时由囚犯制造）

OAP /ˌəʊ eɪ 'piː; *NAmE* ˌoʊ/ *noun* (*BrE, becoming old-fashioned*) the abbreviation for OLD-AGE PENSIONER 领养老金者（全写为 old-age pensioner）

oar /ɔː(r)/ *noun* a long pole with a flat blade at one end that is used for ROWING a boat 船桨；桨: *He pulled as hard as he could on the oars.* 他拼命地划桨。 ➲ VISUAL VOCAB PAGE V59 ➲ COMPARE PADDLE *n.* (1)

IDM **put/stick your 'oar in** (*BrE, informal*) to give your opinion, advice, etc. without being asked and when it is probably not wanted 多管闲事；横插一杠子 SYN **interfere**

oar·lock /'ɔːlɒk; *NAmE* 'ɔːrlɑːk/ (*NAmE*) (*BrE* **row·lock**) *noun* a device fixed to the side of a boat for holding an OAR（固定在小船边缘的）桨架

oars·man /'ɔːzmən; *NAmE* 'ɔːrz-/, **oars·woman** /'ɔːzwʊmən; *NAmE* 'ɔːrz-/ *noun* (*pl.* **-men** /-mən/, **-women** /-wɪmɪn/) a person who ROWS a boat, especially as a member of a CREW (= team) 桨手；划桨人；（尤指）划艇队员

OAS /ˌəʊ eɪ 'es; *NAmE* ˌoʊ/ *abbr.* (*CanE*) OLD AGE SECURITY（加拿大）老年保障金，养老金

oasis /əʊ'eɪsɪs; *NAmE* oʊ-/ *noun* (*pl.* **oases** /-siːz/) **1** an area in the desert where there is water and where plants grow（沙漠中的）绿洲 **2** a pleasant place or period of time in the middle of sth unpleasant or difficult（困苦中）令人快慰的地方（或时刻）；乐土；乐事 SYN **haven**: *an oasis of calm* 宁静的一刻 ◇ *a green oasis in the heart of the city* 都市中心的绿茵

oast house /'əʊst haʊs; *NAmE* 'oʊst/ *noun* (*especially BrE*) a building made of bricks with a round roof that was built to contain an oven used for drying HOPS（啤酒花）烘干室

oat /əʊt; *NAmE* oʊt/ *adj.* [only before noun] made from or containing OATS 燕麦制的；含燕麦的: *oat cakes* 燕麦饼 ◇ *oat bran* 燕麦麸 ➲ SEE ALSO OATMEAL

oat·cake /'əʊtkeɪk; *NAmE* 'oʊt-/ *noun* a Scottish biscuit made with oats, which is not sweet（苏格兰不带甜味的）燕麦饼

oater /'əʊtə(r); *NAmE* 'oʊtər/ *noun* (*NAmE, informal*) a film/movie about life in the western US in the 19th century（以 19 世纪美国西部生活为题材的）西部影片

oath /əʊθ; *NAmE* oʊθ/ *noun* (*pl.* **oaths** /əʊðz; *NAmE* oʊðz/) **1** a formal promise to do sth or a formal statement that sth is true 宣誓；誓言: *to* ***take/swear an oath*** *of allegiance* 宣誓效忠 ◇ *Before giving evidence, witnesses in court have to* ***take the oath*** (= promise to tell the truth). 作证之前，证人必须当庭宣誓据实作证。 ➲ COLLOCATIONS AT VOTE **2** (*old-fashioned*) an offensive word or phrase used to express anger, surprise, etc.; a swear word（表示愤怒、惊异等的）咒骂，诅咒的话: *She heard the sound of breaking glass, followed by a muttered oath.* 她听到打碎玻璃的响声，接着是低声的咒骂。

IDM **on/under 'oath** (*law* 律) having made a formal promise to tell the truth in court（在法庭上）宣誓说实话，经宣誓: *Is she prepared to give evidence on oath?* 她愿意宣誓据实作证吗? ◇ *The judge reminded the witness that he was still under oath.* 法官提醒证人，他仍然受宣誓的约束。

oat·meal /'əʊtmiːl; *NAmE* 'oʊt-/ *noun* [U] **1** flour made from crushed oats, used to make biscuits/cookies, PORRIDGE, etc. 燕麦粉；燕麦片 **2** (*NAmE*) = PORRIDGE (1) **3** a pale brown colour 浅棕色；淡棕色；燕麦黄 ▸ **oat·meal** *adj.*: *an oatmeal carpet* 一块燕麦黄地毯

oats /əʊts; *NAmE* oʊts/ *noun* [pl.] grain grown in cool countries as food for animals and for making flour, PORRIDGE/OATMEAL, etc. 燕麦 ➲ VISUAL VOCAB PAGE V35 ➲ SEE ALSO OAT IDM SEE SOW[1]

ob·bli·gato (*NAmE also* **ob·li·gato**) /ˌɒblɪ'gɑːtəʊ; *NAmE* ˌɑːblɪ'gɑːtoʊ/ *noun* (*pl.* **-os**) (*music* 音, *from Italian*) an important part for an instrument in a piece of music which cannot be left out 必需声部；助奏

ob·dur·ate /'ɒbdjərət; *NAmE* 'ɑːbdər-/ *adj.* (*formal, usually disapproving*) refusing to change your mind or your actions in any way 顽固的；固执的；执拗的 SYN **stubborn** ▸ **ob·dur·acy** /'ɒbdjərəsi; *NAmE* 'ɑːbdər-/ *noun* [U] **ob·dur·ate·ly** *adv.*

OBE /ˌəʊ biː 'iː; *NAmE* ˌoʊ/ *noun* the abbreviation for 'Officer of the Order of the British Empire' (an award given in Britain for a special achievement) 英帝国勋位军官，英帝国官佐勋衔获得者（全写为 Officer of the Order of the British Empire，英国授予有特殊贡献者的勋章）: *She was made an OBE.* 她荣获英帝国官佐勋衔。◇ *Matthew Silk OBE* 英帝国官佐勋衔获得者马修•西尔克

obedi·ent /ə'biːdiənt/ *adj.* doing what you are told to do; willing to obey 顺从的；忠顺的；唯命是从的: *an obedient child* 听话的孩子 ◇ **~ to sb/sth** *He was always obedient to his father's wishes.* 他一向顺从父亲的意愿。 OPP **disobedient** ▸ **obedi·ence** /-əns/ *noun* [U]: ***blind/complete/unquestioning/total obedience*** 盲目 / 绝对 / 无条件 / 完全的服从 ◇ **~ to sb/sth** *He has acted* ***in obedience to*** *the law.* 他是依法行事的。 **obedi·ent·ly** *adv.*

IDM **your obedient servant** (*old use*) used to end a formal letter（用作正式信函的结束语）您恭顺的仆人

obei·sance /əʊ'beɪsns; *NAmE* oʊ'biːsns/ *noun* (*formal*) **1** [U] respect for sb/sth or willingness to obey sb 景仰；尊敬；忠顺；顺从 **2** [C] the act of bending your head or the upper part of your body in order to show respect for sb/sth 鞠躬示敬；颔首行礼

ob·el·isk /'ɒbəlɪsk; *NAmE* 'ɑːb-; 'oʊb-/ *noun* a tall pointed stone column with four sides, put up in memory of a person or an event 方尖碑 ➲ VISUAL VOCAB PAGE V14

O

obese /əʊˈbiːs; *NAmE* oʊ-/ *adj.* (*formal* or *medical* 医) (of people 人) very fat, in a way that is not healthy 臃肿的；虚胖的；病态肥胖的 ➲ COLLOCATIONS AT DIET ▸ **obes·ity** /əʊˈbiːsəti; *NAmE* oʊ-/ *noun* [U]: *Obesity can increase the risk of heart disease.* 肥胖会增加患心脏病的风险。

obey 🔑 /əˈbeɪ/ *verb* [T, I] ~ (**sb/sth**) to do what you are told or expected to do 服从；遵守；顺从：*to obey a command/an order/rules/the law* 服从指挥 / 命令；遵守规章 / 法律 ◇ *He had always obeyed his parents without question.* 他对父母一向绝对服从。◇ *'Sit down!' Meekly, she obeyed.* "坐下！" 她乖乖地顺从了。OPP **disobey**

ob·fus·cate /ˈɒbfʌskeɪt; *NAmE* ˈɑːb-/ *verb* [I, T] ~ (**sth**) (*formal*) to make sth less clear and more difficult to understand, usually deliberately（故意地）混淆，使困惑，使模糊不清 SYN **obscure** ▸ **ob·fus·ca·tion** *noun* [U, C]

ob-gyn /ˌəʊ biː ˌdʒiː waɪ ˈen; *NAmE* ˌoʊ/ *noun* (*NAmE, informal*) **1** [U] the branches of medicine concerned with the birth of children (= OBSTETRICS) and the diseases of women (= GYNAECOLOGY) 妇产科 **2** [C] a doctor who is trained in this type of medicine 妇产科医生

obi /ˈəʊbi; *NAmE* ˈoʊ-/ *noun* (*from Japanese*) a wide piece of cloth worn around the waist of a Japanese KIMONO（日本和服的）宽腰带

ob·itu·ary /əˈbɪtʃuəri; *NAmE* oʊˈbɪtʃueri/ *noun* (*pl.* **-ies**) an article about sb's life and achievements, that is printed in a newspaper soon after they have died 讣闻；讣告 ➲ WORDFINDER NOTE AT NEWSPAPER

ob·ject 🔑 *noun, verb*

▪ ***noun*** /ˈɒbdʒɪkt; *NAmE* ˈɑːbdʒekt; -dʒɪkt/ **1** 🔑 a thing that can be seen and touched, but is not alive 物体；物品；东西：*everyday objects such as cups and saucers* 诸如杯碟之类的日用品 ◇ *Glass and plastic objects lined the shelves.* 架子上排列着玻璃和塑料制品。➲ SEE ALSO UFO **2** ~ **of desire, study, attention, etc.** a person or thing that sb DESIRES, studies, pays attention to, etc.（极欲得到、研究、注意等的）对象 ➲ SEE ALSO SEX OBJECT **3** 🔑 an aim or a purpose 宗旨；目的；目标：*Her sole object in life is to become a travel writer.* 她人生的唯一目标就是当游记作家。◇ *The object is to educate people about road safety.* 目的是教育人们注意交通安全。◇ *If you're late, you'll defeat the whole* ***object of the exercise.*** 如果你迟到了，便不能达到整个活动的目的。➲ SYNONYMS AT TARGET **4** (*grammar* 语法) a noun, noun phrase or pronoun that refers to a person or thing that is affected by the action of the verb (called the DIRECT OBJECT), or that the action is done to or for (called the INDIRECT OBJECT) 宾语（包括直接宾语、间接宾语）➲ COMPARE SUBJECT *n.* (5) ➲ MORE LIKE THIS 21, page R27

IDM **expense, money, etc. is no ˈobject** used to say that you are willing to spend a lot of money 费用不在话下；钱不成问题：*He always travels first class—expense is no object.* 他总是乘头等舱旅行，从不计较花费多少。

▪ ***verb*** /əbˈdʒekt/ **1** 🔑 [I] to say that you disagree with, disapprove of or oppose sth 不同意；不赞成；反对：~ (**to sb/sth**) *Many local people object to the building of the new airport.* 许多当地的居民反对兴建新机场。◇ *If nobody objects, we'll postpone the meeting till next week.* 如果没有人反对，我们就把会议推迟到下周。◇ ~ **to doing sth/to sb doing sth** *I really object to being charged for parking.* 我非常反对收停车费。**2** [T] ~ **that...** | **+ speech** to give sth as a reason for opposing sth 提出…作为反对的理由；抗辩说 SYN **protest**: *He objected that the police had arrested him without sufficient evidence.* 他抗辩说警察没有充分的证据就逮捕了他。➲ SYNONYMS AT COMPLAIN ➲ MORE LIKE THIS 21, page R27

ob·ject·ifi·ca·tion /əbˌdʒektɪfɪˈkeɪʃn/ *noun* [U] (*formal*) the act of treating people as if they are objects, without rights or feelings of their own 人格物化（把人当成没有权利或感情的物体）

ob·ject·ify /əbˈdʒektɪfaɪ/ *verb* (**ob·ject·ifies, ob·ject·ify·ing, ob·ject·ified, ob·ject·ified**) ~ **sb/sth** (*formal*) to treat sb/sth as an object 将…物化；使…人格物化：*magazines that objectify women* 将妇女人格物化的杂志

ob·jec·tion /əbˈdʒekʃn/ *noun* ~ (**to sth/to doing sth**) | ~ (**that...**) a reason why you do not like or are opposed to sth; a statement about this 反对的理由；反对；异议：*I* ***have no objection*** *to him coming to stay.* 我不反对他来小住。◇ *I'd like to come too, if you* ***have no objection.*** 如果你不反对，我也想来。◇ *The main objection to the plan was that it would cost too much.* 反对这个计划的主要理由是费用过高。◇ *to* ***raise an objection*** *to sth* 对某事提出异议 ◇ *No objections were raised at the time.* 当时没人提出异议。◇ *The proposal will go ahead despite strong objections from the public.* 尽管公众强烈反对，这项提案仍将付诸实施。

ob·jec·tion·able /əbˈdʒekʃənəbl/ *adj.* (*formal*) unpleasant or offensive 令人不快的；令人反感的；讨厌的：*objectionable people/odours* 讨厌的人 / 气味 ◇ *Why are you being so objectionable today?* 你今天怎么这么别扭？

ob·ject·ive 🔑 AW /əbˈdʒektɪv/ *noun, adj.*

▪ ***noun*** **1** 🔑 something that you are trying to achieve 目标；目的 SYN **goal**: *the* ***main/primary/principal objective*** 主要 / 首要 / 重要目标 ◇ *to* ***meet/achieve*** *your* ***objectives*** 达到 / 实现你的目标 ◇ *You must set realistic* ***aims and objectives*** *for yourself.* 你必须给自己确定切实可行的目的和目标。◇ *The main objective of this meeting is to give more information on our plans.* 这次会议的主要目的是进一步介绍我们的规划。➲ SYNONYMS AT TARGET **2** (*also* **obˌjective ˈlens**) (*specialist*) the LENS in a TELESCOPE or MICROSCOPE that is nearest to the object being looked at（望远镜或显微镜的）物镜 ➲ VISUAL VOCAB PAGE V72

▪ ***adj.*** **1** 🔑 not influenced by personal feelings or opinions;

▼ **VOCABULARY BUILDING** 词汇扩充

Objects you can use 表示用具、物品的词

It is useful to know some general words to help you describe objects, especially if you do not know the name of a particular object. 有些一般性词汇可用于描述物品，尤其是不知道名称的东西。

- A **device** is something that has been designed to do a particular job. * device 指为特定用途设计的装置、器具、器械：*There is a new device for cars that warns drivers of traffic jams ahead.* 有一种新的汽车装置可提醒司机前面交通拥堵。
- A **gadget** is a small object that does something useful, but is not really necessary. * gadget 指有用、但不一定必需的小器具、小装置：*His kitchen is full of gadgets he never uses.* 他厨房里到处是他从不使用的小器具。
- An **instrument** is used especially for delicate or scientific work. * instrument 尤指用于精密或科学工作的仪器、器械、器具：*'What do you call the instrument that measures temperature?' 'A thermometer.'* "测量温度的仪器叫什么？" "温度计。"
- A **tool** is something that you use for making and repairing things. * tool 指制造或修理用的工具、用具：*'Have you got one of those tools for turning screws?' 'Do you mean a screwdriver?'* "你有拧螺丝钉的工具吗？" "你是指螺丝刀吗？"
- A **machine** has moving parts and is used for a particular job. It usually stands on its own. * machine 指有特定用途的机器，通常为独立设备：*'What's a blender?' 'It's an electric machine for mixing soft food or liquid.'* "搅拌器是什么？" "是搅和软食物或液汁的电动机器。"
- An **appliance** is a large machine that you use in the house, such as a washing machine. * appliance 指大型家用机器，如洗衣机。
- **Equipment** means all the things you need for a particular activity. * equipment 统称某项活动所需的设备、装备：*climbing equipment* 攀登活动的装备
- **Apparatus** means all the tools, machines or equipment that you need for something. * apparatus 统称做某事所用的设备、用具、器械、装置：*firefighters wearing breathing apparatus* 戴着呼吸装置的消防人员

considering only facts 客观的；就事论事的；不带个人感情的 SYN unbiased：*an objective analysis/assessment/report* 客观的分析 / 评价 / 报告 ◇ *objective criteria* 客观标准 ◇ *I find it difficult to be objective where he's concerned.* 只要涉及他，我就难以做到保持客观。 OPP subjective **2** (*philosophy* 哲) existing outside the mind; based on facts that can be proved 客观存在的；基于事实的：*objective reality* 客观现实 OPP subjective **3** [only before noun] (*grammar* 语法) the **objective** case is the one which is used for the object of a sentence 宾格的 ▶ **ob·ject·ive·ly** AW *adv.*：*Looked at objectively, the situation is not too bad.* 客观地看，局面并不算太糟。◇ *Can these effects be objectively measured?* 这些结果能客观地衡量吗？ **ob·ject·iv·ity** AW /ˌɒbdʒekˈtɪvəti; *NAmE* ˌɑːb-/ *noun* [U]：*There was a lack of objectivity in the way the candidates were judged.* 对候选人的评定缺乏客观性。◇ *scientific objectivity* 科学的客观性 OPP subjectivity

ˈobject language *noun* **1** [C] (*linguistics* 语言) = TARGET LANGUAGE (1) **2** [U] (*computing* 计) = OBJECT CODE

ˈobject lesson *noun* [usually sing.] a practical example of what you should or should not do in a particular situation 借鉴；经验教训

ob·ject·or /əbˈdʒektə(r)/ *noun* ~ (**to sth**) a person who objects to sth 反对者：*There were no objectors to the plan.* 没有人反对这个计划。 ➲ SEE ALSO CONSCIENTIOUS OBJECTOR

objet d'art /ˌɒbʒeɪ ˈdɑː; *NAmE* ˌɔːbdʒeɪ ˈdɑːr/ *noun* (*pl.* **ob·jets d'art** /ˌɒbʒeɪ ˈdɑː; *NAmE* ˌɔːbdʒeɪ ˈdɑːr/) (*from French*) a small artistic object, used for decoration（装饰性的）小艺术品，小工艺品

ob·li·gated /ˈɒblɪɡeɪtɪd; *NAmE* ˈɑːb-/ *adj.* ~ (**to do sth**) (*NAmE* or *BrE, formal*) having a moral or legal duty to do sth（道义或法律上）有义务的，有责任的，必须的 SYN obliged：*He felt obligated to help.* 他觉得有义务帮忙。

ob·li·ga·tion /ˌɒblɪˈɡeɪʃn; *NAmE* ˌɑːb-/ *noun* **1** [U] ~ (**to do sth**) the state of being forced to do sth because it is your duty, or because of a law, etc. 义务；职责；责任：*You are* **under no obligation** *to buy anything.* 你不必非买什么东西不可。◇ *She did not feel* **under any obligation** *to tell him the truth.* 她觉得没有义务告诉他实情。◇ *I don't want people coming to see me out of a* **sense of obligation**. 我不想让别人迫于无奈来看我。◇ *We will send you an estimate for the work* **without obligation** (= you do not have to accept it). 我们将寄上工程估算，仅供参考。 **2** [C] something which you must do because you have promised, because of a law, etc.（已承诺的或法律等规定的）义务，责任 SYN commitment：*to fulfil your* **legal/professional/financial obligations** 履行法律 / 职业 / 财务责任 ◇ *They reminded him of his contractual obligations.* 他们提醒他注意合同规定的义务。◇ ~ **to do sth** *We have a* **moral obligation** *to protect the environment.* 我们有道义责任保护环境。 ➲ EXPRESS YOURSELF AT HAVE TO

ob·li·gato = OBBLIGATO

ob·liga·tory /əˈblɪɡətri; *NAmE* -tɔːri/ *adj.* **1** ~ (**for sb**) (**to do sth**) (*formal*) that you must do because of the law, rules, etc.（按法律、规定等）必须的，强制的 SYN compulsory：*It is obligatory for all employees to wear protective clothing.* 所有员工必须穿防护服装。 OPP optional **2** (*often humorous*) that you do because you always do it, or other people in the same situation always do it 习惯性的；随大溜的；赶时髦的：*In the mid-60s he took the almost obligatory trip to India.* * 60 年代中期，他也赶时髦到印度一游。

ob·lige /əˈblaɪdʒ/ *verb* (*formal*) **1** [T, usually passive] ~ **sb to do sth** to force sb to do sth, by law, because it is a duty, etc.（以法律、义务等）强迫，迫使：*Parents are obliged by law to send their children to school.* 法律规定父母必须送子女入学。◇ *I* **felt obliged** *to ask them to dinner.* 我不得不请他们吃饭。◇ *He suffered a serious injury that obliged him to give up work.* 他受伤严重，不得已只好放弃工作。 **2** [I, T] to help sb by doing what they ask or what you know they want（根据要求或需要）帮忙，效劳：*Call me if you need any help—I'd be* **happy to oblige**. 若有需要，尽管给我打电话。我很乐意帮忙。◇ ~ **sb** (**with sth**) *Would you oblige me with some information?* 拜托您给我透露些消息好吗？◇ ~ **sb** (**by doing sth**) *Oblige me by keeping your suspicions to yourself.* 拜托你不要把你的怀疑声张出去。

ob·liged /əˈblaɪdʒd/ *adj.* [not before noun] ~ (**to sb**) (**for sth/for doing sth**) (*formal*) used when you are expressing thanks or asking politely for sth, to show that you are grateful to sb 感激；感谢：*I'm* **much obliged** *to you for helping us.* 承蒙相助，本人不胜感激。◇ *I'd be obliged if you would keep this to yourself.* 如蒙保守这个秘密，我将感激不尽。

ob·li·ging /əˈblaɪdʒɪŋ/ *adj.* (*formal*) very willing to help 乐于助人的；热情的 SYN accommodating, helpful：*They were very obliging and offered to wait for us.* 他们非常热情，主动提出等候我们。 ▶ **ob·li·ging·ly** *adv.*

ob·lique /əˈbliːk/ *adj., noun*

■ *adj.* **1** not expressed or done in a direct way 间接的；不直截了当的；拐弯抹角的 SYN indirect：*an oblique reference/approach/comment* 隐约提及；间接途径；婉转的评论 **2** (of a line 线) sloping at an angle 斜的；倾斜的 **3** ~ **angle** an angle that is not an angle of 90° 斜角 ▶ **ob·lique·ly** *adv.*：*He referred only obliquely to their recent problems.* 他只是隐约提到他们最近遇到的问题。◇ *Always cut stems obliquely to enable flowers to absorb more water.* 一定要斜剪花茎，让花能多吸收些水分。

■ *noun* (*BrE*) = SLASH (3)

ob·lit·er·ate /əˈblɪtəreɪt/ *verb* [often passive] ~ **sth** to remove all signs of sth, either by destroying or covering it completely 毁掉；覆盖；清除：*The building was completely obliterated by the bomb.* 炸弹把那座建筑物彻底摧毁了。◇ *The snow had obliterated their footprints.* 白雪覆盖了他们的足迹。◇ *Everything that happened that night was obliterated from his memory.* 那天夜里发生的一切都从他的记忆中消失了。 ▶ **ob·lit·er·ation** /əˌblɪtəˈreɪʃn/ *noun* [U]

ob·liv·ion /əˈblɪviən/ *noun* [U] **1** a state in which you are not aware of what is happening around you, usually because you are unconscious or asleep 无意识状态；沉睡；昏迷：*He often drinks himself into oblivion.* 他常常喝酒喝得不省人事。◇ *Sam longed for the oblivion of sleep.* 萨姆恨不得一睡不醒，了无心事。 **2** the state in which sb/sth has been forgotten and is no longer famous or important 被遗忘；被忘却；湮没 SYN obscurity：*An unexpected victory saved him from political oblivion.* 一次意外的胜利使得他在政治上不再默默无闻。◇ *Most of his inventions have been consigned to oblivion.* 他的大部分发明都湮没无闻了。 **3** a state in which sth has been completely destroyed 被摧毁；被毁灭；被夷平：*Hundreds of homes were bombed into oblivion during the first weeks of the war.* 在战争的最初几周内，数以百计的房屋被炸毁。

ob·livi·ous /əˈblɪviəs/ *adj.* [not usually before noun] not aware of sth 不知道；未注意；未察觉：~ (**of sth**) *He drove off, oblivious of the damage he had caused.* 他驾车而去，没有注意到他所造成的损害。◇ ~ (**to sth**) *You eventually become oblivious to the noise.* 你终究会变得不在意吵闹声的。 ▶ **ob·livi·ous·ly** *adv.*

ob·long /ˈɒblɒŋ; *NAmE* ˈɑːblɔːŋ; ˈɑːblɑːŋ/ *adj.* **1** an **oblong** shape has four straight sides, two of which are longer than the other two, and four angles of 90° 矩形的；长方形的 **2** (*NAmE*) used to describe any shape that is longer than it is wide 椭圆形的；椭圆体的；长方形的：*an oblong melon* 椭圆形的瓜 ▶ **ob·long** *noun*：*a tiny oblong of glass in the roof* 嵌在屋顶上的一小块矩形玻璃 ➲ SEE ALSO RECTANGLE

ob·lo·quy /ˈɒbləkwi; *NAmE* ˈɑːb-/ *noun* [U] (*formal*) **1** strong public criticism 公开的抨击；公开的谴责；辱骂 **2** loss of respect and honour 耻辱；不名誉

ob·nox·ious /əbˈnɒkʃəs; *NAmE* -ˈnɑːk-/ *adj.* extremely unpleasant, especially in a way that offends people 极讨厌的；可憎的；令人作呕的 SYN offensive：*obnoxious behaviour* 讨厌的行为 ◇ *a thoroughly obnoxious little man*

可恶至极的家伙 ◇ *obnoxious odours* 难闻的气味 ▶ **ob·nox·ious·ly** *adv.*

obo (*also* **o.b.o.**) *abbr.* (*NAmE*) or best offer (used in small advertisements to show that sth may be sold at a lower price than the price that has been asked) 价格可商议：*$800 obo* * 800 美元（可议价） ➲ SEE ALSO O.N.O.

oboe /ˈəʊbəʊ; *NAmE* ˈoʊboʊ/ *noun* a musical instrument of the WOODWIND group. It is shaped like a pipe and has a double REED at the top that you blow into. 双簧管 ➲ VISUAL VOCAB PAGE V38

obo·ist /ˈəʊbəʊɪst; *NAmE* ˈoʊboʊɪst/ *noun* a person who plays the oboe 双簧管吹奏者

ob·scene /əbˈsiːn/ *adj.* **1** connected with sex in a way that most people find offensive 淫秽的；猥亵的；下流的：*obscene gestures/language/books* 淫秽的姿势 / 语言 / 书籍 ◇ *an obscene phone call* (= in which sb says obscene things) 色情骚扰电话 **2** extremely large in size or amount in a way that most people find unacceptable and offensive（数量等）大得惊人的，骇人听闻的 **SYN outrageous**：*He earns an obscene amount of money.* 他赚钱多得吓人。◇ *It's obscene to spend so much on food when millions are starving.* 当数以百万的人忍饥挨饿时，饮食上挥霍无度是天理难容的。▶ **ob·scene·ly** *adv.*：*to behave obscenely* 举止下流 ◇ *obscenely rich* 富得流油

ob·scen·ity /əbˈsenəti/ *noun* (*pl.* **-ies**) **1** [U] obscene language or behaviour 淫秽的语言；下流的行为：*The editors are being prosecuted for obscenity.* 几个编辑因刊载污秽文字而被起诉。◇ *the laws on obscenity* 禁止淫秽的言语及行为的法规 **2** [C, usually pl.] an obscene word or act 下流话（或动作）：*She screamed a string of obscenities at the judge.* 她冲着法官高声骂了一连串的脏话。

ob·scur·ant·ism /ˌɒbskjuˈræntɪzəm; *NAmE* ɑːbˈskjʊr-/ *noun* [U] (*formal*) the practice of deliberately preventing sb from understanding or discovering sth 故弄玄虚；蒙蔽主义；蒙骗政策 ▶ **ob·scur·ant·ist** *adj.*

ob·scure /əbˈskjʊə(r); *NAmE* əbˈskjʊr/ *adj., verb*

■ *adj.* **1** not well known 无名的；鲜为人知的 **SYN unknown**：*an obscure German poet* 一个名不见经传的德国诗人 ◇ *He was born around 1650 but his origins remain obscure.* 他生于 1650 年前后，但身世不详。**2** difficult to understand 费解的；难以理解的：*I found her lecture very obscure.* 我觉得她的讲座非常费解。◇ ***For some obscure reason,*** *he failed to turn up.* 他莫名其妙地没有如期露面。▶ **ob·scure·ly** *adv.*：*They were making her feel obscurely worried* (= for reasons that were difficult to understand). 他们让她无缘无故地担忧起来。

■ *verb* ~ **sth** to make it difficult to see, hear or understand sth 使模糊；使隐晦；使费解：*The view was obscured by fog.* 雾中景色朦胧。◇ *We mustn't let these minor details obscure the main issue.* 我们不能让枝节问题掩盖主要问题。

ob·scur·ity /əbˈskjʊərəti; *NAmE* -ˈskjʊr-/ *noun* (*pl.* **-ies**) **1** [U] the state in which sb/sth is not well known or has been forgotten 默默无闻；无名：*The actress was only 17 when she was plucked from obscurity and made a star.* 这个演员受到提携从无名少女一跃成为明星时年仅 17 岁。◇ *He spent most of his life working in obscurity.* 他在默默无闻的工作中度过了大半生。**2** [U, C, usually pl.] the quality of being difficult to understand; something that is difficult to understand 费解；晦涩；难懂的事：*The course teaches students to avoid ambiguity and obscurity of expression.* 这门课程教学生避免表达上的模棱两可、含混不清。◇ *a speech full of obscurities* 一篇晦涩难懂的演说 **3** [U] (*literary*) the state of being dark 昏暗；黑暗 **SYN darkness**

ob·se·quies /ˈɒbsəkwiz; *NAmE* ˈɑːb-/ *noun* [pl.] (*formal*) funeral ceremonies 葬礼：*state obsequies* 国葬

ob·se·qui·ous /əbˈsiːkwiəs/ *adj.* (*formal, disapproving*) trying too hard to please sb, especially sb who is important 谄媚的；巴结奉迎的 **SYN servile**：*an obsequious manner* 谄媚的态度 ▶ **ob·se·qui·ous·ly** *adv.*：*smiling obsequiously* 谄媚地微笑着 **ob·se·qui·ous·ness** *noun* [U]

ob·serv·able /əbˈzɜːvəbl; *NAmE* -ˈzɜːrv-/ *adj.* that can be seen or noticed 能看得到的；能察觉到的：*observable differences* 可以察觉到的差异 ◇ *Similar trends are observable in mainland Europe.* 类似的趋势在欧洲大陆也能见到。▶ **ob·serv·ably** /əbˈzɜːvəbli; *NAmE* -ˈzɜːrv-/ *adv.*

ob·ser·vance /əbˈzɜːvəns; *NAmE* -ˈzɜːrv-/ *noun* **1** [U, sing.] the practice of obeying a law, celebrating a festival or behaving according to a particular custom（对法律、习俗的）遵守，奉行；（节日的）庆祝：~ (**of sth**) *observance of the law* 守法 ◇ *a strict observance of the Sabbath* 对安息日的严格遵守 **OPP non-observance** **2** [C, usually pl.] an act performed as part of a religious or traditional ceremony 宗教（或传统节日）的仪式：*religious observances* 宗教仪式

ob·ser·vant /əbˈzɜːvənt; *NAmE* -ˈzɜːrv-/ *adj.* **1** good at noticing things around you 善于观察的；观察力敏锐的 **SYN sharp-eyed**：*Observant walkers may see red deer along this stretch of the road.* 观察敏锐的步行者能在这一路段看到赤鹿。◇ *How very observant of you!* 你真有眼力！**2** (*formal*) careful to obey religious laws and customs 谨慎遵守教规和习俗的

ob·ser·va·tion 🔑 /ˌɒbzəˈveɪʃn; *NAmE* ˌɑːbzərˈv-/ *noun* **1** 🔑 [U, C] the act of watching sb/sth carefully for a period of time, especially to learn sth 观察；观测；监视：*Most information was collected by direct observation of the animals' behaviour.* 大部分信息都是通过直接观察动物的行为收集到的。◇ *results based on scientific observations* 根据科学观测得来的结果 ◇ *We managed to escape observation* (= we were not seen). 我们设法避开了人们的注意。◇ *The suspect is being kept* ***under observation*** (= watched closely by the police). 嫌疑人正受到监视。◇ *She has outstanding* ***powers of observation*** (= the ability to notice things around her). 她有超人的观察力。◇ *an* ***observation post/tower*** (= a place from where sb, especially an enemy, can be watched) 瞭望哨；瞭望塔 ➲ COLLOCATIONS AT SCIENTIFIC **2** 🔑 [C] ~ (**about/on sth**) (*formal*) a comment, especially based on sth you have seen, heard or read（尤指据所见、所闻、所读而作的）评论 **SYN remark**：*He began by making a few general observations about the report.* 开头他先对这个报告作了几点概括性的评论。◇ *She has some interesting observations on possible future developments.* 她对未来可能的发展有一些饶有兴味的论述。➲ SYNONYMS AT STATEMENT ▶ **ob·ser·va·tion·al** *adj.*

ˌobserˈvation car *noun* a coach/car on a train with large windows, designed to give passengers a good view of the passing landscape 观光车厢，游览车厢（火车车厢，有大窗）

ob·serv·a·tory /əbˈzɜːvətri; *NAmE* əbˈzɜːrvətɔːri/ *noun* (*pl.* **-ies**) a special building from which scientists watch the stars, the weather, etc. 天文台；气象台

ob·serve 🔑 /əbˈzɜːv; *NAmE* əbˈzɜːrv/ *verb* **1** 🔑 [T] (*formal*) to see or notice sb/sth 看到；注意到；观察到：~ **sb/sth** *Have you observed any changes lately?* 最近你注意到什么变化没有？◇ *All the characters in the novel are closely observed* (= seem like people in real life). 小说中的人物个个栩栩如生。◇ ~ **sb/sth do sth** *The police observed a man enter the bank.* 警察注意到一个男人走进了银行。◇ ~ **sb/sth doing sth** *They observed him entering the bank.* 他们看见他走进银行。◇ ~ **that…** *She observed that all the chairs were already occupied.* 她发现所有的椅子都有人坐了。◇ **be observed to do sth** *He was observed to follow her closely.* 有人看到他紧跟着她。**HELP** This pattern is only used in the passive. 此句型仅用于被动语态。➲ SYNONYMS AT COMMENT, NOTICE **2** 🔑 [T, I] (*formal*) to watch sb/sth carefully, especially to learn more about them 观察；注视；监视 **SYN monitor**：~ (**sb/sth**) *I felt he was observing everything I did.* 我觉得他正在注视着我做的每一件事。◇ *The patients were observed over a period of several months.* 这些病人被观察了数月之久。◇ *He observes keenly, but says little.* 他观察敏锐，但言语寥寥。◇ ~ **how, what, etc.…** *They observed how the parts of the machine fitted together.* 他们观看了机器零件的组装过程。➲ SYNONYMS AT LOOK **3** [T] ~ **that…** | **+ speech** (*formal*) to make a remark 说话；评论 **SYN comment**：*She observed that it was getting late.* 她说天色晚了。**4** [T] ~ **sth** to obey rules, laws, etc. 遵守（规则、法律等）： *Will the rebels observe the ceasefire?* 叛乱者会遵守停火协议吗？ ◇ *The crowd **observed a minute's silence*** (= were silent for one minute) *in memory of those who had died.* 众人为死者默哀一分钟。 **5** [T] **~ sth** (*formal*) to celebrate festivals, birthdays, etc. 庆祝；庆贺；欢度：*Do they observe Christmas?* 他们过不过圣诞节？

ob,served 'trials *noun* [U+sing./pl. v.] = TRIALS RIDING

ob·ser·ver /əb'zɜːvə(r); *NAmE* əb'zɜːrvər/ *noun* **1** a person who watches sb/sth 观察者；观测者；目击者： *According to observers, the plane exploded shortly after take-off.* 据目击者说，飞机起飞后不久就爆炸了。 ◇ ***To the casual observer*** (= somebody who does not pay much attention), *the system appears confusing.* 乍看起来，这个系统好像条理不清。 ➲ SYNONYMS AT WITNESS **2** a person who attends a meeting, lesson, etc. to listen and watch but not to take part 观察员；旁听者： *A team of British officials were sent as observers to the conference.* 一组英国官员被派去做大会观察员。 **3** a person who watches and studies particular events, situations, etc. and is therefore considered to be an expert on them 观察家；观察员；评论员： *a royal observer* 王室观察家

ob·sess /əb'ses/ *verb* **1** [T, usually passive] **~ sb** to completely fill your mind so that you cannot think of anything else, in a way that is not normal 使痴迷；使迷恋；使着迷：*He's obsessed by computers.* 他迷上了电脑。 ◇ *She's completely obsessed with him.* 他让她神魂颠倒。 ◇ *The need to produce the most exciting newspaper story obsesses most journalists.* 大多数记者梦寐以求的就是要写出最撼动人心的新闻报道来。 **2** [I] **~ (about sth)** to be always talking or worrying about a particular thing, especially when this annoys other people 唠叨；挂牵；念念不忘：*I think you should try to stop obsessing about food.* 我看你该歇歇了，别没完没了地唠叨吃的东西。

O

ob·ses·sion /əb'seʃn/ *noun* **1** [U] the state in which a person's mind is completely filled with thoughts of one particular thing or person in a way that is not normal 痴迷；着魔；困扰：*Her fear of flying is bordering on obsession.* 她怕乘飞机几乎到了不可救药的地步。 ◇ **~ with sb/sth** *The media's obsession with the young prince continues.* 新闻媒体继续对小王子进行连篇累牍的报道。 **2** [C] **~ (with sb)** a person or thing that sb thinks about too much 使人痴迷的人（或物）： *Fitness has become an obsession with him.* 他迷上了健身。

ob·ses·sion·al /əb'seʃənl/ *adj.* thinking too much about one particular person or thing, in a way that is not normal 痴迷的；迷恋的；耿耿于怀的： *She is obsessional about cleanliness.* 她有洁癖。 ◇ *obsessional behaviour* 痴迷的行为 ▸ **ob·ses·sion·al·ly** *adv.*

ob·ses·sive /əb'sesɪv/ *adj., noun*
- *adj.* thinking too much about one particular person or thing, in a way that is not normal 着迷的；迷恋的；难以释怀的： *He's becoming more and more obsessive about punctuality.* 他对守时要求越来越过分了。 ◇ *an obsessive attention to detail* 过分注重细枝末节 ▸ **ob·ses·sive·ly** *adv.* : *obsessively jealous* 嫉妒得要命 ◇ *He worries obsessively about his appearance.* 他过于在意自己的外表。
- *noun* (*psychology* 心) a person whose mind is filled with thoughts of one particular thing or person so that they cannot think of anything else 强迫症患者

ob,sessive com'pulsive disorder *noun* [U] = OCD

ob·sid·ian /əb'sɪdiən/ *noun* [U] a type of dark rock that looks like glass and comes from VOLCANOES 黑曜岩；黑曜石

ob·so·les·cence /,ɒbsə'lesns; *NAmE* ,ɑːb-/ *noun* [U] (*formal*) the state of becoming old-fashioned and no longer useful 过时；陈旧；淘汰： *products with **built-in/planned obsolescence*** (= designed not to last long so that people will have to buy new ones) 内在 / 计划陈旧产品（故意设计成不耐使用而迫使人购买新的产品） ▸ **ob·so·les·cent** /,ɒbsə'lesnt; *NAmE* ,ɑːb-/ *adj.*

ob·so·lete /'ɒbsəliːt; *NAmE* ,ɑːbsə'liːt/ *adj.* no longer used because sth new has been invented 淘汰的；废弃的；过时的 SYN **out of date**：*obsolete technology* 过时技术 ◇ *With technological changes many traditional skills have become obsolete.* 随着技术的革新，许多传统技艺已被淘汰。

obs·tacle /'ɒbstəkl; *NAmE* 'ɑːb-/ *noun* **1** **~ (to sth/to doing sth)** a situation, an event, etc. that makes it difficult for you to do or achieve sth 障碍；阻碍；绊脚石 SYN **hindrance**： *A lack of qualifications can be a major obstacle to finding a job.* 学历不足可能成为谋职的主要障碍。 ◇ *So far, we have managed to overcome all the obstacles that have been placed in our path.* 到目前为止，我们已设法排除了前进道路上的一切人为障碍。 **2** an object that is in your way and that makes it difficult for you to move forward 障碍物；绊脚石： *The area was full of streams and bogs and other natural obstacles.* 此地遍布小溪、泥潭和其他天然障碍。 **3** (in SHOWJUMPING 障碍赛马) a fence, etc. for a horse to jump over 障碍栅栏；障碍

'obstacle course *noun* **1** a series of objects that people taking part in a race have to climb over, under, through, etc. 障碍赛跑场地 **2** a series of difficulties that people have to deal with in order to achieve a particular aim 艰险；重重困难 **3** (*NAmE*) (*BrE* **as'sault course**) an area of land with many objects that are difficult to climb, jump over or go through, which is used, especially by soldiers, for improving physical skills and strength 近战训练场；障碍场

'obstacle race *noun* a race in which the people taking part have to climb over, under, through, etc. various objects 障碍赛跑

ob·stet·ri·cian /,ɒbstə'trɪʃn; *NAmE* ,ɑːb-/ *noun* a doctor who is trained in obstetrics 产科医生 ➲ WORDFINDER NOTE AT SPECIALIST

ob·stet·rics /əb'stetrɪks/ *noun* [U] the branch of medicine concerned with the birth of children 产科学 ➲ WORDFINDER NOTE AT BIRTH ▸ **ob·stet·ric** /əb'stetrɪk/ *adj.* : *obstetric medicine* 产科学

ob·stin·ate /'ɒbstɪnət; *NAmE* 'ɑːb-/ *adj.* **1** (*often disapproving*) refusing to change your opinions, way of behaving, etc. when other people try to persuade you to; showing this 执拗的；固执的；顽固的 SYN **stubborn**： *He can be very obstinate when he wants to be!* 他的犟劲儿一上来，简直执拗得要命！ ◇ *her obstinate refusal to comply with their request* 她拒不服从他们的要求 **2** [usually before noun] difficult to get rid of or deal with 棘手的；难以去除的；难以对付的 SYN **stubborn**： *the obstinate problem of unemployment* 失业这个棘手的问题 ◇ *an obstinate stain* 顽固斑渍 ▸ **ob·stin·acy** /'ɒbstɪnəsi; *NAmE* 'ɑːb-/ *noun* [U]： *an act of sheer obstinacy* 纯属固执的举动 **ob·stin·ate·ly** *adv.* : *He obstinately refused to consider the future.* 他执意拒不考虑未来。

ob·strep·er·ous /əb'strepərəs/ *adj.* (*formal* or *humorous*) noisy and difficult to control 喧闹的；桀骜不驯的；任性的

ob·struct /əb'strʌkt/ *verb* (*formal*) **1** **~ sth** to block a road, an entrance, a passage, etc. so that sb/sth cannot get through, see past, etc. 阻挡；阻塞；遮断： *You can't park here, you're obstructing my driveway.* 你不能在这里停车，你挡住了我家的车道。 ◇ *First check that the accident victim doesn't have an obstructed airway.* 首先要确保事故受伤者的气道通畅。 ◇ *The pillar obstructed our view of the stage.* 柱子挡着，我们看不见舞台。 **2** **~ sb/sth** to prevent sb/sth from doing sth or making progress, especially when this is done deliberately（故意）妨碍，阻挠，阻碍 SYN **hinder**： *They were charged with obstructing the police in the course of their duty.* 他们被指控妨碍警察执行公务。 ◇ *terrorists attempting to obstruct the peace process* 企图阻碍和平进程的恐怖分子

IDM **ob,struct 'justice** (*NAmE*) (*BrE* **per,vert the course of 'justice**) (*law* 律) to tell a lie or to do sth in order to prevent the police, etc. from finding out the truth about a crime 妨碍司法（如作伪证等）

ob·struc·tion /əb'strʌkʃn/ *noun* **1** [U, C] the fact of trying to prevent sth/sb from making progress 阻挡；阻碍；

妨碍：*the obstruction of justice* 妨碍司法公正 ◇ *He was arrested for obstruction of a police officer in the execution of his duty.* 他因妨碍警察执行公务而被逮捕。 **2** [U, C] the fact of blocking a road, an entrance, a passage, etc. 堵塞，阻挡（通道等）：*obstruction of the factory gates* 对工厂大门的堵塞 ◇ *The abandoned car was causing an obstruction.* 这辆被遗弃的汽车堵住了道路。 **3** [C] something that blocks a road, an entrance, etc. 路障；障碍；障碍物：*It is my job to make sure that all pathways are clear of obstructions.* 保证所有的道路通畅是我的职责。 **4** [C, U] (*medical* 医) something that blocks a passage or tube in your body; a medical condition resulting from this 梗阻；阻塞；栓塞 **SYN** **blockage**: *He had an operation to remove an obstruction in his throat.* 他做了手术，取出喉头的阻塞物。◇ ***bowel/intestinal obstruction*** 肠梗阻 **5** [U] (*sport* 体育) the offence of unfairly preventing a player of the other team from moving to get the ball（球类运动）阻挡犯规

ob·struc·tion·ism /əbˈstrʌkʃənɪzəm/ *noun* [U] (*formal*) the practice of trying to prevent a parliament or committee from making progress, passing laws, etc.（对议会或委员会工作的）阻挠行为，妨碍 ▸ **ob·struc·tion·ist** /-ɪst/ *noun, adj.*

ob·struct·ive /əbˈstrʌktɪv/ *adj.* **1** trying to prevent sb/sth from making progress 阻挠；妨碍；阻止：*Of course she can do it. She's just being deliberately obstructive.* 这事她当然能做。她只是在刻意阻挠罢了。 ➲ COMPARE CONSTRUCTIVE **2** [only before noun] (*medical* 医) connected with a passage, tube, etc. in your body that has become blocked 梗阻的；阻塞的；栓塞的：*obstructive lung disease* 肺阻塞疾病

ob·tain 🔑 **AW** /əbˈteɪn/ *verb* (*formal*) **1** 🔑 [T] ~ **sth** to get sth, especially by making an effort（尤指经努力）获得，赢得：*to obtain advice/information/permission* 得到忠告 / 信息 / 许可 ◇ *I finally managed to obtain a copy of the report.* 我终于设法弄到了这份报告的一个副本。◇ *To obtain the overall score, add up the totals in each column.* 要得出总计得分，就把各栏的小计加起来。 **2** [I] (not used in the progressive tenses 不用于进行时) (of rules, systems, customs, etc. 规则、制度、习俗等) to exist 存在；流行；沿袭 **SYN** **apply**: *These conditions no longer obtain.* 这些条件不再适用。

ob·tain·able **AW** /əbˈteɪnəbl/ *adj.* [not usually before noun] that can be obtained 可获得；可得到 **SYN** **available**: *Full details are obtainable from any post office.* 详情可至任何邮局索取。

ob·trude /əbˈtruːd/ *verb* [I, T] ~ (**sth/yourself**) (**on/upon sb**) (*formal*) to become or make sth/yourself noticed, especially in a way that is not wanted 强行闯入；搅扰：*Music from the next room obtruded upon his thoughts.* 隔壁的音乐声打扰了他的思绪。

ob·tru·sive /əbˈtruːsɪv/ *adj.* noticeable in an unpleasant way 扎眼的；过分炫耀的；显眼的：*The sofa would be less obtrusive in a paler colour.* 沙发的颜色再浅一点就不那么扎眼了。◇ *They tried to ensure that their presence was not too obtrusive.* 他们尽量做到在场时不引人注目。 ▸ **ob·tru·sive·ly** *adv.*

ob·tuse /əbˈtjuːs; *NAmE* -ˈtuːs/ *adj.* (*formal, disapproving*) slow or unwilling to understand sth 迟钝的；愚蠢的；态度勉强的：*Are you being deliberately obtuse?* 你是不是故意装傻？ ▸ **ob·tuse·ness** *noun* [U]

ob,tuse 'angle *noun* an angle between 90° and 180° 钝角 ➲ PICTURE AT ANGLE ➲ COMPARE ACUTE ANGLE, REFLEX ANGLE, RIGHT ANGLE

obv /ɒv; *NAmE* ɑːv/ *adv.* (*informal*) = OBVS

ob·verse /ˈɒbvɜːs; *NAmE* ˈɑːbvɜːrs/ *noun* (*usually* **the obverse**) [sing.] **1** (*formal*) the opposite of sth 对立面；对应的事物：*The obverse of love is hate.* 爱的反面是恨。 **2** (*specialist*) the side of a coin or MEDAL that has the head or main design on it（硬币或奖章的）正面

ob·vi·ate /ˈɒbvieɪt; *NAmE* ˈɑːb-/ *verb* ~ **sth** (*formal*) to remove a problem or the need for sth 消除；排除；打消 **SYN** **preclude**: *This new evidence* ***obviates the need for*** *any further enquiries.* 这项新证据排除了继续调查的必要。

ob·vi·ous 🔑 **AW** /ˈɒbviəs; *NAmE* ˈɑːb-/ *adj.* **1** 🔑 ~ (**to sb**) (**that...**) easy to see or understand 明显的；显然的；易理解的 **SYN** **clear**: *It was obvious to everyone that the child had been badly treated.* 人人一看便知那个孩子受过虐待。◇ *It's obvious from what she said that something is wrong.* 根据她所说的，显然是出问题了。◇ *I know you don't like her but try not to make it so obvious.* 我知道你不喜欢她，但尽量别表现得那么明显。◇ *He agreed with obvious pleasure.* 他同意了，显然很高兴。◇ ***For obvious reasons****, I'd prefer not to give my name.* 因为显而易见的原因，我不愿披露自己的姓名。◇ *The reasons for this decision were* ***not immediately obvious****.* 作出这一决定的理由暂时还不清楚。 ➲ SYNONYMS AT CLEAR **2** 🔑 that most people would think of or agree to 公认的；当然的：*She was the obvious choice for the job.* 她是这一工作的当然人选。◇ *There's no obvious solution to the problem.* 这个问题尚无公认的解决办法。◇ *This seemed the most obvious thing to do.* 这似乎是最顺理成章的做法。 **3** 🔑 (*disapproving*) not interesting, new or showing imagination; unnecessary because it is clear to everyone 平淡无奇的；无创意的；因显而易见而不必要的：*The ending was pretty obvious.* 结尾十分平淡。◇ *I may be* ***stating the obvious*** *but without more money the project cannot survive.* 我这话可能多余，但是不投入更多资金，项目就难以为继。 ▸ **ob·vi·ous·ness** *noun* [U]

ob·vi·ous·ly 🔑 **AW** /ˈɒbviəsli; *NAmE* ˈɑːb-/ *adv.* **1** 🔑 used when giving information that you expect other people to know already or agree with（用于陈述认为别人已知道或希望别人同意的事）显然，明显地 **SYN** **clearly**: *Obviously, we don't want to spend too much money.* 很明显，我们不想花太多的钱。◇ *Diet and exercise are obviously important.* 显然，饮食和运动是重要的。 **2** 🔑 used to say that a particular situation or fact is easy to see or understand（用于说明某种情况或事实）显而易见，明显，不言而喻：*He was obviously drunk.* 他显然是喝醉了。◇ *They're obviously not coming.* 他们显然不会来了。◇ *'I didn't realise it was a formal occasion.' 'Obviously!'* (= I can see by the way you are dressed) "我没想到这是个正式场合。" "看得出来！"（= 看你的衣着就知道）

obvs /ɒvz; *NAmE* ɑːvz/ (*also* **obv**) *adv.* (*informal*) (in TEXT MESSAGES, emails, etc. 用于短信、电邮等) obviously 显然；明显地

oca·rina /ˌɒkəˈriːnə; *NAmE* ˌɑːk-/ *noun* a small egg-shaped musical instrument that you blow into, with holes for the fingers 奥卡里纳，小鹅笛，陶笛（管身椭圆形）

oc·ca·sion 🔑 /əˈkeɪʒn/ *noun, verb*

■ ***noun*** **1** 🔑 [C] a particular time when sth happens 某次；…的时候：*on this/that occasion* 这次；那次 ◇ *I've met him on several occasions.* 我曾见过他几次。◇ *I can remember very few* ***occasions when*** *he had to cancel because of ill health.* 我记得他因为健康不佳而被迫取消的情况绝无仅有。◇ *They have been seen together on two* ***separate occasions****.* 他们有两次被人看见在一起。◇ *On one occasion, she called me in the middle of the night.* 有一次她深更半夜打电话给我。◇ *He used the occasion to announce further tax cuts.* 他利用这个机会宣布再次减税。 **2** 🔑 [C] a special event, ceremony or celebration 特别的事情（或仪式、庆典）：*a great/memorable/happy occasion* 伟大的 / 难忘的 / 欢乐的庆典 ◇ *Turn every meal into* ***a special occasion****.* 要把每一顿饭都弄得特别一些。 ◇ *They* ***marked the occasion*** (= celebrated it) *with an open-air concert.* 他们举办了露天音乐会来庆祝。◇ *Their wedding turned out to be quite an occasion.* 他们的婚礼办得相当隆重。◇ *He was presented with the watch* ***on the occasion of*** *his retirement.* 他在退休仪式上获赠这块手表。 ➲ WORDFINDER NOTE AT CELEBRATE **3** 🔑 [sing.] ~ (**for sth/doing sth**) a suitable time for sth 适当的机会；时机：*It should have been an occasion for rejoicing, but she could not feel any real joy.* 原本应该是高兴的时刻，她却丝毫未感到快乐。◇ *I'll speak to him about it* ***if the occasion arises*** (= if I get a chance). 有机会的话，我要跟他谈谈这件事。 **4** [U, sing.] (*formal*) a reason

O

or cause 理由；原因：~ (**to do sth**) *I've had no occasion to visit him recently.* 我最近无缘去拜访他。◇ ~ (**of/for sth**) *Her death was the occasion of mass riots.* 她的逝世引发了大规模的骚乱。◇ *I'm willing to go to court over this **if the occasion arises*** (= if it becomes necessary). 如果必要的话，我愿意就此出庭。

IDM **on oc'casion(s)** sometimes but not often 偶尔；偶然；有时：*He has been known on occasion to lose his temper.* 大家都知道他有时会发脾气。➲ MORE AT SENSE *n.*

■ *verb* (*formal*) to cause sth 使发生；造成；导致：~ **sth** *The flight delay was occasioned by the need for a further security check.* 这次航班的延误是由于必须做进一步的安全检查。◇ ~ **sb sth** *The decision occasioned us much anxiety.* 这个决定让我们忧虑不堪。

oc·ca·sion·al /əˈkeɪʒənl/ *adj.* [only before noun] happening or done sometimes but not often 偶尔的；偶然的；临时的：*He works for us on an occasional basis.* 他在我们这里做临时工。◇ *I enjoy the occasional glass of wine.* 我喜欢偶尔喝一杯葡萄酒。◇ *He spent five years in Paris, with occasional visits to Italy.* 他在巴黎待过五年，偶尔去一去意大利。◇ *an occasional smoker* (= a person who smokes, but not often) 偶尔吸烟的人

oc·ca·sion·al·ly /əˈkeɪʒnəli/ *adv.* sometimes but not often 偶然；偶尔；有时候：*We occasionally meet for a drink after work.* 我们下班后偶尔相聚小酌。◇ *This type of allergy can very occasionally be fatal.* 这类过敏症在极个别情况下有可能是致命的。

oc'casional table *noun* a small light table that is easy to move, used for different things at different times 临时茶几；轻便小桌 ➲ VISUAL VOCAB PAGE V22

the Oc·ci·dent /ˈɒksɪdənt; *NAmE* ˈɑːk-/ *noun* [sing.] (*formal*) the western part of the world, especially Europe and America 西方，西洋，西方世界（尤指欧洲和美洲）➲ COMPARE ORIENT ▸ **oc·ci·den·tal** /ˌɒksɪˈdentl; *NAmE* ˌɑːksɪ-/ *adj.*

O

oc·clude /əˈkluːd/ *verb* ~ **sth** (*specialist*) to cover or block sth 使闭塞；堵塞：*an occluded artery* 闭塞的动脉 ▸ **oc·clu·sion** /əˈkluːʒn/ *noun* [U]

oc·cult /əˈkʌlt; *BrE also* ˈɒkʌlt/ *adj.* **1** [only before noun] connected with magic powers and things that cannot be explained by reason or science 神秘的；玄妙的；超自然的；不可思议的 **SYN** **supernatural**：*occult practices* 神秘的习俗 **2 the occult** *noun* [sing.] everything connected with occult practices, etc. 神秘的事物；玄机：*He's interested in witchcraft and the occult.* 他对巫术魔法情有独钟。

oc·cultist /əˈkʌltɪst; ˈɒkʌltɪst; *NAmE* ˈɑːk-/ *noun* a person who is involved in the occult 神秘学者；玄虚术士

oc·cu·pancy **AW** /ˈɒkjəpənsi; *NAmE* ˈɑːk-/ *noun* [U] (*formal*) the act of living in or using a building, room, piece of land, etc.（房屋、土地等的）占用，使用，居住：*Prices are based on full occupancy of an apartment.* 公寓租金按整套租用计算。◇ *to be in sole occupancy* 单独占用

oc·cu·pant **AW** /ˈɒkjəpənt; *NAmE* ˈɑːk-/ *noun* **1** a person who lives or works in a particular house, room, building, etc.（房屋、建筑等的）使用者，居住者：*All outstanding bills will be paid by the previous occupants.* 所有未支付的账单都将由前住户偿付。**2** a person who is in a vehicle, seat, etc. at a particular time（汽车等内的）乘坐者，占用者：*The car was badly damaged but the occupants were unhurt.* 汽车严重损坏，但车内人员安然无恙。

oc·cu·pa·tion **AW** /ˌɒkjuˈpeɪʃn; *NAmE* ˌɑːk-/ *noun* **1** [C] a job or profession 工作；职业：*Please state your name, age and occupation below.* 请在下面写明姓名、年龄和职业。➲ SYNONYMS AT WORK **2** [C] the way in which you spend your time, especially when you are not working 消遣；业余活动：*Her main occupation seems to be shopping.* 逛商店购物似乎是她的主要消遣。**3** [U] the act of moving into a country, town, etc. and taking control of it using military force; the period of time during which a country, town, etc. is controlled in this way 侵占；占领；占领期：*the Roman occupation of Britain* 罗马人对不列颠的占领 ◇ *The zones **under occupation** contained major industrial areas.* 被占领地区里有主要的工业区。◇ *occupation forces* 占领军 **4** [U] (*formal*) the act of living in or using a building, room, piece of land, etc.（土地、房屋、建筑等的）使用，居住，占用：*The offices will be ready for occupation in June.* 办公室将于六月交付使用。◇ *The following applies only to tenants in occupation after January 1, 2010.* 以下规定仅适用于 2010 年 1 月 1 日后入住的房客。◇ *The level of **owner occupation*** (= people owning their homes) *has increased rapidly in the last 30 years.* 拥有住房的人数在过去 30 年间急剧攀升。

oc·cu·pa·tion·al **AW** /ˌɒkjuˈpeɪʃənl; *NAmE* ˌɑːk-/ *adj.* [only before noun] connected with a person's job or profession 职业的：*occupational health* 职业健康问题 ◇ ***an occupational risk/hazard*** 职业性危害 ◇ *an occupational pension scheme* 职业退休金计划 ▸ **oc·cu·pa·tion·al·ly** *adv.*：*occupationally induced disease* 职业病

ˌoccuˌpational ˈtherapist *noun* a person whose job is to help people get better after illness or injury by giving them special activities to do 职业治疗师（利用特定的技能训练帮助病患者或受伤者恢复健康）

ˌoccuˌpational ˈtherapy *noun* [U] the work of an occupational therapist 职业疗法

oc·cu·pied **AW** /ˈɒkjupaɪd; *NAmE* ˈɑːk-/ *adj.* **1** [not before noun] being used by sb 使用中；有人使用（或居住）：*Only half of the rooms are occupied at the moment.* 目前只有半数的房间有人居住。➲ SEE ALSO OWNER-OCCUPIED **2** [not before noun] busy 忙于：~ (**doing sth/in doing sth/in sth**) *He's fully occupied looking after three small children.* 照顾三个小孩把他忙得不可开交。◇ ~ (**with sth/with doing sth**) *Only half her time is occupied with politics.* 她只用自己一半的时间从事政治活动。◇ *The most important thing is to **keep yourself occupied.*** 最重要的就是别让自己闲着。**3** (of a country, etc. 国家等) controlled by people from another country, etc., using military force 被占领的；被侵占的：*He spent his childhood in occupied Europe.* 他在被占领的欧洲度过了童年。**OPP** **unoccupied**

oc·cu·pier **AW** /ˈɒkjupaɪə(r); *NAmE* ˈɑːk-/ *noun* **1** ~ (**of sth**) (*formal*) a person who lives in or uses a building, room, piece of land, etc. 居住人；（土地、房屋等的）占有者，占用者 **SYN** **occupant**：*The letter was addressed to the occupier of the house.* 这封信是写给这所房子的住户的。➲ SEE ALSO OWNER-OCCUPIER **2** [usually pl.] a member of an army that is occupying a foreign country, etc. 占领者；占领军的一员

oc·cupy **AW** /ˈɒkjupaɪ; *NAmE* ˈɑːk-/ *verb* (**oc·cu·pies, oc·cu·py·ing, oc·cu·pied, oc·cu·pied**) **1** ~ **sth** to fill or use a space, an area or an amount of time 使用，占用（空间、面积、时间等）**SYN** **take up**：*The bed seemed to occupy most of the room.* 床似乎占去了大半个屋子。◇ *How much memory does the program occupy?* 这个程序占用多少内存？◇ *Administrative work occupies half of my time.* 行政事务占用了我一半的时间。**2** ~ **sth** (*formal*) to live or work in a room, house or building 使用（房屋、建筑）；居住：*He occupies an office on the 12th floor.* 他在 12 楼有一间办公室。**3** ~ **sth** to enter a place in a large group and take control of it, especially by military force 侵占；占领；占据：*The capital has been occupied by the rebel army.* 叛军已占领了首都。◇ *Protesting students occupied the TV station.* 抗议的学生占领了电视台。➲ WORDFINDER NOTE AT PROTEST **4** to fill your time or keep you busy doing sth 使忙于（做某事）；忙着（做某事）：~ **sb/sth/yourself** *a game that will occupy the kids for hours* 能让小孩一玩就是几个小时的游戏 ◇ *Problems at work continued **to occupy his mind** for some time.* 工作上的问题继续在他的脑海中萦绕了一段时间。◇ ~ **sb/sth/yourself with sb/sth** *She occupied herself with routine office tasks.* 她忙于办公室的日常工作。◇ ~ **sb/sth/yourself (in) doing sth** *She occupied herself doing routine office tasks.* 她忙于办公室的日常工作。**5** ~ **sth** to have an official job or position 任职；执政 **SYN** **hold**：*The president occupies the position for four years.* 总统任期四年。

occur **AW** /əˈkɜː(r)/ *verb* (**-rr-**) **1** [I] (*formal*) to happen 发生；出现：*When exactly did the incident occur?*

这一事件究竟是什么时候发生的? ◇ *Something unexpected occurred.* 发生了一件出乎意料的事。 **2** [I] + adv./prep. to exist or be found somewhere 存在于；出现在： *Sugar occurs naturally in fruit.* 水果天然含糖分。 ➲ MORE LIKE THIS 36, page R29

PHR V **oc'cur to sb** (of an idea or a thought 观念或想法) to come into your mind 被想到；出现在头脑中： *The idea occurred to him in a dream.* 这个主意是他在梦中想到的。◇ **occur to sb that...** *It didn't occur to him that his wife was having an affair.* 他没有想到自己的妻子有婚外情。◇ **~ to do sth** *It didn't occur to her to ask for help.* 她没想到请别人帮忙。

oc·cur·rence AW /ə'kʌrəns; NAmE ə'kɜːr-/ noun (formal) **1** [C] something that happens or exists 发生的事情；存在的事物： *a **common/everyday/frequent/regular occurrence*** 司空见惯的 / 每天发生的 / 经常发生的 / 定期发生的事情 ◇ *Vandalism used to be a **rare occurrence** here.* 过去这里很少发生故意破坏公物的事。◇ *The program counts the number of occurrences of any word within the text.* 这个程序可以统计任何单词在文本中出现的次数。 **2** [U] ~ (of sth) the fact of sth happening or existing 发生；出现；存在： *a link between the occurrence of skin cancer and the use of computer monitors* 皮肤癌的发生与使用电脑显示器之间的关联

OCD /ˌəʊ siː 'diː; NAmE ˌoʊ/ noun [U] the abbreviation for 'obsessive compulsive disorder' (a mental DISORDER in which sb feels they have to repeat certain actions or activities to get rid of fears or unpleasant thoughts) 强迫性神经（官能）症，强迫症（全写为 obsessive compulsive disorder）： *to suffer from OCD* 患有强迫症

ocean /'əʊʃn; NAmE 'oʊʃn/ noun **1** (usually **the ocean**) [sing.] (especially NAmE) the mass of salt water that covers most of the earth's surface 大海；海洋： *the depths of the ocean* 海洋的深处 ◇ *People were swimming in the ocean despite the hurricane warning.* 尽管有飓风警报，人们仍然在大海里游泳。◇ *The plane hit the ocean several miles offshore.* 飞机在距离海岸数英里处坠入大海。◇ *Our beach house is just a couple of miles from the ocean.* 我家滨海的房子离大海只有几英里。◇ *an ocean liner* 远洋客轮 ◇ *Ocean levels are rising.* 海平面正在上升。 **2** (usually **Ocean**) [C] one of the five large areas that the ocean is divided into（五大洋之一的）洋： ***the Antarctic/Arctic/Atlantic/Indian/Pacific Ocean*** 南极海；北冰洋；大西洋；印度洋；太平洋 ➲ NOTE AT SEA ➲ VISUAL VOCAB PAGE V5

IDM **an ocean of sth** (also **oceans of sth**) (informal) a large amount of sth 众多；大量 ➲ MORE AT DROP n.

ocean·arium /ˌəʊʃə'neəriəm; NAmE ˌoʊʃə'neriəm/ noun an extremely large container in which fish and other sea creatures are kept to be seen by the public or to be studied by scientists 大型海洋水族馆 ➲ SEE ALSO AQUARIUM

ocean·front /'əʊʃnfrʌnt; NAmE 'oʊ-/ adj. (NAmE) located on land near the ocean 滨海的；临海的；在海边的： *an oceanfront hotel* 海滨旅馆

'ocean-going adj. [only before noun] (of ships 船) made for crossing the sea or ocean, not for journeys along the coast or up rivers 远洋航行的；远洋的

Ocea·nia /ˌəʊsi'ɑːniə; -ʃi-; NAmE ˌoʊʃi-/ noun [U] a large region of the world consisting of the Pacific islands and the seas around them 大洋洲

ocean·ic /ˌəʊʃi'ænɪk; NAmE ˌoʊʃi-/ adj. [usually before noun] (specialist) living in or connected with the ocean 生活在海洋里的；海洋的；大海的： *oceanic fish* 海洋鱼类

ocean·og·raphy /ˌəʊʃə'nɒgrəfi; NAmE ˌoʊʃə'nɑːg-/ noun [U] the scientific study of the ocean 海洋学 ▸ **ocean·og·raph·er** noun

ˌocean 'trench noun = TRENCH (3)

oce·lot /'ɒsəlɒt; NAmE 'ɑːsəlɑːt; 'oʊs-/ noun a wild animal of the cat family, that has yellow fur with black lines and spots, found in Central and S America 豹猫（产于中南美洲的野生猫科动物，毛黄，有黑色斑纹和斑点）

och /ɒk; ɒx; NAmE ɑːk; ɑːx/ exclamation (ScotE, IrishE) used to express the fact that you are surprised, sorry, etc. （用于表示惊奇、遗憾等）啊，哦： *Och, aye* (= Oh, yes). 啊，对。

oche /'ɒki; NAmE 'ɑːki/ noun [sing.] the line which players must stand behind in the game of DARTS（掷镖游戏的）投掷线

ochre (US also **ocher**) /'əʊkə(r); NAmE 'oʊ-/ noun [U] **1** a type of red or yellow earth used in some paints and DYES 赭土；赭石 **2** the red or yellow colour of ochre 赭色；土黄色

ocker /'ɒkə(r); NAmE 'ɑːk-/ noun (AustralE, informal) a rude or aggressive Australian man 粗鲁（或无教养）的澳大利亚人 ▸ **ocker** adj.

o'clock /ə'klɒk; NAmE ə'klɑːk/ adv. used with the numbers 1 to 12 when telling the time, to mean an exact hour（表示整点）…点钟： *He left between five and six o'clock.* 他是五点到六点之间离开的。◇ *at/after/before eleven o'clock* 十一点整 / 后 / 前

OCR abbr. (computing 计) OPTICAL CHARACTER RECOGNITION 光符识别（用光学方法识别印刷字符）

octa·gon /'ɒktəgən; NAmE 'ɑːktəgɑːn/ noun (geometry 几何) a flat shape with eight straight sides and eight angles 八边形；八角形 ➲ PICTURE AT POLYGON ▸ **oc·tag·on·al** /ɒk'tægənl; NAmE ɑːk't-/ adj. : *an octagonal coin* 八角形硬币

oc·tane /'ɒkteɪn; NAmE 'ɑːk-/ noun a chemical substance in petrol/gas, used as a way of measuring its quality 辛烷（汽油中的化学物质，用于检测汽油的质量）： *high-octane fuel* 高辛烷值的燃料

oct·ave /'ɒktɪv; NAmE 'ɑːk-/ noun (music 音) the difference (the INTERVAL) between the first and last notes in a series of eight notes on a SCALE 八度： *to play an octave higher* 高八度演奏 ◇ *Orbison's vocal range spanned three octaves.* 奥毕森的音域跨越三个八度。

oc·tavo /ɒk'teɪvəʊ; -'tɑːv-; NAmE ɑːk-; -voʊ/ noun (pl. **-os**) (specialist) a size of a book page that is made by folding each sheet of paper into eight LEAVES (= 16 pages) 八开本

octet /ɒk'tet; NAmE ɑːk-/ noun **1** [C+sing./pl. v.] a group of eight singers or musicians 八重唱组合；八重奏乐团 **2** [C] a piece of music for eight singers or musicians 八重奏（曲）；八重唱（曲）

octo- /'ɒktəʊ; NAmE 'ɑːktoʊ/ (also **oct-**) combining form (in nouns, adjectives and adverbs 构成名词、形容词和副词) eight; having eight 八；八…的： *octagon* 八角形

Oc·to·ber /ɒk'təʊbə(r); NAmE ɑːk'toʊ-/ noun [U, C] (abbr. **Oct.**) the 10th month of the year, between September and November 十月 HELP To see how **October** is used, look at the examples at **April**. * October 的用法见词条 April 下的示例。

oc·to·gen·ar·ian /ˌɒktədʒə'neəriən; NAmE ˌɑːktədʒə'ner-/ noun a person between 80 and 89 years old 八旬老人；80 至 89 岁的人

octo·pus /'ɒktəpəs; NAmE 'ɑːk-/ noun [C, U] (pl. **octo·puses**) a sea creature with a soft round body and eight long arms, that is sometimes used for food 章鱼

octo·syl·lable /'ɒktəʊsɪləbl; NAmE 'ɑːktoʊ-/ noun (specialist) a line of poetry consisting of eight syllables 八音节诗行 ▸ **octo·syl·lab·ic** /ˌɒktəʊsɪ'læbɪk; NAmE ˌɑːktoʊ-/ adj.

ocu·lar /'ɒkjələ(r); NAmE 'ɑːk-/ adj. [only before noun] **1** (specialist) connected with the eyes 眼的；眼睛的： *ocular muscles* 眼部肌肉 **2** (formal) that can be seen 可以看见的；看得到的： *ocular proof* 看得见的证据

ocu·list /'ɒkjəlɪst; NAmE 'ɑːk-/ noun (old-fashioned) a doctor who examines and treats people's eyes 眼科医生

OD /ˌəʊ 'diː; NAmE ˌoʊ/ verb (**OD's**, **OD'ing**, **OD'd**, **OD'd**) [I] ~ (on sth) (informal) = OVERDOSE

O

odd 🔑 AW /ɒd; NAmE ɑːd/ *adj.* (**odder, oddest**)
• STRANGE 奇怪 **1** 🔑 strange or unusual 奇怪的；怪异的；反常的：*They're very odd people.* 他们那些人都很古怪。◇ *There's something odd about that man.* 那个人有点儿怪。◇ *It's* ***most odd that*** (= very odd that) *she hasn't written.* 真怪了，她一直没写信。◇ *The* ***odd thing*** *was that he didn't recognize me.* 怪就怪在他没认出我来。◇ *She had the oddest feeling that he was avoiding her.* 她有种异样的感觉，觉得他在躲着她。➲ COMPARE PECULIAR (1)
• ODD- （某方面）怪异 **2** (in compounds 构成复合词) strange or unusual in the way mentioned（某方面）怪异的，奇怪的：*an odd-looking house* 样子怪异的房子 ◇ *an odd-sounding name* 听起来奇怪的名字
• NOT REGULAR/OFTEN 不规则；不常 **3 the odd** [only before noun] (no comparative or superlative 无比较级或最高级) happening or appearing occasionally; not very regular or frequent 偶然出现的；偶尔发生的；不规律的 SYN **occasional**：*He makes the odd mistake—nothing too serious.* 他偶尔会犯错误，但不怎么严重。
• VARIOUS 各种各样 **4** [only before noun] (no comparative or superlative 无比较级或最高级) of no particular type or size; various 奇形怪状的；各种各样的：*decorations made of odd scraps of paper* 用各种各样的纸片做的装饰
• NOT MATCHING 不相配 **5** [usually before noun] (no comparative or superlative 无比较级或最高级) not with the pair or set that it belongs to; not matching 不成对的；不相配的：*You're wearing odd socks!* 你穿的袜子不成双呀！
• NUMBERS 数字 **6** 🔑 (no comparative or superlative 无比较级或最高级) (of numbers 数字) that cannot be divided exactly by the number two 奇数的：*1, 3, 5 and 7 are odd numbers.* * 1、3、5 和 7 是奇数。OPP **even**
• AVAILABLE 可得到的 **7** [only before noun] available; that sb can use 可得到的；可用的 SYN **spare**：*Could I see you when you've got an* ***odd moment?*** 你有空时，我能不能见见你？
• APPROXIMATELY 约略 **8** (no comparative or superlative; usually placed immediately after a number 无比较级或最高级；通常紧接在数字后面) approximately or a little more than the number mentioned 大约；略多：*How old is she—seventy odd?* 她多大年纪？七十出头？◇ *He's worked there for twenty-odd years.* 他在那里工作了二十多年。
▶ **odd·ness** *noun* [U]：*the oddness of her appearance* 她那怪样子 ◇ *His oddness frightened her.* 他的反常把她吓坏了。
IDM **the odd man/one 'out** a person or thing that is different from others or does not fit easily into a group or set 与其他不同（或合不来）的人（或物）；异类：*At school he was always the odd man out.* 在学校里他总是与别人格格不入。◇ *Dog, cat, horse, shoe—which is the odd one out?* 狗、猫、马、鞋，哪一个不属同类？➲ MORE AT FISH *n.*

odd·ball /'ɒdbɔːl; NAmE 'ɑːd-/ *noun* (*informal*) a person who behaves in a strange or unusual way 行为古怪者；反常者；怪人 ▶ **odd·ball** *adj.*：*oddball characters* 古怪的人物

odd·ity /'ɒdəti; NAmE 'ɑːd-/ *noun* (*pl.* **-ies**) **1** [C] a person or thing that is strange or unusual 古怪反常的人（或事物）；怪现象：*The book deals with some of the oddities of grammar and spelling.* 这本书专讲语法和拼写方面的某些不规则现象。 **2** [U] the quality of being strange or unusual 古怪；怪异；反常：*She suddenly realized the oddity of her remark and blushed.* 她突然意识到自己的话很奇怪，脸一下子红了。

,odd-'job man *noun* (*especially BrE*) a person paid to do odd jobs 打零工的人；散工；短工

,odd 'jobs *noun* [pl.] small jobs of various types 零散的工作；杂活；零活儿：*to do odd jobs around the house* 在家里干杂活

oddly 🔑 /'ɒdli; NAmE 'ɑːd-/ *adv.* **1** 🔑 in a strange or unusual way 古怪地；怪异地；反常地 SYN **strangely**：*She's been behaving very oddly lately.* 她最近行为极其反常。◇ *oddly coloured clothes* 颜色古怪的衣裳 ◇ *He looked at her in a way she found oddly disturbing.* 他异样地望着她，令她局促不安。 **2** 🔑 used to show that sth is surprising 令人奇怪地；令人惊奇地 SYN **surprisingly**：*She felt, oddly, that they had been happier when they had no money.* 她感到奇怪的是，他们没钱时反倒生活得更幸福。◇ ***Oddly enough,*** *the most expensive tickets sold fastest.* 奇怪极了，最贵的票居然卖得最快。

odd·ments /'ɒdmənts; NAmE 'ɑːd-/ *noun* [pl.] (*especially BrE*) **1** small pieces of cloth, wood, etc. that are left after a larger piece has been used to make sth 布头；零木料；边角料 SYN **remnant** **2** small items that are not valuable or are not part of a larger set（无价值或派不上用场的）小物品，零碎 SYN **bits and pieces/bobs**

odds AW /ɒdz; NAmE ɑːdz/ *noun* [pl.] **1** (*usually* **the odds**) the degree to which sth is likely to happen（事物发生的）可能性，概率，几率，机会：***The odds are*** *very much* ***in our favour*** (= we are likely to succeed). 我方胜算的几率极大。◇ ***The odds are*** *heavily* ***against him*** (= he is not likely to succeed). 他成功的几率很小。◇ ***The odds are that*** (= it is likely that) *she'll win.* 她有可能会赢。◇ ***What are the odds*** (= how likely is it) *he won't turn up?* 他不会露面的可能性有多大？ **2** something that makes it seem impossible to do or achieve sth 不利条件；掣肘的事情；逆境：*They secured a victory in the face of overwhelming odds.* 尽管情况非常不利，他们仍得到了胜利。◇ ***Against all (the) odds,*** *he made a full recovery.* 在凶多吉少的情形下，他终于完全康复了。 **3** (in betting 打赌) the connection between two numbers that shows how much money sb will receive if they win a bet 投注赔率：*odds of ten to one* (= ten times the amount of money that has been bet by sb will be paid to them if they win) 十比一的赔率 ◇ *They are offering* ***long/short odds*** (= the prize money will be high/low because there is a high/low risk of losing) *on the defending champion.* 他们为卫冕者开出了高 / 低赔率。◇ (*figurative*) *I'll* ***lay odds*** *on him getting the job* (= I'm sure he will get it). 我敢说他能得到这份工作。➲ WORDFINDER NOTE AT GAMBLING
IDM **be at 'odds (with sth)** to be different from sth, when the two things should be the same（与…）有差异，相矛盾 SYN **conflict**：*These findings are at odds with what is going on in the rest of the country.* 这些研究结果与国内其他地区的实际情况并不相符。 **be at 'odds (with sb) (over/on sth)** to disagree with sb about sth（就某事）（与某人）有分歧：*He's always at odds with his father over politics.* 他在政治上总是与他父亲的意见相左。 **it makes no 'odds** (*informal, especially BrE*) used to say that sth is not important 没关系；无所谓；无差别：*It makes no odds to me whether you go or stay.* 你的去留与我无关。 **over the 'odds** (*BrE, informal*) more money than you would normally expect（比期望的）价钱高：*Many collectors are willing to pay over the odds for early examples of his work.* 许多收藏家都肯出高价买他早期的作品。➲ MORE AT STACKED

,odds and 'ends (*BrE also* **,odds and 'sods**) *noun* [pl.] (*informal*) small items that are not valuable or are not part of a larger set 零碎；琐碎的东西；小玩意：*She spent the day sorting through a box full of odds and ends.* 她花一天工夫整理装满小玩意儿的箱子。◇ *I've got a few odds and ends* (= small jobs) *to do before leaving.* 我临行之前还有些杂事要处理。

,odds-'on *adj.* very likely to happen, win, etc. 很可能发生（或取胜等）的：*the* ***odds-on favourite*** (= the person, horse, etc. that is most likely to succeed, to win a race, etc.) 被看好会赢的人或马等 ◇ ***It's odds-on that*** *he'll be late.* 他多半要迟到。◇ *Arazi is odds-on to win the Kentucky Derby.* 阿拉兹十有八九会在肯塔基赛马会上获胜。

ode /əʊd; NAmE oʊd/ *noun* a poem that speaks to a person or thing or celebrates a special event 颂诗；颂歌：*Keats's 'Ode to a Nightingale'* 济慈的《夜莺颂》

odi·ous /'əʊdiəs; NAmE 'oʊ-/ *adj.* (*formal*) extremely unpleasant 令人作呕的；令人讨厌的；可憎的 SYN **horrible**：*What an odious man!* 真是个讨厌透顶的家伙！

odium /'əʊdiəm; NAmE 'oʊ-/ *noun* [U] (*formal*) a feeling of hatred that a lot of people have towards sb, because of sth they have done 憎恶；厌恶；公愤

odom·eter /əʊ'dɒmɪtə(r); *NAmE* oʊ'dɑːm-/ (*NAmE*) (*BrE* **mil·om·eter, mile·ometer**) (*also informal* **the clock** *US, BrE*) *noun* an instrument in a vehicle that measures the number of miles it has travelled 里程表；计程器 ➲ VISUAL VOCAB PAGE V56

odon·tol·ogy /ˌəʊdɒn'tɒlədʒi; ˌɒd-; *NAmE* ˌoʊdɑːn'tɑːlədʒi/ *noun* [U] the scientific study of the diseases and structure of teeth 牙科学 ▶ **odon·tolo·gist** /ˌəʊdɒn'tɒlədʒɪst; ˌɒd-; *NAmE* ˌoʊdɑːn'tɑːlədʒɪst/ *noun*

odor·ous /'əʊdərəs; *NAmE* 'oʊ-/ *adj.* (*literary* or *specialist*) having a smell 有气味的：*odorous gases* 有味儿的气体

odour (*especially US* **odor**) /'əʊdə(r); *NAmE* 'oʊ-/ *noun* [C, U] (*formal*) a smell, especially one that is unpleasant（尤指难闻的）气味；臭味：*a **foul/musty/pungent, etc. odour*** 难闻的气味、难闻的霉味、刺鼻的气味等 ◇ *the stale odour of cigarette smoke* 香烟的臭味 ◇ (*figurative*) *the odour of suspicion* 启人疑窦 ➲ SEE ALSO BODY ODOUR

IDM **be in good/bad 'odour (with sb)** (*formal*) to have/not have sb's approval and support 得到 / 不得（某人的）青睐；受 / 不受（某人的）赞同

odour·less (*especially US* **odor·less**) /'əʊdələs; *NAmE* 'oʊdərləs/ *adj.* without a smell 无气味的：*an odourless liquid* 无臭的液体

odys·sey /'ɒdəsi; *NAmE* 'ɑːd-/ *noun* [sing.] (*literary*) a long journey full of experiences 艰苦的跋涉；漫长而充满风险的历程 ➲ MORE LIKE THIS 16, page R27 ORIGIN From the **Odyssey**, a Greek poem that is said to have been written by Homer, about the adventures of **Odysseus**. After a battle in Troy, Odysseus had to spend ten years travelling before he could return home. 源自希腊史诗《奥德赛》，相传为荷马所作，描述了奥德修斯在特洛伊战争后，辗转十年返回家园的种种经历。

OECD /ˌəʊ iː siː 'diː; *NAmE* ˌoʊ/ *abbr.* Organization for Economic Cooperation and Development (an organization of industrial countries that encourages trade and economic growth) 经合组织，经济合作与发展组织（工业化国家鼓励贸易和经济发展的组织）

oe·dema (*BrE*) (*NAmE* **edema**) /ɪ'diːmə/ *noun* [U] (*medical* 医) a condition in which liquid collects in the spaces inside the body and makes it swell 水肿

Oedi·pal /'iːdɪpl; *US usually* 'ed-/ *adj.* [usually before noun] connected with an Oedipus complex 恋母情结的

Oedi·pus com·plex /'iːdɪpəs kɒmpleks; *NAmE* 'iːdɪpəs kɑːm-; *usually* 'edɪpəs kɑːm-/ *noun* [sing.] (*psychology* 心) feelings of sexual desire that a boy has for his mother and the jealous feelings towards his father that this causes 恋母情结 ORIGIN From the Greek story of **Oedipus**, whose father Laius had been told by the oracle that his son would kill him. Laius left Oedipus on a mountain to die, but a shepherd rescued him. Oedipus returned home many years later but did not recognize his parents. He killed his father and married his mother, Jocasta. 源自希腊故事《俄狄浦斯》。拉伊俄斯由神谕得知，儿子俄狄浦斯将会杀害他，便将儿子置于山野，任其自灭。但俄狄浦斯为牧羊人所救，多年后返回家园，却不认得父母。他杀死了父亲，娶了母亲伊俄卡斯塔。

o'er /ɔː(r)/ *adv., prep.* (*old use*) over 在…上面；越过

oe·sopha·gus (*BrE*) (*NAmE* **esopha·gus**) /i'sɒfəgəs; *NAmE* i'sɑː-/ *noun* (*pl.* **-ph·agi**) (*anatomy* 解) the tube through which food passes from the mouth to the stomach 食道；食管 SYN **gullet** ➲ VISUAL VOCAB PAGE V64

oes·tro·gen (*BrE*) (*NAmE* **es·tro·gen**) /'iːstrədʒən; *NAmE* 'es-/ *noun* [U] a HORMONE produced in women's OVARIES that causes them to develop the physical and sexual features that are characteristic of females and that causes them to prepare their body to have babies 雌激素 ➲ COMPARE PROGESTERONE, TESTOSTERONE

oes·trus (*BrE*) (*NAmE* **es·trus**) /'iːstrəs; *NAmE* 'estrəs/ *noun* [U] (*specialist*) a period of time in which a female animal is ready to have sex （雌性动物的）动情期

oeuvre /'ɜːvrə/ *noun* [sing.] (*from French, formal*) all the works of a writer, artist, etc.（作家、艺术家等的）全部作品：*Picasso's oeuvre* 毕加索的全部作品

of 🔑 /əv; *strong form* ɒv; *NAmE strong form* ʌv/ *prep.* **1** 🔑 belonging to sb; relating to sb 属于（某人）；关于（某人）：*a friend of mine* 我的一个朋友 ◇ *the love of a mother for her child* 母亲对孩子的爱 ◇ *the role of the teacher* 教师的角色 ◇ *Can't you throw out that old bike of Tommy's?* 难道你就不能把汤米那辆旧自行车给扔掉？ ◇ *the paintings of Monet* 莫奈的画作 HELP When you are talking about everything someone has painted, written, etc., use **of**. When you are referring to one or more examples of somebody's work, use **by**. 指某人所画或所著等的全部作品时，用 of；指其作品中的一部或多部时，则用 by：*a painting by Monet* 莫奈的一幅画 **2** 🔑 belonging to sth; being part of sth; relating to sth 属于（某物）；（某事）部分的；关于（某物）：*the lid of the box* 盒子盖 ◇ *the director of the company* 公司的董事 ◇ *a member of the team* 一名队员 ◇ *the result of the debate* 辩论的结果 **3** 🔑 coming from a particular background or living in a place 出身于（某背景）；住在（某地）：*a woman of Italian descent* 意大利裔女子 ◇ *the people of Wales* 威尔士人民 **4** 🔑 concerning or showing sb/sth 关于，反映（某人或某事）：*a story of passion* 爱情故事 ◇ *a photo of my dog* 我那只狗的照片 ◇ *a map of India* 印度地图 **5** 🔑 used to say what sb/sth is, consists of, or contains（用于表示性质、组成或涵盖）即，由…组成：*the city of Dublin* 都柏林市 ◇ *the issue of housing* 住房问题 ◇ *a crowd of people* 一群人 ◇ *a glass of milk* 一杯牛奶 **6** 🔑 used with measurements and expressions of time, age, etc.（用于表示计量、时间或年龄等）：*2 kilos of potatoes* 两公斤马铃薯 ◇ *an increase of 2%* * 2% 的增长 ◇ *a girl of 12* * 12 岁的女孩 ◇ *the fourth of July* 七月四日 ◇ *the year of his birth* 他出生的那一年 ◇ (*old-fashioned*) *We would often have a walk of an evening.* 我们过去常在晚上散步。 **7** 🔑 used to show sb/sth belongs to a group, often after *some, a few*, etc.（常用在 some、a few 等词语之后，表示人或物的所属）属于…的：*some of his friends* 他的几位朋友 ◇ *a few of the problems* 其中的几个问题 ◇ *the most famous of all the stars* 最知名的一位明星 **8** 🔑 used to show the position of sth/sb in space or time（表示人或事的时空位置）在，当：*just north of Detroit* 就在底特律以北 ◇ *at the time of the revolution* 在革命的年代 ◇ (*NAmE*) *at a quarter of eleven tonight* (= 10.45 p.m.) 在今晚十一点差一刻 **9** 🔑 used after nouns formed from verbs. The noun after 'of' can be either the object or the subject of the action.（用于由动词转化的名词之后，of 之后的名词可以是受动者，也可以是施动者）：*the arrival of the police* (= they arrive) 警察的到来 ◇ *criticism of the police* (= they are criticized) 对警察的批评 ◇ *fear of the dark* 对黑暗的惧怕 ◇ *the howling of the wind* 狂风的呼啸 **10** 🔑 used after some verbs before mentioning sb/sth involved in the action（用于某些动词后，后接动作所涉及的人或事）：*to deprive sb of sth* 剥夺某人的东西 ◇ *He was cleared of all blame.* 他所受的一切责难都澄清了。 ◇ *Think of a number, any number.* 想一个数字，随便一个。 **11** 🔑 used after some adjectives before mentioning sb/sth that a feeling relates to（用于某些形容词后，后接与感情相关的人或事）因为，由于：*to be proud of sth* 为某事自豪 **12** 🔑 used to give your opinion of sb's behaviour（用于对某人的行为发表看法）：*It was kind of you to offer.* 感谢你的好意。 **13** used when one noun describes a second one（用于一个名词修饰另一个名词时）：*Where's that idiot of a boy* (= the boy that you think is stupid)? 那个傻小子在哪儿？

IDM **of 'all** used before a noun to say that sth is very surprising（用于名词前，表示某事着实令人吃惊）竟然，偏偏：*I'm surprised that you of all people should say that.* 你竟然那么说，真让我吃惊！ **of all the...** used to express anger（用以表示愤怒）：*Of all the nerve!* 竟然如此厚颜无耻！

off 🔑 /ɒf; *NAmE* ɔːf; ɑːf/ *adv., prep., adj., noun, verb*

▪ *adv.* HELP For the special uses of **off** in phrasal verbs, look at the entries for the verbs. For example **come off** is in the phrasal verb section at **come**. * off 在短语动词中的

O

特殊用法见有关动词词条。如 come off 在词条 come 的短语动词部分。 **1** 🔑 away from a place; at a distance in space or time 离开（某处）；（在时间或空间上）距，离：*I called him but he ran off.* 我喊他，可他跑开了。◇ *Sarah's off in India somewhere.* 萨拉远在印度某地。◇ *I must be off soon* (= leave). 我得赶紧走了。◇ *Off you go!* 你走吧！◇ *Summer's not far off now.* 夏天已近在眼前了。◇ *A solution is still some way off.* 解决办法尚需时日。 **2** 🔑 used to say that sth has been removed（用以表示除去了某物）：*He's had his beard shaved off.* 他把胡子刮掉了。◇ *Take your coat off.* 脱了外衣吧。◇ *Don't leave the toothpaste with the top off.* 用完了牙膏别不盖盖。 **3** starting a race 起跑：*They're off* (= the race has begun). 他们起跑了。 **4** 🔑 no longer going to happen; cancelled 不再会发生；被取消：*The wedding is off.* 婚礼被取消了。 **5** 🔑 not connected or functioning 未连接；不工作：*The water is off.* 停水了。◇ *Make sure the TV is off.* 请注意关掉电视机。 **6** (*especially BrE*) (of an item on a menu 菜单中的项目) no longer available or being served 没有；不再供应：*Sorry, the duck is off.* 对不起，鸭子卖光了。 **7** 🔑 away from work or duty 休假；休息：*She's off today.* 她今天休假。◇ *I've got three days off next week.* 我下周有三天休假。◇ *How many days did you* ***take off****?* 你休了几天假？◇ *I need some* ***time off****.* 我需要休息一段时间。 **8** 🔑 taken from the price 减价的；削价的：*shoes with $20 off* 减价 20 美元的鞋 ◇ *All shirts have/are 10% off.* 衬衣全部减价 10%。 **9** behind or at the sides of the stage in a theatre 在剧院舞台的后面（或旁边）**SYN** offstage

IDM **be well/better/badly, etc. ˈoff** 🔑 used to say how much money sb has（用于表示经济情况）：*Families will be better off under the new law* (= will have more money). 这项新法律将使每个家庭的经济较前宽裕。◇ *They are both comfortably off* (= have enough money to be able to buy what they want without worrying too much about the cost). 他们俩的生活都很宽裕。 **be better/worse off (doing sth)** 🔑 to be in a better or worse situation（做某事）会较好 / 较糟：*She's better off without him.* 他不在身边她反倒更快乐。◇ *The weather was so bad we'd have been better off staying at home.* 天气太糟了，我们要是待在家里就好了。◇ *We can't be any worse off than we are already.* 我们的状况已经糟得不能再糟了。 **be ˌoff for ˈsth** (*informal*) to have a particular amount of sth 有一定数量的东西：*How are we off for coffee* (= how much do we have)? 我们还有多少咖啡？➲ SEE ALSO BADLY OFF **ˌoff and ˈon / ˌon and ˈoff** from time to time; now and again 不时地；有时；断断续续地：*It rained on and off all day.* 雨断断续续地下了一整天。

■ ***prep.*** **HELP** For the special uses of **off** in phrasal verbs, look at the entries for the verbs. For example **take sth off sth** is in the phrasal verb section at **take**. * off 在短语动词中的特殊用法见有关动词词条。如 take sth off sth 在词条 take 的短语动词部分。 **1** 🔑 down or away from a place or at a distance in space or time 从（某处）落下；离开；（时空上）离，距：*I fell off the ladder.* 我从梯子上跌了下来。◇ *Keep off the grass!* 勿践踏草坪！◇ *an island off the coast of Spain* 西班牙海岸附近的岛 ◇ *They were still 100 metres off the summit.* 他们距山顶还有 100 米远。◇ *Scientists are still a long way off finding a cure.* 科学家要找到一个治疗方法，还早着呢。◇ *We're getting right off the subject.* 我们完全离题了。 **2** 🔑 leading away from sth, for example a road or room 离开；偏离：*We live off Main Street.* 我们住在大街附近。◇ *There's a bathroom off the main bedroom.* 主卧室旁边有一个卫生间。 **3** 🔑 used to say that sth has been removed 从…去掉；从…移开：*You need to take the top off the bottle first!* 你得先把瓶盖子打开！◇ *I want about an inch off the back of my hair.* 我想把脑后的头发剪短约一英寸。 **4** 🔑 away from work or duty 休假；休息：*He's had ten days off school.* 他有十天没上学了。 **5** 🔑 away from a price 偏离…价格；削价；杀价：*They knocked £500 off the car.* 他们对这辆汽车杀价 500 英镑。 **6 off of** (*non-standard or NAmE, informal*) off; from 离开；来源于；从：*I got it off of my brother.* 这是我从我弟弟那里弄到的。 **7** not wanting or liking sth that you usually eat or use 不想；戒除：*I'm off* (= not drinking) *alcohol for a week.* 我有一星期没喝酒了。◇ *He's finally off drugs* (= he no longer takes them). 他终于把毒戒了。

■ ***adj.*** [not before noun] **1** (*BrE*) (of food 食物) no longer fresh enough to eat or drink 不新鲜；变质：*This fish has gone off.* 这条鱼已变质了。◇ *The milk smells off.* 这奶的味道不对劲。◇ *It's off.* 那东西坏了。 **2 ~ (with sb)** (*informal, especially BrE*) not polite or friendly 不礼貌；不热情；冷淡：*He was a bit off with me this morning.* 他今天早晨对我有点冷淡。 **3** (*informal, especially BrE*) not acceptable 不能接受；难以容忍；不行：*It's a bit off expecting us to work on Sunday.* 让我们星期天上班工作，那可不太行吧。

■ ***noun*** [sing.] **the off** the start of a race 起跑：*They're ready for the off.* 他们准备起跑了。

■ ***verb*** **~ sb** (*informal, especially NAmE*) to kill sb 杀死（某人）

off- /ɒf; *NAmE* ɔːf; ɑːf/ *prefix* (in nouns, adjectives, verbs and adverbs 构成名词、形容词、动词和副词) not on; away from 不在…上；离开；去掉：*offstage* 幕后 ◇ *offload* 卸掉 ➲ MORE LIKE THIS 6, page R25

ˌoff-ˈair *adj.* (in radio and television 广播及电视) not being broadcast 不在广播中的：*off-air recording* 非广播实况录制 **OPP** on-air ▶ **ˌoff-ˈair** *adv.*：*to record off-air* 预先录制广播节目

offal /ˈɒfl; *NAmE* ˈɔːfl; ˈɑːfl/ *noun* [U] (*US also* **vaˈriety meats** [pl.]) the inside parts of an animal, such as the heart and LIVER, cooked and eaten as food（食用的）动物内脏

off·beat /ˌɒfˈbiːt; *NAmE* ˌɔːf-; ˌɑːf-/ *adj.* [usually before noun] (*informal*) different from what most people expect 不寻常的；不落俗套的；标新立异的 **SYN** **unconventional**：*offbeat humour* 另类的幽默 ◇ *an offbeat approach to interviewing* 别开生面的采访

ˌoff-ˈBroadway *adj.* (*NAmE*) **1** (of a theatre 剧院) not on Broadway, New York's main theatre district 不在百老汇的；外百老汇的 **2** (of a play 戏剧) unusual in some way and often by a new writer 不落俗的；有新意的；出自新人之手的 ➲ COMPARE FRINGE THEATRE

ˌoff-ˈcentre (*especially US* **ˌoff-ˈcenter**) *adv.*, *adj.* not exactly in the centre of sth 不居中（的）

ˌoff ˈcolour (*especially US* **ˌoff ˈcolor**) *adj.* **1** [not before noun] (*BrE, informal*) not in good health; looking or feeling ill/sick 身体不舒服；气色不佳；不适 **2** [usually before noun] (*especially NAmE*) an **off-colour** joke is one that people think is rude, usually because it is about sex（笑话）粗俗的，下流的

off·cut /ˈɒfkʌt; *NAmE* ˈɔːf-; ˈɑːf-/ *noun* (*especially BrE*) a piece of wood, paper, etc. that remains after the main piece has been cut 下脚料；边角材料

ˈoff day *noun* (*informal*) a day when you do not do things as well as usual 不顺利的日子；倒霉的一天

ˌoff-ˈduty *adj.* not at work 非值勤的；歇班的：*an off-duty policeman* 休班警察

of·fence 🔑 (*especially US* **of·fense**) /əˈfens/ *noun* **1** 🔑 [C] **~ (against sb/sth)** an illegal act 违法行为；犯罪；罪行 **SYN** **crime**：*a* ***criminal/serious/minor/sexual, etc. offence*** 刑事罪、重罪、轻罪、性犯罪等 ◇ ***a first offence*** (= the first time that sb has been found guilty of a crime) 初犯 ◇ ***a capital offence*** (= one for which sb may be punished by death) 死罪 ◇ *He was not aware that he had* ***committed an offence****.* 他没有意识到自己犯罪了。◇ ***an offence against society/humanity/the state*** 妨害社会 / 人类 / 国家的罪行 ◇ *New legislation makes it an offence to carry guns.* 新法律规定持枪为犯罪行为。➲ WORDFINDER NOTE AT TRIAL **2** 🔑 [U] the act of upsetting or insulting sb 冒犯；搅扰；侮辱：*I'm sure he* ***meant no offence*** *when he said that.* 我相信他那么说并无冒犯的意思。◇ *The photo may* ***cause offence*** *to some people.* 这张照片可能会引起一些人的反感。◇ *No one will* ***take offence*** (= feel upset or insulted) *if you leave early.* 你若早退谁也不会介意的。◇ *Don't be so quick to* ***take offence****.* 别动不动就生气。

IDM **no ofˈfence** (*informal*) used to say that you do not mean to upset or insult sb by sth you say or do 无冒犯之意：*No offence, but I'd really like to be on my own.* 我无意冒犯，但我确实想自己一个人待着。

of·fend /ə'fend/ *verb* **1** [T, often passive, I] ~ (**sb**) to make sb feel upset because of sth you say or do that is rude or embarrassing 得罪；冒犯：*They'll be offended if you don't go to their wedding.* 你若不参加他们的婚礼，他们会生气的。◇ *Neil did not mean to offend anybody with his joke.* 尼尔开那个玩笑并非想冒犯谁。◇ *A TV interviewer must be careful not to offend.* 电视采访者必须小心别得罪人。 **2** [T] ~ **sb/sth** to seem unpleasant to sb 令人不适：*The smell from the farm offended some people.* 农场散发的气味让一些人闻了不舒服。◇ *an ugly building that **offends the eye*** 一座丑陋碍眼的建筑物 **3** [I] (*formal*) to commit a crime or crimes 犯罪；犯法：*He started offending at the age of 16.* 他 16 岁就开始犯法。 **4** [I] ~ (**against sb/sth**) (*formal*) to be against what people believe is morally right 违背（人情）；违反（常理）；有悖于：*comments that offend against people's religious beliefs* 有悖人民宗教信仰的评论 ▶ **of·fend·ed** *adj.* : *Alice looked rather offended.* 艾丽斯显得愤愤不已。

of·fend·er /ə'fendə(r)/ *noun* **1** (*rather formal*) a person who commits a crime 犯罪者；违法者；罪犯：*a **persistent/serious/violent, etc. offender*** 惯犯、重犯、暴力犯等 ◇ *a young offender institution* 青少年罪犯管教所 ⊃ SEE ALSO FIRST OFFENDER, SEX OFFENDER **2** a person or thing that does sth wrong 妨害…的人（或事物）：*When it comes to pollution, the chemical industry is a major offender.* 谈到环境污染问题，化工产业是一大祸害。

of·fend·ing /ə'fendɪŋ/ *adj.* [only before noun] **1** causing you to feel annoyed or upset; causing problems 烦人的；令人不安的；惹麻烦的：*The offending paragraph was deleted.* 令某些人不悦的那段话已经删除。◇ *The traffic jam soon cleared once the offending vehicle had been removed.* 肇事车辆一经移走，交通拥堵很快就消除了。 **2** guilty of a crime 有罪的；违法的：*The offending driver received a large fine.* 肇事司机被判以大额罚款。

of·fense *noun* (*NAmE*) **1** /ə'fens/ [C] = OFFENCE : *to commit an offense* 犯罪 ◇ *The new law makes it a criminal offense to drink alcohol in public places.* 新法律将在公共场所饮酒定为刑事犯罪。◇ *a minor/serious offense* 轻罪；重罪 ◇ *She pleaded guilty to five traffic offenses.* 她承认曾五次违反交通法规。 **2** /'ɒfens; *NAmE* 'ɔːf-; 'ɑːf-/ [sing.+sing./pl. v., U] (*BrE* **at·tack** [sing.]) (*sport* 体育) the members of a team whose main aim is to score points against the other team; a method of attack（球队的）前锋，锋线队员；进攻方法；攻势：*The Redskins' offense is stronger than their defense.* 红皮队的进攻强于防守。◇ *He played offense for the Chicago Bulls.* 他在芝加哥公牛队打前锋。 ⊃ COMPARE DEFENCE (7)

of·fen·sive /ə'fensɪv/ *adj., noun*

■ ***adj.*** **1** rude in a way that causes you to feel upset, insulted or annoyed 冒犯的；得罪人的；无礼的：*offensive remarks* 冒犯的言论 ◇ *The programme contains language which some viewers may find offensive.* 节目里使用了某些观众可能认为是犯忌的语言。◇ ~ **to sb** *His comments were deeply offensive to a large number of single mothers.* 他的评论严重触怒了众多的单身母亲。 OPP **inoffensive** **2** (*formal*) extremely unpleasant 极其讨厌的；令人不适的 SYN **obnoxious**: *an offensive smell* 刺鼻的气味 ⊃ SYNONYMS AT DISGUSTING **3** [only before noun] connected with the act of attacking sb/sth 攻击性的；进攻性的：*an offensive war* 侵略战争 ◇ *offensive action* 进攻行动 ◇ *He was charged with carrying an **offensive weapon**.* 他被指控携带攻击性武器。 ⊃ COMPARE DEFENSIVE *adj.* (1) **4** (*NAmE, sport* 体育) connected with the team that has control of the ball; connected with the act of scoring points 攻方的；进攻型的；攻击型的：*offensive play* 进攻打法 ⊃ COMPARE DEFENSIVE *adj.* (3) ▶ **of·fen·sive·ly** *adv.* **of·fen·sive·ness** *noun* [U]

■ ***noun*** **1** a military operation in which large numbers of soldiers, etc. attack another country 进攻；攻击；侵犯 SYN **strike**: *an air offensive* 空中攻击 ◇ *They **launched the offensive** on January 10.* 他们于 1 月 10 日发动了进攻。 **2** a series of actions aimed at achieving sth in a way that attracts a lot of attention（引人注意的）系列行动；运动；攻势 SYN **campaign**: *The government has launched a new offensive against crime.* 政府发动了新的打击犯罪攻势。◇ *a sales offensive* 销售攻势 ◇ *The public seems unconvinced by their latest **charm offensive*** (= their attempt to make people like them). 公众看起来并没被他们最近的魅力攻势所打动。

IDM **be on the of'fensive** to be attacking sb/sth rather than waiting for them to attack you 发动攻势；主动出击 **go on** (**to**) **the of'fensive** | **take the of'fensive** to start attacking sb/sth before they start attacking you 先发制人

offer /'ɒfə(r); *NAmE* 'ɔːf-; 'ɑːf-/ *verb, noun*

■ ***verb*** **1** [T, I] to say that you are willing to do sth for sb or give sth to sb 主动提出；自愿给予：~ (**sth**) *Josie had offered her services as a guide.* 乔西曾表示愿意当向导。◇ *He offered some useful advice.* 他提出了一些有益的建议。◇ *I don't think they need help, but I think I should offer anyway.* 我想他们不需要帮助，但我认为我还是应该主动提出来。◇ ~ **sth** (**to sb**) (**for sth**) *He offered $4 000 for the car.* 他出价 4 000 美元买这辆汽车。◇ *They decided to offer the job to Jo.* 他们决定把这份工作给乔。◇ ~ **sb sth** *They decided to offer Jo the job.* 他们决定让乔做这件工作。◇ *I gratefully took the cup of coffee she offered me.* 我感激地接过她递来的一杯咖啡。◇ *Taylor offered him 500 dollars to do the work.* 泰勒愿出 500 美元雇他做这件工作。◇ ~ **to do sth** *The kids offered to do the dishes.* 孩子们主动要求洗盘子。◇ + **speech** *'I'll do it,' she offered.* "这个我来做吧。"她提议道。 ⊃ EXPRESS YOURSELF AT SHALL ⊃ MORE LIKE THIS 26, page R28 **2** [T] ~ **sth** to make sth available or to provide the opportunity for sth 提供（东西或机会）；供应：*The hotel offers excellent facilities for families.* 本旅馆提供适合家庭的优良设施。◇ *The job didn't offer any prospects for promotion.* 这份工作没有任何升迁的希望。◇ *He did not offer any explanation for his behaviour.* 他没有对自己的行为作出任何解释。 **3** [T] ~ **sth/sb** (**up**) (**to sb**) (*formal*) to give sth to God 奉献，祭献（给上帝）：*We offered up our prayers for the men's safe return.* 我们祈求上苍保佑他们平安归来。 ⊃ MORE LIKE THIS 33, page R28

IDM **have sth to offer** to have sth available that sb wants 能提供；能适合要求：*Oxford has a lot to offer visitors in the way of entertainment.* 牛津向来访者提供各式各样的娱乐活动。◇ *a young man with a great deal to offer* (= who is intelligent, has many skills, etc.) 一个多才多艺的年轻人 **offer your 'hand** (*formal*) to hold out your hand for sb to shake 伸出手（以便同别人握手）

▼ **EXPRESS YOURSELF** 情景表达

Offering somebody something 主动提供某物

Particularly when you are the host, you may want to make polite offers to your guests. 尤其是作为主人招待宾客时，礼貌地主动提供某物或帮助可以这么说：

- ***Would you like** a magazine to read?* 您想看杂志吗?
- ***Can I get you** a coffee?* 我给你来杯咖啡好吗?
- ***Can I offer you** something to drink?* 我给你拿点喝的好吗?
- ***How about** something to eat? I could make some sandwiches.* 吃点东西怎么样？我可以做些三明治。
- ***If you'd like to use/If you need** the bathroom, it's the second door on the right.* 如果你想用洗手间，右边第二个门就是。
- ***Feel free to** go upstairs and have a rest if you'd like to.* 你想要的话，请随时上楼休息。

Responses 回应：

- ***That would be nice.** I'd like a cup of tea, please.* 那太好了，我想要一杯茶，谢谢。
- ***Yes, please.** A glass of orange juice would be lovely.* 好的，一杯橙汁就很好。
- ***If you're sure it's no trouble,** I'd love a coffee.* 若真不给您添麻烦的话，我想来杯咖啡。
- ***No, thank you.** I'm fine for now.* 不用了，谢谢。我暂时不需要。
- ***Not for me, thanks.*** 我不用，谢谢。
- ***I'm fine, thanks.** Maybe later.* 我不用，谢谢。稍后再说吧。

O

■ ***noun*** **1** 🔑 an act of saying that you are willing to do sth for sb or give sth to sb 主动提议；建议：**~ (of sth)** *Thank you for your kind offer of help.* 谢谢你的好心帮助。◇ *to **accept/refuse/decline an offer*** 接受 / 拒绝 / 谢绝好意 ◇ *I took him up on his offer of a loan.* 他主动借钱给我，我接受了。◇ *You can't just turn down offers of work like that.* 人家给你工作，你不能就那样一一谢绝呀。◇ *an offer of marriage* 求婚 ◇ **~ to do sth** *I accepted her offer to pay.* 她要付款，我同意了。 **2** 🔑 **~ (for sth)** an amount of money that sb is willing to pay for sth 出价；报价：*I've had an offer of $2 500 for the car.* 有人向我出价 2 500 美元买这辆汽车。◇ *They've decided to accept our original offer.* 他们已决定接受我们最初的报价。◇ *The offer has been withdrawn.* 那个报价已经撤销了。◇ *They made me an offer I couldn't refuse.* 他们提出了一个使我不好拒绝的报价。◇ *The original price was £3 000, but I'm **open to offers*** (= willing to consider offers that are less than that). 原价为 3 000 英镑，但价钱还可以商量。 ➲ WORDFINDER NOTE AT DEAL ➲ SEE ALSO O.N.O. **3** 🔑 a reduction in the normal price of sth, usually for a short period of time（通常为短期的）减价，削价；处理价；特价：*This **special offer** is valid until the end of the month.* 这个特价优惠月底前有效。◇ *See next week's issue for details of more **free offers**.* 有关更多免费赠品的详情请见下期周刊。◇ *They have an offer on beer at the moment.* 他们目下正在打折卖啤酒。

IDM **on 'offer 1** that can be bought, used, etc. 提供的；可买到；可使用：*The following is a list of courses currently on offer.* 以下是目前所开设课程的清单。◇ *Prizes worth more than £20 000 are on offer.* 优胜者奖品总值逾 20 000 英镑。 **2** (*especially BrE*) on sale at a lower price than normal for a short period of time 短期内打折销售；削价出售：*Italian wines are on (special) offer this week.* 意大利葡萄酒本周特价销售。 **under 'offer** (*BrE*) if a house or other building is **under offer**, sb has agreed to buy it at a particular price（房屋或其他建筑物）已有买主出价，在洽售中

of·fer·ing /ˈɒfərɪŋ; *NAmE* ˈɔːf-; ˈɑːf-/ *noun* **1** something that is produced for other people to use, watch, enjoy, etc. 用品；剧作；作品；供消遣的产品：*the latest offering from the Canadian-born writer* 在加拿大出生的那位作家的最新作品 **2** something that is given to a god as part of religious worship 祭品；供品 ➲ SEE ALSO BURNT OFFERING, PEACE OFFERING

of·fer·tory /ˈɒfətri; *NAmE* ˈɔːfərtɔːri; ˈɑːf-/ *noun* (*pl.* **-ies**) **1** the offering of bread and wine to God at a church service 祭品（奉献给上帝的饼和酒） **2** an offering or a collection of money during a church service 献金（礼拜中收集的捐款）

ˌoff-ˈgrid *adj.* = OFF-THE-GRID

off·hand /ˌɒfˈhænd; *NAmE* ˌɔːf-; ˌɑːf-/ *adj., adv.*

■ ***adj.*** (*disapproving*) not showing much interest in sb/sth 漫不经心的；不在乎的：*an offhand manner* 随随便便的态度 ◇ *He was very offhand with me.* 他完全是在敷衍我。 ▶ **off·hand·ed·ly** /ˌɒfˈhændɪdli; *NAmE* ˌɔːf-; ˌɑːf-/ *adv.*：*He spoke offhandedly, making it clear I had no say in the matter.* 他自说自话，清楚表明这件事我无权发言。

■ ***adv.*** without being able to check sth or think about it 未经核实地；不假思索地；即席地：*I don't know offhand how much we made last year.* 我一时还真说不清我们去年赚了多少钱。

of·fice 🔑 /ˈɒfɪs; *NAmE* ˈɔːf-; ˈɑːf-/ *noun*

• ROOM/BUILDING 房屋；建筑物 **1** 🔑 [C] a room, set of rooms or building where people work, usually sitting at desks 办公室；办公楼：*The company is moving to new offices on the other side of town.* 公司要迁往城另一边的新办公楼。◇ *Are you going to the office today?* 你今天去办公室吗？◇ *an **office job*** 办公室工作 ◇ ***office workers*** 办公室人员 ➲ COLLOCATIONS AT JOB ➲ VISUAL VOCAB PAGE V71 ➲ SEE ALSO BACK OFFICE, HEAD OFFICE **2** 🔑 [C] a room in which a particular person works, usually at a desk（某人的）办公室：*Some people have to share an office.* 有些人只好合用一间办公室。◇ *Come into my office.* 到我的办公室里来。 **3** [C] (*NAmE*) (*BrE* **sur·gery**) a place where a doctor, dentist or VET sees patients 诊室；门诊处：*a **doctor's/dentist's office*** 诊室；牙医诊所 **4** 🔑 [C] (often in compounds 常构成复合词) a room or building used for a particular purpose, especially to provide information or a service 办事处；（尤指）问询处，服务处：*the local tourist office* 当地旅游办事处 ◇ *a ticket office* 售票处 ➲ SEE ALSO BOX OFFICE, REGISTRY OFFICE

• GOVERNMENT DEPARTMENT 政府部门 **5 Office** [C] used in the names of some British government departments（用于英国某些政府部门的名称中）：*the Foreign Office* 外交部 ◇ *the Home Office* 内政部

• IMPORTANT POSITION 重要职位 **6** 🔑 [U, C] an important position of authority, especially in government; the work and duties connected with this 要职；重要官职；重要职务：*She **held office** as a cabinet minister for ten years.* 她担任内阁部长长达十年。◇ *How long has he been **in office**?* 他任职多久了？◇ *The party has been **out of office*** (= has not formed a government) *for many years.* 那个党已在野多年了。◇ *The present government **took office** in 2009.* 现政府于 2009 年上台执政。◇ *to **seek/run for office*** 谋求 / 竞选公职 ◇ (*BrE*) *to **stand for office*** 竞选要职 ◇ *the office of treasurer* 司库的职务 ➲ COLLOCATIONS AT VOTE

IDM **through sb's good 'offices** (*formal*) with sb's help 经某人斡旋；承某人协助

'office block (*BrE*) (*also* **'office building** *NAmE, BrE*) *noun* a large building that contains offices, usually belonging to more than one company 办公大楼（通常为几家公司合用的） ➲ VISUAL VOCAB PAGE V3

'office boy, **'office girl** *noun* (*old-fashioned*) a young person employed to do simple tasks in an office 办公室勤杂员

'office-holder (*also* **'office-bearer**) *noun* a person who is in a position of authority, especially in the government or a government organization 官员；公务员；高级职员

'office hours *noun* [pl.] the time when people in offices are normally working 办公时间：*Our telephone lines are open during normal office hours.* 我们的电话在正常办公时间一直开通。

of·fi·cer 🔑 /ˈɒfɪsə(r); *NAmE* ˈɔːf-; ˈɑːf-/ *noun* **1** 🔑 a person who is in a position of authority in the armed forces 军官：***army/air-force/naval, etc. officers*** 陆军、空军、海军等军官 ◇ *a **commissioned/non-commissioned officer*** 军官；军士 ◇ *The matter was passed on to me, as your **commanding officer**.* 这件事转到了你的指挥官我这里。 ➲ WORDFINDER NOTE AT ARMY ➲ SEE ALSO FLYING OFFICER, PETTY OFFICER, PILOT OFFICER, WARRANT OFFICER **2** 🔑 (often in compounds 常构成复合词) a person who is in a position of authority in the government or a large organization（政府或大机构的）官员，高级职员：*an environmental health officer* 环境卫生官员 ◇ *a customs/prison/welfare officer* 海关 / 典狱 / 福利官员 ◇ *officers of state* (= ministers in the government)（政府各部）部长 ➲ SEE ALSO CHIEF EXECUTIVE OFFICER, MEDICAL OFFICER, PRESS OFFICER, PROBATION OFFICER, RETURNING OFFICER **3** 🔑 (often used as a form of address 常用作称谓) = POLICE OFFICER：*the officer in charge of the case* 负责本案的警察 ◇ *the investigating officer* 进行调查工作的警察 ◇ *Yes, officer, I saw what happened.* 是，警察先生，我看到了发生的事。 **4** (*NAmE*) a title for a police officer 警察的头衔：*Officer Dibble* 迪布尔警官

'office worker *noun* a person who works in the offices of a business or company（公司、企业的）办事人员；公司职员；上班族

of·fi·cial 🔑 /əˈfɪʃl/ *adj., noun*

■ ***adj.*** **1** 🔑 [only before noun] connected with the job of sb who is in a position of authority 公务的；公职的；公事的：*official responsibilities* 公务 ◇ *the Prime Minister's official residence* 首相官邸 ◇ *He attended in his official capacity as mayor.* 他以市长的官方身份莅临。◇ *This was her first official engagement.* 这是她的首桩公务。◇ *He made an official visit to Tokyo in March.* 他于三月到东京进行了一次公务访问。 **2** 🔑 [usually before noun] agreed to, said, done, etc. by sb who is in a position of authority 正式的；官方的；官方授权的：*an official announcement/*

decision/statement 官方公告 / 决定 / 声明 ◇ *according to official statistics/figures* 根据官方统计 / 数字 ◇ *An official inquiry has been launched into the cause of the accident.* 当局已对事故的原因展开调查。◇ *The country's official language is Spanish.* 这个国家的官方语言为西班牙语。◇ *I intend to lodge an official complaint* (= to complain to sb in authority). 我打算正式提出申诉。◇ *The news is not yet official.* 这消息尚未经官方证实。 **3** [only before noun] that is told to the public but may not be true 公开的；公布的；据官方的：*I only knew the official version of events.* 我对事情的了解仅限于官方的版本。◇ *The official story has always been that they are just good friends.* 官方一直说他们只不过是好朋友。 **4** [only before noun] formal and attended by people in authority 正式的；公务的；官方场合的：*an official function/reception* 官方活动 / 招待会 ◇ *The official opening is planned for October.* 正式开幕拟在十月。 **OPP unofficial**

■ *noun* (often in compounds 常构成复合词) a person who is in a position of authority in a large organization 要员；官员；高级职员：*a bank/company/court/government official* 银行 / 公司 / 法院 / 政府要员 ◇ *a senior official in the State Department* 国务院的高级官员

of·fi·cial·dom /əˈfɪʃldəm/ *noun* [U] (*disapproving*) people who are in positions of authority in large organizations when they seem to be more interested in following rules than in being helpful 官僚；当官的人

of·fi·cial·ese /əˌfɪʃəˈliːz/ *noun* [U] (*disapproving*) language used in official documents that is thought by many people to be too complicated and difficult to understand 公文体（复杂而难以理解）

of·fi·cial·ly /əˈfɪʃəli/ *adv.* **1** publicly and by sb who is in a position of authority 正式地；官方地；公开地：*The library will be officially opened by the local MP.* 图书馆将由当地下院议员正式揭幕。◇ *We haven't yet been told officially about the closure.* 我们尚未接到关闭的正式通知。◇ *The college is not an officially recognized English language school.* 那所学院不是官方认可的英语学校。 **2** according to a particular set of rules, laws, etc. 依据法规等：*Many of those living on the streets are not officially homeless.* 根据法律定义，许多流浪街头的人并非无家可归者。◇ *I'm not officially supposed to be here.* 按公事说，我是不该到这里来的。 **3** according to information that has been told to the public but that may not be true 据传；据公布：*Officially, he resigned because of bad health.* 据官方说法，他是因健康状况不佳而辞职的。 **OPP unofficially**

ofˌficial reˈceiver *noun* (*law* 律, *BrE*) = RECEIVER (3)

ofˌficial ˈsecret *noun* (in Britain) a piece of information known only to the government and its employees, which it is illegal for them to tell anyone under the Official Secrets Act 公务秘密（英国“公务秘密法”禁止政府工作人员泄露的信息）

the Ofˌficial ˈSecrets Act *noun* (in Britain) a law that prevents people giving information if the government wants it to remain secret 公务秘密法（英国禁止泄露政府机密的法规）

of·fi·ci·ate /əˈfɪʃieɪt/ *verb* **1** [I, T] **~ (at sth) | ~ sth** to act as an official in charge of sth, especially a sports event 主持（工作）；（尤指体育比赛）担任裁判：*A referee from a neutral country will officiate (at) the game.* 一名来自中立国的裁判将担任这场比赛的裁判。 **2** [I] **~ (at sth)** (*formal*) to do the official duties at a public or religious ceremony 主持（仪式）；履行职务

of·fi·cious /əˈfɪʃəs/ *adj.* (*disapproving*) too ready to tell people what to do or to use the power you have to give orders 爱指手画脚的；爱发号施令的 **SYN self-important**: *a nasty officious little man* 讨厌、好管闲事的家伙 ▸ **of·fi·cious·ly** *adv.*: *'You can't park here,' he said officiously.* “此处不准停车。”他装腔作势地说。 **of·fi·cious·ness** *noun* [U]

off·ing /ˈɒfɪŋ; *NAmE* ˈɔːf-; ˈɑːf-/ *noun*

IDM in the offing (*informal*) likely to appear or happen soon 即将发生：*I hear there are more staff changes in the offing.* 我听说有更多的人事变动在酝酿中。

ˌoff-ˈkey *adj.* **1** (of a voice or a musical instrument 声音或乐器) not in tune 走调 **2** not suitable or correct in a particular situation 不得体；不相宜；不恰当；不适当 **SYN inappropriate**: *Some of his remarks were very off-key.* 他有些话说得很不得体。 ▸ **ˌoff-ˈkey** *adv.*: *to sing off-key* 唱走了调

ˌoff-ˈlabel *adj.* relating to the use of a drug for sth other than what it was originally created for（药物）有标签外作用的，未按标签说明使用的：*A number of people suffered reactions due to off-label prescriptions.* 许多人因为将药物作标识以外用途的处方药而有不良反应。 ▸ **ˌoff-ˈlabel** *adv.*: *The antidepressant was prescribed off-label to treat an eating disorder.* 这种抗抑郁药曾被处方用来治疗饮食失调，这是未标明的用途。

ˈoff-licence (*BrE*) (*US* **ˈliquor store, ˈpackage store**) *noun* a shop that sells alcoholic drinks in bottles and cans to take away 外卖酒馆

ˌoff-ˈlimits *adj.* **1 ~ (to sb)** (of a place 地方) where people are not allowed to go 不准进入的；禁止入内的：*The site is off-limits to the general public.* 这个场所不对公众开放。 **2** not allowed to be discussed 不许谈论的；禁止探讨的：*The subject was ruled off-limits.* 规定禁止谈论这个话题。

off·line /ˌɒfˈlaɪn; *NAmE* ˌɔːf-; ˌɑːf-/ *adj.* (*computing* 计) not directly controlled by or connected to a computer or to the Internet 未联机的；未连线的；脱机的；离线的：*For offline orders, call this number.* 离线订货请拨打这个号码。 ▸ **off·line** *adv.*: *How do I write an email offline?* 如何在离线时写电子邮件？ ⊃ SEE ALSO ONLINE

IDM ˌtake sth offˈline to talk about sth on a later occasion, perhaps because it does not interest the other people who are present at a meeting 以后再谈（可能因会议上其他人对该话题不感兴趣）：*Could you two take that offline so we can move onto the other items on the agenda?* 你们二位以后再谈这个话题好吗？这样我们就可以继续讨论议程上的其他事项了。

off·load /ˌɒfˈləʊd; *NAmE* ˌɔːfˈloʊd; ˌɑːf-/ *verb* to get rid of sth/sb that you do not need or want by passing it/them to sb else 把（担子等）转移（给别人）；减轻（负担）；卸（包袱）：**~ sth/sb** *They should stop offloading waste from oil tankers into the sea.* 他们应当停止从油轮上往海里倾倒废弃物。◇ **~ sth/sb on/onto sb** *It's nice to have someone you can offload your problems onto.* 有个能分忧的人真是不错。

ˌoff-ˈpeak *adj.* [only before noun] happening or used at a time that is less popular or busy, and therefore cheaper 非高峰期的；淡季的：*off-peak electricity/travel* 非高峰时间的电力；淡季旅游 ▸ **ˌoff-ˈpeak** *adv.*: *Phone calls cost 20c per unit off-peak.* 非高峰时间电话费每单位 20 美分。 ⊃ COMPARE PEAK *adj.*

ˌoff-ˈpiste *adj.* away from the tracks of firm snow that have been prepared for SKIING on 在滑雪道外的；非滑雪场地的：*off-piste skiing* 道外滑雪 ▸ **ˌoff-ˈpiste** *adv.*: *We enjoy skiing off-piste.* 我们喜欢在滑道外滑雪。

off·print /ˈɒfprɪnt; *NAmE* ˈɔːf-; ˈɑːf-/ *noun* a separate printed copy of an article that first appeared as part of a newspaper, magazine, etc.（报纸、杂志等文章的）单行本

ˈoff-putting *adj.* (*informal, especially BrE*) not pleasant, in a way that prevents you from liking sb/sth 令人烦恼的；令人讨厌的：*I find his manner very off-putting.* 我觉得他的举止令人颇为厌恶。

ˈoff-ramp *noun* (*NAmE, SAfrE*) a road used for driving off a major road such as an INTERSTATE（高速公路等的）出口匝道，驶出坡道 ⊃ COMPARE ON-RAMP

ˈoff-road *adj.* [usually before noun] not on the public road 非公路上的；越野的：*an* ***off-road vehicle*** (= one for driving on rough ground) 越野车

ˌoff-ˈroader *noun* **1** a vehicle which is driven across rough ground as a sport 越野赛车 **2** a person who drives a vehicle across rough ground as a sport 越野赛车手 ▶ ˌ**off-ˈroading** *noun* [U]

ˌ**off-ˈscreen** *adj.* [only before noun] in real life, not in a film/movie 真实的；生活中的；非屏幕上的：*They were off-screen lovers.* 他们是真实生活中的情侣。▶ ˌ**off-ˈscreen** *adv.*：*She looks totally different off-screen.* 她在现实生活中看上去判若两人。➲ COMPARE ON-SCREEN

ˈ**off season** *noun* [sing.] **1** the time of the year that is less busy in business and travel（生意和旅游的）淡季 **SYN** **low season** **2** (*NAmE*) (*BrE* **close season**) (*sport* 体育) the time during the summer when teams do not play important games（夏季的）比赛淡季 ▶ ˌ**off-ˈseason** *adj.* [only before noun]：*off-season prices* 淡季价格 ˌ**off-ˈseason** *adv.*：*We prefer to travel off-season.* 我们喜欢在淡季旅游。

off·set **AW** /ˈɒfset; *NAmE* ˈɔːf-; ˈɑːf-/ *verb, adj.*

■ *verb* (**off·set·ting**, **off·set**, **off·set**) to use one cost, payment or situation in order to cancel or reduce the effect of another 抵消；弥补；补偿：**~ sth** *Prices have risen in order to offset the increased cost of materials.* 为补偿原料成本的增加而提高了价格。◇ **~ sth against sth** (*BrE*) *What expenses can you* ***offset against tax****?* 什么开支可以获得税项减免?

■ *adj.* [only before noun] used to describe a method of printing in which ink is put onto a metal plate, then onto a rubber surface and only then onto the paper 胶印的 ➲ SEE ALSO CARBON OFFSET

off·shoot /ˈɒfʃuːt; *NAmE* ˈɔːf-; ˈɑːf-/ *noun* **1** a thing that develops from sth, especially a small organization that develops from a larger one 分支；（尤指）分支机构 **2** (*specialist*) a new STEM that grows on a plant 蘖枝；分枝

O

off·shore /ˌɒfˈʃɔː(r); *NAmE* ˌɔːf-; ˌɑːf-/ *adj.* [usually before noun] **1** happening or existing in the sea, not far from the land 海上的；近海的：*offshore drilling* 近海钻探 ◇ *an offshore island* 近海岛屿 **2** (of winds 风) blowing from the land towards the sea 向海的；离岸的：*offshore breezes* 习习陆风 **3** (*business* 商) (of money, companies, etc. 资金、公司等) kept or located in a country that has more generous tax laws than other places 设在海外（尤指税制较宽松的国家）的；投放国外的；离岸的：*offshore investments* 境外投资 ▶ **off·shore** *adv.*：*a ship anchored offshore* 一艘泊在海上的船 ◇ *profits earned offshore* 境外赢利 ➲ COMPARE INSHORE, ONSHORE

off·shor·ing /ˌɒfˈʃɔːrɪŋ; *NAmE* ˌɔːf-; ˌɑːf-/ *noun* [U] the practice of a company in one country arranging for people in another country to do work for it（公司的）离岸外包业务，外包国外业务：*the offshoring of call-centre jobs to India* 电话客户服务中心业务对印度的离岸外包 ▶ **off·shore** *verb* **~ sth**

off·side *adj., noun*

■ *adj.* /ˌɒfˈsaɪd; *NAmE* ˌɔːf-; ˌɑːf-/ **1** (*US also* **off·sides**) in some sports, for example football (SOCCER) and HOCKEY, a player is **offside** if he or she is in a position, usually ahead of the ball, that is not allowed（足球、曲棍球等体育运动中）越位的：*He was offside when he scored.* 他进球时已越位了。◇ *the offside rule* 越位规则 **OPP** **onside** **2** (*BrE*) on the side of a vehicle that is furthest from the edge of the road（车辆）外侧的，右侧的：*the offside mirror* 右侧镜 **OPP** **nearside**

■ *noun* [U] **1** /ˌɒfˈsaɪd; *NAmE* ˌɔːf-; ˌɑːf-/ (*US also* **off·sides**) the fact of being offside in a game such as football (SOCCER) or HOCKEY（足球、曲棍球等体育运动中的）越位：*The goal was disallowed for offside.* 因为越位，进球无效。**2** /ˈɒfsaɪd; *NAmE* ˈɔːf-; ˈɑːf-/ (*BrE*) the side of a vehicle that is furthest from the edge of the road（车辆的）外侧，远侧，右侧：*The offside was damaged.* 车辆外侧受损。**OPP** **nearside**

off·sider /ɒfˈsaɪdə(r); *NAmE* ɔːf-; ɑːf-/ *noun* (*AustralE, NZE, informal*) a person who works with or helps sb else 同事；工友；帮手

off·spring /ˈɒfsprɪŋ; *NAmE* ˈɔːf-; ˈɑːf-/ *noun* (*pl.* **off·spring**) (*formal* or *humorous*) **1** a child of a particular person or couple 孩子；子女；后代：*the problems parents have with their teenage offspring* 父母与青少年子女之间的问题 ◇ *to* ***produce/raise offspring*** 生育 / 抚养后代 **2** the young of an animal or plant 崽兽；幼崽；幼苗

off·stage /ˌɒfˈsteɪdʒ; *NAmE* ˌɔːf-; ˌɑːf-/ *adj.* **1** not on the stage in a theatre; not where the audience can see 舞台外的；幕后的：*offstage sound effects* 幕后音响效果 **2** happening to an actor in real life, not on the stage（演员的）现实生活的，私生活的；舞台下的：*The stars were having an offstage relationship.* 这对明星在现实生活中发展出恋情。▶ **off·stage** *adv.*：*The hero dies offstage.* 剧中主角并非死在台上。**OPP** **onstage**

ˈ**off-street** *adj.* [usually before noun] not on the public road 不在大街上的；大街以外的；路外的；后街的：*an apartment with* ***off-street parking*** 后街街边可停车的公寓 **OPP** **on-street**

ˌ**off-the-ˈcuff** ➲ CUFF *n.* **HELP** You will also find other compounds beginning **off-the-** at the entry for the last word in the compound. 其他以 off-the- 开头的复合词可在最后一个词的词条下找到。

ˌ**off-the-ˈgrid** (*also* ˌ**off-ˈgrid**) *adj.* (*especially NAmE*) not using the public supplies of electricity, gas, water, etc. 不入网的（不使用公用输电网、煤气输送网、自来水网等）：*an off-the-grid house, independent of traditional utility services* 一所不依赖传统公用服务设施的网外房子 ➲ SEE ALSO GRID

ˌ**off-the-ˈshelf** *adj.* [only before noun] (of a product 产品) that can be bought immediately and does not have to be specially designed or ordered 从货架直接取下买走的；现成的：*off-the-shelf software packages* 现买软件包 ➲ SEE ALSO SHELF

ˌ**off-ˈwhite** *adj.* very pale yellowish-white in colour 米色的；米黄色的 ▶ ˌ**off-ˈwhite** *noun* [U]

ˈ**off year** *noun* (*US*) a year in which there are no important elections, especially no election for president 无重要选举的年份；（尤指）非大选年 ▶ ˈ**off-year** *adj.*

OFSTED /ˈɒfsted; *NAmE* ˈɔːf-/ *abbr.* the Office for Standards in Education (a British government department that is responsible for checking that standards in schools are acceptable) 教育标准局（英国负责评鉴学校标准的政府部门）

oft /ɒft; *NAmE* ɔːft; ɑːft/ *adv.* (*old use*) often 时常

oft- /ɒft; *NAmE* ɔːft; ɑːft/ *prefix* (in adjectives 构成形容词) often 时常：*an oft-repeated claim* 一再重复的说法 ➲ MORE LIKE THIS 6, page R25

often 🔑 /ˈɒfn; ˈɒftən; *NAmE* ˈɔːfn; ˈɑːf-; ˈɔːftən/ *adv.* **1** 🔑 many times 时常；常常 **SYN** **frequently**：*We often go there.* 我们常去那里。◇ *I've often wondered what happened to him.* 我时常纳闷他出了什么事。◇ ***How often*** *do you go to the theatre?* 你多长时间看一次戏？◇ *I see her quite often.* 我常常见到她。◇ *Try to exercise as often as possible.* 尽可能经常锻炼。◇ *We should meet for lunch more often.* 我们应该多多一起吃午饭。◇ ***It is not often*** *that you get such an opportunity.* 你得到这样的机会，可不是常有的事。**2** 🔑 in many cases 往往；大多 **SYN** **commonly**：*Old houses are often damp.* 老房子大多都潮湿。◇ *People are often afraid of things they don't understand.* 人往往对自己不懂的东西感到恐惧。◇ ***All too often*** *the animals die through neglect.* 动物因缺乏照料而死亡的事司空见惯。

IDM **as ˌoften as ˈnot | more ˌoften than ˈnot** usually; in a way that is typical of sb/sth 通常；往往；一贯：*As often as not, he's late for work.* 他上班往往迟到。ˌ**every so ˈoften** occasionally; sometimes 有时；偶尔 ➲ MORE AT ONCE *adv.*

often·times /ˈɒfntaɪmz; ˈɒftən-; *NAmE* ˈɔːfn-; ˈɑːf-; ˈɔːftən-/ *adv.* (*old use* or *NAmE*) often 常常

ogham (*also* **ogam**) /ˈɒgəm; *NAmE* ˈɑːg-/ *noun* [U] an ancient British and Irish alphabet of twenty characters 欧甘字母表（古英国和爱尔兰字母表，有 20 个字母）

ogle /ˈəʊɡl; *NAmE* ˈoʊɡl/ *verb* [T, I] ~ (**sb**) to look hard at sb in an offensive way, usually showing sexual interest（色迷迷地）盯着看，痴痴地看：*He was not in the habit of ogling women.* 他没有盯着女人看个没完的习惯。

ˈO grade (*also* **ˈordinary grade**) *noun* [C, U] (in Scotland in the past) an exam in a particular subject, at a lower level than HIGHERS, usually taken at the age of 16. In 1988 it was replaced by the STANDARD GRADE. 普通等级考试（苏格兰旧时的单科考试，低于高级考试，通常在 16 岁时参加。1988 年由标准等级考试取代）

ogre /ˈəʊɡə(r); *NAmE* ˈoʊ-/ *noun* **1** (in stories) a cruel and frightening giant who eats people（传说中的）食人恶魔 **2** a very frightening person 凶恶的人；可怕的人：*My boss is a real ogre.* 我的上司是个十足的恶魔。

ogress /ˈəʊɡres; *NAmE* ˈoʊ-/ *noun* a female ogre 吃人女妖

OH *abbr.* (*BrE, informal*) (especially in TEXT MESSAGES, emails, etc.) other half (a person's wife, husband or partner) 另一半，伴侣（全写为 other half，尤用于短信、电邮等）

oh 🔑 (*also especially literary* **O**) /əʊ; *NAmE* oʊ/ *exclamation* **1** 🔑 used when you are reacting to sth that has been said, especially if you did not know it before（表示领悟）哦，唔：*'I saw Ben yesterday.' 'Oh yes, how is he?'* "我昨天看见本了。""哦，他好吗？" ◇ *'Emma has a new job.' 'Oh, has she?'* "埃玛新找了一份工作。""噢，是吗？" **2** 🔑 used to express surprise, fear, joy, etc.（表示惊奇、恐惧、高兴等）啊，哈，哎哟：*Oh, how wonderful!* 啊，真是妙极了！◇ *Oh no, I've broken it!* 哎哟，我把它给打碎了！ **3** 🔑 used to attract sb's attention（用以引起注意）喂，嘿，嗨：*Oh, Sue! Could you help me a moment?* 嘿，休！你帮会儿忙行不行？ **4** 🔑 used when you are thinking of what to say next（用于思索想说的话时）嗯：*I've been in this job for, oh, about six years.* 我做这项工作，嗯，有六年左右了吧。➲ MORE LIKE THIS 2, page R25

ohm /əʊm; *NAmE* oʊm/ *noun* (*physics* 物) a unit for measuring electrical RESISTANCE 欧姆（电阻单位）

ohm·meter /ˈəʊmmiːtə(r); *NAmE* ˈoʊm-/ *noun* (*physics* 物) a device for measuring electrical RESISTANCE 欧姆计；电阻表

oho /əʊˈhəʊ; *NAmE* oʊˈhoʊ/ *exclamation* used for showing that you are surprised in a happy way, or that you recognize sb/sth（表示惊喜或辨认出）啊哈，哦嗬 ➲ MORE LIKE THIS 2, page R25

ˈoh-oh *exclamation* = UH-OH

OHP /ˌəʊ eɪtʃ ˈpiː; *NAmE* ˌoʊ eɪtʃ ˈpiː/ *noun* the abbreviation for OVERHEAD PROJECTOR 投影仪（全写为 overhead projector）：*Will you be using an OHP?* 你要用投影仪吗？

ˈoh-so *adv.* (*informal*) extremely 极其；非常：*their oh-so ordinary lives* 他们极其平凡的生活

OHT /ˌəʊ eɪtʃ ˈtiː; *NAmE* ˌoʊ eɪtʃ ˈtiː/ *noun* the abbreviation for 'overhead transparency' (a transparent plastic sheet that you can write or print sth on and show on a screen using an OVERHEAD PROJECTOR) 投影胶片（全写为 overhead transparency，用于投影仪）

oi (*also* **oy**) /ɔɪ/ *exclamation* (*BrE, informal*) used to attract sb's attention, especially in an angry way（用以引起注意，尤指愤怒地）嘿，嗨：*Oi, you! What do you think you're doing?* 嗨，你！你以为你在干什么？ ➲ MORE LIKE THIS 2, page R25

-oid *suffix* (in adjectives and nouns 构成形容词和名词) similar to 类似的；相像的：*humanoid* 类人的 ◇ *rhomboid* 长菱形 ➲ MORE LIKE THIS 7, page R25

oik /ɔɪk/ *noun* (*BrE, slang*) an offensive way of referring to a person that you consider rude or stupid, especially a person of a lower social class 蠢货；大老粗

oil 🔑 /ɔɪl/ *noun, verb*
▪ *noun* **1** 🔑 [U] a thick liquid that is found in rock underground 石油；原油 SYN **petroleum**: *drilling for oil* 钻探石油 ➲ WORDFINDER NOTE AT ENERGY **2** 🔑 [U] a form of PETROLEUM that is used as fuel and to make parts of machines move smoothly 燃油；润滑油：*engine oil* 发动机油 ◇ *an* ***oil lamp/heater*** 油灯；用燃油的暖气机 ◇ *Put some oil in the car.* 给汽车加点润滑油。 **3** 🔑 [U, C] a smooth thick liquid that is made from plants or animals and is used in cooking 食用油：*olive oil* 橄榄油 ◇ *vegetable oils* 植物油 **4** [U, C] a smooth thick liquid that is made from plants, minerals, etc. and is used on the skin or hair 防护油；润肤油；护发油：*lavender bath oil* 薰衣草沐浴油 ◇ *suntan oil* 防晒油 ➲ SEE ALSO ESSENTIAL OIL **5** [U] (*also* **oils** [pl.]) coloured paint containing oil used by artists（绘画用）油彩：*a painting done* ***in oils*** 一幅油画 ◇ *landscapes in oil* 风景油画 ➲ COLLOCATIONS AT ART ➲ SEE ALSO OIL PAINT **6** [C] = OIL PAINTING：*Among the more important Turner oils was 'Venus and Adonis'.*《维纳斯和阿多尼斯》是透纳比较重要的油画作品之一。 ➲ SEE ALSO OILY, CASTOR OIL, COD LIVER OIL, LINSEED OIL IDM SEE BURN *v.*, POUR
▪ ***verb*** ~ **sth** to put oil onto or into sth, for example a machine, in order to protect it or make it work smoothly 给…加润滑油：*He oiled his bike and pumped up the tyres.* 他给自己的自行车上了油，给轮胎充了气。
IDM **oil the ˈwheels** (*BrE*) (*NAmE* **grease the ˈwheels**) to help sth to happen easily and without problems, especially in business or politics（尤指在商业上或政治上）起促进作用

ˈoil-bearing *adj.* [only before noun] producing or containing oil 产油的；含油的

oil·can /ˈɔɪlkæn/ *noun* a metal container for oil, especially one with a long thin SPOUT, used for putting oil onto machine parts 油壶；（尤指）长嘴油壶

oil·cloth /ˈɔɪlklɒθ; *NAmE* -klɔːθ/ *noun* [U] a type of cotton cloth that is covered on one side with a layer of oil so that water cannot pass through it, used especially in the past for covering tables 油布（一面涂上油以防水防湿，旧时尤用作桌布）

ˈoil colour (*especially US* **ˈoil color**) *noun* [C, U] = OIL PAINT

oiled /ɔɪld/ *adj.* **well ~** (*BrE, informal*) drunk 喝醉酒的

oil·field /ˈɔɪlfiːld/ *noun* an area where oil is found in the ground or under the sea 油田

ˌoil-ˈfired *adj.* (of a heating system, etc. 暖气系统等) burning oil as fuel 燃油的

oil·man /ˈɔɪlmæn/ *noun* (*pl.* **-men** /-men/) a man who owns an oil company or works in the oil industry 石油商；石油大亨；石油工人

ˈoil paint (*also* **ˈoil colour**) *noun* [C, U] a type of paint that contains oil 油漆；油画颜料

ˈoil painting *noun* **1** (*also* **oil**) [C] a picture painted in OIL PAINT 油画 **2** [U] the art of painting in OIL PAINT 油画艺术
IDM **be no ˈoil painting** (*BrE, humorous*) used when you are saying that a person is not attractive to look at 相貌平平；非美人儿

ˈoil pan *noun* (*NAmE*) = SUMP (2)

ˈoil rig (*also* **ˈoil platform**) *noun* a large structure with equipment for getting oil from under the ground or under the sea 石油钻塔；钻油平台；油井设备 ➲ VISUAL VOCAB PAGE V15

ˌoilseed ˈrape *noun* [U] = RAPE (3)

oil·skin /ˈɔɪlskɪn/ *noun* **1** [U] a type of cotton cloth that has had oil put on it in a special process so that water cannot pass through it, used for making WATERPROOF clothing 防水油布，防雨布（用于制作防水衣） **2** [C] a coat or jacket made of oilskin 防水外衣 **3 oilskins** [pl.] a set of clothes made of oilskin, worn especially by sailors（尤指水手穿的）防水服装

ˈoil slick *noun* = SLICK (1)

'**oil tanker** *noun* a large ship with containers for carrying oil 油轮

'**oil well** (*also* **well**) *noun* a hole made in the ground to obtain oil 油井

oily /'ɔɪli/ *adj.* (**oil·ier**, **oili·est**) **1** containing or covered with oil 含油的；油污的；涂油的：*oily fish* 含油多的鱼 ◇ *an oily rag* 油污的抹布 **2** feeling, tasting, smelling or looking like oil （质地、味道、气味、形态）像油的：*an oily substance* 油状物质 **3** (*disapproving*) (of a person or their behaviour 人或行为) trying to be too polite, in a way that is annoying 油滑的；油腔滑调的；奉迎的 SYN **obsequious**：*an oily smile* 谄媚的微笑 ▶ **oili·ness** *noun* [U]

oink /ɔɪŋk/ *exclamation, noun* used to represent the sound a pig makes （猪叫声）哼 ➲MORE LIKE THIS 4, page R25

oint·ment /'ɔɪntmənt/ *noun* [U, C] a smooth substance that you rub on the skin to heal a wound or sore place 药膏；软膏；油膏 SYN **cream**：*antiseptic ointment* 抗菌软膏 IDM SEE FLY *n.*

OJ /'əʊ dʒeɪ; *NAmE* 'oʊ/ *noun* [U] (*NAmE, informal*) the abbreviation for 'orange juice' 橙汁（全写为 orange juice）

Ojibwa /əʊ'dʒɪbwɑː; *NAmE* oʊ-/ (*pl.* **Ojibwa** or **Ojib·was**) *noun* a member of a Native American people, many of whom live in the US states of Michigan, Wisconsin and Minnesota and in Ontario in Canada 奥吉布瓦人（美洲土著，很多居于美国密歇根、威斯康星、明尼苏达诸州以及加拿大安大略省）

OK 🔑 (*also* **okay**) /əʊ'keɪ; *NAmE* oʊ-/ *exclamation, adj., adv., noun, verb*

■*exclamation* (*informal*) **1** 🔑 yes; all right 对；好；行：*'Shall we go for a walk?' 'OK.'* "咱们去散散步，好不好？" "好。" **2** 🔑 used to attract sb's attention or to introduce a comment （用以引起注意或引入话题）好了，对了：*Okay, let's go.* 好了，咱们走吧。 **3** 🔑 used to check that sb agrees with you or understands you（用于弄清别人是否赞同或明白）好吗，行不：*The meeting's at 2, OK?* 两点开会，明白吗？ ◇ *I'll do it my way, OK?* 我想用我的方式做，行吗？ **4** 🔑 used to stop people arguing with you or criticizing you （用以制止对方争辩或批评）得了，行了，好了：*OK, so I was wrong. I'm sorry.* 行了，是我不对。对不起。

■*adj., adv.* (*informal*) **1** 🔑 safe and well; in a calm or happy state 安然无恙；平安；快活：*Are you OK?* 你没事吧？ ➲ SYNONYMS AT WELL **2** 🔑 ~ (**for sb**) (**to do sth**) all right; acceptable; in an acceptable way 可以；可行；尚可；不错：*Is it OK if I leave now?* 我现在离开，可以吗？ ◇ *Is it OK for me to come too?* 我也去，行吗？ ◇ *Does my hair look okay?* 我的头发还看得过去吗？ ◇ *I think I did OK in the exam.* 我觉得我考得还可以。 ◇ *Whatever you decide, it's* **okay by me**. 无论你怎么决定对我来说都行。 ◇ *an okay movie* 一部不错的电影 ➲EXPRESS YOURSELF AT PERMISSION

■*noun* [sing.] (*informal*) permission 允许；准许；同意 SYN **go-ahead**：*I'm still waiting for the boss to give me the OK.* 我还在等上司点头呢。

■*verb* (**OK's**, **OK'ing**, **OK'd**, **OK'd**) ~ **sth** (*informal*) to officially agree to sth or allow it to happen 正式批准；同意 SYN **approve**：*She filled in an expenses claim and her manager OK'd it.* 她填写了一张费用申请单，她的经理批准了。

okapi /əʊ'kɑːpi; *NAmE* oʊ-/ *noun* an African animal that belongs to the same family as the GIRAFFE, but is smaller with a dark body and white lines across its legs 獾狮狓（栖于非洲，长颈鹿科动物，皮肤深色，腿部有白纹）

oke /əʊk; *NAmE* oʊk/ (*also* **ou**) *noun* (*SAfrE, informal*) a man or a boy 小伙子；男孩：*He's quite a big oke.* 他是个大小伙子了。

okey-doke /ˌəʊki 'dəʊk; *NAmE* ˌoʊki 'doʊk/ (*also* **okey-dokey** /ˌəʊki 'dəʊki; *NAmE* ˌoʊki 'doʊki/) *exclamation* (*informal*) used to express agreement （用以表示同意）好吧，好了 SYN **OK**

okra /'əʊkrə; 'ɒkrə; *NAmE* 'oʊkrə/ (*also* **bhindi**) *noun* [U] (*also* ˌ**ladies'** '**fingers** [pl.]) the green seed cases of the okra plant, eaten as a vegetable 秋葵，黄秋葵（一种蔬菜） ➲VISUAL VOCAB PAGE V33

old 🔑 /əʊld; *NAmE* oʊld/ *adj.* (**old·er**, **old·est**)

• AGE 年龄 **1** 🔑 **be... years, months, etc. ~** of a particular age 具体年龄；（多少）岁；年纪：*The baby was only a few hours old.* 婴儿才出生几个小时。 ◇ *In those days most people left school when they were only fifteen years old.* 那时候，大多数人上学只上到十五岁。 ◇ *At thirty years old, he was already earning £40 000 a year.* 他三十岁时已拿到4万英镑的年薪了。 ◇ *two fourteen-year-old boys* 两个十四岁的男孩 ◇ *a class for five-year-olds* (= children who are five) 为五岁儿童开的班 ◇ *I didn't think she was* **old enough** *for the responsibility.* 我认为她尚年轻，不足以担当此任。 ◇ **How old** *is this building?* 这座建筑已有多少年了？ ◇ *He's the oldest player in the team.* 他是队里年龄最大的队员。 ◇ *She's much older than me.* 她的年龄比我大得多。

• NOT YOUNG 不年轻 **2** 🔑 having lived for a long time; no longer young 老的；年纪大的；不年轻的：*to* **get/grow old** 上年纪 ◇ *The old man lay propped up on cushions.* 老人靠在垫子上躺着。 ◇ *She was a woman grown* **old before her time** (= who looked older than she was). 她显得未老先衰。 OPP **young** **3 the old** *noun* [pl.] old people 老年人：*The old feel the cold more than the young.* 老年人比年轻人怕冷。 ➲MORE LIKE THIS 24, page R28

> **WORDFINDER 联想词：** care home, dementia, frail, geriatric, mobility, pensioner, retire, sprightly, widow

• NOT NEW 旧 **4** 🔑 having existed or been used for a long time 存在（或使用）时间长的；陈旧的；古老的：*old habits* 旧习惯 ◇ *He always gives the* **same old** *excuses.* 他总是重复那些老掉牙的借口。 ◇ *This carpet's getting pretty old now.* 这块地毯现在已经很旧了。 OPP **new** **5** 🔑 [only before noun] former; belonging to past times or a past time in your life 过去的；从前的：*Things were different in* **the old days**. 从前的情况可不一样。 ◇ *I went back to visit my old school.* 我重访了母校。 ◇ *Old and Middle English* 古英语和中古英语 **6** 🔑 [only before noun] used to refer to sth that has been replaced by sth else（用于指称被替代的东西）原来的，原先的：*We had more room in our old house.* 我们原先的房子比较宽敞。 OPP **new** **7** 🔑 [only before noun] known for a long time 相识时间长的；结识久的：*She's an old friend of mine* (= I have known her for a

---

▼ **SYNONYMS 同义词辨析**

old

elderly • **aged** • **long-lived** • **mature**

These words all describe sb/sth that has lived for a long time or that usually lives for a long time. 以上各词均形容人年纪大、长寿或事物古老、持久。

old having lived for a long time; no longer young 指年老、年纪大：*She's getting old—she's 75 next year.* 她上年纪了，明年就 75 岁了。

elderly (*rather formal*) used as a polite word for 'old' * old 的委婉语，指年纪较大的、上了年纪的：*She is very busy caring for two elderly relatives.* 她在忙着照顾两个年老的亲戚。

aged (*formal*) very old 指年迈的、年老的：*Having aged relatives to stay in your house can be quite stressful.* 年迈的亲戚住在家里有时压力相当大。

long-lived having a long life; lasting for a long time 指寿命长的、长寿的、经久耐用的、持久的：*Everyone in my family is exceptionally long-lived.* 我们家每个人都特别长寿。

mature used as a polite or humorous way of saying that sb is no longer young 礼貌或幽默的说法，指某人已成年或不再年轻：*clothes for the mature woman* 成年妇女的服装

PATTERNS

- a(n) old/elderly/aged/long-lived/mature **man/woman**
- a(n) old/elderly/aged/mature **gentleman/lady/couple**

---

long time). 她是我的一个老朋友。◇ *We're old rivals.* 我们是老对头。➲ COMPARE RECENT
• **GOOD OLD/POOR OLD** 可爱；可怜 **8** [only before noun] (*informal*) used to show affection or a lack of respect（表示亲昵或不敬）: ***Good old** Dad!* 可爱的老爸！◇ *You **poor old** thing!* 你这可怜的家伙！◇ *I hate her, the silly old cow!* 我恨她，那个笨蛋老女人！

IDM **'any old how** (*informal*) in a careless or untidy way 随便地；凌乱地：*The books were piled up all over the floor any old how.* 地板上书堆得乱七八糟的，到处都是。**'any old…** (*informal*) any item of the type mentioned (used when it is not important which particular item is chosen) 任何一个；随便哪个：*Any old room would have done.* 随便哪间屋子都行。**as old as the 'hills** very old; ancient 古老的；悠久的 ➲ MORE LIKE THIS 14, page R26 **for 'old times' sake** if you do sth **for old times' sake**, you do it because it is connected with sth good that happened to you in the past 看在旧日的情分上；念及老交情 **the 'good/'bad old days** an earlier period of time in your life or in history that is seen as better/worse than the present 往昔的好 / 苦日子：*That was in the bad old days of rampant inflation.* 那是在物价飞涨、生活艰难的往昔。**of 'old** (*formal* or *literary*) in or since past times 在往昔；从以前：*in days of old* 从前 ◇ *We know him of old* (= we have known him for a long time). 我们认识他很久了。**old 'boy, 'chap, 'man, etc.** (*old-fashioned, BrE, informal*) used by older men of the middle and upper classes as a friendly way of addressing another man（中上阶层男子对其他男子的友好称呼）老兄，伙计，哥们儿 **old enough to be sb's 'father/'mother** (*disapproving*) very much older than sb (especially used to suggest that a romantic or sexual relationship between the two people is not appropriate) 论年龄足以当某人的爹 / 娘（尤指双方在爱情或性关系方面不相配）**old enough to know 'better** old enough to behave in a more sensible way than you actually did 已长大，该懂事了 **(have) an old head on young 'shoulders** used to describe a young person who acts in a more sensible way than you would expect for a person of their age 年轻老练；少年老成 **the (ˌsame) old 'story** what usually happens 惯常的事情；（仍旧是）那么回事：*It's the same old story of a badly managed project with inadequate funding.* 又是一桩资金短缺、经营不善的老故事。**an old 'wives' tale** (*disapproving*) an old idea or belief that has been proved not to be scientific 不经之谈；不科学的陈腐思想 **one of the 'old school** an old-fashioned person who likes to do things as they were done in the past 守旧的人；保守派人物 ➲ SEE ALSO OLD SCHOOL ➲ MORE AT CHIP *n.*, FOOL *n.*, GRAND *adj.*, HEAVE-HO, HIGH *adj.*, MONEY, RIPE, SETTLE *v.*, TEACH, TOUGH *adj.*, TRICK *n.*

▼ **WHICH WORD?** 词语辨析

older / elder

• The usual comparative and superlative forms of **old** are **older** and **oldest**. * old 的比较级和最高级通常为 older 和 oldest：*My brother is older than me.* 我哥哥比我大。◇ *The palace is the oldest building in the city.* 这宫殿是城里最古老的建筑。In *BrE* you can also use **elder** and **eldest** when comparing the ages of people, especially members of the same family, although these words are not common in speech now. As adjectives they are only used before a noun and you cannot say 'elder than'. 在英式英语中，比较人的年龄，尤其是家庭成员的年龄时亦可用 elder 和 eldest，不过这种说法在口语中已不常见；作形容词时它们只能用于名词前，而且不说 elder than：*my older/elder sister* 我的姐姐 ◇ *the elder/older of their two children* 他们的两个孩子中大的一个 ◇ *I'm the eldest/oldest in the family.* 我是家中的老大。

ˌold 'age *noun* [U] the time of your life when you are old 老年；暮年：*Old age can bring many problems.* 人老麻烦多。◇ *He lived alone **in his old age**.* 他孑然一身度过晚年。➲ COLLOCATIONS AT AGE

ˌold-age 'pension *noun* (*BrE, CanE*) a regular income paid by the state to people above a particular age 养老金；老年抚恤金

ˌold-age 'pensioner *noun* (*abbr.* **OAP**) (*BrE, becoming old-fashioned, CanE*) a person who receives an old-age pension 领养老金者 ➲ SEE ALSO SENIOR CITIZEN

ˌold age se'curity *noun* [U] (*abbr.* **OAS**) (*CanE*) a regular income paid by the government to people above the age of 65（加拿大政府给 65 岁以上的人定期发放的）老年保障金，养老金

the Old Bai·ley /ˌəʊld ˈbeɪli; *NAmE* ˌoʊld/ *noun* [sing.] the main criminal court in London 老贝利（伦敦中央刑事法院）

ˌold 'bat *noun* (*BrE, informal, disapproving*) a silly or annoying old person 愚蠢的老人；傻老帽儿

the ˌOld 'Bill *noun* [sing.] (*BrE, informal*) the police 警方

old boy *noun* **1** **'old boy** a man who used to be a student at a particular school, usually a private one（通常指私立学校的）校友 **2** **ˌold 'boy** (*informal, especially BrE*) an old man 老人；老头：*The old boy next door has died.* 隔壁的老头去世了。➲ SEE ALSO OLD GIRL

IDM **the ˌold 'boy network** (*BrE, informal*) the practice of men who went to the same school using their influence to help each other at work or socially 校友关系网；老同学间的互相关照

ˌold 'buffer *noun* (*BrE, old-fashioned*) = BUFFER (4)

the 'old country *noun* [sing.] the country where you were born, especially when you have left it to live somewhere else 祖国；故国

ˌold 'dear *noun* (*BrE, informal*) an old woman 老太太；老婆婆

olde /əʊld; ˈəʊldi; *NAmE* oʊld; ˈoʊldi/ *adj.* [only before noun] (*old use*) a way of spelling 'old' that was used in the past and is now sometimes used in names and advertisements to give the impression that sth is traditional（old 的旧式拼法，现有时用于名称或广告，以使人感到某物是传统的）：*a pub that tries to recreate the flavour of olde England* 一家力图重现古英格兰风情的酒馆

olden /ˈəʊldən; *NAmE* ˈoʊldən/ *adj.* [only before noun] existing a long time ago in the past 古老的；悠久的：*What was life like **in the olden days**, Gran?* 从前的生活是什么样的，奶奶？

ˌOld 'English (*also* **ˌAnglo-'Saxon**) *noun* [U] the English language before about 1150, which is very different from modern English 古英语（约公元 1150 年前的英语，与现代英语差异很大）

ˌOld ˌEnglish 'sheepdog *noun* a very large dog with very long grey and white hair 英格兰牧羊犬

ˌold-e'stablished *adj.* [only before noun] that has existed for a long time 年代久远的；古老的；悠久的；固有的

olde worlde /ˌəʊldi ˈwɜːldi; *NAmE* ˌoʊldi ˈwɜːrldi/ *adj.* [usually before noun] (*BrE, humorous*) (of a place or its atmosphere 地方或其气氛) trying deliberately to seem old-fashioned（故意显得）古色古香的，古朴的：*the olde worlde atmosphere of the tea room with its log fire* 壁炉中燃烧着木柴的茶室的古朴气氛

ˌold-'fashioned *adj.* (*sometimes disapproving*) **1** not modern; no longer fashionable 陈旧的；过时的；不时髦的 SYN **dated**: *old-fashioned clothes/styles/methods/equipment* 过时的衣服 / 式样 / 方法 / 设备 ➲ COMPARE FASHIONABLE **2** (of a person 人) believing in old or traditional ways; having traditional ideas 保守的；守旧的；迂腐的：*My parents are old-fashioned about relationships and marriage.* 我父母对男女关系和婚姻问题思想保守得很。

ˌold 'flame *noun* a former lover 旧情人：*She met an old flame at the party.* 她在聚会上遇到了旧情郎。

O

old girl *noun* **1 'old girl** (*BrE*) a woman who used to be a student at a particular school, usually a private one（通常指私立学校的）女校友 **2 ˌold 'girl** (*informal, especially BrE*) an old woman 老婆婆；老太太：*The old girl next door has died.* 隔壁的老太太去世了。

ˌOld 'Glory *noun* (*NAmE*) a name for the flag of the US 古老的荣耀（指美国国旗）；星条旗

the ˌold 'guard *noun* [sing.+sing./pl. v.] the original members of a group or an organization, who are often against change（守旧的）元老派；保守派；卫道士

ˌold 'hand *noun* ~ **(at sth/at doing sth)** a person with a lot of experience and skill in a particular activity 老手；经验丰富的人；在行的人：*She's an old hand at dealing with the press.* 她是与新闻界打交道的老手。

ˌold 'hat *noun* [U] something that is old-fashioned and no longer interesting 陈腐的事物；过时的东西：*Today's hits rapidly become old hat.* 今日红极一时的东西，很快就会过时。

oldie /'əʊldi; *NAmE* 'oʊldi/ *noun* (*informal*) an old person or thing 老人；旧事物 ➲SEE ALSO GOLDEN OLDIE

old·ish /'əʊldɪʃ; *NAmE* 'oʊldɪʃ/ *adj.* fairly old 相当老的；相当旧的

ˌold 'lady *noun* (*informal*) a person's wife or mother 老婆；老妈

ˌold 'lag *noun* (*BrE, informal*) a person who has been in prison many times 多次坐牢的人；惯犯

ˌold 'maid *noun* (*old-fashioned, disapproving*) a woman who has never married and is now no longer young 老姑娘；老处女

ˌold 'man *noun* (*informal*) a person's husband or father 老公；老爸

ˌold 'master *noun* **1** a famous painter, especially of the 13th–17th centuries in Europe（尤指欧洲 13 至 17 世纪的）绘画大师，名画家 **2** a picture painted by an old master 绘画大师的作品

ˌOld 'Nick *noun* (*old-fashioned, humorous*) the DEVIL 魔王；撒旦

ˌold 'people's home (*BrE*) (*also* **re'tirement home** *NAmE, BrE*) *noun* a place where old people live and are cared for 养老院；敬老院

'old school *adj.* old-fashioned or traditional 古老的；古旧的；传统的

ˌold school 'tie *noun* (*BrE*) **1** [C] a tie worn by former students of a particular school, especially a private one（尤指私立学校的）校友领带 **2 the old school tie** [sing.] used to refer to the fact of men who went to the same private school using their influence to help each other at work or socially, and to the traditional attitudes they share（私立学校校友间的）相互关照，校友情谊，共有的思想观念

ˌold 'stager *noun* (*informal*) a person who has great experience in a particular activity 老手；老资格

old·ster /'əʊldstə(r); *NAmE* 'oʊld-/ *noun* (*informal*) an old person 老人；老者

'old-style *adj.* [only before noun] typical of past fashions or times 老派的；陈腐的；迂腐的：*an old-style dress shop* 老派服装店 ◇ *old-style politics* 陈旧的政治观点

the ˌOld 'Testament *noun* [sing.] the first part of the Bible, that tells the history of the Jews, their beliefs and their relationship with God before the birth of Christ《〈圣经〉旧约》 ➲COMPARE NEW TESTAMENT

'old-time *adj.* [only before noun] typical of the past 昔日的；过去的；旧式的：*old-time dancing* 古典舞蹈

ˌold-'timer *noun* **1** a person who has been connected with a club or an organization, or who has lived in a place, for a long time 老会员；老成员；老居民；老资格的人 SYN **veteran** **2** (*NAmE*) an old man 老人

ˌold 'woman *noun* **1** (*informal, especially BrE*) a person's wife or mother 老婆；老妈 **2** (*BrE, disapproving*) a man who worries too much about things that are not important 像管家婆似的男人

the ˌOld 'World *noun* [sing.] Europe, Asia and Africa 旧世界（指欧洲、亚洲和非洲） ➲COMPARE NEW WORLD

'old-world *adj.* [only before noun] (*approving*) belonging to past times; not modern 古式的；非现代的：*an old-world hotel with character and charm* 一家风格典雅的古式饭店

ole /əʊl; *NAmE* oʊl/ *adj.* used in written English to represent how some people say the word 'old'（用于书面英语，代表有些人说 old 一词的方式）老的：*My ole man used to work there.* 我老爸曾在那儿做事。

olé /əʊ'leɪ; *NAmE* oʊ'leɪ/ *exclamation* (*from Spanish, informal*) used for showing approval or happiness（表示赞成或高兴）好哇，哇

ole·agin·ous /ˌəʊli'ædʒɪnəs; *NAmE* ˌoʊ-/ *adj.* (*formal*) covered in or containing a lot of oil or GREASE 涂油脂的；油腻的；油质的

ole·an·der /ˌəʊli'ændə(r); *NAmE* ˌoʊli-/ *noun* [C, U] a Mediterranean bush or tree with white, pink or red flowers and long pointed thick leaves 夹竹桃

Ol·es·tra™ /ɒ'lestrə; *NAmE* oʊ'l-/ *noun* [U] a substance which is used instead of fat in some foods 奥利斯特拉油（食物油脂替代品）

'O level (*also* **'ordinary level**) *noun* [C, U] (in England and Wales in the past) an exam in a particular subject, at a lower level than A LEVEL, usually taken at the age of 16. In 1988 it was replaced by the GCSE. 普通证书考试（过去英格兰、威尔士对某科目的考试，低于高级证书考试，通常在 16 岁时参加。1988 年被普通中等教育证书 (GCSE) 取代）：*O level French* 法语普通证书考试 ◇ *She took six subjects at O level.* 她参加了六门课程的普通证书考试。◇ *He's got an O level in Russian.* 他通过了俄语普通证书考试。➲ COMPARE GCE

ol·fac·tory /ɒl'fæktəri; *NAmE* ɑːl-; oʊl-/ *adj.* [only before noun] (*specialist*) connected with the sense of smell 嗅觉的：*olfactory cells/nerves/organs* 嗅觉细胞 / 神经 / 器官

oli·garch /'ɒlɪɡɑːk; *NAmE* 'ɑːləɡɑːrk/ *noun* **1** a member of an oligarchy 寡头政治家；寡头统治集团成员 **2** an extremely rich and powerful person, especially a Russian who became rich in business after the end of the former Soviet Union 大亨（尤指苏联解体后发迹的俄罗斯人）

oli·garchy /'ɒlɪɡɑːki; *NAmE* 'ɑːləɡɑːrki/ *noun* (*pl.* **-ies**) **1** [U] a form of government in which only a small group of people hold all the power 寡头政治 **2** [C+sing./pl. v.] the people who hold power in an oligarchy 寡头统治集团 **3** [C] a country governed by an oligarchy 寡头统治的国家

olive /'ɒlɪv; *NAmE* 'ɑːlɪv/ *noun, adj.*

■ *noun* **1** [C] a small green or black fruit with a strong taste, used in cooking and for its oil 油橄榄；齐墩果；橄榄 **2** (*also* **'olive tree**) [C] a tree on which olives grow 橄榄树：*olive groves* 橄榄树丛 **3** (*also* **ˌolive 'green**) [U] a yellowish-green colour 橄榄绿 ➲MORE LIKE THIS 15, page R26

■ *adj.* **1** (*also* **ˌolive-'green**) yellowish-green in colour 橄榄绿的 **2** (of skin 皮肤) yellowish-brown in colour 黄褐色的；淡褐色的：*an olive complexion* 浅褐色的面容

'olive branch *noun* [usually sing.] a symbol of peace; sth you say or do to show that you wish to make peace with sb 橄榄枝；和平的象征：*Management is holding out an olive branch to the strikers.* 资方向罢工者伸出了橄榄枝。

ˌolive 'drab *noun* [U] a dull green colour, used in some military uniforms 草绿色，草黄色，灰橄榄色（用于军服）

ˌolive 'oil *noun* [U] oil produced from OLIVES, used in cooking and on salad 橄榄油（用于烹饪和凉拌色拉）➲ SEE ALSO EXTRA VIRGIN

ollie /ˈɒli; *NAmE* ˈɑːli/ *noun* (in SKATEBOARDING 滑板运动) a jump that is done by pushing one foot down hard on the back of the board 翻骊，豚跳（一脚猛踩滑板后部的带板起跳动作） ➲ COMPARE NOLLIE

ology /ˈɒlədʒi; *NAmE* ˈɑːl-/ *noun* (*pl.* **-ies**) (*informal, humorous*) a subject of study 学科：*They come here with their ologies knowing nothing about life.* 他们带着自己的种种学问来到这里，对人生却一无所知。

-ology, **-logy** *combining form* (in nouns 构成名词) **1** a subject of study 学科；科目：*sociology* 社会学 ◇ *genealogy* 宗谱学 **2** a characteristic of speech or writing 用语特征；写作特点：*phraseology* 措辞 ◇ *trilogy* 三部曲 ▶ **-ological**, **-logical** (*also* **-ologic**, **-logic**) (in adjectives 构成形容词)：*pathological* 病理学的 **-ologist**, **-logist** (in nouns 构成名词)：*biologist* 生物学家

Olym·piad /əˈlɪmpiæd/ *noun* **1** an occasion when the modern Olympic games are held 奥林匹克运动会；奥运会：*The 26th Olympiad took place in Atlanta, Georgia.* 第 26 届奥运会是在佐治亚州的亚特兰大举办的。 **2** an international competition in a particular subject, especially a science 奥林匹克大赛（常用于科学有关的国际比赛）：*the 14th International Physics Olympiad* 第 14 届国际奥林匹克物理竞赛

Olym·pian /əˈlɪmpiən/ *noun, adj.* (*formal*)
- ■ ***noun*** a person who takes part or has taken part in the Olympic Games 奥林匹克运动员：*the greatest Olympian of all time* 历史上最伟大的奥运选手
- ■ ***adj.*** **1** [only before noun] relating to the ancient or modern Olympic games 奥林匹克运动会的：*Olympian gymnasts* 奥林匹克体操运动员 **2** like a god; powerful and impressive 似神的；威严的；超凡的

Olym·pic /əˈlɪmpɪk/ *adj.* [only before noun] connected with the Olympic Games 奥林匹克运动会的：*an Olympic athlete/medallist* 奥林匹克运动员 / 奖牌获得者

the Oˌlympic ˈGames (*also* **the Olym·pics**) *noun* [pl.] an international sports festival held every four years in a different country 奥林匹克运动会；奥运会：*the London Olympics, held in 2012* * 2012 年在伦敦举行的奥林匹克运动会

om·buds·man /ˈɒmbʊdzmən; -mæn; *NAmE* ˈɑːm-/ *noun* (*pl.* **-men** /-mən; -men/) an official whose job is to examine and report on complaints made by ordinary people about companies, the government or public authorities 政府巡查员（政府处理民众诉愿的官员）

omega /ˈəʊmɪɡə; *NAmE* oʊˈmeɡə/ *noun* the last letter of the Greek alphabet (Ω, ω) 希腊字母表的最后一个字母

ˌOmega-ˈ3 /ˌəʊmɪɡə ˈθriː; *NAmE* oʊˌmeɪɡə/ (*also* **ˌOmega-3 fatty ˈacid**) *noun* any of a group of acids, found mainly in fish oils, that many people think are important for human health * ω-3 脂肪酸（鱼油中多含，据信有利于人体健康）

om·elette (*NAmE also* **om·elet**) /ˈɒmlət; *NAmE* ˈɑːm-/ *noun* a hot dish of eggs mixed together and fried, often with cheese, meat, vegetables, etc. added 煎蛋卷，摊鸡蛋，鸡蛋饼（常加入奶酪、肉和蔬菜等）：*a cheese and mushroom omelette* 奶酪、蘑菇蛋饼

IDM **you can't make an ˌomelette without breaking ˈeggs** (*saying*) you cannot achieve sth important without causing a few small problems 不打破鸡蛋就做不成蛋饼；不花代价就难成大事

omen /ˈəʊmən; *NAmE* ˈoʊ-/ *noun* a sign of what is going to happen in the future 预兆；前兆；征兆 SYN **portent**：*a good/bad omen* 吉祥的 / 不祥的预兆 ◇ *an omen of death/disaster* 死亡 / 灾难的征兆 ◇ **~ for sth** *The omens for their future success are not good.* 他们未来成功的预兆不祥。

omena /əʊˈmemə; *NAmE* oʊ-/ *noun* [C, U] (*pl.* **omena**) (*EAfrE*) small fish that are dried to preserve them, and often fried and then cooked with tomatoes and milk to make a STEW 小鱼干（常炸过后与番茄和牛奶同煮，做成炖菜）

OMG *abbr.* (especially in TEXT MESSAGES, emails, etc.) oh my God (used to express surprise, excitement, etc.) 我的天啊（全写为 oh my God，尤用于短信、电邮等，表示惊讶、兴奋等）：*OMG—I can't believe your parents are letting you go to Thailand on your own!* 天啊，我无法相信你父母会让你独自一人去泰国！

omi·cron /əʊˈmaɪkrɒn; *NAmE* ˈɑːməkrɑːn/ *noun* the 15th letter of the Greek alphabet (Ο, ο) 希腊字母表的第 15 个字母

omi·god /ˌəʊmaɪˈɡɒd; *NAmE* ˌoʊmaɪˈɡɑːd/ *exclamation* (*also* **omigosh** /ˌəʊmaɪˈɡɒʃ; *NAmE* ˌoʊmaɪˈɡɑːʃ/) (*informal*) used to show that you are shocked or cannot believe sth（表示震惊或难以置信）天啊：*Omigod, we're going out of business!* 天啊，我们要倒闭了！ ◇ *Omigod, is that really his wife?* 天啊，那真是他妻子吗？

om·in·ous /ˈɒmɪnəs; *NAmE* ˈɑːm-/ *adj.* suggesting that sth bad is going to happen in the future 不祥的；恶兆的；不吉利的 SYN **foreboding**：*There were ominous dark clouds gathering overhead.* 不祥的黑云在头顶上汇聚。◇ *She picked up the phone but there was an ominous silence at the other end.* 她拿起电话，但对方只有不祥的沉默。▶ **om·in·ous·ly** *adv.*

omis·sion /əˈmɪʃn/ *noun* (*formal*) **1** [U] **~ (from sth)** the act of not including sb/sth or not doing sth; the fact of not being included/done 省略；删除；免除：*Everyone was surprised at her omission from the squad.* 她未入选该小组使大家感到惊讶。◇ *The play was shortened by the omission of two scenes.* 此剧删减了两场戏。◇ *sins of omission* (= not doing things that should be done) 渎职罪 **2** [C] a thing that has not been included or done 遗漏；疏忽：*There were a number of errors and omissions in the article.* 这篇文章中有多处错误和疏漏。

omit /əˈmɪt/ *verb* (**-tt-**) (*formal*) **1** to not include sth/sb, either deliberately or because you have forgotten it/them 删除；忽略；漏掉；遗漏 SYN **leave sb/sth out**：**~ sth/sb** *If you are a student, you can omit questions 16–18.* 学生可以免答 16–18 题。◇ **~ sth/sb from sth** *People were surprised that Smith was omitted from the team.* 人们感到惊讶，史密斯竟未入选该队。 **2 ~ to do sth** to not do or fail to do sth 不做；未能做：*She omitted to mention that they were staying the night.* 她没说他们当晚要留宿的事。

omni- /ˈɒmnɪ; *NAmE* ˈɑːmnɪ/ *combining form* (in nouns, adjectives and adverbs 构成名词、形容词和副词) of all things; in all ways or places 总；全部；遍：*omnivore* 杂食动物 ◇ *omnipresent* 无所不在的

omni·bus /ˈɒmnɪbəs; *NAmE* ˈɑːm-/ *noun, adj.*
- ■ ***noun*** **1** (*BrE*) a television or radio programme that combines several recent programmes in a series（广播、电视）综合节目：*the 90-minute Sunday omnibus edition* * 90 分钟节目的星期天综合版 **2** a large book that contains a number of books, for example novels by the same author（若干种作品的）汇编，选集 **3** (*old-fashioned*) a bus 公共汽车
- ■ ***adj.*** (*NAmE*) including many things or different types of thing 综合性的；选编的：*an omnibus law*（含多项法令的）综合法令

omni·dir·ec·tion·al /ˌɒmnɪdəˈrekʃənl; -dɪˈr-; -daɪˈr-; *NAmE* ˌɑːmnɪ-/ *adj.* (*specialist*) receiving or sending signals in all directions（接收或发射信号）全向的：*an omnidirectional microphone* 全向传声器

om·nipo·tent /ɒmˈnɪpətənt; *NAmE* ɑːm-/ *adj.* (*formal*) having total power; able to do anything 万能的；全能的；无所不能的：*an omnipotent God* 全能的上帝 ▶ **om·nipo·tence** /-təns/ *noun* [U]：*the omnipotence of God* 上帝的全能

omni·pres·ent /ˌɒmnɪˈpreznt; *NAmE* ˌɑːm-/ *adj.* (*formal*) present everywhere 无所不在的；遍及各处的：*These days the media are omnipresent.* 现在新闻媒体无处不在。▶ **omni·pres·ence** /ˌɒmnɪˈprezns; *NAmE* ˌɑːm-/ *noun* [U]

om·nis·ci·ent /ɒmˈnɪsiənt; *NAmE* ɑːm-/ *adj.* (*formal*) knowing everything 无所不知的；全知全能的；博闻广识的：*The novel has an omniscient narrator.* 这部小说采用全知叙述方式。▶ **om·nis·ci·ence** /-siəns/ *noun* [U]

omni·vore /ˈɒmnɪvɔː(r); *NAmE* ˈɑːm-/ *noun* an animal or a person that eats all types of food, especially both plants and meat 杂食动物；杂食的人 ➲ COMPARE CARNIVORE, HERBIVORE, INSECTIVORE

om·niv·or·ous /ɒmˈnɪvərəs; *NAmE* ɑːm-/ *adj.* **1** (*specialist*) eating all types of food, especially both plants and meat 杂食的；（尤指）动植物都吃的 ➲ COMPARE CARNIVOROUS at CARNIVORE, HERBIVOROUS at HERBIVORE **2** (*formal*) having wide interests in a particular area or activity 兴趣广泛的：*She has always been an omnivorous reader.* 她一向阅读兴趣广泛。

on /ɒn; *NAmE* ɑːn; ɔːn/ *prep., adv.*

■ *prep.* HELP For the special uses of **on** in phrasal verbs, look at the entries for the verbs. For example **turn on sb** is in the phrasal verb section at **turn**. * on 在短语动词中的特殊用法见有关动词词条。如 turn on sb 在词条 turn 的短语动词部分。 **1** in or into a position covering, touching or forming part of a surface（覆盖、附着）在…上（意指接触物体表面或构成物体表面的一部分）：*a picture on a wall* 墙上的画 ◇ *There's a mark on your skirt.* 你裙子上有一块污斑。◇ *the diagram on page 5* 第 5 页上的图解 ◇ *Put it down on the table.* 把它放在桌子上。◇ *He had been hit on the head.* 他被打中了脑袋。◇ *She climbed on to the bed.* 她爬上了床。HELP This could also be written 此句亦可写作：*onto the bed* **2** supported by sb/sth 由…支撑着：*She was standing on one foot.* 她单脚站立着。◇ *Try lying on your back.* 试着仰卧。◇ *Hang your coat on that hook.* 把衣服挂在衣钩上。 **3** used to show a means of transport 在（交通工具）上：*He was on the plane from New York.* 他在从纽约来的飞机上。◇ *to travel on the bus/tube/coach* 乘公共汽车 / 地铁 / 长途汽车 ◇ *I came on my bike.* 我骑自行车来的。◇ *a woman on horseback* 骑马的女郎 **4** used to show a day or date 在（某一天）：*He came on Sunday.* 他是星期天来的。◇ *We meet on Tuesdays.* 我们每星期二见面。◇ *on May the first/the first of May* 在五月一日 ◇ *on the evening of May the first* 在五月一日的晚上 ◇ *on one occasion* 曾经有一次 ◇ *on your birthday* 在你生日那天 **5** immediately after sth 就在…之后；一…就：*On arriving home I discovered they had gone.* 我一到家就发现他们已经离开了。◇ *Please report to reception on arrival.* 到达后请立即到接待处报到。◇ *There was a letter waiting for him on his return.* 他一回来就有一封信在等着他看。 **6** about sth/sb 关于（事或人）：*a book on South Africa* 一本关于南非的书 ◇ *She tested us on irregular verbs.* 她考了我们的不规则动词。 **7** being carried by sb; in the possession of sb （身上）带着；有：*Have you got any money on you?* 你带钱了没有？ **8** used to show that sb belongs to a group or an organization 为（某团体或组织）的一员：*to be on the committee/staff/jury/panel* 为委员会 / 全体职员 / 陪审团 / 专家组的成员 ◇ *Whose side are you on* (= which of two or more different views do you support)? 你支持哪一方的观点？ **9** eating or drinking sth; using a drug or a medicine regularly 吃；喝；按时服用（药物）：*He lived on a diet of junk food.* 他把垃圾食品当饭吃。◇ *The doctor put me on antibiotics.* 医生要我服用抗生素。 **10** used to show direction（表示方向）在，向，对：*on the left/right* 在左边 / 右边 ◇ *He turned his back on us.* 他转过身去背对着我们。 **11** at or near a place 在，接近（某地）：*a town on the coast* 沿海的城镇 ◇ *a house on the Thames* 泰晤士河畔的房子 ◇ *We lived on an estate.* 我们住在一处庄园上。 **12** used to show the basis or reason for sth 根据；由于：*a story based on fact* 基于事实的小说 ◇ *On their advice I applied for the job.* 我听从他们的建议申请了这份工作。 **13** paid for by sth 以…支付；由…支付：*to live on a pension/a student grant* 靠养老金 / 助学金生活 ◇ *to be on a low wage* 挣低工资 ◇ *You can't feed a family on £50 a week.* 你无法靠每周 50 英镑养活一家人。◇ *Drinks are* **on me** (= I am paying). 饮料钱由我付。 **14** by means of sth; using sth 通过；使用；借助于：*She played a tune on her guitar.* 她用她的吉他弹了一支曲子。◇ *The information is available on the Internet.* 从互联网上可以得到这个信息。◇ *We spoke on the phone.* 我们通过电话谈了谈。◇ *What's on TV?* 电视上有什么节目？◇ *The programme's on Channel 4.* 这个节目在 4 频道。 **15** used with some nouns or adjectives to say who or what is affected by sth（与某些名词或形容词连用，表示影响到）：*a ban on smoking* 对吸烟的禁令 ◇ *He's hard on his kids.* 他对自己的孩子很严厉。◇ *Go easy on the mayo!* (= do not take/give me too much) 少放一点蛋黄酱！ **16** compared with sb/sth 与…相比：*Sales are up on last year.* 销售量比去年增长了。 **17** used to describe an activity or a state（用于说明活动或状态）：*to be on business/holiday/vacation* 在工作 / 度假中 ◇ *The book is currently on loan.* 该书已借出。 **18** used when giving a telephone number （用于提供电话号码）：*You can get me on 020 7946 0887.* 你找我可以拨打 020 7946 0887。◇ *She's on extension 2401.* 她的分机号是 2401。

■ *adv.* HELP For the special uses of **on** in phrasal verbs, look at the entries for the verbs. For example **get on** is in the phrasal verb section at **get**. * on 在短语动词中的特殊用法见有关动词词条。如 get on 在词条 get 的短语动词部分。 **1** used to show that sth continues （表示持续性）：*He worked on without a break.* 他毫不停歇地继续工作。◇ *If you like a good story, read on.* 欲知故事的趣味所在，请往下读。 **2** used to show that sb/sth moves or is sent forward 向前（移动）：*She stopped for a moment, then walked on.* 她停了一会儿，然后又向前走。◇ *Keep straight on for the beach.* 一直向前走到海滩。◇ *From then on he never trusted her again.* 从那时起，他再也不信任她了。◇ *Please send the letter on to my new address.* 请把信件转寄到我的新地址。 **3** on sb's body; being worn 穿在身上；穿着；戴着：*Put your coat on.* 把外衣穿上。◇ *I didn't have my glasses on.* 我没戴眼镜。◇ *What did she have on* (= what was she wearing)? 她穿着什么衣服？ **4** covering, touching or forming part of sth（表示覆盖、接触某物或成为某物的一部分）：*Make sure the lid is on.* 要注意盖上盖子。 **5** connected or operating; being used（表示已连接、处于工作状态或使用中）：*The lights were all on.* 灯都亮着。◇ *The TV is always on in their house.* 他们家的电视总是开着。◇ *We were without electricity for three hours but it's on again now.* 我们停电三个小时了，不过现在又来电了。 **6** happening （表示发生）：*There was a war on at the time.* 当时正值战争。◇ *What's on at the movies?* 电影院在上演什么片子？◇ *The band are on* (= performing) *in ten minutes.* 乐队再过十分钟开始演奏。 **7** planned to take place in the future（预先安排的事）将发生：*The game is still on* (= it has not been cancelled). 比赛仍将举行。◇ *I don't think we've got anything on this weekend.* 我想这个周末我们没安排活动。◇ *I'm sorry we can't come—we've got* **a lot on**. 很抱歉我们去不了，我们安排得太满了。 **8** on duty; working 值班；执行任务中：*I'm on now till 8 tomorrow morning.* 我正在值班，要值到明早 8 点钟。 **9** in or into a vehicle 登上（车辆）：*The bus stopped and four people got on.* 公共汽车停下来，四个人上了车。◇ *They hurried on to the plane.* 他们匆忙登上了飞机。➲ SEE ALSO ONTO

IDM **be 'on about sth** (*informal*) to talk about sth; to mean sth 谈论（某事）；有…的意思：*I didn't know what he was on about. It didn't make sense.* 我不知道他说的是什么，他说得不清不楚的。 **be/go/keep 'on about sth** (*informal, disapproving*) to talk in a boring or complaining way about sth 抱怨；唠叨；发牢骚：*Stop keeping on about it!* 别再唠叨那件事了！ **be/go/keep 'on at sb (to do sth)** (*informal, disapproving*) to keep asking or telling sb sth so that they become annoyed or tired（对某人）絮叨；说（或问）得令人生厌：*He was on at me again to lend him money.* 他又来缠着我借钱给他。 **be 'on for sth** (*informal*) to want to do sth 想要做某事：*Is anyone on for a drink after work?* 有人想下班后喝一杯吗？ **it isn't 'on** (*informal*) used to say that sth is not acceptable 不行；没门儿 **,on and 'on** without stopping; continuously 连续不停地；持续地：*She went on and on about her trip.* 她没完没了地谈她的旅行。 **what are you, etc. 'on?** (*informal*) used when you are very surprised at sb's behaviour and are suggesting that they are acting in a similar way to sb using drugs 你鬼迷心窍了吧；你吃错药了吧 **you're 'on** (*informal*) used when you are accepting a bet（用于接受打赌时）赌就赌吧 ➲ MORE AT OFF *adv.*

,on-'air *adj.* (in radio and television 用于广播及电视) being broadcast 正在播放：*She explains how she deals with*

on-air technical problems. 她解释了她是如何处理播放中的技术问题的。 OPP **off-air** IDM SEE AIR *n.*

onan·ism /ˈəʊnənɪzəm; *NAmE* ˈoʊ-/ *noun* [U] (*formal*) **1** = MASTURBATION **2** = COITUS INTERRUPTUS

ˌon-ˈboard *adj.* [only before noun] **1** on a ship, aircraft or vehicle 在船（或飞机、车）上的：*an on-board motor* 舷内发动机 **2** (*also* **onboard**) (*computing* 计) relating to, or controlled by, part of the main CIRCUIT BOARD 主板（控制）的；板上的：*a PC with onboard sound* 有板载声卡的个人电脑

ˌon-ˈcall [only before noun] (*especially NAmE*) (of a doctor, police officer, etc. 医生、警察等) available for work if necessary, especially in an emergency （尤指紧急情况下）随叫随到的：*on-call doctors* 随时应诊的医生 ➲ SEE ALSO CALL *n.*

once /wʌns/ *adv., conj.*

■ ***adv.*** **1** on one occasion only; one time 仅一次；一次：*I've only been there once.* 我只去过那里一次。◇ *He cleans his car* ***once a*** *week.* 他每周洗一次汽车。◇ *She only sees her parents* ***once every*** *six months.* 她每半年只探望一次父母。◇ (*informal*) *He only did it* ***the once.*** 这种事儿他仅仅干过一次。 **2** at some time in the past 曾；曾经：*I once met your mother.* 我曾经见过你母亲。◇ *He once lived in Zambia.* 他曾在赞比亚生活过。◇ *This book was famous once, but nobody reads it today.* 这本书曾名噪一时，但现在却无人问津。 **3** used in negative sentences and questions, and after *if* to mean 'ever' or 'at all'（用于否定句、疑问句和 if 后）曾，根本：*He never once offered to help.* 他从没有主动提出过帮忙。◇ *If she once decides to do something, you won't change her mind.* 她一旦决定干什么，谁也改变不了她的主意。

IDM **ˌall at ˈonce 1** suddenly 突然；骤然；忽然：*All at once she lost her temper.* 她突然大发脾气。 **2** all together; at the same time 一起；同时 SYN **simultaneously**：*I can't do everything all at once—you'll have to be patient.* 我不能万事一把抓呀。你可急不得。 **at ˈonce 1** immediately; without delay 立即；马上：*Come here at once!* 马上到这里来！ **2** at the same time 同时 SYN **simultaneously**：*Don't all speak at once!* 大家不要同时讲！◇ *I can't do two things at once.* 我不能同时做两件事。 **(just) for ˈonce | just this ˈonce** (*informal*) on this occasion (which is in contrast to what happens usually) 仅此一次（与通常情况对比而言）：*Just for once he arrived on time.* 只有这一次他按时到了。◇ *Can't you be nice to each other just this once?* 难道你们就不能彼此客气哪怕一次？ **going ˈonce, going ˈtwice, ˈsold** (*especially NAmE*) (*BrE also* **ˌgoing, ˌgoing, ˈgone**) said by an AUCTIONEER to show that an item has been sold（拍卖师用语）一次，二次，成交 **once aˈgain | once ˈmore** one more time; another time 再一次；再次：*Once again the train was late.* 火车又一次晚点了。◇ *Let me hear it just once more.* 让我再听一遍。 **once a…, always a…** used to say that sb cannot change（表示一个人不能改变）一次为…便永远是…：*Once an actor, always an actor.* 一朝从艺，永为艺人。 **once and for ˈall** now and for the last time; finally or completely 最终地；最后地；彻底地；一次了结地：*We need to settle this once and for all.* 我们需要把这事一次解决。 **ˌonce ˈbitten, ˌtwice ˈshy** (*saying*) after an unpleasant experience you are careful to avoid sth similar 一朝被蛇咬，十年怕井绳 **once in a blue ˈmoon** (*informal*) very rarely 极少地；难得地；破天荒地 **(every) ˌonce in a ˈwhile** occasionally 偶尔地；间或 **ˌonce or ˈtwice** a few times 一两次；几次：*I don't know her well, I've only met her once or twice.* 我跟她不很熟，我只见过她一两次。 **ˌonce too ˈoften** used to say that sb has done sth wrong or stupid again, and this time they will suffer because of it 侥幸难再：*You've tried that trick once too often.* 你故伎重施，可这次再逃不脱了。 **ˌonce upon a ˈtime** used, especially at the beginning of stories, to mean 'a long time in the past'（用于故事的开头）从前，很久以前：*Once upon a time there was a beautiful princess.* 从前，有一位美丽的公主。

■ ***conj.*** as soon as; when 一…就；一旦；当…时候：*We didn't know how we would cope once the money had gone.* 一旦钱花光了，我们就不知道该怎么办了。◇ *The water is fine once you're in!* 你一旦下了水，就会觉得水里挺舒适。

ˈonce-over *noun*

IDM **give sb/sth a/the ˈonce-over** (*informal*) **1** to look at sb/sth quickly to see what they or it are like 匆匆打量；随便看一眼 **2** to clean sth quickly 匆匆打扫：*She gave the room a quick once-over before the guests arrived.* 趁客人还没来，她匆匆把屋子打扫了一下。

on·col·ogy /ɒŋˈkɒlədʒi; *NAmE* ɑnˈkɑːl-/ *noun* [U] the scientific study of and treatment of TUMOURS in the body 肿瘤学 ▶ **on·colo·gist** /ɒŋˈkɒlədʒɪst; *NAmE* ɑːnˈkɑːl-/ *noun*

on·com·ing /ˈɒnkʌmɪŋ; *NAmE* ˈɑːn-; ˈɔːn-/ *adj.* [only before noun] coming towards you 迎面而来的；即将来临的 SYN **approaching**：*Always walk facing the oncoming traffic.* 走路一定要面向驶来的车辆。

ˈon-deˈmand *adj.* [only before noun] done or happening whenever sb asks 按需的；随选即行提供的：*The new network promises lightning-fast access to on-demand video.* 新的网络会以闪电般的速度接入视频点播。➲ SEE ALSO DEMAND *n.*, PRINT ON DEMAND

one /wʌn/ *number, det., pron.*

■ ***number, det.*** **1** the number 1 一：*Do you want one or two?* 你要一个还是两个？◇ *There's only room for one person.* 只有一个人的空间。◇ *One more, please!* 请再来一个！◇ *a one-bedroomed apartment* 一间卧室的公寓房 ◇ *I'll see you at one* (= one o'clock). 我一点钟见你。 **2** used in formal language or for emphasis before *hundred*, *thousand*, etc., or before a unit of measurement（正式用语或表示强调，用在 hundred、thousand 等或度量单位之前）一：*It cost one hundred and fifty pounds.* 那东西花了一百五十英镑。◇ *He lost by less than one second.* 他以不到一秒钟的差距输了比赛。 **3** used for emphasis to mean 'a single' or 'just one'（表示强调）单独一个，仅仅一个：*There's only one thing we can do.* 我们能做的只有一件事。 **4** a person or thing, especially when they are part of a group（尤指一组中的）一个人，一件事物：*One of my friends lives in Brighton.* 我有一个朋友住在布赖顿。◇ *One place I'd really like to visit is Bali.* 我真正想去的一个地方就是巴厘岛。 **5** used for emphasis to mean 'the only one' or 'the most important one'（表示强调）唯一的一个，最重要的一个：*He's the one person I can trust.* 他是我唯一可以信赖的人。◇ *Her one concern was for the health of her baby.* 她唯一操心的就是孩子的健康。◇ *It's the one thing I can't stand about him.* 这是我最不能容忍他的一件事。 **6** used when you are talking about a time in the past or the future, without actually saying which one（用于一般地谈论过去或将来的某个时间）：*I saw her one afternoon last week.* 我在上周的一个下午见到了她。◇ ***One day*** (= at some time in the future) *you'll understand.* 总有一天你会明白的。 **7** the same 同一个：*They all went off in one direction.* 他们都朝同一个方向走了。 **8** (*informal, especially NAmE*) used for emphasis instead of *a* or *an*（代替 a 或 an，表示强调）：*That was one hell of a game!* 那一场比赛简直不得了！◇ *She's one snappy dresser.* 她的穿着很入时。 **9** used with a person's name to show that the speaker does not know the person（与人名连用，表示说话人不认识的人）某一个 SYN **certain**：*He worked as an assistant to one Mr Ming.* 他给一位明先生当助手。

IDM **as ˈone** (*formal*) in agreement; all together 一致；一齐：*We spoke as one on this matter.* 在这个问题上我们口径一致。 **(be) at ˈone (with sb/sth)** (*formal*) to feel that you completely agree with sb/sth, or that you are part of sth 完全一致；是…的一部分：*a place where you can feel at one with nature* 一个能让你感到与大自然融为一体的地方 **for ˈone** used to emphasize that a particular person does sth and that you believe other people do too 就是其中之一（表达意见时用以加强语气）：*I, for one, would prefer to postpone the meeting.* 主张推迟会期的，我就是一个。 **get sth in ˈone** to understand or guess sth immediately 立即明白（或猜到） **get one ˈover (on) sb/sth** (*informal*) to get an advantage over sb/sth 占上风；胜过；占优势：*I'm not going to let them get one over on me!* 我决不让他们胜过我！ **go one ˈbetter (than sb/sth)** to do sth better than sb else or than you have done before 胜人一筹；（比自己过去）做得更好 SYN **outdo**：*She did well this*

O

year and next year she hopes to go one better. 今年她干得不错，她希望明年更上一层楼。 **in 'one** used to say that sb/sth has different roles, contains different things or is used for different purposes 集于一身（或一体）；多功能；多用途：*She's a mother and company director in one.* 她既是母亲又是公司董事。◇ *It's a public relations office, a press office and a private office* ***all in one.*** 那儿既是公关办公室，也是新闻办公室，又是私人办公室：三合一。➲ SEE ALSO ALL-IN-ONE **ˌone after aˈnother/the ˈother** first one person or thing, and then another, and then another, up to any number or amount 一个接一个地；陆续地；络绎不绝地：*The bills kept coming in, one after another.* 账单纷至沓来。 **ˌone and ˈall** (*old-fashioned, informal*) everyone 各位；大家；每个人：*Happy New Year to one and all!* 祝各位新年快乐！ **ˌone and ˈonly** used to emphasize that sb is famous 绝无仅有的；唯一的；有名的：*Here he is, the one and only Van Morrison!* 他来了，这盖世无双的范·莫里森！ **ˌone and the ˈsame** used for emphasis to mean 'the same'（表示强调）同一个：*I never realized Ruth Rendell and Barbara Vine were one and the same* (= the same person using two different names). 我从未意识到鲁思·兰德尔和芭芭拉·瓦因原来是同一个人。 **ˌone by ˈone** 🔑 separately and in order 逐个地；逐一地：*I went through the items on the list one by one.* 我逐条看了清单上的条目。 **ˌone or ˈtwo** 🔑 a few 一些；一二：*We've had one or two problems—nothing serious.* 我们有一些问题，不过没什么大不了的。 **ˌone ˈup (on sb)** having an advantage over sb 略胜一筹；强过（某人） **when you've seen, heard, etc. ˈone, you've seen, heard, etc. them ˈall** (*saying*) used to say that all types of the things mentioned are very similar 所有的…都大同小异；知其一便知其全部：*I don't like science fiction novels much. When you've read one, you've read them all.* 我不太喜欢科幻小说。读过一本，就知道其他的内容了。➲ MORE AT ALL *pron.*, MINORITY, SQUARE *n.*

O

■ *pron.* **1** 🔑 used to avoid repeating a noun, when you are referring to sb/sth that has already been mentioned, or that the person you are speaking to knows about（用来避免重复已提过的或是听者已知的事物的名称）：*I'd like an ice cream. Are you having one, too?* 我想买份冰淇淋，你也要一份吗？◇ *Our car's always breaking down. But we're getting a new one soon.* 我们的汽车老出毛病，但我们快要买新的了。◇ *She was wearing her new dress, the red one.* 她穿着她的新衣服，那件红的。◇ *My favourite band? Oh, that's a hard one* (= a hard question). 我最喜爱的乐队？哦，这可就难说了。◇ *What made you choose the one rather than the other?* 你怎么选了这个而不是那个？◇ (*BrE*) *How about those ones over there?* 你看那边那些怎么样？ **2** 🔑 used when you are identifying the person or thing you are talking about（用于辨别所谈的人或事）：*Our house is the one next to the school.* 我家的房子就是学校旁边的那座。◇ *The students who are most successful are usually the ones who come to all the classes.* 成绩最好的学生往往是出全勤的那些。 **3** 🔑 **~ of** a person or thing belonging to a particular group 其中的一个人（或事物）：*It's a present for one of my children.* 这是送给我的一个孩子的礼物。◇ *We think of you as one of the family.* 我们把你看作家中的一员。 **4** 🔑 a person of the type mentioned（某类人中的）一个：*10 o'clock is too late for the* ***little ones.*** 十点钟对那些小家伙来说就太晚了。◇ *He ached to be home with his* ***loved ones.*** 他渴望着回家与亲人团聚。◇ **~ to do sth** *She was never one to criticize.* 她是个从不爱批评人的人。 **5** 🔑 (*formal*) used to mean 'people in general' or 'I', when the speaker is referring to himself or herself 人们；本人：*One should never criticize if one is not sure of one's facts.* 一个人如果对自己掌握的事实没有把握，就绝不该随便批评。◇ *One gets the impression that they disapprove.* 据本人观察，他们不赞成。 HELP This use of **one** is very formal and now sounds old-fashioned. It is much more usual to use **you** for 'people in general' and **I** when you are talking about yourself. * one 的这一用法颇为正式，现在听起来过时了。现在更常用 you 指一般人，用 I 指自己。 **6 a ˈone** (*old-fashioned, especially BrE*) a person whose behaviour is amusing or surprising（举止）有趣的人，令人惊奇的人：*Oh, you are a one!* 哈！你这个活宝！ **7 the ~ about sth** the joke 玩笑；笑话：*Have you heard the one about the Englishman, the Irishman and the Scotsman?* 你听没听过那个关于英格兰人、爱尔兰人和苏格兰人的笑话？

IDM **be (a) one for (doing) sth** to be a person who enjoys sth, or who does sth often or well 乐于（或长于）做某事的人：*I've never been a great one for fish and chips.* 我一向对炸鱼薯条不热衷。

▼GRAMMAR POINT 语法说明

one / ones

One / ones is used to avoid repeating a countable noun, but there are some times when you should not use it, especially in formal speech or writing. * one / ones 用以避免重复可数名词；但有时候，尤其在正式谈话或书面语中，不应使用：

- After a possessive (*my, your, Mary's*, etc.), *some, any, both* or a number, unless it is used with an adjective. 在所有格（如 my、your、Mary's 等）、some、any、both 或数字之后不用 one / ones，除非与形容词连用：*'Did you get any postcards?' 'Yes, I bought four nice ones.'* "你买明信片了吗？" "买了，我买了四张很漂亮的。" ◇ ~~*I bought four ones.*~~
- It can be left out after superlatives, *this, that, these, those, either, neither, another, which*, etc. 在形容词最高级、this、that、these、those、either、neither、another、which 等词后可省略 one / ones：*'Here are the designs. Which (one) do you prefer?' 'I think that (one) looks the most original.'* "图样在这里。你喜欢哪（一）张？" "我认为那张看上去最有创意。"
- *These ones* and *those ones* are not used in *NAmE*, and are unusual in *BrE*. 美式英语中不用 these ones 和 those ones，英式英语也很少用：*Do you prefer these designs or those?* 你喜欢这些图样还是那些？
- It is never used to replace uncountable nouns and is unusual with abstract countable nouns: *The Scottish legal system is not the same as the English system*, is better than *…as the English one.* * one / ones 不用以替代不可数名词，与抽象可数名词连用也很少见：用 The Scottish legal system is not the same as the English system（苏格兰法制与英格兰法制不同）胜于用 … as the English one。

ˌone aˈnother 🔑 *pron.* **one another** is used when you are saying that each member of a group does sth to or for the other people in the group 互相：*We all try and help one another.* 我们都尽力互相帮助。◇ *I think we've learned a lot about one another in this session.* 我认为这一学年我们相互有了很多了解。

ˌone-armed ˈbandit *noun* = SLOT MACHINE

ˌone-horse ˈtown *noun* (*informal*) a small town with not many interesting things to do or places to go to 简朴小镇

ˌone-ˈliner *noun* (*informal*) a short joke or funny remark 小笑话；俏皮话；风趣的话：*He came out with some good one-liners.* 他讲了几个很有趣的小笑话。

ˌone-ˈman *adj.* [only before noun] done or controlled by one person only; suitable for one person 适于一个人的；由一个人操作的：*a* ***one-man show/business*** 独角戏；一个人经营的生意 ◇ *a one-man tent* 单人帐篷 ➲ SEE ALSO ONE-WOMAN

ˌone-man ˈband *noun* a street musician who plays several instruments at the same time 一人乐队（一个人同时演奏几种乐器的街头艺人）；(*figurative*) *He runs the business as a one-man band* (= one person does everything). 他是单枪匹马办企业。

one·ness /ˈwʌnnəs/ *noun* [U] (*formal*) the state of being completely united with sb/sth, or of being in complete agreement with sb 一体；一致；和谐：*a sense of oneness with the natural world* 与自然界的和谐感

ˌone-night ˈstand *noun* (*informal*) a sexual relationship that lasts for a single night; a person that sb has this relationship with 一夜情；露水情缘；曾与之有一夜情

的人：*I wanted it to be more than a one-night stand.* 我要的不只是一夜情缘。◇ *For her I was just a one-night stand.* 我不过是她玩一夜情的对象而已。

ˌone-ˈoff *adj., noun*
■ ***adj.*** (*BrE*) (*NAmE* **ˈone-shot**) [only before noun] made or happening only once and not regularly 一次性的；非经常的：*a one-off payment* 一次性付款
■ ***noun*** (*BrE*) a thing that is made or that happens only once and not regularly 绝无仅有的事物；仅出现一次的事物：*It was just a one-off; it won't happen again.* 这事绝无仅有，不会再发生了。

ˌone-on-ˈone *adj.* [usually before noun] (*NAmE*) = ONE-TO-ONE

ˌone-parent ˈfamily (*also* **ˌlone-parent ˈfamily**) *noun* a family in which the children live with one parent rather than two 单亲家庭 ⇨ SEE ALSO SINGLE PARENT

ˈone-piece *adj.* [only before noun] (especially of clothes 尤指衣服) consisting of one piece, not separate parts 上下一件式的；连体式的：*a one-piece swimsuit* 连体式游泳衣

oner·ous /ˈəʊnərəs; *NAmE* ˈɑːn-; ˈoʊ-/ *adj.* (*formal*) needing great effort; causing trouble or worry 费力的；艰巨的；令人焦虑的 **SYN** **taxing**: *an onerous duty/task/responsibility* 繁重的义务 / 工作 / 职责

one's /wʌnz/ *det.* the possessive form of *one* (one 的所有格) 个人的，自己的：*One tries one's best.* 一个人尽其所能。

one·self /wʌnˈself/ *pron.* (*formal*) **1** (the reflexive form of *one* * one 的反身形式) used as the object of a verb or preposition when 'one' is the subject of the verb or is understood as the subject (one 作动词的主语时，oneself 作动词或介词的宾语) 自己，自身：*One has to ask oneself what the purpose of the exercise is.* 大家必须问一问自己，这个锻炼的目的是什么。◇ *One cannot choose freedom for oneself without choosing it for others.* 人不能光为了自己的自由而不顾别人的自由。◇ *It is difficult to make oneself concentrate for long periods.* 让自己长时间聚精会神是很困难的。 **2** used to emphasize *one* (用以强调 one) 亲自，自己：*One likes to do it oneself.* 人都喜欢亲自去做。 **HELP** **One** and **oneself** are very formal words and now sound old-fashioned. It is much more usual to use **you** and **yourself** for referring to people in general and **I** and **myself** when the speaker is referring to himself or herself. * one 和 oneself 是非常正式的字眼，现在听起来过时了。现在更常用 you 和 yourself 泛指一般人，用 I 和 myself 指说话人自己。
IDM **be oneˈself** to be in a normal state of body and mind, not influenced by other people 身心自在；怡然自得：*One needs space to be oneself.* 人要有空间才能怡然自得。 **(all) by oneˈself 1** alone; without anyone else (某人) 独自，单独 **2** without help (某人) 独立地 **(all) to oneˈself** not shared with anyone 独享的；独自拥有的

ˈone-shot (*NAmE*) (*BrE* **ˌone-ˈoff**) *adj.* [only before noun] made or happening only once and not regularly 一次性的；非经常性的

ˌone-ˈsided *adj.* **1** (*disapproving*) (of an argument, opinion, etc. 论点、意见等) showing only one side of the situation; not balanced 片面的；偏颇的 **SYN** **biased**: *The press were accused of presenting a very one-sided picture of the issue.* 新闻界被指责对这件事的报道非常片面。 **2** (of a competition or a relationship 竞争或关系) involving people who have different abilities; involving one person more than another 实力悬殊的；一边倒的：*a totally one-sided match* 实力非常悬殊的比赛 ◇ *a one-sided conversation* (= in which one person talks most of the time) 一边倒的交谈

one·sie /ˈwʌnzi/ *noun* a piece of clothing that covers the top half of the body and the legs 连体服

Onesies™ /ˈwʌnziz/ *noun* (*NAmE*) a piece of clothing for babies that covers the top half of the body and sometimes also the legs. It fastens between the legs. (婴儿) 连体衣，连裤衣；宝宝衫 ⇨ COMPARE BABYGRO™

ˌone-size-fits-ˈall *adj.* [only before noun] designed to be suitable for a wide range of situations or needs 通用的；一体适用的：*a one-size-fits-all monetary policy* 通用的货币政策

ˌone-ˈstar *adj.* [usually before noun] **1** having one star in a system that measures quality. The highest standard is usually represented by four or five stars (服务质量) 一星级的：*a one-star hotel* 一星级宾馆 **2** (*NAmE*) having the fifth-highest military rank, and wearing uniform which has one star on it (军阶) 一星的：*a one-star general* 一星少将

ˈone-stop *adj.* in which you can buy or do everything you want in one place 综合性的；全方位服务的；一站式的；一切全包的：*Our agency is a one-stop shop for all your travel needs.* 我社为您的旅游提供全方位服务。

ˈone-time *adj.* [only before noun] **1** former 原先的；从前的；一度的：*her one-time best friend, Anna* 她以前的挚友安娜 **2** not to be repeated 一次性的；一次全包的 **SYN** **one-off**: *a one-time fee of $500* * 500 美元的一次性总费用

ˌone-to-ˈone (*especially BrE*) (*NAmE usually* **ˌone-on-ˈone**) *adj.* [usually before noun] **1** between two people only 一对一的；仅限两人之间的：*a one-to-one meeting* 一对一的会见 **2** matching sth else in an exact way 一一对应的；完全对应的：*There is no one-to-one correspondence between sounds and letters.* 发音与字母之间没有一对一的关系。 ▶ **ˌone-to-ˈone** *adv.*: *He teaches one-to-one.* 他一对一地个别教学。

ˌone-track ˈmind *noun* [usually sing.] if sb has a **one-track mind**, they can only think about one subject (often used to refer to sb thinking about sex) 单向褊狭的思路；一根筋；满脑子只想着一件事 (常指性爱)

ˌone-trick ˈpony *noun* (*becoming old-fashioned, disapproving*) a performer who is only famous for one song, etc.; a person or business that is only good at doing one thing "一招鲜" (指只有一首成名曲的歌手、单一特长的人或单一经营的企业)：*This comedian is no one-trick pony.* 这位喜剧演员并不只有一招绝活。

one-upmanship /wʌn ˈʌpmənʃɪp/ *noun* [U] (*disapproving*) the skill of getting an advantage over other people 取巧占上风的伎俩

ˌone-ˈway *adj.* [usually before noun] **1** moving or allowing movement in only one direction 单行的；单向的：*one-way traffic* 单向交通 ◇ *a one-way street* 单行道 ◇ *a one-way valve* 单向阀门 **2** (*especially NAmE*) (*BrE also* **sin·gle**) a **one-way** ticket, etc. can be used for travelling to a place but not back again 单程的 ⇨ COMPARE RETURN *n.* (7) **3** operating in only one direction 单方面的；单向进行的：*Theirs was a one-way relationship* (= one person made all the effort). 他们的关系是一头热。◇ *They observed the prisoners through a* ***one-way mirror*** (= a mirror that allows a person standing behind it to see through it). 他们透过单向镜子监视犯人。

ˌone-ˈwoman *adj.* [only before noun] done or controlled by one woman only 一个女人做的；由一个女人控制的：*a one-woman show* 女独角戏

ˌon-ˈfield *adj.* at or on a sports field 运动场上的：*on-field medical treatment* 场上治疗

on·going **AW** /ˈɒnɡəʊɪŋ; *NAmE* ˈɑːnɡoʊ-; ˈɔːn-/ *adj.* [usually before noun] continuing to exist or develop 持续存在的；仍在进行的；不断发展的：*an ongoing debate/discussion/process* 持续的辩论 / 讨论 / 过程 ◇ *The police investigation is ongoing.* 警方的调查在持续进行中。

onion 🔑 /ˈʌnjən/ *noun* [C, U] a round vegetable with many layers inside each other and a brown, red or white skin. Onions have a strong smell and flavour. 洋葱；葱头：*Chop the onions finely.* 把洋葱切细。◇ *French onion soup* 法式洋葱汤 ⇨ VISUAL VOCAB PAGE V33

on·line 🔑 /ˌɒnˈlaɪn; *NAmE* ˌɑːn-; ˌɔːn-/ *adj.* (*computing* 计) 🔑 controlled by or connected to a computer or to the Internet 在线的；联网的；联机的：*Online shopping is*

O

both cheap and convenient. 网上购物既便宜又方便。◇ *an online database* 在线数据库 ◇ *He spends hours playing online games.* 他花很长时间玩网络游戏。 ▶ **on·line** ⚷ *adv.* : *The majority of small businesses now do their banking online.* 大多数小企业现在都在网上办理银行业务。 ➲ COLLOCATIONS AT EMAIL ➲ WORDFINDER NOTE AT WEBSITE ➲ SEE ALSO OFFLINE, BE, COME, ETC. ON LINE at LINE *n.* **onliner** /ˌɒnˈlaɪnə(r); *NAmE* ˌɑːn-; ˌɔːn-/ *noun* : *What percentage of onliners use e-commerce?* 网民使用电子商务的比例是多少？

ˌonline ˈdating (*also* **ˈInternet dating**) using the Internet to arrange to meet sb and possibly begin a romantic relationship with them 网上交友（服务），网恋（通过网上结识对象，开始恋情）: *an online dating service/site* 网上交友服务 / 网站

on·look·er /ˈɒnlʊkə(r); *NAmE* ˈɑːn-; ˈɔːn-/ *noun* a person who watches sth that is happening but is not involved in it 旁观者 SYN **bystander**: *A crowd of onlookers gathered at the scene of the crash.* 在撞车现场聚集了一大群围观者。 ➲ SYNONYMS AT WITNESS

only ⚷ /ˈəʊnli; *NAmE* ˈoʊnli/ *adj., adv., conj.*

■ *adj.* [only before noun] **1** ⚷ used to say that no other or others of the same group exist or are there 仅有的；唯一的：*She's their only daughter.* 她是他们的独生女。◇ *We were the only people there.* 我们是唯一在场的人。◇ *His only answer was a grunt.* 他唯一的回答就只是哼了一声。 **2** ⚷ used to say that sb/sth is the best and you would not choose any other 最好的；最适当的：*She's the only person for the job.* 她是这项工作最合适的人选。

IDM **the only thing ˈis...** ⚷ (*informal*) used before mentioning a worry or problem you have with sth 问题是；麻烦的是；只是；不过：*I'd love to come—the only thing is I might be late.* 我很想去，只不过我可能会迟到。 ➲ MORE AT NAME *n.*, ONE *number*

■ *adv.* **1** ⚷ nobody or nothing except 只；只有；仅：*There are only a limited number of tickets available.* 剩下的票数量很有限。◇ *The bar is for* ***members only***. 这间酒吧只对会员开放。◇ ***You only have to*** *look at her to see she doesn't eat enough.* 你只消看一眼就知道她吃得不够多。◇ *Only five people turned up.* 只来了五个人。 **2** ⚷ in no other situation, place, etc. 仅在…情况下（或地点等）: *I agreed, but only because I was frightened.* 我当时同意只是因为我很害怕。 ◇ *Children are admitted only if accompanied by an adult.* 儿童必须有成年人陪同方可入场。 HELP In formal written English **only** (or **only if** and its clause) can be placed first in the sentence. In the second part of the sentence, **be**, **do**, **have**, etc. come before the subject and the main part of the verb. 在正式书面英语中，only 或 only if 及其从句可置于句首。在句子的其余部分，be、do、have 等置于主语及主要动词前：*Only in Paris* ***do*** *you find bars like this.* 只有在巴黎才会看到这样的酒吧。◇ ***Only if*** *these conditions are fulfilled* ***can*** *the application proceed to the next stage.* 只有这些条件都满足，申请才能进入下一程序。 **3** ⚷ no more important, interesting, serious, etc. than 只不过；仅…而已：*It was only a suggestion.* 这只是个提议罢了。◇ *Don't blame me, I'm only the messenger!* 别责怪我，我只不过是个传话的！ ◇ *He was only teasing you.* 他只是逗你玩玩罢了。 **4** ⚷ no more than; no longer than 只有；仅；刚刚：*She's only 21 and she runs her own business.* 她只有 21 岁，就经营起自己的企业了。◇ *It only took a few seconds.* 那只需要几秒钟。◇ *It took only a few seconds.* 那只需要几秒钟。 **5** ⚷ not until（直到）…才；（只是）…才：*We only got here yesterday.* 我们昨天才到这里。◇ (*formal*) ***Only then did*** *she realize the stress he was under.* 直到那时她才意识到他所承受的压力。 HELP When **only** begins a sentence **be**, **do**, **have**, etc. come before the subject and the main part of the verb. 当句子以 only 开始时，be、do、have 等词要置于主语和主要动词之前。 **6** ⚷ used to say that sb can do no more than what is mentioned, although this is probably not enough 仅此而已；只能：*We can only guess what happened.* 我们只能猜测发生了什么事。◇ *He could only watch helplessly as the car plunged into the ravine.* 他只能眼睁睁地看着汽车冲落峡谷。◇ *I only hope that she never finds out.* 我唯有希望永远别被她知道。 **7** ⚷ used to say that sth will have a bad effect （用于说明事情的恶果）只会，愈加：*If you do that, it will only make matters worse.* 如果你那样做，只会乱上加乱。◇ *Trying to reason with him only enrages him even more.* 跟他讲理只会使他更加生气。 **8 ~ to do sth** used to mention sth that happens immediately afterwards, especially sth that causes surprise, disappointment, etc. 不料；竟然：*She turned up the driveway, only to find her way blocked.* 她开上自家车道，不料发现路已被堵。

IDM **not only... but (also)...** ⚷ both... and... 不但…而且…：*He not only read the book, but also remembered what he had read.* 他不但读了这本书，而且记得所读的内容。 ➲ LANGUAGE BANK AT ADDITION **only ˈjust 1** not long ago/before 刚才；刚刚：*We've only just arrived.* 我们刚到。 **2** almost not 险些没；差点没；刚好：*He only just caught the train.* 他差点没赶上火车。◇ *I can afford it, but only just.* 这东西我刚好买得起。 **only too...** very 很；非常：*I was only too pleased to help.* 我非常乐意帮忙。◇ *Children can be difficult as we know only too well.* 小孩子往往很难对付，对此我们都非常清楚。 **you're only young ˈonce** (*saying*) young people should enjoy themselves as much as possible, because they will have to work and worry later in their lives 行乐当及年少时；青春只有一次 ➲ MORE AT EYE *n.*, IF *conj.*

■ *conj.* (*informal*) except that; but 不过；但是；可是：*I'd love to come, only I have to work.* 我很想去，但是我要上班。◇ *It tastes like chicken, only stronger.* 这东西尝起来像鸡肉，只是味道浓一点。

ˌonly ˈchild *noun* a child who has no brothers or sisters 独生子（或女）：*I'm an only child.* 我是独生子。

o.n.o. *abbr.* (*BrE*) or near/nearest offer (used in small advertisements to show that sth may be sold at a lower price than the price that has been asked) 或接近买方出价，可还价（用于小广告中，表示某物可减价出售）：*Guitar £200 o.n.o.* 吉他 200 英镑，可还价。 ➲ SEE ALSO OBO

ˌon-ˈoff *adj.* [only before noun] **1** (of a switch 开关) having the positions 'on' and 'off' 开 − 关的；双位的；通断的；离合的：*an on-off switch* 通断开关 **2** (of a relationship 关系) interrupted by periods when the relationship is not continuing 断断续续的；间断的

ono·mato·poeia /ˌɒnəˌmætəˈpiːə; *NAmE* ˌɑːn-/ *noun* [U] (*specialist*) the fact of words containing sounds similar to the noises they describe, for example *hiss*; the use of words like this in a piece of writing 象声；拟声；拟声法 ➲ WORDFINDER NOTE AT IMAGE ▶ **ono·mato·poe·ic** /-ˈpiːɪk/ *adj.* : *Bang and pop are onomatopoeic words.* * bang 和 pop 是拟声词。

ˈon-ramp *noun* (*NAmE, SAfrE*) a road used for driving onto a major road such as an INTERSTATE（高速公路等的）驶进匝道，驶进坡道 ➲ COMPARE OFF-RAMP

on·rush /ˈɒnrʌʃ; *NAmE* ˈɑːn-; ˈɔːn-/ *noun* [sing.] a strong movement forward; the sudden development of sth 猛然向前；突如其来

ˌon-ˈscreen *adj.* [only before noun] **1** appearing or written on the screen of a computer, television or cinema/movie theater 屏幕上的；荧屏的；影视的：*on-screen courtroom dramas* 荧屏播映的法庭戏 ◇ *on-screen messages* 屏幕上的信息 **2** connected with the imaginary story of a film/movie and not with real life 扮演的；屏幕上的；非现实生活的：*His on-screen father is also his father in real life.* 他那荧幕上的父亲也是他现实生活中的父亲。 ➲ COMPARE OFF-SCREEN ▶ **ˌon-ˈscreen** *adv.*

onset /ˈɒnset; *NAmE* ˈɑːn-; ˈɔːn-/ *noun* [sing.] the beginning of sth, especially sth unpleasant 开端，发生，肇始（尤指不快的事件）：*the onset of disease/old age/winter* 疾病的发作；老年的开始；冬天的来临

on·shore /ˈɒnʃɔː(r); *NAmE* ˈɑːn-; ˈɔːn-/ *adj.* [usually before noun] **1** on the land rather than at sea 陆上的：*an onshore oil field* 陆上油田 **2** (of wind 风) blowing from the sea towards the land 吹向陆地的；向岸的 ▶ **on·shore** *adv.* ➲ COMPARE OFFSHORE

on·side /ˌɒnˈsaɪd; *NAmE* ˌɑːn-; ˌɔːn-/ *adj.* (in football (SOCCER), HOCKEY, etc. 足球、曲棍球等) in a position on the field where you are allowed to play the ball 未越位；非越位 ▸ **on·side** *adv.* OPP **offside**

IDM ▸ **get/keep sb onˈside** (*BrE*) to get/keep sb's support 得到（或保持）某人的支持： *The party needs to keep the major national newspapers onside if it's going to win the next election.* 这个政党要想在下次大选中获胜，就需要得到全国各大报纸的继续支持。

on·slaught /ˈɒnslɔːt; *NAmE* ˈɑːn-; ˈɔːn-/ *noun* [C, usually sing.] a strong or violent attack 攻击；猛攻： ~ **(against/on sb/sth)** *the enemy onslaught on our military forces* 敌军对我军的进攻 ◇ ~ **(of sth)** *The town survives the onslaught of tourists every summer.* 每年夏天，这座小城都要熬过一段旅游者蜂拥而至的苦日子。 ◇ *an onslaught of abuse* 一阵谩骂

on·stage /ˌɒnˈsteɪdʒ; *NAmE* ˌɑːn-; ˌɔːn-/ *adj.* on the stage in a theatre; in front of an audience 舞台上的；表演的： *onstage fights* 舞台上的打斗 ▸ **on·stage** *adv.* OPP **offstage**

ˌon-ˈstreet *adj.* [only before noun] (of parking facilities 停车设施) located at the side of a public road rather than in a garage, a drive, etc. 街边的；路边的 OPP **off-street**

onto /ˈɒntə; *NAmE* ˈɑːn-; ˈɔːn-; *before vowels* ˈɒntu/ (*also* **on to**) *prep.* **1** used with verbs to express movement on or to a particular place or position（与动词连用，表示朝某处或某位置运动）向，朝： *Move the books onto the second shelf.* 把书移到第二层架子上。 ◇ *She stepped down from the train onto the platform.* 她走下火车来到站台上。 **2** used to show that sth faces in a particular direction 朝向，面向（某个方向）： *The window looked out onto the terrace.* 窗户外对着的是露天平台。

PHR V **be ˈonto sb 1** (*informal*) to know about what sb has done wrong 发现（某人做了坏事）： *She knew the police would be onto them.* 她知道警方将追查他们。 **2** to be talking to sb, usually in order to ask or tell them sth 与…谈话；询问： *They've been onto me for ages to get a job.* 很久以来，他们一直催促我找份工作。 **be ˈonto sth** to know about sth or be in a situation that could lead to a good result for you 了解；掌握；处于有利地位： *Scientists believe they are onto something big.* 科学家相信，他们将会有重大发现。 ◇ *She's onto a good thing with that new job.* 她在新工作中将大有作为。

ontol·ogy /ɒnˈtɒlədʒi; *NAmE* ɑːnˈtɑːl-/ *noun* **1** [U] a branch of philosophy that deals with the nature of existence 本体论 **2** [C] a list of concepts and categories in a subject area that shows the relationships between them 本体（一个主题下不同概念及类别）： *a guide to creating a marketing ontology* 市场本体构建指南 ▸ **onto·logic·al** /ˌɒntəˈlɒdʒɪkl; *NAmE* ˌɑːntəˈlɑːdʒ-/ *adj.*

ˌon-ˈtrend *adj.* very fashionable 时髦的；流行的： *That jacket is bang on-trend.* 那种夹克衫非常流行。 ◇ *an on-trend haircut* 流行发型

onus /ˈəʊnəs; *NAmE* ˈoʊnəs/ *noun* (*usually* **the onus**) [sing.] (*formal*) the responsibility for sth 职责；责任： *The onus is on employers to follow health and safety laws.* 雇主有义务遵行健康安全法。

on·ward /ˈɒnwəd; *NAmE* ˈɑːnwərd; ˈɔːn-/ *adj.* [only before noun] (*formal*) continuing or moving forward 继续的；向前的： *Ticket prices include your flight and onward rail journey.* 票价包括您的机票和接续的铁路旅费。

on·wards /ˈɒnwədz; *NAmE* ˈɑːnwərdz; ˈɔːn-/ (*especially BrE*) (*NAmE usually* **on·ward** /ˈɒnwəd; *NAmE* ˈɑːnwərd; ˈɔːn-/) *adv.* **1 from... onwards** continuing from a particular time 从（某时）起一直： *They lived there from the 1980s onwards.* 他们从 20 世纪 80 年代起一直住在那里。 ◇ *The pool is open from 7 a.m. onwards.* 游泳池从早上 7 点起开放。 **2** (*formal*) forward 向前；前往： *We drove onwards towards the coast.* 我们驱车前往海滨。

onyx /ˈɒnɪks; *NAmE* ˈɑːn-/ *noun* [U] a type of stone that has layers of different colours in it, usually used for decorative objects 缟玛瑙

oo·dles /ˈuːdlz/ *noun* [pl.] ~ **(of sth)** (*old-fashioned, informal*) a large amount of sth 大量；很多 SYN **load**

oo-er /ˌuː ˈɜː(r)/ *exclamation* (*humorous*) used for expressing surprise, especially about sth sexual（表示惊讶，尤指对性方面）啊，哎呀

ooh /uː/ *exclamation* used for expressing surprise, happiness or pain（表示惊讶、高兴或疼痛）哎呀，啊哈，哎哟 ➲ MORE LIKE THIS 2, page R25

oom·pah /ˈʊmpɑː; ˈuːm-/ (*also* **ˈoompah-pah**) *noun* (*informal*) used to refer to the sound produced by a group of BRASS instruments（铜管乐器组发出的）嗡姆吧声： *an oompah band* 铜管乐队

oomph /ʊmf/ *noun* [U] (*informal*) energy; a special good quality 精力；特质；气质： *a styling product to give your hair more oomph* 使头发更靓丽的一种定型剂

oops /ʊps; uːps/ *exclamation* **1** used when sb has almost had an accident, broken sth, etc.（差点出事故、摔破物品等时说）哎： *Oops! I almost spilled the wine.* 哎！我差点把酒洒了。 **2** used when you have done sth embarrassing, said sth rude by accident, told a secret, etc.（做了令人尴尬的事、说了无理的话或泄露了秘密等时说）哎： *Oops, I shouldn't have said that.* 哎，我不应该那么说。 ➲ MORE LIKE THIS 2, page R25

oops-a-daisy /ˈʊpsə deɪzi; ˈʌpsə/ *exclamation* = UPSY-DAISY

ooze /uːz/ *verb, noun*

■ *verb* **1** [I, T] if a thick liquid **oozes** from a place, or if sth **oozes** a thick liquid, the liquid flows from the place slowly（浓液体）渗出，慢慢流出： ~ **from/out of/through sth** | ~ **out** *Blood oozed out of the wound.* 血从伤口慢慢流出来。 ◇ ~ **with sth** *an ugly swelling oozing with pus* 流着脓水的烂疮 ◇ ~ **sth** *The wound was oozing blood.* 伤口流着血。 ◇ *a plate of toast oozing butter* 一盘渗着黄油的烤面包片 **2** [T, I] if sb/sth **oozes** a particular characteristic, quality, etc., they show it strongly 洋溢着，充满（特质、气质等） SYN **exude**： ~ **sth** *She walked into the party oozing confidence.* 她信心十足地来到聚会上。 ◇ ~ **with sth** *His voice oozed with sex appeal.* 他的声音充溢着性感。

■ *noun* **1** [U] very soft mud, especially at the bottom of a lake or river（河床、湖底的）泥浆，稀泥 **2** [sing.] the very slow flow of a thick liquid（浓液的）缓慢渗出 ▸ **oozy** *adj.*

op /ɒp; *NAmE* ɑːp/ *noun* (*BrE, informal*) = OPERATION (1)： *I'm going in for my op on Monday.* 星期一我要住院动手术。

Op. (*also* **op.**) *abbr.* OPUS（按作曲家的创作时间排列的）编号乐曲： *Webern's Five Pieces, Op. 10* 韦伯恩的第十号作品的五首小曲

opa·city /əʊˈpæsəti; *NAmE* oʊ-/ *noun* [U] **1** (*specialist*) the fact of being difficult to see through; the fact of being OPAQUE 不透明性；模糊 **2** (*formal*) the fact of being difficult to understand; the fact of being OPAQUE 费解；难懂；模糊 OPP **transparency**

opal /ˈəʊpl; *NAmE* ˈoʊpl/ *noun* [C, U] a white or almost clear SEMI-PRECIOUS stone in which changes of colour are seen, used in jewellery 蛋白石；猫眼石： *an opal ring* 蛋白石戒指

opal·es·cent /ˌəʊpəˈlesnt; *NAmE* ˌoʊpə-/ *adj.* (*formal* or *literary*) changing colour like an opal 像猫眼石般变色的；色彩变幻的

opaque /əʊˈpeɪk; *NAmE* oʊ-/ *adj.* **1** (of glass, liquid, etc. 玻璃、液体等) not clear enough to see through or allow light through 不透明的；不透光的；浑浊的： *opaque glass* 不透明的玻璃 ◇ *opaque tights* 不透明的连裤袜 **2** (of speech or writing 说话或写作) difficult to understand; not clear 难懂；模糊；隐晦；不清楚 SYN **impenetrable**： *The jargon in his talk was opaque to me.* 他谈话中使用的行话对我是一团迷雾。 OPP **transparent**

ˈop art *noun* [U] a style of modern art that uses patterns and colours in a way that makes the images seem to move as you look at them 欧普艺术，光效应艺术（利用色彩图形使画面产生动感的现代艺术）

O

op. cit. *abbr.* used in formal writing to refer to a book or an article that has already been mentioned（用于正式文章中，指前文提到的书或文章）同上

op·code /ˈɒpkəʊd; *NAmE* ɑːpkoʊd/ *noun* = OPERATION CODE

OPEC /ˈəʊpek; *NAmE* ˈoʊ-/ *abbr.* Organization of Petroleum Exporting Countries (an organization of countries that produce and sell oil) 石油输出国组织；欧佩克

ˈop-ed (*also* **op-ˈed page**) *noun* (*NAmE*) the page in a newspaper opposite the EDITORIAL page that contains comment on the news and articles on particular subjects（报章上与社论版位置相对的）评论版

open /ˈəʊpən; *NAmE* ˈoʊ-/ *adj., verb, noun*

■ *adj.*

• **NOT CLOSED** 开着 **1** allowing things or people to go through 开放的；敞开的：*A wasp flew in the open window.* 一只黄蜂飞进了开着的窗子。◇ *She had left the door* ***wide open***. 她把房门敞开着。**OPP closed** **2** (of sb's eyes, mouth, etc. 人的眼睛、嘴等) with EYELIDS or lips apart 张开的；张着的：*She had difficulty keeping her eyes open* (= because she was very tired). 她连睁开眼睛的力气都没有了。◇ *He was breathing through his open mouth.* 他张着嘴呼吸。**OPP closed** **3** spread out; with the edges apart 展开的；开放的：*The flowers are all open now.* 花现在都开了。◇ *The book lay open on the table.* 书摊开在桌子上。**OPP closed** **4** not blocked by anything 畅通的；开放的：*The pass is* ***kept open*** *all the year.* 关口一年到头都是开放的。**OPP closed**

• **NOT FASTENED** 未系着 **5** not fastened or covered, so that things can easily come out or be put in 敞口的；未封的：*Leave the envelope open.* 别封上信封。◇ *The bag burst open and everything fell out.* 袋子爆开了，里边的东西都散落出来。**6** (of clothes 衣服) not fastened 没扣上的；敞开的：*Her coat was open.* 她的外衣敞着。

• **NOT ENCLOSED** 未围着 **7** not surrounded by anything; not confined 开阔的；未围上的：***open country*** (= without forests, buildings, etc.) 空旷的田野 ◇ *a city with a lot of parks and* ***open spaces*** 有很多公园和空地的城市 ◇ *driving along the* ***open road*** (= part of a road in the country, where you can drive fast) 沿开阔的道路开车

• **NOT COVERED** 敞开 **8** with no cover or roof on 敞开的；露天的；裸露的：*an open drain* 一条明沟 ◇ *people working* ***in the open air*** (= not in a building) 在户外作业的人 ◇ *The hall of the old house was open to the sky.* 旧房子的门厅是露天的。◇ *an open wound* (= with no skin covering it) 开放性伤口 ◇ (*NAmE*) *an open flame* 明火 **HELP** In British English this is called a *naked flame*. 英式英语称作 naked flame。

• **FOR CUSTOMERS/VISITORS** 对宾客 **9** [not usually before noun] if a shop/store, bank, business, etc. is **open**, it is ready for business and will admit customers or visitors 开放；营业：*Is the museum open on Sundays?* 博物馆每星期天都开放吗？◇ *The new store will be open in the spring.* 新商店将在春天开业。◇ *The house had been* ***thrown open*** *to the public.* 这所宅院已向公众开放。◇ *I declare this festival open.* 我宣布庆祝活动开始。**OPP closed**

• **OF COMPETITION/BUILDING** 比赛；建筑物 **10** if a competition, etc. is **open**, anyone can enter it 对大众开放的；公开的；人人可以参加的 **SYN public**：*an open debate/championship/scholarship* 公开的辩论会；人人可以参加的锦标赛；人人均可申请的奖学金 ◇ *She was tried in* ***open court*** (= the public could go and listen to the trial). 她被公开审判。◇ *The debate was* ***thrown open*** *to the audience.* 辩论会对听众开放。**11** [not before noun] **~ to sb** if a competition, building, etc. is **open** to particular people, those people can enter it（比赛、建筑物等）对特定群体开放：*The competition is open to young people under the age of 18.* 这项比赛让 18 岁以下的青少年参加。◇ *The house is not open to the public.* 这所住宅不对外开放。**OPP closed**

• **AVAILABLE** 备有 **12** [not before noun] ~ (**to sb**) to be available and ready to use 可得到；可使用：*What options are open to us?* 我们有什么选择？◇ *Is the offer still open?* 这个报价还有效吗？◇ *I want to keep my Swiss bank account open.* 我想保留我的瑞士银行账户。**OPP closed**

• **NOT PROTECTED** 无防范 **13** ~ (**to sth**) likely to suffer sth such as criticism, injury, etc. 易受损害；脆弱 **SYN vulnerable**：*The system is open to abuse.* 这项制度容易被滥用。◇ *He has* ***laid himself wide open*** *to political attack.* 他在政治上已经处于极易受到攻击的境地。

• **NOT HIDDEN** 不隐匿 **14** known to everyone; not kept hidden 人人皆知的；不保密的；公开的：*an open quarrel* 公开的争吵 ◇ *open government* 透明的管理 ◇ *their open display of affection* 他们的公开秀恩爱 ◇ *His eyes showed open admiration as he looked at her.* 他看她的时候，眼神里明显流露着敬佩之情。

• **PERSON'S CHARACTER** 性格 **15** honest; not keeping thoughts and feelings hidden 诚恳；坦诚；直率 **SYN frank**：*She was always open with her parents.* 她总是与父母无话不谈。◇ *He was quite open about his reasons for leaving.* 他对离开的原因完全未加隐瞒。➲ SYNONYMS AT HONEST **16** **~ to sth** (of a person 人) willing to listen to and think about new ideas 思想开明的；不固执己见的：*I'm open to suggestions for what you would like to do in our classes.* 我很乐意听听你们对课堂活动的建议。

• **NOT YET DECIDED** 待定 **17** ~ (**to sth**) not yet finally decided or settled 未决定的；待决定的：*The race is still* ***wide open*** (= anyone could win). 赛跑胜负未定。◇ *The price is not open to negotiation.* 价格不容商议。◇ *Some phrases in the contract are open to interpretation.* 合同中的某些条文容有不同诠释。◇ *Which route is better remains* ***an open question*** (= it is not decided). 哪条路线较好尚待决定。◇ *In an interview try to ask* ***open questions*** (= to which the answer is not just 'yes' or 'no'). 主持面试时要尽量问一些开放式的问题。

• **CLOTH** 织物 **18** with wide spaces between the threads 稀疏的；不密的：*an open weave* 稀疏织法

• **PHONETICS** 语音学 **19** (*also* **low**) (of a vowel 元音) produced by opening the mouth wide 开的；开口的 ➲ COMPARE CLOSE² *adj.*

IDM **be an ˌopen ˈsecret** if sth is **an open secret**, many people know about it, although it is supposed to be a secret 是公开的秘密 **have/keep an ˌopen ˈmind (about/on sth)** to be willing to listen to or accept new ideas or suggestions 愿意聆听（或接受）意见；（对…）不怀成见；思想开明 **keep your ˈears/ˈeyes open (for sth)** to be quick to notice or hear things（对…）保持警觉；注意；留心 **an ˌopen ˈbook** if you describe sb or their life as **an open book**, you mean that you can easily understand them and know everything about them 容易被了解的人（或事） **an ˌopen inviˈtation (to sb)** **1** an invitation to sb to visit you at any time（给…）随时可以来访的邀请 **2** if sth is **an open invitation** to criminals, etc., it encourages them to commit a crime by making it easier 容易引诱人犯罪的行为：*Leaving your camera on the seat in the car is an open invitation to thieves.* 把照相机留在汽车座位上无异于开门揖盗。**with ˌopen ˈarms** if you welcome sb **with open arms**, you are extremely happy and pleased to see them 热烈地；热情地；诚挚地 ➲ MORE AT BURST *v.*, DOOR, EYE *n.*, MARKET *n.*, OPTION *n.*

■ *verb*

• **DOOR/WINDOW/LID** 门窗；盖子 **1** [T] **~ sth** to move a door, window, lid, etc. so that it is no longer closed 开；打开；开启：*Mr Chen opened the car door for his wife.* 陈先生为妻子打开车门。**OPP close¹** **2** [I] to move or be moved so that it is no longer closed 打开；（使）开：*The door opened and Alan walked in.* 门开了，艾伦走了进去。**OPP close¹**

• **CONTAINER/PACKAGE** 容器；包 **3** [T] **~ sth** to remove the lid, undo the FASTENING, etc. of a container, etc. in order to see or get what is inside 打开，开启（瓶盖、封口等）：*Shall I open another bottle?* 要不要我再开一瓶？◇ *He opened the letter and read it.* 他拆开信读起来。

• **EYES** 眼睛 **4** [T, I] **~ (sth)** if you **open** your eyes or your eyes **open**, you move your EYELIDS upwards so that you can see 睁开 **OPP close¹**

• **MOUTH** 嘴 **5** [T, I] **~ (sth)** if you **open** your mouth or your mouth **opens**, you move your lips, for example in order to speak 张开：*He hardly ever opens his mouth* (= speaks). 他几乎从不开口。

• **BOOK** 书籍 **6** [T] **~ sth** to turn the cover or the pages of a book so that it is no longer closed 打开；翻开：*Open your books at page 25.* 把书翻到第 25 页。OPP **close**[1]
• **SPREAD OUT** 展开 **7** [I, T] to spread out or UNFOLD; to spread sth out or UNFOLD it 展开；打开：*What if the parachute doesn't open?* 降落伞打不开怎么办？◇ *The flowers are starting to open.* 花开始绽放了。◇ **~ sth** *Open the map on the table.* 把地图摊在桌子上。◇ *He opened his arms wide to embrace her.* 他张开双臂拥抱她。
• **BORDER/ROAD** 边界；道路 **8** [T] **~ sth** to make it possible for people, cars, goods, etc. to pass through a place 让（行人、车辆、货物等）通行；开放：*When did the country open its borders?* 这个国家是何时开放边界的？◇ *The road will be opened again in a few hours after police have cleared it.* 待警察清理完以后，道路在几小时内就会重新开放。OPP **close**[1]
• **FOR CUSTOMERS/VISITORS** 对宾客 **9** [I, T] (of a shop/store, business, etc. 商店、企业等) to start business for the day; to start business for the first time 开始营业；开业；开门：*What time does the bank open?* 这家银行什么时候开门？◇ **~ sth** *The company **opened its doors** for business a month ago.* 该公司一个月前开业。OPP **close**[1] **10** [I] to be ready for people to go to 开始接待：*The new hospital opens on July 1st.* 这家新医院七月一日开诊。◇ *When does the play open?* 这个剧什么时候上演？OPP **close**[1]
• **START STH** 开始某事 **11** [T] to start an activity or event 着手；开始：**~ sth** *You need just one pound to **open a bank account** with us.* 你只需一英镑就可在我行开立一个账户。◇ *The police have opened an investigation into the death.* 警察已开始对这桩命案进行调查。◇ *Troops **opened fire on*** (= started shooting) *the crowds.* 军队向人群开火了。◇ **~ sth with sth** *They will open the new season with a performance of 'Carmen'.* 他们将以上演《卡门》来开启新的戏剧季。➲ SYNONYMS AT START **12** [I] **~ (with sth)** (of a story, film/movie, etc. 故事、电影等) to start in a particular way 以…开篇；以…开头：*The story opens with a murder.* 这个故事以谋杀案开始。
• **WITH CEREMONY** 以仪式 **13** [T] **~ sth** to perform a ceremony showing that a building can start being used 为（建筑物）揭幕；宣布启用：*The bridge was opened by the Queen.* 女王为大桥开通揭幕。
• **COMPUTING** 计算机技术 **14** [T, I] **~ (sth)** to start a computer program or file so that you can use it on the screen 启动，打开（计算机程序或文件）➲ WORDFINDER NOTE AT FILE

IDM **open 'doors for sb** to provide opportunities for sb to do sth and be successful 为…敞开大门；提供良机 **open your/sb's 'eyes (to sth)** to realize or make sb realize the truth about sth （使人）长见识（或开眼界、认清事实）：*Travelling really opens your eyes to other cultures.* 旅游真正能使人开阔眼界，认识其他文化。**open your/sb's mind to sth** to become or make sb aware of new ideas or experiences （使人）思想开阔，意识到某事 **open the way for sb/sth (to do sth)** to make it possible for sb to do sth or for sth to happen 开方便之门 ➲ MORE AT HEART, HEAVEN

PHR V **'open into/onto sth** to lead to another room, area or place 通向，通往（他处） **,open 'out** to become bigger or wider 变大；变宽：*The street opened out into a small square.* 街道豁然变宽，形成一个小广场。**,open 'out (to sb)** (*BrE*) = OPEN UP (TO SB) **,open 'up 1** to begin shooting 开火：*Anti-aircraft guns opened up.* 高射炮开始射击。**2** (often used in orders 常用于命令) to open a door, container, etc. 打开（门、容器等）：*Open up or we'll break the door down!* 开门！不然就砸门了！ **,open 'up (to sb)** (*BrE also* **,open 'out (to sb)**) to talk about what you feel and think; to become less shy and more willing to communicate 直抒胸臆；畅所欲言：*It helps to discuss your problems but I find it hard to open up.* 与人谈谈自己面对的问题固然有益，但我觉得很难说得出口。**,open sth↔'up | ,open 'up 1** to become or make sth possible, available or able to be reached （使某事物）成为可能，可得到，可达到：*The railway opened up the east of the country.* 铁路使这个国家的东部不再闭塞。◇ *Exciting possibilities were opening up for her in the new job.* 新工作为她带来了令人兴奋的发展前途。**2** to begin business for the day 开门；营业；开业：*I open up the store for the day at around 8.30.* 我的店每天早上大约 8:30 开门。OPP **close up 3** to start a new business 开张；开业：*There's a new Thai restaurant opening up in town.* 城里有一家新的泰国餐馆开张了。OPP **close down 4** to develop or start to happen or exist; to develop or start sth 发展；开始发生；出现：*A division has opened up between the two ministers over the issue.* 两位部长在这个问题上出现了分歧。◇ *Scott opened up a 3-point lead in the first game.* 斯科特在第一局就以 3 分领先。**5** to appear and become wider; to make sth wider when it is narrow or closed 张开；裂开；拓展；打开：*The wound opened up and started bleeding.* 伤口裂开，开始流血。◇ *The operation will open up the blocked passages around his heart.* 手术将把他心脏周围被堵塞的通道打开。OPP **close up ,open sth↔'up** to make sth open that is shut, locked, etc. 打开；翻开：*She laid the book flat and opened it up.* 她把书平摊开。

▼**EXPRESS YOURSELF** 情景表达

Conversation openers 打开话题

What can you say when you have to speak to someone for the first time or when you have to open a meeting? Here are some possible ways of starting a conversation or getting the audience's attention before a talk or speech. 与人初次交谈时打开话题，会议开始要讲话，或者演讲之前引起听众注意，可用以下方式：

- ***Do you mind if I sit here?*** 我坐在这儿可以吗？
- ***Hello, is this seat taken?*** 你好，这个座位有人吗？
- ***May I join you? Can I get you a coffee?*** 可以和你一起吗？我给你拿杯咖啡好吗？
- ***Lovely weather we're having!/Can you believe this rain/wind/cold/sunshine?*** 多好的天气呀！/真想不到会下这么大雨/刮这么大风/这么冷/阳光这么灿烂！
- ***Excuse me, could I ask you a question?*** 打扰一下，可以问您一个问题吗？
- ***Shall we make a start? I think it's almost three o'clock.*** (*BrE*) 我们马上开始好吗？我看都快三点了。
- ***Shall we get started? I'd like to introduce our speaker.*** (*especially NAmE*) 我们开始吧？我来介绍一下演讲人。
- ***I think everyone's here, so I'd like to welcome you to this conference.*** 我想大家都到齐了，在此我对出席本次会议的各位表示欢迎。

■ *noun* **the open** [sing.]
• **OUTDOORS** 户外 **1** outdoors; the countryside 户外；野外；旷野：*Children need to play out **in the open**.* 孩子需要在户外玩耍。
• **NOT HIDDEN** 不隐匿 **2 in/into the ~** not hidden or secret 公开；非秘密：*Government officials do not want these comments **in the open**.* 政府官员不想公开这些评论。◇ *They intend to **bring** their complaints **out into the open**.* 他们想把心中的种种不满公开讲出来。

the ,open 'air *noun* [sing.] a place outside rather than in a building 户外；露天：*He likes to cook in the open air.* 他喜欢在户外做饭。

,open-'air *adj.* [only before noun] happening or existing outside rather than inside a building 户外的；露天的：*an open-air swimming pool* 露天游泳池

,open-and-shut 'case *noun* a legal case or other matter that is easy to decide or solve 容易解决的案件（或问题）：*The murder was an open-and-shut case.* 这桩谋杀案很容易侦破。

,open 'bar *noun* [U, C] an occasion when all the drinks at a party or other event have been paid for by sb else or are included in the ticket price（聚会等场合的）酒水免费，酒水已付

open·cast /ˈəʊpənkɑːst; *NAmE* ˈoʊpənkæst/ (*BrE*) (*NAmE* **,open-'pit**) *adj.* [usually before noun] in **opencast** mines coal is taken out of the ground near the surface 露天开采的 ➲ SEE ALSO STRIP MINING

O

ˈopen day (*BrE*) (*NAmE* ˌ**open** ˈ**house**) *noun* a day when people can visit a school, an organization, etc. and see the work that is done there（学校、机关等的）开放参观日，开放日

ˌ**open** ˈ**door** *noun, adj.*

■ ***noun*** [sing.] a situation that allows sth to happen, or that allows people to go to a place or get information without restrictions 门户开放；自由往来：*The government's policy is **an open door to** disaster.* 政府的政策为灾难敞开了大门。◇ *An insecure computer system is an open door to criminals.* 不安全的电脑系统给罪犯提供了可乘之机。

■ ***adj.*** ˌ**open-**ˈ**door** [only before noun] **1** (of a policy, system, principle, etc. 政策、制度、原则等) allowing people or goods freedom to come into a country; allowing people to go to a place or get information without restrictions 门户开放的；自由往来的：*the country's **open-door policy** for refugees* 这个国家对难民的开放政策 **2** a policy within a company or other organization designed to allow people to freely communicate with the people in charge（公司或机构中下属与主管）直接沟通的；政策开明的：*We operate an **open-door policy** here, and are always willing to listen to our students' suggestions.* 我们这里实行"开门政策"，愿意随时听取学生的建议。

ˌ**open-**ˈ**ended** *adj.* without any limits, aims or dates fixed in advance 无限制的；无确定目标的；无期限的：*an open-ended discussion* 无限制的自由讨论 ◇ *The contract is open-ended.* 本合同是无限期的。

open·er /ˈəʊpnə(r); *NAmE* ˈoʊ-/ *noun* **1** (usually in compounds 通常构成复合词) a tool that is used to open things 开启的工具：*a can opener* 罐头起子 ◇ *a bottle-opener* 开瓶器 ➲ SEE ALSO EYE-OPENER **2** the first in a series of things such as sports games; the first action in an event, a game, etc. 揭幕赛；开场戏：*They won the opener 4–2.* 他们以 4:2 赢了揭幕赛。◇ *Jones scored the opener.* 琼斯首先得分。◇ *a good conversation opener* 一个很好的开场白 **3** (in CRICKET 板球) either of the two BATSMEN who start play 开球员；首位击球员

IDM **for** ˈ**openers** (*informal, especially NAmE*) as a beginning or first part of a process 首先；作为开始；开端 SYN **for starters**

ˌ**open-faced** ˈ**sandwich** (*also* ˌ**open-face** ˈ**sandwich**) *noun* (*NAmE*) a slice of bread with meat, cheese, etc. on top but without a second slice of bread to cover this 单片三明治，露馅三明治（顶层无面包片覆盖）

ˌ**open-**ˈ**handed** *adj.* **1** generous and giving willingly 慷慨的；大方的：*an open-handed host* 一位慷慨大方的东道主 **2** using the flat part of the hand 用手掌的：*an open-handed blow* 用巴掌打

ˌ**open-**ˈ**hearted** *adj.* kind and friendly 善良诚恳的

ˌ**open-heart** ˈ**surgery** *noun* [U] a medical operation on the heart, during which the patient's blood is kept flowing by a machine 体外循环心脏手术；心脏直视手术；开心术

ˌ**open** ˈ**house** *noun* **1** [U, sing.] a place or a time at which visitors are welcome 开放；开放时间：*It's always open house at their place.* 他们的房舍随时对外开放参观。**2** (*NAmE*) (*BrE* ˈ**open day**) [C] a day when people can visit a school, an organization, etc. and see the work that is done there（学校、机关等的）开放日，开放参观日 **3** [C] (*NAmE*) a time when people who are interested in buying a particular house or apartment can look around it（为欲购房者而设的）看房时间

open·ing /ˈəʊpnɪŋ; *NAmE* ˈoʊ-/ *noun, adj.*

■ ***noun*** **1** [C] a space or hole that sb/sth can pass through 孔；洞；缺口：*We could see the stars through an opening in the roof.* 我们从屋顶的小洞能看见星星。**2** [C, usually sing.] the beginning or first part of sth 开始；开端：*The movie has an exciting opening.* 电影的开头非常刺激。OPP **ending** **3** [C, usually sing.] a ceremony to celebrate the start of a public event or the first time a new building, road, etc. is used 开幕式；落成典礼：*the opening of the Olympic Games* 奥林匹克运动会开幕式 ◇ *the official opening of the new hospital* 新建医院的落成典礼 **4** [C, U] the act or process of making sth open or of becoming open 开；开放；展开：*the opening of a flower* 花朵的绽放 ◇ *the opening of the new play* 新剧的开演 ◇ *Late opening of supermarkets is common in Britain now.* 现在超市营业至很晚在英国司空见惯。OPP **closing** **5** [C] a job that is available 空缺的职位 SYN **vacancy**：*There are several openings in the sales department.* 销售部有几个空缺。**6** [C] a good opportunity for sb 良机：*Winning the competition was the opening she needed for her career.* 在这次比赛中获胜是她未来事业发展的良好开端。**7** [C] part of a piece of clothing that is made to open and close so that it can be put on easily 开襟；开口：*The skirt has a side opening.* 这裙子是侧面开口的。

■ ***adj.*** [only before noun] first; beginning 开始的；开篇的；第一：*his opening remarks* 他的开场白 ◇ *the opening chapter of the book* 该书的第一章 OPP **closing**

ˈ**opening hours** *noun* [pl.] the time during which a shop/store, bank, etc. is open for business（商店、银行等的）营业时间

ˌ**opening** ˈ**night** *noun* [usually sing.] the first night that, for example, a play is performed or a film/movie is shown to the public（戏剧的）首夜演出；（电影的）首夜放映 ➲ WORDFINDER NOTE AT PERFORMANCE

ˈ**opening time** *noun* [U] (*BrE*) the time when pubs can legally open and begin to serve drinks（酒吧的法定）开始营业时间 OPP **closing time**

ˌ**opening** ˈ**up** *noun* [sing.] **1** the process of removing restrictions and making sth such as land or jobs available to more people 解禁；开放；供开发：*the opening up of new opportunities for women in business* 企业为妇女提供的新的工作机会 **2** the process of making sth ready for use 启用；落成：*the opening up of a new stretch of highway* 一段新公路的开通启用

ˌ**open-**ˈ**jaw** *adj.* [only before noun] (of a plane ticket or FARE 机票或票价) allowing sb to fly to one place and fly back from another place 开口的，缺口的，不同点进出的（可选择回程出发地）

ˌ**open** ˈ**letter** *noun* a letter of complaint or protest to an important person or group that is printed in a newspaper so that the public can read it 公开信

ˌ**open** ˈ**line** *noun, adj.*

■ ***noun*** a telephone communication in which conversations can be heard or recorded by others 可被监听（或录音）的电话；开放线路电话

■ ***adj.*** ˌ**open-**ˈ**line** [only before noun] relating to a radio or television programme that the public can take part in by telephone（电台或电视节目）公众可打电话参与的，开放式的，互动式的：*an open-line radio show* 互动式电台节目

open·ly /ˈəʊpənli; *NAmE* ˈoʊ-/ *adv.* without hiding any feelings, opinions or information 公开地；毫不隐瞒地：*Can you talk openly about sex with your parents?* 你可以跟父母敞开谈性的问题吗？◇ *The men in prison would never cry openly* (= so that other people could see). 狱中犯人从不当众哭泣。

ˌ**open** ˈ**market** *noun* [sing.] a situation in which companies can trade without restrictions, and prices depend on the amount of goods and the number of people buying them 公开市场；自由市场：*to buy/sell/trade **on the open market*** 在自由市场上买 / 卖 / 交易

ˌ**open** ˈ**mike** *noun* [U] an occasion in a club when anyone can sing, play music or tell jokes 即兴表演式聚会（出席者都可上台唱歌、演奏或表演滑稽说笑）：*open-mike night* 即兴表演晚会

ˌ**open-**ˈ**minded** *adj.* willing to listen to, think about or accept different ideas 愿意考虑不同意见的；思想开明的 OPP **narrow-minded** ► ˌ**open-**ˈ**minded·ness** *noun* [U]

ˌ**open-ˈmouthed** *adj.* with your mouth open because you are surprised or shocked（因惊愕）张着口的，瞠目结舌的，目瞪口呆的

ˌ**open-ˈnecked** (*also* ˌ**open-ˈneck**) *adj.* (of a shirt 衬衣) worn without a tie and with the top button undone 未打领带也未扣领扣的；敞领的

open·ness /ˈəʊpənnəs; *NAmE* ˈoʊ-/ *noun* [U] **1** the quality of being honest and not hiding information or feelings 诚实；率真；坦率 **2** the quality of being able to think about, accept or listen to different ideas or people 虚心的品质；开明 **3** the quality of not being confined or covered 开阔；开放；未遮盖

ˌ**open-ˈpit** (*NAmE*) (*BrE* **open·cast**) *adj.* [usually before noun] in **open-pit** mines coal is taken out of the ground near the surface 露天开采的 ➲SEE ALSO STRIP MINING

ˌ**open-ˈplan** *adj.* an **open-plan** building or area does not have inside walls dividing it up into rooms 开放式的；敞开式的；未隔间的：*an open-plan office* 敞开式的办公室

ˌ**open ˈprison** (*BrE*) (*NAmE* ˌ**minimum seˈcurity prison**) *noun* a prison in which prisoners have more freedom than in ordinary prisons 开放式监狱（对犯人的自由限制较少）

ˌ**open ˈsandwich** *noun* a SANDWICH which is served on a plate with no top piece of bread 单片三明治（无顶层面包片）

ˈ**open season** *noun* [sing.] **1** ~ (**for sth**) the time in the year when it is legal to hunt and kill particular animals or birds, or to catch fish, for sport （法定）渔猎开放季节 OPP **close season** ➲ WORDFINDER NOTE AT HUNT **2** ~ **for/on sb/sth** a time when there are no restrictions on criticizing particular groups of people or treating them unfairly （针对某些团体的）言论开放期，自由评论期：*It seems to be open season on teachers now.* 现在好像是自由评论教师的开放期。

ˌ**open ˈsesame** *noun* [sing.] an easy way to gain or achieve sth that is usually very difficult to get 开门咒语；通行手段；通行证：*Academic success is not always an open sesame to a well-paid job.* 在校成绩好并非总是获得高薪职位的敲门砖。 ORIGIN From the fairy tale *Ali Baba and the Forty Thieves*, in which the magic words **open sesame** had to be said to open the cave where the thieves kept their treasure. 源自童话故事《阿里巴巴和四十大盗》。只有念出咒语"芝麻，开门"，大盗藏宝洞的大门才能打开。

ˌ**open ˈslather** *noun* [U] (*AustralE, disapproving*) freedom to act without restrictions or limits 行动自由；无约束：*The changes will give developers open slather.* 这些变革将为开发商大开方便之门。

ˌ**open-ˈsource** *adj.* (*computing* 计) used to describe software for which the original SOURCE CODE is made available to anyone （软件）开放源代码的，提供源程序的

ˈ**open syllable** *noun* (*phonetics* 语音) a syllable which does not end with a consonant, for example *so* 开音节（以元音结束，如 so）

ˌ**open-ˈtoed** *adj.* (of shoes 鞋) not covering the toes 露趾的：*open-toed sandals* 露趾凉鞋

ˌ**open-ˈtop** (*also* ˌ**open-ˈtopped**) *adj.* (*BrE*) (of a vehicle 机动车) having no roof 敞篷的

ˌ**open ˈverdict** *noun* an official decision in a British court stating that the exact cause of a person's death is not known 死因未详的裁决，存疑判决（英国法庭宣称死因不明的判决）

opera /ˈɒprə; *NAmE* ˈɑːprə/ *noun* **1** [C, U] a dramatic work in which all or most of the words are sung to music; works of this type as an art form or entertainment 歌剧；歌剧剧本；歌剧艺术：*Puccini's operas* 普契尼的歌剧 ◇ *to go to the opera* 去看歌剧 ◇ *an opera singer* 歌剧演员 ◇ ***light/grand opera*** 轻歌剧；大歌剧 ➲SEE ALSO SOAP OPERA

> **WORDFINDER** 联想词：aria, chorus, coloratura, diva, libretto, orchestra pit, recitative, score, surtitles

2 [C] a company that performs opera; a building in which operas are performed 歌剧团；歌剧院：*the Vienna State Opera* 维也纳国家歌剧院 ▶ **op·er·at·ic** /ˌɒpəˈrætɪk; *NAmE* ˌɑːp-/ *adj.*：*operatic arias/composers* 歌剧咏叹调 / 作曲家

op·er·able /ˈɒpərəbl; *NAmE* ˈɑːp-/ *adj.* **1** that functions; that can be used 运作的；可实行的；可使用的：*When will the single currency be operable?* 什么时候实行单一货币？ **2** (of a medical condition 医疗状况) that can be treated by an operation 可以动手术的 OPP **inoperable**

ˈ**opera glasses** *noun* [pl.] small BINOCULARS that people use in a theatre to see the actors or singers on the stage 观剧小望远镜

ˈ**opera house** *noun* a theatre where operas are performed 歌剧院

op·er·and /ˈɒpərænd; *NAmE* ˈɑːp-/ *noun* (*mathematics* 数) the number on which an operation is to be done 操作数；运算对象

op·er·ate /ˈɒpəreɪt; *NAmE* ˈɑːp-/ *verb*

• MACHINE 机器 **1** [I] + **adv./prep.** to work in a particular way 运转；工作 SYN **function**：*Most domestic freezers operate at below –18°C.* 多数家用冰柜能制冷到零下 18 摄氏度以下。◇ *Solar panels can only operate in sunlight.* 太阳能电池板只能在日光下起作用。◇ (*figurative*) *Some people can only operate well under pressure.* 有些人只有在压力下才工作得好。 **2** [T] ~ **sth** to use or control a machine or make it work 操作；控制；使运行：*What skills are needed to operate this machinery?* 操作这种机器需要什么技能？

• SYSTEM/PROCESS/SERVICE 系统；过程；服务 **3** [I, T] to be used or working; to use sth or make it work （被）使用；（使）运转：*A new late-night service is now operating.* 现在推出一项新的深夜服务。◇ *The regulation operates in favour of married couples.* 这一规定的实施有利于已婚夫妇。◇ ~ **sth** *The airline operates flights to 25 countries.* 这家航空公司经营飞往 25 个国家的航班。◇ *France operates a system of subsidized loans to dairy farmers.* 法国对奶农实行补贴贷款制度。

• OF BUSINESS/ORGANIZATION 企业；机构 **4** [I] + **adv./prep.** to work in a particular way or from a particular place （以某方式或从某地方）经营，营业：*They plan to operate from a new office in Edinburgh.* 他们计划由爱丁堡的新办事处经营。◇ *Illegal drinking clubs continue to operate in the city.* 非法饮酒俱乐部继续在城内营业。

• MEDICAL 医疗 **5** [I] to cut open sb's body in order to remove a part that has a disease or to repair a part that is damaged 动手术：*The doctors operated last night.* 医生昨夜做手术了。◇ ~ (**on sb**) (**for sth**) *We will have to operate on his eyes.* 我们得给他的眼睛动手术。

• OF SOLDIERS 士兵 **6** [I] (+ **adv./prep.**) to be involved in military activities in a place （在某地）采取军事行动：*Troops are operating from bases in the north.* 部队正从北部基地发动军事行动。

ˈ**operating system** *noun* (*abbr.* **OS**) a set of programs that controls the way a computer works and runs other programs （计算机）操作系统 ➲WORDFINDER NOTE AT PROGRAM

ˈ**operating table** *noun* a special table that you lie on to have a medical operation in a hospital 手术台：*The patient died **on the operating table*** (= during an operation). 病人死在手术台上。

ˈ**operating theatre** (*also* **theatre**) (*both BrE*) (*NAmE* ˈ**operating room**) *noun* a room in a hospital used for medical operations 手术室

op·er·ation /ˌɒpəˈreɪʃn; *NAmE* ˌɑːp-/ *noun*

• MEDICAL 医疗 **1** (*also BrE, informal* **op**) [C] the process of cutting open a part of a person's body in order to remove or repair a damaged part 手术：*Will I need to **have an operation**?* 我需要动手术吗？ ◇ *He underwent a three-hour heart operation.* 他接受了三个小时的心脏手术。◇ ~ (**on sb/sth**) (**to do sth**) *an operation on her lung to* remove a tumour 为她做的肺部肿瘤切除手术 ◇ ~ (**on sb/sth**) (**for sth**) *Doctors **performed an** emergency **operation** for appendicitis last night.* 医生昨天夜里做了紧急阑尾炎手术。 ➲ WORDFINDER NOTE AT HOSPITAL ➲ COLLOCATIONS AT ILL

WORDFINDER 联想词: amputate, anaesthetic, graft, procedure, scalpel, scrubs, stitch, surgery, transplant

- **ORGANIZED ACTIVITY** 有组织的活动 **2** [C] an organized activity that involves several people doing different things（有组织的）活动，行动：*a security operation* 安全行动 ◇ *The police have launched a major operation against drug suppliers.* 警方展开了一次打击毒贩的大规模行动。◇ *the UN peacekeeping operations* 联合国维持和平行动
- **BUSINESS** 商务 **3** [C, usually pl.] a business or company involving many parts（包括许多部分的）企业，公司：*a huge multinational operation* 庞大的跨国公司 **4** [C] the activity or work done in an area of business or industry（工商业）活动，业务：*the firm's banking operations overseas* 这家公司的国外银行业务
- **COMPUTER** 计算机 **5** [C, U] an act performed by a machine, especially a computer 运算；运作：*The whole operation is performed in less than three seconds.* 全部运算在三秒内完成。
- **MACHINE/SYSTEM** 机器；系统 **6** [U] the way that parts of a machine or a system work; the process of making sth work 运转；运行；操作：*Regular servicing guarantees the smooth operation of the engine.* 定期维修可保持发动机的顺畅运转。◇ *Operation of the device is extremely simple.* 这个装置的操作非常简单。
- **MILITARY ACTIVITY** 军事行动 **7** [C, usually pl.] military activity 军事行动：*He was the officer in charge of operations.* 他是负责指挥作战行动的军官。
- **MATHEMATICS** 数学 **8** [C] a process in which a number or quantity is changed by adding, multiplying, etc. 运算

IDM **in ope'ration** working, being used or having an effect 工作中；使用中；有效：*The system has been in operation for six months.* 这个系统已经运行六个月了。◇ *Temporary traffic controls are in operation on New Road.* 新路正在实施临时交通管制。 **come into ope'ration** to start working; to start having an effect 开始工作；开始生效 SYN **come/enter into force**: *The new rules come into operation from next week.* 新规定从下周起实施。 **put sth into ope'ration** to make sth start working; to start using sth 实施；使…运转；启用：*It's time to put our plan into operation.* 现在应该执行我们的计划了。

op·er·ation·al /ˌɒpəˈreɪʃənl; *NAmE* ˌɑːp-/ *adj.* **1** [usually before noun] connected with the way in which a business, machine, system, etc. works 操作的；运转的；运营的；业务的：*operational activities/costs/difficulties* 营运活动 / 成本 / 困难 **2** [not usually before noun] ready to be used 可使用：*The new airport is now **fully operational**.* 新机场现在可全面投入运营。 **3** [only before noun] connected with a military operation 军事行动的：*operational headquarters* 作战指挥部 ▸ **op·er·ation·al·ly** *adv.*

ˌoperational ˈresearch (*also* **ˈoperations research**) *noun* [U] (*specialist*) the study of how businesses are organized, in order to make them more efficient 运筹学

ˌopeˈration code (*also* **op·code**) *noun* [U, C] (*computing* 计) an instruction written in MACHINE CODE which relates to a particular task 操作码；运算码

opeˈrations room *noun* a room from which military or police activities are controlled（军队或警方的）作战指挥室，行动指挥室

op·era·tive /ˈɒpərətɪv; *NAmE* ˈɑːpərətɪv; -reɪt-/ *noun, adj.*

■ *noun* **1** (*specialist*) a worker, especially one who works with their hands 工作人员；（尤指）技术工人，操作员：*a factory operative* 工厂工人 ◇ ***skilled/unskilled operatives*** 技术 / 非技术工人 **2** (*especially NAmE*) a person who does secret work, especially for a government organization 密探；（尤指政府的）特工人员：*an intelligence operative* 情报人员

■ *adj.* **1** [not usually before noun] ready to be used; in use 可使用；在使用中 SYN **functional**: *This law becomes operative immediately.* 本法规即时生效。◇ *The station will be **fully operative** again in January.* 该站将于一月份全部恢复运营。 **2** [only before noun] (*medical* 医) connected with a medical operation 手术的：*operative treatment* 手术治疗 ➲ SEE ALSO POST-OPERATIVE

IDM **the operative word** used to emphasize that a particular word or phrase is the most important one in a sentence 关键词；最重要的词语：*I was in love with her—'was' being the operative word.* 在 I was in love with her 这句话中，was 是关键词。

op·er·ator /ˈɒpəreɪtə(r); *NAmE* ˈɑːp-/ *noun* **1** (often in compounds 常构成复合词) a person who operates equipment or a machine 操作人员；技工：*a computer/machine operator* 电脑 / 机器操作员 **2** (*BrE also* **tel·eph·on·ist**) a person who works on the telephone SWITCHBOARD of a large company or organization, especially at a TELEPHONE EXCHANGE 电话员；接线员 **3** (often in compounds 常构成复合词) a person or company that runs a particular business（某企业的）经营者，专业公司：*a tour operator* 经营旅游业者 ◇ *a bus operator* 公共汽车公司 **4** (*informal, especially disapproving*) a person who is skilful at getting what they want, especially when this involves behaving in a dishonest way 投机取巧者；善于钻营的人；骗子：*a **smooth/slick/shrewd operator*** 一个八面玲珑 / 油嘴滑舌 / 工于心计的取巧者 **5** (*mathematics* 数) a symbol or function which represents an operation in mathematics 算子

op·er·etta /ˌɒpəˈretə; *NAmE* ˌɑːpə-/ *noun* a short OPERA, usually with a humorous subject 轻歌剧；小歌剧

oph·thal·mic /ɒfˈθælmɪk; *NAmE* ɑːf-/ *adj.* (*medical* 医) connected with the eye 眼科的；与眼睛有关的：*ophthalmic surgery* 眼科手术

ophˌthalmic opˈtician *noun* (*BrE*) = OPTICIAN

oph·thal·molo·gist /ˌɒfθælˈmɒlədʒɪst; *NAmE* ˌɑːfθælˈmɑːl-/ *noun* a doctor who studies and treats the diseases of the eye 眼科医生 ➲ WORDFINDER NOTE AT SPECIALIST

oph·thal·mol·ogy /ˌɒfθælˈmɒlədʒi; *NAmE* ˌɑːfθælˈmɑːl-/ *noun* [U] the scientific study of the eye and its diseases 眼科学

opi·ate /ˈəʊpiət; *NAmE* ˈoʊ-/ *noun* (*formal*) a drug derived from OPIUM. Opiates are used in medicine to reduce severe pain. 阿片制剂

opine /əʊˈpaɪn; *NAmE* oʊ-/ *verb* ~ **that...** (*formal*) to express a particular opinion 表达，发表（意见）：*He opined that Prague was the most beautiful city in Europe.* 他认为布拉格是欧洲最美丽的城市。

opin·ion /əˈpɪnjən/ *noun* **1** [C] your feelings or thoughts about sb/sth, rather than a fact 意见；想法；看法 SYN **view**: ~ (**about/of/on sb/sth**) *We were invited to **give our opinions** about how the work should be done.* 我们应邀就如何开展工作提出意见。◇ *I've recently **changed my opinion of** her.* 我最近改变了对她的看法。◇ *Everyone **had an opinion** on the subject.* 大家对这个问题都有自己的看法。◇ ~ (**that...**) *The chairman **expressed the opinion** that job losses were inevitable.* 主席认为，失业在所难免。◇ *He has very strong political opinions.* 他的政见颇为坚定。◇ ***In my opinion**, it's a very sound investment.* 依我看，这是十分稳当的投资。◇ (*formal*) *It is our opinion that he should resign.* 我们认为他应该辞职。◇ *If you want my opinion, I think you'd be crazy not to accept.* 既然要我说嘛，我认为你不接受那才傻呢。 ➲ LANGUAGE BANK AT ACCORDING TO ➲ EXPRESS YOURSELF AT THINK **2** [U] the beliefs or views of a group of people（群体的）观点，信仰：*legal/medical/political opinion* (= the beliefs of people working in the legal, etc. profession) 法学界 / 医学界 / 政界的观点 ◇ *There is **a difference of opinion*** (= people disagree) *as to the merits of the plan.* 关于这个计划的优缺点，大家有意见分歧。◇ ***Opinion is divided*** (= people disagree) *on the issue.* 大家对这件事意见分歧。◇ *There is a wide body of opinion that supports this proposal.* 支持这项提议的大有人在。◇ *Which is the better is a **matter of opinion*** (= people have different opinions about it). 哪一个比较好只是看法问题。 ➲ SEE ALSO PUBLIC OPINION **3** [C] advice from a professional person 专家意见: *They called in a psychologist to give an independent opinion.* 他们征询一位心理学家的独立意见。◇ *I'd like a* ***second opinion*** (= advice from another person) *before I make a decision.* 我在作决定之前，想听听别人的意见。

IDM be of the opinion that… (*formal*) to believe or think that… 相信；认为 **have a good, bad, high, low, etc. opinion of sb/sth** to think that sb/sth is good, bad, etc. 对…评价好 / 不好 / 高 / 低: *The boss has a very high opinion of her.* 老板对她评价很高。➲ MORE AT CONSIDER

▼ LANGUAGE BANK 用语库

opinion

Giving your personal opinion 表达个人意见

- ***In my opinion****, everyone should have some understanding of science.* 依我看，每个人都应该懂一点科学。
- *Everyone should,* ***in my opinion****, have some understanding of science.* 依我看，每个人都应该懂一点科学。
- ***It seems to me that*** *many people in this country have a poor understanding of science.* 在我看来，这个国家许多人都不太懂科学。
- *This is,* ***in my view****, the result of a failure of the scientific community to get its message across.* 依我看，这是科学界未能清楚传达讯息所致。
- *Another reason why so many people have such a poor understanding of science is,* ***I believe****, the lack of adequate funding for science in schools.* 我认为，如此多的人对科学缺乏认识的另一个原因是学校对科学教育投入的资金不足。
- *Smith argues that science is separate from culture.* ***My own view is that*** *science belongs with literature, art, philosophy and religion as an integral part of our culture.* 史密斯认为科学与文化是互不相干的。我的观点是科学与文学、艺术、哲学以及宗教一起都是我们文化的不可或缺的一部分。
- ***In this writer's opinion****, the more the public know about science, the less they will fear and distrust it.* 在这个作家看来，公众对科学了解得越多，他们就越不会惧怕科学并且会更加相信科学。

➲ SYNONYMS AT THINK
➲ LANGUAGE BANK AT ACCORDING TO, ARGUE, IMPERSONAL, NEVERTHELESS, PERHAPS

opin·ion·ated /ə'pɪnjəneɪtɪd/ (*also* **,self-o'pinion·ated**) *adj.* (*disapproving*) having very strong opinions that you are not willing to change 固执己见的；顽固的

o'pinion poll *noun* = POLL (1)

opium /'əʊpiəm; *NAmE* 'oʊ-/ *noun* [U] a powerful drug made from the juice of a type of POPPY (= a kind of flower), used in the past in medicines to reduce pain and help people sleep. Some people take opium illegally for pleasure and can become ADDICTED to it. 鸦片

opos·sum /ə'pɒsəm; *NAmE* ə'pɑːs-/ (*AustralE, NZE* or *NAmE, informal* **pos·sum**) *noun* a small American or Australian animal that lives in trees and carries its young in a POUCH (= a pocket of skin on the front of the mother's body) 负鼠（产于美洲或澳大利亚的小动物，在树上生活，携幼崽于母兽育儿袋中）

op·pon·ent /ə'pəʊnənt; *NAmE* ə'poʊ-/ *noun* **1** a person that you are playing or fighting against in a game, competition, argument, etc. 对手；竞争者 **SYN adversary**: *a political opponent* 政敌 ◇ *a* ***dangerous/worthy/formidable opponent*** 危险的 / 可敬的 / 强大的对手 ◇ *The team's opponents are unbeaten so far this season.* 该队的竞争对手本赛季尚无败绩。 **2** ~ (**of sth**) a person who is against sth and tries to change or stop it 反对者；阻止者: *opponents of abortion* 反对堕胎的人 ◇ *opponents of the regime* 反对政权的人

op·por·tune /'ɒpətjuːn; *NAmE* ,ɑːpər'tuːn/ *adj.* (*formal*) **1** (of a time 时间) suitable for doing a particular thing, so that it is likely to be successful 恰好的；适当的；恰当的 **SYN favourable**: *The offer could not have come at a more opportune moment.* 那个建议提得正是时候。 **2** (of an action or event 行动或事情) done or happening at the right time to be successful 及时的；适时的: *an opportune remark* 适时的言辞 **OPP inopportune** ▸ **op·por·tune·ly** *adv.*

op·por·tun·ism /,ɒpə'tjuːnɪzəm; *NAmE* ,ɑːpər'tuː-/ *noun* [U] (*disapproving*) the practice of using situations unfairly to gain advantage for yourself without thinking about how your actions will affect other people 机会主义

op·por·tun·ist /,ɒpə'tjuːnɪst; *NAmE* ,ɑːpər'tuː-/ (*also* **op·por·tun·is·tic**) *adj.* [usually before noun] (*often disapproving*) making use of an opportunity, especially to get an advantage for yourself; not done in a planned way 机会主义的；投机的；见风转舵的: *an opportunist crime* 临时起意的偶发犯罪 ▸ **op·por·tun·ist** *noun*: *80% of burglaries are committed by casual opportunists.* * 80% 的入室行窃都是临时起意者所为。

op·por·tun·is·tic /,ɒpətjuː'nɪstɪk; *NAmE* ,ɑːpərtuː'n-/ *adj.* **1** (*disapproving*) = OPPORTUNIST **2** [only before noun] (*medical* 医) harmful to people whose IMMUNE SYSTEM has been made weak by disease or drugs 机会致病性的（对免疫系统差的人有害）: *an opportunistic infection* 机会性感染

op·por·tun·ity /,ɒpə'tjuːnəti; *NAmE* ,ɑːpər'tuː-/ *noun* [C, U] (*pl.* **-ies**) a time when a particular situation makes it possible to do or achieve sth 机会；时机 **SYN chance**: ~ (**to do sth**) *You'll have the opportunity to ask any questions at the end.* 你们最后将有机会提问任何问题。◇ ~ (**for sth/for doing sth**) *There was no opportunity for further discussion.* 没有机会进行深入讨论了。◇ ~ (**of doing sth**) *At least give him the opportunity of explaining what happened.* 至少要给他机会解释一下发生了什么事。◇ *Our company promotes* ***equal opportunities*** *for women* (= women are given the same jobs, pay, etc. as men). 本公司提倡男女机会均等。◇ ***career/employment/job opportunities*** 职业发展 / 就业 / 工作机会 ◇ *I'd like to* ***take this opportunity*** *to thank my colleagues for their support.* 我谨借此机会感谢同事的支持。◇ *He is rude to me* ***at every opportunity*** (= whenever possible). 他动不动就对我粗鲁无礼。◇ *They intend to close the school* ***at the earliest opportunity*** (= as soon as possible). 他们打算尽早关闭学校。◇ ***a window of opportunity*** (= a period of time when the circumstances are right for doing sth) 行事的良机 ➲ SEE ALSO PHOTO OPPORTUNITY

oppor'tunity shop (*also* **'op shop**) *noun* (*AustralE, NZE*) a shop/store that sells clothes and other goods given by people to raise money for a charity 义卖商店（为慈善事业募资）**SYN charity shop, thrift shop**

op·pose /ə'pəʊz; *NAmE* ə'poʊz/ *verb* **1** to disagree strongly with sb's plan, policy, etc. and try to change it or prevent it from succeeding 反对（计划、政策等）；抵制；阻挠: ~ **sb/sth** *This party would bitterly oppose the re-introduction of the death penalty.* 该党会强烈反对恢复死刑。◇ *He threw all those that opposed him into prison.* 他把所有反对他的人都投进了监狱。◇ ~ (**sb/sth**) **doing sth** *I would oppose changing the law.* 我将反对改变这个法规。➲ COMPARE PROPOSE (4) **2** ~ **sb** to compete with sb in a contest（在竞赛中）与…对垒，与…角逐: *He intends to oppose the prime minister in the leadership election.* 在领导层选举中，他欲与首相一决高下。

op·posed /ə'pəʊzd; *NAmE* ə'poʊzd/ *adj.* [not usually before noun] ~ (**to sth**) **1** (of a person 人) disagreeing strongly with sth and trying to stop it 强烈反对: *She remained bitterly opposed to the idea of moving abroad.* 她仍然强烈反对移居国外。◇ *They are totally opposed to abortion.* 他们完全反对堕胎。 **2** (of ideas, opinions, etc. 意见、看法等) very different from sth 截然不同: *Our*

O

*views are **diametrically opposed** on this issue.* 在这个问题上，我们的观点大相径庭。

IDM **as opposed to** (*formal*) used to make a contrast between two things（表示对比）而，相对于：*200 attended, as opposed to 300 the previous year.* 出席的有 200 人，而前一年是 300 人。◇ *This exercise develops suppleness as opposed to* (= rather than) *strength.* 这项锻炼不是增强力量，而是增强柔韧性的。

op·pos·ing /əˈpəʊzɪŋ; *NAmE* əˈpoʊzɪŋ/ *adj.* [only before noun] **1** (of teams, armies, forces, etc. 队组、军队、力量等) playing, fighting, working, etc. against each other 对立的；相竞争的；对抗的：*a player from the opposing side* 对方的运动员 ◇ *It is time for opposing factions to unite and work towards a common goal.* 现在是对立各派联合起来、为共同目标而奋斗的时候了。 **2** (of attitudes, views, etc. 态度、观点等) very different from each other 相反的；极不相同的

op·pos·ite /ˈɒpəzɪt; -sɪt; *NAmE* ˈɑːpəzət/ *adj., adv., noun, prep.*

■***adj.*** **1** [only before noun] on the other side of a particular area from sb/sth and usually facing them 对面的；另一边的：*Answers are given on the opposite page.* 答案在对页上。◇ *We live further down on the opposite side of the road.* 我们住在马路对面再远一点的地方。◇ *It's not easy having a relationship when you live at opposite ends of the country.* 人虽同国却各处东西；在这种情况下保持交往，谈何容易。 **2** (used after the noun 用于名词后) facing the speaker or sb/sth that has been mentioned 对面的：*I could see smoke coming from the windows of the house directly opposite.* 我能看到烟从正对面的窗户里冒出来。◇ *He sat down in the chair opposite.* 他在对面的椅子上坐了下来。 **3** [usually before noun] as different as possible from sth 相反的；迥然不同的：*I watched them leave and then drove off in the opposite direction.* 我目送他们离开，然后开车向相反的方向驶去。◇ *She tried calming him down but it seemed to be having the opposite effect.* 她试着让他平静下来，却似乎适得其反了。◇ *students at opposite ends of the ability range* 能力差距两极的学生

IDM **your ˌopposite ˈnumber** (*informal*) a person who does the same job as you in another organization（另一个单位内）与自己职位相当的人：*The Foreign Secretary is currently having talks with his opposite number in the White House.* 外交大臣现正和白宫的对等官员会谈。 **the ˌopposite ˈsex** the other sex 异性：*He found it difficult to talk to members of the opposite sex.* 他觉得很难与异性交谈。 ➲ MORE AT PULL *v.*

■***adv.*** on the other side of a particular area from sb/sth and usually facing them 对面；相反：*There's a newly married couple living opposite* (= on the other side of the road). 有一对新婚夫妇住在马路对面。◇ *See opposite* (= on the opposite page) *for further details.* 详情见对页。

■***noun*** a person or thing that is as different as possible from sb/sth else 对立的人（或物）；对立面；反面：*Hot and cold are opposites.* 热和冷是对立面。◇ *What is **the opposite of** heavy?* 重的反义词是什么？◇ *I thought she would be small and blonde but she's **the complete opposite**.* 我原以为她是一位身材娇小的金发女郎，但她恰恰相反。◇ *Exactly the opposite is true.* 事实恰恰相反。◇ *'Is it better now?' '**Quite the opposite**, I'm afraid.'* "现在好点了吗？" "恐怕正相反。"

IDM **ˌopposites atˈtract** used to say that people who are very different are often attracted to each other 相反相成；相异相吸

■***prep.*** **1** on the other side of a particular area from sb/sth, and usually facing them 与…相对；在…对面：*I sat opposite him during the meal* (= on the other side of the table). 席间我坐在他的对面。◇ *The bank is opposite the supermarket* (= on the other side of the road). 银行在超市的正对面。◇ *Write your address opposite* (= next to) *your name.* 在姓名旁边写上你的地址。 **2** acting in a film/movie or play as the partner of sb 与…合演；与…联袂演出：*She starred opposite Tom Hanks.* 她与汤姆·汉克斯联袂主演。

op·pos·ition /ˌɒpəˈzɪʃn; *NAmE* ˌɑːpə-/ *noun* **1** [U] ~ (**to sb/sth**) the act of strongly disagreeing with sb/sth, especially with the aim of preventing sth from happening（强烈的）反对，反抗，对抗：*Delegates expressed **strong opposition** to the plans.* 代表强烈反对这些计划。◇ *The army **met with fierce opposition** in every town.* 军队在每一座城镇都遭遇到了顽强的抵抗。◇ *He spent five years in prison for his opposition to the regime.* 他因为反对那个政权而过了五年的铁窗生活。◇ ***opposition forces*** (= people who are arguing, fighting, etc. with another group) 反对势力 **2 the opposition** [sing.+sing./pl. v.] the people you are competing against in business, a competition, a game, etc.（事业、竞赛、游戏等的）对手，敌手，竞争者：*He's gone to work for the opposition.* 他去为竞争对手工作了。◇ *The opposition is/are mounting a strong challenge to our business.* 对方正对我方企业逐渐形成强大的挑战。◇ *Liverpool couldn't match the opposition in the final and lost 2–0.* 利物浦队在决赛中不敌对手，以 0:2 输掉比赛。 **3 the Opposition** (*NAmE* **the opposition**) [sing.+sing./pl. v.] the main political party that is opposed to the government; the political parties that are in a parliament but are not part of the government 反对党；在野党：*the **leader of the Opposition*** 反对党领袖 ◇ ***Opposition MPs/parties*** 反对党议员；反对党派 ◇ *the Opposition spokesman on education* 反对党教育事务发言人 ➲ WORDFINDER NOTE AT GOVERNMENT **4** [U, C] (*formal*) the state of being as different as possible; two things that are as different as possible 对立；对立的事物：*the opposition between good and evil* 善与恶的对立 ◇ *His poetry is full of oppositions and contrasts.* 他的诗歌充满了对立与对比。 ▶ **op·pos·ition·al** /-ʃənl/ *adj.* [usually before noun] (*formal*)：*oppositional groups/tactics* 反对团体 / 策略

IDM **in oppoˈsition** (of a political party 政党) forming part of a parliament but not part of the government 反对党的；在野的 **in oppoˈsition to sb/sth** **1** disagreeing strongly with sb/sth, especially with the aim of preventing sth from happening 强烈反对（或抵制）某人 / 某事物：*Protest marches were held in opposition to the proposed law.* 为抗议新提出的法案举行了示威游行。 **2** contrasting two people or things that are very different 对比；对照：*Leisure is often defined in opposition to work.* 休闲常被定义为工作的反面。

op·press /əˈpres/ *verb* **1** ~ **sb** to treat sb in a cruel and unfair way, especially by not giving them the same freedom, rights, etc. as other people 压迫；欺压；压制：*The regime is accused of oppressing religious minorities.* 人们指控这个政权压迫少数宗教群体。 ➲ WORDFINDER NOTE AT FREEDOM **2** ~ **sb** to make sb only able to think about sad or worrying things 压抑；使窒息；使烦恼 SYN **weigh down**：*The gloomy atmosphere in the office oppressed her.* 办公室的低沉气氛使她感到郁闷。 ▶ **op·pres·sion** /əˈpreʃn/ *noun* [U]：*victims of oppression* 受压迫者

op·pressed /əˈprest/ *adj.* **1** treated in a cruel and unfair way and not given the same freedom, rights, etc. as other people 被压迫的；受迫害的：*oppressed minorities* 被压迫的少数群体 **2 the oppressed** *noun* [pl.] people who are oppressed 被压迫者

op·pres·sive /əˈpresɪv/ *adj.* **1** treating people in a cruel and unfair way and not giving them the same freedom, rights, etc. as other people 压迫的；压制的；高压的：*oppressive laws* 对部分人的压制性法律 ◇ *an oppressive regime* 残暴的政权 **2** (of the weather 天气) extremely hot and unpleasant and lacking fresh air 闷热的；令人窒息的 SYN **stifling**：*oppressive heat* 难熬的酷暑 **3** making you feel unhappy and anxious 令人苦恼的；令人焦虑的 SYN **stifling**：*an oppressive relationship* 令人苦恼的关系 ▶ **op·pres·sive·ly** *adv.*：*to behave oppressively* 表现得盛气凌人 ◇ *oppressively hot* 热得令人窒息 ◇ *He suffered from an oppressively dominant mother.* 他那武断专横的母亲令他苦不堪言。 **op·pres·sive·ness** *noun* [U]

op·press·or /əˈpresə(r)/ *noun* a person or group of people that treats sb in a cruel and unfair way, especially by not giving them the same rights, etc. as other people 压迫者；残暴的统治者；暴君

op·pro·brium /əˈprəʊbriəm; *NAmE* əˈproʊ-/ *noun* [U] (*formal*) severe criticism of a person, country, etc. by a large group of people（众人的）谴责，责难，抨击 ▶ **op·pro·bri·ous** /əˈprəʊbriəs; *NAmE* əˈproʊ-/ *adj.*：*an opprobrious remark* 众人的指摘

ˈop shop *noun* (*AustralE, NZE*) = OPPORTUNITY SHOP

opt /ɒpt; *NAmE* ɑːpt/ *verb* [I, T] to choose to take or not to take a particular course of action 选择；挑选：**~ for/against sth** *After graduating she opted for a career in music.* 毕业后她选择了从事音乐工作。◇ **~ to do sth** *Many workers opted to leave their jobs rather than take a pay cut.* 许多工人宁愿离职也不接受减薪。➲ SYNONYMS AT CHOOSE

PHR V **ˌopt ˈin (to sth)** to choose to be part of a system or an agreement 决定加入；选择参与 **ˌopt ˈout (of sth)** **1** to choose not to take part in sth 决定退出；选择不参与：*Employees may opt out of the company's pension plan.* 雇员可选择不参加该公司的养老金计划。 **2** (of a school or hospital in Britain 英国的学校或医院) to choose not to be under the control of the local authority 选择不受地方当局管理 ➲ RELATED NOUN OPT-OUT

optic /ˈɒptɪk; *NAmE* ˈɑːp-/ *adj., noun*

■ ***adj.*** [usually before noun] (*specialist*) connected with the eye or the sense of sight 眼的；视觉的：*the optic nerve* (= from the eye to the brain) 视神经

■ ***noun*** a device for measuring amounts of strong alcoholic drinks in a bar 奥普蒂克量杯（酒吧用以量烈性酒）

op·tic·al /ˈɒptɪkl; *NAmE* ˈɑːp-/ *adj.* [usually before noun] **1** connected with the sense of sight or the relationship between light and sight 视力的；视觉的；光学的：*optical effects* 视觉效果 **2** used to help you see sth more clearly 有助于视力的；光学的：*optical aids* 助视器 ◇ *optical instruments such as microscopes and telescopes* 显微镜和望远镜等光学仪器 **3** (*computing* 计) using light for reading or storing information 光读取的；光存储的：*optical storage* 光存储器 ◇ *an optical disk* 光盘 ▶ **op·tic·al·ly** /-kli/ *adv.*

ˌoptical ˈcharacter recognition *noun* [U] (*abbr.* **OCR**) (*computing* 计) the process of using light to record printed information onto disks for use in a computer system 光符识别（用光学方法识别印刷字符，以便用于计算机系统）

ˌoptical ˈfibre (*BrE*) (*NAmE* **ˌoptical ˈfiber**) *noun* [C, U] a thin glass thread through which light can be TRANSMITTED (= sent) 光导纤维；光纤

optical illusions 视错觉

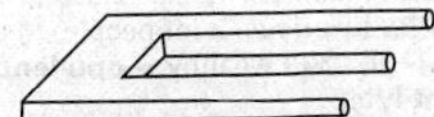

Are there two prongs or three?
有两个还是三个叉子齿？

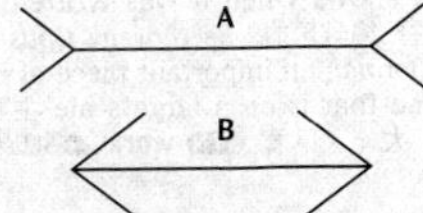

Horizontal line A and horizontal line B are of equal length, but horizontal line A appears to be longer.
水平线 A 和 B 长度相同，但 A 看起来要长些。

ˌoptical ilˈlusion *noun* something that tricks your eyes and makes you think that you can see sth that is not there, or makes you see sth as different from what it really is 视错觉；错视；视觉幻象

op·tic·als /ˈɒptɪklz; *NAmE* ˈɑːp-/ *noun* [pl.] (*IndE*) a pair of glasses 一副眼镜

op·ti·cian /ɒpˈtɪʃn; *NAmE* ɑːp-/ *noun* **1** (*also* **ophˌthalmic opˈtician**) (*BrE*) (*also* **op·tom·etrist** *NAmE, BrE*) a person whose job is to examine people's eyes and to recommend and sell glasses 眼镜商；验光师 **2** **op·ti·cian's** (*pl.* **op·ti·cians**) the shop/store where an optician works 眼镜商店：*to go to the optician's* 去配眼镜 ➲ MORE LIKE THIS 34, page R29 **3** a person who makes LENSES, glasses, etc. 光学仪器制造者

op·tics /ˈɒptɪks; *NAmE* ˈɑːp-/ *noun* [U] the scientific study of sight and light 光学 ➲ SEE ALSO FIBRE OPTICS ➲ MORE LIKE THIS 29, page R28

op·ti·mal /ˈɒptɪməl; *NAmE* ˈɑːp-/ *adj.* = OPTIMUM (1) ➲ COMPARE SUBOPTIMAL ▶ **op·ti·mal·ly** *adv.*

op·ti·mism /ˈɒptɪmɪzəm; *NAmE* ˈɑːp-/ *noun* [U] **~ (about/for sth)** a feeling that good things will happen and that sth will be successful; the tendency to have this feeling 乐观；乐观主义：*optimism about/for the future* 对未来的乐观 ◇ *We may now look forward* ***with optimism***. 我们现在可以乐观地展望未来。◇ *a mood of* ***cautious optimism*** 谨慎乐观的心情 ◇ *There are very real grounds for optimism.* 的确有理由可以乐观。**OPP** **pessimism**

op·ti·mist /ˈɒptɪmɪst; *NAmE* ˈɑːp-/ *noun* a person who always expects good things to happen or things to be successful 乐观的人；乐天派 **OPP** **pessimist**

op·ti·mis·tic /ˌɒptɪˈmɪstɪk; *NAmE* ˌɑːp-/ *adj.* expecting good things to happen or sth to be successful; showing this feeling 乐观的；抱乐观看法的 **SYN** **positive**：**~ (about sth)** *She's not very optimistic about the outcome of the talks.* 她对会谈的结果不太乐观。◇ **~ (that…)** *They are cautiously optimistic that the reforms will take place.* 他们对是否实行改革表示审慎的乐观。◇ *We are now taking a more optimistic view.* 我们现在抱较乐观的态度。◇ *in an optimistic mood* 以乐观的情绪 ◇ *I think you're being a little over-optimistic.* 我看你是有点过于乐观了。 **OPP** **pessimistic** ▶ **op·ti·mis·tic·al·ly** /-kli/ *adv.*

op·ti·mize (*BrE also* **-ise**) /ˈɒptɪmaɪz; *NAmE* ˈɑːp-/ *verb* **1** **~ sth** to make sth as good as it can be; to use sth in the best possible way 使最优化；充分利用：*to optimize the use of resources* 充分利用资源 **2** (*computing* 计) to change data, software, etc. in order to make it work more efficiently or to make it suitable for a particular purpose 优化（数据、软件等）：*It is important that websites are optimized for mobile devices.* 重要的是，网站要为适应移动设备而进行优化。

op·ti·mum /ˈɒptɪməm; *NAmE* ˈɑːp-/ *adj.* [only before noun] **1** (*also* **op·ti·mal**) the best possible; producing the best possible results 最佳的；最适宜的：*optimum growth* 最佳增长 ◇ *the optimum use of resources* 对资源的充分利用 ◇ *the optimum conditions for effective learning* 保证学习效果的最佳条件 **2** **the optimum** *noun* [sing.] the best possible result, set of conditions, etc. 最佳结果；最好的条件 **SYN** **ideal**

op·tion 🔑 **AW** /ˈɒpʃn; *NAmE* ˈɑːp-/ *noun, verb*

■ ***noun*** **1** 🔑 [C, U] something that you can choose to have or do; the freedom to choose what you do 可选择的事物；选择；选择权；选择的自由：*As I see it, we have two options…* 据我看，我们有两种选择… ◇ *There are various options open to you.* 你有多种选择。◇ *Going to college was not an option for me.* 上大学不是我能选的道路。◇ *I* ***had no option but to*** (= I had to) *ask him to leave.* 我别无选择，只有请他离开。◇ **~ (of doing sth)** *Students have the option of studying abroad in their second year.* 学生在二年级时可以选择出国学习。◇ **~ (to do sth)** *A savings plan that gives you the option to vary your monthly payments.* 一项允许可调每月存款额度的储蓄方案。◇ *This particular model comes with a wide range of options* (= things you can choose to have when buying sth but which you will have to pay extra for). 这一型号有各式各样的配件可供选择。 **2** 🔑 [C] a

O

subject that a student can choose to study, but that they do not have to do 选修课: *The course offers options in design and computing.* 这一课程开了设计和计算机技术的选修科目。**3** [C] the right to buy or sell sth at some time in the future （未来的）买卖选择权；期权：**~ (on sth)** *We have an option on the house.* 我们有权购买这所房子。◇ *He has promised me first option on his car* (= the opportunity to buy it before anyone else). 他答应我可以优先买他的汽车。◇ **~ (to do sth)** *The property is for rent with an option to buy at any time.* 这房子供出租，但可随时买下。◇ *share options* (= the right to buy shares in a company) 认股选择权 **4** [C] (*computing* 计) one of the choices you can make when using a computer program 选项；选择：*Choose the 'Cut' option from the Edit menu.* 从编辑选单上选"剪切"项。

IDM keep/leave your 'options open to avoid making a decision now so that you still have a choice in the future 保留选择余地；暂不决定 **the ˌsoft/ˌeasy 'option** (*often disapproving*) a choice which is thought to be easier because it involves less effort, difficulty, etc. 轻松的选择；捷径：*They are anxious that the new course should not be seen as a soft option.* 他们盼望新办法不会被视为捷径。◇ *He decided to* ***take the easy option*** *and give them what they wanted.* 他决定顺水推舟，他们要什么就给什么。

■*verb* **~ sth** to buy or sell the right to own or use sth, at some time in the future 购买（或出售）…的选择权：*The novel has been optioned for the screen by his production company.* 这部小说改编成影视作品的权利已经被他的制作公司买下了。

▼ **SYNONYMS 同义词辨析**

option

choice • alternative • possibility

These are all words for sth that you choose to do in a particular situation. 以上各词均指某种情况下的选择。

option something that you can choose to have or do; the freedom to choose what you do 指可选择的事物、选择、选择权、选择的自由：*As I see it, we have two options...* 据我看，我们有两种选择…◇ *Students have the option of studying abroad in their second year.* 学生在二年级时可以选择出国学习。**NOTE Option** is also the word used in computing for one of the choices you can make when using a computer program. * option 亦指计算机程序里的选项、选择：*Choose the 'Cut' option from the Edit menu.* 从编辑选单上选择"剪切"项。

choice the freedom to choose what you do; something that you can choose to have or do 指选择权、选择的自由、选择、可选择的事物：*If I had the choice, I would stop working tomorrow.* 如果让我选择，我明天就停止工作。◇ *There is a wide range of choices open to you.* 你有很多选择。

alternative something that you can choose to have or do out of two or more possibilities 指可供选择的事物、其中一种选择：*You can be paid in cash weekly or by cheque monthly: those are the two alternatives.* 你的工资可以按周以现金支取，或按月以支票支取。二者可选其一。

OPTION, CHOICE OR ALTERNATIVE? 用 option、choice 还是 alternative?

Choice is slightly less formal than **option** and **alternative** is slightly more formal. **Choice** is most often used for 'the freedom to choose', although you can sometimes also use **option** (but not usually **alternative**). * choice 较 option 稍非正式，而 alternative 更正式些。表示选择权或选择的自由最常用 choice，不过有时也可用 option，但通常不用 alternative：*If I had the choice/option, I would...* 如果让我选择，我会…◇ ~~*If I had the alternative, I would...*~~ ◇ *parental choice in education* 父母在教育方面的选择权 ◇ ~~*parental option/alternative in education*~~ Things that you can choose are **options, choices** or **alternatives**. However, **alternative** is more frequently used to talk about choosing between two things rather than several. 表示可选择的事物用 option、choice 或 alternative 均可。不过，alternative 较常用以指两个而非多个可选项。

possibility one of the different things that you can do in a particular situation 指某种情况下可选择的事物：*We need to explore a wide range of possibilities.* 我们需要探究各种可能的情况。◇ *The possibilities are endless.* 可想的办法是无穷的。**NOTE Possibility** can be used in a similar way to **option, choice** and **alternative**, but the emphasis here is less on the need to make a choice, and more on what is available. * possibility 的用法与 option、choice 和 alternative 相似，不过其重点主要在于可选择的事物而非需要作出选择。

PATTERNS

- **with/without** the option/choice/possibility **of** sth
- a(n) **good/acceptable/reasonable/possible** option/choice/alternative
- the **only** option/choice/alternative/possibility **open to** sb
- to **have** a(n)/the option/choice **of doing sth**
- to **have no** option/choice/alternative **but to** do sth
- a **number/range of** options/choices/alternatives/possibilities

op·tion·al AW /ˈɒpʃənl; NAmE ˈɑːp-/ *adj.* that you can choose to do or have if you want to 可选择的；选修的：*Certain courses are compulsory; others are optional.* 有些课程是必修的，其他是选修的。◇ *This model comes with a number of* ***optional extras*** (= things you can choose to have but which you will have to pay extra for). 这一型号有一系列可供选择的附件，价格另计。

op·tom·etrist /ɒpˈtɒmətrɪst; NAmE ɑːpˈtɑːm-/ (*BrE also* **op·ti·cian, ophˌthalmic opˈtician**) *noun* a person whose job is to examine people's eyes and to recommend and sell glasses 眼镜商；验光师

op·tom·etry /ɒpˈtɒmətri; NAmE ɑːpˈtɑːm-/ *noun* [U] the job of measuring how well people can see and checking their eyes for disease 验光；视力测定

ˈopt-out *noun* (often used as an adjective 常用作形容词) **1** (in Britain) the action of a school or hospital that decides to manage its own money and is therefore no longer controlled by a LOCAL AUTHORITY or similar organization（英国学校、医院从地方当局财政管辖的）退出，脱离 **2** the act of choosing not to be involved in an agreement 不参与协议的决定：*an opt-out clause* 退出的条款 ◇ *MPs hoped to reverse Britain's opt-out from the treaty.* 国会议员希望推翻英国退出该条约的决定。

opu·lent /ˈɒpjələnt; NAmE ˈɑːp-/ *adj.* (*formal*) **1** made or decorated using expensive materials 豪华的；富丽堂皇的；华丽的 SYN **luxurious 2** (of people 人) extremely rich 极富有的；阔气的 SYN **wealthy** ▸ **opu·lence** /-ləns/ *noun* [U] **opu·lent·ly** *adv.*

opus /ˈəʊpəs; NAmE ˈoʊ-/ *noun* (*pl.* **opera** /ˈɒpərə; NAmE ˈɑːp-/) [usually sing.] **1** (*abbr.* **op.**) a piece of music written by a famous COMPOSER and usually followed by a number that shows when it was written（按作曲家的创作时间排列的）编号乐曲：*Beethoven's Opus 18* 贝多芬第十八号作品 **2** (*formal*) an important piece of literature, etc., especially one that is on a large scale 主要（文学等）作品；（尤指）大作，巨著 SYN **work** ⇨ SEE ALSO MAGNUM OPUS

or /ɔː(r)/ *conj.* **1** used to introduce another possibility（用以引出另一种可能性）或，或者，还是：*Is your sister older or younger than you?* 你有姐姐还是妹妹？◇ *Are you coming or not?* 你来还是不来？◇ *Is it a boy or a girl?* 是个男孩还是女孩？◇ *It can be black, white or grey.* 它可能是黑的、白的或灰的。⇨ COMPARE EITHER... OR... **2** used in negative sentences when mentioning two or more things（用于否定句，提出两种或多种事物时）也不：*He can't read or write.* 他不会读，也不会写。◇ *There are people without homes, jobs or family.* 有人既无房屋，又无工作，又无家庭。⇨ COMPARE NEITHER... NOR... **3** (*also* **or else**) used to warn or advise sb that sth bad could happen; otherwise（用于警告或忠告）否则，不然：*Turn the heat down or it'll burn.* 把炉火开小一些，不然

就烧焦了。 **4** 🔑 used between two numbers to show approximately how many（用于两个数字之间表示约略数目）大约：*There were six or seven of us there.* 我们约有六七个人在场。 **5** 🔑 used to introduce a word or phrase that explains or means the same as another（用于引出解释性词语）或者说：*geology, or the science of the earth's crust* 地质学，或者说地壳的科学 ◇ *It weighs a kilo, or just over two pounds.* 这东西重一公斤，或者说两磅多一点儿。 **6** 🔑 used to say why sth must be true（用于说明原因）不然，否则：*He must like her, or he wouldn't keep calling her.* 他一定喜欢她，不然他不会老给她打电话。 **7** 🔑 used to introduce a contrasting idea（用于引出对比的概念）：*He was lying—or was he?* 他在说谎，还是没有说谎？

IDM **or so** 🔑 about 大约：*It'll cost €100 or so.* 这大约要花 100 欧元。 **or somebody/something/somewhere | somebody/something/somewhere or other** 🔑 (*informal*) used when you are not exactly sure about a person, thing or place（表示对人、事、地点不太有把握）：*He's a factory supervisor or something.* 他是工厂监督一类的人吧。 ◇ *'Who said so?' 'Oh, somebody or other. I can't remember who it was.'* "这是谁说的？" "啊，某一个人吧，我记不清是谁了。"

-or *suffix* (in nouns 构成名词) a person or thing that …的人（或物）：*actor* 演员 ➲ COMPARE -EE (1), -ER (1) ➲ MORE LIKE THIS 7, page R25

or·acle /ˈɒrəkl; *NAmE* ˈɔːr-/ *noun* [C] **1** (in ancient Greece) a place where people could go to ask the gods for advice or information about the future; the priest or PRIESTESS through whom the gods were thought to give their message（古希腊的）神示所；（传达神谕的）牧师，女祭司：*They consulted the oracle at Delphi.* 他们在德尔斐神示所向神请示。 **2** (in ancient Greece) the advice or information that the gods gave, which often had a hidden meaning（古希腊常有隐含意义的）神谕，神示 **3** [usually sing.] a person or book that gives valuable advice or information 能提供宝贵信息的人（或书）；权威；智囊：*My sister's the oracle on investment matters.* 我姐姐是个万无一失的投资顾问。

or·acu·lar /əˈrækjələ(r)/ *adj.* (*formal* or *humorous*) of or like an oracle; with a hidden meaning 神谕般的；天书般的；晦涩难懂的

oral /ˈɔːrəl/ *adj.*, *noun*

■ ***adj.*** **1** [usually before noun] spoken rather than written 口头的：*a test of both oral and written French* 法语口试和笔试 ◇ *oral evidence* 口头证据 ◇ *He was interested in **oral history*** (= history that is collected from interviews with people who have personal knowledge of past events). 他对口述历史感兴趣。 ➲ SYNONYMS AT SPOKEN ➲ COMPARE VERBAL (2) **2** [only before noun] connected with the mouth 用口的；口腔的；口服的：*oral hygiene* 口腔卫生 ◇ *oral sex* (= using the mouth to STIMULATE sb's sex organs) 口交 **3** (*phonetics* 语音) (of a speech sound 语音) produced without the air in the nose VIBRATING 口腔发声的；口腔的 ➲ COMPARE NASAL (3) ▶ **or·al·ly** /ˈɔːrəli/ *adv.*：*Answers can be written or presented orally on tape.* 答案可以写下来或口述录在磁带上。 ◇ *Not to be taken orally* (= a warning on some medicines to show that they must not be swallowed). 不得口服。

■ ***noun*** **1** (*especially BrE*) a spoken exam, especially in a foreign language（尤指外语考试中的）口试：*a French oral* 法语口试 ◇ *He failed the oral.* 他口试不及格。 **2** (*NAmE*) a spoken exam in a university（大学里的）口试 ➲ WORDFINDER NOTE AT EXAM

ˌoral ˈhistory *noun* [U] the collection and study of historical information using sound recordings of interviews with people who remember past events 口述历史（用访谈录音方法）；口述历史学

oral·ism /ˈɔːrəlɪzəm/ *noun* [U] the system of teaching deaf people to communicate using speech and LIP-READING 口语教学法（教聋人通过讲话和唇读来交际） ▶ **oral·ist** /-ɪst/ *adj.*

or·ange 🔑 /ˈɒrɪndʒ; *NAmE* ˈɔːr-; ˈɑːr-/ *noun*, *adj.*

■ ***noun*** [C, U] **1** 🔑 a round CITRUS fruit with thick reddish-yellow skin and a lot of sweet juice 橙子；柑橘：*orange peel* 柑橘皮 ◇ *an orange tree* 橙树 ◇ *freshly squeezed orange juice* 鲜榨橙汁 ◇ *orange groves* (= groups of orange trees) 橙树丛 ◇ *orange blossom* 香橙花 ➲ VISUAL VOCAB PAGE V33 ➲ SEE ALSO BLOOD ORANGE **2** (*BrE*) orange juice, or a drink made from or tasting of oranges 橙汁；橘汁饮料：*Would you like some orange?* 您想喝点橙汁吗？ ◇ *A vodka and orange, please.* 请来一份橙汁伏特加酒。 **3** 🔑 a bright reddish-yellow colour 橙红色；橘黄色 IDM SEE APPLE

■ ***adj.*** **1** 🔑 bright reddish-yellow in colour 橙红色的；橘黄色的：*yellow and orange flames* 黄色和橙色的火焰 **2 Orange** related to or belonging to a Protestant political group which believes that Northern Ireland should remain part of the UK 奥兰治党的，奥兰治社团的（新教政治团体，主张北爱尔兰继续隶属英国）：*an Orange march* 奥兰治党的游行

or·ange·ade /ˌɒrɪndʒˈeɪd; *NAmE* ˌɔːr-; ˌɑːr-/ *noun* **1** [U, C] a sweet drink with an orange flavour. In Britain it always has bubbles in it; in the US it can be with or without bubbles. 橙汁饮料；橘子汁；橙汁汽水 **2** [C] a glass of orangeade 一杯橙汁汽水 ➲ COMPARE LEMONADE

Or·ange·man /ˈɒrɪndʒmən; *NAmE* ˈɔːr-; ˈɑːr-/ *noun* (*pl.* **-men** /-mən/) a member of the Orange Order, a Protestant political organization that wants Northern Ireland to remain part of the United Kingdom 奥兰治党员，奥兰治人（主张北爱尔兰继续隶属英国的新教政治组织成员）

or·an·gery /ˈɒrɪndʒəri; *NAmE* ˈɔːr-; ˈɑːr-/ *noun* (*pl.* **-ies**) a glass building where orange trees are grown 柑橘暖房

ˌorange ˈsquash *noun* (*BrE*) **1** [U, C] a thick sweet liquid made with orange juice and sugar; a drink made from this with water added 加糖（或加水）橙汁饮料：*a bottle of orange squash* 一瓶橙子水饮料 **2** [C] a glass of orange squash 一杯橙汁饮料：*Two orange squashes, please.* 请来两杯橙汁饮料。

orang-utan /ɔːˌræŋ uːˈtæn; əˈræŋ uːtæn; *NAmE* əˈræŋ ətæn/ *noun* a large APE (= an animal like a large MONKEY with no tail) with long arms and reddish hair, that lives in Borneo and Sumatra 猩猩，褐猿（产于婆罗洲和苏门答腊） ORIGIN From Malay *orang utan/hutan*, meaning 'person of the forest'. 源自马来语 orang utan/hutan，意为"森林人"。

ora·tion /ɔːˈreɪʃn/ *noun* (*formal*) a formal speech made on a public occasion, especially as part of a ceremony 演说，致辞（尤指作为仪式的一部分）

ora·tor /ˈɒrətə(r); *NAmE* ˈɔːr-; ˈɑːr-/ *noun* (*formal*) a person who makes formal speeches in public or is good at public speaking 讲演者；雄辩家；善于演说的人：*a fine political orator* 优秀的政治演说家

ora·tor·ic·al /ˌɒrəˈtɒrɪkl; *NAmE* ˌɔːrəˈtɔːr-/ *adj.* (*formal*, *sometimes disapproving*) connected with the art of public speaking 演说的；讲演术的：*oratorical skills* 演说技能

ora·torio /ˌɒrəˈtɔːriəʊ; *NAmE* ˌɔːrəˈtɔːrioʊ; ˌɑːrə-/ *noun* (*pl.* **-os**) a long piece of music for singers and an ORCHESTRA, usually based on a story from the Bible 清唱剧，神剧（通常以《圣经》故事为主题） ➲ COMPARE CANTATA

ora·tory /ˈɒrətri; *NAmE* ˈɔːrətɔːri; ˈɑːr-/ *noun* (*pl.* **-ies**) **1** [U] the skill of making powerful and effective speeches in public 讲演术；雄辩术 SYN **rhetoric** **2** [C] a room or small building that is used for private prayer or worship（私人）祈祷室，小礼拜堂

orb /ɔːb; *NAmE* ɔːrb/ *noun* **1** (*literary*) an object shaped like a ball, especially the sun or moon 球体；（尤指）日，月 **2** a gold ball with a cross on top, carried by a king or queen at formal ceremonies as a symbol of power 王权宝球（国王或女王在正式仪式上携带的顶部饰十字架的金球，是权力的象征） ➲ COMPARE SCEPTRE

orbit /ˈɔːbɪt; *NAmE* ˈɔːrbɪt/ *noun*, *verb*

■ ***noun*** **1** [C, U] a curved path followed by a planet or an object as it moves around another planet, star, moon, etc.（天体等运行的）轨道：*the earth's orbit around the sun* 地球环绕太阳的轨道 ◇ *a space station **in orbit** round* the moon 绕月球运行的一个空间站 ◇ *A new satellite has been **put into orbit** around the earth.* 一颗新的人造卫星被送上了环绕地球的轨道。 ➲ WORDFINDER NOTE AT SPACE, UNIVERSE **2** [sing.] an area that a particular person, organization, etc. deals with or is able to influence (人、组织等的)影响范围，势力范围: *to **come/fall/be within sb's orbit*** 进入 / 落入 / 属于某人的势力范围

■ ***verb*** [T, I] **~ (around) sth** to move in an orbit (= a curved path) around a much larger object, especially a planet, star, etc. 沿轨道运行；围绕…运动: *The earth takes a year to orbit the sun.* 地球绕太阳一周要一年的时间。

or·bit·al /ˈɔːbɪtl; *NAmE* ˈɔːrb-/ *adj., noun*

■ ***adj.*** [only before noun] **1** connected with the orbit of a planet or object in space (行星或空间物体)轨道的 **2** (*BrE*) (of a road 道路) built around the edge of a town or city to reduce the amount of traffic travelling through the centre (城市)外环路的

■ ***noun*** (*BrE*) a very large RING ROAD, especially if it is a MOTORWAY 高速环行路: *the M25 London orbital* 伦敦 M25 高速环行路

or·bit·er /ˈɔːbɪtə(r); *NAmE* ˈɔːrb-/ *noun* a SPACECRAFT designed to move around a planet or moon rather than to land on it (绕天体作轨道运行的)宇宙飞船；轨道飞行器

orca /ˈɔːkə; *NAmE* ˈɔːrkə/ *noun* = KILLER WHALE

Or·ca·dian /ɔːˈkeɪdiən; ɔːrˈk-/ *noun* a person from the islands of Orkney in Scotland (苏格兰奥克尼群岛的)奥克尼人 ▶ **Or·ca·dian** *adj.*

orch·ard /ˈɔːtʃəd; *NAmE* ˈɔːrtʃərd/ *noun* a piece of land, normally separated from the surrounding area, in which fruit trees are grown 果园 ➲ VISUAL VOCAB PAGE V3

or·ches·tra /ˈɔːkɪstrə; *NAmE* ˈɔːrk-/ *noun* **1** [C+sing./pl. v.] a large group of people who play various musical instruments together, led by a CONDUCTOR 管弦乐队: *She plays the flute in the school orchestra.* 她在校管弦乐队里吹长笛。 ◇ *the Scottish Symphony Orchestra* 苏格兰交响乐团 ➲ SEE ALSO CHAMBER ORCHESTRA, SYMPHONY ORCHESTRA **2 the orchestra** [sing.] (*NAmE*) (*BrE* **the ˈorchestra stalls, the stalls**) the seats that are nearest to the stage in a theatre (剧场的)正厅前排座位

or·ches·tral /ɔːˈkestrəl; *NAmE* ɔːrˈk-/ *adj.* connected with an orchestra 管弦乐的；管弦乐队的: *orchestral music* 管弦乐曲

ˈorchestra pit (*also* **pit**) *noun* the place in a theatre just in front of the stage where the orchestra sits and plays for an OPERA, a BALLET, etc. 乐池，乐队席(舞台前乐队演奏的地方) ➲ WORDFINDER NOTE AT OPERA

or·ches·trate /ˈɔːkɪstreɪt; *NAmE* ˈɔːrk-/ *verb* **1 ~ sth** to arrange a piece of music in parts so that it can be played by an orchestra 编配(或创作)管弦乐曲 **2 ~ sth** to organize a complicated plan or event very carefully or secretly 精心安排；策划；密谋 SYN **stage-manage**: *a carefully orchestrated publicity campaign* 精心策划的一场宣传运动 ▶ **or·ches·tra·tion** /ˌɔːkɪˈstreɪʃn; *NAmE* ˌɔːrk-/ *noun* [C, U]

or·chid /ˈɔːkɪd; *NAmE* ˈɔːrkɪd/ *noun* a plant with brightly coloured flowers of unusual shapes. There are many different types of orchid and some of them are very rare. 兰科植物；兰花 ➲ VISUAL VOCAB PAGE V11

or·dain /ɔːˈdeɪn; *NAmE* ɔːrˈd-/ *verb* **1 ~ sb (as sth) | ~ sb + noun** to make sb a priest, minister or RABBI 授予圣秩(品)；授予圣职: *He was ordained (as) a priest last year.* 他去年被授以神父圣职。 ➲ SEE ALSO ORDINATION **2 ~ sth | ~ that…** (*formal*) (of God, the law or FATE 神、法律或命运) to order or command sth; to decide sth in advance 主宰；掌握；规定: *Fate had ordained that they would never meet again.* 他们命里注定永远不会再相见。

or·deal /ɔːˈdiːl; ˈɔːdiːl; *NAmE* ɔːrˈd-/ *noun* [usually sing.] **~ (of sth/of doing sth)** a difficult or unpleasant experience 磨难；折磨；煎熬；严酷的考验: *They are to be spared the ordeal of giving evidence in court.* 他们将免受出庭作证的难堪。 ◇ *The hostages spoke openly about the terrible ordeal they had been through.* 人质公开陈述了他们所遭受的非人的折磨。 ◇ *The interview was less of an ordeal than she'd expected.* 面试并非如她想象的那样可怕。

order 🔑 /ˈɔːdə(r); *NAmE* ˈɔːrd-/ *noun, verb*

■ ***noun***

• **ARRANGEMENT** 安排 **1** 🔑 [U, C] the way in which people or things are placed or arranged in relation to each other 顺序；次序: *The names are listed **in alphabetical order**.* 姓名是按字母顺序排列的。 ◇ ***in chronological/numerical order*** 按时间 / 数字顺序 ◇ *arranged **in order of** priority/importance/size* 按优先次序 / 重要性 / 大小排列 ◇ *The results, ranked **in descending/ascending order**, are as follows:* 结果按降序 / 升序排列如下: ◇ *All the procedures must be done in the correct order.* 一切手续必须按正确顺序办理。 ◇ *Let's take the problems in a different order.* 咱们换一个顺序来处理这些问题吧。 **2** 🔑 [U] the state of being carefully and neatly arranged 条理: *It was time she **put** her life **in order**.* 她到了该好好安排自己生活的时候了。 ◇ *The house had been kept in good order.* 房子保持得井井有条。 ◇ *Get your ideas into some sort of order before beginning to write.* 落笔之前，先要理清思路。 ◇ *It is one of the functions of art to bring order out of chaos.* 艺术的功能之一就是在于呈现纷乱中的秩序。 OPP **disorder**

• **CONTROLLED STATE** 有序状态 **3** 🔑 [U] the state that exists when people obey laws, rules or authority 治安；秩序；规矩: *The army has been sent in to maintain order in the capital.* 军队被调进首都维持治安。 ◇ *Some teachers find it difficult to **keep** their classes **in order**.* 有些教师觉得难以维持课堂秩序。 ◇ *The police are trying to restore public order.* 警察正在努力恢复公共秩序。 ◇ *The argument continued until the chairman **called** them both **to order*** (= ordered them to obey the formal rules of the meeting). 争论持续不休，直到主席要求双方遵守议事规则。 ➲ COMPARE DISORDER (2) ➲ SEE ALSO POINT OF ORDER

• **INSTRUCTIONS** 指示 **4** 🔑 [C] something that sb is told to do by sb in authority 指示；命令: **~ (for sb/sth to do sth)** *He **gave orders** for the work to be started.* 他下令开始工作。 ◇ **~ (to do sth)** *The general **gave the order** to advance.* 将军下令前进。 ◇ *I'm **under orders** not to let anyone in.* 我奉命不准任何人进入。 ◇ *She **takes orders** only from the president.* 她只听从总裁的吩咐。 ◇ *Dogs can be trained to **obey orders**.* 狗可以训练得听从命令。 ◇ (*informal*) *No sugar for me—**doctor's orders**.* 我不要糖，谨遵医嘱嘛。 ◇ *Interest rates can be controlled **by order of** the central bank.* 利率可由中央银行指示控制。

• **GOODS** 货品 **5** 🔑 [C, U] **~ (for sth)** a request to make or supply goods 订货；订购；订单: *I would like to **place an order** for ten copies of this book.* 这本书我想订购十册。 ◇ *an order form* 订货单 ◇ *The machine parts are still **on order*** (= they have been ordered but have not yet been received). 机器零件尚在订购之中。 ◇ *These items can be made **to order*** (= produced especially for a particular customer). 这几项可以定做。 ➲ SEE ALSO MAIL ORDER **6** [C] goods supplied in response to a particular order that sb has placed 所订的货物；交付的订货: *The stationery order has arrived.* 订购的文具到货了。

• **FOOD/DRINKS** 食物；饮料 **7** 🔑 [C] a request for food or drinks in a restaurant, bar, etc.; the food or drinks that you ask for 点菜；所点的饮食菜肴: *May I **take your order**?* 您现在点菜吗? ◇ ***Last orders** at the bar now please!* (= because the bar is going to close) 本店(打烊前)最后一次点酒了! ◇ *an order for steak and fries* 点一份牛排炸薯条 ◇ *a **side order*** (= for example, vegetables or salad that you eat with your main dish) 配菜(主菜以外的蔬菜、色拉等) ➲ WORDFINDER NOTE AT RESTAURANT ➲ COLLOCATIONS AT RESTAURANT

• **MONEY** 钱 **8** [C] a formal written instruction for sb to be paid money or to do sth 付款指令(或委托书)；书面指令；汇票 ➲ SEE ALSO BANKER'S ORDER, COURT ORDER, MONEY ORDER, POSTAL ORDER, STANDING ORDER

• **SYSTEM** 制度 **9** [C, usually sing.] (*formal*) the way that a society, the world, etc. is arranged, with its system of rules and customs 秩序；结构: *a change in the political and social order* 政治和社会结构的改变 ◇ *the natural order of things* 天地万物的自然秩序 ◇ *He was seen as a threat to* *the established order.* 他被视为现存制度的大敌。◇ *A new order seems to be emerging.* 新的秩序似乎正在显现。

• SOCIAL CLASS 社会阶级 **10** [C, usually pl.] (*disapproving* or *humorous*) a social class 阶级；等级；阶层：*the lower orders* 底层社会

• BIOLOGY 生物 **11** [C] a group into which animals, plants, etc. that have similar characteristics are divided, smaller than a CLASS and larger than a FAMILY（生物分类的）目：*the order of primates* 灵长目 ➲ COMPARE GENUS ➲ WORDFINDER NOTE AT BREED

• RELIGIOUS COMMUNITY 宗教团体 **12** [C+sing./pl. v.] a group of people living in a religious community, especially MONKS or NUNS（按照一定的规范生活的）宗教团体；（尤指）修会：*religious orders* 修会 ◇ *the Benedictine order* 本笃会

• SPECIAL HONOUR 特殊荣誉 **13** [C+sing./pl. v.] a group of people who have been given a special honour by a queen, king, president, etc. （获国王、女王、总统等）授勋的人；勋位；勋爵士团：*The Order of the Garter is an ancient order of chivalry.* 嘉德勋位是古老的骑士勋位。 **14** [C] a BADGE or RIBBON worn by members of an order who have been given a special honour 勋章；绶带

• SECRET SOCIETY 秘密社团 **15** [C+sing./pl. v.] a secret society whose members meet for special ceremonies（秘密）社团，集团，结社：*the Ancient Order of Druids* 古德鲁伊特共济会

IDM **be in/take (holy) 'orders** to be/become a priest 已领受 / 领受神品（或圣秩）；为 / 成为神职人员 **in 'order 1** (of an official document 正式文件) that can be used because it is all correct and legal（依法）有效的 SYN **valid**: *Is your work permit in order?* 你的工作许可证有效吗？ **2** (*formal*) as it should be 正常；准备好；就绪：*Is everything in order, sir?* 一切都正常吗，先生？ **3** if sth is **in order**, it is a suitable thing to do or say on a particular occasion 妥当；适宜：*I think a drink would be in order.* 我想应该喝杯饮料了吧。 **in 'order (to do sth)** (*formal*) allowed according to the rules of a meeting, etc. 符合议事规则：*Is it in order to speak now?* 依规定现在可以发言了吗？ **in order that** (*formal*) so that sth can happen 目的在于；为了；以便：*All those concerned must work together in order that agreement can be reached on this issue.* 一切有关人员必须通力合作，以便能在这个问题上达成协议。 **in order to do sth** with the purpose or intention of doing or achieving sth 目的是；以便；为了：*She arrived early in order to get a good seat.* 她早早到场，好找个好位置。◇ *In order to get a complete picture, further information is needed.* 为掌握全面情况，还需要详细资料。 ➲ LANGUAGE BANK AT PROCESS[1] **in running/working 'order** (especially of machines 尤指机器) working well 运转正常；运转良好：*The engine is now in perfect working order.* 发动机现在运转完全正常。 **of a high order | of the highest/first order** of a high quality or degree; of the highest quality or greatest degree 高质量的；高品质的；一流的：*The job requires diplomatic skills of a high order.* 这项工作要求高超的外交技巧。◇ *She was a snob of the first order.* 她是天字第一号势利鬼。 **of/in the order of sth** (*BrE*) (*NAmE* **on the order of**) (*formal*) about sth; approximately sth 大约；差不多：*She earns something in the order of £80 000 a year.* 她的年收入为 8 万英镑左右。 **the ˌorder of the 'day** common, popular or suitable at a particular time or for a particular occasion 常见的；流行的；适宜的：*Pessimism seems to be the order of the day.* 悲观失望似乎是当今司空见惯的情形。 **Order! Order!** used to remind people to obey the rules of a formal meeting or debate（用于提醒人们遵守会议、辩论的规则）安静！安静！；别吵！别吵！ **ˌout of 'order 1** (of a machine, etc. 机器等) not working correctly 有毛病；出故障：*The phone is out of order.* 电话坏了。 **2** not arranged correctly or neatly 安排不当；不整洁：*I checked the files and some of the papers were out of order.* 我检查过案卷，其中有些未按顺序编排。 **3** (*BrE*) (*NAmE* **ˌout of 'line**) (*informal*) behaving in a way that is not acceptable or right 行为不当；举止令人难以接受：*You were well out of order taking it without asking.* 你不问一声就把它拿走，这是很不妥当的。 **4** (*formal*) not allowed by the rules of a formal meeting or debate 违反规程的；不合乎（会议或辩论）规则的：*His objection was ruled out of order.* 他的反对被裁定为违反会议规则。 ➲ MORE AT CALL *v.*, HOUSE *n.*, LAW, MARCH *v.*, PECK *v.*, SHORT *adj.*, STARTER, TALL

■ *verb*

• GIVE INSTRUCTIONS 下达指令 **1** [T] to use your position of authority to tell sb to do sth or say that sth must happen 命令；指挥；要求：**~ sb to do sth** *The company was ordered to pay compensation to its former employees.* 公司被勒令向以前的员工作出补偿。◇ *The officer ordered them to fire.* 军官命令他们开火。◇ **~ sb + adv./prep.** *They were ordered out of the class for fighting.* 他们因打架被勒令退出课堂。◇ **~ sth** *The government has ordered an investigation into the accident.* 政府要求对事故进行调查。◇ **~ that...** *They ordered that for every tree cut down two more be planted.* 他们要求每砍伐一棵树就要补栽两棵树。◇ (*BrE also*) *They ordered that for every tree cut down two more should be planted.* 他们要求每砍伐一棵树就要补栽两棵树。◇ **~ (sb) + speech** *'Sit down and be quiet,' she ordered.* “坐下，安静点！”她命令道。 ➲ EXPRESS YOURSELF AT TELL

• GOODS/SERVICE 货物；服务 **2** [T] to ask for goods to be made or supplied; to ask for a service to be provided 订购；订货；要求提供（服务）：**~ sth (from sb)** *These boots can be ordered direct from the manufacturer.* 这些靴子可向厂方直接订货。◇ **~ sb sth** *Shall I order you a taxi?* 要我给你叫辆出租车吗？◇ **~ sth for sb** *Shall I order a taxi for you?* 要我给你叫辆出租车吗？

▼ **SYNONYMS 同义词辨析**

order

tell • instruct • direct • command

These words all mean to use your position of authority to say to sb that they must do sth. 以上各词均含命令、指挥、要求之义。

order to use your position of authority to tell sb to do sth 指命令、指挥、要求：*The company was ordered to pay compensation to its former employee.* 公司被勒令向以前的员工作出补偿。◇ *'Come here at once!' she ordered.* “马上过来！”她命令道。

tell to say to sb that they must or should do sth 指命令、指示、吩咐：*He was told to sit down and wait.* 有人吩咐他坐下等着。◇ *Don't tell me what to do!* 别对我指手画脚的！

instruct (*rather formal*) to tell sb to do sth, especially in a formal or official way 尤指以正式或官方的方式指示、命令、吩咐：*The letter instructed him to report to headquarters immediately.* 那封信指示他立即向总部汇报。

direct (*formal*) to give an official order 指正式发出指示、命令：*The judge directed the jury to return a verdict of not guilty.* 法官指示陪审团作出无罪裁决。

command to use your position of authority to tell sb to do sth 指利用权力命令：*He commanded his men to retreat.* 他命令手下撤退。

ORDER OR COMMAND? 用 order 还是 command?

Order is a more general word than **command** and can be used about anyone in a position of authority, such as a parent, teacher or government telling sb to do sth. **Command** is slightly stronger than **order** and is the normal word to use about an army officer giving orders, or in any context where it is normal to give orders without any discussion about them. It is less likely to be used about a parent or teacher. * order 含义较 command 宽泛，可指任何有权威的人，如父母、老师或政府下命令。command 的语气稍强于 order，是指部队长官发布命令的常规用词，或者用于没有商量余地的命令。command 不大用于父母或老师下命令的情况。

PATTERNS

- to order/tell/instruct/direct/command sb **to do sth**
- to order/instruct/direct/command **that...**
- to **do** sth **as** ordered/told/instructed/directed/commanded

O

• **FOOD/DRINK** 食物；饮料 **3** [T, I] to ask for sth to eat or drink in a restaurant, bar, etc. 点（酒菜等）：~ **(sth)** *I ordered a beer and a sandwich.* 我要了一杯啤酒，一个三明治。◇ *Have you ordered yet?* 你点菜了没有？◇ ~ **sb/yourself sth** *He ordered himself a double whisky.* 他为自己点了一杯双份威士忌。◇ ~ **(sth) (for sb)** *Will you order for me while I make a phone call?* 我打个电话，你帮我点下菜可以吗？

• **ORGANIZE/ARRANGE** 组织；安排 **4** [T] ~ **sth** (*formal*) to organize or arrange sth 组织；安排；整理：*I need time to order my thoughts.* 我需要时间梳理一下思路。➲ SEE ALSO ORDERED, DISORDERED **IDM** SEE DOCTOR *n.*

PHR V ˌ**order sb aˈbout/aˈround** (*disapproving*) to keep telling sb what to do in a way that is annoying or unpleasant （不断地）支使，命令，使唤

ˈorder book *noun* a record kept by a business of the products it has agreed to supply to its customers, often used to show how well the business is doing （公司业绩的）订货簿：*We have a full order book for the coming year.* 我们来年的订货簿已经记满了。

or·dered /ˈɔːdəd; *NAmE* ˈɔːrdərd/ *adj.* [usually before noun] carefully arranged or organized 精心安排的；组织有序的 **SYN** **orderly**: *an ordered existence* 井井有条的生活 ◇ *a well-ordered society* 井然有序的社会 **OPP** **disordered**

ˈorder form *noun* a document filled in by customers when ordering goods 订货单

order·ing /ˈɔːdərɪŋ; *NAmE* ˈɔːrdər-/ *noun* [C, U] the way in which sth is ordered or arranged; the act of putting sth into an order 次序；组合；排列 **SYN** **arrangement**: *Many possible orderings may exist.* 组合方式可能有许多种。◇ *the successful ordering of complex data* 复杂数据的成功排列

or·der·ly /ˈɔːdəli; *NAmE* ˈɔːrdərli/ *adj., noun*

■ *adj.* **1** arranged or organized in a neat, careful and logical way 整洁的；有秩序的；有条理的 **SYN** **tidy**: *a calm and orderly life* 平静有序的生活 ◇ *vegetables planted in orderly rows* 一行行栽种整齐的蔬菜 **2** behaving well; peaceful 表现良好的；守秩序的：*an orderly demonstration* 秩序井然的示威 **OPP** **disorderly** ▶ **or·der·li·ness** /ˈɔːdəlinəs; *NAmE* ˈɔːrdər-/ *noun* [U]

■ *noun* (*pl.* **-ies**) **1** a person who works in a hospital, usually doing jobs that do not need any special training （医院的）护工，勤杂工 **2** a soldier who does jobs that do not need any special training 勤务兵

ˌ**order of ˈmagnitude** *noun* (*mathematics* 数) a level in a system of ordering things by size or amount, where each level is higher by a FACTOR of ten 数量级（量度物理量大小的标准，用以 10 为底的指数表达）：*The actual measurement is two orders of magnitude* (= a hundred times) *greater than we expected.* 实际测量结果比我们预料的大两个量级（即一百倍）。◇ (*figurative*) *The problem is of the same order of magnitude for all concerned.* 这个问题对有关各方的影响是一样大的。

ˈOrder Paper *noun* (*BrE*) a list of the subjects to be discussed by Parliament on a particular day （议会的）议事日程表

or·din·al /ˈɔːdɪnl; *NAmE* ˈɔːrdənl/ (*also* ˌ**ordinal ˈnumber**) *noun* a number that refers to the position of sth in a series, for example 'first', 'second', etc. 序数词（如第一、第二等）➲ COMPARE CARDINAL *n.* (2) ▶ **or·din·al** *adj.*

or·din·ance /ˈɔːdɪnəns; *NAmE* ˈɔːrd-/ *noun* [C, U] (*formal*) an order or a rule made by a government or sb in a position of authority 法令；条例；指示；训令

or·din·and /ˈɔːdɪnænd; *NAmE* ˈɔːrd-/ *noun* a person who is preparing to become a priest, minister or RABBI 待领圣职的人；领圣秩者

or·din·ar·ily /ˈɔːdnrəli; *NAmE* ˌɔːrdnˈerəli/ *adv.* **1** in a normal way 普通地；平常地；正常地 **SYN** **normally**: *To the untrained eye, the children were behaving ordinarily.* 在外行人眼里，这些孩子表现正常。 **2** used to say what normally happens in a particular situation, especially because sth different is happening this time 一般情况下；通常地 **SYN** **usually**: *Ordinarily, she wouldn't have bothered arguing with him.* 一般情况下，她一定懒得跟他理论。◇ *We do not ordinarily carry out this type of work.* 我们通常不会实际去做这类工作。

or·din·ary /ˈɔːdnri; *NAmE* ˈɔːrdneri/ *adj.* **1** [usually before noun] not unusual or different in any way 普通的；平常的；一般的；平凡的：*an ordinary sort of day* 平平常常的一天 ◇ *in the ordinary course of events* 在一般情况下 ◇ *ordinary people like you and me* 像你我这等普通人 ◇ *This was no ordinary meeting.* 这次会议非同寻常。 **2** (*disapproving*) having no unusual or interesting features 平庸的；平淡无奇的：*The meal was very ordinary.* 这顿饭平常得很。➲ COMPARE EXTRAORDINARY (2) ▶ **or·din·ari·ness** *noun* [U]

IDM **in the ordinary way** (*BrE*) used to say what normally happens in a particular situation 一般地；通常地：*In the ordinary way, she's not a nervous person.* 一般而言，她是个不爱紧张的人。 **out of the ˈordinary** unusual or different 不寻常；特殊；超凡脱俗：*I'm looking for something a little more out of the ordinary.* 我正在找些稍不寻常的东西。

ˈordinary grade *noun* = O GRADE

ˈordinary level *noun* = O LEVEL

ˌ**ordinary ˈseaman** *noun* (*abbr.* **OS**) a sailor of the lowest rank in the British navy （英国的）二等水兵

ˌ**ordinary ˈshare** *noun* a fixed unit of a company's capital. People who own ordinary shares have voting rights in the company. 普通股（公司资本的固定单位，持有人在公司有投票权）

or·din·ate /ˈɔːdɪnət; *NAmE* ˈɔːrd-/ *noun* (*mathematics* 数) the COORDINATE that gives the distance along the vertical AXIS 纵坐标 ➲ COMPARE ABSCISSA

or·din·ation /ˌɔːdɪˈneɪʃn; *NAmE* ˌɔːrdnˈeɪʃn/ *noun* [U, C] the act or ceremony of making sb a priest, minister or RABBI （圣职的）授予；派立礼；按立圣职；授神职礼 ➲ SEE ALSO ORDAIN (1)

ord·nance /ˈɔːdnəns; *NAmE* ˈɔːrd-/ *noun* [U] **1** large guns on wheels （可移动的）大炮 **SYN** **artillery** **2** military supplies and materials 军备物资；军需品；军用器材：*an ordnance depot* 军械库

ˌ**Ordnance ˈSurvey map** *noun* a very detailed map of an area of Britain or Ireland, prepared by an organization called the **Ordnance Survey**, which is supported by the government （由英国或爱尔兰政府资助的全国地形测量局所绘制的）全国地形测绘详图

ord·ure /ˈɔːdjʊə(r); *NAmE* ˈɔːrdʒər/ *noun* [U] (*formal*) solid waste from the body of a person or an animal （人或动物的）粪便 **SYN** **faeces**

ore /ɔː(r)/ *noun* [U, C] rock, earth, etc. from which metal can be obtained 矿石；矿砂；矿：*iron ore* 铁矿石

ore·gano /ˌɒrɪˈɡɑːnəʊ; *NAmE* əˈreɡənoʊ/ *noun* [U] a plant with leaves that have a sweet smell and are used in cooking as a HERB 牛至（叶可用于调味）➲ VISUAL VOCAB PAGE V35

organ /ˈɔːɡən; *NAmE* ˈɔːrɡən/ *noun* **1** a part of the body that has a particular purpose, such as the heart or the brain; part of a plant with a particular purpose （人体或动植物的）器官：*the internal organs* 内脏 ◇ *the sense organs* (= the eyes, ears, nose, etc.) 感觉器官 ◇ *the sexual/reproductive organs* 生殖器官 ◇ *an organ transplant/donor* 器官移植 / 捐赠者 ➲ COLLOCATIONS AT ILL ➲ VISUAL VOCAB PAGE V64 **2** (*especially humorous*) a PENIS 阴茎；阳物：*the male organ* 雄性性器官 **3** (*also* **ˈpipe organ**) a large musical instrument with keys like a piano. Sounds are produced by air forced through pipes. 管风琴：*She plays the organ in church.* 她在教堂负责弹奏管风琴。◇ *organ music* 管风琴曲 ➲ COMPARE HARMONIUM **4** a musical instrument similar to a pipe organ, but without pipes 风琴：*an electric organ* 电子琴 ➲ SEE ALSO BARREL ORGAN, MOUTH ORGAN **5** (*formal*) an official organization that is part of a larger organization and has a

O

special purpose（官方的）机构，机关：*the organs of government* 政府机关 **6** (*formal*) a newspaper or magazine that gives information about a particular group or organization; a means of communicating the views of a particular group 机关报刊；（某团体的）宣传工具：*The People's Daily is the official organ of the Chinese Communist Party.*《人民日报》是中国共产党的官方报纸。

or·gan·die (*NAmE also* **or·gandy**) /ˈɔːɡəndi; *NAmE* ˈɔːrɡ-/ *noun* [U] a type of thin cotton cloth that is slightly stiff, used especially for making formal dresses 蝉翼纱（细薄而稍硬的棉布，用于制作礼服）

ˈorgan grinder *noun* a person who plays a BARREL ORGAN (= a large musical instrument played by turning a handle) 手摇风琴手；手摇风琴演奏者：(*humorous*) *He's only the* ***organ grinder's monkey*** (= an unimportant person who does what he is told to do). 他不过是个听人使唤的。

or·gan·ic /ɔːˈɡænɪk; *NAmE* ɔːrˈɡ-/ *adj.* [usually before noun] **1** (of food, farming methods, etc. 食品、耕作方式等) produced or practised without using artificial chemicals 有机的；不使用化肥的；绿色的：***organic cheese/vegetables/wine, etc.*** 有机奶酪、蔬菜、酒等 ◇ ***an organic farmer/gardener*** 实行有机栽培的农民 / 园艺师 ◇ ***organic farming/horticulture*** 有机耕作 / 园艺 ➲ WORDFINDER NOTE AT CROP ➲ VISUAL VOCAB PAGE V9 **2** produced by or from living things 有机物的；生物的：*Improve the soil by adding* ***organic matter.*** 加入有机物以改良土壤。◇ ***organic compounds*** 有机化合物 OPP **inorganic 3** (*specialist*) connected with the organs of the body 器官的；器质性的；官能的：*organic disease* 器官疾病 **4** (*formal*) consisting of different parts that are all connected to each other 有机的；统一的；关联的：*the view of society as an organic whole* 视社会为一有机体的观点 **5** (*formal*) happening in a slow and natural way, rather than suddenly 逐渐的；演进的；自然的：*the organic growth of foreign markets* 国外市场的逐步发展 ▸ **or·gan·ic·al·ly** /-kli/ *adv.*：*organically grown fruit* 用有机方式种植的水果 ◇ *The cardboard disintegrates organically.* 硬纸板是会自然分解的。◇ *Doctors could find nothing organically wrong with her.* 医生查不出她的器官有什么毛病。◇ *The organization should be allowed to develop organically.* 应该让这个组织逐步发展。

orˌganic ˈchemistry *noun* [U] the branch of chemistry that deals with substances that contain CARBON 有机化学 ➲ COMPARE INORGANIC CHEMISTRY

or·gan·ism /ˈɔːɡənɪzəm; *NAmE* ˈɔːrɡ-/ *noun* **1** (*biology* 生 or *formal*) a living thing, especially one that is extremely small 生物；有机体；（尤指）微生物 ➲ SEE ALSO MICRO-ORGANISM ➲ WORDFINDER NOTE AT BIOLOGY **2** (*formal*) a system consisting of parts that depend on each other 有机组织；有机体系：*the social organism* (= society) 社会机体

or·gan·ist /ˈɔːɡənɪst; *NAmE* ˈɔːrɡ-/ *noun* a person who plays the organ 风琴演奏者；风琴手

or·gan·iza·tion 🔑 (*BrE also* **-isa·tion**) /ˌɔːɡənaɪˈzeɪʃn; *NAmE* ˌɔːrɡənəˈz-/ *noun* **1** 🔑 [C] a group of people who form a business, club, etc. together in order to achieve a particular aim 组织；团体；机构：*to work for a business/political/voluntary organization* 为一个商业 / 政治 / 志愿机构工作 ◇ *the World Health Organization* 世界卫生组织 ◇ *He's the president of a large international organization.* 他是一个大型国际组织的主席。**2** 🔑 [U] the act of making arrangements or preparations for sth 组织工作；筹备工作 SYN **planning**：*I leave most of the organization of these conferences to my assistant.* 我把这些会议的大部分筹备工作留给我的助手。**3** 🔑 [U] the way in which the different parts of sth are arranged 安排；配置；分配 SYN **structure**：*The report studies the organization of labour within the company.* 这个报告研究了公司内部的人力分配问题。**4** 🔑 [U] the quality of being arranged in a neat, careful and logical way 条理；系统性：*She is highly intelligent but her work lacks organization.* 她聪明绝顶，工作却缺乏条理。▸ **or·gan·iza·tion·al**, **-isa·tion·al** /-ʃənl/ *adj.*：*organizational skills* 组织技巧 ◇ *organizational change* 组织上的变化 **or·gan·iza·tion·al·ly**, **-isa·tion·al·ly** *adv.*

ˌorganiˈzation chart (*also* **or·gano·gram**) *noun* a diagram of the structure of an organization, especially a large business, showing the relationships between all the jobs in it（大企业等的）组织机构图，组织架构图

or·gan·ize 🔑 (*BrE also* **-ise**) /ˈɔːɡənaɪz; *NAmE* ˈɔːrɡ-/ *verb* **1** 🔑 [T] ~ **sth** to arrange for sth to happen or to be provided 组织；筹备：*to organize a meeting/party/trip* 组织会议 / 聚会 / 旅行 ◇ *I'll invite people if you can organize food and drinks.* 如果你能备办饮食，我就负责邀请人。**2** 🔑 [T] ~ **sth** to arrange sth or the parts of sth into a particular order or structure 安排；处理；分配：*Modern computers can organize large amounts of data very quickly.* 现代计算机能迅速处理大量的信息资料。◇ *You should try and organize your time better.* 你应该尽量更有效地分配你的时间。◇ *We do not fully understand how the brain is organized.* 我们不完全了解大脑是怎样构成的。**3** [T] ~ **yourself/sb** to plan your/sb's work and activities in an efficient way 规划；管理；照料：*I'm sure you don't need me to organize you.* 我相信你用不着我为你安排。**4** [T, I] ~ (**sb/yourself**) (**into sth**) to form a group of people with a shared aim, especially a union or political party（使）成立，组建，建立（联盟、党派等）：*the right of workers to organize themselves into unions* 工人自行组织工会的权利 ➲ SEE ALSO DISORGANIZED ▸ **or·gan·izer**, **-iser** *noun*：*the organizers of the festival* 节日活动的筹划者 ➲ SEE ALSO PERSONAL ORGANIZER

or·gan·ized 🔑 (*BrE also* **-ised**) /ˈɔːɡənaɪzd; *NAmE* ˈɔːrɡ-/ *adj.* **1** 🔑 [only before noun] involving large numbers of people who work together to do sth in a way that has been carefully planned 有组织的；系统的：*an organized body of workers* 一个有组织的工人团体 ◇ ***organized religion*** (= traditional religion followed by large numbers of people who obey a fixed set of rules) 组织严密的传统宗教信仰 ◇ ***organized crime*** (= committed by professional criminals working in large groups) 有组织的犯罪 ➲ COMPARE UNORGANIZED (3) **2** 🔑 arranged or planned in the way mentioned 有条理的；有安排的：*a carefully organized campaign* 精心策划的运动 ◇ *a well-organized office* 井然有序的办公室 ➲ COMPARE DISORGANIZED **3** 🔑 (of a person 人) able to plan your work, life, etc. well and in an efficient way 有条理的；有效率的：*a very organized person* 很有条理的人 ◇ *Isn't it time you started to get organized?* 你该提高点效率了吧？ ➲ COMPARE DISORGANIZED

ˈorgan loft *noun* a place where there is an organ high above the ground in a church or concert hall（教堂或音乐厅内的）管风琴楼厢

or·gano·gram (*also* **or·gani·gram**) /ɔːˈɡænəɡræm; *NAmE* ɔːrˈɡ-/ *noun* (*business* 商) = ORGANIZATION CHART

or·gano·phos·phate /ˌɔːɡənəʊˈfɒsfeɪt; ɔːˌɡænəʊ-; *NAmE* ˌɔːrɡənoʊˈfɑːsfeɪt; ɔːrˌɡænoʊ-/ *noun* a chemical containing CARBON and PHOSPHORUS 有机磷酸酯

or·ganza /ɔːˈɡænzə; *NAmE* ɔːrˈɡ-/ *noun* [U] a type of thin stiff transparent cloth, used for making formal dresses 透明硬纱，欧根纱（用于制作礼服）

or·gasm /ˈɔːɡæzəm; *NAmE* ˈɔːrɡ-/ *noun* [U, C] the moment during sexual activity when feelings of sexual pleasure are at their strongest 性高潮：*to achieve/reach orgasm* 达到性高潮 ◇ *to have an orgasm* 出现性高潮

or·gas·mic /ɔːˈɡæzmɪk; *NAmE* ɔːrˈɡ-/ *adj.* [only before noun] connected with or like an orgasm 性高潮的；似性高潮的

or·gi·as·tic /ˌɔːdʒiˈæstɪk; *NAmE* ˌɔːrdʒ-/ *adj.* [usually before noun] (*formal*) typical of an orgy 纵欲的；放纵的；放荡的

orgy /ˈɔːdʒi; *NAmE* ˈɔːrdʒi/ *noun* (*pl.* **-ies**) **1** a party at which there is a lot of eating, drinking and sexual activity 淫乐的聚会；狂欢会：*a drunken orgy* 纵酒狂欢会 **2** ~ (**of sth**) (*disapproving*) an extreme amount of a particular activity 放纵；放荡：*The rebels went on an orgy of killing.* 叛乱者肆意杀人。

O

oriel /ˈɔːriəl/ *noun* (*architecture* 建) a part of a building, like a small room with windows, that sticks out from a wall above the ground 突出主体墙外的建筑；凸肚窗：*an oriel window* 凸肚窗；飘窗

Ori·ent /ˈɔːriənt/ **the Orient** *noun* [sing.] (*literary*) the eastern part of the world, especially China and Japan 东方（尤指中国和日本）➲ COMPARE OCCIDENT

ori·ent AW /ˈɔːrient/ (*also* **orien·tate**) *verb* **1** [usually passive] **~ sb/sth (to/towards sb/sth)** to direct sb/sth towards sth; to make or adapt sb/sth for a particular purpose 使朝向；使面对；确定方向；使适应：*Our students are oriented towards science subjects.* 我们教的学生都是理科方向的。◇ *policies oriented to the needs of working mothers* 针对在职母亲的需要而制定的政策 ◇ *We run a commercially oriented operation.* 我们经营一个商业性的企业。◇ *profit-orientated organizations* 以赢利为目的的机构 ◇ *Neither of them is politically oriented* (= interested in politics). 他们两人都无意涉足政治。 **2 ~ yourself** to find your position in relation to your surroundings 确定方位；认识方向：*The mountaineers found it hard to orient themselves in the fog.* 登山者在大雾中很难辨认方向。 **3 ~ yourself** to make yourself familiar with a new situation 熟悉；适应：*It took him some time to orient himself in his new school.* 他经过了一段时间才熟悉新学校的环境。➲ COMPARE DISORIENTATE

Orien·tal /ˌɔːriˈentl/ *noun* (*old-fashioned, often offensive*) a person from China, Japan or other countries in E Asia 东方人；东亚国家的人

orien·tal /ˌɔːriˈentl/ *adj.* connected with or typical of the eastern part of the world, especially China and Japan, and the people who live there 东方（尤指中国和日本）的；东方人的：*oriental languages* 东方语言

O

orien·tal·ist /ˌɔːriˈentəlɪst/ *noun* a person who studies the languages, arts, etc. of ORIENTAL countries 东方学专家；东方学者

orien·tate AW /ˈɔːrienteɪt/ *verb* = ORIENT

orien·ta·tion AW /ˌɔːrienˈteɪʃn/ *noun* **1** [U, C] the type of aims or interests that a person or an organization has; the act of directing your aims towards a particular thing 方向；目标；定向：*The course is essentially theoretical in orientation.* 该课程的定位是以理论为主。◇ **~ to/towards sth** *Companies have been forced into a greater orientation to the market.* 各公司不得不转型，更加面向市场。 **2** [U, C] a person's basic beliefs or feelings about a particular subject（个人的）基本信仰，态度，观点：***religious/political orientation*** 宗教信仰；政治取向 ◇ ***a person's sexual orientation*** (= whether they are attracted to men, women or both) 某人的性取向 **3** [U] training or information that you are given before starting a new job, course, etc.（任职等前的）培训，训练；迎新会：*an orientation course* 上岗培训课 **4** [C] (*specialist*) the direction in which an object faces 方向：*The orientation of the planet's orbit is changing continuously.* 该行星轨道的方向不断变化。

orien·teer·ing /ˌɔːrienˈtɪərɪŋ; *NAmE* -ˈtɪr-/ *noun* [U] the sport of following a route across country on foot, as quickly as possible, using a map and COMPASS 定向运动，定向越野，野外定向（利用指南针和地图，徒步穿越旷野的运动）➲ VISUAL VOCAB PAGE V44

ori·fice /ˈɒrɪfɪs; *NAmE* ˈɔːr-/ *noun* (*formal* or *humorous*) a hole or opening, especially one in the body（尤指身体上的）孔，穴，腔：*the nasal orifice* 鼻孔

ori·gami /ˌɒrɪˈɡɑːmi; *NAmE* ˌɔːr-/ *noun* [U] the Japanese art of folding paper into attractive shapes 日本折纸艺术

ori·gin 🔑 /ˈɒrɪdʒɪn; *NAmE* ˈɔːr-/ *noun* [C, U] (*also* **origins** [pl.]) **1** 🔑 the point from which sth starts; the cause of sth 起源；源头；起因：*the origins of life on earth* 地球上生命的起源 ◇ *Most coughs are viral **in origin*** (= caused by a virus). 咳嗽大多是由病毒引发的。◇ *The origin of the word remains obscure.* 该词的来源尚不清楚。◇ *This particular custom **has its origins in** Wales.* 这一特殊风俗起源于威尔士。 **2** 🔑 a person's social and family background 出身；来历：*She has risen from humble origins to immense wealth.* 她出身卑微，终成巨富。◇ *children of various ethnic origins* 各族裔的儿童 ◇ *people of German origin* 德裔民众 ◇ *a person's country **of origin*** (= where they were born) 某人的出生国

ori·gin·al 🔑 /əˈrɪdʒənl/ *adj., noun*

■ ***adj.*** **1** 🔑 [only before noun] existing at the beginning of a particular period, process or activity 原来的；起初的；最早的：*The room still has many of its original features.* 房间还保留着当初的许多特点。◇ *I think you should go back to your original plan.* 我认为你应该回头执行你原来的计划。 **2** 🔑 new and interesting in a way that is different from anything that has existed before; able to produce new and interesting ideas 首创的；独创的；有独创性的：*an original idea* 独到的见解 ◇ *That's not a very original suggestion.* 那个建议没什么新意。◇ *an original thinker* 有创意的人 **3** 🔑 [usually before noun] painted, written, etc. by the artist rather than copied 原作的；真迹的；非复制的：*an original painting by local artist Graham Tovey* 一幅本土艺术家格雷厄姆·托维的绘画创作 ◇ *The original manuscript has been lost.* 原稿已经遗失。◇ *Only original documents* (= not photocopies) *will be accepted as proof of status.* 只有文件正本才能用作身份证明。

■ ***noun*** **1** 🔑 a document, work of art, etc. produced for the first time, from which copies are later made 原件；正本；原稿；原作：*This painting is a copy; the original is in Madrid.* 这幅画是复制品，原画在马德里。◇ *Send out the photocopies and keep the original.* 寄复印本，保留原件。 **2** (*formal*) a person who thinks, behaves, dresses, etc. in an unusual way（思想、行为、衣着等）不同寻常的人，独特的人，怪人

IDM **in the oˈriginal** in the language in which a book, etc. was first written, before being translated 用原著的语言；未经翻译：*I studied Italian so that I would be able to read Dante in the original.* 我学习意大利语以便能读但丁的原著。

ori·gin·al·ity /əˌrɪdʒəˈnæləti/ *noun* [U] the quality of being new and interesting in a way that is different from anything that has existed before 独创性；创意；独特构思：*This latest collection lacks style and originality.* 这本最新选集既无风格，又无创意。

ori·gin·al·ly 🔑 /əˈrɪdʒənəli/ *adv.* used to describe the situation that existed at the beginning of a particular period or activity, especially before sth was changed 原来；起初：*The school was originally very small.* 这所学校当初很小。◇ *She comes originally from York.* 她原本来自约克郡。◇ *Originally, we had intended to go to Italy, but then we won the trip to Greece.* 我们本来打算去意大利，但后来赢得机会去了希腊。

oˌriginal ˈsin *noun* [U] (in Christianity 基督教) the tendency to be evil that is believed to be present in everyone from birth 原罪

ori·gin·ate /əˈrɪdʒɪneɪt/ *verb* (*formal*) **1** [I] **(+ adv./prep.)** to happen or appear for the first time in a particular place or situation 起源；发源；发端于：*The disease is thought to have originated in the tropics.* 这种疾病据说起源于热带地区。 **2** [T] **~ sth** to create sth new 创立；创建；发明：*Locke originated this theory in the 17th century.* 洛克于 17 世纪创立了这个理论。▶ **ori·gin·ator** *noun*

ori·ole /ˈɔːriəʊl; *NAmE* -oʊl/ *noun* **1** a N American bird: the male is black and orange and the female is yellow-green 拟鹂（产于北美洲，雄鸟毛色黑色橘色相间，雌鸟黄绿色） **2** a European bird, the male of which is bright yellow with black wings 黄鹂（产于欧洲，雄鸟毛色鲜黄，双翼黑色）

Oriya /ɒˈriːjə; *NAmE* ɔːˈr-/ *noun* [U] a language spoken in Orissa in eastern India 奥里雅语（印度东部奥里萨邦的语言）

or·molu /ˈɔːməluː; *NAmE* ˈɔːrm-/ *noun* [U] a gold metal made of a mixture of other metals, used to decorate furniture, make decorative objects, etc. 仿金铜；金色黄铜；铜锌锡合金

or·na·ment *noun, verb*

■ ***noun*** /ˈɔːnəmənt; *NAmE* ˈɔːrn-/ **1** [C] (*especially BrE*) an object that is used as decoration in a room, garden/yard, etc. rather than for a particular purpose 装饰品：*a china/glass ornament* 瓷器 / 玻璃装饰品 ◇ (*BrE, NAmE*) *Christmas tree ornaments* 圣诞树装饰品 **2** [C] (*formal*) an object that is worn as jewellery 首饰；饰物 **3** [U] (*formal*) the use of objects, designs, etc. as decoration 装饰；摆设；点缀：*The clock is simply for ornament; it doesn't work any more.* 这架时钟纯属摆设，它再也不走了。**4 ~ to sth** (*NAmE*) a person or thing whose good qualities improve sth 为…增添光彩的人（或事物）：*The building is an ornament to the city.* 这座建筑物为整个城市增色不少。**5 ornaments** [pl.] (*music* 音) features that are added when playing individual notes to make them more beautiful or interesting 装饰音

■ ***verb*** /ˈɔːnəment; *NAmE* ˈɔːrn-/ [usually passive] **~ sth** (*formal*) to add decoration to sth 装饰；点缀；美化 **SYN** **decorate**：*a room richly ornamented with carving* 雕饰得富丽堂皇的屋子

or·na·men·tal /ˌɔːnəˈmentl; *NAmE* ˌɔːrn-/ *adj.* used as decoration rather than for a practical purpose 装饰性的；点缀的 **SYN** **decorative**：*an ornamental fountain* 装饰性喷泉 ◇ *The chimney pots are purely ornamental.* 这些烟囱管帽纯属装饰。

or·na·men·ta·tion /ˌɔːnəmenˈteɪʃn; *NAmE* ˌɔːrn-/ *noun* [U] the use of objects, designs, etc. to decorate sth 装饰；点缀

or·nate /ɔːˈneɪt; *NAmE* ɔːrˈn-/ *adj.* covered with a lot of decoration, especially when this involves very small or complicated designs 华美的；富丽的；豪华的：*a mirror in an ornate gold frame* 镶着豪华金框的镜子 ▶ **or·nate·ly** *adv.*：*ornately carved chairs* 精雕细刻的椅子

or·nery /ˈɔːnəri; *NAmE* ˈɔːrn-/ *adj.* (*NAmE, informal*) bad-tempered and difficult to deal with 脾气暴躁的；难对付的；别扭的

or·ni·tholo·gist /ˌɔːnɪˈθɒlədʒɪst; *NAmE* ˌɔːrnɪˈθɑːl-/ *noun* a person who studies birds 鸟类学家 ➲ COMPARE BIRD-WATCHER

or·ni·thol·ogy /ˌɔːnɪˈθɒlədʒi; *NAmE* ˌɔːrnɪˈθɑːl-/ *noun* [U] the scientific study of birds 鸟类学 ▶ **or·ni·tho·logic·al** /ˌɔːnɪθəˈlɒdʒɪkl; *NAmE* ˌɔːrnɪθəˈlɑːdʒ-/ *adj.*

or·ogeny /ɒˈrɒdʒəni; *NAmE* ɔːˈrɑːdʒ-/ *noun* [U] (*geology* 地) a process in which the outer layer of the earth is folded to form mountains 造山运动（地层褶皱形成山脉的过程）

oro·graph·ic /ˌɒrəˈɡræfɪk; *NAmE* ˌɔːrəˈɡræfɪk/ *adj.* (*geology* 地) connected with mountains, especially with their position and shape 地形的；山形的

oro·tund /ˈɒrətʌnd; *NAmE* ˈɔːrə-/ *adj.* (*formal*) (of the voice or the way something is said 嗓音或说话方式) using full and impressive sounds and language 洪亮的；令人难忘的 ▶ **oro·tund·ity** /ˌɒrəˈtʌndɪti; *NAmE* ˌɔːrə-/ *noun* [U]

orphan /ˈɔːfn; *NAmE* ˈɔːrfn/ *noun, verb*

■ ***noun*** a child whose parents are dead 孤儿：*He was an orphan and lived with his uncle.* 他是个孤儿，和他叔叔一起生活。◇ *orphan boys/girls* 父母双亡的男孩 / 女孩

■ ***verb*** [usually passive] **~ sb** to make a child an orphan 使成为孤儿：*She was orphaned in the war.* 战争使她成为孤儿。

or·phan·age /ˈɔːfənɪdʒ; *NAmE* ˈɔːrf-/ *noun* a home for children whose parents are dead 孤儿院

ortho- /ˈɔːθəʊ; *NAmE* ˈɔːrθoʊ/ *combining form* (in nouns, adjectives and adverbs 构成名词、形容词和副词) correct; standard 正确的；标准的：*orthodox* 正统的 ◇ *orthography* 正字法

ortho·don·tics /ˌɔːθəˈdɒntɪks; *NAmE* ˌɔːrθəˈdɑːn-/ *noun* [U] the treatment of problems concerning the position of the teeth and JAWS 口腔正畸术 ➲ **MORE LIKE THIS** 29, page R28 ▶ **ortho·don·tic** *adj.*：*orthodontic treatment* 口腔正畸治疗

ortho·don·tist /ˌɔːθəˈdɒntɪst; *NAmE* ˌɔːrθəˈdɑːn-/ *noun* a dentist who treats problems concerning the position of the teeth and JAWS 口腔正畸医生

ortho·dox /ˈɔːθədɒks; *NAmE* ˈɔːrθədɑːks/ *adj.* **1** (especially of beliefs or behaviour 尤指信仰或行为) generally accepted or approved of; following generally accepted beliefs 普遍接受的；正统的；规范的 **SYN** **traditional**：*orthodox medicine* 传统医学 **OPP** **unorthodox** ➲ COMPARE HETERODOX **2** following closely the traditional beliefs and practices of a religion 正统信仰的；正宗教义的：*an orthodox Jew* 正统的犹太教徒 **3 Orthodox** belonging to or connected with the Orthodox Church 正教的；东正教派的

the ˌOrthodox ˈChurch (*also* **the ˌEastern ˌOrthodox ˈChurch**) *noun* [sing.] a branch of the Christian Church in eastern Europe and Greece 东正教会；正教

ortho·doxy /ˈɔːθədɒksi; *NAmE* ˈɔːrθədɑːksi/ *noun* (*pl.* **-ies**) **1** [C, U] (*formal*) an idea or view that is generally accepted 正统观念；普遍接受的观点：*an economist arguing against the current financial orthodoxy* 一位批驳现行正统金融观念的经济学家 **2** [U, C, usually pl.] the traditional beliefs or practices of a religion, etc. 正统的信仰（或做法） **3 Orthodoxy** [U] the Orthodox Church, its beliefs and practices 正教会；正教信仰与做法

orth·og·raphy /ɔːˈθɒɡrəfi; *NAmE* ɔːrˈθɑːɡ-/ *noun* [U] (*formal*) the system of spelling in a language （文字的）拼写体系，正字法 ▶ **or·tho·graph·ic** /ˌɔːθəˈɡræfɪk; *NAmE* ˌɔːrθ-/ *adj.*

ortho·paed·ics (*especially US* **ortho·ped·ics**) /ˌɔːθəˈpiːdɪks; *NAmE* ˌɔːrθə-/ *noun* [U] the branch of medicine concerned with injuries and diseases of the bones or muscles 矫形外科 ➲ **MORE LIKE THIS** 29, page R28 ▶ **ortho·paed·ic** (*especially US* **ortho·ped·ic**) *adj.*：*an orthopaedic surgeon/hospital* 矫形外科医生 / 医院

Or·well·ian /ɔːˈweliən; *NAmE* ɔːrˈw-/ *adj.* used to describe a political system in which a government tries to have complete control over people's behaviour and thoughts （政治制度）奥威尔式的，极权的 ➲ **MORE LIKE THIS** 17, page R27 **ORIGIN** From the name of the English writer George Orwell, whose novel *Nineteen Eighty-Four* describes a government that has total control over the people. 源自英国作家乔治 • 奥威尔。他在小说《一九八四》中描写对人民实行极权统治的政府。

-ory *suffix* **1** (in adjectives 构成形容词) that does…; involving the action concerned 起…作用的；包含相关动作的：*explanatory* 解释性的 **2** (in nouns 构成名词) a place for …的地方：*observatory* 天文台

oryx /ˈɒrɪks; *NAmE* ˈɔːr-/ *noun* a large ANTELOPE with long straight horns 大羚羊（有长角）

OS /ˌəʊ ˈes; *NAmE* ˌoʊ/ *abbr.* **1** (*computing* 计) OPERATING SYSTEM 操作系统 **2** ORDINARY SEAMAN （英国）二等水兵

Oscar™ /ˈɒskə(r); *NAmE* ˈɑːs-/ *noun* = ACADEMY AWARD™：*The movie was nominated for an Oscar.* 这部电影获奥斯卡金像奖提名。◇ *an* ***Oscar nomination/winner*** 奥斯卡金像奖提名 / 获奖者

os·cil·late /ˈɒsɪleɪt; *NAmE* ˈɑːs-/ *verb* **1** [I] **~ (between A and B)** (*formal*) to keep changing from one extreme of feeling or behaviour to another, and back again （情感或行为）摇摆，波动，变化 **SYN** **swing**：*Her moods oscillated between depression and elation.* 她的情绪时而抑郁，时而亢奋。**2** [I] (*physics* 物) to keep moving from one position to another and back again 振动；摆动：*Watch how the needle on the dial oscillates.* 仔细看仪表盘上的指针如何摆动。 **3** [I] (*physics* 物) (of an electric current, radio waves, etc. 电流、无线电波等) to change in strength or direction at regular intervals 振荡；波动

os·cil·la·tion /ˌɒsɪˈleɪʃn; *NAmE* ˌɑːs-/ *noun* (*formal*) **1** [U, sing.] a regular movement between one position and another or between one amount and another 摆动；摇

O

摆；振动：*the oscillation of the compass needle* 罗盘指针的摆动 ◇ **~ between A and B** *the economy's continual oscillation between growth and recession* 经济增长与衰退之间的持续波动 **2** [C] **~ (between A and B)** | **~ (of sth) (against sth)** a single movement from one position to another of sth that is oscillating 一次波动；浮动；振幅：*the oscillations of the pound against foreign currency* 英镑兑外币汇价的波动 **3** [U, C] **~ (between A and B)** a repeated change between different feelings, types of behaviour or ideas （情感、行为、思想的）摇摆不定，变化无常，犹豫不定：*his oscillation, as a teenager, between science and art* 十几岁的他对学文科还是学理科的犹豫不决

os·cil·la·tor /ˈɒsɪleɪtə(r); *NAmE* ˈɑːs-/ *noun* (*physics* 物) a piece of equipment for producing OSCILLATING electric currents 振荡器

os·cil·lo·scope /əˈsɪləskəʊp; *NAmE* -skoʊp/ *noun* (*physics* 物) a piece of equipment that shows changes in electrical current as waves in a line on a screen 示波器

osier /ˈəʊziə(r); *NAmE* ˈoʊʒər/ *noun* a type of WILLOW tree, with thin branches that bend easily and are used for making BASKETS 蒿柳

os·mium /ˈɒzmiəm; *NAmE* ˈɑːzmiəm/ *noun* [U] (*symb.* **Os**) a chemical element. Osmium is a hard silver-white metal. 锇

os·mo·sis /ɒzˈməʊsɪs; *NAmE* ɑːzˈmoʊ-/ *noun* [U] **1** (*biology* 生 or *chemistry* 化) the gradual passing of a liquid through a MEMBRANE (= a thin layer of material) as a result of there being different amounts of dissolved substances on either side of the membrane 渗透：*Water passes into the roots of a plant by osmosis.* 水渗透至植物根部。 **2** the gradual process of learning or being influenced by sth, as a result of being in close contact with it 耳濡目染；潜移默化 ▶ **os·mot·ic** /ɒzˈmɒtɪk; *NAmE* ɑːzˈmɑːtɪk/ *adj.*：*osmotic pressure* 渗透压力

O

os·prey /ˈɒspreɪ; *NAmE* ˈɑːs-/ *noun* a large BIRD OF PREY (= a bird that kills other creatures for food) that eats fish 鹗；鱼鹰

os·se·ous /ˈɒsiəs; *NAmE* ˈɑːs-/ *adj.* (*specialist*) made of or turned into bone 骨的；骨质的；骨化的

os·sify /ˈɒsɪfaɪ; *NAmE* ˈɑːs-/ *verb* [usually passive] (**os·si·fies, os·si·fy·ing, os·si·fied, os·si·fied**) **1** [I, T, usually passive] **~ (sth)** (*formal, disapproving*) to become or make sth fixed and unable to change （使）僵化；（使）固定不变：*an ossified political system* 僵化的政治制度 **2** [I, T, usually passive] **~ (sth)** (*specialist*) to become or make sth hard like bone 使骨化；骨质化 ▶ **os·si·fi·ca·tion** *noun* [U]

os·ten·sible /ɒˈstensəbl; *NAmE* ɑːˈst-/ *adj.* [only before noun] (*formal*) seeming or stated to be real or true, when this is perhaps not the case 表面的；宣称的；假托的 SYN **apparent**：*The ostensible reason for his absence was illness.* 他假托生病缺勤。 ▶ **os·ten·sibly** /-əbli/ *adv.*：*Troops were sent in, ostensibly to protect the civilian population.* 谎称为保护平民而派驻了军队。

os·ten·ta·tion /ˌɒstenˈteɪʃn; *NAmE* ˌɑːs-/ *noun* [U] (*disapproving*) an exaggerated display of wealth, knowledge or skill that is made in order to impress people （对财富、知识、技能的）炫耀，卖弄，夸示

os·ten·ta·tious /ˌɒstenˈteɪʃəs; *NAmE* ˌɑːs-/ *adj.* **1** (*disapproving*) expensive or noticeable in a way that is intended to impress people 摆阔的；铺张的；浮华的 SYN **showy** **2** (*disapproving*) behaving in a way that is meant to impress people by showing how rich, important, etc. you are 炫耀的；卖弄的；夸示的 **3** (of an action 举动) done in a very obvious way so that people will notice it 夸张的；招摇的：*He gave an ostentatious yawn.* 他夸张地打了个哈欠。 ▶ **os·ten·ta·tious·ly** *adv.*：*ostentatiously dressed* 招摇的打扮

osteo- /ˈɒstiəʊ; *NAmE* ˈɑːstioʊ/ *combining form* (in nouns and adjectives 构成名词和形容词) connected with bones 骨的：*osteopath* 骨疗医师；正骨医生

osteo·arth·ritis /ˌɒstiəʊɑːˈθraɪtɪs; *NAmE* ˌɑːstioʊɑːrˈθ-/ *noun* [U] (*medical* 医) a disease that causes painful swelling and permanent damage in the joints of the body, especially the hips, knees and thumbs 骨关节炎；骨性关节炎

osteo·path /ˈɒstiəpæθ; *NAmE* ˈɑːs-/ *noun* a person whose job involves treating some diseases and physical problems by pressing and moving the bones and muscles 骨疗医师；正骨医生；骨医士 ⊃ COMPARE CHIROPRACTOR

oste·op·athy /ˌɒstiˈɒpəθi; *NAmE* ˌɑːstiˈɑːp-/ *noun* [U] the treatment of some diseases and physical problems by pressing and moving the bones and muscles 骨疗学；正骨术 ⊃ WORDFINDER NOTE AT CURE ▶ **osteo·path·ic** /ˌɒstiəˈpæθɪk; *NAmE* ˌɑːs-/ *adj.*

osteo·por·osis /ˌɒstiəʊpəˈrəʊsɪs; *NAmE* ˌɑːstioʊpəˈroʊ-/ (*also* ˌ**brittle** ˈ**bone disease**) *noun* [U] (*medical* 医) a condition in which the bones become weak and are easily broken, usually when people get older or because they do not eat enough of certain substances 骨质疏松；骨质疏松症

ost·ler /ˈɒslə(r); *NAmE* ˈɑːs-/ (*NAmE also* **host·ler**) *noun* (in the past) a man who took care of guests' horses at an INN （昔日客栈的）马夫

os·tra·cism /ˈɒstrəsɪzəm; *NAmE* ˈɑːs-/ *noun* [U] (*formal*) the act of deliberately not including sb in a group or activity; the state of not being included 排挤；排斥

os·tra·cize (*BrE also* **-ise**) /ˈɒstrəsaɪz; *NAmE* ˈɑːs-/ *verb* **~ sb** (*formal*) to refuse to let sb be a member of a social group; to refuse to meet or talk to sb 排挤；排斥 SYN **shun**：*He was ostracized by his colleagues for refusing to support the strike.* 他因拒绝支持罢工而受到同事的排斥。

os·trich /ˈɒstrɪtʃ; *NAmE* ˈɑːs-; ˈɔːs-/ *noun* **1** a very large African bird with a long neck and long legs, that cannot fly but can run very fast 鸵鸟 **2** (*informal*) a person who prefers to ignore problems rather than try and deal with them 逃避现实的人；不愿正视现实者

OTC /ˌəʊ tiː ˈsiː; *NAmE* ˌoʊ/ *abbr.* = OVER-THE-COUNTER：*OTC medicines and food supplements* 非处方药和膳食补充剂 ◇ *OTC trading of securities* 证券的场外交易

other /ˈʌðə(r)/ *adj., pron.* **1** used to refer to people or things that are additional or different to people or things that have been mentioned or are known about 另外；其他：*Mr Harris and Mrs Bate and three other teachers were there.* 哈里斯老师、贝特老师和其他三位老师在场。 ◇ *Are there any other questions?* 还有其他问题没有？ ◇ *I can't see you now—some other time, maybe.* 我现在不能见你，也许别的时候吧。 ◇ *Two buildings were destroyed and many others damaged in the blast.* 在这次爆炸中，两座建筑物被摧毁，还有许多建筑物遭损坏。 ◇ *This option is preferable to any other.* 这个选择比其他任何一个都好。 ◇ ***Some** designs **are better than others.*** 有一些设计比其他的好。 ⊃ COMPARE ANOTHER (1) **2** **the, my, your, etc. ~** used to refer to the second of two people or things （指两个人或事物中的第二个）那个，另一个：*My other sister is a doctor.* 我的另一个妹妹是医生。 ◇ *One son went to live in Australia and **the other one** was killed in a car crash.* 一个儿子移居澳大利亚，另一个在撞车事故中身亡。 ◇ *He raised one arm and then the other.* 他先举起一只胳膊，然后举起另一只。 ◇ *You must ask **one or other** of your parents.* 你必须问你的父亲或母亲。 **3** **the, my, your, etc. ~** used to refer to the remaining people or things in a group （指一组中其余的人或事物）其余的，另外的：*I'll wear my other shoes—these are dirty.* 这双鞋脏了，我要穿别的鞋。 ◇ *'I like this one.' 'What about the other ones?'* "我喜欢这个。" "其他那些怎么样？" ◇ *I went swimming while the others played tennis.* 我去游泳，而其他人去打网球了。 **4** **the other…** used to refer to a place, direction, etc. that is the opposite to where you are, are going, etc. （指与说话人所在位置等相反的方向或地点）另一边，对面，相反的方向：*I work on the other* *side of town.* 我在城的另一边工作。◇ *He crashed into a car coming the other way.* 他撞上了迎面开来的汽车。◇ *He found me, not **the other way round/around**.* 他发现了我，而不是我发现了他。

IDM HELP Most idioms containing **other** are at the entries for the nouns and verbs in the idioms, for example **in other words** is at **word**. 大多数含 other 的习语，都可在该等习语中的名词及动词相关词条找到，如 in other words 在词条 word 下。 **the ˌother 'day/'morning/'evening/'week** recently 那天，那天早上，那天晚上，那个星期（用于指说话前不久的日子）：*I saw Jack the other day.* 我前几天看到杰克了。 **other than** (usually used in negative sentences 通常用于否定句) **1** except 除…以外：*I don't know any French people other than you.* 除了你，我不认识别的法国人。◇ *We're going away in June but **other than that** I'll be here all summer.* 我们六月份外出；除此以外，我整个夏天都在这里。 **2** (*formal*) different or in a different way from; not 不同；不同于；不：*I have never known him to behave other than selfishly.* 我从没见过他不自私。

ˌother 'half (*also* **ˌbetter 'half**) *noun* (*informal, humorous*) the person that you are married to, or your boyfriend or girlfriend 另一半（指配偶或男友、女友）

other·ness /'ʌðənəs; *NAmE* 'ʌðərnəs/ *noun* [U] (*formal*) the quality of being different or strange 相异；奇特性；特别：*the otherness of an alien culture* 异域文化的不同情调

other·wise /'ʌðəwaɪz; *NAmE* 'ʌðərwaɪz/ *adv.* **1** used to state what the result would be if sth did not happen or if the situation were different 否则；不然：*My parents lent me the money. Otherwise, I couldn't have afforded the trip.* 我父母借钱给我了。否则，我可付不起这次旅费。◇ *Shut the window, otherwise it'll get too cold in here.* 把窗户关好，不然屋子里就太冷了。◇ *We're committed to the project. We wouldn't be here otherwise.* 我们是全心全意投入这项工作的，否则我们就不会到这里来了。 **2** apart from that 除此以外：*There was some music playing upstairs. Otherwise the house was silent.* 楼上有些音乐声。除此以外，房子里静悄悄的。◇ *He was slightly bruised but otherwise unhurt.* 他除了一点青肿之外没有受伤。 **3** in a different way to the way mentioned; differently 以其他方式；另；亦：*Bismarck, **otherwise known as** 'the Iron Chancellor'* 俾斯麦，亦称为"铁血宰相"◇ *It is not permitted to sell or otherwise distribute copies of past examination papers.* 不准出售或以其他方式散发过去的试卷。◇ *You know what this is about. Why **pretend otherwise*** (= that you do not)? 你明明知道这是怎么回事，为什么装作不知道？◇ *I wanted to see him but he was **otherwise engaged*** (= doing sth else). 我想见他，但他正忙着别的事情。

IDM **or otherwise** used to refer to sth that is different from or the opposite of what has just been mentioned 或其他情况；或相反：*It was necessary to discover the truth or otherwise of these statements.* 有必要查证这些说法是真是假。◇ *We insure against all damage, accidental or otherwise.* 我们的保险涵盖一切意外损失及其他各种损失。➲ MORE AT KNOW *v.*

ˌother 'woman *noun* [usually sing.] a woman with whom a man is having a sexual relationship, although he already has a wife or partner 情妇；女第三者

ˌother-'worldly *adj.* concerned with spiritual thoughts and ideas rather than with ordinary life 超脱世俗的；断绝尘缘的；超凡入圣的；出世的 ▸ **ˌother-'worldli·ness** *noun* [U]

oti·ose /'əʊtiəʊs; *NAmE* 'oʊʃioʊs/ *adj.* (*formal*) having no useful purpose 多余的；无用的 SYN **unnecessary**：*an otiose round of meetings* 一轮无用的会议

ot·itis /əʊ'taɪtɪs; *NAmE* oʊ-/ *noun* [U] (*medical* 医) a painful swelling of the ear, caused by an infection 耳炎

OTT /ˌəʊ tiː 'tiː; *NAmE* ˌoʊ/ *adj.* (*BrE, informal*) = OVER THE TOP：*Her make-up was a bit OTT.* 她化的妆有些过浓。

otter /'ɒtə(r); *NAmE* 'ɑːtər/ *noun* a small animal that has four WEBBED feet (= with skin between the toes), a tail and thick brown fur. Otters live in rivers and eat fish. 水獭

otto /'ɒtəʊ; *NAmE* 'ɑːtoʊ/ *noun* (*NAmE*) = ATTAR

ot·to·man /'ɒtəmən; *NAmE* 'ɑːt-/ *noun* a piece of furniture like a large box with a soft top, used for storing things in and sitting on 褥榻，箱式凳（箱子式的坐凳，有软垫）

OU /ˌəʊ 'juː; *NAmE* ˌoʊ/ *abbr.* (in Britain) Open University（英国的）开放大学，公开大学

ou /əʊ; *NAmE* oʊ/ *noun* (*pl.* **os** or **ouens** /'əʊənz; *NAmE* 'oʊ-/) (*SAfrE*) = OKE

ouch /aʊtʃ/ *exclamation* used to express sudden pain（表示突然的疼痛）哎呦：*Ouch! That hurt!* 哎呦！疼死了！➲ MORE LIKE THIS 2, page R25

oud /uːd/ *noun* a musical instrument similar to a LUTE played mainly in Arab countries 厄乌德琴（拨弦乐器，流行于阿拉伯国家）

ought to /'ɔːt tə; *before vowels and finally* 'ɔːt tu/ *modal verb* (*negative* **ought not to**, *short form especially BrE* **oughtn't to**) **1** used to say what is the right thing to do 应该；应当：*They ought to apologize.* 他们应该道歉。◇ *'Ought I to write to say thank you?' 'Yes, I think you ought (to).'* "我应该写信致谢吗？""对，我觉得你应该。"◇ *They ought to have apologized* (= but they didn't). 他们本该道歉的。◇ *Such things ought not to be allowed.* 这种事应该禁止。◇ *He oughtn't to have been driving so fast.* 他本不该把车开得那么快。 ➲ NOTE AT SHOULD **2** used to say what you expect or would like to happen（表示期望或可能发生的事）应该：*Children ought to be able to read by the age of 7.* 儿童 7 岁时应该识字了。◇ *Nurses ought to earn more.* 护士的薪资应该多一点。 **3** used to say what you advise or recommend（表示劝告或建议）应该：*We ought to be leaving now.* 我们现在该动身了。◇ *This is delicious. You ought to try some.* 这个菜很可口，你可得尝尝。◇ *You ought to have come to the meeting. It was interesting.* 会议可有意思了，你真该参加。 **4** used to say what has probably happened or is probably true（表示可能发生的或真实的事情）应该：*If he started out at nine, he ought to be here by now.* 他如果九点出发，现在应该到这里了。◇ *That ought to be enough food for the four of us.* 这些食物应该够咱们四个人吃了。◇ *Oughtn't the water to have boiled by now?* 水现在该开了吧？ ➲ NOTE AT MODAL

Ouija board™ /'wiːdʒə bɔːd; *NAmE* bɔːrd/ *noun* a board marked with letters of the alphabet and other signs, used in SEANCES to receive messages said to come from people who are dead 灵应牌（刻有字母和其他符号的板牌，用于降灵会中接收亡魂传递的信息）

ounce /aʊns/ *noun* **1** [C] (*abbr.* **oz**) a unit for measuring weight, 1⁄16 of a pound, equal to 28.35 grams 盎司（重量单位，1⁄16 磅，等于 28.35 克） ➲ SEE ALSO FLUID OUNCE **2** [sing.] **~ of sth** (*informal*) (used especially with negatives 尤与否定词连用) a very small quantity of sth 少许；少量；一点点；丝毫：*There's not an ounce of truth in her story.* 她所说的一点儿都不真实。 IDM SEE PREVENTION

our /ɑː(r); 'aʊə(r)/ *det.* (the possessive form of *we* * we 的所有格) **1** belonging to us; connected with us 我们的：*our daughter/dog/house* 我们的女儿／狗／房子 ◇ *We showed them some of our photos.* 我们给他们看了我们的一些照片。◇ *Our main export is rice.* 我们主要出口大米。◇ *And now, over to our Rome correspondent…* 现在是驻罗马记者的报道… **2 Our** used to refer to or address God or a holy person（用于称上帝或圣人）：*Our Father* (= God) 上帝 ◇ *Our Lady* (= the Virgin Mary) 圣母马利亚

ours /ɑːz; 'aʊəz; *NAmE* ɑːrz; 'aʊərz/ *pron.* **1** the one or ones that belong to us 我们的：*Their house is very similar to ours, but ours is bigger.* 他们的房子和我们的十分相像，但我们的要大些。◇ *No, those are Ellie's kids. Ours are upstairs.* 不，那些是埃利的孩子。我们的都在楼上。◇ *He's a friend of ours.* 他是我们的朋友。 **2** (*BrE, informal*) our home 我们的住处：*Do you fancy coming to ours for Sunday dinner?* 周日来我们家吃晚饭怎么样？

our·selves /ɑː'selvz; ˌaʊə's-; *NAmE* ɑːr's-; ˌaʊər's-/ *pron.* **1** the reflexive form of *we*; used when you and another person or other people together cause and are affected by an action（we 的反身形式）我们自己：*We shouldn't blame ourselves for what happened.* 我们不应该为发生的事责怪自己。◇ *Let's just relax and enjoy ourselves.* 咱们轻松一下，好好享受享受。◇ *We'd like to see it for ourselves.* 我们想亲眼看看它。 **2** 🔑 used to emphasize *we* or *us*; sometimes used instead of these words（用于强调或代替 we 或 us）我们自己，亲自：*We've often thought of going there ourselves.* 我们常想亲自到那里去一趟。◇ *The only people there were ourselves.* 那里除了我们，没有别人。

IDM **(all) by our'selves 1** alone; without anyone else（我们）独自，单独 **2** without help（我们）独力地 **(all) to our'selves** for us alone; not shared with anyone（完全）属于我们自己：*We had the pool all to ourselves.* 这个游泳池完全供我们自己使用。

-ous *suffix* (in adjectives 构成形容词) having the nature or quality of 有…性质的：*poisonous* 有毒的 ◇ *mountainous* 多山的 ➲ MORE LIKE THIS 7, page R25 ▸ **-ously** (in adverbs 构成副词)：*gloriously* 光荣地 **-ousness** (in nouns 构成名词)：*spaciousness* 宽敞

oust /aʊst/ *verb* to force sb out of a job or position of power, especially in order to take their place 剥夺；罢免；革职：**~ sb (as sth)** *He was ousted as chairman.* 他的主席职务被革除了。◇ **~ sb (from sth)** *The rebels finally managed to oust the government from power.* 反叛者最后总算推翻了政府。

oust·er /ˈaʊstə(r)/ *noun* (*NAmE*) the act of removing sb from a position of authority in order to put sb else in their place; the fact of being removed in this way 罢免；废黜；革职：*the president's ouster by the military* 军方对总统的废黜

O

out 🔑 /aʊt/ *adv., prep., noun, adj., verb*

■ ***adv., prep.*** HELP For the special uses of **out** in phrasal verbs, look at the entries for the verbs. For example **burst out** is in the phrasal verb section at **burst**. * out 在短语动词中的特殊用法见有关动词词条。如 burst out 在词条 burst 的短语动词部分。 **1** 🔑 **~ (of sth)** away from the inside of a place or thing（从…里）出来：*She ran out into the corridor.* 她跑出来，冲进走廊。◇ *She shook the bag and some coins fell out.* 她抖了抖袋子，几个硬币掉了出来。◇ *I got out of bed.* 我起了床。◇ *He opened the box and **out** jumped a frog.* 他打开盒子，从里面跳出一只青蛙来。◇ ***Out you go!*** (= used to order sb to leave a room) 滚出去！◇ (*informal*) *He ran out the door.* 他跑出门去。 **2** 🔑 **~ (of sth)** (of people 人) away from or not at home or their place of work 不在家；不在工作地点；外出：*I called Liz but she was out.* 我打电话给利兹，但她不在家。◇ *Let's go out this evening* (= for example to a restaurant or club). 咱们今天晚上出去吧。◇ *We haven't had a **night out** for weeks.* 我们已经好几个星期晚上没出去过了。◇ *Mr Green is out of town this week.* 格林先生本周到外地去了。 **3** 🔑 **~ (of sth)** away from the edge of a place 出去；离开（某地）边缘：*The boy dashed out into the road.* 男孩子向路中间冲去。◇ *Don't lean out of the window.* 不要探出窗外。 **4** 🔑 **~ (of sth)** a long or a particular distance away from a place or from land 远离（某地或陆地）；离（某地或陆地）：*She's working out in Australia.* 她远在澳大利亚工作。◇ *He lives right out in the country.* 他住在远离此地的乡间。◇ *The boats are all out at sea.* 船只全都出海了。◇ *The ship sank ten miles out of Stockholm.* 那艘船在距离斯德哥尔摩十英里处沉入海中。 **5** 🔑 **~ (of sth)** used to show that sth/sb is removed from a place, job, etc. 除掉；清除：*This detergent is good for getting stains out.* 这种洗涤剂能清除斑渍。◇ *We want this government out.* 我们想要这届政府下台。◇ *He got thrown out of the restaurant.* 他被逐出了餐馆。 **6** 🔑 **~ of sth/sb** used to show that sth comes from or is obtained from sth/sb（表示来源）从，用…制作：*He drank his beer out of the bottle.* 他从瓶口直接喝啤酒。◇ *a statue made out of bronze* 一尊青铜像 ◇ *a romance straight out of a fairy tale* 童话故事般的爱情 ◇ *I paid for the damage out of my savings.* 我用自己的积蓄赔偿了损失。◇ *We'll get the truth out of her.* 我们会从她那里套出实情。 **7** 🔑 **~ of sth** used to show that sb/sth does not have any of sth 没有；缺少：*We're out of milk.* 我们没有牛奶了。◇ *He's been **out of work** for six months.* 他已经失业六个月了。◇ *You're **out of luck**—she left ten minutes ago.* 你真不走运，她十分钟前才离开。 **8** 🔑 **~ of sth** used to show that sb/sth is not or no longer in a particular state or condition（表示不在原状态）脱离，离开：*Try and stay out of trouble.* 尽量别惹麻烦。◇ *I watched the car until it was **out of sight**.* 我目送汽车，直到看不见为止。 **9** 🔑 **~ (of sth)** used to show that sb is no longer involved in sth（表示不再参与某事）脱离：*It was an awful job and I'm glad to be out of it.* 那件差事简直是受罪，我很高兴摆脱掉了。◇ *He gets out of the army in a few weeks.* 几周之后他就要离开部队。◇ *They'll be out* (= of prison) *on bail in no time.* 他们马上就要获得保释出狱。◇ *Brown goes on to the semi-finals but Lee is out.* 布朗进入了半决赛，但李被淘汰了。 **10 ~ of sth** used to show the reason why sth is done（表示原因）因为，出于：*I asked out of curiosity.* 我因为好奇问了问。◇ *She did it out of spite.* 她那么做是出于恶意。 **11** 🔑 **~ of sth** from a particular number or set 从（某个数目或集）中：*You scored six out of ten.* 总分十分你得了六分。◇ *Two out of three people think the President should resign.* 有三分之二的人认为总统应当辞职。 **12** 🔑 (of a book, etc. 书籍等) not in the library; borrowed by sb else 不在图书馆；已借出：*The book you wanted is out on loan.* 你要的那本书借出去了。 **13** 🔑 (of the TIDE 海潮) at or towards its lowest point on land 在退潮期；退潮：*I like walking on the wet sand when the tide is out.* 我喜欢退潮后走在湿润的沙滩上。 **14** 🔑 if the sun, moon or stars are or come **out**, they can be seen from the earth and are not hidden by clouds（日、月、星辰）出现，未被云遮住 **15** (of flowers 花朵) fully open 开放：*There should be some snowdrops out by now.* 现在应该有雪花莲开放了。 **16** 🔑 available to everyone; known to everyone 公开；发行：*When does her new book come out?* 她的新书什么时候出版？◇ ***Word** always **gets out*** (= people find out about things) *no matter how careful you are.* 无论你多么小心，总会有消息走漏。◇ ***Out with it!*** (= say what you know) 你就说出来吧！ **17** 🔑 clearly and loudly so that people can hear 大声地：*to call/cry/shout out* 大声叫 / 哭 / 喊 ◇ *Read it **out loud**.* 请大声朗读。◇ *Nobody **spoke out** in his defence.* 没有人站出来替他辩护。 **18** (*informal*) having told other people that you are HOMOSEXUAL 已公开同性恋身份：*I had been out since I was 17.* 我从 17 岁起就公开我是同性恋。 **19** (in CRICKET, BASEBALL, etc. 板球、棒球等) if a team or team member is **out**, it is no longer their turn with the BAT 出局：*The West Indies were **all out** for 364* (= after scoring 364 RUNS in CRICKET). 西印度群岛队以 364 分全队出局。 **20** (in TENNIS, etc. 网球等) if the ball is **out**, it landed outside the line 出界：*The umpire said the ball was out.* 裁判员判球出界。 **21** 🔑 **~ (in sth)** not correct or exact; wrong 错误；不准确：*I was slightly out in my calculations.* 我的计算出了点小错。◇ *Your guess was a long way out* (= completely wrong). 你的猜测完全错了。◇ *The estimate was **out by** more than $100.* 这个估计差了 100 多美元。 **22** not possible or not allowed 不可能；不允许：*Swimming is out until the weather gets warmer.* 天气转暖前，游泳是不可能的。 **23** not fashionable 过时：*Black is out this year.* 今年黑色不时兴了。 **24** 🔑 (of fire, lights or burning materials 火、灯光、燃烧物等) not or no longer burning or lit 熄灭：*Suddenly all the lights went out.* 突然间所有的灯光都灭了。◇ *The fire had burnt itself out.* 炉火烧尽熄灭了。 **25** at an end 结束：*It was summer and school was out.* 夏天，学校放假了。◇ *She was to regret her words **before the day was out**.* 她到不了天黑就会为自己说的话后悔。 **26** unconscious 无知觉；昏迷：*He was out for more than an hour and came round in the hospital.* 他昏迷了一个多小时，在医院才苏醒过来。◇ *She was knocked **out cold**.* 她完全被打昏了。 **27** (*BrE, informal*) on strike 罢工 **28** to the end; completely 到底；完全地：***Hear me out** before you say anything.* 你听我说完再讲话。◇ *We left them to **fight it out*** (= settle a disagreement by fighting or arguing). 我们让他们争吵下去，争出个输赢。 ➲ SEE ALSO ALL-OUT

IDM **be out for sth/to do sth** to be trying to get or do sth 试图得到（或做）：*I'm not out for revenge.* 我不是来寻报复的。◇ *She's **out for what she can get*** (= trying to get something for herself). 她力图得到自己能得的。◇ *The* *company is out to capture the Canadian market.* 这家公司竭尽全力抢占加拿大市场。 **ˌout and aˈbout 1** able to go outside again after an illness 病愈后能外出走动 **2** travelling around a place 遍游某地： *We've been out and about talking to people all over the country.* 我们游遍了全国，和各地的人交谈。 **ˈout of here** (*informal*) going or leaving 走；离去；离开： *As soon as I get my money I'm out of here!* 我一拿到钱就走！ **ˈout of it** (*informal*) **1** sad because you are not included in sth（觉得自己是外人而）不是味儿： *We've only just moved here so we feel a little out of it.* 我们刚搬到这里，所以心里觉得有点不适应。 **2** not aware of what is happening, usually because of drinking too much alcohol, or taking drugs（因酒或药物作用而对周围事情）茫然不觉，昏昏然

▪*noun* [sing.] a way of avoiding having to do sth 回避的方法；托辞；出路： *She was desperately looking for an out.* 她在拼命找一条脱身之计。 IDM ➤ SEE IN *adv.*

▪*adj.* (*informal*) having told other people that you are HOMOSEXUAL 已公开同性恋身份的： *an out gay man* 已公开同性恋身份的男子

▪*verb* **1 ~ sb** to say publicly that sb is HOMOSEXUAL, especially when they would prefer to keep the fact a secret 揭露，公布（同性恋者）： *He is the latest politician to be outed by gay activists.* 他是被同性恋维权人士新近揭露的同性恋政治人物。 **2 ~ sb/sth (as sth)** to say sth publicly about sb/sth that they would prefer to keep secret 揭露，公布（别人想要保守的秘密）： *The man who claimed to have found the diaries has been outed as a fraud.* 声称找到日记的人被揭露是个骗子。

out- /aʊt/ *prefix* **1** (in verbs 构成动词) greater, better, further, longer, etc. 超越；超过： *outnumber* 在数量上压倒 ◇ *outwit* 在智慧上胜过 ◇ *outgrow* 长得比…快 ◇ *outlive* 活得比…长 **2** (in nouns and adjectives 构成名词和形容词) outside; OUTWARD; away from 在外面；向外；离开： *outbuildings* 附属建筑物 ◇ *outpatient* 门诊病人 ◇ *outlying* 偏远的 ◇ *outgoing* 向外的 ➲ MORE LIKE THIS 6, page R25

out·age /ˈaʊtɪdʒ/ *noun* (*especially NAmE*) a period of time when the supply of electricity, etc. is not working 停电（等）期间： *a power outage* 停电期间

ˌout-and-ˈout *adj.* [only before noun] in every way 十足的；完全的；彻头彻尾的 SYN **complete**: *What she said was an out-and-out lie.* 她说的是个弥天大谎。

out·back /ˈaʊtbæk/ *noun* **the outback** [sing.] the area of Australia that is a long way from the coast and the towns, where few people live（澳大利亚的）内地，内陆地区

out·bid /ˌaʊtˈbɪd/ *verb* (**out·bid·ding**, **out·bid**, **out·bid**) **~ sb (for sth)** to offer more money than sb else in order to buy sth, for example at an AUCTION（在拍卖等中）出价高于…

out·board /ˈaʊtbɔːd; *NAmE* -bɔːrd/ *adj.* (*specialist*) on, towards or near the outside of a ship or an aircraft（船或飞机）舷外的，外侧的，靠近外侧的

ˌoutboard ˈmotor (*also* **ˌoutboard ˈengine**, **out·board**) *noun* an engine that you can fix to the back of a small boat 舷外挂机

out·bound /ˈaʊtbaʊnd/ *adj.* (*formal*) travelling from a place rather than arriving in it 向外的；出港的；离开某地的： ***outbound flights/passengers*** 出港航班 / 旅客 OPP **inbound**

out·box /ˈaʊtbɒks; *NAmE* -bɑːks/ *noun* **1** (*computing* 计) the place on a computer where new email messages that you write are stored before they are sent（电子邮件）发件箱 **2** (*US*) = OUT TRAY

out·break /ˈaʊtbreɪk/ *noun* the sudden start of sth unpleasant, especially violence or a disease（暴力、疾病等坏事的）爆发，突然发生： *the outbreak of war* 战争的爆发 ◇ *an outbreak of typhoid* 伤寒的爆发 ◇ *Outbreaks of rain are expected in the afternoon.* 下午将有暴雨。 ➲ COLLOCATIONS AT ILL ➲ WORDFINDER NOTE AT HEALTH

out·build·ing /ˈaʊtbɪldɪŋ/ *noun* [usually pl.] a building such as a SHED or STABLE that is built near to, but separate from, a main building 附属建筑物

out·burst /ˈaʊtbɜːst; *NAmE* -bɜːrst/ *noun* **1** a sudden strong expression of an emotion（感情的）爆发，迸发： *an outburst of anger* 突然大怒 ◇ *She was alarmed by his violent outburst.* 他暴跳如雷，令她惊恐万状。 **2** a sudden increase in a particular activity or attitude（活动的）激增；（态度的）激化： *an outburst of racism* 种族主义的突然高涨

out·cast /ˈaʊtkɑːst; *NAmE* -kæst/ *noun* a person who is not accepted by other people and who sometimes has to leave their home and friends 被抛弃者；被排斥者： *People with the disease were often treated as social outcasts.* 患有这种疾病的人常被社会摈弃。 ► **out·cast** *adj.*

out·class /ˌaʊtˈklɑːs; *NAmE* -ˈklæs/ *verb* [often passive] **~ sb/sth** to be much better than sb you are competing against 远远高出，远远超过（对手）： *Kennedy was outclassed 0–6 0–6 in the final.* 肯尼迪在决赛中以 0:6 和 0:6 连输两盘落败。

out·come AW /ˈaʊtkʌm/ *noun* the result or effect of an action or event 结果；效果： *We are waiting to hear the final outcome of the negotiations.* 我们在等待谈判的最终结果。 ◇ *These costs are payable whatever the outcome of the case.* 无论讼案结果如何，这些费用都应照付。 ◇ *We are confident of a successful outcome.* 我们相信会有圆满的结果。 ◇ *Four possible outcomes have been identified.* 现已确定有四种可能的结果。 ➲ SYNONYMS AT RESULT

out·crop /ˈaʊtkrɒp; *NAmE* -krɑːp/ *noun* a large mass of rock that stands above the surface of the ground（岩石）露出地面的部分；露头

out·cry /ˈaʊtkraɪ/ *noun* [C, U] (*pl.* **-ies**) **~ (at/over/against sth)** a reaction of anger or strong protest shown by people in public 呐喊；怒吼；强烈的抗议： *an outcry over the proposed change* 对拟议的改革所发出的强烈抗议 ◇ *The new tax provoked a* ***public outcry***. 新税项引起了公众的强烈抗议。 ◇ *There was outcry at the judge's statement.* 法官的陈辞引起一片哗然。

out·dated /ˌaʊtˈdeɪtɪd/ *adj.* no longer useful because of being old-fashioned 过时的；陈旧的： *outdated equipment* 过时的设备 ◇ *These figures are now outdated.* 这些数字现在已经过时。 ➲ COMPARE OUT OF DATE (1)

out·dis·tance /ˌaʊtˈdɪstəns/ *verb* **~ sb/sth** to leave sb/sth behind by going faster, further, etc.; to be better than sb/sth 远远超过；超越；优于 SYN **outstrip**

outdo /ˌaʊtˈduː/ *verb* (**out·does** /-ˈdʌz/, **out·did** /-ˈdɪd/, **out·done** /-ˈdʌn/) **~ sb/sth** to do more or better than sb else 胜过；优于 SYN **beat**: *Sometimes small firms can outdo big business when it comes to customer care.* 在顾客服务方面，有时小企业可能优于大企业。 ◇ ***Not to be outdone*** (= not wanting to let sb else do better), *she tried again.* 她不甘落后，又试了一次。

out·door /ˈaʊtdɔː(r)/ *adj.* [only before noun] used, happening or located outside rather than in a building 户外的；室外的： ***outdoor clothing/activities*** 户外穿的衣服 / 活动 ◇ *an outdoor swimming pool* 室外游泳池 ◇ *I'm not really the* ***outdoor type*** (= I prefer indoor activities). 我不是那种真正喜爱户外活动的人。 OPP **indoor**

out·doors /ˌaʊtˈdɔːz; *NAmE* -ˈdɔːrz/ *adv., noun*

▪*adv.* outside, rather than in a building 在户外；在野外： *The rain prevented them from eating outdoors.* 雨天使他们无法户外用餐。 OPP **indoors**

▪*noun* **the outdoors** [sing.] the countryside, away from buildings and busy places 野外；旷野；郊外： *They both have a love of the outdoors.* 他们俩都喜爱郊外的环境。 ◇ *Come to Canada and enjoy* ***the great outdoors***. 到加拿大来享受蓝天碧野吧！ ➲ COLLOCATIONS AT TOWN

outer /ˈaʊtə(r)/ *adj.* [only before noun] **1** on the outside of sth 外表的；外边的 SYN **external**: *the outer layers of the skin* 皮肤表层 **2** furthest from the inside or centre of sth 远离中心的；外围的： *I walked along the outer edge of the track.* 我沿着跑道的外缘走。 ◇ *the outer*

O

suburbs of the city 城市的远郊 ◇ *Outer London* 伦敦的外围地区 ◇ (*figurative*) *to explore the outer* (= most extreme) *limits of human experience* 探索人类经验的极限 OPP **inner**

ˌ**outer belt** (*US*) (*BrE* ˈ**ring road**) *noun* a road that is built around a city or town to reduce traffic in the centre 环路；环城路

outer·most /ˈaʊtəməʊst; *NAmE* ˈaʊtərmoʊst/ *adj.* [only before noun] furthest from the inside or centre 最外边的；最远的：*the outermost planet* 最远的行星 ◇ *He fired and hit the outermost ring of the target.* 他开枪射中了靶子的最外一环。OPP **innermost**

ˌ**outer** ˈ**space** *noun* [U] = SPACE (6)：*radio waves from outer space* 来自外层空间的无线电波

outer·wear /ˈaʊtəweə(r); *NAmE* ˈaʊtərwer/ *noun* [U] clothes such as coats, hats, etc. that you wear outside 外衣；户外的穿着

out·face /ˌaʊtˈfeɪs/ *verb* ~ **sb** (*formal*) to defeat an enemy or opponent by being brave and remaining confident 凛然面对；吓退

out·fall /ˈaʊtfɔːl/ *noun* (*specialist*) the place where a river, pipe, etc. flows out into the sea（河流、管道等的）排放口，出水口；入海口；河口：*a sewage outfall* 污水排放口

out·field /ˈaʊtfiːld/ *noun, adv.*

■ *noun* [sing.] the outer part of the field in BASEBALL, CRICKET and some other sports（棒球、板球等体育运动的）外场，外野 ➲ COMPARE INFIELD *n.*

■ *adv.* in or to the outfield 在外场；向外场

out·field·er /ˈaʊtfiːldə(r)/ *noun* (in CRICKET and BASEBALL 板球及棒球) a player in the outfield 外场手；外场员；外野手

O

out·fit /ˈaʊtfɪt/ *noun, verb*

■ *noun* **1** [C] a set of clothes that you wear together, especially for a particular occasion or purpose 全套服装，装束（尤指为某场合或目的）：*She was wearing an expensive new outfit.* 她穿着一身昂贵的新衣裳。◇ *a wedding outfit* 一套结婚礼服 ◇ *a cowboy/Superman outfit* (= one that you wear for fun in order to look like the type of person mentioned) 一套牛仔 / 超人服装 **2** [C+sing./pl. v.] (*informal*) a group of people working together as an organization, business, team, etc. 团队；小组；分队：*a market research outfit* 市场调查组 ◇ *This was the fourth album by the top rock outfit.* 这是这个顶级摇滚乐队的第四张唱片专辑。**3** [C] a set of equipment that you need for a particular purpose 全套装备；成套工具：*a bicycle repair outfit* 修自行车的整套工具

■ *verb* (-tt-) [often passive] ~ **sth/sb** (**with sth**) (*especially NAmE*) to provide sb/sth with equipment or clothes for a special purpose 装备；配置设备；供给服装 SYN **equip**：*The ship was outfitted with a 12-bed hospital.* 这艘船配备了一所有12个床位的医院。

out·fit·ter (*also* **out·fit·ters**) /ˈaʊtfɪtə(r)/ *noun* **1** (*old-fashioned, BrE*) a shop/store that sells men's clothes or school uniforms（出售男装或校服的）服装店 **2** (*NAmE*) a shop/store that sells equipment for camping and other outdoor activities 户外用品店；露营装备店

out·flank /ˌaʊtˈflæŋk/ *verb* **1** ~ **sb/sth** to move around the side of an enemy or opponent, especially in order to attack them from behind 包抄；侧翼包围 **2** ~ **sb/sth** to gain an advantage over sb, especially by doing sth unexpected（尤指出其不意地）胜过，占先 SYN **outmanoeuvre**

out·flow /ˈaʊtfləʊ; *NAmE* -floʊ/ *noun* [usually sing.] ~ (**of sth/sb**) (**from sth**) the movement of a large amount of money, liquid, people, etc. out of a place 外流；流出量：*There was a capital outflow of $22 billion in 2008.* * 2008 年的资本外流量为 220 亿美元。◇ *a steady outflow of oil from the tank* 石油从油罐里不断的流出 ◇ *the outflow of refugees* 难民涌出 OPP **inflow**

out·fox /ˌaʊtˈfɒks; *NAmE* -ˈfɑːks/ *verb* ~ **sb** to gain an advantage over sb by being more clever than they are 以智力胜过（或超过）SYN **outwit**

out·going /ˈaʊtgəʊɪŋ; *NAmE* -goʊ-/ *adj.* **1** liking to meet other people, enjoying their company and being friendly towards them 爱交际的；友好的；外向的 SYN **sociable**：*an outgoing personality* 外向的性格 **2** [only before noun] leaving the position of responsibility mentioned 将卸任的；离职的：*the outgoing president/government* 即将下台的总统 / 政府 OPP **incoming** **3** [only before noun] going away from a particular place rather than arriving in it 向外的；离开的：*This telephone should be used for outgoing calls.* 这部电话用来往外拨打电话。◇ *outgoing flights/passengers* 离港航班 / 旅客 ◇ *the outgoing tide* 退潮 OPP **incoming**

out·goings /ˈaʊtgəʊɪŋz; *NAmE* -goʊ-/ *noun* [pl.] (*BrE*) the amount of money that a person or a business has to spend regularly, for example every month 开支；经常性费用 SYN **expenditure**：*low/high outgoings* 开支低 / 高 ◇ *Write down your incomings and outgoings.* 把你的收入与支出记下来。

ˈ**out-group** *noun* the people who do not belong to a particular IN-GROUP in a society 外群体；外团体

out·grow /ˌaʊtˈgrəʊ; *NAmE* -ˈgroʊ/ *verb* (**out·grew** /-ˈgruː/, **out·grown** /-ˈgrəʊn; *NAmE* -ˈgroʊn/) **1** ~ **sth** to grow too big to be able to wear or fit into sth 长得穿不下（衣服）；增长得容不进（某地）SYN **grow out of sth**：*She's already outgrown her school uniform.* 她已经长得连校服都不能穿了。◇ *The company has outgrown its offices.* 公司发展得办公室都不够用了。**2** ~ **sb** to grow taller, larger or more quickly than another person 比…长得高（或大、快）：*He's already outgrown his older brother.* 他已长得比他哥哥还高。**3** ~ **sth** to stop doing sth or lose interest in sth as you become older 因长大而放弃；年增志移 SYN **grow out of sth**：*He's outgrown his passion for rock music.* 随着年龄的增长，他已对摇滚乐失去了热情。

out·growth /ˈaʊtgrəʊθ; *NAmE* -groʊθ/ *noun* **1** (*specialist*) a thing that grows out of sth else 长出物；分支：*The eye first appears as a cup-shaped outgrowth from the brain.* 眼睛最初看上去是从大脑长出，呈杯状。**2** (*formal*) a natural development or result of sth 自然发展（或结果）：*The law was an outgrowth of the 2008 presidential election.* 这项法律是 2008 年总统选举的自然产物。

out·gun /ˌaʊtˈgʌn/ *verb* (-nn-) [often passive] ~ **sb/sth** to have greater military strength than sb（军事上）胜过，超过：(*figurative*) *The England team was completely outgunned.* 英格兰队毫无还手之力。

out·house /ˈaʊthaʊs/ *noun* **1** (*BrE*) a small building, such as a SHED, outside a main building（主建筑的）外围建筑，附属建筑 **2** (*especially NAmE*) a toilet in a small building of its own 屋外厕所

out·ing /ˈaʊtɪŋ/ *noun* **1** [C] ~ (**to**...) a trip that you go on for pleasure or education, usually with a group of people and lasting no more than one day（集体）出外游玩（或学习等）；远足 SYN **excursion**：*We went on an outing to London.* 我们游览了伦敦。◇ *a family outing* 全家远足 ➲ SYNONYMS AT TRIP **2** [C] (*sport* 体育, *informal*) an occasion when sb takes part in a competition 参赛；比赛 **3** [U, C] the practice of naming people as HOMOSEXUALS in public, when they do not want anyone to know（违背同性恋者本人意愿）对（其）身份的公开挑明

out·land·ish /aʊtˈlændɪʃ/ *adj.* (*usually disapproving*) strange or extremely unusual 古怪的；极不寻常的；奇特的 SYN **bizarre**：*outlandish costumes/ideas* 奇装异服；古怪的想法 ▸ **out·land·ish·ly** *adv.*

out·last /ˌaʊtˈlɑːst; *NAmE* -ˈlæst/ *verb* ~ **sb/sth** to continue to exist or take part in an activity for a longer time than sb/sth 比…持续时间长：*He can outlast anyone on the dance floor.* 在舞场上，他比谁都能跳。

out·law /ˈaʊtlɔː/ *verb, noun*

■ *verb* **1** ~ **sth** to make sth illegal 宣布…不合法；使…成为非法 SYN **ban**：*plans to outlaw the carrying of knives* 宣布携带刀具为非法的方案 ◇ *the outlawed nationalist party*

被宣布为非法的民族主义党 **2 ~ sb** (in the past) to make sb an outlaw（旧时）剥夺（某人的）法律权益

■ *noun* (used especially about people in the past) a person who has done sth illegal and is hiding to avoid being caught; a person who is not protected by the law（尤指过去的人）亡命徒，逃犯，草莽英雄，被剥夺法律权益者：*Robin Hood, the world's most famous outlaw* 罗宾汉，蜚声世界的绿林好汉

out·lay /ˈaʊtleɪ/ *noun* [C, U] ~ (**on sth**) the money that you have to spend in order to start a new project（启动新项目的）开支，费用：*The business quickly repaid the initial outlay on advertising.* 这家公司很快偿付了初期的广告费。◇ *a massive* ***financial/capital outlay*** 大量的财政 / 资本开支 ➲ SYNONYMS AT COST

out·let /ˈaʊtlet/ *noun* **1** ~ (**for sth**) a way of expressing or making good use of strong feelings, ideas or energy（感情、思想、精力发泄的）出路；表现机会：*She needed to find an outlet for her many talents and interests.* 她多才多艺、兴趣广泛，需要找个施展的机会。◇ *Sport became the perfect outlet for his aggression.* 运动成为他攻击性情绪的最佳释放途径。 **2** (*business* 商) a shop/store or an organization that sells goods made by a particular company or of a particular type 专营店；经销店：*The business has 34 retail outlets in this state alone.* 那家商号仅在本州就有 34 个零售店。 **3** a shop/store that sells goods of a particular make at reduced prices（某品牌的）折扣店：*the Nike outlet in the outlet mall* 折扣品商场里的耐克折扣店 **4** a pipe or hole through which liquid or gas can flow out 出口；排放管：*a sewage outlet* 污水排放口 ◇ *an outlet pipe* 排水管道 OPP **inlet** **5** (*also* **re·cep·tacle, socket**) (*both NAmE*) (*BrE* **ˈpower point**) a device in a wall that you put a plug into in order to connect electrical equipment to the power supply of a building（电源）插座 ➲ PICTURE AT PLUG

out·line /ˈaʊtlaɪn/ *verb, noun*

■ *verb* **1** ~ **sth** (**to sb**) | ~ **what, how, etc....** to give a description of the main facts or points involved in sth 概述；略述 SYN **sketch**：*We outlined our proposals to the committee.* 我们向委员会提纲挈领地讲了讲我们的提案。 **2** [usually passive] ~ **sth** (**against sth**) to show or mark the outer edge of sth 显示…的轮廓；勾勒…的外形：*They saw the huge building outlined against the sky.* 他们看见了在天空的映衬下那座巨大建筑的轮廓。

■ *noun* [C, U] **1** a description of the main facts or points involved in sth 概述；梗概：*This is a brief outline of the events.* 这就是事件的简要情况。◇ *You should draw up a plan or outline for the essay.* 你应该为文章草拟个计划或提纲。◇ *The book describes* ***in outline*** *the main findings of the research.* 本书扼要叙述了主要的研究结果。◇ ***an outline agreement/proposal*** 协议 / 建议纲要 **2** the line that goes around the edge of sth, showing its main shape but not the details 轮廓线；略图：*At last we could see the dim outline of an island.* 我们终于能看到一小岛朦胧的轮廓了。◇ *an* ***outline map/sketch*** 略图；草图 ◇ *She drew the figures* ***in outline.*** 她简略地勾勒出人物的轮廓。

out·live /ˌaʊtˈlɪv/ *verb* **1** ~ **sb** to live longer than sb 比…活得长：*He outlived his wife by three years.* 他比妻子多活了三年。 **2** ~ **sth** to continue to exist after sth else has ended or disappeared（在…结束或消失后）继续存在：*The machine had* ***outlived its usefulness*** (= was no longer useful). 这机器已无用了。

out·look /ˈaʊtlʊk/ *noun* [usually sing.] **1** ~ (**on sth**) the attitude to life and the world of a particular person, group or culture 观点；见解；世界观；人生观：*He had a practical outlook on life.* 他的人生观很实际。◇ *Most Western societies are liberal* ***in outlook.*** 西方社会大多思想观念开放。 **2** ~ (**for sth**) the probable future for sb/sth; what is likely to happen 前景；可能性 SYN **prospect**：*The outlook for jobs is bleak.* 就业市场前景暗淡。◇ *the country's economic outlook* 国家的经济前景 ◇ *The outlook* (= the probable weather) *for the weekend is dry and sunny.* 周末天气可望晴朗干燥。 **3** (*formal*) a view from a particular place 景色；景致；景观：*The house has a pleasant outlook over the valley.* 房子俯瞰山谷，景色宜人。

out·ly·ing /ˈaʊtlaɪɪŋ/ *adj.* [only before noun] far away from the cities of a country or from the main part of a place 边远的；偏远的；远离市镇的：*outlying areas* 偏远地区

out·man·oeuvre (*especially US* **out·ma·neu·ver**) /ˌaʊtməˈnuːvə(r)/ *verb* ~ **sb/sth** to do better than an opponent by acting in a way that is cleverer or more skilful 比…高明；比…技高一筹：*The president has so far managed to outmanoeuvre his critics.* 到目前为止，总统面对批评者都能够应付裕如。

out·moded /ˌaʊtˈməʊdɪd; *NAmE* -ˈmoʊd-/ *adj.* (*disapproving*) no longer fashionable or useful 过时的；已无用的：*an outmoded attitude* 陈腐的观点

out·num·ber /ˌaʊtˈnʌmbə(r)/ *verb* ~ **sb/sth** to be greater in number than sb/sth（在数量上）压倒，比…多：*The demonstrators were heavily outnumbered by the police.* 示威者人数远不及警察人数。◇ *In this profession, women outnumber men by two to one* (= there are twice as many women as men). 在这个行业，女性人数是男性的两倍。

ˌout-of-ˌbody exˈperience *noun* a feeling of being outside your own body, especially when you feel that you are watching yourself from a distance 离体体验，灵魂出窍体验（尤指从远处观看自己的感觉）

ˌout of ˈdate *adj.* **1** old-fashioned or without the most recent information and therefore no longer useful 过时的；缺乏新信息的；陈腐的：*These figures are very out of date.* 这些数字早已过时。◇ *Suddenly she felt old and out of date.* 她猛然觉得自己老了，跟不上时代了。◇ *an out-of-date map* 已过时的地图 ◇ *out-of-date technology* 落伍的技术 ➲ COMPARE OUTDATED **2** no longer valid 失效的；过期的：*an out-of-date driving licence* 过期的驾驶执照 ➲ SEE ALSO UP TO DATE

ˈout-of-pocket *adj.* ~ **expenses/costs/expenditure/spending** small business expenses that you pay yourself, with your employer paying you back later（小额商务费用）垫付的：*On business trips she has some travel and other out-of-pocket expenses.* 她出差要垫付一些差旅费和其他费用。➲ COMPARE POCKET *n.* (3)

ˌout-of-ˈstate *adj.* [only before noun] (*US*) coming from or happening in a different state 外州的；州外的：*out-of-state license plates* 外州的汽车牌照

ˌout-of-the-ˈway *adj.* far from a town or city 偏僻的；偏远的：*a little out-of-the-way place on the coast* 海边一个偏远的小地方

ˌout-of-ˈtown *adj.* [only before noun] **1** located away from the centre of a town or city 城外的；郊野的：*out-of-town superstores* 市郊超级商场 **2** coming from or happening in a different place 外地的；外来的：*an out-of-town guest* 外来客 ◇ *an out-of-town performance* 外地演出

ˌout-of-ˈwork *adj.* [only before noun] unemployed 失业的；下岗的：*an out-of-work actor* 待业演员

out·pace /ˌaʊtˈpeɪs/ *verb* ~ **sb/sth** to go, rise, improve, etc. faster than sb/sth（在速度上）超过；比…快 SYN **outstrip**：*He easily outpaced the other runners.* 他轻而易举地超过了其他赛跑选手。◇ *Demand is outpacing production.* 需求正在超过生产。

out·pa·tient /ˈaʊtpeɪʃnt/ *noun* a person who goes to a hospital for treatment but does not stay there 门诊病人：*an outpatient clinic* 门诊部 ➲ COMPARE INPATIENT

out·per·form /ˌaʊtpəˈfɔːm; *NAmE* -pərˈfɔːrm/ *verb* ~ **sb/sth** to achieve better results than sb/sth 超过；胜过 ▶ **out·per·form·ance** *noun* [U]

out·place·ment /ˈaʊtpleɪsmənt/ *noun* [U] (*business* 商) the process of helping people to find new jobs after they have been made unemployed（对失业人员的）安置，再就业服务

out·play /ˌaʊtˈpleɪ/ *verb* ~ **sb** to play much better than sb you are competing against（技胜一筹）战胜，击败：

We were totally outplayed and lost 106–74. 我们以 74:106 惨败。

out·point /ˌaʊtˈpɔɪnt/ *verb* **~ sb** (especially in boxing 尤用于拳击运动) to defeat sb by scoring more points 以点数取胜

out·post /ˈaʊtpəʊst; *NAmE* -poʊst/ *noun* **1** a small military camp away from the main army, used for watching an enemy's movements, etc. 前哨（基地） **2** a small town or group of buildings in a lonely part of a country 偏远村镇；孤零住区：*a remote outpost* 偏远的村镇 ◇ *the last outpost of civilization* 文明的边缘地区

out·pour·ing /ˈaʊtpɔːrɪŋ/ *noun* **1** [usually pl.] a strong and sudden expression of feeling（感情的）迸发，倾泻：*spontaneous outpourings of praise* 一片自然迸发的赞美声 **2** a large amount of sth produced in a short time 涌现；喷涌：*a remarkable outpouring of new ideas* 新思想的大量涌现

out·put 🔑 AW /ˈaʊtpʊt/ *noun, verb*

■ ***noun*** [U, sing.] **1** 🔑 the amount of sth that a person, a machine or an organization produces（人、机器、机构的）产量，输出量：*Manufacturing output has increased by 8%.* 工业产量增长了 8%。 ➲ WORDFINDER NOTE AT INDUSTRY **2** (*computing* 计) the information, results, etc. produced by a computer 输出：*data output* 数据输出 ◇ *an output device* 输出装置 ➲ COMPARE INPUT *n.* **3** the power, energy, etc. produced by a piece of equipment 输出功率；输出量：*an output of 100 watts* 输出功率 100 瓦 **4** a place where energy, power, information, etc. leaves a system 输出端：*Connect a cable to the output.* 把缆线接到输出端上。

■ ***verb*** (**out·put·ting**, **out·put**, **out·put** or **out·put·ting**, **out·put·ted**, **out·put·ted**) **~ sth** (*computing* 计) to supply or produce information, results, etc. 输出：*Computers can now output data much more quickly.* 现在计算机能更快地输出数据。 ➲ COMPARE INPUT *v.*

O

out·rage /ˈaʊtreɪdʒ/ *noun, verb*

■ ***noun*** **1** [U] a strong feeling of shock and anger 愤怒；义愤；愤慨：*The judge's remarks caused public outrage.* 裁判的话引起了公愤。 ◇ *Environmentalists have expressed outrage at the ruling.* 环境保护主义者对这一裁决表示愤慨。 **2** [C] an act or event that is violent, cruel or very wrong and that shocks people or makes them very angry 暴行；骇人听闻的事 SYN **atrocity**：*No one has yet claimed responsibility for this latest bomb outrage.* 迄今还没有人宣称对最近的爆炸丑行负责。

■ ***verb*** [often passive] **~ sb** to make sb very shocked and angry 使震怒；激怒：*He was outraged at the way he had been treated.* 他对所遭受的待遇感到非常愤怒。

out·ra·geous /aʊtˈreɪdʒəs/ *adj.* **1** very shocking and unacceptable 骇人的；无法容忍的 SYN **scandalous**：*outrageous behaviour* 极端无礼的行为 ◇ *'That's outrageous!' he protested.* "简直骇人听闻！"他抗议说。 **2** very unusual and slightly shocking 反常的；令人惊讶的：*She says the most outrageous things sometimes.* 她有时候尽说些耸人听闻的事。 ◇ *outrageous clothes* 怪里怪气的服装 ▸ **out·ra·geous·ly** *adv.*：*an outrageously expensive meal* 贵得吓人的一顿饭 ◇ *They behaved outrageously.* 他们的行为表现让人难以容忍。

out·ran PAST TENSE OF OUTRUN

out·rank /ˌaʊtˈræŋk/ *verb* **~ sb** to be of higher rank, quality, etc. than sb（在职衔、质量等上）超过，在…之上

outré /ˈuːtreɪ; *NAmE* uːˈtreɪ/ *adj.* (*from French, formal*) very unusual and slightly shocking 反常的；惊人的；古怪的

out·reach /ˈaʊtriːtʃ/ *noun* [U] the activity of an organization that provides a service or advice to people in the community, especially those who cannot or are unlikely to come to an office, a hospital, etc. for help 外展服务（在服务机构以外的场所提供的社区服务等）：*an outreach and education programme* 外展服务及教育计划 ◇ *outreach workers* 外展服务人员 ◇ *efforts to expand the outreach to black voters* 扩大对黑人选民外展服务的努力

out·rider /ˈaʊtraɪdə(r)/ *noun* a person who rides a motorcycle or a horse in front of or beside the vehicle of an important person in order to give protection（要人座车周围的）骑士护卫，摩托护卫

out·rig·ger /ˈaʊtrɪɡə(r)/ *noun* a wooden structure that is fixed to the side of a boat or ship in order to keep it steady in the water; a boat fitted with such a structure 舷外托架；有舷外托架的小船

out·right /ˈaʊtraɪt/ *adj., adv.*

■ ***adj.*** [only before noun] **1** complete and total 完全的；彻底的；绝对的：*an outright ban/rejection/victory* 完全禁止；断然拒绝；彻底胜利 ◇ *She was the outright winner.* 她是绝对的优胜者。 ◇ *No one party is expected to gain an outright majority.* 没有任何政党可望获得绝对多数。 **2** open and direct 公开的；直率的；直截了当的：*There was outright opposition to the plan.* 该计划遭到公开直接反对。

■ ***adv.*** **1** in a direct way and without trying to hide anything 公开地；直率地；毫无保留地：*Why don't you ask him outright if it's true?* 你为什么不直截了当地问他那是否属实？ ◇ *She couldn't help herself and she laughed outright.* 她忍不住大笑起来。 **2** clearly and completely 完全彻底；干净利落：*Neither candidate won outright.* 两个候选人谁也没干脆利落地获胜。 ◇ *The group rejects outright any negotiations with the government.* 这个团体断然拒绝与政府进行任何谈判。 **3** not gradually; immediately 一下子；骤然间；立即：*Most of the crash victims were **killed outright**.* 飞机坠毁的遇难者大都是当场死亡。 ◇ *We had saved enough money to buy the house outright.* 我们存了足够的钱，能一次付清款项买下这所房子。

out·run /ˌaʊtˈrʌn/ *verb* (**out·run·ning**, **out·ran** /ˌaʊtˈræn/, **out·run**) **1** **~ sb/sth** to run faster or further than sb/sth 跑得比…快（或远）；超过：*He couldn't outrun his pursuers.* 他跑不过追他的人。 **2** **~ sth** to develop faster than sth 发展更快；超过 SYN **outstrip**：*Demand for the new model is outrunning supply.* 新型号的产品供不应求。

out·sell /ˌaʊtˈsel/ *verb* (**out·sold**, **out·sold** /-ˈsəʊld; *NAmE* -ˈsoʊld/) **~ sb/sth** to sell more or to be sold in larger quantities than sb/sth 比…卖得多：*We are now outselling all our competitors.* 我们现在比所有竞争对手都卖得多。 ◇ *This year the newspaper has outsold its main rival.* 今年该报的发行量已超过了它的主要对手。

out·set /ˈaʊtset/ *noun*

IDM **at/from the 'outset (of sth)** at/from the beginning of sth 从开始：*I made it clear right from the outset that I disapproved.* 从一开始我就明确地说我不赞成。

out·shine /ˌaʊtˈʃaɪn/ *verb* (**out·shone**, **out·shone** /-ˈʃɒn; *NAmE* -ˈʃoʊn/) **~ sb/sth** to be more impressive than sb/sth; to be better than sb/sth 比…做得好；使逊色；高人一筹

out·side 🔑 *noun, adj., prep., adv.*

■ ***noun*** /ˌaʊtˈsaɪd/ (*usually* **the outside**) **1** 🔑 [C, usually sing.] the outer side or surface of sth 外部；外表 SYN **exterior**：*The outside of the house needs painting.* 房子的外墙需要油漆一下。 ◇ *You can't open the door from the outside.* 你从外边打不开这个门。 **2** 🔑 [sing.] the area that is near or around a building, etc.（建筑物等的）周围，外围：*I walked around the outside of the building.* 我绕着这座建筑四周散步。 ◇ *I didn't go into the temple—I only saw it from the outside.* 我没有走进庙宇，只是从外面看了一下。 **3** 🔑 [sing.] the part of a road nearest to the middle（靠近路中央的）外侧，外手：*Always overtake **on the outside**.* 超车务必走外侧道。 **4** [sing.] the part of a curving road or track furthest from the inner or shorter side of the curve（弯曲路面或轨道的）外道，外缘 OPP **inside**

IDM **at the outside** at the most; as a maximum 至多：*There was room for 20 people at the outside.* 最多只能容纳 20 个人。 **on the outside 1** used to describe how sb appears or seems 从表面；从外表：*On the outside she seems calm, but I know she's worried.* 她貌似镇定，但我知道她有心事。 **2** not in prison 不在狱中：*Life on the outside took some getting used to again.* 费了很大劲儿才慢慢适应了狱后的生活。

■ ***adj.*** /ˈaʊtsaɪd/ [only before noun] **1** ⚷ of, on or facing the outer side 外部的；在外面的；向外的 **SYN** **external**: *The outside walls are damp.* 外墙潮湿。 **2** ⚷ not located in the main building; going out of the main building 主建筑物以外的；向外面的 **SYN** **external**: *an outside toilet* 户外厕所 ◇ *You have to pay to make outside calls.* 打外线电话必须付费。◇ *I can't get an outside line.* 我接不通外线。 **3** ⚷ not included in or connected with your group, organization, country, etc. 不属于本团体（或机构、国家等）的；外部的；不相关的: *We plan to use an outside firm of consultants.* 我们计划利用外面的咨询公司。◇ *She has a lot of* ***outside interests*** (= not connected with her work). 她有许多业余爱好。◇ *They felt cut off from the* ***outside world*** (= from other people and from other things that were happening). 他们觉得与外界隔绝了。 **4** used to say that sth is very unlikely 不可能的；可能性极小的: *They have only an* ***outside chance*** *of winning.* 他们的胜算极小。◇ *150 is an outside estimate* (= it is very likely to be less). 估计最多不超过 150。

■ ***prep.*** /ˌaʊtˈsaɪd/ (*also* **out·side of** *especially in NAmE*) **1** ⚷ on or to a place on the outside of sth 在…外面；向…外面: *You can park your car outside our house.* 你可以把汽车停在我们家屋外。 **OPP** **inside** **2** ⚷ away from or not in a particular place 离开；不在: *It's the biggest theme park outside the United States.* 这是美国以外最大的主题游乐园。◇ *We live in a small village* ***just outside*** *Leeds.* 我们就住在利兹市外的一个小村子里。 **3** ⚷ not part of sth 不在…范围内；不属于: *The matter is outside my area of responsibility.* 此事不属于我的职责范围。◇ *You may do as you wish outside working hours.* 上班时间以外，你爱干什么就干什么。 **OPP** **within** **4** **outside of** apart from 除了: *There was nothing they could do, outside of hoping things would get better.* 除了盼望情况好转，他们无能为力。

■ ***adv.*** /ˌaʊtˈsaɪd/ **1** ⚷ not in a room, building or container but on or to the outside of it 在外面；向外面: *I'm seeing a patient—please wait outside.* 我正在给病人看病，请在外面等候。◇ *The house is painted green outside.* 房子的外墙漆成了绿色。 **2** ⚷ not inside a building 在户外: *It's warm enough to eat outside.* 天气暖和了，可以露天吃饭了。◇ *Go outside and see if it's raining.* 去外边看看是否下雨了。 **OPP** **inside**

ˌoutside ˈbroadcast *noun* (*BrE*) a programme filmed or recorded away from the main studio 实地拍摄的节目；现场录制的节目

ˌoutside ˈlane (*BrE*) (*NAmE* **ˌpassing ˈlane**) *noun* the part of a major road such as a MOTORWAY or INTERSTATE nearest the middle of the road, where vehicles drive fastest and can go past vehicles ahead（高速公路等靠近路中心的）外车道，超车道

out·sider /ˌaʊtˈsaɪdə(r)/ *noun* **1** a person who is not accepted as a member of a society, group, etc. 外人；局外人: *Here she felt she would always be an outsider.* 她在这里总觉得是个外人。 ➲ WORDFINDER NOTE AT SOCIETY **2** a person who is not part of a particular organization or profession （组织、行业）外部的人；外来者: *They have decided to hire outsiders for some of the key positions.* 他们决定在某些关键职位上聘任外来人员。◇ *To an outsider it may appear to be a glamorous job.* 在外面的人看来，这似乎是一份令人向往的工作。 **3** a person or an animal taking part in a race or competition that is not expected to win（比赛中）不被看好的人（或动物）: *The race was won by a 20–1 outsider.* 比赛获胜者是匹不被看好、1 赔 20 的赛马。◇ *To everyone's surprise, the post went to* ***a rank outsider*** (= a complete outsider). 出人意料的是，那个职位竟然落到一个毫不起眼的人头上。

out·size /ˈaʊtsaɪz/ (*also* **out·sized** /ˈaʊtsaɪzd/) *adj.* [usually before noun] **1** larger than the usual size 较大的；超过一般型号的: *an outsize desk* 一张特大号桌子 **2** designed for large people 特体的；特大号的: *outsize clothes* 特大号服装

out·skirts /ˈaʊtskɜːts; *NAmE* -skɜːrts/ *noun* [pl.] the parts of a town or city that are furthest from the centre（市镇的）边缘地带；市郊: *They live* ***on the outskirts*** *of Milan.* 他们住在米兰市郊。 ➲ WORDFINDER NOTE AT LOCATION

out·smart /ˌaʊtˈsmɑːt; *NAmE* -ˈsmɑːrt/ *verb* **~ sb** to gain an advantage over sb by acting in a clever way 比…精明；智胜 **SYN** **outwit**: *She always managed to outsmart her political rivals.* 她总有办法表现得比她的政敌智高一筹。

out·source /ˈaʊtsɔːs; *NAmE* -sɔːrs/ *verb* [T, I] **~ (sth)** (*business* 商) to arrange for sb outside a company to do work or provide goods for that company 交外办理；外包；外购: *We outsource all our computing work.* 我们把全部计算工作包给外边去做。 ▶ **out·sourc·ing** *noun* [U]

out·spoken /aʊtˈspəʊkən; *NAmE* -ˈspoʊkən/ *adj.* saying exactly what you think, even if this shocks or offends people 直率的，直言不讳的（不怕得罪人） **SYN** **blunt**: *an outspoken opponent of the leader* 一个直言不讳反对领导的人 ◇ *outspoken comments* 直率的评论 ◇ **~ in sth** *She was outspoken in her criticism of the plan.* 她直言不讳批评该计划。 ➲ SYNONYMS AT HONEST ▶ **out·spoken·ly** *adv.* **out·spoken·ness** *noun* [U]

out·spread /ˌaʊtˈspred/ *adj.* (*formal*) spread out completely 展开的；舒展的: *The bird soared high, with outspread wings.* 鸟儿展翅高飞。

out·stand·ing 🔑 /aʊtˈstændɪŋ/ *adj.* **1** ⚷ extremely good; excellent 优秀的；杰出的；出色的: *an outstanding player/achievement/success* 杰出的运动员 / 成绩 / 成就 ◇ *an area of* ***outstanding natural beauty*** 自然风景极美的地区 ➲ SYNONYMS AT EXCELLENT **2** ⚷ [usually before noun] very obvious or important 突出的；明显的；重要的 **SYN** **prominent**: *the outstanding features of the landscape* 这一景观的突出特征 **3** (of payment, work, problems, etc. 款项、工作、困难等) not yet paid, done, solved, etc. 未支付的；未完成的；未解决的: *She has outstanding debts of over £500.* 她未清偿的债务超过 500 英镑。◇ *A lot of work is still outstanding.* 许多工作尚未完成。

out·stand·ing·ly /aʊtˈstændɪŋli/ *adv.* **1** used to emphasize the good quality of sth （用于正面强调）非常，极其 **SYN** **remarkably**: *outstandingly successful* 非常成功 **2** extremely well 优异；极好: *He performed well but not outstandingly.* 他表演得还不错，但算不上非常出色。

out·sta·tion /ˈaʊtsteɪʃn/ *noun, adj.*

■ ***noun*** a branch of a company or an organization that is far from the HEADQUARTERS (= the place from which the company or organization is controlled) （远离总部的）外设分公司，外设分部

■ ***adj.*** (*IndE*) working or studying in a place where you do not live （工作或学习）在非居住地的；离家在外的: *The business school has accommodation for outstation students.* 商学院为外地学生提供住宿。

ˈoutstation cheque *noun* (*IndE*) a CHEQUE from a bank account in one place that is exchanged for money in another city, state, etc. 异地支票

out·stay /ˌaʊtˈsteɪ/ *verb* **IDM** ▶ SEE WELCOME *n.*

out·stretched /ˌaʊtˈstretʃt/ *adj.* (of parts of the body 身体部位) stretched or spread out as far as possible 伸展的；张开的: *He ran towards her* ***with arms outstretched/with outstretched arms.*** 他张开双臂朝她飞奔而去。

out·strip /ˌaʊtˈstrɪp/ *verb* (**-pp-**) **1** **~ sth** to become larger, more important, etc. than sb/sth 比…大（或重要等）；超过；胜过: *Demand is outstripping supply.* 需求快超过供给了。 **2** **~ sth** to be faster, better or more successful than sb you are competing against 超过，超越（竞争对手） **SYN** **surpass**: *Their latest computer outstrips all its rivals.* 他们最新型的计算机超越了所有的对手。 **3** **~ sb** to run faster than sb in a race so that you pass them 比…跑得快；超越

outta (*also* **outa**) /ˈaʊtə/ *prep.* used for writing the way 'out of' is sometimes pronounced in informal speech （用于书写，表示 out of 在非正式口语中的发音）: *I'm outta here!* (= I'm leaving now.) 我要走了！

O

ˈout-take *noun* a piece of a film that is removed before the film/movie is shown, for example because it contains a mistake（电影的）不选用镜头，剪掉的镜头

ˈout-there *adj.* (*NAmE, informal*) (of people) different, confident, having strong opinions, and attracting attention to yourself; (of ideas) different from what most people consider normal, but exciting（人）特立独行的；（想法）吸引他人瞩目的，让人耳目一新的；自成一格的：*Wow, this is such an out-there character. This role is definitely going to be cool.* 哇，这是个如此个性鲜明的人物。这个角色一定很酷。◇ *It may be totally out-there but I think it could work.* 这可能离经叛道，但我认为行得通。

ˈout tray (*BrE*) (*US* **out-box**) *noun* (in an office) a container on your desk for letters or documents that are waiting to be sent out or passed to sb else（办公室的）待发信件盘 ➲COMPARE IN TRAY ➲VISUAL VOCAB PAGE V71

out·vote /ˌaʊtˈvəʊt; *NAmE* -ˈvoʊt/ *verb* [usually passive] **~ sb/sth** to defeat sb/sth by winning a larger number of votes 得票超过 SYN **vote sb/sth↔down**: *His proposal was outvoted by 10 votes to 8.* 他的提案以 10 比 8 票被否决。

out·ward /ˈaʊtwəd; *NAmE* -wərd/ *adj., adv.*
■*adj.* [only before noun] **1** connected with the way people or things seem to be rather than with what is actually true 表面的；外表的：*Mark showed no outward signs of distress.* 马克在外表上没有现出沮丧的神色来。◇ *She simply observes the outward forms of religion.* 她只是表面上信教而已。◇ ***To all outward appearances*** (= as far as it was possible to judge from the outside) *they were perfectly happy.* 从外表上怎么看他们都显得无比幸福。OPP **inward** **2** going away from a particular place, especially one that you are going to return to 外出的；向外的：*the outward voyage/journey* 外出航程 / 旅程 **3** away from the centre or a particular point 朝外面的；向外的：*outward movement* 向外的运动 ◇ ***outward investment*** (= in other countries) 对外投资 ◇ *Managers need to become more **outward-looking*** (= more open to new ideas). 管理人员需要有更广阔的视野。OPP **inward**
■*adv.* = OUTWARDS

O

ˌoutward ˈbound *adj.* going away from home or a particular place 离家的；外出的

the ˌOutward ˌBound ˈTrust [sing.] (*also* **ˌOutward ˈBound™** [U]) *noun* an international organization that provides training in outdoor activities including sports for young people 野外拓展训练信托，外展信托（为年轻人等提供野外活动培训的国际组织）

out·ward·ly /ˈaʊtwədli; *NAmE* -wərd-/ *adv.* on the surface; in appearance 表面上；外表上：*Though badly frightened, she remained outwardly composed.* 她虽然非常害怕，但表面上依然很镇静。◇ *Outwardly, the couple seemed perfectly happy.* 表面上看，这对夫妇似乎幸福美满。OPP **inwardly**

out·wards /ˈaʊtwədz; *NAmE* -wərdz/ (*BrE*) (*also* **out·ward** *NAmE, BrE*) *adv.* **~ (from sth)** towards the outside; away from the centre or from a particular point 向外；朝外：*The door opens outwards.* 这个门向外开。◇ *Factories were spreading outwards from the old heart of the town.* 工厂从旧城中心逐渐向外扩展。OPP **inwards**

out·weigh /ˌaʊtˈweɪ/ *verb* **~ sth** to be greater or more important than sth 重于；大于；超过：*The advantages **far outweigh** the disadvantages.* 利远大于弊。

out·wit /ˌaʊtˈwɪt/ *verb* (**-tt-**) **~ sb/sth** to defeat sb/sth or gain an advantage over them by doing sth clever（智力上）超过，胜过 SYN **outsmart**: *Somehow he always manages to outwit his opponents.* 他反正总能设法智胜对手。

out·with /ˌaʊtˈwɪθ/ *prep.* (*ScotE*) outside of sth; not within sth 在…外面

out·work /ˈaʊtwɜːk; *NAmE* -wɜːrk/ *noun* [U] (*BrE, business* 商) work that is done by people at home 外包活 ▶ **out·work·er** *noun*

out·work·ing /ˈaʊtwɜːkɪŋ; *NAmE* -wɜːrk-/ *noun* [U] (*BrE, business* 商) the activity of doing work away from the office or factory that provides the work（由单位或公司发包的）外包工作

out·worn /ˈaʊtwɔːn; *NAmE* -wɔːrn/ *adj.* [usually before noun] old-fashioned and no longer useful 过时的；陈腐的；无用的 SYN **obsolete**: *outworn institutions* 陈腐的习俗 ➲ COMPARE WORN OUT

ouzo /ˈuːzəʊ; *NAmE* ˈuːzoʊ/ *noun* [U, C] a strong alcoholic drink from Greece, made from ANISEED and usually drunk with water 茴香烈酒（希腊产，通常兑水饮用）

ova PL. OF OVUM

oval /ˈəʊvl; *NAmE* ˈoʊvl/ *adj., noun*
■*adj.* shaped like an egg 椭圆形的；卵形的：*an oval face* 鹅蛋脸
■*noun* **1** an oval shape 椭圆形；卵形 **2** (*AustralE*) a ground for Australian Rules football 澳大利亚式橄榄球球场

the ˌOval ˈOffice *noun* [sing.] **1** the office of the US President in the White House（美国白宫的）椭圆形办公室，总统办公室 **2** a way of referring to the US President and the part of the government that is controlled by the President（美国）总统及政府行政部门：*Congress is waiting to see how the Oval Office will react.* 国会正观望总统方面的反应。➲MORE LIKE THIS 19, page R27

ovary /ˈəʊvəri; *NAmE* ˈoʊ-/ *noun* (*pl.* **-ies**) **1** either of the two organs in a woman's body that produce eggs; a similar organ in female animals, birds and fish 卵巢 **2** the part of a plant that produces seeds（植物的）子房 ➲VISUAL VOCAB PAGE V11 ▶ **ovar·ian** /əʊˈveəriən; *NAmE* oʊˈver-/ *adj.* [only before noun]: *ovarian cancer* 卵巢癌

ova·tion /əʊˈveɪʃn; *NAmE* oʊ-/ *noun* enthusiastic clapping by an audience as a sign of their approval 热烈鼓掌；热烈欢迎：*to give sb a **huge/rapturous/rousing ovation*** 对某人表示万分的 / 狂热的 / 热烈的欢迎 ◇ *The soloist got a ten-minute **standing ovation*** (= in which people stand up from their seats). 独奏演员受到了长达十分钟的起立鼓掌欢呼。➲WORDFINDER NOTE AT PERFORMANCE

oven 🔑 /ˈʌvn/ *noun* the part of a cooker/stove shaped like a box with a door on the front, in which food is cooked or heated 烤箱；烤炉：*Take the cake out of the oven.* 把蛋糕从烤箱中取出来。◇ *a gas/an electric oven* 煤气 / 电烤箱 ◇ ***a cool/hot/moderate oven*** 低温 / 高温 / 中温烤箱 ◇ *Open a window, it's **like an oven** in here!* 打开窗户。这儿热得像火炉！➲VISUAL VOCAB PAGES V26, V28 ➲ COMPARE MICROWAVE *n.* (1) IDM ▶SEE BUN

ˈoven glove (*also* **ˈoven mitt**) *noun* a glove made of thick material, used for holding hot dishes from an oven 烤箱手套；隔热手套 ➲VISUAL VOCAB PAGE V26

oven·proof /ˈʌvnpruːf/ *adj.* suitable for use in a hot oven 适于烤箱内用的；耐热的：*an ovenproof dish* 耐热碟子

ˌoven-ˈready *adj.* [usually before noun] (of food 食物) bought already prepared and ready for cooking 已调制好的；加工过的；可直接入炉的

oven·ware /ˈʌvnweə(r); *NAmE* -wer/ *noun* [U] dishes that can be used for cooking food in an oven 烤箱器皿；烤盘

over 🔑 /ˈəʊvə(r); *NAmE* ˈoʊ-/ *adv., prep., noun*
■**adv.** HELP For the special uses of **over** in phrasal verbs, look at the entries for the verbs. For example **take sth over** is in the phrasal verb section at **take**. * over 在短语动词中的特殊用法见有关动词词条。如 take sth over 在词条 take 的短语动词部分。 **1** 🔑 downwards and away from a vertical position 从直立位置向下和向外；落下；倒下：*Try not to knock that vase over.* 小心别把那个花瓶碰倒了。◇ *The wind must have blown it over.* 准是风把它吹倒了。 **2** 🔑 from one side to another side 从一侧到另一侧；翻转：*She turned over onto her front.* 她翻过身俯卧着。◇ *The car skidded off the road and rolled over and over.* 汽车滑出路面不断翻滚。 **3** 🔑 across a street, an open space, etc. 穿过（街道、开阔的空间等）：*I stopped and crossed over.* 我停下来，走到对面。◇ *He rowed us over to the other side of the lake.* 他把我们摆渡到湖的对岸。◇ *They have gone over to France.* 他们渡海到法国去了。◇ *This is my aunt who's*

over from Canada. 这是我姑姑，她是从加拿大过来的。◇ *I went over (= across the room) and asked her name.* 我走过去问她叫什么名字。◇ *Put it down* ***over there.*** 把东西放到那边去。 **4** so as to cover sb/sth completely 完全覆盖（某人或某物）: *The lake was frozen over.* 湖面完全封冻了。◇ *Cover her over with a blanket.* 给她盖条毯子。 **5** above; more 以上；大于；多于: *children of 14 and over* * 14 岁及 14 岁以上的儿童 ◇ *You get an A grade for scores of 75 and over.* * 75 分及 75 分以上的分数就是优等。 **6** remaining; not used or needed 剩余的；未用的；不需要的: *If there's any food left over, put it in the fridge.* 要是有剩下的饭菜，就放到冰箱里。 **7** again 再；又: *He repeated it several times over until he could remember it.* 他重复了几遍直到能记住为止。◇ (*NAmE*) *It's all wrong—you'll have to do it over.* 完全错了。你得重做一遍。 **8** ended 结束: *By the time we arrived the meeting was over.* 我们到达时，会议已经结束了。◇ *Thank goodness that's over!* 谢天谢地，事情总算过去了！◇ *I was glad when it was* ***over and done with.*** 事情终告了结，我很高兴。 **9** used to talk about sb/sth changing position（表示位置变换）改变，掉换: *He's gone over to the enemy* (= joined them). 他已变节投敌。◇ *Please change the wheels over* (= for example, put the front wheels at the back). 请把轮子调个个儿。◇ *Let's ask some friends over* (= to our home). 咱们邀请几个朋友来家里吧。◇ *Hand over the money!* 把钱交出来！ **10** used when communicating by radio（用于无线通话）完毕: *Message received. Over* (= it is your turn to speak). 消息收到了。完毕。◇ *Message understood.* ***Over and out.*** 消息听懂了。通话完毕。

IDM **(all) over aˈgain** a second time from the beginning 再；重新: *He did the work so badly that I had to do it all over again myself.* 他活儿做得太糟糕了，我只好亲自从头再做一次。 **over against sth** in contrast with sth 与…对比（或相对） **ˌover and ˈover (aˈgain)** many times; repeatedly 多次；反复地；一再: *I've told you over and over again not to do that.* 我已一再跟你讲不要再那么做了。 **ˌover to ˈyou** used to say that it is sb's turn to do sth 轮到你了；该你了

■ ***prep.*** HELP For the special uses of **over** in phrasal verbs, look at the entries for the verbs. For example **get over sth** is in the phrasal verb section at **get**. * over 在短语动词中的特殊用法见有关动词词条。如 get over sth 在词条 get 的短语动词部分。 **1** resting on the surface of sb/sth and partly or completely covering them/it（部分或全部覆盖）在…上面: *She put a blanket over the sleeping child.* 她给熟睡的孩子盖上毯子。◇ *He wore an overcoat over his suit.* 他在西服外面再加了一件大衣。◇ *She put her hand over her mouth to stop herself from screaming.* 她用手捂住嘴，以免叫出声来。 **2** in or to a position higher than but not touching sb/sth; above sb/sth 悬在…上面；向…上方: *They held a large umbrella over her.* 他们给她撑起一把大伞。◇ *The balcony juts out over the street.* 阳台伸出在街道上方。◇ *There was a lamp hanging over the table.* 桌子上方吊着一盏灯。 **3** from one side of sth to the other; across sth 从一边到另一边；穿越: *a bridge over the river* 横跨河面的桥 ◇ *They ran over the grass.* 他们跑过草地。◇ *They had a wonderful view over the park.* 他们放眼望去，把公园美丽的景色尽收眼底。 **4** on the far or opposite side of sth 在…的远端（或对面）: *He lives over the road.* 他住在马路对面。 **5** so as to cross sth and be on the other side 到另一边；翻越: *She climbed over the wall.* 她翻过墙去。 **6** falling from or down from a place 从…落下: *The car had toppled over the cliff.* 汽车从山崖上跌落下去了。◇ *He didn't dare look over the edge.* 他不敢从边缘向下看。 **7** **all ~** in or on all or most parts of sth 遍及: *Snow is falling all over the country.* 全国各地都在下雪。◇ *They've travelled all over the world.* 他们游遍了全世界。◇ *There were papers lying around* ***all over the place.*** 文件散落一地。 **8** more than a particular time, amount, cost, etc. 多于（某时间、数量、花费等）: *over 3 million copies sold* 售出三百多万册 ◇ *She stayed in Lagos for over a month.* 她在拉各斯待了一个多月。◇ *He's over sixty.* 他六十多岁了。 **9** used to show that sb has control or authority（表示能控制、有权威）: *She has only the director over her.* 她的上司只有主任一个。◇ *He ruled over a great empire.* 他统治着一个大帝国。◇ *She has editorial control over what is included.* 她有权决定编辑的内容。 **10** during sth 在…期间: *We'll discuss it over lunch.* 我们将在吃午饭时商量此事。◇ *Over the next few days they got to know the town well.* 在以后几天中，他们逐渐熟悉了这个小镇。◇ *She has not changed much over the years.* 这些年来她没有多大变化。◇ *He built up the business over a period of ten years.* 他用了十年时间把这个企业创建起来。◇ *We're away over* (= until after) *the New Year.* 新年期间我们不在家。 **11** past a particular difficult stage or situation 渡过（困难阶段或局面）: *We're over the worst of the recession.* 我们已渡过了经济衰退的最艰难时期。◇ *It took her ages to get over her illness.* 她花了很长时间才把病治好。 **12** because of or concerning sth; about sth 由于；关于: *an argument over money* 为了钱的争吵 ◇ *a disagreement over the best way to proceed* 在如何最好地推进工作这一问题上出现的分歧 **13** using sth; by means of sth 利用；通过: *We heard it over the radio.* 我们从广播中听到的。◇ *She wouldn't tell me over the phone.* 她不肯在电话里告诉我。 **14** louder than sth 声音大于: *I couldn't hear what he said over the noise of the traffic.* 交通噪声太大，我听不清他说的话。 ➲ NOTE AT ABOVE

IDM **ˌover and aˈbove** in addition to sth 此外；另外: *There are other factors over and above those we have discussed.* 除了我们所讨论的之外，还有其他因素。

■ ***noun*** (in CRICKET 板球) a series of six balls BOWLED by the same person 一轮投球（同一个投球手连续投出的六个球）

over- /ˈəʊvə(r); *NAmE* ˈoʊ-/ *prefix* (in nouns, verbs, adjectives and adverbs 构成名词、动词、形容词和副词) **1** more than usual; too much 太；过于: *overproduction* 生产过剩 ◇ *overload* 使超载 ◇ *over-optimistic* 过分乐观的 ◇ *overconfident* 过分自信的 ◇ *overanxious* 过于急切 **2** completely 完全地: *overjoyed* 十分高兴 **3** upper; outer; extra 上面；外面；额外: *overcoat* 长大衣 ◇ *overtime* 加班 **4** over; above 上方；上空: *overcast* 阴云密布 ◇ *overhang* 悬挂 ➲ MORE LIKE THIS 6, page R25

over·achieve /ˌəʊvərəˈtʃiːv; *NAmE* ˌoʊ-/ *verb* **1** [I] to do better than expected in your studies or work 学习（或工作）得比预期好；取得比预期好的成绩 **2** [I] to try too hard to be successful in your work 过于努力；过于进取 ▸ **over·achiever** *noun*

over·act /ˌəʊvərˈækt; *NAmE* ˌoʊ-/ *verb* [I, T] ~ (**sth**) (*disapproving*) to behave in a way that is exaggerated and not natural, especially when you are acting a part in a play 举止过火；表现做作；过分夸张地表演

over·active /ˌəʊvərˈæktɪv; *NAmE* ˌoʊvər-/ *adj.* [usually before noun] **1** (of an organ or part of the body 器官或身体部位) causing harm by doing sth too much 过度活动的: *an overactive thyroid* 亢进的甲状腺 **2** (of sb's imagination 想象力) too active, especially so that they imagine things that are not true 过于活跃的；（尤指）想入非非的: *She suffers from an overactive imagination.* 她患上了狂想症。

over·age /ˌəʊvərˈeɪdʒ; *NAmE* ˌoʊ-/ *adj.* too old to be allowed to do a particular thing 超龄的；年龄过大的

over·all AW *adj., adv., noun*

■ ***adj.*** /ˌəʊvərˈɔːl; *NAmE* ˌoʊ-/ [only before noun] including all the things or people that are involved in a particular situation; general 全面的；综合的；总体的: *the person with* ***overall responsibility*** *for the project* 全面负责本项目的人 ◇ *There will be winners in each of three age groups, and one* ***overall winner.*** 三个年龄组将各产生一位优胜者，另有一位总优胜者。◇ *an* ***overall improvement*** *in standards of living* (= affecting everyone) 生活水平的全面提高 ◇ *When she finished painting, she stepped back to admire the* ***overall effect.*** 画完以后，她退后一步，以审视总体效果。

■ ***adv.*** /ˌəʊvərˈɔːl; *NAmE* ˌoʊ-/ **1** including everything or everyone; in total 全部；总计: *The company will invest $1.6m overall in new equipment.* 这个公司将总计投资 160 万美元购置新设备。 **2** generally; when you consider everything 一般来说；大致上；总体上: *Overall, this is a very useful book.* 总的来说，这是一本很有用的书。 ➲ LANGUAGE BANK AT CONCLUSION

■ ***noun*** /ˈəʊvərɔːl; *NAmE* ˈoʊ-/ **1** (*BrE*) [C] a loose coat worn

O

over other clothes to protect them from dirt, etc. 外套；罩衣：*The lab assistant was wearing a white overall.* 实验室助手穿着一件白罩衣。**2 overalls** (*BrE*) (*NAmE* **cov·er·alls**) [pl.] a loose piece of clothing like a shirt and trousers/pants in one piece, made of heavy cloth and usually worn over other clothing by workers doing dirty work 工装服；连身工作服：*The mechanic was wearing a pair of blue overalls.* 机修工穿着一件蓝色工装连衣裤。➲ COMPARE BOILER SUIT **3 overalls** (*also* **'bib overalls**) (*both NAmE*) (*BrE* **dun·garees**) [pl.] a piece of clothing that consists of trousers/pants with an extra piece of cloth covering the chest, held up by strips of cloth over the shoulders 工装裤

overalls 工装服

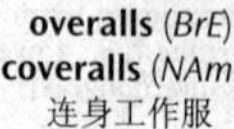

overalls (*BrE*) **coveralls** (*NAmE*) 连身工作服

dungarees (*BrE*) **overalls** (*NAmE*) 工装裤

,overall ma'jority *noun* [usually sing.] **1** more votes in an election or vote than all the other people or parties together 总体多数（票数超过其他人或政党票数的总和）**2** the difference between the number of members that the government has in a parliament and the number that all the other political parties have together 总体优势（执政党在议会中的议员人数与所有其他政党议员总数的差额）：*a huge 101-seat overall majority* 多达 101 个席位的总体优势

over·am·bi·tious /ˌəʊvəræmˈbɪʃəs; *NAmE* ˌoʊ-/ *adj.* **1** (of a person 人) too determined to be successful, rich, powerful, etc. 进取心过强的；野心过大的 **2** (of a plan, task, etc. 计划、任务等) unsuccessful or likely to be unsuccessful because of needing too much effort, money or time 所需投入过大的，目标过高的（因而未成功或成功机会甚微）：*Her plans were overambitious.* 她的计划都过于宏大。

over·arch·ing /ˌəʊvərˈɑːtʃɪŋ; *NAmE* ˌoʊvərˈɑːrtʃɪŋ/ *adj.* [usually before noun] (*formal*) very important, because it includes or influences many things 非常重要的；首要的；概莫能外的

over·arm /ˈəʊvərɑːm; *NAmE* ˈoʊvərɑːrm/ (*especially BrE*) (*also* **over·hand** *especially in NAmE*) *adv.* if you throw a ball **overarm**, you throw it with your arm swung backwards and then lifted high above your shoulder 肩上投球（投球时举手过肩） ▸ **over·arm** (*especially BrE*) (*also* **over·hand** *especially in NAmE*) *adj.*：*an overarm throw* 上手投球 ➲ COMPARE UNDERARM *adv.*

over·ate PAST TENSE OF OVEREAT

over·awe /ˌəʊvərˈɔː; *NAmE* ˌoʊ-/ *verb* [usually passive] ~ **sb** to impress sb so much that they feel nervous or frightened 使极为敬畏；使胆怯 ▸ **over·awed** *adj.*

over·bal·ance /ˌəʊvəˈbæləns; *NAmE* ˌoʊvərˈb-/ *verb* [I, T] ~ (**sb/sth**) (*especially BrE*) to lose your balance and fall; to make sb/sth lose their balance and fall（使）失去平衡，摔倒：*He overbalanced and fell into the water.* 他失去了平衡，落入水中。

over·bear·ing /ˌəʊvəˈbeərɪŋ; *NAmE* ˌoʊvərˈber-/ *adj.* (*disapproving*) trying to control other people in an unpleasant way 专横的；飞扬跋扈的 **SYN** **domineering**: *an overbearing manner* 专断的作风

over·bite /ˈəʊvəbaɪt; *NAmE* ˈoʊvərb-/ *noun* [usually sing.] (*specialist*) a condition in which a person or animal's upper JAW is too far forward in relation to their lower JAW 覆殆

over·blown /ˌəʊvəˈbləʊn; *NAmE* ˌoʊvərˈbloʊn/ *adj.* **1** that is made to seem larger, more impressive or more important than it really is 过分的；夸张的；虚饰过度的 **SYN** **exaggerated** **2** (of flowers 花朵) past the best, most beautiful stage 残败的；盛期已过的

over·board /ˈəʊvəbɔːd; *NAmE* ˈoʊvərbɔːrd/ *adv.* over the side of a boat or a ship into the water 从船上落下：*to fall/jump overboard* 从船上落入 / 跳入水中 ◇ *Huge waves washed him overboard.* 巨浪把他冲下甲板卷入海中。

IDM **go 'overboard** (*informal*) to be too excited or enthusiastic about sth or about doing sth 过分热情；过分热衷：*Don't go overboard on fitness.* 别过分热衷健身运动。**throw sb/sth 'overboard** to get rid of sb/sth that you think is useless 抛弃；扔掉

over·book /ˌəʊvəˈbʊk; *NAmE* ˌoʊvərˈbʊk/ *verb* [T, I] ~ (**sth**) to sell more tickets on a plane or reserve more rooms in a hotel than there are places available 超额预订（飞机座位或旅馆客房）：*The flight was heavily overbooked.* 该班机售票大大超出机位数量。➲ COMPARE DOUBLE-BOOK

over·bridge /ˈəʊvəbrɪdʒ; *NAmE* ˈoʊvərb-/ *noun* a bridge over a railway/railroad or road 天桥；上跨桥

over·bur·den /ˌəʊvəˈbɜːdn; *NAmE* ˌoʊvərˈbɜːrdn/ *verb* [usually passive] ~ **sb/sth** (**with sth**) to give sb/sth more work, worry, etc. than they can deal with 使负担过重

over·came PAST TENSE OF OVERCOME

over·cap·acity /ˌəʊvəkəˈpæsəti; *NAmE* ˌoʊvərkə-/ *noun* [U, sing.] (*business* 商) the situation in which an industry or a factory cannot sell as much as it is designed to produce 生产能力过剩

over·cast /ˌəʊvəˈkɑːst; *NAmE* ˌoʊvərˈkæst/ *adj.* covered with clouds; dull 阴天的；多云的；阴暗的：*an overcast sky/day* 阴沉的天空 / 天气 ◇ *Today it will be dull and overcast.* 今天将为阴天。

over·cau·tious /ˌəʊvəˈkɔːʃəs; *NAmE* ˌoʊvərˈk-/ *adj.* too careful 过于谨慎的；过分小心的

over·charge /ˌəʊvəˈtʃɑːdʒ; *NAmE* ˌoʊvərˈtʃɑːrdʒ/ *verb* [T, I] ~ (**sb**) (**for sth**) to make sb pay too much for sth 多收（某人的）钱：*Make sure they don't overcharge you for the drinks.* 注意别让他们多收饮料费。◇ *We were overcharged by £5.* 我们让人家多收了 5 英镑。**OPP** **undercharge**

over·coat /ˈəʊvəkəʊt; *NAmE* ˈoʊvərkoʊt/ *noun* a long warm coat worn in cold weather 长大衣 ➲ VISUAL VOCAB PAGE V66

over·come 🔑 /ˌəʊvəˈkʌm; *NAmE* ˌoʊvərˈkʌm/ *verb* (**over·came** /-ˈkeɪm/, **over·come**) **1** 🔑 ~ **sth** to succeed in dealing with or controlling a problem that has been preventing you from achieving sth 克服；解决：*She overcame injury to win the Olympic gold medal.* 她战胜了伤痛，赢得了奥运会金牌。◇ *The two parties managed to overcome their differences on the issue.* 两个政党设法弥合了在这个问题上的分歧。**2** 🔑 ~ **sb/sth** to defeat sb 战胜：*In the final game Sweden easily overcame France.* 在决赛中，瑞典队轻松战胜了法国队。**3** 🔑 [usually passive] ~ **sb** to be extremely strongly affected by sth 受到…的极大影响 **SYN** **overwhelm**: *Her parents were overcome with grief at the funeral.* 在葬礼上她的父母悲痛欲绝。◇ *The dead woman had been overcome by smoke.* 这个女人是被烟呛死的。

over·com·pen·sate /ˌəʊvəˈkɒmpenseɪt; *NAmE* ˌoʊvərˈkɑːm-/ *verb* [I] ~ (**for sth**) (**by doing sth**) to do too much when trying to correct a problem and so cause a different problem 过度补偿（为纠正某事而做得过分）；矫枉过正：*She overcompensated for her shyness by talking* *too much and laughing too loud.* 她努力克服羞怯，却矫枉过正，说话太多，笑声太大。

over·con·fi·dent /ˌəʊvəˈkɒnfɪdənt; *NAmE* ˌoʊvərˈkɑːn-/ *adj.* too confident 过分自信的；自负的

over·cook /ˌəʊvəˈkʊk; *NAmE* ˌoʊvərˈkʊk/ *verb* **~ sth** to cook food for too long 煮得过熟；煮得过久

over·crit·ic·al /ˌəʊvəˈkrɪtɪkl; *NAmE* ˌoʊvərˈk-/ *adj.* too critical 过分挑剔的；吹毛求疵的

over·crowd·ed /ˌəʊvəˈkraʊdɪd; *NAmE* ˌoʊvərˈk-/ *adj.* (of a place 地方) with too many people or things in it 过于拥挤的：*overcrowded cities/prisons* 拥挤不堪的城市 / 监狱 ◇ *Too many poor people are living in* ***overcrowded conditions.*** 有太多贫民生活在十分拥挤的条件下。

over·crowd·ing /ˌəʊvəˈkraʊdɪŋ; *NAmE* ˌoʊvərˈk-/ *noun* [U] the situation when there are too many people or things in one place 过度拥挤；拥挤的状况

over·de·veloped /ˌəʊvədɪˈveləpt; *NAmE* ˌoʊvərd-/ *adj.* that has grown too large 发育过度的；过于发达的：*overdeveloped muscles* 过于发达的肌肉 ◇ *an overdeveloped sense of humour* 过分的幽默感 ▸ **over·de·velop** *verb* **~ sth** **over·devel·op·ment** *noun* [U]

over·do /ˌəʊvəˈduː; *NAmE* ˌoʊvərˈduː/ *verb* (**over·does** /-ˈdʌz/, **over·did** /-ˈdɪd/, **over·done** /-ˈdʌn/) **1 ~ sth** to do sth too much; to exaggerate sth 做得过分；做得过火；夸张：*She really overdid the sympathy* (= and so did not seem sincere). 她真是同情得过火了。 **2 ~ sth** to use too much of sth 过多使用；滥用：*Don't overdo the salt in the food.* 菜里别放太多盐。◇ *Use illustrations where appropriate but don't* ***overdo it.*** 要适当地使用插图，但不宜过多。 **3** [usually passive] **~ sth** to cook sth for too long 烹煮（饭菜）时间过长：*The fish was overdone and very dry.* 这鱼烧的时间太长，都干掉了。

IDM **overˈdo it/things** to work, study, etc. too hard or for too long （工作、学习等）过分努力：*He's been overdoing things recently.* 他最近过于努力了。◇ *I overdid it in the gym and hurt my back.* 我在健身房练得过火了，结果弄伤了背。

over·dog /ˈəʊvədɒg; *NAmE* ˈoʊvərdɔːg/ *noun* (*disapproving*) a person, organization or country that is successful or in a stronger position than others, especially when they seem to have an unfair advantage（尤指不公正地）占上风者，占优势者；特权阶层：*political leaders who support the interests of the overdog* 支持特权阶层利益的政治领导人 **OPP** **underdog**

over·dose /ˈəʊvədəʊs; *NAmE* ˈoʊvərdoʊs/ *noun, verb*

- ***noun*** too much of a drug taken at one time（一次用药）过量；剂量过大：*a* ***drug/drugs overdose*** 药物剂量过大 ◇ *She took a massive overdose of sleeping pills.* 她服用了过量的安眠药。 ➲ **WORDFINDER NOTE AT DRUG**
- ***verb*** (*also informal* **OD**) [I] **~ (on sth)** to take too much of a drug at one time, so that it is dangerous 一次用药过量：*He had overdosed on heroin.* 他过量服用了海洛因。◇ (*figurative*) *I had overdosed on sun.* 我晒太阳的时间过长了。

over·draft /ˈəʊvədrɑːft; *NAmE* ˈoʊvərdræft/ *noun* the amount of money that you owe to a bank when you have spent more money than is in your bank account; an arrangement that allows you to do this 透支额；透支安排：***to run up/pay off an overdraft*** 透支；付清透支 ➲ **WORDFINDER NOTE AT LOAN** ➲ **COLLOCATIONS AT FINANCE**

over·draw /ˌəʊvəˈdrɔː; *NAmE* ˌoʊvərˈdrɔː/ *verb* (**over·drew** /-ˈdruː/, **over·drawn** /-ˈdrɔːn/) [T, I] **~ (sth)** (*especially BrE*) to take out more money from a bank account than it contains 透支：*Customers who overdraw their accounts will be charged a fee.* 透支的客户须付手续费。

over·drawn /ˌəʊvəˈdrɔːn; *NAmE* ˌoʊvərˈd-/ *adj.* **1** [not usually before noun] (of a person 人) having taken more money out of your bank account than you have in it 已透支；有透支：*I'm overdrawn by £100.* 我透支了 100 英镑。 **2** (of a bank account 银行账户) with more money taken out than was paid in or left in 被透支的：*an overdrawn account* 透支的账户 ◇ *Your account is £200 overdrawn.* 您的账户已透支 200 英镑。

over·dressed /ˌəʊvəˈdrest; *NAmE* ˌoʊvərˈd-/ *adj.* (*usually disapproving*) wearing clothes that are too formal or too elegant for a particular occasion 穿着太正式的；打扮过分的

over·drive /ˈəʊvədraɪv; *NAmE* ˈoʊvərd-/ *noun* [U] an extra high gear in a vehicle, that you use when you are driving at high speeds（汽车的）超速挡：*to be in overdrive* 在超速挡驾驶

IDM **go into ˈoverdrive** to start being very active and working very hard 加劲；加倍努力；拼命工作：*As the wedding approached, the whole family went into overdrive.* 随着婚礼将近，全家人都忙得不亦乐乎。

over·dub /ˌəʊvəˈdʌb; *NAmE* ˌoʊvərˈd-/ *verb* (**-bb-**) **~ sb/sth** to record new sounds over the sounds on an original recording so that both can be heard 把（录音）配到原带上；叠录

over·due /ˌəʊvəˈdjuː; *NAmE* ˌoʊvərˈduː/ *adj.* **1** not paid, done, returned, etc. by the required or expected time（到期）未付的，未做的，未还的；过期的：*an overdue payment/library book* 逾期的欠款；逾期未还图书馆的书 ◇ *The rent is now overdue.* 现在房租已属拖欠。◇ *Her baby is two weeks overdue.* 她的胎儿已超过预产期两周了。◇ *This car is overdue for a service.* 这辆汽车早就该保养了。 **2** that should have happened or been done before now 早该发生的；早应完成的：*overdue reforms* 迟来的改革 ◇ *A book like this is* ***long overdue.*** 像这样的书早就该有人出版了。

ˌover ˈeasy *adj.* (*NAmE*) (of fried eggs 煎蛋) turned over when almost cooked and fried for a short time on the other side 两面煎而蛋黄半熟的

over·eat /ˌəʊvərˈiːt; *NAmE* ˌoʊ-/ *verb* (**over·ate** /ˌəʊvərˈet; *NAmE* ˌoʊvərˈeɪt/, **over·eaten** /-ˈiːtn/) [I] to eat more than you need or more than is healthy 吃得过量；吃撑了 ▸ **over·eat·ing** *noun* [U]: *She went through periods of compulsive overeating.* 她经历过几个阶段的强迫性暴食。

ˌover-ˈegg *verb*

IDM **ˌover-egg the ˈpudding** used to say that you think sb has done more than is necessary, or has added unnecessary details to make sth seem better or worse than it really is 做事过分；画蛇添足：*If you're telling lies, keep it simple—never over-egg the pudding.* 如果撒谎，措辞要简短，千万别画蛇添足。

over·empha·sis /ˌəʊvərˈemfəsɪs; *NAmE* ˌoʊ-/ *noun* [U, sing.] **~ (on sth)** too much emphasis or importance 过分强调；过于重视：*an overemphasis on curing illness rather than preventing it* 过分强调治病而不是预防 ▸ **over·empha·size, -ise** /ˌəʊvərˈemfəsaɪz; *NAmE* ˌoʊ-/ *verb* : **~ sth** *The importance of preparation* ***cannot be overemphasized.*** 准备工作的重要性怎么强调也不过分。

over·esti·mate **AW** *verb, noun*

- ***verb*** /ˌəʊvərˈestɪmeɪt; *NAmE* ˌoʊ-/ **~ sth** to estimate sth to be larger, better, more important, etc. than it really is 高估：*They overestimated his ability when they promoted him.* 他们提拔他的时候高估了他的能力。◇ *The importance of these findings* ***cannot be overestimated*** (= is very great). 这些发现的重要性是无法充分估量的。 **OPP** **underestimate** ▸ **over·esti·mation** *noun* [U, C]
- ***noun*** /ˌəʊvərˈestɪmət; *NAmE* ˌoʊ-/ [usually sing.] an estimate about the size, cost, etc. of sth that is too high 过高的评估 **OPP** **underestimate**

over·ex·cited /ˌəʊvərɪkˈsaɪtɪd; *NAmE* ˌoʊ-/ *adj.* too excited and not behaving in a calm or sensible way 过度兴奋的；兴奋得忘乎所以的：*Don't get the children overexcited just before bedtime.* 临睡前不要让孩子过于兴奋。

over·ex·pose /ˌəʊvərɪkˈspəʊz; *NAmE* ˌoʊvərɪkˈspoʊz/ *verb* [usually passive] **1 ~ sth** to affect the quality of a photograph or film by allowing too much light to enter the camera 使（胶片等）曝光过度 **OPP** **underexpose** **2 ~ sb/sth** to allow sb/sth to be seen too much on television, in the newspapers, etc. 对…报道过频：*The club is careful*

O

not to let the younger players be overexposed, and rarely allows them to be interviewed. 俱乐部不想让年轻队员过度曝光，因而很少允许他们接受采访。 ▶ **over·ex·pos·ure** /ˌəʊvərɪk'spəʊʒə(r); *NAmE* ˌoʊvərɪk'spoʊ-/ *noun* [U]

over·ex·tend·ed /ˌəʊvərɪk'stendɪd; *NAmE* ˌoʊ-/ *adj.* [not usually before noun] involved in more work or activities, or spending more money, than you can manage without problems 承担过多工作；开支过大 ▶ **over·ex·tend** *verb* : **~ yourself** *They should not overextend themselves on the mortgage.* 他们不应该用抵押借款过多。

over·feed /ˈəʊvəfiːd; *NAmE* ˈoʊvərfiːd/ *verb* (**over·fed**, **over·fed** /-fed/) **~ sb/sth** to give sb/sth too much food 给…喂食过度 ▶ **over·fed** *adj.* OPP **underfed**

over·fish·ing /ˌəʊvəˈfɪʃɪŋ; *NAmE* ˌoʊvərˈf-/ *noun* [U] the process of taking so many fish from the sea, a river, etc. that the number of fish in it becomes very low 过度捕捞

over·flow *verb, noun*

■ ***verb*** /ˌəʊvəˈfləʊ; *NAmE* ˌoʊvərˈfloʊ/ **1** [I, T] to be so full that the contents go over the sides 漫出；溢出：*The bath is overflowing* 浴盆溢水了！ ◇ **~ with sth** *Plates overflowed with party food.* 聚会上的食物碟满盘盈。 ◇ (*figurative*) *Her heart overflowed with love.* 她的心里充满了爱。 ◇ **~ sth** *The river overflowed its banks.* 河水涨出了堤岸。 **2** [I] **~ (with sth)** (of a place 地方) to have too many people in it 挤满了人：*The streets were overflowing with the crowds.* 街上到处挤满了人。 ◇ *The hospitals are **filled to overflowing*** (= with patients). 医院都人满为患。 **3** [I, T] **~ (into sth) | ~ (sth)** to spread beyond the limits of a place or container that is too full 扩展出界；过度延伸：*The meeting overflowed into the street.* 集会的人群延伸到了大街上。

■ ***noun*** /ˈəʊvəfləʊ; *NAmE* ˈoʊvərfloʊ/ **1** [U, sing.] a number of people or things that do not fit into the space available 容纳不下的人（或物）：*A new office block was built to accommodate the overflow of staff.* 新建了一座办公大楼以便容纳多出的员工。 ◇ *an overflow car park* 备用停车场 **2** [U, sing.] the action of liquid flowing out of a container, etc. that is already full; the liquid that flows out 溢出；漫出；溢出的液体：*an overflow of water from the lake* 漫出的湖水 ◇ (*figurative*) *an overflow of powerful emotions* 横流的激情 **3** (*also* **'overflow pipe**) [C] a pipe that allows extra liquid to escape 溢流管 **4** [C, usually sing.] (*computing* 计) a fault that happens because a number or data item (for example, the result of a calculation) is too large for the computer to represent it exactly 溢出，溢流（运算产生的数值位数或字的长度等超过存储单元的长度）

over·fly /ˌəʊvəˈflaɪ; *NAmE* ˌoʊvərˈf-/ *verb* (**over·flies**, **over·fly·ing**, **over·flew** /-ˈfluː/, **over·flown** /-ˈfləʊn; *NAmE* -ˈfloʊn/) [T, I] **~ (sth)** to fly over a place 飞越；飞过：*We overflew the war zone, taking photographs.* 我们飞越战区摄影。 ◇ *the noise from overflying planes* 过往飞机发出的噪声 ▶ **over·flight** *noun*

over·fond /ˌəʊvəˈfɒnd; *NAmE* ˌoʊvərˈfɑːnd/ *adj.* **~ of sb/sth** liking sb/sth too much（对…）过于喜欢，过分喜爱

over·gar·ment /ˈəʊvəɡɑːmənt; *NAmE* ˈoʊvərɡɑːrm-/ *noun* (*formal*) an item of clothing that is worn over other clothes 罩袍；大衣

over·gen·er·al·ize (*BrE also* **-ise**) /ˌəʊvəˈdʒenrəlaɪz; *NAmE* ˌoʊvərˈdʒ-/ *verb* [I] to make a statement that is not accurate because it is too general 做过分概括的陈述；说话过于笼统 ▶ **over·gen·er·al·iza·tion, -isa·tion** /ˌəʊvədʒenrəlaɪˈzeɪʃn; *NAmE* ˌoʊvərdʒenrələˈzeɪʃn/ *noun* [C, U]

over·gen·er·ous /ˌəʊvəˈdʒenərəs; *NAmE* ˌoʊvərˈdʒ-/ *adj.* **~ (with sth)** giving too much of sth（施与某物时）过于慷慨，过分大方：*She is not overgenerous with praise.* 她不说过头的恭维话。

over·graze /ˌəʊvəˈɡreɪz; *NAmE* ˌoʊvərˈɡ-/ *verb* **~ sth** if land is **overgrazed**, it is damaged by having too many animals feeding on it 在（土地）上过度放牧

over·ground /ˈəʊvəɡraʊnd; *NAmE* ˈoʊvərɡ-/ *adv.* (*BrE*) on or above the surface of the ground, rather than under it 在地面上；高出地面：*The new railway line will run overground.* 新铁路线将采用地上铺设。 ▶ **over·ground** *adj.* : *overground trains* 地面火车 ➲ COMPARE UNDERGROUND *adv.*

over·grown /ˌəʊvəˈɡrəʊn; *NAmE* ˌoʊvərˈɡroʊn/ *adj.* **1** (of gardens, etc. 花园等) covered with plants that have been allowed to grow wild and have not been controlled 植物蔓生的；杂草丛生的：*an overgrown path* 长满野草的小径 ◇ **~ with sth** *The garden's completely overgrown with weeds.* 花园里长满了杂草。 **2** (*often disapproving*) that has grown too large 发展过快的；长得过大的：*an overgrown village* 膨胀过大的村庄 ◇ *They act like a pair of overgrown children* (= they are adults but they behave like children). 他俩的举动就像一对大孩子。

over·growth /ˈəʊvəɡrəʊθ; *NAmE* ˈoʊvərɡroʊθ/ *noun* [U, sing.] (*specialist*) too much growth of sth, especially sth that grows on or over sth else 增生；疯长

over·hand /ˈəʊvəhænd; *NAmE* ˈoʊvərh-/ *adj., adv.* (*especially NAmE*) = OVERARM

over·hang *verb, noun*

■ ***verb*** /ˌəʊvəˈhæŋ; *NAmE* ˌoʊvərˈh-/ (**over·hung**, **over·hung** /-ˈhʌŋ/) [T, I] **~ (sth)** to stick out over and above sth else 悬垂；悬挂；突出于某物之上：*His big fat belly overhung his belt.* 他那硕大肥胖的肚子垂在腰带上面。 ◇ *The path was cool and dark with overhanging trees.* 小路树木掩映，凉爽幽暗。

■ ***noun*** /ˈəʊvəhæŋ; *NAmE* ˈoʊvərh-/ **1** the part of sth that sticks out over and above sth else（…上的）伸出物，外伸物，悬垂物：*The roof has an overhang to protect the walls from the rain.* 屋顶有飞檐突出，保护墙壁不受雨淋。 **2** the amount by which sth hangs over and above sth else 外伸量；突出量 **3** [usually sing.] (*business* 商, *especially NAmE*) the state of being extra to what is required; the things that are extra 过剩（物）；积压（物）：*attempts to reduce the overhang of unsold goods* 减少滞销商品积压的尝试

over·hasty /ˌəʊvəˈheɪsti; *NAmE* ˌoʊvərˈh-/ *adj.* done too soon or doing sth too soon, especially without enough thought 过于匆忙的；过急的；过于草率的：*an overhasty decision* 过于草率的决定 ◇ *We were overhasty in making the choice.* 我们当初作选择时太仓促了。

over·haul *noun, verb*

■ ***noun*** /ˈəʊvəhɔːl; *NAmE* ˈoʊvərh-/ an examination of a machine or system, including doing repairs on it or making changes to it 检修；大修；改造：***a complete/major overhaul*** 彻底检修；大修 ◇ *A radical overhaul of the tax system is necessary.* 有必要彻底改革税制。

■ ***verb*** /ˌəʊvəˈhɔːl; *NAmE* ˌoʊvər-/ **1 ~ sth** to examine every part of a machine, system, etc. and make any necessary changes or repairs 彻底检修：*The engine has been completely overhauled.* 发动机已彻底检修过了。 **2 ~ sb** to come from behind a person you are competing against in a race and go past them 赶上，超过（赛跑对手） SYN **overtake**：*He managed to overhaul the leader on the final lap.* 他在最后一圈发力超过了领先的选手。

over·head *adv., adj., noun*

■ ***adv.*** /ˌəʊvəˈhed; *NAmE* ˌoʊvərˈhed/ above your head; in the sky 在头上方；在空中：*Planes flew overhead constantly.* 飞机不断从头顶上飞过。 ◇ *Thunder boomed in the sky overhead.* 雷声在天空中隆隆作响。

■ ***adj.*** /ˈəʊvəhed; *NAmE* ˈoʊvərhed/ **1** above your head; raised above the ground 头上方的；地面以上的；高架的：*overhead power lines* 高架输电线 **2** [only before noun] connected with the general costs of running a business or an organization, for example paying for rent or electricity 经费的；管理费用的：*overhead costs* 营运开支

■ ***noun*** [U] (*especially NAmE*) = OVERHEADS

ˌoverhead proˈjector *noun* (*abbr.* **OHP**) a piece of equipment that projects an image onto a wall or screen so that many people can see it 投影仪 ➲ COMPARE DATA PROJECTOR, SLIDE PROJECTOR

over·heads /ˈəʊvəhedz; *NAmE* ˈoʊvərh-/ *noun* [pl.] (*especially BrE*) (*also* **over·head** [U] *especially in NAmE*) regular costs that you have when you are running a business or an organization, such as rent, electricity, wages, etc. 经费；营运费用；经常性开支 ➲ SYNONYMS AT COST

over·hear /ˌəʊvəˈhɪə(r); *NAmE* ˌoʊvərˈhɪr/ *verb* (**over·heard, over·heard** /-ˈhɜːd; *NAmE* -ˈhɜːrd/) to hear, especially by accident, a conversation in which you are not involved 偶然听到；无意中听到： **~ sb/sth** *We talked quietly so as not to be overheard.* 我们低声交谈，以免别人听到。◇ *I overheard a conversation between two boys on the bus.* 我在公共汽车上无意中听到两个男孩的对话。◇ **~ sb doing sth** *We overheard them arguing.* 我们碰巧听到他们吵嘴。◇ **~ sb do sth** *I overheard him say he was going to France.* 我偶然听见他说他要去法国。 ➲ COMPARE EAVESDROP

over·heat /ˌəʊvəˈhiːt; *NAmE* ˌoʊvərˈh-/ *verb* **1** [I, T] to become or to make sth become too hot 变得过热；使过热： *The engine is overheating.* 发动机过热了。◇ **~ sth** *It's vital not to overheat the liquid.* 最关键的是不要让液体过热。 **2** [I] (of a country's economy 国家经济) to be too active, with rising prices 发展过热，过于活跃（以致物价高涨） ▶ **over·heat·ing** *noun* [U]

over·heated /ˌəʊvəˈhiːtɪd; *NAmE* ˌoʊvərˈh-/ *adj.* **1** too hot 太热的；过热的： *Don't sleep in an overheated room.* 不要在太热的屋子里睡觉。 **2** too interested or excited 过于热心的；过于兴奋的；痴迷的： *the figment of an overheated imagination* 想入非非而虚构的事物 **3** (of a country's economy 国家经济) too active in a way that may cause problems 过热的；增长过快的

over·hung PAST TENSE OF OVERHANG

over·in·dulge /ˌəʊvərɪnˈdʌldʒ; *NAmE* ˌoʊ-/ *verb* **1** [I] **~ (in sth)** to have too much of sth nice, especially food or drink 过多地享用（尤指食物或饮料） **2** [T] **~ sb** to give sb more than is good for them 过分放任；过于纵容： *His mother overindulged him.* 他母亲对他过于溺爱。

over·in·flated /ˌəʊvərɪnˈfleɪtɪd; *NAmE* ˌoʊ-/ *adj.* **1** (of a price or value 价格或价值) too high 过高的；过于高涨的： *overinflated house prices* 过高的房价 **2** made to seem better, worse, more important, etc. than it really is 夸张的；夸大的；言过其实的 SYN **exaggerated** **3** filled with too much air 过度充气的： *Overinflated tyres burst more easily.* 充气过量的轮胎更容易爆裂。

over·joyed /ˌəʊvəˈdʒɔɪd; *NAmE* ˌoʊvərˈdʒ-/ *adj.* [not before noun] extremely happy or pleased 非常高兴；欣喜若狂 SYN **delighted**: **~ (at sth)** *He was overjoyed at my success.* 我的成功使他欣喜若狂。◇ **~ (to do sth)** *We were overjoyed to hear their good news.* 听到他们的好消息，我们都大喜过望。◇ **~ (that...)** *She was overjoyed that her article had been published.* 她的文章发表了，这使她高兴极了。

over·kill /ˈəʊvəkɪl; *NAmE* ˈoʊvərkɪl/ *noun* [U] (*disapproving*) too much of sth that reduces the effect it has 过犹不及；做得过火的事： *There is a danger of overkill if you plan everything too carefully.* 如果事事过分谨小慎微，那结果难免有适得其反的危险。

over·laid PAST TENSE, PAST PART. OF OVERLAY

over·land /ˈəʊvəlænd; *NAmE* ˈoʊvərl-/ *adj.* across the land; by land, not by sea or by air 横跨陆地的；通过陆路的： *an overland route* 陆上路线 ▶ **over·land** *adv.* : *to travel overland* 作陆上旅行

over·lap AW *verb, noun*

■ *verb* /ˌəʊvəˈlæp; *NAmE* ˌoʊvərˈlæp/ (**-pp-**) **1** [T, I] **~ (sth)** if one thing **overlaps** another, or the two things **overlap**, part of one thing covers part of the other（物体）部分重叠，交叠： *A fish's scales overlap each other.* 鱼鳞一片片上下交叠。◇ *The floor was protected with overlapping sheets of newspaper.* 地板用一张搭着一张的报纸保护着。 **2** [T] **~ sth** to make two or more things overlap 使部分重叠： *You will need to overlap the pieces of wood slightly.* 你得使这些木片像鱼鳞片似的搭叠起来。 **3** [I, T] **~ (sth)** if two events **overlap** or **overlap** each other, the second one starts before the first one has finished（时间上）部分重叠 **4** [I, T] to cover part of the same area of interest, knowledge, responsibility, etc.（范围方面）部分重叠： *Our jobs overlap slightly, which sometimes causes difficulties.* 我们的工作略有重叠，所以有时引起一些困难。◇ **~ (with) sth** *The language of science overlaps with that of everyday life.* 有些科学用语也用于日常生活。

■ *noun* /ˈəʊvəlæp; *NAmE* ˈoʊvərlæp/ **1** [C, U] **~ (between sth and sth)** a shared area of interest, knowledge, responsibility, etc.（范围方面的）重叠部分： *There is (a) considerable overlap between the two subjects.* 两门科目之间有相当多的共通之处。 **2** [C, U] the amount by which one thing covers another thing（物体的）重叠部分，重叠量： *an overlap of 5 cm on each roof tile* 每片房瓦上 5 厘米的重叠度 **3** [U, sing.] a period of time in which two events or activities happen together（两事发生的）重叠时间，交接时期： *There will be an overlap of a week while John teaches Ann the job.* 将有一周的交接期可以让约翰教导安如何接手工作。

over·lay *verb, noun*

■ *verb* /ˌəʊvəˈleɪ; *NAmE* ˌoʊvərˈleɪ/ (**over·laid, over·laid** /-ˈleɪd/) [usually passive] **1 ~ sth (with sth)** (*specialist*) to put sth on top of a surface so as to cover it completely; to lie on top of a surface 覆盖；包；铺；镀： *wood overlaid with gold* 包金木 **2 ~ sth (with sth)** (*literary*) to add sth, especially a feeling or quality, to sth else so that it seems to cover it（尤指以感情或品质）撒满，遮掩： *The place was overlaid with memories of his childhood.* 这个地方处处都装点着他童年的回忆。

■ *noun* /ˈəʊvəleɪ; *NAmE* ˈoʊvərleɪ/ **1** a transparent sheet with drawings, figures, etc. on it that can be placed on top of another sheet in order to change it 套图透明膜；上衬： *An overlay showing population can be placed on top of the map.* 可以在地图上加一层显示人口的透明膜。 **2** a thing that is laid on top of or covers sth else 覆盖物；涂层： *an overlay of fibreglass insulation* 玻璃纤维绝缘层

over·leaf /ˌəʊvəˈliːf; *NAmE* ˌoʊvərˈliːf/ *adv.* on the other side of the page of a book, etc. 在（书页等的）背面；在后面： *Complete the form overleaf.* 填好背面的表格。◇ *The changes are explained in detail overleaf.* 修改处在背面有详细的说明。

over·lie /ˌəʊvəˈlaɪ; *NAmE* ˌoʊvərˈlaɪ/ *verb* (**over·ly·ing, over·lay** /-ˈleɪ/, **over·lain** /-ˈleɪn/) [I, T] **~ (sth)** (*specialist*) to lie over sth 叠加于；置于…上面： *overlying rock* 压在上面的岩石

over·load *verb, noun*

■ *verb* /ˌəʊvəˈləʊd; *NAmE* ˌoʊvərˈloʊd/ [often passive] **1 ~ sth** to put too great a load on sth 使超载；使负荷过重： *an overloaded truck* 一辆超载的卡车 **2 ~ sb (with sth)** to give sb too much of sth 使…负担过重： *He's overloaded with responsibilities.* 他担负的责任过多。◇ *Don't overload the students with information.* 不要给学生灌输过多的信息。 **3 ~ sth** to put too great a demand on a computer, an electrical system, etc. causing it to fail 使（计算机）超载运行；使（电路）超负荷

■ *noun* /ˈəʊvələʊd; *NAmE* ˈoʊvərloʊd/ [U, sing.] too much of sth 过多；过量；超负荷： *In these days of technological change we all suffer from* **information overload**. 在这科技日新月异的时代，过多的信息使人人都应接不暇。

over·long /ˌəʊvəˈlɒŋ; *NAmE* ˌoʊvərˈlɔːŋ; ˌoʊvərˈlɑːŋ/ (*NAmE also* **ˈoverly long**) *adj.* too long 过长的： *an overlong agenda* 过长的议程表

over·look /ˌəʊvəˈlʊk; *NAmE* ˌoʊvərˈlʊk/ *verb* **1 ~ sth** to fail to see or notice sth 忽略；未注意到 SYN **miss**: *He seems to have overlooked one important fact.* 他好像忽略了一个重要的事实。 **2 ~ sth** to see sth wrong or bad but decide to ignore it（对不良现象等）不予理会，视而不见 SYN **turn a blind eye**: *We could not afford to overlook such a serious offence.* 对这样严重的违法行为，我们决不能视若无睹。 **3 ~ sth** if a building, etc. **overlooks** a place, you can see that place from the building 俯视；眺望： *a restaurant overlooking the lake* 一家濒湖餐厅 ◇ *Our back yard is overlooked by several houses.* 好几栋房子都看得见我家的后院。 **4 ~ sb (for sth)** to not consider sb for a

O

job or position, even though they might be suitable（提拔等时）对（某人）不予考虑 **SYN pass over**: *She's been overlooked for promotion several times.* 几次提职时都没有考虑她。

over·lord /ˈəʊvəlɔːd; *NAmE* ˈoʊvərlɔːrd/ *noun* (especially in the past) a person who has power over many other people（尤指旧时的）领主，庄主，大王：*feudal overlords* 封建领主

over·ly /ˈəʊvəli; *NAmE* ˈoʊvərli/ *adv.* (before an adjective 用于形容词前) too; very 很；十分；过于 **SYN excessively**: *I'm not overly fond of pasta.* 我不怎么喜欢吃意大利面食。◇ *We think you are being overly optimistic.* 我们认为你过于乐观了。

over·manned /ˌəʊvəˈmænd; *NAmE* ˌoʊvərˈm-/ *adj.* (of a company, office, etc. 公司、办公室等) having more workers than are needed 人浮于事的；人员过多的 **SYN overstaffed OPP undermanned** ▶ **over·man·ning** /ˌəʊvəˈmænɪŋ; *NAmE* ˌoʊvərˈm-/ *noun* [U]: *the problems of overmanning in industry* 产业界从业人员过多的问题

over·much /ˌəʊvəˈmʌtʃ; *NAmE* ˌoʊvərˈm-/ (*NAmE also* **ˈoverly much**) *adv.* (especially with a negative verb 尤与否定动词连用) too much; very much 很多；过多；非常：*She didn't worry overmuch about it.* 她对此不太担忧。▶ **over·much** *adj.*

over·night *adv., adj.*
- *adv.* /ˌəʊvəˈnaɪt; *NAmE* ˌoʊvərˈn-/ **1** during or for the night 在夜间；在晚上：*We **stayed overnight** in London after the theatre.* 我们看完戏后在伦敦住了一晚。 **2** suddenly or quickly 突然；一夜之间；旋即：*Don't expect it to improve overnight.* 不要指望这事一下子就改善了。
- *adj.* /ˈəʊvənaɪt; *NAmE* ˈoʊvərn-/ [only before noun] **1** happening during the night; for a night 夜间的；晚上的；只供一夜的：*an overnight flight* 夜间飞行 ◇ *overnight accommodation* 一夜住宿 ◇ *She took only **an overnight bag*** (= containing the things needed for a night spent away from home). 她只带了一个外出住宿一晚的用品旅行袋。 **2** happening suddenly or quickly 突然的；很快的；一夜之间的：*The play was an overnight success.* 这部剧作一夜成名。

ˌover-optiˈmis·tic *adj.* **1** too confident that sth will be successful 过分乐观的：*I'm not over-optimistic about my chances of getting the job.* 我对获得这份工作不抱太大希望。 **2** showing more confidence that sth will be successful than is justified by later events 期望过高的；过于乐观的：*The sales forecasts turned out to be over-optimistic.* 结果证明销售预测过于乐观。

over·pass /ˈəʊvəpɑːs; *NAmE* ˈoʊvərpæs/ (*NAmE*) (*BrE* **fly-over**) *noun* a bridge that carries one road over another one 跨线桥；上跨式立交桥 ➲ COMPARE UNDERPASS

over·pay /ˌəʊvəˈpeɪ; *NAmE* ˌoʊvərˈpeɪ/ *verb* (**over·paid**, **over·paid** /-ˈpeɪd/) [usually passive] **~ sb** to pay sb too much; to pay sb more than their work is worth 付款过多；多付报酬 **OPP underpay** ▶ **over·pay·ment** /-ˈpeɪmənt/ *noun* [C, U]

over·play /ˌəʊvəˈpleɪ; *NAmE* ˌoʊvərˈp-/ *verb* **~ sth** to give too much importance to sth 过分强调；过分重视 **OPP underplay**

IDM overplay your ˈhand to spoil your chance of success by judging your position to be stronger than it really is 因不自量力而毁掉胜机；高估自己的地位；错估形势

over·popu·lated /ˌəʊvəˈpɒpjuleɪtɪd; *NAmE* ˌoʊvərˈpɑːp-/ *adj.* (of a country or city 国家或城市) with too many people living in it 人口过多的 ▶ **over·popu·la·tion** /ˌəʊvəˌpɒpjuˈleɪʃn; *NAmE* ˌoʊvərˌpɑːp-/ *noun* [U]: *the problems of overpopulation* 人口过剩问题

over·power /ˌəʊvəˈpaʊə(r); *NAmE* ˌoʊvərˈp-/ *verb* **1 ~ sb** to defeat or gain control over sb completely by using greater strength（以较强力量）征服，制胜：*Police finally managed to overpower the gunman.* 警察最终制伏了持枪歹徒。 **2 ~ sb/sth** to be so strong or great that it affects or disturbs sb/sth seriously 压倒；令人折服；使难以忍受 **SYN overwhelm**: *Her beauty overpowered him.* 她的美貌令他倾倒。◇ *The flavour of the garlic overpowered the meat.* 大蒜的味道盖过了肉味。

over·power·ing /ˌəʊvəˈpaʊərɪŋ; *NAmE* ˌoʊvərˈp-/ *adj.* very strong or powerful 强烈的；极强大的；坚强的：*an overpowering smell of fish* 浓烈的鱼腥味儿 ◇ *an overpowering personality* 极强的个性 ◇ *The heat was overpowering.* 酷热难当。▶ **over·power·ing·ly** *adv.*

over·priced /ˌəʊvəˈpraɪst; *NAmE* ˌoʊvərˈp-/ *adj.* too expensive; costing more than it is worth 价格太高的；过于昂贵的 ➲ SYNONYMS AT EXPENSIVE

over·print /ˌəʊvəˈprɪnt; *NAmE* ˌoʊvərˈp-/ *verb* **~ A (on B) | ~ B with A** to print sth on a document, etc. that already has printing on it（在印刷品上）套印，加印

over·pro·duce /ˌəʊvəprəˈdjuːs; *NAmE* ˌoʊvərprəˈduːs/ *verb* [T, I] **~ (sth)** to produce more of sth than is wanted or needed 过多地生产；过度生产 ▶ **over·pro·duc·tion** /ˌəʊvəprəˈdʌkʃn; *NAmE* ˌoʊvərp-/ *noun* [U]

over·pro·tect·ive /ˌəʊvəprəˈtektɪv; *NAmE* ˌoʊvərp-/ *adj.* too anxious to protect sb from being hurt, in a way that restricts their freedom 过分保护的；袒护的；溺爱有加的：*overprotective parents* 溺爱子女的父母

over·quali·fied /ˌəʊvəˈkwɒlɪfaɪd; *NAmE* ˌoʊvərˈkwɑːl-/ *adj.* having more experience or training than is necessary for a particular job, so that people do not want to employ you（对某职位而言）资历过高的

over·ran PAST TENSE OF OVERRUN

over·rate /ˌəʊvəˈreɪt; *NAmE* ˌoʊvərˈr-/ *verb* [usually passive] **~ sb/sth** to have too high an opinion of sb/sth; to put too high a value on sb/sth 对…评价过高；高估：*In my opinion, Hirst's work has been vastly overrated.* 依我看，赫斯特的作品被大大地高估了。**OPP underrate**

over·reach /ˌəʊvəˈriːtʃ; *NAmE* ˌoʊvərˈr-/ *verb* [T, I] **~ (yourself)** to fail by trying to achieve more than is possible 贪功致败；不自量力：*In making these promises, the company had clearly overreached itself.* 这家公司作出这些承诺，显然是不自量力。

over·react /ˌəʊvəriˈækt; *NAmE* ˌoʊ-/ *verb* [I] **~ (to sth)** to react too strongly, especially to sth unpleasant 反应过激，反应过火（尤指对不愉快的事情）：*The financial markets overreacted to the news.* 金融市场对这条消息反应过于强烈。▶ **over·reac·tion** /-ˈækʃn/ *noun* [sing., U]

over·ride /ˌəʊvəˈraɪd; *NAmE* ˌoʊvərˈr-/ *verb* (**over·rode** /-ˈrəʊd; *NAmE* -ˈroʊd/, **over·rid·den** /-ˈrɪdn/) **1 ~ sth** to use your authority to reject sb's decision, order, etc.（以权力）否决，推翻，不理会 **SYN overrule**: *The chairman overrode the committee's objections and signed the agreement.* 主席不顾委员会的反对，径行签署了协议。 **2 ~ sth** to be more important than sth 比…更重要；凌驾：*Considerations of safety override all other concerns.* 对安全的考虑高于一切。 **3 ~ sth** to stop a process that happens automatically and control it yourself 超驰控制，超控（使自动控制暂时失效，改用手工控制）：*A special code is needed to override the time lock.* 这定时锁要用特定密码才能打开。

over·rid·ing /ˌəʊvəˈraɪdɪŋ; *NAmE* ˌoʊvərˈr-/ *adj.* [only before noun] more important than anything else in a particular situation 最重要的；首要的；凌驾一切的：*the **overriding factor/consideration/concern*** 首要因素 / 考虑 / 关注的事 ◇ *Their overriding aim was to keep costs low.* 他们的首要目标是维持低成本。

over·ripe /ˌəʊvərˈraɪp; *NAmE* ˌoʊvərˈr-/ *adj.* too RIPE 过熟的：*overripe fruit* 熟过头的水果

over·rule /ˌəʊvəˈruːl; *NAmE* ˌoʊvərˈr-/ *verb* [often passive] **~ sb/sth** to change a decision or reject an idea from a position of greater power（以权力）否定，拒绝，更改决定 **SYN override**: *to overrule a decision/an objection*（以权力）推翻决议 / 异议 ◇ *The verdict was overruled by the Supreme Court.* 最高法院驳回了那个裁决。

over·run /ˌəʊvəˈrʌn; *NAmE* ˌoʊ-/ *verb* (**over·ran** /-ˈræn/, **over·run**) **1** [T, often passive] ~ **sth** (especially of sth bad or not wanted 尤指坏事或不欲之事) to fill or spread over an area quickly, especially in large numbers 泛滥；横行；肆虐：*The house was completely overrun with mice.* 这房子简直成了老鼠的天下。◇ *Enemy soldiers had overrun the island.* 敌军士兵侵占了该岛。**2** [I, T] to take more time or money than was intended 多用（时间、钱财等）；超时：*Her lectures never overrun.* 她讲课从不拖堂。◇ ~ **sth** *You've overrun your time by 10 minutes.* 你超时 10 分钟了。▶ **over·run** *noun*：*a cost overrun* 超出的成本

over·seas AW /ˌəʊvəˈsiːz; *NAmE* ˌoʊvərˈs-/ *adj., adv.*

■ *adj.* connected with foreign countries, especially those separated from your country by the sea or ocean 外国的；海外的：*overseas development/markets/trade* 海外发展 / 市场 / 贸易 ◇ *overseas students/visitors* 外国留学生 / 游客 ➲ COMPARE HOME *adj.* (3)

■ *adv.* to or in a foreign country, especially those separated from your country by the sea or ocean 在国外；向海外 SYN **abroad**：*to live/work/go overseas* 在国外生活 / 工作；出国 ◇ *The product is sold both at home and overseas.* 这个产品行销国内外。

over·see /ˌəʊvəˈsiː; *NAmE* ˌoʊvərˈsiː/ *verb* (**over·saw** /-ˈsɔː/, **over·seen** /-ˈsiːn/) ~ **sb/sth** to watch sb/sth and make sure that a job or an activity is done correctly 监督；监视 SYN **supervise**

over·seer /ˈəʊvəsɪə(r); *NAmE* ˈoʊvərsɪr/ *noun* **1** (*old-fashioned*) a person whose job is to make sure that other workers do their work 监工；工头 **2** a person or an organization that is responsible for making sure that a system is working as it should（某体系的）监督者，监督机构，督察

over·sell /ˌəʊvəˈsel; *NAmE* ˌoʊvərˈsel/ *verb* (**over·sold**, **over·sold** /-ˈsəʊld; *NAmE* -ˈsoʊld/) [often passive] **1** ~ **sb/sth/yourself** to say that sb/sth is better than they really are 吹嘘；过分颂扬：*He has a tendency to oversell himself.* 他爱自我吹嘘。**2** ~ **sth** (*business* 商) to sell too much or more of sth than is available 过多销售；空头销售：*The seats on the plane were oversold.* 飞机上的座位超卖了。

over·sen·si·tive /ˌəʊvəˈsensətɪv; *NAmE* ˌoʊvərˈs-/ *adj.* too easily upset or offended 过于敏感的；爱生气的；动不动就发脾气的

over·sexed /ˌəʊvəˈsekst; *NAmE* ˌoʊvərˈs-/ *adj.* having stronger sexual desire than is usual 性欲过盛的

over·shadow /ˌəʊvəˈʃædəʊ; *NAmE* ˌoʊvərˈʃædoʊ/ *verb* [often passive] **1** ~ **sb/sth** to make sb/sth seem less important, or successful 使显得逊色；使黯然失色：*He had always been overshadowed by his elder sister.* 他与他姐姐相比总是相形见绌。**2** ~ **sth** to make an event less enjoyable than it should be 使扫兴；使蒙上阴影 SYN **cloud**：*News of the accident overshadowed the day's events.* 出事的消息给这一天的活动蒙上了阴影。**3** ~ **sth** to throw a shadow over sth 掩盖；遮蔽：*The garden is overshadowed by tall trees.* 花园中大树浓荫密布。

over·share /ˌəʊvəˈʃeə(r); *NAmE* ˌoʊvərˈʃer/ *verb* [I] to give more information than people want to hear about your personal life 过度分享（私生活）：*Her tendency to overshare is sometimes embarrassing!* 她喜欢过度分享自己的私生活，有时真叫人尴尬！▶ **over·sharing** *noun* **over·sharer** *noun*

over·shoe /ˈəʊvəʃuː; *NAmE* ˈoʊvərʃuː/ *noun* a shoe worn over another shoe, especially in wet weather or to protect a floor 套鞋，罩鞋（在雨天时或为保护地板而穿）

over·shoot /ˌəʊvəˈʃuːt; *NAmE* ˌoʊvərˈʃ-/ *verb* (**over·shot**, **over·shot** /-ˈʃɒt; *NAmE* -ˈʃɑːt/) **1** [T, I] to go further than the place you intended to stop or turn 超过，越过（预定地点）：~ **sth** *The aircraft overshot the runway.* 飞机冲出了跑道。◇ ~ (**sth**) (**by sth**) *She had overshot by 20 metres.* 她超过了 20 米。**2** [T] ~ **sth** (**by sth**) to do more or to spend more money than you originally planned 超过（原计划）；突破（预计费用）：*The department may overshoot its cash limit this year.* 这个部门今年可能要突破现金限额。

over·sight /ˈəʊvəsaɪt; *NAmE* ˈoʊvərs-/ *noun* **1** [C, U] the fact of making a mistake because you forget to do sth or you do not notice sth 疏忽；忽略；失察：*I didn't mean to leave her name off the list; it was an oversight.* 我不是有意在名单上漏掉她的名字的，这是个疏忽。**2** [U] (*formal*) the state of being in charge of sb/sth 负责；照管：*The committee has oversight of finance and general policy.* 该委员会负责处理财政和一般性政策。

over·sim·plify /ˌəʊvəˈsɪmplɪfaɪ; *NAmE* ˌoʊvərˈs-/ *verb* (**over·sim·pli·fies**, **over·sim·pli·fy·ing**, **over·sim·pli·fied**, **over·sim·pli·fied**) [T, I] ~ (**sth**) to describe a situation, a problem, etc. in a way that is too simple and ignores some of the facts 陈述过于简略；说明过于简单化：*It's easy to oversimplify the issues involved.* 很容易把涉及的问题看得太简单。◇ *an oversimplified view of human nature* 对人性过于简单化的看法 ▶ **over·sim·pli·fi·ca·tion** /ˌəʊvəˌsɪmplɪfɪˈkeɪʃn; *NAmE* ˌoʊvərˌs-/ *noun* [C, usually sing., U]：*This is a gross oversimplification of the facts.* 这显然把事实过分简单化了。➲ COMPARE SIMPLIFICATION

over·sized /ˈəʊvəsaɪzd; *NAmE* ˈoʊvərs-/ (*also less frequent* **over·size** /-saɪz/) *adj.* bigger than the normal size; too big 过大的；硕大的；大得超过正常的

over·sleep /ˌəʊvəˈsliːp; *NAmE* ˌoʊvərˈs-/ *verb* (**over·slept**, **over·slept** /-ˈslept/) [I] to sleep longer than you intended 睡过头；睡得太久：*I overslept and missed the bus.* 我睡过了头，因此误了班车。➲ WORDFINDER NOTE AT SLEEP

over·spend /ˌəʊvəˈspend; *NAmE* ˌoʊvərˈs-/ *verb* (**over·spent**, **over·spent** /-ˈspent/) [I, T] to spend too much money or more than you planned 花钱过多；比（预计的）花得多；超支：~ (**on sth**) *The company has overspent on marketing.* 这个公司在市场推广方面开支过多。◇ ~ **sth** *Many departments have overspent their budgets this year.* 许多部门今年开支都超过了预算。▶ **over·spend** /ˈəʊvəspend; *NAmE* ˈoʊvərs-/ *noun* [sing.] (*BrE*)：*a £1 million overspend* * 100 万英镑的超支额 **over·spent** /ˌəʊvəˈspent; *NAmE* ˌoʊvərˈs-/ *adj.*：*The organization is heavily overspent.* 这个机构严重超支。

over·spill /ˈəʊvəspɪl; *NAmE* ˈoʊvərs-/ *noun* [U, sing.] (*BrE*) people who move out of a city because it is too crowded to an area where there is more space 迁出城市的过剩人口：*New towns were designed to house London's overspill.* 新的城镇是为容纳伦敦的过剩人口而设计的。

over·staffed /ˌəʊvəˈstɑːft; *NAmE* ˌoʊvərˈstæft/ *adj.* (of a company, office, etc. 公司、办公室等) having more workers than are needed 人手过多；人浮于事 SYN **overmanned** OPP **understaffed**

over·state /ˌəʊvəˈsteɪt; *NAmE* ˌoʊvərˈs-/ *verb* ~ **sth** to say sth in a way that makes it seem more important than it really is 夸大；夸张；言过其实 SYN **exaggerate**：*He tends to* ***overstate his case*** *when talking politics.* 他一谈政治便流于夸夸其谈。◇ *The seriousness of the crime* ***cannot be overstated.*** 这一罪行的严重性怎么说也不为过。OPP **understate** ▶ **over·state·ment** /ˈəʊvəsteɪtmənt; *NAmE* ˈoʊvərs-/ *noun* [C, U]：*It is not an overstatement to say a crisis is imminent.* 说危机当头绝非危言耸听。

over·stay /ˌəʊvəˈsteɪ; *NAmE* ˌoʊvərˈs-/ *verb* ~ **sth** to stay longer than the length of time you are expected or allowed to stay 停留过久：*They overstayed their visa.* 他们居留超过了签证期限。IDM SEE WELCOME *n.*

over·step /ˌəʊvəˈstep; *NAmE* ˌoʊvərˈs-/ *verb* (**-pp-**) ~ **sth** to go beyond what is normal or allowed 超越（正常或允许的）范围；越权；僭越：*to overstep your authority* 越权 ◇ *He tends to* ***overstep the boundaries of*** *good taste.* 他往往文雅过度而流于庸俗。

IDM **overstep the ˈmark/ˈline** to behave in a way that people think is not acceptable（行为）越轨

over·stock /ˌəʊvəˈstɒk; *NAmE* ˌoʊvərˈstɑːk/ *verb* **1** [T, I] ~ (**sth**) to buy or make more of sth than you need or can sell 库存过多（货物）；进（货）过多 **2** [T, I] ~ (**sth**) to put too many animals in a place where there is not enough

O

room or food for them（在空间、食物不足的地方）畜养过多的动物

over·stretch /ˌəʊvəˈstretʃ; NAmE ˌoʊvərˈs-/ *verb* ~ **sb/sth/yourself** (*especially BrE*) to do more than you are capable of; to make sb/sth do more than they are capable of （使）勉强维持，硬撑着，超负荷运转：*This will overstretch the prison service's resources.* 这将使监狱的资源不堪负荷。◇ *Credit cards can tempt you to overstretch yourself* (= spend more money than you can afford). 信用卡能诱使你超额消费。▶ **over·stretched** *adj.*：*overstretched muscles* 过度疲劳的肌肉 ◇ *overstretched services* 扩展过度的服务

over·sub·scribed /ˌəʊvəsəbˈskraɪbd; NAmE ˌoʊvərs-/ *adj.* if an activity, service, etc. is **oversubscribed**, there are fewer places, tickets, etc. than the number of people who are asking for them（活动、服务等）供不应求的，未能达到需求量的

overt /əʊˈvɜːt; ˈəʊvɜːt; NAmE oʊˈvɜːrt; ˈoʊvɜːrt/ *adj.* [usually before noun] (*formal*) done in an open way and not secretly 公开的；明显的；不隐瞒的：*There was little overt support for the project.* 对这个项目公开表示支持的很少。➲ COMPARE COVERT *adj.* ▶ **overt·ly** *adv.*：*overtly political activities* 公开的政治活动

over·take /ˌəʊvəˈteɪk; NAmE ˌoʊvərˈt-/ *verb* (**over·took** /-ˈtʊk/, **over·taken** /-ˈteɪkən/) **1** [T, I] ~ (**sb/sth**) (*especially BrE*) to go past a moving vehicle or person ahead of you because you are going faster than they are 超过；赶上：*He pulled out to overtake a truck.* 他驶出车流，以超过一辆卡车。◇ *It's dangerous to overtake on a bend.* 在弯道强行超车是危险的。 **2** [T] ~ **sb/sth** to become greater in number, amount or importance than sth else（在数量或重要性方面）大于，超过 SYN **outstrip**：*Nuclear energy may overtake oil as the main fuel.* 核能可能会超过石油成为主要燃料。◇ *We mustn't let ourselves be overtaken by our competitors.* 我们决不能让竞争对手超过我们。 **3** [T, often passive] ~ **sb/sth** if sth unpleasant **overtakes** a person, it unexpectedly starts to happen and to affect them（不愉快的事情）突然发生，突然降临：*The climbers were overtaken by bad weather.* 登山者突然遭遇了恶劣天气。◇ *Sudden panic overtook her.* 她突然感到一阵恐慌。◇ *Our original plan was* ***overtaken by events*** (= the situation changed very rapidly) *and we had to make a new one.* 我们原来的计划没赶上变化，只好再订一个新的。

over·tax /ˌəʊvəˈtæks; NAmE ˌoʊvərˈt-/ *verb* **1** ~ **sb/sth/yourself** to do more than you are able or want to do; to make sb/sth do more than they are able or want to do 使用过度；（使）超负荷工作：*to overtax your strength* 透支体力 ◇ *Take it easy. Don't overtax yourself.* 轻松一点，别让自己劳累过度。 **2** ~ **sb/sth** to make a person or an organization pay too much tax（对人或机构）课税过重，多收税款

ˌover-the-ˈcounter *adj.* (*abbr.* **OTC**) [only before noun] **1** (of drugs and medicines 药品) that can be obtained without a PRESCRIPTION (= a written order from a doctor) 无需处方可买到的；非处方的 **2** (*business* 商, *NAmE*) (of stocks and shares 股票及证券) not appearing in an official STOCK EXCHANGE list 场外交易的

over·think /ˌəʊvəˈθɪŋk; NAmE ˌoʊvərˈθ-/ *verb* [T, I] (**over·thought**, **over·thought** /-ˈθɔːt/) to think about sth too much or for too long 过度思虑；考虑时间过长：*He has a tendency to overthink things.* 他总是过度思虑。

over·throw *verb, noun*

■ *verb* /ˌəʊvəˈθrəʊ; NAmE ˌoʊvərˈθroʊ/ (**over·threw** /-ˈθruː/, **over·thrown** /-ˈθrəʊn; NAmE -ˈθroʊn/) ~ **sb/sth** to remove a leader or a government from a position of power by force 推翻；打倒；赶下台：*The president was overthrown in a military coup.* 总统在军事政变中被赶下台。

■ *noun* /ˈəʊvəθrəʊ; NAmE ˈoʊvərθroʊ/ [usually sing.] the act of taking power by force from a leader or government 推翻；打倒

over·time /ˈəʊvətaɪm; NAmE ˈoʊvərt-/ *noun* [U] **1** time that you spend working at your job after you have worked the normal hours 加班；加班的时间：*to* ***do/work overtime*** 加班 ◇ ***overtime pay/earnings/hours*** 加班费；加班收入；加班时间 ◇ *The union announced a ban on overtime.* 工会宣布禁止加班。➲ WORDFINDER NOTE AT PAY ➲ COLLOCATIONS AT JOB **2** the money sb earns for doing overtime 加班费：*They pay $150 a day plus overtime.* 他们支付每天 150 美元的报酬，外加加班费。 **3** (*NAmE*) (*BrE* **ˌextra ˈtime**) (*sport* 体育) a set period of time that is added to the end of a sports game, etc., if there is no winner at the end of the normal period（体育比赛等的）加时，加时赛

IDM **be working ˈovertime** (*informal*) to be very active or too active 非常活跃；过分活跃：*There was nothing to worry about. It was just her imagination working overtime.* 没什么可担心的。那只是她的想象力太丰富了。

over·tired /ˌəʊvəˈtaɪəd; NAmE ˌoʊvərˈtaɪərd/ *adj.* extremely tired, so that you become irritated easily 劳累过度（而烦躁）的

over·tone /ˈəʊvətəʊn; NAmE ˈoʊvərtoʊn/ *noun* [usually pl.] an attitude or an emotion that is suggested and is not expressed in a direct way 弦外之音；言外之意；暗示：*There were political overtones to the point he was making.* 他的论点有政治寓意。➲ COMPARE UNDERTONE

over·took PAST TENSE OF OVERTAKE

over·train /ˌəʊvəˈtreɪn; NAmE ˌoʊvərˈt-/ *verb* [I] (of an ATHLETE 运动员) to train too hard or for too long 过度训练

over·ture /ˈəʊvətʃʊə(r); ˈəʊvətjʊə(r); NAmE ˈoʊvərtʃər; -tʃʊr/ *noun* **1** a piece of music written as an introduction to an OPERA or a BALLET（歌剧或芭蕾舞的）序曲，前奏曲：*Prokofiev's overture to 'Romeo and Juliet'* 普罗科菲耶夫《罗密欧与朱丽叶序曲》 **2** [usually pl.] ~ (**to sb**) a suggestion or an action by which sb tries to make friends, start a business relationship, have discussions, etc. with sb else 友好姿态；建议：*He began* ***making overtures to*** *a number of merchant banks.* 他开始主动同一些投资银行接触。

over·turn /ˌəʊvəˈtɜːn; NAmE ˌoʊvərˈtɜːrn/ *verb* **1** [I, T] if sth **overturns**, or if sb **overturns** it, it turns upside down or on its side 倾倒；倾覆；翻掉：*The car skidded and overturned.* 汽车打滑翻倒了。◇ ~ **sth** *He stood up quickly, overturning his chair.* 他猛然站起来，弄翻了椅子。 **2** [T] ~ **sth** to officially decide that a legal decision, etc. is not correct, and to make it no longer valid 推翻，撤销（判决等）：***to overturn a decision/conviction/verdict*** 撤销决定 / 定罪 / 裁决 ◇ *His sentence was overturned by the appeal court.* 上诉法庭撤销了对他的判决。

over·use /ˌəʊvəˈjuːz; NAmE ˌoʊvərˈj-/ *verb* ~ **sth** to use sth too much or too often 使用过度；滥用：*'Nice' is a very overused word.* * nice 一词用得实在太滥了。▶ **over·use** *noun* [U, sing.]

over·value /ˌəʊvəˈvæljuː; NAmE ˌoʊvərˈv-/ *verb* [often passive] ~ **sth** to put too high a value on sth 估计过高；过于重视：*Intelligence cannot be overvalued.* 智力是无比重要的。◇ (*business* 商) *overvalued currencies/stocks* 估价过高的货币 / 股票

over·view /ˈəʊvəvjuː; NAmE ˈoʊvərv-/ *noun* a general description or an outline of sth 概述；纵览；概论；概况 SYN **survey, helicopter view** ➲ LANGUAGE BANK AT ABOUT

over·ween·ing /ˌəʊvəˈwiːnɪŋ; NAmE ˌoʊvərˈw-/ *adj.* [only before noun] (*formal, disapproving*) showing too much confidence or pride 傲慢的；自负的；过于自信的 SYN **arrogant**

over·weight /ˌəʊvəˈweɪt; NAmE ˌoʊvərˈw-/ *adj.* **1** (of people 人) too heavy and fat 太胖的；超重的：*She was only a few pounds overweight.* 她只是超重几磅而已。OPP **underweight** ➲ COLLOCATIONS AT DIET **2** above an allowed weight 超过限制重量的；过重的：*overweight baggage* 超重的行李

over·whelm /ˌəʊvəˈwelm; NAmE ˌoʊvərˈw-/ *verb* [often passive] **1** ~ **sb** to have such a strong emotional effect on sb

O

that it is difficult for them to resist or know how to react （感情或感觉）充溢，难以承受 SYN **overcome**: *She was overwhelmed by feelings of guilt.* 她感到愧疚难当。◇ *The beauty of the landscape overwhelmed me.* 秀丽的风光令我深深地陶醉。 **2 ~ sb** to defeat sb completely 压倒；击败；征服 SYN **overpower**: *The army was overwhelmed by the rebels.* 军队被叛乱者完全击败了。 **3 ~ sb** to be so bad or so great that a person cannot deal with it; to give too much of a thing to a person 压垮；使应接不暇: *We were overwhelmed by requests for information.* 各方的问讯使我们应接不暇。 **4 ~ sb/sth** (*literary*) (of water 水) to cover sb/sth completely 淹没；漫过 SYN **flood**

over·whelm·ing /ˌəʊvəˈwelmɪŋ; *NAmE* ˌoʊvərˈw-/ *adj.* very great or very strong; so powerful that you cannot resist it or decide how to react 巨大的；压倒性的；无法抗拒的: *The evidence against him was overwhelming.* 对他不利的证据确凿，无法抵赖。◇ *The **overwhelming majority** of those present were in favour of the plan.* 绝大多数与会者都赞同这个计划。◇ *an **overwhelming sense of** loss* 莫大的失落感 ◇ *She had the almost overwhelming desire to tell him the truth.* 她恨不得要告诉他实情。◇ *You may find it somewhat overwhelming at first.* 起初你可能觉得它有些无法抗拒。 ▶ **over·whelm·ing·ly** *adv.*: *They voted overwhelmingly against the proposal.* 他们以压倒多数票反对这项提案。

over·winter /ˌəʊvəˈwɪntə(r); *NAmE* ˌoʊvərˈw-/ *verb* [I, T] ~ (sth) (of animals, birds and plants 鸟兽和植物) to spend the winter months in a place; to stay alive or to keep sth alive during the winter （使）越冬，度过冬天 ➲ COMPARE WINTER *v.*

over·work /ˌəʊvəˈwɜːk; *NAmE* ˌoʊvərˈwɜːrk/ *verb, noun*

■ *verb* [I, T] to work too hard; to make a person or an animal work too hard （使）过度劳累，过分努力: *You look tired. Have you been overworking?* 你似乎很疲倦，是不是近来劳累过度了？ ◇ **~ sb/sth** *She overworks her staff.* 她让员工过度劳累。

■ *noun* [U] the fact of working too hard 劳累过度；过分辛苦: *His illness was brought on by money worries and overwork.* 他的病是因操心钱和劳累过度而造成的。

over·worked /ˌəʊvəˈwɜːkt; *NAmE* ˌoʊvərˈwɜːrkt/ *adj.* **1** made to work too hard or too much 工作过多的；劳累过度的: *overworked nurses* 劳累过度的护士 **2** (of words or phrases 词语) used too often so that the meaning or effect has become weaker 用得过滥的；滥而无效的

over·write /ˌəʊvəˈraɪt; *NAmE* ˌoʊvərˈr-/ *verb* (**over·wrote** /-ˈrəʊt; *NAmE* -ˈroʊt/, **over·writ·ten** /-ˈrɪtn/) **~ sth** (*computing* 计) to replace information on the screen or in a file by putting new information over it 盖写；重写

over·wrought /ˌəʊvəˈrɔːt; *NAmE* ˌoʊvərˈr-/ *adj.* very worried and upset; excited in a nervous way 过度紧张的；过分忧烦的；紧张激动的 SYN **distraught**

over·zeal·ous /ˌəʊvəˈzeləs; *NAmE* ˌoʊvərˈz-/ *adj.* showing too much energy or enthusiasm 过于热心的；激情过高的: *An overzealous fan ran onto the stage during the concert.* 音乐会上，一名狂热的歌迷冲到了台上。

ovi·duct /ˈəʊvɪdʌkt; *NAmE* ˈoʊ-/ *noun* (*anatomy* 解) either of the tubes that carry eggs from the OVARIES in women and female animals 输卵管

ovine /ˈəʊvaɪn; *NAmE* ˈoʊ-/ *adj.* (*specialist*) relating to sheep 羊的；与羊有关的

ovip·ar·ous /əʊˈvɪpərəs; *NAmE* oʊ-/ *adj.* (*biology* 生) (of an animal 动物) producing eggs rather than live babies 卵生的 ➲ COMPARE OVOVIVIPAROUS, VIVIPAROUS

ovoid /ˈəʊvɔɪd; *NAmE* ˈoʊ-/ *adj.* (*formal*) shaped like an egg 蛋形的；卵形的 ▶ **ovoid** *noun*

ovo·vi·vip·ar·ous /ˌəʊvəʊvɪˈvɪpərəs; *NAmE* ˌoʊvoʊ-/ *adj.* (*biology* 生) (of an animal 动物) producing babies by means of eggs that are HATCHED inside the body of the parent, like some snakes 卵胎生的 ➲ COMPARE OVIPAROUS, VIVIPAROUS

ovu·late /ˈɒvjuleɪt; *NAmE* ˈɑːv-/ *verb* [I] (of a woman or a female animal 女性或雌性动物) to produce an egg (called an OVUM), from the OVARY 排卵；产卵 ▶ **ovu·la·tion** /ˌɒvjuˈleɪʃn; *NAmE* ˌɑːv-/ *noun* [U]: *methods of predicting ovulation* 预测排卵的方法

ovule /ˈɒvjuːl; ˈəʊ-; *NAmE* ˈoʊ-/ *noun* (*biology* 生) the part of the OVARY of a plant containing the female cell, which becomes the seed when it is FERTILIZED 胚珠 ➲ VISUAL VOCAB PAGE V11

ovum /ˈəʊvəm; *NAmE* ˈoʊ-/ *noun* (*pl.* **ova** /ˈəʊvə; *NAmE* ˈoʊvə/) (*biology* 生) a female cell of an animal or a plant that can develop into a young animal or plant when FERTILIZED 卵；卵子；卵细胞

ow /aʊ/ *exclamation* used to express sudden pain （表示疼痛）哎呦: *Ow! That hurt!* 哎呦！疼死我了！ ➲ MORE LIKE THIS 2, page R25

owe 🔑 /əʊ; *NAmE* oʊ/ *verb* (not used in the progressive tenses 不用于进行时) **1** to have to pay sb for sth that you have already received or return money that you have borrowed 欠（债）；欠（账）: **~ sb sth** *She still owes her father £3 000.* 她还欠她父亲 3 000 英镑。◇ (*figurative*) *I'm still owed three days' leave.* 还欠我三天假。◇ **~ sb sth for sth** *How much do I owe you for the groceries?* 买这些杂货我得给你多少钱？ ◇ **~ sth (to sb) (for sth)** *She still owes £3 000 to her father.* 她还欠她父亲 3 000 英镑。◇ *The country owes billions of dollars to foreign creditors.* 这个国家欠外国债主数十亿美元。 **2** to feel that you ought to do sth for sb or give them sth, especially because they have done sth for you 欠（情）: **~ sth to sb** *I owe a debt of gratitude to all my family.* 我很感激我的全家人。◇ *You owe it to your staff to be honest with them.* 与下属坦诚相待，这是你对他们应有的态度。 ◇ **~ sb sth** *You owe me a favour!* 你还欠我一个人情！ ◇ *Thanks for sticking up for me—I owe you one* (= I owe you a favour). 谢谢你支持我，我欠你一个情。◇ *I think you owe us an explanation.* 我认为你应当给我们一个解释。 ◇ *I think we're owed an apology.* 我认为得有人向我们道歉。 HELP The passive is not used in this meaning except with a person as the subject. 除了以人作主语外，这一义项不用被动语态: ~~*An apology is owed to us.*~~ **3** to exist or be successful because of the help or influence of sb/sth 归因于；归功于；起源于: **~ sth to sb/sth** *He owes his success to hard work.* 他的成功是靠勤奋工作。◇ *The play owes much to French tragedy.* 这部戏颇受法国悲剧的影响。◇ *I owe everything to him.* 我的一切都归功于他。 ◇ **~ sb sth** *I owe him everything.* 我的一切都归功于他。◇ *I knew that I owed the surgeon my life.* 我明白外科医生救了我的命。 **4 ~ allegiance/loyalty/obedience (to sb)** (*formal*) to have to obey or be loyal to sb who is in a position of authority or power （对位高权重者）忠诚，服从 ➲ MORE LIKE THIS 33, page R28

owing /ˈəʊɪŋ; *NAmE* ˈoʊɪŋ/ *adj.* [not before noun] money that is **owing** has not been paid yet 拖欠；未付；未偿还: *£100 is still owing on the loan.* 还有 100 英镑贷款未还。

ˈowing to *prep.* because of 因为；由于: *The game was cancelled owing to torrential rain.* 比赛因大雨取消了。

owl /aʊl/ *noun* a BIRD OF PREY (= a bird that kills other creatures for food) with large round eyes, that hunts at night. Owls are traditionally thought to be wise. 猫头鹰，鸮（传统上认为是智慧的象征）: *An owl hooted nearby.* 一只猫头鹰在附近啼叫。 ➲ SEE ALSO BARN OWL, NIGHT OWL, TAWNY OWL

owlet /ˈaʊlət/ *noun* a young OWL 鸮类幼体

owl·ish /ˈaʊlɪʃ/ *adj.* looking like an owl, especially because you are wearing round glasses, and therefore seeming serious and intelligent （尤指因戴圆形眼镜而显得）似猫头鹰的，儒雅的 ▶ **owl·ish·ly** *adv.*: *She blinked at them owlishly.* 她斯文地向他们眨了眨眼。

own 🔑 /əʊn; *NAmE* oʊn/ *adj., pron., verb*

■ ***adj., pron.*** **1** used to emphasize that sth belongs to or is connected with sb （用于强调）自己的，本人的: *It was her own idea.* 那是她自己的主意。◇ *I saw it with my own eyes* (= I didn't hear about it from somebody else). 我亲

O

眼看见的。◇ *Is the car your own?* 这辆汽车是你自己的吗？◇ *Your day off is your own* (= you can spend it as you wish). 你的假日归你自己支配。◇ *Our children are grown up and have children **of their own**.* 我们的子女都已长大成人，有了自己的孩子。◇ ***For reasons of his own*** (= particular reasons that perhaps only he knew about), *he refused to join the club.* 由于他个人的原因，他谢绝加入俱乐部。◇ *The accident happened **through no fault of her own**.* 这一事故的发生不是她本人的过错。◇ *He wants to come into the business **on his own terms**.* 他想依自己开出的条件加入该公司。◇ *I need a room **of my own**.* 我需要有一间自己的房间。◇ *I have my **very own** room at last.* 我终于有了我自己的房间了！ HELP **Own** cannot be used after an article. * own 不能用在冠词之后：*I need my own room.* 我需要有一间自己的房间。◇ ~~*I need an own room.*~~ ◇ *It's good to have your own room.* 有一间自己的房间真好。◇ ~~*It's good to have the own room.*~~ **2** done or produced by and for yourself 自己做的；为自己的：*She makes all her own clothes.* 她的衣服都是自己做。◇ *He has to cook his own meals.* 他必须自己做饭。

IDM **come into your/its 'own** to have the opportunity to show how good or useful you are or sth is 得到充分的发挥：*When the traffic's this bad, a bicycle really comes into its own.* 在交通如此拥堵的时候，自行车就显出了它的价值。 **get your 'own back (on sb)** (*informal*) to do sth to sb in return for harm they have done to you; to get REVENGE 报复：*I'll get my own back on him one day, I swear!* 我发誓，我总有一天要报复他的！ **hold your 'own (against sb/sth) (in sth)** to remain in a strong position when sb is attacking you, competing with you, etc. 坚守立场；（使自己）立于不败之地：*Business isn't good but we're managing to hold our own.* 生意不景气，但我们正设法坚持下去。◇ *She can hold her own against anybody in an argument.* 她在辩论中不会让任何人占上风。◇ *The patient is holding her own although she is still very sick.* 病人的病情仍然很重，但她还在支持着。 **(all) on your 'own 1** alone; without anyone else 独自；单独：*I'm all on my own today.* 今天就我一个人。◇ *She lives on her own.* 她一个人生活。 **2** without help 独立地：*He did it on his own.* 这件事他独立完成了。 ➲ MORE AT DEVIL, MIND *n.*, SAKE[1], SOUND *n.*

■ ***verb*** (not used in the progressive tenses 不用于进行时) **1** [T] **~ sth** to have sth that belongs to you, especially because you have bought it 拥有，有（尤指买来的东西）：*Do you own your house or do you rent it?* 你的房子是自己的，还是租的？◇ *I don't own anything of any value.* 我没有任何值钱的东西。◇ *Most of the apartments are privately owned.* 多数公寓房都是私人的。◇ *an American-owned company* 一家美资公司 **2** [I, T] (*old-fashioned*) to admit that sth is true 承认：**~ to sth/to doing sth** *He owned to a feeling of guilt.* 他承认有歉疚感。◇ **~ (that)...** *She owned (that) she had been present.* 她承认她当时在场。

IDM **,behave/,act as if you 'own the place | think you 'own the place** (*disapproving*) to behave in a very confident way that annoys other people, for example by telling them what to do （言行）喧宾夺主

PHR V **,own 'up (to sth/to doing sth)** to admit that you are responsible for sth bad or wrong 承担责任；认错；坦白 SYN **confess**：*I'm still waiting for someone to own up to the breakages.* 我还在等着有人承认把东西打碎了。

,own-'brand (*also* **,own-'label**) (*both BrE*) (*US* **'store-brand**) *adj.* used to describe goods that are marked with the name of the shop/store in which they are sold rather than with the name of the company that produced them 自有品牌的（指产品以商店自定的品牌出售）

owner /'əʊnə(r); *NAmE* 'oʊ-/ *noun* a person who owns sth 物主；所有权人；主人：*a dog/factory owner* 狗的主人；工厂主 ◇ *The painting has been returned to its **rightful owner**.* 这幅画已归还给合法所有权人。◇ *He's now **the proud owner of** a cottage in Wales.* 现在他很得意自己在威尔士有一座小别墅。 ➲ SEE ALSO HOMEOWNER, LANDOWNER

,owner-'occupied *adj.* (of a house, etc. 房子等) lived in by the owner rather than rented to sb else 房主自用的

,owner-'occupier *noun* a person who owns the house, flat/apartment, etc. that they live in 住自家房屋者；房屋自用者

own·er·ship /'əʊnəʃɪp; *NAmE* 'oʊnərʃɪp/ *noun* [U] the fact of owning sth 所有权；产权；物主身份：*a growth in home ownership* 拥有房产的人数的增加 ◇ *Ownership of the land is currently being disputed.* 这块土地的所有权现在还有争议。◇ *to be in **joint/private/public ownership*** 为共有 / 私有 / 公有产权 ◇ *The restaurant is under new ownership.* 这家餐厅易主了。

,own 'goal *noun* [usually sing.] **1** (in football (SOCCER) 足球) a goal that is scored by mistake by a player against his or her own team 乌龙球；射进自家球门的球 **2** something that you do that achieves the opposite of what you wanted and that brings you a disadvantage 帮倒忙的事；无意中让自己吃亏的事

,own-'label *adj.* (*BrE*) = OWN-BRAND

owt /aʊt/ *pron.* (*BrE, dialect, informal*) anything 任何事物；任何东西：*I didn't say owt.* 我什么也没说。

ox /ɒks; *NAmE* ɑːks/ *noun* (*pl.* **oxen** /'ɒksn; *NAmE* 'ɑːksn/) **1** a BULL (= a male cow) that has been CASTRATED (= had part of its sex organs removed), used, especially in the past, for pulling farm equipment, etc. （阉割的）公牛；犍牛 ➲ COMPARE BULLOCK, STEER *n.* **2** (*old-fashioned*) any cow or BULL on a farm 饲养的牛 ➲ SEE ALSO CATTLE

oxbow 曲流湾

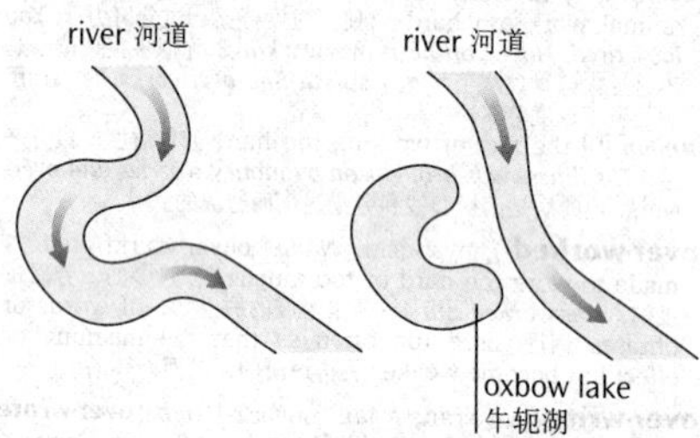

oxbow /'ɒksbəʊ; *NAmE* 'ɑːksboʊ/ *noun* (*specialist*) a bend in a river that almost forms a full circle; a lake that forms when this bend is separated from the river 牛轭湖；河道曲流湾

Ox·bridge /'ɒksbrɪdʒ; *NAmE* 'ɑːks-/ *noun* [U] the universities of Oxford and Cambridge, when they are thought of together 牛津剑桥大学：*an Oxbridge education* 牛津剑桥的教育 ➲ COMPARE IVY LEAGUE, RED-BRICK (2)

ox·ford /'ɒksfəd; *NAmE* 'ɑːksfərd/ *noun* **1 oxfords** [pl.] (*especially NAmE*) leather shoes that fasten with LACES 牛津鞋（一种系鞋带的皮鞋）➲ COMPARE LACE-UP **2** [U] = OXFORD CLOTH：*an oxford shirt* 一件牛津布衬衣

,oxford 'cloth (*also* **ox·ford**) *noun* [U] (*NAmE*) a type of heavy cotton cloth used mainly for making shirts 牛津布（厚棉布，主要做衬衫用）

oxi·dant /'ɒksɪdənt; *NAmE* 'ɑːks-/ *noun* (*chemistry* 化) a substance that makes another substance combine with oxygen 氧化剂

oxide /'ɒksaɪd; *NAmE* 'ɑːk-/ *noun* [U, C] (*chemistry* 化) a COMPOUND of OXYGEN and another chemical element 氧化物：*iron oxide* 氧化铁 ◇ *an oxide of tin* 氧化锡

oxi·dize (*BrE also* **-ise**) /'ɒksɪdaɪz; *NAmE* 'ɑːk-/ *verb* [T, I] **~ (sth)** (*chemistry* 化) to remove one or more ELECTRONS from a substance, or to combine or to make sth combine with OXYGEN, especially when this causes metal to become covered with RUST （使）氧化；（尤指使）生锈

▸ **oxi·da·tion** /ˌɒksɪˈdeɪʃn; *NAmE* ˌɑːk-/ *noun* [U] ⊃COMPARE REDUCE (4), REDUCTION (4)

Oxon /ˈɒksɒn; *NAmE* ˈɑːksɑːn/ *abbr.* (used after degree titles) of Oxford University（用于学位名称后）牛津大学的：*Alice Tolley MA (Oxon)* 文科硕士艾丽斯·托利（牛津大学）

Oxon·ian /ɒkˈsəʊniən; *NAmE* ɑːkˈsoʊ-/ *adj.* (*formal* or *humorous*) relating to Oxford in England, or to Oxford University（英格兰）牛津的，牛津大学的

ox·tail /ˈɒksteɪl; *NAmE* ˈɑːks-/ *noun* [U, C] meat from the tail of a cow, used especially for making soup 牛尾肉（通常用于做汤）：*oxtail soup* 牛尾汤

oxter /ˈɒkstə(r); *NAmE* ˈɑːks-/ *noun* (*BrE, dialect, informal*) a person's ARMPIT 夹肢窝；腋窝

oxy·acet·yl·ene /ˌɒksiəˈsetəliːn; *NAmE* ˌɑːk-/ *adj.* connected with a mixture of oxygen and ACETYLENE gas which produces a very hot flame, used especially for cutting or joining metal 氧乙炔的（尤用于切割或焊接金属）：*an oxyacetylene torch* 氧乙炔炬

oxy·gen /ˈɒksɪdʒən; *NAmE* ˈɑːk-/ *noun* [U] (*symb.* **O**) a chemical element. Oxygen is a gas that is present in air and water and is necessary for people, animals and plants to live. 氧；氧气

oxy·gen·ate /ˈɒksɪdʒəneɪt; *NAmE* ˈɑːk-/ *verb* ~ **sth** (*specialist*) to supply sth with oxygen 供氧；输氧 ▸ **oxy·gen·ation** *noun* [U]

oxy·gen·ator /ˈɒksɪdʒəneɪtə(r); *NAmE* ˈɑːks-/ *noun* **1** (*medical* 医) a device for putting oxygen into the blood 氧合器；人工肺 **2** a water plant that puts oxygen into the water around it 充氧水生植物

ˈ**oxygen bar** *noun* a place where you can pay to breathe pure oxygen in order to improve your health and help you relax 氧吧

ˈ**oxygen mask** *noun* a device placed over the nose and mouth through which a person can breathe OXYGEN, for example in an aircraft or a hospital 氧气面具；氧气面罩

ˈ**oxygen tent** *noun* (*medical* 医) a structure like a tent which can be used to increase sb's supply of oxygen and help them to breathe（急救输氧用的）氧幕；氧气帐

oxy·moron /ˌɒksɪˈmɔːrɒn; *NAmE* ˌɑːksɪˈmɔːrɑːn/ *noun* (*specialist*) a phrase that combines two words that seem to be the opposite of each other, for example *a deafening silence* 矛盾修辞法

oy *exclamation* = OI

oyez (*also* **oyes**) /əʊˈjeɪ; *NAmE* oʊ-/ *exclamation* used by a TOWN CRIER or an officer in court to tell people to be quiet and pay attention（街头公告员或法庭官员用语）肃静

oys·ter /ˈɔɪstə(r)/ *noun* a large flat SHELLFISH. Some types of oyster can be eaten and others produce shiny white JEWELS called PEARLS. 牡蛎；蚝：*Oyster beds, on the mudflats, are a form of fish farming.* 滩涂牡蛎养殖是一种水产养殖方式。 ⊃PICTURE AT SHELLFISH IDM SEE WORLD

oys·ter·catch·er /ˈɔɪstəkætʃə(r); *NAmE* ˈɔɪstərk-/ *noun* a black bird with long legs and a long red beak that lives near the coast and feeds on SHELLFISH 蛎鹬（捕食贝类的滨鸟）

ˈ**oyster mushroom** *noun* a type of wide, flat FUNGUS that grows on trees and that you can eat 糙皮侧耳；平菇

oy vey /ˌɔɪ ˈveɪ/ *exclamation* used for showing disappointment or sadness (mainly by Yiddish speakers or Jewish people)（主要为讲依地语者或犹太人使用，表示失望或悲伤）哎呀，天哪

Oz /ɒz; *NAmE* ɑːz/ *noun* [U] (*BrE, AustralE, NZE, informal*) Australia 澳大利亚；澳洲

oz *abbr.* (in writing 书写形式) OUNCE(S) 盎司（重量单位）：*4oz sugar* * 4 盎司的糖

ozone /ˈəʊzəʊn; *NAmE* ˈoʊzoʊn/ *noun* [U] **1** (*chemistry* 化) a poisonous gas with a strong smell that is a form of OXYGEN 臭氧 **2** (*BrE, informal*) air near the sea that smells fresh and pure 海边的清新空气

ozone-ˈfriend·ly *adj.* not containing substances that will damage the OZONE LAYER 无害臭氧层的；不含损害臭氧层物质的

ˈ**ozone hole** *noun* an area in the ozone layer where the amount of OZONE has been very much reduced so that harmful RADIATION from the sun can pass through it 臭氧洞

ˈ**ozone layer** *noun* [sing.] a layer of OZONE high above the earth's surface that helps to protect the earth from harmful RADIATION from the sun 臭氧层 ⊃COLLOCATIONS AT ENVIRONMENT

Oz·zie = AUSSIE

O

Pp

P (*also* **p**) /piː/ *noun* [C, U] (*pl.* **Ps**, **P's**, **p's** /piːz/) the 16th letter of the English alphabet 英语字母表的第 16 个字母：*'Pizza' begins with (a) P/'P'.* * pizza 一词以字母 p 开头。IDM SEE MIND *v.*

p (*also* **p.**) *abbr.* **1** (*pl.* **pp.**) page 页：*See p.34 and pp.63–72.* 见第 34 页及第 63–72 页。 **2** /piː/ PENNY, PENCE 便士：*a 30p stamp* 一枚 30 便士的邮票 **3** (*music* 音) quietly (from Italian 'piano') 轻柔地；安静地；弱 ➲ SEE ALSO P. AND H., P. AND P.

PA /ˌpiː ˈeɪ/ *noun* **1** PUBLIC ADDRESS SYSTEM 广播系统：*Announcements were made over the PA.* 通告是从广播系统播出的。 **2** (*especially BrE*) the abbreviation for 'personal assistant' (a person who works as a secretary or an assistant for one person) 私人助理，私人秘书（全写为 personal assistant）：*She's the Managing Director's PA.* 她是总经理的私人助理。

Pa *abbr.* (in writing 书写形式) PASCAL 帕（斯卡）（标准压强单位）

pa /pɑː/ *noun* (*old-fashioned, informal*) father 爹；爸爸：*I used to know your pa.* 我过去跟你爸爸很熟。

p.a. *abbr.* per year (from Latin 'per annum') 每年（源自拉丁语 per annum）：*an increase of 3% p.a.* 每年 3% 的增长

paan (*also* **pan**) /pɑːn/ *noun* [U, C] (*IndE*) a BETEL leaf, usually folded into a shape with three sides and filled with spices for eating 蒌叶，蒟酱叶包槟榔，包叶槟榔（通常折成粽子状食用）

PAC /ˌpiː eɪ ˈsiː/ *abbr.* POLITICAL ACTION COMMITTEE 政治行动委员会（美国组织，为所支持的公职候选人筹集资金）

pace¹ /peɪs/ *noun, verb* ➲ SEE ALSO PACE²

■ ***noun*** **1** [sing., U] the speed at which sb/sth walks, runs or moves （移动的）速度；步速：*to set off at a steady/gentle/leisurely pace* 以稳定的 / 徐缓的 / 悠闲的步子出发 ◇ *Congestion frequently reduces traffic to **walking pace**.* 交通阻塞经常把车流的速度降低得如步行般缓慢。◇ *The ball **gathered pace** as it rolled down the hill.* 球向山下滚去，速度越来越快。◇ *The runners have noticeably quickened their pace.* 赛跑者明显加快了脚步。 **2** [sing., U] ~ (**of sth**) the speed at which sth happens 发生的速度；步伐；节奏：*It is difficult to keep up with the rapid pace of change.* 跟上快速的变化是很困难的。◇ *We encourage all students to work **at their own pace*** (= as fast or as slow as they can). 我们鼓励学生都按自己的节奏学习。◇ *I prefer the relaxed **pace of life** in the country.* 我喜爱乡间那悠闲的生活节奏。◇ *Rumours of corruption and scandal **gathered pace*** (= increased in number). 腐化堕落的传闻日益增多。 **3** [C] an act of stepping once when walking or running; the distance travelled when doing this （走或跑时）迈出的一步，一步的距离；步幅 SYN **step**：*She took two paces forward.* 她向前走了两步。 **4** [U] the fact of sth happening, changing, etc. quickly 迅速出现（或变化等）；快节奏：*He gave up his job in advertising because he couldn't **stand the pace**.* 他辞去了广告业的工作，因为他承受不了那种快节奏。◇ *The novel lacks pace* (= it develops too slowly). 这部小说缺乏节奏感。 ➲ SEE ALSO PACY

IDM **go through your 'paces | show your 'paces** to perform a particular activity in order to show other people what you are capable of doing 展示自己的能力 **keep 'pace (with sb/sth)** to move, increase, change, etc. at the same speed as sb/sth （与…）并驾齐驱；（与…）步调一致：*She found it hard to keep pace with him as he strode off.* 他大步走开了，她感到很难跟上他。◇ *Until now, wage increases have always kept pace with inflation.* 到目前为止，工资的增长与通货膨胀始终保持同步。 **off the 'pace** (in sport 体育运动) behind the leader or the leading group in a race or a competition （赛跑或比赛中）在领头人之后，在领头队之后：*Tiger Woods is still three shots off the pace* (= in GOLF). 泰格 • 伍兹仍落后领先选手三杆。 **put sb/sth through their/its 'paces** to give sb/sth a number of tasks to perform in order to see what they are capable of doing 考察，考验（某人的能力） **set the 'pace** **1** to do sth at a particular speed or to a particular standard so that other people are then forced to copy it if they want to be successful 确定速度；确立标准；领先：*The company is no longer setting the pace in the home computer market.* 这家公司再也不能在国内计算机市场上独领风骚了。 **2** (in a race 跑步比赛) to run faster than the other people taking part, at a speed that they then try to copy 领跑 ➲ MORE AT FORCE *v.*, SNAIL

■ ***verb*** **1** [I, T] to walk up and down in a small area many times, especially because you are feeling nervous or angry 来回踱步；走来走去：**+ adv./prep.** *She **paced up and down** outside the room.* 她在屋子外面来回走着。◇ **~ sth** *Ted paced the floor restlessly.* 特德焦躁地在屋里走来走去。 **2** [T] **~ sth** to set the speed at which sth happens or develops 确定速度；调整节奏：*He paced his game skilfully.* 他巧妙地控制着自己的比赛节奏。 **3** [T] **~ yourself** to find the right speed or rhythm for your work or an activity so that you have enough energy to do what you have to do 调整自己的工作（或活动）节奏：*He'll have to learn to pace himself in this job.* 他必须学会使自己适应这项工作的节奏。

PHR V **ˌpace sth↔ˈoff/ˈout** to measure the size of sth by walking across it with regular steps 以步丈量

pace² /ˈpɑːkeɪ; ˈpɑːtʃeɪ; ˈpeɪsi/ *prep.* (*from Latin, formal*) used before a person's name to express polite disagreement with what they have said （用于人名前，委婉提出不同意见）请…原谅：*The evidence suggests, pace Professor Jones, that...* (= Professor Jones has a different opinion). 请琼斯教授原谅，证据表明… ➲ SEE ALSO PACE¹

ˌpace ˈbowler *noun* = FAST BOWLER

pace·maker /ˈpeɪsmeɪkə(r)/ *noun* **1** an electronic device that is put inside a person's body to help their heart beat regularly （心脏）起搏器 **2** (*also* **pace·setter** *especially in NAmE*) a person or an animal that begins a race quickly so that the other people taking part will try to copy the speed and run a fast race 领跑人；领跑动物：(*figurative*) *The big banks have been the pacesetters in developing the system.* 大银行是发展这一体系的先驱。 **3** (*also* **pace·setter** *especially in NAmE*) a person or team that is winning in a sports competition （竞赛中的）领先者，领先队伍：*The local club are now only one point off the pacemakers.* 当地俱乐部与领先者只差一分。

pace·man /ˈpeɪsmæn/ *noun* (*pl.* **-men** /-men/) = FAST BOWLER

pace·setter /ˈpeɪssetə(r)/ *noun* (*especially NAmE*) = PACEMAKER (2), (3)

pacey = PACY

pa·chinko /pəˈtʃɪŋkəʊ; *NAmE* -koʊ/ *noun* [U] (*from Japanese*) a Japanese form of PINBALL, in which you can win prizes 弹球盘，柏青哥（一种日本赌博游戏）

pachy·derm /ˈpækɪdɜːm; *NAmE* -dɜːrm/ *noun* (*specialist*) a type of animal with a very thick skin, for example, an ELEPHANT 厚皮动物（如大象）

pa·cif·ic /pəˈsɪfɪk/ *adj.* [usually before noun] (*literary*) peaceful or loving peace 平静的；和平的；爱和平的

Paˌcific ˈDaylight Time *noun* [U] (*abbr.* **PDT**) the time used in summer in the western parts of Canada and the US that is seven hours behind UTC 太平洋夏令时间（加拿大西部和美国西部的夏季时间，比协调世界时晚七个小时）

the Paˌcific ˈRim *noun* [sing.] the countries around the Pacific Ocean, especially the countries of eastern Asia, considered as an economic group 太平洋周边地区，环太平洋圈（尤指被视为经济体的东亚诸国）

Paˌcific ˈStandard Time *noun* [U] (*abbr.* **PST**) the time used in winter in the western parts of Canada and the US that is eight hours behind UTC 太平洋标准时间（加拿大西部和美国西部的冬季时间，比协调世界时晚八个小时）

Pa'cific time *noun* [U] the standard time on the west coast of the US and Canada 太平洋时间（加拿大和美国西海岸的标准时间）

paci·fier /ˈpæsɪfaɪə(r)/ (*NAmE*) (*BrE* **dummy**) *noun* a specially shaped rubber or plastic object for a baby to suck 安抚奶嘴

paci·fism /ˈpæsɪfɪzəm/ *noun* [U] the belief that war and violence are always wrong 和平主义；绥靖主义；反战主义

paci·fist /ˈpæsɪfɪst/ *noun* a person who believes in pacifism and who refuses to fight in a war 和平主义者；绥靖主义者；反战主义者 ➲ COMPARE CONSCIENTIOUS OBJECTOR ▶ **paci·fist** *adj.* [usually before noun]: *pacifist beliefs* 和平主义信仰

pacify /ˈpæsɪfaɪ/ *verb* (**paci·fies**, **paci·fy·ing**, **paci·fied**, **paci·fied**) **1** ~ **sb** to make sb who is angry or upset become calm and quiet 使平静；平息；抚慰 SYN **placate**: *The baby could not be pacified.* 婴儿怎么也不能平静下来。◇ *The speech was designed to pacify the irate crowd.* 讲话的目的是安抚愤怒的群众。 **2** ~ **sth** to bring peace to an area where there is fighting or a war 平息战争；使实现和平 ▶ **paci·fi·ca·tion** /ˌpæsɪfɪˈkeɪʃn/ *noun* [U]

pack /pæk/ *verb*, *noun*

■ *verb*

• **PUT INTO CONTAINER** 装入容器 **1** [I, T] to put clothes, etc. into a bag in preparation for a trip away from home 收拾（行李）；装（箱）：*I haven't packed yet.* 我还没收拾行李呢。◇ ~ **sth** *I haven't packed my suitcase yet.* 我的行李箱还没收拾好呢。◇ *He packed a bag with a few things and was off.* 他装了几件衣物就走了。◇ *He packed a few things into a bag.* 他装了几件衣物。◇ *Did you pack the camera?* 你装进照相机了吗？◇ ~ **sb sth** *I've packed you some food for the journey.* 我给你打点了些路上吃的食物。 **2** [T] ~ **sth** (**up**) (**in/into sth**) to put sth into a container so that it can be stored, transported or sold 打包；包装：*The pottery was packed in boxes and shipped to the US.* 陶器已装箱运往美国。◇ *I carefully packed up the gifts.* 我小心翼翼地把礼品包好。 OPP **unpack**

• **PROTECT** 保护 **3** [T] ~ **sth** (**in/with sth**) to protect sth that breaks easily by surrounding it with soft material （在四周填入软料以）包装（易损物品）：*The paintings were carefully packed in newspaper.* 这些画被仔细地用报纸裹了起来。

• **PRESERVE FOOD** 保存食品 **4** [T] ~ **sth** (**in sth**) to preserve food in a particular substance （用某物）保存，保藏：*fish packed in ice* 用冰块保存的鱼

• **FILL** 填入 **5** [I, T] to fill sth with a lot of people or things 塞进；挤进：**+ adv./prep.** *We all packed together into one car.* 我们大家挤进一辆汽车里。◇ ~ **sth** (**with sth**) *Fans packed the hall to see the band.* 乐迷为了一睹乐队风采，把大厅挤得水泄不通。 ➲ SEE ALSO PACKED, PACKED OUT

• **SNOW/SOIL** 雪；土壤 **6** [T] ~ **sth** (**down**) to press sth such as snow or soil to form a thick hard mass 堆积；压实：*Pack the earth down around the plant.* 把植物周围的土压实。◇ *a patch of packed snow* 一片压实的雪地

• **CARRY GUN** 携枪 **7** [T, I] ~ (**sth**) (*NAmE*, *informal*) to carry a gun 佩带，携带（枪支）：*to pack a gun* 佩带枪支 ◇ *Is he packing?* 他带着枪吗？

• **STORM** 暴风雨 **8** [T] ~ **sth** to have sth 夹带着：*A storm packing 75 mph winds swept across the area last night.* 昨晚暴雨和着每小时 75 英里的狂风横扫该地区。

IDM **pack a** (**powerful**, **real**, **etc.**) **'punch** (*informal*) **1** (of a BOXER 拳击手) to be capable of hitting sb very hard 能重拳出击；能重击 **2** to have a powerful effect on sb 产生巨大影响；十分有效力：*The advertising campaign packs quite a punch.* 这次广告造势产生了相当大的影响。 **pack your 'bags** (*informal*) to leave a person or place permanently, especially after a disagreement （尤指产生分歧后）永远离开 ➲ MORE AT SEND

PHR V **ˌpack a'way** to be capable of being folded up small when it is not being used 能折叠（以缩小体积）：*The tent packs away in a small bag.* 帐篷可以折叠装进小袋子里。 **ˌpack sth↔a'way** to put sth in a box, etc. when you have finished using it （用后）收拾好：*We packed away the summer clothes.* 我们把夏装收起来了。 **ˌpack sb↔'in** [no passive] (of plays, performers, etc. 戏剧、演员等) to attract a lot of people to see it/them 吸引（大批观众）：*The show is still **packing them in**.* 演出仍然吸引着大批观众。 **ˌpack sth↔'in** (*informal*) to stop doing sth 停止做某事 SYN **give up**: *She decided to pack in her job.* 她决定辞职不干了。◇ (*especially BrE*) ***Pack it in*** (= stop behaving badly or annoying me), *you two!* 别闹了，你们俩！ **ˌpack sb/sth 'in/'into sth** **1** to do a lot of things in a limited period of time 在（有限时间里）做（大量工作）：*You seem to have packed a lot into your life!* 你生活中好像有做不完的事情！ **2** to put a lot of things or people into a limited space 在（有限空间里）塞进（大量的人或物）；塞满 SYN **cram**: *They've managed to pack a lot of information into a very small book.* 他们在一本很小的书中囊括了大量的信息。 **ˌpack 'into sth** to go somewhere in large numbers so that all available space is filled 使爆满 SYN **cram**: *Over 80 000 fans packed into the stadium to watch the final.* * 8 万多名球迷涌入了体育场观看决赛。 ➲ SEE ALSO PACK *v.* (5) **ˌpack sb↔'off** (**to…**) (*informal*) to send sb somewhere, especially because you do not want them with you 把…打发走：*My parents always packed me off to bed early.* 我父母总是早早就打发我上床。 **ˌpack sth↔'out** (of shows, performers, etc. 表演、演员等) to attract enough people to completely fill a theatre, etc. 吸引（足够的观众）；使…满座：*The band can still pack out concert halls.* 这支乐队仍能使音乐厅爆满。 ➲ SEE ALSO PACKED OUT **ˌpack 'up** (*informal*, *especially BrE*) (of a machine 机器) to stop working 停止工作；坏了：*The TV's packed up again.* 电视机又坏了。 **ˌpack 'up** | **ˌpack sth↔'up** **1** to put your possessions into a bag, etc. before leaving a place 打行李；收拾行装：*Are you packing up already? It's only 4 o'clock.* 你已经开始打点行李了？现在才刚刚 4 点钟。◇ *We arrived just as the musicians were packing up their instruments.* 我们到场时乐队已开始收拾乐器了。 **2** (*BrE*, *informal*) to stop doing sth, especially a job 停止；放弃；辞掉 SYN **give up**: *What made you pack up a good job like that?* 什么原因使你辞去了那么好的工作？ ➲ SEE ALSO PACK *v.* (2)

■ *noun*

• **CONTAINER** 容器 **1** [C] (*especially NAmE*) a container, usually made of paper, that holds a number of the same thing or an amount of sth, ready to be sold （商品的）纸包，纸袋，纸盒：*a pack of cigarettes/gum* 一盒香烟 / 口香糖 ◇ *You can buy the envelopes in packs of ten.* 你可以整沓地买信封，每沓十个。 ➲ VISUAL VOCAB PAGE V36 ➲ COMPARE PACKAGE *n.* (1), PACKET (1) ➲ SEE ALSO FLAT-PACK, SIX-PACK

• **SET** 套 **2** [C] a set of different things that are supplied together for a particular purpose 全套东西：*Send for your free information pack today.* 今天就来信索取免费资讯包。

• **THINGS TIED FOR CARRYING** 成捆携带的东西 **3** [C] a number of things that are wrapped or tied together, especially for carrying 一捆，一包（尤指适于携带的东西）：*donkeys carrying packs of wool* 驮着成捆羊毛的驴 ◇ (*figurative*) *Everything she told us is a **pack of lies*** (= a story that is completely false). 她对我们说的全是一派谎言。

• **LARGE BAG** 大包 **4** [C] a large bag that you carry on your back 大背包：*We passed a group of walkers, carrying huge packs.* 我们与一批背着超大行囊的步行者擦肩而过。 ➲ SEE ALSO BACKPACK *n.*, FANNY PACK

• **OF ANIMALS** 动物 **5** [C+sing./pl. v.] a group of animals that hunt together or are kept for hunting 一群（动物或猎狗）：*packs of savage dogs* 成群的野狗 ◇ *wolves hunting in packs* 成群猎食的狼 ◇ *a pack of hounds* 一群猎犬 ➲ WORDFINDER NOTE AT HUNT

• **OF PEOPLE** 人 **6** [C+sing./pl. v.] a group of similar people or things, especially one that you do not like or approve of 群；帮；团伙：*We avoided a pack of journalists waiting outside.* 我们避开了等在门外的一群记者。◇ *He's the leader of the pack.* 他是那个团伙的头目。 **7** [C+sing./pl. v.] all the people who are behind the leaders in a race, competition, etc. （统称）竞赛中的落后者：*measures aimed at keeping the company ahead of the pack* 旨在使公司领先所有竞争对手的措施

P

• **OF CARDS** 纸牌 **8** (*especially BrE*) (*also* **deck** *NAmE, BrE*) [C] a complete set of 52 PLAYING CARDS 一副（为 52 张）: *a pack of cards* 一副纸牌 ➲VISUAL VOCAB PAGE V41

• **OF CUBS/BROWNIES** 男 / 女幼童军 **9** [C+sing./pl. v.] an organized group of CUBS/CUB SCOUTS or BROWNIES 一队（男或女幼童军）: *to join a Brownie pack* 加入一队幼女童军

• **FOR WOUND** 用于伤口 **10** [C] a hot or cold piece of soft material that absorbs liquid, used for treating a wound （治创伤用的）裹布，填塞物，敷料 ➲SEE ALSO FACE PACK, ICE PACK, MUD PACK IDM ➲SEE JOKER

pack·age /ˈpækɪdʒ/ *noun, verb*

■*noun* **1** (*especially NAmE*) = PARCEL (1): *A large package has arrived for you.* 你有一个大包裹来了。 ➲ COMPARE PACK *n.* (1) **2** (*NAmE*) a box, bag, etc. in which things are wrapped or packed; the contents of a box, etc. 包；盒；袋；包装好的东西: *Check the list of ingredients on the side of the package.* 检查一下包装盒侧面的成分清单。◇ *a package of hamburger buns* 一袋做汉堡包用的圆面包 ➲ VISUAL VOCAB PAGE V36 ➲ COMPARE PACKET (1) **3** (*also* **ˈpackage deal**) a set of items or ideas that must be bought or accepted together （必须整体接收的）一套东西，一套建议；一揽子交易: *a benefits package* 一套福利措施 ◇ *an aid package* 综合援助计划 ◇ *a package of measures to help small businesses* 扶助小企业的整套措施 **4** (*also* **ˈsoftware package**) (*computing* 计) a set of related programs for a particular type of task, sold and used as a single unit 软件包: *The system came with a database software package.* 本系统配有数据库软件包。

■*verb* [often passive] **1** to put sth into a box, bag, etc. to be sold or transported 将…包装好: **~ sth** *packaged food/goods* 包装好的食品 / 商品 ◇ *We package our products in recyclable materials.* 我们用可回收的材料包装我们的产品。◇ **~ sth up** *The orders were already packaged up, ready to be sent.* 订货已包装好待运。 **2 ~ sb/sth (as sth)** to present sb/sth in a particular way 包装成；使改头换面；把…装扮为: *an attempt to package news as entertainment* 把新闻包装成娱乐形式的尝试

ˈpackage store *noun* (*US*) = LIQUOR STORE

ˈpackage tour (*BrE also* **ˈpackage holiday**) *noun* a holiday/vacation that is organized by a company at a fixed price and that includes the cost of travel, hotels, etc. 包价旅游（费用固定、一切由旅行社代办的度假旅游） ➲WORDFINDER NOTE AT HOLIDAY

pack·aging /ˈpækɪdʒɪŋ/ *noun* [U] **1** materials used to wrap or protect goods that are sold in shops/stores 包装材料；外包装: *Attractive packaging can help to sell products.* 精美的包装有助于产品的销售。 ➲ VISUAL VOCAB PAGE V36 **2** the process of wrapping goods 包装工作；包装: *His company offers a flexible packaging service for the food industry.* 他的公司为食品工业提供灵活的包装业务。

ˈpack animal *noun* an animal used for carrying loads, for example a horse 驮畜；役畜

packed /pækt/ *adj.* **1** extremely full of people 异常拥挤的；挤满人的 SYN **crowded**: *The restaurant was packed.* 餐馆里坐满了客人。◇ *The show played to* ***packed houses*** (= large audiences). 演出场场爆满。 **2** containing a lot of a particular thing 有大量…的；…极多的: **~ with sth** *The book is packed with information.* 这本书资料丰富。◇ **-packed** *an information-packed book* 一本资料丰富的书 **3 tightly ~** pressed closely together 紧密压在一起的: *The birds' nests are lined with tightly packed leaves.* 鸟巢有一层压得密密实实的树叶。 **4** [not before noun] (*informal*) having put everything you need into cases, boxes, etc. before you go somewhere 收拾好行李: *I'm all packed and ready to go.* 我已打点好行装，准备出发了。

ˌpacked ˈlunch *noun* (*BrE*) a meal of SANDWICHES, fruit, etc. that is prepared at home and eaten at school, work, etc. 自备的午餐 ➲COMPARE BAG LUNCH, BOX LUNCH

ˌpacked ˈout *adj.* [not before noun] (*informal, especially BrE*) completely full of people or things 爆满；挤满人（或物）: *Opera houses are packed out wherever she sings.* 她演唱所到的歌剧院都是场场爆满。

pack·er /ˈpækə(r)/ *noun* a person, machine or company that puts food, goods, etc. into containers to be sold or sent to sb 包装工；包装机；包装公司

packet /ˈpækɪt/ *noun* **1** (*BrE*) a small paper or cardboard container in which goods are packed for selling （商品的）小包装纸袋，小硬纸板盒: *a packet of biscuits/cigarettes/crisps* 一包饼干 / 香烟 / 炸薯片 ➲VISUAL VOCAB PAGE V36 ➲ COMPARE PACK *n.* (1), PACKAGE *n.* (2) ➲ SEE ALSO PAY PACKET **2** a small object wrapped in paper or put into a thick envelope so that it can be sent by mail, carried easily or given as a present （邮政）小件包裹: *A packet of photographs arrived with the mail.* 一包照片邮寄来了。 **3** (*NAmE*) (*BrE* **sa·chet**) a closed plastic or paper package that contains a very small amount of liquid or a powder （塑料或纸质）密封小袋: *a packet of instant cocoa mix* 一袋混合速溶可可粉 ➲ VISUAL VOCAB PAGE V36 **4** [sing.] (*BrE, informal*) a large amount of money 一笔巨款: *That car must have cost a packet.* 买那辆汽车一定花了一大笔钱。 **5** (*computing* 计) a piece of information that forms part of a message sent through a computer network 信息包；数据包 **6** (*NAmE*) a set of documents that are supplied together for a particular purpose 一套文件；一套资料: *a training packet* 一套培训材料

ˈpacket switching *noun* [U] (*computing* 计) a process in which data is separated into parts before being sent, and then joined together after it arrives 包交换，分组交换（将数据分组发送后再连接）

pack·horse /ˈpækhɔːs; *NAmE* -hɔːrs/ *noun* a horse that is used to carry heavy loads 驮马

ˈpack ice *noun* [U] a large mass of ice floating in the sea, formed from smaller pieces that have frozen together 聚集的浮冰；大块的浮冰

pack·ing /ˈpækɪŋ/ *noun* [U] **1** the act of putting your possessions, clothes, etc. into bags or boxes in order to take or send them somewhere 打行李；收拾行囊: *Have you finished your packing?* 你收拾好行李了吗？ **2** material used for wrapping around delicate objects in order to protect them, especially before sending them somewhere 包装材料: (*BrE*) *The price includes* ***postage and packing.*** 本价格包括邮资和包装费。

ˈpacking case *noun* (*BrE*) a large strong box for packing or transporting goods in 包装箱；装货箱

ˈpack rat *noun* **1** (*NAmE*) a person who collects and stores things that they do not really need 驮鼠（指爱收藏杂物的人） **2** a small N American animal like a mouse that collects small sticks, etc. in its hole 驮鼠；林鼠

pact /pækt/ *noun* **~ (between A and B) | ~ (with sb) (to do sth)** a formal agreement between two or more people, groups or countries, especially one in which they agree to help each other 条约；协议；公约: *a non-aggression pact* 互不侵犯条约 ◇ *They have* ***made a pact*** *with each other not to speak about their differences in public.* 他们彼此达成协议，不公开谈论他们的歧见。◇ *a* ***suicide pact*** (= an agreement by two or more people to kill themselves at the same time) 自杀协议（两人或多人约定同时自杀）

pacy (*also* **pacey**) /ˈpeɪsi/ *adj.* (*BrE, informal*) **1** (of a book, film/movie, etc. 书、电影等) having a story that develops quickly 快节奏的；剧情发展快的 **2** able to run quickly （奔跑）速度快的；能跑快的 SYN **fast**: *a pacy winger who can also score goals* 能射门得分的快速边锋

pad /pæd/ *noun, verb*

■*noun*

• **OF SOFT MATERIAL** 软材料 **1** a thick piece of soft material that is used, for example, for absorbing liquid, cleaning or protecting sth （吸收液体、保洁或保护用的）软垫，护垫，垫状物: *medicated cleansing pads for sensitive skin* 敏感皮肤药物清洗棉 ◇ *sanitary pads* (= that a woman uses during her PERIOD) 卫生棉垫 ➲SEE ALSO SHOULDER PAD

• **OF PAPER** 纸张 **2** a number of pieces of paper for writing or drawing on, that are fastened together at one edge 便笺本；拍纸簿：*a* ***sketch/writing pad*** 速写簿；拍纸簿 ➲ SEE ALSO NOTEPAD, SCRATCH PAD
• **OF ANIMAL'S FOOT** 动物的足 **3** the soft part under the foot of a cat, dog, etc. 爪垫；肉掌
• **FOR CLEANING** 用于清洗 **4** a small piece of rough material used for cleaning pans, surfaces, etc. 百洁布，菜瓜布（刷锅等的小块粗糙材料）：*a scouring pad* 刷洗用的金属丝球
• **FOR SPACECRAFT/HELICOPTER** 航天器；直升机 **5** a flat surface where a SPACECRAFT or a HELICOPTER takes off and lands 发射台；停机坪 ➲ SEE ALSO HELIPAD, LAUNCH PAD
• **FOR PROTECTION** 用于防护 **6** [usually pl.] a piece of thick material that you wear in some sports, for example football and CRICKET, to protect your legs, elbows, etc.（运动用）防护垫（如护腿、护肘等）➲ VISUAL VOCAB PAGE V48
• **OF WATER PLANTS** 水生植物 **7** the large flat leaf of some water plants, especially the WATER LILY 浮叶（尤见于睡莲）：*floating lily pads* 睡莲的浮叶
• **FLAT/APARTMENT** 公寓 **8** [usually sing.] (*old-fashioned, informal*) the place where sb lives, especially a flat/apartment 住所；（尤指）公寓 ➲ SEE ALSO INK PAD, KEYPAD

■ ***verb*** (**-dd-**)
• **ADD SOFT MATERIAL** 添加软材料 **1** [T, often passive] **~ sth (with sth)** to put a layer of soft material in or on sth in order to protect it, make it thicker or change its shape（用软材料）填充，覆盖，保护：*All the sharp corners were padded with foam.* 所有的棱角都垫上了泡沫塑料。◇ *a padded jacket* 有夹层的外套 ◇ *a* ***padded envelope*** (= for sending delicate objects) 有垫料层的封套
• **WALK QUIETLY** 轻步行走 **2** [I] **+ adv./prep.** to walk with quiet steps 蹑手蹑脚地走：*She padded across the room to the window.* 她蹑手蹑脚地穿过屋子走到窗前。
• **BILLS** 账单 **3** [T] **~ sth** (*NAmE*) to dishonestly add items to bills to obtain more money 虚报（账目）；做黑账：*to* ***pad bills/expense accounts*** 在账单上 / 开支账上做手脚 ➲ MORE LIKE THIS 36, page R29

PHR V **,pad sth↔'out 1** to put soft material into a piece of clothing in order to change its shape 给（衣服）加衬垫 **2** to make sth such as an article, seem longer or more impressive by adding things that are unnecessary（用多余的话）延长（文章等）；充篇幅：*The report was padded out with extracts from previous documents.* 该报告摘抄过去的文件而加长了篇幅。

,padded 'cell *noun* a room in a hospital for mentally ill people, with soft walls to prevent violent patients from injuring themselves（精神病院的）软壁病房

pad·ding /ˈpædɪŋ/ *noun* [U] **1** soft material that is placed inside sth to make it more comfortable or to change its shape 衬料；衬垫 **2** words that are used to make a speech, piece of writing, etc. longer, but that do not contain any interesting information 赘语；废话；凑篇幅的文字

pad·dle /ˈpædl/ *noun, verb*
■ ***noun*** **1** [C] a short pole with a flat wide part at one or both ends, that you hold in both hands and use for moving a small boat, especially a CANOE, through water 桨；船桨 ➲ VISUAL VOCAB PAGE V60 ➲ COMPARE OAR **2** [C] a tool or part of a machine shaped like a paddle, especially one used for mixing food（机具的）桨状部分；（尤指）食物搅拌器的桨叶 **3 a paddle** [sing.] (*BrE*) an act or period of walking in shallow water with no shoes or socks 蹚水；赤脚涉水：*Let's go for a paddle.* 咱们去玩水吧。➲ SEE ALSO DOG-PADDLE **4** [C] (*NAmE*) a BAT used for playing TABLE TENNIS 乒乓球拍 **5** [C] (*NAmE*) a piece of wood with a handle, used for hitting children as a punishment 戒尺（体罚儿童的工具）IDM SEE CREEK
■ ***verb*** **1** [I, T] to move a small boat through water using a paddle 用桨划船：**(+ adv./prep.)** *We paddled downstream for about a mile.* 我们划船顺流而下约一英里。◇ **~ sth (+ adv./prep.)** *We paddled the canoe along the coast.* 我们划着独木舟沿海岸而行。**2** (*BrE*) (*NAmE* **wade**) [I] to walk or stand with no shoes or socks in shallow water in the sea, a lake, etc. 蹚水；赤足涉水：*The children have gone paddling.* 孩子们戏水去了。**3** [I] to swim with short movements of your hands or feet up and down 狗爬式游泳 ➲ WORDFINDER NOTE AT SWIM **4** [T] **~ sb/sth** (*NAmE*) to hit a child with a flat piece of wood as a punishment 用戒尺打（孩子）

paddle·board·ing /ˈpædlbɔːdɪŋ; *NAmE* -bɔːrd-/ *noun* [U] the sport of moving on the water while lying, KNEELING or standing on a board, using your arms or a PADDLE (1) to move yourself along 冲浪舟运动（在冲浪板上或卧、或跪坐、或站立，用双手或桨划水前进）▸ **paddle·board** *noun*

'paddle steamer (*BrE*) (*also* **paddle·boat** *NAmE, BrE*) *noun* an old-fashioned type of boat driven by steam and moved forward by a large wheel or wheels at the side 桨轮蒸汽船；明轮船 ➲ VISUAL VOCAB PAGE V59

'paddling pool (*BrE*) (*NAmE* **'wading pool**) *noun* a shallow swimming pool for children to play in, especially a small plastic one that you fill with water（尤指小型的塑料）浅水池，戏水池

pad·dock /ˈpædək/ *noun* **1** a small field in which horses are kept（牧马的）小围场 ➲ WORDFINDER NOTE AT HORSE **2** (in horse racing or motor racing 赛马或赛车) an area where horses or cars are taken before a race and shown to the public 检阅场 **3** (*AustralE, NZE*) any field or area of land that has fences around it 设有围栏的一片土地

Paddy /ˈpædi/ *noun* (*pl.* **-ies**) (*informal*) an offensive word for a person from Ireland 帕迪（对爱尔兰人的蔑称）

paddy /ˈpædi/ *noun* (*pl.* **-ies**) **1** (*also* **'paddy field**) a field in which rice is grown 稻田；水田：*a rice paddy* 水稻田 **2** [usually sing.] (*BrE, informal*) a state of being angry or in a bad mood 发火；发怒 SYN **temper**: *The news put him in a bit of a paddy.* 这消息让他肝火上升。

'paddy wagon *noun* (*informal, NAmE*) = PATROL WAGON

pad·kos /ˈpʌtkɒs; *NAmE* -kɑːs/ *noun* [U] (*SAfrE*) food that you take with you to eat while on a journey 旅行食物；干粮

padlock 挂锁

pad·lock /ˈpædlɒk; *NAmE* -lɑːk/ *noun, verb*
■ ***noun*** a type of lock that is used to fasten two things together or to fasten one thing to another. Padlocks are used with chains on gates, etc. 挂锁
■ ***verb*** to lock sth with a padlock 用挂锁锁住：**~ sth to sth** *She always padlocked her bike to the railings.* 她总是用挂锁把自行车锁在栏杆上。◇ **~ sth** *The doors were padlocked.* 门都用挂锁锁着。

padre /ˈpɑːdreɪ/ *noun* (often used as a form of address 常用于称谓) a priest, or other Christian minister, especially in the armed forces 牧师；神父；（尤指）随军牧师 ➲ COMPARE CHAPLAIN

paean /ˈpiːən/ *noun* (*literary*) a song of praise or victory 赞歌；凯歌

P

paed- (BrE) (NAmE **ped-**) /piːd/ *combining form* (in nouns and adjectives 构成名词和形容词) connected with children 与儿童有关的；儿童的：*paediatrician* 儿科医生

paed·er·ast, **paed·er·asty** *noun* (BrE) = PEDERAST, PEDERASTY

paedi·at·ri·cian (BrE) (NAmE **pedi·at·ri·cian**) /ˌpiːdiəˈtrɪʃn/ *noun* a doctor who studies and treats the diseases of children 儿科医生；儿科学家 ➲ WORDFINDER NOTE AT SPECIALIST

paedi·at·rics (BrE) (NAmE **pedi·at·rics**) /ˌpiːdiˈætrɪks/ *noun* [U] the branch of medicine concerned with children and their diseases 儿科学 ▶ **paedi·at·ric** (BrE) (NAmE **pedi-**) *adj.* [only before noun]：*paediatric surgery* 小儿外科

paedo·phile (BrE) (NAmE **pedo-**) /ˈpiːdəʊfaɪl; NAmE -doʊ-/ *noun* a person who is sexually attracted to children 恋童癖者

paedo·philia (BrE) (NAmE **pedo-**) /ˌpiːdəˈfɪliə/ *noun* [U] the condition of being sexually attracted to children; sexual activity with children 恋童癖；与儿童的性行为

pa·ella /paɪˈelə/ *noun* [U, C] a Spanish dish of rice, chicken, fish and vegetables, cooked and served in a large shallow pan 西班牙炖饭（用大米、鸡肉、鱼肉和蔬菜以平底锅烹制而成）

pagan /ˈpeɪɡən/ *noun* (*often disapproving*) **1** a person who holds religious beliefs that are not part of any of the world's main religions 异教徒（信奉非主流宗教者） **2** used in the past by Christians to describe a person who did not believe in Christianity 教外人（旧时的基督徒用以指非基督徒） ▶ **pagan** *adj.*：*a pagan festival* 异教节日 **pa·gan·ism** /ˈpeɪɡənɪzəm/ *noun* [U]

P

page 🔑 /peɪdʒ/ *noun, verb*

■ ***noun*** **1** 🔑 (*abbr.* **p**) one side or both sides of a sheet of paper in a book, magazine, etc.（书刊或纸张的）页，面，张，版：*Turn to page 64.* 翻到第 64 页。◇ *Someone has torn a page out of this book.* 有人从这本书里撕掉了一张。◇ ***a blank/new page*** 空白页；新的一页 ◇ ***the sports/financial pages** of the newspaper* 报纸的体育 / 财经版 ◇ *on the **opposite/facing page*** 在对面的一页上 ◇ ***over the page*** (= on the next page) 在下一页 ➲ SEE ALSO FRONT PAGE, FULL-PAGE, YELLOW PAGES™ **2** 🔑 a section of data or information that can be shown on a computer screen at any one time（计算机的）页面，版面 ➲ SEE ALSO HOME PAGE **3** (*literary*) an important event or period of history 历史篇章，历史篇页（指历史大事或时期）：*a glorious page of Arab history* 阿拉伯历史上光辉的篇章 **4** (*especially NAmE*) = PAGEBOY (1) **5** (*NAmE*) a student who works as an assistant to a member of the US Congress（美国议员的）青年助理（本身为学生） **6** (in the Middle Ages 中世纪) a boy or young man who worked for a KNIGHT while training to be a knight himself 学习骑士（接受训练期间做侍从，可晋升骑士）

IDM **on the same ˈpage** if two or more people or groups are **on the same page**, they agree about what they are trying to achieve 目标一致；就目标达成共识 **turn the ˈpage** to begin doing things in a different way and thinking in a more positive way after a period of difficulties（经过困难后）翻开新的一页，开始新的生活 ➲ MORE AT PRINT *v.*

■ ***verb*** **1** ~ **sb** to call sb's name over a PUBLIC ADDRESS SYSTEM in order to find them and give them a message（在公共传呼系统上）呼叫：*Why don't you have him paged at the airport?* 你为何不在机场扩音喇叭上呼叫他呢？ **2** ~ **sb** to contact sb by sending a message to their PAGER 用传呼机传呼（某人）：*Page Dr Green immediately.* 立即传呼格林医生。

PHR V **ˌpage ˈthrough sth** (*NAmE*) to quickly turn the pages of a book, magazine, etc. and look at them without reading them carefully or in detail 随意翻阅；浏览 SYN **flick through sth, leaf through sth**

pa·geant /ˈpædʒənt/ *noun* **1** a public entertainment in which people dress in historical COSTUMES and give performances of scenes from history 穿古代服装的游行；再现历史场景的娱乐活动 **2** (*NAmE*) a competition for young women in which their beauty, personal qualities and skills are judged 选美比赛：*a beauty pageant* 选美比赛 ➲ COMPARE BEAUTY CONTEST (1) **3** ~ **(of sth)** (*literary*) something that is considered as a series of interesting and different events 内容繁杂有趣的场面；盛大华丽的情景：*life's rich pageant* 丰富的人生画卷

pa·geant·ry /ˈpædʒəntri/ *noun* [U] impressive and exciting events and ceremonies involving a lot of people wearing special clothes 壮观的场面；隆重的仪式；盛典：*the pageantry of royal occasions* 王室庆典的盛况

page·boy /ˈpeɪdʒbɔɪ/ *noun* **1** (*also* **page** *especially in NAmE*) a small boy who helps or follows a BRIDE during a marriage ceremony 新娘的伴童；小男傧相 ➲ COMPARE BRIDESMAID **2** (*also* **page**) (*old-fashioned*) a boy or young man, usually in uniform, employed in a hotel to open doors, deliver messages for people, etc.（旅馆的）行李员，门童 **3** a HAIRSTYLE for women in which the hair is shoulder-length and turned under at the ends 女子齐肩内鬈发；扣边女式发型

pager /ˈpeɪdʒə(r)/ *noun* a small electronic device that you carry around with you and that shows a message or lets you know when sb is trying to contact you, for example by making a sound 寻呼机；传呼机；BP 机 ➲ SEE ALSO BEEPER, BLEEPER

ˌpage-ˈthree girl *noun* (BrE) a naked or partly naked young woman whose picture is printed in a newspaper 三版女郎（报纸上裸体或半裸体年轻女子） ORIGIN From page three of the *Sun* newspaper, where one of these pictures is or was printed every day. 源自《太阳报》第三版，每日印有裸女或半裸女照片。

ˈpage-turner *noun* (*informal*) a book that is very exciting 令人欲罢不能的书；扣人心弦的读物

ˈpage view *noun* one visit to a single page on a website（一次）网页浏览：*a surge in page views* 网页浏览量的激增

pa·gin·ate /ˈpædʒɪneɪt/ *verb* ~ **sth** (*specialist*) to give a number to each page of a book, piece of writing, etc. 给（书等）标页码，编页码

pa·gin·ation /ˌpædʒɪˈneɪʃn/ *noun* [U] (*specialist*) the process of giving a page number to each page of a book; the page numbers given 标页码；编页码；页码

pa·goda /pəˈɡəʊdə; NAmE -ˈɡoʊ-/ *noun* a TEMPLE (= religious building) in S or E Asia in the form of a tall tower with several levels, each of which has its own roof that extends beyond the walls（南亚或东亚的）佛塔 ➲ VISUAL VOCAB PAGE V15

pah /pɑː/ *exclamation* used to represent the sound that people make when they disagree with sth or disapprove of sth strongly（表示强烈不满或不同意）哼！ ➲ MORE LIKE THIS 2, page R25

paid /peɪd/ *adj.* [usually before noun] **1** (of work, etc. 工作等) for which people receive money 有偿的；付费的：*Neither of them is currently in paid employment.* 他们俩目前都没有挣钱的差事。◇ *a well-paid job* 报酬不菲的工作 OPP **unpaid** **2** (of a person 人) receiving money for doing work 有报酬的；有薪金的：*Men still outnumber women in the paid workforce.* 在上班挣钱的人口中，男性仍然多于女性。◇ *a poorly paid teacher* 收入微薄的教师 OPP **unpaid** ➲ SEE ALSO PAY *v.*

IDM **put ˈpaid to sth** (*informal*) to stop or destroy sth, especially what sb plans or wants to do 使终止；使（希望等）破灭

ˈpaid-up *adj.* [only before noun] **1** having paid all the money necessary to be a member of a club or an organization 已付清会费的；已缴款的：*a fully paid-up member* 会费完全付清的会员 **2** (*BrE, informal*) strongly supporting sb/sth 坚决支持的；付出全部心力的：*a fully paid-up environmental campaigner* 全力投入的环保运动者

pail /peɪl/, **pail·ful** /ˈpeɪlfʊl/ *noun* (*NAmE* or *old-fashioned*) = BUCKET (1), (3)

pain /peɪn/ *noun, verb*

■ ***noun*** SEE ALSO PAINS **1** [U, C] the feelings that you have in your body when you have been hurt or when you are ill/sick （身体上的）疼痛：*a cry of pain* 痛苦的喊叫 ◇ *She was clearly **in a lot of pain**.* 她显然疼痛万分。◇ *He felt a sharp pain in his knee.* 他感到膝盖一阵剧痛。◇ *patients suffering from acute back pain* 患剧烈背痛的病人 ◇ ***stomach/chest pains*** 胃痛；胸痛 ◇ *You get more **aches and pains** as you get older.* 年纪越大，病痛就越多。◇ *The booklet contains information on **pain relief** during labour.* 这本小册子介绍了减轻分娩疼痛的知识。◇ *This cream should help to **relieve the pain**.* 这种药膏应有助于止痛。SEE ALSO GROWING PAINS (1) WORDFINDER NOTE AT HEALTH **2** [U, C] mental or emotional suffering 痛苦；苦恼；烦恼：*the pain of separation* 离别的痛苦 ◇ *I never meant to cause her pain.* 我从没有让她痛苦之意。◇ *the **pleasures and pains** of growing old* 变老的苦与乐 **3** [C] (*informal*) a person or thing that is very annoying 讨厌的人（或事）；令人头痛的人（或事）：*She can be a real pain when she's in a bad mood.* 她脾气不好时，真是令人头痛。◇ ***It's a pain** having to go all that way for just one meeting.* 就为了见一面，要跑那么远的路，真烦死人了。

IDM **no ˌpain, no ˈgain** (*saying*) used to say that you need to suffer if you want to achieve sth 不劳则无获 **on/under pain of sth** (*formal*) with the threat of having sth done to you as a punishment if you do not obey 违则受到某种惩罚；违则以…论处：*They were required to cut pollution levels, on pain of a £10 000 fine if they disobeyed.* 他们被要求降低污染水平，违则罚款 1 万英镑。 **a pain in the ˈneck** (*BrE also* **a pain in the ˈarse/ˈbackside**) (*NAmE also* **a pain in the ˈass/ˈbutt**) (*informal*) a person or thing that is very annoying 极讨厌的人（或事物）

■ ***verb*** (not used in the progressive tenses 不用于进行时) (*formal*) to cause sb pain or make them unhappy 使痛苦；使苦恼 SYN **hurt**: **~ sb** *She was deeply pained by the accusation.* 这一指控使她极为痛苦。◇ (*old use*) *The wound still pained him occasionally.* 他还是感到伤口不时疼痛。◇ **it pains sb to do sth** *It pains me to see you like this.* 看到你这副模样真令我难过。◇ **it pains sb that…** *It pained him that she would not acknowledge him.* 让他难过的是，她不愿意理睬他。

ˈpain barrier *noun* [usually sing.] the moment at which sb doing hard physical activity feels the greatest pain, after which the pain becomes less 痛苦极限，痛障（艰苦体力活动的最痛苦时刻，此后疼痛会减轻）：*He broke through the pain barrier at 25 kilometres and went on to win his first marathon.* 他克服了 25 公里时的痛苦极限，进而赢得了他的第一个马拉松冠军。

pained /peɪnd/ *adj.* showing that sb is feeling annoyed or upset 显出痛苦（或难过、苦恼）的：*a **pained expression/voice*** 痛苦的表情 / 声音

pain·ful /ˈpeɪnfl/ *adj.* **1** causing you pain 令人疼痛的：*Is your back still painful?* 你的背还疼吗？◇ *a painful death* 痛苦的死亡 ◇ *My ankle is still too painful to walk on.* 我的脚腕子还是疼得不能走路。 **2** **~ (for sb) (to do sth) | ~ (doing sth)** causing you to feel upset or embarrassed 令人痛苦（或难过、难堪）的：*a **painful experience/memory*** 痛苦的经历 / 回忆 ◇ *Their efforts were painful to watch.* 看着他们辛劳真是令人心痛。 **3** unpleasant or difficult to do 不愉快的；困难的；艰难的 SYN **trying**: *Applying for jobs can be a long and painful process.* 求职会是一个漫长而又艰难的历程。

pain·ful·ly /ˈpeɪnfəli/ *adv.* **1** extremely, and in a way that makes you feel annoyed, upset, etc. 非常地；令人痛苦地；令人烦恼地：*Their son was **painfully** shy.* 他们的儿子非常害羞。◇ *The dog was **painfully** thin.* 那条狗瘦得可怜。◇ *He was **painfully aware** of his lack of experience.* 他痛苦地意识到自己缺乏经验。◇ *Progress has been **painfully** slow.* 进度慢得令人焦急。 **2** in a way that causes you physical or emotional pain 使人疼痛地；令人苦恼地：*He banged his knee painfully against the desk.* 他的膝盖撞到桌子上，疼得很。 **3** with a lot of effort and difficulty 吃力地；艰难地：*painfully acquired experience* 艰难获得的经验

pain·kill·er /ˈpeɪnkɪlə(r)/ *noun* a drug that reduces pain 止痛药：*She's on (= taking) painkillers.* 她在服止痛药。 ▸ **pain·kill·ing** *adj.* [only before noun]: ***painkilling drugs/injections*** 止痛药物 / 注射剂

pain·less /ˈpeɪnləs/ *adj.* **1** causing you no pain 无痛的：*a painless death* 无痛死亡 ◇ *The treatment is painless.* 这种治疗无疼痛。 **2** not unpleasant or difficult to do 愉快的；轻松的；不难的；不讨厌的：*The interview was relatively painless.* 此次面试相对轻松。 ▸ **pain·less·ly** *adv.*

pains /peɪnz/ *noun* [pl.]

IDM **be at pains to do sth** to put a lot of effort into doing sth correctly 下苦功；花大力气：*She was at great pains to stress the advantages of the new system.* 她极力强调新制度的优点。 **for your ˈpains** (*especially BrE, often ironic*) as payment, reward or thanks for sth you have done 作为回报；作为答谢：*I told her what I thought and got a mouthful of abuse for my pains!* 我跟她讲了我的想法，而得到的回报竟是破口大骂！ **take (great) pains (to do sth) | go to great pains (to do sth)** to put a lot of effort into doing sth 兢兢业业地做某事；费力地做某事：*The couple went to great pains to keep their plans secret.*

▼ **SYNONYMS** 同义词辨析

painful

sore • raw • inflamed • excruciating • burning • itchy

These words all describe sth that causes you physical pain. 以上各词均指使人肉体上疼痛的。

painful causing you physical pain 指使人肉体上疼痛的

NOTE **Painful** can describe a part of the body, illness, injury, treatment or death. * painful 可用于描述身体部位、疾病、受伤、治疗或死亡等：*Is your knee still painful?* 你的膝盖还疼吗？◇ *a series of painful injections* 一次又一次令人痛苦的注射 ◇ *a slow and painful death* 缓慢而痛苦的死亡

sore (of a part of the body) painful and often red, especially because of infection or because a muscle has been used too much 指（身体部位）发炎疼痛的、肌肉酸痛的：*a sore throat* 咽喉疼 ◇ *Their feet were sore after hours of walking.* 他们走了几小时的路，脚都走疼了。

raw (of a part of the body) red and painful, for example because of an infection or because the skin has been damaged 指（身体部位）红肿疼痛的、破损的、擦伤的：*The skin on her feet had been rubbed raw.* 她脚上的皮磨破了。

inflamed (of a part of the body) painful, red and hot because of an infection or injury 指（身体部位）发炎的、红肿的：*The wound had become inflamed.* 伤口发炎了。

excruciating extremely painful 指极痛苦的、极苦恼的

NOTE **Excruciating** can describe feelings, treatments or death but not parts of the body. * excruciating 可用于描述情感、治疗或死亡，而非身体部位：~~an excruciating throat/back/knee~~

burning painful and giving a feeling of being very hot 指火辣辣地痛的：*She felt a burning sensation in her throat.* 她感到咽喉火辣辣的疼。

itchy giving an uncomfortable feeling on your skin that makes you want to scratch; having this feeling 指发痒的：*an itchy rash* 发痒的皮疹 ◇ *I feel itchy all over.* 我觉得浑身发痒。

PATTERNS

- sore/inflamed/itchy **eyes**
- raw/inflamed/itchy **skin**
- a painful/an excruciating **death**
- a painful/burning **sensation**
- excruciating/burning **pain**

P

这对夫妇煞费苦心，对计划守口如瓶。 **take (great) pains with/over sth** to do sth very carefully 小心翼翼地做某事： *He always takes great pains with his lectures.* 他总是仔细用心地准备讲稿。

pains·tak·ing /ˈpeɪnzteɪkɪŋ/ *adj.* [usually before noun] needing a lot of care, effort and attention to detail 需细心的；辛苦的；需专注的 SYN **thorough**: *painstaking research* 细心的研究 ◇ *The event had been planned with painstaking attention to detail.* 这次活动的细节是经过精心计划的。 ▸ **pains·tak·ing·ly** *adv.*

paint /peɪnt/ *noun, verb*

■ *noun* **1** [U] a liquid that is put on surfaces to give them a particular colour; a layer of this liquid when it has dried on a surface 油漆；油漆涂层： *white paint* 白漆 ◇ ***gloss/matt/acrylic paint*** 亮光漆；亚光漆；树脂漆 ◇ *The woodwork has recently been given a fresh **coat of paint**.* 木建部分最近新刷了一层漆。 ◇ ***Wet paint!*** (= used as a sign) 油漆未干！ ◇ *The paint is starting to peel off.* 油漆开始起皮剥落了。 ➲ SEE ALSO GREASEPAINT, OIL PAINT, WARPAINT **2** **paints** [pl.] tubes or blocks of paint used for painting pictures 绘画颜料： *oil paints* 油画颜料

■ *verb* **1** [T, I] ~ **sth (with sth)** to cover a surface or object with paint 在…上刷油漆： ~ **(sth)** *We've had the house painted.* 我们已经把房子油漆过了。 ◇ *Paint the shed with weather-resistant paint.* 用抗风雨的油漆把棚子漆一漆。 ◇ *a brightly painted barge* 涂得很鲜艳的画舫 ◇ **~ sth + adj./noun** *The walls were painted yellow.* 墙壁漆成了黄色。 ➲ COLLOCATIONS AT DECORATE **2** [T, I] to make a picture or design using paints 用颜料画： **~ sth/sb** *to paint portraits* 画肖像 ◇ *A friend painted the children for me* (= painted a picture of the children). 一位朋友给我画了这张孩子们的画像。 ◇ **~ sth on sth** *Slogans had been painted on the walls.* 标语涂在墙上。 ◇ **~ (in sth)** *She paints in oils.* 她画油画。 ◇ *My mother paints well.* 我母亲很会画画。 ➲ COLLOCATIONS AT ART **3** [T] to give a particular impression of sb/sth 把…描绘成 SYN **portray**: **~ sb/sth as sth** *The article paints them as a bunch of petty criminals.* 文章把他们描绘成一伙小犯罪分子。 ◇ **~ sb/sth in...** *The documentary painted her in a bad light.* 纪录片的描绘对她很不利。 **4** [T] **~ sth** to put coloured make-up on your nails, lips, etc. 往（指甲、嘴唇等上）施化妆品；染（指甲）；涂（唇膏）

IDM **paint a (grim, gloomy, rosy, etc.) ˈpicture of sb/sth** to describe sb/sth in a particular way; to give a particular impression of sb/sth 给人以…印象；把…描绘成： *The report paints a vivid picture of life in the city.* 报告生动地描绘了都市生活。 ◇ *Journalists paint a grim picture of conditions in the camps.* 记者描绘了营里的恶劣状况。 **paint the town ˈred** (*informal*) to go to a lot of different bars, clubs, etc. and enjoy yourself 花天酒地地玩乐；出没于各娱乐场所 **paint sth with a ˌbroad ˈbrush** to describe sth in a general way, ignoring the details 大致地描述 ➲ MORE AT BLACK *adj.*

PHR V **ˌpaint sth↔ˈout** to cover part of a picture, sign, etc. with another layer of paint 用油漆等涂掉 **ˌpaint ˈover sth** to cover sth with a layer of paint 刷油漆覆盖： *We painted over the dirty marks on the wall.* 我们把墙上的脏印子用油漆盖上了。

paint·ball /ˈpeɪntbɔːl/ *noun* [U] a game in which people shoot balls of paint at each other 彩弹游戏

paint·box /ˈpeɪntbɒks; *NAmE* -bɑːks/ *noun* a box containing a set of paints 颜料盒

paint·brush /ˈpeɪntbrʌʃ/ *noun* a brush that is used for painting 画笔；漆刷 ➲ VISUAL VOCAB PAGE V21

ˌpaint-by-ˈnumbers *adj.* [only before noun] **1** (of pictures 图画) having sections with different numbers showing which colours should be used to fill them in 用数字标明填色区域的 **2** (*disapproving*) used to describe sth that is produced without using the imagination 缺乏想象力的；呆板的；刻板的： *He accused the government of relying on paint-by-numbers policies.* 他指责政府依赖一成不变的政策。

ˈpaint chip *noun* **1** a small piece of paint that has broken off sth or the small area where the paint has come off 剥落的油漆；油漆剥落处 **2** (*NAmE*) a strip of card with samples of paint in different colours, provided in shops/stores to help customers decide what paint to buy （供选购者用的）油漆色样条，油漆色卡

paint·er /ˈpeɪntə(r)/ *noun* **1** a person whose job is painting buildings, walls, etc. 油漆匠： *He works as a painter and decorator.* 他的职业是油漆匠和装潢匠。 **2** an artist who paints pictures 画家： *a famous painter* 著名画家 ◇ *a **portrait/landscape painter*** 肖像 / 风景画家 **3** a rope fastened to the front of a boat, used for tying it to a post, ship, etc. （系船的）缆绳

paint·er·ly /ˈpeɪntəli; *NAmE* -ərli/ *adj.* typical of artists or painting 有画家（或绘画）特征的 SYN **artistic**

paint·ing /ˈpeɪntɪŋ/ *noun* **1** [C] a picture that has been painted 绘画；油画： *a collection of paintings by American artists* 美国艺术家绘画作品集 ◇ *cave paintings* 洞窟里的壁画 ➲ SYNONYMS AT PICTURE ➲ COLLOCATIONS AT ART ➲ SEE ALSO OIL PAINTING

WORDFINDER 联想词： **art**, background, canvas, exhibition, foreground, frame, fresco, portrait, watercolour

2 [U] the act or art of using paint to produce pictures 作画；绘画： *Her hobbies include music and painting.* 她的爱好包括音乐和绘画。 ➲ VISUAL VOCAB PAGE V45 **3** [U] the act of putting paint onto the surface of objects, walls, etc. 涂漆；刷油漆： *painting and decorating* 油漆和装潢

ˈpaint stripper *noun* [U] a liquid used to remove old paint from surfaces 脱漆剂；除漆剂

paint·work /ˈpeɪntwɜːk; *NAmE* -wɜːrk/ *noun* [U] (*especially BrE*) the layer of paint on the surface of a door, wall, car, etc. 漆面；油漆层： *The paintwork is beginning to peel.* 漆面已经开始剥落了。

pair /peə(r); *NAmE* per/ *noun, verb*

■ ***noun***

• **TWO THINGS THE SAME** 相同的两样东西 **1** [C] two things of the same type, especially when they are used or worn together 一双；一对： *a **pair of gloves/shoes/earrings, etc.*** 一副手套、一双鞋、一对耳环等 ◇ *a huge pair of eyes* 一双大眼睛 ◇ *The vase is one of a **matching pair**.* 这只花瓶是一对中的一只。

• **TWO PARTS JOINED** 连接的两部分 **2** [C] an object consisting of two parts that are joined together 分两个相连接部分的物体： *a **pair of trousers/pants/jeans, etc.*** 一条长裤、裤子、牛仔裤等 ◇ *a **pair of glasses/binoculars/scissors, etc.*** 一副眼镜、一架双筒望远镜、一把剪刀等 HELP A plural verb is sometimes used with **pair** in the singular in senses 1 and 2. In informal *NAmE* some people use **pair** as a plural form. 在第 1 及第 2 义中，pair 有时以单数形式与复数动词搭配。在非正式的美式英语中，有些人把 pair 作为复数： *three pair of shoes* 三双鞋子 This is not considered correct in written English. 在书面语中，这种用法被认为不正确。

• **TWO PEOPLE** 两个人 **3** [C+sing./pl. v.] two people who are doing sth together or who have a particular relationship 两个共事（或有特殊关系）的人；俩；对： *Get pairs of students to act out the dialogue in front of the class.* 叫学生两人一组在课堂上演出这个对话。 ◇ *Get the students to do the exercise as **pair work*** (= two students work together). 让学生两人一组做练习。 ◇ (*informal*) *I've had enough of the pair of you!* 你们俩让我烦透了！ HELP In *BrE* a plural verb is usually used. 在英式英语中常用复数动词： *A pair of children were kicking a ball about.* 两个孩子在踢球。 ◇ *The pair are planning a trip to India together.* 这俩人计划一起去印度旅行。

• **TWO ANIMALS/BIRDS** 两个动物；两只鸟 **4** [C+sing./pl. v.] two animals or birds of the same type that are breeding together （同时驯养的）两个同类的鸟（或兽）；一对： *a breeding pair* 用于繁殖的一对 ◇ *a pair of swans* 一对天鹅

• **TWO HORSES** 两匹马 **5** [C] two horses working together to pull a CARRIAGE 一起拉车的两匹马： *a carriage and pair* 双驾马车 ➲ SEE ALSO AU PAIR

IDM **a pair of ˈhands** (*informal*) a person who can do, or is doing, a job 一个能做事的人；人手；正在工作的人： *We* *need an extra pair of hands if we're going to finish on time.* 要想按时完成，我们就要再增加一个人。◇ *Colleagues regard him as a **safe pair of hands*** (= sb who can be relied on to do a job well). 同事认为他办事可靠。 **in 'pairs** in groups of two objects or people 成对的；成双的： *Students worked in pairs on the project.* 学生两人一组做这个项目。 **I've only got one pair of 'hands** (*informal*) used to say that you are too busy to do anything else 我只有一双手 ➲ MORE AT SAFE *adj.*

■ ***verb***

• **MAKE GROUPS OF TWO** 配对 **1** [T, usually passive] to put people or things into groups of two 使成对；配对： **~ A with B** *Each blind student was paired with a sighted student.* 每个盲人学员都与一个视力正常的同学配对。◇ **~ A (and B) (together)** *All the shoes on the floor were neatly paired.* 地板上的鞋子都整齐成双地摆着。

• **OF ANIMALS/BIRDS** 兽；鸟 **2** [I] (*specialist*) to come together in order to breed 配对（以繁殖）；交配： *Many of the species pair for life.* 许多物种都终生配对。

PHR V ˌ**pair 'off (with sb)** | ˌ**pair sb↔off (with sb)** to come together, especially in order to have a romantic relationship; to bring two people together for this purpose （使）结对，配对： *It seemed that all her friends were pairing off.* 好像她的朋友全都成双结对了。◇ *He's always trying to pair me off with his cousin.* 他总想把我和他表弟配成一对。 ˌ**pair 'up (with sb)** | ˌ**pair sb↔up (with sb)** to come together or to bring two people together to work, play a game, etc. （使两人）结组工作（或游戏等）

pair·ing /ˈpeərɪŋ; *NAmE* ˈper-/ *noun* **1** [C] two people or things that work together or are placed together; the act of placing them together 结对的两个人（或物）；配对；搭配： *Tonight they take on a Chinese pairing in their bid to reach the final tomorrow.* 今晚他们将挑战一对中国选手，争取进入明天的决赛。 **2** [U] (in the British Parliament) the practice of an MP agreeing with an MP of a different party that neither of them will vote in a debate so that they do not need to attend the debate 配对，结对（英国议会中来自不同政党的两名议员约定放弃投票从而不必参加辩论进行表决）

paisa /ˈpaɪsɑː; -sə/ *noun* (*pl.* **paise** /-seɪ; -sə/) a coin of India, Pakistan and Nepal. There are one hundred paise in a RUPEE. 派士（印度、巴基斯坦和尼泊尔的硬币，100派士等于 1 卢比）

pais·ley /ˈpeɪzli/ *noun* [U] a detailed pattern of curved shapes that look like feathers, used especially on cloth 佩斯利（羽状）图案： *a paisley tie* 一条佩斯利花纹领带

Pai·ute /ˈpaɪuːt/ *noun* (*pl.* **Pai·ute** or **Pai·utes**) a member of a Native American people many of whom live in the south-western US 派尤特人（美洲土著，很多居于美国西南部）

pa·ja·mas (*NAmE*) (*BrE, CanE* **py·ja·mas**) /pəˈdʒɑːməz; *NAmE* -ˈdʒæm-/ *noun* [pl.] a loose jacket and pants/trousers worn in bed （一套）睡衣裤 ➲ VISUAL VOCAB PAGE V68

pak choi /ˌpæk ˈtʃɔɪ/ (*BrE*) (*NAmE* ˌ**bok 'choy**) *noun* [U] a type of CHINESE CABBAGE with long dark green leaves and thick white STEMS 白菜；小白菜

Pak·eha /ˈpɑːkɪhɑː/ *noun* (*NZE*) a white person from New Zealand (that is, not a Maori) 新西兰白种人

Paki /ˈpæki/ *noun* (*BrE, informal, taboo*) a very offensive word for a person from Pakistan, especially one living in Britain. The word is often also used for people from India or Bangladesh. 巴基斯坦佬（对巴基斯坦人，尤指在英国居住者的蔑称，也常用于印度人和孟加拉人）

pa·kora /pəˈkɔːrə/ *noun* a flat piece of spicy S Asian food consisting of meat or vegetables fried in BATTER （南亚）油炸辣肉菜片

PAL /pæl/ *noun* [U] a television broadcasting system that is used in most of Europe * PAL 制（欧洲大部分地区使用的电视广播系统） ➲ COMPARE NTSC

pal /pæl/ *noun, verb*

■ ***noun* 1** (*informal, becoming old-fashioned*) a friend 朋友；伙伴；哥们儿： *We've been pals for years.* 我们是多年的哥们儿了。 ➲ SEE ALSO PEN PAL **2** (*informal*) used to address a man in an unfriendly way （对男子的不友好的称呼）家伙，小子： *If I were you, pal, I'd stay away from her!* 我要是你呀，小子，我就离她远远的！ ▶ **pally** *adj.*： *I got very pally (= friendly) with him.* 我跟他的关系铁着呢。

■ ***verb*** (**-ll-**)

PHR V ˌ**pal a'round (with sb)** (*informal, especially NAmE*) to do things with sb as a friend （和某人）一起共事，结伙出没： *I palled around with him and his sister at school.* 我上学时常常与他和他姐姐在一起。 ˌ**pal 'up (with sb)** (*BrE*) (*NAmE* ˌ**buddy 'up (to/with sb)**) (*informal*) to become friendly with sb （和某人）成为朋友： *They palled up while they were at college.* 他们上大学时成了朋友。

pal·ace /ˈpæləs/ *noun* **1** [C] the official home of a king, queen, president, etc. 王宫；宫殿；总统府： *Buckingham Palace* 白金汉宫 ◇ *the royal/presidential palace* 王宫；总统府 ➲ VISUAL VOCAB PAGE V15 **2** (*often* **the Palace**) [sing.] the people who live in a palace, especially the British royal family 住在王宫里的人；（尤指英国的）王室： *The Palace last night refused to comment on the reports.* 昨晚王室拒绝对报道作出评论。◇ *a Palace spokesman* 王室发言人 ➲ MORE LIKE THIS 19, page R27 **3** [C] any large impressive house 豪华住宅；宫殿： *The Old Town has a whole collection of churches, palaces and mosques.* 旧城区汇集了许多教堂、大宅院和清真寺。 **4** [C] (*old-fashioned*) (sometimes used in the names of buildings 有时用于建筑物名称) a large public building, such as a hotel or cinema/movie theater 大的公共建筑（如旅馆、影剧院）： *the Strand Palace Hotel* 滨河王宫饭店

ˌ**palace 'coup** (*also* ˌ**palace revo'lution**) *noun* a situation in which a ruler or leader has their power taken away from them by sb within the same party, etc. 宫廷政变；宫廷革命

palaeo- (*especially BrE*) (*NAmE usually* **paleo-**) /ˈpæliəʊ; ˈpeɪl-; *NAmE* -ioʊ/ *combining form* (in nouns, adjectives and adverbs 构成名词、形容词和副词) connected with ancient times 古代的

palae·og·raphy (*BrE*) (*NAmE* **pale·og·raphy**) /ˌpæliˈɒɡrəfi; ˌpeɪl-; *NAmE* -ˈɑːɡ-/ *noun* [U] the study of ancient writing systems 古文字学 ▶ **palae·og·rapher** (*also* **pale·og·rapher**) /ˌpæliˈɒɡrəfə(r); ˌpeɪl-; *NAmE* -ˈɑːɡ-/ *noun*

Palaeo·lith·ic (*especially BrE*) (*NAmE usually* **Paleo-**) /ˌpæliəˈlɪθɪk; ˌpeɪl-/ *adj.* from or connected with the early part of the Stone Age 旧石器时代的

palae·on·tolo·gist (*especially BrE*) (*NAmE usually* **paleo-**) /ˌpæliɒnˈtɒlədʒɪst; ˌpeɪl-; *NAmE* ˌpeɪliɑːnˈtɑːl-/ *noun* a person who studies FOSSILS 古生物学家；化石学家

palae·on·tology (*especially BrE*) (*NAmE usually* **paleo-**) /ˌpæliɒnˈtɒlədʒi; ˌpeɪl-; *NAmE* ˌpeɪliɑːnˈtɑːl-/ *noun* [U] the study of FOSSILS (= the remains of animals or plants in rocks) as a guide to the history of life on earth 古生物学；化石学

pal·ais /ˈpæleɪ/ (*also* ˌ**palais de 'danse** /ˌpæleɪ də ˈdɑːns/) *noun* (*BrE*) (in the past) a large public building used for dancing; a dance hall （旧时的）舞场，舞厅

pal·at·able /ˈpælətəbl/ *adj.* **1** (of food or drink 食物或饮料) having a pleasant or acceptable taste 可口的；味美的 **2 ~ (to sb)** pleasant or acceptable to sb 宜人的；可意的；可接受的： *Some of the dialogue has been changed to make it more palatable to an American audience.* 有些对白有所修改以适应美国观众的口味。 **OPP** **unpalatable**

pal·atal /ˈpælətl/ *noun* (*phonetics* 语音) a speech sound made by placing the tongue against or near the hard PALATE of the mouth, for example /j/ at the beginning of *yes* 腭音 ▶ **pal·atal** *adj.*

pal·at·al·ize (*BrE also* **-ise**) /ˈpælətəlaɪz/ *verb* **~ sth** (*phonetics* 语音) to make a speech sound by putting your tongue against or near your hard PALATE 使（语音）腭

P

化 ▸ **pal·at·al·iza·tion, -isation** /ˌpælətəlaɪˈzeɪʃn; NAmE -ləˈz-/ *noun* [U]

pal·ate /ˈpælət/ *noun* **1** the top part of the inside of the mouth 腭；上腭： *the **hard/soft palate*** (= the hard/soft part at the front/back of the palate) 硬腭；软腭 ➲ SEE ALSO CLEFT PALATE **2** [usually sing.] the ability to recognize and/or enjoy good food and drink 味觉；品尝力： *a menu to tempt even the most **jaded palate*** 能引起最没胃口的人食欲的食谱

pa·la·tial /pəˈleɪʃl/ *adj.* [usually before noun] (of a room or building 房间或建筑物) very large and impressive, like a palace 宫殿般的；富丽堂皇的 **SYN splendid**

pa·lat·in·ate /pəˈlætɪnət/ *noun* **1** [C] the area ruled by a Count Palatine (= a ruler with the power of a king or queen) 巴拉丁领地（行使王权的巴拉丁伯爵的辖地） **2 the Palatinate** [sing.] the land of the German Empire that was ruled over by the Count Palatine of the Rhine 巴拉丁领地（莱恩的巴拉丁伯爵统辖的德意志帝国领地）

pal·at·ine /ˈpælətaɪn/ *adj.* [only before noun] **1** (of an official, etc. in the past 旧时官员等) having the power in a particular area that a king or queen usually has （在领地内）行使王权的 **2** (of an area of land 地域) ruled over by sb who has the power of a king or queen 归行使王权者统辖的；属于巴拉丁领地的

pa·la·ver /pəˈlɑːvə(r); NAmE also -ˈlæv-/ *noun* (*informal*) **1** [U, sing.] (*BrE*) a lot of unnecessary activity, excitement or trouble, especially caused by sth that is unimportant 麻烦；琐事；忙乱 **SYN fuss**: *What's all the palaver about?* 这些鸡毛蒜皮的事到底是为什么？ ◇ *What a palaver it is, trying to get a new visa!* 申请新签证真烦死人了！ **2** [U] (*NAmE*) talk that does not have any meaning; nonsense 空话；废话： *He's talking palaver.* 他在信口开河。

pa·lazzo pants /pəˈlætsəʊ pænts; NAmE pəˈlɑːtsoʊ/ *noun* [pl.] women's trousers/pants with wide loose legs 宽腿女裤

P

pale /peɪl/ *adj., verb, noun*

▪ ***adj.*** (**paler, pal·est**) **1** (of a person, their face, etc. 人、面孔等) having skin that is almost white; having skin that is whiter than usual because of illness, a strong emotion, etc. 灰白的；苍白的；白皙的： *a pale complexion* 惨白的面容 ◇ *pale with fear* 害怕得脸色苍白 ◇ *to **go/turn pale*** 变得苍白 ◇ *You look pale. Are you OK?* 你气色不好，没事吧？ ◇ *The ordeal left her looking **pale and drawn**.* 这场磨难使她看起来苍白而又憔悴。 **2** light in colour; containing a lot of white 浅色的；淡色的： *pale blue eyes* 淡蓝色的眼睛 ◇ *a paler shade of green* 淡绿的色调 ◇ *a pale sky* 天色昏暗 **OPP dark, deep** **3** (of light 光线) not strong or bright 暗淡的；微弱的： *the cold pale light of dawn* 破晓时分的鱼白寒光 ➲ SEE ALSO PALLID, PALLOR ▸ **pale·ly** /ˈpeɪlli/ *adv.*: *Mark stared palely* (= with a pale face) *at his plate.* 马克面色苍白，呆呆地望着盘子。 **pale·ness** *noun* [U]

▪ ***verb*** [I] ~ (**at sth**) to become paler than usual 变得比平常白；变苍白： *She* (= her face) *paled visibly at the sight of the police car.* 她一看见警车，脸色就刷地变白了。 ◇ *The blue of the sky paled to a light grey.* 天空的蓝色渐变成了浅灰色。

IDM **ˈpale beside/next to sth | ˈpale in/by comparison (with/to sth) | ˈpale into insignificance** to seem less important when compared with sth else 相形见绌；显得逊色： *Last year's riots pale in comparison with this latest outburst of violence.* 去年的骚乱与最近这次暴乱相比，可说是小巫见大巫。

▪ ***noun***

IDM **beˌyond the ˈpale** considered by most people to be unacceptable or unreasonable 出格；出圈；越轨；令人不能容忍： *His remarks were clearly beyond the pale.* 他的话显然过分了。

pale·face /ˈpeɪlfeɪs/ *noun* (used in films/movies, etc. 用于电影等) a name for a white person, said to have been used by Native Americans 白脸人（据说美洲土著称呼白人曾使用的名称）

paleo- (*NAmE*) = PALAEO-

pal·ette /ˈpælət/ *noun* **1** a thin board with a hole in it for the thumb to go through, used by an artist for mixing colours on when painting 调色板 ➲ VISUAL VOCAB PAGE V45 **2** [usually sing.] (*specialist*) the colours used by a particular artist （画家使用的）主要色彩，主色调： *Greens and browns are typical of Ribera's palette.* 绿色和棕色是里贝拉的主色调。

ˈpalette knife *noun* a knife with a blade that bends easily and has a round end, used by artists and in cooking 调色刀；画刀；（炊具中的）铲刀 ➲ VISUAL VOCAB PAGE V27

pali·mony /ˈpælɪməni/ *noun* [U] (*informal, especially NAmE*) money that a court orders sb to pay regularly to a former partner when they have lived together without being married （法院判定定期付给前未婚同居对象的）生活费 ➲ COMPARE ALIMONY

pal·imp·sest /ˈpælɪmpsest/ *noun* **1** an ancient document from which some or all of the original text has been removed and replaced by a new text 再生羊皮纸卷，重写羊皮书卷（全部或部分原有文字被刮去，在上面另行书写） **2** (*formal*) something that has many different layers of meaning or detail 具有多重意义的事物；多层次的东西

pal·in·drome /ˈpælɪndrəʊm; NAmE -droʊm/ *noun* a word or phrase that reads the same backwards as forwards, for example *madam* or *nurses run* 回文（正反读都一样的词语）

pal·ing /ˈpeɪlɪŋ/ *noun* [C, usually pl., U] a metal or wooden post that is pointed at the top; a fence made of these posts 尖木桩；尖铁条；围栏

pal·is·ade /ˌpælɪˈseɪd/ *noun* **1** a fence made of strong wooden or metal posts that are pointed at the top, especially used to protect a building in the past 木栅栏；金属栅栏 **2 palisades** [pl.] (*US*) a line of high steep CLIFFS, especially along a river or by the sea or ocean （尤指河边、海边的）绝壁，峭壁

pall /pɔːl/ *noun, verb*

▪ ***noun*** **1** [usually sing.] **~ of sth** a thick dark cloud of sth 浓密的云烟；尘烟： *a **pall of smoke/dust*** 一团烟雾 / 沙尘 ◇ (*figurative*) *News of her death **cast a pall** over the event.* 她死亡的消息给这件事蒙上了阴影。 **2** a cloth spread over a COFFIN (= a box used for burying a dead person in) 柩衣；棺材罩布

▪ ***verb*** [I] (not used in the progressive tenses 不用于进行时) ~ (**on sb**) to become less interesting to sb over a period of time because they have done or seen it too much （因见或做得过多而）失去魅力，使人厌倦： *Even the impressive scenery began to pall on me after a few hundred miles.* 行经了数百英里以后，即使秀丽风光也使我感到索然无味了。

pal·la·dium /pəˈleɪdiəm/ *noun* [U] (*symb.* **Pd**) a chemical element. Palladium is a rare silver-white metal that looks like PLATINUM. 钯（银白色稀有化学元素）

ˈpall-bearer *noun* a person who walks beside or helps to carry the COFFIN at a funeral 扶灵者；抬棺者

pal·let /ˈpælət/ *noun* **1** a heavy wooden or metal base that can be used for moving or storing goods 托盘；平台；运货板 **2** a cloth bag filled with STRAW, used for sleeping on （睡觉用的）草垫子

pal·li·asse /ˈpæliæs; NAmE pælˈjæs/ *noun* a cloth bag filled with STRAW, used for sleeping on 草荐；草褥 **SYN pallet**

pal·li·ate /ˈpælieɪt/ *verb* ~ **sth** (*formal*) to make a disease or an illness less painful or unpleasant without curing it 减轻，缓和（疾病或不适）

pal·lia·tive /ˈpæliətɪv/ *noun* **1** (*medical* 医) a medicine or medical treatment that reduces pain without curing its cause 治标药物；缓解剂；治标措施；保守疗法 ➲ WORDFINDER NOTE AT CURE **2** (*formal, usually disapproving*) an action, a decision, etc. that is designed to make a difficult situation seem better without actually solving the cause of the problems 权宜之计；消极措施；缓冲剂

▸ **pal·lia·tive** *adj.* [usually before noun]: *palliative treatment* 保守疗法 ◇ *short-term palliative measures* 短期的权宜之计

pal·lid /ˈpælɪd/ *adj.* **1** (of a person, their face, etc. 人、面色等) pale, especially because of illness （尤指因病）苍白的： *a pallid complexion* 苍白的脸色 **2** (of colours or light 颜色或光线) not strong or bright, and therefore not attractive 暗淡的；微弱的；乏味的： *a pallid sky* 暗淡的天空

pal·lor /ˈpælə(r)/ *noun* [U] pale colouring of the face, especially because of illness or fear 苍白的脸色（尤指因病或恐惧）： *Her cheeks had an unhealthy pallor.* 她面色苍白，显得虚弱。

pally /ˈpæli/ *adj.* ➲ PAL

palm /pɑːm/ *noun, verb*

▪ *noun* **1** the inner surface of the hand between the wrist and the fingers 手掌；手心： *He held the bird gently in* ***the palm of his hand.*** 他把小鸟轻轻地托在掌心。◇ *sweaty palms* 汗涔涔的手掌 ◇ ***to read sb's palm*** (= to say what you think will happen to sb by looking at the lines on their palm) 看手相 ➲ VISUAL VOCAB PAGE V64 **2** (*also* ˈ**palm tree**) a straight tree with a mass of long leaves at the top, growing in tropical countries. There are several types of palm tree, some of which produce fruit. 棕榈树： *a date palm* 枣椰树 ◇ *a coconut palm* 椰子树 ◇ ***palm leaves/fronds/groves*** 棕榈叶；棕榈树丛 ➲ VISUAL VOCAB PAGE V10

IDM **have sb in the ˌpalm of your ˈhand** to have complete control or influence over sb 完全控制某人；把某人攥在手心里 ➲ MORE AT CROSS *v.*, GREASE *v.*

▪ *verb* **~ sth** to hide a coin, card, etc. in your hand, especially when performing a trick 把…藏在手中（尤指玩戏法）

PHR V **ˌpalm sb↔ˈoff (with sth)** (*informal*) to persuade sb to believe an excuse or an explanation that is not true, in order to stop them asking questions or complaining （借口某事）欺骗搪塞某人，骗过某人 **ˌpalm sth↔ˈoff (on/onto sb)** | **ˌpalm sb↔ˈoff (with sth)** (*informal*) to persuade sb to accept sth that has no value or that you do not want, especially by tricking them 哄骗他人接受（无价值或自己不要的东西）；用假货行骗： *She's always palming the worst jobs off on her assistant.* 她总是哄骗她的助手做最苦的差事。◇ *Make sure he doesn't try to palm you off with faulty goods.* 当心别上当让他把残次品卖给你。 **ˌpalm sth ˈoff as sth** (*informal*) to tell sb that sth is better than it is, especially in order to sell it 推销假货；以假乱真： *They were trying to palm the table off as a genuine antique.* 他们在设法把那张普通桌子当真正的古董推销出去。

Palm·cord·er™ /ˈpɑːmkɔːdə(r); *NAmE* -kɔːrd-/ *noun* a small CAMCORDER (= video camera that records pictures and sound) that can be held in the PALM of one hand 掌上摄像机

pal·metto /pælˈmetəʊ; *NAmE* -toʊ/ *noun* (*pl.* **-os**) a small PALM tree that grows in the south-eastern US 矮棕榈（生长于美国东南部）

palm·ist /ˈpɑːmɪst/ *noun* a person who claims to be able to tell what a person is like and what will happen to them in the future, by looking at the lines on the PALM of their hand 手相术士；看手相的人

palm·is·try /ˈpɑːmɪstri/ *noun* [U] the art of telling what a person is like and what will happen to them by looking at the lines on the PALM of their hand 手相术

ˈ**palm oil** *noun* [U] oil obtained from the fruit of some types of PALM tree, used in cooking and in making soap, CANDLES, etc. 棕榈油

ˌ**Palm ˈSunday** *noun* [U, C] (in the Christian Church) the Sunday before Easter 棕枝主日，圣枝主日（复活节前的星期日）

palmy /ˈpɑːmi/ *adj.* (**palm·ier**, **palmi·est**) used to describe a time in the past when life was good （指昔日）繁荣昌盛的，美好年华的： *That's a picture of me in my palmier days.* 那是我风华正茂时的照片。

palo·mino /ˌpæləˈmiːnəʊ; *NAmE* -noʊ/ *noun* (*pl.* **-os**) a horse that is a cream or gold colour with a white MANE and tail 帕洛米诺马（体毛奶白色或金黄色、鬃毛和尾毛为白色）

palp·able /ˈpælpəbl/ *adj.* that is easily noticed by the mind or the senses 易于察觉的；可意识到的；明显的： *a* ***palpable*** *sense of relief* 如释重负 ◇ *The tension in the room was almost palpable.* 屋子里的紧张气氛几乎能感觉到。▸ **palp·ably** /-əbli/ *adv.*: *It was palpably clear what she really meant.* 她的本意是什么，那是一清二楚的。

pal·pate /pælˈpeɪt/ *verb* **~ sth** (*medical* 医) to examine part of the body by touching it 触诊；触摸检查 ▸ **pal·pa·tion** *noun* [U]

pal·pi·tate /ˈpælpɪteɪt/ *verb* [I] (of the heart 心脏) to beat rapidly and/or in an IRREGULAR way especially because of fear or excitement 急速跳动，悸动（尤指因恐惧或兴奋）

pal·pi·ta·tions /ˌpælpɪˈteɪʃnz/ *noun* [pl.] a physical condition in which your heart beats very quickly and in an IRREGULAR way 心悸： *Just the thought of flying gives me palpitations* (= makes me very nervous). 一想到飞行我的心就怦怦地跳。

palsy /ˈpɔːlzi/ *noun* [U] (*old-fashioned*) PARALYSIS (= loss of control or feeling in part or most of the body), especially when the arms and legs shake without control 瘫痪，麻痹（尤指四肢颤动类） ➲ SEE ALSO CEREBRAL PALSY ▸ **pal·sied** /ˈpɔːlzid/ *adj.*

pal·try /ˈpɔːltri/ *adj.* [usually before noun] **1** (of an amount 数量) too small to be considered as important or useful 可忽略不计的；微小的；微不足道的 **SYN** **meagre**: *This account offers a paltry 1% return on your investment.* 这个账户给你投资的回报仅是微不足道的 1%。◇ *a paltry sum* 小得可怜的数额 **2** having no value or useful qualities 无价值的；无用的： *a paltry gesture* 没有意义的姿态

pam·pas /ˈpæmpəs; *NAmE also* -pəz/ *noun* (*usually* **the pampas**) [sing.+sing./pl. v.] the large area of land in S America that has few trees and is covered in grass （南美洲的）大草原，草甸

ˈ**pampas grass** *noun* [U] a type of tall grass from S America that is often grown in gardens/yards for its long silver-white flowers that look like feathers 潘帕斯草，蒲苇（产于南美洲，开银白色长羽毛状花，常植于庭园）

pam·per /ˈpæmpə(r)/ *verb* **~ sb** (*sometimes disapproving*) to take care of sb very well and make them feel as comfortable as possible 细心照顾；精心护理；娇惯；纵容 **SYN** **cosset**: *Pamper yourself with our new range of beauty treatments.* 尽情享受一下我们的新系列美容服务吧。◇ *a spoilt and pampered child* 一个娇生惯养的孩子

pamph·let /ˈpæmflət/ *noun* a very thin book with a paper cover, containing information about a particular subject 小册子；手册 **SYN** **leaflet**

pamph·let·eer /ˌpæmfləˈtɪə(r); *NAmE* -ˈtɪr/ *noun* a person who writes pamphlets on particular subjects 撰写小册子的人；小册子作者

pan[1] 🔑 /pæn/ *noun, verb*

▪ *noun* **1** 🔑 a container, usually made of metal, with a handle or handles, used for cooking food in 平锅；平底锅： *pots and pans* 锅碗瓢盆 ◇ *a large stainless steel pan* 一只不锈钢大平锅 ➲ SEE ALSO FRYING PAN, SAUCEPAN **2** 🔑 the amount contained in a pan 一锅的量： *a pan of boiling water* 一锅开水 **3** (*NAmE*) (*BrE* **tin**) a metal container used for cooking food in （烘煮食物用的）烤盘，烤模： *a cake pan* 蛋糕烤盘 ➲ VISUAL VOCAB PAGE V28 **4** either of the dishes on a pair of SCALES that you put things into in order to weigh them （天平的）秤盘 **5** (*BrE*) the bowl of a toilet 马桶 ➲ SEE ALSO BEDPAN, DUSTPAN, SKIDPAN, WARMING PAN

IDM **go down the 'pan** (*BrE, informal*) to be wasted or spoiled 被浪费；被糟蹋：*That's another brilliant idea down the pan.* 又一个好主意被糟践了！➲ MORE AT FLASH *n.*

■ *verb* (-nn-) **1** [T, usually passive] ~ **sth** (*informal*) to severely criticize sth such as a play or a film/movie 严厉批评，抨击（戏剧、电影等）**SYN** **slate** **2** [I, T] if a television or video camera **pans** somewhere, or a person **pans** or **pans a camera**, the camera moves in a particular direction, to follow an object or to film a wide area （移动摄像机）追拍，摇摄：**+ adv./prep.** *The camera panned back to the audience.* 摄像机摇回拍摄观众。◇ **~ sth + adv./prep.** *He panned the camera along the row of faces.* 他移动摄像机顺着这一排面孔拍摄。**3** [I, T] ~ (**for**) **sth** to wash soil or small stones in a pan to find gold or other valuable minerals （用淘选盘）淘洗；淘（金）：*panning for gold* 淘金

PHR V **,pan 'out** (*informal*) (of events or a situation 事情或局面) to develop in a particular way 以一定方式发展：*I'm happy with the way things have panned out.* 我对事情的发展趋势感到很满意。

pan² = PAAN

pan- /pæn/ *combining form* (in adjectives and nouns 构成形容词和名词) including all of sth; connected with the whole of sth 包含一切的；全部的；泛：*pan-African* 泛非洲的 ◇ *pandemic* 大流行病

pana·cea /,pænə'siːə/ *noun* ~ (**for sth**) something that will solve all the problems of a particular situation 万灵药；万能之计

pan·ache /pə'næʃ; pæ'n-; *NAmE* pæ'næʃ; *also* -'nɑːʃ/ *noun* [U] the quality of being able to do things in a confident and elegant way that other people find attractive 神气十足；潇洒气质 **SYN** **flair, style**

pan·ama /'pænəmɑː/ (*also* **,panama 'hat**) *noun* a man's hat made from fine STRAW 巴拿马草帽 ➲ VISUAL VOCAB PAGE V70

pan·cake /'pænkeɪk/ *noun* **1** [C] a thin flat round cake made from a mixture of flour, eggs and milk that is fried on both sides, usually eaten hot for breakfast in the US, and in Britain either as a DESSERT with sugar, jam, etc. or as a main course with meat, cheese, etc. 烙饼；薄饼 **2** [U] thick make-up for the face, used especially in the theatre （尤指舞台化妆用的）粉饼 **IDM** SEE FLAT *adj.*

'Pancake Day *noun* (*informal*) the day before the beginning of Lent, when people traditionally eat PANCAKES 薄饼日（大斋期的前一天，按传统习惯吃薄饼）➲ COMPARE SHROVE TUESDAY

'pancake race *noun* a traditional race in Britain on Pancake Day, in which each runner keeps throwing a PANCAKE into the air from a pan 薄饼赛跑（薄饼日举行的英国传统赛跑，参加者不断将平底锅中的薄烤饼抛向空中）

pan·cetta /pæn'tʃetə/ *noun* [U] (*from Italian*) meat from the belly of a pig that has been CURED (= preserved using salt or smoke) 意大利咸猪肉，意大利熏猪肉（用猪腹部的肉制成）

pan·chay·at /pʌn'tʃaɪjət/ *noun* (in some S Asian countries 某些南亚国家) **1** a village council 潘查耶特；村务委员会 **2** the official organization that governs local areas in the country, outside large towns （大市镇以外的）地方当局；村（或县、地区）评议会

pan·creas /'pæŋkriəs/ *noun* an organ near the stomach that produces INSULIN and a liquid that helps the body to DIGEST food 胰；胰腺 ➲ VISUAL VOCAB PAGE V64 ▶ **pan·cre·at·ic** /,pæŋkri'ætɪk/ *adj.* [only before noun]

panda /'pændə/ *noun* **1** (*also* **,giant 'panda**) a large black and white animal like a BEAR, that lives in China and is very rare 大熊猫；猫熊 **2** (*also* **,red 'panda**) an Asian animal like a RACCOON, with reddish-brown fur and a long thick tail 小熊猫，小猫熊（产于亚洲，毛棕红色，尾巴粗长）

pan·dal /'pændl; *BrE also* -'dɑːl/ *noun* (*IndE*) a large tent used at social events （大型活动用的）临时棚舍

pan·dem·ic /pæn'demɪk/ *noun* a disease that spreads over a whole country or the whole world （全国或全球性）流行病；大流行病 ▶ **pan·dem·ic** *adj.*：*a pandemic disease* 大范围流行的疾病 ➲ COMPARE ENDEMIC, EPIDEMIC

pan·de·mon·ium /,pændə'məʊniəm; *NAmE* -'moʊ-/ *noun* [U] a situation in which there is a lot of noise, activity and confusion, especially because people are feeling angry or frightened 骚动；群情沸腾 **SYN** **chaos**：*Pandemonium broke out when the news was announced.* 这消息一宣布，立即乱成一片。

pan·der /'pændə(r)/ *verb*

PHR V **'pander to sth/sb** (*disapproving*) to do what sb wants, or try to please them, especially when this is not acceptable or reasonable 迎合；奉迎；投其所好：*to pander to sb's wishes* 迎合某人的愿望 ◇ *The speech was pandering to racial prejudice.* 这篇讲话是在纵容种族偏见。

p. and h. (*also* **p. & h.**) /,piː ənd 'eɪtʃ/ *abbr.* (*NAmE*) postage and handling 邮资和手续费 ➲ COMPARE P. AND P.

pan·dit /'pændɪt/ (*also* **pun·dit**) *noun* **1** a Hindu priest or wise man （印度教的）祭司，哲人 **2** (*IndE*) a teacher 教师 **3** (*IndE*) a skilled musician 乐师

Pandora's box /pæn,dɔːrəz 'bɒks; *NAmE* 'bɑːks/ *noun* [sing., U] a process that, if started, will cause many problems 潘多拉魔盒（指邪恶之源）：*This court case could open a Pandora's box of similar claims.* 这宗诉讼案会为类似的索赔开启潘多拉魔盒。➲ MORE LIKE THIS 16, page R27

ORIGIN From the Greek myth in which **Pandora** was created by the god Zeus and sent to the earth with a box containing many evils. When she opened the box, the evils came out and infected the earth. 源自希腊神话。主神宙斯创造了潘多拉并派其带着装满邪恶的盒子下凡。当她打开盒子时，各种邪恶奔涌而出，泛滥人间。

pan·dowdy /pæn'daʊdi/ *noun* (*pl.* **-ies**) [C, U] (*US*) a sweet dish of apples and spices covered with a mixture of butter, milk and eggs, that is baked 苹果布丁（用黄油、牛奶和鸡蛋覆盖苹果和香料烤制而成）

p. and p. (*also* **p. & p.**) /,piː ən 'piː/ *abbr.* (*BrE*) postage and packing (= the cost of packing sth and sending it by post) 邮资与包装费：*Add £2 for p. and p.* 另加邮资及包装费 2 英镑。➲ COMPARE P. AND H., S AND H

pane /peɪn/ *noun* a single sheet of glass in a window （一片）窗玻璃：*a pane of glass* 一片窗玻璃 ◇ *a windowpane* 一块窗玻璃

pan·eer (*also* **panir**) /pæ'nɪə(r); *NAmE* -'nɪr/ *noun* [U] a type of soft cheese used in Asian cooking 奶豆腐（亚洲烹饪用软干酪）

pan·egyr·ic /,pænə'dʒɪrɪk/ *noun* (*formal*) a speech or piece of writing praising sb/sth 颂词；颂文

panel 🔑 **AW** /'pænl/ *noun, verb*

■ *noun* **1** 🔑 [C] a square or RECTANGULAR piece of wood, glass or metal that forms part of a larger surface such as a door or wall （门、墙等上面的）嵌板，镶板，方格板块：*One of the glass panels in the front door was cracked.* 前门的一块方玻璃破裂了。➲ VISUAL VOCAB PAGE V25 ➲ SEE ALSO SOLAR PANEL **2** [C] a piece of metal that forms part of the outer frame of a vehicle （车身的）金属板，钣金 **3** [C] a piece of cloth that forms part of a piece of clothing （衣服上的）镶条，嵌条，饰片：*The trousers have double thickness knee panels for extra protection.* 这条裤子上有双倍厚的护膝片以加强保护。**4** 🔑 [C+sing./pl. v.] a group of specialists who give their advice or opinion about sth; a group of people who discuss topics of interest on television or radio 专家咨询组；（广播、电视上的）讨论小组：*an advisory panel* 顾问组 ◇ *a panel of experts* 专家组 ◇ *We have two politicians on tonight's panel.* 今天晚上出席座谈会的有两位政界人士。◇ *a panel discussion* 专家小组讨论 **5** (*also* **'jury panel**) [C] (*both especially NAmE*) = JURY (1) **6** [C] a flat board in a vehicle or on a piece of machinery where the controls and instruments are fixed （汽车或其他机械的）控制板，仪表盘：*an **instrument panel*** 仪表盘 ◇ *a **control/display panel*** 控制 / 显示面板

■ ***verb*** (**-ll-**, *especially US* **-l-**) [usually passive] **~ sth** to cover or decorate a surface with flat strips of wood, glass, etc. 镶板（用木或玻璃板等镶嵌或装饰）：*The walls were panelled in oak.* 墙壁镶了橡木饰片。◇ *a **glass-/wood-panelled** door* 镶玻璃 / 木板的门

'panel beater *noun* (*BrE*) a person whose job is to remove the DENTS from the outer frame of a vehicle that has been in an accident （汽车）钣金工

'panel game *noun* (*BrE*) a game in which a team of people try to answer questions correctly, especially on television or radio （尤指电视或电台的）分组答题竞赛，分组智力竞赛

pan·el·ling AW (*especially US* **pan·el·ing**) /'pænəlɪŋ/ *noun* [U] square or RECTANGULAR pieces of wood used to cover and decorate walls, ceilings, etc. （装饰墙壁、天花板等的）嵌板，饰块

pan·el·list (*especially US* **pan·el·ist**) /'pænəlɪst/ *noun* a person who is a member of a panel answering questions during a discussion, for example on radio or television （广播、电视节目中的）讨论会成员

'panel van (*AustralE, NZE, SAfrE*) (*NAmE* **'panel truck**) *noun* a small van/truck, especially one without windows at the sides or seats for passengers （密封式）小货车，厢式货车

'pan-fry *verb* (**pan-fries**, **pan-frying**, **pan-fried**, **pan-fried**) **~ sth** to fry food in a pan in shallow fat 用平锅煎：*pan-fried chicken* 用平锅摊煎的鸡肉

pang /pæŋ/ *noun* a sudden strong feeling of physical or emotional pain突然的疼痛（或痛苦）；一阵剧痛：***hunger pangs/pangs of hunger*** 饥饿之苦 ◇ *a sudden **pang of jealousy*** 突然涌来的嫉妒

panga /'pæŋgə/ *noun* (*EAfrE, SAfrE*) a large heavy knife that is used for cutting grass or small sticks or for removing WEEDS 大砍刀

Pan·gaea /pæn'dʒiːə/ *noun* [sing.] (*geology* 地) an extremely large area of land which existed millions of years ago, made up of all the present continents 泛大陆（原始大陆，由现在的所有大陆组成）

pan·go·lin /'pæŋgəlɪn; *BrE also* pæŋ'gəʊlɪn/ (*also* **ˌscaly 'anteater**) *noun* a small animal from Africa or Asia that eats insects, and has a long nose, tongue and tail, and hard SCALES on its body 穿山甲，有鳞食蚁兽（见于非洲和亚洲）

pan·han·dler /'pænhændlə(r)/ *noun* (*NAmE, informal*) a person who asks other people for money in the street 叫花子；乞丐 ▶ **pan·han·dle** *verb* [I]

panic /'pænɪk/ *noun, verb*

■ ***noun*** [U, C, usually sing.] **1** a sudden feeling of great fear that cannot be controlled and prevents you from thinking clearly 惊恐；恐慌：*a moment of panic* 一时惊慌 ◇ *They were in a state of panic.* 他们惊恐万状。◇ *Office workers fled **in panic** as the fire took hold.* 火势起来时，办公室人员惊慌逃出。◇ *There's no point **getting into a panic** about the exams.* 对考试惊惶失措是没有用的。◇ *a **panic attack*** (= a condition in which you suddenly feel very anxious, causing your heart to beat faster, etc.) 一阵心慌意乱 ◇ *a panic decision* (= one that is made when you are in a state of panic) 慌乱中作出的决定 ➲ SYNONYMS AT FEAR **2** a situation in which people are made to feel very anxious, causing them to act quickly and without thinking carefully 人心惶惶的局面；惶恐不安：*News of the losses caused* (*a*) *panic among investors.* 亏损的消息令投资者人心惶惶。◇ *Careful planning at this stage will help to avoid a last-minute panic.* 现在精心规划，就可以避免事到临头手忙脚乱。◇ ***There's no panic*** (= we do not need to rush), *we've got plenty of time.* 不用着急，我们有的是时间。◇ ***panic buying/selling*** (= the act of buying/selling things quickly and without thinking carefully because you are afraid that a particular situation will become worse) 恐慌性抢购 / 抛售

IDM **'panic stations** (*BrE, informal*) a situation in which people feel anxious and there is a lot of confused activity, especially because there is a lot to do in a short period of time 慌乱的状态；（尤指）忙乱的状况

■ ***verb*** (**-ck-**) [I, T] to suddenly feel frightened so that you cannot think clearly and you say or do sth stupid, dangerous, etc.; to make sb do this （使）惊慌，惊慌失措：*I panicked when I saw smoke coming out of the engine.* 我看见发动机冒烟时，吓得手足无措。◇ **~ sb/sth** *The gunfire panicked the horses.* 枪声惊吓到马匹。

PHR V **'panic sb into doing sth** [usually passive] to make sb act too quickly because they are afraid of sth 使仓惶行事；使仓促行动

'panic button *noun* a button that sb working in a bank, etc. can press to call for help if they are in danger （银行等的）紧急呼救按钮

IDM **press/push the 'panic button** to react in a sudden or extreme way to sth unexpected that has frightened you 惊慌失措；仓促行事；采取紧急行动

pan·icky /'pænɪki/ *adj.* (*informal*) anxious about sth; feeling or showing panic 焦虑不安的；惊慌的 SYN **hysterical**

'panic room (*also* **'safe room**) *noun* a room in a home or an office building where people can go to avoid a dangerous situation （家中或办公楼中的）紧急避险室，避难室

'panic-stricken *adj.* extremely anxious about sth, in a way that prevents you from thinking clearly 惊慌失措的 SYN **hysterical**

pa·nini /pə'niːni/ (*also* **pa·nino** /pə'niːnəʊ; *NAmE* -noʊ/) *noun* (*pl.* **pa·nini** or **pa·ninis**) a sandwich made with Italian bread, usually toasted 意式帕尼尼三明治（通常面包经烘烤）

panir = PANEER

pan·nier /'pæniə(r)/ *noun* each of a pair of bags or boxes carried on either side of the back wheel of a bicycle or motorcycle; each of a pair of BASKETS carried on either side of its back by a horse or DONKEY （自行车、摩托车后架两侧的）挂篮，货筐；（牲畜背上驮的）驮笼，驮篮

pan·oply /'pænəpli/ *noun* [sing., U] (*formal*) a large and impressive number or collection of sth 巨大的数量（或收藏品） SYN **array**

pan·or·ama /ˌpænə'rɑːmə; *NAmE* -'ræmə/ *noun* **1** a view of a wide area of land 全景 SYN **vista**：*There is a superb panorama of the mountains from the hotel.* 从旅馆可饱览峰峦叠嶂的雄伟景观。 ➲ SYNONYMS AT VIEW **2** a description, study or set of pictures that presents all the different aspects or stages of a particular subject, event, etc. （某专题或事件的）全面叙述，综合研究；全景画卷 ▶ **pan·or·am·ic** /ˌpænə'ræmɪk/ *adj.* [usually before noun]：*a panoramic view over the valley* 山谷的全景

'pan pipes *noun* [pl.] (*BrE*) (*NAmE also* **'pan·pipe** [C]) a musical instrument made of a row of pipes of different lengths that you play by blowing across the open ends 排箫；牧神箫

pansy /'pænzi/ *noun* (*pl.* **-ies**) **1** a small garden plant with brightly coloured flowers 三色堇；蝴蝶花 **2** (*taboo, slang*) an offensive word for a HOMOSEXUAL man 娘娘腔的男人，脂粉男子，男妖（对同性恋男人的蔑称）

pant /pænt/ *verb* [I, T] (+ **speech**) to breathe quickly with short breaths, usually with your mouth open, because you have been doing some physical exercise, or because it is very hot 气喘；喘息：*She finished the race panting heavily.* 她跑完比赛气喘吁吁的。◇ *She could hear him panting up the stairs* (= running up and breathing quickly). 她听见他气喘吁吁地跑上楼。◇ *He found her **panting for breath** at the top of the hill.* 上到山顶，他发现她上气不接下气。 ▶ **pant** *noun* [usually pl.]：*His breath came in short pants.* 他气息急促。 ➲ SEE ALSO PANTS IDM SEE PUFF *v.*

PHR V **'pant for/after sb/sth** to want sth/sb very much 渴望：*The end of the novel leaves you panting for more.* 小说的结尾让人感到意犹未尽。

pan·ta·loons /ˌpæntəˈluːnz/ *noun* [pl.] **1** women's loose trousers/pants with wide legs that fit tightly at the ankles 女式灯笼裤 **2** (in the past) men's tight trousers/pants fastened at the foot （旧时的）男式紧身裤，马裤

pan·tech·nicon /pænˈteknɪkən/ *noun* (*old-fashioned, BrE*) = REMOVAL VAN

pan·the·ism /ˈpænθiɪzəm/ *noun* [U] **1** the belief that God is present in all natural things 泛神论（认为神存在于万事万物） **2** belief in many or all gods 泛神崇拜；泛神信仰 ▶ **pan·the·ist** /-θiɪst/ *noun* **pan·the·ist·ic** /ˌpænθiˈɪstɪk/ *adj.*

pan·theon /ˈpænθiən; *NAmE* -θiɑːn/ *noun* **1** (*specialist*) all the gods of a nation or people （一国或一个民族信仰的）众神，诸神：*the ancient Egyptian pantheon* 古埃及众神 **2** (*formal*) a group of people who are famous within a particular area of activity （统称某一领域的）名人，名流 **3** a TEMPLE (= religious building) built in honour of all the gods of a nation; a building in which famous dead people of a nation are buried or HONOURED 万神庙；先贤祠；伟人祠

pan·ther /ˈpænθə(r)/ *noun* **1** a black LEOPARD (= a large wild animal of the cat family) 黑豹 **2** (*NAmE*) = PUMA

pantie girdle *noun* = PANTY GIRDLE

pan·ties /ˈpæntiz/ (*especially NAmE*) (*BrE also* **knick·ers**) *noun* [pl.] a piece of women's underwear that covers the body from the waist to the tops of the legs 女式内裤

pan·tile /ˈpæntaɪl/ *noun* a curved TILE used for roofs 波形瓦；筒瓦

P

panto /ˈpæntəʊ; *NAmE* -toʊ/ *noun* (*pl.* **-os** /-təʊz; *NAmE* -toʊz/) (*BrE, informal*) = PANTOMIME

panto·graph /ˈpæntəɡrɑːf; *NAmE* -ɡræf/ *noun* a device used for copying a drawing in a bigger or smaller size 缩放仪；比例绘图仪

panto·mime /ˈpæntəmaɪm/ *noun* **1** (*also BrE, informal* **panto**) [C, U] (in Britain) a type of play with music, dancing and jokes, that is based on a FAIRY TALE and is usually performed at Christmas （英国多在圣诞节期间上演的）童话剧 **2** [U, C, usually sing.] the use of movement and the expression of your face to communicate sth or to tell a story 哑剧；默剧 SYN **mime** **3** [C, usually sing.] (*BrE*) a ridiculous situation, usually with a lot of confusion 滑稽可笑的局面 SYN **farce**

ˌpantomime ˈdame (*also* **dame**) *noun* (*BrE*) a female character in a PANTOMIME (1), that is usually played by a man 童话剧中的女性（通常由男人扮演）

ˌpantomime ˈhorse *noun* (*BrE*) a character in a PANTOMIME (1) that is supposed to be a horse, played by two people in a special COSTUME 童话剧中的马（由两人共穿一件特制戏装扮演）

pan·try /ˈpæntri/ *noun* (*pl.* **-ies**) a cupboard/closet or small room in a house, used for storing food 食品贮藏室；食品贮藏柜 SYN **larder**

pants 🔑 /pænts/ *noun* [pl.] **1** 🔑 (*BrE*) UNDERPANTS or KNICKERS 内裤；短裤：*a pair of pants* 一件内裤 **2** 🔑 (*especially NAmE*) trousers 裤子：*a new pair of pants* 一条新裤子 ◇ *ski pants* 滑雪裤 ➲ VISUAL VOCAB PAGE V66 ➲ SEE ALSO CARGO PANTS **3** (*BrE, slang*) (also used as an adjective 也用作形容词) something you think is of poor quality 次品；劣质品 SYN **rubbish**: *Their new album is absolute pants!* 他们的新专辑简直是垃圾！◇ *Do we have to watch this pants programme?* 我们非要看这种烂节目吗？
IDM **bore, scare, etc. the ˈpants off sb** (*informal*) to make sb extremely bored, frightened, etc. 把…烦死（或吓死等） ➲ MORE AT ANT, CATCH *v.*, SEAT *n.*, WEAR *v.*, WET *v.*

pant·suit /ˈpæntsuːt; *BrE also* -sjuːt/ (*NAmE*) (*BrE* **ˈtrouser suit**) *noun* a woman's suit of jacket and trousers/pants （女子的）衣裤套装

pant·sula /ˌpæntˈsuːlə/ *noun* [U] a style of South African dancing in which each person takes a turn to perform dance movements in front of a group of other dancers who are in a circle 潘祖拉圈舞（南非舞，参加者依次在围成一圈的其他舞者前跳舞）

panty girdle (*also* **pantie girdle**) /ˈpænti ɡɜːdl; *NAmE* ɡɜːrdl/ *noun* a tight piece of women's underwear that combines KNICKERS/PANTIES and a GIRDLE （女式）紧身搭短裤

panty·hose /ˈpæntihəʊz; *NAmE* -hoʊz/ (*NAmE*) (*BrE* **tights**) *noun* [pl.] a piece of clothing made of very thin cloth that fits closely over a woman's hips, legs and feet （女用）连裤袜，紧身裤 ➲ COMPARE STOCKING (1)

pap /pæp/ (*BrE*) *noun, verb*
■ *noun* **1** [U] (*disapproving*) books, magazines, television programmes, etc. that have no real value 无价值的读物（或电视节目等） **2** [U] soft or almost liquid food eaten by babies or people who are ill/sick （婴儿或病人吃的）软食，流食 **3** [U] (*SAfrE*) PORRIDGE made with flour from MAIZE (CORN) 玉米面粥 **4** [C] = PAPARAZZO
■ *verb* (**-pp-**) **~ sb** to follow a famous person around and take a photograph of them without their permission 跟踪并偷拍（名人）：*She can't even go to the gym without being papped.* 她连去健身房都会被偷拍。

papa /pəˈpɑː; *NAmE* ˈpɑːpə/ *noun* (*BrE, old-fashioned* or *NAmE*) used to talk about or to address your father 爸爸

pap·acy /ˈpeɪpəsi/ *noun* **1 the papacy** [sing.] the position or the authority of the POPE 教皇的职位（或权力） **2** [C, usually sing.] the period of time when a particular POPE is in power （某教皇）在位期

papad /ˈpɑːpəd/ *noun* (*IndE*) a POPPADOM 印度脆饼

papal /ˈpeɪpl/ *adj.* [only before noun] connected with the POPE 教皇的：*papal authority* 教皇的权力 ◇ *a papal visit to Mexico* 教皇对墨西哥的访问

pap·ar·azzo /ˌpæpəˈrætsəʊ; *NAmE* -ˈrɑːtsoʊ/ (*also* **pap**) *noun* (*pl.* **pap·ar·azzi** /-tsi/) [usually pl.] a photographer who follows famous people around in order to get interesting photographs of them to sell to a newspaper 猎奇名流的摄影记者；狗仔队

pa·paya /pəˈpaɪə/ (*BrE also* **paw·paw**) *noun* a tropical fruit with yellow and green skin, sweet orange or red flesh and round black seeds 番木瓜；（俗称）木瓜 ➲ VISUAL VOCAB PAGE V33

paper 🔑 /ˈpeɪpə(r)/ *noun, verb*
■ *noun*
• FOR WRITING/WRAPPING 供书写 / 包装 **1** 🔑 [U] (often in compounds 常构成复合词) the thin material that you write and draw on and that is also used for wrapping and packing things 纸；纸张：*a piece/sheet of paper* 一片 / 一张纸 ◇ *a package wrapped in brown paper* 一个用牛皮纸包扎的包裹 ◇ *recycled paper* 再生纸 ◇ *She wrote her name and address on a slip* (= a small piece) *of paper.* 她把姓名和地址写在一张纸条上。◇ *Experience is more important for this job than paper qualifications* (= that exist on paper, but may not have any real value). 就这项工作而言，经验比纸面上的资格重要。◇ *paper losses/profits* (= that are shown in accounts but which may not exist in reality) 账面亏损 / 利润 ◇ *This journal is available in paper and electronic form.* 这份刊物有印刷版本和电子版本。➲ SEE ALSO NOTEPAPER, WRAPPING PAPER, WRITING PAPER
• NEWSPAPER 报纸 **2** 🔑 [C] a newspaper 报纸：*a local/national paper* 地方性 / 全国性报纸 ◇ *a daily/an evening/a Sunday paper* 日报；晚报；星期日报 ◇ *I read about it in the paper.* 我从报上得知这件事。◇ *Have you seen today's paper?* 你看到今天的报纸没有？◇ *The papers* (= newspapers in general) *soon got hold of the story.* 报纸很快就获悉了这件事。
• DOCUMENTS 文件 **3** 🔑 **papers** [pl.] pieces of paper with writing on them, such as letters, pieces of work or

private documents 文件；文献： *His desk was covered with books and papers.* 他的办公桌上全是书籍和文件。**4** **papers** [pl.] official documents that prove your identity, give you permission to do sth, etc. 证明；证件： ***divorce/identification papers*** 离婚 / 身份证件 ➲SEE ALSO WALKING PAPERS, WORKING PAPER (2)

• **EXAM** 考试 **5** [C] (*BrE*) a set of exam questions on a particular subject; the answers that people write to the questions 试卷；试题；答卷： *The Geography paper was hard.* 地理试题难极了。◇ *She spent the evening marking exam papers.* 她用一个晚上批阅试卷。➲WORDFINDER NOTE AT EXAM

• **ARTICLE** 文章 **6** [C] an academic article about a particular subject that is written by and for specialists 论文： *a recent paper in the Journal of Medicine* 最近刊在《医学学报》上的一篇论文 ◇ *She was invited to **give a paper*** (= a talk) *on the results of her research.* 她应邀发表一篇论文，报告她的研究结果。➲COLLOCATIONS AT SCIENTIFIC ➲SEE ALSO GREEN PAPER, ORDER PAPER, POSITION PAPER, WHITE PAPER, WORKING PAPER **7** [C] (*NAmE*) a piece of written work done by a student （学生的）研究报告，论文： *Your grade will be based on four papers and a final exam.* 你的成绩将根据四篇论文和期末考试决定。➲SEE ALSO TERM PAPER

• **ON WALLS** 墙壁上 **8** [C, U] paper that you use to cover and decorate the walls of a room 壁纸： *The room was damp and the paper was peeling off.* 屋子很潮湿，壁纸都一片片剥落了。 **HELP** There are many other compounds ending in **paper**. You will find them at their place in the alphabet. 以 paper 结尾的复合词还有很多，可在各字母中的适当位置查到。

IDM **on paper 1** when you put sth **on paper**, you write it down 写下来；笔录 **2** judged from written information only, but not proved in practice 仅照字面看；理论上： *The idea **looks good on paper**.* 仅就字面看，这个主意不错。➲MORE AT PEN *n.*, WORTH *adj.*

■*verb* ~ sth to decorate the walls of a room by covering them with WALLPAPER 贴壁纸

PHR V **ˌpaper ˈover sth 1** to cover a wall with WALLPAPER in order to hide sth 糊壁纸遮盖 **SYN** **wallpaper**: *The previous owners had obviously papered over any damp patches.* 原先的房主显然是用壁纸把潮斑都盖起来了。 **2** to try to hide a problem or disagreement in a way that is temporary and not likely to be successful 暂时掩盖，权且掩饰（问题或分歧）： *The government is trying to **paper over the cracks** in the cabinet.* 政府正竭力掩饰内阁出现的裂痕。◇ *We can't just paper over the problem.* 我们不能就这么掩饰这个问题。

paper·back /ˈpeɪpəbæk; *NAmE* -pərb-/ *noun* [C, U] a book that has a thick paper cover 平装书；简装书： *a cheap paperback* 一本廉价的简装书 ◇ *When is it coming out in **paperback**?* 这本书的平装本什么时候出版？◇ ***a paperback book/edition*** 平装书；平装版本 ➲COMPARE HARDBACK

ˈpaper boy, **ˈpaper girl** *noun* a boy or girl who delivers newspapers to people's houses 男（或女）报童

pa·per·chase /ˈpeɪpətʃeɪs; *NAmE* -pərtʃ-/ *noun* **1** (*BrE*) a game in which one runner drops pieces of paper for the other runners to follow 撒纸追逐游戏（领头者沿途撒下纸屑，供追赶者寻踪追逐） **2** (*NAmE, informal*) the fact of producing too much work on paper 过多的书面工作；文牍追求

ˈpaper clip *noun* a piece of bent wire or plastic that is designed to hold loose sheets of paper together 回形针；曲别针；纸夹 ➲VISUAL VOCAB PAGE V71

ˈpaper cutter (*US*) (*BrE* **guil·lo·tine**) *noun* [C] a device with a long blade for cutting paper 裁纸机；切纸机

paper·knife /ˈpeɪpənaɪf; *NAmE* ˈpeɪpər-/ *noun* (*pl.* **-knives**) (*especially BrE*) (*NAmE usually* **ˈletter opener**) a knife used for opening envelopes 拆信刀；开信刀

paper·less /ˈpeɪpələs; *NAmE* -pərləs/ *adj.* using computers, telephones, etc. rather than paper to exchange information 无纸的；不用纸交换信息的： *the paperless office* 无纸办公室 ◇ *a system of paperless business transactions* 无纸商业交易系统

ˌpaper ˈmoney *noun* [U] money that is made of paper, not coins 纸币；钞票 **SYN** **note**

ˌpaper ˈplate *noun* a cardboard plate that can be thrown away after it is used （一次性）纸盘子

ˈpaper-pusher *noun* (*disapproving*) a person who does unimportant office work as their job 办公室小职员；小文书

ˈpaper round (*BrE*) (*NAmE* **ˈpaper route**) *noun* the job of delivering newspapers to houses; the route taken when doing this 送报；送报路线

ˈpaper shop *noun* (*BrE*) = NEWSAGENT (2)

ˌpaper-ˈthin *adj.* (of objects 物品) very thin and delicate 薄如纸的；极薄的： *paper-thin slices of meat* 像纸一样薄的肉片 ➲COMPARE WAFER-THIN

ˌpaper ˈtiger *noun* a person, a country or a situation that seems or claims to be powerful or dangerous but is not really （指人、国家或局势）纸老虎，外强中干者

ˌpaper ˈtowel *noun* **1** [C] a thick sheet of paper that you use to dry your hands or to absorb water 厚纸巾 **2** [U] (*NAmE*) (*BrE* **ˈkitchen paper**, **ˈkitchen roll**, **ˈkitchen towel**) thick paper on a roll, used for cleaning up liquid, food, etc. 厨房用卷纸 ➲VISUAL VOCAB PAGE V26

ˈpaper trail *noun* (*informal*) a series of documents that provide evidence of what you have done or what has happened （揭示来龙去脉的）系列文件： *He was a shrewd lawyer with a talent for uncovering paper trails of fraud.* 他是个精明能干的律师，能从一连串文件中找出诈骗的蛛丝马迹。

paper·weight /ˈpeɪpəweɪt; *NAmE* -pərw-/ *noun* a small heavy object that you put on top of loose papers to keep them in place 镇纸

paper·work /ˈpeɪpəwɜːk; *NAmE* ˈpeɪpərwɜːrk/ *noun* [U] **1** the written work that is part of a job, such as filling in forms or writing letters and reports 文书工作： *We're trying to cut down on the amount of paperwork involved.* 我们正在努力降低相关的文书工作量。 **2** all the documents that you need for sth, such as a court case or buying a house （诉讼案件、购置房产等所需的）全部文件，全部资料： *How quickly can you prepare the paperwork?* 你要多久才能把全部文件备好？

pa·pery /ˈpeɪpəri/ *adj.* like paper; thin and dry 纸一样的；薄而干的

pa·pier mâché /ˌpæpieɪ ˈmæʃeɪ; *NAmE* ˌpeɪpər məˈʃeɪ; ˌpæpjeɪ/ *noun* [U] (*from French*) paper mixed with glue or flour and water, that is used to make decorative objects 混凝纸，制型纸（加进胶水等经浆状处理的纸，用以做装饰品）

pap·il·loma /ˌpæpɪˈləʊmə; *NAmE* -ˈloʊ-/ *noun* (*medical* 医) a small lump like a WART that grows on the skin and is usually harmless 乳头状瘤（通常为良性）

pap·ist /ˈpeɪpɪst/ *noun* (*taboo*) an offensive word for a Roman Catholic, used by some Protestants 教皇党人（某些新教教徒对天主教徒的蔑称） ▸ **pap·ist** *adj.*

pa·poose /pəˈpuːs/ *noun* a type of bag that can be used for carrying a baby in, on your back or in front of you 婴儿袋，婴儿兜（可背负或放在胸前）

pap·rika /pəˈpriːkə; *BrE also* ˈpæprɪkə/ *noun* [U] a red powder made from a type of PEPPER, used in cooking as a spice 红辣椒粉 ➲VISUAL VOCAB PAGE V35

ˈPap smear (*NAmE*) (*BrE* **ˈsmear test**, **smear**, **ˌcervical ˈsmear**) *noun* a medical test in which a very small amount of TISSUE from a woman's CERVIX is removed and examined for cancer cells 涂片试验（从妇女子宫颈取少许组织，以检查是否有癌细胞）

pa·pyrus /pəˈpaɪrəs/ *noun* (*pl.* **pa·pyri** /pəˈpaɪriː/) **1** [U] a tall plant with thick STEMS that grows in water 纸莎草

P

2 [U] paper made from the STEMS of the papyrus plant, used in ancient Egypt for writing and drawing on（古埃及用的）纸莎草纸 3 [C] a document or piece of paper made of papyrus （写在纸莎草纸上的）文献，文稿

par /pɑː(r)/ *noun* [U] **1** (in GOLF 高尔夫球) the number of strokes a good player should need to complete a course or to hit the ball into a particular hole 标准杆: *a par five hole* 标准杆为五杆的球洞 ◇ *Par for the course is 72.* 这个球场的标准杆是72杆。 **2** (*also* **'par value**) (*business* 商) the value that a share in a company had originally （股票的）面值，票面价值: *to be redeemed* ***at par*** 以面值兑换

IDM **below/under 'par** less well, good, etc. than is usual or expected 不太好；不佳；不及平常好；不如预期: *Teaching in some subjects has been well below par.* 一些科目的教学一直远达不到标准。 **be ˌpar for the 'course** (*disapproving*) to be just what you would expect to happen or expect sb to do in a particular situation 不出所料；果不其然 SYN **norm**: *Starting early and working long hours is par for the course in this job.* 开工早、工时长是这份工作的常态。 **on a par with sb/sth** as good, bad, important, etc. as sb/sth else 与…同样好（或坏、重要等）；不相上下；伯仲之间 **up to 'par** as good as usual or as good as it should be 达到通常（或应有）的水准 SYN **up to scratch**

par. (*also* **para.**) *abbr.* (in writing 书写形式) paragraph 段；段落: *See par. 3.* 参见第3段。

para /'pærə/ *noun* (*informal*) = PARATROOPER

para- /'pærə/ *prefix* (in nouns and adjectives 构成名词和形容词) **1** beyond 超越: *paranormal* 超常的 **2** similar to but not official or not fully qualified 准；近似: *paramilitary* 准军事的 ◇ *a paramedic* 医务辅助人员 ➲ MORE LIKE THIS 6, page R25

par·able /'pærəbl/ *noun* a short story that teaches a moral or spiritual lesson, especially one of those told by Jesus as recorded in the Bible （尤指《圣经》中的）寓言故事

para·bola /pə'ræbələ/ *noun* (*geometry* 几何) a curve like the path of an object thrown into the air and falling back to earth 抛物线 ➲ PICTURE AT CONIC SECTION ▸ **para·bol·ic** /ˌpærə'bɒlɪk; *NAmE* -'bɑːlɪk/ *adj.*: *parabolic curves* 抛物曲线

para·ceta·mol /ˌpærə'siːtəmɒl; -'set-; *NAmE* -mɑːl/ (*BrE*) (*NAmE* **acet·amino·phen**) *noun* [U, C] (*pl.* **para·ceta·mol** or **para·ceta·mols**) a drug used to reduce pain and fever 对乙酰氨基酚；扑热息痛: *Do you have any paracetamol?* 你有扑热息痛吗？ ◇ *Take two paracetamol(s) and try to sleep.* 服两片扑热息痛，好好睡一觉。

para·chute /'pærəʃuːt/ *noun, verb*

■ *noun* (*also informal* **chute**) a device that is attached to people or objects to make them fall slowly and safely when they are dropped from an aircraft. It consists of a large piece of thin cloth that opens out in the air to form an umbrella shape. 降落伞: *Planes dropped supplies by parachute.* 飞机用降落伞空投补给。 ◇ *a* ***parachute drop/jump*** 空投；跳伞 ◇ *a parachute regiment* 空降兵团 ➲ WORDFINDER NOTE AT AIRCRAFT

■ *verb* **1** [I] (+ **adv./prep.**) to jump from an aircraft using a parachute 跳伞: *The pilot was able to parachute to safety.* 飞行员得以跳伞脱险。 ◇ *She regularly* ***goes parachuting.*** 她经常去从事跳伞活动。 **2** [T] **~ sb/sth + adv./prep.** to drop sb/sth from an aircraft by parachute 伞降；空投

para·chut·ist /'pærəʃuːtɪst/ *noun* a person who jumps from a plane using a parachute 跳伞者

para·clin·ical /ˌpærə'klɪnɪkl/ *adj.* (*specialist*) related to the parts of medicine, especially laboratory sciences, that are not directly involved in the care of patients 临床旁学的，辅助临床的（关于实验室科学等）

par·ade /pə'reɪd/ *noun, verb*

■ *noun*

• **PUBLIC CELEBRATION** 公共庆典 **1** [C] a public celebration of a special day or event, usually with bands in the streets and decorated vehicles 游行 SYN **procession**: *the Lord Mayor's parade* 欢迎新市长大游行 ◇ *St Patrick's Day parade in New York* 纽约市圣帕特里克节庆祝游行 ➲ WORDFINDER NOTE AT CELEBRATE

• **OF SOLDIERS** 士兵 **2** [C, U] a formal occasion when soldiers march or stand in lines so that they can be examined by their officers or other important people 检阅；阅兵: *a military parade* 军事检阅 ◇ *They stood as straight as soldiers* ***on parade.*** 他们像接受检阅的士兵一样站得笔直。 ◇ (*figurative*) *The latest software will be on parade at the exhibition.* 最新软件将在展览会上展出。 ➲ SEE ALSO IDENTIFICATION PARADE

• **SERIES** 系列 **3** [C] a series of things or people 一系列（人或事）: *Each generation passes through a similar parade of events.* 每一代人都要经历一系列类似的事。

• **WEALTH/KNOWLEDGE** 财富；知识 **4** [C, usually sing.] **~ of wealth, knowledge, etc.** (*often disapproving*) an obvious display of sth, particularly in order to impress other people 夸示；炫耀

• **ROW OF SHOPS** 一排商店 **5** [C] (*especially BrE*) (often in names 常用于名称) a street with a row of small shops 有一排小商店的街道: *a shopping parade* 购物街 IDM SEE RAIN *v.*

■ *verb*

• **WALK TO CELEBRATE/PROTEST** 游行庆祝 / 抗议 **1** [I] (**+ adv./prep.**) to walk somewhere in a formal group of people, in order to celebrate or protest about sth 游行；游行庆祝；游行示威: *The victorious team will parade through the city tomorrow morning.* 明天上午获胜队将在城内举行庆祝游行。

• **SHOW IN PUBLIC** 公开展示 **2** [I] **+ adv./prep.** to walk around in a way that makes other people notice you 招摇过市；大摇大摆: *People were parading up and down showing off their finest clothes.* 人们走来走去，炫耀着他们最漂亮的服装。 **3** [T] **~ sb/sth + adv./prep.** to show sb/sth in public so that people can see them/it 展览；展示: *The trophy was paraded around the stadium.* 奖杯被环绕着体育场进行展示。 ◇ *The prisoners were paraded in front of the crowd.* 囚犯被押解示众。 ◇ (*figurative*) *He is not one to parade his achievements.* 他不是一个爱炫耀自己成就的人。

• **OF SOLDIERS** 士兵 **4** [I, T] to come together, or to bring soldiers together, in order to march in front of other people （使）列队行进，接受检阅: **+ adv./prep.** *The crowds applauded as the guards paraded past.* 卫队列队走过时，人群鼓掌欢迎。 ◇ **~ sb + adv./prep.** *The colonel paraded his men before the Queen.* 上校指挥士兵列队行进，接受女王的检阅。

• **PRETEND** 佯装 **5** [I, T] to pretend to be, or to make sb/sth seem to be, good or important when they are not （使）冒充，伪装，打扮成: **~ as sth** *myth parading as fact* 外表看似真实的神话 ◇ **~ sb/sth/yourself as sth** *He paraded himself as a loyal supporter of the party.* 他把自己伪装成该党的忠实支持者。

pa'rade ground *noun* a place where soldiers gather to march or to be INSPECTED by an officer or an important visitor 阅兵场

para·digm AW /'pærədaɪm/ *noun* **1** (*specialist* or *formal*) a typical example or pattern of sth 范式；范例；典范；样式: *a paradigm for students to copy* 供学生效法的榜样 ◇ *The war was a paradigm of the destructive side of human nature.* 那场战争尽显人性中具有破坏性的一面。 **2** (*grammar* 语法) a set of all the different forms of a word 词形变化表: *verb paradigms* 动词词形变化表 ▸ **para·dig·mat·ic** /ˌpærədɪɡ'mætɪk/ *adj.*

'paradigm shift *noun* a great and important change in the way sth is done or thought about 范式转移（指行事或思维方式的重大变化）

para·dise /'pærədaɪs/ *noun* **1** (*often* **Paradise**) [U] (in some religions) a perfect place where people are said to go when they die （某些宗教所指的）天堂，天国 SYN **heaven**: *The ancient Egyptians saw paradise as* *an idealized version of their own lives.* 古埃及人把天堂视为他们自身现实生活的理想形式。 **2** [C] a place that is extremely beautiful and that seems perfect, like heaven 天堂，乐土，乐园（指美好的环境）： *a tropical paradise* 一处热带的人间乐土 **3** [C] a perfect place for a particular activity or kind of person（某类活动或某类人的）乐园，完美去处： *The area is a birdwatcher's paradise.* 这一地区是鸟类观察者的乐园。 **4** [U] a state of perfect happiness 至福；极乐 SYN **bliss**: *Being alone is his idea of paradise.* 他视独处为至乐之事。 **5 Paradise** [U] (in the Bible《圣经》) the garden of Eden, where Adam and Eve lived 伊甸园

para·dox /'pærədɒks; *NAmE* -dɑːks/ *noun* **1** [C] a person, thing or situation that has two opposite features and therefore seems strange 矛盾的人（或事物、情况）： *He was a paradox—a loner who loved to chat to strangers.* 他真是个矛盾人物，生性孤僻却又喜欢和陌生人闲聊。◇ *It is a curious paradox that professional comedians often have unhappy personal lives.* 这真是个奇怪的矛盾现象：职业喜剧演员的私人生活往往并不快乐。 **2** [C, U] a statement containing two opposite ideas that make it seem impossible or unlikely, although it is probably true; the use of this in writing 似非而是的隽语；悖论；悖论修辞： *'More haste, less speed' is a well-known paradox.* "欲速则不达"是人们熟知的似非而是的隽语。◇ *It's a work full of paradox and ambiguity.* 这部作品充满了似非而是及模棱两可之处。 ➲ WORDFINDER NOTE AT IMAGE ▶ **para·dox·ical** /ˌpærə'dɒksɪkl; *NAmE* -'dɑːks-/ *adj.*: *It is paradoxical that some of the poorest people live in some of the richest areas of the country.* 某些最贫穷的人却住在这个国家一些最富有的地区，这似乎很矛盾。 **para·dox·ic·al·ly** /-kli/ *adv.*: *Paradoxically, the less she ate, the fatter she got.* 很矛盾的是，她吃得越少，就变得越胖。

par·af·fin /'pærəfɪn/ (*also* **'paraffin oil**) (*both BrE*) (*NAmE* **kero·sene**) *noun* [U] a type of oil obtained from PETROLEUM and used as a fuel for heat and light 煤油： *a paraffin heater/lamp/stove* 煤油取暖器；煤油灯；煤油炉

'paraffin wax *noun* [U] a soft white substance that is made from PETROLEUM or coal, and is used especially for making CANDLES 石蜡（尤用以制造蜡烛）

para·glider /'pærəglaɪdə(r)/ *noun* **1** a structure consisting of a big thin piece of cloth like a PARACHUTE, and a HARNESS which is attached to a person when they jump from a high place in the sport of PARAGLIDING 滑翔伞 **2** a person who does paragliding 滑翔伞运动者

para·glid·ing /'pærəglaɪdɪŋ/ *noun* [U] a sport in which you wear a special structure like a PARACHUTE, jump from a high place and are carried along by the wind before coming down to earth 滑翔伞运动： *to go paragliding* 去伞翼滑翔 ➲ VISUAL VOCAB PAGE V53

para·gon /'pærəgən; *NAmE* -gɑːn/ *noun* a person who is perfect or who is a perfect example of a particular good quality 完人；典范： *I make no claim to be a paragon.* 我没有说过自己是完人。◇ *He wasn't the* ***paragon of virtue*** *she had expected.* 他不是她想象中的那种美德典范。

para·graph AW /'pærəgrɑːf; *NAmE* -græf/ *noun* (*abbr.* **par.**, **para.**) a section of a piece of writing, usually consisting of several sentences dealing with a single subject. The first sentence of a paragraph starts on a new line. 段；段落： *an* ***opening/introductory paragraph*** 开头的 / 导引的一段 ◇ *Write a paragraph on each of the topics given below.* 就下面所列主题各写一个段落。 ◇ *See paragraph 15 of the handbook.* 参见手册第 15 段。

para·graph·ing AW /'pærəgrɑːfɪŋ; *NAmE* -græf-/ *noun* [U] the way that a piece of writing is divided into paragraphs 段落划分；分段（方式）

para·keet (*also* **parra·keet**) /'pærəkiːt/ *noun* a small bird of the PARROT family, usually with a long tail 长尾鹦鹉

para·legal /ˌpærə'liːgl/ *noun* (*especially NAmE*) a person who is trained to help a lawyer 律师助理 ▶ **para·legal** *adj.*

para·lin·guis·tic /ˌpærəlɪŋ'gwɪstɪk/ *adj.* (*linguistics* 语言) relating to communication through ways other than words, for example tone of voice, expressions on your face and actions 副语言的，辅助语言的，伴随语言的（通过声调、表情、行动等交流）

par·all·ax /'pærəlæks/ *noun* [U] (*specialist*) the effect by which the position or direction of an object appears to change when the object is seen from different positions 视差（从不同位置观察物体所产生的位置或方向上的差别）

par·al·lel 🔑 AW /'pærəlel/ *adj., noun, verb*

■ ***adj.*** **1** 🔑 two or more lines that are **parallel** to each other are the same distance apart at every point 平行（的）： *parallel lines* 平行线 ◇ **~ to/with sth** *The road and the canal are parallel to each other.* 道路与运河平行。 **2** very similar or taking place at the same time 极相似的；同时发生的；相应的；对应的： *a parallel case* 同类型事例 ◇ *parallel trends* 并行发展的趋势 **3** (*computing* 计) involving several computer operations at the same time 并行的： *parallel processing* 并行处理 ▶ **par·al·lel** *adv.*: *The road and the canal* ***run parallel*** *to each other.* 道路与运河平行。◇ *The plane flew parallel to the coast.* 飞机沿海岸线飞行。

■ ***noun*** **1** [C, U] a person, a situation, an event, etc. that is very similar to another, especially one in a different place or time（尤指不同地点或时间的）极其相似的人（或情况、事件等） SYN **equivalent**: *These ideas have parallels in Freud's thought too.* 这些观念与弗洛伊德思想中的某些观点也非常相似。 ◇ *This is an achievement* ***without parallel*** *in modern times.* 这一成就在当代无人可及。◇ *This tradition* ***has no parallel*** *in our culture.* 这种传统在我们的文化中是没有的。 **2** [C, usually pl.] similar features 相似特征；相似特点： *There are interesting parallels between the 1960s and the late 1990s.* * 20 世纪 60 年代和 90 年代后期有些颇有意思的相似之处。 ◇ *It is possible to* ***draw a parallel between*** (= find similar features in) *their experience and ours.* 在他们的经历和我们的经历之间找到相似点是可能的。 **3** (*also* ˌ**parallel of 'latitude**) [C] an imaginary line around the earth that is always the same distance from the EQUATOR; this line on a map（地球或地图的）纬线，纬（度）圈： *the 49th parallel* * 49 度纬线

IDM **in 'parallel (with sth/sb)** with and at the same time as sth/sb else （与…）同时： *The new degree and the existing certificate courses would run in parallel.* 新的学位课程和现有的证书课程将同时开设。

■ ***verb*** **1 ~ sth** to be similar to sth; to happen at the same time as sth 与…相似；与…同时发生： *Their legal system parallels our own.* 他们的法律制度与我们的相似。 ◇ *The rise in unemployment is paralleled by an increase in petty crime.* 在失业率上升的同时，轻微罪行也跟着增长。 **2 ~ sth** to be as good as sth 与…媲美；比得上 SYN **equal**: *a level of achievement that has never been paralleled* 绝无仅有的最高成就 ➲ COMPARE UNPARALLELED

ˌ**parallel 'bars** *noun* [pl.] two bars on posts that are used for doing GYMNASTIC exercises 双杠

ˌ**parallel 'imports** *noun* [pl.] (*economics* 经) goods that are imported into a country without the permission of the company that produced them, and sold at a lower price than the company sells them at 平行进口货物，水货（未经厂家许可进口并低价销售的产品）

par·al·lel·ism /'pærəlelɪzəm/ *noun* [U, C] (*formal*) the state of being similar; a similar feature 相似；相似的特点： *I think he exaggerates the parallelism between the two cases.* 我认为他夸大了两件事的相似之处。

par·al·lelo·gram /ˌpærə'leləgræm/ *noun* (*geometry* 几何) a flat shape with four straight sides, the opposite sides being parallel and equal to each other 平行四边形 ➲ PICTURE ON NEXT PAGE

ˌ**parallel 'processing** *noun* [U] (*computing* 计) the division of a process into different parts, which are performed at the same time by different PROCESSORS in a computer 并行处理

ˌparallel ˈruler *noun* a device for drawing lines that are always the same distance apart, consisting of two connected rulers 平行线尺（由两把相连接的尺子组成）

Para·lym·pian (*also* **paralympian**) /ˌpærəˈlɪmpiən/ *noun* a person who competes in the Paralympics 残奥会运动员 ▸ **Paralympian** (*also* **paralympian**) *adj.*

the Para·lym·pics /ˌpærəˈlɪmpɪks/ *noun* [pl.] an international ATHLETICS competition for people who are disabled 残疾人奥运会；残奥会

para·lyse (*BrE*) (*NAmE* **para·lyze**) /ˈpærəlaɪz/ *verb* [often passive] **1 ~ sb** to make sb unable to feel or move all or part of their body 使瘫痪；使麻痹：*The accident left him **paralysed from the waist down**.* 那场事故使他腰部以下都瘫痪了。◇ (*figurative*) *paralysing heat* 令人头昏脑涨的炎热 ◇ (*figurative*) *She stood there, paralysed with fear.* 她站在那里，吓得呆若木鸡。 **2 ~ sth** to prevent sth from functioning normally 使不能正常工作：*The airport is still paralysed by the strike.* 机场仍因罢工而陷于瘫痪。

par·aly·sis /pəˈræləsɪs/ *noun* (*pl.* **par·aly·ses** /-siːz/) **1** [U, C] a loss of control of, and sometimes feeling in, part or most of the body, caused by disease or an injury to the nerves 麻痹；瘫痪：*paralysis of both legs* 双腿瘫痪 **2** [U] a total inability to move, act, function, etc. （活动、工作等）能力的完全丧失，瘫痪：*The strike caused total paralysis in the city.* 罢工使这座城市完全瘫痪。

para·lyt·ic /ˌpærəˈlɪtɪk/ *adj.* **1** [not before noun] (*BrE, informal*) very drunk 烂醉；酩酊大醉 **2** [usually before noun] (*formal*) suffering from PARALYSIS; making sb unable to move 瘫痪的；麻痹的；使动弹不得的：*a paralytic illness* 一种麻痹症 ◇ *paralytic fear* 令人不知所措的恐惧

para·med·ic /ˌpærəˈmedɪk/ *noun* a person whose job is to help people who are sick or injured, but who is not a doctor or a nurse 急救医士；护理人员；医务辅助人员：*Paramedics treated the injured at the roadside.* 护理人员在路旁为伤者治疗。 ➲ WORDFINDER NOTE AT ACCIDENT ▸ **para·med·ic·al** /-ɪkl/ *adj.*：*paramedical staff* 医务辅助人员

par·am·eter AW /pəˈræmɪtə(r)/ *noun* [usually pl.] (*formal*) something that decides or limits the way in which sth can be done 决定因素；规范；范围：*to **set/define the parameters*** 制订 / 设定规范 ◇ *We had to work within the parameters that had already been established.* 我们必须在已设定的范围内工作。

para·mili·tary /ˌpærəˈmɪlətri; *NAmE* -teri/ *adj.*, *noun*
■ *adj.* [usually before noun] **1** a **paramilitary** organization is an illegal group that is organized like an army 非法军事组织的：*a right-wing paramilitary group* 一个右翼非法军事集团 **2** helping the official army of a country 辅助军事的；准军事的：*paramilitary police, such as the CRS in France* 法国的共和国保安部队之类的军事辅助警察
■ *noun* [usually pl.] (*pl.* **-ies**) **1** a member of an illegal paramilitary group or organization 非法军事集团（或组织）的成员 **2** a member of an organization that helps the official army of a country 辅助军事组织的成员；准军事组织的成员

parallelograms 平行四边形

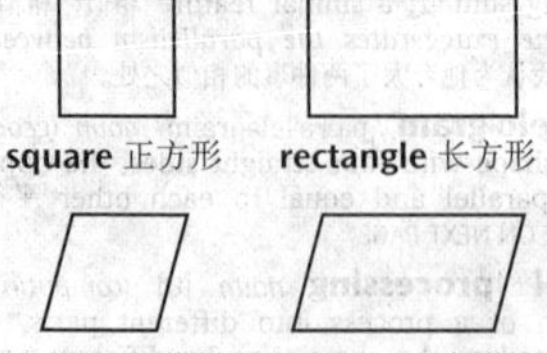

para·mount /ˈpærəmaʊnt/ *adj.* **1** more important than anything else 至为重要的；首要的：*This matter is **of paramount importance**.* 此事至关重要。◇ *Safety is paramount.* 安全至上。➲ LANGUAGE BANK AT VITAL **2** (*formal*) having the highest position or the greatest power 至高无上的；至尊的；权力最大的：*China's paramount leader* 中国的最高领导人 ▸ **para·mount·cy** /-maʊntsi/ *noun* [U]

par·amour /ˈpærəmʊə(r); *NAmE* -mʊr/ *noun* (*old-fashioned* or *literary*) a person that sb is having a romantic or sexual relationship with 情人；情妇；情夫 SYN **lover**

para·noia /ˌpærəˈnɔɪə/ *noun* [U] **1** (*medical* 医) a mental illness in which a person may wrongly believe that other people are trying to harm them, that they are sb very important, etc. 偏执狂；妄想症 ➲ WORDFINDER NOTE AT CONDITION **2** (*informal*) fear or suspicion of other people when there is no evidence or reason for this （对别人的）无端恐惧，多疑

para·noid /ˈpærənɔɪd/ *adj.*, *noun*
■ *adj.* (*also less frequent* **para·noiac** /ˌpærəˈnɔɪɪk; -ˈnɔɪæk/) **1** afraid or suspicious of other people and believing that they are trying to harm you, in a way that is not reasonable 多疑的；恐惧的：*She's getting really paranoid about what other people say about her.* 她开始对别人怎么议论她变得十分猜疑。➲ SYNONYMS AT AFRAID **2** suffering from a mental illness in which you wrongly believe that other people are trying to harm you or that you are very important 患偏执症的；有妄想狂的：*paranoid delusions* 偏执妄想 ◇ *paranoid schizophrenia* 偏执型精神分裂症 ◇ *a paranoid killer* 偏执型杀人凶手
■ *noun* (*also* **para·noiac** /ˌpærəˈnɔɪɪk; -ˈnɔɪæk/) a person who suffers from paranoia 偏执狂；妄想症患者

para·nor·mal /ˌpærəˈnɔːml; *NAmE* -ˈnɔːrml/ *adj.* **1** that cannot be explained by science or reason and that seems to involve mysterious forces 超自然的；无法用科学解释的；超常的 SYN **supernatural** **2 the paranormal** *noun* [sing.] events or subjects that are paranormal 超常事件（或话题）SYN **supernatural**

para·pet /ˈpærəpɪt; -pet/ *noun* a low wall along the edge of a bridge, a roof, etc. to stop people from falling 防护矮墙：(*figurative*) *He was not prepared to **put his head above the parapet** and say what he really thought* (= he did not want to risk doing it). 他不想贸然出头说出自己的真实想法。

para·pher·na·lia /ˌpærəfəˈneɪliə; *NAmE also* -fərˈn-/ *noun* [U] a large number of objects or personal possessions, especially the equipment that you need for a particular activity （尤指某活动所需的）装备，大量用品，私人物品：*skiing paraphernalia* 滑雪装备 ◇ *an electric kettle and all the paraphernalia for making tea and coffee* 电水壶及沏茶冲咖啡的全套用具

para·phrase /ˈpærəfreɪz/ *verb*, *noun*
■ *verb* [T, I] **~ (sth)** to express what sb has said or written using different words, especially in order to make it easier to understand （用更容易理解的文字）解释，释义，意译：*Try to paraphrase the question before you answer it.* 先试着解释一下问题再作回答。
■ *noun* a statement that expresses sth that sb has written or said using different words, especially in order to make it easier to understand 解释；释义；意译

para·ple·gia /ˌpærəˈpliːdʒə/ *noun* [U] PARALYSIS (= loss of control or feeling) in the legs and lower body 截瘫；下身麻痹

para·ple·gic /ˌpærəˈpliːdʒɪk/ *noun* a person who suffers from paraplegia 截瘫病人；下身麻痹患者 ▸ **para·ple·gic** *adj.*

para·psych·ology /ˌpærəsaɪˈkɒlədʒi; *NAmE* -ˈkɑːl-/ *noun* [U] the study of mental powers that seem to exist but that cannot be explained by scientific knowledge 心灵学；超心理学

para·quat /ˈpærəkwɒt; *NAmE* -kwɑːt/ *noun* [U] an extremely poisonous liquid used to kill plants that are growing where they are not wanted （剧毒）灭草剂；百草枯

para·sail·ing /ˈpærəseɪlɪŋ/ *noun* [U] the sport of being pulled up into the air behind a boat while wearing a special PARACHUTE 帆伞运动；水上拖伞运动

par·as·cend·ing /ˈpærəsendɪŋ/ *noun* [U] (*BrE*) a sport in which you wear a PARACHUTE and are pulled along behind a boat, car, etc. so that you rise up into the air （汽船、汽车等牵引的）伞翼滑翔运动：*to go parascending* 进行伞翔运动

para·site /ˈpærəsaɪt/ *noun* **1** a small animal or plant that lives on or inside another animal or plant and gets its food from it 寄生物；寄生植物；寄生虫 **2** (*disapproving*) a person who always relies on or benefits from other people and gives nothing back 寄生虫；依赖他人过活者

para·sit·ic /ˌpærəˈsɪtɪk/ (*also less frequent* **para·sit·ical** /ˌpærəˈsɪtɪkl/) *adj.* **1** caused by a parasite 寄生生物引起的：*a* ***parasitic disease/infection*** 寄生虫病 / 感染 **2** living on another animal or plant and getting its food from it 寄生的；依附性的：*a parasitic mite* 寄生螨 **3** (*disapproving*) (of a person 人) always relying on or benefiting from other people and giving nothing back 寄生虫似的；依赖他人的 ▶ **para·sit·ic·al·ly** /-kli/ *adv.*

para·sol /ˈpærəsɒl; *NAmE* -sɔːl; -sɑːl/ *noun* **1** a type of light umbrella that women in the past carried to protect themselves from the sun （旧时的）女用阳伞 **2** a large umbrella that is used for example on beaches or outside restaurants to protect people from hot sun （海滩上、餐馆外等处的）大遮阳伞 ➲ VISUAL VOCAB PAGE V20 ➲ COMPARE SUNSHADE (1)

para·statal /ˌpærəˈsteɪtl/ *adj.* (*specialist*) (of an organization 机构) having some political power and serving the state 国有的；部分国有的

para·taxis /ˌpærəˈtæksɪs/ *noun* [U] (*grammar* 语法) the placing of clauses and phrases one after the other, without words to link them or show their relationship 无连词并列；意合连接 ➲ COMPARE HYPOTAXIS

par·atha /pəˈrɑːtə/ *noun* a type of S Asian bread made without YEAST, usually fried on a GRIDDLE 抛饼（南亚食品，不发酵，通常用鏊子煎成）

para·troop·er /ˈpærətruːpə(r)/ (*also informal* **para**) *noun* a member of the paratroops 伞兵；空降兵

para·troops /ˈpærətruːps/ *noun* [pl.] soldiers who are trained to jump from planes using a PARACHUTE 空降兵部队；伞兵部队 ▶ **para·troop** *adj.* [only before noun]: *a paratroop regiment* 伞兵团

par·boil /ˈpɑːbɔɪl; *NAmE* ˈpɑːrb-/ *verb* ~ **sth** to boil food, especially vegetables, until it is partly cooked （尤指将蔬菜）煮成半熟

par·cel /ˈpɑːsl; *NAmE* ˈpɑːrsl/ *noun, verb*

■ *noun* **1** (*especially BrE*) (*NAmE usually* **pack·age**) something that is wrapped in paper or put into a thick envelope so that it can be sent by mail, carried easily, or given as a present 包裹；小包：*There's a parcel and some letters for you.* 有你的一个包裹和几封信。◇ *She was carrying a parcel of books under her arm.* 她腋下夹着一包书。◇ *The prisoners were allowed food parcels.* 囚犯可以收食物包裹。 **2** a piece of land 一块地；一片地：*50 five-acre parcels have already been sold.* 五英亩一块的土地已经售出 50 块。 **3** (*especially BrE*) a small amount of food that is wrapped in sth, usually pastry, before it is cooked 油酥包（通常以油酥皮包裹少许食物烹制）：*filo pastry parcels* 千层油酥包 IDM SEE PART *n.*

■ *verb* (*especially BrE*) (**-ll-**, *especially US* **-l-**) ~ **sth** (**up**) to wrap sth up and make it into a parcel 包；裹好；打包：*She parcelled up the books to send.* 她把要寄走的书包了起来。

PHR V **ˌparcel sth↔ˈout** to divide sth into parts or between several people 把某物分开；把某物（在几个人之间）分：*The land was parcelled out into small lots.* 这块地被分成了若干小块。

ˈparcel bomb *noun* (*BrE*) a bomb that is sent to sb in a package and that explodes when the package is opened 邮包炸弹；包裹炸弹

parch /pɑːtʃ; *NAmE* pɑːrtʃ/ *verb* ~ **sth** (especially of hot weather 尤指炎热天气) to make an area of land very dry 使（土地）极干燥

parched /pɑːtʃt; *NAmE* pɑːrtʃt/ *adj.* **1** very dry, especially because the weather is hot 焦干的；晒焦的：*dry parched land* 焦干的土地 ◇ *soil parched by drought* 旱灾造成的焦干的土壤 ◇ *She licked her parched lips.* 她舔了舔干裂的双唇。 **2** (*informal*) very thirsty 干渴的；极渴的：*Let's get a drink—I'm parched.* 咱们喝点儿饮料吧，我嗓子都干得冒烟儿了。

ˌparched ˈrice *noun* [U] rice that has been pressed flat and dried, used in Asian cooking 大米片（扁平干燥）

Par·cheesi™ /pɑːˈtʃiːzi; *NAmE* pɑːrˈtʃ-/ *noun* [U] (*NAmE*) a simple game played with DICE and COUNTERS on a special board, similar to the British game, LUDO 巴棋戏（一种用骰子和筹码在棋盘上玩的游戏，类似英国的"卢多"）

parch·ment /ˈpɑːtʃmənt; *NAmE* ˈpɑːrtʃ-/ *noun* **1** [U] material made from the skin of a sheep or GOAT, used in the past for writing on 羊皮纸：*parchment scrolls* 羊皮纸卷 **2** [U] a thick yellowish type of paper 仿羊皮纸 **3** [C] a document written on a piece of parchment 羊皮纸文献

pard·ner /ˈpɑːdnə(r); *NAmE* ˈpɑːrd-/ *noun* (*NAmE, informal, non-standard*) a way of saying or writing 'partner' in informal speech 搭档，伙伴（partner 的非正式表达方式）

par·don /ˈpɑːdn; *NAmE* ˈpɑːrdn/ *exclamation, noun, verb*

■ *exclamation* **1** (*also* **ˌpardon ˈme** *especially in NAmE*) used to ask sb to repeat sth because you did not hear it or did not understand it （用于请求别人重复某事）什么，请再说一遍：*'You're very quiet today.' 'Pardon?' 'I said you're very quiet today.'* "你今天话很少啊。""什么？""我说你今天话很少。" **2** (*also* **ˌpardon ˈme**) used by some people to say 'sorry' when they have accidentally made a rude noise, or said or done sth wrong 抱歉；对不起

■ *noun* **1** (*BrE also* **ˌfree ˈpardon**) (*law* 律) [C] an official decision not to punish sb for a crime, or to say that sb is not guilty of a crime 赦免；特赦：*to* ***ask/grant/receive a pardon*** 请求 / 准予 / 获得赦免 ◇ *a* ***royal/presidential pardon*** 皇家 / 总统特赦 **2** [U] (*formal*) ~ (**for sth**) the action of forgiving sb for sth 原谅；宽恕 SYN **forgiveness**: *He asked her pardon for having deceived her.* 他欺骗了她，向她请求原谅。 IDM SEE BEG

■ *verb* (not usually used in the progressive tenses 通常不用于进行时) **1** ~ **sb** to officially allow sb who has been found guilty of a crime to leave prison and/or avoid punishment 赦免；特赦：*She was pardoned after serving ten years of a life sentence.* 她被判终身监禁，服刑十年后被赦免了。 **2** to forgive sb for sth they have said or done (used in many expressions when you want to be polite) 原谅（表示礼貌时常用的词语） SYN **excuse**: ~ **sth** *Pardon my ignorance, but what is a 'duplex'?* 请原谅我无知，duplex 是什么呢？ ◇ *The place was,* ***if you'll pardon the expression,*** *a dump.* 那个地方，请恕我直言，简直是个垃圾场。◇ ~ **sb** (**for sth/for doing sth**) *You could be pardoned for thinking* (= it is easy to understand why people think) *that education is not the government's priority.* 人们认为政府没有优先考虑教育，这是不难理解的。 ◇ *Pardon me for interrupting you.* 对不起，打扰您了。◇ ~ **sb doing sth** *Pardon my asking, but is that your husband?* 请原谅我多问，那位是您的先生吗？

IDM **ˌpardon ˈme** (*informal*) **1** (*especially NAmE*) used to ask sb to repeat sth because you did not hear it or do not understand it （用于请求别人重复某事）什么，请再说一次 **2** used by some people to say 'sorry' when they have accidentally made a rude noise or done sth wrong （为偶尔的冒失响声或过失表示歉意）对不起 ➲ SEE ALSO I BEG YOUR PARDON at BEG **ˌpardon me for ˈdoing sth** used to show that you are upset or offended by the way that sb has spoken to you （对别人的说话方式表示烦恼或生气）原谅我不得不做某事：*'Oh, just shut up!' 'Well, pardon me for breathing!'* "你给我闭嘴！""嗬，不能让人不呼吸吧！" ➲ MORE AT FRENCH *n.*

P

par·don·able /ˈpɑːdnəbl; *NAmE* ˈpɑːrdn-/ *adj.* that can be forgiven or excused 可原谅的；可以宽恕的 SYN **excusable** OPP **unpardonable**

pare /peə(r); *NAmE* per/ *verb* **1** to remove the thin outer layer of sth, especially of fruit 削皮，去皮（尤指果皮）：**~ sth** *She pared the apple.* 她削了苹果。◇ **~ sth from sth** *First, pare the rind from the lemon.* 首先把柠檬皮剥掉。◇ **~ sth off/away** *He pared away the excess glue with a razor blade.* 他用剃须刀刀片将溢胶刮去。➲ SEE ALSO PARING KNIFE **2 ~ sth (back/down)** to gradually reduce the size or amount 逐步减小（体积或数量）；使缩小：*The training budget has been pared back to a minimum.* 培训预算已被削减到最低限度。◇ *The workforce has been* ***pared to the bone*** (= reduced to the lowest possible level). 公司员工已被裁减到极限。 **3 ~ sth** (*especially BrE*) to cut away the edges of sth, especially your nails, in order to make them smooth and neat 修剪（指甲等） ➲ SEE ALSO PARINGS

par·ent 🔑 /ˈpeərənt; *NAmE* ˈper-/ *noun* **1** 🔑 [usually pl.] a person's father or mother 父亲；母亲：*He's still living with his parents.* 他还和父母住在一起。◇ *her adoptive parents* 她的养父母 ◇ *Sue and Ben have recently become parents.* 休和本最近当了爸爸妈妈了。➲ SEE ALSO ONE-PARENT FAMILY, SINGLE PARENT, STEP-PARENT ➲ WORDFINDER NOTE AT FAMILY **2** an animal or a plant which produces other animals or plants（动、植物的）亲本，亲代，父本，母本：*the parent bird/tree* 亲代鸟；亲代树 **3** (often used as an adjective 常用作形容词) an organization that produces and owns or controls smaller organizations of the same type 创始机构；母公司；总部：*a parent bank and its subsidiaries* 总行及其附属银行 ◇ *the parent company* 母公司

par·ent·age /ˈpeərəntɪdʒ; *NAmE* ˈper-/ *noun* [U] the origin of a person's parents and who they are 出身；世系；家世：*a young American of German parentage* 一个年轻的德裔美国人 ◇ *Nothing is known about her parentage and background.* 她的家世和来历不明。

par·en·tal /pəˈrentl/ *adj.* [usually before noun] connected with a parent or parents 父亲的；母亲的；父母的；双亲的：*parental responsibility/rights* 父母的职责 / 权利 ◇ *parental choice in education* 父母在教育上的选择 ◇ *the parental home* 父母的家

pa,rental con'trols *noun* [pl.] (*also* **pa,rental 'lock** [C]) a feature that is offered in some computer, mobile/ cell phone and digital television services, that enables parents or other adults to control children's access to material that is not suitable for them 家长监护（一些计算机、手机、数字电视所提供的功能，保护孩子不接触"儿童不宜"的内容） ▶ **parental control** *adj.* [only before noun]: *parental control software* 家长监护软件

pa,rental 'leave *noun* [U] time when a parent is allowed to be away from work to care for a child（照顾孩子的）父母假，家长假，育儿假：*paid/unpaid parental leave* 带薪 / 不带薪家长假 ◇ *fathers who take parental leave* 休育儿假的父亲们 ➲ SEE ALSO MATERNITY LEAVE, PATERNITY LEAVE

par·en·thesis /pəˈrenθəsɪs/ *noun* (*pl.* **par·en·theses** /-əsiːz/) **1** a word, sentence, etc. that is added to a speech or piece of writing, especially in order to give extra information. In writing, it is separated from the rest of the text using brackets, commas or DASHES. 插入语 **2** (*formal* or *NAmE*) (*BrE* **bracket, 'round bracket**) [usually pl.] either of a pair of marks, ( ), placed around extra information in a piece of writing or part of a problem in mathematics 括号：*Irregular forms are given* ***in parentheses.*** 不规则形式标注在括号内。

par·en·thet·ical /ˌpærənˈθetɪkl/ (*also* **par·en·thet·ic** /-ɪk/) *adj.* [usually before noun] (*formal*) given as extra information in a speech or piece of writing 插入的；插入成分的：*parenthetical remarks* 补充的话 ▶ **par·en·thet·ic·al·ly** /-kli/ *adv.*

par·ent·hood /ˈpeərənthʊd; *NAmE* ˈper-/ *noun* [U] the state of being a parent 做父母的身份：*the* ***responsibilities/ joys of parenthood*** 做父母的责任 / 欢乐

par·ent·ing /ˈpeərəntɪŋ; *NAmE* ˈper-/ *noun* [U] the process of caring for your child or children 养育；抚养；教养：***good/poor parenting*** 教养有方 / 无方 ◇ ***parenting skills*** 教养子女的技巧 ➲ COLLOCATIONS AT CHILD

par·en·tis ➲ IN LOCO PARENTIS

'parents-in-law *noun* [pl.] the parents of your husband or wife 配偶的双亲；公婆；岳父母 ➲ SEE ALSO IN-LAWS

,parent-'teacher association *noun* = PTA

par excellence /ˌpɑːr ˈeksəlɑːns; *NAmE* ˌeksəˈlɑːns/ *adj.* (*from French*) (only used after the noun it describes 仅用于所修饰的名词之后) better than all the others of the same kind; a very good example of sth 最好的；最优秀的；典型的；卓越的：*She turned out to be an organizer par excellence.* 结果她是一个非常出色的组织者。 ▶ **par excellence** *adv.*: *Chemistry was par excellence the laboratory science of the early nineteenth century.* 化学是 19 世纪初期最杰出的实验室科学。

par·iah /pəˈraɪə/ *noun* a person who is not acceptable to society and is avoided by everyone 被社会遗弃者；贱民 SYN **outcast**

'paring knife *noun* a small sharp knife, used especially for cutting and PEELING fruit 水果刀；削皮小尖刀 ➲ SEE ALSO PARE (1) ➲ VISUAL VOCAB PAGE V27

par·ings /ˈpeərɪŋz; *NAmE* ˈper-/ *noun* [pl.] thin pieces that have been cut off sth 削下之物；切下的碎屑：*cheese parings* 奶酪碎屑 ➲ SEE ALSO PARE (3)

par·ish /ˈpærɪʃ/ *noun* **1** [C] an area that has its own church and that a priest is responsible for 堂区；教区：***a parish church/priest*** 堂区的教堂 / 神父 ◇ *He is vicar of a large rural parish.* 他是乡下一个大教区的代牧。 **2** [C] (in England) a small country area that has its own elected local government（英格兰）乡村行政小区：*the parish council* 行政区议会 **3** [C+sing./pl. v.] the people living in a particular area, especially those who go to church 教区居民；（尤指）教区教徒 **4** [C] (in the US state of Louisiana 美国路易斯安那州) a county 县

par·ish·ad /ˈpɑrɪʃʌd/ *noun* (*IndE*) a council 委员会；议会

,parish 'clerk *noun* an official who organizes the affairs of a church in a particular area 教区秘书

pa·rish·ion·er /pəˈrɪʃənə(r)/ *noun* a person living in a parish, especially one who goes to church regularly 教区居民；（尤指）教区教徒

,parish-'pump *adj.* [only before noun] (*BrE, disapproving*) connected with local affairs only (and therefore not thought of as being very important) 地方主义的；区域性的；地方性的 SYN **parochial**: *parish-pump politics* 地方主义政治

,parish 'register *noun* a book that has a list of all the BAPTISMS, marriages and funerals that have taken place at a particular PARISH church 教区记事册（记录洗礼、婚丧等事）

par·ity /ˈpærəti/ *noun* (*pl.* **-ies**) **1** [U] **~ (with sb/sth) | ~ (between A and B)** (*formal*) the state of being equal, especially the state of having equal pay or status（尤指薪金或地位）平等，相同，对等：*Prison officers are demanding pay parity with the police force.* 狱警正要求与警察同工同酬。 **2** [U, C] (*finance* 财) the fact of the units of money of two different countries being equal（两国货币的）平价：*to achieve parity with the dollar* 取得与美元的平价

park 🔑 /pɑːk; *NAmE* pɑːrk/ *noun, verb*

■ ***noun*** **1** 🔑 [C] an area of public land in a town or a city where people go to walk, play and relax 公园：*Hyde Park* 海德公园 ◇ *We went for a walk in the park.* 我们去公园散了散步。◇ *a park bench* 公园的长凳 **2** 🔑 [C] (in compounds 构成复合词) an area of land used for a particular purpose 专用区；园区：*a business/science park*

商业 / 科学园区 ◇ *a wildlife park* 野生动物园 ➲ SEE ALSO AMUSEMENT PARK, CAR PARK, NATIONAL PARK, RETAIL PARK, SAFARI PARK, THEME PARK **3** [C] (in Britain) an area of land, usually with fields and trees, attached to a large country house （英国）庄园，庭院 **4** [C] (*NAmE*) a piece of land for playing sports, especially BASEBALL 运动场；（尤指）棒球场 ➲ SEE ALSO BALLPARK (1) **5 the park** [sing.] (*BrE*) a football (SOCCER) or RUGBY field 足球场；橄榄球场：*the fastest man on the park* 足球场上速度最快的人 IDM SEE WALK *n.*

■ ***verb*** **1** [I, T] ~ (**sth**) to leave a vehicle that you are driving in a particular place for a period of time 停（车）；泊（车）：*You can't park here.* 此处不准停车。◇ *You can't park the car here.* 此处禁止停车。◇ *He's parked very badly.* 他的车停放得很不好。◇ *a badly parked truck* 一辆没有停放好的卡车 ◇ *A red van was parked in front of the house.* 一辆红色面包车停在房前。◇ *a parked car* 一辆停放的轿车 ◇ (*informal, figurative*) *Just park your bags in the hall until your room is ready.* 你的房间收拾好之前，请先把行李放在大厅。➲ SEE ALSO DOUBLE-PARK **2** [T] **~ yourself + adv./prep.** (*informal*) to sit or stand in a particular place for a period of time （在某处）坐下（或站着）：*She parked herself on the edge of the bed.* 她坐在床沿上。 **3** [T] **~ sth** (*business* 商, *informal*) to decide to leave an idea or issue to be dealt with or considered at a later meeting 把…搁置，推迟（在以后的会议上讨论或处理）：*Let's park that until our next meeting.* 咱们把这留到下次开会时再处理吧。

PHR V **ˌpark ˈup | ˌpark sth↔ˈup** (*especially BrE* or *AustralE*) to find a place where you can park your vehicle 泊车；停放（车辆）：*People want to be able to park up and pop into the shop.* 人们希望有地方可以停车，然后进店看看。◇ *I couldn't **get parked up** anywhere near the restaurant.* 在这家餐馆附近我找不到地方停车。

parka /ˈpɑːkə; *NAmE* ˈpɑːrkə/ *noun* a very warm jacket or coat with a HOOD that often has fur inside 派克大衣；风雪外套

park·ade /pɑːˈkeɪd; *NAmE* pɑːrˈk-/ *noun* (*CanE*) a parking garage for many cars 停车场

ˌpark and ˈride *noun* a system designed to reduce traffic in towns in which people park their cars on the edge of a town and then take a special bus or train to the town centre; the area where people park their cars before taking the bus 存车换乘系统，驻车换乘系统（把汽车停在城外，然后乘公交车到市中心，以减少市区的车辆）；转乘停车场：*Use the park and ride.* 请使用驻车换乘系统。◇ *I've left my car in the park and ride.* 我把汽车停在转乘停车场了。◇ *a park-and-ride service* 停车转乘服务

par·kin /ˈpɑːkɪn; *NAmE* ˈpɑːrkɪn/ *noun* [U] (*BrE*) a dark brown sticky cake made with OATMEAL and TREACLE, flavoured with GINGER 燕麦姜饼

park·ing /ˈpɑːkɪŋ; *NAmE* ˈpɑːrk-/ *noun* [U] **1** the act of stopping a vehicle at a place and leaving it there for a period of time 停车；泊车：*There is no parking here between 9 a.m. and 6 p.m.* 上午 9 时至下午 6 时此处禁止停车。◇ *I managed to find a **parking space**.* 我终于找到了一个停车位。◇ *a parking fine* (= for parking illegally) 违章停车罚款 **2** a space or an area for leaving vehicles 停车场；停车位：*The hotel is centrally situated with ample free parking.* 旅馆坐落在市中心，有充裕的免费停车位。

ˈparking brake *noun* (*NAmE*) = HANDBRAKE

ˈparking garage (*NAmE*) (*BrE* **ˌmulti-storey ˈcar park, ˌmulti-ˈstorey**) *noun* a large building with several floors for parking cars in 多层停车场；立体停车场

ˈparking lot *noun* (*NAmE*) an area where people can leave their cars 停车场 ➲ COMPARE CAR PARK

ˈparking meter (*also* **meter**) *noun* a machine beside the road that you put money into when you park your car next to it 停车计时器 ➲ VISUAL VOCAB PAGE V3

ˈparking ticket (*also* **ticket**) *noun* an official notice that is put on your car when you have parked illegally, ordering you to pay money 违章停车罚单

Par·kin·son's dis·ease /ˈpɑːkɪnsnz dɪziːz; *NAmE* ˈpɑːrk-/ (*also* **par·kin·son·ism** /ˈpɑːkɪnsənɪzəm; *NAmE* ˈpɑːrk-/) *noun* [U] a disease of the nervous system that gets worse over a period of time and causes the muscles to become weak and the arms and legs to shake 帕金森病（神经系统疾病，能致肌肉无力和四肢颤抖）

ˈParkinson's law *noun* [U] (*humorous*) the idea that work will always take as long as the time available for it 帕金森定律（工作总是到时限最后一刻才会完成）

park·land /ˈpɑːklænd; *NAmE* ˈpɑːrk-/ *noun* [U] open land with grass and trees, for example around a large house in the country （如乡村大宅院周围的）有草木的开阔地

par·kour /pɑːˈkʊə(r); *NAmE* pɑːrˈkʊr/ *noun* [U] the sport of moving through a city by running, jumping and climbing under, around and through things 跑酷，城市疾走（在城市中奔跑、跳跃、攀爬、蛇行、穿越的运动）➲ COMPARE FREERUNNING ORIGIN From French *parcours du combattant*, a type of military training. 源自法语 parcours du combattant，一种军事训练课程。➲ VISUAL VOCAB PAGE V54

park·way /ˈpɑːkweɪ; *NAmE* ˈpɑːrk-/ *noun* (*NAmE*) a wide road with trees and grass along the sides or middle （有草木的）大路；绿化道路；林荫大道

parky /ˈpɑːki; *NAmE* ˈpɑːrki/ *adj.* (*BrE, informal, old-fashioned* or *humorous*) (of the weather 天气) cold 寒冷的

par·lance /ˈpɑːləns; *NAmE* ˈpɑːrl-/ *noun* [U] (*formal*) a particular way of using words or expressing yourself, for example one used by a particular group 说法；术语；用语：*in **common/legal/modern parlance*** 用普通 / 法律 / 现代用语 ◇ *A Munro, in climbing parlance, is a Scottish mountain exceeding 3 000 feet.* "芒罗"在登山术语里是指高度超过 3 000 英尺的苏格兰山峰。

par·lay /ˈpɑːleɪ; *NAmE* ˈpɑːrleɪ/ *verb*

PHR V **ˈparlay sth into sth** (*NAmE*) to use or develop sth such as money or a skill to make it more successful or worth more 成功地利用；有效发展；使增值：*She hopes to parlay her success as a model into an acting career.* 她希望利用自己当模特儿的成功经历进而发展演艺事业。

par·ley /ˈpɑːli; *NAmE* ˈpɑːrli/ *noun, verb*

■ ***noun*** (*old-fashioned*) a discussion between enemies or people who disagree, in order to try and find a way of solving a problem （敌对或有异议的双方间的）和谈，会谈，对话

■ ***verb*** [I] **~ (with sb)** (*old-fashioned*) to discuss sth with sb in order to solve a disagreement （和某人）和谈，谈判，会谈

par·lia·ment /ˈpɑːləmənt; *NAmE* ˈpɑːrl-/ *noun* **1** [C, sing.+sing./pl. v.] the group of people who are elected to make and change the laws of a country 议会；国会：*The German parliament is called the 'Bundestag'.* 德国的议会称为 Bundestag。➲ COLLOCATIONS AT POLITICS **2** **Parliament** [U+sing./pl. v.] the parliament of the United Kingdom, consisting of the House of Commons and the House of Lords 英国议会（包括下议院和上议院）：*a Member of Parliament* 议会议员 ◇ *The issue was debated **in Parliament**.* 议会就这个问题进行了辩论。◇ *an Act of Parliament* 议会法案 ◇ *to **win a seat in Parliament*** 赢得议会中的一个席位 ◇ *to **be elected to Parliament*** 当选为议会议员 **3** (*also* **Parliament**) [C, U] a particular period during which a parliament is working; Parliament as it exists between one GENERAL ELECTION and the next 一届议会的会期；（两次大选之间的）一届议会：*We are now into the second half of the parliament.* 我们现已进入了本届议会的后半任期。◇ *to dissolve Parliament* (= formally end its activities) *and call an election* 解散议会并举行大选 ➲ SEE ALSO HOUSES OF PARLIAMENT, HUNG ➲ WORDFINDER NOTE AT GOVERNMENT

WORDFINDER 联想词： act, bill, Chamber, coalition, **election**, **law**, legislation, politician, **vote**

P

par·lia·men·tar·ian /ˌpɑːləmən'teəriən; *NAmE* ˌpɑːrləmən'ter-/ *noun* a member of a parliament, especially one with a lot of skill and experience 议会议员；（尤指）资深议员，老道的议员

par·lia·men·tary /ˌpɑːlə'mentri; *NAmE* ˌpɑːrl-/ *adj.* [usually before noun] connected with a parliament; having a parliament 议会的；国会的；设有议会的：*parliamentary elections* 议会选举 ◇ *a parliamentary democracy* 议会民主政体 ➲ COMPARE UNPARLIAMENTARY

ˌparliamentary private 'secretary *noun* = PPS

ˌparliamentary 'privilege *noun* [U] the special right of Members of Parliament to speak freely in Parliament, especially about another person, without risking legal action 议员特权，言论免责权（在议会中针对他人等自由发言而不会被起诉）：*He made the allegation under the protection of parliamentary privilege.* 他是在议员特权的保护下做出那种指控的。

ˌparliamentary 'secretary *noun* a Member of Parliament who works in a government department below the minister 政务次官（大臣掌管的政府部门的议员）➲ COMPARE PARLIAMENTARY PRIVATE SECRETARY, PARLIAMENTARY UNDERSECRETARY

parliaˌmentary ˌunder'secretary *noun* (in the UK) a Member of Parliament in a government department, below a minister in rank 政务次长（英国政府部门任职的议员，级别低于大臣）

par·lour (*especially US* **par·lor**) /'pɑːlə(r); *NAmE* 'pɑːrl-/ *noun* **1** (*old-fashioned*) a room in a private house for sitting in, entertaining visitors, etc. （私人住房的）起居室，客厅 **2** (in compounds 构成复合词) (*especially NAmE*) a shop/store that provides particular goods or services （专营某种商品或业务的）店铺：*a beauty/an ice-cream parlour* 美容院；冰淇淋店 ➲ SEE ALSO FUNERAL PARLOUR, MASSAGE PARLOUR

'parlour game (*especially US* **'parlor game**) *noun* a game played in the home, especially a word game or guessing game 室内游戏；（尤指）填字游戏，猜谜游戏

par·lour·maid (*especially US* **par·lor·maid**) /'pɑːləmeɪd; *NAmE* 'pɑːrlərmeɪd/ *noun* (*old use*) a female servant who was employed in the past to serve food at the dinner table （旧时侍候用餐的）客厅侍女

par·lous /'pɑːləs; *NAmE* 'pɑːrləs/ *adj.* (*formal*) (of a situation 形势) very bad and very uncertain; dangerous 恶劣的；动荡的；危险的 SYN **perilous**

Parma vio·let /ˌpɑːmə 'vaɪələt; *NAmE* ˌpɑːrmə/ *noun* a strong-smelling plant with light purple flowers 帕尔马紫罗兰

Par·mesan /'pɑːmɪzæn; ˌpɑːmɪ'zæn; *NAmE* 'pɑːrməzɑːn; -zæn/ (*also* **ˌParmesan 'cheese**) *noun* [U] a type of very hard Italian cheese that is usually GRATED and eaten on Italian food 帕尔马干酪（一种意大利硬奶酪，常磨碎撒在食品上）

pa·ro·chial /pə'rəʊkiəl; *NAmE* -'roʊ-/ *adj.* **1** [usually before noun] (*formal*) connected with a church PARISH 教区的；堂区的：*parochial schools* 教区学校 ◇ *a member of the parochial church council* 教区教堂理事会成员 **2** (*disapproving*) only concerned with small issues that happen in your local area and not interested in more important things 只关心本地区的；地方观念的 ▶ **pa·ro·chial·ism** /-ɪzəm/ *noun* [U]：*the parochialism of a small community* 小圈子的狭隘观念

pa'rochial school *noun* (*NAmE*) a private school supported by a particular Christian church （由某个基督教教派办的）教区学校 ➲ COMPARE FAITH SCHOOL

par·od·ist /'pærədɪst/ *noun* a person who writes parodies 滑稽模仿作品作者

par·ody /'pærədi/ *noun, verb*

■ *noun* (*pl.* **-ies**) ~ (**of sth**) **1** [C, U] a piece of writing, music, acting, etc. that deliberately copies the style of sb/sth in order to be amusing 滑稽模仿作品（文章、音乐作品或表演等的滑稽模仿）：*a parody of a horror film* 一部恐怖电影的仿作 ➲ WORDFINDER NOTE AT COMEDY **2** [C] (*disapproving*) something that is such a bad or an unfair example of sth that it seems ridiculous 拙劣的模仿；荒诞不经的事 SYN **travesty**：*The trial was a parody of justice.* 那次审判是对正义的嘲弄。

■ *verb* (**par·odies**, **par·ody·ing**, **par·odied**, **par·odied**) ~ **sb/sth** to copy the style of sb/sth in an exaggerated way, especially in order to make people laugh 滑稽地模仿；夸张地演绎 SYN **lampoon**

par·ole /pə'rəʊl; *NAmE* pə'roʊl/ *noun, verb*

■ *noun* [U] **1** permission that is given to a prisoner to leave prison before the end of their SENTENCE on condition that they behave well 假释；有条件的释放：*to be eligible for parole* 符合假释条件 ◇ *She was released* **on parole**. 她获得假释。➲ WORDFINDER NOTE AT PRISON ➲ COLLOCATIONS AT JUSTICE **2** (*linguistics* 语言) language considered as the words individual people use, rather than as the communication system of a particular community 言语 ➲ COMPARE LANGUE

■ *verb* [usually passive] ~ **sb** to give a prisoner permission to leave prison before the end of their SENTENCE on condition that they behave well 假释；有条件地释放：*She was paroled after two years.* 她两年后获假释。

par·ox·ysm /'pærəksɪzəm/ *noun* ~ (**of sth**) **1** a sudden strong feeling or expression of an emotion that cannot be controlled 突然发作：*paroxysms of hate* 突然满腔仇恨 ◇ *a paroxysm of laughter* 一阵狂笑 **2** (*medical* 医) a sudden short attack of pain, causing physical shaking that cannot be controlled 阵发痛

par·quet /'pɑːkeɪ; *NAmE* pɑːr'keɪ/ *noun* [U] a floor covering made of flat pieces of wood fixed together in a pattern 拼花地板；镶木地板：*parquet flooring* 拼花地板 ➲ COMPARE WOODBLOCK (1)

parra·keet ➲ PARAKEET

parri·cide /'pærɪsaɪd/ *noun* [U, C] (*formal*) the crime of killing your father, mother or a close relative; a person who is guilty of this crime 杀父（或母、近亲）罪；杀父（或母、近亲）者 ➲ COMPARE FRATRICIDE (1), MATRICIDE, PATRICIDE

par·rot /'pærət/ *noun, verb*

■ *noun* a tropical bird with a curved beak. There are several types of parrot, most of which have bright feathers. Some are kept as pets and can be trained to copy human speech. 鹦鹉 IDM SEE SICK *adj.*

■ *verb* ~ **sb/sth** (*disapproving*) to repeat what sb else has said without thinking about what it means 鹦鹉学舌地说…

'parrot-fashion *adv.* (*BrE, disapproving*) if sb learns or repeats sth **parrot-fashion**, they do it without thinking about it or understanding what it means 鹦鹉学舌般地；盲从地；亦步亦趋地

parry /'pæri/ *verb* (**par·ries**, **parry·ing**, **par·ried**, **par·ried**) **1** [T, I] ~ (**sth**) to defend yourself against sb who is attacking you by pushing their arm, weapon, etc. to one side 挡开，拦挡（攻击等）SYN **deflect**：*He parried a blow to his head.* 他挡开了砸向头部的一击。◇ *The shot was parried by the goalie.* 射门的球被守门员挡出去了。**2** [T] ~ **sth** | + **speech** to avoid having to answer a difficult question, criticism, etc., especially by replying in the same way 逃避，躲避，回避（难题、批评等）SYN **fend off**：*She parried all questions about their relationship.* 她回避了关于他们之间关系的所有问题。▶ **parry** *noun* (*pl.* **-ies**)

parse /pɑːz; *NAmE* pɑːrs/ *verb* ~ **sth** (*grammar* 语法) to divide a sentence into parts and describe the grammar of each word or part （对句子）作语法分析；作句法分析

Par·see (*also* **Parsi**) /ˌpɑː'siː; 'pɑːsiː; *NAmE* ˌpɑːr'siː; 'pɑːrsiː/ *noun* a member of a religious group whose ANCESTORS originally came from Persia and whose religion is Zoroastrianism 帕西人（拜火教徒后裔，祖先为波斯人）

par·si·mo·ni·ous /ˌpɑːsɪˈməʊniəs; *NAmE* ˌpɑːrsəˈmoʊ-/ *adj.* (*formal*) extremely unwilling to spend money 悭吝的；吝啬的；小气的 SYN **mean** ▶ **par·si·mo·ni·ous·ly** *adv.*

par·si·mony /ˈpɑːsɪməni; *NAmE* ˈpɑːrsəmoʊni/ *noun* [U] (*formal*) the fact of being extremely unwilling to spend money 悭吝；吝啬；小气 SYN **meanness**

pars·ley /ˈpɑːsli; *NAmE* ˈpɑːrsli/ *noun* [U] a plant with curly green leaves that are used in cooking as a HERB and to decorate food 欧芹；荷兰芹：*fish with parsley sauce* 欧芹沙司鱼 ➲ VISUAL VOCAB PAGE V35 ➲ SEE ALSO COW PARSLEY

pars·nip /ˈpɑːsnɪp; *NAmE* ˈpɑːrs-/ *noun* [C, U] a long pale yellow root vegetable 欧洲防风；欧洲萝卜 ➲ VISUAL VOCAB PAGE V34

par·son /ˈpɑːsn; *NAmE* ˈpɑːrsn/ *noun* **1** (*old-fashioned*) an Anglican VICAR or PARISH priest 圣公会教区牧师；教区牧师 **2** (*informal*) a Protestant CLERGYMAN 新教牧师

par·son·age /ˈpɑːsənɪdʒ; *NAmE* ˈpɑːrs-/ *noun* a parson's house 教区牧师的住所

ˌparson's ˈnose (*NAmE also* ˌ**pope's ˈnose**) *noun* the piece of flesh at the tail end of a cooked bird, usually a chicken （烹调过的禽类、尤指鸡的）尾部的肉

part 🔑 /pɑːt; *NAmE* pɑːrt/ *noun, verb, adv.*

■ ***noun***

• SOME 一些 **1** 🔑 [U] **~ of sth** some but not all of a thing 部分：*We spent part of the time in the museum.* 我们花了一部分时间在博物馆。◇ *Part of the building was destroyed in the fire.* 大楼的一部分毁于火灾。◇ *Voters are given **only part of the story*** (= only some of the information). 只对选民透露了部分情况。◇ ***Part of me** feels sorry for him* (= I feel partly, but not entirely, sorry for him). 我有点儿同情他。

• PIECE 片段 **2** 🔑 [C] a section, piece or feature of sth 片段；部分；一点：*The early part of her life was spent in Paris.* 她年轻时生活在巴黎。◇ *The novel is good **in parts**.* 小说的一些章节不错。◇ *We've done the difficult part of the job.* 我们已完成了工作的困难部分。◇ *The procedure can be divided into two parts.* 这一程序可以分为两部分。◇ *The worst part was having to wait three hours in the rain.* 最糟糕的是必须在雨中等待三个小时。

• MEMBER 成员 **3** 🔑 [U] a member of sth; a person or thing that, together with others, makes up a single unit 成员；成分：*You need to be able to work as part of a team.* 你必须能作为团队的一员去工作。

• OF MACHINE 机器 **4** 🔑 [C] a piece of a machine or structure 部件；零件：*aircraft parts* 飞行器零件 ◇ *the working parts of the machinery* 机器的运作部件 ◇ ***spare parts*** 备用零件

• OF BODY/PLANT 身体；植物 **5** 🔑 [C] a separate piece or area of a human or animal body or of a plant 器官；部位；组成部分：*the parts of the body* 身体各部位 ➲ SEE ALSO PRIVATE PARTS

• REGION/AREA 地区；区域 **6** 🔑 [C] an area or a region of the world, a country, a town, etc. （世界、国家或城镇等的）区域，地区：*the northern part of the country* 这个国家的北部地区 ◇ *a plant that grows in many parts of the world* 生长在世界许多地区的一种植物 ◇ *Which part of Japan do you come from?* 你是日本哪个地区的人？◇ *Come and visit us if you're ever in our part of the world.* 什么时候到我们这个地方来，请来看看我们。 **7 parts** [pl.] (*old-fashioned, informal*) a region or an area 区域；地区：*She's not from these parts.* 她不是这一带的人。◇ *He's just arrived back from foreign parts.* 他刚从外地回来。

• OF BOOK/SERIES 书；系列片 **8** 🔑 [C] (*abbr.* **pt**) a section of a book, television series, etc., especially one that is published or broadcast separately （书、电视剧等的、尤指单独发行或播出的）部，集，部分：*an encyclopedia published in 25 weekly parts* 每周出版一部，共 25 部的百科全书 ◇ *Henry IV, Part II* 《亨利四世》第二篇 ◇ *The final part will be shown next Sunday evening.* 最后一集将于下星期天晚上播出。

• FOR ACTOR 演员 **9** 🔑 [C] a role played by an actor in a play, film/movie, etc.; the words spoken by an actor in a particular role 角色；台词：*She was very good in the part.* 她这个角色演得很好。◇ *Have you learned your part yet?* 你记住你的台词了吗？◇ (*figurative*) *He's always playing a part* (= pretending to be sth that he is not). 他总是装模作样的。

• INVOLVEMENT 参与 **10** [C, usually sing., U] the way in which sb/sth is involved in an action or situation 参加；参与：*He **had no part in** the decision.* 他没有参与这项决定。

• IN MUSIC 音乐 **11** [C] music for a particular voice or instrument in a group singing or playing together 部；声部；音部；段落：*the clarinet part* 单簧管部 ◇ *four-part harmony* 四部和声

• EQUAL PORTION 等份 **12** [C] a unit of measurement that allows you to compare the different amounts of substances in sth （度量单位的）等份，份：*Add three parts wine to one part water.* 一份水兑上三份葡萄酒。

• IN HAIR 发式 **13** (*NAmE*) (*BrE* **part·ing**) [C] a line on a person's head where the hair is divided with a COMB （头发的）分缝，发缝，分线 ➲ VISUAL VOCAB PAGE V65

IDM **the best/better part of sth** most of sth, especially a period of time; more than half of sth （事物、时间的）绝大部分，多半：*The journey took her the better part of an hour.* 旅程花去了她半个多小时。 **for the ˈmost part** 🔑 mostly; usually 多半；通常：*The contributors are, for the most part, professional scientists.* 投稿者大多是专业科学家。 ➲ LANGUAGE BANK AT GENERALLY **for ˈmy, ˈhis, ˈtheir, etc. part** speaking for myself, etc. 就我（或他、他们等）而言 SYN **personally** **have a part to ˈplay (in sth)** to be able to help sth 能帮助，能在…中发挥作用：*We all have a part to play in the fight against crime.* 打击犯罪，我们大家都有一份责任。 **have/play a ˈpart (in sth)** to be involved in sth 参与某事：*She plays an active part in local politics.* 她积极参与地方政治。 **have/play/take/want no ˈpart in/of sth** to not be involved or refuse to be involved in sth, especially because you disapprove of it 不参与，不卷入，拒绝加入（尤指不赞成的事情）：*I want no part of this sordid business.* 我不想卷入这一卑鄙勾当。 **in ˈpart** 🔑 partly; to some extent 部分地；在某种程度上：*Her success was due in part to luck.* 她的成功在某种程度上是由于运气好。 **look/dress the ˈpart** to have an appearance or wear clothes suitable for a particular job, role or position 外貌 / 穿着与工作（或身份、职务）相宜 **a man/woman of (many) ˈparts** a person with many skills 多才多艺的人；多面手 **on the part of sb/on sb's part** made or done by sb 由某人所为：*It was an error on my part.* 那是我的过失。 **part and parcel of sth** an essential part of sth 重要部分；基本部分：*Keeping the accounts is part and parcel of my job.* 记账是我的主要工作。 ➲ MORE LIKE THIS 13, page R26 **part of the ˈfurniture** a person or thing that you are so used to seeing that you no longer notice them 见惯了的人（或东西）；存在已久故不为人注意的人（或事物）：*I worked there so long that I became part of the furniture.* 我在那里工作得太久，都不为人注意了。 **take sth in good ˈpart** (*BrE*) to accept sth slightly unpleasant without complaining or being offended 从容面对，不介意地接受（不太愉快的事） **take ˈpart (in sth)** 🔑 to be involved in sth 参与某事 SYN **participate**：*to take part in a discussion/demonstration/fight/celebration* 参加讨论 / 示威 / 战斗 / 庆祝 ◇ *How many countries took part in the last Olympic Games?* 有多少国家参加了上届奥运会？ **take sb's ˈpart** (*BrE*) to support sb, for example in an argument （在辩论等中）支持某人，站在某人一边 SYN **side with**：*His mother always takes his part.* 他母亲总是向着他。 ➲ MORE AT DISCRETION, LARGE *adj.*, SUM *n.*

■ ***verb***

• LEAVE SB 离开某人 **1** [I] (*formal*) if a person **parts** from another person, or two people **part**, they leave each other 离开；分别：*We parted at the airport.* 我们在机场分手了。◇ *I hate to part on such bad terms.* 我不愿分手时关系闹得这么僵。◇ **~ from sb** *He has recently parted from his wife* (= they have started to live apart). 他最近与妻子分居了。 ➲ SEE ALSO PARTING

• KEEP APART 隔离 **2** [T, often passive] **~ sb (from sb)** (*formal*) to prevent sb from being with sb else 分离；分开；隔离：*I hate being parted from the children.* 我不愿与孩子们分开。◇ *The puppies were parted from their mother at birth.* 小狗崽儿一出生就和它们的妈妈分开了。

P

• **MOVE AWAY** 移开 **3** [I, T] if two things or parts of things **part** or you **part** them, they move away from each other 分散；分开；解散： *The crowd parted in front of them.* 人群在他们面前分开了。◇ *The elevator doors parted and out stepped the President.* 电梯门打开了，总统从里面步出。◇ ~ **sth** *Her lips were slightly parted.* 她的嘴唇微微张开。◇ *She parted the curtains a little and looked out.* 她扒开窗帘，向外张望。

• **HAIR** 头发 **4** [T] ~ **sth** to divide your hair into two sections with a COMB, creating a line that goes from the back of your head to the front 分开；梳成分头： *He parts his hair in the middle.* 他梳着中分头。➲ SEE ALSO PARTING *n.* (2)

IDM **part 'company (with/from sb)** **1** to leave sb; to end a relationship with sb 离开；分手；断绝关系： *This is where we part company* (= go in different directions). 这就是我们分手的地方。◇ *The band have parted company with their manager.* 乐队与其经理人已散伙了。◇ *The band and their manager have parted company.* 乐队与其经理人已散伙了。 **2** to disagree with sb about sth （与某人）有意见分歧： *Weber parted company with Marx on a number of important issues.* 韦伯与马克思在若干重大问题上意见有分歧。➲ MORE AT FOOL *n.*

PHR V **'part with sth** to give sth to sb else, especially sth that you would prefer to keep 放弃，交出（尤指不舍得的东西）： *Make sure you read the contract before parting with any money.* 一定要注意先看清合约再交钱。

■ ***adv.*** (often in compounds 常构成复合词) consisting of two things; to some extent but not completely 由两部分构成；在一定程度上；部分地： *She's part French, part English.* 她是英法血统各半。◇ *His feelings were part anger, part relief.* 他感到既愤怒，又解脱。◇ *The course is part funded by the European Commission.* 这个课程由欧洲委员会部分资助。◇ *He is part owner of a farm in France.* 他拥有法国某农场的一部分。

par·take /pɑːˈteɪk; *NAmE* pɑːrˈt-/ *verb* (**par·took** /pɑːˈtʊk; *NAmE* pɑːrˈtʊk/, **par·taken** /-ˈteɪkən/) (*formal*) **1** [I] ~ (**of sth**) (*old-fashioned* or *humorous*) to eat or drink sth especially sth that is offered to you 吃，喝，享用（尤指给予的东西）： *Would you care to partake of some refreshment?* 你想吃些东西吗？ **2** [I] ~ (**in sth**) (*old-fashioned*) to take part in an activity 参加；参与： *They preferred not to partake in the social life of the town.* 他们不想参加这个镇的社交活动。

PHR V **par'take of sth** (*formal*) to have some of a particular quality 具有（部分特性）；有点儿： *His work partakes of the aesthetic fashions of his time.* 他的作品具有当时的某些审美时尚。

par·terre /pɑːˈteə(r); *NAmE* pɑːrˈter/ *noun* (*from French*) **1** a flat area in a garden, with plants arranged in a formal design 花坛；花圃 **2** (*especially NAmE*) the lower level in a theatre where the audience sits, especially the area underneath the BALCONY （尤指戏院楼厅底下的）正厅观众席

ˌpart exˈchange *noun* [U] (*BrE*) a way of buying sth, such as a car, in which you give the old one as part of the payment for a more expensive one 部分抵价交易；以旧换新交易： *We'll take your car **in part exchange**.* 我们收下你的旧车，以抵付购买新车的部分款额。 ▶ **ˌpart-exˈchange** *verb* ~ **sth**

par·theno·gen·esis /ˌpɑːθənəʊˈdʒenɪsɪs; *NAmE* ˌpɑːrθənoʊ-/ *noun* [U] (*biology* 生) the process of producing new plants or animals from an OVUM that has not been FERTILIZED 孤雌生殖 ▶ **par·theno·gen·et·ic** /ˌpɑːθənəʊdʒəˈnetɪk; *NAmE* ˌpɑːrθənoʊ-/ *adj.*： *parthenogenetic species* 单性生殖物种 **par·theno·gen·et·ic·ally** /-kli/ *adj.*： *These organisms reproduce parthenogenetically.* 这些生物通过单性生殖进行繁殖。

par·tial /ˈpɑːʃl; *NAmE* ˈpɑːrʃl/ *adj.* **1** not complete or whole 部分的；不完全的： *It was only a partial solution to the problem.* 那只是部分地解决了这个问题。◇ *a partial eclipse of the sun* 日偏食 **2** [not before noun] ~ **to sb/sth** (*old-fashioned*) liking sb/sth very much 热爱；钟爱： *I'm not partial to mushrooms.* 我不太爱吃蘑菇。 **3** [not usually before noun] ~ (**towards sb/sth**) (*disapproving*) showing or feeling too much support for one person, team, idea, etc., in a way that is unfair 偏颇；偏袒 SYN **biased** OPP **impartial**

par·ti·al·ity /ˌpɑːʃiˈæləti; *NAmE* ˌpɑːrʃ-/ *noun* (*formal*) **1** [U] (*disapproving*) the unfair support of one person, team, idea, etc. 偏袒 SYN **bias** OPP **impartiality** **2** [sing.] ~ **for sth/sb** a feeling of liking sth/sb very much 特别喜爱；酷爱 SYN **fondness**： *She has a partiality for exotic flowers.* 她特别喜爱异国花卉。

par·tial·ly /ˈpɑːʃəli; *NAmE* ˈpɑːrʃ-/ *adv.* partly; not completely 部分地；不完全地： *The road was partially blocked by a fallen tree.* 倒下的一棵树挡住了部分道路。◇ *a society for the blind and **partially sighted*** (= people who can see very little) 一个盲人及弱视者协会 ➲ NOTE AT PARTLY

par·tici·pant AW /pɑːˈtɪsɪpənt; *NAmE* pɑːrˈt-/ *noun* ~ (**in sth**) a person who is taking part in an activity or event 参与者；参加者： *He has been an active participant in the discussion.* 他一直积极参与这次讨论。

par·tici·pate AW /pɑːˈtɪsɪpeɪt; *NAmE* pɑːrˈt-/ *verb* [I] ~ (**in sth**) (*rather formal*) to take part in or become involved in an activity 参加；参与： *She didn't participate in the discussion.* 她没有参加讨论。◇ *We encourage students to participate fully in the running of the college.* 我们鼓励学生全面参与学院的运作。◇ *Details of the competition are available at all participating stores.* 比赛的详情可在各参与商店取阅。

par·tici·pa·tion AW /pɑːˌtɪsɪˈpeɪʃn; *NAmE* pɑːrˌt-/ *noun* [U] the act of taking part in an activity or event 参加；参与： *a show with lots of **audience participation*** 观众热烈参与的演出 ◇ ~ **in sth** *A back injury prevented active participation in any sports for a while.* 背伤曾一度妨碍积极参加任何体育运动。

par·tici·pa·tory AW /pɑːˌtɪsɪˈpeɪtəri; *NAmE* pɑːrˈtɪsəpətɔːri/ *adj.* [usually before noun] allowing everyone in a society, business, etc. to give their opinions and to help make decisions 参与式的（允许所有成员参与）： *Participatory democracy is a fundamental principle of cooperative businesses.* 参与式民主制是合作企业的基本原则。

par·ti·ciple /pɑːˈtɪsɪpl; *NAmE* ˈpɑːrt-/ *noun* (*grammar* 语法) (in English) a word formed from a verb, ending in *-ing* (= the PRESENT PARTICIPLE) or *-ed, -en,* etc. (= the PAST PARTICIPLE) 分词（现在分词或过去分词） ▶ **par·ti·ci·pial** /ˌpɑːtɪˈsɪpiəl; *NAmE* ˌpɑːrt-/ *adj.*

par·ticle /ˈpɑːtɪkl; *NAmE* ˈpɑːrt-/ *noun* **1** a very small piece of sth 颗粒；微粒： *particles of dust/gold* 灰尘；金屑 **2** (*physics* 物) a very small piece of matter, such as a PHOTON, an ELECTRON or a PROTON, that is part of an atom 粒子 ➲ SEE ALSO ALPHA PARTICLE, ELEMENTARY PARTICLE ➲ WORDFINDER NOTE AT ATOM **3** (*grammar* 语法) an adverb or a preposition that can combine with a verb to make a phrasal verb 小品词（与动词构成短语动词的副词或介词）： *In 'She tore up the letter', the word 'up' is a particle.* 在 She tore up the letter 句中，up 是小品词。➲ SEE ALSO ADVERBIAL PARTICLE

'particle physics *noun* [U] the scientific study of very small pieces of matter that are parts of an atom 粒子物理（学）

par·ticu·lar 🔑 /pəˈtɪkjələ(r); *NAmE* pərˈt-/ *adj., noun*

■ ***adj.*** **1** 🔑 [only before noun] used to emphasize that you are referring to one individual person, thing or type of thing and not others 专指的，特指的（与泛指相对） SYN **specific**： *There is one particular patient I'd like you to see.* 我想让你见一个病人。◇ *Is there a particular type of book he enjoys?* 他特别喜爱哪一类的书籍吗？ **2** 🔑 [only before noun] greater than usual; special 不寻常的；格外的；特别的： *We must pay particular attention to this point.* 我们必须特别注意这一点。◇ *These documents are of particular interest.* 这些文件让人尤其感兴趣。 **3** ~ (**about/over sth**) very definite about what you like and careful about what you choose 讲究；挑剔 SYN **fussy**： *She's very particular about her clothes.* 她对衣着特别挑剔。

IDM **in parˈticular 1** especially or particularly 尤其；特别；格外：*He loves science fiction in particular.* 他特别喜爱科幻小说。➲ LANGUAGE BANK AT EMPHASIS **2** special or specific 特殊的；专门的；具体的：*Peter was lying on the sofa doing* ***nothing in particular****.* 彼得躺在沙发上，无所事事。◇ *Is there* ***anything in particular*** *you'd like for dinner?* 晚饭你有具体想吃的吗？◇ *She directed the question at* ***no one in particular****.* 她的问题并没有针对任何个人。

■ ***noun*** *(formal)* **1** [usually pl.] a fact or detail, especially one that is officially written down （正式记下的）细节，详情：*The police officer took down all the particulars of the burglary.* 这名警察记下了窃案发生的详细情况。◇ *The nurse asked me for my particulars* (= personal details such as your name, address, etc.). 护士向我询问了我的个人资料。◇ *The new contract will be the same in every particular as the old one.* 新合同与旧合同的各项细节将完全相同。 **2 particulars** [pl.] written information and details about a property, business, job, etc. 详细资料；详细介绍材料：*Application forms and further particulars are available from the Personnel Office.* 申请表格及其他详细资料可向人事部索取。

par·ticu·lar·ity /pəˌtɪkjuˈlærəti; *NAmE* pərˌt-/ *noun* *(pl.* **-ies***)* *(formal)* **1** [U] the quality of being individual or unique 个性；独特性：*the particularity of each human being* 每个人的独特性 **2** [U] attention to detail; being exact 考究；准确；精确 **3 particularities** [pl.] the special features or details of sth 特征；特性；细节；详情

par·ticu·lar·ize (*BrE also* **-ise**) /pəˈtɪkjələraɪz; *NAmE* pərˈt-/ *verb* [I, T] ~ **(sth)** *(formal)* to give details of sth, especially one by one; to give particular examples of sth 详细说明；逐一列举；以具体的例子说明

par·ticu·lar·ly /pəˈtɪkjələli; *NAmE* pərˈtɪkjələrli/ *adv.* especially; more than usual or more than others 特别；尤其：*particularly good/important/useful* 特别好 / 重要 / 有用 ◇ *Traffic is bad, particularly in the city centre.* 交通状况很差，尤其是在市中心。◇ *I enjoyed the play particularly the second half.* 我很喜欢那部剧，特别是下半段。◇ *The lecture was* ***not particularly*** (= not very) *interesting.* 讲座并不特别精彩。◇ *'Did you enjoy it?' 'No,* ***not particularly****'* (= not very much).' "你玩得开心吗？" "不很开心。"

par·ticu·late /pɑːˈtɪkjələt; -leɪt; *NAmE* pɑːrˈt-/ *adj., noun* *(chemistry* 化*)*

■ ***adj.*** relating to, or in the form of, PARTICLES 微粒（形式）的；颗粒（状）的：*particulate pollution* 颗粒污染物

■ ***noun*** **particulates** [pl.] matter in the form of PARTICLES 微粒；颗粒；粒子

part·ing /ˈpɑːtɪŋ; *NAmE* ˈpɑːrt-/ *noun, adj.*

■ ***noun*** **1** [U, C] the act or occasion of leaving a person or place 离别；分手；分别：*the moment of parting* 离别的时刻 ◇ *We had a tearful parting at the airport.* 我们在机场洒泪而别。 **2** *(BrE)* *(NAmE* **part***)* [C] a line on a person's head where the hair is divided with a COMB （头发的）分缝，发缝，分线：*a* ***side/centre parting*** 偏分；中分 ➲ VISUAL VOCAB PAGE V65 **3** [U, C] the act or result of dividing sth into parts 分开；分离；散开：*the parting of the clouds* 云破天开

IDM **a/the ˌparting of the ˈways** a point at which two people or groups of people decide to separate 岔路口；分道扬镳处；分手处

■ ***adj.*** [only before noun] said or done by sb as they leave 离别时说的（或做的）：*a parting kiss* 临别之吻 ◇ *His parting words were 'I love you.'* 他临别的话是"我爱你"。

IDM **ˌparting ˈshot** a final remark, especially an unkind one, that sb makes as they leave 临去的放话（尤指不友善的）

par·ti·san /ˌpɑːtɪˈzæn; ˈpɑːtɪzæn; *NAmE* ˈpɑːrtəzn/ *adj., noun*

■ ***adj.*** *(often disapproving)* showing too much support for one person, group or idea, especially without considering it carefully （对个别人、团体或思想）过分支持的，偏护的，盲目拥护的 **SYN** **one-sided**：*Most newspapers are politically partisan.* 大多数报纸都有政治倾向。

■ ***noun*** **1** a person who strongly supports a particular leader, group or idea 坚定的支持者；铁杆拥护者 **SYN** **follower** **2** a member of an armed group that is fighting secretly against enemy soldiers who have taken control of its country 游击队员 ▸ **par·ti·san·ship** /-ʃɪp/ *noun* [U]

par·ti·tion /pɑːˈtɪʃn; *NAmE* pɑːrˈt-/ *noun, verb*

■ ***noun*** **1** [C] a wall or screen that separates one part of a room from another 隔断；隔扇；隔板墙：*a glass partition* 玻璃隔板 ◇ *partition walls* 隔断墙 ➲ VISUAL VOCAB PAGE V71 **2** [U] the division of one country into two or more countries 分割；分治；瓜分：*the partition of Germany after the war* 战后对德国的分割

■ ***verb*** [often passive] to divide sth into parts 分割；使分裂：**~ sth** *to partition a country* 分割一个国家 ◇ **~ sth into sth** *The room is partitioned into three sections.* 这间屋子被隔为三小间。

PHR V **parˌtition sth↔ˈoff** to separate one area, one part of a room, etc. from another with a wall or screen （把地方、房间等）分隔，隔开

par·ti·tive /ˈpɑːtətɪv; *NAmE* ˈpɑːrt-/ *noun* *(grammar* 语法*)* a word or phrase that shows a part or quantity of sth 表示部分的词（或词组）；表量词语：*In 'a spoonful of sugar', the word 'spoonful' is a partitive.* 在 a spoonful of sugar 中，spoonful 一词是表量词。▸ **par·ti·tive** *adj.*

part·ly /ˈpɑːtli; *NAmE* ˈpɑːrt-/ *adv.* to some extent; not completely 一定程度上；部分地：*Some people are unwilling to attend the classes* ***partly because*** *of the cost involved.* 有些人不愿来上课，部分原因是所需的费用问题。◇ *He was only partly responsible for the accident.* 他对这次事故只负有部分责任。

▼ **WHICH WORD? 词语辨析**

partly / partially

- **Partly** and **partially** both mean 'not completely'. * partly 和 partially 均指部分：*The road is partly/partially finished.* 道路完工了一部分。 **Partly** is especially used to talk about the reason for something, often followed by *because* or *due to*. * partly 尤用以说明原因，其后常跟 because 或 due to：*I didn't enjoy the trip very much, partly because of the weather.* 我旅行过得不太愉快，部分是因为天气的缘故。 **Partially** should be used when you are talking about physical conditions. 指身体状况时应用 partially：*His mother is partially blind.* 他的母亲失去了部分视力。

part·ner **AW** /ˈpɑːtnə(r); *NAmE* ˈpɑːrt-/ *noun, verb*

■ ***noun*** **1** the person that you are married to or having a sexual relationship with 配偶；性伴侣：*Come to the New Year disco and bring your partner!* 携伴来参加新年迪斯科舞会吧！◇ *a marriage partner* 配偶 ➲ WORDFINDER NOTE AT LOVE ➲ COLLOCATIONS AT MARRIAGE **2** one of the people who owns a business and shares the profits, etc. 合伙人：*a partner in a law firm* 律师事务所的合伙人 ◇ *a* ***junior/senior partner*** 次要 / 主要合伙人 ➲ SEE ALSO SLEEPING PARTNER **3** a person that you are doing an activity with, such as dancing or playing a game 搭档；同伴；舞伴：*a* ***dancing/tennis, etc. partner*** 舞伴、网球搭档等 ➲ WORDFINDER NOTE AT DANCE ➲ SEE ALSO SPARRING PARTNER **4** a country or an organization that has an agreement with another country 伙伴（与另一国家有协议关系的国家或组织）：*a trading partner* 贸易伙伴

■ ***verb*** **~ sb** to be sb's partner in a dance, game, etc. （在跳舞、游戏等中）结成伙伴，做搭档，配对：*Gerry offered to partner me at tennis.* 格里提出和我搭档打网球。

part·ner·ship **AW** /ˈpɑːtnəʃɪp; *NAmE* ˈpɑːrtnərʃɪp/ *noun* **1** [U] the state of being a partner in business 伙伴关系；合伙人身份：*to* ***be in/to go into partnership*** 结成合作关系 ◇ **~ with sb/sth** *He developed his own program* ***in partnership*** *with an American expert.* 他与一位美国专家合作开发出自己的程序。 **2** [C, U] a relationship

P

between two people, organizations, etc.; the state of having this relationship 合作关系；合作：*Marriage should be an equal partnership.* 婚姻应当是平等的伴侣关系。◇ **~ with sb/sth** *the school's partnership with parents* 学校与家长的合作 ◇ **~ between A and B** *a partnership between the United States and Europe* 美国与欧洲的合作 **3** [C] a business owned by two or more people who share the profits 合伙企业：*a junior member of the partnership* 企业的次要合伙人

ˌpart of ˈspeech *noun* (*grammar* 语法) one of the classes into which words are divided according to their grammar, such as noun, verb, adjective, etc. 词类；词性 SYN **word class** ➲ WORDFINDER NOTE AT DICTIONARY, GRAMMAR

par·took PAST TENSE OF PARTAKE

par·tridge /ˈpɑːtrɪdʒ; *NAmE* ˈpɑːrt-/ *noun* [C, U] (*pl.* **par·tridges** or **par·tridge**) a brown bird with a round body and a short tail, that people hunt for sport or food; the meat of this bird 山鹑；山鹑肉

ˌpart-ˈtime *adj., adv.* (*abbr.* **PT**) for part of the day or week in which people work 部分时间的；兼职的：*She's looking for a part-time job.* 她在寻找兼职工作。◇ *to study on a part-time basis* 在职学习 ◇ *part-time workers* 兼职工作者 ◇ *I'm only part-time at the moment.* 我现在只是兼职。◇ *Liz works part-time from 10 till 2.* 利兹的兼职时间是 10 点到 2 点。➲ COMPARE FULL-TIME ➲ WORDFINDER NOTE AT WORK

ˌpart-ˈtimer *noun* a person who works part-time 兼职者；部分时间工作的人

par·tur·ition /ˌpɑːtjʊˈrɪʃn; *NAmE* ˌpɑːrt-/ *noun* [U] (*specialist*) the act of giving birth 分娩

ˈpart-way *adv.* some of the way 半途；部分地：*They were part-way through the speeches when he arrived.* 他到达的时候讲演已经进行一段时间了。

ˈpart-work *noun* (*BrE*) a book that is published in several parts that people can collect over a period of time 分期发表的作品；分册出版的书

party /ˈpɑːti; *NAmE* ˈpɑːrti/ *noun, verb*

■ ***noun*** (*pl.* **-ies**) **1** (*also* **Party**) [C+sing./pl. v.] a political organization that you can vote for in elections and whose members have the same aims and ideas 政党；党派：*the Democratic and Republican Parties in the United States* 美国的民主党和共和党 ◇ *She belongs to the Labour Party.* 她是工党党员。◇ *the **ruling/opposition party*** 执政党；反对党 ◇ *the **party leader/manifesto/policy*** 党的领袖 / 宣言 / 政策 ➲ COLLOCATIONS AT POLITICS **2** [C] (especially in compounds 尤用于构成复合词) a social occasion, often in a person's home, at which people eat, drink, talk, dance and enjoy themselves 聚会；宴会；联欢会；派对：*a **birthday/dinner/garden, etc.** party* 生日聚会、晚宴、园会等 ◇ ***to give/have/throw a party*** 搞聚会 ◇ ***Did you go to the party?*** 你去参加聚会了吗？◇ *party games* 联欢会游戏 ➲ SEE ALSO HEN PARTY, HOUSE PARTY, STAG PARTY at STAG NIGHT (2) ➲ WORDFINDER NOTE AT CELEBRATE **3** [C+sing./pl. v.] a group of people who are doing sth together such as travelling or visiting somewhere （一起旅行或参观等的）群，队，组：*The school is taking a party of 40 children to France.* 学校将带领一个 40 人的儿童团队前往法国。◇ *The theatre gives a 10% discount to parties of more than ten.* 剧场给十人以上的团体打九折。➲ SEE ALSO SEARCH PARTY, WORKING PARTY **4** [C] (*formal*) one of the people or groups of people involved in a legal agreement or argument （契约或争论的）当事人，一方：*the **guilty/innocent party*** 有罪的 / 无罪的一方 ◇ *The contract can be terminated by either party with three months' notice.* 合同的任何一方如提前三个月通知，均可终止本合同。➲ SEE ALSO INJURED PARTY, THIRD PARTY

IDM **be (a) ˈparty to sth** (*formal*) to be involved in an agreement or action 参与，参加（协议或行动）：*to be party to a decision* 参与作出决议 ◇ *He refused to be a party to any violence.* 他拒绝参与任何暴力活动。**ˌbring sth to the ˈparty/ˈtable** to contribute sth useful to a discussion, project, etc. 为（讨论、项目等）作出贡献：*What Hislop brought to the party was real commitment and energy.* 希斯洛普对党的贡献是他全身心的投入和十足的干劲。

■ ***verb*** (**par·ties**, **party·ing**, **par·tied**, **par·tied**) [I] (*informal*) to enjoy yourself, especially by eating, drinking alcohol and dancing 寻欢作乐；吃喝玩乐：*They were out partying every night.* 他们每晚都外出寻欢作乐。

ˌparty ˈfavors (*also* **favors**) (*both NAmE*) *noun* [pl.] small gifts that are often given to children at a party （聚会上赠给儿童的）小礼品

ˈparty-goer *noun* a person who enjoys going to parties or who is a guest at a particular party 爱参加聚会的人；聚会的客人

ˌparty ˈline *noun* [usually sing.] the official opinions and policies of a political party, which members are expected to support 政党的路线 IDM SEE TOE *v.*

ˈparty piece *noun* (*BrE, informal*) a thing that sb does to entertain people, especially at parties, for example singing a song （聚会上的某项）娱乐活动

ˌparty poˈlitical *adj.* [only before noun] (*especially BrE*) made by or relating to a political party 政党的；党派政治的：*a party political broadcast* 党派政治广播

ˌparty ˈpolitics *noun* [U+sing./pl. v.] political activity that involves political parties 政党政治：*The President should stand above party politics.* 总统应当置身于政党政治之上。◇ *Many people think that party politics should not enter into local government.* 许多人都认为，地方政府内不应拉帮结派。

ˈparty pooper /ˈpɑːti puːpə(r); *NAmE* ˈpɑːrti puːpər/ *noun* (*informal*) a person who does not want to take part in an enjoyable activity and spoils the fun for other people （在聚会等上）令众人扫兴者

ˌparty ˈspirit *noun* [U] the sort of mood in which you can enjoy a party and have fun 社交情结；爱社交的心情

ˌparty ˈwall *noun* a wall that divides two buildings or rooms and belongs to both owners 界墙；隔断墙；共用墙

par·venu /ˈpɑːvənjuː; *NAmE* ˈpɑːrvənuː/ *noun* (*pl.* **-us**) (*formal, disapproving*) a person from a low social or economic position who has suddenly become rich or powerful 暴发户；新贵

pas·cal /ˈpæskl/ *noun* **1** (*abbr.* **Pa**) the standard unit for measuring pressure 帕（斯卡）（标准压强单位）**2 Pascal, PASCAL** a language used for writing programs for computer systems 帕斯卡语言；Pascal（计算机系统编程）语言

pas·chal /ˈpɑːskl; *NAmE* ˈpæskl/ *adj.* (*formal*) **1** relating to Easter 复活节的 **2** relating to the Jewish Passover 逾越节的

pas de deux /ˌpɑː də ˈdɜː/ *noun* (*pl.* **pas de deux** /ˌpɑː də ˈdɜː/) (*from French*) a dance, often part of a BALLET, that is performed by two people （芭蕾舞等中的）双人舞

pash·mi·na /pæʃˈmiːnə/ *noun* a long piece of cloth made of fine soft wool from a type of GOAT and worn by a woman around the shoulders 羊绒披肩

Pashto /ˈpæʃtəʊ; *NAmE* -toʊ/ *noun* [U] the official language of Afghanistan, also spoken in northern Pakistan 普什图语（阿富汗官方语言，也用于巴基斯坦北部地区）

pass /pɑːs; *NAmE* pæs/ *verb, noun*

■ ***verb***

• **MOVE** 移动 **1** [I, T] to move past or to the other side of sb/sth 通过；走过：*Several people were passing but nobody offered to help.* 有几个人路过，却没有人主动伸出援手。◇ *I hailed a passing taxi.* 我招手叫了一辆路过的出租车。◇ *The road was so narrow that cars were unable to pass.* 道路太窄，汽车无法通过。◇ **~ sb/sth** *to pass a barrier/sentry/checkpoint* 通过障碍 / 岗哨 / 检查站 ◇ *You'll pass a bank on the way to the train station.* 你在去火车站的路上会经过一家银行。◇ *She passed me in the street*

P

without even saying hello. 她在街上与我擦肩而过，却连一声招呼也没打。◇ (*especially NAmE*) *There was a truck behind that was trying to pass me.* 后面有一辆卡车想要超过我。 **HELP** The usual word in British English in the last example is **overtake**. 在上一例句中，英式英语通常用 overtake。 **2** ⚷ [I] **+ adv./prep.** to go or move in the direction mentioned 沿某方向前进；向某方向移动：*The procession passed slowly along the street.* 队伍沿街缓缓行进。◇ *A plane passed low overhead.* 一架飞机从头上低空飞过。 **3** [T] **~ sth + adv./prep.** to make sth move in the direction or into the position mentioned 使沿（某方向）移动；使达到（某位置）：*He passed the rope around the post three times to secure it.* 他把绳索在柱子上绕了三匝缠紧。

• **GIVE** 给予 **4** ⚷ [T] to give sth to sb by putting it into their hands or in a place where they can easily reach it 给；递；传递：**~ sth (to sb)** *Pass the salt, please.* 请把盐递过来。◇ *Pass that book over.* 把那本书递过来。◇ **~ sb sth** *Pass me over that book.* 递给我那本书。

• **BALL** 球 **5** ⚷ [T, I] (in ball games 球类运动) to kick, hit or throw the ball to a player of your own side 传球：**~ sth (to sb)** *He passed the ball to Rooney.* 他把球传给了鲁尼。◇ **~ (to sb)** *Why do they keep passing back to the goalie?* 他们为什么老是把球回传给守门员？

• **AFTER DEATH** 死后 **6** [I] **~ to sb** to be given to another person after first belonging to sb else, especially after the first person has died 转移给，遗留给（继承人等）：*On his death, the title passed to his eldest son.* 他死后，封号传给长子。

• **BECOME GREATER** 变大 **7** ⚷ [T] **~ sth** (of an amount 数量) to become greater than a particular total 大于；超过 **SYN** **exceed**：*Unemployment has now **passed the three million mark**.* 失业人数现已突破三百万大关。

• **CHANGE** 变化 **8** [I] **~ from sth to/into sth** to change from one state or condition to another 转变；变化；过渡：*She had passed from childhood to early womanhood.* 她已由童年进入了少女期。

• **TIME** 时间 **9** ⚷ [I] when time **passes**, it goes by 推移；逝去：*Six months passed and we still had no news of them.* 半年过去了，我们仍然没有他们的音讯。◇ *We grew more anxious **with every passing day**.* 一天天过去，我们的焦虑与日俱增。 **10** ⚷ [T] **~ sth** to spend time, especially when you are bored or waiting for sth 消磨；度过；打发：*We sang songs to **pass the time**.* 我们借唱歌消磨时间。◇ *How did you pass the evening?* 你是怎么打发那个晚上的？

• **END** 结束 **11** ⚷ [I] to come to an end; to be over 结束；完结：*They waited for the storm to pass.* 他们等待暴风雨过去。

• **TEST/EXAM** 测验；考试 **12** ⚷ [I, T] to achieve the required standard in an exam, a test, etc. 及格；合格：*I'm not really expecting to pass first time.* 我真不指望第一次就能合格。◇ **~ sth** *She hasn't passed her driving test yet.* 她还没有通过驾驶执照考试。 **OPP** **fail** **13** [T] **~ sb** to test sb and decide that they are good enough, according to an agreed standard 准予通过；承认合格：*The examiners passed all the candidates.* 主考人评定考生全部及格。 **OPP** **fail**

• **LAW/PROPOSAL** 法律；建议 **14** ⚷ [T] **~ sth** to accept a proposal, law, etc. by voting 经表决通过（动议、法律等）：*The bill was passed by 360 votes to 280.* 这个法案以 360 票对 280 票获得通过。

• **HAPPEN** 发生 **15** [I] to be allowed 得到允许：*I don't like it, but I'll **let it pass*** (= will not object). 我不喜欢，但我也不会反对。◇ *Her remarks **passed without comment*** (= people ignored them). 人们对她的言论未予理睬。 **16** [I] to happen; to be said or done 发生；说出（或做出）：**~ (between A and B)** *They'll never be friends again after all that has passed between them.* 经过了这么多事情，他们已经友谊难再了。◇ **+ adj.** *His departure **passed unnoticed**.* 他神不知、鬼不觉地离开了。

• **NOT KNOW** 不知 **17** [I] **~ (on sth)** to say that you do not know the answer to a question, especially during a QUIZ 不知道，过（尤在回答竞赛问题时所用）：*'What's the capital of Peru?' 'I'll have to pass on that one.'* "秘鲁的首都是哪里？" "过。" ◇ *'Who wrote 'Catch-22'?' 'Pass* (= I don't know).' "谁写了《第二十二条军规》？" "不知道。"

• **NOT WANT** 不要 **18** [I] **~ (on sth)** to say that you do not want sth that is offered to you 不要；免掉：*Thanks. I'm going to pass on dessert, if you don't mind.* 谢谢，您若不介意，我就免了饭后甜点吧。

• **SAY/STATE STH** 陈述 **19** [T] **~ sth (on sb/sth)** to say or state sth, especially officially 宣布；声明：*The court waited in silence for the judge to **pass sentence**.* 全体出庭人员默默等待法官宣判。◇ *It's not for me to **pass judgement** on your behaviour.* 我无权评判你的行为。◇ *The man smiled at the girl and passed a friendly remark.* 男子对姑娘微微一笑，又说了句亲切的话。

• **BELIEF/UNDERSTANDING** 相信；理解 **20** [T] **~ belief, understanding, etc.** (*formal*) to go beyond the limits of what you can believe, understand, etc. 超出…的限度：*It passes belief* (= is impossible to believe) *that she could do such a thing.* 很难相信她会做出这等事来。

• **IN CARD GAMES** 纸牌游戏 **21** [I] to refuse to play a card or make a BID[1] (4) when it is your turn 不出牌；不叫牌；过

• **FROM THE BODY** 排出体外 **22** [T] **~ sth** to send sth out from the body as or with waste matter 排泄；排出：*If you're passing blood you ought to see a doctor.* 如果便中带血，你就应该找大夫看看。 ➲ MORE LIKE THIS 33, page R28

IDM **ˌcome to ˈpass** (*old use*) to happen 发生；出现 **not pass your ˈlips 1** if words do **not pass your lips**, you say nothing 未说话；未开口 **2** if food or drink does **not pass your lips**, you eat or drink nothing 未吃；未喝；（水米）未沾 **pass the ˈhat round/around** (*informal*) to collect money from a number of people, for example to buy a present for sb 凑份子（送礼）；凑集金钱 **pass ˈmuster** to be accepted as of a good enough standard 达到要求；获得接受 **pass the time of ˈday (with sb)** to say hello to sb and have a short conversation with them （与某人）寒暄，打招呼，闲谈一会儿 **pass ˈwater** (*formal*) to URINATE 小便；小解；解小手

PHR V **ˌpass sth↔aˈround/ˈround** ⚷ to give sth to another person, who gives it to sb else, etc. until everyone has seen it 挨个传递某物；传阅：*Can you pass these pictures around for everyone to look at, please?* 请你把这些画传给每个人看一看好吗？ **ˈpass as sb/sth** = PASS FOR/AS SB/STH **ˌpass aˈway 1** ⚷ (*also* **ˌpass ˈon**) to die. People say 'pass away' to avoid saying 'die'. （婉辞，指去世）亡故：*His mother passed away last year.* 他母亲去年去世了。 **2** to stop existing 消失；消逝：*civilizations that have passed away* 不复存在的文明 **ˌpass ˈby (sb/sth)** ⚷ to go past 通过；经过（…旁边）：*The procession passed right by my front door.* 队伍正好从我家前门经过。 **ˌpass sb/sth ˈby** to happen without affecting sb/sth 未影响（某人/某事）：*She feels that life is passing her by* (= that she is not enjoying the opportunities and pleasures of life). 她觉得人生毫不眷顾她。 **ˌpass sth↔ˈdown** [often passive] to give or teach sth to your children or people younger than you, who will then give or teach it to those who live after them, and so on 使世代相传；流传 **SYN** **hand down** **ˈpass for/as sb/sth** to be accepted as sb/sth 被认为是；被当作：*He speaks the language so well he could easily pass for a German.* 他德语讲得好极了，很容易被当成德国人。◇ *We had some wine—or what passes for wine in that area.* 我们喝了一些酒，或是在那个地区被当作酒的东西。 **ˈpass into sth** to become a part of sth 变为其中一部分；融入；纳入：*Many foreign words have passed into the English language.* 许多外来词语已变成英语的一部分。 **ˌpass ˈoff** (*BrE*) (of an event 事情) to take place and be completed in a particular way （以某方式）发生并完成：*The demonstration passed off peacefully.* 示威游行始终和平地进行。 **ˌpass sb/yourself/sth ˈoff as sb/sth** to pretend that sb/sth is sth they are not 装作；佯装；假装：*He escaped by passing himself off as a guard.* 他伪装成看守人而得以脱逃。 **ˌpass ˈon** = PASS AWAY **ˌpass sth↔ˈon (to sb)** ⚷ to give sth to sb else, especially after receiving it or using it yourself 转交；（用后）递给，传给：*Pass the book on to me when you've finished with it.* 你看完那本书后请传给我。◇ *I passed your message on to my mother.* 我把你的留言转给我妈了。◇ *Much of the discount is pocketed by retailers instead of being passed on to customers.* 折扣的大部分进了零售商的腰包，而顾客没有得到实惠。 **ˌpass ˈout** ⚷ to become unconscious

P

昏迷；失去知觉 SYN **faint** ˌ**pass ˈout (of sth)** (*BrE*) to leave a military college after finishing a course of training 从军校毕业：*a passing-out ceremony* 军校毕业典礼 ˌ**pass sb↔ˈover** to not consider sb for promotion in a job, especially when they deserve it or think that they deserve it （考虑提职等时）跳过某人：*He was passed over in favour of a younger man.* 他未被擢升，一个比他年轻的人却获得了提拔。 ˌ**pass ˈover sth** to ignore or avoid sth 避免提及；不考虑 SYN **overlook**: *They chose to pass over her rude remarks.* 他们决定不计较她的粗鲁言辞。 ˌ**pass ˈthrough...** to go through a town, etc., stopping there for a short time but not staying 经过；路过：*We were passing through, so we thought we'd come and say hello.* 我们路过此地，所以想来问候一声。 ˌ**pass sth↔ˈup** (*informal*) to choose not to make use of a chance, an opportunity, etc. 放弃，不要（机会等）：*Imagine passing up an offer like that!* 真想不到居然拒绝这样的好意！

■ ***noun***

• **IN EXAM** 考试 **1** (*especially BrE*) a successful result in an exam 及格；合格；通过：*She got a pass in French.* 她法语考试及格了。◇ *12 passes and 3 fails* * 12 门及格，3 门不及格 ◇ *Two A-level passes are needed for this course.* 本课程要求有两个高级证书考试的及格成绩。◇ *The* ***pass mark*** *is 50%.* * 50% 为及格成绩。◇ *The school has a 90%* ***pass rate*** (= 90% of students pass their exams). 该校学生的及格率为 90%。

• **OFFICIAL DOCUMENT** 正式文件 **2** an official document or ticket that shows that you have the right to enter or leave a place, to travel on a bus or train, etc. 通行证；车票；乘车证：*a boarding pass* (= for a plane) 登机牌 ◇ *There is no admittance without a security pass.* 无保安通行证不得入内。➲ SEE ALSO BUS PASS

• **OF BALL** 球类运动 **3** (in some sports) an act of hitting or throwing the ball to another player in your team （某些运动中）传球：*a long pass to Turner* 给特纳的一个长传 ◇ *a back pass to the goalkeeper* 回传给守门员

• **THROUGH MOUNTAINS** 穿越山脉 **4** a road or way over or through mountains 关口；关隘；山路：*a mountain pass* 山口 ➲ VISUAL VOCAB PAGE V5

• **MOVING PAST/OVER** 经过；越过 **5** an act of going or moving past or over sth 越过；飞跃：*The helicopter made several passes over the village before landing.* 直升机在村落上空盘旋数次才降落。

• **STAGE IN PROCESS** 阶段 **6** a stage in a process, especially one that involves separating things from a larger group 阶段；步骤：*In the first pass all the addresses are loaded into the database.* 第一步，所有地址均输入数据库。

IDM **come to such a ˈpass | come to a pretty ˈpass** (*old-fashioned* or *humorous*) to reach a sad or difficult state 陷于不妙的（或困难的）境地；落到这步田地 **make a pass at sb** (*informal*) to try to start a sexual relationship with sb 勾引；与某人调情

pass·able /ˈpɑːsəbl; *NAmE* ˈpæs-/ *adj.* **1** fairly good but not excellent 过得去的；尚可的 SYN **satisfactory** **2** [not usually before noun] if a road or a river is **passable**, it is not blocked and you can travel along or across it 通行无阻 OPP **impassable**

pass·ably /ˈpɑːsəbli; *NAmE* ˈpæs-/ *adv.* in a way that is acceptable or good enough 过得去；尚可；还可以 SYN **reasonably**: *He speaks passably good French.* 他法语讲得还可以。

pas·sage /ˈpæsɪdʒ/ *noun*

• **LONG NARROW WAY** 狭长通路 **1** (*also* **pas·sage·way** /ˈpæsɪdʒweɪ/) [C] a long narrow area with walls on either side that connects one room or place with another 通道；走廊 SYN **corridor**: *a secret underground passage* 地下秘密通道 ◇ *A dark narrow passage led to the main hall.* 一条阴暗狭窄的走廊通向大厅。

• **IN THE BODY** 体内 **2** [C] a tube in the body through which air, liquid, etc. passes （体内通气、输液等的）管路，通道：*blocked nasal passages* 鼻道堵塞 ➲ SEE ALSO BACK PASSAGE

• **SECTION FROM BOOK** 章节 **3** [C] a short section from a book, piece of music, etc. 章节；段落；乐段 SYN **excerpt, extract**: *Read the following passage and answer the questions below.* 阅读下面这段文章并回答后面的问题。➲ COLLOCATIONS AT LITERATURE

• **OF TIME** 时间 **4** [sing.] **the ~ of time** (*literary*) the process of time passing （时间的）流逝，推移：*Her confidence grew with the passage of time.* 她的信心与日俱增。

• **OF BILL IN PARLIAMENT** 议会的议案 **5** [sing.] the process of discussing a BILL in a parliament so that it can become law 通过：*The bill is now guaranteed an easy passage through the House of Representatives.* 现在该法案保证能在众议院顺利通过。

• **JOURNEY BY SHIP** 海程 **6** [sing.] a journey from one place to another by ship （乘船的）航程，旅程：*Her grandfather had* ***worked his passage*** (= worked on a ship to pay for the journey) *to America.* 她的祖父一路在船上打工支付船费来到美国。

• **GOING THROUGH** 通过 **7** [sing.] **a ~ (through sth)** a way through sth 通路；通道：*The officers forced a passage through the crowd.* 警察在人群中辟开一条通路。 **8** [U] (*formal*) the action of going across, through or past sth 穿过；穿越：*Large trees may obstruct the passage of light.* 大树可能阻挡光线穿过。 **9** [U, C, usually sing.] the permission to travel across a particular area of land 通行许可：*We were promised (a) safe passage through the occupied territory.* 我们得到保证，可以安全通过占领区。➲ SEE ALSO BIRD OF PASSAGE (2), RITE OF PASSAGE

pas·sant ➲ EN PASSANT

pass·book /ˈpɑːsbʊk; *NAmE* ˈpæs-/ *noun* a small book containing a record of the money you put into and take out of an account at a BUILDING SOCIETY or a bank 银行存折；房屋互助协会借贷簿

passé /ˈpæseɪ; ˈpɑːs-; *NAmE* pæˈseɪ/ *adj.* [not usually before noun] (*from French, disapproving*) no longer fashionable 过时；陈旧；不再流行 SYN **outmoded**

pas·sen·ger /ˈpæsɪndʒə(r)/ *noun* **1** a person who is travelling in a car, bus, train, plane or ship and who is not driving it or working on it 乘客；旅客：*a passenger train* (= carrying passengers, not goods) 客运列车 **2** (*informal, disapproving, especially BrE*) a member of a group or team who does not do as much work as the others 白吃饭的人；闲散人员：*The firm cannot afford to carry passengers.* 公司养不起白吃饭的人。

ˈpassenger seat *noun* the seat in a car which is next to the driver's seat （汽车驾驶员旁边的）乘客座位，副驾驶座 ➲ VISUAL VOCAB PAGE V56

ˌ**passer-ˈby** *noun* (*pl.* **passers-by**) a person who is going past sb/sth by chance, especially when sth unexpected happens 路人；过路的人：*Police asked passers-by if they had seen the accident.* 警察询问过路的人是否目击了这次事故。➲ SYNONYMS AT WITNESS

ˌ**pass-ˈfail** *adj.* (*US*) connected with a grading system for school classes, etc. in which a student passes or fails rather than receiving a grade as a letter (for example, A or B) 及格－不及格评分制的（不细分为 A、B 之类的等级）▶ ˌ**pass-ˈfail** *adv.*: *to take a class pass-fail* 选修一门只给及格－不及格两种评分的课程

pas·sim /ˈpæsɪm/ *adv.* (*from Latin*) used in the notes to a book or an article to show that a particular name or subject appears in several places in it （用于书、文章注释，表示某个名称或题目出现于该书、该文的）各处，多处

pass·ing /ˈpɑːsɪŋ; *NAmE* ˈpæs-/ *noun, adj.*

■ ***noun*** [U] **1** **the ~ of time/the years** the process of time going by （时间、岁月的）流逝，推移 **2** (*formal*) the fact of sth ending or of sb dying （事物的）结束，消亡；（人的）亡故，逝世：*When the government is finally brought down, no one will mourn its passing.* 当政府最终垮台，将不会有人为它的消亡而悲哀。◇ *the passing of the old year* (= on New Year's Eve) 除夕日 ◇ *Many will mourn her passing* (= her death, when you do not want to say this directly). 很多人将会为她的过世而悲伤。 **3** **the ~ of sth** the act of making sth become a law （法律等的）通过：*the passing of a resolution/law* 决议 / 法律的通过

IDM **in passing** done or said while you are giving your attention to sth else 顺便；随便 SYN **casually**: *He only mentioned it in passing and didn't give any details.* 他只是随口提及而已，并没有谈任何细节。

■ *adj.* [only before noun] **1** lasting only for a short period of time and then disappearing 暂时的；瞬间的 SYN **brief**: *a **passing** phase/thought/interest* 过渡阶段；一闪念；一时之兴 ◇ *He makes only a **passing reference** to the theory in his book* (= it is not the main subject of his book). 他在书中对这个理论只是一笔带过。◇ *She bears more than **a passing resemblance to*** (= looks very like) *your sister.* 她酷似你姐姐。 **2** going past 经过的；过往的：*I love him more with each passing day.* 随着时间的流逝，我越发爱他了。◇ *the noise of passing cars* 过往车辆的嘈杂 **3 ~ grade/mark** (*NAmE*) a grade/mark that achieves the required standard in an exam, a test, etc. （考试、测验等）及格的

ˈpassing lane (*NAmE*) (*BrE* **ˌoutside ˈlane**) *noun* the part of a major road such as a MOTORWAY or INTERSTATE nearest the middle of the road, where vehicles drive fastest and can go past vehicles ahead （高速公路等靠近路中央的）超车车道，快车道

ˈpassing shot *noun* (in TENNIS 网球) a shot which goes past your opponent, and which he or she cannot reach 超身球，穿越球（越过对手使其无法接住）

pas·sion /ˈpæʃn/ *noun* **1** [C, U] a very strong feeling of love, hatred, anger, enthusiasm, etc. 强烈情感；激情：*He's a man of violent passions.* 他是个性情暴烈的人。◇ *a **crime of passion*** 激情犯罪 ◇ *She argued her case with considerable passion.* 她相当激动地为自己的主张提出论据。◇ ***Passions were running high*** (= people were angry and emotional) *at the meeting.* 会上群情激愤。 **2** [sing.] (*formal*) a state of being very angry 盛怒；激愤 SYN **rage**: *She **flies into a passion** if anyone even mentions his name.* 哪怕是有人提到他的名字，她也会勃然大怒。 **3** [U] **~ (for sb)** a very strong feeling of sexual love 强烈的爱（尤指两性间的）：*His passion for her made him blind to everything else.* 他迷恋她，达到了不顾一切的地步。 **4** [C] **~ (for sth)** a very strong feeling of liking sth; a hobby, an activity, etc. that you like very much 酷爱；热衷的爱好（或活动等）：*The English have a passion for gardens.* 英格兰人酷爱花园。◇ *Music is a passion with him.* 他对音乐情有独钟。 **5 the Passion** [sing.] (in Christianity 基督教) the suffering and death of Jesus Christ 耶稣的受难

pas·sion·ate /ˈpæʃənət/ *adj.* **1** having or showing strong feelings of sexual love or of anger, etc. 拥有（或表现出）强烈性爱的；情意绵绵的；怒不可遏的：*to have a passionate nature* 天性易激动 ➲ WORDFINDER NOTE AT LOVE **2** having or showing strong feelings of enthusiasm for sth or belief in sth 热诚的；狂热的：*a passionate interest in music* 对音乐的浓厚兴趣 ◇ *a passionate defender of civil liberties* 公民自由权利的积极捍卫者 ▶ **pas·sion·ate·ly** *adv.*: *He took her in his arms and kissed her passionately.* 他把她搂在怀里狂热地亲吻。◇ *They are all passionately interested in environmental issues.* 他们都热衷于环境问题。

ˈpassion flower *noun* a tropical climbing plant with large brightly coloured flowers 西番莲

ˈpassion fruit *noun* [C, U] (*pl.* **passion fruit**) a small tropical fruit with a thick purple skin and many seeds inside, produced by some types of passion flower 鸡蛋果，百香果（一种西番莲果实） ➲ VISUAL VOCAB PAGE V33

pas·sion·less /ˈpæʃnləs/ *adj.* without emotion or enthusiasm 冷淡的；冷漠的；无情的

ˈPassion play *noun* a play about the suffering and death of Jesus Christ 耶稣受难剧

pas·sive AW /ˈpæsɪv/ *adj.*, *noun*

■ *adj.* **1** accepting what happens or what people do without trying to change anything or oppose them 消极的；被动的：*He played a passive role in the relationship.* 他在他们的关系中处于被动地位。◇ *a passive observer of events* 列席观察员 **2** (*grammar* 语法) connected with the form of a verb used when the subject is affected by the action of the verb, for example *He was bitten by a dog.* is a passive sentence （动词形式）被动语态的 ➲ COMPARE ACTIVE *adj.* (6) ▶ **pas·sive·ly** AW *adv.*

■ *noun* (*also* **ˌpassive ˈvoice**) [sing.] (*grammar* 语法) the form of a verb used when the subject is affected by the action of the verb 动词被动形式；被动语态 ➲ COMPARE ACTIVE *n.*

ˌpassive-agˈgressive *adj.* being angry without expressing your anger openly, but resisting people in authority by refusing to do what they want or to accept responsibility for your actions 消极对抗的：*He exhibited passive-aggressive tendencies.* 他表现出了消极抵抗倾向。

ˌpassive reˈsistance *noun* [U] a way of opposing a government or an enemy by peaceful means, often by refusing to obey laws or orders 消极反抗；和平抵抗

ˌpassive ˈsmoking *noun* [U] the act of breathing in smoke from other people's cigarettes 被动吸烟；吸二手烟

pas·siv·ity AW /pæˈsɪvəti/ *noun* [U] the state of accepting what happens without reacting or trying to fight against it 被动；消极状态

pas·siv·ize (*BrE also* **-ise**) /ˈpæsɪvaɪz/ *verb* **~ sth** (*grammar* 语法) to put a verb into the passive form 将（动词）变成被动语态形式；使被动化

ˈpass key *noun* = MASTER KEY

Pass·over /ˈpɑːsəʊvə(r); *NAmE* ˈpæsoʊ-/ *noun* [U, C] the Jewish religious festival and holiday in memory of the escape of the Jews from Egypt 逾越节（犹太人的宗教节日）

pass·port /ˈpɑːspɔːt; *NAmE* ˈpæspɔːrt/ *noun* **1** an official document that identifies you as a citizen of a particular country, and that you may have to show when you enter or leave a country 护照：*a valid passport* 有效护照 ◇ *a South African passport* 南非护照 ◇ *I was stopped as I went through **passport control*** (= where passports are checked). 在经过护照查验卡时，我被叫住了。◇ *a passport photo* 护照相片 ➲ WORDFINDER NOTE AT AIRPORT, TOURIST **2** **~ to sth** a thing that makes sth possible or enables you to achieve sth 途径；路子；手段 SYN **key**: *The only passport to success is hard work.* 获得成功的唯一途径就是艰苦奋斗。

pass·word /ˈpɑːswɜːd; *NAmE* ˈpæswɜːrd/ *noun* **1** a secret word or phrase that you need to know in order to be allowed into a place 暗语；暗号；口令 **2** (*computing* 计) a series of letters or numbers that you must type into a computer or computer system in order to be able to use it 口令（字）；密码：*Enter a username and password to get into the system.* 进入系统请键入用户名和密码。 ➲ WORDFINDER NOTE AT FILE

past /pɑːst; *NAmE* pæst/ *adj.*, *noun*, *prep.*, *adv.*

■ *adj.* **1** gone by in time 过去的；昔日的：*in past years/centuries/ages* 在过去的岁月 / 世纪 / 时代 ◇ *in times past* 在过去 ◇ *The time for discussion is past.* 讨论的时间已过。 **2** [only before noun] gone by recently; just ended 刚过去的；刚结束的：*I haven't seen much of her in the past few weeks.* 近几周来我很少见到她。◇ *The past month has been really busy at work.* 上个月工作实在是忙。 **3** [only before noun] belonging to an earlier time 从前的；以往的：*past events* 以往的事件 ◇ *From past experience I'd say he'd probably forgotten the time.* 根据过去的经验，我想他可能把时间忘了。◇ ***past and present students** of the college* 学院的老校友和在校生 ◇ *Let's forget about who was more to blame—it's all **past history**.* 咱们且忘掉更该责怪谁吧，那都是陈年旧账了。 **4** [only before noun] (*grammar* 语法) connected with the form of a verb used to express actions in the past （动词）过去式的

■ *noun* **1 the past** [sing.] the time that has gone by; things that happened in an earlier time 过去；昔日；过去的事情：*I used to go there often in the past.* 过去我常去那里。◇ ***the recent/distant past*** 较近的 / 遥远的过去 ◇ *She looked back on the past without regret.* 她回首往事毫无遗憾。◇ *Writing letters seems to be **a thing of the past**.* 写信好像已是昔日的事情了。 **2** [C] a person's past life

P

or career （某人）过去的经历（或事业）: *We don't know anything about his past.* 我们对他的经历一无所知。◇ *They say she has a 'past'* (= bad things in her past life that she wishes to keep secret). 据说她有一段"过去"（不名誉的秘史）。 **3 the past** [sing.] (*grammar* 语法) = PAST TENSE

IDM SEE BLAST *n.*, DISTANT, LIVE[1]

■ ***prep.*** **1** (*NAmE also* **after**) later than sth 晚于；在…之后: *half past two* 两点半 ◇ *ten (minutes) past six* 六点过十分 ◇ *There's a bus at twenty minutes past the hour* (= at 1.20, 2.20, etc.). 每小时逢二十分发一班公共汽车。◇ *We arrived at two o'clock and left at ten past* (= ten minutes past two). 我们两点钟到达，十分钟后离开。◇ *It was past midnight when we got home.* 我们到家已是午夜之后了。 **2** on or to the other side of sb/sth 在另一边；到另一侧: *We live in the house just past the church.* 我们就住在挨着教堂那边的房子里。◇ *He hurried past them without stopping.* 他匆匆走过他们身边，连停都没停。◇ *He just walked **straight past** us!* 他与我们擦肩而过！ **3** above or further than a particular point or stage 多于；超过: *Unemployment is now past the 3 million mark.* 失业人数现在已超过了 300 万大关。◇ *The flowers are past their best.* 这些花已过了盛开的季节。◇ *He's past his prime.* 他已不再年富力强了。◇ *She's long past retirement age.* 她早已超过了退休年龄。◇ *Honestly, I'm **past caring** what happens* (= I can no longer be bothered to care). 老实说，我已什么事都不关心了。

IDM **'past it** (*BrE, informal*) too old to do what you used to be able to do; too old to be used for its normal function （人）过老而无用；（物）旧得不宜使用: *In some sports you're past it by the age of 25.* 在某些运动中，人过 25 岁就难有作为了。◇ *That coat is looking decidedly past it.* 那件外衣看来绝对穿不出去了。

■ ***adv.*** **1** from one side of sth to the other 从一侧到另一侧；经过: *I called out to him as he ran past.* 他跑过时，我大声喊他。 **2** used to describe time passing （时间）过去，逝去 SYN **by**: *A week went past and nothing had changed.* 一个星期过去了，情况毫无变化。

P

pasta /'pæstə; *NAmE* 'pɑːstə/ *noun* [U] an Italian food made from flour, water and sometimes eggs, formed into different shapes and usually served with a sauce. It is hard when dry and soft when cooked. 意大利面食

paste /peɪst/ *noun, verb*

■ ***noun*** **1** [sing.] a soft wet mixture, usually made of a powder and a liquid 面糊: *She mixed the flour and water to a smooth paste.* 她把面粉和水和成细滑的面糊。 **2** [C] (especially in compounds 尤用于构成复合词) a smooth mixture of crushed meat, fish, etc. that is spread on bread or used in cooking 肉（或鱼等）酱（作涂抹料或烹饪用） **3** [U] a type of glue that is used for sticking paper to things 糨糊: *wallpaper paste* 贴壁纸的糨糊 **4** [U] a substance like glass, that is used for making artificial JEWELS, for example diamonds （制作人造宝石的）铅质玻璃

■ ***verb*** **1** [T] **~ sth + adv./prep.** to stick sth to sth else using glue or paste 粘贴；粘合: *He pasted the pictures into his scrapbook.* 他把画片贴到他的剪贴簿里。◇ *Paste the two pieces together.* 把这两片粘在一起。◇ *Paste down the edges.* 把边缘贴合起来。 **2** [T] **~ sth** to make sth by sticking pieces of paper together 拼贴: *The children were busy cutting and pasting paper hats.* 孩子们忙着剪裁和粘贴纸帽子。 **3** [T, I] **~ (sth)** (*computing* 计) to copy or move text into a document from another place or another document 粘贴；贴入；插入: *This function allows you to **cut and paste** text.* 本功能可使你剪切并粘贴文本。◇ *It's quicker to cut and paste than to retype.* 剪切和粘贴比重新打字要快。

paste·board /'peɪstbɔːd; *NAmE* -bɔːrd/ *noun* [U] a type of thin board made by sticking sheets of paper together （用多层纸粘贴的）硬纸板

pas·tel /'pæstl; *NAmE* pæ'stel/ *noun* **1** [U] soft coloured CHALK, used for drawing pictures 彩色粉笔；蜡笔: *drawings in pastel* 蜡笔画 **2 pastels** [pl.] small sticks of CHALK 粉笔: *a box of pastels* 一盒粉笔 **3** [C] a picture drawn with pastels 彩色粉笔画；蜡笔画 ➲ COLLOCATIONS AT ART **4** [C] a pale delicate colour 淡雅的色彩: *The whole house was painted in soft pastels.* 整座房屋都漆成柔和淡雅的色彩。

pas·tern /'pæstən; *NAmE* -tərn/ *noun* (*anatomy* 解) the part of a horse's foot between the FETLOCK and the HOOF （马足部的）骹

pas·teur·ize (*BrE also* **-ise**) /'pɑːstʃəraɪz; *NAmE* 'pæs-/ *verb* **~ sth** to heat a liquid, especially milk, to a particular temperature and then cool it, in order to kill harmful bacteria 用巴氏杀菌法消毒 ▶ **pas·teur·iza·tion, -isa·tion** /ˌpɑːstʃəraɪ'zeɪʃn; *NAmE* ˌpæstʃərə'zeɪʃn/ *noun* [U]

pas·tiche /pæ'stiːʃ/ *noun* **1** [C] a work of art, piece of writing, etc. that is created by deliberately copying the style of sb/sth else 刻意模仿的文艺作品；模仿作品: *a pastiche of the classic detective story* 经典侦探故事的仿作 **2** [C] a work of art, etc. that consists of a variety of different styles （集多种风格于一身的）混成作品，集锦 **3** [U] the art of creating a pastiche 模仿艺术；模仿技艺

pas·tille /'pæstəl; *NAmE* pæ'stiːl/ *noun* (*especially BrE*) a small sweet/candy that you suck, especially one that is flavoured with fruit or that contains medicine for a sore throat 含片；含片状药物: *fruit pastilles* 果味含片 ◇ *throat pastilles* 喉片

pas·time /'pɑːstaɪm; *NAmE* 'pæs-/ *noun* something that you enjoy doing when you are not working 消遣；休闲活动 SYN **hobby** ➲ SYNONYMS AT INTEREST

past·ing /'peɪstɪŋ/ *noun* [sing.] (*especially BrE*) **1** a heavy defeat in a game or competition （比赛中的）惨败，大败 **2** an instance of being hit very hard as a punishment 遭受痛打；受体罚 SYN **thrashing**

pas·tis /pæ'stiːs/ *noun* [U, C] (*pl.* **pas·tis**) (*from French*) a strong alcoholic drink usually drunk before a meal, that has the flavour of ANISEED 法国茴香酒（常作开胃酒）

ˌpast 'master *noun* **~ (at sth/at doing sth)** a person who is very good at sth because they have a lot of experience in it 老手；内行；专家 SYN **expert**: *She's a past master at getting what she wants.* 她可是个老练的人，想要什么就能得到什么。

pas·tor /'pɑːstə(r); *NAmE* 'pæs-/ *noun* a minister in charge of a Christian church or group, especially in some NONCONFORMIST churches （尤指非英国国教的）牧师

pas·tor·al /'pɑːstərəl; *NAmE* 'pæs-/ *adj.* **1** relating to the work of a priest or teacher in giving help and advice on personal matters, not just those connected with religion or education 牧灵的，牧师的，教牧的（有关圣职人员及教师对个人幸福的关顾）: *pastoral care* 牧师对教友的关怀 **2** showing country life or the countryside, especially in a romantic way 田园的；乡村生活的；村野风情的: *a pastoral scene/poem/symphony* 田园风光 / 诗 / 交响乐 **3** relating to the farming of animals 畜牧的: *agricultural and pastoral practices* 农牧业活动

pas·tor·al·ism /'pɑːstərəlɪzəm; *NAmE* 'pæs-/ *noun* [U] a way of keeping animals such as CATTLE, sheep, etc. that involves moving them from place to place to find water and food 游牧（牧者带着牲口逐水草而居） ▶ **pas·tor·al·ist** *noun, adj.*

ˌpast 'participle *noun* (*grammar* 语法) the form of a verb that in English ends in *-ed*, *-en*, etc. and is used with the verb *have* to form PERFECT tenses such as *I have eaten*, with the verb *be* to form passive sentences such as *It was destroyed*, or sometimes as an adjective as in *an upset stomach* 过去分词 ➲ COMPARE PRESENT PARTICIPLE

the ˌpast 'perfect (*also* **the ˌpast ˌperfect 'tense, the plu·per·fect**) *noun* [sing.] (*grammar* 语法) the form of a verb that expresses an action completed before a particular point in the past, formed in English with *had* and the past participle 过去完成时；过去完成式

pas·trami /pæ'strɑːmi/ *noun* [U] cold spicy smoked beef 五香熏牛肉

pas·try /ˈpeɪstri/ *noun* (*pl.* **-ies**) **1** [U] a mixture of flour, fat and water or milk that is rolled out flat and baked as a base or covering for PIES, etc. 油酥面团；油酥面皮 ➲ SEE ALSO CHOUX PASTRY, FILO PASTRY, PUFF PASTRY, SHORTCRUST PASTRY **2** [C] a small cake made using pastry 油酥糕点 ➲ SEE ALSO DANISH PASTRY

ˈpastry cook *noun* a professional cook whose main job is to make pastry, cakes, etc. 糕点师傅；糕点厨师

the ˌpast ˈtense (*also* **the past**) *noun* [sing.] (*grammar* 语法) the form of a verb used to describe actions in the past 过去时；过去式：*The past tense of 'take' is 'took'.* * take 的过去式是 took。

pas·tur·age /ˈpɑːstʃərɪdʒ; *NAmE* ˈpæs-/ *noun* [U] (*specialist*) land covered with grass for animals to eat 牧场

pas·ture /ˈpɑːstʃə(r); *NAmE* ˈpæs-/ *noun, verb*

■ ***noun*** **1** [U, C] land covered with grass that is suitable for feeding animals on 牧场；牧草地：*an area of permanent/rough/rich pasture* 一片永久的/高低不平的/富饶的牧场 ◇ *high mountain pastures* 高山牧场 ◇ *The cattle were put **out to pasture**.* 牛群放牧在牧场草地上。 ➲ VISUAL VOCAB PAGE V3 **2 pastures** [pl.] the circumstances of your life, work, etc. 生活状况；工作条件；个人发展的机遇：*I felt we were off to **greener pastures*** (= a better way of life). 我觉得我们在迈向更好的生活。◇ (*BrE*) *She decided it was time to move on to **pastures new*** (= a new job, place to live, etc.). 她认定做出改变的时候到了。

■ ***verb*** **~ sth** to put animals in a field to feed on grass 放牧

pas·ture·land /ˈpɑːstʃəlænd; *NAmE* ˈpæstʃərl-/ *noun* [U, pl.] (*also* **pas·tur·age** [U]) land where animals can feed on grass 牧场；牧草地

pasty¹ /ˈpæsti/ *noun* (*pl.* **-ies**) (*BrE*) a small PIE containing meat and vegetables 馅饼 ➲ SEE ALSO CORNISH PASTY

pasty² /ˈpeɪsti/ *adj.* pale and not looking healthy 面色苍白的 SYN **pallid**：*a pasty face/complexion* 苍白的面孔/容颜

pat /pæt/ *verb, noun, adj., adv.*

■ ***verb*** (**-tt-**) to touch sb/sth gently several times with your hand flat, especially as a sign of affection（喜爱地）轻拍：**~ sth** *She patted the dog on the head.* 她轻轻地拍着狗的头。◇ *He patted his sister's hand consolingly.* 他轻拍着妹妹的手安慰她。◇ **~ sth + adj.** *Pat your face dry with a soft towel.* 用软毛巾把脸搌干。 ➲ MORE LIKE THIS 36, page R29

IDM **pat sb/yourself on the ˈback** (*informal*) to praise sb or yourself for doing sth well 表扬，称赞（某人或自己）

■ ***noun*** **1** [usually sing.] a gentle friendly touch with your open hand or with a flat object（友善的）轻拍，拍打：*a pat on the head* 轻轻拍一下头 ◇ *He gave her knee an affectionate pat.* 他温情地拍了拍她的膝盖。 **2 ~ of butter** a small, soft, flat lump of butter 一小块黄油 ➲ SEE ALSO COWPAT

IDM **a ˌpat on the ˈback (for sth/for doing sth)** (*informal*) praise or approval for sth that you have done well 表扬；赞许：*He deserves a pat on the back for all his hard work.* 他工作兢兢业业，值得嘉许。

■ ***adj.*** (*usually disapproving*) (of an answer, a comment, etc. 答案、评论等) too quick, easy or simple; not seeming natural or realistic 过于简易的；不自然的；油滑的 SYN **glib**：*The ending of the novel is a little too pat to be convincing.* 小说的结尾有点过于简单，不能令人信服。◇ *There are no pat answers to these questions.* 这些问题没有简单的答案。

■ ***adv.***

IDM **have/know sth off ˈpat** (*BrE*) (*NAmE* **have/know sth down ˈpat**) to know sth perfectly so that you can repeat it at any time without having to think about it 了如指掌；滚瓜烂熟：*He had all the answers off pat.* 所有的答案他都胸有成竹。 **stand ˈpat** (*especially NAmE*) to refuse to change your mind about a decision you have made or an opinion you have 固执己见；拒不改变决定

patch /pætʃ/ *noun, verb*

■ ***noun***

• SMALL AREA 小块 **1** a small area of sth, especially one which is different from the area around it 色斑；斑点；（与周围不同的）小块，小片：*a black dog with a white patch on its back* 背上有一块白斑的黑狗 ◇ *a bald patch on the top of his head* 他头顶的秃块 ◇ *damp patches on the wall* 墙上的片片湿渍 ◇ *patches of dense fog* 团团浓雾

• PIECE OF MATERIAL 小片材料 **2** a small piece of material that is used to cover a hole in sth or to make a weak area stronger, or as decoration 补丁；补块：*I sewed patches on the knees of my jeans.* 我在我的牛仔裤膝部打了补丁。 **3** a piece of material that you wear over an eye, usually because the eye is damaged 眼罩：*He had a black patch over one eye.* 他一只眼戴着黑眼罩。 ➲ SEE ALSO EYEPATCH **4** (*NAmE*) (*BrE* **badge**) a piece of material that you sew onto clothes as part of a uniform（制服上的）标记，标识 **5** a piece of material that people can wear on their skin to help them to stop smoking 戒烟贴片：*nicotine patches* 尼古丁戒烟贴片

• PIECE/AREA OF LAND 地块 **6** a small piece of land, especially one used for growing vegetables or fruit 小块土地；（尤指）菜地，果园：*a vegetable patch* 一块菜地 ➲ VISUAL VOCAB PAGE V20 **7** (*BrE, informal*) an area that sb works in, knows well or comes from 工作地；熟悉的地区；家乡：*He knows every house in his patch.* 他熟悉他那地区的每一座房子。◇ *She has had a lot of success in her **home patch**.* 她在自己的家乡地区真是成绩斐然。

• DIFFICULT TIME 艰难时刻 **8** (*informal, especially BrE*) a period of time of the type mentioned, usually a difficult or unhappy one 一段（艰难）岁月；一段（痛苦）日子：*to go through a **bad/difficult/sticky patch*** 经历艰难/困难/不幸的时期 ➲ SEE ALSO PURPLE PATCH

• IN COMPUTING 计算机技术 **9** a small piece of code (= instructions that a computer can understand) which can be added to a computer program to improve it or to correct a fault 修补（程序）；补丁：*Follow the instructions below to download and install the patch.* 按照下面的说明下载并安装修补程序。

IDM **be not a ˈpatch on sb/sth** (*informal, especially BrE*) to be much less good, attractive, etc. than sb/sth else 远不如；远比…逊色

▼ **SYNONYMS 同义词辨析**

patch

dot • mark • spot

These are all words for a small part on a surface that is a different colour from the rest. 以上各词均指斑点、色斑。

patch an area of sth, especially one which is different from the area around it 指色斑、斑点、（与周围不同的）小块、小片：*a white dog with a black patch on its head* 头上有一块黑斑的白狗 ◇ *patches of dense fog* 团团浓雾

dot a small round mark on sth, especially one that is printed 指点、小点、小圆点，尤指印出来的点：*The letters 'i' and 'j' have dots over them.* 字母 i 和 j 上面都有一点。◇ *The island is a small green dot on the map.* 这个岛在地图上是一个小绿点。

mark a noticeable area of colour on the body of a person or animal 指人或动物身上的斑、记号、色斑：*The horse had a white mark on its head.* 这匹马头上有块白斑。

spot a small round area that is a different colour or feels different from the surface it is on 指斑点：*Which has spots, a leopard or a tiger?* 有斑点的是豹还是虎？

PATTERNS

- a patch/dot/mark/spot **on** sth
- **with** patches/dots/marks/spots
- a **blue/black/red, etc.** patch/dot/mark/spot

■ ***verb*** **~ sth (with sth)** to cover a hole or a worn place, especially in clothes, with a piece of cloth or other material 打补丁；缝补；修补 SYN **mend**：*patched jeans*

P

带补丁的牛仔裤 ◇ *to patch a hole in the roof* 修补屋顶的漏洞

PHR V ˌ**patch sb/sth ˈthrough** (**to sb/sth**) to connect telephone or electronic equipment temporarily （临时把电话、电子设备）接通，连通：*She was patched through to London on the satellite link.* 她经卫星线路与伦敦接通了。 ˌ**patch sth↔toˈgether** to make sth from several different parts, especially in a quick careless way 拼凑；草草拼合：*They hope to be able to patch together a temporary settlement.* 他们希望能快速搭好一个临时安置区。 ˌ**patch sth/sb↔ˈup** (*rather informal*) **1** to repair sth, especially in a temporary way by adding a new piece of material or a patch 修理；（尤指）临时修补：*Just to patch the boat up will cost £10 000.* 小船简单地修一下就得花 1 万英镑。 **2** to treat sb's injuries, especially quickly or temporarily 临时包扎（伤口）；仓促处理（损伤）：*The doctor will soon patch you up.* 大夫很快就会给你处理好的。 **3** to try to stop arguing with sb and be friends again 言归于好：*They've managed to patch up their differences.* 他们终于弥合了分歧。 ◇ *Have you tried* **patching things up** *with her?* 你有没有试试跟她和好？ **4** to agree on sth, especially after long discussions and even though the agreement is not exactly what everyone wants 勉强同意：*They managed to patch up a deal.* 他们勉强达成交易。

patch·ouli /ˈpætʃʊli; pəˈtʃuːli/ *noun* [U] a PERFUME made with oil from the leaves of a SE Asian bush 广藿香水

patch·work /ˈpætʃwɜːk; *NAmE* -wɜːrk/ *noun* **1** [U] a type of NEEDLEWORK in which small pieces of cloth of different colours or designs are sewn together （不同图案杂色布块的）拼缝物；拼布工艺：*a patchwork quilt* 拼布绗缝盖被 ➲ COMPARE CRAZY QUILT ➲ **VISUAL VOCAB** PAGE V24 **2** [sing.] a thing that is made up of many different pieces or parts 拼凑之物：*a patchwork of different styles and cultures* 不同风格和文化的拼合 ◇ *From the plane, the landscape was just a patchwork of fields.* 从飞机上俯瞰，满目是田园交错的景色。

patchy /ˈpætʃi/ *adj.* **1** existing or happening in some places and not others 零散的；散落的；分布不匀的 SYN **uneven**：*patchy fog* 团团的雾 ◇ *The grass was dry and patchy.* 草都干了，东一片西一片的。 **2** (*NAmE also* **spotty**) not complete; good in some parts, but not in others 不完整的；参差不齐的：*a patchy knowledge of Spanish* 对西班牙语一知半解 ◇ *It was a patchy performance.* 那是一场水准参差的演出。 ▸ **patch·ily** *adv.* **patchi·ness** *noun* [U]

pate /peɪt/ *noun* (*old use* or *humorous*) the top part of the head, especially when there is no hair on it 头顶；（尤指）秃顶，光顶：*The sun beat down on his bald pate.* 灼热的阳光直射到他那光光的秃顶上。

pâté /ˈpæteɪ; *NAmE* pɑːˈteɪ/ *noun* [U] a soft mixture of very finely chopped meat or fish, served cold and used for spreading on bread, etc. 鱼酱，肉酱（用作冷盘、涂于面包等上）

pâté de foie gras /ˌpæteɪ də fwʌ ˈɡrɑː; *NAmE* pɑːˌteɪ/ (*also* ˌ**foie ˈgras**) *noun* [U] (*from French*) an expensive type of pâté made from the LIVER of a GOOSE 鹅肝酱

pa·tel·la /pəˈtelə/ *noun* (*pl.* **pa·tel·lae** /-liː/) (*anatomy* 解) the KNEECAP 髌骨；膝盖骨

pa·tent *noun, adj., verb*

■ *noun* /ˈpætnt; *BrE also* ˈpeɪtnt/ [C, U] an official right to be the only person to make, use or sell a product or an invention; a document that proves this 专利；专利证书：*to* **apply for/obtain a patent** *on an invention* 申请 / 获得发明专利 ◇ *The device was protected* **by patent**. 这一装置受专利保护。

■ *adj.* /ˈpeɪtnt; *NAmE also* ˈpætnt/ [only before noun] **1** connected with a patent 有专利的；受专利保护的：*patent applications/laws* 专利申请；专利法 ◇ *the US Patent Office* 美国专利局 **2** (of a product 产品) made or sold by a particular company 专利生产的；专利经销的：*patent medicines* 专利药 **3** (*formal*) used to emphasize that sth bad is very clear and obvious 明显的；赤裸裸的 SYN **blatant**：*It was a patent lie.* 那是赤裸裸的谎言。

■ *verb* /ˈpætnt; *BrE also* ˈpeɪtnt/ **~ sth** to obtain a patent for an invention or a process 获得专利

pa·tent·ee /ˌpætənˈtiː; *BrE also* ˌpeɪt-/ *noun* a person or an organization that holds the patent for sth 专利权（所有）人；专利获得者

patent leather /ˌpeɪtnt ˈleðə(r); *NAmE usually* ˈpætnt/ *noun* [U] a type of leather with a hard shiny surface, used especially for making shoes and bags 漆革；漆皮

pa·tent·ly /ˈpeɪtəntli; ˈpætəntli; *NAmE* ˈpæt-/ *adv.* (*formal*) without doubt 毫无疑问；显然 SYN **clearly**：*Her explanation was patently ridiculous.* 她的解释显然是荒唐可笑的。 ◇ *It was* **patently obvious** *that she was lying.* 她显然是在撒谎。

pater /ˈpeɪtə(r)/ *noun* (*old-fashioned, BrE*) father 父亲

pater·famil·ias /ˌpeɪtəfəˈmɪliæs; *NAmE* ˌpætərf-/ *noun* [sing.] (*formal* or *humorous*) the man who is the head of a family （男性）家长

pa·ter·nal /pəˈtɜːnl; *NAmE* -ˈtɜːrnl/ *adj.* **1** connected with being a father; typical of a kind father 父亲的；慈父般的：*paternal love* 父爱 ◇ *He gave me a piece of paternal advice.* 他给了我慈父般的忠告。 **2** related through the father's side of the family 父系的：*my paternal grandmother* (= my father's mother) 我的祖母 ▸ **pa·ter·nal·ly** /-nəli/ *adv.*：*He smiled paternally at them.* 他像慈父一样对他们微笑。 ➲ COMPARE MATERNAL

pa·ter·nal·ism /pəˈtɜːnəlɪzəm; *NAmE* -ˈtɜːrn-/ *noun* [U] (*sometimes disapproving*) the system in which a government or an employer protects the people who are governed or employed by providing them with what they need, but does not give them any responsibility or freedom of choice 家长作风；家长式管理；专制 ▸ **pa·ter·nal·is·tic** /pəˌtɜːnəˈlɪstɪk; *NAmE* -ˌtɜːrn-/ (*also* **pa·ter·nal·ist**) *adj.*：*a paternalistic employer* 家长式雇主

pa·ter·nity /pəˈtɜːnəti; *NAmE* -ˈtɜːrn-/ *noun* [U] the fact of being the father of a child 父亲的身份（或地位）：*He refused to admit paternity of the child.* 他拒不承认是那孩子的父亲。 ➲ COMPARE MATERNITY

paˈternity leave *noun* [U] time that the father of a new baby is allowed to have away from work 陪产假（父亲照顾新生儿的休假） ➲ **COLLOCATIONS** AT CHILD ➲ SEE ALSO MATERNITY LEAVE, PARENTAL LEAVE

paˈternity suit (*also* **paˈternity case**) *noun* a court case that is intended to prove who a child's father is, especially so that he can be ordered to give the child financial support 确认生父的诉讼（请求法院确认生父并使其承担抚养义务）

path 🔑 /pɑːθ; *NAmE* pæθ/ (*pl.* **paths** /pɑːðz; *NAmE* pæðz/) (*also* **path·way**) *noun* **1** 🔑 a way or track that is built or is made by the action of people walking 小路；小径：*a concrete path* 混凝土小路 ◇ *the* **garden path** 花园小径 ◇ **Follow the path** *through the woods.* 沿着这条小路穿过树林。 ◇ *to walk along a path* 沿小径前行 ◇ *The* **path led** *up a steep hill.* 小路通向一座陡峭的山丘。 ◇ *a* **coastal path** 海边的小路 ➲ SEE ALSO FOOTPATH **2** 🔑 [usually sing.] a line along which sb/sth moves; the space in front of sb/sth as they move 路线；道路 SYN **way**：*He threw himself* **into the path of** *an oncoming vehicle.* 他冲入迎面有汽车驶来的路中。 ◇ *The avalanche forced its way down the mountain, crushing everything* **in its path**. 雪崩冲下山来，摧毁了沿途的一切。 ◇ *Three men blocked her path.* 三个男人挡住了她的去路。 ➲ SEE ALSO FLIGHT PATH **3** 🔑 a plan of action or a way of achieving sth 行动计划；成功的途径：*a career path* 职业道路 ◇ *the path to success* 成功之道 IDM SEE BEAT *v.*, CROSS *v.*, LEAD[1] *v.*, PRIMROSE, SMOOTH *v.*

path·et·ic /pəˈθetɪk/ *adj.* **1** making you feel pity or sadness 可怜的；可悲的；令人怜惜的 SYN **pitiful**：*a pathetic and lonely old man* 可怜又孤独的老翁 ◇ *The starving children were a pathetic sight.* 饥饿的儿童看起来是一幅凄惨的景象。 **2** (*informal, disapproving*) weak and not

successful 无力的；不成功的 SYN **feeble**: *a pathetic excuse* 牵强的借口 ◇ *She made a pathetic attempt to smile.* 她勉强地微微一笑。◇ *You're pathetic!* 你真是没用！
▶ **path·et·ic·al·ly** /-kli/ *adv.*: *He cried pathetically.* 他哭得很悲伤。◇ *a pathetically shy woman* 令人怜悯的腼腆女人

pa,thetic 'fallacy *noun* [U, sing.] (in art and literature 用于艺术和文学) the act of describing animals and things as having human feelings 拟人谬化（对动物或物体赋予人类感情）

path·find·er /ˈpɑːθfaɪndə(r); *NAmE* ˈpæθ-/ *noun* **1** a person, group or thing that goes before others and shows the way over unknown land 探路者；开路人 **2** a person, group or thing that finds a new way of doing sth 先锋；开拓者 SYN **trailblazer**: *The company is a pathfinder in computer technology.* 这家公司是计算机技术的开拓者。

patho- /ˈpæθəʊ; *NAmE* -θoʊ/ *combining form* (in nouns, adjectives and adverbs 构成名词、形容词和副词) connected with disease 与疾病相关: *pathogenesis* (= the development of a disease) 发病机制 ◇ *pathophysiology* 病理生理学

patho·gen /ˈpæθədʒən/ *noun* (*specialist*) a thing that causes disease 病原体 ▶ **patho·gen·ic** /-ˈdʒenɪk/ *adj.*

patho·gen·esis /ˌpæθəˈdʒenɪsɪs/ *noun* (*medical* 医) the way in which a disease develops 发病机制；病机

patho·logic·al /ˌpæθəˈlɒdʒɪkl; *NAmE* -ˈlɑːdʒ-/ *adj.* **1** not reasonable or sensible; impossible to control 不理智的；无道理的；无法控制的: *pathological fear/hatred/violence* 无理由的恐惧／憎恨／暴行 ◇ *a* ***pathological liar*** (= a person who cannot stop telling lies) 说谎成性者 **2** caused by, or connected with, disease or illness 病态的；与疾病有关的: *pathological depression* 病态的抑郁 **3** (*specialist*) connected with PATHOLOGY 病理学的；与病理学相关的
▶ **patho·logic·al·ly** /-kli/ *adv.*: *pathologically jealous* 有嫉妒狂的

path·olo·gist /pəˈθɒlədʒɪst; *NAmE* -ˈθɑːl-/ *noun* a doctor who studies pathology and examines dead bodies to find out the cause of death 病理学医生；病理学家 ➲ COMPARE MEDICAL EXAMINER

path·ology /pəˈθɒlədʒi; *NAmE* -ˈθɑːl-/ *noun* **1** [U] (*medical* 医) the scientific study of diseases 病理学 **2** [C] an aspect of sb's behaviour that is extreme and unreasonable and that they cannot control 变态；反常

pathos /ˈpeɪθɒs; *NAmE* -θɑːs; -θɔːs/ *noun* [U] (in writing, speech and plays 文章、讲话和戏剧) the power of a performance, description, etc. to produce feelings of sadness and sympathy 感染力；令人产生悲悯共鸣的力量

path·way /ˈpɑːθweɪ; *NAmE* ˈpæθ-/ *noun* = PATH

pa·tience 🔑 /ˈpeɪʃns/ *noun* [U] **1** 🔑 ~ (**with sb/sth**) the ability to stay calm and accept a delay or sth annoying without complaining 耐心；忍耐力: *She* ***has little patience with*** (= will not accept or consider) *such views.* 她很难接受这类观点。◇ *People have* ***lost patience with*** (= have become annoyed about) *the slow pace of reform.* 人们对改革的缓慢速度已经失去耐性。◇ *I have run out of patience with her.* 我对她已失去耐性了。◇ *My patience is wearing thin.* 我要忍耐不住了。◇ *Teaching children with special needs requires patience and understanding.* 教导有特殊需要的儿童需要耐心和体谅。 **2** 🔑 the ability to spend a lot of time doing sth difficult that needs a lot of attention and effort 毅力；坚忍；恒心: *It takes time and patience to photograph wildlife.* 拍摄野生生物要肯花时间，还要有毅力。◇ *I* ***don't have the patience to*** *do jigsaw puzzles.* 我没有耐性玩拼图游戏。 **3** (*BrE*) (*NAmE* **soli·taire**) a card game for only one player 单人纸牌游戏 IDM SEE JOB, TRY *v.*

pa·tient 🔑 /ˈpeɪʃnt/ *noun, adj.*
■ ***noun*** **1** 🔑 a person who is receiving medical treatment, especially in a hospital 接受治疗者，病人（尤指医院里的）: *cancer patients* 癌症病人 ➲ WORDFINDER NOTE AT DOCTOR **2** 🔑 a person who receives treatment from a particular doctor, dentist, etc.（某个医生或牙医等的）病人: *He's one of Dr Shaw's patients.* 他是肖医生的病人之一。 **3** (*grammar* 语法) the person or thing that is affected by the action of the verb. In the sentence 'I started the car', the patient is *car*. 受动者 ➲ COMPARE AGENT (6)
■ ***adj.*** 🔑 ~ (**with sb/sth**) able to wait for a long time or accept annoying behaviour or difficulties without becoming angry 有耐心的；能忍耐的: *She's very patient with young children.* 她对幼儿特别有耐心。◇ *You'll just have to be patient and wait till I'm finished.* 你只能耐心点儿，等我把事情做完。▶ **pa·tient·ly** *adv.*: *She sat patiently waiting for her turn.* 她耐心地坐着等候轮到自己。

pat·ina /ˈpætɪnə; *NAmE* pəˈtiːnə/ *noun* [usually sing.] **1** a green, black or brown layer that forms on the surface of some metals （金属表面的）绿锈，铜锈，氧化层 **2** a thin layer that forms on other materials; the shiny surface that develops on wood or leather when it is polished 薄层；（木器或皮革的）光泽: (*figurative*) *He looked relaxed and elegant and had the patina of success.* 他神态轻松潇洒，给人成功的印象。

pat·in·ation /ˌpætɪˈneɪʃn/ *noun* [U, C] (*specialist*) a shiny layer on the surface of metal, wood, etc.; the process of covering sth with a shiny layer 包浆；（金属、木器等的）光泽，生成光泽

patio /ˈpætiəʊ; *NAmE* -oʊ/ *noun* (*pl.* **-os**) a flat hard area outside, and usually behind, a house where people can sit（房屋外面或后面的）露台，平台: *Let's have lunch* ***out on the patio.*** 咱们在外面平台上吃午饭吧。 ➲ VISUAL VOCAB PAGE V20

ˌpatio 'door *noun* [usually pl.] (*especially BrE*) a large glass sliding door that leads to a garden or BALCONY （通往花园或阳台的）玻璃推拉门

pa·tis·serie /pəˈtiːsəri/ *noun* (*from French*) **1** [C] a shop/store that sells cakes, etc. 糕点店 **2** [U] (*also* **pa·tis·series** [pl.]) (*formal*) cakes 糕点

Pat Malone /ˌpæt məˈləʊn; *NAmE* -ˈloʊn/ *noun*
IDM **on your Pat Ma'lone** (*AustralE, NZE, informal*) alone; without anybody else 单独；独自

pat·ois /ˈpætwɑː/ *noun* (*pl.* **pat·ois** /-twɑːz/) a form of a language, spoken by people in a particular area, that is different from the standard language of the country 方言；土语；土话

patri·arch /ˈpeɪtriɑːk; *NAmE* -ɑːrk/ *noun* **1** the male head of a family or community （男性）家长，族长，酋长 ➲ COMPARE MATRIARCH **2** an old man that people have a lot of respect for 德高望重的男性长者 **3** **Patriarch** the title of a most senior BISHOP (= a senior priest) in the Orthodox or Roman Catholic Church （东正教和天主教的）牧首，宗主教

patri·arch·al /ˌpeɪtriˈɑːkl; *NAmE* -ˈɑːrkl/ *adj.* **1** ruled or controlled by men; giving power and importance only to men 男人统治的；男性主宰的: *a patriarchal society* 男权社会 **2** connected with a patriarch 族长的；家长的 ➲ COMPARE MATRIARCHAL

patri·arch·ate /ˈpeɪtriɑːkət; *NAmE* -ɑːrk-/ *noun* (*formal*) **1** the title, position or period of office of a Patriarch 宗主教（或牧首）的职务（或任期等） **2** the area governed by a Patriarch 宗主教（或牧首）区

patri·archy /ˈpeɪtriɑːki; *NAmE* -ɑːrki/ *noun* [C, U] (*pl.* **-ies**) a society, system or country that is ruled or controlled by men 男性统治的社会（或制度、国家）；男权政治；父权制 ➲ COMPARE MATRIARCHY

pa·tri·cian /pəˈtrɪʃn/ *adj.* (*formal*) connected with or typical of the highest social class 贵族的；上流社会的 SYN **aristocratic** ▶ **pa·tri·cian** *noun* ➲ COMPARE PLEBEIAN *adj.*

patri·cide /ˈpætrɪsaɪd/ *noun* [U, C] (*formal*) the crime of killing your father; a person who is guilty of this crime 弑父罪；弑父者 ➲ COMPARE FRATRICIDE (1), MATRICIDE, PARRICIDE

P

patri·lin·eal /ˌpætrɪˈlɪniəl/ *adj.* (*formal*) used to describe the relationship between father and child that continues in a family with each generation, or sth that is based on this relationship 父子相传的；父系的： *In that society, inheritance of land is patrilineal* (= the children get the land that their father owned). 在那个社会，土地继承是父传子的。 ➲ COMPARE MATRILINEAL

patri·mony /ˈpætrɪməni; *NAmE* -moʊni/ *noun* [sing.] (*formal*) **1** property that is given to sb when their father dies 遗产；祖传财产 **SYN** **inheritance** **2** the works of art and TREASURES of a nation, church, etc. 文化遗产；文物；国家（或教堂等）的财产 **SYN** **heritage**

pat·riot /ˈpeɪtriət; *BrE also* ˈpæt-/ *noun* a person who loves their country and who is ready to defend it against an enemy 爱国者

pat·ri·ot·ic /ˌpeɪtriˈɒtɪk; ˌpæt-; *NAmE* ˌpeɪtriˈɑːtɪk/ *adj.* having or expressing a great love of your country 爱国的： *a patriotic man who served his country well* 为国尽忠的爱国者 ◇ *patriotic songs* 爱国歌曲 ▶ **pat·ri·ot·ic·al·ly** /-kli/ *adv.*

pat·ri·ot·ism /ˈpeɪtriətɪzəm; *BrE also* ˈpæt-/ *noun* [U] love of your country and willingness to defend it 爱国主义；爱国精神

pa·trol /pəˈtrəʊl; *NAmE* pəˈtroʊl/ *verb, noun*

■ *verb* (**-ll-**) **1** [T, I] ~ (**sth**) to go around an area or a building at regular times to check that it is safe and that there is no trouble 巡逻；巡查： *Troops patrolled the border day and night.* 军队日夜在边境地区巡逻。 ◇ *Guards can be seen patrolling everywhere.* 到处都能见到卫兵在巡逻。 **2** [T] ~ **sth** to drive or walk around a particular area, especially in a threatening way （尤指威胁性地）逛荡，闲逛： *Gangs of youths patrol the streets at night.* 夜里成帮结伙的年轻人在街上闲逛。

■ *noun* **1** [C, U] the act of going to different parts of a building, an area, etc. to make sure that there is no trouble or crime 巡逻；巡查： *Security guards make regular patrols at night.* 夜间保安人员定时巡逻。 ◇ *a police car* ***on patrol*** 巡逻的警车 **2** [C] a group of soldiers, vehicles, etc. that patrol an area 巡逻队；巡逻车队： *a naval/police patrol* 海军/警察巡逻队 ◇ *a patrol car/boat* 巡逻车；巡逻船 **3** [C] a group of about six BOY SCOUTS or GIRL GUIDES/GIRL SCOUTS that forms part of a larger group 童子军小队

pa·trol·man /pəˈtrəʊlmən; *NAmE* -ˈtroʊ-/, **pa·trol·woman** /pəˈtrəʊlwʊmən; *NAmE* -ˈtroʊ-/ *noun* (*pl.* **-men** /-mən/, **-women** /-wɪmɪn/) **1** (in the US) a police officer who walks or drives around an area to make sure that there is no trouble or crime （美国的）巡警： *Patrolman Don Lilly* 巡警唐·利利 **2** (in Britain) an official of an association for car owners who goes to give help to drivers who have a problem with their cars （英国汽车协会帮助车主解决困难的）公路巡查员，巡视员 ➲ MORE LIKE THIS 25, page R28

paˈtrol wagon (*also informal* **ˈpaddy wagon**) (*both NAmE*) *noun* a police van for transporting prisoners in 囚车

pat·ron /ˈpeɪtrən/ *noun* **1** a person who gives money and support to artists and writers （艺术家、作家的）赞助人，资助者： *Frederick the Great was the patron of many artists.* 腓特烈大帝是许多艺术家的赞助人。 **2** a famous person who supports an organization such as a charity and whose name is used in the advertisements, etc. for the organization 名义赞助人（支持慈善组织等的名人，名字常用于有关的广告宣传中） **3** (*formal*) a person who uses a particular shop/store, restaurant, etc. 老主顾；顾客；常客： *Patrons are requested not to smoke.* 请顾客不要吸烟。

pat·ron·age /ˈpætrənɪdʒ; ˈpeɪt-/ *noun* [U] **1** the support, especially financial, that is given to a person or an organization by a patron 资助；赞助： *Patronage of the arts comes from businesses and private individuals.* 对艺术的资助来自企业和个人。 **2** the system by which an important person gives help or a job to sb in return for their support （掌权者给予提挈以换取支持的）互惠互利 **3** (*especially NAmE*) the support that a person gives a shop/store, restaurant, etc. by spending money there 惠顾；光顾

pat·ron·ess /ˌpeɪtrənˈes/ *noun* a female PATRON (1) 女赞助人；女资助人 ➲ NOTE AT GENDER

pat·ron·ize (*BrE also* **-ise**) /ˈpætrənaɪz; *NAmE* ˈpeɪt-/ *verb* **1** [T, I] ~ (**sb**) (*disapproving*) to treat sb in a way that seems friendly, but which shows that you think that they are not very intelligent, experienced, etc. 屈尊俯就地对待；摆出高人一等的派头： *Some television programmes tend to patronize children.* 有些电视节目往往以大人的观点对待儿童。 **2** [T] ~ **sth** (*formal*) to be a regular customer of a shop/store, restaurant, etc. 经常光顾： *The club is patronized by students and locals alike.* 学生和当地居民都经常去那家俱乐部。 **3** [T] ~ **sb/sth** to help a particular person, organization or activity by giving them money 赞助；资助： *She patronizes many contemporary British artists.* 她赞助许多英国当代艺术家。

pat·ron·iz·ing (*BrE also* **-is·ing**) /ˈpætrənaɪzɪŋ; *NAmE* ˈpeɪt-/ *adj.* (*disapproving*) showing that you think you are better or more intelligent than sb else 自以为高人一等的；摆架子的 **SYN** **superior**： *a patronizing smile* 屈尊俯就的一笑 ◇ *I was only trying to explain; I didn't want to sound patronizing.* 我只是想解释一下而已，绝无自诩清高之意。 ▶ **pat·ron·iz·ing·ly, -is·ing·ly** *adv.* ： *He patted her hand patronizingly.* 他以上级姿态拍了拍她的手。

ˌ**patron ˈsaint** *noun* a Christian SAINT who is believed to protect a particular place or group of people 主保圣人；守护圣人： *St Patrick, Ireland's patron saint* 圣帕特里克，爱尔兰的主保圣人 ◇ *St Christopher, patron saint of travellers* 圣克利斯托弗，旅行主保

patro·nym·ic /ˌpætrəˈnɪmɪk/ *noun* (*specialist*) a name formed from the name of your father or a male ANCESTOR, especially by adding sth to the beginning or end of their name 从父名衍生出的名字（尤指在父亲或父系祖先之名上加前、后缀） ➲ COMPARE MATRONYMIC

patsy /ˈpætsi/ *noun* (*pl.* **-ies**) (*informal, especially NAmE*) a weak person who is easily cheated or tricked, or who is forced to take the blame for sth that sb else has done wrong 容易吃亏上当者；容易成为替罪羊者

pat·ter /ˈpætə(r)/ *noun, verb*

■ *noun* **1** [sing.] the sound that is made by sth repeatedly hitting a surface quickly and lightly 吧嗒吧嗒的响声；急速的轻拍声： *the patter of feet/footsteps* 哒哒的脚步声 ◇ *the patter of rain on the roof* 雨打屋顶的啪哒声 **2** [U, sing.] fast continuous talk by sb who is trying to sell you sth or entertain you （为推销或娱乐的）不间断说话： *sales patter* 为了推销一口气说的话

IDM **the patter of tiny feet** (*informal* or *humorous*) a way of referring to children when sb wants, or is going to have, a baby （用于想要或即将有孩子时）小宝宝的脚步声： *We can't wait to hear the patter of tiny feet.* 我们恨不得早点儿有个小宝宝。

■ *verb* **1** [I] + **adv./prep.** to make quick, light sounds as a surface is being hit several times 发出轻快的拍打声： *Rain pattered against the window.* 雨点啪哒啪哒地敲击着窗子。 **2** [I] + **adv./prep.** to walk with light steps in a particular direction 轻盈地走： *I heard her feet pattering along the corridor.* 我听到她步履轻盈地在走廊上走过。

pat·tern 🔑 /ˈpætn; *NAmE* -tərn/ *noun, verb*

■ *noun* **1** 🔑 the regular way in which sth happens or is done 模式；方式： ***changing patterns*** *of behaviour* 变化行为模式 ◇ *an irregular sleeping pattern* 不规律的睡眠模式 ◇ *The murders all seem to* ***follow a (similar) pattern*** (= happen in the same way). 这些凶杀案似乎同出一辙。 **2** 🔑 [usually sing.] an excellent example to copy 范例；典范；榜样；样板： *This system* ***sets the pattern*** *for others to follow.* 这个系统堪为他人仿效的典范。 **3** 🔑 a regular arrangement of lines, shapes, colours, etc. as a design on material, carpets, etc. 图案；花样；式样： *a pattern of* *diamonds and squares* 菱形和正方形构成的图案 ◇ *a shirt with a floral pattern* 一件花衬衣

WORDFINDER 联想词： band, check, dot, fleck, speckle, splash, spot, streak, stripe

4 a design, set of instructions or shape to cut around that you use in order to make sth 模型；底样；纸样： *a knitting pattern* 编织图样 ◇ *She bought a dress pattern and some material.* 她买了一幅衣服纸样和一些衣料。 **5** a small piece of material, paper, etc. that helps you choose the design of sth 样品；样本 **SYN** **sample**: *wallpaper patterns* 壁纸样品

■ ***verb*** **1** **~ sth** to form a regular arrangement of lines or shapes on sth 构成图案（或花样）： *Frost patterned the window.* 霜在窗子上形成了图案。 ◇ *a landscape patterned by vineyards* 由一片片葡萄园构成的风景图 **2** **~ sth** (*specialist*) to cause a particular type of behaviour to develop 使形成，促成（某行为模式）： *Adult behaviour is often patterned by childhood experiences.* 成年人的行为模式往往受童年经历影响。

PHR V **'pattern sth on sth** (*BrE*) (*NAmE* **'pattern sth after sth**) [usually passive] to use sth as a model for sth; to copy sth 模仿；仿效： *a new approach patterned on Japanese ideas* 模仿日本概念而设计的新方法

pat·terned /ˈpætənd; *NAmE* -tərnd/ *adj.* decorated with a pattern 有图案的；带花样的： *patterned wallpaper* 印有图案的壁纸 ◇ **~ with sth** *cups patterned with yellow flowers* 有黄花图案的杯子 ➲ VISUAL VOCAB PAGE V66

pat·tern·ing /ˈpætənɪŋ; *NAmE* -tərn-/ *noun* [U] **1** (*specialist*) the forming of fixed ways of behaving by copying or repeating sth 固有行为方式的形成： *cultural patterning* 文化形态的形成 ◇ *the patterning of husband-wife roles* 夫妻角色的形成 **2** the arrangement of shapes or colours to make patterns （形状、色彩的）排列，造型： *a red fish with black patterning* 有黑色花纹的红鱼

patty /ˈpæti/ *noun* (*pl.* **-ies**) (*especially NAmE*) finely chopped meat, fish, etc. formed into a small round flat shape 碎肉饼；鱼肉饼： *a hamburger patty* 汉堡包肉饼

pau·city /ˈpɔːsəti/ *noun* [sing.] **~ (of sth)** (*formal*) a small amount of sth; less than enough of sth 少量；少许；贫乏： *a paucity of information* 信息的短缺

paunch /pɔːntʃ/ *noun* a fat stomach on a man （男人的）大肚子，啤酒肚 ▸ **paunchy** *adj.*

pau·per /ˈpɔːpə(r)/ *noun* (*old use*) a very poor person 穷人；贫民；乞丐

pause /pɔːz/ *verb, noun*

■ ***verb*** **1** [I] to stop talking or doing sth for a short time before continuing 暂停；停顿： *Anita paused for a moment, then said: 'All right'.* 安尼塔略停了一会儿，然后说："好吧"。 ◇ *The woman spoke almost without* ***pausing for breath*** (= very quickly). 那女人说话像放连珠炮似的。 ◇ *I paused at the door and looked back.* 我停在门口，回头看了看。 ◇ ***Pausing only to*** *pull on a sweater, he ran out of the house.* 他只停下来穿了件毛衣就冲出了屋外。 **2** [T] **~ sth** to stop a DVD, etc. for a short time using the pause button （按暂停键）暂停播放： *She paused the DVD and went to answer the phone.* 她暂停了 DVD 去接电话。

■ ***noun*** **1** [C] **~ (in sth)** a period of time during which sb stops talking or stops what they are doing 停顿；停顿的时间： *There was a long pause before she answered.* 她停了好一会儿才回答。 ◇ *David waited for a pause in the conversation so he could ask his question.* 戴维等着谈话停下来，好问个问题。 ◇ *After a brief pause, they continued climbing.* 他们略停了一下就继续爬山。 ◇ *The rain fell* ***without pause***. 雨不停地下着。 **2** [C] (*especially BrE*) (*also* **fer·mata** *especially in NAmE*) (*music* 音) a sign (𝄐) over a note or a REST to show that it should be longer than usual 延长记号 **3** [U] (*also* **'pause button**) a control that allows you to stop a DVD PLAYER, etc. for a short time 暂停键： *Press pause to stop the tape.* 按暂停键停下磁带。

IDM **give (sb) 'pause** (*also* **give (sb) pause for 'thought**) (*formal*) to make sb think seriously about sth or hesitate before doing sth 使认真考虑；使犹豫 ➲ MORE AT PREGNANT

pav·ane /pəˈvæn; -ˈvɑːn/ (*also* **pavan** /ˈpævən/) *noun* a slow dance popular in the 16th and 17th centuries; a piece of music for this dance 帕凡舞（流行于 16 和 17 世纪的慢步舞）；帕凡舞曲

pave /peɪv/ *verb* [often passive] **~ sth (with sth)** to cover a surface with flat stones or bricks （用砖石）铺（地）： *a paved area near the back door* 后门旁一块石板地

IDM **,pave the 'way (for sb/sth)** to create a situation in which sb will be able to do sth or sth can happen （为…）铺平道路，创造条件： *This decision paved the way for changes in employment rights for women.* 这项决议为修改妇女就业权利创造了条件。 ➲ MORE AT ROAD, STREET *n.*

pave·ment /ˈpeɪvmənt/ *noun* **1** [C] (*BrE*) (*NAmE* **side·walk**) a flat part at the side of a road for people to walk on （马路边的）人行道： *a pavement cafe* 路边咖啡馆 ➲ VISUAL VOCAB PAGE V3 **2** [C, U] any area of flat stones on the ground 石板铺的地面： *a mosaic pavement* 马赛克地面 **3** [U] (*NAmE*) the surface of a road 路面： *Two cars skidded on the icy pavement.* 两辆汽车在结冰的路面上打滑。

'pavement artist (*BrE*) (*NAmE* **'sidewalk artist**) *noun* an artist who draws pictures in CHALK on the PAVEMENT/SIDEWALK, hoping to get money from people who pass 街头画家，马路画家（在人行道上用粉笔作画讨钱）

pa·vil·ion /pəˈvɪliən/ *noun* **1** a temporary building used at public events and exhibitions （公共活动或展览用的）临时建筑物： *the US pavilion at the Trade Fair* 交易会上的美国展览馆 **2** (*BrE*) a building next to a sports ground, used by players and people watching the game （运动场旁设立的）运动员席，看台： *a cricket pavilion* 板球场看台 **3** (*NAmE*) a large building used for sports or entertainment 大型文体馆： *the Pauley Pavilion, home of the university's basketball team* 普莱文体中心，这所大学篮球队的主场 **4** a building that is meant to be more beautiful than useful, built as a shelter in a park or used for concerts and dances （公园中的）亭，阁；（音乐会、舞会的）华美建筑： *his first show at the Winter Gardens Pavilion, Blackpool* 他在布莱克浦冬园阁的首次演出

pav·ing /ˈpeɪvɪŋ/ *noun* [U] **1** a surface of flat stones or material like stone on the ground 石板等铺的地面： *Weeds grew through the cracks in the paving.* 杂草从铺石路面的缝隙中长出来。 ➲ SEE ALSO CRAZY PAVING **2** the stones or material that are used to make a flat surface on the ground 铺料；铺地的材料： *We'll use concrete paving.* 我们将使用混凝土铺地面。

'paving stone *noun* a flat, usually square, piece of stone that is used to make a hard surface for walking on 铺地石板；方石板 **SYN** **flagstone**

pav·lova /pævˈləʊvə; *NAmE* -ˈloʊ-/ *noun* a cold DESSERT (= sweet dish) made of MERINGUE, cream and fruit 巴甫洛娃蛋糕（用蛋白酥、奶油和水果制成）

Pav·lov·ian /pævˈləʊviən; *NAmE* -ˈloʊ-/ *adj.* (of an animal's or human's reaction 动物或人的反应) happening in response to a particular STIMULUS 巴甫洛夫氏条件作用的；经典条件反射的： *Her yawn was a Pavlovian response to my yawn.* 她打哈欠是对我打哈欠的条件反射。 **ORIGIN** From the name of the Russian scientist, I P Pavlov, who carried out experiments on dogs, showing how they could be conditioned to react to certain stimuli. 源自俄罗斯科学家巴甫洛夫的名字，他对狗做的实验表明：它们经过训练能够对某些刺激作出反应。

paw /pɔː/ *noun, verb*

■ ***noun*** **1** the foot of an animal that has CLAWS or nails （动物的）爪 ➲ VISUAL VOCAB PAGE V12 **2** (*informal*) a person's hand （人的）手： *Take your filthy paws off me!* 把你的脏手从我身上拿开！

■ ***verb*** **1** [I, T] (of an animal 动物) to scratch or touch sth repeatedly with a paw （不断地）挠，抓： **~ at sth** *The dog pawed at my sleeve.* 狗一直挠我的衣袖。 ◇ **~ sth** *The stallion pawed the ground impatiently.* 种马焦躁地用蹄刨

P

着地面。 **2** [T] **~ sb** (*sometimes humorous*) to touch sb in a rough sexual way that they find offensive 猥亵地乱摸；动手动脚；动手挑逗

pawn /pɔːn/ *noun, verb*

■ ***noun*** **1** a CHESS piece of the smallest size and least value. Each player has eight pawns at the start of a game.（国际象棋的）兵，卒 ➲ **VISUAL VOCAB PAGE V42** **2** a person or group whose actions are controlled by more powerful people 被利用的人；走卒：*The hostages are being used as political pawns.* 人质正被用作政治卒子。

IDM **in pawn** if sth is **in pawn**, it has been pawned 被抵押；被典当：*All her jewellery was in pawn.* 她的首饰全典当了。

■ ***verb*** **~ sth** to leave an object with a pawnbroker in exchange for money. The object is returned to the owner if he or she pays back the money within an agreed period of time. If not, it can be sold. 质押；典当

pawn·broker /ˈpɔːnbrəʊkə(r); *NAmE* -broʊ-/ *noun* a person who lends money in exchange for articles left with them. If the money is not paid back by a particular time, the pawnbroker can sell the article. 典当商人；当铺老板

Paw·nee /ˈpɔːniː/ *noun* (*pl.* **Paw·nee** or **Paw·nees**) a member of a Native American people, many of whom live in the US state of Oklahoma 波尼人（美洲土著，很多居于美国俄克拉何马州）

pawn·shop /ˈpɔːnʃɒp; *NAmE* -ʃɑːp/ *noun* a pawnbroker's shop/store 当铺

paw·paw /ˈpɔːpɔː/ *noun* (*BrE*) = PAPAYA

pay 🔑 /peɪ/ *verb, noun*

■ ***verb*** (**paid**, **paid** /peɪd/) **1** 🔑 [I, T] to give sb money for work, goods, services, etc. 付费；付酬：**~ (for sth)** *I'll pay for the tickets.* 我来买票。◇ *Are you **paying in cash** or **by credit card**?* 您付现金还是用信用卡？◇ *My company **pays well*** (= pays high salaries). 我公司给的工资很高。◇ **~ for sb to do sth** *Her parents paid for her to go to Canada.* 她父母出钱送她去加拿大。◇ **~ sth** *to **pay cash*** 付现金 ◇ **~ sth for sth** *She pays £200 a week for this apartment.* 这套房子她每周要付租金 200 英镑。◇ **~ sb (for sth)** *Would you mind paying the taxi driver?* 您付出租车费好吗？◇ **~ sb sth** *He still hasn't **paid** me **the money** he owes me.* 他还没归还欠我的钱呢。◇ *I'm paid $100 a day.* 我每天工资 100 美元。◇ **~ sb/sth to do sth** *I don't pay you to sit around all day doing nothing!* 我不是花钱雇你整天闲坐着的！ ➲ SEE ALSO LOW-PAID, PRE-PAY, WELL PAID ➲ **WORDFINDER NOTE** AT EMPLOY **2** 🔑 [T] to give sb money that you owe them 交纳；偿还：**~ sth** *to **pay a bill/debt/fine/ransom, etc.*** 缴付账单、债款、罚金、赎金等 ◇ **~ sth to sb** *Membership fees should be paid to the secretary.* 会员费应交给秘书。◇ **~ sb sth** *Have you paid him the rent yet?* 你向他付房租了没有？ **3** 🔑 [I] (of a business, etc. 企业等) to produce a profit 赢利；创收：*It's hard to make farming pay.* 种庄稼获利很不容易。 **4** 🔑 [I, T] to result in some advantage or profit for sb 受益；划算：*Crime doesn't pay.* 犯罪是划不来的。◇ **it pays to do sth** *It pays to keep up to date with your work.* 工作能跟上时代是有利的。◇ **it pays sb to do sth** *It would probably pay you to hire an accountant.* 聘一名会计师或许对你有好处。 **5** 🔑 [I] to suffer or be punished for your beliefs or actions 付代价；遭受惩罚：**~ (for sth)** *You'll pay for that remark!* 你会为你的话付出代价的！◇ **~ (with sth)** *Many people paid with their lives* (= they died). 许多人付出了生命。 **6** 🔑 [T] used with some nouns to show that you are giving or doing the thing mentioned（与某些名词结合使用，表示将要做或付出某事物）：**~ sth** *I didn't **pay attention** to what she was saying.* 我没有注意她在说什么。◇ *The director **paid tribute** to all she had done for the charity.* 董事赞扬她为慈善事业所做的一切。◇ *I'll **pay a call on*** (= visit) *my friends.* 我将去看朋友。◇ **~ sb sth** *I'll pay you a call when I'm in town.* 我在城里的时候将去拜访你。◇ *He's always **paying me compliments**.* 他总是夸奖我。 ➲ **MORE LIKE THIS** 33, page R28

IDM **the ˈdevil/ˈhell to pay** (*informal*) a lot of trouble 大麻烦；大乱子：*There'll be hell to pay when he finds out.* 一旦他发现了真相，那麻烦就大了。 **he who pays the piper calls the ˈtune** (*saying*) the person who provides the money for sth can also control how it is spent 花钱的人说了算；财大者气粗 **pay ˈcourt to sb** (*old-fashioned*) to treat sb with great respect in order to gain favour with them 献殷勤；奉迎；讨好 **pay ˈdividends** to produce great advantages or profits 有所收获；产生效益：*Exercising regularly will pay dividends in the end.* 经常运动最终会对身体大有好处。 **ˌpay for itˈself** (of a new system, sth you have bought, etc. 新系统、所买的东西等) to save as much money as it cost 使损益相当；够本：*The rail pass will pay for itself after about two trips.* 火车通票大约只需乘两次车就够本了。 **pay good ˈmoney for sth** used to emphasize that sth cost(s) a lot of money, especially if the money is wasted 为…花费很多钱（尤指钱白花了）：*I paid good money for this jacket, and now look at it—it's ruined!* 这件夹克是我花大价钱买的。瞧瞧，全给毁了！ **pay its ˈway** (of a business, etc. 企业等) to make enough money to pay what it costs to keep it going 赢利运作；不负债；收支平衡：*The bridge is still not paying its way.* 这座桥现在还入不敷出。 **pay the ˈpenalty (for sth/for doing sth) | pay a/the ˈprice (for sth/for doing sth)** to suffer because of bad luck, a mistake or sth you have done 因…受害 / 付代价：*He looked terrible this morning. I think he's paying the penalty for all those late nights.* 他今天上午脸色很不好，我想这是他一直熬夜造成的。◇ *They're now paying the price for past mistakes.* 他们现在正为过去的错误付出代价。 **pay your reˈspects (to sb)** (*formal*) to visit sb or to send a message of good wishes as a sign of respect for them（拜访或问候某人）表示敬意：*Many came to **pay their last respects*** (= by attending sb's funeral). 许多人前来参加葬礼向逝者告别。 **pay through the ˈnose (for sth)** (*informal*) to pay too much money for sth（为…）付过高的价 **pay your ˈway** to pay for everything yourself without having to rely on anyone else's money 独立偿付一切；自食其力 **you pays your ˌmoney and you takes your ˈchoice** (*informal, especially BrE*) used for saying that there is very little difference between two or more things that you can choose 如何选择由你做主（表示各种选择的分别不大） ➲ MORE AT ARM *n.*, HEED *n.*, ROB

PHR V **ˌpay sb ˈback (sth) | ˌpay sth↔ˈback (to sb)** 🔑 to return money that you borrowed from sb（向某人）还钱 **SYN** **repay**：*I'll pay you back next week.* 我下周把钱还给你。◇ *You can pay back the loan over a period of three years.* 你可以在三年内分期归还贷款。◇ *Did he ever pay you back that $100 he owes you?* 他把欠你的 100 美元还给你没有？ **ˌpay sb ˈback (for sth)** 🔑 to punish sb for making you or sb else suffer 报复；惩罚：*I'll pay him back for making me look like a fool in front of everyone.* 他让我当众出丑，我非治治他不可。 ➲ RELATED NOUN PAYBACK **ˌpay sth↔ˈdown** (*especially NAmE*) to reduce an amount of money that you owe by paying some of it（分期或部分）支付，偿还：*She used the money to pay down her mortgage.* 她把这笔钱用于偿还她的部分抵押贷款。 **ˌpay sth↔ˈin | ˌpay sth ˈinto sth** to put money into a bank account 存款；存入账户：*I paid in a cheque this morning.* 我今天上午存入一张支票。◇ *I'd like to pay some money into my account.* 我想在我的账户里存一些钱。 **ˌpay ˈoff** (*informal*) (of a plan or an action, especially one that involves risk 尤指冒险的计划或行动) to be successful and bring good results 成功；奏效；达到目的：*The gamble paid off.* 这一把赌对了。 **ˌpay sb↔ˈoff 1** to pay sb what they have earned and tell them to leave their job 付清工资后解雇；遣散：*The crew were paid off as soon as the ship docked.* 船一泊港，船员就被付酬解雇了。 **2** (*informal*) to give sb money to prevent them from doing sth or talking about sth illegal or dishonest that you have done 用钱封某人的口；买通某人：*All the witnesses had been paid off.* 所有的证人都被买通了。 ➲ RELATED NOUN PAY-OFF **ˌpay sth↔ˈoff** to finish paying money owed for sth 付清；偿清：*We paid off our mortgage after fifteen years.* 我们历经十五年的时间还清了抵押借款。 **ˌpay sth↔ˈout 1** 🔑 to pay a large sum of money for sth 付巨款：*I had to pay out £500 to get my car repaired.* 我只好花 500 英镑的高价修理我的汽车。 ➲ RELATED NOUN PAYOUT **2** to pass a length of rope through your hands

（从手中）放出绳索 ˌ**pay ˈup** to pay all the money that you owe to sb, especially when you do not want to or when the payment is late 总算付清全部欠款：*I had a hard time getting him to pay up.* 我好不容易让他还清了全部欠款。

■ ***noun*** [U] the money that sb gets for doing regular work 工资；薪水：*Her job is hard work, but the pay is good.* 她工作虽辛苦，但薪水不低。◇ *a* ***pay increase*** 加薪 ◇ (*BrE*) *a* ***pay rise*** 加薪 ◇ (*NAmE*) *a* ***pay raise*** 加薪 ◇ *a 3%* ***pay offer*** 愿出 3% 的酬劳 ◇ *holiday pay* 假日薪金 ◇ *to make a* ***pay claim*** (= to officially ask for an increase in pay) 正式要求加薪 ➲ SYNONYMS AT INCOME ➲ SEE ALSO SICK PAY

WORDFINDER 联想词：bonus, commission, deduction, earn, overtime, rise, salary, tax, wage

IDM **in the pay of sb/sth** (*usually disapproving*) working for sb or for an organization, often secretly 秘密（为某人或某组织）工作；由…豢养；被…收买

pay·able /ˈpeɪəbl/ *adj.* [not before noun] **1** that must be paid or can be paid 应付；可偿付：*A 10% deposit is payable in advance.* 须预付 10% 的押金。◇ *The price is payable in monthly instalments.* 本价格可按月分期付款。**2** when a cheque, etc. is made **payable to** sb, their name is written on it and they can then pay it into their bank account 应付予（抬头人、收款人等）

ˌ**pay and disˈplay** *noun* [U] (*BrE*) a system of car parking in which you buy a ticket from a machine for a period of time and put it in the window of the car 停车付费系统（从售票机购得停车证置于车窗）

ˌ**pay as you ˈearn** *noun* [U] = PAYE ➲ COMPARE WITHHOLDING TAX

ˌ**pay-as-you-ˈgo** *adj.* connected with a system of paying for a service just before you use it rather than paying for it later 付费后使用的；预付费的：*pay-as-you-go phones* 预先付费电话

pay·back /ˈpeɪbæk/ *noun* [C, U] **1** the money that you receive back on money that you have invested (especially when this is equal to the amount that you invested to start with); the time that it takes to get your money back 本金返还；还本；投资的回收期：*a 10-year payback* * 10 年的投资回收期 **2** the advantage or reward that sb receives for sth they have done; the act of paying sth back 报偿；回报：*His victory was seen as payback for all the hard work he'd put in during training.* 他的胜利被视为训练期间所有辛苦努力的回报。◇ (*informal*) *It's* ***payback*** *time!* (= a person will have to suffer for what they have done) 现在该遭到报应了！

ˈ**pay bed** *noun* (in the UK) a bed for private patients that they pay to use in a free public hospital （英国免费公立医院的）自费病床，私人病床

ˈ**pay channel** *noun* a television channel that you must pay for separately in order to watch it 付费电视频道

ˈ**pay cheque** (*BrE*) (*US* **pay·check** /ˈpeɪtʃek/) *noun* **1** the cheque that you are given when your wages are paid to you 工资支票 **2** (*especially NAmE*) a way of referring to the amount of money that you earn 收入；进项；进账：*a huge paycheck* 巨额收入

pay·day /ˈpeɪdeɪ/ *noun* [U, C] the day on which you get your wages or salary 发薪日；发工资日：*Friday is payday.* 星期五是发薪日。

ˌ**payday ˈloan** *noun* a small amount of money that sb borrows for a short time at a high rate of interest, agreeing that they will pay it back when they receive their next wages 发薪日贷款（小额短期高利贷，借贷人承诺在下一个发薪日偿还） ▶ ˌ**payday ˈlender** *noun* ˌ**payday ˈlending** *noun* [U]

ˈ**pay dirt** *noun* [U] (*especially NAmE*) earth that contains valuable minerals or metal such as gold （含贵重矿物或金属的）矿石，矿砂

IDM **hit/strike ˈpay dirt** (*informal*) to suddenly be in a successful situation, especially one that makes you rich 骤然成功；暴富

PAYE /ˌpiː eɪ waɪ ˈiː/ *abbr.* pay as you earn (a British system of paying income tax in which money is taken from your wages by your employer and paid to the government) 预扣所得税（英国制度，雇主从职工工资中扣除应缴税款，直接上缴政府）

payee /ˌpeɪˈiː/ *noun* (*specialist*) a person that money or a cheque is paid to 受款人；收款人

ˈ**pay envelope** (*NAmE*) (*BrE* ˈ**pay packet**, ˈ**wage packet**) *noun* an envelope containing your wages; the amount a person earns 工资袋；所得工资

payer /ˈpeɪə(r)/ *noun* a person who pays or who has to pay for sth 付款人；交款人：*mortgage payers* 按揭付款人 ◇ *The company are not very good payers* (= they are slow to pay their bills, or they do not pay their employees well). 这家公司财务支付信誉不佳。

ˌ**pay-for-perˈformance** *adj.* [only before noun] (*NAmE*) paying more or less money depending on how well a person does their job 按工作表现付酬的；按绩效付酬的：*There has been an increase in pay-for-performance plans all over the US.* 绩效付酬计划在全美各地已经日益普及。➲ COMPARE PERFORMANCE (3), PERFORMANCE-RELATED

ˌ**paying ˈguest** *noun* a person who pays to live in sb's house with them, usually for a short time （付费并同在一处居住的）临时住宿者

pay·load /ˈpeɪləʊd; *NAmE* -loʊd/ *noun* (*specialist*) **1** the passengers and goods on a ship or an aircraft for which payment is received （飞机、船只的）商载，酬载，有酬载荷 **2** the goods that a vehicle, for example a lorry/truck, is carrying; the amount it is carrying （车辆等的）装载货物，装载量 **3** the EXPLOSIVE power of a bomb or a MISSILE （炸弹、导弹的）爆炸力，炸药量 **4** the equipment carried by a SPACECRAFT or SATELLITE （航天器、卫星的）装备

pay·mas·ter /ˈpeɪmɑːstə(r); *NAmE* -mæs-/ *noun* **1** (*usually disapproving*) a person or group of people that pays another person or organization and therefore can control their actions 操纵者；后台老板 **2** an official who pays the wages in the army, a factory, etc. （军队、工厂等的）工薪出纳员

pay·ment /ˈpeɪmənt/ *noun* **1** [U] ~ (**for sth**) the act of paying sb/sth or of being paid 付款；支付；收款：***payment in instalments/in advance/by cheque/in cash*** 分期 / 预先 / 支票 / 现金付款 ◇ *There will be a penalty for late payment of bills.* 账单拖延付款要收滞纳金。**2** [C] ~ (**for sth**) a sum of money paid or expected to be paid （将付或应付的）款额，款项：*a* ***cash payment*** 现金付款 ◇ *They are finding it difficult to* ***meet the payments*** *on their car.* 他们感到很难偿付汽车款。◇ *He agreed to make ten* ***monthly payments*** *of £50.* 他同意每月付款 50 英镑，十次付清。➲ SYNONYMS ON NEXT PAGE ➲ COLLOCATIONS AT FINANCE ➲ SEE ALSO BALANCE OF PAYMENTS, DOWN PAYMENT **3** [U, sing.] ~ (**for sth**) a reward or an act of thanks for sth you have done 报答；报偿 SYN **recompense**：*We'd like you to accept this gift* ***in payment for*** *your kindness.* 谨以薄礼答谢厚爱，敬请笑纳。◇ *Is this all the payment I get for my efforts?* 这就是对我辛劳的全部报偿吗？

IDM **on payment of sth** when sth has been paid 付款后：*Entry is only allowed on payment of the full registration fee.* 缴付全数登记费用方可进入。

ˈ**pay-off** *noun* (*informal*) **1** a payment of money to sb so that they will not cause you any trouble or to make them keep a secret （用以买通别人的）黑钱；行贿钱 SYN **bribe** **2** a payment of money to sb to persuade them to leave their job 辞退金；遣散费 **3** an advantage or a reward from sth you have done 回报；报偿

pay·ola /peɪˈəʊlə; *NAmE* -ˈoʊlə/ *noun* [U] (*NAmE, informal*) the practice of giving or taking payments for doing sth illegal, especially for illegally influencing the sales of a particular product 买通，贿赂（尤指为非法影响销售）SYN **bribery**

pay·out /ˈpeɪaʊt/ *noun* a large amount of money that is given to sb 付出的巨款： *an insurance payout* 巨额保险偿付 ◇ *a lottery payout* 彩票大额奖金

ˈpay packet (*also* **ˈwage packet**) (*both BrE*) (*NAmE* **ˈpay envelope**) *noun* an envelope containing your wages; the amount a person earns 工资袋；所得工资

ˌpay-per-ˈview *noun* [U] a system of television broadcasting in which you pay an extra sum of money to watch a particular programme, such as a film/movie or a sports event （电视节目的）付费收看

pay·phone /ˈpeɪfəʊn; *NAmE* -foʊn/ *noun* a telephone, usually in a public place, that is operated using coins or a card 公用（付费）电话

pay·roll /ˈpeɪrəʊl; *NAmE* -roʊl/ *noun* **1** a list of people employed by a company showing the amount of money to be paid to each of them （公司员工的）工资名单：

▼SYNONYMS 同义词辨析

payment

premium • contribution • subscription • repayment • deposit • instalment

These are all words for an amount of money that you pay or are expected to pay, or for the act of paying. 以上各词均指款额、款项、付款。

payment an amount of money that you pay or are expected to pay; the act of paying 指款额、款项、付款： *ten monthly payments of $50* 每月付款 50 美元，十次付清 ◇ *payment in advance* 预先付款

premium an amount of money that you pay once or regularly for an insurance policy; an extra payment added to the basic rate; a higher amount of money than usual 指保险费、额外费用、附加费、溢价： *an insurance premium* 保险费 ◇ *a premium for express delivery* 快递附加费

contribution a sum of money that you pay regularly to your employer or the government in order to pay for benefits such as health insurance, a pension, etc. 指（给雇主或政府用作医疗保险、养老金等福利的）定期缴款： *You can increase your monthly contributions to the pension plan.* 你可以增加你的养老金计划每月供款。

subscription an amount of money you pay in advance to receive regular copies of a newspaper or magazine or to receive a service 指（报刊、杂志的）订阅费、订购款，（服务的）用户费： *a subscription to 'Newsweek'* 《新闻周刊》的订阅费

repayment (*BrE*) an amount of money that you pay regularly to a bank, etc. until you have returned all the money that you owe; the act of paying this money 指按期偿还的款项、分期偿还额、偿还债务、归还借款： *the repayments on the loan* 贷款的分期偿还额

deposit an amount of money that you pay as the first part of a larger payment 指订金： *We've put down a 5% deposit on the house.* 我们已支付了房款的 5% 作为订金。

instalment one of a number of payments that you make regularly over a period of time until you have paid for sth 指分期付款的一期付款： *We paid for the car by/in instalments.* 我们以分期付款买了这辆车。

PATTERNS

- (a/an) **annual/monthly/regular** payment/premium/contributions/subscription/repayment/deposit/instalment
- payment/repayment **in full**
- to **pay** a(n) premium/contribution/subscription/deposit/instalment
- to **make** a payment/repayment/deposit
- to **meet/keep up** (**with**) (the) payment(s)/the premiums/(the) repayment(s)/the instalments

We have 500 people on the payroll. 我们在编员工有 500 人。 **2** [usually sing.] the total amount paid in wages by a company （公司的）工资总支出

pay·slip /ˈpeɪslɪp/ *noun* (*BrE*) a piece of paper given to an employee that shows how much money they have been paid and how much has been taken away for tax, etc. （给员工的）工资明细表，工资计算单

ˌpay TˈV (*also* **ˈpay television**) *noun* [U] a system of television broadcasting in which you pay extra money to watch particular television programmes or channels 收费电视

pay·wall /ˈpeɪwɔːl/ *noun* a feature of a website that prevents users from accessing certain web pages unless they have paid to use the website 付费墙，收费墙（对网站内容设限，须付费才能访问）： *The most interesting pages on the site are behind a paywall.* 这个网站最有趣的网页都在付费专区里。

PB /ˌpiː ˈbiː/ *abbr.* PERSONAL BEST 个人最好成绩

ˈp-book (*also* **ˈP-book**) *noun* a book that is printed on paper 纸质书 ➲ COMPARE E-BOOK

PBS /ˌpiː biː ˈes/ *abbr.* the Public Broadcasting Service (an organization in the US that broadcasts television programmes to local stations that do not show advertisements) （美国）公共电视网（给不播广告的地方台播放电视节目）

PC /ˌpiː ˈsiː/ *noun, abbr.*

■ ***noun*** the abbreviation for 'personal computer' (a computer that is designed for one person to use at work or at home) 个人电脑，个人计算机（全写为 personal computer） ➲ **VISUAL VOCAB** PAGES V71, V73

■ ***abbr.*** **1** (*BrE*) POLICE CONSTABLE 警员 ➲ SEE ALSO WPC **2** POLITICALLY CORRECT 政治上正确的

PCB /ˌpiː siː ˈbiː/ *noun* printed circuit board 印制电路板

ˌPˈC card *noun* (*computing* 计) a plastic card with a PRINTED CIRCUIT on it that can be put into a computer to allow it to work with other devices 印制电路卡；PC 卡

PCP /ˌpiː siː ˈpiː/ *noun* **1** PRIMARY CARE PHYSICIAN 初级护理医师；基础医疗医师 **2** PRIMARY CARE PROVIDER 初级护理机构；基础医疗机构

PC Plod /ˌpiː siː ˈplɒd; *NAmE* ˈplɑːd/ *noun* (*BrE, informal, humorous*) a junior police officer 初级警员 ➲ MORE LIKE THIS 18, page R27

PCSO /ˌpiː siː es ˈəʊ; *NAmE* ˈoʊ/ *noun* (in England and Wales) the abbreviation for 'police community support officer' (a person who is not a police officer but works in an area to help the work of the police) （英格兰和威尔士的）社区服务警察（全写为 police community support officer）

PDF /ˌpiː diː ˈef/ (*also* **ˌPDˈF file**) *noun* (*computing* 计) the abbreviation for 'Portable Document Format' (a type of computer file that can contain words or pictures. It can be read using any system, can be sent from one computer to another, and will look the same on any computer.) 可移植文档格式，可携式文件格式（全写为 Portable Document Format）： *I'll send it to you as a PDF.* 我会用 PDF 格式把它发给你。

p.d.q. /ˌpiː diː ˈkjuː/ *abbr.* pretty damn/damned quick (= very fast) 火速；马上；立即： *Make sure you get here p.d.q.* 你马上给我赶到这儿来。

PDT /ˌpiː diː ˈtiː/ *abbr.* PACIFIC DAYLIGHT TIME 太平洋夏令时间

PE (*BrE*) (*US* **P.E.**) /ˌpiː ˈiː/ *noun* [U] the abbreviation for 'physical education' (sport and exercise that is taught in schools) 体育（课）（全写为 physical education）： *a PE class* 一堂体育课

pea /piː/ *noun* a small round green seed, eaten as a vegetable. Several peas grow together inside a long thin POD on a climbing plant also called a pea. 豌豆；豌豆粒： *frozen peas* 冷冻豌豆 ◇ *pea soup* 豌豆汤 ➲ **VISUAL**

P

VOCAB PAGE V34 ➲ SEE ALSO CHICKPEA, MUSHY PEAS, SPLIT PEA, SWEET PEA

peace /piːs/ *noun* **1** [U, sing.] a situation or a period of time in which there is no war or violence in a country or an area 和平；太平：*war and peace* 战争与和平 ◇ ***peace talks/negotiations*** 和平谈判 / 协商 ◇ *The negotiators are trying to **make peace** between the warring factions.* 谈判者正努力使交战各派议和。◇ *A UN force has been sent to **keep the peace*** (= to prevent people from fighting). 一支联合国部队被派出维护和平。◇ *After years of war, the people long for a lasting peace.* 历经多年战乱之后，人民渴望永久和平。◇ *the Peace of Utrecht, 1713* (= the agreement ending the war) * 1713 年的乌得勒支和平协议 ◇ *The two communities live together **in peace**.* 这两个社区和平相处。◇ *The countries have been **at peace** for more than a century.* 这些国家和平共处已有一个多世纪。◇ *the **peace movement*** (= that tries to prevent war by protesting, persuading politicians, etc.) 争取和平运动 ➲ COLLOCATIONS AT WAR

WORDFINDER 联想词：agreement, armistice, ceasefire, disengage, negotiate, reparations, surrender, treaty, truce

2 [U] the state of being calm or quiet 平静；安静；宁静：*She lay back and enjoyed the peace of the summer evening.* 她轻松地躺着享受夏日傍晚的宁静。◇ *I would work better if I had some **peace and quiet**.* 四周若再安静一些，我会干得更好。◇ *He just wants to be **left in peace*** (= not to be disturbed). 他只希望不受打扰。◇ *I need to check that she is all right, just for my own **peace of mind*** (= so that I do not have to worry). 我必须看到她安然无恙，心里才踏实。◇ *He never felt really **at peace** with himself.* 他从未真正感到心里平静过。 **3** [U] the state of living in friendship with sb without arguing 和睦；融洽；和谐：*They simply can't seem to live in peace with each other.* 他们好像就是不能和睦相处。◇ *She felt **at peace with** the world.* 她感觉与世无争。➲ SEE ALSO BREACH *n.*, JUSTICE OF THE PEACE

IDM ˌ**hold your ˈpeace/ˈtongue** (*old-fashioned*) to say nothing although you would like to give your opinion （想说却）保持沉默，缄口不语 **make (your) peace with sb** to end an argument with sb, usually by saying you are sorry （经道歉）与人和解，言归于好 ➲ MORE AT WICKED *n.*

▼ **WHICH WORD?** 词语辨析

peace / peacefulness

- The noun **peace** can be used to talk about a peaceful state or situation. 名词 peace 指和平、平静、安宁的状态或形势：*world peace* 世界和平 ◇ *I just need some peace and quiet.* 我需要的只是平静与安宁。
  Peacefulness is not a common word. It means 'the quality of being peaceful'. * peacefulness 不常用，指和平、平静、安宁的性质。

peace·able /ˈpiːsəbl/ *adj.* **1** not involving or causing argument or violence 不惹事的；和平的；安宁的 SYN **peaceful**：*A peaceable settlement has been reached.* 已经达成和解。 **2** not liking to argue; wishing to live in peace with others 不爱争吵的；爱好和平的；温和的 SYN **peaceful, calm**：*a peaceable character* 性格温和的人 ▸ **peace·ably** /-əbli/ *adv.*

the ˈPeace Corps *noun* [sing.] a US organization that sends young Americans to work in other countries without pay in order to create international friendship 和平队，和平工作团（美国组织，派遣年轻人去其他国家做志愿工作以建立国际友谊）

ˈ**peace dividend** *noun* [usually sing.] money previously spent on weapons and the defence of a country and now available to be used for other things because of a reduction in a country's military forces 和平红利，和平增益（指国家因裁军而得以用于其他方面的原军备和国防费用）

peace·ful /ˈpiːsfl/ *adj.* **1** not involving a war, violence or argument 不诉诸战争（或暴力、争论）的；和平的：*a **peaceful protest/demonstration/solution*** 和平抗议 / 示威 / 解决办法 ◇ *They hope for a **peaceful settlement** of the dispute.* 他们希望和平解决争端。 **2** quiet and calm; not worried or disturbed in any way 安静的；平静的 SYN **tranquil**：*a peaceful atmosphere* 宁静的气氛 ◇ *peaceful sleep* 安静的睡眠 ◇ *It's so peaceful out here in the country.* 这里的郊外一切都是那么宁静。◇ *He had a peaceful life.* 他过着平静的生活。 **3** trying to create peace or to live in peace; not liking violence or disagreement 爱好和平的；和睦的；寻求和平的 SYN **peaceable**：*a peaceful society* 和谐的社会 ◇ *The aims of the organization are wholly peaceful.* 这个组织的宗旨完全是追求和平。 ▸ **peace·ful·ly** /-fəli/ *adv.*：*The siege has ended peacefully.* 围城已经和平地结束了。◇ *The baby slept peacefully.* 婴儿睡得很安稳。 **peace·ful·ness** *noun* [U] ➲ NOTE AT PEACE

peace·keep·er /ˈpiːskiːpə(r)/ *noun* **1** a member of a military force who has been sent to help stop people fighting in a place where war or violence is likely 维和部队成员 **2** a person who tries to stop people arguing or fighting 调解人；劝架者：*She's the peacekeeper in that family.* 那个家庭的纠纷都由她来调解。

peace·keep·ing /ˈpiːskiːpɪŋ/ *adj.* [only before noun] intended to help stop people fighting and prevent war or violence in a place where this is likely 维护和平的：*peacekeeping operations* 维和行动 ◇ *a United Nations peacekeeping force* 联合国维持和平部队 ➲ COLLOCATIONS AT WAR

ˈ**peace-loving** *adj.* preferring to live in peace and to avoid arguments and fighting 爱好和平的 SYN **peaceable**

peace·maker /ˈpiːsmeɪkə(r)/ *noun* a person who tries to persuade people or countries to stop arguing or fighting and to make peace 调解人；调停人

peace·nik /ˈpiːsnɪk/ *noun* (*informal, sometimes disapproving*) a PACIFIST (= sb who believes war and violence are always wrong and refuses to fight) 反战分子；和平主义分子

ˈ**peace offering** *noun* a present given to sb to show that you are sorry for sth or want to make peace after an argument 表示和解的礼物；致歉的礼物

ˈ**peace pipe** *noun* a TOBACCO pipe offered and smoked as a symbol of peace by Native Americans 和平烟斗（美洲土著作为和平象征请人抽的）

ˈ**peace process** *noun* [usually sing.] a series of talks and agreements designed to end war or violence between two groups 和平进程

peace·time /ˈpiːstaɪm/ *noun* [U] a period of time when a country is not at war 和平时期 ➲ COMPARE WARTIME

peach /piːtʃ/ *noun, adj.*

■ ***noun*** **1** [C] a round fruit with soft red and yellow skin, yellow flesh and a large rough seed inside 桃；桃子：*a peach tree* 桃树 ➲ VISUAL VOCAB PAGE V32 ➲ COMPARE NECTARINE **2** [sing.] ~ (**of a...**) (*old-fashioned, informal*) a particularly good or attractive person or thing 极好的人（或物）；特别漂亮的东西（或人） **3** [U] a pinkish-orange colour 桃红色；粉红色

■ ***adj.*** pinkish-orange in colour 粉红色的；桃红色的

peach Melba /ˌpiːtʃ ˈmelbə/ *noun* [U, C] a cold DESSERT (= a sweet dish) made from half a PEACH, ice cream and RASPBERRY sauce 山莓酱桃子冰淇淋（用半个桃子、冰淇淋和山莓酱制成）

peachy /ˈpiːtʃi/ *adj.* **1** like a peach in colour or appearance （颜色或外形）像桃的：*pale peachy skin* 白里透红的皮肤 **2** (*NAmE, informal*) fine; very nice 顺利；很好：*Everything is just peachy.* 一切顺利。

ˈ**pea coat** (*also* ˈ**pea jacket**) *noun* a type of thick short coat 水手短外套（一种厚呢短大衣）

pea·cock /ˈpiːkɒk; NAmE -kɑːk/ *noun* a large male bird with long blue and green tail feathers that it can spread out like a fan 雄孔雀：*as proud as a peacock* 孔雀般的骄傲 ➲ SEE ALSO PEAHEN

ˌpeacock ˈblue *adj.* deep greenish-blue in colour 孔雀蓝的；暗绿光蓝的 ▸ **ˌpeacock ˈblue** *noun* [U] ➲ MORE LIKE THIS 15, page R26

pea·fowl /ˈpiːfaʊl/ *noun* (*pl.* **pea·fowl**) a large PHEASANT found mainly in Asia. The male is called a PEACOCK and the female is called a PEAHEN. 孔雀（主要见于亚洲，peacock 指雄孔雀，peahen 指雌孔雀）

ˌpea-ˈgreen *adj.* bright green in colour, like PEAS 浅绿色的；豆绿的 ➲ MORE LIKE THIS 15, page R26

pea·hen /ˈpiːhen/ *noun* a large brown bird, the female of the peacock 雌孔雀

peak 🔑 /piːk/ *noun, verb, adj.*

■ ***noun*** **1** 🔑 [usually sing.] the point when sb/sth is best, most successful, strongest, etc. 顶峰；高峰 SYN **height**: *Traffic* ***reaches its peak*** *between 8 and 9 in the morning.* 上午 8、9 点钟之间是交通高峰期。◇ *She's* ***at the peak of*** *her career.* 她正处在事业的巅峰。◇ *the* ***peaks and troughs*** *of married life* 婚后生活的起起伏伏 ➲ COMPARE OFF-PEAK **2** 🔑 the pointed top of a mountain; a mountain with a pointed top 山峰；峰峦：*a* ***mountain peak*** 山峰 ◇ *snow-capped/jagged peaks* 积雪覆盖的 / 嶙峋怪异的群峰 ◇ *The climbers made camp halfway up the peak.* 登山者在半山腰设置营地。➲ WORDFINDER NOTE AT MOUNTAIN ➲ VISUAL VOCAB PAGE V5 **3** any narrow and pointed shape, edge, etc. 尖形；尖端；尖头：*Whisk the egg whites into stiff peaks.* 把蛋清搅成硬尖状。**4** (*BrE*) (*NAmE* **bill, visor**) the stiff front part of a cap that sticks out above your eyes 帽舌；帽檐 ➲ VISUAL VOCAB PAGE V70

■ ***verb*** [I] to reach the highest point or value 达到高峰；达到最高值：*Oil production peaked in the early 1980s.* * 20 世纪 80 年代初期，石油产量达到了最高峰。◇ *Unemployment peaked at 17%.* 失业率达到 17% 的最高点。◇ *an athlete who peaks* (= produces his or her best performance) *at just the right time* 一位恰在最佳时刻缔造出最佳成绩的运动员 ➲ WORDFINDER NOTE AT TREND

■ ***adj.*** [only before noun] used to describe the highest level of sth, or a time when the greatest number of people are doing sth or using sth 最高度的；高峰时期的；巅峰状态的：*It was a time of* ***peak demand*** *for the product.* 那是对该产品需求最旺的时期。◇ *March is one of the* ***peak periods*** *for our business.* 三月是我们公司业务最繁忙的时期之一。◇ *The athletes are all in* ***peak condition***. 所有运动员都处在巅峰状态。◇ *We need extra help during the* ***peak season***. 我们在最繁忙的季节需要额外人手。➲ COMPARE OFF-PEAK

peaked /ˈpiːkt/ *adj.* **1** having a PEAK (4) 有帽檐的；有帽舌的 **2** (*NAmE*) (*BrE* **peaky**) ill/sick or pale 有病的；憔悴的；苍白的

ˌpeak ˈoil *noun* [U] the point in time when world oil production reaches its highest rate, after which it goes into permanent decline 石油峰值（指世界石油生产达到峰值的时间点）

ˌpeak ˈrate *noun* the busiest time, which is therefore charged at the highest rate 高峰期，高峰时段（收费最高）：*peak-rate phone calls* 高峰时段通话

ˈpeak time (*also* **ˌpeak ˈviewing time**) *noun* (*BrE*) = PRIME TIME

peaky /ˈpiːki/ (*BrE, informal*) (*NAmE* **peaked**) *adj.* ill/sick or pale 有病的；憔悴的；苍白的：*You're looking a little peaky. Are you OK?* 你看来有点憔悴。你没事吧？

peal /piːl/ *noun, verb*

■ ***noun*** **1** ~ (**of sth**) a loud sound or series of sounds 响亮的声音；轰轰的响声：*She burst into peals of laughter.* 她忽然哈哈大笑起来。**2** the loud ringing sound of a bell 洪亮的钟声：*a peal of bells rang out* 洪亮的钟声响了起来 **3** a set of bells that all have different notes; a musical pattern that can be rung on a set of bells 编钟；编钟音乐

■ ***verb*** **1** [I] ~ (**out**) (of bells 钟或铃) to ring loudly 大声作响：*The bells of the city began to peal out.* 都市的钟声齐鸣。**2** [I] ~ (**with sth**) to suddenly laugh loudly 轰然大笑：*Ellen pealed with laughter.* 埃伦忽然大笑起来。

pea·nut /ˈpiːnʌt/ *noun* **1** (*BrE also* **ground·nut**) [C] a nut that grows underground in a thin shell 花生：*a packet of salted peanuts* 一包咸花生 ◇ *peanut oil* 花生油 ➲ VISUAL VOCAB PAGE V35 **2 peanuts** [pl.] (*informal*) a very small amount of money 很少的钱：*He gets paid peanuts for doing that job.* 他干那件工作报酬很低。

ˌpeanut ˈbutter *noun* [U] a thick soft substance made from very finely chopped PEANUTS, usually eaten spread on bread 花生酱：(*NAmE*) *a peanut butter and jelly sandwich* 一份花生酱加果酱三明治

pear /peə(r); NAmE per/ *noun* a yellow or green fruit that is narrow at the top and wide at the bottom 梨：*a pear tree* 梨树 ➲ SEE ALSO PRICKLY PEAR

pearl /pɜːl; NAmE pɜːrl/ *noun* **1** [C] a small hard shiny white ball that forms inside the shell of an OYSTER and is of great value as a JEWEL 珍珠：*a string of pearls* 一挂珍珠 ◇ *a pearl necklace* 珍珠项链 ◇ *She was wearing her pearls* (= a NECKLACE of pearls). 她戴着她的珍珠项链。➲ VISUAL VOCAB PAGE V70 ➲ SEE ALSO SEED PEARL **2** [C] a copy of a pearl that is made artificially 人造珍珠 **3** [U] = MOTHER-OF-PEARL：*pearl buttons* 珍珠母纽扣 **4** [C, usually sing.] a thing that looks like a pearl in shape or colour （形状或颜色）像珍珠之物：*pearls of dew on the grass* 草上的露珠 **5** [C] a thing that is very highly valued 极有价值的东西：*She is a pearl among women.* 她是女中豪杰。

IDM **cast, throw, etc. pearls before ˈswine** to give or offer valuable things to people who do not understand their value 明珠暗投；对牛弹琴 **a ˌpearl of ˈwisdom** (*usually ironic*) a wise remark 睿智的语言；隽语；妙语：*Thank you for those pearls of wisdom.* 谢谢你的金玉良言。

ˌpearl ˈbarley *noun* [U] smooth grains of BARLEY, which are added to soups and other dishes 珍珠大麦，大麦粉粒（添加于汤和菜中）

pearly /ˈpɜːli; NAmE ˈpɜːrli/ *adj.* of or like a pearl 珍珠的；似珍珠的：*pearly white teeth* 珍珠般的皓齿

the ˌPearly ˈGates *noun* [pl.] (*humorous*) the gates of heaven 天堂之门

ˈpear-shaped *adj.* **1** shaped like a pear 梨形的；像梨一样的 **2** a **pear-shaped** person is wider around their waist and hips than around the top part of their body （指人）罐子状的，腹大腰圆的

IDM **go ˈpear-shaped** (*BrE, informal*) if things **go pear-shaped**, they go wrong 出毛病；出问题

peas·ant /ˈpeznt/ *noun* **1** (especially in the past, or in poorer countries) a farmer who owns or rents a small piece of land （尤指旧时或贫穷国家的）农民，小农，佃农：*peasant farmers* 自耕农 **2** (*informal, disapproving*) a person who is rude, behaves badly, or has little education 老粗；土包子；没教养的人 SYN **lout**

peas·ant·ry /ˈpezntri/ *noun* [sing.+sing./pl. v.] all the peasants in a region or country （统称）（一个地区或国家的）农民：*the local peasantry* 当地的农民

pease pudding /ˌpiːz ˈpʊdɪŋ/ *noun* [U] (*BrE*) a hot dish made from dried PEAS that are left in water and then boiled until they form a soft mass, usually served with HAM or PORK 豌豆布丁（用煮烂的干豌豆制成，通常和火腿或猪肉一起吃）

ˈpea-shooter *noun* (*BrE*) a small tube that children use to blow small objects such as dried PEAS at sb/sth, in order to hit them or it 射豆吹管；射豆枪

pea-souper /ˌpiː ˈsuːpə(r)/ *noun* (*old-fashioned, BrE, informal*) a very thick yellowish FOG 黄色浓雾

peat /piːt/ *noun* [U] a soft black or brown substance formed from decaying plants just under the surface of the ground, especially in cool wet areas. It is burned as a fuel or used to improve garden soil. 泥煤；泥炭：*peat bogs* 泥炭沼 ▶ **peaty** *adj.*：*peaty soils* 泥炭土

peb·ble /ˈpebl/ *noun* a smooth, round stone that is found in or near water 鹅卵石；砾石

ˈpebble-dash *noun* [U] (*BrE*) CEMENT mixed with small stones used for covering the outside walls of houses（抹房屋外墙的）小砾石灰浆

pebbly /ˈpebli/ *adj.* covered with pebbles 砾石覆盖的：*a pebbly beach* 遍布卵石的海滩

pecan /ˈpiːkən; pɪˈkæn; *NAmE* pɪˈkɑːn/ *noun* the nut of the American **pecan tree** with a smooth pinkish-brown shell 美国山核桃；碧根果 ➲ VISUAL VOCAB PAGE V35

pecca·dillo /ˌpekəˈdɪləʊ; *NAmE* -ˈdɪloʊ/ *noun* (*pl.* **-oes** or **-os**) a small unimportant thing that sb does wrong 过失；岔子；轻罪

pec·cary /ˈpekəri/ (*pl.* **-ies**) *noun* an animal like a pig, which lives in the southern US, Mexico and Central and S America 西貒，矛牙野猪（见于美国南部、墨西哥和美洲中南部）

peck /pek/ *verb, noun*

■ *verb* **1** [I, T] (of birds 鸟) to move the beak forward quickly and hit or bite sth 啄；鹐：**~ (at sth)** *A robin was pecking at crumbs on the ground.* 一只知更鸟在地上啄食面包渣。◇ **~ sth** *A bird had pecked a hole in the sack.* 一只鸟把袋子啄了个洞。◇ **~ sth out** *Vultures had pecked out the dead goat's eyes.* 秃鹫啄出了死羊的眼睛。 **2** [T] (*informal*) to kiss sb lightly and quickly 匆匆地轻吻：**~ sb on sth** *He pecked her on the cheek as he went out.* 他出门时匆匆轻吻了一下她的面颊。◇ **~ sth** *She pecked his cheek.* 她轻吻了一下他的脸。

IDM **a/the ˈpecking order** (*informal, often humorous*) the order of importance in relation to one another among the members of a group 等级排序 SYN **hierarchy**：*New Zealand is at the top of the pecking order of rugby nations.* 新西兰在橄榄球国家中首屈一指。

PHR V **ˈpeck at sth** to eat only a very small amount of a meal because you are not hungry（因不饿而）浅尝几口 SYN **pick at**

■ *noun* **1** (*informal*) a quick kiss 匆匆的吻：*He gave her a friendly peck on the cheek.* 他友好地在她脸上轻轻一吻。 **2** an act of pecking sb/sth 啄：*The budgerigar gave a quick peck at the seed.* 虎皮鹦鹉匆匆地啄了一下种子。

peck·er /ˈpekə(r)/ *noun* (*slang, especially NAmE*) a PENIS 阴茎；鸡巴

IDM **ˌkeep your ˈpecker up** (*BrE, informal*) to remain cheerful despite difficulties（在困难中）振作精神，打起精神

peck·ish /ˈpekɪʃ/ *adj.* (*BrE, informal*) slightly hungry 有点饿的

pecs /peks/ *noun* [pl.] (*informal*) = PECTORALS

pec·tin /ˈpektɪn/ *noun* [U] (*chemistry* 化) a substance similar to sugar that forms in fruit that is ready to eat, and is used to make jam/jelly firm as it is cooked 果胶

pec·toral /ˈpektərəl/ *adj., noun*

■ *adj.* (*anatomy* 解) relating to or connected with the chest or breast 胸部的；胸的：*pectoral muscles* 胸肌

■ *noun* **pectorals** (*also informal* **pecs**) [pl.] the muscles of the chest 胸肌

pe·cu·liar /pɪˈkjuːliə(r)/ *adj.* **1** strange or unusual, especially in a way that is unpleasant or worrying 怪异的；奇怪的；不寻常的：*a peculiar smell/taste* 奇怪的气味 / 味道 ◇ *There was something peculiar in the way he smiled.* 他笑起来有点怪。◇ *I had a peculiar feeling we'd met before.* 我有一种奇怪的感觉，觉得我们以前见过面。 ◇ *For some peculiar reason, she refused to come inside.* 出于某种奇怪的原因，她拒绝到里面来。 ➲ COMPARE ODD (1) **2 ~ (to sb/sth)** belonging or relating to one particular place, situation, person, etc., and not to others（某人、某地、某种情况等）特有的，特殊的：*a humour that is peculiar to American sitcoms* 美国情景喜剧特有的幽默 ◇ *a species of bird peculiar to Asia* 亚洲独有的鸟类 ◇ *He has his own peculiar style which you'll soon get used to.* 他有自己独特的风格，你会很快习惯的。◇ *the peculiar properties of mercury* 水银的特殊性质 **3** (*BrE, informal*) slightly ill/sick 不适；不舒服 IDM SEE FUNNY

pe·cu·li·ar·ity /pɪˌkjuːliˈærəti/ *noun* (*pl.* **-ies**) **1** [C] a strange or unusual feature or habit 怪异的性质（或习惯）；怪癖：*a physical peculiarity* 身体上的特征 **2** [C] a feature that only belongs to one particular person, thing, place, etc.（人、物、地等的）个性，特色，特点 SYN **characteristic**：*the cultural peculiarities of the English* 英格兰人的文化特点 **3** [U] the quality of being strange or unusual 奇怪；怪异

pe·cu·li·ar·ly /pɪˈkjuːliəli; *NAmE* -ərli/ *adv.* **1** very; more than usually 很；不寻常地；特别 SYN **particularly, especially**：*These plants are peculiarly prone to disease.* 这些植物特别容易发生病变。 **2** in a way that relates to or is especially typical of one particular person, thing, place, etc. 独特地；特有地 SYN **uniquely**：*He seemed to believe that it was a peculiarly British problem.* 他似乎认为那是英国独有的问题。 **3** in a strange or unusual way 奇怪地；异常地

pe·cu·ni·ary /pɪˈkjuːniəri; *NAmE* -ieri/ *adj.* (*formal*) relating to or connected with money 金钱的；与钱相关的：*pecuniary advantage* 金钱方面的好处

ped- (*NAmE*) (*BrE* **paed-**) /piːd/ *combining form* (in nouns and adjectives 构成名词和形容词) connected with children 与儿童有关的；儿童的

peda·gogic /ˌpedəˈɡɒdʒɪk; *NAmE* -ˈɡɑːdʒ-/ (*also* **peda·gogic·al** /-ɪkl/) *adj.* (*formal*) concerning teaching methods 教学法的：*pedagogic principles* 教学法原则 ▶ **peda·gogic·al·ly** /ˌpedəˈɡɒdʒɪkli; *NAmE* -ˈɡɑːdʒ-/ *adv.*

peda·gogue /ˈpedəɡɒɡ; *NAmE* -ɡɑːɡ/ *noun* (*old use* or *formal*) a teacher; a person who likes to teach people things, especially because they think they know more than other people 教师；好为人师的人

peda·gogy /ˈpedəɡɒdʒi; *NAmE* -ɡɑːdʒ-/ *noun* [U] (*specialist*) the study of teaching methods 教育学；教学法

pedal /ˈpedl/ *noun, verb*

■ *noun* **1** a flat bar on a machine such as a bicycle, car, etc. that you push down with your foot in order to make parts of the machine move or work（自行车、汽车等的）脚蹬子，踏板：*I couldn't reach the pedals on her bike.* 我骑她的车够不到脚蹬子。◇ *She pressed her foot down sharply on the brake pedal.* 她猛踩刹车踏板。➲ WORDFINDER NOTE AT CYCLING ➲ VISUAL VOCAB PAGE V55 **2** a bar on a musical instrument such as a piano or an organ that you push with your foot in order to control the sound（钢琴、风琴等的）踏板，踏瓣，脚踏键 ➲ VISUAL VOCAB PAGE V40

IDM **put the pedal to the metal | with the pedal to the metal** (*NAmE, informal*) **1** (to go) at full speed; (to drive) with the ACCELERATOR of the car pressed to the floor 全速（前进）；（开车时）将油门踩到底：*We drove through the night flat-out, with the pedal to the metal.* 我们将油门踩到底，在夜色里全速前进。 **2** to use as much effort as possible; with as much effort as possible 竭尽全力；尽最大努力：*I'm still putting the pedal to the metal here at work.* 我还在这里竭尽全力地工作。

■ *verb* (**-ll-**, *US* **-l-**) **1** [I, T] to ride a bicycle somewhere 骑自行车：**+ adv./prep.** *I saw her pedalling along the towpath.* 我看见她在纤道上骑自行车。◇ *He jumped on his bike and pedalled off.* 他跳上自行车就骑走了。◇ **~ sth + adv./prep.** *She pedalled her bicycle up the track.* 她骑车上了小路。 **2** [I, T] to turn or press the pedals on a bicycle or other machine 踩踏板：(**+ adv./prep.**) *You'll have to pedal hard up this hill.* 走上坡时你必须用力蹬车。◇ **~ sth** *She had been pedalling her exercise bike all morning.* 她整个上午都在蹬健身车。 ➲ SEE ALSO BACK-PEDAL (2), SOFT-PEDAL ➲ MORE LIKE THIS 36, page R29

ˈpedal bin *noun* (*BrE*) a container for rubbish, usually in a kitchen, with a lid that opens when a pedal is pressed 脚踏式垃圾桶

ped·alo /ˈpedələʊ; *NAmE* -loʊ/ *noun* (*pl.* **-oes** or **-os**) (*BrE*) a small pleasure boat that you move through the water by pushing PEDALS with your feet 脚踏游船；脚踏轮桨船

ˈpedal pushers *noun* [pl.] women's trousers/pants that reach just below the knee 长及小腿的女裤；女式六分裤

ped·ant /ˈpednt/ *noun* (*disapproving*) a person who is too concerned with small details or rules especially when learning or teaching 迂夫子；书呆子；学究

pe·dan·tic /prˈdæntɪk/ *adj.* (*disapproving*) too worried about small details or rules 迂腐的；学究气的 ▸ **pe·dan·tic·al·ly** /-kli/ *adv.*

ped·ant·ry /ˈpedntri/ *noun* [U] (*disapproving*) too much attention to small details or rules 迂腐；谨小慎微

ped·dle /ˈpedl/ *verb* **1** **~ sth** to try to sell goods by going from house to house or from place to place 挨户销售；巡回销售：*He worked as a door-to-door salesman peddling cloths and brushes.* 他的工作是上门推销抹布和刷子。◇ *to peddle illegal drugs* 贩卖毒品 **2** **~ sth** to spread an idea or story in order to get people to accept it 兜售，宣传，传播（思想、消息）：*to peddle malicious gossip* 散布恶意的流言蜚语 ◇ *This line* (= publicly stated opinion) *is being peddled by all the government spokesmen.* 所有的政府发言人都在宣扬这个官方路线。

ped·dler /ˈpedlə(r)/ *noun* **1** (*also* **ˈdrug peddler**) (*both BrE*) a person who sells illegal drugs 毒品贩子 **2** (*NAmE*) (*BrE* **ped·lar**) a person who in the past travelled from place to place trying to sell small objects （旧时的）流动小贩

ped·er·ast (*BrE also* **paed·er·ast**) /ˈpedəræst/ *noun* (*formal*) a man who has sex with a boy （与男童发生性关系的）恋童癖男子 ▸ **ped·er·asty** (*BrE also* **paed·er·asty**) /ˈpedəræsti/ *noun* [U]

ped·es·tal /ˈpedɪstl/ *noun* the base that a column, statue, etc. rests on （柱子或雕塑等的）底座，基座：*a pedestal basin* (= a WASHBASIN supported by a column) 有底座的洗脸盆 ◇ *I replaced the vase carefully on its pedestal.* 我小心地把花瓶放回基座上。➲ VISUAL VOCAB PAGE V14

IDM **to put/place sb on a ˈpedestal** to admire sb so much that you do not see their faults 把某人奉为完人；盲目崇拜某人 ➲ MORE AT KNOCK *v.*

ped·es·trian /pəˈdestriən/ *noun, adj.*

■ *noun* a person walking in the street and not travelling in a vehicle 行人；步行者 ➲ COMPARE MOTORIST ➲ WORDFINDER NOTE AT TRAFFIC

■ *adj.* **1** [only before noun] used by or for the use of pedestrians; connected with pedestrians 行人使用的；行人的：*pedestrian areas* 步行区 ◇ *Pedestrian accidents are down by 5%.* 行人受伤事故下降了 5%。**2** without any imagination or excitement; dull 缺乏想象的；乏味的；无趣的 SYN **unimaginative**

peˌdestrian ˈcrossing (*BrE*) (*NAmE* **cross·walk**) *noun* a part of a road where vehicles must stop to allow people to cross 人行横道；行人穿越道 ➲ VISUAL VOCAB PAGE V3 ➲ SEE ALSO ZEBRA CROSSING

ped·es·tri·an·ize (*BrE also* **-ise**) /pəˈdestriənaɪz/ *verb* **~ sth** to make a street or part of a town into an area that is only for people who are walking, not for vehicles 使为行人专用；行人专用化 ▸ **ped·es·tri·an·iza·tion, -isa·tion** /pəˌdestriənaɪˈzeɪʃn; *NAmE* -nəˈz-/ *noun* [U]

peˌdestrian ˈprecinct (*BrE*) (*NAmE* **peˌdestrian ˈmall**) *noun* a part of a town, especially a shopping area, that vehicles are not allowed to enter 步行区；行人专用区 ➲ VISUAL VOCAB PAGE V3

pedi·at·ri·cian (*NAmE*) (*BrE* **paedi·at·ri·cian**) /ˌpiːdiəˈtrɪʃn/ *noun* a doctor who studies and treats the diseases of children 儿科医生；儿科专家

pedi·at·rics (*NAmE*) (*BrE* **paedi·at·rics**) /ˌpiːdiˈætrɪks/ *noun* [U] the branch of medicine concerned with children and their diseases 儿科学 ▸ **pedi·at·ric** (*NAmE*) (*BrE* **paedi-**) *adj.*

pedi·cab /ˈpedɪkæb/ *noun* a small vehicle with three wheels, operated by PEDALS like a bicycle, used as a taxi in some countries （某些国家用作出租的）脚踏三轮车，人力三轮车 ➲ SEE ALSO RICKSHAW

pedi·cure /ˈpedɪkjʊə(r); *NAmE* -kjʊr/ *noun* [C, U] care and treatment of the feet and TOENAILS 足部保养；足部护理 ➲ COMPARE MANICURE *n.*

pedi·gree /ˈpedɪgriː/ *noun, adj.*

■ *noun* **1** [C] knowledge of or an official record of the animals from which an animal has been bred 动物血统记录；动物纯种系谱：*dogs with good pedigrees* (= their ANCESTORS are known and of the same breed) 纯种的狗 **2** [C, U] a person's family history or the background of sth, especially when this is impressive 家谱；门第；世系；起源：*She was proud of her long pedigree.* 她为自己源远流长的家世而自豪。◇ *The product has a pedigree going back to the last century.* 这项产品的渊源可追溯到上个世纪。

■ *adj.* (*BrE*) (*NAmE usually* **pedi·greed**) [only before noun] (of an animal 动物) coming from a family of the same breed that has been officially recorded for a long time and is thought to be of a good quality 优良品种的；纯种的：*pedigree sheep* 纯种绵羊

pedi·ment /ˈpedɪmənt/ *noun* (*architecture* 建) the part in the shape of a triangle above the entrance of a building in the ancient Greek style （古典希腊式建筑入口处上方的）山花

ped·lar (*BrE*) (*NAmE* **ped·dler**) /ˈpedlə(r)/ *noun* a person who in the past travelled from place to place trying to sell small objects （旧时的）流动小贩

ped·ometer /peˈdɒmɪtə(r); *NAmE* -ˈdɑːm-/ *noun* an instrument for measuring how far you have walked 计步器；步程计

pedo·phile (*NAmE*) (*BrE* **paedo-**) /ˈpiːdəʊfaɪl; *NAmE* -doʊ-/ *noun* a person who is sexually attracted to children 恋童癖者

pedo·philia (*NAmE*) (*BrE* **paedo-**) /ˌpiːdəˈfɪliə/ *noun* [U] the condition of being sexually attracted to children; sexual activity with children 恋童癖；与儿童的性行为

pee /piː/ *verb, noun*

■ *verb* (**peed, peed**) [I] (*informal*) to pass waste liquid from your body 撒尿 SYN **urinate**：*I need to pee.* 我要撒尿。

■ *noun* (*informal*) **1** [sing.] an act of passing liquid waste from your body 撒尿：(*BrE*) *to go for a pee* 去撒尿 ◇ *to have a pee* 去小便 ◇ (*NAmE*) *to take a pee* 尿尿 **2** [U] liquid waste passed from your body; URINE 尿；小便

peek /piːk/ *verb* **1** [I] to look at sth quickly and secretly because you should not be looking at it 窥视；偷看 SYN **peep**：*No peeking!* 禁止窥探！◇ **+ adv./prep.** *She peeked at the audience from behind the curtain.* 她从帷幕后面窥视了一下观众。◇ *I couldn't resist peeking in the drawer.* 我不由得偷看了一下抽屉里面。**2** [I] **~ out/over/through, etc.** to be just visible 微露出；探出：*Her feet peeked out from the end of the blanket.* 她的脚从毯子一端露了出来。▸ **peek** *noun* [sing.]：*I took a quick peek inside.* 我匆匆向里面偷看了一眼。

peek·aboo /ˌpiːkəˈbuː/ (*BrE also* **ˈpeep-bo**) *noun* [U] a simple game played to amuse young children, in which you keep hiding your face and then showing it again, saying 'Peekaboo!' or 'Peep-bo!' 藏猫猫（把脸隐藏而后闪现以逗幼儿的游戏）；（做这种游戏时发的声音）猫儿

peel /piːl/ *verb, noun*

■ *verb* **1** [T] **~ sth** to take the outer layer off fruit, vegetables, etc. 剥（水果、蔬菜等的）皮；给…去皮：*to peel an orange/a banana* 剥橙子 / 香蕉 ◇ *Have you peeled the potatoes?* 你给土豆刮皮了吗？➲ COLLOCATIONS AT COOKING **2** [T, I] **~ (sth) away/off/back** to remove a layer, covering, etc. from the surface of sth; to come off the surface of sth 剥掉；揭掉；剥落：*Carefully peel away the lining paper.* 小心剥掉衬着的那层纸。◇ *The label will peel off if you soak it in water.* 标签浸到水中就会脱落。**3** [I]

~ (**off**) (of a covering 覆盖层) to come off in strips or small pieces 脱落；剥落：*The wallpaper was beginning to peel.* 壁纸开始剥落了。 **4** [I] (of a surface 表面) to lose strips or small pieces of its covering 起皮；剥落：*Put on some cream to stop your nose from peeling.* 抹点乳霜，以免你的鼻子再脱皮。◇ *The walls have begun to peel.* 墙壁开始破皮了。 IDM SEE EYE *n.*

PHR V ˌ**peel ˈoff** to leave a group of vehicles, aircraft, etc. and turn to one side（车辆、飞机等）离队，转向一侧：*The leading car in the motorcade peeled off to the right.* 汽车队的先导车转向右侧。 ˌ**peel ˈoff** | ˌ**peel** (**sth**)↔ˈ**off** (*informal*) to remove some or all of your clothes 脱衣服：*You look hot—why don't you peel off?* 你看来很热，为何不脱掉衣服？◇ *He peeled off his shirt.* 他脱下了衬衣。 ˌ**peel ˈout** (*NAmE*, *informal*) to leave quickly and in a noisy way, especially in a car, on a motorcycle, etc.（尤指乘汽车、摩托车等）喧嚣地迅速离去

■ ***noun*** **1** [U, C] the thick outer layer of some fruits and vegetables（某些水果、蔬菜的）外皮；果皮：*orange/lemon peel* 橙子皮；柠檬皮 ◇ (*NAmE also*) *an orange/a lemon peel* 一片橙子皮 / 柠檬皮 ➲ VISUAL VOCAB PAGE V33 ➲ COMPARE RIND (1), SKIN *n.* (4), ZEST (3) **2 peels** [pl.] (*NAmE*) = PEELINGS

peel·er /ˈpiːlə(r)/ *noun* (usually in compounds 通常构成复合词) a special type of knife for taking the skin off fruit and vegetables 去皮器；削皮器：*a potato peeler* 土豆去皮器 ➲ VISUAL VOCAB PAGE V27

peel·ings /ˈpiːlɪŋz/ (*NAmE also* **peels**) *noun* [pl.] the skin of fruit or vegetables that has been removed 刮掉的果皮（或菜皮）

peep /piːp/ *verb, noun*

■ ***verb*** **1** [I] (+ **adv./prep.**) to look quickly and secretly at sth, especially through a small opening（尤指通过小孔）窥视，偷看：*We caught her peeping through the keyhole.* 她从锁孔偷看时被我们撞着了。◇ *Could I just peep inside?* 我能不能看一眼里边？◇ *He was peeping at her through his fingers.* 他从指缝偷看她。 **2** [I] + **adv./prep.** to be just visible 微露出；部分现出：*The tower peeped above the trees.* 塔尖从树梢上露出来。◇ *The sun peeped out from behind the clouds.* 太阳从云层里露了一下脸。 **3** [I, T] ~ (**sth**) to make a short high sound; to make sth make this sound（使）发出尖细的声音，发出吱吱声 ➲ MORE LIKE THIS 3, page R25

■ ***noun*** **1** [C, usually sing.] a quick or secret look at sth 偷偷一瞥：*Dave **took a quick peep** at the last page.* 戴夫迅速地瞟了一下最后一页。 **2** [sing.] (*informal*) something that sb says or a sound that sb makes 说话；出声音：*We did **not hear a peep out of** the baby all night.* 我们整夜都没听到婴儿出声。 **3** [C] a short high sound like the one made by a young bird or by a whistle 啾啾声；嘟嘟声 **4** (*also* **peep ˈpeep**) [C] (*BrE*) a word for the sound of a car's horn, used especially by children 嘟嘟（儿语，指汽车喇叭声） **5 peeps** [pl.] (*informal*) people, especially friends, colleagues or people that you are addressing in a group email, BLOG, etc. 朋友，同事，各位（对群发邮件的收件人或博客订阅者等的称呼）：*I spoke to the marketing peeps this morning.* 今天上午我和营销部的同事谈过了。

peep-bo /ˈpiːpbəʊ; ˈpiːpəʊ; *NAmE* -boʊ; -poʊ/ *noun* [U] (*BrE*) = PEEKABOO

peep·hole /ˈpiːphəʊl; *NAmE* -hoʊl/ *noun* a small opening in a wall, door, etc. that you can look through（墙或门上等的）窥视孔

ˌ**Peeping ˈTom** *noun* (*disapproving*) a person who likes to watch people secretly when they are taking off their clothes 窥视者汤姆；有窥裸癖者 SYN **voyeur**

ˈ**peep show** *noun* **1** a series of moving pictures in a box that you look at through a small opening 拉洋片；西洋镜 **2** a type of show in which sb pays to watch a woman take off her clothes in a small room 偷窥式脱衣表演

peer /pɪə(r); *NAmE* pɪr/ *noun, verb*

■ ***noun*** **1** [usually pl.] a person who is the same age or who has the same social status as you 身份（或地位）相同的人；同龄人；同辈：*She enjoys the respect of her peers.* 她受到同侪的尊敬。◇ *Children are worried about failing in front of their peers.* 儿童都怕在同伴面前失败。◇ ***Peer pressure*** *is strong among young people* (= they want to be like other people of the same age). 年轻人受到强大的同辈压力。 **2** (in Britain) a member of the NOBILITY（英国）贵族成员 ➲ SEE ALSO LIFE PEER, PEERESS

■ ***verb*** [I] (+ **adv./prep.**) to look closely or carefully at sth, especially when you cannot see it clearly 仔细看；端详：*We peered into the shadows.* 我们往阴暗处仔细瞧。◇ *He went to the window and peered out.* 他走到窗前仔细往外瞧。◇ *She kept peering over her shoulder.* 她不停地回头看。◇ *He peered closely at the photograph.* 他聚精会神地端详着相片。 ➲ SYNONYMS AT STARE

peer·age /ˈpɪərɪdʒ; *NAmE* ˈpɪr-/ *noun* **1** [sing.] all the peers as a group（统称）贵族：*a member of the peerage* 一位贵族成员 **2** [C] the rank of a peer (2) or peeress 贵族的爵位

peer·ess /ˈpɪəres; *NAmE* ˈpɪrəs/ *noun* a female PEER (2) 女贵族

ˈ**peer group** *noun* a group of people of the same age or social status 同龄群体；社会地位相同的群体：*She gets on well with her peer group.* 她和同龄人相处融洽。◇ *peer-group pressure* 同侪压力

peer·less /ˈpɪələs; *NAmE* ˈpɪrləs/ *adj.* better than all others of its kind 无双的；杰出的；出众的 SYN **unsurpassed**：*a peerless performance* 出色的表演

ˌ**peer reˈview** *noun* [U, C] a judgement on a piece of scientific or other professional work by others working in the same area（对科研、专业成果等作出的）同行评议，同行评估，同侪审查：*All research proposals are subject to peer review before selection.* 所有研究建议均须经过同行评议后再行筛选。 ▶ ˌ**peer-reˈviewed** *adj.*：*peer-reviewed journals* 实行同行评审制的期刊

ˌ**peer-to-ˈpeer** *adj.* [only before noun] (*computing* 计) (of a computer system 计算机系统) in which each computer can act as a SERVER for the others, allowing data to be shared without the need for a central server 对等的，点对点的（系统中的任何一台计算机均可用作服务器，允许文件共享） ➲ COMPARE CLIENT-SERVER

peeve /piːv/ *noun*

IDM **sb's pet ˈpeeve** (*NAmE*) (*BrE* **sb's pet ˈhate**) something that you particularly dislike 特别厌恶的东西

peeved /piːvd/ *adj.* ~ (**about sth**) (*informal*) annoyed 恼怒的；生气的：*He sounded peeved about not being told.* 没人通知他，为此他气哼哼的。

peev·ish /ˈpiːvɪʃ/ *adj.* easily annoyed by unimportant things; bad-tempered 爱生气的；易怒的；脾气坏的 SYN **irritable** ▶ **peev·ish·ly** *adv.*

pee·wit /ˈpiːwɪt/ *noun* = LAPWING

peg /peg/ *noun, verb*

■ ***noun*** **1** a short piece of wood, metal or plastic used for holding things together, hanging things on, marking a position, etc.（木、金属或塑料）钉子，楔子，橛子，短桩：*There's a peg near the door to hang your coat on.* 门边有个钩子可以挂衣服。 **2** (*also* ˈ**tent peg**) a small pointed piece of wood or metal that you attach to the ropes of a tent and push into the ground in order to hold the tent in place（木制或金属）帐篷短桩，橛子 **3** (*also* ˈ**clothes peg**) (*both BrE*) (*NAmE* **clothes·pin**) a piece of wood or plastic used for attaching wet clothes to a clothes line 晾衣夹子 **4** (*also* ˈ**tuning peg**) a wooden, metal or plastic screw used for making the strings of a musical instrument tighter or looser 弦钮；琴栓 ➲ VISUAL VOCAB PAGE V38 **5** (*IndE*) a small amount of a drink, especially a strong alcoholic one 少量饮料；（尤指）少量烈酒：*a peg of whisky* 一点威士忌

IDM ˌ**off the ˈpeg** (*BrE*) (*NAmE* ˌ**off the ˈrack**) (of clothes 衣服) made to a standard average size and not made especially to fit you 成品的；现成的：*He buys his clothes off the peg.* 他买的是成衣。◇ *off-the-peg fashions* 成衣的流行式样 ˌ**bring/ˌtake sb ˈdown a peg** (**or two**) to make sb realize that they are not as good, important, etc. as they

P

think they are 杀某人的威风；挫某人的锐气：*He needed to be taken down a peg or two.* 需要杀杀他的威风。**a peg to 'hang sth on** something that gives you an excuse or opportunity to discuss or explain sth 借口；理由；话头 ➲ MORE AT SQUARE *adj.*

pegs 钩；楔；栓；桩

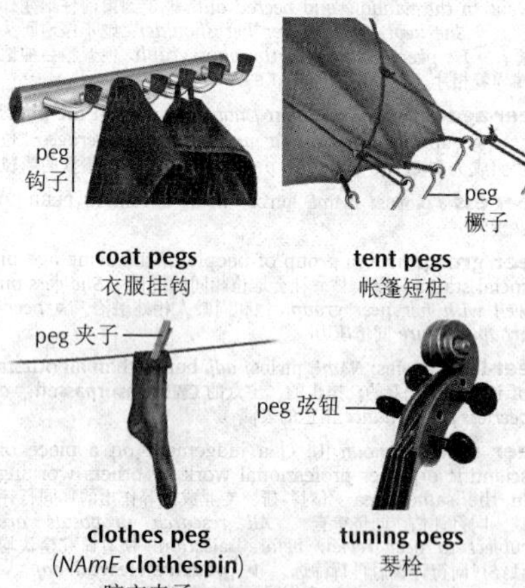

■ *verb* (-gg-) **1** to fasten sth with pegs 用夹子夹住；用楔子钉住：**~ sth (out) + adv./prep.** *All their wet clothes were pegged out on the line.* 他们的湿衣服都夹在绳子上晾着。◇ **~ sth to sth** *She was busy pegging her tent to the ground.* 她忙着用橛子把帐篷钉牢在地上。**2** [usually passive] to fix or keep prices, wages, etc. at a particular level 使工资、价格等固定于某水平（或与…挂钩）：**~ sth (at sth)** *Pay increases will be pegged at 5%.* 工资调升率将限定在 5%。◇ **~ sth (to sth)** *Loan repayments are pegged to your income.* 分期付还贷款按你的收入计算。**3 ~ sb as sth** (*NAmE, informal*) to think of sb in a particular way 视为；看作：*She pegged him as a big spender.* 她觉得他是个大手大脚的人。IDM SEE LEVEL *adj.*

PHR V **,peg a'way (at sth)** (*informal, especially BrE*) to continue working hard at sth or trying to achieve sth difficult 坚持不懈地工作（或努力）**,peg sb/sth↔'back** (*especially BrE*) (especially in sport 尤用于体育运动) to stop sb/sth from winning or increasing the amount by which they are ahead 扼止；止住；拖住：*Each time we scored we were pegged back minutes later.* 每次我们得分，几分钟后便被追上。**,peg 'out** (*BrE, informal*) to die 死；断气

'peg leg *noun* (*informal*) an artificial leg, especially one made of wood 假腿（尤指木制的）

pe·jora·tive /pɪ'dʒɒrətɪv; *NAmE* -'dʒɔːr-; -'dʒɑːr-/ *adj.* (*formal*) a word or remark that is **pejorative** expresses disapproval or criticism 贬损的；轻蔑的 SYN **derogatory**：*I'm using the word 'academic' here in a pejorative sense.* 我这里使用的"学术"一词是贬义的。▶ **pe·jora·tive·ly** *adv.*

Pe·kin·ese (*also* **Pe·king·ese**) /,piːkɪ'niːz/ *noun* (*pl.* **Pe·kin·ese** or **Pe·kin·eses**) a very small dog with long soft hair, short legs and a flat nose 北京狗；狮子狗

pe·la·gic /pə'lædʒɪk/ *adj.* (*specialist*) connected with, or living in, the parts of the sea that are far from land 远海的；远洋的

peli·can /'pelɪkən/ *noun* a large bird that lives near water, with a bag of skin under its long beak for storing food 鹈鹕

,pelican 'crossing *noun* (in Britain) a place on a road where you can stop the traffic and cross by operating a set of TRAFFIC LIGHTS （英国由行人控制红绿灯的）人行横道，行人穿越道

pel·lagra /pə'lægrə/ *noun* [U] a disease caused by a lack of good food, that causes the skin to crack and may lead to mental illness 糙皮病，玉米红斑病（因缺乏营养而引起的皮肤皲裂，可导致精神障碍）

pel·let /'pelɪt/ *noun* **1** a small hard ball of any substance, often of soft material that has become hard 小球；团粒；丸：*food pellets for chickens* 团粒鸡食 **2** a very small metal ball that is fired from a gun 小弹丸

pell-mell /,pel 'mel/ *adv.* (*old-fashioned*) very quickly and in a way that is not controlled 匆忙地；仓促地；混乱地

pel·lu·cid /pə'luːsɪd/ *adj.* (*literary*) extremely clear 清澈的；清晰的 SYN **transparent**

Pel·man·ism /'pelmənɪzəm/ *noun* [U] a game in which players must remember cards or other objects that they have seen 佩尔曼记忆训练游戏（参加者必须记住所见到的纸牌或其他物品）

pel·met /'pelmɪt/ (*also* **val·ance** *especially in NAmE*) *noun* a strip of wood or cloth above a window that hides the curtain rail 窗帘盒；窗帘短帷幔

pe·lota /pə'lɒtə; -'ləʊ-; *NAmE* -'loʊ-/ *noun* **1** [U] a game from Spain in which players hit a ball against a wall using a kind of BASKET attached to their hand 西班牙回力球运动（运动员戴篮状手套对墙击球）**2** [C] the ball used in the game of pelota 回力球

the pel·oton /'pelətɒn; *NAmE* -tɑːn/ *noun* [sing.] (*from French*) the main group of riders in a bicycle race （自行车赛中的）主车群

pelt /pelt/ *verb, noun*

■ *verb* **1** [T] **~ sb (with sth)** to attack sb by throwing things at them 投物攻击；向…投掷：*The children pelted him with snowballs.* 孩子们向他投掷雪球。**2** [I] **~ (down)** (of rain 雨) to fall very heavily 倾泻；下得很大 **3** [I] **+ adv./prep.** (*informal*) to run somewhere very fast 飞跑 SYN **dash**：*We pelted down the hill after the car.* 我们飞奔下山追赶那辆汽车。

■ *noun* the skin of an animal, especially with the fur or hair still on it （动物的）皮，毛皮

IDM **(at) full 'pelt/'tilt** as fast as possible 急速；疾速；尽快

,pelvic 'floor *noun* (*anatomy* 解) the muscles at the base of the ABDOMEN, attached to the pelvis 骨盆底

pel·vis /'pelvɪs/ *noun* the wide curved set of bones at the bottom of the body that the legs and SPINE are connected to 骨盆 ➲ VISUAL VOCAB PAGE V64 ▶ **pel·vic** /'pelvɪk/ *adj.* [only before noun]：*the pelvic bones* 骨盆骨

pem·mican /'pemɪkən/ *noun* [U] a food made from crushed dried meat, originally made by Native Americans 干肉饼，肉糜饼（最初为美洲土著的食品）

pen 🔑 /pen/ *noun, verb*

■ *noun* **1** 🔑 (often in compounds 常构成复合词) an instrument made of plastic or metal used for writing with ink 笔；钢笔：*pen and ink* 钢笔和墨水 ◇ *a new book from the pen of Martin Amis* 马丁·埃米斯写的新书 ➲ SEE ALSO BALLPOINT PEN at BALLPOINT, FELT-TIP PEN, FOUNTAIN PEN **2** a small piece of land surrounded by a fence in which farm animals are kept 圈；围栏；畜栏：*a sheep pen* 羊圈 **3** (*NAmE, slang*) = PENITENTIARY

IDM **the ,pen is ,mightier than the 'sword** (*saying*) people who write books, poems, etc. have a greater effect on history and human affairs than soldiers and wars 笔诛胜于剑伐 **put pen to 'paper** to write or start to write sth 写；动笔 ➲ MORE AT SLIP *n.*

■ *verb* (-nn-) **1 ~ sth** (*formal*) to write sth 写：*He penned a letter to the local paper.* 他给当地报纸写了一封信。**2 ~ sb/sth (in/up)** to shut an animal or a person in a small space （把…）关起来，圈起来：*At clipping time sheep need to be penned.* 在剪羊毛时，需要把羊圈起来。◇ *The* *whole family were penned up in one room for a month.* 全家人被关在一间屋子里达一个月之久。

penal /ˈpiːnl/ *adj.* [usually before noun] **1** connected with or used for punishment, especially by law 惩罚的；刑罚的： *penal reforms* 刑罚改革 ◇ *the* ***penal system*** 刑罚制度 ◇ *Criminals could at one time be sentenced to* ***penal servitude*** (= prison with hard physical work). 曾经有个时期，罪犯可以被判服劳役刑。 ◇ *a* ***penal colony*** (= a place where criminals were sent as a punishment in the past) 罪犯流放地 **2** that can be punished by law 应受刑罚的： *a penal offence* 刑事犯罪 **3** very severe 严重的；严厉的： *penal rates of interest* 很重的利率

ˈpenal code *noun* a system of laws connected with crime and punishment 刑法典

pen·al·ize (*BrE also* **-ise**) /ˈpiːnəlaɪz/ *verb* **1 ~ sb (for sth)** to punish sb for breaking a rule or law by making them suffer a disadvantage 处罚；惩罚；处以刑罚： *You will be penalized for poor spelling.* 你拼写不好将会扣分。 **2** to punish sb for breaking a rule in a sport or game by giving an advantage to their opponent （体育运动中）判罚： **~ sb (for sth)** *He was penalized for time-wasting.* 他因拖延时间而受罚。 ◇ **~ sth** *Foul play will be severely penalized.* 比赛犯规将受到严厉处罚。 **3 ~ sb** to put sb at a disadvantage by treating them unfairly 置于不利地位；不公正地对待： *The new law appears to penalize the poorest members of society.* 新法规似乎不利于社会中的最贫困者。

pen·alty /ˈpenəlti/ *noun* (*pl.* **-ies**) **1** a punishment for breaking a law, rule or contract 惩罚；处罚；刑罚： *to impose a penalty* 予以惩罚 ◇ *Assault* ***carries a*** *maximum* ***penalty*** *of seven years' imprisonment.* 侵犯人身罪可判处最高七年的监禁。 ◇ **~ (for sth)** *The penalty for travelling without a ticket is £200.* 无票乘车的罚款为 200 英镑。 ◇ *Contractors who fall behind schedule incur heavy financial penalties.* 承包商如延误工期将被处以巨额罚款。 ◇ *a penalty clause in a contract* 合同中的惩罚条款 ◇ *You can withdraw money from the account at any time* ***without penalty***. 您可以随时从账户中提款，不收罚金。 ➲ SEE ALSO DEATH PENALTY **2 ~ (of sth)** a disadvantage suffered as a result of sth 害处；不利： *One of the penalties of fame is loss of privacy.* 成名的弊端之一是失掉了隐私。 **3** (in sports and games 体育运动) a disadvantage given to a player or a team when they break a rule （对犯规者的）判罚，处罚： *He incurred a ten-second penalty in the first round.* 他在第一轮受到停赛十秒钟的处罚。 **4** (in football (SOCCER) and some other similar sports 足球和其他类似体育运动) a chance to score a goal or point without any defending players, except the GOALKEEPER, trying to stop it; the goal or point that is given if it is successful. This chance is given because the other team has broken the rules. 点球；罚点球得分： *Two minutes later Ford equalized with a penalty.* 两分钟后，福特以一记点球将比分扳平。 ◇ *We* ***were awarded a penalty*** *after a late tackle.* 对方铲球犯规后，我们得到了一个点球。 ◇ *I volunteered to* ***take the penalty*** (= be the person who tries to score the goal/point). 我自愿主罚点球。 ◇ *He* ***missed a penalty*** *in the last minute of the game.* 在比赛的最后一刻，他罚失了点球。 **IDM** SEE PAY *v.*

ˈpenalty area (*BrE also* **ˈpenalty box, area**) *noun* (in football (SOCCER) 足球) the area in front of the goal. If the defending team breaks the rules within this area, the other team is given a penalty. 罚球区；禁区

ˈpenalty box *noun* **1** (*BrE*) = PENALTY AREA **2** (in ICE HOCKEY 冰上曲棍球) an area next to the ice where a player who has broken the rules must wait for a short time 犯规队员临时座席；受罚席

ˈpenalty kick (*BrE also* **ˈspot kick**) *noun* a kick that is taken as a PENALTY in the game of football (SOCCER) （足球比赛的）罚点球，罚球

ˈpenalty point *noun* (*BrE*) a note on sb's DRIVING LICENCE showing they have committed an offence while driving （司机的）违章驾驶记录

ˌpenalty ˈshoot-out *noun* (in football (SOCCER) 足球) a way of deciding the winner when both teams have the same score at the end of a game. Each team is given a number of chances to kick the ball into the goal and the team that scores the most goals wins. 罚点球决定胜负

pen·ance /ˈpenəns/ *noun* **1** [C, usually sing., U] (especially in particular religions 尤见于某些宗教) an act that you give yourself to do, or that a priest gives you to do in order to show that you are sorry for sth you have done wrong 补赎；悔罪；修和圣事： *an act of penance* 赎罪善功 ◇ **~ for sth** *to do penance for your sins* 为自己的罪过做补赎 ➲ COLLOCATIONS AT RELIGION **2** [sing.] something that you have to do even though you do not like doing it 苦差事；被迫做的事： *She regards living in New York as a penance; she hates big cities.* 她把住在纽约视为苦事，她讨厌大都市。

ˌpen-and-ˈink *adj.* [usually before noun] drawn with a pen 用钢笔画的： *pen-and-ink drawings* 钢笔画

pence /pens/ (*BrE*) (*abbr.* **p**) PL. OF PENNY

pen·chant /ˈpɒ̃ʃɒ̃; *NAmE* ˈpentʃənt/ *noun* **~ for sth** a special liking for sth 爱好；嗜爱 **SYN** **fondness**: *She* ***has a penchant for*** *champagne.* 她酷爱香槟酒。

pen·cil /ˈpensl/ *noun, verb*

■ ***noun*** [C, U] a narrow piece of wood, or a metal or plastic case, containing a black or coloured substance, used for drawing or writing 铅笔： *a pencil drawing* 铅笔画 ◇ *I'll get a pencil and paper.* 我去拿铅笔和纸。 ◇ *She scribbled a note* ***in pencil***. 她用铅笔草草写了张便条。 ◇ *coloured pencils* 彩色铅笔 ➲ VISUAL VOCAB PAGE V71 ➲ SEE ALSO EYEBROW PENCIL, PROPELLING PENCIL

■ ***verb*** (**-ll-**, *especially US* **-l-**) **~ sth** to write, draw or mark sth with a pencil 用铅笔写（或画、做记号）： *a pencilled portrait* 铅笔画像 ◇ *A previous owner had pencilled 'First Edition' inside the book's cover.* 这本书过去的主人在书的封二上用铅笔写了"第一版"。

PHR V **ˌpencil sth/sb↔ˈin** to write down sb's name or details of an arrangement with them that you know might have to be changed later 临时记下（约会的人名或安排细节）： *We've pencilled in a meeting for Tuesday afternoon.* 我们暂定星期二下午开会。 ◇ *Shall I pencil you in for Friday?* (= for a meeting) 我要不要先记下你星期五开会？

ˈpencil case *noun* a small bag, etc. for holding pencils and pens 铅笔盒；铅笔袋 ➲ VISUAL VOCAB PAGE V72

ˈpencil pusher *noun* (*NAmE*) = PEN-PUSHER

ˈpencil sharpener *noun* a small device with a blade inside, used for making pencils sharp 削铅笔器；转笔刀 ➲ VISUAL VOCAB PAGE V71

ˈpencil skirt *noun* a narrow straight skirt 窄身直筒裙；铅笔裙

pen·dant /ˈpendənt/ *noun* a piece of jewellery that you wear around your neck on a chain （项链上的）垂饰，饰坠 ➲ VISUAL VOCAB PAGE V70

pend·ing /ˈpendɪŋ/ *prep., adj.*

■ ***prep.*** (*formal*) while waiting for sth to happen; until sth happens 在等待…时期；直到…为止： *He was released on bail pending further inquiries.* 他获得保释，等候进一步调查。

■ ***adj.*** (*formal*) **1** waiting to be decided or settled 待定的；待决的： *Nine cases are still pending.* 尚有九宗案件待决。 ◇ *a* ***pending file/tray*** (= where you put letters, etc. you are going to deal with soon) 待办卷宗 / 文件盘 **2** going to happen soon 即将发生的 **SYN** **imminent**: *An election is pending in Italy.* 意大利即将举行选举。 ◇ *his pending departure* 他即将离开

ˈpen drive *noun* = FLASH DRIVE

pen·du·lous /ˈpendjələs; *NAmE* -dʒələs/ *adj.* (*formal*) hanging down loosely and swinging from side to side 悬垂摆动的

P

pen·du·lum /ˈpendjələm; *NAmE* -dʒələm/ *noun* a long straight part with a weight at the end that moves regularly from side to side to control the movement of a clock 钟摆：(*figurative*) *In education, the pendulum has swung back to traditional teaching methods.* 教育界又恢复了传统教学法。◇ (*figurative*) *the pendulum of public opinion* 舆论的转变 ➲ PICTURE AT CLOCK

pene·trable /ˈpenətrəbl/ *adj.* (*formal*) that allows sth to be pushed into or through it; that can have a way made through it 可被穿透的；能穿透的：*soil that is easily penetrable with a fork* 能轻易下耙的土壤 OPP **impenetrable**

pene·trate /ˈpenətreɪt/ *verb* **1** [T, I] to go into or through sth 穿过；进入：**~ sth** *The knife had penetrated his chest.* 刀子刺入了他的胸膛。◇ *The sun's radiation penetrates the skin.* 太阳的辐射能透进皮肤。◇ (*figurative*) *The war penetrates every area of the nation's life.* 战争波及全国国民生活的各个领域。◇ **~ into/through/to sth** *These fine particles penetrate deep into the lungs.* 这些微小的尘埃可深深地吸入肺部。 **2** [T, I] to succeed in entering or joining an organization, a group, etc. especially when this is difficult to do 渗透，打入（组织、团体等）：**~ sth** *They had penetrated airport security.* 他们已打入机场保安组织。◇ *The party has been penetrated by extremists.* 极端分子已经打入了这个党。◇ *This year the company has been trying to penetrate new markets* (= to start selling their products there). 今年这家公司一直试图打入新市场。◇ **~ into sth** *The troops had penetrated deep into enemy lines.* 部队已经深入敌军防线。 **3** [T] **~ sth** to see or show a way into or through sth 看透；透过…看见：*Our eyes could not penetrate the darkness.* 我们的眼睛在黑暗中什么也看不见。◇ *The flashlights barely penetrated the gloom.* 手电筒勉强照见那幽暗处。 **4** [T] **~ sth** to understand or discover sth that is difficult to understand or is hidden 洞察；发现；揭示：*Science can penetrate many of nature's mysteries.* 科学能揭示自然界的许多奥秘。 **5** [I, T] to be understood or realized by sb 被领悟；被理解：*I was at the door before his words penetrated.* 我走到门口才听懂了他说的话。◇ **~ sth** *None of my advice seems to have penetrated his thick skull* (= he has not listened to any of it). 他那木脑袋似乎一点也听不进我的忠告。 **6** [T] **~ sb/sth** (of a man 男人) to put the PENIS into the VAGINA or ANUS of a sexual partner （以阴茎）插入

pene·trat·ing /ˈpenətreɪtɪŋ/ *adj.* **1** (of sb's eyes or the way they look at you 眼睛或眼神) making you feel uncomfortable because the person seems to know what you are thinking 锐利的；犀利的；尖利的：*penetrating blue eyes* 锐利的蓝眼睛 ◇ *a* ***penetrating gaze/look/stare*** 洞察一切的凝视 / 目光 / 注视 **2** (of a sound or voice 声音或嗓音) loud and hard 响亮的；尖厉的 SYN **piercing**: *Her voice was shrill and penetrating.* 她的声音尖厉刺耳。 **3** showing that you have understood sth quickly and completely 深刻的；精辟的：*a* ***penetrating comment/criticism/question*** 精辟的评论；入木三分的批评；尖锐的问题 **4** spreading deeply or widely 弥漫的；渗透的：*a penetrating smell* 刺鼻的气味 ◇ *the* ***penetrating cold/damp*** 刺骨的寒气；很重的湿气

pene·tra·tion /ˌpenəˈtreɪʃn/ *noun* [U] **1** the act or process of making a way into or through sth 穿透；渗透；进入：*The floor is sealed to prevent water penetration.* 地板加了密封涂料防止渗水。◇ *the company's successful penetration of overseas markets* 公司对海外市场的顺利开拓 **2** the act of a man putting his PENIS into his partner's VAGINA or ANUS （男人阴茎的）插入

pene·tra·tive /ˈpenətrətɪv; *NAmE* -treɪtɪv/ *adj.* **1** (of sexual activity 性行为) involving putting the PENIS into sb's VAGINA or ANUS 行房的；交媾的：*penetrative sex* 行房事 **2** able to make a way into or through sth 能穿透的；能进入的：*penetrative weapons* 穿透性武器 **3** deep and thorough 深入的；彻底的：*a penetrative survey* 全面深入的调查

pen·friend /ˈpenfrend/ (*BrE*) (*also* ˈ**pen pal** *NAmE, BrE*) *noun* a person that you make friends with by writing letters, often sb you have never met 笔友

pen·guin /ˈpeŋɡwɪn/ *noun* a black and white bird that lives in the Antarctic. Penguins cannot fly but use their wings for swimming. There are several types of penguin, some of them very large but some of them quite small. 企鹅

peni·cil·lin /ˌpenɪˈsɪlɪn/ *noun* [U] a substance obtained from MOULD, used as a drug to treat or prevent infections caused by bacteria; a type of ANTIBIOTIC 青霉素；盘尼西林

pen·ile /ˈpiːnaɪl/ *adj.* [only before noun] (*specialist*) relating to the PENIS 阴茎的

pen·in·sula /pəˈnɪnsjələ; *NAmE* -sələ/ *noun* an area of land that is almost surrounded by water but is joined to a larger piece of land 半岛：*the Iberian peninsula* (= Spain and Portugal) 伊比利亚半岛

pen·in·su·lar /pəˈnɪnsjələ(r); *NAmE* -sələr/ *adj.* on or connected with a peninsula 半岛上的；与半岛有关的：*peninsular Spanish* (= that is spoken in Spain, not in Latin America) 半岛本土西班牙语

penis /ˈpiːnɪs/ *noun* the organ on the body of a man or male animal that is used for URINATING and sex 阴茎

peni·tence /ˈpenɪtəns/ *noun* [U] a feeling of being sorry because you have done sth wrong 忏悔；悔罪；愧疚

peni·tent /ˈpenɪtənt/ *adj., noun*
■ *adj.* feeling or showing that you are sorry for having done sth wrong 忏悔的；后悔的；愧疚的 SYN **remorseful**
■ *noun* a person who shows that they are sorry for doing sth wrong, especially a religious person who wants God to forgive them 忏悔者；（尤指宗教）悔罪者

peni·ten·tial /ˌpenɪˈtenʃl/ *adj.* (*formal*) showing that you are sorry for having done sth wrong 悔悟的；悔罪的；忏悔的

peni·ten·tiary /ˌpenɪˈtenʃəri/ *noun* (*pl.* **-ies**) (*also slang* **pen**) (*both NAmE*) a prison 监狱

penknife 小折刀

pen·knife /ˈpennaɪf/ *noun* (*pl.* **-knives** /-naɪvz/) (*also* **pock·et·knife** *especially in NAmE*) a small knife with one or more blades that fold down into the handle 小折刀 ➲ VISUAL VOCAB PAGE V21

pen·man·ship /ˈpenmənʃɪp/ *noun* [U] (*formal*) the art of writing by hand; skill in doing this 书写艺术；书法；书写技巧

ˈ**pen name** *noun* a name used by a writer instead of their real name 笔名 SYN **nom de plume** ➲ COMPARE PSEUDONYM

pen·nant /ˈpenənt/ *noun* **1** a long narrow pointed flag, for example one used on a ship to give signals （船上用作信号等的）三角旗 **2** (in the US 美国) a flag given to the winning team in a sports league, especially in BASEBALL （奖给棒球等联赛优胜队的）锦旗

pen·ni·less /ˈpeniləs/ *adj.* having no money; very poor 一文不名的；穷困的 SYN **destitute** ➲ SYNONYMS AT POOR

penn'orth /ˈpenəθ; *NAmE* -nərθ/ *noun* [usually sing.] (*old-fashioned, BrE*) = PENNYWORTH

Penn·syl·va·nia Dutch /ˌpensɪlveɪniə ˈdʌtʃ/ *noun* **1 the Pennsylvania Dutch** [pl.] a group of people originally

P

from Germany and Switzerland who settled in Pennsylvania in the 17th and 18th centuries 德裔宾州人（17 至 18 世纪定居在宾夕法尼亚州的德国人和瑞士人后裔） **2** [U] a type of German mixed with English spoken by the Pennsylvania Dutch 宾州德语（德裔宾州人讲的德语与英语的混合语）

penny /ˈpeni/ *noun* (*pl.* **pen·nies** or **pence**) HELP In senses 1 and 2, **pennies** is used to refer to the coins, and **pence** to refer to an amount of money. In sense 3, the plural is **pennies**. 在第 1 及第 2 义中，pennies 指硬币，pence 指款额。在第 3 义中，复数形式为 pennies。 **1** (*abbr.* **p**) a small British coin and unit of money. There are 100 pence in one pound (£1). 便士（英国的小硬币和货币单位，1 英镑为 100 便士）: *He had a few pennies in his pocket.* 他口袋里有几个便士的硬币。◇ *That will be 45 pence, please.* 一共是 45 便士。◇ *They cost 20p each.* 这些东西每个要 20 便士。 **2** (*abbr.* **d**) a British coin in use until 1971. There were twelve pennies in one SHILLING. 便士（英国 1971 年前使用的硬币，十二便士为一先令） **3** (*NAmE*) a cent 分

IDM **ˌevery ˈpenny** all of the money 所有的钱；每一分钱: *We collected £700 and every penny went to charity.* 我们募集了 700 英镑，悉数捐给了慈善机构。 **ˌin for a ˈpenny, ˌin for a ˈpound** (*saying*) used to say that since you have started to do sth, it is worth spending as much time or money as you need to in order to complete it 一不做，二不休；有始有终 **not a ˈpenny** no money at all 分文没有；根本不用钱: *It didn't cost a penny.* 那东西没花一分钱。 **the ˈpenny drops** (*informal, especially BrE*) used to say that sb has finally understood or realized sth that they had not understood or realized before 恍然大悟；终于明白；茅塞顿开 **a ˌpenny for your ˈthoughts | a penny for them** (*saying*) used to ask sb what they are thinking about（用于询问别人想什么）你在呆呆地寻思什么呢 **turn up like a bad ˈpenny** (*informal*) (of a person 人) to appear when they are not welcome or not wanted, especially when this happens regularly（不愿碰上的）却总出现；冤家路窄 **ˌtwo/ˌten a ˈpenny** (*BrE*) (*NAmE* **a ˌdime a ˈdozen**) very common and therefore not valuable 普通得不值钱；（因常见而）价值低 ➲ MORE AT PINCH *v.*, PRETTY *adj.*, SPEND *v.*

ˌpenny ˈblack *noun* an old British stamp worth one penny, first used in 1840. It was the first stamp in the world that could be stuck to an envelope. 黑便士（英国 1840 年首次发行的 1 便士邮票，是世界上第一枚可粘贴在信封上的邮票）

ˌpenny-ˈfarthing *noun* (*BrE*) an early type of bicycle with a very large front wheel and a very small back wheel 早期的自行车（前轮大，后轮小）

ˈpenny-pinching *adj.* (*disapproving*) unwilling to spend money 吝啬的；悭吝的；小气的 SYN **mean** ▸ **ˈpenny-pinching** *noun* [U]

ˌpenny ˈwhistle *noun* = TIN WHISTLE

penny·worth /ˈpeniwɜːθ; *NAmE* -wɜːrθ/ *noun* [sing.] (*old-fashioned, BrE*) as much as you can buy with a penny; a small amount of sth 值一便士的量；少量；些许

IDM **put in your two ˈpennyworth** (*also* **put in your two ˈpenn'orth**) (*both BrE*) (*NAmE* **put in your two ˈcents' worth**) (*informal*) to give your opinion about sth, even if other people do not want to hear it 发表意见（即使别人不想听）

pen·ology /piːˈnɒlədʒi; pɪ-; *NAmE* -ˈnɑːl-/ *noun* [U] the scientific study of the punishment of criminals and the operation of prisons 刑罚学；监狱管理学 ▸ **pen·olo·gist** /piːˈnɒlədʒɪst; pɪ-; *NAmE* -ˈnɑːl-/ *noun*

ˈpen pal (*especially NAmE*) (*BrE also* **pen·friend**) *noun* a person that you make friends with by writing letters, often sb you have never met 笔友

ˈpen-pusher (*especially BrE*) (*NAmE usually* **ˈpencil pusher**) *noun* (*informal, disapproving*) a person with a boring job, especially in an office, that involves a lot of writing 抄写匠；文书

ˈpen scanner *noun* a small device in the shape of a pen, which you move over text to copy it so that it can be stored on a computer 笔式扫描器；扫描笔

pen·sion¹ /ˈpenʃn/ *noun, verb* ➲ SEE ALSO PENSION²

■ *noun* an amount of money paid regularly by a government or company to sb who is considered to be too old or too ill/sick to work 养老金；退休金；抚恤金: *to receive an old-age/a retirement pension* 领养老金 / 退休金 ◇ *a disability/widow's pension* 残疾 / 遗孀抚恤金 ◇ *a state pension* 国家抚恤金 ◇ *to live on a pension* 靠退休金生活 ◇ *to take out a personal/private pension* 获得个人 / 私人抚恤金 ◇ *a pension fund* 退休金基金 ➲ COLLOCATIONS AT AGE, FINANCE

■ *verb*

PHR V **ˌpension sb ˈoff** (*especially BrE*) [usually passive] to allow or force sb to retire and to pay them a pension 准许某人退休，强迫某人退休（并发给养老金）: *He was pensioned off and his job given to a younger man.* 他被迫退休，工作交给了一个比他年轻的人。 ◇ (*informal, figurative*) *That car of yours should have been pensioned off years ago.* 你那辆汽车早就该报废了。

pen·sion² /ˈpɒ̃sjɒ̃; *NAmE* pɑːnsiˈoʊn/ *noun* (*from French*) a small, usually cheap, hotel in some European countries, especially France（欧洲，尤指法国的）廉价小旅店 ➲ SEE ALSO PENSION¹ *n.*

pen·sion·able /ˈpenʃənəbl/ *adj.* giving sb the right to receive a pension 有权享受养老金（或抚恤金、退休金）的: *people of pensionable age* 达到领养老金年龄的人 ◇ *pensionable pay* 可供计算退休金的薪酬

pen·sion·er /ˈpenʃənə(r)/ *noun* (*especially BrE*) a person who is receiving a pension, especially from the government 领养老金（或退休金、抚恤金）者: *an old-age pensioner* 领养老金的人 ➲ SEE ALSO OAP, SENIOR CITIZEN ➲ WORDFINDER NOTE AT OLD

ˈpension plan (*BrE usually* **ˈpension scheme**) (*NAmE also* **reˈtirement plan**) *noun* a system in which you, and usually your employer, pay money regularly into a fund while you are employed. You are then paid a PENSION¹ when you retire. 退休金计划，养老金计划（通常雇员与雇主定期缴款，雇员退休后可领取退休金）

pen·sive /ˈpensɪv/ *adj.* thinking deeply about sth, especially because you are sad or worried 沉思的；忧伤的；忧戚的: *a pensive mood* 沉重的心情 ◇ *to look pensive* 神情忧伤 ▸ **pen·sive·ly** *adv.*

penta- /ˈpentə/ *combining form* (in nouns, adjectives and adverbs 构成名词、形容词和副词) five; having five 五；五…的: *pentagon* 五边形 ◇ *pentathlon* 现代五项运动

penta·gon /ˈpentəgən; *NAmE* -gɑːn/ *noun* **1** [C] (*geometry* 几何) a flat shape with five straight sides and five angles 五边形；五角形 ➲ PICTURE AT POLYGON **2 the Pentagon** [sing.] the building near Washington DC that is the HEADQUARTERS of the US Department of Defense and the military leaders 五角大楼（指美国国防部）: *a spokesman for the Pentagon* 美国国防部发言人

pen·tagon·al /penˈtægənl/ *adj.* (*geometry* 几何) having five sides 五边形的；五角形的

penta·gram /ˈpentəgræm/ *noun* a flat shape of a star with five points, formed by five straight lines. Pentagrams are often used as magic symbols. 五角星形（常用于象征魔力）

pen·tam·eter /penˈtæmɪtə(r)/ *noun* [C, U] (*specialist*) a line of poetry with five stressed syllables; the rhythm of poetry with five stressed syllables to a line 五音步诗行；五音步诗律

pent·ath·lon /penˈtæθlən/ *noun* a sporting event in which people compete in five different sports (running, riding, swimming, shooting and FENCING) 现代五项运动，五项全能运动（赛跑、骑马、游泳、射击、击

P

剑） ➲ COMPARE BIATHLON, DECATHLON, HEPTATHLON, TRIATHLON

penta·tonic /ˌpentəˈtɒnɪk; *NAmE* -ˈtɑːn-/ *adj.* (*music* 音) related to or based on a SCALE of five notes 五声音阶的；五音的

Pente·cost /ˈpentɪkɒst; *NAmE* -kɔːst; -kɑːst/ *noun* [U, C] **1** (*BrE also* ˌ**Whit** ˈ**Sunday**) (in the Christian Church) the 7th Sunday after Easter when Christians celebrate the Holy Spirit coming to the APOSTLES 圣灵降临节，五旬节（基督教节日，在复活节后的第 7 个星期日） **2** = SHAVUOTH

Pente·cos·tal /ˌpentɪˈkɒstl; *NAmE* -ˈkɔːs-; -ˈkɑːs-/ *adj.* connected with a group of Christian Churches that emphasize the gifts of the Holy Spirit, such as the power to heal the sick 五旬节派的（强调神恩作用，如治病的能力） ▶ **Pente·costal·ism** /ˌpentɪˈkɒstəlɪzəm; *NAmE* -ˈkɔːs-; -ˈkɑːs-/ *noun* [U] **Pente·costal·ist** *noun*

pent·house /ˈpenthaʊs/ *noun* an expensive and comfortable flat/apartment or set of rooms at the top of a tall building 顶层豪华公寓；阁楼套房

pent-up /ˌpent ˈʌp/ *adj.* **1** (of feelings, energy, etc. 感情、精力等) that cannot be expressed or released 压抑的；积压的： *pent-up frustration/energy* 郁积的挫折感；被抑制的精力 **2** having feelings that you cannot express 感情抑郁的；难以抒怀的： *She was too pent-up to speak.* 她闷闷不乐，不想说话。

pen·ul·ti·mate /penˈʌltɪmət/ *adj.* [only before noun] immediately before the last one 倒数第二的 **SYN** **next/second to last**： *the penultimate chapter/day/stage* 倒数第二章 / 天 / 阶段

pen·um·bra /pəˈnʌmbrə/ *noun* (*specialist*) **1** an area of shadow which is between fully dark and fully light（黑暗与光明之间的）半影 **2** (*astronomy* 天) the shadow made by the earth or the moon during a PARTIAL ECLIPSE（偏食期间的）半影 ➲ COMPARE UMBRA

pen·uri·ous /pəˈnjʊəriəs; *NAmE* -ˈnʊr-/ *adj.* (*formal*) very poor 贫穷的；穷困的；赤贫的 **SYN** **destitute, penniless**

pen·ury /ˈpenjəri/ *noun* [U] (*formal*) the state of being very poor 贫困；贫穷 **SYN** **poverty**

peon /ˈpiːən/ *noun* **1** a worker on a farm in Latin America（拉丁美洲的）农场工人 **2** (*NAmE*, *humorous*) a person with a hard or boring job that is not well paid and not considered important 苦力；苦工

peony /ˈpiːəni/ *noun* (*pl.* **-ies**) a garden plant with large round white, pink or red flowers 牡丹；芍药

people 🔑 /ˈpiːpl/ *noun, verb*

■ *noun* **1** 🔑 [pl.] persons; men, women and children 人： *At least ten people were killed in the crash.* 至少有十人在撞车事故中丧生。◇ *There were a lot of people at the party.* 有许多人参加聚会。◇ *Many young people are out of work.* 很多年轻人失业。 **2** 🔑 [pl.] persons in general or everyone 人们；大家： *He doesn't care what people think of him.* 他不在乎人们怎样看他。◇ *She tends to annoy people.* 她的举止往往惹人烦。 **HELP** Use **everyone** or **everybody** instead of 'all people'. 用everyone或everybody，不用all people。 **3** 🔑 [C] all the persons who live in a particular place or belong to a particular country, race, etc.（统称）人民，国民；民族；种族： *the French people* 法国人 ◇ *the native peoples of Siberia* 西伯利亚原住民 ➲ SEE ALSO TOWNSPEOPLE **4** 🔑 **the people** [pl.] the ordinary men and women of a country rather than those who govern or have a special position in society 平民；百姓；大众： *the life of the common people* 普通人的生活 ◇ *It was felt that the government was no longer in touch with the people.* 人们觉得政府已脱离了民众。 ➲ SEE ALSO LITTLE PEOPLE (1) **5** 🔑 [pl.] men and women who work in a particular type of job or are involved in a particular area of activity（统称某行业或领域的）人： *a meeting with business people and bankers* 与商界和银行界人士的会晤 ◇ *These garments are intended for professional sports people.* 这些服装是为专业运动员制作的。 **6** [pl.] (*literary*) the men, women and children that a person leads 国民；人民；臣民；群众： *The king urged his people to prepare for war.* 国王呼吁臣民准备作战。 **7** [pl.] the men and women who work for you or support you 雇员；支持者；下属人员： *I've had my people watching the house for a few days.* 我让佣人照看了几天房子。 **8** [pl.] (*informal*) guests or friends 客人；朋友： *I'm having people to dinner this evening.* 今晚我在家里宴请客人。 **9** [pl.] (*old-fashioned*) the men, women and children that you are closely related to, especially your parents, grandparents, etc. 家人；亲人；家属；（尤指）父母，祖父母： *She's spending the holidays with her people.* 她正与家人一起度假。 ➲ SEE ALSO BOAT PEOPLE, STREET PEOPLE, TRADESPEOPLE

IDM **of 'all people** when you say **of all people**, you are emphasizing that sb is the person you would most or least expect to do sth（在所有的人中）偏偏，唯有： *She of all people should know the answer to that.* 在所有的人中，她是最应知道那个问题的答案的。 **people (who live) in glass houses shouldn't throw 'stones** (*saying*) you should not criticize other people, because they will easily find ways of criticizing you 身居玻璃房，投石招祸殃；自身毛病多，勿挑他人错 ➲ MORE AT MAN *n.*, THING

■ *verb* [usually passive] **~ sth** (**with sth**) to live in a place or fill it with people 居住在；把…挤满人；住满居民： *The town was peopled largely by workers from the car factory and their families.* 这个镇上的居民大部分都是汽车厂的工人及其家属。◇ *The ballroom was peopled with guests.* 舞厅里满堂宾客。

'people carrier (*also* **'people mover**) (*both BrE*) (*NAmE*, *BrE* **mini·van, Mini Van™**) *noun* a large car, like a van, designed to carry up to eight people 小型面包车；（八人）小客车 ➲ VISUAL VOCAB PAGE V56

'people person *noun* (*informal*) a person who enjoys, and is good at, being with and talking to other people 喜欢（或擅长）交际的人

Pe·oria /piˈɔːriə/ *noun* a small city in the US state of Illinois. The opinions of the people who live there are considered to be typical of opinions in the whole of the US. 皮奥里亚（美国伊利诺伊州小城，据信此地居民的观点在美国很有代表性）： *Ask yourself what the folks in Peoria will think of it.* 想一想皮奥里亚的人会如何看待这件事。

pep /pep/ *verb, noun*

■ *verb* (**-pp-**)

PHR V ˌ**pep sb/sth↔'up** (*informal*) to make sb/sth more interesting or full of energy 增加…的趣味；使兴致勃勃；激励；使活跃 **SYN** **liven up**： *Pep up meals by adding more unusual spices.* 加些特别的调料使饭菜味道更佳。◇ *A walk in the fresh air will pep you up.* 在清新空气中散散步会使你精神振奋。

■ *noun* [U] energy and enthusiasm 精力；活力；热情

pep·per 🔑 /ˈpepə(r)/ *noun, verb*

■ *noun* **1** 🔑 [U] a powder made from dried BERRIES (called PEPPERCORNS), used to give a hot flavour to food 胡椒粉： *Season with* ***salt and pepper*** 用盐和胡椒粉调味 ◇ *freshly* ***ground pepper*** 新研磨的胡椒粉 ➲ SEE ALSO BLACK PEPPER, CAYENNE, WHITE PEPPER **2** (*BrE*) (*also* ˌ**sweet 'pepper** *BrE, NAmE*) (*NAmE* **'bell pepper**) [C, U] a hollow fruit, usually red, green or yellow, eaten as a vegetable either raw or cooked 甜椒；柿子椒；灯笼椒 ➲ VISUAL VOCAB PAGE V34

■ *verb* **~ sth** to put pepper on food（在食物上）撒胡椒粉： *peppered steak* 撒了胡椒粉的牛排 ◇ *Salt and pepper the potatoes.* 给土豆放上盐和胡椒粉。

PHR V **'pepper sb/sth with sth** [usually passive] to hit sb/sth with a series of small objects, especially bullets（以小物体）频繁击打；（尤指）向…不断射击 **SYN** **spray** **'pepper sth with sth** [often passive] to include large numbers of sth in sth 大量加入： *He peppered his speech with jokes.* 他在讲演中插入了许多笑话。

ˌ**pepper-and-'salt** (*also* ˌ**salt-and-'pepper**) *adj.* (especially of hair 尤指头发) having two colours that are

P

mixed together, especially a dark colour and a light one 两色相间的；（尤指）深浅色相间的，花白的

pep·per·corn /ˈpepəkɔːn; *NAmE* -pərkɔːrn/ *noun* a dried BERRY from a tropical plant, that is crushed to make pepper 胡椒粒；干胡椒籽 ⊃ VISUAL VOCAB PAGE V35

ˌpeppercorn ˈrent *noun* (*BrE*) a very low rent 极低的租金；象征性租金

pep·per·mint /ˈpepəmɪnt; *NAmE* -pərm-/ *noun* **1** [U] a type of MINT (= a plant used to give flavour to food that produces an oil with a strong flavour) 胡椒薄荷；薄荷 ⊃ COMPARE SPEARMINT **2** [C] a sweet/candy flavoured with peppermint oil 薄荷糖

pep·per·oni /ˌpepəˈrəʊni; *NAmE* -ˈroʊ-/ *noun* [U] a type of spicy SAUSAGE 意大利辣肉肠：*a pepperoni pizza* 辣香肠比萨饼

ˈpepper pot (*especially BrE*) (*NAmE usually* **ˈpepper shaker**) *noun* a small container with holes in the top, used for putting pepper on food 胡椒瓶 ⊃ VISUAL VOCAB PAGE V23

pep·pery /ˈpepəri/ *adj.* **1** tasting of pepper 胡椒味的；辣的 **2** bad-tempered 脾气不好的；爱发火的：*a peppery old man* 脾气暴躁的老头儿

ˈpep pill *noun* (*informal*) a pill containing a drug that gives you more energy or makes you happy for a short time 兴奋药丸

peppy /ˈpepi/ *adj.* (**pep·pier**, **pep·pi·est**) (*informal, especially NAmE*) lively and full of energy or enthusiasm 生机勃勃的；精力充沛的；满腔热情的：*a peppy advertising jingle* 热情洋溢的广告歌

ˈpep rally *noun* (*NAmE, informal*) a meeting of school students before a sports event to encourage support for the team （竞赛前的）动员会，誓师集会：(*figurative*) *The Democrats held a pep rally on Capitol Hill yesterday.* 民主党昨天在国会山召开了竞选誓师大会。

pep·sin /ˈpepsɪn/ *noun* [U] (*biology* 生) a substance in the stomach that breaks down PROTEINS in the process of DIGESTION 胃蛋白酶

ˈpep talk *noun* (*informal*) a short speech intended to encourage sb to work harder, try to win, have more confidence, etc. 激励的话；鼓舞士气的话

pep·tic ulcer /ˌpeptɪk ˈʌlsə(r)/ *noun* an ULCER in the DIGESTIVE SYSTEM, especially in the stomach 消化性溃疡；（尤指）胃溃疡

pep·tide /ˈpeptaɪd/ *noun* (*chemistry* 化) a chemical consisting of two or more AMINO ACIDS joined together 肽

per 🔑 /pə(r); *strong form* pɜː(r)/ *prep.* used to express the cost or amount of sth for each person, number used, distance travelled, etc. 每；每一：*Rooms cost £50 per person, per night.* 房价每人每晚 50 英镑。◇ *60 miles per hour* 每小时 60 英里

IDM **as per sth** following sth that has been decided 按照；依据：*The work was carried out as per instructions.* 工作是按指示进行的。 **as per ˈnormal/ˈusual** (*informal*) in the way that is normal or usual; as often happens 照常；按惯例；一如既往：*Everyone blamed me as per usual.* 大家照例是责怪我。

per·am·bu·la·tion /pəˌræmbjuˈleɪʃn/ *noun* [C] (*formal or humorous*) a slow walk or journey around a place, especially one made for pleasure 漫步；散步；遛弯；兜风 ▸ **per·am·bu·late** /pəˈræmbjuleɪt/ *verb* [I, T] ~ (**sth**)

per·am·bul·ator /pəˈræmbjuleɪtə(r)/ *noun* **1** (*specialist*) a device consisting of a wheel on a long handle, which is pushed along the ground to measure distances 测距仪 **2** (*old-fashioned, BrE*) = PRAM

per annum /pər ˈænəm/ *adv.* (*abbr.* **p.a.**) (*from Latin*) for each year 每年：*earning £30 000 per annum* 每年赚 3 万英镑

per·cale /pəˈkeɪl; *NAmE* pərˈkeɪl/ *noun* [U] a type of cotton or POLYESTER cloth used for making sheets 高级密织棉布（用以制作被单）

per cap·ita /pə ˈkæpɪtə; *NAmE* pər/ *adj., adv.* (*from Latin*) for each person 每人的；人均的：*Per capita income rose sharply last year.* 去年人均收入猛增。◇ *average earnings per capita* 人均收益

per·ceive AW /pəˈsiːv; *NAmE* pərˈs-/ *verb* (*formal*) **1** to notice or become aware of sth 注意到；意识到；察觉到：**~ sth** *I perceived a change in his behaviour.* 我注意到他举止有些改变。◇ **~ that…** *She perceived that all was not well.* 她意识到一切都不顺利。◇ **~ sb/sth to be/have sth** *The patient was perceived to have difficulty in breathing.* 发现病人呼吸困难。 HELP This pattern is usually used in the passive. 此句型通常用于被动语态。 **2** to understand or think of sb/sth in a particular way 将…理解为；将…视为；认为 SYN see：**~ sb/sth/yourself (as sth)** *This discovery was perceived as a major breakthrough.* 这一发现被视为一项重大突破。◇ *She did not perceive herself as disabled.* 她没有把自己看成残疾人。◇ **~ sb/sth to be/have sth** *They were widely perceived to have been unlucky.* 人们普遍认为他们的运气不佳。 HELP This pattern is usually used in the passive. 此句型通常用于被动语态。

> **WORD FAMILY**
> **perceive** *verb*
> **perception** *noun*
> **perceptive** *adj.*
> **perceptible** *adj.*
> (≠ imperceptible)

per cent 🔑 (*especially BrE*) (*NAmE usually* **per·cent**) /pə ˈsent; *NAmE* pər ˈsent/ (*symb.* **%**) *noun, adj., adv.*

■ ***noun*** 🔑 (*pl.* **per cent**, **per·cent**) one part in every hundred 百分之…：*Poor families spend about 80 to 90 per cent of their income on food.* 贫困家庭大约花费收入的 80% 到 90% 购买食物。◇ *It is often stated that we use only 10 per cent of our brain.* 常有报告称人只运用了大脑的 10%。◇ *What per cent of the population is/are overweight?* 体重超重的人占人口多大的百分比？

> ▼ **GRAMMAR POINT 语法说明**
>
> **expressing percentages**
>
> - Percentages (= numbers of per cent) are written in words as *twenty-five per cent* and in figures as *25%*. 百分比用文字表示为 twenty-five per cent，用数字表示为 25%。
> - If a percentage is used with an uncountable or a singular noun the verb is generally singular. 百分比与不可数名词或单数名词连用时，动词一般为单数：*90% of the land is cultivated.* * 90% 的土地为可耕地。
> - If the noun is singular but represents a group of people, the verb is singular in *NAmE* but in *BrE* it may be singular or plural. 如果是单数集合名词，美式英语动词用单数，英式英语用单、复数均可：*Eighty per cent of the work force* ***is/are*** *against the strike.* 百分之八十的劳动力都反对这次罢工。
> - If the noun is plural, the verb is plural. 如果名词为复数，动词用复数：*65% of children* ***play*** *computer games.* * 65% 的孩子玩电脑游戏。

■ ***adj., adv.*** 🔑 by, in or for every hundred 每一百中：*a 15 per cent rise in price* 价格上扬 15%◇ *House prices rose five per cent last year.* 去年房价上涨了百分之五。

per·cent·age AW /pəˈsentɪdʒ; *NAmE* pərˈs-/ *noun* **1** [C+sing./pl. v.] the number, amount, rate of sth, expressed as if it is part of a total which is 100; a part or share of a whole 百分率；百分比：*What percentage of the population is/are overweight?* 身体超重的人占人口多大的百分比？◇ *A high percentage of the female staff are part-time workers.* 女职员中，兼职工作的人占很高的比例。◇ *Interest rates are expected to rise by one* ***percentage point*** (= a unit of one per cent). 利率预计提高一个百分点。◇ *Tax rates fell by 3.4 percentage points.* 税率下降了 3.4 个百分点。◇ *The figure is* ***expressed as a percentage.*** 数字是用百分率表示的。◇ *The results were analysed* ***in***

P

percentage terms. 结果是按百分比分析的。 **2** [C, usually sing.] a share of the profits of sth 利润的分成；提成： *He gets a percentage for every car sold.* 他每售出一辆车便可得到一份提成。

per·cent·ile /pəˈsentaɪl; *NAmE* pərˈs-/ *noun* (*specialist*) one of the 100 equal groups that a larger group of people can be divided into, according to their place on a scale measuring a particular value 百分位数： *Overall these students rank in the 21st percentile on the tests—that is, they did worse than 79 per cent of all children taking the test.* 这些考生的总体百分位排名占第 21 位。就是说，79% 的应试儿童比他们考得好。

per·cep·tible /pəˈseptəbl; *NAmE* pərˈs-/ *adj.* **1** (*formal*) great enough for you to notice it 可察觉到的；看得出的 **SYN** **noticeable**： *a perceptible change/increase/decline/impact* 可以察觉的变化 / 增长 / 下降 / 影响 ◇ *The price increase has had no perceptible effect on sales.* 这次提价没有对销售产生明显的影响。◇ *Her foreign accent was* ***barely perceptible.*** 她的外国口音几乎听不出来。 **2** (*specialist*) that you can notice or feel with your senses 可感知的；可感觉的： *the perceptible world* 可感知的世界 **OPP** **imperceptible** ▸ **per·cep·tibly** /-əbli/ *adv.*： *Income per head rose perceptibly.* 人均收入明显提高了。◇ *It was perceptibly colder.* 天气明显地冷了。

per·cep·tion **AW** /pəˈsepʃn; *NAmE* pərˈs-/ *noun* **1** [U] (*specialist* or *formal*) the way you notice things, especially with the senses 知觉；感知： *our perception of reality* 我们对现实的认识 ◇ *visual perception* 视觉 ➲ SEE ALSO EXTRASENSORY PERCEPTION **2** [U] (*formal*) the ability to understand the true nature of sth 洞察力；悟性 **SYN** **insight**： *She showed great perception in her assessment of the family situation.* 她对家庭状况的分析显示出敏锐的洞察力。 **3** [U, C] (*formal*) an idea, a belief or an image you have as a result of how you see or understand sth 看法；见解： *a campaign to change public perception of the police* 改变警察公众形象的运动 ◇ **~ that…** *There is a general public perception that standards in schools are falling.* 公众普遍认为，学校的水平都在下降。

per·cep·tive /pəˈseptɪv; *NAmE* pərˈs-/ *adj.* **1** (*approving*) having or showing the ability to see or understand things quickly, especially things that are not obvious 理解力强的；有洞察力的；思维敏捷的： *a* ***highly perceptive*** *comment* 见地高明的评论 ◇ *It was very perceptive of you to notice that.* 你能注意到此事，真够敏锐的。 **2** (*specialist* or *formal*) connected with seeing, hearing and understanding 感知的；视觉的；听觉的；感觉的；知觉的： *our innate perceptive abilities* 我们天生的五官感觉能力 ▸ **per·cep·tive·ly** *adv.* **per·cep·tive·ness** *noun* [U]

per·cep·tual /pəˈseptʃuəl; *NAmE* pərˈs-/ *adj.* [only before noun] (*specialist*) relating to the ability to PERCEIVE things or the process of PERCEIVING 知觉的；感知的： *perceptual skills* 知觉技能

perch /pɜːtʃ; *NAmE* pɜːrtʃ/ *verb, noun*

■ *verb* **1** [I] **~ (on sth)** (of a bird 鸟) to land and stay on a branch, etc. 栖息；停留： *A robin was perching on the fence.* 一只知更鸟落在篱笆上。 **2** [I, T] (*informal*) to sit or to make sb sit on sth, especially on the edge of it （使）坐，坐在…边沿： **~ (on sth)** *We perched on a couple of high stools at the bar.* 我们坐在酒吧的几张高脚凳上。◇ **~ sb/yourself (on sth)** *She perched herself on the edge of the bed.* 她坐在床沿上。 ➲ SYNONYMS AT SIT **3** [I] **~ (on sth)** to be placed on the top or the edge of sth 置于（顶上或边上）： *The hotel perched precariously on a steep hillside.* 旅店立在陡峭的山坡上状似摇摇欲坠。

■ *noun* **1** a place where a bird rests, especially a branch or bar for this purpose, for example in a bird's CAGE （鸟的）栖息处，栖木 **2** a high seat or position 高座；高处： *He watched the game from his precarious perch on top of the wall.* 他无视安全，高坐在墙头上观看比赛。 **3** (*pl.* **perch**) a FRESHWATER fish that is sometimes used for food 鲈鱼；河鲈 **IDM** SEE KNOCK *v.*

per·chance /pəˈtʃɑːns; *NAmE* pərˈtʃæns/ *adv.* (*old use*) perhaps 也许；可能

perched /pɜːtʃt; *NAmE* pɜːrtʃt/ *adj.* **~ on, etc. sth** **1** (especially of a bird 尤指鸟) sitting or resting on sth 栖息；停留： *There was a bird perched on the roof.* 有一只鸟落在屋顶上。 **2** placed in a high and/or dangerous position 被置于高处（或危险处）： *a hotel perched high on the cliffs* 高高矗立在悬崖上的旅馆

per·cipi·ent /pəˈsɪpiənt; *NAmE* pərˈs-/ *adj.* (*formal*) having or showing the ability to understand things, especially things that are not obvious 敏锐的；理解透彻的；明察秋毫的 **SYN** **perceptive**

per·co·late /ˈpɜːkəleɪt; *NAmE* ˈpɜːrk-/ *verb* **1** [I] (+ **adv./prep.**) (of a liquid, gas, etc. 液体、气体等) to move gradually through a surface that has very small holes or spaces in it 渗入；渗透；渗漏： *Water had percolated down through the rocks.* 水从岩缝间渗漏下去。 **2** [I] to gradually become known or spread through a group or society 逐渐流传；传开： *It had percolated through to us that something interesting was about to happen.* 我们听到传言说，将要发生一件有趣的事。 **3** [T, I] **~ (sth)** to make coffee in a percolator; to be made in this way （用渗滤式咖啡壶）滤煮；滤煮咖啡 ▸ **per·co·la·tion** /ˌpɜːkəˈleɪʃn; *NAmE* ˌpɜːrk-/ *noun* [U]

per·co·la·tor /ˈpɜːkəleɪtə(r); *NAmE* ˈpɜːrk-/ *noun* a pot for making coffee, in which boiling water is forced up a central tube and then comes down again through the coffee 渗滤式咖啡壶

per·cus·sion /pəˈkʌʃn; *NAmE* pərˈk-/ *noun* **1** [U] musical instruments that you play by hitting them with your hand or with a stick, for example drums 打击乐器；敲击乐器： *percussion instruments* 打击乐器 ◇ *The track features Joey Langton* ***on percussion.*** 唱片的这段乐曲的打击乐部分是由乔伊 • 兰顿演奏的。 ➲ VISUAL VOCAB PAGE V37 **2 the percussion** [sing.] (*also* **perˈcussion section** [C]) the players of percussion instruments in an ORCHESTRA （管弦乐团的）打击乐器组 ➲ COMPARE BRASS (2), STRING *n.* (5), WOODWIND

per·cus·sion·ist /pəˈkʌʃənɪst; *NAmE* pərˈk-/ *noun* a person who plays percussion instruments 打击乐器演奏员

per·cus·sive /pəˈkʌsɪv; *NAmE* pərˈk-/ *adj.* (*specialist*) connected with sounds made by hitting things, especially PERCUSSION instruments 打击声的；打击乐器声的

per·cu·tan·eous /ˌpɜːkjuːˈteɪniəs; *NAmE* ˌpɜːrk-/ *adj.* (*medical* 医) made or done through the skin 经皮的；通过皮肤的： *a percutaneous injection* 皮下注射

per diem /ˌpɜː ˈdiːem; *NAmE* ˌpɜːr/ *adj., noun* (*from Latin, especially NAmE*)

■ *adj.* [only before noun] (of money 钱) for each day 每日的；按日计的： *a per diem allowance* 每日津贴 ▸ **per diem** *adv.*： *He agreed to pay at specified rates per diem.* 他同意每天按规定的数额付款。

■ *noun* [U, C] money paid, for example to employees, for things they need to buy every day 日补贴；日津贴： *He will get $14 000 a year in per diem to help with the higher costs of living in Washington.* 他每年将得到 14 000 美元的日补贴，以弥补华盛顿较高的生活费。

per·di·tion /pɜːˈdɪʃn; *NAmE* pɜːrˈd-/ *noun* [U] (*formal*) punishment that lasts for ever after death 永劫不复；堕入地狱

pere·grin·ation /ˌperəɡrɪˈneɪʃn/ *noun* [usually pl.] (*literary* or *humorous*) a journey, especially a long slow one （尤指漫长而缓慢的）旅程

pere·grine /ˈperɪɡrɪn/ (*also* ˌ**peregrine ˈfalcon**) *noun* a grey and white BIRD OF PREY (= a bird that kills other creatures for food) that can be trained to hunt for sport 游隼

per·emp·tor·ily /pəˈremptrəli/ *adv.* (*formal, disapproving*) in a way that allows no discussion or refusal 专横地；霸道地；不容商量地： *She peremptorily rejected the request.* 她断然拒绝了请求。

P

per·emp·tory /pəˈremptəri/ *adj.* (*formal, disapproving*) (especially of sb's manner or behaviour 尤指态度、举止) expecting to be obeyed immediately and without question or refusal 强硬的；强制的；不容分辩的： *a peremptory summons* 强制性传票 ◇ *The letter was peremptory in tone.* 信中的语气强硬。

per·en·nial /pəˈreniəl/ *adj., noun*

■ ***adj.*** **1** continuing for a very long time; happening again and again 长久的；持续的；反复出现的： *the perennial problem of water shortage* 缺水这个老问题 ◇ *that perennial favourite, hamburgers* 汉堡包，永远受人喜爱的食品 **2** (of plants 植物) living for two years or more 多年生的 ► **per·en·ni·al·ly** /-niəli/ *adv.*： *a perennially popular subject* 长年的热门话题

■ ***noun*** any plant that lives for more than two years 多年生植物 ➲ COMPARE ANNUAL *n.* (2), BIENNIAL *n.*

per·fect *adj., verb, noun*

■ ***adj.*** /ˈpɜːfɪkt; *NAmE* ˈpɜːrf-/ **1** having everything that is necessary; complete and without faults or weaknesses 完备的；完美的；完全的： *in perfect condition* 状况极佳 ◇ *a perfect set of teeth* 一副完美的牙齿 ◇ *Well I'm sorry—but **nobody's perfect*** (= used when sb has criticized you). 呃，对不起。不过，人无完人嘛。 **2** completely correct; exact and accurate 完全正确的；准确的；地道的： *She speaks perfect English.* 她讲一口地道的英语。 ◇ *a **perfect copy/fit/match*** 精确的副本；绝对合身；天作之合 ◇ *What **perfect timing**!* 时机掌握得恰到好处！ ➲ SEE ALSO WORD-PERFECT **3** the best of its kind 优秀的；最佳的： *a **perfect example** of the painter's early style* 这位画家早期风格的典范 ◇ *the **perfect crime*** (= one in which the criminal is never discovered) 一桩无头案 **4** excellent; very good 极好的；很好的： *The weather was perfect.* 天气好极了。 ➲ SYNONYMS AT EXCELLENT **5** ~ **for sb/sth** exactly right for sb/sth 正合适 SYN **ideal**： *It was a perfect day for a picnic.* 那是野餐最理想的天气。 ◇ *She's the perfect candidate for the job.* 她是这项工作的最佳人选。 ◇ *'Will 2.30 be OK for you?' 'Perfect, thanks.'* "2:30 对你合适吗？" "正合适，谢谢。" **6** [only before noun] total; complete 全部的；完全的；纯然的： *I don't know him—he's a perfect stranger.* 我不认识他，他是百分之百的陌生人。 **7** (*grammar* 语法) connected with the form of a verb that consists of part of the verb *have* with the past participle of the main verb, used to express actions completed by the present or a particular point in the past or future （动词）完成时的，完成体的： *'I have eaten' is the present perfect tense of the verb 'to eat', 'I had eaten' is the past perfect and 'I will have eaten' is the future perfect.* * I have eaten 是动词 eat 的现在完成时；I had eaten 是过去完成时；I will have eaten 是将来完成时。 ➲ SEE ALSO FUTURE PERFECT, PAST PERFECT, PRESENT PERFECT IDM SEE PRACTICE *n.*, WORLD

■ ***verb*** /pəˈfekt; *NAmE* pərˈf-/ ~ **sth** to make sth perfect or as good as you can 使完善；使完美；使完备： *As a musician, she has spent years perfecting her technique.* 身为音乐家，她多年来不断在技艺上精益求精。

■ ***noun*** /ˈpɜːfɪkt; *NAmE* ˈpɜːrf-/ **the perfect** (*also* **the ˌperfect ˈtense**) [sing.] (*grammar* 语法) the form of a verb that expresses actions completed by the present or a particular point in the past or future, formed in English with part of the verb *have* and the past participle of the main verb （动词的）完成时（态） ➲ SEE ALSO FUTURE PERFECT, PAST PERFECT, PRESENT PERFECT

per·fec·tion /pəˈfekʃn; *NAmE* pərˈf-/ *noun* [U, sing.] **1** the state of being perfect 完善；完美： *physical perfection* 体格健全 ◇ *The fish was cooked **to perfection**.* 这鱼烹得恰到好处。 ◇ *The novel achieves a perfection of form that is quite new.* 小说的形式新颖完美。 ◇ *His performance was perfection* (= sth perfect). 他的表演真是炉火纯青。 **2** the act of making sth perfect by doing the final improvements 最后加工；完美；圆满： *They have been working on the perfection of the new model.* 他们一直在努力完善新型号。 IDM SEE COUNSEL *n.*

per·fec·tion·ist /pəˈfekʃənɪst; *NAmE* pərˈf-/ *noun* (*sometimes disapproving*) a person who likes to do things perfectly and is not satisfied with anything less 完美主义者；至善论者 ► **per·fec·tion·ism** /pəˈfekʃənɪzəm; *NAmE* pərˈf-/ *noun* [U]

per·fect·ly /ˈpɜːfɪktli; *NAmE* ˈpɜːrf-/ *adv.* **1** completely 完全地；非常；十分： *It's perfectly normal to feel like this.* 有这样的感觉是完全正常的。 ◇ *It's perfectly good as it is* (= it doesn't need changing). 现在这样已经非常好了。 ◇ *You **know perfectly well** what I mean.* 我的意思你是一清二楚的。 ◇ *To be **perfectly honest**, I didn't want to go anyway.* 说真心话，反正我不想去。 ◇ *He stood perfectly still until the danger had passed.* 他一动不动地站在那里，直到危险解除。 ◇ *'Do you understand?' 'Perfectly.'* "你明白吗？" "完全明白。" ◇ (*old-fashioned*) *How perfectly awful!* 简直是一塌糊涂！ **2** in a perfect way 完美地；完好地；圆满地： *The TV works perfectly now.* 这台电视机现在状况好极了。 ◇ *It fits perfectly.* 那正合适。

ˌperfect ˈpitch *noun* [U] (*music* 音) the ability to identify or sing a musical note correctly without the help of an instrument 绝对音高，绝对音感（指不须借助乐器准确识别或唱出音符的能力）

ˌperfect ˈstorm *noun* [sing.] (*especially NAmE*) an occasion when several bad things happen at the same time, creating a situation that could not be worse 祸不单行；屋漏偏逢连夜雨

per·fidi·ous /pəˈfɪdiəs; *NAmE* pərˈf-/ *adj.* (*literary*) that cannot be trusted 不可信任的；背叛的；不忠的 SYN **treacherous**

per·fidy /ˈpɜːfədi; *NAmE* ˈpɜːrf-/ *noun* [U] (*literary*) unfair treatment of sb who trusts you 背叛；背信弃义 SYN **treachery**

per·for·ate /ˈpɜːfəreɪt; *NAmE* ˈpɜːrf-/ *verb* ~ **sth** to make a hole or holes through sth 打孔；穿孔；打眼： *The explosion perforated his eardrum.* 爆炸震破了他的耳膜。 ◇ *a perforated line* (= a row of small holes in paper, made so that a part can be torn off easily) 齿孔线

per·for·ation /ˌpɜːfəˈreɪʃn; *NAmE* ˌpɜːrf-/ *noun* **1** [C, usually pl.] a small hole in a surface, often one of a series of small holes 齿孔： *Tear the sheet of stamps along the perforations.* 沿齿孔把邮票撕开。 **2** [U] (*medical* 医) the process of splitting or tearing in such a way that a hole is left 穿孔；穿通： *Excessive pressure can lead to perforation of the stomach wall.* 过大的压力会导致胃壁穿孔。

per·force /pəˈfɔːs; *NAmE* pərˈfɔːrs/ *adv.* (*old use* or *formal*) because it is necessary or cannot be avoided 必须；必定；势必 SYN **necessarily**

per·form /pəˈfɔːm; *NAmE* pərˈfɔːrm/ *verb* **1** [T] ~ **sth** to do sth, such as a piece of work, task or duty 做；履行；执行 SYN **carry out**： *to perform an experiment/a miracle/a ceremony* 做实验；创奇迹；举行仪式 ◇ *She performs an important role in our organization.* 她在我们的组织中发挥着重要的作用。 ◇ *This operation has never been performed in this country.* 这个国家从未做过这种手术。 ◇ *A computer can perform many tasks at once.* 电脑能同时执行多项任务。 **2** [T, I] ~ (**sth**) to entertain an audience by playing a piece of music, acting in a play, etc. 演出；表演： *to perform somersaults/magic tricks* 表演空翻 / 魔术 ◇ *The play was first performed in 2007.* 这部剧于 2007 年首次上演。 ◇ *I'd like to hear it performed live.* 我希望听现场演出。 ◇ *to perform on the flute* 吹奏长笛 ◇ *I'm looking forward to seeing you perform.* 我期待着看你演出。 ➲ WORDFINDER NOTE AT CONCERT **3** [I] ~ (**well/badly/poorly**) to work or function well or badly 工作，运转（好 / 不好）： *The engine seems to be performing well.* 发动机看起来运转良好。 ◇ *The company has been performing poorly over the past year.* 这家公司过去一年业绩欠佳。 IDM SEE MIRACLE

per·form·ance /pəˈfɔːməns; *NAmE* pərˈfɔːrm-/ *noun* **1** [C] the act of performing a play, concert or some other form of entertainment 表演；演出： *The performance starts at seven.* 演出七点开始。 ◇ *an evening performance* 晚场演出 ◇ *a performance of Ravel's String Quartet*

P

拉威尔弦乐四重奏的演出 ◇ *a series of performances by the Kirov Ballet* 基洛夫芭蕾舞团的系列演出 ◇ *one of the band's rare **live performances*** 那个乐队少见的一次现场演出 ➲ COLLOCATIONS AT MUSIC

WORDFINDER 联想词：cue, dresser, matinee, opening night, ovation, prompter, rehearsal, stage manager

2 [C] the way a person performs in a play, concert, etc. 艺术上的表现；演技：*She **gave the greatest performance** of her career.* 她做了演艺生涯中最精彩的表演。◇ *an Oscar-winning performance from Kate Winslet* 凯特·温斯莱特荣获奥斯卡奖的演出 ➲ COLLOCATIONS AT CINEMA **3** [U, C] how well or badly you do sth; how well or badly sth works 表现；性能；业绩；工作情况：*the country's economic performance* 国家的经济状况 ◇ *It was an impressive performance by the French team.* 那是法国队一次令人叹服的表现。◇ *The new management techniques aim to improve performance.* 新的管理技术旨在提高效率。◇ *He criticized the recent poor performance of the company.* 他批评公司近期业绩不佳。◇ ***high-performance*** (= very powerful) *cars* 高性能汽车 ◇ ***performance indicators*** (= things that show how well or badly sth is working) 性能指标 ➲ COMPARE PAY-FOR-PERFORMANCE, PERFORMANCE-RELATED **4** [U, sing.] (*formal*) the act or process of performing a task, an action, etc. 做；执行；履行：*She has shown enthusiasm in the performance of her duties.* 她在工作中表现出了热忱。◇ *He did not want **a repeat performance** of the humiliating defeat he had suffered.* 他不想让失败的耻辱重演。**5** [sing.] (*informal, especially BrE*) an act that involves a lot of effort or trouble, sometimes when it is not necessary (不必要的) 麻烦，忙乱 SYN **carry-on**：*It's such a performance getting the children off to school in the morning.* 早上打发孩子上学可要忙乱一阵子呢。

per'formance art *noun* [U] an art form in which an artist gives a performance, rather than producing a physical work of art 行为艺术（通过行为表现而非实物创作所展示的艺术形式）

per'formance-enhancing *adj.* [only before noun] (of a substance, especially a drug) that people take so that they will be more successful in a sports competition (尤指药物) 兴奋性的 (以提高在体育竞赛的表现)：*steroids and other performance-enhancing drugs* 类固醇等兴奋剂

per,formance-re'lated *adj.* [only before noun] depending on how well a person does their job 基于工作表现的；按绩效的：*Is there any evidence that **performance-related pay** actually improves performance?* 是否有证据表明绩效工资确实会提高业绩？ ➲ COMPARE PAY-FOR-PERFORMANCE, PERFORMANCE (3)

per·forma·tive /pə'fɔːmətɪv; NAmE pər'fɔːrm-/ *adj.* (*grammar* 语法) when sb uses a performative word or expression, for example 'I promise' or 'I apologize', they are also doing sth (promising or apologizing) 表述行为的（如说 I promise 或 I apologize，同时表示许诺或道歉）➲ SEE ALSO CONSTATIVE

per·form·er /pə'fɔːmə(r); NAmE pər'fɔːrm-/ *noun* **1** a person who performs for an audience in a show, concert, etc. 表演者；演出者；演员：*a brilliant/polished/seasoned performer* 卓越的 / 优雅的 / 娴熟的表演者 **2** a person or thing that behaves or works in the way mentioned 表现得…者；表现了…者：*He was a poor performer at school and left with no qualifications.* 他在校学习成绩不好，没有毕业就离开学校。◇ *VW is the **star performer** of the motor industry this year.* 大众汽车在本年度汽车行业中出类拔萃。

the per,forming 'arts *noun* [pl.] arts such as music, dance and drama which are performed for an audience 表演艺术

per·fume /'pɜːfjuːm; NAmE pər'fjuːm/ *noun, verb*

■ *noun* [C, U] **1** a liquid, often made from flowers, that you put on your skin to make yourself smell nice 香水：*a bottle of expensive perfume* 一瓶昂贵的香水 ◇ *We stock a wide range of perfumes.* 我们备有各种各样的香水。◇ *the perfume counter of the store* 商店的香水柜台 ◇ *She was wearing too much perfume.* 她喷了太多的香水。**2** a pleasant, often sweet, smell 芳香；香味；馨香 SYN **scent**：*the heady perfume of the roses* 玫瑰扑鼻的香味

■ *verb* [often passive] **1 ~ sth (with sth)** (*literary*) (especially of flowers 尤指花) to make the air in a place smell pleasant 使香气弥漫 SYN **scent**：*The garden was perfumed with the smell of roses.* 花园里弥漫着玫瑰的芳香。**2 ~ sth (with sth)** to put perfume in or on sth 在…上洒香水；抹香水：*She perfumed her bath with fragrant oils.* 她沐浴时在浴缸内洒了些芳香油。▶ **per·fumed** *adj.*：*perfumed soap* 香皂

per·fumery /pə'fjuːməri; NAmE pər'f-/ *noun* (*pl.* **-ies**) **1** [C] a place where perfumes are made and/or sold 香水制造厂；香水商店 **2** [U] the process of making perfume 香水制造

per·func·tory /pə'fʌŋktəri; NAmE pər'f-/ *adj.* (*formal*) (of an action 行为) done as a duty or habit, without real interest, attention or feeling 敷衍的；例行公事般的；潦草的：*a perfunctory nod/smile* 敷衍的点头 / 微笑 ◇ *They only made a perfunctory effort.* 他们只是敷衍了事。▶ **per·func·tor·ily** /-trəli/ *adv.*：*to nod/smile perfunctorily* 漫不经心地点头 / 微笑

per·gola /'pɜːɡələ; NAmE 'pɜːrɡ-/ *noun* an ARCH in a garden/yard with a frame for plants to grow over and through 花架；蔓藤架 ➲ VISUAL VOCAB PAGE V20

per·haps /pə'hæps; præps; NAmE pər'h-/ *adv.* **1** possibly 可能；大概；也许 SYN **maybe**：*'Are you going to come?' 'Perhaps. I'll see how I feel.'* "你来不来？" "也许来。要看我身体情况了。" ◇ *Perhaps he's forgotten.* 也许是他忘掉了。**2** used when you want to make a statement or opinion less definite (表示不确定) 也许，可能：*This is perhaps his best novel to date.* 这也许是他迄今最好的小说。**3** used when making a rough estimate (用于粗略的估计) 或许，可能：*a change which could affect perhaps 20% of the population* 一项可能影响 20% 的人口的改革 **4** used when you agree or accept sth unwillingly, or do not want to say strongly that you disapprove (表示勉强同意或其实不赞成) 也许，大概：*'You could do it yourself.' 'Yeah, perhaps.'* "你可以自己做。" "嗯，也许吧。" **5** used when making a polite request, offer or suggestion (用于委婉的请求、主动承诺或提出建议) 也许，如果：*Perhaps*

▼ **LANGUAGE BANK** 用语库

perhaps

Making an opinion sound less definite 以不确定的语气表达意见

- *Most cybercrime involves traditional crimes, such as theft and fraud, being committed in new ways. Phishing is **perhaps/possibly/probably** the best-known example of this.* 大多数网络犯罪都包含盗窃、诈骗等传统犯罪，只是犯罪的方式有了新的变化。网络钓鱼大概是这类犯罪中最著名的例子。
- *It **seems/appears** that the more personal data which organizations collect, the more opportunity there is for this data to be lost or stolen.* 看来各种机构收集的个人资料越多，这些资料丢失或被盗的可能性就越大。
- ***It seems clear that** introducing national ID cards would do little to prevent identity theft.* 看来很明显的是，采用全国通用身份证对防止身份盗用起不了什么作用。
- ***It could be argued that** the introduction of national ID cards might actually make identity theft easier.* 可以说采用全国通用身份证实际上可能使身份盗用更容易。
- ***It is possible that/It may be that** the only way to protect ourselves against DNA identity theft is to avoid the creation of national DNA databases.* 或许保护自己免遭 DNA 身份盗用的唯一途径就是不要建立全国 DNA 数据库。

➲ LANGUAGE BANK AT IMPERSONAL, OPINION

it would be better if you came back tomorrow. 如果你明天回来，也许更好。◇ *I think perhaps you've had enough to drink tonight.* 我想今晚你已经喝得够多了。

per·igee /ˈperɪdʒiː/ *noun* (*astronomy* 天) the point in the ORBIT of the moon, a planet or other object in space when it is nearest the planet, for example the earth, around which it turns 近地点（绕地运动的天体轨道上离地心最近点）➲ COMPARE APOGEE (2)

peril /ˈperəl/ *noun* (*formal* or *literary*) **1** [U] serious danger 严重危险：*The country's economy is now in grave peril.* 现在，这个国家的经济陷入了严重危机。 **2** [C, usually pl.] ~ (**of sth**) the fact of sth being dangerous or harmful 祸害；险情：*a warning about the perils of drug abuse* 对吸毒之害的警告

IDM **do sth at your** (**own**) **ˈperil** used to warn sb that if they do sth, it may be dangerous or cause them problems （警告对方）自冒风险

per·il·ous /ˈperələs/ *adj.* (*formal* or *literary*) very dangerous 危险的；艰险的 SYN **hazardous** ▸ **per·il·ous·ly** *adv.*：*We came* ***perilously close*** *to disaster.* 我们险些出了大乱子。

per·im·eter /pəˈrɪmɪtə(r)/ *noun* **1** the outside edge of an area of land （土地的）外缘，边缘：*Guards patrol the perimeter of the estate.* 保安人员在庄园四周巡逻。◇ *a* ***perimeter fence/track/wall*** 围绕四周的栅栏 / 小径 / 墙 **2** (*mathematics* 数) the total length of the outside edge of an area or a shape 周长 ➲ COMPARE CIRCUMFERENCE

peri·natal /ˌperɪˈneɪtl/ *adj.* (*specialist*) at or around the time of birth 围生期的；围产期的；临产的：*perinatal care* 围生期护理 ◇ *perinatal mortality* 围生期死亡率

peri·neum /ˌperɪˈniːəm/ *noun* (*pl.* **peri·nea** /-ˈniːə/) (*anatomy* 解) the area between the ANUS and the SCROTUM or VULVA 会阴

period 🔑 AW /ˈpɪəriəd; *NAmE* ˈpɪr-/ *noun*, *adv.*, *adj.*

▪ ***noun***

• **LENGTH OF TIME** 时间长度 **1** 🔑 a particular length of time 一段时间；时期：*a period of consultation/mourning/uncertainty* 磋商 / 哀悼 / 形势不明朗的期间 ◇ *The factory will be closed down over a 2-year period/a period of two years.* 这家工厂将在两年内关闭。◇ *This compares with a 4% increase for the same period last year.* 这个数字与去年同期的 4% 升幅相近。◇ *This offer is available for a* ***limited period*** *only.* 这项优惠仅在限期内有效。◇ *All these changes happened over* ***a period of time.*** 所有这些变化都是在一段时间内发生的。 ◇ *The aim is to reduce traffic at* ***peak periods.*** 目的是降低高峰时段的交通流量。◇ *You can have it for a* ***trial period*** (= in order to test it). 这东西你可以试用一段时间。 ➲ SEE ALSO COOLING-OFF PERIOD **2** 🔑 a length of time in the life of a particular person or in the history of a particular country （人生或国家历史的）阶段，时期，时代：*Which period of history would you most like to have lived in?* 你最喜欢生活在哪一个历史时期？◇ *the post-war period* 战后时期 ◇ *Like Picasso, she too had a blue period.* 和毕加索一样，她也有过一段以蓝色为主调的创作时期。◇ *Most teenagers go through a period of rebelling.* 大多数青少年都要经历一段叛逆期。 **3** (*geology* 地) a length of time which is a division of an ERA. A period is divided into EPOCHS. 纪（地质年代，代下分纪，纪下分世）：*the Jurassic period* 侏罗纪

• **LESSON** 课时 **4** any of the parts that a day is divided into at a school, college, etc. for study 节；学时；课：*'What do you have next period?' 'French.'* "你下一节是什么课？" "法语。" ◇ *a* ***free/study period*** (= for private study) 自习课

• **WOMAN** 妇女 **5** the flow of blood each month from the body of a woman who is not pregnant 月经；经期；例假：*period pains* 痛经 ◇ *monthly periods* 月经 ◇ *When did you last* ***have a period?*** 你上一次月经是什么时候？➲ COMPARE MENSTRUATION

• **PUNCTUATION** 标点 **6** (*NAmE*) (*BrE* ˌ**full ˈstop**) the mark (.) used at the end of a sentence and in some abbreviations, for example *e.g.* 句点；句号

▪ ***adv.*** (*especially NAmE*) (*BrE also* ˌ**full ˈstop**) (*informal*) used at the end of a sentence to emphasize that there is nothing more to say about a subject （用于句末，强调不再多说）到此为止，就是这话：*The answer is no, period!* 答复是不，不再说了！

▪ ***adj.*** [only before noun] having a style typical of a particular time in history 具有某个时代特征的：*period costumes/furniture* 代表某一时期的服装 / 家具

peri·od·ic AW /ˌpɪəriˈɒdɪk; *NAmE* ˌpɪriˈɑːdɪk/ (*also less frequent* **peri·od·ical** /ˌpɪəriˈɒdɪkl; *NAmE* ˌpɪriˈɑːd-/) *adj.* [usually before noun] happening fairly often and regularly 间发性的；定期的；周期的：*Periodic checks are carried out on the equipment.* 设备定期进行检查。 ▸ **peri·od·ic·al·ly** AW /-kli/ *adv.*：*Mailing lists are updated periodically.* 邮寄名单定期更新。

peri·od·ical AW /ˌpɪəriˈɒdɪkl; *NAmE* ˌpɪriˈɑːd-/ *noun* a magazine that is published every week, month, etc., especially one that is concerned with an academic subject （学术）期刊

the ˌ**periodic ˈtable** *noun* [sing.] (*chemistry* 化) a list of all the chemical elements, arranged according to their ATOMIC NUMBER 元素周期表

peri·odon·tal /ˌperiəˈdɒntl; *NAmE* -ˈdɑːn-/ *adj.* (*medical* 医) related to or affecting the parts of the mouth that surround and support the teeth 牙周的

peri·odon·titis /ˌperiədɒnˈtaɪtɪs; *NAmE* -dɑːn-/ (*BrE also* **pyor·rhoea**) (*NAmE also* **pyor·rhea**) *noun* [U] (*medical* 医) a condition in which the area around the teeth becomes sore and swollen, which may make the teeth fall out 牙周炎

ˈ**period piece** *noun* **1** a play, film/movie, etc. that is set in a particular period of history 古装戏剧（或电影等） **2** a decorative object, piece of furniture, etc. that was made during a particular period of history and is typical of that period 具有某个时代特征的装饰品（或家具等）

peri·pat·et·ic /ˌperipəˈtetɪk/ *adj.* (*formal*) going from place to place, for example in order to work 巡回工作的；流动的：*a peripatetic music teacher* 一名流动的音乐教师

per·iph·eral /pəˈrɪfərəl/ *adj.*, *noun*

▪ ***adj.*** **1** (*formal*) not as important as the main aim, part, etc. of sth 次要的；附带的：*peripheral information* 辅助信息 ◇ ~ **to sth** *Fund-raising is peripheral to their main activities.* 相对于他们的主要活动，筹集资金是次要的。 **2** (*specialist*) connected with the outer edge of a particular area 外围的；周边的：*the peripheral nervous system* 周围神经系统 ◇ *peripheral vision* 周边视觉 **3** (*computing* 计) (of equipment 设备) connected to a computer 与计算机相连的：*a peripheral device* 外围设备 ▸ **per·iph·er·al·ly** /pəˈrɪfərəli/ *adv.*

▪ ***noun*** (*computing* 计) a piece of equipment that is connected to a computer 外围设备；外部设备：*monitors, printers and other peripherals* 显示器、打印机及其他外围设备

per·iph·ery /pəˈrɪfəri/ *noun* [usually sing.] (*pl.* **-ies**) (*formal*) **1** the outer edge of a particular area 边缘；周围；外围：*industrial development* ***on the periphery of*** *the town* 城镇周边地区工业的发展 ◇ *The condition makes it difficult for patients to see objects at the periphery of their vision.* 这种病症使患者难于看见视觉边缘的物体。 **2** the less important part of sth, for example of a particular activity or of a social or political group 次要部分；次要活动；边缘：*minor parties* ***on the periphery of*** *American politics* 处于美国政治边缘的小党派

peri·phrasis /pəˈrɪfrəsɪs/ *noun* [U] **1** (*specialist*) the use of an indirect way of speaking or writing 迂回表达；迂说 **2** (*grammar* 语法) the use of separate words to express a GRAMMATICAL relationship, instead of verb endings, etc. 加词表达法，迂说法（非通过词缀等表示语法关系） ▸ **peri·phras·tic** /ˌperɪˈfræstɪk/ *adj.*

peri·scope /ˈperɪskəʊp; *NAmE* -skoʊp/ *noun* a device like a long tube, containing mirrors which enable the user to see over the top of sth, used especially in a SUBMARINE (= a ship that can operate underwater) to see above the surface of the sea 潜望镜

P

per·ish /ˈperɪʃ/ *verb* **1** [I] (*formal* or *literary*) (of people or animals 人或动物) to die, especially in a sudden violent way 死亡；暴死：*A family of four perished in the fire.* 一家四口死于此次火灾之中。 **2** [I] (*formal*) to be lost or destroyed 丧失；湮灭；毁灭：*Early buildings were made of wood and have perished.* 早期建筑物为木质结构，已经消失殆尽。 **3** [I, T] ~ (**sth**) (*BrE*) if a material such as rubber **perishes** or **is perished**, it becomes damaged, weaker or full of holes （使橡胶等）老化，脆裂

IDM ˌ**perish the** ˈ**thought** (*informal* or *humorous*) used to say that you find a suggestion unacceptable or that you hope that sth will never happen （用于拒绝一项建议或希望某事永不发生）没门儿，甭想了，下辈子吧：*Me get married? Perish the thought!* 我结婚？下辈子再说吧！

per·ish·able /ˈperɪʃəbl/ *adj.* (especially of food 尤指食物) likely to decay or go bad quickly 易腐烂的；易变质的：***perishable goods/foods*** 易腐烂变质的商品 / 食物

per·ish·ables /ˈperɪʃəblz/ *noun* [pl.] (*specialist*) types of food that decay or go bad quickly 易腐食物

per·ished /ˈperɪʃt/ *adj.* [not before noun] (*BrE, informal*) (of a person 人) very cold 极冷：*We were perished.* 我们冷极了。

per·ish·er /ˈperɪʃə(r)/ *noun* (*old-fashioned, BrE, informal*) a child, especially one who behaves badly 小孩；（尤指）淘气包，讨厌鬼

per·ish·ing /ˈperɪʃɪŋ/ *adj.* (*BrE, informal*) **1** extremely cold 冰冷的；酷寒的 **SYN** **freezing**：*It's perishing outside!* 外边冷极了。◇*I'm perishing!* 我都快冻死了！ **2** [only before noun] (*old-fashioned*) used to show that you are annoyed about sth 讨厌的；可恶的：*I've had enough of this perishing job!* 这讨厌的差事，我真受够了！

peri·stal·sis /ˌperɪˈstælsɪs/ *noun* [U] (*biology* 生) the wave-like movements of the INTESTINE, etc. caused when the muscles contract and relax （肠等的）蠕动

peri·ton·eum /ˌperɪtəˈniːəm/ *noun* (*pl.* **peri·ton·eums** or **peri·ton·ea** /-ˈniːə/) (*anatomy* 解) the MEMBRANE (= very thin layer of TISSUE) on the inside of the ABDOMEN that covers the stomach and other organs 腹膜

peri·ton·itis /ˌperɪtəˈnaɪtɪs/ *noun* [U] (*medical* 医) a serious condition in which the inside wall of the body becomes swollen and infected 腹膜炎

peri·win·kle /ˈperiwɪŋkl/ *noun* **1** [C, U] a small plant that grows along the ground 蔓长春花 **2** (*BrE also* **win·kle**) [C] a small SHELLFISH, like a SNAIL, that can be eaten 滨螺，蛾螺，玉黍螺（可食用）

per·jure /ˈpɜːdʒə(r); *NAmE* ˈpɜːrdʒ-/ *verb* ~ **yourself** (*law* 律) to tell a lie in court after you have sworn to tell the truth 作伪证；发假誓 ▸ **per·jurer** /ˈpɜːdʒərə(r); *NAmE* ˈpɜːrdʒ-/ *noun*

per·jury /ˈpɜːdʒəri; *NAmE* ˈpɜːrdʒ-/ *noun* [U] (*law* 律) the crime of telling a lie in court 伪证；伪誓；伪证罪

perk /pɜːk; *NAmE* pɜːrk/ *noun, verb*

■ ***noun*** (*also formal* **per·quis·ite**) [usually pl.] something you receive as well as your wages for doing a particular job （工资之外的）补贴，津贴，额外待遇：*Perks offered by the firm include a car and free health insurance.* 公司给予的额外待遇包括一辆汽车和免费健康保险。◇ (*figurative*) *Not having to get up early is just one of the perks of being retired.* 不必早起只是退休生活的好处之一。

■ ***verb***

PHR V ˌ**perk** ˈ**up** | ˌ**perk sb↔**ˈ**up** (*informal*) to become or to make sb become more cheerful or lively, especially after they have been ill/sick or sad （使）振奋，活跃，快活 **SYN** **brighten**：*He soon perked up when his friends arrived.* 朋友一来他就精神起来了。 ˌ**perk** ˈ**up** | ˌ**perk sth↔**ˈ**up** (*informal*) to increase, or to make sth increase in value, etc. 上扬；增加；使增值：*Share prices had perked up slightly by close of trading.* 收盘时股价略有上扬。 ˌ**perk sth↔**ˈ**up** (*informal*) to make sth more interesting, more attractive, etc. 使更有趣；使更诱人 **SYN** **liven up**：*ideas for perking up bland food* 给无味的食品增添味道的主意

perky /ˈpɜːki; *NAmE* ˈpɜːrki/ *adj.* (**perk·ier**, **perki·est**) (*informal*) cheerful and full of energy 高兴的；快活的；精力充沛的 ▸ **perki·ness** *noun* [U]

perm /pɜːm; *NAmE* pɜːrm/ *noun, verb*

■ ***noun*** a way of changing the style of your hair by using chemicals to create curls that last for several months 卷发；烫发：*to have a perm* 烫鬈发

■ ***verb*** ~ **sth** to give sb's hair a perm 烫（发）：*to have your hair permed* 烫鬈发 ◇ *a shampoo for permed hair* 适用于烫过的头发的洗发液 ➲ VISUAL VOCAB PAGE V65

perma·frost /ˈpɜːməfrɒst; *NAmE* ˈpɜːrməfrɔːst; ˈpɜːrməfrɑːst/ *noun* [U] (*specialist*) a layer of soil that is permanently frozen, in very cold regions of the world （寒带）永久冻土，永冻土，多年冻土

perma·link /ˈpɜːməlɪŋk; *NAmE* ˈpɜːr-/ *noun* a HYPERLINK that is always linked to the same electronic document, even if the document is replaced 永久链接，固定链接（固定指向同一电子文件）：*On my homepage you can click on the permalink to any of my blog posts.* 在我的主页，你可以点击永久链接连到我的任何一篇博文。

per·man·ence /ˈpɜːmənəns; *NAmE* ˈpɜːrm-/ (*also less frequent* **per·man·ency** /-nənsi/) *noun* [U] the state of lasting for a long time or for all time in the future 永久；持久性：*The spoken word is immediate but lacks permanence.* 口头之言便捷，但不持久。◇*We no longer talk of the permanence of marriage.* 如今，再没有人说婚姻要天长地久了。

per·man·ent 🔑 /ˈpɜːmənənt; *NAmE* ˈpɜːrm-/ *adj., noun*

■ ***adj.*** 🔑 lasting for a long time or for all time in the future; existing all the time 永久的；永恒的；长久的：*a permanent job* 固定工作 ◇ *permanent staff* 固定职工 ◇ *They are now living together on a permanent basis.* 他们现在是长期同住。 ◇ *The accident has not done any permanent damage.* 那场事故没有造成什么永久性损伤。◇*a permanent fixture* (= a person or an object that is always in a particular place) 固定于某处的人 / 东西 **OPP** **impermanent**, **temporary** ▸ **per·man·ent·ly** 🔑 *adv.*：*The stroke left his right side permanently damaged.* 中风使他的右半身永久受损。◇ *She had decided to settle permanently in France.* 她已经决定永久定居法国。

■ ***noun*** (*old-fashioned, NAmE*) = PERM

ˌ**Permanent** ˈ**Resident Card** *noun* an official card that shows that sb from another country is allowed to live and work in Canada （加拿大）永久居民卡

ˌ**Permanent** ˈ**Undersecretary** (*also* ˌ**Permanent** ˈ**Secretary**) *noun* (in Britain) a person of high rank in the CIVIL SERVICE, who advises a SECRETARY OF STATE （英国）常务次官 ➲ COMPARE UNDERSECRETARY (1)

ˌ**permanent** ˈ**wave** *noun* (*old-fashioned*) = PERM

perma·tan /ˈpɜːmətæn; *NAmE* ˈpɜːrmə-/ *noun* (*informal, humorous*) the brown skin colour that a person with pale skin gets from being in the sun, when they have this skin colour all year 持久古铜色（指晒黑后终年不退的肤色）

per·me·able /ˈpɜːmiəbl; *NAmE* ˈpɜːrm-/ *adj.* ~ (**to sth**) (*specialist*) allowing a liquid or gas to pass through 可渗透的；可渗入的：*The skin of amphibians is permeable to water.* 两栖动物的皮肤是透水的。◇ *permeable rocks* 渗透性岩石 **OPP** **impermeable** ▸ **per·mea·bil·ity** /ˌpɜːmiəˈbɪləti; *NAmE* ˌpɜːrm-/ *noun* [U]

per·me·ate /ˈpɜːmieɪt; *NAmE* ˈpɜːrm-/ *verb* (*formal*) **1** [T, I] (of a liquid, gas, etc. 液体、气体等) to spread to every part of an object or a place 渗透；弥漫；扩散：~ **sth** *The smell of leather permeated the room.* 屋子里弥漫着皮革的气味。◇ **+ adv./prep.** *rainwater permeating through the ground* 渗入地下的雨水 **2** [T, I] (of an idea, an influence, a feeling, etc. 思想、影响、感情等) to affect every part of sth 感染；传播；扩散：~ **sth** *a belief that permeates all levels of society* 深入社会各阶层的看法 ◇ **+ adv./prep.** *Dissatisfaction among the managers soon permeated down* *to members of the workforce.* 管理人员的不满情绪很快传染给了全体职工。 ▸ **per·me·ation** /ˌpɜːmiˈeɪʃn; *NAmE* ˌpɜːrm-/ *noun* [U] (*formal*)

per·mis·sible /pəˈmɪsəbl; *NAmE* pərˈm-/ *adj.* (*formal*) acceptable according to the law or a particular set of rules 容许的；许可的：*permissible levels of nitrates in water* 水中硝酸盐含量的容许度 ◇ ~ (**for sb**) (**to do sth**) *It is not permissible for employers to discriminate on grounds of age.* 资方不得以年龄为由歧视职工。

per·mis·sion /pəˈmɪʃn; *NAmE* pərˈm-/ *noun* **1** [U] the act of allowing sb to do sth, especially when this is done by sb in a position of authority 准许；许可；批准：~ (**for sth**) *You must* ***ask permission*** *for all major expenditure.* 一切重大开支均须报请批准。 ◇ ~ (**for sb/sth**) (**to do sth**) *The school has been refused permission to expand.* 学校扩充未得到许可。 ◇ *No official* ***permission*** *has been* ***given*** *for the event to take place.* 这项活动未得到正式批准，不能举行。 ◇ *She took the car* ***without permission.*** 她未经许可擅自使用了汽车。 ◇ *poems reprinted* ***by kind permission of*** *the author* 经作者惠允后重印的诗歌 ◇ (*formal*) *With your permission, I'd like to say a few words.* 如蒙允许，我想讲几句话。 **2** [C, usually pl.] an official written statement allowing sb to do sth 许可证；书面许可：*The publisher is responsible for obtaining the necessary permissions to reproduce illustrations.* 出版者负责取得准许复制插图的必要许可文件。 ➲ SEE ALSO PLANNING PERMISSION

▼ **EXPRESS YOURSELF 情景表达**

Asking for permission/a favour 请求允许或帮助

You are more likely to get what you want if you can ask for it politely. Here are some ways of asking whether you may do something. 礼貌的请求更可能达成愿望，以下是询问是否可以做某事的一些表达方式：

- ***Would you mind if*** *I opened the window?* 你会介意我开窗吗？
- ***Could I possibly*** *borrow your phone?* 我借你的电话用一下好吗？
- ***I hate to ask, but could I please*** *borrow your phone?* (*NAmE*) 冒昧打扰了，我能借你的电话用一下吗？
- ***Do you happen to have*** *a pair of gloves* ***I could borrow*** *for the evening?* 你有没有适合出席晚会的手套可以借给我？
- ***Would it be all right if*** *I left five minutes early?* 我提前五分钟离开可以吗？
- ***Is there any chance that we could*** *stay at your house the night before our flight?* 我们有没有可能在航班出发的前一天晚上住在你家？
- ***Would it be OK to*** *leave my bag here?* 我把包留在这儿行吗？

Responses 回应：

- ***Yes, of course.*** 好的。当然可以。
- ***Go ahead.*** 可以。
- ***That's fine.*** 没问题。
- ***I'd rather you didn't, if you don't mind.*** 如果你不介意的话，最好别这么做。
- ***I'd prefer it*** *if you asked somebody else.* 也许你问问别人更好。
- ***If there's someone else you can ask, I'd be grateful.*** 请您再问问其他人。

per·mis·sive /pəˈmɪsɪv; *NAmE* pərˈm-/ *adj.* allowing or showing a freedom of behaviour that many people do not approve of, especially in sexual matters 放任的；纵容的；姑息的；（尤指两性关系）放纵的：*permissive attitudes* 纵容的态度 ◇ *permissive parents* (= who allow their children a lot of freedom) 放任的父母 ▸ **per·mis·sive·ness** *noun* [U]

the perˌmissive soˈciety *noun* [sing.] (*often disapproving*) the changes towards greater freedom in attitudes and behaviour that happened in many countries in the 1960s and 1970s, especially the greater freedom in sexual matters 宽容社会，（尤指）性开放社会（20 世纪 60 和 70 年代出现在很多国家）

per·mit *verb, noun*

■ ***verb*** /pəˈmɪt; *NAmE* pərˈm-/ (**-tt-**) (*formal*) **1** [T] to allow sb to do sth or to allow sth to happen 允许；准许：~ **sth** *Radios are not permitted in the library.* 图书馆内不许使用收音机。 ◇ *There are fines for exceeding permitted levels of noise pollution.* 噪音超标会处以罚款。 ◇ ~ **sb/yourself sth** *We were not permitted any contact with each other.* 我们被禁止跟对方有任何接触。 ◇ *Jim permitted himself a wry smile.* 吉姆勉强苦笑了一下。 ◇ ~ **sb/yourself to do sth** *Visitors are not permitted to take photographs.* 参观者请勿拍照。 ◇ *She would not permit herself to look at them.* 她避免看他们。 ◇ (*formal*) *Permit me to offer you some advice.* 请允许我向你提些建议。 ➲ EXPRESS YOURSELF AT FORBID **2** [I, T] to make sth possible 允许；使有可能：*We hope to visit the cathedral, if time permits.* 如果时间允许，我们希望能参观一下主教座堂。 ◇ *I'll come tomorrow,* ***weather permitting*** (= if the weather is fine). 天气许可的话，我明天过来。 ◇ ~ **sth** *The password permits access to all files on the hard disk.* 这个密码可调出硬盘上的所有文档。 ◇ ~ **sb/sth to do sth** *Cash machines permit you to withdraw money at any time.* 取款机可让你随时取款。

■ ***noun*** /ˈpɜːmɪt; *NAmE* ˈpɜːrmɪt/ an official document that gives sb the right to do sth, especially for a limited period of time 许可证，特许证（尤指限期的）：*a* ***fishing/residence/parking, etc. permit*** 钓鱼、居住、停车等许可证 ◇ *to* ***apply for a permit*** 申请许可证 ◇ *to* ***issue a permit*** 签发许可证 ➲ SEE ALSO WORK PERMIT ➲ **MORE LIKE THIS** 21, page R27

per·mu·ta·tion /ˌpɜːmjuˈteɪʃn; *NAmE* ˌpɜːrm-/ *noun* [usually pl.] any of the different ways in which a set of things can be ordered 排列（方式）；组合（方式）；置换：*The possible permutations of x, y and z are xyz, xzy, yxz, yzx, zxy and zyx.* * x、y 和 z 的可能的组合方式为 xyz、xzy、yxz、yzx、zxy 和 zyx。

per·ni·cious /pəˈnɪʃəs; *NAmE* pərˈn-/ *adj.* (*formal*) having a very harmful effect on sb/sth, especially in a way that is gradual and not easily noticed 有害的，恶性的（尤指潜移默化地）

per·nick·ety /pəˈnɪkəti; *NAmE* pərˈn-/ (*especially BrE*) (*NAmE usually* **per·snick·ety**) *adj.* (*informal, disapproving*) worrying too much about unimportant details; showing this 爱挑剔的；吹毛求疵的 SYN **fussy**

per·or·ation /ˌperəˈreɪʃn/ *noun* (*formal*) **1** the final part of a speech in which the speaker gives a summary of the main points（讲话的）结尾，结论，总结 **2** (*disapproving*) a long speech that is not very interesting 冗长乏味的演说

per·ox·ide /pəˈrɒksaɪd; *NAmE* -ˈrɑːk-/ (*also* ˌ**hydrogen peˈroxide**) *noun* [U] a clear liquid used to kill bacteria and to BLEACH hair (= make it lighter) 过氧化物；过氧化氢；双氧水：*a woman with peroxide blonde hair* 漂染金发的女子

perp /pɜːp; *NAmE* pɜːrp/ *noun* (*NAmE, informal*) = PERPETRATOR：*The perp stole a police car and got away.* 那个罪犯偷了一辆警车逃跑了。

per·pen·dicu·lar /ˌpɜːpənˈdɪkjələ(r); *NAmE* ˌpɜːrp-/ *adj., noun*

■ ***adj.*** **1** ~ (**to sth**) (*specialist*) forming an angle of 90° with another line or surface; vertical and going straight up 垂直的；成直角的：*Are the lines perpendicular to each other?* 这些直线相互垂直吗？ ◇ *The staircase was almost perpendicular* (= very steep). 楼梯几乎成垂直的了。 **2** **Perpendicular** (*architecture* 建) connected with a style of ARCHITECTURE common in England in the 14th and 15th centuries 垂直式的（英格兰 14、15 世纪盛行的建筑风格）

■ ***noun*** **the perpendicular** [sing.] a line, position or direction that is exactly perpendicular 垂直线（或位置、方向）：*The wall is a little out of the perpendicular.* 墙壁有点倾斜。

P

per·pet·rate /ˈpɜːpətreɪt; *NAmE* ˈpɜːrp-/ *verb* (*formal*) to commit a crime or do sth wrong or evil 犯（罪）；做（错事）；干（坏事）：**~ sth** *to* **perpetrate** *a crime/fraud/ massacre* 犯罪；行骗；进行屠杀 ◇ **~ sth against/upon/ on sb** *violence perpetrated against women and children* 针对妇女和儿童的暴力行为 ▸ **per·pet·ra·tion** /ˌpɜːpəˈtreɪʃn; *NAmE* ˌpɜːrp-/ *noun* [U]

per·pet·ra·tor /ˈpɜːpətreɪtə(r); *NAmE* ˈpɜːrp-/ (*also NAmE, informal* **perp**) *noun* a person who commits a crime or does sth that is wrong or evil 作恶者；行凶者；犯罪者：*the perpetrators of the crime* 该项罪行的犯案者

per·pet·ual /pəˈpetʃuəl; *NAmE* pərˈp-/ *adj.* **1** [usually before noun] continuing for a long period of time without interruption 不间断的；持续的；长久的 **SYN** **continuous**：*the perpetual noise of traffic* 持续不断的交通噪声 ◇ *We lived for years in a perpetual state of fear.* 多年来我们一直生活在恐惧中。**2** [usually before noun] frequently repeated, in a way that is annoying 一再反复的；无尽无休的；没完没了的 **SYN** **continual**：*How can I work with these perpetual interruptions?* 打扰不断，让我怎么工作？ **3** [only before noun] (of a job or position 工作或职位) lasting for the whole of sb's life 终身的；永久的：*He was elected perpetual president.* 他被选为终身会长。◇ (*humorous*) *She's a perpetual student.* 她是个终身学习者。▸ **per·petu·al·ly** /-tʃuəli/ *adv.*

perˌpetual ˈmotion *noun* [U] a state in which sth moves continuously without stopping, or appears to do so 永动：*We're all in a state of* **perpetual motion** *in this office* (= we're always moving around or changing things). 我们这个办公室里大家总在忙得团团转。

per·petu·ate /pəˈpetʃueɪt; *NAmE* pərˈp-/ *verb* **~ sth** (*formal*) to make sth such as a bad situation, a belief, etc. continue for a long time 使永久化；使持久化；使持续：*to perpetuate injustice* 持续造成不公正 ◇ *This system perpetuated itself for several centuries.* 这一制度维持了几个世纪。◇ *Comics tend to perpetuate the myth that 'boys don't cry'.* 连环画往往在延续着"男儿有泪不轻弹"的神话。▸ **per·petu·ation** /pəˌpetʃuˈeɪʃn; *NAmE* pərˌp-/ *noun* [U]

per·petu·ity /ˌpɜːpəˈtjuːəti; *NAmE* ˌpɜːrpəˈtuː-/ *noun* [U] **IDM** **in perpetuity** (*formal*) for all time in the future 永远；永久 **SYN** **forever**：*They do not own the land in perpetuity.* 他们并不永久拥有这片土地。

per·plex /pəˈpleks; *NAmE* pərˈp-/ *verb* [usually passive] **~ sb | it perplexes sb that…** if sth **perplexes** you, it makes you confused or worried because you do not understand it 迷惑；使困惑 **SYN** **puzzle**：*They were perplexed by her response.* 她的答复令他们困惑不解。▸ **per·plex·ing** *adj.*：*a perplexing problem* 令人不解的问题

per·plexed /pəˈplekst; *NAmE* pərˈp-/ *adj.* confused and anxious because you are unable to understand sth; showing this 困惑的；迷惑不解的：*a perplexed expression* 困惑的表情 ◇ *She looked perplexed.* 她看来茫然若失。▸ **per·plex·ed·ly** /pəˈpleksɪdli; *NAmE* pərˈp-/ *adv.*

per·plex·ity /pəˈpleksəti; *NAmE* pərˈp-/ *noun* (*pl.* **-ies**) (*formal*) **1** [U] the state of feeling confused and anxious because you do not understand sth 困惑；迷惘 **SYN** **confusion**：*Most of them just stared at her in perplexity.* 他们多数人茫然地凝视着她。**2** [C, usually pl.] something that is difficult to understand 难以理解的事物；疑团：*the perplexities of life* 人生的困惑

ˈperp walk *noun* (*NAmE, informal*) the act of walking into or out of a police station, COURTHOUSE, etc., that the police force a person they have arrested to do, so that the media can show it to the public 罪犯示众（警方押解被拘捕者出入警察局、法庭等处，以便媒体公示）

per·quis·ite /ˈpɜːkwɪzɪt; *NAmE* ˈpɜːrk-/ *noun* (*formal*) **1** [usually pl.] = PERK **2** **~ (of sb)** something to which sb has a special right because of their social position 特权；利益：*Politics used to be the perquisite of the property-owning classes.* 政治曾经是有产阶级的特权。

perry /ˈperi/ *noun* [U, C] a slightly sweet alcoholic drink made from the juice of PEARS 梨酒 ➲ COMPARE CIDER

per se /ˌpɜː ˈseɪ; *NAmE* ˌpɜːr/ *adv.* (*from Latin*) used meaning 'by itself' to show that you are referring to sth on its own, rather than in connection with other things 本身；本质上：*The drug is not harmful per se, but is dangerous when taken with alcohol.* 这种药本身无害，但与酒同服就危险了。

per·se·cute /ˈpɜːsɪkjuːt; *NAmE* ˈpɜːrs-/ *verb* [often passive] **1 ~ sb (for sth)** to treat sb in a cruel and unfair way, especially because of their race, religion or political beliefs（因种族、宗教或政治信仰）迫害，残害，压迫：*Throughout history, people have been persecuted for their religious beliefs.* 人们因宗教信仰而受迫害的情况贯穿了整个历史。◇ *persecuted minorities* 被迫害的少数群体 ➲ WORDFINDER NOTE AT EQUAL **2 ~ sb** to deliberately annoy sb all the time and make their life unpleasant 骚扰；打扰；为…找麻烦 **SYN** **harass**：*Why are the media persecuting him like this?* 新闻媒体为什么总这样揪住他不放？ ▸ **per·se·cu·tion** /ˌpɜːsɪˈkjuːʃn; *NAmE* ˌpɜːrs-/ *noun* [U, C]：*the victims of religious persecution* 宗教迫害的受难者 ➲ COLLOCATIONS AT RACE

perseˈcution complex *noun* a type of mental illness in which sb believes that other people are trying to harm them 受迫害妄想症

per·se·cu·tor /ˈpɜːsɪkjuːtə(r); *NAmE* ˈpɜːrs-/ *noun* a person who treats another person or group of people in a cruel and unfair way 迫害者；残害者

per·se·ver·ance /ˌpɜːsɪˈvɪərəns; *NAmE* ˌpɜːrsəˈvɪr-/ *noun* [U] (*approving*) the quality of continuing to try to achieve a particular aim despite difficulties 毅力；韧性；不屈不挠的精神：*They showed great perseverance in the face of difficulty.* 他们面对困难表现了坚强的毅力。◇ *The only way to improve is through hard work and dogged perseverance.* 要更上一层楼，唯一的途径就是艰苦奋斗，不屈不挠。

per·se·vere /ˌpɜːsɪˈvɪə(r); *NAmE* ˌpɜːrsəˈvɪr/ *verb* [I] (*approving*) to continue trying to do or achieve sth despite difficulties 坚持；孜孜以求：**~ (in sth/in doing sth)** *Despite a number of setbacks, they persevered in their attempts to fly around the world in a balloon.* 虽屡遭挫折，他们仍不断尝试乘气球环游世界。◇ **~ (with sth/sb)** *She persevered with her violin lessons.* 她孜孜不倦地学习小提琴。◇ *You have to persevere with difficult students.* 对难教的学生你必须坚持诲人不倦的精神。

per·se·ver·ing /ˌpɜːsɪˈvɪərɪŋ; *NAmE* ˌpɜːrsəˈvɪrɪŋ/ *adj.* [usually before noun] (*approving*) showing determination to achieve a particular aim despite difficulties 坚韧不拔的；不屈不挠的

Per·sian /ˈpɜːʃn; -ʒn; *NAmE* ˈpɜːrʒn/ *noun* **1** [C] a person from ancient Persia, or modern Persia, now called Iran 波斯人 **2** (*also* **Farsi**) [U] the official language of Iran 波斯语 **3** [C] = PERSIAN CAT ▸ **Per·sian** *adj.*

ˌPersian ˈcarpet (*also* **ˌPersian ˈrug**) *noun* a carpet of traditional design from the Near East, made by hand from silk or wool 波斯地毯

ˌPersian ˈcat (*also* **Per·sian**) *noun* a breed of cat with long hair, short legs and a round flat face 波斯猫

per·si·flage /ˈpɜːsɪflɑːʒ; *NAmE* ˈpɜːrs-/ *noun* [U] (*formal*) comments and jokes in which people laugh at each other in a fairly unkind but not serious way 取笑；插科打诨

per·sim·mon /pəˈsɪmən; *NAmE* pərˈs-/ *noun* a sweet fruit that looks like a large orange tomato 柿子 ➲ VISUAL VOCAB PAGE V32

per·sist **AW** /pəˈsɪst; *NAmE* pərˈs-/ *verb* **1** [I, T] to continue to do sth despite difficulties or opposition, in a way that can seem unreasonable 顽强地坚持；执着地做：**~ (in doing sth)** *Why do you persist in blaming yourself for what happened?* 你何必为已发生的事没完没了地自责？ ◇ **~ (in sth)** *She persisted in her search for the truth.* 她执着地追求真理。◇ **~ (with sth)** *He persisted with his questioning.* 他问个不停。◇ **+ speech** *'So, did you agree or not?' he persisted.* "那么你同意了没有？"他叮问道。**2** [I] to continue to exist 维持；保持；持续存在： *If the symptoms persist, consult your doctor.* 如果症状持续，就去看医生。

per·sist·ence AW /pəˈsɪstəns; *NAmE* pərˈs-/ *noun* [U] **1** the fact of continuing to try to do sth despite difficulties, especially when other people are against you and think that you are being annoying or unreasonable 坚持；锲而不舍： *His persistence was finally rewarded when the insurance company agreed to pay for the damage.* 保险公司同意赔偿损失，他的坚持不懈终于得到了回报。◇ *It was her sheer persistence that wore them down in the end.* 最终把他们拖垮的是她的不屈不挠。 **2** the state of continuing to exist for a long period of time 持续存在；维持： *the persistence of unemployment in the 1970s and 1980s* * 20 世纪 70 年代和 80 年代的持续失业状况

per·sist·ent AW /pəˈsɪstənt; *NAmE* pərˈs-/ *adj.* **1** determined to do sth despite difficulties, especially when other people are against you and think that you are being annoying or unreasonable 执着的；不屈不挠的；坚持不懈的： *How do you deal with persistent salesmen who won't take no for an answer?* 你怎么对付那些志在必得、一直纠缠下去的推销员？ ◇ *a **persistent offender*** (= a person who continues to commit crimes after they have been caught and punished) 惯犯 **2** continuing for a long period of time without interruption, or repeated frequently, especially in a way that is annoying and cannot be stopped 连绵的；持续的；反复出现的 SYN **unrelenting**: *persistent rain* 阴雨连绵 ◇ *a persistent cough* 持续不断的咳嗽 ▶ **per·sist·ent·ly** AW *adv.*: *They have persistently denied claims of illegal dealing.* 他们一再否认进行非法交易的说法。 ◇ *persistently high interest rates* 居高不下的利率

per,sistent ,vegetative 'state *noun* (*medical* 医) a condition in which a person's body is kept working by medical means but the person shows no sign of brain activity 持续植物状态；植物人状态

per·snick·ety /pəˈsnɪkəti; *NAmE* pərˈs-/ *adj.* (*NAmE*) = PERNICKETY

per·son 🔑 /ˈpɜːsn; *NAmE* ˈpɜːrsn/ *noun* (*pl.* **people** /ˈpiːpl/) HELP The plural form **persons** is used in some formal language. 在某些正式用语中复数形式用 persons。 **1** 🔑 a human as an individual 人；个人： *What sort of person would do a thing like that?* 什么人会干那样的事呢？ ◇ *He's a fascinating person.* 他是个魅力十足的人。 ◇ *What is she like as a person?* 她的人品怎么样？ ◇ *He's just the person we need for the job.* 他正是我们需要的适合这项工作的人。 ◇ *I had a letter from the people who used to live next door.* 我接到了过去的邻居写来的一封信。 ◇ *I'm not really a city person* (= I don't really like cities). 我不是一个很喜欢城市生活的人。 ➲ SEE ALSO PEOPLE PERSON HELP Use **everyone** or **everybody** instead of 'all people'. 可用 everyone 或 everybody，不用 all people。 **2** 🔑 (*formal* or *disapproving*) a human, especially one who is not identified 人；某人： *A certain person* (= somebody that I do not wish to name) *told me about it.* 有人告诉了我这件事。 ◇ *The price is $40 per person.* 价格为每人 40 美元。 ◇ *This vehicle is licensed to carry 4 persons.* (= in a notice) 此车准乘 4 人。 ◇ (*law* 律) *The verdict was murder by a person or persons unknown.* 裁断是一人或多人谋杀，凶手身份未明。 ➲ SEE ALSO VIP **3** 🔑 **-person** (in compounds 构成复合词) a person working in the area of business mentioned; a person concerned with the thing mentioned 从事…工作（或担任…职务）的人；人员： *a salesperson* 推销员 ◇ *a spokesperson* 发言人 **4** (*grammar* 语法) any of the three classes of personal pronouns. The **first person** (*I/we*) refers to the person(s) speaking; the **second person** (*you*) refers to the person(s) spoken to; the **third person** (*he/she/it/they*) refers to the person(s) or thing(s) spoken about. 人称（第一人称 I / we 指说话人，第二人称 you 指听话的人，第三人称 he / she / it / they 指谈到的人或事物）

IDM **about/on your 'person** if you have or carry sth **about/on your person**, you carry it about with you, for example in your pocket 随身带着；身上有 **in 'person** 🔑 if you do sth **in person**, you go somewhere and do it yourself, instead of doing it by letter, asking sb else to do it, etc. 亲自；亲身 **in the person of sb** (*formal*) in the form or shape of sb 以某人的形骸；通过某人体现： *Help arrived in the person of his mother.* 来帮忙的是他的母亲。 ➲ MORE AT RESPECTER

per·sona /pəˈsəʊnə; *NAmE* pərˈsoʊnə/ *noun* (*pl.* **per·son·ae** /-niː; -naɪ/ or **per·so·nas**) (*formal*) the aspects of a person's character that they show to other people, especially when their real character is different 伪装；假象；人格面具： *His public persona is quite different from the family man described in the book.* 他的公开形象与书中描写的恋家男人相去甚远。 ➲ SEE ALSO DRAMATIS PERSONAE

per·son·able /ˈpɜːsənəbl; *NAmE* ˈpɜːrs-/ *adj.* (of a person 人) attractive to other people because of having a pleasant appearance and character 品貌兼优的；英俊潇洒的

per·son·age /ˈpɜːsənɪdʒ; *NAmE* ˈpɜːrs-/ *noun* (*formal*) an important or famous person 要人；名人： *a royal personage* 王室要人

per·son·al 🔑 /ˈpɜːsənl; *NAmE* ˈpɜːrs-/ *adj.*

• **YOUR OWN** 自己 **1** 🔑 [only before noun] your own; not belonging to or connected with anyone else 个人的；私人的： ***personal effects/belongings/possessions*** 私人物品 / 财产 / 财物 ◇ ***personal details*** (= your name, age, etc.) 个人基本资料 ◇ *Of course, this is just a personal opinion.* 当然了，这只是个人意见。 ◇ *Coogan has run a **personal best** of just under four minutes.* 库根跑出了刚好低于四分钟的个人最好成绩。 ◇ *The novel is written from **personal experience**.* 这部小说是根据个人亲身经历写成的。 ◇ *Use stencils to add a few **personal touches** to walls and furniture.* 用型板给墙壁和家具增添些个人风格。 ◇ *All hire cars are for **personal use** only.* 所有租赁车辆仅供个人使用。

• **FEELINGS/CHARACTER/RELATIONSHIPS** 感情；性格；关系 **2** 🔑 [only before noun] connected with individual people, especially their feelings, characters and relationships 人际的；个性的： *Having good **personal relationships** is the most important thing for me.* 拥有良好的人际关系对我最为重要。 ◇ *He was popular as much for his personal qualities as for his management skills.* 他的人品和他的管理技巧同样受到人们的喜爱。

• **NOT OFFICIAL** 非公事 **3** 🔑 not connected with a person's job or official position 私人的；私事的： *The letter was marked 'Personal'.* 信上标注着"私人"字样。 ◇ *I'd like to talk to you about a personal matter.* 我想和你谈点私事。 ◇ *I try not to let work interfere with my **personal life**.* 我尽量不让工作干扰我的私生活。 ◇ *She's a personal friend of mine* (= not just somebody I know because of my job). 她是我的私人朋友。

• **DONE BY PERSON** 本人做 **4** 🔑 [only before noun] done by a particular person rather than by sb who is acting for them 亲自做的： *The President made a personal appearance at the event.* 总统亲临现场。 ◇ *I shall give the matter my personal attention.* 我将亲自处理此事。

• **DONE FOR PERSON** 为个人 **5** 🔑 [only before noun] made or done for a particular person rather than for a large group of people or people in general 为某人做的；个别的： *We offer a **personal service** to all our customers.* 我们为所有顾客提供个人服务。 ◇ *a **personal pension plan*** (= a pension organized by a private company for one particular person) （私营公司的）个人养老金计划

• **OFFENSIVE** 冒犯 **6** 🔑 referring to a particular person's character, appearance, opinions, etc. in a way that is offensive 针对个人的；人身攻击的： *Try to avoid making personal remarks.* 要尽量避免针对个人的言论。 ◇ *There's no need to **get personal**!* 没有必要搞人身攻击嘛！ ◇ ***Nothing personal*** (= I do not wish to offend you), *but I do have to go now.* 我没有得罪之意，不过我现在不得不告辞了。

• **CONNECTED WITH BODY** 身体 **7** 🔑 [only before noun] connected with a person's body 人身的；身体的： ***personal cleanliness/hygiene*** 个人卫生

'personal ad *noun* a private advertisement in a newspaper, etc., especially from sb who is looking for a romantic or sexual partner （尤指交友或寻性伴侣的）私人广告

P

ˌ**personal alˈlowance** (*BrE*) (*NAmE* ˌ**personal exˈemption**) *noun* the amount of money you are allowed to earn each year before you have to pay INCOME TAX 个人免税额

ˌ**personal asˈsistant** *noun* ➲ PA (2)

ˌ**personal ˈbest** *noun* (*abbr.* **PB**) the best result that you have ever had in an event such as a race or other competition 个人最好成绩: *She won the race with a* ***personal best*** *of 2 minutes 22.* 她以 2 分 22 秒的个人最好成绩赢了比赛。

ˈ**personal column** *noun* a part of a newspaper or magazine for private messages or small advertisements （报刊的）私人广告栏

ˌ**personal comˈputer** *noun* (*abbr.* **PC**) a computer that is designed for one person to use at work or at home 个人电脑；个人计算机 ➲ COMPARE MICROCOMPUTER

ˈ**personal day** *noun* (*NAmE*) a day that you take off work for personal reasons, but not because you are ill/sick or on holiday/vacation （非病假或节假日的）事假日 ➲ COMPARE DUVET DAY

ˌ**personal exˈemption** (*NAmE*) (*BrE* ˌ**personal alˈlowance**) *noun* the amount of money you are allowed to earn each year before you have to pay INCOME TAX 个人免税额

ˌ**personal ˈinjury** *noun* [U] (*law* 律) physical injury, rather than damage to property or to sb's reputation 人身伤害；人身损害

per·son·al·ity 🔑 /ˌpɜːsəˈnæləti; *NAmE* ˌpɜːrs-/ *noun* (*pl.* **-ies**) **1** 🔑 [C, U] the various aspects of a person's character that combine to make them different from other people 性格；个性；人格: *His wife has a strong personality.* 他妻子的个性很强。◇ *The children all have very different personalities.* 孩子们的性格各不相同。◇ *He maintained order by sheer force of personality.* 他凭借强大的人格力量维护秩序。◇ *There are likely to be tensions and* ***personality clashes*** *in any social group.* 任何社会团体都容易出现关系紧张和性格冲突。 **2** 🔑 [U] the qualities of a person's character that make them interesting and attractive 魅力；气质；气度: *We need someone with lots of personality to head the project.* 我们需要一位富有魅力的人来主持这个项目。 **3** 🔑 [C] a famous person, especially one who works in entertainment or sport 名人，风云人物（尤指娱乐界或体育界的）**SYN** **celebrity**: *personalities from the world of music* 音乐界名流 ◇ *a* ***TV/sports personality*** 电视圈 / 体育界名人 **4** [C] a person whose strong character makes them noticeable 性格鲜明的人；有突出个性的人: *Their son is a real personality.* 他们的儿子真是有个性。 **5** [U] the qualities of a place or thing that make it interesting and different 特色；特征 **SYN** **character**: *The problem with many modern buildings is that they lack personality.* 许多现代建筑物的问题在于缺乏特色。

persoˈnality cult *noun* (*disapproving*) a situation in which people are encouraged to show extreme love and admiration for a famous person, especially a political leader 个人迷信；个人崇拜

persoˈnality disorder *noun* (*specialist*) a serious mental condition in which sb's behaviour makes it difficult for them to have normal relationships with other people or a normal role in society 人格障碍，性格障碍（有严重异常人格特质，以致难以与人正常交往或影响社会功能）

per·son·al·ize (*BrE also* **-ise**) /ˈpɜːsənəlaɪz; *NAmE* ˈpɜːrs-/ *verb* **1** [usually passive] **~ sth** to mark sth in some way to show that it belongs to a particular person 在…上标明主人姓名: *All the towels were personalized with their initials.* 所有毛巾上都标有物主姓名的首字母。 **2 ~ sth** to design or change sth so that it is suitable for the needs of a particular person 为个人特制（或专设）: *All our courses are personalized to the needs of the individual.* 我们的全部课程都是针对个人需要设计的。 **3 ~ sth** to refer to particular people when discussing a general subject 针对个人；个人化: *The mass media tends to personalize politics.* 大众传媒往往把政治个人化。 ▶ **per·son·al·ized, -ised** *adj.*: *a highly personalized service* 高度个性化的服务 ◇ (*BrE*) *a personalized number plate* (= on a car) 个性化的车牌

per·son·al·ly 🔑 /ˈpɜːsənəli; *NAmE* ˈpɜːrs-/ *adv.* **1** 🔑 used to show that you are giving your own opinion about sth 就本人而言；就个人意见: *Personally, I prefer the second option.* 就我个人而言，我倾向第二种选择。◇ *'Is it worth the effort?' 'Speaking personally, yes.'* "值得为它费功夫吗？" "就本人而言，值得。" **2** 🔑 by a particular person rather than by sb acting for them 本人；亲自: *All letters will be answered personally.* 一切信函都将由本人亲自答复。◇ *Do you know him personally* (= have you met him, rather than just knowing about him from other people)? 你本人认识他吗？ **3** 🔑 in a way that is connected with one particular person rather than a group of people 个别地；单个地 **SYN** **individually**: *He was personally criticized by inspectors for his incompetence.* 他因不称职而受到检查员的个别批评。◇ *You will be held personally responsible for any loss or breakage.* 如有丢失或损坏，将由你个人负责。 **4** 🔑 in a way that is intended to be offensive 无礼地；冒犯地: *I'm sure she didn't mean it personally.* 我相信她绝无冒犯之意。 **5** 🔑 in a way that is connected with sb's personal life rather than with their job or official position 私人地（与工作相对）: *Have you had any dealings with any of the suspects, either personally or professionally?* 你是否与任何嫌疑人有过私人或业务来往？
IDM **take sth ˈpersonally** to be offended by sth 认为某事针对自己而不悦: *I'm afraid he took your remarks personally.* 恐怕你的话激怒了他。

ˌ**personal ˈorganizer** (*BrE also* **-iser**) *noun* a small file with loose sheets of paper in which you write down information, addresses, what you have arranged to do, etc.; a very small computer for the same purpose 私人记事本；电子记事簿 ➲ SEE ALSO FILOFAX™

ˌ**personal ˈpronoun** *noun* (*grammar* 语法) any of the pronouns *I, you, he, she, it, we, they, me, him, her, us, them* 人称代词

ˌ**personal ˈshopper** *noun* a person whose job is to help sb else buy things, either by going with them around a shop/store or by doing their shopping for them （私人）购物助理，购物代理人

ˌ**personal ˈspace** *noun* [U] the space directly around where you are standing or sitting 个人空间（站立或坐着时与他人保持的距离范围）: *He leaned towards her and she stiffened at this invasion of her personal space.* 他向她俯过身去，这种侵犯她个人空间的举动让她绷紧了身子。

ˌ**personal ˈtrainer** *noun* a person who is paid by sb to help them exercise, especially by deciding what types of exercise are best for them 私人健身教练 ➲ WORDFINDER NOTE AT FIT

persona non grata /pɜːˌsəʊnə nɒn ˈɡrɑːtə; nəʊn; *NAmE* pɜːrˌsoʊnə nɑːn/ *noun* [U] (*from Latin*) a person who is not welcome in a particular place because of sth they have said or done, especially one who is told to leave a country by the government 不受欢迎的人（尤指遭政府驱逐出境的）

per·soni·fi·ca·tion /pəˌsɒnɪfɪˈkeɪʃn; *NAmE* pərˌsɑːn-/ *noun* **1** [C, usually sing.] **~ of sth** a person who has a lot of a particular quality or characteristic 体现某品质或特点的人；化身；典型 **SYN** **epitome**: *She was the personification of elegance.* 她是典雅的化身。 **2** [U, C] the practice of representing objects, qualities, etc. as humans, in art and literature; an object, quality, etc. that is represented in this way 拟人；人格化；拟人化的东西（或品质等）: *the personification of autumn in Keats's poem* 济慈诗歌中对秋天的拟人化

per·son·ify /pəˈsɒnɪfaɪ; *NAmE* pərˈsɑːn-/ *verb* (**per·soni·fies, per·soni·fy·ing, per·soni·fied**) **1 ~ sth** to be an example of a quality or characteristic, or to have a lot of it 是…的典型；集中表现 **SYN** **typify**: *These children* *personify all that is wrong with the education system.* 这些儿童充分体现了教育制度的缺陷。◇ *He is kindness personified.* 他是仁慈的化身。 **2** [usually passive] **~ sth (as sb)** to show or think of an object, quality, etc. as a person 拟人化；把…人格化：*The river was personified as a goddess.* 这条河被人格化为一位女神。

per·son·nel /ˌpɜːsəˈnel; *NAmE* ˌpɜːrs-/ *noun* **1** [pl.] the people who work for an organization or one of the armed forces （组织或军队中的）全体人员，职员：*skilled personnel* 熟练人员 ◇ ***sales/technical/medical/security/military, etc. personnel*** 推销、技术、医务、保安、军事等人员 **2** [U+sing./pl. v.] the department in a company that deals with employing and training people 人事部门 **SYN** **human resources**: *the personnel department/manager* 人事部门 / 经理 ◇ *She works in personnel.* 她在人事部工作。◇ *Personnel is/are currently reviewing pay scales.* 人事部现在正审核工资级别。

ˌperson'nel carrier *noun* a military vehicle for carrying soldiers 运兵车；士兵运输车

ˌperson-to-'person *adj.* [usually before noun] **1** happening between two or more people who deal directly with each other rather than through another person 人对人的；个人之间的：*Technical support is offered on a person-to-person basis.* 技术支持是向个人直接提供的。 **2** (*especially NAmE*) (of a telephone call 电话) made by calling the OPERATOR (= a person who works at a telephone exchange) and asking to speak to a particular person. If that person is not available, the call does not have to be paid for. 指定受话人的，叫人的（请接线员接通；如果指定受话人不在，可免交电话费）：*a person-to-person call* 叫人的电话

per·spec·tive **AW** /pəˈspektɪv; *NAmE* pərˈs-/ *noun* **1** [C] a particular attitude towards sth; a way of thinking about sth 态度；观点；思考方法 **SYN** **viewpoint**: *a global perspective* 全球的视角 ◇ *Try to see the issue **from** a different **perspective**.* 试以不同的角度看待这件事。◇ *a report that looks at the education system **from the perspective** of deaf people* 从聋人的角度看待教育制度的报告 ◇ **~ on sth** *His experience abroad provides a wider perspective on the problem.* 他在国外的经历使他以更广阔的视角看待这个问题。 **2** [U] the ability to think about problems and decisions in a reasonable way without exaggerating their importance 客观判断力；权衡轻重的能力：*She was aware that she was losing all sense of perspective.* 她意识到自己正在失掉一切正确判断的能力。◇ *Try to **keep** these issues **in perspective**.* 要尽量恰当地处理这些问题。◇ *Talking to others can often help to **put** your own problems **into perspective**.* 跟别人谈谈往往有助于正确处理自己的问题。◇ *It is important not to let things **get out of perspective**.* 重要的是不要把事情轻重倒置。 **3** [U] the art of creating an effect of depth and distance in a picture by representing people and things that are far away as being smaller than those that are nearer the front 透视法：*We learnt how to draw buildings **in perspective**.* 我们学习如何用透视法画建筑物。◇ *The tree on the left is **out of perspective**.* 左侧的树不成比例。 **4** [C] (*formal*) a view, especially one in which you can see far into the distance 景观；远景：*a perspective of the whole valley* 山谷全景

Per·spex™ /ˈpɜːspeks; *NAmE* ˈpɜːrs-/ (*BrE*) (*NAmE* **Plexiglas™**) *noun* [U] a strong transparent plastic material that is often used instead of glass 珀斯佩有机玻璃

per·spi·ca·cious /ˌpɜːspɪˈkeɪʃəs; *NAmE* ˌpɜːrs-/ *adj.* (*formal*) able to understand sb/sth quickly and accurately; showing this 敏锐的；有洞察力的；精辟的：*a perspicacious remark* 入木三分的评论 ▶ **per·spi·ca·city** /ˌpɜːspɪˈkæsəti; *NAmE* ˌpɜːrs-/ *noun* [U]

per·spir·ation /ˌpɜːspəˈreɪʃn; *NAmE* ˌpɜːrs-/ *noun* [U] **1** drops of liquid that form on your skin when you are hot 汗；汗珠 **SYN** **sweat**: *Beads of perspiration stood out on his forehead.* 他的前额上挂着汗珠。◇ *Her skin was damp with perspiration.* 她的皮肤上汗津津的。 **2** the act of perspiring 排汗；出汗：*Perspiration cools the skin in hot weather.* 热天出汗可使皮肤降温。

per·spire /pəˈspaɪə(r); *NAmE* pərˈs-/ *verb* [I] (*formal*) to produce sweat on your body 出汗；排汗；发汗 **SYN** **sweat**

per·suade /pəˈsweɪd; *NAmE* pərˈs-/ *verb* **1** to make sb do sth by giving them good reasons for doing it 劝说；说服：**~ sb to do sth** *Try to persuade him to come.* 尽量劝他来。◇ **~ sb** *Please try and persuade her.* 请尽力说服她。◇ *She's always easily persuaded.* 她向来禁不住劝。◇ *I'm sure he'll come with a bit of persuading.* 我相信，劝一劝他就会来的。◇ **~ sb into sth/into doing sth** *I allowed myself to be persuaded into entering the competition.* 我搁不住人家的劝说，就参加了比赛。 **2** to make sb believe that sth is true 使信服；使相信 **SYN** **convince**: **~ sb/yourself that…** *It will be difficult to persuade them that there's no other choice.* 很难让他们相信别无选择。◇ *She had persuaded herself that life was not worth living.* 她自认为人生没有价值。◇ **~ sb** *No one was persuaded by his arguments.* 没人相信他的论点。◇ **~ sb of sth** (*formal*) *I am still not fully persuaded of the plan's merits.* 我还不能完全信服这个计划的优点。

▼ **WHICH WORD?** 词语辨析

persuade / convince

- The main meaning of **persuade** is to make someone agree to do something by giving them good reasons for doing it. * persuade 的主要意思为说服、劝说：*I tried to persuade her to see a doctor.* 我极力劝她去看医生。 The main meaning of **convince** is to make someone believe that something is true. * convince 的主要意思为使确信、信服：*He convinced me he was right.* 他使我相信他是正确的。
- It is quite common, however, for each of these words to be used with both meanings, especially for **convince** to be used as a synonym for **persuade**. 不过，上述两词两种含义都用的情况相当普遍，尤其是 convince 常作同义词替代 persuade：*I persuaded/convinced her to see a doctor.* 我劝她去看医生。 Some speakers of *BrE* think that this is not correct. 有些说英式英语的人认为此用法不正确。

per·sua·sion /pəˈsweɪʒn; *NAmE* pərˈs-/ *noun* **1** [U] the act of persuading sb to do sth or to believe sth 说服；劝说：*It didn't take much persuasion to get her to tell us where he was.* 我们没费什么口舌就让她说出了他的下落。◇ *After a little gentle persuasion, he agreed to come.* 耐心劝说一下，他同意来了。◇ *She has great powers of persuasion.* 她的游说能力极强。 **2** [C, U] a particular set of beliefs, especially about religion or politics （宗教或政治）信仰：*politicians of all persuasions* 信仰各异的政治人物 ◇ *every shade of religious persuasion* 形形色色的宗教信仰

per·sua·sive /pəˈsweɪsɪv; *NAmE* pərˈs-/ *adj.* able to persuade sb to do or believe sth 有说服力的；令人信服的：*persuasive arguments* 令人信服的论点 ◇ *He can be very persuasive.* 他有时很会说服人。 ▶ **per·sua·sive·ly** *adv.*: *They argue persuasively in favour of a total ban on handguns.* 他们以雄辩的论据支持全面禁用手枪。 **per·sua·sive·ness** *noun* [U]

pert /pɜːt; *NAmE* pɜːrt/ *adj.* **1** (especially of a girl or young woman 尤指青少年女子) showing a lack of respect, especially in a cheerful and amusing way 无礼的；冒失的；轻佻的 **SYN** **impudent**: *a pert reply* 无礼的答复 **2** (of a part of the body 身体部位) small, firm and attractive 小巧玲珑的；诱人的；硬实的：*a pert nose* 小巧笔挺的鼻子 ◇ *pert features* 俊俏的面庞 ▶ **pert·ly** *adv.*

per·tain /pəˈteɪn; *NAmE* pərˈt-/ *verb* [I] (*formal*) to exist or to apply in a particular situation or at a particular time 存在；适用：*Living conditions are vastly different from those pertaining in their country of origin.* 生活条件与

P

他们的出生国大不相同。◇ *Those laws no longer pertain.* 那些法律已不适用了。

PHR V **per'tain to sth/sb** (*formal*) to be connected with sth/sb 与…相关；关于：*the laws pertaining to adoption* 有关收养的法律

per·tin·acious /ˌpɜːtɪˈneɪʃəs; *NAmE* ˌpɜːrtnˈeɪ-/ *adj.* (*formal*) determined to achieve a particular aim despite difficulties or opposition 坚定不移的；坚决的；义无反顾的 ▶ **per·tin·acity** /ˌpɜːtɪˈnæsəti; *NAmE* ˌpɜːrtnˈæ-/ *noun* [U]

per·tin·ent /ˈpɜːtɪnənt; *NAmE* ˈpɜːrtnənt/ *adj.* (*formal*) appropriate to a particular situation 有关的；恰当的；相宜的 SYN **relevant**：*a **pertinent question/fact*** 有关的问题 / 事实◇ **~ to sth** *Please keep your comments pertinent to the topic under discussion.* 请勿发表与讨论主题无关的言论。 ▶ **per·tin·ent·ly** *adv.* **per·tin·ence** /-əns/ *noun* [U]

per·turb /pəˈtɜːb; *NAmE* pərˈtɜːrb/ *verb* **~ sb** (*formal*) to make sb worried or anxious 使焦虑；使不安 SYN **alarm**：*Her sudden appearance did not seem to perturb him in the least.* 她的突然出现似乎一点也没有令他不安。 ▶ **per·turbed** /-ˈtɜːbd; *NAmE* -ˈtɜːrbd/ *adj.*：*a perturbed young man* 烦恼的年轻人◇ **~ at/about sth** *She didn't seem perturbed at the change of plan.* 她对改变计划似乎毫不在意。 OPP **unperturbed**

per·turb·ation /ˌpɜːtəˈbeɪʃn; *NAmE* ˌpɜːrtərˈb-/ *noun* **1** [U] (*formal*) the state of feeling anxious about sth that has happened 忧虑；不安；烦恼 SYN **alarm** **2** [C, U] (*specialist*) a small change in the quality, behaviour or movement of sth 摄动；微扰；扰动；小变异：*temperature perturbations* 温度的些微变化

per·use /pəˈruːz/ *verb* **~ sth** (*formal* or *humorous*) to read sth, especially in a careful way 细读；研读：*A copy of the report is available for you to peruse at your leisure.* 此报告有副本，供你闲暇时细读。 ▶ **per·usal** /pəˈruːzl/ *noun* [U, sing.]：*The agreement was signed after careful perusal.* 合同是仔细阅读以后才签署的。

perv (*also* **perve**) /pɜːv; *NAmE* pɜːrv/ *noun* (*informal*) **1** = PERVERT **2** (*AustralE, NZE*) a look at sb/sth that shows sexual interest in them or it, in an unpleasant way 色眯眯的瞥；淫欲的目光

per·vade /pəˈveɪd; *NAmE* pərˈv-/ *verb* **~ sth** (*formal*) to spread through and be noticeable in every part of sth 渗透；弥漫；遍及 SYN **permeate**：*a pervading mood of fear* 普遍的恐惧情绪 ◇ *the sadness that pervades most of her novels* 充斥她大部分小说的悲怆情绪◇ *The entire house was pervaded by a sour smell.* 整栋房子都充满了酸味。

per·va·sive /pəˈveɪsɪv; *NAmE* pərˈv-/ *adj.* existing in all parts of a place or thing; spreading gradually to affect all parts of a place or thing 遍布的；充斥各处的；弥漫的：*a pervasive smell of damp* 四处弥漫的潮湿味儿 ◇ *A sense of social change is pervasive in her novels.* 她的小说里充满社会变化的意识。 ▶ **per·va·sive·ly** *adv.* **per·va·sive·ness** *noun* [U]

per·verse /pəˈvɜːs; *NAmE* pərˈvɜːrs/ *adj.* showing deliberate determination to behave in a way that most people think is wrong, unacceptable or unreasonable 执拗的；任性的；不通情理的：*a perverse decision* (= one that most people do not expect and think is wrong) 悖谬的决定 ◇ *She finds a perverse pleasure in upsetting her parents.* 她让父母担惊受怕，从任性中得到快乐。◇ *Do you really mean that or are you just being **deliberately perverse**?* 你是真要那样，还是故意作对？ ▶ **per·verse·ly** *adv.*：*She seemed perversely proud of her criminal record.* 她似乎不通人事，拿自己的犯罪前科当荣耀。 **per·vers·ity** *noun* [U]：*He refused to attend out of sheer perversity.* 他拒不出席，纯属任性固执。

per·ver·sion /pəˈvɜːʃn; *NAmE* pərˈvɜːrʒn/ *noun* [U, C] **1** behaviour that most people think is not normal or acceptable, especially when it is connected with sex; an example of this type of behaviour 反常行为；（性）变态：*sexual perversion* 性变态 ◇ *sadomasochistic perversions* 施虐受虐的变态行为 **2** the act of changing sth that is good or right into sth that is bad or wrong; the result of this 颠倒；歪曲；颠倒是非：*the perversion of justice* 对正义的歪曲 ◇ *Her account was a perversion of the truth.* 她的报告颠倒了是非。

per·vert *verb, noun*

■ *verb* /pəˈvɜːt; *NAmE* pərˈvɜːrt/ **1 ~ sth** to change a system, process, etc. in a bad way so that it is not what it used to be or what it should be 败坏；使走样；误导；误用：*Some scientific discoveries have been perverted to create weapons of destruction.* 某些科学发明被滥用来生产毁灭性武器。 **2 ~ sb/sth** to affect sb in a way that makes them act or think in an immoral or unacceptable way 腐蚀；侵害；使堕落 SYN **corrupt**：*Some people believe that television can pervert the minds of children.* 有些人认为，电视会腐蚀儿童的心灵。

IDM **perˌvert the course of ˈjustice** (*BrE*) (*NAmE* **obˈstruct justice**) (*law* 律) to tell a lie or to do sth in order to prevent the police, etc. from finding out the truth about a crime 妨碍司法（如作伪证等）

■ *noun* /ˈpɜːvɜːt; *NAmE* ˈpɜːrvɜːrt/ (*also informal* **perv**) a person whose sexual behaviour is not thought to be normal or acceptable by most people 性变态者 SYN **deviant**：*a sexual pervert* 性变态者

per·verted /pəˈvɜːtɪd; *NAmE* pərˈvɜːr-/ *adj.* not thought to be normal or acceptable by most people 反常的；变态的：*sexual acts, normal and perverted* 正常的和变态的性行为 ◇ *She was having difficulty following his perverted logic.* 她很难理解他那反常的逻辑。 ◇ *They clearly take a perverted delight in watching others suffer.* 他们看别人受罪时显然得到一种病态的快感。

pe·seta /pəˈseɪtə/ *noun* the former unit of money in Spain (replaced in 2002 by the euro) 比塞塔（西班牙以前的货币单位，于 2002 年为欧元所取代）

pesky /ˈpeski/ *adj.* [only before noun] (*informal, especially NAmE*) annoying 恼人的；讨厌的：*pesky insects* 讨厌的昆虫

peso /ˈpeɪsəʊ; *NAmE* -soʊ/ *noun* (*pl.* **-os**) the unit of money in many Latin American countries and the Philippines 比索（多个拉美国家和菲律宾货币单位）

pes·sary /ˈpesəri/ *noun* (*pl.* **-ies**) **1** a small piece of solid medicine that is placed inside a woman's VAGINA and left to dissolve, used to cure an infection or to prevent her from becoming pregnant （治疗炎症或避孕用的）阴道栓剂 ➲ SEE ALSO SUPPOSITORY **2** a device that is placed inside a woman's VAGINA to support the WOMB 子宫托

pes·sim·ism /ˈpesɪmɪzəm/ *noun* [U] **~ (about/over sth)** a feeling that bad things will happen and that sth will not be successful; the tendency to have this feeling 悲观；悲观情绪；悲观主义：*There is a mood of pessimism in the company about future job prospects.* 公司中有一种对工作前景悲观的情绪。 OPP **optimism**

pes·sim·ist /ˈpesɪmɪst/ *noun* a person who always expects bad things to happen 悲观主义者；悲观论者：*You don't have to be a pessimist to realize that we're in trouble.* 不是悲观论者也能意识到我们有了麻烦。 OPP **optimist**

pes·sim·is·tic /ˌpesɪˈmɪstɪk/ *adj.* **~ (about sth)** expecting bad things to happen or sth not to be successful; showing this 悲观的；悲观主义的：*They appeared surprisingly pessimistic about their chances of winning.* 他们对胜利的可能性显得出奇地悲观。 ◇ *a pessimistic view of life* 对人生悲观的看法 ◇ *I think you're being far too pessimistic.* 我觉得你过于悲观了。 OPP **optimistic** ▶ **pes·sim·is·tic·al·ly** /-kli/ *adv.*

pest /pest/ *noun* **1** an insect or animal that destroys plants, food, etc. 害虫；害兽；害鸟：*pest control* 害虫防治 ◇ ***insect/plant/garden pests*** 害虫；作物 / 花园害虫 **2** (*informal*) an annoying person or thing 讨厌的人（或物）：*That child is being a real pest.* 那个孩子真讨厌。

pes·ter /ˈpestə(r)/ *verb* [T, I] to annoy sb, especially by asking them sth many times 打扰；纠缠；烦扰 SYN **badger**：**~ sb for sth** *Journalists pestered neighbours for information.* 记者缠着邻居打听消息。 ◇ **~ sb with sth** *He* *has been pestering her with phone calls for over a week.* 他打电话骚扰她有一个多星期了。◇ ~ **sb/sth** *The horses were continually pestered by flies.* 马不断地被苍蝇叮咬。◇ ~ (**sb to do sth**) *The kids kept pestering me to read to them.* 孩子们老缠着我给他们读故事书。

ˈ**pester power** *noun* [U] (*informal*) the ability that children have to make their parents buy things, by repeatedly asking them until they agree （孩子要求父母买东西的）缠磨力，缠功

pesti·cide /ˈpestɪsaɪd/ *noun* [C, U] a chemical used for killing pests, especially insects 杀虫剂；除害药物：*vegetables grown without the use of pesticides* 未用杀虫剂种植的蔬菜 ◇ *crops sprayed with pesticide* 喷洒过杀虫剂的庄稼 ➲ SEE ALSO HERBICIDE, INSECTICIDE

pesti·lence /ˈpestɪləns/ *noun* [U, sing.] (*old use* or *literary*) any infectious disease that spreads quickly and kills a lot of people 瘟疫

pesti·len·tial /ˌpestɪˈlenʃl/ *adj.* **1** [only before noun] (*literary*) extremely annoying 极讨厌的；极烦人的 **2** (*old use*) connected with or causing a pestilence 瘟疫的；引起瘟疫的

pes·tle /ˈpesl/ *noun* a small heavy tool with a round end used for crushing things in a special bowl called a MORTAR 杵，碾槌（研磨食品工具） ➲ VISUAL VOCAB PAGES V27, V72

pesto /ˈpestəʊ; *NAmE* ˈpestoʊ/ *noun* [U] an Italian sauce made of BASIL leaves, PINE NUTS, cheese and oil 意大利松子青酱（用罗勒叶、松子、干酪和油调制而成）

PET *noun* [U] **1** /ˌpiː iː ˈtiː/ the abbreviation for 'polyethylene terephthalate' (an artificial substance used to make materials for packaging food, including plastic drinks bottles) 聚对苯二甲酸乙二醇酯（全写为 polyethylene terephthalate，可做食品饮料包装材料） **2** /pet/ (*medical* 医) the abbreviation for 'positron emission tomography' (a process that produces an image of your brain or of another part inside your body) 正电子发射断层扫描（全写为 positron emission tomography，大脑或其他体内部位的成像）：*a PET scan* 正电子发射断层扫描 **3** /pet/ the abbreviation for 'Preliminary English Test' (a British test now called 'Cambridge English: Preliminary', set by the University of Cambridge, that measures a person's ability to speak and write English as a foreign language at an INTERMEDIATE level) 初级英语考试，剑桥英语第二级认证（全写为 Preliminary English Test，现称 Cambridge English: Preliminary，英国考试，检测英语作为外语者的中级口语和写作能力）

pet 🔑 /pet/ *noun, verb, adj.*

■ ***noun*** **1** 🔑 an animal, a bird, etc. that you have at home for pleasure, rather than one that is kept for work or food 宠物：*Do you have any pets?* 你有没有养宠物？◇ ***a pet dog/hamster, etc.*** 养作宠物的狗、仓鼠等 ◇ ***a family/domestic pet*** 家庭宠物 ◇ ***pet food*** 宠物食品 ◇ ***a pet shop*** (= where animals are sold as pets) 宠物店 **2** (*usually disapproving*) a person who is given special attention by sb, especially in a way that seems unfair to other people 宠儿；宝贝；红人 SYN **favourite**：*She's the teacher's pet.* 她是老师的宠儿。 **3** (*BrE, informal*) used when speaking to sb to show affection or to be friendly （昵称）宝贝儿，乖乖：*What's wrong, pet?* 怎么啦，宝贝儿？◇ *Be a pet* (= be kind) *and post this letter for me.* 乖啊，替我把这封信寄了。

■ ***verb*** (**-tt-**) **1** [T] ~ **sb/sth** (*especially NAmE*) to touch or move your hand gently over an animal or a child in a kind and loving way 抚摸；（爱抚地）摩挲 **2** [I] (*informal*) (of two people 两人) to kiss and touch each other in a sexual way 亲吻；调情；爱抚 ➲ SEE ALSO PETTING

■ ***adj.*** [only before noun] that you are very interested in 很喜欢的；钟爱的；很感兴趣的：*his* ***pet subject/theory/project, etc.*** 他所喜爱的学科、理论、项目等 ➲ SEE ALSO PET NAME

IDM **sb's pet ˈhate** (*BrE*) (*NAmE* **sb's pet ˈpeeve**) something that you particularly dislike 特别厌恶的东西

petal /ˈpetl/ *noun* a delicate coloured part of a flower. The head of a flower is usually made up of several petals around a central part. 花瓣 ➲ VISUAL VOCAB PAGE V11

pe·tard /pəˈtɑːd; *NAmE* pəˈtɑːrd/ *noun* IDM SEE HOIST *v.*

Peter /ˈpiːtə(r)/ *noun* IDM SEE ROB

peter /ˈpiːtə(r)/ *verb*

PHR V **ˌpeter ˈout** to gradually become smaller, quieter, etc. and then end 逐渐减少；逐渐减弱；慢慢消失：*The campaign petered out for lack of support.* 那场运动因缺乏支持者而最终不了了之。◇ *The road petered out into a dirt track.* 大道延伸到一条泥土小径。

ˌPeter ˈPan *noun* a person who looks unusually young for their age, or who behaves in a way that would be more appropriate for sb younger 外表异常年轻的人；行为像孩子的成人 ➲ MORE LIKE THIS 17, page R27 ORIGIN From a story by J M Barrie about a boy with magic powers who never grew up. 源自詹姆斯·巴里的小说《彼得·潘》，主人公是个永远长不大的有魔力的男孩。

ˈ**Peters projection** *noun* [sing.] a map of the world on which the relative size, but not the shape of countries is more accurate than on more traditional maps 彼得斯投影世界地图（其中各国的相对面积而不是形状比传统地图更准确） ➲ COMPARE MERCATOR PROJECTION

peth·id·ine /ˈpeθədiːn/ *noun* [U] a drug used to reduce severe pain, especially for women giving birth 哌替啶，度冷丁（一种镇痛药）

petit bourgeois /ˌpeti ˈbʊəʒwɑː; *NAmE* ˈbʊrʒ-/ (*also* **ˌpetty ˈbourgeois**) *noun* (*pl.* **petits/petty bourgeois**) (*disapproving*) a member of the lower middle class in society, especially one who thinks that money, work and social position are very important 小资产阶级分子 ▸ **ˌpetit ˈbourgeois** (*also* **ˌpetty ˈbourgeois**) *adj.* [usually before noun]

pe·tite /pəˈtiːt/ *adj.* (*approving*) (of a girl, woman or her figure 女孩、妇女或其身材) small and thin 纤弱的；娇小的：*a petite blonde* 娇小的金发女郎

the peˌtite ˌbourgeoiˈsie (*also* **ˌpetty ˌbourgeoiˈsie**) *noun* [sing.] the lower middle class in society 小资产阶级

petit four /ˌpeti ˈfɔː(r)/ *noun* [usually pl.] (*pl.* **petits fours** /ˌpeti ˈfɔː(r)/) (*from French*) a very small decorated cake or biscuit/cookie that is served with coffee or tea 花式小点心；小茶点

pe·ti·tion /pəˈtɪʃn/ *noun, verb*

■ ***noun*** **1** ~ (**against/for sth**) a written document signed by a large number of people that asks sb in a position of authority to do or change sth 请愿书：*a petition against experiments on animals* 反对用动物做实验的请愿书 ◇ *The workers are getting up* (= starting) *a petition for tighter safety standards.* 工人正发起请愿，要求提高安全标准。 **2** (*law* 律) an official document asking a court to take a particular course of action 申诉书；申请书 **3** (*formal*) a formal prayer to God or request to sb in authority 祈祷；祈求

■ ***verb*** **1** [I, T] to make a formal request to sb in authority, especially by sending them a petition 祈求；请求；请愿：~ **for/against sth** *Local residents have successfully petitioned against the siting of a prison in their area.* 当地居民反对在区内兴建监狱的请愿成功了。◇ ~ **sb/sth** (**for sth**) *The group intends to petition Parliament for reform of the law.* 这个团体准备请求议会修改法律。◇ ~ **sb/sth to do sth** *Parents petitioned the school to review its admission policy.* 家长请愿恳求学校修订招生政策。 **2** [I, T] ~ (**sb**) (**for sth**) | ~ **sb/sth to do sth** to formally ask for sth in court （向法庭）请求，申请：*to petition for divorce* 申请离婚

pe·ti·tion·er /pəˈtɪʃənə(r)/ *noun* **1** a person who organizes or signs a petition 请愿者 **2** (*law* 律) a person who asks a court to take a particular course of action 诉愿人；上诉人 **3** (*formal*) a person who makes a formal request to sb in authority 恳求者；请求者

P

petit mal /ˌpeti ˈmæl/ *noun* [U] a form of EPILEPSY that is not very serious, in which sb becomes unconscious only for very short periods 癫痫小发作

ˈ**pet name** *noun* a name you use for sb instead of their real name, as a sign of affection 昵称；爱称

pet·rel /ˈpetrəl/ *noun* a black and white bird that can fly over the sea a long way from land 圆尾鹱；海燕

Petri dish /ˈpetri dɪʃ; ˈpiːtri/ *noun* a shallow covered dish used for growing bacteria, etc. in 培养皿（培养细菌等用的有盖玻璃碟） ➲ VISUAL VOCAB PAGE V72

petri·fied /ˈpetrɪfaɪd/ *adj.* **1** extremely frightened 非常害怕的；恐慌的 SYN **terrified**: *a petrified expression* 惶恐的表情 ◊ ~ (**of sth**) *I'm petrified of snakes.* 我特别怕蛇。◊ *They were petrified with fear* (= so frightened that they were unable to move or think). 他们都吓呆了。◊ ~ (**that…**) *She was petrified that the police would burst in at any moment.* 她感到惧怕的是警察随时都可能破门而入。 **2** [only before noun] **petrified** trees, insects, etc. have died and been changed into stone over a very long period of time 石化的：*a petrified forest* 石化林

pet·rify /ˈpetrɪfaɪ/ *verb* (**petri·fies**, **petri·fy·ing**, **petri·fied**, **petri·fied**) **1** [T] ~ **sb** to make sb feel extremely frightened 使吓呆；使惊呆 SYN **terrify** **2** [I, T] ~ (**sth**) to change or to make sth change into a substance like stone （使）石化

petro- /ˈpetrəʊ; NAmE ˈpetroʊ/ *combining form* (in nouns, adjectives and adverbs 构成名词、形容词和副词) **1** connected with rocks 岩石的：*petrology* 岩石学 **2** connected with petrol/gas 石油的；汽油的：*petrochemical* 石油化学产品

petro·chem·ical /ˌpetrəʊˈkemɪkl; NAmE ˌpetroʊ-/ *noun* any chemical substance obtained from PETROLEUM oil or natural gas 石油化学产品：*the petrochemical industry* 石油化学工业

P

petro·dol·lar /ˈpetrəʊdɒlə(r); NAmE ˈpetroʊdɑːlər/ *noun* a unit of money that is used for calculating the money earned by countries that produce and sell oil 石油美元（计算石油生产及销售国收入的单位）

pet·rol 🔑 /ˈpetrəl/ (*BrE*) (*NAmE* **gas**, **gas·oline**) *noun* [U] a liquid obtained from PETROLEUM, used as fuel in car engines, etc. 汽油：*to fill a car up with petrol* 给汽车油箱装满汽油 ◊ *to run out of petrol* 用光汽油 ◊ *the petrol tank of a car* 汽车的油箱 ◊ *an increase in petrol prices* 汽油价格的上涨 ◊ *leaded/unleaded petrol* 含铅 / 无铅汽油 ➲ COMPARE DIESEL

ˌ**petrol ˈblue** *adj.* a deep greenish blue in colour 深蓝绿色的：*petrol-blue eyes* 藏蓝色的双眸 ▸ ˌ**petrol ˈblue** *noun* [U] ➲ MORE LIKE THIS 15, page R26

ˈ**petrol bomb** *noun* (*BrE*) = MOLOTOV COCKTAIL

ˈ**petrol bunk** *noun* (*IndE*) a petrol station 汽车加油站

pet·rol·eum /pəˈtrəʊliəm; NAmE -ˈtroʊ-/ *noun* [U] mineral oil that is found under the ground or the sea and is used to produce petrol/gas, PARAFFIN, DIESEL oil, etc. 石油；原油

peˌtroleum ˈjelly (*NAmE also* **pet·rol·atum** /ˌpetrəˈleɪtəm/) *noun* [U] a soft clear substance obtained from petroleum, used to heal injuries on the skin or to make machine parts move together more smoothly 矿脂；凡士林 SYN **Vaseline™**

pet·rology /pəˈtrɒlədʒi; NAmE -ˈtrɑːl-/ *noun* [U] the scientific study of how rocks are made and what they are made of 岩石学

ˈ**petrol station** (*BrE*) (*NAmE* ˈ**gas station**) (*also* ˈ**filling station**, ˈ**service station** *NAmE, BrE*) *noun* a place at the side of a road where you take your car to buy petrol/gas, oil, etc. 汽车加油站

petti·coat /ˈpetɪkəʊt; NAmE -koʊt/ *noun* (*old-fashioned*) a piece of women's underwear like a thin dress or skirt, worn under a dress or skirt 衬裙 SYN **slip**

petti·fog·ging /ˈpetɪfɒgɪŋ; NAmE -fɔːg-; -fɑːg-/ *adj.* [only before noun] (*old-fashioned*) paying too much attention to unimportant details; concerned with unimportant things 吹毛求疵的；挑剔的；琐碎的 SYN **petty**

pet·ting /ˈpetɪŋ/ *noun* [U] the activity of kissing and touching sb, especially in a sexual way 亲吻抚摸；调情：*heavy petting* (= sexual activity which avoids PENETRATION) 热烈的爱抚

ˈ**petting zoo** *noun* (*NAmE*) a zoo with animals that children can touch （允许儿童触摸动物的）爱畜动物园

pet·tish /ˈpetɪʃ/ *adj.* behaving in a bad-tempered or unreasonable way, especially because you cannot have or do what you want 发脾气的（尤因未能遂愿）；使性子的 ▸ **pet·tish·ly** *adv.*

petty /ˈpeti/ *adj.* (*usually disapproving*) **1** [usually before noun] small and unimportant 小的；琐碎的；次要的 SYN **minor**: *petty squabbles* 小口角 ◊ *petty crime/theft* (= that is not very serious) 轻微罪行；小偷小摸 ◊ ***a petty criminal/thief*** 轻罪犯；小窃贼 ◊ ***a petty bureaucrat/official*** (= who does not have much power or authority, although they might pretend to) 小官僚；小官员 **2** caring too much about small and unimportant matters, especially when this is unkind to other people 小气的；狭隘的 SYN **small-minded**: *How could you be so petty?* 你怎么那么小气呢？ ▸ **petti·ness** *noun* [U]

ˌ**petty ˈbourgeois** *noun, adj.* = PETIT BOURGEOIS

the ˌpetty ˌbourgeoiˈsie *noun* [sing.] = PETITE BOURGEOISIE

ˌ**petty ˈcash** *noun* [U] a small amount of money kept in an office for small payments （办公室的）小额备用现金

ˌ**petty ˈofficer** *noun* (*abbr.* **PO**) a sailor of middle rank in the navy 海军军士

petu·lant /ˈpetjulənt; NAmE ˈpetʃə-/ *adj.* bad-tempered and unreasonable, especially because you cannot do or have what you want 闹脾气的；爱耍性子的；赌气的；任性的 ▸ **petu·lant·ly** *adv.* **petu·lance** /-əns/ *noun* [U]

pe·tu·nia /pəˈtjuːniə; NAmE -ˈtuː-/ *noun* a garden plant with white, pink, purple or red flowers 矮牵牛

pew /pjuː/ *noun* a long wooden seat in a church 教堂长椅
IDM ˌ**take a ˈpew!** (*BrE, informal, humorous*) used to tell sb to sit down 坐下！

pew·ter /ˈpjuːtə(r)/ *noun* [U] a grey metal made by mixing tin with LEAD² (1), used especially in the past for making cups, dishes, etc.; objects made from pewter 白镴；锡镴；白镴制品

pey·ote /peɪˈəʊti; NAmE -ˈoʊ-/ *noun* **1** (*also* **mes·cal**) [C, U] a small, blue-green CACTUS that contains a powerful drug that affects people's minds 佩奥特掌（蓝绿色小仙人掌，具致幻作用） **2** [U] the drug that comes from this plant 佩奥特碱（从佩奥特掌中提取的致幻剂）

PG /ˌpiː ˈdʒiː/ *abbr.* (*BrE*) parental guidance. A film that has the label 'PG' is not suitable for children to watch without an adult. * PG 类影片，家长引导（建议家长对儿童加以引导）

PGCE /ˌpiː dʒiː siː ˈiː/ *noun* the abbreviation for 'Postgraduate Certificate in Education' (a British teaching qualification taken by people who have a university degree) 研究生教育证书（全写为 Postgraduate Certificate in Education，有大学学位者取得的英国教师资格证书）

pH /ˌpiː ˈeɪtʃ/ *noun* [sing.] (*chemistry* 化) a measurement of the level of acid or ALKALI in a SOLUTION or substance. In the pH range of 0 to 14 a reading of below 7 shows an acid and of above 7 shows an alkali. * pH 值（溶液或物质的酸碱度。pH 值介于 0 至 14，7 以下为酸，7 以上为碱）：*a pH of 7.5* * pH 值 7.5 ◊ *to test the pH level of the soil* 测试土壤的酸碱度 ➲ WORDFINDER NOTE AT CHEMISTRY

phago·cyte /ˈfæɡəsaɪt/ *noun* (*biology* 生) a type of cell present in the body that is able to absorb bacteria and other small cells 吞噬细胞

phal·anx /ˈfælæŋks/ *noun* (*formal*) a group of people or things standing very close together 密集的人（或事物）

phal·lic /ˈfælɪk/ *adj.* of or like a phallus 似阴茎的；阴茎的：*phallic symbols* 阴茎的象征物

phal·locen·tric /ˌfæləʊˈsentrɪk; *NAmE* -loʊˈs-/ *adj.* (*formal*) related to men, male power, or the phallus as a symbol of male power 男性中心的；阳具中心的 ▸ **phal·locen·trism** /ˌfæləʊˈsentrɪzəm; *NAmE* -loʊˈs-/ *noun* [U]

phal·lus /ˈfæləs/ *noun* **1** (*specialist*) the male sexual organ, especially when it is ERECT (= stiff) （尤指勃起的）阴茎 **2** a model or an image of the male sexual organ that represents power and FERTILITY 阴茎模型，阴茎图像（力量与生殖力的象征）

phan·tasm /ˈfæntæzəm/ *noun* (*formal*) a thing seen in the imagination 幻觉；幻影；幻想 **SYN** **illusion**

phan·tas·ma·goria /ˌfæntæzməˈɡɒriə; *NAmE* -ˈɡɔːr-/ *noun* [sing.] (*formal*) a changing scene of real or imagined figures, for example as seen in a dream or created as an effect in a film/movie （真实或幻觉形象的）变换情景，幻觉效应 ▸ **phan·tas·ma·gor·ical** /-ˈɡɒrɪkl; *NAmE* -ˈɡɔːr-/ *adj.*

phan·tasy *noun* [C, U] (*old use*) = FANTASY

phantom /ˈfæntəm/ *noun, adj.*

■ ***noun*** **1** a GHOST 鬼；鬼魂；幽灵：*the phantom of his dead father* 他已故父亲的幽灵 **2** a thing that exists only in your imagination 幻觉；幻象

■ ***adj.*** [only before noun] **1** like a GHOST 像鬼的；幽灵似的：*a phantom horseman* 幽灵似的骑士 **2** existing only in your imagination 幻觉的；幻象的；虚幻的：*phantom profits* 虚幻的利润 ◇ *phantom illnesses* 幻觉疾病 ◇ *a* ***phantom pregnancy*** (= a condition in which a woman seems to be pregnant but in fact is not) 假妊娠

phar·aoh /ˈfeərəʊ; *NAmE* ˈferoʊ/ *noun* a ruler of ancient Egypt 法老（古埃及国王）

Phari·see /ˈfærɪsiː/ *noun* **1** a member of an ancient Jewish group who followed religious laws and teaching very strictly 法利赛人（严守律法的古犹太教派成员） **2** (*disapproving*) a person who is very proud of the fact that they have high religious and moral standards, but who does not care enough about other people 自诩圣洁者；自恃清高者；伪善者 **SYN** **hypocrite**

pharma·ceut·ical /ˌfɑːməˈsuːtɪkl; -ˈsjuː-; *NAmE* ˌfɑːrməˈsuː-/ *adj., noun*

■ ***adj.*** [only before noun] connected with making and selling drugs and medicines 制药的；配药的；卖药的：*pharmaceutical products* 药物 ◇ *the pharmaceutical industry* 制药业

■ ***noun*** [usually pl.] (*specialist*) a drug or medicine 药物：*the development of new pharmaceuticals* 新药的开发 ◇ *the pharmaceuticals industry* 制药业

pharma·cist /ˈfɑːməsɪst; *NAmE* ˈfɑːrm-/ *noun* **1** (*NAmE also, old-fashioned* **drug·gist**) a person whose job is to prepare medicines and sell or give them to the public in a shop/store or in a hospital 药剂师：*We had to wait for the pharmacist to make up her prescription.* 我们只得等药剂师给她配好药。➲ COMPARE CHEMIST (1) **2 pharma·cist's** (*pl.* **pharma·cists**) (*BrE*) a shop that sells medicines 药店；药房：*They sell vitamin supplements at the pharmacist's.* 那药店卖维生素补充剂。➲ COMPARE CHEMIST (2) ➲ SEE ALSO PHARMACY

pharma·colo·gist /ˌfɑːməˈkɒlədʒɪst; *NAmE* ˌfɑːrməˈkɑːl-/ *noun* a scientist who studies pharmacology 药物学家；药理学家

pharma·col·ogy /ˌfɑːməˈkɒlədʒi; *NAmE* ˌfɑːrməˈkɑːl-/ *noun* [U] the scientific study of drugs and their use in medicine 药理学 ▸ **pharma·co·logic·al** /ˌfɑːməkəˈlɒdʒɪkl; *NAmE* ˌfɑːrməkəˈlɑːdʒ-/ *adj.*：*pharmacological research* 药物学研究

pharma·co·poeia (*NAmE also* **pharma·co·peia**) /ˌfɑːməkəˈpiːə; *NAmE* ˌfɑːrmə-/ *noun* (*specialist*) an official book containing a list of medicines and drugs and instructions for their use 药典

phar·macy /ˈfɑːməsi; *NAmE* ˈfɑːrm-/ *noun* (*pl.* **-ies**) **1** [C] a shop/store, or part of one, that sells medicines and drugs 药房；药店；医药柜台 ➲ COMPARE CHEMIST (2), DRUGSTORE **2** [C] a place in a hospital where medicines are prepared （医院的）药房，配药室 ➲ SEE ALSO DISPENSARY (1) **3** [U] the study of how to prepare medicines and drugs 药剂学；制药学 ➲ WORDFINDER NOTE AT MEDICINE

pharm·ing /ˈfɑːmɪŋ; *NAmE* ˈfɑːrmɪŋ/ *noun* [U] **1 pharming™** the process of changing the GENES of an animal or a plant so that it produces large quantities of a substance, especially for use in medicine 药耕（指通过改变动植物基因大量生产某种物质，尤为医用） **ORIGIN** From **farming** and **pharmaceutical**. 源自 farming 和 pharmaceutical 的缩合。 **2** the practice of secretly changing computer files or software so that visitors to a popular website are sent to a different website instead, without their knowledge, where their personal details are stolen and used to steal money from them 域欺骗，网址嫁接（指暗中修改计算机文件或软件将网站访客骗到其他网站，从而盗取其个人资料并进而盗取钱财） ➲ COMPARE PHISHING

pha·ryn·geal *adj.* /fəˈrɪndʒiəl; ˌfærɪnˈdʒiːəl/ *adj., noun*

■ ***adj.*** (*medical* 医) relating to the pharynx 咽的

■ ***noun*** (*also* **phaˌryngeal ˈconsonant**) (*phonetics* 语音) a speech sound produced by the root of the tongue using the PHARYNX 咽音

pha·ryn·gitis *adj.* /ˌfærɪnˈdʒaɪtɪs/ *noun* [U] (*medical* 医) a condition in which the throat is red and sore 咽炎

phar·ynx /ˈfærɪŋks/ *noun* (*pl.* **pha·ryn·ges** /fəˈrɪndʒiːz/) (*anatomy* 解) the soft area at the top of the throat where the passages to the nose and mouth connect with the throat 咽 ➲ VISUAL VOCAB PAGE V64

phase 🔑 **AW** /feɪz/ *noun, verb*

■ ***noun*** **1** 🔑 a stage in a process of change or development 阶段；时期：*during the first/next/last phase* 在第一/下一/最后阶段 ◇ *the* ***initial/final phase*** *of the project* 工程的初始/最后阶段 ◇ *a* ***critical/decisive phase*** 关键性/决定性阶段 ◇ *the* ***design phase*** 设计阶段 ◇ *His anxiety about the work was just* ***a passing phase****.* 他对工作的担心只是暂时的。◇ *She's going through* ***a difficult phase****.* 她正处于困难时期。◇ *The wedding marked the beginning of* ***a new phase*** *in Emma's life.* 婚礼标志着埃玛生活新阶段的开始。 **2** each of the shapes of the moon as we see it from the earth at different times of the month 月相；（月亮的）盈亏

IDM **in phase/out of phase (with sth)** (*BrE*) working/not working together in the right way 协调；不协调：*The traffic lights were out of phase.* 红绿灯信号不协调。

■ ***verb*** [usually passive] **~ sth** to arrange to do sth gradually in stages over a period of time 分阶段进行；逐步做：*the phased withdrawal of troops from the area* 从该地区分期逐步的撤军 ◇ *Closure of the hospitals was phased over a three-year period.* 这些医院的关闭是在三年期间逐步进行的。

PHR V **ˌphase sth↔ˈin** to introduce or start using sth gradually in stages over a period of time 逐步引入；分阶段开始：*The new tax will be phased in over two years.* 新税种将在两年内逐步实行。 **ˌphase sth↔ˈout** to stop using sth gradually in stages over a period of time 逐步废除：*Subsidies to farmers will be phased out by next year.* 对农民的补贴将在明年之前逐步取消。

phat /fæt/ *adj.* (*slang, especially NAmE*) very good 精彩的；极棒的

phat·ic /ˈfætɪk/ *adj.* (*linguistics* 语言) relating to language used for social purposes rather than to give information or ask questions 纯交际性的；用于寒暄交际的：*phatic communication* 客套话

P

PhD (*also* **Ph.D.** *especially in NAmE*) /ˌpiː eɪtʃ ˈdiː/ *noun* the abbreviation for 'Doctor of Philosophy' (a university degree of a very high level that is given to sb who has done research in a particular subject) 哲学博士学位，博士学位（全写为 Doctor of Philosophy，授予完成某学科研究者的高级学位）：*to **be/have/do a PhD*** 是一位博士；有博士学位；攻读博士学位 ◇ *Anne Thomas, PhD* 安妮・托马斯博士 ➲ COLLOCATIONS AT EDUCATION

phea·sant /ˈfeznt/ *noun* [C, U] (*pl.* **phea·sants** or **phea·sant**) a large bird with a long tail, the male of which is brightly coloured. People sometimes shoot pheasants for sport or food. Meat from this bird is also called pheasant. 野鸡；雉；野鸡肉：(*BrE*) *to shoot pheasant* 射猎野鸡 ◇ (*NAmE*) *to hunt pheasant* 打野鸡 ◇ *roast pheasant* 烤野鸡 ➲ VISUAL VOCAB PAGE V12

phe·nol /ˈfiːnɒl; *NAmE* -nɔːl; -nɑːl/ *noun* [U] (*chemistry* 化) a poisonous white chemical. When dissolved in water it is used as an ANTISEPTIC and DISINFECTANT, usually called CARBOLIC ACID. 酚；苯酚；石炭酸

phen·ology /fəˈnɒlədʒi; *NAmE* -ˈnɑːl-/ *noun* [U] the study of patterns of events in nature, especially in the weather and in the behaviour of plants and animals 物候学

phe·nom /fəˈnɒm; ˈfiːnɒm; *NAmE* -nɑːm/ *noun* (*NAmE, informal*) a person or thing that is very successful or impressive 非凡的人（或事物）；了不起的人（或事物）**SYN** **phenomenon**

phe·nom·enal **AW** /fəˈnɒmɪnl; *NAmE* -ˈnɑːm-/ *adj.* very great or impressive 了不起的；非凡的 **SYN** **extraordinary**: *The product has been a phenomenal success.* 这一产品获得了极大的成功。

phe·nom·en·al·ly /fəˈnɒmɪnəli; *NAmE* -ˈnɑːm-/ *adv.* **1** in a very great or impressive way 了不起地；非凡地；难以置信地 **SYN** **extraordinarily**: *This product has been phenomenally successful.* 这种产品获得了极大的成功。 **2** extremely; very 极其；十分：*phenomenally bad weather* 非常糟糕的天气

phe·nom·en·ology /fɪˌnɒmɪˈnɒlədʒi; *NAmE* -nɑːməˈnɑːl-/ *noun* [U] the branch of philosophy that deals with what you see, hear, feel, etc. in contrast to what may actually be real or true about the world 现象学 ▸ **phe·nom·eno·logic·al** /fɪˌnɒmɪnəˈlɒdʒɪkl; *NAmE* -nɑːmənəˈlɑːdʒ-/ *adj.*

phe·nom·enon **AW** /fəˈnɒmɪnən; *NAmE* fəˈnɑːm-/ *noun* (*pl.* **phe·nom·ena** /-mə/) **1** a fact or an event in nature or society, especially one that is not fully understood 现象：***cultural/natural/social phenomena*** 文化／自然／社会现象 ◇ *Globalization is a phenomenon of the 21st century.* 全球化是 21 世纪的现象。 **2** ((*NAmE*) *pl.* **phe·nom·enons**) a person or thing that is very successful or impressive 杰出的人；非凡的人（或事物）➲ MORE LIKE THIS 30, page R28

phe·no·type /ˈfiːnətaɪp/ *adj., noun* (*biology* 生) the set of characteristics of a living thing, resulting from its combination of GENES and the effect of its environment 表型（的），表现型（的）（基因和环境作用的结合而形成的一组生物特征）➲ COMPARE GENOTYPE

phero·mone /ˈferəməʊn; *NAmE* -moʊn/ *noun* (*biology* 生) a substance produced by an animal as a chemical signal, often to attract another animal of the same SPECIES 外激素；信息素

phew /fjuː/ *exclamation* a sound that people make to show that they are hot, tired, or happy that sth bad has finished or did not happen 哦（表示热、累或宽慰）：*Phew, it's hot in here!* 哦，这里真热呀！◇ *Phew, I'm glad that's all over.* 哦，这档事总算结束了！➲ COMPARE WHEW ➲ MORE LIKE THIS 2, page R25

phi /faɪ/ *noun* the 21st letter of the Greek alphabet (Φ, φ) 希腊字母表的第 21 个字母

phial /ˈfaɪəl/ (*also* **vial** *especially in NAmE*) *noun* (*formal*) a small glass container, for medicine or PERFUME 管形瓶；小药瓶

ˌ**Phi** ˌ**Beta** ˈ**Kappa** *noun* (in the US) a society for college and university students who are very successful in their studies * ΦBK 联谊会（美国大学高材生组织）

phil·an·der·er /fɪˈlændərə(r)/ *noun* (*old-fashioned, disapproving*) a man who has sexual relationships with many different women 色鬼；玩弄女性者

phil·an·dering /fɪˈlændərɪŋ/ *noun* [U] (*old-fashioned, disapproving*) (of a man 男人) the fact of having sexual relationships with many different women 淫乱；玩弄女性 **SYN** **womanizing** ▸ **phil·an·dering** *adj.* [only before noun]

phil·an·throp·ist /fɪˈlænθrəpɪst/ *noun* a rich person who helps the poor and those in need, especially by giving money 慈善家；乐善好施的人

phil·an·thropy /fɪˈlænθrəpi/ *noun* [U] the practice of helping the poor and those in need, especially by giving money 博爱；慈善；乐善好施 ▸ **phil·an·throp·ic** /ˌfɪlənˈθrɒpɪk; *NAmE* -ˈθrɑːp-/ *adj.*：*philanthropic work* 慈善工作 **phil·an·throp·ic·al·ly** /ˌfɪlənˈθrɒpɪkli; *NAmE* -ˈθrɑːp-/ *adv.*

phila·tel·ist /fɪˈlætəlɪst/ *noun* (*specialist*) a person who collects or studies stamps 集邮爱好者；邮票专家

phil·ately /fɪˈlætəli/ *noun* [U] (*specialist*) the collection and study of stamps 集邮；邮票研究 ▸ **phila·tel·ic** /ˌfɪləˈtelɪk/ *adj.*

-phile *combining form* (in nouns and adjectives 构成名词和形容词) liking a particular thing; a person who likes a particular thing 爱好…的；…爱好者：*Anglophile* 亲英者 ◇ *bibliophile* 藏书家 ➲ COMPARE -PHOBE

phil·har·mon·ic /ˌfɪlɑːˈmɒnɪk; *NAmE* ˌfɪlərˈmɑːnɪk/ *adj.* used in the names of ORCHESTRAS, music societies, etc.（用于乐队、音乐团体等名称中）爱乐的：*the Berlin Philharmonic (Orchestra)* 柏林爱乐（管弦）乐团

-philia *combining form* (in nouns 构成名词) love of sth, especially connected with a sexual attraction that is not considered normal（尤指不正常的）性嗜好；癖好；怪癖：*paedophilia* 恋童癖 ➲ COMPARE -PHOBIA

phil·is·tine /ˈfɪlɪstaɪn; *NAmE* -stiːn/ *noun* (*disapproving*) a person who does not like or understand art, literature, music, etc. 对文化艺术无知的人；文化修养低的人 ▸ **phil·is·tine** *adj.*：*philistine attitudes* 厌恶艺术的态度 **phil·is·tin·ism** /-tɪnɪzəm/ *noun* [U]：*the philistinism of the tabloid press* 小报之庸俗

Phil·lips /ˈfɪlɪps/ *adj.* (of a screw or SCREWDRIVER 螺丝钉或螺丝刀) with a cross-shaped part for turning 十字形的 ➲ COMPARE FLATHEAD, SLOTTED (2)

philo- /ˈfɪləʊ; *NAmE* ˈfɪloʊ/ (*also* **phil-**) *combining form* (in nouns, adjectives, verbs and adverbs 构成名词、形容词、动词和副词) liking 爱好；喜爱：*philanthropy* 博爱

phil·olo·gist /fɪˈlɒlədʒɪst; *NAmE* -ˈlɑːl-/ *noun* a person who studies philology 语文学家；语文研究者

phil·ology /fɪˈlɒlədʒi; *NAmE* -ˈlɑːl-/ *noun* [U] the scientific study of the development of language or of a particular language 语文学；语文研究 ▸ **phil·olo·gic·al** /ˌfɪləˈlɒdʒɪkl; *NAmE* -ˈlɑːdʒ-/ *adj.*

phil·oso·pher **AW** /fəˈlɒsəfə(r); *NAmE* -ˈlɑːs-/ *noun* **1** a person who studies or writes about philosophy 哲学家：*the Greek philosopher Aristotle* 希腊哲学家亚里士多德 **2** a person who thinks deeply about things 深思的人；善于思考的人：*He seems to be a bit of a philosopher.* 他像个思想家似的。

the phiˌ**losopher's** ˈ**stone** *noun* [sing.] an imaginary substance that, in the past, people believed could change any metal into gold or silver, or could make people live for ever 点金石，哲人石（旧时被认为能使其他金属变为金银或能使人长生不老的仙石）

philo·soph·ic·al AW /ˌfɪləˈsɒfɪkl; *NAmE* -ˈsɑːf-/ (*also* **philo·soph·ic** /-ˈsɒfɪk; *NAmE* -ˈsɑːfɪk/) *adj.* **1** connected with philosophy 哲学的：*the philosophical writings of Kant* 康德的哲学论著 ◇ *philosophic debate* 哲学辩论 **2 ~ (about sth)** (*approving*) having a calm attitude towards a difficult or disappointing situation 达观的；处乱不惊的 SYN **stoic**: *He was philosophical about losing and said that he'd be back next year to try again.* 他对失败处之泰然，声称来年将再来一试身手。▶ **philo·soph·ic·al·ly** AW /-kli/ *adv.*: *This kind of evidence is philosophically unconvincing.* 这类证据在哲学上是不足为信的。◇ *She took the bad news philosophically.* 她镇定地面对这个坏消息。

phil·oso·phize AW (*BrE also* **-ise**) /fəˈlɒsəfaɪz; *NAmE* -ˈlɑːs-/ *verb* [I] **~ (about/on sth)** to talk about sth in a serious way, especially when other people think this is boring 郑重论述；高谈阔论：*He spent the evening philosophizing on the meaning of life.* 他整个晚上大谈人生的意义。▶ **phil·oso·phiz·ing, -is·ing** AW *noun* [U]

phil·oso·phy 🔑 AW /fəˈlɒsəfi; *NAmE* -ˈlɑːs-/ *noun* **1** 🔑 [U] the study of the nature and meaning of the universe and of human life 哲学：*moral philosophy* 伦理学 ◇ *the philosophy of science* 科学哲学 ◇ *a professor of philosophy* 哲学教授 ◇ *a degree in philosophy* 哲学学位 **2** 🔑 [C] a particular set or system of beliefs resulting from the search for knowledge about life and the universe 哲学体系；思想体系：*the philosophy of Jung* 荣格的哲学体系 **3** 🔑 [C] a set of beliefs or an attitude to life that guides sb's behaviour 人生哲学；生活的信条（或态度）：*Her philosophy of life is to take every opportunity that presents itself.* 她的处世态度是不放过任何呈现眼前的机会。

phil·tre (*especially US* **phil·ter**) /ˈfɪltə(r)/ *noun* (*literary*) a magic drink that is supposed to make people fall in love 春药

phish·ing /ˈfɪʃɪŋ/ *noun* [U] the activity of tricking people by getting them to give their identity, bank account numbers, etc. over the Internet or by email, and then using these to steal money from them 网络仿冒，网络钓鱼（通过互联网或电邮骗取他人身份信息、银行账号等以盗取金钱） ➲ COMPARE PHARMING (2)

phle·bitis /fləˈbaɪtɪs/ *noun* [U] (*medical* 医) a condition in which the walls of a VEIN become sore and swollen 静脉炎

phle·bot·omy /fləˈbɒtəmi; *NAmE* -ˈbɑːt-/ *noun* [C, U] (*pl.* **-ies**) (*medical* 医) the opening of a VEIN in order to remove blood or put another liquid in 静脉切开术

phlegm /flem/ *noun* [U] **1** the thick substance that forms in the nose and throat, especially when you have a cold 痰 **2** the ability to remain calm in a situation that is difficult or upsetting 冷静；镇定；自制力

phleg·mat·ic /flegˈmætɪk/ *adj.* not easily made angry or upset 冷静的；镇定的；不易冲动的 SYN **calm**: *a phlegmatic temperament* 平和的性情 ▶ **phleg·mat·ic·al·ly** /-kli/ *adv.*

phloem /ˈfləʊem; *NAmE* ˈfloʊ-/ *noun* [U] (*biology* 生) the material in a plant containing very small tubes that carry sugars produced in the leaves around the plant 韧皮部（由筛管等将叶制造的糖分输送到各部位的植物组织） ➲ COMPARE XYLEM

phlox /flɒks; *NAmE* flɑːks/ *noun* **1** a tall garden plant with groups of white, blue or red flowers with a sweet smell 福禄考（高大开花植物，可种植在花园） **2** a low, spreading plant with small white, blue or pink flowers 从生福禄考（低矮蔓生开花植物）

-phobe *combining form* (in nouns 构成名词) a person who dislikes a particular thing or particular people 厌恶…的人：*Anglophobe* 仇英者 ◇ *xenophobe* 仇外者 ➲ COMPARE -PHILE

pho·bia /ˈfəʊbiə; *NAmE* ˈfoʊ-/ *noun* **1** a strong unreasonable fear of sth 恐怖症，恐惧症（无名的极度恐惧）：*He has a phobia about flying.* 他有飞行恐惧症。 **2 -phobia** (in nouns 构成名词) a strong unreasonable fear or hatred of a particular thing 对…的恐惧症：*claustrophobia* 幽闭恐怖症 ◇ *xenophobia* 恐外症 ➲ COMPARE -PHILIA

pho·bic /ˈfəʊbɪk; *NAmE* ˈfoʊ-/ *noun* **1** a person who has a strong unreasonable fear or hatred of sth 恐惧症患者；极端仇视者：*cat phobics* 特别怕猫的人 **2 -phobic** (in adjectives 构成形容词) having a strong unreasonable fear or hatred of a particular thing 恐惧…的；仇恨…的：*claustrophobic* 幽闭恐怖的 ◇ *xenophobic* 仇外的 ▶ **pho·bic** *adj.*: *phobic anxiety* 由恐惧而生的焦虑

phoe·nix /ˈfiːnɪks/ *noun* (in stories) a magic bird that lives for several hundred years before burning itself and then being born again from its ASHES（传说中的）凤凰，长生鸟：*to rise like a phoenix from the ashes* (= to be powerful or successful again) 雄起如再生的凤凰

phone 🔑 /fəʊn; *NAmE* foʊn/ *noun, verb*

■ *noun* **1** 🔑 [U, C] a system for talking to sb else over long distances using wires or radio; a machine used for this; a telephone 电话；电话系统；电话机：*I have to make **a phone call**.* 我得打个电话。◇ *The **phone rang** and Pat answered it.* 电话响起，帕特接了。◇ *They like to do business **by phone/over the phone**.* 他们喜欢用电话谈生意。◇ *His phone must be switched off.* 他的电话一定是关机了。◇ *I hadn't got my phone with me.* 我没有带手机。◇ *a phone bill* 电话费单 ➲ SEE ALSO CELL PHONE, ENTRYPHONE™, MOBILE PHONE, PAYPHONE, TELEPHONE *n.* ➲ **EXPRESS YOURSELF** AT MESSAGE **2** 🔑 [C] the part of a phone that you hold in your hand and speak into; a telephone 电话听筒；电话：*to **pick up the phone*** 拿起电话 ◇ *to **put the phone down*** 放下电话 ◇ *He left the phone off the hook as he didn't want to be disturbed.* 他不想被电话打扰，就把电话听筒摘下来了。 ➲ SEE ALSO ANSWERPHONE, TELEPHONE *n.* **3 -phone** (in nouns 构成名词) an instrument that uses or makes sound（发声或使用声音的）工具，仪器：*dictaphone* 口述录音机 ◇ *xylophone* 木琴 **4 -phone** (in adjectives and nouns 构成形容词和名词) speaking a particular language; a person who does this 说某种语言的；讲某种语言的人：*anglophone* 讲英语的（人）◇ *francophone* 讲法语的（人） **5** (*phonetics* 语音) a sound made in speech, especially when not considered as part of the sound system of a particular language 音子；音素 ➲ COMPARE PHONEME

IDM **be on the ˈphone 1** to be using the telephone 在打电话：*He's been on the phone to Kate for more than an hour.* 他给凯特打电话讲了一个多小时了。 **2** (*BrE*) to have a telephone in your home or place of work（在家中或工作单位）有电话，安了电话：*They're not on the phone at the holiday cottage.* 他们的度假别墅没装电话。

▼ **BRITISH/AMERICAN** 英式 / 美式英语

phone / call / ring

Verbs 动词

- In *BrE*, **to phone**, **to ring** and **to call** are the usual ways of saying **to telephone**. In *NAmE* the most common word is **call**, but **phone** is also used. Speakers of *NAmE* do not say **ring**. **Telephone** is very formal and is used mainly in *BrE*. 在英式英语中，phone、ring 和 call 为表示打电话的惯常用语。在美式英语中，call 最常用，但也用 phone。说美式英语的人不用 ring。telephone 非常正式，主要用于英式英语。

Nouns 名词

- You can use **call** or **phone call** (more formal) in both *BrE* and *NAmE*. 在英式英语和美式英语中，用 call 或 phone call（较正式）均可：*Were there any phone calls for me?* 有我的电话吗？◇ *How do I make a local call?* 本地电话怎么打？ The idiom **give sb a call** is also common. 习语 give sb a call 亦常用：*I'll give you a call tonight.* 我今晚会给你打电话。 In informal *BrE* you could also say 非正式英式英语中亦可说：*I'll give you a ring tonight.* 我今晚会给你打电话。

P

■ *verb* (*especially BrE*) (*BrE also* ˌ**phone ˈup**) [I, T] to make a telephone call to sb 打电话 SYN **call**: *I was just phoning up for a chat.* 我只是打电话聊聊天。◇ *He phoned to invite me out for dinner.* 他打电话请我外出吃饭。◇ *Someone phone for an ambulance!* 谁打电话叫辆救护车！◇ *Could you **phone back** later?* 您过一会儿再打电话来好吗？◇ ***He phoned home**, but there was no reply.* 他往家里打电话，但没有人接。◇ ~ **sb/sth** *Don't forget to phone New York.* 别忘了往纽约打电话。◇ *For reservations, phone 020 281 3964.* 预订请拨打 020 281 3964。◇ *Phone them up and find out when they are coming.* 给他们打个电话，问问他们什么时候来。➲ WORDFINDER NOTE AT CALL

▼ **COLLOCATIONS 词语搭配**

Phones 电话

Making and receiving phone calls 打 / 接电话
- the phone/telephone **rings** 电话铃响了
- **answer/pick up/hang up** the phone/telephone 接 / 挂电话
- **lift/pick up/hold/replace** the receiver 拿起 / 拿着 / 放回听筒
- **dial** a (phone/wrong) number/an extension number/an area code 拨打（电话）号码；拨错号码；拨打分机号码；拨打区号
- **call sb/talk (to sb)/speak (to sb)** on the phone/telephone; from home/work/the office 给某人打电话；从家里 / 工作地点 / 办公室给某人打电话
- **make/get/receive** a phone call 打 / 接电话
- **take** the phone **off the hook** (= remove the receiver so that the phone does not ring) 摘下电话听筒
- the line is (*BrE*) **engaged**/ (*especially NAmE*) **busy** 占线
- the phones have been (*NAmE*) **ringing off the hook** (= ringing frequently) 电话铃声不断
- **put sb through/get through** to the person you want to speak to 给某人接通另一人的电话；打通电话
- **put sb** on hold (= so that they must wait for the person they want to speak to) 让某人不要挂上电话（以便等想找的人接电话）
- **call from/use** a landline 用座机打电话

Mobile/cell phones 手机
- **be/talk** on a (*both BrE*) mobile phone/mobile/(*especially NAmE*) cell phone/(*informal, especially NAmE*) cell 用手机讲电话
- **use/answer/call** (**sb on**)/**get a message on** your mobile phone/mobile/cell phone/cell 使用 / 接听 / 拨打某人的手机；用手机接收信息
- **switch/turn on/off** your mobile phone/mobile/cell phone/cell 开启 / 关闭手机
- **charge/recharge** your mobile phone/mobile/cell phone/cell 给手机充电
- a mobile/cell phone **is on/is off/rings/goes off** 手机开机 / 关机 / 响铃 / 没电关机
- (*BrE*) **top up** your mobile (phone) 给手机充值
- **send/receive** a text (message)/an SMS (message)/a fax 发送 / 接收信息 / 短信 / 传真
- **insert/remove/change** a SIM card 插入 / 取出 / 更换 SIM 卡

PHR V ˌ**phone ˈin** (*especially BrE*) **1** to make a telephone call to the place where you work 往工作单位打电话: + **adj.** *Three people have **phoned in sick** already this morning.* 今天上午已有三个人打电话来请病假。 **2** to make a telephone call to a radio or television station 往（电台或电视台）打电话；打热线电话: *Listeners are invited to phone in with their comments.* 听众被鼓励拨打热线电话发表意见。➲ RELATED NOUN PHONE-IN ˌ**phone sth**↔ˈ**in** (*especially BrE*) to make a telephone call to the place where you work in order to give sb some information 往工作单位打电话通报某事: *I need you to phone the story in before five.* 我要你在五点钟前把整件事电告单位。

ˈ**phone book** *noun* = TELEPHONE DIRECTORY

ˈ**phone booth** (*also* ˈ**telephone booth**) *noun* a place that is partly separated from the surrounding area, containing a public telephone, in a hotel, restaurant, in the street, etc. （半封闭的）公用电话间，电话亭

ˈ**phone box** (*also* ˈ**telephone box**, ˈ**telephone kiosk**, ˈ**call box**) (*all BrE*) *noun* a small unit with walls and a roof, containing a public telephone, in the street, etc. （全封闭的）公用电话亭，电话间

ˈ**phone call** *noun* = CALL (1)

phone·card /ˈfəʊnkɑːd; *NAmE* ˈfoʊnkɑːrd/ *noun* (*NAmE also* ˈ**calling card**) **1** a plastic card that you can use in some public telephones instead of money （公共电话用）电话卡 **2** (*NAmE*) a card with a number on it that you use in order to pay to make a call from any phone. The cost of the call is charged to your account and you pay it later. （转账付费）电话卡

ˈ**phone hacking** *noun* [U] the activity of finding a way to access the information stored on sb else's phone without their permission, especially to listen to their VOICEMAIL 电话窃听，窃取他人电话信息（尤指窃听电话留言）: *£1 million in damages has been paid out to victims of phone hacking.* 已经向电话窃听受害者支付 100 万英镑的损害赔偿金。▸ ˈ**phone hacker** *noun*

ˈ**phone-in** (*BrE*) (*NAmE* ˈ**call-in**) *noun* a radio or television programme in which people can telephone and make comments or ask questions about a particular subject （广播、电视的）热线直播节目，听众来电直播节目 ➲ WORDFINDER NOTE AT RADIO

phon·eme /ˈfəʊniːm; *NAmE* ˈfoʊ-/ *noun* (*phonetics* 语音) any one of the set of smallest units of speech in a language that distinguish one word from another. In English, the /s/ in *sip* and the /z/ in *zip* represent two different phonemes. 音位，音素（区分单词的最小语音单位，英语 sip 中的 /s/ 和 zip 中的 /z/ 是两个不同的音位） ▸ **phon·em·ic** /fəˈniːmɪk/ *adj.*

ˈ**phone number** *noun* = TELEPHONE NUMBER

ˈ**phone tapping** *noun* = TELEPHONE TAPPING

phon·et·ic /fəˈnetɪk/ *adj.* **1** using special symbols to represent each different speech sound 表示语音的；音标的: *the International Phonetic Alphabet* 国际音标 ◇ *a phonetic symbol/transcription* 音标；注音 **2** (of a spelling or spelling system 拼写或拼写系统) that closely matches the sounds represented 与发音近似的: *Spanish spelling is phonetic, unlike English spelling.* 与英语不同，西班牙语的拼写与发音相近。 **3** connected with the sounds of human speech 语音的 ▸ **phon·et·ic·al·ly** /-kli/ *adv.*

phon·et·ics /fəˈnetɪks/ *noun* [U] the study of speech sounds and how they are produced 语音学 ➲ WORDFINDER NOTE AT PRONUNCIATION ➲ MORE LIKE THIS 29, page R28 ▸ **phon·et·ician** /ˌfəʊnəˈtɪʃn; ˌfɒn-; *NAmE* ˌfoʊn-; ˌfɑːn-/ *noun*

pho·ney (*also* **phony** *especially in NAmE*) /ˈfəʊni; *NAmE* ˈfoʊni/ *adj.*, *noun*

■ *adj.* (**pho·nier**, **pho·ni·est**) (*informal, disapproving*) not real or true; false, and trying to trick people 假的；冒充的；欺骗的 SYN **fake**: *She spoke with a phoney Russian accent.* 她用一种伪装的俄国腔调说话。

■ *noun* (*pl.* **-neys** or **-nies**) (*informal*) a person who is not honest or sincere; a thing that is not real or true 不诚实的人；冒充的人（或东西）；冒牌货

ˌ**phoney ˈwar** *noun* [sing.] (*BrE*) a period of time when two groups are officially at war but not actually fighting （战争时期并未真正交战的）假战争

phon·ic /ˈfɒnɪk; *NAmE* ˈfɑːnɪk/ *adj.* **1** (*specialist*) relating to sound; relating to sounds made in speech 声音的；语音的 **2** **-phonic** (in adjectives 构成形容词) connected with an instrument that uses or makes sound 用…传声的；用…发声的: *telephonic* 电话的

phon·ics /ˈfɒnɪks; *NAmE* ˈfɑːn-/ *noun* [U] a method of teaching people to read based on the sounds that letters represent 语音教学法；拼读法 ➲ MORE LIKE THIS 29, page R28

phono- /ˈfəʊnəʊ; *NAmE* ˈfoʊnoʊ/ (*also* **phon-**) *combining form* (in nouns, adjectives and adverbs 构成名词、形容词和副词) connected with sound or sounds 声的；声音的；语音的：*phonetic* 语音的

phono·graph /ˈfəʊnəɡrɑːf; *NAmE* ˈfoʊnəɡræf/ *noun* (*old-fashioned*) = RECORD PLAYER

phon·ology /fəˈnɒlədʒi; *NAmE* -ˈnɑːl-/ *noun* [U] (*linguistics* 语言) the speech sounds of a particular language; the study of these sounds 音系；音系学 ▸ **phono·logic·al** /ˌfəʊnəˈlɒdʒɪkl; ˌfɒn-; *NAmE* ˌfoʊnəˈlɑːdʒ-; ˌfɑːn-/ *adj.*：*phonological analysis* 音系分析 **phon·olo·gist** /fəˈnɒlədʒɪst; *NAmE* fəˈnɑːl-/ *noun*

phony (*especially NAmE*) = PHONEY

phooey /ˈfuːi/ *exclamation* used when you think sb/sth is wrong or silly （表示不信、轻蔑等）错了，真傻，呸，啐 ▸ **phooey** *noun* [U]：*It's all phooey!* 全错了！

phos·gene /ˈfɒzdʒiːn; *NAmE* ˈfɑːz-/ *noun* [U] a poisonous gas that was used as a CHEMICAL WEAPON during the First World War 光气，碳酰氯（第一次世界大战中用作化学武器）

phos·phate /ˈfɒsfeɪt; *NAmE* ˈfɑːs-/ *noun* [C, U] (*chemistry* 化) any COMPOUND containing phosphorus, used in industry or for helping plants to grow 磷酸盐；磷酸酯：*phosphate-free washing powder* 无磷洗衣粉

phos·phor·es·cent /ˌfɒsfəˈresnt; *NAmE* ˌfɑːs-/ *adj.* (*specialist*) **1** producing a faint light in the dark （在黑暗中）发微光的，发荧光的 ➲ COMPARE FLUORESCENT **2** producing light without heat or with so little heat that it cannot be felt 发磷光的 ▸ **phos·phor·es·cence** /-sns/ *noun* [U]

phos·phor·ic acid /fɒsˌfɒrɪk ˈæsɪd; *NAmE* fɑːsˌfɔːrɪk/ *noun* [U] an acid used in FERTILIZERS and in the production of DETERGENTS and food 磷酸（用于化肥，以及生产洗涤剂和食品）

phos·phorus /ˈfɒsfərəs; *NAmE* ˈfɑːs-/ *noun* [U] (*symb.* **P**) a chemical element. Phosphorus is found in several different forms, including as a poisonous, pale yellow substance that shines in the dark and starts to burn as soon as it is placed in air. 磷

phot·ic /ˈfəʊtɪk; *NAmE* ˈfoʊ-/ *adj.* (*specialist*) **1** relating to, or caused by, light 光的；光引起的 **2** relating to the part of the ocean which receives enough light for plants to grow （海洋）光照充足的，透光的：*the photic zone* 透光带

photo ⚷ /ˈfəʊtəʊ; *NAmE* ˈfoʊtoʊ/ *noun* (*pl.* **-os**) = PHOTOGRAPH：*a* ***colour/black-and-white photo*** 彩色/黑白照片 ◇ *a* ***passport photo*** 护照照片 ◇ *a* ***photo album*** (= a book for keeping your photos in) 相册 ◇ ***I'll take a photo*** *of you.* 我来给你拍个照。 HELP The usual phrase in *NAmE* is **take a picture**. 美式英语常用 take a picture。 ➲ SYNONYMS AT PHOTOGRAPH ➲ EXPRESS YOURSELF AT DESCRIBE

photo- /ˈfəʊtəʊ; *NAmE* ˈfoʊtoʊ/ *combining form* (in nouns, adjectives, verbs and adverbs 构成名词、形容词、动词和副词) **1** connected with light 光的；关于光的：*photosynthesis* 光合作用 **2** connected with photography 摄影的；照相的：*photogenic* 上相的

photo·bomb /ˈfəʊtəʊbɒm; *NAmE* ˈfoʊtoʊbɑːm/ *verb* (*informal*) **1** [T, I] ~ (**sth**) to spoil a photograph by suddenly appearing or doing sth unexpected as the picture is taken （在拍照时）乱入镜头 **2** [T] ~ **sb** to suddenly appear or do sth unexpected while a photograph is being taken of sb 在（某人）拍照时闯入镜头：*He photobombed the actress as she was posing for the press.* 那名女演员摆姿势给媒体拍照时，他突然闯入镜头。 ▸ **photo·bomb** *noun*：*A fan decided to drop a photobomb on the reporter.* 一名粉丝决定在记者拍照时闯入镜头。 **photo·bomb·er** *noun* **photo·bomb·ing** *noun* [U]

ˈ**photo booth** *noun* a small structure with walls and a roof where you can put money in a machine and get a photograph of yourself in a few minutes 自助快照亭

photo·call /ˈfəʊtəʊkɔːl; *NAmE* ˈfoʊtoʊ-/ *noun* a time that is arranged in advance when newspaper photographers are invited to take photographs of sb （摄影记者预约的）拍照时间；媒体拍照时间：*The president joined the team for a photocall.* 总统加入到团队中接受媒体拍照。

photo·cell /ˈfəʊtəʊsel; *NAmE* ˈfoʊtoʊ-/ *noun* = PHOTOELECTRIC CELL

photo·chem·ical /ˌfəʊtəʊˈkemɪkl; *NAmE* ˌfoʊtoʊ-/ *adj.* (*chemistry* 化) caused by or relating to the chemical action of light 光化作用的；光化学的：*photochemical smog* 光化烟雾

photo·copier /ˈfəʊtəʊkɒpiə(r); *NAmE* ˈfoʊtoʊkɑːp-/ (*also* **copier** *especially in NAmE*) *noun* a machine that makes copies of documents, etc. by photographing them 复印机；影印机 ➲ VISUAL VOCAB PAGE V71

photo·copy ⚷ /ˈfəʊtəʊkɒpi; *NAmE* ˈfoʊtoʊkɑːpi/ *noun, verb*

■ *noun* ⚷ (*also* **copy**) (*pl.* **-ies**) a copy of a document, etc. made by the action of light on a specially treated surface 影印本；复印件：*Make as many photocopies as you need.* 你需要多少复印件就复印多少吧。

■ *verb* (**photo·cop·ies**, **photo·copy·ing**, **photo·cop·ied**, **photo·cop·ied**) (*also* **copy** *especially in BrE*) **1** ⚷ [T, I] ~ (**sth**) to make a photocopy of sth 影印；复制；复印：*a photocopied letter* 复印的信 ◇ *Can you get these photocopied for me by 5 o'clock?* 你能不能在 5 点钟前把这些给我复印好？ ◇ *I seem to have spent most of the day photocopying.* 我这一天的大部分时间似乎都花在复印上了。 **2** [I] ~ **well/badly** (of printed material 印刷品) to produce a good/bad photocopy 影印得好/不好：*The comments in pencil haven't photocopied very well.* 用铅笔写的评语没有复印清楚。

photo·elec·tric /ˌfəʊtəʊɪˈlektrɪk; *NAmE* ˌfoʊtoʊ-/ *adj.* using an electric current that is controlled by light 光电的

ˌ**photoelectric** ˈ**cell** (*also* **photo·cell**) *noun* an electric device that uses a stream of light. When the stream is broken it shows that sb/sth is present, and can be used to control alarms, machinery, etc. 光电池；光电感应器；光电管

ˌ**photo** ˈ**finish** *noun* [usually sing.] the end of a race in which the leading runners or horses are so close together that only a photograph of them passing the finishing line can show which is the winner 摄影定名次（竞赛成绩十分接近，以终点线摄影决定结果）

photo·fit /ˈfəʊtəʊfɪt; *NAmE* ˈfoʊtoʊfɪt/ *noun* (*BrE*) a picture of a person who is wanted by the police, made by putting together photographs of different features of faces from information that is given by sb who has seen the person 通缉犯拼像（根据目击者提供的信息拼凑而成） ➲ COMPARE E-FIT™, IDENTIKIT™

photo·gen·ic /ˌfəʊtəʊˈdʒenɪk; *NAmE* ˌfoʊtoʊ-/ *adj.* looking attractive in photographs 上镜的；上相的：*I'm not very photogenic.* 我不大上相。

photo·graph ⚷ /ˈfəʊtəɡrɑːf; *NAmE* ˈfoʊtəɡræf/ *noun, verb*

■ *noun* ⚷ (*also* **photo**) a picture that is made by using a camera that stores images in digital form or that has a film sensitive to light inside it 照片；相片：***aerial/satellite photographs*** 飞机航拍/卫星照片 ◇ *colour photographs* 彩色照片 ◇ *Please enclose a recent passport-sized photograph of yourself.* 请附寄一张近照，大小同护照用相片。 ◇ *I spent the day* ***taking photographs*** *of the city.* 我花了一天时间拍摄这座城市的照片。 HELP The usual phrase in *NAmE* is **take pictures**. 美式英语常用 take pictures。

P

▼SYNONYMS 同义词辨析

photograph

picture • photo • shot • snapshot/snap • print

These are all words for a picture that has been made using a camera. 以上各词均指照片、相片。

photograph a picture that has been made using a camera 指照片、相片： *a photograph of the house* 这座房子的照片 ◇ *Can I take a photograph?* 我可以拍个照吗？

picture a photograph 指照片、相片： *We had our picture taken in front of the hotel.* 我们在旅馆前照了相。

photo a photograph 指照片、相片： *a passport photo* 护照照片

PHOTOGRAPH, PICTURE OR PHOTO? 用 photograph、picture 还是 photo?

Photograph is slightly more formal and **photo** is slightly less formal. **Picture** is used especially in the context of photographs in newspapers, magazines and books.
* photograph 较正式而 photo 较非正式。picture 尤指报纸、杂志和书籍中的照片。

shot a photograph 指照片、相片： *I tried to get a shot of him in the water.* 我试着给他拍一张在水中的照片。
NOTE **Shot** often places more emphasis on the process of taking the photograph, rather than the finished picture.
* shot 通常更强调拍摄照片的过程，而非已拍出的照片。

snapshot/snap an informal photograph that is taken quickly, and not by a professional photographer 指非专业摄影师随手抓拍的照片： *holiday snaps* 度假时随手拍的照片

print a copy of a photograph that is produced from film or from a digital camera 指由胶片或数码相机洗印的照片： *a set of prints* 一套照片

PATTERNS
- a **colour** photograph/picture/photo/snap/print
- to **take** a photograph/picture/photo/shot/snapshot

■ *verb* **1** [T] to take a photograph of sb/sth 拍照；照相： ~ **sb/sth** *He has photographed some of the world's most beautiful women.* 他为几位倾世佳丽拍过照片。◇ *a beautifully photographed book* (= with good photographs in it) 一本有精美照片的书 ◇ ~ **sb/sth + adj.** *She refused to be photographed nude.* 她拒拍裸体照片。◇ ~ **sb/sth doing sth** *They were photographed playing with their children.* 他们跟孩子一起嬉戏的情景被拍成了照片。 **2** [I] ~ **well, badly, etc.** to look or not look attractive in photographs（很、不等）上相，上镜： *Some people just don't photograph well.* 有些人就是不上相。

pho·tog·raph·er /fəˈtɒɡrəfə(r); *NAmE* fəˈtɑːɡ-/ *noun* a person who takes photographs, especially as a job 拍照者；摄影师： *a wildlife/fashion/portrait photographer* 野生动物 / 时装 / 人像摄影师

photo·graph·ic /ˌfəʊtəˈɡræfɪk; *NAmE* ˌfoʊ-/ *adj.* connected with photographs or photography 摄影的；摄制的；照片的： *photographic equipment/film/images* 摄影设备 / 胶片 / 图像 ◇ *They produced a photographic record of the event.* 他们为这一事件制作了一套照片实录。◇ *His paintings are almost photographic in detail.* 他的绘画细致得简直和照片一样逼真。 ▶ **photo·graph·ic·al·ly** /-kli/ *adv.*

ˌphotographic ˈmemory *noun* [usually sing.] the ability to remember things accurately and in great detail after seeing them 精确的记忆力

pho·tog·raphy /fəˈtɒɡrəfi; *NAmE* fəˈtɑːɡ-/ *noun* [U] the art, process or job of taking photographs or filming sth 照相术；摄影： *colour/flash/aerial, etc. photography* 彩色、闪光、空中等摄影 ◇ *fashion photography by David Burn* 戴维•伯恩的时装摄影 ◇ *Her hobbies include hiking and photography.* 她的业余爱好包括徒步旅行和摄影。◇ *the director of photography* (= the person who is in charge of the actual filming of a film/movie, programme, etc.) 摄影导演 ◇ *Did you see the film about Antarctica? The photography was superb!* 你看了关于南极的那部电影没有？摄影棒极了！ ➲ VISUAL VOCAB PAGE V45

photo·jour·nal·ism /ˌfəʊtəʊˈdʒɜːnəlɪzəm; *NAmE* ˌfoʊtoʊˈdʒɜːrn-/ *noun* [U] the work of giving news using mainly photographs, especially in a magazine 图片新闻报道；摄影新闻报道；摄影新闻工作

photo·mon·tage /ˌfəʊtəʊmɒnˈtɑːʒ; *NAmE* ˌfoʊtoʊmɑːnˈtɑːʒ/ *noun* [C, U] a picture which is made up of different photographs put together; the technique of producing these pictures 合成照片（术）；照相剪接

pho·ton /ˈfəʊtɒn; *NAmE* ˈfoʊtɑːn/ *noun* (*physics* 物) a unit of ELECTROMAGNETIC energy 光子

ˈphoto opportunity *noun* an occasion when a famous person arranges to be photographed doing sth that will impress the public（名人）拍照的时机；（名人）接受拍照的时间

photo·real·ism /ˌfəʊtəʊˈriːəlɪzəm; -ˈrɪəl-; *NAmE* ˌfoʊtoʊˈriːəlɪzəm/ *noun* [U] an artistic style that represents a subject in an accurate and detailed way, like a photograph 照相写实主义（如照片一般精确细致地表现主题）

photo·recep·tor /ˈfəʊtəʊrɪseptə(r); *NAmE* ˈfoʊtoʊ-/ *noun* (*biology* 生) a cell or an organ that is sensitive to light 光感受器

photo·sensi·tive /ˌfəʊtəʊˈsensətɪv; *NAmE* ˌfoʊtoʊ-/ *adj.* (*specialist*) reacting to light, for example by changing colour or producing an electrical signal 光敏的；感光的

ˈphoto shoot *noun* an occasion when a photographer takes pictures of sb, for example a famous person, fashion model, etc. for use in a magazine, etc.（以名人、时装模特等为对象的）专业摄影： *I went on a photo shoot to Rio with him.* 我和他一起去里约拍照了。

photo·shop /ˈfəʊtəʊʃɒp; *NAmE* ˈfoʊtoʊʃɑːp/ (*also* **Photo·shop**) *verb* (**-pp-**) ~ **sth** to change a picture or photograph using a computer 用计算机修改（图片或照片）： *I'm sure this picture has been photoshopped.* 我敢说这张图片准用电脑修改过。

photo·stat /ˈfəʊtəstæt; *NAmE* ˈfoʊ-/ *noun* a photocopy or a machine that produces them 直接影印本；直接复印机

photo·syn·thesis /ˌfəʊtəʊˈsɪnθəsɪs; *NAmE* ˌfoʊtoʊ-/ *noun* [U] (*biology* 生) the process by which green plants turn CARBON DIOXIDE and water into food using energy obtained from light from the sun 光合作用 ➲ COLLOCATIONS AT LIFE

photo·syn·the·size (*BrE also* **-ise**) /ˌfəʊtəʊˈsɪnθəsaɪz; *NAmE* ˌfoʊtoʊ-/ *verb* [I, T] ~ (**sth**) (*biology* 生) (of plants 植物) to make food by means of PHOTOSYNTHESIS 通过光合作用产生（养料）；进行光合作用

photo·trop·ism /ˌfəʊtəʊˈtrəʊpɪzəm; *NAmE* ˌfoʊtoʊˈtroʊ-/ *noun* [U] (*biology* 生) the action of a plant turning towards or away from light（植物的正或负）向光性 ▶ **photo·trop·ic** /-ˈtrɒpɪk; *NAmE* -ˈtrɑːpɪk/ *adj.*

phrasal /ˈfreɪzl/ *adj.* of or connected with a phrase 短语的；词组的

ˌphrasal ˈverb *noun* (*grammar* 语法) a verb combined with an adverb or a preposition, or sometimes both, to give a new meaning, for example *go in for*, *win over* and *see to* 短语动词；动词词组

phrase /freɪz/ *noun*, *verb*

■ *noun* **1** (*grammar* 语法) a small group of words without a FINITE verb that together have a particular meaning and that typically form part of a sentence. 'the green car' and 'on Friday morning' are phrases. 短语；词组 ➲ SYNONYMS AT WORD ➲ SEE ALSO NOUN PHRASE **2** a group of words which have a particular meaning when used together 成语；习语；惯用法；警句： *a memorable phrase* 易记的警句 ◇ *She was, in her own favourite phrase, 'a woman without a past'.* 用她自己最喜欢的字眼说，她是个"没有不清白过去的女人"。 ➲ SEE ALSO CATCHPHRASE

3 (*music* 音) a short series of notes that form a unit within a longer passage in a piece of music 乐句；乐节 IDM SEE COIN *v.*, TURN *n.*

■ ***verb* 1** [T] to say or write sth in a particular way （以某种方式）表达，措辞，推敲： **~ sth (+ adv./prep.)** *a carefully phrased remark* 措辞谨慎的话语 ◇ *I agree with what he says, but I'd have phrased it differently.* 我赞同他说的，但我会以不同的方式表述。 ◇ **~ sth as sth** *Her order was phrased as a suggestion.* 她的命令表述得像是一项建议。 **2** [I, T] **~ (sth)** to divide a piece of music into small groups of notes; to play or sing these in a particular way, especially in an effective way 划分乐句，分乐节（尤指为奏乐或歌唱）

ˈphrase book *noun* a book containing lists of common expressions translated into another language, especially for people visiting a foreign country 常用语手册，会话手册（尤指为出国旅游者使用）

phrase·ology /ˌfreɪziˈɒlədʒi; *NAmE* -ˈɑːlə-/ *noun* [U] (*formal*) the particular way in which words and phrases are arranged when saying or writing sth 措辞；遣词造句

phras·ing /ˈfreɪzɪŋ/ *noun* [U] **1** the words used to express sth 措辞；用语： *The phrasing of the report is ambiguous.* 这份报告的措辞模棱两可。 **2** (*music* 音) the way in which a musician or singer divides a piece of music into phrases by pausing in suitable places 乐句划分法；分句法

phreak·ing /ˈfriːkɪŋ/ *noun* [U] (*informal, especially NAmE*) the act of getting into a communications system illegally, usually in order to make telephone calls without paying 非法窃入通信系统；（通常指）窃用电话 ▶ **phreak·er** *noun*

phren·ology /frəˈnɒlədʒi; *NAmE* -ˈnɑːl-/ *noun* [U] the study of the shape of the human head, which some people think is a guide to a person's character 颅相学 ▶ **phren·olo·gist** /frəˈnɒlədʒɪst; *NAmE* -ˈnɑːl-/ *noun*

phwoah (*also* **phwoor, phwoar**) /ˈfwɔːə/ *exclamation* (*BrE, informal*) used when you find sth or sb very impressive and attractive, especially in a sexual way （对某事物或某人的性感魅力等表示赞叹）哇噻

phylum /ˈfaɪləm/ *noun* (*pl.* **phyla** /-lə/) (*biology* 生) a group into which animals, plants, etc. are divided, smaller than a KINGDOM and larger than a CLASS （生物分类学的）门 ➲ COMPARE GENUS ➲ **WORDFINDER NOTE** AT BREED

phys·ic·al 🔑 AW /ˈfɪzɪkl/ *adj., noun*

■ ***adj.***

• **THE BODY** 身体 **1** 🔑 [usually before noun] connected with a person's body rather than their mind 身体的；肉体的；躯体的： *physical fitness* 健康体魄 ◇ *physical appearance* 外貌 ◇ *The ordeal has affected both her mental and physical health.* 痛苦的经历损害了她的身心健康。 ◇ *He tends to avoid all physical contact.* 他倾向于避免一切身体接触。 ➲ COLLOCATIONS ON NEXT PAGE

• **REAL THINGS** 实物 **2** 🔑 [only before noun] connected with things that actually exist or are present and can be seen, felt, etc. rather than things that only exist in a person's mind 客观存在的；现实的；物质的；有形的： *the* ***physical world/universe/environment*** 客观世界 / 宇宙 / 环境 ◇ *the* ***physical properties*** (= the colour, weight, shape, etc.) *of copper* 铜的物理性质

• **NATURE/SCIENCE** 自然；科学 **3** 🔑 [only before noun] according to the laws of nature 根据自然规律的；符合自然法则的： *It is a physical impossibility to be in two places at once.* 同时身处两地在自然法则上是不可能的。 **4** 🔑 [only before noun] connected with the scientific study of forces such as heat, light, sound, etc. and how they affect objects 物理学的： *physical laws* 物理定律

• **SEX** 性 **5** 🔑 involving sex 性欲的；肉欲的： *physical love* 性爱 ◇ *They are having a physical relationship.* 他们有着性关系。

• **PERSON** 人 **6** (*informal*) (of a person 人) liking to touch other people a lot 爱触摸他人的；爱动手动脚的： *She's not very physical.* 她不爱摩摩挲挲的。

• **VIOLENT** 暴力 **7** (*informal*) violent (used to avoid saying this in a direct way) 使用武力的；粗暴的： *Are you going to cooperate or do we have to get physical?* 你是合作呢，还是要我们动粗？

■ ***noun*** (*also* ˌ**physical examiˈnation**) a medical examination of a person's body, for example, to check that they are fit enough to do a particular job 体检；体格检查

ˌ**physical eduˈcation** *noun* = PE

ˌ**physical geˈography** *noun* [U] **1** the scientific study of the natural features on the surface of the earth, for example mountains and rivers 自然地理学 **2** the way in which the natural features of a place are arranged 地貌特征；地形；地势： *the physical geography of Scotland* 苏格兰的地形

phys·ic·al·ity /ˌfɪzɪˈkæləti/ *noun* [U] (*formal*) the quality of being physical rather than emotional or spiritual 肉体性

phys·ic·al·ly 🔑 AW /ˈfɪzɪkli/ *adv.* **1** 🔑 in a way that is connected with a person's body rather than their mind 身体上；肉体上： *mentally and physically handicapped* 身心俱残 ◇ *physically and emotionally exhausted* 身心交瘁 ◇ *I felt physically sick before the exam.* 考前我感到身体不适。 ◇ *I don't find him physically attractive.* 我不觉得他外表吸引人。 ◇ *They were physically prevented from entering the building.* 他们被挡在大楼门外。 **2** 🔑 according to the laws of nature or what is probable 依据自然规律；按自然法则；根本上： *It's physically impossible to finish by the end of the week.* 根本不可能在本周末之前完成。

ˌ**physical ˈscience** *noun* [U] (*also* **the physical sciences** [pl.]) the areas of science concerned with studying natural forces and things that are not alive, for example physics and chemistry 自然科学；物理科学 ➲ COMPARE LIFE SCIENCES

ˌ**physical ˈtherapist** (*US*) (*BrE* **physio·ther·ap·ist**, *informal* **physio**) *noun* a person whose job is to give patients physical therapy 物理治疗师；理疗师

ˌ**physical ˈtherapy** (*US*) (*BrE* **physio·ther·apy**, *informal* **physio**) *noun* [U] the treatment of disease, injury or weakness in the joints or muscles by exercises, MASSAGE and the use of light and heat 物理疗法；理疗

ˌ**physical ˈtraining** *noun* = PT (1)

phys·ician /fɪˈzɪʃn/ *noun* (*especially NAmE*) a doctor, especially one who is a specialist in general medicine and not SURGERY 医师；（尤指）内科医生 ➲ COMPARE SURGEON HELP This word is now old-fashioned in *BrE*. **Doctor** or **GP** is used instead. 在英式英语中，本词现已过时，而代之以 doctor 或 GP。

physi·cist /ˈfɪzɪsɪst/ *noun* a scientist who studies physics 物理学家；物理学研究者： *a nuclear physicist* 核物理学家

phys·ics 🔑 /ˈfɪzɪks/ *noun* [U] the scientific study of matter and energy and the relationships between them, including the study of forces, heat, light, sound, electricity and the structure of atoms 物理学： *a degree in physics* 物理学学位 ◇ ***particle/nuclear/theoretical physics*** 粒子 / 核 / 理论物理学 ◇ *the laws of physics* 物理定律 ◇ *a school physics department* 学校的物理系 ◇ *to study the physics of the electron* 研究电子物理 ➲ SEE ALSO ASTROPHYSICS, GEOPHYSICS ➲ **MORE LIKE THIS** 29, page R28

WORDFINDER 联想词： amplitude, **atom**, energy, fission, force, frequency, gravity, molecule, nuclear

physio /ˈfɪziəʊ; *NAmE* ˈfɪzioʊ/ *noun* (*pl.* **-os**) (*BrE, informal*) **1** [U] = PHYSIOTHERAPY **2** [C] = PHYSIOTHERAPIST

physio- /ˈfɪziəʊ; *NAmE* ˈfɪzioʊ/ *combining form* (in nouns, adjectives and adverbs 构成名词、形容词和副词) **1** connected with nature 自然的 **2** connected with PHYSIOLOGY 生理学的

physi·ognomy /ˌfɪziˈɒnəmi; *NAmE* -ˈɑːnə-/ *noun* (*pl.* **-ies**) (*formal*) the shape and features of a person's face 容貌；相貌；面相

physi·olo·gist /ˌfɪziˈɒlədʒɪst; *NAmE* -ˈɑːlə-/ *noun* a scientist who studies physiology 生理学家；生理学研究者

P

physi·ology /ˌfɪziˈɒlədʒi; *NAmE* -ˈɑːlə-/ *noun* **1** [U] the scientific study of the normal functions of living things 生理学：*the department of anatomy and physiology* 解剖生理学系 **2** [U, sing.] the way in which a particular living thing functions 生理机能：*plant physiology* 植物的生理机能 ◇ *the physiology of the horse* 马的生理机能 ▸ **physio·logic·al** /ˌfɪziəˈlɒdʒɪkl; *NAmE* -ˈlɑːdʒ-/ *adj.*：*the physiological effect of space travel* 宇宙航行的生理影响 **physio·lo·gic·al·ly** /-ɪkli/ *adv.*

physio·ther·ap·ist /ˌfɪziəʊˈθerəpɪst; *NAmE* ˌfɪzioʊ-/ (*also informal* **physio**) (*both BrE*) (*US* ˌ**physical** ˈ**therapist**) *noun* a person whose job is to give patients physiotherapy 物理治疗师；理疗师

physio·ther·apy /ˌfɪziəʊˈθerəpi; *NAmE* ˌfɪzioʊ-/ (*also informal* **physio**) (*both BrE*) (*US* ˌ**physical** ˈ**therapy**) *noun* [U] the treatment of disease, injury or weakness in the joints or muscles by exercises, MASSAGE and the use of light and heat 物理疗法；理疗 ⊃ **WORDFINDER NOTE AT CURE** ⊃ **COLLOCATIONS AT INJURY**

phys·ique /fɪˈziːk/ *noun* [C, U] the size and shape of a person's body 体格；体形 **SYN** **build**：*He has the physique of a rugby player.* 他有橄榄球运动员的体形。◇ *a powerful physique* 健壮的体格

pi /paɪ/ *noun* **1** (*geometry* 几何) the symbol π used to show the RATIO of the CIRCUMFERENCE of (= distance around) a circle to its DIAMETER (= distance across), that is 3.14159... 圆周率 **2** the 16th letter of the Greek alphabet (Π, π) 希腊字母表的第 16 个字母

pi·an·is·simo /ˌpiəˈnɪsɪməʊ; *NAmE* -moʊ/ *adv.* (*abbr.* **pp**) (*music* 音, *from Italian*) very quietly 很弱 **OPP** **fortissimo** ▸ **pi·an·is·simo** *adj.*

pi·an·ist /ˈpɪənɪst/ *noun* a person who plays the piano 钢琴弹奏者；钢琴家：*a concert pianist* 音乐会的钢琴演奏者 ◇ *a jazz pianist* 爵士乐钢琴演奏者

▼ **COLLOCATIONS** 词语搭配

Physical appearance 外貌

- A person may be described as **having** 描述一个人的长相可用 have 一词：

Eyes 眼睛

- (bright) blue/green/(dark/light) brown/hazel **eyes** （明亮的）蓝 / 绿 / （深 / 浅）棕色 / 浅绿褐色眼睛
- deep-set/sunken/bulging/protruding **eyes** 凹陷的 / 凸出的眼睛
- small/beady/sparkling/twinkling/(*informal*) shifty **eyes** 小的 / 小珠般圆亮的 / 亮晶晶的 / 闪闪发亮的 / 贼溜溜的眼睛
- piercing/penetrating/steely **eyes** 敏锐的 / 锐利的眼睛；冷冰冰的眼神
- bloodshot/watery/puffy **eyes** 布满血丝的 / 水汪汪的 / 肿胀的眼睛
- bushy/thick/dark/raised/arched **eyebrows** 浓密的 / 扬起的 / 弓形的眉毛
- long/dark/thick/curly/false **eyelashes**/**lashes** 长长的 / 浓密的 / 弯曲的 / 假的眼睫毛

Face 脸

- a flat/bulbous/pointed/sharp/snub **nose** 塌 / 蒜头 / 尖头 / 尖 / 短平而上翘的鼻子
- a straight/a hooked/a Roman/(*formal*) an aquiline **nose** 挺直的鼻子；鹰钩鼻；高鼻梁；鹰钩鼻
- full/thick/thin/pouty **lips** 丰满的 / 厚 / 薄 / 翘嘴唇
- dry/chapped/cracked **lips** 干的 / 皲裂的 / 干裂的嘴唇
- flushed/rosy/red/ruddy/pale **cheeks** 发红的 / 红润的 / 苍白的面颊
- soft/chubby/sunken **cheeks** 柔嫩的 / 胖乎乎的 / 凹陷的面颊
- white/perfect/crooked/protruding **teeth** 洁白的 / 完好无缺的 / 参差不齐的 / 凸出来的牙齿
- a large/high/broad/wide/sloping **forehead** 大大的 / 高高的 / 宽大的 / 后倾的前额
- a strong/weak/pointed/double **chin** 硬朗的 / 瘦削的 / 尖 / 双下巴
- a long/full/bushy/wispy/goatee **beard** 长 / 大 / 浓密的 / 一小撮 / 山羊胡子
- a long/thin/bushy/droopy/handlebar/pencil **moustache**/(*especially US*) **mustache** 长长的 / 稀疏的 / 浓密的 / 耷拉着的 / 翘 / 细直的八字胡

Hair and skin 头发和皮肤

- pale/fair/olive/dark/tanned **skin** 苍白的 / 白皙的 / 橄榄色的 / 黝黑的 / 晒黑的皮肤
- dry/oily/smooth/rough/leathery/wrinkled **skin** 干性的 / 油性的 / 光滑的 / 粗糙的 / 有皱纹的皮肤
- a dark/a pale/a light/a sallow/a ruddy/an olive/a swarthy/a clear **complexion** 黝黑的 / 苍白的 / 白皙的 / 蜡黄的 / 红润的 / 浅褐色的 / 黝黑的 / 无瑕的面容
- deep/fine/little/facial **wrinkles** 深深的 / 细小的 / 小的 / 面部的皱纹
- blonde/blond/fair/(light/dark) brown/(jet-)black/auburn/red/(*BrE*) ginger/grey **hair** 金黄色的 / 浅色的 / （浅 / 深）棕色的 / 乌黑的 / 红褐色的 / 红色的 / 姜黄色的 / 灰白色的头发
- straight/curly/wavy/frizzy/spiky **hair** 直发；鬈发；波浪形的 / 鬈曲的 / 刺猬式的头发
- thick/thin/fine/bushy/thinning **hair** 厚密的 / 稀疏的 / 纤细的 / 浓密的 / 逐渐稀少的头发
- dyed/bleached/soft/silky/dry/greasy/shiny **hair** 染了色的 / 漂白了的 / 柔顺的 / 丝滑的 / 干性的 / 油性的 / 有光泽的头发
- long/short/shoulder-length/cropped **hair** 长 / 短 / 齐肩 / 剪短了的头发
- a bald/balding/shaved **head** 秃头；开始秃顶的头；剃光了的头
- a receding **hairline** 后移的发际线
- a bald **patch**/**spot** 秃了的一块
- a side/centre/(*US*) center (*BrE*) **parting**/ (*NAmE*) **part** 偏分；中分

Body 身体

- a long/short/thick/slender/(*disapproving*) scrawny **neck** 长 / 短 / 粗 / 细 / 干瘦的脖子
- broad/narrow/sloping/rounded/hunched **shoulders** 宽 / 窄 / 斜 / 圆 / 耸肩膀
- a bare/broad/muscular/small/large **chest** 赤裸的 / 宽阔的 / 肌肉发达的胸膛；小胸；大胸
- a flat/swollen/bulging **stomach** 扁平的 / 鼓胀的 / 鼓起的肚子
- a small/tiny/narrow/slim/slender/28-inch **waist** 纤细的 / 28 英寸的腰
- big/wide/narrow/slim **hips** 大的 / 宽的 / 窄小的 / 苗条的臀部
- a straight/a bent/an arched/a broad/a hairy **back** 直的 / 弯曲的 / 弓着的 / 宽大的 / 多毛的背部
- thin/slender/muscular **arms** 瘦削的 / 细长的 / 肌肉发达的臂膀
- big/large/small/manicured/calloused/gloved **hands** 大的 / 小的 / 修剪整齐的 / 有老茧的 / 戴着手套的手
- long/short/fat/slender/delicate/bony **fingers** 长的 / 短的 / 粗的 / 细长的 / 纤细的 / 瘦削的手指
- long/muscular/hairy/shapely/(*both informal, often disapproving*) skinny/spindly **legs** 长的 / 肌肉发达的 / 多毛的 / 有曲线美的 / 皮包骨的 / 干瘦的腿
- muscular/chubby/(*informal, disapproving*) flabby **thighs** 肌肉发达的 / 胖乎乎的 / 肥胖的大腿
- big/little/small/dainty/wide/narrow/bare **feet** 大的 / 小的 / 娇小可爱的 / 宽的 / 窄的 / 光着的脚
- a good/a slim/a slender/an hourglass **figure** 好的 / 修长的 / 苗条的 / 沙漏形身材
- **be of** slim/medium/average/large/athletic/stocky **build** 有着苗条的 / 中等的 / 普通的 / 大块头的 / 健壮的 / 矮壮的身材

piano 🔑 *noun, adv.*

■ ***noun*** 🔑 /pi'ænəʊ; *NAmE* -noʊ/ (*pl.* **-os**) (*also old-fashioned, formal* **pi·ano·forte** /pi,ænəʊ'fɔːti; *NAmE* pi,ænoʊ'fɔːr-/) a large musical instrument played by pressing the black and white keys on the keyboard. The sound is produced by small HAMMERS hitting the metal strings inside the piano. 钢琴：*to play the piano* 弹钢琴 ◇ *playing jazz* ***on the piano*** 用钢琴弹奏爵士乐 ◇ *piano music* 钢琴曲 ◇ *a* ***piano teacher/lesson*** 钢琴教师 / 课 ◇ *Ravel's piano concerto in G* 拉威尔的 G 大调钢琴协奏曲 ➲ SEE ALSO GRAND PIANO, THUMB PIANO, UPRIGHT PIANO

■ ***adv.*** /'pjɑːnəʊ; *NAmE* -noʊ/ (*abbr.* **p**) (*music* 音, *from Italian*) played or sung quietly 轻柔地；安静地；弱 **OPP** **forte**

▸ **piano** *adj.*

pi,ano ac'cordion *noun* a type of ACCORDION that you press buttons and keys on to produce the different notes （键盘式）手风琴

Pi·an·ola™ /,piə'nəʊlə; *NAmE* -'noʊ-/ *noun* a piano that plays automatically by means of a PIANO ROLL 皮阿诺拉自动钢琴 **SYN** **player piano**

pi'ano roll *noun* a roll of paper full of very small holes that controls the movement of the keys in a PLAYER PIANO 自动钢琴打孔纸卷（用于自动钢琴琴键弹奏）

pi·azza /pi'ætsə; *NAmE* pi'ɑːzə/ *noun* a public square, especially in an Italian town （尤指意大利城镇中的）广场

pi·broch /'piːbrɒk; -brɒx; *NAmE* -brɑːk; -brɑːx/ *noun* [C, U] a piece of music played on the BAGPIPES, especially at military occasions or funerals; music of this type 风笛变奏曲（常在军事场合或葬礼上吹奏）

pic /pɪk/ *noun* (*informal*) a picture 图片；画片

pica /'paɪkə/ *noun* (*specialist*) a unit for measuring the size of printed letters and the length of a line of printed text 派卡（印刷字母规格和字行长度单位）

pi·can·te /pɪ'kɑːnteɪ/ *adj.* (*from Spanish, NAmE*) (of food 食物) hot and spicy 香辣的：*tortilla chips dipped in a picante sauce* 蘸香辣调味汁的玉米薄片

pic·ar·esque /,pɪkə'resk/ *adj.* (*formal*) connected with literature that describes the adventures of a person who is sometimes dishonest but easy to like 流浪汉小说题材的：*a picaresque novel* 一部流浪汉小说

Pic·ca·dilly Cir·cus /,pɪkədɪli 'sɜːkəs; *NAmE* 'sɜːrkəs/ *noun* (*BrE*) used to describe a place that is very busy or crowded 热闹忙碌的地方；拥挤的地方：*It's been like Piccadilly Circus in this house all morning.* 这房子里整个上午都忙乱得像皮卡迪利广场。**ORIGIN** From the name of a busy area in the centre of London where several large roads meet and where there is always a lot of traffic. 源自伦敦市中心繁忙地带皮卡迪利广场，几条大街在此交汇，车辆川流不息。➲ COMPARE GRAND CENTRAL STATION

pic·ca·ninny (*also* **picka·ninny**) /,pɪkə'nɪni/ *noun* (*pl.* **-ies**) (*old-fashioned*) an offensive word for a small black child （含冒犯意）小黑人，小黑崽

pic·colo /'pɪkələʊ; *NAmE* -loʊ/ *noun* (*pl.* **-os**) a musical instrument of the WOODWIND group, like a small FLUTE that plays high notes 短笛 ➲ VISUAL VOCAB PAGE V38

pick 🔑 /pɪk/ *verb, noun*

■ ***verb*** **1** 🔑 [T] (*rather informal*) to choose sb/sth from a group of people or things 选择；挑选：**~ sb/sth** *Pick a number from one to twenty.* 从一至二十中挑选一个数。◇ *She picked the best cake for herself.* 她为自己挑了一块最好的蛋糕。◇ *He* ***picked his words*** *carefully.* 他用词细心谨慎。◇ *Have I picked a bad time to talk to you?* 我是不是挑了个不恰当的时间跟你谈话？◇ **~ sb/sth to do sth** *He has been picked to play in this week's game.* 他已入选参加本周的比赛。➲ SYNONYMS AT CHOOSE ➲ SEE ALSO HAND-PICKED **2** 🔑 [T] **~ sth** to take flowers, fruit, etc. from the plant or the tree where they are growing 采；摘：*to pick grapes* 摘葡萄 ◇ *flowers freshly picked from the garden* 刚从花园采的鲜花 ◇ *to go blackberry picking* 去采黑莓 **3** 🔑 [T] to pull or remove sth or small pieces of sth from sth else, especially with your fingers （用手指）摘掉，剔除，掐去：**~ sth + adv./prep.** *She picked bits of fluff from his sweater.* 她摘掉他毛衣上的绒毛。◇ *He picked the nuts off the top of the cake.* 他把蛋糕上面的果仁拿掉。◇ **~ sth** *to* ***pick your nose*** (= put your finger inside your nose to remove dried MUCUS) 抠鼻子 ◇ *to* ***pick your teeth*** (= use a small sharp piece of wood to remove pieces of food from your teeth) 剔牙 ◇ **~ sth + adj.** *The dogs picked the bones clean* (= ate all the meat from the bones). 狗把骨头啃得干干净净。**4** [I, T] **~ (sth)** (*NAmE*) = PLUCK (3)

IDM **,pick and 'choose** to choose only those things that you like or want very much 挑拣；精挑细选：*You have to take any job you can get—you can't pick and choose.* 你只能有什么工作就干什么，不能挑三拣四了。 **pick sb's 'brains** (*informal*) to ask sb a lot of questions about sth because they know more about the subject than you do 讨教；请教；不断地问（以向别人学习） **pick a 'fight/'quarrel (with sb)** to deliberately start a fight or an argument with sb 找茬儿；找麻烦；挑衅 **pick 'holes in sth** to find the weak points in sth such as a plan, suggestion, etc. 挑刺儿；挑毛病；找漏洞：*It was easy to pick holes in his arguments.* 找他论据中的漏洞很容易。 **pick a 'lock** to open a lock without a key, using sth such as a piece of wire （用铁丝等）捅开锁 **pick sb's 'pocket** to steal sth from sb's pocket without them noticing 扒窃；掏包儿 ➲ RELATED NOUN PICKPOCKET **pick up the 'bill, 'tab, etc. (for sth)** (*informal*) to pay for sth 付账：*The company picked up the tab for his hotel room.* 公司为他付旅馆费。◇ *The government will continue to pick up college fees for some students.* 政府将继续替一些学生缴纳学费。 **pick up the 'pieces** to return or to help sb return to a normal situation, particularly after a shock or a disaster （使）恢复；补救；收拾残局：*You cannot live your children's lives for them; you can only be there to pick up the pieces when things go wrong.* 你不能替孩子过活，只能在出现问题时帮忙解决。 **pick up 'speed** to go faster 加速 **pick up the 'threads** to return to an earlier situation or way of life after an interruption 恢复原状 **pick your 'way (across, along, among, over, through sth)** to walk carefully, choosing the safest, driest, etc. place to put your feet 择路而行；小心看着路行走：*She picked her way delicately over the rough ground.* 她小心翼翼地在高低不平的地面上行走。 **pick a 'winner 1** to choose a horse, etc. that you think is most likely to win a race 认定胜利者（如赛马中） **2** (*informal*) to make a very good choice 挑选得当；选得很准 ➲ MORE AT BONE *n.*, PIECE *n.*, SHRED *n.*

PHR V **'pick at sth 1** to eat food slowly, taking small amounts or bites because you are not hungry 磨蹭着吃；（因为不饿而）小口吃 **2** to pull or touch sth several times （反复地）揪，扯：*He tried to undo the knot by picking at it with his fingers.* 他用手指不停地扯，想把绳结解开。

,pick sb↔'off (*informal*) to aim carefully at a person, an animal or an aircraft, especially one of a group, and then shoot them 选择（目标）射击：*Snipers were picking off innocent civilians.* 狙击手专拣无辜的平民射击。 **,pick sth↔'off** to remove sth from sth such as a tree, a plant, etc. 去除；剪除：*Pick off all the dead leaves.* 把枯叶全部摘掉。

'pick on sb/sth 1 to treat sb unfairly, by blaming, criticizing or punishing them （跟某人）闹别扭；故意刁难挑剔：*She was picked on by the other girls because of her size.* 她因为个头关系被其他女孩欺负。 **2** to choose sb/sth 挑选；选中：*He picked on two of her statements which he said were untrue.* 他从她的话中挑出了两处他认为不真实的地方。

,pick sb/sth↔'out 1 to choose sb/sth carefully from a group of people or things 精心挑选 **SYN** **select**：*She was picked out from dozens of applicants for the job.* 她从大批的求职者中被选中承担这项工作。◇ *He picked out the ripest peach for me.* 他给我挑了个熟透了的桃子。 **2** to recognize sb/sth from among other people or things 认出来；辨别出：*See if you can pick me out in this photo.* 看你能不能把我从这张照片上认出来。 **,pick sth↔'out 1** to play a tune on a musical instrument slowly without using written music （不用乐谱）慢慢地弹奏（乐曲）：*He picked out the tune on the piano with one finger.* 他凭记忆用

P

一个手指在钢琴上慢慢弹出了那支曲子。 **2** to discover or recognize sth after careful study（经仔细研究）找出，认识到： *Read the play again and pick out the major themes.* 请重读剧本，把主题找出来。 **3** to make sth easy to see or hear 使显著；使容易看见（或听见）： *a sign painted cream, with the lettering picked out in black* 印着醒目黑字的乳白色标牌

ˌpick sth↔ˈover | ˌpick ˈthrough sth to examine a group of things carefully, especially to choose the ones you want 用心挑选；筛选： *Pick over the lentils and remove any little stones.* 仔细挑拣豆子，把小石子拣出去。 ◇ *I picked through the facts of the case.* 我仔细审查本案的事实。

ˌpick ˈup 1 to get better, stronger, etc.; to improve 改善；好转；增强： *Trade usually picks up in the spring.* 贸易一般在春天回升。 ◇ *The wind is picking up now.* 现在风愈刮愈大了。 ◇ *Sales have picked up 14% this year.* 今年销售额增长了 14%。 ➲ RELATED NOUN PICKUP (3) **2** (*informal*) to start again; to continue 重新开始；继续： *Let's* **pick up where we left off** *yesterday.* 咱们从昨天停下的地方继续吧。 **3** (*informal, especially NAmE*) to put things away and make things neat, especially for sb else（为某人）收拾，整理： *All I seem to do is cook, wash and pick up after the kids.* 烧饭、洗衣、跟在孩子屁股后头收拾东西，好像这就是我全部的活儿。 **ˌpick ˈup | ˌpick sth ˈup** to answer a phone 接电话： *The phone rang and rang and nobody picked up.* 电话铃响了又响，但没人接。 **ˌpick sb↔ˈup 1** 🔑 to go somewhere in your car and collect sb who is waiting for you（开车）接人 SYN **collect**： *I'll pick you up at five.* 我五点钟来接你。 **2** to allow sb to get into your vehicle and take them somewhere 让人乘车；搭载： *The bus picks up passengers outside the airport.* 公共汽车在机场外接送乘客。 **3** to rescue sb from the sea or from a dangerous place, especially one that is difficult to reach（从海里或危险处）营救，搭救： *A lifeboat picked up survivors.* 救生艇把幸存者救起来。 **4** (*informal, often disapproving*) to start talking to sb you do not know because you want to have a sexual relationship with them（猥亵地与生人）搭讪，勾搭： *He goes to clubs to pick up girls.* 他到俱乐部去泡妞。 ➲ RELATED NOUN PICKUP (2) **5** (*informal*) (of the police 警察) to arrest sb 逮捕；抓捕： *He was picked up by police and taken to the station for questioning.* 警察把他抓到局子里问话去了。 **6** to make sb feel better 使人觉得舒服；提神： *Try this—it will pick you up.* 尝尝这个，能让你提提神的。 ➲ RELATED NOUN PICK-ME-UP **ˌpick sb/sth↔ˈup** 🔑 to take hold of sb/sth and lift them/it up 拿起；举起；提起： *She went over to the crying child and picked her up.* 她走到啼哭的孩子身边，把她抱了起来。 **ˌpick sth↔ˈup 1** 🔑 to get information or a skill by chance rather than by making a deliberate effort（偶然）得到，听到，学会： *to pick up bad habits* 染上坏习惯 ◇ *Here's a tip I picked up from my mother.* 告诉你一个窍门，是我从妈妈那里学来的。 ◇ *She picked up Spanish when she was living in Mexico.* 她旅居墨西哥时顺便学会了西班牙语。 **2** to identify or recognize sth 辨认；识别出： *Scientists can now pick up early signs of the disease.* 现在科学家能够辨认这种疾病的早期症状。 **3** 🔑 to collect sth from a place 取回；收集： *I picked up my coat from the cleaners.* 我从干洗店取回了外衣。 ➲ RELATED NOUN PICKUP (4) **4** 🔑 to receive an electronic signal, sound or picture 接收（信号、声音、图像等）： *We were able to pick up the BBC World Service.* 我们能收到英国广播公司国际广播节目。 **5** (*informal*) to buy sth, especially cheaply or by chance（碰巧或廉价地）买到： *We managed to pick up a few bargains at the auction.* 我们从拍卖场买到了几件便宜货。 **6** (*informal*) to get or obtain sth 得；感染；得到： *I seem to have picked up a terrible cold from somewhere.* 我似乎从什么地方染上了重感冒。 ◇ *I picked up £30 in tips today.* 我今天得到 30 英镑的小费。 **7** to find and follow a route 找到；跟踪；追寻： *to pick up the scent of an animal* 追踪动物的臭迹 ◇ *We can pick up the motorway in a few miles.* 经过几英里以后我们就能上高速公路。 **8** to return to an earlier subject or situation in order to continue it 回到（本题）；恢复原状 SYN **take up**： *He picks up this theme again in later chapters of the book.* 在该书的后几章，他又重回到这个主题上。 **9** to notice sth that is not very obvious; to see sth that you are looking for 察觉；发现；注意到： *I picked up the faint sound of a car in the distance.* 我听到远处传来微弱的汽车声。 **10** (*especially NAmE*) to put things away neatly 收拾；整理： *Will you pick up all your toys?* 把你的玩具都收起来好不好？ **11** (*NAmE*) to put things away and make a room neat 收拾房间： *to pick up a room* 整理房间 **ˌpick ˈup on sth 1** to notice sth and perhaps react to it 领略；意会；意识到： *She failed to pick up on the humour in his remark.* 她没有领悟他话中的幽默。 **2** to return to a point that has already been mentioned or discussed 回到（某问题等）；重提（要点等）： *If I could just pick up on a question you raised earlier.* 请允许我重提一下您早先提出的问题。 **ˌpick sb ˈup on sth** to mention sth that sb has said or done that you think is wrong 提到某人的错误；挑毛病；算旧账： *I knew he would pick me up on that slip sooner or later.* 我知道他迟早会提起我那个小过失的。 **ˌpick your·self ˈup** to stand up again after you have fallen（跌倒后）爬起来： *He just picked himself up and went on running.* 他爬起来继续跑。 ◇ (*figurative*) *She didn't waste time feeling sorry for herself—she just picked herself up and carried on.* 她没有浪费时间自怜，而是振作起来继续干。

■ ***noun* 1** [sing.] (*rather informal*) an act of choosing sth 挑选；选择： ***Take your pick*** (= choose). 自己选吧。 ◇ *The winner gets first pick of the prizes.* 获胜者可先挑奖品。 **2** [C] (*informal*) a person or thing that is chosen 选中的人（或物）： *She was his pick for best actress.* 她是他选中的最佳女演员。 ➲ SYNONYMS AT CHOICE **3** [sing.] **the ~ of sth** (*rather informal*) the best thing or things in a group 精品；精华；最好的东西： *We're reviewing the pick of this month's new books.* 我们正在做本月的精品新书评介。 ◇ *I think we got* **the pick of the bunch** (= the best in the group). 我认为我们得到了其中的极品。 **4** [C] = PICKAXE： *picks and shovels* 镐与平锹 **5** [C] (*informal*) = PLECTRUM ➲ SEE ALSO ICE PICK, TOOTHPICK IDM SEE BUNCH *n.*

ˈpick-and-mix *adj.* (*BrE*) used to describe a way of putting sth together by choosing things from among a large variety of different items 组合的；综合的；拼合的： *a pick-and-mix programme of study* 综合课程

picka·ninny = PICCANINNY

pick·axe (*NAmE also* **pick·ax**) /ˈpɪkæks/ (*also* **pick**) *noun* a large heavy tool that has a curved metal bar with sharp ends fixed at the centre to a wooden handle. It is used for breaking rocks or hard ground. 镐；尖嘴镐；鹤嘴锄 ➲ PICTURE AT AXE

pick·er /ˈpɪkə(r)/ *noun* a person or machine that picks flowers, vegetables, etc. 采摘者；采摘机；采摘工具： *cotton pickers* 采棉人

picket /ˈpɪkɪt/ *noun, verb*

■ ***noun* 1** a person or group of people who stand outside the entrance to a building in order to protest about sth, especially in order to stop people from entering a factory, etc. during a strike; an occasion at which this happens（罢工期间纠察妥协分子的）纠察员，纠察队；罢工警戒： *Five pickets were arrested by police.* 五名纠察队员被警方逮捕。 ◇ *I was on picket duty at the time.* 当时我正执行罢工的纠察工作。 ◇ *a mass picket of the factory* 工厂的大规模罢工纠察队 ➲ SEE ALSO FLYING PICKET, PICKETER ➲ WORDFINDER NOTE AT UNION **2** a soldier or group of soldiers guarding a military base（军营的）警戒哨，警戒队，哨兵 **3** a pointed piece of wood that is fixed in the ground, especially as part of a fence（尤指栅栏的）尖木桩，尖板条： *a picket fence* 尖板条栅栏

■ ***verb*** [T, I] **~ (sth)** to stand outside somewhere such as your place of work to protest about sth or to try and persuade people to join a strike 在…外抗议；进行罢工纠察： *200 workers were picketing the factory.* * 200 名工人在工厂外罢工抗议。 ◇ *Striking workers picketed outside the gates.* 罢工工人围在大门外担任纠察（禁止出入）。

pick·et·er /ˈpɪkɪtə(r)/ *noun* (*NAmE*) a person who takes part in a picket（罢工行动的）纠察队员

picket·ing /ˈpɪkɪtɪŋ/ *noun* [U] the activity of standing outside the entrance to a building in order to protest about sth and stop people from entering the building 进行纠察封锁；担任警戒；围厂抗议： *mass picketing of the factory* 罢工工人集体对工厂的封锁

ˈpicket line *noun* a line or group of PICKETS (1) 纠察线；纠察队人墙： *Fire crews refused to cross the picket line.* 消防人员拒不冲破围厂队伍的人墙。

pick·ings /ˈpɪkɪŋz/ *noun* [pl.] something, especially money, that can be obtained from a particular situation in an easy or a dishonest way 油水；（不正当的）外快；不义之财： *There were only **slim pickings** to be made at the fair.* 在交易会上只能捞些小油水。◇ *There are **rich pickings** to be had by investing in this sort of company.* 向这类公司投资大有油水可捞。◇ *The strike affecting the country's largest airline is producing **easy pickings** for smaller companies.* 罢工给全国最大航空公司带来的影响使得较小的航空公司轻易捡到便宜。

pickle /ˈpɪkl/ *noun, verb*

■ ***noun* 1** [C, usually pl.] (*BrE*) a vegetable that has been preserved in VINEGAR or salt water and has a strong flavour, served cold with meat, salads, etc. 泡菜；腌菜 **2** [U] (*BrE*) a cold thick spicy sauce made from fruit and vegetables that have been boiled, often sold in JARS and served with meat, cheese, etc. 菜酱 **3** (*NAmE*) (*BrE* **gher·kin**) [U, C] a small CUCUMBER that has been preserved in VINEGAR before being eaten 醋泡小黄瓜

IDM **in a ˈpickle** (*informal*) in a difficult or unpleasant situation 处于困境；处境窘迫

■ ***verb*** ~ sth to preserve food in VINEGAR or salt water 腌渍

pickled /ˈpɪkld/ *adj.* **1** (of food 食物) preserved in VINEGAR 腌渍的： *pickled cabbage/herring/onions* 腌渍洋白菜 / 鲱鱼 / 洋葱 **2** (*old-fashioned, informal*) drunk 醉醺醺的

ˈpick-me-up *noun* (*informal*) something that makes you feel better, happier, healthier, etc., especially medicine or an alcoholic drink 提神物品，兴奋剂（尤指药物或酒精饮料）： (*figurative*) *This deal would offer the best possible pick-me-up to the town's ailing economy.* 这笔交易对该镇每况愈下的经济是一服最好的强心剂。

pick·off /ˈpɪkɒf; *NAmE* -ɔːf; -ɑːf/ *noun* (*NAmE*) (in BASEBALL 棒球) a situation in which a player running to a BASE is out because a FIELDER or the PITCHER suddenly throws the ball to that base 牵制出局（指守场员或投手对跑垒员突然传杀致使其出局）

pick·pocket /ˈpɪkpɒkɪt; *NAmE* -pɑːkɪt/ *noun* a person who steals money, etc. from other people's pockets, especially in crowded places 扒手；小偷

pick·up /ˈpɪkʌp/ *noun, adj.*

■ ***noun* 1** (*also* **ˈpickup truck**) [C] a vehicle with low sides and no roof at the back used, for example, by farmers 轻型货车；敞篷小货车；皮卡货车 ➲ VISUAL VOCAB PAGE V62 **2** [C] a person sb meets for the first time, for example in a bar, with whom they start a sexual relationship 偶然结识的调情者： *casual pickups* 游戏鸳鸯 **3** [C] ~ (**in sth**) an improvement 改进；好转；改善： *a pickup in the housing market* 房市的好转 **4** [U, C] an occasion when sb/sth is collected 接人；收取物品；提货： *Goods are delivered not later than noon on the day after pickup.* 货物递送不迟于收件后的第二天中午。 **5** [C] the part of a record player or musical instrument that changes electrical signals into sound, or sound into electrical signals （唱机的）唱头，磁头 **6** [U] (*NAmE*) a vehicle's ability to ACCELERATE (= increase in speed) （车辆的）加速能力

■ ***adj.*** [only before noun] (*NAmE*) (of a sports game 体育比赛) often not planned in advance and that anyone who wants to can join in 临时拼凑的；临时组织的： *A group of kids started a pickup game of basketball on the street outside.* 一群孩子在外面开始了即兴街头篮球赛。

picky /ˈpɪki/ *adj.* (*informal*) (of a person 人) liking only particular things and difficult to please 挑剔的；难伺候的 SYN **fussy**

ˌpick-your-ˈown *adj.* [only before noun] (of fruit or vegetables 水果或蔬菜) picked by the customer on the farm where they are grown （顾客到农田）自己采摘的： *pick-your-own strawberries* 供采摘的草莓

pic·nic /ˈpɪknɪk/ *noun, verb*

■ ***noun* 1** an occasion when people pack a meal and take it to eat outdoors, especially in the countryside 野餐： *It's a nice day. Let's **go for a picnic**.* 天气不错；咱们去野餐吧。◇ *We **had a picnic** beside the river.* 我们在河边野餐。 **2** the meal, usually consisting of SANDWICHES, salad and fruit, etc. that you take with you when you go on a picnic 野餐食物： *Let's eat our picnic by the lake.* 咱们到湖边去吃野餐吧。◇ *a picnic lunch* 午间野餐 ◇ *a picnic basket* 野餐提篮

IDM **be no ˈpicnic** (*informal*) to be difficult and cause a lot of problems 可不容易；不是好玩的： *Bringing up a family when you're unemployed is no picnic.* 失了业还要抚养孩子可不是容易的事。

■ ***verb*** (**-ck-**) [I] to have a picnic 野餐： *No picnicking allowed* (= on a sign) 禁止野餐

pic·nick·er /ˈpɪknɪkə(r)/ *noun* a person who is having a picnic 野餐者

pico- /ˈpiːkəʊ; ˈpaɪkəʊ; *NAmE* ˈpiːkoʊ; ˈpaɪkoʊ/ *combining form* (in nouns; used in units of measurement 构成名词，用于计量单位) 10^{-12}; one million millionth 皮（可）；微微；万亿分之一

picto·gram /ˈpɪktəgræm/ *noun* **1** a picture representing a word or phrase 图画文字 **2** a diagram that uses pictures to represent amounts or numbers of a particular thing 统计图表

pic·tor·ial /pɪkˈtɔːriəl/ *adj.* [usually before noun] **1** using or containing pictures 用图片的；有插图的： *a **pictorial account/record** of the expedition* 对远征的图片记述 / 记录 **2** connected with pictures 画片的；图画的： *pictorial traditions* 绘图传统 ▶ **pic·tori·al·ly** /-əli/ *adv.*

pic·ture /ˈpɪktʃə(r)/ *noun, verb*

■ ***noun***

• **PAINTING/DRAWING** 绘画 **1** [C] a painting or drawing, etc. that shows a scene, a person or thing 图画；绘画： *A picture of flowers hung on the wall.* 墙上挂着一张花卉的图画。◇ *The children were **drawing pictures** of their pets.* 孩子们在画他们的宠物。◇ *She wanted a famous artist to **paint her picture*** (= a picture of herself). 她想请一位名画家为自己画像。◇ *a book with lots of pictures in it* 一本有大量插图的书

• **PHOTOGRAPH** 照片 **2** [C] a photograph 相片；照片： *We had our **picture taken** in front of the hotel.* 我们在旅馆前照了相。◇ *The picture shows the couple together on their yacht.* 照片显示这对情侣一同在他们的游艇上。◇ *Have you got any pictures of your trip?* 你有这次旅行的照片吗？

➲ SYNONYMS AT PHOTOGRAPH ➲ EXPRESS YOURSELF AT DESCRIBE

• **ON TV** 电视 **3** [C] an image on a television screen 电视图像： *harrowing television pictures of the famine* 电视上悲惨的饥荒画面 ◇ *satellite pictures* 卫星图像 ◇ *The picture isn't very clear tonight.* 今晚电视画面不怎么清楚。

• **DESCRIPTION** 描述 **4** [C, usually sing.] a description that gives you an idea in your mind of what sth is like 描绘；描述： *The writer paints a gloomy picture of the economy.* 作者把经济状况描绘得一片惨淡。◇ *The police are trying to **build up a picture** of what happened.* 警方正试图掌握事情发生的经过。

• **MENTAL IMAGE** 印象 **5** [C, usually sing.] a mental image or memory of sth 头脑中的情景；记忆；印象： *I have a vivid picture of my grandfather smiling down at me when I was very small.* 我清楚地记得很小的时候祖父低头向我微笑的情景。

• **GENERAL SITUATION** 局面 **6 the picture** [sing.] the general situation concerning sb/sth 状况；情形；形势： *Just a few years ago the picture was very different.* 几年前的情况就大不相同。◇ *The overall picture for farming is encouraging.* 农业的总体形势是令人鼓舞的。

• MOVIES 电影 **7** [C] a film/movie 电影：*The movie won nine Academy Awards, including Best Picture.* 这部电影荣获九项奥斯卡金像奖，包括最佳影片奖。◇ (*especially NAmE*) *I believe her husband's* **in pictures** (= he acts in movies or works in the movie industry). 我想她丈夫是在电影圈工作。➲ SEE ALSO MOTION PICTURE **8 the pictures** [pl.] (*old-fashioned, informal*) the cinema/the movies 电影院；影剧院：*Shall we go to the pictures tonight?* 今晚我们去看电影好吗？

▼ SYNONYMS 同义词辨析

picture

painting • drawing • portrait • print • sketch

These are all words for a scene, person or thing that has been represented on paper by drawing, painting, etc. 以上各词均表示图画、绘画。

picture a scene, person or thing that has been represented on paper using a pencil, a pen or paint 指用铅笔、钢笔或颜料画出的图画、绘画：*The children were drawing pictures of their pets.* 孩子在画他们的宠物。

painting a picture that has been made using paint 指用颜料画出的图画、绘画：*a collection of paintings by American artists* 美国艺术家的绘画作品集

drawing a picture that has been made using a pencil or pen, not paint 指用铅笔或钢笔而非颜料画出的图画、素描画：*a pencil/charcoal drawing* 铅笔画；炭笔画

portrait a painting, drawing or photograph of a person, especially of the head and shoulders 指肖像、半身画像、半身照：*Vermeer's 'Portrait of the artist in his studio'* 弗美尔的"艺术家在工作室的肖像" ◇ *a self-portrait* (= a painting that you do of yourself) 自画像

print a picture that has been copied from a painting using photography 指（用照相制版法制作的）绘画复制品：*a Renoir print* 一张雷诺阿画作的影印件

sketch a simple picture that is drawn quickly and does not have many details 指素描、速写、草图：*I usually do a few very rough sketches before I start on a painting.* 我开始作画之前通常会画几幅草图。

PATTERNS
- to **draw** a picture/portrait/sketch
- to **paint** a picture/portrait
- to **make** a painting/drawing/portrait/print/sketch
- to **do** a painting/drawing/portrait/sketch

IDM **be/look a 'picture** to look very beautiful or special 好看；悦目 **be the picture of 'health, 'guilt, 'misery, etc.** (*informal*) to look extremely healthy, guilty, unhappy, etc. 显得非常健康（或内疚、不愉快等） **get the 'picture** (*informal*) to understand a situation, especially one that sb is describing to you 明白，了解（别人描述的情形）：*'I pretended that I hadn't heard.' 'I get the picture.'* "我装作没听见。""我明白了。" **in/out of the 'picture** (*informal*) involved/not involved in a situation 在局内/局外：*Morris is likely to win, with Jones out of the picture now.* 琼斯现已出局，莫里斯极有可能胜出。 **put/keep sb in the 'picture** (*informal*) to give sb the information they need in order to understand a situation 介绍情况；使了解情况：*Just to put you in the picture—there have been a number of changes here recently.* 只是让你了解一下情况吧，最近这里出现了许多变化。➲ MORE AT BIG *adj.*, PAINT *v.*, PRETTY *adj.*

■ *verb*

• IMAGINE 想象 **1** to imagine sb/sth; to create an image of sb/sth in your mind 想象；设想；忆起：**~ sb/sth** *I can still picture the house I grew up in.* 我还能回忆起我童年时住的那座房子。◇ **~ sb/sth as sth** *We found it hard to picture him as the father of teenage sons.* 我们很难想象他居然是有几个十几岁儿子的父亲了。◇ **~ sb/sth doing sth** *When he did not come home she pictured him lying dead on the roadside somewhere.* 他还没回家的时候，她想象着他已横尸路边了。◇ **~ what, how, etc....** *I tried to picture what it would be like to live alone.* 我努力设想一个人单独生活是什么情景。

• DESCRIBE 描绘 **2** [often passive] **~ sb/sth as sth** to describe or present sb/sth in a particular way 描述；描写 SYN **portray**：*Before the trial Liz had been pictured as a frail woman dominated by her husband.* 审讯之前，利兹被描绘成受丈夫操纵的孱弱女子。

• SHOW IN PHOTOGRAPH 照片显示 **3** [usually passive] to show sb/sth in a photograph or picture 显示在照片上；用图片显示：**~ sb/sth (+ adv./prep/adj.)** *She is pictured here with her parents.* 这张照片是她和父母的合影。◇ **~ sb/sth doing sth** *The team is pictured setting off on their European tour.* 图片显示，这个队正开始欧洲之行。

'picture book *noun* a book with a lot of pictures, especially one for children 画册；图画书

'picture messaging *noun* [U] a system of sending images from one mobile/cell phone to another（手机的）图像传输系统；彩信 SYN EMS

ˌpicture-'perfect *adj.* (*NAmE*) exactly right in appearance or in the way things are done 完美的；圆满的

ˌpicture 'postcard *noun* (*old-fashioned*) a POSTCARD with a picture on one side 美术明信片；风景明信片

ˌpicture-'postcard *adj.* [only before noun] (*especially BrE*) (of places 地方) very pretty 优美的；漂亮的：*a picture-postcard village* 风景如画的村庄

'picture rail *noun* a narrow strip of wood attached to the walls of a room below the ceiling and used for hanging pictures from 挂画的板条；挂画线

pic·tur·esque /ˌpɪktʃəˈresk/ *adj.* **1** (of a place, building, scene, etc. 地方、建筑物、景色等) pretty, especially in a way that looks old-fashioned 优美的；古色古香的 SYN **quaint**：*a picturesque cottage/setting/village* 画儿一般的小屋/环境/村落 **2** (of language 语言) producing strong mental images by using unusual words 生动的；栩栩如生的：*a picturesque description of life at sea* 对海上生活生动的描述 ▶ **pic·tur·esque·ly** *adv.*：*The inn is picturesquely situated on the banks of the river.* 小客栈坐落在河畔，构成一幅美丽的图画。

'picture window *noun* a very large window made of a single piece of glass（整块玻璃做的）大观景窗；落地窗

pic·tur·ize (*BrE also* **-ise**) /ˈpɪktʃəraɪz/ *verb* **~ sth** (*IndE*) to adapt a story or play as a film/movie; to create a film SEQUENCE to accompany a song 将…改编成电影；为（歌曲）配电影镜头：*The novel has been picturized twice.* 这部小说已两度改编为电影。▶ **pic·tur·iza·tion, -isa·tion** /ˌpɪktʃəraɪˈzeɪʃn; *NAmE* -rəˈz-/ *noun* [C, U]: *It was one of the few song picturizations that created magic with both music and visuals.* 那是创造音乐和视觉神奇效果的少数音乐电影之一。

pid·dle /ˈpɪdl/ *verb* [I] (*old-fashioned, informal*) to URINATE 撒尿

pid·dling /ˈpɪdlɪŋ/ *adj.* [only before noun] (*informal, disapproving*) small and unimportant 琐碎的；鸡毛蒜皮的 SYN **trivial**

pidgin /ˈpɪdʒɪn/ *noun* [U] **1** a simple form of a language, especially English, Portuguese or Dutch, with a limited number of words, that are used together with words from a local language. It is used when people who do not speak the same language need to talk to each other. 洋泾浜语；皮钦语 **2 Pidgin** = TOK PISIN **3 ~ English, French, Japanese, etc.** a way of speaking a language that uses simple words and forms, used when a person does not speak the language well, or when he or she is talking to sb who does not speak the language well 洋泾浜英语（或法语、日语等）；洋泾浜式；混杂语式：*I tried to get my message across in my pidgin Italian.* 我尝试用我的洋泾浜意大利语表达出我的意思。

pi-dog = PYE-DOG

pie /paɪ/ *noun* [C, U] **1** fruit baked in a dish with PASTRY on the bottom, sides and top 果馅饼；果馅派：*a slice of* *apple pie* 一块苹果派 ◇ *Help yourself to some more pie.* 请随意再吃些果馅饼吧。◇ *a pie dish* 一份果馅饼 ➲ SEE ALSO CUSTARD PIE **2** (*especially BrE*) meat, vegetables, etc. baked in a dish with PASTRY on the bottom, sides and top 肉馅饼；蔬菜馅饼： *a steak and kidney pie* 牛肉腰子馅饼 ➲ SEE ALSO MINCE PIE, PORK PIE, SHEPHERD'S PIE

IDM **a ˌpiece/ˌslice/ˌshare of the ˈpie** a share of sth such as money, profits, etc. （金钱、利润等的）一份；一杯羹 **ˌpie in the ˈsky** (*informal*) an event that sb talks about that seems very unlikely to happen 难以实现的事；幻想的事；空中楼阁： *This talk of moving to Australia is all just pie in the sky.* 移居澳大利亚之说纯属异想天开。➲ MORE AT AMERICAN *adj.*, EASY *adj.*, EAT, FINGER *n.*, NICE

pie·bald /ˈpaɪbɔːld/ *adj.* (of a horse 马) with areas on it of two colours, usually black and white 花斑的；有黑白两色的 ➲ COMPARE SKEWBALD

piece /piːs/ *noun, verb*

■ *noun*

• **SEPARATE AMOUNT** 分离的量 **1** [C] ~ (**of sth**) (used especially with *of* and uncountable nouns 尤与 of 和不可数名词连用) an amount of sth that has been cut or separated from the rest of it; a standard amount of sth 片；块；段；截；标准的量： *a piece of string/wood* 一截绳子；一块木头 ◇ *She wrote something on a small piece of paper.* 她在一小片纸上写了点什么。◇ *a large piece of land* 一大片土地 ◇ *a piece of cake/cheese/meat* 一块蛋糕 / 奶酪 / 肉 ◇ *He cut the pizza into bite-sized pieces.* 他把比萨饼切成一口一块的小块。◇ *I've got a piece of grit in my eye.* 我眼里进了一粒沙子。

▼ **VOCABULARY BUILDING 词汇扩充**

Pieces

If you want to talk about a small amount or one example of something that is normally an uncountable noun, there is a range of words you can use. You must choose the right one to go with the substance you are talking about. 许多表示少量、一个等的词可用以修饰不可数名词，但必须选择能与该物质名词搭配得当的词。

- **Piece** and (*BrE, informal*) **bit** are very general words and can be used with most uncountable nouns. * piece 和 bit（英式英语的非正式用语）是十分通用的词，可与大多数不可数名词连用： *a piece of paper/wood/string/cake/fruit/meat/work/research/advice* 一张纸；一块木头；一根绳子；一块蛋糕；一个水果；一块肉；一件工作；一项研究；一个忠告 ◇ *a bit of paper/work/chocolate/luck* 一小片纸；一点工作；一小块巧克力；一点运气
- A **slice** is a thin flat piece. * slice 指薄片： *a slice of bread/cake/salami/cheese/pie/apple* 一片面包 / 蛋糕 / 萨拉米香肠 / 干酪 / 馅饼 / 苹果 ◇ (*figurative*) *a slice of life* 反映现实生活的电影（或戏剧、书）
- A **chunk** is a thick, solid piece. * chunk 指厚厚的一块： *a chunk of cheese/bread/rock* 一块厚干酪 / 面包 / 岩石 ◇ *a chunk of land* (= a fairly large piece) 一大块土地
- A **lump** is a piece of something solid without any particular shape. * lump 指无一定形状的一块、一团： *a lump of coal/rock/mud* 一块煤 / 岩石；一团泥
- A **fragment** is a very small piece of something that is broken or damaged. * fragment 指碎片、破片： *fragments of glass* 玻璃碎片 ◇ (*figurative*) *fragments of conversation* 谈话片断 It can also be used with countable nouns to mean a small part of something. 该词亦可与可数名词连用表示小部分： *a fragment of the story* 故事的一个片段
- A **speck** is a tiny piece of powder. * speck 指小颗粒、微粒： *a speck of dust/dirt* 一点灰尘 / 污垢 You can also say 也可以说： *a speck of light* 一点光
- **Drop** is used with liquids. * drop 用于液体： *a drop of water/rain/blood/milk/whisky* 一滴水 / 雨 / 血 / 牛奶 / 威士忌酒
- A **pinch** is as much as you can hold between your finger and thumb. * pinch 指一撮、一捏、一掐： *a pinch of salt/cinnamon* 一撮盐 / 肉桂粉
- A **portion** is enough for one person. * portion 指够一人用的一份、一客： *a portion of chicken* 一份鸡肉

• **PART** 部分 **2** [C, usually pl.] one of the bits or parts that sth breaks into 碎片；碎块： *There were tiny pieces of glass all over the road.* 道路上满是碎玻璃渣。◇ *The boat had been smashed* ***to pieces*** *on the rocks.* 小船在岩石上撞得粉碎。◇ *The vase lay* ***in pieces*** *on the floor.* 花瓶碎片散落在地上。**3** [C] one of the parts that sth is made of 零件；部件： *He* ***took*** *the clock* ***to pieces.*** 他把钟拆散了。◇ *a missing piece of the puzzle* 拼图玩具未拼上的一片 ◇ *The bridge was taken down* ***piece by piece.*** 桥梁被一部分一部分地拆下。◇ *a 500-piece jigsaw* 一副 500 片的拼图玩具 ➲ SEE ALSO ONE-PIECE, TWO-PIECE, THREE-PIECE

• **SINGLE ITEM** 单件 **4** [C] (used especially with *of* and uncountable nouns 尤与 of 和不可数名词连用) a single item of a particular type, especially one that forms part of a set（尤指一套中的）一件，一台： *a piece of clothing/furniture/luggage* 一件衣服 / 家具 / 行李 ◇ *a piece of equipment/machinery* 一台设备 / 机器 ◇ *a 28-piece dinner service* 一套 28 件的餐具 **5** [C] ~ **of sth** used with many uncountable nouns to describe a single example or an amount of sth 条；项；点： *a* ***piece of advice/information/news*** 一条建议 / 信息 / 消息 ◇ *an interesting piece of research* 一项有趣的研究 ◇ *Isn't that a* ***piece of luck?*** 那难道不是有点运气？ **6** [C] ~ (**of sth**) a single item of writing, art, music, etc. that sb has produced or created（文章、艺术品、音乐作品等的）一件，一篇，一首，一支： *a* ***piece of art/music/poetry, etc.*** 一件艺术品、一支乐曲、一首诗歌等 ◇ *They performed pieces by Bach and Handel.* 他们演奏了巴赫和亨德尔的几支曲子。◇ (*formal*) *They have some beautiful pieces* (= works of art, etc.) *in their home.* 他们家中珍藏了一些精美的艺术品。➲ SEE ALSO MASTERPIECE, MUSEUM PIECE, PARTY PIECE, PERIOD PIECE, SHOWPIECE

• **NEWS ARTICLE** 新闻报道 **7** [C] an article in a newspaper or magazine or a broadcast on television or radio（新闻传媒的）文章，报道： *Did you see her piece about the Internet in the paper today?* 你看了今天报纸上她写的关于互联网的文章没有？ ➲ SEE ALSO SET PIECE

• **COIN** 硬币 **8** [C] a coin of the value mentioned（某价值的）硬币： *a 50p piece* 一枚 50 便士的硬币 ◇ *a five-cent piece* 一枚五分的硬币

• **IN CHESS, ETC.** 国际象棋等 **9** [C] one of the small figures or objects that you move around in games such as CHESS 棋子

• **SHARE OF STH** 份额 **10** [sing.] ~ **of sth** (*especially NAmE*) a part or share of sth 部分；份额： *companies seeking a piece of the market* 争取市场份额的公司

• **GUN** 枪 **11** [C] (*NAmE, slang*) a gun 枪支；枪

• **DISTANCE** 距离 **12** **a piece** [sing.] (*old-fashioned, NAmE, informal*) a short distance 短距离；一小段距离： *She lives down the road a piece from here.* 她住在路那头离这里不远的地方。 HELP You will find other compounds ending in **piece** at their place in the alphabet. 其他以 piece 结尾的复合词可在各字母中的适当位置查到。

IDM **a/some ˌpiece of ˈwork** (*NAmE, informal*) used to express the fact that you admire sb or find them amusing, often when they have done sth that surprises you 了不起的人；与众不同的人： *You're some piece of work, Jack, do you know that?* 你知道吗，杰克？你真了不起。 **fall to ˈpieces** **1** (usually used in the progressive tenses 通常用于进行时) (of things 东西) to become very old and in bad condition because of long use 变得破旧不堪 SYN **fall apart**: *Our car is falling to pieces, we've had it so long.* 我们的汽车已破旧不堪，我们已用了它很久了。 **2** (of a person, an organization, a plan, etc. 人、机构、计划等) to stop working; to be destroyed 停止运作；崩溃；瓦解： *He's worried the business will fall to pieces without him.* 他担心没有了他企业将会倒闭。 **give sb a piece of your ˈmind** (*informal*) to tell sb that you disapprove of their behaviour or are angry with them 表明对某人的行为不满；向某人表示恼火 **go to ˈpieces** (*informal*) (of a person 人) to be so upset or afraid that you cannot manage to live or work normally 身心崩溃；沮丧至极 **(all) in one ˈpiece** (*informal*) safe; not damaged or hurt, especially after a journey or dangerous experience 安然无恙（尤指旅行或经历危险之后）： *They* were lucky to get home in one piece. 他们能平安返家真是幸运。 **(all) of a 'piece** (*formal*) **1** all the same or similar 一模一样；相仿：*The houses are all of a piece.* 这些房子千篇一律。 **2** all at the same time 同时；一起：*The house was built all of a piece in 1754.* 整所房子是在 1754 年建造完成的。 **pick/pull/tear sb/sth to 'pieces/'shreds** (*informal*) to criticize sb, or their work or ideas, very severely 严厉斥责；痛斥；批评得体无完肤 **a ˌpiece of 'cake** (*informal*) a thing that is very easy to do 轻而易举的事；举手之劳 **a ˌpiece of 'piss** (*BrE, taboo, slang*) a thing that is very easy to do 小菜一碟；轻而易举的事 ➲ MORE AT ACTION *n.*, BIT, LONG *adj.*, NASTY, PICK *v.*, PIE, SAY *v.*, VILLAIN

■ *verb*

PHR V **ˌpiece sth↔to'gether 1** to understand a story, situation, etc. by taking all the facts and details about it and putting them together 组合资料（以便了解情况）：*Police are trying to piece together the last hours of her life.* 警方正努力理清她在死亡之前数小时的情况。 **2** to put all the separate parts of sth together to make a complete whole 拼凑；拼合 **SYN** **assemble**：*to piece together a jigsaw* 拼合拼图

pièce de ré·sist·ance /ˌpjes də reˈzɪstɒ̃s; *NAmE* ˌreziː-ˈstɑːns/ *noun* [usually sing.] (*pl.* **pièces de ré·sist·ance** /ˌpjes də reˈzɪstɒ̃s; *NAmE* ˌreziːˈstɑːns/) (*from French*) the most important or impressive part of a group or series of things 成功之作；最重要的项目

piece·meal /ˈpiːsmiːl/ *adj.* [usually before noun] (*often disapproving*) done or happening gradually at different times and often in different ways, rather than carefully planned at the beginning 逐渐做成（或发生）的；零敲碎打的；零散的：*a piecemeal approach to dealing with the problem* 全无章法的解决问题的方式 ◇ *piecemeal changes* 零星的变化 ▸ **piece·meal** *adv.*：*The reforms were implemented piecemeal.* 改革在零零星星地进行。

ˌpiece of 'eight *noun* (*pl.* **pieces of eight**) an old Spanish coin 八里亚尔币比索（西班牙旧币名）

'piece rate *noun* an amount of money paid for each thing or amount of sth that a worker produces 计件酬金；计件工资

piece·work /ˈpiːswɜːk; *NAmE* -wɜːrk/ *noun* [U] work that is paid for by the amount done and not by the hours worked 计件工作 ▸ **piece·work·er** *noun*

'pie chart *noun* a diagram consisting of a circle that is divided into sections to show the size of particular amounts in relation to the whole 饼形图；饼分图 ➲ LANGUAGE BANK AT ILLUSTRATE, PROCESS[1]

pied /paɪd/ *adj.* (especially of birds 尤指鸟) of two or more different colours, especially black and white 黑白双色的；多色的；杂色的

pied-à-terre /ˌpjeɪd ɑː ˈteə(r); *NAmE* ˈter/ *noun* (*pl.* **pieds-à-terre** /ˌpjeɪd ɑː/) (*from French*) a small flat/apartment, usually in a town, that you do not live in as your main home but keep for use when necessary 备用小公寓；备用房

pie-dog = PYE-DOG

ˌPied 'Piper *noun* a person who persuades a lot of other people to follow them or do sth with them 有感召力的人；有号召力的人 ➲ MORE LIKE THIS 17, page R27 **ORIGIN** From the old German story of the Pied Piper of Hamelin, who made first rats and later children follow him by playing beautiful music on his pipe. 源自古老的德国传说，哈默尔恩的花衣魔笛手吹奏美妙的乐曲，先后诱走老鼠和孩子。

ˌpie-'eyed *adj.* (*informal*) very drunk 烂醉的

pier /pɪə(r); *NAmE* pɪr/ *noun* **1** a long structure built in the sea and joined to the land at one end, often with places of entertainment on it （常设有娱乐场所的）突堤 ➲ WORDFINDER NOTE AT SEA **2** a long low structure built in a lake, river or the sea and joined to the land at one end, used by boats to allow passengers to get on and off （突入湖、河、海中的）码头；突码头 **SYN** **landing stage** **3** (*specialist*) a large strong piece of wood, metal or stone that is used to support a roof, wall, bridge, etc. 墙墩；桥墩

pierce /pɪəs; *NAmE* pɪrs/ *verb* **1** [T, I] to make a small hole in sth, or to go through sth, with a sharp object 扎；刺破；穿透：**~ sth** *The arrow pierced his shoulder.* 箭头射入他的肩膀。◇ *He pierced another hole in his belt with his knife.* 他用刀子在皮腰带上又扎了一个洞。◇ *to have your ears/nose, etc. pierced* (= to have a small hole made in your ears/nose, etc. so that you can wear jewellery there) 在耳朵、鼻子等上扎洞眼 ◇ **~ sb** (*figurative*) *She was pierced to the heart with guilt.* 她万般愧疚，心如刀割。◇ **~ through sth** *The knife pierced through his coat.* 刀子刺穿了他的外衣。 **2** [T, I] **~ (through) sth** (*literary*) (of light, sound, etc. 光、声等) to be suddenly seen or heard 刺破；穿过；透入：*Sirens pierced the silence of the night.* 警笛声划破了夜晚的宁静。◇ *Shafts of sunlight pierced the heavy mist.* 缕缕阳光穿透了浓雾。 **3** [T, I] **~ (through) sth** to force a way through a barrier 冲破；突破 **SYN** **penetrate**：*They failed to pierce the Liverpool defence.* 他们未能突破利物浦队的防线。

pier·cing /ˈpɪəsɪŋ; *NAmE* ˈpɪrsɪŋ/ *adj., noun*

■ *adj.* **1** [usually before noun] (of eyes or the way they look at sb 眼睛或眼神) seeming to notice things about another person that would not normally be noticed, especially in a way that makes that person feel anxious or embarrassed 锐利的；逼人的；尖利的：*She looked at me with piercing blue eyes.* 她用一双敏锐的蓝眼睛盯着我。◇ *a piercing look* 洞悉一切的目光 **2** [usually before noun] (of sounds 声音) very high, loud and unpleasant 尖厉的；刺耳的 **SYN** **shrill**：*a piercing shriek* 尖厉的叫声 ◇ *She has such a* ***piercing voice***. 她的声音是那么刺耳。 **3** [only before noun] (of feelings 感情) affecting you very strongly, especially in a way that causes you pain 深切的；刻骨的：*piercing sadness* 深深的悲哀 **4** (of the wind or cold 风或寒气) very strong and feeling as if it can pass through your clothes and skin 刺骨的；凛冽的 **5** [only before noun] sharp and able to make a hole in sth 锋利的；锐利的：*The animal is covered in long piercing spines.* 这种动物浑身长满了锋利的长刺。 ▸ **pier·cing·ly** *adv.*：*His eyes were piercingly blue.* 他有一双敏锐的蓝眼睛。◇ *The weather remained piercingly cold.* 天气依旧彻骨地寒冷。

■ *noun* **1** [U] = BODY PIERCING **2** [C] the hole that is made in your ear, nose or some other part of your body so that you can wear jewellery there （耳朵、鼻子或其他身体部位为戴首饰打的）穿孔，洞眼：*She has a tongue piercing.* 她为佩戴首饰穿了个舌洞。

Pier·rot /ˈpɪərəʊ; ˈpjerəʊ; *NAmE* ˈpɪəroʊ/ *noun* a male character in traditional French plays, with a sad white face and a pointed hat （法国传统剧中表情哀伤、脸上用粉涂成白色、头戴尖顶帽的）白面男丑角

pietà /pjerˈtɑː/ *noun* (*art* 美术) a picture or SCULPTURE of the Virgin Mary holding the dead body of Christ 圣母怜子图，圣母恸子图（或雕像）（显示圣母抱着耶稣的遗体）

piety /ˈpaɪəti/ *noun* [U] the state of having or showing a deep respect for sb/sth, especially for God and religion; the state of being PIOUS 虔诚 **OPP** **impiety**

pif·fle /ˈpɪfl/ *noun* [U] (*old-fashioned, informal*) nonsense 胡言乱语；废话；蠢话 **SYN** **rubbish**

pif·fling /ˈpɪflɪŋ/ *adj.* (*informal, disapproving*) small and unimportant 渺小的；微不足道的：*piffling amounts* 微不足道的数量

pig 🔑 /pɪg/ *noun, verb*

■ *noun* **1** 🔑 (*also* **hog** *especially in NAmE*) an animal with pink, black or brown skin, short legs, a broad nose and a short tail which curls round itself. Pigs are kept on farms for their meat (called PORK) or live in the wild. 猪：*a pig farmer* 养猪的农民 ◇ *Pigs were grunting and squealing in the yard.* 猪在院子里哼哼地叫个不停。 ➲ SEE ALSO BOAR, PIGLET, SOW[2], SWINE (3), GUINEA PIG (1) **2** (*informal*, *disapproving*) an unpleasant or offensive person; a person who is dirty or GREEDY 令人不快（或讨厌）的人；贪婪（或肮脏）的人：*Arrogant pig!* 傲慢的家伙！◇ *Don't be such a pig!* 别那么讨厌嘛！◇ *The greedy pig's eaten all the biscuits!* 那个馋猫把饼干都吃光了！◇ *She* ***made a pig of herself*** *with the ice cream* (= ate too much). 她大吃了一通冰淇淋。◇ *He's a real* ***male chauvinist pig*** (= a man who does not think women are equal to men). 他是个彻头彻尾的大男子主义者。 **3** (*slang*) an offensive word for a police officer（对警察的蔑称）

IDM **make a 'pig's ear (out) of sth** (*BrE, informal*) to do sth badly; to make a mess of sth 把事情办砸；弄得一团糟 **(buy) a pig in a 'poke** if you **buy a pig in a poke**, you buy sth without seeing it or knowing if it is good enough（买）未看过的东西；（买）不知优劣的东西 **a pig of a sth** (*BrE, informal*) a difficult or unpleasant thing or task 挠头的事；烦人的事；苦差：*I've had a pig of a day.* 我这一天倒霉透了。 **pigs might 'fly** (*BrE*) (*NAmE* **when pigs 'fly**) (*ironic, saying*) used to show that you do not believe sth will ever happen（表示不相信某事会发生）太阳从西出：*'With a bit of luck, we'll be finished by the end of the year.' 'Yes, and pigs might fly!'* "运气不错的话，我们年底就能完成。" "是啊，太阳能打西边出嘛！"

■ ***verb*** (**-gg-**) (*BrE, informal*) to eat too much of sth 吃得过量；大吃特吃：**~ sth** *I had a whole box of chocolates and pigged the lot!* 我把一整盒巧克力吃了个精光！◇ **~ yourself (on sth)** *Don't give me cakes—I'll just pig myself.* 可别给我拿糕点，那我会吃个没够的。

PHR V **,pig 'out (on sth)** (*informal*) to eat too much food 大吃；猛吃：*They pigged out on pizza.* 他们猛抢着吃比萨饼。

pi·geon /ˈpɪdʒɪn/ *noun* a fat grey and white bird with short legs. Pigeons are common in cities and also live in woods and fields where people shoot them for sport or food. 鸽子：*the sound of pigeons cooing* 鸽子咕咕的叫声 ➲ COMPARE DOVE[1] (1) ➲ SEE ALSO CARRIER PIGEON, CLAY PIGEON SHOOTING, HOMING PIGEON, WOOD PIGEON

IDM **be sb's pigeon** (*old-fashioned, BrE*) to be sb's responsibility or business 是某人的职责（或事情） ➲ MORE AT CAT

pi·geon·hole /ˈpɪdʒɪnhəʊl; *NAmE* -hoʊl/ *noun, verb*

■ ***noun*** one of a set of small boxes that are fixed on a wall and open at the front, used for putting letters, messages, etc. in; one of a similar set of boxes that are part of a desk, used for keeping papers, documents, etc. in 信件格；开口文件格：*If you can't come, leave a note in my pigeonhole.* 你若不能来，就在我的信件格里留张便条。

■ ***verb*** **1 ~ sb (as sth)** to decide that sb belongs to a particular group or type without thinking deeply enough about it and considering what other qualities they might have 将（某人）轻率分类；主观划分（某人）为 SYN **categorize, label**：*He has been pigeonholed as a children's writer.* 他硬被归入儿童文学作家之列。 **2 ~ sth** to decide to deal with sth later or to forget it 搁置；将…束之高阁；不予处理 SYN **shelve**：*Plans for a new school have been pigeonholed.* 建新学校的计划搁在一边了。

,pigeon-'toed *adj.* having feet that point towards each other and not straight forward 足内翻的；内八字脚的

pig·gery /ˈpɪɡəri/ *noun* (*pl.* **-ies**) a place where pigs are kept or bred 猪圈；猪栏；养猪场

piggy /ˈpɪɡi/ *noun, adj.*

■ ***noun*** (*pl.* **-ies**) a child's word for a pig（儿童用语）猪猪，小猪

■ ***adj.*** [only before noun] (*informal, disapproving*) (of a person's eyes 人的眼睛) like those of a pig 像猪一样的

pig·gy·back /ˈpɪɡibæk/ *noun, verb*

■ ***noun*** a ride on sb's back, while he or she is walking 背着；肩驮：*Give me a piggyback, Daddy!* 背背我，爸爸！◇ *a piggyback ride* 肩驮 ▶ **pig·gy·back** *adv.*：*to ride piggyback* 骑在肩上

■ ***verb***

PHR V **'piggyback on sb/sth** to use sth that already exists as a support for your own work; to use a larger organization, etc. for your own advantage 利用；借助；攀附利用

'piggy bank *noun* a container in the shape of a pig, with a narrow opening in the top for putting coins in, used by children to save money 猪形储钱罐；扑满 ➲ COMPARE MONEY BOX

,piggy in the 'middle (*also* **,pig in the 'middle**) (*both BrE*) (*NAmE* **,monkey in the 'middle**) *noun* **1** a children's game where two people throw a ball to each other over the head of another person who tries to catch it 过顶传球（儿童游戏，由两人抛传球，中间一人争抢） **2** a person who is caught between two people or groups who are fighting or arguing（被夹在中间而）左右为难的人

,pig-'headed *adj.* unwilling to change your opinion about sth, in a way that other people think is annoying and unreasonable 顽固的；固执的 SYN **obstinate, stubborn** ▶ **,pig-'headed·ness** *noun* [U]

,pig-'ignorant *adj.* (*informal*) very stupid or badly educated 蠢笨的；粗鄙的

'pig iron *noun* [U] a form of iron that is not pure 生铁；铸铁

pig·let /ˈpɪɡlət/ *noun* a young pig 猪仔；小猪

pig·ment /ˈpɪɡmənt/ *noun* [U, C] **1** a substance that exists naturally in people, animals and plants and gives their skin, leaves, etc. a particular colour 色素 **2** a coloured powder that is mixed with a liquid to produce paint, etc. 颜料

pig·men·ta·tion /ˌpɪɡmenˈteɪʃn/ *noun* [U] the presence of pigments in skin, hair, leaves, etc. that causes them to be a particular colour 色素沉着；天然颜色

pig·ment·ed /pɪɡˈmentɪd/ *adj.* (especially of skin 尤指皮肤) having a natural colour 天然色的；本色的

pigmy *noun, adj.* = PYGMY

pig·skin /ˈpɪɡskɪn/ *noun* **1** [U] leather made from the skin of a pig 猪皮革 **2** [sing.] (*NAmE, informal*) the ball used in AMERICAN FOOTBALL（美式足球使用的）球

pig·sty /ˈpɪɡstaɪ/ (*also* **sty**) *noun* (*pl.* **-ies**) (*NAmE also* **pig·pen** /ˈpɪɡpen/) **1** [C] a small building or a confined area where pigs are kept 猪圈；猪场 **2** [sing.] (*informal*) a very dirty or untidy place 肮脏的地方；猪窝般邋遢的地方

pig·swill /ˈpɪɡswɪl/ *noun* [U] = SWILL (1)

pig·tail /ˈpɪɡteɪl/ (*BrE*) (*also* **braid** *NAmE, BrE*) *noun* hair that is tied together into one or two bunches and twisted into a PLAIT or PLAITS, worn either at the back of the head or one on each side of the head 辫子：*She wore her hair* ***in pigtails***. 她梳着两条辫子。 ➲ VISUAL VOCAB PAGE V65 ➲ COMPARE PONYTAIL

pike /paɪk/ *noun, verb*

■ ***noun*** **1** (*pl.* **pike**) a large FRESHWATER fish with very sharp teeth 狗鱼；梭子鱼 **2** a weapon with a sharp blade on a long wooden handle, used in the past by soldiers on foot 长矛 **3** (*NAmE*) = TURNPIKE **4** (*dialect*) a pointed top of a hill in the north of England（英格兰北部的）山峰，陡峰

IDM **come down the 'pike** (*NAmE, informal*) to happen; to become noticeable 发生；显现：*We're hearing a lot about new inventions coming down the pike.* 我们经常听说新发明不断问世。

■ ***verb*** (*AustralE, NZE, informal*)

PHR V **,pike 'out** to decide not to do sth that you had agreed to do 背约；退出；出尔反尔 **'pike on sb** to fail to help or support sb as they had hoped or expected 未能如某人所愿提供帮助（或支持）；辜负别人的期望

pike·staff /ˈpaɪkstɑːf; *NAmE* -stæf/ *noun* IDM SEE PLAIN *adj.*

pikey /ˈpaɪki/ *noun* (*BrE, informal, offensive*) **1** a name for a GYPSY 吉卜赛鬼 **2** a person who is poor and not educated 没教养的穷鬼：*He referred to them as dirty pikey scum.* 他称他们是肮脏又没教养的人渣。

pilaf (also **pilaff**) /ˈpiːlæf; NAmE prɪˈlɑːf/ (also **pilau** /ˈpiːlaʊ/) noun [U, C] a hot spicy Eastern dish of rice and vegetables and often pieces of meat or fish 辣味菜肉饭

pi·las·ter /pɪˈlæstə(r)/ noun (specialist) a flat column that sticks out from the wall of a building, used as decoration 壁柱；半露柱

Pi·la·tes /pɪˈlɑːtiːz/ noun [U] a system of stretching and pushing exercises using special equipment, which help make your muscles stronger and make you able to bend parts of your body more easily 普拉提（用特殊设备进行健身和柔韧性训练的伸展式锻炼方法）

pil·chard /ˈpɪltʃəd; NAmE -tʃərd/ noun a small sea fish that is used for food 欧洲沙丁鱼；沙丁鱼

pile /paɪl/ noun, verb

■**noun** ➲ SEE ALSO PILES **1** [C] a number of things that have been placed on top of each other 摞；垛；沓：*a pile of books/clothes/bricks* 一摞书 / 衣物 / 砖块 ◇ *He arranged the documents in neat piles.* 他把文件一摞摞地码得整整齐齐。◇ *She looked in horror at the mounting pile of letters on her desk.* 她惶恐地望着桌子上堆积如山的信函。 **2** [C] a mass of sth that is high in the middle and wider at the bottom than at the top 堆；成堆的东西 **SYN** **heap**: *a pile of sand* 一堆沙 ◇ *piles of dirty washing* 成堆待洗的脏衣物 **3** [C, usually pl.] **~ of sth** (informal) a lot of sth 大量；许多：*I have got piles of work to do.* 我有大量工作要做。◇ *He walked out leaving a pile of debts behind him.* 他出走了，留下累累债务。 **4** [U, sing.] the short threads, pieces of wool, etc. that form the soft surface of carpets and some types of cloth such as VELVET 绒头；绒毛：*a deep-pile carpet* 一块厚绒地毯 **5** [C] a large wooden, metal or stone post that is fixed into the ground and used to support a building, bridge, etc. 桩；桩柱 **6** [C] (formal or humorous) a large impressive building 宏伟建筑物

IDM **(at the) bottom/top of the 'pile** in the least/most important position in a group of people or things 处于无足轻重的 / 举足轻重的地位 **make a/your 'pile** (informal) to make a lot of money 赚很多钱

■**verb** **1** [T] to put things one on top of another; to form a pile 堆放；摞起；叠放：**~ sth** *She* ***piled*** *the boxes* ***one on top of the other.*** 她把盒子一个个地摞起来。◇ *The clothes were* ***piled high*** *on the chair.* 衣服在椅子上堆得高高的。◇ **~ sth up** *Snow was piled up against the door.* 积雪封门。 **2** [T] to put sth on/into sth; to load sth with sth 放置；装入：**~ A with B** *The sofa was* ***piled high*** *with cushions.* 沙发上高高地堆着一些垫子。◇ *He piled his plate with as much food as he could.* 他把食物猛往自己盘子里堆。◇ **~ B on(to) A** *He piled as much food as he could onto his plate.* 他把食物猛往自己盘子里堆。◇ **~ B in(to) A** *She piled everything into her suitcase.* 她把一应物品装进衣箱。 ➲ SEE ALSO STOCKPILE v. **3** [I] **+ adv./prep.** (informal) (of a number of people 许多人) to go somewhere quickly without order or control 蜂拥；拥挤：*The coach finally arrived and we all piled on.* 长途汽车终于开来了，我们一拥而上。

IDM **pile on the 'agony/'gloom** (informal, especially BrE) to make an unpleasant situation worse 使雪上加霜；伤口上撒盐：*Bosses piled on the agony with threats of more job losses.* 老板威胁要削减更多的职位，令情况更加恶化。

PHR V **ˌpile 'on** (especially of a person's weight 尤指体重) to increase quickly 剧增；猛增：*The weight just piled on while I was abroad.* 我出国期间体重一个劲地增加。 **ˌpile sth↔'on** **1** to make sth increase rapidly 使迅速增加；猛增：*The team piled on the points in the first half of the game.* 球队在上半场连连得分。◇ *I've been piling on the pounds* (= I have put on weight) *recently.* 我最近体重猛增。 **2** to express a feeling in a much stronger way than is necessary 夸张；夸大其词：*Don't pile on the drama!* 别再添油加醋了！◇ *Things aren't really that bad—she does tend to* ***pile it on.*** 事情并没有那么糟糕，她的确有意夸张。 **3** to give sb more or too much of sth 过度施加；猛增某物：*The German team* ***piled on the pressure*** *in the last 15 minutes.* 在最后 15 分钟，德国队施加了强大的压力。 **ˌpile sth 'on(to) sb** to give sb a lot of sth to do, carry, etc. 给…增加工作；使负担加重：*He felt his boss was piling too much work on him.* 他觉得上司派给他的工作太多。 **ˌpile 'up** to become larger in quantity or amount 堆积；积压 **SYN** **accumulate**: *Work always piles up at the end of the year.* 年底总是积压一大堆工作。

pile·driver /ˈpaɪldraɪvə(r)/ noun **1** (BrE, informal) a very heavy kick or blow 狠踢；重击 **2** a machine for forcing heavy posts into the ground 打桩机

piles /paɪlz/ noun [pl.] painful swollen VEINS at or near the ANUS 痔；痔疮 **SYN** **haemorrhoids**

ˈpile-up noun a road accident involving several vehicles crashing into each other 连环车祸；连续撞车：*Three people died in a multiple pile-up in freezing fog.* 有三人死于冻雾引起的连环车祸中。

pil·fer /ˈpɪlfə(r)/ verb [I, T] to steal things of little value or in small quantities, especially from the place where you work 偷窃（小东西）；小偷小摸；（尤指员工）偷窃：**~ (from sb/sth)** *He was caught pilfering.* 他行窃时被抓个正着。◇ **~ sth (from sb/sth)** *She regularly pilfered stamps from work.* 她常从工作单位顺手牵羊拿走邮票。 ▸ **pil·fer·age** /ˈpɪlfərɪdʒ/ noun [U] (formal): *pilferage of goods* 货物盗窃 **pil·fer·er** noun: *Certain types of goods are preferred by pilferers.* 某些类型的商品较为小偷所喜欢。 **pil·fer·ing** noun [U]: *We know that pilfering goes on.* 我们知道常有小偷小摸的事情。

pil·grim /ˈpɪlgrɪm/ noun **1** a person who travels to a holy place for religious reasons 朝觐者；朝圣的人；香客：*Muslim pilgrims on their way to Mecca* 前往麦加的穆斯林朝觐者 ◇ *Christian pilgrims visiting Lourdes* 赴卢尔德朝圣的基督徒 **2** **Pilgrim** a member of the group of English people (**the Pilgrim Fathers**) who sailed to America on the ship *The Mayflower* in 1620 and started a COLONY in Massachusetts 清教徒前辈移民（1620 年乘五月花号赴美洲，在马萨诸塞建立英国殖民地）

pil·grim·age /ˈpɪlgrɪmɪdʒ/ noun [C, U] **1** a journey to a holy place for religious reasons 朝圣之旅：*to go on/make a pilgrimage* 前往朝圣 ➲ COLLOCATIONS AT RELIGION **2** a journey to a place that is connected with sb/sth that you admire or respect 参拜之行；瞻仰之旅：*His grave has become a* ***place of pilgrimage.*** 他的陵墓成了参拜之地。 ➲ WORDFINDER NOTE AT JOURNEY

pill /pɪl/ noun, verb

■**noun** **1** [C] a small flat round piece of medicine that you swallow without chewing it 药丸；药片：*a vitamin pill* 维生素片 ➲ SEE ALSO PEP PILL, SLEEPING PILL **2** **the pill** or **the Pill** [sing.] a pill that some women take to prevent them becoming pregnant 口服避孕药：*the contraceptive pill* 避孕药丸 ◇ *to be/go* ***on the pill*** 在服用避孕药 ➲ SEE ALSO MORNING-AFTER PILL **3** [C] (NAmE) an annoying person 讨厌的人；讨厌鬼

IDM **sugar/sweeten the pill** to do sth that makes an unpleasant situation seem less unpleasant 药里加糖；缓和情况；缓解苦感 **SYN** **sugar-coat** ➲ MORE AT BITTER adj.

■**verb** [I] (of a piece of clothing, especially one made of wool 尤指毛织衣物) to become covered in very small balls of FIBRE 起球；结绒

pil·lage /ˈpɪlɪdʒ/ verb [I, T] to steal things from a place or region, especially in a war, using violence 抢劫；劫掠；掠夺 **SYN** **plunder**: *The rebels went looting and pillaging.* 叛乱者趁火打劫，掠夺财物。◇ **~ sth** *The town had been pillaged and burned.* 这座城镇被洗劫焚毁。◇ **~ sth from sth** *Works of art were pillaged from churches and museums.* 教堂和博物馆的艺术品被劫掠一空。 ▸ **pil·lage** noun [U]: *They brought back horrific accounts of murder and pillage.* 他们带回了残杀掳掠的可怕消息。 **pil·la·ger** noun ➲ COMPARE LOOT v., PLUNDER v.

pil·lar /ˈpɪlə(r)/ noun **1** a large round stone, metal or wooden post that is used to support a bridge, the roof of a building, etc., especially when it is also decorative（尤指兼作装饰的）柱子，桥墩 **2** a large round stone, metal or wooden post that is built to remind people of a famous person or event 纪念柱 **SYN** **column** **3** **~ of sth** a mass of sth that is shaped like a pillar 柱状物：*a pillar of smoke/rock* 烟柱；石柱 **4** **~ of sth** a strong supporter of sth; an important member of sth 台柱子；主心骨；中流砥柱：*a pillar of the Church* 教会的骨干分子 ◇ *a pillar of society* 社会中坚 **5 ~ of sth** a person who has a lot of a particular quality 富有某种素质的人；某种素质的化身：*She is a **pillar of strength** in a crisis.* 她在危难中表现非常坚强。 **6** a basic part or feature of a system, organization, belief, etc. （组织、制度、信仰等的）核心，基础，支柱：*the central pillar of this theory* 这一理论的核心支柱

IDM **be driven, pushed, etc. from ˌpillar to ˈpost** to be forced to go from one person or situation to another without achieving anything 被迫四处碰壁（或到处奔波）

ˈpillar box *noun* (*old-fashioned, BrE*) a tall red metal box in the street, used for putting letters in which are being sent by post 邮筒；信筒 ➲ COMPARE LETTER BOX, POSTBOX

ˌpillar-box ˈred *adj.* (*BrE*) very bright red in colour 鲜红的 ▶ **ˌpillar-box ˈred** *noun* [U] ➲ MORE LIKE THIS 15, page R26

pil·lared /ˈpɪləd; *NAmE* -ərd/ *adj.* [only before noun] (of a building or part of a building 建筑物) having PILLARS 有立柱的；柱式的

pill·box /ˈpɪlbɒks; *NAmE* -bɑːks/ *noun* a small shelter for soldiers, often partly underground, from which a gun can be fired （士兵的）掩体，隐蔽所，碉堡

pil·lion /ˈpɪliən/ *noun* a seat for a passenger behind the driver of a motorcycle 摩托车后座：*a pillion passenger/seat* 摩托车后座乘客；摩托车后座 ▶ **pil·lion** *adv.*：*to ride pillion* 坐在摩托车的后座上

pil·lock /ˈpɪlək/ *noun* (*BrE, slang*) a stupid person 蠢材；笨蛋

pil·lory /ˈpɪləri/ *verb, noun*

■ *verb* (**pil·lor·ies, pil·lory·ing, pil·lor·ied, pil·lor·ied**) [often passive] **~ sb** to criticize sb strongly in public 公开批评；抨击：*He was regularly pilloried by the press for his radical ideas.* 他因观点极端而经常受到新闻界的抨击。

■ *noun* (*pl.* **-ies**) a wooden frame, with holes for the head and hands, which people were locked into in the past as a punishment （古刑具）木枷，颈手枷 ➲ COMPARE STOCK *n.* (9)

pil·low /ˈpɪləʊ; *NAmE* -loʊ/ *noun, verb*

■ *noun* **1** a square or RECTANGULAR piece of cloth filled with soft material, used to rest your head on in bed 枕头：*She lay back against the pillows.* 她半躺半坐靠在枕头上。◇ ***pillow talk*** (= conversations in bed between lovers) 枕边细语 ◇ *He lay back on the grass using his backpack as a pillow.* 他用背包当枕头仰卧在草地上。 ➲ VISUAL VOCAB PAGE V24 **2** (*NAmE*) = CUSHION (1)

■ *verb* **~ sth** (**+ adv./prep.**) (*literary*) to rest sth, especially your head, on an object 枕着（某物）：*She lay on the grass, her head pillowed on her arms.* 她头枕着胳膊躺在草地上。

pil·low·case /ˈpɪləʊkeɪs; *NAmE* -loʊ-/ (*also* **pil·low·slip** /ˈpɪləʊslɪp; *NAmE* -loʊ-/) *noun* a cloth cover for a PILLOW, that can be removed 枕头套 ➲ VISUAL VOCAB PAGE V24

pilot 🔑 /ˈpaɪlət/ *noun, verb, adj.*

■ *noun* **1** 🔑 a person who operates the controls of an aircraft, especially as a job 飞行员；（航空器）驾驶员：*an airline pilot* 民航飞机飞行员 ◇ *a fighter pilot* 战斗机飞行员 ◇ *The accident was caused by pilot error.* 这场事故是飞行员的失误造成的。 ➲ SEE ALSO AUTOMATIC PILOT, AUTOPILOT, CO-PILOT, TEST PILOT ➲ WORDFINDER NOTE AT AIRCRAFT **2** a person with special knowledge of a difficult area of water, for example, the entrance to a HARBOUR, whose job is to guide ships through it 领航员；引水员；领港员 **3** a single television programme that is made in order to find out whether people will like it and want to watch further programmes （电视的）试播节目 **4** = PILOT LIGHT

■ *verb* **1 ~ sth** to fly an aircraft or guide a ship; to act as a pilot 驾驶（航空器）；领航（船只）：*The plane was piloted by the instructor.* 飞机由教练员驾驶。◇ *The captain piloted the boat into a mooring.* 船长把船驶向泊位。 **2 ~ sth** (**through sth**) to guide sb/sth somewhere, especially through a complicated place or system 引导；使通过（尤指复杂的地方或系统）：*She piloted a bill on the rights of part-time workers through parliament.* 她几经周折终于使兼职人员权利法案在议会中得以通过。 **3 ~ sth** to test a new product, idea, etc. with a few people or in a small area before it is introduced everywhere 试点；试行

■ *adj.* [only before noun] done on a small scale in order to see if sth is successful enough to do on a large scale 试验性的；试点的：*a **pilot project/study/survey*** 试验性项目／研究／调查 ◇ *a **pilot episode*** (= of a radio or television series) （广播剧或电视剧的）试播集

ˈpilot light (*also* **pilot**) *noun* a small flame that burns all the time, for example on a gas BOILER, and lights a larger flame when the gas is turned on 引火火种；长明火

ˈpilot officer *noun* (*abbr.* **PO**) an officer of the lowest rank in the British AIR FORCE 英国空军少尉

ˈpilot whale *noun* a small WHALE that lives in warm seas 巨头鲸；领航鲸

Pils /pɪlz; pɪls/ (*also* **Pilsner** /ˈpɪlznə(r); ˈpɪls-/) *noun* [U] a type of strong light-coloured beer originally made in what is now the Czech Republic 比尔森啤酒（原产于现在的捷克共和国境内）

Pima /ˈpiːmə/ *noun* (*pl.* **Pima** or **Pimas**) *noun* a member of a Native American people, many of whom live in the US state of Arizona 皮马人（美洲土著，很多居于美国亚利桑那州）

pi·mento /pɪˈmentəʊ; *NAmE* -toʊ/ *noun* (*pl.* **-os**) a small red PEPPER with a mild taste 西班牙甜椒

pimp /pɪmp/ *noun, verb*

■ *noun* a man who controls PROSTITUTES and lives on the money that they earn 拉皮条的男人

■ *verb* **1** [I] **~ (for sb)** to get customers for a PROSTITUTE 拉嫖客；做淫媒；拉皮条 **2** [T] (*informal*) to add things to sth to make it look or sound better, especially by making it more individual 修饰，改装，加工（尤指使事物更具个人特色）：**~ sth** *Pimp your car with stylish custom wheels!* 给你的车装上时尚的订制车轮！ ◇ **~ sth up** *I would love to pimp the songs up.* 我很想让这些歌曲更具特色。

pim·per·nel /ˈpɪmpənel; *NAmE* -pərnel/ *noun* a small wild plant with red, white or blue flowers 海绿（开红、白或蓝花的矮小野生植物）

pim·ple /ˈpɪmpl/ *noun* a small raised red spot on the skin 丘疹；粉刺；小脓包 ➲ COMPARE SPOT *n.* (3) ➲ SEE ALSO GOOSE PIMPLES ▶ **pim·ply** /ˈpɪmpli/ *adj.*：*pimply skin* 长丘疹的皮肤 ◇ *a pimply youth* 长粉刺的青年人

PIN /pɪn/ (*also* **ˈPIN number**) *noun* the abbreviation for 'personal identification number' (a number given to you, for example by a bank, so that you can use a plastic card to take out money from a cash machine) 个人识别号码，个人密码（全写为 personal identification number，银行等向顾客提供的可与提款卡配合使用的号码） ➲ SEE ALSO CHIP AND PIN

pin 🔑 /pɪn/ *noun, verb*

■ *noun*

• **FOR FASTENING/JOINING** 用于固定／连接 **1** 🔑 a short thin piece of stiff wire with a sharp point at one end and a round head at the other, used especially for fastening together pieces of cloth when sewing 大头针 ➲ SEE ALSO BOBBY PIN, DRAWING PIN, HAIRPIN, LINCHPIN, PINS AND NEEDLES, SAFETY PIN

• **JEWELLERY** 首饰 **2** a short thin piece of stiff wire with a sharp point at one end and an item of decoration at the other, worn as jewellery 胸针；饰针：*a diamond pin* 一枚钻石胸针 ➲ SEE ALSO TIEPIN **3** (*especially NAmE*) = BROOCH

• **BADGE** 徽章 **4** (*especially NAmE*) a type of BADGE that is fastened with a pin at the back （有别针的）徽章：*He supports the group and wears its pin on his lapel.* 他支持这个团体，为此在翻领上佩戴该团体的徽章。

• MEDICAL 医疗 **5** a piece of steel used to support a bone in your body when it has been broken （接骨用的）钢钉
• ELECTRICAL 电器 **6** one of the metal parts that stick out of an electric plug and fit into a SOCKET （插头的）销：*a 2-pin plug* 双芯插头 ➲ PICTURE AT PLUG
• IN GAMES 游戏 **7** a wooden or plastic object that is shaped like a bottle and that players try to knock down in games such as BOWLING （保龄球等的）木瓶，瓶柱 ➲ VISUAL VOCAB PAGE V44 ➲ SEE ALSO NINEPINS, TENPIN
• IN GOLF 高尔夫球 **8** a stick with a flag on top of it, placed in a hole so that players can see where they are aiming for 旗杆
• LEGS 腿 **9 pins** [pl.] (*informal*) a person's legs （人的）双腿
• ON SMALL BOMB 小炸弹上 **10** a small piece of metal on a HAND GRENADE that stops it from exploding and is pulled out just before the HAND GRENADE is thrown （手榴弹上的）保险栓，保险针 ➲ SEE ALSO LINCHPIN

IDM **for two 'pins** (*old-fashioned, BrE*) used to say that you would like to do sth, even though you know that it would not be sensible 恨不得；恨不能：*I'd kill him for two pins.* 我恨不得杀了他。 ➲ MORE AT HEAR

■ *verb* (-nn-)
• FASTEN/JOIN 固定；连接 **1** **~ sth + adv./prep.** to attach sth onto another thing or fasten things together with a pin, etc. （用大头钉等）固定，别上，钉住：*She pinned the badge onto her jacket.* 她把徽章别到外衣上。◇ *A message had been pinned to the noticeboard.* 布告牌上钉着一条消息。◇ *Pin all the pieces of material together.* 把这些材料都钉到一起。◇ *She always wears her hair pinned back.* 她总是把头发往后别。
• PREVENT MOVEMENT 阻碍 **2** **~ sb/sth + adv./prep.** to make sb unable to move by holding them or pressing them against sth 使不能动弹；按住；钳住：*They pinned him against a wall and stole his wallet.* 他们把他按在墙上，偷走了他的钱包。◇ *He grabbed her arms and pinned them to her sides.* 他抓住她的双臂，按在她身体两侧。◇ *They found him pinned under the wreckage of the car.* 人们发现他被卡在汽车残骸下。

IDM **,pin (all) your 'hopes on sb/sth | ,pin your 'faith on sb/sth** to rely on sb/sth completely for success or help 完全依赖；寄希望于；指望：*The company is pinning its hopes on the new project.* 这家公司对此新项目寄予厚望。

PHR V **,pin sb↔'down 1** to make sb unable to move by holding them firmly 按住；使动弹不得：*Two men pinned him down until the police arrived.* 两个人按住他直到警察赶来。 **2** to find sb and make them answer a question or tell you sth you need to know 找某人查问；使说清楚：*I need the up-to-date sales figures but I can never pin him down at the office.* 我需要最新的销售数字，可就是不能在办公室找到他问清楚。 **,pin sb↔'down (to sth/doing sth)** to make sb make a decision or say clearly what they think or what they intend to do 使决定；使说明意向：*It's difficult to pin her down to fixing a date for a meeting.* 让她确定个开会日期实在是难。 **,pin sth↔'down** to explain or understand sth exactly 确切说明（或理解）：*The cause of the disease is difficult to pin down precisely.* 病因目前还难以解释清楚。 **'pin sth on sb** to make sb be blamed for sth, especially for sth they did not do 让（无辜的人）受过：*No one would admit responsibility. They all tried to* ***pin the blame on*** *someone else.* 谁也不肯负责，大家都竭力把过失推给别人。◇ *You can't pin this one on me—I wasn't even there!* 这事你不能怪罪我。我当时根本不在场！

pina co·lada /ˌpiːnə kəˈlɑːdə/ *noun* [C, U] an alcoholic drink made by mixing RUM with PINEAPPLE juice and COCONUT 菠萝汁朗姆酒（用朗姆酒和菠萝汁、椰汁调制而成）

pina·fore /ˈpɪnəfɔː(r)/ *noun* **1** (*also* **'pinafore dress**) (*both especially BrE*) (*NAmE usually* **jumper**) a loose dress with no sleeves, usually worn over a BLOUSE or sweater 无袖女装（通常套在衬衣或针织套衫外面）；围裙装 **2** (*old-fashioned*) (*also informal* **pinny**) (*both BrE*) a long loose piece of clothing without sleeves, worn by women over the front of their clothes to keep them clean, for example when cooking （女用）围裙 ➲ COMPARE APRON (1) **3** a loose piece of clothing like a dress without sleeves, worn by children over their clothes to keep them clean, or by young girls over a dress （小孩）围裙，围嘴；（女孩的）连胸围裙

pi·ña·ta (*also* **pi·na·ta**) /pɪnˈjɑːtə/ *noun* (*especially NAmE*) (*from Spanish*) a brightly decorated figure, filled with toys and sweets/candy, which children try to hit with a stick with their eyes covered in order to break it open, as a party game 彩色礼品包（内装玩具和糖果，儿童聚会玩游戏时蒙眼用小棍戳破）

pin·ball /ˈpɪnbɔːl/ *noun* [U] a game played on a **pinball machine**, in which the player sends a small metal ball up a sloping board and scores points as it BOUNCES off objects. The player tries to prevent the ball from reaching the bottom of the machine by pressing two buttons at the side. 弹球游戏

pin·board /ˈpɪnbɔːd; *NAmE* -bɔːrd/ *noun* (*BrE*) a board made of CORK that is fixed to an indoor wall, on which you can display messages, notices, etc. 软木告示牌（用于留言、发布通知等）

pince-nez /ˌpæs ˈneɪ/ *noun* (*pl.* **pince-nez**) (*from French*) a pair of glasses, worn in the past, with a spring that fits on the nose, instead of parts at the sides that fit over the ears （旧时的）夹鼻眼镜

pin·cer /ˈpɪnsə(r)/ *noun* **1 pincers** [pl.] a tool made of two crossed pieces of metal, used for holding things firmly and pulling things, for example nails out of wood 钳子：*a pair of pincers* 一把钳子 **2** [C] one of a pair of curved CLAWS of some types of animal, for example CRABS and LOBSTERS （蟹、虾等的）螯 ➲ VISUAL VOCAB PAGE V13

ˈpincer movement *noun* [usually sing.] a military attack in which an army attacks the enemy from two sides at the same time 钳形运动；钳形攻势

pinch /pɪntʃ/ *verb, noun*
■ *verb*
• WITH THUMB AND FINGER 用拇指和手指 **1** [T] **~ sb/sth/yourself** to take a piece of sb's skin between your thumb and first finger and squeeze hard, especially to hurt the person 拧；捏；掐：*My sister's always pinching me and it really hurts.* 我姐姐老拧我，真的很痛。◇ *He pinched the baby's cheek playfully.* 他捏着宝宝的脸颊逗着玩。◇ (*figurative*) *She had to pinch herself to make sure she was not dreaming.* 她不得不掐一下自己，弄清楚自己不是在做梦。 **2** [T] **~ sth (+ adv./prep.)** to hold sth tightly between the thumb and finger or between two things that are pressed together 捏住；夹紧：*Pinch the nostrils together between your thumb and finger to stop the bleeding.* 用手指捏住鼻孔止血。◇ *a pinched nerve in the neck* 脖子上一条被挤压的神经 **3** [I, T] to place the thumb and a finger of one hand on the screen of an electronic device such as a mobile/cell phone or small computer and move them together or apart, to make the image on the screen appear smaller or larger （在手机等电子装置上）两指张合以放大（或缩小）图像 ➲ SEE ALSO FLICK *v.* (6), SPREAD *v.* (3), TAP
• OF A SHOE 鞋 **4** [I, T] **~ (sb/sth)** if sth such as a shoe **pinches** part of your body, it hurts you because it is too tight 夹（脚）；夹痛：*These new shoes pinch.* 这双新鞋夹脚。
• STEAL 偷窃 **5** [T] **~ sth (from sb/sth)** (*BrE, informal*) to steal sth, especially sth small and not very valuable 偷摸；行窃 SYN **nick**：*Who's pinched my pen?* 谁拿了我的笔？
• COST TOO MUCH 昂贵 **6** [T] **~ sb/sth** to cost a person or an organization a lot of money or more than they can spend 使花费过多；使入不敷出：*Higher interest rates are already pinching the housing industry.* 提高利率已使住房产业不堪负荷。
• ARREST 拘捕 **7** [T] **~ sb** (*old-fashioned, BrE, informal*) to arrest sb 逮捕：*I was pinched for dangerous driving.* 我因危险驾驶而被抓。

IDM **pinch 'pennies** (*informal*) to try to spend as little money as possible 一毛不拔；吝啬

PHR V **,pinch 'in/'out** to place usually the thumb and a finger of one hand on the screen of a device such as a mobile/cell phone or small computer and move them together or apart, to make the image or text on the screen appear smaller or larger（在手机等电子装置的屏幕上）两指合拢以缩小图文，两指张开以放大图文：*Pinch in on the home page.* 在主页上两指合拢将图文缩小。◇ *You can pinch out to zoom in on the map.* 你可以两指外滑放大地图。 **,pinch sth↔'off/'out** to remove sth by pressing your fingers together and pulling 掐掉；摘掉

■ *noun*

• **WITH THUMB AND FINGER** 用拇指和手指 **1** an act of squeezing a part of sb's skin tightly between your thumb and finger, especially in order to hurt them 捏；掐；拧：*She gave him a pinch on the arm to wake him up.* 她拧了一下他的胳膊把他唤醒。

• **SMALL AMOUNT** 少量 **2** the amount of sth that you can hold between your finger and thumb 一撮：*a pinch of salt* 一撮盐

IDM **at a 'pinch** (*BrE*) (*NAmE* **in a 'pinch**) used to say that sth could be done or used in a particular situation if it is really necessary 必要时；不得已时：*We can get six people round this table at a pinch.* 必要时，这张桌子可以坐六个人。 **take sth with a pinch of 'salt** to be careful about believing that sth is completely true 不完全相信；半信半疑 ➲ MORE AT FEEL *v.*

pinched /pɪntʃt/ *adj.* (of a person's face 人的脸) pale and thin, especially because of illness, cold or worry（因疾病、寒冷、愁苦等）苍白清瘦的，清癯的

'pinch-hit *verb* (*NAmE*) **1** [I] (in BASEBALL 棒球) to hit the ball for another player 代击球；替补击球 **2** [I] ~ (**for sb**) (*informal*) to do sth for sb else who is suddenly unable to do it 临时顶替；紧急替代

'pinch run *verb* [I] (in BASEBALL 棒球) to take the place of a player who is on a BASE 替补（跑垒员）：*Gordon pinch ran for Gomez.* 戈登上场替补跑垒员戈麦斯。

pin·cush·ion /'pɪnkʊʃn/ *noun* a small thick PAD made of cloth, used for sticking pins in when they are not being used 针垫；针插

pine /paɪn/ *noun, verb*

■ *noun* **1** [C, U] (*also* **'pine tree** [C]) an EVERGREEN forest tree with leaves like needles 松树：*pine forests* 松树林 ◇ *pine needles* 松针 ◇ *a Scots pine* 欧洲赤松 **2** (*also* **pine-wood**) [U] the pale soft wood of the pine tree, used in making furniture, etc. 松木：*a pine table* 松木桌子

■ *verb* [I] to become very sad because sb has died or gone away（因死亡、离别）难过，悲伤：*She pined for months after he'd gone.* 他走了以后，她难过了好几个月。

PHR V **,pine a'way** to become very sick and weak because you miss sb/sth very much（因思念等）病重虚弱，憔悴：*After his wife died, he just pined away.* 妻子死后，他日渐憔悴。 **'pine for sb/sth** to want or miss sb/sth very much 怀念；思念；渴望：*She was pining for the mountains of her native country.* 她对祖国的青山思念不已。

pin·eal /paɪ'ni:əl/ (*also* **pi'neal gland**) *noun* (*anatomy* 解) a small organ in the brain that releases a HORMONE 松果体；松果腺

pine·apple /'paɪnæpl/ *noun* [C, U] a large tropical fruit with thick rough skin, sweet yellow flesh with a lot of juice and stiff leaves on top 菠萝；凤梨：*fresh pineapple* 新鲜菠萝 ◇ *a tin of pineapple chunks* 一罐菠萝块 ◇ *pine-apple juice* 菠萝汁 ➲ VISUAL VOCAB PAGE V33 **IDM** SEE ROUGH *adj.*

'pine cone *noun* the hard dry fruit of the PINE tree 松球；松果

'pine marten *noun* a small wild animal with a long body, short legs and sharp teeth. Pine martens live in forests and eat smaller animals. 松貂

'pine nut (*BrE also* **'pine kernel**) *noun* the white seed of some PINE trees, used in cooking 松子；松仁

pine·wood /'paɪnwʊd/ *noun* = PINE (2)

ping /pɪŋ/ *noun, verb*

■ *noun* a short high sound made when a hard object hits sth that is made of metal or glass（硬物碰击金属或玻璃发出的响声）乒，砰 ➲ MORE LIKE THIS 3, page R25

■ *verb* **1** [I, T] ~ (**sth**) to make a short, high ringing sound; to make sth produce this sound（使）乒乒作响，发乒乒声 **2** (*NAmE*) (*BrE* **pink**) [I] (of a car engine 汽车发动机) to make knocking sounds because the fuel is not burning correctly 发爆声；敲缸 **3** [T] ~ **sth** to test whether an Internet connection is working by sending a signal to a computer and waiting for a reply 乒网（向计算机发送信号等待回复，以测试是否连通互联网） **4** [T] ~ **sth** (**to sb**) | ~ **sb** (*informal*) to send an email or TEXT MESSAGE to sb 发送（电子邮件、手机短信）：*I'll ping it to you later.* 我随后把它发送给你。

ping·er /'pɪŋə(r)/ *noun* a device that makes a series of short high sounds, for example on a cooker/stove to tell you that the cooking time has ended（厨灶等的）响铃定时器

'ping-pong (*BrE, informal*) (*NAmE* **'Ping-Pong™**) (*also* **table tennis**) *noun* [U] a game played like TENNIS with BATS and a small plastic ball on a table with a net across it 乒乓球运动 ➲ VISUAL VOCAB PAGE V49 ➲ MORE LIKE THIS 11, page R26

pin·head /'pɪnhed/ *noun* the very small flat surface at one end of a pin 大头针的平头

pin·hole /'pɪnhəʊl; *NAmE* -hoʊl/ *noun* a very small hole, especially one made by a pin 针刺的孔；针孔

pin·ion /'pɪnjən/ *verb* ~ **sb/sth + adv./prep.** to hold or tie sb, especially by their arms, so that they cannot move 捆住，缚住（双臂）；固定住：*His arms were pinioned to his sides.* 他的双臂被绑在身体两侧。◇ *They were pinioned against the wall.* 他们被牢牢地靠墙绑着。

pink 🔑 /pɪŋk/ *adj., noun, verb*

■ *adj.* **1** 🔑 pale red in colour 粉红色的：*pale pink roses* 淡粉色的玫瑰 ◇ *She went bright pink with embarrassment.* 她尴尬得满脸绯红。 **2** [only before noun] (*BrE*) connected with HOMOSEXUAL people 与同性恋者有关的：*the pink pound* (= money spent by HOMOSEXUALS as an influence in the economy) 同性恋群体消费力 **3** (*politics* 政, *informal, disapproving*) having or showing slightly LEFT-WING political views 政治观点偏左的；略呈左倾的 ➲ COMPARE RED *adj.* (5) ▸ **pink·ness** *noun* [U] **IDM** SEE TICKLE *v.*

■ *noun* **1** 🔑 [U, C] the colour that is produced when you mix red and white together 粉红色：*She was dressed in pink.* 她穿着粉红色的衣服。◇ *The bedroom was decorated in pale pinks.* 卧室涂成了淡粉红色。 **2** [C] a garden plant with pink, red or white flowers that have a sweet smell 香石竹；石竹

IDM **in the 'pink** (*old-fashioned, informal*) in good health 满面红光；容光焕发

■ *verb* (*BrE*) (*NAmE* **ping**) [I] (of a car engine 汽车发动机) to make knocking sounds because the fuel is not burning correctly 发爆声；敲缸

,pink-'collar *adj.* [only before noun] (*especially NAmE*) connected with low-paid jobs done mainly by women, for example in offices and restaurants（办公室、餐馆等）以女性为主低薪职业的；粉领的：*pink-collar workers* 粉领工人 ➲ COMPARE BLUE-COLLAR, WHITE-COLLAR

,pink 'gin *noun* **1** [U, C] an alcoholic drink made from GIN mixed with ANGOSTURA that gives it a bitter flavour 苦味杜松子酒；红杜松子酒 **2** [C] a glass of pink gin 一杯苦味杜松子酒

'pink·ing shears *noun* [pl.] special scissors used for cutting cloth so that it will not FRAY at the edges 锯齿形布边剪刀；花齿剪

pink·ish /'pɪŋkɪʃ/ *adj.* fairly pink in colour 浅粉色的；略带桃红色的

pinko /'pɪŋkəʊ; *NAmE* -koʊ/ *noun* (*pl.* **-os** or **-oes**) **1** (*NAmE, informal, disapproving*) a COMMUNIST or a SOCIALIST 共产主义者，社会主义者（含贬义） **2** (*BrE, informal*) a person who is slightly LEFT-WING in their ideas, but not very 观点偏左的人；左倾分子 ➲ COMPARE RED *n.* (3) ▸ **pinko** *adj.*

P

ˌ**pink ˈslip** *noun* (*NAmE, informal*) a letter given to sb to say that they must leave their job 解雇通知书

pinky (*also* **pinkie**) /ˈpɪŋki/ *noun* (*pl.* **-ies**) (*NAmE, ScotE*) the smallest finger of the hand （手的）小指： *a pinky ring* (= worn on the smallest finger) 戴在小指上的戒指 SYN **little finger**

ˈ**pin money** *noun* [U] a small amount of money that you earn, especially when this is used to buy things that you want rather than things that you need 小额闲钱

pin·na·cle /ˈpɪnəkl/ *noun* **1** [usually sing.] ~ **of sth** the most important or successful part of sth 顶点；顶峰；鼎盛时期： *the pinnacle of her career* 她事业的顶峰 **2** a small pointed stone decoration built on the roof of a building （建筑物）尖顶 **3** a high pointed piece of rock, especially at the top of a mountain （尤指山顶的）尖岩，兀立岩石

pinny /ˈpɪni/ *noun* (*pl.* **-ies**) (*BrE, informal*) = PINAFORE (2)

Pinoc·chio /pɪˈnəʊkiəʊ; *NAmE* -ˈnoʊkioʊ/ *noun* a character in a children's story who changes from a wooden figure into a boy. Whenever he tells a lie, his nose grows longer. 皮诺曹（从木偶变成男孩的童话人物，说谎时鼻子就变长）： *Cartoons showed the Minister as a long-nosed Pinocchio.* 漫画把部长描画成长鼻子皮诺曹。

pin·point /ˈpɪnpɔɪnt/ *verb, adj., noun*
▪ *verb* **1** ~ **sth** to find and show the exact position of sb/sth or the exact time that sth happened 明确指出，确定（位置或时间）： *He was able to pinpoint on the map the site of the medieval village.* 他能在地图上准确找出那个中世纪村庄的位置。 **2** ~ **sth** to be able to give the exact reason for sth or to describe sth exactly 准确解释（或说明）： *The report pinpointed the areas most in need of help.* 报告精确说明了亟待援助的地区。
▪ *adj.* if sth is done with **pinpoint accuracy**, it is done exactly and in exactly the right position 准确的；精确的： *The pilots bombed strategic targets with pinpoint accuracy.* 飞行员准确地轰炸了战略目标。
▪ *noun* a very small area of sth, especially light 极小的范围；光点

pin·prick /ˈpɪnprɪk/ *noun* **1** a very small area of sth, especially light （光等的）点： *His eyes narrowed to two small pinpricks.* 他把眼睛眯成了两条细缝。 **2** a very small hole in sth, especially one that has been made by a pin 小孔；针孔 **3** something that annoys you even though it is small and unimportant 烦心的小事；令人不快的琐事

ˌ**pins and ˈneedles** *noun* [U] an uncomfortable feeling in a part of your body, caused when a normal flow of blood returns after it has been partly blocked, especially because you have been sitting or lying in an awkward position 发麻；麻木： *to have pins and needles* 感觉麻木
IDM **be on ˌpins and ˈneedles** (*NAmE*) = (BE) ON TENTERHOOKS

pin·stripe /ˈpɪnstraɪp/ *noun* **1** [C] one of the white vertical lines printed on dark cloth that is used especially for making business suits （深色西装衣料上）白色细条纹 **2** [U, C] dark cloth with white vertical lines printed on it; a suit made from this cloth 带有白色细条纹的深色衣料；细条纹西服： *a pinstripe suit* 一套细条纹西装 ▸ **pin·striped** *adj.* [only before noun]: *a pinstriped suit* 一套细条纹西装 ◇ *a pinstriped official* (= who is wearing a pinstriped suit) 一个穿细条纹西装的官员

pint /paɪnt/ *noun* **1** (*abbr.* **pt**) a unit for measuring liquids and some dry goods. There are 8 pints in a gallon, equal to 0.568 of a litre in the UK and some other countries, and 0.473 of a litre in the US. 品脱（容量单位，为 ⅛ 加仑，在英国等国家约合 0.568 升，在美国约合 0.473 升）： ***a pint of beer/milk*** 一品脱啤酒 / 牛奶 ◇ *We'd better get a couple of extra pints (= of milk) tomorrow.* 明天我们最好再多买几品脱牛奶。 ◇ *Add half a pint of cream.* 加上半品脱奶油。 **2** (*BrE*) a pint of beer (especially in a pub) 一品脱啤酒（尤用于酒吧）： *Do you want to go for a pint later?* 待会儿你想去喝杯啤酒吗？

pinta /ˈpaɪntə/ *noun* (*old-fashioned, BrE, informal*) a pint of milk 一品脱牛奶

pinto /ˈpɪntəʊ; *NAmE* -toʊ/ *adj.* (*NAmE*) (of a horse 马) with areas on it of two colours, usually black and white 有两色花斑的；（通常指）黑白斑纹的 SYN **piebald** ▸ **pinto** *noun* (*pl.* **-os**)

ˈ**pinto bean** *noun* a type of curved BEAN with coloured marks on the skin 斑豆；花腰豆

ˌ**pint ˈpot** *noun* a beer glass, often with a handle, that holds one pint 一品脱啤酒杯（常带柄） IDM SEE QUART

ˈ**pint-sized** *adj.* (*informal*) (of people 人) very small 矮小的

ˈ**pin-up** *noun* **1** a picture of an attractive person, especially one who is not wearing many clothes, that is put on a wall for people to look at 名人（或美人）海报；挂在墙上的半裸美人像 **2** a person who appears in a pin-up 半裸海报画中的模特儿；海报中的名人（或美女）

pin·wheel /ˈpɪnwiːl/ *noun* (*NAmE*) **1** (*BrE* **wind·mill**) a toy with curved plastic parts that form the shape of a flower which turns round on the end of a stick when you blow on it 玩具风车 **2** = CATHERINE WHEEL

Pin·yin /pɪnˈjɪn/ *noun* [U] the standard system of ROMAN spelling in Chinese 汉语拼音

pi·on·eer /ˌpaɪəˈnɪə(r); *NAmE* -ˈnɪr/ *noun, verb*
▪ *noun* **1** ~ (**in/of sth**) a person who is the first to study and develop a particular area of knowledge, culture, etc. that other people then continue to develop 先锋；先驱；带头人 SYN **trailblazer**： *a pioneer in the field of microsurgery* 显微外科领域的创始人 ◇ *a computer pioneer* 计算机方面的先驱 ◇ *a pioneer aviator* 航空探索者 ◇ *a pioneer design* (= one that introduces new ideas, methods, etc.) 开创性设计 **2** one of the first people to go to a particular area in order to live and work there 开发者；拓荒者： *the pioneer spirit* 拓荒者的精神 ➔ WORDFINDER NOTE AT EXPLORE
▪ *verb* ~ **sth** when sb **pioneers** sth, they are one of the first people to do, discover or use sth new 当开拓者；做先锋；倡导： *a new technique pioneered by surgeons in a London hospital* 由伦敦一家医院的外科医生率先采用的新技术

pi·on·eer·ing /ˌpaɪəˈnɪərɪŋ; *NAmE* -ˈnɪr-/ *adj.* [usually before noun] introducing ideas and methods that have never been used before 开拓性的；先驱性的；探索性的： *pioneering work on infant mortality* 婴儿死亡率方面的探索性研究工作 ◇ *the pioneering days of radio* 无线电的初创时期

pious /ˈpaɪəs/ *adj.* **1** having or showing a deep respect for God and religion 虔诚的；虔敬的 SYN **devout**： *pious acts* 虔诚之举 OPP **impious** ➔ SEE ALSO PIETY **2** (*disapproving*) pretending to be religious, moral or good in order to impress other people 道貌岸然的；伪善的；假正经的 SYN **sanctimonious**： *pious sentiments* 虚情假意 **3** ~ **hope** something that you want to happen but is unlikely to be achieved 可望而不可即的；难以实现的： *Such reforms seem likely to remain little more than pious hopes.* 这类改革可能只是画饼充饥而已。 ▸ **pi·ous·ly** *adv.*

pip /pɪp/ *noun, verb*
▪ *noun* **1** (*especially BrE*) (*NAmE usually* **seed**) the small hard seed that is found in some types of fruit （某些水果的）种子，籽： ***an apple/orange pip*** 苹果籽；橙子籽 ➔ VISUAL VOCAB PAGE V32 **2 the pips** [pl.] (*old-fashioned, BrE*) a series of short high sounds, especially those used when giving the exact time on the radio 嘟嘟声；（尤指电台的）报时信号 **3** (*NAmE*) one of the dots showing the value on DICE and DOMINOES; one of the marks showing the value and SUIT of a PLAYING CARD （色子、骨牌、纸牌上的）点
▪ *verb* (**-pp-**) ~ **sb** (*BrE, informal*) to beat sb in a race, competition, etc. by only a small amount or at the last moment 以微弱优势击败；险胜；终于战胜： *She pipped her rival for the gold medal.* 她险胜对手，夺得金牌。 ◇ *He was **pipped at/to the post** for the top award.* 他到终点时以些微之差被超越，失去了冠军。

pipe /paɪp/ *noun, verb*
▪ *noun* **1** [C, U] a tube through which liquids and gases can flow 管子；管道： *hot and cold water pipes* 冷、热

水管 ◇ *lead/plastic pipes* 铅 / 塑料管子 ◇ *a leaking gas pipe* 漏气的煤气管 ◇ *Copper pipe is sold in lengths.* 铜管按长度出售。 ◇ *a* **burst pipe** 爆裂的管子 ➲ COLLOCATIONS AT DECORATE ➲ SEE ALSO DRAINPIPE (1), EXHAUST *n.* (2), WINDPIPE **2** [C] a narrow tube with a bowl at one end, used for smoking TOBACCO 烟斗；烟袋：*to smoke a pipe* 抽烟斗 ◇ *He puffed on his pipe.* 他吸着烟斗。◇ *pipe tobacco* 烟斗丝 **3** [C] a musical instrument in the shape of a tube, played by blowing 管乐器 ➲ SEE ALSO PAN PIPES **4** [C] any of the tubes from which sound is produced in an organ （管风琴的）音管 **5 pipes** [pl.] = BAGPIPES

pipes 管；烟斗

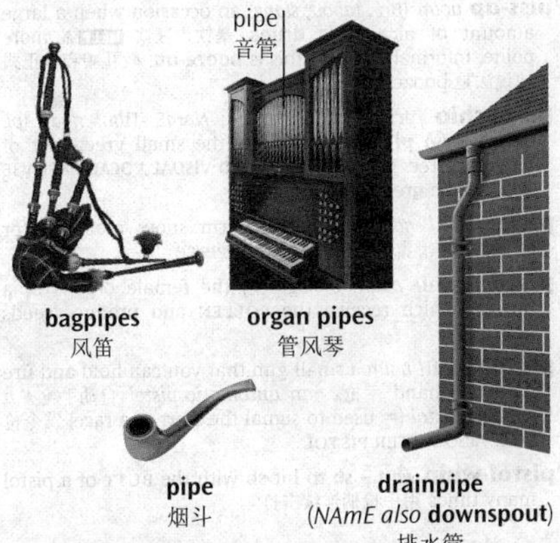

bagpipes 风笛 **organ pipes** 管风琴 **pipe** 烟斗 **drainpipe** (*NAmE also* **downspout**) 排水管

■ *verb* **1** [T] ~ **sth** (+ **adv./prep.**) to send water, gas, oil, etc. through a pipe from one place to another 用管道输送：*to pipe oil across the desert* 用管子把石油输送过沙漠 ◇ *Water is piped from the reservoir to the city.* 水用管子从水库输送到城市。 **2** [T] ~ **sth** (+ **adv./prep.**) [usually passive] to send sounds or signals through a wire or cable from one place to another 用线路系统传输（或传送）：*The speech was piped over a public address system.* 讲话经广播系统传送出去。 **3** [T, I] ~ (**sb**) to play music on a pipe or the BAGPIPES, especially to welcome sb who has arrived 用管乐器演奏（尤指迎宾曲）：*Passengers were piped aboard ship at the start of the cruise.* 游客在管乐迎宾曲中登船开始巡游。◇ *a prize for piping and drumming* 笛鼓演奏奖 **4** [I, T] (+ **speech**) to speak or sing in a high voice or with a high sound 尖声地说（或唱）；尖声啼鸣：*Outside a robin piped.* 外面有一只知更鸟在啼鸣。 **5** [T] ~ **sth** (**on sth**) to decorate food, especially a cake, with thin lines of ICING, etc. by squeezing it out of a special bag or tube 裱花（用裱花袋把糖霜等裱在糕点上）：*The cake had 'Happy Birthday' piped on it.* 蛋糕上裱了"生日快乐"的字样。

PHR V **,pipe 'down** (*informal*) used especially in orders, to tell sb to stop talking or to be less noisy 安静些；别说话；别嚷嚷 **,pipe 'up (with sth)** (*informal*) to begin to speak 开始说；说起来：*The person next to me piped up with a silly comment.* 我旁边那位愚蠢地评论起来。◇ + **speech** *'I know the answer,' piped up a voice at the back of the room.* "我知道答案。"房间后边有个声音叫起来。

'pipe band *noun* a marching band consisting of BAGPIPES and drums （行进）风笛鼓乐队

'pipe cleaner *noun* a short piece of wire, covered with soft material, used for cleaning inside a TOBACCO pipe 烟斗通条

,piped 'music *noun* [U] (*BrE*) recorded music that is played continuously in shops, restaurants, etc. （商店、餐馆等处不断播放的）背景音乐

'pipe dream *noun* a hope or plan that is impossible to achieve or not practical 脱离实际的愿望；行不通的计划；妄想

pipe·line /'paɪplaɪn/ *noun* a series of pipes that are usually underground and are used for carrying oil, gas, etc. over long distances 输油管道，输气管道，输送管线（通常指地下的）

IDM **in the 'pipeline** something that is **in the pipeline** is being discussed, planned or prepared and will happen or exist soon 在讨论（或规划、准备）中；在酝酿中

'pipe organ *noun* = ORGAN

piper /'paɪpə(r)/ *noun* a person who plays music on a pipe or the BAGPIPES 吹笛者；风笛吹奏者 IDM SEE PAY *v.*

pip·ette /pɪ'pet; *NAmE* paɪ'p-/ *noun* (*specialist*) a narrow tube used in a laboratory for measuring or transferring small amounts of liquids （实验室用的）移液管 ➲ VISUAL VOCAB PAGE V72

pipe·work /'paɪpwɜːk; *NAmE* -wɜːrk/ *noun* [U] the pipes used for carrying oil, gas or water around a machine, building, etc. （统称机器、建筑物等的）管道；管路系统

pip·ing /'paɪpɪŋ/ *noun, adj.*

■ *noun* [U] **1** a pipe or pipes of the type or length mentioned （某种或某长度的）管道，管子：*ten metres of lead piping* 十米长的铅管 **2** a folded strip of cloth, often with a length of string inside, used to decorate a piece of clothing, a CUSHION, etc. （衣服、靠垫等的）绲边：*a uniform with gold piping* 带金色绲边的制服 **3** lines of cream or ICING/FROSTING as decoration on a cake （用糖霜等裱成的）糕点条纹花饰 **4** the sound of a pipe or pipes being played 笛声；管乐器声

■ *adj.* (of a person's voice 人的声音) high 尖的；高的

,piping 'hot *adj.* (of liquids or food 液体或食物) very hot 滚烫的；烫手的；炙热的

pipit /'pɪpɪt/ *noun* (often in compounds 常构成复合词) a small brown bird with a pleasant song 鹨；小百灵：*a meadow/rock/tree pipit* 草地鹨；岩石鹨；树鹨

pip·squeak /'pɪpskwiːk/ *noun* (*old-fashioned, informal*) a person that you think is unimportant or does not deserve respect because they are small or young 无足轻重的人；小人物；小子

pi·quancy /'piːkənsi/ *noun* [U] the quality of being piquant 趣味；兴奋；辛辣：*The tart flavour of the cranberries adds piquancy.* 越橘的酸味很可口。◇ *The situation has an added piquancy since the two men are also rivals in love.* 事情更加有趣的是，这两个人也是情敌。

pi·quant /'piːkənt/ *adj.* **1** having a pleasantly strong or spicy taste 辛辣的；开胃的 **2** exciting and interesting 刺激的；令人兴奋的；有趣的

pique /piːk/ *noun, verb*

■ *noun* [U] (*formal*) annoyed or bitter feelings that you have, usually because your pride has been hurt 怨恨；愤恨；恼怒：*When he realized nobody was listening to him, he left in a* **fit of pique**. 他发觉他说话无人理睬，就愤然离去。

■ *verb* ~ **sb/sth** (*formal*) to make sb annoyed or upset 使愤恨；使恼怒 SYN **wound**[1] ▸ **piqued** *adj.* [not before noun]: *She couldn't help feeling a little piqued by his lack of interest.* 她不禁对他的淡漠感到有些不悦。

IDM **,pique sb's 'interest, curi'osity, etc.** to make sb very interested in sth 使…兴趣盎然；引起…的好奇

piqué /'piːkeɪ/ *noun* [U] a type of stiff cloth with a raised pattern 凸纹坚挺布料；珠地布；凹凸织物

pir·acy /'paɪrəsi/ *noun* [U] **1** the crime of attacking ships at sea in order to steal from them 海上抢劫 **2** the act of making illegal copies of DVDs, computer programs, books, etc., in order to sell them 盗版行为；非法复制：*software piracy* 软件盗版行为 ➲ SEE ALSO PIRATE *n.*

P

pi·ranha /pɪˈrɑːnə/ *noun* a small S American FRESHWATER fish that attacks and eats live animals 水虎鱼，锯脂鲤（南美的一种捕食动物的小淡水鱼）

pir·ate /ˈpaɪrət/ *noun, verb*
■ ***noun*** **1** (especially in the past) a person on a ship who attacks other ships at sea in order to steal from them （尤指旧时的）海盗： *a pirate ship* 海盗船 **2** (often used as an adjective 常用作形容词) a person who makes illegal copies of DVDs, computer programs, books, etc., in order to sell them 盗版者；盗印者： *a pirate edition* 盗版 ◇ *software pirates* 软件盗版者 **3** (often used as an adjective 常用作形容词) a person or an organization that broadcasts illegally 非法播音的人（或组织）： *a pirate radio station* 非法电台 ➲ SEE ALSO PIRACY ▶ **pir·at·ical** /ˌpaɪˈrætɪkl/ *adj.*
■ ***verb*** **~ sth** to copy and use or sell sb's work or a product without permission and without having the right to do so 盗印；窃用： *pirated computer games* 盗版电脑游戏

piri-piri /ˌpɪri ˈpɪri/ *noun* [U] a type of spicy sauce made from CHILLIES 辣椒酱

pirou·ette /ˌpɪruˈet/ *noun* a fast turn or spin that a person, especially a BALLET dancer, makes on one foot （尤指芭蕾舞中的）皮鲁埃特旋转，单脚尖旋转 ▶ **pirou·ette** *verb* [I]: *She pirouetted across the stage.* 她用皮鲁埃特旋转，从舞台的一边转到另一边。

pisca·tor·ial /ˌpɪskəˈtɔːriəl/ (*also* **pisca·tory** /ˈpɪskətəri; *NAmE* -tɔːri/) *adj.* (*formal*) relating to fishing or to FISHERMEN 捕鱼的；渔业的；渔民的

Pis·ces /ˈpaɪsiːz/ *noun* **1** [U] the 12th sign of the ZODIAC, the Fishes 黄道第十二宫；双鱼宫；双鱼（星）座 **2** [sing.] a person born when the sun is in this sign, that is between 20 February and 20 March 属双鱼座的人（约出生于 2 月 20 日至 3 月 20 日）▶ **Pis·cean** /ˈpaɪsiən/ *noun, adj.*

P

pis·cine /ˈpɪsaɪn; ˈpaɪsiːn/ *adj.* (*formal* or *specialist*) of or related to fish 鱼的；鱼类的

piss /pɪs/ *verb, noun* (*taboo, slang*)
■ ***verb*** [I] to URINATE 撒尿 HELP A more polite way of expressing this is **go to the toilet/loo** (*BrE*), **go to the bathroom** (*NAmE*) or simply **go** (*NAmE, BrE*). 较委婉的表达方式为 go to the toilet/loo（英式英语）、go to the bathroom（美式英语）或直接用 go（美式和英式英语均可）。
IDM **ˈpiss yourself (laughing)** to laugh very hard 大笑不止；笑破肚皮
PHR V **ˌpiss aˈbout/aˈround** (*BrE*) to waste time by behaving in a silly way 浪费时间；混日子 HELP A more polite, informal way of saying this is **mess about** (*BrE*) or **mess around** (*NAmE, BrE*). 较礼貌和非正式的说法是 mess about（英式英语）或 mess around（美式和英式英语均可）。 **ˌpiss sb aˈbout/aˈround** (*BrE*) to treat sb in a way that is deliberately not helpful to them or wastes their time 存心折腾（某人）；故意捣乱 HELP A more polite, informal way of saying this is **mess sb about/around**. 较礼貌和非正式的说法是 mess sb about/around。 **ˈpiss down** (*BrE*) to rain heavily 下大雨 **ˌpiss ˈoff** (*especially BrE*) (usually used in orders 通常用于命令) to go away 走开： *Why don't you just piss off and leave me alone?* 你就不能滚开，让我一个人待会儿？ **ˌpiss sb↔ˈoff** to make sb annoyed or bored 使生气；使厌烦： *Her attitude really pisses me off.* 她的态度让我厌烦极了。
■ ***noun*** **1** [U] = URINE **2** [sing.] an act of URINATING 撒尿： *to go for a piss* 去撒尿
IDM **be on the ˈpiss** (*BrE*) to be out at a pub, club, etc. and drinking a large amount of alcohol （在酒馆等）暴饮 **take the ˈpiss (out of sb/sth)** (*BrE*) to make fun of sb, especially by copying them or laughing at them for reasons they do not understand 拿…开心；嘲弄模仿 ➲ MORE AT PIECE *n.*

ˈpiss artist *noun* (*BrE, taboo, slang*) **1** a person who drinks too much alcohol 酒鬼 SYN **alcoholic** **2** a person who behaves in a stupid way 傻瓜；蠢猪；笨蛋

pissed /pɪst/ *adj.* **1** (*BrE, taboo, slang*) drunk 烂醉的；醉醺醺的 **2** (*NAmE, slang*) (*also* **ˌpissed ˈoff** *BrE, NAmE*) very angry or annoyed 气疯了；怒冲冲的： *I'm pissed off with the way they've treated me.* 他们那样对待我使我很生气。
IDM **(as) pissed as a ˈnewt** (*BrE*) very drunk 烂醉如泥

ˌpiss-ˈpoor *adj.* (*taboo, slang*) **1** of a very low standard 差劲的；水平极低的： *That band really was piss-poor.* 那支乐队糟糕透顶。 **2** not having enough money for basic needs 拮据的；贫穷的

piss·pot /ˈpɪspɒt; *NAmE* -pɑːt/ *noun* (*slang, offensive*) = CHAMBER POT

ˈpiss-take *noun* (*BrE, taboo, slang*) a joke that is intended to make sb/sth seem ridiculous 挖苦的笑话；戏谑的玩笑

ˈpiss-up *noun* (*BrE, taboo, slang*) an occasion when a large amount of alcohol is drunk 暴饮；狂饮 HELP A more polite, informal word for this is **booze-up**. 较礼貌和非正式的说法是 booze-up。

pis·ta·chio /pɪˈstæʃiəʊ; -ˈstɑːʃiəʊ; *NAmE* -ʃioʊ/ *noun* (*pl.* **-os**) **1** (*also* **piˈstachio nut**) [C] the small green nut of an Asian tree 开心果；阿月浑子 ➲ VISUAL VOCAB PAGE V35 **2** [U] a pale green colour 淡绿色

piste /piːst/ *noun* a track of firm snow prepared for SKIING on 滑雪道 ➲ SEE ALSO OFF-PISTE

pis·til /ˈpɪstɪl/ *noun* (*biology* 生) the female organs of a flower, which receive the POLLEN and produce seeds 雌蕊

pis·tol /ˈpɪstl/ *noun* a small gun that you can hold and fire with one hand 手枪： *an automatic pistol* 自动手枪 ◇ *a starting pistol* (= used to signal the start of a race) 发令枪 ➲ SEE ALSO WATER PISTOL

ˈpistol-whip *verb* **~ sb** to hit sb with the BUTT of a pistol many times 用手枪柄连续击打

piston 活塞

pis·ton /ˈpɪstən/ *noun* a part of an engine that consists of a short CYLINDER that fits inside a tube and moves up and down or backwards and forwards to make other parts of the engine move 活塞

pit /pɪt/ *noun, verb*
■ ***noun***
• **DEEP HOLE** 深洞 **1** [C] a large deep hole in the ground 深洞；深坑： *We dug a deep pit in the yard.* 我们在院子中挖了个深洞。 ◇ *The body had been dumped in a pit.* 尸体被扔进了深坑。 **2** [C] (especially in compounds 尤用于构成复合词) a deep hole in the ground from which minerals are dug out 矿井： *a chalk/gravel pit* 白垩/沙砾矿坑
• **MINE** 矿 **3** [C] = COAL MINE： *pit closures* 煤矿关闭 ◇ (*BrE*) *He went down the pit* (= started work as a MINER) *when he left school.* 他中学一毕业就当矿工了。
• **IN SKIN** 皮肤 **4** [C] a small shallow hole in the surface of sth, especially a mark left on the surface of the skin

by some disease, such as CHICKENPOX 麻子；痘瘢 ➲ SEE ALSO PITTED
- **IN FRUIT** 水果 **5** [C] (*especially NAmE*) = STONE (5)： *a peach pit* 桃核
- **IN MOTOR RACING** 汽车赛 **6 the pits** [pl.] (*BrE*) (*NAmE usually* **the pit** [C]) a place near the track where cars can stop for fuel, new tyres, etc. during a race（赛车道旁的）维修站 ➲ SEE ALSO PIT STOP (1)
- **IN THEATRE** 剧场 **7** [C] = ORCHESTRA PIT
- **PART OF BODY** 身体部位 **8** [C] (*NAmE, informal*) = ARMPIT
- **IN BUSINESS** 商业 **9** [C] (*NAmE*) the area of a STOCK EXCHANGE where a particular product is traded（交易所中某一商品的）交易场所： *the corn pit* 玉米交易厅 ➲ COMPARE FLOOR *n.* (6) ➲ SEE ALSO SANDPIT

IDM **be the 'pits** (*informal*) to be very bad or the worst example of sth 是坏典型；是拙劣典型；最糟糕 **the pit of your/the 'stomach** the bottom of the stomach where people say they feel strong feelings, especially fear 心窝；心底： *He had a sudden sinking feeling in the pit of his stomach.* 他内心深处突然有一种不祥之感。 ➲ MORE AT BOTTOMLESS

■ *verb* (-tt-) [usually passive]
- **MAKE HOLES** 打洞 **1 ~ sth** to make marks or holes on the surface of sth 使…表面有斑点；在…上打洞： *The surface of the moon is pitted with craters.* 月亮的表面布满陨石坑。◇ *Smallpox scars had pitted his face.* 他满脸是天花疤痕。
- **FRUIT** 水果 **2** (*BrE also* **stone**) **~ sth** to remove the stone from the inside of a fruit 去掉…的果核： *pitted olives* 去核橄榄

PHR V **'pit sb/sth against sth** to test sb or their strength, intelligence, etc. in a struggle or contest against sb/sth else 使竞争；使较量；使经受考验： *Lawyers and accountants felt that they were being pitted against each other.* 律师和会计师都觉得他们要一争高下。◇ *a chance to* **pit your wits** *against the world champions* (= in a test of your intelligence) 一次与世界冠军斗智的机会

pita, 'pita bread *noun* [U] (*NAmE*) = PITTA

pit-a-pat /ˌpɪt ə ˈpæt/ (*also* **'pitter-patter**) *adv.* with quick light steps or beats 扑扑的响声；噼啪声；哒哒声： *Her heart went pit-a-pat.* 她心里扑扑直跳。 ▸ **ˌpit-a-'pat** (*also* **'pitter-patter**) *noun* [sing.]： *I could hear the pit-a-pat of feet in the corridor.* 我能听见走廊上啪哒啪哒的脚步声。 ➲ MORE LIKE THIS 11, page R26

ˌpit ˌbull 'terrier (*also* **'pit bull**) *noun* a small strong aggressive dog, sometimes used in dog fights where people bet on which dog will win 比特犬（有时用于斗狗）

pitch 🔑 /pɪtʃ/ *noun, verb*

■ *noun*
- **FOR SPORT** 体育运动 **1** 🔑 (*BrE*) (*also* **field** *NAmE, BrE*) [C] an area of ground specially prepared and marked for playing a sports game（体育比赛的）场地；球场： *a football/cricket/rugby pitch* 足球 / 板球 / 橄榄球场 ◇ *The rugby tour was a disaster both on and off the pitch.* 这次橄榄球巡回赛在场上、场下都彻底失败。 ➲ VISUAL VOCAB PAGE V47
- **OF SOUND** 声音 **2** 🔑 [sing., U] how high or low a sound is, especially a musical note（尤指乐音的）音高： *A basic sense of rhythm and pitch is essential in a music teacher.* 基本的韵律感和音高感是音乐教师的必备素质。 ➲ SEE ALSO PERFECT PITCH
- **DEGREE/STRENGTH** 程度；强度 **3** [sing., U] the degree or strength of a feeling or activity; the highest point of sth（感情、活动等的）程度，力度；（事物的）最高点： *a frenetic pitch of activity* 活动的狂热极点 ◇ *Speculation has reached such a pitch that a decision will have to be made immediately.* 种种猜测甚嚣尘上，以致必须立即作出决定。 ➲ SEE ALSO FEVER PITCH
- **TO SELL STH** 销售 **4** [C, usually sing.] talk or arguments used by a person trying to sell things or persuade people to do sth 推销的话；说教；宣传论点： *an aggressive* **sales pitch** 强有力的推销行话 ◇ *the candidate's campaign pitch* 候选人的竞选宣传 ◇ *Each company was given ten minutes to* **make its pitch**. 每个公司有十分钟时间做推销宣传。
- **IN BASEBALL** 棒球 **5** [C] an act of throwing the ball; the way in which it is thrown 投球；投球方法
- **BLACK SUBSTANCE** 黑色物质 **6** [U] a black sticky substance made from oil or coal, used on roofs or the wooden boards of a ship to stop water from coming through 沥青；柏油
- **IN STREET/MARKET** 街道；市场 **7** [C] (*BrE*) a place in a street or market where sb sells things, or where a street entertainer usually performs 街头售货摊点；街头艺人表演地点
- **OF SHIP/AIRCRAFT** 船；飞机 **8** [U] (*specialist*) the movement of a ship up and down in the water or of an aircraft in the air（船在水上的）上下颠簸，纵摇；（飞机在空中的）俯仰 ➲ COMPARE ROLL *n.* (6)
- **OF ROOF** 屋顶 **9** [sing., U] (*specialist*) the degree to which a roof slopes 倾斜度

IDM **make a 'pitch for sb/sth | make a 'pitch to sb** to make a determined effort to get sth or to persuade sb of sth 决心获得；决心劝服 ➲ MORE AT QUEER *v.*

■ *verb*
- **THROW** 抛 **1** [T] **~ sb/sth + adv./prep.** to throw sb/sth with force 用力扔；投；抛： *The explosion pitched her violently into the air.* 爆炸把她猛烈地抛向空中。◇ (*figurative*) *The new government has already been pitched into a crisis.* 新政府已被抛入危机之中。
- **IN SPORTS** 体育运动 **2** [I, T] **~ (sth)** (in BASEBALL 棒球) to throw the ball to the person who is BATTING 将（球）投给击球员；投球；当投手 ➲ SYNONYMS AT THROW **3** [I, T] **~ (sth) + adv./prep.** (of the ball in the games of CRICKET or GOLF 板球或高尔夫球) to hit the ground; to make the ball hit the ground 触地；（使球）定点落地： *The ball pitched a yard short.* 球差一码落了地。 **4** [T, I] **~ (sth)** (in GOLF 高尔夫球) to hit the ball in a high curve 劈高球；击高球
- **FALL** 倒下 **5** [I] **+ adv./prep.** to fall heavily in a particular direction 重跌；跟跄倒下： *With a cry she pitched forward.* 她大叫一声向前跌倒了。
- **OF SHIP/AIRCRAFT** 船；飞机 **6** [I] to move up and down on the water or in the air 纵摇；颠簸；上下飘荡： *The sea was rough and the ship pitched and rolled all night.* 大海波涛汹涌，船整夜颠簸摇晃。
- **SET LEVEL** 定标准 **7** [T] to set sth at a particular level 确定标准： **~ sth (+ adv./prep./adj.)** *They have pitched their prices too high.* 他们把价格定得太高了。◇ **~ sth (at sth)** *The test was pitched at too low a level for the students.* 这次考试太低估学生的程度了。
- **TRY TO SELL** 推销 **8** [T] to aim or direct a product or service at a particular group of people（使产品或服务）针对，面向；确定销售对象（或目标市场）： **~ sth (at sb)** *The new software is being pitched at banks.* 这种新软件以银行为目标市场。◇ **~ sth (as sth)** *Orange juice is to be pitched as an athlete's drink.* 橙汁将作为运动员饮料进行推销。 **9** [T, I] to try to persuade sb to buy sth, to give you sth or to make a business deal with you 推销；争取支持（或生意等）： **~ sth** *Representatives went to Japan to pitch the company's newest products.* 销售代表前往日本推销公司的最新产品。◇ **~ (for sth)** *We were pitching against a much larger company for the contract.* 我们在与一家比我们大得多的公司竞争这项合同。
- **SOUND/MUSIC** 声音；音乐 **10** [T] **~ sth + adj.** to produce a sound or piece of music at a particular level 定音高： *You pitched that note a little flat.* 你把那个音符定得有点低了。◇ *The song was pitched too low for my voice.* 这首歌起调太低，不适合我的嗓音。 ➲ SEE ALSO HIGH-PITCHED, LOW-PITCHED
- **TENT** 帐篷 **11** [T] **~ sth** to set up a tent or a camp for a short time 搭（帐篷）；扎（营）： *We could* **pitch our tent** *in that field.* 我们可以临时把帐篷搭在那块地上。◇ *They* **pitched camp** *for the night near the river.* 他们靠河边扎营过夜。 ➲ SEE ALSO PITCHED

IDM **ˌpitch a 'story/'line/'yarn (to sb)** (*informal*) to tell sb a story or make an excuse that is not true（对某人）编谎话

PHR V **ˌpitch 'in (with sb/sth)** (*informal*) to join in and help with an activity, by doing some of the work or by giving money, advice, etc. 投入；参与；支援： *Everyone pitched in with the work.* 每个人都投入了这项工作。◇ *Local companies pitched in with building materials*

P

and labour. 当地的公司支援了建筑材料和劳动力。 **ˌpitch sth↔ˈin** to give a particular amount of money in order to help with sth 参与；出力；出份子： *We all pitched in $10 to buy her a gift.* 我们每人出 10 美元，凑钱给她买礼物。 **ˌpitch ˈinto sb** (*informal*) to attack or criticize sb 攻击；批判；批评： *She started pitching into me as soon as I arrived.* 我刚一到她就劈头盖脸地批评起我来。 **ˌpitch ˈinto sth** (*informal*) to start an activity with enthusiasm 蓬勃开展；大干： **pitch into doing sth** *I rolled up my sleeves and pitched into cleaning the kitchen.* 我卷起袖子，给厨房做大扫除。 **ˌpitch ˈup** (*BrE, informal*) to arrive somewhere, especially late or without planning 到达（尤指迟到或不约而至） **SYN turn up**: *You can't just pitch up and expect to get in without a ticket.* 你可不能说来就来，还想无票入场。

ˌpitch and ˈputt *noun* [U] GOLF played on a very small course 小场地高尔夫球

ˌpitch-ˈblack *adj.* completely black or dark 漆黑的；乌黑的 ➲ MORE LIKE THIS 15, page R26

ˌpitch-ˈdark *adj.* completely dark 漆黑的

pitched /pɪtʃt/ *adj.* (of a roof 屋顶) sloping; not flat 倾斜的

ˌpitched ˈbattle *noun* **1** a fight that involves a large number of people 群殴；聚众打斗： *The demonstration escalated into a pitched battle with the police.* 示威逐步升级，演变成了一场同警察的混战。 **2** a military battle fought with soldiers arranged in prepared positions （军事上的）对阵战

pitch·er /ˈpɪtʃə(r)/ *noun* **1** (*NAmE*) (*BrE* **jug**) a container with a handle and a LIP, for holding and pouring liquids （有柄有嘴的）壶，罐： *a pitcher of water* 一罐水 **2** (*BrE*) a large CLAY container with a small opening and one or two handles, used, especially in the past, for holding liquids （尤指旧时的）带柄的陶罐 ➲ PICTURE AT JUG **3** (in BASEBALL 棒球) the player who throws the ball to the BATTER 投球手

pitch·fork /ˈpɪtʃfɔːk; *NAmE* -fɔːrk/ *noun* a farm tool in the shape of a large fork with a long handle and two or three sharp metal points, used especially for lifting and moving HAY (= dried grass), etc. 杈；干草叉

ˈpitch invasion *noun* (*BrE*) an occasion when a crowd of people who are watching a sports game run onto the field, for example to celebrate sth or protest about sth （观众为庆祝或抗议等的）闯入比赛场地，侵入运动场

pitch·out /ˈpɪtʃaʊt/ *noun* **1** (in BASEBALL 棒球) a BALL deliberately thrown so that it is too far away to hit so that the CATCHER can throw it to get a player out who is running between BASES 战术坏球 **2** (in AMERICAN FOOTBALL 美式足球) a ball thrown sideways 横传球

pit·eous /ˈpɪtiəs/ *adj.* [usually before noun] (*literary*) deserving pity or causing you to feel pity 可怜的；令人怜悯的；令人同情的 **SYN pathetic**: *a piteous cry/sight* 可怜的哭声 / 景象 ▶ **pit·eous·ly** *adv.*

pit·fall /ˈpɪtfɔːl/ *noun* a danger or difficulty, especially one that is hidden or not obvious at first 危险；困难；（尤指）陷阱，隐患： *the potential pitfalls of buying a house* 购买房屋可能遇到的圈套

pith /pɪθ/ *noun* [U] **1** a soft dry white substance inside the skin of oranges and some other fruits （橙子等水果中的）中果皮 ➲ VISUAL VOCAB PAGE V33 **2** the essential or most important part of sth 精髓；核心；要点： *the pith of her argument* 她论据的核心

pit·head /ˈpɪthed/ *noun* the entrance to a coal mine and the offices, machinery, etc. in the area around it 矿井井口；坑口周围设施

ˈpith helmet *noun* a light hard hat worn to give protection from the sun in very hot countries （热带国家用的）木髓遮阳帽

pithy /ˈpɪθi/ *adj.* (*approving*) (**pith·ier**, **pithi·est**) (of a comment, piece of writing, etc. 说话或文章等) short but expressed well and full of meaning 言简意赅的；精练的 ▶ **pith·ily** /-ɪli/ *adv.*： *pithily expressed* 简洁地表达的

piti·able /ˈpɪtiəbl/ *adj.* (*formal*) **1** deserving pity or causing you to feel pity 值得同情的；可怜的： *The refugees were in a pitiable state.* 难民处境可怜。 **2** not deserving respect 卑鄙的；卑劣的： *a pitiable lack of talent* 令人遗憾的无能表现 ▶ **piti·ably** /-əbli/ *adv.*

piti·ful /ˈpɪtɪfl/ *adj.* **1** deserving pity or causing you to feel pity 可怜的；令人怜悯的；令人同情的 **SYN pathetic**: *The horse was a* ***pitiful sight*** (= because it was very thin or sick). 这匹马看上去可怜兮兮的。 **2** not deserving respect 卑微的；卑鄙的 **SYN poor**: *a pitiful effort/excuse/performance* 不值一提的努力 / 借口 / 表现 ▶ **piti·fully** /-fəli/ *adv.*： *The dog was whining pitifully.* 那条狗可怜巴巴地哀叫着。 ◇ *She was pitifully thin.* 她瘦骨嶙峋，令人怜悯。 ◇ *The fee is pitifully low.* 酬金低得可怜。

piti·less /ˈpɪtiləs/ *adj.* **1** showing no pity; cruel 冷酷的；无情的 **SYN callous**: *a pitiless killer/tyrant* 残忍的凶手 / 暴君 **2** very cruel or severe, and never ending 严酷而无尽的 **SYN relentless**: *a scorching, pitiless sun* 灼热的骄阳 ▶ **piti·less·ly** *adv.*

piton /ˈpiːtɒn; *NAmE* -tɑːn/ *noun* a short pointed piece of metal used in rock-climbing. The piton is fixed into the rock and has a rope attached to it through a ring at the other end. （登山用的）钢锥，岩钉

ˈpit pony *noun* a small horse that was used in the past for moving coal in a mine （旧时煤矿的）驮煤小马

ˈpit prop *noun* a large piece of wood used to support the roof of part of a coal mine from which coal has been removed （煤矿的）木支架，坑木，坑柱

ˈpit stop *noun* **1** (in motor racing 赛车运动) an occasion when a car stops during a race for more fuel, etc. 进站加油（或修理等） **2** (*NAmE, informal*) a short stop during a long trip for a rest, a meal, etc. （长途旅行中的）短暂休息，歇脚

pitta (*BrE*) (*NAmE* **pita**) /ˈpiːtə; *BrE also* ˈpɪtə/ (*also* **ˈpitta bread**, **ˈpita bread**) *noun* [U, C] a type of flat bread in the shape of an OVAL that can be split open and filled 皮塔饼，填馅面包，口袋面包（一种扁平的椭圆面包，可加入馅料）

pit·tance /ˈpɪtns/ *noun* [usually sing.] a very small amount of money that sb receives, for example as a wage, and that is hardly enough to live on 微薄的工资；极少的报酬： *to pay sb a pittance* 付给某人菲薄的工资 ◇ *to work for a pittance* 为一点小钱而工作

pit·ted /ˈpɪtɪd/ *adj.* **1** having small marks or holes in the surface 表面有小点（或小洞）的；坑坑洼洼的 **2** (of fruit 水果) having had the large hard seed (= the PIT) removed 去核的： *pitted olives* 去核橄榄

pitter-patter /ˈpɪtə pætə(r)/ *adv.*, *noun* = PIT-A-PAT

pi·tu·it·ary /pɪˈtjuːɪtəri; *NAmE* -ˈtuːəteri/ (*also* **piˈtuitary gland**) *noun* a small organ at the base of the brain that produces HORMONES that influence growth and sexual development 脑垂体；垂体

pity 🔑 /ˈpɪti/ *noun, verb*

WORD FAMILY
pity *noun, verb*
pitiful *adj.*
pitiless *adj.*
pitiable *adj.*
piteous *adj.*

■ *noun* **1** 🔑 [U] ~ (**for sb/sth**) a feeling of sympathy and sadness caused by the suffering and troubles of others 同情；怜悯： *I could only feel pity for what they were enduring.* 对他们所受的苦难我唯有同情而已。 ◇ *a* ***look/feeling/surge of pity*** 怜悯的表情 / 感觉 / 涌动 ◇ ***I took pity on*** *her and lent her the money.* 我同情她，就把钱借给了她。 ◇ (*formal*) *I beg you to* ***have pity on him.*** 请你可怜可怜他吧。 ◇ *I don't want your pity.* 我用不着你可怜。 **2** 🔑 [sing.] used to show that you are disappointed about sth （用于表示失望）遗憾，可惜 **SYN shame**: **a ~ (that…)** ***It's a pity*** *that you can't stay longer.* 你不能再多停留些时间，真是遗憾。 ◇ *'I've lost it!'*

'Oh, what a pity.' “我把东西弄丢了！”“哎呀，真可惜。” ◇ *What a pity that she didn't tell me earlier.* 真遗憾，她没有早点告诉我。◇ **a ~ (to do sth)** *It seems a pity to waste this food.* 浪费这些食物真可惜。◇ *This dress is really nice. Pity it's so expensive.* 这件连衣裙真不错，只可惜太贵了。◇ *Oh, that's a pity.* 唉，那可真遗憾。◇ *It would be a **great pity** if you gave up now.* 你要是现在放弃，那就太可惜了。

IDM **more's the 'pity** (*informal*) unfortunately 不幸地：*'Was the bicycle insured?' 'No, more's the pity!'* “自行车上保险没有？”“没有。真倒霉！”

■ ***verb*** (**pit·ies, pit·ied, pit·ied**) (not used in the progressive tenses 不用于进行时) to feel sorry for sb because of their situation; to feel pity for sb 同情；怜悯；可怜： **~ sb** *He pitied people who were stuck in dead-end jobs.* 他很同情那些工作上毫无前途的人。◇ *Compulsive gamblers are more **to be pitied** than condemned.* 对嗜赌成瘾者要多些同情，少些谴责。◇ **~ sb doing sth** *I pity her having to work such long hours.* 她不得不加班加点工作，真让我同情。

pity·ing /ˈpɪtiɪŋ/ *adj.* [usually before noun] showing pity for sb, often in a way that shows that you think you are better than them 怜悯的，同情的（常带优越感）： *a **pitying look/smile*** 垂怜的眼神 / 微笑 ▶ **pity·ing·ly** *adv.*

pivot /ˈpɪvət/ *noun, verb*

■ ***noun*** **1** the central point, pin or column on which sth turns or balances 支点；枢轴；中心点 **2** the central or most important person or thing 最重要的人（或事物）；中心；核心： *West Africa was the pivot of the cocoa trade.* 西非曾是可可豆贸易的中心。◇ *The pivot on which the old system turned had disappeared.* 维系旧制度的支柱已经消失了。

■ ***verb*** [I, T] **~ (sth) (+ adv./prep.)** to turn or balance on a central point (= a pivot); to make sth do this （使）在枢轴上旋转（或转动）： *Windows that pivot from a central point are easy to clean.* 沿中轴转动的窗子容易擦洗。◇ *She pivoted around and walked out.* 她一转身走了出去。

PHR V **'pivot on/around sth** (of an argument, a theory, etc. 论点、理论等) to depend completely on sth 围绕（主旨）；以…为核心 **SYN** **hinge on**

piv·otal /ˈpɪvətl/ *adj.* of great importance because other things depend on it 关键性的；核心的： *a pivotal role in European affairs* 在欧洲事务中的关键作用

pixel /ˈpɪksl/ *noun* (*computing* 计) any of the small individual areas on a computer screen, which together form the whole display 像素（组成屏幕图像的最小独立元素）

pix·el·ate (*also* **pix·el·late**) /ˈpɪksəleɪt/ *verb* **1 ~ sth** to divide an image into PIXELS 使像素化；将（图像）分解成像素 **2 ~ sth** to show an image on television as a small number of large PIXELS, especially in order to hide sb's identity（尤指为了不透露当事人身份而）使电视图像模糊，打上马赛克

pixie /ˈpɪksi/ *noun* (in stories) a creature like a small person with pointed ears, who has magic powers （传说中的）小精灵，小仙子，小妖怪

pizza /ˈpiːtsə/ *noun* [C, U] an Italian dish consisting of a flat round bread base with cheese, tomatoes, vegetables, meat, etc. on top 比萨饼；意大利饼： *a ham and mushroom pizza* 火腿蘑菇比萨饼 ◇ *Is there any pizza left?* 还有比萨饼吗？

pizz·azz /pɪˈzæz/ *noun* [U] (*informal*) a lively and exciting quality or style 激情；活泼；风度 **SYN** **flair**: *We need someone with youth, glamour and pizzazz.* 我们需要一位年富力强、魅力十足、风度翩翩的人。

piz·zeria /ˌpiːtsəˈriːə/ (*NAmE also* **'pizza parlor**) *noun* a restaurant that serves mainly pizzas 比萨饼店；比萨饼餐厅

pizzi·cato /ˌpɪtsɪˈkɑːtəʊ; *NAmE* -toʊ/ *adj., adv.* (*music* 音, *from Italian*) played using the fingers instead of a BOW[2] (3) to pull at the strings of a musical instrument such as a VIOLIN 弹拨的（地）；拨奏的（地）

Pl. *abbr.* (used in written addresses) PLACE （用于书写地址）街道，广场： *Grosvenor Pl.* 格罗夫诺街

pl. *abbr.* (in writing 书写形式) plural 复数；复数形式

plac·ard /ˈplækɑːd; *NAmE* -kɑːrd/ *noun* a large written or printed notice that is put in a public place or carried on a stick in a march 标语牌；广告牌；招贴；海报： *They were carrying placards and banners demanding that he resign.* 人们手持标语牌和横幅，要求他下台。 ➲ WORDFINDER NOTE AT PROTEST

pla·cate /pləˈkeɪt; *NAmE* ˈpleɪkeɪt/ *verb* **~ sb** to make sb feel less angry about sth 安抚；平息（怒气） **SYN** **pacify**: *a placating smile* 安抚的微笑 ◇ *The concessions did little to placate the students.* 让步根本未能平息学生的愤怒。

pla·ca·tory /pləˈkeɪtəri; *NAmE* ˈpleɪkətɔːri/ *adj.* (*formal*) designed to make sb feel less angry by showing that you are willing to satisfy or please them 和解的；安抚性的；安慰的： *a **placatory remark/smile/gesture*** 抚慰的话 / 微笑 / 姿态

place 🔑 /pleɪs/ *noun, verb*

■ ***noun***

• **POSITION/POINT/AREA** 位置；地点；区域 **1** 🔑 [C] a particular position, point or area 位置；地点；场所；地方： *Is this the place where it happened?* 这就是事发现场吗？◇ *This would be a good place for a picnic.* 这可是个野餐的好地方。◇ *I can't be in two places at once.* 我不能同时身处两地。

• **CITY/TOWN/BUILDING** 城；镇；建筑物 **2** 🔑 [C] a particular city, town, building, etc. 某处地方（如城镇或建筑物等）： *I can't remember all the places we visited in Thailand.* 我记不清在泰国参观过的所有地方。◇ *I used to live in York and I'm still fond of the place.* 我以前住在约克，现在仍然喜欢那里。◇ *The police searched the place.* 警察搜查了那个地方。◇ *We were looking for a **place to eat**.* 我们想找个吃饭的地方。◇ *Let's get out of this place!* 咱们离开这儿吧！ **3** 🔑 [C] (especially in compounds or phrases 尤用于构成复合词或词组) a building or an area of land used for a particular purpose 有某用途的建筑（或土地）： *a **meeting place*** 聚会地点 ◇ *The town has many excellent **eating places**.* 镇上有许多很棒的餐馆。◇ (*formal*) *churches and other **places of worship*** 教堂和其他礼拜场所 ◇ *He can usually be contacted at his **place of work**.* 一般都能在他的工作单位找到他。 ➲ SEE ALSO RESTING PLACE

• **AREA ON SURFACE** 表面区域 **4** 🔑 [C] a particular area on a surface, especially on a person's body 表面的某处；（尤指）身体某处： *He broke his arm in three places.* 他胳膊上有三处骨折。◇ *The paint was peeling off the wall **in places**.* 墙上有几处油漆剥落了。

• **IN BOOK/SPEECH, ETC.** 书、讲话等 **5** 🔑 [C] a point in a book, speech, piece of music, etc., especially one that sb has reached at a particular time 段；点；节；（尤指）读到的（或说到的）某点： *She had marked her place with a bookmark.* 她把书签夹在读到的地方。◇ *Excuse me, I seem to have **lost my place**.* 对不起，我好像忘记说到哪里了。

• **SEAT** 座位 **6** 🔑 [C] a position, seat, etc., especially one that is available for or being used by a person or vehicle （尤指占用或空着的）座位，位置，泊位： *Come and sit here—I've **saved you a place**.* 到这儿来坐吧。我给你留了个座位。◇ *I don't want to **lose my place** in the line.* 我可不想失去排队的位置。◇ *Would you like to **change places** with me so you can see better?* 你想跟我换个位子看得更清楚点吗？◇ *I've **set a place** for you at the table.* 我在餐桌上给你安排好了座位。

• **ROLE/IMPORTANCE** 角色；重要性 **7** [sing.] **~ (in sth)** the role or importance of sb/sth in a particular situation, usually in relation to others 身份；地位；资格： *He is assured of his place in history.* 他必定会被载入史册。◇ *Accurate reporting **takes second place** to lurid detail.* 准确的报道在其次，耸人听闻的细节最重要。◇ *My father believed that people should **know their place*** (= behave according to their social position). 我父亲认为人应该安分守己。◇ *It's **not your place*** (= your role) *to give advice.* 还轮不到你来做指导。◇ *Anecdotes **have no place in*** (= are not acceptable in) *an academic essay.* 学术文章容不得奇闻逸事。

• **AT UNIVERSITY/SCHOOL** 学校 **8** 🔑 [C] an opportunity to take part in sth, especially to study at a school or university

P

or on a course 求学机会；进修机会；入学名额：*She's been offered a place at Bath to study Business.* 她已被录取到巴斯大学读商科。◇ *There are very few places left on the course.* 这门课程没剩几个名额了。

• **IN SPORTS TEAM** 运动队 **9** [C] the position of being a member of a sports team 队员身份；队员资格：*She has **won a place** in the Olympic team.* 她已获得奥运代表队的队员资格。◇ *He **lost his place** in the first team.* 他失去了在一队的资格。

• **CORRECT POSITION** 正确位置 **10** ⚷ [C] the natural or correct position for sth 恰当位置；适当的地方：*Is there a place on the form to put your address?* 表格上有填写地址的位置吗？◇ *Put it back in its place when you've finished with it.* 用毕放回原处。

• **SAFE AREA** 安全地区 **11** [C] (usually with a negative 通常与否定词连用) a suitable or safe area for sb to be 适当的（或安全的）处所：*These streets are **no place for** a child to be out alone at night.* 这些街道可不是小孩子夜间单独去的地方。

• **HOME** 家 **12** ⚷ [sing.] (*informal*) a house or flat/apartment; a person's home 家；住处：*What about dinner at **my place?*** 到我家吃晚饭好不好？◇ *I'm fed up with living with my parents, so I'm looking for **a place of my own.*** 我腻烦跟父母同住了，所以正在找一个属于自己的住处。

• **IN RACE/COMPETITION** 竞赛 **13** ⚷ [C, usually sing.] a position among the winners of a race or competition （速度比赛或竞赛获胜者的）名次：*He finished in third place.* 他得了第三名。

• **MATHEMATICS** 数学 **14** [C] the position of a figure after a DECIMAL POINT （小数点后的）位：*The number is correct to three decimal places.* 这个数目精确到小数点后三位数。

• **STREET/SQUARE** 街道；广场 **15 Place** [sing.] (*abbr.* **Pl.**) used as part of a name for a short street or square （作短街道或广场名称的一部分）：*66 Portland Place* 波特兰街 66 号

IDM **all 'over the place** (*BrE also* **all 'over the shop**) (*US also* **all 'over the lot**) (*informal*) **1** everywhere 到处；各处：*New restaurants are appearing all over the place.* 新餐馆如雨后春笋般纷纷出现了。 **2** not neat or tidy; not well organized 凌乱；狼藉；杂乱无章：*Your calculations are all over the place* (= completely wrong). 你的计算错得一塌糊涂。 **change/swap 'places (with sb)** (usually used in negative sentences 通常用于否定句) to be in sb else's situation （与某人）交换位置，交换处境：*I'm perfectly happy—I wouldn't change places with anyone.* 我幸福极了，谁也甭想跟我交换位置。 **fall/slot into 'place** if sth complicated or difficult to understand **falls** or **slots into place**, it becomes organized or clear in your mind 明朗化；清晰；理出头绪 **give 'place to sb/sth** (*formal*) to be replaced by sb/sth 让位于；被…代替 SYN **give way to**：*Houses and factories gave place to open fields as the train gathered speed.* 火车逐渐加速驶过了房屋和工厂进入旷野。 **be 'going places** (*informal*) to be getting more and more successful in your life or career 事业顺利；春风得意：*a young architect who's really going places* 一个春风得意的青年建筑师 **if ˌI was/were in 'your place** used to introduce a piece of advice you are giving to sb 若是换了我呀；我若在你的位置：*If I were in your place, I'd resign immediately.* 我要是你呀，我就立即辞职。 **in the 'first place** used at the end of a sentence to talk about why sth was done or whether it should have been done or not （用于句尾，谈论某事为何或是否应该做）究竟，到底，当初：*I still don't understand why you chose that name in the first place.* 我仍不明白你究竟为什么取了这么个名字。◇ *I should never have taken that job in the first place.* 我当初就不该接受那份工作。 **in the 'first, 'second, etc. place** used at the beginning of a sentence to introduce the different points you are making in an argument （用于句首）第一、第二等等：*Well, in the first place he has all the right qualifications.* 嗯，首先，他符合一切条件。 **be in a good, bad, dark, etc. 'place** (*also less frequent* **be in a good, bad, dark, etc. 'space**) to be feeling positive, sad, worried, etc. about sth; to be in a good, bad, worrying state 感觉…；处于…的状态：*I'm happy now. I'm in a good place.* 我现在很高兴，感觉良好。 **in 'my, 'your, etc. place in my, your, etc. situation** 处于我（或你等）的境况：*I wouldn't like to be in your place.* 我可不想处于你的境地。 **in 'place 1** ⚷ (*also* **into 'place**) in the correct position; ready for sth 在正确位置；准备妥当：*Carefully lay each slab in place.* 要仔细铺好每一块石板。◇ *The receiver had already clicked into place.* 听筒咔的一声放回原位了。 **2** ⚷ working or ready to work 在工作；准备就绪：*All the arrangements are now in place for their visit.* 他们来访的一切事宜都安排好了。 **3** (*NAmE*) = ON THE SPOT (3) **in place of sb/sth | in sb's/sth's 'place** ⚷ instead of sb/sth 代替；顶替：*You can use milk in place of cream in this recipe.* 这道食谱可以用牛奶代替

▼ **SYNONYMS 同义词辨析**

place

site • area • position • point • location • scene • spot • venue

These are all words for a particular area or part of an area, especially one used for a particular purpose or where sb/sth is situated or happens. 以上各词均表示地点、场所、位置。

place a particular point, area, city, town, building, etc., especially one used for a particular purpose or where a particular thing happens 指有特定用途或事情发生的地点、场所、城镇、建筑物、地方：*This would be a good place for a picnic.* 这可是个野餐的好地方。

site the place where sth, especially a building, is or will be situated; a place where sth happened or that is used for a particular purpose 尤指建筑物的地点、位置，事情发生或有特定用途的地点、场所：*They've chosen a site for the new school.* 他们为新学校选了校址。

area a part of a room, building or particular space that is used for a special purpose; a particular place on an object 指（房间、建筑物、处所内划为某用途的）地方、场地，物体上的区、部位：*the hotel reception area* 旅馆接待处 ◇ *Move the cursor to a blank area on the screen.* 把光标移至电脑屏幕的空白区。

position the place where a person or thing is situated; the place where sb/sth is meant to be 指位置、方位、恰当的位置：*From his position at the top of the hill, he could see the harbour.* 他在山头那个位置可以俯瞰海港。

NOTE The **position** of sb/sth is often temporary: the place where sb/sth is at a particular time. * position 指人 / 物所处的位置常常是暂时性的，即在某段时间所在的位置。

point a particular place within an area, where sth happens or is supposed to happen 指某事发生或将要发生的地点、某个地方：*the point at which the river divides* 河流分岔点

location a place where sth happens or exists, especially a place that is not named or not known 指事情发生或存在的地方、地点、位置，尤指无名或鲜为人知的地方：*The company is moving to a new location.* 公司准备迁移新址。

scene a place where sth happens, especially sth unpleasant 尤指不愉快事件发生的地点、现场：*the scene of the accident* 事故现场

spot a particular point or area, especially one that has a particular character or where sth particular happens 尤指具有某种特点或某一事件发生的地点、场所：*The lake is one of the local **beauty spots**.* 这个湖是当地的一个风景点。

venue the place where people meet for an organized event such as a performance or sports event 指演出、体育比赛等的聚会地点、场馆、会场

PATTERNS

- **at** a place/site/position/point/location/scene/spot/venue
- **in** a(n) place/area/position/location/venue
- the place/site/point/location/spot/venue **where…**
- the **right** place/site/position/location/spot/venue
- a **central** site/position/location/venue
- the/sb's/sth's **exact**/**precise** place/site/position/point/location/spot

奶油。◇ *He was unable to come to the ceremony, but he sent his son to accept the award in his place.* 他不能亲自来参加仪式，但派了他儿子前来代他领奖。 **out of 'place 1** 🔑 not in the correct place 位置不当： *Some of these files seem to be out of place.* 有些档案似乎没放对地方。 **2** 🔑 not suitable for a particular situation 不得体；不适当： *Her remarks were out of place.* 她出言不当。◇ *I felt completely out of place among all these successful people.* 夹在这些事业有成的人中间我觉得自己格格不入。 **a place in the 'sun** a position in which you are comfortable or have an advantage over other people 舒适的状态；有利地位；优越境况 **put yourself in sb else's/sb's 'place** to imagine that you are in sb else's situation 设身处地替别人着想；设想自己处于别人的境地： *Of course I was upset—just put yourself in my place.* 我当然不高兴，你设身处地为我想想。 **put sb in their 'place** to make sb feel stupid or embarrassed for showing too much confidence 挫某人的锐气；杀某人的威风；使明白自己的身份： *At first she tried to take charge of the meeting but I soon put her in her place.* 起初她试图主导会议，但我很快就把她轰下去了。 **take 'place** 🔑 to happen, especially after previously being arranged or planned （尤指根据安排或计划）发生，进行： *The film festival takes place in October.* 电影节将于十月举行。◇ *We may never discover what took place that night.* 我们可能永远不会知道那一夜发生了什么事。 **take sb's/sth's 'place | take the place of sb/sth** 🔑 to replace sb/sth 代替；替换： *She couldn't attend the meeting so her assistant took her place.* 她不能参加会议，所以她的助手代她出席。◇ *Computers have taken the place of typewriters in most offices.* 在大多数办公室，电脑已经取代了打字机。 **take your 'place 1** to go to the physical position that is necessary for an activity 就位；入座： *Take your places for dinner.* 请各位入席。 **2** to take or accept the status in society that is correct or that you deserve 得到应有的社会地位；名副其实 ➲ MORE AT HAIR, HEART, LIGHTNING *n.*, OWN *v.*, PRIDE *n.*, ROCK *n.*

■ ***verb***

- **IN POSITION** 位置 **1** 🔑 [T] **~ sth + adv./prep.** to put sth in a particular place, especially when you do it carefully or deliberately （小心或有意）放置，安放： *He placed his hand on her shoulder.* 他把手搭在她的肩上。◇ *A bomb had been placed under the seat.* 座位下面放了一枚炸弹。◇ *The parking areas in the town are few, but strategically placed.* 城内停车场虽少，但都设在关键地方。
- **IN SITUATION** 境况 **2** [T] **~ sb/yourself + adv./prep.** (more formal than *put* 比 put 正式) to put sb/yourself in a particular situation 使（人）处于某位置；安置；安顿： *to place sb in command* 让某人指挥 ◇ *She was placed in the care of an uncle.* 她由一位叔父照顾。◇ *His resignation placed us in a difficult position.* 他的辞职使我们不知所措。◇ *The job places great demands on me.* 这项工作对我的要求很高。
- **ATTITUDE** 态度 **3** 🔑 [T] **~ sth on sth/doing sth** used to express the attitude sb has towards sb/sth 以某种态度对待（或看待）： *Great emphasis is placed on education.* 教育受到高度重视。◇ *They place a high value on punctuality.* 他们对守时极为重视。
- **RECOGNIZE** 辨认 **4** [T] **~ sb/sth** (usually used in negative sentences 通常用于否定句) to recognize sb/sth and be able to identify them/it 认出；辨认；识别： *I've seen her before but I just can't place her.* 我从前见过她，不过现在认不出她来。◇ *His accent was impossible to place.* 他的口音无法辨认。
- **BET/ORDER/ADVERTISEMENT** 打赌；订单；广告 **5** 🔑 [T] **~ sth** to give instructions about sth or make a request for sth to happen 下指示；请求： *to place a bet/an order* 下注；下订单 ◇ *We placed an advertisement for a cleaner in the local paper.* 我们在本地报纸上登了广告，招一名清洁工。
- **FIND HOME/JOB** 找家 / 工作 **6** [T] to find a suitable home, job, etc. for sb 为…安置家庭（或工作等）： **~ sb (with sb/sth)** *The children were placed with foster parents.* 这些小孩已安顿好，交给寄养父母了。◇ **~ sb (in sth)** *The agency placed about 2 000 secretaries last year.* 去年，这家中介所为大约 2 000 名秘书找到了工作。
- **GIVE RANK** 排档次 **7** [T] **~ sb/sth + adv./prep.** to decide that sb/sth has a particular position or rank compared with other people or things （经比较）归类，划分，排名次： *I would place her among the top five tennis players in the world.* 我会把她排在世界五名顶尖网球选手之列。◇ *Nursing attracts people who place relationships high on their list of priorities.* 护理工作对重视人际关系的人具有吸引力。
- **IN RACE** 体育竞赛 **8** [T, I] used to describe a person, a team, a horse, etc. finishing in a particular position in a race 排名；获名次： **~ sb/sth + adj.** *He was placed fifth in last Saturday's race.* 在上周六的径赛中，他名列第五。◇ **~ (sth)** (*BrE*) *My horse has been placed several times* (= it was among the first three or four to finish the race). 我的马在竞赛中屡获名次。◇ (*NAmE*) *His horse placed in the last race* (= it was among the first three to finish the race, usually in second place). 他的马在上次比赛中得了名次（常指亚军）。

IDM **be well, ideally, uniquely, better, etc. placed for sth/to do sth 1** to be in a good, very good, etc. position or have a good, etc. opportunity to do sth 有良好的（或理想的、独特的等）机遇；处于有利等的位置： *Engineering graduates are well placed for a wide range of jobs.* 工程科毕业生在很多职业中处于优势。◇ *The company is ideally placed to take advantage of the new legislation.* 这家公司条件理想得很，恰好可以充分利用新法规。 **2** to be located in a pleasant or convenient place 坐落在方便宜人的地方；位于合宜的地点： *The hotel is well placed for restaurants, bars and clubs.* 这家宾馆位置很好，附近有很多餐厅、酒吧和俱乐部。 ➲ MORE AT PEDESTAL, PREMIUM *n.*, RECORD *n.*

pla·cebo /plə'siːbəʊ; *NAmE* -boʊ/ *noun* (*pl.* **-os**) a substance that has no physical effects, given to patients who do not need medicine but think that they do, or used when testing new drugs 安慰剂，安慰药（给无实际治疗需要者或测试新药时使用）： *the **placebo effect*** (= the effect of taking a placebo and feeling better) 安慰剂效应 ➲ WORDFINDER NOTE AT MEDICINE

'place card *noun* a small card with a person's name on it, placed on a table to show where they are to sit （标有姓名的）座位卡

place·hold·er /'pleɪshəʊldə(r); *NAmE* -hoʊld-/ *noun* **1** (*specialist*) a symbol or piece of text which replaces sth that is missing （替代缺失部分的）占位符，占位文字 **2** (*linguistics* 语言) an item which is necessary in a sentence, but does not have real meaning, for example the word 'it' in 'It's a pity she left.' 位标（句子中必要但无实际意义的词项，如 It's a pity she left 中的 it）

'place kick *noun* (in RUGBY and AMERICAN FOOTBALL 橄榄球和美式足球) a kick made by putting the ball on the ground first 定位球

place·man /'pleɪsmən/ *noun* (*pl.* **-men** /-mən/) (*BrE, disapproving*) a person who is given an official position as a reward for supporting a politician or government 获赠官禄者（因支持某从政者或政府而得官职）

'place mat *noun* a MAT on a table on which a person's plate is put 餐具垫

place·ment /'pleɪsmənt/ *noun* **1** [U] the act of finding sb a suitable job or place to live （对人的）安置，安排： *a job placement service* 职业介绍所 ◇ *placement with a foster family* 安置到寄养家庭 **2** (*also* **'work placement**) [U, C] (*BrE*) a job, often as part of a course of study, where you get some experience of a particular kind of work 实习工作；实习课： *The third year is spent **on placement** in selected companies.* 第三年是在选定的公司里实习。◇ *The course includes a placement in Year 3.* 本课程第 3 年有实习课。 ➲ COMPARE INTERNSHIP (1), WORK EXPERIENCE (2) **3** [U] the act of placing sth somewhere （对物件的）安置，放置： *This procedure ensures correct placement of the catheter.* 这个程序可保证导液管的正确置入。 ➲ SEE ALSO ADVANCED PLACEMENT, PRODUCT PLACEMENT

'placement test *noun* a test which is designed to find the appropriate level for students in a course or programme of study （课程等的）分班考试，分级考试

'place name *noun* a name of a town or other place 地名

P

pla·centa /plə'sentə/ (*usually* **the placenta**) *noun* (*anatomy* 解) the material that comes out of a woman or female animal's body after a baby has been born, and which was necessary to feed and protect the baby 胎盘 SYN **afterbirth**

pla·cen·tal /plə'sentl/ *adj.* [usually before noun] **1** (*medical* 医) of or related to the PLACENTA 胎盘的 **2** (*biology* 生) having a PLACENTA 有胎盘的；有胎座的：*placental mammals* 胎盘哺乳动物

'place setting *noun* a set or an arrangement of knives, forks and spoons, and/or plates and dishes for one person （供一人用的）一套餐具

pla·cid /'plæsɪd/ *adj.* **1** (of a person or an animal 人或动物) not easily excited or irritated 温和的；平和的；文静的：*a placid baby/horse* 安静的婴儿；驯良的马 OPP **high-spirited** **2** calm and peaceful, with very little movement 平静的；宁静的；安静的 SYN **tranquil**：*the placid waters of the lake* 平静的湖水 ▶ **pla·cid·ity** /plə'sɪdəti/ *noun* [U] **pla·cid·ly** *adv.*

pla·cing /'pleɪsɪŋ/ *noun* the position of sb/sth in a race or a competition or in a list arranged in order of success 名次；排名：*He needs a high placing in today's qualifier to reach the final.* 在今天的资格赛中，他必须排名靠前才能进入决赛。

pla·giar·ism /'pleɪdʒərɪzəm/ *noun* [U, C] (*disapproving*) an act of plagiarizing sth; sth that has been plagiarized 剽窃；抄袭；剽窃作品：*There were accusations of plagiarism.* 曾有过剽窃的指控。◇ *a text full of plagiarisms* 满篇剽窃他人著作的文章 ▶ **pla·giar·ist** /'pleɪdʒərɪst/ *noun*

pla·giar·ize (*BrE also* **-ise**) /'pleɪdʒəraɪz/ *verb* [T, I] ~ (**sth**) (*disapproving*) to copy another person's ideas, words or work and pretend that they are your own 剽窃；抄袭：*He was accused of plagiarizing his colleague's results.* 他被指控剽窃同事的成果。

P

plague /pleɪg/ *noun, verb*

■ ***noun*** **1** (*also* **the plague**) [U] = BUBONIC PLAGUE：*an outbreak of plague* 鼠疫的爆发 **2** [C] any infectious disease that kills a lot of people 死亡率高的传染病；瘟疫 SYN **epidemic**：*the plague of AIDS* 艾滋病这种严重的传染病 **3** [C] ~ **of sth** large numbers of an animal or insect that come into an area and cause great damage （大批动物或昆虫肆虐造成的）灾害，祸患：*a plague of locusts/rats, etc.* 蝗灾、鼠害等 IDM SEE AVOID

■ ***verb*** **1** ~ **sb/sth** (**with sth**) to cause pain or trouble to sb/sth over a period of time 给…造成长时间的痛苦（或麻烦）；困扰；折磨；使受煎熬 SYN **trouble**：*to be plagued by doubt* 为疑虑所困扰 ◇ *Financial problems are plaguing the company.* 财政问题使这家公司焦头烂额。◇ *The team has been plagued by injury this season.* 本赛季这支队一直为队员受伤所困扰。 **2** ~ **sb** (**with sth**) to annoy sb or create problems, especially by asking for sth, demanding attention, etc. 纠缠；缠磨；缠扰 SYN **hound**：*Rock stars have to get used to being plagued by autograph hunters.* 摇滚歌星必须习惯歌迷要求签名的纠缠。

plaice /pleɪs/ *noun* [C, U] (*pl.* **plaice**) a flat sea fish that is used for food 鲽（一种可食用的比目海鱼）

plaid /plæd/ *noun* **1** [U] a type of thick cloth with a pattern of lines and squares of different colours and widths, especially a TARTAN pattern 格子呢；毛呢 ➲ VISUAL VOCAB PAGE V66 **2** [C] a long piece of plaid made of wool, worn over the shoulders as part of the Scottish national dress 方格花呢长披肩（苏格兰民族服饰的一部分）

Plaid Cymru /ˌplaɪd 'kʌmri:/ *noun* [U+sing./pl. v.] (*WelshE*) a Welsh political party that wants Wales to be an independent state 威尔士党，威尔士民族主义党（主张威尔士独立）

plain 🔑 /pleɪn/ *adj., noun, adv.*

■ ***adj.*** (**plain·er**, **plain·est**) **1** 🔑 easy to see or understand 清楚的；明显的；浅白的 SYN **clear**：*He made it plain that we should leave.* 他明确表示要我们离开。◇ *She made her annoyance plain.* 她满脸不耐烦。◇ *The facts were **plain to see**.* 事实显而易见。◇ *It was a rip-off, **plain and simple**.* 这是一个不折不扣的冒牌货。➲ SYNONYMS AT CLEAR **2** 🔑 not trying to trick anyone; honest and direct 坦诚的；直率的；直接的：***The plain fact** is that nobody really knows.* 事实很明显，没有人真正了解。◇ *a politician with a reputation for **plain speaking*** 说话直率出了名的一个政治人物 **3** 🔑 not decorated or complicated; simple 不尚修饰的；朴素的；简单的：*a plain but elegant dress* 朴素淡雅的连衣裙 ◇ *plain food* 清淡的食物 ◇ *The interior of the church was plain and simple.* 教堂内部朴素无华。◇ *plain yogurt* (= without sugar or fruit) 原味酸奶 ➲ COMPARE FANCY *adj.* (2) **4** 🔑 without marks or a pattern on it

▼ **SYNONYMS** 同义词辨析

plain

simple • stark • bare • unequivocal

These words all describe statements, often about sth unpleasant, that are very clear, not trying to hide anything, and not using more words than necessary. 以上各词常形容令人不快的陈述清楚明白、直截了当、简单明了。

plain used for talking about a fact that other people may not like to hear; honest and direct in way that other people may not like 用于他人可能不乐意听的事实，或指直率、直接得让人不喜欢：*The plain fact is that nobody really knows.* 事实很明显，没有人真正了解。

simple [only before noun] used for talking about a fact that other people may not like to hear; very obvious and not complicated by anything else 用于他人可能不乐意听的事实，或指事物简单明了：*The simple truth is that we just can't afford it.* 事实很简单，我们就是付不起。

PLAIN OR SIMPLE? 用 plain 还是 simple?

When it is being used to emphasize facts that other people may not like to hear, **plain** is usually used in the expression *the plain fact/truth is that…*. **Simple** can be used in this way too, but it can also be used in a wider variety of structures and collocations (such as *reason* and *matter*). 用以强调他人可能不乐意听的事实时，plain 通常用于 the plain fact/truth is that... 短语中。simple 也可用这种表达方式，但是还可用于更多种类的句型结构，与更多的词语（如 reason 和 matter）搭配：*The problem was due to the simple fact that…* 问题源于这一简单的事实…◇ ~~*The problem was due to the plain fact that…*~~ ◇ ~~*for the plain reason that…*~~ ◇ ~~*It's a plain matter of…*~~ Expressions with **simple** often suggest impatience with other people's behaviour. 与 simple 构成的表达法通常暗指对别人的行为不耐烦。

stark (*rather formal*) used for describing an unpleasant fact or difference that is very obvious 用于描述令人不快的事实或区别十分明显、鲜明：*The stark truth is that there is not enough money left.* 明摆着的事实是剩下的钱已经不够了。 NOTE The *simple/plain truth* may be sth that some people do not want to hear, but it may be good for them to hear it anyway. The *stark truth* is sth particularly unpleasant and has no good side to it at all. * simple/plain truth 指所谈的事尽管不中听，但听了可能会有好处。stark truth 指所谈之事特别令人不快，而且没有任何好处。

bare [only before noun] the most basic or simple, with nothing extra 指最基本的、最简单的：*She gave me only the bare facts of the case.* 她只给我介绍了这个案件的一些基本情况。

unequivocal (*formal*) expressing your opinion or intention very clearly and firmly 指表达明确的、毫不含糊的、斩钉截铁的：*The reply was an unequivocal 'no'.* 回答是个干脆利落的"不"字。

PATTERNS

- the plain/simple/stark/bare/unequivocal **truth**
- a(n) plain/simple/stark/bare/unequivocal **fact**/**statement**
- a(n) plain/simple/unequivocal **answer**

素的；无花纹的；单色的： *covers in plain or printed cotton* 单色或印花的罩布 ◇ *Write on plain paper* (= without lines). 用无格白纸书写。 **5** [only before noun] used to emphasize that sth is very ordinary, not special in any way 极普通的；平庸的；平凡的 SYN **everyday**: *You don't need any special skills for this job, just plain common sense.* 这项工作不需要任何特殊技能，只要有普通常识就够了。 **6** (especially of a woman 尤指女人) not beautiful or attractive 相貌平平的；无姿色的 **7** describing a simple STITCH used in knitting （编织）平针的，平纹的 ▶ **plain·ness** *noun* [U]

IDM **be plain 'sailing** (*NAmE* **be clear/smooth 'sailing**) to be simple and free from trouble 顺利；一帆风顺 **in plain 'English** simply and clearly expressed, without using technical language 用平白的言语（或文字） **(as) plain as a 'pikestaff | (as) plain as 'day | (as) plain as the nose on your 'face** very obvious 一清二楚；一目了然；显而易见

■ *noun* (*also* **plains** [pl.]) a large area of flat land 平原： *the flat coastal plain of Thassos* 萨索斯岛平坦的滨海平原 ◇ *the Great Plains* 北美洲大平原 ➲ SEE ALSO FLOODPLAIN

■ *adv.* (*informal*) used to emphasize how bad, stupid, etc. sth is （用于强调）简直，绝对地： *plain stupid/wrong* 简直愚蠢至极；绝对错误

plain·chant /'pleɪntʃɑːnt; *NAmE* -tʃænt/ *noun* [U] = PLAINSONG

,plain 'chocolate *noun* [U] (*BrE*) = DARK CHOCOLATE

,plain 'clothes *noun* [pl.] ordinary clothes, not uniform, when worn by police officers on duty （警察执行任务时穿的）便衣，便服： *officers in plain clothes* 便衣警察 ➲ WORDFINDER NOTE AT POLICE ▶ **,plain-'clothes** *adj.* [only before noun]: *plain-clothes police officers* 便衣警察

,plain 'flour (*BrE*) (*NAmE* **,all-purpose 'flour**) *noun* [U] flour that does not contain BAKING POWDER （不含发酵粉的）普通面粉 ➲ COMPARE SELF-RAISING FLOUR

plain·ly /'pleɪnli/ *adv.* **1** in a way that is easy to see, hear, understand or believe 清晰地；明显地；清楚地 SYN **clearly**: *The sea was plainly visible in the distance.* 大海在远处清晰可见。◇ *The lease plainly states that all damage must be paid for.* 租约明确规定，一切损坏必须赔偿。◇ *She had no right to interfere in what was plainly a family matter.* 这事明摆着是别人的家事，她无权干涉。 ◇ *Plainly* (= obviously) *something was wrong.* 很显然什么地方出了问题。 **2** using simple words to say sth in a direct and honest way 简单明了地；直截了当地： *To put it plainly, he's a crook.* 实话实说吧，他是个骗子。 **3** in a simple way, without decoration 简朴地；朴素地： *She was plainly dressed and wore no make-up.* 她衣着朴素，粉黛不施。

plain·song /'pleɪnsɒŋ; *NAmE* -sɔːŋ; -sɑːŋ/ (*also* **plain·chant**) *noun* [U] a type of church music for voices alone, used since the Middle Ages 宗教圣咏，素歌（中世纪以来的教堂音乐）

plaint /pleɪnt/ *noun* **1** (*BrE, law* 律) a complaint made against sb in court 起诉；诉状 **2** (*literary*) a sad cry or sound 凄凉的哭泣（或声音）

'plain text *noun* [U] (*specialist*) data that is stored in the form of ASCII (= a standard code used so that data can be moved between computers that use different programs). Plain text cannot be FORMATTED (= displayed in a particular way on the screen). 明文，纯文本数据（以 ASCII 形式储存的数据）

plain·tiff /'pleɪntɪf/ (*also less frequent* **com·plain·ant**) *noun* (*law* 律) a person who makes a formal complaint against sb in court 原告；起诉人 ➲ COMPARE DEFENDANT

plaint·ive /'pleɪntɪv/ *adj.* sounding sad, especially in a weak complaining way （声音）悲伤的，哀怨的 SYN **mournful**: *a plaintive cry/voice* 凄楚的哭泣 / 声音 ▶ **plaint·ive·ly** *adv.*

plait /plæt/ (*BrE*) (*also* **braid** *NAmE, BrE*) *noun, verb*

■ *noun* a long piece of sth, especially hair, that is divided into three parts and twisted together 辫状物；发辫；辫子： *She wore her hair in plaits.* 她梳着辫子。 ➲ VISUAL VOCAB PAGE V65

■ *verb* **~ sth** to twist three or more long pieces of hair, rope, etc. together to make one long piece 将（头发、绳子等）编成辫

plan 🔑 /plæn/ *noun, verb*

■ *noun*

• **INTENTION** 意图 **1** 🔑 something that you intend to do or achieve 计划；打算： **~ (for sth)** *Do you have any plans for the summer?* 这个夏天你有什么打算？ ◇ **~ (to do sth)** *There are no plans to build new offices.* 现在没有建新办公楼的计划。 ◇ *Your* ***best plan*** (= the best thing to do) *would be to go by car.* 你开车去是上策。 ◇ *There's been* ***a change of plan.*** 计划有变。 ◇ *We can't change our plans now.* 我们现在不能改变计划了。 ➲ SYNONYMS AT PURPOSE

• **ARRANGEMENT** 安排 **2** 🔑 a set of things to do in order to achieve sth, especially one that has been considered in detail in advance （详细）规划，方案；精心安排： **~ (for sth)** *Both sides agreed to a detailed plan for keeping the peace.* 双方都同意维护和平的详细方案。 ◇ **~ (to do sth)** *The government has announced plans to create one million new training places.* 政府已经宣布开设一百万个新培训名额的计划。 ◇ *a* ***development/business/peace, etc. plan*** 发展计划、营业规划、和平规划等 ◇ *a five-point plan* 五点规划 ◇ *a three-year plan* 三年计划 ◇ *We need to* ***make plans*** *for the future.* 我们必须规划未来。 ◇ *a* ***plan of action/campaign*** 行动 / 运动方案 ◇ *Let's hope everything will go* ***according to plan.*** 但愿一切都会按计划进行。 ➲ SEE ALSO MASTER PLAN

• **MAP** 地图 **3** 🔑 a detailed map of a building, town, etc. （建筑、城镇等的）详图： *a plan of the museum* 博物馆详图 ◇ *a street plan of the city* 城市街道详图

• **DRAWING** 绘图 **4** 🔑 [usually pl.] **~ (for/of sth)** (*specialist*) a detailed drawing of a machine, building, etc. that shows its size, shape and measurements （机器、建筑等的）设计图，平面图；图解： *The architect is* ***drawing up plans*** *for the new offices.* 建筑师正在绘制新办公楼的设计图。 ➲ COMPARE ELEVATION (4), GROUND PLAN (1) **5** 🔑 a diagram that shows how sth will be arranged 分布图；示意图： *a* ***seating plan*** (= showing where each person will sit, for example at a dinner) 座位安排示意图 ◇ *a* ***floor plan*** (= showing how furniture is arranged) 楼层平面图

• **MONEY** 钱 **6** 🔑 (especially in compounds 尤用于构成复合词) a way of investing money for the future 投资方式： *a savings plan* 储蓄计划

IDM **,make a 'plan** (*SAfrE*) to think of sth you can do to solve a problem or make sth happen 想办法；设法解决： *It's going to be difficult to find the time but I'll make a plan.* 要抽出时间很难，不过我会想办法的。 ➲ MORE AT SOUND *v.*

■ *verb* (**-nn-**)

• **MAKE ARRANGEMENTS** 安排 **1** 🔑 [T, I] to make detailed arrangements for sth you want to do in the future 精心安排；计划；谋划： **~ sth** *to plan a trip* 计划一次旅行 ◇ *Everything* ***went*** *exactly* ***as planned.*** 一切都严格地按计划进行。 ◇ *We planned the day down to the last detail.* 我们极为详细地安排了这一天的日程。 ◇ **~ sth for sth** *A meeting has been planned for early next year.* 计划明年年初召开一次会议。 ◇ **~ (for sth)** *to plan for the future* 规划未来 ◇ **~ how, what, etc....** *I've been planning how I'm going to spend the day.* 我一直在筹划怎样度过这一天。 ◇ **~ that...** *They planned that the two routes would connect.* 他们计划让两条路接上。

• **INTEND/EXPECT** 意欲；期待 **2** 🔑 [I, T] to intend or expect to do sth 打算；期待： **~ on sth/on doing sth** *We hadn't planned on going anywhere this evening.* 我们今晚没打算外出。 ◇ **~ to do sth** *They plan to arrive some time after three.* 他们预计在三点钟以后到达。 ◇ **~ sth** *We're planning a trip to France in the spring—are you interested?* 我们打算春天去法国旅游。你有意去吗？

• **DESIGN** 设计 **3** 🔑 [T] **~ sth** to make a design or an outline for sth 设计；安排；组织；策划： *to plan an essay/a garden* 构思一篇文章；设计一个花园 ◇ *a well-planned campaign* 一场精心策划的活动

PHR V **,plan sth↔'out** to plan carefully and in detail sth that you are going to do in the future 精心安排；筹划：

P

Plan out your route before you go. 出发前要仔细设计好你的路线。◇ *She has her career all planned out.* 她对自己的职业已作了精心规划。

Plan 'A *noun* [sing.] the thing or things sb intends to do if everything happens as they expect（一切如所预料的情况下使用的）第一行动方案，甲案

pla·nar /ˈpleɪnə(r)/ *adj.* (*specialist*) of or related to a flat surface 平面的

Plan 'B *noun* [sing.] the thing or things sb intends to do if their first plan is not successful（第一方案不可行的情况下使用的）第二行动方案，次选方案，乙案：*If Plan A fails, go to Plan B.* 假如第一方案失败了，就执行第二方案。

plane /pleɪn/ *noun, adj., verb*

■ ***noun*** **1** (*BrE also* **aero·plane**) (*also* **air·plane** *especially in NAmE*) a flying vehicle with wings and one or more engines 飞机：*She left* ***by plane*** *for Berlin.* 她乘飞机去柏林了。◇ *a* ***plane crash*** 飞机坠毁 ◇ ***I caught the next plane*** *to Dublin.* 我赶上了下一班飞机去都柏林。◇ ***The plane took off*** *an hour late.* 飞机延迟了一小时起飞。◇ ***The plane landed*** *at Geneva.* 飞机在日内瓦降落。➲ COLLOCATIONS AT TRAVEL ➲ VISUAL VOCAB PAGE V57

> **WORDFINDER** 联想词：cabin crew, charter, flight path, in-flight, land, long-haul, refuel, take-off, **travel**

2 (*geometry* 几何) any flat or level surface, or an imaginary flat surface through or joining material objects 平面：*the* ***horizontal/vertical plane*** 水平 / 垂直平面 **3** a level of thought, existence or development（思想、存在或发展的）水平，程度，阶段，境界：*to reach a higher plane of achievement* 取得更高的成就 **4** a tool with a blade set in a flat surface, used for making the surface of wood smooth by shaving very thin layers off it 木工刨；刨子 ➲ VISUAL VOCAB PAGE V21

■ ***adj.*** [only before noun] (*specialist*) completely flat; level 平的；平坦的：*a plane surface* 平面

■ ***verb*** **1** [T] to make a piece of wood smoother or flatter with a PLANE (4)（用刨子）刨平：**~ sth** *Plane the surface down first.* 首先要把表面刨平。◇ **~ sth + adj.** *Then plane the wood smooth.* 然后把木头刨光。 **2** [I] (of a bird 鸟) to fly without moving the wings, especially high up in the air 滑翔 **3** [I] (of a boat, etc. 小船等) to move quickly across water, only just touching the surface 擦着水面疾驶

plane·load /ˈpleɪnləʊd; *NAmE* -loʊd/ *noun* the number of people or the amount of goods that can be carried in a plane 飞机载客量（或装载量）：*two planeloads of refugees* 两飞机的难民

planer /ˈpleɪnə(r)/ *noun* an electric tool for making wooden surfaces smooth 平刨机；刨床

planet /ˈplænɪt/ *noun* **1** [C] a large round object in space that moves around a star (such as the sun) and receives light from it 行星：*the planets of our solar system* 太阳系的行星 ◇ *the planet Earth/Venus/Mars* 地球；金星；火星 **2** **the planet** [sing.] used to mean 'the world', especially when talking about the environment 地球（尤指环境）：*the battle to save the planet* 拯救地球的战斗 ➲ WORDFINDER NOTE AT EARTH

IDM **to be on another 'planet | what 'planet is sb on?** (*informal, humorous*) used to suggest that sb's ideas are not realistic or practical（指某人的想法完全不切实际）：*He thinks being a father is easy. What planet is he on?* 他认为做父亲很容易，他真是天真！

plan·et·arium /ˌplænɪˈteəriəm; *NAmE* -ˈter-/ *noun* (*pl.* **-iums**) a building with a curved ceiling to represent the sky at night, with moving images of the planets and stars, used to educate and entertain people 天文馆

plan·et·ary /ˈplænətri; *NAmE* -teri/ *adj.* [only before noun] (*specialist*) relating to a planet or planets 行星的：*a planetary system* 行星系

'plane tree *noun* a tree with spreading branches and broad leaves, that is often found in towns in northern countries 悬铃木

plan·gent /ˈplændʒənt/ *adj.* **1** (*formal*) (of sounds 声音) loud, with a strong beat 洪亮的；轰鸣的 **2** (*literary*) (of sounds or images 声音或图像) expressing sadness 哀婉的；凄凉的 SYN **plaintive**：*the plangent sound of the harpsichord* 拨弦键琴如泣如诉的声音

plank /plæŋk/ *noun* **1** a long narrow flat piece of wood that is used for making floors, etc. 木板；板条：*a plank of wood* 一块木板条 ◇ *a wooden plank* 一条木板 **2** a main point in the policy of an organization, especially a political party（政党等的）政策准则，政纲的核心：*The* ***central plank*** *of the bill was rural development.* 这一法案的核心是农村发展。IDM SEE THICK *adj.*, WALK *v.*

plank·ing /ˈplæŋkɪŋ/ *noun* [U] **1** planks used to make a floor, etc. 板材；地板木料 **2** the activity of lying face down with your arms by your sides in an unusual or dangerous place in order to take a photograph to put on the Internet or SOCIAL NETWORKING sites 趴街（双臂放在身体两侧，趴在不寻常或危险之地，拍照传到互联网或社交网站上）：*Recent tragedies did little to decrease the popularity of planking.* 最近发生的悲剧并未减少趴街的风行。

plank·ton /ˈplæŋktən/ *noun* [U+sing./pl. v.] the very small forms of plant and animal life that live in water 浮游生物

ˌplanned e'conomy (*also* **comˌmand e'conomy**) *noun* an economy in which production, prices and incomes are decided and fixed by the central government 计划经济

plan·ner /ˈplænə(r)/ *noun* **1** (*also* **ˌtown 'planner**) a person whose job is to plan the growth and development of a town 城市规划师 **2** a person who makes plans for a particular area of activity 设计者；规划者：*curriculum planners* 课程规划人员 **3** a book, chart, computer program, etc. that contains dates and is used for recording information, arranging meetings, etc. 记事簿；规划簿：*a journey planner* 旅程安排表 ◇ *a wall planner* 壁挂记事簿 ➲ VISUAL VOCAB PAGE V71

plan·ning /ˈplænɪŋ/ *noun* [U] **1** the act or process of making plans for sth 计划制订；规划过程：*financial planning* 财政计划 ➲ SEE ALSO FAMILY PLANNING **2** = TOWN PLANNING

'planning permission *noun* [U] (*BrE*) official permission to build a new building or change one that already exists 规划许可；建筑（或改建）许可

plant /plɑːnt; *NAmE* plænt/ *noun, verb*

■ ***noun***

• LIVING THING 生物 **1** [C] a living thing that grows in the earth and usually has a STEM, leaves and roots, especially one that is smaller than a tree or bush 植物；花草：*All plants need light and water.* 一切植物都需要阳光和水。◇ ***flowering/garden/indoor plants*** 开花 / 园林 / 室内植物 ◇ *a tomato/potato plant* 番茄秧；马铃薯秧 ◇ *the animal and plant life of the area* 本地区的动植物 ➲ COLLOCATIONS AT LIFE ➲ VISUAL VOCAB PAGE V11 ➲ SEE ALSO BEDDING PLANT, HOUSEPLANT, POT PLANT, RUBBER PLANT

• FACTORY 工厂 **2** [C] a factory or place where power is produced or an industrial process takes place 发电厂；工厂：*a nuclear reprocessing plant* 核物质再处理厂 ◇ *Japanese car plants* 日本汽车制造厂 ◇ *a chemical plant* 化工厂 ➲ SEE ALSO SEWAGE PLANT ➲ SYNONYMS AT FACTORY ➲ WORDFINDER NOTE AT FACTORY

• MACHINERY 机械 **3** [U] the large machinery that is used in industrial processes（工业用的）大型机器，设备：*The company has been investing in new plant and equipment.* 这家公司一直在投资购置新机器和设备。

• STH ILLEGAL 不合法的事物 **4** [C, usually sing.] (*informal*) something that sb has deliberately placed among another person's clothes or possessions in order to make them appear guilty of a crime 栽赃物品

• PERSON 人 **5** [C] a person who joins a group of criminals or enemies in order to get and secretly report information about their activities 坐探；内线；卧底

■ ***verb***
• **SEEDS/PLANTS** 种子；植物 **1** ~ **sth** to put plants, seeds, etc. in the ground to grow 栽种；种植；播种：*to plant and harvest rice* 栽种并收割水稻 ◇ *Plant these shrubs in full sun.* 把这些灌木栽在阳光充足的地方。 **2** to cover or supply a garden/yard, area of land, etc. with plants 在（某处）栽种：**~ sth** *a densely planted orange grove* 栽植稠密的橘树林 ◇ **~ sth with sth** *The field had been ploughed and planted with corn.* 这块地已犁过并种上了玉米。
• **PUT IN POSITION** 安放 **3 ~ sth/yourself + adv./prep.** to place sth or yourself firmly in a particular place or position 立稳；竖立；安放：*They planted a flag on the summit.* 他们在山顶上插了一面旗子。◇ *He planted himself squarely in front of us.* 他稳稳地站在我们面前。
• **BOMB** 炸弹 **4 ~ sth (+ adv./prep.)** to hide sth such as a bomb in a place where it will not be found （秘密）放置，安置
• **STH ILLEGAL** 不合法的事物 **5 ~ sth (on sb)** to hide sth, especially sth illegal, in sb's clothing, possessions, etc. so that when it is found it will look as though they committed a crime （给某人）栽（赃）：*He claims that the drugs were planted on him.* 他声称这些毒品是别人给他栽的赃。
• **PERSON** 人 **6 ~ sb (in sth)** to send sb to join a group, etc., especially in order to make secret reports on its members 使卧底；安插（密探）
• **THOUGHT/IDEA** 思想；意见 **7 ~ sth (in sth)** to make sb think or believe sth, especially without them realizing that you gave them the idea 使（思想、信念等）植根于：*He planted the first seeds of doubt in my mind.* 是他最初启发我起疑心的。

PHR V **ˌplant sth↔ˈout** to put plants in the ground so that they have enough room to grow 栽植于土地（以获得足够的生长空间）

plan·tain /ˈplæntɪn/ *noun* **1** [C, U] a fruit like a large BANANA, but less sweet, that is cooked and eaten as a vegetable 大蕉 **2** [C] a wild plant with small green flowers and broad flat leaves that spread out close to the ground 车前草

plan·tar /ˈplæntə(r)/ *adj.* [only before noun] (*anatomy* 解) of or related to the bottom of the foot 跖的；足底的

ˌplantar ˈwart (*NAmE*) (*BrE* **ver·ruca**) *noun* a small hard lump like a WART on the bottom of the foot, which can be easily spread from person to person 跖疣；足底疣

plan·ta·tion /plɑːnˈteɪʃn; *NAmE* plæn-/ *noun* **1** a large area of land, especially in a hot country, where crops such as coffee, sugar, rubber, etc. are grown 种植园，种植场（尤指热带国家种植咖啡、甘蔗、橡胶等的大庄园）：*a banana plantation* 香蕉种植园 **2** a large area of land that is planted with trees to produce wood 木材林地；人造林：*conifer/forestry plantations* 针叶树林地；种植林

plant·er /ˈplɑːntə(r); *NAmE* ˈplæn-/ *noun* **1** an attractive container to grow a plant in 花盆 ➲ VISUAL VOCAB PAGE V20 **2** a person who owns or manages a PLANTATION in a tropical country 种植园主；种植园经营者：*a tea planter* 茶园园主 **3** a machine that plants seeds, etc. 播种机；插秧机

plant·ing /ˈplɑːntɪŋ; *NAmE* ˈplæn-/ *noun* [U, C] an act of planting sth; sth that has just been planted 种植；栽种；栽种物：*The Tree Council promotes tree planting.* 林木委员会倡导植树造林。◇ *These bushes are fairly recent plantings.* 这些灌木丛是最近栽植的。

ˈplant pot *noun* a container for growing plants in 花盆 ➲ VISUAL VOCAB PAGE V22

plants·man /ˈplɑːntsmən; *NAmE* ˈplænts-/, **plants·woman** /ˈplɑːntswʊmən; *NAmE* ˈplænts-/ *noun* (*pl.* **-men** /-mən/, **-women** /-wɪmɪn/) an expert in garden plants and GARDENING 花卉栽培技术员；园艺师

plaque /plæk; *BrE also* plɑːk/ *noun* **1** [C] a flat piece of stone, metal, etc., usually with a name and dates on, attached to a wall in memory of a person or an event （纪念性的）牌匾，匾额；纪念匾 **2** [U] a soft substance that forms on teeth and encourages the growth of harmful bacteria 牙菌斑 ➲ COMPARE SCALE *n.* (10)

plasma /ˈplæzmə/ (*also* **plasm** /ˈplæzəm/) *noun* [U] **1** (*biology* 生 or *medical* 医) the clear liquid part of blood, in which the blood cells, etc. float 血浆 **2** (*physics* 物) a gas that contains approximately equal numbers of positive and negative electric charges and is present in the sun and most stars 等离子体

ˈplasma screen *noun* a type of television or computer screen that is larger and thinner than most screens and produces a very clear image （电视机或电脑的）等离子屏幕

ˌplasma TˈV *noun* a television set with a plasma screen 等离子电视

plas·ter /ˈplɑːstə(r); *NAmE* ˈplæs-/ *noun, verb*
■ ***noun*** **1** [U] a substance made of LIME, water and sand, that is put on walls and ceilings to give them a smooth hard surface 灰泥：*an old house with crumbling plaster and a leaking roof* 一所灰泥剥落、屋顶漏水的老房子 ➲ WORDFINDER NOTE AT CONSTRUCTION **2** (*also less frequent* **ˌplaster of ˈParis**) [U] a white powder that is mixed with water and becomes very hard when it dries, used especially for making copies of statues or holding broken bones in place 建筑石膏；熟石膏：*a plaster bust of Julius Caesar* 一尊尤利乌斯・恺撒的半身石膏塑像 ◇ (*BrE*) *She broke her leg a month ago and it's still* **in plaster**. 她一个月前腿骨骨折，至今仍打着石膏。 **3** (*also* **ˈsticking plaster**) (*both BrE*) (*also* **ˈBand-Aid™** *NAmE, BrE*) [C, U] a piece of material that can be stuck to the skin to protect a small wound or cut; this material 膏药；创可贴；护创胶布 ➲ WORDFINDER NOTE AT HURT ➲ COLLOCATIONS AT INJURY
■ ***verb*** **1 ~ sth** to cover a wall, etc. with plaster 抹灰于，用灰泥抹（墙等） ➲ COLLOCATIONS AT DECORATE **2 ~ sb/sth/yourself in/with sth** to cover sb/sth with a wet or sticky substance 往…上涂抹：*She plastered herself in suntan lotion.* 她往身上抹防晒液。◇ *We were plastered from head to foot with mud.* 我们浑身上下都沾满了泥。 **3 ~ sth + adv./prep.** to make your hair flat and stick to your head 把（头发）梳平；使（头发）粘在（头上）：*His wet hair was plastered to his head.* 他那湿透的头发紧贴在头皮上。 **4 ~ sth + adv./prep.** to completely cover a surface with pictures or POSTERS 贴满，遍贴（画片或招贴画）：*Her bedroom wall was plastered with photos of him.* 她卧室的墙上贴满了他的照片。◇ *She had photos of him plastered all over her bedroom wall.* 她把他的照片贴满了卧室的墙。◇ *The next day their picture was plastered all over the newspapers.* 第二天，他们的照片被刊登在各家报纸上。

PHR V **ˌplaster ˈover sth** to cover sth such as a crack or an old wall with plaster 用灰泥抹（裂缝或旧墙）

plas·ter·board /ˈplɑːstəbɔːd; *NAmE* ˈplæstərbɔːrd/ (*NAmE also* **drywall**) *noun* [U] a building material made of sheets of cardboard with plaster between them, used for inside walls and ceilings 灰泥板；纸面石膏板

ˈplaster cast *noun* **1** (*also* **cast**) a case made of PLASTER OF PARIS that covers a broken bone and protects it （固定骨折部位的）管形石膏 **2** a copy of sth, made from PLASTER OF PARIS 石膏模型：*They took a plaster cast of the teeth for identification purposes.* 他们做了这副牙的石膏模型作鉴别之用。

plas·tered /ˈplɑːstəd; *NAmE* ˈplæstərd/ *adj.* [not before noun] (*informal*) drunk 醉：*to be/get plastered* 喝醉酒

plas·terer /ˈplɑːstərə(r); *NAmE* ˈplæs-/ *noun* a person whose job is to put plaster on walls and ceilings 抹灰工；泥水匠；粉刷工

plaster of Paris /ˌplɑːstər əv ˈpærɪs; *NAmE* ˌplæs-/ *noun* [U] = PLASTER (2)

ˌplaster ˈsaint *noun* a person who tries to appear to have no moral faults or weaknesses, especially when this appearance is false 道貌岸然者；（尤指）伪圣人，伪君子

P

plas·ter·work /ˈplɑːstəwɜːk; *NAmE* ˈplæstərwɜːrk/ *noun* [U] the dry PLASTER on ceilings when it has been formed into shapes and patterns for decoration （天花板的）灰泥装饰图案

plas·tic 🔑 /ˈplæstɪk/ *noun, adj.*

■ ***noun*** **1** 🔑 [U, C, usually pl.] a light strong material that is produced by chemical processes and can be formed into shapes when heated. There are many different types of plastic, used to make different objects and FABRICS. 塑料： *The pipes should be* ***made of plastic****.* 这些管子应该是用塑料制作的。◇ *a sheet of clear plastic* 一张透明的塑料 ◇ *the plastic industry* 塑料工业 **2 plastics** [U] the science of making plastics 塑料学 **3** [U] (*informal*) a way of talking about CREDIT CARDS 信用卡： *Do they take plastic?* 他们收信用卡吗？

■ ***adj.*** **1** 🔑 made of plastic 塑料制的；塑料的： *a plastic bag/cup/toy* 塑料袋／杯／玩具 **2** (of a material or substance 材料或物质) easily formed into different shapes 可塑的；有塑性的 SYN **malleable**： *Clay is a plastic substance.* 黏土是可塑物质。 **3** (*disapproving*) that seems artificial; false; not real or sincere 做作的；虚伪的；矫饰的 SYN **false**： *TV game show hosts with their banal remarks and plastic smiles* 语言陈腐、笑容刻板的电视竞赛节目主持人

ˌplastic ˈarts *noun* [pl.] (*specialist*) art forms that involve making models or representing things so that they seem solid 造型艺术： *The plastic arts include sculpture, pottery and painting.* 造型艺术包括雕塑、陶艺和绘画。

ˌplastic ˈbullet *noun* a bullet made of plastic, that is intended to injure but not to kill people 塑料子弹；橡皮子弹

ˌplastic exˈplosive *noun* [U, C] an EXPLOSIVE that is used to make bombs 塑性炸药

Plas·ti·cine™ /ˈplæstəsiːn/ *noun* [U] (*BrE*) a soft substance like CLAY that is made in different colours, used especially by children for making models 橡皮泥

plas·ti·city /plæˈstɪsəti/ *noun* [U] (*specialist*) the quality of being easily made into different shapes 可塑性；塑性

plas·ti·cize (*BrE also* **-ise**) /ˈplæstɪsaɪz/ *verb* **~ sth** (*specialist*) to add sth to a substance so that it becomes easy to bend and form into different shapes 使增塑；使塑化；使可塑

ˌplastic ˈsurgeon *noun* a doctor who is qualified to perform plastic surgery 整形外科医生

ˌplastic ˈsurgery *noun* [U] medical operations to repair injury to a person's skin, or to improve a person's appearance 整形外科

ˈplastic wrap (*also* **Saran Wrap™**) (*both NAmE*) (*BrE* **ˈcling film**) *noun* [U] a thin transparent plastic material that sticks to a surface and to itself, used especially for wrapping food （尤指包装食物的）塑料保鲜膜，透明薄膜

plate 🔑 /pleɪt/ *noun, verb*

■ ***noun***

• **FOOD** 食物 **1** 🔑 [C] a flat, usually round, dish that you put food on 盘子；碟子： *sandwiches on a plate* 盘子上的三明治 ◇ *a pile of dirty plates* 一摞脏盘子 ◇ *dinner plates* 餐盘 ➲ VISUAL VOCAB PAGE V23 **2** 🔑 [C] the amount of food that you can put on a plate 一盘所盛之量；一盘： *a plate of sandwiches* 一盘三明治 ◇ *two large plates of pasta* 两大盘意大利面 ➲ COMPARE PLATEFUL **3** [C] (*especially NAmE*) a whole main course of a meal, served on one plate 一道主菜： *Try the seafood plate.* 尝尝这道海鲜吧。

• **FOR STRENGTH** 强化用 **4** 🔑 [C] a thin flat piece of metal, used especially to join or make sth stronger （金属）板条，板： *The tanks were mainly constructed of steel plates.* 这些坦克车主要是用钢板制造的。◇ *She had a metal plate inserted in her arm.* 她的胳膊里嵌着一块接骨板。

• **FOR INFORMATION** 提供信息 **5** [C] a flat piece of metal with some information on it, for example sb's name （刻有名字等的）金属牌子： *A brass plate beside the door said 'Dr Alan Tate'.* 门旁的铜牌上写着"艾伦·泰特医生"。 ➲ SEE ALSO NAMEPLATE

• **ON VEHICLE** 车辆上 **6** [usually pl.] the pieces of metal or plastic at the front and back of a vehicle with numbers and letters on it （车辆）牌照，号牌；车牌 ➲ SEE ALSO L-PLATE, LICENSE PLATE, NUMBER PLATE

• **SILVER/GOLD** 银；金 **7** [U] ordinary metal that is covered with a thin layer of silver or gold 镀金（或镀银）的金属： *The cutlery is plate, not solid silver.* 这套餐具是镀银的，不是纯银的。 ➲ SEE ALSO GOLD PLATE, SILVER PLATE, TINPLATE **8** [U] dishes, bowls, etc. that are made of silver or gold 金质（或银质）餐具

• **ON ANIMAL** 动物 **9** [C] (*biology* 生) one of the thin flat pieces of horn or bone that cover and protect an animal 板；骨板： *the armadillo's protective shell of bony plates* 犰狳的一层防护性骨板

• **GEOLOGY** 地质学 **10** [C] one of the very large pieces of rock that form the earth's surface and move slowly 板块： *the Pacific plate* 太平洋板块 ◇ *Earthquakes are caused by two* ***tectonic plates*** *bumping into each other.* 地震是由两块地壳构造板块互相碰撞造成的。 ➲ SEE ALSO PLATE TECTONICS

• **PRINTING/PHOTOGRAPHY** 印刷；摄影 **11** [C] a photograph that is used as a picture in a book, especially one that is printed on a separate page on high quality paper 书籍插图照片；（尤指优质纸上的）整页插图： *The book includes 55 colour plates.* 本书有 55 幅彩色插图。◇ *See plate 4.* 见彩图 4。 **12** [C] a sheet of metal, plastic, etc. that has been treated so that words or pictures can be printed from it （印刷用的）印版，图版： *a printing plate* 印版 **13** [C] a thin sheet of glass, metal, etc. that is covered with chemicals so that it reacts to light and can form an image, used in larger or older cameras （玻璃、金属等）底片，感光板

• **IN MOUTH** 口内 **14** [C] a thin piece of plastic with wire or artificial teeth attached to it which fits inside your mouth in order to make your teeth straight 假牙托；托牙板；假牙床 ➲ COMPARE BRACE *n.* (2), DENTURES

• **IN BASEBALL** 棒球 **15** [sing.] (*NAmE*) = HOME PLATE

• **IN CHURCH** 教堂 **16** (*usually* **the plate**) [sing.] a flat dish that is used to collect money from people in a church 奉献盘；捐款盘 ➲ SEE ALSO BOOKPLATE, BREASTPLATE, FOOTPLATE, HOTPLATE

IDM **have enough/a lot/too much on your ˈplate** (*informal*) to have a lot of work or problems, etc. to deal with 问题（或工作等）成堆 ➲ MORE AT HAND *v.*, STEP *v.*

■ ***verb*** [usually passive] **1 ~ sth (with sth)** to cover a metal with a thin layer of another metal, especially gold or silver 电镀（尤指镀金、镀银）： *a silver ring plated with gold* 一枚镀金的银戒指 ➲ SEE ALSO GOLD-PLATED, SILVER PLATE **2 ~ sth (with sth)** to cover sth with sheets of metal or another hard substance 为…加设护板；（用金属板等）覆盖： *The walls of the vault were plated with steel.* 保险库的墙壁都装了钢板。 ➲ SEE ALSO ARMOUR-PLATED

plat·eau /ˈplætəʊ; *NAmE* plæˈtoʊ/ *noun, verb*

■ ***noun*** (*pl.* **plat·eaux** or **plat·eaus** /-təʊz; *NAmE* -ˈtoʊz/) **1** an area of flat land that is higher than the land around it 高原 ➲ VISUAL VOCAB PAGE V5 **2** a time of little or no change after a period of growth or progress （发展、增长后的）稳定期，停滞期： *Inflation has reached a plateau.* 通货膨胀停了下来。 ➲ WORDFINDER NOTE AT TREND

■ ***verb*** [I] **~ (out)** to stay at a steady level after a period of growth or progress （在一段时期的发展后）保持稳定水平，处于停滞状态： *Unemployment has at last plateaued out.* 失业情况终于稳定了下来。

plate·ful /ˈpleɪtfʊl/ *noun* the amount that a plate holds 一盘之量；盘： *She ate three platefuls of spaghetti.* 她吃了三盘意大利面。 ➲ COMPARE PLATE *n.* (2)

ˌplate ˈglass *noun* [U] very clear glass of good quality, made in thick sheets, used for doors, windows of shops/stores, etc. 平板玻璃

ˌplate-ˈglass *adj.* (*BrE*) (used about universities in Britain 英国大学) built in the United Kingdom in the 1960s, in contrast to older universities "平板玻璃"的（建于 20 世纪 60 年代，与较古老的大学形成对照） ➲ COMPARE RED-BRICK (2), OXBRIDGE

plate·lay·er /ˈpleɪtleɪə(r)/ *noun* (*BrE*) a person whose job is to lay and repair railway tracks （铁路）铺轨工，养路工

plate·let /ˈpleɪtlət/ *noun* a very small part of a cell in the blood, shaped like a disc. Platelets help to CLOT the blood from a cut or wound. 血小板

ˌplate tecˈtonics *noun* [U] (*geology* 地) the movements of the large sheets of rock (called PLATES) that form the earth's surface; the scientific study of these movements 板块运动；板块构造学；大地构造学

plat·form /ˈplætfɔːm; *NAmE* -fɔːrm/ *noun*
- **AT TRAIN STATION** 火车站 **1** the raised flat area beside the track at a train station where you get on or off the train 站台；月台：(*BrE*) *What platform does it go from?* 火车从哪个站台发车？◇ (*BrE*) *The train now standing at platform 1 is for Leeds.* 停靠在 1 号站台的火车是开往利兹的。➲ COMPARE TRACK *n.* (4) ➲ WORDFINDER NOTE AT TRAIN ➲ VISUAL VOCAB PAGE V63
- **FOR PERFORMERS** 表演用 **2** a flat surface raised above the level of the ground or floor, used by public speakers or performers so that the audience can see them 讲台；舞台 SYN **rostrum**：*Coming onto the platform now is tonight's conductor, Jane Glover.* 现在出场的是今晚的指挥简·格洛弗。◇ *Representatives of both parties shared a platform* (= they spoke at the same meeting). 两党的代表同台发言。
- **RAISED SURFACE** 凸起的平面 **3** a raised level surface, for example one that equipment stands on or is operated from 平台：*an oil/a gas platform* 石油 / 天然气钻井平台 ◇ *a launch platform* (= for SPACECRAFT) 发射平台 ◇ *a viewing platform giving stunning views over the valley* 纵览山谷美景的观景台
- **POLITICS/OPINIONS** 政治；观点 **4** [usually sing.] the aims of a political party and the things that they say they will do if they are elected to power （政党的）纲领，政纲，宣言：*They are campaigning on an anti-immigration platform.* 他们正在宣传反对外来移民的政纲。 **5** an opportunity or a place for sb to express their opinions publicly or make progress in a particular area （公开表达意见或在某方面发展的）机会，阵地，讲坛：*She used the newspaper column as a platform for her feminist views.* 她以这个报纸专栏为讲坛，宣传她的女权主义观点。
- **COMPUTING** 计算机技术 **6** the type of computer system or the software that is used 计算机平台：*a multimedia platform* 多媒体平台 ◇ *a mobile gaming platform* 移动游戏平台 ➲ WORDFINDER NOTE AT COMPUTER
- **SHOES** 鞋子 **7** a type of shoe with a high, thick SOLE; the sole on such a shoe 厚底鞋；厚鞋底：*platform shoes* 厚底鞋 ➲ VISUAL VOCAB PAGE V69
- **ON BUS** 公共汽车 **8** (*BrE*) the open part at the back of a DOUBLE-DECKER bus where you get on or off （双层汽车的）上下车出入口，入口平台

▼ BRITISH/AMERICAN 英式 / 美式英语

platform / track
- In British stations the platforms, where passengers get on and off trains, have numbers. 在英国火车站，旅客上下火车的站台 (platform) 有编号：*The Edinburgh train is waiting at platform 4.* 去爱丁堡的火车在 4 号站台等候。
- In stations in the USA, it is the track that the train travels along that has a number. 在美国火车站，以火车的轨道 (track) 编号作为站台号：*The train for Chicago is on track 9.* 开往芝加哥的列车停靠在 9 号站台。

ˈplatform game (*also* **plat·form·er** /ˈplætfɔːmə(r); *NAmE* -fɔːrm-/) *noun* a computer game in which the player controls a character who jumps and climbs between platforms at different positions on the screen （电脑）平台游戏，跳爬游戏

plat·ing /ˈpleɪtɪŋ/ *noun* [U] **1** a thin covering of a metal, especially silver or gold, on another metal 镀层（镀在金属上的其他金属薄层） **2** a layer of coverings, especially of metal plates 外层；（尤指）金属板护层：*armour plating* 装甲敷板

plat·inum /ˈplætɪnəm/ *noun* [U] (*symb.* **Pt**) a chemical element. Platinum is a silver-grey PRECIOUS METAL, used in making expensive jewellery and in industry. 铂；白金

ˌplatinum ˈblonde *noun* (*informal*) a woman whose hair is a very pale silver colour, especially because it has been coloured with chemicals; this colour of hair 银发女郎（尤指染发的）；（头发的）银色 ▶ **ˌplatinum ˈblonde** *adj.*

ˌplatinum ˈdisc *noun* a platinum record in a frame, given to a singer, etc. who has sold a very high number of records （给唱片销售量极高的歌手等颁发的）白金唱片

plati·tude /ˈplætɪtjuːd; *NAmE* -tuːd/ *noun* (*disapproving*) a comment or statement that has been made very often before and is therefore not interesting 陈词滥调；老生常谈 ▶ **plati·tud·in·ous** /ˌplætɪˈtjuːdɪnəs; *NAmE* -ˈtuːdənəs/ *adj.* (*formal*)

pla·ton·ic /pləˈtɒnɪk; *NAmE* -ˈtɑːn-/ *adj.* (of a relationship 关系) friendly but not involving sex 柏拉图式的（指不含性爱）：*platonic love* 柏拉图式的爱 ◇ *Their relationship is strictly platonic.* 他们的关系是纯友谊。➲ WORDFINDER NOTE AT FRIEND

Pla·ton·ism /ˈpleɪtənɪzəm/ *noun* [U] (*philosophy* 哲) the ideas of the ancient Greek PHILOSOPHER Plato and those who followed him 柏拉图主义；柏拉图学说 ▶ **Pla·ton·ist** /ˈpleɪtənɪst/ *adj., noun*

pla·toon /pləˈtuːn/ *noun* a small group of soldiers that is part of a COMPANY and commanded by a LIEUTENANT （军队的）排

plat·ter /ˈplætə(r)/ *noun* a large plate that is used for serving food 大平盘：*a silver platter* 大银盘子 ◇ *I'll have the fish platter* (= several types of fish and other food served on a large plate). 我来一份什锦鱼拼盘。IDM SEE SILVER *n.*

platy·pus /ˈplætɪpəs/ (*also* **ˌduck-billed ˈplatypus**) *noun* an Australian animal that is covered in fur and has a beak like a DUCK, WEBBED feet (= with skin between the toes) and a flat tail. Platypuses lay eggs but give milk to their young. 鸭嘴兽，鸭獭（栖于澳大利亚）

plau·dits /ˈplɔːdɪts/ *noun* [usually pl.] (*formal*) praise and approval 赞誉；称赞；褒扬：*His work **won him plaudits** from the critics.* 他的作品赢得了评论家的赞赏。

plaus·ible /ˈplɔːzəbl/ *adj.* **1** (of an excuse or explanation 借口或解释) reasonable and likely to be true 有道理的；可信的：*Her story sounded perfectly plausible.* 她的说辞听起来言之有理。◇ *The only plausible explanation is that he forgot.* 唯一合理的解释就是他忘掉了。OPP **implausible** **2** (*disapproving*) (of a person 人) good at sounding honest and sincere, especially when trying to trick people 巧言令色的；花言巧语的：*She was a plausible liar.* 她是个巧言令色的说谎高手。▶ **plausi·bil·ity** /ˌplɔːzəˈbɪləti/ *noun* [U] **plaus·ibly** /-əbli/ *adv.*：*He argued very plausibly that the claims were true.* 他花言巧语地辩解说那些说法属实。

play /pleɪ/ *verb, noun*
■ *verb*
- **OF CHILDREN** 儿童 **1** [I, T] to do things for pleasure, as children do; to enjoy yourself, rather than work 玩耍；游戏；玩乐：*You'll have to play inside today.* 你今天只能在屋里玩耍。◇ *There's a time to work and a time to play.* 工作、玩耍皆有时。◇ **~ with sb/sth** *A group of kids were playing with a ball in the street.* 一群孩子在街上玩球。◇ *I haven't got anybody to play with!* 没有人跟我玩儿！◇ **~ sth** *Let's play a different game.* 咱们玩点别的游戏吧。 **2** [T, no passive, I] to pretend to be or do sth for fun （为玩耍）假装，假扮：**~ sth** *Let's play pirates.* 咱们假扮海盗玩吧。◇ **~ at doing sth** *They were playing at being cowboys.* 他们装扮成牛仔玩。

P

- **TRICK** 把戏 **3** [T] **~ a trick/tricks (on sb)** to trick sb for fun 捉弄；戏弄
- **SPORTS/GAMES** 运动；比赛 **4** [T, I] **~ (sth) (with/against sb)** to be involved in a game; to compete against sb in a game 参加比赛；（同某人）比赛：**~ sth** *to **play football/chess/cards, etc.*** 踢足球、下棋、玩纸牌等 ◇ **~ sb** *France are playing Wales tomorrow.* 明天法国队和威尔士队比赛。◇ **~ sb at sth** *Have you played her at squash yet?* 你跟她打过壁球没有？◇ **~ for sb** *He plays for Cleveland.* 他代表克利夫兰参赛。◇ **~ against sb** *France are playing against Wales on Saturday.* 星期六法国队迎战威尔士队。◇ **+ adv./prep.** *Evans played very well.* 埃文斯比赛很出色。 **5** [I] to take a particular position in a sports team（在运动队中）担当，充任：**+ adv./prep.** *Who's playing on the wing?* 谁担任边锋？ ◇ **+ noun** *I've never played right back before.* 我过去从来未当过右后卫。 **6** [T] **~ sb (+ adv./prep.)** to include sb in a sports team 派…出场；让…加入运动队：*I think we should play Matt on the wing.* 我认为我们应该让麦特打边锋。 **7** [T] **~ sth** to make contact with the ball and hit or kick it in the way mentioned 触，带，踢，击（球）：*She played the ball and ran forward.* 她带球向前冲。◇ *He played a backhand volley.* 他用反手截击球。 **8** [T] **~ sth** (in CHESS 国际象棋) to move a piece in CHESS, etc. 走（子）；行（棋）：*She played her bishop.* 她走象。 **9** [T, I] **~ (sth)** (in card games 纸牌游戏) to put a card face upwards on the table, showing its value 出牌：*to play your ace/a trump* 出 A / 王牌 ◇ *He played out of turn!* 他抢出牌！
- **MUSIC** 音乐 **10** [T, I] **~ (sth) (on sth)** to perform on a musical instrument; to perform music 弹拨，吹奏（乐器）；演奏：**~ (sth)** *to **play the piano/violin/flute, etc.*** 弹钢琴、拉小提琴、吹长笛等 ◇ *In the distance a band was playing.* 远处有个乐队在演奏。◇ **~ sth (on sth)** *He played a tune on his harmonica.* 他用口琴吹奏了一支曲子。◇ **~ sth to sb** *Play that new piece to us.* 给我们演奏那支新曲子吧。◇ **~ sb sth** *Play us that new piece.* 给我们演奏那支新曲子吧。 **11** [T] to use an MP3 player, a CD player, etc. to make it possible to hear a song, an album, a CD, etc. 播放：**~ sth (for sb)** *Play their new CD for me, please.* 请把他们的新唱片放给我听一下吧。 ◇ *They're always playing that song on the radio.* 电台总是播放那首歌。◇ **~ (sb sth)** *Play me their new album, please.* 请给我放他们的新专辑。 **12** [I] (of a song, an album, etc.) to be heard（歌曲、专辑等）被播放：*My favourite song was playing on the radio.* 收音机里播放着我最喜爱的歌曲。
- **DVD/VIDEO** * DVD 光盘；视频 **13** [I, T] (of a DVD or video * DVD 光盘或视频) to start working; to make a DVD or video start working 开始播放；播放（光盘或视频）：*These videos won't play on my computer.* 这些视频在我的电脑上不能播放。◇ **~ sth** *Click below to play videos.* 点击下方播放视频。
- **ACT/PERFORM** 扮演；演出 **14** [T] **~ sth** to act in a play, film/movie, etc.; to act the role of sb （在电影、话剧中）扮角色，扮演，表演：*The part of Elizabeth was played by Cate Blanchett.* 伊丽莎白这一角色由凯特 • 布兰切特扮演。◇ *He had always wanted to play Othello.* 他一直想扮演奥赛罗。 **15** [I] to pretend to be sth that you are not 佯装；假装：**+ adj.** *I decided it was safer to **play dead**.* 我拿定主意装死会更安全些。◇ **+ noun** *She enjoys playing the wronged wife.* 她很喜欢扮演受委屈的妻子。 **16** [I] **~ (to sb)** to be performed 上演；演出：*A production of 'Carmen' was playing to packed houses.* 《卡门》一剧上演场场爆满。
- **HAVE EFFECT** 起作用 **17** [T] **~ a part/role (in sth)** to have an effect on sth （在…中）发挥作用：*The media played an important part in the last election.* 大众传媒在上一次选举中发挥了重要作用。
- **SITUATION** 局面 **18** [T] **~ sth + adv./prep.** to deal with a situation in the way mentioned （以某种方式）应付，处理：*He played the situation carefully for maximum advantage.* 他谨慎应付局面以获得最大利益。
- **OF LIGHT/A SMILE** 光；微笑 **19** [I] **+ adv./prep.** to move or appear quickly and lightly, often changing direction or shape 闪烁；浮现；掠过：*Sunlight played on the surface of the lake.* 阳光在湖面上闪烁。
- **OF FOUNTAIN** 喷泉 **20** [I] when a FOUNTAIN **plays,** it produces a steady stream of water 喷涌；涌流 ➲ MORE LIKE THIS 33, page R28

IDM **HELP** Most idioms containing **play** are at the entries for the nouns and adjectives in the idioms, for example **play the game** is at **game**. 大多数含 play 的习语，都可在该等习语中的名词及形容词相关词条找到，如 play the game 在词条 game 下。 **have money, time, etc. to 'play with** (*informal*) to have plenty of money, time, etc. for doing sth 有的是金钱（或时间等） **what is sb 'playing at?** used to ask in an angry way about what sb is doing（气愤时的质问语）某人在搞什么名堂？：*What do you think you are playing at?* 你以为你在搞什么名堂？ **'play with yourself** (*informal*) to MASTURBATE 手淫

PHR V **,play a'bout/a'round (with sb/sth) 1** to behave or treat sth in a careless way 玩弄；乱弄；胡弄：*Don't play around with my tools!* 别瞎摆弄我的工具！ **2** (*informal*) to have a sexual relationship with sb, usually with sb who is not your usual partner 鬼混；厮混：*Her husband is always playing around.* 她的丈夫总是在外拈花惹草。 **,play a'long (with sb/sth)** to pretend to agree with sb/sth 假意顺从：*I decided to play along with her idea.* 我决定假意听从她的意见。 **'play at sth/at doing sth** (*often disapproving*) to do sth without being serious about it or putting much effort into it 敷衍应付；虚与委蛇 **play a'way (from home) 1** (of a sports team 体育运动队) to play a match at the opponent's ground or STADIUM 在客场打比赛 **2** (*BrE*) (of a person who is married or who has a regular sexual partner 已婚或有固定性伴侣者) to have a secret sexual relationship with sb else 有外遇；搞婚外恋 **,play sth↔'back (to sb)** to play music, film, etc. that has been recorded on a tape, video, etc. 播放录音（或录像等）：*Play that last section back to me again.* 把最后一节再给我放一次。 ➲ RELATED NOUN PLAYBACK **,play sth↔'down** to try to make sth seem less important than it is 减低…的重要性；贬低；淡化 **SYN** **downplay** **OPP** **play sth↔up** **,play A 'off against B** (*BrE*) (*NAmE also* **'play A off B**) to put two people or groups in competition with each other, especially in order to get an advantage for yourself 挑拨离间（以便渔利）：*She played her two rivals off against each other and got the job herself.* 她挑拨两个对手相争，使自己弄到了那份工作。 ➲ RELATED NOUN PLAY-OFF **,play 'on** (*sport* 体育) to continue to play; to start playing again 继续比赛；恢复比赛：*The home team claimed a penalty but the referee told them to play on.* 主队要求判罚，但裁判却要他们继续比赛。 **'play on/upon sth** to take advantage of sb's feelings, etc. 利用（感情等） **SYN** **exploit**：*Advertisements often play on people's fears.* 广告常利用人们的恐惧心理。 **,play sth↔'out** when an event **is played out**, it happens 发生；出现 **SYN** **enact**：*Their love affair was played out against the backdrop of war.* 他们在战争的背景下发生恋情。 **,play yourself/itself 'out** to become weak and no longer useful or important 消耗净尽；使精疲力竭 **,play 'up | ,play sb 'up** (*informal, especially BrE*) to cause sb problems or pain （给某人）添麻烦；使痛苦：*The kids have been playing up all day.* 孩子们整天价惹麻烦。◇ *My shoulder is playing me up today.* 我的肩膀今天疼起来了。 **,play sth↔'up** to try to make sth seem more important than it is 夸大…的重要性；渲染；吹嘘 **SYN** **overplay** **OPP** **play sth↔down** **'play with sb/sth** to treat sb who is emotionally attached to you in a way that is not serious and which can hurt their feelings 玩弄人；玩弄感情：*She tends to play with men's emotions.* 她总是玩弄男人的感情。◇ *She realized that Patrick was merely playing with her.* 她意识到帕特里克只是和她逢场作戏而已。 **'play with sth 1** to keep touching or moving sth 摆弄；玩弄：*She was playing with her hair.* 她在抚弄自己的头发。 ◇ *Stop playing with your food!* 别老是摆弄食物！ **2** to use things in different ways to produce an interesting or humorous effect, or to see what effect they have 巧妙地利用；新奇（或幽默等地）运用：*In this poem Fitch plays with words which sound alike.* 在这首诗中，菲奇巧妙地运用了些近音词。◇ *The composer plays with the exotic sounds of Japanese instruments.* 作曲者运用了日本乐器的异国音调。

■ ***noun***

- **CHILDREN** 儿童 **1** [U] things that people, especially children, do for pleasure rather than as work 游戏；玩

耍；娱乐： *the happy sounds of children* ***at play*** 儿童嬉戏的欢闹声 ◇ *the importance of learning through play* 寓教于乐的重要性 ◇ *a play area* 游戏的场地 ➲ SYNONYMS AT ENTERTAINMENT

• **IN THEATRE** 剧院 **2** [C] a piece of writing performed by actors in a theatre or on television or radio 戏剧；剧本： *to* ***put on*** (= perform) *a play* 演出戏剧 ◇ *a play by Shakespeare* 一出莎士比亚的戏剧 ◇ *a radio play* 广播剧 ➲ SEE ALSO MORALITY PLAY, MYSTERY PLAY, PASSION PLAY ➲ WORDFINDER NOTE AT ACTOR, DRAMA

WORDFINDER 联想词： act, cast, **drama**, entrance, exit, line, role, scene, speech

• **IN SPORT** 体育运动 **3** [U] the playing of a game 比赛；赛风；比赛中的表现： *Rain stopped play.* 因雨停赛。◇ *There was some excellent play in yesterday's match.* 昨天的比赛有精彩的场面。 ➲ SEE ALSO FAIR PLAY, FOUL PLAY (2) **4** [C] (*NAmE*) an action or move in a game 比赛中的动作： *a defensive play* 防守动作

• **IN ROPE** 绳索 **5** [U] the possibility of free and easy movement 间隙；活动空间： *We need more play in the rope.* 我们需要再松一松绳子。

• **ACTIVITY/INFLUENCE** 活动；影响 **6** [U] the activity or operation of sth; the influence of sth on sth else 活动；作用；影响： *the free play of market forces* 市场力量的自由调节作用 ◇ *The financial crisis has* ***brought*** *new factors* ***into play***. 财政危机已引发了新的变数。 ◇ *Personal feelings should not* ***come into play*** *when you are making business decisions.* 为公事作决策不应掺入个人感情。

• **OF LIGHT/A SMILE** 光；笑容 **7** [U] (*literary*) a light, quick movement that keeps changing 轻快变幻的动作；闪烁；闪现： *the play of sunlight on water* 阳光在水面上的闪烁

IDM **have a 'play (with sth)** to spend time playing with a toy, game, etc. 玩（玩具、游戏等）： *I had a play with the new computer game.* 我玩了一下这个新的电脑游戏。 **in/out of 'play** (*sport* 体育) (of a ball 球) inside/outside the area allowed by the rules of the game 在死球 / 非死球区域；在可继续 / 不能继续比赛区域： *She just managed to keep the ball in play.* 她把球勉强保持在界内。 **make a 'play for sb/sth** to try to obtain sth; to do things that are intended to produce a particular result 企图得到；处心积虑做事： *She was making a play for the sales manager's job.* 她千方百计要取得销售部经理的位置。 **make great/much 'play of sth** to emphasize the importance of a particular fact 强调；着重说明： *He made great play of the fact that his uncle was a duke.* 他特别强调自己的叔叔是位公爵。 **a play on 'words** the humorous use of a word or phrase that can have two different meanings 双关语；语带双关 **SYN** **pun** ➲ MORE AT CALL *v.*, CHILD, STATE *n.*, WORK *n.*

play·able /ˈpleɪəbl/ *adj.* **1** (of a piece of music or a computer game 乐曲或电脑游戏) easy to play 容易演奏的；容易掌握的 **2** (of a sports field 运动场) in a good condition and suitable for playing on 适于使用的；可用以比赛的 **OPP** **unplayable**

ˈplay-acting *noun* [U] behaviour that seems to be honest and sincere when in fact the person is pretending 假装；伪善；演戏 ▶ **ˈplay-act** *verb* [I]: *He thought she was play-acting but in fact she had really hurt herself.* 他以为她是装出来的，但实际上她真的受了伤。

play·back /ˈpleɪbæk/ *noun* [U, C, usually sing.] the act of playing music, showing a film/movie or listening to a telephone message that has been recorded before; a recording that you listen to or watch again 录音（或录像、电话留言等的）播放；（回放的）录音，录像

ˈplayback singer *noun* (*IndE*) a singer who records songs to be used in a film where actors pretend to sing （电影）配唱歌手，幕后歌手

play·bill /ˈpleɪbɪl/ *noun* **1** a printed notice advertising a play 戏剧海报 **2** (*NAmE*) a theatre programme 戏单；戏剧演出节目单

play·boy /ˈpleɪbɔɪ/ *noun* a rich man who spends his time enjoying himself 寻欢作乐的有钱男子；花花公子；纨绔子弟

ˌplay-by-ˈplay *noun* [usually sing.] (*NAmE*) a report on what is happening in a sports game, given as the game is being played 体育比赛现场解说

ˈplay date *noun* an arrangement that parents make for their children to play together at a particular time and place （家长为孩子安排的）游戏约会，玩耍约会

ˌplayed ˈout *adj.* [not before noun] (*informal*) no longer having any influence or effect 失去影响（或作用）

play·er /ˈpleɪə(r)/ *noun* **1** a person who takes part in a game or sport 游戏者；运动员；参赛选手： ***a tennis/rugby/chess, etc. player*** 网球、橄榄球、国际象棋等选手 ◇ *a game for four players* 四人玩的游戏 ◇ *a midfield player* 中场球员 **2** a company or person involved in a particular area of business or politics （商业或政治方面的）参与者，竞争者，玩家： *The company has emerged as a* ***major player*** *in the London property market.* 那家公司已崭露头角，成为伦敦房地产市场的主要竞争者。 ➲ SEE ALSO TEAM PLAYER **3** (in compounds 构成复合词) a machine for reproducing sound or pictures that have been recorded on CDs, etc. 播放机： ***a CD/DVD/cassette/record player*** 激光唱片 / 数字光碟 / 盒式磁带 / 唱片播放机 **4** (usually in compounds 通常构成复合词) a person who plays a musical instrument 演奏者： *a trumpet player* 小号手 **5** (*old-fashioned*) (especially in names 尤用于名称) an actor 演员： *Phoenix Players present 'Romeo and Juliet'.* 凤凰剧社献演《罗密欧与朱丽叶》。

ˈplayer piano *noun* a piano that plays automatically by means of a PIANO ROLL 自动钢琴（用打孔纸卷控制琴键） **SYN** **Pianola™**

play·ful /ˈpleɪfl/ *adj.* **1** full of fun; wanting to play 有趣的；爱嬉戏的；爱玩的： *a playful puppy* 顽皮的小狗 **2** (of a remark, an action, etc. 话语、动作等) made or done in fun; not serious 打趣的；闹着玩的；嬉戏的 **SYN** **light-hearted**: *He gave her a playful punch on the arm.* 他开玩笑地捶了一下她的胳膊。 ▶ **play·ful·ly** /-fəli/ *adv.* **play·ful·ness** *noun* [U]

play·goer /ˈpleɪɡəʊə(r); *NAmE* -ɡoʊər/ *noun* = THEATRE-GOER

play·ground /ˈpleɪɡraʊnd/ *noun* **1** an outdoor area where children can play, especially at a school or in a park （尤指公园中的）游戏场，游乐场；（学校）操场 ➲ COMPARE SCHOOLYARD ➲ SEE ALSO ADVENTURE PLAYGROUND **2** a place where a particular type of people go to enjoy themselves （某些集体聚会游乐的）园地，天地，活动场所： *The resort is a playground of the rich and famous.* 这个度假胜地是富翁名流的娱乐场所。

play·group /ˈpleɪɡruːp/ (*also* **play·school**) (*both BrE*) *noun* [C, U] a place where children who are below school age go regularly to play together and to learn through playing （学龄前儿童的）幼儿游戏班 ➲ COMPARE NURSERY SCHOOL

play·house /ˈpleɪhaʊs/ *noun* **1** used in names of theatres （用于剧场名称）剧院： *the Liverpool Playhouse* 利物浦剧院 **2** (*BrE also* **ˈWendy house**) a model of a house large enough for children to play in 游戏房（供儿童进入玩耍的大模型房子）

play·ing /ˈpleɪɪŋ/ *noun* **1** [U] the way in which sb plays sth, especially a musical instrument （演奏等的）表现，风格： *The orchestral playing is superb.* 这个管弦乐团的演奏棒极了。 **2** [C] the act of playing a piece of music （乐曲）演奏： *repeated playings of the National Anthem* 国歌反复的演奏

ˈplaying card (*also* **card**) *noun* any one of a set of 52 cards with numbers and pictures printed on one side, which are used to play various card games 纸牌；扑克牌： (*BrE*) *a pack of (playing) cards* 一副纸牌 ◇ (*NAmE*) *a deck of (playing) cards* 一副纸牌 ➲ VISUAL VOCAB PAGE V41

ˈplaying field *noun* a large area of grass, usually with lines marked on it, where people play sports and games

P

运动场；操场：*the school playing fields* 学校的运动场 IDM SEE LEVEL *adj.*

play·let /ˈpleɪlət/ *noun* a short play 短剧

play·list /ˈpleɪlɪst/ *noun* a list of all the songs and pieces of music that are played by a radio station or on a radio programme （电台节目的）音乐播放清单

play·maker /ˈpleɪmeɪkə(r)/ *noun* a player in a team game who starts attacks or brings other players on the same side into a position in which they could score 组织进攻的队员

play·mate /ˈpleɪmeɪt/ *noun* a friend with whom a child plays （儿童的）玩伴 ➲ WORDFINDER NOTE AT FRIEND

ˈplay-off *noun* a match/game, or a series of them, between two players or teams with equal points or scores to decide who the winner is （平局后决出胜负的）附加赛；季后赛：*They lost to Chicago in the play-offs.* 在季后赛中他们负于芝加哥队。

play·pen /ˈpleɪpen/ *noun* a frame with wooden bars or NETTING that surrounds a small area in which a baby or small child can play safely （幼儿）玩耍护栏

play·room /ˈpleɪruːm; -rʊm/ *noun* a room in a house for children to play in 游戏室

play·scheme /ˈpleɪskiːm/ *noun* (*BrE*) a project that provides organized activities for children, especially during school holidays （尤指学校放假期间为儿童制订的）组织活动计划

play·school /ˈpleɪskuːl/ *noun* (*BrE*) = PLAYGROUP

play·suit /ˈpleɪsuːt; *BrE also* -sjuːt/ *noun* **1** a piece of clothing for babies or small children that covers the body, arms and legs 宝宝连身衣；幼儿连裤装 **2** (*BrE*) a set of clothes that children wear for fun so that they look like a particular person （儿童）模仿套装：*a Spiderman playsuit* 蜘蛛侠装扮套装 **3** a piece of women's underwear that covers the upper body to the tops of the legs （长及大腿根部的）女式连体内衣

play·thing /ˈpleɪθɪŋ/ *noun* **1** a person or thing that you treat like a toy, without really caring about them or it 玩物；玩乐对象：*She was an intelligent woman who refused to be a rich man's plaything.* 她是个有头脑的女性，拒不做富人的玩物。**2** (*old-fashioned*) a toy 玩具：*The teddy bear was his favourite plaything.* 软毛玩具熊是他最心爱的玩具。

play·time /ˈpleɪtaɪm/ *noun* [U, C] **1** (*especially BrE*) a time at school when teaching stops for a short time and children can play （学校的）游戏时间，课间休息时间 **2** a time for playing and having fun 娱乐时间：*With so much homework to do, her playtime is now very limited.* 因为作业太多，她现在的娱乐时间很少。

play·wright /ˈpleɪraɪt/ *noun* a person who writes plays for the theatre, television or radio 剧作家 SYN **dramatist** ➲ COMPARE SCREENWRITER, SCRIPTWRITER

plaza /ˈplɑːzə; *NAmE* ˈplæzə/ *noun* (*especially NAmE*) **1** a public outdoor square especially in a town where Spanish is spoken （尤指通行西班牙语的城镇的）露天广场 **2** a small shopping centre, sometimes also with offices 购物中心：*a downtown shopping plaza* 市中心的购物区

plc /ˌpiː el ˈsiː/ (*also* **PLC**) *abbr.* (*BrE*) public limited company (used after the name of a company or business) 公开股份有限公司（用于公司、企业名称之后）：*Lloyd's Bank plc* 劳埃德银行

plea /pliː/ *noun* **1** (*formal*) an urgent emotional request 请求；恳求：**~ (for sth)** *She made an impassioned plea for help.* 她恳切地求助。◇ **~ (to sb) (to do sth)** *a plea to industries to stop pollution* 请求生产企业停止污染 ◇ *He refused to listen to her tearful pleas.* 他对她声泪俱下的恳求置之不理。**2** (*law* 律) a statement made by sb or for sb who is accused of a crime （被告或被告律师的）诉讼抗辩，答辩：*a plea of guilty/not guilty* 承认/不承认有罪 ◇ *to enter a guilty plea* 正式表示认罪 ➲ WORDFINDER NOTE AT TRIAL **3 ~ of sth** (*law* 律) a reason given to a court for doing or not doing sth （向法庭提供的）理由，借口，辩解：*He was charged with murder, but got off on a plea of insanity.* 他被指控犯了谋杀罪，但以精神错乱为由逃过惩罚。

ˈplea bargain·ing *noun* [U] (*law* 律) an arrangement in court by which a person admits to being guilty of a smaller crime in the hope of receiving less severe punishment for a more serious crime 诉辩，辩诉交易，控辩交易（在法庭上由被告承认轻罪以期减轻刑罚的安排）➲ COMPARE COP A PLEA at COP *v.*, TURN KING'S/QUEEN'S EVIDENCE at EVIDENCE *n.* ▶ **ˈplea bargain** *noun*：*He reached a plea bargain with the authorities.* 他和当局达成了辩诉交易。

plead /pliːd/ *verb* (**pleaded**, **pleaded**, *NAmE also* **pled**, **pled** /pled/) **1** [I, T] to ask sb for sth in a very strong and serious way 乞求；恳求 SYN **beg**：**~ (with sb) (to do sth)** *She pleaded with him not to go.* 她恳求他不要离开。◇ **~ (with sb) (for sth)** *I was forced to plead for my child's life.* 我被迫苦苦哀求给我的孩子一条生路。◇ *pleading eyes* 乞求的眼神 ◇ **~ to do sth** *He pleaded to be allowed to see his mother one more time.* 他恳求准许他再看妈妈一眼。◇ **+ speech** *'Do something!' she pleaded.* "帮帮忙吧！" 她央求道。**2** [I, T, no passive] to state in court that you are guilty or not guilty of a crime （向法庭）表明认罪（或不认罪）：**(+ adj.)** *to plead guilty/not guilty* 认罪；不认罪 ◇ *How do you plead?* (= said by the judge at the start of the trial) 你是否认罪？（法官在庭审开始时间被告）◇ **~ sth** *He advised his client to plead insanity* (= say that he/she was mentally ill and therefore not responsible for his/her actions). 他建议他的当事人以精神不正常作为辩护理由。**3** [T] **~ sth** to present a case to a court （在法庭上）申辩，辩护：*They hired a top lawyer to plead their case.* 他们聘请了一位顶级律师帮他们辩护。**4** [T, no passive] **~ sth (for sth)** | **~ that...** to give sth as an explanation or excuse for sth 解释；推说；找借口：*He pleaded family problems for his lack of concentration.* 他解释说他不能集中精神是因为有家庭问题。**5** [T, I] to argue in support of sb/sth 为…辩护；声援；支持：**~ sth** *She appeared on television to plead the cause of political prisoners everywhere.* 她出现在电视上为所有政治犯声援请命。◇ **~ for sb/sth** *The United Nations has pleaded for a halt to the bombing.* 联合国已呼吁停止轰炸。

plead·ing /ˈpliːdɪŋ/ *noun* **1** [C, U] an act of asking for sth that you want very much, in an emotional way 恳求；央求：*He refused to give in to her pleadings.* 他拒不接受她的请求。**2** [C, usually pl.] (*law* 律) a formal statement of sb's case in court 诉状；答辩状 ➲ SEE ALSO SPECIAL PLEADING

plead·ing·ly /ˈpliːdɪŋli/ *adv.* in an emotional way that shows that you want sth very much but are not certain that sb will give it to you 恳求地；乞求地：*He looked pleadingly at her.* 他以乞求的目光望着她。

pleas·ant /ˈpleznt/ *adj.* (**pleas·ant·er**, **pleas·ant·est**) HELP **more pleasant** and **most pleasant** are more common * more pleasant 和 most pleasant 较常见。**1** enjoyable, pleasing or attractive 令人愉快的；可喜的；宜人的；吸引人的：*a pleasant climate/evening/place* 令人愉快的气候/夜晚/地方 ◇ *What a pleasant surprise!* 这真是一桩令人又惊又喜的事！◇ *to live in pleasant surroundings* 生活在宜人的环境中 ◇ *music that is pleasant to the ear* 悦耳的音乐 ◇ *a pleasant environment to work in* 舒适的工作环境 ◇ ***It was pleasant to** be alone again.* 又是一个人了，真自在。**2** friendly and polite 友好的；和善的；文雅的：*a pleasant young man* 彬彬有礼的年轻人 ◇ *a pleasant smile/voice/manner* 和蔼可亲的笑容/声音/态度 ◇ **~ to sb** *Please try to be pleasant to our guests.* 请尽量对我们的客人客气点。OPP **unpleasant** ▶ **pleas·ant·ly** *adv.*：*a pleasantly cool room* 凉爽宜人的房间 ◇ *I was pleasantly surprised by my exam results.* 我的考试成绩真让我喜出望外。◇ *'Can I help you?' he asked pleasantly.* "需要帮忙吗？" 他和悦地问道。**pleas·ant·ness** *noun* [U]：*She remembered the pleasantness of the evening.* 她对那个愉快的夜晚记忆犹新。

pleas·ant·ry /ˈplezntri/ *noun* [C, usually pl., U] (*pl.* **-ies**) (*formal*) a friendly remark made in order to be polite 客气话；客套：*After exchanging the usual pleasantries, they got down to serious discussion.* 互致寒暄之后，他们便开始严肃的讨论了。

please /pliːz/ *exclamation, verb*

■ ***exclamation*** **1** used as a polite way of asking for sth or telling sb to do sth（用于客气地请求或吩咐时）请，请问：*Please sit down.* 请坐。◇ *Two coffees, please.* 请来两杯咖啡。◇ *Quiet please!* 请安静！◇ *Please could I leave early today?* 请问我今天早走一会儿行吗？ **2** used to add force to a request or statement（用于加强请求或陈述的语气）请千万，请务必，的确：*Please don't leave me here alone.* 请千万别把我一个人留在这儿。◇ *Please, please don't forget.* 请务必务必不要忘记呀。◇ *Please, I don't understand what I have to do.* 我的确不明白我该做什么。 **3** used as a polite way of accepting sth（表示接受的客气话）太感谢了，太好了：*'Would you like some help?' 'Yes, please.'* "您需要帮忙吗？""是的。太感谢了。"◇ *'Coffee?' 'Please.'* "要咖啡吗？""那太好了。" **4 Please!** (*informal, often humorous*) used to ask sb to stop behaving badly（用于让别人停止不规矩行为）别闹了，收敛点儿：*Children, please! I'm trying to work.* 孩子们，别闹了！我在干活呢。◇ *John! Please!* 约翰！老实点儿吧！ **5 Please/P-lease** /pəˈliːz/ used when you are replying to sb who has said sth that you think is stupid（认为对方说话荒唐时用）得了吧，算了吧：*Oh, please! You cannot be serious.* 喔，得了吧！你准是在打哈哈。

> **▼ EXPRESS YOURSELF 情景表达**
>
> **Asking for something 请求给予某物**
>
> Whether you are in shops or restaurants or in somebody's home, you can use polite questions to get what you want. 在店铺、餐馆或别人家礼貌地请求给予某物，可用以下方式：
>
> - *Could I have a glass of water, please?* 请给我一杯水好吗？
> - *Do you have any decaffeinated coffee?* 你们有没有不含咖啡因的咖啡？
> - *I'd like tea with sugar, please.* 请来一杯加糖的茶。
> - *I'll have the pasta with salad, please.* 请给我来份意大利面配色拉。
>
> Responses 回应：
>
> - *Certainly.* 当然可以。
> - *I'm sorry, we don't have any left.* 抱歉，已经没有了。
> - *Yes, of course. Here you are/go.* 好的，给你。

■ ***verb*** **1** [T, I] ~ (sb) | **it pleases sb to do sth** to make sb happy 使满意；使愉快：*You can't please everybody.* 你无法让每个人都满意。◇ *He's a difficult man to please.* 他是个难以取悦的人。◇ ***There's just no pleasing some people*** (= some people are impossible to please). 有些人你是没法让他们满意的。◇ *I did it to please my parents.* 我这么做是要让父母高兴。◇ *She's always very eager to please.* 她总是急欲取悦别人。 OPP **displease** **2** [I] often used after *as* or *what, where*, etc. to mean 'to want', 'to choose' or 'to like' to do sth（常用在 as 或 what、where 等词后）想，选择，喜欢：*You may stay as long as you please.* 你想待多久就待多久。◇ *She always does exactly as she pleases.* 她总是我行我素。◇ *I'm free now to live wherever I please.* 我现在想住哪里就住哪里。

IDM **if you ˈplease** **1** (*old-fashioned, formal*) used when politely asking sb to do sth（表示客气时用）请：*Take a seat, if you please.* 请坐吧。 **2** (*old-fashioned, especially BrE*) used to say that you are annoyed or surprised at sb's actions（用于对某人的行为表示气愤或惊异）你们听听，岂有此理：*And now, if you please, he wants me to rewrite the whole thing!* 哼！你们听听，他竟要我全部重写！ **please the ˈeye** to be very attractive to look at 十分悦目 **ˌplease ˈGod** used to say that you very much hope or wish that sth will happen（表示殷切期望）但愿老天帮忙，上帝保佑：*Please God, don't let him be dead.* 老天爷呀！千万别让他死啊。 **ˌplease yourˈself** (*informal*) used to tell sb that you are annoyed with them and do not care what they do（表示恼怒和不关心）随你的便，悉听尊便：*'I don't think I'll bother finishing this.' 'Please yourself.'* "我想我不会费力做完这件事。""随你的便。" **ˌplease yourˈself** | **ˌdo as you ˈplease** to be able to do whatever you like 能够随心所欲：*There were no children to cook for, so we could just please ourselves.* 因为不用给孩子做饭，我们就可以自便了。

pleased /pliːzd/ *adj.* **1** feeling happy about sth 高兴；满意；愉快：~ **(with sb/sth)** *She was very pleased with her exam results.* 她对她的考试成绩非常满意。◇ *The boss should be pleased with you.* 上司应该对你满意了。◇ ~ **(that…)** *I'm really pleased that you're feeling better.* 你觉得好些了，我真高兴。◇ ~ **(to hear, know, etc. sth)** *I'm pleased to hear about your news.* 听到你的消息我很高兴。◇ *You're coming? I'm so pleased.* 你要来呀？我太高兴了。◇ *He did not look too pleased when I told him.* 我告诉他时，他似乎不是很高兴。 ➲ SYNONYMS AT GLAD **2** ~ **to do sth** happy or willing to do sth 高兴，乐于（做某事）：*We are always pleased to be able to help.* 我们一向乐意能帮忙。◇ *I was **pleased to hear** you've been promoted.* 听说你高升了，我很高兴。◇ *Aren't you pleased to see me?* 见到我你不高兴吗？◇ (*especially BrE*) ***Pleased to meet you*** (= said when you are introduced to sb). 很高兴认识您。◇ *Thank you for your invitation, which I am very pleased to accept.* 承蒙邀请，我欣然接受。◇ *I am pleased to inform you that the book you ordered has arrived.* 谨此欣然奉告，您所订的书已到。

IDM (as) **ˌpleased as ˈPunch** very pleased 称心满意；自满自足 ➲ MORE LIKE THIS 14, page R26 **far from ˈpleased** | **none too ˈpleased** not pleased; angry 不悦；气愤：*She was none too pleased at having to do it all again.* 工作必须重做，这使她气愤不已。 **only too ˈpleased (to do sth)** very happy or willing to do sth 十分情愿，巴不得（做某事）：*We're only too pleased to help.* 我们非常愿意帮忙。 **ˈpleased with yourself** (*often disapproving*) too proud of sth you have done 自鸣得意；飘飘然：*He was looking very pleased with himself.* 他显得沾沾自喜。

pleas·ing /ˈpliːzɪŋ/ *adj.* that gives you pleasure or satisfaction 令人高兴的；令人满意的：*a pleasing design* 令人满意的设计 ◇ ~ **to sb/sth** *The new building was **pleasing to the eye**.* 这座新楼真漂亮。 ➲ SYNONYMS AT SATISFYING ▸ **pleas·ing·ly** *adv.*：*She had a pleasingly direct manner.* 她为人直爽，令人愉快。

pleas·ur·able /ˈpleʒərəbl/ *adj.* (*formal*) giving pleasure 愉快的；快活的；适意的 SYN **enjoyable**：*a pleasurable experience* 愉快的经历 ◇ *We do everything we can to make your trip pleasurable.* 我们会尽力使你的旅途愉快。

pleas·ur·ably /ˈpleʒərəbli/ *adv.* with pleasure 愉快地；怡然：*He sipped his coffee pleasurably.* 他怡然地品着咖啡。

pleas·ure /ˈpleʒə(r)/ *noun* **1** [U] a state of feeling or being happy or satisfied 高兴；快乐；愉快；欣慰；满意 SYN **enjoyment**：*to read **for pleasure*** 读书以自娱 ◇ ~ **(in sth/in doing sth)** *He **takes** no **pleasure in** his work.* 他从他的工作中得不到丝毫乐趣。◇ ~ **(of sth/of doing sth)** *She **had the pleasure of** seeing him look surprised.* 看他好像吃了一惊，她感到开心。◇ (*formal*) *We request the pleasure of your company at the marriage of our daughter Lisa.* 敬请光临小女莉萨的婚礼。◇ ***It gives me great pleasure** to introduce our guest speaker.* 我很荣幸来介绍我们的特约演讲人。 ➲ SYNONYMS AT FUN **2** [U] the activity of enjoying yourself, especially in contrast to working 玩乐；休闲：*Are you in Paris on business or pleasure?* 你来巴黎是公干还是游玩？ ➲ SYNONYMS AT ENTERTAINMENT **3** [C] a thing that makes you happy or satisfied 乐事；快事：*the pleasure and pains of everyday life* 日常生活的苦与乐 ◇ *the simple pleasures of the countryside* 乡村淳朴的乐趣 ◇ ***It's a pleasure** to meet you.* 很高兴认识你。◇ *'Thanks for doing that.' **'It's a pleasure.'*** "这事真劳您大驾了。""不客气。" ➲ COMPARE DISPLEASURE

IDM **at your/sb's ˈpleasure** (*formal*) as you want; as sb else wants 根据你的（或某人的）意愿；随意：*The land*

P

can be sold at the owner's pleasure. 这块地可随主人的意愿出售。 **my 'pleasure** used as a polite way of replying when sb thanks you for doing sth, to show that you were happy to do it（对别人表示感谢的一种礼貌回答）不客气，很乐意效劳 **with 'pleasure** 🔑 used as a polite way of accepting or agreeing to sth（客气地接受或同意）当然了，很愿意： *'May I sit here?' 'Yes, with pleasure.'* "我可以坐在这儿吗？" "当然可以。"

▼ **SYNONYMS** 同义词辨析

pleasure

delight • joy • privilege • treat • honour

These are all words for things that make you happy or bring you enjoyment. 以上各词均指令人愉快、高兴的事。

pleasure a thing that brings you enjoyment or satisfaction 指乐事、快事： *the pleasures and pains of everyday life* 日常生活的苦与乐 ◇ ***It's been a pleasure** meeting you.* 很高兴认识您。

delight a thing or person that brings you great enjoyment or satisfaction 指令人高兴的事或人、乐事、乐趣： *the delights of living in the country* 生活在乡村的乐趣

joy a thing or person that brings you great enjoyment or happiness 指令人高兴的事或人、乐事、乐趣： *the joys and sorrows of childhood* 童年的欢乐与悲伤

PLEASURE, DELIGHT OR JOY? 用 pleasure、delight 还是 joy?

A **delight** or **joy** is greater than a **pleasure**; a person, especially a child, can be a **delight** or **joy**, but not a **pleasure**; **joys** are often contrasted with **sorrows**, but **delights** are not. * delight 和 joy 语气较 pleasure 强。令人高兴的人，尤其是孩子，可以是一种 delight 或 joy，但不能是一种 pleasure。joys 常与 sorrows 形成对比，但 delights 无这种对比。

privilege (*rather formal*) something that you are proud and lucky to have the opportunity to do 指荣幸、荣耀、光荣： *It was a great privilege to hear her sing.* 听她唱歌是莫大的荣幸。

treat (*informal*) a thing that sb enjoyed or is likely to enjoy very much 指乐事、乐趣： *You've never been to this area before? Then you're **in for a real treat**.* 你以前从来没有到过这一地区？那么你一定会喜之不尽。

honour/honor (*formal*) something that you are very pleased or proud to do because people are showing you great respect 指荣幸、光荣： *It was a great honour to be invited here today.* 今天承蒙邀请到此，深感荣幸。

PATTERNS

- the pleasures/delights/joys **of** sth
- **It's a** great pleasure/joy **to me that**...
- **It's a(n)** pleasure/delight/joy/privilege/treat/honour **to do sth**
- **It's a** pleasure/delight/joy **to see/find**...
- a pleasure/delight/joy **to behold/watch**
- a **real** pleasure/delight/joy/privilege/treat
- a **great** pleasure/joy/privilege/honour
- a **rare** joy/privilege/treat/honour

'pleasure boat (*also* **'pleasure craft**) *noun* a boat used for short pleasure trips 游艇；游船

pleat /pliːt/ *noun* a permanent fold in a piece of cloth, made by sewing the top or side of the fold（布料上缝的）褶

pleat·ed /ˈpliːtɪd/ *adj.* having pleats 打褶的；有褶的： *a pleated skirt* 有褶的裙子

plea·ther /ˈpleðə(r)/ *noun* [U] a plastic material that looks like leather 塑料皮革；人造革： *a pleather jacket* 塑料皮革上衣 **ORIGIN** From **plastic** and **leather**. 源自 plastic 和 leather 的缩合。 ➲ **MORE LIKE THIS** 1, page R25

pleb *noun* (*disapproving*) an ordinary person, especially one who is poor or not well educated 普通人；（尤指）社会地位低下的人

plebe /pliːb/ *noun* (*US, informal*) a first-year student at a military or NAVAL college in the US（美国军校）一年级学生，新生

ple·beian /pləˈbiːən/ *adj., noun*

■ *adj.* **1** connected with ordinary people or people of the lower social classes 平民的；百姓的；下层社会的 **2** (*disapproving*) lacking in culture or education 粗俗的；俗鄙的： *plebeian tastes* 庸俗的趣味

■ *noun* (*usually disapproving*) a person from a lower social class (used originally in ancient Rome) 下层人；平民；庶民 ➲ COMPARE PATRICIAN

pleb·is·cite /ˈplebɪsɪt; -saɪt/ *noun* ~ (**on sth**) (*politics* 政) a vote by the people of a country or a region on an issue that is very important 公民投票；全民公决 **SYN** **referendum**: *to **hold a plebiscite** on the country's future system of government* 就国家未来的政府体制举行公民投票

plebs /plebz/ *noun* (*usually* **the plebs**) [pl.] (*informal*) an offensive way of referring to ordinary people, especially those of the lower social classes 平头百姓；市井小民；贱民

plec·trum /ˈplektrəm/ *noun* (*pl.* **plec·trums** *or* **plec·tra** /-trə/) (*also informal* **pick**) a small piece of metal, plastic, etc. used for PLUCKING the strings of a GUITAR or similar instrument（弹拨琴弦用的）琴拨，拨子

pled (*US*) PAST TENSE, PAST PART. OF PLEAD

pledge /pledʒ/ *noun, verb*

■ *noun* **1** a serious promise 保证；诺言；誓约 **SYN** **commitment**: ~ (**of sth**) *a pledge of support* 支援的许诺 ◇ ~ (**to do sth**) *Will the government **honour its** election **pledge** not to raise taxes?* 政府会履行其竞选诺言，不增加税收吗？ ◇ ~ (**that**...) *Management has **given a pledge** that there will be no job losses this year.* 资方保证今年不会削减工作职位。 **2** a sum of money or sth valuable that you leave with sb to prove that you will do sth or pay back money that you owe 质钱；抵押品

IDM **sign/take the 'pledge** (*old-fashioned*) to make a promise never to drink alcohol 发誓戒酒

■ *verb* **1** [T] to formally promise to give or do sth 保证给予（或做）；正式承诺： ~ **sth** *Japan has pledged $100 million in humanitarian aid.* 日本已承诺提供一亿美元人道主义援助。 ◇ *The government **pledged their support** for the plan.* 政府保证支持这个计划。 ◇ ~ **sth to sb/sth** *We all had to **pledge allegiance** to the flag* (= state that we are loyal to our country). 我们都必须对国旗宣誓效忠。 ◇ ~ **to do sth** *The group has pledged to continue campaigning.* 这个组织发誓继续投入运动。 ◇ ~ (**that**)... *The group has pledged that they will continue campaigning.* 这个组织发誓他们将继续投入运动。 **2** [T] to make sb or yourself formally promise to do sth 使保证；使发誓 **SYN** **swear**: ~ **sb/yourself** (**to sth**) *They were all pledged to secrecy.* 他们都宣誓保密。 ◇ ~ **sb/yourself to do sth** *The government has pledged itself to root out corruption.* 政府已承诺铲除腐败。 **3** [T] ~ **sth** to leave sth with sb as a pledge (2) 抵押；典当 **4** [I, T] (*NAmE*) to promise to become a junior member of a FRATERNITY or SORORITY 宣誓参加美国大学生联谊会： *Do you think you'll pledge this semester?* 这学期你会加入大学生联谊会吗？ ◇ ~ **sth** *My brother pledged Sigma Nu.* 我哥哥宣誓加入 ΣN 联谊会。

the ˌPledge of Alˈlegiance *noun* [sing.] a formal promise to be loyal to the US, which Americans make standing in front of the flag with their right hand on their heart 宣誓效忠（美国人站在国旗前右手贴左胸宣誓）

plen·ary /ˈpliːnəri/ *adj., noun*

■ *adj.* [only before noun] (*formal*) **1** (of meetings, etc. 会议等) to be attended by everyone who has the right to attend 全体参加的： *The new committee holds its first **plenary session** this week.* 新委员会本周举行第一次全会。 ➲ **WORDFINDER NOTE AT** CONFERENCE **2** without any limit; complete 无限的；完全的；绝对的： *The Council has* *plenary powers to administer the agreement.* 理事会拥有全权执行这项协议。

■ **noun** (*pl.* **-ies**) a plenary meeting 全体会议；全会

pleni·po·ten·tiary /ˌplenɪpəˈtenʃəri; *NAmE also* -ʃieri/ *noun* (*pl.* **-ies**) (*specialist*) a person who has full powers to take action, make decisions, etc. on behalf of their government, especially in a foreign country （尤指在国外代表政府的）全权代表；全权大使 ▶ **pleni·po·ten·tiary** *adj.*: *plenipotentiary powers* 全权

pleni·tude /ˈplenɪtjuːd; *NAmE* -tuːd/ *noun* [sing., U] (*formal*) a large amount of sth 大量；充裕；众多 SYN **abundance**

plent·eous /ˈplentiəs/ *adj.* (*literary*) = PLENTIFUL

plen·ti·ful /ˈplentɪfl/ (*also* **plent·eous**) *adj.* available or existing in large amounts or numbers 大量的；众多的；充足的；丰富的 SYN **abundant**: *a* ***plentiful supply*** *of food* 充足的食物供应 ◇ *In those days jobs were plentiful.* 那个时期工作岗位多得很。 ▶ **plen·ti·ful·ly** /-fəli/ *adv.*: *Evidence is plentifully available.* 证据俯拾即是。◇ *She kept them plentifully supplied with gossip.* 她不断向他们散播大量的流言蜚语。

plenty 🔑 /ˈplenti/ *pron., adv., noun, det.*

■ **pron.** 🔑 ~ (**of sth**) a large amount; as much or as many as you need 大量；众多；充足：*plenty of eggs/money/time* 充裕的鸡蛋 / 钱 / 时间 ◇ *'Do we need more milk?' 'No, there's plenty in the fridge.'* “我们要不要再买些牛奶？”“不必了。冰箱里还多着呢。”◇ *They always gave us plenty to eat.* 他们总是给我们好多东西吃。◇ *We had plenty to talk about.* 我们有说不完的话。 ➲ NOTE AT MANY, MUCH

■ **adv.** **1** 🔑 **~ more (of) (sth)** a lot 大量；很多：*We have plenty more of them in the warehouse.* 我们仓库里这些东西还多得很。◇ *There's plenty more paper if you need it.* 你要是需要纸，还有很多。 **2 ~ big, long, etc. enough (to do sth)** (*informal*) more than big, long, etc. enough 足够有余：*The rope was plenty long enough to reach the ground.* 这根绳子长及地面依然有余。 **3** (*NAmE*) a lot; very 非常；十分；很：*We talked plenty about our kids.* 我们谈了很多关于孩子的事。◇ *You can be married and still be plenty lonely.* 结了婚也可能非常孤寂。 IDM SEE FISH *n.*

■ **noun** [U] (*formal*) a situation in which there is a large supply of food, money, etc. 富裕；充裕：*Everyone is happier* ***in times of plenty.*** 在富足的岁月里，每个人都比较快乐。◇ *We had food and drink* ***in plenty.*** 我们的食物和饮料十分充足。

■ **det.** (*NAmE* or *informal*) a lot of 很多；大量：*There's plenty room for all of you!* 这里有足够的地方容纳你们所有人！

ple·num /ˈpliːnəm/ *noun* a meeting attended by all the members of a committee, etc.; a PLENARY meeting （委员会等的）全体会议，全会

ple·on·asm /ˈpliːənæzəm/ *noun* [U, C] (*specialist*) the use of more words than are necessary to express a meaning. For example, 'see with your eyes' is a pleonasm because the same meaning can be expressed using 'see'. 冗笔；冗述；赘述 ▶ **ple·on·as·tic** /ˌpliːəˈnæstɪk/ *adj.*

pleth·ora /ˈpleθərə/ *noun* [sing.] (*formal*) an amount that is greater than is needed or can be used 过多；过量；过剩 SYN **excess**

pleura /ˈplʊərə; *NAmE* ˈplʊrə/ *noun* (*pl.* **pleurae** /-riː/) (*anatomy* 解) one of the two MEMBRANES that surround the lungs 胸膜

pleur·isy /ˈplʊərəsi; *NAmE* ˈplʊr-/ *noun* [U] a serious illness that affects the inner covering of the chest and lungs, causing severe pain in the chest or sides 胸膜炎；肋膜炎

Plexi·glas™ /ˈpleksiglɑːs; *NAmE* -glæs/ (*NAmE*) (*BrE* **Per·spex™**) *noun* [U] a strong transparent plastic material that is often used instead of glass 珀斯佩有机玻璃

plexus ➲ SOLAR PLEXUS

pli·able /ˈplaɪəbl/ *adj.* **1** easy to bend without breaking 易弯曲的；柔韧的 SYN **flexible** **2** (of people 人) easy to influence or control 易受影响的；可塑的；容易摆布的 SYN **impressionable**

pli·ant /ˈplaɪənt/ *adj.* **1** (of a person or their body 人或人体) soft and giving way to sb, especially in a sexual way 绵软顺从的；柔顺的：*her pliant body* 她那柔软的肢体 ◇ *She lay pliant in his arms.* 她顺从地偎依在他的怀中。 **2** (*sometimes disapproving*) willing to accept change; easy to influence or control 温顺的；容易摆布的：*He was deposed and replaced by a more pliant successor.* 他被赶下台，由一个比较容易摆布的继任者取代。 ▶ **pli·ancy** /ˈplaɪənsi/ *noun* [U]

pli·ers /ˈplaɪəz; *NAmE* -ərz/ *noun* [pl.] a metal tool with handles, used for holding things firmly and twisting and cutting wire 钳子；夹钳：*a pair of pliers* 一把钳子 ➲ VISUAL VOCAB PAGE V21

plight /plaɪt/ *noun, verb*

■ **noun** [sing.] a difficult and sad situation 苦难；困境；苦境：*the plight of the homeless* 无家可归者的艰难困苦 ◇ *The African elephant is in a desperate plight.* 非洲象正面临绝境。

■ **verb**

IDM **plight your 'troth** (*old use* or *humorous*) to make a promise to a person saying that you will marry them; to marry sb 许婚；以身相许

plim·soll /ˈplɪmsəl/ (*also* **pump**) (*both BrE*) (*also* **'gym shoe** *BrE, NAmE*) *noun* a light simple sports shoe made of CANVAS (= strong cotton cloth) with a rubber SOLE 橡胶底帆布鞋；体操鞋：*a pair of plimsolls* 一双体操鞋

'Plimsoll line (*also* **'load line**) *noun* a line on the side of a ship showing the highest point that the water can safely reach when the ship is loaded （船的）载重线，吃水线

plinth /plɪnθ/ *noun* a block of stone on which a column or statue stands （雕像或柱子的）底座，柱基 ➲ VISUAL VOCAB PAGE V14

plod /plɒd; *NAmE* plɑːd/ *verb* (**-dd-**) [I, T] to walk slowly with heavy steps, especially because you are tired 艰难地行走；吃力地行进 SYN **trudge**: **+ adv./prep.** *Our horses plodded down the muddy track.* 我们的马沿着泥泞小路蹒跚而行。◇ *We plodded on through the rain.* 我们冒雨艰难地跋涉。◇ **~ your way + adv./prep.** *I watched her plodding her way across the field.* 我注视着她步履艰难地穿过田野。 ➲ MORE LIKE THIS 36, page R29 ▶ **plod** *noun* [sing.]

PHR V ˌ**plod a'long/'on** to make very slow progress, especially with difficult or boring work 进展缓慢（尤指艰难枯燥的工作） SYN **slog**

plod·der /ˈplɒdə(r); *NAmE* ˈplɑːd-/ *noun* a person who works slowly and steadily but without imagination 缺乏想象力的苦干者；沉闷苦干者

plod·ding /ˈplɒdɪŋ; *NAmE* ˈplɑːd-/ *adj.* working or doing sth slowly and steadily, especially in a way that other people think is boring 老牛拖破车似的；做事慎重而呆板的

plonk /plɒŋk; *NAmE* plɑːŋk/ *verb, noun*

■ **verb** (*especially BrE*) (*NAmE usually* **plunk**) (*informal*) **1 ~ sth + adv./prep.** to put sth down on sth, especially noisily or carelessly 随意放下；砰然扔下：*He plonked the books down on the table.* 他砰的一声把书扔到了桌子上。◇ *Just plonk your bag anywhere.* 把你的袋子随便搁在哪儿吧。 **2 ~ yourself (down)** to sit down heavily or carelessly 重重地坐下；不经意地坐下：*He just plonked himself down and turned on the TV.* 他一屁股坐下来，打开了电视。

■ **noun** (*informal, especially BrE*) **1** [U] cheap wine that is not of good quality 廉价劣质酒；便宜酒 **2** [C, usually sing.] a low sound like that of sth heavy falling and hitting a surface （重物落下碰到物体表面发出的）砰的声响，扑通声：*She sat down with a plonk.* 她扑通一声坐下来。

plonk·er /ˈplɒŋkə(r); *NAmE* ˈplɑːŋk-/ *noun* (*BrE, slang*) a stupid person 傻子；呆子；笨蛋

plop /plɒp; *NAmE* plɑːp/ *noun, verb*

■ **noun** [usually sing.] a short sound like that of a small object dropping into water （物体落入水的）扑通声，咚

■ *verb* (-pp-) **1** [I] + **adv./prep.** to fall, making a plop 咚的落下：*The frog plopped back into the water.* 青蛙扑通一声跳回水中。◇ *A tear plopped down onto the page she was reading.* 一滴眼泪啪哒一声落在她正在读的书页上。 **2** [T] ~ **sth** + **adv./prep.** to drop sth into sth, especially a liquid, so that it makes a plop 扑通一声把…放入（尤指液体）：*Can you just plop some ice in my drink?* 能在我的饮料中放点冰块吗？ **3** [T, I] ~ (**yourself**) (**down**) to sit or lie down heavily or in a relaxed way （重重地或懒洋洋地）坐下，躺下 ➲ MORE LIKE THIS 3, page R25

plo·sive /ˈpləʊsɪv; *NAmE* ˈploʊ-/ *noun* (*phonetics* 语音) a speech sound made by stopping the flow of air coming out of the mouth and then suddenly releasing it, for example /t/ and /p/ in *top* 爆破音（如 top 中的 /t/ 和 /p/） ▶ **plo·sive** *adj.*

plot /plɒt; *NAmE* plɑːt/ *noun, verb*

■ *noun* **1** [C, U] the series of events that form the story of a novel, play, film/movie, etc. 故事情节；布局：*a conventional plot about love and marriage* 传统的婚恋故事情节 ◇ *The book is well organized in terms of plot.* 这本书的故事布局十分严谨。 ➲ WORDFINDER NOTE AT BOOK ➲ COLLOCATIONS AT LITERATURE

> WORDFINDER 联想词：dialogue, ending, flashback, narrate, scenario, scene, storyline, tension, twist

2 [C] ~ (**to do sth**) a secret plan made by a group of people to do sth wrong or illegal 阴谋；密谋 SYN **conspiracy** **3** [C] a small piece of land that is used or intended for a special purpose （专用的）小块土地：*She bought a small plot of land to build a house on.* 她买了一小块地盖房子。◇ *a vegetable plot* 一块菜圃 ➲ SYNONYMS AT LAND

IDM **ˌlose the ˈplot** (*BrE, informal*) to lose your ability to understand or deal with what is happening 迷惘；不知所措 **the plot ˈthickens** used to say that a situation is becoming more complicated and difficult to understand 情况变得复杂起来

■ *verb* (-tt-) **1** [I, T] to make a secret plan to harm sb, especially a government or its leader 密谋；暗中策划 SYN **conspire**：~ (**with sb**) (**against sb**) *They were accused of plotting against the state.* 他们被指控密谋叛国。◇ ~ **sth** *Military officers were suspected of plotting a coup.* 人们怀疑军方在策划政变。◇ ~ **to do sth** *They were plotting to overthrow the government.* 他们在密谋颠覆政府。 **2** [T] ~ **sth** (**on sth**) to mark sth on a map, for example the position or course of sth （在地图上）画出，标出：*The earthquake centres had been plotted on a world map.* 地震震中均被标示在一张世界地图上。 **3** [T] ~ **sth** (**on sth**) to make a diagram or chart from some information 绘制（图表）：*We carefully plotted each patient's response to the drug on a chart.* 我们仔细绘出了每个病人对这种药物反应的图表。 **4** [T] ~ **sth** (**on sth**) to mark points on a GRAPH and draw a line or curve connecting them 绘制（图表的曲线）：*First, plot the temperature curve on the graph.* 首先，在图表上绘出温度曲线来。 **5** [T] ~ **sth** to write the plot of a novel, play, etc. （为小说、戏剧等）设计情节，布局：*a tightly-plotted thriller* 情节丝丝入扣的惊险刺激小说

plot·ter /ˈplɒtə(r); *NAmE* ˈplɑːtər/ *noun* **1** a person who makes a secret plan to harm sb 阴谋家；秘密策划者 SYN **conspirator** **2** a device that turns data from a computer into a GRAPH, usually on paper （计算机）绘图机，描绘器

plough (*NAmE* **plow**) /plaʊ/ *noun, verb*

■ *noun* **1** [C] a large piece of farming equipment with one or several curved blades, pulled by a TRACTOR or by animals. It is used for digging and turning over soil, especially before seeds are planted. 犁 ➲ SEE ALSO SNOW-PLOUGH *n.* **2 the Plough** (*BrE*) (*NAmE* **the ˌBig ˈDipper**) [sing.] a group of seven bright stars that can only be seen from the northern half of the world 北斗星

IDM **under the ˈplough** (*BrE, formal*) (of land 土地) used for growing crops, not for keeping animals on 用于耕作的；作农田的 SYN **arable**

■ *verb* [T, I] ~ (**sth**) to dig and turn over a field or other area of land with a plough 犁（田）；耕（地）；翻（土）：*ploughed fields* 犁过的田地 ➲ COLLOCATIONS AT FARMING

IDM **ˌplough a lonely, your own, etc., ˈfurrow** (*literary*) to do things that other people do not do, or be interested in things that other people are not interested in 自耕孤畴（指自行其是或自得其乐）

PHR V **ˌplough sth↔ˈback (in/into sth)** | **ˌplough sth↔back ˈin** **1** to turn over growing crops, grass, etc. with a plough and mix them into the soil to improve its quality 犁埋；使秸秆还田 **2** to put money made as profit back into a business in order to improve it 把（利润）再投资：*The money was all ploughed back into the company.* 所有的钱都再投资到这个公司。 **ˈplough into sb/sth** (especially of a vehicle or its driver 尤指汽车或司机) to crash violently into sth, especially because you are driving too fast or not paying enough attention 猛撞（尤因开车太快或不小心所致）：*A truck ploughed into the back of the bus.* 一辆卡车猛撞到公共汽车的尾部。 **ˌplough sth ˈinto sth** to invest a large amount of money in a company or project 把（大批资金）投入；大量投资于：*The government has ploughed more than $20 billion into building new schools.* 政府已投放200多亿美元兴建新学校。 **ˌplough ˈon (with sth)** to continue doing sth that is difficult or boring 坚持做，继续进行（艰难或乏味的事）；苦撑：*No one was listening to her, but she **ploughed on regardless**.* 没有人在听她讲话，但她仍不加理会，喋喋不休。 **ˌplough (your way) ˈthrough sth** **1** to force a way through sth 费劲地穿越（或通过）：*She ploughed her way through the waiting crowds.* 她从等候的人群中挤过去。 **2** (of a vehicle or an aircraft 车辆或飞机) to go violently through sth, out of control 猛冲过；失控地穿过：*The plane ploughed through the trees.* 飞机猛冲过树林。 **3** to make slow progress through sth difficult or boring, especially a book, a report, etc. 艰难地进行，缓慢地推进（尤指读书、做报告等）；埋头苦干：*I had to plough through dozens of legal documents.* 我得慢慢地埋头阅读几十份法律文件。 **ˌplough sth↔ˈup** **1** to turn over a field or other area of land with a plough to change it from grass, for example, to land for growing crops （用犁）开垦；犁地 **2** to break up the surface of the ground by walking or driving across it again and again 轧翻，碾坏（地面）：*The paths get all ploughed up by motorbikes.* 小路全让摩托车给轧坏了。

plough·man (*NAmE* **plow·man**) /ˈplaʊmən/ *noun* (*pl.* **-men** /-mən/) a man whose job is guiding a plough, especially one pulled by animals 扶犁者（尤指畜力拉的犁）

ˌploughman's ˈlunch (*also* **ˈploughman's**) *noun* (*BrE*) a cold meal of bread, cheese, PICKLE and salad, often served in pubs 农夫午餐（包括面包、奶酪、泡菜和色拉，常在酒馆供应）

plough·share (*NAmE* **plow·share**) /ˈplaʊʃeə(r); *NAmE* -ʃer/ (*NAmE also* **share**) *noun* the broad curved blade of a plough 犁铧；铧 IDM SEE SWORD

plover /ˈplʌvə(r)/ *noun* a bird with long legs and a short tail that lives on wet ground 鸻；千鸟

plow, **plow·man**, **plow·share** (*NAmE*) = PLOUGH, PLOUGHMAN, PLOUGHSHARE

ploy /plɔɪ/ *noun* words or actions that are carefully planned to get an advantage over sb else 计谋；策略；手法；花招 SYN **manoeuvre**：*a clever marketing ploy* 机智的销售策略 ◇ ~ **to do sth** *It was all a ploy to distract attention from his real aims.* 那全是障眼法，借以转移对他真实目的的注意。

pluck /plʌk/ *verb, noun*

■ *verb*

• **HAIR** 毛发 **1** [T] ~ **sth** (**out**) to pull out hairs with your fingers or with TWEEZERS 摘；拔：*She plucked out a grey hair.* 她拔掉了一根灰白头发。◇ *expertly plucked eyebrows* 拔得精巧的眉毛

• **CHICKEN, ETC.** 鸡等 **2** [T] ~ **sth** to pull the feathers off a dead bird, for example a chicken, in order to prepare it for cooking 拔掉，煺去（死禽的毛）

• **MUSICAL INSTRUMENT** 乐器 **3** (*NAmE also* **pick**) [T, I] ~ (**at**) **sth** to play a musical instrument, especially a GUITAR,

P

by pulling the strings with your fingers 弹，弹拨（乐器的弦）：*to pluck the strings of a violin* 弹拨小提琴的弦 ◇ *He took the guitar and plucked at the strings.* 他拿起吉他拨动起琴弦来。

• **REMOVE SB/STH** 移开人 / 物 **4** [T] ~ **sb** (**from sth**) (**to sth**) to remove sb from a place or situation, especially one that is unpleasant or dangerous 解救；搭救：*Police plucked a drowning girl from the river yesterday.* 昨天警方从河里救起了一名溺水少女。◇ *Survivors of the wreck were **plucked to safety** by a helicopter.* 沉船的幸存者被直升机营救脱险。◇ *She was plucked from obscurity to instant stardom.* 她得到提携，从默默无闻转瞬成为明星。 **5** [T] ~ **sth** (**from sth**) to take hold of sth and remove it by pulling it 抢夺：*He plucked the wallet from the man's grasp.* 他抢走了那个男人紧抓着的钱包。

• **FRUIT/FLOWER** 果；花 **6** [T] ~ **sth** (**from sth**) (*old-fashioned* or *literary*) to pick a fruit, flower, etc. from where it is growing 摘；掐；采摘：*I plucked an orange from the tree.* 我从树上摘了一个橙子。

IDM **pluck sth out of the 'air** to say a name, number, etc. without thinking about it, especially in answer to a question 脱口而出；随意回答：*I just plucked a figure out of the air and said: 'Would £1 000 seem reasonable to you?'* 我随口说出一个数字问道："你看 1 000 英镑合适吗？" **pluck up** (**the**) **'courage** (**to do sth**) to make yourself do sth even though you are afraid to do it 鼓起勇气（做某事）：*I finally plucked up the courage to ask her for a date.* 我终于鼓起勇气约她出去。

PHR V **'pluck at sth** to hold sth with the fingers and pull it gently, especially more than once 揪；拽；拉；抻 SYN **tug**：*The child kept plucking at his mother's sleeve.* 小孩不停地拉扯着他妈妈的衣袖。◇ (*figurative*) *The wind plucked at my jacket.* 风不时地吹动着我的上衣。

■ ***noun*** [U] (*informal*) courage and determination 胆识；胆量；意志：*It takes a lot of pluck to do what she did.* 她这么做需要很大的胆量。

plucky /ˈplʌki/ *adj.* (*informal*) (**pluck·ier**, **plucki·est**) having a lot of courage and determination 勇敢的；有胆量的；刚毅的 SYN **brave** ▶ **pluck·ily** *adv.*

plugs 插头；塞子

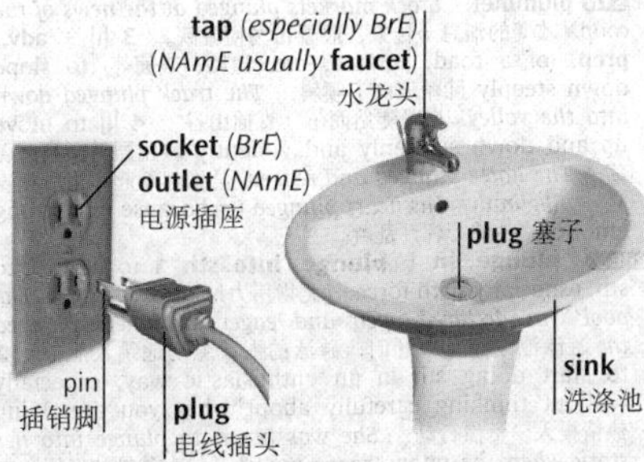

plug /plʌɡ/ *noun, verb*

■ ***noun***

• **ELECTRICAL EQUIPMENT** 电气设备 **1** a small plastic object with two or three metal pins that connects a piece of electrical equipment to the main supply of electricity 插头：*a three-pin plug* 三相插头 ◇ *I'll have to **change the plug** on my hairdryer.* 我必须更换吹风机的插头。 **2** (*informal, especially BrE*) a small opening in a wall, by which you connect a piece of electrical equipment to the main supply of electricity （电源）插座 SYN **socket**：*Can I use this plug for my iron?* 我能用这个插座插熨斗吗？ **3** a small object that connects a wire from one piece of electrical equipment to an opening in another 转换插头：*the plug from the computer to the printer* 连接电脑和打印机的转换插头

• **IN ENGINE** 发动机 **4** = SPARK PLUG

• **IN BATH/SINK** 浴缸；水池 **5** a thick round piece of plastic, rubber or metal that you put in the hole in a bath/BATHTUB or a SINK to stop the water flowing out 塞子：*She **pulled out the plug** and let the water drain away.* 她拔起塞子放掉了水。 ➲ SYNONYMS AT LID

• **IN HOLE** 洞 **6** a round piece of material that fits into a hole and blocks it 堵塞物；塞子：*She took the plug of cotton wool from her ear.* 她从耳朵中取出棉毛耳塞来。 ➲ SEE ALSO EARPLUG **7** (*NAmE*) = STOPPER ➲ SYNONYMS AT LID

• **FOR SCREW** 螺丝 **8** a small plastic tube that you put into a hole in a wall so that it will hold a screw 螺钉楔子，螺钉塞栓（塞入洞中用来固定螺丝的小塑料管）

• **FOR BOOK/MOVIE** 书籍；电影 **9** (*informal*) praise or attention that sb gives to a new book, film/movie, etc. in order to encourage people to buy or see it 推销；宣传：*He managed to get in a plug for his new book.* 他设法为自己的新书插入了一条宣传信息。 IDM SEE PULL *v.*

■ ***verb*** (**-gg-**)

• **FILL HOLE** 堵洞 **1** ~ **sth** (**up**) to fill a hole with a substance or piece of material that fits tightly into it 堵塞；封堵：*He plugged the hole in the pipe with an old rag.* 他用一块旧破布把管子上的那个洞塞住了。

• **PROVIDE STH MISSING** 弥补不足 **2** ~ **sth** to provide sth that has been missing from a particular situation and is needed in order to improve it 补足；补充；供给：*A cheaper range of products was introduced to **plug the gap** at the lower end of the market.* 推出相对廉价的一系列产品是为了填补较低端市场的缺口。

• **BOOK/MOVIE** 书籍；电影 **3** ~ **sth** (*informal*) to give praise or attention to a new book, film/movie, etc. in order to encourage people to buy it or see it 推广；宣传 SYN **promote**：*She came on the show to plug her latest album.* 她上电视节目宣传她的新唱片专辑。

• **SHOOT** 射击 **4** ~ **sb** (*old-fashioned, NAmE, informal*) to shoot sb 射击；射杀 ➲ MORE LIKE THIS 36, page R29

PHR V **ˌplug aˈway** (**at sth**) to continue working hard at sth, especially sth that you find difficult 坚持不懈地做（尤指困难的事） **ˌplug sth↔ˈin** | **ˌplug sth ˈinto sth** to connect a piece of electrical equipment to the main supply of electricity or to another piece of electrical equipment 接通（电源）；把（插头）插进（插座）：*Is the printer plugged in?* 打印机接上电源没有？ OPP **unplug** **ˌplug sth ˈinto sth 1** = PLUG STH↔IN **2** to connect a computer to a computer system 把（计算机）联网：*All our computers are plugged into the main network.* 我们所有的电脑都和主网络联网了。 **ˌplug ˈinto sth 1** (of a piece of electrical equipment 电器) to be able to be connected to the main supply of electricity or to another piece of electrical equipment 能与（电源或其他电器）连接：*The DVD player plugs into the back of the television.* * DVD 播放机在电视机的后部连接。 **2** to become involved with a particular activity or group of people 参与；加入：*The company has doubled its profits since plugging into lucrative overseas markets.* 自从这家公司进入赚钱的海外市场以后，利润翻了一番。

ˌPlug and ˈPlay *noun* [U] (*computing* 计) a system that makes it possible for a piece of equipment, such as a printer, to be connected to a computer and to work immediately, without the user needing to do anything 即插即用（系统） ▶ **ˌplug-and-ˈplay** *adj.*：*plug-and-play peripherals* 即插即用式外围设备

plug·hole /ˈplʌɡhəʊl; *NAmE* -hoʊl/ (*BrE*) (*US* **drain**) *noun* a hole in a bath/BATHTUB, SINK, etc. where the water flows away and into which a plug fits （水池、浴缸等的）排水孔，漏眼，渗水孔 ➲ VISUAL VOCAB PAGE V25

IDM (**go**) **down the ˈplughole** (*BrE*) = (GO) DOWN THE DRAIN

ˈplug-in *adj., noun*

■ ***adj.*** [only before noun] **1** able to be connected using a plug 可插入插头的；插入式的：*a plug-in kettle* 电源插入式水壶 **2** (*computing* 计) able to be added to a computer system so that it can do more things 插入（以扩展功能）的；外挂的：*a plug-in graphics card* 插入式图形卡

■ ***noun*** **1** (*computing* 计) a piece of computer software that can be added to a system so that it can do more things 插件；外挂程序 **2** (*CanE*) a connection to an electricity supply in a garage, etc. so that you can use an electric HEATER to warm the engine of a car, so that it starts more easily（连接车库等电源的）发动机预热器接线

ˌplug-ˈugly *adj.* (*informal*) very ugly 极丑陋的；很难看的

plum /plʌm/ *noun, adj.*

■ ***noun*** **1** [C] a soft round fruit with smooth red or purple skin, sweet flesh and a large flat seed inside 李子；梅子：*a plum tree* 李树 **2** [U, C] a dark reddish-purple colour 紫红色

■ ***adj.*** [only before noun] (of a job, etc. 工作等) considered very good and worth having 称心的；值得拥有的：*She's landed a plum job at the BBC.* 她在英国广播公司谋得一份称心如意的工作。

plum·age /ˈpluːmɪdʒ/ *noun* [U] the feathers covering a bird's body（鸟的）全身羽毛

plumb /plʌm/ *verb, adv.*

■ ***verb*** ~ **sth** (*literary*) to try to understand or succeed in understanding sth mysterious 探索；钻研；探究 **SYN** **fathom**：*She spent her life plumbing the mysteries of the human psyche.* 她毕生探索人类心灵的奥秘。

IDM **plumb the depths of sth** to be or to experience an extreme example of sth unpleasant 陷入（痛苦等的）深渊；深入…深处：*His latest novel plumbs the depths of horror and violence.* 他最新的小说充斥着极端恐怖和暴力。◇ *The team's poor performances* ***plumbed new depths*** *last night when they lost 10–2.* 昨晚这个队的糟糕表现达到了新低纪录，以 2:10 输掉了。

PHR V **ˌplumb sth↔ˈin** (*especially BrE*) to connect a WASHING MACHINE, toilet, etc. to the water supply in a building 把（洗衣机、马桶等）与水管连接

■ ***adv.*** **1** (used before prepositions 用于介词前) exactly 恰恰；正好：*He was standing plumb in the middle of the road.* 他站在路正中间。 **2** (*old-fashioned, NAmE, informal*) completely 完全；彻底：*He's plumb crazy.* 他彻底疯了。

plumb·er /ˈplʌmə(r)/ *noun* a person whose job is to fit and repair things such as water pipes, toilets, etc. 水暖工；管子工；铅管工

plumb·ing /ˈplʌmɪŋ/ *noun* [U] **1** the system of pipes, etc. that supply water to a building（建筑物的）管路系统，自来水管道 ➲ COLLOCATIONS AT DECORATE **2** the work of a plumber 水暖工的工作

ˈplumb line *noun* a piece of thick string with a weight attached to one end, used to find the depth of water or to test whether a wall, etc. is straight（测水深或垂直面用的）铅垂线，重锤线

plume /pluːm/ *noun* **1** a cloud of sth that rises and curves upwards in the air 飘升之物：*a plume of smoke* 一缕青烟 **2** a large feather 翎；羽毛：*a black hat with an ostrich plume* 饰有一根鸵鸟羽毛的黑帽子 **3** a group of feathers or long thin pieces of material tied together and often used as a decoration（常用作饰物的）连在一起的羽毛，羽状物；羽饰 ➲ SEE ALSO NOM DE PLUME

plumed /pluːmd/ *adj.* having or decorated with a plume or plumes 有羽毛的；用羽毛装饰的：*a plumed helmet* 一副羽饰头盔

plum·met /ˈplʌmɪt/ *verb* [I] to fall suddenly and quickly from a high level or position 暴跌；速降 **SYN** **plunge**：*Share prices plummeted to an all-time low.* 股票价格暴跌到历史最低点。◇ *Her spirits plummeted at the thought of meeting him again.* 一想到又要见到他，她的心情便直往下沉。◇ *The jet plummeted into a row of houses.* 那架喷气式飞机一头栽进一排房子里。➲ WORDFINDER NOTE AT TREND

plummy /ˈplʌmi/ *adj.* **1** (*BrE, informal, usually disapproving*) (of a voice 嗓音) having a sound that is typical of upper-class English people 拿腔拿调的；做作的：*a plummy accent* 一副矫揉造作的腔调 **2** like a PLUM in colour, taste, etc.（颜色、味道等）像梅子的

plump /plʌmp/ *adj., verb*

■ ***adj.*** (**plump·er, plump·est**) **1** having a soft, round body; slightly fat 丰腴的；微胖的：*a short, plump woman* 一个矮胖的女人 ◇ *a plump face* 饱满的面庞 **2** looking soft, full and attractive to use or eat 松软的；丰满的；饱满的：*plump cushions* 松软的垫子 ◇ *plump tomatoes* 滚圆的番茄 ▶ **plump·ness** *noun* [U]

■ ***verb*** ~ **sth** (**up**) to make sth larger, softer and rounder 使变大；使更软；使更圆：*He leaned forward while the nurse plumped up his pillows.* 他往前够了够身子，让护士把枕头拍松了。

PHR V **ˈplump for sb/sth** (*informal*) to choose sb/sth from a number of people or things, especially after thinking carefully 慎重挑选；筛选

ˌplum ˈpudding *noun* [U, C] (*old-fashioned, BrE*) = CHRISTMAS PUDDING

ˌplum toˈmato *noun* an Italian tomato that is long and thin, rather than round（意大利）李形番茄

plun·der /ˈplʌndə(r)/ *verb, noun*

■ ***verb*** [I, T] to steal things from a place, especially using force during a time of war（尤指战乱时用武力）抢劫，掠夺 **SYN** **loot**：*The troops crossed the country, plundering and looting as they went.* 部队经过乡村，一路抢劫掳掠。◇ ~ **sth** (**of sth**) *The abbey had been plundered of its valuables.* 教堂的珍宝被洗劫一空。◇ ~ **sth** (**from sth**) *Only a small amount of the money that he plundered from his companies has been recovered.* 他从公司搜刮的钱只有一小部分被追回。➲ COMPARE PILLAGE ▶ **plun·der·er** *noun*

■ ***noun*** [U] **1** the act of plundering 抢掠；掠夺 **2** things that have been stolen, especially during a war, etc.（尤指战争中）掠夺的财物 ➲ COMPARE PILLAGE

plunge /plʌndʒ/ *verb, noun*

■ ***verb*** **1** [I, T] to move or make sb/sth move suddenly forwards and/or downwards 使突然前冲（或下落）：**+ adv./prep.** *She lost her balance and plunged 100 feet to her death.* 她没有站稳，从 100 英尺的高处跌下摔死了。◇ **~ sb/sth + adv./prep.** *The earthquake plunged entire towns over the edge of the cliffs.* 地震将整座整座的城镇掀到悬崖之下。 **2** [I] (of prices, temperatures, etc. 价格、温度等) to decrease suddenly and quickly 暴跌；骤降；突降 **SYN** **plummet**：*Stock markets plunged at the news of the coup.* 政变的消息一传来，股票市场便暴跌。 **3** [I] **+ adv./prep.** (of a road, surface, etc. 道路、表面等) to slope down steeply 陡峭地向下倾斜：*The track plunged down into the valley.* 小路陡然而下，直插山谷。 **4** [I] to move up and down suddenly and violently（剧烈）颠簸，震荡：*The horse plunged and reared.* 马猛然跃起，用后腿直立。◇ (*figurative*) *His heart plunged* (= because of a strong emotion). 他的心怦怦乱跳。

PHR V **ˌplunge ˈin | ˌplunge ˈinto sth** **1** to jump into sth, especially with force（尤指用力地）投入，跳进：*The pool was declared open and eager swimmers plunged in.* 游泳池刚刚宣布开门，游泳的人就急切地跳入池中。 **2** to start doing sth in an enthusiastic way, especially without thinking carefully about what you are doing 热情投入；贸然行动：*She was about to plunge into her story when the phone rang.* 她刚要开始大谈她的经历，电话响了。◇ *He's always plunging in at the deep end* (= becoming involved in difficult situations without being well enough prepared). 他总是贸然行动，屡屡陷入困境。

ˌplunge sth ˈin | ˌplunge sth ˈinto sth to push sth quickly and with force into sth else 猛力插入；扎进：*She plunged the knife deep into his chest.* 她把刀子深深地刺进他的胸膛。 **ˌplunge ˈinto sth** **1** = PLUNGE IN **2** to experience sth unpleasant 经历，陷入（不快的事）：*The country plunged deeper into recession.* 那个国家进一步陷入经济衰退之中。 **ˌplunge sb/sth ˈinto sth** to make sb/sth experience sth unpleasant 使经历，使陷入（不快的事情）：*The news plunged them into deep depression.* 这条消息立即使他们深感沮丧。◇ *There was a flash of lightning and the house was* ***plunged into darkness.*** 雷电闪过，房子陷入一片黑暗之中。

■ ***noun*** [usually sing.] **1** a sudden movement downwards or away from sth 突然跌落；突然分离 **SYN** **drop**：*The calm water ends there and the river begins a headlong plunge.* 平静的河水突然中断，开始奔腾直泻而下。 **2** ~ (**in** sth) a sudden decrease in an amount or the value of sth （数量、价格的）暴跌，猛降，骤减 SYN **drop**: *a dramatic plunge in profits* 利润锐减 **3 ~ into sth** the act of becoming involved in a situation or activity 卷入；参与：*The company is planning a deeper plunge into the commercial market.* 这家公司正计划进一步投入商业市场。**4** an act of jumping or DIVING into water; a quick swim 跳水；快速游泳：*He took the plunge into the deep end.* 他跳入深水区。◇ *She went for a plunge.* 她去游泳了。

IDM **take the 'plunge** (*informal*) to decide to do sth important or difficult, especially after thinking about it for a long time （尤指深思熟虑后）果断行事，毅然决定

'plunge pool *noun* a small deep artificial pool filled with cold water, especially one that you jump into in order to get cooler after a SAUNA （尤指洗完桑拿浴后跳入的）冷水池

plun·ger /ˈplʌndʒə(r)/ *noun* **1** a part of a piece of equipment that can be pushed down 柱塞；活塞 ➲ VISUAL VOCAB PAGE V26 **2** a piece of equipment used for clearing kitchen and bathroom pipes, that consists of a rubber cup fixed to a handle （疏通管道用的）搋子

plun·ging /ˈplʌndʒɪŋ/ *adj.* [only before noun] (of a dress, BLOUSE, etc. 连衣裙、女衬衫等) cut in a deep V shape at the front 低领的；凹领的；深开领的：*a plunging neckline* 深开式领口

plunk /plʌŋk/ *verb* (*informal*) **1 ~ sth + adv./prep.** (*NAmE*) = PLONK：*He plunked the package down on the desk.* 他把包裹砰地撂到桌子上。**2 ~ sth** to play a GUITAR, a keyboard, etc. with your fingers and produce a rough unpleasant sound 弹拨，刮奏（吉他、琴键等）▶ **plunk** *noun*：*the plunk, plunk of the banjo* 班卓琴咚咚的弦声

PHR V **'plunk down sth** to pay money for sth, especially a large amount 重金买下；付钱买

plu·per·fect /ˌpluːˈpɜːfɪkt; *NAmE* -ˈpɜːrf-/ *noun* (*grammar* 语法) = PAST PERFECT

plural /ˈplʊərəl; *NAmE* ˈplʊrəl/ *noun, adj.*

■ *noun* (*grammar* 语法) (*abbr.* **pl.**) a form of a noun or verb that refers to more than one person or thing （名词或动词的）复数，复数形式：*The plural of 'child' is 'children'.* * child 一词的复数形式是 children。◇ *The verb should be in the plural.* 这个动词应该用复数形式。➲ COMPARE SINGULAR *n.*

■ *adj.* **1** (*grammar* 语法) (*abbr.* **pl.**) connected with or having the plural form 复数的；复数形式的：*Most plural nouns in English end in 's'.* 英语中多数复数名词以 s 结尾。**2** relating to more than one 多样的；多元的：*a plural society* (= one with more than one RACIAL, religious, etc. group) 多元社会

plur·al·ism /ˈplʊərəlɪzəm; *NAmE* ˈplʊr-/ *noun* [U] (*formal*) **1** the existence of many different groups of people in one society, for example people of different races or of different political or religious beliefs 多元化，多元性（不同种族、不同政治或宗教信仰的多种群体共存）：*cultural pluralism* 文化的多元性 **2** the belief that it is possible and good for different groups of people to live together in peace in one society 多元主义（不同群体可以有益地在同一社会中和平共处的主张）**3** (*usually disapproving*) the fact of having more than one job or position at the same time, especially in the Church 兼职；（尤指）兼任神职

plur·al·ist /ˈplʊərəlɪst; *NAmE* ˈplʊr-/ *adj., noun*

■ *adj.* (*also* **plur·al·is·tic** /ˌplʊərəˈlɪstɪk; *NAmE* ˌplʊr-/) **1** (of a society 社会) having many different groups of people and different political parties in it 多元性的；多元化的：*a pluralist democracy* 多元化的民主 **2** (*philosophy* 哲) not based on a single set of principles or beliefs 多元主义的；多元论的：*a pluralist approach to politics* 多元主义的政治手段

■ *noun* **1** a person who believes that it is possible and good for different groups of people to live together in peace in our society 多元主义者（认为社会中不同群体可以有益地和平共处的人）**2** a person who has more than one job or position at the same time, especially in the Church 兼职者；（尤指）兼任神职者（同时担任两个或以上的职务）

plur·al·ity /plʊəˈræləti; *NAmE* plʊˈr-/ *noun* (*pl.* **-ies**) **1** [C, usually sing.] (*formal*) a large number 众多；大量：*a plurality of influences* 众多的影响 **2** [C, usually sing.] (*US*) (*politics* 政) the number of votes given to one person, political party, etc. when this number is less than 50% but more than any other single person, etc. receives （未超过半数的）相对较多：*In order to be elected, a candidate needs only a plurality of the votes cast.* 候选人只需要得到相对多数票就能当选。➲ COMPARE MAJORITY (3) **3** [U] (*grammar* 语法) the state of being plural 复数

plur·al·ize (*BrE also* **-ise**) /ˈplʊərəlaɪz; *NAmE* ˈplʊrə-/ *verb* **~ sth** to make a word plural 使（单词）成复数；使构成复数 ▶ **plur·al·iza·tion, -isa·tion** /ˌplʊərəlaɪˈzeɪʃn; *NAmE* ˌplʊrələˈz-/ *noun* [U]

plus[1] 🔑 AW /plʌs/ *prep., noun, adj., conj.*

■ *prep.* **1** 🔑 used when the two numbers or amounts mentioned are being added together 加：*Two plus five is seven.* 二加五等于七。◇ *The cost is £22, plus £1 for postage.* 费用为 22 英镑，另加 1 英镑的邮费。**2** 🔑 as well as sth/sb; and also 和；也；外加：*We have to fit five of us plus all our gear in the car.* 我们五人和全部用具都得塞进车里。OPP **minus**

IDM **plus or 'minus** used when the number mentioned may actually be more or less by a particular amount 或多或少；左右；大约 SYN **give or take**：*The margin of error was plus or minus three percentage points.* 误差幅度在三个百分点左右。

■ *noun* **1** (*informal*) an advantage; a good thing 优势；好处；长处：*Knowledge of French is a plus in her job.* 通晓法文使她在工作中占优势。◇ *There were a lot of pluses in the performance.* 这次演出有多处值得嘉许。**2** (*also* **'plus sign**) the symbol (+), used in mathematics 加号：*He put a plus instead of a minus.* 他填了个加号而不是减号。OPP **minus**

■ *adj.* **1** used after a number to show that the real number or amount is more than the one mentioned （用于数字后表示实际数量较大）多，余：*The work will cost £10 000 plus.* 这项工作将耗资万余英镑。**2** 🔑 above zero 零度以上；零上：*The temperature is plus four degrees.* 温度为零上四度。OPP **minus 3** 🔑 [only before noun] used to describe an aspect of sth that you consider to be a good thing 优点的；好的：*One of the hotel's* ***plus points*** *is that it is very central.* 那个旅馆的优势之一是它位于市中心。◇ ***On the plus side****, all the staff are enthusiastic.* 好的方面是职员的工作热忱都很高。OPP **minus 4** [not before noun] (used in a system of marks/grades 用于记分系统) slightly higher than the mark/grade A, B, etc. 略高于（A、B 等）：*I got B plus (B+) in the test.* 我考试得了个 B+。OPP **minus**

■ *conj.* 🔑 (*informal*) used to add more information 而且；此外；况且 SYN **furthermore**：*I've got too much on at work. Plus my father is not well.* 我工作负担太重了，而且我父亲身体也不好。

plus[2] /pluː/

IDM **plus ça change** /ˌpluː sæ ˈʃɒ̃ʒ; *NAmE* sɑː ˈʃɑːnʒ/ (*saying, from French*) used as a way of saying that people and situations never really change over time, although they may appear to 变来变去还是老样子；表面虽变本质犹存

ˌplus 'fours *noun* [pl.] (*BrE*) wide loose trousers/pants that end just below the knees, where they fit closely, and that used to be worn, for example, by men playing GOLF （过膝下四英寸的）灯笼裤；宽大运动裤：*a pair of plus fours* 一条灯笼裤

plush /plʌʃ/ *noun, adj.*

■ *noun* [U] a type of silk or cotton cloth with a thick soft surface made of a mass of threads （丝或棉的）长毛绒：*red plush armchairs* 红色长毛绒扶手椅

■ *adj.* (*informal*) very comfortable; expensive and of good quality 舒适的；豪华的 SYN **luxurious**：*a plush hotel* 豪华的旅馆

ˌplus-ˈminus *adv.* (*SAfrE*) (used when you are giving a figure that is not exact) approximately（表示数字不十分准确）大约，差不多： *'How many people were there?' 'Plus-minus thirty.'* "当时有多少人？""三十人上下。"

Pluto /ˈpluːtəʊ; *NAmE* -toʊ/ *noun* one of a number of round objects in space that are not as large as planets but which go around the sun. In August 2006, the International Astronomical Union declared that Pluto should be called a DWARF PLANET because it is smaller and has different characteristics from the other planets in our SOLAR SYSTEM; in 2008 it declared that DWARF PLANETS further from the sun than Neptune could also be called plutoids. 冥王星（比行星小但围绕太阳旋转的星体之一。2006 年 8 月，国际天文学联合会宣布应将其称为矮行星，因为它比我们太阳系的其他行星小，而且有着不同的特点。2008 年，国际天文学联合会宣布较海王星离太阳更远的矮行星也可称为类冥矮行星。）

plu·toc·racy /pluːˈtɒkrəsi; *NAmE* -ˈtɑːk-/ *noun* (*pl.* **-ies**) **1** [U] government by the richest people of a country 富豪统治；财阀当政 **2** [C] a country governed by the richest people in it 富豪统治的国家

plu·to·crat /ˈpluːtəkræt/ *noun* (*often disapproving*) a person who is powerful because of their wealth 有钱有势的人；财阀

plu·toid /ˈpluːtɔɪd/ *noun* any DWARF PLANET that is further from the sun than the planet Neptune 类冥矮行星（指比海王星离太阳更远的矮行星）

plu·to·nium /pluːˈtəʊniəm; *NAmE* -ˈtoʊ-/ *noun* [U] (*symb.* **Pu**) a chemical element. Plutonium is RADIOACTIVE and is used in nuclear weapons and in producing nuclear energy. 钚（放射性化学元素）

ply /plaɪ/ *verb, noun*

■ *verb* (**plies, ply·ing, plied, plied**) **1** [I, T] (*literary* or *IndE*) (of ships, buses, etc. 船、公共汽车等) to travel regularly along a particular route or between two particular places 定时往来；定期行驶： **+ adv./prep.** *Ferries ply across a narrow strait to the island.* 渡船定时穿越狭窄的海峡驶向海岛。◇ *Buses ply regularly to and from these places.* 公交车定时往返于这些地方。◇ **~ sth** *canals plied by gondolas and steam boats* 有小划船和蒸汽船往来的运河 **2** [T] **~ sth** (*formal*) to use a tool, especially in a skilful way（娴熟地）使用： *The tailor delicately plied his needle.* 裁缝精巧地飞针走线。

IDM **ply your ˈtrade** to do your work or business 从事工作；做事 **ply for ˈhire/ˈtrade/ˈbusiness** (*BrE*) to look for customers, passengers, etc. in order to do business 招徕顾客；等生意： *taxis plying for hire outside the theatre* 在剧院外招揽乘客的出租车

PHRV **ˈply sb with sth 1** to keep giving sb large amounts of sth, especially food and/or drink 持续大量提供（食物、饮料等） **2** to keep asking sb questions 不停地提问： *He plied me with questions from the moment he arrived.* 他一到就不断地向我提问题。

■ *noun* [U] (especially in compounds 尤用于构成复合词) a measurement of wool, rope, wood, etc. that tells you how thick it is（毛线、绳子、木板等的计量单位）股，层，厚： *four-ply knitting yarn* 四股毛线

Ply·mouth Breth·ren /ˌplɪməθ ˈbreðrən/ *noun* [pl.] a strict Protestant group started in England around 1830 普利茅斯兄弟会（约 1830 年成立于英格兰的严格的基督教新教派别）

ply·wood /ˈplaɪwʊd/ *noun* [U] board made by sticking thin layers of wood on top of each other 胶合板；压合板；夹板： *plywood furniture* 胶合板家具

PM /ˌpiː ˈem/ *noun* (*informal, especially BrE*) the abbreviation for PRIME MINISTER 首相，总理（全写为 prime minister）： *an interview with the PM* 对首相的采访

p.m. 🔑 (*NAmE also* **P.M.**) /ˌpiː ˈem/ *abbr.* after 12 o'clock NOON (from Latin 'post meridiem') 下午，午后（源自拉丁文 post meridiem）： *The appointment is at 3 p.m.* 约会定于下午 3 点。➲ COMPARE A.M.

PMP /ˌpiː em ˈpiː/ *noun* the abbreviation for 'portable media player' (a piece of equipment that stores and plays sound and pictures) 便携式媒体播放器，PMP 播放器（全写为 portable media player，用于存储与播放声音和图像）

PMS /ˌpiː em ˈes/ (*also* **PMT** /ˌpiː em ˈtiː/ *BrE*) *noun* [U] physical and emotional problems such as pain and feeling depressed that many women experience before their PERIOD (= flow of blood) each month. PMS/PMT are abbreviations for 'premenstrual syndrome/tension'. 月经前综合征，经前紧张症（又称 PMT，全写为 premenstrual syndrome 或 premenstrual tension） ➲ SEE ALSO PREMENSTRUAL

pneu·mat·ic /njuːˈmætɪk; *NAmE* nuː-/ *adj.* [usually before noun] **1** filled with air 充气的： *a pneumatic tyre* 充气轮胎 **2** worked by air under pressure 由压缩空气操作的；气动的；风动的： *pneumatic tools* 风动工具

pneuˌmatic ˈdrill (*BrE*) (*NAmE* **jack·ham·mer**) *noun* a large powerful tool, worked by air pressure, used especially for breaking up road surfaces 气钻

pneu·mo·nia /njuːˈməʊniə; *NAmE* nuːˈmoʊ-/ *noun* [U] a serious illness affecting one or both lungs that makes breathing difficult 肺炎

PO /ˌpiː ˈəʊ; *NAmE* ˈoʊ/ *abbr.* **1** THE POST OFFICE 邮政部门；邮政系统 ➲ SEE ALSO PO BOX **2** POSTAL ORDER 汇票

poach /pəʊtʃ; *NAmE* poʊtʃ/ *verb* **1** [T] **~ sth** to cook food, especially fish, gently in a small amount of liquid 水煮，炖，煨（尤指鱼）： *poached salmon* 清炖鲑鱼 **2** [T] **~ sth** to cook an egg gently in nearly boiling water after removing its shell 水煮（荷包蛋） **3** [T, I] **~ (sth)** to illegally hunt birds, animals or fish on sb else's property or without permission（在他人地界）偷猎，偷捕： *The elephants are poached for their tusks.* 为获取象牙而偷猎大象。➲ WORDFINDER NOTE AT HUNT **4** [T, I] **~ (sb/sth) (from sb/sth)** to take and use sb/sth that belongs to sb/sth else, especially in a secret, dishonest or unfair way 盗用；挖走（人员等）： *The company poached the contract from their main rivals.* 这家公司窃取了其主要竞争对手的合同。◇ *Several of our employees have been poached by a rival firm.* 我们公司有好几名职员被对手公司给挖走了。◇ *I hope I'm not* **poaching on your territory** (= doing sth that is actually your responsibility). 但愿我没有侵犯你的职权。

poach·er /ˈpəʊtʃə(r); *NAmE* ˈpoʊtʃ-/ *noun* **1** a person who illegally hunts birds, animals or fish on sb's else's property 偷猎者；非法捕猎的人 **2** a special pan for POACHING eggs 水煮荷包蛋锅 **3** (*also* **ˈgoal poacher**) (especially in football (SOCCER) 尤指足球) a player who waits near the opposite team's goal in order to try to score if they get the ball（在对方球门附近伺机进球的）偷袭球员

IDM **poacher turned ˈgamekeeper** (*especially BrE*) a person who has changed from one situation or attitude to the opposite one, especially sb who used to oppose people in authority but is now in a position of authority 经过角色转换的人；当年造反今天掌权的人

ˌPˈO box (*also* **ˈpost office box**) *noun* used as a kind of address, so that mail can be sent to a post office where it is kept until it is collected 邮政信箱： *Radio Netherlands, PO Box 222, Hilversum* 希尔弗瑟姆邮政信箱 222 号，荷兰广播电台

pocked /pɒkt; *NAmE* pɑːkt/ *adj.* having holes or hollow marks on the surface （表面）有洞的，有坑的 SYN **pitted**

pocket 🔑 /ˈpɒkɪt; *NAmE* ˈpɑːk-/ *noun, verb*

■ *noun*

• **IN CLOTHING** 衣服 **1** 🔑 a small piece of material like a small bag sewn into or onto a piece of clothing so that you can carry things in it 衣袋；口袋；兜： *a coat pocket* 上衣口袋 ◇ *I put the note in my pocket.* 我把纸币装进了衣袋。◇ ***Turn out your pockets*** (= empty your pockets). 把口袋里的东西通通拿出来。◇ *Take your hands out of your pockets!* 不要把手插在口袋里！◇ *a pocket dictionary* (= one that is small enough to fit in your pocket) 袖珍词典 ➲ VISUAL VOCAB PAGE V68

• **SMALL CONTAINER** 小容器 **2** a small bag or container fastened to sth so that you can put things in it, for example, in a car door or in a bag（附在车门上、提包内等的）小口袋，小容器：*Information about safety procedures is in the pocket in front of you* (= on a plane). 安全求生的资料放在您前方的小袋子里。
• **MONEY** 钱 **3** [usually sing.] used to talk about the amount of money that you have to spend 钱财；财力；资金：*We have holidays to **suit every pocket**.* 我们有适合各种程度消费的度假方式。◇ *He had no intention of paying for the meal **out of his own pocket**.* 他不想自己掏腰包付饭钱。◇ *The Foundation is reputed to have very **deep pockets*** (= to have a lot of money). 据说这个基金会资金雄厚。
• **SMALL GROUP/AREA** 小团体 / 范围 **4** a small group or area that is different from its surroundings（与周围不同的）小组织，小区域：*There are still a few isolated pockets of resistance to the new regime.* 现在仍有零星孤立的势力反对新政权。◇ *a pocket of air* 气井 ➲ SEE ALSO AIR POCKET
• **IN BILLIARDS, ETC.** 台球等 **5** any of the holes or nets around the edges of the table used in the games of BILLIARDS, POOL or SNOOKER, which you have to hit the ball into 球袋；网袋 ➲ VISUAL VOCAB PAGE V44

IDM **be in sb's 'pocket** to be controlled or strongly influenced by sb 受某人的控制（或极大影响）；在某人掌握之中 **be/live in each other's 'pockets** (*BrE*) if two people are **in each other's pockets**, they are too close to each other or spend too much time with each other 过从甚密；形影不离 **have sb in your 'pocket** to have influence or power over sb, for example, a police officer or a politician, especially by threatening them or by offering them money 驾驭，让…听使唤（尤指通过恐吓或贿赂）**have sth in your 'pocket** to be certain to win sth 胜利在握；稳操胜券 **,in/,out of 'pocket** (*especially BrE*) having gained/lost money as a result of sth 得到 / 损失钱财：*That one mistake left him thousands of pounds out of pocket.* 那一次失误让他损失了数千英镑。➲ COMPARE OUT-OF-POCKET ➲ MORE AT BURN *v.*, DIP *v.*, HAND *n.*, LINE *v.*, PICK *v.*

■ *verb*
• **PUT INTO POCKET** 放入衣袋 **1** ~ **sth** to put sth into your pocket 把…放进衣袋：*She paid for the drink and pocketed the change without counting it.* 她付了饮料费，把找回的零钱数都没数就装进了口袋。
• **MONEY** 钱 **2** ~ **sth** to take or keep sth, especially an amount of money, that does not belong to you 攫取；揩油；中饱私囊：*He regularly charges passengers more than the normal fare and pockets the difference.* 他经常多收乘客票钱，把差额塞进自己的腰包。 **3** ~ **sth** to earn or win an amount of money 挣；赚下：*Last year, she pocketed over $1 million in advertising contracts.* 去年，她从广告合同中赚了 100 多万美元。
• **IN BILLIARDS, ETC.** 台球等 **4** ~ **sth** (in the games of BILLIARDS, POOL and SNOOKER 台球、普尔和斯诺克) to hit a ball into a POCKET (5) 击（球）入球袋 SYN **pot**

pock·et·book /ˈpɒkɪtbʊk; *NAmE* ˈpɑːk-/ *noun* **1** (*NAmE*) used to refer to the financial situation of a person or country. (In the past it was a small flat case for carrying papers or money.)（个人或国家的）财政状况，财力，钱袋子：*Many foreign goods are too expensive for American pocketbooks.* 许多外国货都太贵，与一般美国人的财力不符。◇ *The increase is likely to hit the pocketbooks of consumers.* 提价可能会砸到消费者的钱袋子。 **2** (*especially BrE*) a small book for writing in 记事本；小笔记本 SYN **notebook 3** (*old-fashioned, NAmE*) = HANDBAG

pock·et·ful /ˈpɒkɪtfʊl; *NAmE* ˈpɑːk-/ *noun* the amount a pocket holds 一衣袋（的量）：*a pocketful of coins* 一衣袋硬币

pock·et·knife /ˈpɒkɪtnaɪf; *NAmE* ˈpɑːk-/ *noun* (*especially NAmE*) = PENKNIFE

'pocket money *noun* [U] **1** (*especially BrE*) (*also* **al·low·ance** *especially in NAmE*) a small amount of money that parents give their children, usually every week or every month（父母给孩子的）零花钱 **2** a small amount of money that you can spend on things you need or want 零用钱；小额私用款 ➲ COMPARE SPENDING MONEY

'pocket-sized (*also* **'pocket-size**) *adj.* small enough to fit into your pocket or to be carried easily 袖珍的；便携的

,pocket 'veto *noun* (in the US) a method by which the President can stop a new law from being introduced by not signing it and keeping it until a session of Congress has finished 搁置否决（美国总统阻止新法律实施的一种方法，即不予签字并将其保留至国会休会后）

pock·mark /ˈpɒkmɑːk; *NAmE* ˈpɑːkmɑːrk/ *noun* a hollow mark on the skin, often caused by disease or infection（皮肤上的）痘痕，麻子，麻点，麻坑

'pock-marked *adj.* covered with hollow marks or holes 有麻子的；布满坑洞的：*a pock-marked face* 一张麻子脸 ◇ *The district is pock-marked with caves.* 这个地区布满了坑洞。

pod /pɒd; *NAmE* pɑːd/ *noun* **1** a long thin case filled with seeds that develops from the flowers of some plants, especially PEAS and BEANS 荚；豆荚；荚果：*a pea pod* 豌豆荚 ◇ *a vanilla pod* 香子兰蒴果 ➲ VISUAL VOCAB PAGES V34, V35 **2** a long narrow container that is hung under an aircraft and used to carry fuel, equipment, weapons, etc.（飞机的）吊舱，发射架 **3** part of a SPACECRAFT or a boat that can be separated from the main part 分离舱 **4** [C] a small group of sea animals, such as DOLPHINS or WHALES, swimming together（海豚或鲸等海洋动物的）一小群：*a pod of adult dolphins* 一小群成年海豚

pod·cast /ˈpɒdkɑːst; *NAmE* ˈpɑːdkæst/ *noun* a digital AUDIO file that can be taken from the Internet and played on a computer or a device that you can carry with you 播客：*To listen to the podcast, click on the link below.* 点击下面的链接收听播客。➲ WORDFINDER NOTE AT RADIO ➲ COLLOCATIONS AT EMAIL ➲ MORE LIKE THIS 1, page R25 ▸ **pod·caster** *noun*：*The US has an estimated 60 million podcasters.* 美国约有 6 000 万播客发布者。**pod·cast·ing** *noun* [U]: *Podcasting could turn into an audio form of blogging.* 播客制作可变成博客的有声形式。

podgy /ˈpɒdʒi; *NAmE* ˈpɑːdʒi/ (*BrE*) (*also* **pudgy** *NAmE, BrE*) *adj.* (*informal, usually disapproving*) slightly fat 微胖的：*podgy arms* 胖乎乎的胳膊

po·dia·trist /pəˈdaɪətrɪst/ *noun* (*especially NAmE*) = CHIROPODIST

po·dia·try /pəˈdaɪətri/ *noun* [U] (*especially NAmE*) = CHIROPODY

po·dium /ˈpəʊdiəm; *NAmE* ˈpoʊ-/ *noun* **1** a small platform that a person stands on when giving a speech or CONDUCTING an ORCHESTRA, etc. 讲台；讲坛；（乐队的）指挥台 SYN **rostrum 2** (*NAmE*) = LECTERN

Po·dunk /ˈpəʊdʌŋk; *NAmE* ˈpoʊ-/ *adj.* (*US, informal*) (of a town 小镇) small, dull and not important 无生气的；无足轻重的 ORIGIN From a place name of southern New England. 源自新英格兰南部地名波敦克。

poem /ˈpəʊɪm; *NAmE* ˈpoʊəm/ *noun* a piece of writing in which the words are chosen for their sound and the images they suggest, not just for their obvious meanings. The words are arranged in separate lines, usually with a repeated rhythm, and often the lines RHYME at the end. 诗；韵文 ➲ COLLOCATIONS AT LITERATURE

poesy /ˈpəʊəzi; -si; *NAmE* ˈpoʊ-/ *noun* [U] (*literary*) poetry 诗；诗篇

poet /ˈpəʊɪt; *NAmE* ˈpoʊət/ *noun* a person who writes poems 诗人

poet·ess /ˌpəʊɪˈtes; *NAmE* ˌpoʊəˈtes/ *noun* (*old-fashioned*) a woman who writes poems 女诗人

poet·ic /pəʊˈetɪk; *NAmE* poʊ-/ (*also less frequent* **poet·ical** /-ɪkl/) *adj.* **1** [only before noun] connected with poetry; being poetry 诗歌的；诗的：*poetic language* 诗歌语言 ◇ *Byron's Poetical Works* 拜伦诗作 **2** (*approving*) like or suggesting poetry, especially because it shows imagination and deep feeling 像诗一般的；富有诗意的 SYN **lyrical**: *There is a poetic quality to her playing.* 她的演奏富有诗意。IDM SEE LICENCE ▸ **poet·ic·al·ly** /-kli/ *adv.*

P

po,etic 'justice *noun* [U] a situation in which sth bad happens to sb, and you think that this is what they deserve 报应；应得的惩罚

po,etic 'licence (*NAmE* **po,etic 'license**) *noun* [U] the freedom to change facts, the normal rules of language, etc. in a special piece of writing or speech in order to achieve a particular effect （写作或演讲中的）破格修辞法，破格用语

poet·ics /pəʊ'etɪks; *NAmE* poʊ-/ *noun* [U] **1** the art of writing poetry 诗歌写作；诗艺 **2** the study of poetry, literature, etc. 诗学

,Poet 'Laureate *noun* **1** (especially in Britain) a person who has been officially chosen to write poetry for the country's important occasions 桂冠诗人（尤指英国正式选定为国家重要场合赋诗者） **2** (*especially NAmE*) a person whose poetry is considered to be the best, or most typical of their country or region （某国或地区的）最杰出诗人，代表诗人

poet·ry /'pəʊətri; *NAmE* 'poʊ-/ *noun* **1** [U] a collection of poems; poems in general 诗集；诗歌；诗作 SYN **verse**: *epic/lyric/pastoral, etc. poetry* 史诗、抒情诗、田园诗等 ◇ *Maya Angelou's poetry* 玛雅·安吉罗的诗作 ◇ *a poetry reading* 诗歌朗诵 ➲ COLLOCATIONS AT LITERATURE ➲ COMPARE PROSE ➲ WORDFINDER NOTE AT WRITE

> WORDFINDER 联想词： couplet, **image**, lyric, recite, refrain, rhyme, scansion, stanza, verse

2 [U, sing.] (*approving*) a beautiful and elegant quality 美好的品质；优雅的气质；诗意： *There was poetry in all her gestures.* 她一举一动都很优美。

po-faced /'pəʊ feɪst; *NAmE* 'poʊ/ *adj.* (*BrE, informal, disapproving*) looking very serious and as though you do not approve of sb/sth 一本正经的；不以为然的；孤傲的；板着脸的

pogo stick /'pəʊgəʊ stɪk; *NAmE* 'poʊgoʊ/ *noun* a pole with a bar to stand on and a spring at the bottom, that you jump around on for fun 蹦蹦跷；弹簧单高跷

pog·rom /'pɒgrəm; *NAmE* 'poʊg-/ *noun* the organized killing of large numbers of people, because of their race or religion (originally the killing of Jews in Russia) 大屠杀，集体迫害（因种族或宗教原因，原指沙俄时对犹太人的杀戮）

poign·ant /'pɔɪnjənt/ *adj.* having a strong effect on your feelings, especially in a way that makes you feel sad 令人沉痛的；悲惨的；酸楚的 SYN **moving**: *a* ***poignant*** *image/moment/memory, etc.* 悲惨的形象、时刻、回忆等 ◇ *Her face was a* ***poignant reminder*** *of the passing of time.* 她的容颜显示了时间的流逝，令人感伤。 ▶ **poign·ancy** /-jənsi/ *noun* [U]: *the poignancy of parting and separation* 别离的痛苦 ◇ *Of particular poignancy was the photograph of their son with his sisters, taken the day before he died.* 特别令人感伤的是他们的儿子去世前一天和姐妹们的合影。 **poign·ant·ly** /-jəntli/ *adv.*

poin·set·tia /,pɔɪn'setiə/ *noun* a tropical plant with large red or pink leaves that grow to look like flowers, often grown indoors in pots 一品红；猩猩木

point /pɔɪnt/ *noun, verb*

■ *noun*

• **OPINION/FACT** 看法；事实 **1** [C] a thing that sb says or writes giving their opinion or stating a fact 论点；观点；见解： *She* ***made*** *several interesting* ***points*** *in the article.* 她在文章中提出了几个有趣的观点。 ◇ ***I take your point*** (= understand and accept what you are saying). 我赞同你的看法。 ◇ *He's just saying that to* ***prove a point*** (= to show his idea is right). 他那样说只是为了证明他的看法。 ◇ *OK, you've* ***made your point!*** 好了，你已经把话说清楚了！ ➲ SEE ALSO TALKING POINT

• **MAIN IDEA** 要点 **2** [C] (*usually* **the point**) the main or most important idea in sth that is said or done 重点；要点；核心问题： ***The point is*** *you shouldn't have to wait so long to see a doctor.* 关键是看病不该等那么长时间。 ◇ *I wish he would* ***get to the point*** (= say it quickly). 但愿他快点说正题。 ◇ *I'll* ***come straight to the point:*** *we need more money.* 我就直说吧：我们还需要钱。 ◇ *Do you* ***see my point*** (= understand)? 你明白我的意思吗？ ◇ *I think I* ***missed the point*** (= did not understand). 我想我没听懂。 ◇ *You* ***have a point*** (= your idea is right)—*it would be better to wait till this evening.* 你说的有道理，还是等到今天晚上比较好。 ◇ *'There won't be anywhere to park.' 'Oh,* ***that's a (good) point.'*** (= I had not thought of that) "会找不到地方停车。" "嗯，还真是。" ◇ *It just isn't true. That's* ***the whole point*** (= the only important fact). 最重要的是，那根本不是事实。 ◇ *'He's been married before.'* ***'That's beside the point*** (= not important).' "他结过婚。" "那不重要。" ◇ *I know it won't cost very much but* ***that's not the point*** (= not the important thing). 我知道那花不了多少钱，但这不是重点。

• **PURPOSE** 目的 **3** [U, sing.] the purpose or aim of sth 意图；目的；理由： *What's the point of all this violence?* 这些暴行的意图何在？ ◇ *There's* ***no point*** *in getting angry.* 发火是没有用的。 ◇ ***I don't see the point of*** *doing it all again.* 我就不明白，再做一次有什么意义。 ◇ *The point of the lesson is to compare the two countries.* 本课的目的是比较这两个国家。 ➲ SYNONYMS AT PURPOSE

• **DETAIL** 细节 **4** [C] a particular detail or fact 具体细节（或事实）： *Here are the* ***main points*** *of the news.* 以下是新闻摘要。 ◇ *Can you explain that point again?* 你能再解释一下那一点吗？

• **QUALITY** 素质 **5** [C] a particular quality or feature that sb/sth has 特点；特性；特征： *Tact is not one of her* ***strong points.*** 她不善于圆通处事。 ◇ *Read the manual to learn the program's* ***finer points*** (= small details). 读一下指南，以了解这一程序的细节。 ◇ *Living in Scotland* ***has its good points*** *but the weather is not one of them.* 在苏格兰生活有其优点，但天气不好。 ◇ *One of the hotel's* ***plus points*** (= good features) *is that it is very central.* 这个旅馆的一大优点是它位于市中心。 ➲ SEE ALSO SELLING POINT

• **TIME** 时间 **6** [C] a particular time or stage of development 时刻；关头；瞬间；阶段： *The climber was* ***at/on the point of*** *death when they found him.* 当他们发现那个登山者的时候，他已奄奄一息。 ◇ *We were* ***on the point of*** *giving up.* 我们当时几乎要放弃了。 ◇ *Many people suffer from mental illness* ***at some point*** *in their lives.* 许多人在人生的某个阶段都会得精神疾病。 ◇ *We had* ***reached the point*** *when there was no money left.* 我们曾落到身无分文的地步。 ◇ ***At this point in time*** *we just have to wait.* 到这种时刻，我们只好等待了。 ◇ ***At this point*** *I don't care what you decide to do.* 到这个时候，我不在乎你决定要怎么做了。 ➲ SEE ALSO HIGH POINT, LOW POINT, SATURATION POINT, STARTING POINT, STICKING POINT, TURNING POINT

• **PLACE** 地方 **7** [C] a particular place or area 某地方；地点： *I'll wait for you at the meeting point in the arrivals hall.* 我将在到港大厅的迎接处等你。 ◇ *the point at which the river divides* 河流分叉点 ◇ *Draw a line from point A to point B.* 从 A 点到 B 点画一条线。 ◇ *No parking beyond this point.* 请勿越界停车。 ➲ SYNONYMS AT PLACE ➲ SEE ALSO FOCAL POINT, JUMPING-OFF POINT, THREE-POINT TURN, VANISHING POINT, VANTAGE POINT

• **DIRECTION** 方向 **8** [C] one of the marks of direction around a COMPASS （罗盘上的）罗经点，方位点： *the points of the compass* (= N, S, E, W, etc.) 罗盘上的罗经点

• **IN COMPETITION** 竞赛 **9** [C] (*abbr.* **pt**) an individual unit that adds to a score in a game or sports competition 得分；点： *to* ***win/lose a point*** 赢 / 输一分 ◇ *Australia finished 20 points ahead.* 澳大利亚队终局领先 20 分。 ◇ *They won* ***on points*** (= by scoring more points rather than by completely defeating their opponents). 他们以点数取胜。 ➲ SEE ALSO BROWNIE POINT, MATCH POINT

• **MEASUREMENT** 计量 **10** [C] a mark or unit on a scale of measurement （单位）点；标度： *The party's share of the vote fell by ten percentage points.* 该党的得票率下跌了十个百分点。 ➲ SEE ALSO BOILING POINT, FREEZING POINT, MELTING POINT

• **SHARP END** 尖儿 **11** [C] the sharp thin end of sth 尖端；尖头： *the point of a pencil/knife/pin* 铅笔 / 刀 / 大头针尖 ➲ VISUAL VOCAB PAGE V27 ➲ SEE ALSO BALLPOINT, GUNPOINT, KNIFEPOINT

- **LAND** 土地 **12** [C] (*also* **Point**) a narrow piece of land that stretches into the sea 岬角；尖地；海角：*The ship sailed around the point.* 那条船绕过了岬角。◇*Pagoda Point* 宝塔角
- **PUNCTUATION** 标点 **13** [C] a small dot used in writing, especially the dot that separates a whole number from the part that comes after it 小数点；点：*two point six* (*2.6*) 二点六 ◇ *a decimal point* 小数点 ◇ *We broadcast on ninety-five point nine* (*95.9*) *FM.* 我们以调频 95.9 播音。➲ SEE ALSO BULLET POINT, FULL STOP *n.*
- **OF LIGHT/COLOUR** 光；色 **14** [C] a very small dot of light or colour 光点；色点：*The stars were points of light in the sky.* 天空中的点点光亮就是星星。
- **FOR ELECTRICITY** 电 **15** [C] (*BrE*) a place in a wall, etc. where a piece of equipment can be connected to electricity（电源）插座：*a power/shaver/telephone point* 电源 / 剃须刀 / 电话插座
- **IN BALLET** 芭蕾舞 **16 points** [pl.] = POINTE
- **ON RAILWAY TRACK** 铁轨 **17 points** [pl.] (*BrE*) (*NAmE* **switch** [C]) a piece of track at a place where a railway/railroad line divides that can be moved to allow a train to change tracks 转辙器；道岔；尖轨
- **SIZE OF LETTERS** 字符大小 **18** [C] a unit of measurement for the size of letters in printing or on a computer screen, etc.（印刷物或计算机屏幕上字体大小的单位）点，磅值：*Change the text to 10 point.* 把文本字体大小变为10点。

IDM **if/when it comes to the 'point** used when you have to decide sth or say what you really think 必须作决定（或亮明观点）时：*When it comes to the point, he always changes his mind.* 他总是关键时候变卦。 **in point of 'fact** used to say what is true in a situation 实际上；其实：*In point of fact, she is their adopted daughter.* 实际上，她是他们的养女。 **make a 'point of doing sth** to be or make sure you do sth because it is important or necessary（因重要或必要）保证做，必定做：*I made a point of closing all the windows before leaving the house.* 我离家前必定要把所有的窗子都关好。 **ˌmore to the 'point** used to say that sth is more important than sth else 更为重要的是：*I couldn't do the job—I've never been to Spain and, more to the point, I don't speak Spanish.* 这个工作我做不了——我从未去过西班牙；而更重要的是，我不会说西班牙语。 **on point** (*NAmE*) appropriate or relevant to the situation 适合的；相关的；相符的：*The quotation was directly on point.* 这段话引用得恰到好处。◇ *Let's stay on point.* 咱们不要偏离主题。 **ˌpoint of 'contact** a place where you go or a person that you speak to when you are dealing with an organization 联系地点；联系人：*The receptionist is the first point of contact most people have with the clinic.* 多数人与诊所接触的第一个人是接待员。 **a ˌpoint of de'parture 1** a place where a journey starts 出发点 **2** (*formal*) an idea, a theory or an event that is used to start a discussion, an activity, etc. 抛砖引玉的事物；起点 **a ˌpoint of 'honour** a thing that sb considers to be very important for their honour or reputation 事关名誉的大事 **the ˌpoint of ˌno re'turn** the time when you must continue with what you have decided to do, because it is not possible to get back to an earlier situation 欲罢不能的时刻；已无退路；不可能回头 **ˌpoint 'taken** used to say that you accept that sb else is right when they have disagreed with you or criticized you（接受相反的意见）同意，好吧，算你有理：*Point taken. Let's drop the subject.* 好吧。咱们就抛开这个话题吧。 **to the 'point** expressed in a simple, clear way without any extra information or feelings 简明恰当；简洁中肯 **SYN** **pertinent**：*The letter was short and to the point.* 这封信简短扼要。 **to the 'point of** (**doing**) **sth** to a degree that can be described as sth 达到某种程度；近乎：*He was rude to the point of being aggressive.* 他粗鲁到蛮不讲理的地步。 **up to a** (**certain**) **'point** to some extent; to some degree but not completely 在某种程度上：*I agree with you up to a point.* 我在某种程度上同意你的看法。➲ MORE AT BELABOUR, CASE *n.*, FINE *adj.*, LABOUR *v.*, MOOT *adj.*, SCORE *v.*, SORE *adj.*, STRETCH *v.*

■ ***verb***

- **SHOW WITH FINGER** 用手指示意 **1** 🔑 [I, T, no passive] to stretch out your finger or sth held in your hand towards sb/sth in order to show sb where a person or thing is（用手指头或物体）指，指向：**~ (at/to/towards sb/sth)** *'What's your name?' he asked, pointing at the child with his pen.* 他用笔指着小孩问："你叫什么名字？"◇ *He pointed to the spot where the house used to stand.* 他指出那所房子原来所在的地方。◇ *She pointed in my direction.* 她指向我这边。◇ *It's rude to point!* 用手指人很不礼貌啊！◇ **~ sth** *She pointed her finger in my direction.* 她指着我这个方向。
- **AIM** 瞄准 **2** 🔑 [T] **~ sth** (**at sb/sth**) to aim sth at sb/sth 瞄准：*He pointed the gun at her head.* 他举枪对准了她的头。
- **FACE DIRECTION** 朝向 **3** 🔑 [I] **+ adv./prep.** to face in or be directed towards a particular direction 对着；朝向：*The telescope was pointing in the wrong direction.* 望远镜对错了方向。◇ *The signpost pointed straight ahead.* 路标直指前方。◇ *A compass needle points north.* 罗盘指针指向北方。
- **LEAD TO** 指引 **4** [I, T] to lead to or suggest a particular development or logical argument（意思上）指向；引导；指引：**+ adv./prep.** *The evidence seems to point in that direction.* 证据似乎指向那个方向。◇ **~ the way + adv./prep.** *The fans are looking to the new players to point the way to victory.* 球迷都在指望新球员打出胜利之路。
- **SHOW THE WAY** 指路 **5** [T] to show sb which way to go 指路；指点：**~ sb + adv./prep.** *I wonder if you could point me in the right direction for the bus station.* 请问您能指点我到公共汽车站往哪个方向走吗？◇ **~ the way + adv./prep.** *A series of yellow arrows pointed the way to reception.* 连续的黄色箭头标出了通往接待处的路。
- **WALL** 墙壁 **6** [T] **~ sth** to put MORTAR between the bricks of a wall（用灰泥）抹砖缝，勾缝

IDM **point a/the 'finger** (**at sb**) to accuse sb of doing sth 指责：*The article points an accusing finger at the authorities.* 那篇文章谴责了当局。

PHR V **ˌpoint sb/sth↔'out** (**to sb**) 🔑 to stretch your finger out towards sb/sth in order to show sb which person or thing you are referring to 指（给某人）看：*I'll point him out to you next time he comes in.* 他下次进来的时候，我指给你看。 **ˌpoint 'out** (**to sb**) | **ˌpoint sth↔'out** (**to sb**) 🔑 to mention sth in order to give sb information about it or make them notice it（向某人）指出：*She tried in vain to point out to him the unfairness of his actions.* 她试图向他指出他的做法不公正，但无济于事。◇ *He pointed out the dangers of driving alone.* 他指出单独驾车的危险性。◇ **point out** (**to sb**) **that...** *I should point out that not one of these paintings is original.* 我应当指出，这些画中没有一幅是真迹。◇ **+ speech** *'It's not very far,' she pointed out.* "那里不太远。"她说道。➲ LANGUAGE BANK AT ARGUE **'point to sth 1** to mention sth that you think is important and/or the reason why a particular situation exists 提出，指出（重要的事或理由）：*The board of directors pointed to falling productivity to justify their decision.* 董事会指出生产率下降一事为其决策辩护。 **2** to suggest that sth is true or likely 暗示；预示：*All the signs point to a successful year ahead.* 一切迹象都预示着来年将一帆风顺。 **ˌpoint sth↔'up** (*formal*) to emphasize sth so that it becomes more noticeable 强调；明确显示 **SYN** **highlight**：*The conference merely pointed up divisions in the party.* 这次会议只是显现了该党内部的分歧。

ˌpoint-and-'click *adj.* [usually before noun] (*computing* 计) able to be used with a mouse 可用鼠标的；可点击的

ˌpoint-and-'shoot *adj.* (of a camera 照相机) easy to use, without a person needing to adjust controls on it "傻瓜"型的；全自动的

ˌpoint-'blank *adj.* [only before noun] **1** (of a shot 射击) fired with the gun touching or very close to the person or thing it is aimed at 挨着的；近身的；近距离的：*The officer was shot dead **at point-blank range**.* 这位军官被近距离开枪打死。 **2** (of sth that is said 说的话) very definite and direct and not very polite 直截了当（缺乏礼貌）的 **SYN** **blunt**：*a point-blank refusal* 断然拒绝 ▶ **ˌpoint-'blank** *adv.*：*She fired point-blank at his chest.* 她抵住他的胸口开了枪。◇ *He refused point-blank to be photographed.* 他断然拒绝被拍照。

P

'point duty *noun* [U] (*BrE*) the job of controlling traffic that is done by a police officer standing in the middle of the road （交通警察的）站岗，值勤：*to be on point duty* 指挥交通

pointe /pwæ̃t/ *noun* [U] (*also* **pointes** /pwæ̃t/, **points** [pl.]) the hard tops of the toes of a kind of shoe that a BALLET dancer balances on （芭蕾舞鞋的）硬鞋尖

point·ed /ˈpɔɪntɪd/ *adj.* **1** having a sharp end 尖的；有尖头的：*a pointed chin* 尖下巴 ◇ *pointed teeth* 尖尖的牙齿 ◇ *a pointed instrument* 锐器 ➲ SEE ALSO POINTY **2** aimed in a clear and often critical way against a particular person or their behaviour 尖锐的；尖刻的；明确的：*a **pointed comment/remark*** 一针见血的评论 / 言论 ◇ *His words were a pointed reminder of her position.* 他的话刻意提醒了她的身份。

point·ed·ly /ˈpɔɪntɪdli/ *adv.* in a way that is clearly intended to show what you mean or to express criticism 明确地；尖锐地；直言不讳地：*She yawned and looked pointedly at her watch.* 她打了个哈欠，又刻意看了看手表。

point·er /ˈpɔɪntə(r)/ *noun* **1** (*informal*) a piece of advice 提示；建议：*Here are some pointers on how to go about the writing task.* 关于这项写作任务，有以下几点建议。 **2** ~ (**to sth**) a sign that sth exists; a sign that shows how sth may develop in the future 标志；迹象；兆头；动向：*The surge in car sales was regarded as an encouraging pointer to an improvement in the economy.* 汽车销售量的激增被视为经济回升的指标。 **3** a thin strip of metal that points to the numbers on a DIAL on a piece of equipment for measuring sth （刻度盘的）指针 **4** a stick used to point to things on a map or picture on a wall 指示杆 **5** (*computing* 计) a small symbol, for example an arrow, that marks a point on a computer screen 指针（光标） **6** a large dog used in hunting, trained to stand still with its nose pointing towards the birds that are being hunted 指示猎狗，指示犬（经训练用以指示猎物等）

'pointer finger *noun* (*NAmE*) a child's word for the INDEX FINGER （儿语）食指

'point guard *noun* (in BASKETBALL 篮球) the player who directs the team's attacking players （球队进攻的）控球后卫，组织后卫

poin·til·lism /ˈpɔɪntɪlɪzəm; ˈpwænt-/ *noun* [U] a style of painting that was developed in France in the late 19th century in which very small dots of colour are used to build up the picture 点彩画法，点描技法（19 世纪末叶兴起于法国的绘画风格） ▶ **poin·til·list** /-lɪst/ *adj.* **poin·til·list** /-lɪst/ *noun*：*Seurat, the French pointillist* 修拉，法国点彩派画家

point·ing /ˈpɔɪntɪŋ/ *noun* [U] the MORTAR that is put in the spaces between the bricks or stones in a wall; the method of filling in the spaces with MORTAR （勾墙砖、石缝用的）砂浆，灰浆；勾缝

'pointing device *noun* (*computing* 计) a mouse or other device which allows you to move the CURSOR on a computer screen 点击设备（如鼠标等）

point·less /ˈpɔɪntləs/ *adj.* having no purpose; not worth doing 无意义的；无目标的；不值得做的：*We searched until we knew it would be pointless to continue.* 我们搜索又搜索，直到觉得继续下去也枉然时才罢手。 ▶ **point·less·ly** *adv.*：*He argued pointlessly with his parents.* 他无谓地和父母争论。 **point·less·ness** *noun* [U]：*the pointlessness of war* 战争的无意义

'point man *noun* a soldier who goes in front of the others to look for danger 尖兵；先遣兵：(*figurative, NAmE*) *the President's point man on education* (= the person who is responsible for it) 总统在教育方面的特派员

ˌpoint of 'order *noun* (*pl.* **points of order**) (*formal*) a question about whether the rules of behaviour in a formal discussion or meeting are being followed correctly 议事规划问题；议事程序问题

ˌpoint of 'reference *noun* (*pl.* **points of reference**) something that you already know that helps you understand a situation or explain sth to sb 参照物；参考依据

ˌpoint of 'sale *noun* [usually sing.] the place where a product is sold 销售点；售货点：*More information on healthy foods should be provided **at the point of sale**.* 销售点应提供更多有关健康食品的资料。

ˌpoint of 'use *noun* [usually sing.] the place where a product or a service is actually used （产品的）使用地点；（服务的）提供地点：*Medical care is still free **at the point of use**.* 医疗保健在实际提供点仍然是免费的。

ˌpoint of 'view *noun* (*pl.* **points of view**) **1** the particular attitude or opinion that sb has about sth 观点；态度；意见；看法：*Why can't you ever see my point of view?* 你怎么老不明白我的观点呢？ ◇ *There are a number of different points of view on this issue.* 在这个问题上意见纷纭。 ◇ ***From my point of view*** (= as far as I was concerned), *the party was a complete success.* 依我看，这次聚会非常圆满。 **2** a particular way of considering or judging a situation 考虑角度；判断方法 SYN **angle**：*These statistics are important from an ecological point of view.* 从生态学的角度看，这些统计数字很重要。 ◇ *The book is written from the father's point of view.* 这本书是从父亲的角度写的。

ˌpoint-to-'point *noun* (*BrE*) a race on horses that goes over a marked course across fields and has fences or walls for the horses to jump over 定点越野赛马

pointy /ˈpɔɪnti/ *adj.* (*informal*) with a point at one end 尖的；有尖头的 SYN **pointed**：*pointy ears* 尖耳朵 ◇ (*humorous*) *Don't try to argue when you find yourself at the **pointy end** of a knife* (= when sb is threatening you with a knife). 有人用刀尖顶着你时，不要试图去争辩。

poise /pɔɪz/ *noun, verb*

■ ***noun*** [U] **1** a calm and confident manner with control of your feelings or behaviour 沉着自信；稳重；自若 **2** the ability to move or stand in an elegant way with good control of your body 优雅的举止；仪态

■ ***verb*** [I, T] to be or hold sth steady in a particular position, especially above sth else （尤指在…上方）保持（某种姿势）；（使）保持平稳：**+ adv./prep.** *The hawk poised in mid-air ready to swoop.* 老鹰在半空中盘旋，准备俯冲。 ◇ **~ sth/yourself to do sth** *He was poising himself to launch a final attack.* 他稳定住自己，以发动最后攻击。 ◇ **~ sth/yourself + adv./prep.** *She poised the javelin in her hand before the throw.* 她把标枪握稳，然后投了出去。

poised /pɔɪzd/ *adj.* **1** [not before noun] in a position that is completely still but is ready to move at any moment 处于准备状态；蓄势待发：**~ (on, above, over, etc. sth)** *Tina was tense, her hand poised over the telephone.* 蒂娜心情紧张，手悬在电话机上。 ◇ *He stopped writing and looked at me, pen poised.* 他不写了，手握钢笔望着我。 ◇ **~ to do sth** *The cat crouched in the grass, poised to jump.* 猫儿蹲踞在草丛中，准备跳跃。 **2** [not before noun] **~ (in, on, above, etc. sth)** in a position that is balanced but likely to change in one direction or another （暂时）平衡，稳固：*The cup was poised on the edge of the chair.* 杯子放在椅子边上，不稳当。 ◇ (*figurative*) *The world stood poised between peace and war.* 世界处于战争与和平之间。 **3** [not before noun] completely ready for sth or to do sth 有充分准备；准备好；蓄势待发 SYN **set**：**~ for sth** *The economy is poised for recovery.* 经济呈复苏之势。 ◇ **~ to do sth** *Kate is poised to become the highest-paid supermodel in the fashion world.* 凯特已准备好成为时装界最高薪的超级模特儿。 **4** having a calm and confident manner and in control of your feelings and behaviour 泰然自若的；沉着自信的；稳健的 SYN **assured**：*He is a remarkably poised young man.* 他是个特别稳健的年轻人。

poi·son /ˈpɔɪzn/ *noun, verb*

■ ***noun*** [C, U] **1** a substance that causes death or harm if it is swallowed or absorbed into the body 毒物；毒药；毒素：*Some mushrooms contain a deadly poison.* 有些蘑菇含有致命毒素。 ◇ *How did he die? Was it poison?* 他是怎么死的？是中毒吗？ ◇ *The dog was killed by rat poison* (= poison intended to kill RATS). 狗被耗子药毒死了。 ◇ *to hunt with poison arrows* 用毒箭狩猎 ◇ *bombs* *containing poison gas* 毒气弹 **2** an idea, a feeling, etc. that is extremely harmful 极有害的思想（或心情等）；精神毒药：*the poison of racial hatred* 种族仇恨这种害人的思想

IDM **what's your 'poison?** (*informal, humorous*) used to ask sb what alcoholic drink they would like （用于问别人想喝什么酒） ➲ MORE AT MAN *n.*

■ *verb* **1** ~ **sb/yourself** (**with sth**) to harm or kill a person or an animal by giving them poison 毒死；毒害 **2** ~ **sth** to put poison in or on sth 下毒；在…中放毒：*a poisoned arrow* 毒箭 ◇ *Someone had been poisoning his food.* 有人一直在他的食物里下毒。◇ *Large sections of the river have been poisoned by toxic waste from factories.* 工厂的有毒废弃物污染了大段大段的河流。 **3** ~ **sth** to have a bad effect on sth 毒化；败坏；使恶化：*His comment served only to poison the atmosphere still further.* 他的评论只是令气氛更加恶化了。◇ *She succeeded in* ***poisoning their minds*** *against me.* 她成功地令他们仇视我。

IDM **a poisoned 'chalice** (*especially BrE*) a thing that seems attractive when it is given to sb but which soon becomes unpleasant 金杯毒酒

poi·son·er /'pɔɪzənə(r)/ *noun* a person who murders sb by using poison 投毒杀人者；毒死别人的人

poi·son·ing /'pɔɪzənɪŋ/ *noun* [U, C] **1** the fact or state of having swallowed or absorbed poison 中毒；服毒：*a series of deaths caused by carbon monoxide poisoning* 一氧化碳中毒引起的一连串死亡 ◇ *At least 10 000 children are involved in accidental poisonings every year.* 每年至少有 1 万名儿童意外中毒。 **2** the act of killing or harming sb/sth by giving them poison 毒害；毒杀；投毒：*The police suspected poisoning.* 警方怀疑有人下毒。◇ *The rats were controlled by poisoning.* 用毒杀法使老鼠受到控制。 ➲ SEE ALSO BLOOD POISONING, FOOD POISONING

ˌpoison 'ivy *noun* [U] a N American climbing plant that causes painful spots on the skin when you touch it 毒常春藤，气根毒藤（原产于北美，接触后会引起皮炎）

ˌpoison 'oak *noun* [U] a N American bush that causes painful spots on the skin when you touch it 栎叶漆，毒栎（原产于北美，接触后会引起皮炎）

poi·son·ous /'pɔɪzənəs/ *adj.* **1** causing death or illness if swallowed or absorbed into the body 引起中毒的；有毒的 SYN **toxic**：*poisonous chemicals/plants* 有毒化学品 / 植物 ◇ *This gas is highly poisonous.* 这种气体有剧毒。◇ *The leaves of certain trees are poisonous to cattle.* 某些树的叶子会毒害牛。 **2** (of animals and insects 动物和昆虫) producing a poison that can cause death or illness if the animal or insect bites you 分泌毒素的；能毒伤人的 SYN **venomous**：*poisonous snakes* 毒蛇 **3** extremely unpleasant or unfriendly 极端讨厌（或不友善）的；恶毒的；邪恶的：*the poisonous atmosphere in the office* 办公室里的恶劣气氛

ˌpoison 'pen letter *noun* an unpleasant letter that is not signed and is intended to upset the person who receives it 恶意的匿名信；匿名诽谤信

ˌpoison 'pill *noun* (*informal, business* 商) a form of defence used by a company to prevent, or to reduce the effect of, a TAKEOVER bid that they do not want, for example by selling some of their important possessions （公司为防止被兼并而采取的）自戕式防御；（出售某些重要财产以求最终自保的）掏空政策

poke /pəʊk; *NAmE* poʊk/ *verb, noun*

■ *verb* **1** [T] to quickly push your fingers or another object into sb/sth （用手指或其他东西）捅，戳，杵 SYN **prod**：~ **sb/sth with sth** *She poked him in the ribs with her elbow.* 她用胳膊肘顶他的肋部。◇ ~ **sth into sth** *She poked her elbow into his ribs.* 她用胳膊肘顶他的肋部。◇ ~ **sb/sth** *I'm sick of being poked and prodded by doctors.* 我讨厌让医生在我身上戳戳点点的。◇ *She got up and poked the fire* (= to make it burn more strongly). 她起来拨了拨火。 **2** [T] ~ **sth + adv./prep.** to push sth somewhere or move it in a particular direction with a small quick movement 推；捅；戳；探：*He poked his head around the corner to check that nobody was coming.* 他从转角处探出头来，查看有没有人过来。◇ *Someone had poked a message under the door.* 有人从门底下塞进了一张纸条。◇ *Don't poke her eye out with that stick!* 别让那根棍子戳着她的眼睛！ **3** [I] **+ adv./prep.** if an object is **poking out of, through, etc.** sth, you can see a part of it that is no longer covered by sth else 露出；伸出；探出：*The end of the cable was left poking out of the wall.* 电缆头从墙里露出来了。◇ *Clumps of grass poked up through the snow.* 一簇簇的草破雪而出。 **4** [T] ~ **a hole in sth** (**with sth**) to make a hole in sth by pushing your finger or another object into it 捅窟窿；扎洞：*The kids poked holes in the ice with sticks.* 孩子们用棍子在冰上戳洞。 **5** [T] ~ **sb** (*taboo, slang*) (of a man 男人) to have sex with sb 与（某人）性交

IDM **poke 'fun at sb/sth** to say unkind things about sb/sth in order to make other people laugh at them 拿…开心；奚落；嘲弄 SYN **ridicule**：*Her novels poke fun at the upper class.* 她的小说嘲弄上流社会。 ➲ MORE AT NOSE *n.*

PHR V **ˌpoke a'bout/a'round** (*informal*) to look for sth, especially sth that is hidden among other things that you have to move 搜查；翻找：*The police spent the day poking around in his office but found nothing.* 警察花了一天时间搜查他的办公室，但一无所获。◇ (*figurative*) *We've had journalists poking around and asking a lot of questions.* 我们让记者追着问了许多问题。 **'poke at sth** to push a pointed object, your finger, etc. at sth repeatedly with small quick movements （用手指、物件等反复地）捅，戳，扎：*He poked at the spaghetti with a fork.* 他用叉子拨弄着意大利细面条。

■ *noun* **1** [C, usually sing.] the action of quickly pushing your fingers or another object into sb/sth 捅；戳；拨；挑：*to give the fire a poke* 拨一拨火 ◇ *He gave me a poke in the ribs to wake me up.* 他捅了一下我的肋部把我叫醒。 **2** [U] (*BrE*) power in a car （汽车的）马力，推进力：*I prefer something with a bit more poke.* 我想要马力再大些的。

IDM **have a ˌpoke a'round** (*informal*) to look carefully around a place to see what you can find; to try to find out information about sb/sth 仔细寻觅；探究；打探 **take a 'poke at sb/sth** (*old-fashioned, NAmE, informal*) to make an unkind remark about sb/sth; to laugh at sb/sth 嘲弄；奚落；嘲笑 ➲ MORE AT PIG *n.*

poker /'pəʊkə(r); *NAmE* 'poʊ-/ *noun* **1** [U] a card game for two or more people, in which the players bet on the values of the cards they hold 扑克牌游戏 **2** [C] a metal stick for moving or breaking up coal in a fire 通条；拨火棍

'poker-faced *adj.* (*informal*) with an expression on your face that does not show what you are thinking or feeling 不露声色的；毫无表情的 ▶ **'poker face** *noun*：*He maintained a poker face.* 他一直面无表情。

poky /'pəʊki; *NAmE* 'poʊki/ *adj.* (*informal*) (**poki·er, poki·est**) **1** (*especially BrE*) (of a room or a building 屋子或建筑物) too small; without much space 狭窄的；窄小的 SYN **cramped**：*a poky little room* 窄小的屋子 **2** (*also* **pokey**) (*both NAmE*) extremely slow and annoying 极慢的；迟钝的；拖沓的；慢腾腾的

pol /pɒl; *NAmE* pɑːl/ *noun* (*NAmE, informal*) = POLITICIAN (1)

Po·lack /'pəʊlæk; *NAmE* 'poʊ-/ *noun* (*taboo, slang, especially NAmE*) an offensive word for a person from Poland, or a person of Polish origin 波兰佬（含冒犯意，指波兰人或波兰后裔）

polar /'pəʊlə(r); *NAmE* 'poʊ-/ *adj.* [only before noun] **1** connected with, or near the North or South Pole 极地的；近地极的；南极（或北极）的：*the polar regions* 极区 ◇ *polar explorers* 极地探险家 **2** (*specialist*) connected with the POLES (= the positive and negative ends) of a MAGNET 磁极的：*polar attraction* 极向引力 **3** (*formal*) used to describe sth that is the complete opposite of sth else 完全相反的；截然对立的：*The parents' position is often the polar opposite of the child's.* 父母的观点常与孩子的完全相反。

'polar bear *noun* a white BEAR that lives near the North Pole 北极熊；白熊

po·lar·ity /pəˈlærəti/ *noun* [U] **1** ~ **(between A and B)** (*formal*) the situation when two tendencies, opinions, etc. oppose each other（两种倾向、意见等的）截然对立，两极化：*the growing polarity between the left and right wings of the party* 党内左右两派间日益明显的对立 **2** [U, C] (*physics* 物) the condition of having two POLES with opposite qualities 极性（两极并存的状态）

po·lar·ize (*BrE also* **-ise**) /ˈpəʊləraɪz; *NAmE* ˈpoʊ-/ *verb* **1** [I, T] to separate or make people separate into two groups with completely opposite opinions （使）两极化，截然对立：*Public opinion has polarized on this issue.* 在这个问题上公众意见已呈两极化。◇ ~ **sth** *The issue has polarized public opinion.* 这个问题已使公众意见两极化。 **2** [T] ~ **sth** (*physics* 物) to make waves of light, etc. VIBRATE in a single direction 使（光波等）偏振 **3** [T] ~ **sth** (*physics* 物) to give polarity to sth 使（物体）极化：*to polarize a magnet* 使磁体极化 ▶ **po·lar·iza·tion, -isa·tion** /ˌpəʊləraɪˈzeɪʃn; *NAmE* ˌpoʊlərəˈz-/ *noun* [U, C]

Po·lar·oid™ /ˈpəʊlərɔɪd; *NAmE* ˈpoʊ-/ *noun* **1** [C] (*also* ˌ**Polaroid** ˈ**camera**) a camera that can produce a photograph within a few seconds 宝丽来照相机；拍立得照相机 **2** [C] a photograph that has been taken with a Polaroid camera 宝丽来一次成像照片；拍立得相片 **3** [U] a transparent substance that is put on SUNGLASSES and car windows to make the sun seem less bright（太阳镜或汽车玻璃上的）偏光薄膜：*Polaroid sunglasses* 偏光膜太阳镜 **4** **Polaroids** [pl.] (*also* ˌ**Polaroid** ˈ**sunglasses**) SUNGLASSES that have a layer of Polaroid on them 偏光膜太阳镜；贴膜太阳镜

pole /pəʊl; *NAmE* poʊl/ *noun, verb*

■ ***noun*** **1** a long thin straight piece of wood or metal, especially one with the end placed in the ground, used as a support 竿；杆子；杖；篙：*a tent pole* 帐篷支柱 ◇ *a ski pole* 滑雪杖 ◇ *a curtain pole* 窗帘杆 ⊃ VISUAL VOCAB PAGES V22, V60 ⊃ SEE ALSO BARGEPOLE, FLAGPOLE, TELEGRAPH POLE, TOTEM POLE (1) **2** either of the two points at the opposite ends of the line on which the earth or any other planet turns （行星的）极；地极：*the North/South Pole* 北极；南极 **3** (*physics* 物) either of the two ends of a MAGNET, or the positive or negative points of an electric battery 磁极；电极 **4** either of two opposite or contrasting extremes （对立或相反的）任何一方；极端：*Their opinions were at opposite poles of the debate.* 他们的意见在辩论中截然相反。

IDM **be ˈpoles apart** to be widely separated; to have no interests that you share 天南地北；南辕北辙；截然相反 **up the ˈpole** (*old-fashioned, BrE, informal*) crazy 发狂的；疯狂的 ⊃ MORE AT GREASY, TOUCH *v.*

■ ***verb*** [T, I] ~ **(sth)** + **adv./prep.** to move a boat by pushing on the bottom of a river, etc. with a pole 用篙撑船；摆船

pole·axe (*BrE*) (*US* **pole·ax**) /ˈpəʊlæks; *NAmE* ˈpoʊl-/ *verb* **1** ~ **sb** to hit sb very hard so that they fall down and cannot stand up again 打垮；击倒 **2** [usually passive] ~ **sb** to surprise or shock you so much that you do not know what to say or do 使惊慌失措；使手足无措 SYN **dumbfound**

pole·cat /ˈpəʊlkæt; *NAmE* ˈpoʊl-/ *noun* **1** a small European wild animal with a long thin body, dark brown fur and a strong unpleasant smell 艾鼬，臭貂（体长，有臭味） **2** (*NAmE*) = SKUNK

ˈ**pole dancing** *noun* [U] sexually exciting dancing that is performed in a bar or club, with the dancer moving his or her body around a long pole 钢管舞（在酒吧或夜总会跳的艳舞，舞者绕长杆扭动身体） ▶ ˈ**pole dancer** *noun*

po·lem·ic /pəˈlemɪk/ *noun* (*formal*) **1** [C] a speech or a piece of writing that argues very strongly for or against sth/sb 激烈争论；辩论文章；论战 **2** [U] (*also* **polemics** [pl.]) the practice or skill of arguing strongly for or against sth/sb 辩论术；辩论法：*Her speech was memorable for its polemic rather than its substance.* 她的演说之所以令人难忘，不是因其内容而是因其辩论方法。

po·lem·ic·al /pəˈlemɪkl/ (*also less frequent* **po·lem·ic**) *adj.* (*formal*) involving strong arguments for or against sth, often in opposition to the opinion of others 争论的；挑起辩论的

po·lemi·cist /pəˈlemɪsɪst/ *noun* (*formal*) a person who makes skilful use of POLEMIC 善于辩论的人；善辩者；有辩才的人

po·lenta /pəˈlentə/ *noun* [U] **1** a yellow food made with MAIZE (CORN) flour, used in Italian cooking （意大利烹饪中的）玉米糊 **2** the flour used to make polenta 玉米粉

ˈ**pole position** *noun* [U, C] the leading position at the start of a race involving cars or bicycles （汽车、自行车比赛的）杆位，首发位置

the ˈPole Star *noun* [sing.] the star that is above the North Pole in the sky 北极星

the ˈpole vault *noun* [sing.] a sporting event in which people try to jump over a high bar, using a long pole to push themselves off the ground 撑竿跳高 ⊃ VISUAL VOCAB PAGE V50 ▶ ˈ**pole-vaulter** *noun* ˈ**pole-vaulting** *noun* [U]

po·lice /pəˈliːs/ *noun, verb*

■ ***noun*** (*often* **the police**) [pl.] an official organization whose job is to make people obey the law and to prevent and solve crime; the people who work for this organization 警察部门；警方：*A man was arrested by the police and held for questioning.* 一名男子被警方逮捕并拘押讯问。◇ *Get out of the house or **I'll call the police**.* 滚出这所房子，不然我就叫警察了。◇ *Police suspect a local gang.* 警方怀疑当地的一个不良帮派。◇ ***a police car*** 警车 ◇ *Hundreds of police in riot gear struggled to control the violence.* 数以百计的警察身披防暴装备，奋力镇压暴乱。 ⊃ SEE ALSO SECRET POLICE ⊃ WORDFINDER NOTE AT LAW

> **WORDFINDER** 联想词：arrest, charge, cordon, detain, detective, interrogate, plain clothes, raid, undercover

■ ***verb*** **1** ~ **sth** (of the police, army, etc. 警察、军队等) to go around a particular area to make sure that nobody is breaking the law there 巡查；维护治安：*The border will be policed by UN officials.* 边境将由联合国官员巡查。 **2** ~ **sth** (of a committee, etc. 委员会等) to make sure that a particular set of rules is obeyed 监督；监管 SYN **monitor**：*The profession is policed by its own regulatory body.* 这个行业由其自律机构监督。

poˈlice commissioner *noun* (*especially NAmE*) = COMMISSIONER (2)

poˌlice ˈconstable (*also* **constable**) *noun* (*abbr.* **PC**) (in Britain and some other countries) a police officer of the lowest rank （英国和其他一些国家的）警察，警员：*Police Constable Jordan* 警员乔丹

poˈlice department *noun* (in the US) the police organization of a particular city （美国城市中的）警察局

poˈlice dog *noun* a dog that is trained to find or attack suspected criminals 警犬

poˈlice force *noun* the police organization of a country, district or town （国家、地区或城镇的）警力，警察部队

po·lice·man /pəˈliːsmən/ *noun* (*pl.* **-men** /-mən/) a male police officer （男）警察 ⊃ NOTE AT GENDER ⊃ MORE LIKE THIS 25, page R28

poˈlice officer (*also* **officer**) *noun* a member of the police 警察；警员 ⊃ MORE LIKE THIS 25, page R28

poˈlice state *noun* (*disapproving*) a country where people's freedom, especially to travel and to express political opinions, is controlled by the government, with the help of the police 警察国家（通过警察部门控制人民旅行及言论等自由）

poˈlice station (*NAmE also* ˈ**station house**) *noun* the office of a local police force 警察局；派出所：*The suspect was taken to the nearest police station for questioning.* 嫌疑犯被带到最近的警察局讯问。

po·lice·wo·man /pəˈliːswʊmən/ *noun* (*pl.* **-women** /-wɪmɪn/) a female police officer 女警察 ➲ NOTE AT GENDER ➲ **MORE LIKE THIS** 25, page R28

po·licing /pəˈliːsɪŋ/ *noun* [U] **1** the activity of keeping order in a place with police （用警察）维护治安；治安保卫： *community policing* 社区治安维护 **2** the activity of controlling an industry, an activity, etc. to make sure that people obey the rules （对行业、活动等的）监督，管理，检查

pol·icy 🔑 AW /ˈpɒləsi; *NAmE* ˈpɑːl-/ *noun* (*pl.* **-ies**) **1** 🔑 [C, U] ~ (**on sth**) a plan of action agreed or chosen by a political party, a business, etc. 政策；方针： *the present government's policy on education* 现政府的教育政策 ◇ *The company has **adopted a firm policy** on shoplifting.* 那家公司对店内行窃采取了严厉的措施。 ◇ *We have tried to **pursue a policy** of neutrality.* 我们设法奉行中立的政策。 ◇ *US **foreign/domestic policy*** 美国的外交 / 国内政策 ◇ *They have had a significant **change in policy** on paternity leave.* 他们对男人陪产假制度作了重大改变。 ◇ *a policy document* 政策文件 ➲ **COLLOCATIONS** AT POLITICS **2** [C, U] (*formal*) a principle that you believe in that influences how you behave; a way in which you usually behave 原则；为人之道： *She is following her usual policy of ignoring all offers of help.* 她遵循着自己的一贯原则，对于他人的主动帮助一概不予理睬。 ◇ (*saying*) *Honesty is the best policy.* 诚实为上。 **3** 🔑 [C] a written statement of a contract of insurance 保险单： *Check the terms of the policy before you sign.* 仔细阅读保险单的条款后再签字。 ➲ **WORDFINDER NOTE** AT INSURANCE

pol·icy·hold·er /ˈpɒləsihəʊldə(r); *NAmE* ˈpɑːləsihoʊl-/ *noun* (*formal*) a person or group that holds an insurance policy 保险单持有人（或机构）

polio /ˈpəʊliəʊ; *NAmE* ˈpoʊlioʊ/ (*also formal* **polio·my·el·itis** /ˌpəʊliəʊˌmaɪəˈlaɪtɪs; *NAmE* ˌpoʊlioʊ-/) *noun* [U] an infectious disease that affects the central nervous system and can cause temporary or permanent PARALYSIS (= loss of control or feeling in part or most of the body) 脊髓灰质炎；小儿麻痹症

pol·ish 🔑 /ˈpɒlɪʃ; *NAmE* ˈpɑːl-/ *noun, verb*

■ ***noun*** **1** 🔑 [U, C] a substance used when rubbing a surface to make it smooth and shiny 擦光剂；上光剂；亮光剂： ***furniture/floor/shoe/silver polish*** 家具上光漆；地板蜡；鞋油；银光剂 ◇ *wax polish* 亮光蜡 ➲ SEE ALSO FRENCH POLISH, NAIL POLISH ➲ **VISUAL VOCAB** PAGE V65 **2** 🔑 [sing.] an act of polishing sth 抛光；上光；擦亮： *I give it a polish now and again.* 我不时把它抛一抛光。 **3** [sing.] the shiny appearance of sth after it has been polished 擦光的面；打磨光亮的面 SYN **lustre, sheen** **4** [U] a high quality of performance achieved with great skill （表演的）完美，娴熟，精湛 SYN **brilliance**： *She played the cello with the polish of a much older musician.* 她演奏大提琴颇有资深演奏家的风范。 **5** [U] high standards of behaviour; being polite 文雅；优雅；品味；礼貌 SYN **refinement** IDM SEE SPIT *n.*

■ ***verb*** **1** 🔑 [T, I] to make sth smooth and shiny by rubbing it 擦光；磨光；抛光： ~ (**sth**) *Polish shoes regularly to protect the leather.* 要经常擦鞋，以保护皮革。 ◇ ~ **sth** (**up**) (**with sth**) *He polished his glasses with a handkerchief.* 他用手绢揩拭眼镜。 ➲ SEE ALSO FRENCH POLISH **2** [T] to make changes to sth in order to improve it 修改；润饰；润色： ~ **sth** *The statement was carefully polished and checked before release.* 这项声明是经仔细润色检查后才发表的。 ◇ ~ **sth up** *The hotel has polished up its act* (= improved its service) *since last year.* 这家酒店自去年以来已经改善了服务水平。

PHR V ˌ**polish sb**↔ˈ**off** (*informal, especially NAmE*) to kill sb 干掉；杀死 ˌ**polish sth**↔ˈ**off** (*informal*) to finish sth, especially food, quickly 很快做完；（尤指）迅速吃光： *He polished off the remains of the apple pie.* 他把剩下的苹果派赶快吃完。

pol·ished /ˈpɒlɪʃt; *NAmE* ˈpɑːl-/ *adj.* **1** shiny as a result of polishing 抛光的；磨光的；擦亮的 SYN **gleaming** **2** elegant, confident and/or highly skilled 优雅的；娴熟的 SYN **fine**

pol·ish·er /ˈpɒlɪʃə(r); *NAmE* ˈpɑːl-/ *noun* a machine for polishing sth 上光机；磨光机；打蜡机： *a floor polisher* 地板上光机

pol·it·buro /ˈpɒlɪtbjʊərəʊ; *NAmE* ˈpɑːlɪtbjʊroʊ/ *noun* (*pl.* **-os**) the most important committee of a Communist party, with the power to decide on policy （共产党的）政治局

po·lite 🔑 /pəˈlaɪt/ *adj.* (**po·liter, po·litest**) HELP **more polite** and **most polite** are also common * more polite 和 most polite 也常用。 **1** 🔑 having or showing good manners and respect for the feelings of others 有礼貌的；客气的；儒雅的 SYN **courteous**： *Please be polite to our guests.* 请礼貌待客。 ◇ *We were all too polite to object.* 我们都太客气了，没有反对。 OPP **impolite** **2** 🔑 socially correct but not always sincere 应酬的；礼节性的；客套的： *I don't know how to make **polite conversation**.* 我不晓得怎么说应酬话。 ◇ *The performance was greeted with polite applause.* 这场演出得到了礼貌性的掌声。 **3** [only before noun] from a class of society that believes it is better than others 上流社会的： *'Bum' is not a word we use in polite company.* "屁股"可不是我们当着文雅人的面说的字眼。 ▶ **po·lite·ly** 🔑 *adv.* **po·lite·ness** *noun* [U]

poli·tesse /ˌpɒlɪˈtes; *NAmE* ˌpɑːl-/ *noun* [U] (*from French, literary*) formal politeness 正规礼节

pol·it·ic /ˈpɒlətɪk; *NAmE* ˈpɑːl-/ *adj.* (*formal*) (of actions 行为) based on good judgement 谨慎的；得当的；明智的 SYN **prudent, wise**： *It seemed politic to say nothing.* 沉默似乎是上策。 ➲ SEE ALSO BODY POLITIC

pol·it·ical 🔑 /pəˈlɪtɪkl/ *adj.* **1** 🔑 connected with the state, government or public affairs 政治的；政府的；政权的： *a monarch without political power* 没有政治权力的君主 ◇ *He was a **political prisoner*** (= one who was put in prison because he was thought to be harmful to the state). 他曾是个政治犯。 **2** 🔑 connected with the different groups working in politics, especially their policies and the competition between them 政党的；党派的： *a political debate/party/leader* 政治辩论 / 党派 / 领袖 ◇ *What are your political sympathies?* 你认同哪个政党？ **3** (of people 人) interested in or active in politics 关心政治的；政治上活跃的： *She became very political at university.* 她上大学时开始十分热衷于政治。 ◇ *I'm not a **political animal*** (= person who is interested in politics). 我对政治没兴趣。 **4** concerned with power, status, etc. within an organization, rather than with matters of principle 争权夺利的；人事纠纷的： *I suspect that he was dismissed for political reasons.* 我怀疑他被解职是人事上的原因。 ➲ SEE ALSO POLITICALLY

poˌ**litical** ˈ**action committee** *noun* (*abbr.* **PAC**) (in the US) a group of people who collect money to support the candidates and policies that will help them achieve their political and social aims 政治行动委员会（美国组织，为所支持的公职候选人筹集资金）

poˌ**litical a**ˈ**sylum** *noun* [U] (*formal*) = ASYLUM (1)

poˌ**litical cor**ˈ**rectness** *noun* [U] (*sometimes disapproving*) the principle of avoiding language and behaviour that may offend particular groups of people 政治上正确，政治正确性（指言行上避免有歧视之嫌）

poˌ**litical e**ˈ**conomy** *noun* [U] the study of how nations organize the production and use of wealth 政治经济学

poˌ**litical ge**ˈ**ography** *noun* [U] the way in which the world is divided into different countries, especially as a subject of study 政治地理学

pol·it·ic·al·ly 🔑 /pəˈlɪtɪkli/ *adv.* in a way that is connected with politics 政治上： *a politically sensitive issue* 一个政治上敏感的议题 ◇ *politically motivated crimes* 政治犯罪 ◇ *It makes sense politically as well as economically.* 这在经济上和政治上都有道理。

P

po,litically cor'rect *adj.* (*abbr.* **PC**) used to describe language or behaviour that deliberately tries to avoid offending particular groups of people 政治上正确的（指言行上避免有歧视之嫌）

po,litically incor'rect *adj.* failing to avoid language or behaviour that may offend particular groups of people 政治上不正确的（指言行上有歧视之嫌）

po,litical 'science (*also* **pol·it·ics**) *noun* [U] the study of government and politics 政治学

po,litical 'scientist *noun* an expert in political science 政治学家

pol·it·ician /ˌpɒləˈtɪʃn; *NAmE* ˌpɑːl-/ *noun* **1** (*also NAmE, informal* **pol**) a person whose job is concerned with politics, especially as an elected member of parliament, etc. 从政者；政治家 ➲ WORDFINDER NOTE AT PARLIAMENT **2** (*disapproving*) a person who is good at using different situations in an organization to try to get power or advantage for himself or herself 政客；见风使舵者；投机钻营者

pol·iti·cize (*BrE also* **-ise**) /pəˈlɪtɪsaɪz/ *verb* [often passive] **1** ~ sth to make sth a political issue 使政治化；使带有政治色彩：*the highly politicized issue of unemployment* 高度政治化的失业问题 **2** ~ sb/sth to make sb/sth become more involved in politics 使参与（或卷入）政治；使对政治敏感：*The rural population has become increasingly politicized in recent years.* 近年来，农村人口对政治愈来愈感兴趣。 ▶ **pol·iti·ciza·tion, -isa·tion** /pəˌlɪtɪsaɪˈzeɪʃn; *NAmE* -səˈz-/ *noun* [U]: *the politicization of education* 教育的政治化

pol·it·ick·ing /ˈpɒlətɪkɪŋ; *NAmE* ˈpɑːl-/ *noun* [U] (*often disapproving*) political activity, especially to win support for yourself 政治活动；（尤指）拉拢活动

pol·it·ico /pəˈlɪtɪkəʊ; *NAmE* -koʊ/ *noun* (*pl.* **-os**) (*informal, disapproving*) a politician; a person who is active in politics 政客；热衷政治的人

pol·it·ics /ˈpɒlətɪks; *NAmE* ˈpɑːl-/ *noun* **1** [U+sing./pl. v.] the activities involved in getting and using power in public life, and being able to influence decisions that affect a country or a society 政治；政治事务（或活动）：*party politics* 党派政治 ◇ *local politics* 地方政治活动 ◇ *He's thinking of **going into politics*** (= trying to become a Member of Parliament, Congress, etc.) 他打算步入政坛。◇ *a major figure in British politics* 英国政坛的重要人物 **2** [U+sing./pl. v.] (*disapproving*) matters concerned with getting or using power within a particular group or organization 权术；钩心斗角：*I don't want to get involved in office politics.* 我不想卷入办公室的钩心斗角。 ◇ *the internal politics of the legal profession* 法律界内部的钩心斗角 ◇ *sexual politics* (= concerning relationships of power between the sexes) 两性间的权势之争 **3** [pl.] a person's political views or beliefs （个人的）政治观点，

▼ **COLLOCATIONS 词语搭配**

Politics 政治

Power 权力

- **create/form/be the leader of** a political party 创建／组建／领导政党
- **gain/take/win/lose/regain** control of Congress 获得／失去／夺回对国会的控制权
- **start/spark/lead/be on the brink of** a revolution 发起／引发／领导一场革命；革命一触即发
- **be engaged/locked in** an internal power struggle 参与／陷入内部权力斗争
- **lead/form** a rival/breakaway faction 领导／组建反对派／分裂派
- **seize/take** control of the government/power 夺取／接手对政府／政权的控制权
- **bring down/overthrow/topple** the government/president/regime 推翻政府／总统／政权
- **abolish/overthrow/restore** the monarchy 废除／推翻／恢复君主制
- **establish/install** a military dictatorship/a stable government 建立军事独裁／稳定的政府
- **be forced/removed/driven from** office/power 被迫离职／下台；被免职／赶下台
- **resign/step down as** party leader/an MP/president/prime minister 辞去政党领袖／议员／总统／总理的职位
- **enter/retire from/return to** political life 开始／退出／重回政治生涯

Political debate 政治辩论

- **spark/provoke** a heated/hot/intense/lively debate 引发激烈的辩论
- **engage in/participate in/contribute to** (the) political/public debate (on/over sth) 参与（关于某事的）政治／公开辩论
- **get involved in/feel excluded from** the political process 参与／感觉被排挤出政治进程
- **launch/start/lead/spearhead** a campaign/movement 发起／领导一场运动
- **join/be linked with** the peace/anti-war/feminist/civil rights movement 参与和平／反战／女权／民权运动；与和平／反战／女权／民权运动有联系
- **criticize/speak out against/challenge/support** the government 批评／公开反对／质疑／支持政府
- **lobby/put pressure on** the government (to do sth) 游说／施压于政府（去做某事）
- **come under fire/pressure from** opposition parties 受到来自反对党的抨击／压力

Policy 政策

- **call for/demand/propose/push for/advocate** democratic/political/land reform(s) 呼吁／强烈要求／提议／敦促／倡导民主／政治／土地改革
- **formulate/implement** domestic economic policy 制定／执行国内经济政策
- **change/influence/shape/have an impact on** government/economic/public policy 改变／影响政府／经济／公共政策
- **be consistent with/be in line with/go against/be opposed to** government policy 符合／违背政府政策
- **reform/restructure/modernize** the tax system 改革／重组／革新税收制度
- **privatize/improve/deliver/make cuts in** public services 私有化／改善／提供／削减公共服务
- **invest (heavily) in/spend sth on** schools/education/public services/(the) infrastructure 在学校／教育／公共服务／基础设施上投入（大量）资金
- **nationalize** the banks/the oil industry 使银行／石油产业国有化
- **promise/propose/deliver/give** ($80 billion in/significant/substantial/massive) tax cuts 承诺／提议／兑现／实行（800 亿美元／大幅度的）减税
- a/the budget is **approved**/ (*especially NAmE*) **passed** by parliament/congress 预算经议会／国会通过

Making laws 制定法律

- **have a majority in/have seats in** Parliament/Congress/the Senate 在议会／国会／参议院中占多数席位／占有席位
- **propose/sponsor** a bill/legislation/a resolution 提交议案／法规／决议
- **introduce/bring in/draw up/draft/adopt/pass** a bill/a law/legislation/measures 推出／提出／拟定／起草／采用／通过议案／法律／法规／措施
- **amend/repeal** an act/a law/legislation 修正／废除法案／法律／法规
- **veto/vote against/oppose** a bill/legislation/a measure/a proposal/a resolution 否决／投票反对／反对议案／法规／措施／提议／决议
- **get/require/be decided by** a majority vote 获得／需要多数票；由多数票决定

➲ COLLOCATIONS AT ECONOMY, VOTE

P

政见，政治信仰： *His politics are extreme.* 他的政治观点偏激。 **4** [U] = POLITICAL SCIENCE： *a degree in Politics* 政治学学位 **5** [sing.] a system of political beliefs; a state of political affairs 政治思想体系；政治局势： *A politics of the future has to engage with new ideas.* 未来的政治制度必须同新思想结合。 ➲ WORDFINDER NOTE AT GOVERNMENT

pol·ity /ˈpɒləti; *NAmE* ˈpɑːl-/ *noun* (*pl.* **-ies**) (*specialist*) **1** [C] a society as a political unit 政治组织；国家组织 **2** [U] the form or process of government 政体；政权形态；政治制度

polka /ˈpɒlkə; *NAmE* ˈpoʊlkə/ *noun* a fast dance for two people together that was popular in the 19th century; a piece of music for this dance 波尔卡舞（盛行于 19 世纪的一种轻快的双人舞）；波尔卡舞曲

ˈ**polka dot** *noun* one of many dots that together form a pattern, especially on cloth （织物等圆点图案中的）圆点： *a polka-dot tie* 圆点领带 ➲ VISUAL VOCAB PAGE V66 ➲ COMPARE SPOT *n.* (1)

poll /pəʊl; *NAmE* poʊl/ *noun, verb*

■ *noun* **1** (*also* **oˈpinion poll**) [C] the process of questioning people who are representative of a larger group in order to get information about the general opinion 民意测验；民意调查 SYN **survey**： *to* ***carry out/conduct*** *a poll* 进行民意测验 ◊ *A recent poll suggests some surprising changes in public opinion.* 最近的调查表明，民意有了出人意表的变化。 **2** [C] (*also* **the polls** [pl.]) the process of voting at an election; the process of counting the votes 选举投票；计票： *The final result of the poll will be known tomorrow.* 投票结果将于明天公布。 ◊ *Thursday is traditionally the day when Britain* ***goes to the polls*** (= when elections are held). 英国传统的投票选举日是星期四。 ◊ *Polls close* (= voting ends) *at 9 p.m.* 投票于晚上 9 点结束。 ➲ SYNONYMS AT ELECTION **3** [sing.] the number of votes given in an election 投票数 SYN **ballot**： *Labour is ahead in the poll.* 工党的得票数领先。 ◊ *They gained 20% of the poll.* 他们得到了 20% 的选票。 ➲ SEE ALSO DEED POLL, EXIT POLL, STRAW POLL ➲ WORDFINDER NOTE AT DEMOCRACY

■ *verb* **1** [T, I] to receive a particular number of votes in an election 获得（票数）： **~ sth** *They polled 39% of the vote in the last election.* 在上届选举中，他们获得了 39% 的选票。 ◊ **+ adv./prep.** *The Republicans have polled well* (= received many votes) *in recent elections.* 共和党在最近的选举中得票数都很高。 **2** [T, usually passive] **~ sb** to ask a large number of members of the public what they think about sth 对…进行民意调查 SYN **survey**： *Over 50% of those polled were against the proposed military action.* 民调中有超过 50% 的人反对拟议的军事行动。

pol·lard /ˈpɒləd; -lɑːd; *NAmE* ˈpɑːlərd/ *verb* [usually passive] **~ sth** (*specialist*) to cut off the branches at the top of a tree so that the lower branches will grow more thickly 给（树木）去顶；截梢

pol·len /ˈpɒlən; *NAmE* ˈpɑːlən/ *noun* [U] fine powder, usually yellow, that is formed in flowers and carried to other flowers of the same kind by the wind or by insects, to make those flowers produce seeds 花粉 ➲ COLLOCATIONS AT LIFE

ˈ**pollen count** *noun* [usually sing.] a number that shows the amount of pollen in the air, used to warn people whose health is affected by it 花粉计数（用于警示花粉过敏者空气中花粉的含量）

ˈ**pollen tube** *noun* (*biology* 生) a tube that grows when pollen lands on the STIGMA (= a part of the female organ) of a flower to carry the male cell to the OVULE (= the part that contains the female cell) 花粉管

pol·lin·ate /ˈpɒləneɪt; *NAmE* ˈpɑːl-/ *verb* **~ sth** to put POLLEN into a flower or plant so that it produces seeds 授粉；传粉： *flowers pollinated by bees/the wind* 由蜜蜂/风传粉的花卉 ▸ **pol·lin·ation** /ˌpɒləˈneɪʃn; *NAmE* ˌpɑːl-/ *noun* [U]

poll·ing /ˈpəʊlɪŋ; *NAmE* ˈpoʊ-/ *noun* [U] **1** the activity of voting 投票： *Polling has been heavy since 8 a.m.* 从早上 8 点开始，投票一直很踊跃。 **2** the act of asking questions as part of an opinion POLL 民意测验

ˈ**polling booth** (*especially BrE*) (*NAmE usually* ˈ**voting booth**) *noun* a small place in a POLLING STATION, separated from the surrounding area, where people vote by marking a card, etc. 投票亭，写票间（设在投票站）

ˈ**polling day** *noun* [U, C] (*BrE*) a day on which people vote in an election 投票日；选举日： *a week before polling day* 投票日前一周（的那天）

ˈ**polling station** (*especially BrE*) (*NAmE usually* ˈ**polling place**) *noun* a building where people go to vote in an election 投票站；投票点 ➲ COLLOCATIONS AT VOTE

polli·wog (*also* **polly·wog**) /ˈpɒliwɒɡ; *NAmE* ˈpɑːliwɑːɡ/ *noun* (*NAmE*) = TADPOLE

poll·ster /ˈpəʊlstə(r); *NAmE* ˈpoʊl-/ *noun* a person who makes or asks the questions in an OPINION POLL 民意测验主办人；民意调查员

ˈ**poll tax** *noun* a tax that must be paid at the same rate by every person or every adult in a particular area 人头税

pol·lu·tant /pəˈluːtənt/ *noun* (*formal*) a substance that pollutes sth, especially air and water 污染物；污染物质

pol·lute /pəˈluːt/ *verb* to add dirty or harmful substances to land, air, water, etc. so that it is no longer pleasant or safe to use 污染；弄脏： **~ sth** *the exhaust fumes that are polluting our cities* 污染我们城市的废气 ◊ **~ sth by/with sth** *The river has been polluted with toxic waste from local factories.* 当地工厂排放的有毒废弃物污染了这条河。 ◊ (*figurative*) *a society polluted by racism* 受种族主义污染的社会 ➲ COLLOCATIONS AT ENVIRONMENT

pol·luter /pəˈluːtə(r)/ *noun* a person, company, country, etc. that causes pollution 污染者；污染源

pol·lu·tion 🔑 /pəˈluːʃn/ *noun* [U] **1** 🔑 the process of making air, water, soil, etc. dirty; the state of being dirty 污染；玷污；弄脏： ***air/water pollution*** 空气 / 水污染 ◊ *to reduce levels of environmental pollution* 降低环境污染的程度 ➲ COLLOCATIONS AT ENVIRONMENT **2** 🔑 substances that make air, water, soil, etc. dirty 污染物；秽物；垃圾： *beaches covered with pollution* 秽物狼藉的海滩 **3** **noise/light ~** harmful or annoying levels of noise, or of artificial light at night 噪音污染；（夜间扰人的）强烈灯光

Polly·anna /ˌpɒliˈænə; *NAmE* ˌpɑːl-/ *noun* [usually sing.] a person who is always cheerful and expects only good things to happen 盲目乐观的人；无忧无虑的人 ➲ MORE LIKE THIS 17, page R27 ORIGIN From the name of a character created by the US writer of children's stories, Eleanor Hodgman Porter. 源自美国儿童文学作家埃莉诺・霍奇曼・波特所创作的人物波莉亚娜。

polly·wog = POLLIWOG

polo /ˈpəʊləʊ; *NAmE* ˈpoʊloʊ/ *noun* [U] a game in which two teams of players riding on horses try to hit a ball into a goal using long wooden hammers (called MALLETS) 马球（运动） ➲ VISUAL VOCAB PAGE V51 ➲ SEE ALSO WATER POLO

pol·on·aise /ˌpɒləˈneɪz; *NAmE* ˌpɑːl-/ *noun* a slow Polish dance that was popular in the 19th century; a piece of music for this dance 波洛内兹舞（盛行于 19 世纪的波兰慢步舞）；波洛内兹舞曲

ˈ**polo neck** (*BrE*) (*NAmE* **turtle·neck**) *noun* a high round COLLAR made when the neck of a piece of clothing is folded over; a piece of clothing with a polo neck 高圆翻领；高圆翻领衣服： *a polo-neck sweater* 高翻领套衫 ◊ *You can wear a polo neck with that jacket.* 你可以穿件高圆翻领衫配那件外衣。 ➲ VISUAL VOCAB PAGE V68

po·lo·nium /pəˈləʊniəm; *NAmE* -ˈloʊ-/ *noun* [U] (*symb.* **Po**) a chemical element. Polonium is a RADIOACTIVE metal that is present in nature when URANIUM decays. 钋（放射性化学元素）

P

ˈ**polo shirt** *noun* an informal shirt with short sleeves, a COLLAR and a few buttons at the neck 马球衫（开领短袖）➲ VISUAL VOCAB PAGE V68

pol·ter·geist /ˈpəʊltəgaɪst; ˈpɒl-; *NAmE* ˈpoʊltərg-/ *noun* a GHOST that makes loud noises and throws objects 促狭鬼（有时发怪声、乱扔东西）

pol·troon /pɒlˈtruːn; *NAmE* pɑːlˈt-/ *noun* (*old use, disapproving*) a COWARD (= a person who lacks courage) 胆小鬼；懦夫

poly /ˈpɒli; *NAmE* ˈpɑːli/ *noun* (*pl.* **polys**) (*BrE, informal*) = POLYTECHNIC

poly- /ˈpɒli; *NAmE* ˈpɑːli/ *combining form* (in nouns, adjectives and adverbs 构成名词、形容词和副词) many 多；复：*polygamy* 一夫多妻 ◇ *polyphonic* 复调的

poly·an·dry /ˌpɒliˈændri; *NAmE* ˌpɑːl-/ *noun* [U] (*specialist*) the custom of having more than one husband at the same time 一妻多夫（制）➲ COMPARE POLYGAMY ▸ **poly·an·drous** /ˌpɒliˈændrəs; *NAmE* ˌpɑːl-/ *adj.*

poly·an·thus /ˌpɒliˈænθəs; *NAmE* ˌpɑːl-/ *noun* [C, U] a small garden plant with round brightly coloured flowers, several of which grow at the end of each STEM 西洋樱草（矮小花园植物，开鲜艳圆形花）

poly·car·bon·ate /ˌpɒliˈkɑːbənət; *NAmE* ˌpɑːliˈkɑːrb-/ *noun* [U, C] (*specialist*) a very strong transparent plastic used, for example, in windows and LENSES 聚碳酸酯（坚硬透明塑料，用于窗子和镜头等）

poly·clinic /ˈpɒliklɪnɪk; *NAmE* ˈpɑːl-/ *noun* (*BrE*) a medical centre that is not part of a hospital, where both general doctors and specialists work 综合诊所；综合诊疗中心

poly·es·ter /ˌpɒliˈestə(r); *NAmE* ˌpɑːli-; ˈpɑːliestər/ *noun* [U] a strong material made of FIBRES (called polyesters) which are produced by chemical processes, often mixed with other materials and used especially for making clothes 聚酯（纤维）；涤纶：*a cotton and polyester shirt* 涤棉混纺衬衫

P

poly·ethyl·ene /ˌpɒliˈeθəliːn; *NAmE* ˌpɑːl-/ (*NAmE*) (*BrE* **poly·thene**) *noun* [U] a strong thin plastic material, used especially for making bags or for wrapping things in 聚乙烯

pol·yg·amy /pəˈlɪgəmi/ *noun* [U] (*specialist*) the custom of having more than one wife at the same time 一夫多妻（制）➲ COMPARE POLYANDRY ▸ **pol·yg·am·ist** /pəˈlɪgəmɪst/ *noun* **pol·yg·am·ous** /pəˈlɪgəməs/ *adj.*：*a polygamous marriage/society* 一夫多妻制婚姻 / 社会

poly·glot /ˈpɒliglɒt; *NAmE* ˈpɑːliglɑːt/ *adj.* (*formal*) knowing, using or written in more than one language 通晓（或使用）多种语言的；用多种语言写成的 SYN **multilingual**：*a polyglot nation* 多语种民族 ▸ **poly·glot** *noun*

polygons 多边形

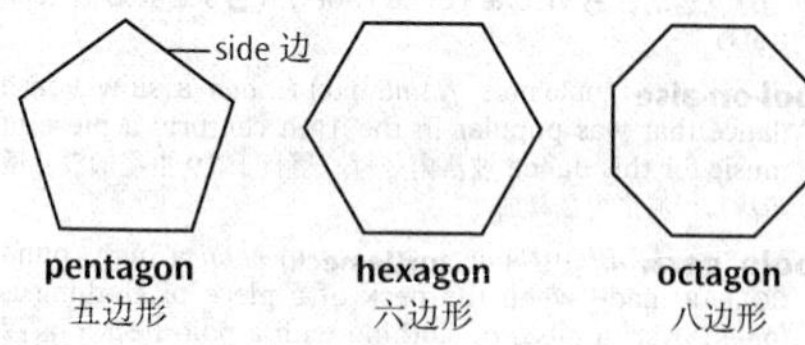

poly·gon /ˈpɒlɪgən; *NAmE* ˈpɑːligɑːn/ *noun* (*geometry* 几何) a flat shape with at least three straight sides and angles, and usually five or more 多边形；多角形 ▸ **pol·yg·on·al** /pəˈlɪgənl/ *adj.*

poly·graph /ˈpɒligræf; *BrE also* -grɑːf; *NAmE* ˈpɑːli-/ *noun* (*specialist, formal*) = LIE DETECTOR

poly·he·dron /ˌpɒliˈhiːdrən; -ˈhed-; *NAmE* ˌpɑːli-/ *noun* (*pl.* **poly·he·dra** /-ˈhiːdrə; -ˈhed-/ or **poly·he·drons**) (*geometry* 几何) a solid shape with many flat sides, usually more than six 多面体（通常多于六面）▸ **poly·he·dral** *adj.*

poly·math /ˈpɒlimæθ; *NAmE* ˈpɑːl-/ *noun* (*formal, approving*) a person who knows a lot about many different subjects 博学家；博学大师

poly·mer /ˈpɒlɪmə(r); *NAmE* ˈpɑːl-/ *noun* (*chemistry* 化) a natural or artificial substance consisting of large MOLECULES (= groups of atoms) that are made from combinations of small simple MOLECULES 聚合物；多聚体

poly·mer·ize (*BrE also* **-ise**) /ˈpɒlɪməraɪz; *NAmE* ˈpɑːlɪ-/ *verb* [I, T] ~ (**sth**) (*chemistry* 化) to combine, or to make units of a chemical combine, to make a POLYMER（使）聚合：*The substance polymerizes to form a hard plastic.* 这种物质聚合形成坚硬的塑料。▸ **poly·mer·iza·tion, -isa·tion** /ˌpɒlɪməraɪˈzeɪʃn; *NAmE* ˌpɑːlɪmərəˈz-/ *noun* [U]

poly·morph·ous /ˌpɒliˈmɔːfəs; *NAmE* ˌpɑːliˈmɔːrfəs/ (*also* **poly·morph·ic** /-fɪk/) *adj.* (*formal* or *specialist*) having or passing through many stages of development（发展）呈多种形式的，多态的

polyp /ˈpɒlɪp; *NAmE* ˈpɑːlɪp/ *noun* **1** (*medical* 医) a small lump that grows inside the body, especially in the nose, that is caused by disease but is usually harmless 息肉；（尤指）鼻息肉 **2** a small and very simple sea creature with a body shaped like a tube 水螅（体）；（水螅型）珊瑚虫

pol·yph·ony /pəˈlɪfəni/ *noun* [U] (*music* 音) the combination of several different patterns of musical notes sung together to form a single piece of music 复调 SYN **counterpoint** ▸ **poly·phon·ic** /ˌpɒliˈfɒnɪk; *NAmE* ˌpɑːliˈfɑːnɪk/ *adj.*

poly·pro·pyl·ene /ˌpɒliˈprəʊpəliːn; *NAmE* ˌpɑːliˈproʊ-/ *noun* [U] a strong plastic often used for objects such as toys or chairs that are made in a MOULD 聚丙烯

poly·sem·ous /ˌpɒliˈsiːməs; *NAmE* ˌpɑːl-/ *adj.* (*linguistics* 语言) (of a word 词) having more than one meaning（一词）多义的

poly·semy /pəˈlɪsɪmi/ *noun* [U] (*linguistics* 语言) the fact of having more than one meaning（一词）多义；多义性；多义现象

poly·styr·ene /ˌpɒliˈstaɪriːn; *NAmE* ˌpɑːl-/ (*also* **Styrofoam™** *especially in NAmE*) *noun* [U] a very light soft plastic that is usually white, used especially for making containers that prevent heat loss 聚苯乙烯：*polystyrene cups* 聚苯乙烯杯子

poly·syl·lable /ˈpɒlisɪləbl; *NAmE* ˈpɑːl-/ *noun* (*specialist*) a word of several (usually more than three) syllables 多音节词 ▸ **poly·syl·lab·ic** /ˌpɒlisɪˈlæbɪk; *NAmE* ˌpɑːl-/ *adj.*

poly·tech·nic /ˌpɒliˈteknɪk; *NAmE* ˌpɑːl-/ (*also BrE, informal* **poly**) *noun* (in Britain in the past) a college for higher education, especially in scientific and technical subjects. Most polytechnics are now called, and have the same status as, universities.（旧时英国的）理工学院（现在多已改为大学）

poly·the·ism /ˈpɒliθiɪzəm; *NAmE* ˈpɑːl-/ *noun* [U] the belief that there is more than one god 多神论；多神信仰 ➲ COMPARE MONOTHEISM ▸ **poly·the·is·tic** /ˌpɒliθiˈɪstɪk; *NAmE* ˌpɑːl-/ *adj.*

poly·thene /ˈpɒlɪθiːn; *NAmE* ˈpɑːl-/ (*BrE*) (*NAmE* **poly·ethyl·ene**) *noun* [U] a strong thin plastic material, used especially for making bags or for wrapping things in 聚乙烯：*a polythene bag* 聚乙烯袋

poly·tun·nel /ˈpɒlitʌnl; *NAmE* ˈpɑːl-/ *noun* a long low structure covered with plastic, used for growing seeds or young plants outdoors 塑料大棚；塑料暖房 ➲ VISUAL VOCAB PAGE V3

poly·un·sat·ur·ated fat /ˌpɒliʌnˌsætʃəreɪtɪd ˈfæt; *NAmE* ˌpɑːl-/ *noun* [C, U] a type of fat found, for example, in seeds and vegetable oils, which does not encourage the harmful development of CHOLESTEROL 多不饱和脂肪

（存在于种子和植物油等中，不促进胆固醇的有害增长）：*foods that are high in polyunsaturated fats* 富含多不饱和脂肪的食物 ➲ SEE ALSO MONOUNSATURATED FAT, SATURATED FAT, TRANS-FATTY ACID, UNSATURATED FAT ▸ **poly·un·sat·ur·ates** /ˌpɒliʌnˈsætʃərəts; *NAmE* ˌpɑːl-/ *noun* [pl.]: *foods that are high in polyunsaturates* (= polyunsaturated fats) 富含多不饱和脂肪的食物

poly·ureth·ane /ˌpɒliˈjʊərəθeɪn; *NAmE* ˌpɑːliˈjʊr-/ *noun* [U] (*specialist*) a type of plastic material used in making paints, glues, etc. 聚氨酯；聚氨基甲酸酯

poly·va·lent /ˌpɒliˈveɪlənt; *NAmE* ˌpɑːl-/ *adj.* **1** (*chemistry* 化) having a VALENCY of 3 or more 多价的 **2** (*formal*) having many different functions or forms 多功能的；多形式的：*polyvalent managerial skills* 多方面的管理技能 ▸ **poly·va·lence** /ˌpɒliˈveɪləns; *NAmE* ˌpɑːl-/ *noun* [U]

pom /pɒm; *NAmE* pɑːm/ *noun* = POMMY

Poma™ /ˈpəʊmə; *NAmE* ˈpoʊmə/ *noun* (*BrE*) = BUTTON LIFT

pom·ade /pəˈmeɪd; -ˈmɑːd/ *noun* (*old-fashioned*) [U, C] a liquid that is put on the hair to make it look shiny and smell nice 发油

po·man·der /pəˈmændə(r); *NAmE* ˈpoʊmændər/ *noun* a round container filled with dried flowers, leaves, etc. that is used to give a pleasant smell to rooms or clothes 香盒（圆形，盛干的馨香花叶等）

pom·egran·ate /ˈpɒmɪɡrænɪt; *NAmE* ˈpɑːm-/ *noun* a round fruit with thick smooth skin and red flesh full of large seeds 石榴 ➲ VISUAL VOCAB PAGE V32

pom·elo /ˈpɒmələʊ; *NAmE* ˈpɑːməloʊ/ (*also* **pum·melo**) *noun* (*pl.* **-os**) a large CITRUS fruit that has thick yellow skin and that tastes similar to a GRAPEFRUIT, but sweeter 柚子

pom·mel /ˈpɒml; *NAmE* ˈpɑːml/ *noun* **1** the higher front part of a SADDLE on a horse （马鞍的）鞍桥，鞍头 **2** the round part on the end of the handle of a SWORD （剑柄顶端的）圆球

ˈpommel horse *noun* a large object on four legs with two handles on top, which GYMNASTS put their hands on and swing their body and legs around 鞍马

pommy /ˈpɒmi; *NAmE* ˈpɑːmi/ *noun* (*pl.* **-ies**) (*also* **pom**) (*AustralE, NZE, informal*) an offensive word for a British person 英国佬

pomp /pɒmp; *NAmE* pɑːmp/ *noun* [U] the impressive clothes, decorations, music, etc. and traditional customs that are part of an official occasion or ceremony 排场；气派；盛况：*all the pomp and ceremony of a royal wedding* 王室婚礼的盛大场面与仪式
IDM **ˌpomp and ˈcircumstance** formal and impressive ceremony 隆重的仪式

pom·pom /ˈpɒm pɒm; *NAmE* ˈpɑːm pɑːm/ (*also* **pom·pon** /ˈpɒmpɒn; *NAmE* ˈpɑːmpɑːn/) *noun* **1** a small ball made of wool, used for decoration, especially on a hat 小绒球（尤用以装饰帽子）SYN **bobble** ➲ VISUAL VOCAB PAGE V70 **2** (especially in the US) a large round bunch of strips of plastic, tied to a handle, used by CHEERLEADERS （美国啦啦队常用的）绒球，丝球

pom·pous /ˈpɒmpəs; *NAmE* ˈpɑːm-/ *adj.* (*disapproving*) showing that you think you are more important than other people, especially by using long and formal words 虚华的；言辞浮夸的 SYN **pretentious**：*a pompous official* 自负的官员 ▸ **pom·pos·ity** /pɒmˈpɒsəti; *NAmE* pɑːmˈpɑːs-/ *noun* [U]：*The prince's manner was informal, without a trace of pomposity.* 王子态度平易谦和，没有一点傲气。**pom·pous·ly** *adv.*

ponce /pɒns; *NAmE* pɑːns/ *noun, verb*
▪ *noun* (*BrE, informal*) **1** a man who controls one or several PROSTITUTES and the money that they earn 男鸨；拉皮条者 SYN **pimp 2** an offensive word for a man whose appearance and behaviour seem similar to a woman's, or who is thought to be HOMOSEXUAL 娘娘腔的男人；同性恋男子
▪ *verb*
PHR V **ˌponce aˈbout/aˈround** (usually used in the progressive tenses 通常用于进行时) (*BrE, informal*) to waste time when you are doing sth so that you achieve nothing; to do silly things in a way that looks ridiculous 无事忙；干些无聊的事

poncey (*also* **poncy**) /ˈpɒnsi; *NAmE* ˈpɑːnsi/ *adj.* (*BrE, disapproving, informal*) trying to be impressive in a way that is silly and not natural 虚夸的；张扬而做作的：*I don't want to go to some poncey restaurant—I just want something to eat!* 我不想去什么花里胡哨的餐馆，我只想吃点东西！

pon·cho /ˈpɒntʃəʊ; *NAmE* ˈpɑːntʃoʊ/ *noun* (*pl.* **-os**) a type of coat without sleeves, made from one large piece of cloth with a hole in the middle for the head to go through 庞乔斗篷（在大块织物正中开领口制成）

pond /pɒnd; *NAmE* pɑːnd/ *noun* a small area of still water, especially one that is artificial 池塘；水池（尤指人工的）：*a fish pond* 养鱼池 ➲ VISUAL VOCAB PAGES V3, V20
IDM **across the ˈpond** (*informal*) on the other side of the Atlantic Ocean from Britain/the US 在大西洋彼岸 ➲ MORE AT BIG *adj.*

pon·der /ˈpɒndə(r); *NAmE* ˈpɑːn-/ *verb* [I, T] (*formal*) to think about sth carefully for a period of time 沉思；考虑；琢磨 SYN **consider**：**~ (about/on/over sth)** *She pondered over his words.* 她反复琢磨他的话。◇ *They were left to ponder on the implications of the announcement.* 交由他们去琢磨这项宣告的含义。◇ **~ sth** *The senator pondered the question for a moment.* 这位参议员考虑了一下这个问题。◇ **~ whether, what, etc.…** *They are pondering whether the money could be better used elsewhere.* 他们正在斟酌能否把钱花到其他更适当的地方。◇ **+ speech** *'I wonder why,' she pondered aloud.* "我想知道为什么。"她边想边说。

pon·der·ous /ˈpɒndərəs; *NAmE* ˈpɑːn-/ *adj.* (*formal*) **1** (*disapproving*) (of speech and writing 言语或文字) too slow and careful; serious and boring 慢条斯理的；沉闷乏味的 SYN **tedious 2** moving slowly and heavily; able to move only slowly 缓慢的；笨拙的；笨重的 SYN **laboured**：*She watched the cow's ponderous progress.* 她看着牛迟缓地向前走着。▸ **pon·der·ous·ly** *adv.* **pon·der·ous·ness** *noun* [U]

ˈpond skater (*BrE*) (*NAmE* **ˈwater strider**) *noun* an insect that moves quickly across the surface of water 黾蝽；水黾

pone /pəʊn; *NAmE* poʊn/ *noun* [U] (*US*) = CORN PONE

pong /pɒŋ; *NAmE* pɔːŋ; pɑːŋ/ *noun* (*BrE, informal*) a strong unpleasant smell 强烈难闻的气味；臭味；恶臭 ▸ **pong** *verb* [I]：*That cheese pongs!* 那奶酪熏死人了！

pon·tiff /ˈpɒntɪf; *NAmE* ˈpɑːn-/ *noun* (*formal*) the POPE (= the leader of the Roman Catholic Church) 教皇；宗座

pon·tif·ic·al /pɒnˈtɪfɪkl; *NAmE* pɑːn-/ *adj.* (*formal*) connected with a POPE 教皇的；宗座的

pon·tifi·cate *verb, noun*
▪ *verb* /pɒnˈtɪfɪkeɪt; *NAmE* pɑːn-/ [I] **~ (about/on sth)** (*disapproving*) to give your opinions about sth in a way that shows that you think you are right 自以为是地谈论；目空一切地议论
▪ *noun* /pɒnˈtɪfɪkət; *NAmE* pɑːn-/ the official position or period in office of a POPE 教皇职务（或在任时期）

pon·toon /pɒnˈtuːn; *NAmE* pɑːn-/ *noun* **1** [C] a temporary floating platform built across several boats or hollow structures, especially one used for tying boats to 浮码头；浮桥平台 **2** [C] a boat or hollow structure that is one of several used to support a floating platform or bridge （支撑浮桥的）浮筒，趸船：*a pontoon bridge* 浮桥 **3** [U] (*BrE*) = BLACKJACK

pony /ˈpəʊni; *NAmE* ˈpoʊni/ *noun, verb*
▪ *noun* (*pl.* **-ies**) **1** a type of small horse 小型马；矮马 ➲ SEE ALSO SHETLAND PONY **2** (*BrE, slang*) £25 * 25 英镑 IDM SEE DOG *n.*, SHANK

■ *verb* (**po·nies**, **pony·ing**, **po·nied**, **po·nied**)

PHR V **,pony 'up sth** (*NAmE, informal*) to pay money for sth 为…付款：*Each guest had to pony up $40 for the meal.* 每位来宾都得为这顿饭付 40 美元。

pony·tail /ˈpəʊniteɪl; *NAmE* ˈpoʊ-/ *noun* a bunch of hair tied at the back of the head so that it hangs like a horse's tail 马尾辫 ➲ VISUAL VOCAB PAGE V65 ➲ COMPARE PIGTAIL

'pony-trekking *noun* [U] (*BrE*) the activity of riding PONIES in the countryside for pleasure 骑矮马兜风（或野游）：*to go pony-trekking* 骑矮马出游

Ponzi scheme /ˈpɒnzi skiːm; *NAmE* ˈpɑːnzi/ *noun* a plan for making money that involves encouraging people to invest by offering them a high rate of interest and using their money to pay earlier INVESTORS. When there are not enough new INVESTORS, people who have recently invested lose their money. 庞氏骗局，非法集资（指提供高息以吸引人们投资，将得来的钱用于偿还之前的投资者，而当没有足够的新投资者时，就会给最近的投资者造成损失） ORIGIN From Charles Ponzi, who organized the first scheme of this kind in the US in 1919. 源自查尔斯•庞兹。他于 1919 年在美国首次策划了此类骗局。

poo (*also* **pooh**) /puː/ (*both BrE*) *noun* [U, C] (*also* **poop** *NAmE, BrE*) a child's word for the solid waste that is passed through the BOWELS（儿童用语）㞎㞎 SYN **faeces**：*dog poo* 狗屎 ◇ *I want to do a poo!* 我要拉㞎㞎！
▸ **poo** (*also* **pooh**) *verb* [I]

pooch /puːtʃ/ *noun* (*informal*) a dog 狗

poo·dle /ˈpuːdl/ *noun* **1** a dog with thick curly hair that is sometimes cut into special shapes 鬈毛狗 **2** (*BrE, informal*) a person who is too willing to do what sb else tells them to do 百依百顺的人

poof /pʊf/ *noun, exclamation*

■ *noun* (*also* **poof·ter** /ˈpʊftə(r)/) (*BrE, taboo, slang*) an offensive word for a HOMOSEXUAL man （指男同性恋者）假鸳鸯，鸡公对

■ *exclamation* used when talking about sth disappearing suddenly （描述事物突然消失）嗖的一声，刺溜一下：*He walked through—and vanished. Poof! Like that.* 他走了过去，然后就嗖的一下子不见了。

pooh /puː/ *exclamation, noun, verb*

■ *exclamation* (*especially BrE*) **1** used to express disgust at a bad smell （表示对臭味的厌恶）噗，呸：*It stinks! Pooh!* 好臭！噗！ **2** used to say that you think sb's idea, suggestion, etc. is not very good or that you do not believe what sb has said （表示对别人的意见等不屑一顾或不相信）嘁，得了吧：*'I might lose my job for this.' 'Oh, pooh, nobody will care.'* "这下子我可能会丢饭碗了。""嘁，得了吧！谁会在乎！"

■ *noun, verb* = POO

,pooh-'pooh *verb* ~ **sth** (*informal*) to say that a suggestion, an idea, etc. is not true or not worth thinking about 说…不真实；对…不屑一顾（或嗤之以鼻）

pool 🔑 /puːl/ *noun, verb*

■ *noun*

• **FOR SWIMMING** 游泳 **1** 🔑 [C] = SWIMMING POOL：*Does the hotel have a pool?* 这家旅馆有没有游泳池？ ◇ *relaxing by the pool* 在游泳池边休息 ➲ SEE ALSO PLUNGE POOL

• **OF WATER** 水 **2** 🔑 [C] a small area of still water, especially one that has formed naturally 水坑，水塘，池塘（尤指自然形成的）：*freshwater pools* 淡水池塘 ◇ *a rock pool* (= between rocks by the sea) （海边岩石间的）潮水潭

• **OF LIQUID/LIGHT** 液体；光 **3** 🔑 [C] ~ (**of sth**) a small amount of liquid or light lying on a surface 一摊（液体）；一小片（液体或光）：*The body was lying in a pool of blood.* 尸体倒卧在血泊之中。 ◇ *a pool of light* 一小片亮光

• **GROUP OF THINGS/PEOPLE** 众人；事物 **4** [C] ~ (**of sth**) a supply of things or money that is shared by a group of people and can be used when needed 共用的资源（或资金）：*a pool of cars used by the firm's sales force* 公司销售人员共用的车辆 ◇ *a pool car* 一辆共用的汽车 **5** [C] ~ (**of sth**) a group of people available for work when needed （统称）备用人员：*a pool of cheap labour* 廉价后备劳力

• **GAME** 游戏 **6** [U] a game for two people played with 16 balls on a table, often in pubs and bars. Players use CUES (= long sticks) to try to hit the balls into pockets at the edge of the table. 普尔；落袋台球；弹子球：*a pool table* 普尔球台 ◇ *to shoot* (= play) *pool* 打普尔 ➲ VISUAL VOCAB PAGE V44 ➲ COMPARE BILLIARDS, SNOOKER *n.* (1)

• **FOOTBALL** 足球 **7 the pools** [pl.] = FOOTBALL POOLS：*He does the pools every week.* 他每周都去赌足球普尔。 ◇ *a pools winner* 赌普尔获胜者 ➲ SEE ALSO GENE POOL

■ *verb* ~ **sth** to collect money, information, etc. from different people so that it can be used by all of them 集中资源（或材料等）：*The students work individually, then pool their ideas in groups of six.* 学生先分头工作，然后六人一组交流心得。 ◇ *Police forces across the country are pooling resources in order to solve this crime.* 全国各地警方通力合作以侦破这宗罪案。

pool·room /ˈpuːlruːm; -rʊm/ *noun* (*NAmE*) **1** a place for playing a game of POOL 台球室 **2** a BETTING SHOP 彩票经销点；（赌注）投注站

pool·side /ˈpuːlsaɪd/ *noun* [sing.] the area around a swimming pool 游泳池池边：*lazing at the poolside* 在游泳池边消闲 ◇ *a poolside bar* 游泳池边酒吧

poop /puːp/ *noun, verb*

■ *noun* **1** (*also* **'poop deck**) [C] the raised part at the back end of a ship 船尾楼甲板 ➲ COMPARE STERN *n.* **2** [U] (*especially NAmE*) (*BrE also* **poo**) (*informal*) a child's word for the solid waste that is passed through the BOWELS （儿童用语）㞎㞎：*dog poop on the sidewalk* 便道上的狗屎 **3** [U] (*old-fashioned, informal, especially NAmE*) information about sth, especially the most recent news 信息；（尤指）最新消息

■ *verb* (*NAmE, informal*) **1** [I] to pass solid waste from the BOWELS 拉屎；大便：*The dog just pooped in the kitchen!* 狗刚在厨房拉屎了！ **2** [T] ~ **sb** (**out**) to make sb very tired 累垮（某人）；使筋疲力尽

PHR V **,poop 'out** to stop working or functioning 停止工作；抛锚；丧失功能

pooped /puːpt/ (*also* **,pooped 'out**) *adj.* [not before noun] (*informal, especially NAmE*) very tired 疲惫不堪；筋疲力尽

pooper scoop·er /ˈpuːpə skuːpə(r)/ (*also* **'poop scoop**) *noun* (*informal*) a tool used by dog owners for removing their dogs' solid waste from the streets, parks, etc. 狗粪铲；狗粪夹

poor 🔑 /pɔː(r); *BrE also* pʊə(r); *NAmE also* pʊr/ *adj.* (**poor·er**, **poor·est**)

• **HAVING LITTLE MONEY** 拮据 **1** 🔑 having very little money; not having enough money for basic needs 贫穷的；贫寒的；清贫的：*They were too poor to buy shoes for the kids.* 他们穷得没钱给孩子买鞋穿。 ◇ *We aim to help the poorest families.* 我们的目标是接济最贫困的家庭。 ◇ *It's among the poorer countries of the world.* 它是世界上的贫穷国家之一。 OPP **rich** **2 the poor** *noun* [pl.] people who have very little money 贫困者；穷人：*They provided food and shelter for the poor.* 他们为贫困者提供食物和住所。 OPP **rich** ➲ MORE LIKE THIS 24, page R28

WORDFINDER 联想词：beg, benefit, **charity**, homeless, hostel, poverty, shanty town, sweatshop, **unemployment**

• **UNFORTUNATE** 不幸 **3** 🔑 [only before noun] deserving pity and sympathy 可怜的；不幸的；令人同情的：*Have you heard about poor old Harry? His wife's left him.* 你听说了老哈里的惨况吗？他妻子离他而去了。 ◇ *It's hungry—the poor little thing.* 它饿了，这可怜的小家伙。 ◇ *'I have stacks of homework to do.' 'Oh, you poor thing.'* "我有一大堆的作业要做哪。""唉呦，你好可怜哦。"

• **NOT GOOD** 不好 **4** 🔑 not good; of a quality that is low or lower than expected 劣质的；差的；次的：*the party's poor performance in the election* 该党在选举中的表现欠佳 ◇ *to be in poor health* 身体不好 ◇ *It was raining heavily and visibility was poor.* 当时天下着大雨，能见度很低。 ◇ *poor food/light/soil* 劣质食品；昏暗的光线；贫瘠的土地 ◇ *to have a poor opinion of sb* (= to not think well of sb) 对某人评价很低 **5** 🔑 (of a person 人) not good or

skilled at sth 不擅长的；不熟练的： *a poor swimmer* 不擅游泳的人 ◇ *a poor judge of character* 看人不准的人 ◇ *She's a good teacher but a poor manager.* 她长于教学，却拙于管理。◇ *a poor sailor* (= sb who easily gets sick at sea) 易晕船的人
- **HAVING LITTLE OF STH** 匮乏 **6** ~ **in sth** having very small amounts of sth 缺乏；贫乏；缺少： *a country poor in natural resources* 自然资源贫乏的国家 ◇ *soil poor in nutrients* 养分不足的土壤 OPP **rich**

IDM **be/come a poor second, third, etc.** (*especially BrE*) to finish a long way behind the winner in a race, competition, etc. （在体育竞赛等中）远远落后 **the ˌpoor man's 'sb/'sth** a person or thing that is similar to but of a lower quality than a particular famous person or thing （比同类的名人显物）逊色的人（或物）；次级货色： *Sparkling white wine is the poor man's champagne.* 白葡萄汽酒是廉价的香槟。 ➲ MORE AT ACCOUNT *n.*

▼ SYNONYMS 同义词辨析

poor

disadvantaged • needy • impoverished • deprived • penniless • hard up

These words all describe sb who has very little or no money and therefore cannot satisfy their basic needs. 以上各词均形容人贫穷、贫寒。

poor having very little money; not having enough money for basic needs 指贫穷的、贫寒的、清贫的： *They were too poor to buy shoes for the kids.* 他们穷得没钱给孩子买鞋穿。

disadvantaged having less money and fewer opportunities than most people in society 指生活条件差的、贫困的、社会地位低下的： *socially disadvantaged sections of the community* 该社区社会地位低下的贫困阶层

needy poor 指缺乏生活必需品的、贫困的： *It's a charity that provides help for needy children.* 这是一个为贫困孩子提供援助的慈善机构。

impoverished (*journalism*) poor 指赤贫的、不名一文的： *Thousands of impoverished peasants are desperate to move to the cities.* 成千上万赤贫的农民急切盼望搬到城里去。

deprived [usually before noun] without enough food, education, and all the things that are necessary for people to live a happy and comfortable life 指贫穷的、穷困的、穷苦的

POOR, NEEDY, IMPOVERISHED OR DEPRIVED? 用 poor、needy、impoverished 还是 deprived?

Poor is the most general of these words and can be used to describe yourself, another individual person, people as a group, or a country or an area. **Needy** is mostly used to describe people considered as a group: it is not used to talk about yourself or individual people. * poor 在这组词中最通用，可用以描述自己、另一个人、某个群体、国家或地区。needy 主要用以描述群体，不用以描述自己或个人： *poor/needy children/families* 贫困的孩子／家庭 ◇ ~~*They were too needy to buy shoes for the kids.*~~

Impoverished is used, especially in journalism, to talk about poor countries and the people who live there. To talk about poor areas in rich countries, use **deprived**. * impoverished 尤用于新闻，指贫穷国家和生活在贫穷国家的人。指富裕国家的贫困地区用 deprived。

penniless (*literary*) having no money; very poor 指一文不名的、穷困的： *He died penniless in Paris.* 他死于巴黎，死时身无分文。

hard up (*informal*) having very little money, especially for a short period of time 尤指暂时拮据、缺钱： *I was always hard up as a student.* 我当学生时总是很拮据。

PATTERNS
- poor/disadvantaged/needy/impoverished/deprived/penniless/hard-up **people/families**
- poor/disadvantaged/needy/impoverished/deprived **areas**
- poor/disadvantaged/impoverished **countries**
- a(n) poor/disadvantaged/impoverished/deprived **background**

poor·house /ˈpɔːhaʊs; ˈpʊə-; *NAmE* ˈpɔːr-; ˈpʊr-/ (*BrE also* **work·house**) *noun* (in Britain in the past) a building where very poor people were sent to live and given work to do （英国旧时的）济贫院，劳动救济所

the 'Poor Law *noun* a group of laws used in Britain in the past to control the help that was given to poor people （英国旧时的）济贫法

poor·ly /ˈpɔːli; ˈpʊəli; *NAmE* ˈpʊrli; ˈpɔːrli/ *adv., adj.*
■ *adv.* in a way that is not good enough 糟糕地；不如意；不足 SYN **badly**： *a poorly attended meeting* (= at which there are not many people) 寥寥几个人参加的会议 ◇ *poorly designed* 设计不周的 ◇ *The job is relatively poorly paid.* 相对而言，这工作报酬很低。◇ *Our candidate **fared** poorly in the election* (= did not get many votes). 我们的候选人在选举中得票不多。
■ *adj.* [not usually before noun] (*BrE, informal*) ill/sick 有病；不适；不舒服： *She felt poorly.* 她感到身体不适。

poor·ness /ˈpɔːnəs; ˈpʊənəs; *NAmE* ˈpɔːrnəs; ˈpʊrnəs/ *noun* [U] the state of lacking a good quality or feature （优点等的）匮乏，缺乏，贫乏： *The poorness of the land makes farming impossible.* 土地贫瘠以致无法耕作。

ˌpoor re'lation *noun* something that is not treated with as much respect as other similar things because it is not thought to be as good, important or successful 略逊一筹的事物；不受青睐的事物： *The short story is often considered to be a poor relation to the novel.* 人们通常认为短篇小说远不如长篇小说受青睐。

poo·tle /ˈpuːtl/ *verb* [I] + **adv./prep.** (*BrE, informal*) to move or travel without any hurry 不慌不忙地移动（或行进）： *She pootled along in her old car.* 她开着她那辆旧车缓缓而行。

P

pop /pɒp; *NAmE* pɑːp/ *noun, verb, adj., adv.*
■ *noun*
- **MUSIC** 音乐 **1** (*also* **'pop music**) [U] popular music of the sort that has been popular since the 1950s, usually with a strong rhythm and simple tunes, often contrasted with rock, SOUL and other forms of popular music 流行音乐，流行乐曲（通常与摇滚乐、灵乐和其他形式的流行音乐相对）： *rock, pop and soul* 摇滚乐、流行音乐和灵乐 ➲ COLLOCATIONS AT MUSIC
- **SOUND** 声音 **2** [C] a short sharp EXPLOSIVE sound （短促清脆的爆裂声）砰： *The cork came out of the bottle with a loud pop.* 软木塞砰的一声从瓶口迸了出来。 ➲ MORE LIKE THIS 3, page R25
- **DRINK** 饮料 **3** [U] (*old-fashioned, informal*) a sweet FIZZY drink (= with bubbles) that is not alcoholic 汽水
- **FATHER** 父亲 **4** [sing.] (*old-fashioned, informal, especially NAmE*) used as a word for 'father', especially as a form of address （尤用作称呼）爸，爹： *Hi, Pop!* 嗨，爸！

IDM **have/take a 'pop (at sb)** (*BrE, informal*) to attack sb physically or in words 攻击，抨击（某人） **...a pop** (*informal, especially NAmE*) costing a particular amount for each one 每个…钱： *We can charge $50 a pop.* 我们可以每个收费 50 美元。

■ *verb* (**-pp-**)
- **MAKE SOUND** 发声 **1** [I, T] ~ (**sth**) to make a short EXPLOSIVE sound; to cause sth to make this sound （使）发砰砰声： *the sound of corks popping* 瓶塞被拔起时发出的砰砰声 **2** [T, I] ~ (**sth**) to burst, or make sth burst, with a short EXPLOSIVE sound （使）爆裂，发爆裂声： *She jumped as someone popped a balloon behind her.* 有人在她背后弄爆了一个气球，把她吓了一跳。
- **GO QUICKLY** 速去 **3** [I] + **adv./prep.** (*informal*) to go somewhere quickly, suddenly or for a short time （突然或匆匆）去： *I'll pop over and see you this evening.* 我今晚就赶去看你。◇ *Why don't you pop in (= visit us) for a drink next time you're in the area?* 下次来到这一带时，就到我们这儿小酌一杯如何？

- **PUT QUICKLY** 迅速放置 **4** [T] **~ sth/sb + adv./prep.** (*informal, especially BrE*) to put sth/sb somewhere quickly, suddenly or for a short time （迅速或突然）放置：*He popped his head around the door and said hello.* 他从门后探一探头，打了声招呼。◇ *I'll pop the books in* (= deliver them) *on my way home.* 我回家时顺便把书送过去吧。◇ *Pop your bag on here.* 把你的包放在这上面。
- **APPEAR SUDDENLY** 突然出现 **5** [I] **+ adv./prep.** to suddenly appear, especially when not expected 突然出现；冷不防冒出：*The window opened and a dog's head popped out.* 窗子打开了，冷不防一只狗探出头来。◇ *An idea suddenly popped into his head.* 他突然想到了一个主意。◇ (*computing* 计) *The dialog box pops up every time I try to close the browser.* 我每次想要关闭浏览器时这个对话框都会弹出。
- **OF EARS** 耳朵 **6** [I] if your ears **pop** when you are going up or down in a plane, etc., the pressure in them suddenly changes （乘飞机等升降时）耳压变化；（耳）胀
- **OF EYES** 眼睛 **7** [I] if your eyes **pop** or **pop out**, they suddenly open fully because you are surprised or excited （因激动、惊奇）张大，睁大，瞪起：*Her eyes nearly popped out of her head when she saw them.* 她一看到他们，眼睛瞪得快要掉出来了。
- **TAKE DRUGS** 服药 **8** [T] **~ sth** (*informal*) to take a lot of a drug, regularly （经常大量地）服药，用毒品：*She's been popping pills for months.* 她大量服药已有几个月了。 **9** [T] **~ the hood** (*NAmE*) to open the HOOD/BONNET of a car 打开汽车的引擎盖

IDM **pop your 'clogs** (*BrE, humorous*) to die 翘辫子；上西天；一命呜呼 **pop the 'question** (*informal*) to ask sb to marry you 开口求婚

PHR V **,pop 'off** (*informal*) to die 上西天；一命呜呼 **,pop sth↔'on** (*BrE, informal*) **1** to put on a piece of clothing 穿（衣）：*I'll just pop on a sweater and meet you outside.* 我套件毛衣就出来见你。 **2** to turn on a piece of electrical equipment 开启（电器）

■ ***adj.*** [only before noun] **MUSIC/STYLE** 音乐；风格 **1** connected with modern popular music 流行音乐的；通俗风格的：*a pop song* 流行歌曲 ◇ *a pop band/group* 流行音乐乐队 / 组合 ◇ *a pop star* 流行音乐歌星 ◇ *a pop concert* 流行音乐会 **2** made in a modern popular style 通俗的；现代的：*pop culture* 通俗文化

■ ***adv.***

IDM **go 'pop** to burst or explode with a sudden short sound 爆裂；爆炸：*The balloon went pop.* 气球砰的一声爆了。

pop. *abbr.* population 人口：*pop. 200 000* 人口 20 万

'pop art (*also* **Pop Art**) *noun* [U] a style of art, developed in the 1960s, that was based on popular culture and used material such as advertisements, film/movie images, etc. 波普艺术，通俗艺术，大众艺术（20 世纪 60 年代兴起，以通俗文化为基础，以广告和电影形象等为素材）

pop·corn /ˈpɒpkɔːn; *NAmE* ˈpɑːpkɔːrn/ *noun* [U] a type of food made from grains of MAIZE (CORN) that are heated until they burst, forming light whitish balls that are then covered with salt or sugar 爆（玉）米花

pope /pəʊp; *NAmE* poʊp/ (*often* **the Pope**) *noun* the leader of the Roman Catholic Church, who is also the Bishop of Rome 教皇：*the election of a new pope* 新教皇的选举 ◇ *Pope Francis* 教皇方济各 ◇ *a visit from the Pope* 教皇的来访 ➲ SEE ALSO PAPACY, PAPAL

IDM **Is the Pope a 'Catholic?** (*humorous*) used to say that there is no doubt that sth is true 这还用问吗；当然是：*'Will they arrive late?' 'Is the Pope a Catholic?'* "他们会迟到吗？" "这还用问吗？"

popery /ˈpəʊpəri; *NAmE* ˈpoʊ-/ *noun* [U] (*taboo*) an offensive way of referring to Roman Catholicism 教皇主义（对天主教的贬称）

,pope's 'nose *noun* (*NAmE*) = PARSON'S NOSE

'pop-eyed *adj.* (*informal*) having eyes that are wide open, especially because you are very surprised, excited or frightened （因惊恐或激动）瞪大眼睛的，双目圆睁的

pop·gun /ˈpɒpɡʌn; *NAmE* ˈpɑːp-/ *noun* a toy gun that fires small objects such as CORKS and makes a short sharp noise 玩具气枪

pop·ish /ˈpəʊpɪʃ; *NAmE* ˈpoʊ-/ *adj.* [usually before noun] (*taboo, offensive*) used by some people to describe sb/sth that is connected with Roman Catholicism 天主教的，教皇制度的（某些人用以形容与天主教有关的人或事物）

pop·lar /ˈpɒplə(r); *NAmE* ˈpɑːp-/ *noun* a tall straight tree with soft wood 杨，杨树（树干高，木质较软）

pop·lin /ˈpɒplɪn; *NAmE* ˈpɑːp-/ *noun* [U] a type of strong cotton cloth used for making clothes 府绸；毛葛

'pop music *noun* = POP (1)

pop·over /ˈpɒpəʊvə(r); *NAmE* ˈpɑːpoʊvər/ *noun* (*NAmE*) a type of food made from a mixture of eggs, milk and flour which rises to form a hollow shell when it is baked 空心松饼，膨松饼（将蛋、奶、面粉调和后烘焙而成）

poppa /ˈpɒpə; *NAmE* ˈpɑːpə/ *noun* (*NAmE, informal*) used by children to talk about or to address their father （儿童用语）爸 ➲ SEE ALSO PAPA, POP *n.* (4)

pop·pa·dom /ˈpɒpədəm; *NAmE* ˈpɑːp-/ *noun* a type of thin round crisp S Asian bread that is fried in oil and often served with CURRY 印度脆饼（常佐以咖喱）

pop·per /ˈpɒpə(r); *NAmE* ˈpɑːp-/ *noun* (*BrE*) = PRESS STUD

pop·pet /ˈpɒpɪt; *NAmE* ˈpɑːp-/ *noun* (*BrE, informal*) used to talk to or about sb you like or love, especially a child 宝贝儿；乖乖；心肝儿

,pop psy'chology *noun* [U] the use by ordinary people of simple or fashionable ideas from PSYCHOLOGY in order to understand or explain people's feelings and emotional problems 大众心理学（普通人运用心理学中简单或流行的概念来理解或解释情感问题）

poppy /ˈpɒpi; *NAmE* ˈpɑːpi/ *noun* (*pl.* **-ies**) a wild or garden plant, with a large delicate flower that is usually red, and small black seeds. OPIUM is obtained from one type of poppy. 罂粟：*poppy fields/seeds* 罂粟田 / 籽 ➲ **VISUAL VOCAB PAGE V11**

poppy·cock /ˈpɒpikɒk; *NAmE* ˈpɑːpikɑːk/ *noun* [U] (*old-fashioned, informal*) nonsense 废话；胡说

'pop quiz *noun* (*NAmE*) a short test that is given to students without any warning （给学生的）突击小测验

Pop·sicle™ /ˈpɒpsɪkl; *NAmE* ˈpɑːp-/ (*NAmE*) (*BrE* **,ice 'lolly**, *informal* **lolly**) *noun* a piece of ice flavoured with fruit, served on a stick 冰棍；冰棒

pop·sock /ˈpɒpsɒk; *NAmE* ˈpɑːpsɑːk/ *noun* a short STOCKING that covers the foot and the lower part of the leg to the ankle or knee 女式短袜；中筒袜

pop·tas·tic /pɒpˈtæstɪk; *NAmE* pɑːp-/ *adj.* (*informal, especially BrE*) very good 呱呱叫的：*She's the most poptastic pop star of the lot.* 她是这批流行歌星中最棒的。

popu·lace /ˈpɒpjələs; *NAmE* ˈpɑːp-/ (*usually* **the populace**) *noun* [sing.+sing./pl. v.] (*formal*) all the ordinary people of a particular country or area 平民百姓；民众：*He had the support of large sections of the local populace.* 他受到当地大部分百姓的拥护。◇ *The populace at large is/are opposed to sudden change.* 民众普遍反对突然的改变。

popu·lar 🔑 /ˈpɒpjələ(r); *NAmE* ˈpɑːp-/ *adj.* **1** 🔑 liked or enjoyed by a large number of people 大众喜爱的；广受欢迎的；当红的：*a **hugely/immensely popular** singer* 一个十分 / 非常受欢迎的歌手 ◇ *This is one of our most popular designs.* 这是我们最受欢迎的设计之一。◇ *Skiing has become very popular recently.* 滑雪运动最近盛行起来。◇ **~ (with sb)** *These policies are unlikely to **prove popular** with middle-class voters.* 这些政策不大可能博得中产阶级选民的欢心。◇ *I'm not very popular with my parents* (= they are annoyed with me) *at the moment.* 眼下爸妈对我都很不高兴。◇ (*ironic*) *'Our dog got into the neighbour's garden again!' 'You'll be popular.'* "我们的狗又钻进邻居家的花园了！" "你要有好受的了。" **OPP** **unpopular** **2** 🔑 [only before noun] (*sometimes disapproving*) suited to the taste and knowledge of ordinary people 通俗的；大众化的：***popular music/culture/fiction*** 流行音乐 / 文化 / 小说 ◇ *the popular press* 通俗报刊 **3** [only before noun] (of ideas, beliefs and opinions 概念、信仰、意见) shared by a large number of people 普遍的；大众的；流行的：*a popular misconception* 普遍的错误观念 ◇ ***Contrary to popular belief****, women cause fewer road accidents than men.* 与普遍的看法相反，女性引发的交通事故比男性少。◇ ***Popular opinion*** *was divided on the issue.* 在这个议题上，民众意见有分歧。◇ *By* ***popular demand****, the tour has been extended by two weeks.* 应大家要求，这次旅游延长了两周。 **4** [only before noun] connected with the ordinary people of a country 民众的；百姓的：*The party still has widespread popular support.* 这个政党仍得到民众的广泛支持。

ˌpopular etyˈmology *noun* = FOLK ETYMOLOGY

ˌpopular ˈfront *noun* a political group or party that has SOCIALIST aims 人民阵线（指有社会主义目标的政治团体或政党）

popu·lar·ity /ˌpɒpjuˈlærəti; *NAmE* ˌpɑːp-/ *noun* [U] the state of being liked, enjoyed or supported by a large number of people 受欢迎；普及；流行：*the increasing popularity of cycling* 自行车运动的日益风行 ◇ *Her novels have* ***gained in popularity*** *over recent years.* 近年来她的小说渐受欢迎。◇ **~ with/among sb** *to win/lose popularity with the students* 受到 / 不受学生的欢迎

popu·lar·ize (*BrE also* **-ise**) /ˈpɒpjələraɪz; *NAmE* ˈpɑːp-/ *verb* **1 ~ sb/sth** to make a lot of people know about sth and enjoy it 宣传；宣扬；推广：*The programme did much to popularize little-known writers.* 这个节目大力宣扬不太知名的作家。 **2 ~ sth** to make a difficult subject easier to understand for ordinary people 使通俗化；使普及：*He spent his life popularizing natural history.* 他毕生致力于普及博物学。 ▶ **popu·lar·iza·tion, -isa·tion** /ˌpɒpjələraɪˈzeɪʃn; *NAmE* ˌpɑːpjələrəˈz-/ *noun* [U]

popu·lar·ly /ˈpɒpjələli; *NAmE* ˈpɑːpjələrli/ *adv.* **1** by a large number of people 普遍地；广泛地；一般地 SYN **commonly**：*a popularly held belief* 大多数人持有的看法 ◇ *the UN Conference on Environment and Development, popularly known as the 'Earth Summit'* 联合国环境与发展会议，即一般所称的"地球高峰会议" **2** by the ordinary people of a country（一国）民众作出的 SYN **democratically**：*a popularly elected government* 民选政府

popu·late /ˈpɒpjuleɪt; *NAmE* ˈpɑːp-/ *verb* **1** [often passive] **~ sth** to live in an area and form its population 居住于；生活于；构成…的人口 SYN **inhabit**：*a* ***heavily/densely/sparsely/thinly populated*** *country* 人口密集 / 稠密 / 稀疏 / 稀少的国家 ◇ *The island is populated largely by sheep.* 这个岛的主要生物是绵羊。◇ (*figurative*) *the amazing characters that populate her novels* 常见于她小说中的令人惊叹的人物 **2 ~ sth** to move people or animals to an area to live there 迁移；移居；殖民于：*The French began to populate the island in the 15th century.* 法国人于 15 世纪开始迁移到这个岛。 **3 ~ sth** (*computing* 计) to add data to a document（给文件）增添数据，输入数据

popu·la·tion /ˌpɒpjuˈleɪʃn; *NAmE* ˌpɑːp-/ *noun* **1** [C+sing./pl. v., U] all the people who live in a particular area, city or country; the total number of people who live there（地区、国家等的）人口，人口数量：*One third of the world's population consumes/consume two thirds of the world's resources.* 世界上三分之一的人口消耗着全球三分之二的资源。◇ *The entire population of the town was at the meeting.* 全镇的居民都出席了集会。◇ *countries with ageing populations* 人口老龄化的国家 ◇ *Muslims make up 55% of the population.* 穆斯林占人口的 55%。◇ *an increase in population* 人口的增长 ◇ *areas of* ***dense/sparse population*** (= where many/not many people live) 人口稠密 / 稀少的地区 ◇ *The population is increasing at about 6% per year.* 人口以每年约 6% 的速度增加。◇ *Japan has a population of nearly 130 million.* 日本有近 1.3 亿人口。 **2** [C+sing./pl. v.] a particular group of people or animals living in a particular area（统称）某领域的生物；族群；人口：*the* ***adult/working/rural, etc. population*** *of the country* 一国的成年人口、劳动人口、农村人口等 ➲ WORDFINDER NOTE AT CITY

popuˈlation explosion *noun* a sudden large increase in the number of people in an area 人口激增；人口爆炸

popu·lism /ˈpɒpjəlɪzəm; *NAmE* ˈpɑːp-/ *noun* [U] a type of politics that claims to represent the opinions and wishes of ordinary people 平民政治；民粹主义；民意论 ▶ **popu·list** /-ɪst/ *noun*：*a party of populists* 民粹党 **popu·list** *adj.* [usually before noun]：*a populist leader* 民粹主义领袖

popu·lous /ˈpɒpjələs; *NAmE* ˈpɑːp-/ *adj.* (*formal*) where a large number of people live 人口众多的；人口密集的：*one of America's most populous states* 美国人口大州之一

ˈpop-up *adj., noun*

■ ***adj.*** [only before noun] **1** (of a book, etc. 书籍等) containing a picture that stands up when the pages are opened 有立体活动图的：*a pop-up birthday card* 立体生日卡 **2** (of an electric TOASTER 吐司炉) that pushes the bread quickly upwards when it is ready 弹出烤面包片的 **3** (of a computer menu, etc. 计算机选单等) that can be brought to the screen quickly while you are working on another document 有弹出功能的；能迅速显示的：*a* ***pop-up menu/window*** 弹出式选单 / 视窗 **4** a pop-up shop, restaurant, etc. is a business that opens quickly somewhere and is designed to only use that location for a short period of time（店铺、餐馆等）临时的，短期经营的：*The airline opened a pop-up shop to promote its winter sale.* 该航空公司开了一家临时店进行冬季促销。

■ ***noun*** **1** a computer menu, window, etc. that can be brought to the screen quickly while you are working on another document; a computer window, especially one containing an advert, that appears on the screen, although it has not been requested（计算机）弹出式选单，弹出式窗口，弹出式广告：*an advertising pop-up* 弹出式广告 **2** a shop, restaurant, etc. that opens quickly somewhere and is designed to only use that location for a short period of time 短期经营的店铺；快闪店：*The designers opened a pop-up in the main shopping area as part of the fashion event.* 作为时尚活动的一部分，设计师在主购物区开了一家临时店。

por·cel·ain /ˈpɔːsəlɪn; *NAmE* ˈpɔːrs-/ *noun* [U, C] a hard white shiny substance made by baking CLAY and used for making delicate cups, plates and decorative objects; objects that are made of this 瓷；瓷器：*a porcelain figure* 瓷像

porch /pɔːtʃ; *NAmE* pɔːrtʃ/ *noun* **1** a small area at the entrance to a building, such as a house or a church, that is covered by a roof and often has walls 门廊；门厅 ➲ VISUAL VOCAB PAGE V18 **2** (*NAmE*) = VERANDA (1)

por·cine /ˈpɔːsaɪn; *NAmE* ˈpɔːrs-/ *adj.* (*formal*) like a pig; connected with pigs 像猪的；猪的

por·cu·pine /ˈpɔːkjupaɪn; *NAmE* ˈpɔːrk-/ *noun* an animal covered with long stiff parts like needles (called QUILLS), which it can raise to protect itself when it is attacked 豪猪；箭猪

pore /pɔː(r)/ *noun, verb*

■ ***noun*** one of the very small holes in your skin that sweat can pass through; one of the similar small holes in the surface of a plant or a rock（皮肤上的）毛孔；（植物的）气孔；孔隙 ➲ SEE ALSO POROUS

■ ***verb***

PHR V **ˈpore over sth** to look at or read sth very carefully 仔细打量；审视；认真研读；审阅 SYN **examine**：*His lawyers are poring over the small print in the contract.* 他的律师们正在审阅合同上的小号字。

pork /pɔːk; *NAmE* pɔːrk/ *noun* [U] **1** meat from a pig that has not been CURED (= preserved using salt or smoke) 猪肉：*roast pork* 烤猪肉 ◇ *pork chops* 猪排 ◇ *a leg of pork* 猪腿肉 ➲ COMPARE BACON, GAMMON, HAM *n.* (1) **2** (*NAmE, informal*) = PORK BARREL

P

ˈpork barrel *noun* [U] (*NAmE, slang*) local projects that are given a lot of government money in order to win votes; the money that is used 分肥项目，分肥拨款（议员等为争取选票而促使政府拨款给所属地区的发展项目）

porker /ˈpɔːkə(r); *NAmE* ˈpɔːrk-/ *noun* a pig that is made fat and used as food 育肥的猪；食用猪

ˌpork ˈpie *noun* [C, U] (*BrE*) a small PIE filled with PORK and usually eaten cold 猪肉馅饼（通常冷吃）

ˌpork ˈscratchings (*BrE*) (*US* **ˈpork rinds**) *noun* [pl.] crisp pieces of pig skin that are fried and eaten cold, often sold in bags as a SNACK 脆猪皮片（小吃）

porky /ˈpɔːki; *NAmE* ˈpɔːrki/ *noun, adj.*
■ *noun* (*pl.* **-ies**) (*also* **ˌporky ˈpie**) (*BrE, slang*) a statement that is not true; a lie 假话；谎言：*to tell porkies* 编瞎话
■ *adj.* (*informal, disapproving*) (of people 人) fat 肥胖的

porn /pɔːn; *NAmE* pɔːrn/ *noun* [U] (*informal*) = PORNOGRAPHY ➲ SEE ALSO HARD PORN, SOFT PORN

porno /ˈpɔːnəʊ; *NAmE* ˈpɔːrnoʊ/ *adj.* [usually before noun] (*informal*) = PORNOGRAPHIC：*a porno movie* 色情电影

porn·og·raph·er /pɔːˈnɒɡrəfə(r); *NAmE* pɔːrˈnɑːɡ-/ *noun* (*disapproving*) a person who produces or sells pornography 色情作品的制作者（或发行者、销售者）

porno·graph·ic /ˌpɔːnəˈɡræfɪk; *NAmE* ˌpɔːrn-/ (*also informal* **porno**) *adj.* [usually before noun] (*disapproving*) intended to make people feel sexually excited by showing naked people or sexual acts, usually in a way that many other people find offensive 下流的；黄色的；色情的：*pornographic movies/magazines* 黄色电影 / 杂志

porn·og·raphy /pɔːˈnɒɡrəfi; *NAmE* pɔːrˈnɑːɡ-/ (*also informal* **porn**) *noun* [U] (*disapproving*) books, magazines, DVDs, etc. that describe or show naked people and sexual acts in order to make people feel sexually excited, especially in a way that many other people find offensive 淫秽作品；色情书刊（或影碟等）：*child pornography* 儿童色情作品

por·os·ity /pɔːˈrɒsəti; *NAmE* -ˈrɑːs-/ *noun* [U] (*specialist*) the quality or state of being porous 孔隙度；孔隙率；疏松

por·ous /ˈpɔːrəs/ *adj.* having many small holes that allow water or air to pass through slowly 多孔的；透水的；透气的：*porous material/rocks/surfaces* 渗透性材料 / 岩石 / 表面

por·phy·ria /pɔːˈfɪriə; *NAmE* pɔːrˈf-/ *noun* [U] (*medical* 医) a disease of the blood that causes mental problems and makes the skin sensitive to light 卟啉病，紫质症（引发精神症状和皮肤对光过敏的血液病）

por·poise /ˈpɔːpəs; *NAmE* ˈpɔːrpəs/ *noun* a sea animal that looks like a large fish with a pointed mouth. Porpoises are similar to DOLPHINS but smaller. 钝吻海豚；鼠海豚

por·ridge /ˈpɒrɪdʒ; *NAmE* ˈpɔːr-/ *noun* [U] **1** (*especially BrE*) (*NAmE usually* **oat·meal**) a type of soft thick white food made by boiling OATS in milk or water, eaten hot, especially for breakfast 麦片粥 **2** (*EAfrE*) a type of thick drink made by boiling flour with water 面糊；粥

port 🔑 /pɔːt; *NAmE* pɔːrt/ *noun, verb*
■ *noun* **1** 🔑 [C] a town or city with a HARBOUR, especially one where ships load and unload goods 港口城市；口岸城市：*fishing ports* 渔港 ◇ *Rotterdam is a major port.* 鹿特丹是一个重要的港口城市。 **2** 🔑 [C, U] (*abbr.* **Pt.**) a place where ships load and unload goods or shelter from storms 港口；避风港：*a naval port* 军港 ◇ *The ship spent four days **in port**.* 这艘船在港口停泊了四天。◇ *They reached port at last.* 他们终于抵达港口。◇ ***port of entry*** (= a place where people or goods can enter a country) 入境口岸 ➲ SEE ALSO AIRPORT, FREE PORT, HELIPORT, SEAPORT **3** (*also* **port ˈwine**) [U] a strong sweet wine, usually dark red, that is made in Portugal. It is usually drunk at the end of a meal. 波尔图葡萄酒（葡萄牙产） **4** [C] a glass of port 一杯波尔图葡萄酒 **5** [U] the side of a ship or aircraft that is on the left when you are facing forward（船、飞机等的）左舷：*the port side* 左舷 ➲ COMPARE STARBOARD **6** [C] (*computing* 计) a place on a computer where you can attach another piece of equipment, often using a cable（输出或输入）端口，接口：*the modem port* 调制解调器端口 ➲ VISUAL VOCAB PAGE V73
IDM **any port in a ˈstorm** (*saying*) if you are in great trouble, you take any help that is offered 慌不择路；饥不择食；有病乱投医
■ *verb* **1 ~ sth (from sth) (to sth)** (*computing* 计) to copy software from one system or machine to another 移植（软件）：*Is there a problem with apps ported from another platform?* 从另一个平台移入的应用程序是否会有问题？ **2 ~ sth (to sth)** to continue to use the same number when you change from one phone company to another（更换电话公司时）携带（电话号码）：*how to port your number to a new mobile phone* 如何携号使用新手机

port·able /ˈpɔːtəbl; *NAmE* ˈpɔːrt-/ *adj., noun*
■ *adj.* that is easy to carry or to move 便携式的；手提的；轻便的：*a portable TV* 手提电视机 ◇ (*figurative*) *a portable loan/pension* (= that can be moved if you change banks, jobs, etc.) 可转移贷款 / 养老金 ◇ *portable software* 可移植软件 ▸ **port·abil·ity** /ˌpɔːtəˈbɪləti; *NAmE* ˌpɔːrt-/ *noun* [U]: *The new light cover increases this model's portability.* 新型的轻质外壳使这种型号携带更轻便。
■ *noun* a small type of machine that is easy to carry, especially a computer or a television 便携机；（尤指）手提电脑，便携式电视机

port·age /ˈpɔːtɪdʒ; *NAmE* ˈpɔːrt-/ *noun* [U] the act of carrying boats or goods between two rivers（在两条河之间运送船只或货物的）陆上运输，陆上搬运

Porta-john™ /ˈpɔːtə dʒɒn; *NAmE* ˈpɔːrtə dʒɑːn/ *noun* = PORTAPOTTY

Porta·kabin™ /ˈpɔːtəkæbɪn; *NAmE* ˈpɔːrt-/ *noun* (*BrE*) a small building that can be moved from place to place by a vehicle, designed to be used as a temporary office, etc. 波特凯宾房；移动办公室；移动房

por·tal /ˈpɔːtl; *NAmE* ˈpɔːrtl/ *noun* **1** [usually pl.] (*formal or literary*) a large, impressive gate or entrance to a building 壮观的大门；豪华的入口 **2** (*computing* 计) a website that is used as a point of entry to the Internet, where information has been collected that will be useful to a person interested in particular kinds of things 门户；入口站点：*a business/news/shopping portal* 商务 / 新闻 / 购物门户

Porta·loo™ /ˈpɔːtəluː; *NAmE* ˈpɔːrt-/ (*BrE*) (*NAmE* **porta-potty**, **Porta-john™**) *noun* (*pl.* **-oos**) a toilet inside a small light building that can be moved from place to place 波特庐移动厕所

ˈportal vein (*also* **hepatic ˈportal vein**) *noun* (*anatomy* 解) a VEIN that takes blood from the stomach and other organs near the stomach to the LIVER 门静脉

porta·potty (*also* **Porta Potti™**) /ˈpɔːtəpɒti; *NAmE* ˈpɔːrtəpɑːti/ *noun* (*pl.* **-ies**) **1** (*NAmE*) (*BrE* **Portaloo™**) (*NAmE also* **Porta-john™**) a toilet inside a small light building that can be moved from place to place 移动厕所 **2** (*BrE*) a toilet that you can take with you when you are travelling 户外便携式坐便器

port·cul·lis /pɔːtˈkʌlɪs; *NAmE* pɔːrt-/ *noun* a strong, heavy iron gate that can be raised or let down at the entrance to a castle（城堡入口可升降的）铁闸门，吊闸门

por·tend /pɔːˈtend; *NAmE* pɔːrˈt-/ *verb* **~ sth** (*formal*) to be a sign or warning of sth that is going to happen in the future, especially sth bad or unpleasant 预兆，预示，预告（尤指坏事） SYN **foreshadow**

por·tent /ˈpɔːtent; *NAmE* ˈpɔːrt-/ *noun* (*literary*) a sign or warning of sth that is going to happen in the future, especially when it is sth unpleasant 预兆；征兆；先兆；（尤指）恶兆，凶兆 SYN **omen**

por·tent·ous /pɔːˈtentəs; *NAmE* pɔːrˈt-/ *adj.* **1** (*literary*) important as a sign or a warning of sth that is going to happen in the future, especially when it is sth unpleasant 预示（坏事）的；先兆的：*a portentous sign* 不祥的征兆 **2** (*formal, disapproving*) very serious and intended to impress people 煞有介事的；装腔作势的；装模作样的 SYN **pompous**：*a portentous remark* 装腔作势的言论 ▶ **por·tent·ous·ly** *adv.* **por·tent·ous·ness** *noun* [U]

por·ter /'pɔːtə(r); *NAmE* 'pɔːrt-/ *noun* **1** a person whose job is carrying people's bags and other loads, especially at a train station, an airport or in a hotel （尤指火车站、机场或旅馆）行李员，搬运工 ➲ SEE ALSO KITCHEN PORTER **2** (*BrE*) a person whose job is to move patients from one place to another in a hospital （医院里护送病人的）护工 **3** (*BrE*) a person whose job is to be in charge of the entrance to a hotel, large building, college, etc. 门卫；门房：*the night porter* 夜班门卫 ◊ *The hotel porter will get you a taxi.* 旅馆的门卫会给你叫出租车的。➲ COMPARE DOORMAN **4** (*NAmE*) a person whose job is helping passengers on a train, especially in a SLEEPING CAR （尤指卧铺车厢的）列车服务员

port·folio /pɔːt'fəʊliəʊ; *NAmE* pɔːrt'foʊlioʊ/ *noun* (*pl.* **-os**) **1** a thin flat case used for carrying documents, drawings, etc. 文件夹；公事包 **2** a collection of photographs, drawings, etc. that you use as an example of your work, especially when applying for a job （求职时用以证明资历的）作品，整套照片 **3** (*finance* 财) a set of shares owned by a particular person or organization （个人或机构的）投资组合，有价证券组合：***an investment/a share portfolio*** 投资 / 股份组合 ➲ WORDFINDER NOTE AT INVEST **4** (*formal, especially BrE*) the particular area of responsibility of a government minister （部长或大臣的）职责，职务：*the defence portfolio* 国防部长职责 ◊ *She resigned her portfolio.* 她辞去了部长职务。◊ *He was asked to join as a **minister without portfolio*** (= one without responsibility for a particular government department). 他获邀出任不管部大臣。**5** the range of products or services offered by a particular company or organization （公司或机构提供的）系列产品，系列服务：*a portfolio of wines* 系列葡萄酒

port·hole /'pɔːthəʊl; *NAmE* 'pɔːrthoʊl/ *noun* a round window in the side of a ship or an aircraft （船、飞机等的）舷窗

por·tico /'pɔːtɪkəʊ; *NAmE* 'pɔːrtɪkoʊ/ *noun* (*pl.* **-oes** or **-os**) (*formal*) a roof that is supported by columns, especially one that forms the entrance to a large building 门廊；柱廊 ➲ VISUAL VOCAB PAGE V14

por·tion AW /'pɔːʃn; *NAmE* 'pɔːrʃn/ *noun, verb*

■ ***noun*** **1** one part of sth larger 部分：*a **substantial/significant portion** of the population* 人口中的一大部分 / 重要部分 ◊ *Only a small portion of the budget is spent on books.* 购书只占预算的一小部分。◊ *The central portion of the bridge collapsed.* 桥的中段坍塌了。**2** an amount of food that is large enough for one person （食物的）一份，一客：*a generous portion of meat* 一大份肉 ◊ *She cut the cake into six small portions.* 她把蛋糕切成了六小份。**3** [usually sing.] a part of sth that is shared with other people 分享的部分；分担的责任 SYN **share**：*You must accept a portion of the blame for this crisis.* 你必须承担这次危机的一部分责任。

■ ***verb*** to divide sth into parts or portions 把…分成若干份（或部分）：**~ sth** *The factory portions and packs over 12 000 meals a day.* 这个工厂每天分装 12 000 多份饭食。◊ **~ sth out** *Land was portioned out among the clans.* 土地已分给了各个家族。

port·ly /'pɔːtli; *NAmE* 'pɔːrt-/ *adj.* [usually before noun] (especially of an older man 尤指年长男子) rather fat 发福的；发胖的 SYN **stout**

port·man·teau /pɔːt'mæntəʊ; *NAmE* pɔːrt'mæntoʊ/ *noun, adj.*

■ ***noun*** (*pl.* **portmanteaus** or **portmanteaux**) (*old-fashioned*) a large heavy suitcase that opens into two parts 两格式旅行衣箱

■ ***adj.*** [only before noun] consisting of a number of different items that are combined into a single thing 综合的；复合式的：*a portmanteau course* 综合课程 ◊ *'Depression' is a portmanteau condition.* "抑郁症"是一种综合症状。

port'manteau word *noun* a word that is invented by combining the beginning of one word and the end of another and keeping the meaning of each. For example *motel* is a portmanteau word that is a combination of *motor* and *hotel*. 缩合词，合并词（由一个词的词首和另一个词的词尾合成）

ˌport of 'call *noun* (*pl.* **ports of call**) **1** a port where a ship stops during a journey （航行途中的）停靠港，停泊港 **2** (*informal*) a place where you go or stop for a short time, especially when you are going to several places （旅途中的）落脚处，落脚点：*My first port of call in town was the bank.* 我进城的第一站是银行。

por·trait /'pɔːtreɪt; -trət; *NAmE* 'pɔːrtrət/ *noun, adj.*

■ ***noun*** **1** a painting, drawing or photograph of a person, especially of the head and shoulders 肖像；半身画像；半身照：*He had his portrait painted in uniform.* 他让人画了一幅身着制服的画像。◊ *a full-length portrait* 全身画像 ◊ *a portrait painter* 肖像画家 ➲ SYNONYMS AT PICTURE ➲ WORDFINDER NOTE AT PAINTING ➲ COLLOCATIONS AT ART ➲ SEE ALSO SELF-PORTRAIT **2** a detailed description of sb/sth 详细的描述；描绘 SYN **depiction**：*a portrait of life at the French court* 对法国宫廷生活的详细描述

■ ***adj.*** (*computing* 计) (of a page of a document 文件页面) printed so that the top of the page is one of the shorter sides 竖向的；纵向打印格式的 ➲ COMPARE LANDSCAPE *n.* (3)

por·trait·ist /'pɔːtreɪtɪst; -trət-; *NAmE* 'pɔːrtrət-/ *noun* a person who makes portraits 肖像画家（或摄影师等）

por·trait·ure /'pɔːtrətʃə(r); *NAmE* 'pɔːrt-/ *noun* [U] the art of making portraits; the portraits that are made 画像技法；人像摄影法；肖像；画像；照片

por·tray /pɔː'treɪ; *NAmE* pɔːr't-/ *verb* **1 ~ sb/sth** to show sb/sth in a picture; to describe sb/sth in a piece of writing 描绘；描画；描写 SYN **depict** **2 ~ sb/sth (as sb/sth)** to describe or show sb/sth in a particular way, especially when this does not give a complete or accurate impression of what they are like 将…描写成；给人以某种印象；表现 SYN **represent**：*Throughout the trial, he portrayed himself as the victim.* 在审讯过程中，他始终把自己说成是受害者。**3 ~ sb/sth** to act a particular role in a film/movie or play 扮演（某角色）SYN **play**：*Her father will be portrayed by Sean Connery.* 肖恩·康纳利将饰演她的父亲。

por·tray·al /pɔː'treɪəl; *NAmE* pɔːr't-/ *noun* [C, U] the act of showing or describing sb/sth in a picture, play, book, etc.; a particular way in which this is done 描绘；描述；描写；展现方式：*The article examines the portrayal of gay men in the media.* 这篇文章剖析了传媒对男同性恋者的描述。◊ *He is best known for his chilling portrayal of Hannibal Lecter.* 他以饰演令人毛骨悚然的汉尼拔·莱克特而著称。

Por·tu·guese /ˌpɔːtʃu'giːz; *NAmE* ˌpɔːrt-/ *adj., noun*

■ ***adj.*** from or connected with Portugal 葡萄牙的

■ ***noun*** **1** [C] (*pl.* **Por·tu·guese**) a person from Portugal 葡萄牙人 **2** [U] the language used in Portugal and Brazil and some other countries 葡萄牙语

pose 🔑 AW /pəʊz; *NAmE* poʊz/ *verb, noun*

■ ***verb*** **1** 🔑 [T] **~ sth** to create a threat, problem, etc. that has to be dealt with 造成（威胁、问题等）；引起；产生：*to **pose a threat/challenge/danger/risk*** 构成威胁 / 挑战 / 危险 / 风险 ◊ *The task **poses no special problems**.* 这项任务不会造成特别的问题。**2** [T] **~ a question** (*formal*) to ask a question, especially one that needs serious thought 提问；质询 **3** 🔑 [I] **~ (for sb/sth)** to sit or stand in a particular position in order to be painted, drawn or photographed （为画像、摄影）摆好姿势：*The delegates posed for a group photograph.* 代表们摆好姿势准备拍集体照。**4** 🔑 [I] **~ as sb** to pretend to be sb in order to trick other people 佯装；冒充；假扮：*The gang entered the building posing as workmen.* 这伙匪徒冒充工人混进了大楼。**5** [I] (usually used in the progressive tenses 通常用

P

于进行时) (*disapproving*) to dress or behave in a way that is intended to impress other people 招摇；炫耀；拿姿作态：*I saw him out posing in his new sports car.* 我看见他开着他的崭新跑车招摇过市。

■ ***noun*** **1** a particular position in which sb stands, sits, etc., especially in order to be painted, drawn or photographed （为画像、拍照等摆的）姿势：*He adopted a relaxed pose for the camera.* 他摆了个悠闲的姿势拍照。**2** (*disapproving*) a way of behaving that is not sincere and is only intended to impress other people 装腔作势；故作姿态 SYN **affectation** IDM SEE STRIKE *v.*

poser /ˈpəʊzə(r); *NAmE* ˈpoʊ-/ *noun* **1** (*informal*) a difficult question or problem 难题；困难；棘手的事 SYN **puzzler** **2** (*also* **pos·eur**) (*disapproving*) a person who behaves or dresses in a way that is intended to impress other people and is not sincere 装腔作势的人；装模作样的人

pos·eur /pəʊˈzɜː(r); *NAmE* poʊ-/ *noun* = POSER (2)

posey /ˈpəʊzi; *NAmE* ˈpoʊzi/ *adj.* (*informal*) trying to impress other people, especially in a way that is silly or not natural 竭力表现的；虚夸的；张扬而做作的

posh /pɒʃ; *NAmE* pɑːʃ/ *adj.* (**posh·er, posh·est**) (*informal*) **1** elegant and expensive 优雅豪华的；富丽堂皇的：*a posh hotel* 豪华旅馆 ◇ *You look very posh in your new suit.* 你穿上新套装显得雍容华贵。**2** (*BrE, sometimes disapproving*) typical of or used by people who belong to a high social class 上流社会的；上等人的 SYN **stylish**：*a posh accent/voice* 上等人的腔调 / 嗓音 ◇ *They live in the posh part of town.* 他们生活在市内的富人区。◇ *They pay for their children to go to a posh school.* 他们花钱让子女上贵族学校。▸ **posh** *adv.*：(*BrE*) *to talk posh* 谈吐高雅

posho /ˈpɒʃəʊ; *NAmE* ˈpɑːʃoʊ/ *noun* **1** [C] (*pl.* **-os**) (*BrE, informal, disapproving*) a person from a high social class 上等人；贵人 **2** [U] (*EAfrE*) a type of flour made from MAIZE (CORN) 玉米粉：*a posho mill* 玉米粉研磨机

P

ˈ**posing pouch** *noun* (*BrE*) an item of men's clothing that covers only the GENITALS （只遮盖生殖器的）一点式男内裤

posit /ˈpɒzɪt; *NAmE* ˈpɑːz-/ *verb* **~ sth | ~ that...** (*formal*) to suggest or accept that sth is true so that it can be used as the basis for an argument or a discussion 假设；认定；认为…属实 SYN **postulate**：*Most religions posit the existence of life after death.* 大多数宗教都假定人死后生命仍存在。

pos·ition /pəˈzɪʃn/ *noun, verb*

■ ***noun***

• **PLACE** 地方 **1** [C] the place where sb/sth is located 位置；地方：*From his position on the cliff top, he had a good view of the harbour.* 他在悬崖之巅，海港景色一览无余。◇ *Where would be the best position for the lights?* 这些灯装在什么位置最好？ ➲ SYNONYMS AT PLACE **2** [U] the place where sb/sth is meant to be; the correct place 恰当位置；正确位置：*Is everybody **in position**?* 大家都就位了吗？ ◇ *He took up his position by the door.* 他到门边就位。

• **WAY SB/STH IS PLACED** 安置方式 **3** [C, U] the way in which sb is sitting or standing, or the way in which sth is arranged （坐或站的）姿态，姿势；放置方式：*a **sitting/kneeling/lying position*** 坐姿；跪姿；卧姿 ◇ *Keep the box in an upright position.* 把盒子竖着放。◇ *Make sure that you are working in a comfortable position.* 工作时一定要保持舒适的姿势。◇ *My arms were aching so I shifted (my) position slightly.* 我胳膊疼了，所以稍微变了变姿势。➲ SEE ALSO MISSIONARY POSITION

• **SITUATION** 情势 **4** [C, usually sing.] the situation that sb is in, especially when it affects what they can and cannot do 处境；地位；状况：*to be in a **position of power/strength/authority*** 处于有权力 / 有实力 / 有权威的地位 ◇ *What would you do in my position?* 你要是碰到我这样的情况会怎么办？ ◇ *This put him and his colleagues in a difficult position.* 这使他和他的同事陷于困境。◇ *The company's financial position is not certain.* 这家公司的财务状况不明朗。◇ **~ to do sth** *I'm afraid I am **not in a position** to help you.* 我恐怕帮不了你。➲ SYNONYMS AT SITUATION

• **OPINION** 看法 **5** [C] **~ (on sth)** an opinion on or an attitude towards a particular subject 观点；态度；立场：*to **declare/reconsider/shift/change your position*** 表明 / 重新考虑 / 转变 / 改变立场 ◇ *the party's position on education reforms* 这个党对教育改革的态度 ◇ *She has made her position very clear.* 她明确表示了自己的立场。◇ *My parents always **took the position** that early nights meant healthy children.* 我的父母总是认为孩子早睡就会身体健康。

• **LEVEL OF IMPORTANCE** 重要程度 **6** [C, U] a person or organization's level of importance when compared with others 地位；等级：*the position of women in society* 妇女的社会地位 ◇ *the company's dominant position in the world market* 那个公司在全球市场中的主导地位 ◇ *Wealth and position* (= high social status) *were not important to her.* 财富与地位对她并不重要。

• **JOB** 工作 **7** [C] (*formal*) a job 职位；职务 SYN **post**：*He held a senior position in a large company.* 他在一家大公司担任高级职务。◇ *I should like to apply for the position of Sales Director.* 我想申请销售总监一职。➲ SYNONYMS AT JOB

• **IN RACE/COMPETITION** 竞赛；竞争 **8** [C] a place in a race, competition, or test, when compared to others 名次：*United's 3–0 win moved them up to third position.* 联队 3:0 的胜利使他们排名升至第三。

• **IN SPORT** 体育运动 **9** [C] the place where sb plays and the responsibilities they have in some team games （队员的）职责，位置，角色：*What position does he play?* 他打哪个位置？

• **IN WAR** 战争 **10** [C, usually pl.] a place where a group of people involved in fighting have put men and guns 阵地：*They attacked the enemy positions at dawn.* 黎明时分，他们向敌军阵地发起进攻。

■ ***verb*** **~ sth** (+ **adv./prep.**) to put sb/sth in a particular position 安装；安置；使处于 SYN **place**：*Large television screens were positioned at either end of the stadium.* 体育场的两端安装了大型电视屏幕。◇ *She quickly positioned herself behind the desk.* 她迅速在桌子后面她的位置上坐好。◇ *The company is now well positioned to compete in foreign markets.* 现在这家公司已准备好在国外市场竞争。▸ **pos·ition·ing** *noun* [U]

pos·ition·al /pəˈzɪʃənəl/ *adj.* [only before noun] (*specialist or sport* 体育) connected with the position of sb/sth 位置上的；地位上的；职位上的：*The team has made some positional changes because two players are injured.* 因有两名队员受伤，这个队将队员做了些位置上的调整。

poˈsition paper *noun* a written report from an organization or a government department that explains or recommends a particular course of action （机构或政府部门的）行动报告，施政说明，建议书

posi·tive AW /ˈpɒzətɪv; *NAmE* ˈpɑːz-/ *adj., noun*

■ ***adj.***

• **CONFIDENT** 有信心 **1** thinking about what is good in a situation; feeling confident and sure that sth good will happen 积极乐观的；自信的：*a **positive attitude/outlook*** 乐观的态度 / 前景 ◇ *the power of positive thought* 乐观思想的力量 ◇ **~ (about sth)** *She tried to be more positive about her new job.* 她努力更积极地投入新工作。◇ ***On the positive side**, profits have increased.* 从好的方面看，利润增加了。◇ *The report ended on a positive note.* 报告的结尾显得很乐观。OPP **negative**

• **EFFECTIVE/USEFUL** 有效；有用 **2** directed at dealing with sth or producing a successful result 积极的；建设性的；朝着成功的：*We must take **positive steps** to deal with the problem.* 我们必须采取积极措施处理这个问题。◇ *It will require **positive action** by all in the industry.* 这将需要业内全体同人和衷共济。OPP **negative** **3** expressing agreement or support 表示赞同的；拥护的：*We've had a very positive response to the idea.* 我们这个想法反响很好。OPP **negative** **4** good or useful 良好的；有助益的；正面的：*to make a positive contribution to a discussion* 给讨论会提出好的建言 ◇ *His family have been a very positive influence on him.* 他的家庭对他有十分良好的影响。◇ *Overseas investment has had a positive effect on exports.* 海外投资对出口有积极影响。OPP **negative**

- **SURE/DEFINITE** 确信；肯定 **5** [not before noun] (of a person 人) completely sure that sth is correct or true 有绝对把握；确信；肯定： **~ (about sth)** *I can't be positive about what time it happened.* 我说不准这事是什么时间发生的。◇ **~ (that...)** *She was positive that he had been there.* 她确信他曾在场。◇ *'Are you sure?' 'Positive.'* "你敢肯定吗？" "绝对肯定。" ➲ SYNONYMS AT SURE **6** [only before noun] (*informal*) complete and definite 完全的；绝对的 SYN **absolute**: *He has a positive genius for upsetting people.* 他气人的本事可大呢。◇ *It was a positive miracle that we survived.* 我们能够生还，完全是个奇迹。 **7** giving clear and definite proof or information 证据确凿的；明确的 SYN **conclusive**: *We have no positive evidence that she was involved.* 我们没有确凿证据证明她参与其事。◇ (*formal*) *This is **proof positive** that he stole the money.* 这就是他偷钱的确证。
- **SCIENTIFIC TEST** 科学试验 **8** showing clear evidence that a particular substance or medical condition is present 阳性的；证明…存在的： *a positive pregnancy test* 呈阳性反应的怀孕检测 ◇ *The athlete **tested positive** for steroids.* 这个运动员类固醇检测呈阳性。◇ *to be HIV positive* 艾滋病病毒化验呈阳性 OPP **negative**
- **NUMBER/QUANTITY** 数目；数量 **9** greater than zero 正数的 OPP **negative**
- **ELECTRICITY** 电 **10** (*specialist*) containing or producing the type of electricity that is carried by a PROTON 正电的；正极的： *a **positive charge*** 正电荷 ◇ *the **positive terminal** of a battery* 电池的正极 OPP **negative**

■ *noun*

- **GOOD QUALITY** 优点 **1** [C, U] a good or useful quality or aspect 优势；优点： *Take your weaknesses and translate them into positives.* 把你的弱点变成优点。
- **IN PHOTOGRAPHY** 摄影 **2** [C] (*specialist*) a developed film showing light and dark areas and colours as they actually were, especially one printed from a NEGATIVE 正片
- **RESULT OF TEST** 化验结果 **3** [C] the result of a test or an experiment that shows that a substance or condition is present 阳性结果（或反应） OPP **negative**

ˌpositive disˌcriminˈation (*BrE*) (*also* **afˌfirmative ˈaction** *NAmE, BrE*) *noun* [U] the practice or policy of making sure that a particular number of jobs, etc. are given to people from groups that are often treated unfairly because of their race, sex, etc. 积极区别对待政策（对因种族、性别等原因遭歧视的群体在就业等方面给予特别照顾） ➲ COLLOCATIONS AT RACE ➲ COMPARE REVERSE DISCRIMINATION

posi·tive·ly AW /ˈpɒzətɪvli; *NAmE* ˈpɑːz-/ *adv.* **1** used to emphasize the truth of a statement, especially when this is surprising or when it contrasts with a previous statement 绝对地；肯定地： *The instructions were not just confusing, they were positively misleading.* 这些指示不单令人费解，而且肯定会误导人。 **2** in a way that shows you are thinking of the good things about a situation, not the bad 乐观地；肯定地；积极地： *Very few of those interviewed spoke positively about their childhood.* 接受采访的人当中，很少有人说他们的童年是快乐的。◇ *Thinking positively is one way of dealing with stress.* 保持乐观是对付压力的一种方法。 OPP **negatively** **3** in a way that shows you approve of or agree with sth/sb 赞成地；积极地： *Investors reacted positively to news of the takeover.* 投资者对公司收购的消息反应积极。 OPP **negatively** **4** in a way that leaves no possibility of doubt 明确地；明白无误地 SYN **conclusively**: *Her attacker has now been positively identified by police.* 袭击她的人现在已被警方确认。 **5** (*specialist*) in a way that contains or produces the type of electricity that is opposite to that carried by an ELECTRON 带（或产生）正电地： *positively charged protons* 带正电的质子 OPP **negatively**

ˌpositive ˈvetting *noun* [U, C] (*BrE*) the process of checking everything about a person's background and character when they apply for a job in which they will have to deal with secret information, especially in the CIVIL SERVICE 道德审查（对申请从事保密工作者的背景和品行进行检查）

posi·tiv·ism /ˈpɒzətɪvɪzəm; *NAmE* ˈpɑːz-/ *noun* [U] a system of philosophy based on things that can be seen or proved, rather than on ideas 实证主义；实证哲学；实证论 ▸ **posi·tiv·ist** /-vɪst/ *noun* **posi·tiv·ist** *adj.*: *a positivist approach* 实证主义方式

posi·tron /ˈpɒzɪtrɒn; *NAmE* ˈpɑːzɪtrɑːn/ *noun* (*physics* 物) a PARTICLE in an atom which has the same mass as an ELECTRON and an equal but positive charge 正电子；阳电子 ➲ WORDFINDER NOTE AT ATOM

poss /pɒs; *NAmE* pɑːs/ *adj.* [not before noun] (*BrE, informal*) possible 可能： *I'll be there **if poss**.* 如果可能，我会去那里的。◇ *as soon **as poss*** 尽快

posse /ˈpɒsi; *NAmE* ˈpɑːsi/ *noun* **1** (*informal*) a group of people who are similar in some way, or who spend time together 一群，一队，一伙（有共同之处的人）： *a little posse of helpers* 一小伙帮忙的人 **2** (in the US in the past) a group of people who were brought together by a SHERIFF (= an officer of the law) in order to help him catch a criminal （美国旧时由县治安官调集、协助捉拿罪犯的）地方武装团队 **3** (*informal*) a group of young men involved in crime connected with drugs （与毒品有关的）青年犯罪团伙

pos·sess /pəˈzes/ *verb* (not used in the progressive tenses 不用于进行时) **1** **~ sth** (*formal*) to have or own sth 有；拥有： *He was charged with possessing a shotgun without a licence.* 他被控无照拥有猎枪。◇ *The gallery possesses a number of the artist's early works.* 这家画廊藏有那位画家的一些早期作品。 **2** **~ sth** (*formal*) to have a particular quality or feature 具有（特质）： *I'm afraid he doesn't possess a sense of humour.* 恐怕他没有什么幽默感。 **3** [usually passive] **~ sb** (*literary*) (of a feeling, an emotion, etc. 感觉、情绪等) to have a powerful effect on sb and control the way that they think, behave, etc. 攫住；支配；控制 **4** **~ sb to do sth** (used in negative sentences and questions 用于否定句和疑问句) to make sb do sth that seems strange or unreasonable 使言行失常： *What possessed him to say such a thing?* 他着了什么魔竟说出这种话来？

pos·sessed /pəˈzest/ *adj.* [not before noun] **~ (by sth)** (of a person or their mind 人或头脑) controlled by an evil spirit 着了魔： *She has convinced herself that she is possessed by the devil.* 她确信自己被魔鬼附了身。

IDM **be possessed of sth** (*formal*) to have a particular quality or feature 具有某种品质（或特征）： *She was possessed of exceptional powers of concentration.* 她有高超的专注能力。 **like a man/woman posˈsessed | like one posˈsessed** with a lot of force or energy 着了魔似的；拼命地；猛烈地： *He flew out of the room like a man possessed.* 他猛然冲出房门，像着了魔似的。

pos·ses·sion /pəˈzeʃn/ *noun*

- **HAVING/OWNING** 拥有 **1** [U] (*formal*) the state of having or owning sth 具有；拥有： *The manuscript is just one of the treasures **in their possession**.* 这部手稿只是他们的珍藏之一。◇ *The gang was caught **in possession of** stolen goods.* 这伙人被逮住，人赃俱获。 ◇ *The possession of a passport is essential for foreign travel.* 出国旅行必须持有护照。◇ *On her father's death, she **came into possession of*** (= received) *a vast fortune.* 她父亲死后，她继承了一大笔财产。◇ *You cannot legally **take possession of** the property* (= start using it after buying it) *until three weeks after the contract is signed.* 契约签署三周以后，你才能合法取得这份产业的所有权。 ➲ SEE ALSO VACANT POSSESSION **2** [C, usually pl.] something that you own or have with you at a particular time 个人财产；私人物品 SYN **belongings**: *personal possessions* 私人物品 ◇ *The ring is one of her most treasured possessions.* 这只戒指是她最珍贵的财产之一。 ➲ SYNONYMS AT THING
- **IN SPORT** 体育运动 **3** [U] the state of having control of the ball 控球状态： *to **win/get/lose possession** of the ball* 赢得 / 得到 / 失去对球的控制
- **LAW** 法律 **4** [U] the state of having illegal drugs or weapons with you at a particular time 持有违禁物；私藏毒品（或武器）： *She was charged with possession.* 她被控持有违禁物品。

P

• COUNTRY 国家 **5** [C] (*formal*) a country that is controlled or governed by another country 殖民地；托管地；属地

• BY EVIL SPIRIT 受恶魔控制 **6** [U] the situation when sb's mind is believed to be controlled by the DEVIL or by an evil spirit 鬼魂缠身；着魔

IDM **possession is nine tenths of the 'law** (*saying*) if you already have or control sth, it is difficult for sb else to take it away from you, even if they have the legal right to it 现实占有，败一胜九；占有者在诉讼中总占上风 ➲ MORE AT FIELD *n.*

pos·ses·sive /pəˈzesɪv/ *adj., noun*

■ *adj.* **1** ~ (**of/about sb/sth**) demanding total attention or love; not wanting sb to be independent 要求悉心关爱的；占有欲强的：*Some parents are too possessive of their children.* 有些父母过分要求子女百依百顺。 **2** ~ (**of/about sth**) not liking to lend things or share things with others 不愿分享的；有独占欲望的：*Jimmy's very possessive about his toys.* 吉米的玩具谁也碰不得。 **3** [usually before noun] (*grammar* 语法) showing that sth belongs to sb/sth 表示所属关系的；所有格的：*possessive pronouns* (= yours, theirs, etc.) 物主代词 ▶ **pos·ses·sive·ly** *adv.*：*'That's mine!' she said possessively.* "那是我的！"她霸道地说。 **pos·ses·sive·ness** *noun* [U]：*I couldn't stand his jealousy and possessiveness.* 我受不了他的嫉妒与霸道作风。

■ *noun* (*grammar* 语法) **1** [C] a pronoun or a form of a word that expresses the fact that sth belongs to sb/sth 所有格；属有词：*'Ours' and 'their' are possessives.* * ours 和 their 是所有格形式。 **2 the possessive** *noun* [sing.] the special form of a word that expresses belonging 所有格 ➲ COMPARE GENITIVE

pos·ses·sor /pəˈzesə(r)/ *noun* (*formal* or *humorous*) a person who owns or has sth 持有人；所有者 SYN **owner**：*He is now **the proud possessor** of a driving licence.* 他现在有了驾驶执照，颇有些飘飘然。

pos·set /ˈpɒsɪt; *NAmE* ˈpɑːs-/ *noun, verb*

■ *noun* [U] **1** in the past, a drink made with hot milk and beer or wine 牛奶甜酒（旧时用热牛奶加啤酒或葡萄酒调制而成） **2** a dessert made with cream and fruit, often lemons 奶油水果甜点（水果常用柠檬）

■ *verb* (*BrE*) (**-tt-**, *NAmE also* **-t-**) [I] if a baby **possets**, milk comes back up from its stomach and out through its mouth （婴儿）漾奶，吐奶

pos·si·bil·ity 🔑 /ˌpɒsəˈbɪləti; *NAmE* ˌpɑːs-/ *noun* (*pl.* **-ies**)

1 🔑 [U, C] the fact that sth might exist or happen, but is not certain to 可能；可能性：~ (**that…**) *There is now no possibility that she will make a full recovery.* 她现在已不可能完全康复。 ◇ ~ (**of sth/of doing sth**) *He refused to rule out the possibility of a tax increase.* 他拒绝排除增税的可能性。 ◇ *It is not **beyond the bounds of possibility** that we'll all meet again one day.* 我们大家将来有一天再度聚在一起，并非绝不可能。 ◇ *Bankruptcy is a real possibility if sales don't improve.* 如果销售情况得不到改善，真有破产的可能。 ◇ *What had seemed impossible now seemed a **distinct possibility**.* 过去看似不可能的事，现在显然有可能了。 OPP **impossibility** **2** 🔑 [C, usually pl.] one of the different things that you can do in a particular situation 可选择的方法：*to **explore/consider/investigate** a wide **range of possibilities*** 探究／考虑／调查各种可能的情况 ◇ *to **exhaust** all the **possibilities*** 用尽一切可能的手段 ◇ *Selling the house is just one possibility that is open to us.* 卖掉房子只是我们可以选择的其中一种做法。 ◇ ***The possibilities are endless.*** 可想的办法是无穷的。 ➲ SYNONYMS AT OPTION **3** 🔑 [C, usually pl.] something that gives you a chance to achieve sth 机会；契机 SYN **opportunity**：*The course offers a range of exciting possibilities for developing your skills.* 这门课程可提供一整套新鲜活泼的技能训练。 **4 possibilities** [pl.] if sth **has possibilities**, it can be improved or made successful 潜力；改进的余地 SYN **potential**：*The house is in a bad state of repair but it has possibilities.* 这房子虽亟待修缮，但仍有可资利用的价值。

pos·sible 🔑 /ˈpɒsəbl; *NAmE* ˈpɑːs-/ *adj., noun*

■ *adj.* **1** 🔑 [not usually before noun] that can be done or achieved 可能；能做到（或取得）：*It is possible to get there by bus.* 可以乘公共汽车到那里。 ◇ *Would it be possible for me to leave a message for her?* 我可以给她留个话儿吗？ ◇ *This wouldn't have been possible without you.* 若没有你，这事恐怕就办不成了。 ◇ *Try to avoid losing your temper **if at all possible*** (= if you can). 尽可能别发脾气。 ◇ *Use public transport **whenever possible*** (= when you can). 只要可能，就利用公共交通。 ◇ *It's just not **physically possible** to finish all this by the end of the week.* 要在本周末完成这一切，这在客观上是办不到的。 ◇ *We spent every possible moment on the beach.* 我们一有时间就到海滩边去。 OPP **impossible** ➲ EXPRESS YOURSELF AT FORBID, PERMISSION **2** 🔑 that might exist or happen but is not certain to 可能存在（或发生）的：*a possible future president* 未来可能当选总统的人 ◇ *the possible side effects of the drug* 这种药可能产生的副作用 ◇ *Frost is possible, although unlikely, at this time of year.* 每年这个时节都有可能下霜，只是并不常见。 ◇ *It's just possible that I gave them the wrong directions.* 我也许给他们指错了方向。 ◇ *With the possible exception of the Beatles, no other band has become so successful so quickly.* 可能除了披头士乐队这个例外，还没有哪个乐队如此转瞬走红的。 ➲ LANGUAGE BANK AT PERHAPS **3** 🔑 reasonable or acceptable in a particular situation 合理的；可接受的：*There are several possible explanations.* 有几种合理的解释。 **4** used after adjectives to emphasize that sth is the best, worst, etc. of its type （用于形容词后表示强调）最…的：*It was the **best possible** surprise anyone could have given me.* 那是我曾感受过的最大惊喜。 ◇ *Don't leave your packing until the **last possible** moment.* 打点行李不要拖到最后一刻。

IDM **as quickly, much, soon, etc. as 'possible** 🔑 as quickly, much, soon, etc. as you can 尽量快（或多、早等）：*We will get your order to you as soon as possible.* 我们将会把您的订货尽早送达。 ➲ MORE AT WORLD, WORST *n.*

■ *noun* a person or thing that is suitable for a particular job, purpose, etc. and might be chosen 合适的人（或物）；恰当人选（或事项）：*Out of all the people interviewed, there are only five possibles.* 在所有面试过的人中，仅有五个合适的人选。

pos·sibly 🔑 /ˈpɒsəbli; *NAmE* ˈpɑːs-/ *adv.* **1** 🔑 used to say that sth might exist, happen or be true, but you are not certain 可能；或许 SYN **perhaps**：*It was possibly their worst performance ever.* 这也许是他们迄今为止最糟糕的表现。 ◇ *She found it difficult to get on with her, possibly because of the difference in their ages.* 她觉得很难与她相处，这可能是因为她们年龄上的差距。 ◇ *'Will you be around next week?' 'Possibly.'* "你下周过来吗？" "也许吧。" ➲ LANGUAGE BANK AT PERHAPS ➲ EXPRESS YOURSELF AT LIKELY **2** 🔑 used to emphasize that you are surprised, annoyed, etc. about sth （强调惊奇、恼怒等）：*You can't possibly mean that!* 你绝不会是那个意思吧！ **3** 🔑 used to ask sb politely to do sth （表示委婉的请求）：*Could you possibly open that window?* 请你把那扇窗子打开好吗？ **4** 🔑 used to say that sb will do or has done as much as they can in order to make sth happen 尽量；尽可能：*I will come as soon as I possibly can.* 我会尽快赶来的。 ◇ *They tried everything they possibly could to improve the situation.* 他们为改善局面用尽了一切办法。 **5** used with negatives, especially 'can't' and 'couldn't', to say strongly that you cannot do sth or that sth cannot or could not happen or be done （与 can't、couldn't 等否定词连用，以加强语气）：*I can't possibly tell you that!* 我绝不会把那件事告诉你的！ ◇ *You can't possibly carry all those bags.* 你绝拿不了所有这些包包袋袋的。 ◇ *'Let me buy it for you.' 'That's very kind of you, but I couldn't possibly* (= accept).' "这个，我买给你吧。" "您太客气了。可我决不能让您破费呀。"

pos·sum /ˈpɒsəm; *NAmE* ˈpɑːsəm/ *noun* (*AustralE, NZE* or *NAmE, informal*) = OPOSSUM

IDM **play 'possum** (*informal*) to pretend to be asleep or not aware of sth, in order to trick sb 装睡；装蒜；装傻；装糊涂

post 🔑 /pəʊst; *NAmE* poʊst/ *noun, verb*

■ *noun*

• LETTERS 信函 **1** 🔑 (*BrE*) (*also* **mail** *NAmE, BrE*) [U] the official system used for sending and delivering letters, packages, etc. 邮政；邮递；邮寄：*I'll send the original to* *you* **by post**. 我将把原件邮寄给你。◇ *I'll put the information* **in the post** *to you tomorrow.* 我明天会把资料邮寄给你。◇ *My application* **got lost in the post**. 我的申请书寄丢了。 **2** (*BrE*) (*also* **mail** *NAmE, BrE*) [U] letters, packages, etc. that are sent and delivered 邮寄的信函（或包裹等）；邮件： *There was a lot of post this morning.* 今天上午邮件很多。◇ *Have you opened your post yet?* 你拆开你的邮件了没有？ **3** (*BrE*) [U, sing.] an occasion during the day when letters, etc. are collected or delivered 收集（或投递）邮件的时间；邮班： *to* **catch/miss the post** 赶上 / 错过邮班 ◇ *The parcel came in this morning's post.* 这个包裹是今天上午邮送来的。◇ *Payment should be sent* **by return of post** (= immediately). 请立即付款。

• **JOB** 工作 **4** [C] a job, especially an important one in a large organization 职位；（尤指）要职 **SYN** **position**: *an academic/a government post* 教学 / 政府职位 ◇ *to* **take up a post** 就职 ◇ *to* **resign (from) a post** 辞职 ◇ *We will be creating 15 new posts next year.* 明年我们将增设 15 个新职位。◇ *The company has been unable to* **fill the post**. 公司的这个空缺还未能填补。◇ *He has* **held the post** *for three years.* 他担任这个职务已经三年了。 ➲ SYNONYMS AT JOB **5** (*especially NAmE*) (*BrE usually* **post·ing**) an act of sending sb to a particular place to do their job, especially for a limited period of time 派驻： *an overseas post* 派驻海外

• **FOR SOLDIER/GUARD** 士兵；警卫 **6** [C] the place where sb, especially a soldier, does their job 哨所；岗位： *a* **police/customs/military post** 警察岗亭；海关关卡；军事哨所 ◇ *an observation post* 观察哨所 ◇ *The guards were ordered not to leave their posts.* 警卫受命不得擅离岗位。 ➲ SEE ALSO LAST POST, STAGING POST, TRADING POST

• **WOOD/METAL** 木头；金属 **7** [C] (often in compounds 常构成复合词) a piece of wood or metal that is set in the ground in a vertical position, especially to support sth or to mark a point 柱；桩；标志杆： *corner posts* (= that mark the corners of a sports field) 运动场的角杆 ➲ SEE ALSO BEDPOST, GATEPOST, LAMP POST, SIGNPOST *n.*

• **END OF RACE** 速度比赛终点 **8 the post** [sing.] the place where a race finishes, especially in horse racing （尤指赛马的）终点，终点标志 ➲ SEE ALSO FIRST-PAST-THE-POST, WINNING POST

• **FOOTBALL** 足球 **9** [C, usually sing.] = GOALPOST： *The ball hit the post and bounced in.* 球击在门柱上弹进了球门。

• **INTERNET** 互联网 **10** (*also* **post·ing**) [C] (*computing* 计) a message sent to a discussion group on the Internet; a piece of writing that forms part of a BLOG （发送到互联网讨论组的）帖子，信息；博文；网志文章： *The forum does not allow posts from non-members.* 该论坛不允许非会员发帖。 **IDM** SEE DEAF, PILLAR

■ ***verb***

• **LETTERS** 信函 **1** (*BrE*) (*NAmE* **mail**) [T] to send a letter, etc. to sb by post/mail 寄；邮寄： **~ sth (off) (to sb)** *Have you posted off your order yet?* 你把订单寄出去没有？◇ *Is it OK if I post the cheque to you next week?* 我下周把支票寄给你行不行？ ◇ **~ sb sth** *Is it OK if I post you the cheque next week?* 我下周寄给你支票可以吗？ ➲ COMPARE MAIL *v.* **2** (*BrE*) (*NAmE* **mail**) [T] **~ sth** to put a letter, etc. into a POSTBOX 把（信件等）投入邮筒；投递；邮寄： *Could you post this letter for me?* 请把这封信替我寄了好吗？

• **STH THROUGH HOLE** 塞入孔中 **3** [T] **~ sth + adv./prep.** to put sth through a hole into a container 把…放入（或塞入）： *Let yourself out and post the keys through the letter box.* 你先出去，再把这些钥匙塞进信箱吧。

• **SB FOR JOB** 委派 **4** [T, usually passive] **~ sb + adv./prep.** to send sb to a place for a period of time as part of their job 派驻： *She's been posted to Washington for two years.* 她被派往华盛顿工作两年。 ◇ *Most of our employees get posted abroad at some stage.* 我们的大部分雇员都会在某一时期派驻国外。

• **SOLDIER/GUARD** 士兵；警卫 **5** [T] **~ sb + adv./prep.** to put sb, especially a soldier, in a particular place so that they can guard a building or area 使驻守；布置…站岗： *Guards have been posted along the border.* 边界上已部署了边防岗哨。

• **PUBLIC NOTICE** 公告 **6** [T, often passive] **~ sth + adv./prep.** to put a notice, etc. in a public place so that people can see it 张贴；公布 **SYN** **display**: *A copy of the letter was posted on the noticeboard.* 布告牌上张贴了这封信的内容。

• **GIVE INFORMATION** 发布信息 **7** [T] (*especially NAmE*) to announce sth publicly or officially, especially financial information or a warning 发布，公布，宣布（尤指财经信息或警告）： **~ sth** *The company posted a $1.1 billion loss.* 这家公司公布了 11 亿美元的亏损。◇ *A snow warning was posted for Ohio.* 俄亥俄州已发出大雪警报。 ◇ **~ sb/sth + adj.** *The aircraft and its crew were* **posted missing**. 据报这架飞机和机组人员已失踪。 **8** [T, I] to put information or pictures on a website （在网站上）发布（信息或图片）： **~ sth (on sth)** *The results will be posted on the Internet.* 结果将在互联网上公布。 ◇ **~ (on sth)** *The photos have been provided by fans who post on the message board.* 这些照片由那些在留言板上发布信息的粉丝提供。

• **PAY MONEY TO COURT** 向法院交款 **9** [T] **~ bail/(a) bond** (*especially NAmE*) to pay money to a court so that a person accused of a crime can go free until their trial 交付（保释金）： *She was released after posting $100 cash bond and her driver's license.* 交了 100 美元现款保释金及驾驶执照以后，她获得保释了。 ➲ MORE LIKE THIS 33, page R28

IDM **keep sb 'posted (about/on sth)** to regularly give sb the most recent information about sth and how it is developing 定期通报；及时报告

▼ **BRITISH/AMERICAN** 英式 / 美式英语

post / mail

Nouns 名词

- In *BrE* the official system used for sending and delivering letters, parcels/packages, etc. is usually called the **post**. In *NAmE* it is usually called the **mail**. 邮政系统在英式英语中通常叫做 post，在美式英语中通常称为 mail： *I'll put an application form in the post/mail for you today.* 我今天会把申请表邮寄给你。◇ *Send your fee by post/mail to this address.* 将费用邮寄到此地址。 **Mail** is sometimes used in *BrE* in such expressions as: *the Royal Mail*. **Post** occurs in *NAmE* in such expressions as: *the US Postal Service*. 在英式英语中，mail 有时用于 the Royal Mail（皇家邮政）等短语中。在美式英语中，post 出现在 the US Postal Service（美国邮政管理局）等短语中。
- In *BrE* **post** is also used to mean the letters, parcels/packages, etc. that are delivered to you. **Mail** is the usual word in *NAmE* and is sometimes also used in *BrE*. 在英式英语中，post 亦指邮件。mail 在美式英语中为常用词，有时亦用于英式英语： *Was there any post/mail this morning?* 今早有邮件吗？◇ *I sat down to open my post/mail.* 我坐下来打开我的邮件。

Verbs 动词

- Compare 比较： *I'll post the letter when I go out.* (*BrE*) 我出门时去寄这封信。（英式英语） and 与 *I'll mail the letter when I go out.* (*NAmE*) 我出门时去寄这封信。（美式英语）

Compounds 复合词

- Note these words: **postman** (*BrE*), **mailman/mail carrier** (both *NAmE*); **postbox** (*BrE*), **mailbox** (*NAmE*) Some compounds are used in both *BrE* and *NAmE*. **post office**, **postcard**, **mail order**. 注意下列词汇：邮递员英式英语为 postman，美式英语为 mailman/mail carrier；邮筒英式英语为 postbox，美式英语为 mailbox。有些复合词既用于英式英语，也用于美式英语，如 post office（邮局）、postcard（明信片）、mail order（邮购）。

post- /pəʊst; *NAmE* poʊst/ *prefix* (in nouns, verbs and adjectives 构成名词、动词和形容词) after 后；以后： *a postgraduate* 研究生 ◇ *a post-Impressionist* 后印象主义者 ◇ *the post-1945 period* * 1945 年以后的时期 ➲ COMPARE ANTE-, PRE- ➲ MORE LIKE THIS 6, page R25

post·age /ˈpəʊstɪdʒ; *NAmE* ˈpoʊ-/ *noun* [U] the cost of sending a letter, etc. by post 邮资；邮费： *an increase in postage rates* 邮费的增加 ◇ *How much was the postage on*

P

that letter? 寄那封信要多少钱? ◇ (BrE) All prices include **postage and packing**. 所有的价格都包括邮资和包装费。◇ (NAmE) All prices include **postage and handling**. 所有的价格都包括邮资和手续费。

ˈpostage meter noun (NAmE) = FRANKING MACHINE

ˈpostage stamp noun (formal) = STAMP (1)

pos·tal /ˈpəʊstl; NAmE ˈpoʊstl/ adj. [only before noun] **1** connected with the official system for sending and delivering letters, etc. 邮政的；邮递的：your full **postal address** 你邮政地址的全写 ◇ the **postal service/system** 邮政业务 / 系统 ◇ postal charges 邮费 **2** (especially BrE) involving things that are sent by post 邮寄物品的；邮寄的：postal bookings 邮寄预订

IDM **go ˈpostal** (informal, especially NAmE) to become very angry 大怒：He went postal when he found out. 他发现后勃然大怒。

ˈpostal ballot noun (BrE) a system of voting on a particular issue in which everyone sends their vote by post 邮寄式投票

ˈpostal code noun (BrE, CanE) = POSTCODE

ˈpostal order (BrE) (also **ˈmoney order** NAmE, BrE) noun (abbr. **PO**) an official document that you can buy at a bank or a post office and send to sb so that they can exchange it for money （银行或邮政）汇票

ˈpostal service noun **1** a system of collecting and delivering letters, etc. 邮政业务：a good postal service 良好的邮政服务 **2 the Postal Service** (US) (BrE **the ˈPost Office**) the national organization in many countries that is responsible for collecting and delivering letters, etc. 邮政部门；邮政系统

ˈpostal vote (BrE) (US **ˌabsentee ˈballot**) noun a vote in an election that you can send when you cannot be present 邮寄的选票；邮寄投票

post·bag /ˈpəʊstbæg; NAmE ˈpoʊst-/ noun (BrE) **1** (also **mail·bag** NAmE, BrE) [usually sing.] all the letters, emails, etc. received by a newspaper, a TV station, a website, or an important person at a particular time or about a particular subject （寄给报纸、电视台、网站、要人等的）公众来信：We had a huge postbag on the subject from our readers. 我们收到了读者关于这个问题的大量来函。 **2** = MAILBAG (1)

post·box /ˈpəʊstbɒks; NAmE ˈpoʊstbɑːks/ (also **ˈletter box**) (both BrE) (NAmE **mail·box**) noun a public box, for example in the street, that you put letters into when you send them 邮筒；邮箱 ➲ PICTURE AT LETTER BOX ➲ VISUAL VOCAB PAGE V3 ➲ COMPARE PILLAR BOX

post·card /ˈpəʊstkɑːd; NAmE ˈpoʊstkɑːrd/ (also **card**) noun a card used for sending messages by post without an envelope, especially one that has a picture on one side 明信片：colourful postcards of California 五颜六色的加利福尼亚州明信片 ◇ Send us a postcard from Venice! 从威尼斯给我们寄张明信片来！ ◇ Send your answers on a postcard to the above address. 把答案写在明信片上，寄到上述地址。 ➲ SEE ALSO PICTURE POSTCARD

post·code /ˈpəʊstkəʊd; NAmE ˈpoʊstkoʊd/ (BrE) (also **ˈpostal code** BrE, CanE) noun a group of letters and numbers that are used as part of an address so that post/mail can be separated into groups and delivered more quickly 邮政编码；邮编 ➲ SEE ALSO ZIP CODE

ˌpostcode ˈlottery noun [sing.] (BrE) a situation in which the amount or type of medical treatment that is provided to people depends on the particular area of the country they live in 邮编幸运医疗（在英国指能得到的医保程度或方式取决于居住的地区）

post-coital /ˌpəʊst ˈkɔɪtl; ˈkəʊɪtl; NAmE ˌpoʊst; ˈkoʊɪtl/ adj. [usually before noun] happening or done after SEXUAL INTERCOURSE 性交后发生（或做）的；性交后的

ˌpost-ˈdate verb **1 ~ sth** to write a date on a cheque that is later than the actual date so that the cheque cannot be CASHED (= exchanged for money) until that date 把（支票日期）填迟；预填（支票）日期；签迟日期 ➲ COMPARE BACKDATE (1) **2 ~ sth** to happen, exist or be made at a later date than sth else in the past 发生（或存在、造出）得较晚；发生在…之后 OPP **predate**

post·doc·tor·al /ˌpəʊstˈdɒktərəl; NAmE ˌpoʊstˈdɑːk-/ adj. [usually before noun] connected with advanced research or study that is done after a PhD has been completed 博士后的

pos·ter /ˈpəʊstə(r); NAmE ˈpoʊ-/ noun **1** a large notice, often with a picture on it, that is put in a public place to advertise sth 招贴画；海报 SYN **placard**：election posters 选举海报 ◇ a poster campaign (= an attempt to educate people about sth by using posters) 招贴宣传运动 ➲ WORDFINDER NOTE AT ADVERTISE **2** a large picture that is printed on paper and put on a wall as decoration （大幅）装饰画：posters of her favourite pop stars 她所喜爱的流行歌星的大幅画片 ➲ VISUAL VOCAB PAGE V72 **3** a person who posts a message on a MESSAGE BOARD (= a place on a website where people can read or write messages) （在网络留言板上）发布消息的人，张贴信息的人

ˈposter child (also **ˈposter boy, ˈposter girl**) noun (especially NAmE) **1** a child with a particular illness or other problem whose picture appears on a poster advertising an organization that helps children with that illness or problem （为慈善等目的）出现在海报上的儿童 **2** (often humorous) a person who is seen as representing a particular quality or activity 代表人物；典型：He is the poster child for incompetent government. 他是无能政府的典型人物。

poste rest·ante /ˌpəʊst ˈrestɑːnt; NAmE ˌpoʊst reˈst-/ (BrE) (NAmE **ˌgeneral deˈlivery**) noun [U] an arrangement in which a post office keeps a person's mail until they go to collect it, used especially when sb is travelling （邮局的）邮件寄存服务；存局候领

pos·ter·ior /pɒˈstɪəriə(r); NAmE pɑːˈstɪr-/ adj., noun
■ **adj.** [only before noun] (specialist) located behind sth or at the back of sth 在后面的；在后部的 OPP **anterior**
■ **noun** (humorous) the part of your body that you sit on; your bottom 臀部；屁股

pos·teri·ori ➲ A POSTERIORI

pos·ter·ity /pɒˈsterəti; NAmE pɑːˈs-/ noun [U] (formal) all the people who will live in the future 后代；后裔；子孙；后世：Their music has been **preserved for posterity**. 他们的音乐已为后世保存起来。 ◇ Posterity will remember him as a great man. 后人将会记住他是个伟人。

ˈposter paint noun [U, C] a thick paint used especially for children's paintings 广告颜料

ˌpost exˈchange noun = PX

ˌpost-ˈfree adj. [only before noun] (BrE) used to describe sth that you can send by post without having to pay anything 免付邮资的 ▶ **ˌpost-ˈfree** adv.：Information will be sent post-free to any interested readers. 有意索取资料的读者可免付邮资。

post·grad /ˈpəʊstgræd; NAmE ˈpoʊst-/ noun (informal) a POSTGRADUATE 研究生

post·gradu·ate /ˌpəʊstˈgrædʒuət; NAmE ˌpoʊst-/ (also informal **post·grad**) noun (especially BrE) a person who already holds a first degree and who is doing advanced study or research; a GRADUATE student 研究生：postgraduate students 研究生 ◇ a postgraduate course 研究生课程 ➲ NOTE AT STUDENT

ˌpost-ˈhaste adv. (literary) as quickly as you can 尽快；从速：to depart post-haste 火速动身

post hoc /ˌpəʊst ˈhɒk; NAmE ˌpoʊst ˈhɑːk/ adj. (from Latin, formal) (of an argument, etc. 论点等) happening after the event, especially when one event is the cause of another 以先后为因果的；事后归因的：a post hoc explanation 事后归因的解释 ▶ **post hoc** adv.

post·hu·mous /ˈpɒstjʊməs; *NAmE* ˈpɑːstʃəməs/ *adj.* [usually before noun] happening, done, published, etc. after a person has died 死后发生（或做、出版等）的：*a posthumous award for bravery* 死后荣膺的英勇奖 ▶ **post·hu·mous·ly** *adv.*

post·ie /ˈpəʊsti; *NAmE* ˈpoʊ-/ *noun* (*BrE, informal*) = POSTMAN

ˌpost-inˈdustrial *adj.* [only before noun] (of a place or society 地方或社会) no longer relying on heavy industry (= the production of steel, large machinery, etc.) 后工业化的；不再依赖重工业的

post·ing /ˈpəʊstɪŋ; *NAmE* ˈpoʊ-/ *noun* **1** (*especially BrE*) (*NAmE usually* **post**) an act of sending sb to a particular place to do their job, especially for a limited period of time 派驻：*an overseas posting* 派驻海外 **2** = POST (10)

ˈPost-it™ (*also* **ˈPost-it note**) *noun* a small piece of coloured, sticky paper that you use for writing a note on, and that can be easily removed 报事贴；黏胶便条纸；便利贴 ➲ **VISUAL VOCAB** PAGE V71

post·man /ˈpəʊstmən; *NAmE* ˈpoʊst-/, **post·woman** /ˈpəʊstwʊmən; *NAmE* ˈpoʊst-/ *noun* (*pl.* **-men** /-mən/, **-women** /-wɪmɪn/) (*also informal* **post·ie**) (*especially BrE*) a person whose job is to collect and deliver letters, etc. 邮递员；邮差 ➲ SEE ALSO MAILMAN ➲ NOTE AT GENDER

ˌpostman's ˈknock (*BrE*) (*NAmE* **ˈpost office**) *noun* [U] a children's game in which imaginary letters are exchanged for kisses 邮差敲门游戏（儿童用假托的信件换取亲吻）

post·mark /ˈpəʊstmɑːk; *NAmE* ˈpoʊstmɑːrk/ *noun* an official mark placed over the stamp on a letter, etc. that shows when and where it was posted and makes it impossible to use the stamp again 邮戳 ▶ **post·mark** *verb* [usually passive]: **~ sth** *The card was postmarked Tokyo 9th March.* 明信片上盖着东京 3 月 9 日的邮戳。

post·mas·ter /ˈpəʊstmɑːstə(r); *NAmE* ˈpoʊstmæstər/, **post·mist·ress** /ˈpəʊstmɪstrəs; *NAmE* ˈpoʊst-/ *noun* a person who is in charge of a post office 邮政局长

post·mod·ern /ˌpəʊstˈmɒdn; *NAmE* ˌpoʊstˈmɑːdərn/ *adj.* connected with or influenced by postmodernism 后现代主义的；受后现代主义影响的

post·mod·ern·ism /ˌpəʊstˈmɒdənɪzəm; *NAmE* ˌpoʊstˈmɑːdərn-/ *noun* [U] a style and movement in art, ARCHITECTURE, literature, etc. in the late 20th century that reacts against modern styles, for example by mixing features from traditional and modern styles 后现代主义（20 世纪后期在艺术、建筑、文学等方面对抗现代风格，如融合传统与现代风格） ➲ COMPARE MODERNISM (2) ▶ **post·mod·ern·ist** *noun, adj.* [usually before noun]

post·modi·fier /ˌpəʊstˈmɒdɪfaɪə(r); *NAmE* ˌpoʊstˈmɑːd-/ *noun* (*grammar* 语法) a word or group of words that describes a noun phrase or restricts its meaning in some way, and is placed after it 后置修饰语；后修饰成分：*In 'the house on the corner', 'on the corner' is a postmodifier.* 在 the house on the corner 中，on the corner 是后置修饰语。 ➲ COMPARE MODIFIER, PREMODIFIER

post-mortem /ˌpəʊst ˈmɔːtəm; *NAmE* ˌpoʊst ˈmɔːrtəm/ *noun* **1** (*also* **post-ˌmortem examiˈnation**) a medical examination of the body of a dead person in order to find out how they died 验尸；尸体解剖 **SYN** **autopsy**：*to do/conduct/carry out a post-mortem* 进行剖尸验证 ◇ **~ on sb** *The post-mortem on the child revealed that she had been poisoned.* 验尸证明这孩子是被人毒死的。 **2 ~ (on sth)** a discussion or an examination of an event after it has happened, especially in order to find out why it failed 事后反思（或剖析）：*to hold a post-mortem on the party's election defeat* 对该党竞选失败进行检讨

post·natal /ˌpəʊstˈneɪtl; *NAmE* ˌpoʊst-/ (*NAmE* **post·partum**) *adj.* [only before noun] connected with the period after the birth of a child 产后的；分娩后的：*postnatal care* 产后护理 ➲ COMPARE ANTENATAL, PRENATAL

ˌpostˌnatal deˈpression (*BrE*) (*NAmE* **ˌpost-ˌpartum deˈpression**) *noun* [U] a medical condition in which a woman feels very sad and anxious in the period after her baby is born 产后抑郁（症）

ˈpost office 🔑 *noun* **1** 🔑 [C] a place where you can buy stamps, send letters, etc. 邮局：*Where's the main post office?* 邮政总局在哪儿？ ◇ *You can buy your stamps at the post office.* 你可以在邮局买邮票。 ◇ *a post office counter* 邮局的柜台 **2** 🔑 **the ˈPost Office** [sing.] (*abbr.* **PO**) the national organization in many countries that is responsible for collecting and delivering letters, etc. 邮政部门；邮政系统：*He works for the Post Office.* 他在邮政部门工作。 **3** (*NAmE*) (*BrE* **ˌpostman's ˈknock**) [U] a children's game in which imaginary letters are exchanged for kisses 邮差敲门游戏（儿童用假托的信件换取亲吻）

ˈpost office box *noun* = PO BOX

ˌpost-ˈoperative *adj.* [only before noun] (*medical* 医) connected with the period after a medical operation 手术后的：*post-operative complications/pain/care* 手术后并发症 / 疼痛 / 护理

ˌpost-ˈpaid *adj.* [only before noun] that you can send free because the charge has already been paid 邮资已付的：*a post-paid envelope* 已付邮资的信封 ▶ **ˌpost-ˈpaid** *adv.*

post-partum /ˌpəʊst ˈpɑːtəm; *NAmE* ˌpoʊst ˈpɑːrtəm/ (*NAmE also* **post·par·tum**) (*BrE also* **post·natal**) *adj.* [only before noun] connected with the period after the birth of a child 产后的；分娩后的 ➲ COMPARE ANTENATAL, PRENATAL

ˌpost-ˌpartum deˈpression (*NAmE also* **ˌpostˌpartum deˈpression**) (*BrE also* **ˌpostˌnatal deˈpression**) *noun* [U] a medical condition in which a woman feels very sad and anxious in the period after her baby is born 产后抑郁（症）

post·pone /pəˈspəʊn; *NAmE* poʊˈspoʊn/ *verb* to arrange for an event, etc. to take place at a later time or date 延迟；延期；展缓 **SYN** **put off**：**~ sth** *The game has already been postponed three times.* 这场比赛已经三度延期了。 ◇ **~ sth to/until sth** *We'll have to postpone the meeting until next week.* 我们将不得不把会议推迟到下周举行。 ◇ **~ doing sth** *It was an unpopular decision to postpone building the new hospital.* 延迟兴建新医院的决定是不得人心的。 ➲ COMPARE CANCEL (1) ➲ **MORE LIKE THIS** 27, page R28 ▶ **post·pone·ment** *noun* [U, C]: *Riots led to the postponement of local elections.* 骚乱致使地方选举延期了。

post·pos·ition /ˌpəʊstpəˈzɪʃn; *NAmE* ˌpoʊst-/ *noun* (*grammar* 语法) a word or part of a word that comes after the word it relates to, for example '-ish' in 'greenish' 后置词；后置成分 ▶ **post·pos·ition·al** /-ʃənl/ *adj.*

post·pran·dial /ˌpəʊstˈprændiəl; *NAmE* ˌpoʊst-/ *adj.* [usually before noun] (*formal* or *humorous*) happening immediately after a meal 饭后的；餐后的

ˌpost-proˈduc·tion *adj.* [usually before noun] post-production work on music or on films/movies is done after recording or filming （音乐或电影制作）录制之后的，后期的：*post-production editing* 后期剪辑 ▶ **ˌpost-proˈduc·tion** *noun* [U]: *The movie is now in post-production and will be released next month.* 这部电影目前正在进行后期制作，将于下月发行。

ˈpost room *noun* (*BrE*) the department of a company that deals with sending and receiving mail （公司的）邮件收发部，收发室

post·script /ˈpəʊstskrɪpt; *NAmE* ˈpoʊst-/ *noun* **1** (*abbr.* **PS**) **~ (to sth)** an extra message that you add at the end of a letter after your signature （加于信末的）附言，又及 **2 ~ (to sth)** extra facts or information about a story, an event, etc. that are added after it has finished 补充；补编；后话；跋

P

ˌpost-ˈsync (*also* **ˌpost-ˈsynch**) *verb* **~ sth** (*specialist*) to add sound to a film/movie after it has been filmed 给（电影）后期配音；为…后期录音

ˌpost-ˌtraumatic ˈstress disorder *noun* [U] (*medical* 医) a medical condition in which a person suffers mental and emotional problems resulting from an experience that shocked them very much 创伤后精神紧张性障碍

pos·tu·late *verb, noun*

■ *verb* /ˈpɒstjuleɪt; *NAmE* ˈpɑːstʃəl-/ **~ sth | ~ that...** (*formal*) to suggest or accept that sth is true so that it can be used as the basis for a theory, etc. 假定；假设 **SYN posit**: *They postulated a 500-year lifespan for a plastic container.* 他们假定塑料容器的寿命为 500 年。

■ *noun* /ˈpɒstjulət; *NAmE* ˈpɑːstʃəl-/ (*formal*) a statement that is accepted as true, that forms the basis of a theory, etc. 假定；假设

pos·tural /ˈpɒstʃərəl; *NAmE* ˈpɑːs-/ *adj.* (*formal*) connected with the way you hold your body when sitting or standing（坐、立）姿势的

pos·ture /ˈpɒstʃə(r); *NAmE* ˈpɑːs-/ *noun, verb*

■ *noun* **1** [U, C] the position in which you hold your body when standing or sitting（坐、立的）姿势：*a comfortable/relaxed posture* 舒适的/轻松的姿势 ◇ ***upright/sitting/supine postures*** 直立的/坐着的/仰卧的姿势 ◇ ***Good posture** is essential when working at the computer.* 用电脑工作时良好的姿势极其重要。◇ *Back pains can be the result of **bad posture**.* 腰背疼可能是不良姿势造成的。 **2** [C, usually sing.] your attitude to a particular situation or the way in which you deal with it 态度；看法；立场；处理方式：*The government has adopted an aggressive posture on immigration.* 政府对移民入境采取了强硬的态度。

■ *verb* [I] **~ (as sth)** (*formal*) to pretend to be sth that you are not by saying and doing things in order to impress or trick people 故作姿态；装样子

pos·tur·ing /ˈpɒstʃərɪŋ; *NAmE* ˈpɑːs-/ *noun* [U, C] (*disapproving*) behaviour that is not natural or sincere but is intended to attract attention or to have a particular effect 做作的举止；忸怩作态；虚伪表现

post·viral syn·drome /ˌpəʊstˈvaɪrəl sɪndrəʊm; *NAmE* ˌpoʊstˈvaɪrəl sɪndroʊm/ (*also* **ˌpostˌviral faˈtigue syndrome**) *noun* [U] a condition that follows a VIRAL infection, in which sb feels extremely weak and tired, and which can last for a long time 病毒后综合征（受病毒性感染后长时间虚弱疲劳）

ˌpost-ˈwar *adj.* [usually before noun] existing, happening or made in the period after a war, especially the Second World War 战后的；（尤指）第二次世界大战以后的：*the post-war years* 战后的年代

post·woman ➲ POSTMAN

posy /ˈpəʊzi; *NAmE* ˈpoʊzi/ *noun* (*pl.* **-ies**) a small bunch of flowers 小花束

pot /pɒt; *NAmE* pɑːt/ *noun, verb*

■ *noun*

• **FOR COOKING** 烹饪 **1** [C] a deep round container used for cooking things in 锅：*pots and pans* 锅碗瓢盆

• **CONTAINER** 容器 **2** [C] (*especially BrE*) a container made of glass, CLAY or plastic, used for storing food in（盛食品的）罐，瓶，壶，盒：*a pot of jam* 一罐果酱 ◇ *a yogurt pot* 酸奶瓶 ➲ VISUAL VOCAB PAGE V36 **3** [C] (especially in compounds 尤用于构成复合词) a container of various kinds, made for a particular purpose（某种用途的）容器：*a coffee pot* 咖啡壶 ◇ *a pepper pot* 胡椒瓶 ◇ *a teapot* 茶壶 ◇ *Is there any more tea in the pot?* 茶壶里还有茶吗？ ➲ SEE ALSO CHAMBER POT, CHIMNEY POT, FLOWERPOT, LOBSTER POT, MELTING POT, POTTED (3) **4** [C] the amount contained in a pot 一罐，一瓶，一壶（的量）：*They drank a pot of coffee.* 他们喝了一壶咖啡。 **5** [C] a bowl, etc. that is made by a POTTER 陶盆；陶罐；碗

• **MONEY** 钱 **6 the pot** [sing.] (*especially NAmE*) the total amount of money that is bet in a card game（一局纸牌游戏的）赌注总额，全部赌注 **7 the pot** [sing.] (*especially NAmE*) all the money given by a group of people in order to do sth together, for example to buy food 凑集的资金；凑集的钱 ➲ SEE ALSO KITTY

• **DRUG** 毒品 **8** [U] (*informal*) = MARIJUANA：*pot smoking* 吸大麻

• **SHOT** 发射 **9** [C] = POTSHOT：*He took a pot at the neighbour's cat with his air rifle.* 他用气枪向邻居的猫打了一枪。

• **IN BILLIARDS, ETC.** 台球等 **10** [C] (in the game of BILLIARDS, POOL or SNOOKER 台球、普尔或斯诺克) the act of hitting a ball into one of the pockets around the edge of the table 击球入袋

• **STOMACH** 腹部 **11** [C] (*informal*) = POT BELLY

IDM go to ˈpot (*informal*) to be spoiled because people are not working hard or taking care of things 荒废；荒疏；疏懒：*Her handwriting's gone to pot since she started using a computer all the time.* 自从她开始完全使用电脑后，她的书法就荒疏了。 **the pot calling the kettle ˈblack** (*saying, informal*) used to say that you should not criticize sb for a fault that you have yourself 锅笑壶黑；五十步笑百步；乌鸦说猪黑 **ˌpot ˈluck** when you take **pot luck**, you choose sth or go somewhere without knowing very much about it, but hope that it will be good, pleasant, etc. 碰运气；撞大运：*It's pot luck whether you get good advice or not.* 能不能得到好的指点那就全靠运气了。◇ *You're welcome to stay to supper, but you'll have to take pot luck* (= eat whatever is available). 欢迎你留下来吃晚饭，不过你得有什么就吃什么了。 ➲ SEE ALSO POTLUCK **ˈpots of money** (*BrE, informal*) a very large amount of money 大笔的金钱；巨额款项 ➲ MORE AT GOLD *n.*, MELTING POT, QUART, WATCH *v.*

■ *verb* (**-tt-**)

• **PLANT** 植物 **1 ~ sth** to put a plant into a FLOWERPOT filled with soil 把…栽入盆中；种盆栽

• **IN BILLIARDS, ETC.** 台球等 **2 ~ sth** (in the games of BILLIARDS, POOL and SNOOKER 台球、普尔和斯诺克) to hit a ball into one of the pockets (= holes at the corners and edges of the table) 击（球）入袋 **SYN pocket**: *He potted the black to take a 7–3 lead.* 他把黑球击入袋中，以 7:3 领先。

• **SHOOT** 射击 **3 ~ sth** to kill an animal or a bird by shooting it 射杀，射猎（飞禽或走兽） ➲ SEE ALSO POTTED

pot·able /ˈpəʊtəbl; *NAmE* ˈpoʊ-/ *adj.* (*formal*) (of water 水) safe to drink 可饮用的；适于饮用的

pot·ash /ˈpɒtæʃ; *NAmE* ˈpɑːt-/ *noun* [U] a chemical containing potassium, used to improve soil for farming and in making soap 钾碱

po·tas·sium /pəˈtæsiəm/ *noun* [U] (*symb.* **K**) a chemical element. Potassium is a soft silver-white metal that exists mainly in COMPOUNDS which are used in industry and farming. 钾

po·tato /pəˈteɪtəʊ; *NAmE* -toʊ/ *noun* [C, U] (*pl.* **-oes**) a round white vegetable with a brown or red skin that grows underground as the root of a plant also called a potato 马铃薯；土豆；洋芋：*Will you peel the potatoes for me?* 你给我削土豆皮好不好？◇ ***roast/boiled/baked/fried potatoes*** 烘/煮/烤/炸土豆 ➲ VISUAL VOCAB PAGE V33 ➲ SEE ALSO COUCH POTATO, HOT POTATO, JACKET (4), MASHED POTATO, MEAT AND POTATOES, MEAT-AND-POTATOES, SMALL POTATOES, SWEET POTATO

poˌtato ˈcrisp (*BrE*), **poˈtato chip** (*NAmE*) *noun* = CRISP (1), CHIP (4)

poˈtato masher *noun* a kitchen UTENSIL (= tool) for MASHING potatoes 土豆捣烂器；马铃薯捣烂器 ➲ VISUAL VOCAB PAGE V27

ˌpot-ˈbellied *adj.* (of people and animals 人或动物) having a large stomach that sticks out 肚子大的；大腹便便的；啤酒肚的

ˌpot ˈbelly *noun* (*informal* **pot**) a large stomach that sticks out 突出的腹部；大肚子

pot·boil·er /ˈpɒtbɔɪlə(r); *NAmE* ˈpɑːt-/ *noun* (*disapproving*) a book, a play, etc. that is produced only to earn money quickly 为赚钱创作的书籍（或戏剧等）；营利文艺

'pot-bound (*also* **'root-bound**) *adj.* (of a plant 植物) having roots that fill the flower pot, with no more room for them to grow 根满盆的；盆缚的

'pot cheese *noun* [U] (*US*) a type of soft white cheese with lumps in it 大颗粒松软白干酪

po·teen (*also* **po·theen**) /pə'tiːn; pə'tʃiːn/ *noun* [U] (*IrishE*) strong alcoholic drink made illegally, usually from potatoes 卜丁酒（爱尔兰私酒，常用土豆酿制）

po·tency /'pəʊtnsi; *NAmE* 'poʊ-/ *noun* (*pl.* **-ies**) **1** [U, C] the power that sb/sth has to affect your body or mind 影响力；支配力；效力：*the potency of desire* 欲望的支配力 ◇ *If you keep a medicine too long, it may lose its potency.* 药物存放太久，可能会失去效力。 **2** [U] the ability of a man to have sex （男子）性能力，性机能

po·tent /'pəʊtnt; *NAmE* 'poʊ-/ *adj.* **1** having a strong effect on your body or mind 有强效的；有力的；烈性的；影响身心的：*a potent drug* 猛药 ◇ *a very potent alcoholic brew* 烈性酒精饮料 ◇ *a potent argument* 有力的论据 **2** powerful 强大的；强有力的：*a potent force* 强大的力量 ➲ SEE ALSO IMPOTENT ▶ **po·tent·ly** *adv.*

po·ten·tate /'pəʊtnteɪt; *NAmE* 'poʊ-/ *noun* (*literary, often disapproving*) a ruler who has a lot of power, especially when this is not restricted by a parliament, etc. 权力大的统治者；（尤指不受国会等约束的）君主，统治者

po·ten·tial 🔑 AW /pə'tenʃl/ *adj., noun*
■ ***adj.*** 🔑 [only before noun] that can develop into sth or be developed in the future 潜在的；可能的 SYN **possible**: *potential customers* 潜在的客户 ◇ *a potential source of conflict* 潜在的冲突根源 ◇ *a potential prime minister* 未来的首相 ◇ *First we need to identify actual and potential problems.* 首先，我们需要弄清实际的问题和潜在的问题。 ▶ **po·ten·tial·ly** 🔑 AW /-ʃəli/ *adv.*：*a potentially dangerous situation* 有潜在危险的局势
■ ***noun*** **1** 🔑 [U] the possibility of sth happening or being developed or used 可能性；潜在性：~ (**for**) *the potential for change* 变革的可能性 ◇ ~ (**for doing sth**) *The European marketplace offers excellent potential for increasing sales.* 欧洲市场带来了扩销的大好机遇。 **2** 🔑 [U] qualities that exist and can be developed 潜力；潜质 SYN **promise**: *All children should be encouraged to* ***realize their full potential.*** 应当鼓励所有的儿童充分发挥他们的潜能。 ◇ *She has great potential as an artist.* 她很有潜质，是一位可造就的艺术家。 ◇ *He has the potential to become a world-class musician.* 他有潜力成为世界级的音乐家。 ◇ *The house has a lot of potential.* 这所房子颇具潜力。 **3** [U, C] (*physics* 物) the difference in VOLTAGE between two points in an electric field or CIRCUIT 电位；电势；电压

po,tential 'energy *noun* [U] (*physics* 物) the form of energy that an object gains as it is lifted 势能

po·ten·ti·al·ity /pə,tenʃi'æləti/ *noun* (*pl.* **-ies**) (*formal*) a power or a quality that exists and is capable of being developed 潜力；潜在的可能性：*We often underestimate our potentialities.* 我们常常低估自己的潜力。

po·tenti·om·eter /pə,tenʃi'ɒmɪtə(r); *NAmE* -'ɑːm-/ *noun* **1** a device for measuring differences in electrical POTENTIAL 电势差计；电位器 **2** a device for varying electrical RESISTANCE, used, for example, in volume controls 分压器

po·theen = POTEEN

pot·hole /'pɒthəʊl; *NAmE* 'pɑːthoʊl/ *noun* **1** a large rough hole in the surface of a road that is formed by traffic and bad weather （路面的）坑洼 **2** a deep hole that is formed in rock, especially by the action of water 岩石中的溶洞；地壶；瓯穴

pot·hol·ing /'pɒthəʊlɪŋ; *NAmE* 'pɑːthoʊlɪŋ/ (*BrE*) *noun* [U] = CAVING：*to go potholing* 去探索洞穴 ▶ **pot·holer** *noun* = CAVER

po·tion /'pəʊʃn; *NAmE* 'poʊʃn/ *noun* (*literary*) a drink of medicine or poison; a liquid with magic powers 药水；毒液；魔水：*a* ***magic/love potion*** 魔水；春药饮剂 ◇ (*humorous*) *I've tried all sorts of drugs, creams, pills and potions.* 我已试过各种各样的药物、药膏、药片和药水。

potjie /'pɔɪki/ *noun* (*SAfrE*) **1** a round pot, usually with three legs, that is made from CAST IRON and used for cooking food slowly over a fire 波基锅，鼎锅（通常有三足的铸铁圆罐焖烧锅） **2** a meal that is prepared in a pot like this 波基锅炖菜：*a chicken potjie* 波基锅炖鸡

'pot liquor *noun* [U] (*especially US*) the liquid in which meat, fish, or vegetables have been cooked 肉汁；菜卤；高汤

pot·luck /pɒt'lʌk; *NAmE* pɑːt-/ *noun* (*NAmE*) a meal to which each guest brings some food, which is then shared out among the guests 百味餐（参加者带食物分享）

'pot plant *noun* (*BrE*) = HOUSEPLANT

pot·pourri /,pəʊpʊ'riː; *NAmE* ,poʊ-/ *noun* (*from French*) **1** [U, C] a mixture of dried flowers and leaves used for making a room smell pleasant 百花香（房间熏香用的干花和叶子的混合物） **2** [sing.] a mixture of various things that were not originally intended to form a group 杂烩；集锦：*a potpourri of tunes* 乐曲集锦

'pot roast *noun* a piece of meat cooked with vegetables in a pot 蔬菜炖肉块 ▶ **'pot-roast** *verb* ~ **sth**

pot·shot /'pɒtʃɒt; *NAmE* 'pɑːtʃɑːt/ (*also* **pot**) *noun* (*informal*) a shot that sb fires without aiming carefully 乱射；盲目射击：*Somebody* ***took a potshot at*** *him as he drove past.* 他开车经过的时候，有人向他乱开了一枪。 ◇ (*figurative*) *The newspapers* ***took constant potshots at*** (= criticized) *the president.* 报界经常恣意批评总统。

pot·tage /'pɒtɪdʒ; *NAmE* 'pɑːt-/ *noun* [U] (*old use*) soup or STEW 汤；炖菜

pot·ted /'pɒtɪd; *NAmE* 'pɑːt-/ *adj.* [only before noun] **1** planted in a pot 盆栽的：*potted plants* 盆栽植物 **2** (*BrE*) (of a book, or a story 书籍或故事) in a short simple form 简本的；缩略的：*a potted history of England* 英格兰简史 **3** (*BrE*) **potted** meat or fish has been cooked and preserved in a small container （鱼、肉等熟食）罐装的

pot·ter /'pɒtə(r); *NAmE* 'pɑːt-/ *verb, noun*
■ ***verb*** (*BrE*) (*NAmE* **putt·er**) [I] + **adv./prep.** to do things or move without hurrying, especially when you are doing sth that you enjoy and that is not important 悠然地做事，慢条斯理地做事（尤为喜欢的小事）：*I spent the day pottering around the house.* 我在家里做做这、做做那，悠然自得地过了一天。
■ ***noun*** a person who makes CLAY pots by hand 陶工

,potter's 'wheel *noun* a piece of equipment with a flat disc that goes around, on which potters put wet CLAY in order to shape it into pots 陶钧（制陶用的转轮） ➲ VISUAL VOCAB PAGE V45

pot·tery /'pɒtəri; *NAmE* 'pɑːt-/ *noun* (*pl.* **-ies**) **1** [U] pots, dishes, etc. made with CLAY that is baked in an oven, especially when they are made by hand 陶器（尤指手工制的）：*Roman pottery* 罗马时期的陶器 ◇ *a piece of pottery* 一件陶制品 **2** [U] the CLAY that some dishes and pots are made of 陶土：*a jug made of blue-glazed pottery* 一把蓝釉陶壶 **3** [U] the skill of making pots and dishes from CLAY, especially by hand 制陶手艺；制陶技艺：*a pottery class* 陶艺班 ➲ VISUAL VOCAB PAGE V45 **4** [C] a place where CLAY pots and dishes are made 制陶作坊；陶窑；陶器工厂

'potting compost *noun* [U] good quality soil, used for growing plants in flower pots 盆栽用土

'potting shed *noun* a small building where seeds and young plants are grown in pots before they are planted outside 盆栽育秧棚

potto /'pɒtəʊ; *NAmE* 'pɑːtoʊ/ *noun* (*pl.* **-os**) an animal like a MONKEY with a pointed face, found in tropical W Africa 树熊猴，波特懒猴（生活于非洲西部热带地区）

potty /'pɒti; *NAmE* 'pɑːti/ *adj., noun*
■ ***adj.*** (*BrE, informal, becoming old-fashioned*) (**pot·tier**, **pot·ti·est**) **1** crazy 发疯的；癫狂的：*The kids are driving*

me potty! 这群小崽子烦死我了！ **2** **~ about sb/sth** liking sb/sth a lot 喜爱；对…痴迷

■ ***noun*** (*pl.* **-ies**) (*informal*) a bowl that very young children use when they are too small to use a toilet （幼儿的）便盆 ➲ COMPARE CHAMBER POT

ˌpotty-ˈmouthed *adj.* (*informal, especially NAmE*) using rude, offensive language 满口脏话的；粗口的：*a potty-mouthed comedian* 爆粗口的喜剧演员

ˈpotty-train *verb* **~ sb** to teach a small child to use a potty or toilet 训练（幼儿）使用便器 ▸ **ˈpotty-trained** *adj.* **ˈpotty-training** *noun* [U]

pouch /paʊtʃ/ *noun* **1** a small bag, usually made of leather, and often carried in a pocket or attached to a belt 小袋子；荷包：*a tobacco pouch* 烟丝荷包 ◇ *She kept her money in a pouch around her neck.* 她把钱装在脖子上挂的荷包里。 **2** a large bag for carrying letters, especially official ones 邮袋 ➲ SEE ALSO DIPLOMATIC POUCH at DIPLOMATIC BAG **3** a pocket of skin on the stomach of some female MARSUPIAL animals, such as KANGAROOS, in which they carry their young （有袋目动物腹部的）育儿袋 ➲ VISUAL VOCAB PAGE V12 **4** a pocket of skin in the cheeks of some animals, such as HAMSTERS, in which they store food （某些动物贮存食物的）颊袋，喉囊

pouffe (*also* **pouf**) /puːf/ (*both BrE*) (*NAmE* **has·sock**) *noun* a large thick CUSHION used as a seat or for resting your feet on （厚实的）坐垫，脚垫

poult·ice /ˈpəʊltɪs; *NAmE* ˈpoʊ-/ *noun* a soft substance spread on a cloth, sometimes heated, and put on the skin to reduce pain or swelling 泥敷剂（涂于敷料上，有时用以热敷）

poult·ry /ˈpəʊltri; *NAmE* ˈpoʊ-/ *noun* **1** [pl.] chickens, DUCKS and GEESE, kept for their meat or eggs 家禽：*to keep poultry* 饲养家禽 ◇ *poultry farming* 养禽业 ➲ VISUAL VOCAB PAGE V12 **2** [U] meat from chickens, DUCKS and GEESE 禽肉：*Eat plenty of fish and poultry.* 要多吃鱼和禽肉。

P

pounce /paʊns/ *verb* [I] to move suddenly forwards in order to attack or catch sb/sth 猛扑；突袭：*The lion crouched ready to pounce.* 狮子蹲下身，准备猛扑。 ◇ **~ on/upon sb/sth** *The muggers pounced on her as she got out of the car.* 她一下汽车，劫匪便向她扑上去。 ◇ *Rooney pounced on the loose ball and scored.* 鲁尼对准无人控制的球就是一脚，破门得分。

PHR V **ˈpounce on/upon sth** to quickly notice sth that sb has said or done, especially in order to criticize it 一眼看出，抓紧机会（以便批评） SYN **seize on/upon**：*His comments were pounced upon by the press.* 他的评论立即被新闻界揪住。

pound 🔑 /paʊnd/ *noun, verb*

■ ***noun***

• **MONEY** 钱 **1** 🔑 [C] (*also specialist* **ˌpound ˈsterling**) (*symb.* **£**) the unit of money in the UK, worth 100 pence 英镑（英国货币单位，等于 100 便士）：*a ten-pound note* 一张十英镑的钞票 ◇ *a pound coin* 一英镑的硬币 ◇ *I've spent £25 on food today.* 我今天的餐费花了 25 英镑。 ◇ *What would you do if you won a million pounds?* 你要是赢了一百万英镑，你想怎么用？ ➲ SEE ALSO STERLING *n.* **2** 🔑 [C] the unit of money of several other countries 镑（英国以外某些国家的货币单位） **3** **the pound** [sing.] (*finance* 财) the value of the British pound compared with the value of the money of other countries 英镑与外币的比值：*the **strength/weakness of the pound** (against other currencies)* 英镑坚挺 / 疲软 ◇ *The pound closed slightly down at $1.534.* 英镑的汇价略跌，收盘时为 1.534 美元。

• **WEIGHT** 重量 **4** 🔑 [C] (*abbr.* **lb**) a unit for measuring weight, equal to 0.454 of a kilogram 磅（重量单位，合 0.454 千克）：*half a pound of butter* 半磅黄油 ◇ *They cost two dollars **a pound**.* 这些东西每磅两美元。 ◇ *I've lost six and a half pounds since I started my diet.* 从节食以来，我体重已减轻了六磅半。

• **FOR CARS** 汽车 **5** [C] a place where vehicles that have been parked illegally are kept until their owners pay to get them back 违章停车车辆扣留场

• **FOR DOGS** 狗 **6** [C] a place where dogs that have been found in the street without their owners are kept until their owners claim them 流浪狗收留所

IDM **(have, get, want, etc.) your pound of ˈflesh** the full amount that sb owes you, even if this will cause them trouble or suffering （不顾别人死活要讨回）应得的东西 ORIGIN From Shakespeare's *Merchant of Venice*, in which the moneylender Shylock demanded a pound of flesh from Antonio's body if he could not pay back the money he borrowed. 源自莎士比亚的《威尼斯商人》。如果安东尼奥不能偿还借款，放债者夏洛克就要割他身上的一磅肉抵债。 ➲ MORE AT PENNY, PREVENTION

■ ***verb***

• **HIT** 击打 **1** [I, T] to hit sth/sb hard many times, especially in a way that makes a lot of noise 反复击打；连续砰砰地猛击 SYN **hammer**：**~ at/against/on sth** *Heavy rain pounded on the roof.* 暴雨唧唧地砸在屋顶上。 ◇ *Someone was pounding at the door.* 有人在砰砰地敲门。 ◇ **~ away (at/against/on sth)** *The factory's machinery pounded away day and night.* 工厂的机器昼夜轰隆作响。 ◇ **~ sb/sth (with sth)** *She pounded him with her fists.* 她用拳头一个劲地擂他。 ➲ SYNONYMS AT BEAT

• **WALK NOISILY** 咚咚走动 **2** [I] **+ adv./prep.** to move with noisy steps 咚咚地走：*She pounded along the corridor after him.* 她跟着他在走廊里咚咚地走过。

• **OF HEART/BLOOD** 心脏；血液 **3** [I] to beat quickly and loudly （心脏）狂跳，怦怦地跳：*Her heart was pounding with excitement.* 她激动得心脏怦怦直跳。 ◇ *The blood was pounding* (= making a beating noise) *in his ears.* 他听到血液在耳中怦怦搏动的声音。 ◇ *Her head began to pound.* 她的头开始怦怦地抽痛。 ◇ *a pounding headache* 锤击般的头痛

• **BREAK INTO PIECES** 粉碎 **4** [T] **~ sth (to/into sth)** to hit sth many times in order to break it into smaller pieces 捣碎；击碎：*The seeds were pounded to a fine powder.* 籽粒被捣成了细粉。

• **ATTACK WITH BOMBS** 轰炸 **5** [T] **~ sth** to attack an area with a large number of bombs over a period of time 狂轰滥炸：*The area is still being pounded by rebel guns.* 这个地区仍然遭受着叛军炮火的轰击。

• **OF MUSIC** 音乐 **6** [I] **~ (out)** to be played loudly 大声播放：*Rock music was pounding out from the jukebox.* 自动点唱机高声播放着摇滚乐。

PHR V **ˌpound sth↔ˈout** to play music loudly on a musical instrument （用乐器）大声弹奏：*to pound out a tune on the piano* 在钢琴上用力弹奏曲子

pound·age /ˈpaʊndɪdʒ/ *noun* [U] **1** (*specialist*) a charge that is made for every pound in weight of sth, or for every £1 in value 按每磅重量的收费；按每英镑价值计算的收费 **2** (*informal*) weight 重量：*to carry extra poundage* 超重负载

ˈpound cake (*NAmE*) (*BrE* **Maˈdeira cake**) *noun* [C, U] a plain yellow cake made with eggs, fat, flour and sugar 磅饼

pound·er /ˈpaʊndə(r)/ *noun* (in compounds 构成复合词) **1** something that weighs the number of pounds mentioned 重…磅的东西：*a three-pounder* (= a fish, for example, that weighs 3lb) 三磅重的东西（如 3 磅重的鱼） **2** a gun that fires a SHELL that weighs the number of pounds mentioned 发射…磅炮弹的大炮：*an eighteen-pounder* 发射十八磅炮弹的大炮

pound·ing /ˈpaʊndɪŋ/ *noun* [usually sing.] **1** a very loud repeated noise, such as the sound of sth hitting sth else hard; the sound or the feeling of your heart beating strongly 连续的重击声；剧烈的心跳（声）：*We were awoken by a pounding at the door.* 我们被砰砰的敲门声吵醒。 ◇ *There was a pounding in his head.* 他觉得头嗡嗡直响。 **2** an occasion when sth is hit hard or attacked and severely damaged 遭重创的情景；严重破损的情况 SYN **battering**：*The boat **took a pounding** in the gale.* 这条船在狂风中严重受损。 ◇ (*figurative*) *The team **took a pounding*** (= were badly defeated). 这支队遭到惨败。

'pound sign *noun* **1** the symbol (£) that represents a pound in British money 英镑符号 **2** (*NAmE*) (*BrE* **hash, 'hash sign**) the symbol (#), especially one on a telephone （尤指电话上的）#号

pour /pɔː(r)/ *verb* **1** [T] ~ sth (+ adv./prep.) to make a liquid or other substance flow from a container in a continuous stream, especially by holding the container at an angle 使（液体）连续流出；倾倒；倒出： *Pour the sauce over the pasta.* 把酱汁浇在意大利面食上。◇ *Although I poured it carefully, I still managed to spill some.* 尽管我倒这东西很小心，还是洒了一些。 **2** [I] + adv./prep. (of liquid, smoke, light, etc. 液体、烟、光等) to flow quickly in a continuous stream 涌流；倾泻；喷发： *Tears poured down his cheeks.* 眼泪顺着他的面颊簌簌地落下。◇ *Thick black smoke was pouring out of the roof.* 黑色浓烟从屋顶滚滚冒出。 **3** [T, I] to serve a drink by letting it flow from a container into a cup or glass 倒，斟（饮料）：~ (sth) *Will you pour the coffee?* 你来倒咖啡好吗？◇ *Shall I pour?* 我来倒好吗？◇ ~ **sth out** *I was in the kitchen, pouring out drinks.* 我在厨房里倒饮料。◇ ~ **sth for sb** *I've poured a cup of tea for you.* 我给你倒了一杯茶。◇ ~ **sb sth** *I've poured you a cup of tea.* 我倒了杯茶给你。 **4** [I, T] when rain **pours** down or when **it's pouring** (**with**) rain, rain is falling heavily （雨）倾盆而下；下大雨： ~ (**down**) *The rain continued to pour down.* 大雨哗哗地下个不停。◇ *It's pouring outside.* 外面下着瓢泼大雨。◇ (*BrE*) ~ **with rain** *It's pouring with rain.* 大雨滂沱。◇ (*NAmE*) ~ (**down**) **rain** *It's pouring rain outside.* 外面下着瓢泼大雨。 **5** [I] + adv./prep. to come or go somewhere continuously in large numbers 不断涌向（或涌现） SYN **flood**: *Letters of complaint continue to pour in.* 投诉信纷至沓来。◇ *Commuters came pouring out of the station.* 通勤上班者涌出车站。

IDM **pour oil on troubled 'water(s)** to try to settle a disagreement or argument 调解争端；排解纠纷 ➲ MORE AT COLD *adj.*, HEART, RAIN *v.*, SCORN *n.*

PHR V **,pour sth 'into sth** to provide a large amount of money for sth 向…投入大量金钱；大量投资于： *The government has poured millions into the education system.* 政府已在教育系统投入数百万。 **,pour 'out** when feelings or sb's words **pour out** they are expressed, usually after they have been kept hidden for some time （感情或话语）奔涌，迸发： *The whole story then came pouring out.* 接着，事情的来龙去脉被和盘托出。 **,pour sth↔'out** to express your feelings or give an account of sth, especially after keeping them or it secret or hidden 毫无保留地表达感情（或思想等）；表露无遗；畅所欲言： *She poured out her troubles to me over a cup of coffee.* 她一面喝着咖啡，一面向我倾吐着她的烦恼。 ➲ RELATED NOUN OUTPOURING

pout /paʊt/ *verb* [I, T] ~ (**sth**) | + **speech** if you **pout**, **pout** your lips or if your lips **pout**, you push out your lips, to show you are annoyed or to look sexually attractive （恼怒或性感地）噘嘴： *He pouted angrily.* 他生气地噘起嘴。◇ *Her lips pouted invitingly.* 她挑逗地撮起双唇。◇ *models pouting their lips for the camera* 隆唇拍照的模特儿 ▶ **pout** *noun*： *Her lips were set in a pout of annoyance.* 她愠恼地噘起了双唇。 **pouty** *adj.*： *pouty lips* 噘起的嘴唇

pout·ine /puː'tiːn/ *noun* [U] (*CanE*) a dish of FRENCH FRIES with melted cheese on top, served with a sauce (usually GRAVY) 肉汁乳酪薯条（以软乳酪覆盖，浇肉汁等食用）

pov·erty /'pɒvəti; *NAmE* 'pɑːvərti/ *noun* **1** [U] the state of being poor 贫穷；贫困： *conditions of* ***abject/extreme poverty*** 极度贫穷的状况 ◇ *to* ***alleviate/relieve poverty*** 缓解 / 解除贫困 ◇ *Many elderly people live* ***in poverty***. 许多老年人生活于贫困之中。 ➲ WORDFINDER NOTE AT POOR ➲ COLLOCATIONS AT INTERNATIONAL **2** [U, sing.] a lack of sth; poor quality 贫乏；短缺；劣质： *There is a poverty of colour in her work.* 她的作品缺乏色彩。

the 'poverty line (*also* **the 'poverty level** *especially in US*) *noun* [sing.] the official level of income that is necessary to be able to buy the basic things you need such as food and clothes and to pay for somewhere to live 贫困线（政府规定维持最低生活水平所需的收入标准）： *A third of the population is living* ***at*** *or* ***below the poverty line***. 三分之一的人口生活在贫困线或以下。

'poverty-stricken *adj.* extremely poor; with very little money 赤贫的；一贫如洗的

'poverty trap *noun* [usually sing.] a situation in which a person stays poor even when they get a job because the money they receive from the government is reduced 贫困的牢笼（即使找到工作也依旧贫困，因为政府补贴相应减少）

POW /ˌpiː əʊ 'dʌbljuː; *NAmE* oʊ/ *noun* the abbreviation for PRISONER OF WAR 战俘，俘虏（全写为 prisoner of war）： *a POW camp* 战俘营

pow /paʊ/ *exclamation* used to express the sound of an explosion, a gun firing or sb hitting sb else （爆炸声、枪声或打人的声音）嘭，乒，砰

pow·der /'paʊdə(r)/ *noun, verb*

▪ ***noun*** **1** [U, C] a dry mass of very small fine pieces or grains 粉末；细面： *chilli powder* 辣椒粉 ◇ *lumps of chalk crushed to (a) fine white powder* 白垩块被碾成白色细粉 ◇ *The snow was like powder.* 雪像粉末一样。◇ *A wide range of cleaning fluids and powders is available.* 有各种各样的清洗液和去污粉供应。◇ *The mustard is sold in* ***powder form***. 芥末是以粉末状出售的。 ➲ SEE ALSO BAKING POWDER, CURRY POWDER, SOAP POWDER, TALCUM POWDER, WASHING POWDER **2** [U] a very fine, soft, dry substance that you can put on your face to make it look smooth and dry 扑面粉；美容粉 ➲ VISUAL VOCAB PAGE V65 **3** [U] = GUNPOWDER

IDM **keep your 'powder dry** (*old-fashioned*) to remain ready for a possible emergency 时刻准备应急；枕戈待旦；有备无患 **take a 'powder** (*NAmE, informal*) to leave suddenly; to run away 突然离开；跑掉；溜掉

▪ ***verb*** ~ **sth** to put powder on sth 傅粉；抹粉： *She powdered her face and put on her lipstick.* 她往脸上搽了粉，又涂上了口红。

IDM **powder your 'nose** (*old-fashioned*) a polite way of referring to the fact that a woman is going to the toilet/bathroom （女士如厕的委婉说法）补妆，净手： *I'm just going to powder my nose.* 我想去补补妆。

,powder 'blue *adj.* very pale blue in colour 浅蓝色的 ▶ **,powder 'blue** *noun* [U] ➲ MORE LIKE THIS 15, page R26

pow·dered /'paʊdəd; *NAmE* -dərd/ *adj.* **1** (of a substance that is naturally liquid 原为液体的物质) dried and made into powder 制成粉状的；干燥成粉的： *powdered milk* 奶粉 **2** crushed and made into a powder 研成粉末的： *powdered chalk* 白垩粉 **3** covered with powder 涂粉的；傅粉的： *her powdered cheeks* 她那搽了粉的面颊

,powdered 'milk *noun* [U] = MILK POWDER

'powdered sugar *noun* [U] (*US*) = CONFECTIONER'S SUGAR

'powder keg *noun* a dangerous situation that may suddenly become very violent 危险的局面；一触即发的情势；火药桶

'powder puff *noun* a round thick piece of soft material that you use for putting powder on your face 粉扑

'powder room *noun* **1** a polite word for a women's toilet/bathroom in a public building （委婉语）女洗手间 **2** (*NAmE*) a small room in a house containing a WASHBASIN and a toilet, usually for guests to use （常为客人用）盥洗室 SYN **half-bath**

pow·dery /'paʊdəri/ *adj.* like powder; covered with powder 粉状的；傅了粉的： *a light fall of powdery snow* 细雪轻轻飘落 ◇ *powdery cheeks* 傅粉的面颊

power /'paʊə(r)/ *noun, verb*

▪ ***noun***

• **CONTROL** 操纵 **1** [U] the ability to control people or things 控制力；影响力；操纵力： ~ (**over sb/sth**) *The aim is to give people more power over their own lives.* 目的是让人们更能主宰自己的生活。◇ ~ (**to do sth**) *He has the*

P

power to make things very unpleasant for us. 他掌握着我们的命运，可以把我们搞得狼狈不堪。◇ *to have sb* ***in your power*** (= to be able to do what you like with sb) 能支配某人 **2** [U] political control of a country or an area 统治；政权：*to* ***take/seize/lose power*** 掌握 / 夺取 / 失掉政权 ◇ *The present regime has been* ***in power*** *for two years.* 现政权已经执政两年了。◇ *The party* ***came to power*** *at the last election.* 这个政党是在上次大选中当选执政的。◇ *They are hoping to return to power.* 他们希望重掌政权。◇ *a* ***power struggle*** *between rival factions within the party* 党内对立派别之间的权力斗争 ➲ COLLOCATIONS AT POLITICS ➲ SEE ALSO BALANCE OF POWER

• **ABILITY** 能力 **3** [U] (in people 人的) the ability or opportunity to do sth 能力；机会：*It is not* ***within my power*** (= I am unable or not in a position) *to help you.* 我是爱莫能助啊。◇ *I will* ***do everything in my power*** *to help you.* 我将尽全力帮助你。 **4** [U] (*also* **powers** [pl.]) a particular ability of the body or mind （身体、心智的）某种能力：*He had lost the power of speech.* 他丧失了语言能力。◇ *The drug may affect your powers of concentration.* 这种药可能会影响你的注意力集中。◇ *He had to use all his powers of persuasion.* 他只好使出说服人的全部本领。 **5 powers** [pl.] all the abilities of a person's body or mind （全部）体力，智力：*At 26, he is* ***at the height of his powers*** *and ranked fourth in the world.* * 26 岁时，他处于巅峰状态，排名世界第四。

• **AUTHORITY** 权威 **6** [U, C, usually pl.] the right or authority of a person or group to do sth 权力；职权；权势：**~ (to do sth)** *The Secretary of State has the power to approve the proposals.* 国务卿有权批准这些提案。◇ *The powers of the police must be clearly defined.* 警察的职权必须明确界定。◇ **~ (of sth)** *The president has the power of veto over all new legislation.* 总统有权否决一切新法规。➲ SEE ALSO POWER OF ATTORNEY

• **COUNTRY** 国家 **7** [C] a country with a lot of influence in world affairs, or with great military strength 有影响力的大国；军事强国：*world powers* 世界列强 ◇ *an* ***allied/enemy power*** 同盟国；敌对国 ➲ SEE ALSO SUPERPOWER

• **INFLUENCE** 影响 **8** [U] (in compounds 构成复合词) strength or influence in a particular area of activity 某方面的力量（或影响）；实力：*economic power* 经济实力 ◇ ***air/sea power*** (= military strength in the air/at sea) 空中 / 海上军事力量 ◇ *purchasing power* 购买力 **9** [U] the influence of a particular thing or group within society （某事物或社会集团的）影响力，势力：*the power of the media* 媒体的影响力 ◇ *parent power* 父母的影响力

• **ENERGY** 能量 **10** [U] the strength or energy contained in sth 力；力量；能量：*The ship was helpless against the power of the storm.* 那艘船只能任凭强大的暴风雨肆虐。◇ *It was a performance of great power.* 那是巨大能量的作用。 ➲ SEE ALSO FIREPOWER, STAYING POWER **11** [U] physical strength used in action; physical strength that sb possesses and might use （身体的）力量；体力：*He hit the ball with as much power as he could.* 他用尽全力击球。◇ *the sheer physical power of the man* 那个男人惊人的体力 **12** [U] energy that can be collected and used to operate a machine, to make electricity, etc. 能；能量；动力：***nuclear/wind/solar power*** 核能；风能；太阳能 ◇ *engine power* 发动机的功率 ➲ **WORDFINDER NOTE** AT ELECTRICITY ➲ SEE ALSO HORSEPOWER

• **ELECTRICITY** 电 **13** [U] the public supply of electricity 电力供应：*They've switched off the power.* 他们关掉了电源。◇ *a power failure* 停电

• **MATHEMATICS** 数学 **14** [C, usually sing.] the number of times that an amount is to be multiplied by itself 乘方；幂：*4 to the power of 3 is* 4^3 (= $4 \times 4 \times 4 = 64$). * 4 的 3 次方是 4^3。

• **OF LENS** 透镜 **15** [U] the amount by which a LENS can make objects appear larger 放大倍数；放大率：*the power of a microscope/telescope* 显微镜 / 望远镜的放大率

• **GOOD/EVIL SPIRIT** 善良的 / 邪恶的精灵 **16** [C] a good or evil spirit that controls the lives of others 正义（或邪恶）力量：*the powers of darkness* (= the forces of evil) 黑暗势力

IDM **do sb a 'power of good** (*old-fashioned, informal*) to be very good for sb's physical or mental health 对身心大为有益 **more power to sb's 'elbow** (*old-fashioned, BrE, informal*) used to express support or encouragement for sb to do sth （表示支持或鼓励）再加把劲，加油，祝…成功 **the (real) power behind the 'throne** the person who really controls an organization, a country, etc. in contrast to the person who is legally in charge 太上皇；幕后操纵者 **the ˌpowers that 'be** (*often ironic*) the people who control an organization, a country, etc. 当权派；权力集团 ➲ MORE AT CORRIDOR, SWEEP *v.*

■ ***verb***

• **SUPPLY ENERGY** 提供动力 **1** [T, usually passive] **~ sth** to supply a machine or vehicle with the energy that makes it work 驱动，推动（机器或车辆）：*The aircraft is powered by a jet engine.* 这架飞机由喷气发动机驱动。

• **MOVE QUICKLY** 快速移动 **2** [I, T] to move or move sth very quickly and with great power in a particular direction （使）迅猛移动，快速前进：**+ adv./prep.** *He powered through the water.* 他在水中迅速游动。◇ **~ sth + adv./prep.** *She* ***powered her way*** *into the lead.* 她迅速用力冲到最前面。◇ *He powered his header past the goalie.* 他用力把球顶过了守门员。

PHR V **ˌpower 'down | ˌpower sth↔'down** (*also* **ˌpower 'off, ˌpower sth↔'off**) to stop a machine, especially a computer, by turning off the electricity supply 使（机器）停止工作；关机（尤指计算机）；关闭电源：*We were told to power down at 9.45.* 我们收到通知，9:45 要关闭电源。◇ *Log off or power down your system.* 注销或关闭系统。◇ *Do not power off or reboot in the middle of the update.* 更新过程中不要关闭电源或重新启动。◇ *Power off your PC.* 关闭电脑。 **OPP** **power sth↔up** ➲ RELATED NOUN POWER-DOWN **ˌpower sth↔'up** (*also* **ˌpower sth↔'on**) to prepare a machine to start working by supplying it with electricity, etc. 给…供电（等）；使（机器）启动 **OPP** **power down**

ˌpower-assisted 'steering *noun* [U] (*BrE*) = POWER STEERING

'power base *noun* the area or the people that provide the main support for a politician or a political party （政治人物或政党的）权力基础，后盾

power·boat /'paʊəbəʊt; *NAmE* 'paʊərboʊt/ *noun* a fast boat with a powerful engine that is used especially for racing 摩托艇；汽艇；快艇

'power breakfast *noun* a meeting that business people have early in the morning while they eat breakfast （商界人士）早餐会

'power broker *noun* a person who has a strong influence on who has political power in an area 能左右当权者的人；权力经纪人

'power cut (*BrE*) (*NAmE* **'power outage**) *noun* an interruption in the supply of electricity; a period of time when this happens 供电中断；停电（的一段时间）

'power-down (*also* **power·down**) *noun* [C, U] a time when a machine or system stops working （机器或系统的）停止运行：*a power-down of the whole building* 整座大楼的瘫痪 ◇ *The internal clock and date were not stored after power-down.* 内置时钟和日期在停机之后没有保存下来。

'power dressing *noun* [U] a style of dressing in which people in business wear formal and expensive clothes to emphasize how important they and their jobs are （为显示身份的）显贵穿着，商界要员打扮

powered /'paʊəd; *NAmE* 'paʊərd/ *adj.* (usually in compounds 通常构成复合词) operated by a form of energy such as electricity or by the type of energy mentioned 由…驱动的；电动的：*a powered wheelchair* 电动轮椅 ◇ *a solar-powered calculator* 太阳能电池计算器 ➲ SEE ALSO HIGH-POWERED (3)

power·ful /'paʊəfl; *NAmE* 'paʊərfl/ *adj.* **1** (of people 人) being able to control and influence people and events 有权势的；有影响力的 **SYN** **influential**：*an* ***immensely powerful*** *organization* 有巨大影响力的组织 ◇ *a rich and powerful man* 一个有钱有势的人 ◇ *Only the intervention of powerful friends obtained her release.* 经过

P

有影响力的朋友们斡旋，她才得以获释。 **2** ⚷ having great power or force; very effective 强有力的；力量大的；很有效的：*powerful weapons* 威力强大的武器 ◇ *a powerful engine* 大功率引擎 ◇ *a powerful voice* 洪亮的嗓音 **3** ⚷ having a strong effect on your mind or body（对身心）有强烈作用的，效力大的：*a powerful image/drug/speech* 鲜明的形象；疗效显著的药物；有力的演说 **4** ⚷ (of a person or an animal 人或动物) physically strong 健壮的；强壮的 SYN **muscular**：*a powerful body* 健壮的体魄 ◇ *a powerful athlete* 矫健的运动员 ▶ **power·ful·ly** /-fəli/ *adv.*：*a powerfully emotive song* 激动人心的歌曲 ◇ *He is powerfully built* (= he has a large strong body). 他身体魁梧健壮。◇ *She argued powerfully for reform.* 她雄辩滔滔，力主改革。

power·house /ˈpaʊəhaʊs; *NAmE* ˈpaʊərh-/ *noun* **1** a group or an organization that has a lot of power 强大的集团（或组织）：*China has been described as an 'emerging economic powerhouse'.* 中国被称为"崛起中的经济强国"。**2** a person who is very strong and full of energy 精力充沛的人；身强力壮的人

power·less /ˈpaʊələs; *NAmE* ˈpaʊərləs/ *adj.* **1** without power to control or to influence sb/sth 无影响力的；无权的 SYN **helpless**：*powerless minorities* 弱势的少数族群 ◇ *When the enemy attacked, we were completely powerless against them.* 敌人进攻的时候，我们毫无抵御能力。**2 ~ to do sth** completely unable to do sth 无能为力：*I saw what was happening, but I was powerless to help.* 我眼看着事情发生，却无力相助。▶ **power·less·ness** *noun* [U]：*a feeling/sense of powerlessness* 无能为力的感觉

power·lift·ing /ˈpaʊəlɪftɪŋ; *NAmE* ˈpaʊər-/ *noun* [U] the sport of lifting weights in three different ways, in a set order（分三项依次进行的）力量举重 ▶ **power·lift·er** *noun*

ˈpower line *noun* a thick wire that carries electricity 输电线；电力线：*overhead power lines* 架空输电线

ˈpower nap *noun* a short sleep that sb has during the day in order to get back their energy 恢复精力的小睡 ▶ **ˈpower-nap** *verb* [I] (-pp-)

ˌpower of atˈtorney *noun* [U, C] (*pl.* **powers of attorney**) (*law* 律) the right to act as the representative of sb in business or financial matters; a document that gives sb this right（商业或金融等事务的）代表权，代理权；授权书；委托书

ˈpower outage (*NAmE*) (*BrE* **ˈpower cut**) *noun* an interruption in the supply of electricity; a period of time when this happens 供电中断；停电（的一段时间）

ˈpower plant (*BrE also* **ˈpower station**) *noun* a building or group of buildings where electricity is produced 发电厂；发电站

ˈpower play *noun* [U] **1** (in ICE HOCKEY 冰上曲棍球) a situation in which one team has more players than another because a player is off the ice as a punishment 以多打少（队员被罚下场造成一队的队员人数比另一队多）**2** a way of behaving that shows or increases a person's power, especially in a relationship 强权行为；高压行动：*political power play* 政治强权行为

ˈpower point *noun* (*BrE*) = SOCKET (1)

ˈpower politics *noun* [U+sing./pl. v.] a situation in which a country tries to achieve its aims by using or threatening to use its military or economic power against another country 强权政治；强权外交

ˈpower-sharing *noun* [U] a policy or system in which different groups or political parties share responsibility for making decisions, taking political action, etc. 权力分掌（按联盟成员或政党分配决策和政治行动等的权力）

ˈpower shower *noun* (*BrE*) a shower that has an electric PUMP to make the water come out fast 电泵淋浴器；强力淋浴器

ˈpower station (*BrE*) (*also* **ˈpower plant** *NAmE, BrE*) *noun* a building or group of buildings where electricity is produced 发电厂；发电站：*a coal-fired power station* 燃煤火力发电厂 ◇ *a nuclear power station* 核电站 ➲ WORDFINDER NOTE AT ENERGY

ˈpower steering (*BrE also* **ˌpower-assisted ˈsteering**) *noun* [U] (in a vehicle 车辆) a system that uses power from the engine to help the driver change direction 动力转向系统

ˈpower-up *noun* **1** [U] the moment when a machine is switched on and starts working（机器的）启动；开机：*Does the computer beep on power-up?* 电脑开机时发出"哔"的响声吗？ **2** [C] in computer games, an advantage that a character can get if a player wins a certain number of points, for example more strength 威力升级（玩电脑游戏者赢得一定点数时人物获得力量提升等）

ˈpower user *noun* (*computing* 计) a person who can use the more advanced features of computer software（计算机软件）高级功能使用者，高级用户

ˈpower walking *noun* [U] the activity of walking very quickly as a form of exercise（为锻炼而进行的）快走，疾走，暴走

pow·wow /ˈpaʊwaʊ/ *noun* **1** a meeting of Native Americans 帕瓦（美洲土著的一种集会） **2** (*informal* or *humorous*) a meeting for discussion 讨论会；议事会

pox /pɒks; *NAmE* pɑːks/ *noun* **the pox** [sing.] (*old use*) **1** an infectious disease spread by sexual contact 梅毒 SYN **syphilis 2** = SMALLPOX

poxy /ˈpɒksi; *NAmE* ˈpɑːksi/ *adj.* [only before noun] (*BrE, informal*) if sb describes sth as **poxy**, they think it has little value or importance 无价值的；无足轻重的；鸡毛蒜皮的

pp *abbr.* **1 pp.** pages 页；页码：*See pp. 100–117.* 参阅第100–117 页。**2** (*also* **p.p.**) (*especially BrE*) used in front of a person's name when sb signs a business letter on his/her behalf（信末署名时置于另一人的名字前，表示代其发函）：*pp Chris Baker* (= from Chris Baker, but signed by sb else because Chris Baker is away) 代表克里斯·贝克 **3** (*music* 音) very quietly (from Italian 'pianissimo') 很弱（源于意大利语 pianissimo）

ppi /ˌpiː piː ˈaɪ/ *abbr.* (*computing* 计) pixels per inch (a measure of the quality of images)（图像质量度量单位）每英寸像素

PPS /ˌpiː piː ˈes/ *noun* the abbreviation for 'Parliamentary Private Secretary' (a Member of Parliament in Britain who is given the job of helping a minister) 议会私人秘书（全写为 Parliamentary Private Secretary，协助各大臣工作的议员）

PPV /ˌpiː piː ˈviː/ *abbr.* PAY-PER-VIEW（电视节目的）每收视一次付费

PR /ˌpiː ˈɑː(r)/ *noun* [U] **1** the abbreviation for PUBLIC RELATIONS 公关，公共关系（全写为 public relations）：*a PR department/agency/campaign* 公关部门 / 机构 / 活动 ◇ *The article is very good PR for the theatre.* 这篇文章有助于加强该剧院的公共关系。**2** the abbreviation for PROPORTIONAL REPRESENTATION 比例代表制（全写为 proportional representation）

prac·tic·able /ˈpræktɪkəbl/ *adj.* (*formal*) able to be done; likely to be successful 可行的；行得通的 SYN **feasible, workable**：*at the earliest practicable opportunity* 在尽可能早的时机 ◇ *as soon as (is) practicable* 尽快 ◇ *The only practicable alternative is to postpone the meeting.* 另外唯一可行的办法就是推迟会期。◇ *Employers should provide a safe working environment, as far as is reasonably practicable.* 只要条件许可，雇主就须提供安全的工作环境。➲ COMPARE IMPRACTICABLE ▶ **prac·tic·abil·ity** /ˌpræktɪkəˈbɪləti/ *noun* [U]：*We were doubtful about the practicability of the plan.* 我们怀疑这个计划是否切实可行。 **prac·tic·ably** /-əbli/ *adv.*：*Please reply as soon as is practicably possible.* 请尽早回复。

prac·tical ⚷ /ˈpræktɪkl/ *adj., noun*

■ *adj.*

• CONNECTED WITH REAL THINGS 真实 **1** ⚷ connected with real situations rather than with ideas or theories 实

P

际的；真实的；客观存在的：*to have gained* ***practical experience*** *of the work* 获得实际工作经验 ◇ ***practical advice/help/support*** 切实的忠告 / 帮助 / 支持 ◇ *practical problems* 实际问题 ◇ *There are some obvious practical applications of the research.* 这项研究有一些明显的实际用途。◇ ***In practical terms,*** *it means spending less.* 具体点说，那意味着少花些钱。◇ *From a practical point of view, it isn't a good place to live.* 实际一点看，这里不是理想的住处。➲ COMPARE THEORETICAL

• **LIKELY TO WORK** 可行 **2** ⚷ (of an idea, a method or a course of action 想法、方法或行动) right or sensible; likely to be successful 切实可行的 **SYN** **workable**：*It wouldn't be practical for us to go all that way just for the weekend.* 我们跑那么远只为了去度个周末实在很不切实际。**OPP** **impractical**

• **USEFUL** 有用 **3** ⚷ (of things 东西) useful or suitable 有用的；适用的：*a practical little car, ideal for the city* 理想的城市实用小汽车 **OPP** **impractical**

• **SENSIBLE** 理智 **4** ⚷ (of a person 人) sensible and realistic 明智的；实事求是的：*Let's be practical and work out the cost first.* 咱们实际一点儿，先计算一下成本费用。**OPP** **impractical**

• **GOOD AT MAKING THINGS** 长于制作 **5** ⚷ (of a person 人) good at making or repairing things 心灵手巧的；善于制作（或修补）的 **SYN** **handy**：*Bob's very practical. He does all the odd jobs around the house.* 鲍勃心灵手巧，家里的零活他都包了。

• **ALMOST TOTAL** 几乎全部 **6** [only before noun] almost complete or total 几乎完全的；实际上的 **SYN** **virtual**：*She married a practical stranger.* 她等于是嫁了个陌生人。

IDM **for (all) ˈpractical purposes** used when you are stating what the reality of a situation is 事实上；其实：*There's still another ten minutes of the game to go, but for practical purposes it's already over.* 比赛虽然还有十分钟，但实际上等于已经结束了。

■ ***noun*** (*BrE, informal*) a lesson or an exam in science or technology in which students have to do or make things, not just read or write about them 实习课；实践课；实验考核 ➲ WORDFINDER NOTE AT EXAM

prac·ti·cal·ity /ˌpræktɪˈkæləti/ *noun* **1** [U] the quality of being suitable, or likely to be successful 可行性；适用性 **SYN** **feasibility**：*I have doubts about the practicality of their proposal.* 我怀疑他们的建议是否行得通。**2** [U] the quality of being sensible and realistic 实事求是：*I was impressed by her practicality.* 她做事踏实，着实令我赞佩。**3 practicalities** [pl.] the real facts and circumstances rather than ideas or theories 实际事物；实际情况：*It sounds like a good idea; let's look at the practicalities and work out the costs.* 这个主意听起来不错。咱们来看看实际运作，计算一下费用。

ˌpractical ˈjoke *noun* a trick that is played on sb to make them look stupid and to make other people laugh 恶作剧；捉弄人的把戏 ▶ **ˌpractical ˈjoker** *noun*

prac·tic·al·ly ⚷ /ˈpræktɪkli/ *adv.* **1** ⚷ almost; very nearly 几乎；差不多；很接近 **SYN** **virtually**：*The theatre was practically empty.* 剧院几乎是空的。◇ *I meet famous people practically every day.* 我几乎每天都见到名人。◇ *My essay is practically finished now.* 我的论文现在差不多写完了。◇ *There's practically no difference between the two options.* 这两种选择几乎没什么差别。➲ NOTE AT ALMOST **2** ⚷ in a realistic or sensible way; in real situations 实事求是地；实际地：*Practically speaking, we can't afford it.* 实际说来，我们买不起这东西。◇ *It sounds like a good idea, but I don't think it will work practically.* 这个主意听起来不错，但我认为它实际上行不通。➲ COMPARE THEORETICALLY at THEORETICAL

ˌpractical ˈnurse *noun* (*NAmE*) a nurse with practical experience but less training than a REGISTERED NURSE 职业护士（有实际经验，但所受训练不及注册护士）

prac·tice ⚷ /ˈpræktɪs/ *noun, verb*

■ ***noun***

• **ACTION NOT IDEAS** 实践 **1** ⚷ [U] action rather than ideas 实践；实际行动：*the* ***theory and practice*** *of teaching* 教学的理论与实践 ◇ *She's determined to* ***put*** *her new ideas* ***into practice.*** 她决心要把自己的新想法付诸实践。

• **WAY OF DOING STH** 做法 **2** ⚷ [U, C] a way of doing sth that is the usual or expected way in a particular organization or situation 通常的做法；惯例；常规：***common/current/standard practice*** 一般 / 现行 / 常规做法 ◇ *guidelines for* ***good practice*** 优良做法的指导原则 ◇ *a review of pay and* ***working practices*** 对薪金和工作制度的审查 ◇ *religious practices* 宗教习俗 ➲ SEE ALSO BEST PRACTICE, CODE OF PRACTICE, RESTRICTIVE PRACTICES

• **HABIT/CUSTOM** 习惯；风俗 **3** [C] a thing that is done regularly; a habit or a custom 惯常做的事；习惯；习俗：*the German practice of giving workers a say in how their company is run* 德国人在公司经营上给予工人发言权的做法 ◇ *It is his practice to read several books a week.* 他习惯于每周读几本书。

• **FOR IMPROVING SKILL** 提高技巧 **4** ⚷ [U, C] doing an activity or training regularly so that you can improve your skill; the time you spend doing this 训练；练习（时间）：*conversation practice* 会话练习 ◇ *It takes a lot of practice to play the violin well.* 拉好小提琴需要多加练习。◇ *There's a basketball practice every Friday evening.* 每星期五晚上有篮球训练。◇ *She does an hour's piano practice every day.* 她每天练一小时钢琴。➲ SEE ALSO TEACHING PRACTICE

• **OF DOCTOR/LAWYER** 医生；律师 **5** [U, C] the work or the business of some professional people such as doctors, dentists and lawyers; the place where they work（医生、律师的）工作，业务活动，工作地点：*the practice of medicine* 行医 ◇ *Students should have prior experience of veterinary practice.* 学生应有兽医工作的经验。◇ *My solicitor is no longer in practice.* 我的律师已不再执业了。◇ *a successful* ***medical/dental/law practice*** 成功的诊所 / 牙医诊所 / 律师事务所 ➲ SEE ALSO GENERAL PRACTICE, GROUP PRACTICE, PRIVATE PRACTICE ➲ WORDFINDER NOTE AT DOCTOR

IDM **in ˈpractice** ⚷ in reality 实际上；事实上：*Prisoners have legal rights, but in practice these rights are not always respected.* 囚犯虽有合法的权利，但实际上这些权利常未受到尊重。**be/get ˌout of ˈpractice** to be/become less good at doing sth than you were because you have not spent time doing it recently 生疏；荒疏；疏于练习：*Don't ask me to speak French! I'm out of practice.* 可别让我讲法语！我已经生疏了。**ˌpractice makes ˈperfect** (*saying*) a way of encouraging people by telling them that if you do an activity regularly and try to improve your skill, you will become very good at it 熟能生巧

■ ***verb*** ⚷ (*especially US*) = PRACTISE：*to practice the piano every day* 每天练习弹钢琴 ◇ *The team is practicing for their big game on Friday.* 球队正在训练，备战星期五的重大比赛。◇ *They practiced the dance until it was perfect.* 他们反复练舞，直到尽善尽美为止。◇ *She's practicing medicine in Philadelphia.* 她在费城行医。

prac·tise ⚷ (*especially US* **prac·tice**) /ˈpræktɪs/ *verb* **1** ⚷ [I, T] to do an activity or train regularly so that you can improve your skill 练习；实习；训练：*You need to practise every day.* 你需要每天练习。◇ **~ for sth** *She's practising for her piano exam.* 她在练习准备钢琴考试。◇ **~ sth** *I've been practising my serve for weeks.* 我练发球有好几周了。◇ **~ (sth) on sb/sth** *He usually wants to practise his English on me.* 他通常想跟我练习英语。◇ **~ doing sth** *Practise reversing the car into the garage.* 练习倒车入车库。➲ MORE LIKE THIS 27, page R28 **2** ⚷ [T] **~ sth** (*formal*) to do sth regularly as part of your normal behaviour 经常做；养成…的习惯：*to practise self-restraint/safe sex* 培养自制力；实行安全性行为 ◇ *Do you still practise your religion?* 你还奉行你的宗教信仰吗？ **3** ⚷ [I, T] to work as a doctor, lawyer, etc. 从事（医务工作、律师职业等）；执业：*There are over 50 000 solicitors practising in England and Wales.* 英格兰和威尔士共有 5 万多名律师执业。◇ **~ as sth** *She practised as a barrister for many years.* 她从事出庭律师工作多年。◇ **~ sth** *He was banned from practising medicine.* 他被禁止行医。

IDM **ˌpractise what you ˈpreach** to do the things yourself that you tell other people to do 身体力行；躬行所言；言行一致

P

prac·tised (*especially US* **-ticed**) /ˈpræktɪst/ *adj.* good at doing sth because you have been doing it regularly 熟练的；老到的；内行的：*She's only 18 but she's already a practised composer.* 她才 18 岁，但已成了老练的作曲家。◇ *It took* ***a practised eye*** *to spot the difference.* 只有内行人才能看出其中的差异。◇ **~ in sth** *He has good ideas but he isn't practised in the art of marketing.* 他有好的构想，但市场营销技巧却嫌稚嫩。

prac·tis·ing (*especially US* **-ticing**) /ˈpræktɪsɪŋ/ *adj.* [only before noun] taking an active part in a particular religion, profession, etc. 积极参加宗教活动的：*a practising Christian/teacher* 虔诚的基督徒；热心的教师

prac·ti·tion·er AW /prækˈtɪʃənə(r)/ *noun* **1** (*specialist*) a person who works in a profession, especially medicine or law（尤指医学或法律界的）从业人员：*dental practitioners* 牙医 ◇ *a qualified practitioner* 合格执业者 ➲ SEE ALSO GENERAL PRACTITIONER **2** (*formal*) a person who regularly does a particular activity, especially one that requires skill 习艺者；专门人才：*one of the greatest practitioners of science fiction* 最了不起的科幻小说家之一

prae·sid·ium (*especially BrE*) = PRESIDIUM

prag·mat·ic /prægˈmætɪk/ *adj.* solving problems in a practical and sensible way rather than by having fixed ideas or theories 实用的；讲求实效的；务实的 SYN **realistic**：*a pragmatic approach to management problems* 对管理问题采取的务实做法 ▶ **prag·mat·ic·al·ly** /-kli/ *adv.*

prag·mat·ics /prægˈmætɪks/ *noun* [U] (*linguistics* 语言) the study of the way in which language is used to express what sb really means in particular situations, especially when the actual words used may appear to mean sth different 语用学（研究语言使用及其和语境的关系）

prag·ma·tism /ˈprægmətɪzəm/ *noun* [U] (*formal*) thinking about solving problems in a practical and sensible way rather than by having fixed ideas and theories 实用主义；务实思想；实用观点 ▶ **prag·ma·tist** /-tɪst/ *noun*

prairie /ˈpreəri; *NAmE* ˈpreri/ *noun* [C, U] a flat wide area of land in N America and Canada, without many trees and originally covered with grass 北美草原；新大陆北部草原（美国北部和加拿大）

ˈprairie dog *noun* a small brown N American animal of the SQUIRREL family that lives in holes on the prairies 草原犬鼠（生活于北美地穴）

ˌprairie ˈoyster *noun* **1** a drink containing raw egg, used as a treatment for a HANGOVER (= the bad feeling sb has the day after drinking too much alcohol) 生鸡蛋醒酒汤（用于解除宿醉） **2 prairie oysters** [pl.] (*especially NAmE*) a dish consisting of cooked TESTICLES from a young cow 煮小牛睾丸

ˈprairie wolf *noun* = COYOTE

praise 🔑 /preɪz/ *noun, verb*

▪ *noun* [U] **1** 🔑 (*also less frequent* **praises** [pl.]) words that show approval of or admiration for sb/sth 赞扬；称赞；赞美：*His teachers are* ***full of praise for*** *the progress he's making.* 老师们对他的进步赞不绝口。◇ *She wrote poems* ***in praise of*** *freedom.* 她写诗讴歌自由。◇ *His latest movie has* ***won high praise from*** *the critics.* 他的最新电影得到了评论家的高度赞扬。◇ *We have* ***nothing but praise*** *for the way they handled the investigation.* 对于他们处理调查的方式我们唯有赞赏。◇ *The team coach singled out two players for special praise.* 教练提出两名队员给予特别表扬。◇ *She left with their praises ringing in her ears.* 她离开了，耳边回荡着大家的赞美声。◇ *They always* ***sing his praises*** (= praise him very highly). 他们总是对他大加赞扬。 **2** 🔑 the expression of worship to God（对上帝的）颂扬，赞颂：***hymns/songs of praise*** 赞美诗；颂歌 ◇ *Praise be (to God)!* (= expressing belief or joy) 愿主受赞美！ IDM SEE DAMN *v.*

▪ *verb* **1** 🔑 to express your approval or admiration for sb/sth 表扬；赞扬；称赞 SYN **compliment**：**~ sb/sth** *She praised his cooking.* 她称赞他的烹调技术。◇ **~ sb/sth for sth/for doing sth** *He praised his team for their performance.* 他称赞了队员们的表现。◇ **~ sb/sth as sth** *Critics praised the work as highly original.* 评论家称赞这部作品独树一帜。 **2** 🔑 **~ sb** to express your thanks to or your respect for God 颂扬，赞颂（上帝）：*Praise the Lord.* 赞美上帝！◇ *Allah be praised.* 感谢真主！

IDM **praise sb/sth to the ˈskies** to praise sb/sth a lot 高度赞扬

ˈpraise singer *noun* (*SAfrE*) (*also* **ˈpraise poet**) (in traditional African society) a person who writes and performs music and poetry in order to praise a chief or other important person（非洲传统的）赞歌表演者，赞歌艺人（创作并表演赞颂酋长或其他要人的音乐和诗歌）

praise·worthy /ˈpreɪzwɜːði; *NAmE* -wɜːrði/ *adj.* (*formal*) deserving praise 值得称赞的；值得表扬的 SYN **commendable**：*a praiseworthy achievement* 值得称颂的成就

pra·line /ˈprɑːliːn; ˈpreɪliːn/ *noun* [U] a sweet substance made of nuts and boiled sugar, often used to fill chocolates 果仁糖（常用作巧克力糖芯）

pram /præm/ (*BrE*) (*NAmE* **ˈbaby carriage**) *noun* a small vehicle on four wheels for a baby to go out in, pushed by a person on foot 婴儿车 ➲ WORDFINDER NOTE AT BABY ➲ PICTURE AT PUSHCHAIR

prana /ˈprɑːnə/ *noun* [U] (in Hindu philosophy) the force that keeps all life in existence（印度教哲学中的）息，生命气息

prance /prɑːns; *NAmE* præns/ *verb* **1** [I] **+ adv./prep.** to move quickly with exaggerated steps so that people will look at you 阔步行走；神气地快速走动：*The lead singer was prancing around with the microphone.* 首席歌手手执麦克风，神气地走来走去。 **2** [I] (of a horse 马) to move with high steps 腾跃；腾跳

prang /præŋ/ *verb* **~ sth** (*BrE, informal*) to damage a vehicle in an accident 使（汽车）碰撞 ▶ **prang** *noun*

prank /præŋk/ *noun* a trick that is played on sb as a joke 玩笑；恶作剧：*a childish prank* 幼稚的恶作剧 ▶ **prank·ster** /ˈpræŋkstə(r)/ *noun*：*Student pranksters have done considerable damage to the school buildings.* 恶作剧的学生对学校的建筑造成相当大的损坏。

praseo·dym·ium /ˌpreɪziəʊˈdɪmiəm; *NAmE* -zioʊ-/ *noun* [U] (*symb.* **Pr**) a chemical element. Praseodymium is a soft silver-white metal used in ALLOYS and to colour glass. 镨

prat /præt/ *noun* (*BrE, informal*) a stupid person 笨蛋；蠢驴；傻瓜

prate /preɪt/ *verb* [I] **~ (on) (about sth)** (*old-fashioned, disapproving*) to talk too much in a stupid or boring way 胡扯；瞎吹；唠叨

prat·fall /ˈprætfɔːl/ *noun* (*especially NAmE*) **1** an embarrassing mistake 丢人现眼；出丑 **2** a fall on your bottom 屁股蹲儿；坐跌

prat·tle /ˈprætl/ *verb* [I] **~ (on/away) (about sb/sth)** (*old-fashioned, often disapproving*) to talk a lot about unimportant things 闲扯；唠叨：*She prattled on about her children all evening.* 她整个晚上没完没了地唠叨她的孩子们的事。 ▶ **prat·tle** *noun* [U]

prawn /prɔːn/ *noun* [C, U] (*especially BrE*) (*NAmE usually* **shrimp**) a SHELLFISH with ten legs and a long tail, that can be eaten. Prawns turn pink when cooked. 对虾；大虾；明虾 ➲ VISUAL VOCAB PAGE V13

ˌprawn ˈcracker *noun* (*BrE*) a small piece of food made from rice flour with a PRAWN flavour, that is fried until it is crisp 虾片（用米粉制成的虾味薄片，油炸至酥脆后食用）

praxis /ˈpræksɪs/ *noun* [U] (*philosophy* 哲) a way of doing sth; the use of a theory or a belief in a practical way 做事方法；实践；实际运用

pray 🔑 /preɪ/ *verb, adv.*

▪ *verb* **1** 🔑 [I, T] to speak to God, especially to give thanks or ask for help 祈祷；祷告：*They knelt down and prayed.* 他们跪下来祷告。◇ **~ for sb/sth** *I'll pray for you.* 我将为你祈祷。◇ *to pray for peace* 祈求和平 ◇ **~ to sb (for sb/sth)**

P

She prayed to God for an end to her sufferings. 她祈求上帝结束她的苦难。◇ ~ **(that)**… *We prayed (that) she would recover from her illness.* 我们为她的康复祈祷。◇ ~ **to do sth** *He prayed to be forgiven.* 他祈求宽恕。◇ + **speech** *'Please God don't let it happen,' she prayed.* "请求上帝不要让这事发生。"她祈祷说。**2** [I, T] to hope very much that sth will happen 企盼；祈望：~ **(for sth)** *We're praying for good weather on Saturday.* 我们十分企盼星期六是个晴天。◇ ~ **that**… *I prayed that nobody would notice my mistake.* 我但愿没人注意到我的错误。

■ ***adv.*** (*old use* or *ironic*) used to mean 'please' when you are asking a question or telling sb to do sth（用于询问或指示）请问，请：*What, pray, is the meaning of this?* 请问，这是什么意思？◇ *Pray continue.* 请继续。

pray·er /preə(r); *NAmE* prer/ *noun* **1** [C] ~ **(for sb/sth)** words that you say to God giving thanks or asking for help 祷告，祈祷（的内容）：*to say your prayers* 祷告 ◇ *prayers for the sick* 为病人的祈祷 ◇ *He arrived at that very moment, as if **in answer to her prayer**.* 他就在那一刻到了，好像是她的祈祷应验了。◇ *Their **prayers were answered** and the child was found safe and well.* 他们的祷告应验了：小孩找到了，安然无恙。➲ COLLOCATIONS AT RELIGION **2** [C] a fixed form of words that you can say when you speak to God 祈祷文；经文：*It was a prayer she had learnt as a child.* 这是她儿时就学会了的祈祷文。➲ SEE ALSO LORD'S PRAYER **3** [U] the act or habit of praying 祷告，祈祷（的行为）：*They knelt in prayer.* 他们跪下祈祷。◇ *We believe in the power of prayer.* 我们相信祈祷的力量。**4 prayers** [pl.] a religious meeting that takes place regularly in which people say prayers 祈祷会；祷告式 **5** [C, usually sing.] a thing that you hope for very much 企盼的事；祈望：*My prayer is that one day he will walk again.* 我的企盼就是有一天他能重新走路。

IDM **not have a 'prayer (of doing sth)** to have no chance of succeeding (in doing sth)（做某事）没有成功的机会 ➲ MORE AT WING *n.*

'prayer book *noun* a book that contains prayers, for use in religious services 祈祷书（礼拜时用）

'prayer meeting *noun* a religious meeting when people say prayers to God 祷告会；祈祷会

'prayer rug (*also* **'prayer mat**) *noun* a small carpet on which Muslims rest their knees when they are saying prayers 礼拜垫（穆斯林礼拜时用）

'prayer wheel *noun* (in Tibetan Buddhism 藏传佛教) an object that is turned as a way of saying a prayer or MEDITATING 转经筒（转动经筒即表示诵经或冥思）

,praying 'mantis (*also* **mantis**) *noun* a large green insect that eats other insects. The female praying mantis often eats the male. 螳螂

pre- /priː/ *prefix* (in verbs, nouns and adjectives 构成动词、名词和形容词) before 先于；在…前：*preheat* 预热 ◇ *precaution* 预防 ◇ *pre-war* 战前的 ◇ *preseason training* (= before a sports season starts) 赛季前的训练 ➲ COMPARE ANTE-, POST- ➲ MORE LIKE THIS 6, page R25

preach /priːtʃ/ *verb* **1** [I, T] to give a religious talk in a public place, especially in a church during a service 布道，讲道（尤指教堂中礼拜时）：*She preached to the congregation about forgiveness.* 她向会众宣讲宽恕的道理。◇ ~ **sth** *The minister preached a sermon on the parable of the lost sheep.* 牧师讲道时用了亡羊的比喻。**2** [T, I] to tell people about a particular religion, way of life, system, etc. in order to persuade them to accept it 宣传，宣扬，宣讲（教义、生活方式、体制等）：~ **sth** *to preach the word of God* 传布上帝的道 ◇ *He preached the virtues of capitalism to us.* 他向我们宣扬资本主义的优点。◇ ~ **(about sth)** *She preached about the benefits of a healthy lifestyle.* 她宣讲了健康生活的好处。➲ COLLOCATIONS AT RELIGION **3** [I] (*disapproving*) to give sb advice on moral standards, behaviour, etc., especially in a way that they find annoying or boring 说教：*I'm sorry, I didn't mean to preach.* 很抱歉，我并没有说教的意思。◇ ~ **at sb** *You're preaching at me again!* 你又在对我说教了！

IDM **preach to the con'verted** to speak to people in support of views that they already hold 向教徒宣教；教读书人写大字 ➲ MORE AT PRACTISE

preach·er /ˈpriːtʃə(r)/ *noun* a person, often a member of the CLERGY, who gives religious talks and often performs religious ceremonies, for example in a church 传道者；牧师：*a preacher famous for her inspiring sermons* 以发人深省的讲道出名的传道者 ◇ *a **lay preacher*** (= who is not a priest, etc. but who has been trained to give religious talks) 在俗传道员

preachy /ˈpriːtʃi/ *adj.* (*informal, disapproving*) trying to give advice or to persuade people to accept an opinion on what is right and wrong 说教的；劝诫的

pre·amble /priˈæmbl; ˈpriːæmbl/ *noun* [C, U] (*formal*) an introduction to a book or a written document; an introduction to sth you say 序言；导言；前言；开场白：*The aims of the treaty are stated in its preamble.* 条约的宗旨已在序言中说明。◇ *She gave him the bad news **without preamble**.* 她开门见山地把坏消息告诉了他。

pre·ar·ranged /ˌpriːəˈreɪndʒd/ *adj.* planned or arranged in advance 预先安排的；预先准备的；预定的 SYN **predetermined**

,pre-'book *verb* [I, T] (*BrE*) to arrange to have sth such as a room, table, seat, or ticket in advance 预订（房间、餐桌、座位或票等）；预约：*You are advised to pre-book.* 敬请预约。◇ ~ **sth** *Accommodation is cheaper if you pre-book it.* 预订住宿要便宜些。

pre·but·tal /ˈpriːbʌtl/ *noun* [C, U] (*informal*) a statement saying or proving that a criticism is false or unfair before the criticism has actually been made（对未提出的指责等的）预先驳斥

pre·can·cer·ous /ˌpriːˈkænsərəs/ *adj.* (*medical* 医) that will develop into cancer if not treated 癌前的；癌变前的：*precancerous cells* 癌前细胞

pre·car·ious /prɪˈkeəriəs; *NAmE* -ˈker-/ *adj.* **1** (of a situation 情势) not safe or certain; dangerous 不稳的；不确定的；不保险的；危险的：*He earned a precarious living as an artist.* 作为一个艺术家，他过的是朝不保夕的生活。◇ *The museum is in a financially precarious position.* 这家博物馆的财政状况不稳定。**2** likely to fall or cause sb to fall 摇摇欲坠的；不稳固的：*That ladder looks very precarious.* 那梯子看来摇摇晃晃的。◇ *The path down to the beach is very precarious in wet weather.* 通往海滨的小路在雨天非常湿滑危险。▶ **pre·car·ious·ly** *adv.*：*The economy is precariously close to recession.* 经济濒于衰退的边缘。◇ *He balanced the glass precariously on the arm of his chair.* 他把杯子放在椅子的扶手上，随时可能摔下。**pre·car·ious·ness** *noun* [U]

pre·cast /ˌpriːˈkɑːst; *NAmE* -ˈkæst/ *adj.* (of some building materials 某些建筑材料) made into blocks ready to use 预制的；预先浇铸的：*precast concrete slabs* 混凝土预制板

pre·cau·tion /prɪˈkɔːʃn/ *noun* [usually pl.] **1** ~ **(against sth)** something that is done in advance in order to prevent problems or to avoid danger 预防措施；预防；防备：*safety precautions* 安全防范措施 ◇ *precautions against fire* 防火措施 ◇ *You must **take all reasonable precautions** to protect yourself and your family.* 你必须采取一切合理的预防措施，保护自己和家人。◇ *I'll keep the letter **as a precaution**.* 我要保存这封信，以防万一。**2 precautions** [pl.] a way of referring to CONTRACEPTION 避孕措施：*We didn't **take any precautions** and I got pregnant.* 我们没有采取任何避孕措施，所以我怀孕了。▶ **pre·cau·tion·ary** /prɪˈkɔːʃənəri; *NAmE* -neri/ *adj.*：*He was kept in the hospital overnight **as a precautionary measure**.* 为了谨慎起见，他被安排整晚留院观察。

pre·cede AW /prɪˈsiːd/ *verb* (*formal*) **1** [T, I] ~ **(sb/sth)** to happen before sth or come before sth/sb in order 在…之前发生（或出现）；先于：*the years preceding the war* 战前的几年 ◇ *His resignation was preceded by weeks of speculation.* 在他辞职之前，有关的猜测已持续了几个星期。◇ *She preceded me in the job.* 她是我这工作的前任。◇ *See* *the preceding chapter.* 参见前一章。 **2** [T] ~ **sb + adv./prep.** to go in front of sb 走在…前面： *She preceded him out of the room.* 她先于他走出屋子。

PHR V **pre'cede sth with sth** to do or say sth to introduce sth else 以…开始（或引导）： *She preceded her speech with a vote of thanks to the committee.* 她讲话的开头是对委员会的鸣谢。

pre·ce·dence AW /ˈpresɪdəns/ *noun* [U] ~ (**over sb/sth**) the condition of being more important than sb else and therefore coming or being dealt with first 优先；优先权 SYN **priority**: *She had to learn that her wishes did not* ***take precedence over*** *other people's needs.* 她必须懂得，自己的愿望不能先于别人的需要。◇ *The speakers came on to the platform* ***in order of precedence*** (= the most important one first). 演讲人按级别鱼贯上台。

pre·ce·dent AW /ˈpresɪdənt/ *noun* **1** [C, U] an official action or decision that has happened in the past and that is seen as an example or a rule to be followed in a similar situation later 可援用参考的具体例子；实例；范例： *The ruling* ***set a precedent*** *for future libel cases.* 这项裁决为今后的诽谤案提供了判例。 **2** [C, U] a similar action or event that happened earlier 先前出现的事例；前例；先例： *historical precedents* 历史前例 ◇ *There is no precedent for a disaster of this scale.* 这种规模的灾难是空前的。◇ *Such protests are* ***without precedent*** *in recent history.* 这类抗议事件在近代史上没有发生过。 **3** [U] the way that things have always been done 传统；常例；常规 SYN **tradition**: *to break with precedent* (= to do sth in a different way) 打破常规 ➲ SEE ALSO UNPRECEDENTED

pre·cept /ˈpriːsept/ *noun* [C, U] (*formal*) a rule about how to behave or what to think （思想、行为的）准则，规范 SYN **principle**

pre·cinct /ˈpriːsɪŋkt/ *noun* **1** (*BrE*) a commercial area in a town where cars cannot go 步行商业区： *a* ***pedestrian/shopping precinct*** 步行区；购物区 **2** (*NAmE*) one of the parts into which a town or city is divided in order to organize elections 选区 **3** (*NAmE*) a part of a city that has its own police station; the police station in this area 警区；分区警察局；派出所： *Detective Hennessy of the 44th precinct* 第 44 警区的亨尼西警探 ◇ *The murder occurred just a block from the precinct.* 谋杀案就发生在和警察分局相隔一个街区的地方。 **4** [usually pl.] (*formal*) the area around a place or a building, sometimes surrounded by a wall （建筑物等的）外围，围墙内区域： *the* ***cathedral/college precincts*** 大教堂 / 学院周围 ◇ *within the precincts of the castle* 在城堡的围墙内

pre·cious /ˈpreʃəs/ *adj., adv.*

■ ***adj.*** **1** rare and worth a lot of money 珍奇的；珍稀的： *a precious vase* 稀世花瓶 ◇ *The crown was set with precious jewels—diamonds, rubies and emeralds.* 王冠上镶嵌着稀世宝石，有钻石、红宝石和绿宝石。 ➲ SEE ALSO PRECIOUS METAL, PRECIOUS STONE ➲ SYNONYMS AT VALUABLE **2** valuable or important and not to be wasted 宝贵的；珍贵的： *Clean water is a precious commodity in that part of the world.* 在世界的那个地方，洁净的水是宝贵的东西。◇ *You're wasting precious time!* 你在浪费宝贵的时间！ **3** loved or valued very much 受珍爱的；被珍惜的 SYN **treasured**: ***precious memories/possessions*** 珍贵的回忆 / 财物 **4** [only before noun] (*informal*) used to show you are angry that another person thinks sth is very important （表示气愤）宝贝似的： *I didn't touch your precious car!* 我没碰你那辆宝贝车！ **5** (*disapproving*) (especially of people and their behaviour 尤指人及其行为) very formal, exaggerated and not natural in what you say and do 道貌岸然的；矫揉造作的 SYN **affected** ▶ **pre·cious·ness** *noun* [U]: *the preciousness of an old friendship* 悠久友谊的可贵 ◇ *His writings reveal an unattractive preciousness of style.* 他的文章流露出不讨好的做作风格。

■ ***adv.*** (*informal*) ~ **little/few** used to emphasize the fact that there is very little of sth or that there are very few of sth （强调极少或太少）： *There's precious little to do in this town.* 这个镇上没有多少可做的事。

ˌprecious 'metal *noun* [C, U] a very valuable metal such as gold or silver 贵金属

ˌprecious 'stone (*also* **stone**) *noun* a rare valuable stone, such as a diamond, that is used in jewellery 宝石 ➲ SEE ALSO SEMI-PRECIOUS

preci·pice /ˈpresəpɪs/ *noun* a very steep side of a high CLIFF, mountain or rock 悬崖；峭壁： (*figurative*) *The country was now* ***on the edge of a precipice*** (= very close to disaster). 这个国家现在情势岌岌可危。 ➲ VISUAL VOCAB PAGE V5 ➲ SEE ALSO PRECIPITOUS ➲ WORDFINDER NOTE AT MOUNTAIN

pre·cipi·tate *verb, adj., noun*

■ ***verb*** /prɪˈsɪpɪteɪt/ (*formal*) **1** ~ **sth** to make sth, especially sth bad, happen suddenly or sooner than it should 使…突然降临；加速（坏事的发生） SYN **bring on, spark**: *His resignation precipitated a leadership crisis.* 他的辞职立即引发了领导层的危机。 **2** ~ **sb/sth into sth** to suddenly force sb/sth into a particular state or condition 使突然陷入（某种状态）： *The assassination of the president precipitated the country into war.* 总统被暗杀使国家骤然陷入战争状态。

■ ***adj.*** /prɪˈsɪpɪtət/ (*formal*) (of an action or a decision 行动或决定) happening very quickly or suddenly and usually without enough care and thought 鲁莽的；草率的；仓促的 ▶ **pre·cipi·tate·ly** *adv.*： *to act precipitately* 贸然行事

■ ***noun*** /prɪˈsɪpɪteɪt/ (*chemistry* 化) a solid substance that has been separated from a liquid in a chemical process 沉淀物；析出物

pre·cipi·ta·tion /prɪˌsɪpɪˈteɪʃn/ *noun* **1** [U] (*specialist*) rain, snow, etc. that falls; the amount of this that falls 降水，降水量（包括雨、雪、冰等）： *an increase in annual precipitation* 年降水量的增加 ➲ WORDFINDER NOTE AT RAIN **2** [U, C] (*chemistry* 化) a chemical process in which solid material is separated from a liquid 沉淀；淀析

pre·cipit·ous /prɪˈsɪpɪtəs/ *adj.* (*formal*) **1** very steep, high and often dangerous 陡峭的；险峻的；峭拔的 SYN **sheer**: *precipitous cliffs* 险峻的峭壁 ◇ *a precipitous drop at the side of the road* 道路一旁陡降的坡面 **2** sudden and great 突然的；骤然的；急剧的 SYN **abrupt**: *a precipitous decline in exports* 出口的急剧下降 **3** done very quickly, without enough thought or care 草率的；仓促的；贸然的 SYN **hasty**: *a precipitous action* 贸然行动 ▶ **pre·cipit·ous·ly** *adv.*： *The land dropped precipitously down to the rocky shore.* 地面陡降，下方是布满岩石的岸边。◇ *The dollar plunged precipitously.* 美元直线下跌。◇ *We don't want to act precipitously.* 我们不想仓促行事。 ➲ SEE ALSO PRECIPICE

pre·cis /ˈpreɪsiː; *NAmE* preɪˈsiː/ *noun* [C, U] (*pl.* **pre·cis** /-siːz/) a short version of a speech or a piece of writing that gives the main points or ideas 概要；摘要；大纲 SYN **summary**: *to* ***write/give/make a precis*** *of a report* 写 / 提供 / 做一份报告摘要 ▶ **pre·cis** *verb* (**pre·cises, pre·cis·ing** /-siːɪŋ/, **pre·cised** /-siːd/, **pre·cised**)： ~ **sth** *to precis a scientific report* 写科研报告摘要

pre·cise 🔑 AW /prɪˈsaɪs/ *adj.* **1** 🔑 clear and accurate 准确的；确切的；精确的；明确的 SYN **exact**: *precise details/instructions/measurements* 确切的细节；明确的指令；精确的尺寸 ◇ *Can you give a more precise definition of the word?* 你能给这个词下个更确切的定义吗？◇ *I can be reasonably precise about the time of the incident.* 我可以相当准确地说出这件事发生的时间。 **2** 🔑 [only before noun] used to emphasize that sth happens at a particular time or in a particular way （强调时间或方式等）就，恰好： *We were just talking about her when,* ***at that precise moment,*** *she walked in.* 我们正谈论着她，恰好在这个时候，她走进来了。◇ *Doctors found it hard to establish the precise nature of her illness.* 医生们难以判定她的确切病因。 **3** 🔑 taking care to be exact and accurate, especially about small details 细致的；精细的；认真的；一丝不苟的 SYN **meticulous**: *a skilled and precise worker* 熟练而认真的工人 ◇ *small, precise movements* 细微的动作 ◇ (*disapproving*) *She's rather prim and precise.* 她拘谨严肃，一丝不苟。

IDM **to be (more) pre'cise** used to show that you are giving more detailed and accurate information about sth

P

you have just mentioned 确切地说；准确地说：*The shelf is about a metre long—well, 98cm, to be precise.* 架子长约一米。嗯，精确地说，是 98 厘米。

pre·cise·ly 🔑 AW /prɪˈsaɪsli/ *adv.* **1** 🔑 exactly 准确地；恰好地：*They look precisely the same to me.* 依我看，他们的长相一模一样。◇ *That's precisely what I meant.* 那恰恰是我的意思。◇ *It's not clear precisely how the accident happened.* 事故究竟是怎么发生的不是很清楚。◇ *The meeting starts at 2 o'clock precisely.* 会议在两点整开始。**2** 🔑 accurately; carefully 精确地；细心地；仔细地：*to describe sth precisely* 精确地描述某事物 ◇ *She pronounced the word very slowly and precisely.* 她缓慢而清晰地读出这个字。**3** 🔑 used to emphasize that sth is very true or obvious（强调真实或明显）正是，确实：*It's* ***precisely because*** *I care about you that I don't like you staying out late.* 正因为我关心你，我才不要你太晚回家。**4** used to emphasize that you agree with a statement, especially because you think it is obvious or is similar to what you have just said（加强同意的语气）对，的确如此，一点也不错：*'It's not that easy, is it?' 'No, precisely.'* "事情并不那么容易吧？" "对，的确不容易。"

IDM **more preˈcisely** used to show that you are giving more detailed and accurate information about sth you have just mentioned 更确切地说；更严格地说：*The problem is due to discipline, or, more precisely, the lack of discipline, in schools.* 问题出在纪律上，或者更确切地说，是学校缺乏纪律。⇨ LANGUAGE BANK AT I.E.

pre·ci·sion AW /prɪˈsɪʒn/ *noun* [U] the quality of being exact, accurate and careful 精确；准确；细致 SYN **accuracy**：*done with mathematical precision* 以数学般的精准完成的 ◇ *Historians can't estimate the date* ***with any (degree of) precision.*** 历史学家无法准确估算这个日期。◇ *He chose his words* ***with precision.*** 他用词确切。◇ ***precision instruments/tools*** 精密仪器 / 工具

pre·clude /prɪˈkluːd/ *verb* (*formal*) to prevent sth from happening or sb from doing sth; to make sth impossible 使行不通；阻止；妨碍；排除：**~ sth** *Lack of time precludes any further discussion.* 由于时间不足，不可能深入讨论。◇ **~ sb from doing sth** *My lack of interest in the subject precluded me from gaining much enjoyment out of it.* 由于对这个科目缺乏兴趣，我没有从中获得多少乐趣。◇ **~ (sb) doing sth** *His religious beliefs precluded him/his serving in the army.* 他的宗教信仰不允许他服兵役。

pre·co·cious /prɪˈkəʊʃəs; *NAmE* -ˈkoʊ-/ *adj.* (*sometimes disapproving*) (of a child 儿童) having developed particular abilities and ways of behaving at a much younger age than usual（能力或行为）早熟的：*a precocious child who started her acting career at the age of 5* * 5 岁便开始演艺生涯的超常儿童 ◇ *sexually precocious* 性早熟 ◇ *From an early age she displayed a precocious talent for music.* 她年纪轻轻就表现出不凡的音乐天赋。▶ **pre·co·cious·ly** *adv.*：*a precociously talented child* 有超常天才的儿童 **pre·co·city** /prɪˈkɒsəti; *NAmE* -ˈkɑː-/ (*also* **pre·co·cious·ness**) *noun* [U]：*his unusual precocity* 他的异常早熟

pre·cog·ni·tion /ˌpriːkɒɡˈnɪʃn; *NAmE* -kɑːɡ-/ *noun* [U] (*formal*) the knowledge that sth will happen in the future, which sb has because of a dream or a sudden feeling 预知，早知，先知（由梦境或突如其来的感觉感知到未来会发生的事）

pre-Columbian /ˌpriː kəˈlʌmbiən/ *adj.* connected with N and S America and their cultures before the arrival of Columbus in 1492 哥伦布到达之前的美洲的；前哥伦布的

pre·con·ceived /ˌpriːkənˈsiːvd/ *adj.* [only before noun] (of ideas, opinions, etc. 思想、观点等) formed before you have enough information or experience of sth 事先形成的；预想的：*Before I started the job, I had no preconceived notions of what it would be like.* 开始做这工作之前，我并未预想过它的实际情况。

pre·con·cep·tion /ˌpriːkənˈsepʃn/ *noun* [C, usually pl., U] an idea or opinion that is formed before you have enough information or experience 事先形成的观念；先入之见；预想；成见 SYN **assumption**：*a book that will challenge your preconceptions about rural life* 一本改变你对农村生活成见的书 ⇨ COMPARE MISCONCEPTION

pre·con·di·tion /ˌpriːkənˈdɪʃn/ *noun* **~ (for/of sth)** something that must happen or exist before sth else can exist or be done 先决条件；前提 SYN **prerequisite**：*A ceasefire is an essential precondition for negotiation.* 停火是谈判的必要前提。

pre·con·scious /ˌpriːˈkɒnʃəs; *NAmE* -ˈkɑːn-/ *adj.* (*psychology* 心) associated with a part of the mind from which memories and thoughts that have not been REPRESSED can be brought to the surface 前意识的（指能被带到意识区域的未受压抑的记忆和思想）

pre·cooked /ˌpriːˈkʊkt/ *adj.* (of food 食物) prepared and partly cooked in advance so that it can be quickly heated and eaten later 预煮的；预先烹调的

pre·cur·sor /priːˈkɜːsə(r); *NAmE* -ˈkɜːrs-/ *noun* **~ (of/to sth)** (*formal*) a person or thing that comes before sb/sth similar and that leads to or influences its development 先驱；先锋；前身 SYN **forerunner**

ˌpre-ˈcut *adj.* cut in advance and ready to use 预先剪切的；经剪切随时可用的

pre·date /ˌpriːˈdeɪt/ (*also* **ante·date**) *verb* **~ sth** to be built or formed, or to happen, at an earlier date than sth else in the past 早于；先于…建成（或形成、发生等）：*Few of the town's fine buildings predate the earthquake of 1755.* 该城那些精美的建筑很少是 1755 年大地震前建成的。OPP **post-date**

pre·da·tion /prɪˈdeɪʃn/ *noun* [U] (*specialist*) the act of an animal killing and eating other animals（动物的）捕食

preda·tor /ˈpredətə(r)/ *noun* [C, U] **1** an animal that kills and eats other animals 捕食者；捕食性动物：*Some animals have no natural predators.* 有些动物没有天敌。**2** (*disapproving*) a person or an organization that uses weaker people for their own advantage 弱肉强食的人（或机构）；剥削者；掠夺者：*to protect domestic industry from foreign predators* 保护本国工业不受外来剥削

preda·tory /ˈpredətri; *NAmE* -tɔːri/ *adj.* **1** (*specialist*) (of animals 动物) living by killing and eating other animals 捕食性的 **2** (of people 人) using weaker people for their own financial or sexual advantage（在金钱或性关系上）欺负弱小的，压榨他人的：*a predatory insurance salesman* 用高压手段推销的保险推销员 ◇ *a predatory look* 狞视

ˌpredatory ˈpricing *noun* [U] (*business* 商) the fact of a business company selling its goods at such a low price that other companies can no longer compete and have to stop selling similar goods 掠夺性定价；为挤垮对手的大削价

pre·de·cease /ˌpriːdɪˈsiːs/ *verb* **~ sb** (*law* 律) to die before sb 先于…去世：*His wife predeceased him.* 他的妻子先于他去世。

pre·de·ces·sor /ˈpriːdɪsesə(r); *NAmE* ˈpredəs-/ *noun* **1** a person who did a job before sb else 前任：*The new president reversed many of the policies of his predecessor.* 新任总统彻底改变了其前任的许多政策。**2** a thing, such as a machine, that has been followed or replaced by sth else 原先的东西；被替代的事物 ⇨ COMPARE SUCCESSOR

pre·des·tin·ation /ˌpriːdestɪˈneɪʃn/ *noun* [U] the theory or the belief that everything that happens has been decided or planned in advance by God or by FATE and that humans cannot change it 宿命论；命定说

pre·des·tined /ˌpriːˈdestɪnd/ *adj.* **~ (to do sth)** (*formal*) already decided or planned by God or by FATE 命中注定的；上天安排的：*It seems she was predestined to be famous.* 她好像是命中注定要出名似的。

pre·de·ter·mine /ˌpriːdɪˈtɜːmɪn; *NAmE* -ˈtɜːrm-/ *verb* **~ sth** (*formal*) to decide sth in advance so that it does not happen by chance 预先决定；事先安排：*The sex of the embryo is predetermined at fertilization.* 胚胎的性别早在受精时就决定了。▶ **pre·de·ter·mined** *adj.*：*An alarm* *sounds when the temperature reaches a predetermined level.* 温度一达到预设的度数，警报就会响起来。

pre·de·ter·miner /ˌpriːdɪˈtɜːmɪnə(r); *NAmE* -ˈtɜːrm-/ *noun* (*grammar* 语法) a word that can be used before a determiner, such as *all* in *all the students* or *twice* in *twice the price* 前位限定词，前位限定成分（置于限定词前，如 all the students 中的 all 和 twice the price 中的 twice）

pre·dica·ment /prɪˈdɪkəmənt/ *noun* a difficult or an unpleasant situation, especially one where it is difficult to know what to do 尴尬的处境；困境；窘境 **SYN quandary**: *the club's financial predicament* 俱乐部的财政困境 ◇ *I'm in a terrible predicament.* 我的处境十分尴尬。

predi·cate *noun, verb*

▪ ***noun*** /ˈpredɪkət/ (*grammar* 语法) a part of a sentence containing a verb that makes a statement about the subject of the verb, such as *went home* in *John went home.* 谓语（句子成分，对主语加以陈述，如 John went home 中的 went home） ➲ COMPARE OBJECT *n.* (4)

▪ ***verb*** /ˈpredɪkeɪt/ (*formal*) **1** [usually passive] **~ sth on/upon sth** to base sth on a particular belief, idea or principle 使基于；使以…为依据： *Democracy is predicated upon the rule of law.* 民主是以法治为基础的。 **2 ~ that... | ~ sth** to state that sth is true 表明；阐明；断言： *The article predicates that the market collapse was caused by weakness of the dollar.* 这篇文章声言，市场的崩溃是美元疲软造成的。

pre·dica·tive /prɪˈdɪkətɪv; *NAmE* ˈpredɪkeɪtɪv/ *adj.* (*grammar* 语法) (of an adjective 形容词) coming after a verb such as *be, become, get, seem, look.* Many adjectives, for example *old* can be either predicative as in *The man is very old,* or ATTRIBUTIVE as in *an old man.* Some, like *asleep,* can only be predicative. 作表语的，谓语性的（例如 asleep，用于 be、become、get、seem、look 等动词后；与 attributive 相对） ▸ **pre·dica·tive·ly** *adv.*

pre·dict 🔑 **AW** /prɪˈdɪkt/ *verb* to say that sth will happen in the future 预言；预告；预报 **SYN forecast**: **~ sth** *a reliable method of predicting earthquakes* 预报地震的可靠方法 ◇ *Nobody could predict the outcome.* 谁也无法预料结果如何。 ◇ **~ what, whether, etc....** *It is impossible to predict what will happen.* 预知未来的事是不可能的。 ◇ **~ (that)...** *She predicted (that) the election result would be close.* 她预言选举结果将很接近。 ◇ **it is predicted that...** *It was predicted that inflation would continue to fall.* 据预报，通货膨胀率将继续下降。 ◇ **sb/sth is predicted to do sth** *The trial is predicted to last for months.* 预料审讯将持续数月之久。 ➲ LANGUAGE BANK AT EXPECT

pre·dict·able **AW** /prɪˈdɪktəbl/ *adj.* **1** if sth is **predictable**, you know in advance that it will happen or what it will be like 可预见的；可预料的： *a predictable result* 可预见的结果 ◇ *The ending of the book was entirely predictable.* 那本书的结局是完全预料得到的。 ◇ *In March and April, the weather is much less predictable.* 三、四月份的天气非常不好预测。 **2** (*often disapproving*) behaving or happening in a way that you would expect and therefore boring 意料之中的；老套乏味的： *He's very nice, but I find him rather dull and predictable.* 他为人很不错，但我觉得他相当呆板乏味。 ▸ **pre·dict·abil·ity** **AW** /prɪˌdɪktəˈbɪləti/ *noun* [U] **pre·dict·ably** **AW** /-əbli/ *adv.*: *Prices were predictably high.* 价格高昂是意料中的事。 ◇ *Predictably, the new regulations proved unpopular.* 正如所料，新规定果然不得人心。

pre·dic·tion **AW** /prɪˈdɪkʃn/ *noun* [C, U] a statement that says what you think will happen; the act of making such a statement 预言；预测；预告： *Not many people agree with the government's prediction that the economy will improve.* 没有多少人赞同政府认为经济将会有所改善的预测。 ◇ *The results of the experiment confirmed our predictions.* 实验结果证实了我们的预测。 ◇ *Skilled readers make use of context and prediction.* 阅读能力强的人会利用上下文及推测来理解文意。 ◇ *It's difficult to make accurate predictions about the effects on the environment.* 很难准确预测对环境产生的影响。 ➲ COLLOCATIONS AT SCIENTIFIC ➲ LANGUAGE BANK AT EXPECT

pre·dict·ive /prɪˈdɪktɪv/ *adj.* [usually before noun] **1** (*formal*) connected with the ability to show what will happen in the future 预测的；预言的；前瞻的： *the predictive power of science* 科学的预测能力 **2** (of a computer program 计算机程序) allowing you to enter text on a computer or a mobile/cell phone more quickly by using the first few letters of each word to predict what you want to say 预测输入的（根据输入的字母来预测可能的字词）： ***predictive text input*** 预测文字输入 ◇ ***predictive messaging*** 可预测输入的信息传送

pre·dic·tor /prɪˈdɪktə(r)/ *noun* (*formal*) something that can show what will happen in the future 有预测作用的事物；预示物： *Cholesterol level is not a strong predictor of heart disease in women.* 胆固醇水平在预示女性患心脏病方面并不是一个很准确的因素。

pre·digest·ed /ˌpriːdaɪˈdʒestɪd/ *adj.* (of information 信息) put in a simple form that is easy to understand 简化的；使易于理解的

pre·di·lec·tion /ˌpriːdɪˈlekʃn; *NAmE* ˌpredlˈek-/ *noun* [usually sing.] **~ (for sth)** (*formal*) if you **have a predilection for** sth, you like it very much 喜爱；偏爱；钟爱 **SYN liking, preference**

pre·dis·pose /ˌpriːdɪˈspəʊz; *NAmE* -ˈspoʊz/ *verb* (*formal*) **1** to influence sb so that they are likely to think or behave in a particular way 使倾向于；使受…的影响： **~ sb to sth** *He believes that some people are predisposed to criminal behaviour.* 他认为有些人容易犯罪。 ◇ **~ sb to do sth** *Her good mood predisposed her to enjoy the play.* 她当时兴致高，所以一定喜欢那出戏。 **2 ~ sb to sth** to make it likely that you will suffer from a particular illness 使易于患（某种病）；容易诱发： *Stress can predispose people to heart attacks.* 压力容易使人患心脏病。

pre·dis·pos·ition /ˌpriːdɪspəˈzɪʃn/ *noun* [C, U] **~ (to/towards sth) | ~ (to do sth)** (*formal*) a condition that makes sb/sth likely to behave in a particular way or to suffer from a particular disease 倾向；癖性；（易患某种病的）体质： *a genetic predisposition to liver disease* 易患肝病的遗传体质

pre·dom·in·ance **AW** /prɪˈdɒmɪnəns; *NAmE* -ˈdɑːm-/ *noun* **1** [sing.] the situation of being greater in number or amount than other things or people （数量上的）优势 **SYN preponderance**: *a predominance of female teachers in elementary schools* 小学里女教师居多的现象 **2** [U] the state of having more power or influence than others 主导地位；支配地位 **SYN dominance**

pre·dom·in·ant **AW** /prɪˈdɒmɪnənt; *NAmE* -ˈdɑːm-/ *adj.* **1** most obvious or noticeable 显著的；明显的；盛行的： *a predominant feature* 显著特征 ◇ *Yellow is the predominant colour this spring in the fashion world.* 黄色是今春时装界的流行色。 **2** having more power or influence than others 占优势的；主导的 **SYN dominant**: *a predominant culture* 主流文化

pre·dom·in·ant·ly **AW** /prɪˈdɒmɪnəntli; *NAmE* -ˈdɑːm-/ (*also less frequent* **pre·dom·in·ate·ly** /prɪˈdɒmɪnətli; *NAmE* -ˈdɑːm-/) *adv.* mostly; mainly 主要地；多数情况下： *She works in a predominantly male environment.* 她在一个男性居多的环境里工作。 ➲ LANGUAGE BANK AT GENERALLY

pre·dom·in·ate **AW** /prɪˈdɒmɪneɪt; *NAmE* -ˈdɑːm-/ *verb* **1** [I] to be greater in amount or number than sth/sb else in a place, group, etc. （数量上）占优势；居多： *a colour scheme in which red predominates* 以红色为主的色彩组合 ◇ *Women predominated in the audience.* 观众以妇女为主。 **2** [I] **~ (over sb/sth)** to have the most influence or importance 占主导地位；有最大影响（或重要性）： *Private interest was not allowed to predominate over the public good.* 私人利益不得凌驾于公众利益之上。

pre·eˈclamp·sia *noun* [U] (*medical* 医) a condition in which a pregnant woman has high BLOOD PRESSURE, which can become serious if it is not treated 先兆子痫，水肿蛋白尿高血压综合征（由怀孕引起）

pree·mie /ˈpriːmi/ *noun* (*NAmE, informal*) a PREMATURE baby 早产儿

P

ˌpre-ˈeminent *adj.* (*formal*) more important, more successful or of a higher standard than others 杰出的；出类拔萃的；卓越的 **SYN** **outstanding**: *Dickens was pre-eminent among English writers of his day.* 狄更斯在其同时期英国作家中最为出色。 ▶ **ˌpre-ˈeminence** *noun* [U]: *to achieve pre-eminence in public life* 成为出色的公众人物

ˌpre-ˈeminent·ly *adv.* to a very great degree; especially 极大地；特别地；格外地

pre-empt /priˈempt/ *verb* **1** ~ **sth** to prevent sth from happening by taking action to stop it 预先制止；防止；避免: *A good training course will pre-empt many problems.* 良好的培训课程会防止许多问题产生。 **2** ~ **sb/sth** to do or say sth before sb else does 抢在…之前做（或说）；先发制人: *She was just about to apologize when he pre-empted her.* 她正想道歉，他却抢先说了。 **3** ~ **sth** (*NAmE*) to replace a planned programme on the television 临时取代（电视节目表上的节目）: *The scheduled programme will be pre-empted by a special news bulletin.* 预定的节目将临时换成特别新闻简报。

pre-emption /priˈempʃn/ *noun* [U] (*business* 商) the opportunity given to one person or group to buy goods, shares, etc. 优先采购；先行购买: *Existing shareholders will have pre-emption rights.* 现有股东将有优先购买权。

pre-emptive /priˈemptɪv/ *adj.* [usually before noun] done to stop sb taking action, especially action that will be harmful to yourself 先发制人的: *a* ***pre-emptive attack/strike*** *on the military base* 对军事基地先发制人的进攻

preen /priːn/ *verb* **1** [T, I] ~ (**yourself**) (*usually disapproving*) to spend a lot of time making yourself look attractive and then admiring your appearance 刻意打扮，精心修饰（并自我欣赏）: *Will you stop preening yourself in front of the mirror?* 你别对着镜子打扮个没完行不行？ **2** [T] ~ **yourself** (**on sth**) (*usually disapproving*) to feel very pleased with yourself about sth and show other people how pleased you are 顾盼自雄；沾沾自喜；得意扬扬 **3** [I, T] ~ (**itself**) (of a bird 鸟) to clean itself or make its feathers smooth with its beak （用喙）整理羽毛

ˌpre-eˈxist *verb* [I] to exist from an earlier time 早先存在；在先出现: *a pre-existing medical condition* 宿疾 ▶ **ˌpre-eˈxistent** *adj.*

pre·fab /ˈpriːfæb/ *noun* (*informal*) a prefabricated building 预制建筑: *prefabs built after the war* 战后修建的预制房屋

pre·fab·ri·cated /ˌpriːˈfæbrɪkeɪtɪd/ *adj.* (especially of a building 尤指建筑) made in sections that can be put together later 预制的；用预制构件组装的 ▶ **pre·fab·ri·ca·tion** /ˌpriːfæbrɪˈkeɪʃn/ *noun* [U]

pref·ace /ˈprefəs/ *noun, verb*

■ ***noun*** an introduction to a book, especially one that explains the author's aims （书的）前言，序言 ➲ COMPARE FOREWORD

■ ***verb*** **1** ~ **sth** (**with sth**) to provide a book or other piece of writing with a preface 为…写序言: *He prefaced the diaries with a short account of how they were discovered.* 他在前言中简要叙述了发现日记的经过。 **2** ~ **sth by/with sth** | ~ **sth by doing sth** (*formal*) to say sth before you start making a speech, answering a question, etc. 以…为开端；作…的开场白: *I must preface my remarks with an apology.* 讲话前，我必须先表示歉意。

prefa·tory /ˈprefətri; *NAmE* -tɔːri/ *adj.* [only before noun] (*formal*) acting as a PREFACE or an introduction to sth 序言性的；前言性的；导言性的: *a prefatory note* 卷首语

pre·fect /ˈpriːfekt/ *noun* **1** (in some British schools) an older student with some authority over younger students and some other responsibilities and advantages （某些英国学校中负责维持纪律等的）学长 **2** (*also* **Prefect**) an officer responsible for an area of local government in some countries, for example France, Italy and Japan （法、意、日等国家的）地方行政长官；省长；县长

pre·fec·ture /ˈpriːfektʃə(r)/ *noun* an area of local government in some countries, for example France, Italy and Japan （法、意、日等国的）地方行政区域；省；县

pre·fer 🔑 /prɪˈfɜː(r)/ *verb* (**-rr-**) (not used in the progressive tenses 不用于进行时) to like one thing or person better than another; to choose one thing rather than sth else because you like it better 较喜欢；喜欢…多于…: ~ **sth** *'Coffee or tea?' 'I'd prefer tea, thanks.'* "要咖啡还是茶？""我要茶，谢谢。" ◇ *I much prefer jazz to rock music.* 我喜欢爵士乐远胜过摇滚乐。 ◇ ***I would prefer it if*** *you didn't tell anyone.* 我希望你别告诉任何人。 ◇ *A local firm* ***is to be preferred.*** 选一家当地的公司更好。 ◇ ~ **sth** + **adj.** *I prefer my coffee black.* 我喜欢不加奶的咖啡。 ◇ ~ **to do sth** *The donor prefers to remain anonymous.* 捐赠者希望自己的姓名不被公开。 ◇ *I prefer not to think about it.* 我不想考虑此事。 ◇ ~ **sb/sth to do sth** *Would you prefer me to stay?* 你愿意我留下来吗？ ◇ ~ **doing sth** *I prefer playing in defence.* 我喜欢打防守。 ◇ ~ **that...** (*formal*) *I would prefer that you did not mention my name.* 我希望你不要说出我的名字。 **IDM** SEE CHARGE *n.* ➲ MORE LIKE THIS 36, page R29

▼ **EXPRESS YOURSELF 情景表达**

Expressing a preference 表达喜好

These are ways of stating what your preferred choice is. Note that we sometimes discount our own expertise or authority before expressing our preference. 面对选择时，表达自己更喜欢某事物，可用以下方式。需要注意的是在表达喜好之前，有时会先表明自己的选择并非代表专家或权威的意见：

- ***I like*** *the red one* ***better than/more than*** *the green one.* 比起那个绿色的，我更喜欢红的。
- ***I prefer*** *beef to lamb.* 我喜欢牛肉胜于羊肉。
- ***I'd prefer*** *to wait here.* 我宁愿在这儿等。
- ***I'd rather*** *go to the concert than the play.* 与看戏相比，我更愿意去听音乐会。
- ***I think I'd rather*** *stay in than go out tonight.* 今晚我想待在家里，不想外出。
- ***I like*** *swimming* ***better than*** *jogging.* 比起慢跑，我更喜欢游泳。
- ***I think*** *that colour's* ***much more attractive.*** 我觉得那种颜色好看多了。
- ***It doesn't really matter to me*** *whether we eat here or go out.* (*especially NAmE*) 我们在这儿吃还是出去吃，我真无所谓。
- ***I don't really mind*** *whether we talk now or later.* (*BrE*) 我们是现在谈还是以后谈，我不大在意。
- ***I'm happy either way.*** (*NAmE*) （两个之中）无论哪一个我都乐意。
- ***I don't really care either way.*** （这两个）我都无所谓。
- ***If it were up to me, I'd choose*** *the green one.* 如果让我来选，我会选那个绿色的。
- ***If you ask me,*** *the old one looks better than the new one.* 要问我的话，旧的那个看起来比新的好。
- ***I'm not an expert but*** *Design B seems more eye-catching.* 我不是专家，但 B 设计似乎更抢眼。

pref·er·able /ˈprefrəbl/ *adj.* more attractive or more suitable; to be preferred to sth 较适合；更可取: ~ (**to sth**) *Anything was preferable to the tense atmosphere at home.* 什么都比家里的紧张气氛好。 ◇ ~ (**to doing sth**) *He finds country life* ***infinitely preferable*** *to living in the city.* 他觉得乡村生活比都市生活称心得多。 ◇ ~ (**to do sth**) *It would be preferable to employ two people, not one.* 雇请两个人比雇请一个更好。 ▶ **pref·er·ably** /ˈprefrəbli/ *adv.*: *We're looking for a new house, preferably one near the school.* 我们正在找新房子，最好是靠近学校的。

pref·er·ence 🔑 /ˈprefrəns/ *noun* **1** 🔑 [U, sing.] ~ (**for sb/sth**) a greater interest in or desire for sb/sth than sb/sth else 偏爱；爱好；喜爱: *It's a matter of* ***personal preference.*** 那是个人的爱好问题。 ◇ *Many people* ***expressed a strong preference*** *for the original plan.* 许多人表示尤为喜欢原计划。 ◇ *I can't say that I have any particular* *preference.* 我说不出自己有什么特别偏好。◇ *Let's make a list of possible speakers, **in order of preference**.* 咱们按优先顺序列出一份可能请到的发言者名单。 **2** [C] a thing that is liked better or best 偏爱的事物；最喜爱的东西：*a study of consumer preferences* 消费者偏好调查 ➲ SYNONYMS AT CHOICE

IDM **give (a) preference to sb/sth** to treat sb/sth in a way that gives them an advantage over other people or things 给…以优惠；优待：*Preference will be given to graduates of this university.* 这所大学的毕业生会获得优先考虑。 **in preference to sb/sth** rather than sb/sth 而不是：*She was chosen in preference to her sister.* 她被选中了，而不是她妹妹。

pref·er·en·tial /ˌprefəˈrenʃl/ *adj.* [only before noun] giving an advantage to a particular person or group 优先的；优惠的；优待的：*Don't expect to get **preferential treatment**.* 不要指望受到优待。▶ **pref·er·en·tial·ly** /-ʃəli/ *adv.*

pre·fer·ment /prɪˈfɜːmənt; *NAmE* -ˈfɜːrm-/ *noun* [U] (*formal*) the fact of being given a more important job or a higher rank 晋升；提升 SYN **promotion**

pre·fig·ure /ˌpriːˈfɪɡə(r); *NAmE* -ɡjər/ *verb* **~ sth** (*formal*) to suggest or show sth that will happen in the future 预示；预兆

pre·fix /ˈpriːfɪks/ *noun, verb*

■ ***noun*** **1** (*grammar* 语法) a letter or group of letters added to the beginning of a word to change its meaning, such as *un-* in *unhappy* and *pre-* in *preheat* 前缀（缀于单词前以改变其意义的字母或字母组合） ➲ COMPARE AFFIX *n.*, SUFFIX **2** a word, letter or number that is put before another 前置代号（置于前面的单词或字母、数字）：*Car insurance policies have the prefix MC (for motor car).* 汽车保险单标有 MC 代号（表示汽车）。 **3** (*old-fashioned*) a title such as *Dr* or *Mrs* used before a person's name （人名前的）称谓

■ ***verb*** to add letters or numbers to the beginning of a word or number 在…前面加（字母或数字）：**~ A to B** *American members have the letters US prefixed to their code numbers.* 美国会员的代码前加了字母 US。◇ **~ B with A** *Their code numbers are prefixed with US.* 他们的代码前加上了字母 US。

preg·gers /ˈpreɡəz; *NAmE* -ɡərz/ *adj.* [not before noun] (*BrE, informal*) pregnant 怀孕；怀胎

preg·nancy /ˈpreɡnənsi/ *noun* [U, C] (*pl.* **-ies**) the state of being pregnant 妊娠；怀孕：*Many women experience sickness **during pregnancy**.* 许多妇女在怀孕期都会有恶心现象。◇ *a **pregnancy test*** 妊娠检查 ◇ ***unplanned/unwanted pregnancies*** 计划外 / 非意愿妊娠 ◇ *the increase in teenage pregnancies* 十几岁少女怀孕率的上升 ➲ COLLOCATIONS AT CHILD

preg·nant /ˈpreɡnənt/ *adj.* **1** (of a woman or female animal 女人或雌性动物) having a baby or young animal developing inside her/its body 妊娠的；怀孕的：*My wife is pregnant.* 我妻子怀孕了。◇ *I was pregnant with our third child at the time.* 当时我正怀着我们的第三个孩子。◇ *a **heavily pregnant** woman* (= one whose baby is nearly ready to be born) 临产期孕妇 ◇ *to **get/become pregnant*** 怀孕 ◇ *He got his girlfriend pregnant and they're getting married.* 他让女友怀孕了，因此他们即将结婚。◇ *She's six months pregnant.* 她怀孕六个月了。 ➲ COLLOCATIONS AT CHILD

WORDFINDER 联想词：antenatal, **child**, conception, fetus, maternity leave, miscarriage, morning sickness, scan, womb

2 **~ with sth** (*formal*) full of a quality or feeling 饱含；充溢着：*Her silences were pregnant with criticism.* 她的沉默里充满了批评之意。

IDM **a pregnant ˈpause/ˈsilence** an occasion when nobody speaks, although people are aware that there are feelings or thoughts to express 耐人寻味的停顿；心照不宣的沉默

pre·heat /ˌpriːˈhiːt/ *verb* **~ sth** to heat an oven to a particular temperature before you put food in it to cook 使（烤箱）预热

pre·hen·sile /prɪˈhensaɪl; *NAmE* -sl/ *adj.* (*specialist*) (of a part of an animal's body 动物肢体的一部分) able to hold things 能抓住东西的；缠绕性的：*the monkey's prehensile tail* 猴子的长卷尾 ➲ VISUAL VOCAB PAGE V12

pre·his·toric /ˌpriːhɪˈstɒrɪk; *NAmE* -ˈstɔːr-/ *adj.* connected with the time in history before information was written down 史前的；有文字记载以前的；远古的：*in prehistoric times* 在史前时期 ◇ *prehistoric man/remains/animals/burial sites* 史前人类 / 遗迹 / 动物 / 葬地

pre·his·tory /ˌpriːˈhɪstri/ *noun* **1** [U] the period of time in history before information was written down 史前时期；远古时期 **2** [sing.] the earliest stages of the development of sth （事物发展的）初期，开始阶段，萌芽时期：*the prehistory of capitalism* 资本主义发展的初期

ˌpre-inˈstall *verb* = PRELOAD

pre·judge /ˌpriːˈdʒʌdʒ/ *verb* **~ sth** (*formal*) to make a judgement about a situation before you have all the necessary information 预先判断；过早判断：*They took care not to **prejudge the issue**.* 他们态度谨慎，不过早对此事下判断。

preju·dice /ˈpredʒudɪs/ *noun, verb*

■ ***noun*** [U, C] an unreasonable dislike of or preference for a person, group, custom, etc., especially when it is based on their race, religion, sex, etc. 偏见；成见：*a victim of **racial prejudice*** 种族偏见的受害者 ◇ *Their decision was based on ignorance and prejudice.* 他们的决定是基于无知和偏见。◇ **~ against sb/sth** *There is little prejudice against workers from other EU states.* 对来自其他欧盟国家的劳工可说并无偏见。◇ **~ in favour of sb/sth** *I must admit to a prejudice in favour of British universities.* 我得承认我对英国大学有所偏爱。 ➲ COLLOCATIONS AT RACE

IDM **without ˈprejudice (to sth)** (*law* 律) without affecting any other legal matter 不损害其他权益；无损于合法权利：*They agreed to pay compensation without prejudice* (= without admitting GUILT). 他们同意赔偿，但不承认有罪。

■ ***verb*** **1** **~ sb (against sb/sth)** to influence sb so that they have an unfair or unreasonable opinion about sb/sth 使怀有（或产生）偏见 SYN **bias**：*The prosecution lawyers have been trying to prejudice the jury against her.* 控方律师一直力图使陪审团对她产生偏见。 **2** **~ sth** (*formal*) to have a harmful effect on sth 损害；有损于：*Any delay will prejudice the child's welfare.* 任何延误都会损及这个孩子的身心健康。

preju·diced /ˈpredʒədɪst/ *adj.* having an unreasonable dislike of or preference for sb/sth, especially based on their race, religion, sex, etc. 有偏见的；带成见的；偏爱的；偏心的：*Few people will admit to being racially prejudiced.* 很少有人会承认自己有种族偏见。◇ **~ (against/in favour of sb/sth)** *They are prejudiced against older applicants.* 他们对年长一些的申请人抱有成见。◇(*humorous*) *I think it's an excellent article, but then I'm prejudiced—I wrote it.* 我认为那篇文章相当出色；不过，我有些偏心，那是我写的嘛！

preju·di·cial /ˌpredʒuˈdɪʃl/ *adj.* **~ (to sth)** (*formal*) harming or likely to harm sb/sth 有害的；不利的；会造成损害的 SYN **damaging**：*developments prejudicial to the company's future* 不利于公司未来发展的新形势

prel·ate /ˈprelət/ *noun* (*formal*) a priest of high rank in the Christian Church, such as a BISHOP or CARDINAL （基督教会的）高级教士，高级神职人员

pre·lim·in·ary AW /prɪˈlɪmɪnəri; *NAmE* -neri/ *adj., noun*

■ ***adj.*** happening before a more important action or event 预备性的；初步的；开始的 SYN **initial**：*After a few preliminary remarks he announced the winners.* 说了几句开场白之后，他即宣布优胜者名单。◇ *preliminary results/findings/enquiries* 初步结果 / 发现 / 调查 ◇ *the preliminary rounds of the contest* 预赛 ◇ **~ to sth** *pilot studies preliminary to a full-scale study* 全面研究前的试验性初步研究

■ ***noun*** (*pl.* **-ies**) **~ (to sth)** a **preliminary** is an action or event that is done in preparation for sth 初步行动（或活

P

动）；预备性措施： *Research will be needed as a preliminary to taking a decision.* 做决定之前需要进行研究。◇ *I'll skip the usual preliminaries and come straight to the point.* 闲话少说，我就直接进入正题。◇ *England was lucky to get through the preliminaries* (= the preliminary stages in a sports competition). 英格兰队幸运地通过了预选赛。

pre·load /ˌpriːˈləʊd; NAmE -ˈloʊd/ (*also* ˌ**pre·in'stall**) *verb* ~ **sth** to load sth in advance 预载；预装： *The PC comes with office software preloaded.* 这台电脑随机预装了办公软件。▸ **pre·load** *noun*

prel·ude /ˈpreljuːd/ *noun* **1** a short piece of music, especially an introduction to a longer piece 前奏曲 **2** ~ (**to sth**) an action or event that happens before another more important one and forms an introduction to it 序幕；前奏；先声

pre·mar·ital /ˌpriːˈmærɪtl/ *adj.* [only before noun] happening before marriage 婚前的： *premarital sex* 婚前性行为

pre·ma·ture /ˈpremətʃə(r); NAmE ˌpriːməˈtʃʊr; -ˈtʊr/ *adj.* **1** happening before the normal or expected time 未成熟的；过早的；提前的： *his premature death at the age of 37* 他 37 岁时早逝 **2** (of a birth or a baby 生产或婴儿) happening or being born before the normal length of PREGNANCY has been completed 早产的： *The baby was four weeks pre-mature.* 这个婴儿早产了四周。◇ *a premature birth after only thirty weeks* 怀孕仅三十周的早产 ➲ WORDFINDER NOTE AT BABY **3** happening or made too soon 草率的；仓促的： *a premature conclusion/decision/judgement* 草率的结论 / 决定 / 判断 ◇ ***It is premature** to talk about success at this stage.* 现阶段就谈成功尚为时过早。▸ **pre·ma·ture·ly** *adv.* : *The child was born prematurely.* 这孩子是早产的。◇ *Her hair became prematurely white.* 她的头发过早地苍白了。

ˈ**pre-med** *noun* (*informal*) **1** [U] (*especially NAmE*) a course or set of classes that students take in preparation for medical school 医学预科（课程） **2** [C] (*especially NAmE*) a student who is taking classes in preparation for medical school 医学预科生 **3** [U] = PREMEDICATION

pre·medi·ca·tion /ˌpriːˌmedɪˈkeɪʃn/ (*also informal* **pre-med**) *noun* [U] drugs given to sb in preparation for an operation or other medical treatment 麻醉前用药；（治疗）前驱药

pre·medi·tated /ˌpriːˈmedɪteɪtɪd/ *adj.* (of a crime or bad action 罪案或恶行) planned in advance 预谋的；事先策划的： *a premeditated attack* 事先策划的攻击 ◇ *The killing had not been premeditated.* 这次杀人不是预谋的。**OPP** **unpremeditated** ▸ **pre·medi·ta·tion** /ˌpriːˌmedɪˈteɪʃn/ *noun* [U]

pre·men·strual /ˌpriːˈmenstruəl/ *adj.* happening or experienced before MENSTRUATION 月经前的： *Many women suffer from **premenstrual tension/syndrome**, causing headaches and depression.* 许多妇女患月经前紧张 / 综合征，引起头疼和情绪低落。➲ SEE ALSO PMS

prem·ier /ˈpremiə(r); NAmE prɪˈmɪr; -ˈmjɪr/ *adj., noun*
▪ ***adj.*** [only before noun] most important, famous or successful 首要的；最著名的；最成功的；第一的： *one of the country's premier chefs* 国家名厨之一 ◇ (*BrE, sport* 体育) *the Premier League/Division* 超级联赛
▪ ***noun*** **1** used especially in newspapers, etc. to mean 'prime minister'（尤用于报章等）首相，总理 **2** (in Canada) the first minister of a PROVINCE or TERRITORY （加拿大的）省总理，地区总理

premi·ere /ˈpremieə(r); NAmE prɪˈmɪr; -ˈmjɪr/ *noun, verb*
▪ ***noun*** the first public performance of a film/movie or play（电影、戏剧的）首次公演，首映： *the **world premiere** of his new play* 他的新戏在全世界的首次公演 ◇ *The movie will have its premiere in July.* 这部电影将于七月首映。
▪ ***verb*** [T, I] ~ (**sth**) to perform a play or piece of music or show a film/movie to an audience for the first time; to be performed or shown to an audience for the first time 首次公演（戏剧、音乐、电影）： *The play was premiered at the Birmingham Rep in 2014.* 这出戏于 2014 年在伯明翰轮演剧场首次公演。◇ *His new movie premieres in New York this week.* 他的新电影本周在纽约首映。

prem·ier·ship /ˈpremiəʃɪp; NAmE prɪˈmɪrʃɪp; -ˈmjɪr-/ *noun* [sing.] **1** the period or position of being prime minister 首相职位（或任期）；总理职位（或任期）： *during Gordon Brown's premiership* 在戈登 • 布朗的首相任期内 **2** (*often* **the Premiership**) the former name for the football (SOCCER) league in England and Wales which has the best teams in it, now called the PREMIER LEAGUE 英格兰足球超级联赛（现称 the Premier League） **3** a professional league for the best RUGBY UNION teams in England 英格兰橄榄球超级联赛

prem·ise (*BrE also, less frequent* **prem·iss**) /ˈpremɪs/ *noun* (*formal*) a statement or an idea that forms the basis for a reasonable line of argument 前提；假定： *the basic premise of her argument* 她的论证的基本前提 ◇ *a false premise* 错误的前提 ◇ *His reasoning is based on the premise that all people are equally capable of good and evil.* 他的推理是以人可以为善亦可以为恶为前提的。

prem·ised /ˈpremɪst/ *adj.* ~ **on/upon sth** (*formal*) based on a particular idea or belief that is considered to be true 根据，基于（观点、信念等）： *Traditional economic analysis is premised on the assumption that more is better.* 传统的经济分析是以多多益善的设想为依据的。

prem·ises 🔑 /ˈpremɪsɪz/ *noun* [pl.] the building and land near to it that a business owns or uses （企业的）房屋建筑及附属场地，营业场所： ***business/commercial/industrial premises*** 经营场所；工业用房屋场地 ◇ *No alcohol may be consumed **on the premises**.* 场区内禁止饮酒。◇ *Police were called to escort her **off the premises**.* 召来警察护送她离场。➲ SYNONYMS AT BUILDING

pre·mium /ˈpriːmiəm/ *noun, adj.*
▪ ***noun*** **1** an amount of money that you pay once or regularly for an insurance policy 保险费： *a monthly premium of £6.25* 每月 6.25 英镑的保险费 ➲ SYNONYMS AT PAYMENT ➲ WORDFINDER NOTE AT INSURANCE **2** an extra payment added to the basic rate 额外费用；附加费： *You have to pay a high premium for express delivery.* 快递须付高额的附加费。◇ *A premium of 10% is paid out after 20 years.* * 20 年后要付清 10% 的额外费用。
IDM **at a ˈpremium 1** if sth is **at a premium**, there is little of it available and it is difficult to get 稀少；难得： *Space is at a premium in a one-bedroomed apartment.* 单居室公寓的空间是很有限的。 **2** at a higher than normal price 超出平常价；溢价： *Shares are selling at a premium.* 这种股票以高于面值的价格出售。 **put/place/set a premium on sb/sth** to think that sb/sth is particularly important or valuable 重视；珍视
▪ ***adj.*** [only before noun] very high (and higher than usual); of high quality 高昂的；优质的： *premium prices/products* 奇高的价格；优质产品

pre·modi·fier /ˌpriːˈmɒdɪfaɪə(r); NAmE -ˈmɑːd-/ *noun* (*grammar* 语法) a word, especially an adjective or a noun, that is placed before a noun and describes it or restricts its meaning in some way 前置修饰语；前修饰成分： *In 'a loud noise', the adjective 'loud' is a premodifier.* 在 a loud noise 中，形容词 loud 是前置修饰语。➲ COMPARE MODIFIER, POSTMODIFIER

pre·mon·ition /ˌpriːməˈnɪʃn; ˌprem-/ *noun* a feeling that sth is going to happen, especially sth unpleasant （尤指不祥的）预感： ~ (**of sth**) *a premonition of disaster* 大祸临头的预感 ◇ ~ (**that...**) *He had a premonition that he would never see her again.* 他有一种再也见不到她的预感。▸ **pre·moni·tory** /prɪˈmɒnɪtəri; NAmE -ˈmɑːnɪtɔːri/ *adj.* (*formal*) : *a premonitory dream* 预兆性的梦

pre·natal /ˌpriːˈneɪtl/ (*especially NAmE*) (*BrE also* **ante·natal**) *adj.* relating to the medical care given to pregnant women 产前的 ➲ COMPARE POSTNATAL

pre·nup·tial agreement /priːˌnʌpʃl əˈɡriːmənt/ (*also informal* **pre·nup** /ˈpriːnʌp/) *noun* an agreement made by a couple before they get married in which they say how their money and property is to be divided if they get divorced 婚前协议（关于倘若离婚财产如何分割等）

pre·occu·pa·tion /priˌɒkjuˈpeɪʃn; *NAmE* -ˌɑːk-/ *noun* **1** [U, C] ~ (**with sth**) a state of thinking about sth continuously; sth that you think about frequently or for a long time 盘算；思虑；长久思考的事情 **SYN** **obsession**: *She found his preoccupation with money irritating.* 她对他一心只想着钱感到很厌烦。◇ *His current preoccupation is the appointment of the new manager.* 他目前操心的是新经理的任命。**2** [U] a mood created by thinking or worrying about sth and ignoring everything else 心事重重；忧心忡忡；全神贯注：*She spoke slowly, in a state of preoccupation.* 她说话慢吞吞的，显得心事重重。

pre·occu·pied /priˈɒkjupaɪd; *NAmE* -ˈɑːk-/ *adj.* ~ (**with sth**) thinking and/or worrying continuously about sth so that you do not pay attention to other things 专注；心事重重；一门心思：*He was too preoccupied with his own thoughts to notice anything wrong.* 他只顾着想心事，没注意到有什么不对。

pre·occupy /priˈɒkjupaɪ; *NAmE* -ˈɑːk-/ *verb* (**pre·occu·pies, pre·occu·py·ing, pre·occu·pied, pre·occu·pied**) ~ **sb** if sth is **preoccupying** you, you think or worry about it very often or all the time 使日夜思考；使忧心忡忡

pre·or·dained /ˌpriːɔːˈdeɪnd; *NAmE* -ɔːrˈd-/ *adj.* (*formal*) already decided or planned by God or by FATE 命中注定的；上天安排的 **SYN** **predestined**: *Is everything we do preordained?* 我们做的事都是天意吗？◇ ~ **to do sth** *They seemed preordained to meet.* 他们似乎命中注定要相逢。

ˌpre-ˈowned *adj.* (*NAmE*) not new; owned by sb else before 旧的；二手的；转手的 **SYN** **second-hand**

prep /prep/ *noun, verb*

■ ***noun*** [U] (*BrE*) (in some private schools) school work that is done at the end of the day after lessons （某些私立学校的）课外作业

■ ***verb*** (-**pp**-) **1** [T, I] (*especially NAmE, informal*) to prepare (sth) 把…准备好；预备：~ **sth** *Prep the vegetables in advance.* 提前把蔬菜准备好。◇ ~ (**for sth**) *They're prepping for college.* 他们正为上大学做准备。**2** [T] ~ **sb** (*specialist*) to prepare sb for a medical operation 为（患者）做手术前准备

ˌpre-ˈpacked (*also* **ˌpre-ˈpackaged**) *adj.* (of goods, especially food 商品，尤指食物) put into packages before being sent to shops/stores to be sold 包装好的；已包装的：*pre-packed sandwiches* 预先包装的三明治

pre·paid /ˌpriːˈpeɪd/ (*BrE also* **ˌpre-ˈpay**) *adj.* paid for in advance 预付款的；资费已付的：*a prepaid mobile phone* 预付话费的移动电话 ◇ *A prepaid envelope is enclosed* (= so you do not have to pay the cost of sending a letter). 内附邮资已付的信封一个。

prep·ar·ation 🔑 /ˌprepəˈreɪʃn/ *noun* **1** 🔑 [U] ~ (**for sth**) the act or process of getting ready for sth or making sth ready 准备；预备：*Preparation for the party started early.* 聚会的准备工作很早就开始了。◇ *food preparation* 食物制作 ◇ *Careful preparation for the exam is essential.* 认真准备考试十分必要。◇ *The third book in the series is currently **in preparation**.* 丛书的第三册现在正准备出版。◇ *The team has been training hard **in preparation for** the big game.* 为备战这场重要比赛，队伍一直在严格训练。**2** 🔑 [C, usually pl.] things that you do to get ready for sth or make sth ready 准备工作：~ (**for sth**) *The country is **making preparations** for war.* 这个国家正在备战。◇ *Was going to college a good preparation for your career?* 上大学是否为你的事业打下了良好基础？◇ ~ (**to do sth**) *We made preparations to move to new offices.* 我们为搬新办公室做好了准备。◇ *wedding preparations* 婚礼的筹备工作 **3** [C] a substance that has been specially prepared for use as a medicine, COSMETIC, etc. （医药、化妆品等）配制品，制剂：*a pharmaceutical preparation* 药剂 ◇ *preparations for the hair and skin* 护发护肤制剂

pre·para·tory /prɪˈpærətri; *NAmE* -tɔːri/ *adj.* (*formal*) done in order to prepare for sth 预备的；筹备的：*preparatory meetings* 预备会议 ◇ *Security checks had been carried out **preparatory to*** (= to prepare for) *the President's visit.* 为迎接总统来访，当局已预先进行了安全检查。

preˈparatory school (*also* **ˈprep school**) *noun* **1** (in Britain) a private school for children between the ages of 7 and 13 预备学校（英国为准备升入公学者而设的私立小学）➲ COMPARE PUBLIC SCHOOL (1) **2** (in the US) a school, usually a private one, that prepares students for college 预备学校（美国为准备升入高等院校者而设的私立中学）

pre·pare 🔑 /prɪˈpeə(r); *NAmE* -ˈper/ *verb* **1** 🔑 [T] to make sth or sb ready to be used or to do sth 使做好准备；把…预备好：~ **sth/sb** *to prepare a report* 撰写报告 ◇ ~ **sth/sb for sb/sth** *A hotel room is being prepared for them.* 正在为他们准备一间旅馆客房。◇ *The college prepares students for a career in business.* 这个学院是培养商务人才的。**2** 🔑 [I, T] to make yourself ready to do sth or for sth that you expect to happen 使（自己）有准备；防范：*I had no time to prepare.* 我当时没时间准备。◇ ~ **for sth** *The whole class is working hard preparing for the exams.* 全班都在努力用功准备考试。◇ ~ **yourself** (**for sth**) *The police are preparing themselves for trouble at the demonstration.* 警察正在准备防范示威时可能出现的骚乱。◇ ~ **to do sth** *I was preparing to leave.* 我正准备离开。◇ ~ **yourself to do sth** *The troops prepared themselves to go into battle.* 部队准备开赴战场。➲ MORE LIKE THIS 26, page R28 **3** 🔑 [T] ~ **sth** to make food ready to be eaten 预备（饭菜）；做（饭）：*He was in the kitchen preparing lunch.* 他在厨房做午饭。**4** [T] ~ **sth** (**from sth**) to make a medicine or chemical substance, for example by mixing other substances together 调制，配制（药品等）：*remedies prepared from herbal extracts* 用草药提取成分配制的药物

IDM **prepare the ˈground** (**for sth**) to make it possible or easier for sth to be achieved （为…）准备条件，铺路：*The committee will prepare the ground for next month's meeting.* 这个委员会将为下个月的会议做好准备。

pre·pared 🔑 /prɪˈpeəd; *NAmE* -ˈperd/ *adj.* **1** 🔑 [not before noun] ~ (**for sth**) ready and able to deal with sth 准备好；有所准备：*I was not prepared for all the problems it caused.* 我对这事引起的诸多麻烦毫无防备。◇ *We'll be better prepared next time.* 下次我们会准备得更充分。◇ *When they set out they were well prepared.* 他们出发时有很充分的准备。**OPP** **unprepared** ➲ SEE ALSO ILL-PREPARED **2** 🔑 ~ **to do sth** willing to do sth 愿意：*We are not prepared to accept these conditions.* 我们无意接受这些条件。◇ *How much are you prepared to pay?* 你愿意出多少钱？**OPP** **unwilling** **3** 🔑 done, made, written, etc. in advance 事先做好（或写好等）的：*The police officer read out a prepared statement.* 那个警察宣读了一份事先写好的声明。

pre·pared·ness /prɪˈpeərɪdnəs; *NAmE* -ˈperd-/ *noun* [U] ~ (**to do sth**) (*formal*) the state of being ready or willing to do sth 准备好的状态；愿意：*I was surprised by his preparedness to break the law.* 我对他打算以身试法感到惊讶。◇ *The troops are in a state of preparedness.* 军队已进入备战状态。

ˌpre-ˈpay *adj.* (*BrE*) = PREPAID: *pre-pay phones* 预付费电话

pre·pay·ment /ˌpriːˈpeɪmənt/ *noun* [U] payment in advance 预先支付；预付款：*a prepayment plan* 预付款计划

pre·pon·der·ance /prɪˈpɒndərəns; *NAmE* -ˈpɑːn-/ *noun* [sing.] if there is a **preponderance** of one type of people or things in a group, there are more of them than others 优势；多数；主体 **SYN** **predominance**

pre·pon·der·ant /prɪˈpɒndərənt; *NAmE* -ˈpɑːn-/ *adj.* [usually before noun] (*formal*) larger in number or more important than other people or things in a group 主要的；占多数的；主导的；占优势的 ▶ **pre·pon·der·ant·ly** *adv.*

pre·pone /priːˈpəʊn; *NAmE* -ˈpoʊn/ *verb* ~ **sth** (*IndE, informal*) to move sth to an earlier time than was originally planned 将…提前

P

prep·os·ition /ˌprepəˈzɪʃn/ *noun* (*grammar* 语法) a word or group of words, such as *in, from, to, out of* and *on behalf of*, used before a noun or pronoun to show place, position, time or method 介词 ▸ **prep·os·ition·al** /-ʃənl/ *adj.*: *a prepositional phrase* (= a preposition and the noun following it, for example *at night* or *after breakfast*) 介词短语

pre·pos·sess·ing /ˌpriːpəˈzesɪŋ/ *adj.* (especially after a negative 尤用于否定词后) (*formal*) attractive in appearance 外表吸引人的；妩媚的；漂亮的 SYN **appealing**: *He was not a prepossessing sight.* 他长相不怎么样。➲ COMPARE UNPREPOSSESSING

pre·pos·ter·ous /prɪˈpɒstərəs; *NAmE* -ˈpɑːs-/ *adj.* (*formal*) **1** completely unreasonable, especially in a way that is shocking or annoying 荒唐的；极不合情理的 SYN **outrageous**: *These claims are absolutely preposterous!* 这些要求简直荒谬绝伦！ **2** unusual in a silly or shocking way 怪诞的；离奇古怪的 SYN **outrageous**: *The band were famous for their preposterous clothes and haircuts.* 这支乐队以怪异的服装和发式而闻名。 ▸ **pre·pos·ter·ous·ly** *adv.*: *a preposterously expensive bottle of wine* 一瓶天价的葡萄酒

prep·py (*also* **prep·pie**) /ˈprepi/ *noun* (*pl.* **-ies**) (*NAmE, informal*) a young person who goes or went to an expensive private school and who dresses and acts in a way that is thought to be typical of such a school 预备学校学生，预备学校毕业生（指有私立学校学生派头的人） ▸ **prep·py** (*also* **prep·pie**) *adj.*: *a preppy image* 私立学校学生形象 ◇ *preppy clothes* 私立学校学生的衣着

pre·pran·dial /ˌpriːˈprændiəl/ *adj.* [only before noun] (*formal* or *humorous*) happening immediately before a meal 餐前的；饭前的：*a preprandial drink* 餐前饮料

ˌpre-proˈduc·tion *adj.* [usually before noun] done before the process of producing sth, especially a film/movie, begins 生产前的；（尤指电影拍摄）准备期的：*the pre-production script* 开拍前的剧本 ▸ **ˌpre-proˈduc·tion** *noun* [U]

ˈprep school *noun* = PREPARATORY SCHOOL

ˌpre-ˈqualify·ing *adj.* [only before noun] relating to a competition or game in which teams or players take part to decide if they are good enough to be in another competition 预选赛的；资格赛的：*players who fail at the pre-qualifying stage* 在预选赛中淘汰掉的选手 ▸ **ˌpre-ˈqualifier** *noun*

pre·quel /ˈpriːkwəl/ *noun* a book or a film/movie about events that happened before those in a popular book or film/movie 先篇，前篇，前传（叙述某流行图书或电影中的故事之前的事情）: *Fans waited for years for the first Star Wars prequel.* 《星球大战》的第一部前传让影迷期待了多年。➲ COMPARE SEQUEL (1)

Pre-Raphael·ite /ˌpriː ˈræfəlaɪt/ *noun, adj.*

■ *noun* a member of a group of British 19th century artists who painted in a style similar to Italian artists of the 14th and 15th centuries, before the time of Raphael 拉斐尔前派画家（英国 19 世纪的画家，风格近似拉斐尔之前的 14、15 世纪意大利画家）

■ *adj.* **1** connected with or in the style of the Pre-Raphaelites 拉斐尔前派绘画风格的：*Pre-Raphaelite paintings* 拉斐尔前派风格的绘画 **2** (especially of a woman 尤指女人) looking like a person in a painting by one of the Pre-Raphaelites, for example with pale skin and long thick dark red hair 似拉斐尔前派绘画中人物的（如皮肤白皙，有浓密的深红色长发）

ˌpre-reˈcord *verb* ~ **sth** to record music, a television programme, etc. in advance, so that it can be broadcast or used later 预先录制（音乐、电视节目等）

pre·regis·ter /ˌpriːˈredʒɪstə(r)/ *verb* [I] ~ (**for sth**) (*especially NAmE*) to register for sth before the usual time or before sth starts 预先注册；提前登记 ▸ **pre·regis·tra·tion** /ˌpriːredʒɪˈstreɪʃn/ *noun* [U]

pre·requis·ite /ˌpriːˈrekwəzɪt/ *noun* [usually sing.] ~ (**for/of/to sth**) (*formal*) something that must exist or happen before sth else can happen or be done 先决条件；前提；必备条件 SYN **precondition**: *A degree is an essential prerequisite for employment at this level.* 学位是做这级工作必备的先决条件。➲ COMPARE REQUISITE *n.* ▸ **pre·requis·ite** *adj.* [only before noun]: *prerequisite knowledge* 必备的知识

pre·roga·tive /prɪˈrɒɡətɪv; *NAmE* -ˈrɑːɡ-/ *noun* (*formal*) a right or advantage belonging to a particular person or group because of their importance or social position 特权；优先权：*In many countries education is still the prerogative of the rich.* 在许多国家接受教育仍然是富人的特权。◇ *the royal prerogative* (= the special rights of a king or queen) 君主特权

pres·age /ˈpresɪdʒ; prɪˈseɪdʒ/ *verb* ~ **sth** (*literary*) to be a warning or sign that sth will happen, usually sth unpleasant 预兆，警示，预言（尤指不祥之事） ▸ **pre·sage** /ˈpresɪdʒ/ *noun*: *the first presages of winter* 第一丝冬意

Pres·by·ter·ian /ˌprezbɪˈtɪəriən; *NAmE* -ˈtɪr-/ *noun* a member of a branch of the Christian Protestant Church that is the national Church of Scotland and one of the largest Churches in the US. It is governed by ELDERS who are all equal in rank. 长老会成员（长老会为苏格兰国教及美国最大教会之一） ▸ **Pres·by·ter·ian** *adj.* **Pres·by·ter·ian·ism** /ˌprezbɪˈtɪəriənɪzəm; *NAmE* -ˈtɪr-/ *noun* [U]

pres·by·tery /ˈprezbɪtri; *NAmE* -teri/ *noun* (*pl.* **-ies**) **1** a local council of the Presbyterian Church 教务评议会 **2** a house where a Roman Catholic priest lives 本堂神父住宅 **3** part of a church, near the east end, beyond the CHOIR 司祭席

pre·school /ˈpriːskuːl/ *noun* a school for children between the ages of about two and five 幼儿园 SYN **nursery school**

pres·ci·ent /ˈpresiənt/ *adj.* (*formal*) knowing or appearing to know about things before they happen 预知的；先觉的 ▸ **pres·ci·ence** /-əns/ *noun* [U]

pre·scribe /prɪˈskraɪb/ *verb* **1** (of a doctor 医生) to tell sb to take a particular medicine or have a particular treatment; to write a PRESCRIPTION for a particular medicine, etc. 给…开（药）；让…采用（疗法）；开（处方）: ~ **sth** *Valium is usually prescribed to treat anxiety.* 安定剂通常用于治疗焦躁。◇ ~ (**sb**) **sth** (**for sth**) *He may be able to prescribe you something for that cough.* 他也许能给你开一些咳嗽药。➲ WORDFINDER NOTE AT DOCTOR **2** (of a person or an organization with authority 当局) to say what should be done or how sth should be done 规定；命令；指示 SYN **stipulate**: ~ **sth** *The prescribed form must be completed and returned to this office.* 必须把指定的表格填好并交回本办事处。◇ ~ **that…** *Police regulations prescribe that an officer's number must be clearly visible.* 警政制度规定，警察的编号必须清晰可见。◇ ~ **which, what, etc.…** *The syllabus prescribes precisely which books should be studied.* 教学大纲明确规定了哪些是必读的书。

pre·scrip·tion /prɪˈskrɪpʃn/ *noun* **1** [C] ~ (**for sth**) an official piece of paper on which a doctor writes the type of medicine you should have, and which enables you to get it from a chemist's shop/drugstore 处方；药方：*The doctor gave me a prescription for antibiotics.* 医生给我开了抗生素。◇ (*BrE*) *Antibiotics are only available* **on prescription**. 抗生素只能凭处方购买。◇ (*NAmE*) *Antibiotics are only available* **by prescription**. 抗生素只能凭处方购买。◇ *They are not available without a prescription.* 这些药没有处方不能出售。◇ ***prescription drugs/medication(s)*** 处方药 **2** [C] medicine that your doctor has ordered for you 医生开的药：*The pharmacist will make up your prescription.* 药剂师会给你依处方配药。◇ *a* ***prescription charge*** (= in Britain, the money you must pay for a medicine your doctor has ordered for you) 处方药费 **3** [U] the act of prescribing medicine 开处方；开药：*The prescription of drugs is a doctor's responsibility.* 开药是医生的责任。**4** [C] ~ (**for sth**) (*formal*) a plan or a suggestion for making sth happen or for improving it 计划；建议；秘诀：*a prescription for happiness* 增进幸福的秘诀

pre·scrip·tive /prɪˈskrɪptɪv/ *adj.* **1** (*formal*) telling people what should be done 指定的；规定的：*prescriptive methods of teaching* 灌输式教学法 **2** (*linguistics* 语言) telling people how a language should be used, rather than describing how it is used 规定的；规范的 OPP **descriptive 3** (*specialist*) (of rights and institutions 权利和制度) made legal or acceptable because they have existed for a long time 约定俗成的；相沿成习的：*prescriptive powers* 相沿成习的权力

pre·select /ˌpriːsɪˈlekt/ *verb* **~ sth** to choose sth in advance so it is ready to be used 预先选择；预先挑选：*You can preselect programmes you want to watch, and program your VCR to record them.* 你可以预选想看的节目并设定录像机录下来。

pre·sell /ˌpriːˈsel/ *verb* (**pre·sold**, **pre·sold** /ˌpriːˈsəʊld; *NAmE* -ˈsoʊld/) **1 ~ sth** to help sell a product, service, etc., especially one that is not yet available, by using advertising and other techniques to attract consumers' attention （通过广告等）提前促销（尤指未上市的产品、服务等）：*Putting a trial version on your website is a great way of preselling your product.* 将试用版放到网站上是一种很好的提前促销产品的方式。 **2 ~ sth** to sell sth in advance of when it is available 预售：*These farmers presell their crops.* 这些农民预售他们的作物。

pres·ence 🔑 /ˈprezns/ *noun* **1** 🔑 [U] (of a person 人) the fact of being in a particular place 在场；出席：*He hardly seemed to notice my presence.* 他似乎没有注意到我在场。◇ *Her presence during the crisis had a calming effect.* 危难时有她在，对大家的心情有稳定作用。◇ (*formal*) *Your presence is requested at the meeting.* 务请出席会议。OPP **absence 2** 🔑 [U] (of a thing or a substance 事物或物质) the fact of being in a particular place or thing 存在；出现：*The test can identify the presence of abnormalities in the unborn child.* 这项检查能鉴定胎儿是否有不正常现象。OPP **absence 3** [sing.] a group of people, especially soldiers, who have been sent to a place to deal with a particular situation （派遣的）一个队；（尤指执行任务的）部队：*The government is maintaining a heavy police presence in the area.* 政府在这地区派驻了大批警察。◇ *a military presence* 驻军 **4** [C, usually sing.] (*literary*) a person or spirit that you cannot see but that you feel is near 感觉在附近的人（或鬼魂）：*She felt a presence behind her.* 她觉得有什么东西跟在背后。 **5** [U] (*approving*) the quality of making a strong impression on other people by the way you talk or behave 仪态；风度；气质：*a man of great presence* 风度翩翩的男子

IDM **in the ˈpresence of sb | in sb's ˈpresence** with sb in the same place 在…面前；有…在场：*The document was signed in the presence of two witnesses.* 本文件是有两位证人见证签署的。◇ *She asked them not to discuss the matter in her presence.* 她要求他们不要当着她的面讨论这个问题。 **in the ˈpresence of sth** when sth exists in a particular place 存在…的情况下；有…的存在：*Litmus paper turns red in the presence of an acid.* 石蕊试纸遇到酸就变红。 **make your presence ˈfelt** to do sth to make people very aware of the fact that you are there; to have a strong influence on a group of people or a situation 突显自己；对（人群或局势）发挥作用

ˌpresence of ˈmind *noun* [U] the ability to react quickly and stay calm in a difficult or dangerous situation 镇定；处变不惊；遇事不慌：*The boy **had the presence of mind to** turn off the gas.* 那男孩子镇定地关掉了煤气。

pres·ent 🔑 *adj., noun, verb*

■ **adj.** /ˈpreznt/ **1** 🔑 [only before noun] existing or happening now 现存的；当前的：*in the present situation* 在当前形势下 ◇ *the present owner of the house* 现在的房主 ◇ *a list of all club members, **past and present*** 过去和现在的全部会员名单 ◇ *We do not have any more information **at the present time**.* 目前我们没有进一步的消息。◇ *A few brief comments are sufficient **for present purposes**.* 就当前而言，几句简短的话已经足够了。➲ NOTE AT ACTUAL ➲ SEE ALSO PRESENT DAY **2** 🔑 [not before noun] **~ (at sth)** (of a person 人) being in a particular place 出现；在场；出席：*There were 200 people present at the meeting.* 有 200 人出席会议。OPP **absent 3** 🔑 [not before noun] **~ (in sth)** (of a thing or a substance 事物或物质) existing in a particular place or thing 存在：*Levels of pollution present in the atmosphere are increasing.* 大气中的污染程度正在加深。◇ *Analysis showed that traces of arsenic were present in the body.* 分析显示，尸体中有微量砷。OPP **absent**

IDM **all ˌpresent and corˈrect** (*BrE*) (*NAmE* **all present and acˈcounted for**) used to say that all the things or people who should be there are now there 全到无误；应在场的都在场了 **present company exˈcepted** (*informal*) used after being rude or critical about sb to say that the people you are talking to are not included in the criticism 在座诸位除外；与这里的各位无关

■ ***noun*** /ˈpreznt/ **1** 🔑 a thing that you give to sb as a gift 礼物；礼品：***birthday/Christmas/wedding, etc. presents*** 生日、圣诞节、结婚等礼物 ◇ *What can I get him for a birthday present?* 我给他送点什么生日礼物呢？ **2** 🔑 (*usually* **the present**) [sing.] the time now 目前；现在：*You've got to forget the past and start living in the present.* 你必须忘掉过去，开始现在的生活。◇ *I'm sorry he's out **at present*** (= now). 很抱歉他这会儿不在。 **3 the present** [sing.] (*grammar* 语法) = PRESENT TENSE IDM SEE MOMENT, TIME *n.*

■ ***verb*** /prɪˈzent/

• **GIVE** 给 **1** 🔑 to give sth to sb, especially formally at a ceremony 把…交给；颁发；授予：**~ sth** *The local MP will start the race and present the prizes.* 当地议员将鸣枪开赛，并颁发奖品。◇ **~ sb with sth** *On his retirement, colleagues presented him with a set of golf clubs.* 在他退休之际，同事们赠给他一套高尔夫球杆。◇ **~ sth to sb** *The sword was presented by the family to the museum.* 这家人把宝剑捐赠给了博物馆。

• **STH TO BE CONSIDERED** 考虑的事 **2** 🔑 to show or offer sth for other people to look at or consider 提出；提交：**~ sth (to sb)** *The committee will present its final report to Parliament in June.* 委员会将于六月向议会提交最后的报告。◇ **~ sth (for sth)** *Eight options were presented for consideration.* 已提出八项备选方案供审议。◇ *Are you presenting a paper at the conference?* 你要在大会上宣读论文吗？

• **STH IN PARTICULAR WAY** 方式 **3** 🔑 to show or describe sth/sb in a particular way （以某种方式）展现，显示，表现：**~ sth** *The company has decided it must present a more modern image.* 公司已决定，必须展现出更加现代的形象。◇ *It is essential that we present a united front* (= show that we all agree). 至关重要的是我们要表现得团结一致。◇ **~ yourself + adv./prep.** *You need to present yourself better.* 你需要更善于展示自己。◇ **~ sth/sb/yourself as sth** *He likes to present himself as a radical politician.* 他喜欢表现出一副激进政治家的样子。◇ *The article presents these proposals as misguided.* 文章认为这些提案失当。

• **SB WITH PROBLEM** 麻烦 **4** to cause sth to happen or be experienced 使发生；使经历：**~ sb with sth** *Your request shouldn't present us with any problems.* 你的请求应该不会给我们造成任何问题。◇ **~ sth** *Use of these chemicals may present a fire risk.* 使用这些化学品有可能导致失火。

• **ITSELF** 本身 **5** (of an opportunity, a solution, etc. 机会、答案等) to suddenly happen or become available 突然出现；显露；产生 SYN **arise**：**~ itself** *One major problem did present itself, though.* 不过，确实出现了一个重大问题。◇ *As soon as the opportunity presented itself, she would get another job.* 一有机会，她就会另谋新职 。◇ **~ itself to sb** *Thankfully, a solution presented itself to him surprisingly soon.* 谢天谢地，他意外地很快就找到了答案。

• **RADIO/TV PROGRAMME** 广播 / 电视节目 **6 ~ sth** (*BrE*) to appear in a radio or television programme and introduce the different items in it 主持播放；主持（节目）：*She used to present a gardening programme on TV.* 她曾在电视上主持一个园艺节目。

• **PLAY/BROADCAST** 戏剧；广播 **7 ~ sth** to produce a show, play, broadcast, etc. for the public 上演；公演；推出：*Compass Theatre Company presents a new production of 'King Lear'.* 罗经剧团推出了全新制作的《李尔王》。

P

• **INTRODUCE SB** 介绍 **8 ~ sb (to sb)** (*formal*) to introduce sb formally, especially to sb of higher rank or status 正式介绍；引见：*May I present my fiancé to you?* 请允许我向您介绍我的未婚夫。

• **YOURSELF** 自己 **9 ~ yourself at, for, in, etc.** (*formal*) to officially appear somewhere 正式出席；莅临；出现：*You will be asked to present yourself for interview.* 将请你到场面试。◊ *She was ordered to present herself in court on 20 May.* 她被传唤于 5 月 20 日出庭。

• **EXPRESS STH** 表达 **10 ~ sth (to sb)** (*formal*) to offer or express sth in speech or writing（口头或书面）表达，表示：*Please allow me to present my apologies.* 请允许我致歉。

• **CHEQUE/BILL** 支票；账单 **11 ~ sth** to give sb a cheque or bill that they should pay 交付；提交：*A cheque presented by Mr Jackson was returned by the bank.* 银行退回了杰克逊先生提交的支票。◊ *The builders presented a bill for several hundred pounds.* 承建商送来了一份数百英镑的账单。

IDM **pre͵sent 'arms** (of soldiers 士兵) to hold a RIFLE vertical in front of the body as a mark of respect 持枪敬礼 ➲ MORE LIKE THIS 21, page R27

pre·sent·able /prɪˈzentəbl/ *adj.* **1** looking clean and attractive and suitable to be seen in public 像样的；体面的：*I must go and **make myself presentable** before the guests arrive.* 趁客人还没到，我得去打扮一下好见人。 **2** acceptable 可接受的；符合要求的：*You're going to have to do a lot more work on this essay before it's presentable.* 你的这篇文章还得多加润饰才能交得出手。

pre·sen·ta·tion 🔑 /ˌpreznˈteɪʃn; *NAmE* ˌpriːzen-/ *noun* **1** 🔑 [U] the act of showing sth or of giving sth to sb 提交；授予；颁发；出示：*The trial was adjourned following the presentation of new evidence to the court.* 新证据呈到庭上后，审讯就宣告暂停。◊ *The presentation of prizes began after the speeches.* 讲话结束后就开始颁奖了。◊ *The Mayor will **make the presentation*** (= hand over the gift) *herself.* 市长将亲自颁发礼品。◊ *Members will be admitted **on presentation of** a membership card.* 会员出示会员证便可入场。 **2** 🔑 [U] the way in which sth is offered, shown, explained, etc. to others 提出（或展示、解释等）的方式：*Improving the product's presentation* (= the way it is wrapped, advertised, etc.) *should increase sales.* 改进产品的包装形式会提高销售量。◊ *I admire the clear, logical presentation of her arguments.* 我很欣赏她的论证，言辞清晰且有条理。 **3** 🔑 [C] a meeting at which sth, especially a new product or idea, or piece of work, is shown to a group of people 展示会；介绍会；发布会：*The sales manager will **give a presentation** on the new products.* 营销经理将举行一次新产品推介会。 **4** [C] the series of computer SLIDES (= images) that accompany the talk when sb gives a presentation at a meeting 幻灯片演示：*I've put my presentation on a memory stick.* 我已经把我的幻灯片演示文件存在 U 盘里了。 **5** [C] a ceremony or formal occasion during which a gift or prize is given 颁奖仪式；赠送仪式 **6** [C] a performance of a play, etc. in a theatre（戏剧等的）上演，演出 **7** [C, U] (*medical* 医) the position in which a baby is lying in the mother's body just before birth 先露（胎儿的临产胎位）

pre·sen·ta·tion·al /ˌpreznˈteɪʃənl; *NAmE* ˌpriːzen-/ *adj.* [only before noun] connected with the act of showing, explaining or offering sth to other people, especially a new product, a policy or a performance 展示的；介绍的；提交的；表演的：*a course on developing presentational skills* 展示技巧训练课程

the ͵present 'day *noun* [sing.] the situation that exists in the world now, rather than in the past or the future 当代；现代；当今：*a study of European drama, from Ibsen **to the present day*** 从易卜生到现代欧洲戏剧的研究 ▸ **͵present-'day** *adj.* [only before noun]: *present-day fashions* 现代时装 ◊ *present-day America* 今日美国

pre·sent·ee·ism /ˌpreznˈtiːɪzəm/ *noun* [U] (*BrE*) the practice of spending more time at your work than you need to according to your contract 超时工作 ➲ COMPARE ABSENTEEISM

pre·sent·er /prɪˈzentə(r)/ *noun* **1** (*BrE*) a person who introduces the different sections of a radio or television programme（广播、电视）节目主持人：*a TV presenter* 电视节目主持人 ➲ SEE ALSO ANNOUNCER (1), HOST *n.* (3) **2** a person who makes a speech or talks to an audience about a particular subject 演讲人；发言人：*conference presenters* 会议发言人 **3** (*NAmE*) a person who gives sb a prize at a ceremony（仪式上的）颁奖人

pre·sen·ti·ment /prɪˈzentɪmənt/ *noun* (*formal*) a feeling that sth is going to happen, especially sth unpleasant 预感；（尤指）不祥之感 **SYN** **foreboding**：*a presentiment of disaster* 大难临头的预感

pres·ent·ly /ˈprezntli/ *adv.* **1** (*especially NAmE*) at the time you are speaking or writing; now 此刻；现在；眼下 **SYN** **currently**：*The crime is presently being investigated by the police.* 警方目前正在调查这起案件。◊ *These are the courses presently available.* 这些就是现有的课程。 **HELP** In this meaning **presently** usually comes before the verb, adjective or noun that it refers to. 作此义时 presently 通常放在所修饰的动词、形容词或名词之前。 **2** used to show that sth happened after a short time（表示很快就发生了）：*Presently, the door opened again and three men stepped out.* 不久，门又打开了，走出来三个人。 **HELP** In this meaning **presently** usually comes at the beginning of a sentence. 作此义时 presently 通常置于句首。 **3** used to show that sth will happen soon（表示即将发生）**SYN** **shortly**：*She'll be here presently.* 她马上就会到这儿。 **HELP** In this meaning **presently** usually comes at the end of a sentence. 作此义时 presently 通常置于句末。

▼ **BRITISH/AMERICAN** 英式 / 美式英语

presently

- In both *BrE* and *NAmE*, **presently** can mean 'soon' or 'after a short time'. 在英式英语和美式英语中，presently 均含不久、一会儿之意：*I'll be with you presently.* 我一会儿就来。 In *NAmE* the usual meaning of **presently** is 'at the present time' or 'now'. 在美式英语中，presently 通常表示目前、现在：*She is presently living in Milan.* 她现住在米兰。◊ *There is presently no cure for the disease.* 目前这种疾病无药可医。 This use is becoming more accepted in *BrE*, but **at present** or **currently** are usually used. 此用法在英式英语中正逐渐被接受，不过通常用的还是 at present 或 currently。

͵present 'participle *noun* (*grammar* 语法) the form of the verb that in English ends in *-ing* and is used with the verb *to be* to form progressive tenses such as *I was running* or sometimes as an adjective as in *running water* 现在分词 ➲ COMPARE PAST PARTICIPLE

the ͵present 'perfect *noun* [sing.] (*grammar* 语法) the form of a verb that expresses an action done in a time period up to the present, formed in English with the present tense of *have* and the past participle of the verb, as in *I have eaten* 现在完成时

͵present 'tense (*also* **the present**) *noun* [usually sing.] (*grammar* 语法) the form of a verb that expresses an action that is happening now or at the time of speaking 现在时

pre·ser·va·tion /ˌprezəˈveɪʃn; *NAmE* -zərˈv-/ *noun* [U] **1** the act of keeping sth in its original state or in good condition 保护；维护；保存：*building/environmental/food preservation* 建筑物的维护；环境保护；食物的保存 ◊ *a preservation group/society* 环保团体 **2** the act of making sure that sth is kept 保留；维持；保持：*The central issue in the strike was the preservation of jobs.* 罢工的核心问题是工作职位的保留。 **3** the degree to which sth has not been changed or damaged by age, weather, etc. 保存的状况；保养的程度：*The paintings were in an* excellent state of preservation. 这些绘画保存得非常好。➲ SEE ALSO SELF-PRESERVATION

pre·ser·va·tion·ist /ˌprezəˈveɪʃənɪst; NAmE -zərˈv-/ *noun* a person who works to keep old buildings or areas of the countryside in their original condition and to prevent them from being destroyed 文物保护者；环境保护者

preserˈvation order *noun* (in Britain) a document that makes it illegal to change or destroy a building, a tree or part of the countryside, because of its beauty or historical interest （英国）文物及环境保护令

pre·ser·va·tive /prɪˈzɜːvətɪv; NAmE -ˈzɜːrv-/ *noun* [C, U] a substance used to prevent food or wood from decaying 防腐剂；保护剂：*The juice contains no artificial preservatives.* 这种果汁不含人工防腐剂。◇ *(a) wood preservative* 木材防腐剂 ➲ COLLOCATIONS AT DIET ▶ **pre·ser·va·tive** *adj.* [only before noun]

pre·serve 🔑 /prɪˈzɜːv; NAmE -ˈzɜːrv/ *verb, noun*

■ *verb* **1** 🔑 **~ sth** to keep a particular quality, feature, etc.; to make sure that sth is kept 保护；维护；保留：*He was anxious to preserve his reputation.* 他急于维护自己的名声。◇ *Efforts to preserve the peace have failed.* 维护和平的努力失败了。 **2** 🔑 [often passive] to keep sth in its original state in good condition 维持…的原状；保存；保养：**~ sth/sb** *a perfectly preserved 14th century house* 保存完好的 14 世纪宅第 ◇ *(humorous) Is he really 60? He's remarkably* ***well preserved.*** 他真有 60 岁了吗？他真会保养啊。◇ **~ sth + adj.** *This vase has been preserved intact.* 这个花瓶保存得完好无损。 **3** 🔑 **~ sth** to prevent sth, especially food, from decaying by treating it in a particular way 贮存；保鲜：*olives preserved in brine* 盐水橄榄 ◇ *Wax polish preserves wood and leather.* 上光蜡可保护木材和皮革。 **4** 🔑 **~ sb/sth (from sth)** to keep sb/sth alive, or safe from harm or danger 使继续存活；保护；保全 SYN **save**：*The society was set up to preserve endangered species from extinction.* 成立这个协会是为了保护濒危物种不致灭绝。➲ COMPARE CONSERVE *v.*

■ *noun* **1** [sing.] **~ (of sb)** an activity, a job, an interest, etc. that is thought to be suitable for one particular person or group of people （某人或群体活动、工作等的）专门领域：*Football is no longer the preserve of men.* 足球再也不是男人的专利了。◇ *in the days when nursing was a female preserve* 在护理工作为女性所专有的时代 **2** [C, usually pl., U] a type of jam made by boiling fruit with a large amount of sugar 果酱 **3** [C, usually pl., U] *(especially BrE)* a type of PICKLE made by cooking vegetables with salt or VINEGAR 腌菜；泡菜 **4** [C] *(NAmE)* = RESERVE (2) **5** [C] an area of private land or water where animals and fish are kept for people to hunt 私人渔猎场（或保留地）

pre·server /prɪˈzɜːvə(r); NAmE -ˈzɜːrv-/ *noun* **1** [C] a person who makes sure that a particular situation does not change 保护人；维护者；保存者：*The police are the preservers of law and order.* 警察负责维持治安。 **2** [C, U] a substance used to prevent wood from decaying 木材防腐剂 ➲ SEE ALSO LIFE PRESERVER

pre·set /ˌpriːˈset/ *verb* (**pre·setting**, **pre·set**, **pre·set**) **1** to set the controls of a piece of electrical equipment so that it will start to work at a particular time 预调；预置；给…预定时间：**~ sth to do sth** *You can preset the radiators to come on when you need them to.* 你可以预先调好暖气，使它在你需要的时候启动。◇ **~ sth** *to preset TV channels/radio stations* (= to set the controls so that particular channels are selected when you press particular buttons) 预调电视频道 / 广播电台 **2** [usually passive] **~ sth** to decide sth in advance 预先决定；事先安排：*They kept to the preset route.* 他们沿着事先规划的路线前进。

pre·side /prɪˈzaɪd/ *verb* [I] *(formal)* to lead or be in charge of a meeting, ceremony, etc. 主持（会议、仪式等）；担任（会议）主席：*the presiding judge* 首席法官 ◇ **~ at/over sth** *They asked if I would preside at the committee meeting.* 他们问我是否会主持委员会会议。◇ *(figurative) The party presided over one of the worst economic declines in the country's history* (= it was in power when the decline happened). 该党执政时期，国家经历了历史上最严重的经济衰退。

presi·dency /ˈprezɪdənsi/ *noun* [usually sing.] (*pl.* **-ies**) the job of being president of a country or an organization; the period of time sb holds this job 总统（或主席）的职位；总统（或主席）任期：*the current holder of the EU presidency* 现任欧盟主席 ◇ *He was a White House official during the Bush presidency.* 他是布什任总统时的白宫官员。

presi·dent 🔑 /ˈprezɪdənt/ *noun* **1** 🔑 (*also* **President**) the leader of a REPUBLIC, especially the US 总统；国家主席：*Several presidents attended the funeral.* 好几位总统参加了葬礼。◇ *the President of the United States* 美国总统 ◇ *President Obama is due to visit the country next month.* 奥巴马总统定于下月访问该国。◇ *Do you have any comment, Mr President?* 总统先生，您有何评论？➲ WORDFINDER NOTE AT CONGRESS ➲ COLLOCATIONS AT POLITICS **2** 🔑 (*also* **President**) the person in charge of some organizations, clubs, colleges, etc. （机构、俱乐部、学院等的）会长，院长，主席：*to be made president of the students' union* 当选学生会主席 **3** 🔑 *(especially NAmE)* the person in charge of a bank or a commercial organization 银行行长；总经理；董事长；总裁：*the bank president* 银行行长 ◇ *the president of Columbia Pictures* 哥伦比亚影业公司董事长 ▶ **presi·den·tial** /ˌprezɪˈdenʃl/ *adj.*：*a presidential campaign/candidate/election* 总统竞选活动 / 候选人 / 选举 ◇ *a presidential system of government* 总统制政体

ˌpresident-eˈlect *noun* (*pl.* **presidents-elect**) a person who has been elected to be president but who has not yet begun the job 当选总统

ˈPresidents' Day *noun* (in the US) a legal holiday on the third Monday in February, in memory of the birthdays of George Washington and Abraham Lincoln 总统日（美国法定假日，二月的第三个星期一，纪念美国总统乔治·华盛顿和亚伯拉罕·林肯的诞辰）

pre·sid·ium (*also* **prae·sid·ium** *especially in BrE*) /prɪˈsɪdiəm/ *noun* a permanent committee that makes important decisions as part of a government or large political organization, especially in COMMUNIST countries （尤指共产主义国家的）常务委员会，主席团

press 🔑 /pres/ *noun, verb*

■ *noun*

• **NEWSPAPERS** 报章 **1** 🔑 (*often* **the Press**) [sing.+sing./pl. v.] newspapers and magazines 报章杂志；报刊；平面媒体：*the* ***local/national/foreign press*** 地方 / 全国 / 外国报刊 ◇ *the* ***popular/tabloid press*** (= smaller newspapers with a lot of pictures and stories about famous people) 通俗报刊；小报 ◇ *The story was reported* ***in the press*** *and on television.* 这件事已在报刊和电视上报道了。◇ *the* ***music/sporting press*** (= newspapers and magazines about music/sport) 音乐 / 体育报刊 ◇ *Unlike the American, the British press operates on a national scale.* 与美国不同，英国报刊都是行销全国的。◇ *the* ***freedom of the Press/press freedom*** (= the freedom to report any events and express opinions) 新闻自由 ◇ *The event is bound to attract wide* ***press coverage*** (= it will be written about in many newspapers). 这个事件一定会在各报刊广泛报道。➲ SEE ALSO GUTTER PRESS **2** 🔑 **the press, the Press** [sing.+sing./pl. v.] the journalists and photographers who work for newspapers and magazines 记者；新闻工作者；新闻界：*The Press was/were not allowed to attend the trial.* 庭审谢绝新闻采访。 **3** [sing., U] the type or amount of reports that newspapers write about sb/sth 报道；评论：*The airline has* ***had a bad press*** *recently* (= journalists have written unpleasant things about it). 这家航空公司最近受到新闻界的责难。

• **PUBLISHING/PRINTING** 出版；印刷 **4** [C, U] a machine for printing books, newspapers, etc.; the process of printing them 印刷机；印刷：*We were able to watch the books rolling off the presses.* 我们可以看到书本从印刷机上源源不断地印出。◇ *These prices are correct at the time of* ***going to press.*** 这些价格在付印时是准确无误的。◇ *a story that is* ***hot off the press*** (= has just appeared in the newspapers) 刚刚见报的新闻报道 ➲ SEE ALSO PRINTING PRESS, STOP PRESS **5** [C] a business that prints and publishes books

P

出版社；印刷所：*Oxford University Press* 牛津大学出版社
- **EQUIPMENT FOR PRESSING** 挤压设备 **6** [C] (especially in compounds 尤用于构成复合词) a piece of equipment that is used for creating pressure on things, to make them flat or to get liquid from them 压平机；压榨机；榨汁机：*a trouser press* 烫裤机 ◇ *a garlic press* 压蒜器 ➲ VISUAL VOCAB PAGE V27
- **ACT OF PUSHING** 推压 **7** [C, usually sing.] an act of pushing sth with your hand or with a tool that you are holding 挤压；推；按：*He gave the bell another press.* 他又按了一下铃。◇ *Those shirts need a press* (= with an iron). 这些衬衣需要熨一熨。
- **CROWD** 群集 **8** [sing.] a large number of people or things competing for space or movement 拥挤的人群（或大批事物）SYN **throng**：*the press of bodies all moving the same way* 拥向同一方向的人群
- **CUPBOARD** 橱柜 **9** [C] (*IrishE, ScotE*) a large cupboard, usually with shelves, for holding clothes, books, etc.（分层）大壁橱，衣柜，书柜，碗柜

■ *verb*
- **PUSH/SQUEEZE** 推；挤 **1** [T, I] to push sth closely and firmly against sth; to be pushed in this way（被）压，挤，推，施加压力：**~ sth/sb/yourself against sth** *She pressed her face against the window.* 她把脸贴在窗子上。◇ **~ sth to sth** *He pressed a handkerchief to his nose.* 他用手绢捂住鼻子。◇ **~ sth together** *She pressed her lips together.* 她紧抿着双唇。◇ **~ against sth** *His body was pressing against hers.* 他的身体紧贴着她。**2** [T, I] to push or squeeze part of a device, etc. in order to make it work 按，压（使启动）：**~ sth** *to press a button/switch/key* 按下按钮 / 开关 / 按键 ◇ **~ sth + adj.** *He pressed the lid firmly shut.* 他把盖子盖得紧紧的。◇ **(+ adv./prep.)** *Press here to open.* 请按此处打开。◇ *She pressed down hard on the gas pedal.* 她用力踩下油门踏板。➲ PICTURE AT SQUEEZE **3** [T] **~ sth into/onto sth** to put sth in a place by pushing it firmly 将…塞进；把…按入：*He pressed a coin into her hand and moved on.* 他把一枚硬币塞进她手里，然后继续向前走。**4** [T] **~ sth** to squeeze sb's hand or arm, especially as a sign of affection（深情地）紧握（某人的手或臂）**5** [I] **+ adv./prep.** (of people in a crowd 人群) to move in the direction mentioned by pushing（向…）拥挤，推搡着移动：*The photographers pressed around the royal visitors.* 摄影记者们在王室贵宾周围挤来挤去。◇ (*figurative*) *A host of unwelcome thoughts were pressing in on him.* 一大堆恼人的心事涌上他的心头。
- **TRY TO PERSUADE** 劝说 **6** [T] to make strong efforts to persuade or force sb to do sth 催促；敦促；逼迫 SYN **push, urge**：**~ sb** *If pressed, he will admit that he knew about the affair.* 如果逼问他，他就会承认对此事知情。◇ **~ sb for sth** *The bank is pressing us for repayment of the loan.* 银行正在催我们偿还贷款。◇ **~ sb to do sth** *They are pressing us to make a quick decision.* 他们正催促我们尽快做决定。◇ **~ sb into sth/into doing sth** *Don't let yourself be pressed into doing something you don't like.* 不要勉强自己做不喜欢的事情。
- **POINT/CLAIM/CASE** 观点；要求；事情 **7** [T] **~ sth** to express or repeat sth with force 坚持；反复强调：*I don't want to* ***press the point****, but you do owe me $200.* 我不想老提这一点，但你确实欠我 200 美元。◇ *She is still* ***pressing her claim*** *for compensation.* 她仍然坚持索赔。◇ *They were determined to* ***press their case*** *at the highest level.* 他们决心把事情闹到最高层。
- **MAKE FLAT/SMOOTH** 弄平 **8** [T] to make sth flat or smooth by using force or putting sth heavy on top 把…压平；压扁：**~ sth** *pressed flowers* (= pressed between the pages of a book) 夹在书页中间压扁的花 ◇ **~ sth + adj.** *Press the soil flat with the back of a spade.* 用铁锹背把土拍平。**9** [T] **~ sth** to make clothes smooth using a hot iron 熨平；烫平 SYN **iron**：*My suit needs pressing.* 我的西服该熨了。
- **FRUIT/VEGETABLES** 蔬果 **10** [T] **~ sth** to squeeze the juice out of fruit or vegetables by using force or weight 把…榨汁；压榨
- **METAL** 金属 **11** [T] to make sth from a material, using pressure 把…压成；压制：**~ sth** *to press a CD* 压制一张光盘 ◇ **~ sth from/out of sth** *The car bodies are pressed out of sheets of metal.* 汽车车身是用钣金压制成的。

IDM **,press (the) 'flesh** (*informal*) (of a famous person or politician 名人或政治人物) to say hello to people by shaking hands 和群众握手致意 **,press sth 'home** to get as much advantage as possible from a situation by attacking or arguing in a determined way 坚持不懈；争辩到底：*to press home an attack/an argument/a point* 把进攻 / 论证 / 论点坚持到底 ◇ *Simon saw she was hesitating and pressed home his advantage.* 西蒙见她犹豫不决，便趁机占尽优势。**,press sb/sth into 'service** to use sb/sth for a purpose that they were not trained or intended for because there is nobody or nothing else available 姑且使用；临时凑合：*Every type of boat was pressed into service to rescue passengers from the sinking ferry.* 为了营救正在下沉的渡轮上的旅客，各类船只都被临时征用了。➲ MORE AT BUTTON *n.*, CHARGE *n.*, PANIC BUTTON

PHR V **,press a'head/'on (with sth)** to continue doing sth in a determined way; to hurry forward 坚决继续进行；匆忙前进；加紧：*The company is pressing ahead with its plans for a new warehouse.* 这家公司正加紧推动设置新仓库的计划。◇ *'Shall we stay here for the night?' 'No, let's press on.'* "我们今晚在这里住下好吗？""不，咱们继续走。" **'press for sth** to keep asking for sth 不断要求 SYN **demand, push for**：*They continued to press for a change in the law.* 他们不断要求修改这项法律。**'press sth on sb** to try to make sb accept sth, especially food or drink, although they may not want it 勉强某人接受；强迫某人吃（或喝）：*She kept pressing cake on us.* 她非要我们吃蛋糕不可。

'press agency *noun* = NEWS AGENCY

'press agent (*also NAmE, informal* **flack**) *noun* a person whose job is to supply information and advertising material about a particular actor, musician, theatre, etc. to newspapers, radio or television（剧团等雇用的）广告宣传人员

'press box *noun* a special area or a room at a sports ground where sports journalists sit（体育场的）新闻工作室，记者席

'press conference (*especially BrE*) (*NAmE usually* **'news conference**) *noun* a meeting at which sb talks to a group of journalists in order to answer their questions or to make an official statement 记者招待会；新闻发布会：*to hold/give a press conference* 举行 / 召开记者招待会

'press corps *noun* (*pl.* **press corps**) a group of journalists who work in or go to a particular place to report on an event 记者团；特派记者组

'press cutting (*BrE*) (*also* **'press clipping** *NAmE, BrE*) *noun* = CUTTING (1)

pressed /prest/ *adj.* **1** [not before noun] **~ (for sth)** not having enough of sth, especially time or money（时间、资金等）紧缺，短绌：*I'm really pressed for cash at the moment.* 眼下我真的缺钱。➲ SEE ALSO HARD-PRESSED **2** made flat using force or a heavy object 压平的；压扁的：*pictures made with pressed flowers* 用压花制作的画 ◇ *neatly pressed trousers* 熨得平平整整的裤子

'press gallery *noun* an area in a parliament building or a court for journalists to sit in（议会或法庭的）记者席

'press gang *noun* a group of people who were employed in the past to force men to join the army or navy 抓丁团，拉夫队（旧时受雇抓人当兵）

'press-gang *verb* **~ sb (into sth/into doing sth)** (*informal*) to force sb to do sth that they do not want to do 迫使自己，勉强别人（做某事）

pres·sie *noun* = PREZZIE

press·ing /ˈpresɪŋ/ *adj., noun*

■ *adj.* [usually before noun] **1** needing to be dealt with immediately 紧急的；急迫的 SYN **urgent**：*I'm afraid I have some pressing business to attend to.* 很抱歉，我有些急事需要处理。**2** difficult to refuse or to ignore 难以推却的；不容忽视的：*a pressing invitation* 难以推却的邀请

■ *noun* an object, especially a record, made by using pressure or weight to shape a piece of metal, plastic, etc.; a number of such objects that are made at one time 模压制品，同批次的模压产品（尤指唱片）：*The initial pressing of the group's album has already sold out.* 这个乐队的首批专辑唱片已售罄。

press·man /'presmæn/ *noun* (*pl.* **-men** /-men/) (*BrE, informal*) a journalist 记者；报人；新闻工作者

'press office *noun* the office of a large organization, political party or government department that answers questions from journalists and provides them with information （组织、政党或政府的）新闻办公室

'press officer *noun* a person who is in charge of or works for a press office 新闻发言人；新闻发布官；新闻局长

'press release *noun* an official statement made to journalists by a large organization, a political party or a government department （向媒体发布的）新闻稿

'press secretary *noun* a person who works for a politician or a political organization and gives information about them to journalists, the newspapers, etc. 新闻秘书

'press stud (*also* **pop·per**) (*both BrE*) (*NAmE* **snap**) *noun* a type of button used for fastening clothes, consisting of two metal or plastic sections that can be pressed together 摁扣；子母扣 ➲ **VISUAL VOCAB** PAGE V68

'press-up (*BrE*) (*also* **'push-up** *NAmE, BrE*) *noun* [usually pl.] an exercise in which you lie on your stomach and raise your body off the ground by pressing down on your hands until your arms are straight 俯卧撑 ➲ **VISUAL VOCAB** PAGE V46

pres·sure /'preʃə(r)/ *noun, verb*

■ ***noun***

• **WHEN STH PRESSES** 挤压时 **1** [U] the force or weight with which sth presses against sth else 压力；挤压：*The nurse applied pressure to his arm to stop the bleeding.* 护士压住他的胳膊止血。◇ *The barriers gave way under the pressure of the crowd.* 拥挤的人群把路障推倒了。

• **OF GAS/LIQUID** 气体；液体 **2** [U, C] the force produced by a particular amount of gas or liquid in a confined space or container; the amount of this 压力；压强：*air/water pressure* 空气/水的压力 ◇ *Check the tyre pressure* (= the amount of air in a tyre) *regularly.* 要定期检查轮胎的气压。➲ SEE ALSO BLOOD PRESSURE

• **OF ATMOSPHERE** 大气 **3** [U] the force of the atmosphere on the earth's surface 大气压：*A band of* ***high/low pressure*** *is moving across the country.* 一股高/低气压正经过这个国家。➲ SEE ALSO ATMOSPHERIC (1)

• **PERSUASION/FORCE** 劝说；强迫 **4** [U] the act of trying to persuade or to force sb to do sth 催促；要求；呼吁；强迫：~ (**for sth**) *The pressure for change continued to mount.* 改革的呼声持续高涨。◇ ~ (**on sb**) (**to do sth**) *There is a great deal of pressure on young people to conform.* 年轻人被大力要求顺应社会。◇ *The government eventually bowed to* ***popular pressure*** (= they agreed to do what people were trying to get them to do). 政府最终向群众的压力低头。◇ *Teenagers may find it difficult to resist* ***peer pressure.*** 青少年可能觉得很难抗拒同侪的压力。

• **STRESS** 紧张 **5** [U] (*also* **pressures** [pl.]) difficulties and feelings of anxiety that are caused by the need to achieve or to behave in a particular way 心理压力；紧张：*She was unable to attend because of the pressure of work.* 由于工作紧张，她不能出席。◇ *You need to be able to handle pressure in this job.* 你要能应付这一工作的压力。◇ *How can anyone enjoy the pressures of city life?* 怎么会有人喜欢都市生活的压力呢？

IDM **put 'pressure on sb** (**to do sth**) to force or to try to persuade sb to do sth 强迫；促使；劝说 **under 'pressure** **1** if a liquid or a gas is kept **under pressure**, it is forced into a container so that when the container is opened, the liquid or gas escapes quickly （液体或气体）受压力，压缩 **2** being forced to do sth 被迫：*The director is under increasing pressure to resign.* 主任面对被迫请辞的压力越来越大。**3** made to feel anxious about sth you have to do 承受着（急于完成某事的）压力：*The team performs well under pressure.* 这个队在压力下表现良好。

■ ***verb*** [often passive] (*especially NAmE*) (*BrE also* **pres·sur·ize**) ~ **sb** (**into sth/into doing sth**) | ~ **sb to do sth** to persuade sb to do sth, especially by making them feel that they have to or should do it 逼迫；使迫不得已：*Don't let yourself be pressured into making a hasty decision.* 不要勉强自己仓促作决定。

▼ **SYNONYMS** 同义词辨析

pressure

stress • tension • strain

These are all words for the feelings of anxiety caused by the problems in sb's life. 以上各词均指生活上的心理压力、精神紧张。

pressure difficulties and feelings of anxiety that are caused by the need to achieve sth or to behave in a particular way 指为达到某一目标或有某种行为表现而产生的心理压力、紧张：*She was unable to attend because of the pressures of work.* 由于工作紧张，她不能出席。

stress pressure or anxiety caused by the problems in sb's life 指因生活问题引起的精神压力、心理负担、紧张：*stress-related illnesses* 与精神压力有关的疾病

PRESSURE OR STRESS? 用 pressure 还是 stress?

It is common to say that sb *is suffering from stress*, while **pressure** may be the thing that causes **stress**. 承受精神压力常用 suffer from stress，而 pressure 可指造成压力(stress) 的事物。

tension a feeling of anxiety and stress that makes it impossible to relax 指情绪上的紧张、烦躁：*nervous tension* 神经紧张

strain pressure on sb/sth because they have too much to do or manage; the problems, worry or anxiety that this produces 指压力、重负、重压之下出现的问题、担忧：*I found it a strain looking after four children.* 我觉得照料四个孩子挺累的。

PATTERNS

- to be **under** pressure/stress/strain
- **considerable** pressure/stress/tension/strain
- to **cause** stress/tension/strain
- to **cope with** the pressure/stress/tension/strain
- to **relieve**/**release** the pressure/stress/tension/strain
- to be **suffering from** stress/tension

'pressure cooker *noun* **1** a strong metal pot with a tight lid, that cooks food quickly by steam under high pressure 高压锅；压力锅 **2** a situation that is difficult or dangerous because people are likely to become anxious or violent 一触即发的危险局势；剑拔弩张的形势

'pressure group *noun* a group of people who try to influence the government and ordinary people's opinions in order to achieve the action they want, for example a change in a law 压力集团（向政府和公众施加影响的团体）：*the environmental pressure group 'Greenpeace'* "绿色和平"这个环保压力集团 ➲ COMPARE ADVOCACY GROUP, LOBBY *n.* (3) ➲ SEE ALSO INTEREST GROUP

'pressure hose *noun* a long tube that is strong enough for liquid to pass through it at high pressure 高压软管；耐压胶管

'pressure point *noun* **1** a place on the surface of the body that is sensitive to pressure, for example where an artery can be pressed against a bone to stop the loss of blood 压迫止血点；压觉点 **2** a place or situation where there is likely to be trouble 危机地点（或局面）

'pressure suit *noun* a suit which can be filled with air, used to protect the person wearing it from low air

P

pressure, for example while flying a plane very high in the atmosphere 增压服，加压服（高空飞行等用）

'pressure washer *noun* a machine that cleans things by spraying them with water under high pressure 高压喷洗机；高压清洗机

pres·sur·ize (*BrE also* **-ise**) /ˈpreʃəraɪz/ *verb* **1** (*BrE*) (*also* **pres·sure** *NAmE, BrE*) [often passive] to persuade sb to do sth, especially by making them feel that they have to or should do it 逼迫；使迫不得已：**~ sb (into sth/into doing sth)** *She was pressurized into accepting the job.* 她被迫接受了这份工作。◇ **~ sb to do sth** *He felt that he was being pressurized to resign.* 他觉得被迫要辞职。**2** [usually passive] **~ sth** to keep the air pressure in a SUBMARINE, an aircraft, etc. the same as it is on earth 使（潜艇、飞机等内）保持正常气压 ▶ **pres·sur·iza·tion, -isa·tion** /ˌpreʃəraɪˈzeɪʃn; *NAmE* -rəˈz-/ *noun* [U]

pres·tige /preˈstiːʒ/ *noun, adj.*

■ ***noun*** [U] the respect and admiration that sb/sth has because of their social position, or what they have done 威信；声望；威望 **SYN** **status**：*personal prestige* 个人声望 ◇ *There is a lot of prestige attached to owning a car like this.* 拥有这样一部汽车会显得很气派。◇ *jobs with low prestige* 地位低微的工作

■ ***adj.*** [only before noun] **1** that brings respect and admiration; important 令人敬仰的；受尊重的；重要的：*a prestige job* 体面的工作 **2** admired and respected because it looks important and expensive 名贵的；贵重的；讲究派头的 **SYN** **luxury**：*a prestige car* 豪华的汽车

pres·ti·gious /preˈstɪdʒəs/ *adj.* [usually before noun] respected and admired as very important or of very high quality 有威望的；声誉高的：*a prestigious award* 赫赫有名的奖项 ◇ *a prestigious university* 名牌大学

presto /ˈprestəʊ; *NAmE* ˈprestoʊ/ *exclamation, adv., adj., noun*

■ ***exclamation*** (*NAmE*) (*BrE* **ˌhey ˈpresto**) **1** something that people say when they have just done sth so quickly and easily that it seems to have been done by magic 嘿，瞧（变魔术般迅速而轻松地做完某事时所说） **2** something that people say just before they finish a magic trick 变（变魔术完成之前所说）

■ ***adv., adj.*** (used as an instruction in a piece of music 用作乐曲指示语) very quickly 急板

■ ***noun*** (*pl.* **-os**) a piece of music that should be performed very quickly 急板乐曲（或乐章、乐段）

pre·sum·ably 🔑 **AW** /prɪˈzjuːməbli; *NAmE* -ˈzuː-/ *adv.* used to say that you think that sth is probably true 很可能；大概；想必是：*Presumably this is where the accident happened.* 这大概就是事故现场。◇ *You'll be taking the car, presumably?* 想必您是要买这辆汽车了？◇ *I couldn't concentrate, presumably because I was so tired.* 我的精神集中不起来，大概是太累了吧。

pre·sume **AW** /prɪˈzjuːm; *NAmE* -ˈzuːm/ *verb* **1** [I, T] to suppose that sth is true, although you do not have actual proof 假设；假定 **SYN** **assume**：*They are very expensive, I presume?* 我想这些东西很贵吧？◇ *'Is he still abroad?' 'I* ***presume so****.'* "他还在国外吗？" "我想是吧。" ◇ **~ (that)...** *I presumed (that) he understood the rules.* 我相信他明白这些规则。◇ **it is presumed that...** *Little is known of the youngest son; it is presumed that he died young.* 对于最小的儿子一般所知甚少，据推测他已经夭亡。◇ **~ sb/sth to be/have sth** *I presumed him to be her husband.* 我料想那就是她丈夫。**2** [T] to accept that sth is true until it is shown not to be true, especially in court（尤指法庭上）推定，假定：**~ sb/sth + adj.** *Twelve passengers are missing,* ***presumed dead****.* 有十二名旅客失踪，并已推定罹难。◇ *In English law, a person is* ***presumed innocent*** *until proved guilty.* 英国法律规定，一个人被证明有罪前假定为无罪。◇ **~ sth** *We must presume innocence until we have proof of guilt.* 在证实一个人有罪之前，我们必须假定其无罪。◇ **~ sb/sth to be/have sth** *We must presume them to be innocent until we have proof of guilt.* 在证实他们有罪之前，我们必须假定其无罪。**3** [T] **~ sth** (*formal*) to accept sth as true or existing and to act on that basis 设定；设想；假设：*The course seems to presume some previous knowledge of the subject.* 这门课程似乎是以具备某些基础知识为前提的。**4** [I] **~ to do sth** (*formal*) to behave in a way that shows a lack of respect by doing sth that you have no right to do 妄行；越权行事：*I wouldn't presume to tell you how to run your own business.* 我不会僭越去指点你该如何经营你自己的事业。

PHR V **preˈsume on/upon sb/sth** (*formal*) to make use of sb's friendship by asking them for more than you should 利用（友谊）作过分的要求：**presume on/upon sb/sth to do sth** *I felt it would be presuming on our personal relationship to keep asking her for help.* 我觉得总要她帮忙就是过分利用了我们的私人交情。

pre·sump·tion **AW** /prɪˈzʌmpʃn/ *noun* **1** [C] something that is thought to be true or probable 可能的事；认为真实的事：*There is a general presumption that the doctor knows best.* 一般人都以为医生最了解情况。**2** [U] (*formal*) behaviour that is too confident and shows a lack of respect for other people 非分的行为；妄自尊大 **3** [U, C] (*law* 律) the act of supposing that sth is true, although it has not yet been proved or is not certain 推定；假定；假设：*Everyone is entitled to the presumption of innocence until they are proved to be guilty.* 在被证明有罪之前，每个人都应被假定无罪。

pre·sump·tive /prɪˈzʌmptɪv/ *adj.* [usually before noun] (*formal* or *specialist*) likely to be true, based on the facts that are available 很可能的；假设的；推断的 ➲ SEE ALSO HEIR PRESUMPTIVE

pre·sump·tu·ous **AW** /prɪˈzʌmptʃuəs/ *adj.* [not usually before noun] too confident, in a way that shows a lack of respect for other people 自负；冒昧；放肆

pre·sup·pose /ˌpriːsəˈpəʊz; *NAmE* -ˈpoʊz/ *verb* (*formal*) **1** **~ sth** to accept sth as true or existing and act on that basis, before it has been proved to be true 姑且认为；假设 **SYN** **presume**：*Teachers sometimes presuppose a fairly high level of knowledge by the students.* 教师有时候假定学生的知识水平相当高。**2** **~ that... | ~ sth** to depend on sth in order to exist or be true 以…为前提；依…而定 **SYN** **assume**：*His argument presupposes that it does not matter who is in power.* 他的论点前提是，谁掌权都无关紧要。

pre·sup·pos·ition /ˌpriːsʌpəˈzɪʃn/ *noun* [C, U] (*formal*) something that you believe to be true and use as the beginning of an argument even though it has not been proved; the act of believing it is true 假设的事情；假定；预设 **SYN** **assumption**：*theories based on presupposition and coincidence* 基于假设和偶合的理论

ˌpre-ˈtax *adj.* [only before noun] before the tax has been taken away 未扣税的；税前的：***pre-tax profits/losses/income*** 税前利润 / 亏损 / 收入

ˌpre-ˈteach *verb* **~ sth** to teach sth, especially new words, to students before a test or exercise 考试（或练习）前教授（新词等）；先期教授

ˌpre-ˈteen *noun* a young person of about 11 or 12 years of age（约 11 或 12 岁的）大儿童，小少年；10 岁出头的儿童 ▶ **ˌpre-ˈteen** *adj.* [usually before noun]：*the pre-teen years* 十岁出头的几年

pre·tence (*BrE*) (*NAmE* **pre·tense**) /prɪˈtens; *NAmE* ˈpriːtens/ *noun* **1** [U, sing.] the act of behaving in a particular way, in order to make other people believe sth that is not true 假象；伪装；虚伪的表现：*Their friendliness was only pretence.* 他们的友善态度只不过是装出来的。◇ **~ of doing sth** *By the end of the evening she had abandoned all pretence of being interested.* 到晚会结束时，她已将假装的兴趣抛得一干二净。◇ **~ of sth** *He made no pretence of great musical knowledge.* 他未敢妄称音乐知识丰富。◇ **~ that...** *She was unable to* ***keep up the pretence*** *that she loved him.* 她无法继续假装爱他了。**2** [U, C, usually sing.] (*formal* or *literary*) a claim that you have a particular quality or skill 妄称；自称；标榜：**~ (to sth)** *a woman with some pretence to beauty* 自诩有几分姿色的女人 ◇ **~ (to**

P

doing sth) *I make no pretence to being an expert on the subject.* 我不敢自诩为这方面的专家。 IDM SEE FALSE

pre·tend /prɪˈtend/ *verb, adj.*

■ ***verb*** **1** [I, T] to behave in a particular way, in order to make other people believe sth that is not true 假装；佯装：*I'm tired of having to pretend all the time.* 我讨厌老得装假。◇ *Of course I was wrong; it would be hypocritical to* ***pretend otherwise.*** 当然是我错了，混充正确就是虚伪了。◇ **~ (to sb) (that…)** *He pretended to his family that everything was fine.* 他对家人佯称一切都好。◇ *We pretended (that) nothing had happened.* 我们假装什么事情也没发生。◇ **~ to do sth** *He pretended not to notice.* 他假装没注意。◇ *She didn't love him, though she* ***pretended to.*** 她并不爱他，虽然她装出爱的样子。◇ **~ sth** (*formal*) *She pretended an interest she did not feel.* 她毫无兴趣却装作有。 **2** [I, T] (especially of children 尤指儿童) to imagine that sth is true as part of a game （在游戏中）装扮，扮作，模拟：*They didn't have any real money so they had to pretend.* 他们没有真钱，就用假的代替。◇ **~ (that)…** *Let's pretend (that) we're astronauts.* 咱们假装是太空人吧。 **3** [I, T] (usually used in negative sentences and questions 通常用于否定句和疑问句) to claim to be, do or have sth, especially when this is not true 自诩；自称；自认为：**~ to sth** *I can't pretend to any great musical talent.* 我不能妄称自己多有音乐天赋。◇ **~ (that)…** *I don't pretend (that) I know much about the subject, but…* 我不敢说自己对这个主题有多了解，但是…◇ **~ to be/do/have sth** *The book doesn't pretend to be a great work of literature.* 这本书并未自封为文学杰作。 ➲ MORE LIKE THIS 26, page R28

■ ***adj.*** [usually before noun] (*informal*) (often used by children 常为儿童用语) not real, imaginary 假装的；想象的：*pretend cakes* 假糕点

pre·tend·er /prɪˈtendə(r)/ *noun* **~ (to sth)** a person who claims they have a right to a particular title even though other people disagree with them （头衔的）觊觎者，冒充者

pre·tense (*NAmE*) = PRETENCE

pre·ten·sion /prɪˈtenʃn/ *noun* [C, usually pl., U] **1** the act of trying to appear more important, intelligent, etc. than you are in order to impress other people 虚饰；虚夸：*intellectual pretensions* 装作有知识 ◇ *The play mocks the pretensions of the new middle class.* 这出戏讽刺了新中产阶级的装模作样。◇ *He spoke without pretension.* 他有话直说，不装相。 **2** a claim to be or to do sth 自命；声称；标榜：**~ (to sth/to doing sth)** *a building with no pretensions to architectural merit* 没有刻意表现建筑特色的楼房 ◇ **~ (to do sth)** *The movie makes no pretension to reproduce life.* 这部电影并未标榜重现了真实生活。

pre·ten·tious /prɪˈtenʃəs/ *adj.* (*disapproving*) trying to appear important, intelligent, etc. in order to impress other people; trying to be sth that you are not, in order to impress 炫耀的；虚夸的；自命不凡的：*That's a pretentious name for a dog!* 狗叫这个名字真够炫的！◇ *It was just an ordinary house—nothing pretentious.* 那只是一座普通的房子，没有故作特别。◇ *He's so pretentious!* 他太自命不凡了！ ➲ COMPARE UNPRETENTIOUS ▶ **pre·ten·tious·ly** *adv.* **pre·ten·tious·ness** *noun* [U]

the pret·er·ite (*NAmE also* **pret·erit**) /ˈpretərət/ *noun* [sing.] (*grammar* 语法) a form of a verb that expresses the past 过去时；过去式

pre·term /ˌpriːˈtɜːm; *NAmE* -ˈtɜːrm/ *adj.* born or happening after a short PREGNANCY, especially one that is less than 37 weeks早产的，不满妊娠期的（尤指怀孕少于 37 周的）：*caring for low birthweight and preterm babies* 对体重不足和早产婴儿的护理 ◇ *a preterm birth/delivery* 早产 ▶ **preterm** *adv.*：*Babies born preterm are at greater risk of needing hospitalization.* 早产儿更有需要入院治疗的危险。

pre·ter·nat·ural /ˌpriːtəˈnætʃrəl; *NAmE* -tərˈn-/ *adj.* [only before noun] (*formal*) that does not seem natural; that cannot be explained by natural laws 不寻常的；超自然的；难以解释的 ▶ **pre·ter·nat·ur·al·ly** /-rəli/ *adv.*：*The city was preternaturally quiet.* 这座城市显得异样的宁静。

pre·test /ˈpriːtest/ *noun* a test that you take to find out how much you already know or can do before learning or doing sth （学习或做某事前的）预先测试 ▶ **pre·test** *verb* **~ sb**

pre·text /ˈpriːtekst/ *noun* **~ (for sth/for doing sth)** | **~ (to do sth)** a false reason that you give for doing sth, usually sth bad, in order to hide the real reason; an excuse 借口；托辞：*The incident was used as a pretext for intervention in the area.* 这次事件成了干涉那个地区的借口。◇ *He left the party early* ***on the pretext of*** *having work to do.* 他借口有事要处理，早早离开了聚会。 ➲ SYNONYMS AT REASON

pret·tify /ˈprɪtifaɪ/ *verb* (**pret·ti·fies, pret·ti·fy·ing, pret·ti·fied, pret·ti·fied**) **~ sth** (*usually disapproving*) to try to make sth pretty, often with the result that it looks worse or false 粉饰，美化（常弄巧成拙）

pretty /ˈprɪti/ *adv., adj.*

■ ***adv.*** (with adjectives and adverbs 与形容词和副词连用) (*rather informal*) **1** to some extent; fairly 颇；相当：*I'm pretty sure I'll be going.* 我相当肯定会去的。◇ *The game was pretty good.* 这个游戏相当不错。◇ *It's pretty hard to explain.* 这事很难解释清楚。◇ *I'm going to have to find a new apartment pretty soon.* 我很快就得找个新住处了。 ➲ NOTE AT QUITE **2** very 十分；非常；极；很：*That performance was pretty impressive.* 那场表演很出色。◇ *Things are looking pretty good!* 形势看来很不错！

IDM **pretty ˈmuch/ˈwell** (*BrE also* **pretty ˈnearly**) (*NAmE also* **pretty ˈnear**) (*informal*) almost; almost completely 几乎；差不多：*One dog looks pretty much like another to me.* 在我看来，狗长得都差不多。 ➲ MORE AT SIT

■ ***adj.*** (**pret·tier, pret·ti·est**) **1** (especially of a woman, or a girl 尤指女子或女孩) attractive without being very beautiful 漂亮的；标致的；妩媚的；动人的：*a pretty face* 俏丽的脸 ◇ *a pretty little girl* 俊俏的小姑娘 ◇ *You look so pretty in that dress!* 你穿那件连衣裙真漂亮！ ➲ SYNONYMS AT BEAUTIFUL **2** (of places or things 地方或事物) attractive and pleasant to look at or to listen to without being large, beautiful or impressive 赏心悦目的；动听的；美观的；精致的：*pretty clothes* 漂亮的衣服 ◇ *a pretty garden* 赏心悦目的花园 ◇ *a pretty name* 优美的名字 ▶ **pret·tily** /ˈprɪtɪli/ *adv.* (*especially BrE*)：*She laughed prettily.* 她的笑声很迷人。◇ *The rooms are simply but prettily furnished.* 房间都布置得简朴而美观。 **pret·ti·ness** *noun* [U]：*the prettiness of youth* 青春的美好

IDM **as ˌpretty as a ˈpicture** (*old-fashioned*) very pretty 美丽如画；非常漂亮 ➲ MORE LIKE THIS 14, page R26 **not just a pretty ˈface** (*humorous*) used to emphasize that you have particular skills or qualities 并非徒有其表；不只脸蛋漂亮：*'I didn't know you could play the piano.' 'I'm not just a pretty face, you know!'* "我不知道你还会弹钢琴呢。" "我可不只是脸蛋儿漂亮，对吧！" **ˌnot a pretty ˈsight** (*humorous*) not pleasant to look at 不顺眼；有碍观瞻：*You should have seen him in his swimming trunks—not a pretty sight!* 你应该见识见识他穿游泳裤的样子，真是一景呢！ **a pretty ˈpenny** (*old-fashioned*) a lot of money 很多钱；一大笔钱 ➲ MORE AT PASS *n.*

pret·zel /ˈpretsl/ *noun* a crisp salty biscuit in the shape of a knot or stick, often served with drinks at a party 椒盐脆饼（常作小吃）

pre·vail /prɪˈveɪl/ *verb* (*formal*) **1** [I] **~ (in/among sth)** to exist or be very common at a particular time or in a particular place 普遍存在；盛行；流行：*We were horrified at the conditions prevailing in local prisons.* 地方监狱的普遍状况让我们震惊。◇ *Those beliefs still prevail among certain social groups.* 那些信念在某些社会群体中仍很盛行。 **2** [I] **~ (against/over sth)** (of ideas, opinions, etc. 思想、观点等) to be accepted, especially after a struggle or an argument 被接受；战胜；压倒 SYN **triumph**：*Justice will prevail over tyranny.* 正义必将战胜暴虐。◇ *Fortunately, common sense prevailed.* 幸而理智占了上风。 **3** [I] **~ (against/over sb)** to defeat an opponent, especially after a long struggle （尤指长时间斗争后）战胜，挫败

P

PHR V **pre'vail on/upon sb to do sth** to persuade sb to do sth 劝说：*I'm sure he could be prevailed upon to give a talk.* 我相信能说服他来做一次报告。

pre·vail·ing /prɪˈveɪlɪŋ/ *adj.* [only before noun] **1** existing or most common at a particular time 普遍的；盛行的；流行的 SYN **current, predominant**: *the prevailing economic conditions* 普遍的经济状况 ◇ *the attitude towards science prevailing at the time* 当时对科学的流行看法 ◇ *The prevailing view seems to be that they will find her guilty.* 普遍的看法似乎认为她会被判有罪。 **2 the prevailing wind** in an area is the one that blows over it most frequently （指风）某地区常刮的，盛行的 ➲ WORDFINDER NOTE AT WIND[1]

preva·lent /ˈprevələnt/ *adj.* ~ **(among sb)** | ~ **(in sb/sth)** (*formal*) that exists or is very common at a particular time or in a particular place 流行的；普遍存在的；盛行的 SYN **common, widespread**: *a prevalent view* 普遍的观点 ◇ *These prejudices are particularly prevalent among people living in the North.* 这些偏见在北方人中尤为常见。 ▶ **preva·lence** /-əns/ *noun* [U]

pre·vari·cate /prɪˈværɪkeɪt/ *verb* [I, T] (+ **speech**) (*formal*) to avoid giving a direct answer to a question in order to hide the truth 支吾搪塞；闪烁其词；吞吞吐吐 SYN **beat about the bush**: *Stop prevaricating and come to the point.* 别吞吞吐吐的，有话快说吧。 ▶ **pre·vari·ca·tion** /prɪˌværɪˈkeɪʃn/ *noun* [U, C]

pre·vent 🔑 /prɪˈvent/ *verb* to stop sb from doing sth; to stop sth from happening 阻止；阻碍；阻挠：~ **sth/sb** *The accident could have been prevented.* 这次事故本来是可以防止的。 ◇ ~ **sb/sth from doing sth** *He is prevented by law from holding a licence.* 法律不准他持有执照。 ◇ *Nothing would prevent him from speaking out against injustice.* 什么都不能阻止他鸣不平。 ◇ ~ **(sb/sth) doing sth** (*BrE*) *Nothing would prevent him/his speaking out against injustice.* 什么也阻挡不了他为不平之事鸣冤叫屈。 ▶ **pre·vent·able** /prɪˈventəbl/ *adj.*: *preventable diseases/accidents* 可以防止的疾病／事故

pre·ven·tion /prɪˈvenʃn/ *noun* [U] the act of stopping sth bad from happening 预防；防止；防范：***accident/crime prevention*** 防止事故／犯罪 ◇ *the prevention of disease* 疾病的预防 ◇ *a fire prevention officer* 消防官员

IDM **preˌvention is better than 'cure** (*BrE*) (*US* **an ounce of preˌvention is better than a pound of 'cure**) (*saying*) it is better to stop sth bad from happening rather than try to deal with the problems after it has happened 预防优于补救；防患于未然是上策

pre·vent·ive /prɪˈventɪv/ (*also* **pre·venta·tive** /prɪˈventətɪv/) *adj.* [only before noun] intended to try to stop sth that causes problems or difficulties from happening 预防性的；防备的：*preventive medicine* 预防医学 ◇ *The police were able to take preventive action and avoid a possible riot.* 警方得以及时采取防范措施，避免了可能发生的骚乱。 ➲ COMPARE CURATIVE

pre·ver·bal /ˌpriːˈvɜːbl; *NAmE* -ˈvɜːrbl/ *adj.* [usually before noun] (*specialist*) connected with the time before a child learns to speak （幼儿）前语言期的，习得语言能力前的：*preverbal communication* 前语言期交流

pre·view /ˈpriːvjuː/ *noun, verb*

■ *noun* **1** an occasion at which you can see a film/movie, a show, etc. before it is shown to the general public 预映；预演；预展：*a press preview* (= for journalists only) 招待新闻界的预展 ◇ *a special preview of our winter fashion collection* 我们冬季时装系列的特别预展 ➲ SEE ALSO SNEAK PREVIEW **2** a description in a newspaper or a magazine that tells you about a film/movie, a television programme, etc. before it is shown to the public （报刊上有关电影、电视节目等的）预先评述，预告：*Turn to page 12 for a preview of next week's programmes.* 下周节目预告请见第 12 页。 **3** (*NAmE*) = TRAILER (4)

■ *verb* **1** ~ **sth** to see a film/movie, a television programme, etc. before it is shown to the general public and write an account of it for a newspaper or magazine 为（影视节目）写预评：*The exhibition was previewed in last week's issue.* 本刊上周对展览作了预评。 **2** ~ **sth** (*especially NAmE*) to give sb a short account of sth that is going to happen, be studied, etc. 概述；扼要介绍：*The professor previewed the course for us.* 教授为我们扼要介绍了这门课程。

pre·vi·ous 🔑 AW /ˈpriːviəs/ *adj.* [only before noun] **1** 🔑 happening or existing before the event or object that you are talking about 先前的；以往的 SYN **prior**: *No previous experience is necessary for this job.* 这一工作无需相关的经验。 ◇ *The car has only had one previous owner.* 这辆汽车以前没换过车主。 ◇ *She is his daughter from a previous marriage.* 她是他与前妻生的女儿。 ◇ *I was unable to attend because of a previous engagement.* 我因有约在先，无法出席。 ◇ *The judge will take into consideration any previous convictions.* 任何前科法官都将予以考虑。 **2** 🔑 immediately before the time you are talking about （时间上）稍前的 SYN **precede**: *I couldn't believe it when I heard the news. I'd only seen him the previous day.* 听到这消息时，我不敢相信；我就在前一天还见到过他。 ▶ **pre·vi·ous·ly** 🔑 AW *adv.*: *The building had previously been used as a hotel.* 这座楼房早先曾用作旅馆。 ◇ *I had visited them three days previously.* 三天前我曾探访过他们。 **pre·vi·ous to** *prep.*: *Previous to this, she'd always been well.* 这以前，她身体一向很好。

ˌpre-'war *adj.* [usually before noun] happening or existing before a war, especially before the Second World War 战前的；（尤指）第二次世界大战以前的：*the pre-war years* 战前的年代 ◇ *pre-war Britain* 战前的英国

ˌpre-'wash *verb, noun*

■ *verb* **1** ~ **sth** to wash cloth before it is used, or clothing before it is sold 预洗（未使用或待售的布料或衣物） **2** ~ **sth** to give clothing an extra wash before the main wash, especially in a machine （尤指用洗衣机等在常规洗涤程序前）预洗

■ *noun* **'pre-wash** **1** [C] an extra wash before the main wash （主洗之前的）预洗 **2** [U] a substance which is applied to clothing before washing, in order to make it cleaner （洗涤之前使用的）衣物除渍精

prey /preɪ/ *noun, verb*

■ *noun* [U, sing.] **1** an animal, a bird, etc. that is hunted, killed and eaten by another 猎物：*The lion will often stalk its prey for hours.* 狮子经常悄然跟踪猎物达几个小时。 ◇ ***birds of prey*** (= birds that kill for food) 猛禽 ➲ WORDFINDER NOTE AT HUNT ➲ COLLOCATIONS AT LIFE **2** a person who is harmed or tricked by sb, especially for dishonest purposes 受害者；受骗者：*Elderly people are easy prey for dishonest salesmen.* 老年人容易上狡诈推销员的当。

IDM **be/fall 'prey to sth** (*formal*) **1** (of an animal 动物) to be killed and eaten by another animal or bird 被捕食；成为猎物 **2** (of a person 人) to be harmed or affected by sth bad 受害；受坏影响

■ *verb*

IDM **prey on sb's 'mind** (of a thought, problem, etc. 想法、问题等) to make sb think and worry about it all the time 萦绕心头；使耿耿于怀

PHR V **'prey on/upon sb/sth** **1** (of an animal or a bird 兽或鸟) to hunt and kill another animal for food 捕食；猎获 **2** to harm sb who is weaker than you, or make use of them in a dishonest way to get what you want 欺凌，坑骗，敲诈（弱者）：*Bogus social workers have been preying on old people living alone.* 冒牌社会福利工作者不断坑害独居老人。

prez /prez/ *noun* (*slang*) = PRESIDENT

prez·zie (*also* **pres·sie**) /ˈprezi/ *noun* (*BrE, informal*) a present that you give sb, for example for their birthday 礼物；礼品

pri·ap·ic /praɪˈæpɪk; *NAmE also* -ˈeɪp-/ *adj.* **1** (*formal*) connected with or like a PENIS （似）阴茎的 **2** (*formal*) connected with male sexual activity 男子性活动的 **3** (*medical* 医) having a PENIS which is always ERECT (= stiff) 阴茎异常勃起的

P

pri·ap·ism /'praɪəpɪzəm/ *noun* [U] (*medical* 医) a condition in which a man's PENIS remains ERECT (= stiff) 阴茎异常勃起

price /praɪs/ *noun, verb*

■ ***noun* 1** [C, U] the amount of money that you have to pay for sth 价格；价钱；物价：*Boat for sale, price £2 000* 小船，售价 2 000 英镑 ◇ *house/retail/oil/share prices* 房屋 / 零售 / 石油 / 股票价格 ◇ *to charge a **high/reasonable/low price** for sth* 索要很高 / 适中 / 很低的价格 ◇ *The price of cigarettes is set to rise again.* 香烟又要涨价。◇ *He managed to get a good price for the car.* 他终于把汽车卖了个好价钱。◇ ***rising/falling prices*** 攀升 / 下跌的价格 ◇ *Can you **give me a price** for the work* (= tell me how much you will charge)? 请问做这件工作要多少钱？◇ *I'm only buying it if it's the **right price*** (= a price that I think is reasonable). 只有价钱合理我才会买这东西。◇ *Children over five must pay (the) **full price** for the ticket.* 五岁以上的儿童须买全票。◇ *How much are these? They don't have a price on them.* 这些东西卖多少钱？它们都没有标价。◇ *It's amazing how much computers have come down **in** price over the past few years.* 过去这几年，电脑的价格大大降低，简直令人惊讶。◇ ***price rises/increases/cuts*** 价格上升 / 提高 / 降低 ◇ *a price list* 价目表 ➲ SEE ALSO ASKING PRICE, COST PRICE, CUT-PRICE, HALF-PRICE, MARKET PRICE, LIST PRICE, PURCHASE PRICE, SELLING PRICE **2** [sing.] the unpleasant things that you must do or experience in order to achieve sth or as a result of achieving sth 代价：**~ (of sth)** *Criticism is part of the price of leadership.* 挨批评是当领导要付出的部分代价。◇ **~ (for sth/for doing sth)** *Loneliness is **a high price to pay** for independence in your old age.* 孤寂是老年独自生活要付出的高昂代价。◇ *Giving up his job was **a small price to pay** for his children's happiness.* 放弃工作是他为子女幸福所付出的小小代价。**3** [C] (in horse racing 赛马) the numbers that tell you how much money you will receive if the horse that you bet on wins the race 投注赔率 SYN **odds**: *Six to one is a good price for that horse.* 那匹马有六比一的赔率很不错。➲ SEE ALSO STARTING PRICE

> **▼ SYNONYMS 同义词辨析**
>
> **price**
>
> **cost • value • expense • worth**
>
> These words all refer to the amount of money that you have to pay for sth. 以上各词均指价值、价钱。
>
> **price** the amount of money that you have to pay for an item or service 指商品或服务的价格、价钱：*house prices* 房屋价格 ◇ *How much are these? They don't have a price on them.* 这些东西卖多少钱？它们都没有标价。◇ *I can't afford it **at that price**.* 这样的价格我付不起。
>
> **cost** the amount of money that you need in order to buy, make or do sth 指购买、制造某物或做某事所需的成本、费用、花费：*A new computer system has been installed **at a cost of** £80 000.* 新的计算机系统已安装，费用为 8 万英镑。
>
> **value** how much sth is worth in money or other goods for which it can be exchanged 指价值：*The winner will receive a prize **to the value of** £1 000.* 获胜者将得到价值为 1 000 英镑的奖品。NOTE Especially in British English, **value** can also mean how much sth is worth compared with its price. 尤其在英式英语中，value 亦表示划算程度：*This restaurant is excellent value* (= is worth the money it costs). 这家餐馆很合算。
>
> **PRICE, COST OR VALUE?** 用 price、cost 还是 value？
>
> The **price** is what sb asks you to pay for an item or service. * price 指商品或服务的要价：*to ask/charge a high price* 要价高；收费高 ◇ ~~*to ask/charge a high cost/value*~~ Obtaining or achieving sth may have a **cost**; the **value** of sth is how much other people would be willing to pay for it. * cost 指获取某物或达到某目的所需的费用；value 指别人愿意为某物付出的价值：*house prices* 房屋价格 ◇ *the cost of moving house* 搬家费用 ◇ *The house now has a market value of one million pounds.* 这栋房子目前的市场价值为 100 万英镑。
>
> **expense** the money that you spend on sth; sth that makes you spend money 指所花费用、花钱的东西、开销：*The garden was transformed **at great expense**.* 花园改建花了一大笔费用。◇ *Running a car is a big expense.* 养一辆车开销很大。
>
> **worth** the financial value of sb/sth 指人或物的价值：*He has a personal net worth of $10 million.* 他有价值 1 000 万美元的个人净资产。NOTE **Worth** is more often used to mean the practical or moral value of sth. * worth 较常用以指某事物的实际作用或道德意义。
>
> **PATTERNS**
>
> - the **high** price/cost/value
> - the **real**/**true** price/cost/value/worth
> - to **put**/**set** a price/value **on** sth
> - to **increase**/**reduce** the price/cost/value/expense
> - to **raise**/**double**/**lower** the price/cost/value
> - to **cut** the price/cost

IDM **at 'any price** whatever the cost or the difficulties may be 不惜任何代价；无论如何：*We want peace at any price.* 为了争取和平，我们不惜任何代价。**at a 'price 1** costing a lot of money 以高价；花大钱：*You can buy strawberries all year round, but at a price.* 草莓一年到头都买得到，不过很贵。**2** involving sth unpleasant 付代价：*He'll help you—at a price!* 他会帮助你的，但要付出代价！**beyond 'price** (*formal* or *literary*) extremely valuable or important 无价的；极宝贵的；极重要的 **everyone has their 'price** (*saying*) you can persuade anyone to do sth by giving them more money or sth that they want 重赏之下，必有勇夫；人皆有价；有钱能使鬼推磨 **not at 'any price** used to say that no amount of money would persuade you to do or to sell sth 无论如何也不；给多少钱也不：*I wouldn't work for her again—not at any price!* 我再也不替她做事了，给多少钱也不做！**a 'price on sb's head** an amount of money that is offered for capturing or killing sb 缉拿（或杀害）某人的悬赏金 **put a 'price on sth** to say how much money sth valuable is worth （为贵重物）定价，作价：*They haven't yet put a price on the business.* 他们还没有给这笔生意开价。◇ *You can't put a price on that sort of loyalty.* 那样的忠心是无法用金钱衡量的。**'what price...?** (*BrE, informal*) **1** used to say that you think that sth you have achieved may not be worth all the problems and difficulties it causes （认为得不偿失）…不值得，…有什么用？：*What price fame and fortune?* 名利的代价何其大。**2** used to say that sth seems unlikely （认为可能性不大）…可能吗，…不可能吧：*What price England winning the World Cup?* 英格兰队夺得世界杯冠军，这可能吗？➲ MORE AT CHEAP *adj.*, PAY *v.*

■ ***verb* 1** [usually passive] to fix the price of sth at a particular level 给…定价；为…作价：**~ sth + adv./prep.** *a reasonably priced house* 定价合理的一座房子 ◇ *These goods are priced too high.* 这些货品定价过高。◇ **~ sth at sth** *The tickets are priced at $100 each.* 每张票定价 100 美元。**2 ~ sth (up)** to write or stick tickets on goods to show how much they cost （在商品上）标价，贴价格标签 **3 ~ sth** to compare the prices of different types of the same thing 比较…的价格：*We priced various models before buying this one.* 我们比较了多种型号的价格以后才买了这一款。

IDM **price yourself/sth out of the 'market** to charge such a high price for your goods, services, etc. that nobody wants to buy them 因索价过高而无人问津

'price controls *noun* [pl.] (*economics* 经) restrictions that a government puts on the price of goods at particular times, such as when there is not enough of sth, when there is a war, etc. （物品短缺或战时等的）物价控制，价格管制

'price-fixing *noun* [U] the practice of companies agreeing not to sell goods below a particular price 价格垄断（公司之间协议不低于某价位销售货品）

'price index *noun* = RETAIL PRICE INDEX

price·less /'praɪsləs/ *adj.* **1** extremely valuable or important 无价的；极珍贵的；极重要的：*a priceless collection of*

P

antiques 价值连城的古文物收藏 ◇ *priceless information* 极有价值的信息 ➲ SYNONYMS AT VALUABLE **2** (*informal*) extremely amusing 极有趣的：*You should have seen his face—it was priceless!* 你真该见识见识他那副尊容，可笑极了！

ˈprice tag *noun* a label on sth that shows how much you must pay 价格标签：(*figurative*) *There is a £2 million price tag on the team's star player.* 这个球队的明星球员身价为200万英镑。➲ PICTURE AT LABEL

ˈprice war *noun* a situation in which companies or shops/stores keep reducing the prices of their products and services in order to attract customers away from their COMPETITORS 价格战（以减价来吸引顾客）

pricey /ˈpraɪsi/ *adj.* (**prici·er**, **prici·est**) (*informal*) expensive 昂贵的 ➲ SYNONYMS AT EXPENSIVE

pri·cing /ˈpraɪsɪŋ/ *noun* [U] the act of deciding how much to charge for sth 定价；作价；计价：*competitive pricing* 有竞争力的定价 ◇ *pricing policy* 定价政策 ➲ SEE ALSO ROAD PRICING

prick /prɪk/ *verb, noun*

■ ***verb*** **1** [T] to make a very small hole in sth with a sharp point 扎；刺；戳：**~ sth** *He pricked the balloon and burst it.* 他把气球扎爆了。◇ **~ sth with sth** *Prick holes in the paper with a pin.* 用大头针在纸上扎洞。 **2** [T] **~ sth (on sth)** to make a small hole in the skin so that it hurts or blood comes out 扎破，刺破（皮肤）：*She pricked her finger on a needle.* 她的手指被针扎了。 **3** [I, T] to make sb feel a slight pain as if they were being pricked 使感到刺痛：*He felt a pricking sensation in his throat.* 他感觉喉咙有点刺痛。◇ **~ sth** *Tears pricked her eyes.* 泪水刺激了她的双眼。

IDM **prick your ˈconscience | your ˈconscience pricks you** to make you feel guilty about sth; to feel guilty about sth 唤醒良心；受到良心谴责：*Her conscience pricked her as she lied to her sister.* 她对姐姐撒谎时良心上感到很不安。 **prick (up) your ˈears 1** (of an animal, especially a horse or dog 动物，尤指马或狗) to raise the ears 竖起耳朵 **2** (*also* **your ˈears prick up**) (of a person 人) to listen carefully, especially because you have just heard sth interesting 倾耳细听：*Her ears pricked up at the sound of his name.* 一听到他的名字她的耳朵就立刻竖了起来。

■ ***noun*** **1** (*taboo, slang*) a PENIS 鸡巴；屌 **2** (*taboo, slang*) an offensive word for a stupid or unpleasant man 鸟人；笨蛋：*Don't be such a prick!* 别那么笨！ **3** an act of making a very small hole in sth with a sharp point 扎；穿刺：*I'm going to give your finger a little prick with this needle.* 我将用这根针在你手指上轻轻扎一下。 **4** a slight pain caused by a sharp point or sth that feels like a sharp point 针刺感；刺痛（感）：*You will feel a tiny prick in your arm.* 你会觉得胳膊上有一点点刺痛。◇ (*figurative*) *He could feel the hot prick of tears in his eyes.* 他眼里噙着泪水，火辣辣的。

prickle /ˈprɪkl/ *verb, noun*

■ ***verb*** **1** [T, I] **~ (sth)** to give sb an unpleasant feeling on their skin, as if a lot of small sharp points are pushing into it 刺痛；扎疼：*The rough cloth prickled my skin.* 粗布扎我的皮肤。◇ *His moustache prickled when he kissed me.* 他吻我的时候胡子扎人。 **2** [I] **~ (with sth)** (of skin, eyes, etc. 皮肤、眼睛等) to sting or feel strange and unpleasant because you are frightened, angry, excited, etc. 有刺痛感：*Her eyes prickled with tears.* 泪水刺疼了她的眼睛。◇ *The hairs on the back of my neck prickled when I heard the door open.* 听到开门声，我颈后汗毛倒竖。◇ (*figurative*) *He prickled* (= became angry) *at the suggestion that it had been his fault.* 一听说过错在他，他马上火儿了。

■ ***noun*** **1** a small sharp part on the STEM or leaf of a plant or on the skin of some animals （植物的）芒刺，刺；（动物的）皮刺，刺毛：*a cactus covered in prickles* 长满刺的仙人掌 **2** a slight stinging feeling on the skin 刺痒；轻微的刺痛感：*a prickle of fear/excitement* 恐惧/激动的刺痒感

prick·ly /ˈprɪkli/ *adj.* (**prick·lier**, **prick·li·est**) **1** covered with prickles 多刺的：*a prickly bush* 多刺的灌木 **2** causing you to feel as if your skin is touching sth that is covered with prickles 引起刺痛的；扎疼的；刺痒的：*a prickly feeling* 刺痛感 **3** (*informal*) (of a person 人) easily annoyed or offended 易怒的；爱生气的 SYN **touchy** **4** (of a decision, an issue, etc. 决定、问题等) difficult to deal with because people have very different ideas about it 棘手的；难处理的；烫手的 SYN **thorny**：*Let's move on to the prickly subject of taxation reform.* 咱们继续讨论下一项税制改革这个棘手的问题吧。

ˌprickly ˈheat *noun* [U] a skin condition, common in hot countries, that causes small red spots that ITCH 痱子

ˌprickly ˈpear *noun* **1** a type of CACTUS with PRICKLES (= sharp parts like needles), and yellow flowers 仙人果，刺梨（仙人掌属植物，花黄色） **2** the reddish fruit of the prickly pear that is shaped like a PEAR and can be eaten 仙人果（梨状，红色，可食用）

ˈprick-teaser (*also* **ˈprick-tease**) *noun* (*taboo, slang*) = COCK-TEASER

pride 🔑 /praɪd/ *noun, verb*

■ ***noun***

• **PLEASURE/SATISFACTION** 愉悦；满足 **1** 🔑 [U, sing.] a feeling of pleasure or satisfaction that you get when you or people who are connected with you have done sth well or own sth that other people admire 自豪；骄傲；得意感：*The sight of her son graduating filled her with pride.* 看到儿子毕业她充满了自豪。◇ **~ (in sth)** *I take (a) pride in my work.* 我为自己的工作感到骄傲。◇ **~ (in doing sth)** *We take great pride in offering the best service in town.* 我们以能够提供全城最好的服务而自豪。◇ *I looked* **with pride** *at what I had achieved.* 回顾过去的成就，我感到十分光荣。◇ *Success in sport is a source of national pride.* 体育成就是民族自豪的源泉。➲ SYNONYMS AT SATISFACTION **2** [sing.] **the ~ of sth** a person or thing that gives people a feeling of pleasure or satisfaction 值得自豪的人（或事物）：*The new sports stadium is the pride of the town.* 新体育场是这个城市的骄傲。

• **RESPECT FOR YOURSELF** 自尊 **3** 🔑 [U] the feeling of respect that you have for yourself 自尊心；自尊；尊严：*Pride would not allow him to accept the money.* 自尊心不容他接受这笔钱。◇ *Her pride was hurt.* 她的自尊心受到了伤害。◇ *Losing his job was a real* **blow to his pride**. 失掉工作对他的自尊是个沉重的打击。◇ *It's time to* **swallow your pride** (= hide your feelings of pride) *and ask for your job back.* 这时候你应该收起自尊，讨回那份工作。 **4** 🔑 [U] (*disapproving*) the feeling that you are better or more important than other people 自负；傲慢：*Male pride forced him to suffer in silence.* 男性的自尊迫使他隐忍不言。➲ SEE ALSO PROUD

• **LIONS** 狮子 **5** [C+sing./pl. v.] a group of LIONS 狮群

IDM **sb's pride and ˈjoy** a person or thing that causes sb to feel great pleasure or satisfaction 某人引以为荣的人（或事物） **pride comes/goes before a ˈfall** (*saying*) if you have too high an opinion of yourself or your abilities, sth will happen to make you look stupid 骄傲使人失败 **pride of ˈplace** the position in which sth is most easily seen, that is given to the most important thing in a particular group 显要位置；最突出（或最重要）的位置

■ ***verb***

PHR V **ˈpride yourself on sth/on doing sth** [no passive] to be proud of sth 引以为荣；为…而骄傲：*She had always prided herself on her appearance.* 她总是对自己的外貌感到得意。

priest 🔑 /priːst/ *noun* **1** 🔑 a person who is qualified to perform religious duties and ceremonies in the Roman Catholic, Anglican and Orthodox Churches （天主教、圣公会、东正教的）司祭，神父，司铎：*a parish priest* 堂区司铎 ◇ *the ordination of women priests* 女司祭的授职礼 ➲ COMPARE CHAPLAIN, CLERGYMAN, MINISTER *n.* (2), VICAR **2** 🔑 (*feminine* **priest·ess** /ˈpriːstes/) a person who performs religious ceremonies in some religions that are not Christian （非基督教会的）教士，祭司，僧侣

priest·hood /ˈpriːsthʊd/ *noun* **1 the priesthood** [sing.] the job or position of being a priest 牧师（或教士、神

父、司铎）的职位；司祭品： *to enter the priesthood* (= to become a priest) 接受司祭职 ➲ COLLOCATIONS AT RELIGION **2** all the priests of a particular religion or country （总称教会或国家的）全体教士，全体神职人员；司祭团

priest·ly /ˈpriːstli/ *adj.* [usually before noun] connected with a priest; like a priest 神职人员的；像神职人员的

ˈpriest's hole *noun* a secret space in a house where Catholic priests hid in the past at times when Catholicism was against the law in England （旧时天主教在英国属违法时的）司铎藏身处

prig /prɪɡ/ *noun* (*disapproving*) a person who behaves in a morally correct way and who shows that they disapprove of what other people do 自命清高的人 ▶ **prig·gish** *adj.* **prig·gish·ness** *noun* [U]

prim /prɪm/ *adj.* (**prim·mer**, **prim·mest**) (*disapproving*) **1** (of a person 人) always behaving in a careful and formal way, and easily shocked by anything that is rude 一本正经的；循规蹈矩的；古板的： *You can't tell her that joke—she's much too* **prim and proper**. 你可别跟她讲那个笑话；她这个人古板正经得要命。 **2** formal and neat 正式的；端庄的 SYN **demure**: *a prim suit with a high-necked collar* 端庄的高领西服 ▶ **prim·ly** *adv.*： *'You're not supposed to say that,' she said primly.* "你不该讲那样的话。"她一本正经地说。

prima ballerina /ˌpriːmə ˌbæləˈriːnə/ *noun* the main woman dancer in a BALLET company （芭蕾舞团的）首席女舞蹈演员

pri·macy AW /ˈpraɪməsi/ *noun* (*pl.* **-ies**) (*formal*) **1** [U] the fact of being the most important person or thing 首要；至高无上： *a belief in the primacy of the family* 家庭至上论 **2** [C] the position of an ARCHBISHOP 总主教职

prima donna /ˌpriːmə ˈdɒnə; *NAmE* ˈdɑːnə/ *noun* **1** the main woman singer in an OPERA performance or an OPERA company （歌剧演出或歌剧团的）首席女歌唱演员，女主角演员 **2** (*disapproving*) a person who thinks they are very important because they are good at sth, and who behaves badly when they do not get what they want 妄自尊大而爱闹脾气者；恃才傲物者

prim·aeval *adj.* = PRIMEVAL

prima facie /ˌpraɪmə ˈfeɪʃi/ *adj.* [only before noun] (*from Latin, law* 律) based on what at first seems to be true, although it may be proved false later 基于初步印象的；初步认定的： *prima facie evidence* 初步的证据 ▶ **prima facie** *adv.*： *Prima facie, there is a strong case against him.* 据初步认定，证据对他极其不利。

primal /ˈpraɪml/ *adj.* [only before noun] (*formal*) connected with the earliest origins of life; very basic 原始的；最初的；根源的；根本的 SYN **primeval**: *the primal hunter-gatherer* 原始狩猎采集者 ◇ *a primal urge/fear* 本能的欲望 / 恐惧

pri·mar·ily 🔑 AW /praɪˈmerəli; *BrE also* ˈpraɪmərəli/ *adv.* mainly 主要地；根本地 SYN **chiefly**: *a course designed primarily for specialists* 主要为专业人员开设的课程 ◇ *The problem is not primarily a financial one.* 这个问题基本上不是财政问题。

pri·mary 🔑 AW /ˈpraɪməri; *NAmE* -meri/ *adj.*, *noun*

■ ***adj.*** **1** 🔑 [usually before noun] main; most important; basic 主要的；最重要的；基本的 SYN **prime**: *The primary aim of this course is to improve your spoken English.* 这门课的主要目的是提高英语会话能力。 ◇ *Our primary concern must be the children.* 我们首先要关心的必须是儿童。 ◇ *Good health care is of primary importance.* 良好的医疗保健是重中之重。 **2** 🔑 [usually before noun] (*formal* or *specialist*) developing or happening first; earliest 最初的；最早的： *primary causes* 最初的原因 ◇ *The disease is still in its primary stage.* 这病尚处于初始阶段。 **3** 🔑 [only before noun] (*especially BrE*) connected with the education of children between the ages of about five and eleven 初等教育的；小学教育的： *primary teachers* 小学教师 ➲ COMPARE ELEMENTARY (1), SECONDARY (3), TERTIARY

■ ***noun*** (*pl.* **-ies**) (*also* **ˌprimary eˈlection**) (in the US) an election in which people in a particular area vote to choose a candidate for a future important election （美国）初选： *the Illinois primary* 伊利诺伊州的初选 ◇ *the presidential primaries* 总统候选人初选 ➲ WORDFINDER NOTE AT CONGRESS

ˌprimary ˈcare (*also* **ˌprimary ˈhealth care**) *noun* [U] the medical treatment that you receive first when you are ill/sick, for example from your family doctor 初级护理；基础医疗；初始的治疗

primary ˌcare phyˈsician *noun* (*abbr.* **PCP**) (*especially NAmE*) a doctor who provides primary care 初级护理医师；基础医疗医师

primary ˌcare proˈvider *noun* (*abbr.* **PCP**) a company or organization that provides primary care 初级护理机构；基础医疗机构

ˌprimary ˈcolour (*especially US* **ˌprimary ˈcolor**) *noun* one of the three colours, red, yellow and blue, that can be mixed together to make all other colours 原色，基色（指能混合成其他各种颜色的红、黄、蓝三色之一）

ˌprimary ˈhealth care *noun* = PRIMARY CARE

ˈprimary industry *noun* [U, C] (*economics* 经) the section of industry that provides RAW MATERIALS to be made into goods, for example farming and MINING 第一产业（指农业、矿业等生产原材料的产业） ➲ COMPARE SECONDARY INDUSTRY, TERTIARY INDUSTRY

ˈprimary school *noun* **1** (*BrE*) a school for children between the ages of 4 or 5 and 11 小学 **2** (*old-fashioned, NAmE*) = ELEMENTARY SCHOOL ➲ COMPARE SECONDARY SCHOOL

ˈprimary source *noun* a document, etc. that contains information obtained by research or observation, not taken from other books, etc. 第一手资料；（通过研究或观察等获得的）直接材料 ➲ COMPARE SECONDARY SOURCE

ˌprimary ˈstress *noun* [C, U] (*phonetics* 语音) the strongest stress that is put on a syllable in a word or a phrase when it is spoken 主重音；第一重音 ➲ COMPARE SECONDARY STRESS

pri·mate *noun* **1** /ˈpraɪmeɪt/ any animal that belongs to the group of MAMMALS that includes humans, APES and MONKEYS 灵长类；灵长目动物 ➲ VISUAL VOCAB PAGE V12 **2** /ˈpraɪmət; ˈpraɪmeɪt/ an ARCHBISHOP (= a priest of very high rank in the Christian Church) 大主教；总主教： *the Primate of all England* (= the Archbishop of Canterbury) 全英格兰主教长（坎特伯雷大主教）

prime AW /praɪm/ *adj.*, *noun*, *verb*

■ ***adj.*** [only before noun] **1** main; most important; basic 主要的；首要的；基本的： *My prime concern is to protect my property.* 我最关心的是保护自己的财产。 ◇ *Winning is not the prime objective in this sport.* 获胜不是这项体育运动的主要目的。 ◇ *The care of the environment is of prime importance.* 保护环境是最重要的。 ◇ *He's the police's* **prime suspect** *in this case.* 他是该案中警方的主要怀疑对象。 ➲ SYNONYMS AT MAIN **2** of the best quality; excellent 优质的；上乘的；优异的： *prime (cuts of) beef* 上等的牛肉（块） ◇ *The store has a prime position in the mall.* 这家商店位于购物广场一个非常理想的位置。 **3** a **prime example** of sth is one that is typical of it 典型的；有代表性的： *The building is a prime example of 1960s architecture.* 这座大楼是 20 世纪 60 年代的典型建筑。 **4** most likely to be chosen for sth; most suitable 最可能的；首选的；最适宜的： *The house is isolated and a prime target for burglars.* 这座孤零零的房子是盗贼的首选目标。 ◇ *He's a prime candidate for promotion.* 他是最有望获得晋升的人选。

■ ***noun*** [sing.] the time in your life when you are strongest or most successful 盛年；年富力强的时期；鼎盛时期： *a young woman in her prime* 正当妙龄的女郎 ◇ *He was barely 30 and* **in the prime of (his) life**. 他才 30 岁，正是英姿勃发的年华。 ◇ *These flowers are long* **past their prime**. 这些花的鼎盛花期早过了。

■ ***verb*** **1** to prepare sb for a situation so that they know what to do, especially by giving them special

P

information 事先指点；使（某人）做好准备 SYN **brief**: ~ **sb** (**with sth**) *They had been primed with good advice.* 他们事先得到了高人指点。◇ ~ **sb** (**for sth**) *She was ready and primed for action.* 她已胸有成竹、跃跃欲试了。◇ ~ **sb to do sth** *He had primed his friends to give the journalists as little information as possible.* 他已经知会他的朋友，尽量少向记者透露消息。 **2** ~ **sth** to make sth ready for use or action 把（事物）准备好：*The bomb was primed, ready to explode.* 炸弹已准备好，可随时引爆。 **3** ~ **sth** to prepare wood, metal, etc. for painting by covering it with a special paint that helps the next layer of paint to stay on 在（金属、木材等上）打底漆

IDM **prime the 'pump** to encourage the growth of a new or weak business or industry by putting money into it 投资以振兴（新的或不景气的企业或行业）

'prime cost (*also* **'first cost**) *noun* [C, U] (*business* 商) the cost of sth calculated by adding the cost of materials used to make it and the cost of paying sb to make it, but not including costs that are connected with running a business, such as rent and electricity 主要成本（包括原材料和劳动力）

,prime 'minister (*also* **,Prime 'Minister**) *noun* (*abbr.* **PM**) the main minister and leader of the government in some countries 首相；总理

,prime 'mover *noun* a person or thing that starts sth and has an important influence on its development 发起者；推动者；原动力

,prime 'number *noun* (*mathematics* 数) a number that can be divided exactly only by itself and 1, for example 7, 17 and 41 素数，质数（只能被 1 和其自身整除）

primer /'praɪmə(r)/ *noun* **1** [U, C] a type of paint that is put on wood, metal, etc. before it is painted to help the paint to stay on the surface 底漆；底层涂料 **2** [C] /'praɪmə(r); *NAmE* 'prɪmər/ (*NAmE*) a book that contains basic instructions 初级读本；入门书：*The President doesn't need a primer on national security.* 总统对于国家安全是不需要读入门书的。 **3** [C] /'praɪmə(r); *NAmE* 'prɪmər/ (*old-fashioned*) a book for teaching children how to read, or containing basic facts about a school subject 识字课本；启蒙读本

'prime rate *noun* (in the US) the lowest rate of interest at which business customers can borrow money from banks（美国银行的）最优惠贷款利率 ➲ COMPARE BASE RATE

'prime time (*BrE also* **'peak time**, **,peak 'viewing time**) *noun* [U] the time when the greatest number of people are watching television or listening to the radio（广播、电视的）黄金时间：*prime-time television* 黄金时间的电视节目

pri·meval (*also* **prim·aeval**) /praɪ'miːvl/ *adj.* [usually before noun] **1** from the earliest period of the history of the world, very ancient 远古的；原始的：*primeval forests* 原始森林 **2** (*formal*) (of a feeling, or a desire 感觉或欲望) very strong and not based on reason, as if from the earliest period of human life 出于原始天性的：*primeval urges* 本能的欲望

primi·tive /'prɪmətɪv/ *adj.*, *noun*

■ *adj.* **1** [usually before noun] belonging to a very simple society with no industry, etc. 原始的；远古的：*primitive tribes* 原始部落 ◇ *primitive beliefs* 原始的信仰 **2** [usually before noun] belonging to an early stage in the development of humans or animals 原始的；（人类或动物）发展早期的：*primitive man* 原始人 **3** very simple and old-fashioned, especially when sth is also not convenient and comfortable 简陋的；落后的；发展水平低的 SYN **crude**: *The methods of communication used during the war were primitive by today's standards.* 按今天的标准，大战时期使用的通讯方法非常落后。◇ *The facilities on the campsite were very primitive.* 营地的设施非常简陋。 **4** [usually before noun] (of a feeling or a desire 感觉或欲望) very strong and not based on reason, as if from the earliest period of human life 出于原始天性的：*a primitive instinct* 原始本能 ▶ **primi·tive·ly** *adv.* **primi·tive·ness** *noun* [U]

■ *noun* **1** an artist of the period before the Renaissance; an example of work from this period 文艺复兴前的艺术家（或作品） **2** an artist who paints in a very simple style like a child; an example of the work of such an artist 原始派画家（或作品）

primi·tiv·ism /'prɪmɪtɪvɪzəm/ *noun* [U] a belief that simple forms and ideas are the most valuable, expressed as a philosophy or in art or literature（哲学、艺术或文学的）原始主义，尚古主义，原始风格

primo·geni·ture /,praɪməʊ'dʒenɪtʃə(r); *NAmE* -moʊ-/ *noun* [U] **1** (*formal*) the fact of being the first child born in a family 长子身份；长嗣身份 **2** (*law* 律) the system in which the oldest son in a family receives all the property when his father dies 长子继承权

prim·or·dial /praɪ'mɔːdiəl; *NAmE* -'mɔːrdiəl/ *adj.* [usually before noun] (*formal*) **1** existing at or from the beginning of the world 原生的；原始的 SYN **primeval** **2** (of a feeling or a desire 感觉或欲望) very basic 基本的 SYN **primeval**: *primordial impulses* 本能的冲动

primp /prɪmp/ *verb* [I, T] ~ (**sth/yourself**) (*often disapproving*) to make yourself look attractive by arranging your hair, putting on make-up, etc. 打扮；修饰

prim·rose /'prɪmrəʊz; *NAmE* -roʊz/ *noun* **1** [C] a small wild plant that produces pale yellow flowers in spring 报春花（开黄色花） ➲ VISUAL VOCAB PAGE V11 **2** (*also* **,primrose 'yellow**) [U] a pale yellow colour 淡黄色 ➲ MORE LIKE THIS 15, page R26 ▶ **prim·rose** (*also* **,primrose 'yellow**) *adj.*

IDM **the primrose 'path** (*literary*) an easy life that is full of pleasure but that causes you harm in the end 追求享乐（招致恶果）

prim·ula /'prɪmjələ/ *noun* a type of primrose that is often grown in gardens/yards 报春花属植物（广泛栽种于庭园）

Pri·mus™ /'praɪməs/ (*also* **'Primus stove**) *noun* a small cooker/stove that you can move around that burns oil. It is used especially by people who are camping. 普赖默斯便携式燃油炉

prince /prɪns/ *noun* **1** a male member of a royal family who is not king, especially the son or grandson of the king or queen 王子；王孙；亲王：*the royal princes* 亲王 ◇ *the Prince of Wales* 威尔士亲王 **2** the male ruler of a small country or state that has a royal family; a male member of this family, especially the son or grandson of the ruler（小国的）国王，王室男性成员，王子，王孙：*Prince Albert of Monaco* 摩纳哥国王阿尔伯特 **3** (in some European countries) a NOBLEMAN（某些欧洲国家的）贵族 **4** ~ **of/among sth** (*literary*) a man who is thought to be one of the best in a particular field（某一领域的）杰出人物，巨子，大王：*the prince of comedy* 喜剧大师

,Prince 'Charming *noun* [sing.] (*usually humorous*) a man who seems to be a perfect boyfriend or husband because he is very attractive, kind, etc. 白马王子；（女子的）梦中情人 ➲ MORE LIKE THIS 16, page R27 ORIGIN From the hero of some European fairy tales, for example *Cinderella* and *Sleeping Beauty*. 源自《灰姑娘》和《睡美人》等欧洲童话中的男主角。

,Prince 'Consort *noun* a title sometimes given to the husband of a queen who is himself a prince 王夫：*Prince Albert, the Prince Consort* 王夫艾伯特亲王

prince·ling /'prɪnslɪŋ/ *noun* (*usually disapproving*) a prince who rules a small or unimportant country（小国的）国王，国君，大公

prince·ly /'prɪnsli/ *adj.* [usually before noun] **1** (*usually ironic*) if you say that an amount of money is **princely**, you are usually saying the opposite and that it is not very large 巨额的；庞大的：*I bought a bike for the*

P

princely sum of £20! 我花 20 英镑巨款买了一辆自行车! **2** (*old-fashioned, formal*) very grand; generous 雄伟的; 堂皇的; 慷慨的: *princely buildings* 宏伟的建筑 ◇ *a princely gift* 一份丰厚的礼物 **3** connected with a prince; like a prince 王子王孙的; 王公贵族的; 似王子的

prin·cess /ˌprɪnˈses; ˈprɪnses/ *noun* **1** a female member of a royal family who is not a queen, especially the daughter or granddaughter of the king or queen (除女王或王后外的) 王室女成员; (尤指) 公主: *the royal princesses* 王室女成员 ◇ *Princess Anne* 安妮公主 **2** the wife of a prince 王妃; 王公贵族夫人: *the Princess of Wales* 威尔士王妃 ◇ *Princess Michael of Kent* 肯特迈克尔王妃 **3** (*disapproving*) a young woman who has always been given everything that she wants, and who thinks that she is better than other people (受宠溺而自以为优越的) 娇小姐 **4** (*BrE, informal*) used as a form of address by a man to a girl or young woman (男子对女孩或年轻女子的称呼) 大小姐: *Is something the matter, princess?* 有什么事吗, 大小姐?

ˌPrincess ˈRoyal *noun* a title often given to the oldest daughter of a British king or queen 长公主, 大公主 (英国授予君主长女的称号)

prin·ci·pal AW /ˈprɪnsəpl/ *adj., noun*

■ ***adj.*** [only before noun] most important; main 最重要的; 主要的: *The principal reason for this omission is lack of time.* 跳过它的主要原因是时间不足。◇ *New roads will link the principal cities of the area.* 新建道路将连通这个地区的主要城市。➲ SYNONYMS AT MAIN

■ ***noun*** **1** (*BrE*) the person who is in charge of a college or a university 大学校长; 学院院长: *Peter Brown, principal of St John's College* 彼得 · 布朗, 圣约翰学院院长 ➲ SEE ALSO DEAN **2** (*NAmE*) (*BrE* **ˌhead ˈteacher**) a teacher who is in charge of a school (中小学) 校长: *Principal Ray Smith* 雷 · 史密斯校长 **3** [usually sing.] (*finance* 财) an amount of money that you lend to sb or invest to earn interest 本金; 资本 **4** the person who has the most important part in a play, an OPERA, etc. 主要演员; 主角 **5** (*specialist*) a person that you are representing, especially in business or law (尤指商务或法律事务的) 当事人, 委托人

ˌprincipal ˈboy *noun* (*BrE*) the main male role in a PANTOMIME, usually played by a woman 英国童话剧男主角 (通常由女演员扮演)

prin·ci·pal·ity /ˌprɪnsɪˈpæləti/ *noun* (*pl.* **-ies**) **1** [C] a country that is ruled by a prince 王公治理的国家; 公国; 侯国: *the principality of Monaco* 摩纳哥公国 **2 the Principality** [sing.] (*BrE*) Wales 威尔士

prin·ci·pal·ly AW /ˈprɪnsəpli/ *adv.* mainly 主要地 SYN **chiefly**: *The book is aimed principally at beginners.* 这本书主要是为初学者编写的。◇ *No new power stations have been built, principally because of the cost.* 没有新建的发电站, 主要是因为经费问题。

ˌprincipal ˈparts *noun* [pl.] (*grammar* 语法) the forms of a verb from which all the other forms can be made. In English these are the infinitive (for example *swim*), the past tense (*swam*) and the past participle (*swum*). (动词) 主要部分, 主要形式 (英语中有动词的不定式、过去时和过去分词)

prin·ciple AW /ˈprɪnsəpl/ *noun* **1** [C, usually pl., U] a moral rule or a strong belief that influences your actions 道德原则; 行为准则; 规范: *He has high moral principles.* 他道德高尚。◇ *I refuse to lie about it; **it's against my principles**.* 我绝不为此事撒谎; 那是违背我的原则的。◇ ***Stick to your principles** and tell him you won't do it.* 要恪守自己的原则, 告诉他你绝不会干的。◇ *She refuses to allow her family to help her as **a matter of principle**.* 她不要家人帮忙, 对她来说这是个原则问题。◇ *He doesn't invest in the arms industry **on principle**.* 他根据自己的信条, 不投资军火工业。 **2** [C] a law, a rule or a theory that sth is based on 法则; 原则; 原理: *the principles and practice of writing reports* 报告写作的理论与实践 ◇ *The principle behind it is very simple.* 其中的原理十分简单。◇ *There are three fundamental principles of teamwork.* 团队合作有三个基本原则。◇ *Discussing all these details will get us nowhere; we must get back to **first principles*** (= the most basic rules). 一直谈这些细节不会有结果的; 我们必须回到根本原则上来。 **3** [C] a belief that is accepted as a reason for acting or thinking in a particular way 观念; (行动、思想的) 理由, 信条: *the principle that free education should be available for all children* 所有儿童都应该能享受免费教育的观念 **4** [sing.] a general or scientific law that explains how sth works or why sth happens 定律; 工作原理: *the principle that heat rises* 热气上升的定律

IDM **in ˈprinciple** **1** if something can be done **in principle**, there is no good reason why it should not be done although it has not yet been done and there may be some difficulties 原则上; 理论上: *In principle there is nothing that a human can do that a machine might not be able to do one day.* 原则上, 总会有一天, 凡是人能做的事, 机器就能做。 **2** in general but not in detail 大体上; 基本上: *They have agreed to the proposal in principle but we still have to negotiate the terms.* 他们已基本同意了这项提议, 但我们还得磋商各项条款。

prin·cipled AW /ˈprɪnsəpld/ *adj.* **1** having strong beliefs about what is right and wrong; based on strong beliefs 是非观念强的; 原则性强的; 基于坚定信念的: *a principled woman* 坚持原则的女人 ◇ *to take a principled stand against abortion* 采取反堕胎的原则性立场 OPP **unprincipled** **2** based on rules or truths 根据规则 (或事实) 的: *a principled approach to language teaching* 有理论基础的语言教学法

print /prɪnt/ *verb, noun*

■ ***verb***

• **LETTERS/PICTURES** 图文 **1** [T, I] ~ (**sth**) to produce letters, pictures, etc. on paper using a machine that puts ink on the surface 在纸上印; 打印: *Do you want your address printed at the top of the letter?* 你要不要把地址印在信的顶端? ◇ *I'm printing a copy of the document for you.* 我正在给你印一份这个文件。◇ *Each card is printed with a different message.* 每张卡片都印着不同的信息。◇ (*computing* 计) *Click on the icon when you want to print.* 你想打印时就点击一下这个图标。➲ WORDFINDER NOTE AT FILE

• **BOOKS/NEWSPAPERS** 书报 **2** [T] ~ **sth** to produce books, newspapers, etc. by printing them in large quantities 印刷: *They printed 30 000 copies of the book.* 这本书他们印了 3 万册。

• **PUBLISH** 出版 **3** [T] ~ **sth** to publish sth in printed form 登载; 刊登; 发表: *The photo was printed in all the national newspapers.* 这张照片被刊登在各全国性报纸上。

• **PHOTOGRAPH** 照片 **4** [T] ~ **sth** to produce a photograph from a film 洗印; 冲洗: *I'm having the pictures developed and printed.* 我已把照片送去冲印。

• **WRITE** 书写 **5** [I, T] to write without joining the letters together 用印刷体写 (字母之间笔画不相连接): *In some countries children learn to print when they first go to school.* 在有些国家, 儿童刚上学时学习用印刷体书写。◇ ~ **sth** *Print your name and address clearly in the space provided.* 请用印刷体在空白处填写你的姓名和住址。

• **MAKE MARK** 留痕迹 **6** [T] ~ **sth** (**in/on sth**) to make a mark on a soft surface by pressing (在松软的表面) 压印, 印出: *The tracks of the large animal were clearly printed in the sand.* 这只大动物的足迹清晰地印在沙滩上。◇ (*figurative*) *The memory of that day was indelibly printed on his brain.* 那天的记忆永不磨灭地深印在他的脑海里。

• **MAKE DESIGN** 印图案 **7** [T] to make a design on a surface or cloth by pressing a surface against it which has been coloured with ink or DYE 印 (图案); 印染: *They had printed their own design on the T-shirt.* 他们在 T 恤衫上印了自己设计的图案。

IDM **the ˌprinted ˈword/ˈpage** what is published in books, newspapers, etc. 印在书报上的文字; 书刊文字; 印刷品: *the power of the printed word* 书刊文字的力量 ➲ MORE AT LICENCE, WORTH *adj.*

PHR V **ˌprint sth↔ˈoff/ˈout** to produce a document or information from a computer in printed form (从计算机中) 打印出 ➲ RELATED NOUN PRINTOUT

P

■ *noun*
• LETTERS/NUMBERS 文字；数字 **1** [U] letters, words, numbers, etc. that have been printed onto paper 印刷字体：*in **large/small/bold print*** 用大号 / 小号 / 粗字体 ◇ *The print quality of the new laser printer is superb.* 新激光打印机的打印质量好极了。➲ SEE ALSO SMALL PRINT
• NEWSPAPERS/BOOKS 书报 **2** [U] used to refer to the business of producing newspapers, magazines and books 印刷行业；出版界：*the print media* 印刷媒体 ◇ *print unions* 出版业工会
• MARK 痕迹 **3** [C, usually pl.] a mark left by your finger, foot, etc. on the surface of sth 指纹；手印；脚印；足迹：*His prints were found on the gun.* 在枪上发现了他的指纹。➲ SEE ALSO FINGERPRINT, FOOTPRINT (1)
• PICTURE 图片 **4** [C] a picture that is cut into wood or metal then covered with ink and printed onto paper; a picture that is copied from a painting using photography 版画；（用照相制版法制作的）绘画复制品：*a framed set of prints* 一组镶框的版画 ➲ SYNONYMS AT PICTURE ➲ COLLOCATIONS AT ART
• PHOTOGRAPH 照片 **5** [C] a photograph produced from film（用底片洗印的）相片：*How many sets of prints would you like?* 你想洗几套照片？◇ *a colour print* 一张彩色照片 ➲ SYNONYMS AT PHOTOGRAPH
• CLOTH 织物 **6** [U, C] cotton cloth that has a pattern printed on it; this pattern 印花棉布（或图案）；花样：*a cotton print dress* 花布连衣裙 ◇ *a floral print* 花卉图案 ➲ SEE ALSO BLUEPRINT

IDM **get into 'print** to be published 被出版；被发表：*By the time this gets into print, they'll already have left the country.* 这篇东西发表的时候，他们将已经离开这个国家了。 **in print** **1** (of a book 书籍) still available from the company that publishes it 继续印行 **2** (of a person's work 作品) printed in a book, newspaper, etc. 已刊印；已出版：*It was the first time he had seen his name in print.* 那是他第一次见到自己的名字被刊印出来。 **,out of 'print** (of a book 书籍) no longer available from the company that publishes it 绝版；不再印行

P

print·able /'prɪntəbl/ *adj.* (usually used with a negative 通常与否定词连用) suitable to be repeated in writing and read by people 适宜刊印（或阅读）的：*His comment when he heard the news was not printable* (= was very rude). 他听到这消息时下的评语不宜刊登。OPP **unprintable**

,printed 'circuit *noun* a CIRCUIT for electricity that uses thin strips of metal instead of wires to carry the current 印制电路

print·er /'prɪntə(r)/ *noun* **1** a machine for printing text on paper, especially one connected to a computer 打印机（尤指与计算机相连的）：*a colour/laser printer* 彩色 / 激光打印机 ➲ VISUAL VOCAB PAGE V71 **2** a person or a company whose job is printing books, etc. 印刷商；印刷工人；印刷公司 **3** **printer's** (*pl.* **printers**) a place where books, etc. are printed 印刷厂

print·ing /'prɪntɪŋ/ *noun* **1** [U] the act of producing letters, pictures, patterns, etc. on sth by pressing a surface covered with ink against it 印刷；印刷术：*the invention of printing* 印刷术的发明 ◇ *the printing trade* 印刷业 ◇ *colour printing* 彩色印刷 **2** [C] the act of printing a number of copies of a book at one time（书籍的）一次印刷：*The book is in its sixth printing.* 这本书是第六次印刷了。**3** [U] a type of writing when you write all the letters separately and do not join them together 印刷字体

'printing press *noun* a machine that produces books, newspapers, etc. by pressing a surface covered in ink onto paper 印刷机

print·maker /'prɪntmeɪkə(r)/ *noun* an artist who prints pictures or designs 版画匠；版画家

,print on de'mand *noun* (*abbr.* **POD**) [U] a system of printing books only when a customer wants one 按需印刷；随选印刷：*The titles are available through print on demand.* 这些书刊可按需印刷。◇ *This is a print-on-demand title.* 这是按需印刷的书。

print·out /'prɪntaʊt/ *noun* [U, C] a page or set of pages containing information in printed form from a computer（计算机）打印件，打印资料：*a printout of text downloaded from the Internet* 从互联网下载文本的打印件 ➲ VISUAL VOCAB PAGE V71 ➲ COMPARE READ-OUT

'print run *noun* (*specialist*) the number of copies of a book, magazine, etc. printed at one time（书刊等的）一次印数，每次印数

print·works /'prɪntwɜːks; *NAmE* -wɜːrks/ *noun* (*pl.* **print·works**) (*BrE*) a factory where patterns are printed on cloth 印染厂；印花厂

prion /'priːɒn; *NAmE* -ɑːn/ *noun* (*biology* 生) a very small unit of PROTEIN that is believed to be the cause of brain diseases such as BSE, CJD and SCRAPIE 普里昂，蛋白质感染粒，朊病毒（能导致脑病）

prior AW /'praɪə(r)/ *adj., noun*
■ *adj.* [only before noun] (*formal*) **1** happening or existing before sth else or before a particular time 先前的；较早的；在前的：*Although not essential, some **prior knowledge** of statistics is desirable.* 统计学的知识虽非必要，但最好是学过一点。◇ *This information must not be disclosed without **prior written consent**.* 未事先征得书面许可，此消息不得泄露。◇ *Visits are by **prior arrangement**.* 参观需要事先安排。◇ *Please give us **prior notice** if you need an evening meal.* 需用晚餐者，请预先通知我们。◇ *She will be unable to attend because of a **prior engagement**.* 因事先有别的安排，她将不能出席。**2** already existing and therefore more important 优先的；占先的；较重要的：*They have a **prior claim** to the property.* 他们有权优先获得该处房产。 **3** **'prior to** before sth 在…前面的：*during the week prior to the meeting* 在开会前的一周内
■ *noun* (*feminine* **pri·or·ess** /'praɪərəs; *BrE also* ˌpraɪə'res/) **1** a person who is in charge of a group of MONKS or NUNS living in a PRIORY（小隐修院）院长 **2** (in an ABBEY) a person next in rank below an ABBOT or ABBESS（隐修院）会长，副院长

pri·ori ➲ A PRIORI

pri·ori·tize AW (*BrE also* **-ise**) /praɪ'ɒrətaɪz; *NAmE* -'ɔːr-/ *verb* **1** [T, I] ~ (**sth**) to put tasks, problems, etc. in order of importance, so that you can deal with the most important first 按重要性排列；划分优先顺序：*You should make a list of all the jobs you have to do and prioritize them.* 你应该把所有要做的事都列出来，并按轻重缓急排个顺序。 **2** [T] **~ sth** (*formal*) to treat sth as being more important than other things 优先处理：*The organization was formed to prioritize the needs of older people.* 这个机构是为优先满足老年人的需要而成立的。▶ **pri·ori·tiza·tion, -isa·tion** AW /praɪˌɒrətaɪ'zeɪʃn; *NAmE* -ˌɔːrətə'z-/ *noun* [U]

pri·or·ity AW /praɪ'ɒrəti; *NAmE* -'ɔːr-/ *noun* (*pl.* **-ies**) **1** [C] something that you think is more important than other things and should be dealt with first 优先事项；最重要的事；首要事情：*a **high/low priority*** 重点 / 非重点项目 ◇ *Education is a **top priority**.* 教育是当务之急。◇ *Our **first priority** is to improve standards.* 我们的头等大事是提高标准。◇ *Financial security was high on his **list of priorities**.* 在他的心目中，金融安全是十分重要的一环。◇ *You need to **get your priorities right*** (= decide what is important to you). 你需要把自己的事情分出轻重缓急。◇ (*NAmE*) *You need to **get your priorities straight**.* 你需要把个人事情的轻重缓急分清楚。 **2** [U] ~ (**over sth**) the most important place among various things that have to be done or among a group of people 优先；优先权；重点 SYN **precedence**：*Club members will be **given priority**.* 俱乐部成员享有优先权。◇ *The search for a new vaccine will **take priority over** all other medical research.* 研制新的疫苗将排在其他一切医学研究之前。◇ *Priority cases, such as homeless families, get dealt with first.* 优先事项，比如无住房家庭的问题，得到优先处理。 **3** [U] (*BrE*) the right of a vehicle to go before other traffic at a particular place on a road（车辆的）优先通行权 SYN **right of way**：*Buses have priority at this junction.* 在这个路口，公共汽车有优先通行权。

pri·ory /ˈpraɪəri/ *noun* (*pl.* **-ies**) a building where a community of MONKS or NUNS lives, which is smaller and less important than an ABBEY 小修道院；小隐道院

prise (*especially BrE*) (*US* **prize**) /praɪz/ (*also* **pry** *especially in NAmE*) *verb* to use force to separate sth from sth else 强行使分开；撬开： **~ sth + adv./prep.** *He prised her fingers from the bag and took it from her.* 他掰开她的手指，把她手中的袋子抢走了。 ◇ **~ sth + adj.** *She used a knife to prise open the lid.* 她用刀把盖子撬开了。

PHR V ˌ**prise sth**↔ˈ**out** (**of sb**) | ˈ**prise sth from sb** to force sb to give you information about sb/sth（向某人）逼问情况；强迫…透露消息

prism /ˈprɪzəm/ *noun* **1** (*geometry* 几何) a solid figure with ends that are parallel and of the same size and shape, and with sides whose opposite edges are equal and parallel 棱柱体；棱柱 ➲ PICTURE AT SOLID **2** a transparent glass or plastic object, often with ends in the shape of a triangle, which separates light that passes through it into the colours of the RAINBOW 棱镜；三棱镜

pris·mat·ic /prɪzˈmætɪk/ *adj.* **1** (*specialist*) using or containing a prism; in the shape of a prism 用棱柱体（或棱镜）的；棱柱形的 **2** (*literary*) (of colours 颜色) formed by a prism; very bright and clear 棱镜折射的；分光的；绚丽的；五光十色的

prison 🔑 /ˈprɪzn/ *noun* **1** 🔑 [C, U] a building where people are kept as a punishment for a crime they have committed, or while they are waiting for trial 监狱；牢狱；看守所 **SYN** **jail**: *He was* ***sent to prison*** *for five years.* 他被关押了五年。 ◇ *She is* ***in prison****, awaiting trial.* 她正在拘押候审中。 ◇ *to* ***be released from prison*** 被释放出狱 ◇ *a* ***maximum-security prison*** 最高度戒备的监狱 ◇ *the* ***prison population*** (= the total number of prisoners in a country) 在押人数 ◇ *the problem of overcrowding in prisons* 监狱人满为患的问题 ◇ *Ten prison officers and three inmates needed hospital treatment following the riot.* 骚乱之后，有十名狱警和三名囚犯需入院治疗。 ➲ COLLOCATIONS AT JUSTICE ➲ NOTE AT SCHOOL

> **WORDFINDER** 联想词： cell, death row, discharge, **justice**, parole, probation, remission, sentence, warder

2 🔑 [U] the system of keeping people in prisons 监禁；关押；关押制度： *the* ***prison service/system*** 监狱管理机构 / 制度 ◇ *The government insists that 'prison works' and plans to introduce a tougher sentencing policy for people convicted of violent crime.* 政府坚持认为"关押有效"，并计划对暴力犯罪者实行更严厉的判刑政策。 **3** [C] a place or situation from which sb cannot escape 难以脱身的地方（或处境）；牢笼；樊笼： *His hospital room had become a prison.* 他的病房变成了牢笼。

ˈ**prison camp** *noun* a guarded camp where prisoners, especially prisoners of war or political prisoners, are kept 集中营；战俘营

pris·on·er 🔑 /ˈprɪznə(r)/ *noun* **1** 🔑 a person who is kept in prison as a punishment, or while they are waiting for trial 囚犯；犯人；羁押候审者： *The number of prisoners serving life sentences has fallen.* 被判无期徒刑的囚犯数目下降了。 ◇ *They are demanding the release of all* ***political prisoners***. 他们正在要求释放所有的政治犯。 **2** 🔑 a person who has been captured, for example by an enemy, and is being kept somewhere 被（敌人等）关起来的人；俘虏；战俘： *He was* ***taken prisoner*** *by rebel soldiers.* 他被叛军俘虏了。 ◇ *They are* ***holding her prisoner*** *and demanding a large ransom.* 他们把她劫持了，并索要巨额赎金。 ◇ (*figurative*) *She is afraid to go out and has become a virtual prisoner in her own home.* 她不敢出门，实际上已成了关在家中的囚犯。

ˌ**prisoner of ˈconscience** *noun* (*pl.* **prisoners of conscience**) a person who is kept in prison because of his or her political or religious beliefs（因政治或宗教信仰）被关押的人；政治犯；宗教犯

ˌ**prisoner of ˈwar** *noun* (*pl.* **prisoners of war**) (*abbr.* **POW**) a person, usually a member of the armed forces, who is captured by the enemy during a war and kept in a prison camp until the war has finished 战俘；俘虏

ˌ**prison ˈvisitor** *noun* (in Britain) a person who visits people in prison in order to help them, and who does not get paid for doing so（英国）义务探监者，探监义工

prissy /ˈprɪsi/ *adj.* (*informal, disapproving*) too careful to always behave correctly and appearing easily shocked by rude behaviour, etc. 谨小慎微的；大惊小怪的；拘泥谨慎的 **SYN** **prudish**

pris·tine /ˈprɪstiːn/ *adj.* **1** fresh and clean, as if new 崭新的；清新的 **SYN** **immaculate**: *The car is* ***in pristine condition***. 这辆汽车是全新的。 **2** not developed or changed in any way; left in its original condition 未开发的；处于原始状态的 **SYN** **unspoiled**: *pristine, pollution-free beaches* 没有污染的原始海滩

pri·thee /ˈprɪðiː/ *exclamation* (*old use*) used when asking sb politely to do sth 请；求求您

priv·acy /ˈprɪvəsi; *NAmE* ˈpraɪv-/ *noun* [U] **1** the state of being alone and not watched or disturbed by other people 隐私；私密： *She was longing for some peace and privacy.* 她渴望过清静的私人生活。 ◇ *I value my privacy.* 我重视自己的隐私。 ◇ *He read the letter later* ***in the privacy of*** *his own room.* 稍后，他在自己房间里私下读了那封信。 **2** the state of being free from the attention of the public 不受公众干扰的状态： *freedom of speech and the* ***right to privacy*** 言论自由与隐私权

pri·vate 🔑 /ˈpraɪvət/ *adj., noun*

■ *adj.*

- **NOT PUBLIC** 非公开 **1** 🔑 [usually before noun] belonging to or for the use of a particular person or group; not for public use 私有的；私用的；自用的： *The sign said, 'Private property. Keep out.'* 标牌上写着："私人领地，禁止进入。" ◇ *Those are my father's private papers.* 那些都是我父亲的私人文件。 ◇ *The hotel has 110 bedrooms, all with private bathrooms.* 这家旅馆有 110 间客房，各有独立卫生间。
- **CONVERSATION/MEETING** 谈话；会晤 **2** 🔑 intended for or involving a particular person or group of people, not for people in general or for others to know about 为一部分人的；私人的；秘密的： *a private conversation* 私人交谈 ◇ *They were sharing a private joke.* 他们讲着外人听不懂的笑话。 ◇ *Senior defence officials held private talks.* 高级防务官员举行了秘密会谈。
- **FEELINGS/INFORMATION** 情感；信息 **3** 🔑 that you do not want other people to know about 内心的；隐秘的；私下的 **SYN** **secret**: *her private thoughts and feelings* 她私下的想法和感情
- **NOT OWNED/RUN BY STATE** 非国有 **4** 🔑 [usually before noun] owned or managed by an individual person or an independent company rather than by the state 私立的；私营的；民营的： ***private banks*** 私营银行 ◇ *a programme to return many of the state companies to* ***private ownership*** 把众多国营公司转为民营的计划 **OPP** **public** **5** 🔑 [only before noun] working or acting for yourself rather than for the state or for a group or company, especially in health or education 个体的，独立的，私人的（尤指医疗或教育）： *private doctors* 私人医生 ◇ (*BrE*) *If I can afford it, I think I'll go private* (= pay for medical care rather than use the government service). 如果负担得起，我想我会自费医疗的。
- **NOT WORK** 非工作 **6** 🔑 [usually before noun] not connected with your work or official position 与工作（或官职）无关的；个人的；私人的： *a politician's* ***private life*** 政界人物的私生活
- **QUIET** 清静 **7** 🔑 where you are not likely to be disturbed; quiet 僻静的；不受打扰的： *Let's go somewhere a bit more private.* 咱们另找个僻静些的地方吧。 **OPP** **public**
- **PERSON** 人 **8** [usually before noun] not wanting to share thoughts and feelings with other people 不愿吐露心思的；内向的；不爱交流思想感情的： *He's a very private person.* 他是个闷葫芦。
- **LESSONS** 课堂 **9** [usually before noun] given by a teacher, etc. to one person or a small group of people for payment 私人教授的；个别传授的： *She gives private English lessons at weekends.* 她周末做私人英语家教。

• MONEY 钱 **10** that you receive from property or other sources but do not have to earn 由财产增溢的；间接收入的；非劳动所得的：*He has a private income.* 他有一笔私人收入。

▸ **pri·vate·ly** *adv.*：*Can we speak privately?* 我们能单独谈谈吗？◇ *In public he supported the official policy, but privately he was sure it would fail.* 他明里支持这项官方政策，但暗中却确信它会失败。◇ *a privately owned company* 私营公司 ◇ *Their children were educated privately.* 他们的子女都是上私立学校的。◇ *She smiled, but privately she was furious.* 她面露微笑，但心里却十分恼火。

■ *noun* **1** [C] (*abbr.* **Pte**) a soldier of the lowest rank in the army 二等兵，列兵（级别最低的士兵）：*Private (John) Smith* 列兵（约翰·）史密斯 **2 privates** [pl.] (*informal*) = PRIVATE PARTS

IDM **in 'private** with nobody else present 私下地；没外人在场：*Is there somewhere we can discuss this in private?* 有没有什么地方能让我们单独谈谈这件事？ ➲ COMPARE IN PUBLIC at PUBLIC *n.*

ˌprivate 'company (*also* **ˌprivate ˌlimited 'company**) *noun* (*business* 商) a business that may not offer its shares for sale to the public 私营公司；私人持股公司 ➲ COMPARE PUBLIC COMPANY, PLC

ˌprivate de'tective (*also* **ˌprivate in'vestigator**) (*also informal* **ˌprivate 'eye**) *noun* a DETECTIVE who is not in the police, but who can be employed to find out information, find a missing person, follow sb, etc. 私人侦探

ˌprivate 'enterprise *noun* [U] the economic system in which industry or business is owned by independent companies or private people and is not controlled by the government 私营企业；民营企业 ➲ COMPARE FREE ENTERPRISE

ˌprivate 'equity *noun* [U] (*finance* 财) investment made in a company, usually a small one, whose shares are not bought and sold by the public （通常指小公司的）私募股权，私人权益资本，私人股权投资

pri·vat·eer /ˌpraɪvəˈtɪə(r); *NAmE* -ˈtɪr/ *noun* a ship used in the past for attacking and stealing from other ships 武装民船，私掠船（旧时用以攻击和劫掠其他船只）

ˌprivate 'law *noun* [U] (*law* 律) the part of the law that concerns individual people and their property 私法（涉及个人权益、财产等）

ˌprivate 'member *noun* (in the British political system) a member of parliament who is not a minister in the government 普通议员（英国议会中不担任政府部长职位的议员）

ˌprivate 'member's bill *noun* (in the British political system) a law that is suggested by a member of parliament who is not a minister in the government and that is not part of the government's plans （英国政体）普通议员提案

ˌprivate 'parts (*also informal* **pri·vates**) *noun* [pl.] a polite way of referring to the sexual organs without saying their names 私处

ˌprivate 'patient *noun* (in Britain) a person who is treated by a doctor outside the National Health Service and who pays for their treatment 自费病人（不受英国国民医疗服务体系补助者）

ˌprivate 'practice *noun* **1** [U] (of a profession 职业) the fact of working on your own or in a small independent company rather than as an employee of the government or a large company 私人开业：*Most solicitors in England and Wales are **in private practice**.* 英格兰和威尔士的大多数律师都是私人执业者。 **2** [U, C] (in Britain) the fact of providing medical care outside the National Health Service, which people must pay for; a place providing this care 私人医生开业，私营医疗院所（不属于英国国民医疗服务体系）

ˌprivate 'school (*also* **indeˌpendent 'school**) *noun* a school that receives no money from the government and where the education of the students is paid for by their parents 私立学校 ➲ COMPARE PUBLIC SCHOOL, STATE SCHOOL

ˌprivate 'secretary *noun* **1** a secretary whose job is to deal with the more important and personal affairs of a business person 私人秘书 **2** a CIVIL SERVANT who acts as an assistant to a senior government official 政府高级官员的助理

the ˌprivate 'sector *noun* [sing.] the part of the economy of a country that is not under the direct control of the government （国家经济的）私营企业 ➲ COLLOCATIONS AT ECONOMY ➲ COMPARE PUBLIC SECTOR, THIRD SECTOR

ˌprivate 'soldier *noun* a soldier of the lowest rank 列兵；二等兵

ˌprivate 'view (*also* **ˌprivate 'viewing**) *noun* an occasion when a few people are invited to look at an exhibition of paintings before it is open to the public （局限于少数参观者的）画作预展

pri·va·tion /praɪˈveɪʃn/ *noun* [C, usually pl., U] (*formal*) a lack of the basic things that people need for living 贫困；匮乏；艰难 SYN **hardship**：*the privations of poverty* 艰难困苦 ◇ *They endured years of suffering and privation.* 他们饱受多年的煎熬与贫困。

pri·vat·ize (*BrE also* **-ise**) /ˈpraɪvətaɪz/ *verb* ~ **sth** to sell a business or an industry so that it is no longer owned by the government 使私有化；将…私营化 SYN **denationalize** OPP **nationalize** ▸ **pri·vat·iza·tion, -isa·tion** /ˌpraɪvətaɪˈzeɪʃn; *NAmE* -təˈz-/ *noun* [U]：*There were fears that privatization would lead to job losses.* 人们担心私有化会导致失业。

privet /ˈprɪvɪt/ *noun* [U] a bush with small dark green leaves that remain on the bush and stay green all year, often used for garden HEDGES 女贞（常绿灌木，常用作花园绿篱）：*a privet hedge* 女贞树篱

priv·il·ege /ˈprɪvəlɪdʒ/ *noun, verb*

■ *noun* **1** [C] a special right or advantage that a particular person or group of people has 特殊利益；优惠待遇：*Education should be a universal right and not a privilege.* 教育应当是全民共有的而非少数人独享的权利。◇ *You can enjoy all the benefits and privileges of club membership.* 你可以享受俱乐部成员的一切福利和优惠。 **2** [U] (*disapproving*) the rights and advantages that rich and powerful people in a society have （有钱有势者的）特权，特殊待遇：*As a member of the nobility, his life had been one of wealth and privilege.* 身为贵族中的一员，他过着有钱有势的生活。 **3** [sing.] something that you are proud and lucky to have the opportunity to do 荣幸；荣耀；光荣 SYN **honour**：*I hope to have the privilege of working with them again.* 但愿有幸与他们再度合作。◇ *It was a great privilege to hear her sing.* 听她唱歌真是三生有幸。 ➲ SYNONYMS AT PLEASURE **4** [C, U] (*specialist*) a special right to do or say things without being punished 免责特权：*parliamentary privilege* (= the special right of members of parliament to say particular things without risking legal action) 议会言论免责权

■ *verb* ~ **sb/sth** (*formal*) to give sb/sth special rights or advantages that others do not have 给予特权；特别优待 SYN **favour**：*education policies that privilege the children of wealthy parents* 特别优遇富家子弟的教育政策

priv·il·eged /ˈprɪvəlɪdʒd/ *adj.* **1** (*sometimes disapproving*) having special rights or advantages that most people do not have 有特权的；受特别优待的：*Those in authority were in a privileged position.* 过去，当权者自有特权。◇ *She comes from a privileged background.* 她出身特权阶层。◇ *In those days, only **a privileged few** had the vote.* 在那个时代，只有少数特殊的人才享有选举权。 **2** [not before noun] having an opportunity to do sth that makes you feel proud 荣幸；幸运 SYN **honoured**：*We are privileged to welcome you as our speaker this evening.* 我们荣幸地欢迎您今晚来讲演。 **3** (*law* 律) (of information 信息) known only to a few people and legally protected so that it does not have to be made public 特许保密的 SYN **confidential**

privy /ˈprɪvi/ *adj., noun*

■ *adj.* (*formal*) ~ **to sth** allowed to know about sth secret 准许知情；可参与秘事：*She was not privy to any information contained in the letters.* 她未获准接触那些信的内容。

■ *noun* (*pl.* **-ies**) (*old-fashioned*) a toilet, especially an outdoor one （户外）厕所，茅房

the ˌPrivy ˈCouncil *noun* [sing.+sing./pl. v.] (in Britain) a group of people who advise the king or queen on political affairs （英国）枢密院 ▸ **ˌPrivy ˈCouncillor** *noun*

the ˌprivy ˈpurse *noun* [sing.] (in Britain) an amount of money that the government gives to the king or queen to pay his or her private expenses plus some official expenses （由英国政府拨的）女王私用金，国王私用金

prize 🔑 /praɪz/ *noun, adj., verb*

■ *noun* **1** 🔑 an award that is given to a person who wins a competition, race, etc. or who does very good work 奖；奖赏；奖励；奖品；奖金：*She was awarded the Nobel Peace Prize.* 她获颁诺贝尔和平奖。◇ *He **won first prize** in the woodwind section.* 他获得木管乐器组一等奖。◇ *There are **no prizes for guessing** (= it is very easy to guess) who she was with.* 一下子就能猜出她和谁在一起了。◇ *I won £500 in **prize money**.* 我获得了 500 英镑的奖金。◇ *Win a car in our grand **prize draw**!* 参加我们的大抽奖，赢取一辆汽车！ ➲ SEE ALSO CONSOLATION PRIZE ➲ **WORDFINDER NOTE** AT COMPETITION **2** something very important or valuable that is difficult to achieve or obtain 难能可贵的事物；难以争取的重要事物：*World peace is the greatest prize of all.* 世界和平是最可贵的。

■ *adj.* [only before noun] **1** (especially of an animal, a flower or a vegetable 尤指动物、花或蔬菜) good enough to win a prize in a competition 好得足以得奖的；应获奖的：*prize cattle* 能获奖的牛 **2** being a very good example of its kind 优秀的；典范性的；出类拔萃的：*a prize student* 模范学生 ◇ *He's a **prize specimen** of the human race!* 他是人中楷模！◇ (*informal*) *She's a **prize idiot*** (= very silly). 她是十足的蠢猪。

■ *verb* **1** [usually passive] to value sth highly 珍视；高度重视 SYN **treasure**：~ **sth** *an era when honesty was prized above all other virtues* 尊诚实为美德之首的时代 ◇ ~ **sth for sth** *Oil of cedarwood is **highly prized** for its use in perfumery.* 雪松油可用于制香水，因此十分珍贵。 **2** (*NAmE*) = PRISE

prized /praɪzd/ *adj.* [only before noun] very valuable to sb 珍贵的；宝贵的：*I lost some of my most **prized possessions** in the fire.* 大火吞噬了我的一些最珍贵的物品。

prize·fight /ˈpraɪzfaɪt/ *noun* a BOXING competition that is fought for money 职业拳击赛 ▸ **prize·fight·er** *noun* **prize·fight·ing** *noun* [U]

ˈprize-giving *noun* (*BrE*) a ceremony at which prizes are given to people who have done very good work 颁奖仪式；颁奖典礼

prize·win·ner /ˈpraɪzwɪnə(r)/ *noun* a person who has won a prize 获奖者；优胜者 ▸ **prize·win·ning** *adj.* [only before noun]：*a prizewinning story* 获奖故事

pro /prəʊ; *NAmE* proʊ/ *noun, adj., prep.*

■ *noun* (*pl.* **pros**) (*informal*) a person who works as a professional, especially in a sport 从事某职业的人；职业运动员；职业选手；老手：*a golf pro* 职业高尔夫球选手 ◇ *He handled the situation like an **old pro*** (= sb who has a lot of experience). 他像行家一般处理了这一局面。

IDM **the ˌpros and ˈcons** the advantages and disadvantages of sth 事物的利与弊；支持与反对：*We weighed up the pros and cons.* 我们权衡了利弊得失。

■ *adj.* (*especially NAmE*) (in sport 体育运动) professional 职业的；专业的：*a pro wrestler* 职业摔跤手 ◇ *pro football* 职业足球 ◇ *a young boxer who's just **turned pro*** 刚转为职业选手的年轻拳击手

■ *prep.* (*informal*) if sb is **pro** sb/sth, they are in favour of or support that person or thing 赞成；支持：*He has always been pro the environment.* 他一向支持环境保护。 ➲ COMPARE ANTI

pro- /prəʊ; *NAmE* proʊ/ *prefix* (in adjectives 构成形容词) in favour of; supporting 拥护；支持；亲：*pro-democracy* 拥护民主 ➲ COMPARE ANTI- ➲ **MORE LIKE THIS** 6, page R25

pro·active /ˌprəʊˈæktɪv; *NAmE* ˌproʊ-/ *adj.* (of a person or policy 人或政策) controlling a situation by making things happen rather than waiting for things to happen and then reacting to them 积极主动的；主动出击的；先发制人的 ➲ COMPARE REACTIVE (1) ▸ **pro·active·ly** *adv.*

ˌpro-ˈam *adj.* [only before noun] (in sport 体育运动) involving both professional and AMATEUR players 包括职业和业余选手的：*a pro-am golf tournament* 包括职业和业余选手参加的高尔夫球锦标赛 ▸ **ˌpro-ˈam** *noun*：*to play in a pro-am* 参加公开赛

prob·abil·ist·ic /ˌprɒbəbɪˈlɪstɪk; *NAmE* ˌprɑːb-/ *adj.* [usually before noun] (*specialist*) (of methods, arguments, etc. 方法、论点等) based on the idea that, as we cannot be certain about things, we can base our beliefs or actions on what is probable 基于概率的；或然的；盖然性的

prob·abil·ity /ˌprɒbəˈbɪləti; *NAmE* ˌprɑːb-/ *noun* (*pl.* **-ies**) **1** [U, C] how likely sth is to happen 可能性；或然性 SYN **likelihood**：*The probability is that prices will rise rapidly.* 物价有可能会迅速上升。◇ *There seemed to be a high probability of success.* 成功的几率似乎很高。 **2** [C] a thing that is likely to happen 很可能发生的事：*A fall in interest rates is a **strong probability** in the present economic climate.* 在目前的经济形势下，降低利率大有可能。◇ *It now seems a probability rather than just a possibility.* 这件事似乎十拿九稳，而不是仅有可能。 **3** [C, U] (*mathematics* 数) a RATIO showing the chances that a particular thing will happen 概率；几率；或然率：*There is a 60% probability that the population will be infected with the disease.* 民众感染这种疾病的概率为 60%。

IDM **in ˌall probaˈbility...** it is very likely that 很可能：*In all probability he failed to understand the consequences of his actions.* 他很可能未了解到行动的后果。 ➲ MORE AT BALANCE *n.*

prob·able 🔑 /ˈprɒbəbl; *NAmE* ˈprɑːb-/ *adj., noun*

■ *adj.* 🔑 likely to happen, to exist or to be true 很可能发生（或存在等）的：*the probable cause/explanation/outcome* 可能的原因 / 解释 / 结果 ◇ ***highly/quite/most probable*** 极其 / 相当 / 最可能的 ◇ ***It is probable that** the disease has a genetic element.* 这种疾病很可能有遗传因素。 ➲ COMPARE IMPROBABLE

■ *noun* ~ **(for sth)** (*especially BrE*) a person or an animal that is likely to win a race or to be chosen for a team 可能获胜的人（或动物）；可能入选者

prob·ably 🔑 /ˈprɒbəbli; *NAmE* ˈprɑːb-/ *adv.* used to say that sth is likely to happen or to be true 几乎肯定；很可能；大概：*You're probably right.* 你很可能是对的。◇ *It'll probably be OK.* 这大概没有问题。◇ *It was the best known and probably the most popular of her songs.* 这是她最著名的、大概也是她最受欢迎的歌曲。 ◇ *'Is he going to be there?' 'Probably.'* "他会去那里吗？" "大概吧。" ◇ *'Do we need the car?' '**Probably not.**'* "我们需要开车吗？" "大概不需要吧。" ◇ *As you probably know, I'm going to be changing jobs soon.* 你或许知道，我不久就要换工作了。◇ *The two cases are **most probably** connected.* 这两桩案件极有可能互相关联。 ➲ **LANGUAGE BANK** AT PERHAPS

pro·bate /ˈprəʊbeɪt; *NAmE* ˈproʊ-/ *noun, verb*

■ *noun* [U] (*law* 律) the official process of proving that a WILL (= a legal document that says what is to happen to a person's property when they die) is valid 遗嘱认证；遗嘱检验

■ *verb* ~ **sth** (*NAmE, law* 律) to prove that a WILL is valid 核实（或检验）遗嘱

pro·ba·tion /prəˈbeɪʃn; *NAmE* proʊ-/ *noun* [U] **1** (*law* 律) a system that allows a person who has committed a crime not to go to prison if they behave well and if they see an official (called a PROBATION OFFICER) regularly for a fixed period of time 缓刑制；缓刑：*The prisoner*

P

was put **on probation**. 犯人已获缓刑。◇ *He was given two years' probation.* 他被判缓刑两年。➲ WORDFINDER NOTE AT PRISON **2** a time of training and testing when you start a new job to see if you are suitable for the work 试用期；见习期；考察期：*a period of probation* 试用期 ➲ WORDFINDER NOTE AT TRAINING **3** (*NAmE*) a fixed period of time during which a student who has behaved badly or not worked hard must improve their work or their behaviour 试读，试读期（为表现不理想的学生而设）▶ **pro·ba·tion·ary** /prəˈbeɪʃnri; *NAmE* proʊˈbeɪʃəneri/ *adj.*：*a probationary period* 试用期 ◇ *young probationary teachers* 年轻的见习教师

pro·ba·tion·er /prəˈbeɪʃnə(r); *NAmE* proʊ-/ *noun* **1** a person who is new in a job and is being watched to see if they are suitable 见习生；试用员工 **2** a person who is seeing a PROBATION OFFICER because of having committed a crime 缓刑犯

proˈbation officer *noun* a person whose job is to check on people who are on probation and help them 缓刑监督官

probe /prəʊb; *NAmE* proʊb/ *verb, noun*

■ *verb* **1** [I, T] to ask questions in order to find out secret or hidden information about sb/sth 盘问；追问；探究 SYN **investigate**: ~ (into sth) *He didn't like the media probing into his past.* 他不喜欢媒体追问他的过去。◇ ~ **sth** *a TV programme that probed government scandals in the 1990s* 追查 20 世纪 90 年代政府丑闻的电视节目 ◇ + **speech** *'Then what happened?' he probed.* "后来发生了什么事？"他追问道。**2** [T] ~ **sth** to touch, examine or look for sth, especially with a long thin instrument（用细长工具）探查，查看：*The doctor probed the wound for signs of infection.* 医生检查伤口是否有感染的迹象。◇ *Searchlights probed the night sky.* 探照灯扫视着夜空。

■ *noun* **1** ~ (into sth) (used especially in newspapers 尤用于报章) a thorough and careful investigation of sth 探究；详尽调查：*a police probe into the financial affairs of the company* 警方对这家公司的财务进行的详细调查 **2** (*also* ˈ**space probe**) a SPACECRAFT without people on board which obtains information and sends it back to earth（不载人）空间探测器 **3** (*specialist*) a long thin metal tool used by doctors for examining inside the body（医生用的）探针 **4** (*specialist*) a small device put inside sth and used by scientists to test sth or record information 探测仪；传感器；取样器

prob·ing /ˈprəʊbɪŋ; *NAmE* ˈproʊ-/ *adj.* **1** intended to discover the truth 探查性的；追根究底的：*They asked a lot of **probing questions**.* 他们提了许多盘根问底的问题。**2** examining sb/sth closely 逼视的；仔细观察的：*She looked away from his dark probing eyes.* 她转移目光，避开他那双锐利的黑眼睛。▶ **prob·ing** *noun* [U, C]：*the journalist's unwanted probings* 记者不受欢迎的追问

pro·biot·ic /ˌprəʊbaɪˈɒtɪk; *NAmE* ˌproʊbaɪˈɑːtɪk/ *adj.* [only before noun] encouraging the growth of bacteria that have a good effect on the body 促进有益菌生长的；益生菌的；益生素的：*probiotic products/yogurt/cheese* 益生菌产品 / 酸奶 / 乳酪

prob·ity /ˈprəʊbəti; *NAmE* ˈproʊ-/ *noun* [U] (*formal*) the quality of being completely honest 正直；诚实：*financial probity* 在钱财方面的诚实

prob·lem 🔑 /ˈprɒbləm; *NAmE* ˈprɑːb-/ *noun, adj.*

■ *noun* **1** 🔑 a thing that is difficult to deal with or to understand 棘手的问题；难题；困难：***big/major/serious problems*** 重大 / 主要 / 严重的问题 ◇ ***health/family, etc. problems*** 健康、家庭等问题 ◇ ***financial/practical/technical problems*** 财政 / 实际 / 技术困难 ◇ *to **address/tackle/solve a problem*** 处理 / 应付 / 解决难题 ◇ (*especially NAmE*) *to **fix a problem*** 解决问题 ◇ *the problem of drug abuse* 吸毒的问题 ◇ *If he chooses Mary it's bound to **cause problems**.* 如果他选玛丽，肯定要招来后患。◇ *Let me know if you have any problems.* 你若有困难就告诉我。◇ *Most students **face the problem** of funding themselves while they are studying.* 大多数学生在求学期间都会面临经济来源的问题。◇ *The problem first arose in 2008.* 这个问题首次出现在 2008 年。◇ *Unemployment is a very real problem for graduates now.* 现在，失业对大学毕业生是个实质问题。◇ *It's a nice table! **The only problem is (that)** it's too big for our room.* 这张桌子的确不错！唯一的问题是放在我们的屋子里太大了。◇ *Stop worrying about their marriage—it isn't your problem.* 别替他们的婚事操心了，那不关你的事。◇ *There's no history of heart problems* (= disease connected with the heart) *in our family.* 我们家族里没有心脏病史。◇ *the magazine's **problem page*** (= containing letters about readers' problems and advice about how to solve them) 这本杂志的解疑专栏 **2** a question that can be answered by using logical thought or mathematics 逻辑题；数学题：*mathematical problems* 数学题 ◇ *to find the answer to the problem* 找出问题的答案 ➲ WORDFINDER NOTE AT MATHS

IDM **have a ˈproblem with sth** to disagree with or object to sth 对…有异议；不同意；反对：*I have no problem with you working at home tomorrow.* 你明天在家里工作，我没有意见。◇ (*informal*) *We are going to do this my way. **Do you have a problem with that?*** (= showing that you are impatient with the person that you are speaking to) 这件事将按照我的方法来做，你有什么意见吗？**no ˈproblem** (*informal*) **1** 🔑 (*also* **not a ˈproblem**) used to show that you are happy to help sb or that sth will be easy to do（表示乐于相助或事情容易做）没问题：*'Can I pay by credit card?' 'Yes, no problem.'* "我能用信用卡付款吗？" "行，没问题。" **2** 🔑 used after sb has thanked you or said they are sorry for sth（回答别人的道谢或道歉）没什么，不客气，没关系：*'Thanks for the ride.' 'No problem.'* "谢谢你载我一程。" "不客气。" **ˌit's/ˌthat's not ˈmy problem** (*informal*) used to show that you do not care about sb else's difficulties 那不关我的事 **that's ˈher/ˈhis/ˈtheir/ˈyour problem** (*informal*) used to show that you think a person should deal with their own difficulties 那是她 / 他 / 他们 / 你自己的问题 **what's your problem?** (*informal*) used to show that you think sb is being unreasonable（认为对方不讲道理时说）你怎么了，你犯啥病啊：*What's your problem?—I only asked if you could help me for ten minutes.* 你有毛病啊？我只是问问你能不能抽十分钟帮个忙而已。

■ *adj.* [only before noun] causing problems for other people 找麻烦的；成问题的；惹乱子的：*She was a **problem child**, always in trouble with the police.* 她曾是个问题儿童，总是给警察找麻烦。

prob·lem·at·ic /ˌprɒbləˈmætɪk; *NAmE* ˌprɑːb-/ (*also less frequent* **prob·lem·at·ical** /-ɪkl/) *adj.* difficult to deal with or to understand; full of problems; not certain to be successful 造成困难的；存在问题的 OPP **unproblematic**

ˈproblem-solving *noun* [U] the act of finding ways of dealing with problems 寻求答案；解决问题

pro bono /ˌprəʊ ˈbəʊnəʊ; *NAmE* ˌproʊ ˈboʊnoʊ/ *adj.* [only before noun] (*from Latin*) (especially of legal work 尤指法律工作) done without asking for payment 无偿服务的；公益性的 ▶ **pro bono** *adv.*

pro·bos·cis /prəˈbɒsɪs; *NAmE* -ˈbɑːs-; *also* -ˈbɑːskɪs/ *noun* (*pl.* **pro·bos·ces** /-siːz/, **pro·bos·cises**) (*specialist*) **1** the long FLEXIBLE nose of some animals, such as an ELEPHANT（某些动物的）长鼻子；象鼻 **2** the long thin mouth, like a tube, of some insects（某些昆虫的）喙，吻，管状长嘴 **3** (*humorous*) a large human nose（人的）大鼻子

probs /prɒbz; *NAmE* prɑːbz/ *noun* [pl.]

IDM **no ˈprobs** (*informal*) used to mean 'there is no problem' 没问题；一定：*I can let you have it by next week. No probs.* 我下周就会给你。没问题。

pro·caine /ˈprəʊkeɪn; *NAmE* ˈproʊ-/ (*also* **novo·caine**) *noun* [U] (*medical* 医) a substance used to stop sb from feeling pain in a particular part of their body, especially by a dentist 普鲁卡因（牙医等用的局部麻醉药）

pro·ced·ure 🔑 AW /prəˈsiːdʒə(r)/ *noun* **1** 🔑 [C, U] ~ (**for sth**) a way of doing sth, especially the usual or correct way（正常）程序，手续，步骤：*maintenance procedures* 维修程序 ◇ ***emergency/safety/disciplinary***

procedures 紧急状况 / 安全事务 / 纪律问题的处理程序 ◇ *to follow **normal/standard/accepted procedure*** 遵循正常的 / 标准的 / 认可的步骤 ◇ *Making a complaint is quite a simple procedure.* 申诉的手续相当简单。 **2** [U] the official or formal order or way of doing sth, especially in business, law or politics （商业、法律或政治上的）程序: ***court/legal/parliamentary procedure*** 法庭 / 司法 / 议会程序 **3** [C] (*medical* 医) a medical operation 手术: *to perform a routine surgical procedure* 做常规的外科手术 ➲ WORDFINDER NOTE AT OPERATION ▶ **pro·ced·ural** AW /prəˈsiːdʒərəl/ *adj.* (*formal*): *procedural rules* 程序性规则

pro·ceed 🔑 AW /prəˈsiːd; *NAmE* proʊ-/ *verb* **1** 🔑 [I] ~ (**with sth**) to continue doing sth that has already been started; to continue being done 继续做（或从事、进行）: *We're not sure whether we still want to proceed with the sale.* 我们不确定是否还要继续减价促销。 ◇ *Work is proceeding slowly.* 工作进展缓慢。 **2** [I] **~ to do sth** to do sth next, after having done sth else first 接着做；继而做 SYN **go on**: *He outlined his plans and then proceeded to explain them in more detail.* 他简单介绍了他的计划，接着又作了更详细的解释。 ◇ (*humorous*) *Having said she wasn't hungry, she then proceeded to order a three-course meal.* 她先说不饿，接着却要了一份三道菜的大餐。 **3** [I] **+ adv./prep.** (*formal*) to move or travel in a particular direction 行进；前往: *The marchers proceeded slowly along the street.* 游行者沿着街道缓缓行进。 ◇ *Passengers for Rome should proceed to Gate 32 for boarding.* 前往罗马的旅客，请到 32 号登机口登机。

PHR V **proˈceed against sb** (*law* 律) to start a court case against sb 起诉（某人） **proˈceed from sth** (*formal*) to be caused by or be the result of sth 由…引起；起因于；是…的结果

pro·ceed·ing AW /prəˈsiːdɪŋ/ *noun* (*formal*) **1** [C, usually pl.] ~ (**against sb**) (**for sth**) the process of using a court to settle a disagreement or to deal with a complaint 诉讼；诉讼程序: ***bankruptcy/divorce/extradition, etc. proceedings*** 破产、离婚、引渡等诉讼 ◇ *to bring **legal proceedings** against sb* 向某人提起法律诉讼 **2 proceedings** [pl.] an event or a series of actions 事件；过程；一系列行动: *The Mayor will open the proceedings at the City Hall tomorrow.* 明天市长将在市政厅宣布开幕。 ◇ *We watched the proceedings from the balcony.* 我们从阳台上观看仪式。 **3 proceedings** [pl.] the official written report of a meeting, etc. （会议等的）正式记录；公报

pro·ceeds AW /ˈprəʊsiːdz; *NAmE* ˈproʊ-/ *noun* [pl.] ~ (**of/from sth**) the money that you receive when you sell sth or organize a performance, etc.; profits （售物或演出等的）收入，收益，进款: *She sold her car and bought a piano with the proceeds.* 她卖掉了汽车，然后用这笔收入买了一架钢琴。 ◇ *The proceeds of the concert will go to charity.* 这次音乐会的收入将捐给慈善机构。

pro·cess[1] 🔑 AW /ˈprəʊses; *NAmE* ˈprɑːses; ˈproʊ-/ *noun, verb* ➲ SEE ALSO PROCESS[2]

■ ***noun*** **1** 🔑 a series of things that are done in order to achieve a particular result （为达到某一目标的）过程；进程: *a consultation process* 磋商过程 ◇ *to begin the difficult process of reforming the education system* 开始改革教育制度的艰难历程 ◇ *I'm afraid getting things changed will be a slow process.* 做任何改革恐怕都会是个缓慢的过程。 ◇ *mental processes* 思维过程 ◇ *Coming off the drug was a long and painful* (= difficult) *process for him.* 戒毒对他是个漫长、痛苦的过程。 ◇ *Find which food you are allergic to by **a process of elimination**.* 用排除法找出你对哪种食物过敏。 ◇ *We're **in the process of** selling our house.* 我们正在出售自家的住宅。 ◇ *I was moving some furniture and I twisted my ankle **in the process*** (= while I was doing it). 我在搬动家具时把脚给崴了。 ➲ SEE ALSO PEACE PROCESS **2** 🔑 a series of things that happen, especially ones that result in natural changes （事物发展，尤指自然变化的）过程，步骤，流程: *the ageing process* 老化过程 ◇ *It's a normal part of the **learning process**.* 那是学习过程中的正常现象。 **3** 🔑 a method of doing or making sth, especially one that is used in industry 做事方法；工艺流程；工序: *manufacturing processes* 制造方法 ➲ WORDFINDER NOTE AT FACTORY

■ ***verb*** **1** 🔑 **~ sth** to treat raw material, food, etc. in order to change it, preserve it, etc. 加工；处理: *Most of the food we buy is processed in some way.* 我们买的大部分食品都用某种方法加工过。 ◇ *processed cheese* 加工好的干酪 **2 ~ sth** to deal officially with a document, request, etc. 审阅，审核，处理（文件、请求等）: *It will take a week for your application to be processed.* 审核你的申请需要一周时间。 **3 ~ sth** (*computing* 计) to perform a series of operations on data in a computer 数据处理 ▶ **pro·cess·ing** AW *noun* [U]: *the food processing industry* 食品加工业 ◇ *a sewage processing plant* 污水处理厂 ➲ SEE ALSO DATA PROCESSING, WORD PROCESSING

▼ LANGUAGE BANK 用语库

process

Describing a process 描述过程

- *This diagram **illustrates the process of** paper-making./ This diagram **shows how** paper is made.* 这个图说明了造纸的过程。
- ***First/First of all**, logs are delivered to a paper mill, where the bark is removed and the wood is cut into small chips.* 首先，原木被运送到造纸厂，在那里去掉树皮，然后被切成木片。
- ***Next/Second**, the wood chips are pulped, either using chemicals or in a pulping machine.* 接下来，用化学品或磨浆机把木片化成浆。
- *Pulping breaks down the internal structure of the wood and **enables/allows** the natural oils **to be removed**.* 制浆过程使木材的内部结构分解，从而去除木材里的天然油。
- ***Once/After** the wood has been pulped, the pulp is bleached **in order to** remove impurities./...is bleached **so that** impurities **can** be removed.* 木材制成浆后，将其漂白以去除杂质。
- ***The next stage is to** feed the pulp into the paper machine, where it is mixed with water **and then** poured onto a wire conveyor belt.* 下一步便是将纸浆送入制纸机，与水混合后再倒入金属传送带。
- ***As** the pulp travels along the conveyor belt, the water drains away. **This causes** the solid material **to** sink to the bottom, forming a layer of paper.* 当纸浆沿传送带传送时，水分蒸发，使得固体物质沉到底部，形成一层纸。
- ***At this point** the new paper is still wet, **so** it is passed between large heated rollers, which press out the remaining water and **simultaneously** dry the paper/... dry the paper **at the same time**.* 这时，新出的纸仍然是湿的，故让其经过几个巨大的热滚筒，挤压脱水并同时烘干。
- ***The final stage is to** wind the paper onto large rolls./ **Finally**, the paper is wound onto large rolls.* 最后一步是将纸卷在巨大的卷轴上。

➲ NOTE AT FIRSTLY, LASTLY

➲ LANGUAGE BANK AT CONCLUSION, FIRST

pro·cess[2] /prəˈses/ *verb* [I] **+ adv./prep.** (*formal*) to walk or move along slowly, in or as if in, a procession 列队行进；缓缓前进 ➲ SEE ALSO PROCESS[1] *v.*

pro·ces·sion /prəˈseʃn/ *noun* **1** [C, U] a line of people or vehicles that move along slowly, especially as part of a ceremony; the act of moving in this way （人或车辆的）队列，行列；列队行进；游行: *a funeral procession* 送葬的队列 ◇ *a torchlight procession* 火炬游行队伍 ◇ *The procession made its way down the hill.* 队伍走下山了。 ◇ *Groups of unemployed people from all over the country marched **in procession** to the capital.* 来自全国的失业群众列队向首都进发。 **2** [C] a number of people who come one after the other （一个接着一个而来的）一队人，一列人: *A procession of waiters appeared bearing trays of food.* 一长列服务生端着一盘一盘饭菜出现了。

P

pro·ces·sion·al /prəˈseʃənl/ *adj.* [only before noun] used in a procession, especially a religious one; connected with a procession 供（宗教）游行用的；列队行进的

pro·ces·sor /ˈprəʊsesə(r); *NAmE* ˈprɑː-; ˈproʊ-/ *noun* **1** a machine or person that processes things 加工机（或工人） **2** (*computing* 计) a part of a computer that controls all the other parts of the system 处理器；处理机 SYN **central processing unit** ➲ SEE ALSO FOOD PROCESSOR, MICROPROCESSOR, WORD PROCESSOR

ˌpro-ˈchoice *adj.* believing that a pregnant woman should be able to choose to have an ABORTION if she wants 提倡堕胎合法的；主张自由选择人工流产的 ➲ COMPARE ANTI-CHOICE, PRO-LIFE

pro·claim /prəˈkleɪm/ *verb* (*formal*) **1** to publicly and officially tell people about sth important 宣布；宣告；声明 SYN **declare**: **~ sth** *The president proclaimed a state of emergency.* 总统宣布了紧急状态。◇ **~ that...** *The charter proclaimed that all states would have their own government.* 宪章规定，所有各州皆可建立各自的政府。◇ **~ sb/sth/yourself + noun** *He proclaimed himself emperor.* 他自封为皇帝。◇ **~ sb/sth/yourself to be/have sth** *Steve checked the battery and proclaimed it to be dead.* 史蒂夫检查了电池后宣布它没电了。◇ **~ how, what, etc....** *The senator proclaimed how shocked he was at the news.* 那名参议员声称他听到这消息时是多么的震惊。◇ **+ speech** *'We will succeed,' she proclaimed.* "我们会成功的。"她宣称。 **2** to show sth clearly; to be a sign of sth 明确显示；成为标志；表明：**~ sth** *This building, more than any other, proclaims the character of the town.* 这座建筑比任何其他建筑都能代表本城的特色。◇ **~ sb/sth + noun** *His accent proclaimed him a Scot.* 他的口音表明他是苏格兰人。◇ **~ sb/sth to be/have sth** *His accent proclaimed him to be a Scot.* 他的口音表明他是苏格兰人。

P

proc·lama·tion /ˌprɒkləˈmeɪʃn; *NAmE* ˌprɑːk-/ *noun* [C, U] an official statement about sth important that is made to the public; the act of making an official statement 宣言；公告；声明

pro·cliv·ity /prəˈklɪvəti/ *noun* (*pl.* **-ies**) **~ (for sth/for doing sth)** (*formal*) a natural tendency to do sth or to feel sth, often sth bad （常指对坏事的）倾向，癖好 SYN **propensity**: *his sexual/criminal proclivities* 他的性倾向 / 犯罪倾向 ◇ *the government's proclivity for spending money* 政府花钱的倾向

pro·cras·tin·ate /prəʊˈkræstɪneɪt; *NAmE* proʊ-/ *verb* [I] (*formal, disapproving*) to delay doing sth that you should do, usually because you do not want to do it 拖延；耽搁 ▶ **pro·cras·tin·ation** /prəʊˌkræstɪˈneɪʃn; *NAmE* proʊ-/ *noun* [U]

pro·cre·ate /ˈprəʊkrieɪt; *NAmE* ˈproʊ-/ *verb* [I, T] **~ (sth)** (*formal*) to produce children or baby animals 繁殖；生育；生殖 SYN **reproduce** ▶ **pro·cre·ation** /ˌprəʊkriˈeɪʃn; *NAmE* ˌproʊ-/ *noun* [U]: *They believe that sex is primarily for procreation.* 他们认为，性交主要是为了繁衍。

Pro·crus·tean /ˌprəʊˈkrʌstiən; *NAmE* ˌproʊ-/ *adj.* (of a system, a set of rules, etc. 体系或系列规章等) treating all people or things as if they are the same, without considering individual differences and in a way that is too strict and unreasonable 强求一致的；一刀切的 ➲ MORE LIKE THIS 16, page R27 ORIGIN From the Greek story of **Procrustes**, a robber who forced people to lie on a bed and made them fit it by stretching their bodies or cutting off part of their legs. 源自有关强盗普洛克路斯忒斯 (Procrustes) 的希腊神话，他迫使人们躺在一张床上并通过拽拉身体或截腿使其适合床的长度。

proc·tor /ˈprɒktə(r); *NAmE* ˈprɑːk-/ (*NAmE*) (*BrE* **in·vigi·la·tor**) *noun* a person who watches people while they are taking an exam to make sure that they have everything they need, that they keep to the rules, etc. 监考人员 ▶ **proc·tor** (*NAmE*) (*BrE* **in·vigi·late**) *verb* [T, I] **~ (sth)**

proc·ur·ator fis·cal /ˌprɒkjureɪtə ˈfɪskl; *NAmE* ˌprɑːkjəreɪtər/ *noun* (*pl.* **proc·ur·ators fis·cal**) (in Scotland) a public official whose job is to decide whether people who are suspected of a crime should be brought to trial （苏格兰）地方检察官

pro·cure /prəˈkjʊə(r); *NAmE* -ˈkjʊr/ *verb* **1** [T] (*formal*) to obtain sth, especially with difficulty （设法）获得，取得，得到：**~ sth (for sb/sth)** *She managed to procure a ticket for the concert.* 她好不容易弄到一张音乐会入场券。◇ *They procured a copy of the report for us.* 他们为我们弄到了一份报告。◇ **~ sb sth** *They procured us a copy of the report.* 他们给我们弄到了一份报告。 **2** [T, I] **~ (sb)** to provide a PROSTITUTE for sb 诱使（妇女）卖淫：*He was accused of procuring under-age girls.* 他被控唆使未成年女性卖淫。

pro·cure·ment /prəˈkjʊəmənt; *NAmE* -ˈkjʊrm-/ *noun* [U] (*formal*) the process of obtaining supplies of sth, especially for a government or an organization （尤指为政府或机构）采购，购买

prod /prɒd; *NAmE* prɑːd/ *verb, noun*
■ *verb* (**-dd-**) **1** [T, I] to push sb/sth with your finger or with a pointed object 戳；杵；捅 SYN **poke**: **~ sb/sth (+ adv./prep.)** *She prodded him in the ribs to wake him up.* 她用手指杵他的肋部把他叫醒。◇ **~ at sb/sth** *He prodded at his breakfast with a fork.* 他拿叉子戳弄着早餐。 **2** [T] **~ sb (into sth/into doing sth)** to try to make sb do sth, especially when they are unwilling 催促；督促；鼓动：*She finally prodded him into action.* 她终于促使他行动起来。➲ MORE LIKE THIS 36, page R29
■ *noun* **1** the act of pushing sb with your finger or with a pointed object 戳；杵；捅 SYN **dig**: *She gave him a sharp prod with her umbrella.* 她用雨伞使劲捅了他一下。 **2** (*informal*) an act of encouraging sb or of reminding sb to do sth 催促；鼓励；提醒：*If they haven't replied by next week, you'll have to call them and* ***give them a prod.*** 如果下周他们还没答复，你就得打电话催催他们。 **3** an instrument like a stick that is used for prodding animals （赶牲畜用的）尖棒，刺棒 **4 Prod** (*also* **Prod·die** /ˈprɒdi; *NAmE* ˈprɑːdi/) (*informal*) an offensive word for a Protestant （贬称）新教徒

prod·ding /ˈprɒdɪŋ; *NAmE* ˈprɑːd-/ *noun* [U] encouragement to do sth 催促；督促；鼓励；激励：*He needed no prodding.* 他不用督促。

prod·igal /ˈprɒdɪgl; *NAmE* ˈprɑːd-/ *adj.* (*formal, disapproving*) too willing to spend money or waste time, energy or materials 浪费的；挥霍的；大手大脚的 SYN **extravagant** ▶ **prod·ig·al·ity** /ˌprɒdɪˈgæləti; *NAmE* ˌprɑːd-/ *noun* [U]
IDM **the/a ˌprodigal (ˈson)** a person who leaves home and wastes their money and time on a life of pleasure, but who later is sorry about this and returns home 回头的浪子；改邪归正的人

pro·di·gious /prəˈdɪdʒəs/ *adj.* [usually before noun] (*formal*) very large or powerful and causing surprise or admiration 巨大的；伟大的 SYN **colossal, enormous**: *a prodigious achievement/memory/talent* 惊人的成就 / 记忆力 / 才华 ◇ *DVDs can store* ***prodigious amounts*** *of information.* * DVD 光盘能够存储大量信息。 ▶ **pro·di·gious·ly** *adv.*: *a prodigiously talented musician* 有惊人天赋的音乐家

prod·igy /ˈprɒdədʒi; *NAmE* ˈprɑːd-/ *noun* (*pl.* **-ies**) a young person who is unusually intelligent or skilful for their age （年轻的）天才，奇才，精英；神童：***a child/an infant prodigy*** 天才儿童；神童 ◇ *a musical prodigy* 音乐奇才

pro·duce 🔑 *verb, noun*

WORD FAMILY
produce *verb*
producer *noun*
production *noun*
productive *adj.* (≠ unproductive)
productively *adv.*
product *noun*
produce *noun*

■ *verb* /prəˈdjuːs; *NAmE* -ˈduːs/
• GOODS 商品 **1** 🔑 **~ sth** to make things to be sold, especially in large quantities 生产；制造 SYN **manufacture**: *a factory that produces microchips* 微芯片制造厂 ➲ SYNONYMS AT MAKE ➲ SEE ALSO MASS-PRODUCE

• **MAKE NATURALLY** 自然生产 **2** 🔑 **~ sth** to grow or make sth as part of a natural process; to have a baby or young animal 生长；出产；繁育： *The region produces over 50% of the country's wheat.* 这个地区出产全国 50% 以上的小麦。◇ *Our cat produced kittens last week.* 我家的猫上周生小猫咪了。◇ *Her duty was to produce an heir to the throne.* 她的任务就是生育王位继承人。

• **CREATE WITH SKILL** 巧妙制作 **3** 🔑 **~ sth** to create sth, especially when skill is needed（运用技巧）制作，造出： *She produced a delicious meal out of a few leftovers.* 她用几样剩菜烹制出美味的一餐。

• **RESULT/EFFECT** 结果；效果 **4** 🔑 **~ sth** to cause a particular result or effect 引起；导致；使产生 SYN **bring about**: *A phone call to the manager produced the result she wanted.* 她给经理打了个电话便如愿以偿。◇ *The drug produces a feeling of excitement.* 这种药能使人产生兴奋的感觉。

• **SHOW/BRING OUT** 展示；出示 **5** **~ sth (from/out of sth)** to show sth or make sth appear from somewhere 出示；展现；使出现： *He produced a letter from his pocket.* 他从口袋里掏出一封信来。◇ *At the meeting the finance director produced the figures for the previous year.* 会上，财务总监出示了前一年的数字。

• **PERSON** 人 **6** **~ sb** if a town, country, etc. **produces** sb with a particular skill or quality, the person comes from that town, country, etc. 栽培；培养： *He is the greatest athlete this country has ever produced.* 他是这个国家培养的最了不起的运动员。

• **MOVIE/PLAY** 电影；戏剧 **7** **~ sth** to be in charge of preparing a film/movie, play, etc. for the public to see 制作，拍摄（电影、戏剧等）；监督： *She produced a TV series about adopted children.* 她拍了一部描写收养儿童的电视系列片。

▪ ***noun*** /ˈprɒdjuːs; *NAmE* ˈprɑːduːs; ˈproʊ-/ [U] things that have been made or grown, especially things connected with farming 产品；（尤指）农产品： *farm produce* 农产品 ◇ *The shop sells only fresh local produce.* 这家商店只售当地的新鲜农产品。◇ *It says on the label 'Produce of France'.* 标签上写着"法国出产"。➲ SYNONYMS AT PRODUCT

pro·du·cer 🔑 /prəˈdjuːsə(r); *NAmE* -ˈduː-/ *noun* **1** 🔑 a person, a company or a country that grows or makes food, goods or materials 生产商；制造商；产地： *French wine producers* 法国葡萄酒酿造商 ◇ *Libya is a major oil producer.* 利比亚是主要石油生产国之一。➲ COMPARE CONSUMER **2** 🔑 a person who is in charge of the practical and financial aspects of making a film/movie or a play（电影的）制片人，监制人；舞台监督： *Hollywood screenwriters, actors and producers* 好莱坞的剧作家、演员和制片人 ➲ COMPARE DIRECTOR (3) **3** a person or company that arranges for sb to make a programme for radio or television, or a record, CD, etc.（广播、电视、唱片等的）制作人，制作公司，监制： *an independent television producer* 独立电视节目制作人

prod·uct 🔑 /ˈprɒdʌkt; *NAmE* ˈprɑːd-/ *noun* **1** 🔑 [C, U] a thing that is grown or produced, usually for sale 产品；制品： ***dairy/meat/pharmaceutical, etc. products*** 乳制品、肉制品、药物产品等 ◇ *investment in* ***product development*** 产品开发投资 ◇ *to* ***launch a new product*** *on to the market* 把新产品推向市场 ◇ (*business* 商) *We need new product to sell* (= a new range of products). 我们需要新产品供销售。➲ COLLOCATIONS AT BUSINESS ➲ SEE ALSO END PRODUCT, GROSS NATIONAL PRODUCT **2** 🔑 [C] a thing produced during a natural, chemical or industrial process（自然、化学或工业过程的）产物，生成物，产品： *the products of the reaction* 反应的生成物 ➲ SEE ALSO BY-PRODUCT (1), WASTE PRODUCT **3** [C] **~ of sth** a person or thing that is the result of sth 产儿；产物；结果： *The child is the product of a broken home.* 这孩子是一个破裂家庭的产儿。 **4** [C, U] a cream, jelly or liquid that you put on your hair or skin to make it look better 美容（或美发）用品（指发乳、发胶、润肤霜、润肤水等）： *This product can be used on wet or dry hair.* 这种美发用品可用在湿发或干发上。 **5** (*mathematics* 数) [C] a quantity obtained by multiplying one number by another 积；乘积： *The product of 21 and 16 is 336.* * 21 和 16 的乘积是 336。

pro·duc·tion 🔑 /prəˈdʌkʃn/ *noun* **1** 🔑 [U] the process of growing or making food, goods or materials, especially large quantities 生产；制造；制作： ***wheat/oil/car, etc. production*** 小麦、石油、汽车等的生产 ◇ *land available for* ***food production*** 可用于食品生产的土地 ◇ *The new model will be* ***in production*** *by the end of the year.* 新型号将于年底投产。◇ *Production of the new aircraft will start next year.* 新飞机的生产将于明年开始。◇ *The car* ***went out of production*** *in 2007.* 这款汽车已于 2007 年停产。◇ *production costs* 生产成本 ◇ *a production process* 生产工序 ➲ SEE ALSO MASS PRODUCTION at MASS-PRODUCE ➲ WORDFINDER NOTE AT FACTORY **2** 🔑 [U] the quantity of goods that is produced 产量： ***a decline/an increase in production*** 产量的下降 / 上升 ◇ *It is important not to let* ***production levels*** *fall.* 重要的是别让产量滑落。 **3** 🔑 [U] the act or process of making sth naturally（自然的）产生，分泌： *drugs to stimulate the body's production of hormones* 刺激身体分泌荷尔蒙的药物 **4** 🔑 [C, U] a film/movie, a play or a broadcast that is prepared for the public; the act of preparing a film or a play, etc.（电影、戏剧或广播节目的）出品，制作： *a new production of 'King Lear'* 新制作的《李尔王》◇ *He wants a career in film production.* 他想从事电影制作。

IDM **on production of sth** (*formal*) when you show sth

▼ **SYNONYMS** 同义词辨析

product

goods • commodity • merchandise • produce

These are all words for things that are produced to be sold. 以上各词均指产品、商品。

product a thing that is produced or grown, usually to be sold 指制造或种植的产品： *to create/develop/launch a new product* 创造 / 开发 / 推出新产品

goods things that are produced to be sold 指商品、货品： *cotton/leather goods* 棉织 / 皮革商品 ◇ *electrical goods* 电器商品

commodity (*economics*) a product or raw material that can be bought and sold, especially between countries 尤指国家间贸易的商品： *rice, flour and other basic commodities* 稻米、面粉和其他基本商品

merchandise [U] goods that are bought or sold; things that you can buy that are connected with or advertise a particular event or organization 指商品、货品、相关商品、指定商品： *official Olympic merchandise* 奥林匹克运动会官方指定商品

GOODS OR MERCHANDISE? 用 goods 还是 merchandise?

Choose **goods** if the emphasis is on what the product is made of or what it is for. 强调商品制作的原料或用途用 goods： *leather/household goods* 皮革商品；家居用品
Choose **merchandise** if the emphasis is less on the product itself and more on its brand or the fact of buying/selling it. 如果不太强调商品本身，而更强调品牌或买卖用 merchandise。

produce [U] things that have been grown or made, especially things connected with farming 尤指农产品，也包括其他种植或制造的产品： *We sell only fresh local produce.* 我们只售当地的新鲜农产品。

PATTERNS

- **consumer/industrial** products/goods/commodities
- **household** products/goods
- **farm** products/produce
- **luxury** products/goods/commodities
- to **sell/market** a product/goods/a commodity/merchandise/produce
- to **export** a product/goods/a commodity/merchandise
- to **buy/purchase** a product/goods/a commodity/merchandise/produce

P

经出示（某物）：*Discounts only on production of your student ID card.* 须出示学生证方可打折。

pro'duction line (*also* **as'sembly line**) *noun* a line of workers and machines in a factory, along which a product passes, having parts made, put together or checked at each stage until the product is finished 生产线；装配线；流水线：*Cars are checked as they come off the production line.* 汽车下了生产线立即作检验。

pro'duction number *noun* a scene in a musical play or a film/movie where a lot of people sing and dance（音乐剧、电影中的）集体歌舞

pro·duct·ive /prəˈdʌktɪv/ *adj.* **1** making goods or growing crops, especially in large quantities 生产的；（尤指）多产的：***highly productive** farming land* 高产农田 ◇ *productive workers* 高效工人 OPP **unproductive** **2** doing or achieving a lot 有效益的；富有成效的 SYN **fruitful**：*a productive meeting* 有成效的会议 ◇ *My time spent in the library was very productive.* 我花在图书馆的时间很有收获。 ⊃ COMPARE COUNTERPRODUCTIVE **3 ~ of sth** (*formal*) resulting in sth or causing sth 引起；导致；唤起：*a play productive of the strongest emotions* 唤起强烈感情的一出戏 ▸ **pro·duct·ive·ly** *adv.*：*to use land more productively* 更有效地利用土地 ◇ *It's important to spend your time productively.* 重要的是要有效地利用时间。

prod·uct·iv·ity /ˌprɒdʌkˈtɪvəti; *NAmE* ˌprɑːd-; ˌproʊd-/ *noun* [U] the rate at which a worker, a company or a country produces goods, and the amount produced, compared with how much time, work and money is needed to produce them 生产率；生产效率：***high/improved/increased productivity*** 高的 / 提高了的 / 增长了的生产率 ◇ *Wage rates depend on levels of productivity.* 工资水平取决于生产量的多寡。

ˌproduct ˈplacement *noun* [U, C] the use of particular products in films/movies or television programmes in order to advertise them 植入式广告，置入性行销（为了广告目的而在电影或电视节目中使用某些产品） ⊃ WORDFINDER NOTE AT ADVERTISE

Prof. *abbr.* (in writing 书写形式) PROFESSOR 教授：*Prof. Mike Harrison* 迈克·哈里森教授

prof /prɒf; *NAmE* prɑːf/ *noun* (*informal*) = PROFESSOR：*a college prof* 大学教授

pro·fane /prəˈfeɪn/ *adj., verb*

■ ***adj.*** **1** (*formal*) having or showing a lack of respect for God or holy things 亵渎神灵的；亵圣的：*profane language* 亵渎上帝的语言 **2** (*specialist*) not connected with religion or holy things 非宗教的；世俗的 SYN **secular**：*songs of sacred and profane love* 歌唱圣洁与世俗爱情的歌曲

■ ***verb*** **~ sth** (*formal*) to treat sth holy with a lack of respect 亵渎神灵；亵圣

pro·fan·ity /prəˈfænəti; *NAmE also* proʊˈf-/ *noun* (*pl.* **-ies**) (*formal*) **1** [U] behaviour that shows a lack of respect for God or holy things 亵圣；对神灵的亵渎 **2** [C, usually pl.] swear words, or religious words used in a way that shows a lack of respect for God or holy things（亵圣的）诅咒语：*He uttered a stream of profanities.* 他脏话连篇。

pro·fess /prəˈfes/ *verb* (*formal*) **1** to claim that sth is true or correct, especially when it is not 妄称；伪称；声称：**~ sth** *She still professes her innocence.* 她仍然声称自己无辜。 ◇ **~ to be/have sth** *I don't profess to be an expert in this subject.* 我不敢自诩为这方面的专家。 **2** to state openly that you have a particular belief, feeling, etc. 宣称；公开表明 SYN **declare**：**~ sth** *He professed his admiration for their work.* 他表示钦佩他们的工作。 ◇ **~ yourself + adj.** *She professed herself satisfied with the progress so far.* 她表示对目前为止的进度很满意。 **3 ~ sth** to belong to a particular religion 信奉，信仰（某一宗教）：*to profess Christianity/Islam/Judaism* 信仰基督教 / 伊斯兰教 / 犹太教

pro·fessed /prəˈfest/ *adj.* [only before noun] (*formal*) **1** used to describe a belief or a position that sb has publicly made known 公开表明的：*a professed Christian/anarchist* 公开表明信仰的基督教徒；公开表明立场的无政府主义者 **2** used to describe a feeling or an attitude that sb says they have but which may not be sincere 自称的；自诩的；假充的：*These, at least, were their professed reasons for pulling out of the deal.* 至少这些是他们自称退出这宗交易的理由。

pro·fes·sion 🔑 /prəˈfeʃn/ *noun* **1** 🔑 [C] a type of job that needs special training or skill, especially one that needs a high level of education（需要专门技能，尤指需要较高教育水平的某一）行业，职业：***the medical/legal/teaching, etc. profession*** 医疗、法律、教学等行业 ◇ ***to enter/go into/join a profession*** 加入一个行业 ◇ (*BrE*) ***the caring professions*** (= that involve looking after people) 护理行业 ◇ *He was an electrician **by profession**.* 他的职业是电工。 ◇ *She was at the very top of her profession.* 她是她那个行业中的佼佼者。 ⊃ SYNONYMS AT WORK ⊃ COLLOCATIONS AT JOB **2** 🔑 **the profession** [sing.+sing./pl. v.] all the people who work in a particular type of profession（某）职业界；业内人士；同业；同行；同人：*The legal profession has/have always resisted change.* 法律界向来抗拒变革。 **3 the professions** [pl.] the traditional jobs that need a high level of education and training, such as being a doctor or a lawyer（统称，指需要较高教育水平的）职业：*employment in industry and the professions* 实业界与专业界的工作 **4** [C] **~ of sth** a statement about what you believe, feel or think about sth, that is sometimes made publicly 声明；宣称；表白 SYN **declaration**：*a profession of faith* 信仰的表白

pro·fes·sion·al 🔑 AW /prəˈfeʃənl/ *adj., noun*

■ ***adj.*** **1** 🔑 [only before noun] connected with a job that needs special training or skill, especially one that needs a high level of education 职业的；专业的：*professional qualifications/skills* 专业资格 / 技能 ◇ *professional standards/practice* 专业标准；行业惯例 ◇ *an opportunity for professional development* 专业进修的机会 ◇ *If it's a legal matter you need **to seek professional advice**.* 如果这属于法律问题，你就需要寻求专业意见了。 **2** 🔑 (of people 人) having a job which needs special training and a high level of education 有职业的；专业的：*Most of the people on the course were professional women.* 参加本课程的大多数人是职业女性。 **3** 🔑 showing that sb is well trained and extremely skilled 娴熟的；训练有素的；精通业务的 SYN **competent**：*He dealt with the problem in a highly professional way.* 他处理这个问题非常专业。 OPP **amateur** **4** 🔑 suitable or appropriate for sb working in a particular profession 职业上的；专业上的：***professional conduct/misconduct*** 职业操守；失职 OPP **unprofessional** **5** 🔑 doing sth as a paid job rather than as a hobby 职业性的；专业的；非业余的：*a professional golfer* 职业高尔夫球运动员 ◇ *After he won the amateur championship he **turned professional**.* 他获得业余赛冠军后就转为职业运动员了。 OPP **amateur** **6** 🔑 (of sport 体育运动) done as a paid job rather than as a hobby 职业性的；专业的；非业余的：*the world of professional football* 职业足球界 OPP **amateur** ⊃ COMPARE NON-PROFESSIONAL

■ ***noun*** **1** 🔑 a person who does a job that needs special training and a high level of education 专门人员；专业人士；专家：*the terms that doctors and other health professionals use* 医师和其他保健专业人员使用的术语 **2** 🔑 (*also informal* **pro**) a person who does a sport or other activity as a paid job rather than as a hobby 职业运动员；（从事某活动的）专业人员：*a top golf professional* 顶尖高尔夫球职业选手 OPP **amateur** **3** 🔑 (*also informal* **pro**) a person who has a lot of skill and experience 内行；专门人才；技术精湛者；老练的人：*This was clearly a job for a real professional.* 这显然是真正的专家才能干的工作。 OPP **amateur**

proˌfessional deˈvelopment day *noun* (*especially CanE*) a day on which classes at schools are cancelled so that teachers can get further training in their subjects 专职进修日，教师发展日（学校停课）

proˌfessional ˈfoul *noun* (*BrE*) (in sport, especially football (SOCCER) 体育运动，尤指足球) a rule that sb breaks deliberately so that their team can gain an advantage, especially to prevent a player from the other team from scoring a goal 故意犯规

pro·fes·sion·al·ism AW /prəˈfeʃənəlɪzəm/ *noun* [U] **1** the high standard that you expect from a person who is well trained in a particular job 专业水平；专业素质：*We were impressed by the professionalism of the staff.* 职员的专业素质给我们的印象很深。**2** great skill and ability 精湛的技艺；高超的技能；专长：*the power and professionalism of her performance* 她的表演的感染力和精湛技艺 **3** the practice of using professional players in sport 职业化（在体育运动中使用职业运动员）：*Increased professionalism has changed the game radically.* 职业运动员日益增加，彻底改变了这项运动。

pro·fes·sion·al·ize (*BrE also* **-ise**) /prəˈfeʃənəlaɪz/ *verb* [usually passive] **~ sth** to make an activity more professional, for example by paying people who take part in it 使专业化；使职业化 ▸ **pro·fes·sion·al·iza·tion, -isa·tion** /prəˌfeʃənəlaɪˈzeɪʃn; *NAmE* -ləˈz-/ *noun* [U]: *the increasing professionalization of sports* 体育运动的日益职业化

pro·fes·sion·al·ly AW /prəˈfeʃənəli/ *adv.* **1** in a way that is connected with a person's job or training 在工作上；在职业上：*You need a complete change, both professionally and personally.* 你需要在工作上和自身两方面有彻底的改变。**2** in a way that shows skill and experience 娴熟地；老练地；内行地：*The product has been marketed very professionally.* 这项产品的推销一直很讲究专业技巧。**3** by a person who has the right skills and qualifications 专业人员做的；内行人干的：*The burglar alarm should be professionally installed.* 防盗警报应当由专业人员安装。**4** as a paid job, not as a hobby 作为职业；非业余地：*After the injury, he never played professionally again.* 受伤以后，他再也没有参加职业比赛。

pro·fes·sor /prəˈfesə(r)/ (*also informal* **prof**) *noun* (*abbr.* **Prof.**) **1** (*especially BrE*) (*NAmE* **ˈfull professor**) a university teacher of the highest rank 教授：*Professor (Ann) Williams* （安·）威廉斯教授 ◇ *a chemistry professor* 化学教授 ◇ *to be appointed Professor of French at Cambridge* 被任命为剑桥大学的法文教授 ◇ *He was made (a) professor at the age of 40.* 他 40 岁时就成为了教授。HELP **Full professor** is used to describe a rank of university teacher, and not as a title. * full professor 是大学教师的级别，不用作称呼。**2** (*NAmE*) a teacher at a university or college （大学的）讲师，教员 ➲ COMPARE ASSISTANT PROFESSOR, ASSOCIATE PROFESSOR

pro·fes·sor·ial /ˌprɒfəˈsɔːriəl; *NAmE* ˌprɑːf-/ *adj.* connected with a professor; like a professor 教授的；教授似的：*professorial duties* 教授的职责 ◇ *His tone was almost professorial.* 他说话的口气简直像个教授。

pro·fes·sor·ship /prəˈfesəʃɪp; *NAmE* -sərʃ-/ *noun* the rank or position of a university professor 教授的级别（或职位等）：*a visiting professorship* 客座教授职位 ◇ *She was appointed to a professorship in Economics at Princeton.* 她获聘为普林斯顿大学经济学教授。

prof·fer /ˈprɒfə(r); *NAmE* ˈprɑːf-/ *verb* (*formal*) **1 ~ sth (to sb)** | **~ sb sth** to offer sth to sb, by holding it out to them 端着（给…）；递上：*'Try this,' she said, proffering a plate.* "尝尝这个吧。"她端上一盘菜说。**2** to offer sth such as advice or an explanation 提出，提供（建议、解释等）：**~ sth (to sb)** *What advice would you proffer to someone starting up in business?* 您对初入商界的人有何建议？◇ **~ sb sth** *What advice would you proffer her?* 您对她有什么忠告？◇ **~ itself** *A solution proffered itself.* 一个解答自然出现了。

pro·fi·cient /prəˈfɪʃnt/ *adj.* able to do sth well because of training and practice 熟练的；娴熟的；精通的；训练有素的：*I'm a reasonably proficient driver.* 我开车的技术还算不错。◇ **~ in sth/in doing sth** *She's proficient in several languages.* 她精通好几种语言。◇ **~ at sth/at doing sth** *He's proficient at his job.* 他的工作效率很高。▸ **pro·fi·ciency** /-nsi/ *noun* [U]: *to develop proficiency* 提高熟练程度 ◇ *a certificate of language proficiency* 语言水平证书 ◇ **~ in sth/in doing sth** *a high level of oral proficiency in English* 一口流利的英语

pro·file /ˈprəʊfaɪl; *NAmE* ˈproʊ-/ *noun, verb*

■ ***noun*** **1** the outline of a person's face when you look from the side, not the front 面部的侧影；侧面轮廓：*his strong profile* 他轮廓清晰的侧影 ◇ *a picture of the president **in profile*** 总统的侧面画像 **2** a description of sb/sth that gives useful information 概述；简介；传略：*a **job/employee profile*** 工作 / 雇员简介 ◇ *We first build up a detailed profile of our customers and their requirements.* 首先，我们建立起我们的客户及其需求的详细资料。◇ *You can update your Facebook profile* (= your description of yourself on a SOCIAL NETWORKING website). 你可以更新你在"脸书"网站上的个人资料。**3** the general impression that sb/sth gives to the public and the amount of attention they receive 印象；形象：*The deal will certainly raise the company's international profile.* 这宗交易肯定会提高这家公司的国际形象。**4** the edge or outline of sth that you see against a background 外形；轮廓：*the profile of the tower against the sky* 天空映衬下塔楼的轮廓

IDM **a ˌhigh/ˌlow ˈprofile** the amount of attention sb/sth has from the public 惹人 / 不惹人注目；高 / 低姿态：*This issue has had a high profile in recent months.* 近几个月来，这个议题一直是关注的焦点。◇ *I advised her to **keep a low profile** for the next few days* (= not to attract attention). 我建议她未来几天保持低调。

■ ***verb*** **~ sb/sth** to give or write a description of sb/sth that gives the most important information 扼要介绍；概述；写简介：*His career is profiled in this month's journal.* 这期月刊概述了他的工作生涯。

pro·fil·ing /ˈprəʊfaɪlɪŋ; *NAmE* ˈproʊ-/ *noun* [U] the act of collecting useful information about sb/sth so that you can give a description of them or it （有关人或事物的）资料搜集：*customer profiling* 客户情况汇集 ◇ *offender profiling* 犯人资料收集 ➲ SEE ALSO RACIAL PROFILING ▸ **pro·fil·er** /ˈprəʊfaɪlə(r); *NAmE* ˈproʊ-/ *noun*

profit /ˈprɒfɪt; *NAmE* ˈprɑːfɪt/ *noun, verb*

■ ***noun*** **1** [C, U] the money that you make in business or by selling things, especially after paying the costs involved 利润；收益；赢利：*a rise/an increase/a drop/a fall in profits* 收益的上升 / 增长 / 跌落 / 下降 ◇ **~ (on sth)** *The company **made a** healthy **profit** on the deal.* 公司在这笔生意中获利颇丰。◇ **~ (from sth)** *Profit from exports rose 7.3%* 出口利润增长了 7.3%。◇ ***Net profit*** (= after you have paid costs and tax) *was up 16.1%.* 纯利润上升了 16.1%。◇ *The sale generated **record profits**.* 这笔生意带来了创纪录的收益。◇ *We should be able to sell the house **at a profit**.* 我们卖掉这座房子应该可以获利。◇ *The agency is voluntary and not run **for profit**.* 这个机构是义务性的，不是为了赢利。OPP **loss** ➲ WORDFINDER NOTE AT MONEY ➲ COLLOCATIONS AT BUSINESS **2** [U] (*formal*) the advantage that you get from doing sth 好处；利益；裨益：*Future lawyers could study this text with profit.* 未来的律师研读这一文本也许会有裨益。

■ ***verb*** [I, T] (*formal*) to get sth useful from a situation; to be useful to sb or give them an advantage 获益；得到好处；对…有用（或有益）：**~ (from sth)** *Farmers are profiting from the new legislation.* 新法规使农民受益。◇ **~ (by sth)** *We tried to profit by our mistakes* (= learn from them). 我们努力从错误中吸取教训。◇ **~ sth** *Many local people believe the development will profit them.* 当地的许多人认为，这项开发将对他们有利。

prof·it·able /ˈprɒfɪtəbl; *NAmE* ˈprɑːf-/ *adj.* **1** that makes or is likely to make money 有利润的；赢利的：*a highly profitable business* 一家赢利很高的企业 ◇ *It is usually more profitable to sell direct to the public.* 向社会大众直销往往获利较高。➲ SYNONYMS AT SUCCESSFUL **2** that gives sb an advantage or a useful result 有益的；有好处的 SYN **rewarding**：*She spent a profitable afternoon in the library.* 她在图书馆待了一个下午，颇有收获。▸ **prof·it·abil·ity** /ˌprɒfɪtəˈbɪləti; *NAmE* ˌprɑːf-/ *noun* [U]: *to increase profitability* 增加收益 **prof·it·ably** /-əbli/ *adv.*: *to run a business profitably* 把企业经营得有盈余 ◇ *He spent the weekend profitably.* 他过了一个有收获的周末。

P

ˌprofit and ˈloss account *noun* (*business* 商) a list that shows the amount of money that a company has earned and the total profit or loss that it has made in a particular period of time 损益账

prof·it·eer·ing /ˌprɒfɪˈtɪərɪŋ; *NAmE* ˌprɑːfəˈtɪr-/ *noun* [U] (*disapproving*) the act of making a lot of money in an unfair way, for example by asking very high prices for things that are hard to get 牟取暴利 ▶ **prof·it·eer** *noun*

pro·fit·er·ole /prəˈfɪtərəʊl; *NAmE* -roʊl/ (*especially BrE*) (*NAmE usually* ˌ**cream** ˈ**puff**) *noun* a small cake in the shape of a ball, made of light PASTRY, filled with cream and usually with chocolate on top 奶心巧克力酥球

prof·it·less /ˈprɒfɪtləs; *NAmE* ˈprɑːf-/ *adj.* (*formal*) producing no PROFIT or useful result 无利可图的；无益的

ˈ**profit-making** *adj.* [usually before noun] (of a company or a business 公司或企业) that makes or will make a profit 赢利的；能赚钱的

ˈ**profit margin** (*also* **margin**) *noun* (*business* 商) the difference between the cost of buying or producing sth and the price that it is sold for 利润率

ˈ**profit-sharing** *noun* [U] the system of dividing all or some of a company's profits among its employees （公司内部的）利润分成，利润分配，分红

ˈ**profit-taking** *noun* [U] (*business* 商) the sale of shares in companies whose value has increased 获利回吐（股价上升时售出股票）

prof·li·gate /ˈprɒflɪɡət; *NAmE* ˈprɑːf-/ *adj.* (*formal, disapproving*) using money, time, materials, etc. in a careless way 挥霍的；浪费的 SYN **wasteful**: *profligate spending* 恣意挥霍的开支 ▶ **prof·li·gacy** /ˈprɒflɪɡəsi; *NAmE* ˈprɑːf-/ *noun* [U]

ˈ**pro-form** *noun* (*grammar* 语法) a word that depends on another part of the sentence or text for its meaning, for example 'her' in 'I like Ruth but I don't love her.' 替代形式（意义依上下文而定，如 I like Ruth but I don't love her 中的 her）

pro forma /ˌprəʊ ˈfɔːmə; *NAmE* ˌproʊ ˈfɔːrmə/ *adj.* (*from Latin*) [usually before noun] **1** (especially of a document 尤指文件) prepared in order to show the usual way of doing sth or to provide a standard method 按惯例的；惯常的；例行的: *a pro forma letter* 格式信件 ◇ *pro forma instructions* 常规指示 **2** (of a document 文件) sent in advance 预开的；预先通知性的；形式上的: *a pro forma invoice* (= a document that gives details of the goods being sent to a customer) 形式发票 **3** done because it is part of the usual way of doing sth, although it has no real meaning 流于形式的；摆样子的: *a pro forma debate* 流于形式的辩论 ▶ **pro forma** *noun*: *I enclose a pro forma for you to complete, sign and return.* 谨附估价单一份，请填好并签字后寄回。

pro·found /prəˈfaʊnd/ *adj.* **1** very great; felt or experienced very strongly 巨大的；深切的；深远的: *profound changes in the earth's climate* 地球气候的巨大变化 ◇ *My father's death had a profound effect on us all.* 父亲的去世深深地影响了我们全家。 **2** showing great knowledge or understanding 知识渊博的；理解深刻的；深邃的: *profound insights* 精辟的见解 ◇ *a profound book* 深奥的书 **3** needing a lot of study or thought 艰深的；玄奥的: *profound questions about life and death* 生死方面的玄奥问题 **4** (*medical* 医) very serious; complete 严重的；完全的；彻底的: *profound disability* 严重残疾

pro·found·ly /prəˈfaʊndli/ *adv.* **1** in a way that has a very great effect on sb/sth 极大地；深刻地: *We are profoundly affected by what happens to us in childhood.* 童年发生的事深深地影响着我们。 **2** (*medical* 医) very seriously; completely 严重地；完全地；彻底地: *profoundly deaf* 完全失聪

pro·fund·ity /prəˈfʌndəti/ *noun* (*pl.* **-ies**) (*formal*) **1** [U] the quality of understanding or dealing with a subject at a very serious level （理解或处理问题的）深刻性，彻底性 SYN **depth**: *He lacked profundity and analytical precision.* 他缺乏深度和分析的精确性。 **2** [U] the quality of being very great, serious or powerful 巨大；严重；强大: *the profundity of her misery* 她的苦难之深 **3** [C, usually pl.] something that sb says that shows great understanding 深奥的话；意味深长的话: *His profundities were lost on the young audience.* 他语重心长，但年轻的听众却没有领会。

pro·fuse /prəˈfjuːs/ *adj.* produced in large amounts 大量的；众多的；丰富的: *profuse apologies/thanks* 一再道歉；千恩万谢 ◇ *profuse bleeding* 血流如注 ▶ **pro·fuse·ly** *adv.*: *to bleed profusely* 大量出血 ◇ *to apologize profusely* 连连道歉

pro·fu·sion /prəˈfjuːʒn/ *noun* [sing.+sing./pl. v., U] (*formal* or *literary*) a very large quantity of sth 大量；众多 SYN **abundance**: *a profusion of colours* 色彩斑斓 ◇ *Roses grew in profusion against the old wall.* 老旧墙边遍生玫瑰。

pro·geni·tor /prəʊˈdʒenɪtə(r); *NAmE* proʊ-/ *noun* (*formal*) **1** a person or thing from the past that a person, animal or plant that is alive now is related to （人或动、植物等的）祖先，祖代 SYN **ancestor**: *He was the progenitor of a family of distinguished actors.* 他是一个著名演艺世家的先辈。 **2** a person who starts an idea or a development 创始人；先驱: *the progenitors of modern art* 现代艺术的先驱

pro·geny /ˈprɒdʒəni; *NAmE* ˈprɑːdʒ-/ *noun* [pl.] (*formal* or *humorous*) a person's children; the young of animals and plants 子孙；幼崽；幼兽；幼苗: *He was surrounded by his numerous progeny.* 众多的子孙簇拥着他。

pro·ges·ter·one /prəˈdʒestərəʊn; *NAmE* -roʊn/ *noun* [U] a HORMONE produced in the bodies of women and female animals which prepares the body to become pregnant and is also used in CONTRACEPTION 孕酮；黄体酮 ➲ COMPARE OESTROGEN, TESTOSTERONE

prog·no·sis /prɒɡˈnəʊsɪs; *NAmE* prɑːɡˈnoʊ-/ *noun* (*pl.* **prog·no·ses** /-siːz/) **1** (*medical* 医) an opinion, based on medical experience, of the likely development of a disease or an illness （对病情的）预断，预后 **2** (*formal*) a judgement about how sth is likely to develop in the future 预测；预言；展望 SYN **forecast**: *The prognosis is for more people to work part-time in the future.* 预计将来会有更多人从事兼职工作。 ▶ **prog·nos·tic** /prɒɡˈnɒstɪk; *NAmE* prɑːɡˈnɑːs-/ *adj.*

prog·nos·ti·ca·tion /prɒɡˌnɒstɪˈkeɪʃn; *NAmE* prɑːɡˌnɑːs-/ *noun* (*formal*) a thing that sb says will happen in the future 预言；预告；预报: *gloomy prognostications* 悲观的预言

pro·gram 🔑 /ˈprəʊɡræm; *NAmE* ˈproʊ-/ *noun, verb*

■ *noun* **1** 🔑 (*computing* 计) a set of instructions in CODE that control the operations or functions of a computer 程序；编码指令: *Load the program into the computer.* 把程序装入电脑。 ➲ WORDFINDER NOTE AT COMPUTER

> **WORDFINDER** 联想词: code, data, functionality, input, interface, keyword, operating system, retrieve, **software**

2 🔑 (*NAmE*) = PROGRAMME: *an intense training program* 强化培训方案 ◇ *the university's graduate programs* 大学研究生课程 ◇ *a TV program* 电视节目

■ *verb* (**-mm-**, *NAmE also* **-m-**) **1** 🔑 [I, T] (*computing* 计) to give a computer, etc. a set of instructions to make it perform a particular task 编写程序: *In this class, students will learn how to program.* 这节课学生将学习编程。 ◇ **~ sth (to do sth)** *The computer is programmed to warn users before information is deleted.* 这台计算机编程时已设计在信息删除前提醒用户。 ➲ COMPARE PROGRAMME *v.* **2** 🔑 (*NAmE*) = PROGRAMME

pro·gram·mable /ˈprəʊɡræməbl; prəʊˈɡræm-; *NAmE* ˈproʊ-; proʊˈɡ-/ *adj.* (of a computer or electrical device 计算机或电器) able to accept instructions that control how it operates or functions 程控的；可编程序的

pro·gram·mat·ic /ˌprəʊɡrəˈmætɪk; *NAmE* ˌproʊ-/ *adj.* [usually before noun] (*formal*) connected with, suggesting or following a plan 计划的；有关计划的；按计划的：*programmatic reforms* 按计划进行的改革

pro·gramme (*BrE*) (*NAmE* **pro·gram**) /ˈprəʊɡræm; *NAmE* ˈproʊ-/ *noun, verb*

■ *noun*

• **PLAN** 计划 **1** a plan of things that will be done or included in the development of sth 计划；方案；活动安排：*to launch a research programme* 开展科研计划 ◇ *a training programme for new staff* 新职员培训方案 ◇ *a programme of economic reform* 经济改革方案

• **ON TV/RADIO** 电视；广播 **2** something that people watch on television or listen to on the radio 节目：*a news programme* 新闻节目 ◇ *Did you see that programme on India last night?* 昨晚关于印度的那个节目你看了没有？ ➲ WORDFINDER NOTE AT RADIO ➲ COLLOCATIONS AT TELEVISION

> **WORDFINDER** 联想词：chat show, documentary, **drama**, game show, news, quiz, reality TV, sitcom, **television**

• **FOR PLAY/CONCERT** 戏剧；音乐会 **3** a thin book or a piece of paper that gives you information about a play, a concert, etc. 节目单；演出介绍：*a theatre programme* 剧场节目表 ➲ WORDFINDER NOTE AT CONCERT

• **ORDER OF EVENTS** 活动程序 **4** an organized order of performances or events （演出或活动的）程序 SYN **line-up**：*an exciting musical programme* 一场激动人心的音乐演出 ◇ *a week-long programme of lectures* 持续一周的讲座安排 ◇ *What's the programme for* (= what are we going to do) *tomorrow?* 明天安排了什么活动？

• **COURSE OF STUDY** 课程 **5** (*NAmE*) a course of study 课程：*a school programme* 学校课程 ➲ NOTE AT COURSE

• **OF MACHINE** 机器 **6** a series of actions done by a machine, such as a WASHING MACHINE （机器工作的）程序：*Select a cool programme for woollen clothes.* 洗毛衣要选择凉水程序。

IDM **get with the ˈprogramme** (*BrE*) (*NAmE* **get with the ˈprogram**) (*informal*) (usually in orders 通常用于命令) used to tell sb that they should change their attitude and do what they are supposed to be doing （让人改变态度）按计划行事，做应该做的事

■ *verb* [usually passive]

• **PLAN** 计划 **1** **~ sth (for sth)** to plan for sth to happen, especially as part of a series of planned events 计划；规划；安排：*The final section of road is programmed for completion next month.* 最后一段道路计划于下月竣工。

• **PERSON/ANIMAL** 人；动物 **2** **~ sb/sth to do sth** to make a person, an animal, etc. behave in a particular way, so that it happens automatically 训练；培养：*Human beings are genetically programmed to learn certain kinds of language.* 人类生来有学习某几种语言的遗传因素。

• **MACHINE** 机器 **3** **~ sth (to do sth)** to give a machine instructions to do a particular task 预调；预设：*She programmed the central heating to come on at eight.* 她把中央供暖系统设定为八点启动。

ˌprogrammed ˈlearning *noun* [U] a method of study in which a subject is divided into very small parts and the student must be successful in one part before he or she can go on to the next 程序化学习，循序渐进学习（按个别学生的进度，分阶段设定目标）

pro·gram·mer /ˈprəʊɡræmə(r); *NAmE* ˈproʊ-/ *noun* a person whose job is writing programs for computers （计算机）程序设计员，编程人员

pro·gram·ming /ˈprəʊɡræmɪŋ; *NAmE* ˈproʊ-/ *noun* [U] **1** the process of writing and testing programs for computers （计算机）程序设计，程序编制，编程：*a high-level programming language* 高级编程语言 **2** the planning of which television or radio programmes to broadcast （广播、电视节目的）编排，选编：*politically balanced programming* 政治上均衡报道的节目编选

pro·gress *noun, verb*

■ *noun* /ˈprəʊɡres; *NAmE* ˈprɑːɡ-; -ɡrəs/ [U] **1** the process of improving or developing, or of getting nearer to achieving or completing sth 进步；进展；进程：*to make progress* 取得进步 ◇ ***slow/steady/rapid/good progress*** 缓慢的／平稳的／迅速的／良好的进展 ◇ *We have made great progress in controlling inflation.* 我们在抑制通货膨胀方面取得了巨大进展。◇ ***economic/scientific/technical progress*** 经济的／科学的／技术的进步 ◇ *They asked for **a progress report** on the project.* 他们索要工程进度报告。**2** movement forwards or towards a place 前进；行进：*She watched his slow progress down the steep slope.* 她望着他慢慢走下陡坡。◇ *There wasn't much traffic so we made good progress.* 来往车辆不多，所以我们开得很快。➲ MORE LIKE THIS 28, page R28

IDM **in progress** (*formal*) happening at this time 进行中：*Work on the new offices is now in progress.* 新办公楼正在施工。◇ *Please be quiet—examination in progress.* 考试正在进行，请安静。

■ *verb* /prəˈɡres/ **1** [I] to improve or develop over a period of time; to make progress 进步；改进；进展 SYN **advance**：*The course allows students to progress at their own speed.* 本课程允许学生按各自的速度学习。◇ *Work on the new road is progressing slowly.* 新路的修建工作在缓慢进行。**2** [I] + **adv./prep.** (*formal*) to move forward 前进；行进：*The line of traffic progressed slowly through the town.* 车流缓慢地穿过城镇。◇ (*figurative*) *Cases can take months to progress through the courts.* 案件可能需要好几个月才能审结。**3** [I] to go forward in time （时间上）推移，流逝 SYN **go on**：*The weather became colder as the day progressed.* 天色越晚，天气就越冷。

PHR V **proˈgress to sth** to move on from doing one thing to doing sth else 接着做（另一件事）：*She started off playing the recorder and then progressed to the clarinet.* 她起初吹竖笛，继而吹单簧管。

pro·gres·sion /prəˈɡreʃn/ *noun* **1** [U, C] the process of developing gradually from one stage or state to another （进入另一阶段的）发展；前进；进程：*opportunities for career progression* 事业发展的机遇 ◇ *the rapid progression of the disease* 病情的迅速发展 ◇ **~ (from sth) (to sth)** *a natural progression from childhood to adolescence* 从童年到青少年的自然过渡 **2** [C] a number of things that come in a series 系列；序列；连续 ➲ SEE ALSO ARITHMETIC PROGRESSION, GEOMETRIC PROGRESSION

pro·gres·sive /prəˈɡresɪv/ *adj., noun*

■ *adj.* **1** in favour of new ideas, modern methods and change 进步的；先进的；开明的：*progressive schools* 开明的学校 OPP **retrogressive** **2** happening or developing steadily 稳步的；逐步的；稳定发展的：*a progressive reduction in the size of the workforce* 劳力数量的逐步减少 ◇ *a progressive muscular disease* 逐渐严重的肌肉病症 **3** (*also* **con·tinu·ous**) (*grammar* 语法) connected with the form of a verb (for example *I am waiting* or *It is raining*) that is made from a part of *be* and the present participle. Progressive forms are used to express an action that continues for a period of time. （动词）进行时的，进行式的 ▸ **pro·gres·siv·ism** *noun* [U]：*political progressivism* 政治进步主义

■ *noun* [usually pl.] a person who is in favour of new ideas, modern methods and change 进步人士；开明人士；改革派：*political battles between progressives and conservatives* 改革派与保守派之间的政治斗争

pro·gres·sive·ly /prəˈɡresɪvli/ *adv.* (often with a comparative 常与比较级连用) steadily and continuously 持续稳定地；逐步地；愈益：*The situation was becoming progressively more difficult.* 局势变得愈发困难起来。◇ *The pain got progressively worse.* 疼痛越来越厉害。

prog rock /ˌprɒɡ ˈrɒk; *NAmE* ˌprɑːɡ ˈrɑːk/ (*also* **proˌgressive ˈrock**) *noun* [U] a style of rock music that includes elements of other kinds of music, including JAZZ 前卫摇滚乐（包括爵士乐等其他音乐元素）

pro·hibit AW /prəˈhɪbɪt; *NAmE also* proʊˈh-/ *verb* (*formal*) **1** [often passive] to stop sth from being done or used especially by law （尤指以法令）禁止 SYN **forbid**：**~ sth** *a law prohibiting the sale of alcohol* 禁止售酒的法令 ◇ **~ sb from doing sth** *Soviet citizens were prohibited from*

P

travelling abroad. 苏联时代国民被禁止出国旅行。◇ ~ (**sb**) **doing sth** *The policy prohibits smoking on school grounds.* 该政策禁止在校内吸烟。**2** ~ **sth/sb from doing sth** to make sth impossible to do 阻止；使不可能 SYN **prevent**: *The high cost of equipment prohibits many people from taking up this sport.* 昂贵的装备令许多人对这项运动望而却步。

pro·hib·ition AW /ˌprəʊɪˈbɪʃn; *NAmE* ˌproʊəˈb-/ *noun* **1** [U] (*formal*) the act of stopping sth being done or used, especially by law（尤指通过法律的）禁止，阻止：*the prohibition of smoking in public areas* 禁止在公共场所吸烟的规定 **2** [C] ~ (**against/on sth**) (*formal*) a law or a rule that stops sth being done or used 禁令；禁律：*a prohibition against selling alcohol to people under the age of 18* 禁止向 18 岁以下青少年售酒的法令 **3 Prohibition** [U] (in the US) the period of time from 1920 to 1933 when it was illegal to make and sell alcoholic drinks（1920 至 1933 年美国的）禁酒时期

pro·hib·ition·ist /ˌprəʊɪˈbɪʃənɪst; *NAmE* ˌproʊəˈb-/ *noun* a person who supports the act of making sth illegal, especially the sale of alcoholic drinks 禁止令拥护者；禁止论者（尤指禁酒主义者）

pro·hibi·tive AW /prəˈhɪbətɪv; *NAmE also* proʊˈh-/ *adj.* **1** (of a price or a cost 价格或费用) so high that it prevents people from buying sth or doing sth 高昂得令人难以承受的；贵得买不起的 SYN **exorbitant**: *prohibitive costs* 难以承受的费用 ◇ *The price of property in the city is prohibitive.* 城市的房地产价格令人望而却步。**2** preventing people from doing sth by law（以法令）禁止的：*prohibitive legislation* 禁律 **3** (*NAmE*) (of a person taking part in an election or a competition 参加竞选或比赛的人) extremely likely to win 极可能获胜的：*Miami began the day a prohibitive Super Bowl favorite.* 迈阿密队今天从一开始就表现出是美国橄榄球超级碗大赛的夺冠热门。 ▸ **pro·hibi·tive·ly** *adv.*: *Car insurance can be prohibitively expensive for young drivers.* 汽车保险费有时高得让年轻开车人承受不起。

pro·ject AW *noun, verb*

■ ***noun*** /ˈprɒdʒekt; *NAmE* ˈprɑːdʒ-/
- **PLANNED WORK** 规划的工作 **1** a planned piece of work that is designed to find information about sth, to produce sth new, or to improve sth 生产（或研究等）项目；方案；工程：*a research project* 研究计划 ◇ *a building project* 建筑工程 ◇ *to set up a project to computerize the library system* 开展一个图书馆系统电脑化的项目
- **SCHOOL/COLLEGE WORK** 学校的课题 **2** a piece of work involving careful study of a subject over a period of time, done by school or college students（大、中学学生的）专题研究：*a history project* 历史科的专题研究 ◇ *The final term will be devoted to project work.* 最后一学期的时间将全部用于专题研究。
- **SET OF AIMS/ACTIVITIES** 方案 **3** a set of aims, ideas or activities that sb is interested in or wants to bring to people's attention 方案；计划：*The party attempted to assemble its aims into a focussed political project.* 这个党试图把订立的目标综合为一个政治方案。
- **HOUSING** 住房 **4** (*NAmE*) = HOUSING PROJECT: *Going into the projects alone is dangerous.* 只身进入公房区是危险的。

■ ***verb*** /prəˈdʒekt/
- **PLAN** 计划 **1** [T, usually passive] ~ **sth** to plan an activity, a project etc. for a time in the future 规划；计划；拟订方案：*The next edition of the book is projected for publication in March.* 本书的下一版计划于三月发行。◇ *The projected housing development will go ahead next year.* 计划中的住宅建设将于明年动工。
- **ESTIMATE** 估计 **2** [T, usually passive] to estimate what the size, cost or amount of sth will be in the future based on what is happening now 预测；预计；推想 SYN **forecast**: ~ **sth** *A growth rate of 4% is projected for next year.* 预计明年的增长率为 4%。◇ ~ **sth to do sth** *The unemployment rate has been projected to fall.* 据预测失业率将下降。 HELP This pattern is usually used in the passive. 此句型通常用于被动语态：**it is projected that...** *It is projected that the unemployment rate will fall.* 据预测失业率将会下降。
- **LIGHT/IMAGE** 光；影像 **3** [T] ~ **sth** (**on/onto sth**) to make light, an image, etc. fall onto a flat surface or screen 放映；投射；投影：*Images are projected onto the retina of the eye.* 影像被投射到眼睛的视网膜上。
- **STICK OUT** 突出 **4** [I] + **adv./prep.** to stick out beyond an edge or a surface 突出；外伸；伸出 SYN **protrude**: *a building with balconies projecting out over the street* 阳台伸出到街上的楼房
- **PRESENT YOURSELF** 表现 **5** [T] to present sb/sth/yourself to other people in a particular way, especially one that gives a good impression 展现；表现；确立（好印象）：~ **sth** *They sought advice on how to project a more positive image of their company.* 他们就如何树立公司更正面的形象征询意见。◇ *She projects an air of calm self-confidence.* 她表现出镇定自若的神态。◇ ~ **sb/sth/yourself** (**as sb/sth**) *He projected himself as a man worth listening to.* 他装成很有见地的样子。
- **SEND/THROW UP OR AWAY** 发出；抛射 **6** [T] ~ **sth/sb** (+ **adv./prep.**) to send or throw sth up or away from yourself 投掷；抛射；发送：*Actors must learn to project their voices.* 演员必须学会放开声音。◇ (*figurative*) *the powerful men who would project him into the White House* 能使他平步进入白宫的有力人士

PHR V **proˈject sth onto sb** (*psychology* 心) to imagine that other people have the same feelings, problems, etc. as you, especially when this is not true（不自觉地）把（自己的感觉或问题等）投射到别人身上

pro·ject·ile /prəˈdʒektaɪl; *NAmE* -tl/ *noun, adj.*

■ ***noun*** (*formal* or *specialist*) **1** an object, such as a bullet, that is fired from a gun or other weapon 射弹（如子弹、炮弹等） **2** any object that is thrown as a weapon（作为武器的）发射物；导弹

■ ***adj.*** (*formal* or *specialist*) very fast and with a lot of force 迅速有力的；猛烈的：*projectile motion* 迅速有力的动作 ◇ *The virus causes projectile* (= sudden and violent) *vomiting.* 该病毒可引起突然的剧烈呕吐。

pro·jec·tion AW /prəˈdʒekʃn/ *noun*
- **ESTIMATE** 估计 **1** [C] an estimate or a statement of what figures, amounts, or events will be in the future, or what they were in the past, based on what is happening now 预测；推断；设想：*to make **forward/backward projections** of population figures* 推断未来/过去的人口数量 ◇ *Sales have exceeded our projections.* 销售量超过了我们的预测。
- **OF IMAGE** 影像 **2** [U, C] the act of putting an image of sth onto a surface; an image that is shown in this way 投射；放映；投影；放映的影像：*the projection of three-dimensional images on a computer screen* 在电脑屏幕上显示的立体影像 ◇ *laser projections* 激光影像
- **OF SOLID SHAPE** 立体图形 **3** [C] (*specialist*) a solid shape or object as represented on a flat surface 投影图：*map projections* 投影地图
- **STH THAT STICKS OUT** 突出物 **4** [C] something that sticks out from a surface 突起物；隆起物：*tiny projections on the cell* 细胞上的小尖突出物
- **OF VOICE/SOUND** 声音 **5** [U] the act of making your voice, a sound, etc. AUDIBLE (= able to be heard) at a distance（嗓音或声音的）发送，传送，放开：*voice projection* 嗓音的放开
- **PSYCHOLOGY** 心理学 **6** [U] the act of imagining that sb else is thinking the same as you and is reacting in the same way 投射（不自觉地把自己的思想等加诸他人）
- **OF THOUGHTS/FEELINGS** 思想感情 **7** [C, U] the act of giving a form and structure to inner thoughts and feelings（思想感情的）体现，形象化：*The idea of God is a projection of humans' need to have something greater than themselves.* 人类需要有强于自身的形象，上帝就是这个需要的体现。

pro·jec·tion·ist /prəˈdʒekʃənɪst/ *noun* a person whose job is to show films/movies by operating a projector 电影放映员

pro·ject·or /prəˈdʒektə(r)/ *noun* a piece of equipment for projecting photographs, films/movies or computer SLIDES onto a screen 放映机；投影仪 ➲ VISUAL VOCAB PAGES V71, V72 ➲ SEE ALSO DATA PROJECTOR, OVERHEAD PROJECTOR, SLIDE PROJECTOR

pro·lapse /ˈprəʊlæps; *NAmE* ˈproʊ-/ *noun* (*medical* 医) a condition in which an organ of the body has slipped forward or down from its normal position (身体器官的）脱垂，下垂，脱出

prole /prəʊl; *NAmE* proʊl/ *noun* (*old-fashioned, BrE, informal*) an offensive word for a person （含冒犯意，指无产阶级工人）

pro·le·tar·ian /ˌprəʊləˈteəriən; *NAmE* ˌproʊləˈter-/ *adj.* connected with ordinary people who earn money by working, especially those who do not own any property 无产者的；无产阶级的；工人阶级的 ➲ COMPARE BOURGEOIS (1) ▶ **pro·le·tar·ian** *noun*

the pro·le·tar·iat /ˌprəʊləˈteəriət; *NAmE* ˌproʊləˈter-/ *noun* [sing.+sing./pl. v.] (*specialist*) (used especially when talking about the past 尤用以指过去) the class of ordinary people who earn money by working, especially those who do not own any property 无产阶级；工人阶级；普罗阶级 ➲COMPARE BOURGEOISIE

ˌpro-ˈlife *adj.* [usually before noun] opposed to ABORTION 反堕胎的；反对人工流产的：*the pro-life movement* 反堕胎运动 ◇ *a pro-life campaigner* 反堕胎运动成员 ➲ COMPARE PRO-CHOICE

pro·lif·er·ate /prəˈlɪfəreɪt/ *verb* [I] to increase rapidly in number or amount 迅速繁殖（或增殖）；猛增 SYN **multiply**: *Books and articles on the subject have proliferated over the last year.* 过去一年以来，论及这一专题的书和文章大量涌现。

pro·lif·er·ation /prəˌlɪfəˈreɪʃn/ *noun* [U, sing.] the sudden increase in the number or amount of sth; a large number of a particular thing 激增；增殖；增生；大量的事物：*attempts to prevent cancer cell proliferation* 防止癌细胞扩散的努力 ◇ *a proliferation of personal computers* 个人电脑的激增

pro·lif·ic /prəˈlɪfɪk/ *adj.* **1** (of an artist, a writer, etc. 艺术家、作家等) producing many works, etc. 多产的；创作丰富的：*a prolific author* 多产的作家 ◇ *a prolific goalscorer* 杰出射门手 ◇ *one of the most prolific periods in her career* 她的创作生涯中成果最丰的时期之一 **2** (of plants, animals, etc. 植物、动物等) producing a lot of fruit, flowers, young, etc. 丰硕的；多产的；多育的 **3** able to produce enough food, etc. to keep many animals and plants alive 富饶的；富庶的；肥沃的：*prolific rivers* 富饶的河川 **4** existing in large numbers 众多的；大批的：*a pop star with a prolific following of teenage fans* 拥有大批少男少女歌迷的流行歌星 ▶ **pro·lif·ic·al·ly** *adv.*: *to write prolifically* 著作等身 ◇ *animals that breed prolifically* 多产的动物

pro·lix /ˈprəʊlɪks; *NAmE* ˈproʊ-/ *adj.* (*formal*) (of writing, a speech, etc. 文章、讲话等) using too many words and therefore boring 冗长乏味的；繁琐的；啰嗦的 ▶ **pro·lix·ity** /prəʊˈlɪksəti; *NAmE* proʊ-/ *noun* [U]

pro·logue /ˈprəʊlɒg; *NAmE* ˈproʊlɔːg; -lɑːg/ *noun* a speech, etc. at the beginning of a play, book, or film/movie that introduces it 序言；序幕；开场白 ➲COMPARE EPILOGUE

pro·long /prəˈlɒŋ; *NAmE* -ˈlɔːŋ; -ˈlɑːŋ/ *verb* ~ **sth** to make sth last longer 延长 SYN **extend**: *The operation could prolong his life by two or three years.* 这次手术可使他多活两三年。◇ *Don't* ***prolong the agony*** (= of not knowing sth)—*just tell us who won!* 别卖关子了，快说谁赢了！

pro·longa·tion /ˌprəʊlɒŋˈgeɪʃn; *NAmE* ˌproʊlɔːŋ-/ *noun* [U, sing.] (*formal*) the act of making sth last longer 延长；延伸：*the artificial prolongation of human life* 对人类寿命的人为的延长

pro·longed /prəˈlɒŋd; *NAmE* -ˈlɔːŋd; -ˈlɑːŋd/ *adj.* continuing for a long time 持久的；长期的：*a prolonged illness* 长期的病 ◇ *a prolonged period of dry weather* 长期的干旱天气

prom /prɒm; *NAmE* prɑːm/ *noun* **1** (especially in the US) a formal dance, especially one that is held at a HIGH SCHOOL（尤指美国高中的）正式舞会：*the senior prom* 高年级毕业舞会 **2** (*BrE, informal, becoming old-fashioned*) = PROMENADE (1): *to walk along the prom* 沿步行道散步 **3** (*BrE*) = PROMENADE CONCERT: *the last night of the proms* 逍遥音乐会的最后夜场

prom·en·ade /ˌprɒməˈnɑːd; *NAmE* ˌprɑːməˈneɪd/ *noun, verb*
■ *noun* **1** (*also informal* **prom**) (*both BrE, becoming old-fashioned*) a public place for walking, usually a wide path beside the sea 公共散步场所；（常指）滨海步行大道 **2** (*old-fashioned*) a walk that you take for pleasure or exercise, especially by the sea, in a public park, etc.（尤指在海滨、公园等的）散步，漫步
■ *verb* [I] (*old-fashioned*) to walk up and down in a relaxed way, by the sea, in a public park, etc.（在海滨、公园等）散步，漫步

ˌpromenade ˈconcert (*also informal* **prom**) (*both BrE*) *noun* a concert at which many of the audience stand up or sit on the floor 逍遥音乐会（听众可随意走动）

Pro·me·thean /prəˈmiːθiən/ *adj.* doing things in an individual and original way and showing no respect for authority and rules 勇于开创的；不畏权势的；不受约束的 ➲MORE LIKE THIS 16, page R27 ORIGIN From the Greek myth in which **Prometheus**, a Titan, stole fire from the gods and gave it to humans. 源自提坦巨神普罗米修斯 (Prometheus) 盗取火种送到人间的希腊神话。

pro·me·thium /prəˈmiːθiəm/ *noun* [U] (*symb.* **Pm**) a chemical element. Promethium is a RADIOACTIVE metal that was first produced artificially in a nuclear REACTOR and is found in small amounts in nature. 钷（放射性化学元素）

prom·in·ence /ˈprɒmɪnəns; *NAmE* ˈprɑːm-/ *noun* [U, sing.] the state of being important, well known or noticeable 重要；突出；卓越；出名：*a young actor who has recently risen to prominence* 最近崭露头角的一名年轻演员 ◇ *The newspapers have given undue prominence to the story.* 报章对这件事的报道太多了。◇ *She has achieved a prominence she hardly deserves.* 她实在不配享有这么大的名声。

prom·in·ent /ˈprɒmɪnənt; *NAmE* ˈprɑːm-/ *adj.* **1** important or well known 重要的；著名的；杰出的：*a prominent politician* 杰出的政治家 ◇ *He* ***played a prominent part*** *in the campaign.* 他在这次运动中发挥了重要作用。◇ *She was prominent in the fashion industry.* 她曾在时装界名噪一时。**2** easily seen 显眼的；显著的；突出的 SYN **noticeable**: *The church tower was a prominent feature in the landscape.* 教堂的尖塔曾经是此地景观的重要特色。◇ *The story was given a prominent position on the front page.* 这则报道刊登在头版的显著位置。**3** sticking out from sth 突出的；凸现的：*a prominent nose* 高鼻子 ◇ *prominent cheekbones* 突出的颧骨 ▶ **prom·in·ent·ly** *adv.*: *The photographs were prominently displayed on her desk.* 几张照片摆在她桌子上显眼的位置。◇ *Problems of family relationships feature prominently in her novels.* 关注家庭纠葛是她小说的显著特点。

pro·mis·cu·ous /prəˈmɪskjuəs/ *adj.* (*disapproving*) **1** having many sexual partners 淫乱的；滥交的：*promiscuous behaviour* 淫乱行为 ◇ *a promiscuous lifestyle* 不检点的生活 ◇ *to be sexually promiscuous* 性生活淫乱 **2** (*formal*) taken from a wide range of sources, especially without careful thought 大杂烩的；杂乱的：*promiscuous reading* 读书庞杂 ◇ *a stylistically promiscuous piece of music* 一支风格杂乱的乐曲 ▶ **prom·is·cu·ity** /ˌprɒmɪsˈkjuːəti; *NAmE* ˌprɑːməs-/ *noun* [U]: *sexual promiscuity* 淫乱 **prom·is·cu·ous·ly** *adv.*

prom·ise /ˈprɒmɪs; *NAmE* ˈprɑːm-/ *verb, noun*
■ *verb* **1** [I, T] to tell sb that you will definitely do or not do sth, or that sth will definitely happen 许诺；承诺；答应；保证：~ **(to do sth)** *The college principal promised to look into the matter.* 学院院长答应调查这个问题。◇ *'Promise not to tell anyone!' 'I promise.'* "你要保证不告诉别人！""我保证。" ◇ *They arrived at 7.30* ***as they had promised.*** 他们按说定的 7:30 到达了。◇ ~ **sth** *The government has promised a full investigation into the disaster.* 政府已承诺对这次灾难进行全面调查。◇ *I'll see what I can do but* ***I can't promise anything.*** 我会看看我能做什么，但

不能给予任何承诺。◇ ~ (that)… *The brochure promised (that) the local food would be superb.* 旅游指南中保证说当地有上佳的美食。◇ ~ sb (that)… *You promised me (that) you'd be home early tonight.* 你曾向我保证今晚会早回家的。◇ ~ sth to sb *He promised the money to his grandchildren.* 他答应把这笔钱给孙儿孙女们。◇ ~ sb sth *He promised his grandchildren the money.* 他答应给孙儿孙女们这笔钱。◇ ~ yourself sth *I've promised myself some fun when the exams are over.* 等考试完了，我打算好好玩玩。◇ ~ (sb) + speech *'I'll be back soon,' she promised.* "我马上回来。" 她答应说。 ➲ MORE LIKE THIS 33, page R28 **2** [T] to make sth seem likely to happen; to show signs of sth 使很可能；预示： **it promises to be sth** *It promises to be an exciting few days.* 那可望是兴奋刺激的几天。◇ ~ sth *There were dark clouds overhead promising rain.* 天上乌云密布，预示就要下雨。 ➲ MORE LIKE THIS 26, page R28

IDM **I (can) 'promise you** (*informal*) used as a way of encouraging or warning sb about sth （用于鼓励或警告）保证，保管： *I can promise you, you'll have a wonderful time.* 我保证你会玩得很痛快。◇ *If you don't take my advice, you'll regret it, I promise you.* 你若不听我的劝告，保管你会后悔的。 **promise (sb) the 'earth/'moon/'world** (*informal*) to make promises that will be impossible to keep 作出不可能实现的承诺

■ ***noun*** **1** [C] a statement that tells sb that you will definitely do or not do sth 诺言；许诺；承诺： *to **make/keep/break a promise*** 许下 / 信守 / 违背诺言 ◇ ~ (to do sth) *She kept her promise to visit her aunt regularly.* 她信守诺言，定期去看望姑妈。◇ ~ (of sth) *The government failed to keep its promise of lower taxes.* 政府未能兑现减税的承诺。◇ ~ (that…) *Do I have your promise that you won't tell anyone about this?* 你保证不把这事告诉任何人吗？◇ *You haven't gone back on your promise, have you?* 你该不会反悔了吧？ IDM SEE LICK *n.* **2** [U] a sign that sb/sth will be successful 获得成功的迹象 SYN **potential**： *Her work **shows** great **promise**.* 她的作品显示她大有前途。◇ *He failed to fulfil his **early promise**.* 他没有像小时候表现的那样有出息。◇ *Their future was **full of promise**.* 他们的未来充满希望。 **3** [U, sing.] ~ of sth a sign, or a reason for hope that sth may happen, especially sth good 吉兆；迹象： *The day dawned bright and clear, with the promise of warm, sunny weather.* 拂晓时晴空万里，预示着温暖晴朗的天气。

the ˌPromised 'Land *noun* [sing.] a place or situation where you expect to be happy, safe, etc. 福地；乐土；安乐境界

prom·is·ing /'prɒmɪsɪŋ; *NAmE* 'prɑːm-/ *adj.* showing signs of being good or successful 有希望的；有前途的；有出息的： *He was voted the most promising new actor for his part in the movie.* 他因在该电影中扮演的角色而获评为最有前途的新演员。◇ *The weather doesn't look very promising.* 天气看起来不会太好。 ▶ **prom·is·ing·ly** *adv.*： *The day began promisingly with bright sunshine.* 晨曦灿烂，预示了一个大好的晴天。

prom·is·sory note /'prɒmɪsəri nəʊt; *NAmE* 'prɑːmɪsɔːri noʊt/ *noun* (*specialist*) a signed document containing a promise to pay a stated amount of money before a particular date 本票；期票

promo /'prəʊməʊ; *NAmE* 'proʊmoʊ/ *adj.* [only before noun] (*informal*) connected with advertising (= PROMOTING) sb/sth, especially a new pop record 推销（新流行唱片等）的；广告宣传的： *a promo video* 促销录像 ▶ **promo** *noun* (*pl.* **-os**)： *to make pop promos* 做流行音乐促销

prom·on·tory /'prɒməntri; *NAmE* 'prɑːməntɔːri/ *noun* (*pl.* **-ies**) a long narrow area of high land that goes out into the sea 岬，岬角（深入海中的狭长高地） SYN **headland** ➲ WORDFINDER NOTE AT COAST ➲ VISUAL VOCAB PAGE V5

pro·mote AW /prə'məʊt; *NAmE* -'moʊt/ *verb* **1** ~ sth to help sth to happen or develop 促进；推动 SYN **encourage**： *policies to promote economic growth* 促进经济增长的政策 ◇ *a campaign to promote awareness of environmental issues* 提高环保意识的运动 **2** to help sell a product, service, etc. or make it more popular by advertising it or offering it at a special price 促销；推销： ~ sth *The band has gone on tour to promote their new album.* 这个乐队已开始巡回宣传他们的新唱片。◇ ~ sth as sth *The area is being promoted as a tourist destination.* 这个地区正被推广为旅游点。 **3** [often passive] to move sb to a higher rank or more senior job 提升；晋升： ~ sb *She worked hard and was soon promoted.* 她工作勤奋，不久就得到提升了。◇ ~ sb (from sth) (to sth) *He has been promoted to sergeant.* 他已晋升为巡佐。 OPP **demote** **4** ~ sth (from sth) (to sth) to move a sports team from playing with one group of teams to playing in a better group 将（体育运动队）晋级： *They were promoted to the First Division last season.* 上个赛季他们晋升为甲级队。 OPP **relegate**

pro·moter AW /prə'məʊtə(r); *NAmE* -'moʊ-/ *noun* **1** a person or company that organizes or provides money for an artistic performance or a sporting event （艺术演出或体育比赛的）筹办人，发起者，赞助者 **2** ~ of sth a person who tries to persuade others about the value or importance of sth 倡导者；支持者 SYN **champion**： *She became a leading promoter of European integration.* 她成为欧洲一体化的主要支持者。

pro·mo·tion AW /prə'məʊʃn; *NAmE* -'moʊʃn/ *noun* **1** [U, C] ~ (to sth) a move to a more important job or rank in a company or an organization 提升；提拔；晋升： *Her promotion to Sales Manager took everyone by surprise.* 竟然提拔她当销售经理，叫每个人都感到意外。◇ *The new job is a promotion for him.* 这一新职务对他是擢升。◇ *a job with excellent **promotion prospects*** 有充分晋升机会的职务 ➲ COLLOCATIONS AT JOB **2** [U] ~ (to sth) a move by a sports team from playing in one group of teams to playing in a better group （体育运动队的）晋级，升级： *the team's promotion to the First Division* 这个球队晋升为甲级队 OPP **relegation** **3** [U, C] activities done in order to increase the sales of a product or service; a set of advertisements for a particular product or service 促销活动；广告宣传： *Her job is mainly concerned with sales and promotion.* 她的工作主要是销售和广告宣传方面的。◇ *We are doing a special promotion of Chilean wines.* 我们正在做智利葡萄酒的特别促销活动。 ➲ SEE ALSO CROSS-PROMOTION ➲ SYNONYMS AT ADVERTISEMENT ➲ WORDFINDER NOTE AT SHOP **4** [U] ~ of sth (*formal*) activity that encourages people to believe in the value or importance of sth, or that helps sth to succeed 推广；促进： *a society for the promotion of religious tolerance* 一个促进宗教包容的团体

pro·mo·tion·al /prə'məʊʃənl; *NAmE* -'moʊ-/ *adj.* connected with advertising 广告宣传的；推销的： *promotional material* 广告宣传资料

prompt /prɒmpt; *NAmE* prɑːmpt/ *adj., verb, noun, adv.*

■ ***adj.*** **1** done without delay 立即的；迅速的；及时的 SYN **immediate**： *Prompt action was required as the fire spread.* 由于火势蔓延，须要立即采取行动。◇ *Prompt payment of the invoice would be appreciated.* 见发票即付款，将不胜感激。 **2** [not before noun] (of a person 人) acting without delay; arriving at the right time 敏捷；迅速；准时 SYN **punctual**： *Please be prompt when attending these meetings.* 参加上述会议，请准时出席。 ▶ **prompt·ness** *noun* [U]

■ ***verb*** **1** [T] to make sb decide to do sth; to cause sth to happen 促使；导致；激起 SYN **provoke**： ~ sth *The discovery of the bomb prompted an increase in security.* 此次发现炸弹促使当局加强了安全工作。◇ *His speech prompted an angry outburst from a man in the crowd.* 他的讲话激起了人群中一男子的愤怒。◇ ~ sb to do sth *The thought of her daughter's wedding day prompted her to lose some weight.* 对女儿婚期的操心使她消瘦不少。 **2** [T] to encourage sb to speak by asking them questions or suggesting words that they could say 鼓励，提示，提醒（某人说话）： ~ sb *She was too nervous to speak and had to be prompted.* 她紧张得说不出话来，只好听人提示。◇ ~ sb to do sth (*computing* 计) *The program will prompt you to enter data where required.* 这个程序在必要时将提醒你输入数据。◇ ~ (sb) + speech *'And then what happened?' he prompted.* "后来怎样了？" 他鼓励对方继续说下去。 **3** [T, I] ~ (sb) to follow

P

the text of a play and remind the actors what the words are if they forget their lines 给（演员）提词

■ *noun* **1** a word or words said to an actor, to remind them what to say next when they have forgotten（给演员的）提词，提示 **2** (*computing* 计) a sign on a computer screen that shows that the computer has finished doing sth and is ready for more instructions 提示符

■ *adv.* exactly at the time mentioned 准时地：*The meeting will begin at ten o'clock prompt.* 会议将于十点钟准时开始。

prompt·er /ˈprɒmptə(r); *NAmE* ˈprɑːm-/ *noun* a person who prompts actors in a play 提词人（给演员提示台词）➲ WORDFINDER NOTE AT PERFORMANCE

prompt·ing /ˈprɒmptɪŋ; *NAmE* ˈprɑːm-/ *noun* [U] (*also* **promptings** [pl.]) an act of persuading sb to do sth 劝说；催促；督促：*He wrote the letter without further prompting.* 他不用人再催促就写了信。◇ *Never again would she listen to the promptings of her heart.* 她再也不会冲动行事了。

prompt·ly 🔑 /ˈprɒmptli; *NAmE* ˈprɑːm-/ *adv.* **1** 🔑 without delay 迅速地；立即：*She deals with all the correspondence promptly and efficiently.* 她迅速有效地处理全部来往信件。 **2** 🔑 exactly at the correct time or at the time mentioned 及时地；准时地 SYN **punctually**：*They arrived promptly at two o'clock.* 他们于两点钟准时到达。 **3** (always used before the verb 总置于动词前) immediately 立即；马上：*She read the letter and promptly burst into tears.* 她一看信眼泪就夺眶而出。

pro·mul·gate /ˈprɒmlgeɪt; *NAmE* ˈprɑːm-/ *verb* (*formal*) **1** [usually passive] **~ sth** to spread an idea, a belief, etc. among many people 传播；传扬；宣传 **2 ~ sth** to announce a new law or system officially or publicly 宣布，颁布，发布（新法律或制度） ▶ **pro·mul·ga·tion** /ˌprɒmlˈgeɪʃn; *NAmE* ˌprɑːm-/ *noun* [U]

prone /prəʊn; *NAmE* proʊn/ *adj.* **1** likely to suffer from sth or to do sth bad 易于遭受；有做（坏事）的倾向 SYN **liable**：**~ to sth** *prone to injury* 容易受伤 ◇ *Working without a break makes you more prone to error.* 连续工作不停歇使人更容易出错。◇ **~ to do sth** *Tired drivers were found to be particularly prone to ignore warning signs.* 据调查，疲劳驾车时特别容易忽视警示标志。 **2 -prone** (in adjectives 构成形容词) likely to suffer or do the thing mentioned 有做…倾向的；易于遭受…的：*error-prone* 容易出错的 ◇ *injury-prone* 容易受伤的 ➲ SEE ALSO ACCIDENT-PRONE **3** (*formal*) lying flat with the front of your body touching the ground 俯卧的 SYN **prostrate**：*The victim lay prone without moving.* 受害人趴在地上一动不动。◇ *He was found lying in a prone position.* 人们发现他俯卧着。➲ COMPARE SUPINE (1) ▶ **prone·ness** *noun* [U]：*proneness to depression* 易消沉倾向

prong /prɒŋ; *NAmE* prɔːŋ/ *noun* **1** each of the two or more long pointed parts of a fork 叉子齿；叉齿 ➲ VISUAL VOCAB PAGE V23 **2** each of the separate parts of an attack, argument, etc., that move towards a place, subject, etc. from different positions（进攻、论点等的）方面 **3 -pronged** (in adjectives 构成形容词) having the number or type of prongs mentioned 有…齿的；分…方面的：*a two-pronged fork* 二齿叉 ◇ *a three-pronged attack* 三路进攻

pro·nom·inal /prəʊˈnɒmɪnl; *NAmE* proʊˈnɑːm-/ *adj.* (*grammar* 语法) relating to a pronoun 代词的

pro·noun /ˈprəʊnaʊn; *NAmE* ˈproʊ-/ *noun* (*grammar* 语法) a word that is used instead of a noun or noun phrase, for example *he, it, hers, me, them,* etc. 代词（代替名词或名词词组的单词）：*demonstrative/interrogative/possessive/relative pronouns* 指示 / 疑问 / 物主 / 关系代词 ➲ SEE ALSO PERSONAL PRONOUN

pro·nounce 🔑 /prəˈnaʊns/ *verb* **1** 🔑 **~ sth** to make the sound of a word or letter in a particular way 发音；读（音）：*Very few people can pronounce my name correctly.* 很少人能把我的名字念正确。◇ *The 'b' in lamb is not pronounced.* * lamb 中的 b 不发音。➲ SEE ALSO PRONUNCIATION, UNPRONOUNCEABLE **2** (*formal*) to say or give sth formally, officially or publicly 正式宣布（或公布、授予等）：**~ sth** *to pronounce an opinion* 发表意见 ◇ *The judge will* ***pronounce sentence*** *today.* 法官将于今天宣判。◇ **~ sb/sth + noun** *She pronounced him the winner of the competition.* 她宣布他是竞赛的优胜者。◇ *I now pronounce you man and wife* (= in a marriage ceremony). 现在正式宣布你们结为夫妻。◇ **~ sb/sth + adj.** *She was pronounced dead on arrival at the hospital.* 到达医院时她被宣布已经死亡。◇ **~ sb/sth to be/have sth** *He pronounced the country to be in a state of war.* 他宣布全国进入战争状态。◇ **~ that…** *She pronounced that an error had been made.* 她宣称曾经有个错误。◇ **+ speech** *'It's pneumonia,' he pronounced gravely.* "是肺炎。"他沉重地宣布。

> **WORD FAMILY**
> pronounce *verb*
> pronunciation *noun*
> unpronounceable *adj.*
> mispronounce *verb*

PHR V **proˈnounce for/against sb** (*law* 律) to give a judgement in court for or against sb 作出有利（或不利）于…的判决；判…胜诉（或败诉）：*The judge pronounced for* (= in favour of) *the defendant.* 法官宣布被告胜诉。 **proˈnounce on/upon sth** (*formal*) to state your opinion on sth, or give a decision about sth 就…表态（或作决定）：*The minister will pronounce on further security measures later today.* 今天稍后，部长将发表进一步的安全措施。

pro·nounce·able /prəˈnaʊnsəbl/ *adj.* (of sounds or words 声音或词语) that can be pronounced 发音的；读得出的 OPP **unpronounceable**

pro·nounced /prəˈnaʊnst/ *adj.* very noticeable, obvious or strongly expressed 显著的；很明显的；表达明确的 SYN **definite**：*He walked with a pronounced limp.* 他走路明显跛足。◇ *She has very pronounced views on art.* 她有非常明确的艺术观。

pro·nounce·ment /prəˈnaʊnsmənt/ *noun* **~ (on sth)** (*formal*) a formal public statement 声明；公告；宣告

pronto /ˈprɒntəʊ; *NAmE* ˈprɑːntoʊ/ *adv.* (*informal*) quickly; immediately 立即；马上；火速：*I expect to see you back here, pronto!* 我要你立即回到这里来！

pro·nun·ci·ation 🔑 /prəˌnʌnsiˈeɪʃn/ *noun* **1** 🔑 [U, C] the way in which a language or a particular word or sound is pronounced 发音；读音：*a guide to English pronunciation* 英语发音指南 ◇ *There is more than one pronunciation of 'garage'.* * garage 的读音不止一种。

> **WORDFINDER** 联想词：cluster, consonant, diphthong, elide, intonation, phonetics, stress, tone, voiced

2 🔑 [sing.] the way in which a particular person pronounces the words of a language（某人的）发音：*Your pronunciation is excellent.* 你的发音好极了。➲ WORDFINDER NOTE AT DICTIONARY, LANGUAGE, WORD

proof 🔑 /pruːf/ *noun, adj., verb*

■ *noun* **1** 🔑 [U, C] information, documents, etc. that show that sth is true 证据；证明 SYN **evidence**：***positive/conclusive proof*** 确切的 / 确凿的证据 ◇ **~ of sth** *Can you provide any* ***proof of identity****?* 你能提供什么身份证明吗？◇ *Keep the receipt as* ***proof of purchase****.* 保存收据，作为购物证明。◇ *These results are a further proof of his outstanding ability.* 这些成果进一步证明了他的杰出才干。◇ **~ that…** *There is no proof that the knife belonged to her.* 没有证据证明那把刀子是属于她的。 **2** [U] the process of testing whether sth is true or a fact 检验；证实：*Is the claim capable of proof?* 这个说法能证明是正确的吗？➲ SEE ALSO BURDEN OF PROOF **3** [C] (*mathematics* 数) a way of proving that a statement is true or that what you have calculated is correct 证明；求证；验算 **4** [C, usually pl.] a copy of printed material which is produced so that mistakes can be corrected 校样：*She was checking the proofs of her latest novel.* 她正在审阅她的新小说的校样。 **5** [U] a standard used to measure the strength of alcoholic drinks（酒的）标准酒精度

IDM **the proof of the ˈpudding (is in the ˈeating)** (*saying*) you can only judge if sth is good or bad when you have tried it 只有通过体验才能判断事物的好坏 ➲ MORE AT LIVING *adj.*

P

■ *adj.* **1 ~ against sth** (*formal*) that can resist the damaging or harmful effects of sth 能抵御；能防范；可防护：*The sea wall was not proof against the strength of the waves.* 海堤挡不住海浪的力量。 **2** (in compounds 构成复合词) that can resist or protect against the thing mentioned 防…的；抗…的：***rainproof/windproof** clothing* 防雨 / 防风服装 ◇ *The car has childproof locks on the rear doors.* 汽车后门装有防止儿童开启的锁。◇ *an inflation-proof pension plan* 已考虑通货膨胀的养老金计划

■ *verb* **1 ~ sth** to put a special substance on sth, especially cloth, to protect it against water, fire, etc. 给（织物等）做防护处理；使防水（或防火等）：*proofed canvas* 做过防水处理的帆布 **2 ~ sth** to produce a test copy of a piece of printed work so that mistakes can be corrected 印…的校样：*colour proofing* 印彩色校样

proof·read /ˈpruːfriːd/ *verb* (**proof·read**, **proof·read** /-red/) [T, I] ~ (**sth**) to read and correct a piece of written or printed work 校阅；校对；勘校：*Has this document been proofread?* 这份文件校对过没有？ ▶ **proof·read·er** *noun*：*to work as a proofreader for a publishing company* 给一家出版公司当校对员

prop /prɒp; *NAmE* prɑːp/ *noun*, *verb*

■ *noun* **1** a piece of wood, metal, etc. used to support sth or keep it in position 支柱；支撑物：*Rescuers used props to stop the roof of the tunnel collapsing.* 救援人员用支柱防止隧道塌方。◇ *a pit prop* (= one used in a coal mine) 煤矿坑木 **2** a person or thing that gives help or support to sb/sth that is weak 支持者；支柱；后盾 **3** [usually pl.] a small object used by actors during the performance of a play or in a film/movie 道具：*He is responsible for all the stage props and lighting.* 他负责全部舞台道具和灯光。 ➲ WORDFINDER NOTE AT STAGE **4** (*also* ˈ**prop forward**) (in RUGBY 橄榄球) a player on either side of the front row of a SCRUM 支柱前锋

IDM **give props to sb** (*informal*) used to say that people should appreciate what sb has done because it is good 对（某人）表示感激（或敬佩）：*I gotta give props to the bass player.* 我得向低音电吉他演奏者表示感谢。 ORIGIN **Props** here means 'proper respect or recognition'. 在这里 props 意为"应得的尊重或认可"。

■ *verb* (**-pp-**) to support an object by leaning it against sth, or putting sth under it etc.; to support a person in the same way 支撑：**~ sth/sb/yourself** (**up**) (**against sth**) *He propped his bike against the wall.* 他把自行车靠在墙边。◇ *She propped herself up on one elbow.* 她单肘撑起身子。◇ *He lay propped against the pillows.* 他靠着枕头躺着。◇ **~ sth + adj.** *The door was propped open.* 门被支开着。

PHR V ˌ**prop sth↔ˈup 1** to prevent sth from falling by putting sth under it to support it 撑起；支起 SYN **shore sth↔up 2** (*often disapproving*) to help sth that is having difficulties 帮助；扶持；救济：*The government was accused of propping up declining industries.* 人们指责政府贴补日趋衰落的产业。

propa·ganda /ˌprɒpəˈɡændə; *NAmE* ˌprɑːpə-/ *noun* [U] (*usually disapproving*) ideas or statements that may be false or exaggerated and that are used in order to gain support for a political leader, party, etc. 宣传；鼓吹：*enemy propaganda* 敌方的宣传 ◇ *a propaganda campaign* 宣传运动

propa·gand·ist /ˌprɒpəˈɡændɪst; *NAmE* ˌprɑːpə-/ *noun* (*formal, usually disapproving*) a person who creates or spreads propaganda 鼓吹者；宣传者 ▶ **propa·gand·ist** *adj.* [only before noun]：*a propagandist organization* 宣传机构

propa·gand·ize (*BrE also* **-ise**) /ˌprɒpəˈɡændaɪz; *NAmE* ˌprɑːpə-/ *verb* [I, T] ~ (**sb/sth**) (*formal, disapproving*) to spread PROPAGANDA; to influence people using PROPAGANDA 宣传；大肆鼓吹；煽动

propa·gate /ˈprɒpəɡeɪt; *NAmE* ˈprɑːp-/ *verb* **1** [T] **~ sth** (*formal*) to spread an idea, a belief or a piece of information among many people 传播；宣传：*Television advertising propagates a false image of the ideal family.* 电视广告传播着理想家庭的一种假象。 **2** [T, I] ~ (**sth**) (*specialist*) to produce new plants from a parent plant 繁殖；增殖：*The plant can be propagated from seed.* 这种植物可由种子繁殖。◇ *Plants won't propagate in these conditions.* 植物在这种条件下不能繁殖。 ▶ **propa·ga·tion** /ˌprɒpəˈɡeɪʃn; *NAmE* ˌprɑːp-/ *noun* [U]

prop·aga·tor /ˈprɒpəɡeɪtə(r); *NAmE* ˈprɑːp-/ *noun* a box for propagating plants in （植物）繁殖盒

pro·pane /ˈprəʊpeɪn; *NAmE* ˈproʊ-/ *noun* [U] a gas found in natural gas and PETROLEUM and used as a fuel for cooking and heating 丙烷：*a propane gas cylinder* 丙烷气钢瓶

pro·pel /prəˈpel/ *verb* (**-ll-**) [often passive] **1 ~ sth** (**+ adv./prep.**) to move, drive or push sth forward or in a particular direction 推动；驱动；推进：*mechanically propelled vehicles* 机动车辆 ◇ *He succeeded in propelling the ball across the line.* 他成功地把球带过线。 **2 ~ sb + adv./prep.** to force sb to move in a particular direction or to get into a particular situation 驱使；迫使；推搡：*He was grabbed from behind and propelled through the door.* 有人从后面抓住他，把他推过门去。◇ *Fury propelled her into action.* 怒火驱使她行动起来。 ➲ SEE ALSO PROPULSION

pro·pel·lant /prəˈpelənt/ *noun* [C, U] **1** a gas that forces out the contents of an AEROSOL 喷射剂（如喷雾器中的压缩气体） **2** a thing or substance that propels sth, for example the fuel that fires a ROCKET 推进剂（如发射火箭用的燃料）

pro·pel·ler /prəˈpelə(r)/ *noun* a device with two or more blades that turn quickly and cause a ship or an aircraft to move forward 螺旋桨（飞机或轮船的推进器） ➲ VISUAL VOCAB PAGE V57

proˌpelling ˈpencil *noun* a pencil with a LEAD² (2) that can be moved down for writing by turning or pushing the top of the pencil 自动铅笔；活动铅笔

pro·pen·sity /prəˈpensəti/ *noun* (*pl.* **-ies**) (*formal*) a tendency to a particular kind of behaviour （行为方面的）倾向；习性 SYN **inclination**：**~** (**for sth/for doing sth**) *He showed a propensity for violence.* 他表现出暴力倾向。◇ **~** (**to do sth**) *She has a propensity to exaggerate.* 她老是言过其实。

proper /ˈprɒpə(r); *NAmE* ˈprɑːp-/ *adj.* **1** [only before noun] (*especially BrE*) right, appropriate or correct; according to the rules 正确的；恰当的；符合规则的：*We should have had a proper discussion before voting.* 我们本应在表决之前好好讨论一下才是。◇ *Please follow the proper procedures for dealing with complaints.* 请按规定手续处理投诉。◇ *Nothing is in its proper place.* 东西都放得乱七八糟。 **2** [only before noun] (*BrE, informal*) that you consider to be real and of a good enough standard 真正的；像样的；名副其实的：*Eat some proper food, not just toast and jam!* 吃点正常的食物，别净吃烤面包加果酱！◇ *When are you going to get a proper job?* 你打算什么时候去找一份正经的工作呀？ **3** socially and morally acceptable 符合习俗（或体统）的；正当的；规矩的：*It is **right and proper** that parents take responsibility for their children's attendance at school.* 父母负责督促子女上学上课，这是天经地义的事。◇ *The development was planned without proper regard to the interests of local people.* 新开发区的规划没有恰当考虑当地居民的利益。◇ *He is always perfectly proper in his behaviour.* 他的行为举止向来是无可挑剔的。 OPP **improper** ➲ SEE ALSO PROPRIETY **4** [after noun] according to the most exact meaning of the word 严格意义上的；狭义的：*The celebrations proper always begin on the last stroke of midnight.* 正式庆典总是在午夜钟声的最后一响开始。 **5** [only before noun] (*BrE, informal*) complete 完全的；彻底的：*We're in a proper mess now.* 我们现在真是一团糟。 **6 ~ to sth** (*formal*) belonging to a particular type of thing; natural in a particular situation or place 独具的；天然享有的；特有的：*They should be treated with the dignity proper to all individuals created by God.* 他们应当享有上帝赋予每一个受造物的尊严。

IDM ˌ**good and ˈproper** (*BrE, informal*) completely; thoroughly 完全；彻底：*That's messed things up good and proper.* 这就把事情彻底弄砸了。

ˌ**proper ˈfraction** *noun* (*mathematics* 数) a FRACTION that is less than one, with the bottom number greater than the top number, for example ¼ or ⅝ 真分数

prop·er·ly /ˈprɒpəli; *NAmE* ˈprɑːpərli/ *adv.* **1** (*especially BrE*) in a way that is correct and/or appropriate 正确地；适当地：*How much money do we need to do the job properly?* 我们需要多少钱才能做好这件事？◇ *The television isn't working properly.* 这台电视机出故障了。◇ *Make sure the letter is properly addressed.* 一定要正确书写信上的地址。 **2** in a way that is socially or morally acceptable 得体地；恰当地；符合习俗地：*You acted perfectly properly in approaching me first.* 你先来找我是完全对的。◇ *When will these kids learn to behave properly?* 这些孩子何时才能学会规矩些？ **OPP** **improperly** **3** really; in fact 真正地；实际上：*He had usurped powers that properly belonged to parliament.* 他僭夺了实际上属于议会的权力。◇ *The subject is not,* ***properly speaking*** (= really), *a science.* 严格地说，这门学科不是科学。

ˌ**proper ˈnoun** (*also* ˌ**proper ˈname**) *noun* (*grammar* 语法) a word that is the name of a person, a place, an institution, etc. and is written with a capital letter, for example *Tom, Mrs Jones, Rome, Texas, the Rhine, the White House* 专有名词（人、地、机构等的名称） ➲ COMPARE ABSTRACT NOUN, COMMON NOUN

prop·er·tied /ˈprɒpətid; *NAmE* ˈprɑːpərtid/ *adj.* [only before noun] (*formal*) owning property, especially land 有财产的；（尤指）有地产的

prop·erty /ˈprɒpəti; *NAmE* ˈprɑːpərti/ *noun* (*pl.* **-ies**) **1** [U] a thing or things that are owned by sb; a possession or possessions 所有物；财产；财物：*This building is government property.* 这座大楼是政府的财产。◇ *Be careful not to damage other people's property.* 小心别损及别人的财物。 ➲ SEE ALSO INTELLECTUAL PROPERTY, LOST PROPERTY, PUBLIC PROPERTY ➲ **SYNONYMS** AT THING **2** [U] land and buildings 不动产；房地产：*The price of property has risen enormously.* 房地产的价格大幅上升了。◇ *property prices* 房地产价格 ◇ *a property developer* 房地产开发商 ➲ **SYNONYMS** AT BUILDING **3** [C] a building or buildings and the surrounding land 房屋及院落；庄园；房地产：*There are a lot of empty properties in the area.* 这个地区有大量的闲置房地产。 ➲ **SYNONYMS** AT BUILDING ➲ **COLLOCATIONS** AT HOUSE **4** [C, usually pl.] (*formal*) a quality or characteristic that sth has 性质；特性：*Compare the physical properties of the two substances.* 比较一下这两种物质的物理性质。◇ *a plant with medicinal properties* 药用植物

proph·ecy /ˈprɒfəsi; *NAmE* ˈprɑːf-/ *noun* (*pl.* **-ies**) **1** [C] a statement that sth will happen in the future, especially one made by sb with religious or magic powers 预言：*to fulfil a prophecy* (= make it come true) 实现预言 **2** [U] (*formal*) the power of being able to say what will happen in the future 预言能力：*She was believed to have the gift of prophecy.* 据信她有预言的天赋。

proph·esy /ˈprɒfəsaɪ; *NAmE* ˈprɑːf-/ *verb* (**proph·es·ies, proph·esy·ing, proph·es·ied, proph·es·ied**) to say what will happen in the future (done in the past using religious or magic powers) 预告；预言：**~ sth** *to prophesy war* 预言有战争 ◇ **~ that…** *She prophesied that she would win a gold medal.* 她预言自己将赢得金牌。◇ **+ speech** *'It will end in disaster,' he prophesied.* "这将以灾难而告终。"他预言道。

prophet /ˈprɒfɪt; *NAmE* ˈprɑːf-/ *noun* **1** [C] (in the Christian, Jewish and Muslim religions) a person sent by God to teach the people and give them messages from God （基督教、犹太教和伊斯兰教的）先知 **2 the Prophet** [sing.] Muhammad, who founded the religion of Islam 先知穆罕默德（伊斯兰教的创始人） **3** [C] a person who claims to know what will happen in the future 预言家；预言者 **4** [C] **~ (of sth)** a person who teaches or supports a new idea, theory, etc. 倡导者；拥护者；鼓吹者：*William Morris was one of the early prophets of socialism.* 威廉·莫里斯是社会主义的早期传播者之一。 **5 the Prophets** [pl.] the name used for some books of the Old Testament and the Hebrew Bible （《〈圣经〉旧约》和《希伯来圣经》中的）先知书 **IDM** SEE DOOM *n.*

proph·et·ess /ˈprɒfɪtes; ˌprɒfɪˈtes; *NAmE* ˈprɑːfətes/ *noun* a woman who is a prophet (1,3,4) 女预言家；女倡导者

proph·et·ic /prəˈfetɪk/ *adj.* (*formal*) **1** correctly stating or showing what will happen in the future 正确预言的；有预见的：*Many of his warnings proved prophetic.* 他的许多警告都证明是有先见之明的。 **2** like or connected with a prophet or prophets 预言家的；像预言家的；似先知的：*the prophetic books of the Old Testament* 《〈圣经〉旧约》先知书 ▶ **proph·et·ic·al·ly** /prəˈfetɪkli/ *adv.*

prophy·lac·tic /ˌprɒfɪˈlæktɪk; *NAmE* ˌproʊfəˈlæktɪk/ *adj., noun*

■ **adj.** (*medical* 医) done or used in order to prevent a disease 预防疾病的：*prophylactic treatment* 预防性治疗 ▶ **prophy·lac·tic·al·ly** /-kli/ *adv.*

■ **noun** **1** (*medical* 医) a medicine, device or course of action that prevents disease 预防性药物（或器具、措施） **2** (*NAmE, formal*) = CONDOM (1)

prophy·laxis /ˌprɒfɪˈlæksɪs; *NAmE* ˌprɑːf-/ *noun* [U] (*medical* 医) action that is taken in order to prevent disease （疾病）预防

pro·pin·quity /prəˈpɪŋkwəti/ *noun* [U] (*formal*) the state of being near in space or time （空间或时间上的）临近，接近 **SYN** **proximity**

pro·piti·ate /prəˈpɪʃieɪt/ *verb* **~ sb** (*formal*) to stop sb from being angry by trying to please them 使息怒 **SYN** **placate**：*Sacrifices were made to propitiate the gods.* 人们供奉祭品以求神灵息怒。 ▶ **pro·piti·ation** /prəˌpɪʃiˈeɪʃn/ *noun* [U]

pro·piti·atory /prəˈpɪʃiətri; *NAmE* -tɔːri/ *adj.* (*formal*) intended to win back the friendship and approval of an angry or aggressive person 为和解的；为赢回好感的；安抚的：*She saw the flowers as a propitiatory offering.* 在她看来，送花是主动和解的表示。

pro·pi·tious /prəˈpɪʃəs/ *adj.* **~ (for sth/sb)** (*formal*) likely to produce a successful result 吉利的；吉庆的；吉祥的：*It was not a propitious time to start a new business.* 那不是开张营业的吉时佳日。

pro·pon·ent /prəˈpəʊnənt; *NAmE* -ˈpoʊ-/ *noun* **~ (of sth)** (*formal*) a person who supports an idea or course of action 倡导者；支持者；拥护者 **SYN** **advocate**

pro·por·tion **AW** /prəˈpɔːʃn; *NAmE* -ˈpɔːrʃn/ *noun*

• **PART OF WHOLE** 部分 **1** [C+sing./pl. v.] a part or share of a whole 部分；份额：*Water covers a large proportion of the earth's surface.* 水覆盖了地球表面的大部分。◇ *Loam is a soil with roughly equal proportions of clay, sand and silt.* 壤土是由大约等份的黏土、沙和粉砂合成的。◇ *The proportion of regular smokers increases with age.* 习惯吸烟的人口比重随年龄的增长而上升。◇ *A higher proportion of Americans go on to higher education than is the case in Britain.* 美国人上大学的比例大于英国。

• **RELATIONSHIP** 关系 **2** [U] **~ (of sth to sth)** the relationship of one thing to another in size, amount, etc. 比例；倍数关系 **SYN** **ratio**：*The proportion of men to women in the college has changed dramatically over the years.* 近年来，这个学院的男女学生比例出现了剧变。◇ *The basic ingredients are limestone and clay in the proportion 2:1.* 基本成分是石灰石和黏土，比例为 2:1。◇ *The room is very long* ***in proportion to*** (= relative to) *its width.* 这房间的长度比宽度大很多。 **3** [U, C, usually pl.] the correct relationship in size, degree, importance, etc. between one thing and another or between the parts of a whole 正确的比例；均衡；匀称：*You haven't drawn the figures in the foreground* ***in proportion.*** 你的前景人物画得不合比例。◇ *The head is* ***out of proportion with*** *the body.* 头部和身体不成比例。◇ *an impressive building with fine proportions* 比例协调的雄伟建筑物 ◇ *Always try to keep* ***a sense of proportion*** (= of the relative importance of different things). 事有轻重缓急之分，这要常记在心。

P

- **SIZE/SHAPE** 大小；形状 **4 proportions** [pl.] the measurements of sth; its size and shape 面积；体积；规模；程度：*This method divides the task into more manageable proportions.* 这个方法把要完成的任务划分成较易操作的步骤。◇ *a food shortage that could soon* ***reach crisis proportions*** 可能会很快达到危机程度的粮食短缺 ◇ *a room of fairly generous proportions* 相当宽敞的屋子
- **MATHEMATICS** 数学 **5** [U] the equal relationship between two pairs of numbers, as in the statement '4 is to 8 as 6 is to 12' 等比关系；比例

IDM **ˌkeep sth in proˈportion** to react to sth in a sensible way and not think it is worse or more serious than it really is 恰当地处事；看待事物恰如其分 **out of (all) proˈportion (to sth)** larger, more serious, etc. in relation to sth than is necessary or appropriate 不相称；不协调：*They earn salaries out of all proportion to their ability.* 他们挣的工资与其能力不相称。◇ *The media have blown the incident up out of all proportion.* 媒体大肆渲染这件事。

▼ GRAMMAR POINT 语法说明

proportion

- If **proportion** is used with an uncountable or a singular noun, the verb is generally singular. * proportion 与不可数名词或单数名词连用时，动词一般用单数：*A proportion of the land* ***is*** *used for agriculture.* 一部分土地作农用。
- If **the proportion of** is used with a plural countable noun, or a singular noun that represents a group of people, the verb is usually singular, but with **a (large, small, etc.) proportion of** a plural verb is often used, especially in *BrE*. * the proportion of 与复数可数名词或单数集合名词连用时，动词通常为单数；但如果是 a (large, small etc.) proportion of，则常用复数动词，尤其在英式英语中：*The proportion of small cars on America's roads* ***is*** *increasing.* 美国公路上小型车的比例在逐渐增加。◇ *A high proportion of five-year-olds* ***have*** *teeth in poor condition.* 有较高比例的五岁儿童牙齿不健康。

▼ LANGUAGE BANK 用语库

proportion

Describing fractions and proportions 描述分数和份额

- *According to this pie chart,* ***a third of*** *students' leisure time is spent watching TV.* 如饼分图所示，学生的闲暇时间有三分之一都花在看电视上。
- ***One in five*** *hours* ***is/are*** *spent socializing.* 每五个小时中有一个小时花在社交活动上。
- *Socializing* ***accounts for/makes up/comprises*** *about 20% of leisure time.* 社交活动占去大约百分之二十的闲暇时间。
- *Students spend* ***twice as much*** *time playing computer games as doing sport.* 学生们玩电脑游戏的时间是做运动时间的两倍。
- ***Three times as many*** *hours are spent playing computer games as reading.* 玩电脑游戏的时间是阅读时间的三倍。
- *The figure for playing computer games is* ***three times higher than*** *the figure for reading.* 玩电脑游戏的时间比阅读时间多两倍。
- ***The largest proportion of*** *time is spent playing computer games.* 大部分时间都花在玩电脑游戏上。

➲ NOTE AT HALF
➲ SYNONYMS AT CONSIST
➲ LANGUAGE BANK AT EXPECT, FALL, ILLUSTRATE, INCREASE

pro·por·tion·al AW /prəˈpɔːʃənl; *NAmE* -ˈpɔːrʃ-/ *adj.* ~ **(to sth)** increasing or decreasing in size, amount or degree according to changes in sth else 成比例的；相称的：*Salary is proportional to years of experience.* 薪金视资历而定。◇ *to be* ***directly/inversely proportional*** *to sth* 与某事物成正比/反比 ▶ **pro·por·tion·al·ly** AW *adv.*：*Families with children spend proportionally less per person than families without children.* 有子女家庭比无子女家庭的人均开销相对地少。

pro·por·tion·al·ity /prəˌpɔːʃəˈnæləti; *NAmE* -pɔːrʃ-/ *noun* [U] (*formal*) the principle that an action, a punishment, etc. should not be more severe than is necessary（行动、处罚等的）相称原则，恰当性

proˌportional ˌrepresenˈtation *noun* [U] (*abbr.* **PR**) a system that gives each party in an election a number of seats in relation to the number of votes its candidates receive 比例代表制（按参选各党派的得票比例分配席位）➲ COMPARE FIRST-PAST-THE-POST

pro·por·tion·ate AW /prəˈpɔːʃənət; *NAmE* -ˈpɔːrʃ-/ *adj.* ~ **(to sth)** (*formal*) increasing or decreasing in size, amount or degree according to changes in sth else 成比例的；相应的；相称的 **SYN** **proportional**：*The number of accidents is proportionate to the increased volume of traffic.* 交通事故的数字与交通量的增长成正比。➲ COMPARE DISPROPORTIONATE ▶ **pro·por·tion·ate·ly** AW *adv.*：*Prices have risen but wages have not risen proportionately.* 物价上涨了，但是工资并没有相应增加。

pro·por·tioned /prəˈpɔːʃənd; *NAmE* -ˈpɔːrʃ-/ *adj.* (used especially after an adverb 尤用于副词后) having parts that relate in size to other parts in the way that is described 按比例的；有某种比例关系的：*a well-proportioned living room* 比例合理的起居室 ◇ *She was tall and perfectly proportioned.* 她身材高挑且十分匀称。

pro·posal 🔑 /prəˈpəʊzl; *NAmE* -ˈpoʊzl/ *noun* **1** 🔑 [C, U] a formal suggestion or plan; the act of making a suggestion 提议；建议；动议：*to* ***submit/consider/accept/reject a proposal*** 提交/审议/接受/拒绝一项建议 ◇ **~ to do sth** *a proposal to build more office accommodation* 增建办公楼的建议 ◇ **~ that...** *His proposal that the system should be changed was rejected.* 他提的关于修改制度的建议被拒绝了。◇ **~ for sth** *The proposal for a new high-speed railway met with strong opposition.* 新建一条高速铁路的提议遭到了强烈反对。➲ WORDFINDER NOTE AT DEAL **2** 🔑 [C] an act of formally asking sb to marry you 求婚

pro·pose 🔑 /prəˈpəʊz; *NAmE* -ˈpoʊz/ *verb*
- **SUGGEST PLAN** 建议 **1** 🔑 [T] (*formal*) to suggest a plan, an idea, etc. for people to think about and decide on 提议；建议：**~ sth** *The government proposed changes to the voting system.* 政府建议修改表决制度。◇ *What would you propose?* 你想提什么建议？◇ **~ that...** *She proposed that the book be banned.* 她提议查禁这本书。◇ (*BrE also*) *She proposed that the book should be banned.* 她提议查禁这本书。◇ **it is proposed that...** *It was proposed that the president be elected for a period of two years.* 有人提议选出的主席任期为两年。◇ **~ doing sth** *He proposed changing the name of the company.* 他建议更改公司的名称。◇ **it is proposed to do sth** *It was proposed to pay the money from public funds.* 有人提议用公款支付这笔钱。
- **INTEND** 意欲 **2** 🔑 [T] (*formal*) to intend to do sth 打算；希冀；计划：**~ to do sth** *What do you propose to do now?* 现在你打算做什么？◇ **~ doing sth** *How do you propose getting home?* 你打算怎么回家？
- **MARRIAGE** 婚姻 **3** 🔑 [I, T] to ask sb to marry you 求婚：*He was afraid that if he proposed she might refuse.* 他担心他若求婚，她会拒绝。◇ **~ to sb** *She proposed to me!* 她向我求婚了！◇ **~ sth (to sb)** *to propose marriage* 求婚 ➲ WORDFINDER NOTE AT WEDDING
- **AT FORMAL MEETING** 正式会议 **4** [T] to suggest sth at a formal meeting and ask people to vote on it 提名；提出…供表决：**~ sb (for/as sth)** *I propose Tom Ellis for chairman.* 我提名汤姆·埃利斯做主席。◇ **~ sth** *to* ***propose a motion*** (= to be the main speaker in support of an idea at a formal debate) 提出动议 ➲ COMPARE OPPOSE (1), SECOND[1] *v.* ➲ WORDFINDER NOTE AT DEBATE

• SUGGEST EXPLANATION 提出解释 **5** [T] ~ sth (*formal*) to suggest an explanation of sth for people to consider 提供（解释） SYN **propound**: *She proposed a possible solution to the mystery.* 她提出了对这个奥秘的一种可能的解答。

IDM **propose a 'toast (to sb) | propose sb's 'health** to ask people to wish sb health, happiness and success by raising their glasses and drinking （为某人）祝酒： *I'd like to propose a toast to the bride and groom.* 我提议为新郎新娘的幸福干杯！

pro·poser /prəˈpəʊzə(r); *NAmE* -ˈpoʊz-/ *noun* a person who formally suggests sth at a meeting 提议人；建议人 ➲ COMPARE SECONDER

prop·os·ition /ˌprɒpəˈzɪʃn; *NAmE* ˌprɑːp-/ *noun, verb*

■ *noun* **1** an idea or a plan of action that is suggested, especially in business 提议，建议，计划（尤指业务上的）： *I'd like to put a business proposition to you.* 我想向您提个业务上的建议。◇ *He was trying to make it look like an **attractive proposition**.* 他正设法使他的计划显得吸引人。 **2** a thing that you intend to do; a problem or task to be dealt with 欲做的事；待处理的问题；任务 SYN **matter**: *Getting a work permit in the UK is not always a simple proposition.* 在英国获得工作许可证往往不是一件简单的事情。 **3** (*also* **Proposition**) (in the US) a suggested change to the law that people can vote on （美国）法律修正议案： *How did you vote on Proposition 8?* 对于第 8 项修正案你是怎么投的票？ **4** (*formal*) a statement that expresses an opinion 见解；主张；观点： *Her assessment is based on the proposition that power corrupts.* 她的分析是建立在权力使人堕落的观点上的。 **5** (*mathematics* 数) a statement of a THEOREM, and an explanation of how it can be proved 命题 ▸ **prop·os·ition·al** *adj.*

■ *verb* ~ sb to say in a direct way to sb that you would like to have sex with them 求欢： *She was propositioned by a strange man in the bar.* 酒吧里有个陌生男人向她求欢。

pro·pound /prəˈpaʊnd/ *verb* ~ sth (*formal*) to suggest an idea or explanation of sth for people to consider 提出（主意或解释）供考虑 SYN **propose, put forward**: *the theory of natural selection, first propounded by Charles Darwin* 查尔斯·达尔文首先提出的自然选择理论

pro·pri·etary /prəˈpraɪətri; *NAmE* -teri/ *adj.* [usually before noun] **1** (of goods 商品) made and sold by a particular company and protected by a REGISTERED TRADEMARK 专卖的；专营的；专利的： *a proprietary medicine* 专卖药品 ◇ *proprietary brands* 专利品牌 ◇ *a proprietary name* 专利商标名 **2** relating to an owner or to the fact of owning sth 所有的；所有权的： *The company has a proprietary right to the property.* 公司拥有这笔财产的所有权。

pro·pri·etor /prəˈpraɪətə(r)/ *noun* (*formal*) the owner of a business, a hotel, etc. 业主；所有人： *newspaper proprietors* 报业老板 ▸ **pro·pri·etor·ship** /prəˈpraɪətəʃɪp; *NAmE* -tərʃ-/ *noun* [U] ➲ SEE ALSO PROPRIETRESS

pro·pri·etor·ial /prəˌpraɪəˈtɔːriəl/ *adj.* (*formal*) relating to an owner or to the fact of owning sth 业主的；所有者的；所有权的： *proprietorial rights* 所有权 ◇ *He laid a proprietorial hand on her arm* (= as if he owned her). 他紧紧攥住她的胳膊不放。 ▸ **pro·pri·etor·ial·ly** *adv.*

pro·pri·etress /prəˈpraɪətres/ *noun* (*old-fashioned*) a woman who owns a business, hotel, etc. 女业主；女所有人 ➲ SEE ALSO PROPRIETOR ➲ NOTE AT GENDER

pro·pri·ety /prəˈpraɪəti/ *noun* (*formal*) **1** [U] moral and social behaviour that is considered to be correct and acceptable 得体的举止；有分寸的行为： *Nobody questioned the propriety of her being there alone.* 没人认为她只身出现在那里不得体。 OPP **impropriety** **2 the proprieties** [pl.] the rules of correct behaviour 行为规范；礼节；规矩 SYN **etiquette**: *They were careful to observe the proprieties.* 他们恪守规矩。

pro·pul·sion /prəˈpʌlʃn/ *noun* [U] (*specialist*) the force that drives sth forward 推进；推动力： *wind/steam/jet propulsion* 风力／蒸汽／喷气推进 ➲ SEE ALSO PROPEL ▸ **pro·pul·sive** /prəˈpʌlsɪv/ *adj.*

pro rata /ˌprəʊ ˈrɑːtə; *NAmE* ˌproʊ/ *adj.* (*from Latin, formal*) (of a payment or share of sth 付款或份额) calculated according to how much of sth has been used, the amount of work done, etc. 按比例的；成比例的；相应的 SYN **proportionate**: *If costs go up, there will be a pro rata increase in prices.* 如果成本增加，价格就会相应上涨。 ▸ **pro rata** *adv.*: *Prices will increase pro rata.* 价格将相应提高。

pro·sa·ic /prəˈzeɪɪk/ *adj.* (*usually disapproving*) **1** ordinary and not showing any imagination 平庸的；没有诗意（或美感）的 SYN **unimaginative**: *a prosaic style* 平淡的风格 **2** dull; not romantic 平淡的；乏味的；无聊的 SYN **mundane**: *the prosaic side of life* 生活平淡的一面 ▸ **pro·saic·al·ly** /-kli/ *adv.*

pro·scen·ium /prəˈsiːniəm/ *noun* the part of the stage in a theatre that is in front of the curtain 台口（剧场舞台帷幕前的部分）： *a traditional theatre with a **proscenium arch*** (= one that forms a frame for the stage where the curtain is opened) 舞台有拱形框架的传统剧场 ➲ WORDFINDER NOTE AT STAGE

pro·scribe /prəˈskraɪb; *NAmE* proʊˈs-/ *verb* ~ sth (*formal*) to say officially that sth is banned 宣布禁止： *proscribed organizations* 被查禁的组织 ▸ **pro·scrip·tion** /prəˈskrɪpʃn; *NAmE* proʊˈs-/ *noun* [U, C]

prose /prəʊz; *NAmE* proʊz/ *noun* [U] writing that is not poetry 散文： *the author's clear elegant prose* (= style of writing) 作者清雅的散文

pros·ecute /ˈprɒsɪkjuːt; *NAmE* ˈprɑːs-/ *verb* **1** [T, I] ~ (sb/sth) (for sth/doing sth) to officially charge sb with a crime in court 起诉；控告；检举： *The company was prosecuted for breaching the Health and Safety Act.* 这家公司被控违反《卫生安全法》。◇ *Trespassers will be prosecuted* (= a notice telling people to keep out of a particular area). 闲人莫入，违者必究。◇ *The police decided not to prosecute.* 警方决定不予起诉。 ➲ WORDFINDER NOTE AT LAW **2** [I, T] ~ (sb) to be a lawyer in a court case for a person or an organization that is charging sb with a crime 担任控方律师： *the **prosecuting counsel/lawyer/attorney*** 原告律师 ◇ *James Spencer, prosecuting, claimed that the witness was lying.* 原告律师詹姆斯·斯潘塞称证人在撒谎。 **3** [T] ~ sth (*formal*) to continue taking part in or doing sth 继续从事（或参与）： *They had overwhelming public support to prosecute the war.* 绝大多数民众支持他们继续这场战争。

pros·ecu·tion /ˌprɒsɪˈkjuːʃn; *NAmE* ˌprɑːs-/ *noun* **1** [U, C] the process of trying to prove in court that sb is guilty of a crime (= of prosecuting them); the process of being officially charged with a crime in court （被）起诉，检举，诉讼： *Prosecution for a first minor offence rarely leads to imprisonment.* 因初犯轻罪被控者很少被判监禁。◇ *He threatened to bring a private prosecution against the doctor.* 他威胁要对医生提起自诉。 ➲ WORDFINDER NOTE AT TRIAL ➲ COLLOCATIONS AT JUSTICE **2 the prosecution** [sing.+sing./pl. v.] a person or an organization that prosecutes sb in court, together with the lawyers, etc. 原告，控方（包括原告和原告律师等）： *He was a **witness for the prosecution**.* 他是原告证人。◇ *The prosecution has/have failed to prove its/their case.* 控方未能证明所控属实。◇ *defence and prosecution* 被告和原告 ◇ *a prosecution lawyer* 控方律师 **3** [U] (*formal*) the act of making sth happen or continue 实施；从事；继续进行

pros·ecu·tor /ˈprɒsɪkjuːtə(r); *NAmE* ˈprɑːs-/ *noun* **1** a public official who charges sb officially with a crime and prosecutes them in court 公诉人；检察官： *the **public/state prosecutor*** 公诉人；州检察官 **2** a lawyer who leads the case against a DEFENDANT in court 原告律师；控方律师

pros·elyt·ize (*BrE also* **-ise**) /ˈprɒsələtaɪz; *NAmE* ˈprɑːs-/ *verb* [I] (*formal, often disapproving*) to try to persuade other people to accept your beliefs, especially about religion or politics 使（在宗教、政治等方面）归附

ˈprose poem *noun* a piece of writing that uses the language and ideas associated with poetry, but is not in VERSE form 散文诗

P

'pro shop *noun* a shop/store at a GOLF club that sells or repairs golf equipment, usually run by a professional player who works at that club（高尔夫球俱乐部中通常由职业球员经营的）球具店

pros·ody /'prɒsədi; *NAmE* 'prɑːs-/ *noun* [U] **1** (*specialist*) the patterns of sounds and rhythms in poetry; the study of this 韵律；韵律学 **2** (*phonetics* 语音) the part of PHONETICS which is concerned with stress and INTONATION as opposed to individual speech sounds 重音和语调模式；韵律结构 ▸ **pro·sodic** /prəʊ'sɒdɪk; *NAmE* prə'sɑːdɪk/ *adj.*

pro·spect AW *noun, verb*

■ ***noun*** /'prɒspekt; *NAmE* 'prɑːs-/ **1** [U, sing.] the possibility that sth will happen 可能性；希望：~ **(of sth/of doing sth)** *There is no immediate prospect of peace.* 短期内没有和平的可能。◇ *A place in the semi-finals is* ***in prospect*** (= likely to happen). 可望争得半决赛权。◇ ~ **(that...)** *There's a reasonable prospect that his debts will be paid.* 有理由相信他会偿还债务的。 **2** [sing.] an idea of what might or will happen in the future 前景；展望；设想：*an exciting prospect* 令人兴奋的前景 ◇ *Travelling alone around the world is a daunting prospect.* 想象着将要只身走遍世界颇令人心悸。◇ ~ **(of sth/of doing sth)** *The prospect of becoming a father filled him with alarm.* 一想到将为人父他就满怀忧思。 **3** **prospects** [pl.] the chances of being successful 成功的机会；前景；前途：***good job/employment/career prospects*** 美好的工作 / 就业 / 事业前途 ◇ *At 25 he was an unemployed musician with no prospects.* * 25 岁的他是个没有工作、前途渺茫的乐师。◇ ~ **for sth** *Long-term prospects for the economy have improved.* 长期的经济前景已有所改善。◇ ~ **of sth** *What are the prospects of promotion in this job?* 做这份工作有多少晋升的机会？ **4** [C] ~ **(for sth)** a person who is likely to be successful in a competition（竞赛中的）有望获胜者：*She is one of Canada's best prospects for a gold medal.* 她是加拿大最有希望夺金的选手之一。 **5** [C] (*formal*) a wide view of an area of land, etc. 风景；景色：*a delightful prospect of the lake* 令人心旷神怡的湖上风光

■ ***verb*** /prə'spekt; *NAmE* 'prɑːs-/ [I] ~ **(for sth)** to search an area for gold, minerals, oil, etc. 探矿；勘探：*Thousands moved to the area to prospect for gold.* 数以千计的人涌入那个地区淘金。◇ (*figurative*) *to prospect for new clients* 寻找新客户

pro·spect·ive AW /prə'spektɪv/ *adj.* [usually before noun] **1** expected to do sth or to become sth 有望的；可能的；预期的；潜在的 SYN **potential**：*a prospective buyer* 可能的买主 **2** expected to happen soon 即将发生的；行将来临的 SYN **forthcoming**：*They are worried about prospective changes in the law.* 他们担心即将修改法律。

pro·spect·or /prə'spektə(r); *NAmE* 'prɑːspektər/ *noun* a person who searches an area for gold, minerals, oil, etc. 勘探者；探矿者

pro·spec·tus /prə'spektəs/ *noun* **1** a book or printed document that gives information about a school, college, etc. in order to advertise it（学校的）简章，简介 ➲ WORDFINDER NOTE AT ADVERTISE **2** (*business* 商) a document that gives information about a company's shares before they are offered for sale（企业的）招股说明书，募股章程

pros·per /'prɒspə(r); *NAmE* 'prɑːs-/ *verb* [I] to develop in a successful way; to be successful, especially in making money 繁荣；兴旺；成功；发达 SYN **thrive**

pros·per·ity /prɒ'sperəti; *NAmE* prɑː's-/ *noun* [U] the state of being successful, especially in making money 兴旺；繁荣；成功；昌盛 SYN **affluence**：*Our future prosperity depends on economic growth.* 我们未来的繁荣昌盛依赖经济的发展。◇ *The country is enjoying a period of* ***peace and prosperity***. 国家正值太平盛世。

pros·per·ous /'prɒspərəs; *NAmE* 'prɑːs-/ *adj.* (*formal*) rich and successful 繁荣的；成功的；兴旺的 SYN **affluent**：*prosperous countries* 繁荣的国家 ➲ SYNONYMS AT RICH

pro·state /'prɒsteɪt; *NAmE* 'prɑːs-/ (*also* **'prostate gland**) *noun* a small organ in men, near the BLADDER, that produces a liquid in which SPERM is carried 前列腺

pros·thesis /prɒs'θiːsɪs; *NAmE* prɑːs-/ *noun* (*pl.* **pros·theses** /-'θiːsiːz/) (*medical* 医) an artificial part of the body, for example a leg, an eye or a tooth 假体（如假肢、假眼或假牙） ▸ **pros·thet·ic** /prɒs'θetɪk; *NAmE* prɑːs-/ *adj.*：*a prosthetic arm* 假臂

pros·thet·ics /prɒs'θetɪks; *NAmE* prɑːs-/ *noun* **1** [pl.] artificial parts of the body 假体（人造的身体部分）；义肢 **2** [U] the activity of making or attaching artificial body parts 假体制作（或安装）；义肢制作（或安装）

pros·ti·tute /'prɒstɪtjuːt; *NAmE* 'prɑːstətuːt/ *noun, verb*

■ ***noun*** a person who has sex for money 卖淫者；娼妓；妓女；男妓

■ ***verb*** **1** ~ **sth/yourself** to use your skills, abilities, etc. to do sth that earns you money but that other people do not respect because you are capable of doing sth better 滥用才能；糟蹋自己：*Many felt he was prostituting his talents by writing Hollywood scripts.* 许多人觉得他给好莱坞写剧本是滥用自己的才华。 **2** ~ **yourself** to work as a prostitute 卖淫；出卖肉体

pros·ti·tu·tion /ˌprɒstɪ'tjuːʃn; *NAmE* ˌprɑːstə'tuːʃn/ *noun* [U] **1** the work of a prostitute 卖淫；为娼；当男妓：*Many women were forced into prostitution.* 许多妇女被迫为娼。◇ *child prostitution* 儿童卖淫 **2** ~ **of sth** (*formal*) the use of your abilities on sth of little value 才能的滥用（或糟蹋）

pros·trate *adj., verb*

■ ***adj.*** /'prɒstreɪt; *NAmE* 'prɑːs-/ (*formal*) **1** lying on the ground and facing downwards 俯卧的；趴着的；俯伏的：*They fell prostrate in worship.* 他们拜倒在地。◇ *He stumbled over Luke's prostrate body.* 他绊倒在卢克俯卧的身躯上。 **2** ~ **(with sth)** so shocked, upset, etc. that you cannot do anything 给（悲伤等）压倒：*She was* ***prostrate with grief*** *after her son's death.* 她因丧子悲痛欲绝。

■ ***verb*** /prɒ'streɪt; *NAmE* 'prɑːs-/ **1** ~ **yourself** to lie on your front with your face looking downwards, especially as an act of worship 俯伏；拜倒 **2** [usually passive] ~ **sb** to make sb feel weak, shocked, and unable to do anything 使一筹莫展；使无能为力 SYN **overcome**：*He was expecting to find her prostrated by the tragedy.* 他以为这场悲剧会使她一蹶不振。◇ *For months he was* ***prostrated with grief***. 他好几个月都悲痛不已。

pros·tra·tion /prɒ'streɪʃn; *NAmE* prɑː's-/ *noun* [U] (*formal*) **1** extreme physical weakness 筋疲力尽；极度虚弱；虚脱：*a state of prostration brought on by the heat* 暑热导致的虚脱状态 **2** the action of lying with your face downwards, especially in worship 拜倒；俯伏

prot·ac·tin·ium /ˌprəʊtæk'tɪniəm; *NAmE* ˌproʊ-/ *noun* [U] (*symb.* **Pa**) a chemical element. Protactinium is a RADIOACTIVE metal found naturally when URANIUM decays. 镤（放射性化学元素）

prot·ag·on·ist /prə'tægənɪst/ *noun* (*formal*) **1** the main character in a play, film/movie or book（戏剧、电影、书的）主要人物，主人公，主角 ➲ COMPARE HERO (2) ➲ WORDFINDER NOTE AT CHARACTER **2** one of the main people in a real event, especially a competition, battle or struggle（比赛、斗争中的）主要人物，主要参与者 **3** an active supporter of a policy or movement, especially one that is trying to change sth（政策、运动的）倡导者，拥护者 SYN **champion**：*a leading protagonist of the conservation movement* 资源保护运动的急先锋

pro·tea /'prəʊtiə; *NAmE* 'proʊ-/ *noun* **1** a type of bush found in South Africa with large flowers with thick orange or pink outer leaves 普罗蒂亚木（南非灌木，开外层花瓣为橙色或粉红色的大花） **2** the flower itself, which is one of South Africa's national symbols 普罗蒂亚花，帝王花（南非国花）

pro·tean /'prəʊtiən; prəʊ'tiːən; *NAmE* 'proʊ-; proʊ't-/ *adj.* (*literary*) able to change quickly and easily 多变的；易变的；变幻无常的：*a protean character* 多变的性格

pro·te·ase /ˈprəʊtieɪz; *NAmE* ˈproʊ-/ *noun* (*biology* 生) a substance in the body that breaks down PROTEINS and PEPTIDES 蛋白（水解）酶

pro·tect 🔑 /prəˈtekt/ *verb* **1** 🔑 [T, I] to make sure that sb/sth is not harmed, injured, damaged, etc. 保护；防护：**~ sb/sth/yourself (against/from sth)** *Troops have been sent to protect aid workers against attack.* 已经派出部队保护援助工作人员免遭袭击。◇ *They huddled together to protect themselves from the wind.* 他们挤在一起，免受风吹。◇ *Each company is fighting to protect its own commercial interests.* 每家公司都在奋力保护自己的商业利益。◇ **~ (against/from sth)** *a paint that helps protect against rust* 防锈漆 **2** 🔑 [T, usually passive] **~ sth** to introduce laws that make it illegal to kill, harm or damage a particular animal, area of land, building, etc. （制定法律）保护：*a protected area/species* 受保护的地区 / 物种 **3** [T, usually passive] **~ sth** to help an industry in your own country by taxing goods from other countries so that there is less competition （通过征关税）保护（国内企业）；实行贸易保护：*protected markets* 受保护的市场 **4** [T, I] **~ (sb/sth) (against sth)** to provide sb/sth with insurance against fire, injury, damage, etc. 投保；为…买保险：*Many policies do not protect you against personal injury.* 许多保单都不保障人身伤害。

pro·tec·tion 🔑 /prəˈtekʃn/ *noun* **1** 🔑 [U] **~ (for/of sb/sth) (against/from sth)** the act of protecting sb/sth; the state of being protected 保护；防卫：*Wear clothes that provide adequate protection against the wind and rain.* 穿上足以防风雨的衣服。◇ *He asked to be put **under police protection**.* 他请求警方保护。◇ *the conservation and protection of the environment* 环境的维护与保护 ◇ ***data protection** laws* 数据保护法 **2** 🔑 [C] **~ (against sth)** a thing that protects sb/sth against sth 保护物；护身符：*They wore the charm as a protection against evil spirits.* 他们戴着护身符以驱邪。 **3** [U] **~ (against sth)** insurance against fire, injury, damage, etc. 保险：*Our policy offers complete protection against fire and theft.* 我们的保单全面承保火灾及盗窃风险。 **4** [U] the system of helping an industry in your own country by taxing foreign goods 贸易保护；关税保护制：*The government is ready to introduce protection for the car industry.* 政府准备对汽车工业实行贸易保护。 **5** [U] the system of paying criminals so that they will not attack your business or property 保护费（付给歹徒金钱以免受骚扰或破坏）：*to pay **protection money*** 交保护费 ◇ *to run a **protection racket*** 干敲诈保护费的勾当

pro·tec·tion·ism /prəˈtekʃənɪzəm/ *noun* [U] the principle or practice of protecting a country's own industry by taxing foreign goods （贸易）保护主义 ▶ **pro·tec·tion·ist** /-ʃənɪst/ *adj.*：*protectionist policies* 贸易保护政策

pro·tect·ive /prəˈtektɪv/ *adj.* **1** [only before noun] providing or intended to provide protection 保护的；防护的：*Workers should wear full **protective clothing**.* 工人应该穿着全套防护服。◇ *a protective layer of varnish* 清漆防护层 ◇ *a protective barrier against the sun's rays* 防晒屏障 **2** having or showing a wish to protect sb/sth 出于（对…的）保护：**~ (towards sb/sth)** *She had been fiercely protective towards him as a teenager.* 她过去曾极力呵护他这个十几岁的孩子。◇ **~ (of sb/sth)** *He was extremely protective of his role as advisor.* 他极力保护自己的顾问角色。◇ *He put a protective arm around her shoulders.* 他呵护地用胳膊搂住她的肩膀。◇ *Parents can easily become over-protective of their children* (= want to protect them too much). 父母容易过度保护孩子。 **3** intended to give an advantage to your own country's industry 贸易保护的；实行关税保护的：*protective tariffs* 保护性关税 ▶ **pro·tect·ive·ly** *adv.*：*She clutched her bag protectively.* 她用力抓紧护着自己的提包。 **pro·tect·ive·ness** *noun* [U]

pro,tective ˈcustody *noun* [U] the state of being kept in prison for your own safety 保护性拘留；保护性监禁

pro·tect·or /prəˈtektə(r)/ *noun* a person, an organization or a thing that protects sb/sth 保护人（或组织、装置等）：*I regarded him as my friend and protector.* 我视他为我的朋友和保护者。◇ *the company's image as a protector of the environment* 这个公司作为环境保护者的形象 ◇ *Hard hats and ear protectors are provided.* 提供了安全帽和护耳。

pro·tect·or·ate /prəˈtektərət/ *noun* **1** [C] a country that is controlled and protected by a more powerful country 受保护国；受保护领地 ➲ COMPARE COLONY (1) **2** [U] the state or period of being controlled and protected by another country （一国对另一国的）保护关系

pro·tégé (*feminine* **pro·té·gée**) /ˈprɒtəʒeɪ; *NAmE* ˈproʊt-/ *noun* (*from French*) a young person who is helped in their career and personal development by a more experienced person 受提携的后进：*a protégé of the great violinist Yehudi Menuhin* 伟大的小提琴家耶胡迪•梅纽因的门生

pro·tein /ˈprəʊtiːn; *NAmE* ˈproʊ-/ *noun* [C, U] a substance, found within all living things, that forms the structure of muscles, organs, etc. There are many different proteins and they are an essential part of what humans and animals eat to help them grow and stay healthy. 蛋白质：*essential proteins and vitamins* 必不可少的蛋白质和维生素 ◇ *protein deficiency* 蛋白质缺乏 ◇ *Peas, beans and lentils are a good source of vegetable protein.* 豌豆、豆荚和扁豆是植物蛋白质的丰富来源。 ➲ SEE ALSO ENZYME ➲ WORDFINDER NOTE AT BIOLOGY

pro tem /ˌprəʊ ˈtem; *NAmE* ˌproʊ/ *adv.* (*from Latin*) for now, but not for a long time 暂时；临时 **SYN** **temporarily**：*A new manager will be appointed pro tem.* 将临时任命一位新经理。 ▶ **pro tem** *adj.*：*A pro tem committee was formed from existing members.* 由现有的委员组成了一个临时委员会。

pro·test 🔑 *noun, verb*

■ ***noun*** 🔑 /ˈprəʊtest; *NAmE* ˈproʊ-/ [U, C] the expression of strong disagreement with or opposition to sth; a statement or an action that shows this 抗议；抗议书（或行动）；反对：*The director resigned **in protest** at the decision.* 主任辞职以示抗议这项决定。◇ *The announcement **raised a storm of protest**.* 这个声明引起了一场抗议风潮。◇ *a protest march* 抗议游行 ◇ *She accepted the charge **without protest**.* 她一声未吭地接受了指控。◇ **~ (against sth)** *The workers staged a protest against the proposed changes in their contracts.* 工人们发起抗议，反对拟议中的对他们合同的修改。◇ *The building work will go ahead, despite protests from local residents.* 尽管当地居民反对，建筑工程将照样进行。◇ *The riot began as a peaceful protest.* 暴乱是从一场和平抗议开始的。 ➲ WORDFINDER NOTE AT UNION

> **WORDFINDER** 联想词：civil disobedience, demonstrate, hunger strike, march, occupy, placard, riot, sabotage, uprising

IDM **under ˈprotest** unwillingly and after expressing disagreement 无奈地；不服气地；不甘心地：*She wrote a letter of apology but only under protest.* 她无奈之下写了一封致歉信。

■ ***verb*** /prəˈtest; *NAmE also* ˈproʊ-/ **1** 🔑 [I, T] to say or do sth to show that you disagree with or disapprove of sth, especially publicly （公开）反对；抗议：**~ (about/against/at sth)** *Students took to the streets to protest against the decision.* 学生们走上街头，抗议这项决定。◇ *The victim's widow protested at the leniency of the sentence.* 受害人的遗孀抗议判决太轻。◇ *There's no use protesting, I won't change my mind.* 抗议没有用，我决不改变主意。◇ **~ sth** (*NAmE*) *They fully intend to protest the decision.* 他们决意反对这项决定。 ➲ SYNONYMS AT COMPLAIN **2** [T] to say firmly that sth is true, especially when you have been accused of sth or when other people do not believe you 坚决地表示；申辩：**~ sth** *She has always **protested her innocence**.* 她一直坚持说自己是无辜的。◇ **~ that...** *He protested that the journey was too far by car.* 他坚持说路途太远，不宜开汽车去。◇ **+ speech** *'That's not what you said earlier!' Jane protested.* "你当初不是这么说的！"简争辩说。 ➲ MORE LIKE THIS 21, page R27

P

Prot·est·ant /ˈprɒtɪstənt; *NAmE* ˈprɑːt-/ *noun* a member of a part of the Western Christian Church that separated from the Roman Catholic Church in the 16th century 新教教徒（16 世纪脱离天主教）: *He's a Protestant.* 他是新教教徒。 ▶ **Prot·est·ant** *adj.*: *The majority of the population is Protestant.* 这里的人大多数都信奉新教。◇ *a Protestant church/country* 新教教堂 / 国家 **Prot·est·ant·ism** /ˈprɒtɪstəntɪzəm; *NAmE* ˈprɑːt-/ *noun* [U]

ˌProtestant ˈethic (*also* **ˌProtestant ˈwork ethic**) *noun* [sing.] the idea that a person has a duty to work hard and spend their time and money in a careful, responsible way, sometimes thought to be typical of Protestants 新教伦理（强调勤奋工作、有效利用时间与节俭）

pro·test·ation /ˌprɒtəˈsteɪʃn; *NAmE* ˌprɑːt-/ *noun* [C, U] (*formal*) a strong statement that sth is true, especially when other people do not believe you 郑重的声明；坚决的表示: *She repeated her protestation of innocence.* 她再度强调自己是清白的。◇ *Despite his protestation to the contrary, he was extremely tired.* 尽管他极力否认，但他确实筋疲力尽了。

pro·test·er /prəˈtestə(r); *BrE also* ˈprəʊtestə(r); *NAmE* ˈproʊ-/ *noun* a person who makes a public protest （公开）抗议者，反对者 **SYN** **demonstrator**: *Thousands of protesters marched through the city.* 数千人游行抗议，走过全城。

proto- /ˈprəʊtəʊ; *NAmE* ˈproʊtoʊ/ *combining form* (in nouns and adjectives 构成名词和形容词) original; from which others develop 原始的；最初的: *prototype* 原型 ◇ *proto-modernist painters* 原始现代派画家

proto·col **AW** /ˈprəʊtəkɒl; *NAmE* ˈproʊtəkɔːl; -kɑːl/ *noun* **1** [U] a system of fixed rules and formal behaviour used at official meetings, usually between governments 礼仪；外交礼节: *a breach of protocol* 违反外交礼节 ◇ *the protocol of diplomatic visits* 外交访问的礼仪 **2** [C] (*specialist*) the first or original version of an agreement, especially a TREATY between countries, etc.; an extra part added to an agreement or TREATY 条约草案；议定书；（协议或条约的）附件: *the first Geneva Protocol*《日内瓦四公约》第一议定书 ◇ *It is set out in a legally binding protocol which forms part of the treaty.* 这在有法律约束力的、构成条约一部分的附件中有说明。 **3** [C] (*computing* 计) a set of rules that control the way data is sent between computers （数据传输的）协议 **4** [C] (*specialist*) a plan for performing a scientific experiment or medical treatment 科学实验计划；医疗方案

ˌProto-ˌIndo-ˌEuroˈpean *noun* [U] the ancient language on which all Indo-European languages are thought to be based. There are no written records of Proto-Indo-European, but experts have tried to construct it from the evidence of modern languages. 原始印欧语（据信为所有印欧语言之源头）

pro·ton /ˈprəʊtɒn; *NAmE* ˈproʊtɑːn/ *noun* (*physics* 物) a very small piece of matter (= a substance) with a positive electric charge that forms part of the NUCLEUS (= central part) of an atom 质子 ➲ SEE ALSO ELECTRON, NEUTRON ➲ WORDFINDER NOTE AT ATOM

proto·plasm /ˈprəʊtəplæzəm; *NAmE* ˈproʊ-/ *noun* [U] (*biology* 生) a clear substance like jelly which forms the living part of an animal or plant cell 原生质 ➲ COMPARE CYTOPLASM

proto·type /ˈprəʊtətaɪp; *NAmE* ˈproʊ-/ *noun* ~ (**for/of sth**) the first design of sth from which other forms are copied or developed 原型；雏形；最初形态: *the prototype of the modern bicycle* 现代自行车的雏形 ▶ **proto·typ·ical** /ˌprəʊtəˈtɪpɪkl; *NAmE* ˌproʊ-/ *adj.*

proto·zoan /ˌprəʊtəˈzəʊən; *NAmE* ˌproʊtəˈzoʊən/ *noun* (*pl.* **proto·zoans** or **proto·zoa** /-ˈzəʊə; *NAmE* -ˈzoʊə/) (*biology* 生) a very small living thing, usually with only one cell, that can only be seen under a MICROSCOPE 原生动物 ▶ **proto·zoan** *adj.*

pro·tract·ed /prəˈtræktɪd; *NAmE also* proʊˈt-/ *adj.* (*formal*) lasting longer than expected or longer than usual 延长的；拖延的；持久的 **SYN** **prolonged**: ***protracted delays/disputes/negotiations*** 持久的延误 / 争论 / 谈判

pro·tract·or /prəˈtræktə(r); *NAmE also* proʊˈt-/ *noun* an instrument for measuring and drawing angles, usually made from a half circle of clear plastic with degrees (0° to 180°) marked on it 量角器；分度规 ➲ VISUAL VOCAB PAGE V72

pro·trude /prəˈtruːd; *NAmE* proʊ-/ *verb* [I] (*formal*) to stick out from a place or a surface 突出；伸出；鼓出: *protruding teeth* 龅牙 ◇ ~ **from sth** *He hung his coat on a nail protruding from the wall.* 他把上衣挂在凸出墙面的一根钉子上。

pro·tru·sion /prəˈtruːʒn; *NAmE* proʊˈt-/ *noun* [C, U] (*formal*) a thing that sticks out from a place or surface; the fact of doing this 突出物；凸起；伸出: *a protrusion on the rock face* 岩石表面的突起部分

pro·tu·ber·ance /prəˈtjuːbərəns; *NAmE* proʊˈtuː-/ *noun* (*formal*) a round part that sticks out from a surface 突出物；隆起部分 **SYN** **bulge**

pro·tu·ber·ant /prəˈtjuːbərənt; *NAmE* proʊˈtuː-/ *adj.* (*formal*) curving or swelling out from a surface 隆起的；鼓出的；凸起的 **SYN** **bulging**: *protuberant eyes* 凸出的眼睛

proud /praʊd/ *adj., adv.*

■ ***adj.*** (**proud·er**, **proud·est**)

• **PLEASED** 满意 **1** feeling pleased and satisfied about sth that you own or have done, or are connected with 骄傲的；自豪的；得意的；满足的: *proud parents* 自豪的父母 ◇ *the proud owner of a new car* 得意扬扬的新汽车主人 ◇ ~ **of sb/sth/yourself** *Your achievements are **something to be proud of**.* 你的成就是值得骄傲的。◇ *He was proud of himself for not giving up.* 他为自己没有放弃而深感自豪。◇ ~ **to be/have sth** *I feel very proud to be a part of the team.* 能成为队中的一员我感到十分荣幸。◇ ~ **that...** *She was proud that her daughter had so much talent.* 女儿这么有天赋令她喜不自胜。 ➲ SEE ALSO HOUSE-PROUD ➲ SYNONYMS AT GLAD **2** [only before noun] causing sb to feel pride 引以为荣的；令人自豪的: *This is the proudest moment of my life.* 这是我生命中最荣耀的时刻。◇ *The car had been his **proudest possession**.* 这辆汽车是他最引以自豪的财产。

• **FEELING TOO IMPORTANT** 自负 **3** (*disapproving*) feeling that you are better and more important than other people 傲慢的；骄傲自大的 **SYN** **arrogant**: *She was too proud to admit she could be wrong.* 她自视甚高，不愿承认自己也会有错。

• **HAVING SELF-RESPECT** 自尊的 **4** having respect for yourself and not wanting to lose the respect of others 自尊的；自重的: *They were a proud and independent people.* 他们是一个独立而自尊的民族。◇ *Don't be too proud to ask for help.* 不要自尊心太强而羞于求人帮忙。

• **BEAUTIFUL/TALL** 秀丽；颀长 **5** (*literary*) beautiful, tall and impressive 秀丽的；挺拔的；壮观的: *The sunflowers stretched tall and proud to the sun.* 向日葵在阳光中亭亭玉立。 ➲ SEE ALSO PRIDE

■ ***adv.***

IDM **do sb ˈproud** (*old-fashioned, BrE*) to treat sb very well by giving them a lot of good food, entertainment, etc. 盛情款待；给某人隆重礼遇 **do yourself/sb ˈproud** to do sth that makes you proud of yourself or that makes other people proud of you 做令自己风光（或自豪）的事；做赢得赞誉的事

proud·ly /ˈpraʊdli/ *adv.* **1** in a way that shows that sb is proud of sth 得意地；自豪地；骄傲地: *She proudly displayed her prize.* 她得意地展示所获的奖品。 **2** (*literary*) in a way that is large and impressive 雄伟地；壮观地；高大地: *The Matterhorn rose proudly in the background.* 马特峰巍然屹立在背景中。

prov·able /ˈpruːvəbl/ *adj.* that can be shown to be true 可以证明的；能证实的 **SYN** **verifiable**

prove /pruːv/ *verb* (**proved**, **proved** or **proved**, **proven** /ˈpruːvn/ *especially in NAmE*) HELP In *BrE* **proved** is the more common form. Look also at **proven**. 英式英语中 proved 是较常见的形式。另见 proven。

WORD FAMILY
prove *verb* (≠ disprove)
proof *noun*
proven *adj.* (≠ unproven)

• SHOW STH IS TRUE 证明 **1** [T] to use facts, evidence, etc. to show that sth is true 证明；证实：~ **sth** *They hope this new evidence will prove her innocence.* 他们希望这一新证据能证明她无罪。◇ *'I know you're lying.' 'Prove it!'* "我知道你在撒谎。" "拿出证据来！" ◇ *He felt he needed to* **prove his point** (= show other people that he was right). 他觉得有必要证明自己的想法是对的。◇ *Are you just doing this to* **prove a point**? 你这么做就是为证明自己对吗？◇ **What are you trying to prove?** 你想证明什么？◇ *I certainly* **don't have anything to prove**—*my record speaks for itself.* 我当然不用证明，我的记录就可说明一切。◇ ~ **sth to sb** *Just give me a chance and I'll prove it to you.* 只要给我个机会，我会证明给你看。◇ ~ (**that**)... *This proves (that) I was right.* 这证明我是对的。◇ ~ **sb/sth/yourself** + **adj./noun** *She was determined to prove everyone wrong.* 她决心证明大家都错了。◇ *In this country, you are innocent until proved guilty.* 在这个国家，一个人在被证明有罪之前是清白的。◇ ~ **sb/sth/yourself to be/have sth** *You've just proved yourself to be a liar.* 你恰恰证明了自己是撒谎者。◇ ~ **what, how, etc**.... *This just proves what I have been saying for some time.* 这恰好证实了我长久以来所说的。◇ **it is proved that**... *Can it be proved that he did commit these offences?* 能证明他确实犯了这些罪吗？ OPP **disprove** ⇨ LANGUAGE BANK AT EVIDENCE ⇨ SEE ALSO PROOF *v.*

• BE 是 **2** *linking verb* if sth **proves** dangerous, expensive, etc. or if it **proves to be** dangerous, etc., you discover that it is dangerous, etc. over a period of time 后来被发现是；最终显现为 SYN **turn out**: + **adj.** *The opposition proved too strong for him.* 这个对手过于强劲，使得他难以招架。◇ + **noun** *Shares in the industry proved a poor investment.* 事实证明投资这个行业的股票是一个失败。◇ ~ **to be sth** *The promotion proved to be a turning point in his career.* 这次提升最后证明是他职业生涯的一个转折点。

• YOURSELF 自己 **3** [T] ~ **yourself** (**to sb**) to show other people how good you are at doing sth or that you are capable of doing sth 展现，展示，显示（自己的才能）：*He constantly feels he has to prove himself to others.* 他时常觉得自己必须向人一展身手。 **4** [T] ~ **yourself** + **adj./noun** | ~ **yourself to be sth** to show other people that you are a particular type of person or that you have a particular quality 显示（自己）是；向人证明（自己）是：*He proved himself determined to succeed.* 他向人证明了自己不达目的不罢休。

• OF BREAD 面包 **5** [I] to swell before being baked because of the action of YEAST 发酵 SYN **rise** IDM SEE EXCEPTION

proven /ˈpruːvn; ˈprəʊvn; *NAmE* ˈproʊ-/ *adj.* [only before noun] tested and shown to be true 被证明的；已证实的：*a student of proven ability* 确有才华的学生 ◇ *It is a proven fact that fluoride strengthens growing teeth.* 氟化物可以强化生长中的牙齿，这是已证明的事实。⇨ SEE ALSO PROVE (1) OPP **unproven**

IDM **not ˈproven** (in Scottish law 苏格兰法律) a VERDICT (= decision) at a trial that there is not enough evidence to show that sb is guilty or innocent, and that they must be set free 证据不足（不予起诉）

prov·en·ance /ˈprɒvənəns; *NAmE* ˈprɑːv-/ *noun* [U, C] (*specialist*) the place that sth originally came from 原产地；发源地；起源；出处 SYN **origin**: *All the furniture is of English provenance.* 所有这些家具都是英国货。◇ *There's no proof about the provenance of the painting* (= whether it is genuine or not). 这幅画的真伪无法鉴别。

ˈpro-verb *noun* (*grammar* 语法) a verb that depends on another verb for its meaning for example 'do' in 'She likes chocolate and so do I.' 代动词（意义依另一动词而定，如 She likes chocolate and so do I 中的 do）

prov·erb /ˈprɒvɜːb; *NAmE* ˈprɑːvɜːrb/ *noun* a well-known phrase or sentence that gives advice or says sth that is generally true, for example 'Waste not, want not.' 谚语；格言

pro·verb·ial /prəˈvɜːbiəl; *NAmE* -ˈvɜːrb-/ *adj.* **1** [only before noun] used to show that you are referring to a particular proverb or well-known phrase 谚语的；谚语表达的；如谚语所说的：*Let's not count our proverbial chickens.* 我们还是不要过分乐观。 **2** [not usually before noun] well known and talked about by a lot of people 众所周知；著名 SYN **famous**: *Their hospitality is proverbial.* 他们的热情好客人人皆知。▸ **pro·verbi·al·ly** /-biəli/ *adv.*

pro·vide /prəˈvaɪd/ *verb* **1** to give sth to sb or make it available for them to use 提供；供应；给予 SYN **supply**: ~ **sth** *The hospital has a commitment to provide the best possible medical care.* 这家医院承诺要提供最好的医疗服务。◇ *The report was not expected to provide any answers.* 人们没有指望这个报告会提供什么答案。◇ *Please answer questions in the space provided.* 请在留出的空白处答题。◇ ~ **sth for sb** *We are here to provide a service for the public.* 我们来这里是为公众服务。◇ ~ **sb with sth** *We are here to provide the public with a service.* 我们来这里是为公众服务。◇ ~ **sth to sb** *The charity aims to provide assistance to people in need.* 这家慈善机构的宗旨是向贫困者提供帮助。 **2** ~ **that**... (*formal*) (of a law or rule 法律或规则) to state that sth will or must happen 规定 SYN **stipulate**: *The final section provides that any work produced for the company is thereafter owned by the company.* 最后一节规定，此后为公司创作的一切作品均为该公司所有。⇨ SEE ALSO PROVISION

PHR V **proˈvide against sth** (*formal*) to make preparations to deal with sth bad or unpleasant that might happen in the future 预防；防备 **proˈvide for sb** to give sb the things that they need to live, such as food, money and clothing 提供生活所需 **proˈvide for sth** (*formal*) **1** to make preparations to deal with sth that might happen in the future 为…做好准备 **2** (of a law, rule, etc. 法律、规定等) to make it possible for sth to be done 作出规定；使有据可依；使可以做：*The legislation provides for the detention of suspected terrorists for up to seven days.* 法律规定，对嫌疑恐怖分子最多可拘留七天。

pro·vided /prəˈvaɪdɪd/ (*also* **pro·vid·ing**) *conj.* ~ (**that**)... used to say what must happen or be done to make it possible for sth else to happen 如果；假如；在…条件下 SYN **if**: *We'll buy everything you produce, provided of course the price is right.* 我们将采购你们的全部产品，当然价格得合适。◇ *Provided that you have the money in your account, you can withdraw up to £100 a day.* 只要账户存款足够，每天可提取不超过 100 英镑。

provi·dence /ˈprɒvɪdəns; *NAmE* ˈprɑːv-/ (*also* **Providence**) *noun* [U] (*formal*) God, or a force that some people believe controls our lives and the things that happen to us, usually in a way that protects us 上帝；苍天；天佑 SYN **fate**: *to trust in divine providence* 相信上苍 IDM SEE TEMPT

provi·dent /ˈprɒvɪdənt; *NAmE* ˈprɑːv-/ *adj.* (*formal*) careful in planning for the future, especially by saving money 精打细算的；未雨绸缪的 SYN **prudent** OPP **improvident**

provi·den·tial /ˌprɒvɪˈdenʃl; *NAmE* ˌprɑːv-/ *adj.* (*formal*) lucky because it happens at the right time, but without being planned 天缘巧合的；及时的；适时的 SYN **timely** ▸ **provi·den·tial·ly** /-ʃəli/ *adv.*

pro·vider /prəˈvaɪdə(r)/ *noun* a person or an organization that supplies sb with sth they need or want 供应者；提供者；供养人：*training providers* 提供训练的人 ◇ *We are one of the largest providers of employment in the area.* 我们是本地区最大的雇主之一。◇ *The eldest son is* **the family's sole provider** (= the only person who earns money). 这家的长子是唯一养家糊口的人。⇨ SEE ALSO SERVICE PROVIDER

pro·vid·ing /prəˈvaɪdɪŋ/ *conj.* = PROVIDED

prov·ince /ˈprɒvɪns; *NAmE* ˈprɑːv-/ *noun* **1** [C] one of the areas that some countries are divided into with its own local government 省份；（某些国家的）一级行政区：*the*

P

provinces of Canada 加拿大各省 **2 the provinces** [pl.] all the parts of a country except the capital city 首都以外的地区；外省；外地： *The show will tour the provinces after it closes in London.* 伦敦的演出结束后，将到全国各地巡回演出。◇ *a shy young man from the provinces* 腼腆的外地男青年 **3** [sing.] (*formal*) a person's particular area of knowledge, interest or responsibility 知识（或兴趣、职责）范围；领域： *Such decisions are normally the province of higher management.* 这类决定一般属于高层管理的职责范围。◇ *I'm afraid the matter is **outside my province*** (= I cannot or need not deal with it). 很抱歉，这事不归我管。

pro·vin·cial /prəˈvɪnʃl/ *adj., noun*

■ ***adj.*** **1** [only before noun] connected with one of the large areas that some countries are divided into, with its own local government 省的；一级行政区的： ***provincial assemblies/elections*** 省议会；省选举 **2** [only before noun] (*sometimes disapproving*) connected with the parts of a country that do not include the capital city 首都以外的；外省的；外地的；地方上的： *a provincial town* 首都以外的城镇 ➲ WORDFINDER NOTE AT LOCATION **3** (*disapproving*) unwilling to consider new or different ideas or things 心胸狭隘的；守旧的；迂腐的 SYN **narrow-minded** ▸ **pro·vin·cial·ly** /-ʃəli/ *adv.*

■ ***noun*** (*often disapproving*) a person who lives in or comes from a part of the country that is not near the capital city 都城以外的人；外省人；外地人；乡巴佬

pro·vin·cial·ism /prəˈvɪnʃlɪzəm/ *noun* [U] (*disapproving*) the attitude of people who are unwilling to consider new or different ideas or things 胸襟狭隘；陈腐态度；排外主义

ˈproving ground *noun* a place where sth such as a new machine, vehicle or weapon can be tested 实验场；试验地： *It's an ideal proving ground for the new car.* 这里是个理想的新车试验场。◇ (*figurative*) *The club is the proving ground for young boxers.* 这个俱乐部是年轻拳击手的摇篮。

pro·vi·sion /prəˈvɪʒn/ *noun, verb*

■ ***noun*** **1** [U, C, usually sing.] the act of supplying sb with sth that they need or want; sth that is supplied 提供；供给；给养；供应品： *housing provision* 住房供应 ◇ *The government is responsible for the provision of health care.* 政府负责提供医疗服务。◇ *There is no provision for anyone to sit down here.* 这里没有可坐的地方。◇ *The provision of specialist teachers is being increased.* 当局正在增加设置专门师资。 **2** [U, C] **~ for sb/sth** preparations that you make for sth that might or will happen in the future （为将来做的）准备： *He had already **made provisions for*** (= planned for the financial future of) *his wife and children before the accident.* 意外事故发生之前，他已为妻子、儿女做好了经济安排。◇ *You should **make provision for** things going wrong.* 你要采取措施，以防不测。 **3 provisions** [pl.] supplies of food and drink, especially for a long journey 饮食供应；（尤指旅途中的）粮食 **4** [C] a condition or an arrangement in a legal document （法律文件的）规定，条款： *Under the provisions of the lease, the tenant is responsible for repairs.* 按契约规定，房客负责房屋维修。➲ SEE ALSO PROVIDE

■ ***verb*** [often passive] **~ sb/sth** (**with sth**) (*formal*) to supply sb/sth with enough of sth, especially food, to last for a particular period of time 为…提供所需物品（尤指食物）

pro·vi·sion·al /prəˈvɪʒənl/ *adj.* **1** arranged for the present time only and likely to be changed in the future 临时的；暂时的 SYN **temporary**： *a provisional government* 临时政府 ◇ *provisional arrangements* 暂时性安排 **2** arranged, but not yet definite 暂定的： *The booking is only provisional.* 这只是暂定的预订。 ▸ **pro·vi·sion·al·ly** /-nəli/ *adv.*： *The meeting has been provisionally arranged for Friday.* 会议暂定于星期五举行。

proˌvisional ˈlicence (*BrE*) (*NAmE* **ˈlearner's permit**) *noun* an official document that you must have when you start to learn to drive 实习驾驶执照；学员驾照

pro·viso /prəˈvaɪzəʊ; *NAmE* -zoʊ/ *noun* (*pl.* **-os**) (*formal*) a condition that must be accepted before an agreement can be made 限制条款；附文；但书 SYN **provision**： *Their participation is subject to a number of important provisos.* 他们的参与受一些重要条款的限制。◇ *He agreed to their visit **with the proviso that** they should stay no longer than one week.* 他同意他们来做客，但条件是逗留不得超过一周。

pro·voca·teur /prəˌvɒkəˈtɜː(r); *NAmE* -ˌvɑːkə-/ *noun* = AGENT PROVOCATEUR

provo·ca·tion /ˌprɒvəˈkeɪʃn; *NAmE* ˌprɑːv-/ *noun* [U, C] the act of doing or saying sth deliberately in order to make sb angry or upset; something that is done or said to cause this 挑衅；刺激；激怒： *He reacted violently only **under provocation**.* 只因为被激怒，他才暴力相向。◇ *The terrorists can strike at any time **without provocation**.* 恐怖分子可能无缘无故地随时攻击。◇ *She bursts into tears **at the slightest provocation**.* 稍一招惹，她就大哭起来。◇ *So far the police have refused to respond to their provocations.* 截至目前为止，警方并未对他们的挑衅作出反应。

pro·voca·tive /prəˈvɒkətɪv; *NAmE* -ˈvɑːkə-/ *adj.* **1** intended to make people angry or upset; intended to make people argue about sth 挑衅的；煽动性的；激起争端的： *a provocative remark* 煽动性的言论 ◇ *He doesn't really mean that—he's just being deliberately provocative.* 他不是真有此意，只不过是存心挑逗一下罢了。 **2** intended to make sb sexually excited 引诱的；激起性欲的： *a provocative smile* 撩人的一笑 ▸ **pro·voca·tive·ly** *adv.*

pro·voke /prəˈvəʊk; *NAmE* -ˈvoʊk/ *verb* **1 ~ sth** to cause a particular reaction or have a particular effect 激起；引起；引发： *The announcement provoked a storm of protest.* 这个声明激起了抗议的风潮。◇ *The article was intended to provoke discussion.* 这篇文章旨在引发讨论。◇ *Dairy products may provoke allergic reactions in some people.* 乳制品可能会引起某些人的过敏反应。 **2 ~ sb** (**into sth/into doing sth**) | **~ sb to do sth** to say or do sth that you know will annoy sb so that they react in an angry way 挑衅；激怒；刺激 SYN **goad**： *The lawyer claimed his client was provoked into acts of violence by the defendant.* 律师声称，他的当事人是受到被告的挑衅才采取暴力行动的。◇ *Be careful what you say—he's easily provoked.* 说话要小心，他这个人一惹就火儿。

prov·ost /ˈprɒvəst; *NAmE* ˈproʊvoʊst/ (*also* **Provost**) *noun* **1** (in Britain) the person in charge of a college at some universities （英国某些大学的）学院院长 **2** (in the US) a senior member of the staff who organize the affairs of some universities （美国某些大学的）教务长 **3** (in Scotland) the head of a council in some towns, cities and districts （苏格兰的）市长，镇长，区长 ➲ COMPARE MAYOR (1) **4** the head of a group of priests belonging to a particular CATHEDRAL 座堂主任；教区长

prow /praʊ/ *noun* (*formal* or *literary*) the pointed front part of a ship or boat 船头

prow·ess /ˈpraʊəs/ *noun* [U] (*formal*) great skill at doing sth 非凡的技能；高超的技艺；造诣： *academic/sporting prowess* 学术 / 体育运动造诣

prowl /praʊl/ *verb, noun*

■ ***verb*** **1** [I, T] (+ **adv./prep.**) | **~ sth** (of an animal 动物) to move quietly and carefully around an area, especially when hunting 潜行（为捕猎等）： *The tiger prowled through the undergrowth.* 老虎悄然穿过矮树丛。 **2** [I, T] (+ **adv./prep.**) | **~ sth** to move quietly and carefully around an area, especially with the intention of committing a crime 潜行（图谋不轨等）： *A man was seen prowling around outside the factory just before the fire started.* 就在起火之前，有人看到一个男子在工厂外踱来踱去。 **3** [T, I] **~ sth** | (+ **adv./prep.**) to walk around a room, an area, etc., especially because you are bored, anxious, etc., and cannot relax （因无聊、焦躁等）徘徊，走来走去： *He prowled the empty rooms of the house at night.* 夜里，他在家中的空屋子里踱来踱去。

■ ***noun***

IDM **(be/go) on the ˈprowl** (of an animal or a person 人或动物) moving quietly and carefully, hunting or looking for sth 悄然潜行（以捕猎或寻找）： *There was a fox on the prowl near the chickens.* 有一只狐狸在鸡群附近徘徊。◇ *an intruder on the prowl* 一个蹑足潜入的人

prowl·er /ˈpraʊlə(r)/ *noun* a person who follows sb or who moves around quietly outside their house, especially at night, in order to frighten them, harm them or steal sth from them （图谋不轨的）潜行者

prox·imal /ˈprɒksɪməl; *NAmE* ˈprɑːk-/ *adj.* (*anatomy* 解) located towards the centre of the body 近端的；近身体中心的

prox·im·ate /ˈprɒksɪmət; *NAmE* ˈprɑːk-/ *adj.* [usually before noun] (*specialist*) nearest in time, order, etc. to sth （时间、顺序等）最接近的，最邻近的

prox·im·ity /prɒkˈsɪməti; *NAmE* prɑːk-/ *noun* [U] ~ (**of sb/sth**) (**to sb/sth**) (*formal*) the state of being near sb/sth in distance or time （时间或空间）接近，邻近，靠近： *a house **in the proximity of*** (= near) *the motorway* 靠近高速公路的一座房子 ◇ *The proximity of the college to London makes it very popular.* 这所学院因靠近伦敦而备受欢迎。◇ *The area has a number of schools **in close proximity** to each other.* 这个地区有许多学校比邻而立。◇ *the death of two members of her family in close proximity* 她的两个亲人在短时间内的相继去世

proxy /ˈprɒksi; *NAmE* ˈprɑːksi/ *noun* (*pl.* **-ies**) **1** [U] the authority that you give to sb to do sth for you, when you cannot do it yourself 代理权；代表权： *You can vote either in person or **by proxy**.* 你可以亲自投票或请人代理。◇ ***a proxy vote*** 由他人代投的票 **2** [C, U] a person who has been given the authority to represent sb else 代理人；受托人；代表： *Your proxy will need to sign the form on your behalf.* 你的代理人将须代表你在表格上签字。◇ *They were like proxy parents to me.* 他们待我如同父母。◇ **~ for sb** *She is acting as proxy for her husband.* 她做她丈夫的代表。 **3** [C] **~ for sth** (*formal* or *specialist*) something that you use to represent sth else that you are trying to measure or calculate （测算用的）代替物，指标： *The number of patients on a doctor's list was seen as a good proxy for assessing how hard they work.* 医生诊单上的病人数被看作是衡量他们工作努力程度的可靠指标。

Pro·zac™ /ˈprəʊzæk; *NAmE* ˈproʊ-/ *noun* [C, U] a drug used to treat the illness of DEPRESSION 氟西三丁；百忧解（抗抑郁药）： *She's been **on Prozac** for two years.* 她服用百忧解已经两年了。

prude /pruːd/ *noun* (*disapproving*) a person that you think is too easily shocked by things connected with sex 正经过度的人；对性问题大惊小怪者；谈性色变者

pru·dent /ˈpruːdnt/ *adj.* (*formal*) sensible and careful when you make judgements and decisions; avoiding unnecessary risks 谨慎的；慎重的；精明的： *a prudent businessman* 精明的商人 ◇ *a prudent decision/investment* 审慎的决定 / 投资 ◇ *It might be more prudent to get a second opinion before going ahead.* 行动之前再征求一下意见也许更为慎重。 OPP **imprudent** ▶ **pru·dence** /-dns/ *noun* [U] (*formal*) ➲ SYNONYMS AT CARE **pru·dent·ly** *adv.*

prud·ery /ˈpruːdəri/ *noun* [U] (*formal, disapproving*) the attitude or behaviour of people who seem very easily shocked by things connected with sex 谈性色变的态度（或行为）；（对性问题的）大惊小怪，假正经

prud·ish /ˈpruːdɪʃ/ *adj.* (*disapproving*) very easily shocked by things connected with sex （对性问题）大惊小怪的，迂腐守旧的，伪善的 SYN **strait-laced** ▶ **prud·ish·ness** *noun* [U]

prune /pruːn/ *noun, verb*

■ ***noun*** a dried PLUM that is often eaten cooked 干梅子；西梅干；李子干： *stewed prunes* 炖梅脯

■ ***verb*** **1** to cut off some of the branches from a tree, bush, etc. so that it will grow better and stronger 修剪树枝；打杈： **~ sth** *When should you prune apple trees?* 苹果树应该什么时候剪枝？◇ *He pruned the longer branches off the tree.* 他把较长的树枝剪掉了。◇ **~ sth back** *The hedge needs pruning back.* 树篱需要修剪了。 **2 ~ sth** (**back**) to make sth smaller by removing parts; to cut out parts of sth 裁减；削减；精简： *Staff numbers have been pruned back to 175.* 员工的数量已精减到 175 人。◇ *Prune out any unnecessary details.* 把无关紧要的细节统统删掉。 ▶ **prun·ing** *noun* [U]: *All roses require annual pruning.* 玫瑰都要年年修剪。◇ *The company would benefit from a little pruning here and there.* 公司如能处处精简一点，必将获益。

pruri·ent /ˈprʊəriənt; *NAmE* ˈprʊr-/ *adj.* (*formal, disapproving*) having or showing too much interest in things connected with sex 好色的；下作的；淫亵的 ▶ **pruri·ence** /-əns/ *noun* [U]

Prus·sian blue /ˌprʌʃn ˈbluː/ *noun* [U] a deep blue colour used in paints 普鲁士蓝；深蓝色

pry /praɪ/ *verb* (**pries, pry·ing, pried, pried** /praɪd/) **1** [I] **~ (into sth)** to try to find out information about other people's private lives in a way that is annoying or rude 探听，打听，探查（隐私）： *I'm sick of you prying into my personal life!* 我讨厌你刺探我的私生活！◇ *I'm sorry. I didn't mean to pry.* 对不起，我并不想刺探别人的私事。◇ *She tried to keep the children away from **the prying eyes** of the world's media.* 她尽量使孩子们躲开世界上媒体猎奇的目光。 **2** (*especially NAmE*) = PRISE

PS /ˌpiː ˈes/ *noun* something written at the end of a letter to introduce some more information or sth that you have forgotten. PS is the abbreviation for 'postscript'. 附言，又及（全写为 postscript，用于信末）： *PS Could you send me your fax number again?* 又及：请再把您的传真号码发给我好吗？◇ *She added a PS asking me to water the plants.* 她加了一句附言，要我浇花。

psalm /sɑːm/ *noun* a song, poem or prayer that praises God, especially one in the Bible （《圣经》中的）圣咏；赞美诗；赞美歌： *the Book of Psalms* 《〈圣经〉诗篇》 ➲ **MORE LIKE THIS** 20, page R27

psal·ter /ˈsɔːltə(r)/ *noun* a book containing a collection of songs and poems, (called PSALMS), with their music, that is used in a church 圣咏集；诗篇集

pseph·ology /siˈfɒlədʒi; *NAmE* -ˈfɑːl-/ *noun* [U] the study of how people vote in elections 选举学 ➲ **MORE LIKE THIS** 20, page R27 ▶ **pseph·olo·gist** /siˈfɒlədʒɪst; *NAmE* -ˈfɑːl-/ *noun*

pseud /suːd; *BrE also* sjuːd/ *noun* (*BrE, informal, disapproving*) a person who pretends to know a lot about a particular subject in order to impress other people 假博士；冒牌学问家 ▶ **pseud** *adj.*

pseudo- /ˈsuːdəʊ; ˈsjuː-; *NAmE* ˈsuːdoʊ/ *combining form* (in nouns, adjectives and adverbs 构成名词、形容词和副词) not genuine; false or pretended 假的；伪的；冒牌的： *pseudo-intellectual* 假知识分子 ◇ *pseudo-science* 伪科学

pseudo·nym /ˈsuːdənɪm; *BrE also* ˈsjuː-/ *noun* a name used by sb, especially a writer, instead of their real name 假名；化名；笔名： *She writes **under a pseudonym**.* 她用笔名写作。 ➲ COMPARE PEN NAME ▶ **pseud·onym·ous** /suːˈdɒnɪməs; sjuː-; *NAmE* suːˈdɑːn-/ *adj.*

PSHEE /ˌpiː es eɪtʃ ˌiː ˈiː/ *noun* [U] the abbreviation for 'personal, social, health and economic education' (a subject taught in British schools that deals with a person's emotional and social development and discusses such issues as health, sex, drugs, relationships with other people, work and finance) 个人、社会、健康和经济教育（全写为 personal, social, health and economic education，英国学校课程） HELP In secondary schools the subject also includes 'economic education' that deals with managing personal finances. 在中学，这门课还包括涉及个人财务管理的"经济教育"内容。

psi /psaɪ; saɪ/ *noun* the 23rd letter of the Greek alphabet (Ψ, ψ) 希腊字母表的第 23 个字母

p.s.i. /ˌpiː es ˈaɪ/ *abbr.* pounds per square inch (used for giving the pressure of tyres, etc.) 磅 / 平方英寸（胎压等的单位）

P

psit·ta·cosis /ˌsɪtəˈkəʊsɪs; *NAmE* -ˈkoʊ-/ *noun* [U] (*medical* 医) a disease of birds, especially PARROTS, which causes PNEUMONIA (= a disease of the lungs) in humans 鹦鹉热，鸟热（可传染人类引起肺炎）

psor·ia·sis /səˈraɪəsɪs/ *noun* [U] (*medical* 医) a skin disease that causes rough red areas where the skin comes off in small pieces 银屑病；牛皮癣

psst /pst/ *exclamation* the way of writing the sound people say when they want to attract sb's attention quietly（书写形式，表示轻声引人注意的声音）嘶，嘘：*Psst! Let's get out now before they see us!* 嘘！咱们现在趁别人没看见时走吧！ ➲ MORE LIKE THIS 2, page R25

PST /ˌpiː es ˈtiː/ *abbr.* **1** PACIFIC STANDARD TIME 太平洋标准时间 **2** provincial sales tax (a tax that is added to the price of goods in some parts of Canada)（加拿大部分地区征收的）省销售税

psych /saɪk/ *verb*
PHR V **ˌpsych sb↔ˈout (of sth)** (*informal*) to make an opponent feel less confident by saying or doing things that make you seem better, stronger, etc. than them 使（对手）心虚；震慑（对手） **ˌpsych sb/yourself ˈup (for sth)** (*informal*) to prepare sb/yourself mentally for sth difficult or unpleasant 为（困难或不快的事）做好思想准备：*I'd got myself all psyched up for the interview and then it was called off at the last minute.* 我为这次面试做好了万全的心理准备，可最后它临时取消了。 ➲ SEE ALSO PSYCHED

psy·che /ˈsaɪki/ *noun* (*formal*) the mind; your deepest feelings and attitudes 灵魂；心灵；精神；心态：*the human psyche* 人的心灵 ◇ *She knew, at some deep level of her psyche, that what she was doing was wrong.* 她在内心深处还是知道自己当时正在做错误的事。

psyched /saɪkt/ *adj.* [not before noun] (*informal, especially NAmE*) excited, especially about sth that is going to happen 兴奋；殷切期待

psy·che·delia /ˌsaɪkəˈdiːliə/ *noun* [U] music, art, fashion, etc. that is created as a result of the effects of psychedelic drugs （迷幻药物作用下创作的）迷幻音乐，迷幻艺术，迷幻文化

psy·che·del·ic /ˌsaɪkəˈdelɪk/ *adj.* [usually before noun] **1** (of drugs 药物) causing the user to see and hear things that are not there or that do not exist (= to HALLUCINATE) 引起幻觉的；使人精神恍惚的 **2** (of art, music, clothes, etc. 艺术、音乐、服装等) having bright colours, strange sounds, etc. like those that are experienced when taking psychedelic drugs 产生迷幻效果的

psy·chi·at·ric /ˌsaɪkiˈætrɪk/ *adj.* relating to PSYCHIATRY or to mental illness 精神病的；精神病学的：*a psychiatric hospital/nurse* 精神病医院 / 护理人员 ◇ *psychiatric treatment* 精神病治疗 ◇ *psychiatric disorders* 精神紊乱 ➲ COMPARE MENTAL (2)

psych·iatrist /saɪˈkaɪətrɪst/ *noun* a doctor who studies and treats mental illnesses 精神病学家；精神科医生 ➲ WORDFINDER NOTE AT SPECIALIST

psych·iatry /saɪˈkaɪətri/ *noun* [U] the study and treatment of mental illness 精神病学；精神病治疗

psy·chic /ˈsaɪkɪk/ *adj., noun*
■ *adj.* **1** (*also less frequent* **psych·ical** /ˈsaɪkɪkl/) connected with strange powers of the mind and not able to be explained by natural laws 关于通灵的；超自然的 SYN **paranormal**: *psychic energy/forces/phenomena/powers* 超自然的能量；超自然力量；超自然的现象；心灵力 ◇ *psychic healing* 心灵治疗法 **2** (of a person 人) seeming to have strange mental powers and to be able to do things that are not possible according to natural laws 有特异功能的；通灵的：*She claims to be psychic and helps people to contact the dead.* 她自称有通灵术，能帮助活人与死者沟通。 ◇ *How am I supposed to know—I'm not psychic!* 我怎么会知道呢，我又没有特异功能！ **3** (*also less frequent* **psych·ical**) (*formal*) connected with the mind rather than the body 心灵的；灵魂的 ➲ MORE LIKE THIS 20, page R27 ▸ **psych·ic·al·ly** /-kli/ *adv.*
■ *noun* a person who claims to have strange mental powers so that they can do things that are not possible according to natural laws, such as predicting the future and speaking to dead people （自称）有特异功能的人，有通灵术的人

psy·cho /ˈsaɪkəʊ; *NAmE* -koʊ/ *noun* (*pl.* **-os**) (*informal*) a person who is mentally ill and who behaves in a very strange violent way 精神病患者；精神病人 ▸ **psy·cho** *adj.*

psycho- /ˈsaɪkəʊ; *NAmE* -koʊ/ (*also* **psych-**) *combining form* (in nouns, adjectives and adverbs 构成名词、形容词和副词) connected with the mind 精神的；灵魂的；心灵的；心理的：*psychology* 心理学 ◇ *psychiatric* 精神病学的

psy·cho·active /ˌsaɪkəʊˈæktɪv; *NAmE* -koʊ-/ *adj.* (*specialist*) (of a drug 药) affecting the mind 作用于精神的

psy·cho·ana·lyse (*BrE*) (*NAmE* **-yze**) /ˌsaɪkəʊˈænəlaɪz; *NAmE* -koʊ-/ (*also* **ana·lyse, ana·lyze**) *verb* **~ sb** to treat or study sb using psychoanalysis 对…进行精神分析（或治疗）；对…做心理分析（或治疗）

psy·cho·analy·sis /ˌsaɪkəʊəˈnæləsɪs; *NAmE* -koʊə-/ (*also* **an·aly·sis**) *noun* [U] a method of treating sb who is mentally ill by asking them to talk about past experiences and feelings in order to try to find explanations for their present problems 精神分析（疗法）；心理分析（疗法） ▸ **psy·cho·ana·lyt·ic** /ˌsaɪkəʊˌænəˈlɪtɪk; *NAmE* -koʊ-/ *adj.* [only before noun]: *a psychoanalytic approach* 精神分析法 **psy·cho·ana·lyt·ic·al·ly** /-ɪkli/ *adv.*

psy·cho·ana·lyst /ˌsaɪkəʊˈænəlɪst; *NAmE* -koʊ-/ (*also* **ana·lyst**) *noun* a person who treats patients using psychoanalysis 精神分析学家（或医生）

psy·cho·bab·ble /ˈsaɪkəʊbæbl; *NAmE* -koʊ-/ *noun* [U] (*informal, disapproving*) the language that people use when they talk about feelings and emotional problems, that sounds very scientific, but really has little meaning 心理学呓语（谈论感情问题时使用的用词深奥但空洞的语言）

psy·cho·drama /ˈsaɪkəʊdrɑːmə; *NAmE* -koʊ-/ *noun* **1** a way of treating people who are mentally ill by encouraging them to act events from their past to help them understand their feelings 心理剧疗法，精神表演疗法（重演旧事以帮助精神病患者了解自己） **2** a play or film/movie that makes the minds and feelings of the characters more important than the events 心理戏剧，心理电影（着重人物心理）

psy·cho·kin·esis /ˌsaɪkəʊkɪˈniːsɪs; -kaɪˈn-; *NAmE* -koʊ-/ *noun* [U] the act of moving an object by using the power of the mind 心灵致动，传心致动（精神集中于物体使之移动）

psy·cho·lin·guis·tics /ˌsaɪkəʊlɪŋˈɡwɪstɪks; *NAmE* -koʊ-/ *noun* [U] the study of how the mind processes and produces language 心理语言学 ▸ **psy·cho·lin·guis·tic** /ˌsaɪkəʊlɪŋˈɡwɪstɪk; *NAmE* -koʊ-/ *adj.*

psy·cho·logic·al AW /ˌsaɪkəˈlɒdʒɪkl; *NAmE* -ˈlɑːdʒ-/ *adj.* **1** [usually before noun] connected with a person's mind and the way in which it works 心灵的；心理的；精神上的：*the psychological development of children* 儿童的心理发展 ◇ *Abuse can lead to both psychological and emotional problems.* 虐待可造成心理和情绪上的问题。 ◇ *Her symptoms are more psychological than physical* (= imaginary rather than real). 她的病症是臆想的，而不是真实的。 ◇ *Victory in the last game gave them **a psychological advantage** over their opponents.* 上一场比赛的胜利使他们比对手有心理优势。 ◇ *a psychological novel* (= one that examines the minds of the characters) 心理小说 **2** [only before noun] connected with the study of PSYCHOLOGY 心理学的；关于心理学的：*psychological research* 心理学研究 ▸ **psy·cho·logic·al·ly** AW /-kli/ *adv.*: *psychologically harmful* 精神上有害的 ◇ *Psychologically, the defeat was devastating.* 就心理而言，这次失败是致命的。

IDM the ˌpsychological ˈmoment the best time to do sth in order for it to be successful 最佳时机；最适当时机

ˌpsychological ˈwarfare *noun* [U] things that are said and done in order to make an opponent believe that they cannot win a war, a competition, etc. 心理战

psych·olo·gist AW /saɪˈkɒlədʒɪst; *NAmE* -ˈkɑːl-/ *noun* a scientist who studies and is trained in psychology 心理学家；心理学研究者：*an educational psychologist* 教育心理学家 ◇ *a clinical psychologist* (= one who treats people with mental DISORDERS or problems) 心理医生

psych·ology AW /saɪˈkɒlədʒi; *NAmE* -ˈkɑːl-/ *noun* **1** [U] the scientific study of the mind and how it influences behaviour 心理学：***social/educational/child psychology*** 社会 / 教育 / 儿童心理学 ➲ COMPARE POP PSYCHOLOGY **2** [sing.] the kind of mind that sb has that makes them think or behave in a particular way 心理；心理特征：*the psychology of small boys* 小男孩的心理特征 ◇ *Watching the shoppers at the sales gave her a first-hand insight into crowd psychology.* 在大减价时观察购物者使她对群体心理有了第一手了解。 **3** [sing.] how the mind influences behaviour in a particular area of life 心理影响：*the psychology of interpersonal relationships* 人际关系的心理影响 ➲ MORE LIKE THIS 20, page R27

psy·cho·met·ric /ˌsaɪkəˈmetrɪk/ *adj.* [only before noun] (*specialist*) used for measuring mental abilities and processes 心理测量的；精神测定的：*psychometric testing* 心理测试

psy·cho·path /ˈsaɪkəpæθ/ *noun* a person suffering from a serious mental illness that causes them to behave in a violent way towards other people 精神变态者；精神病患者 ▶ **psy·cho·path·ic** /ˌsaɪkəˈpæθɪk/ *adj.*：*a psychopathic disorder/killer* 精神错乱；精神变态杀人者

psy·cho·path·ology /ˌsaɪkəʊpəˈθɒlədʒi; *NAmE* ˌsaɪkoʊpəˈθɑːlədʒi/ *noun* **1** [U] the scientific study of mental DISORDERS 精神病理学；心理病理学 **2** [C] a DISORDER that affects sb's mind or their behaviour 精神机能障碍

psych·osis /saɪˈkəʊsɪs; *NAmE* -ˈkoʊ-/ *noun* [C, U] (*pl.* **psych·oses** /-siːz/) a serious mental illness that makes a person lose contact with reality 精神病 ➲ SEE ALSO PSYCHOTIC ➲ WORDFINDER NOTE AT CONDITION

psy·cho·somat·ic /ˌsaɪkəʊsəˈmætɪk; *NAmE* -koʊ-/ *adj.* **1** (of an illness 疾病) caused by mental problems, such as stress and worry, rather than physical problems 由心理负担导致的；由精神压力引起的 **2** (*specialist*) connected with the relationship between the mind and the body 心身的

psy·cho·ther·apy /ˌsaɪkəʊˈθerəpi; *NAmE* -koʊ-/ (*also* **ther·apy**) *noun* [U] the treatment of mental illness by discussing sb's problems with them rather than by giving them drugs 心理治疗；精神治疗 ▶ **psy·cho·ther·ap·ist** /-pɪst/ (*also* **ther·ap·ist**) *noun*

psych·ot·ic /saɪˈkɒtɪk; *NAmE* -ˈkɑːt-/ *noun* (*medical* 医) a person suffering from severe mental illness 精神病患者 ▶ **psych·ot·ic** *adj.*：*a psychotic disorder/illness* 精神错乱；精神病 ◇ *a psychotic patient* 精神病患者 ➲ SEE ALSO PSYCHOSIS ➲ SYNONYMS AT MENTALLY

psy·cho·trop·ic /ˌsaɪkəˈtrəʊpɪk; *NAmE* -ˈtroʊpɪk/ *adj.* [usually before noun] (*medical* 医) relating to drugs or substances that affect a person's mental state (药物等) 精神 (类) 的：*psychotropic medication/drugs* 精神药物

PT *abbr.* **1** /ˌpiː ˈtiː/ (*BrE*) physical training (sport and physical exercise that is taught in schools, in the army, etc.) 体育；体格锻炼 **2** (*also* **P/T**) (in writing 书写形式) PART-TIME 部分时间的；兼职（的）：*The course is 1 year FT, 2 years PT.* 这门课程全读生修一年，半读生修两年。

pt (*also* **pt.** *especially in NAmE*) *abbr.* (in writing 书写形式) **1** part 部分：*Shakespeare's Henry IV Pt 2* 莎士比亚《亨利四世》下篇 **2** pint 品脱 **3** point 得分；点：*The winner scored 10 pts.* 获胜者得了 10 分。 **4 Pt.** (especially on a map) port （尤用于地图）港口：*Pt. Moresby* 莫尔兹比港

PTA /ˌpiː tiː ˈeɪ/ *abbr.* parent-teacher association (a group run by parents and teachers in a school that organizes social events and helps the school in different ways) 家长教师联谊会，家长教师会（全写为 parent-teacher association）

ptar·migan /ˈtɑːmɪɡən; *NAmE* ˈtɑːrm-/ *noun* a type of GROUSE (= a bird with a fat body and feathers on its legs), found in mountain areas and in Arctic regions 雷鸟（栖息于山区和北极地区） ➲ MORE LIKE THIS 20, page R27

Pte *abbr.* (*BrE*) (in writing 书写形式) PRIVATE 二等兵：*Pte Jim Hill* 二等兵吉姆・希尔

ptero·dac·tyl /ˌterəˈdæktɪl/ *noun* a flying REPTILE that lived millions of years ago 翼指龙（数百万年前的飞行爬行动物） ➲ MORE LIKE THIS 20, page R27

PTO /ˌpiː tiː ˈəʊ; *NAmE* ˈoʊ/ *abbr.* (*BrE*) please turn over (written at the bottom of a page to show that there is more on the other side) （页末字样）请见下页，见反面

Pty *abbr.* proprietary (used in the names of some companies in Australia and South Africa) 公司（用于澳大利亚和南非的一些公司名称）：*Computer Software Packages Pty Ltd* 电脑软件包有限公司

pub 🔑 /pʌb/ (*also formal* **ˌpublic ˈhouse**) (*both BrE*) *noun* a building where people go to drink and meet their friends. Pubs serve alcoholic and other drinks, and often also food. 酒吧；酒馆：*They've gone down the pub for a drink.* 他们下酒馆喝酒去了。◇ *a pub lunch* 酒馆供的午餐 ◇ *the landlord of the local pub* 当地酒馆的老板 ➲ VISUAL VOCAB PAGE V15

ˈpub crawl *noun* (*BrE, informal*) a visit to several pubs, going straight from one to the next, drinking at each of them 挨店喝酒；串酒馆

pube /pjuːb/ *noun* [usually pl.] (*informal*) a pubic hair 阴毛

pu·berty /ˈpjuːbəti; *NAmE* -bərti/ *noun* [U] the period of a person's life during which their sexual organs develop and they become capable of having children 青春期：*to reach puberty* 进入青春期 ➲ WORDFINDER NOTE AT YOUNG ➲ COLLOCATIONS AT AGE ➲ SEE ALSO ADOLESCENCE

pubes /ˈpjuːbiːz/ *noun* (*pl.* **pubes**) the lower front part of the body, above the legs, covered by hair in adults 耻骨区

pu·bes·cent /pjuːˈbesnt/ *adj.* [usually before noun] (*formal*) in the period of a person's life when they are changing physically from a child to an adult 青春期的；到达发育期的

pubic /ˈpjuːbɪk/ *adj.* [only before noun] connected with the part of a person's body near their sexual organs 阴部的：*pubic hair* 阴毛 ◇ *the pubic bone* 耻骨

pubis /ˈpjuːbɪs/ *noun* (*pl.* **pubes** /ˈpjuːbiːz/) one of the two bones that form the sides of the PELVIS 耻骨

pub·lic 🔑 /ˈpʌblɪk/ *adj., noun*

■ *adj.*

• **OF ORDINARY PEOPLE** 普通人 **1** 🔑 [only before noun] connected with ordinary people in society in general 平民的；大众的；公众的；百姓的：*The campaign is designed to increase public awareness of the issues.* 这场运动旨在提高民众对这些问题的认识。 ◇ *Levels of waste from the factory may be a danger to public health.* 工厂废弃物的排放量可能危及大众的健康。 ◇ *Why would the closure of hospitals be* ***in the public interest*** (= useful to ordinary people)? 关闭医院怎么会对民众有利呢？ ◇ *The government had to bow to public pressure.* 政府不得不向公众的压力低头。

• **FOR EVERYONE** 公众 **2** 🔑 [only before noun] provided, especially by the government, for the use of people in general 公共的；公立的：*a public education system* 公共教育体系 ◇ *a public library* 公共图书馆 OPP **private**

• **OF GOVERNMENT** 政府 **3** 🔑 [only before noun] connected with the government and the services it provides 政府的；有关政府所提供服务的：***public money/spending/***

P

funding/expenditure 公款；公共开支；政府拨款；政府开支 ◇ *He spent much of his career in* ***public office*** (= working in the government). 他的职业生涯中大部分时间从事政府工作。◇ (*BrE*) *the* ***public purse*** (= the money that the government can spend) 国库 ◇ *The rail industry is no longer in* ***public ownership*** (= controlled by the government). 铁路业不再归国有了。**OPP** **private**

- **SEEN/HEARD BY PEOPLE** 公开 **4** known to people in general 人人皆知的；公开的： *a* ***public figure*** (= a person who is well known because they are often on the television, radio, etc.) 公众人物 ◇ *Details of the government report have not yet been* ***made public***. 政府报告的细节尚未公布。◇ *She entered* ***public life*** (= started a job in which she became known to the public) *at the age of 25.* 她 25 岁时开始了面对公众的工作。 **5** open to people in general; intended to be seen or heard by people in general 公之于众的；公开的： *a public apology* 公开的道歉 ◇ *The painting will be put on* ***public display*** *next week.* 这幅画将于下周公开展出。◇ *This may be the band's last* ***public appearance*** *together.* 这可能是这个乐队最后一次全体公开亮相。
- **PLACE** 地方 **6** where there are a lot of people who can see and hear you 公开场合的；大庭广众的： *Let's go somewhere a little less public.* 咱们找一个僻静些的地方吧。**OPP** **private**

▶ **pub·lic·ly** /-kli/ *adv.* ： *a publicly owned company* 股票上市公司 ◇ *He later publicly apologized for his comments.* 后来他对自己的言论作了公开道歉。◇ *This information is not publicly available.* 这个消息没有对外公开。

IDM **go 'public** **1** to tell people about sth that is a secret 公之于世；公开（秘密等） **2** (of a company 公司) to start selling shares on the STOCK EXCHANGE 上市；公开出售股份 **in the public 'eye** well known to many people through newspapers and television（通过报纸、电视）让公众熟知的，广为人知的： *She doesn't want her children growing up in the public eye.* 她不想让子女在众人瞩目中成长。➲ MORE AT KNOWLEDGE

■ ***noun*** [sing.+sing./pl. v.]

- **ORDINARY PEOPLE** 普通人 **1** **the public** ordinary people in society in general 平民；百姓；民众： *The palace is now* ***open to the public.*** 这座宫殿现在向大众开放了。◇ *There have been many complaints from* ***members of the public***. 现在已有大量的民众投诉。◇ *The public has/have a right to know what is contained in the report.* 民众有权了解报告的内容。➲ SEE ALSO GENERAL PUBLIC
- **GROUP OF PEOPLE** 民众 **2** a group of people who share a particular interest or who are involved in the same activity 志趣相同（或从事同一类活动）的群体： *the theatre-going public* 爱看戏的民众 ◇ *She knows how to keep her public* (= for example, the people who buy her books) *satisfied.* 她知道如何迎合受众的兴趣。

IDM **in 'public** when other people, especially people you do not know, are present 公开地；在别人（尤指生人）面前： *She doesn't like to be seen in public without her make-up on.* 她不愿意未化妆就公开露面。➲ COMPARE IN PRIVATE at PRIVATE *n.* ➲ MORE AT WASH *v.*

ˌpublic 'access *noun* [U] **1** the right of people in general to go into particular buildings or areas of land or to obtain particular information（进入公共场所的）大众通行权；（对信息的）公众知情权，公众使用权： *public access to the countryside* 乡村通行权 **2** (in the US and some other countries) the right of people in general to use television or radio channels to present their own programmes（美国及其他一些国家的）公共频道播放权： *a public access channel* 公共频道

ˌpublic ad'dress system *noun* (*abbr.* **PA system, PA**) an electronic system that uses MICROPHONES and LOUDSPEAKERS to make music, voices, etc. louder so that they can be heard by everyone in a particular place or building 广播系统

ˌpublic af'fairs *noun* [pl.] issues and questions about social, economic, political or business activities, etc. that affect ordinary people in general 公共事务

pub·lican /ˈpʌblɪkən/ *noun* **1** (*BrE, formal*) a person who owns or manages a pub 酒馆老板（或经理） **2** (*AustralE, NZE*) a person who owns or manages a hotel 旅馆老板（或经理）

pub·li·ca·tion **AW** /ˌpʌblɪˈkeɪʃn/ *noun* **1** [U, C] the act of printing a book, a magazine, etc. and making it available to the public; a book, a magazine, etc. that has been published（书刊等的）出版，发行；出版物： *the publication date* 出版日期 ◇ *the publication of his first novel* 他首部小说的出版 ◇ *specialist publications* 专业出版物 **2** [U] the act of printing sth in a newspaper, report, etc. so that the public knows about it 发表；刊登；公布： *a delay in the publication of the exam results* 考试成绩的延期公布 ◇ *The newspaper continues to defend its publication of the photographs.* 这家报纸继续为刊登这些照片辩护。

ˌpublic 'bar *noun* (in Britain) a bar in a pub with simple or less comfortable furniture than the other bars（英国酒馆中的）廉价酒吧，大众酒吧 ➲ COMPARE LOUNGE BAR

ˌpublic 'company (*also* **ˌpublic ˌlimited 'company**) (*both BrE*) (*NAmE* **ˌpublic corpo'ration**) *noun* (*abbr.* **plc, PLC**) a company that sells shares in itself to the public 公开招股公司

ˌpublic con'venience *noun* (*BrE, formal*) a public building containing toilets that are provided for anyone to use 公共厕所

ˌpublic corpo'ration *noun* **1** (*NAmE*) (*BrE* **ˌpublic 'company, ˌpublic ˌlimited 'company**) a company that sells shares in itself to the public 公开招股公司；上市公司 **2** (*BrE*) an organization that is owned by the government and that provides a national service 公营机构；国有公司

ˌpublic de'fender *noun* (*law* 律) (in the US) a lawyer who is paid by the government to defend people in court if they cannot pay for a lawyer themselves（美国）公设辩护人，公设辩护律师

ˌpublic 'domain *noun* [sing.] something that is in the **public domain** is available for everyone to use or to discuss and is not secret（用于不受版权保护的财产）公有领域，公有产业： *The information has been placed in the public domain.* 这资料不受版权保护。◇ *public domain software* 无版权软件

ˌpublic 'enemy *noun* a person who has done, or is believed to have done, a very bad thing, especially sth that is harmful to society 人民公敌；社会公敌： *public enemy number one* (= the person or thing that is most frightening or that is most hated) 头号公敌（最可怕或最可恶的人或事物）

ˌpublic 'holiday *noun* a day on which most of the shops/stores, businesses and schools in a country are closed, often to celebrate a particular event 公共假日；公休日 ➲ COMPARE BANK HOLIDAY

ˌpublic 'house *noun* (*BrE, formal*) = PUB

ˌpublic 'housing *noun* [U] (in the US) houses and flats/apartments that are built by the government for people who do not have enough money to pay for private accommodation（美国政府为低收入者修建的）公共住房

pub·li·cist /ˈpʌblɪsɪst/ *noun* a person whose job is to make sth known to the public, for example a new product, actor, etc. 推介人员；宣传员；广告人员

pub·li·city /pʌbˈlɪsəti/ *noun* [U] **1** the attention that is given to sb/sth by newspapers, television, etc.（媒体的）关注，宣传，报道： ***good/bad/adverse publicity*** 有利的 / 不利的 / 反面的报道 ◇ *There has been a great deal of publicity surrounding his disappearance.* 他的失踪已为传媒广泛报道。◇ *The trial took place amid a* ***blaze of*** (= a lot of) ***publicity***. 审讯在媒体的广泛关注下进行。 **2** the business of attracting the attention of the public to sth/sb; the things that are done to attract attention 宣传业；广告宣传工作；传播工作： *She works in publicity.* 她从事宣传工作。◇ *There has been a lot of*

P

advance publicity for her new film. 她的新电影尚未上映即大加宣传。◇ *publicity material* 宣传材料 ◇ *a* ***publicity campaign*** 宣传运动 ◇ *The band dressed up as the Beatles as a* ***publicity stunt.*** 乐队扮作披头士乐队作为宣传噱头。➲ SYNONYMS AT ADVERTISEMENT

pub·li·cize (*BrE also* **-ise**) /'pʌblɪsaɪz/ *verb* **~ sth** to make sth known to the public; to advertise sth 宣传；推广；宣扬；传播：*They flew to Europe to publicize the plight of the refugees.* 他们飞往欧洲报道难民的惨状。◇ *a* ***much/highly/widely publicized*** *speech* (= that has received a lot of attention on television, in newspapers, etc.) 一篇受到媒体广泛报道的讲话 ◇ *He was in London publicizing his new biography of Kennedy.* 他在伦敦推销他新出版的肯尼迪传。➲ WORDFINDER NOTE AT ADVERTISE

ˌpublic ˌlimited 'company *noun* (*BrE*) (*abbr.* **plc**) = PUBLIC COMPANY

ˌpublic 'nuisance *noun* **1** [sing., U] (*law* 律) an illegal act that causes harm to people in general 公害；妨害大众的行为：*He was charged with committing (a) public nuisance.* 他被控妨害公众利益。**2** [C, usually sing.] (*informal*) a person or thing that annoys a lot of people 妨害大众的人（或事物）；公害；蠹虫

ˌpublic o'pinion *noun* [U] the opinions that people in society have about an issue 舆论；民意：*The media has a powerful influence on public opinion.* 传媒对于舆论有很大的影响。

ˌpublic 'property *noun* [U] **1** (*law* 律) land, buildings, etc. that are owned by the government and can be used by everyone 公共财产；公产；公物 **2** a person or thing that everyone has a right to know about 公众人物；公众有权了解的人（或事情）：*Sophie became public property when she married into the royal family.* 索菲嫁入王室后，即成为公众人物。

ˌpublic 'prosecutor *noun* (*BrE*) a lawyer who works for the government and tries to prove people guilty in court 公诉人；检察官 ➲ SEE ALSO DISTRICT ATTORNEY

ˌpublic re'lations *noun* **1** [U] (*abbr.* **PR**) the business of giving the public information about a particular organization or person in order to create a good impression 公关工作（或活动）：*She works in public relations.* 她从事公关工作。◇ *a public relations exercise* 一项公关活动 **2** [pl.] the state of the relationship between an organization and the public 公共关系：*Sponsoring the local team is good for public relations.* 赞助当地球队有利于公共关系。

ˌpublic 'school *noun* [C, U] **1** (in Britain, especially in England) a private school for young people between the ages of 13 and 18, whose parents pay for their education. The students often live at the school while they are studying. 公学（在英国，尤其是英格兰，为 13 到 18 岁青少年开办的私立付费学校，学生常寄宿）：*He was educated at (a) public school.* 他出身英国公学。➲ COMPARE PREPARATORY SCHOOL (1), PRIVATE SCHOOL **2 'public school** (in the US, Australia, Scotland and other countries) a free local school paid for by the government（美国、澳大利亚、苏格兰及其他国家免费的）公立学校 ➲ COMPARE STATE SCHOOL

the ˌpublic 'sector *noun* [sing.] (*economics* 经) the part of the economy of a country that is owned or controlled by the government 公营部门；公共部门 ➲ COMPARE PRIVATE SECTOR, THIRD SECTOR

ˌpublic 'servant *noun* a person who is employed by the state or in local government or who is an elected representative 公务员；公仆：*pay increases for public servants* 公务员的加薪 ◇ *a long and outstanding career as a public servant* 任公务员时间长且表现优秀

ˌpublic 'service *noun* **1** [C] a service such as transport or health care that a government or an official organization provides for people in general in a particular society 公共事业；公营事业：*to improve public services in the area* 改进本地区的公用事业 ◇ *a public service broadcast* 公营广播 **2** [C, U] something that is done to help people rather than to make a profit 公益事业（或服务）：*to perform a public service* 从事一项公益服务 **3** [U] the government and government departments 政府；政府部门：*to work in public service* 在政府机关工作 ◇ *public service workers* 公务人员

ˌpublic 'service broadcasting *noun* [U] radio and television programmes broadcast by organizations such as the BBC in Britain that are independent of government but are financed by public money 公共服务广播（由英国广播公司等受公款资助的非政府独立机构播放的节目）➲ WORDFINDER NOTE AT RADIO

ˌpublic-'spirit·ed *adj.* willing to do things that will help other people in society 有公益精神的；热心公益的；助人为乐的：*a public-spirited act* 助人为乐的行为 ◇ *That was very public-spirited of you.* 你那样做真是热心公益啊！▸ **ˌpublic 'spirit** *noun* [U]

ˌpublic 'television *noun* [U] (*NAmE*) a television service that shows mainly EDUCATIONAL programmes and is paid for by the government, the public and some companies 大众文化教育电视（由政府、公众以及某些公司赞助）

ˌpublic 'transport (*BrE*) (*NAmE* **ˌpublic transpor'tation**) *noun* [U] the system of buses, trains, etc. provided by the government or by companies, which people use to travel from one place to another 公共交通；公交车辆：*to* ***travel on/by public transport*** 乘公交车 ◇ *Most of us use public transport to get to work.* 我们大多数人都乘公共交通工具上班。➲ COLLOCATIONS AT TOWN ➲ VISUAL VOCAB PAGE V9

ˌpublic u'tility *noun* (*formal*) a private company that must obey government rules, that supplies essential services such as gas, water and electricity to the public 公用事业（公司）

ˌpublic 'works *noun* [pl.] building work, such as that of hospitals, schools and roads, that is paid for by the government 公共工程（或建设）

pub·lish 🔑 AW /'pʌblɪʃ/ *verb* **1** 🔑 [T] **~ sth** to produce a book, magazine, CD-ROM, etc. and sell it to the public 出版；发行：*The first edition was published in 2007.* 第一版于 2007 年发行。◇ *He works for a company that publishes reference books.* 他在一家工具书出版公司工作。◇ *Most of our titles are also published on CD-ROM.* 我们的大部分书籍也制成光盘发行。➲ WORDFINDER NOTE AT BOOK **2** 🔑 [T] **~ sth** to print a letter, an article, etc. in a newspaper or magazine（在报刊）发表，刊登，登载：*Pictures of the suspect were published in all the daily papers.* 嫌疑人的照片刊登在各家日报上了。**3** 🔑 [T] **~ sth** to make sth available to the public on the Internet（在互联网上）发表，公布：*The report will be published on the Internet.* 报告将在互联网上公布。**4** 🔑 [T, I] **~ (sth)** (of an author 作者) to have your work printed and sold to the public 发表（作品）；使（作品）出版：*She hasn't published anything for years.* 她好几年没有发表作品了。◇ *University teachers are under pressure to publish.* 大学教师有不得不发表作品的压力。**5** [T] **~ sth** (*formal*) to make official information known to the public 公布；发布 SYN **release**：*The findings of the committee will be published on Friday.* 委员会的调查结果将于星期五公布。

pub·lish·er AW /'pʌblɪʃə(r)/ *noun* a person or company that prepares and prints books, magazines, newspapers or electronic products and makes them available to the public 出版人（或机构）；发行人（或机构）

pub·lish·ing 🔑 AW /'pʌblɪʃɪŋ/ *noun* [U] the profession or business of preparing and printing books, magazines, CD-ROMs, etc. and selling or making them available to the public 出版（业）；发行（业）：*a publishing house* (= company) 出版社 ➲ SEE ALSO DESKTOP PUBLISHING

puce /pjuːs/ *adj.* reddish-purple in colour 紫红色的：*His face was puce with rage.* 他气得脸色发紫。▸ **puce** *noun* [U]

puck /pʌk/ *noun* **1** a hard flat rubber disc that is used as a ball in ICE HOCKEY（冰球运动使用的）冰球 ➲ VISUAL

VOCAB PAGE V48 **2** (*computing* 计) a pointing device that looks like a computer mouse and is used to control the movement of the CURSOR on a computer screen 手持游标器；光标定位器；定标器

puck·er /ˈpʌkə(r)/ *verb* [I, T] ~ (**sth**) (**up**) to form or to make sth form small folds or lines 皱起；使起褶子；噘起：*His face puckered, and he was ready to cry.* 他的脸一皱，像要哭了。◇ *She puckered her lips.* 她噘起嘴唇。◇ *puckered fabric* 有褶皱的织物

puck·ish /ˈpʌkɪʃ/ *adj.* [usually before noun] (*literary*) enjoying playing tricks on other people 顽皮的；淘气的；爱恶作剧的 SYN **mischievous**

pud /pʊd/ *noun* (*BrE, informal*) = PUDDING

pud·ding /ˈpʊdɪŋ/ (*BrE, informal* **pud**) *noun* [U, C] **1** (*BrE*) a sweet dish eaten at the end of a meal （餐末的）甜食，甜点：*What's for pudding?* 有什么甜点？◇ *I haven't made a pudding today.* 我今天没做甜点。 SYN **afters, dessert, sweet** **2** (*BrE*) a hot sweet dish, often like a cake, made from flour, fat and eggs with fruit, jam, etc. in or on it 热布丁糕（用面粉、油、蛋制作，加水果、果酱等）：*treacle pudding* 糖浆布丁 ◇ *bread and butter pudding* (= made with bread, butter and milk) 面包黄油布丁 ⇨ SEE ALSO CHRISTMAS PUDDING, RICE PUDDING, SPONGE PUDDING, SUMMER PUDDING **3** (*BrE*) a hot dish like a PIE with soft PASTRY made from flour, fat and eggs and usually filled with meat 热布丁饼（用面粉、油、蛋制作，通常用肉填充）：*a steak and kidney pudding* 牛肉腰子布丁 **4** (*especially NAmE*) a cold DESSERT (= a sweet dish) like cream flavoured with fruit, chocolate, etc. 冷布丁（有水果、巧克力等口味）：*chocolate pudding* 巧克力布丁 ⇨ SEE ALSO BLACK PUDDING, YORKSHIRE PUDDING IDM SEE OVER-EGG, PROOF *n.*

ˈpudding basin *noun* (*BrE*) a deep round bowl that is used for mixing food or for cooking puddings in （调拌食物的）深盆；布丁蒸盘

P

pud·dle /ˈpʌdl/ *noun* a small amount of water or other liquid, especially rain, that has collected in one place on the ground 水洼；小水坑；（尤指）雨水坑 ⇨ WORDFINDER NOTE AT RAIN

pu·denda /pjuːˈdendə/ *noun* [pl.] (*old-fashioned, formal*) the sexual organs that are outside the body, especially those of a woman 阴部；（尤指）女阴

pudgy /ˈpʌdʒi/ (*BrE also* **podgy**) *adj.* (*informal, usually disapproving*) slightly fat 微胖的

Pue·blo /ˈpwebləʊ; *NAmE* -loʊ/ *noun* (*pl.* **Pue·blo** or **Pue·blos**) *noun* a member of a group of Native American people who live in the US states of Arizona and New Mexico 普韦布洛人（美洲土著，居于美国亚利桑那州和新墨西哥州）

pue·blo /ˈpwebləʊ; *NAmE* -bloʊ/ *noun* (*pl.* **-os**) (*from Spanish*) a town or village in Latin America or the south-western US, especially one with traditional buildings 普韦布洛村落（在拉丁美洲或美国西南部，尤指有传统建筑的村落）

pu·er·ile /ˈpjʊəraɪl; *NAmE* ˈpjʊrəl/ *adj.* (*disapproving*) silly; suitable for a child rather than an adult 愚蠢的；幼稚的；孩子气的 SYN **childish**

puff /pʌf/ *verb, noun*

■ ***verb*** **1** [I, T] to smoke a cigarette, pipe, etc. 吸，抽（香烟、烟斗等）：~ (**at/on sth**) *He puffed* (*away*) *on his pipe.* 他（一口一口地）吸着烟斗。◇ ~ **sth** *I sat puffing my cigar.* 我坐着抽雪茄。 **2** [T, I] to make smoke or steam blow out in clouds; to blow out in clouds 使喷出，冒出（烟或蒸汽）：~ **sth** (**out**) *Chimneys were puffing out clouds of smoke.* 烟囱冒着滚滚浓烟。◇ ~ (**out**) *Steam puffed out.* 蒸汽向外喷出。 **3** [I, T] (+ **speech**) (*informal*) to breathe loudly and quickly, especially after you have been running 急促喘息；气喘吁吁 SYN **gasp**：*I was starting to puff a little from the climb.* 爬坡弄得我有点喘息起来。⇨ SEE ALSO PUFFED **4** [I] + **adv./prep.** to move in a particular direction, sending out small clouds of smoke or steam 喷着汽（或烟）移动：*The train puffed into the station.* 火车喷着蒸汽驶进车站。

IDM **be puffed up with ˈpride, etc.** to be too full of pride, etc. 自满；自负 **ˌpuff and ˈpant** (*also* **ˌpuff and ˈblow** *informal*) to breathe quickly and loudly through your mouth after physical effort 气喘吁吁；呼哧呼哧地喘 ⇨ MORE LIKE THIS 13, page R26 ⇨ MORE AT HUFF *v.*

PHR V **ˌpuff sth↔ˈout** to make sth bigger and rounder, especially by filling it with air 吹胀；使鼓起来：*She puffed out her cheeks.* 她鼓起了腮帮子。 **ˌpuff ˈup** | **ˌpuff sth↔ˈup** to swell or to make sth swell 膨胀；使膨胀：*Her cheeks puffed up.* 她的腮帮子鼓了起来。◇ *The frog puffed itself up.* 这只青蛙胀得鼓鼓的。

■ ***noun*** **1** [C] an act of breathing in sth such as smoke from a cigarette, or drugs 吸，抽（把气体经口或鼻引到体内的动作）：*He had a few puffs at the cigar.* 他吸了几口雪茄。◇ *Take two puffs from the inhaler every four hours.* 每隔四小时从吸药器中吸两口药。 **2** [C] a small amount of air, smoke, etc. that is blown from somewhere （烟、气等的）一缕，少量：*a puff of wind* 一丝清风 ◇ *Puffs of white smoke came from the chimney.* 烟囱冒出了袅袅白烟。◇ *Any chance of success seemed to vanish in a puff of smoke* (= to disappear quickly). 成功的机会犹如一缕青烟，瞬息即逝。 **3** [C] a hollow piece of light PASTRY that is filled with cream, jam, etc. 千层酥；奶油酥；泡芙 ⇨ SEE ALSO CREAM PUFF **4** (*NAmE also* **ˈpuff piece**) [C] (*informal, usually disapproving*) a piece of writing or speech that praises sb/sth too much 吹捧的文章（或讲话） **5** [U] (*informal, especially BrE*) breath 呼吸；喘息：*The hill was very steep and I soon* ***ran out of puff.*** 山坡陡峭，我很快就气喘吁吁了。⇨ SEE ALSO POWDER PUFF

puff·ball /ˈpʌfbɔːl/ *noun* a FUNGUS with a round brown head, that bursts when it is ready to release its seeds 马勃（菌）

puffed /pʌft/ (*also* **ˌpuffed ˈout**) *adj.* [not before noun] (*BrE, informal*) breathing quickly and with difficulty because you have been having a lot of physical exercise 气喘吁吁；上气不接下气

puff·er /ˈpʌfə(r)/ *noun* **1** (*informal*) = INHALER **2** = PUFFERFISH

puff·er·fish /ˈpʌfəfɪʃ; *NAmE* -fərf-/ *noun* (*pl.* **puffer·fish** or **puffer·fishes**) (*also* **puff·er**) a poisonous fish that lives in warm seas and fills with air when it is in danger 河豚

puf·fin /ˈpʌfɪn/ *noun* a black and white bird with a large, brightly coloured beak that lives near the sea, common in the N Atlantic 角嘴海雀，海鹦（常见于北大西洋，喙大而色艳） ⇨ VISUAL VOCAB PAGE V12

ˌpuff ˈpastry *noun* [U] a type of light PASTRY that forms many thin layers when baked, used for making PIES, cakes, etc. 千层酥面团；油酥面团

ˈpuff piece *noun* (*NAmE*) = PUFF (4)

ˌpuff ˈsleeve (*also* **ˌpuffed ˈsleeve**) *noun* a type of sleeve on a piece of clothing that fits close to the body at the shoulder and the lower edge and is wider in the middle, forming a round shape 泡泡袖

puffy /ˈpʌfi/ *adj.* (**puff·ier, puffi·est**) **1** (of eyes, faces, etc. 眼睛、面部等) looking swollen (= larger, rounder, etc. than usual) 鼓胀的；肿胀的：*Her eyes were puffy from crying.* 她眼睛都哭肿了。 **2** (of clouds, etc. 云等) looking soft, round and white 松软洁白的；白绒团状的 ▸ **puf·fi·ness** *noun* [U]

pug /pʌg/ *noun* a small dog with short hair and a wide flat face with deep folds of skin 哈巴狗

pu·gil·ist /ˈpjuːdʒɪlɪst/ *noun* (*old-fashioned*) a BOXER 拳击手 ▸ **pu·gil·ism** /-lɪzəm/ *noun* [U] **pu·gil·is·tic** /ˌpjuːdʒɪˈlɪstɪk/ *adj.*

pug·na·cious /pʌgˈneɪʃəs/ *adj.* (*formal*) having a strong desire to argue or fight with other people 爱争执的；好斗的；爱滋事的 SYN **bellicose** ▸ **pug·na·cious·ly** *adv.* **pug·na·city** /pʌgˈnæsəti/ *noun* [U]

puis·sance /ˈpwiːsɒ̃s; *NAmE* ˈpwɪsəns/ *noun* **1 Puissance** [sing.] a competition in SHOWJUMPING to test a horse's ability to jump high fences （马的）越障能力测试赛 **2** [U] (*literary*) great power or influence 大权；权势；影响力

puja /ˈpuːdʒɑː/ *noun* **1** a Hindu ceremony of worship 普阇（印度教的礼拜） **2** an OFFERING (= a gift that is given to a god) at the ceremony 普阇祭品；印度教礼拜祭品

pu·jari /puːˈdʒɑːri/ *noun* a Hindu priest 印度教祭司

puke /pjuːk/ *verb* [I, T] ~ (**sth**) (**up**) (*informal*) to VOMIT 吐；呕吐：*The baby puked all over me this morning.* 宝宝今天早上吐了我一身。◇ *That guy makes me puke!* (= makes me angry) 那个家伙气死我了！◇ *I puked up my dinner.* 我把吃的饭都吐了。▶ **puke** *noun* [U]: *to be covered in puke* 到处是吐的东西

pukka /ˈpʌkə/ *adj.* (*BrE*) **1** (*old-fashioned*) genuine; not a copy; appropriate in a particular social situation 真品的；适用于社交场合的 **2** (*informal*) of very good quality 高质量的；上等的；一流的

pul·chri·tude /ˈpʌlkrɪtjuːd; *NAmE also* -tuːd/ *noun* [U] (*literary*) beauty 美丽；标致

Pul·it·zer Prize /ˈpʊlɪtsə praɪz; *NAmE* ˈpʊlɪtsər praɪz; *also* ˈpjuːl-/ *noun* [C, usually sing.] in the US, one of the prizes that are given each year for excellent work in literature, music, or JOURNALISM 普利策奖（美国年度奖，颁发给文学、音乐或新闻业优秀作品的奖项之一）

pull 🔑 /pʊl/ *verb, noun*

■ *verb*

• **MOVE/REMOVE STH** 移动 / 挪走某物 **1** 🔑 [I, T] to hold sth firmly and use force in order to move it or try to move it towards yourself 拉；拽；扯；拖：*You push and I'll pull.* 你推，我拉。◇ *Don't pull so hard or the handle will come off.* 别太使劲拉，不然把手会脱落。◇ **~ at/on sth** *I pulled on the rope to see if it was secure.* 我抻了抻绳子看看是否牢固。◇ **~ sth** *Stop pulling her hair!* 别揪她头发！◇ **~ sb/sth + adv./prep.** *She pulled him gently towards her.* 她把他轻轻地拉到身边。◇ **~ sth + adj.** *Pull the door shut.* 把门拉上。 **2** 🔑 [T] **~ sth** (**+ adv./prep.**) to remove sth from a place by pulling 拔出；抽出：*Pull the plug out.* 把插头拔掉。◇ *She pulled off her boots.* 她脱下了靴子。◇ *He pulled a gun on me* (= took out a gun and aimed it at me). 他拔出枪来指着我。 **3** 🔑 [T] **~ sb/sth + adv./prep.** to move sb/sth in a particular direction by pulling （向某方向）拖，拉动：*Pull your chair nearer the table.* 把你的椅子再往桌子拉近些。◇ *He pulled on his sweater.* 他套上了毛衣。◇ *She took his arm and pulled him along.* 她抓起他的胳膊，拉着他往前走。 **4** 🔑 [T] **~ sth** to hold or be attached to sth and move it along behind you 将…拖在身后；拉；牵引：*In this area oxen are used to pull carts.* 这个地区用牛拉车。

• **BODY** 身体 **5** 🔑 [I, T] to move your body or a part of your body in a particular direction, especially using force 扭转；移开；抽回：**+ adv./prep.** *He tried to kiss her but she pulled away.* 他想吻她，但她却扭开了身子。◇ **~ sth/yourself + adv./prep.** *The dog snapped at her and she quickly pulled back her hand.* 那狗要咬她，她马上把手缩了回来。◇ **~ sth/yourself + adj.** *John pulled himself free and ran off.* 约翰脱身跑掉了。

• **CURTAINS** 帘；幔 **6** 🔑 [T] **~ sth** to open or close curtains, etc. 拉上；收拢 **SYN draw**: *Pull the curtains—it's dark outside.* 外边天黑了，把窗帘拉上。

• **MUSCLE** 肌肉 **7** 🔑 [T] **~ sth** to damage a muscle, etc. by using too much force 拉伤；扭伤；抻：*to pull a muscle/ligament/tendon* 扭伤肌肉 / 肌腱 / 韧带 ➲ SYNONYMS AT INJURE

• **SWITCH** 开关 **8** 🔑 [T] **~ sth** to move a switch, etc. towards yourself or down in order to operate a machine or piece of equipment 扳动；拉；扣：*Pull the lever to start the motor.* 拉动手柄启动马达。◇ *Don't pull the trigger!* 别扣扳机！

• **VEHICLE/ENGINE** 车辆；引擎 **9** [I, T] **~ (sth) to the right/the left/one side** to move or make a vehicle move sideways （使车辆）转向，打斜：*The wheel is pulling to the left.* 方向盘正在向左打。◇ *She pulled the car to the right to avoid the dog.* 她把汽车向右一闪，好躲开那条狗。 **10** [I] (of an engine 发动机) to work hard and use a lot of power 吃力地运转：*The old car pulled hard as we drove slowly up the hill.* 老旧的汽车吃力地向前爬，把我们缓缓地拖上了山坡。

• **BOAT** 小船 **11** [I, T] **~ (sth)** (**+ adv./prep.**) to use OARS to move a boat along 划；划动：*They pulled towards the shore.* 他们向岸边划去。

• **CROWD/SUPPORT** 群众；支持 **12** [T] **~ sb/sth** (**in**) to attract the interest or support of sb/sth 吸引；博取：*They pulled in huge crowds on their latest tour.* 最近巡回演出时，他们吸引了大批观众。

• **ATTRACT SEXUALLY** 吸引异性 **13** [T, I] **~ (sb)** (*BrE, informal*) to attract sb sexually 吸引异性：*He can still pull the girls.* 他仍然能让姑娘们着迷。◇ *She's hoping to pull tonight.* 她希望今晚风采迷人。

• **TRICK/CRIME** 计谋；罪行 **14** [T] **~ sth** (*informal*) to succeed in playing a trick on sb, committing a crime, etc. （耍手腕）得逞；犯下（罪行）：*He's pulling some sort of trick on you.* 他在耍花招骗你呢。

• **CANCEL** 撤销 **15** [T] **~ sth** (*informal*) to cancel an event; to stop showing an advertisement, etc. 取消，撤销（活动、广告等）：*The gig was pulled at the last moment.* 音乐会临时取消了。

IDM **pull a ˈfast one (on sb)** (*slang*) to trick sb 蒙骗；捉弄 **pull in different/opposite diˈrections** to have different

▼ **SYNONYMS 同义词辨析**

pull

drag • draw • haul • tow • tug

These words all mean to move sth in a particular direction, especially towards or behind you. 以上各词均含拖、拉、拽之意。

pull to hold sth and move it in a particular direction; to hold or be attached to a vehicle and move it along behind you 指向某方向拖、拉、牵引：*Pull the chair nearer the table.* 把椅子再往桌子这边拉近些。◇ *They use oxen to pull their carts.* 他们用牛拉车。

drag to pull sb/sth in a particular direction or behind you, usually along the ground, and especially with effort 通常指使劲在地上拖、拉、拽：*The sack is too heavy to lift—you'll have to drag it.* 这麻袋太重了，提不起来。你得拖着走。

draw (*formal*) to move sb/sth by pulling them/it gently; to pull a vehicle such as a carriage 指拖动、拉动、牵引、拖车：*I drew my chair closer to the fire.* 我把椅子向火旁拉近了点。◇ *a horse-drawn carriage* 马车

haul to pull sb/sth to a particular place with a lot of effort 指用力拖、拉、拽：*Fishermen were hauling in their nets.* 渔民在拉网。

DRAG OR HAUL? 用 drag 还是 haul?

You usually **drag** sth behind you along the ground; you usually **haul** sth towards you, often upwards towards you. **Dragging** sth often needs effort, but **hauling** sth always does. * drag 通常指在身后的地上拖，haul 通常指朝面前拉、向上拽。drag 常需要用力，而 haul 总是要用力。

tow to pull a car, boat or light plane behind another vehicle, using a rope or chain 指用绳索拖、拉、牵引（汽车、船或轻型飞机）：*Our car was towed away by the police.* 我们的汽车被警察拖走了。

tug to pull sb/sth hard in a particular direction 指朝某一方向用力拖、拉、拽：*She tried to escape but he tugged her back.* 她试图逃跑，但他把她拽了回来。

PATTERNS

- to pull/drag/draw/haul/tow/tug sb/sth **along/down/towards** sth
- to pull/drag/draw/haul/tow sb/sth **behind you**
- to pull/drag/draw/haul a **cart/sledge**
- to pull/draw a **coach/carriage**
- to pull/haul/tow a **truck**
- **horses** pull/draw/haul sth
- **dogs** pull/drag/haul sth

P

aims that cannot be achieved together without causing problems 目标迥异；各行其是 **pull sb's 'leg** (*informal*) to play a joke on sb, usually by making them believe sth that is not true 捉弄；和…开玩笑 **pull the 'other one (—it's got 'bells on)** (*BrE, informal*) used to show that you do not believe what sb has just said （表示不相信对方的话）别打哈哈了 **pull out all the 'stops** (*informal*) to make the greatest effort possible to achieve sth 竭尽全力；费九牛二虎之力 **pull the 'plug on sb/sth** (*informal*) to put an end to sb's project, a plan, etc. 阻止；制止；终止 **pull your 'punches** (*informal*) (usually used in negative sentences 通常用于否定句) to express sth less strongly than you are able to, for example to avoid upsetting or shocking sb 言辞婉转；委婉表示： *Her articles certainly don't pull any punches.* 她的文章确实一针见血。 **pull sth/a ˌrabbit out of the 'hat** (*informal*) to suddenly produce sth as a solution to a problem 突然提出解决方法；突施妙计 **pull 'rank (on sb)** to make use of your place or status in society or at work to make sb do what you want 凭借地位指使（某人）；弄权 **pull the rug (out) from under sb's 'feet** (*informal*) to take help or support away from sb suddenly 突然停止帮助（或支援） **pull your 'socks up** (*BrE, informal*) to try to improve your performance, work, behaviour, etc. 力求做好；努力向上： *You're going to have to pull your socks up.* 你可得加把劲儿了。 **pull 'strings (for sb)** (*NAmE also* **pull 'wires**) (*informal*) to use your influence in order to get an advantage for sb 凭影响（为某人）谋利益；（为某人）活动，走后门 **pull the 'strings** to control events or the actions of other people 幕后操纵；暗中控制 **ˌpull up 'stakes** (*NAmE*) (*BrE* **ˌup 'sticks**) to suddenly move from your house and go to live somewhere else 突然迁居 **pull your 'weight** to work as hard as everyone else in a job, an activity, etc. 尽本分；尽职责 **pull the 'wool over sb's eyes** (*informal*) to try to trick sb; to hide your real actions or intentions from sb 蒙蔽某人；欺骗某人 ➲ MORE AT BOOTSTRAP, FACE *n.*, HORN *n.*, PIECE *n.*, SHRED *n.*

P

PHR V **ˌpull a'head (of sb/sth)** to move in front of sb/sth 抢先；领先： *The cyclists were together until the bend, when Tyler pulled ahead.* 自行车选手们原本胶着在一起，直到转弯处泰勒才超前领先。 **ˌpull sb/sth a'part** to separate people or animals that are fighting 分开，拉开（打斗的人或动物） **ˌpull sth a'part** 🔑 to separate sth into pieces by pulling different parts of it in different directions 拆散；拆卸 **'pull at sth** = PULL ON/AT STH **ˌpull a'way (from sth)** (of a vehicle 车辆) to start moving 开动： *They waved as the bus pulled away.* 公共汽车开动时他们挥手告别。 **ˌpull 'back 1** (of an army 军队) to move back from a place 撤退；撤离 SYN **withdraw** **2** to decide not to do sth that you were intending to do, because of possible problems 退出；退却 SYN **withdraw**: *Their sponsors pulled back at the last minute.* 他们的赞助人在最后时刻打了退堂鼓。 **ˌpull sb↔'back** to make an army move back from a place 撤回部队；撤兵 **ˌpull 'back | ˌpull sth↔'back** (*sport* 体育) to improve a team's position in a game （比赛中）挽回局势，翻盘，扳回： *Rangers pulled back to 4–3.* 流浪者队以 4:3 反败为胜。 ◇ *They pulled back a goal just before half-time.* 在上半场临结束时，他们扳回一球。 **ˌpull sb 'down** (*especially US*) to make sb less happy, healthy or successful 使扫兴；贬低某人 **ˌpull sth↔'down 1** 🔑 to destroy a building completely 捣毁，拆毁，摧毁（建筑物） SYN **demolish** **2** = PULL STH↔IN/DOWN **ˌpull sb↔'in** (*informal*) to bring sb to a police station in order to ask them questions about a crime 拘留（问话） **ˌpull sth↔'in/'down** (*informal*) to earn the large amount of money mentioned 赚（大笔钱） SYN **make**: *I reckon she's pulling in over $100 000.* 我估计她要赚 10 多万美元。 **ˌpull 'in (to sth)** 🔑 **1** (of a train 火车) to enter a station and stop 进站停靠 **2** (*BrE*) (of a vehicle or its driver 车辆或司机) to move to the side of the road or to the place mentioned and stop 驶向路边（或某处）停靠： *The police car signalled to us to pull in.* 警车发出信号，要我们驶向路边停靠。 **ˌpull 'off | ˌpull 'off sth** 🔑 (of a vehicle or its driver 车辆或司机) to leave the road in order to stop for a short time 驶向路边短暂停车 **ˌpull sth↔'off** (*informal*) to succeed in doing sth difficult 做成，完成（困难的事情）： *We pulled off the deal.* 我们做成了这笔交易。 ◇ *I never thought you'd pull it off.* 我真没想到你把这事办成了。 **'pull on/at sth** to take long deep breaths from a cigarette, etc. 猛吸，狠抽（香烟等） **ˌpull 'out** 🔑 (of a vehicle or its driver 车辆或司机) to move away from the side of the road, etc. 驶离路边；驶出： *A car suddenly pulled out in front of me.* 一辆汽车突然由路边冲到我前面。 **ˌpull 'out (of sth) 1** 🔑 (of a train 火车) to leave a station 驶离车站；出站 **2** 🔑 to move away from sth or stop being involved in it 脱离；退出 SYN **withdraw**: *The project became so expensive that we had to pull out.* 这个项目变得耗资巨大，我们只得退出。 **ˌpull sb/sth 'out (of sth)** 🔑 to make sb/sth move away from sth or stop being involved in it 使脱离；使退出 SYN **withdraw**: *They are pulling their troops out of the war zone.* 他们正从战区撤出军队。 ➲ RELATED NOUN PULL-OUT **ˌpull 'over** 🔑 (of a vehicle or its driver 车辆或司机) to move to the side of the road in order to stop or let sth pass 驶向路边；向路边停靠（或让车） **ˌpull sb/sth↔'over** 🔑 (of the police 警察) to make a driver or vehicle move to the side of the road 令（司机或车辆）停靠路边 **ˌpull 'through | ˌpull 'through sth 1** 🔑 to get better after a serious illness, operation, etc. （大病、手术等后）康复，痊愈： *The doctors think she will pull through.* 医生相信她将康复。 **2** to succeed in doing sth very difficult 完成，做成（十分困难的事）： *It's going to be tough but we'll pull through it together.* 这件事会很棘手，但我们将协力把它完成。 **ˌpull sb 'through | ˌpull sb 'through sth 1** to help sb get better after a serious illness, operation, etc. 帮…复原（或康复） **2** to help sb succeed in doing sth very difficult 协助…完成（十分困难的事）： *I relied on my instincts to pull me through.* 我全靠本能闯了过来。 **ˌpull to'gether** to act, work, etc. together with other people in an organized way and without fighting 齐心协力；通力合作 **ˌpull yourself to'gether** 🔑 to take control of your feelings and behave in a calm way 使自己镇定自若（或冷静）： *Stop crying and pull yourself together!* 别哭了，振作起来！ **ˌpull 'up** 🔑 (of a vehicle or its driver 车辆或司机) to stop 停车；停止： *He pulled up at the traffic lights.* 他在红绿灯处停了车。 **ˌpull sb 'up** (*BrE, informal*) to criticize sb for sth that they have done wrong 训斥；斥责

■ ***noun***

- **TRYING TO MOVE STH** 试图移动 **1** 🔑 [C] an act of trying to make sth move by holding it firmly and bringing it towards you 拉；拽；扯： *I gave the door a sharp pull and it opened.* 我猛地一拉，门开了。
- **PHYSICAL FORCE** 自然力 **2** 🔑 [sing.] **the ~ (of sth)** a strong physical force that makes sth move in a particular direction 力；引力；磁力： *the earth's gravitational pull* 地球的引力
- **ATTRACTION** 吸引 **3** 🔑 [C, usually sing.] **the ~ (of sth)** the fact of sth attracting you or having a strong effect on you 吸引力；诱惑；影响： *The magnetic pull of the city was hard to resist.* 都市的强大魅力难以抗拒。
- **INFLUENCE** 影响 **4** [U] (*informal*) power and influence over other people （对他人的）影响，影响力： *people who have a lot of pull with the media* 能左右传媒的人物
- **ON CIGARETTE/DRINK** 香烟；饮料 **5** [C] **~ (at/on sth)** an act of taking a deep breath of smoke from a cigarette, etc. or a deep drink of sth 深吸；大口喝： *She* ***took a long pull*** *on her cigarette.* 她深深地吸了口烟。
- **WALK UP HILL** 登山 **6** [C, usually sing.] (*BrE*) a difficult walk up a steep hill 艰难攀登： *It's* ***a long pull*** *up to the summit.* 登上山顶要攀爬很久。
- **MUSCLE INJURY** 肌肉损伤 **7** [C] an injury to a muscle caused by using too much force 拉伤；扭伤
- **HANDLE/ROPE** 手柄；绳索 **8** [C] (especially in compounds 尤用于构成复合词) something such as a handle or rope that you use to pull sth 拉手；拉绳；拉环： *a bell/door pull* 钟绳；门把手 ➲ SEE ALSO RING PULL

IDM **on the 'pull** (*BrE, slang*) (of a person 人) trying to find a sexual partner 寻觅性伴侣

pull·back /'pʊlbæk/ *noun* **1** an act of taking soldiers away from an area 撤兵；撤回部队 **2** a time when prices are reduced, or when fewer people want to buy sth 价格下跌；需求减少

ˈpull date (*US*) (*BrE* **ˈsell-by date**) *noun* the date printed on food packages, etc. after which the food must not be sold （食品等的）最迟销售日期，保质期

ˈpull-down *adj.* **1** designed to be used by being pulled down 下拉式的；拉下使用的：*a pull-down bed* 下拉式床 **2 ~ menu** (*computing* 计) a list of possible choices that appears on a computer screen below a menu title 下拉式选单；下拉选项屏；下拉选单 ➲ VISUAL VOCAB PAGE V74

ˌpulled ˈpork *noun* [U] meat from a pig that is cooked very slowly, often with smoke, until it is so soft you can pull it into small pieces with your hands 手撕猪肉（慢火烹至松软，常熏制）

pul·let /ˈpʊlɪt/ *noun* a young chicken, especially one that is less than one year old （尤指不足一年的）小母鸡

pul·ley /ˈpʊli/ *noun* a wheel or set of wheels over which a rope or chain is pulled in order to lift or lower heavy objects 滑轮；滑轮组；滑车：*a system of ropes and pulleys* 绳索滑轮系统 ➲ PICTURE AT BLOCK AND TACKLE

ˈpulling power (*BrE*) (*NAmE* **ˈdrawing power**) *noun* [U] the ability of sb/sth to attract people 吸引力；诱惑力

Pull·man /ˈpʊlmən/ *noun* (*pl.* **Pull·mans**) a type of very comfortable coach/car on a train 普尔曼豪华火车车厢

ˈpull-out *noun, adj.*
- *noun* **1** a part of a magazine, newspaper, etc. that can be taken out easily and kept separately （报刊等的）可取出插页：*an eight-page pull-out on health* 八页的保健插页 ◇ *a pull-out guide* 活页指南 **2** an act of taking an army away from a particular place; an act of taking an organization out of a system （军队的）转移，撤离；（机构的）撤销
- *adj.* [only before noun] (*especially NAmE*) a **pull-out** bed, couch, etc. can be kept hidden when not in use and pulled out when it is needed （床、沙发等）抽拉式的，伸缩的

pull·over /ˈpʊləʊvə(r); *NAmE* -oʊ-/ *noun* (*especially BrE*) a knitted piece of clothing made of wool or cotton for the upper part of the body, with long sleeves and no buttons 套头毛衣；套衫 SYN **jumper, sweater**

ˈpull tab (*also* **tab**) (*both NAmE*) (*BrE* **ˈring pull**) *noun* a small piece of metal with a ring attached which is pulled to open cans of food, drink, etc. （易拉罐等的）拉环；易拉环 ➲ VISUAL VOCAB PAGE V36

pul·lu·late /ˈpʌljuleɪt/ *verb* (*formal*) **1** [I] to breed or spread quickly 迅速繁殖；大量扩散 **2** [I] to be full of life or activity 充满生机；生机勃勃；生机盎然 ▸ **pul·lu·lat·ing** *adj.*：*a pullulating mass of people* 活跃的人群

ˈpull-up (*also* **ˈchin-up** *especially in NAmE*) *noun* [usually pl.] an exercise in which you hold onto a high bar above your head and pull yourself up towards it 引体向上（单杠运动）

pul·mon·ary /ˈpʌlmənəri; *NAmE* -neri/ *adj.* [only before noun] (*medical* 医) connected with the lungs 肺的；肺部的；与肺有关的

pulp /pʌlp/ *noun, verb, adj.*
- *noun* **1** [sing., U] a soft wet substance that is made especially by crushing sth 浆状物：*Cook the fruit gently until it forms a pulp.* 用文火把水果煮烂。◇ *His face had been **beaten to a pulp*** (= very badly beaten). 他的脸被打得稀巴烂。 **2** [U] a soft substance that is made by crushing wood, cloth or other material and then used to make paper 纸浆：***paper/wood pulp*** 纸浆；木浆 **3** [U] the soft part inside some fruit and vegetables （瓜果等的）肉质部分，髓 SYN **flesh** **4** writing that is of poor quality but popular and often SENSATIONAL (2) （常哗众取宠的）低俗流行作品 ▸ **pulpy** *adj.*：*Cook the fruit slowly until soft and pulpy.* 把水果慢慢地煮成软糊状。
- *verb* **~ sth** to crush or beat sth so that it becomes soft and wet 将…捣成浆：*Unsold copies of the novel had to be pulped.* 没卖出去的小说只好化成纸浆。◇ *pulped fruit* 果泥
- *adj.* [only before noun] (of books, magazines, etc. 书刊等) badly written and often intended to shock people 粗制滥造的；庸俗刺激的：*pulp fiction* 粗制滥造的小说

pul·pit /ˈpʊlpɪt/ *noun* a small platform in a church that is like a box and is high above the ground, where a priest, etc. stands to speak to the people （教堂中的）小讲坛

pul·sar /ˈpʌlsɑː(r)/ *noun* (*astronomy* 天) a star that cannot be seen but that sends out regular rapid radio signals 脉冲星 ➲ COMPARE QUASAR

pul·sate /pʌlˈseɪt; *NAmE* ˈpʌlseɪt/ *verb* **1** [I] to make strong regular movements or sounds 有规律地跳动（或发声）；均匀震动；搏动：*pulsating rhythms* 均匀的节奏 ◇ *a pulsating headache* 阵阵的头痛 ◇ *Lights were pulsating in the sky.* 天空有闪烁的光。 **2** [I] to be full of excitement or energy 洋溢，充满（激情或活力） SYN **buzz**：*a pulsating game* 令人兴奋的游戏 ◇ **~ with sth** *The streets were pulsating with life.* 街上生机勃勃。 ▸ **pul·sa·tion** /pʌlˈseɪʃn/ *noun* [C, U]

pulse /pʌls/ *noun, verb*
- *noun* **1** [usually sing.] the regular beat of blood as it is sent around the body, that can be felt in different places, especially on the inside part of the wrist; the number of times the blood beats in a minute 脉搏；脉率：*a **strong/weak pulse*** 强 / 弱脉搏 ◇ *an abnormally high pulse rate* 异常高的脉率 ◇ *The doctor **took/felt my pulse**.* 医生给我量了脉搏 / 把了脉。◇ *Fear sent her **pulse racing*** (= made it beat very quickly). 她吓得脉搏急速跳动。 **2** a strong regular beat in music 强劲的音乐节拍 SYN **rhythm**：*the throbbing pulse of the drums* 阵阵强劲的鼓点 **3** a single short increase in the amount of light, sound or electricity produced by a machine, etc. 脉冲：*pulse waves* 脉冲波 ◇ *sound pulses* 声脉冲 **4 pulses** [pl.] the seeds of some plants that are eaten as food, such as PEAS and LENTILS 豆果果实；荚果；豆子 IDM SEE FINGER *n.*
- *verb* **1** [I] to move, beat or flow with strong regular movements or sounds 搏动；跳动；震动 SYN **throb**：*A vein pulsed in his temple.* 他太阳穴上的静脉在搏动。◇ *the pulsing rhythm of the music* 这乐曲的强烈节奏 **2** [I] **~ (with sth)** to be full of a feeling such as excitement or energy 洋溢着；充满（激情等） SYN **buzz**：*The auditorium pulsed with excitement.* 礼堂里洋溢着热烈的气氛。

pul·ver·ize (*BrE also* **-ise**) /ˈpʌlvəraɪz/ *verb* **1 ~ sth** (*formal*) to crush sth into a fine powder 粉碎；将…磨成粉 **2 ~ sb/sth** (*informal, especially BrE*) to defeat or destroy sb/sth completely 彻底击败（或战胜）；摧毁 SYN **crush**：*We pulverized the opposition.* 我们彻底击败了对手。

puma /ˈpjuːmə; *NAmE* ˈpuːmə/ (*especially BrE*) (*NAmE usually* **cou·gar**) (*NAmE also* **ˈmountain lion, pan·ther**) *noun* a large American wild animal of the cat family, with yellowish-brown or greyish fur 美洲狮

pum·ice /ˈpʌmɪs/ (*also* **ˈpumice stone**) *noun* [U] a type of grey stone that comes from VOLCANOES and is very light in weight. It is used in powder form for cleaning and polishing, and in pieces for rubbing on the skin to make it softer. 浮岩，浮石（一种火山玻璃，其粉末用于清洁抛光以及使皮肤光滑）

pum·mel /ˈpʌml/ *verb* (**-ll-**, *US* **-l-**) [T, I] to keep hitting sb/sth hard, especially with your FISTS (= tightly closed hands) 连续猛击；反复拳打；捶打：**~ sb/sth (with sth)** *He pummelled the pillow with his fists.* 他用双拳不停地捶打枕头。◇ (*figurative*) *She pummelled* (= strongly criticized) *her opponents.* 她严厉抨击了对手。◇ **~ (at sth)** *Her fists pummelled at his chest.* 她用拳头连连捶打他的胸膛。

pum·melo /ˈpʌmələʊ; *NAmE* -loʊ/ *noun* = POMELO

pump /pʌmp/ *noun, verb*
- *noun* **1** a machine that is used to force liquid, gas or air into or out of sth 抽水机；泵；打气筒：*She washed her face at the pump in front of the inn.* 她在客栈前的水泵旁洗了洗脸。◇ (*BrE*) *a petrol pump* 汽油泵 ◇ (*NAmE*) *a gas pump* 汽油泵 ◇ *a **foot/hand pump*** (= that you work by using your foot or hand) 脚踏泵；手摇泵 ◇ *a bicycle*

P

pump 自行车打气筒 ➲ VISUAL VOCAB PAGES V24, V55 ➲ SEE ALSO STOMACH PUMP **2** (*BrE*) = PLIMSOLL **3** (*especially NAmE*) (*BrE* **'court shoe**) a woman's formal shoe that is plain and does not cover the top part of the foot 船鞋，无带低帮女鞋，无带半高跟女鞋（正式场合穿的朴素女鞋）➲ VISUAL VOCAB PAGE V69 **4** (*BrE*) a woman's light soft flat shoe worn for dancing or exercise; a similar style of shoe worn as a fashion item 轻软舞鞋，休闲女鞋（女子跳舞、运动时穿或用作时装）: *ballet pumps* 芭蕾舞鞋 ➲ VISUAL VOCAB PAGE V69 IDM SEE HAND *n.*, PRIME *v.*

■ *verb* **1** [T, I] to make water, air, gas, etc. flow in a particular direction by using a pump or sth that works like a pump 用泵（或泵样器官等）输送: **~ (sth) (+ adv./prep.)** *The engine is used for pumping water out of the mine.* 这台发动机是用来从矿井中抽水的。◇ *The heart pumps blood around the body.* 心脏把血液输送到全身。◇ **~ sth + adj.** *The lake had been pumped dry.* 湖水已被抽干。**2** [I] **+ adv./prep.** (of a liquid 液体) to flow in a particular direction as if it is being forced by a pump 涌出；涌流；奔流: *Blood was pumping out of his wound.* 血从他的伤口喷出。**3** [T] **~ sth (+ adv./prep.)** to move sth quickly up and down or in and out 上下（或内外）快速摇动；急速摇晃: *He kept pumping my hand up and down.* 他不停地摇动着我的手。◇ *I pumped the handle like crazy.* 我拼命地来回摇动手柄。**4** [I] to move quickly up and down or in and out 快速上下（或内外）运动: *She sprinted for the line, legs pumping.* 她双腿紧蹬，奔向终点线。◇ *My heart was pumping with excitement.* 我激动得心里怦怦直跳。**5** [T] **~ sb (for sth)** (*informal*) to try to get information from sb by asking them a lot of questions 盘问；追问；一再探问: *See if you can pump him for more details.* 看你能不能向他再探问出些细节来。

IDM **pump 'bullets, 'shots, etc. into sb** to fire a lot of bullets into sb 向…连续发射 **pump sb full of sth** to fill sb with sth, especially drugs 给…大量（服用药物等）: *They pumped her full of painkillers.* 他们给她服用大量的止痛药。**pump 'iron** (*informal*) to do exercises in which you lift heavy weights in order to make your muscles stronger 举重（锻炼） **pump sb's 'stomach** to remove the contents of sb's stomach using a pump, because they have swallowed sth harmful 给…洗胃

PHR V **,pump sth 'into sth | ,pump sth 'in** to put a lot of money into sth 向…大量投资；注入大量资金: *He pumped all his savings into the business.* 他把全部积蓄都投入了该企业。 **,pump sth 'into sb** to force a lot of sth into sb 强行向…灌输: *It's difficult to pump facts and figures into tired students.* 把事实和数字硬灌输给疲惫的学生太难了。 **,pump sth↔'out** (*informal*) to produce sth in large amounts 大量生产（或制造）: *loudspeakers pumping out rock music* 大播摇滚乐的扩音器 ◇ *Our cars pump out thousands of tonnes of poisonous fumes every year.* 我们的汽车每年排放出数千吨的有毒尾气。 **,pump sb↔'up** [usually passive] to make sb feel more excited or determined 给（某人）打气；鼓励 **,pump sth↔'up** **1** to fill a tyre, etc. with air using a pump 为（轮胎等）充气；打气 **2** (*informal*) to increase the amount, value or volume of sth 增加…的量（或价值、体积等）；提高: *Interest rates were pumped up last week.* 上周利率提高了。

'pump-action *adj.* [only before noun] (of a gun or other device 枪或其他设备) worked by quickly pulling or pressing part of it in and out or up and down 唧筒式的；压动式的: *a pump-action shotgun* 唧筒式猎枪 ◇ *a pump-action spray* 手压式喷雾器

pum·per·nickel /ˈpʌmpənɪkl; *NAmE* -pərn-/ *noun* [U] (*from German*) a type of heavy dark brown bread made from RYE, originally from Germany and often sold in slices 黑麦粗面包（源于德国，常切片出售）

pump·kin /ˈpʌmpkɪn/ *noun* [U, C] a large round vegetable with thick orange skin. The seeds can be dried and eaten and the soft flesh can be cooked as a vegetable or in sweet PIES. 南瓜；南瓜大果: *Pumpkin pie is a traditional American dish served on Thanksgiving.* 南瓜馅饼是美国传统的感恩节食物。➲ VISUAL VOCAB PAGE V34

'pump-priming *noun* [U] the act of investing money to encourage growth in an industry or a business, especially by a government （政府）注资刺激经济

'pump room *noun* (especially in the past) the room at a SPA where people go to drink the special water （尤指旧时设在矿泉地的）矿泉水供应室

pun /pʌn/ *noun, verb*

■ *noun* **~ (on sth)** the clever or humorous use of a word that has more than one meaning, or of words that have different meanings but sound the same 双关语: *We're banking on them lending us the money—no pun intended!* 我们正指望他们借给我们钱呢 —— bank 绝无双关之意！➲ COMPARE WORDPLAY ➲ WORDFINDER NOTE AT COMEDY

■ *verb* **(-nn-)** [I] to make a pun 使用双关语

Punch /pʌntʃ/ *noun* IDM SEE PLEASED

punch 🔑 /pʌntʃ/ *verb, noun*

■ *verb* **1** 🔑 to hit sb/sth hard with your FIST (= closed hand) 拳打；以拳痛击: **~ sb/sth** *He was kicked and punched as he lay on the ground.* 他倒在地上，被拳打脚踢。◇ *He was* **punching the air** *in triumph.* 他得意扬扬地挥舞着拳头。◇ **~ sb/sth in/on sth** *She punched him on the nose.* 她一拳打在他的鼻子上。**2** to make a hole in sth with a PUNCH (3) or some other sharp object 给…打孔；（用打孔器等）打孔: **~ sth** *to punch a time card* 在记时卡上打孔 ◇ **~ sth in/through sth** *The machine punches a row of holes in the metal sheet.* 机器在金属薄板上冲出一排孔。**3 ~ sth** to press buttons or keys on a computer, telephone, etc. in order to operate it 按（键）；压（按钮）: *I punched the button to summon the elevator.* 我按电钮叫电梯。▶ **punch·er** *noun*: *He's one of boxing's strongest punchers.* 他是拳坛的铁榔头之一。

IDM **,punch above your 'weight** to be or try to be more successful than others in doing sth that normally requires more skill, experience, money, etc. than you have 超常发挥取胜；以小搏大: *This player seems to be able to constantly punch above his weight.* 这名选手似乎总有本事击败实力比他强的对手。

PHR V **,punch 'in/'out** (*NAmE*) to record the time you arrive at/leave work by putting a card into a special machine 用记时卡登录（上、下班）时间；刷记时卡 ➲ SEE ALSO CLOCK IN/ON, CLOCK OUT/OFF at CLOCK **,punch sth↔'in | ,punch sth 'into sth** to put information into a computer by pressing the keys 将（信息）键入计算机: *He punched in the security code.* 他把密码输入电脑。 **,punch sb 'out** (*NAmE, informal*) to hit sb so hard that they fall down 将某人击倒 **,punch sth↔'out 1** to press a combination of buttons or keys on a computer, telephone, etc. 按键（输入号码等）: *He picked up the telephone and punched out his friend's number.* 他拿起电话，拨打朋友的电话号码。 **2** to make a hole in sth or knock sth out by hitting it very hard 在…上打孔；打掉: *I felt as if all my teeth had been punched out.* 我觉得好像我满口牙齿都被打掉了。**3** to cut sth from paper, wood, metal, etc. with a special tool 冲压

■ *noun* **1** 🔑 [C] a hard hit made with the FIST (= closed hand) 重拳击打；用力的捶打: *a punch in the face* 打在脸上的一记重拳 ◇ *Hill* **threw a punch** *at the police officer.* 希尔对警察挥了一拳。◇ *a knockout punch* 将对手击倒的一拳 ◇ *He shot out his right arm and* **landed a punch** *on Lorrimer's nose.* 他突然抡起右臂，一拳打在洛里默的鼻子上。**2** [U] the power to interest people 吸引力: *It's a well-constructed crime story, told with speed and punch.* 这篇描写犯罪的故事构思精巧，情节紧凑，引人入胜。**3** [C] a tool or machine for cutting holes in paper, leather or metal 打孔机；穿孔器；冲床: *a hole punch* 打孔器 ➲ VISUAL VOCAB PAGE V71 **4** [U] a hot or cold drink made by mixing water, fruit juice, spices, and usually wine or another alcoholic drink 潘趣酒，宾治酒（用水、果汁、香料及葡萄酒或其他酒类勾兑成的冷或热的饮料） IDM SEE BEAT *v.*, PACK *v.*, PULL *v.*, ROLL *v.*

Punch and Judy show /ˌpʌntʃ ən ˈdʒuːdi ʃəʊ; *NAmE* ʃoʊ/ *noun* (in Britain) a traditional type of entertainment for children in which PUPPETS are used to tell stories about Punch, who is always fighting with his wife Judy

《庞奇和朱迪》傀儡戏（英国传统木偶剧，讲述总和妻子朱迪打闹的庞奇的故事）

punch·bag /ˈpʌntʃbæg/ (*BrE*) (*NAmE* **ˈpunching bag**) *noun* a heavy leather bag, hung on a rope, which is punched, especially by BOXERS as part of training, or as a form of exercise 沙袋（悬吊式，用于拳击训练）

punch·ball /ˈpʌntʃbɔːl/ *noun* a heavy leather ball, fixed on a spring, which is punched, especially by BOXERS as a part of training, or as a form of exercise 梨球（用弹簧等固定，用于拳击等训练）

punch·bowl /ˈpʌntʃbəʊl; *NAmE* -boʊl/ *noun* a bowl used for serving PUNCH (4) 潘趣酒碗

punch·card /ˈpʌntʃkɑːd; *NAmE* -kɑːrd/ (*also* ˌ**punched ˈcard**) *noun* a card on which, in the past, information was recorded as lines of holes and used for giving instructions, etc. to computers and other machines 穿孔卡（旧时把信息打成一排排的小孔，用以将指令输入计算机等）

ˈ**punch-drunk** (*also* ˌ**slap-ˈhappy** *especially in NAmE*) *adj.* **1** (of a BOXER 拳击手) confused as a result of being punched on the head many times 被击晕的；晕头转向的 **2** unable to think clearly; in a confused state 思维混乱的；糊涂的

ˈ**punching bag** (*NAmE*) (*BrE* **punch·bag**) *noun* a heavy leather bag, hung on a rope, which is punched, especially by BOXERS as part of training, or as a form of exercise （用于拳击训练的悬吊式）沙袋 ➲ MORE LIKE THIS 9, page R26

punch·line /ˈpʌntʃlaɪn/ (*also NAmE, informal* **ˈtag line**) *noun* the last few words of a joke that make it funny （笑话最后的）妙趣横生的语句，妙语；画龙点睛之语

ˈ**punch-up** *noun* (*BrE, informal*) a physical fight 打架；斗殴；动拳脚 SYN **brawl**

punchy /ˈpʌntʃi/ *adj.* (**punch·ier**, **punchi·est**) (of a speech, song, etc. 演说、歌曲等) having a strong effect because it expresses sth clearly in only a few words 简洁有力的；言简意赅的；简练的

punc·tili·ous /pʌŋkˈtɪliəs/ *adj.* (*formal*) very careful to behave correctly or to perform your duties exactly as you should 一丝不苟的；循规蹈矩的：*a punctilious host* 一丝不苟的主人 ▸ **punc·tili·ous·ly** *adv.* **punc·tili·ous·ness** *noun* [U]

punc·tual /ˈpʌŋktʃuəl/ *adj.* happening or doing sth at the arranged or correct time; not late 按时的；准时的；守时的：*She has been reliable and punctual.* 她一直可靠守时。◇ *a punctual start at 9 o'clock* * 9 点钟准时开始 ▸ **punc·tu·al·ity** /ˌpʌŋktʃuˈæləti/ *noun* [U] **punc·tu·al·ly** /ˈpʌŋktʃuəli/ *adv.*：*They always pay punctually.* 他们一向按时付款。

punc·tu·ate /ˈpʌŋktʃueɪt/ *verb* **1** [T, often passive] **~ sth (with sth)** to interrupt sth at intervals 不时打断：*Her speech was punctuated by bursts of applause.* 她的讲演不时被阵阵掌声打断。 **2** [I, T] **~ (sth)** to divide writing into sentences and phrases by using special marks, for example commas, question marks, etc. 给…加标点符号

punc·tu·ation /ˌpʌŋktʃuˈeɪʃn/ *noun* [U] the marks used in writing that divide sentences and phrases; the system of using these marks 标点符号；标点符号用法

ˌ**punctuˈation mark** *noun* a sign or mark used in writing to divide sentences and phrases 标点符号

punc·ture /ˈpʌŋktʃə(r)/ *noun, verb*

■ *noun* **1** (*BrE*) a small hole in a tyre made by a sharp point （轮胎上刺破的）小孔，小洞：*I had a puncture on the way and arrived late.* 我在路上扎破了轮胎，所以迟到了。➲ SEE ALSO FLAT *n.* (6) **2** a small hole, especially in the skin, made by a sharp point （尤指皮肤上被刺破的）扎孔；刺伤

■ *verb* **1** [T, I] **~ (sth)** to make a small hole in sth; to get a small hole 在…上扎孔（或穿孔）；（被）刺破：*to puncture a tyre* 扎破轮胎 ◇ *She was taken to the hospital with broken ribs and a punctured lung.* 她肋骨骨折、肺部穿孔，被送往医院。◇ *One of the front tyres had punctured.* 一个前轮被扎破了。 **2** [T] **~ sth** to suddenly make sb feel less confident, proud, etc. 使突然泄气；挫伤（锐气等）：*to puncture sb's confidence* 打击某人的信心

pun·dit /ˈpʌndɪt/ *noun* **1** a person who knows a lot about a particular subject and who often talks about it in public 行家；权威；专家 SYN **expert** **2** = PANDIT

pun·gent /ˈpʌndʒənt/ *adj.* **1** having a strong taste or smell 味道（或气味）强烈的；刺激性的：*the pungent smell of burning rubber* 烧橡胶的刺鼻气味 ➲ SYNONYMS AT BITTER ➲ WORDFINDER NOTE AT TASTE **2** direct and having a strong effect 说穿的；一语道破的；一针见血的：*pungent criticism* 一针见血的批评 ▸ **pun·gency** /-nsi/ *noun* [U] **pung·ent·ly** *adv.*

pun·ish 🔑 /ˈpʌnɪʃ/ *verb* **1** 🔑 to make sb suffer because they have broken the law or done sth wrong 处罚；惩罚：**~ sb** *Those responsible for this crime will be severely punished.* 犯下这宗罪行的人将受到严厉惩罚。◇ *My parents used to punish me by not letting me watch TV.* 过去我父母常以不让我看电视来惩罚我。◇ **~ sb for sth/for doing sth** *He was punished for refusing to answer their questions.* 他拒不回答他们的问题，受到了惩罚。 ➲ WORDFINDER NOTE AT LAW **2 ~ sth (by/with sth)** to set the punishment for a particular crime 对…判罪；判定…的处罚方式：*In those days murder was always punished with the death penalty.* 那个时候，谋杀总是判死罪。 **3 ~ yourself (for sth)** to blame yourself for sth that has happened 责怪（自己）；自责

pun·ish·able /ˈpʌnɪʃəbl/ *adj.* **~ (by/with sth)** (of a crime 罪行) that can be punished, especially by law 可以惩罚的；可以处罚的；（尤指）应法办的：*a crime punishable by/with imprisonment* 可判监禁的罪行 ◇ *Giving false information to the police is a punishable offence.* 向警方谎报情况是应受惩处的罪行。

pun·ish·ing /ˈpʌnɪʃɪŋ/ *adj.* [usually before noun] long and difficult and making you work hard so you become very tired 艰难持久的；令人筋疲力尽的：*The President has a punishing schedule for the next six months.* 总统今后六个月的工作日程十分繁忙。

pun·ish·ment 🔑 /ˈpʌnɪʃmənt/ *noun* **1** 🔑 [U, C] an act or a way of punishing sb 惩罚；处罚；刑罚：*to* ***inflict/impose/mete out punishment*** 予以惩罚 ◇ **~ (for sth)** *What is the punishment for murder?* 谋杀应处以什么刑罚？◇ *There is little evidence that harsher punishments deter any better than more lenient ones.* 甚少证据显示严惩比宽待更能遏止犯罪。◇ *The punishment should fit the crime.* 罚宜当罪。◇ *He was sent to his room* ***as a punishment.*** 他被罚回到他的房间。 ➲ SEE ALSO CAPITAL PUNISHMENT, CORPORAL PUNISHMENT **2** [U] rough treatment 粗暴对待；虐待：*The carpet by the door takes the most punishment.* 门边的地毯磨损得最厉害。

pu·ni·tive /ˈpjuːnətɪv/ *adj.* [usually before noun] (*formal*) **1** intended as punishment 惩罚性的；刑罚的；处罚的：*There are calls for more* ***punitive measures*** *against people who drink and drive.* 有人呼吁对酒后驾车的人要有更具处罚性的措施。◇ (*NAmE*) *He was awarded* ***punitive damages*** (= in a court of law). 法庭判给他处罚性的损害赔偿。 **2** very severe and that people find very difficult to pay （租税等）苛刻的：*punitive taxes* 惩罚性征税 ▸ **pu·ni·tive·ly** *adv.*

Pun·jabi /pʊnˈdʒɑːbi/ *noun* **1** [C] a person from the Punjab area in NW India and Pakistan 旁遮普人（印度西北部和巴基斯坦的旁遮普地区的人） **2** [U] the language of people from the Punjab 旁遮普语 ▸ **Pun·jabi** *adj.*

punk /pʌŋk/ *noun* **1** (*also* ˌ**punk ˈrock**) [U] a type of loud and aggressive rock music popular in the late 1970s and early 1980s 朋克摇滚乐（流行于 20 世纪 70 年代后期和 80 年代初期）：*a punk band* 朋克摇滚乐队 **2** (*also* ˌ**punk ˈrocker**) [C] a person who likes punk music and dresses like a punk musician, for example

P

by wearing metal chains, leather clothes and having brightly coloured hair 朋克摇滚乐迷: *a punk haircut* 朋克发式 **3** [C] (*informal, especially NAmE*) a young man or boy who behaves in a rude or violent way 小流氓; 小混混; 小阿飞 SYN **lout**

pun·kah /ˈpʌŋkə; -kɑː/ *noun* **1** (*IndE*) an electric fan 电风扇 **2** (in India in the past) a large cloth fan that hung from the ceiling and that was moved by pulling a string 拉风（印度旧时悬挂于天花板用绳子拉动的布屏风扇）

pun·net /ˈpʌnɪt/ *noun* (*BrE*) a small box or BASKET that soft fruit is often sold in（盛软质水果的）小果盒，小果篮 ➲ VISUAL VOCAB PAGE V36

pun·ster /ˈpʌnstə(r)/ *noun* a person who often makes PUNS 爱说双关语的人

punt[1] /pʌnt/ *noun, verb* ➲ SEE ALSO PUNT[2]

■ *noun* **1** a long shallow boat with a flat bottom and square ends which is moved by pushing the end of a long pole against the bottom of a river 方头平底船（用篙撑） ➲ VISUAL VOCAB PAGE V60 **2** (*BrE, informal*) a bet 赌博; 打赌: *The investment is little more than a punt.* 这项投资无异于一场赌博。 **3** (in RUGBY or AMERICAN FOOTBALL 橄榄球或美式足球) a long kick made after dropping the ball from your hands 弃踢; 碰踢

■ *verb* **1** [I, T] ~ (**sth**) (+ **adv./prep.**) to travel in a punt[1] (1), especially for pleasure 乘方头平底船游览: *We spent the day punting on the river.* 我们乘方头平底小船在河上游览了一天。 ◇ *to go punting* 坐方头平底船游玩 **2** [T] ~ **sth** (+ **adv./prep.**) to kick a ball hard so that it goes a long way, sometimes after it has dropped from your hands and before it reaches the ground 踢凌空长球; 踢脱手球

punt[2] /pʊnt/ *noun* the former unit of money in the Republic of Ireland (replaced in 2002 by the euro) 爱尔兰镑（爱尔兰共和国以前的货币单位，于 2002 年为欧元所取代） ➲ SEE ALSO PUNT[1]

P

punt·er /ˈpʌntə(r)/ *noun* (*BrE, informal*) **1** a person who buys or uses a particular product or service 顾客; 主顾; 客户 SYN **customer**: *It's important to keep the punters happy.* 重要的是让顾客满意。 **2** a person who gambles on the result of a horse race 赌马的人

puny /ˈpjuːni/ *adj.* (**puni·er, puni·est**) (*disapproving*) **1** small and weak 弱小的; 孱弱的 SYN **feeble**: *The lamb was a puny little thing.* 羊羔瘦小孱弱。 **2** not very impressive 不起眼的; 可怜的; 微不足道的: *They laughed at my puny efforts.* 他们嘲笑我微不足道的努力。

pup /pʌp/ *noun* **1** = PUPPY **2** a young animal of various SPECIES (= types) 幼小动物: *a seal pup* 一只小海豹

IDM **sell sb/buy a pup** (*old-fashioned, BrE, informal*) to sell sb or be sold sth that has no value or is worth much less than the price paid 卖给…（或买到）伪劣货

pupa /ˈpjuːpə/ *noun* (*pl.* **pupae** /ˈpjuːpiː/) an insect in the stage of development between a LARVA and an adult insect 蛹 ➲ COMPARE CHRYSALIS ▶ **pupal** /ˈpjuːpəl/ *adj.* [usually before noun]

pu·pate /pjuːˈpeɪt; *NAmE* ˈpjuːpeɪt/ *verb* [I] (*biology* 生) to develop into a pupa 化蛹

pupil 🔑 /ˈpjuːpl/ *noun* **1** 🔑 (*especially BrE, becoming old-fashioned*) a person who is being taught, especially a child in a school 学生; （尤指）小学生: *How many pupils does the school have?* 这所小学有多少学生? ◇ *She now teaches only private pupils.* 她现在只当私人教师。 ➲ SYNONYMS AT STUDENT **2** 🔑 a person who is taught artistic, musical, etc. skills by an expert 弟子; 门生; 门徒: *The painting is by a pupil of Rembrandt.* 这幅画为伦勃朗的一位弟子所作。 **3** the small round black area at the centre of the eye 瞳孔; 眸子; 瞳仁: *Her pupils were dilated.* 她的瞳孔扩大了。 ➲ VISUAL VOCAB PAGE V64 ➲ COMPARE IRIS (1)

pu·pil·lage (*especially US* **pu·pil·age**) /ˈpjuːpɪlɪdʒ/ *noun* [U, C, sing.] **1** (*formal*) a period during which you are a student, especially when you are being taught by a particular person 学生时期（尤指接受某人教育） **2** (*BrE*) a period during which a lawyer trains to become a BARRISTER by studying with a qualified barrister; the system which allows this training 大律师见习期（或制度）; 大律师实习期（或制度）

pup·pet /ˈpʌpɪt/ *noun* **1** a model of a person or an animal that can be made to move, for example by pulling strings attached to parts of its body or by putting your hand inside it. A puppet with strings is also called a MARIONETTE. 玩偶; 木偶: *a hand puppet* 手偶 ◇ *a puppet show* 木偶表演 ➲ SEE ALSO GLOVE PUPPET **2** (*usually disapproving*) a person or group whose actions are controlled by another 傀儡: *The occupying forces set up a* ***puppet government.*** 占领军建立了一个傀儡政府。

pup·pet·eer /ˌpʌpɪˈtɪə(r); *NAmE* -ˈtɪr/ *noun* a person who performs with puppets 演木偶戏的人; 操纵木偶的人

pup·pet·ry /ˈpʌpɪtri/ *noun* [U] the art and skill of making and using puppets 木偶制作（或表演）艺术

puppy /ˈpʌpi/ *noun* (*pl.* **-ies**) (*also* **pup**) **1** a young dog 小狗; 幼犬: *a litter of puppies* 一窝小狗 ◇ *a Labrador puppy* 拉布拉多小狗 **2** (*old-fashioned, informal*) a proud or rude young man 傲慢小子; 自负无礼的青年

ˈ**puppy fat** (*BrE*) (*NAmE* ˈ**baby fat**) *noun* [U] fat on a child's body that disappears as the child grows older 小儿虚胖（长大后消失）

ˈ**puppy love** *noun* [U] feelings of love that a young person has for sb else and that adults do not think is very serious 青少年的初恋; 少年不成熟的恋爱

ˈ**pup tent** *noun* (*NAmE*) a small tent for two people 三角形小帐篷

pur·chase 🔑 AW /ˈpɜːtʃəs; *NAmE* ˈpɜːrtʃəs/ *noun, verb*

■ *noun* (*formal*) **1** 🔑 [U, C] the act or process of buying sth 购买; 采购: *to* ***make a purchase*** (= buy sth) 采购 ◇ *Keep your receipt as* ***proof of purchase.*** 保存好收据作为购货凭证。 ◇ *The company has just announced its £27 million purchase of Park Hotel.* 这家公司刚刚宣布以 2 700 万英镑买下了帕克酒店。 ➲ WORDFINDER NOTE AT BUY ➲ COLLOCATIONS AT SHOPPING ➲ SEE ALSO HIRE PURCHASE **2** 🔑 [C] something that you have bought 购买的东西; 购买项目: *major purchases, such as a new car* 新汽车之类的巨额购买项目 ◇ *If you are not satisfied with your purchase we will give you a full refund.* 所购之物若不合意，我们将全额退款。 **3** [U, sing.] (*specialist*) a firm hold on sth with the hands or feet, for example when you are climbing 握紧; 抓牢; 蹬稳 SYN **grip**: *She tried to get a purchase on the slippery rock.* 她设法抓牢光滑的岩石。

■ *verb* 🔑 ~ **sth** (**from sb**) (*formal*) to buy sth 买; 购买; 采购: *The equipment can be purchased from your local supplier.* 这种设备可以从您当地的供应商购买。 ◇ *They purchased the land for $1 million.* 他们以 100 万美元买下了这块土地。 ◇ (*figurative*) *Victory was purchased* (= achieved) *at too great a price.* 这次胜利的代价太大了。

ˈ**purchase price** *noun* [usually sing.] (*formal*) the price that is paid for sth you buy 买价

pur·chaser AW /ˈpɜːtʃəsə(r); *NAmE* ˈpɜːrtʃ-/ *noun* (*formal*) a person who buys sth 购买人; 采购人员; 买主 ➲ COMPARE BUYER (1)

pur·chas·ing AW /ˈpɜːtʃəsɪŋ; *NAmE* ˈpɜːrtʃ-/ *noun* [U] (*business* 商) the activity of buying things, especially for a company 购买; 采购

ˈ**purchasing power** *noun* [U] **1** money that people have available to buy goods with （人民的）购买力 **2** the amount that a unit of money can buy （货币的）购买力: *the peso's purchasing power* 比索的购买力

pur·dah /ˈpɜːdə; *NAmE* ˈpɜːrdə/ *noun* [U] the system in some Muslim societies by which women live in a separate part of a house or cover their faces so that men do not see them（某些穆斯林社会妇女不见外男的）内房制度: ***to be in purdah*** 不公开露面 ◇ *He kept his daughters in virtual purdah.* 他让女儿们恪守不见外男的习俗。

pure 🔑 /pjʊə(r); *NAmE* pjʊr/ *adj.* (**purer** /ˈpjʊərə(r); *NAmE* ˈpjʊr-/, **purest** /ˈpjʊərɪst; *NAmE* ˈpjʊr-/)
- **NOT MIXED** 纯的 **1** 🔑 [usually before noun] not mixed with anything else; with nothing added 纯的；纯净的；纯粹的：*pure gold/silk, etc.* 纯金、真丝等 ◇ *These shirts are 100% pure cotton.* 这些衬衫是 100% 的纯棉。◇ *Classical dance in its purest form requires symmetry and balance.* 纯正的古典舞蹈要求对称与平衡。◇ *One movie is classified as pure art, the other as entertainment.* 一部电影被列为纯艺术片，另一部被列为娱乐片。
- **CLEAN** 洁净 **2** 🔑 clean and not containing any harmful substances 干净的；不含有害物质的：*a bottle of pure water* 一瓶纯净水 ◇ *The air was sweet and pure.* 空气清新而纯净。**OPP** **impure**
- **COMPLETE** 完全 **3** 🔑 [only before noun] complete and total 完全的；纯粹的：*They met by pure chance.* 他们相遇纯属偶然。◇ *She laughed with pure joy.* 她由衷地笑起来。
- **COLOUR/SOUND/LIGHT** 色；声；光 **4** 🔑 very clear; perfect 清晰的；纯正的：*beaches of pure white sand* 洁白的沙滩 ◇ *a pure voice* 纯净的嗓音
- **MORALLY GOOD** 纯良 **5** without evil thoughts or actions, especially sexual ones; morally good 纯真的；无邪的；贞洁的；正派的：*to lead a pure life* 过纯洁的生活 ◇ *His motives were pure.* 他动机纯正。◇ (*literary*) *to be pure in body and mind* 身心纯洁 **OPP** **impure**
- **SUBJECT YOU STUDY** 学科 **6** [only before noun] concerned with increasing knowledge of the subject rather than with using knowledge in practical ways 纯理论的；非应用的：*pure mathematics* 纯粹数学 ◇ *technology as opposed to pure science subjects* 相对于纯理论学科的技术 ⊃ COMPARE APPLIED
- **BREED/RACE** 品种；种族 **7** not mixed with any other breed or race, etc. 血统纯的；纯种的：*These cattle are one of the purest breeds in Britain.* 这些牛是英国最纯的品种之一。⊃ SEE ALSO PURE-BRED, PURIFY, PURITY

IDM ˌ**pure and** ˈ**simple** used after the noun that it refers to in order to emphasize that there is nothing but the thing you have just mentioned involved in sth（用于名词后表示强调）纯粹，全然：*It's laziness, pure and simple.* 这全然是懒惰。

ˈ**pure-bred** *adj.* (of an animal 动物) born from parents of the same breed, not from a mix of two or more breeds 纯种的

purée /ˈpjʊəreɪ; *NAmE* pjʊˈreɪ/ *noun, verb*
- ▪ ***noun*** [U, C] food in the form of a thick liquid made by crushing fruit or cooked vegetables in a small amount of water（用水果、熟的蔬菜压成的）酱，糊，泥：*apple purée* 苹果泥
- ▪ ***verb*** (**pur·éed**, **pur·éed**) **~ sth** to make food into a purée 把（食物）研成糊状

pure·ly 🔑 /ˈpjʊəli; *NAmE* ˈpjʊrli/ *adv.* only; completely 仅仅；完全：*I saw the letter purely by chance.* 我看见这封信纯属偶然。◇ *The charity is run on a purely voluntary basis.* 这个慈善团体完全是义务性质的。◇ *She took the job **purely and simply** for the money.* 她做这份工作图的就是钱。

pur·ga·tive /ˈpɜːɡətɪv; *NAmE* ˈpɜːrɡ-/ *noun* a substance, especially a medicine, that causes your BOWELS to empty 泻药；通便药物 ▸ **pur·ga·tive** *adj.*

pur·ga·tory /ˈpɜːɡətri; *NAmE* ˈpɜːrɡətɔːri/ *noun* [U] **1** (*usually* **Purgatory**) (in Roman Catholic teaching 天主教教义) a place or state in which the souls of dead people suffer for the bad things they did when they were living, so that they can become pure enough to go to heaven 炼狱 **2** (*informal, humorous*) any place or state of suffering 受难的处所（或状态）；惩戒所；折磨；磨难 **SYN** **hell**：*Getting up at four o'clock every morning is sheer purgatory.* 每天早上四点起床简直是活受罪。

purge /pɜːdʒ; *NAmE* pɜːrdʒ/ *verb, noun*
- ▪ ***verb*** **1** to remove people from an organization, often violently, because their opinions or activities are unacceptable to the people in power 清除，清洗（组织中的异己分子）：**~ sth** (**of sb**) *His first act as leader was to purge the party of extremists.* 他当上领导的第一件事就是清除党内的极端分子。◇ **~ sb** (**from sth**) *He purged extremists from the party.* 他把极端分子清除出党。 **2** (*formal*) to make yourself/sb/sth pure, healthy or clean by getting rid of bad thoughts or feelings 净化（心灵、风气等）；涤荡（污秽）：**~ yourself/sb/sth** (**of sth**) *We need to purge our sport of racism.* 我们必须消除体育界的种族主义。◇ **~ sth** (**from sth**) *Nothing could purge the guilt from her mind.* 她内心的愧疚是无法消除的。
- ▪ ***noun*** the act of removing people, often violently, from an organization because their views are unacceptable to the people who have power（对异己的）清洗，清除，暴力铲除

puri·fier /ˈpjʊərɪfaɪə(r); *NAmE* ˈpjʊr-/ *noun* a device that removes substances that are dirty, harmful or not wanted 清洁器；净化器：*an air/a water purifier* 空气 / 水净化器

pur·ify /ˈpjʊərɪfaɪ; *NAmE* ˈpjʊr-/ *verb* (**puri·fies**, **puri·fy·ing**, **puri·fied**, **puri·fied**) **1 ~ sth** to make sth pure by removing substances that are dirty, harmful or not wanted 使（某物）洁净；净化：*One tablet will purify a litre of water.* 一丸即可净化一升水。 **2 ~ sb/sth/yourself** to make sb pure by removing evil from their souls 洗涤（思想）；净化（心灵）：*Hindus purify themselves by bathing in the River Ganges.* 印度教徒在恒河中浸泡借以涤罪。 **3 ~ sth** (**from sth**) (*specialist*) to take a pure form of a substance out of another substance that contains it 提纯；精炼 ▸ **puri·fi·ca·tion** /ˌpjʊərɪfɪˈkeɪʃn; *NAmE* ˌpjʊr-/ *noun* [U]: *a water purification plant* 滤水厂

Pu·rim /ˈpʊərɪm; pʊˈriːm; *NAmE* ˈpʊr-/ *noun* [U] a Jewish festival that is celebrated in the spring 普林节，普珥节（犹太教春季的节日）

pur·ist /ˈpjʊərɪst; *NAmE* ˈpjʊr-/ *noun* a person who thinks things should be done in the traditional way and who has strong opinions on what is correct in language, art, etc.（语言、艺术等方面的）纯粹主义者，正统主义者 ▸ **pur·ism** /ˈpjʊərɪzəm; *NAmE* ˈpjʊr-/ *noun* [U]

pur·itan /ˈpjʊərɪtən; *NAmE* ˈpjʊr-/ *noun, adj.*
- ▪ ***noun*** **1** (*usually disapproving*) a person who has very strict moral attitudes and who thinks that pleasure is bad 禁欲者；苦行者 **2 Puritan** a member of a Protestant group of Christians in England in the 16th and 17th centuries who wanted to worship God in a simple way 清教徒（属于 16 和 17 世纪的英国教会）
- ▪ ***adj.*** **1 Puritan** connected with the Puritans and their beliefs 清教徒的；清教主义的；禁欲的；苦行的 **2** = PURITANICAL

pur·it·an·ical /ˌpjʊərɪˈtænɪkl; *NAmE* ˌpjʊr-/ (*also* **pur·itan**) *adj.* (*usually disapproving*) having very strict moral attitudes 清教徒式的；道德极严格的：*Their parents had a puritanical streak and didn't approve of dancing.* 他们的父母管教颇严格，不赞成跳舞。

pur·itan·ism /ˈpjʊərɪtənɪzəm; *NAmE* ˈpjʊr-/ *noun* [U] **1 Puritanism** the beliefs and practices of the Puritans 清教主义；清教徒的教义和行为 **2** very strict moral attitudes 十分严格的道德观

pur·ity /ˈpjʊərəti; *NAmE* ˈpjʊr-/ *noun* [U] the state or quality of being pure 纯洁；纯净；纯粹：*The purity of the water is tested regularly.* 水的纯度定期检测。◇ *spiritual purity* 心灵纯洁 **OPP** **impurity**

purl /pɜːl; *NAmE* pɜːrl/ *noun* [U] a STITCH used in knitting（编织的）反针，倒针 ▸ **purl** *verb* [T, I]

pur·lieus /ˈpɜːljuːz; *NAmE* ˈpɜːrluːz/ *noun* [pl.] (*literary*) the area near or surrounding a place 临近地区；周围地区

pur·loin /pɜːˈlɔɪn; ˈpɜːlɔɪn; *NAmE* pɜːrˈl-; ˈpɜːrl-/ *verb* **~ sth** (**from sb/sth**) (*formal* or *humorous*) to steal sth or use it without permission 偷窃；擅自使用

pur·ple 🔑 /ˈpɜːpl; *NAmE* ˈpɜːrpl/ *adj.* **1** 🔑 having the colour of blue and red mixed together 紫色的：*a purple flower* 紫色的花 ◇ *His face was purple with rage.* 他气得脸色发紫。 **2 ~ prose/passage** writing or a piece of

P

writing that is too grand in style 华丽的文辞；雕琢的章句 ▶ **pur·ple** noun [U, C]: *She was dressed in purple.* 她穿一身紫色衣裳。

ˌPurple 'Heart noun a MEDAL given to a member of the armed forces of the US who has been wounded in battle (美国授予作战负伤军人的) 紫心勋章

'purple patch noun (BrE) a period of success or good luck 成功的时期；红运

purp·lish /ˈpɜːpəlɪʃ; NAmE ˈpɜːrp-/ adj. similar to purple in colour 带紫色的；发紫的：*purplish lips* 发紫的嘴唇

pur·port verb, noun
■ **verb** /pəˈpɔːt; NAmE pərˈpɔːrt/ ~ **to be/have sth** (formal) to claim to be sth or to have done sth, when this may not be true 自称；标榜 SYN **profess**: *The book does not purport to be a complete history of the period.* 本书无意标榜为那个时期的全史。
■ **noun** /ˈpɜːpɔːt; NAmE ˈpɜːrpɔːrt/ [sing.] **the ~ of sth** (formal) the general meaning of sth 主要意思；大意；主旨

pur·ported /pəˈpɔːtɪd; NAmE pərˈpɔːrt-/ adj. [only before noun] (formal) that has been stated to have happened or to be true, when this might not be the case 据称的；传言的：*the scene of the purported crime* 传闻中的罪案发生地点 ▶ **pur·port·ed·ly** adv. : *a letter purportedly written by Mozart* 一封据传是莫扎特的亲笔信

pur·pose /ˈpɜːpəs; NAmE ˈpɜːrpəs/ noun **1** [C] the intention, aim or function of sth; the thing that sth is supposed to achieve 意图；目的；用途；目标：*Our campaign's main purpose is to raise money.* 我们这次活动的主要目的就是募款。◇ *The purpose of the book is to provide a complete guide to the university.* 本书旨在全面介绍这所大学。◇ *A meeting was called **for the purpose of** appointing a new treasurer.* 为任命新财务主管而召开了一次会议。◇ *The experiments **serve no useful purpose*** (= are not useful). 这些实验毫无用处。◇ *The building is used for religious purposes.* 这座建筑是用于宗教活动的。**2** **purposes** [pl.] what is needed in a particular situation 情势的需要：*These gifts count as income for tax purposes.* 这些礼物应属于纳税的收入。◇ ***For the purposes of** this study, the three groups have been combined.* 为了这项研究工作，三个小组业已合并。**3** [C, U] meaning that is important and valuable to you 重要意义；有价值的意义：*Volunteer work gives her life* (*a sense of*) ***purpose***. 做志愿工作使她的生活有了意义。**4** [U] the ability to plan sth and work successfully to achieve it 意志；毅力；决心 SYN **determination**: *He has enormous confidence and **strength of purpose**.* 他信心十足，意志坚强。➲ SEE ALSO CROSS PURPOSES
IDM **on 'purpose** not by accident; deliberately 故意；有意地：*He did it on purpose, knowing it would annoy her.* 他明知会激怒她，却故意那么做。 **to little/no 'purpose** (formal) with little/no useful effect or result 作用不大；徒劳 ➲ MORE AT FIT adj., INTENT n., PRACTICAL adj.

ˌpurpose-'built adj. (BrE) designed and built for a particular purpose 定做的；专门设置的

pur·pose·ful /ˈpɜːpəsfl; NAmE ˈpɜːrp-/ adj. having a useful purpose; acting with a clear aim and with determination 目的明确的；有目的的；目标清晰而坚定的：*Purposeful work is an important part of the regime for young offenders.* 使从事有意义的劳动是管理少年犯的重要一环。◇ *She looked purposeful and determined.* 她看来目标明确，意志坚定。 ▶ **pur·pose·ful·ly** /-fəli/ adv. **pur·pose·ful·ness** noun [U]

pur·pose·less /ˈpɜːpəsləs; NAmE ˈpɜːrp-/ adj. having no meaning, use or clear aim 无目的的；无用的；无意义的 SYN **meaningless, pointless**: *purposeless destruction* 盲目的破坏

pur·pose·ly /ˈpɜːpəsli; NAmE ˈpɜːrp-/ adv. on purpose; deliberately 故意地；蓄意地：*He sat down, purposely avoiding her gaze.* 他坐了下来，有意避开她的目光。

pur·pos·ive /ˈpɜːpəsɪv; NAmE ˈpɜːrp-/ adj. (formal) having a clear and definite purpose 目标明确的；有目的的 SYN **purposeful**

P

▼ **SYNONYMS** 同义词辨析

purpose
aim • intention • plan • point • idea

These are all words for talking about what sb/sth intends to do or achieve. 以上各词均指意图、目的、目标。

purpose what sth is supposed to achieve; what sb is trying to achieve 指目的、目标：*Our campaign's main purpose is to raise money.* 我们这次活动的主要目的是募款。

aim what sb is trying to achieve; what sth is supposed to achieve 指目标、目的：*She went to London with the aim of finding a job.* 她去伦敦是为了找工作。◇ *Our main aim is to increase sales in Europe.* 我们的主要目标是增加在欧洲的销售量。

PURPOSE OR AIM? 用 purpose 还是 aim?

Your **purpose** for doing something is your reason for doing it; your **aim** is what you want to achieve. **Aim** can suggest that you are only trying to achieve sth; **purpose** gives a stronger sense of achievement being certain. **Aim** can be *sb's aim* or *the aim of sth*. **Purpose** is more usually *the purpose of sth*: you can talk about *sb's purpose* but that is more formal. * purpose 指做某事的原因，aim 指要达到的目的。aim 可意味着做成某事尚在尝试阶段，purpose 表示达成目标的把握更大。aim 可指某人的目的 (sb's aim)，也可指某事的目的 (the aim of sth)，purpose 更常指做某事的原因 (the purpose of sth)，也可指某人的目的 (sb's purpose)，但这样用较正式。

intention what you intend to do 指打算、计划、意图：*I have no intention of going to the wedding.* 我无意去参加婚礼。◇ *She's full of **good intentions** but they rarely work out.* 她虽然处处出于善意，却很少行的通。

plan what you intend to do or achieve 指计划、打算：*There are no plans to build new offices.* 现在没有建新办公楼的计划。

INTENTION OR PLAN? 用 intention 还是 plan?

Your **intentions** are what you want to do, especially in the near future; your **plans** are what you have decided or arranged to do, often, but not always, in the longer term. * intention 尤指近期的打算、意图；plan 通常但不总是指较长远的计划、安排。

point (rather informal) the purpose or aim of sth 指意图、目的、理由：***What's the point** of all this violence?* 这些暴行的意图何在？◇ *The point of the lesson is to compare the two countries.* 本课的目的是比较这两个国家。

idea (rather informal) the purpose of sth; sb's aim 指目的、意图：*The whole idea of going was so that we could meet her new boyfriend.* 我们去的唯一目的就是要见她的新男朋友。◇ ***What's the idea behind this?*** 这背后的意图是什么？

POINT OR IDEA? 用 point 还是 idea?

Point is a more negative word than **idea**. If you say *What's the point...?* you are suggesting that there is no point; if you say *What's the idea...?* you are genuinely asking a question. **Point**, but not **idea**, is used to talk about things you feel annoyed or unhappy about. * point 比 idea 有更多的否定含义：what's the point ...? 暗指毫无意义；what's the idea ...? 用于真正询问目的。用 point 而非 idea 表示对所谈论的事情感到不快：~~*There's no idea in...*~~ ◇ ~~*I don't see the idea of...*~~

PATTERNS
- **with the** purpose/aim/intention/idea **of doing sth**
- sb's intention/plan **to do sth**
- **to have** a(n) purpose/aim/intention/plan/point
- **to achieve/fulfil** a(n) purpose/aim

purr /pɜː(r)/ *verb* **1** [I] when a cat **purrs**, it makes a low continuous sound in the throat, especially when it is happy or comfortable （猫）发出呼噜声，惬意地打呼噜 **2** [I] (of a machine or vehicle 机器或机动车) to make a low continuous sound; to move making such a sound 轰隆作响；轰鸣着移动：*a purring engine* 轰隆作响的发动机 ◇ *The car purred away.* 汽车咕隆着开走了。 **3** [I, T] (+ **speech**) to speak in a low and gentle voice, for example to show you are happy or satisfied, or because you want to attract sb or get them to do sth （愉快或满意地）低沉柔和地讲话；轻声招呼：*He was purring with satisfaction.* 他满足地轻声低语。 ▸ **purr** (*also* **pur·ring**) *noun* [sing.]: *the purr of a cat/a car engine* 猫发出的呼噜声；汽车发动机的隆隆声

purse /pɜːs; *NAmE* pɜːrs/ *noun, verb*

▪ ***noun*** **1** [C] (*especially BrE*) a small bag made of leather, plastic, etc. for carrying coins and often also paper money, cards, etc., used especially by women 钱包，皮夹子（尤指女用的）：*I took a coin out of my purse and gave it to the child.* 我从钱包取出一枚硬币给那个小孩。 ➲ VISUAL VOCAB PAGE V69 ➲ COMPARE CHANGE PURSE, WALLET **2** [C] (*NAmE*) = HANDBAG **3** [sing.] the amount of money that is available to a person, an organization or a government to spend 资金；财源；备用款：*We have holidays to suit every purse.* 我们有适合不同消费计划的度假安排。 ◇ *Should spending on the arts be met out of the* ***public purse*** (= from government money)? 花在艺术活动的开支应该由政府支付吗？ **4** [C] (*sport* 体育) a sum of money given as a prize in a BOXING match （拳击赛的）奖金 **IDM** SEE SILK

▪ ***verb*** **~ your lips** to form your lips into a small tight round shape, for example to show disapproval 噘嘴，噘起嘴唇（以表示反对等）

pur·ser /ˈpɜːsə(r); *NAmE* ˈpɜːrs-/ *noun* an officer on a ship who is responsible for taking care of the passengers, and for the accounts （轮船上的）事务长

the ˈpurse strings *noun* [pl.] a way of referring to money and how it is controlled or spent 资金管理；开支管理：*Who* ***holds the purse strings*** *in your house?* 你们家里谁管钱？ ◇ *The government will have to* ***tighten the purse strings*** (= spend less). 政府将不得不紧缩开支。

pur·su·ance /pəˈsjuːəns; *NAmE* pərˈsuː-/ *noun*

IDM **in pursuance of sth** (*formal* or *law* 律) in order to do sth; in the process of doing sth 为了；在…过程中：*They may need to borrow money in pursuance of their legal action.* 他们在诉讼过程中可能需要借贷。

pur·su·ant /pəˈsjuːənt; *NAmE* pərˈsuː-/ *adj.* **~ to sth** (*formal* or *law* 律) according to or following sth, especially a rule or law 依照，根据，按照（尤指规则或法律） **SYN** **accordance**

pur·sue 🔑 **AW** /pəˈsjuː; *NAmE* pərˈsuː/ *verb* (*formal*) **1** 🔑 **~ sth** to do sth or try to achieve sth over a period of time 追求；致力于；执行；贯彻：*to pursue a goal/an aim/an objective* 追求目标；贯彻宗旨；实现目标 ◇ *We intend to pursue this policy with determination.* 我们准备坚决贯彻这项政策。 ◇ *She wishes to pursue a medical career.* 她希望从事医学工作。 **2** 🔑 **~ sth | + speech** to continue to discuss, find out about or be involved in sth 继续探讨（或追究、从事）：*to pursue legal action* 进行诉讼 ◇ *We have decided not to pursue the matter.* 我们决定不再追究这件事。 **3** 🔑 **~ sb/sth** to follow or chase sb/sth, especially in order to catch them 追逐；跟踪；追赶：*She left the theatre, hotly pursued by the press.* 她离开剧场，被记者穷追不舍。 ◇ *Police pursued the car at high speed.* 警察高速追赶那辆汽车。

pur·suer /pəˈsjuːə(r); *NAmE* pərˈsuː-/ *noun* a person who is following or chasing sb 追赶者；追寻者；追捕者

pur·suit **AW** /pəˈsjuːt; *NAmE* pərˈsuːt/ *noun* **1** [U] **~ of sth** the act of looking for or trying to find sth 追求；寻找：*the* ***pursuit of*** *happiness/knowledge/profit* 对幸福/知识/利润的追求 ◇ *She travelled the world* ***in pursuit of*** *her dreams.* 她走遍天下，追寻她的梦想。 **2** [U] the act of following or chasing sb 追赶；跟踪；追捕：*We drove away with two police cars* ***in pursuit*** (= following). 我们驾车离开，后面有两辆警车跟着追赶。 ◇ *I galloped off on my horse with Rosie* ***in hot pursuit*** (= following quickly behind). 我纵马而去，罗西紧追不舍。 **3** [C, usually pl.] something that you give your time and energy to, that you do as a hobby 事业；消遣；爱好 **SYN** **hobby, pastime**: ***outdoor/leisure/artistic pursuits*** 户外活动；休闲活动；艺术爱好

puru·lent /ˈpjʊərələnt; *NAmE* ˈpjʊr-/ *adj.* (*medical* 医) containing or producing PUS 化脓的；流脓的：*a purulent discharge from the wound* 从伤口中流出的脓

pur·vey /pəˈveɪ; *NAmE* pərˈveɪ/ *verb* **~ sth** (*formal*) to supply food, services or information to people 提供，供应（食物、服务或信息）

pur·vey·or /pəˈveɪə(r); *NAmE* pərˈv-/ *noun* (*formal*) a person or company that supplies sth 提供者；供应商；供应公司

pur·view /ˈpɜːvjuː; *NAmE* ˈpɜːrv-/ *noun* [U]

IDM **within/outside the purview of sth** (*formal*) within/outside the limits of what a person, an organization, etc. is responsible for; dealt/not dealt with by a document, law, etc. 在（个人或组织等的）权限之内/之外；在（文件、法律等的）范围内/外

pus /pʌs/ *noun* [U] a thick yellowish or greenish liquid that is produced in an infected wound 脓

push 🔑 /pʊʃ/ *verb, noun*

▪ ***verb***

• **USING HANDS/ARMS/BODY** 用手/胳膊/身体 **1** 🔑 [I, T] to use your hands, arms or body in order to make sb/sth move forward or away from you; to move part of your body into a particular position 推动（人或物）；移动（身体部位）：*We pushed and pushed but the piano wouldn't move.* 我们推了又推，但钢琴一动不动。 ◇ *Push hard when I tell you to.* 我叫你推时，你就使劲推。 ◇ *You push and I'll pull.* 你推，我拉。 ◇ **~ at sth** *She pushed at the door but it wouldn't budge.* 她推了推门，但门纹丝不动。 ◇ **~ sth** *He walked slowly up the hill pushing his bike.* 他推着自行车缓缓爬上山。 ◇ **~ sb/sth + adv./prep.** *She pushed the cup towards me.* 她把杯子推向我这边。 ◇ *He pushed his chair back and stood up.* 他向后挪挪椅子，站了起来。 ◇ *He tried to kiss her but she pushed him away.* 他想吻她，但她把他推开了。 ◇ *She pushed her face towards him.* 她把脸凑近了他。 ◇ **~ sth + adj.** *I pushed the door open.* 我推开了门。 **2** 🔑 [I, T] to use force to move past sb/sth using your hands, arms, etc. 推进（道路）；挤开：*People were* ***pushing and shoving*** *to get to the front.* 人们推推搡搡，向最前面挤。 ◇ **+ adv./prep.** *The fans pushed against the barrier.* 球迷们推挤着栅栏门。 ◇ **~ your way + adv./prep.** *Try and push your way through the crowd.* 试着从人群中挤过去。

• **AFFECT STH** 影响 **3** 🔑 [T] **~ sth + adv./prep.** to affect sth so that it reaches a particular level or state 推动；促使（达到某程度或状态）：*This development could push the country into recession.* 这种新情况可能使国家陷入萧条。 ◇ *The rise in interest rates will push prices up.* 利率的提高将促使价格上扬。

• **SWITCH/BUTTON** 开关；按钮 **4** 🔑 [T] **~ sth** to press a switch, button, etc., for example in order to make a machine start working 按；揿；摁：*I pushed the button for the top floor.* 我按了到顶层的按钮。

• **PERSUADE** 劝说 **5** 🔑 [T] to persuade or encourage sb to do sth that they may not want to do 说服；劝解；鼓励；敦劝：**~ sb (into sth/into doing sth)** *My teacher pushed me into entering the competition.* 我的老师劝我参加比赛。 ◇ **~ sb to do sth** *No one pushed you to take the job, did they?* 谁也没推着你接受这份工作，对不对？

• **WORK HARD** 辛勤工作 **6** 🔑 [T] **~ sb/yourself** to make sb work hard *The music teacher really pushes her pupils.* 这个音乐老师对学生督促得很严。 ◇ *Lucy should push herself a little harder.* 露西应该鞭策自己多加把劲了。

• **PUT PRESSURE ON SB** 施压 **7** [T] **~ sb (+ adv./prep.)** (*informal*) to put pressure on sb and make them angry or upset 迫使…生气（或不安）：*Her parents are very tolerant, but*

P

sometimes she pushes them too far. 她的父母十分宽容，但她有时也让他们忍无可忍。

• NEW IDEA/PRODUCT 新主意 / 产品 **8** [T] ~ **sth** (*informal*) to try hard to persuade people to accept or agree with a new idea, buy a new product, etc. 力劝…接受；推销：*The interview gave him a chance to push his latest movie.* 这次采访使他有机会推销他的新电影。◇ *She didn't want to **push the point** any further at that moment.* 当时她不想继续强调那个观点。

• SELL DRUGS 贩毒 **9** [T] ~ **sth** (*informal*) to sell illegal drugs 贩卖毒品

• OF ARMY 军队 **10** [I] + **adv./prep.** to move forward quickly through an area 挺进；推进：*The army pushed (on) towards the capital.* 军队向首都挺进。

IDM **be ˌpushing ˈ40, ˈ50, etc.** (*informal*) to be nearly 40, 50, etc. years old 接近 40 岁（或 50 岁等） **be ˌpushing up (the) ˈdaisies** (*old-fashioned, humorous*) to be dead and in a grave 葬入地下；正忙着滋养冢上黄花 **push the ˈboat out** (*BrE, informal*) to spend a lot of money on enjoying yourself or celebrating sth 挥霍享乐；铺张庆贺 SYN **splash out** ˈ**push the envelope** (*informal*) to go beyond the limits of what is allowed or thought to be possible 超越界线；突破：*He is a performer who consistently pushes the envelope of TV comedy.* 他是一个在电视喜剧表演中不断寻求突破的演员。 **push your ˈluck | ˈpush it/things** (*informal*) to take a risk because you have successfully avoided problems in the past （由于过去的成功过关）再冒一次险，继续碰运气：*You didn't get caught last time, but don't push your luck!* 上次没被逮住，但你不要再心存侥幸了！ **push sth to the back of your ˈmind** to try to forget about sth unpleasant 刻意忘掉（不愉快的事）；把…丢到脑后：*I tried to push the thought to the back of my mind.* 我尽量把这个念头忘掉。➲ MORE AT BUTTON *n.*, PANIC BUTTON

PHR V **ˌpush sb aˈbout/aˈround** 🔑 to give orders to sb in a rude or unpleasant way 粗暴命令；任意摆布 **ˌpush aˈhead/ˈforward (with sth)** 🔑 to continue with a plan in a determined way 毅然推行（计划）：*The government is pushing ahead with its electoral reforms.* 政府正坚定地推行选举改革。 **ˌpush sth↔ˈaside** to avoid thinking about sth 不考虑；不去想：*He pushed aside the feelings of fear.* 他排除了恐惧。 **ˌpush ˈback (on sth)** (*especially NAmE*) to oppose or resist a plan, an idea or a change 反对，抵制（计划、想法或变革） **ˌpush sth ˈback** to make the time or date of a meeting, etc. later than originally planned 推迟；延迟：*The start of the game was pushed back from 2 p.m. to 4 p.m.* 比赛从午后两点延迟到 4 点才开始。 **ˈpush for sth | ˈpush sb for sth** to repeatedly ask for sth or try to make sth happen because you think it is very important （向某人）反复要求，施压争取…：*The pressure group is pushing for a ban on GM foods.* 压力集团正强烈要求取缔转基因食品。◇ *I'm going to have to push you for an answer.* 我将不得不催促你答复了。 **ˌpush ˈforward** to continue moving or travelling somewhere, especially when it is a long distance or difficult 继续前进；继续跋涉 **ˌpush yourself/sb ˈforward** to make other people think about and notice you or sb else 使引人注目；使出风头；突显：*She had to push herself forward to get a promotion.* 她必须努力表现自己以求得升迁机会。 **ˌpush ˈin** (*BrE*) (*NAmE* **ˌcut ˈin**) to go in front of other people who are waiting 加塞儿；插队 **ˌpush ˈoff** **1** (*BrE, informal*) used to tell sb rudely to go away 滚开；一边去：*Hey, what are you doing? Push off!* 嘿，你在干什么？滚开！ **2** to move away from land in a boat, or from the side of a swimming pool, etc. （乘船）离岸；离开（游泳池边等） **ˌpush ˈon** to continue with a journey or an activity 继续前进（或进行活动）：*We rested for a while then pushed on to the next camp.* 我们休息了一会儿，然后继续朝下一个营地迈进。 **ˌpush sb↔ˈout** to make sb leave a place or an organization 驱逐；开除 **ˌpush sb/sth↔ˈout** to make sth less important than it was; to replace sth 减少…的重要性；使失势；替换 **ˌpush sth↔ˈout** to produce sth in large quantities 大量生产：*factories pushing out cheap cotton shirts* 大量生产廉价棉衬衣的工厂 **ˌpush sb/sth ˈover** to make sb/sth fall to the ground by pushing them 推倒；推翻：*Sam pushed me over in the playground.* 萨姆在运动场上把我推倒了。➲ SEE ALSO PUSHOVER **ˌpush sth↔ˈthrough** to get a new law or plan officially accepted 使通过；使得到批准：*The government is pushing the changes through before the election.* 政府正努力推动，要在选举前促成这些变革。

▪ ***noun***

• USING HANDS/ARMS/BODY 用手 / 胳膊 / 身体 **1** 🔑 an act of pushing sth/sb 推；搡：*She gave him a gentle push.* 她轻轻地推了他一下。◇ *The car won't start. Can you give it a push?* 汽车发动不起来。你推一下好不好？◇ ***At the push of a button*** (= very easily) *he could get a whole list of names.* 他一按键就能得到完整的名单。

• OF ARMY 军队 **2** 🔑 a large and determined military attack 进攻；攻势；挺进：*a final push against the enemy* 对敌军的最后猛攻 ◇ (*figurative*) *The firm has begun a major push into the European market.* 这家公司已大举进攻欧洲市场。

• EFFORT 努力 **3** 🔑 ~ **for sth** a determined effort to achieve sth 矢志的追求；坚定的努力：*The push for reform started in 2007.* 推行改革的努力始于 2007 年。 **4** 🔑 encouragement to do sth 鼓励；激励：*He wants to open his own business, but needs a push in the right direction to get him started.* 他想创业，但还需要适当的鼓励助他起步。

IDM **at a ˈpush** (*BrE, informal*) used to say that sth is possible, but only with difficulty 不得已时；为难地；勉强地：*We can provide accommodation for six people at a push.* 我们勉强可以安排六个人住宿。 **give sb/get the ˈpush 1** (*BrE, informal*) to dismiss sb/to be dismissed from your job （被）解雇，炒鱿鱼 SYN **fire**：*They gave him the push after only six weeks.* 他只干了六周就被开除了。 **2** (*BrE, informal*) to end a romantic relationship with sb; to be told that a romantic relationship with sb is over 与某人结束恋爱关系；把（恋人）甩掉；被甩：*He was devastated when his girlfriend gave him the push.* 女友把他甩了，他感到极度沮丧。 **when ˌpush comes to ˈshove** (*informal*) when there is no other choice; when everything else has failed 别无选择时；须孤注一掷时

push·back /ˈpʊʃbæk/ *noun* [U] (*especially NAmE*) opposition or resistance to a plan, an idea or a change 反对；抵制；反弹：*The plan was abandoned because the pushback from the military was so strong.* 由于军方强烈反对，这一计划中止了。

push·bike /ˈpʊʃbaɪk/ *noun* (*old-fashioned, BrE*) a bicycle 自行车；脚踏车

ˈpush-button *adj.* [only before noun] operated by pressing buttons with your fingers 按键式的；用按钮操作的：*a push-button phone* 按键式电话 ▶ **ˈpush-button** *noun*

pushchair (*BrE*) **stroller** (*NAmE*) 折叠式幼儿车 | **pram** (*BrE*) **baby carriage** (*NAmE*) 婴儿车 | **carrycot** (*BrE*) 手提式婴儿床

push·chair /ˈpʊʃtʃeə(r); *NAmE* -tʃer/ (*BrE*) (*NAmE* **stroll·er**) *noun* a small folding seat on wheels in which a small child sits and is pushed along 折叠式幼儿车；童车 ➲ COMPARE BUGGY (2)

pushed /pʊʃt/ *adj.* [not before noun] (*informal*) **1** ~ **(to do sth)** having difficulty doing sth 有困难；难于；有难处：*You'll be **hard pushed** to finish this today.* 要你今天做完这件事会很难。 **2** ~ **for sth** not having enough of sth 短缺；缺乏：*to **be pushed for money/time*** 缺少资金 / 时间

3 busy 忙碌：*I know you're pushed, but can you make tomorrow's meeting?* 我知道你很忙，可是你能不能参加明天的会议？

push·er /ˈpʊʃə(r)/ *noun* (*informal*) a person who sells illegal drugs 贩毒者；毒品贩子：*drug pushers* 毒品贩子 ➲ SEE ALSO PAPER-PUSHER, PEN-PUSHER

push·over /ˈpʊʃəʊvə(r); *NAmE* -oʊ-/ *noun* (*informal*) **1** a thing that is easy to do or win 轻易的事；容易获得的胜利：*The game will be a pushover.* 赢得这场比赛将会是轻而易举的事。**2** a person who is easy to persuade or influence 容易说服的人；耳软心活的人；好说话的人：*I don't think she'll agree—she's no pushover.* 我想她不会同意，她可不好说话。

push·pin /ˈpʊʃpɪn/ *noun* (*NAmE*) a type of DRAWING PIN with a coloured plastic head that is not flat 彩头图钉 ➲ VISUAL VOCAB PAGE V71

ˈpush poll *noun* (*politics* 政) a way of trying to influence the way people vote by giving them information, often sth bad about an opposing candidate, while seeming to be asking their opinion 导向性民意调查，引导式民调（旨在影响选民投票的调查，常提供有关对手的负面信息）▸ **ˈpush polling** *noun* [U]：*allegations of push polling* 关于导向性民意调查的指控

ˈpush-start *verb* **~ sth** (*especially BrE*) to push a vehicle in order to make the engine start 推车启动（发动机）▸ **ˈpush-start** *noun* ➲ SEE ALSO KICK-START *v.*

ˈpush technology *noun* [U] (*computing* 计) a service that allows Internet users to keep receiving the particular type of information that they describe by completing a form 推送技术（用户能不断接收所选择的某类互联网信息）

ˈpush-up (*especially NAmE*) (*BrE also* **ˈpress-up**) *noun* [usually pl.] an exercise in which you lie on your stomach and raise your body off the ground by pressing down on your hands until your arms are straight 俯卧撑 ➲ VISUAL VOCAB PAGE V46

pushy /ˈpʊʃi/ *adj.* (**push·ier**, **pushi·est**) (*informal, disapproving*) trying hard to get what you want, especially in a way that seems rude 执意强求的；死缠硬磨的：*a pushy salesman* 纠缠不休的推销员 ▸ **pushi·ness** *noun* [U]

pu·sil·lan·im·ous /ˌpjuːsɪˈlænɪməs/ *adj.* (*formal*) frightened to take risks 胆怯的；怯懦的 **SYN** **cowardly**

puss /pʊs/ *noun* **1** (*especially BrE*) used when you are calling or talking to a cat（用于唤猫或对猫说话）咪咪，猫咪 **2** (*informal, especially NAmE*) a person's face or mouth（人的）脸，嘴

pussy /ˈpʊsi/ *noun* (*pl.* **-ies**) **1** a child's word for a cat（儿童用语）猫咪 **2** (*taboo, slang*) the female sexual organs, especially the VULVA 屄；女阴

pussy·cat /ˈpʊsikæt/ *noun* (*informal*) **1** a child's word for a cat（儿童用语）猫咪 **2** a person who is kind and friendly, especially when you would not expect them to be like this（尤指出人意料的）和蔼可亲的人：*He's just a pussycat really, once you get to know him.* 你了解他以后就会发现他实在和蔼可亲。

pussy·foot /ˈpʊsifʊt/ *verb* [I] **~ (about/around)** (*informal, usually disapproving*) to be careful or anxious about expressing your opinion in case you upset sb（说话）慎重，顾虑重重

ˈpussy willow *noun* a small tree with flowers in spring that are like soft fur 飞絮柳；（尤指）退色柳

pus·tule /ˈpʌstjuːl; *NAmE* -tʃuːl/ *noun* (*formal* or *medical* 医) a spot on the skin containing PUS 脓疱

put 🔑 /pʊt/ *verb* (**put·ting**, **put**, **put**)
• **IN PLACE/POSITION** 处所；位置 **1** 🔑 **~ sth + adv./prep.** to move sth into a particular place or position 放；安置：*Put the cases down there, please.* 请把箱子搁在那边。◇ *Did you put sugar in my coffee?* 你在我的咖啡里放糖了没有？◇ *Put your hand up if you need more paper.* 若有人还要纸，请举手。**2** 🔑 **~ sth + adv./prep.** to move sth into a particular place or position using force 猛推；用力插入：*He put his fist through a glass door.* 他用拳头砸穿了玻璃门。**3** 🔑 **~ sb/sth + adv./prep.** to cause sb/sth to go to a particular place 将…送往；使…前往：*Her family put her into a nursing home.* 她的家人把她送进了一家疗养院。◇ *It was the year the Americans put a man on the moon.* 那是美国人把人送上月球的那一年。
• **ATTACH** 附着 **4** 🔑 **~ sth + adv./prep.** to attach or fix sth to sth else 使与…连接；安装：*We had to put new locks on all the doors.* 我们只好把所有的门都安上新锁。
• **WRITE** 写 **5** 🔑 **~ sth (+ adv./prep.)** to write sth or make a mark on sth（在…上）书写，记，做标记：*Put your name here.* 在这里填上姓名。◇ *Friday at 11? I'll put it in my diary.* 星期五 11 点？我要把它记在记事本里。◇ *I couldn't read what she had put.* 她写的什么我辨认不出来。
• **INTO STATE/CONDITION** 状态；情况 **6** 🔑 **~ sb/sth + adv./prep.** to bring sb/sth into the state or condition mentioned 使处于（某状态或情况）：*I was put in charge of the office.* 他们让我负责管理这个办公室。◇ *The incident put her in a bad mood.* 这件事弄得她心情很不好。◇ ***Put yourself in my position.*** *What would you have done?* 你设身处地为我想想，你会怎么办？◇ *I tried to* ***put the matter into perspective.*** 我尽量正确评估这个问题。◇ *Don't go* ***putting yourself at risk.*** 当心不可冒什么风险。◇ *It was time to* ***put*** *their suggestion* ***into practice.*** 那时就该把他们的建议付诸实施了。◇ *This new injury will* ***put him out of action*** *for several weeks.* 这次的新伤将使他几周无法动弹。
• **AFFECT SB/STH** 影响某人 / 某事物 **7** 🔑 **~ sth on/onto/to sth** to make sb/sth feel sth or be affected by sth 使感觉到；使受到…的影响：*Her new job has put a great strain on her.* 她的新工作使她感到负担很重。◇ *They* ***put pressure on*** *her to resign.* 他们向她施加压力，让她自行辞职。◇ *It's time you* ***put a stop to*** *this childish behaviour.* 这种孩子气的行为你该收敛了。
• **GIVE VALUE/RANK** 厘定；划定 **8 ~ sth on sth** to give or attach a particular level of importance, trust, value, etc. to sth 给予（重视、信任、价值等）：*Our company puts the emphasis on quality.* 我们公司重视质量。◇ *He put a limit on the amount we could spend.* 他规定了我们开销的限额。**9 ~ sb/sth + adv./prep.** to consider sb/sth to belong to the class or level mentioned 把…视为（或列为）：*I'd put her in the top rank of modern novelists.* 我认为她应属于一流的当代小说家。
• **EXPRESS** 表述 **10** 🔑 **~ sth + adv./prep.** to express or state sth in a particular way 说；表达：*She put it very tactfully.* 她的话说得很巧妙。◇ ***Put simply,*** *we accept their offer or go bankrupt.* 简单地说吧，我们要么接受他们的条件，要么破产。◇ *I was,* ***to put it mildly,*** *annoyed* (= I was extremely angry). 说得温和点儿，我相当恼火。◇ *He was too trusting—or,* ***to put it another way,*** *he had no head for business.* 他太轻信人了。或者换个说法，他没有商业头脑。◇ *The meat was—***how shall I put it?***—a little overdone.* 这肉嘛，怎么说呢，做得稍微老了点儿。◇ *As T.S. Eliot puts it…* 正如 T.S. 艾略特所说…◇ *She had never tried to* ***put*** *this feeling* ***into words.*** 她从未试图把这种感情说出来。◇ *Can you help me put this letter into good English, please?* 请问你能帮我用通顺的英语来表达这信的内容吗？
• **IN SPORT** 体育运动 **11 ~ sth** to throw the SHOT 推（铅球）

IDM **HELP** Most idioms containing **put** are at the entries for the nouns and adjectives in the idioms, for example **put your foot in it** is at **foot**. 大多数含 put 的习语，都可在该等习语中的名词及形容词相关词条找到，如 put your foot in it 在词条 foot 下。**put it aˈbout** (*BrE, informal*) to have many sexual partners 浪荡胡为；乱搞男女关系 **I wouldn't put it ˈpast sb (to do sth)** (*informal*) used to say that you think sb is capable of doing sth wrong, illegal, etc. 我看…干得出（错的、违法的等事） **put it to sb that…** to suggest sth to sb to see if they can argue against it 与…挑明；对…提出：*I put it to you that you are the only person who had a motive for the crime.* 我跟你说白了，你是唯一有作案动机的人。 **put one ˈover on sb** (*informal*) to persuade sb to believe sth that is not true 蒙骗；诱骗：*Don't try to put one over on me!* 你甭想蒙我！ **put sb ˈthrough it** (*informal, especially BrE*) to force sb to experience sth difficult or unpleasant 折磨；让…难堪：*They really put me through it* (= asked me difficult questions)

P

at the interview. 面试的时候，他们真把我折腾了一番。 **put to'gether** used when comparing or contrasting sb/sth with a group of other people or things to mean 'combined' or 'in total'（用于与一组人或事物作比较）合计，总和，合起来：*Your department spent more last year than all the others put together.* 去年，你们部门的开支比其他所有部门合起来都多。 **,put up or 'shut up** (*especially BrE*) used to tell sb to stop just talking about sth and actually do it, show it, etc. 要么拿出实际行动来，要么就闭嘴；动点儿真格的，别光耍嘴皮子

PHR V **,put sth↔a'bout** (*BrE, informal*) to tell a lot of people news, information, etc. that may be false 散布，传播（不实的消息等）：**put it about that...** *Someone's been putting it about that you plan to resign.* 有人传说你打算辞职。

'put sth above sth = PUT STH BEFORE/ABOVE STH

,put yourself/sth↔a'cross/'over (to sb) to communicate your ideas, feelings, etc. successfully to sb 交流，沟通（思想、感情等）：*She's not very good at putting her views across.* 她不大善于表达自己的观点。

,put sth↔a'side 1 to ignore or forget sth, usually a feeling or difference of opinion 忽视；不理睬；忘记 **SYN** **disregard**: *They decided to put aside their differences.* 他们决定搁置双方的分歧。 **2** to save sth or keep it available to use 储存；保留：*We put some money aside every month for our retirement.* 我们每月都存一些钱供退休后使用。◇ *I put aside half an hour every day to write my diary.* 我每天留出半个小时写日记。

'put sb/sth at sth to calculate sb/sth to be a particular age, weight, amount, etc. 估计；计算：*The damage to the building is put at over $1 million.* 对这座建筑物造成的损坏估计超过 100 万美元。

,put sb↔a'way [often passive] (*informal*) to send sb to prison, to a mental hospital, etc. 把某人送入监狱（或精神病院等） **,put sth↔a'way 1** 🔑 to put sth in the place where it is kept because you have finished using it 将…收起；把…放回原处：*I'm just going to put the car away* (= in the garage). 我正打算把汽车开进车库。 **2** to save money to spend later 积蓄；攒钱：*She has a few thousand dollars put away for her retirement.* 她为退休生活积攒了几千美元。 **3** (*informal*) to eat or drink large quantities of sth 猛吃；猛喝；胡吃海塞：*He must have put away a bottle of whisky last night.* 昨晚他准是喝了一整瓶威士忌。

,put sth↔'back 1 🔑 to return sth to its usual place or to the place where it was before it was moved 将…放回：*If you use something, put it back!* 用过的东西要放回原处！ **2** 🔑 to move sth to a later time or date 推迟；延迟 **SYN** **postpone**: *The meeting has been put back to next week.* 这次会议已延期到下周了。 **3** to cause sth to be delayed 拖延；延缓；使延迟：*Poor trading figures put back our plans for expansion.* 贸易额不佳延缓了我们的扩张计划。 **4** to move the hands of a clock so that they show the correct earlier time 向后拨，拨慢（钟表指针）：*Remember to put your clocks back tonight* (= because the time has officially changed). 记住今晚把时钟拨回去。

'put sth before/above sth to treat sth as more important than sth else 把…看得比…重要

,put sth be'hind you to try to forget about an unpleasant experience and think about the future 把（不愉快的事）置于脑后

,put sth↔'by (*especially BrE*) (*also* **,put sth↔a'side**) to save money for a particular purpose 攒钱；积蓄：*I'm putting by part of my wages every week to buy a bike.* 我每个星期把一部分工资存起来准备买辆自行车。

,put 'down (of an aircraft or its pilot 飞机或飞行员) to land 降落；着陆：*He put down in a field.* 他降落在一块田里。 **,put sb↔'down** (*informal*) to make sb look or feel stupid, especially in front of other people 使（当众）出丑；使出洋相；让某人现眼 ➲ RELATED NOUN PUT-DOWN **,put sth↔'down 1** 🔑 to stop holding sth and place it on a table, shelf, etc. 搁在（桌子上等）；放下：*Put that knife down before you hurt somebody!* 把刀子放下，别伤着人！◇ *It's a great book. I couldn't put it down.* 这本书棒极了。我是爱不释手啊。◇ (*BrE*) *She put the phone down on me* (= ended the call before I had finished speaking). 她没等我把话说完就挂了线。➲ SEE ALSO UNPUTDOWNABLE **2** to write sth; to make a note of sth 写下；（用笔等）记下：*The meeting's on the 22nd. Put it down in your diary.* 会议日期是 22 号。把它记在你的记事本里。 **3** to pay part of the cost of sth 下订金；付部分费用：*We put a 5% deposit down on the house.* 我们给这所房子交了 5% 的订金。 **4** to stop sth by force 镇压；平定 **SYN** **crush**: *to put down a rebellion* 平定叛乱 ◇ *The military government is determined to put down all opposition.* 军政府决心镇压一切反对势力。 **5** [often passive] to kill an animal, usually by giving it a drug, because it is old or sick 药死（衰老或有病的动物）；人道毁灭：*We had to have our cat put down.* 我们只得用药结束了猫的生命。 **6** to put a baby to bed 安置（婴儿）入睡：*Can you be quiet—I've just put the baby down.* 请安静点儿，我刚把小孩哄睡着了。 **7** to present sth formally for discussion by a parliament or committee 将…提请（议会或委员会）审议 **SYN** **table**: *to put down a motion/an amendment* 提交一项动议 / 修正案

,put sb 'down as sth to consider or judge sb to be a particular type of person 把某人视为（或看作）：*I'd put them both down as retired teachers.* 我看他们俩都是退休教师。 **,put sb 'down for sth** to put sb's name on a list, etc. for sth 登记；注册；列入（名单等）：*Put me down for three tickets for Saturday.* 给我登记预订三张星期六的票。◇ *They've put their son down for the local school.* 他们已经给儿子报名上当地的学校。 **'put sth down to sth** to consider that sth is caused by sth 把…归因于 **SYN** **attribute**: *What do you put her success down to?* 你认为她是靠什么成功的？

,put sth↔'forth (*formal*) = PUT STH↔OUT

,put yourself/sb↔'forward to suggest yourself/sb as a candidate for a job or position 推荐；举荐：*Can I put you/your name forward for club secretary?* 我推荐你 / 提名你任俱乐部秘书好不好？ **,put sth↔'forward 1** 🔑 to move sth to an earlier time or date 将…提前：*We've put the wedding forward by one week.* 我们已把婚礼提前了一周。 **2** to move the hands of a clock to the correct later time 向前拨，拨快（时钟指针）：*Remember to put your clocks forward tonight* (= because the time has officially changed). 记住今晚把时钟指针往前拨。 **3** 🔑 to suggest sth for discussion 提出；提议；建议：*to put forward a suggestion* 提出建议

,put sb↔'in to elect a political party to govern a country 选举（政党）执政：*Who will the voters put in this time?* 这次选民会选谁执政呢？ **,put sth↔'in 1** 🔑 to fix equipment or furniture into position so that it can be used 安装 **SYN** **install**: *We're having a new shower put in.* 我们要安装新淋浴设备。 **2** to include sth in a letter, story, etc. 把…写进（信函、故事等）；添上；插入 **3** to interrupt another speaker in order to say sth 打断；插话：*Could I put in a word?* 我可以插句话吗？◇ **+ speech** *'But what about us?' he put in.* "那我们怎么办？"他插嘴说。 **4** to officially make a claim, request, etc. 正式提出（要求等）：*The company has put in a claim for damages.* 这家公司已提出赔偿损失的要求。 **5 put in a (...) performance** to give a performance of sth, especially one of a particular kind 表演：*All the actors put in great performances.* 所有演员都表演得非常好。 **6** (*also* **'put sth into sth**) to spend a lot of time or make a lot of effort doing sth 花费，耗费，投入（时间、心思等）：*She often puts in twelve hours' work a day.* 她时常每天工作十二个小时。◇ **put sth into doing sth** *He's putting a lot of work into improving his French.* 他正下功夫提高他的法语水平。 ➲ RELATED NOUN INPUT **7** (*also* **'put sth into sth**) to use or give money 投入，投放（资金等）：**put sth into doing sth** *He's put all his savings into buying that house.* 他把所有的积蓄都用来买那所房子了。 **,put 'in (at...) | 'put into...** (of a boat or its sailors 船或水手) to enter a port 进港；入港：*They put in at Lagos for repairs.* 他们驶入拉各斯港进行维修。 **OPP** **put out (to.../from...)** **,put 'in for sth** (*especially BrE*) to officially ask for sth 申请：*Are you going to put in for that job?* 你想申请那份工作吗？ **,put yourself/sb/sth 'in for sth** to enter yourself/sb/sth for a competition 报名，给…登记（参加竞赛）

,put sth 'into sth 1 to add a quality to sth 将…注入；使融入：*He put as much feeling into his voice as he could.* 他尽可能把感情融进他的声音。 **2** = PUT STH IN (6), (7)

ˌ**put sb↔ˈoff 1** to cancel a meeting or an arrangement that you have made with sb 取消，撤销（与某人的会晤或安排）: *It's too late to put them off now.* 现在已来不及取消与他们的安排了。 **2** to make sb dislike sb/sth or not trust them/it 使反感；使疏远；使不信任: *She's very clever but her manner does tend to put people off.* 她人很精明，但态度令人反感。◇ *Don't be put off by how it looks—it tastes delicious.* 别看外表就讨厌它，这东西味道可美哩。➲ SEE ALSO OFF-PUTTING **3** (*also* ˌ**put sb ˈoff sth**) to disturb sb who is trying to give all their attention to sth that they are doing 搅扰；使分神: *Don't put me off when I'm trying to concentrate.* 别在我要集中精神时打扰我。◇ *The sudden noise put her off her game.* 突然的嘈杂声干扰了她的比赛。 **4** (*BrE*) (of a vehicle or its driver 车辆或司机) to stop in order to allow sb to leave 停车卸（客）；让…下车: *I asked the bus driver to put me off at the station.* 我请公共汽车司机让我在火车站下车。 ˌ**put sb ˈoff sth/sb** to make sb lose interest in or enthusiasm for sth/sb 使失去兴趣（或热情）: *He was put off science by bad teaching.* 老师教得不好使他失去了对理科的兴趣。◇ **put sb off doing sth** *The accident put her off driving for life.* 那场事故让她一生都不想开车了。 ˌ**put sth↔ˈoff** to change sth to a later time or date 推迟；延迟 SYN **postpone, delay**: *We've had to put off our wedding until September.* 我们只得把婚期推迟到九月。◇ **put off doing sth** *He keeps putting off going to the dentist.* 他把看牙医的事一拖再拖。

ˌ**put sb ˈon** to give sb the telephone so that they can talk to the person at the other end 让某人听电话: *Hi, Dad—can you put Nicky on?* 你好，爸爸。你让尼基接接电话好吗? ˌ**put sth↔ˈon 1** to dress yourself in sth 穿上；戴上: *Hurry up! Put your coat on!* 快点！把外衣穿上！OPP **take sth↔off** **2** to apply sth to your skin, face, etc. 抹；搽；擦；涂: *She's just putting on her make-up.* 她正在化妆呢。 **3** to switch on a piece of equipment 开动；发动；使运行: *I'll put the kettle on for tea.* 我来烧壶水好沏茶。◇ *She put on the brakes suddenly.* 她突然踩了刹车。 **4** to make a tape, CD, DVD, etc. begin to play 播放（磁带、CD、DVD 等）: *Do you mind if I put some music on?* 我放点音乐你不介意吧? ◇ *He put some jazz on the stereo.* 他用立体声音响播放了一点爵士乐。 **5** to become heavier, especially by the amount mentioned 增加（若干）体重；发胖 SYN **gain**: *She looks like she's put on weight.* 她似乎发胖了。◇ *He must have put on several kilos.* 他体重一定增加了好几公斤。 **6** (*BrE*) to provide sth specially 专门提供: *The city is putting on extra buses during the summer.* 今年夏天，这城市将额外增开公共汽车。 **7** to produce or present a play, a show, etc. 举办；上演；展出: *The local drama club is putting on 'Macbeth'.* 当地的剧社正在演出《麦克白》。 **8** to pretend to have a particular feeling, quality, way of speaking, etc. 装作；假装: *He put on an American accent.* 他假操着一口美国腔。◇ *I don't think she was hurt. She was just **putting it on**.* 我想她没有受伤。她只是在装样子。 ˌ**put sth ˈon sth 1** to add an amount of money or a tax to the cost of sth 在（价格等）上加某金额（或税额）: *The government has put ten pence on the price of twenty cigarettes.* 政府在每二十支香烟的价格上加征了十便士的税款。 **2** to bet money on sth 把钱押在；下赌注: *I've never put money on a horse.* 我从未赌过马。◇ *I put £5 on him to win.* 我在他身上押 5 英镑赌他赢。

ˌ**put sb ˈonto sb/sth 1** to tell the police, etc. about where a criminal is or about a crime 向（警方等）揭发，告发，举报: *What first put the police onto the scam?* 警方当初怎么得知这个骗局的? **2** to tell sb about sb/sth that they may like or find useful 告诉；提供信息: *Who put you onto this restaurant—it's great!* 谁告诉你这家餐馆的? 真棒极了！

ˌ**put ˈout (for sb)** (*NAmE, slang*) to agree to have sex with sb 同意性交 ˌ**put yourself ˈout (for sb)** (*informal*) to make a special effort to do sth for sb 特意（为某人）费事: *Please don't put yourself out on my account.* 请别特意为我费事了。 ˌ**put sb ˈout 1** to cause sb trouble, extra work, etc. 给某人添麻烦（或增加额外工作等）SYN **inconvenience**: *I hope our arriving late didn't put them out.* 但愿我们迟到没有给人家添麻烦。 **2 be put out** to be upset or offended 烦恼；生气: *He looked really put out.* 看来他真生气了。 **3** to make sb unconscious 使昏迷；使失去知觉: *These pills should put him out for a few hours.* 这些药片会使他昏迷几个小时。 ˌ**put sth↔ˈout 1** to take sth out of your house and leave it, for example for sb to collect 将…扔到外面；清理掉；扔掉: (*BrE*) *to put the rubbish out* 倒垃圾 ◇ (*NAmE*) *to put the garbage/trash out* 倒垃圾 **2** to place sth where it will be noticed and used 把…摆好；预备好（物品）: *Have you put out clean towels for the guests?* 你为客人预备好干净毛巾没有? **3** to stop sth from burning or shining 熄灭；扑灭: *to put out a candle/cigarette/light* 熄灭蜡烛 / 香烟 / 灯火 ◇ *Firefighters soon put the fire out.* 消防人员很快把火扑灭了。 **4** to produce sth, especially for sale 生产；制造: *The factory puts out 500 new cars a week.* 这家工厂每周生产 500 辆新汽车。➲ RELATED NOUN OUTPUT **5** to publish or broadcast sth 出版；广播；公布: *Police have put out a description of the man they wish to question.* 警方公布了他们想要讯问的那名男子的特征。 **6** to give a job or task to a worker who is not your employee or to a company that is not part of your own group or organization 把（工作）外包: *A lot of the work is put out to freelancers.* 许多工作都外包给自由职业者了。 **7** to make a figure, result, etc. wrong 使出差错: *The rise in interest rates put our estimates out by several thousands.* 利率上升使我们的估算差了好几千。 **8** to push a bone out of its normal position 使脱臼 SYN **dislocate**: *She fell off her horse and put her shoulder out.* 她落下马来，造成肩关节脱位。 **9** (*also formal* ˌ**put sth↔ˈforth**) to develop or produce new leaves, SHOOTS, etc. 长出（叶、芽等）；抽芽 ˌ**put ˈout (to.../from...)** (of a boat or its sailors 船或水手) to leave a port 离港；起航: *to put out to sea* 起航出海 ◇ *We put out from Liverpool.* 我们从利物浦起航。OPP **put in (at...)**

ˌ**put yourself/sth ˈover (to sb)** = PUT YOURSELF/STH↔ACROSS/OVER (TO SB)

ˌ**put sth↔ˈthrough** to continue with and complete a plan, programme, etc. 完成；达成；使成功: *We managed to put the deal through.* 我们设法做成了这笔生意。 ˌ**put sb ˈthrough sth 1** to make sb experience sth very difficult or unpleasant 使经受（磨炼、痛苦）；折磨: *You have put your family through a lot recently.* 最近你让家人受了不少苦。 **2** to arrange or pay for sb to attend a school, college, etc. 安排某人上（学）；供某人上（学）: *He put all his children through college.* 他把子女都送进了大学。 ˌ**put sb/sth ˈthrough (to sb/...)** to connect sb by telephone 给…接通（电话）；把…接到: *Could you put me through to the manager, please?* 请帮我找经理接一下电话好吗?

ˈ**put sb to sth** to cause sb trouble, difficulty, etc. 给某人添麻烦（或增加困难等）: *I hope we're not putting you to too much trouble.* 希望我们没有给你添太多的麻烦。 ˈ**put sth to sb 1** to offer a suggestion to sb so that they can accept or reject it 给…提出（建议）: *Your proposal will be put to the board of directors.* 你的建议将提交董事会裁决。 **2** to ask sb a question 提问: *The audience is now invited to put questions to the speaker.* 现在请听众向讲演者提问。

ˌ**put sth↔toˈgether** to make or prepare sth by fitting or collecting parts together 组装；组织；汇集: *to put together a model plane/an essay/a meal* 组装飞机模型；构思文章；准备饭菜 ◇ *I think we can put together a very strong case for the defence.* 我想我们能够为辩方整理出十分有力的论据。

ˈ**put sth towards sth** to give money to pay part of the cost of sth 为…凑钱: *Here's $100 to put towards your ski trip.* 这是 100 美元，补助你去滑雪用。

ˌ**put ˈup sth 1** to show a particular level of skill, determination, etc. in a fight or contest （在战斗、竞赛中）显示，表现: *They surrendered without putting up much of a fight.* 他们没怎么抵抗就投降了。◇ *The team put up a great performance* (= played very well). 这个队表现好极了。 **2** to suggest an idea, etc. for other people to discuss 提出（意见等）: *to put up an argument/a case/a proposal* 提出论据 / 事例 / 建议 ˌ**put sb↔ˈup 1** to let sb stay at your home 留某人住在家中: *We can put you up for the night.* 今晚我们可以留你过夜。 **2** to suggest

P

or present sb as a candidate for a job or position 推荐；提名： *The Green Party hopes to put up more candidates in the next election.* 绿党希望在下届大选中推出更多的候选人。 **,put sth↔'up 1** to raise sth or put it in a higher position 提升；使升高： *to put up a flag* 升旗 ◇ *She's put her hair up.* 她把头发挽在头上。 **2** to build sth or place sth somewhere 建造；搭建；竖立： *to put up a building/fence/memorial/tent* 盖楼房；架篱笆；修纪念碑；搭帐篷 ➲ SYNONYMS AT BUILD **3** to fix sth in a place where it will be seen 置…于明显处；张贴 SYN **display**: *to put up a notice* 贴出通知 **4** to raise or increase sth 提高；增加： *They've put up the rent by £20 a month.* 他们把每月的租金提高了 20 英镑。 **5** to provide or lend money 提供，借出（资金）： *A local businessman has put up the £500 000 needed to save the club.* 一位当地的商人拿出了拯救该俱乐部所需的 50 万英镑。 **,put 'up** (**at...**) (*especially BrE*) to stay somewhere for the night 投宿；（在…）过夜： *We put up at a motel.* 我们晚间住在一家汽车旅馆。 **,put 'up for sth | ,put yourself 'up for sth** to offer yourself as a candidate for a job or position 自荐为…的候选人；参与甄选： *She is putting up for election to the committee.* 她正在参加委员会委员的竞选。 **,put sb 'up to sth** (*informal*) to encourage or persuade sb to do sth wrong or stupid 怂恿；撺掇；唆使： *Some of the older boys must have put him up to it.* 那件事准是一些大孩子怂恿他干的。 **,put 'up with sb/sth** to accept sb/sth that is annoying, unpleasant, etc. without complaining 容忍；忍受 SYN **tolerate**: *I don't know how she puts up with him.* 我不明白她怎么受得了他。 ◇ *I'm not going to put up with their smoking any longer.* 我再也不能容忍他们抽烟了。

pu·ta·tive /'pju:tətɪv/ *adj.* [only before noun] (*formal* or *law* 律) believed to be the person or thing mentioned 推定的；认定的；公认的 SYN **presumed**: *the putative father of this child* 这孩子的推定的父亲

'put-down *noun* (*informal*) a remark or criticism that is intended to make sb look or feel stupid 令人难堪的话；噎人的话

P

'put-on *noun* [usually sing.] (*NAmE*) something that is done to trick or cheat people 假象；骗局

pu·tong·hua /pu:'tʊŋhwɑ:/ *noun* [U] the standard spoken form of modern Chinese, based on the form spoken in Beijing 普通话（以北京话为基础的标准现代汉语口语） ➲ COMPARE MANDARIN (3)

pu·tre·fac·tion /,pju:trɪ'fækʃn/ *noun* [U] (*formal*) the process of decaying, especially that of a dead body 腐败；腐烂；（尸体）腐化

pu·trefy /'pju:trɪfaɪ/ *verb* (**pu·tre·fies**, **pu·tre·fy·ing**, **pu·tre·fied**, **pu·tre·fied**) [I] (*formal*) to decay and smell very bad 腐烂；腐化 SYN **rot**

pu·trid /'pju:trɪd/ *adj.* **1** (of dead animals or plants 死的动植物) decaying and therefore smelling very bad 腐烂的；腐臭的 SYN **foul**: *the putrid smell of rotten meat* 烂肉的臭味 **2** (*informal*) very unpleasant 令人厌恶（或恶心）的： *a putrid pink colour* 难看的粉红色

putsch /pʊtʃ/ *noun* (*from German*) a sudden attempt to remove a government by force 政变；武力夺取政权

putt /pʌt/ *verb* [I, T] ~ (**sth**) (in GOLF 高尔夫球) to hit the ball gently when it is on the short grass near the hole, so that it rolls across the ground a short distance into or towards the hole 轻击；推球入洞 ▶ **putt** *noun*

putt·er /'pʌtə(r)/ *verb, noun*

■ *verb* **1** [I] (of a boat or vehicle 船或车辆) to make a repeated low sound as it moves slowly 嘟嘟（或咕噜）作响： *the puttering of the engine as it reduced speed* 发动机减速时的咕噜声 **2** (*NAmE*) (*BrE* **pot·ter**) [I] (+ **adv./prep.**) to do things or move without hurrying, especially when you are doing sth that you enjoy and that is not important 从容做事；欣然从事；漫步；闲荡： *I spent the morning puttering around the house.* 我在家磨蹭了一上午。

■ *noun* (in the game of GOLF 高尔夫球运动) the type of CLUB that is used for putting (= hitting the ball short distances) 轻击球杆

'putting green *noun* a small GOLF COURSE on an area of smooth short grass where people can practise PUTTING（高尔夫球的）轻击区；（练习轻击的）小型高尔夫球场

putty /'pʌti/ *noun* [U] a soft sticky substance that becomes hard when it is dry and that is used for fixing glass into window frames （窗用）油灰

IDM (**like**) **putty in sb's 'hands** easily controlled or influenced by another person （像）某人手中的面团；任某人摆布；易受某人的影响： *She'll persuade him. He's like putty in her hands.* 她会说服他的。他就像她手里的面团一样。

,put-up 'job *noun* [usually sing.] (*informal*) a plan or an event that has been arranged secretly in order to trick or cheat sb 骗局；障眼法

'put-upon *adj.* treated in an unfair way by sb because they take advantage of your kindness or willingness to do things 被占便宜的；被利用的： *his much put-upon wife* 他那饱受委屈的妻子

putz /pʌts/ *verb, noun*

■ *verb* [I] ~ **around** (*NAmE, informal*) to waste time not doing anything useful or important 闲荡；游手好闲

■ *noun* (*NAmE, informal*) a stupid person 笨蛋；傻瓜

puz·zle /'pʌzl/ *noun, verb*

■ *noun* **1** a game, etc. that you have to think about carefully in order to answer it or do it 谜；智力游戏： *a crossword puzzle* 纵横字谜 ◇ *a book of puzzles for children* 儿童谜语书 ➲ VISUAL VOCAB PAGE V43 **2** (*especially NAmE*) = JIGSAW **3** [usually sing.] something that is difficult to understand or explain 不解之谜；疑问 SYN **mystery**

■ *verb* ~ **sb** to make sb feel confused because they do not understand sth 迷惑；使困惑 SYN **baffle**: *What puzzles me is why he left the country without telling anyone.* 令我不解的是，他为什么悄悄地离开了这个国家。 ▶ **puz·zling** /'pʌzlɪŋ/ *adj.*： *one of the most puzzling aspects of the crime* 这桩罪案最费解的一面

PHR V **'puzzle over/about sth** to think hard about sth in order to understand or explain it 苦苦思索；仔细琢磨 **,puzzle sth↔'out** to find the answer to a difficult or confusing problem by thinking carefully 琢磨出…的答案 SYN **work out**: **puzzle out why, what, etc....** *He was trying to puzzle out why he had been brought to the house.* 他想弄明白自己为何被带到这所房子。

puz·zled /'pʌzld/ *adj.* unable to understand sth or the reason for sth 困惑的；迷惑不解的 SYN **baffled**: *She had **a puzzled look** on her face.* 她满脸困惑的表情。 ◇ *Scientists are puzzled as to why the whale had swum to the shore.* 科学家们感到不解：为什么这头鲸游到海岸上来。 ◇ *He looked puzzled so I repeated the question.* 他好像没听懂，于是我把问题又重复了一遍。

puzzle·ment /'pʌzlmənt/ *noun* [U] (*formal*) a feeling of being confused because you do not understand sth 迷惘；困惑： *She frowned in puzzlement.* 她迷惑地蹙着眉。

puz·zler /'pʌzlə(r)/ *noun* (*informal*) something that makes you feel confused 费解的事；谜团 SYN **poser**

PVC /,pi: vi: 'si:/ *noun* [U] a strong plastic material used for a wide variety of products, such as clothing, pipes, floor coverings, etc. 聚氯乙烯（用于服装、管材、地板铺料等）

PVR /,pi: vi: 'ɑ:(r)/ *noun* the abbreviation for 'personal video recorder' (a device that records video onto a hard disk or other memory device, using digital technology) 个人视频录像机（全写为 personal video recorder，用数字技术将视频录制到硬盘等存储器的装置） SYN **DVR**

p.w. *abbr.* (*BrE*) per week 每周： *Rent is £100 p.w.* 租金为每周 100 英镑。

PX /,pi: 'eks/ (*pl.* **PXs** /,pi: 'eksɪz/) *noun* post exchange (a shop/store at a US military base that sells food, clothes and other things)（美军军营内）军人服务社，小卖部

pye-dog (*also* **pie-dog, pi-dog**) /ˈpaɪ dɒɡ; *NAmE* dɔːɡ/ (*also* **paˈriah dog**) *noun* (especially in Asia) a dog that has no owner or home and is of no particular breed （尤指亚洲的）无主野狗，流浪狗

pygmy (*also* **pigmy**) /ˈpɪɡmi/ *noun, adj.*
■ ***noun*** (*pl.* **-ies**) **1 Pygmy** a member of a race of very short people living in parts of Africa and SE Asia 俾格米人（生活于非洲和东南亚部分地区，身材矮小） **2** (*disapproving*) a very small person or thing or one that is weak in some way 矮小的人（或物）；侏儒；弱小者：*He regarded them as intellectual pygmies.* 他把他们视为智力上的侏儒。
■ ***adj.*** [only before noun] used to describe a plant or SPECIES (= type) of animal that is much smaller than other similar kinds （比同类动植物）小得多的，矮小的，微小的：*a pygmy shrew* 倭鼩鼱

py·jama /pəˈdʒɑːmə; *NAmE* -ˈdʒæm-/ *noun* loose trousers/pants tied at the waist and worn by men or women in some Asian countries （一些亚洲国家男女围腰而系的）宽松裤：*He was dressed in a pyjama and kurta, ideal for a summer evening.* 他穿着宽松裤和库尔塔衫，是夏日夜晚的理想穿着。

py·ja·mas (*especially US* **pa·ja·mas**) /pəˈdʒɑːməz; *NAmE* -ˈdʒæm-/ *noun* [pl.] a loose jacket and trousers/pants worn in bed （一套）睡衣裤：*a pair of pyjamas* 一套睡衣 ➲ VISUAL VOCAB PAGE V68 ▶ **py·jama** (*especially US* **pa·jama**) *adj.* [only before noun]: *pyjama bottoms* 睡裤 IDM ➤ SEE CAT

pylon /ˈpaɪlən; *NAmE also* -lɑːn/ *noun* a tall metal structure that is used for carrying electricity wires high above the ground 电缆塔

pyra·mid /ˈpɪrəmɪd/ *noun* **1** a large building with a square or TRIANGULAR base and sloping sides that meet in a point at the top. The ancient Egyptians built stone pyramids as places to bury their kings and queens. （古埃及的）金字塔 ➲ VISUAL VOCAB PAGE V15 **2** (*geometry* 几何) a solid shape with a square or TRIANGULAR base and sloping sides that meet in a point at the top 锥体；棱锥体 ➲ PICTURE AT SOLID **3** an object or a pile of things that has the shape of a pyramid 金字塔形的物体（或一堆东西）：*a pyramid of cans in a shop window* 商店橱窗中摆成金字塔形的罐头 **4** an organization or a system in which there are fewer people at each level as you get near the top 金字塔式的组织（或系统）：*a management pyramid* 金字塔式管理系统 ▶ **pyr·am·idal** /ˈpɪrəmɪdl/ *adj.*

ˌpyramid ˈselling *noun* [U] a way of selling things in which sb buys the right to sell a company's goods and then sells the goods to other people. These other people sell the goods again to others. 金字塔式销售；宝塔式营销

pyre /ˈpaɪə(r)/ *noun* a large pile of wood on which a dead body is placed and burned in a funeral ceremony （火葬用的）柴堆

pyr·eth·rum /paɪˈriːθrəm/ *noun* **1** [C] a type of flower grown especially in Kenya 除虫菊（尤见于肯尼亚） **2** [U] a substance made from this flower and used for killing insects 除虫菊杀虫剂

Pyrex™ /ˈpaɪreks/ *noun* [U] a type of hard glass that does not break at high temperatures, and is often used to make dishes for cooking food in 派莱克斯耐高温玻璃（常用以制造炊具）

pyr·ites /paɪˈraɪtiːz; *NAmE* pəˈr-/ *noun* [U] a shiny yellow mineral that is made up of SULPHUR and a metal such as iron 硫化矿物：***iron/copper pyrites*** 黄铁矿；黄铜矿

pyro·mania /ˌpaɪrəʊˈmeɪniə; *NAmE* ˌpaɪroʊ-/ *noun* [U] (*specialist*) a mental illness that causes a strong desire to set fire to things 纵火狂

pyro·maniac /ˌpaɪrəʊˈmeɪniæk; *NAmE* ˌpaɪroʊ-/ *noun* **1** (*specialist*) a person who suffers from pyromania 纵火狂患者 **2** (*informal, humorous*) a person who enjoys making or watching fires 爱玩火（或看火）的人

pyro·tech·nics /ˌpaɪrəˈteknɪks/ *noun* **1** [U+sing./pl. v.] (*specialist*) FIREWORKS or a display of FIREWORKS 烟花；烟火的施放 **2** [pl.] (*formal*) a clever and complicated display of skill, for example by a musician, writer or speaker （音乐家、作家、演讲者等的）技巧的展示：*guitar pyrotechnics* 吉他演奏技巧的展示 ▶ **pyro·tech·nic** *adj.* [usually before noun]

Pyr·rhic vic·tory /ˌpɪrɪk ˈvɪktəri/ *noun* a victory that is not worth winning because the winner has suffered or lost so much in winning it 得不偿失的胜利；以惨重代价换取的胜利 ➲ MORE LIKE THIS 16, page R27 ORIGIN From **Pyrrhus**, the king of Epirus who defeated the Romans in 279 BC but lost many of his own men. 源自伊庇鲁斯国王皮洛士，他于公元前 279 年打败罗马人，但自己的部队也伤亡惨重。

Py·thag·oras' the·orem /paɪˈθæɡərəsɪz θɪərəm; *NAmE* θiːə-; θɪr-/ (*NAmE* **Py·thag·orean the·orem** /paɪˌθæɡəˈriːən θɪərəm; *NAmE* pəˌθæɡəˈriːən θiːərəm; pəˌθæɡəˈriːən θɪrəm/) *noun* (*geometry* 几何) the rule that, in a RIGHT-ANGLED TRIANGLE/RIGHT TRIANGLE, the SQUARE (4) of the HYPOTENUSE (= the side opposite the right angle) is equal to the squares of the other two sides added together 勾股定理；毕达哥拉斯定理

py·thon /ˈpaɪθən; *NAmE* -θɑːn/ *noun* a large tropical snake that kills animals for food by winding its long body around them and crushing them 蟒；蚺蛇

P

Qq

Q /kjuː/ *noun, abbr.*
■ ***noun*** (*also* **q**) [C, U] (*pl.* **Qs**, **Q's**, **q's** /kjuːz/) the 17th letter of the English alphabet 英语字母表的第 17 个字母：*'Queen' begins with (a) Q/'Q'.* * queen 一词以字母 q 开头。➲ SEE ALSO Q-TIP™
■ ***abbr.*** question 问题；疑问 IDM SEE MIND *v.*

QA /ˌkjuː ˈeɪ/ *abbr.* = QUALITY ASSURANCE

Qa·ba·lah = KABBALAH

QC /ˌkjuː ˈsiː/ *noun* (in Britain) the highest level of BARRISTER, who can speak for the government in court. QC is the abbreviation for 'Queen's Counsel' and is used when there is a queen in Britain.（英国）王室法律顾问，御用大律师（全写为 Queen's Counsel，女王在位时使用）➲ COMPARE KC

QE /ˌkjuː ˈiː/ *abbr.* = QUANTITATIVE EASING

QED (*also* **Q.E.D.** *US, BrE*) /ˌkjuː iː ˈdiː/ *abbr.* that is what I wanted to prove and I have proved it (from Latin 'quod erat demonstrandum') 证明完毕，证讫（源自拉丁文 quod erat demonstrandum）

qib·lah (*also* **qibla**, **kiblah**, **kibla**) /ˈkɪblə/ *noun* [sing.] the direction of the Kaaba (the holy building at Mecca), towards which Muslims turn when they are PRAYING 吉布拉，天房方向（即麦加天房克尔白的方向，为穆斯林礼拜朝向）

QR code™ /ˌkjuː ˈɑː kəʊd; *NAmE* ˈɑːr koʊd/ *noun* a pattern of black and white squares that contains information, often a web address, that can be read by the camera on a SMARTPHONE 二维码（包含网址等信息，智能手机的相机可读取）

Q

qt *abbr.* (in writing 书写形式) QUART 夸脱（液量单位）

ˈQ-tip™ *noun* (*NAmE*) = COTTON BUD

qua /kweɪ; kwɑː/ *prep.* (*from Latin, formal*) as sth; in the role of sth 作为；以…身份：*The soldier acted qua soldier, not as a human being.* 那名士兵当时以军人的身份行事，而不是以一般人的身份。➲ SEE ALSO SINE QUA NON

quack /kwæk/ *noun, verb*
■ ***noun*** **1** the sound that a DUCK makes（鸭子的）呱呱声，嘎嘎声 ➲ MORE LIKE THIS 4, page R25 **2** (*informal, disapproving*) a person who dishonestly claims to have medical knowledge or skills 江湖郎中；冒牌医生；庸医：*quack doctors* 庸医 ◇ *I've got a check-up with the quack (= the doctor) next week.* 我下周要到庸医那里检查身体。
■ ***verb*** [I] when a DUCK **quacks**, it makes the noise that is typical of ducks（鸭子）嘎嘎叫，呱呱叫

quack·ery /ˈkwækəri/ *noun* [U] the methods or behaviour of sb who pretends to have medical knowledge 江湖医术；庸医行径

quad /kwɒd; *NAmE* kwɑːd/ *noun* **1** = QUADRANGLE **2** = QUADRUPLET ➲ SEE ALSO QUADS

ˈquad bike (*BrE*) (*NAmE* ˌ**four-ˈwheeler**) *noun* a motorcycle with four large wheels, used for riding over rough ground, often for fun 四轮摩托车（常用于娱乐）➲ VISUAL VOCAB PAGE V55 ➲ SEE ALSO ATV

quad·ran·gle /ˈkwɒdræŋɡl; *NAmE* ˈkwɑːd-/ *noun* (*formal*) (*also rather informal* **quad**) an open square area that has buildings all around it, especially in a school or college 四方院子（四周有建筑的开放场地，常见于校园）

quad·ran·gu·lar /kwɒˈdræŋɡjələ(r); *NAmE* kwɑːˈd-/ *adj.* **1** (*geometry* 几何) (of a shape 形状) having four sides and flat rather than solid 四角形的 **2** (of a sporting competition 体育比赛) involving four teams or individuals who each compete against all the others 四队（或四人）参加的；四方角逐的

quad·rant /ˈkwɒdrənt; *NAmE* ˈkwɑːd-/ *noun* **1** (*geometry* 几何) a quarter of a circle or of its CIRCUMFERENCE (= the distance around it) 四分之一圆（或圆周）；象限 ➲ PICTURE AT CIRCLE **2** an instrument for measuring angles, especially to check your position at sea or to look at stars 象限仪，四分仪（常用于测量海上方位或观看星辰）

quadra·phon·ic (*also* **quadro·phon·ic**) /ˌkwɒdrəˈfɒnɪk; *NAmE* ˌkwɑːdrəˈfɑːn-/ *adj.* (of a system of recording or broadcasting sound 录音或广播系统) coming from four different SPEAKERS at the same time 四声道的；四轨录放音的 ➲ COMPARE MONO *adj.*, STEREO

quad·rat·ic /kwɒˈdrætɪk; *NAmE* kwɑːˈd-/ *adj.* (*mathematics* 数) involving an unknown quantity that is multiplied by itself once only 平方的；二次方的：*a quadratic equation* 二次方程式

quadri- /ˈkwɒdrɪ; *NAmE* ˈkwɑːdrɪ/ (*also* **quadr-**) *combining form* (in nouns, adjectives and adverbs 构成名词、形容词和副词) four; having four 四；四…的：*quadrilateral* 四边形 ◇ *quadruplet* 四胞胎之一

quad·ri·ceps /ˈkwɒdrɪseps; *NAmE* ˈkwɑːd-/ *noun* (*pl.* **quadri·ceps**) (*also informal* **quads**) (*anatomy* 解) the large muscle at the front of the THIGH 四头肌

quad·ri·lat·eral /ˌkwɒdrɪˈlætərəl; *NAmE* ˌkwɑːd-/ *noun* (*geometry* 几何) a flat shape with four straight sides 四边形 ➲ PICTURE AT PARALLELOGRAM, TRAPEZIUM ▶ **quad·ri·lat·eral** *adj.*

quad·rille /kwəˈdrɪl/ *noun* a dance for four or more couples in a square, popular in the past 方阵舞，卡德利尔舞（过去流行，由四对或以上的男女构成方阵）

quad·ril·lion /kwɒˈdrɪljən; *NAmE* kwɑːˈd-/ *number* the number 10^{15}, or 1 followed by 15 zeros 千的五次幂

quadri·ple·gic /ˌkwɒdrɪˈpliːdʒɪk; *NAmE* ˌkwɑːd-/ *noun* a person who is permanently unable to use their arms and legs 四肢瘫痪者 ▶ **quadri·ple·gic** *adj.* **quadri·ple·gia** /ˌkwɒdrɪˈpliːdʒə; *NAmE* ˌkwɑːd-/ *noun* [U]

quadro·phon·ic *adj.* = QUADRAPHONIC

quad·ru·ped /ˈkwɒdruped; *NAmE* ˈkwɑːd-/ *noun* (*specialist*) any creature with four feet 四足动物 ➲ COMPARE BIPED

quad·ru·ple *verb, adj., det.*
■ ***verb*** /kwɒˈdruːpl; *NAmE* kwɑːˈdruːpl/ [I, T] ~ (**sth**) to become four times bigger; to make sth four times bigger（使）变为四倍：*Sales have quadrupled in the last five years.* 在过去五年中，销售额已增长至以前的四倍。
■ ***adj.*** [only before noun], ***det.*** /ˈkwɒdrʊpl; *NAmE* kwɑːˈdruːpl/ **1** consisting of four parts, people or groups 由四部分（或人、群体）构成的；四方面的：*a quadruple alliance* 四方联盟 **2** being four times as much or as many 四倍的：*a quadruple whisky* 一份四倍的威士忌 ◇ *This year we produced quadruple the amount produced in 2013.* 我们今年的产量是 2013 年的四倍。

quad·ru·plet /ˈkwɒdrʊplət; kwɒˈdruːplət; *NAmE* ˈkwɑːdrʊplət; kwɑːˈdruːplət/ (*also* **quad**) *noun* one of four children born at the same time to the same mother 四胞胎之一

quads /kwɒdz; *NAmE* kwɑːdz/ *noun* [pl.] (*informal*) = QUADRICEPS

quaff /kwɒf; *NAmE* kwæf; kwɑːf/ *verb* ~ **sth** (*old-fashioned* or *literary*) to drink a large amount of sth quickly 豪饮；痛饮；开怀畅饮

quag·mire /ˈkwæɡmaɪə(r); *BrE also* ˈkwɒɡ-/ *noun* **1** an area of soft wet ground 泥淖；湿地；泥沼 SYN **bog** **2** a difficult or dangerous situation 困境；险境 SYN **morass**

quail /kweɪl/ *noun, verb*
■ ***noun*** [C, U] (*pl.* **quails** or **quail**) a small brown bird, whose meat and eggs are used for food; the meat of this bird 鹌鹑；鹌鹑肉
■ ***verb*** [I] ~ (**at/before sb/sth**) (*literary*) to feel frightened or to show that you are frightened 感觉（或显出）恐惧；胆怯；畏缩

quaint /kweɪnt/ *adj.* attractive in an unusual or old-fashioned way 新奇有趣的；古色古香的：*quaint old customs* 稀奇的古老习俗 ◇ *a quaint seaside village* 古朴典雅的海滨村庄 ▶ **quaint·ly** *adv.* **quaint·ness** *noun* [U]

quake /kweɪk/ *verb, noun*

■ *verb* **1** [I] ~ (**with sth**) (of a person 人) to shake because you are very frightened or nervous（因恐惧或紧张）发抖，颤抖，哆嗦 SYN **tremble**: *Quaking with fear, Polly slowly opened the door.* 波莉吓得直发抖，慢慢地打开了门。**2** [I] (of the earth or a building 地面或建筑物) to move or shake violently 震动；颤动：*The ground quaked as the bomb exploded.* 炸弹爆炸时，地面都震动了。

■ *noun* (*informal*) = EARTHQUAKE

Quaker /ˈkweɪkə(r)/ *noun* a member of the Society of Friends, a Christian religious group that meets without any formal ceremony and is strongly opposed to violence and war 贵格会教徒，公谊会教徒（属于基督教派，废除礼仪，反对暴力和战争）▶ **Quaker** *adj.*：*a Quaker school* 贵格会学校

quali·fi·ca·tion /ˌkwɒlɪfɪˈkeɪʃn; *NAmE* ˌkwɑːl-/ *noun* **1** [C, usually pl.] (*BrE*) an exam that you have passed or a course of study that you have successfully completed（通过考试或学习课程取得的）资格，学历：***academic/educational/professional/vocational qualifications*** 学术/教育/专业/职业资历 ◇ *a **nursing/teaching, etc. qualification*** 护理、教学等资格 ◇ *He left school with no **formal qualifications**.* 他没有获得正式学历就离校了。◇ *to **acquire/gain/get/obtain/have/hold qualifications*** 获得/取得/得到/拿到/拥有/持有资格 ◇ *In this job, experience counts for more than **paper qualifications**.* 担任这项工作，经验比文凭更重要。➲ WORDFINDER NOTE AT STUDY ➲ COLLOCATIONS AT EDUCATION **2** [C] a skill or type of experience that you need for a particular job or activity（通过经验或具备技能而取得的）资格，资历：*Previous teaching experience is a necessary qualification for this job.* 教学经验是担任这项工作的必备条件。➲ WORDFINDER NOTE AT APPLY **3** [C, U] information that you add to a statement to limit the effect that it has or the way it is applied 限定条件 SYN **proviso**: *I accept his theories, but not without certain qualifications.* 我接受他的理论，但并非毫无保留。◇ *The plan was approved without qualification.* 这项计划获得无条件批准。**4** [U] the fact of passing an exam, completing a course of training or reaching the standard necessary to do a job or take part in a competition 获得资格；合格；达到标准：*Nurses in training should be given a guarantee of employment following qualification.* 接受培训的护士取得资格后应有工作保障。◇ *A victory in this game will earn them qualification for the World Cup.* 这场比赛的胜利将使他们取得世界杯的参赛资格。

quali·fied /ˈkwɒlɪfaɪd; *NAmE* ˈkwɑːl-/ *adj.* **1** having passed the exams or completed the training that are necessary in order to do a particular job; having the experience to do a particular job 具备…的学历（或资历）：*a **qualified accountant/teacher, etc.*** 取得执业资格的会计师、教师等 ◇ *to be **highly/suitably/fully qualified*** 高度/正好/完全符合资格 ◇ ~ **for sth** *She's extremely **well qualified** for the job.* 她完全符合担任这项工作的条件。**2** [not before noun] ~ (**to do sth**) having the practical knowledge or skills to do sth 具备…的知识（或技能）；符合资格：*I don't know much about it, so I don't feel qualified to comment.* 关于此事我所知不多，所以觉得没资格评论。**3** [usually before noun] (of approval, support, etc. 赞同、支持等) limited in some way 有限度的；有保留的；有条件的：*The plan was given only qualified support.* 这项计划只得到有限度的支持。◇ *The project was only a **qualified success**.* 这个项目只取得了一般的效益。

quali·fier /ˈkwɒlɪfaɪə(r); *NAmE* ˈkwɑːl-/ *noun* **1** a person or team that has defeated others in order to enter a particular competition（击败对手可进入某竞赛的）合格者 **2** a game or match that a person or team has to win in order to enter a particular competition 预选赛；资格赛；外围赛：*a World Cup qualifier* 世界杯预选赛 **3** (*grammar* 语法) a word, especially an adjective or adverb, that describes another word in a particular way 修饰词（尤指形容词或副词）：*In 'the open door', 'open' is a qualifier, describing the door.* 在 the open door 中，open 是修饰词，描述 door。

quali·fy /ˈkwɒlɪfaɪ; *NAmE* ˈkwɑːl-/ *verb* (**quali·fies**, **quali·fy·ing**, **quali·fied**, **quali·fied**)

• **FOR JOB** 工作 **1** [I] to reach the standard of ability or knowledge needed to do a particular job, for example by completing a course of study or passing exams 取得资格（或学历）；合格：*How long does it take to qualify?* 需要多长时间才能取得资格？◇ ~ **as sth** *He qualified as a doctor last year.* 他去年获得了医生的资格。➲ WORDFINDER NOTE AT TRAINING

• **GIVE SKILLS/KNOWLEDGE** 传授技能/知识 **2** [T] to give sb the skills and knowledge they need to do sth 使合格；使具备资格：~ **sb** (**for sth**) *This training course will qualify you for a better job.* 本培训课程将使你能胜任更好的工作。◇ ~ **sb to do sth** *The test qualifies you to drive heavy vehicles.* 通过这一考试就有资格驾驶重型车辆。

• **HAVE/GIVE RIGHT** 有/赋予权利 **3** [I, T] to have or give sb the right to do sth 有权，使有权（做某事）：~ (**for sth**) *If you live in the area, you qualify for a parking permit.* 你若在本地区居住，就有权领取停车许可证。◇ *To qualify, you must have lived in this country for at least three years.* 你必须在这个国家居住至少三年才能享有此权利。◇ ~ **sb** (**for sth**) *Paying a fee doesn't automatically qualify you for membership.* 交纳会费并不能使你自动成为会员。

• **FOR COMPETITION** 竞赛 **4** [I] to be of a high enough standard to enter a competition; to defeat another person or team in order to enter or continue in a competition 达标；获得参赛资格：*He failed to qualify.* 他未能获得参赛资格。◇ ~ **for sth** *They qualified for the World Cup.* 他们取得世界杯的参赛资格。

• **FIT DESCRIPTION** 名副其实 **5** [I, T] to have the right qualities to be described as a particular thing 符合，配得上（某称号、名称等）：~ (**as sth**) *Do you think this dress qualifies as evening wear?* 你看这连衣裙适合作晚礼服吗？◇ ~ **sth** (**as sth**) *It's an old building, but that doesn't qualify it as an ancient monument!* 这是一座老建筑，但不足以称为古迹。

• **STATEMENT** 陈述 **6** [T] ~ **sth** | ~ **what…** to add sth to a previous statement to make the meaning less strong or less general 使所说的话语气减弱（或更具体等）：*I want to qualify what I said earlier—I didn't mean he couldn't do the job, only that he would need supervision.* 我想具体说明一下我原先的话，我没有说他不能担任这工作，只是说他需要指导。

• **GRAMMAR** 语法 **7** [T] ~ **sth** (of a word 单词) to describe another word in a particular way 修饰；限定：*In 'the open door', 'open' is an adjective qualifying 'door'.* 在 the open door 中，open 是修饰 door 的形容词。

quali·ta·tive AW /ˈkwɒlɪtətɪv; *NAmE* ˈkwɑːləteɪt-/ *adj.* [usually before noun] connected with what sth is like or how good it is, rather than with how much of it there is 质量的；定性的；性质的：***qualitative analysis/research*** 定性分析/研究 ◇ *There are qualitative differences between the two products.* 这两种产品存在着质的差别。➲ COMPARE QUANTITATIVE ▶ **quali·ta·tive·ly** AW *adv.*：*qualitatively different* 性质上不同的

qual·ity /ˈkwɒləti; *NAmE* ˈkwɑːl-/ *noun, adj.*

■ *noun* (*pl.* **-ies**) **1** [U, C] the standard of sth when it is compared to other things like it; how good or bad sth is 质量；品质：*to **be of good/poor/top quality*** 质量好/差/上乘 ◇ *goods of a **high quality*** 优质商品 ◇ *high-quality goods* 优质商品 ◇ *a decline in water quality* 水质的下降 ◇ *When costs are cut product quality suffers.* 一降低成本，产品质量就会受到影响。◇ *Their **quality of life** improved dramatically when they moved to France.* 他们移居法国以后，生活质量大大提高。**2** [U] a high standard 上乘；优质；高标准 SYN **excellence**: *contemporary writers of **quality*** 当代的优秀作家 ◇ *We aim to provide quality at reasonable prices.* 我们的宗旨是质量上乘、价格合理。**3** [C] a thing that is part of a person's character, especially sth good（尤指好的）人品，素质，品德：***personal qualities** such as honesty and generosity* 诚实、宽容等个人品

Q

质 ◇ *to have **leadership qualities*** 具有领导素质 **4** [C, U] a feature of sth, especially one that makes it different from sth else 特征；特质；特色：*the special quality of light and shade in her paintings* 她绘画中的明、暗特征 **5** [C] (*BrE*) = QUALITY NEWSPAPER

■ ***adj.* 1** [only before noun] used especially by people trying to sell goods or services to say that sth is of a high quality 优质的；高质量的：*We specialize in quality furniture.* 我们专营高档家具。◇ *quality service at a competitive price* 质优价廉的服务 **2** (*BrE, slang*) very good 盖帽儿了；棒极了：*'What was the film like?' 'Quality!'* "这部电影怎么样？" "棒极了！"

ˈquality assurance (*abbr.* **QA**) *noun* [U] the practice of managing the way goods are produced or services are provided to make sure they are kept at a high standard 质量保证

ˈquality control *noun* [U] the practice of checking goods as they are being produced, to make sure that they are of a high standard 质量控制

ˌquality ˈnewspaper (*also less frequent* **qual·ity**) *noun* (*BrE*) a newspaper that is intended for people who are intelligent and educated（供有品位者阅读的）高端报纸 ➲ COMPARE TABLOID (2)

ˈquality time *noun* [U] time spent giving your full attention to sb, especially to your children after work（尤指工作之余关爱子女，增进感情的）黄金时光

qualm /kwɑːm; kwɔːm/ *noun* [usually pl.] ~ (**about sth**) a feeling of doubt or worry about whether what you are doing is right（对自己行为的）顾虑，不安 SYN **misgiving**: *He had been working very hard so he had **no qualms about** taking a few days off.* 他一直辛勤工作，所以休息几天他觉得心安理得。

quan·dary /ˈkwɒndəri; *NAmE* ˈkwɑːn-/ *noun* [usually sing.] (*pl.* **-ies**) the state of not being able to decide what to do in a difficult situation 困惑；进退两难；困窘 SYN **dilemma**: *George was **in a quandary**—should he go or shouldn't he?* 乔治犹豫不定，他是该去呢，还是不该去？

Q

quango /ˈkwæŋɡəʊ; *NAmE* -ɡoʊ/ *noun* (*pl.* **-os**) (*often disapproving*) (in Britain) an organization dealing with public matters, started by the government, but working independently and with its own legal powers（英国）半官方机构

quanta PL. OF QUANTUM

quan·ti·fier /ˈkwɒntɪfaɪə(r); *NAmE* ˈkwɑːn-/ *noun* (*grammar* 语法) a determiner or pronoun that expresses quantity, for example 'all' or 'both' 数量词；数量修饰语；量词

quan·tify /ˈkwɒntɪfaɪ; *NAmE* ˈkwɑːn-/ *verb* (**quan·ti·fies, quan·ti·fy·ing, quan·ti·fied, quan·ti·fied**) ~ **sth** to describe or express sth as an amount or a number 以数量表述；量化：*The risks to health are impossible to quantify.* 健康的风险是无法用数量表示的。▶ **quan·ti·fi·able** *adj.*: *quantifiable data* 可量化的资料 **quan·ti·fi·ca·tion** /ˌkwɒntɪfɪˈkeɪʃn; *NAmE* ˌkwɑːn-/ *noun* [U]

quan·ti·ta·tive /ˈkwɒntɪtətɪv; *NAmE* ˈkwɑːntəteɪt-/ *adj.* connected with the amount or number of sth rather than with how good it is 数量的；量化的；定量的：***quantitative analysis/research*** 定量分析 / 研究 ◇ *There is no difference between the two in quantitative terms.* 两者在数量上毫无差别。➲ COMPARE QUALITATIVE ▶ **quan·ti·ta·tive·ly** *adv.*

ˌquantitative ˈeasing (*abbr.* **QE**) *noun* [U] the introduction of new money into a country's money supply by a central bank 量化宽松（由中央银行引入新资金，增加国家货币供应量的货币政策）

quan·tity 🔑 /ˈkwɒntəti; *NAmE* ˈkwɑːn-/ *noun* (*pl.* **-ies**) **1** 🔑 [C, U] an amount or a number of sth 数量；数额；数目：*a **large/small quantity** of sth* 大量 / 少量的某物 ◇ ***enormous/vast/huge quantities** of food* 大量的食物 ◇ *a product that is cheap to produce **in large quantities*** 可以低成本大批生产的产品 ◇ *Is it available in sufficient quantity?* 这东西能不能足量供应？ **2** 🔑 [U] the measurement of sth by saying how much of it there is 量；数量：*The data is limited in terms of both quality and quantity.* 这份资料在质量和数量上都很有限。 **3** 🔑 [C, U] a large amount or number of sth 大量；大批；众多；大宗：*The police found a quantity of drugs at his home.* 警察在他家发现了大量毒品。◇ *It's cheaper to buy goods **in quantity**.* 大宗购物比较便宜。◇ *I was overwhelmed by the sheer quantity of information available.* 已有的信息量大得令我不知所措。 IDM SEE UNKNOWN *adj.*

ˈquantity surveyor *noun* (*BrE*) a person whose job is to calculate the quantity of materials needed for building sth, how much it will cost and how long it will take（建筑）估价师，估算员

quan·tum /ˈkwɒntəm; *NAmE* ˈkwɑːn-/ *noun* (*pl.* **quanta** /ˈkwɒntə; *NAmE* ˈkwɑːntə/) (*physics* 物) a very small quantity of ELECTROMAGNETIC energy 量子

ˌquantum ˈleap (*also less frequent* **ˌquantum ˈjump**) *noun* a sudden, great and important change, improvement or development 突变；巨变；飞跃

ˌquantum meˈchanics *noun* [U] (*physics* 物) the branch of MECHANICS that deals with movement and force in pieces of matter smaller than atoms 量子力学

ˈquantum theory *noun* [U] (*physics* 物) a theory based on the idea that energy exists in units that cannot be divided 量子理论

quar·an·tine /ˈkwɒrəntiːn; *NAmE* ˈkwɔːr-/ *noun, verb*

■ ***noun*** [U] a period of time when an animal or a person that has or may have a disease is kept away from others in order to prevent the disease from spreading（为防传染的）检疫，隔离期：*The dog was kept **in quarantine** for six months.* 这条狗被检疫隔离了六个月。◇ *quarantine regulations* 检疫的规定

■ ***verb*** ~ **sth/sb** to put an animal or a person into quarantine（对动物或人）进行检疫，隔离

quark /kwɑːk; *NAmE* kwɑːrk/ *noun* **1** [C] (*physics* 物) a very small part of matter (= a substance). There are several types of quark and it is thought that PROTONS, NEUTRONS, etc. are formed from them. 夸克（据信构成质子、中子等的细小粒子） **2** [U] a type of soft cheese from central Europe, similar to CURD CHEESE 夸克干酪；软（质）干酪

quar·rel /ˈkwɒrəl; *NAmE* ˈkwɔːr-; ˈkwɑːr-/ *noun, verb*

■ ***noun* 1** [C] ~ (**with sb/between A and B**) (**about/over sth**) an angry argument or disagreement between people, often about a personal matter 口角；争吵；拌嘴：*a family quarrel* 家庭纷争 ◇ *He did not mention the quarrel with his wife.* 他没有提起和妻子的争吵。◇ *They had a quarrel about money.* 他们为钱吵了一架。◇ *Were you at any time aware of a quarrel between the two of them?* 你什么时候注意到他俩拌过嘴吗？ **2** [U] ~ (**with sb/sth**) (especially in negative sentences 尤用于否定句) a reason for complaining about sb/sth or for disagreeing with sb/sth 抱怨（或不赞成）的理由：*We **have no quarrel with** his methods.* 我们没有理由不赞成他的方法。 IDM SEE PICK *v.*

■ ***verb*** (**-ll-**, *US* **-l-**) [I] to have an angry argument or disagreement 争吵；吵嘴；吵架：*My sister and I used to quarrel all the time.* 我和妹妹过去老是吵架。◇ ~ (**with sb**) (**about/over sth**) *She quarrelled with her brother over their father's will.* 她和弟弟因父亲遗嘱的事起了争执。 ➲ MORE LIKE THIS 36, page R29

PHR V **ˈquarrel with sb/sth** to disagree with sb/sth 不赞同；反对：*Nobody could quarrel with your conclusions.* 你的结论无可辩驳。

quar·rel·some /ˈkwɒrəlsəm; *NAmE* ˈkwɔːr-; ˈkwɑːr-/ *adj.* (of a person 人) liking to argue with other people 爱争吵的；好口角的 SYN **argumentative**

quarry /ˈkwɒri; *NAmE* ˈkwɔːri; ˈkwɑːri/ *noun, verb*

■ ***noun*** (*pl.* **-ies**) **1** [C] a place where large amounts of stone, etc. are dug out of the ground 采石场：*a slate quarry* 板岩采石场 ◇ *the site of a disused quarry* 废弃的采石场 ➲ COMPARE MINE *n.* (1) **2** [sing.] an animal or a person that is being hunted or followed 被追猎的动物（或人）；追捕的对象；猎物 SYN prey: *The hunters lost sight of their quarry in the forest.* 猎人在森林里跟丢了猎物。◇ *The photographers pursued their quarry through the streets.* 摄影师满街捕捉拍摄对象。

■ *verb* (**quar·ries, quarry·ing, quar·ried, quar·ried**) [T, I] to take stone, etc. out of a quarry 从（采石场）采（石等）: **~ sth (from/out of sth)** *The local rock is quarried from the hillside.* 当地的石头都是从那片山坡开采的。◇ **~ (for) sth** *The area is being quarried for limestone.* 这地方正在开采石灰石。▶ **quarry·ing** *noun* [U]: *There has been quarrying in the area for centuries.* 这地方的采石业已有几百年了。

ˈ**quarry tile** *noun* a floor TILE made from stone that has not been GLAZED （未上釉的）缸砖，红地砖

quart /kwɔːt; *NAmE* kwɔːrt/ *noun* (*abbr.* **qt**) a unit for measuring liquids, equal to 2 pints or about 1.14 litres in the UK and Canada, and 0.95 of a litre in the US 夸脱（液量单位，在英国和加拿大等于 2 品脱或 1.14 升，在美国等于 0.95 升）

IDM **put a quart into a pint ˈpot** (*BrE*) to put sth into a space that is too small for it 将…置于容不下之处

quar·ter /ˈkwɔːtə(r); *NAmE* ˈkwɔːrt-/ *noun, verb*

■ *noun*

• **1 OF 4 PARTS** 四分之一 **1** (*also* **fourth** *especially in NAmE*) [C] one of four equal parts of sth 四等份之一: *a quarter of a mile* 四分之一英里 ◇ *The programme lasted an hour and a quarter.* 这个节目历时一小时十五分钟。◇ *Cut the apple into quarters.* 把苹果切成四瓣。◇ *The theatre was about three quarters full.* 剧场大约坐了四分之三的人。➲ NOTE AT HALF

• **15 MINUTES** * 15 分钟 **2** [C] a period of 15 minutes either before or after every hour （正点之前或之后的）15 分钟，一刻钟: *It's (a) quarter to four now—I'll meet you at (a) quarter past.* 现在是差一刻四点，我会在四点一刻和你碰面。◇ (*NAmE also*) *It's quarter of four now—I'll meet you at quarter after.* 现在是差一刻四点，我会在四点一刻和你碰面。

• **3 MONTHS** * 3 个月 **3** [C] a period of three months, used especially as a period for which bills are paid or a company's income is calculated 三个月时间；季度；季

• **PART OF TOWN** 城区 **4** [C, usually sing.] a district or part of a town 城镇的区（或一部分）: *the Latin quarter* 拉丁区 ◇ *the historic quarter of the city* 这座城市具有历史意义的城区

• **PERSON/GROUP** 个人；群体 **5** [C] a person or group of people, especially as a source of help, information or a reaction （尤指能提供帮助、信息或作出反应的）个人，群体: *Support for the plan came from an unexpected quarter.* 支持这一计划的是没料想到的一方。◇ *The news was greeted with dismay* ***in some quarters.*** 有一部分人对这条消息感到泄气。

• **25 CENTS** * 25 分钱 **6** [C] a coin of the US and Canada worth 25 cents （美国和加拿大的）25 分硬币

• **ROOMS TO LIVE IN** 住房 **7 quarters** [pl.] rooms that are provided for soldiers, servants, etc. to live in （供士兵、服务人员等居住的）营房，宿舍，住房: *We were moved to more comfortable* ***living quarters.*** 我们搬进了较舒适的住处。◇ ***married quarters*** 已婚军人宿舍

• **OF MOON** 月亮 **8** [C] the period of time twice a month when we can see a quarter of the moon 半圆的月相；上弦（或下弦）月: *The moon is in its first quarter.* 月亮正处于上弦。

• **IN SPORT** 体育运动 **9** [C] one of the four periods of time into which a game of AMERICAN FOOTBALL is divided （美式足球的）一节

• **WEIGHT** 重量 **10** [C] (*BrE*) a unit for measuring weight, a quarter of a pound; 4 OUNCES 夸特（重量单位，¼ 磅；4 盎司） **11** [C] a unit for measuring weight, 28 pounds in the UK or 25 pounds in the US; a quarter of a HUNDREDWEIGHT 夸特（重量单位，英国为 28 磅，美国为 25 磅；四分之一英担）

• **PITY** 怜悯 **12** [U] (*old-fashioned* or *literary*) pity that sb shows towards an enemy or opponent who is in their power （对掌控中的敌人或对手的）慈悲，同情 SYN **mercy**: *His rivals knew that they could expect no quarter from such a ruthless adversary.* 他的竞争者明白，不能期望如此残忍的对手发善心。IDM SEE CLOSE² *adj.*

■ *verb*

• **DIVIDE INTO 4** 分为 4 份 **1 ~ sth** to cut or divide sth into four parts 把…切成（或分成）四部分: *She peeled and quartered an apple.* 她削去苹果皮，把苹果切成四瓣。

• **PROVIDE ROOMS** 提供房间 **2 ~ sb (+ adv./prep.)** (*formal*) to provide sb with a place to eat and sleep 给…提供食宿: *The soldiers were quartered in the town.* 士兵在镇里宿营。

quar·ter·back /ˈkwɔːtəbæk; *NAmE* ˈkwɔːrtərbæk/ *noun, verb*

■ *noun* (in AMERICAN FOOTBALL 美式足球) the player who directs the team's attacking play and passes the ball to other players at the start of each attack （指挥进攻的）四分卫

■ *verb* **1** [I] (in AMERICAN FOOTBALL 美式足球) to play as a quarterback 打四分卫 **2** [T] **~ sth** to direct or organize sth 指挥；组织

ˈ**quarter day** *noun* (*BrE, specialist*) the first day of a QUARTER (= a period of three months) on which payments must be made, for example at the STOCK EXCHANGE 季度结算日（季度的第一天，证券交易所等的结算日）

quar·ter·deck /ˈkwɔːtədek; *NAmE* ˈkwɔːrtərdek/ *noun* a part of the upper level of a ship, at the back, that is used mainly by officers 上层后甲板区（主要供军官使用）

ˌ**quarter-ˈfinal** *noun* (in sports or competitions 体育运动或竞赛) one of the four games or matches to decide the players or teams for the SEMI-FINALS of a competition 四分之一决赛

ˈ**Quarter Horse** *noun* (*NAmE*) a small breed of horse that can run very fast over short distances 四分之一英里赛马（美国一种在短距离内能疾跑的矮种马）

quar·ter·ly /ˈkwɔːtəli; *NAmE* ˈkwɔːrtərli/ *adj., adv., noun*

■ *adj.* produced or happening every three months 季度的；每季的: *a quarterly meeting of the board* 董事会的季度会议

■ *adv.* every three months 每季: *to pay the rent quarterly* 按季付租金

■ *noun* (*pl.* **-ies**) a magazine, etc. published four times a year 季刊

quar·ter·mas·ter /ˈkwɔːtəmɑːstə(r); *NAmE* ˈkwɔːrtərmæs-/ *noun* an officer in the army who is in charge of providing food, uniforms and accommodation 军需官；军需主任

ˈ**quarter note** (*NAmE*) (*BrE* **crot·chet**) *noun* (*music* 音) a note that lasts half as long as a MINIM/HALF NOTE 四分音符 ➲ PICTURE AT MUSIC

ˈ**quarter sessions** *noun* [pl.] (in England, in the past) a court with limited powers that was held every three months （英格兰旧时每季开庭一次的）季审法院，季审法庭

ˈ**quarter-tone** *noun* (*music* 音) a quarter of a TONE on a musical SCALE, for example half of the INTERVAL (= the difference) between the notes E and F 四分之一音

quar·tet /kwɔːˈtet; *NAmE* kwɔːrˈtet/ *noun* **1** [C+sing./pl. v.] a group of four musicians or singers who play or sing together 四重奏乐团；四重唱组合: *the Amadeus Quartet* 阿玛迪厄斯四重奏乐队 **2** [C] a piece of music for four musicians or singers 四重奏（曲）；四重唱（曲）: *a Beethoven string quartet* 贝多芬弦乐四重奏曲 **3** [C+sing./pl. v.] a set of four people or things 四人组；四件套；四部曲: *the last in a quartet of novels* 四部曲小说的最后一部

quar·tile /ˈkwɔːtaɪl; *NAmE* ˈkwɔːrt-; -tl/ *noun* (*statistics* 统计) one of four equal groups into which a set of things can be divided according to the DISTRIBUTION of a particular VARIABLE 四分位数；四分位值: *women in the fourth quartile of height* (= the shortest 25% of women) 身高在第四个四分位值的妇女（即最矮的 25% 妇女）➲ COMPARE QUINTILE

quarto /ˈkwɔːtəʊ; *NAmE* ˈkwɔːrtoʊ/ *noun* (*pl.* **-os**) (*specialist*) **1** [U] a size of page made by folding a standard sheet of paper twice to make eight pages 四开（标准印张的四分之一大小） **2** [C] a book with pages in quarto size 四开本图书

quartz /kwɔːts; *NAmE* kwɔːrts/ *noun* [U] a hard mineral, often in CRYSTAL form, that is used to make very accurate clocks and watches 石英

qua·sar /ˈkweɪzɑː(r)/ *noun* (*astronomy* 天) a large object like a star, that is far away and that shines very brightly and occasionally sends out strong radio signals 类星体 ➲ COMPARE PULSAR

quash /kwɒʃ; *NAmE* kwɔːʃ; kwɑːʃ/ *verb* **1** ~ **sth** (*law* 律) to officially say that a decision made by a court is no longer valid or correct 宣布（法庭的裁决）无效；撤销（判决） **SYN** **overturn**: *His conviction was later quashed by the Court of Appeal.* 后来，上诉法院撤销了对他的有罪判决。 **2** ~ **sth** to take action to stop sth from continuing 制止；阻止；平息 **SYN** **suppress**: *The rumours were quickly quashed.* 流言很快被制止了。

quasi- /ˈkweɪzaɪ; -saɪ; ˈkwɑːzi/ *combining form* (in adjectives and nouns 构成形容词和名词) **1** that appears to be sth but is not really so 类似：*a quasi-scientific explanation* 貌似科学的解释 **2** partly; almost 半；准：*a quasi-official body* 半官方机构

quat·er·cen·ten·ary /ˌkwætəsenˈtiːnəri; *NAmE* -tərsenˈteneri/ *noun* (*pl.* **-ies**) a 400th anniversary * 400 周年纪念：*to celebrate the quatercentenary of Shakespeare's birth* 庆祝莎士比亚诞辰 400 周年

quat·rain /ˈkwɒtreɪn; *NAmE* ˈkwɑːt-/ *noun* (*specialist*) a poem or VERSE of a poem that has four lines 四行诗；四行的诗节

qua·ver /ˈkweɪvə(r)/ *verb, noun*

■ *verb* [I, T] (+ **speech**) if sb's voice **quavers**, it is unsteady, usually because the person is nervous or afraid（嗓音因紧张或害怕等）颤抖，颤动：*'I'm not safe here, am I?' she asked in a quavering voice.* "我在这里不安全吧？" 她用颤抖的声音问道。▶ **qua·very** /ˈkweɪvəri/ *adj.*: *a quavery voice* 颤抖的嗓音

■ *noun* **1** (*BrE*) (*NAmE* ˈ**eighth note**) (*music* 音) a note that lasts half as long as a CROTCHET/QUARTER NOTE 八分音符 ➲ PICTURE AT MUSIC **2** [usually sing.] a shaking sound in sb's voice 颤抖的嗓音

quay /kiː/ *noun* a platform in a HARBOUR where boats come in to load, etc. 码头；埠头：*A crowd was waiting on the quay.* 有一群人在码头上等着。➲ VISUAL VOCAB PAGE V5

quay·side /ˈkiːsaɪd/ *noun* [usually sing.] a quay and the area near it 码头区：*crowds waiting* **on/at the quayside** *to welcome them* 等在码头边欢迎他们的人群

queasy /ˈkwiːzi/ *adj.* **1** feeling sick; wanting to VOMIT 恶心的；欲吐的 **SYN** **nauseous** **2** slightly nervous or worried about sth 稍感紧张的；略有不安的；心神不定的 ▶ **queas·ily** *adv.* **queasi·ness** *noun* [U]

Que·chua /ˈketʃwə/ *noun* [U] a language originally spoken by the Quechua people of S America, now spoken in Peru, Bolivia, Chile, Colombia and Ecuador 克丘亚语，奇楚瓦语（原为南美克丘亚人的语言，现在秘鲁、玻利维亚、智利、哥伦比亚和厄瓜多尔使用）

queen /kwiːn/ *noun*

• **FEMALE RULER** 女统治者 **1** the female ruler of an independent state that has a royal family 女王；女酋长；女首领：*to* **be crowned queen** 加冕为女王 ◇ *kings and queens* 国王和女王 ◇ *the Queen of Norway* 挪威女王 ◇ *Queen Victoria* 维多利亚女王 **2** (*also* ˌ**queen** ˈ**consort**) the wife of a king 王后

• **BEST IN GROUP** 出类拔萃 **3** ~ (**of sth**) a woman, place or thing that is thought to be one of the best in a particular group or area （某领域的）杰出女性，精髓，精华：*the queen of fashion* 时尚女王 ◇ *a movie queen* 影后 ◇ *Venice, queen of the Adriatic* 威尼斯，亚得里亚海的明珠

• **AT FESTIVAL** 节日 **4** a woman or girl chosen to perform official duties at a festival or celebration（节日或庆典活动中）当选行使庆典职责的女子：*a carnival queen* 狂欢节小姐 ◇ *a May queen* (= at a festival to celebrate the coming of spring) 五朔节王后 ◇ *a homecoming queen* 返校节王后 ➲ SEE ALSO BEAUTY QUEEN

• **IN CHESS** 国际象棋 **5** the most powerful piece used in the game of CHESS that can move any number of squares in any direction 后 ➲ VISUAL VOCAB PAGE V42

• **IN CARDS** 纸牌 **6** a PLAYING CARD with the picture of a queen on it 王后（牌） ➲ VISUAL VOCAB PAGE V42

• **INSECT** 昆虫 **7** a large female insect that lays eggs for the whole group（为群体产卵的）雌性昆虫，王；后：*a queen bee* 蜂王

• **HOMOSEXUAL** 同性恋 **8** (*informal, taboo*) an offensive word for a male HOMOSEXUAL who behaves like a woman（对女性化的男同性恋者的贬称）王后，假娘儿们 **IDM** SEE EVIDENCE *n.*, UNCROWNED

ˌ**queen** ˈ**bee** *noun* **1** a female BEE that produces eggs for the whole group of bees in a HIVE 蜂王；母蜂 ➲ COMPARE DRONE *n.* (3), WORKER (4) **2** a woman who behaves as if she is the most important person in a particular place or group 女强人；大姐大

queen·ly /ˈkwiːnli/ *adj.* of, like or suitable for a queen 女王的；似女王的；适于女王的

ˌ**queen** ˈ**mother** *noun* a title given to the wife of a king who has died and who is the mother of the new king or queen 太后；皇太后；王太后：*Queen Elizabeth, the Queen Mother* 王太后伊丽莎白

ˌ**Queen's** ˈ**Bench** (*also* ˌ**Queen's** ˈ**Bench Division**) *noun* [sing.] part of the UK High Court（英国高等法院的）（女）王座法庭

Queens·berry Rules /ˌkwiːnzbəri ˈruːlz; *NAmE* -beri/ *noun* [pl.] **1** the standard rules of BOXING 昆斯伯里规则（拳击比赛的标准规则） **2** the rules of polite and acceptable behaviour 礼貌行为准则

ˌ**Queen's** ˈ**Counsel** *noun* = QC

the ˌ**Queen's** ˈ**English** *noun* [U] (*old-fashioned*) the English language as written and spoken correctly by educated people in the UK 标准英语；规范英语 **HELP** 'The Queen's English' is used when the United Kingdom has a queen, and 'the King's English' when it has a king. 英国女王在位时用 the Queen's English，国王在位时用 the King's English。

ˌ**Queen's** ˈ**evidence** *noun* [U] (*BrE*) if a criminal **turns Queen's evidence**, he or she gives evidence against the people who committed a crime with him or her（刑事被告向法庭提供的）对同案犯不利的证据

ˈ**queen-size** (*also* ˈ**queen-sized**) *adj.* (*NAmE*) (of beds, sheets, etc. 床、床单等) larger than a standard size but not as big as KING-SIZE 次特大号的；大号的

the ˌ**Queen's** ˈ**Speech** *noun* [sing.] in the UK, a statement read by the Queen at the start of a new Parliament, which contains details of the government's plans 女王致辞（英国议会开幕式上由女王宣读，内容包括政府施政详情）

queer /kwɪə(r); *NAmE* kwɪr/ *adj., noun, verb*

■ *adj.* (**queer·er, queer·est**) **1** (*old-fashioned*) strange or unusual 奇怪的；反常的 **SYN** **odd**: *His face was a queer pink colour.* 他满脸奇怪的粉红色。**2** (*taboo, slang*) an offensive way of describing a HOMOSEXUAL, especially a man, which is, however, also used by some homosexuals about themselves 娘儿们似的；妖里妖气的 **IDM** SEE FISH *n.*

■ *noun* (*taboo, slang*) an offensive word for a HOMOSEXUAL, especially a man, which is, however, also used by some homosexuals about themselves 同性恋者；假娘儿们

■ *verb*

IDM **queer sb's** ˈ**pitch** | **queer the** ˈ**pitch (for sb)** (*BrE, informal*) to spoil sb's plans or their chances of getting sth 破坏…的计划（或机会）

queer·ly /ˈkwɪəli; *NAmE* ˈkwɪrli/ *adv.* in a strange or unusual way 奇怪地；反常地：*He looked at me queerly.* 他异样地望着我。

quell /kwel/ *verb* (*formal*) **1 ~ sth/sb** to stop sth such as violent behaviour or protests 制止；平息；镇压：*Extra police were called in to quell the disturbances.* 已调集了增援警力来平定骚乱。◇ (*figurative*) *She started to giggle, but Bob quelled her with a look.* 她格格地笑了起来，但鲍勃用眼神制止了她。**2 ~ sth** to stop or reduce strong or unpleasant feelings 消除，缓解，减轻（强烈或不快的感情）**SYN** **calm**：*to quell your fears* 消除恐惧

quench /kwentʃ/ *verb* **1 ~ your thirst** to drink so that you no longer feel thirsty 解（渴）；止（渴）**SYN** **slake** **2 ~ sth** (*formal*) to stop a fire from burning 扑灭；熄灭 **SYN** **extinguish**：*Firemen tried to quench the flames raging through the building.* 消防队员奋力扑灭大楼中熊熊的火焰。

queru·lous /ˈkwerələs; -rjə-/ *adj.* (*formal, disapproving*) complaining; showing that you are annoyed 抱怨的；显得恼怒的 **SYN** **peevish** ▶ **queru·lous·ly** *adv.*

query /ˈkwɪəri; *NAmE* ˈkwɪri/ *noun, verb*

■ *noun* (*pl.* **-ies**) **1** a question, especially one asking for information or expressing a doubt about sth 疑问；询问：*Our assistants will be happy to answer your queries.* 我们的助理很乐意回答诸位的问题。◇ *If you have a query about your insurance policy, contact our helpline.* 若对保险单有疑问，请拨打我们的咨询热线。**2** a question mark to show that sth has not been finished or decided 问号：*Put a query against Jack's name—I'm not sure if he's coming.* 在杰克的名字旁边打个问号，我不确定他是否会来。

■ *verb* (**quer·ies, query·ing, quer·ied, quer·ied**) **1 ~ sth | ~ what, whether, etc....** to express doubt about whether sth is correct or not 怀疑；表示疑虑：*We queried the bill as it seemed far too high.* 账单上的费用似乎太高了，我们对此表示怀疑。◇ *I'm not in a position to query their decision.* 我无权怀疑他们的决定。**2 + speech** to ask a question 询问：*'Who will be leading the team?' queried Simon.* "由谁当队长呢？"西蒙问道。

ˈquery language *noun* [C, U] (*computing* 计) a system of words and symbols that you type in order to ask a computer to give you information from a DATABASE or an information system 查询语言

quest /kwest/ *noun, verb*

■ *noun* **~ (for sth)** (*formal* or *literary*) a long search for sth, especially for some quality such as happiness 探索，寻找，追求（幸福等）：*the quest for happiness/knowledge/truth* 对幸福/知识/真理的追求 ◇ *He set off* **in quest of** *adventure.* 他出发探险去了。

■ *verb* [I] **~ (for sth)** (*formal* or *literary*) to search for sth that is difficult to find 探索；探求

ques·tion /ˈkwestʃən/ *noun, verb*

■ *noun* **1** [C] a sentence, phrase or word that asks for information 问题；疑问：*to ask/answer a question* 提出/回答问题 ◇ ***The question is,*** *how much are they going to pay you?* 问题是他们打算付给你多少钱？◇ (*formal*) ***The question arises*** *as to whether or not he knew of the situation.* 问题是，他对局势是否了解。◇ *The key question of what caused the leak remains unanswered.* 泄漏是什么造成的，这一关键问题仍然没有答案。◇ (*formal*) *He* ***put a question to*** *the minister about the recent reforms.* 他就最近的改革措施向部长提了一个问题。◇ *I hope the police don't ask any* ***awkward questions.*** 我希望警方不要提出难应付的问题。◇ *In an interview try to ask* ***open questions*** *that don't just need 'Yes' or 'No' as an answer.* 在面试中要尽量问易于发挥的问题，不要让对方回答"是"或"否"了事。**2** [C] a task or request for information that is intended to test your knowledge or understanding, for example in an exam or a competition 考题；试题：*Question 3 was very difficult.* 第 3 题难极了。◇ *In the exam there's sure to be* ***a question on*** *energy.* 考试时准有关于能量的题目。**3** [C] **~ (of sth)** a matter or topic that needs to be discussed or dealt with（待讨论或处理的）事情，议题，课题：*Let's look at the question of security.* 咱们来看一下保安问题。◇ *The question which needs to be addressed is one of funding.* 需要面对的是资金问题。◇ *Which route is better remains* ***an open question*** (= it is not decided). 哪条路线较好没有定论。**4** [U] doubt or confusion about sth 怀疑；困惑：*Her honesty is* ***beyond question.*** 她的诚实是毋庸置疑的。◇ *His suitability for the job is* ***open to question.*** 他是否适合担任这工作还需要考虑。◇ *Her version of events was accepted* ***without question.*** 她对事情的陈述没有受到任何质疑就被接受了。

IDM **bring/throw sth into ˈquestion** to cause sth to become a matter for doubt and discussion 引起有关…的怀疑（或议论）：*This case brings into question the whole purpose of the law.* 这宗案件引起了对整个法律宗旨的怀疑。**come into ˈquestion** to become a matter for doubt and discussion 成为怀疑（或讨论）的对象 **ˌgood ˈquestion!** (*informal*) used to show that you do not know the answer to a question（表示不知道答案）问得好：*'How much is all this going to cost?' 'Good question!'* "这一切得花多少钱？""问得好！" **in ˈquestion** **1** that is being discussed 讨论（或议论）中的：*On the day in question we were in Cardiff.* 在所说的那一天，我们在加的夫。**2** in doubt; uncertain 有疑问；不确定：*The future of public transport is not in question.* 公共交通的未来发展是不容置疑的。**just/merely/only a question of (sth/doing sth)** used to say that sth is not difficult to predict, explain, do, etc. 只不过是…的问题（指不难预料、解释、做等的事情）：*It's merely a question of time before the business collapses.* 这家企业的倒闭只是时间问题。◇ *It's just a question of deciding what you really want.* 那只是个确定你真正想要什么的问题。**out of the ˈquestion** impossible or not allowed and therefore not worth discussing 不可能；不允许；不值得讨论：*Another trip abroad this year is out of the question.* 今年再度出国是绝无可能的。**there is/was no question of (sth happening/sb doing sth)** there is/was no possibility of sth（某事）是不可能的：*There was no question of his/him cancelling the trip so near the departure date.* 离出发日期这么近，他不可能取消行程。➲ MORE AT BEG, CALL *v.*, MOOT *adj.*, POP *v.*

▼ **EXPRESS YOURSELF 情景表达**

Dealing with questions 应对提问

If you give a talk, for example at a conference, you need to explain to the audience when they can ask questions, and deal with the questions they ask. 在需要发言的场合，比如在会议上，需要告诉听众何时可以提问并应对提问：

- ***There will be time for questions at the end,*** *if you'd like to save them up till then.* 最后会有提问的时间，大家不妨等到那个时候再发问。
- *If you don't mind,* ***we'll take all of your questions at the end of the presentation.*** 如果诸位不介意的话，我们将在演示结束时统一回应大家的提问。
- ***We've set aside/We're saving the last 15 minutes for questions.*** 我们留出最后 15 分钟作为提问时间。
- *If you have questions,* ***please feel free to ask them as we go along.*** 如果大家有问题，请在我们进行的过程中随时提问。
- ***That's an interesting point. Perhaps I can answer it*** *like this...* 这是个有趣的问题，也许我可以这样回答…
- ***I'm not sure I understand*** *your question.* 我不太肯定是否明白你的问题。
- ***If I understand your question correctly,*** *what you're asking is...* 如果我没理解错的话，你的问题是…
- ***That's something we probably need to look into further.*** 这很可能是需要我们进一步调查的事情。
- ***Does that answer your question?*** 这是否回答了你的问题？
- ***I hope that answers your question.*** 我希望这能回答你的问题。
- ***Can I come back to that point later?*** 我稍后再来谈这个问题好吗？

■ *verb* **1 ~ sb (about/on sth) | + speech** to ask sb questions about sth, especially officially 正式提问；质询；问：*She was arrested and questioned about the fire.* 她被

拘留讯问有关火灾的事情。◇ *The students were questioned on the books they had been studying.* 学生被问到有关他们所学课本的问题。◇ *Over half of those questioned said they rarely took any exercise.* 被问到的人有一半以上说他们很少锻炼身体。**2** to have or express doubts or suspicions about sth 表示疑问；怀疑：**~ sth** *I just accepted what he told me. I never thought to question it.* 他说什么我就相信什么。我从未想过要去怀疑。◇ *No one has ever questioned her judgement.* 对她的判断从没有人表示过怀疑。◇ **~ whether, what, etc.…** *He questioned whether the accident was solely the truck driver's fault.* 他怀疑这起事故是否全是卡车司机的责任。

ques·tion·able /ˈkwestʃənəbl/ *adj.* **1** that you have doubts about because you think it is not accurate or correct 可疑的；有问题的；未必准确（或正确）的 SYN **debatable**: *The conclusions that they come to are highly questionable.* 他们得出的结论大有问题。◇ ***It is questionable whether*** *this is a good way of solving the problem.* 这未必是一个解决问题的好办法。**2** likely to be dishonest or morally wrong 可能不诚实（或不道德）的；别有用心的 SYN **suspect**: *Her motives for helping are questionable.* 她帮忙的动机令人生疑。▸ **ques·tion·ably** /-əbli/ *adv.*

ques·tion·er /ˈkwestʃənə(r)/ *noun* a person who asks questions, especially in a broadcast programme or a public debate（广播节目或公开辩论等的）提问人

ques·tion·ing /ˈkwestʃənɪŋ/ *noun, adj.*

■ ***noun*** [U] the activity of asking sb questions 提问；询问；盘问：*He was taken to the police station for questioning.* 他被带到警察局盘问。◇ *They faced some hostile questioning over the cost of the project.* 关于这个项目的费用，他们面临着咄咄逼人的盘问。

■ ***adj.*** showing that you need information, or that you have doubts 询问的；表示怀疑的：*a questioning look* 怀疑的目光 ◇ *She raised a questioning eyebrow.* 她怀疑地挑起眉毛。▸ **ques·tion·ing·ly** *adv.*

ˈquestion mark *noun* the mark (?) used in writing after a question 问号

IDM **a ˈquestion mark over/against sth** used to say that sth is not certain 对…的疑问；画在…上的问号：*There's still a big question mark hanging over his future with the team.* 他在队中的前途还是个大问号。

ˈquestion master (*also* **quiz·master**) *noun* (*both BrE*) a person who asks the questions in a QUIZ, especially on television or the radio（问答比赛的）提问者；问答节目主持人

ques·tion·naire /ˌkwestʃəˈneə(r); *NAmE* -ˈner/ *noun* **~ (on/about sth)** a written list of questions that are answered by a number of people so that information can be collected from the answers 调查表；问卷：*to complete a questionnaire* 填好问卷 ◇ (*BrE*) *to fill in a questionnaire* 填调查表 ◇ (*especially NAmE*) *to fill out a questionnaire* 填调查表

ˈquestion tag (*also* **ˈtag question**) *noun* (*grammar* 语法) a phrase such as *isn't it?* or *don't you?* that you add to the end of a statement in order to turn it into a question or check that the statement is correct, as in *You like mushrooms, don't you?* 附加疑问成分，反意疑问成分（缀于陈述句之后，以将其变为问句或核实陈述句的正确性）

queue /kjuː/ *noun, verb*

■ ***noun*** **1** (*BrE*) (*NAmE* **line**) a line of people, cars, etc. waiting for sth or to do sth（人、汽车等的）队，行列：*the bus queue* 排队等候公共汽车的人 ◇ *I had to join a queue for the toilets.* 我只得排队等着上厕所。◇ *How long were you* ***in the queue****?* 你排多长时间队了？◇ *There was a queue of traffic waiting to turn right.* 有一长列车辆等着右转弯。➲ COLLOCATIONS AT SHOPPING **2** (*computing* 计) a list of items of data stored in a particular order（存储的数据）队列 IDM SEE JUMP *v.*

■ ***verb*** (**queu·ing** or **queue·ing**) **1** [I] (*BrE*) **~ (up) (for sth)** to wait in a line of people, vehicles, etc. in order to do sth, get sth or go somewhere（人、车等）排队等候：*We had to queue up for an hour for the tickets.* 我们只得排一个小时的队买票。◇ *Queue here for taxis.* 等出租车在这里排队。**2** [T, I] **~ (sth)** (*computing* 计) to add tasks to other tasks so that they are ready to be done in order; to come together to be done in order（使）排队；列队等待：*The system queues the jobs before they are processed.* 这系统先把任务排队再进行处理。

PHR V **be ˌqueuing ˈup (for sth/to do sth)** if people are said to be **queuing up** for sth or to do sth, a lot of them want to have it or do it 排长队等待；趋之若鹜：*Italian football clubs are queuing up to sign the young star.* 意大利的足球俱乐部都抢着要与这个年轻球星签约。

ˈqueue-jumping *noun* [U] (*BrE*) a situation in which a person moves to the front of a queue to get served before other people who have been waiting longer 插队；加塞儿

quib·ble /ˈkwɪbl/ *verb, noun*

■ ***verb*** [I] **~ (about/over sth)** to argue or complain about a small matter or an unimportant detail（为小事）争论，发牢骚；斤斤计较；吹毛求疵：*It isn't worth quibbling over such a small amount.* 不值得为这样的小数目斤斤计较。

■ ***noun*** a small complaint or criticism, especially one that is not important（无足轻重的）抱怨，牢骚，批评：*minor quibbles* 小牢骚

quiche /kiːʃ/ *noun* [C, U] an open PIE filled with a mixture of eggs and milk with meat, vegetables, cheese, etc.（以蛋、奶和肉、蔬菜、干酪做馅的）开口馅饼 ➲ COMPARE FLAN (1), TART *n.* (1)

quick /kwɪk/ *adj., adv., noun*

■ ***adj.*** (**quick·er, quick·est**) **1** done with speed; taking or lasting a short time 快的；迅速的；短暂的：*She gave him a quick glance.* 她迅速扫了他一眼。◇ *These cakes are very quick and easy to make.* 这些糕饼做起来又快又简单。◇ *Would you like a quick drink?* 你要不要小饮一杯？◇ *The doctor said she'd make a quick recovery.* 医生说她很快就能康复。◇ *It's quicker by train.* 坐火车比较快。◇ *Are you sure this is the quickest way?* 你确信这是最快捷的方法吗？◇ *Have you finished already? That was quick!* 你已经做完了？真快呀！◇ *His quick thinking saved her life.* 他敏捷的思维救了她一命。◇ *He fired three shots* ***in quick succession****.* 他瞬间连发三枪。➲ SEE ALSO DOUBLE QUICK **2** moving or doing sth fast 敏捷的；迅速的：*a quick learner* 学得快的人 ◇ **~ (to do sth)** *The kids were quick to learn.* 那些孩子学东西很快。◇ *She was quick* (= too quick) *to point out the mistakes I'd made.* 她总迫不及待地挑我的错。◇ *Her quick hands suddenly stopped moving.* 她敏捷的双手突然停下不动了。◇ *Try to* ***be quick****! We're late already.* 尽量快点儿！我们已经晚了。◇ *Once again, his* ***quick wits*** (= quick thinking) *got him out of an awkward situation.* 他的急智使他再次摆脱了窘境。◇ (*NAmE, informal*) *He's* ***a quick study*** (= he learns quickly). 他学东西特别快。**3** [only before noun] happening very soon or without delay 迅速的；立竿见影的：*We need to make a quick decision.* 我们需要当机立断。◇ *The company wants quick results.* 这公司要立竿见影的成果。➲ NOTE AT FAST

IDM **to have a quick ˈtemper** to become angry easily 性子急；容易发脾气 **ˌquick and ˈdirty** (*informal*) used to describe sth that is usually complicated, but is being done quickly and simply in this case 权宜处理；机动安排：*Read our quick-and-dirty guide to creating a website.* 阅读一下我们的网站制作便捷指南。➲ MORE AT BUCK *n.*, DRAW *n.*, MARK *n.*, UPTAKE

■ ***adv.*** (**quick·er, quick·est**) **1** quickly; fast 迅速地；快速地：*Come as quick as you can!* 你尽快过来吧！◇ *Let's see who can get there quickest.* 咱们看看谁最先到达。◇ *It's another of his schemes to* ***get rich quick****.* 那是他迅速致富的另一种计谋。**2** **quick-** (in adjectives 构成形容词) doing the thing mentioned quickly …敏捷的；…迅速的：*quick-thinking* 才思敏捷的 ◇ *quick-growing* 生长迅速的

IDM **(as) quick as a ˈflash** very quickly 极快；神速；旋即：*Quick as a flash she was at his side.* 她旋即来到他身边。➲ MORE LIKE THIS 14, page R26

■ ***noun*** **the quick** [sing.] the soft, sensitive flesh that is under your nails（指甲下的）活肉：*She has bitten her nails down to the quick.* 她咬指甲都咬到了活肉。

IDM **cut sb to the ˈquick** to upset sb very much by doing

or saying sth unkind（以恶意的言行）深深伤害，把…伤害到家

▼WHICH WORD? 词语辨析

quick / quickly / fast

- **Quickly** is the usual adverb from **quick**. * quickly 为源自 quick 的常用副词： *I quickly realized that I was on the wrong train.* 我很快意识到我坐错了火车。◇ *My heart started to beat more quickly.* 我的心开始跳得快起来。
- **Quick** is sometimes used as an adverb in very informal language, especially as an exclamation. 在日常用语中，quick 有时用作副词，尤作感叹语： *Come on! Quick! They'll see us!* 快点儿吧！快！他们会看见我们的！ **Quicker** is used more often. * quicker 更常用： *My heart started to beat much quicker.* 我的心跳开始大大加快。◇ *The quicker I get you away from here, the better.* 我越快送你离开此地越好。
- **Fast** is more often used when you are talking about the speed that somebody or something moves at. 指某人或某物移动的速度多用 fast： *How fast can a cheetah run?* 猎豹奔跑的速度有多快？◇ *Can't you drive any faster?* 你难道不能开快点儿？◇ ~~*You're driving too quickly.*~~ There is no word **fastly**. 没有 fastly 这个词。

quick·en /ˈkwɪkən/ *verb* (*formal*) **1** [I, T] to become quicker or make sth quicker（使）加快，加速: *She felt her heartbeat quicken as he approached.* 随着他的走近，她觉得自己的心跳加速了。◇ **~ sth** *He quickened his pace to catch up with them.* 他加快脚步追赶他们。**2** [I, T] **~ (sth)** to become more active; to make sth more active 变得更活跃；使更活跃: *His interest quickened as he heard more about the plan.* 他越听这个计划越觉得感兴趣。

ˌquick-ˈfire *adj.* [only before noun] (of a series of things 一系列) done or said very fast, one after the other 一个接一个的；连珠炮似的: *a series of quick-fire questions* 一连串连珠炮似的问题

quickie /ˈkwɪki/ *noun* (*informal*) **1** a thing that only takes a short time 简短的事；短暂的事: *I've got a question—it's just a quickie.* 我有个问题，一个简短的问题。◇ *a quickie divorce* 快速离婚 **2** a sexual act that takes a very short time 瞬间完事的性交

quick·lime /ˈkwɪklaɪm/ *noun* [U] = LIME (1)

quick·ly 🔑 /ˈkwɪkli/ *adv.* **1** 🔑 fast 迅速地；很快地: *She walked quickly away.* 她迅速走开了。◇ *We'll repair it as quickly as possible.* 我们会尽快把它修好的。◇ *The last few weeks have **gone quickly*** (= the time seems to have passed quickly). 最近的几个星期过得很快。**2** 🔑 soon; after a short time 不久；立即: *He replied to my letter very quickly.* 他立即答复了我的信。◇ *It quickly became clear that she was dying.* 很快就看得出她当时已生命垂危。➲ NOTE AT QUICK

quick·ness /ˈkwɪknəs/ *noun* [U] the quality of being fast, especially at thinking, etc. 机智；机敏；敏捷: *She was known for the quickness of her wit.* 她以头脑灵活见称。◇ *He amazes me with his quickness and eagerness to learn.* 他敏思好学，令我惊讶。

ˈquick one *noun* (*BrE, informal*) a drink, usually an alcoholic one, taken quickly 一饮而尽的饮料（通常指酒）；小酌

quick·sand /ˈkwɪksænd/ *noun* [U] (*also* **quicksands** [pl.]) **1** deep wet sand that you sink into if you walk on it 流沙 **2** a situation that is dangerous or difficult to escape from 难以摆脱的困境；危险局面

quick·sil·ver /ˈkwɪksɪlvə(r)/ *noun, adj.*
■ ***noun*** [U] (*old use*) = MERCURY
■ ***adj.*** [only before noun] (*literary*) changing or moving very quickly 变化（或移动）极快的；瞬息万变的: *his quicksilver temperament* 他那喜怒无常的性情

quick·step /ˈkwɪkstep/ *noun* a dance for two people together, with a lot of fast steps; a piece of music for this dance 双人快步舞；双人快步舞曲

ˌquick-ˈtempered *adj.* likely to become angry very quickly 火爆脾气的；急性子的: *a quick-tempered woman* 急性子的女人

ˌquick-ˈwitted *adj.* able to think quickly; intelligent 聪颖的；机敏的；机智的: *a quick-witted student/response* 机敏的学生 / 反应 OPP **slow-witted**

quid /kwɪd/ *noun* (*pl.* **quid**) (*BrE, informal*) one pound in money 一英镑: *Can you lend me five quid?* 你借给我五英镑行吗？

IDM **not the full ˈquid** (*AustralE, NZE, informal*) not very intelligent 不聪明；悟性差 **quids ˈin** in a position of having made a profit, especially a good profit 获得利润；获厚利

quid pro quo /ˌkwɪd prəʊ ˈkwəʊ; *NAmE* proʊ ˈkwoʊ/ *noun* [sing.] (*from Latin*) a thing given in return for sth else 报偿；回报

qui·es·cent /kwiˈesnt/ *adj.* **1** (*formal*) quiet; not active 沉寂的；静态的 **2** (*medical* 医) (of a disease, etc. 疾病等) not developing, especially when this is probably only a temporary state 静止的 SYN **dormant** ▸ **qui·es·cence** /-sns/ *noun* [U]

quiet 🔑 /ˈkwaɪət/ *adj., noun, verb*
■ ***adj.*** (**quiet·er, quiet·est**) **1** 🔑 making very little noise 轻声的；轻柔的；安静的: *her quiet voice* 她那轻柔的声音 ◇ *a quieter, more efficient engine* 一台声音更小、效率更高的发动机 ◇ *Could you keep the kids quiet while I'm on the phone?* 我在打电话，你让孩子们安静点好吗？◇ *He **went very quiet*** (= did not say much) *so I knew he was upset.* 他沉默不语了，所以我知道他很烦恼。◇ ***'Be quiet,'** said the teacher.* "安静点儿！"老师说道。◇ *She crept downstairs* **(as) *quiet as a mouse.*** 她蹑手蹑脚，悄声下了楼。 **2** 🔑 without many people or much noise or activity 僻静的；寂静的；清静的: *a quiet street* 寂静的街道 ◇ *They lead a quiet life.* 他们过着平静的生活。◇ *Business is usually quieter at this time of year.* 每年这个时节，生意往往比较清淡。◇ *They had a quiet wedding.* 他们举行了不事铺张的婚礼。**3** 🔑 not disturbed; peaceful 清静的；平静的；恬静的: *to have a quiet drink* 悠闲地饮酒 ◇ *I was looking forward to a quiet evening at home.* 我盼着在家过个恬静的夜晚。**4** 🔑 (of a person 人) tending not to talk very much 寡言少语的；文静的: *She was quiet and shy.* 她文静而又腼腆。 **5** (of a feeling or an attitude 感情或态度) definite but not expressed in an obvious way 克制的；稳重的；不张扬的: *He had an air of quiet authority.* 他神态威严稳重。 ▸ **quiet·ly** 🔑 *adv.*: *to speak/move quietly* 轻轻地说话 / 移动 ◇ *I spent a few hours quietly relaxing.* 我怡然自得地放松了几个小时。◇ *He is **quietly confident** that they can succeed* (= he is confident, but he is not talking about it too much). 他心里相信他们能成功。◇ *a **quietly-spoken** woman* 话语轻柔的女人 **quiet·ness** *noun* [U]: *the quietness of the countryside* 乡村的恬静 ◇ *His quietness worried her.* 他的沉默不语令她不安。

IDM **keep quiet about sth | keep sth quiet** 🔑 to say nothing about sth; to keep sth secret 对…守口如瓶；不声张；保密: *I've decided to resign but I'd rather you kept quiet about it.* 我已决定辞职，但希望你不要声张出去。

■ ***noun*** [U] the state of being calm and without much noise 宁静；寂静；平静；安静: *the quiet of his own room* 他自己房间的宁静 ◇ *the quiet of the early morning* 清晨的寂静 ◇ *I go to the library for a little **peace and quiet**.* 我到图书馆去清静一下。

IDM **on the ˈquiet** without telling anyone 悄悄地 SYN **secretly**

■ ***verb*** [I, T] (*especially NAmE*) to become calmer or less noisy; to make sb/sth calmer or less noisy（使）平静，安静 SYN **calm down**: **~ (down)** *The demonstrators quieted down when the police arrived.* 警察一到，示威者便安静了下来。◇ **~ sb/sth (down)** *He's very good at quieting the kids.* 他很有办法让孩子们安静下来。

quiet·en /ˈkwaɪətn/ *verb* [I, T] **~ (sb/sth) (down)** (*BrE*) to become calmer or less noisy; to make sb/sth calmer or less noisy（使）安静下来，平静些：*The chatter of voices gradually quietened.* 唧唧喳喳的声音渐渐地平静了。◇ *Things seem to have quietened down a bit this afternoon* (= we are not so busy, etc.). 今天下午，事情似乎平静些了。

quiet·ism /ˈkwaɪətɪzəm/ *noun* [U] (*formal*) an attitude to life which makes you calmly accept things as they are rather than try to change them 淡泊无为；沉静；安之若素 ▶ **quiet·ist** /-ɪst/ *noun, adj.*

quiet·ude /ˈkwaɪətjuːd; *NAmE* -tuːd/ *noun* [U] (*literary*) the state of being still and quiet 平静；寂静；宁静；静谧 SYN **calm**

quie·tus /kwaɪˈiːtəs/ *noun* [C, U] (*literary*) **1** death, or sth that causes death, considered as a welcome end to life 寂灭，解脱（指人生的完结或让人生得以完结的事物）**2** something that makes a person or situation calm 有平静（或缓解）作用的东西

quiff /kwɪf/ *noun* (*especially BrE*) a piece of hair at the front of the head that is brushed upwards and backwards 额发（额前向后上梳的一绺头发）

quill /kwɪl/ *noun* **1** (*also* **ˈquill feather**) a large feather from the wing or tail of a bird 翎（鸟的翅膀或尾部的大羽毛）**2** (*also* **ˌquill ˈpen**) a pen made from a quill feather 翎笔；羽管笔 **3** one of the long sharp stiff SPINES on a PORCUPINE（豪猪的）棘刺

quilt /kwɪlt/ *noun* **1** a decorative cover for a bed, made of two layers with soft material between them 加衬芯床罩：*a patchwork quilt* 拼缝床罩 ➲ VISUAL VOCAB PAGE V24 **2** (*BrE*) = DUVET ➲ COMPARE COMFORTER (2)

quilt·ed /ˈkwɪltɪd/ *adj.* (of clothes, etc. 衣服等) made of two layers of cloth with soft material between them, held in place by lines of STITCHES 絮棉的；加衬芯的：*a quilted jacket* 棉袄

Q

quilt·ing /ˈkwɪltɪŋ/ *noun* [U] the work of making a QUILT; cloth that is used for this（被子的）绗缝，衲缝；被褥料

quin /kwɪn/ *noun* (*BrE, informal*) = QUINTUPLET

quince /kwɪns/ *noun* a hard bitter yellow fruit used for making jam, etc. It grows on a tree, also called a quince. 榅桲（果实金黄有涩味，可制果酱）：*quince jelly* 榅桲果冻 ◇ *a flowering quince* 开花的榅桲

quin·cen·ten·ary /ˌkwɪnsenˈtiːnəri; *NAmE* -senˈteneri/ *noun* (*pl.* **-ies**) a 500th anniversary * 500 周年纪念：*the quincentenary of Columbus's voyage to America* 哥伦布航海到达美洲的 500 周年纪念日

quin·ine /kwɪˈniːn; ˈkwɪniːn; *NAmE also* ˈkwaɪnaɪn/ *noun* [U] a drug made from the BARK of a S American tree, used in the past to treat MALARIA 奎宁，金鸡纳霜（过去用于治疗疟疾）

qui·noa /ˈkiːnwɑː; *BrE also* kiˈnəʊə; *NAmE also* kiˈnoʊə/ *noun* [U] a South American plant, grown for its seeds, used as food and to make alcoholic drinks; the seeds of the quinoa plant 昆诺阿藜（产于南美，籽实用作食物和酿酒）；昆诺阿藜籽

quint /kwɪnt/ *noun* (*NAmE, informal*) = QUINTUPLET

quint·es·sence /kwɪnˈtesns/ *noun* [sing.] **the ~ of sth** (*formal*) **1** the perfect example of sth 典范；范例：*It was the quintessence of an English manor house.* 那是典型的英式庄园宅第。**2** the most important features of sth 精髓；精华 SYN **essence**: *a painting that captures the quintessence of Viennese elegance* 一幅尽显维也纳神韵的绘画 ▶ **quint·es·sen·tial** /ˌkwɪntɪˈsenʃl/ *adj.*: *He was the quintessential tough guy.* 他是个典型的硬汉。**quint·es·sen·tial·ly** /-ʃəli/ *adv.*

quin·tet /kwɪnˈtet/ *noun* **1** [C+sing./pl. v.] a group of five musicians or singers who play or sing together 五重奏乐团；五重唱组合：*the Miles Davis Quintet* 戴维斯五重奏乐团 **2** [C] a piece of music for five musicians or singers 五重奏（曲）；五重唱（曲）：*a string quintet* 弦乐五重奏曲

quin·tile /ˈkwɪntaɪl/ *noun* (*statistics* 统计) one of five equal groups into which a set of things can be divided according to the DISTRIBUTION of a particular VARIABLE 五分位数；五分位值：*men in the first quintile of weight* (= the heaviest 20% of men) 体重在第一个五分位组的男性（即最重的 20% 男性）➲ COMPARE QUARTILE

quin·tu·ple /ˈkwɪntjʊpl; kwɪnˈtjuːpl; *NAmE also* -ˈtuːpl/ *adj., det., verb*

■ ***adj.*** [only before noun], ***det.*** **1** consisting of five parts, people, or groups 由五部分（或人、群体）构成的；五方面的 **2** being five times as much or as many 五倍的

■ ***verb*** [I, T] **~ (sth)** to become five times bigger; to make sth five times bigger（使）成为五倍：*Sales have quintupled over the past few years.* 过去几年中销售量较原来的增加了四倍。

quin·tu·plet /ˈkwɪntʊplət; kwɪnˈtjuːplət; -ˈtʌpl-/ (*also BrE, informal* **quin**) (*also NAmE, informal* **quint**) *noun* one of five children born at the same time to the same mother 五胞胎之一

quip /kwɪp/ *noun, verb*

■ ***noun*** a quick and clever remark 俏皮话；妙语：*to make a quip* 说俏皮话

■ ***verb*** **(-pp-)** **+ speech** to make a quick and clever remark 讲俏皮话；讥讽；嘲弄；打趣

quire /ˈkwaɪə(r)/ *noun* (*old-fashioned*) four sheets of paper folded to make eight LEAVES (= 16 pages) 帖；对折的四张纸（有 16 页）

quirk /kwɜːk; *NAmE* kwɜːrk/ *noun, verb*

■ ***noun*** **1** an aspect of sb's personality or behaviour that is a little strange 怪异的性格（或行为）；怪癖 SYN **peculiarity** **2** a strange thing that happens, especially by accident（尤指偶发的）怪事，奇事：*By a strange **quirk of fate** they had booked into the same hotel.* 真是天缘奇遇，他们住进了同一家旅馆。▶ **quirky** *adj.*: *a quirky sense of humour* 怪异的幽默感

■ ***verb*** [T, I] **~ (sth)** (*especially NAmE*) to twist your mouth or eyebrows suddenly; (of your mouth or eyebrows) to move in this way 突然扭曲（嘴或眉毛）；撇嘴；扬眉；皱眉：*David quirked an eyebrow and smirked slightly.* 戴维突然扬了扬眉毛，露出一丝自鸣得意的笑。◇ *Her lips quirked suddenly.* 她的嘴唇突然抽动了一下。

quis·ling /ˈkwɪzlɪŋ/ *noun* (*disapproving*) a person who helps an enemy that has taken control of his or her country 卖国贼；内奸 SYN **collaborator**

quit 🔑 /kwɪt/ *verb* (**quit·ting, quit, quit**) (*BrE also* **quit·ting, quit·ted, quit·ted**) **1** 🔑 [I, T] (*informal*) to leave your job, school, etc. 离开（工作职位、学校等）；离任；离校：*If I don't get more money I'll quit.* 不给我加薪我就辞职。◇ **~ as sth** *He has decided to quit as manager of the team.* 他已决定辞掉球队主教练的职务。◇ **~ sth** *He quit the show last year because of bad health.* 去年他因身体欠佳而退出了表演。◇ (*NAmE*) *She quit school at 16.* 她 16 岁退学。**2** 🔑 [T, I] (*informal, especially NAmE*) to stop doing sth 停止；戒掉：**~ doing sth** *I've quit smoking.* 我戒了烟。◇ **~ (sth)** *Just quit it!* 你就罢手吧！◇ *We only just started. We're not going to quit now.* 我们才刚刚开始，现在决不放弃。**3** [T, I] **~ (sth)** to leave the place where you live 离开，迁出，搬离（住处）：*We decided it was time to quit the city.* 当时我们决定，该离开城市生活了。◇ *The landlord gave them all **notice to quit**.* 房东通知他们都搬出去。**4** 🔑 [I, T] **~ (sth)** to close a computer program or application 关闭，退出（计算机程序等）

quite 🔑 /kwaɪt/ *adv.* **1** 🔑 (*BrE*) (not used with a negative 不与否定词连用) to some degree 颇；相当；某种程度上 SYN **fairly, pretty**: *quite big/good/cold/warm/interesting* 相当大 / 好 / 冷 / 暖和 / 有趣 ◇ *He plays quite well.* 他表现得相当好。◇ *I quite like opera.* 我很喜欢歌剧。HELP When **quite** is used with an adjective before a noun, it comes before *a* or *an*. * quite 同形容词连用修饰名词时，置于 a 或 an 之前。You can say 可以说：*It's quite a small house* or 或：*Their house is quite small* but not 但不说：~~*It's a quite*~~

~~small house.~~ **2** 🔑 to the greatest possible degree 完全；十分；非常；彻底 SYN **completely**, **absolutely**, **entirely**: *quite delicious/amazing/empty/perfect* 非常美味 / 惊人 / 空 / 出众 ◇ *This is quite a different problem.* 这是个截然不同的问题。◇ *I'm* **quite happy** *to wait for you here.* 我非常高兴在此等候您。◇ (*BrE*) *Flying is* **quite the best** *way to travel.* 坐飞机绝对是最佳旅行方式。◇ *It wasn't quite as simple as I thought it would be.* 这事完全不像我想的那么简单。◇ **Quite frankly**, *I don't blame you.* 坦白说，我并不怪你。◇ *I've had* **quite enough** *of your tantrums.* 我已经受够了你那臭脾气！◇ *Are you* **quite sure**? 你有十足把握吗？◇ *I* **quite agree.** 我完全同意。◇ *I don't quite know what to do next.* 我不太清楚下一步该怎么办。◇ **Quite apart from** *all the work, he had financial problems.* 抛开那些工作的事情，他还有财务困难。◇ (*BrE*) *The theatre was* **not quite** (= was almost) *full.* 剧场并未完全满座。◇ *It's like being in the Alps, but not quite.* 那好像是在阿尔卑斯山，但又不尽然。◇ *'I almost think she prefers animals to people.'* **'Quite right too,'** *said Bill.* "我简直认为她喜爱动物胜过喜爱人。" "没错儿。" 比尔说道。◇ *'I'm sorry to be so difficult.'* **'That's quite all right.'** "对不起，我太为难你了。" "没关系。" **3** 🔑 to a great degree; very; really 在很大程度上；很；的确：*You'll be quite comfortable here.* 你在这里会很舒服的。◇ *I can see it quite clearly.* 我能清清楚楚地看见它。◇ (*NAmE*) *'You've no intention of coming back?' 'I'm quite sorry, but no, I have not.'* "你不打算回来了吗？" "是的。非常抱歉，我不想回来了。" **4** (*also formal* **quite so**) (*BrE*) used to agree with sb or show that you understand them（表示赞同或理解）对，正是：*'He's bound to feel shaken after his accident.' 'Quite.'* "那次事故之后，他一定是像惊弓之鸟。" "可不是。"

IDM **'quite a/the sth** (*also informal* **'quite some sth**) used to show that a person or thing is particularly impressive or unusual in some way（强调在某方面很突出）：*She's quite a beauty.* 她可是个大美人啊。◇ *We found it quite a change when we moved to London.* 我们搬到伦敦后，感觉生活变化很大。◇ *He's quite the little gentleman, isn't he?* 他真是个小绅士，不是吗？◇ *It must be quite some car.* 那辆汽车肯定很了不得。**quite a 'lot (of sth)** 🔑 (*BrE also, informal* **quite a 'bit**) a large number or amount of sth 大量；许多；众多：*They drank quite a lot of wine.* 他们喝了好多酒。**'quite some sth 1** a large amount of sth 大量；众多：*She hasn't been seen for quite some time.* 好久没人看见她了。**2** (*informal*) = QUITE A/THE STH ➲ MORE AT CONTRARY[1] *n.*, FEW *pron.*

▼ **WHICH WORD?** 词语辨析

quite / fairly / rather / pretty

Look at these examples. 看下列例句：

- *The exam was fairly difficult.* 这场考试颇难。
- *The exam was quite difficult.* 这场考试相当难。
- *The exam was rather difficult.* 这场考试十分难。
- **Quite** is a little stronger than **fairly**, and **rather** is a little stronger than **quite**. **Rather** is not very common in *NAmE*; **pretty** has the same meaning and this is used in informal *BrE* too. * quite 比 fairly 语气稍强，而 rather 又比 quite 语气稍强。在美式英语中，rather 不太常用。pretty 与 rather 含义相同，也用于非正式英式英语：*The exam was pretty difficult.* 这场考试十分难。
- In *BrE* **quite** has two meanings. 在英式英语中，quite 含义有二：*I feel quite tired today* (= fairly tired). 今天我感到相当累。With adjectives that describe an extreme state ('non-gradable' adjectives) it means 'completely' or 'absolutely'. 与表示极端状态的形容词（即非级差形容词）连用，意为完全地、绝对地：*I feel quite exhausted.* 我感到筋疲力尽。With some adjectives, both meanings are possible. The speaker's stress and intonation will show you which is meant. 与某些形容词连用，两种含义均有可能，究竟属于哪一种由说话者的重音和语调决定：*Your essay is 'quite good* (= fairly good—it could be better). 你的文章还不错（挺好，不过可以更好）；*Your essay is quite 'good* (= very good, especially when this is unexpected). 你的文章简直太好了（非常好，尤指出乎意料）。
- In *NAmE* **quite** usually means something like 'very', not 'fairly' or 'rather'. **Pretty** is used instead for this sense. 在美式英语中，quite 通常为 very 之义，而非 fairly 或 rather。表示后一种意思用 pretty。

quits /kwɪts/ *adj.*

IDM **be quits (with sb)** (*informal*) when two people **are quits**, they do not owe each other anything, especially money 互不相欠；两清；两讫：*I'll give you £5 and then we're quits.* 我给你 5 英镑，那样我们就两清了。➲ MORE AT CALL *v.*, DOUBLE *n.*

quit·ter /ˈkwɪtə(r)/ *noun* (*often disapproving*) a person who gives up easily and does not finish a task they have started 有始无终的人；虎头蛇尾的人；半途而废者

quiver /ˈkwɪvə(r)/ *verb, noun*

■ ***verb*** [I] to shake slightly; to make a slight movement 轻微颤动；抖动；抽动；哆嗦 SYN **tremble**: *Her lip quivered and then she started to cry.* 她嘴唇微微一颤就哭了起来。

■ ***noun*** **1** an emotion that has an effect on your body; a slight movement in part of your body 强烈感情；哆嗦；微颤；抖动：*He felt a quiver of excitement run through him.* 他觉得浑身上下都兴奋起来。◇ *Jane couldn't help the quiver in her voice.* 简不禁声音颤抖。**2** a case for carrying arrows 箭筒；箭套

qui vive /ˌkiː ˈviːv/ *noun*

IDM **on the qui 'vive** paying close attention to a situation, in case sth happens 密切注意着；警惕：*He's always on the qui vive for a business opportunity.* 他总是密切关注商机。

quix·ot·ic /kwɪkˈsɒtɪk; *NAmE* -ˈsɑːtɪk/ *adj.* (*formal*) having or involving ideas or plans that show imagination but are usually not practical 想入非非的；异想天开的；堂吉诃德式的 ORIGIN From the character Don Quixote in the novel by Miguel de Cervantes, whose adventures are a result of him trying to achieve or obtain things that are impossible. 源自米盖尔·塞万提斯的作品《堂吉诃德》，其主人公堂吉诃德为了实现不切实际的理想而到处历险。

quiz /kwɪz/ *noun, verb*

■ ***noun*** (*pl.* **quiz·zes**) **1** a competition or game in which people try to answer questions to test their knowledge 知识竞赛；智力游戏：*a general knowledge quiz* 常识问答竞赛 ◇ *a television quiz show* 电视智力游戏节目 ➲ WORDFINDER NOTE AT PROGRAMME **2** (*especially NAmE*) an informal test given to students 小测验：*a reading comprehension quiz* 阅读理解小测验 ➲ SEE ALSO POP QUIZ ➲ NOTE AT EXAM

■ ***verb*** (**-zz-**) **1** to ask sb a lot of questions about sth in order to get information from them 盘问；查问；询问；讯问 SYN **question**: **~ sb (about sb/sth)** *Four men are being quizzed by police about the murder.* 警察就这起谋杀案正在盘问四个男子。◇ **~ sb (on/over sth)** *We were quizzed on our views about education.* 我们被征询对教育的看法。**2 ~ sb** (*NAmE*) to give students an informal test 测验（学生）：*You will be quizzed on chapter 6 tomorrow.* 明天将考你们第 6 章。

quiz·master /ˈkwɪzmɑːstə(r); *NAmE* -mæs-/ *noun* = QUESTION MASTER

quiz·zical /ˈkwɪzɪkl/ *adj.* (of an expression 表情) showing that you are slightly surprised or amused 诧异的；感到好笑的：*a quizzical expression* 诧异的表情 ▶ **quiz·zi·cal·ly** /-kli/ *adv.*: *She looked at him quizzically.* 她疑惑地望着他。

quoit /kɔɪt; kwɔɪt/ *noun* **1** [C] a ring that is thrown onto a small post in the game of quoits（投环游戏用的）环，圈 **2 quoits** [U] a game in which rings are thrown onto a small post 投环（将圈投向标棍的游戏）

quoll /kwɒl; *NAmE* kwɑːl/ *noun* a small animal with short legs, a long tail and brown fur with white spots, that lives in the forests of Australia and parts of Papua New Guinea 袋鼬（小型动物，腿短，尾长，毛棕色带白色斑点，分布于澳大利亚和巴布亚新几内亚部分地区）

Q

Quonset hut™ /ˈkwɒnset hʌt; NAmE ˈkwɑːn-/ (NAmE) (BrE **Nis·sen hut**) noun a shelter made of metal with curved walls and roof 尼森式半筒形铁皮屋

quor·ate /ˈkwɔːreɪt; -ət/ adj. (BrE, specialist) a meeting that is **quorate** has enough people present for them to make official decisions by voting（会议）够法定人数的 OPP **inquorate**

Quorn™ /kwɔːn; NAmE kwɔːrn/ noun [U] a substance made from a type of FUNGUS, used in cooking instead of meat 阔恩素肉（用一种真菌制成）

quorum /ˈkwɔːrəm/ noun [sing.] the smallest number of people who must be at a meeting before it can begin or decisions can be made（会议的）法定人数

quota /ˈkwəʊtə; NAmE ˈkwoʊtə/ noun **1** [C] the limited number or amount of people or things that is officially allowed 定额；限额；配额：*to introduce a strict import quota on grain* 严格限制谷物进口量 ◇ *a quota system for accepting refugees* 接收难民的限额制度 **2** [C] an amount of sth that sb expects or needs to have or achieve 定量；定额；指标：*I'm going home now—I've done my quota of work for the day.* 我现在要回家了。我已完成了今天的工作量。 **3** [sing.] (politics 政) a fixed number of votes that a candidate needs in order to be elected（候选人当选所需的）规定票数，最低票数：*He was 76 votes short of the quota.* 他比规定当选票数少了 76 票。

quot·able /ˈkwəʊtəbl; NAmE ˈkwoʊ-/ adj. (of a statement 话语) interesting or amusing and worth repeating 值得（或适合）引用的

quota·tion AW /kwəʊˈteɪʃn; NAmE kwoʊ-/ noun **1** (rather formal) (also rather informal **quote**) [C] a group of words or a short piece of writing taken from a book, play, speech, etc. and repeated because it is interesting or useful 引语；引文；语录：*The book began with a quotation from Goethe.* 这本书一开头引用了歌德的隽语。◇ *a dictionary of quotations* 引语词典 ➲ SEE ALSO MISQUOTATION at MISQUOTE **2** [U] the act of repeating sth interesting or useful that another person has written or said 引用；引述；引证：*The writer illustrates his point by quotation from a number of sources.* 作者旁征博引以阐明自己的观点。 **3** [C] (rather formal) (also rather informal **quote**) a statement of how much money a particular piece of work will cost 报价；估价 SYN **estimate**：*You need to get a written quotation before they start work.* 你得在他们开工之前拿到报价单。 **4** [C] (finance 财) a statement of the current value of goods or shares（货物或股票的）行情，市价，牌价：*the latest quotations from the Stock Exchange* 股票交易所的最新行情

quoˈtation marks (also **quotes**, **ˈspeech marks**) (BrE also **in·vert·ed commas**) noun [pl.] a pair of marks (' ') or (" ") placed around a word, sentence, etc. to show that it is what sb said or wrote, that it is a title or that you are using it in an unusual way 引号

quote AW /kwəʊt; NAmE kwoʊt/ verb, noun

■ *verb*

• **REPEAT EXACT WORDS** 引述 **1** [T, I] to repeat the exact words that another person has said or written 引用；引述：**~ sth (from sb/sth)** *He quoted a passage from the minister's speech.* 他引用了部长的一段讲话。◇ *to quote Shakespeare* 引用莎士比亚的话 ◇ *Quote this reference number in all correspondence.* 请在所有函件中标明这个编号。◇ **~ (sb) (as doing sth)** *The President was quoted in the press as saying that he disagreed with the decision.* 报刊援引总统的话，说他不赞成这项决定。◇ *'It will all be gone tomorrow.' 'Can I quote you on that?'* "明天一切将烟消云散。" "我能引用你的这句话吗？" ◇ ***Don't quote me on this*** (= this is not an official statement), *but I think he is going to resign.* 不要说这话是我说的，但我想他打算辞职。◇ *She said, and I quote, 'Life is meaningless without love.'* 我援引她曾说过的话："人生无爱一场空。" ◇ **+ speech** *'The man who is tired of London is tired of life,' he quoted.* "厌倦伦敦等于厌倦生活。" 他引述道。➲ SEE ALSO MISQUOTE

• **GIVE EXAMPLE** 举例 **2** [T] **~ (sb) sth** to mention an example of sth to support what you are saying 举例说明：*Can you quote me an instance of when this happened?* 你能否给我举例说明一下这事发生的时间？ ➲ SYNONYMS AT MENTION

• **GIVE PRICE** 报价 **3** [T, I] **~ (sb) (sth) (for sth/for doing sth)** to tell a customer how much money you will charge them for a job, service or product 开价；出价；报价：*They quoted us £300 for installing a shower unit.* 他们向我们开价 300 英镑安装淋浴设备。 **4** [T] **~ sth (at sth)** (finance 财) to give a market price for shares, gold or foreign money 为（股票、黄金或外汇）报价：*Yesterday the pound was quoted at $1.8285, unchanged from Monday.* 昨天英镑报价为 1.8285 美元，这个价格从星期一以来未变。 **5** [T] **~ sth** (finance 财) to give the prices for a business company's shares on a STOCK EXCHANGE 为（企业的股份）上市，挂牌：*Several football clubs are now quoted on the Stock Exchange.* 目前有几家足球俱乐部在股票交易所上市。

IDM **ˈquote (... ˈunquote)** (informal) used to show the beginning (and end) of a word, phrase, etc. that has been said or written by sb else（用于引文的开始和结尾）引文起（…引文止）：*It was quote, 'the hardest decision of my life', unquote, and one that he lived to regret.* 那是，原话起，"我一生最困难的决定"，原话止，而且是他后来后悔了的决定。

■ *noun* (rather informal)

• **EXACT WORDS** 原话 **1** = QUOTATION (1)：*The essay was full of quotes.* 这篇文章满篇皆是引语。

• **PRICE** 价格 **2** = QUOTATION (3)：*Their quote for the job was way too high.* 他们给这项工作开价太高了。

• **PUNCTUATION** 标点符号 **3 quotes** [pl.] = QUOTATION MARKS：*If you take text from other sources, place it in quotes.* 引用其他来源的资料要放在引号里。

quoth /kwəʊθ; NAmE kwoʊθ/ verb **+ speech** (old use or humorous) used meaning 'said' before 'I', 'he' or 'she'（用于 I、he 或 she 之前）说过，言道

quo·tid·ian /kwɒˈtɪdiən; kwəʊˈt-; NAmE kwoʊˈt-/ adj. (formal) ordinary; typical of what happens every day 寻常的；普通的；司空见惯的 SYN **day-to-day**

quo·tient /ˈkwəʊʃnt; NAmE ˈkwoʊ-/ noun (mathematics 数) a number which is the result when one number is divided by another 商（除法所得的结果）➲ SEE ALSO INTELLIGENCE QUOTIENT

Qur'an = KORAN

q.v. /ˌkjuː ˈviː/ abbr. used in books to tell a reader that there is more information in another part of the book (from Latin 'quod vide') 见该项，参见该条（源自拉丁文 quod vide）

QWERTY /ˈkwɜːti; NAmE ˈkwɜːrti/ adj. [usually before noun] (of a keyboard on a computer or TYPEWRITER 计算机或打字机键盘) with the keys arranged in the usual way with Q, W, E, R, T and Y on the left of the top row of letters 标准键盘的，传统键盘的（Q、W、E、R、T 和 Y 各键分布在左侧上排）

R /ɑː(r)/ *noun, abbr.*

■ ***noun*** (*also* **r**) [C, U] (*pl.* **Rs**, **R's**, **r's** /ɑːz; *NAmE* ɑːrz/) the 18th letter of the English alphabet 英语字母表的第 18 个字母: *'Rose' begins with (an) R/'R'.* * rose 一词以字母 r 开头。 IDM SEE THREE

■ ***abbr.*** **1** (*BrE*) Queen; King (from Latin 'Regina'; 'Rex') 女王，国王（源自拉丁语 Regina、Rex）: *Elizabeth R.* 伊丽莎白女王 **2 R.** (especially on maps) River（尤用于地图）河，江: *R. Trent* 特伦特河 **3** (*also* **R.** *especially in NAmE*) (in politics in the US 美国政治) REPUBLICAN 共和党人；共和党党员 **4** (*BrE*) Royal（用于服务于国王或女王或受其赞助的组织名称）王室的，皇家的: *the RAC* (= Royal Automobile Club) 英国皇家汽车俱乐部 **5** (*NAmE*) the abbreviation for 'restricted' (a label for a film/movie that is not suitable for people under the age of 17 to see without an adult present) 限制级的（全写为 restricted，未满 17 岁者无成人陪同不宜观看的电影的标记） ⊃ SEE ALSO R & B, R & D

rabbi /ˈræbaɪ/ *noun* a Jewish religious leader or a teacher of Jewish law 拉比（犹太教经师或神职人员）: *the Chief Rabbi* (= the leader of Jewish communities in a particular country) 首席拉比 ◇ *Rabbi Sacks* 萨克斯拉比

rab·bin·ical /rəˈbɪnɪkl/ (*also* **rab·bin·ic**) *adj.* connected with rabbis or Jewish law or teaching 犹太教教士（或法规、教义）的

rabbit 兔

hare 野兔

rab·bit /ˈræbɪt/ *noun, verb*

■ ***noun*** **1** [C] a small animal with soft fur, long ears and a short tail. Rabbits live in holes in the ground or are kept as pets or for food. 兔: *a rabbit hutch* 兔笼 ⊃ COMPARE HARE *n.* **2** [U] meat from a rabbit 兔肉 IDM SEE PULL *v.*

■ ***verb*** [I] **go rabbiting** to hunt or shoot rabbits 猎兔；捕兔

PHR V ˌ**rabbit ˈon** (**about sb/sth**) (*BrE, informal, disapproving*) to talk continuously about things that are not important or interesting 没完没了地说废话；闲扯 SYN **chatter**

ˈ**rabbit warren** (*also* **war·ren**) *noun* **1** a system of holes and underground tunnels where wild rabbits live 野兔繁殖区（由地下交错相连的洞穴组成） **2** (*disapproving*) a building or part of a city with many narrow passages or streets 有许多狭小通道的建筑；街道狭窄而密集的城区

rab·ble /ˈræbl/ *noun* [sing.+sing./pl. v.] (*disapproving*) **1** a large group of noisy people who are or may become violent 乌合之众；聚众的暴民 SYN **mob**: *a drunken rabble* 醉酒闹事的人群 **2 the rabble** ordinary people or people who are considered to have a low social position 贱民；下等人 SYN **the masses**: *a speech that appealed to the rabble* 感染贱民的演讲

ˈ**rabble-rouser** *noun* a person who makes speeches to crowds of people intending to make them angry or excited, especially for political aims 煽动民众者 ▸ ˈ**rabble-rousing** *adj.* ˈ**rabble-rousing** *noun* [U]

Rabe·lais·ian /ˌræbəˈleɪziən; -ˈleɪʒn/ *adj.* dealing with sex and the human body in a rude but humorous way 拉伯雷风格的；粗俗幽默的 ORIGIN From the French writer François Rabelais, whose works dealt with sex and the body in this way. 源自作品对性和人体作粗俗幽默描绘的法国作家弗朗索瓦•拉伯雷。

rabid /ˈræbɪd; ˈreɪb-/ *adj.* **1** [usually before noun] (*disapproving*) (of a type of person 某类人) having very strong feelings about sth and acting in an unacceptable way 极端的；疯狂的: *rabid right-wing fanatics* 极端的右翼狂热分子 ◇ *the rabid tabloid press* 偏激的小报 **2** [usually before noun] (*disapproving*) (of feelings or opinions 感情或看法) violent or extreme 激烈的；极端的: *rabid speculation* 非理性推断 **3** suffering from rabies 患狂犬病的: *a rabid dog* 疯狗 ▸ **rabid·ly** *adv.*

ra·bies /ˈreɪbiːz/ *noun* [U] a disease of dogs and other animals that causes MADNESS and death. Infected animals can pass the disease to humans by biting them. 狂犬病；恐水症

RAC /ˌɑːr eɪ ˈsiː/ *abbr.* Royal Automobile Club (a British organization which provides services for car owners)（英国）皇家汽车俱乐部

rac·coon (*also* **ra·coon**) /rəˈkuːn; *NAmE* ræ-/ *noun* **1** [C] a small N American animal with greyish-brown fur, black marks on its face and a thick tail 浣熊；北美浣熊 **2** [U] the fur of the raccoon 浣熊的毛皮

race 🔑 /reɪs/ *noun, verb*

■ ***noun***

• **COMPETITION** 竞赛 **1** 🔑 [C] ~ (**between A and B**) | ~ (**against sb**) a competition between people, animals, vehicles, etc. to see which one is the faster or fastest 赛跑；速度竞赛: *a race between the two best runners of the club* 俱乐部中两名最佳选手的赛跑 ◇ *Who won the race?* 谁赢了赛跑？ ◇ *He's already in training for the big race against Bailey.* 为了跟贝利决一雌雄，他已经着手训练了。 ◇ *Their horse came third in the race last year.* 他们的马在去年的比赛中获得了第三名。 ◇ ***a boat/horse/road, etc. race*** 划船比赛、赛马、公路赛等 ◇ *a five-kilometre race* 五公里赛跑 ◇ *Shall we* ***have a race*** *to the end of the beach?* 咱们比赛跑到海滩那一头，好吗？ ⊃ SEE ALSO DRAG RACE, HORSE RACE **2** 🔑 [sing.] a situation in which a number of people, groups, organizations, etc. are competing, especially for political power or to achieve sth first 竞争；角逐: ~ (**for sth**) *the race for the presidency* 总统竞选 ◇ ~ (**to do sth**) *The race* ***is on*** (= has begun) *to find a cure for the disease.* 人们开始争相寻找这种疾病的疗法。 ⊃ SEE ALSO RAT RACE

• **FOR HORSES** 马 **3 the races** [pl.] a series of horse races that happen at one place on a particular day 赛马会: *to go to the races* 去参加赛马会

• **PEOPLE** 人 **4** 🔑 [C, U] one of the main groups that humans can be divided into according to their physical differences, for example the colour of their skin 人种；种族: *the* ***Caucasian/Mongolian, etc. race*** 白种人、黄种人等 ◇ *people of* ***mixed race*** 混合种族的人 ◇ *This custom is found in people of all races throughout the world.* 这一习俗在全世界各种族中都有。 ◇ *legislation against discrimination on the grounds of race or sex* 反对种族和性别歧视的立法 ⊃ WORDFINDER NOTE AT EQUAL **5** [C] a group of people who share the same language, history, culture, etc. 民族: *the*

R

Nordic races 北欧日耳曼民族 ◊ *He admired Canadians as a hardy and determined race.* 他敬佩加拿大人，因为他们是吃苦耐劳、意志坚定的民族。 ➲ SEE ALSO HUMAN RACE

• ANIMALS/PLANTS 动植物 **6** [C] a breed or type of animal or plant 种；属；类；族：*a race of cattle* 一种牛

IDM **a ˌrace against ˈtime/the ˈclock** a situation in which you have to do sth or finish sth very fast before it is too late 和时间赛跑；抢时间；争分夺秒 **race to the ˈbottom** (*economics* 经) a situation in which companies and countries compete with each other to produce goods as cheaply as possible by paying low wages and giving workers poor conditions and few rights 逐底竞争（企业或国家通过降低工资、劳动条件和工人权利以尽可能降低生产成本的竞争） ➲ MORE AT HORSE *n.*

■ *verb*

• COMPETE 竞赛 **1** [I, T] to compete against sb/sth to see who can go faster or the fastest, do sth first, etc.; to take part in a race or races （和…）比赛；参加比赛：**~ (against sb/sth)** *Who will he be racing against in the next round?* 下一轮他和谁比赛？ ◊ *They raced to a thrilling victory in the relay.* 他们在接力赛中取得了激动人心的胜利。 ◊ *She'll be racing for the senior team next year.* 明年她将参加高级组别的比赛。 ◊ **~ sb/sth** *We raced each other back to the car.* 我们争先恐后地跑回汽车那儿。 ◊ **~ to do sth** *Television companies are racing to be the first to screen his life story.* 几家电视广播公司争着将他的生平抢先搬上荧屏。 **2** [T] **~ sth** to make an animal or a vehicle compete in a race 使比赛；让…参加速度比赛：*to race dogs/horses/pigeons* 赛狗；赛马；赛鸽 ◊ *to race motorbikes* 赛摩托车

• MOVE FAST 快速运动 **3** [I, T] to move very fast; to move sb/sth very fast （使）快速移动，快速运转：**+ adv./prep.** *He raced up the stairs.* 他飞快地冲上楼去。 ◊ *The days seemed to race past.* 日子似乎很快就过去了。 ◊ **~ sb/sth + adv./prep.** *The injured man was raced to the hospital.* 受伤者被迅速送往医院。 ◊ *She raced her car through the narrow streets of the town.* 她开着车在小镇狭窄的街道上飞快地穿行。

• OF HEART/MIND/THOUGHTS 心；头脑；思想 **4** [I] to function very quickly because you are afraid, excited, etc. （因为害怕、兴奋等）急速跳动，快速转动：*My mind raced as I tried to work out what was happening.* 我拼命地转动脑筋，想搞清楚发生了什么事。 ◊ *She took a deep breath to calm her racing pulse.* 她深深地吸了口气，想使急速跳动的脉搏平静下来。

• OF ENGINE 发动机 **5** [I] to run too fast 运转过快；空转：*The truck came to rest against a tree, its engine racing.* 卡车撞上一棵树停了下来，引擎空转着。

ˈrace car (*NAmE*) (*also* **ˈracing car** *BrE, NAmE*) *noun* a car that has been specially designed for motor racing 赛车

ˈrace card *noun*

IDM **play the ˈrace card** (*disapproving*) to criticize people who belong to different races in a way that is meant to make other people feel opposed to them and to gain you a political advantage, especially during an election 打种族牌

race·card /ˈreɪskɑːd; *NAmE* -kɑːrd/ *noun* (*BrE*) a list of all the horse races at a particular event （赛马）赛程表

▼ COLLOCATIONS 词语搭配

Race and immigration 种族与移民

Prejudice and racism 偏见与种族歧视

- **experience/encounter** racism/discrimination/prejudice/anti-semitism 经历 / 遭遇种族歧视 / 歧视 / 偏见 / 反犹太主义
- **face/suffer** persecution/discrimination 面临 / 遭受迫害 / 歧视
- **fear/escape from/flee** racial/political/religious persecution 惧怕 / 逃离种族 / 政治 / 宗教迫害
- **constitute/be a form of** racial/race discrimination 构成 / 是一种种族歧视
- **reflect/reveal/show/have** a racial/cultural bias 反映出 / 揭示出 / 表现出 / 具有种族 / 文化偏见
- **be biased/be prejudiced against** (*especially BrE*) black people/(*both especially NAmE*) people of color/African Americans/Asians/Africans/Indians, etc. 对黑人 / 有色人种 / 非裔美国人 / 亚洲人 / 非洲人 / 印度人等有偏见
- **discriminate against** minority groups/minorities 歧视少数群体 / 少数民族
- **perpetuate/conform to/fit/defy** a common/popular/traditional/negative stereotype 固守 / 遵从 / 符合 / 藐视普遍的 / 流行的 / 传统的 / 负面的模式化观念
- **overcome/be blinded by** deep-seated/racial/(*especially NAmE*) race prejudice 克服根深蒂固的 / 种族的偏见；被根深蒂固的 / 种族的偏见所蒙蔽
- **entrench/perpetuate** racist attitudes 固守种族主义的态度
- **hurl/shout** (*especially BrE*) racist abuse; (*especially NAmE*) a racist/racial/ethnic slur 高声地进行种族污辱
- **challenge/confront** racism/discrimination/prejudice 拒绝接受 / 对抗种族主义 / 歧视 / 偏见
- **combat/fight (against)/tackle** blatant/overt/covert/subtle/institutional/systemic racism 打压 / 反对 / 处理公然的 / 公开的 / 隐蔽的 / 微妙的 / 制度性的种族歧视

Race and society 种族和社会

- **damage/improve** (*especially BrE*) race relations 破坏 / 改善种族关系
- **practise/**(*especially US*) **practice** (racial/religious) tolerance/segregation 实行（种族 / 宗教）容忍 / 隔离政策
- **bridge/break down/transcend** cultural/racial barriers 消除 / 打破 / 超越文化 / 种族隔阂
- **encourage/promote** social integration 鼓励 / 促进社会融合
- **outlaw/end** discrimination/slavery/segregation 取缔 / 终止歧视 / 奴隶制 / 种族隔离
- **promote/embrace/celebrate** cultural diversity 促进 / 欣然接纳 / 颂扬文化多样性
- **conform to/challenge/violate** (accepted/established/prevailing/dominant) social/cultural norms 遵循 / 挑战 / 违背（公认的 / 确立的 / 盛行的 / 占支配地位的）社会 / 文化规范
- **live in** a multicultural society 生活在多元文化社会
- **attack/criticize** multiculturalism 攻击 / 批评多元文化主义
- **fight for/struggle for/promote** racial equality 为种族平等而斗争；促进种族平等
- **perpetuate/reinforce** economic and social inequality 延续 / 加剧经济和社会的不平等
- **introduce/be for/be against** (*BrE*) positive discrimination/(*especially NAmE*) affirmative action 推行 / 支持 / 反对积极性区别对待政策
- **support/be active in/play a leading role in** the civil rights movement 支持 / 积极参与 / 领导民权运动

Immigration 移居

- **control/restrict/limit/encourage** immigration 控制 / 限制 / 鼓励外来移民
- **attract/draw** a wave of immigrants 吸引一批外来移民
- **assist/welcome** refugees 援助 / 欣然接受难民
- **house/shelter** refugees and asylum seekers 安置 / 庇护难民和寻求政治避难者
- **smuggle** illegal immigrants into the UK 偷运非法移民到英国
- **deport/repatriate** illegal immigrants/failed asylum seekers 驱逐 / 遣返非法移民 / 寻求政治避难失败者
- **assimilate/integrate** new immigrants 同化 / 融合新移民
- **employ/hire** migrant workers 雇用流动工人
- **exploit/rely on** (cheap/illegal) immigrant labour/(*especially US*) labor 剥削 / 依赖（廉价的 / 非法的）移民劳动力
- **apply for/gain/obtain/be granted/be denied** (full) citizenship 申请 / 获得 / 准予 / 未准予（完全的）公民身份
- **have/hold** dual citizenship 持有双重国籍

R

race·course /ˈreɪskɔːs; *NAmE* -kɔːrs/ (*NAmE* **race·track**) *noun* a track where horses race and the buildings, etc. that are connected with it 赛马跑道；赛马场 ➲ VISUAL VOCAB PAGE V51

race·goer /ˈreɪsɡəʊə(r); *NAmE* -ɡoʊ-/ *noun* (*BrE*) a person who goes to horse races 观看赛马的人

race·horse /ˈreɪshɔːs; *NAmE* -hɔːrs/ *noun* a horse that is bred and trained to run in races 赛马 ➲ VISUAL VOCAB PAGE V51

ˈ**race meeting** *noun* (*BrE*) a series of races, especially for horses, held at one course over one day or several days 比赛大会；（尤指）赛马大会

racer /ˈreɪsə(r)/ *noun* **1** a person or an animal that competes in races 参赛的人（或动物）: *Italy's champion downhill racer* 意大利的高山滑雪冠军 **2** a car, boat, etc. designed for racing 专供比赛用的车辆（或小艇等）；赛车；赛艇: *an ocean racer* 海上赛艇 ➲ VISUAL VOCAB PAGE V55

ˌ**race reˈlations** *noun* [pl.] the relationships between people of different races who live in the same community 种族关系

ˈ**race riot** *noun* violent behaviour between people of different races living in the same community 种族骚乱；种族暴乱

race·track /ˈreɪstræk/ *noun* **1** a track for races between runners, cars, bicycles, etc. 跑道；赛道: *You can't cross the road—it's like a racetrack.* 那条马路像赛车道一样，让人无法横越。 **2** (*NAmE*) (*BrE* **race·course**) a track where horses race and the buildings, etc. that are connected with it 赛马跑道；赛马场 ➲ VISUAL VOCAB PAGE V51

race·way /ˈreɪsweɪ/ *noun* (*NAmE*) a track for racing cars or horses 赛车道；赛马跑道

ra·cial /ˈreɪʃl/ *adj.* **1** [only before noun] happening or existing between people of different races 种族的；种族间的: ***racial hatred/prejudice/tension/violence*** 种族仇恨/偏见；种族间的紧张状况/暴力 ◇ *racial equality* 种族平等 ◇ *They have pledged to end* ***racial discrimination*** *in areas such as employment.* 他们已经保证在诸如就业等方面终止种族歧视。 **2** [usually before noun] connected with a person's race 人种的；种族的: *racial minorities* 少数民族 ◇ *a person's* ***racial origin*** 某人的种族背景 ▶ **ra·cial·ly** /-ʃəli/ *adv.*: *The attacks were not racially motivated.* 袭击事件不是由种族原因引起的。◇ *racially mixed schools* 不分种族的学校

ra·cial·ism /ˈreɪʃəlɪzəm/ *noun* [U] (*old-fashioned, BrE*) = RACISM

ra·cial·ist /ˈreɪʃəlɪst/ *noun, adj.* (*old-fashioned, BrE*) = RACIST

ˌ**racial ˈprofiling** *noun* [U] (*NAmE*) the fact of police officers, etc. suspecting that sb has committed a crime based on the colour of their skin or their race rather than on any evidence 种族形象定性（指警察等因肤色或种族而不是证据怀疑人犯罪）

ra·cing /ˈreɪsɪŋ/ *noun* [U] **1** (*also* ˈ**horse racing**) the sport of racing horses 赛马: *a racing stable* 赛马马厩 ➲ SEE ALSO FLAT RACING **2** (usually in compounds 通常构成复合词) any sport that involves competing in races 速度比赛: ***motor/yacht/greyhound, etc. racing*** 摩托车赛、快艇赛、赛狗等 ◇ *a racing driver* 赛车选手 ➲ SEE ALSO DRAG RACING at DRAG RACE

ˈ**racing car** (*NAmE* ˈ**race car**) *noun* a car that has been specially designed for motor racing 赛车 ➲ MORE LIKE THIS 9, page R26

ˌ**racing ˈcertainty** *noun* (*BrE, informal*) a thing that is certain to happen 必然发生的事；确定无疑的事: *It's a racing certainty that the vote will go against him.* 投票将对他不利，这是板上钉钉的事。

ra·cism /ˈreɪsɪzəm/ *noun* [U] (*disapproving*) **1** the unfair treatment of people who belong to a different race; violent behaviour towards them 种族歧视；种族迫害: *a victim of racism* 种族歧视的受害者 ◇ *ugly outbreaks of racism* 危险的种族迫害事件 ➲ COLLOCATIONS AT RACE **2** the belief that some races of people are better than others 种族主义；种族偏见: *irrational racism* 非理性的种族主义 ▶ **ra·cist** /ˈreɪsɪst/ *noun*: *He's a racist.* 他是个种族主义者。 **ra·cist** /ˈreɪsɪst/ *adj.*: *racist thugs* 种族主义暴徒 ◇ *racist attitudes/attacks/remarks* 种族主义的态度/攻击/言论

racks 支架；架子

rack /ræk/ *noun, verb*

■ ***noun*** **1** (often in compounds 常构成复合词) a piece of equipment, usually made of metal or wooden bars, that is used for holding things or for hanging things on 支架；架子: ***a vegetable/wine/plate/toast rack*** 蔬菜架；酒瓶架；盘碟架；面包片架 ◇ *I looked through a rack of clothes at the back of the shop.* 我看遍了挂在商场靠里面的一架子衣服。 ➲ VISUAL VOCAB PAGES V22, V72 ➲ SEE ALSO LUGGAGE RACK, ROOF RACK **2** (*usually* **the rack**) an instrument of TORTURE, used in the past for punishing and hurting people. Their arms and legs were tied to the wooden frame and then pulled in opposite directions, stretching the body.（旧时的）拉肢刑具 **3 ~ of lamb/pork** a particular piece of meat that includes the front RIBS and is cooked in the oven（羊、猪等带前肋的）颈脊肉 **4** a part of a machine that consists of a bar with parts that a wheel or gear can fit into（机器的）齿条，齿轨

IDM **go to ˌrack and ˈruin** to get into a bad condition 变得一团糟: *They let the house go to rack and ruin.* 这房子越来越破旧，他们也不管。 ➲ MORE LIKE THIS 13, page R26 ˌ**off the ˈrack** (*NAmE*) (*BrE* ˌ**off the ˈpeg**) (of clothes 衣服) made to a standard average size and not made especially to fit you 成品的；现成的 **on the ˈrack** feeling extreme pressure, anxiety or pain 倍感压力；焦虑万分；痛苦不堪

■ ***verb*** (*also less frequent* **wrack**) [often passive] **~ sb/sth** to make sb suffer great physical or mental pain 使痛苦不堪；使受折磨: *to be racked with/by guilt* 深感内疚 ◇ *Her face was racked with pain.* 她满脸痛苦。◇ *Violent sobs racked her whole body.* 剧烈的抽泣使她全身抽搐。◇ (*BrE*) *a racking cough* 剧烈的咳嗽

IDM **rack your ˈbrain(s)** to think very hard or for a long time about sth 绞尽脑汁；冥思苦想: *She racked her brains, trying to remember exactly what she had said.* 她绞尽脑汁，想要回忆起她到底说过些什么话。

R

PHR V ˌrack ˈup sth (*especially NAmE*) to collect sth, such as profits or losses in a business, or points in a competition 累积；聚集（某物）；累计（得分）：*The company racked up $200 million in losses in two years.* 公司两年内损失累计达 2 亿美元。◇ *In ten years of boxing he racked up a record 176 wins.* 在十年的拳击生涯中，他累计获胜 176 次，创下纪录。

racket /ˈrækɪt/ *noun* **1** [sing.] (*informal*) a loud unpleasant noise 喧哗；吵闹 SYN **din**: *Stop making that terrible racket!* 别吵啦！ **2** [C] (*informal*) a dishonest or illegal way of getting money 诈骗；勒索：***a protection/an extortion/a drugs, etc. racket*** 收取保护费、敲诈、贩毒等勾当 **3** (*also* **rac·quet**) [C] a piece of sports equipment used for hitting the ball, etc. in the games of TENNIS, SQUASH or BADMINTON. It has an OVAL frame, with strings stretched across and down it.（网球、壁球、羽毛球等的）球拍 ➲ VISUAL VOCAB PAGE V48 ➲ COMPARE BAT *n.* (1) **4 rackets, racquets** [U] a game for two or four people, similar to SQUASH, played with rackets and a small hard ball in a COURT with four walls 墙网球

rack·et·eer /ˌrækəˈtɪə(r); *NAmE* -ˈtɪr/ *noun* (*disapproving*) a person who makes money through dishonest or illegal activities 诈骗者；非法获取钱财者 ▸ **rack·et·eer·ing** *noun* [U]

ˈrack rate *noun* (*especially NAmE*) the standard price of a hotel room（旅馆的）标准房租，原定房租

ra·con·teur /ˌrækɒnˈtɜː(r); *NAmE* -kɑːn-/ *noun* a person who is good at telling stories in an interesting and amusing way 善于讲故事的人

ra·coon = RACCOON

rac·quet = RACKET (3)

rac·quet·ball /ˈrækɪtbɔːl/ *noun* [U] a game played especially in the US by two or four players on a COURT with four walls, using RACKETS and a small hollow rubber ball 美式墙网球（二人或四人对垒，场地四面有墙，使用球拍和空心小橡皮球）

racy /ˈreɪsi/ *adj.* (**raci·er**, **raci·est**) having a style that is exciting and amusing, sometimes in a way that is connected with sex（风格）活泼的；不雅的：*a racy novel* 带荤的小说

rad /ræd/ *adj.*, *noun*

■ ***adj.*** (*old-fashioned, slang, especially NAmE*) very good 非常棒的；精彩的

■ ***noun*** (*physics* 物) a unit for measuring the effect of RADIATION 拉德（辐射吸收剂量单位）

radar /ˈreɪdɑː(r)/ *noun* [U] a system that uses radio waves to find the position and movement of objects, for example planes and ships, when they cannot be seen 雷达：*They located the ship by radar.* 他们通过雷达确定了船只的位置。◇ *a radar screen* 雷达显示屏 ➲ COMPARE SONAR

IDM **below/under the ˈradar** used to say that people are not aware of sth 在视线以外的；未引起注意的：*Experts say a lot of corporate crime stays under the radar.* 专家说许多公司犯罪还没有为人所注意到。 **on/off the ˈradar screen** used to say that people's attention is on or not on sth 受 / 不受人关注：*The issue of terrorism is back on the radar screen.* 恐怖主义问题重新受人关注。

ˈradar trap *noun* = SPEED TRAP

rad·dled /ˈrædld/ *adj.* (*BrE*) (of a person, their face, etc. 人、面容等) looking very tired 疲劳的；疲倦的 SYN **worn**

ra·dial /ˈreɪdiəl/ *adj.*, *noun*

■ ***adj.*** having a pattern of lines, etc. that go out from a central point towards the edge of a circle 放射状的；辐射状的：*the radial pattern of public transport facilities* 呈辐射状分布的公共交通设施 ▸ **ra·di·al·ly** /-iəli/ *adv.*

■ ***noun*** (*BrE also* ˌ**radial ˈtyre**) (*NAmE also* ˌ**radial ˈtire**) a car tyre with strong parts inside that point away from the outside part and make the tyre stronger and safer 辐射式轮胎；子午线轮胎

ra·dian /ˈreɪdiən/ *noun* (*geometry* 几何) a unit used to measure an angle, equal to the angle at the centre of a circle whose ARC is the same length as the circle's RADIUS 弧度

ra·di·ance /ˈreɪdiəns/ *noun* [U] **1** a special bright quality that shows in sb's face, for example because they are very happy or healthy 容光焕发；红光满面 **2** warm light shining from sth（散发出来的）光辉

ra·di·ant /ˈreɪdiənt/ *adj.* **1** showing great happiness, love or health 喜气洋洋的；容光焕发的；面色红润的：*a radiant smile* 喜气洋洋的微笑 ◇ *The bride looked radiant.* 新娘看上去满面春风。◇ ~ **with sth** *She was radiant with health.* 她身体健康，容光焕发。 **2** giving a warm bright light 灿烂的；光芒四射的：*The sun was radiant in a clear blue sky.* 湛蓝的天空阳光灿烂。 **3** [only before noun] (*specialist*) sent out in RAYS from a central point 辐射的；放射的：*the **radiant heat/energy** of the sun* 太阳的辐射热 / 辐射能 ▸ **ra·di·ant·ly** *adv.*：*radiantly happy* 喜气洋洋 ◇ *He smiled radiantly.* 他喜笑颜开。

ra·di·ate /ˈreɪdieɪt/ *verb* **1** [T, I] ~ **(sth)** | ~ **(from sb)** if a person **radiates** a particular quality or emotion, or if it **radiates** from them, people can see it very clearly（使品质或情感）显出，流露：*He radiated self-confidence and optimism.* 他显得自信乐观。 **2** [I, T] ~ **(from sth)** | ~ **(sth)** if sth **radiates** heat, light or energy or heat, etc. **radiates** from it, the heat is sent out in all directions（使热、光、能量）辐射，放射，发散 SYN **give off sth**: *Heat radiates from the stove.* 炉子的热向外散发。 **3** [I] + **adv./prep.** (of lines, etc. 直线等) to spread out in all directions from a central point 自中心辐射出；向周围伸展：*Five roads radiate from the square.* 五条道路由广场向外延伸。◇ *The pain started in my stomach and radiated all over my body.* 我起初只是肚子疼，后来全身都疼。

ra·di·ation /ˌreɪdiˈeɪʃn/ *noun* **1** [U, C] powerful and very dangerous RAYS that are sent out from RADIOACTIVE substances 辐射；放射线：***high levels/doses of radiation*** *that damage cells* 损害细胞的高强度辐射 ◇ *the link between exposure to radiation and childhood cancer* 接触辐射与儿童恶性肿瘤之间的联系 ◇ *a radiation leak from a nuclear power station* 核电站的辐射泄漏 ◇ *radiation sickness* 辐射病 ◇ *the radiations emitted by radium* 镭释放出的放射线 **2** [U] heat, energy, etc. that is sent out in the form of RAYS 辐射的热（或能量等）：*ultraviolet radiation* 紫外线辐射 ◇ *electromagnetic radiation from power lines* 输电线的电磁辐射 **3** (*also* ˌ**radiˈation therapy**) [U] the treatment of cancer and other diseases using radiation 放射疗法 ➲ COMPARE CHEMOTHERAPY, RADIOTHERAPY

ra·di·ator /ˈreɪdieɪtə(r)/ *noun* **1** a hollow metal device for heating rooms. Radiators are usually connected by pipes through which hot water is sent. 散热器；暖气片：*a central heating system with a radiator in each room* 每个房间都配有一个散热器的中央供暖系统 ➲ VISUAL VOCAB PAGE V22 **2** a device for cooling the engine of a vehicle or an aircraft（车辆或飞行发动机的）冷却器，水箱

rad·ical AW /ˈrædɪkl/ *adj.*, *noun*

■ ***adj.*** [usually before noun] **1** concerning the most basic and important parts of sth; thorough and complete 根本的；彻底的；完全的 SYN **far-reaching**: *the need for **radical changes** in education* 对教育进行彻底变革的需要 ◇ *demands for radical reform of the law* 彻底改变法律的要求 ◇ *radical differences between the sexes* 两性间的根本差异 **2** new, different and likely to have a great effect 全新的；不同凡响的：*radical ideas* 不同凡响的观点 ◇ *a radical solution to the problem* 解决问题的全新方法 ◇ *radical proposals* 有创见的建议 **3** in favour of thorough and complete political or social change 激进的；极端的：*the radical wing of the party* 党内的激进派 ◇ *radical politicians/students/writers* 激进的政治人物 / 学生 / 作家 ➲ WORDFINDER NOTE AT SYSTEM **4** (*old-fashioned, NAmE, slang*) very good 很好；非常好 ▸ **rad·ic·al·ly** AW /-kli/ *adv.*：*The new methods are radically different from the old.* 新的方法迥然不同于旧的方法。◇ *Attitudes have changed radically.* 态度发生了根本的变化。

R

■ ***noun*** **1** a person with radical opinions 激进分子：*political radicals* 政治激进分子 **2** (*chemistry* 化) a group of atoms that behave as a single unit in a number of COMPOUNDS 游离基；自由基 ➲ SEE ALSO FREE RADICAL

ˌradical ˈchic *noun* [U] fashionable LEFT-WING views; the people, behaviour and way of life connected with these views 时髦的左派观点；时髦左派（或行为、生活方式）

rad·ic·al·ism /ˈrædɪkəlɪzəm/ *noun* [U] belief in RADICAL ideas and principles 激进主义

rad·ic·al·ize (*BrE also* **-ise**) /ˈrædɪkəlaɪz/ *verb* **~ sb/sth** to make people more willing to consider new and different policies, ideas, etc.; to make people more RADICAL in their political opinions 使人标新立异地考虑（政策或观点等）；使激进：*Recent events have radicalized opinion on educational matters.* 最近发生的事使人们对教育问题的看法有了全新的改变。

rad·icchio /ræˈdiːkiəʊ; *NAmE* -kioʊ/ *noun* [U] a type of CHICORY (= a leaf vegetable) with dark red leaves 紫叶菊苣

radii PL. OF RADIUS

radio 🔑 /ˈreɪdiəʊ; *NAmE* -oʊ/ *noun*, *verb*

■ ***noun*** **1** 🔑 (*often* **the radio**) [U, sing.] the activity of broadcasting programmes for people to listen to; the programmes that are broadcast 无线电广播；无线电广播节目：*The interview was broadcast **on radio** and television.* 广播和电视都报道了这次会见。◇ *The play was written specially for radio.* 这出戏是专为无线电广播而写的。◇ ***I listen to the radio** on the way to work.* 我在上班的路上听广播。◇ *Did you hear the interview with him **on the radio**?* 你有没有在广播里听到采访他的情况？◇ ***local/national radio*** 地方 / 国家无线电广播 ◇ ***a radio programme/station*** 广播节目 / 电台

> WORDFINDER 联想词：air, announce, bulletin, jingle, phone-in, podcast, **programme**, public service broadcasting, station

2 🔑 [C] a piece of equipment used for listening to programmes that are broadcast to the public 收音机：*to **turn the radio on/off*** 打开 / 关上收音机 ◇ *a car radio* 汽车收音机 ➲ SEE ALSO CLOCK RADIO **3** 🔑 [U] the process of sending and receiving messages through the air using ELECTROMAGNETIC waves 无线电传送；无线电通信：*He was unable to contact Blake **by radio**.* 他未能通过无线电和布莱克取得联系。◇ *to keep in **radio contact*** 保持无线电联系 ◇ ***radio signals/waves*** 无线电信号 / 电波 **4** 🔑 [C] a piece of equipment, for example on ships or planes, for sending and receiving radio signals 无线电收发报机：*to hear a gale warning on/over the ship's radio* 在船上的无线电收发报机中听到大风警报

■ ***verb*** (**ra·dio·ing**, **ra·dioed**, **ra·dioed**) [I, T] **~ (sth)** | **~ that...** to send a message to sb by radio（用无线电）发送，传送：*The police officer radioed for help.* 警察用无线电呼救。◇ *The warning was radioed to headquarters.* 通过无线电向总部发出了警报。

radio- /ˈreɪdiəʊ; *NAmE* -oʊ/ *combining form* (in nouns, adjectives and adverbs 构成名词、形容词和副词) **1** connected with radio waves or broadcasting 无线电波的；无线电广播的：*radio-controlled* 无线电遥控的 **2** connected with RADIOACTIVITY 放射的；辐射的：*radiotherapy* 放射疗法

radio·active /ˌreɪdiəʊˈæktɪv; *NAmE* -oʊˈæk-/ *adj.* sending out harmful RADIATION caused when the NUCLEI (= central parts) of atoms are broken up 放射性的；有辐射的 ▶ **radio·activ·ity** /ˌreɪdiəʊækˈtɪvəti; *NAmE* -oʊæk-/ *noun* [U]: *the study of radioactivity* 放射性研究 ◇ *a rise in the level of radioactivity* 辐射强度的增加

ˌradio aˈstronomy *noun* [U] the part of ASTRONOMY that studies radio waves sent out by objects in space 射电天文学；电波天文学

ˈradio button *noun* (*computing* 计) a small circle that you click on in order to make a particular choice. The radio button is then marked with a dot to show that it has been selected. 单选按钮

radio·car·bon /ˌreɪdiəʊˈkɑːbən; *NAmE* -oʊˈkɑːrb-/ *noun* [U] (*specialist*) a RADIOACTIVE form of CARBON that is present in the materials of which living things are formed, used in CARBON DATING 放射性碳（碳的放射性同位素，用以测定物体的年代）：*radiocarbon analysis* 放射性碳分析

ˌradiocarbon ˈdating *noun* [U] (*formal*) = CARBON DATING

radio·chem·is·try /ˌreɪdiəʊˈkemɪstri; *NAmE* -oʊˈk-/ *noun* [U] the area of chemistry which is concerned with RADIOACTIVE substances 放射化学 ▶ **radio·chem·ical** /ˌreɪdiəʊˈkemɪkl; *NAmE* -oʊˈk-/ *adj.*

ˌradio-conˈtrolled *adj.* controlled from a distance by radio signals 无线电操纵的；无线电遥控的

radi·og·raph·er /ˌreɪdiˈɒɡrəfə(r); *NAmE* -ˈɑːɡ-/ *noun* a person working in a hospital whose job is to take X-RAY photographs or to use X-RAYS to treat some illnesses, such as cancer * X 光摄影师；放射治疗师

radi·og·raphy /ˌreɪdiˈɒɡrəfi; *NAmE* -ˈɑːɡ-/ *noun* [U] the process or job of taking X-RAY photographs * X 光照相

radio·iso·tope /ˌreɪdiəʊˈaɪsətəʊp; *NAmE* ˌreɪdioʊˈaɪsətoʊp/ *noun* (*chemistry* 化) a form of a chemical element which sends out RADIATION 放射性同位素

ˈradio jockey *noun* (*IndE*) a person whose job is to introduce different sections of a programme or play recorded popular music on the radio 电台（音乐）节目主持人

radi·olo·gist /ˌreɪdiˈɒlədʒɪst; *NAmE* -ˈɑːlə-/ *noun* a doctor who is trained in radiology 放射科医生；X 光科的医生 ➲ WORDFINDER NOTE AT SPECIALIST

radi·ology /ˌreɪdiˈɒlədʒi; *NAmE* -ˈɑːlə-/ *noun* [U] the study and use of different types of RADIATION in medicine, for example to treat diseases 放射学；放射医疗

radio·met·ric /ˌreɪdiəʊˈmetrɪk; *NAmE* -dioʊ-/ *adj.* relating to a measurement of RADIOACTIVITY 辐射度测量的 ▶ **radio·met·ric·ally** /-ɪkli/ *adv.*: *These rocks have been dated radiometrically at two billion years old.* 经辐射能探测，这些岩石形成于 20 亿年前。

ˌradio-ˈtelephone *noun* a telephone that works by sending and receiving radio signals, used especially in cars, boats, etc. 无线电话

ˌradio ˈtelescope *noun* a piece of equipment that receives radio waves from space and is used for finding stars and the position of SPACECRAFT, etc. 射电望远镜

radio·ther·apy /ˌreɪdiəʊˈθerəpi; *NAmE* -oʊˈθe-/ *noun* [U] the treatment of disease by RADIATION 放射疗法：*a course of radiotherapy* 放射疗程 ➲ COMPARE CHEMOTHERAPY ➲ WORDFINDER NOTE AT CURE ▶ **radio·thera·pist** *noun*

ˈradio wave *noun* a low-energy ELECTROMAGNETIC wave, especially when used for long-distance communication 无线电波

rad·ish /ˈrædɪʃ/ *noun* [C, U] a small crisp red or white root vegetable with a strong taste, eaten raw in salads 樱桃萝卜：*a bunch of radishes* 一把樱桃萝卜 ➲ VISUAL VOCAB PAGE V34

ra·dium /ˈreɪdiəm/ *noun* [U] (*symb.* **Ra**) a chemical element. Radium is a white RADIOACTIVE metal used in the treatment of diseases such as cancer. 镭

ra·dius /ˈreɪdiəs/ *noun* (*pl.* **radii** /ˈreɪdiaɪ/) **1** a straight line between the centre of a circle and any point on its outer edge; the length of this line 半径（长度） ➲ PICTURE AT CIRCLE ➲ COMPARE DIAMETER (1) **2** a round area that covers the distance mentioned from a central point 半径范围；周围：*They deliver to within a 5-mile radius of the store.* 他们给店铺方圆 5 英里内送货上门。**3** (*anatomy* 解) the shorter bone of the two bones in the lower part of the arm between the elbow and the wrist, on the same

R

side as the thumb 桡骨 ➲ VISUAL VOCAB PAGE V64 ➲ SEE ALSO ULNA

radon /ˈreɪdɒn; *NAmE* -dɑːn/ *noun* [U] (*symb.* **Rn**) a chemical element. Radon is a RADIOACTIVE gas used in the treatment of diseases such as cancer. 氡（放射性化学元素）

RAF /ˌɑːr eɪ ˈef; ræf/ *abbr.* Royal Air Force (the British AIR FORCE)（英国）皇家空军：*He was an RAF pilot.* 他是皇家空军飞行员。

Raf·fer·ty's rules /ˈræfətiz ruːlz; *NAmE* -fərt-/ *noun* [pl.] (*AustralE, NZE, informal*) no rules at all 毫无章法；全无规则

raf·fia /ˈræfiə/ *noun* [U] soft material that looks like string and is made from the leaves of a type of PALM tree, used for making BASKETS, MATS, etc. or for tying things 酒椰叶纤维（由酒椰棕榈树叶制成，用于编篮子、垫子或捆扎东西等）

raff·ish /ˈræfɪʃ/ *adj.* (of sb's behaviour, clothes, etc. 人的行为、衣着等) not very acceptable according to some social standards, but interesting and attractive 放荡不羁的

raf·fle /ˈræfl/ *noun, verb*

■ *noun* a way of making money for a particular project or organization. People buy tickets with numbers on them and some of these numbers are later chosen to win prizes. 抽彩 ➲ COMPARE LOTTERY (1)

■ *verb* **~ sth** to give sth as a prize in a raffle 抽彩而奖以（物品）

raft /rɑːft; *NAmE* ræft/ *noun* **1** a flat structure made of pieces of wood tied together and used as a boat or floating platform 木排；筏 **2** a small boat made of rubber or plastic that is filled with air 橡皮艇；充气船：*an inflatable raft* 充气橡皮筏 **3** [usually sing.] **~ of sth** (*informal*) a large number or amount of sth 大量；许多：*a whole raft of new proposals* 大量新的提议

raft·er /ˈrɑːftə(r); *NAmE* ˈræf-/ *noun* [C, usually pl.] one of the sloping pieces of wood that support a roof 椽子

raft·ing /ˈrɑːftɪŋ; *NAmE* ˈræft-/ *noun* [U] the sport or activity of travelling down a river on a RAFT 激流划艇（运动）；漂流运动：*We went* ***white-water rafting*** *on the Colorado River.* 我们去了科罗拉多河玩激流漂流。➲ VISUAL VOCAB PAGE V54

rag /ræg/ *noun, verb*

■ *noun* **1** [C, U] a piece of old, often torn, cloth used especially for cleaning things 抹布；破布 ➲ SEE ALSO GLAD RAGS **2** [C] (*informal, usually disapproving*) a newspaper that you believe to be of low quality 质量低劣的报纸；小报：*the local rag* 地方小报 **3** [C] a piece of RAGTIME music 雷格泰姆乐曲 **4** (*BrE*) [U, C] an event or a series of events organized by students each year to raise money for charity（学生每年组织的）慈善募捐活动：*rag week* 学生募捐周

IDM **in ˈrags** wearing very old torn clothes 衣衫褴褛；穿得破旧：*The children were dressed in rags.* 孩子们穿着破衣烂衫。 **(from) ˌrags to ˈriches** from being extremely poor to being very rich 从赤贫到巨富：*a rags-to-riches story* 穷人发迹史 ◇ *Hers was a classic tale of rags to riches.* 她的经历是从赤贫到富有的一个典型例子。 **ˌlose your ˈrag** (*BrE, informal*) to get angry 发怒；生气 ➲ MORE AT WAVE *v.*

■ *verb* (**-gg-**) **~ sb (about sth)** (*old-fashioned*) to laugh at and/or play tricks on sb 嘲笑；捉弄 SYN **tease**

PHR V **ˈrag on sb** (*NAmE, informal*) to complain to sb about their behaviour, work, etc. 向某人抱怨（或埋怨、发牢骚）

raga /ˈrɑːgə/ *noun* a traditional pattern of notes used in Indian music; a piece of music based on one of these patterns 拉加（印度音乐中的传统曲调）；拉加曲

raga·muf·fin (*also* **ragga·muf·fin**) /ˈrægəmʌfɪn/ *noun* **1** [C] a person, usually a child, who is wearing old clothes that are torn and dirty 衣着破旧肮脏的人（尤指儿童） **2** [C] (*especially BrE*) a person who likes or performs RAGGA music 雷戈音乐爱好者；雷戈音乐表演者 **3** [U] = RAGGA

ˌrag-and-ˈbone man *noun* (*BrE*) (especially in the past) a man who travels around buying things that people no longer want and selling them to other people（尤指旧时）沿街买卖旧货的行贩

rag·bag /ˈrægbæg/ *noun* [sing.] a collection of things that appear to have little connection with each other 大杂烩；杂七杂八的东西：*a ragbag of ideas* 杂乱无章的观点

ˌrag ˈdoll *noun* a soft DOLL made from pieces of cloth 碎布制玩偶；布娃娃 ➲ VISUAL VOCAB PAGE V41

rage /reɪdʒ/ *noun, verb*

■ *noun* **1** [U, C] a feeling of violent anger that is difficult to control 暴怒；狂怒：*His face was dark with rage.* 他气得面色铁青。◇ *to* ***be shaking/trembling/speechless with rage*** 气愤得发抖 / 战栗 / 说不出话来 ◇ *Sue stormed out of the room* ***in a rage.*** 休怒气冲冲地走出了房间。◇ *He* ***flies into a rage*** *if you even mention the subject.* 你只要一提起这个话题，他就会暴跳如雷。 **2** [U] (in compounds 构成复合词) anger and violent behaviour caused by a particular situation（某情况引起的）愤怒，暴力行为：*a case of trolley rage in the supermarket* 超市里一起由手推车引起的暴力事件 ➲ SEE ALSO ROAD RAGE

IDM **be all the ˈrage** (*informal*) to be very popular and fashionable 十分流行；成为时尚；风靡一时

■ *verb* **1** [I, T] to show that you are very angry about sth or with sb, especially by shouting 发怒；怒斥 SYN **rail**: **~ (at/against/about sb/sth)** *He raged against the injustice of it all.* 这一切不公正使他大发怒火。◇ **+ speech** *'That's unfair!' she raged.* "这不公平！" 她愤怒地喊道。 **2** [I] **~ (on)** (of a storm, a battle, an argument, etc. 暴风雨、战斗、争论等) to continue in a violent way 猛烈地继续；激烈进行：*The riots raged for three days.* 暴乱持续了三天。◇ *The blizzard was still raging outside.* 外面暴风雪仍在肆虐。 **3** [I] (**+ adv./prep.**) (of an illness, a fire, etc. 疾病、火焰等) to spread very quickly 迅速蔓延；快速扩散：*Forest fires were raging out of control.* 森林大火正迅速蔓延，无法控制。◇ *A flu epidemic raged through Europe.* 一轮流感席卷了整个欧洲。 **4** [I] (*AustralE, NZE, slang*) to go out and enjoy yourself 外出玩个痛快；出去作乐

ragga /ˈrægə/ (*also* **ragga·muf·fin, raga·muf·fin**) *noun* [U] a type of dance music from the West Indies that contains features of REGGAE and HIP HOP 雷戈（一种源自西印度群岛的舞曲，带有雷盖和嘻哈的特征）

ragga·muf·fin = RAGAMUFFIN

rag·ged /ˈrægɪd/ *adj.* **1** (of clothes 衣服) old and torn 破旧的；褴褛的 SYN **shabby** **2** (of people 人) wearing old or torn clothes 衣衫褴褛的；破衣烂衫的：*ragged children* 衣衫褴褛的孩子们 **3** having an outline, an edge or a surface that is not straight or even（轮廓线、边缘或表面）粗糙的，参差不齐的，不规则的：*ragged clouds* 形状不规则的一朵朵云 ◇ *a ragged coastline* 弯弯曲曲的海岸线 **4** not smooth or controlled 不流畅的；不受控制的：*I could hear the sound of his ragged breathing.* 我能够听到他那急促的呼吸声。◇ *Their performance was still very ragged.* 他们的表演仍然很粗糙。 **5** (*informal*) very tired, especially after physical effort 精疲力竭的；疲惫的 ➲ MORE LIKE THIS 22, page R27 ▶ **rag·ged·ly** *adv.*：*raggedly dressed* 衣着破旧 ◇ *She was breathing raggedly.* 她急促地呼吸着。 **rag·ged·ness** *noun* [U]

IDM **ˌrun sb ˈragged** (*informal*) to make sb do a lot of work or make a big effort so that they become tired 使某人疲于奔命

ra·ging /ˈreɪdʒɪŋ/ *adj.* [only before noun] **1** (of feelings or emotions 感觉或情绪) very strong 强烈的：*a raging appetite/thirst* 极强的食欲；口渴难耐 ◇ *raging jealousy* 强烈的忌妒心 **2** (of natural forces 自然力) very powerful 极其强大的；猛烈的：*a raging storm* 狂风暴雨 ◇ *The stream had become a raging torrent.* 小河变成了一条汹涌的急流。◇ *The building was now a raging inferno.* 这座大楼现在正烈焰熊熊。 **3** (of a pain or an illness 疼痛或疾病) very strong or painful 很严重的；很痛苦的：*a raging headache* 剧烈的头痛 **4** very serious and causing strong feelings

严重激烈的；激发强烈感情的：*His speech has provoked a raging debate.* 他的演讲激起了激烈的争论。

rag·lan /ˈræɡlən/ *adj.* [only before noun] **1** (of a sleeve 衣袖) sewn to the front and back of a coat, sweater, etc. in a line that slopes down from the neck to under the arm 插肩的 **2** (of a coat, sweater, etc. 大衣、毛衣等) having raglan sleeves 有插肩袖的

ra·gout /ræˈɡuː; ˈræɡuː/ *noun* [C, U] (*from French*) a hot dish of meat and vegetables boiled together with various spices（加入各种香料的）蔬菜炖肉

rag·tag /ˈræɡtæɡ/ *adj.* [usually before noun] (*informal*) (of a group of people or an organization 一群人或某组织) not well organized; giving a bad impression 组织散漫的；杂乱的；给人印象差的：*a ragtag band of rebels* 一队叛乱的乌合之众

rag·time /ˈræɡtaɪm/ *noun* [U] an early form of JAZZ, especially for the piano, first played by African American musicians in the early 1900s 雷格泰姆音乐（早期爵士音乐，多在钢琴上演奏，20 世纪初由非洲裔美国音乐家发展而成）

the ˈrag trade *noun* [sing.] (*old-fashioned, informal*) the business of designing, making and selling clothes 服装业；服装生意

rag·weed /ˈræɡwiːd/ *noun* [U] a N American plant with small green flowers that contain a lot of POLLEN, which causes HAY FEVER in some people 豚草（北美植物，其绿色小花含大量花粉，可引起枯草热）

rag·wort /ˈræɡwɜːt; *NAmE* -wɜːrt/ *noun* [U] a wild plant with yellow flowers, poisonous to cows and horses 千里光，狗舌草（开黄色小花，能毒害牛马）

raid /reɪd/ *noun, verb*

■ ***noun* 1 ~ (on sth)** a short surprise attack on an enemy by soldiers, ships or aircraft 突然袭击：*They carried out a bombing raid on enemy bases.* 他们突然出击，轰炸了敌军的基地。➲ COLLOCATIONS AT WAR ➲ SEE ALSO AIR RAID **2 ~ (on sth)** a surprise visit by the police looking for criminals or for illegal goods or drugs 突击检查；突然搜查：*They were arrested during a **dawn raid**.* 在一次清晨的突击搜查中，他们都被捕了。➲ WORDFINDER NOTE AT POLICE **3 ~ (on sth)** an attack on a building, etc. in order to commit a crime 抢劫；打劫：*an armed bank raid* 一起持械抢劫银行案 ➲ SEE ALSO RAM-RAIDING

■ ***verb* 1 ~ sth** (of police 警察) to visit a person or place without warning to look for criminals, illegal goods, drugs, etc. 突击搜捕；突然搜查 **2 ~ sth** (of soldiers, fighting planes, etc. 战士、歼击机等) to attack a place without warning 突袭；偷袭：*Villages along the border are regularly raided.* 边境附近的村庄经常遭受突袭。◇ *a **raiding party*** (= a group of soldiers, etc. that attack a place) 突袭队 **3 ~ sth** to enter a place, usually using force, and steal from it 劫掠；打劫 **SYN** **plunder, ransack**：*Many treasures were lost when the tombs were raided in the last century.* 上世纪这些坟墓遭到偷盗，很多财宝都失踪了。◇ (*humorous*) *I caught him raiding the fridge again* (= taking food from it). 我撞见他又在扫荡冰箱里的食物。

raid·er /ˈreɪdə(r)/ *noun* a person who makes a criminal raid on a place 袭击者；抢劫者：***armed/masked raiders*** 武装 / 蒙面袭击者

rail 🔑 /reɪl/ *noun, verb*

■ ***noun* 1** 🔑 [C] a wooden or metal bar placed around sth as a barrier or to provide support 栏杆；扶手；围栏：*She leaned on the ship's rail and gazed out to sea.* 她靠着船上的护栏，凝望大海。➲ SEE ALSO GUARD RAIL, HANDRAIL **2** 🔑 [C] a bar fixed to the wall for hanging things on（固定在墙上用以挂物品的）横杆：*a picture/curtain/towel rail* 挂图画 / 窗帘 / 毛巾用的横杆 ➲ VISUAL VOCAB PAGE V24 **3** 🔑 [C, usually pl.] each of the two metal bars that form the track that trains run on 铁轨；轨道 ➲ VISUAL VOCAB PAGE V63 **4** 🔑 [U] (often before another noun 常用于另一名词前) railways/railroads as a means of transport 铁路；铁道：*to travel **by rail*** 乘火车 ◇ *rail travel/services/fares* 铁路旅行 / 服务 / 费用 ◇ *a rail link/network* 铁路连接；铁路网

IDM **get back on the ˈrails** (*informal*) to become successful again after a period of failure, or to begin functioning normally again 恢复常轨；东山再起 **go off the ˈrails** (*informal*) **1** to start behaving in a strange or unacceptable manner, for example, drinking a lot or taking drugs 举止怪异；行为出轨 **2** to lose control and stop functioning correctly 失去控制；无法正常运行：*The company has gone badly off the rails in recent years.* 这家公司最近几年已经陷于严重瘫痪。➲ MORE AT JUMP *v.*

■ ***verb*** [I, T] **~ (at/against sth/sb)** | **+ speech** (*formal*) to complain about sth/sb in a very angry way 怒斥；责骂；抱怨 **SYN** **rage**：*She railed against the injustice of it all.* 她大骂此事太不公正。

PHR V **ˌrail sth ˈin/ˈoff** to separate an area or object from others by placing rails around it 用围栏围住；用围栏隔开

rail·car /ˈreɪlkɑː(r)/ *noun* = CAR (2)

rail·card /ˈreɪlkɑːd; *NAmE* -kɑːrd/ *noun* (*BrE*) a card that allows sb to travel by train at a reduced price 火车乘坐优惠卡

rail·head /ˈreɪlhed/ *noun* (*specialist*) the point at which a railway/railroad ends 铁路终点站；铁路末端

rail·ing /ˈreɪlɪŋ/ *noun* [C, usually pl.] a fence made of vertical metal bars; one of these bars 金属围栏；金属栏杆：*iron railings* 铁栏杆 ◇ *I chained my bike to the park railings.* 我用链子把自行车锁在公园的围栏上了。◇ *She leaned out over the railing.* 她靠在栏杆上探出身去。➲ VISUAL VOCAB PAGE V3

rail·lery /ˈreɪləri/ *noun* [U] (*formal*) friendly joking about a person 善意的玩笑；戏谑；逗趣

rail·man /ˈreɪlmən/ *noun* (*pl.* **-men** /-mən/) (*BrE*) = RAILWAYMAN

rail·road 🔑 /ˈreɪlrəʊd; *NAmE* -roʊd/ *noun, verb*

■ ***noun*** (*NAmE*) (*BrE* **rail·way**) **1** 🔑 (*BrE also* **ˈrailway line**) a track with rails on which trains run 铁路；铁道：*railroad tracks* 铁路轨道 **2** 🔑 a system of tracks, together with the trains that run on them, and the organization and people needed to operate them 铁路系统；铁路公司；铁道部门：*This town got a lot bigger when the railroad came in the 1860s.* 自从 19 世纪 60 年代通了火车之后，这座城镇变大了许多。

■ ***verb* 1 ~ sb (into sth/into doing sth)** to force sb to do sth before they have had enough time to decide whether or not they want to do it 迫使…仓促行事；强迫…做 **SYN** **bulldoze** **2 ~ sth (through/through sth)** to make a group of people accept a decision, law, etc. quickly by putting pressure on them 强使（决定、法律等）草率通过：*The bill was railroaded through the House.* 议院不得已草率通过了这项提案。 **3 ~ sb** (*NAmE*) to decide that sb is guilty of a crime, without giving them a fair trial 轻率判处

ˈrailroad crossing (*NAmE*) (*BrE* **ˌlevel ˈcrossing**) *noun* a place where a road crosses a railway/railroad line（公路与铁路交会的）道口，平面交叉，平交道

rail·road·er /ˈreɪlrəʊdə(r); *NAmE* -roʊd-/ (*NAmE*) (*BrE* **rail·way·man, rail·man**) *noun* a person who works for a rail company 铁路工人；铁路员工

rail·way 🔑 /ˈreɪlweɪ/ (*NAmE* **rail·road**) *noun* **1** 🔑 (*BrE also* **ˈrailway line**) a track with rails on which trains run 铁路；铁道：*The railway is still under construction.* 这条铁路仍在建设之中。◇ *a disused railway* 被废弃的铁路 **2** 🔑 a system of tracks, together with the trains that run on them, and the organization and people needed to operate them 铁路公司；铁道部门；铁路系统：*Her father worked on the railways.* 她父亲在铁路部门工作。◇ *a **railway station/worker/company*** 火车站；铁路工人 / 公司 ◇ *the Midland Railway* 米德兰铁路公司 ◇ *a model railway* 铁路模型

rail·way·man /ˈreɪlweɪmən/ *noun* (*pl.* **-men** /-mən/) (*also* **rail·man**) (*both BrE*) (*NAmE* **rail·road·er**) a person who works for a rail company 铁路工人；铁路员工

R

rai·ment /ˈreɪmənt/ *noun* [U] (*old use*) clothing 衣服；服装

rain /reɪn/ *noun, verb*

■*noun* **1** [U, sing.] water that falls from the sky in separate drops 雨；雨水：*There will be rain in all parts tomorrow.* 明天，各地区都会有雨。◇ *Rain is forecast for the weekend.* 预报周末有雨。◇ *Don't go out* ***in the rain.*** 下雨呢，别出去了。◇ *It's* ***pouring with rain*** (= raining very hard). 大雨倾盆。◇ ***heavy/torrential/driving rain*** 大雨；倾盆大雨 ◇ *The rain poured down.* 雨瓢泼而下。◇ ***It looks like rain*** (= as if it is going to rain). 好像要下雨。◇ *A light rain began to fall.* 开始下小雨。◇ *I think I felt a drop of rain.* 我好像感觉到掉雨点儿了。 ➲ COLLOCATIONS AT WEATHER ➲SEE ALSO ACID RAIN, RAINY

WORDFINDER 联想词： downpour, drought, flash flood, monsoon, precipitation, puddle, shelter, shower, squall

2 the rains [pl.] the season of heavy continuous rain in tropical countries（热带地区的）雨季：*The rains come in September.* 雨季九月份开始。 **3** [sing.] **~ of sth** a large number of things falling from the sky at the same time 雨点般降落的东西：*a* ***rain of arrows/stones*** 箭密如雨；铺天盖地而来的石头

IDM **come ˌrain, come ˈshine | (come) ˌrain or ˈshine** whether there is rain or sun; whatever happens 不论是雨或是晴；不管发生什么事：*He goes jogging every morning, rain or shine.* 他每天早晨出去跑步，风雨无阻。 ➲ MORE AT RIGHT *adj.*

▼VOCABULARY BUILDING 词汇扩充

Rain and storms 表示雨、下雨和恶劣天气的词

Rain 雨

- **Drizzle** is fine light rain. * drizzle 指毛毛细雨。
- A **shower** is a short period of rain. * shower 指阵雨。
- A **downpour** or a **cloudburst** is a heavy fall of rain that often starts suddenly. * downpour 或 cloudburst 指倾盆大雨、大暴雨、骤雨。
- When it is raining very hard you can say that it is **pouring**. In informal *BrE* you can also say that it is **bucketing down** or **chucking it down**. You can also say: **The heavens opened**. 大雨倾盆可用 it is pouring。非正式英式英语亦可用 it is bucketing down 或者 it is chucking it down。还可以说 The heavens opened。

Storms 暴风雨

- A **cyclone** and a **typhoon** are types of violent tropical storms with very strong winds. * cyclone 指气旋，typhoon 指台风。
- A **hurricane** has very strong winds and is usually at sea. * hurricane 通常指海上的飓风。
- A **monsoon** is a period of very heavy rain in particular countries, or the wind that brings this rain. * monsoon 指某些国家的雨季、季节性暴雨或带来暴雨的季风。
- A **squall** is a sudden strong, violent wind, usually in a rain or snow storm. * squall 通常指在暴风雨或暴风雪中突起的飑。
- A **tornado** (or *informal* **twister**) has very strong winds which move in a circle, often with a long narrow cloud. * tornado（或非正式用语 twister）指龙卷风。
- A **whirlwind** moves very fast in a spinning movement and causes a lot of damage. * whirlwind 指旋风。
- A **blizzard** is a snow storm with very strong winds. * blizzard 指暴风雪。
- **Tempest** is used mainly in literary language to describe a violent storm. * tempest 主要为文学用语，指暴风雨、风暴、暴风雪。

■*verb* **1** [I] when **it rains**, water falls from the sky in drops 下雨：*Is it raining?* 下雨了吗？◇ *It had been raining hard all night.* 大雨下了一整夜。◇ *It hardly rained at all last summer.* 去年夏天几乎没怎么下雨。◇ *It started to rain.* 开始下雨了。 **2** [I, T] to fall or to make sth fall on sb/sth in large quantities （使）大量降落，雨点般落下：**~ (down) (on sb/sth)** *Bombs rained (down) on the city's streets.* 炸弹雨点儿似的落在这座城市的街道上。◇ *Falling debris rained on us from above.* 碎片从上面像雨点儿一样落在我们身上。◇ *He covered his face as the blows rained down on him* (= he was hit repeatedly). 他在遭到雨点般的击打时护住了自己的脸。◇ **~ sth (down) (on sb/sth)** *The volcano erupted, raining hot ash over a wide area.* 火山喷发，将炽热的火山灰洒落在一大片地域上。

IDM **be raining cats and ˈdogs** (*informal*) to be raining heavily 下倾盆大雨 **it never rains but it ˈpours** (*BrE*) (*NAmE* **when it rains, it ˈpours**) (*saying*) used to say that when one bad thing happens to you, other bad things happen soon after 不雨则已，一雨倾盆；祸不单行 **ˌrain on sb's ˈparade** (*NAmE, informal*) to spoil sth for sb 煞风景；破坏原定的计划

PHR V **be ˌrained ˈoff** (*BrE*) (*NAmE* **be ˌrained ˈout**) (of an event 赛事) to be cancelled or to have to stop because it is raining 因雨取消（或中断）：*The game has been rained off again.* 比赛又一次因雨而被取消。

ˈrain barrel (*NAmE*) (*BrE* **ˈwater butt**) *noun* a large BARREL for collecting rain as it flows off a roof（屋檐下的）雨水桶 ➲VISUAL VOCAB PAGE V20

rain·bow /ˈreɪnbəʊ; *NAmE* -boʊ/ *noun* a curved band of different colours that appears in the sky when the sun shines through rain 虹；彩虹：*all the colours of the rainbow* 彩虹的各种颜色

ˌrainbow coaˈlition *noun* a political group formed by different parties who agree to work together, especially one that includes one or more very small parties（由不同政党组成，尤指包括小党派的）彩虹联盟

ˌrainbow ˈnation *noun* [usually sing.] (*approving*) a name used to describe the people of South Africa because of their many races and cultures 彩虹之国（指南非，因其多种族、多文化而得名）

ˌrainbow ˈtrout *noun* [C, U] type of TROUT (= a fish that is often eaten as food, and often caught in the sport of fishing) 虹鳟

ˈrain check *noun* (*especially NAmE*) a ticket that can be used later if a game, show, etc. is cancelled because of rain（比赛、演出等因雨取消时）可延期使用的票

IDM **take a rain check (on sth)** (*informal, especially NAmE*) to refuse an offer or invitation but say that you might accept it later （婉辞邀请）下次吧，以后再说：*'Are you coming for a drink?' 'Can I take a rain check?—I must get this finished tonight.'* "你来喝一杯吧？""下次吧，好吗？今晚我得把这项工作做完。"

rain·coat /ˈreɪnkəʊt; *NAmE* -koʊt/ *noun* a long light coat that keeps you dry in the rain 雨衣 ➲VISUAL VOCAB PAGE V66

ˈrain date *noun* (*NAmE*) an alternative date when an event will take place if it has to be cancelled on the original date because of rain 遇雨改期日：*July 15 is our annual fun day (rain date July 22).* * 7 月 15 日是我们一年一度的游乐日（遇雨则改至 7 月 22 日）。

rain·drop /ˈreɪndrɒp; *NAmE* -drɑːp/ *noun* a single drop of rain 雨点；雨滴

rain·fall /ˈreɪnfɔːl/ *noun* [U, sing.] the total amount of rain that falls in a particular area in a particular amount of time; an occasion when rain falls 降雨量；下雨：*There has been below average rainfall this month.* 这个月的降雨低于平均降雨量。◇ *an average annual rainfall of 10 cm* * 10 厘米的年平均降雨量 ➲WORDFINDER NOTE AT CLIMATE

rain·for·est /ˈreɪnfɒrɪst; *NAmE* -fɔːr-; -fɑːr-/ *noun* [C, U] a thick forest in tropical parts of the world that have a lot of rain（热带）雨林：*the Amazon rainforest* 亚马孙雨林 ➲ COMPARE CLOUD FOREST

rain·maker /ˈreɪnmeɪkə(r)/ *noun* **1** (*especially NAmE, business* 商) a person who makes a business grow and become successful 使公司生意兴隆的人；成功的企业家 **2** a person who is believed to have the power to make rain fall, especially among Native Americans（尤指印第安人的）求雨法师

rain·out /ˈreɪnaʊt/ *noun* (*NAmE*) an occasion when bad weather prevents an event from starting or finishing 因雨取消；因雨中止

rain·proof /ˈreɪnpruːf/ *adj.* that can keep rain out 防雨的：*a rainproof jacket* 防雨夹克

rain·storm /ˈreɪnstɔːm; *NAmE* -stɔːrm/ *noun* a heavy fall of rain 暴风雨

rain·water /ˈreɪnwɔːtə(r); *NAmE also* -wɑːtər/ *noun* [U] water that has fallen as rain 雨水：*a barrel for collecting rainwater* 接雨水的桶

rainy /ˈreɪni/ *adj.* (**rain·ier**, **rain·iest**) having or bringing a lot of rain 阴雨的；多雨的：*a rainy day* 阴雨天 ◇ *the rainy season* 雨季 ◇ *the rainiest place in Britain* 英国最多雨的地区

IDM **save, keep, etc. sth for a ˌrainy ˈday** to save sth, especially money, for a time when you will really need it 有备无患；未雨绸缪

raise /reɪz/ *verb, noun*

■ ***verb***

• **MOVE UPWARDS** 提升 **1** **~ sth** to lift or move sth to a higher level 提升；举起；提起：*She raised the gun and fired.* 她举枪射击。◇ *He raised a hand in greeting.* 他扬起手表示问候。◇ *She raised her eyes from her work.* 她停下工作，抬起头看了看。**OPP** **lower**[1] ➲ NOTE AT RISE **2** **~ sth/sb/yourself (+ adv./prep.)** to move sth/sb/yourself to a vertical position（使）直立，站立：*Somehow we managed to raise her to her feet.* 不管怎样，我们终于让她站了起来。◇ *He raised himself up on one elbow.* 他用一只胳膊肘支起身子。**OPP** **lower**[1]

• **INCREASE** 增加 **3** **~ sth (to sth)** to increase the amount or level of sth 增加，提高（数量、水平等）：*to raise salaries/prices/taxes* 提高薪水 / 价格 / 税金 ◇ *They raised their offer to $500.* 他们将出价抬高到 500 美元。◇ *How can we raise standards in schools?* 我们怎样才能提高学校的水平？◇ *Don't tell her about the job until you know for sure—we don't want to* ***raise her hopes*** (= make her hope too much). 没确定之前别告诉她工作的事，我们不想让她期望过高。◇ *I've never heard him even* ***raise his voice*** (= speak louder because he was angry). 我甚至从没听到他提高过嗓门儿。

• **COLLECT MONEY/PEOPLE** 筹募钱财；征集人员 **4** **~ sth** to bring or collect money or people together; to manage to get or form sth 筹募；征集；召集；组建：*to raise a loan* 筹集贷款 ◇ *We are* ***raising money*** *for charity.* 我们在进行慈善募捐。◇ *He set about* ***raising an army.*** 他着手组建一支部队。➲ SEE ALSO FUNDRAISER

• **MENTION SUBJECT** 提及主题 **5** **~ sth** to mention sth for people to discuss or sb to deal with 提及；提起（课题）**SYN** **broach**: *The book* ***raises*** *many important* ***questions.*** 这本书谈到了许多重要问题。◇ *I'm glad you* ***raised the subject*** *of money.* 我很高兴你提到了钱这个话题。

• **CAUSE** 引起 **6** **~ sth** to cause or produce sth; to make sth appear 引起；导致；使出现：*to raise doubts in people's minds* 引起人们的怀疑 ◇ *The plans for the new development have raised angry protests from local residents.* 新的开发计划惹得当地居民愤怒抗议。◇ *It wasn't an easy audience but he* ***raised a laugh*** *with his joke.* 虽然这些观众很难逗乐，但他的笑话还是引起了一阵笑声。◇ *It had been a difficult day but she managed to* ***raise a smile.*** 尽管这一天很不顺利，但她还是努力露出笑容。◇ *The horses' hooves raised a cloud of dust.* 马蹄翻飞，扬起一片尘土。➲ SEE ALSO CURTAIN-RAISER, FIRE-RAISER

• **CHILD/ANIMAL** 孩子；动物 **7** (*especially NAmE*) to care for a child or young animal until it is able to take care of itself 抚养；养育；培养：**~ sb/sth** *They were both raised in the South.* 他们俩都是在南方长大的。◇ *kids raised on a diet of hamburgers* 吃汉堡包长大的孩子 ◇ **~ sb/sth as sth | ~ sb/sth + noun** *They raised her (as) a Catholic.* 他们把她培养成为天主教徒。◇ *I was* ***born and raised*** *a city boy.* 我是个在都市里出生、长大的男孩。➲ COMPARE BRING SB↔UP at BRING

• **FARM ANIMALS/CROPS** 牲畜；农作物 **8** **~ sth** to breed particular farm animals; to grow particular crops 饲养；培育；种植：*to raise cattle/corn* 养牛；种植玉米

• **END STH** 终止 **9** **~ sth** to end a restriction on sb/sth 终止，解除（约束）：*to* ***raise a blockade/a ban/an embargo/a siege*** 解除封锁 / 禁令 / 禁运 / 包围

• **ON RADIO/PHONE** 无线电；电话 **10** **~ sb** to contact sb and speak to them by radio or telephone（通过无线电或电话）与…取得联系，和…通话：*We managed to raise him on his mobile phone.* 我们打他的移动电话，总算找到了他。

• **DEAD PERSON** 死人 **11** **~ sb (from sth)** to make sb who has died come to life again 使起死回生；使复活 **SYN** **resurrect**: *Christians believe that God raised Jesus from the dead.* 基督教徒相信上帝让耶稣死而复生。

• **IN CARD GAMES** 纸牌游戏 **12** **~ sb sth** to make a higher bet than another player in a card game 在（另一玩牌人）基础上加注：*I'll raise you another hundred dollars.* 我比你再加 100 美元。

• **MATHEMATICS** 数学 **13** **~ sth to the power of sth** to multiply an amount by itself a particular number of times 使自乘（若干次）：*3 raised to the power of 3 is 27 (= 3 × 3 × 3).* * 3 的三次方等于 27。

IDM **raise a/your ˈhand against/to sb** to hit or threaten to hit sb 打人；威胁要打人 **raise the ˈbar** to set a new, higher standard of quality or performance 提高标准：*The factory has raised the bar on productivity, food safety and quality.* 工厂提高了在生产力、食品安全和质量方面的标准。**OPP** **lower**[1] ➲ COMPARE SET THE BAR at BAR *n.* **raise your ˈeyebrows (at sth)** [often passive] to show that you disapprove of or are surprised by sth 扬起眉毛（表示不赞同或惊讶）：*Eyebrows were raised when he arrived without his wife.* 他没有和妻子一起来，大家都很惊讶。**raise your ˈglass (to sb)** to hold up your glass and wish sb happiness, good luck, etc. before you drink 举杯祝酒 **raise ˈhell** (*informal*) to protest angrily, especially in a way that causes trouble for sb 愤怒抗议；（尤指）大吵大闹 **raise the ˈroof** to produce or make sb produce a lot of noise in a building, for example by shouting or CHEERING（在屋内）大声喧闹，闹翻天 **raise sb's ˈspirits** to make sb feel more cheerful or brave 使振奋；使鼓起勇气 **SYN** **cheer up** ➲ MORE AT ANTE, HACKLES, LIFT *v.*, SIGHT *n.*, TEMPERATURE

PHR V **ˈraise sth to sb/sth** to build or place a statue, etc. somewhere in honour or memory of sb/sth（为…）建造，竖立（塑像等）：*The town raised a memorial to those killed in the war.* 这座小镇为战争中牺牲的人竖起了一座纪念碑。

■ ***noun*** (*NAmE*) (*BrE* **rise**) an increase in the money you are paid for the work you do 加薪；工资增长

raised /reɪzd/ *adj.* **1** higher than the area around 凸起的：*a raised platform* 凸起的平台 **2** at a higher level than normal 提高的；升高的：*the sound of raised voices* 提高嗓门的说话声 ◇ *Smokers often have raised blood pressure.* 吸烟者往往血压高。

rai·sin /ˈreɪzn/ *noun* a dried GRAPE, used in cakes, etc. 葡萄干

rais·ing /ˈreɪzɪŋ/ *noun* [U, sing.] the act of raising sth 增加；提高：*consciousness raising* 觉悟的提高 ◇ *a raising of standards in schools* 学校水平的提高 ➲ SEE ALSO FUND-RAISING at FUNDRAISER

rai·son d'être /ˌreɪzɒ̃ ˈdetrə; *NAmE* ˌreɪzoːn/ *noun* [sing.] (*from French*) the most important reason for sb's/sth's existence 存在的理由：*Work seems to be her sole raison d'être.* 工作似乎成了她生存的唯一理由。

raita /ˈraɪtə/ *noun* [U] a S Asian dish of finely chopped raw vegetables mixed with YOGURT（南亚）酸奶色拉

the Raj /rɑːdʒ; rɑːʒ; *NAmE* rɑːdʒ/ *noun* [sing.] British rule in India before 1947（1947 年前）英国对印度的统治

raja (*also less frequent* **rajah**) /ˈrɑːdʒə/ *noun* an Indian king or prince who ruled over a state in the past（旧时印度的）邦主，王公

rake /reɪk/ *noun, verb*

▪ ***noun*** **1** [C] a garden tool with a long handle and a row of metal points at the end, used for gathering fallen leaves and making soil smooth 耙子；耙状工具 ⇨ VISUAL VOCAB PAGE V20 **2** [C] (*old-fashioned*) a man, especially a rich and fashionable one, who is thought to have low moral standards, for example because he drinks or gambles a lot or has sex with a lot of women 浪荡的男人；花花公子 **3** [sing.] (*specialist*) the amount by which sth, especially the stage in a theatre, slopes（尤指剧院舞台）倾斜度

▪ ***verb*** **1** [T, I] to pull a rake over a surface in order to make it level or to remove sth 耙；梳理：**~ (sth) (+ adv./prep.)** *The leaves had been raked into a pile.* 树叶已经用耙子拢成了一堆。◇ (*figurative*) *She raked a comb through her hair.* 她用梳子梳理头发。◇ **~ sth + adj.** *First rake the soil smooth.* 首先把地耙平。 **2** [T] **~ sth (with sth)** to point a camera, light, gun, etc. at sb/sth and move it slowly from one side to the other 扫视；掠过；扫射：*They raked the streets with machine-gun fire.* 他们用机枪在街上扫射。◇ *Searchlights raked the grounds.* 探照灯从场地上掠过。 **3** [I] **+ adv./prep.** to search a place carefully for sth 搜寻；搜索：*She raked around in her bag for her keys.* 她在包里到处找钥匙。 **4** [T, I] **~ (sth)** to scratch the surface of sth with a sharp object, especially your nails 擦；刮；搔；抓

IDM **rake sb over the 'coals** (*NAmE*) (*BrE* **haul sb over the 'coals**) to criticize sb severely because they have done sth wrong 严厉训斥（或斥责）某人

PHR V **,rake 'in sth** (*informal*) to earn a lot of money, especially when it is done easily 赚大钱（尤指轻易地）：*The movie raked in more than $300 million.* 这部电影轻易赚了 3 亿多美元。◇ *She's been* ***raking it in*** *since she started her new job.* 她自从开始新的工作以来，已经赚了很多钱。 **,rake 'over sth** (*informal, disapproving*) to examine sth that happened in the past in great detail and keep talking about it, when it should be forgotten 纠缠往事：*She had no desire to rake over the past.* 她不想旧事重提。 **,rake sth↔'up** (*informal, disapproving*) to mention sth unpleasant that happened in the past and that other people would like to forget 重翻旧账

raked /reɪkt/ *adj.* (*specialist*) placed on a slope 倾斜的；置于斜坡上的：*raked seating* 阶梯式座位

R

'rake-off *noun* (*informal*) a share of profits, especially from dishonest or illegal activity 佣金，回扣（尤指不正当或非法所得）

raki /'rɑːki; rə'kiː/ *noun* [U, C] a strong alcoholic drink from eastern Europe and the Middle East 拉克酒（产于东欧和中东）

rak·ish /'reɪkɪʃ/ *adj.* **1** (of a man 男人) acting like a RAKE (= in an immoral, etc. way) 放荡的；肆无忌惮的 SYN **dissolute** **2** if you wear a hat at a **rakish angle**, it is not straight on your head and it makes you look relaxed and confident（把帽子）潇洒地歪戴着的 SYN **jaunty** ▸ **rak·ish·ly** *adv.*

rally /'ræli/ *noun, verb*

▪ ***noun*** **1** [C] a large public meeting, especially one held to support a particular idea or political party 公众集会，群众大会（尤指支持某信念或政党）：*to* ***attend/hold a rally*** 参加 / 召集大会 ◇ *a* ***peace/protest, etc. rally*** 和平集会、抗议集会等 ◇ *a* ***mass rally*** *in support of the strike* 支持罢工的群众大会 ⇨ SEE ALSO PEP RALLY **2** [C] a race for cars, motorcycles, etc. over public roads 拉力赛车：*the Monte Carlo rally* 蒙特卡洛汽车拉力赛 ◇ *rally driving* 公路赛车 **3** [C] (in TENNIS and similar sports 网球及类似项目) a series of hits of the ball before a point is scored（争夺一分的）多拍，多拍回合 **4** [sing.] (in sport or on the Stock Exchange 体育运动或证券交易) an act of returning to a strong position after a period of difficulty or weakness 止跌回升 SYN **recovery**: *After a furious late rally, they finally scored.* 他们后来状态恢复迅速，终于得分了。◇ *a rally in shares on the stock market* 证券市场股票的止跌回升

▪ ***verb*** (**ral·lies, rally·ing, ral·lied, ral·lied**) **1** [I, T] to come together or bring people together in order to help or support sb/sth 召集；集合：**~ (around/behind/to sb/sth)** *The cabinet rallied behind the Prime Minister.* 内阁团结一致支持首相。◇ *Many national newspapers rallied to his support.* 许多全国性报纸一致对他表示支持。◇ **~ sb/sth (around/behind/to sb/sth)** *They have rallied a great deal of support for their campaign.* 他们为竞选活动征得了大量的支持。 **2** [I] to become healthier, stronger, etc. after a period of illness, weakness, etc. 复原；恢复健康；振作精神 SYN **recover**: *He never really rallied after the operation.* 手术后，他根本没有真正康复。◇ *The champion rallied to win the second set 6–3.* 冠军选手振作精神，以 6:3 赢下第二局。 **3** [I] (*finance* 财) (especially of share prices or a country's money 尤指股票价格或货币) to increase in value after falling in value 价格回升；跌后回升 SYN **recover**: *The company's shares had rallied slightly by the close of trading.* 这家公司的股票价格在收盘前略有回升。◇ *The pound rallied against the dollar.* 英镑对美元汇率有所回升。

PHR V **,rally 'round/a'round** | **,rally 'round/a'round sb** (of a group of people 一群人) to work together in order to help sb who is in a difficult or unpleasant situation 团结一致（支持某人）；齐心协力（帮助某人）

rally·cross /'rælikrɒs; *NAmE* -krɔːs; -krɑːs/ *noun* [U] a form of motor racing in which cars are driven both over rough ground and on roads（汽车）跨界拉力赛 ⇨ COMPARE AUTOCROSS

'rallying cry *noun* a phrase or an idea that is used to encourage people to support sb/sth（团结众人的）战斗口号，信念

'rallying point *noun* a person, a group, an event, etc. that makes people come together in support of sth 有感召力的人（或团体、事件等）；号召力

RAM /ræm/ *noun* [U] the abbreviation for 'random-access memory' (computer memory in which data can be changed or removed and can be looked at in any order) 内存，随机存储器（全写为 random-access memory）：*256 megabytes of RAM* * 256 兆的内存

ram /ræm/ *verb, noun*

▪ ***verb*** (**-mm-**) **1 ~ sth** (of a vehicle, a ship, etc. 汽车、轮船等) to drive into or hit another vehicle, ship, etc. with force, sometimes deliberately 和…相撞；撞击：*Two passengers were injured when their taxi was rammed from behind by a bus.* 公共汽车从后面撞来，出租车上的两位乘客受了伤。 **2 ~ sth + adv./prep.** to push sth somewhere with force 塞进；挤进：*She rammed the key into the lock.* 她将钥匙塞进锁眼。◇ (*figurative*) *The spending cuts had been rammed through Congress.* 削减开支一事在国会强行通过。

IDM **,ram sth↔'home** (*especially BrE*) to emphasize an idea, argument, etc. very strongly to make sure people listen to it 强调（想法、论点等）以使人接受 ⇨ MORE AT THROAT

PHR V **,ram 'into sth** | **,ram sth 'into sth** to hit against sth or to make sth hit against sth with force 猛烈撞击；使猛烈撞上另一物：*He rammed his truck into the back of the one in front.* 他把卡车蓦地撞到前一辆卡车的车尾上。

▪ ***noun*** **1** a male sheep 公羊 ⇨ COMPARE EWE **2** a part in a machine that is used for hitting sth very hard or for lifting or moving things 夯锤；撞击装置：*hydraulic rams* 水力夯锤 ⇨ SEE ALSO BATTERING RAM

Ram·adan /'ræmədæn; ˌræmə'dæn/ *noun* [U, C] the 9th month of the Muslim year, when Muslims do not eat or drink between DAWN and SUNSET 伊斯兰历九月，斋月，莱麦丹（斋月期间，穆斯林从破晓到日落禁食禁饮）

ram·ble /'ræmbl/ *verb, noun*

▪ ***verb*** **1** [I] **+ adv./prep.** (*especially BrE*) to walk for pleasure, especially in the countryside 漫游，漫步，闲逛（尤指在乡间）：*We spent the summer rambling in Ireland.* 我们花了一个夏天漫游爱尔兰。 **2** [I] to talk about sb/sth in a confused way, especially for a long time 漫谈；闲聊；东拉西扯：*He had lost track of what he was saying and began to ramble.* 他忘了自己的话题，开始瞎扯起来。◇ **~ (on) (about sb/sth)** *What is she rambling on about now?* 她现在又在东拉西扯些什么呀？ **3** [I] (**+ adv./prep.**) (of plants

植物) to grow in many different directions, especially over other plants or objects 蔓生；攀附生长：*Climbing plants rambled over the front of the house.* 攀缘植物贴着房子正面的墙到处疯长。 ➲SEE ALSO RAMBLING

■*noun* **1** (*especially BrE*) a long walk for pleasure 漫步；散步：*to go for a ramble in the country* 去乡间散步 **2** a long confused speech or piece of writing 杂乱无章的长篇大论：*She went into a long ramble about the evils of television.* 她开始东拉西扯地大谈电视的弊端。

ram·bler /'ræmblə(r)/ *noun* **1** (*especially BrE*) a person who walks in the countryside for pleasure, especially as part of an organized group 漫步者；（尤指）有组织的乡间漫步者 **2** a plant, especially a ROSE, that grows up walls, fences, etc. 蔓生植物；攀缘植物；蔷薇

ram·bling /'ræmblɪŋ/ *adj., noun*

■*adj.* **1** (of a building 建筑物) spreading in various directions with no particular pattern 向四处延伸的；规划凌乱的 SYN **sprawling** **2** (of a speech or piece of writing 讲话或文章) very long and confused 冗长而含糊的；不切题的 SYN **incoherent**：*a rambling letter* 不知所云的长信 ➲ WORDFINDER NOTE AT STORY **3** (of a plant 植物) growing or climbing in all directions, for example up a wall 蔓生的；攀缘生长的：*a rambling rose* 蔓生的蔷薇

■*noun* **1** [U] the activity of walking for pleasure in the countryside 乡间漫步 **2 ramblings** [pl.] speech or writing that continues for a long time without saying much and seems very confused 漫无目的的讲话；长而离题的文章：*the ramblings of a madman* 疯子的胡言乱语

Rambo /'ræmbəʊ; *NAmE* -boʊ/ *noun* (*informal*) a very strong and aggressive man 强壮好斗的男子；猛男 ORIGIN From the name of the main character in David Morrell's novel *First Blood*, which was made popular in three films/movies in the 1980s. 源自戴维·莫雷尔的小说《第一滴血》中主人公兰博的名字。据此小说改编的三部电影在 20 世纪 80 年代风靡一时。

ram·bunc·tious /ræm'bʌŋkʃəs/ *adj.* (*informal, especially NAmE*) = RUMBUSTIOUS

ram·bu·tan /ræm'bu:tn/ *noun* a red tropical fruit with soft pointed parts on its skin and a slightly sour taste 红毛丹（热带水果，味略酸）

ram·ekin /'ræməkɪn/ *noun* a small dish for baking and serving food for one person （一人份的）小盘子（用于烤制和盛放食物） ➲VISUAL VOCAB PAGE V27

ram·ifi·ca·tion /ˌræmɪfɪ'keɪʃn/ *noun* [usually pl.] one of the large number of complicated and unexpected results that follow an action or a decision（众多复杂而又难以预料的）结果，后果 SYN **complication**：*These changes are bound to have widespread social ramifications.* 这些变化注定会造成许多难以预料的社会后果。

ramp /ræmp/ *noun, verb*

■*noun* **1** a slope that joins two parts of a road, path, building, etc. when one is higher than the other 斜坡；坡道：*Ramps should be provided for wheelchair users.* 应该给轮椅使用者提供坡道。 **2** (*NAmE*) (*BrE* **'slip road**) a road used for driving onto or off a major road such as a MOTORWAY OR INTERSTATE（进出高速公路等的）支路，引路，匝道：*a freeway exit ramp* 高速公路的出口坡道 ➲ SEE ALSO OFF-RAMP, ON-RAMP **3** a slope or set of steps that can be moved, used for loading a vehicle or getting on or off a plane（装车或上下飞机的）活动梯，活动坡道：*a loading ramp* 装货用的活动坡道 **4** (*IndE*) the long stage that models walk on during a fashion show（时装模特走秀的）T 型台 SYN **catwalk, runway**

■*verb*

PHR V **ˌramp sth↔'up** to make sth increase in amount 使…的数量增加

ram·page *noun, verb*

■*noun* /'ræmpeɪdʒ/ [usually sing.] a sudden period of wild and violent behaviour, often causing damage and destruction 暴跳如雷；狂暴行为：*Gangs of youths **went on the rampage** in the city yesterday.* 成群结伙的年轻人昨天在城里横冲直撞。

■*verb* /ræm'peɪdʒ; 'ræmpeɪdʒ/ [I] + **adv./prep.** (of people or animals 人或动物) to move through a place in a group, usually breaking things and causing damage 横冲直撞 SYN **run amok**：*a herd of rampaging elephants* 一群横冲直撞的大象

ram·pant /'ræmpənt/ *adj.* **1** (of sth bad 坏事) existing or spreading everywhere in a way that cannot be controlled 泛滥的；猖獗的 SYN **unchecked**：*rampant inflation* 失控的通胀 ◇ *Unemployment is now rampant in most of Europe.* 在欧洲的大部分地区，失业问题难以控制。 **2** (of plants 植物) growing thickly and very fast in a way that cannot be controlled 疯长的 ▸ **ram·pant·ly** *adv.*

ram·part /'ræmpɑ:t; *NAmE* -pɑ:rt/ *noun* [usually pl.] a high wide wall of stone or earth with a path on top, built around a castle, town, etc. to defend it 壁垒；城墙

'ram-raiding *noun* [U] (*BrE*) the crime of driving a vehicle into a shop/store window in order to steal goods 飙车抢劫（指驾车撞开商店橱窗行窃） ▸ **'ram-raid** *noun* **'ram-raid** *verb* ~ **sth** **'ram-raider** *noun*

ram·rod /'ræmrɒd; *NAmE* -rɑ:d/ *noun* a long straight piece of iron used in the past to push EXPLOSIVE into a gun（旧时用以将火药推进枪支的）推弹杆，通条

IDM **ˌramrod 'straight** | **(as) straight as a 'ramrod** (of a person 人) with a very straight back and looking serious and formal 腰杆笔直的；挺立的

ram·shackle /'ræmʃækl/ *adj.* **1** (of buildings, vehicles, furniture, etc. 建筑物、车辆、家具等) in a very bad condition and needing repair 摇摇欲坠的；破烂不堪的 SYN **tumbledown** **2** (of an organization or a system 组织或体制) badly organized or designed and not likely to last very long 组织松散（而不能持久）的；行将瓦解的 SYN **rickety**

ran PAST TENSE OF RUN

ranch /rɑ:ntʃ; *NAmE* ræntʃ/ *noun* a large farm, especially in N America or Australia, where cows, horses, sheep, etc. are bred（尤指北美或澳大利亚的）牧场，大农场：*a **cattle/sheep ranch*** 牧牛场；牧羊场 ◇ ***ranch hands*** (= the people who work on a ranch) 牧场工人 ➲SEE ALSO DUDE RANCH IDM SEE BET *v.*

ranch·er /'rɑ:ntʃə(r); *NAmE* 'ræntʃər/ *noun* a person who owns, manages or works on a ranch 大农场（或牧场）主；大农场（或牧场）工人：*a cattle rancher* 牧牛场主

'ranch house *noun* **1** a house on a ranch 农场庄园；牧场住宅 **2** (*NAmE*) a house built all on one level, that is very wide but not very deep from front to back and has a roof that is not very steep 平房住宅（矮屋顶单层，开敞长方形） ➲ COMPARE BUNGALOW (1) ➲ VISUAL VOCAB PAGE V17

ranch·ing /'rɑ:ntʃɪŋ; *NAmE* 'ræntʃɪŋ/ *noun* [U] the activity of running a RANCH 牧场经营；农场经营：*cattle/sheep ranching* 牧牛 / 牧羊场的经营

ran·cid /'rænsɪd/ *adj.* if food containing fat is **rancid**, it tastes or smells unpleasant because it is no longer fresh（含油食品）变质的，变味的，哈喇的

ran·cour (*US* **ran·cor**) /'ræŋkə(r)/ *noun* [U] (*formal*) feelings of hatred and a desire to hurt other people, especially because you think that sb has done sth unfair to you 怨恨；怨毒 SYN **bitterness**：*She learned to accept criticism without rancour.* 她学会了坦然接受批评而不怀恨在心。 ▸ **ran·cor·ous** /'ræŋkərəs/ *adj.*：*a rancorous legal battle* 充满敌意的法律争端

rand /rænd; rɑ:nt/ *noun* (*pl.* **rand**) **1** [C] the unit of money in the Republic of South Africa 兰特（南非共和国货币单位） **2 the Rand** [sing.] (in South Africa) a large area around Johannesburg where gold is mined and where there are many cities and towns 兰德（南非约翰内斯堡周围的金矿区）

R & B /ˌɑ:r ən 'bi:/ *abbr.* RHYTHM AND BLUES 节奏布鲁斯；节奏蓝调

R

R & D /ˌɑːr ən ˈdiː/ *abbr.* RESEARCH AND DEVELOPMENT 研究和开发

ran·dom AW /ˈrændəm/ *adj., noun*

■ ***adj.*** **1** [usually before noun] done, chosen, etc. without sb deciding in advance what is going to happen, or without any regular pattern 随机的，随意的（非事先决定或不规则）：*the random killing of innocent people* 对无辜者的随意杀戮 ◇ *a* ***random sample/selection*** (= in which each thing has an equal chance of being chosen) 随机抽样 / 选择 ◇ *The information is processed in a random order.* 信息是按随机顺序处理的。◇ (*informal*) *He grabbed a pair of random jeans and an old red shirt.* 他抓了一条随意拿到的牛仔裤和一件旧的红衬衫。◇ *She dodged the random items that were on the concrete floor.* 她避开了混凝土地上随意散放的物品。 **2** [only before noun] (*informal*) (especially of a person 尤指人) not known or not identified 不认识的；辨认不出的：*Some random guy gave me a hundred bucks.* 有个陌生男人给了我 100 美元。 **3** (*informal*) a thing or person that is **random** is strange and does not make sense, often in a way that amuses or interests you（人或物）不合常理的，出人意料的，不可思议的：*Mom, you are so random!* 妈妈，你太不可思议了！◇ *The humour is great because it's just so random and unhinged from reality.* 幽默之妙在于它如此的出人意料又不受现实的束缚。▶ **ran·dom·ly** AW *adv.*：*The winning numbers are randomly selected by computer.* 中奖号码是由电脑随机选取的。◇ *My phone seems to switch itself off randomly.* 我的手机好像随时自动关机。 **ran·dom·ness** AW *noun* [U]：*It introduced an element of randomness into the situation.* 这就为形势增加了一种不确定因素。

■ ***noun***

IDM **at ˈrandom** without deciding in advance what is going to happen, or without any regular pattern 随意；随机；胡乱：*She opened the book at random* (= not at any particular page) *and started reading.* 她随意翻开书就看了起来。◇ *The terrorists fired into the crowd at random.* 恐怖分子胡乱地向人群开枪。◇ *Names were chosen at random from a list.* 名字是从名单中随便点的。

ˌrandom ˈaccess *noun* [U] (*computing* 计) the ability in a computer to go straight to data items without having to read through items stored previously 随机存取；随机访问

ˌrandom-ˌaccess ˈmemory *noun* [U] (*computing* 计) = RAM

ran·dom·ize (*BrE also* **-ise**) /ˈrændəmaɪz/ *verb* **~ sth** (*specialist*) to use a method in an experiment, a piece of research, etc. that gives every item an equal chance of being considered; to put things in a RANDOM order 使随机化；（使）作任意排列

R & R /ˌɑːr ən ˈɑː(r)/ *abbr.* **1** rest and recreation (doing things for enjoyment rather than working) 休闲娱乐 **2** (*medical* 医) rescue and resuscitation 急救与复苏；救生

randy /ˈrændi/ *adj.* (**ran·dier**, **ran·di·est**) (*BrE, informal*) sexually excited 性兴奋的；性欲冲动的：*to feel/get randy* 感到性冲动

ranee = RANI

rang PAST TENSE OF RING²

range AW /reɪndʒ/ *noun, verb*

■ ***noun***

• **VARIETY** 种类 **1** [C, usually sing.] **~ (of sth)** a variety of things of a particular type 一系列：*The hotel offers* ***a wide range of*** *facilities.* 这家酒店提供各种各样的设施。◇ *There is* ***a full range of*** *activities for children.* 这里有给孩子们提供的各种活动。

• **LIMITS** 界限 **2** [C, usually sing.] the limits between which sth varies（变动或浮动的）范围，界限，区间：*Most of the students are in the 17–20* ***age range.*** 大多数学生都是在 17 至 20 岁的年龄范围内。◇ *There will be an increase* ***in the range of*** *0 to 3 per cent.* 将会有 0 到 3 个百分点的增长幅度。◇ *It's difficult to find a house in our* ***price range*** (= that we can afford). 在我们的价格范围以内，很难找到房子。◇ *This was* ***outside the range of his experience.*** 这超出了他的阅历。

• **OF PRODUCTS** 产品 **3** [C] a set of products of a particular type 类；种：*our new range of hair products* 我们的新的头发产品系列 ➲ SEE ALSO MID-RANGE, TOP OF THE RANGE

• **DISTANCE** 距离 **4** [C, U] the distance over which sth can be seen or heard 视觉（或听觉）范围：*The child was now out of her* ***range of vision*** (= not near enough for her to see). 这孩子已经走出了她的视线。 **5** [C, U] the distance over which a gun or other weapon can hit things 射程；射击距离：*These missiles have a range of 300 miles.* 这些导弹的射程为 300 英里。➲ SEE ALSO CLOSE-RANGE, LONG-RANGE, SHORT-RANGE **6** [C] the distance that a vehicle will travel before it needs more fuel（车辆）加一次油可行驶的路程

• **OF MOUNTAINS** 山 **7** [C] a line or group of mountains or hills 山脉：*the great mountain range of the Alps* 雄伟的阿尔卑斯山脉 ➲ VISUAL VOCAB PAGE V5

• **FOR SHOOTING** 射击 **8** [C] an area of land where people can practise shooting or where bombs, etc. can be tested 靶场；射击场；炸弹试验场：*a shooting range* 射击场 ➲ SEE ALSO DRIVING RANGE, RIFLE RANGE

• **OVEN** 炉子 **9** [C] a large piece of equipment that can burn various fuels and is kept hot all the time, used for cooking, especially in the past（尤指旧时的）炉灶 **10** (*NAmE*) = STOVE：*Cook the meat on a low heat on top of the range.* 把肉放在炉灶上用文火炖着。

• **FOR COWS** 乳牛 **11 the range** [sing.] (*NAmE*) a large open area for keeping cows, etc. 牧场；乳牛场 ➲ SEE ALSO FREE-RANGE

IDM **in/within ˈrange (of sth)** near enough to be reached, seen or heard 在可及的范围内；在视觉（或听觉）范围内：*He shouted angrily at anyone within range.* 他看见谁就对谁吼叫。 **out of ˈrange (of sth)** too far away to be reached, seen or heard 超出…的范围；在视觉（或听觉）范围之外：*The cat stayed well out of range of the children.* 这只猫离孩子们远远的。

■ ***verb***

• **VARY** 变化 **1** [I] to vary between two particular amounts, sizes, etc., including others between them（在一定的范围内）变化，变动：**~ from A to B** *to* ***range*** *in size/length/price from A to B* 尺寸 / 长度 / 价格在 A 到 B 间变动 ◇ *Accommodation ranges from tourist class to luxury hotels.* 住宿档次从经济旅馆至豪华酒店不等。◇ **~ between A and B** *Estimates of the damage range between $1 million and $5 million.* 估计损失在 100 万到 500 万美元之间。 **2** [I] to include a variety of different things in addition to those mentioned 包括（从…到…）之间的各类事物：**~ from A to B** *She has had a number of different jobs, ranging from chef to swimming instructor.* 她做过许多不同的工作，从厨师到游泳教练。◇ **+ adv./prep.** *The conversation ranged widely* (= covered a lot of different topics). 谈话所涉及的范围很广。➲ SEE ALSO WIDE-RANGING

• **ARRANGE** 安排 **3** [T, usually passive] **~ sb/sth/yourself + adv./prep.** (*formal*) to arrange people or things in a particular position or order（按一定位置或顺序）排列，排序：*The delegates ranged themselves around the table.* 代表依次在桌子周围就座。◇ *Spectators were ranged along the whole route of the procession.* 旁观者排列在整个游行路线的两侧。

• **MOVE AROUND** 徘徊 **4** [I, T] to move around an area 徘徊；漫步；四处移动：**+ adv./prep.** *He ranges far and wide in search of inspiration for his paintings.* 他四处漫步，寻找绘画的灵感。◇ **~ sth** *Her eyes ranged the room.* 她的目光在屋子里来回扫视。

PHR V **ˌrange yourself/sb aˈgainst/ˈwith sb/sth** [usually passive] to join with other people to oppose or support sb/sth（使）结伙反对 / 支持⋯：*The whole family seemed ranged against him.* 全家人好像在合伙对付他。 **ˈrange over sth** to include a variety of different subjects 涉及；包括：*His lecture ranged over a number of topics.* 他的讲座涉及许多话题。

range·find·er /ˈreɪndʒfaɪndə(r)/ *noun* an instrument for estimating how far away an object is, used with a camera or gun（照相机、枪炮的）测距仪

ran·ger /ˈreɪndʒə(r)/ *noun* **1** a person whose job is to take care of a park, a forest or an area of countryside 园

林管理员；护林人 **2 Ranger** (**Guide**) a girl who belongs to the part of the Guide Association in Britain for girls between the ages of 14 and 19（英国 14 至 19 岁的）女童子军 **3 Ranger** (*US*) a soldier who is trained to make quick attacks in enemy areas（接受突袭敌战区训练的）突击队员，特别行动队队员 ➲COMPARE COMMANDO

rangy /ˈreɪndʒi/ *adj.* (of a person or an animal 人或动物) having long thin arms and/or legs 四肢瘦长的

rani (*also* **ranee**) /ˈrɑːniː; rɑːˈniː/ *noun* an Indian queen; the wife of a RAJA 印度土邦女邦主；印度邦主（或王公）之妻

rank /ræŋk/ *noun, verb, adj.*

■***noun***

• **POSITION IN ORGANIZATION/ARMY, ETC.** 级别 **1** [U, C] the position, especially a high position, that sb has in a particular organization, society, etc.（尤指较高的）地位，级别：*She was not used to mixing with people of high social rank.* 她不习惯和社会地位很高的人交往。◇ ***He rose through the ranks*** *to become managing director.* 他级级攀升，当上了常务董事。◇ *Within months she was elevated to ministerial rank.* 不出几个月，她就被提升至部级。➲SEE ALSO RANKING *n.* (1) **2** [C, U] the position that sb has in the army, navy, police, etc. 军衔；军阶；警衔：*He was soon promoted to the rank of captain.* 他很快被提升至上尉军阶。◇ *officers of* ***junior/senior rank*** 有低级 / 高级军阶的军官 ◇ *a campaign to attract more women into the military ranks* 吸引更多的女性担任各级军官的运动 ◇ *officers,* ***and other ranks*** (= people who are not officers) 军官及士兵 ◇ *The colonel was stripped of his rank* (= was given a lower position, especially as a punishment). 那名上校被降职了。 **3 the ranks** [pl.] the position of ordinary soldiers rather than officers 普通士兵：*He served in the ranks for most of the war.* 战争期间，他大部分时间都在部队服役。◇ *He* ***rose from the ranks*** (= from being an ordinary soldier) *to become a warrant officer.* 他从普通士兵升至准尉。

• **QUALITY** 质量 **4** [sing.] the degree to which sb/sth is of high quality 等级；级别：*a painter* ***of the first rank*** 一流的画家 ◇ *Britain is no longer* ***in the front rank of*** *world powers.* 英国再也不是位于前列的世界强国。◇ *The findings are arranged* ***in rank order*** *according to performance.* 这些研究结果是根据性能等级排列的。

• **MEMBERS OF GROUP** 成员 **5 the ranks** [pl.] the members of a particular group or organization（团体或组织的）成员：*We have a number of international players in our ranks.* 我们的队员中有好几个国际选手。◇ *At 50, he was forced to* ***join the ranks of*** *the unemployed.* 他 50 岁时被迫加入了失业行列。◇ *There were serious divisions within the party's own ranks.* 这个党内部存在着严重的分歧。

• **LINE/ROW** 行；列 **6** [C] a line or row of soldiers, police, etc. standing next to each other（警察、士兵等的）队列，行列：*They watched as ranks of marching infantry passed the window.* 他们看着步兵列队从窗前走过。 **7** [C] a line or row of people or things 排；行；列：*massed ranks of spectators* 聚集起来的旁观者的行列 ◇ *The trees grew* ***in serried ranks*** (= very closely together). 树木一排靠一排地生长。➲SEE ALSO TAXI RANK

IDM **break 'ranks 1** (of soldiers, police, etc. 士兵、警察等) to fail to remain in line 掉队；未保持队形 **2** (of the members of a group 成员) to refuse to support the group or the organization of which they are members 不支持所属团体（或组织） ➲MORE AT CLOSE[1] *v.*, PULL *v.*

■***verb*** (not used in the progressive tenses 不用于进行时)

• **GIVE POSITION** 分等级 **1** [T, I] to give sb/sth a particular position on a scale according to quality, importance, success, etc.; to have a position of this kind 把…分等级；属于某等级：**~ sb/sth (+ adv./prep.)** *The tasks have been ranked in order of difficulty.* 按照困难程度对工作进行了分类。◇ *She is currently the highest ranked player in the world.* 她是目前居全球榜首的运动员。◇ ***top-ranked*** *players* 一流的选手 ◇ **~ sb/sth as sth** *Voters regularly rank education as being more important than defence.* 投票者通常认为教育比国防更重要。◇ **~ (sb/sth) + adj.** *At the height of her career she ranked second in the world.* 在她事业的顶峰时期，她排名世界第二位。◇ **~ sb/sth + noun** *The university is ranked number one in the country for engineering.* 在工程学领域，这所大学位居本国第一。◇ **~ as sth** *It certainly doesn't rank as his greatest win.* 这肯定算不上他最大的胜利。◇ **(+ adv./prep.)** *The restaurant ranks among the finest in town.* 这家饭店属于城里最好的。◇ *This must rank with* (= be as good as) *the greatest movies ever made.* 这部影片一定可与史上最优秀的影片相媲美。◇ (*NAmE*) *You just don't rank* (= you're not good enough). 你还不够级别。

• **PUT IN LINE/ROW** 排列；排成行 **2** [T, usually passive] **~ sth** to arrange objects in a line or row 排列；使排成行

■***adj.*** **1** having a strong unpleasant smell 难闻的；恶臭的：*The house was full of the rank smell of urine.* 这屋子里到处有一股尿的臊味。 **2** (*informal*) very unpleasant 非常糟糕的：*I think the whole situation's pretty rank.* 我认为整个情况很糟糕。 **3** [only before noun] used to emphasize a particular quality, state, etc.（强调质量、状况等）极端的，糟糕的：*an example of rank stupidity* 极端愚蠢的例子 ◇ *The winning horse was a* ***rank outsider***. 获胜的这匹马，本来谁也没指望它能获胜。 **4** (of plants, etc. 植物) growing too thickly 疯长的

the ˌrank and 'file *noun* [sing.+sing./pl. v.] **1** the ordinary soldiers who are not officers 普通士兵 **2** the ordinary members of an organization 普通成员：*the rank and file of the workforce* 普通劳动力 ◇ *rank-and-file members* 普通成员

'rank correlation *noun* [U] (*statistics* 统计) a method for finding to what extent two sets of numbers, each arranged in order, are connected or have an effect on each other 秩相关；等级相关

rank·ing /ˈræŋkɪŋ/ *noun, adj.*

■***noun*** **1** the position of sb/sth on a scale that shows how good or important they are in relation to other similar people or things, especially in sport 地位，排名，排位（尤指在体育运动中）：*He has improved his ranking this season from 67th to 30th.* 本赛季他将自己的排名从第 67 位提高到了第 30 位。◇ *She has retained her No.1 world ranking.* 她保住了自己世界第一的排名。 **2 the rankings** [pl.] an official list showing the best players of a particular sport in order of how successful they are（某项体育运动的）最佳运动员排名表

■***adj.*** **1** (*especially NAmE*) having a high or the highest rank in an organization, etc. 地位高的；高级的；最高级的：*a ranking diplomat* 高级外交官 ◇ *He was the* ***ranking officer*** (= the most senior officer present at a particular time). 他是到场最高官员。 **2** (in compounds 构成复合词) having the particular rank mentioned …级别的；…等级的：*high-ranking/low-ranking police officers* 高 / 低级别的警官 ◇ *a top-ranking player* 顶尖级选手

ran·kle /ˈræŋkl/ *verb* [I, T] if sth such as an event or a remark **rankles**, it makes you feel angry or upset for a long time 使人耿耿于怀（或怨恨不已、痛苦不已）：**~ (sb)** *Her comments still rankled.* 她的评价仍然让人耿耿于怀。◇ **~ with sb** *His decision to sell the land still rankled with her.* 他要把地卖掉的决定仍然使她痛心。

ran·sack /ˈrænsæk/ *verb* **~ sth (for sth)** to make a place untidy, causing damage, because you are looking for sth 洗劫；（为找东西）把…翻腾得乱七八糟 **SYN** **turn upside down**：*The house had been ransacked by burglars.* 这房子遭到了盗贼的洗劫。

ran·som /ˈrænsəm/ *noun, verb*

■***noun*** [C, U] money that is paid to sb so that they will set free a person who is being kept as a prisoner by them 赎金：*The kidnappers demanded a ransom of £50 000 from his family.* 绑架者向他的家人索要赎金 5 万英镑。◇ *a* ***ransom demand/note*** 索要赎金的要求 / 通知 ◇ *ransom money* 赎金 ◇ *They are refusing to pay ransom for her release.* 他们拒绝支付赎金来解救她。

IDM **hold sb to 'ransom 1** to keep sb as a prisoner and demand that other people pay you an amount of money before you set them free 将…绑票 **2** (*disapproving*) to take action that puts sb in a very difficult situation in order to force them to do what you want 胁迫；要挟 ➲MORE AT KING

■ *verb* ~ sb to pay money to sb so that they will set free the person that they are keeping as a prisoner（为某人）交付赎金：*The kidnapped children were all ransomed and returned home unharmed.* 被绑架的儿童在赎金交付后均安然回到家中。

ran·som·ware /ˈrænsəmweə(r); *NAmE* -wer/ *noun* [U] a type of software that is designed to block access to a computer system until a sum of money is paid 勒索软件，敲诈软件（封锁用户的计算机系统，付钱后方解封）

rant /rænt/ *verb* [I, T] ~ (**on**) (**about sth**) | ~ **at sb** | + **speech** (*disapproving*) to speak or complain about sth in a loud and/or angry way 怒吼；咆哮；大声抱怨 ▶ **rant** *noun*

IDM **ˌrant and ˈrave** (*disapproving*) to show that you are angry by shouting or complaining loudly for a long time 气愤地大叫大嚷；大声吵闹 ➲ MORE LIKE THIS 13, page R26

rant·ings /ˈræntɪŋz/ *noun* [pl.] loud or angry comments or speeches that continue for a long time（长时间的）怒气冲冲的厉声斥责

rap /ræp/ *noun, verb*

■ *noun* **1** [C] a quick sharp hit or knock 叩击；快速的敲击：*There was a sharp rap on the door.* 有人在重重地急促敲门。 **2** [U] a type of popular music with a fast strong rhythm and words which are spoken fast, not sung 说唱音乐（节奏快而强，配有快速念白的流行音乐）：*a* ***rap song/artist*** 说唱歌曲 / 艺术家 **3** [C] a rap song 说唱歌；快板歌 **4** [C] (*NAmE, informal*) a criminal CONVICTION (= the fact of being found guilty of a crime) 有罪判决；罪名；判刑：*a police* ***rap sheet*** (= a record of the crimes sb has committed) 判刑记录 **5** [sing.] (*NAmE, informal*) an unfair judgement on sth or sb 不公正的判决；苛评：*He denounced the criticisms as 'just one* ***bum rap*** *after another.'* 他谴责这样的批评"只不过是一次又一次的横加指斥"。◇ *Wolves* ***get a bad rap****, says a woman who owns three.* "狼的名声不好，这是不公正的。"一个养着三只狼的女人说。

IDM **(give sb/get) a rap on/over/across the ˈknuckles** (*informal*) (to give sb/receive) strong criticism for sth（给某人以 / 受到）严厉谴责，厉声训斥：*We got a rap over the knuckles for being late.* 我们因为迟到而受到严厉训斥。 **take the ˈrap (for sb/sth)** (*informal*) to be blamed or punished, especially for sth you have not done（无辜）受罚；背黑锅 SYN **blame**：*She was prepared to take the rap for the shoplifting, though it had been her sister's idea.* 尽管在商店偷东西是她妹妹的主意，可她甘愿为此受罚。➲ MORE AT BEAT *v.*

■ *verb* (**-pp-**) **1** [I, T] to hit a hard object or surface several times quickly, making a noise 敲击；击打：(**+ adv./prep.**) *She rapped angrily on the door.* 她怒气冲冲地敲着门。◇ ~ **sth** (**+ adv./prep.**) *He rapped the table with his pen.* 他用钢笔敲了敲桌子。 **2** [T] ~ **sth** (**out**) | + **speech** to say sth suddenly and quickly in a loud, angry way 突然大声说出；突然厉声说出：*He walked through the store, rapping out orders to his staff.* 他在商店里一边走一边对他的员工大声发号施令。 **3** [T] ~ **sb/sth** (**for sth/for doing sth**) (used mainly in newspapers 主要用于报章) to criticize sb severely, usually publicly（公开地）严厉批评，严加指责：*Some of the teachers were rapped for poor performance.* 一些老师因为表现差劲而受到严厉批评。 **4** [I, T] ~ (**sth**) (*music* 音) to say the words of a rap（说唱歌中）念白；唱说唱歌 ➲ SEE ALSO RAPPER

IDM **ˌrap sb on/over the ˈknuckles** | **rap sb's ˈknuckles** to criticize sb for sth 批评；指责

ra·pa·cious /rəˈpeɪʃəs/ *adj.* (*formal, disapproving*) wanting more money or goods than you need or have a right to 贪婪的；贪欲的；强取的 SYN **grasping** ▶ **ra·pa·cious·ly** *adv.* **rap·acity** /rəˈpæsəti/ *noun* [U]：*the rapacity of landowners seeking greater profit* 土地拥有者牟取更大利益的贪婪

rape /reɪp/ *verb, noun*

■ *verb* ~ **sb** to force sb to have sex with you when they do not want to by threatening them or using violence 强奸；强暴 ➲ SEE ALSO RAPIST

■ *noun* **1** [U, C] the crime of forcing sb to have sex with you, especially using violence 强奸罪；强奸案：*He was charged with rape.* 他被控犯了强奸罪。◇ *a rape victim* 强奸案的受害者 ◇ *an increase in the number of reported rapes* 强奸案报案数字的增加 ➲ SEE ALSO DATE RAPE, RAPIST **2** [sing.] ~ (**of sth**) (*literary*) the act of destroying or spoiling an area in a way that seems unnecessary 肆意损坏；肆意糟蹋；蹂躏 **3** (*also* **ˌoilseed ˈrape**) [U] a plant with bright yellow flowers, grown as food for farm animals and for its seeds that are used to make oil 油菜

rape·seed /ˈreɪpsiːd/ [U] seeds of the rape plant, used mainly for cooking oil 油菜籽 ➲ SEE ALSO CANOLA™

rapid 🔑 /ˈræpɪd/ *adj.* **1** 🔑 [usually before noun] happening in a short period of time 瞬间的；短时间内发生的：***rapid change/expansion/growth*** 迅速的改变 / 扩张 / 增长 ◇ *a* ***rapid rise/decline*** *in sales* 销售额的急剧上升 / 下降 ◇ *The patient made a* ***rapid recovery****.* 病人很快恢复了健康。 **2** 🔑 done or happening very quickly 迅速的；快速的；快捷的：*a* ***rapid pulse/heartbeat*** 急促的脉搏 / 心跳 ◇ *The guard fired four shots in rapid succession.* 卫兵接连开了四枪。◇ *The disease is spreading at a rapid rate.* 这种疾病正在迅速蔓延。➲ NOTE AT FAST ▶ **rap·id·ity** /rəˈpɪdəti/ *noun* [U]：*the rapidity of economic growth* 经济增长的高速度 ◇ *The disease is spreading with alarming rapidity.* 这种疾病正在以骇人的速度蔓延。 **rap·id·ly** 🔑 *adv.*：*a rapidly growing economy* 迅速增长的经济 ◇ *Crime figures are rising rapidly.* 犯罪数字正在迅速上升。

ˌrapid-ˈfire *adj.* [only before noun] **1** (of questions, comments, etc. 问题、评论等) spoken very quickly, one after the other 连珠炮似的；接二连三的 **2** (of a gun 枪炮) able to shoot bullets very quickly, one after the other 速射的；连续发射的

ˌrapid-reˈsponse *adj.* [only before noun] having the necessary training and equipment to be able to act quickly when there is an emergency such as an accident, an attack or a natural disaster 快速反应的（指训练有素、配有必要装备、能够快速应对紧急情况）：*a UN rapid-response unit* 联合国快速反应小组 ◇ *rapid-response systems for early detection of the virus* 尽早发现病毒的快速反应体系

rapids /ˈræpɪdz/ *noun* [pl.] part of a river where the water flows very fast, usually over rocks（河的）急流；湍急的河水：*to* ***shoot the rapids*** (= to travel quickly over them in a boat) 快速穿过急流

ˌrapid ˈtransit *noun* [U] (*especially NAmE*) the system of fast public transport in cities, especially the SUBWAY（城市）快速交通系统；（尤指）地铁 ➲ SEE ALSO TRANSIT *n.* (3)

ra·pier /ˈreɪpiə(r)/ *noun* a long thin light SWORD that has two sharp edges 轻巧细长的双刃剑：(*figurative*) *rapier wit* (= very quick and sharp) 敏锐的才思

rap·ist /ˈreɪpɪst/ *noun* a person who forces sb to have sex when they do not want to (= RAPES them) 强奸犯；强奸者

rap·pel /ræˈpel/ (*NAmE*) (*BrE* **ab·seil**) *verb* (**-ll-**) [I] ~ (**down, off, etc. sth**) to go down a steep CLIFF or rock while attached to a rope, pushing against the slope or rock with your feet 绕绳下降（用绳缠绕着身体，双脚蹬陡坡或峭壁自己放绳下滑）➲ VISUAL VOCAB PAGE V53 ▶ **rap·pel** (*NAmE*) (*BrE* **ab·seil**) *noun*

rap·per /ˈræpə(r)/ *noun* a person who speaks the words of a RAP song 说唱歌手

rap·port /ræˈpɔː(r)/ *noun* [sing., U] ~ (**with sb**) | ~ (**between A and B**) a friendly relationship in which people understand each other very well 亲善；融洽；和谐：*She understood the importance of establishing a close rapport with clients.* 她懂得与客户建立密切和谐的关系的重要性。

rap·por·teur /ˌræpɔːˈtɜː(r); *NAmE* -pɔːrˈt-/ *noun* (*from French, specialist*) a person officially chosen by an organization to investigate a problem and report on it 特派调

查员：*the UN special rapporteur on human rights* 联合国人权问题特派调查员

rap·proche·ment /ræˈprɒʃmɒ̃; ræˈprəʊʃmɒ̃; *NAmE* ˌræproʊʃˈmɑːn; -prɑːʃ-/ *noun* [sing., U] (*from French, formal*) a situation in which the relationship between two countries or groups of people becomes more friendly after a period during which they were enemies 友好关系的恢复；和解：~ (**with sb**) *policies aimed at bringing about a rapprochement with China* 旨在与中国恢复友好关系的政策 ◇ ~ (**between A and B**) *There now seems little chance of rapprochement between the warring factions.* 目前，敌对双方和解的可能性似乎很渺茫。➲ WORDFINDER NOTE AT ALLY

rapt /ræpt/ *adj.* so interested in one particular thing that you are not aware of anything else 全神贯注的；专心致志的：*a rapt audience* 听得入神的听众 ◇ *She listened to the speaker with rapt attention.* 她全神贯注地听演讲者讲话。▶ **rapt·ly** *adv.*

rap·tor /ˈræptə(r)/ *noun* (*specialist*) any BIRD OF PREY (= a bird that kills other creatures for food) 猛禽；攫禽

rap·ture /ˈræptʃə(r)/ *noun* [U] (*formal*) a feeling of extreme pleasure and happiness 狂喜；欢天喜地；兴高采烈 SYN **delight**：*Charles listened with rapture to her singing.* 查尔斯兴致勃勃地听她演唱。◇ *The children gazed at her in rapture.* 孩子们欣喜若狂地看着她。

IDM **be in, go into, etc. ˈraptures (about/over sb/sth)** to feel or express extreme pleasure or enthusiasm for sb/sth 感到（或显得）极为高兴；热情至极：*The critics went into raptures about her performance.* 评论家们对她的表演赞不绝口。◇ *The last minute goal sent the fans into raptures.* 最后一刻的进球使得球迷们欣喜若狂。

rap·tur·ous /ˈræptʃərəs/ *adj.* [usually before noun] expressing extreme pleasure or enthusiasm for sb/sth 兴高采烈的；狂喜的；热烈的 SYN **ecstatic**：*rapturous applause* 热烈的鼓掌欢呼 ➲ SYNONYMS AT EXCITED ▶ **rap·tur·ous·ly** *adv.*

rare 🔑 /reə(r); *NAmE* rer/ *adj.* (**rarer, rar·est**) **1** 🔑 not done, seen, happening, etc. very often 稀少的；稀罕的：*a rare disease/occurrence/sight* 罕见的疾病 / 事件；难得一见的事物 ◇ ~ (**for sb/sth to do sth**) *It's extremely rare for it to be this hot in April.* 四月份就这样炎热是极其罕见的。◇ ~ (**to do sth**) *It is rare to find such loyalty these days.* 这样忠心耿耿，在今天非常少见。◇ ***On the rare occasions when*** *they met he hardly even dared speak to her.* 彼此难得相见，见了他几乎都不敢跟她说话。◇ *It was a rare* (= very great) *honour to be made a fellow of the college.* 成为这所学院的董事是极大的荣誉。 **2** 🔑 existing only in small numbers and therefore valuable or interesting 稀罕的；珍贵的：*a rare book/coin/stamp* 珍贵的书 / 硬币 / 邮票 ◇ *a rare breed/plant* 珍稀物种 / 植物 ◇ *This species is extremely rare.* 这一物种极为罕见。 **3** (of meat 肉) cooked for only a short time so that the inside is still red 三分熟的 ➲ COMPARE WELL DONE ➲ SEE ALSO RARITY

rare·bit /ˈreəbɪt; *NAmE* ˈrerbɪt/ *noun* = WELSH RAREBIT

rar·efied /ˈreərɪfaɪd; *NAmE* ˈreraf-/ *adj.* [usually before noun] **1** (*often disapproving*) understood or experienced by only a very small group of people who share a particular area of knowledge or activity 高深精妙的；曲高和寡的：*the rarefied atmosphere of academic life* 阳春白雪的学术生活氛围 **2** (of air 空气) containing less OXYGEN than usual 稀薄的；含氧量低的

ˈrare gas *noun* (*chemistry* 化) = NOBLE GAS

rare·ly 🔑 /ˈreəli; *NAmE* ˈrerli/ *adv.* not very often 罕有；很少；不常：*She is rarely seen in public nowadays.* 如今在公共场所很少能见到她。◇ *We rarely agree on what to do.* 我们很少在要做的事情上看法一致。 ◇ *a rarely-performed play* 一部很少上演的戏剧 ◇ (*formal*) *Rarely has a debate attracted so much media attention.* 很少有辩论吸引这么多媒体关注。

rar·ing /ˈreərɪŋ; *NAmE* ˈrer-/ *adj.* ~ **to do sth** (*informal*) very enthusiastic about starting to do sth 热切；渴望：*The new recruits arrived early, all dressed up and **raring to go*** (= to start). 新兵早早地就到了，都穿得整整齐齐，盼着出发。◇ *She is raring to get back to work after her operation.* 动完了手术，她渴望回到工作岗位上去。

rar·ity /ˈreərəti; *NAmE* ˈrer-/ *noun* (*pl.* **-ies**) **1** [C] a person or thing that is unusual and is therefore often valuable or interesting 珍品；稀有物：*Women are still something of a rarity in senior positions in business.* 在商界位居高职的女性仍然十分罕见。◇ *His collection of plants contains many rarities.* 他收藏的植物包括许多稀有品种。 **2** (*also less frequent* **rare·ness**) [U] the quality of being rare 稀有；罕见：*The value of antiques will depend on their condition and rarity.* 古董的价值依它们的保存状况和稀有程度而定。

ras·cal /ˈrɑːskl; *NAmE* ˈræskl/ *noun* **1** (*humorous*) a person, especially a child or man, who shows a lack of respect for other people and enjoys playing tricks on them 无赖；坏蛋；淘气鬼：*Come here, you little rascal!* 过来，你这个小坏蛋！ **2** (*old-fashioned*) a dishonest man 不诚实的人 ▶ **ras·cal·ly** /-kəli/ *adj.* (*old-fashioned*)

rash /ræʃ/ *noun, adj.*

■ ***noun*** **1** [C, usually sing.] an area of red spots on a person's skin, caused by an illness or a reaction to sth 皮疹；疹：*I woke up covered in a rash.* 我醒来时长了一身皮疹。◇ *I **come out in a rash*** (= a rash appears on my skin) *if I eat chocolate.* 我一吃巧克力就长皮疹。◇ *The sun **brought her out in*** (= caused) *an itchy rash.* 太阳晒了她一身痱子，很痒。◇ *a **heat rash*** (= caused by heat) 痱子 ➲ COMPARE SPOT *n.* (3) **2** [sing.] ~ (**of sth**) a lot of sth; a series of unpleasant things that happen over a short period of time 大量；许多；（涌现的）众多令人不快的事物 SYN **spate**：*a rash of movies about life in prison* 大量关于监狱生活的电影 ◇ *There has been a rash of burglaries in the area over the last month.* 近一个月这一带发生了很多起入室行窃案。

■ ***adj.*** (of people or their actions 人或行为) doing sth that may not be sensible without first thinking about the possible results; done in this way 轻率的；鲁莽的 SYN **reckless**：*a rash young man* 鲁莽的年轻人 ◇ ~ (**to do sth**) *It would be rash to assume that everyone will agree with you on this.* 你要是认为在这件事上谁都会同意你的看法，那就太欠考虑了。 ◇ *Think twice before doing anything rash.* 不要草率行事，要三思而行。◇ *This is what happens when you make rash decisions.* 这就是你贸然作决定的后果。 ▶ **rash·ly** *adv.*：*She had rashly promised to lend him the money.* 她轻率地答应借钱给他。 **rash·ness** *noun* [U]：*He bitterly regretted his rashness.* 他对自己的莽撞极其后悔。

rasher /ˈræʃə(r)/ *noun* (*especially BrE*) a thin slice of BACON (= meat from the back or sides of a pig) 咸猪肉薄片

rasp /rɑːsp; *NAmE* ræsp/ *noun, verb*

■ ***noun*** **1** [sing.] a rough unpleasant sound 刺耳的声音；刮擦声 **2** [C] a metal tool with a long blade covered with rows of sharp points, used for making rough surfaces smooth 锉；锉刀

■ ***verb*** **1** [T, I] to say sth in a rough unpleasant voice 用刺耳的声音说 SYN **croak**：**+ speech** *'Where have you been?' she rasped.* "你去哪儿啦？"她尖声问道。◇ ~ (**sth**) (**out**) *He rasped out some instructions.* 他粗声粗气地发出指令。 **2** [I] to make a rough unpleasant sound 发出刺耳的声音；发出刮擦声 SYN **grate**：*a rasping **cough/voice*** 刺耳的咳嗽声 / 嗓音 **3** [T] ~ **sth** to rub a surface with a rasp or with sth rough that works or feels like a rasp 用锉刀锉；用粗糙的东西磨擦：*The wind rasped his face.* 寒风刺疼了他的脸。

rasp·berry /ˈrɑːzbəri; *NAmE* ˈræzberi/ *noun* (*pl.* **-ies**) **1** a small dark red soft fruit that grows on bushes 覆盆子；山莓；悬钩子：*raspberry jam* 山莓酱 ➲ VISUAL VOCAB PAGE V33 **2** (*NAmE also* ˌ**Bronx ˈcheer**) (*informal*) a rude sound made by sticking out the tongue and blowing（将舌头伸出并吹气而发出的粗鲁的声音）呸声，嘘声：*to blow a raspberry at sb* 对某人发出嘘声

raspy /ˈrɑːspi; *NAmE* ˈræspi/ *adj.* (of sb's voice 嗓音) having a rough sound, as if the person has a sore throat 沙哑刺耳的 SYN **croaky**

Ras·ta·far·ian /ˌræstəˈfeəriən; *NAmE* -ˈfer-/ (*also informal* **Rasta**) *noun* a member of a Jamaican religious group which worships the former Emperor of Ethiopia, Haile Selassie, and which believes that black people will one day return to Africa. Rastafarians often wear DREADLOCKS and have other distinguishing patterns of behaviour and dress. 拉斯塔法里教徒（牙买加一教派成员。崇拜前埃塞俄比亚皇帝海尔・塞拉西，并认为黑人将返回非洲大陆）▶ **Ras·ta·far·ian** (*also informal* **Rasta**) *adj.* **Ras·ta·far·ian·ism** *noun* [U]

ras·ter·ize (*BrE also* **-ise**) /ˈræstəraɪz/ (*also* **rip**) *verb* ~ **sth** (*computing* 计) to change text or images into a form in which they can be displayed on a screen or printed 将（文字或图像）光栅化；使栅格化

rat /ræt/ *noun, verb*

■ *noun* **1** a small animal with a long tail, that looks like a large mouse, usually considered a PEST (= an animal which is disliked because it destroys food or spreads disease) 老鼠；耗子：*rat poison* 老鼠药 ➲ COMPARE RUG RAT **2** (*informal, disapproving*) an unpleasant person, especially one who is not loyal or who tricks sb 讨厌的人；卑鄙的小人；骗子 IDM SEE SINK *v.*, SMELL *v.*

■ *verb* (**-tt-**)

PHR V ˈ**rat on sb** (*NAmE also* **rat sb out** (**to sb**)) (*informal, disapproving*) to tell sb in authority about sth wrong that sb else has done 泄露秘密；告密：*Where I come from, you don't rat on your friends.* 在我的老家，谁都不出卖朋友。ˈ**rat on sth** (*BrE, informal*) to not do sth that you have agreed or promised to do 背弃做某事的诺言 SYN **renege**: *The government is accused of ratting on its promises to the unemployed.* 政府被指责对失业者背信弃义。**rat sb ↔ out** (**to sb**) (*especially NAmE, informal, disapproving*) = RAT ON SB: *Someone ratted us out to the police.* 有人向警方告发了我们。

rata ➲ PRO RATA

ˌ**rat-arsed** *adj.* (*BrE, slang*) extremely drunk 烂醉如泥的

ˌ**rat-a-tat-ˈtat** *noun* [sing.] = RAT-TAT

rata·touille /ˌrætəˈtuːiː; -ˈtwiː/ *noun* [U, C] a dish of onions, PEPPERS, AUBERGINES/EGGPLANTS, COURGETTES/ZUCCHINI and tomatoes cooked together 蔬菜杂烩，炖焖蔬菜（用洋葱、辣椒、茄子、小胡瓜以及番茄一同烹制）

rat·bag /ˈrætbæg/ *noun* (*BrE, slang*) an unpleasant or disgusting person 讨厌的人；令人厌烦的人

ratchet 棘轮

ratchet /ˈrætʃɪt/ *noun, verb*

■ *noun* a wheel or bar with teeth along the edge and a metal piece that fits between the teeth, allowing movement in one direction only（防止倒转的）棘轮，棘齿

■ *verb*

PHR V ˌ**ratchet** (**sth**) ↔**up** to increase, or make sth increase, repeatedly and by small amounts（使）逐渐小幅增长：*Overuse of credit cards has ratcheted up consumer debt to unacceptable levels.* 滥用信用卡使消费债务逐渐增加到了难以接受的地步。

rate 🔑 /reɪt/ *noun, verb*

■ *noun* **1** 🔑 [C] a measurement of the speed at which sth happens 速度；进度：*Most people walk at an average rate of 5 kilometres an hour.* 大多数人步行的平均速度为每小时 5 公里。◇ *The number of reported crimes is increasing at an alarming rate.* 报警案件的数量正在以惊人的速度增长。◇ *Figures published today show another fall in the rate of inflation.* 今天公布的数字表明通货膨胀速度又一次下降。◇ *At the rate you work, you'll never finish!* 以你工作的速度，你永远也做不完！ **2** 🔑 [C] a measurement of the number of times sth happens or exists during a particular period 比率；率：*Local businesses are closing* ***at a/the rate of*** *three a year.* 地方企业正在以每年三家的速度关闭。◇ *a* ***high/low/rising rate*** *of unemployment* 高 / 低 / 不断增长的失业率 ◇ *the annual* ***crime/divorce rate*** 年犯罪 / 离婚率 ◇ *His pulse rate dropped suddenly.* 他的脉搏速率突然下降。◇ *a high* ***success/failure rate*** 很高的成功 / 失败率 ➲ SEE ALSO BIRTH RATE, DEATH RATE **3** [C] a fixed amount of money that is charged or paid for sth 价格；费用：***advertising/insurance/postal, etc. rates*** 广告费、保险费、邮费等 ◇ *a* ***low/high hourly rate of pay*** 按小时支付的低 / 高报酬 ◇ *We offer special* ***reduced rates*** *for students.* 我们对学生有特惠价格。◇ *a* ***fixed-rate*** *mortgage* (= one in which the amount of money paid back each month is fixed for a particular period) 定额偿还按揭贷款

▼ **SYNONYMS 同义词辨析**

rate

charge • fee • rent • fine • fare • toll • rental

These are all words for an amount of money that is charged or paid for sth. 以上各词均指所收取或付出的费用。

rate a fixed amount of money that is asked or paid for sth 指所索取或付出的价格、费用：*a low hourly rate of pay* 按小时支付的低报酬 ◇ *interest rates* 利率

charge an amount of money that is asked for goods or services 指商品或服务的要价、收费：*an admission charge* 入场费

fee (*rather formal*) an amount of money that you have to pay for professional advice or services, to go to a school or college, or to join an organization 指专业服务费、咨询费、学费、会费：*legal fees* 诉讼费 ◇ *an annual membership fee* 年度会费

rent an amount of money that you regularly have to pay for use of a building or room 指房屋租金 NOTE In American English, **rent** can be used to mean **rental**. 在美式英语中，rent 可用以表示 rental（租金）：*The weekly rent on the car was over $300.* 这辆汽车每周的租金是 300 多美元。

fine a sum of money that must be paid as punishment for breaking a law or rule 指罚金、罚款：*a parking fine* 违规停车罚款

fare the money that you pay to travel by bus, plane, taxi, etc. 指乘坐公共汽车、飞机、出租车等的费用

toll an amount of money that you have to pay to use a particular road or bridge 指道路、桥梁的通行费

rental an amount of money that you have to pay to use sth for a particular period of time 指租金

RENT OR RENTAL? 用 rent 还是 rental?

In British English **rent** is only money paid to use a building or room: for other items use **rental**. In American English **rent** can be used for both, but **rental** is still more common for other items. 在英式英语中，rent 只指房屋租金，其他物品的租金用 rental。在美式英语中，rent 可指以上两种租金；但指其他物品的租金时，较常用 rental。

PATTERNS

- (a) rate/charge/fee/rent/fine/fare/toll/rental **for** sth
- (a) rate/charge/fee/rent/toll/rental **on** sth
- **at** a rate/charge/fee/rent/fare/rental of...
- **for** a charge/fee
- **to pay** (a) rate/charge/fee/rent/fine/fare/toll/rental
- **to charge** (a) rate/fee/rent/fare/toll/rental

◇ *the basic rate of tax* (= the lowest amount that is paid by everyone) 基本税额 ◇ ***exchange/interest rates*** 汇率；利率 ◇ ***rates of exchange/interest*** 汇率；利率 ➲ SEE ALSO BASE RATE, FLAT RATE, RACK RATE **4 rates** [pl.] (in Britain) a tax paid by businesses to a local authority for land and buildings that they use and in the past also paid by anyone who owned a house（英国地方政府征收的）房地产税，房产税 ➲ SYNONYMS AT TAX ➲ SEE ALSO FIRST-RATE, SECOND-RATE, THIRD-RATE

IDM **at 'any rate** (*informal*) **1** used to say that a particular fact is true despite what has happened in the past or what may happen in the future（强调事情的真实性）无论如何，不管怎样：*Well, that's one good piece of news at any rate.* 不管怎么说，那是个好消息。◇ *I may be away on business next week but at any rate I'll be back by Friday.* 我下周可能要出差，但无论如何，我最晚星期五回来。**2** used to show that you are being more accurate about sth that you have just said（表示说得更加确切）不管怎样，至少：*He said he'll be coming tomorrow. At any rate, I think that's what he said.* 他说他明天要来。至少，我认为他是这么说的。**3** used to show that what you have just said is not as important as what you are going to say（强调下文）总而言之，反正：*There were maybe 60 or 70 people there. At any rate, the room was packed.* 那里也许有六七十人吧。反正屋子里挤得严严实实。**at a rate of 'knots** (*BrE, informal*) very quickly 飞快地；迅速地 **at 'this/'that rate** (*informal*) used to say what will happen if a particular situation continues to develop in the same way 照此情形；如此下去：*At this rate, we'll soon be bankrupt.* 照此情形，我们很快就会破产。➲ MORE AT GOING *adj.*

■ ***verb*** (not used in the progressive tenses 不用于进行时) **1** 🔑 [T, I] **~ sb/sth (as) sth | ~ as sth** to have or think that sb/sth has a particular level of quality, value, etc. 评估；评价；估价：**~ sb/sth (+ adv./prep.)** *The university is **highly rated** for its research.* 这所大学因其研究工作而受到高度评价。◇ *They rated him highly as a colleague.* 作为同事，他们对他评价甚高。◇ **~ sb/sth + adj.** *Voters continue to rate education high on their list of priorities.* 选民继续把教育看作是头等重要的大事。◇ **~ sb/sth (as) sth | ~ sb/sth + noun** *The show was rated (as) a success by critics and audiences.* 评论家和观众都认为这次演出是成功的。◇ **~ as sth** *The match rated as one of their worst defeats.* 这次比赛可以说是他们最为惨重的一次失败。◇ **+ adj.** *I'm afraid our needs do not rate very high with this administration.* 我们的需求恐怕不会受到这届政府多大重视。**2** [T] **~ sth** (*informal*) to think that sb/sth is good 认为…是好的；看好：*What did you think of the movie? I didn't rate it myself.* 你觉得这部电影怎么样？我个人认为不怎么样。**3** 🔑 [T, usually passive] to place sb/sth in a particular position on a scale in relation to similar people or things 划分等级；分等 SYN **rank**: **~ sb/sth (+ adv./prep.)** *The schools were rated according to their exam results.* 这些学校是按考试成绩排名次的。◇ *a top-rated programme* 一级项目 ◇ **~ sb/sth + noun** *She is currently rated number two in the world.* 她目前排名世界第二。**4** [T] **~ sth** to be good, important, etc. enough to be treated in a particular way 值得，配得上（某种对待）SYN **merit**: *The incident didn't even **rate a mention** in the press.* 这件事在报纸上连提都不值得一提。**5** [T, usually passive] **~ sth (+ noun)** to state that a film/movie or video is suitable for a particular audience 对（电影或录像片）分级 ➲ SEE ALSO X-RATED, ZERO-RATED

'rate cap *noun* (in the US) a limit placed on the amount of interest banks, etc. may charge（美国）利息限额

rate·pay·er /ˈreɪtpeɪə(r)/ *noun* (in Britain in the past) a person who paid taxes to the local authority on the buildings and land they owned（英国旧时的）地方税纳税人

ra·ther 🔑 /ˈrɑːðə(r); *NAmE* ˈræðər/ *adv., exclamation*

■ ***adv.*** **1** 🔑 used to mean 'fairly' or 'to some degree', often when you are expressing slight criticism, disappointment or surprise（常用于表示轻微的批评、失望或惊讶）相当，在某种程度上：*The instructions were rather complicated.* 这些说明相当复杂。◇ *She fell and hurt her leg rather badly.* 她跌倒了，腿伤得相当重。◇ *I didn't fail the exam; in fact I did rather well!* 我没有考不及格，事实上，我考得不错！◇ *It was a rather difficult question.* 这是个相当难的问题。◇ *It was **rather a** difficult question.* 这真是个难题。◇ *He looks rather like his father.* 他看上去很像他的父亲。◇ *The patient has responded to the treatment rather better than expected.* 病人对治疗的反应比预想的好得多。◇ *He was conscious that he was talking **rather too** much.* 他意识到他说得实在太多了。➲ NOTE AT QUITE **2** used with a verb to make a statement sound less strong（与动词连用以减弱语气）有点儿，稍微：*I rather suspect we're making a mistake.* 我有点儿怀疑我们正在犯错误。◇ *We were rather hoping you'd be able to do it by Friday.* 我们希望你最好能在星期五之前做这件事。**3** 🔑 used to correct sth you have said, or to give more accurate information（纠正所说的话或提供更确切的信息）更确切地讲，更准确地说：*She worked as a secretary, or rather, a personal assistant.* 她当了秘书；确切地讲，是私人助理。◇ *In the end he had to walk—or rather run—to the office.* 最后他不得不走着，应该说是跑着，去办公室。➲ LANGUAGE BANK AT I.E. **4** 🔑 used to introduce an idea that is different or opposite to the idea that you have stated previously（提出不同或相反的观点）相反，反而，而是：*The walls were not white, but rather a sort of dirty grey.* 墙面不是白的，而是灰不溜秋的。

IDM **rather you, him, etc. than 'me** (*informal*) used for saying that you would not like to do sth that another person is going to do（表明不想做别人要去做的事）：*'I'm going climbing tomorrow.' 'Rather you than me!'* "我明天去爬山。""你去吧，我可不去！" **rather than** 🔑 instead of sb/sth 而不是：*I think I'll have a cold drink rather than coffee.* 我想要冷饮，不要咖啡。◇ *Why didn't you ask for help, rather than trying to do it on your own?* 你干吗非得自己干，而不请人帮忙？**would rather...** **(than)** 🔑 (usually reduced to *'d rather* 通常缩写为 'd rather) would prefer to 宁愿；更喜欢：*She'd rather die than give a speech.* 她宁愿死也不愿意演讲。◇ *'Do you want to come with us?' 'No, I'd rather not.'* "你想跟我们一起来吗？""不，我不想去。" ◇ *Would you rather walk or take the bus?* 你比较喜欢步行还是坐公共汽车？◇ *'Do you mind if I smoke?' 'Well, I'd rather you didn't.'* "你介意我抽烟吗？""嗯，最好别抽。" ➲ EXPRESS YOURSELF AT PREFER

■ ***exclamation*** /ˌrɑːˈðɜː(r)/ (*old-fashioned, BrE*) used to agree with sb's suggestion（表示同意某人的提议）：*'How about a trip to the beach?' 'Rather!'* "去海边旅游怎么样？""太好了！"

rat·ify /ˈrætɪfaɪ/ *verb* (**rati·fies**, **rati·fy·ing**, **rati·fied**, **rati·fied**) **~ sth** to make an agreement officially valid by voting for or signing it 正式批准；使正式生效：*The treaty was ratified by all the member states.* 这个条约得到了所有成员国的批准。▸ **rati·fi·ca·tion** /ˌrætɪfɪˈkeɪʃn/ *noun* [U]

rat·ing /ˈreɪtɪŋ/ *noun* **1** [C] a measurement of how good, popular, important, etc. sb/sth is, especially in relation to other people or things 等级；级别：*The poll gave a popular approval rating of 39% for the President.* 民意调查表明民众对总统的支持率为 39%。◇ *Education has been given a high-priority rating by the new administration.* 新一届政府将教育放在了高度优先的地位。➲ SEE ALSO CREDIT RATING **2 the ratings** [pl.] a set of figures that show how many people watch or listen to a particular television or radio programme, used to show how popular a programme is 收视率；收听率：*The show has gone up in the ratings.* 这个节目的收视率上升了。➲ COLLOCATIONS AT TELEVISION **3** [C] a number or letter that shows which groups of people a particular film/movie is suitable for 表示电影分级的数字（或字母）；电影的等级：*The film was given a 15 rating by British censors.* 英国审查员将这部电影定为 15 岁以上级。◇ *The movie carries an R rating.* 这部电影带有限制级 R 的标志。**4** [C] (*BrE*) a sailor in the navy who is not an officer 海军士兵；水手

ratio AW /ˈreɪʃiəʊ; *NAmE* -oʊ/ *noun* (*pl.* **-os**) **~ (of A to B)** the relationship between two groups of people or things that is represented by two numbers showing how much larger one group is than the other 比率；比例：*What is the ratio of men to women in the department?* 这个部门的

男女比例是多少？ ◇ *The school has a very high teacher-student ratio.* 这所学校的师生比例很高。 ◇ *The ratio of applications to available places currently stands at 100:1.* 目前，申请人数和录取名额的比例为 100:1。

rati·ocin·ation /ˌræti,ɒsɪˈneɪʃn; *NAmE* ˌreɪʃioʊ-/ *noun* [U] (*formal*) the process of thinking or arguing about sth in a logical way 推理；推论

ra·tion /ˈræʃn/ *noun, verb*

■ ***noun*** **1** [C] a fixed amount of food, fuel, etc. that you are officially allowed to have when there is not enough for everyone to have as much as they want, for example during a war（食品、燃料等短缺时的）配给量，定量：*the weekly butter ration* 每周的黄油配给量 **2 rations** [pl.] a fixed amount of food given regularly to a soldier or to sb who is in a place where there is not much food available（给战士或食品短缺地区的人提供的）定量口粮：*We're on **short rations*** (= allowed less than usual) *until fresh supplies arrive.* 在新的补给到达之前，我们的口粮定量不足。◇ *Once these latest rations run out, the country will again face hunger and starvation.* 最后这批口粮一旦用完，国家又要面临饥荒。 **3** [sing.] ~ (**of sth**) an amount of sth that is thought to be normal or fair 正常量；合理的量：*As part of the diet, allow yourself a small daily ration of sugar.* 作为饮食的一部分，每天可以摄入少量的糖。◇ *I've had my ration of problems for one day—you deal with it!* 我手头的问题已经够我忙活一天的了，你来处理这件事吧！

■ ***verb*** [often passive] to limit the amount of sth that sb is allowed to have, especially because there is not enough of it available 限定…的量；定量供应；配给：~ **sth** *Eggs were rationed during the war.* 战争期间，鸡蛋限量供应。◇ ~ **sb to sth** *The villagers are rationed to two litres of water a day.* 村民每天的用水量限定为两升。➲ SEE ALSO RATIONING

ra·tion·al AW /ˈræʃnəl/ *adj.* **1** (of behaviour, ideas, etc. 行为、思想等) based on reason rather than emotions 合理的；理性的；明智的：*a rational argument/choice/decision* 合理的论点 / 选择 / 决定 ◇ *rational analysis/thought* 有道理的分析 / 思考 ◇ *There is no rational explanation for his actions.* 对他的所作所为无法作出合理的解释。 **2** (of a person 人) able to think clearly and make decisions based on reason rather than emotions 理智的；清醒的 SYN **reasonable**: *No rational person would ever behave like that.* 头脑清醒的人都不会这样做。 OPP **irrational** ▶ **ra·tion·al·ity** AW /ˌræʃəˈnæləti/ *noun* [U]: *the rationality of his argument* 他的论点的合理性 **ra·tion·al·ly** AW /ˈræʃnəli/ *adv.*: *to act/behave/think rationally* 行动 / 举止 / 思考合情合理 ◇ *She argued her case calmly and rationally.* 她冷静而又理智地为她的情况辩解。

ra·tion·ale /ˌræʃəˈnɑːl; *NAmE* -ˈnæl/ *noun* ~ (**behind/for/of sth**) (*formal*) the principles or reasons which explain a particular decision, course of action, belief, etc. 基本原理；根本原因 SYN **reason**: *What is the rationale behind these new exams?* 这些新考试的理论依据是什么？

ra·tion·al·ism AW /ˈræʃnəlɪzəm/ *noun* [U] (*philosophy* 哲) the belief that all behaviour, opinions, etc. should be based on reason rather than on emotions or religious beliefs 理性主义；唯理论

ra·tion·al·ist /ˈræʃnəlɪst/ *noun* a person who believes in rationalism 理性主义者；唯理论者 ▶ **ra·tion·al·ist** (*also* **ra·tion·al·is·tic**) *adj.* [usually before noun]: *a rationalistic position* 理性主义立场

ra·tion·al·ize AW (*BrE also* **-ise**) /ˈræʃnəlaɪz/ *verb* **1** [T, I] ~ (**sth**) to find or try to find a logical reason to explain why sb thinks, behaves, etc. in a way that is difficult to understand 对…进行理性的解释；对…加以科学的说明：*an attempt to rationalize his violent behaviour* 对他的暴力行为作出合理解释的尝试 **2** [T, I] ~ (**sth**) (*BrE*) to make changes to a business, system, etc. in order to make it more efficient, especially by spending less money 使合理化；进行合理化改革；使有经济效益：*Twenty workers lost their jobs when the department was rationalized.* 在部门的合理化改革中，有二十名工人失业。➲ SYNONYMS AT CUT ▶ **ra·tion·al·iza·tion, -isa·tion** AW /ˌræʃnəlaɪˈzeɪʃn; *NAmE* -ləˈz-/ *noun* [U, C]: *No amount of rationalization could justify his actions.* 无论怎么解释，他的行为都不能说是正当的。◇ *a need for rationalization of the industry* 对这一行业进行合理化改革的必要性

ˌrational ˈnumber *noun* (*mathematics* 数) a number that can be expressed as the RATIO of two whole numbers 有理数

ra·tion·ing /ˈræʃənɪŋ/ *noun* [U] the policy of limiting the amount of food, fuel, etc. that people are allowed to have when there is not enough for everyone to have as much as they want 定量配给政策；配给制

ˈrat pack *noun* [sing.+sing./pl. v.] (*BrE, disapproving*) journalists and photographers who follow famous people around in a way which makes their lives unpleasant 鼠帮（指追踪骚扰名人的新闻或摄影记者）

the ˈrat race *noun* [sing.] (*disapproving*) the way of life of people living and working in a large city where people compete in an aggressive way with each other in order to be more successful, earn more money, etc.（大城市里人们追求成功、财富等的）疯狂竞争，激烈竞争 ➲ COLLOCATIONS AT TOWN

ˈrat run *noun* (*BrE, informal*) a small road, especially one with houses on it, used by drivers during busy times when the main roads are full of traffic（开车者在高峰时段为避开拥挤的大路而行驶其间的）小路，小街

rats /ræts/ *exclamation* (*informal*) used to show that you are annoyed about sth（表示气恼）该死，可恶：*Rats! I forgot my glasses.* 该死！我忘了带眼镜。

rat·tan /ræˈtæn/ *noun* [U] a SE Asian climbing plant with long thin strong STEMS used especially for making furniture 藤（东南亚蔓生植物，茎干多用于做家具）：*a rattan chair* 藤椅

ˌrat-ˈtat (*also* **ˌrat-a-tat-ˈtat**) *noun* [sing.] the sound of knocking, especially on a door（敲击声，尤指敲门声）吧嗒，嗒嗒 ➲ MORE LIKE THIS 3, page R25

rat·tle /ˈrætl/ *verb, noun*

■ ***verb*** (*informal*) **1** [I, T] ~ (**sth**) to make a series of short loud sounds when hitting against sth hard; to make sth do this（使）发出咔嗒咔嗒的声音：*Every time a bus went past, the windows rattled.* 每次公共汽车经过这里，窗户都格格作响。 **2** [I] + **adv./prep.** (of a vehicle 车辆) to make a series of short loud sounds as it moves somewhere（运行时）发出连续短促的高声：*A convoy of trucks rattled by.* 卡车队隆隆驶过。 **3** [T] ~ **sb** to make sb nervous or frightened 使紧张；使恐惧 SYN **unnerve**: *He was clearly rattled by the question.* 这个问题显然令他感到紧张。➲ SEE ALSO SABRE-RATTLING

IDM **ˌrattle sb's ˈcage** (*informal*) to annoy sb 骚扰；使恼怒：*Who's rattled his cage?* 谁惹他生气了？

PHR V **ˌrattle aˈround** | **ˌrattle aˈround sth** (*informal*) to be living, working, etc. in a room or building that is too big 在空荡的大房子里居住（或工作等）：*She spent the last few years alone, rattling around the old family home.* 她在世的最后几年，一个人居住在空空荡荡的老宅子里。 **ˌrattle sth ↔ˈoff** to say sth from memory without having to think too hard 脱口而出；不假思索地说出：*She can rattle off the names of all the presidents of the US.* 她可以不假思索地说出所有美国总统的名字。 **ˌrattle ˈon** (**about sth**) (*informal*) to talk continuously about sth that is not important or interesting, especially in an annoying way 对…喋喋不休

■ ***noun*** **1** (*also* **rat·tling**) [usually sing.] a series of short loud sounds made when hard objects hit against each other 一连串短促尖厉的撞击声；咔嗒声：*the rattle of gunfire* 轰隆轰隆的炮火声 ◇ *From the kitchen came a rattling of cups and saucers.* 从厨房里传来叮叮当当杯盘相碰的声音。➲ SEE ALSO DEATH RATTLE **2** a baby's toy that makes a series of short loud sounds when it is shaken 拨浪鼓 **3** a wooden object that is held in one hand and makes a series of short loud sounds when you spin it round, used, for example, by people watching a sports game 响板（在体育比赛等中观众用来助阵）

rattle·snake /ˈrætlsneɪk/ (*also informal* **rat·tler** /ˈrætlə(r)/) *noun* a poisonous American snake that makes a noise like a rattle with its tail when it is angry or afraid 响尾蛇（产于美洲）

rat·tling /ˈrætlɪŋ/ *adv.* **~ good** (*old-fashioned, BrE*) very good 很；非常：*This book is a rattling good read.* 这是一本非常好的读物。

ratty /ˈræti/ *adj.* **1** (*BrE, informal*) becoming angry very easily 易怒的；暴躁的 **SYN** **grumpy**, **irritable**：*He gets ratty if he doesn't get enough sleep.* 他要是睡眠不足动不动就发脾气。 **2** (*NAmE, informal*) in bad condition 糟糕的；状况差的 **SYN** **shabby**：*long ratty hair* 乱蓬蓬的长发 ◇ *a ratty old pair of jeans* 破旧的牛仔裤 **3** looking like a RAT 像鼠的

rau·cous /ˈrɔːkəs/ *adj.* sounding loud and rough 刺耳的；尖厉的：*raucous laughter* 刺耳的笑声 ◇ *a raucous voice* 沙哑的声音 ◇ *a group of raucous young men* 一群吵闹的年轻男子 ▸ **rau·cous·ly** *adv.* **rau·cous·ness** *noun* [U]

raunchy /ˈrɔːntʃi/ *adj.* (*informal*) **1** intended to be sexually exciting 淫秽的；下流的 **SYN** **sexy**：*a raunchy magazine* 色情杂志 ◇ *Their stage act is a little too raunchy for television.* 他们的舞台表演有点儿太淫秽了，不适合上电视。 **2** (*NAmE*) looking dirty and untidy 肮脏的；邋遢的：*a raunchy old man* 邋遢的老头子

rav·age /ˈrævɪdʒ/ *verb* [usually passive] **~ sth** to damage sth badly 毁坏；损坏；严重损害 **SYN** **devastate**：*a country ravaged by civil war* 遭受内战重创的国家

rav·ages /ˈrævɪdʒɪz/ *noun* [pl.] **the ~ of sth** (*formal*) the destruction caused by sth 破坏；损害；毁坏：*the ravages of war* 战争造成的灾难 ◇ *Her looks had not survived the **ravages of time**.* 她的容颜未能幸免于岁月的摧残。

rave /reɪv/ *verb, noun*

■ ***verb*** **1** [I, T] **~ (about sb/sth)** | **+ speech** to talk or write about sth in a very enthusiastic way 热烈谈论（或书写）；（热情洋溢地）奋笔疾书：*The critics raved about his performance in 'Hamlet'.* 评论家们热情赞扬了他在《哈姆雷特》中的表演。 **2** [I, T] **~ (at sb)** | **+ speech** to shout in a loud and emotional way at sb because you are angry with them 咆哮；怒吼：*She was shouting and raving at them.* 她冲着他们大喊大叫。 **3** [I, T] **~ (at sb)** | **+ speech** to talk or shout in a way that is not logical or sensible 瞎扯；胡说八道：*He wandered the streets raving at passers-by.* 他在街上闲逛，跟过路的人瞎扯。 **IDM** SEE RANT

■ ***noun*** **1** (in Britain) a large party, held outside or in an empty building, at which people dance to fast electronic music and often take illegal drugs （英国）狂欢晚会：*an all-night rave* 通宵狂欢晚会 **2** (*NAmE*) = RAVE REVIEW

ravel /ˈrævl/ *verb* (**-ll-**, *US* **-l-**) **~ sth** to make a situation or problem more complicated 使更复杂；使更纷乱

PHR V **ravel sth ↔ out** to open sth which has become twisted or which contains knots 拆开（缠结的东西）；解开…的结 **SYN** **unravel**：(*figurative*) *He was trying to ravel out the complicated series of events that had led to this situation.* 他那时正试图把导致这一局面的一系列复杂事件理出个头绪来。

raven /ˈreɪvn/ *noun, adj.*

■ ***noun*** a large bird of the CROW family, with shiny black feathers and a rough unpleasant cry 渡鸦（羽毛亮黑色，鸣声刺耳）

■ ***adj.*** [only before noun] (*literary*) (of hair 毛发) shiny and black 乌黑光亮的：*raven-haired* 毛发乌黑光亮的

raven·ing /ˈrævənɪŋ/ *adj.* (*literary*) (especially of animals 尤指动物) aggressive and hungry 凶猛的；饥饿而富攻击性的：*He says the media are ravening wolves.* 他说媒体就如同饿狼一般。

rav·en·ous /ˈrævənəs/ *adj.* **1** (of a person or an animal 人或动物) extremely hungry 极其饥饿的 **SYN** **starving**：*What's for lunch? I'm absolutely ravenous.* 午饭吃什么？我饿死了。 **2** [only before noun] (of HUNGER 饥饿) very great 严重的；十分的：*a ravenous appetite* 极强的食欲 ▸ **rav·en·ous·ly** *adv.*

raver /ˈreɪvə(r)/ *noun* (*BrE, informal*) **1** (*often humorous*) a person who likes going out and who has an exciting social life 喜欢社交活动的人；喜欢寻欢作乐的人 **2** a person who goes to RAVES 参加狂欢聚会的人

ˌrave reˈview (*NAmE also* **rave**) *noun* an article in a newspaper or magazine that is very enthusiastic about a particular film/movie, book, etc. 热情洋溢的评论文章

ˈrave-up *noun* (*old-fashioned, BrE, informal*) a lively party or celebration 狂欢聚会；热闹的庆典

rav·ine /rəˈviːn/ *noun* a deep, very narrow valley with steep sides 沟壑；溪谷

rav·ing /ˈreɪvɪŋ/ *adj., adv.*

■ ***adj.*** [only before noun] **1** (of a person 人) talking or behaving in a way that shows they are crazy 狂乱的；语无伦次的；疯疯癫癫的：*The man's a raving lunatic.* 那个男子是个语无伦次的疯子。 **2** used to emphasize a particular state or quality （强调某种状态或品质）：*She's no raving beauty.* 她算不上绝色美女。

■ ***adv.***

IDM **(stark) raving ˈmad/ˈbonkers** (*informal*) completely crazy 十分疯狂；彻底疯狂

rav·ings /ˈreɪvɪŋz/ *noun* [pl.] words that have no meaning, spoken by sb who is crazy 疯话；胡言乱语：*He dismissed her words as the ravings of a hysterical woman.* 他不理睬她的话，认为那是一个歇斯底里的女人的胡言乱语。

ravi·oli /ˌræviˈəʊli; *NAmE* -ˈoʊli/ *noun* [U] PASTA in the shape of small squares filled with meat, cheese, etc., usually served with a sauce 意大利方形饺（以肉、奶酪等为馅，通常佐以酱汁食用）

rav·ish /ˈrævɪʃ/ *verb* (*literary*) **1 ~ sb** (of a man 男子) to force a woman to have sex 强暴；强奸 **SYN** **rape** **2** [usually passive] **~ sb** to give sb great pleasure 使狂喜；使销魂

rav·ish·ing /ˈrævɪʃɪŋ/ *adj.* extremely beautiful 极其美丽的 **SYN** **gorgeous**：*a ravishing blonde* 迷人的金发女郎 ▸ **rav·ish·ing·ly** *adv.*：*ravishingly beautiful* 异常美丽

raw 🔑 /rɔː/ *adj., noun*

■ ***adj.***

• **FOOD** 食物 **1** 🔑 not cooked 生的；未烹制的；未煮的：*raw meat* 生肉 ◇ *These fish are often eaten raw.* 这些鱼常常生吃。

• **MATERIALS** 材料 **2** [usually before noun] in its natural state; not yet changed, used or made into sth else 未经加工的；自然状态的：*raw sugar* 原糖

• **INFORMATION** 信息 **3** [usually before noun] not yet organized into a form in which it can be easily used or understood 未经处理的；未经分析的；原始的：*This information is only **raw data** and will need further analysis.* 这些资料只是原始数据，还需要进一步分析。

• **EMOTIONS/QUALITIES** 情感；品质 **4** [usually before noun] powerful and natural; not controlled or trained 未经训练的；粗犷的：*songs full of raw emotion* 充满豪放情感的歌曲 ◇ *He started with nothing but raw talent and determination.* 他起初一无所有，只有天生的才能和决心。

• **PART OF BODY** 身体部位 **5** red and painful because the skin has been damaged 红肿疼痛的；皮肤破损的；擦伤的：*There were raw patches on her feet where the shoes had rubbed.* 她的双脚被鞋子磨破了好几块皮。 ➲ SYNONYMS AT PAINFUL

• **PERSON** 人 **6** [usually before noun] new to a job or an activity and therefore without experience or skill 工作生疏的；不熟练的；无经验的：*a raw beginner* 没有经验的新手 ◇ *raw recruits* (= for example, in the army) 未经训练的新兵

• **WEATHER** 天气 **7** very cold 寒冷的；严寒的：*a raw north wind* 寒冷的北风 ◇ *It had been a wet raw winter.* 那是一个寒冷潮湿的冬天。

• **DESCRIPTION** 描述 **8** honest, direct and sometimes shocking 真实的；反映真实情况的：*a raw portrayal of working-class life* 工人阶级生活的真实写照 ◇ (*NAmE*) *raw language* (= containing many sexual details) 粗鲁的语言

R

▸ **raw·ness** *noun* [U]

IDM **a raw 'deal** the fact of sb being treated unfairly 不公平的待遇；不公正的对待：*Older workers often get a raw deal.* 年纪大的工人经常受到不公正的对待。

▪ *noun*

IDM **catch/touch sb on the 'raw** (*BrE*) to upset sb by reminding them of sth they are particularly sensitive about 触到某人的痛处；揭某人的疮疤 **in the 'raw 1** in a way that does not hide the unpleasant aspects of sth 质朴的；不加掩饰的：*He spent a couple of months on the streets to experience life in the raw.* 他花了几个月时间走街串巷，体验真实的生活。 **2** (*especially NAmE*) with no clothes on 赤条条；赤身裸体；一丝不挂 SYN **naked** ➲ MORE AT NERVE *n.*

raw·hide /ˈrɔːhaɪd/ *noun* [U] natural leather that has not had any special treatment 生皮；未经加工的皮革

Rawl·plug™ /ˈrɔːlplʌg/ *noun* (*also* **'wall plug**) (*both BrE*) (*NAmE* **'wall anchor**) a small plastic tube, closed at one end, that you put into a wall to hold a screw 罗威纤维管（塑料螺钉栓）

ˌraw ma'terial *noun* [C, U] a basic material that is used to make a product 原料：*We have had problems with the supply of raw materials to the factory.* 我们在工厂的原料供应方面遇到过问题。◇ *These trees provide the raw material for high-quality paper.* 这些树是制造优质纸张的原料。◇ (*figurative*) *The writer uses her childhood as raw material for this novel.* 作者将她的童年时代作为这部小说的素材。➲ WORDFINDER NOTE AT INDUSTRY

ray /reɪ/ *noun* **1** a narrow line of light, heat or other energy 光线；（热或其他能量的）射线：*the sun's rays* 太阳的光线 ◇ *ultraviolet rays* 紫外线 ◇ *The windows were shining in the reflected rays of the setting sun.* 窗户上闪耀着落日的余晖。 ➲ WORDFINDER NOTE AT SUN ➲ SEE ALSO COSMIC RAYS, GAMMA RAYS at GAMMA RADIATION, X-RAY *n.* **2 ~ of sth** a small amount of sth good or of sth that you are hoping for（好事或所希望事物的）一点，少量 SYN **glimmer**: *There was just one small **ray of hope**.* 只有一线希望。 **3** a sea fish with a large broad flat body and a long tail, that is used for food 魟，鳐（扁体长尾，可食用） **4** (*also* **re**) (*music* 音) the second note of a MAJOR SCALE 大调音阶的第 2 音

IDM **a ˌray of 'sunshine** (*informal*) a person or thing that makes life brighter or more cheerful 给人带来快乐的人（或事物） **catch/get/grab some 'rays** (*informal*) to sit or lie in the sun, especially in order to get a SUNTAN 晒太阳；沐日光浴

'ray gun *noun* (in SCIENCE FICTION stories) a gun that kills or injures people by sending out harmful rays（科幻小说中的）死光枪，射线枪

rayon /ˈreɪɒn; *NAmE* -ɑːn/ *noun* [U] a FIBRE made from CELLULOSE; a smooth material made from this, used for making clothes 人造丝；人造丝织品

raze /reɪz/ *verb* [usually passive] **~ sth** to completely destroy a building, town, etc. so that nothing is left 彻底摧毁；将…夷为平地：*The village was **razed to the ground**.* 这座村庄被夷为平地。

razor /ˈreɪzə(r)/ *noun* an instrument that is used for shaving 剃须刀；刮脸刀：*an electric razor* 电动剃须刀 ◇ *a **cut-throat/safety/disposable razor*** 开式 / 安全 / 一次性剃刀 ➲ VISUAL VOCAB PAGE V25 ➲ COMPARE SHAVER

IDM **be on the 'razor's edge | be on a 'razor edge** to be in a difficult situation where any mistake may be very dangerous 处于非常危险的困境；境况岌岌可危

razor·bill /ˈreɪzəbɪl; *NAmE* -zərb-/ *noun* a black and white bird with a beak that looks like an old-fashioned RAZOR, found in the N Atlantic and the Baltic Sea 刀嘴海雀（产于北大西洋和波罗的海）

'razor blade *noun* a thin sharp piece of metal that is used in a razor, especially one that can be thrown away when it is no longer sharp（尤指可更换的）剃须刀刀片 ➲ PICTURE AT BLADE

ˌrazor-'sharp *adj.* **1** extremely sharp 极锋利的：*razor-sharp teeth* 十分锋利的牙齿 **2** showing that sb is extremely intelligent 极其敏锐的：*a razor-sharp mind* 极敏锐的头脑

ˌrazor-'thin *adj.* (*NAmE*) (of a victory in an election, etc. 选举等的胜利) won by a very small number of votes 以微弱优势取胜的；险胜的

'razor wire *noun* [U] strong wire with sharp blades sticking out, placed on top of walls and around areas of land to keep people out 尖利铁丝网，刺钢丝（墙头及土地周围防护用）

razz /ræz/ *verb* **~ sb** (*old-fashioned, NAmE, informal*) to TEASE sb by saying or doing things to make people laugh at them 嘲弄；戏弄

raz·zle /ˈræzl/ *noun*

IDM **be/go (out) on the razzle** (*BrE, informal*) to go out drinking, dancing and enjoying yourself 出外纵饮狂欢；外出寻欢作乐

razz·ma·tazz /ˌræzməˈtæz/ (*also* **raz·za·ma·tazz** /ˌræzəməˈtæz/) (*also* **ˌrazzle-'dazzle**) *noun* [U] (*informal*) a lot of noisy exciting activity that is intended to attract people's attention 令人眼花缭乱的活动：*The documentary focuses on the razzmatazz of an American political campaign.* 这部纪录片着重展现一场美国政治运动令人眼花缭乱的一面。

RC /ˌɑː ˈsiː; *NAmE* ˌɑːr/ *abbr.* ROMAN CATHOLIC 天主教

RCMP /ˌɑː siː em ˈpiː; *NAmE* ˌɑːr/ *abbr.* Royal Canadian Mounted Police (the national police force of Canada) 皇家加拿大骑警队（加拿大的国家警力）

Rd (*also* **Rd.** *especially in NAmE*) *abbr.* (used in written addresses) Road（用于书面地址）路：*12 Ashton Rd* 阿什顿路 12 号

RDA /ˌɑː diː ˈeɪ; *NAmE* ˌɑːr/ *abbr.* recommended daily allowance or recommended dietary allowance (the amount of a chemical, for example a VITAMIN or a mineral, which you should have every day)（维生素或矿物质等的）建议每日摄取量（全写为 recommended daily allowance 或 recommended dietary allowance）

RE /ˌɑːr ˈiː/ *noun* [U] the abbreviation for 'religious education' (a school subject in which students learn about different religions) 宗教教育（全写为 religious education，学校里讲授不同宗教知识的课程）：*an RE teacher* 宗教教育科老师

re¹ /reɪ/ = RAY (4)

re² /riː/ *prep.* used at the beginning of a business letter, etc. to introduce the subject that it is about; used on an email that you are sending as a reply（用于商业信函等开头介绍主题或回复电子邮件）关于，事由：*Re your letter of 1 September…* 关于你 9 月 1 日的来信… ◇ *Re: travel expenses* 回复：旅行开支 ➲ WORDFINDER NOTE AT MESSAGE

re- 🔑 /riː/ *prefix* (in verbs and related nouns, adjectives and adverbs 构成动词及相关的名词、形容词和副词) again 又；再；重新：*reapply* 再申请 ◇ *reincarnation* 转世化身 ◇ *reassuring* 使人放心的 ➲ MORE LIKE THIS 6, page R25

reach 🔑 /riːtʃ/ *verb, noun*

▪ *verb*

• **ARRIVE** 到达 **1** 🔑 [T] **~ sth/sb** to arrive at the place that you have been travelling to 到达；抵达：*They didn't reach the border until after dark.* 他们天黑以后才到达边境。◇ *I hope this letter reaches you.* 我希望你能收到这封信。 **2** 🔑 [T] **~ sb** to come to sb's attention 引起…的注意：*The rumours eventually reached the President.* 传闻最终引起了总统的注意。

• **LEVEL/SPEED/STAGE** 水平；速度；阶段 **3** 🔑 [T] **~ sth** to increase to a particular level, speed, etc. over a period of time 增加到，提升到（某一水平、速度等）：*The conflict has now reached a new level of intensity.* 冲突现在已经达到了新的激烈程度。◇ *Daytime temperatures can reach 40°C.* 白天的气温可以达到 40 摄氏度。 **4** 🔑 [T] **~ sth** to

R

arrive at a particular point or stage of sth after a period of time 达到（某点）；进入（某阶段）：*He first reached the finals in 2014.* 他于 2014 年第一次进入决赛。◇ *The negotiations have reached deadlock.* 谈判陷入僵局。

• **ACHIEVE AIM** 实现目标 **5** [T] **~ sth** to achieve a particular aim 实现；达到 SYN **arrive at**: *to reach a conclusion/decision/verdict/compromise* 得出结论；作出决定 / 裁决 / 妥协 ◇ *Politicians again failed to* ***reach an agreement.*** 政治家们又一次没有达成一致。 ➲ SEE ALSO FAR-REACHING

• **WITH HAND/ARM** 用手 / 手臂 **6** [I, T] to stretch your hand towards sth in order to touch it, pick it up, etc. 伸；伸手：**+ adv./prep.** *She reached inside her bag for a pen.* 她把手伸到包里掏钢笔。◇ **~ sth + adv./prep.** *He reached out his hand to touch her.* 他伸出手去摸她。 **7** [I, T] to be able to stretch your hand far enough in order to touch sth, pick sth up, etc. 能伸到；够得着：(**+ adv./prep.**) *'Grab the end of the rope.' 'I can't reach that far!'* "抓住绳子头。" "我够不着！" ◇ **~ sth** *Can you reach the light switch from where you're sitting?* 从你坐的地方够得着灯的开关吗？ **8** [T] to stretch your hand out or up in order to get sth for sb 为某人伸手取（物）：**~ sth (down) for sb** *Can you reach that box down for me?* 你帮我把那个盒子拿下来好吗？ ◇ **~ sb (down) sth** *Can you reach me down that box?* 你帮我把那个盒子拿下来好吗？

• **BE LONG ENOUGH** 够长 **9** [I, T] to be big enough, long enough, etc. to arrive at a particular point （大或长等）足够达到：**+ adv./prep.** *The carpet only reached halfway across the room.* 地毯只够覆盖半间屋。◇ **~ sth** *Is the cable long enough to reach the socket?* 电线够得着插座吗？

• **CONTACT SB** 联系 **10** [T] **~ sb** to communicate with sb, especially by telephone （尤指用电话）联系，与…取得联系：*Do you know where I can reach him?* 你知道我在哪儿能跟他联系上吗？

• **BE SEEN/HEARD BY SB** 被看到 / 听到 **11** [T] **~ sb** to be seen or heard by sb 被…看到（或听到）：*Through television and radio we are able to reach a wider audience.* 通过电视和收音机，我们能够为更加广泛的观众和听众所熟悉。

IDM **reach for the 'stars** to try to be successful at sth that is difficult 有九天揽月之志；努力完成壮举 ➲ MORE AT EAR

PHR V **,reach 'out to sb** to show sb that you are interested in them and/or want to help them 表示对某人感兴趣；表示愿意提供援助：*The church needs to find new ways of reaching out to young people.* 教会需要寻找新途径来为年轻人提供帮助。

■ ***noun***

• **OF ARMS** 手臂 **1** [sing., U] the distance over which you can stretch your arms to touch sth; the distance over which a particular object can be used to touch sth else 手臂展开的长度；臂展：*As a boxer, his long reach gives him a significant advantage.* 作为拳击运动员，他出拳距离长是他很大的优势。◇ *The shot was well* ***beyond the reach of*** *the goalkeeper.* 这次射门使守门员鞭长莫及。◇ *Cleaning fluids should be kept* ***out of the reach of*** *children.* 洗涤剂应该放在儿童够不到的地方。◇ *He lashed out angrily, hitting anyone* ***within his reach.*** 他气急败坏，见人就打。◇ *Use shears with a long reach for cutting high hedges.* 用长柄大剪刀修剪高树篱。

• **OF POWER/INFLUENCE** 权力；影响 **2** [sing., U] the limit to which sb/sth has the power or influence to do sth 波及范围；影响范围：*Such matters are* ***beyond the reach of*** *the law.* 这样的事情不受法律的管辖。◇ *Victory is now* ***out of her reach.*** 胜利现在对于她来说遥不可及。◇ *The basic model is priced well* ***within the reach of*** *most people.* 基本款式的定价大多数人都完全负担得起。◇ *The company has now overtaken IBM in terms of size and reach.* 在规模和影响范围上，这家公司已经超越了 IBM 公司。

• **OF RIVER** 河流 **3** [C, usually pl.] a straight section of water between two bends on a river 河段；直水道：*the* ***upper/lower reaches*** *of the Nile* (= the part that is furthest from/nearest to the sea) 尼罗河上游 / 下游

• **PLACE FAR FROM CENTRE** 边缘 **4 reaches** [pl.] **the outer, further, etc. ~ of sth** the parts of an area or a place that are a long way from the centre 边缘地带；边远地区：*the outer reaches of space* 外层太空 ◇ (*figurative*) *an exploration of the deepest reaches of the human mind* 对人类思想最深处的探索

• **SECTIONS OF ORGANIZATION** 组织部门 **5 reaches** [pl.] **the higher, lower, etc. ~ of sth** the higher, etc. sections of an organization, a system, etc. （组织、体制等的）领域，部门：*There are still few women in the upper reaches of the civil service.* 在高级公务员中，女性仍然寥寥无几。◇ *Many clubs in the lower reaches of the league are in financial difficulty.* 联合会下层的许多俱乐部都处于财政困难之中。

IDM **within (easy) 'reach (of sth)** close to sth 很接近；靠近：*The house is within easy reach of schools and sports facilities.* 这房子距离学校和体育设施都很近。

reach·able /ˈriːtʃəbl/ *adj.* [not before noun] that is possible to reach 可及；可到达；够得到：*The farm is only reachable by car.* 那个农场只能开车去。

re·acquaint /ˌriːəˈkweɪnt/ *verb* **~ sb/yourself with sth** to let sb/yourself find out about sth again or get used to sth again （使）重新了解；（使）再熟悉：*I'll need to reacquaint myself with this program—it's a long time since I've used it.* 我得再熟悉一下这个程序，我已经很长时间没用了。

react AW /riˈækt/ *verb* **1** [I] **~ (to sth) (by doing sth)** to change or behave in a particular way as a result of or in response to sth 起反应；（对…）作出反应；回应：*Local residents have reacted angrily to the news.* 当地居民对这一消息表示愤怒。◇ *I nudged her but she didn't react.* 我用胳膊肘捅了她一下，可她没有反应。◇ *You never know how he is going to react.* 你根本不知道他会作何反应。◇ *The market reacted by falling a further two points.* 股市的反应是再下跌两个百分点。 **2** [I] (**+ adv./prep.**) to become ill/sick after eating, breathing, etc. a particular substance （对食物等）有不良反应，过敏：*People can react badly to certain food additives.* 人们对某些食品添加剂可能会严重过敏。 **3** [I] **~ (with sth)** | **~ (together)** (*chemistry* 化) (of substances 物质) to experience a chemical change when coming into contact with another substance 起化学反应；发生化学变化：*Iron reacts with water and air to produce rust.* 铁和水及空气发生反应产生铁锈。

➲ WORDFINDER NOTE AT CHEMISTRY

PHR V **re,act a'gainst sb/sth** to show dislike or opposition in response to sth, especially by deliberately doing the opposite of what sb wants you to do 反对；反抗：*He reacted strongly against the artistic conventions of his time.* 他强烈反对当时的艺术俗套。

react·ance /riˈæktəns/ *noun* [U, C] (*physics* 物) (*symb.* **X**) the opposition of a piece of electrical equipment, etc. to the flow of an ALTERNATING CURRENT 电抗 ➲ COMPARE RESISTANCE (5)

react·ant /riˈæktənt/ *noun* (*chemistry* 化) a substance that takes part in and is changed by a chemical reaction 反应物

re·ac·tion AW /riˈækʃn/ *noun*

• **TO EVENT/SITUATION** 对于事件 / 局势 **1** [C, U] **~ (to sb/sth)** what you do, say or think as a result of sth that has happened 反应；回应：*What was his reaction to the news?* 他对这消息有何反应？◇ *My* ***immediate reaction*** *was one of shock.* 我当即的反应是大吃一惊。◇ *A spokesman said the changes were not* ***in reaction to*** *the company's recent losses.* 一位发言人说，这些变动不是针对公司最近的亏损而作出的反应。◇ *There has been a* ***mixed reaction*** *to her appointment as director.* 对她获任命为主管一事，人们的反应各不相同。◇ *The decision provoked an angry reaction from local residents.* 这个决定引起了当地居民的愤怒抗议。◇ *I tried shaking him but there was no reaction.* 我试着摇了摇他，但他一动不动。

• **CHANGE IN ATTITUDES** 态度的改变 **2** [C, usually sing., U] **~ (against sth)** a change in people's attitudes or behaviour caused by disapproval of the attitudes, etc. of the past （对旧观念等的）抗拒：*The return to traditional family values is a reaction against the permissiveness of recent decades.* 传统家庭价值观的回归是对近几十年来放纵自由的一种反动。

• **TO DRUGS** 药物 **3** [C, U] a response by the body, usually a bad one, to a drug, chemical substance, etc. 生理反应；副作用：*to have an* ***allergic reaction*** *to a drug* 对某药物有过敏反应

R

• **TO DANGER** 对于危险 **4** 🔑 **reactions** [pl.] the ability to move quickly in response to sth, especially if in danger 反应能力：*a skilled driver with quick reactions* 反应敏捷的熟练司机

• **SCIENCE** 科学 **5** 🔑 [C, U] (*chemistry* 化) a chemical change produced by two or more substances acting on each other 化学反应：*a* ***chemical/nuclear reaction*** 化学 / 核反应 ➲ SEE ALSO CHAIN REACTION (1) **6** [U, C] (*physics* 物) a force shown by sth in response to another force, which is of equal strength and acts in the opposite direction 反（作用）力

• **AGAINST PROGRESS** 反对发展 **7** [U] opposition to social or political progress or change 反对；反动；阻碍：*The forces of reaction made change difficult.* 反动势力使得改革举步维艰。

re·ac·tion·ary AW /riˈækʃənri; *NAmE* -neri/ *noun* (*pl.* **-ies**) (*disapproving*) a person who is opposed to political or social change 反动分子；反对政治（或社会）变革者 ▸ **re·ac·tion·ary** AW *adj.* : *a reactionary government* 反动的政府

re·acti·vate AW /riˈæktɪveɪt/ *verb* **~ sth** to make sth start working or happening again after a period of time 使恢复活动；使重新出现 ▸ **re·acti·va·tion** AW /riˌæktɪˈveɪʃn/ *noun* [U]

re·act·ive AW /riˈæktɪv/ *adj.* **1** (*formal*) showing a reaction or response 反应的；有反应的；回应的：*The police presented a reactive rather than preventive strategy against crime.* 警方对付犯罪的办法，不是事先加以防范，而是事后作出反应。➲ COMPARE PROACTIVE **2** (*chemistry* 化) tending to show chemical change when mixed with another substance 能起化学反应的；易反应的：*highly reactive substances* 很容易起反应的物质

re·activ·ity /ˌriːækˈtɪvəti/ *noun* (*chemistry* 化) the degree to which sth reacts, or is likely to react 反应性：*Oxygen has high reactivity.* 氧的反应性很高。

re·act·or AW /riˈæktə(r)/ (*also* **ˌnuclear reˈactor**) *noun* a large structure used for the controlled production of nuclear energy 核反应堆

R

read 🔑 *verb, noun, adj.*

■ ***verb*** /riːd/ (**read**, **read** /red/)

• **WORDS/SYMBOLS** 文字；符号 **1** 🔑 [I, T] (not used in the progressive tenses 不用于进行时) to look at and understand the meaning of written or printed words or symbols 识字；阅读；读懂：*She's still learning to read.* 她还在学习识字。◇ *Some children can read and write before they go to school.* 有些孩子在上学前就会看书写字了。◇ **~ sth** *I can't read your writing.* 我看不懂你的笔迹。◇ *Can you read music?* 你识谱吗？◇ *I'm trying to read the map.* 我正看地图呢。**2** 🔑 [I, T] to go through written or printed words, etc. in silence or speaking them to other people 读；朗读：*I'm going to go to bed and read.* 我要上床看书去。◇ **~ to sb/yourself** *He liked reading to his grandchildren.* 他喜欢念书给孙子孙女听。◇ **~ sth** *to read a book/a magazine/the newspaper* 读书；看杂志；看报纸 ◇ *Have you read any Steinbeck* (= novels by him)? 你读过斯坦贝克的小说吗？◇ *He read the poem aloud.* 他朗读了这首诗。◇ **~ sth to sb/yourself** *Go on—read it to us.* 念吧，念给我们听听。◇ **~ sb sth** *She read us a story.* 她给我们读了个故事。➲ SEE ALSO PROOFREAD

• **DISCOVER BY READING** 读到 **3** 🔑 [I, T] (not used in the progressive tenses 不用于进行时) to discover or find out about sb/sth by reading 读到；查阅到：**~ about/of sth** *I read about the accident in the local paper.* 我在当地的报纸上看到了这次事故。◇ **~ that...** *I read that he had resigned.* 我看到了他辞职的消息。◇ **~ sth** *Don't believe everything you read in the papers.* 报上看到的东西，不能尽信。

• **SB'S MIND/THOUGHTS** 思想；想法 **4** [T] **~ sb's mind/thoughts** to guess what sb else is thinking 猜测；揣摩

• **SB'S LIPS** 嘴唇 **5** [T] **~ sb's lips** to look at the movements of sb's lips to learn what they are saying 观唇辨意；读唇语 ➲ SEE ALSO LIP-READ

• **UNDERSTAND** 理解 **6** [T] to understand sth in a particular way 懂得；理解 SYN **interpret**：**~ sth** *How do you read the present situation?* 你对目前的形势有何看法？◇ **~ sth as sth** *Silence must not always be read as consent.* 不能总是将沉默理解为同意。

• **OF A PIECE OF WRITING** 书写的东西 **7** [T] **+ speech** to have sth written on it; to be written in a particular way 写着；写成：*The sign read 'No admittance'.* 告示牌上写着"禁止入内"。◇ *I've changed the last paragraph. It now reads as follows…* 我已经修改了最后一段。现在是这样写的… **8** [I] **+ adv./prep.** to give a particular impression when read 读起来（给人以某种印象）：*Generally, the article reads very well.* 总的来说，这篇文章读起来很不错。◇ *The poem reads like* (= sounds as if it is) *a translation.* 这首诗读起来像是译文。

• **MEASURING INSTRUMENT** 测量仪器 **9** [T] **~ sth** (of measuring instruments 测量仪器) to show a particular weight, pressure, etc. 读数为；显示：*What does the thermometer read?* 温度计的读数是多少？ **10** [T] **~ sth** to get information from a measuring instrument 看读数：*A man came to read the gas meter.* 一个男子来查了煤气表。

• **HEAR** 听 **11** [T] **~ sb** to hear and understand sb speaking on a radio set 听到，听明白（用无线电机讲的话）：*'Do you read me?' 'I'm reading you loud and clear.'* "你听得见我的话吗？""听见了，你的声音又大又清楚。"

• **REPLACE WORD** 替换文字 **12** [T] **~ A for B | ~ B as A** to replace one word, etc. with another when correcting a text 替换；将…改为：*For 'madam' in line 3 read 'madman'.* 第 3 行中的 madam 应为 madman。

• **SUBJECT AT UNIVERSITY** 大学课程 **13** [T, I] (*BrE, rather old-fashioned*) to study a subject, especially at a university 学习；攻读；主修：**~ sth** *I read English at Oxford.* 我在牛津攻读英语。◇ **~ for sth** *She's reading for a law degree.* 她在攻读法学学位。

• **COMPUTING** 计算机技术 **14** [T] (of a computer or the person using it 计算机或计算机使用者) to take information from a disk 读（盘）；从磁盘提取信息：**~ sth** *My computer can't read the CD-ROM you sent.* 我的电脑不能读你送来的光盘。◇ **~ sth into sth** *to read a file into a computer* 把文件读入电脑 ➲ MORE LIKE THIS 33, page R28

IDM **ˌread between the ˈlines** to look for or discover a meaning in sth that is not openly stated 领悟隐含的意义；看出言外之意：*Reading between the lines, I think Clare needs money.* 斟酌一下她的言外之意，我觉得克莱尔需要钱。 **ˌread sb like a ˈbook** to understand easily what sb is thinking or feeling 轻易地了解某人的想法（或感受）；看透某人 **ˌread my ˈlips** (*informal*) used to tell sb to listen carefully to what you are saying 请听清楚；请注意听：*Read my lips: no new taxes* (= I promise there will be no new taxes). 注意听我说：不会征新税。 **ˌread (sb) the ˈRiot Act** (*BrE*) to tell sb with force that they must not do sth 警告（某人）不得做某事 ORIGIN From an Act of Parliament passed in 1715 to prevent riots. It made it illegal for a group of twelve or more people to refuse to split up if they were ordered to do so and part of the Act was read to them. 源自 1715 年通过的防止暴乱的议会法案。法案规定如果十二名或以上的人集结，在宣布解散命令并宣读相关条文后仍拒绝解散，则视为非法。 **ˌtake it/sth as ˈread** (*BrE*) to accept sth without discussing it 直接认定为；不经讨论即认可：*Can we take it as read that you want the job?* 我们能不能认为你想要这份工作？

PHR V **ˌread sth↔ˈback** to read a message, etc. to others in order to check that it is correct 读出（以便核对） **ˌread sth ˈinto sth** to think that sth means more than it really does 把本没有的意思加进去解释；对…作过多的理解：*Don't read too much into what she says.* 不要在她的话里加进太多自己的理解。 **ˌread ˈon** to continue reading 继续读；接着读：*That's the story so far. Now read on…* 故事就讲到这里。现在接着读… **ˌread sth↔ˈout** 🔑 to read sth using your voice, especially to other people（尤指向别人）读，朗读 **ˌread sth↔ˈover/ˈthrough** 🔑 to read sth carefully from beginning to end to look for mistakes or check details 认真通读；仔细核对 **ˌread sth↔ˈup | ˌread ˈup on sb/sth** to read a lot about a subject（就某课题）广泛阅读，博览群书：*I'll need to read up on the case before the meeting.* 在开会前，我需要看一些有关这件事的材料。

■ ***noun*** /riːd/ [sing.] (*informal*) **1** (*especially BrE*) an act or a period of reading sth 阅读；读书：*I was having a quiet* *read when the phone rang.* 我在静静地看书，忽然电话铃响了。 **2 a good, interesting, etc. ~** a book, an article, etc. that is good, etc. 好的（或有意思等的）读物；好书（或文章等）：*His thrillers are always a gripping read.* 他的惊险小说向来引人入胜。

■ ***adj.*** /red/ (used after an adverb 用于副词后) (of a person 人) having knowledge that has been gained from reading books, etc. 博学的；熟知的；精通的：*She's very widely read in law.* 她在法律方面知识渊博。 ➲ SEE ALSO WELL READ

read·able /'riːdəbl/ *adj.* **1** (of a book, an article, etc. 书、文章等) that is easy, interesting and enjoyable to read 可读性强的；通俗易懂的 ➲ **WORDFINDER NOTE** AT STORY **2** (of written or printed words 书写或印刷文字) clear and easy to read 清晰可辨的；易于识读的 **SYN legible** ➲ SEE ALSO MACHINE-READABLE ▶ **read·abil·ity** /ˌriːdə'bɪləti/ *noun* [U]

re·address /ˌriːə'dres/ *verb* **~ sth** to change the address written on an envelope because the person the letter is for does not live at the address it has been delivered to 更改（邮件）上的地址

read·er 🔑 /'riːdə(r)/ *noun* **1** 🔑 a person who reads, especially one who reads a lot or in a particular way 读者；读书…的人；阅读量大的人：*an avid reader of science fiction* 科幻小说迷 ◇ *a **fast/slow reader*** 读书快 / 慢的人 ◇ *The reader is left to draw his or her own conclusions.* 读者需要自己去得出结论。 ➲ **COLLOCATIONS** AT LITERATURE **2** 🔑 a person who reads a particular newspaper, magazine, etc.（报刊等的）读者：*readers' letters* 读者来信 ◇ *Are you a 'Times' reader?* 你是《泰晤士报》的读者吗？ **3** an easy book that is intended to help people learn to read their own or a foreign language 简易读物；读本：*a series of graded English readers* 一系列分级英语读物 **4** (*usually* **Reader**) a senior teacher at a British university just below the rank of a professor 准教授（英国大学教师，仅次于教授）：*She is Reader in Music at Edinburgh.* 她是爱丁堡大学的音乐准教授。 **5** (*computing* 计) an electronic device that reads data stored in one form and changes it into another form so that a computer can perform operations on it 电子阅读器；电子识读机 **6** (*specialist*) a machine that produces on a screen a large image of a text stored on a MICROFICHE or MICROFILM 缩微软片阅读机 ➲ SEE ALSO MIND READER, NEWSREADER

read·er·ship /'riːdəʃɪp; *NAmE* -dərʃ-/ *noun* **1** [usually sing.] the number or type of people who read a particular newspaper, magazine, etc.（统称某报刊等的）读者：*a readership of around 10 000* * 1 万左右的读者人数 ◇ *In its new format, the magazine hopes to attract a much wider readership.* 这份杂志希望以新的版式吸引更多的读者。 **2** (*usually* **Readership**) **~ (in sth)** (*BrE*) the position of a READER at a university（英国大学）准教授职位

read·ily /'redɪli/ *adv.* **1** quickly and without difficulty 快捷地；轻而易举地；便利地 **SYN freely**：*All ingredients are **readily available** from your local store.* 所有的原料都可以方便地从你当地的商店买到。 **2** in a way that shows you do not object to sth 欣然地；乐意地 **SYN willingly**：*Most people readily accept the need for laws.* 大多数人都毫不迟疑地认为法律是必要的。

readi·ness /'redinəs/ *noun* **1** [U] **~ (for sth)** the state of being ready or prepared for sth 准备就绪：*Everyone has doubts about their readiness for parenthood.* 对于自己是否准备好了为人父母，人人都会感到疑虑。 **2** [U, sing.] **~ (of sb) (to do sth)** the state of being willing to do sth 愿意；乐意：*Over half the people interviewed expressed their readiness to die for their country.* 半数以上受访者表示愿意为国献身。

read·ing 🔑 /'riːdɪŋ/ *noun*

• **ACTIVITY** 活动 **1** 🔑 [U] the activity of sb who reads 阅读；读书活动：*My hobbies include reading and painting.* 我的业余爱好包括读书和绘画。 ◇ *He needs more help with his reading.* 他在阅读方面需要更多的帮助。 ◇ *Are you any good at map reading?* 你会看地图吗？ ◇ ***reading glasses*** (= worn when reading) 读书用的眼镜 ◇ ***a reading lamp/light*** (= one that can be moved to shine light onto sth that you are reading) 供阅读用的灯 **2** [sing.] an act of reading sth 阅读；宣读：*A closer* (= more detailed) *reading of the text reveals just how desperate he was feeling.* 细读此文就会看出他当时感到多么绝望。

• **BOOKS/ARTICLES** 书；文章 **3** 🔑 [U] books, articles, etc. that are intended to be read 读本；读物；阅读材料：***reading matter/material*** 阅读材料 ◇ *a series of **reading books** for children* 一套儿童读物 ◇ ***a reading list*** (= a list of books, etc. that students are expected to read for a particular subject) 阅读书目 ◇ ***further reading*** (= at the end of a book, a list of other books that give more information about the same subject) 其他阅读参考材料 ◇ *The report makes for interesting reading* (= it is interesting to read) 这篇报道读起来很有意思。 ◇ *The article is not exactly **light reading*** (= it is not easy to read). 这篇文章读起来并不轻松。

• **WAY OF UNDERSTANDING** 理解方法 **4** [C] **~ (of sth)** the particular way in which you understand a book, situation, etc. 理解；解读 **SYN interpretation**：*a literal reading of the text* 对文本的字面理解 ◇ *My own reading of events is less optimistic.* 我本人对事态的看法不怎么乐观。

• **MEASUREMENT** 度量 **5** 🔑 [C] the amount or number shown on an instrument used for measuring sth（仪表的）读数：*Meter readings are taken every three months.* 每三个月查一次表。

• **EVENT** 活动 **6** [C] an event at which sth is read to an audience for entertainment; a piece of literature that is read at such an event 读书会；朗诵会；朗诵的作品：*a poetry reading* 诗歌朗诵会 ◇ *The evening ended with a reading from her latest novel.* 晚会最后朗诵了一段她的最新小说。

• **FROM BIBLE** 《圣经》 **7** [C] a short section from the Bible that is read to people as part of a religious service（在礼拜仪式中朗读的）《圣经》章节：*The reading today is from the Book of Daniel.* 今天朗读的经文选自《但以理书》。

• **IN PARLIAMENT** 议会 **8** [C] one of the stages during which a BILL (= a proposal for a new law) must be discussed and accepted by a parliament before it can become law 议案宣读（法案在成为法律前须经议会讨论通过的步骤）

'reading age *noun* a person's ability to read, measured by comparing it with the average ability of children of a particular age 阅读年龄；某一年龄段的阅读能力：*a 30-year-old man with a reading age of eight* 阅读能力相当于八岁儿童的 30 岁男子

'reading group *noun* = BOOK GROUP

'reading room *noun* a room in a library, club, etc. where people can read or study 阅览室

re·adjust **AW** /ˌriːə'dʒʌst/ *verb* **1** [I] to get used to a changed or new situation 重新适应；再适应：*Children are highly adaptable—they just need time to readjust.* 儿童的适应能力很强，他们只是需要时间重新适应。 ◇ **~ to sth/doing sth** *Once again he had to readjust to living alone.* 他又一次不得不重新适应独居生活。 **2** [T] **~ sth** to change or move sth slightly 稍作改变；微调：*She got out of the car and readjusted her dress.* 她下了车，稍稍整了整裙子。 ▶ **re·adjust·ment** **AW** *noun* [C, U]：*He has made a number of readjustments to his technique.* 他对自己的技术作了不少调整。 ◇ *a painful period of readjustment* 痛苦的适应期

re·admit /ˌriːəd'mɪt/ *verb* (**-tt-**) [often passive] **1 ~ sb (to sth)** to allow sb to join a group, an organization or an institution again 重新接纳；允许再次加入 **2 ~ sb (to sth)** to take sb into a hospital again after they had been allowed to leave 再次接收…住院：*He was readmitted only a week after being discharged.* 他出院仅一个星期又再次住院。 ▶ **re·admis·sion** /ˌriːəd'mɪʃn/ *noun* [U, C] **~ (to sth)**

ˌread-only 'memory *noun* [U] (*computing* 计) = ROM

'read-out *noun* (*computing* 计) a display of information on a computer screen 读出 ➲ COMPARE PRINTOUT

'read-through /'riːd θruː/ *noun* an occasion when the words of a play are spoken by members of a theatre group, before they begin practising acting it（剧组排演之前的）对台词

R

ˌre-ˈadvertise *verb* [T, I] ~ (**sth**) to advertise sth again, especially a job 再做广告；再登（招聘）广告

ready 🔑 /ˈredi/ *adj., verb, adv., noun*

■*adj.* (**read·ier, readi·est**)

• **PREPARED/AVAILABLE** 准备好；可利用 **1** 🔑[not before noun] fully prepared for what you are going to do 准备好；准备完毕：*Are you nearly ready?* 你快准备好了吗？◇ *'Shall we go?' 'I'm* ***ready when you are!'*** "我们可以走了吗？""我准备好了，就等你了！" ◇ **~ for sth** *I'm just* ***getting*** *the kids* ***ready*** *for school.* 我正在让孩子们准备好去上学。◇ *I was twenty years old and* ***ready for anything.*** 我当时二十岁，什么都愿意去做。◇ **~ to do sth** *Right, we're ready to go.* 对，我们准备好了，可以走了。◇ *Volunteers were* ***ready and waiting*** *to pack the food in boxes.* 志愿者已经准备完毕，等着将食物装箱。 **2** 🔑[not before noun] completed and available to be used 已完成；准备好；可利用：*Come on, dinner's ready!* 快过来，饭好了！◇ *The new building should be ready by 2020.* 这座新大楼应该能在 2020 年前交付使用。◇ **~ for sth** *Can you help me* ***get*** *everything* ***ready*** *for the party?* 你能不能帮我把这次聚会准备妥当？◇ **~ to do sth** *The contract will be ready to sign in two weeks.* 这份合同两周后即可签字。 **3** available to be used easily and immediately 方便使用的；现成的：*All the relevant records are easily available* ***ready to hand.*** 所有相关记录都在手边，用起来很方便。◇ *a ready supply of wood* 现成的木材供应 ◇ *a ready source of income* 现成的收入来源 ➲ SEE ALSO READILY, READINESS, ROUGH-AND-READY

• **WILLING** 情愿 **4** [not before noun] willing and quick to do or give sth 愿意迅速做某事（或给某物）；急于行动：**~ for sth** *I was very angry and ready for a fight.* 我非常生气，想打一架。◇ **~ with sth** *She's always ready with advice.* 她总是乐于提出建议。◇ **~ to do sth** *He's always ready to help his friends.* 他总是乐意帮助朋友。◇ *Don't be so ready to believe the worst about people.* 不要总把人往坏处想。

• **LIKELY TO DO STH** 可能做某事 **5** **~ to do sth** likely to do sth very soon 马上要，很可能即将（做某事） SYN **on the point of**：*She looked ready to collapse at any minute.* 她看样子随时都会倒下。

• **NEEDING STH** 需要某事物 **6** **~ for sth** needing sth as soon as possible 急需；需尽快得到：*Right, I'm ready for bed.* 对，我现在就想睡觉。◇ *After the long walk, we were all ready for a drink.* 长途步行之后，我们都急需喝水。

• **QUICK/CLEVER** 机敏；聪明 **7** [only before noun] quick and clever 聪明的；机敏的：*She has great charm and a ready wit.* 她光彩照人，头脑机敏。

IDM **make ˈready** (**for sth**) (*formal*) to prepare 准备：*to make ready for the President's visit* 为总统来访做准备 **ready, steady, ˈgo!** (*BrE*) (*also* (**get**) **ready,** (**get**) **set, ˈgo** *NAmE, BrE*) what you say to tell people to start a race （赛跑口令）各就各位，预备，跑！ **ˌready to ˈroll** (*informal*) ready to start 准备开始；就要开始

■*verb* (**read·ies, ready·ing, read·ied, read·ied**) **~ sb/yourself/sth** (**for sth**) | **~ sb/yourself/sth** (**to do sth**) (*formal*) to prepare sb/yourself/sth for sth 做好…的准备；（为…）做好准备：*Western companies were readying themselves for the challenge from Eastern markets.* 西方的公司正在为迎接来自东方市场的挑战做准备。

■*adv.* (used before a past participle, especially in compounds 用于过去分词前，尤用于构成复合词) already done 已做完；已完成：*ready-cooked meals* 现成的饭菜 ◇ *The concrete was ready mixed.* 混凝土是搅拌好的。

■*noun* **the ready** [sing.] (*also* **read·ies** [pl.]) (*BrE, informal*) money that you can use immediately 现钱

IDM **at the ˈready** available to be used immediately 随时可用；即可使用：*We all had our cameras at the ready.* 我们都准备好了照相机。

ˌready-ˈmade *adj.* **1** prepared in advance so that you can eat or use it immediately 预制的；已做好的；现成的：*ready-made pastry* 现成的油酥面团 **2** (*old-fashioned*) (especially of clothes 尤指衣服) made in standard sizes, not to the measurements of a particular customer 标准尺码的；现成的；成品的：*a ready-made suit* 成品套装 **3** already provided for you so you do not need to produce or think about it yourself 已有的；现成的：*When he married her he also took on a ready-made family.* 他和她结婚，当上了现成的爸爸。

ˌready ˈmeal *noun* (*BrE*) a meal that you buy already prepared and which only needs to be heated before you eat it 预制餐（加热即可食用）

ˌready-ˈmixed *adj.* already mixed and ready to use 预拌的；预先调制的：*ready-mixed concrete* 预拌混凝土

ˌready ˈmoney (*also* **ˌready ˈcash**) *noun* [U] (*informal*) money in the form of coins and notes that you can spend immediately 现金；现钱

ˌready-to-ˈwear *adj.* (of clothes 衣服) made in standard sizes, not to the measurements of a particular customer 标准尺寸的；现成的

re·affirm /ˌriːəˈfɜːm; *NAmE* -ˈfɜːrm/ *verb* **~ sth** to state sth again in order to emphasize that it is still true 重申；再次确定 ▸ **re·affirm·ation** /ˌriːˌæfəˈmeɪʃn; *NAmE* -fərˈm-/ *noun* [C, U]

re·affor·estation /ˌriːəˌfɒrɪˈsteɪʃn; *NAmE* -ˌfɔːr-/ *noun* [U] (*BrE, specialist*) = REFORESTATION

re·agent /riˈeɪdʒənt/ *noun* (*chemistry* 化) a substance used to cause a chemical reaction, especially in order to find out if another substance is present 试剂

real 🔑 /ˈriːəl; *BrE usually* rɪəl/ *adj., adv.*

■*adj.*

• **EXISTING/NOT IMAGINED** 存在；真实 **1** 🔑actually existing or happening and not imagined or pretended 真实的；实际存在的；非凭空想象的：*It wasn't a ghost; it was a real person.* 那不是鬼魂，是实实在在的人。◇ *pictures of animals, both real and mythological* 现实和神话中的动物图片 ◇ *In the movies guns kill people instantly, but it's not like that* ***in real life.*** 电影中，枪能使人在瞬间毙命，而实际情况并非如此。◇ *Politicians seem to be out of touch with* ***the real world.*** 政治家们似乎不接触现实世界。◇ *The growth of violent crime is a very real problem.* 暴力犯罪的增长是个非常实际的问题。◇ *There's no real possibility of them changing their minds.* 他们实际上不可能改变主意。◇ *We have a real chance of success.* 我们确实有获得成功的机会。

• **TRUE/GENUINE** 确实；真正 **2** 🔑 genuine and not false or artificial 真的；正宗的；非假冒的；非人工的：*Are those real flowers?* 那些是真花吗？◇ *real leather* 真皮 **3** 🔑[only before noun] actual or true, rather than what appears to be true 真正的；确实的；真实的：*Tell me the real reason.* 告诉我真正的理由。◇ *Bono's real name is Paul Hewson.* 波诺的真实姓名是保罗•休森。◇ *See the real Africa on one of our walking safaris.* 参加一次我们的观察野兽徒步旅行，看一看真实的非洲吧。◇ *I couldn't resist the opportunity to meet a* ***real live*** *celebrity.* 我不想错过见到名人真人的机会。 **4** 🔑[only before noun] having all the important qualities that it should have to deserve to be called what it is called 真正的；名副其实的：*She never had any real friends at school.* 在学校，她从来没有真正的朋友。◇ *his first real kiss* 他真正的初吻 ◇ *I had no real interest in politics.* 我对政治兴趣不大。◇ *He was making a real effort to be nice to her.* 他费尽心思地对她好。◇ *She has not shown any real regret for what she did.* 她对自己做过的事还没有表现出真正后悔的样子。

• **FOR EMPHASIS** 强调 **5** 🔑[only before noun] used to emphasize a state or quality（强调状态或品质）：*He looks a real idiot.* 他看上去像个十足的白痴。◇ *This accident could have produced a real tragedy.* 这次事故差一点造成一场惨剧。◇ *Her next play was a real contrast.* 她的下一部戏是个鲜明的对比。

• **MONEY/INCOME** 钱；收入 **6** [only before noun] when the effect of such things as price rises on the power of money to buy things is included in the sums 实际的（已按物价指数等调整）；按购买力衡量的：*Real wage costs have risen by 10% in the past year.* 在过去的一年里，实际工资成本增加了 10%。◇ *This represents a reduction of 5%* ***in real terms.*** 这相当于实际减少了 5%。

IDM **for ˈreal** genuine or serious 真实的；严肃的：*This is not a fire drill—it's for real.* 这不是救火演习，是真失火了。◇ (*NAmE*) *He managed to convince voters that he was for real.* 他使得投票者相信了他是严肃认真的。 **get ˈreal!**

R

(*informal*) used to tell sb that they are behaving in a stupid or unreasonable way 现实点吧；别傻了 **keep it ˈreal** (*informal*) to act in an honest and natural way 做事质朴、诚实 **the ˌreal ˈthing** (*informal*) the genuine thing 真品；真正的事物：*Are you sure it's the real thing* (= love), *not just infatuation?* 你能确定这是真爱，而非一时痴迷？ ➲ MORE AT MCCOY, POWER *n.*

■ ***adv.*** (*NAmE, ScotE, informal*) very 非常；很：*That tastes real good.* 味道好极了。◇ *He's a real nice guy.* 他是个非常好的人。◇ *I'm real sorry.* 我很抱歉。

ˌreal ˈale *noun* [U, C] (*BrE*) a type of beer that is made and stored in the traditional way（按传统方法制作和贮存的）啤酒

ˈreal estate *noun* [U] (*especially NAmE*) **1** (*also* **realty**) property in the form of land or buildings 房地产；不动产：*My father sold real estate.* 我父亲经营过房地产。➲ COLLOCATIONS AT HOUSE **2** the business of selling houses or land for building 房地产业；房地产销售业：*to work in real estate* 经营房地产 **3** (especially on a web page) space that is useful or valuable（尤指网页上）有用的空间，有价值的空间：*A company's home page is its most valuable real estate.* 一家公司的主页是其最有价值的网上空间。◇ *You can increase screen real estate by moving the taskbar to the right of the screen.* 将任务栏移到屏幕右侧可以增加屏幕的使用空间。

ˈreal estate agent (*also* **Real·tor™**) (*both NAmE*) (*BrE* **eˈstate agent**) *noun* a person whose job is to sell houses and land for people 房地产经纪人

realia /reɪˈɑːliə; riˈeɪliə/ *noun* [U] ordinary objects used in a class for teaching purposes 实物教具（用于教学的日常用品）

re·align /ˌriːəˈlaɪn/ *verb* **1 ~ sth** to change the position or direction of sth slightly 调整位置（或方向）：*The road was realigned to improve visibility.* 道路做了调整，以提高能见度。 **2 ~ sth** to make changes to sth in order to adapt it to a new situation 对…进行调整；使适应新形势：*The company has been forced to realign its operations in the area.* 公司被迫对这一领域的经营作了调整。 **3 ~ yourself (with sb/sth)** to change your opinions, policies, etc. so that they are the same as those of another person, group, etc. 改变观点，改变策略（以与别人相同）：*The rebel MPs have realigned themselves with the opposition party.* 几个造反的下院议员已与反对党站在一起。 ▸ **re·align·ment** *noun* [U, C]: **~ (of sth)** *the realignment of personal goals* 个人目标的调整 ◇ *political realignments* 政治改组

real·ism /ˈriːəlɪzəm; *BrE also* ˈrɪəl-/ *noun* [U] **1** a way of seeing, accepting and dealing with situations as they really are without being influenced by your emotions or false hopes 务实作风；现实主义方式：*There was a new mood of realism among the leaders at the peace talks.* 参加和平谈判的领导人之间有着一种务实的新气氛。 **2** (of novels, paintings, films/movies, etc. 小说、绘画、电影等) the quality of being very like real life 现实性；逼真 **3** (*also* **Realism**) a style in art or literature that shows things and people as they are in real life（文艺的）现实主义风格，现实主义 ➲ COMPARE IDEALISM, ROMANTICISM (1)

real·ist /ˈriːəlɪst; *BrE also* ˈrɪə-/ *noun* **1** a person who accepts and deals with a situation as it really is and does not try to pretend that it is different 现实主义者；务实的人：*I'm a realist—I know you can't change people overnight.* 我是个务实的人，我知道人不可能一夜之间被改变。 **2** a writer, painter, etc. whose work represents things as they are in real life 现实主义作家（或画家等）

real·is·tic 🔑 /ˌriːəˈlɪstɪk; *BrE also* ˌrɪə-/ *adj.* **1** 🔑 accepting in a sensible way what it is actually possible to do or achieve in a particular situation 现实的；实际的；实事求是的：*a realistic assessment* 实事求是的评估 ◇ *We have to **be realistic** about our chances of winning.* 我们必须实事求是地估计我们获胜的可能性。◇ *It is not realistic to expect people to spend so much money.* 期望人们花那么多的钱是不实际的。 **2** 🔑 sensible and appropriate; possible to achieve 明智的；恰如其分的；能够实现的 SYN **feasible, viable**: *We must set realistic goals.* 我们必须制订可实现的目标。◇ *a realistic target* 切实的目标 ◇ *to pay a realistic salary* 支付合理的薪水 **3** 🔑 representing things as they are in real life 逼真的；栩栩如生的：*a realistic drawing* 逼真的绘画 ◇ *We try to make these training courses as realistic as possible.* 我们努力使这些训练课程尽可能地贴近实际情况。 OPP **unrealistic**

real·is·tic·al·ly /ˌriːəˈlɪstɪkli; *BrE also* ˌrɪə-/ *adv.* **1** used to say what you think can actually be achieved in a particular situation（表明你认为实际实现的可能性）如实地，实际地：*Realistically, there is little prospect of a ceasefire.* 实事求是地讲，停火的希望很渺茫。 **2** in a way that shows sb accepts in a sensible way what it is actually possible to do or achieve 切合实际地；明智地：*How many can you realistically hope to sell?* 实事求是地讲，你希望能卖出多少？◇ *Kate spoke realistically about the task ahead.* 凯特如实地谈了面临的任务。 **3** in a way that represents things as they are in real life 逼真地；栩栩如生地：*a fireplace with realistically glowing coals* 有逼真的炉火闪耀的壁炉

real·ity 🔑 /riˈæləti/ *noun* (*pl.* **-ies**) **1** 🔑 [U] the true situation and the problems that actually exist in life, in contrast to how you would like life to be 现实；实际情况：*She refuses to **face reality**.* 她不肯面对现实。◇ *You're **out of touch with reality**.* 你脱离了现实。◇ *The reality is that there is not enough money to pay for this project.* 实际情况是没有足够的钱花在这个项目上。 **2** 🔑 [C] a thing that is actually experienced or seen, in contrast to what people might imagine 事实；实际经历；见到的事物：*the **harsh realities of** life* 严峻的生活现实 ◇ *This decision reflects the realities of the political situation.* 这一决定反映了政治形势的真实情况。◇ *Will time travel ever **become a reality**?* 时光旅行真的会成为现实吗？ **3** [U] **~ television/TV/shows/series/contestants** television/shows, etc. that use real people (not actors) in real situations, presented as entertainment 真人秀节目：*a reality TV star* 一个真人秀电视明星 ◇ *the reality show 'Big Brother'* 真人秀节目《老大哥》

IDM **in reˈality** 🔑 used to say that a situation is different from what has just been said or from what people believe 实际上；事实上：*Outwardly she seemed confident but in reality she felt extremely nervous.* 表面上看，她显得信心十足，而实际上她紧张得要命。 ➲ SEE ALSO VIRTUAL REALITY

reˈality check *noun* [usually sing.] (*informal*) an occasion when you are reminded of how things are in the real world, rather than how you would like things to be（提醒人面对现实而不再想当然的）现实感检验

reˌality ˈTV *noun* [U] television shows that are based on real people (not actors) in real situations, presented as entertainment（电视）真人秀 ➲ WORDFINDER NOTE AT PROGRAMME

real·iz·able (*BrE also* **-is·able**) /ˈriːəlaɪzəbl; *BrE also* ˈrɪə-/ *adj.* **1** possible to achieve or make happen 可实现的；可实行的 SYN **achievable**: *realizable objectives* 可实现的目标 **2** that can be sold and turned into money 可兑现的；可变为现金的：*realizable assets* 可变现资产

real·iza·tion (*BrE also* **-isa·tion**) /ˌriːəlaɪˈzeɪʃn; ˌrɪəl-; *NAmE* ˌriːələˈz-/ *noun* **1** [U, sing.] the process of becoming aware of sth 认识；领会；领悟 SYN **awareness**: **~ (of sth)** *the sudden realization of what she had done* 突然意识到她自己究竟干了些什么 ◇ **~ (that…)** *There is a growing realization that changes must be made.* 越来越多的人认识到改革势在必行。 **2** [U] **~ (of sth)** the process of achieving a particular aim, etc.（目标等的）实现 SYN **achievement**: *It was the realization of his greatest ambition.* 这就实现了他的宏伟抱负。 **3** [U] **~ of your assets** (*formal*) the act of selling sth that you own, such as property, in order to get the money that you need for sth 变卖；兑换成现金 **4** [U, C] **~ (of sth)** (*formal*) the act of producing a sound, play, design, etc.; or the thing that is produced 发声；（戏剧）演出；设计成果

real·ize (*BrE also* **-ise**) /ˈriːəlaɪz; *BrE also* ˈrɪəl-/ *verb*
• **BE/BECOME AWARE** 察觉 **1** [T, I] (not used in the progressive tenses 不用于进行时) to understand or become aware of a particular fact or situation 理解；领会；认识到；意识到：**~ (that)...** *I didn't realize (that) you were so unhappy.* 我没有察觉到你那么不开心。◇ *The moment I saw her, I realized something was wrong.* 我一看到她，就觉得不太对劲。◇ **~ how, what, etc....** *I don't think you realize how important this is to her.* 我认为你没有意识到这对她是多么重要。◇ **~ (sth)** *I hope you realize the seriousness of this crime.* 我希望你能认识到这一罪行的严重性。◇ *Only later did she realize her mistake.* 只是到了后来她才意识到自己的错误。◇ *The situation was more complicated than they had at first realized.* 形势比他们最初意识到的更为复杂。◇ *They managed to leave without any of us realizing.* 我们谁也没注意，他们悄悄走了。◇ **it is realized that...** *There was a cheer when it was realized that everyone was safely back.* 人们意识到大家都已平安归来的时候便发出了一阵欢呼声。
• **ACHIEVE STH** 实现 **2** [T] **~ sth** to achieve sth important that you very much want to do 实现；将…变为现实：*She never realized her ambition of becoming a professional singer.* 她从未实现成为一名职业歌手的志向。◇ *We try to help all students* ***realize their full potential*** (= be as successful as they are able to be). 我们努力帮助所有的学生充分发挥他们的潜力。
• **HAPPEN** 发生 **3** [T, usually passive] **~ sth** if sb's fears **are realized**, the things that they are afraid will happen, do happen （所担心的事）发生，产生：*His worst fears were realized when he saw that the door had been forced open.* 他一看门被撬了，就知道最担心的事还是发生了。
• **SELL** 出售 **4** [T] **~ your assets** (*formal*) to sell things that you own, for example property, in order to get the money that you need for sth 把（财产等）变卖，变现 **SYN** **convert** **5** [T] **~ sth** (*formal*) (of goods, etc. 货品等) to be sold for a particular amount of money 以…价格卖出 **SYN** **make**：*The paintings realized $2 million at auction.* 这些绘画在拍卖会上以 200 万美元卖出。
• **MAKE STH REAL** 使成为现实 **6** [T] **~ sth** (*formal*) to produce sth that can be seen or heard, based on written information or instructions 把（概念等）具体表现出来：*The stage designs have been beautifully realized.* 舞台设计得到了完美的体现。

R

ˌ**real-ˈlife** *adj.* [only before noun] actually happening or existing in life, not in books, stories or films/movies 真实的；实际发生的；现实生活中的：*a novel based on real-life events* 以真实事件为素材的小说 ◇ *a real-life Romeo and Juliet* 现实生活中的罗密欧与朱丽叶 **OPP** **fictional**

re·allo·cate /ˌriːˈæləkeɪt/ *verb* **~ sth (to sb/sth)** to change the way money or materials are shared between different people, groups, projects, etc. 重新分配；再分配 **SYN** **redistribute** ▶ **re·allo·ca·tion** /ˌriːˌæləˈkeɪʃn/ *noun* [U, C]

real·ly /ˈriːəli; *BrE also* ˈrɪəli/ *adv.* **1** used to say what is actually the fact or the truth about sth（表明事实或真相）事实上，真正地，真实地：*What do you really think about it?* 你到底对这事怎么看？◇ *Tell me what really happened.* 告诉我究竟发生了什么事。◇ *They are not really my aunt and uncle.* 其实他们并不是我的姑姑和姑父。◇ *I can't believe I am really going to meet the princess.* 我不敢相信我真的要去见公主。 **2** used to emphasize sth you are saying or an opinion you are giving（强调观点等）确实，的确：*I want to help, I really do.* 我想帮忙，真的。◇ *Now I really must go.* 我确实得走了。◇ *I really don't mind.* 我一点都不在意。◇ *He really likes you.* 他的确喜欢你。◇ *I* ***really and truly*** *am in love this time.* 我这一次确确实实是恋爱了。 **3** used to emphasize an adjective or adverb（加强形容词或副词的语气）：*a really hot fire* 好热的炉子 ◇ *I'm really sorry.* 我十分抱歉。 **4** used, often in negative sentences, to reduce the force of sth you are saying（常用于否定句以减弱语气）：*I don't really agree with that.* 对此我不太赞同。◇ *It doesn't really matter.* 没什么关系。◇ *'Did you enjoy the book?' 'Not really.'* (= 'no' or 'not very much') "你喜欢那本书吗？" "不怎么喜欢。"

HELP The position of **really** can change the meaning of the sentence. **I don't really know** means that you are not sure about something; **I really don't know** emphasizes that you do not know. (Look at sense 2.) * really 的位置会改变句子的意思。I don't really know 的意思是对某事没有把握；而 I really don't know 则强调不知道。（见第 2 义）

5 used in questions and negative sentences when you want sb to say 'no'（用于疑问句和否定句，期望对方给以否定的答复）：*Do you really expect me to believe that?* 你真以为我会相信吗？◇ *I don't really need to go, do I?* 我并不一定非要去，对吧？ **6** used to express interest in or surprise at what sb is saying（答话时表示感兴趣或惊讶）：*'We're going to Japan next month.' 'Oh, really?'* "我们下个月要去日本。" "哦，真的吗？" ◇ *'She's resigned.' 'Really? Are you sure?'* "她辞职了。" "真的？你肯定吗？" **7** used to show that you disapprove of sth sb has done（表示不赞同某人所为）：*Really, you could have told us before.* 真是的，其实你大可事先跟我们说一声的。

realm /relm/ *noun* **1** an area of activity, interest, or knowledge 领域；场所：*in the realm of literature* 在文学领域内 ◇ *At the end of the speech he seemed to be moving* ***into the realms of fantasy.*** 讲话的最后，他似乎进入了虚幻的境地。 **2** (*formal*) a country ruled by a king or queen 王国 **SYN** **kingdom**：*the defence of the realm* 王国的防卫
IDM **beyond/within the realms of possibility** not possible/possible 超出 / 在可能范围：*A successful outcome is not beyond the realms of possibility.* 最后取得成功并非没有可能。

ˌ**real ˈnumber** *noun* (*mathematics* 数) any number that is not an IMAGINARY NUMBER 实数 ➲ COMPARE COMPLEX NUMBER

real·poli·tik /reɪˈɑːlpɒlɪtiːk; *NAmE* -pɑːl-/ *noun* [U] (*from German*) a system of politics that is based on the actual situation and needs of a country or political party rather than on moral principles 现实政治；实用政治；实力政策

ˈ**real tennis** (*BrE*) (*NAmE* ˈ**court tennis**) (*AustralE* ˈ**royal tennis**) *noun* [U] an old form of tennis played inside a building with a hard ball 庭院网球（使用硬球的旧式室内网球运动）

ˌ**real ˈtime** *noun* [U] (*computing* 计) the fact that there is only a very short time between a computer system receiving information and dealing with it 实时：*To make the training realistic the simulation operates* ***in real time.*** 为使训练真实，模拟是实时运行的。◇ *real-time missile guidance systems* 实时导弹制导系统

real·tone /ˈriːəltəʊn; *NAmE* -toʊn; *usually* ˈrɪəl-/ *noun* (*BrE*) a part of a song or other recording that is used as the sound a mobile/cell phone makes when it rings 原音铃声（使用歌曲等录音片段的手机铃声）：*Get the top realtones from the best artists delivered instantly to your mobile.* 即时取得一流歌手的最佳原声手机铃声。

Real·tor™ (*also* **real·tor**) /ˈriːəltə(r)/ *noun* (*NAmE*) = REAL ESTATE AGENT

realty /ˈriːəlti/ *noun* [U] (*especially NAmE*) = REAL ESTATE

ˈ**real-world** *adj.* existing in the real world and not specially invented for a particular purpose 存在于现实世界的；真实的：*Teachers need to prepare their students to deal with real-world situations outside the classroom.* 教师应该让学生做好应对课堂以外的现实世界的准备。

ream /riːm/ *noun, verb*
■ *noun* **1 reams** [pl.] (*informal*) a large quantity of writing 大量的文字（或写作）：*She wrote reams in the exam.* 她在考试中写得很多。 **2** [C] (*specialist*) 500 sheets of paper 令（纸张的记数单位，等于 500 张）
■ *verb* **~ sb** (*NAmE, informal*) to treat sb unfairly or cheat them 不公平地对待；欺骗：*We got reamed on that deal.* 那笔交易我们上当受骗了。
PHR V ˌ**ream sb↔ˈout** (*NAmE, informal*) to criticize sb strongly because they have done sth wrong 训斥；斥责；责骂

re·ani·mate /riːˈænɪmeɪt/ *verb* **~ sb/sth** (*formal*) to give sb/sth new life or energy 赋予新的生命；使重新充满活力

reap /riːp/ *verb* **1** [T] ~ **sth** to obtain sth, especially sth good, as a direct result of sth that you have done 取得（成果）；收获：*They are now reaping the rewards of all their hard work.* 现在，他们的全部辛劳都得到了回报。 **2** [I, T] ~ (**sth**) to cut and collect a crop, especially WHEAT, from a field 收割（庄稼）；收获 SYN **harvest**

IDM **reap a/the 'harvest** (*BrE*) to benefit or suffer as a direct result of sth that you have done 享受成果；承担后果；种瓜得瓜，种豆得豆 **you ˌreap what you 'sow** (*saying*) you have to deal with the bad effects or results of sth that you originally started 种瓜得瓜，种豆得豆

reap·er /ˈriːpə(r)/ *noun* a person or a machine that cuts and collects crops on a farm 收割者；收割机 ⊃ SEE ALSO GRIM REAPER

re·appear /ˌriːəˈpɪə(r); *NAmE* -ˈpɪr/ *verb* [I] to appear again after not being heard of or seen for a period of time 再次出现；重新出现：*She went upstairs and did not reappear until morning.* 她上了楼，直到第二天早晨才再次露面。 ▶ **re·appear·ance** /-rəns/ *noun* [U, sing.]

re·apply /ˌriːəˈplaɪ/ *verb* (**re·applies**, **re·apply·ing**, **re·applied**, **re·applied**) **1** [T] ~ **sth** to put another layer of a substance on a surface 再敷一层；再涂一层：*Sunblock should be reapplied every hour.* 防晒霜应每隔一小时再抹一次。 **2** [I] ~ (**for sth**) to make another formal request for sth 重新申请；再次申请：*Previous applicants for the post need not reapply.* 申请过这个职位的人不需重新申请。 **3** [T] ~ **sth** to use sth again, especially in a different situation（尤指在不同场合）再利用：*Students are taught a number of skills that can be reapplied throughout their studies.* 教给学生一些方法，让他们在整个学习过程中可以反复使用。

re·appoint /ˌriːəˈpɔɪnt/ *verb* ~ **sb** (**as**) **sth** | ~ **sb** + **noun** | ~ **sb** (**to sth**) to give sb the job that they used to have in the past 使恢复职位；使回到原岗位：*After the trial he was reappointed (as) treasurer.* 审理过后，他被重新任命为财务主管。 ▶ **re·appoint·ment** *noun* [U]

re·appraisal /ˌriːəˈpreɪzl/ *noun* [C, usually sing., U] the act of examining sth again to see if it needs to be changed 重新检查；重新评价 SYN **reassessment**

re·appraise /ˌriːəˈpreɪz/ *verb* ~ **sth/sb** (*formal*) to think again about the value or nature of sth/sb to see if your opinion about it/them should be changed 重新评估；重新评价 SYN **reassess**

rear /rɪə(r); *NAmE* rɪr/ *noun, adj., verb*

■ ***noun*** **1** (*usually* **the rear**) [sing.] the back part of sth 后部：*A trailer was attached to the rear of the truck.* 卡车后面挂了一辆拖车。 ◇ *There are toilets at both* ***front and rear*** *of the plane.* 飞机前后舱都有洗手间。 ◇ *A high gate blocks the only entrance* ***to the rear***. 一座高大的门挡住了通往后面的唯一入口。 ⊃ NOTE AT BACK **2** (*also* ˌ**rear 'end**) [C, usually sing.] (*informal*) the part of the body that you sit on 屁股；臀部 SYN **bottom**：*a kick in the rear* 踢了一下屁股

IDM ˌ**bring up the 'rear** to be at the back of a line of people, or last in a race 站在队尾；落在最后；殿后

■ ***adj.*** [only before noun] at or near the back of sth 后面的；后部的：*front and rear windows* 前面和后面的窗户 ◇ *the rear entrance of the building* 大楼的后门

■ ***verb*** **1** [T] ~ **sb/sth** [often passive] to care for young children or animals until they are fully grown 抚养；养育；培养 SYN **bring up, raise**：*She reared a family of five on her own.* 她一个人养活五个孩子。 **2** [T] ~ **sth** to breed or keep animals or birds, for example on a farm 饲养：*to rear cattle* 养牛 **3** [I] ~ (**up**) (of an animal, especially a horse 动物，尤指马) to raise itself on its back legs, with the front legs in the air 用后腿直立：*The horse reared, throwing its rider.* 这匹马后腿直立，将骑手摔下。 **4** [I] ~ (**up**) (of sth large 大的东西) to seem to lean over you, especially in a threatening way（尤指可怖地）巍然耸立：*The great bulk of the building reared up against the night sky.* 夜幕下，巨大的高楼显得阴森森的。

IDM **sth rears its (ugly) 'head** if sth unpleasant **rears its head** or **rears its ugly head**, it appears or happens（讨厌的事情）出现，发生

PHR V **'rear sb/sth on sth** [usually passive] to give a person or an animal a particular type of food, entertainment, etc. while they are young（用…）喂养；（以…）娱乐，培养：*I was the son of sailors and reared on stories of the sea.* 我是水手的儿子，是听海的故事长大的。

ˌ**rear 'admiral** *noun* an officer of very high rank in the navy 海军少将：*Rear Admiral Baines* 海军少将贝恩斯

'rear-end *verb* ~ **sth/sb** (*informal, especially NAmE*) (of a vehicle or driver 车辆或驾驶员) to drive into the back of another vehicle 与（前车）追尾

rear·guard /ˈrɪəɡɑːd; *NAmE* ˈrɪrɡɑːrd/ *noun* (*usually* **the rearguard**) [sing.+sing./pl. v.] a group of soldiers that protect the back part of an army especially when the army is RETREATING after it has been defeated 后卫部队 OPP **vanguard**

ˌ**rearguard 'action** *noun* [usually sing.] a struggle to change or stop sth even when it is not likely that you will succeed 顽抗到底；最后挣扎：*They have been* ***fighting a rearguard action*** *for two years to stop their house being demolished.* 两年来，为了不让他们的房子被拆除，他们一直在顽强抗争。

rear·ing /ˈrɪərɪŋ; *NAmE* ˈrɪrɪŋ/ *noun* [U] **1** the process of caring for children as they grow up, teaching them how to behave as members of society 抚养；养育；培养 **2** the process of breeding animals or birds and caring for them as they grow 饲养：*livestock rearing* 家畜饲养

rearm /riˈɑːm; *NAmE* -ˈɑːrm/ *verb* [I, T] to obtain, or supply sb with, new or better weapons, armies, etc. 重新武装；重新装备：*The country was forbidden to rearm under the terms of the treaty.* 根据条约规定，这个国家不允许重新武装。 ◇ ~ **sb** *Rebel troops were being rearmed.* 叛军在进行重新装备。 ▶ **re·arma·ment** /riˈɑːməmənt; *NAmE* -ˈɑːrm-/ *noun* [U]

rear·most /ˈrɪəməʊst; *NAmE* ˈrɪrmoʊst/ *adj.* (*formal*) furthest back 最靠后的；最后面的：*the rearmost section of the aircraft* 飞机的最后部

re·arrange /ˌriːəˈreɪndʒ/ *verb* **1** ~ **sth/sb/yourself** to change the position or order of things; to change your position 重新排列；改变位置：*We've rearranged the furniture in the bedroom.* 我们重新摆放了卧室里的家具。 ◇ *She rearranged herself in another pose.* 她重新摆了个姿势。 **2** ~ **sth** to change the time, date or place of an event 重新安排；改变时间（或日期、地点） SYN **reschedule**：*Can we rearrange the meeting for next Tuesday at 2?* 我们把会议改到下周二下午两点好吗？ ▶ **re·arrange·ment** *noun* [C, U]

ˌ**rear-view 'mirror** *noun* a mirror in which a driver can see the traffic behind 后视镜 ⊃ VISUAL VOCAB PAGE V56

rear·ward /ˈrɪəwəd; *NAmE* ˈrɪrwərd/ *adj.* (*formal*) at or near the back of sth 后面的；后部的：*rearward seats* 后面的座位

ˌ**rear-wheel 'drive** *noun* [U] a system in which power from the engine is sent to the back wheels of a vehicle 后轮驱动（系统） ⊃ COMPARE FRONT-WHEEL DRIVE

rea·son /ˈriːzn/ *noun, verb*

■ ***noun*** **1** [C] a cause or an explanation for sth that has happened or that sb has done 原因；理由；解释：~ (**why…**) *I'd like to know the reason why you're so late.* 我想知道你为什么迟到那么长时间。 ◇ *Give me* ***one good reason*** *why I should help you.* 我为什么要帮你？给我一个充分的理由。 ◇ ~ (**that…**) *We aren't going for the* ***simple reason*** *that we can't afford it.* 我们不去，只是因为我们负担不起。 ◇ ~ (**for sth**) *She gave no reasons for her decision.* 她没有对她的决定作出任何解释。 ◇ ~ (**for doing sth**) *I have no particular reason for doubting him.* 我没有什么特别的理由怀疑他。 ◇ *He said no but he didn't* ***give a reason***. 他说不行，但没有说明原因。 ◇ ***For some reason*** (= one that I don't know or don't understand) *we all have to come in early tomorrow.* 出于某种原因，我们大家明天都不得不早点儿来。 ◇ *The man attacked me* ***for no apparent reason***. 那个人不知何故攻击我。 ◇ *She resigned* ***for personal reasons***. 她出于个人原因而辞职。 ◇ ***For reasons of*** *security the door* *is always kept locked.* 为了保证安全，门总是锁着的。◇ *He wants to keep them all in his office* ***for reasons best known to himself.*** 他想把他们都留在他的办公室里，原因只有他自己知道。◇ *people who,* ***for whatever reason,*** *are unable to support themselves* 那些因为种种原因不能自立的人 ◇ *'Why do you want to know?'* ***'No reason.'*** (= I do not want to say why.) "你为什么想知道？" "不为什么。" ◇ *'Why did she do that?' 'She must* ***have her reasons'*** (= secret reasons which she does not want to tell). "她为什么那么做？" "她一定有她的理由。" ◇ (*formal*) *He was excused* ***by reason of*** (= because of) *his age.* 他因为其年龄而得以免除。 ➲ LANGUAGE BANK AT THEREFORE ➲ EXPRESS YOURSELF AT WHY **2** [U] a fact that makes it right or fair to do sth 正当理由；道理；情理：~ (**to do sth**) *They have reason to believe that he is lying.* 他们有理由认为他是在撒谎。◇ *We* ***have every reason*** (= have very good reasons) *to feel optimistic.* 我们完全有理由感到乐观。◇ ~ (**why…**) *There is no reason why we should agree to this.* 我们没有理由同意这点。◇ ~ (**for sth/for doing sth**) *This result gives us* ***all the more reason*** *for optimism.* 这个结果使我们更有理由保持乐观。◇ *She complained,* ***with reason*** (= rightly), *that she had been underpaid.* 她抱怨给她的报酬太低，是有道理的。 **3** [U] the power of the mind to think in a logical way, to understand and have opinions, etc. 思考力；理解力；理性：*Only human beings are capable of reason* (= of thinking in a logical way, etc.). 只有人类才有理性思考的能力。◇ *to lose your reason* (= become mentally ill) 神经失常 **4** [U] what is possible, practical or right 道理；情理；明智：*I can't get her to* ***listen to reason.*** 我没法跟她讲道理。◇ *Why can't they* ***see reason?*** 他们为什么不明事理？◇ *to be open to reason* (= to be willing to accept sensible advice) 广纳良言 ◇ *He's looking for a job and he's willing to do anything* ***within reason.*** 他在找工作，而且只要是正当的事他都愿意做。

IDM **it ˌstands to ˈreason** (*informal*) it must be clear to any sensible person who thinks about it 这是人人都清楚的；这是明摆着的：*It stands to reason that they'll leave if you don't pay them enough.* 这是明摆着的，你不给他们足够的报酬，他们就走人。 ➲ MORE AT RHYME *n.*

■ *verb* **1** [T, I] ~ (**that…**) | + **speech** to form a judgement about a situation by considering the facts and using your power to think in a logical way 推理；推论；推断：*She reasoned that she must have left her bag on the train.* 她断定准是把包落在火车上了。◇ *They couldn't fire him, he reasoned. He was the only one who knew how the system worked.* 他推断他们不会解雇他。他是唯一知道这套系统如何运转的人。 **2** [I] to use your power to think and understand 思考；理解：*the human ability to reason* 人的思考能力

PHR V **ˌreason sth ˈout** to try and find the answer to a problem by using your power to think in a logical way 通过思考想出对策；推理出（结果） SYN **figure out** **ˈreason with sb** to talk to sb in order to persuade them to be more sensible 和某人讲道理；规劝：*I tried to reason with him, but he wouldn't listen.* 我尽量跟他讲道理，可他就是不听。

▼ SYNONYMS 同义词辨析

reason

explanation • grounds • basis • excuse • motive • justification • pretext

These are all words for a cause or an explanation for sth that has happened or that sb has done. 以上各词均指事情发生或做某事的原因、理由、解释。

reason a cause or an explanation for sth that has happened or that sb has done; a fact that makes it right or fair to do sth 指某事发生或做某事的原因、理由、解释、道理：*He said no but he didn't give a reason.* 他说不行，但没有说明原因。

explanation a statement, fact or situation that tells you why sth has happened; a reason given for sth 指解释、说明、阐述：*The most likely explanation is that his plane was delayed.* 最可能的解释是他的飞机晚点了。◇ *She left the room abruptly without explanation.* 她未作解释就突然离开了房间。

grounds (*rather formal*) a good or true reason for saying, doing or believing sth 指说、做或相信某事的充分理由、根据：*You have no grounds for complaint.* 你没有理由抱怨。

basis (*rather formal*) the reason why people take a particular action 指原因、缘由：*On what basis will this decision be made?* 将基于何种原因作出这一决定呢？

excuse a reason, either true or invented, that you give to explain or defend your behaviour; a good reason that you give for doing sth that you want to do for other reasons 指为自己行为所作的辩护、借口、理由：*Late again! What's your excuse this time?* 又迟到了！你这次有什么借口？◇ *It gave me an excuse to take the car.* 这使我有理由开车去了。

motive a reason that explains sb's behaviour 指动机、原因：*There seemed to be no motive for the murder.* 这起谋杀案看不出有什么动机。

justification (*rather formal*) a good reason why sth exists or is done 指事物存在或做某事的正当理由：*I can see no possible justification for any further tax increases.* 我看不出还能提出什么理由来加税了。

GROUNDS OR JUSTIFICATION? 用 grounds 还是 justification?

Justification is used to talk about finding or understanding reasons for actions, or trying to explain why it is a good idea to do sth. It is often used with words like *little, no, some, every, without,* and *not any.* **Grounds** is used more for talking about reasons that already exist, or that have already been decided, for example by law: *moral/economic grounds.* * justification 用来表示找出或明白做事的理由，或解释要做的事，常与 little、no、some、every、without 和 not any 等词连用。grounds 多指已存在的原因或已决定的（如法律上的）根据：moral/economic grounds（道德/经济原因）。

pretext (*rather formal*) a false reason that you give for doing sth, usually sth bad, in order to hide the real reason 指为掩盖做某事（通常为不好的事）的真正理由而找的借口、托辞：*He left the party early on the pretext of having to work.* 他借口有事要处理，早早离开了聚会。

PATTERNS

- (a/an) reason/explanation/grounds/basis/excuse/motive/justification/pretext **for** sth
- the reason/motive **behind** sth
- **on the** grounds/basis/pretext **of/that…**
- (a) **good/valid** reason/explanation/grounds/excuse/motive/justification

---

rea·son·able /ˈriːznəbl/ *adj.* **1** ~ (**to do sth**) fair, practical and sensible 公平的；合理的；有理由的；明智的：***It is reasonable*** *to assume that he knew beforehand that this would happen.* 有理由认为，他事先就知道会发生这样的事。◇ ***Be reasonable!*** *We can't work late every night.* 要讲道理呀！我们不能每天晚上都加班呀。◇ *Any reasonable person would have done exactly as you did.* 任何有头脑的人都会完全像你那样去做的。◇ *The prosecution has to prove* ***beyond reasonable doubt*** *that he is guilty of murder.* 控方必须毫无疑义地证明他犯有谋杀罪。 OPP **unreasonable** **2** acceptable and appropriate in a particular situation 可以接受的；合乎情理的；公道的：*He made us a reasonable offer for the car.* 他给我们出的车价公平合理。◇ *You must submit your claim within a reasonable time.* 你必须在适当的时间内提出要求。 **3** (of prices 价格) not too expensive 不太贵的；公道的 SYN **fair**: *We sell good quality food at reasonable prices.* 我们以公道的价格出售优质食品。 ➲ SYNONYMS AT CHEAP **4** [usually before noun] fairly good, but not very good 不错的；还算好的；过得去的 SYN **average**: *a reasonable standard of living* 还算不错的生活水平 ◇ *The hotel was reasonable, I suppose* (= but not excellent). 我觉得这家酒店还可以。
▸ **rea·son·able·ness** *noun* [U]

rea·son·ably /ˈriːznəbli/ *adv.* **1** to a degree that is fairly good but not very good 尚可；过得去：*The*

R

instructions are reasonably straightforward. 用法说明还算简单易懂。◇ *She seems reasonably happy in her new job.* 她在新的工作岗位上好像还挺开心。 **2** 🔑 in a logical and sensible way 合情合理地；明智地；通情达理地：*We tried to discuss the matter calmly and reasonably.* 我们试图冷静且通情达理地来讨论这个问题。 **3** 🔑 in a fair way 公平合理地；适度地：*He couldn't reasonably be expected to pay back the loan all at once.* 公平合理地讲，不可能指望他一下子归还全部借款。◇ *The apartments are* ***reasonably priced*** (= not too expensive). 这些公寓房价格合理。

rea·soned /ˈriːzənd/ *adj.* [only before noun] (of an argument, opinion, etc. 论点、意见等) presented in a logical way that shows careful thought 合乎逻辑的；缜密的

rea·son·ing /ˈriːzənɪŋ/ *noun* [U] the process of thinking about things in a logical way; opinions and ideas that are based on logical thinking 推想；推理；理性的观点；论证：*What is* ***the reasoning behind*** *this decision?* 作出这个决定的依据是什么？◇ *This* ***line of reasoning*** *is faulty.* 这样的思路有问题。

re·assem·ble /ˌriːəˈsembl/ *verb* **1** [T] **~ sth** to fit the parts of sth together again after it has been taken apart 重新装配（或组装）：*We had to take the table apart and reassemble it upstairs.* 我们只好先把桌子拆开，到楼上再组装起来。 **2** [I] to meet together again as a group after a break 重新集结；再次集合：*The class reassembled after lunch.* 午饭后，全班同学又集合起来。

re·assert /ˌriːəˈsɜːt; *NAmE* -ˈsɜːrt/ *verb* **1 ~ sth** to make other people recognize again your right or authority to do sth, after a period when this has been in doubt 重申；坚持：*She found it necessary to reassert her position.* 她觉得有必要重申她的立场。 **2 ~ itself** to start to have an effect again, after a period of not having any effect 重新发挥作用：*He thought about giving up his job, but then common sense reasserted itself.* 他曾想放弃这份工作，但后来还是理智占了上风。 **3** to state again, clearly and firmly, that sth is true 再次断言；再次声明：**~ that…** *He reasserted that all parties should be involved in the talks.* 他再次声明各方均应参加会谈。◇ **~ sth** *Traditional values have been reasserted.* 传统价值观再次得到肯定。 ▸ **re·asser·tion** *noun* [sing., U]

re·assess AW /ˌriːəˈses/ *verb* **~ sth** to think again about sth to decide if you need to change your opinion of it 重新考虑；再次评价 SYN **reappraise** ▸ **re·assess·ment** AW *noun* [U, C]

re·assign AW /ˌriːəˈsaɪn/ *verb* [often passive] **1 ~ sb (to sth)** to give sb a different duty, position or responsibility 重新委派，再次指派（任务、职位、责任等）：*After his election defeat he was reassigned to the diplomatic service.* 落选之后，他又被派到外交部门工作。 **2 ~ sth (to sb/sth)** to give sth to a different person or organization; to change the status of sth 重新分配…（给某人或机构）；重新指定：*The case was reassigned to a different court.* 这桩案件已交由另一法院审理。 ▸ **re·assign·ment** *noun* [U, C]

re·assur·ance /ˌriːəˈʃʊərəns; -ˈʃɔːr-; *NAmE* -ˈʃʊr-/ *noun* **1** [U] **~ (that…)** the fact of giving advice or help that takes away a person's fears or doubts （能消除疑虑等的）肯定，保证：*to* ***give/provide/offer reassurance*** 表明肯定的态度 **2** [C] **~ (that…)** something that is said or done to take away a person's fears or doubts 能消除疑虑的说话（或行动）；保证：*We have been given reassurances that the water is safe to drink.* 我们得到保证说这水适合饮用。

re·assure /ˌriːəˈʃʊə(r); ˌriːəˈʃɔː(r); *NAmE* -ˈʃʊr/ *verb* to say or do sth that makes sb less frightened or worried 使…安心；打消…的疑虑 SYN **put/set sb's mind at ease/rest**: **~ sb (about sth)** *They tried to reassure her, but she still felt anxious.* 他们设法让她放心，可她还是焦虑不安。◇ **~ sb that…** *The doctor reassured him that there was nothing seriously wrong.* 医生安慰他说，没什么大毛病。

re·assur·ing /ˌriːəˈʃʊərɪŋ; -ˈʃɔːr-; *NAmE* -ˈʃʊr-/ *adj.* making you feel less worried or uncertain about sth 令人感到宽慰的；令人放心的：*a reassuring smile* 使人信心倍增的微笑 ◇ ***It's reassuring*** *(****to know****)* ***that*** *we've got the money if necessary.* 我们有了应急的钱，这下不必担心了。 ▸ **re·assur·ing·ly** *adv.*

re·awaken /ˌriːəˈweɪkən/ *verb* **~ sth** to make you feel a particular emotion again or to make you remember sth again 勾起，唤起，再次引发（感情、回忆等） SYN **rekindle**: *The place reawakened childhood memories.* 这地方唤起了童年的回忆。

re·bar·ba·tive /rɪˈbɑːbətɪv; *NAmE* -ˈbɑːrb-/ *adj.* (*formal*) not attractive 无吸引力的；令人厌恶的 SYN **objectionable**

re·bate /ˈriːbeɪt/ *noun* **1** an amount of money that is paid back to you because you have paid too much 退还款：*a tax rebate* 退还税款 **2** an amount of money that is taken away from the cost of sth, before you pay for it 折扣，返还（退还的部分货价）；折扣 SYN **discount**: *Buyers are offered a cash rebate.* 购买者享受现金折扣。

rebel *noun, verb*

■ ***noun*** /ˈrebl/ **1** a person who fights against the government of their country 反政府的人；叛乱者；造反者：*rebel forces* 叛乱武装 ◇ *Armed rebels advanced towards the capital.* 武装叛乱分子向首都推进。 **2** a person who opposes sb in authority over them within an organization, a political party, etc. 反抗权威者 **3** a person who does not like to obey rules or who does not accept normal standards of behaviour, dress, etc. 叛逆者；不守规矩者：*I've always been the rebel of the family.* 我在家里向来是个叛逆者。

■ ***verb*** /rɪˈbel/ (**-ll-**) [I] **~ (against sb/sth)** to fight against or refuse to obey an authority, for example a government, a system, your parents, etc. 造反；反抗；背叛：*He later rebelled against his strict religious upbringing.* 他后来背叛了他所受的严格的宗教教育。◇ *Most teenagers find something to rebel against.* 大多数青少年都有反抗意识。

re·bel·lion /rɪˈbeljən/ *noun* **~ (against sb/sth)** **1** [U, C] an attempt by some of the people in a country to change their government, using violence 谋反；叛乱；反叛 SYN **uprising**: *The north of the country rose in rebellion against the government.* 这个国家的北方地区发生了反对政府的叛乱。◇ *The army put down the rebellion.* 军队镇压了叛乱。 ➲ COLLOCATIONS AT WAR **2** [U, C] opposition to authority within an organization, a political party, etc. （对权威的）反抗，不服从：*(a) back-bench rebellion* 下院普通议员的反对 **3** [U] opposition to authority; being unwilling to obey rules or accept normal standards of behaviour, dress, etc. 不顺从；叛逆：*teenage rebellion* 青少年的叛逆

re·bel·li·ous /rɪˈbeljəs/ *adj.* **1** unwilling to obey rules or accept normal standards of behaviour, dress, etc. 反叛的；叛逆的；桀骜不驯的：*rebellious teenagers* 叛逆的青少年 ◇ *He has always had* ***a rebellious streak****.* 他总是有点叛逆。 ➲ WORDFINDER NOTE AT YOUNG **2** opposed to the government of a country; opposed to those in authority within an organization 叛乱的；造反的；反对权威的：*rebellious cities/factions* 叛乱的城市；反对派别 ▸ **re·bel·li·ous·ly** *adv.*：*'I don't care!' she said rebelliously.* "我不在乎！"她桀骜不驯地说道。 **re·bel·li·ous·ness** *noun* [U]

re·birth /ˌriːˈbɜːθ; *NAmE* -ˈbɜːrθ/ *noun* [U, sing.] **1** a period of new life, growth or activity 新生；复活；复兴：*the seasonal cycle of death and rebirth* 死而复生的四季轮回 **2** a spiritual change when a person's faith becomes stronger or they convert to another religion （信仰加强或皈依另一宗教后精神上的）新生，再生

re·birth·ing /ˌriːˈbɜːθɪŋ; *NAmE* -ˈbɜːrθ-/ *noun* [U] a type of PSYCHOTHERAPY that involves reproducing the experience of being born using controlled breathing 呼吸重生法，再生疗法（通过控制呼吸重新体验出生的心理疗法）

re·boot /ˌriːˈbuːt/ *verb* [T, I] **~ (sth)** (*computing* 计) if you **reboot** a computer or it **reboots**, you switch it off and then start it again immediately 重新启动 ➲ WORDFINDER NOTE AT COMPUTER

re·born /ˌriːˈbɔːn; *NAmE* -ˈbɔːrn/ *verb, adj.*

■ ***verb*** **be reborn** (used only in the passive without *by* 仅用于不带 by 的被动语态) **1** to become active or popular again 复兴；再次流行 **2** to be born again 再生；轮回：*If*

R

you were reborn as an animal, which animal would you be? 如果你转世成为动物，你愿意做哪种动物？

■ *adj.* **1** having become active again 重生的；复兴的：*a reborn version of social democracy* 一种社会民主主义的翻版 **2** having experienced a complete spiritual change（精神上）再生的，新生的：*reborn evangelical Christians* 获得再生的福音教会信徒 ➲ SEE ALSO BORN-AGAIN

re·bound *verb, noun*

■ *verb* /rɪˈbaʊnd/ **1** [I] ~ (**from/off sth**) to BOUNCE back after hitting sth 弹回；反弹：*The ball rebounded from the goalpost and Podolski headed it in.* 球从门柱弹回，波多尔斯基头球破门。 **2** [I] ~ (**on sb**) (*formal*) if sth that you do **rebounds** on you, it has an unpleasant effect on you, especially when the effect was intended for sb else 报应；反作用于 **SYN** **backfire** **3** [I] (*business* 商) (of prices, etc. 价格等) to rise again after they have fallen 回升；反弹 **SYN** **bounce back**

■ *noun* /ˈriːbaʊnd/ **1** (*sport* 体育) a ball that hits sth and BOUNCES back 反弹球；回弹球 **2** (in BASKETBALL 篮球) the act of catching the ball after a player has thrown it at the BASKET and has not scored a point 抢篮板球 **3** (*business* 商) a positive reaction that happens after sth negative 复兴；振作

IDM **on the ˈrebound** while you are sad and confused, especially after a relationship has ended（尤指关系破裂之后）在伤心困惑之时

re·brand /ˌriːˈbrænd/ *verb* ~ **sth/yourself** to change the image of a company or an organization or one of its products or services, for example by changing its name or by advertising it in a different way 重塑…的形象（如通过改变名称或广告）；将…重塑：*In the 1990s the Labour Party rebranded itself as New Labour.* 工党于 20 世纪 90 年代重塑形象，改称新工党。 ▶ **re·brand·ing** *noun* [sing., U]: *a rebranding exercise* 重塑形象的活动 ◇ *a £5 million rebranding* 投资 500 万英镑的形象重塑工程

re·buff /rɪˈbʌf/ *noun* (*formal*) an unkind refusal of a friendly offer, request or suggestion 粗暴回绝；生硬的拒绝 **SYN** **rejection**: *Her offer of help was met with a sharp rebuff.* 她主动帮忙，却遭到断然拒绝。 ▶ **re·buff** *verb*: ~ **sth** *They rebuffed her request for help.* 他们拒绝了她的请求，不给她帮助。

re·build /ˌriːˈbɪld/ *verb* (**re·built**, **re·built** /ˌriːˈbɪlt/) **1** ~ **sth** to build or put sth together again 重建；重组；重新装配：*After the earthquake, the people set about rebuilding their homes.* 地震过后，人们开始重建家园。 ◇ *He rebuilt the engine using parts from cars that had been scrapped.* 他用废弃的汽车零件重新组装了发动机。 **2** ~ **sth** to make sth/sb complete and strong again 使复原；使恢复：*When she lost her job, she had to **rebuild her life** completely.* 她丢了工作以后，不得不彻底重新安排自己的生活。 ◇ *attempts to rebuild the shattered post-war economy* 为恢复支离破碎的战后经济所作的尝试

re·buke /rɪˈbjuːk/ *verb* [often passive] ~ **sb** (**for sth/for doing sth**) (*formal*) to speak severely to sb because they have done sth wrong 指责；批评 **SYN** **reprimand**: *The company was publicly rebuked for having neglected safety procedures.* 公司因忽略了安全规程而受到公开批评。 ▶ **re·buke** *noun* [C, U]: *He was silenced by her stinging rebuke.* 她的尖锐批评使他哑口无言。

rebus /ˈriːbəs/ *noun* a combination of pictures and letters which represent a word or phrase whose meaning has to be guessed（以图画和字母混合构成的）图形字谜

rebut /rɪˈbʌt/ *verb* (-**tt**-) ~ **sth** (*formal*) to say or prove that a statement or criticism is false 反驳；驳斥；证明（言论等）错误 **SYN** **refute** ▶ **re·but·tal** /-tl/ *noun* [C, U]: *The accusations met with a firm rebuttal.* 这些指控受到了坚决的驳斥。

re·cal·ci·trant /rɪˈkælsɪtrənt/ *adj.* (*formal*) unwilling to obey rules or follow instructions; difficult to control 不守规章的；不服从指挥的；桀骜不驯的；难以控制的 ▶ **re·cal·ci·trance** /-əns/ *noun* [U]

re·call 🔑 *verb, noun*

■ *verb* /rɪˈkɔːl/ **1** 🔑 [T, I] (*formal*) (not used in the progressive tenses 不用于进行时) to remember sth 记起；回想起 **SYN** **recollect**: ~ **sth** *She could not recall his name.* 她想不起他的名字。 ◇ (+ **adv./prep.**) *If I recall correctly, he lives in Luton.* 如果我没记错的话，他住在卢顿。 ◇ ~ (**sb/sth**) **doing sth** *I can't recall meeting her before.* 我想不起来以前曾经见过她。 ◇ ~ **that**... *He recalled that she always came home late on Wednesdays.* 他回想起她星期三总是很晚回家。 ◇ ~ **what, when, etc**.... *Can you recall exactly what happened?* 你能记起到底发生了什么事吗？ ◇ + **speech** *'It was on a Thursday in March,' he recalled.* "那是三月份的一个星期四。" 他回忆道。 **2** [T] ~ **sth** (not used in the progressive tenses 不用于进行时) to make sb think of sth 使想起；使想到；勾起 **SYN** **evoke**: *The poem recalls Eliot's 'The Waste Land'.* 这首诗令人想起艾略特的《荒原》。 **3** [T] to order sb to return 召回：~ **sb** *Both countries recalled their ambassadors.* 两个国家都召回了各自的大使。 ◇ ~ **sb to sth** *He was recalled to military duty.* 他被召回执行军事任务。 ◇ *They have both been recalled to the Welsh squad* (= selected as members of the team after a time when they were not selected). 他们俩都被重新召回了威尔士队。 **4** [T] ~ **sth** to ask for sth to be returned, often because there is sth wrong with it 收回，召回（残损货品等）：*The company has recalled all the faulty hairdryers.* 公司回收了所有有瑕疵的吹风机。

■ *noun* /rɪˈkɔːl; ˈriːkɔːl/ **1** [U] the ability to remember sth that you have learned or sth that has happened in the past 记忆力；记性：*She has amazing powers of recall.* 她有惊人的记忆力。 ◇ *to have **instant recall*** (= to be able to remember sth immediately) 有快速记忆的能力 ◇ *to have **total recall*** (= to be able to remember all the details of sth) 记得所有细节 **2** [sing.] an official order or request for sb/sth to return, or for sth to be given back 召回令；回归请求；回收令：*Thomas's recall to the Welsh team* 让托马斯回归威尔士队的要求

IDM **beyond reˈcall** impossible to bring back to the original state; impossible to remember 不可恢复；想不起来；记不住

re·cant /rɪˈkænt/ *verb* [T, I] ~ (**sth**) (*formal*) to say, often publicly, that you no longer have the same belief or opinion that you had before 公开宣布放弃（原先的信仰、观点等） ▶ **re·can·ta·tion** /ˌriːkænˈteɪʃn/ *noun* [C, U]

recap /ˈriːkæp/ *verb, noun*

■ *verb* (-**pp**-) [I, T] ~ (**on sth**) | ~ **sth** | ~ **what, where, etc**.... = RECAPITULATE: *Let me just recap on what we've decided so far.* 让我来概括一下到目前为止我们所作的决定吧。

■ *noun* = RECAPITULATION

re·cap·itu·late /ˌriːkəˈpɪtʃuleɪt/ *verb* (*formal*) (*also* **recap**) [I, T] ~ (**on sth**) | ~ **sth** | ~ **what, where, etc**.... to repeat or give a summary of what has already been said, decided, etc. 重述；概括：*To recapitulate briefly, the three main points are these...* 简要概括起来，主要有这样三点… ▶ **re·cap·itu·la·tion** /ˌriːkəpɪtʃuˈleɪʃn/ *noun* [C, U] (*formal*) (*also* **recap**)

re·cap·ture /ˌriːˈkæptʃə(r)/ *verb* **1** ~ **sth** to win back a place, position, etc. that was previously taken from you by an enemy or a rival 赢回；夺回：*Government troops soon recaptured the island.* 政府的军队很快夺回了这个岛。 **2** ~ **sb/sth** to catch a person or an animal that has escaped 抓回；再次捕获 **3** ~ **sth** to bring back a feeling or repeat an experience that you had in the past 回忆；再体验；重温：*He was trying to recapture the happiness*

rebus 图形字谜

to be or not to be

of his youth. 他在努力回忆年轻时的快乐。 ▶ **re·cap·ture** *noun* [U]: *the recapture of towns occupied by the rebels* 夺回被叛军占领的城镇

re·cast /ˌriːˈkɑːst; *NAmE* -ˈkæst/ *verb* (**re·cast**, **re·cast**) **1** ~ **sth** (**as sth**) to change sth by organizing or presenting it in a different way 改动；重组；改写：*She recast her lecture as a radio talk.* 她把讲稿修改成了一篇广播讲话。 **2** ~ **sb** (**as sth**) to change the actors or the role of a particular actor in a play, etc. 重新安排（演员阵容）；改变（演员角色）

recce /ˈreki/ *noun* (*BrE, informal*) = RECONNAISSANCE：*to do a quick recce of an area* 对一地区进行快速侦察

re·cede /rɪˈsiːd/ *verb* **1** [I] to move gradually away from sb or away from a previous position 逐渐远离；渐渐远去：*The sound of the truck receded into the distance.* 卡车的声音渐渐在远处消失了。 ◇ *She watched his receding figure.* 她看着他的身影渐渐远去。 **2** [I] (especially of a problem, feeling or quality 尤指问题、感觉或特质) to become gradually weaker or smaller 逐渐减弱；慢慢变小：*The prospect of bankruptcy has now receded* (= it is less likely). 破产的可能性现已减少了。 ◇ *The pain was receding slightly.* 疼痛正在一点一点地减弱。 **3** [I] (of hair 头发) to stop growing at the front of the head（头顶前部）头发停止生长，变秃：*a middle-aged man with **receding hair/a receding hairline*** 发际线后移的中年男子 ➲ VISUAL VOCAB PAGE V65 **4** [I] **a** ~ **chin** a chin that slopes backwards towards the neck 向后缩的下巴

re·ceipt 🔑 /rɪˈsiːt/ *noun* **1** 🔑 (*NAmE also* **ˈsales slip**) [C] ~ (**for sth**) a piece of paper that shows that goods or services have been paid for 收据；收条：*Can I have a receipt, please?* 请给我开个收据，好吗？ ◇ *to make out* (= write) *a receipt* 开收据 ➲ WORDFINDER NOTE AT BUY ➲ COLLOCATIONS AT SHOPPING **2** [U] ~ (**of sth**) (*formal*) the act of receiving sth 接收；收到：*to acknowledge receipt of a letter* 告诉对方已收到信件 ◇ *The goods will be dispatched **on receipt of** an order form.* 订单一到即发货。 ◇ *Are you **in receipt of** any state benefits?* 你目前是否享有政府补助金？ **3 receipts** [pl.] (*business* 商) money that a business, bank or government receives（企业、银行、政府等）收到的款项，收入：***net/gross receipts*** 净收入；总收入

re·ceiv·able /rɪˈsiːvəbl/ *adj.* (*business* 商) (usually following a noun 通常用于名词后) (of bills, accounts, etc. 票据、账目等) for which money has not yet been received 应收款的：*accounts receivable* 应收账款

re·ceiv·ables /rɪˈsiːvəblz/ *noun* [pl.] (*business* 商) money that is owed to a business 应收款项

re·ceive 🔑 /rɪˈsiːv/ *verb*

• **GET/ACCEPT** 得到；接受 **1** 🔑 [T] (*rather formal*) to get or accept sth that is sent or given to you 拿到；接到；收到：~ **sth** *to receive a letter/present/phone call* 收到信 / 礼物；接到电话 ◇ *to receive information/payment/thanks* 接收信息 / 付款；受到感谢 ◇ ~ **sth from sb/sth** *He received an award for bravery from the police service.* 他以其勇敢行为受到警务部门的嘉奖。

• **TREATMENT/INJURY** 待遇；伤害 **2** 🔑 [T] to experience or be given a particular type of treatment or an injury 体验；受到（某种待遇或伤害）：~ **sth from sb** *We received a warm welcome from our hosts.* 我们受到了主人的热情欢迎。 ◇ ~ **sth** *Emergency cases will receive professional attention immediately.* 急诊病人将立即得到诊治。 ◇ *to receive severe injuries* 受重伤

• **REACT TO STH** 作出反应 **3** 🔑 [T, usually passive] to react to sth new, in a particular way 对…作出反应：~ **sth + adv./prep.** *The play was **well received** by the critics.* 这出戏受到剧评家的认可。 ◇ ~ **sth with sth** *The statistics were received with concern.* 这些统计数字受到了关切。

• **GUESTS** 客人 **4** [T, often passive] ~ **sb** (**with sth**) | ~ **sb** (**as sth**) (*formal*) to welcome or entertain a guest, especially formally 接待；欢迎；招待：*He was received as an honoured guest at the White House.* 他在白宫受到贵宾的礼遇。

• **AS MEMBER OF STH** 成员 **5** [T] ~ **sb** (**into sth**) (*formal*) to officially recognize and accept sb as a member of a group 接纳；允许加入：*Three young people were received into the Church at Easter.* 复活节时有三位年轻人入教。

• **TV/RADIO** 电视；收音机 **6** [T] ~ **sth** to change broadcast signals into sounds or pictures on a television, radio, etc. 接收；收看；收听：*to receive programmes via satellite* 通过卫星收看节目 **7** [T] ~ **sth/sb** to be able to hear a radio message that is being sent by sb 接收到，收听到（无线电消息）：*I'm receiving you loud and clear.* 我听得到你的声音，又清晰，又响亮。

• **STOLEN GOODS** 赃物 **8** [T, I] ~ (**sth**) (*especially BrE*) to buy or accept goods that you know have been stolen 购买，接受（赃物）

• **IN SPORT** 体育运动 **9** [I, T] ~ (**sth**) (in TENNIS, etc. 网球等) to be the player that the SERVER hits the ball to 接（发球）：*She won the toss and chose to receive.* 她猜中了掷币结果，选择接发球。

IDM **be at/on the reˈceiving end** (**of sth**) (*informal*) to be the person that an action, etc. is directed at, especially an unpleasant one 承受不愉快之事：*She found herself on the receiving end of a great deal of criticism.* 她发现自己遭到众多的批评。

re·ceived /rɪˈsiːvd/ *adj.* [only before noun] (*formal*) accepted by most people as being correct 被承认的；被一致认可的：*The **received wisdom** is that they cannot win.* 大家一致认为他们不会赢。 IDM SEE WISDOM

reˌceived pronunciˈation *noun* [U] = RP

re·ceiver /rɪˈsiːvə(r)/ *noun* **1** the part of a telephone that you hold close to your mouth and ear（电话）听筒，受话器：*to **pick up/lift/put down/replace the receiver*** 拿起 / 放回听筒 ➲ COLLOCATIONS AT PHONE ➲ COMPARE HANDSET (1) **2** a piece of radio or television equipment that changes broadcast signals into sound or pictures 无线电接收机；收音机；电视机：*a satellite receiver* 卫星信号接收机 ➲ COMPARE TRANSMITTER (1) **3** (*BrE also* **ofˌficial reˈceiver**) (*law* 律) a person who is chosen by a court to be in charge of a company that is BANKRUPT（破产公司的）财产管理人，官方接管人：*to call in the receivers* 申请委派官方接管人 **4** a person who receives sth 接收者：*Molly's more of a giver than a receiver.* 莫莉更乐于给予而不是接受。 **5** a person who buys or accepts stolen goods, knowing that they have been stolen 购买（或接受）赃物的人 **6** (in AMERICAN FOOTBALL 美式足球) a player who plays in a position in which the ball can be caught when it is being passed forward（前传球的）接球手

re·ceiv·er·ship /rɪˈsiːvəʃɪp; *NAmE* -vərʃ-/ *noun* [U] (*law* 律) the state of a business being controlled by an official receiver because it has no money 破产管理；破产产业接管

re·cent 🔑 /ˈriːsnt/ *adj.* [usually before noun] that happened or began only a short time ago 近来的；新近的：*a recent development/discovery/event* 近来的发展 / 发现 / 事件 ◇ *his most recent visit to Poland* 他最近到波兰的访问 ◇ *There have been many changes **in recent years**.* 近几年发生了许多变化。

re·cent·ly 🔑 /ˈriːsntli/ *adv.* not long ago 不久前；最近：*We received a letter from him recently.* 我们不久以前收到了他的一封信。 ◇ *Until recently they were living in York.* 他们不久以前还住在约克。 ◇ *I haven't seen them recently* (= it is some time since I saw them). 我近来没见过他们。 ◇ *Have you used it recently* (= in the recent past)? 你最近用过它吗？

re·cep·tacle /rɪˈseptəkl/ *noun* **1** ~ (**for sth**) (*formal*) a container for putting sth in 容器：(*figurative*) *The seas have been used as a receptacle for a range of industrial toxins.* 海洋成了各种有毒工业废料的大容器。 **2** (*NAmE*) = OUTLET (5)

re·cep·tion 🔑 /rɪˈsepʃn/ *noun* **1** 🔑 [U] (*especially BrE*) the area inside the entrance of a hotel, an office building, etc. where guests or visitors go first when they arrive 接待处；接待区：*the reception area* 接待区 ◇ *We arranged to meet **in reception** at 6.30.* 我们约定 6:30 在接待处会面。 ◇ *You can leave a message **with reception**.* 你可以在接待处留言。 ◇ (*NAmE, BrE*) *the reception desk* 服务台 ➲ COMPARE FRONT DESK ➲ WORDFINDER NOTE AT HOTEL **2** 🔑 [C] a

R

formal social occasion to welcome sb or celebrate sth 接待仪式；欢迎会；招待会：*a wedding reception* 结婚喜筵 ➲ WORDFINDER NOTE AT CELEBRATE, WEDDING **3** [sing.] the type of welcome that is given to sb/sth 欢迎；反应；反响：*Her latest album has met with a* ***mixed reception*** *from fans.* 她的最新唱片在歌迷中间反响不一。◇ *Delegates gave him a* ***warm reception*** *as he called for more spending on education.* 由于他呼吁增加教育经费，代表们向他报以热烈的欢迎。 **4** [U] the quality of radio and television signals that are broadcast （无线电和电视信号的）接收效果：***good/bad reception*** 良好的 / 差的接收效果 ◇ *There was very poor reception on my phone.* 我的电话接收效果很差。 **5** [U] the act of receiving or welcoming sb 接纳；接待；迎接：*the reception of refugees from the war zone* 接纳交战地区来的难民

re'ception centre (*especially US* **re'ception center**) *noun* **1** a place where people can get information or advice 接待处；接待室：*The museum is building a new reception centre for visitors.* 博物馆正在修建新的来宾接待室。 **2** a place where people, for example those without a home, can get help and temporary accommodation 收容所；救助站：*a reception centre for refugees* 难民救助站

re'ception class *noun* (in Britain) the first class at school for children aged 4 or 5（英国学校为 4 至 5 岁儿童开设的）预备班，启蒙班

re·cep·tion·ist /rɪ'sepʃənɪst/ *noun* a person whose job is to deal with people arriving at or telephoning a hotel, an office building, a doctor's SURGERY, etc. 接待员 ➲ WORDFINDER NOTE AT DOCTOR

re'ception room *noun* (*BrE*) (used especially when advertising houses for sale) a room in a house where people can sit, for example a living room or DINING ROOM（尤用于推销房屋时的）接待室，会客室

re·cep·tive /rɪ'septɪv/ *adj.* ~ (**to sth**) willing to listen to or to accept new ideas or suggestions（对新观点、建议等）愿意倾听的，乐于接受的 SYN **responsive**：*She was always receptive to new ideas.* 她总是愿意接受新观点。◇ *He gave an impressive speech to a receptive audience.* 他做了一次感人的讲演，听众深受感动。 ▸ **re·cep·tive·ness** *noun* [U] **re·cep·tiv·ity** /ˌriːsep'tɪvəti/ *noun* [U]：*receptivity to change* 对变化的适应能力

re·cep·tor /rɪ'septə(r)/ *noun* (*biology* 生) a sense organ or nerve ending in the body that reacts to changes such as heat or cold and makes the body react in a particular way 感受器；受体

re·cess *noun, verb*

■ ***noun*** /rɪ'ses; 'riːses/ **1** [C, U] a period of time during the year when the members of a parliament, committee, etc. do not meet 休会期 **2** [C] a short break in a trial in court 休庭：*The judge called a short recess.* 法官宣布短暂休庭。 **3** (*NAmE*) (*BrE* **break**, **'break time**) [U] a period of time between lessons at school 课间休息 **4** [C] a part of a wall that is set further back than the rest of the wall, forming a space 壁龛；壁橱；凹室 SYN **alcove**：*a recess for books* 放书的壁橱 **5** [C, usually pl.] the part of a place that is furthest from the light and hard to see or get to 隐蔽处；幽深处：*He stared into the dark recesses of the room.* 他盯着房间里黑暗的角落。◇ (*figurative*) *The doubt was still there, in the deep recesses of her mind.* 在她的内心深处依然存有疑虑。

■ ***verb*** /rɪ'ses/ [often passive] **1** [T, I] ~ (**sth**) (*NAmE*) to take or to order a recess 休会；暂停；宣布暂停：*The hearing was recessed for the weekend.* 听证会周末暂停。 **2** [T] ~ **sth** (**in/into sth**) to put sth in a position that is set back into a wall, etc. 把…放进壁龛（或壁橱）；将…嵌入墙壁：*recessed shelves* 凹进墙壁的格子架

re·ces·sion /rɪ'seʃn/ *noun* **1** [C, U] a difficult time for the economy of a country, when there is less trade and industrial activity than usual and more people are unemployed 经济衰退；经济萎缩：*the impact of the current recession on manufacturing* 时下经济萎缩对制造业的影响 ◇ *The economy is* ***in deep recession.*** 经济正处于严重的衰退之中。◇ *policies to pull the country out of recession* 引导国家走出经济萎缩的政策 ➲ COLLOCATIONS AT ECONOMY **2** [U] (*formal*) the movement backwards of sth from a previous position 退后；撤回：*the gradual recession of the floodwater* 洪水的渐渐消退

re·ces·sion·ary /rɪ'seʃnri; *NAmE* -neri/ *adj.* [only before noun] connected with a recession or likely to cause one（引起）经济衰退（或萎缩）的

re·ces·sive /rɪ'sesɪv/ *adj.* (*biology* 生) a **recessive** physical characteristic only appears in a child if it has two GENES for this characteristic, one from each parent. It does not appear if a DOMINANT gene is also present. 隐性的

re·charge /ˌriː'tʃɑːdʒ; *NAmE* -'tʃɑːrdʒ/ *verb* **1** [T, I] ~ (**sth**) to fill a battery with electrical power; to be filled with electrical power 给（电池）充电；充电：*He plugged his razor in to recharge it.* 他把剃刀插在插座上，给它充电。◇ *The drill takes about three hours to recharge.* 钻机充满电大约要三个小时。 **2** [I] (*informal*) to get back your strength and energy by resting for a time 恢复体力；恢复精力；休整：*We needed the break in order to recharge.* 我们需要休息一下以恢复体力。 ▸ **re·charge·able** *adj.*：*rechargeable batteries* 可充电电池

IDM **recharge your 'batteries** to get back your strength and energy by resting for a while 养精蓄锐；休整

re·cher·ché /rə'ʃeəʃeɪ; *NAmE* ˌrəʃer'ʃeɪ/ *adj.* (*from French, formal, usually disapproving*) unusual and not easy to understand, chosen in order to impress people 故作艰深的；矫揉造作的

re·cid·iv·ist /rɪ'sɪdɪvɪst/ *noun* (*formal*) a person who continues to commit crimes, and seems unable to stop, even after being punished 惯犯；累犯者 ▸ **re·cid·iv·ism** /-ɪzəm/ *noun* [U]

re·cipe /'resəpi/ *noun* **1** ~ (**for sth**) a set of instructions that tells you how to cook sth and the INGREDIENTS (= items of food) you need for it 烹饪法；食谱：*a recipe for chicken soup* 鸡汤的做法 ◇ *vegetarian recipes* 素菜食谱 ◇ *a recipe book* 烹饪书 ➲ COLLOCATIONS AT COOKING **2** ~ **for sth** a method or an idea that seems likely to have a particular result 方法；秘诀；诀窍 SYN **formula**：*His plans are* ***a recipe for disaster.*** 他的计划后患无穷。◇ *What's her recipe for success?* 她成功的秘诀是什么？

re·cipi·ent /rɪ'sɪpiənt/ *noun* (*formal*) a person who receives sth 受方；接受者：*recipients of awards* 领奖者

re·cip·ro·cal /rɪ'sɪprəkl/ *adj.* involving two people or groups who agree to help each other or behave in the same way to each other 互惠的；相应的：*The two colleges have a reciprocal arrangement whereby students from one college can attend classes at the other.* 两所学院有一项互惠协定，允许学生跨院选课。 ▸ **re·cip·ro·cal·ly** /-kli/ *adv.*

re'ciprocal verb *noun* (*grammar* 语法) a verb that expresses the idea of an action that is done by two or more people or things to each other, for example 'kiss' in the sentence 'Paul and Claire kissed.' 相互动词，交互动词（如 Paul and Claire kissed 中的 kiss）

re·cip·ro·cate /rɪ'sɪprəkeɪt/ *verb* **1** [T, I] to behave or feel towards sb in the same way as they behave or feel towards you 回报；回应：~ **sth** (**with sth**) *Her passion for him was not reciprocated.* 她对他的热情没有得到回应。◇ *He smiled but his smile was not reciprocated.* 他露出微笑，可他的微笑没有得到回应。◇ ~ (**with sth**) *I wasn't sure whether to laugh or to reciprocate with a remark of my own.* 我不知道是该笑一笑还是该说点什么作为回应。 **2** [I] (*specialist*) to move backwards and forwards in a straight line 沿直线往复移动：*a reciprocating action* 往复运动 ▸ **re·cip·ro·ca·tion** /rɪˌsɪprə'keɪʃn/ *noun* [U]

reci·procity /ˌresɪ'prɒsəti; *NAmE* -'prɑːs-/ *noun* [U] (*formal*) a situation in which two people, countries, etc. provide the same help or advantages to each other 互惠；互助；互换

re·cital /rɪ'saɪtl/ *noun* **1** a public performance of music or poetry, usually given by one person or a small group 音

乐演奏会；诗歌朗诵会：*to give a piano recital* 举办钢琴演奏会 ➲ COLLOCATIONS AT MUSIC **2** a spoken description of a series of events, etc. that is often long and boring（口述）逐一列举；赘述

reci·ta·tion /ˌresɪˈteɪʃn/ *noun* **1** [C, U] an act of saying a piece of poetry or literature that you have learned to an audience 朗诵；朗读 **2** [C] an act of talking or writing about a series of things 逐一列举；逐个叙述：*She continued her recitation of the week's events.* 她接着逐一讲述这一周发生的事。

reci·ta·tive /ˌresɪtəˈtiːv/ *noun* [C, U] (*music* 音) a passage in an OPERA or ORATORIO that is sung in the rhythm of ordinary speech with many words on the same note（歌剧或清唱剧中的）宣叙调 ➲ WORDFINDER NOTE AT OPERA

re·cite /rɪˈsaɪt/ *verb* **1** [T, I] ~ **(sth) (to sb)** | ~ **what…** | **+ speech** to say a poem, piece of literature, etc. that you have learned, especially to an audience（尤指对听众）背诵，吟诵，朗诵：*Each child had to recite a poem to the class.* 每个孩子都得在班上背诵一首诗。 ➲ WORDFINDER NOTE AT POETRY **2** [T] ~ **sth (to sb)** | ~ **what…** | **+ speech** to say a list or series of things（口头）列举；逐一讲述：*They recited all their grievances to me.* 他们把所受的委屈都告诉了我。◇ *She could recite a list of all the kings and queens.* 她能一一说出所有的国王和王后的名字。

reck·less /ˈrekləs/ *adj.* showing a lack of care about danger and the possible results of your actions 鲁莽的；不计后果的；无所顾忌的 SYN **rash**: *He showed* ***a reckless disregard for*** *his own safety.* 他全然不顾个人安危。◇ *She was a good rider, but reckless.* 她是个好骑手，但太鲁莽。◇ *He had always been reckless with money.* 他花钱总是大手大脚。◇ *to cause death by* ***reckless driving*** 鲁莽驾驶造成死亡 ▶ **reck·less·ly** *adv.*: *He admitted driving recklessly.* 他承认鲁莽驾驶。 **reck·less·ness** *noun* [U]

reckon 🔑 /ˈrekən/ *verb* **1** 🔑 [T, I] ~ **(that)**… (*informal, especially BrE*) to think sth or have an opinion about sth 想；认为：*I reckon (that) I'm going to get that job.* 我认为我会得到那份工作。◇ *He'll be famous one day.* ***What do you reckon*** (= do you agree)? 总有一天，他会成为名人的。你觉得呢？◇ *It's worth a lot of money, I reckon.* 我想这值很多钱。◇ *'They'll never find out.' 'You reckon?'* (= I think you may be wrong about that) "他们永远不会发现。" "是吗？" ➲ SYNONYMS AT THINK **2** 🔑 **be reckoned** [T] (not used in the progressive tenses 不用于进行时) to be generally considered to be sth 被普遍认为是；被看作是：**~ to be/have sth** *Children are reckoned to be more sophisticated nowadays.* 人们认为今天的孩子比过去世故。◇ **+ noun/adj.** *It was generally reckoned a success.* 大家都认为那是一次成功。 **3** [T] ~ **to do sth** (*BrE, informal*) to expect to do sth 料想；预计；指望：*We reckon to finish by ten.* 我们预计十点钟以前结束。 **4** [T] to calculate an amount, a number, etc. 估算；估计；计算：**~ sth (at sth)** *The age of the earth is reckoned at about 4 600 million years.* 估计地球的年龄大约为 46 亿年。◇ **~ (that)**… *They reckon (that) their profits are down by at least 20%.* 他们估计利润至少下降了 20%。◇ **be reckoned to do sth** *The journey was reckoned to take about two hours.* 路上估计要花大约两个小时。 IDM SEE NAME *n.*

PHR V **ˈreckon on sth** 🔑 to expect sth to happen or to rely on sth happening 指望；依赖：*They hadn't reckoned on a rebellion.* 他们没有料到会发生叛乱。◇ **reckon on doing sth** *We'd reckoned on having good weather.* 我们原指望会有好天气。 **ˌreckon sth↔ˈup** (*especially BrE*) to calculate the total amount or number of sth 统计；合计：*He reckoned up the cost of everything in his mind.* 他在脑子里把所有费用都合计了一下。 **ˈreckon with sb/sth 1** [usually passive] to consider or treat sb/sth as a serious opponent, problem, etc. 重视；认真处理：*They were already a political force* ***to be reckoned with.*** 他们已经成为一支不容忽视的政治力量。 **2** (usually used in negative sentences 通常用于否定句) to consider sth as a possible problem that you should be prepared for 把（可能出现的问题）考虑进去 SYN **take sth into account**: **reckon with doing sth** *I didn't reckon with getting caught up in so much traffic.* 我没有考虑到塞车会这么严重。 **ˈreckon without sb/sth** (*especially BrE*) to not consider sb/sth as a possible problem that you should be prepared for 没考虑到；不把…算在内 SYN **not take sth into account**: *They had reckoned without the determination of the opposition.* 他们没料到会遭到坚决反对。

reck·on·ing /ˈrekənɪŋ/ *noun* **1** [U, C] the act of calculating sth, especially in a way that is not very exact 估计；估算；计算：***By my reckoning*** *you still owe me £5.* 我算计着，你还欠我 5 英镑。 **2** [C, usually sing., U] a time when sb's actions will be judged to be right or wrong and they may be punished 最后审判日；算总账：*In* ***the final reckoning*** *truth is rewarded.* 在最后算总账的时候，诚实的人会有好报。◇ *Officials concerned with environmental policy predict that* ***a day of reckoning*** *will come.* 担心环境政策的官员们预言总有一天人们会遭到报应。

IDM **in/into/out of the ˈreckoning** (*especially BrE*) (especially in sport 尤用于体育运动) among/not among those who are likely to win or be successful 有（或没有）获胜的可能

re·claim /rɪˈkleɪm/ *verb* **1** to get sth back or to ask to have it back after it has been lost, taken away, etc. 取回；拿回；要求归还：**~ sth** *You'll have to go to the police station to reclaim your wallet.* 你得到警察局去认领你的钱包。◇ **~ sth from sb/sth** *The team reclaimed the title from their rivals.* 这个队从对手手中夺回了冠军。 ➲ SEE ALSO BAGGAGE RECLAIM **2** ~ **sth (from sth)** to make land that is naturally too wet or too dry suitable to be built on, farmed, etc. 开垦，利用，改造（荒地）：*The site for the airport will be reclaimed from the swamp.* 这片湿地将会被开发来建机场。◇ *reclaimed marshland* 被开发利用的沼泽地 **3** [usually passive] ~ **sth** if a piece of land **is reclaimed by** desert, forest, etc., it turns back into desert, etc. after being used for farming or building 重新变为沙漠（或森林等）；沙化；荒漠化；抛荒 **4** ~ **sth (from sth)** to obtain materials from waste products so that they can be used again 回收（废品中有用的东西） ➲ SEE ALSO RECYCLE **5** ~ **sb (from sth)** to rescue sb from a bad or criminal way of life 挽救；感化；使纠正；使悔过自新 ▶ **rec·lam·ation** /ˌrekləˈmeɪʃn/ *noun* [U]: *land reclamation* 土地开垦

re·clas·sify /ˌriːˈklæsɪfaɪ/ *verb* (**re·clas·si·fies**, **re·clas·si·fy·ing**, **re·clas·si·fied**, **re·clas·si·fied**) ~ **sth** to put sth in a different class or category 将…重新分类；将…重新归类：*The drug is to be reclassified after trials showed it to be more harmful than previously thought.* 试验显示这种药比先前想象的危害更大，要重新归类。

re·cline /rɪˈklaɪn/ *verb* **1** [I] ~ **(against/in/on sth)** (*formal*) to sit or lie in a relaxed way, with your body leaning backwards 斜倚；斜躺；向后倚靠：*She was reclining on a sofa.* 她倚靠在沙发上。◇ *a reclining figure* (= for example in a painting) 半躺着的人像 **2** [I, T] ~ **(sth)** when a seat **reclines** or when you **recline** a seat, the back of it moves into a comfortable sloping position（使座椅靠背）向后倾：*a reclining chair* 躺椅

re·cliner /rɪˈklaɪnə(r)/ (*also* **reˈcliner chair**) *noun* a soft comfortable chair with a back that can be pushed back at an angle so that you can lean back in it（可调式）躺椅 ➲ VISUAL VOCAB PAGE V22

re·cluse /rɪˈkluːs; *NAmE* ˈrekluːs/ *noun* a person who lives alone and likes to avoid other people 隐居者；喜欢独处的人：*to lead the life of a recluse* 过隐居的生活 ▶ **re·clu·sive** /rɪˈkluːsɪv/ *adj.*: *a reclusive millionaire* 深居简出的富翁

rec·og·ni·tion 🔑 /ˌrekəɡˈnɪʃn/ *noun* **1** 🔑 [U] the act of remembering who sb is when you see them, or of identifying what sth is 认出；认识；识别：*He glanced briefly towards her but there was no sign of recognition.* 他瞥了她一眼，但似乎没认出她来。◇ *the automatic recognition of handwriting and printed text by computer* 计算机对手写和印刷文本的自动识别 **2** 🔑 [sing., U] ~ **(that…)** the act of accepting that sth exists, is true or is official 承认；认可：*a growing recognition that older people have potential too* 越来越多的人认识到老年人也是有潜力的 ◇ *There is a general recognition of the urgent need for reform.* 人们普

R

遍认识到迫切需要改革。◇ *to seek **international/official/formal recognition** as a sovereign state* 寻求国际上的 / 官方的 / 正式的承认，承认它是一个主权国家 **3** [U] ~ (**for sth**) public praise and reward for sb's work or actions 赞誉；赏识；奖赏：*She gained only minimal recognition for her work.* 她的工作仅仅得到极少的赞誉。◇ *He received the award **in recognition of** his success over the past year.* 他受到了奖励，这是对他过去一年的成绩的肯定。

IDM **to change, alter, etc. beyond/out of (all) recog'nition** to change so much that you can hardly recognize it 变得面目全非；沧海桑田：*The town has changed beyond recognition since I was last here.* 自从我上次离开这里以来，这座小镇已经变得让人认不出来了。

rec·og·niz·able (BrE *also* **-is·able**) /ˈrekəgnaɪzəbl; ˌrekəgˈnaɪzəbl/ *adj.* ~ (**as sth/sb**) easy to know or identify 容易认出的；易于识别的：*The building was easily recognizable as a prison.* 很容易看出这座建筑是所监狱。◇ *After so many years she was still instantly recognizable.* 过了这么多年，还是一眼就能认出她。OPP **unrecognizable** ▸ **rec·og·niz·ably, -is·ably** /-əbli/ *adv.*

rec·og·ni·zance (BrE *also* **-i·sance**) /rɪˈkɒgnɪzəns; NAmE -ˈkɑːg-/ *noun* [U] (*law* 律) a promise by sb who is accused of a crime to appear in court on a particular date; a sum of money paid as a guarantee of this promise 保证书；具结；保释金；保证金

rec·og·nize (BrE *also* **-ise**) /ˈrekəgnaɪz/ *verb* (not used in the progressive tenses 不用于进行时) **1** to know who sb is or what sth is when you see or hear them or it, because you have seen or heard them or it before 认识；认出；辨别出：~ **sb/sth** *I recognized him as soon as he came in the room.* 他一进屋我就认出了他。◇ *Do you recognize this tune?* 你能听出这是哪支曲子吗？◇ ~ **sb/sth by/from sth** *I recognized her by her red hair.* 我从她的红头发认出了她。➲ SYNONYMS AT IDENTIFY **2** to admit or to be aware that sth exists or is true 承认；意识到 SYN **acknowledge**：~ **sth** *They recognized the need to take the problem seriously.* 他们承认需要严肃对待这个问题。◇ ~ **sth as sth** *Drugs were not recognized as a problem then.* 那时候还没有把毒品看成是一个问题加以重视。◇ ~ **how, what, etc....** *Nobody recognized how urgent the situation was.* 当时没有人意识到形势有多么紧急。◇ ~ **that...** *We recognized that the task was not straightforward.* 我们意识到这个任务并非轻而易举。◇ **it is recognized that...** *It was recognized that this solution could only be temporary.* 人们意识到这只是个临时的解决方案。◇ ~ **sb/sth to be/have sth** *Drugs were not recognized to be a problem then.* 那时候还没有把毒品看成是一个问题加以重视。➲ SYNONYMS AT ADMIT **3** to accept and approve of sb/sth officially （正式）认可，接受，赞成：~ **sb/sth** (**as sth**) *recognized qualifications* 获得承认的资格 ◇ *The UK has refused to recognize the new regime.* 英国已拒绝承认这个新的政权。◇ **be recognized to be/have sth** *He is recognized to be their natural leader.* 人们都承认他是他们的当然领袖。**4** **be recognized** (**as sth**) to be thought of as very good or important by people in general 赞赏；赏识；看重；公认：*The book is now recognized as a classic.* 这本书现在是一部公认的经典著作。◇ *She's a recognized authority on the subject.* 她在这个学科上是公认的权威。**5** ~ **sb/sth** to give sb official thanks for sth that they have done or achieved 正式向…致谢；正式感谢：*His services to the state were recognized with the award of a knighthood.* 他被封为爵士，以表彰他对国家的贡献。

re·coil *verb, noun*

■ *verb* /rɪˈkɔɪl/ **1** [I] to move your body quickly away from sb/sth because you find them or it frightening or unpleasant 退缩；畏缩 SYN **flinch**：~ (**from sb/sth**) *She recoiled from his touch.* 她躲开他的触摸。◇ ~ (**at sth**) *He **recoiled in horror** at the sight of the corpse.* 他一见到尸体就吓得往后缩了。**2** [I] ~ (**from sth/from doing sth**) | ~ (**at sth**) to react to an idea or a situation with strong dislike or fear 对…作出厌恶（或恐惧）的反应 SYN **shrink**：*She recoiled from the idea of betraying her own brother.* 背叛自己亲兄弟的这个想法使她感到恐惧。**3** [I] (of a gun 枪炮) to move suddenly backwards when you fire it 反冲；产生后坐力

■ *noun* /ˈriːkɔɪl/ [U, sing.] a sudden movement backwards, especially of a gun when it is fired 反冲；（尤指枪炮的）后坐力

rec·ol·lect /ˌrekəˈlekt/ *verb* [T, I] (not used in the progressive tenses 不用于进行时) (*rather formal*) to remember sth, especially by making an effort to remember it 记起；回忆起；记得 SYN **recall**：~ (**sth**) *She could no longer recollect the details of the letter.* 她想不起那封信的细节了。◇ *As far as I can recollect, she wasn't there on that occasion.* 据我回忆，当时她不在场。◇ ~ **what, how, etc....** *I don't recollect what he said.* 我不记得他说过什么。◇ ~ **that...** *I recollect that we were all gathered in the kitchen.* 我记得当时我们都被召集到厨房里。◇ ~ (**sb/sth**) **doing sth** *I recollect him/his saying that it was dangerous.* 我记得他说那很危险。◇ + **speech** *'It was just before the war,' she recollected.* "那是在战争即将发生之际。"她回忆道。

rec·ol·lec·tion /ˌrekəˈlekʃn/ *noun* (*formal*) **1** [U] the ability to remember sth; the act of remembering sth 记忆力；回忆；记忆 SYN **memory**：~ (**of doing sth**) *I have no recollection of meeting her before.* 我不记得以前见过她。◇ ~ (**of sth**) *My recollection of events differs from his.* 我记忆中的情况和他的不一样。◇ ***To the best of my recollection*** (= if I remember correctly) *I was not present at that meeting.* 如果我没记错的话，我没有出席那次会议。**2** [C] a thing that you remember from the past 往事；回忆的事 SYN **memory**：*to have a **clear/vivid/dim/vague recollection** of sth* 对某事的记忆清晰 / 历历在目 / 模糊不清 / 依稀如烟

re·com·mence AW /ˌriːkəˈmens/ *verb* [I, T] (*formal*) to begin again; to start doing sth again 重新开始；再次开始：*Work on the bridge will recommence next month.* 下个月将重新开始这座桥的建造工作。◇ ~ (**doing**) **sth** *The two countries agreed to recommence talks the following week.* 两国同意于随后的一周重新开始会谈。

rec·om·mend /ˌrekəˈmend/ *verb* **1** to tell sb that sth is good or useful, or that sb would be suitable for a particular job, etc. 推荐；举荐；介绍：~ **sb/sth** *Can you recommend a good hotel?* 你能推荐一家好的旅馆吗？◇ ~ **sb/sth** (**to sb**) (**for/as sth**) *I recommend the book to all my students.* 我向我所有的学生都推荐这本书。◇ *She was recommended for the post by a colleague.* 她由同事推荐到这个岗位。◇ *The hotel's new restaurant comes **highly recommended*** (= a lot of people have praised it). 这家酒店的新餐厅得到了人们的普遍赞扬。**2** to advise a particular course of action; to advise sb to do sth 劝告；建议：~ **sth** *The report recommended a 10% pay increase.* 报告提议工资增加 10%。◇ *It is dangerous to exceed the recommended dose.* 超过建议服用的剂量会有危险。◇ *a recommended price of $50* 建议售价 50 美元 ◇ ~ (**that**)... *I recommend (that) he see a lawyer.* 我建议他去找个律师。◇ (*BrE also*) *I recommend (that) he should see a lawyer.* 我建议他去找个律师。◇ **it is recommended that...** *It is strongly recommended that the machines should be checked every year.* 强烈建议每年都要检查机器。◇ ~ **sb to do sth** *We'd recommend you to book your flight early.* 我们建议你早点儿预订航班。◇ ~ (**sb**) **doing sth** *He recommended reading the book before seeing the movie.* 他建议先看这本书，再去看这部电影。◇ ~ **how, what, etc....** *Can you recommend how much we should charge?* 我们该收多少钱，你能给个建议吗？**3** ~ **sb/sth** (**to sb**) to make sb/sth seem attractive or good 使显得吸引人；使受欢迎 SYN **commend**：*This system has **much to recommend it**.* 这套系统有很多可取之处。

rec·om·men·da·tion /ˌrekəmenˈdeɪʃn/ *noun* **1** [C] an official suggestion about the best thing to do 正式建议；提议：*to accept/reject a recommendation* 接受 / 拒绝一项建议 ◇ ~ (**to sb**) (**for/on/about sth**) *The committee **made recommendations** to the board on teachers' pay and conditions.* 委员会就教师的工资和工作条件问题向董事会提出建议。◇ *I had the operation **on the recommendation of** my doctor.* 我根据医生的建议做了手术。**2** [U, C] the act of telling sb that sth is good or useful or that sb would be suitable for a particular job, etc. 推荐；介绍：*We chose the hotel **on their recommendation*** (= because they recommended it). 我们根据他们的推荐选了这家酒店。◇ *It's*

▼ **SYNONYMS 同义词辨析**

recommend

advise • advocate • urge

These words all mean to tell sb what you think they should do in a particular situation. 以上各词均含劝告、建议之义。

recommend to tell sb what you think they should do in a particular situation; to say what you think the price or level of sth should be 指劝告、建议（针对方法、售价、水平等）： *We'd recommend you to book your flight early.* 我们建议你早点儿预订航班。 ◇ *a recommended price of $50* 建议售价 50 美元

advise to tell sb what you think they should do in a particular situation 指劝告、忠告、建议： *I'd advise you not to tell him.* 我劝你别告诉他。

RECOMMEND OR ADVISE? 用 recommend 还是 advise?

Advise is a stronger word than **recommend** and is often used when the person giving the advice is in a position of authority. * advise 语气较 recommend 强烈，通常指权威人士的忠告： *Police are advising fans without tickets to stay away.* 警察正在告诫没有票的球迷离去。 ◇ ~~*Police are recommending fans without tickets to stay away.*~~ *I advise you…* can suggest that you know better than the person you are advising: this may cause offence if they are your equal or senior to you. *I recommend…* mainly suggests that you are trying to be helpful and is less likely to cause offence. **Recommend** is often used with more positive advice to tell sb about possible benefits and **advise** with more negative advice to warn sb about possible dangers. * I advise you 暗含提出忠告者比对方更了解情况，如果对方处于同等或更高的地位就可能引起反感。I recommend 主要含试图帮助之义，不大可能引起反感。recommend 多指正面的建议，告知某人可能得到的益处；advise 多指反面告诫，警告某人可能产生的危险： ~~*He advised reading the book before seeing the movie.*~~ ◇ ~~*I would recommend against going out on your own.*~~

advocate (*formal*) to support or recommend sth publicly 指拥护、公开支持、提倡： *The group does not advocate the use of violence.* 该团体不支持使用暴力。

urge (*formal*) to recommend sth strongly 指大力推荐、竭力主张： *The situation is dangerous and the UN is urging caution.* 局势岌岌可危，联合国力主谨慎行事。

PATTERNS

- to recommend/advise/advocate/urge **that…**
- **It is** recommended/advised/advocated/urged **that…**
- to recommend/advise/urge **sb to do sth**
- to recommend/advise/advocate **doing sth**
- to **strongly** recommend/advise/advocate sb/sth

best to find a builder through ***personal recommendation.*** 最好通过私人介绍寻找施工人员。 ◇ *Here's a list of my top CD recommendations.* 这是我认为最值得推荐的 CD 的清单。 **3** [C] (*especially NAmE*) a formal letter or statement that sb would be suitable for a particular job, etc. 推荐信；求职介绍信 **SYN** **testimonial**

rec·om·pense /ˈrekəmpens/ *noun, verb*

■ ***noun*** [U] ~ (**for sth/sb**) (*formal*) something, usually money, that you are given because you have suffered in some way, or as a payment for sth 赔偿；补偿；报酬： *There must be adequate recompense for workers who lose their jobs.* 必须给失业的工人足够的补偿。 ◇ *I received $1 000 in recompense for loss of earnings.* 我得到了 1 000 美元的收入损失赔偿。

■ ***verb*** ~ **sb** (**for sth**) (*formal*) to do sth for sb or give them a payment for sth that they have suffered 给…以补偿；赔偿 **SYN** **compensate**: *There was no attempt to recompense the miners for the loss of their jobs.* 没有人表示要对失业矿工给予补偿。

recon /ˈriːkɒn; *NAmE* rɪˈkɑːn/ *noun* [C, U] (*US, informal*) = RECONNAISSANCE

rec·on·cile /ˈrekənsaɪl/ *verb* (*formal*) **1** ~ **sth** (**with sth**) to find an acceptable way of dealing with two or more ideas, needs, etc. that seem to be opposed to each other 使和谐一致；调和；使配合： *an attempt to reconcile the need for industrial development with concern for the environment* 协调工业发展的需要和环境保护之间关系的努力 ◇ *It was hard to reconcile his career ambitions with the needs of his children.* 他很难兼顾事业上的抱负和孩子们的需要。 **2** [usually passive] to make people become friends again after an argument or a disagreement 使和解；使和好如初： ~ **sb** *The pair were reconciled after Jackson made a public apology.* 杰克逊公开道歉之后，这两个人又言归于好了。 ◇ ~ **sb with sb** *He has recently been reconciled with his wife.* 他最近已经和妻子和好了。 **3** ~ **sb/yourself** (**to sth**) to make sb/yourself accept an unpleasant situation because it is not possible to change it 将就；妥协 **SYN** **resign yourself to sth**: *He could not reconcile himself to the prospect of losing her.* 他一想到有可能失去她，就觉得难以忍受。 ▸ **rec·on·cil·able** /ˌrekənˈsaɪləbl/ *adj.*

rec·on·cili·ation /ˌrekənsɪliˈeɪʃn/ *noun* **1** [sing., U] ~ (**between A and B**) | ~ (**with sb**) an end to a disagreement and the start of a good relationship again 调解；和解： *Their change of policy brought about a reconciliation with Britain.* 他们的政策改变促成了与英国的和解。 **2** [U] ~ (**between A and B**) | ~ (**with sth**) the process of making it possible for two different ideas, facts, etc. to exist together without being opposed to each other 协调；和谐一致： *the reconciliation between environment and development* 环境保护与发展之间的和谐统一

rec·on·dite /ˈrekəndaɪt/ *adj.* (*formal*) not known about or understood by many people 深奥的；晦涩的 **SYN** **obscure**

re·con·di·tion /ˌriːkənˈdɪʃn/ *verb* [often passive] ~ **sth** to repair a machine so that it is in good condition and works well 修复（机器）；使（机器）恢复正常运转 **SYN** **overhaul**

re·con·fig·ure /ˌriːkənˈfɪɡə(r); *NAmE* -ˈfɪɡjər/ *verb* ~ **sth** to make changes to the way that sth is arranged to work, especially computer equipment or a program 重新配置（计算机设备等）；重新设定（程序等）： *You may need to reconfigure the firewall if you add a new machine to your network.* 如果在网络中增加新计算机，可能就得重新设定防火墙。

re·con·firm /ˌriːkənˈfɜːm; *NAmE* -ˈfɜːrm/ *verb* ~ **sth** to check again that sth is definitely correct or as previously

▼ **EXPRESS YOURSELF 情景表达**

Asking for and making a recommendation 征求和提出建议

When you need help making a choice, you can ask somebody to give you their view. 需要别人帮助选择时，可以请他们提建议：

- ***What would/do you recommend?*** 你会推荐什么呢？
- ***What do you think would be best?*** 你认为什么是最好的？
- ***Which of the options do you favour/prefer?*** 你更喜欢哪一个选项？

Responses 回应：

- ***I can recommend** the steak today.* 我今天向您推荐牛排。
- ***My favourite is** the Corner Cafe.* 我最喜欢的是街角咖啡馆。
- ***I'd recommend** waiting a few months.* 我建议等几个月。
- ***I suggest you** have another look at the house before you make a decision.* 我建议你做决定之前再看看那房子。
- ***If it were up to me/If you ask me/If it were my decision,** I'd go for the cheaper one.* 如果让我来决定／如果你问我，我会选便宜的那个。

R

arranged 再确认；再确定：*You have to reconfirm your flight 24 hours before travelling.* 你必须在乘飞机之前 24 小时再次确认你的航班。

re·con·nais·sance /rɪˈkɒnɪsns; *NAmE* -ˈkɑːn-/ (*also BrE, informal* **recce**) (*US also, informal* **recon**) *noun* [C, U] the activity of getting information about an area for military purposes, using soldiers, planes, etc. 侦察：*to make an aerial reconnaissance of the island* 对这座岛进行空中侦察 ◇ *Time spent on reconnaissance is seldom wasted.* 花在侦察上的时间很少会白费。◇ *a reconnaissance aircraft/mission/satellite* 侦察飞机 / 任务 / 卫星 ➲ WORDFINDER NOTE AT EXPLORE ➲ COLLOCATIONS AT WAR

re·con·nect /ˌriːkəˈnekt/ *verb* [T, I] to connect sth again; to connect to sth again 再连接；再接合：**~ sth (to sth)** *I replaced the taps and reconnected the water supply.* 我更换了水龙头，再次接通了自来水。◇ **~ (to sth)** *Once you have removed the virus it is safe to reconnect to the Internet.* 病毒一清除，就可以安全地重新连接互联网。

re·con·noitre (*especially US* **-ter**) /ˌrekəˈnɔɪtə(r); *NAmE also* ˌriːkə-/ *verb* [I, T] **~ (sth)** to get information about an area, especially for military purposes, by using soldiers, planes, etc. 侦察；勘察；观测

re·con·quer /ˌriːˈkɒŋkə(r); *NAmE* -ˈkɑːŋ-/ *verb* **~ sth** to take control again of a country or city by force, after having lost it 重新占领（国家或城市）；再征服；夺回

re·con·sider /ˌriːkənˈsɪdə(r)/ *verb* [T, I] **~ (sth)** | **~ what, how, etc....** to think about sth again, especially because you might want to change a previous decision or opinion 重新考虑；重新审议：*to* ***reconsider your decision/position*** 重新考虑你的决定 / 立场 ◇ *Recent information may persuade the board to reconsider.* 最近得到的信息也许会使董事会重新考虑。▶ **re·con·sid·er·ation** /ˌriːkənˌsɪdəˈreɪʃn/ *noun* [U, sing.]

re·con·sti·tute /ˌriːˈkɒnstɪtjuːt; *NAmE* -ˈkɑːnstətuːt/ *verb* **1** **~ sth/itself (as sth)** (*formal*) to form an organization or a group again in a different way 重组；重新设立：*The group reconstituted itself as a political party.* 这个团体重新组建为一个政党。**2** [usually passive] **~ sth** to bring dried food, etc. back to its original form by adding water 使（脱水食物等）恢复原状；使还原 ▶ **re·con·sti·tu·tion** /ˌriːˌkɒnstɪˈtjuːʃn; *NAmE* -ˌkɑːnstəˈtuːʃn/ *noun* [U]

re·con·struct AW /ˌriːkənˈstrʌkt/ *verb* **1** **~ sth (from sth)** to build or make sth again that has been damaged or that no longer exists 修复；重建；重造：*They have tried to reconstruct the settlement as it would have been in Iron Age times.* 他们已试着按铁器时代的样子重建这个小村落。**2** **~ sth** to be able to describe or show exactly how a past event happened, using the information you have gathered 重现描述；使重现：*Investigators are trying to reconstruct the circumstances of the crash.* 调查人员正试图重现撞车时的情形。

re·con·struc·tion AW /ˌriːkənˈstrʌkʃn/ *noun* **1** [U] the process of changing or improving the condition of sth or the way it works; the process of putting sth back into the state it was in before 重建；改造；复原：*the post-war reconstruction of Germany* 德国的战后重建 ◇ *a reconstruction period* 重建时期 **2** [U] the activity of building again sth that has been damaged or destroyed 修复；修理：*the reconstruction of the sea walls* 海堤的修复 **3** [C] a copy of sth that no longer exists 重现：*The doorway is a 19th century reconstruction of Norman work.* 门廊是 19 世纪时模仿诺曼式建筑修建的。**4** [C] a short film showing events that are known to have happened, made in order to try and get more information or better understanding, especially about a crime 再现（犯罪过程等的）影片：*Last night police staged a reconstruction of the incident.* 昨天晚上，警方放映了再现事故经过的影片。 **5 Reconstruction** [U] (in the US) the period after the Civil War when the southern states returned to the US and laws were passed that gave rights to African Americans 重建时期（美国南北战争后南方各州重新加入联邦）

re·con·struct·ive /ˌriːkənˈstrʌktɪv/ *adj.* [only before noun] (of medical treatment 医疗) that involves RECONSTRUCTING part of a person's body because it has been badly damaged or because the person wants to change its shape 修复的；整形的；复原的：*reconstructive surgery* 整形手术

re·con·vene /ˌriːkənˈviːn/ *verb* [I, T] **~ (sth)** if a meeting, parliament, etc. **reconvenes** or if sb **reconvenes** it, it meets again after a break 重新集合；重新召集

re·cord 🔑 *noun, verb*

■ ***noun*** /ˈrekɔːd; *NAmE* ˈrekərd/

• **WRITTEN ACCOUNT** 书面记录 **1** 🔑 [C] **~ (of sth)** a written account of sth that is kept so that it can be looked at and used in the future 记录；记载：*You should* ***keep a record*** *of your expenses.* 你应该记下你的各项开支。◇ ***medical/dental records*** 病历；牙科病历 ◇ *Last summer was the* ***wettest on record.*** 去年夏天是有记录以来降雨量最大的。◇ *It was the worst flood* ***since records began.*** 这是有记录以来最严重的水灾。

• **MUSIC** 音乐 **2** 🔑 [C] a thin round piece of plastic on which music, etc. is recorded 唱片：*to* ***play a record*** 播放唱片 ◇ *a* ***record collection*** 收藏的唱片 ➲ SEE ALSO VINYL (2) **3** [C] a piece or collection of music released as a record, or on CD, the Internet, etc. 唱片；专辑：*a* ***record company*** (= one which produces and sells records) 唱片公司 ◇ *During her career Billie Holiday made over 100 records.* 比莉・哈乐黛在她的歌唱生涯中录制了 100 多张唱片。◇ *His new record is available on CD or as a download.* 他的新专辑可以通过购买 CD 或从网上下载获得。➲ COLLOCATIONS AT MUSIC ➲ SEE ALSO ALBUM (2)

• **HIGHEST/BEST** 最高；最好 **4** 🔑 [C] the best result or the highest or lowest level that has ever been reached, especially in sport（尤指体育运动中最高或最低的）纪录：*She* ***holds the world record*** *for the 100 metres.* 她保持着 100 米的世界纪录。◇ *to* ***break the record*** (= to achieve a better result than there has ever been before) 破纪录 ◇ *to* ***set a new record*** 刷新纪录 ◇ *There was a* ***record number*** *of candidates for the post.* 这个职位的候选人数量空前。◇ *I got to work in* ***record time.*** 我以历来最快的速度赶到单位上班。◇ *record profits* 创纪录的利润 ◇ *Unemployment has reached a* ***record high*** (= the highest level ever). 失业数字已经达到了历来的最高纪录。➲ WORDFINDER NOTE AT SPORT

• **OF SB/STH'S PAST** 过去 **5** 🔑 [sing.] **~ (on sth)** the facts that are known about sb/sth's past behaviour, character, achievements, etc.（有关过去的）事实；记录；经历；功过：*The report criticizes the government's record on housing.* 这份报告批评了政府在住房问题上的所作所为。◇ *The airline has a good* ***safety record.*** 这家航空公司的安全记录一向很好。◇ *He has an impressive record of achievement.* 他所取得的一系列成就令人赞叹。➲ SEE ALSO TRACK RECORD

• **OF CRIMES** 罪行 **6** (*also* ˌ**criminal** ˈ**record**) [C] the fact of having committed crimes in the past 前科；犯罪记录：*Does he have a record?* 他有没有前科？

IDM **(just) for the** ˈ**record 1** used to show that you want what you are saying to be officially written down and remembered（希望载入正式记录）（仅）供记录 **2** used to emphasize a point that you are making, so that the person you are speaking to takes notice（强调要点以引起注意）：*And, for the record, he would be the last person I'd ask.* 需要强调的是，他是我最不愿意去找的人。 ˌ**off the** ˈ**record** if you tell sb sth **off the record**, it is not yet official and you do not want them to repeat it publicly 非正式的；私下的；不得发表的 **put/place sth on (the)** ˈ**record** | **be/go on (the)** ˈ**record (as saying...)** to say sth publicly or officially so that it may be written down and repeated 公开发表（意见等）：*He didn't want to go on the record as either praising or criticizing the proposal.* 他不想公开赞扬或批评这项提议。 **put/set the** ˈ**record straight** to give people the correct information about sth in order to make it clear that what they previously believed was in fact wrong 陈述真相；纠正误解 ➲ MORE AT MATTER *n.*

■ ***verb*** /rɪˈkɔːd; *NAmE* rɪˈkɔːrd/

• **KEEP ACCOUNT** 做记录 **1** 🔑 [T] to keep a permanent account of facts or events by writing them down, filming them, storing them in a computer, etc. 记录；记载：**~ sth** *Her childhood is recorded in the diaries of those years.* 她的童年生活都记在当年的日记里。◇ *You should record all your expenses during your trip.* 你应该记下你一路上的所有开支。◇ **~ how, what, etc.…** *His job is to record how politicians vote on major issues.* 他的工作就是要记录政治家是如何对重大问题投票的。◇ **~ that…** *She recorded in her diary that they crossed the Equator on 15 June.* 她在日记中记载他们是在 6 月 15 日越过赤道的。◇ **it is recorded that…** *It is recorded that, by the year 630, four hundred monks were attached to the monastery.* 据记载，到 630 年有 400 个僧侣隶属该寺院。

- **MAKE COPY** 复制 **2** [T, I] to make a copy of music, a film/movie, etc. by storing it on tape or a disc so that you can listen to or watch it again 录制；录（音）；录（像）：**~ (sth)** *Did you remember to record that programme for me?* 你记得为我录下那个节目了吗？◇ *a recorded concert* 录制的音乐会 ◇ *Tell me when the tape starts recording.* 磁带开始录时告诉我一声。◇ **~ sb/sth doing sth** *He recorded the class rehearsing before the performance.* 他录下了演出前班级的排练。
- **MUSIC** 音乐 **3** [T, I] **~ (sth)** to perform music so that it can be copied onto and kept on tape 演奏音乐供录制；灌（唱片）：*The band is back in the US recording their new album.* 乐队回美国录制新唱片去了。
- **MAKE OFFICIAL STATEMENT** 正式声明 **4** [T] **~ sth | ~ that…** to make an official or legal statement about sth 发表正式（或法律方面的）声明；申明：*The coroner recorded a verdict of accidental death.* 验尸官判定这是一次意外死亡。
- **OF MEASURING INSTRUMENT** 测量仪器 **5** [T] **~ sth | ~ what, how, etc.…** to show a particular measurement or amount 标明；显示：*The thermometer recorded a temperature of 40°C.* 温度计显示气温达到了 40 摄氏度。➲ MORE LIKE THIS 21, page R27

ˈrecord-breaker *noun* a person or thing that achieves a better result or higher level than has ever been achieved before 打破纪录者 ▸ **ˈrecord-breaking** *adj.* [only before noun]: *a record-breaking jump* 打破纪录的一跳

reˌcorded deˈlivery (*BrE*) (*NAmE* **ˌcertified ˈmail**) *noun* [U] a method of sending a letter or package in which the person sending it gets an official note to say it has been posted and the person receiving it must sign a form when it is delivered 挂号邮寄（需收件人签收）：*I'd like to send this (by) recorded delivery.* 这个邮件要挂号。➲ COMPARE REGISTERED MAIL

re·cord·er /rɪˈkɔːdə(r); *NAmE* -ˈkɔːrd-/ *noun* **1** (in compounds 构成复合词) a machine for recording sound or pictures or both 录音机；录像机：*a **tape/cassette/video/DVD recorder*** 磁带 / 盒式录音机；录像机；DVD 录像机 ➲ SEE ALSO FLIGHT RECORDER **2** a musical instrument in the shape of a pipe that you blow into, with holes that you cover with your fingers 竖笛；直笛 ➲ VISUAL VOCAB PAGE V38 **3** a judge in a court in some parts of Britain and the US（英国和美国某些地区的）刑事法院法官，法官 **4** a person who keeps a record of events or facts 记录员；书记员

ˈrecord holder *noun* a person who has achieved the best result that has ever been achieved in a sport 纪录保持者

re·cord·ing /rɪˈkɔːdɪŋ; *NAmE* -ˈkɔːrd-/ *noun* **1** [C] sound or pictures that have been recorded on CD, DVD, video, etc. 录制的音像；录音；视频；录像：*a video recording of the wedding* 婚礼的录像 **2** [U] the process of making a record, film/movie, radio or television show, etc. 录制：*during the recording of the show* 在录制这场表演期间 ◇ ***recording equipment*** 录制设备 ◇ *a **recording studio*** 录音棚 ◇ *the **recording industry*** (= the industry that records and sells music) 唱片业 **3** [U] the process or act of writing down and storing information for official purposes（正式的）记录，记载：*the recording of financial transactions* 关于金融交易的记载

re·cord·ist /rɪˈkɔːdɪst; *NAmE* -ˈkɔːrd-/ *noun* a person whose job is making sound recordings, especially in a recording studio（尤指录音棚的）录音员，录音师

ˈrecord player *noun* a piece of equipment for playing records in order to listen to the music, etc. on them 唱机

re·count¹ /rɪˈkaʊnt/ *verb* (*formal*) to tell sb about sth, especially sth that you have experienced 讲述，叙述（亲身经历）：**~ sth (to sb)** *She was asked to recount the details of the conversation to the court.* 她被要求向法庭陈述谈话细节。◇ **~ what, how, etc.…** *They recounted what had happened during those years.* 他们叙述了那些年里发生的事。◇ **+ speech** *'It was before the war,' he recounted.* "那是在战前。" 他叙述道。

re·count² /ˌriːˈkaʊnt/ *verb* **~ sth** to count sth again, especially votes 重数；重新清点（选票）▸ **re·count** *noun* : *The defeated candidate demanded a recount.* 落选的候选人要求重新计票。

re·coup /rɪˈkuːp/ *verb* **~ sth** (*formal*) to get back an amount of money that you have spent or lost 收回（成本）；弥补（亏损）SYN **recover**: *We hope to recoup our initial investment in the first year.* 我们希望我们的前期投资在第一年就能赚回来。

re·course /rɪˈkɔːs; *NAmE* ˈriːkɔːrs/ *noun* [U] (*formal*) the fact of having to, or being able to, use sth that can provide help in a difficult situation 依靠；依赖；求助：*Your only recourse is legal action.* 你的唯一依靠就是诉诸法律。◇ *She made a complete recovery **without recourse to** surgery.* 她未做手术就完全恢复了健康。◇ *The government, when necessary, **has recourse to** the armed forces.* 政府在必要时可以动用军队。

re·cover AW /rɪˈkʌvə(r)/ *verb*
- **FROM ILLNESS** 从疾病中 **1** [I] **~ (from sth)** to get well again after being ill/sick, hurt, etc. 恢复健康；康复；痊愈：*He's still recovering from his operation.* 手术后，他仍在恢复之中。➲ WORDFINDER NOTE AT HEALTH
- **FROM STH UNPLEASANT** 从不愉快的事中 **2** [I] **~ (from sth)** to return to a normal state after an unpleasant or unusual experience or a period of difficulty 复原；恢复常态：*It can take many years to recover from the death of a loved one.* 从心爱的人去世的痛苦中恢复过来可能要花很多年。◇ *The economy is at last beginning to recover.* 经济终于开始复苏了。
- **MONEY** 钱 **3** [T] **~ sth (from sb/sth)** to get back the same amount of money that you have spent or that is owed to you 全额收回；追回 SYN **recoup**: *He is unlikely to ever recover his legal costs.* 他不大可能收回他的诉讼费用了。
- **STH LOST/STOLEN** 丢失 / 失窃的东西 **4** [T] to get back or find sth that was lost, stolen or missing 找回；寻回；找到：**~ sth** *The police eventually recovered the stolen paintings.* 警方最终追回了失窃的油画。◇ **~ sth from sb/sth** *Six bodies were recovered from the wreckage.* 从残骸中找到了六具尸体。
- **POSITION/STATUS** 位置；地位 **5** [T] **~ sth** to win back a position, level, status, etc. that has been lost 赢回；重新获得 SYN **regain**: *The team recovered its lead in the second half.* 下半场这支队再次领先。
- **SENSES/EMOTIONS** 感觉；情感 **6** [T] to get back the use of your senses, control of your emotions, etc. 恢复；重新控制 SYN **regain**: **~ sth** *It took her a few minutes to **recover consciousness**.* 过了几分钟她才恢复知觉。◇ *to recover your sight* 恢复视力 ◇ **~ yourself** *She seemed upset but quickly recovered herself.* 她显得心烦意乱，但很快静下心来。

▸ **re·covered** AW *adj.* [not before noun]: *She is now fully recovered from her injuries.* 她现在已经完全从伤痛中恢复过来了。

re-cover /ˌriː ˈkʌvə(r)/ *verb* **~ sth** to put a new cover on sth 重新遮盖

re·cov·er·able AW /rɪˈkʌvərəbl/ *adj.* **1** that you can get back after it has been spent or lost 可收回的；可重新获得的：*Travel expenses will be recoverable from the company.* 差旅费用可到公司报销。 **2** that can be obtained from the ground 可开采的：*recoverable oil reserves* 可开采的石油资源

re·cov·ery AW /rɪˈkʌvəri/ *noun* (*pl.* **-ies**) **1** [U, C, usually sing.] ~ (**from sth**) the process of becoming well again after an illness or injury 恢复；痊愈：*My father has made* ***a full recovery*** *from the operation.* 我父亲手术后已完全康复了。◇ *to make* ***a remarkable/quick/speedy/slow, etc. recovery*** 恢复显著、很快、迅速、缓慢等 ◇ *She is* ***on the road to*** (= making progress towards) *recovery.* 她正在康复之中。 **2** [U, C, usually sing.] ~ (**in sth**) the process of improving or becoming stronger again 改善；回升；复苏：*The government is forecasting an* ***economic recovery.*** 政府预测经济会复苏。◇ *a recovery in consumer spending* 消费支出的回升 ◇ *The economy is showing signs of recovery.* 经济呈现出复苏的迹象。 **3** [U] ~ (**of sth**) the action or process of getting sth back that has been lost or stolen 取回；收回；复得：*There is a reward for information leading to the recovery of the missing diamonds.* 凡能为找回丢失的钻石提供线索者可获奖赏。 **4** [U] (*also* **reˈcovery room** [C]) the room in a hospital where patients are kept immediately after an operation（供刚做完手术的病人使用的）监护室

reˈcovery position *noun* [sing.] a position lying on the side, with the arms and legs carefully placed, that helps a person who is not conscious to breathe 复原卧位，复原体位（侧卧、四肢稳当放置，以利于昏迷者呼吸）

rec·re·ant /ˈrekriənt/ *adj.* (*literary*) not brave 怯懦的 SYN **cowardly**

re·create AW /ˌriːkriˈeɪt/ *verb* ~ **sth** to make sth that existed in the past exist or seem to exist again 再现；再创造：*The movie recreates the glamour of 1940s Hollywood.* 这部电影再现了 20 世纪 40 年代好莱坞的辉煌。 ▶ **re·cre·ation** /-ˈeɪʃn/ *noun* [C, U]: *The writer attempts a recreation of the sights and sounds of his childhood.* 作家试图再现他童年的所见所闻。

rec·re·ation /ˌrekriˈeɪʃn/ *noun* **1** [U] the fact of people doing things for enjoyment, when they are not working 娱乐；消遣：*the need to improve facilities for leisure and recreation* 改进消遣娱乐设施之必要 ◇ *the increasing use of land for recreation* 把越来越多的土地用于娱乐 **2** [C] a particular activity that sb does when they are not working 娱乐活动；游戏 SYN **hobby, pastime**: *His recreations include golf, football and shooting.* 他的娱乐活动包括打高尔夫球、踢足球和射击。 ➲ SYNONYMS AT ENTERTAINMENT

rec·re·ation·al /ˌrekriˈeɪʃənl/ *adj.* connected with activities that people do for enjoyment when they are not working 娱乐的；消遣的：*recreational activities/facilities* 娱乐活动 / 设施 ◇ *These areas are set aside for public recreational use.* 这些地方已经划出来用于公共娱乐。

recreˈational vehicle (*NAmE*) (*BrE* **camp·er**, **ˈcamper van**) (*also* **motor·home** *NAmE, BrE*) *noun* (*abbr.* **RV**) a large vehicle designed for people to live and sleep in when they are travelling 野营车，旅行房车（供旅行时居住）➲ VISUAL VOCAB PAGE V63

recreˈation ground *noun* (*BrE*) an area of land used by the public for sports and games 公共娱乐场

recreˈation room (*also NAmE, informal* **ˈrec room**) *noun* **1** a room in a school, a hospital, an office building, etc. in which people can relax, play games, etc.（学校、医院、办公楼等处的）娱乐室，活动室 **2** (*NAmE*) a room in a private house used for games, entertainment, etc.（私人住宅里的）康乐室

re·crim·in·ation /rɪˌkrɪmɪˈneɪʃn/ *noun* [C, usually pl., U] an angry statement that sb makes accusing sb else of sth, especially in response to a similar statement from them 指责；反诉；反控：*bitter recriminations* 激烈的反诉 ◇ *We spent the rest of the evening in mutual recrimination.* 我们后来一晚上都在相互指责。 ▶ **re·crim·in·atory** /rɪˈkrɪmɪnətri; *NAmE* -tɔːri/ *adj.*

ˈrec room /ˈrek ruːm; *NAmE* rʊm/ *noun* (*NAmE, informal*) = RECREATION ROOM

re·cru·desce /ˌriːkruːˈdes/ *verb* [I] (*formal*) (especially of sth bad 尤指坏事) to happen again 再发生；复发 SYN **recur** ▶ **re·cru·des·cence** /ˌriːkruːˈdesns/ *noun* [U] **re·cru·des·cent** /ˌriːkruːˈdesnt/ *adj.*

re·cruit /rɪˈkruːt/ *verb, noun*

■ *verb* **1** [T, I] ~ (**sb**) (**to sth**) | ~ **sb to do sth** to find new people to join a company, an organization, the armed forces, etc. 吸收（新成员）；征募（新兵）：*The police are trying to recruit more officers from ethnic minorities.* 警察机关正试图从少数民族中征募更多的新警员。◇ *They recruited several new members to the club.* 他们吸收了几名新成员进入俱乐部。◇ *He's responsible for recruiting at all levels.* 他负责各级征募工作。 ➲ COLLOCATIONS AT JOB **2** [T] ~ **sb to do sth** to persuade sb to do sth, especially to help you 动员…（提供帮助）：*We were recruited to help peel the vegetables.* 我们被找来帮着给蔬菜去皮。 **3** [T] ~ **sth** to form a new army, team, etc. by persuading new people to join it（通过招募）组成，组建：*to recruit a task force* 组建特遣部队 ▶ **re·cruit·er** *noun* **re·cruit·ment** *noun* [U]: *the recruitment of new members* 新成员的招募 ◇ *a recruitment drive* 征兵运动

■ *noun* **1** a person who has recently joined the armed forces or the police 新兵；新警员：*the training of new recruits* 新兵训练 ◇ *He spoke of us scornfully as* ***raw recruits*** (= people without training or experience). 他轻蔑地称我们是新兵娃娃。 **2** a person who joins an organization, a company, etc. 新成员：*attempts to attract new recruits to the nursing profession* 吸引新成员加入护理行业的努力

rec·tal /ˈrektəl/ *adj.* (*anatomy* 解) relating to the RECTUM 直肠的

rect·angle /ˈrektæŋgl/ *noun* a flat shape with four straight sides, two of which are longer than the other two, and four angles of 90° 长方形；矩形 ➲ PICTURE AT PARALLELOGRAM ▶ **rect·angu·lar** /rekˈtæŋgjələ(r)/ *adj.*

rect·ify /ˈrektɪfaɪ/ *verb* (**rec·ti·fies, rec·ti·fy·ing, rec·ti·fied, rec·ti·fied**) ~ **sth** (*formal*) to put right sth that is wrong 矫正；纠正；改正 SYN **correct**: *to rectify a fault* 改正缺点 ◇ *We must take steps to rectify the situation.* 我们一定要采取措施整顿局面。 ▶ **rec·ti·fi·able** /ˌrektɪˈfaɪəbl/ *adj.*：*The damage will be easily rectifiable.* 所受损坏很容易修复。 **rec·ti·fi·ca·tion** /ˌrektɪfɪˈkeɪʃn/ *noun* [U]

rec·ti·lin·ear /ˌrektɪˈlɪniə(r)/ *adj.* (*specialist*) **1** in a straight line 直线的；笔直的：*rectilinear motion* 直线运动 **2** having straight lines 有直线的：*rectilinear forms* 直线图形

rec·ti·tude /ˈrektɪtjuːd; *NAmE* -tuːd/ *noun* [U] (*formal*) the quality of thinking or behaving in a correct and honest way 公正；正直；诚实 SYN **uprightness**

recto /ˈrektəʊ; *NAmE* -toʊ/ *noun* (*pl.* **-os**) (*specialist*) the page on the right side of an open book（打开的书的）右页 OPP **verso**

rec·tor /ˈrektə(r)/ *noun* **1** an Anglican priest who is in charge of a particular area (called a PARISH). In the past a rector received an income directly from this area.（圣公会的）教区牧师，堂区主持人 ➲ COMPARE VICAR **2** (in Britain) the head of certain universities, colleges or schools（英国某些学校的）校长

rec·tory /ˈrektəri/ *noun* (*pl.* **-ies**) *noun* a house where the rector of a church lives, or lived in the past 堂区主持人的住宅

rec·tum /ˈrektəm/ *noun* (*pl.* **rec·tums** or **recta** /ˈrektə/) (*anatomy* 解) the end section of the tube where food waste collects before leaving the body through the ANUS 直肠 ➲ VISUAL VOCAB PAGE V64

re·cum·bent /rɪˈkʌmbənt/ *adj.* [usually before noun] (*formal*) (of a person's body or position 人的身体或姿势) lying down 躺倒的；躺着的 SYN **reclining**

re·cu·per·ate /rɪˈkuːpəreɪt/ *verb* (*formal*) **1** [I] ~ (**from sth**) to get back your health, strength or energy after being ill/sick, tired, injured, etc. 康复；恢复；恢复健康 SYN recover: *He's still recuperating from his operation.* 他动了手术，还在恢复。 **2** [T] ~ **sth** to get back money that you have spent or lost 收回；挽回（损失） SYN **recoup, recover**: *He hoped to recuperate at least some of his losses.* 他希望至少挽回一部分损失。 ▸ **re·cu·per·ation** /rɪˌkuːpəˈreɪʃn/ *noun* [U]: *It was a period of rest and recuperation.* 那是一段休养的时间。

re·cu·pera·tive /rɪˈkuːpərətɪv/ *adj.* (*formal*) helping you to get better after you have been ill/sick, very tired, etc. 有助于恢复的

recur /rɪˈkɜː(r)/ *verb* (**-rr-**) [I] to happen again or a number of times 再发生；反复出现：*This theme recurs several times throughout the book.* 这一主题在整部书里出现了好几次。◇ *a* ***recurring illness/problem/nightmare, etc.*** 反复发作的疾病、反复出现的问题、一再出现的噩梦等

re·cur·rence /rɪˈkʌrəns; *NAmE* -ˈkɜːr-/ *noun* [C, usually sing., U] if there is **a recurrence of** sth, it happens again 重现；复发：*attempts to prevent a recurrence of the problem* 防止问题再次发生的努力

re·cur·rent /rɪˈkʌrənt; *NAmE* -ˈkɜːr-/ *adj.* that happens again and again 反复出现的；重复发生的：*recurrent infections* 重复感染 ◇ *Poverty is a* ***recurrent theme*** *in her novels.* 贫穷是她的小说中惯有的主题。

re·cur·sion /rɪˈkɜːʃn; *NAmE* -ˈkɜːrʒn/ *noun* [U] (*mathematics* 数) the process of repeating a FUNCTION, each time applying it to the result of the previous stage 递归

re·cur·sive /rɪˈkɜːsɪv; *NAmE* -ˈkɜːrs-/ *adj.* (*specialist*) involving a process that is applied repeatedly 递归的；循环的

re·cus·ant /ˈrekjʊzənt; *NAmE* rəˈkjuːzənt/ *noun* (*formal*) a person who refuses to do what a rule or person in authority says they should do 不服从的人；反抗者 ▸ **re·cus·ancy** /ˈrekjʊzənsi/ *noun* [U]

re·cyc·lable /ˌriːˈsaɪkləbl/ *adj.* able to be RECYCLED 可回收利用的；可再循环的

re·cycle /ˌriːˈsaɪkl/ *verb* **1** ~ **sth** to treat things that have already been used so that they can be used again 回收利用；再利用：*Denmark recycles nearly 85% of its paper.* 丹麦的纸张回收率接近 85%。◇ *recycled paper* 再生纸 ➲ COLLOCATIONS AT ENVIRONMENT ➲ VISUAL VOCAB PAGE V8 **2** ~ **sth** to use the same ideas, methods, jokes, etc. again 再次应用，重新使用（概念、方法、玩笑等）：*He recycled all his old jokes.* 他把那些老掉牙的笑话又说了一遍。▸ **re·cyc·ling** *noun* [U]: *the recycling of glass* 玻璃的回收利用 ◇ *a recycling plant* 废品回收加工厂

red 🔑 /red/ *adj., noun*

■ *adj.* (**red·der**, **red·dest**) **1** 🔑 having the colour of blood or fire 红的；红色的：*a red car* 红色的汽车 ◇ *The lights (= traffic lights) changed to red before I could get across.* 我还没来得及通过，红灯又亮了。 **2** (of the eyes 眼睛) BLOODSHOT (= with thin lines of blood in them) or surrounded by red or very pink skin 充血的；布满血丝的；红肿的：*Her eyes were red from crying.* 她的眼睛都哭红了。 **3** 🔑 (of the face 脸) bright red or pink, especially because you are angry, embarrassed or ashamed 涨红的；通红的：*He stammered something and went very red in the face.* 他结结巴巴地说了些什么，脸涨得通红。◇ (*BrE*) *She went* ***red as a beetroot.*** 她的脸涨得通红。◇ (*NAmE*) *She went* ***red as a beet.*** 她的脸涨得通红。 **4** 🔑 (of hair or an animal's fur 头发或动物的毛皮) reddish-brown in colour 红褐色的：*a red-haired girl* 红发女孩 ◇ *red deer* 赤鹿 ➲ SEE ALSO REDHEAD **5** (*informal, politics* 政, *sometimes disapproving*) having very LEFT-WING political opinions 激进的；革命的；左翼的 ➲ COMPARE PINK *adj.* (3) **6** (*politics* 政) (of an area in the US) having more people who vote for the REPUBLICAN candidate than the DEMOCRATIC one（美国某一地区）红色的（支持共和党候选人多于民主党候选人）：*red states/counties* 红州；红县 OPP **blue** ➲ MORE LIKE THIS 35, page R29 ▸ **red·ness** *noun* [U, sing.]: *You may notice redness and swelling after the injection.* 注射后可能会出现红肿。

IDM **red in ˌtooth and ˈclaw** involving opposition or competition that is violent and without pity 残酷无情；血淋淋；决不宽容：*nature, red in tooth and claw* 残酷无情的大自然 **a red rag to a ˈbull** (*BrE*) (*NAmE* **like waving a red flag in front of a ˈbull**) something that is likely to make sb very angry 斗牛的红布；激起人怒火的事物 ➲ MORE AT PAINT *v.*

■ *noun* **1** 🔑 [C, U] the colour of blood or fire 红色：*She often wears red.* 她经常穿红色的衣服。◇ *the reds and browns of the woods in the fall* (= of the leaves) 秋天树林呈现的红色和褐色 ◇ *I've marked the corrections in red* (= in red ink). 我已经用红笔做了改正。◇ *The traffic lights were on red.* 当时是亮红灯。 **2** [U, C] red wine 红葡萄酒：*Would you prefer red or white?* 你喜欢喝红葡萄酒还是白葡萄酒？◇ *an Italian red* 一杯意大利红葡萄酒 **3** [C] (*informal, disapproving, politics* 政) a person with very LEFT-WING political opinions 左翼人士；激进分子 ➲ COMPARE PINKO

IDM **be in the ˈred** (*informal*) to owe money to your bank because you have spent more than you have in your account 负债；亏空：*The company has plunged $37 million into the red.* 公司负债已达 3 700 万美元。➲ COMPARE BE IN THE BLACK at BLACK *n.* **see ˈred** (*informal*) to become very angry 大发脾气；大怒

re·dact /rɪˈdækt/ *verb* ~ **sth** (**from sth**) to remove information from a document because you do not want the public to see it 删除，去掉，辑除（不愿公之于众的信息）：*All sensitive personal information has been redacted from the public documents.* 所有敏感的个人信息都从公开文件中删掉了。▸ **re·dac·tion** /rɪˈdækʃn/ *noun* [C, U]

ˌred ˈadmiral *noun* a BUTTERFLY (= a flying insect with large brightly coloured wings) that has black wings with bright red marks on them 红纹丽蛱蝶；大西洋赤蛱蝶

ˌred aˈlert *noun* [U, sing.] a situation in which you are prepared for sth dangerous to happen; a warning of this 紧急戒备状态；紧急警报：*Following the bomb blast, local hospitals have been* ***put on red alert.*** 炸弹爆炸之后，当地医院一直处于戒备状态。

ˌred ˈblood cell (*also* **ˈred cell**) (*biology* 生 **eryth·ro·cyte**) *noun* any of the red-coloured cells in the blood, that carry OXYGEN 红细胞；红血球

ˌred-ˈblooded *adj.* [usually before noun] (*informal*) full of strength and energy, often sexual energy 充满活力的；性欲旺盛的 SYN **virile**: *red-blooded young males* 血气方刚的年轻男子

ˌred ˈbox *noun* (*BrE*) a box used by a government minister to hold official documents（英国大臣用的）公文匣

red·breast /ˈredbrest/ *noun* (*literary*) a ROBIN 知更鸟

ˈred-brick *adj.* [usually before noun] **1** (of buildings, walls, etc. 建筑物、墙壁等) built with bricks of a reddish-brown colour 用红砖建成的：*red-brick cottages* 红砖建成的村舍 **2** (*becoming old-fashioned*) (of universities in Britain 英国大学) built in the late 19th or early 20th century, in contrast to older universities, such as Oxford and Cambridge "红砖"的（建于 19 世纪末 20 世纪初，与更为古老的大学如牛津和剑桥形成对照） ➲ COMPARE OXBRIDGE

red·bush /ˈredbʊʃ/ *noun* [U] = ROOIBOS

red·cap /ˈredkæp/ *noun* **1** (*BrE*) a member of the MILITARY POLICE 宪兵 **2** (*NAmE*) a railway/railroad PORTER 铁路搬运工

ˌred ˈcard *noun* (in football (SOCCER) 足球) a card shown by the REFEREE to a player who has broken the rules of the game and is not allowed to play for the rest of the game 红牌（裁判员判罚犯规球员不能继续比赛） ➲ COMPARE YELLOW CARD

ˌred ˈcarpet (*usually* **the red carpet**) *noun* [sing.] a strip of red carpet laid on the ground for an important visitor to walk on when he or she arrives（为迎接贵宾铺的）红地毯：*I didn't expect to be given* ***the red carpet treatment!*** 我可没想到会受到隆重接待！

ˈred cell *noun* = RED BLOOD CELL

R

ˌred ˈcent *noun* [sing.] (*NAmE*) (especially after a negative 尤用于否定词后) a very small amount of money 很少的钱：*I didn't get a red cent for all my work.* 我做了那么多工作，可一分钱也没得到。

red·coat /ˈredkəʊt; *NAmE* -koʊt/ *noun* **1** a British soldier in the past（旧时的）英国士兵 **2** (in Britain) a worker at a HOLIDAY CAMP who entertains and helps guests（英国的）度假营地招待员，度假营地服务员

the ˌRed ˈCrescent *noun* [sing.] the name used by national branches in Muslim countries of the International Movement of the Red Cross and the Red Crescent, an organization that takes care of people suffering because of war or natural disasters 红新月会（"红十字会与红新月会国际联合会"中伊斯兰国家分支机构的称谓）

the ˌRed ˈCross *noun* [sing.] an international organization that takes care of people suffering because of war or natural disasters. Its full name is the International Movement of the Red Cross and the Red Crescent. 红十字会

red·cur·rant /ˌredˈkʌrənt; ˈredkʌrənt; *NAmE* -kɜːr-/ *noun* a very small red BERRY that grows in bunches on a bush and can be eaten 红醋栗：*redcurrant jelly* 红醋栗果冻 ◇ *a redcurrant bush* 红醋栗树丛

ˌred ˈdeer *noun* (*pl.* **red deer**) a DEER with large ANTLERS (= horns shaped like branches), which has a reddish-brown coat in summer 马鹿；赤鹿

red·den /ˈredn/ *verb* [I, T] ~ (**sth**) to become red; to make sth red （使）变红：*The sky was reddening.* 天空红霞映照。◇ *He could feel his face reddening with embarrassment.* 他感到自己因为尴尬而脸红了。◇ *He stared at her and she reddened.* 他盯着她看，弄得她脸都红了。

red·dish /ˈredɪʃ/ *adj.* fairly red in colour 微红的；略带红色的

ˌred ˈdwarf *noun* (*astronomy* 天) a small, old star that is not very hot 红矮星

re·dec·or·ate /ˌriːˈdekəreɪt/ *verb* [I, T] to put new paint and/or paper on the walls of a room or house（用涂料或壁纸）重新装饰，再次装修：*We've just redecorated.* 我们刚刚重新装修过。◇ **~ sth** *The house has been fully redecorated.* 这房子已经彻底重新装修过了。▸ **re·dec·or·ation** /ˌriːˌdekəˈreɪʃn/ *noun* [U]

re·deem /rɪˈdiːm/ *verb* **1** **~ sb/sth** to make sb/sth seem less bad 补救；弥补；掩饰…之不足 SYN **compensate**: *The excellent acting wasn't enough to redeem a weak plot.* 精彩的表演不足以掩盖情节的拙劣。◇ *The only* ***redeeming feature*** *of the job* (= good thing about it) *is the salary.* 这份工作唯一的可取之处就是它的工资。➲ SYNONYMS AT SAVE **2** **~ yourself** to do sth to improve the opinion that people have of you, especially after you have done sth bad 挽回影响；改变印象；维护：*He has a chance to redeem himself after last week's mistakes.* 他有机会弥补上星期犯下的错误。**3** **~ sb** (in Christianity 基督教) to save sb from the power of evil 拯救；救赎：*Jesus Christ came to redeem us from sin.* 耶稣基督来将我们从罪恶中拯救出来。**4** **~ sth** to pay the full sum of money that you owe sb; to pay a debt 偿清；付清：*to* ***redeem a loan/mortgage*** 清偿贷款／按揭贷款 **5** **~ sth** to exchange sth such as shares or VOUCHERS for money or goods 兑换；兑现：*This voucher can be redeemed at any of our branches.* 这抵用券在我们的任一分支机构都可以使用。**6** **~ sth** to get back a valuable object from sb by paying them back the money you borrowed from them in exchange for the object 赎回：*He was able to redeem his watch from the pawnshop.* 他得以从当铺赎回他的表。**7** **~ a pledge/promise** (*formal*) to do what you have promised that you will do 履行，遵守（诺言）

re·deem·able /rɪˈdiːməbl/ *adj.* ~ (**against sth**) that can be exchanged for money or goods 可兑换的；可交换的：*These vouchers are redeemable against any future purchase.* 这些优惠券可在以后购物时使用。

the Re·deem·er /rɪˈdiːmə(r)/ *noun* [sing.] (*literary*) Jesus Christ 救世主；耶稣基督

re·define AW /ˌriːdɪˈfaɪn/ *verb* to change the nature or limits of sth; to make people consider sth in a new way 改变…的本质（或界限）；重新定义；使重新考虑：**~ sth** *The new constitution redefined the powers of the president.* 新宪法重新规定了总统的职权。◇ **~ what, how, etc.…** *We need to redefine what we mean by democracy.* 我们需要重新考虑我们对民主的理解。▸ **re·def·in·ition** /ˌriːdefɪˈnɪʃn/ *noun* [U, C]

re·demp·tion /rɪˈdempʃn/ *noun* [U] **1** (*formal*) the act of saving or state of being saved from the power of evil; the act of REDEEMING 拯救；救赎：*the redemption of the world from sin* 将世界从罪恶中拯救出来 **2** (*finance* 财) the act of exchanging shares for money (= of REDEEMING them) 赎回（股票等）

IDM **beyond/past reˈdemption** too bad to be saved or improved 无法挽救；不可救药

re·demp·tive /rɪˈdemptɪv/ *adj.* (*formal*) that saves you from the power of evil 救赎的；拯救的：*the redemptive power of love* 爱情的救赎力量

re·deploy /ˌriːdɪˈplɔɪ/ *verb* to move sb/sth to a new position or job 调配；重新部署：**~ sb/sth** *Our troops are to be redeployed elsewhere.* 我们的部队将被重新部署到其他地区。◇ **~ sb/sth to sth** *Most of the employees will be redeployed to other parts of the company.* 大多数雇员将被调配到公司的其他部门。▸ **re·deploy·ment** *noun* [U, C]: *the redeployment of staff/resources* 员工／资源的重新配置

re·design /ˌriːdɪˈzaɪn/ *verb* **~ sth** to design sth again, in a different way 重新设计 ▸ **re·design** *noun* [U, C]

re·develop /ˌriːdɪˈveləp/ *verb* [T, I] ~ (**sth**) to change an area by building new roads, houses, factories, etc. 改造；重新建设：*The city has plans to redevelop the site.* 这个城市计划重新建设这一地区。▸ **re·devel·op·ment** *noun* [U, C]: *inner-city redevelopment* 内城区的改造

ˈred-eye *noun* **1** (*also* ˌ**red-eye ˈflight**) [C] (*informal, especially NAmE*) a flight in a plane at night, on which you cannot get enough sleep 夜间航班；红眼夜航：*We took the red-eye to Boston.* 我们乘坐夜间航班飞到波士顿。**2** [U] the appearance of having red eyes that people sometimes have in photographs taken using flash（因使用闪光灯照相而在照片上出现的）红眼

ˌred-ˈfaced *adj.* with a red face, especially because you are embarrassed or angry 脸色涨红的；红脸的

ˌred ˈflag *noun* **1** a flag used to warn people of danger 示警红旗 **2** a red flag as a symbol of revolution or COMMUNISM（象征革命或共产主义的）红旗

ˌred ˈgiant *noun* (*astronomy* 天) a large star towards the end of its life that is relatively cool and gives out a reddish light 红巨星

ˌred-ˈhanded *adj.* IDM SEE CATCH *v.*

red·head /ˈredhed/ *noun* (*sometimes offensive*) a person who has red hair 红发人 ➲ COMPARE BLONDE *n.*, BRUNETTE ➲ WORDFINDER NOTE AT BLONDE ▸ ˌ**red-ˈheaded** *adj.*: *a red-headed girl* 红发女孩

ˌred ˈherring *noun* an unimportant fact, idea, event, etc. that takes people's attention away from the important ones 转移注意力的次要事实（或想法、事件等） ORIGIN From the custom of using the smell of a smoked, dried herring (which was red) to train dogs to hunt. 源自用（红色）熏干鲱鱼的气味训练狗狩猎的做法。

ˌred-ˈhot *adj.* **1** (of metal or sth burning 金属或燃烧物) so hot that it looks red 炽热的；赤热的；热得发红的：*Red-hot coals glowed in the fire.* 炽热的煤炭在炉子里发光。**2** showing strong feeling 激烈的；强烈的：*her red-hot anger* 她的暴怒 **3** (*informal*) new, exciting and of great interest to people 热门的：*a red-hot issue* 热点问题 **4** used to describe the person, animal or team that is considered almost certain to win a race, etc. 几乎一定能获胜的人（或动物、运动队）：*The race was won by the* ***red-hot favourite.*** 夺标呼声最高的选手获得了比赛的胜利。

re·dial /ˈriːdaɪəl/ *verb, noun*
■ *verb* (-ll-, *NAmE* -l-) **1** [I, T] ~ (sth) to call a telephone number again by pressing all of the individual numbers again 按键逐一重拨（电话号码） **2** [I] to call a telephone number again, using the button that automatically calls the last number that was called 按键自动重拨（电话号码）；按重拨键
■ *noun* **1** [U] the ability to redial a telephone number automatically 自动重拨功能 **2** (*also* ˈ**redial button**) [sing.] the button that automatically calls the last number that was called 自动重拨按钮；重拨键

redid PAST TENSE OF REDO

ˌ**Red ˈIndian** (*also* **red·skin**) *noun* (*old-fashioned, taboo*) a very offensive word for a Native American （蔑称）印第安人

re·dir·ect *verb, noun*
■ *verb* /ˌriːdəˈrekt; -dɪ-; -daɪ-/ **1** ~ **sth (to sth)** to use sth, for example money, in a different way or for a different purpose （以新的方式或目的）重新使用：*Resources are being redirected to this important new project.* 为这一重要的新项目重新调配了资源。 **2** ~ **sth (to sth)** to send sth to a different address or in a different direction 改寄；改变投递方向：*Enquiries on this matter are being redirected to the press office.* 询问此事的信件一律转到新闻处。◇ *Make sure you get your mail redirected to your new address.* 注意一定要让你的邮件改投到你的新住址。▶ **re·dir·ec·tion** *noun* [sing., U]：*a sudden redirection of economic policy* 经济政策的突然转变 ◇ *the redirection of mail* 邮件改投
■ *noun* /ˈriːdərekt/ (*computing* 计) an instance of redirecting sth from one address to another; a facility which redirects sth （到另一个网址的）重定向；重定向设置：*Spammers are starting to use automatic redirects.* 滥发垃圾邮件者开始启用自动重定向。

re·dis·cover /ˌriːdɪˈskʌvə(r)/ *verb* ~ **sth** to find again sth that had been forgotten or lost 重新发现；重新找到 ▶ **re·dis·cov·ery** /ˌriːdɪˈskʌvəri/ *noun* [U, C] (*pl.* **-ies**)

re·dis·trib·ute AW /ˌriːdɪˈstrɪbjuːt; ˌriːˈdɪs-/ *verb* ~ **sth (from sb/sth) (to sb/sth)** to share sth out among people in a different way 重新分配：*Wealth needs to be redistributed from the rich to the poor.* 需要将财富从富人那里重新分给穷人。▶ **re·dis·tri·bu·tion** AW /ˌriːdɪstrɪˈbjuːʃn/ *noun* [U, sing.]：*the redistribution of wealth* 财富的重新分配 **re·dis·tribu·tive** /ˌriːdɪˈstrɪbjətɪv/ *adj.*

re·dis·trict /ˌriːˈdɪstrɪkt/ *verb* [T, I] ~ (**sth**) (*US*) to change the official borders between districts （把…）重新划区

ˌ**red-ˈletter day** *noun* an important day, or a day that you will remember, because of sth good that happened then 重要纪念日；喜庆日 ORIGIN From the custom of using red ink to mark holidays and festivals on a calendar. 源自在日历上用红色标示假日和节日的习惯。

ˌ**red ˈlight** *noun* a signal telling the driver of a vehicle to stop 红灯（示意车辆停下的信号）：*to go through a red light* (= not stop at one) 闯红灯

ˌ**red-ˈlight district** *noun* a part of a town where there are many PROSTITUTES 红灯区

red ˈline *noun* an issue or a demand that one person or group refuses to change their opinion about during a disagreement or NEGOTIATIONS （争论或谈判中）拒绝改变立场的问题（或要求）：*The issue of sovereignty is a red line that cannot be crossed.* 主权问题是一条不能跨越的红线。

ˌ**red ˈmeat** *noun* [U] meat that is dark brown in colour when it has been cooked, such as beef and LAMB 红肉（指牛肉、羊肉等）⊃ COMPARE WHITE MEAT (1)

red·neck /ˈrednek/ *noun* (*informal*) an offensive word for a person who lives in a country area of the US, has little education and has strong conservative political opinions 乡巴佬，红脖子（对美国受教育不多且政治观点保守的乡下人的贬称）

redo /ˌriːˈduː/ *verb* (**re·does** /-ˈdʌz/, **redid** /-ˈdɪd/, **re·done** /-ˈdʌn/) ~ **sth** to do sth again or in a different way 重做；换一种方式做：*A whole day's work had to be redone.* 一整天的工作都必须重做。◇ *We've just redone the bathroom* (= decorated it again). 我们刚刚重新装修了浴室。

redo·lent /ˈredələnt/ *adj.* [not before noun] ~ **of/with sth** (*literary*) **1** making you think of the thing mentioned 使人想到；使人联想起：*an atmosphere redolent of the sea and ships* 让人联想起大海和船只的氛围 **2** smelling strongly of the thing mentioned 有…的强烈气味：*a kitchen redolent with the smell of baking* 弥漫着烘焙气味的厨房 ▶ **redo·lence** /-əns/ *noun* [U]

re·double /ˌriːˈdʌbl/ *verb* ~ **sth** to increase sth or make it stronger 加倍；增加；加强：*The leading banks are expected to* ***redouble their efforts*** *to keep the value of the dollar down.* 人们预计各大银行会加倍努力以保持美元的低价位。◇ *redoubled enthusiasm* 倍加热情

re·doubt /rɪˈdaʊt/ *noun* **1** (*literary*) a place or situation in which sb/sth is protected when they are being attacked or threatened 藏身之所；堡垒 **2** a small building from which soldiers can fight and defend themselves 掩体；防御工事

re·doubt·able /rɪˈdaʊtəbl/ *adj.* (*formal*) if a person is **redoubtable**, they have very strong qualities that make you respect them and perhaps feel afraid of them 令人敬畏的；可敬的 SYN **formidable**

re·dound /rɪˈdaʊnd/ *verb*
PHR V **reˈdound to sth** (*formal*) to improve the impression that people have of you 改进，提高（印象）：*Their defeat redounds to the glory of those whom they attacked.* 他们的失败提高了那些受到他们攻击的人的声誉。

ˌ**red ˈpanda** *noun* = PANDA (2)

ˌ**red ˈpepper** *noun* **1** [C, U] a hollow red fruit that is eaten, raw or cooked, as a vegetable 辣椒 **2** [U] (*especially NAmE*) = CAYENNE

re·draft AW /ˌriːˈdrɑːft; *NAmE* -ˈdræft/ *verb* ~ **sth** to write an article, a letter, etc. again in order to improve it or make changes 改写；重新起草 ▶ ˈ**re·draft** *noun*

re·draw /ˌriːˈdrɔː/ *verb* (**re·drew** /-ˈdruː/, **re·drawn** /-ˈdrɔːn/) ~ **sth** to make changes to sth such as the borders of a country or region, a plan, an arrangement, etc. 重新描绘，修改（边界、计划、安排等）：*After the war the map of Europe was redrawn.* 战后，欧洲版图被重新划定。◇ *to* ***redraw the boundaries*** *between male and female roles in the home* 重新划分两性在家庭中所扮演的角色

re·dress *verb, noun*
■ *verb* /rɪˈdres/ ~ **sth** (*formal*) to correct sth that is unfair or wrong 纠正；矫正；改正 SYN **right**：*to redress an injustice* 纠正不公
IDM **redress the ˈbalance** to make a situation equal or fair again 恢复公平合理的情况；恢复平衡
■ *noun* /rɪˈdres; ˈriːdres/ [U] ~ (**for/against sth**) (*formal*) payment, etc. that you should get for sth wrong that has happened to you or harm that you have suffered 赔款；损失赔偿 SYN **compensation**：*to seek legal redress for unfair dismissal* 因横遭解雇而提起赔偿诉讼 ◇ *to have little prospect of redress* 几乎没有获赔的希望

red·skin /ˈredskɪn/ *noun* (*old-fashioned, taboo, offensive*) = RED INDIAN

ˌ**red ˈtape** *noun* [U] (*disapproving*) official rules that seem more complicated than necessary and prevent things from being done quickly 繁文缛节；官僚作风 ORIGIN From the custom of tying up official documents with red or pink tape. 源自用红色或粉红色的带子捆扎公文的习俗。

ˈ**red-top** *noun* (*BrE, informal*) a British TABLOID newspaper, whose name is in red at the top of the front page （英国的）红头通俗小报

re·duce /rɪˈdjuːs; *NAmE* -ˈduːs/ *verb* **1** [T] to make sth less or smaller in size, quantity, price, etc. 减少，缩小（尺寸、数量、价格等）：~ **sth** *Reduce speed now* (= on a sign). 减速行驶。◇ *Giving up smoking reduces the risk of*

R

heart disease. 戒烟会降低得心脏病的风险。◇ ~ sth by sth Costs have been reduced by 20% over the past year. 过去一年，成本支出已经减少了 20%。◇ ~ sth (from sth) (to sth) The number of employees was reduced from 40 to 25. 雇员人数从 40 人减少到了 25 人。◇ The skirt was reduced to £10 in the sale. 在大减价期间，这条裙子减价到 10 英镑。 **2** [T, I] ~ (sth) if you **reduce** a liquid or a liquid **reduces**, you boil it so that it becomes less in quantity（使）蒸发 **3** [I] (NAmE, informal) to lose weight by limiting the amount and type of food that you eat 减轻体重；节食：a reducing plan 节食计划 **4** [T] ~ sth (chemistry 化) to add one or more ELECTRONS to a substance or to remove OXYGEN from a substance 使还原；去氧；脱氧 ➲ COMPARE OXIDIZE

IDM **re,duced 'circumstances** the state of being poorer than you were before. People say 'living in reduced circumstances' to avoid saying 'poor'.（委婉说法，与 poor 同义）境况不济

PHR V **re'duce sb/sth (from sth) to sth/to doing sth** [usually passive] to force sb/sth into a particular state or condition, usually a worse one 使陷入（更坏的）境地；使沦落；使陷入窘境：a beautiful building reduced to rubble 已化为残垣断壁的漂亮建筑 ◇ She was **reduced to tears** by their criticisms. 他们的批评使她流下了眼泪。◇ They were reduced to begging in the streets. 他们沦落到沿街乞讨。 **re'duce sth to sth** to change sth to a more general or more simple form 将…概括成（或简化为）：We can reduce the problem to two main issues. 我们可以将这个问题概括成两个要点。

re·du·cible /rɪ'dju:səbl; NAmE -'du:s-/ adj. ~ to sth (formal) that can be described or considered simply as sth 可以简化的：The problem is not reducible to one of money. 这个问题不能简单地看作是钱的问题。

re·duc·tio ad ab·sur·dum /rɪ,dʌktiəʊ æd æb'sɜ:dəm; NAmE rɪ,dʌktioʊ æd æb'sɜ:rdəm/ noun [U, C] (philosophy 哲, from Latin) a method of proving that sth is not true by showing that its result is not logical or sensible 归谬法

re·duc·tion 🔑 /rɪ'dʌkʃn/ noun **1** 🔑 [C, U] ~ (in sth) an act of making sth less or smaller; the state of being made less or smaller 减少；缩小；降低：a 33% reduction in the number of hospital beds available 医院的床位减少 33% ◇ There has been some reduction in unemployment. 失业人数有所减少。◇ a **slight/significant/substantial/drastic reduction** in costs 成本的略微 / 显著 / 大幅度 / 急剧降低 **2** 🔑 [C] an amount of money by which sth is made cheaper 减价；折扣：There are reductions for children sharing a room with two adults. 孩子和两个大人合住一间房可以打折。➲ WORDFINDER NOTE AT BUY **3** [C] a copy of a photograph, map, picture, etc. that is made smaller than the original one（照片、地图、图片等的）缩图，缩版 OPP **enlargement** **4** [U, C] (chemistry 化) the fact of adding one or more ELECTRONS to a substance or of removing OXYGEN from a substance 还原；去氧；脱氧 ➲ COMPARE OXIDATION at OXIDIZE **5** a sauce made by boiling a liquid until it becomes thick 浓缩酱汁（将汤汁熬至浓稠而成）

re·duc·tion·ism /rɪ'dʌkʃənɪzəm/ noun [U] (formal, often disapproving) the belief that complicated things can be explained by considering them as a combination of simple parts 简化论；简单化理论；还原论 ▸ **re·duc·tion·ist** /-ɪst/ adj., noun

re·duc·tive /rɪ'dʌktɪv/ adj. (formal, often disapproving) that tries to explain sth complicated by considering it as a combination of simple parts 简化论的；简化法的；以简释繁的；还原论的

re·dun·dancy /rɪ'dʌndənsi/ noun (pl. -ies) **1** [U, C, usually pl.] (BrE) the situation when sb has to leave their job because there is no more work available for them（因劳动力过剩而造成的）裁员，解雇：Thousands of factory workers are facing redundancy. 数千名工厂工人面临裁汰。◇ to accept/take **voluntary redundancy** (= to offer to leave your job) 接受自愿裁汰 ◇ the threat of **compulsory redundancies** 强制裁员的威胁 ◇ redundancy payments 裁员补偿 ➲ COLLOCATIONS AT UNEMPLOYMENT ➲ SEE ALSO LAY-OFF (1) **2** [U] (formal or specialist) the state of not being necessary or useful 多余；累赘：Natural language is characterized by redundancy (= words are used that are not really necessary for sb to understand the meaning). 自然语言的特点是繁复。

re·dun·dant /rɪ'dʌndənt/ adj. **1** (BrE) (of a person 人) without a job because there is no more work available for you in a company 被裁减的：to be **made redundant** from your job 成为冗员而被裁减 ◇ redundant employees 受裁汰的员工 ➲ COLLOCATIONS AT UNEMPLOYMENT **2** not needed or useful 多余的；不需要的：The picture has too much redundant detail. 这幅画中不必要的细节太多。 ▸ **re·dun·dant·ly** adv.

re·du·pli·cate /ˌri:'dju:plɪkeɪt; NAmE -'du:-/ verb [I, T] ~ (sth/itself) to make a copy of sth in order to form another of the same kind 复制；加倍：These cells are able to reduplicate themselves. 这些细胞能自我复制。

reduplicative /ˌri:'dju:plɪkeɪtɪv; NAmE -'du:-/ adj. (used about words) repeating a syllable or other part of the word, often with a slight change（单词）音节重叠的：Reduplicative expressions like 'mishmash' and 'nitty-gritty' illustrate the playful nature of English. 像 mishmash 和 nitty-gritty 这样的叠声词显示了英语俏皮的一面。

ˌred 'wine noun **1** [U, C] wine that gets its red colour from the skins of the GRAPES 红葡萄酒 **2** [C] a glass of red wine 一杯红葡萄酒 ➲ COMPARE ROSÉ, WHITE WINE

red·wood /'redwʊd/ noun **1** [C] a very tall type of tree that grows especially in California and Oregon 红杉，红木（多生长于加利福尼亚州和俄勒冈州）：giant redwoods 巨大的红杉树 **2** [U] the reddish wood of the redwood tree 红杉木

'red zone noun [sing.] (in AMERICAN FOOTBALL 美式足球) the area within 20 YARDS of a team's GOAL LINE 禁区（距离球门线 20 码以内的区域）

ˌre-'echo verb [I, T] to be repeated many times; to repeat sth many times 反复回响；一再重复：Their shouts re-echoed through the darkness. 他们的喊声回荡在黑暗中。◇ Her words re-echoed in his mind. 她的话萦绕在他的脑海中。◇ ~ sth He has constantly re-echoed the main theme of his acceptance speech: 'We want to be proud again!'. 他一再重申他接受提名时那篇演说的主题："我们要重新辉煌！"

reed /ri:d/ noun **1** a tall plant like grass with a hollow STEM that grows in or near water 芦苇：reed beds (= where they grow) 芦苇荡 ➲ VISUAL VOCAB PAGES V3, V11 **2** a small thin piece of CANE, metal or plastic in some musical instruments such as the OBOE or the CLARINET that moves very quickly when air is blown over it, producing a sound 簧舌，簧片（金属或塑料制成，用于双簧管、单簧管等吹奏乐器） ➲ VISUAL VOCAB PAGE V38

ˌre-'educate verb ~ sb to teach sb to think or behave in a new or different way 再教育；重新教育 ▸ **ˌre-edu'cation** noun [U]

reedy /'ri:di/ adj. [usually before noun] **1** (of a voice or sound 嗓音或声响) high and not very pleasant 尖利刺耳的 **2** full of reeds 芦苇丛生的；长满芦苇的：reedy river banks 芦苇丛生的河岸

reef /ri:f/ noun, verb

■ **noun** **1** a long line of rocks or sand near the surface of the sea 礁；礁脉：a coral reef 珊瑚礁 ➲ VISUAL VOCAB PAGE V5 **2** a part of a sail that can be tied or rolled up to make the sail smaller in a strong wind 缩帆部；帆的可收缩部

■ **verb** ~ sth (specialist) to make a sail smaller by tying or rolling up part of it 收帆；卷起缩帆部；叠起缩帆部

reef·er /'ri:fə(r)/ noun **1** (also **'reefer jacket**) a short thick jacket made of wool, usually dark blue, with two rows of buttons 双排扣厚毛上衣（通常为深蓝色） **2** (old-fashioned, slang) a cigarette containing MARIJUANA 大麻香烟

ˈ**reef knot** (*especially BrE*) (*NAmE usually* ˈ**square knot**) *noun* a type of double knot that will not come undone easily 平结，方结（不易解开）

reek /riːk/ *verb, noun*

■ *verb* **1** [I] ~ (**of sth**) to smell very strongly of sth unpleasant 散发臭气；发出难闻的气味： *His breath reeked of tobacco.* 他满嘴烟臭味。 **2** [I] ~ (**of sth**) (*disapproving*) to suggest very strongly that sth unpleasant or suspicious is involved in a situation 明显带有，强烈地意味着（令人不快或起疑的特性）： *Her denials reeked of hypocrisy.* 她那样否认显然很虚伪。

■ *noun* [sing.] a strong unpleasant smell 恶臭；难闻的气味 **SYN stench**

reel /riːl/ *noun, verb*

■ *noun* **1** (*especially BrE*) (*also* **spool** *especially in NAmE*) a round object around which you wind such things as thread, wire or film; a reel together with the film, wire, thread, etc. that is wound around it 卷轴；卷盘；卷筒；一卷胶卷（或金属丝、线等）： *a cotton reel* 棉线轴 ◇ *a reel on a fishing rod* 钓鱼竿上的绕线轮 ◇ *reels of magnetic tape* 磁带盘 ◇ *a new reel of film* 一卷新的胶卷 ◇ *The hero was killed in the final reel* (= in the final part of the film/movie). 主人公在电影的结尾部分被杀。 ➲ VISUAL VOCAB PAGE V45 **2** a fast Scottish, Irish or American dance, usually for two or four couples; a piece of music for this dance 里尔舞（流行于苏格兰、爱尔兰或美国的一种轻快舞蹈，通常由两对或四对表演）；里尔舞曲

■ *verb* **1** [I] (+ **adv./prep.**) to move in a very unsteady way, for example because you are drunk or have been hit 踉跄；摇摇晃晃地挪动；蹒跚 **SYN stagger**: *I punched him on the chin, sending him reeling backwards.* 我一拳击中他的下巴，打得他向后打了个趔趄。 **2** [I] ~ (**at/from/with sth**) to feel very shocked or upset about sth 感到震惊；感觉心烦意乱： *I was still reeling from the shock.* 我吓得依然晕头转向。 **3** [I] to seem to be spinning around and around 似乎在不停旋转；仿佛天旋地转： *When he opened his eyes, the room was reeling.* 他睁开眼睛时，房间似乎在不停地旋转。

PHR V ˌ**reel sth↔ˈin/ˈout** to wind sth on/off a reel 往卷轴上绕起；从卷轴上放开： *I slowly reeled the fish in.* 我慢慢地收卷鱼线，将鱼拉过来。 ˌ**reel sth↔ˈoff** to say or repeat sth quickly without having to stop or think about it 一口气说出；滔滔不绝地讲（或重复）： *She immediately reeled off several names.* 她立即一口气说出了好几个名字。

ˌ**re-eˈlect** *verb* ~ **sb** (**to sth**) to elect sb again 再次选举；再度选上： ~ **sb** (**to sth**) *She was re-elected to parliament.* 她再次当选为议员。 ◇ ~ **sb** (**as**) **sth** | ~ **sb + noun** *The committee voted to re-elect him (as) chairman.* 委员会投票再次选举他担任主席。 ▸ ˌ**re-eˈlection** *noun* [U]: (*BrE*) *to stand for re-election* 二度参选 ◇ (*NAmE*) *to run for re-election* 争取再次当选

ˌ**re-eˈmerge** *verb* [I] to appear somewhere again（在某处）又出现，再出现： *The cancer may re-emerge years later.* 癌症可能在多年之后复发。

ˌ**re-eˈnact** *verb* ~ **sth** to repeat the actions of a past event, especially as an entertainment（尤指作为表演）重做，再次进行： *Members of the English Civil War Society will re-enact the battle.* 英国内战协会的成员将再次展现那场战斗。 ▸ ˌ**re-eˈnactment** *noun*

ˌ**re-ˈenter** *verb* [T, I] ~ (**sth**) to return to a place or to an area of activity that you used to be in 再次进入；重返；重操（旧业）

ˌ**re-ˈentry** *noun* [U] ~ (**into sth**) **1** the act of returning to a place or an area of activity that you used to be in 再次进入；重返；重操旧业： *She feared she would not be granted re-entry into Britain.* 她担心不会获准再次踏足英国。 ◇ *a re-entry programme for nurses* (= for nurses returning to work after a long time doing sth else) 让护士重返岗位的方案 **2** the return of a SPACECRAFT into the earth's atmosphere（航天器的）重返地球大气层

ˌ**re-eˈvaluate** **AW** *verb* ~ **sth** to think about sth again, especially in order to form a new opinion about it 重新考虑；再评价；再评估 ▸ ˌ**re-evaluˈation** **AW** *noun* [C, U]

reeve /riːv/ *noun* a law officer in England in the past（英格兰旧时的）城镇长官

ˌ**re-eˈxamine** *verb* ~ **sth** to examine or think about sth again, especially because you may need to change your opinion 再次检查；重新考虑 **SYN reassess**: *All the evidence needs to be re-examined.* 所有的证据都需要重新审核。 ▸ ˌ**re-eˈxamination** *noun* [U, sing.]

ref /ref/ *noun, verb* (*informal*)

■ *noun* = REFEREE (1) : *The game's not over till the ref blows the whistle.* 裁判吹响哨子，比赛才算结束。

■ *verb* (**-ff-**) ~ **sth** = REFEREE (1) : *The game was badly reffed.* 这场比赛的裁判糟透了。

ref. *abbr.* reference (used especially in business as a way of identifying sth such as a document) 文件编号（尤用于商业文件分类）： *our ref.: 3498* 我方编号：3498

re·fec·tory /rɪˈfektri/ *noun* (*pl.* **-ies**) a large room in which meals are served, especially in a religious institution and in some schools and colleges in Britain（尤指英国教会团体和学校的）食堂，餐厅

refer 🔑 /rɪˈfɜː(r)/ *verb* (**-rr-**)

PHR V **reˈfer to sb/sth** (**as sth**) 🔑 to mention or speak about sb/sth 提到；谈及；说起： *The victims were not referred to by name.* 没有提到受害人的姓名。 ◇ *Her mother never referred to him again.* 她的母亲再也没有提起过他。 ◇ *You know who I'm referring to.* 你知道我指的是谁。 ◇ *She always referred to Ben as 'that nice man'.* 她总是称本为"那个大好人"。 ◇ *I promised not to refer to the matter again.* 我答应过再也不提这事了。 ➲ SYNONYMS AT MENTION **reˈfer to sb/sth** **1** 🔑 to describe or be connected to sb/sth 描述；涉及；与…相关： *The star refers to items which are intended for the advanced learner.* 标有星号的项目是给高阶学习者的。 ◇ *The term 'Arts' usually refers to humanities and social sciences.* * arts 一词通常指人文和社会科学。 ◇ *This paragraph refers to the events of last year.* 这一段说的是去年发生的事。 ➲ LANGUAGE BANK AT DEFINE **2** 🔑 to look at sth or ask a person for information 查阅；参考；征询 **SYN consult**: *You may refer to your notes if you want.* 如果需要，可以查阅笔记。 ◇ *to refer to a dictionary* 查词典 **reˈfer sb/sth to sb/sth** to send sb/sth to sb/sth for help, advice or a decision 将…送交给（以求获得帮助等）： *My doctor referred me to a specialist.* 我的医生让我去找一位专家诊治。 ◇ *The case was referred to the Court of Appeal.* 这个案子被送交到上诉法院。 ◇ (*formal*) *May I refer you to my letter of 14 May?* 请查看我 5 月 14 日给你的信。 ➲ MORE LIKE THIS 36, page R29

re·fer·able /rɪˈfɜːrəbl; ˈrefrəbl/ *adj.* ~ **to sth** (*formal*) that can be related to sth else 可与…相关的： *These symptoms may be referable to virus infection rather than parasites.* 这些症状也许是由病毒感染引起的，而与寄生虫无关。

ref·er·ee /ˌrefəˈriː/ *noun, verb*

■ *noun* **1** (*also informal* **ref**) the official who controls the game in some sports（某些体育比赛的）裁判，裁判员： *He was sent off for arguing with the referee.* 他因为和裁判发生争执而被罚出场。 ➲ COMPARE UMPIRE *n.* **2** (*BrE*) a person who gives information about your character and ability, usually in a letter, for example when you are applying for a job 介绍人；推荐人 **3** a person who is asked to settle a disagreement 仲裁员；调解人： *to act as a referee between the parties involved* 充当相关各方的调解人 **4** a person who reads and checks the quality of a technical article before it is published（专业性文章的）审阅人，鉴定专家

■ *verb* **1** (*also informal* **ref**) [I, T] to act as the referee in a game 担任裁判；裁判： *a refereeing decision* 裁判决定 ◇ ~ **sth** *Who refereed the final?* 那场决赛谁是裁判？ **2** [T] ~ **sth** to read and check the quality of a technical article before it is published 审阅，鉴定（专业性文章）

ˌ**referee's asˈsistant** *noun* = ASSISTANT REFEREE

ref·er·ence 🔑 /ˈrefrəns/ *noun, verb*

■ *noun*

R

• **MENTIONING SB/STH** 提及 **1** [C, U] ~ (**to sb/sth**) a thing you say or write that mentions sb/sth else; the act of mentioning sb/sth 说到（或写到）的事；提到；谈及；涉及：*The book is full of references to growing up in India.* 这本书谈到许多在印度怎样长大成人的事。◇ *She* ***made*** *no* ***reference to*** *her illness but only to her future plans.* 她没有提到她的病，只说了说她未来的计划。◇ *the President's* ***passing reference to*** (= brief mention of) *the end of the war* 总统对战争的结束一语带过

• **LOOKING FOR INFORMATION** 查询信息 **2** [U] the act of looking at sth for information 参考；查询；查阅：*Keep the list of numbers near the phone for easy reference.* 把电话号码表放在电话旁边，方便查找。◇ *I wrote down the name of the hotel* ***for future reference*** (= because it might be useful in the future). 我记下了这家酒店的名字，以后也许用得着。◇ *The library contains many popular* ***works of reference*** (= reference books). 这家图书馆藏有许多常用的参考书。

• **ASKING FOR ADVICE** 征求意见 **3** [U] ~ (**to sb/sth**) (*formal*) the act of asking sb for help or advice（帮助或意见的）征求，征询：*The emergency nurse can treat minor injuries without reference to a doctor.* 急救护士不必征求医生的意见就可处理轻伤。

• **NUMBER/WORD/SYMBOL** 数字；文字；符号 **4** [C] (*abbr.* **ref.**) a number, word or symbol that shows where sth is on a map, or where you can find a piece of information（为方便查询所用的）标记，标识，编号：*The map reference is Y4.* 地图编号为 Y4。◇ *Please quote your* ***reference number*** *when making an enquiry.* 查询时请报出编号。➲ WORDFINDER NOTE AT MAP

• **FOR NEW JOB** 找工作 **5** [C] a letter written by sb who knows you, giving information about your character and abilities, especially to a new employer 推荐信；介绍信：*We will* ***take up references*** *after the interview.* 我们在面试之后收推荐信。 **6** [C] a person who agrees to write a reference, for you, for example when you are applying for a job 推荐人；介绍人 SYN **referee**: *My previous boss will act as a reference for me.* 我的前任上司将做我的推荐人。➲ WORDFINDER NOTE AT APPLY

• **IN BOOK** 书籍 **7** [C] a note in a book that tells you where a particular piece of information comes from 参考书目：*There is a list of references at the end of each chapter.* 每一章的后面都有参考书目。➲ SEE ALSO CROSS REFERENCE, FRAME OF REFERENCE, TERMS OF REFERENCE

IDM **in/with reference to** (*formal*) used to say what you are talking or writing about（所述内容）关于：*With reference to your letter of July 22…* 关于你 7 月 22 日的来信…

■ **verb** ~ **sth** (*formal*) to refer to sth; to provide a book, etc. with references 查阅；参考；给（书等）附参考资料：*Each chapter is referenced, citing literature up to 2008.* 每一章都附有参考书目，引用文献近至 2008 年。

ˈreference book *noun* a book that contains facts and information, that you look at when you need to find out sth particular 参考书；工具书

ˈreference library *noun* a library containing books that can be read in the library but cannot be borrowed 工具书阅览室（藏书仅供查阅，不外借）➲ COMPARE LENDING LIBRARY

ˈreference point *noun* a standard by which sth can be judged or compared 参比点；参照标准

ref·er·en·dum /ˌrefəˈrendəm/ *noun* (*pl.* **ref·er·en·dums** or **ref·er·enda** /ˌrefəˈrendə/) [C, U] ~ (**on sth**) an occasion when all the people of a country can vote on an important issue 全民公投；全民公决：*Switzerland decided to* ***hold a referendum*** *on joining the EU.* 瑞士决定就加入欧盟问题举行全民公投。◇ *The changes were approved by referendum.* 全民投票赞同这些变革。➲ WORDFINDER NOTE AT DEMOCRACY ➲ COLLOCATIONS AT VOTE ➲ SYNONYMS AT ELECTION

re·fer·ral /rɪˈfɜːrəl/ *noun* [U, C] ~ (**to sb/sth**) the act of sending sb who needs professional help to a person or place that can provide it 送交，转送（到能提供专门帮助的人或地方那里）：*illnesses requiring referral to hospitals* 需要送到医院就诊的疾病 ◇ *to make a referral* 送交

re·fill *verb, noun*

■ **verb** /ˌriːˈfɪl/ ~ **sth** (**with sth**) to fill sth again 再装满；重新装满：*He refilled her glass.* 他又给她斟满了一杯。▸ **re·fill·able** /ˌriːˈfɪləbl/ *adj.*：*a refillable gas cylinder* 可重新灌注的煤气罐

■ **noun** /ˈriːfɪl/ **1** another drink of the same type 又一份同种饮料：*Would you like a refill?* 您要再来一杯吗？ **2** an amount of sth, sold in a cheap container, that you use to fill up a more expensive container that is now empty 补充装材料（用以补充产品容器内用完的物品）

re·fi·nance /ˌriːˈfaɪnæns/ *verb* [T, I] ~ (**sth**) (*finance* 财) to borrow money in order to pay a debt 再筹资金，再融资（以偿还债务）

re·fine AW /rɪˈfaɪn/ *verb* **1** ~ **sth** to make a substance pure by taking other substances out of it 精炼；提纯；去除杂质：*the process of refining oil/sugar* 炼油的 / 炼糖的工序 **2** ~ **sth** to improve sth by making small changes to it 改进；改善；使精练

re·fined AW /rɪˈfaɪnd/ *adj.* **1** [usually before noun] (of a substance 物质) made pure by having other substances taken out of it 精炼的；提纯的；精制的：*refined sugar* 精制糖 **2** (of a person 人) polite, well educated and able to judge the quality of things; having the sort of manners that are considered typical of a high social class 有礼貌的；优雅的；有教养的 SYN **cultured, genteel** OPP **unrefined**

re·fine·ment AW /rɪˈfaɪnmənt/ *noun* **1** [C] a small change to sth that improves it（精细的）改进，改善 SYN **enhancement**: *This particular model has a further refinement.* 这一款式又有了进一步的改进。 **2** [C] ~ **of sth** a thing that is an improvement on an earlier, similar thing 改良品；经过改进的东西：*The new plan is a refinement of the one before.* 新计划比原计划有改进。 **3** [U] the process of improving sth or of making sth pure 精炼；提炼；提纯：*the refinement of industrial techniques* 工业技术的进一步提高 ◇ *the refinement of uranium* 铀的提炼 **4** [U] the quality of being polite and well educated and able to judge the quality of things; the state of having the sort of manners that are considered typical of a high social class 优雅；礼貌；有教养 SYN **gentility**: *a person of considerable refinement* 很有教养的人 ◇ *an atmosphere of refinement* 优雅的气氛

re·finer /rɪˈfaɪnə(r)/ *noun* a person or company that refines substances such as sugar or oil 从事精炼加工的人（或公司）；炼制者：*oil refiners* 炼油公司

re·finery /rɪˈfaɪnəri/ *noun* (*pl.* **-ies**) a factory where a substance such as oil is REFINED (= made pure)（石油等的）精炼厂，提炼厂，精制厂

refit /ˌriːˈfɪt/ *verb* (**-tt-**) ~ **sth** to repair or fit new parts, equipment, etc. to sth 整修；给…安装新配件；改装：*He spent £70 000 refitting his yacht.* 他花了 7 万英镑整修他的游艇。▸ **refit** /ˈriːfɪt/ *noun*：*The ship has undergone a complete refit.* 这条船已经全面整修了。

re·flate /ˌriːˈfleɪt/ *verb* [T, I] ~ (**sth**) (*economics* 经) to increase the amount of money that is used in a country, usually in order to increase the demand for goods 通货再膨胀，通货复胀（增加货币供应以刺激对商品等的需求）➲ COMPARE DEFLATE (3), INFLATE (3) ▸ **re·fla·tion** /ˌriːˈfleɪʃn/ *noun* [U] **re·fla·tion·ary** /ˌriːˈfleɪʃnri; *NAmE* -neri/ *adj.*：*reflationary policies* 通货复胀政策

re·flect /rɪˈflekt/ *verb* **1** [T, usually passive] ~ **sb/sth** (**in sth**) to show the image of sb/sth on the surface of sth such as a mirror, water or glass 反映；映出（影像）：*His face was reflected in the mirror.* 他的脸映照在镜子里。◇ *She could see herself reflected in his eyes.* 她在他的眼中看到了自己的样子。 **2** [T] ~ **sth** to throw back light, heat, sound, etc. from a surface 反射（声、光、热等）：*The windows reflected the bright afternoon sunlight.* 窗户反射着午后明媚的阳光。◇ *When the sun's rays hit the earth,* *a lot of the heat is reflected back into space.* 太阳光线照射到地球时，大量的热被反射回太空。 **3** [T] **~ sth** to show or be a sign of the nature of sth or of sb's attitude or feeling 显示，表明，表达（事物的自然属性或人们的态度、情感等）: *Our newspaper aims to reflect the views of the local community.* 本报的宗旨是表达当地人民的心声。 **4** [I, T] to think carefully and deeply about sth 认真思考；沉思: *Before I decide, I need time to reflect.* 在作出决定以前，我需要时间认真考虑考虑。 ◇ **~ on/upon sth** *She was left to reflect on the implications of her decision.* 由她来考虑她这个决定会牵扯哪些问题。 ◇ **~ that...** *On the way home he reflected that the interview had gone well.* 回家的路上，他琢磨着这次面试非常顺利。 ◇ **~ how, what, etc....** *She reflected how different it could have been.* 她琢磨着那件事本可以有多大的不同。 ◇ **+ speech** *'It could all have been so different,' she reflected.* "那件事本可以完全不同的。" 她思索着。

IDM **reflect well, badly, etc. on sb/sth** to make sb/sth appear to be good, bad, etc. to other people 使给人以好的（或坏的等）印象: *This incident reflects badly on everyone involved.* 这一事件给所有相关人士都造成了恶劣影响。

re·flect·ance /rɪ'flektəns/ *noun* [U, C] (*physics* 物) a measure of how much light is reflected off a surface, considered as a part of the total light that shines onto it （光的）反射比

re,flected 'glory *noun* [U] (*disapproving*) admiration or praise that is given to sb, not because of sth that they have done, but because of sth that sb connected with them has done 仰仗别人而得的荣耀: *She basked in the reflected glory of her daughter's success.* 她尽情地享受她女儿的成功带给她的荣耀。

re·flec·tion (*BrE also, old-fashioned* **re·flex·ion**) /rɪ'flekʃn/ *noun* **1** [C] an image in a mirror, on a shiny surface, on water, etc. 映像；映照出的影像: *He admired his reflection in the mirror.* 他欣赏着自己在镜中的影像。 **2** [U] the action or process of sending back light, heat, sound, etc. from a surface （声、光、热等的）反射 **3** [C] a sign that shows the state or nature of sth 反映；显示；表达: *Your clothes are often a reflection of your personality.* 穿着常常反映出一个人的个性。 ◇ *The increase in crime is a sad* ***reflection on*** (= shows sth bad about) *our society today.* 犯罪的增加令人遗憾地反映了当今社会不太好的一面。 **4** [U] careful thought about sth, sometimes over a long period of time 沉思；深思；审慎的思考: *She decided* ***on reflection*** *to accept his offer after all.* 经过审慎的思考，她还是决定接受他的提议。 ◇ *A week off would give him time for reflection.* 歇上一周会使他有时间考虑考虑。 **5** [C, usually pl.] your written or spoken thoughts about a particular subject or topic （关于某课题的）思考，回忆: *a book of her reflections on childhood* 一本关于她童年生活的回忆录 **6** [C] an account or a description of sth 记录；描述: *The article is an accurate reflection of events that day.* 这篇文章准确地记录了那天发生的事。 IDM SEE MATURE *adj.*

re·flect·ive /rɪ'flektɪv/ *adj.* **1** (*formal*) thinking deeply about things 沉思的；深思的 SYN **thoughtful**: *a quiet and reflective man* 文静而爱沉思的男子 **2 reflective** surfaces send back light or heat （指物体表面）反射热的，反光的: *reflective car number plates* 反光的汽车牌照 ◇ *On dark nights children should wear reflective clothing.* 在漆黑的夜晚，儿童应该穿反光的衣服。 **3 ~ of sth** typical of a particular situation or thing; showing the state or nature of sth 典型的；代表性的；体现状态（或本质）的: *His abilities are not reflective of the team as a whole.* 他的能力并不代表整队的水平。 ◇ *Everything you do or say is reflective of your personality.* 你的一言一行都体现你的个性。 ▶ **re·flect·ive·ly** *adv.*: *She sipped her wine reflectively.* 她若有所思地品着酒。

re·flect·ivity /,riːflek'tɪvəti; rɪ,flek-/ *noun* [U] (*physics* 物) the degree to which a material reflects light or RADIATION （材料对光或辐射的）反射率

re·flect·or /rɪ'flektə(r)/ *noun* **1** a surface that reflects light 反光面 **2** a small piece of special glass or plastic that is put on a bicycle, or on clothing, so that it can be seen at night when light shines on it （夜间光线照射后能反光的）反光玻璃（或塑料），反光体 ➲ VISUAL VOCAB PAGE V55

re·flex /'riːfleks/ *noun* an action or a movement of your body that happens naturally in response to sth and that you cannot control; sth that you do without thinking 反射动作；本能反应；反射作用: *The doctor tested her reflexes.* 医生检测了她的反射动作。 ◇ *to have* ***quick/slow reflexes*** 反射动作快 / 慢 ◇ *a* ***reflex response/reaction*** 反射性反应 ◇ *Only the goalkeeper's reflexes* (= his ability to react quickly) *stopped the ball from going in.* 只是因为守门员反应迅速，球才没有进。 ◇ *Almost as a* ***reflex action***, *I grab my pen as the phone rings.* 几乎是一种本能反应，电话铃一响，我就抓起笔。

,reflex 'angle *noun* an angle of more than 180° 优角（大于 180 度的角） ➲ PICTURE AT ANGLE ➲ COMPARE ACUTE ANGLE, OBTUSE ANGLE, RIGHT ANGLE

re·flex·ion (*BrE*) = REFLECTION

re·flex·ive /rɪ'fleksɪv/ *adj.* a **reflexive** word or form of a word shows that the action of the verb affects the person who performs the action （词或词形）反身的: *In 'He cut himself', 'cut' is a reflexive verb and 'himself' is a reflexive pronoun.* 在 He cut himself 一句中，cut 是反身动词，himself 是反身代词。

re·flex·ology /,riːfleks'ɒlədʒi; *NAmE* ,riːfleks'ɑːl-/ *noun* [U] a type of alternative treatment in which sb's feet are rubbed in a particular way in order to heal other parts of their body or to make them feel mentally relaxed 反射疗法（通过脚部按摩治疗身体其他部位疾病或松弛神经） ➲ WORDFINDER NOTE AT TREATMENT ▶ **re·flex·olo·gist** *noun*

re·float /,riː'fləʊt; *NAmE* -'floʊt/ *verb* **~ sth** to make a boat or ship float again, for example after it has become stuck on the bottom in shallow water 使（搁浅船只）再浮起

re·flow /'riːfləʊ; *NAmE* -floʊ/ *noun* [U] (*specialist*) **1** a method of joining metals together by heating and melting SOLDER (= a soft metal mixture) 软熔焊接 **2** the fact of changing text on a computer screen so that it takes more or less space 文档重整，页面重排（调整文本在计算机屏幕上的显示密度）

re·focus AW /,riː'fəʊkəs; *NAmE* -'foʊ-/ *verb* (**-s-** or **-ss-**) **1** [I, T] to give attention, effort, etc. to sth new or different 将（注意力、精力等）转向；调整…的重点: **~ (on/upon sb/sth)** *Policy must refocus on people instead of places.* 政策重心必须改变，针对人而非地方。 ◇ **~ sth (on/upon sb/sth)** *We need to refocus attention on the real issues facing this country.* 我们需要将注意力转向国家所面临的实际问题。 **2** [I, T] (of your eyes, a camera, etc. 眼睛、相机等) to adapt or be adjusted again so that things can be seen clearly; to adjust sth again so that you can see things clearly （使）重新聚焦；调整…的焦距

re·for·est·ation /,riːfɒrɪ'steɪʃn; *NAmE* -fɔːr-; -fɑːr-/ (*BrE also* **re·affor·est·ation**) *noun* [U] (*specialist*) the act of planting new trees in an area where there used to be a forest 重新造林；植树造林 ➲ VISUAL VOCAB PAGE V9 ➲ COMPARE DEFORESTATION

re·form /rɪ'fɔːm; *NAmE* rɪ'fɔːrm/ *verb, noun*

■ ***verb*** **1** [T] **~ sth** to improve a system, an organization, a law, etc. by making changes to it 改革；改进；改良: *proposals to reform the social security system* 改革社会保障制度的建议 ◇ *The law needs to be reformed.* 法律需要进行改革。 **2** [I, T] to improve your behaviour; to make sb do this （使）改正，改造（行为）；（使）悔改: *He has promised to reform.* 他许诺要改过自新。 ◇ **~ sb** *She thought she could reform him.* 她觉得她可以使他洗心革面。 ▶ **re·formed** *adj.*: *a reformed character* 改过自新的人

■ ***noun*** [U, C] change that is made to a social system, an organization, etc. in order to improve or correct it 改革；变革；改良；改善: *a government committed to reform* 致力于改革的政府 ◇ ***economic/electoral/constitutional, etc.***

R

reform 经济、选举、宪法等改革 ◊ *the reform of the educational system* 教育体制的改革 ◊ *reforms in education* 教育改革 ◊ ***far-reaching/major/sweeping reforms*** 意义深远的 / 重大的 / 彻底的变革

ˌre-ˈform *verb* [I, T] to form again or form sth again, especially into a different group or pattern 再次形成；重新组成： *The band is re-forming after 23 years.* * 23 年后，这个乐队又在重组。 ◊ **~ sth** *The party has recently been re-formed.* 这个政党最近进行了重新组合。

re·format /ˌriːˈfɔːmæt; *NAmE* -ˈfɔːr-/ *verb* (**-tt-**) **~ sth** (*computing* 计) to give a new FORMAT to a computer disk 使重新格式化

ref·or·ma·tion /ˌrefəˈmeɪʃn; *NAmE* -fərˈm-/ *noun* **1** [U] (*formal*) the act of improving or changing sb/sth 改革；改进；变革 **2 the Reformation** [sing.] new ideas in religion in 16th century Europe that led to attempts to reform the Roman Catholic Church and to the forming of the Protestant Churches; the period of time when these changes were taking place 宗教改革（欧洲 16 世纪改革天主教从而导致新教的产生）；宗教改革时期

re·forma·tory /rɪˈfɔːmətri; *NAmE* rɪˈfɔːrmətɔːri/ *noun* (*pl.* **-ies**) (*also* **reˈform school**) (*NAmE*) (*old-fashioned* in British English 英式英语中为老式用法) a type of school that young criminals are sent to instead of prison 少年犯管教所；青少年教养院

Reˈformed Church *noun* [sing.] a church that has accepted the principles of the REFORMATION, especially a Calvinist one（基督教）新教教会归正会，归正宗（尤指加尔文教派）

re·form·er /rɪˈfɔːmə(r); *NAmE* -ˈfɔːrm-/ *noun* a person who works to achieve political or social change 改革者；改良者；改造者

re·form·ist /rɪˈfɔːmɪst; *NAmE* -ˈfɔːrm-/ *adj.* wanting or trying to change political or social situations 主张改革的；改革派的；改良主义的 ▸ **re·form·ist** *noun*

re·for·mu·late AW /ˌriːˈfɔːmjuleɪt; *NAmE* -ˈfɔːrm-/ *verb* **1 ~ sth** to create or prepare sth again 再制订；再规划；再准备： *It is never too late to reformulate your goals.* 重订目标决不会为时过晚。 **2 ~ sth** to say or express sth in a different way 换种方式说（或表达）： *Let me try to reformulate the problem.* 让我换个说法讲这个问题吧。 ▸ **re·for·mu·la·tion** AW /ˌriːˌfɔːmjuˈleɪʃn; *NAmE* -fɔːrm-/ *noun* [U, C]

re·fract /rɪˈfrækt/ *verb* **~ sth** (*physics* 物) (of water, air, glass, etc. 水、空气、玻璃等) to make waves, such as those of light, sound or energy, change direction when they go through at an angle 使（光波、声波、能量波等）折射；使产生折射： *Light is refracted when passed through a prism.* 光通过棱镜时产生折射。 ▸ **re·frac·tion** /rɪˈfrækʃn/ *noun* [U]

re·fract·ive /rɪˈfræktɪv/ *adj.* (*physics* 物) causing, caused by or relating to refraction（由）折射引起的；折射的

reˌfractive ˈindex *noun* (*physics* 物) a measurement of how much an object or a substance refracts light 折射率

re·fract·om·eter /ˌrɪˌfrækˈtɒmɪtə(r); *NAmE* -ˈtɑːm-/ *noun* (*physics* 物) an instrument for measuring a refractive index 折射计

re·fract·or /rɪˈfræktə(r)/ *noun* (*physics* 物) something such as a LENS which REFRACTS light (= causes it to change direction) 折射器

re·frac·tory /rɪˈfræktəri/ *adj.* **1** (*formal*) (of a person 人) difficult to control; behaving badly 难以驾驭的；行为乖戾的 **2** (*medical* 医) (of a disease or medical condition 疾病或身体状况) difficult to treat or cure 难以诊治的；难以治愈的

re·frain /rɪˈfreɪn/ *verb, noun*

■ ***verb*** [I] (*formal*) to stop yourself from doing sth, especially sth that you want to do 克制；节制；避免 SYN **desist**: **~ (from sth)** *Please refrain from smoking.* 请勿吸烟。 ◊ **~ (from doing sth)** *He has refrained from criticizing the government in public.* 他克制住了自己，没有在公开场合批评政府。

■ ***noun*** **1** a comment or complaint that is often repeated 经常重复的评价（或抱怨）： *Complaints about poor food in schools have become a familiar refrain.* 抱怨学校饭菜差已是耳熟能详的老调了。 **2** the part of a song or a poem that is repeated after each VERSE 副歌；迭歌；迭句 SYN **chorus** ➲ **WORDFINDER NOTE AT POETRY**

re·fresh /rɪˈfreʃ/ *verb* **1** [T] **~ sb/yourself** to make sb feel less tired or less hot 使恢复精力；使凉爽： *The long sleep had refreshed her.* 一场酣睡使她重又精力充沛。 ◊ *He refreshed himself with a cool shower.* 他冲了个凉水澡凉快凉快。 **2** [T] **~ sth** (*informal, especially NAmE*) to fill sb's glass or cup again 重新斟满： *Let me refresh your glass.* 我给你再斟一杯吧。 **3** [T] **~ your/sb's memory** to remind yourself/sb of sth, especially with the help of sth that can be seen or heard 提醒；提示；使想起 SYN **jog**: *He had to refresh his memory by looking at his notes.* 他不得不靠看笔记来提醒自己。 **4** [T, I] **~ (sth)** (*computing* 计) to make the most recent information show, for example on an Internet page 刷新（网页等）： *Click here to refresh this document.* 点击此处以刷新文件。 ◊ *The page refreshes automatically.* 页面会自动更新。 ➲ **WORDFINDER NOTE AT COMMAND**

reˈfresher course (*also* **re·fresh·er** *especially in NAmE*) *noun* a short period of training to improve your skills or to teach you about new ideas and developments in your job 进修课程

re·fresh·ing /rɪˈfreʃɪŋ/ *adj.* **1** pleasantly new or different 令人耳目一新的；别具一格的： *It made a* ***refreshing change*** *to be taken seriously for once.* 总算有一次受到认真对待，这变化真是令人耳目一新。 **2** making you feel less tired or hot 使人精力充沛的；使人凉爽的： ***a refreshing drink/shower*** 提神的饮料 / 淋浴 ▸ **re·fresh·ing·ly** *adv.*: *refreshingly different* 焕然一新 ◊ *The house was refreshingly cool inside.* 屋内清凉宜人。

re·fresh·ment /rɪˈfreʃmənt/ *noun* **1 refreshments** [pl.] drinks and small amounts of food that are provided or sold to people in a public place or at a public event（在公共活动场所供应或销售的）饮料，小食： *Light refreshments will be served during the break.* 中间休息时有点心供应。 **2** [U] (*formal*) food and drink 食物和饮料： *In York we had a short stop for refreshment.* 在约克，我们稍作停留，吃了点东西。 ◊ *Can we offer you some refreshment?* 您要吃点什么吗？ ◊ ***a refreshment room/kiosk/tent*** 小吃部；饮食亭；活动小吃摊 ◊ (*humorous*) ***liquid refreshment*** (= alcoholic drink) 酒 **3** [U] (*formal*) the fact of making sb feel stronger or less tired or hot 恢复活力；焕发精神： *a place to rest and find refreshment for mind and body* 休息和恢复身心活力的场所

refried beans /ˌriːfraɪd ˈbiːnz/ *noun* [pl.] BEANS that have been boiled and fried in advance and are heated again when needed, used especially in Mexican cooking（墨西哥）煎豆泥，炒豆

re·friger·ate /rɪˈfrɪdʒəreɪt/ *verb* **~ sth** (*formal*) to make food, etc. cold in order to keep it fresh or preserve it 使冷却；使变冷；冷藏： *Once opened, this product should be kept refrigerated.* 本产品开封后应冷藏。 ◊ ***a refrigerated lorry/truck*** 冷藏卡车 ▸ **re·friger·ation** /rɪˌfrɪdʒəˈreɪʃn/ *noun* [U]: *Keep all meat products under refrigeration.* 把所有的肉制品都冷藏起来。

re·friger·ator 🔑 /rɪˈfrɪdʒəreɪtə(r)/ *noun* (*formal* or *NAmE*) = FRIDGE : *This dessert can be served straight from the refrigerator.* 这甜点从冰箱里拿出后即可食用。 ➲ **VISUAL VOCAB PAGE V26**

re·fuel /ˌriːˈfjuːəl/ *verb* (**-ll-**, *US* **-l-**) [T, I] **~ (sth)** to fill sth, especially a plane, with fuel in order to continue a journey; to be filled with fuel（尤指给飞机）补充燃料，加燃料；加油： *to refuel a plane* 给飞机加油 ◊ *The planes needed to refuel before the next mission.* 这些飞机需要添加燃料才能再次飞行。 ◊ *a refuelling stop* 加油停留 ➲ **WORDFINDER NOTE AT PLANE**

ref·uge /ˈrefjuːdʒ/ *noun* **1** [U] shelter or protection from danger, trouble, etc. 庇护；避难：*A further 300 people have **taken refuge** in the US embassy.* 又有 300 人在美国大使馆避难。◇ **~ (from sb/sth)** *They were forced to **seek refuge** from the fighting.* 他们被迫寻求庇护，以躲避战争。◇ *a place of refuge* 避难所 ◇ *As the situation at home got worse she increasingly took refuge in her work.* 随着家庭情况的恶化，她越来越在工作中寻求慰藉。 **2** [C] **~ (from sb/sth)** a place, person or thing that provides shelter or protection for sb/sth 避难所；庇护者；慰藉：*He regarded the room as a refuge from the outside world.* 他把这个屋子当作是逃避外界的避难所。◇ *a wetland refuge for birds* 湿地鸟类保护区 **3** [C] a building that provides a temporary home for people in need of shelter or protection from sb/sth 收容所；避难所：*a women's refuge* 妇女收容所 ◇ *a refuge for the homeless* 无家可归者的收容所 **4** (*BrE*) = TRAFFIC ISLAND

refu·gee /ˌrefjuˈdʒiː/ *noun* a person who has been forced to leave their country or home, because there is a war or for political, religious or social reasons 避难者；逃亡者；难民：*a steady flow of refugees from the war zone* 从交战地区不断涌出的难民 ◇ ***political/economic refugees*** 政治避难者；由于经济危机而造成的难民 ◇ ***a refugee camp*** 难民营 ➲ COLLOCATIONS AT RACE, WAR

re·ful·gent /rɪˈfʌldʒənt/ *adj.* (*formal*) very bright 十分明亮的；灿烂的

re·fund *noun, verb*

■ ***noun*** /ˈriːfʌnd/ a sum of money that is paid back to you, especially because you paid too much or because you returned goods to a shop/store 退款；返还款；偿还金额：*a tax refund* 税金退款 ◇ *to **claim/demand/receive a refund*** 要求 / 接受退款 ◇ *If there is a delay of 12 hours or more, you will receive a **full refund** of the price of your trip.* 如果耽搁达到或超过 12 小时，你会得到旅费全额退款。 ➲ WORDFINDER NOTE AT BUY ➲ COLLOCATIONS AT SHOPPING

■ ***verb*** /rɪˈfʌnd/ to give sb their money back, especially because they have paid too much or because they are not satisfied with sth they bought 退还；退（款）；偿付 **SYN** **reimburse**：**~ sth** *Tickets cannot be exchanged or money refunded.* 门票不可退换。◇ **~ sth to sb** *We will refund your money to you in full if you are not entirely satisfied.* 如果你并不感到完全满意，我们会退还全部金额。◇ **~ sb sth** *We will refund you your money in full.* 我们会给你全额退款。 ➲ MORE LIKE THIS 21, page R27 ▸ **re·fund·able** *adj.*：*a refundable deposit* 可退还的押金 ◇ *Tickets are not refundable.* 不能退票。

re·fur·bish /ˌriːˈfɜːbɪʃ; *NAmE* -ˈfɜːrb-/ *verb* **~ sth** to clean and decorate a room, building, etc. in order to make it more attractive, more useful, etc. 再装修；清理装修 ➲ COLLOCATIONS AT DECORATE ▸ **re·fur·bish·ment** (*also informal* **re·furb** /ˈriːfɜːb; *NAmE* -fɜːrb/) *noun* [U, C]：*The hotel is closed for refurbishment.* 酒店停业装修。

re·fusal /rɪˈfjuːzl/ *noun* [U, C] an act of saying or showing that you will not do, give or accept sth 拒绝；回绝：**~ (of sth)** *the refusal of a request/an invitation/an offer* 拒绝请求 / 邀请 / 建议 ◇ *a **blunt/flat/curt refusal*** 率直的 / 断然的 / 粗率的拒绝 ◇ **~ to do sth** *His refusal to discuss the matter is very annoying.* 他拒绝商量这件事，令人很恼火。 ➲ SEE ALSO FIRST REFUSAL

re·fuse¹ /rɪˈfjuːz/ *verb* **1** [I, T] to say that you will not do sth that sb has asked you to do 拒绝；回绝：*Go on, ask her; she can hardly refuse.* 去吧，去求她，她不大可能拒绝。◇ **~ to do sth** *He **flatly refused** to discuss the matter.* 他断然拒绝商讨这件事。◇ *She refused to accept that there was a problem.* 她拒不承认有问题存在。 ➲ MORE LIKE THIS 26, page R28 **2** [T] **~ sth** to say that you do not want sth that has been offered to you 推却；回绝 **SYN** **turn sb/sth↔down**：*I politely refused their invitation.* 我礼貌地回绝了他们的邀请。◇ *The job offer was simply too good to refuse.* 这个工作机会太好了，简直无法推掉。 **3** [T] to say that you will not allow sth; to say that you will not give or allow sb sth that they want or need 不准许；拒绝给（所需之物）**SYN** **deny**：**~ sth** *The bank refused his demand for a full refund.* 银行拒绝了他全额退款的要求。◇ *The authorities refused permission for the new housing development.* 当局不允许新住宅开发。◇ **~ sb sth** *They refused him a visa.* 他们拒绝给他签证。◇ *She would never refuse her kids anything.* 她对孩子百依百顺。 ➲ MORE LIKE THIS 21, page R27, 33, page R28

re·fuse² /ˈrefjuːs/ *noun* [U] (*formal*) waste material that has been thrown away 废弃物；垃圾 **SYN** **rubbish**：***domestic/household refuse*** 生活垃圾 ◇ *the city refuse dump* 城市垃圾场 ◇ ***refuse collection/disposal*** 垃圾收集 / 处理 ➲ NOTE AT RUBBISH ➲ MORE LIKE THIS 21, page R27

ˈrefuse collector (*BrE*) (*NAmE* **ˈgarbage collector**) *noun* (*formal*) = DUSTMAN

re·fuse·nik /rɪˈfjuːznɪk/ *noun* a person who refuses to obey an order or law as a protest 拒绝服从指令（或法规）的人；反抗者；抗议者

re·fute /rɪˈfjuːt/ *verb* (*formal*) **1 ~ sth** to prove that sth is wrong 驳斥；批驳 **SYN** **rebut**：*to **refute an argument/a theory, etc.*** 驳斥一个论点、理论等 **2 ~ sth** to say that sth is not true or fair 反驳；否认 **SYN** **deny**：*She refutes any suggestion that she behaved unprofessionally.* 谁要是表示她不在行，她都予以反驳。 ▸ **re·fut·able** /-əbl/ *adj.* **refu·ta·tion** /ˌrefjuˈteɪʃn/ *noun* [C, U]：*a refutation of previously held views* 对过去所坚持的观点的否定

reg /redʒ/ *abbr.* (*BrE, informal*) REGISTRATION 登记；注册：*a V reg car* (= a car with 'V' in its REGISTRATION NUMBER, showing the year that it was registered) 汽车牌照号码含 V 的汽车

re·gain /rɪˈɡeɪn/ *verb* **1 ~ sth** to get back sth you no longer have, especially an ability or a quality 重新获得，恢复（能力或品质等）：*I struggled to regain some dignity.* 我努力恢复自己的一点儿尊严。◇ *The party has regained control of the region.* 这一政党重新获得了这个地区的控制权。◇ *She paused on the edge, trying to **regain her balance**.* 她在边缘上暂停下来，努力恢复平衡。◇ *He did not **regain consciousness*** (= wake up after being unconscious) *for several days.* 他好几天都没有恢复知觉。 **2 ~ sth** (*literary*) to get back to a place that you have left 回到（原位）；返回：*They finally managed to regain the beach.* 他们最后终于回到了海滩。

regal /ˈriːɡl/ *adj.* typical of a king or queen, and therefore impressive 帝王的；王室的；豪华的：*regal power* 王权 ◇ *the regal splendour of the palace* 帝王宫殿之豪华气派 ◇ *She dismissed him with a regal gesture.* 她像女王般挥手打发他离开。 ➲ COMPARE ROYAL *adj.* (1) ▸ **re·gal·ly** /-ɡəli/ *adv.*

re·gale /rɪˈɡeɪl/ *verb*

PHR V **reˈgale sb with sth** to amuse or entertain sb with stories, jokes, etc.（通过讲故事或说笑话等）使愉悦，使高兴：*He regaled us with tales of his days as a jazz pianist.* 他给我们讲述他当爵士乐钢琴师时的事，逗我们开心。

re·galia /rɪˈɡeɪliə/ *noun* [U] the special clothes that are worn or objects that are carried at official ceremonies（正式场合上的）特别服饰，特别物品

re·gard /rɪˈɡɑːd; *NAmE* rɪˈɡɑːrd/ *verb, noun*

■ ***verb*** **1** to think about sb/sth in a particular way 将…认为；把…视为；看待：**~ sb/sth (+ adv./prep.)** *Her work is very highly regarded.* 她的工作受到高度评价。◇ **~ sb/sth/yourself as sth** *Capital punishment was regarded as inhuman and immoral.* 死刑过去被认为是非人道且不道德的。◇ *He regards himself as a patriot.* 他自认为是个爱国者。◇ *She is **widely regarded** as the current leader's natural successor.* 人们普遍认为她是现任领导的当然继任者。 ➲ SYNONYMS ON NEXT PAGE **2** **~ sb/sth (+ adv./prep.)** (*formal*) to look at sb/sth, especially in a particular way（尤指以某种方式）注视，凝视 **SYN** **contemplate**：*He regarded us suspiciously.* 他以怀疑的眼光看着我们。

IDM **as regards sb/sth** (*formal*) concerning or in connection with sb/sth 关于；至于：*I have little information as regards her fitness for the post.* 至于说她是否适合这个职位，我无可奉告。◇ *As regards the first point in your letter…*

R

关于你信中所提到的第一点…

■ *noun* **1** [U] (*formal*) attention to or thought and care for sb/sth 注意；关注；关心：**~ for sb/sth** *to do sth with* ***scant/little/no regard for sb/sth*** 做事不怎么 / 几乎不 / 根本不顾及某人 / 某事物 ◇ *to* ***have/pay/show little regard*** *for other people's property* 不大爱惜别人的财物 ◇ **~ to sb/sth** *He was driving* ***without regard to*** *speed limits.* 他开着车，根本不理会速度限制。◇ *Social services should* ***pay proper regard*** *to the needs of inner-city areas.* 社会服务机构应该对市中心贫民区的需求给予应有的关注。 **2** [U] (*formal*) respect or admiration for sb 尊重；尊敬；敬佩：*He* ***held her in high regard*** (= had a good opinion of her). 他对她非常敬重。◇ **~ for sb/sth** *I had great regard for his abilities.* 我非常敬佩他的能力。 **3 regards** [pl.] used to send good wishes to sb at the end of a letter, or when asking sb to give your good wishes to another person who is not present（用于信函结尾或转达问候）致意，问候：*With kind regards, Yours…* 谨此致意，…敬上 ◇ *Give your brother my regards when you see him.* 看到你哥哥时，代我向他问好。

IDM **have re'gard to sth** (*law* 律) to remember and think carefully about sth 记住；记起；仔细考虑：*It is always necessary to have regard to the terms of the contract.* 记住合同条款总是必要的。 **in this/that re'gard** (*formal*) concerning what has just been mentioned 在这方面；在这一点上：*I have nothing further to say in this regard.* 在这方面，我没什么要说的了。 **in/with regard to sb/sth** (*formal*) concerning sb/sth 关于；至于：*a country's laws in regard to human rights* 一个国家关于人权的法律 ◇ *The company's position with regard to overtime is made clear in their contracts.* 公司关于加班的立场在合同中有明确说明。 ➲ MORE AT AS *conj.*

re·gard·ing /rɪ'ɡɑːdɪŋ; *NAmE* -'ɡɑːrd-/ *prep.* concerning sb/sth; about sb/sth 关于；至于：*She has said nothing regarding your request.* 关于你的要求，她什么也没说。◇ *Call me if you have any problems regarding your work.* 你如果还有什么工作方面的问题就给我打电话。

re·gard·less /rɪ'ɡɑːdləs; *NAmE* -'ɡɑːrd-/ *adv.* paying no attention, even if the situation is bad or there are difficulties 不顾；不加理会：*The weather was terrible but we* ***carried on regardless.*** 天气非常恶劣，但我们并不理会，照常进行。

re'gardless of *prep.* paying no attention to sth/sb; treating sth/sb as not being important 不管；不顾；不理会：*The club welcomes all new members regardless of age.* 俱乐部对所有新成员不分年龄一律欢迎。◇ *He went ahead and did it, regardless of the consequences.* 他说干就干了，没有考虑后果。◇ *The amount will be paid to everyone regardless of whether they have children or not.* 不管有没有孩子，每个人都会得到相同的金额。

re·gatta /rɪ'ɡætə/ *noun* a sporting event in which races between ROWING BOATS or SAILING BOATS are held 赛艇会；划船比赛；帆船比赛

Re·gency /'riːdʒənsi/ *adj.* [usually before noun] of or in the style of the period 1811–20 in Britain, when George, Prince of Wales, was REGENT (= ruled the country in place of the king, his father) 摄政时期的，摄政时期的风格的（英国 1811–1820 年间，威尔士亲王乔治任摄政王，代替父亲管理国家）：*Regency architecture* 摄政时期风格的建筑

re·gency /'riːdʒənsi/ *noun* (*pl.* **-ies**) a period of government by a REGENT (= a person who rules a country in place of the king or queen) 摄政期；摄政

re·gen·er·ate /rɪ'dʒenəreɪt/ *verb* **1** [T] **~ sth** to make an area, institution, etc. develop and grow strong again 使振兴；使复兴；发展壮大：*The money will be used to regenerate the commercial heart of the town.* 这笔钱将用来重振市镇的商业中心。 **2** [I, T] (*biology* 生) to grow again; to make sth grow again 再生；使再生：*Once destroyed, brain cells do not regenerate.* 脑细胞一旦遭到破坏，就不能再生。◇ **~ sth/itself** *If the woodland is left alone, it will regenerate itself in a few years.* 如果林地不受干扰，几年后

▼ **SYNONYMS 同义词辨析**

regard

call • find • consider • see • view

These words all mean to think about sb/sth in a particular way. 以上各词均含认为、视为、看待之义。

regard to think of sb/sth in a particular way 指认为、视为、看待：*He seemed to regard the whole thing as a joke.* 他似乎是把整件事当成玩笑。

call to say that sb/sth has particular qualities or characteristics 指认为…是、把…看作：*I wouldn't call German an easy language.* 我并不认为德语是一门容易学的语言。

find to have a particular feeling or opinion about sth 指认为、感到：*You may find your illness hard to accept.* 你可能觉得难以接受自己患病。

consider to think of sb/sth in a particular way 指认为、视为、觉得：*Who do you consider (to be) responsible for the accident?* 你认为谁对这个事故负有责任？

REGARD OR CONSIDER? 用 regard 还是 consider?

These two words have the same meaning, but they are used in different patterns and structures. In this meaning **consider** must be used with a complement or clause: you can *consider sb/sth to be sth* or *consider sb/sth as sth*, although very often the *to be* or *as* is left out. 上述两词意义相同，但用于不同的句型和结构。用于此义时，consider 必须与补语或从句连用，可说 consider sb/sth to be sth 或 consider sb/sth as sth，不过 to be 或 as 常常省略不用：*He considers himself an expert.* 他认为自己是专家。◇ *They are considered a high-risk group.* 他们被视为高危人群。 You can also *consider that sb/sth is sth* and again, the *that* can be left out. **Regard** is used in a narrower range of structures. The most frequent structure is *regard sb/sth as sth*; the *as* cannot be left out. 用 consider that sb/sth is sth 亦可，that 同样可以省略。regard 可用的句型结构较少，最常用的结构是 regard sb/sth as sth，但 as 不可省略：~~*I regard him a close friend.*~~ You cannot 不能说：~~*regard sb/sth to be sth*~~ or 或：~~*regard that sb/sth is sth*~~ However, **regard** (but not **consider** in this meaning) can also be used without a noun or adjective complement but with just an object and adverb (*sb/sth is highly regarded*) or adverbial phrase (*regard sb/sth with suspicion/jealousy/admiration*). 不过，regard 亦可不与名词或形容词补语连用，只与宾语和副词（如 sb/sth is highly regarded）或副词短语（如 regard sb/sth with suspicion/jealousy/admiration）连用；consider 则不能这样用。

see to have an opinion of sth 指认为、看待：*Try to see things from her point of view.* 设法从她那个角度去看问题。

view to think of sb/sth in a particular way 指视为、认为、看待：*How do you view your position within the company?* 你如何看待你自己在公司中的位置？ NOTE **View** has the same meaning as **regard** and **consider** but is slightly less frequent and slightly less formal. The main structures are *view sb/sth as sb/sth* (you cannot leave out the *as*) and *view sb/sth with sth*. * view 与 regard、consider 意义相同，但略为不常用，也略非正式。主要结构有 view sb/sth as sb/sth（as 不能省略）和 view sb/sth with sth。

PATTERNS

- to regard/consider/see/view sb/sth **as** sth
- to regard/consider/see/view sb/sth **from** a particular point of view
- to find/consider sb/sth **to be** sth
- **generally**/**usually** regarded/considered/seen/viewed as sth
- to regard/consider/view sb/sth **favourably**/**unfavourably**

就会再生。 ▸ **re·gen·er·ation** /rɪˌdʒenəˈreɪʃn/ *noun* [U]: *economic regeneration* 经济复兴 ◇ *the regeneration of cells in the body* 身体细胞的再生 **re·gen·era·tive** /rɪˈdʒenərətɪv/ *adj.* : *the regenerative powers of nature* 大自然的再生力

re·gent /ˈriːdʒənt/ (*also* **Regent**) *noun* a person who rules a country because the king or queen is too young, old, ill/sick, etc. 摄政者；摄政王： *to act as regent* 担任摄政王 ▸ **re·gent** (*also* **Regent**) *adj.* [after noun]: *the Prince Regent* 摄政王

reg·gae /ˈregeɪ/ *noun* [U] a type of popular music with strong rhythms, developed in Jamaica in the 1960s 雷盖乐（20 世纪 60 年代于牙买加兴起的一种节奏强劲的流行音乐）

reg·gae·ton /ˈregeɪtɒn; *NAmE* -tɑːn/ *noun* [U] a type of dance music, developed in Puerto Rico in the 1980s, which is a mixture of REGGAE, SALSA and HIP HOP or RAP, and which often includes words that are sung or spoken in Spanish 雷鬼顿（混合雷盖乐、萨尔萨舞曲和嘻哈或说唱乐的一种舞曲，20 世纪 80 年代兴起于波多黎各，常包含西班牙语唱词或说唱）

reggo = REGO

regi·cide /ˈredʒɪsaɪd/ *noun* [U, C] (*formal*) the crime of killing a king or queen; a person who is guilty of this crime 弑君罪；弑君者

re·gime AW /reɪˈʒiːm/ *noun* **1** a method or system of government, especially one that has not been elected in a fair way （尤指未通过公正选举的）统治方式，统治制度，政权，政体： *a* ***fascist/totalitarian/military, etc. regime*** 法西斯、极权主义、军事等政权 ◇ *an* ***oppressive/brutal regime*** 压迫民众的 / 残暴的政权 ➲ COLLOCATIONS AT POLITICS **2** a method or system of organizing or managing sth 组织方法；管理体制： *Our tax regime is one of the most favourable in Europe.* 我们的税收管理体制是欧洲最受欢迎的税收体制之一。 **3** = REGIMEN : *a dietary regime* 饮食规则

regi·men /ˈredʒɪmən/ (*also* **re·gime**) *noun* (*medical* 医 or *formal*) a set of rules about food and exercise or medical treatment that you follow in order to stay healthy or to improve your health 生活规则；养生之道；养生法

regi·ment /ˈredʒɪmənt/ *noun* [C+sing./pl. v.] **1** a large group of soldiers that is commanded by a COLONEL （军队的）团 ➲ WORDFINDER NOTE AT ARMY **2** (*formal*) a large number of people or things 一大群人（或事物）

regi·men·tal /ˌredʒɪˈmentl/ *adj.* [only before noun] connected with a particular regiment of soldiers 团的；团队的： *a regimental flag* 团旗 ◇ *regimental headquarters* 团部

regi·ment·ed /ˈredʒɪmentɪd/ *adj.* (*disapproving*) **1** involving strict discipline and/or organization 非常严格的；死板的： *The school imposes a very regimented lifestyle on its students.* 学校将非常死板的生活方式强加给学生。 **2** arranged in strict groups, patterns, etc. 严格规划的；排列整齐的： *regimented lines of trees* 排列整齐的树木 ▸ **regi·men·ta·tion** /ˌredʒɪmenˈteɪʃn/ *noun* [U]: *She rebelled against the regimentation of school life.* 她曾反抗刻板的学校生活。

Re·gina /rɪˈdʒaɪnə/ *noun* [U] (*BrE, formal, from Latin*) a word meaning 'queen', used, for example, in the titles of legal cases which are brought by the state when there is a queen in Britain 女王（英国女王在位时用于政府诉讼案案目等）: *Regina v Jones* 女王诉琼斯案 ➲ COMPARE REX

re·gion 🔑 AW /ˈriːdʒən/ *noun* **1** 🔑 [C] a large area of land, usually without exact limits or borders （通常界限不明的）地区，区域，地方： *the* ***Arctic/tropical/desert, etc. regions*** 北极、热带、沙漠等地区 ◇ *one of the most densely populated regions of North America* 北美人口最为稠密的地区之一 **2** 🔑 [C] one of the areas that a country is divided into, that has its own customs and/or its own government 行政区： *the Basque region of Spain* 西班牙的巴斯克自治区 **3 the regions** [pl.] (*BrE*) all of a country except the capital city （一国除首都以外的）全部地区，所有区域 **4** [C] a part of the body, usually one that has a particular character or problem （通常指有某种特性或问题的）身体部位： *pains in the abdominal region* 腹部的疼痛

IDM **in the region of** used when you are giving a number, price, etc. to show that it is not exact （表示不确切的数字等）大约，差不多 SYN **approximately**: *He earns somewhere in the region of €50 000.* 他大约赚 5 万欧元。

re·gion·al 🔑 AW /ˈriːdʒənl/ *adj.* [usually before noun] of or relating to a region 地区的；区域的；地方的： *regional variations in pronunciation* 发音的地区差异 ◇ *the conflict between regional and national interests* 地方利益和国家利益的冲突 ◇ *regional councils/elections/newspapers* 地方议会 / 选举 / 报纸 ▸ **re·gion·al·ly** AW /-nəli/ *adv.* : *regionally based television companies* 地方性的电视公司

re·gion·al·ism /ˈriːdʒənəlɪzəm/ *noun* **1** [C] a feature of a language that exists in a particular part of a country, and is not part of the standard language （语言的）地域特征，地域性 **2** [U] the desire of the people who live in a particular region of a country to have more political and economic independence 地方分权主义；地域主义

regis·ter 🔑 AW /ˈredʒɪstə(r)/ *verb, noun*

■ *verb*

• PUT NAME ON LIST 登记姓名 **1** 🔑 [T, I] to record your/sb's/sth's name on an official list 登记；注册： **~ sth** *to* ***register a birth/marriage/death*** 登记出生 / 结婚 / 死亡 ◇ *to* ***register a company/trademark*** 注册公司 / 商标 ◇ **~ sth in sth** *The ship was registered in Panama.* 这艘船是在巴拿马注册的。 ◇ **~ sb + adj.** | **~ (sb) as sth** *She is officially registered (as) disabled.* 她正式登记为伤残者。 ◇ **~ (with sb/sth)** *to register with a doctor* 向医生登记 ◇ **~ (at/for sth)** *to register at a hotel* 在旅馆登记 ➲ WORDFINDER NOTE AT CONFERENCE

• GIVE OPINION PUBLICLY 公开发表意见 **2** [T] **~ sth** (*formal*) to make your opinion known officially or publicly （正式地或公开地）发表意见，提出主张： *China has registered a protest over foreign intervention.* 中国对外国干涉正式提出了抗议。

• ON MEASURING INSTRUMENT 测量仪器 **3** 🔑 [I] (+ noun) if a measuring instrument **registers** an amount or sth **registers** an amount on a measuring instrument, the instrument shows or records that amount 显示（读数）；记录： *The thermometer registered 32°C.* 温度计显示读数为 32 摄氏度。◇ *The earthquake registered 3 on the Richter scale.* 地震震级为里氏 3 级。 ◇ *The stock exchange has registered huge losses this week.* 本周证券交易遭到重创。

• SHOW FEELING 表达情感 **4** [T, no passive, I] **~ (sth)** (*formal*) to show or express a feeling 流露出；显得；表达出： *Her face registered disapproval.* 她脸上流露出不赞同的神色。 ◇ *Shock registered on everyone's face.* 人人都面露震惊之色。

• NOTICE STH 注意到 **5** [T, no passive, I] (often used in negative sentences 常用于否定句) **~ (sth)** to notice sth and remember it; to be noticed 注意到；记住；受到注意： *He barely registered our presence.* 他几乎没有注意到我们在场。 ◇ *I told her my name, but it obviously didn't register.* 我把名字告诉了她，但她显然没有在意。

• LETTER/PACKAGE 邮件 **6** [T, usually passive] **~ sth** to send sth by mail, paying extra money to protect it against loss or damage 把…挂号邮寄： *Can I register this, please?* 请给我把这个挂号邮寄。 ◇ *a registered letter* 挂号信

■ *noun*

• LIST OF NAMES 名单 **1** 🔑 [C] an official list or record of names, items, etc.; a book that contains such a list 登记表；注册簿；登记簿： *a* ***parish register*** (= of births, marriages and deaths) 教区登记簿 ◇ *to be on the* ***electoral register/register of voters*** 成为登记在册的选民 ◇ *Could you sign the* ***hotel register*** *please, sir?* 先生，请在旅馆登记簿上签字好吗？ ◇ (*BrE*) *The teacher* ***called the register*** (= checked who was present at school). 老师点了名。

• OF VOICE/INSTRUMENT 嗓音；乐器 **2** [C] the range, or part of a range, of a human voice or a musical instrument 声区；音区： *in the* ***upper/middle/lower register*** 在高 / 中 / 低声区

• OF WRITING/SPEECH 书面语；口语 **3** [C, U] (*linguistics* 语言)

the level and style of a piece of writing or speech, that is usually appropriate to the situation that it is used in（适合特定场合使用的）语体风格；语域：*The essay suddenly switches from a formal to an informal register.* 这篇文章的语体风格突然从正式转为非正式。➲ WORDFINDER NOTE AT DICTIONARY
• FOR HOT/COLD AIR 冷／热空气 **4** [C] (*NAmE*) an opening, with a cover that you can have open or shut, that allows hot or cold air from a heating or cooling system into a room（供暖或制冷设备的）调风口，节气门，百叶型风口 ➲ COMPARE VENT *n.*
• MACHINE 机器 **5** [C] (*NAmE*) = CASH REGISTER

ˌregistered ˈmail (*BrE also* **ˌregistered ˈpost**) *noun* [U] a method of sending a letter or package in which the person sending it can claim money if it arrives late or is lost or damaged 挂号邮寄 ➲ COMPARE RECORDED DELIVERY

ˌregistered ˈnurse *noun* (*abbr.* **RN**) **1** (*NAmE*) a nurse who has a degree in NURSING and who has passed an exam to be allowed to work in a particular state 注册护士 **2** (*BrE*) a nurse who has an official qualification（获得正式资格的）注册护士；合格的护士

ˌregistered ˈtrademark *noun* (*symb.* ®) the sign or name of a product, etc. that is officially recorded and protected so that nobody else can use it 注册商标

ˈregister office *noun* the official way of referring to a REGISTRY OFFICE 户籍登记处

regis·trar /ˌredʒɪˈstrɑː(r); ˈredʒɪstrɑː(r)/ *noun* **1** a person whose job is to keep official records, especially of births, marriages and deaths 登记员；户籍管理员 **2** the senior officer who organizes the affairs of a college or university（大学的）教务长，教务主任，注册主任 **3** a doctor working in a British hospital who is training to become a specialist in a particular area of medicine（英国医院的）专科住院医生：*a paediatric registrar* 儿科住院医生 ➲ COMPARE CONSULTANT, RESIDENT *n.* (3)

regis·tra·tion AW /ˌredʒɪˈstreɪʃn/ *noun* **1** [U, C] the act of making an official record of sth/sb 登记；注册；挂号：*the registration of letters and parcels* 信件和包裹的挂号 ◇ *the registration of students for a course* 学生的选课登记 ◇ *registration fees* 注册费 ◇ *vehicle registrations* 车辆登记 ◇ *the registration of a child's birth* 婴儿出生登记 **2** [U, C] a document showing that an official record has been made of sth 登记文档；注册项目 ➲ COMPARE LOGBOOK (1) **3** [C] (*BrE*) = REGISTRATION NUMBER **4** [U] (*BrE*) the time when a teacher looks at the list of students on the class register and checks that the students are present（教师对上课学生的）点名

regiˈstration number (*also* **regis·tra·tion**) (*both BrE*) (*NAmE* **ˈlicense (plate) number**) *noun* the series of letters and numbers that are shown on a NUMBER PLATE at the front and back of a vehicle to identify it 车辆的登记号码；牌照号码

regis·try /ˈredʒɪstri/ *noun* (*pl.* **-ies**) a place where registers are kept 登记处；注册处

ˈregistry office (*also* **ˈregister office**) *noun* (in Britain) a place where CIVIL marriages (= that do not involve a religious ceremony) are performed and where records of births, marriages and deaths are made 户籍登记处（在英国可举办不涉及宗教仪式的婚礼，并负责登记出生及婚丧等事项）：*to get married in/at a registry office* 在户籍登记处登记结婚

rego (*also* **reggo**) /ˈredʒəʊ; *NAmE* -oʊ/ *noun* (*pl.* **-os**) (*AustralE, NZE, informal*) a REGISTRATION for a car, etc.（机动车辆等的）注册

re·gress /rɪˈɡres/ *verb* [I] **~ (to sth)** (*formal, usually disapproving*) to return to an earlier or less advanced form or way of behaving 倒退；回归；退化

re·gres·sion /rɪˈɡreʃn/ *noun* [U, C] **~ (to sth)** the process of going back to an earlier or less advanced form or state 倒退；回归；退化

re·gres·sive /rɪˈɡresɪv/ *adj.* **1** becoming or making sth less advanced 退化的；倒退的；退步的：*The policy has been condemned as a regressive step.* 这项政策被认为是一种倒退而受到谴责。 **2** (*specialist*) (of taxes 税收) having less effect on the rich than on the poor 递减的（对富人的影响比对穷人的小）

re·gret 🔑 /rɪˈɡret/ *verb, noun*
■ *verb* (**-tt-**) **1** 🔑 to feel sorry about sth you have done or about sth that you have not been able to do 感到遗憾；惋惜；懊悔：**~ sth** *If you don't do it now, **you'll** only **regret it**.* 你如果现在不做，以后一定会后悔的。◇ *The decision could be one he **lives to regret**.* 这一决定也许会有让他后悔的一天。◇ *'I've had a wonderful life,' she said, 'I don't regret a thing.'* "我一辈子生活得很好，"她说，"我没什么可遗憾的。" ◇ **~ doing sth** *He bitterly regretted ever having mentioned it.* 他非常懊悔提起那件事。◇ **~ what, how, etc.…** *I deeply regret what I said.* 我非常后悔说了那些话。◇ **~ that…** *I regret that I never got to meet him in person.* 很遗憾我始终没能见到他本人。 **2** 🔑 (*formal*) used to say in a polite or formal way that you are sorry or sad about a situation（有礼貌地或正式地表示抱歉、痛惜或悲伤）：**~ sth** *The airline regrets any inconvenience.* 航空公司对所造成的任何不便表示歉意。◇ **~ that…** *I regret that I am unable to accept your kind invitation.* 很遗憾，我不能接受你的友好邀请。◇ **~ to do sth** *We regret to inform you that your application has not been successful.* 我们很遗憾地通知您，您的申请未获通过。◇ **it is regretted that…** *It is to be **regretted that** so many young people leave school without qualifications.* 遗憾的是那么多年轻人肄业离校。 ➲ WORDFINDER NOTE AT SORRY ➲ MORE LIKE THIS 36, page R29
■ *noun* 🔑 [U, C] a feeling of sadness or disappointment that you have because of sth that has happened or sth that you have done or not done 痛惜；懊悔；遗憾；失望：*It **is with great regret** that I accept your resignation.* 接受你的辞呈，我感到非常遗憾。◇ *She **expressed her regret at** the decision.* 她对这个决定表示失望。◇ ***a pang/twinge of regret*** 一阵痛悔之情 ◇ ***I have no regrets** about leaving Newcastle* (= I do not feel sorry about it). 我一点也不后悔离开纽卡斯尔。◇ *What is your greatest regret* (= the thing that you are most sorry about doing or not doing)? 你最大的遗憾是什么？◇ *He gave up teaching in 2009, **much to the regret of** his students.* 他于 2009 年放弃了教学，这使他的学生深感遗憾。

re·gret·ful /rɪˈɡretfl/ *adj.* feeling or showing sadness or disappointment because of sth that has happened or sth that you have done or not done 后悔的；失望的；令人惋惜的；遗憾的 SYN **rueful**：*a regretful look* 失望的眼神

re·gret·ful·ly /rɪˈɡretfəli/ *adv.* **1** in a way that shows you are sad or disappointed about sth 遗憾地；痛惜地；失望地；懊悔地：*'I'm afraid not,' he said regretfully.* 他遗憾地说："恐怕不行。" ◇ *Emma shook her head regretfully.* 埃玛遗憾地摇了摇头。 **2** used to show that you are sorry that sth is the case and you wish the situation were different 遗憾的是；十分遗憾 SYN **regrettably**：*Regretfully,*

▼ WHICH WORD? 词语辨析

regretfully / regrettably
• **Regretfully** and **regrettably** can both be used as sentence adverbs to show that you are sorry about something and wish the situation were different.
* regretfully 和 regrettably 均可用作副词，修饰整个句子，表示非常抱歉、遗憾、惋惜：*Regretfully, some jobs will be lost.* 遗憾的是有些人将会失去工作。◇ *Regrettably, some jobs will be lost.* 令人遗憾的是有些人将会失去工作。
• **Regretfully** can also be used to mean 'in a way that shows you are sad or disappointed about something'.
* regretfully 亦可指懊丧、沮丧：*He sighed regretfully.* 他懊丧地叹了口气。

mounting costs have forced the museum to close. 遗憾的是，成本不断增加，博物馆不得不关闭。

re·gret·table /rɪˈgretəbl/ *adj.* ~ (**that…**) (*formal*) that you are sorry about and wish had not happened 令人惋惜的；可惜的；令人遗憾的：*It is regrettable that the police were not informed sooner.* 遗憾的是没有早些报警。◇ *The loss of jobs is highly regrettable.* 失去工作非常令人遗憾。 ▸ **re·gret·tably** /-əbli/ *adv.*：*Regrettably, crime has been increasing in this area.* 令人遗憾的是这一地区的犯罪率在不断上升。

re·group /ˌriːˈgruːp/ *verb* **1** [T, I] ~ (**sth**) (**for sth**) to arrange the way people or soldiers work together in a new way, especially in order to continue fighting or attacking sb 重组；重编：*They regrouped their forces and renewed the attack.* 他们重新聚集兵力，再次发动进攻。◇ *After its election defeat, the party needs to regroup.* 选举失败后，这个党需要改组。 **2** [I] (of a person 人) to return to a normal state after an unpleasant experience or a period of difficulty, and become ready to make an effort again with new enthusiasm or strength 重整旗鼓；重新部署：*Summer is a time to relax, regroup and catch up on all those things you've been putting off all year.* 夏天是休养整顿、处理一年中积压事务的时候。

regu·lar 🔑 /ˈregjələ(r)/ *adj., noun*

■ *adj.*

• **FOLLOWING PATTERN** 规律 **1** 🔑 following a pattern, especially with the same time or space in between each thing and the next 规则的；有规律的；间隙均匀的；定时的：*regular breathing* 均匀的呼吸 ◇ ***a regular pulse/heartbeat*** 正常的脉搏 / 心跳 ◇ *A light flashed **at regular intervals**.* 一盏灯有规律地闪着亮光。◇ *There is a regular bus service to the airport.* 有公共汽车定时开往机场。◇ ***regular meetings/visits*** 定期会议 / 访问 ◇ *The equipment is checked **on a regular basis**.* 设备定期进行检查。 OPP **irregular**

• **FREQUENT** 频繁 **2** 🔑 done or happening often 频繁的；经常做（或发生）的：*Do you take regular exercise?* 你经常锻炼吗？◇ *Domestic violence is a regular occurrence in some families.* 在某些家庭中，家庭暴力是常事。 OPP **irregular** **3** 🔑 [only before noun] (of people 人) doing the same thing or going to the same place often 经常做某事的；常去某地的：*our regular customers* 老主顾 ◇ *regular offenders* (= against the law) 惯犯 ◇ *He was a regular visitor to her house.* 他是她家的常客。

• **USUAL** 通常 **4** 🔑 [only before noun] usual 通常的；平常的；惯常的：*I couldn't see my regular doctor today.* 我今天找不到平常给我看病的医生。◇ *On Monday he would have to return to his regular duties.* 星期一，他就得回去正常上班了。◇ *It's important to follow the regular procedure.* 按照惯常的程序行事是很重要的。

• **EVEN** 匀称 **5** 🔑 having an even shape 均匀的；端正的；齐整的：*a face with regular features* 五官端正的脸庞 ◇ *a regular geometric pattern* 正几何图形 OPP **irregular**

• **PERMANENT** 持久 **6** 🔑 lasting or happening over a long period 持久的；稳定的；固定的：*a regular income* 固定的收入 ◇ *She couldn't find any regular employment.* 她找不到任何固定工作。

• **STANDARD SIZE** 标准尺寸 **7** 🔑 (*especially NAmE*) of a standard size 标准尺寸的；中等大小的；中号的：*Regular or large fries?* 中号的还是大号的炸薯条？

• **ORDINARY** 普通 **8** 🔑 [only before noun] (*especially NAmE*) ordinary; without any special or extra features 普通的；平凡的：*Do you want regular or diet cola?* 你要普通的还是低热量的可乐？◇ (*approving*) *He's just a regular guy who loves his dog.* 他也不过是个十分疼爱自己狗儿的平凡人。

• **SOLDIER** 士兵 **9** [only before noun] belonging to or connected with the permanent armed forces or police force of a country 常备军的；正规军的：***a regular army/soldier*** 正规军；正规军士兵 OPP **irregular**

• **GRAMMAR** 语法 **10** (especially of verbs or nouns 尤指动词或名词) changing their form in the same way as most other verbs and nouns 规则的；按规则变化的：*The past participle of regular verbs ends in '-ed'.* 规则动词的过去分词以 -ed 结尾。 OPP **irregular**

• **FOR EMPHASIS** 强调 **11** (*informal*) used for emphasis to show that sb/sth is an exact or clear example of the thing mentioned 完全的；彻底的：*The whole thing was a regular disaster.* 整个事情完全是一场灾难。

IDM (**as**) **regular as 'clockwork** very regularly; happening at the same time in the same way 非常有规律；极有规律：*He is home by six every day, regular as clockwork.* 他每天 6 点前必定准时回到家。 ➲ MORE LIKE THIS 14, page R26

■ *noun*

• **CUSTOMER** 顾客 **1** a customer who often goes to a particular shop/store, pub, restaurant, etc. 常客；老主顾：*He's one of our regulars.* 他是我们的一位老主顾。

• **MEMBER OF TEAM** 队员 **2** a person who often plays in a particular team, takes part in a particular television show, etc. 主力（或正式）队员；（电视节目的）常任主持人；经常参加某项活动的人：*We are missing six first-team regulars because of injury.* 我们有六位一线主力队员因伤不能出场。

• **SOLDIER** 士兵 **3** a professional soldier who belongs to a country's permanent army 正规军人；职业军人

re·gu·lar·ity /ˌregjuˈlærəti/ *noun* **1** [U] the fact that the same thing happens again and again, and usually with the same length of time between each time it happens 规律性；经常性：*Aircraft passed overhead **with monotonous regularity**.* 飞机一次又一次反复从头顶飞过。 **2** [U] the fact that sth is arranged in an even way or in an organized pattern 匀称；端正；有规则的分布：*the striking regularity of her features* 她的五官非常端正 **3** [C] a thing that has a pattern to it 有规则的东西；有规律的事物：*They had observed regularities in the behaviour of the animals.* 他们曾观察过这些动物的习性。 ➲ COMPARE IRREGULARITY

regu·lar·ize (*BrE also* **-ise**) /ˈregjələraɪz/ *verb* ~ **sth** to make a situation that already exists legal or official 使合法化；使正式存在：*Illegal immigrants were given the opportunity to regularize their position.* 非法移民得到了使其身份合法化的机会。

regu·lar·ly 🔑 /ˈregjələli; *NAmE* -lərli/ *adv.* **1** 🔑 at regular intervals or times 有规律地；间隙均匀地：*We meet regularly to discuss the progress of the project.* 我们定期会面，讨论工程进展情况。 **2** 🔑 often 经常：*I go there quite regularly.* 我经常去那儿。 **3** 🔑 in an even or balanced way 均匀地；匀称地：*The plants were spaced regularly, about 50 cm apart.* 这些植株分布均匀，间距大约为 50 厘米。

regu·late AW /ˈregjuleɪt/ *verb* **1** [T, I] ~ (**sth**) to control sth by means of rules （用规则条例）约束，控制，管理：*The activities of credit companies are regulated by law.* 信贷公司的业务受法律的制约。◇ *It is up to the regulating authority to put the measures into effect.* 应该由管理部门落实这些措施。 **2** [T] ~ **sth** to control the speed, pressure, temperature, etc. in a machine or system 调节，控制（速度、压力、温度等）：*This valve regulates the flow of water.* 这个阀门调节水流。

regu·la·tion 🔑 AW /ˌregjuˈleɪʃn/ *noun, adj.*

■ *noun* **1** 🔑 [C, usually pl.] an official rule made by a government or some other authority 章程；规章制度；规则；法规：*too many **rules and regulations*** 过多的规章制度 ◇ ***fire/safety/building, etc. regulations*** 防火条例、安全规章、建筑法规等 ◇ *to comply with the regulations* 遵守章程 ◇ ***Under the new regulations** spending on office equipment will be strictly controlled.* 根据新的规定，办公设备开支将受到严格控制。◇ *the strict regulations governing the sale of weapons* 关于武器销售的严格规定 **2** [U] controlling sth by means of rules （运用规则条例的）管理，控制：*the voluntary regulation of the press* 新闻出版业的自律

■ *adj.* [only before noun] that must be worn or used according to the official rules 规定的；必须穿戴的；必须使用的：*in regulation uniform* 穿着规定的制服

regu·la·tor AW /ˈregjuleɪtə(r)/ *noun* **1** a person or an organization that officially controls an area of business or industry and makes sure that it is operating fairly （某行业等的）监管者，监管机构 **2** a device that automatically controls sth such as speed, temperature or pressure（速度、温度、压力的）自动调节器

R

regu·la·tory AW /ˈregjələtəri; *NAmE* -tɔːri/ *adj.* [usually before noun] having the power to control an area of business or industry and make sure that it is operating fairly （对工商业）具有监管权的，监管的：*regulatory bodies/authorities/agencies* 监管部门 / 机构

re·gur·gi·tate /rɪˈɡɜːdʒɪteɪt; *NAmE* -ˈɡɜːrdʒ-/ *verb* **1 ~ sth** (*formal*) to bring food that has been swallowed back up into the mouth again 使（咽下的食物）返回到口中；反刍 **2 ~ sth** (*disapproving*) to repeat sth you have heard or read without really thinking about it or understanding it 照搬；拾人牙慧 ▸ **re·gur·gi·ta·tion** /rɪˌɡɜːdʒɪˈteɪʃn; *NAmE* -ˌɡɜːrdʒ-/ *noun* [U]

rehab /ˈriːhæb/ *noun* [U] the process of helping to cure sb who has a problem with drugs or alcohol（戒除毒瘾或酒瘾的）康复：*to go into rehab* 进行康复治疗 ◇ *a rehab clinic* 康复诊所 ➲ WORDFINDER NOTE AT DRUG

re·habili·tate /ˌriːəˈbɪlɪteɪt/ *verb* **1 ~ sb** to help sb to have a normal, useful life again after they have been very ill/sick or in prison for a long time 使（重病患者）康复；使（长期服刑者）恢复正常生活：*a unit for rehabilitating drug addicts* 帮助吸毒者恢复正常生活的机构 **2 ~ sb (as sth)** to begin to consider that sb is good or acceptable after a long period during which they were considered bad or unacceptable 恢复…的名誉；给…平反昭雪：*He played a major role in rehabilitating Magritte as an artist.* 他对恢复玛格里特艺术家的名誉起了重要的作用。 **3 ~ sth** to return a building or an area to its previous good condition 使（建筑物或地区）恢复原状；修复 ▸ **re·habili·ta·tion** /ˌriːəˌbɪlɪˈteɪʃn/ *noun* [U]：*a drug rehabilitation centre* 戒毒康复中心 ◇ *the rehabilitation of the steel industry* 钢铁工业的复兴

re·hash /ˌriːˈhæʃ/ *verb* **~ sth** (*disapproving*) to arrange ideas, pieces of writing or pieces of film into a new form but without any great change or improvement（稍微改动）重新推出；以新形式表达旧内容：*He just rehashes songs from the 60s.* 他只是把 60 年代的歌曲稍加改编而已。 ▸ **re·hash** /ˈriːhæʃ/ *noun* [sing.] (*disapproving*)：*The movie is just a rehash of the best TV episodes.* 这部电影不过是把电视剧里最精彩的几集改编了一下。

R

re·hear /ˌriːˈhɪə(r); *NAmE* -ˈhɪr/ *verb* (**re·heard, re·heard** /ˌriːˈhɜːd; *NAmE* -ˈhɜːrd/) **~ sth** (*law* 律) to hear or consider again a case in court 重新审理（案件）

re·hear·ing /ˌriːˈhɪərɪŋ; *NAmE* -ˈhɪr-/ *noun* (*law* 律) an opportunity for a case to be heard or considered again in court（法庭对案件的）重新审理

re·hearsal /rɪˈhɜːsl; *NAmE* rɪˈhɜːrsl/ *noun* **1** [C, U] time that is spent practising a play or piece of music in preparation for a public performance 排演；排练：*to* ***have a rehearsal*** 进行排练 ◇ *We only had six days of rehearsal.* 我们只有六天的排练时间。 ◇ *Our new production of 'Hamlet' is currently* ***in rehearsal.*** 我们的新版《哈姆雷特》正在排练之中。 ◇ *a rehearsal room* 排练房 ➲ SEE ALSO DRESS REHEARSAL ➲ WORDFINDER NOTE AT PERFORMANCE **2** [C, usually sing.] **~ (for sth)** an experience or event that helps to prepare you for sth that is going to happen in the future 预演；演习：*These training exercises are designed to be a rehearsal for the invasion.* 这些训练是为了入侵而进行的演习。 **3** [C, usually sing.] **~ of sth** (*formal*) the act of repeating sth that has been said before 复述；重复；叙述：*We listened to his lengthy rehearsal of the arguments.* 我们听着他没完没了地重复他的论点。

re·hearse /rɪˈhɜːs; *NAmE* rɪˈhɜːrs/ *verb* **1** [I, T] to practise or make people practise a play, piece of music, etc. in preparation for a public performance 排练；排演：**~ (for sth)** *We were given only two weeks to rehearse.* 只给了我们两个星期排练。 ◇ **~ sth/sb** *Today, we'll just be rehearsing the final scene.* 今天，我们只排演最后一幕。 ◇ *The actors were poorly rehearsed.* 演员排练得不够。 **2** [T] **~ sth** to prepare in your mind or practise privately what you are going to do or say to sb 默诵；背诵；默默地练习：*She walked along rehearsing her excuse for being late.* 她一边走一边默诵着她迟到的托辞。 **3** [T] **~ sth** (*formal, usually disapproving*) to repeat ideas or opinions that have often been expressed before 照搬；重复

re·heat /ˌriːˈhiːt/ *verb* **~ sth** to heat cooked food again after it has been left to go cold 重新加热（凉了的熟食）

re·home /ˌriːˈhəʊm; *NAmE* -ˈhoʊm/ *verb* **~ sth** to find a new owner for a pet, especially a dog or cat, usually after caring for it for a time 为（狗、猫等宠物）找新家：*The organization rescues stray dogs and rehomes them.* 这个组织救助流浪狗，并给它们找新主人。

re·house /ˌriːˈhaʊz/ *verb* **~ sb** to provide sb with a different home to live in 给…重新安排住房：*Thousands of earthquake victims are still waiting to be rehoused.* 数千名地震灾民仍在等待安排新住处。

reign /reɪn/ *noun, verb*

▪ ***noun*** **1** the period during which a king, queen, EMPEROR, etc. rules 君主统治时期：***in/during the reign*** *of Charles II* 在查理二世统治期间 ➲ WORDFINDER NOTE AT KING **2** the period during which sb is in charge of an organization, a team, etc. 任期；当政期

▪ ***verb*** **1** [I] to rule as king, queen, EMPEROR, etc. 统治；当政；为王；为君：*the reigning monarch* 当政的君主 ◇ *Queen Victoria reigned from 1837 to 1901.* 维多利亚女王自 1837 年至 1901 年在位。 ◇ **~ over sb/sth** *Herod reigned over Palestine at that time.* 那时，希律王统治巴勒斯坦。 **2** [I] **~ (over sb/sth)** to be the best or most important in a particular situation or area of skill 成为最佳；成为最重要的：*the reigning champion* 冠军称号的保持者 ◇ *In the field of classical music, he still* ***reigns supreme.*** 在古典音乐领域，他仍然是最为杰出的。 **3** [I] (*literary*) (of an idea, a feeling or an atmosphere 想法、情感或氛围) to be the most obvious feature of a place or moment 盛行；成为最显著的：*At last* ***silence reigned*** (= there was complete silence). 最后，万籁俱寂。 ➲ MORE LIKE THIS 20, page R27

re·ig·nite /ˌriːɪɡˈnaɪt/ *verb* [I, T] to start burning again; to make sth start burning again （使）重新燃烧；再点燃：*The oven burners reignite automatically if blown out.* 烤炉的火如果吹灭了会自动再点燃。 ◇ **~ sth** *You may need to reignite the pilot light.* 你得重新点燃长明火。 ◇ (*figurative*) *Their passion was reignited by a romantic trip to Venice.* 去威尼斯的浪漫之旅重新燃起了他们的激情。

ˌreign of ˈterror *noun* (*pl.* **reigns of terror**) a period during which there is a lot of violence and many people are killed by the ruler or people in power 恐怖统治时期

reiki /ˈreɪki/ *noun* [U] (*from Japanese*) a method of healing based on the idea that energy can be directed into a person's body by touch 灵气疗法（通过触摸向人体内输送能量）

re·im·burse /ˌriːɪmˈbɜːs; *NAmE* -ˈbɜːrs/ *verb* (*formal*) to pay back money to sb which they have spent or lost 偿还；补偿：**~ sth** *We will reimburse any expenses incurred.* 我们将付还所有相关费用。 ◇ **~ sb (for sth)** *You will be reimbursed for any loss or damage caused by our company.* 如我公司给您造成损失或有所损坏，您都将得到赔偿。 ▸ **re·im·burse·ment** *noun* [U]

rein /reɪn/ *noun, verb*

▪ ***noun*** **1** [C, usually pl.] a long narrow leather band that is attached to a metal bar in a horse's mouth (= a BIT) and is held by the rider in order to control the horse 缰绳：*She pulled gently on the reins.* 她轻轻地拉着缰绳。 ➲ WORDFINDER NOTE AT HORSE **2 reins** [pl.] (*BrE*) strips of leather, etc. worn by a small child and held by an adult in order to stop the child from walking off and getting lost（幼儿佩带以防走失的）保护带 **3 the reins** [pl.] the state of being in control or the leader of sth 控制；主宰；掌管：*It was time to* ***hand over the reins*** *of power* (= to give control to sb else). 是该让权的时候了。 ◇ *The vice-president was forced to* ***take up the reins*** *of office.* 副总统被迫走马上任。

IDM **give/allow sb/sth free/full ˈrein | give/allow free/full ˈrein to sth** to give sb complete freedom of action; to allow a feeling to be expressed freely 对…不加约束；放任自由；充分表达（感情）：*The designer was given free rein.* 设计者可以自由发挥。 ◇ *The script allows full rein to* *her larger-than-life acting style.* 剧本允许她充分展现她那夸张的表演风格。 ➲ MORE AT TIGHT *adj.*

■ *verb*

PHR V ˌ**rein sb/sth**↔ˈ**back** | ˌ**rein sth**↔ˈ**in** **1** to start to control sb/sth more strictly 严格控制；加强管理 SYN **check**: *We need to rein back public spending.* 我们需要严格控制公共开销。 ◇ *She kept her emotions tightly reined in.* 她尽量克制着自己的感情。 **2** to stop a horse or make it go more slowly by pulling back the reins 用缰绳勒马

re·incar·nate /ˌriːɪnˈkɑːneɪt; *NAmE* -ˈkɑːrn-/ *verb* [often passive, T, I] ~ (**sb/sth**) (**in/as sb/sth**) to be born again in another body after you have died; to make sb be born again in this way 使投胎；转世；使再生: *They believe humans are reincarnated in animal form.* 他们相信人死后转生为动物。

re·incar·na·tion /ˌriːɪnkɑːˈneɪʃn; *NAmE* -kɑːrˈn-/ *noun* **1** [U] the belief that after sb's death their soul lives again in a new body 转世说 ➲ COLLOCATIONS AT RELIGION **2** [C, usually sing.] a person or an animal whose body contains the soul of a dead person（灵魂的）转世化身，化身

rein·deer /ˈreɪndɪə(r); *NAmE* -dɪr/ *noun* (*pl.* **rein·deer** or **rein·deers**) a large DEER with long ANTLERS (= horns shaped like branches), that lives in cold northern regions 驯鹿: *herds of reindeer* 驯鹿群

re·inforce AW /ˌriːɪnˈfɔːs; *NAmE* -ˈfɔːrs/ *verb* **1** ~ **sth** to make a feeling, an idea, etc. stronger 加强；充实；使更强烈: *Such jokes tend to reinforce racial stereotypes.* 这样的笑话往往会进一步加深关于种族的模式化观念。 ◇ *The climate of political confusion has only reinforced the country's economic decline.* 政局混乱只是加速了国家经济的衰退。 ◇ *Success in the talks will reinforce his reputation as an international statesman.* 谈判成功将会增强他作为国际政治家的声望。 **2** ~ **sth** to make a structure or material stronger, especially by adding another material to it 加固；使更结实: *All buildings are now reinforced to withstand earthquakes.* 所有建筑现都已加固，以抗地震。◇ *reinforced steel* 增强钢材 **3** ~ **sth** to send more people or equipment in order to make an army, etc. stronger 给…加强力量（或装备）；使更强大: *The UN has undertaken to reinforce its military presence along the borders.* 联合国已经着手增强边境驻军。

ˌ**reinforced** ˈ**concrete** *noun* [U] concrete with metal bars or wires inside to make it stronger 钢筋混凝土

re·inforce·ment AW /ˌriːɪnˈfɔːsmənt; *NAmE* -ˈfɔːrs-/ *noun* **1** **reinforcements** [pl.] extra soldiers or police officers who are sent to a place because more are needed 援军；增援警力: *to send in reinforcements* 派出增援部队 **2** [U, sing.] the act of making sth stronger, especially a feeling or an idea（感情或思想等的）巩固，加强，强化

re·instate /ˌriːɪnˈsteɪt/ *verb* **1** ~ **sb/sth** (**in/as sth**) to give back a job or position that had been taken away from sb 使恢复原职；使重返岗位: *He was reinstated in his post.* 他重新回到了自己的岗位。 **2** ~ **sth** (**in/as sth**) to return sth to its previous position or status 把…放回原处；使恢复原状 SYN **restore**: *There have been repeated calls to reinstate the death penalty.* 不断有人呼吁恢复死刑。 ▸ **re·instate·ment** *noun* [U]

re·insur·ance /ˌriːɪnˈʃʊərəns; -ˈʃɔːr-; *NAmE* -ˈʃʊr-/ *noun* [U] (*finance* 财) the practice of one insurance company buying insurance from another company against any losses that result from claims that are made against it 再保险，分保保险（指一保险公司向其他公司购买保险以减少索赔损失）

re·inter·pret AW /ˌriːɪnˈtɜːprɪt; *NAmE* -ˈtɜːrp-/ *verb* ~ **sth** to interpret sth in a new or different way 重新解释；重新诠释 ▸ **re·inter·pret·ation** AW /ˌriːɪnˌtɜːprɪˈteɪʃn; *NAmE* -ˌtɜːrp-/ *noun* [C, U]

re·intro·duce /ˌriːɪntrəˈdjuːs; *NAmE* -ˈduːs/ *verb* **1** ~ **sth** to start to use sth again 再次使用；重新引入 SYN **bring back**: *to reintroduce the death penalty* 恢复死刑 ◇ *plans to reintroduce trams to the city* 市内重新启用有轨电车的计划 **2** ~ **sth** to put a type of animal, bird or plant back into a region where it once lived 将…放归自然栖息地 ▸ **re·intro·duc·tion** *noun* [U, C]

re·invent /ˌriːɪnˈvent/ *verb* ~ **sth/yourself** (**as sth**) to present yourself/sth in a new form or with a new image 以新形象示人；以新形式出现: *The former wild man of rock has reinvented himself as a respectable family man.* 过去的那位摇滚狂人已经改变形象，成了一位体面的爱家的男人。

IDM **reinvent the wheel** to waste time creating sth that already exists and works well 重复发明；无谓地重复；浪费时间做无用功

re·invest AW /ˌriːɪnˈvest/ *verb* [T, I] ~ (**sth**) to put profits that have been made on an investment back into the same investment or into a new one 再投资；把（利润）用于再投资 ▸ **re·invest·ment** AW *noun* [U, C]

re·in·vig·or·ate /ˌriːɪnˈvɪɡəreɪt/ *verb* ~ **sth/sb** to give new energy or strength to sth/sb 给…增添精力（或力量）；使再振作: *We need to reinvigorate the economy of the area.* 我们需要给这个地区的经济注入新的活力。 ◇ *I felt reinvigorated after a rest and a shower.* 我休息了一会儿，冲了个淋浴，感到精神焕发。

re·issue /ˌriːˈɪʃuː/ *verb, noun*

■ *verb* ~ **sth** (**as sth**) to publish or produce again a book, record, etc. that has not been available for some time 重新发行；再版: *old jazz recordings reissued on CD* 以激光唱片重新发行的老爵士乐 ◇ *The novel was reissued in paperback.* 这本小说重新发行了平装本。

■ *noun* an old book or record that has been published or produced again after not being available for some time 再版书；重新发行的唱片（或其他录制品）

re·iter·ate /riˈɪtəreɪt/ *verb* (*formal*) to repeat sth that you have already said, especially to emphasize it 反复地说；重申: ~ **sth** *to reiterate an argument/a demand/an offer* 重申论点；重复一项要求 / 建议 ◇ ~ **that**... *Let me reiterate that we are fully committed to this policy.* 我再说一遍，我们对这项政策是全力以赴、坚定不移的。 ◇ + **speech** *'I said "money",' he reiterated.* "我说的是'钱'。" 他重申道。 ▸ **re·iter·ation** /riˌɪtəˈreɪʃn/ *noun* [sing.]: *a reiteration of her previous statement* 重申她说过的话

re·ject 🔑 AW *verb, noun*

■ *verb* /rɪˈdʒekt/

• **ARGUMENT/IDEA/PLAN** 论点；想法；计划 **1** 🔑 ~ **sth** to refuse to accept or consider sth 拒绝接受；不予考虑: *to reject an argument/a claim/a decision/an offer/a suggestion* 拒绝接受一个论点 / 一项要求 / 一个决定 / 一项提议 / 一个建议 ◇ *The prime minister rejected any idea of reforming the system.* 首相对任何改革体制的想法都不予考虑。 ◇ *The proposal was **firmly rejected**.* 这项提议被断然否决。 ◇ *All our suggestions were **rejected out of hand**.* 我们所有的建议都被一口拒绝了。

• **SB FOR JOB** 找工作者 **2** 🔑 ~ **sb** to refuse to accept sb for a job, position, etc. 拒收；不录用；拒绝接纳: *Please reject the following candidates...* 请排除以下候选人… ◇ *I've been rejected by all the universities I applied to.* 所有我申请的大学都没有录取我。

• **NOT USE/PUBLISH** 不用；不出版 **3** 🔑 ~ **sth** to decide not to use, sell, publish, etc. sth because its quality is not good enough（因质量差）不用，不出售，不出版: *Imperfect articles are rejected by our quality control.* 我们严把质量关，不完美的物件都被退回。

• **NEW ORGAN** 新器官 **4** 🔑 ~ **sth** (of the body 身体) to not accept a new organ after a TRANSPLANT operation, by producing substances that attack the organ 排斥，排异（移植的器官）

• **NOT LOVE** 不爱 **5** 🔑 ~ **sb/sth** to fail to give a person or an animal enough care or affection 不够关心；慢待: *The lioness rejected the smallest cub, which died.* 母狮不理会最小的幼狮，任由它死去。 ◇ *When her husband left home she felt rejected and useless.* 丈夫离家后，她觉得遭到了抛弃，且认为自己一无是处。

▸ **re·jec·tion** AW /rɪˈdʒekʃn/ *noun* [U, C]: *Her proposal met with unanimous rejection.* 她的建议遭到一致否决。 ◇ *a rejection letter* (= a letter in which you are told, for example, that you have not been accepted for a job) 回

R

绝信 ◇ *painful feelings of rejection* 受冷落的痛苦感受

■ ***noun*** /ˈriːdʒekt/

• **STH THAT CANNOT BE USED** 无用之物 **1** something that cannot be used or sold because there is sth wrong with it 废品；次品

• **PERSON** 人 **2** a person who has not been accepted as a member of a team, society, etc. 不合格者；被剔除者；被拒收者：*one of society's rejects* 一名社会弃儿

rejig /ˌriːˈdʒɪɡ/ *verb* (**-gg-**) (*BrE*) (*US* **rejig·ger** /ˌriːˈdʒɪɡə(r)/) **~ sth** (*informal*) to make changes to sth; to arrange sth in a different way 更改；重新安排；重新布置

re·joice /rɪˈdʒɔɪs/ *verb* [I, T] (*formal*) to express great happiness about sth 非常高兴；深感欣喜：*When the war ended, people finally had cause to rejoice.* 战争结束，人们终于可以欢欣鼓舞了。◇ **~ at/in/over sth** *The motor industry is rejoicing at the cut in car tax.* 汽车行业对汽车减税感到非常高兴。◇ **~ to do sth** *They rejoiced to see their son well again.* 他们看到儿子恢复了健康，无比高兴。◇ **~ that...** *I rejoice that justice has prevailed.* 我非常高兴正义得到伸张。

IDM **rejoice in the name of...** (*BrE, humorous*) to have a name that sounds funny 有个滑稽的名字：*He rejoiced in the name of Owen Owen.* 他有个滑稽的名字叫欧文•欧文。

re·joi·cing /rɪˈdʒɔɪsɪŋ/ *noun* [U] (*also* **rejoicings** [pl.]) the happy celebration of sth 喜庆；欢庆：*a time of great rejoicing* 尽情欢庆的时光

re·join¹ /ˌriːˈdʒɔɪn/ *verb* [T, I] **~ (sb/sth)** to join sb/sth again after leaving them 重新加入；和…重新在一起：*to rejoin a club* 重新加入俱乐部 ◇ *She turned off her phone and rejoined them at the table.* 她关掉电话，再回到餐桌旁和他们坐在一起。◇ *The path goes through a wood before rejoining the main road.* 这条小路穿过一片树林后与大路交汇。

re·join² /rɪˈdʒɔɪn/ *verb* **+ speech** | **~ that...** (*formal*) to say sth as an answer, especially sth quick, critical or amusing 回答；反驳 **SYN** **retort**：*'You're wrong!' she rejoined.* "你错了！" 她反驳道。

re·join·der /rɪˈdʒɔɪndə(r)/ *noun* [usually sing.] (*formal*) a reply, especially a quick, critical or amusing one 回答；反驳 **SYN** **retort**

re·ju·ven·ate /rɪˈdʒuːvəneɪt/ *verb* **~ sb/sth** to make sb/sth look or feel younger, more lively or more modern 使年轻；使更有活力；使更新潮 ▸ **re·ju·ven·ation** /rɪˌdʒuːvəˈneɪʃn/ *noun* [U]

re·kin·dle /ˌriːˈkɪndl/ *verb* **~ sth** (*formal*) to make sth become active again 使重新活跃；使复苏 **SYN** **reawaken**：*to rekindle feelings/hopes* 再次引发感情；重新点燃希望

re·lapse *noun, verb*

■ ***noun*** /rɪˈlæps; ˈriːlæps/ [C, U] the fact of becoming ill/sick again after making an improvement 旧病复发：*to have/suffer a relapse* 旧病复发 ◇ *a risk of relapse* 旧病复发的危险 ➲ WORDFINDER NOTE AT HEALTH

■ ***verb*** /rɪˈlæps/ [I] **~ (into sth)** to go back into a previous condition or into a worse state after making an improvement 退回原状；（好转后）再倒退：*They relapsed into silence.* 他们又都沉默不语。◇ *He relapsed into his old bad habits.* 他重染恶习。◇ *Two days after leaving the hospital she relapsed into a coma.* 出院两天后，她再度昏迷。

re·late 🔑 /rɪˈleɪt/ *verb* **1** 🔑 show or make a connection between two or more things 联系；使有联系；把…联系起来 **SYN** **connect**：**~ sth** *I found it difficult to relate the two ideas in my mind.* 我觉得很难把这两种想法联系在一起。◇ **~ A to B** *In the future, pay increases will be related to productivity.* 以后，工资的上涨将和业绩挂钩。**2** 🔑 (*formal*) to give a spoken or written report of sth; to tell a story 叙述；讲述；讲（故事）：**~ sth** *She relates her childhood experiences in the first chapters.* 在开始的几章中，她叙述了自己童年的经历。◇ **~ sth to sb** *He related the facts of the case to journalists.* 他给记者们讲述了这件事的实际情况。◇ **~ how, what, etc....** *She related how he had run away from home as a boy.* 她追述了他小时候是如何离家出走的。◇ **~ that...** *The story relates that an angel appeared and told him to sing.* 这个故事讲述一个天使现身，叫他唱歌。

PHR V **reˈlate to sth/sb** **1** 🔑 to be connected with sth/sb; to refer to sth/sb 涉及；与…相关；谈到：*We shall discuss the problem as it relates to our specific case.* 我们应针对我们的具体情况来讨论这个问题。◇ *The second paragraph relates to the situation in Scotland.* 第二段谈到苏格兰的形势。**2** 🔑 to be able to understand and have sympathy with sb/sth 能够理解并同情；了解；体恤 **SYN** **empathize**：*Many adults can't relate to children.* 许多成年人并不了解儿童的想法。◇ *Our product needs an image that people can relate to.* 我们的产品需要一个大家能理解的形象。

re·lated 🔑 /rɪˈleɪtɪd/ *adj.* **1** 🔑 **~ (to sth/sb)** connected with sth/sb in some way 相关的；有联系的：*Much of the crime in this area is related to drug abuse.* 这一地区的许多犯罪都与吸毒有关。◇ *These problems are* ***closely related.*** 这些问题都是密切相关的。◇ *a* ***related issue/question*** 相关的议题 / 问题 ◇ *a stress-related illness* 压力导致的疾病 **2** 🔑 **~ (to sth/sb)** in the same family 属同一家族的；有亲属关系的：*Are you related to Margaret?* 你与玛格丽特是一家人吗？◇ *We're distantly related.* 我们是远亲。**3** 🔑 **~ (to sth)** belonging to the same group 属于同一种类的；同一组别的：*related languages* 同系语言 ◇ *The llama is related to the camel.* 美洲驼和骆驼是亲缘物种。**OPP** **unrelated** ▸ **re·lated·ness** *noun* [U]

re·la·tion 🔑 /rɪˈleɪʃn/ *noun* **1** 🔑 **relations** [pl.] the way in which two people, groups or countries behave towards each other or deal with each other（人、团体、国家之间的）关系，联系，交往：***diplomatic/international/foreign relations*** 外交 / 国际 / 对外关系 ◇ *US-Chinese relations* 美中关系 ◇ *teacher-pupil relations* 师生关系 ◇ **~ (with sb/sth)** *Relations with neighbouring countries are under strain at present.* 目前，与邻国的关系正处于紧张状态。◇ **~ (between A and B)** *We seek to improve relations between our two countries.* 我们寻求改进我们两国间的关系。◇ (*formal*) *to have* ***sexual relations*** (= to have sex) 发生性关系 ➲ COLLOCATIONS AT INTERNATIONAL ➲ SEE ALSO INDUSTRIAL RELATIONS, PUBLIC RELATIONS, RACE RELATIONS **2** 🔑 [U, C] the way in which two or more things are connected（事物之间的）关系，关联，联系：**~ between A and B** *the relation between rainfall and crop yields* 降雨量和农作物产量之间的关系 ◇ **~ to sth** *the relation of the farmer to the land* 农民和土地的关系 ◇ *The fee they are offering* ***bears no relation to*** *the amount of work involved.* 他们支付的酬金和所需的工作量无关。◇ (*formal*) *I have some comments to make* ***in relation to*** (= concerning) *this matter.* 关于这件事我有几点看法。◇ *Its brain is small* ***in relation to*** (= compared with) *its body.* 和它的身体相比，它的大脑很小。**3** 🔑 [C] a person who is in the same family as sb else 亲戚；亲属 **SYN** **relative**：*a* ***close/near/distant relation*** *of mine* 我的一个近亲 / 远亲 ◇ *a relation by marriage* 姻亲 ◇ *a party for friends and relations* 亲戚朋友的聚会 ◇ *He's called Brady too, but we're* ***no relation*** (= not related). 他也叫布雷迪，但我们不是亲戚。◇ *Is he any relation to you?* 他是你的什么亲戚吗？➲ WORDFINDER NOTE AT FAMILY ➲ SEE ALSO BLOOD RELATION, POOR RELATION

WORDFINDER 联想词：ancestor, branch, descent, dynasty, family tree, genealogy, generation, inherit, trace

re·la·tion·al /rɪˈleɪʃənl/ *adj.* (*formal* or *specialist*) existing or considered in relation to sth else 有关的；相关的

reˌlational ˈdatabase *noun* (*computing* 计) a DATABASE that recognizes relationships between different pieces of information 关系数据库

re·la·tion·ship 🔑 /rɪˈleɪʃnʃɪp/ *noun* **1** 🔑 [C] the way in which two people, groups or countries behave towards each other or deal with each other（人、团体、国家之间的）关系，联系：**~ (between A and B)** *The relationship between the police and the local community has improved.* 警察和当地民众之间的关系已经得到改善。◇ **~ (with sb)** *She has a very* ***close relationship*** *with her sister.* 她和她妹妹

非常亲密。◇ *I have established a good **working relationship** with my boss.* 我与老板已经建立起良好的工作关系。◇ *a master-servant relationship* 主仆关系 ➲ SEE ALSO LOVE-HATE RELATIONSHIP ➲ WORDFINDER NOTE AT ALLY **2** [C] ~ **(between A and B)** | ~ **(with sb)** a loving and/or sexual friendship between two people 情爱关系；性爱关系：*Their affair did not develop into a lasting relationship.* 他们的暧昧关系未能发展成为持久的爱情。◇ *She's had a series of miserable relationships.* 她经历了一次又一次的恋爱波折。◇ *Are you **in a relationship**?* 你在恋爱吗？ ➲ WORDFINDER NOTE AT LOVE **3** [C, U] the way in which two or more things are connected（事物之间的）关联，联系，关系：~ **(between A and B)** *the relationship between mental and physical health* 精神健康和身体健康之间的关系 ◇ ~ **(to sth)** *This comment **bore no relationship to** the subject of our conversation.* 这个意见与我们所谈论的话题毫不相干。◇ *People alter their voices **in relationship to** background noise.* 人们根据环境噪音的大小调节自己的声音。**4** [C, U] the way in which a person is related to sb else in a family 血缘关系；姻亲关系：*a father-son relationship* 父子关系 ◇ ~ **between A and B** *I'm not sure of the exact relationship between them—I think they're cousins.* 我不太清楚他们之间的确切关系，我想他们是表亲吧。

rela·tive /ˈrelətɪv/ *adj., noun*

▪ ***adj.*** **1** considered and judged by being compared with sth else 相比较而言的；比较的：*the **relative merits** of the two plans* 相比较之下两个计划各自的优点 **2** ~ **(to sth)** considered according to its position or connection with sth else 相对的；相关联的：*the position of the sun relative to the earth* 太阳与地球的相对位置 **3** [only before noun] that exists or that has a particular quality only when compared with sth else 相比之下存在（或有）的 SYN **comparative**：*They now live in relative comfort* (= compared with how they lived before). 他们现在过得比较舒适。◇ *Given the failure of the previous plan, this turned out to be a relative success.* 由于前面那个计划失败了，这个计划算是比较成功的。◇ ***It's all relative** though, isn't it? We never had any money when I was a kid and $500 was a fortune to us.* 不过，一切都是相对的，不是吗？我小的时候，我们根本没有钱，500 美元对于我们来说就是很大的一笔钱了。➲ COMPARE ABSOLUTE *adj.* (6) **4** ~ **to sth** (*formal*) having a connection with sth; referring to sth 关于（或涉及）…的：*the facts relative to the case* 与这个案件有关的事实 **5** (*grammar* 语法) referring to an earlier noun, sentence or part of a sentence（指代前面的名词、句子或句子的一部分）：*In 'the man who came', 'who' is a **relative pronoun** and 'who came' is a **relative clause**.* 在 the man who came 中，who 是关系代词，而 who came 是关系从句。

▪ ***noun*** **1** a person who is in the same family as sb else 亲戚；亲属 SYN **relation**：*a close/distant relative* 近亲；远亲 ◇ *her friends and relatives* 她的亲友 **2** a thing that belongs to the same group as sth else 同类事物：*The ibex is a distant relative of the mountain goat.* 北山羊与石山羊有较远的亲缘关系。

ˌrelative atomic ˈmass (*also* **aˌtomic ˈmass**, **aˌtomic ˈweight**) *noun* (*chemistry* 化) the average MASS of all the naturally occurring atoms of a chemical element 相对原子质量

ˌrelative ˈdensity (*also* **speˌcific ˈgravity**) *noun* [U] (*chemistry* 化) the mass of a substance divided by the mass of the same volume of water or air 相对密度

rela·tive·ly /ˈrelətɪvli/ *adv.* to a fairly large degree, especially in comparison to sth else 相当程度上；相当地；相对地：*I found the test relatively easy.* 我觉得这次测验比较容易。◇ *We had relatively few applications for the job.* 申请我们这项工作的人相对较少。◇ *Lack of exercise is also a risk factor for heart disease but it's relatively small when compared with the others.* 缺乏锻炼也是导致心脏病的一个因素。但和其他因素相比危险较小。

IDM **ˈrelatively speaking** used when you are comparing sth with all similar things（和所有类似事物比较）相对而言：*Relatively speaking, these jobs provide good salaries.* 相对来说，这些工作报酬都不低。

rela·tiv·ism /ˈrelətɪvɪzəm/ *noun* [U] (*formal*) the belief that truth is not always and generally valid, but can be judged only in relation to other things, such as your personal situation 相对主义（认为真理并非绝对的，只能根据其他事物加以判断） ▶ **rela·tiv·ist** *adj.*：*a relativist view* 相对主义观点 **rela·tiv·ist** *noun*

rela·tiv·ity /ˌreləˈtɪvəti/ *noun* [U] **1** (*physics* 物) Einstein's theory of the universe based on the principle that all movement is relative and that time is a fourth DIMENSION related to space 相对论 **2** (*formal*) the state of being relative and only able to be judged when compared with sth else 相对性

re·launch /ˌriːˈlɔːntʃ/ *verb* ~ **sth** to start or present sth again in a new or different way, especially a product for sale 重新推出；重新发布 ▶ **re·launch** /ˈriːlɔːntʃ/ *noun*

relax AW /rɪˈlæks/ *verb* **1** [I] to rest while you are doing sth enjoyable, especially after work or effort 放松；休息 SYN **unwind**：*Just relax and enjoy the movie.* 休息休息，看看电影吧。◇ *I'm going to spend the weekend just relaxing.* 这个周末，我什么也不干，就是休息。◇ ~ **with sth** *When I get home from work I like to relax with the newspaper.* 我下班回到家里，喜欢看看报纸，放松一下。**2** [I, T] ~ **(sb)** to become or make sb become calmer and less worried 宽慰；（使）冷静，放心，镇定：*I'll only relax when I know you're safe.* 我只有知道你安然无恙才会放心。◇ *Relax! Everything will be OK.* 别着急！一切都会好的。**3** [I, T] to become or make sth become less tight or stiff （使）放松，松懈；松开：*Allow your muscles to relax completely.* 让你的肌肉完全放松。◇ ~ **sth** *The massage relaxed my tense back muscles.* 按摩使得我背部紧张的肌肉松弛下来。◇ *He **relaxed his grip** on her arm.* 他本来抓着她的胳膊，现在松开了手。◇ (*figurative*) *The dictator refuses to relax his grip on power.* 独裁者拒绝放松对权力的控制。**4** [T] ~ **sth** to allow rules, laws, etc. to become less strict 放宽（限制等）：*The council has relaxed the ban on dogs in city parks.* 政务委员会已经放宽了对带狗到市内公园里去的禁令。**5** [T] ~ **sth** to allow your attention or effort to become weaker 放松精神（或思想）：*You cannot afford to relax your concentration for a moment.* 你必须集中精力，一刻都不能松懈。

re·lax·ant /rɪˈlæksənt/ *noun* (*medical* 医) a drug that is used to make the body relax 松弛药：*a muscle relaxant* 肌肉松弛药

re·lax·ation AW /ˌriːlækˈseɪʃn/ *noun* **1** [U] ways of resting and enjoying yourself; time spent resting and enjoying yourself 放松；休息；消遣；用于放松消遣的时间：*I go hill-walking for relaxation.* 我要是想放松一下，就到山上走走。◇ *a few days of relaxation* 几天的休息时间 ◇ *relaxation techniques* 放松的方法 ➲ SYNONYMS AT ENTERTAINMENT **2** [C] something pleasant that you do in order to rest, especially after you have been working 休闲活动；娱乐活动：*Fishing is his favourite relaxation.* 钓鱼是他最喜欢的消遣活动。**3** [U, C, usually sing.] the act of making a rule or some form of control less strict or severe（对规章制度的）放宽，放松：*the relaxation of foreign currency controls* 对外汇管制的放宽 ◇ *a relaxation of travel restrictions* 旅游限制的放宽

re·laxed AW /rɪˈlækst/ *adj.* **1** ~ **(about sth)** (of a person 人) calm and not anxious or worried 放松的；冷静的；镇定的：*He appeared relaxed and confident before the match.* 比赛前，他显得镇定而自信。◇ *She had a very relaxed manner.* 她的举止特别自然。**2** (of a place 地方) calm and informal 安静的；自在的：*a family-run hotel with a **relaxed atmosphere*** 家庭经营的旅店，气氛自由随便 **3** ~ **(about sth)** not caring too much about discipline or making people follow rules 不加以拘束的 SYN **laid-back**：*I take a fairly **relaxed attitude** towards what the kids wear to school.* 孩子穿什么上学，我觉得无所谓。

re·lax·ing AW /rɪˈlæksɪŋ/ *adj.* helping you to rest and become less anxious 有助于休息的；令人放松的；轻松的：*a relaxing evening with friends* 和朋友在一起的轻松夜晚

relay *verb, noun*

■ ***verb*** /ˈriːleɪ; rɪˈleɪ/ **1 ~ sth (to sb)** to receive and send on information, news, etc. to sb 转发（信息、消息等）: *He relayed the message to his boss.* 他将这个消息转给了他的老板。◇ *Instructions were relayed to him by phone.* 通过电话将指令转达给了他。 **2 ~ sth (to sb)** to broadcast television or radio signals 播放，转播（电视或广播信号）: *The game was relayed by satellite to audiences all over the world.* 这场比赛通过卫星向全世界的观众进行了转播。

■ ***noun*** /ˈriːleɪ/ **1** (*also* **ˈrelay race**) a race between teams in which each member of the team runs or swims one section of the race 接力赛: *the 4 × 100m relay* * 4 × 100 米接力赛 ◇ *a relay team* 接力队 ◇ *the sprint relay* 短跑接力赛 **2** a fresh set of people or animals that take the place of others that are tired or have finished a period of work 接班的人（或动物）；轮换者: *Rescuers worked **in relays** to save the trapped miners.* 救援人员轮班营救受困的矿工。 **3** an electronic device that receives radio or television signals and sends them on again with greater strength 中继设备: *a relay station* 中继站

re·lease 🔑 AW /rɪˈliːs/ *verb, noun*

■ ***verb***

• **SET SB/STH FREE** 释放 **1** 🔑 to let sb/sth come out of a place where they have been kept or trapped 释放；放出；放走: **~ sb/sth** *to **release a prisoner/hostage*** 释放囚犯 / 人质 ◇ **~ sb/sth from sth** *Firefighters took two hours to release the driver from the wreckage.* 消防队员花了两个小时将司机从汽车残骸中救出来。

• **STOP HOLDING STH** 松开 **2** 🔑 **~ sth** to stop holding sth or stop it from being held so that it can move, fly, fall, etc. freely 放开；松开；使自由移动（或飞翔、降落等） SYN **let go, let loose**: *He refused to release her arm.* 他不肯放开她的胳膊。◇ *10 000 balloons were released at the ceremony.* 典礼上放飞了一万个气球。◇ *Intense heat is released in the reaction.* 反应过程中产生高热。

• **FEELINGS** 情感 **3** 🔑 **~ sth** to express feelings such as anger or worry in order to get rid of them 发泄；宣泄: *She burst into tears, releasing all her pent-up emotions.* 她放声大哭，发泄出全部郁积起来的情感。

• **FREE SB FROM DUTY** 免除职责 **4** to free sb from a duty, responsibility, contract, etc. 免除，解除（某人的职责、责任、合同等）；解雇: **~ sb** *The club is releasing some of its older players.* 俱乐部正在解聘一些老队员。◇ **~ sb from sth** *The new law released employers from their obligation to recognize unions.* 新的法律免除了雇主承认工会的义务。

• **PART OF MACHINE** 机器部件 **5** 🔑 **~ sth** to remove sth from a fixed position, allowing sth else to move or function 松开；拉开: *to **release the clutch/handbrake/switch, etc.*** 松开离合器、手闸、开关等

• **MAKE LESS TIGHT** 使不紧张 **6 ~ sth** to make sth less tight 使不紧张；使松弛；放松: *You need to release the tension in these shoulder muscles.* 你需要放松肩部肌肉。

• **MAKE AVAILABLE** 使可获得 **7** 🔑 **~ sth** to make sth available to the public 公开；公布；发布: *Police have released no further details about the accident.* 关于这次事故，警方没有透露更多的细节。◇ *to release a movie/book/CD* 发行电影 / 书 / CD ◇ *new products released onto the market* 投放到市场的新产品 **8 ~ sth** to make sth available that had previously been restricted 开放；放开；解禁: *The new building programme will go ahead as soon as the government releases the funds.* 政府一拨付资金，新的建筑项目就动工。

■ ***noun***

• **SETTING SB/STH FREE** 释放 **1** 🔑 [U, sing.] **~ (of sb) (from sth)** the act of setting a person or an animal free; the state of being set free 释放；获释: *The government has been working to secure the release of the hostages.* 政府一直在努力争取使人质获释。◇ *She can expect an early release from prison.* 她有望早一点出狱。

• **MAKING STH AVAILABLE** 使可得到 **2** 🔑 [U, sing.] the act of making sth available to the public 公开；发行；发布: *The new software is planned for release in April.* 新软件计划四月份发行。◇ *The movie **goes on general release*** (= will be widely shown in cinemas/movie theaters) *next week.* 这部电影将于下周公开上映。 **3** 🔑 [C] a thing that is made available to the public, especially a new CD or film/movie 新发行的东西；（尤指）新激光唱片，新电影: *the latest new releases* 最新发行的产品

• **OF GAS/CHEMICAL** 气体；化学品 **4** 🔑 [U, C] the act of letting a gas, chemical, etc. come out of the container where it has been safely held 排放；泄漏；渗漏: *the release of carbon dioxide into the atmosphere* 二氧化碳向大气层的排放 ◇ *to monitor radiation releases* 监测辐射的释放

• **FROM UNPLEASANT FEELING** 不愉快的感觉 **5** [U, sing.] the feeling that you are free from pain, anxiety or some other unpleasant feeling 解脱；轻松感: *a sense of release after the exam* 考试后的解脱感 ◇ *I think her death was a merciful release.* 我认为她的死是一种幸运的解脱。 ⮌ SEE ALSO PRESS RELEASE

rele·gate /ˈrelɪɡeɪt/ *verb* **1 ~ sb/sth (to sth)** to give sb a lower or less important position, rank, etc. than before 使贬职；使降级；降低…的地位: *She was then relegated to the role of assistant.* 随后她被降级做助手了。◇ *He relegated the incident to the back of his mind.* 他将这个事件抛到了脑后。 **2** [usually passive] **~ sth** (*especially BrE*) to move a sports team, especially a football (SOCCER) team, to a lower position within an official league 使（运动队，尤指足球队）降级；使降组 OPP **promote** ▶ **rele·ga·tion** /ˌrelɪˈɡeɪʃn/ *noun* [U]: *teams threatened with relegation* 有降级危险的球队

re·lent /rɪˈlent/ *verb* (*formal*) **1** [I] to finally agree to sth after refusing 终于答应；不再拒绝 SYN **give in (to sb/sth)**: *'Well, just for a little while then,' she said, finally relenting.* "好吧，不过只能待一会儿。"她最后终于答应了。 **2** [I] to become less determined, strong, etc. 变缓和；变温和；减弱: *After two days the rain relented.* 两天后，雨势减弱了。◇ *The police will not relent in their fight against crime.* 警方将继续严厉打击犯罪活动。

re·lent·less /rɪˈlentləs/ *adj.* **1** not stopping or getting less strong 不停的；持续强烈的；不减弱的 SYN **unrelenting**: *her **relentless pursuit of** perfection* 她对完美的不懈追求 ◇ *The sun was relentless.* 太阳还是那么热。 **2** refusing to give up or be less strict or severe 不放弃的；严格的；苛刻的；无情的: *a relentless enemy* 残酷的敌人 ▶ **re·lent·less·ly** *adv.*

rele·vant 🔑 AW /ˈreləvənt/ *adj.* **1** 🔑 closely connected with the subject you are discussing or the situation you are thinking about 紧密相关的；切题的: *a relevant suggestion/question/point* 相关的提议 / 问题 / 观点 ◇ *Do you have the relevant experience?* 你有相关的经验吗？◇ **~ to sth/sb** *These comments are not directly relevant to this inquiry.* 这些意见与这项调查没有直接联系。 OPP **irrelevant** **2** 🔑 **~ (to sth/sb)** having ideas that are valuable and useful to people in their lives and work 有价值的；有意义的: *Her novel is still relevant today.* 她的小说今天仍有现实意义。 ▶ **rele·vance** AW /-əns/ *noun* [U]: *I don't see the relevance of your question.* 我不懂你这个问题有什么意义。◇ *What he said has no direct relevance to the matter in hand.* 他所说的话与眼下的事没有直接关系。◇ *a classic play of contemporary relevance* 在当代仍有价值的古典戏剧 **rele·vant·ly** *adv.* : *The applicant has experience in teaching and, more relevantly, in industry.* 这名申请者有教学经验，更重要的是，还有行业经验。

re·li·able AW /rɪˈlaɪəbl/ *adj.* **1** that can be trusted to do sth well; that you can rely on 可信赖的；可依靠的 SYN **dependable**: *We are looking for someone who is reliable and hard-working.* 我们在物色可靠而又勤奋的人。◇ *a reliable friend* 可信赖的朋友 **2** that is likely to be correct or true 真实可信的；可靠的: *Our information comes from a reliable source.* 我们的消息来源可靠。◇ *a reliable witness* 可信的目击证人 **3** able to work or operate for long periods without breaking down or needing attention 性能可靠的；稳定耐用的: *My car's not as reliable as it used to be.* 我的车不像过去那样耐用了。 OPP **unreliable** ▶ **re·li·abil·ity** AW /rɪˌlaɪəˈbɪləti/ *noun* [U]: *The incident cast doubt on her motives and reliability.* 这件事使人怀疑她有何动机，以及她是否可靠。◇ *The reliability of these results has been questioned.* 这些结果的可信程度已受到质疑。 **re·li·ably** AW /-əbli/ *adv.* : *I am **reliably informed***

R

(= told by sb who knows the facts) *that the company is being sold.* 有可靠知情人告诉我公司要被卖掉。

re·li·ance AW /rɪˈlaɪəns/ *noun* [U, sing.] ~ (**on/upon sb/sth**) the state of needing sb/sth in order to survive, be successful, etc.; the fact of being able to rely on sb/sth 依赖；依靠；信任 SYN **dependence**: *Heavy reliance on one client is risky when you are building up a business.* 创业时过分依赖某一个客户是有风险的。◇ *Such learning methods encourage too great a reliance upon the teacher.* 这样的学习方法会造成对老师的过分依赖。◇ *The study programme concentrates more on group work and* ***places*** *less* ***reliance on*** (= depends less on) *lectures.* 这个学习计划较注重小组活动而不倚重讲座。◇ *I wouldn't* ***place*** *too much* ***reliance on*** (= trust) *these figures.* 我不会太相信这些数字的。

re·li·ant AW /rɪˈlaɪənt/ *adj.* ~ **on/upon sb/sth** needing sb/sth in order to survive, be successful, etc. 依赖性的；依靠的 SYN **dependent**: *The hostel is heavily reliant upon charity.* 这家收容所在很大程度上依赖赞助。➲ SEE ALSO SELF-RELIANT

relic /ˈrelɪk/ *noun* **1** ~ (**of/from sth**) an object, a tradition, a system, etc. that has survived from the past 遗物；遗迹；遗风；遗俗: *The building stands as the last remaining relic of the town's cotton industry.* 这座建筑物是小镇棉纺业仅存的遗迹。◇ *Videotapes may already seem like relics of a bygone era.* 录像带似乎已成为过去时代的遗物。**2** a part of the body or clothing of a holy person, or sth that they owned, that is kept after their death and respected as a religious object 圣髑；圣骨；圣人遗物: *holy relics* 圣人遗物

re·lief 🔑 /rɪˈliːf/ *noun*

• **REMOVAL OF ANXIETY/PAIN** 焦虑 / 痛苦的消除 **1** 🔑 [U, sing.] the feeling of happiness that you have when sth unpleasant stops or does not happen（不快过后的）宽慰，轻松；解脱: *a sense of relief* 解脱感 ◇ *We all* ***breathed a sigh of relief*** *when he left.* 他走了以后，我们大家都如释重负地松了口气。◇ *She sighed with relief.* 她松了口气。◇ ***Much to my relief*** *the car was not damaged.* 令我非常庆幸的是车并没有损坏。◇ *News of their safety came as a great relief.* 他们平安的消息给大家带来了巨大的安慰。◇ *It was a relief to be able to talk to someone about it.* 能和别人谈谈这件事，感到舒心多了。◇ ***What a relief!*** 可轻松了！**2** 🔑 [U] ~ (**from/of sth**) the act of removing or reducing pain, anxiety, etc.（焦虑、痛苦等的）减轻，消除，缓和: *modern methods of* ***pain relief*** 消除疼痛的新办法 ◇ *the relief of suffering* 痛苦的消除

• **HELP** 帮助 **3** 🔑 [U] food, money, medicine, etc. that is given to help people in places where there has been a war or natural disaster（给灾区或交战地区人民提供的）救济，救援物品 SYN **aid**: ***famine relief*** 饥荒救济物资 ◇ *a* ***relief agency/organization/worker*** 救助机构 / 组织 / 工作者 **4** 🔑 [U] (*especially NAmE*) financial help given by the government to people who need it 救济金

• **ON TAX** 税收 **5** [U] = TAX RELIEF: *relief on mortgage interest payments* 支付按揭利息的税收减免

• **STH DIFFERENT** 变化 **6** 🔑 [U, sing.] something that is interesting or enjoyable that replaces sth boring, difficult or unpleasant for a short period of time（暂时替代单调乏味事物的）调剂，轻松场面: *a few moments of* ***light relief*** *in an otherwise dull performance* 沉闷的表演中几处轻松的情节 ◇ *There was little* ***comic relief*** *in his speech.* 他的演讲少有轻松幽默的地方。◇ ~ **from sth** *The calm of the countryside came as a welcome relief from the hustle and bustle of city life.* 离开喧嚣忙碌的城市生活，来到宁静的乡村，是一种令人愉快的调剂。

• **WORKERS** 工人 **7** [C+sing./pl. v.] (often used as an adjective 常用作形容词) a person or group of people that replaces another when they have finished working for the day or when they are sick 替班者；接替人；换班者: *The next crew relief comes on duty at 9 o'clock.* 下一批换班的员工 9 点钟接班。◇ *relief drivers* 换班的司机

• **FROM ENEMY** 从敌人手中 **8** [sing.] ~ **of...** the act of freeing a town, etc. from an enemy army that has surrounded it（被困城镇等的）解困，解围

• **IN ART** 艺术 **9** [U, C] a way of decorating wood, stone, etc. by cutting designs into the surface of it so that some parts stick out more than others; a design that is made in this way 浮雕；浮雕法；浮雕作品: *The column was decorated* ***in high relief*** (= with designs that stick out a lot) *with scenes from Greek mythology.* 柱子上饰有描述希腊神话中的场面的高浮雕。◇ *The bronze doors are covered with sculpted reliefs.* 青铜门上覆有浮雕。➲ VISUAL VOCAB PAGE V14 ➲ SEE ALSO BAS-RELIEF

• **MAKING STH NOTICEABLE** 使醒目 **10** [U] the effect of colours, light, etc. that makes an object more noticeable than others around it（光和色彩等产生的）醒目效果；醒目；光彩夺目: *The snow-capped mountain stood out* ***in sharp relief*** *against the blue sky.* 白雪覆盖的高山在蓝天的映衬下格外醒目。**11** [U] the quality of a particular situation, problem, etc. that makes it more noticeable than before 突出的品质；令人注目的特征: *Their differences have been* ***thrown into sharp relief*** *by the present crisis.* 目前的危机使得他们的分歧更加引人注目。

reˈlief map *noun* a map that uses various colours, etc. to show the different heights of hills, valleys, etc.（用不同颜色表示地势高低的）地形图，地势图，地貌图

reˈlief road *noun* (*BrE*) a road that vehicles can use to avoid an area of heavy traffic, especially a road built for this purpose（交通高峰时减缓拥挤的）疏导路，旁道

re·lieve /rɪˈliːv/ *verb* **1** ~ **sth** to remove or reduce an unpleasant feeling or pain 解除，减轻，缓和（不快或痛苦）: *to relieve the symptoms of a cold* 减轻感冒的症状 ◇ *to* ***relieve anxiety/guilt/stress*** 消除焦虑 / 内疚；缓解压力 ◇ *Being able to tell the truth at last seemed to relieve her.* 最后能够讲出真话似乎使她感到轻松。**2** ~ **sth** to make a problem less serious 减轻（问题的严重性）；缓和；缓解 SYN **alleviate**: *efforts to relieve poverty* 缓解贫困的努力 ◇ *to relieve traffic congestion* 缓解交通拥堵 **3** ~ **sth** to make sth less boring, especially by introducing sth different 调剂；使有趣: *We played cards to relieve the boredom of the long wait.* 长时间等待实在无聊，我们就打扑克来解闷儿。◇ *The black and white pattern is relieved by tiny coloured flowers.* 五彩缤纷的小花使得黑白图案不那么单调。**4** ~ **sb** to replace sb who is on duty 接替；给…换班: *to relieve a sentry* 换岗 ◇ *You'll be relieved at six o'clock.* 六点钟有人来换你的班。**5** ~ **sth** to free a town, etc. from an enemy army that has surrounded it 将（城镇从敌人的围困中）解围 **6** ~ **yourself** a polite way of referring to going to the toilet（去厕所的一种委婉说法）方便，解手: *I had to relieve myself behind a bush.* 我只好在树丛后面方便了一下。

PHR V **reˈlieve sb of sth 1** to help sb by taking sth heavy or difficult from them 替…拿重物；帮助…减轻（负担）: *Let me relieve you of some of your bags.* 我来帮你拿几个袋子吧。◇ *The new secretary will relieve us of some of the paperwork.* 新来的秘书会减轻我们文案工作的一些负担。**2** (*informal, ironic*) to steal sth from sb 偷窃；窃取: *A boy with a knife relieved him of his wallet.* 一个持刀的家伙偷了他的钱包。**3** to dismiss sb from a job, position, etc. 开除；解除…的职务: *General Beale was relieved of his command.* 比尔将军被解除了指挥权。

re·lieved /rɪˈliːvd/ *adj.* feeling happy because sth unpleasant has stopped or has not happened; showing this 感到宽慰的；放心的；显得开心的: *She sounded relieved.* 她听上去很放心。◇ ~ (**to see, hear, find, etc. sth**) *You'll be relieved to know your jobs are safe.* 现在知道你们的工作保住了，可以放心了。◇ ~ (**that...**) *I'm just relieved that nobody was hurt.* 谁都没有受伤，我深感宽慰。◇ *They exchanged relieved glances.* 他们如释重负地彼此看了看。➲ SYNONYMS AT GLAD

re·li·gion 🔑 /rɪˈlɪdʒən/ *noun* **1** 🔑 [U] the belief in the existence of a god or gods, and the activities that are connected with the worship of them, or in the teachings of a spiritual leader 宗教；宗教信仰；精神信仰: *Is there always a conflict between science and religion?* 科学和宗教信仰之间是否永远存在着冲突？**2** 🔑 [C] one of the systems of faith that are based on the belief in the existence of a particular god or gods, or in the teachings of a spiritual leader 宗教；教派: *the Jewish religion* 犹太教 ◇

R

Christianity, Islam and other world religions 基督教、伊斯兰教和其他世界性宗教 ◇ *The law states that everyone has the right to practise their own religion.* 法律规定每个人都有信仰宗教的权利。 **3** [sing.] a particular interest or influence that is very important in your life 特别的兴趣；重大的影响：*For him, football is an absolute religion.* 对于他来说，足球就是他至高无上的追求。

IDM **get re'ligion** (*informal, disapproving*) to suddenly start believing in a religion 突然有了信仰；突然开始信教

re·ligi·os·ity /rɪˌlɪdʒiˈɒsəti; *NAmE* -ˈɑːsəti/ *noun* [U] (*formal, sometimes disapproving*) the state of being religious or too religious 笃信宗教；过度的宗教热忱

re·li·gious /rɪˈlɪdʒəs/ *adj.* **1** [only before noun] connected with religion or with a particular religion 宗教信仰的；宗教的：***religious beliefs/faith*** 宗教信仰；信德 ◇ ***religious education*** (= education about religion) 宗教教育 ◇ ***religious instruction*** (= instruction in a particular religion) 教义讲授 ◇ *religious groups* 宗教团体 ◇ *objects which have a religious significance* 圣物 **2** (of a person 人) believing strongly in a particular religion and obeying its laws and practices 笃信宗教的；虔诚的 **SYN** **devout**：*His wife is very religious.* 他的妻子非常虔诚。 ▸ **re·li·gious·ness** *noun* [U]

re·li·gious·ly /rɪˈlɪdʒəsli/ *adv.* **1** very carefully or regularly 十分认真地；审慎地；很有规律地：*She followed the instructions religiously.* 她非常认真地按照说明操作。 **2** in a way that is connected with religion 与宗教相关地；虔诚地：*Were you brought up religiously?* 你是在宗教的氛围中长大的吗？

re·lin·quish /rɪˈlɪŋkwɪʃ/ *verb* (*formal*) to stop having sth, especially when this happens unwillingly（尤指不情愿地）放弃 **SYN** **give sth↔up**：**~ sth** *He was forced to relinquish control of the company.* 他被迫放弃对公司的控制权。◇ *They had relinquished all hope that she was alive.* 他们已经完全不指望她还活着了。 ◇ **~ sth to sb** *She relinquished possession of the house to her sister.* 她将房子让给了她的妹妹。

reli·quary /ˈrelɪkwəri; *NAmE* -kweri/ *noun* (*pl.* **-ies**) a container in which a RELIC of a holy person is kept 圣髑盒；盛放圣人遗物的容器

rel·ish /ˈrelɪʃ/ *verb, noun*

■ ***verb*** to get great pleasure from sth; to want very much to do or have sth 享受；从…获得乐趣；渴望；喜欢 **SYN** **enjoy**：**~ sth** *to relish a fight/challenge/debate* 喜欢打架 / 挑战 / 争辩 ◇ *to relish the idea/thought of sth* 欣赏某种观点 / 想法 ◇ ***I don't relish the prospect*** *of getting up early tomorrow.* 我可不愿意明天早上早起。 ◇ **~ (sb/sth) doing sth** *Nobody relishes cleaning the oven.* 没有人喜欢清理烤炉。

■ ***noun*** **1** [U] great enjoyment or pleasure 享受；乐趣：*She savoured the moment* ***with obvious relish.*** 她显然津津有味地回味着那一刻。 **2** [U, C] a cold thick spicy sauce made from fruit and vegetables that have been boiled, that is served with meat, cheese, etc. 风味佐料（用水果和蔬菜煮后制成的冷稠酱汁）

re·live /ˌriːˈlɪv/ *verb* **~ sth** to experience sth again, especially in your imagination（尤指在想象中）再次体验，重温；回味：*He relives the horror of the crash every night in his dreams.* 每天晚上他都会梦见那次撞车的可怕情景。

rel·lie /ˈreli/ *noun* (*AustralE, NZE, informal*) a relative 亲戚；亲眷：*All the rellies will be at the party.* 所有亲戚都会来参加聚会。

▼ **COLLOCATIONS** 词语搭配

Religion 宗教

Being religious 笃信宗教的

- **believe in** God/Christ/Allah/free will/predestination/heaven and hell/an afterlife/reincarnation 信仰上帝 / 耶稣基督 / 真主 / 自由意志 / 宿命论 / 天堂与地狱 / 来生 / 转世说
- **be**/**become** a believer/an atheist/an agnostic/a Christian/Muslim/Hindu/Buddhist, etc. 是 / 成为信徒 / 无神论者 / 不可知论者 / 基督徒 / 穆斯林 / 印度教教徒 / 佛教徒等
- **convert to**/**practise**/(*especially US*) **practice** a religion/Buddhism/Catholicism/Christianity/Islam/Judaism, etc. 皈依 / 信奉宗教 / 佛教 / 天主教 / 基督教 / 伊斯兰教 / 犹太教等
- **go to** church/(*NAmE*) temple (= the synagogue) 去教堂 / 会堂做礼拜
- **go to** the local church/mosque/synagogue/gurdwara 去当地的教堂 / 清真寺 / 犹太教会堂 / 谒师所做礼拜
- **belong to** a church/a religious community 是教堂 / 宗教团体的成员
- **join**/**enter** the church/a convent/a monastery/a religious sect/the clergy/the priesthood 成为牧师 / 女修道士 / 僧侣 / 宗教人员 / 神职人员 / 司祭
- **praise**/**worship**/**obey**/**serve**/**glorify** God 赞美 / 敬拜 / 遵从 / 侍奉 / 颂扬上帝

Celebrations and ritual 庆典与仪式

- **attend**/**hold**/**conduct**/**lead** a service 参加 / 举行 / 组织 / 主持礼拜仪式
- **perform** a ceremony/a rite/a ritual/a baptism/the Hajj/a mitzvah 举行典礼 / 仪式 / 宗教仪式 / 洗礼 / 朝觐 / 受戒仪式
- **carry out**/**perform** a sacred/burial/funeral/fertility/purification rite 举行宗教 / 安葬 / 葬礼 / 丰收 / 净化仪式
- **go on**/**make** a pilgrimage 前往朝圣
- **celebrate** Christmas/Easter/Eid/Ramadan/Hanukkah/Passover/Diwali 庆祝圣诞节 / 复活节 / 开斋节 / 斋月 / 修殿节 / 逾越节 / 排灯节
- **observe**/**break** the Sabbath/a fast/Ramadan 守 / 不守安息日 / 斋戒 / 斋月
- **deliver**/**preach**/**hear** a sermon 传道；讲道；听布道
- **lead**/**address** the congregation 带领会众；对会众发表演讲
- **say**/**recite** a prayer/blessing 念诵 / 背诵经文；祝祷

Religious texts and ideas 宗教经文与思想

- **preach**/**proclaim**/**spread** the word of God/the Gospel/the message of Islam 传布 / 颂扬 / 传播上帝的话 / 《福音》/ 伊斯兰教义
- **study**/**follow** the dharma/the teachings of Buddha 研究 / 遵循达摩 / 佛教教义
- **read**/**study**/**understand**/**interpret** scripture/the Bible/the Koran/the gospel/the Torah 阅读 / 研究 / 理解 / 阐释经文 /《圣经》/《古兰经》/《福音》/ 托拉
- **be based on**/**derive from** divine revelation 基于 / 来源于上帝的启示
- **commit**/**consider sth** heresy/sacrilege 犯异端 / 渎圣罪；认为…是异端邪说 / 亵渎圣物

Religious belief and experience 宗教信仰与体验

- **seek**/**find**/**gain** enlightenment/wisdom 寻求 / 找到 / 获得启迪 / 智慧
- **strengthen**/**lose** your faith 增强 / 失去信德
- **keep**/**practise**/**practice**/**abandon** the faith 忠于 / 践行 / 放弃信仰
- **save**/**purify**/**lose** your soul 拯救 / 净化 / 失去灵魂
- **obey**/**follow**/**keep**/**break**/**violate** a commandment/Islamic law/Jewish law 服从 / 遵循 / 恪守 / 违反 / 亵渎诫条 / 伊斯兰教法 / 犹太教法
- **be**/**accept**/**do** God's will 是 / 接受 / 践行上帝的旨意
- **receive**/**experience** divine grace 得到 / 感受神的恩宠
- **achieve**/**attain** enlightenment/salvation/nirvana 获得启迪 / 拯救 / 涅槃
- **undergo** a conversion/rebirth/reincarnation 经历皈依 / 重生 / 转世化身
- **hear**/**answer** a prayer 聆听 / 回应祷告
- **commit**/**confess**/**forgive** a sin 犯罪；忏悔；宽恕罪过
- **do**/**perform** penance 进行补赎

re·load /ˌriːˈləʊd; *NAmE* -ˈloʊd/ *verb* **1** [I, T] ~ (**sth**) to put more bullets into a gun, more film into a camera, etc. 给…再装填（子弹或胶卷等） **2** [T] ~ **sth** to put data or a program into the memory of a computer again 给（计算机）重新装入（数据或程序） **3** [T] ~ **sth** to fill a container, vehicle, machine, etc. again 再装满（容器、车辆、机器等）

re·locate AW /ˌriːləʊˈkeɪt; *NAmE* ˌriːˈloʊkeɪt/ *verb* [I, T] (especially of a company or workers 尤指公司或工人) to move or to move sb/sth to a new place to work or operate （使）搬迁，迁移：*The firm may be forced to relocate from New York to Stanford.* 公司也许会被迫从纽约迁移到斯坦福。◇ ~ **sth** *The company relocated its head office to Stanford.* 公司将总部迁到了斯坦福。▶ **re·loca·tion** AW /ˌriːləʊˈkeɪʃn; *NAmE* ˌriːloʊ-/ *noun* [U]: *relocation costs* 搬迁费用

re·luc·tant AW /rɪˈlʌktənt/ *adj.* hesitating before doing sth because you do not want to do it or because you are not sure that it is the right thing to do 不情愿的；勉强的：*reluctant agreement* 勉强同意 ◇ ~ (**to do sth**) *She was reluctant to admit she was wrong.* 她不愿承认自己有错。◇ *He finally gave a reluctant smile.* 他最后露出了一丝无可奈何的微笑。◇ *a* ***reluctant hero*** (= a person who does not want to be called a hero) 不情愿做英雄的英雄 OPP eager ▶ **re·luc·tance** AW /-əns/ *noun* [U, sing.]: ~ (**to do sth**) *There is still some reluctance on the part of employers to become involved in this project.* 雇主们仍然不太愿意参与这项工程。◇ *They finally agreed to our terms with a certain reluctance.* 他们最终有点勉强地同意了我们的条件。**re·luc·tant·ly** AW *adv.* : *We reluctantly agreed to go with her.* 我们勉强答应跟她一起去。

rely 🔑 AW /rɪˈlaɪ/ *verb* (**re·lies**, **rely·ing**, **re·lied**, **re·lied**)

> **WORD FAMILY**
> rely *verb*
> reliable *adj.* (≠ unreliable)
> reliably *adv.*
> reliability *noun* (≠ unreliability)
> reliance *noun*

PHR V **reˈly on/upon sb/sth** **1** 🔑 to need or depend on sb/sth 依赖；依靠：*As babies, we rely entirely on others for food.* 在婴儿时期，我们完全依赖别人喂食。◇ **rely on/upon sb/sth to do sth** *These days we rely heavily on computers to organize our work.* 现在，我们在很大程度上依赖电脑来安排我们的工作。◇ **rely on/upon sb/sth doing sth** *The industry relies on the price of raw materials remaining low.* 这一产业靠的是原料便宜，不涨价。 **2** 🔑 to trust or have faith in sb/sth 信任；信赖：*You should rely on your own judgement.* 你应该相信你自己的判断。◇ **rely on/upon sb/sth to do sth** *You can rely on me to keep your secret.* 你可以相信我一定会为你保守秘密。◇ *He can't be relied on to tell the truth.* 不能指望他说真话。 ➲ SYNONYMS AT TRUST

REM /ˌɑːr iː ˈem/ *abbr.* rapid eye movement (describes a period of sleep during which you dream and your eyes make many small movements) 快速眼动（夜间做梦时眼睛快速而细微的移动） ➲ WORDFINDER NOTE AT SLEEP

re·made PAST TENSE, PAST PART. OF REMAKE

re·main 🔑 /rɪˈmeɪn/ *verb* (*rather formal*) (not usually used in the progressive tenses 通常不用于进行时) **1** 🔑 *linking verb* to continue to be sth; to be still in the same state or condition 仍然是；保持不变：**+ adj.** *to remain silent/standing/seated/motionless* 依然沉默 / 站着 / 坐着 / 一动不动 ◇ *Train fares are likely to remain unchanged.* 火车票价很可能会保持不变。◇ ***It remains*** *true that sport is about competing well, not winning.* 体育重在勇于竞争而非获胜，一向如此。◇ **+ noun** *In spite of their quarrel, they remain the best of friends.* 尽管有过争吵，他们仍是最好的朋友。◇ *He will remain (as) manager of the club until the end of his contract.* 他将继续担任俱乐部经理，直至合同期满。 **2** 🔑 [I] to still be present after the other parts have been removed, used, etc.; to continue to exist 剩余；遗留；继续存在：*Very little of the house remained after the fire.* 火灾之后，这座房子所剩无几。◇ *There were only ten minutes remaining.* 只剩下十分钟了。 **3** 🔑 [I] ~ (**to do sth**) to still need to be done, said, or dealt with 仍需去做（或说、处理）：*Much remains to be done.* 还有很多事要去做。◇ ***It remains to be seen*** (= it will only be known later) *whether you are right.* 你说得对不对还有待证实。◇ ***There remained*** *one significant problem.* 还有一个非常重要的问题。◇ *Questions remain about the president's honesty.* 总统是否诚实，还有许多疑问。◇ *I feel sorry for her, but* ***the fact remains*** *(****that****) she lied to us.* 我为她感到难过，可事实是她对我们撒了谎。 ➲ LANGUAGE BANK AT NEVERTHELESS **4** 🔑 [I] **+ adv./prep.** to stay in the same place; to not leave 逗留；不离去：*They remained in Mexico until June.* 他们在墨西哥一直住到了六月。◇ *The plane remained on the ground.* 飞机仍未起飞。◇ *She left, but I remained behind.* 她走了，而我留了下来。 IDM SEE ALOOF

re·main·der /rɪˈmeɪndə(r)/ *noun, verb*

■ ***noun*** **1** (*usually* **the remainder**) [sing.+sing./pl. v.] the remaining people, things or time 其他人员；剩余物；剩余时间 SYN **rest**: *I kept some of his books and gave away the remainder.* 我保留了一些他的书，其他的都送人了。 HELP When **the remainder** refers to a plural noun, the verb is plural. * the remainder 作复数名词时，动词用复数：*Most of our employees work in New York; the remainder are in London.* 我们大部分员工在纽约工作，其余的在伦敦。 **2** [C, usually sing.] (*mathematics* 数) the numbers left after one number has been SUBTRACTED from another, or one number has been divided into another 差数；余数：*Divide 2 into 7, and the answer is 3, remainder 1.* * 7 除以 2，商 3 余 1。 ➲ COMPARE DIVISOR **3** [C] a book that has been remaindered 廉价出售的图书；滞销图书

■ ***verb*** [I, T, usually passive] ~ (**sth**) to sell books at a reduced price 廉价出售（书）

re·main·ing 🔑 /rɪˈmeɪnɪŋ/ *adj.* [only before noun] still needing to be done or dealt with 仍需做的；还需处理的：*The remaining twenty patients were transferred to another hospital.* 其余的二十名病人被转送到另一家医院去了。◇ *Any remaining tickets for the concert will be sold on the door.* 其余门票均于音乐会时即场发售。 ➲ SEE ALSO REMAIN

re·mains 🔑 /rɪˈmeɪnz/ *noun* [pl.] **1** 🔑 ~ (**of sth**) the parts of sth that are left after the other parts have been used, eaten, removed, etc. 剩余物；残留物；剩饭菜：*She fed the remains of her lunch to the dog.* 她把剩下的午饭喂狗了。 **2** 🔑 the parts of ancient objects and buildings that have survived and are discovered in the present day 古代遗物；古迹；遗迹；遗址：*prehistoric remains* 史前遗迹 ◇ *the remains of a Roman fort* 罗马要塞的遗址 **3** 🔑 (*formal*) the body of a dead person or animal 遗体；遗骸：*They had discovered* ***human remains****.* 他们发现过人类遗骸。

re·make *noun, verb*

■ ***noun*** /ˈriːmeɪk/ a new or different version of an old film/movie or song（电影或歌曲的）新版，改编版

■ ***verb*** /ˌriːˈmeɪk/ (**re·made**, **re·made** /ˌriːˈmeɪd/) ~ **sth** to make a new or different version of sth such as an old film/movie or song; to make sth again 重新制作，改编（电影或歌曲等）；重做：*'The Seven Samurai' was remade in Hollywood as 'The Magnificent Seven'.* 《七武士》在好莱坞被重新制作成《七侠荡寇志》。

re·mand /rɪˈmɑːnd; *NAmE* -ˈmænd/ *verb, noun*

■ ***verb*** [usually passive] ~ **sb** (**+ adv./prep.**) to send sb away from a court to wait for their trial which will take place at a later date 将（嫌疑人）还押候审：*The two men were charged with burglary and* ***remanded in custody*** (= sent to prison until their trial). 两名男子被控入室偷窃而被还押候审。◇ *She was* ***remanded on bail*** (= allowed to go free until the trial after leaving a sum of money with the court). 她获准取保候审。

■ ***noun*** [U] the process of keeping sb in prison while they are waiting for their trial 还押；押候：*He is currently being held* ***on remand****.* 他正被还押候审。◇ *a remand prisoner* 还押罪犯

R

be detected and remediated quickly. 这些问题得迅速查明并加以纠正。

re'mand centre *noun* (*BrE*) a place where young people are sent when they are accused of a crime and are waiting for their trial 青少年拘留所

re·mark /rɪˈmɑːk; *NAmE* -ˈmɑːrk/ *noun, verb*

▪ ***noun*** **1** [C] something that you say or write which expresses an opinion, a thought, etc. about sb/sth 谈论；言论；评述 SYN **comment**: *to make a remark* 发表评论 ◇ *He made a number of rude remarks about the food.* 关于这里的食物他说了许多无礼的评论。◇ *What exactly did you mean by that last remark?* 你最后那句话究竟是什么意思？ ➲ SYNONYMS AT STATEMENT **2** [U] (*old-fashioned* or *formal*) the quality of being important or interesting enough to be noticed 引人注目；显耀 SYN **note**: *The exhibition contains nothing that is worthy of remark.* 这次展览没有任何值得看的东西。

▪ ***verb*** [I, T] to say or write a comment about sth/sb 说起；谈论；评论 SYN **comment**: **~ on/upon sth/sb** *The judges remarked on the high standard of entries for the competition.* 众评委说参赛作品水准很高。◇ **~ how...** *She remarked how tired I was looking.* 她说我看上去显得特别累。◇ **+ speech** *'It's much colder than yesterday,' he remarked casually.* "今天比昨天冷多了。"他漫不经心地说。◇ **~ that...** *Critics remarked that the play was not original.* 评论家们指出这部戏剧缺乏创意。◇ **be remarked on** *The similarities between the two have often been remarked on.* 人们经常谈到两者的相似之处。➲ SYNONYMS AT COMMENT

re·mark·able /rɪˈmɑːkəbl; *NAmE* -ˈmɑːrk-/ *adj.* unusual or surprising in a way that causes people to take notice 非凡的；奇异的；显著的；引人注目的 SYN **astonishing**: *a remarkable achievement/career/talent* 非凡的成就/事业/才能 ◇ *She was a truly remarkable woman.* 她是一位真正非同凡响的女人。◇ **~ for sth** *The area is remarkable for its scenery.* 这一地区以其优美的景色而引人瞩目。◇ **~ that...** *It is remarkable that nobody noticed sooner.* 竟然没有人早点发现，真有意思。OPP **unremarkable** ▸ **re·mark·ably** /-əbli/ *adv.*: *The car is in remarkably good condition for its age.* 就车龄而论，这辆车的状况好极了。◇ *Remarkably, nobody was killed.* 竟然没有死人，真是万幸。

R

re·marry /ˌriːˈmæri/ *verb* (**re·mar·ries**, **re·marry·ing**, **re·mar·ried**, **re·mar·ried**) [I] to marry again after being divorced or after your husband or wife has died 再婚 ▸ **re·mar·riage** /ˌriːˈmærɪdʒ/ *noun* [U, C]

re·mas·ter /ˌriːˈmɑːstə(r); *NAmE* -ˈmæs-/ *verb* **~ sth** to make a new MASTER copy of a recording in order to improve the sound quality 重新录制（唱片母带）: *All the tracks have been* ***digitally remastered*** *from the original tapes.* 所有的曲子都已经从原始录音带转录到了数码母带上。

re·match /ˈriːmætʃ/ *noun* [usually sing.] a match or game played again between the same people or teams, especially because neither side won the first match or game （尤指因首轮未决出胜负）重赛，复赛

re·medi·able /rɪˈmiːdiəbl/ *adj.* (*formal*) that can be solved or cured 可解决的；可治愈的 SYN **curable**: *remediable problems/diseases* 可以解决的问题；可治愈的疾病

re·med·ial /rɪˈmiːdiəl/ *adj.* [only before noun] **1** aimed at solving a problem, especially when this involves correcting or improving sth that has been done wrong 旨在解决问题的；补救的；纠正的: *remedial treatment* (= for a medical problem) 治疗 ◇ ***Remedial action*** *must be taken now.* 现在必须进行补救。**2** connected with school students who are slower at learning than others （为后进学生）补习的，辅导的: *remedial education* 补习教育 ◇ *a remedial class* 补习班

re·medi·ation /rɪˌmiːdiˈeɪʃn/ *noun* [U] (*NAmE*) the process of improving sth or correcting sth that is wrong, especially changing or stopping damage to the environment 补救；纠正；（尤指对环境破坏的）整改，制止: *remediation of contaminated soil* 受污染土壤的改善 ▸ **remedi·ate** /rɪˈmiːdieɪt/ *verb* **~ sth** (*NAmE*): *The problems need to be detected and remediated quickly.* 这些问题得迅速查明并加以纠正。

rem·edy /ˈremədi/ *noun, verb*

▪ ***noun*** (*pl.* **-ies**) **1** a way of dealing with or improving an unpleasant or difficult situation 处理方法；改进措施；补偿 SYN **solution**: **~ (for sth)** *There is no simple remedy for unemployment.* 失业问题没有简单的解决办法。◇ **~ (to sth)** *There are a number of possible remedies to this problem.* 这个问题有许多可能采取的解决办法。**2** a treatment or medicine to cure a disease or reduce pain that is not very serious 疗法；治疗；药品: *a herbal remedy* 草药 ◇ **~ for sth** *an excellent home remedy for sore throats* 治疗咽喉疼痛的极佳的家庭疗法 **3 ~ (against sth)** (*law* 律) a way of dealing with a problem, using the processes of the law （通过法律程序的）解决方法，救济 SYN **redress**: *Holding copyright provides the only legal remedy against unauthorized copying.* 持有版权是制止盗版的唯一法律手段。

▪ ***verb*** (**rem·ed·ies**, **rem·edy·ing**, **rem·ed·ied**, **rem·ed·ied**) **~ sth** to correct or improve sth 改正；纠正；改进 SYN **right**: *to remedy a problem* 解决问题 ◇ *This situation is easily remedied.* 这种情形易于补救。

re·mem·ber /rɪˈmembə(r)/ *verb* (not usually used in the progressive tenses 通常不用于进行时)

• **SB/STH FROM THE PAST** 过去的人/事物 **1** [T, I] to have or keep an image in your memory of an event, a person, a place, etc. from the past 回想起；记得；记起: **~ (sb/sth)** *This is Carla. Do you remember her?* 这位是卡拉。你记得她吗？◇ *I don't remember my first day at school.* 我已经忘了第一天上学的情景。◇ *He still remembered her as the lively teenager he'd known years before.* 他记忆中的她依然是他多年以前认识的那个活泼的少女。◇ ***As far as I can remember****, this is the third time we've met.* 我记得这是我们第三次会面了。◇ **~ doing sth** *Do you remember switching the lights off before we came out?* 你记得我们出来之前关灯了吗？◇ *I* ***vaguely remember*** *hearing him come in.* 我隐约记得听到他进来。◇ **~ sb/sth doing sth** *I can still vividly remember my grandfather teaching me to play cards.* 爷爷教我打纸牌的情景我记忆犹新。◇ (*formal*) *I can't remember his taking a single day off work.* 我不记得他请过哪怕一天假。◇ **~ (that)...** *I remember (that) we used to go and see them most weekends.* 我记得我们过去经常在周末去看望他们。

• **FACT/INFORMATION** 事实；信息 **2** [T, I] to bring back to your mind a fact, piece of information, etc. that you knew 想起；记起: **~ (sth)** *I'm sorry—I can't remember your name.* 对不起，我想不起你的名字了。◇ *You were going to help me with this. Remember?* 你说要帮着我做的。记得吗？◇ **~ how, what, etc....** *Can you remember how much money we spent?* 你能回忆起我们花了多少钱吗？◇ **~ (that)...** *Remember that we're going out tonight.* 别忘了我们今天晚上要出去。**3** [T] to keep an important fact in your mind 记住；把…牢记在心: **~ (that)...** *Remember (that) you may feel sleepy after taking the pills.* 记住，吃了这些药片之后，你可能会犯困。◇ **it is remembered that...** *It should be remembered that the majority of accidents happen in the home.* 不要忘记大多数事故都是在家里发生的。

• **STH YOU HAVE TO DO** 必做之事 **4** [T] to not forget to do sth; to actually do what you have to do 记着，不忘（去做）；动手做（必须做的事）: **~ to do sth** *Remember to call me when you arrive!* 你到了之后别忘了给我打电话！◇ **~ sth** *Did you remember your homework* (= to bring it)? 你记得带家庭作业了吗？ HELP Notice the difference between **remember doing sth** and **remember to do sth**: *I remember posting the letter* means 'I have an image in my memory of doing it'; *I remembered to post the letter* means 'I didn't forget to do it'. 注意 remember doing sth 和 remember to do sth 之间的区别：I remember posting the letter 的意思是"我记得把信寄出去了"；I remembered to post the letter 的意思是"我没有忘记要寄信"。

• **IN PRAYERS** 祈祷时 **5** [T] **~ sb** to think about sb with respect, especially when saying a prayer 纪念；缅怀；思念 SYN **commemorate**: *a church service to remember the war dead* 纪念战争死难者的教堂礼拜仪式

• **GIVE PRESENT** 送礼 **6** [T] **~ sb/sth** to give money, a present, etc. to sb/sth 给…送钱（或礼品等）: *My aunt* *always remembers my birthday* (= by sending a card or present). 我姨妈在我的生日总要送我礼物。◇ *His grandfather remembered him* (= left him money) *in his will.* 他爷爷在遗嘱中给他留下了一笔钱。

IDM **be re'membered for sth | be re'membered as sth** to be famous or known for a particular thing that you have done in the past 因某事而成名（或名留青史）: *He is best remembered as the man who brought jazz to England.* 他因为将爵士音乐传到英国而为人们所熟知。

PHR V **re'member me to sb** (*especially BrE*) used to ask sb to give your good wishes to sb else 代我问候某人: *Remember me to your parents.* 代我向你的父母问好。

re·mem·brance /rɪˈmembrəns/ *noun* **1** [U] the act or process of remembering an event in the past or a person who is dead 纪念；记忆；回忆: *A service was held* ***in remembrance of*** *local soldiers killed in the war.* 为当地阵亡的战士举行了纪念仪式。◇ *a remembrance service* 纪念仪式 ◇ (*formal*) *He smiled at the remembrance of their first kiss.* 他想起了他们的初吻，露出了微笑。 **2** [C] (*formal*) an object that causes you to remember sb/sth; a memory of sb/sth 纪念品；纪念物；一段记忆: *The cenotaph stands as a remembrance of those killed during the war.* 矗立着的纪念碑是对战争中死难者的纪念。

Re,membrance 'Sunday (*also* **Re'membrance Day**) *noun* the Sunday nearest to the 11 November on which those killed in war, especially the wars of 1914–18 and 1939–45, are remembered in ceremonies and church services in Britain and some other countries 阵亡将士纪念日（最接近11月11日的星期天。英国和其他一些国家为战争中的死难者，尤为两次世界大战中的阵亡者举行纪念仪式和教堂礼拜仪式）➲ SEE ALSO MEMORIAL DAY, VETERANS DAY

re·mind /rɪˈmaɪnd/ *verb* **~ sb (about/of sth)** to help sb remember sth, especially sth important that they must do 提醒；使想起: **~ sb** *I'm sorry, I've forgotten your name. Can you remind me?* 对不起，我忘了你的名字。提醒我一下好吗？◇ ***That*** (= what you have just said, done, etc.) ***reminds me, I must get some cash.*** 那倒提醒了我，我得带上一些现金。◇ *'You need to finish that essay.'* ***'Don't remind me*** (= I don't want to think about it).*'* "你要完成那篇论文。" "别提啦！" ◇ *'Don't forget the camera.' 'Remind me about it nearer the time.'* "别忘了带相机。" "到时候再提醒我一下。" ◇ **~ sb to do sth** *Remind me to phone Alan before I go out.* 提醒我在出去之前给艾伦打电话。◇ **~ sb (that)...** *Passengers are reminded (that) no smoking is allowed on this train.* 乘客们请注意，本次列车禁止吸烟。◇ **~ sb what, how, etc....** *Can someone remind me what I should do next?* 谁能告诉我下一步该做什么？◇ **~ sb + speech** *'You had an accident,' he reminded her.* 他提醒她道："你出过一次事故了。"

PHR V **re'mind sb of sb/sth** if sb/sth **reminds** you of sb/sth else, they make you remember or think about the other person, place, thing, etc. because they are similar in some way 使想起（类似的人、地方、事物等）: *You remind me of your father when you say that.* 你说那样的话，使我想起了你的父亲。◇ *That smell reminds me of France.* 那股气味使我想起了法国。

re·mind·er /rɪˈmaɪndə(r)/ *noun* **1 ~ (of sb/sth) | ~ (that...)** something that makes you think about or remember sb/sth, that you have forgotten or would like to forget 引起回忆的事物；提醒人的事物: *The sheer size of the cathedral is a* ***constant reminder*** *of the power of religion.* 大教堂的宏大规模使人时时感受到宗教的威严。◇ *The incident* ***served as a*** *timely* ***reminder*** *of just how dangerous mountaineering can be.* 这次事故及时地提醒了人们登山运动有时会有多危险。 **2** a letter or note informing sb that they have not done sth （告知该做某事的）通知单，提示信

rem·in·isce /ˌremɪˈnɪs/ *verb* [I] **~ (about sth/sb)** to think, talk or write about a happy time in your past 回忆，追忆，缅怀（昔日的快乐时光）: *We spent a happy evening reminiscing about the past.* 我们一晚上回忆往事，感到很愉快。

rem·in·is·cence /ˌremɪˈnɪsns/ *noun* **1** [C, usually pl.] a spoken or written description of sth that sb remembers about their past life 怀旧的谈话；回忆录 SYN **memory**: *The book is a collection of his reminiscences about the actress.* 这本书辑录了他对那位女演员的回忆。◇ *reminiscences of a wartime childhood* 战时童年生活的回忆录 **2** [U] the act of remembering things that happened in the past 回忆；追忆 SYN **recollection** **3** [C, usually pl.] something that reminds you of sth similar 使人想起类似事物的东西；引起联想的相似事物: *Her music is full of reminiscences of African rhythms.* 她的音乐总是使人联想到非洲音乐的节奏。

rem·in·is·cent /ˌremɪˈnɪsnt/ *adj.* **1 ~ of sb/sth** reminding you of sb/sth 使回忆起（人或事）: *The way he laughed was strongly reminiscent of his father.* 他笑的样子让人很容易想起他的父亲。 **2** [only before noun] (*formal*) showing that you are thinking about the past, especially in a way that causes you pleasure 回忆过去的；怀旧的；缅怀往事的: *a reminiscent smile* 追忆往事时露出的微笑

re·miss /rɪˈmɪs/ *adj.* [not before noun] (*formal*) not giving sth enough care and attention 疏忽；懈怠；玩忽职守 SYN **negligent**: **~ (of sb) (to do sth)** *It was remiss of them not to inform us of these changes sooner.* 他们粗心大意，没有早一些通知我们这些变化。◇ **~ (in sth/in doing sth)** *She had clearly been remiss in her duty.* 她在工作中显然马马虎虎。

re·mis·sion /rɪˈmɪʃn/ *noun* [U, C] **1** a period during which a serious illness improves for a time and the patient seems to get better （重病的）缓解期，减轻期: *The patient has been* ***in remission*** *for the past six months.* 在过去的六个月中，病人的病情已经有所缓解。◇ *The symptoms reappeared after only a short remission.* 短暂的康复之后，症状再次出现。 **2** (*BrE*) a reduction in the amount of time sb spends in prison, especially because they have behaved well 减刑；减少服刑时间 ➲ WORDFINDER NOTE AT PRISON **3** (*formal*) an act of reducing or cancelling the amount of money that sb has to pay （应付费用的）减少，免除: *New businesses may qualify for tax remission.* 新的企业有资格享受税收减免。◇ *There is a partial remission of fees for overseas students.* 对留学生可以减免部分费用。

remit *noun, verb*

■ ***noun*** /ˈriːmɪt; rɪˈmɪt/ [usually sing.] **~ (of sb/sth) | ~ (to do sth)** (*BrE*) the area of activity over which a particular person or group has authority, control or influence 职权范围；控制范围；影响范围: *Such decisions are* ***outside the remit*** *of this committee.* 这样的决定超出了委员会的职权范围。◇ *In future, staff recruitment will* ***fall within the remit*** *of the division manager.* 以后新员工招募将属于部门经理的职责。◇ *a remit to report on medical services* 报告医疗服务情况的权限

■ ***verb*** /rɪˈmɪt/ (**-tt-**) (*formal*) **1** to send money, etc. to a person or place 汇付；汇款 SYN **forward**: **~ sth** *to remit funds* 汇寄资金 ◇ **~ sth to sb** *Payment will be remitted to you in full.* 报酬将会全额汇寄给你。 **2 ~ sth** to cancel or free sb from a debt, duty, punishment, etc. 免除（债务、职责、惩罚等）；赦免 SYN **cancel**: *to remit a fine* 免除罚金 ◇ *to remit a prison sentence* 免除徒刑 ➲ SEE ALSO UNREMITTING

PHR V **re'mit sth to sb** [usually passive] (*law* 律) to send a matter to an authority so that a decision can be made 将…提交（权力部门以便作出决定）: *The case was remitted to the Court of Appeal.* 这个案件被提交给了上诉法院。

re·mit·tance /rɪˈmɪtns/ *noun* **1** [C] (*formal*) a sum of money that is sent to sb in order to pay for sth 汇款金额: *Please return the completed form with your remittance.* 请将填好的表格连同汇款寄回。 **2** [U] the act of sending money to sb in order to pay for sth 汇付；汇款 SYN **payment**: *Remittance can be made by cheque or credit card.* 可通过支票或信用卡汇款。

remix /ˌriːˈmɪks/ *verb* **~ sth** to make a new version of a recorded piece of music by using a machine to arrange the separate parts of the recording in a different way, add new parts, etc. 合成，再混合（音乐录音） ▶ **remix** /ˈriːmɪks/ (*also* **mix**) *noun* **re·mixer** *noun*: *the skills of remixer Tom Moulton* 合成音乐录音师汤姆•莫尔顿的技艺

rem·nant /ˈremnənt/ *noun* **1** [usually pl.] a part of sth that is left after the other parts have been used, removed, destroyed, etc. 残余部分；剩余部分 SYN **remains**: *The woods are remnants of a huge forest which once covered the whole area.* 这片树林只是剩下的一部分，原来这一带是一大片森林。 **2** a small piece of cloth that is left when the rest has been sold（织物的）零头，零料；布头

re·model /ˌriːˈmɒdl; *NAmE* -ˈmɑːdl/ *verb* (**-ll-**, *especially US* **-l-**) ~ **sth** to change the structure or shape of sth 改变…的结构（或形状）

re·mold (*NAmE*) = REMOULD

rem·on·strance /rɪˈmɒnstrəns; *NAmE* -ˈmɑːn-/ *noun* [C, U] (*formal*) a protest or complaint 抗议；抱怨

rem·on·strate /ˈremənstreɪt; *NAmE* rɪˈmɑːnstreɪt/ *verb* [I, T] ~ (**with sb**) (**about sth**) | + **speech** (*formal*) to protest or complain about sth/sb 抗议；抱怨；埋怨: *They remonstrated with the official about the decision.* 他们就这一决定向这位官员提出了抗议。

re·morse /rɪˈmɔːs; *NAmE* rɪˈmɔːrs/ *noun* [U] the feeling of being extremely sorry for sth wrong or bad that you have done 懊悔；非常遗憾；自责: *I felt guilty and full of remorse.* 我感到内疚，并且非常懊悔。◇ ~ **for sth/for doing sth** *He was filled with remorse for not believing her.* 他因为没有相信她而懊悔不已。 ➲ WORDFINDER NOTE AT SORRY
▸ **re·morse·ful** /-fl/ *adj.* **re·morse·ful·ly** /-fəli/ *adv.*

re·morse·less /rɪˈmɔːsləs; *NAmE* -ˈmɔːrs-/ *adj.* **1** (especially of an unpleasant situation 尤指不愉快的情形) seeming to continue or become worse in a way that cannot be stopped 持续恶化的 SYN **relentless**: *the remorseless increase in crime* 犯罪的持续增长 **2** cruel and having or showing no pity for other people 残酷的；无情的；无同情心的 SYN **merciless**: *a remorseless killer* 残酷的杀手
▸ **re·morse·less·ly** *adv.*

re·mort·gage /ˌriːˈmɔːɡɪdʒ; *NAmE* -ˈmɔːrɡ-/ *verb* [I, T] ~ (**sth**) to arrange a second MORTGAGE on your house or apartment, or to increase or change your first one 再按揭；转按揭 ▸ **re·mort·gage** *noun*

R

re·mote 🔑 /rɪˈməʊt; *NAmE* rɪˈmoʊt/ *adj., noun*
■ *adj.* (**re·moter**, **re·mot·est**)
• PLACE 地点 **1** 🔑 far away from places where other people live 偏远的；偏僻的 SYN **isolated**: *a remote beach* 偏远的海滩 ◇ *one of the remotest areas of the world* 世界上最荒僻的地区之一 ◇ ~ **from sth** *The farmhouse is remote from any other buildings.* 这家农舍附近没有别的房屋。
• TIME 时间 **2** 🔑 [only before noun] far away in time 遥远的；久远的 SYN **distant**: *in the* ***remote past/future*** 在遥远的过去 / 将来 ◇ *a* ***remote ancestor*** (= who lived a long time ago) 远祖
• RELATIVES 亲戚 **3** [only before noun] (of people 人) not closely related 关系较远的；远亲的 SYN **distant**: *a remote cousin* 远房表亲
• COMPUTER/SYSTEM 计算机；系统 **4** that you can connect to from far away, using an electronic link 远程的；远程连接的: *a* ***remote terminal/database*** 远程终端 / 数据库
• DIFFERENT 不同 **5** ~ (**from sth**) very different from sth 相差很大的；极不相同的: *His theories are somewhat remote from reality.* 他的理论有点儿脱离现实。
• NOT FRIENDLY 不友好 **6** (of people or their behaviour 人或行为) not very friendly or interested in other people 不很友好的；冷漠的 SYN **aloof, distant**
• VERY SMALL 微小 **7** 🔑 not very great 细微的；微小的 SYN **slight**: *There is still a* ***remote chance*** *that they will find her alive.* 他们仍然有一线希望能把她活着找到。◇ *I don't have* ***the remotest idea*** *what you're talking about.* 你在说什么我一点儿都不懂。
▸ **re·mote·ness** *noun* [U]: *the geographical remoteness of the island* 这座岛地理位置偏远 ◇ *His remoteness made her feel unloved.* 他的冷漠使她觉得他不爱她。
■ *noun* (*informal*) = REMOTE CONTROL (2)

re,mote 'access *noun* [U] the use of a computer system, etc. that is in another place, that you can connect to when you are far away, using an electronic link 远程存取；远程访问

re,mote con'trol *noun* **1** [U] the ability to operate a machine from a distance using radio or electrical signals 遥控: *It works* ***by remote control.*** 它通过遥控工作。◇ *a remote-control camera* 遥控摄像机 **2** (*also informal* **re·mote**, **zap·per**) [C] a device that allows you to operate a television, etc. from a distance 遥控器: *I can't find the remote control.* 我找不到遥控器。 ➲ VISUAL VOCAB PAGE V22 ▸ **re,mote-con'trolled** *adj.* : *remote-controlled equipment* 可遥控的设备

re·mote·ly /rɪˈməʊtli; *NAmE* -ˈmoʊt-/ *adv.* **1** (usually in negative sentences 通常用于否定句) to a very slight degree 微弱地；细微地；程度很低地 SYN **slightly**: *It wasn't even remotely funny* (= it wasn't at all funny). 这一点也不好笑。◇ *The two incidents were only remotely connected.* 两次事件之间无甚关联。 **2** from a distance 远程地: *remotely operated* 远程操作的 **3** far away from places where other people live 在偏僻地方: *The church is remotely situated on the north coast of the island.* 教堂位于这个岛偏僻的北部海岸。

re,mote 'sensing *noun* [U] the use of SATELLITES to search for and collect information about the earth 遥感；遥测

re·mould (*especially US* **re·mold**) /ˌriːˈməʊld; *NAmE* -ˈmoʊld/ *verb* ~ **sth** (*formal*) to change sth such as an idea, a system, etc. 更新，改变（想法、系统等）: *attempts to remould policy to make it more acceptable* 力图改变政策以使其易于为人们所接受

re·mount /ˌriːˈmaʊnt/ *verb* **1** [I, T] ~ (**sth**) to get on a horse, bicycle, etc. again after getting off it or falling off it 再次骑上，重新跨上（马、自行车等） **2** [T] ~ **sth** to organize and begin sth a second time 再次组织；重新开始

re·mov·able AW /rɪˈmuːvəbl/ *adj.* [usually before noun] that can be taken off or out of sth 可去除的；可取出的 SYN **detachable**

re·moval 🔑 AW /rɪˈmuːvl/ *noun* **1** 🔑 [U] ~ (**of sb/sth**) the act of taking sb/sth away from a particular place 移动；调动；去除: *Clearance of the site required the removal of a number of trees.* 清理这一场所需要移走不少树。◇ *the removal of a tumour* 肿瘤切除 **2** 🔑 [U] ~ (**of sth**) the act of getting rid of sth 除去；消除；清除: *stain removal* 清除污渍 ◇ *the removal of trade barriers* 贸易壁垒的消除 **3** 🔑 [U] ~ (**of sb**) the act of dismissing sb from their job 免职；解职 SYN **dismissal**: *events leading to the removal of the president from office* 导致总统下台的一些事件 **4** 🔑 [C] (*BrE*) an act of taking furniture, etc. from one house to another 搬迁；迁移: *house removals* 搬家 ◇ *a* ***removal company/firm*** 搬家公司 ◇ *When are the removal men coming?* 搬家工人什么时候到？

re·mov·al·ist /rɪˈmuːvəlɪst/ *noun* (*AustralE*) a person or company that takes furniture, etc. from one house or premises to another 搬家工人；搬家公司

re'moval van (*also* **'furniture van**) (*both BrE*) (*NAmE* **'moving van**) *noun* a large van used for moving furniture from one house to another 搬家卡车

re·move 🔑 AW /rɪˈmuːv/ *verb, noun*
■ *verb* **1** 🔑 to take sth/sb away from a place 移开；拿开；去掉；从…机构开除: ~ **sth/sb** *Illegally parked vehicles will be removed.* 非法停放的车辆将被拖走。◇ ~ **sth/sb from sth/sb** *He removed his hand from her shoulder.* 他将手从她的肩膀上拿开。◇ *Three children were removed from the school for persistent bad behaviour.* 三个孩子因一再行为不检被学校开除。 **2** 🔑 ~ **sth** to take off clothing, etc. from the body 脱去（衣服等）；摘下: *She removed her glasses and rubbed her eyes.* 她摘下眼镜，揉了揉眼睛。 **3** 🔑 to get rid of sth unpleasant, dirty, etc.; to make sth disappear 去除，排除（污渍、不愉快的事物等）；使消失: ~ **sth** *She has had the tumour removed.* 她已经将肿瘤切除了。◇ *to remove problems/obstacles/objections* 解决问题；排除障

碍；消除异议 ◇ **~ sth from sb/sth** *The news removed any doubts about the company's future.* 这个消息消除了一切有关公司前景的疑虑。 **4** **~ sb from sth** to dismiss sb from their position or job 免除，解除（职务等）：*The elections removed the government from power.* 这几次选举使得政府倒台。

IDM **once, twice, etc. re'moved** (of a cousin 堂亲或表亲) belonging to a different generation 上代的；下代的：*He's my cousin's son so he's my first cousin once removed.* 他是我表兄弟的儿子，所以他是低我一辈的表亲。 **be far/further/furthest removed from sth** to be very different from sth; to not be connected with sth 与…大相径庭；与…不相干：*Many of these books are far removed from the reality of the children's lives.* 很多这样的书都远远地脱离了孩子们的现实生活。

■ ***noun*** [C, U] (*formal*) an amount by which two things are separated 距离；差距；间距：*Charlotte seemed to be living **at one remove** from reality.* 夏洛特好像生活在现实之外。

re·mover /rɪˈmuːvə(r)/ *noun* **1** [U, C] (usually in compounds 通常构成复合词) a substance used for getting rid of marks, paint, etc. 清除剂：*nail varnish remover* 指甲油清除剂 ◇ *stain remover* 去污剂 ➲ SEE ALSO STAPLE REMOVER **2** [usually pl.] (*BrE*) a person or company whose job is to take furniture, etc. from one house to another 搬家工人；搬家公司：*a firm of removers* 搬家公司

re·mu·ner·ate /rɪˈmjuːnəreɪt/ *verb* [usually passive] **~ sb (for sth)** (*formal*) to pay sb for work that they have done 酬劳；付酬给

re·mu·ner·ation /rɪˌmjuːnəˈreɪʃn/ *noun* [U, C] (*formal*) an amount of money that is paid to sb for the work they have done 酬金；薪水；报酬

re·mu·nera·tive /rɪˈmjuːnərətɪv/ *adj.* [usually before noun] (*formal*) paying a lot of money 报酬丰厚的：*remunerative work* 报酬很高的工作

re·nais·sance /rɪˈneɪsns; *NAmE* ˈrenəsɑːns/ *noun* [sing.] **1 the Renaissance** the period in Europe during the 14th, 15th and 16th centuries when people became interested in the ideas and culture of ancient Greece and Rome and used these influences in their own art, literature, etc. 文艺复兴（欧洲 14、15 和 16 世纪时，人们以古希腊罗马的思想文化来繁荣文学艺术）：*Renaissance art* 文艺复兴时期的艺术 **2** a situation when there is new interest in a particular subject, form of art, etc. after a period when it was not very popular（某一学科或艺术形式等衰落后的）复兴 SYN **revival**：*to experience a renaissance* 经历复兴

Reˌnaissance ˈman *noun* a person who is good at a lot of things and has a lot of interests, especially writing and painting 文艺复兴人，全才人（尤指写作和绘画方面多才多艺的人）

renal /ˈriːnl/ *adj.* [usually before noun] (*medical* 医) relating to or involving the KIDNEYS 肾脏的；与肾脏相关的：*renal failure* 肾衰竭

re·name /ˌriːˈneɪm/ *verb* to give sb/sth a new name 重新命名；给…改名：**~ sth** *to rename a street* 给一条街道改名 ◇ **~ sth + noun** *Leningrad was renamed St Petersburg.* 列宁格勒被重新命名为圣彼得堡。

re·nas·cence /rɪˈnæsns; -ˈneɪ-/ *noun* [U, sing.] (*formal*) a situation in which there is new interest in a particular subject, form of art, etc. after a period when it was not very popular 复兴；再度流行 ▶ **re·nas·cent** /rɪˈnæsnt; -ˈneɪ-/ *adj.*：*renascent fascism* 死灰复燃的法西斯主义

rend /rend/ *verb* (**rent, rent** /rent/) **~ sth** (*old use* or *literary*) to tear sth apart with force or violence 撕开；撕碎：*They rent their clothes in grief.* 他们在悲痛之中扯碎了自己的衣服。◇ (*figurative*) *a country rent in two by civil war* 被内战一分为二的国家 ◇ (*figurative*) *Loud screams rent the air.* 高声的尖叫划破了天空。 ➲ SEE ALSO HEART-RENDING

ren·der /ˈrendə(r)/ *verb*

• **CAUSE SB/STH TO BE STH** 使成为 **1 ~ sb/sth + adj.** (*formal*) to cause sb/sth to be in a particular state or condition 使成为；使变得；使处于某状态 SYN **make**：*to render sth harmless/useless/ineffective* 使某事物无害 / 无用 / 无效 ◇ *Hundreds of people were rendered homeless by the earthquake.* 成百上千的人因为地震而无家可归。

• **GIVE HELP** 提供帮助 **2** (*formal*) to give sb sth, especially in return for sth or because it is expected 给予；提供；回报：**~ sth to sb/sth** *They rendered assistance to the disaster victims.* 他们给灾民提供了援助。◇ *to render a service to sb* 给某人提供服务 ◇ **~ sb sth** *to render sb a service* 为某人服务 ◇ **~ sth** *It was payment **for services rendered**.* 这是服务酬金。

• **PRESENT STH** 提交 **3 ~ sth** (*formal*) to present sth, especially when it is done officially 递交；呈献；提交 SYN **furnish**：*The committee was asked to render a report on the housing situation.* 要求委员会提交一份有关住房情况的报告。

• **EXPRESS/PERFORM** 表达；表演 **4 ~ sth** (*formal*) to express or perform sth 表达；表演；演示：*He stood up and rendered a beautiful version of 'Summertime'.* 他站起来表演了一段优美的《夏日时光》。◇ *The artist has rendered the stormy sea in dark greens and browns.* 画家用了深绿色和棕色来表现波涛汹涌的大海。

• **TRANSLATE** 翻译 **5** to express sth in a different language（用不同的语言）表达；翻译；把…译成 SYN **translate**：**~ sth (as sth)** *The Italian phrase can be rendered as 'I did my best'.* 这个意大利语的短语可以译为"我尽力了"。◇ **~ sth (into sth)** *It's a concept that is difficult to render into English.* 这个概念难以用英语来表达。

• **WALL** 墙壁 **6 ~ sth** (*specialist*) to cover a wall with a layer of PLASTER or CEMENT 粉刷；给（墙壁）抹灰

• **MELT** 化开 **7 ~ sth (down)** to make fat liquid by heating it; to melt sth 将（脂肪）熬成油；熔化

ren·der·ing /ˈrendərɪŋ/ *noun* **1** [C] the performance of a piece of music, a role in a play, etc.; the particular way in which sth is performed 演奏；扮演；表演 SYN **interpretation, rendition**：*her dramatic rendering of Lady Macbeth* 她饰演麦克白夫人的生动表演 **2** [C] a piece of writing that has been translated into a different language; the particular way in which it has been translated 翻译作品；翻译：*a faithful rendering of the original text* 对原文的忠实翻译 **3** [U, C] (*specialist*) a layer of PLASTER or CEMENT that is put on a brick or stone wall in order to make it smooth（抹在墙上的）一层灰泥

ren·dez·vous /ˈrɒndɪvuː; -deɪ-; *NAmE* ˈrɑːn-/ *noun, verb*

■ ***noun*** (*pl.* **ren·dez·vous** /-vuːz/) (*from French*) **1 ~ (with sb)** an arrangement to meet sb at a particular time and place 约会 **2** a place where people have arranged to meet 约会地点 **3** a bar, etc. that is a popular place for people to meet（酒吧等）热门聚会场所，聚会处：*a lively Paris rendezvous* 巴黎一处很热闹的公共场所

■ ***verb*** (**ren·dez·voused** /-vuːd/, **ren·dez·voused**) [I] **~ (with sb)** (*from French*) to meet at a time and place that have been arranged in advance（在约定的时间和地点）会面，相会，集合

ren·di·tion /renˈdɪʃn/ *noun* **1** [C] the performance of sth, especially a song or piece of music; the particular way in which it is performed 表演；演唱；演奏 SYN **interpretation** **2** (*also* **exˌtraordinary renˈdition**) [U] (especially in the US) the practice of sending foreign suspects to be questioned in another country where the laws about the treatment of prisoners are less strict（尤指在美国）非常规引渡（将外籍嫌疑犯引渡到其他对待囚犯较宽松的国家受审）

rene·gade /ˈrenɪɡeɪd/ *noun* (*formal, disapproving*) **1** (often used as an adjective 常用作形容词) a person who leaves one political, religious, etc. group to join another that has very different views 变节者；叛徒；背叛者；叛教者 **2** a person who opposes and lives outside a group or society that they used to belong to 叛逆者 SYN **outlaw**

re·nege /rɪˈniːɡ; rɪˈneɪɡ/ *verb* [I] **~ (on sth)** (*formal*) to break a promise, an agreement, etc. 违背（诺言）；背信弃义；食言 SYN **go back on**：*to renege on a deal/debt/contract, etc.* 违背协定、赖债、违背合约等

R

renew /rɪ'nju:; *NAmE* -'nu:/ *verb* **1 ~ sth** to begin sth again after a pause or an interruption 重新开始；中止后继续 **SYN resume**: *The army renewed its assault on the capital.* 军队重新发动对首都的攻击。◇ *We have to renew our efforts to attract young players.* 我们只好重新开始努力吸引年轻队员。◇ *The annual dinner is a chance to renew acquaintance with old friends.* 一年一度的聚餐会是与老朋友叙旧的好机会。 **2 ~ sth** to make sth valid for a further period of time 使继续有效；延长…的期限：*to* ***renew a licence/lease/subscription/contract, etc.*** 延长执照的期限、续签租约、续订、续签合约等 ◇ *How do I go about renewing my passport?* 我该如何去续签护照？◇ *I'd like to renew these library books* (= arrange to borrow them for a further period of time). 我想续借这几本图书馆的书。 **3 ~ sth** to emphasize sth by saying or stating it again 重申；重复强调 **SYN reiterate, repeat**: *to* ***renew an appeal/a request/a complaint, etc.*** 再次呼吁、请求、投诉等 ◇ *Community leaders have renewed calls for a peaceful settlement.* 社区领导人再次呼吁要和平解决。◇ *The project is to go ahead following renewed promises of aid from the UN.* 在得到联合国重申提供援助的承诺以后，这个项目将着手进行。 **4 ~ sth** to change sth that is old or damaged and replace it with sth new of the same kind 更新；更换：*The wiring in your house should be renewed every ten to fifteen years.* 你家里的电线应该每十到十五年更换一次。

re·new·able /rɪ'nju:əbl; *NAmE* -'nu:-/ *adj.* **1** [usually before noun] (of energy and natural resources 能源和自然资源) that is replaced naturally or controlled carefully and can therefore be used without the risk of finishing it all 可更新的；可再生的；可恢复的：*renewable sources of energy such as wind and solar power* 像风力和太阳能这种用之不竭的能源 ➲ COLLOCATIONS AT ENVIRONMENT **2** (of a contract, ticket, etc. 合同、票等) that can be made valid for a further period of time after it has finished 可延长有效期的；可展期的；可续订的：*a renewable lease* 可展期的租约 ◇ *The work permit is not renewable.* 这份工作许可证不能延期。 **OPP non-renewable**

re·new·ables /rɪ'nju:əblz; *NAmE* -'nu:-/ *noun* [pl.] types of energy that can be replaced naturally such as energy produced from wind or water 可再生能源：*renewables such as hydro-electricity and solar energy* 水力发电和太阳能之类的可再生能源 ◇ *investment in renewables* 对可再生能源的投资 **HELP** **Renewables** are more commonly referred to as **renewable energy** (**sources**). * renewables 更常见的说法是 renewable energy (sources)。 ➲ COLLOCATIONS AT ENVIRONMENT

re·newal /rɪ'nju:əl; *NAmE* -'nu:əl/ *noun* [U, C] **1 ~ (of sth)** a situation in which sth begins again after a pause or an interruption 恢复；更新；重新开始：*a renewal of interest in traditional teaching methods* 对传统教学法重新产生兴趣 **2** the act of making a contract, etc. valid for a further period of time after it has finished（对合同等的）有效期延长，展期，续订，更新：*The lease comes* ***up for renewal*** *at the end of the month.* 本租约到月底需要办理展期。◇ *the renewal date* 更新日期 **3** a situation in which sth is replaced, improved or made more successful 更新；改进；复兴；振兴：*economic renewal* 经济复兴 ◇ ***urban renewal*** (= the act of improving the buildings, etc. in a particular area) 市区改造

re·newed /rɪ'nju:d; *NAmE* rɪ'nu:d/ *adj.* [usually before noun] happening again with increased interest or strength 再次发生的；再次兴起的；更新的：*Renewed fighting has been reported on the border.* 据报道，在边境地区战火重燃。◇ *with renewed enthusiasm* 以重燃的热情

ren·min·bi /'renmɪnbi/ *noun* (*pl.* **ren·min·bi**) **1 the renminbi** [sing.] the money system of China 人民币（中国币制） **2** = YUAN

ren·net /'renɪt/ *noun* [U] a substance that makes milk thick and sour and is used in making cheese 凝乳酶（使牛奶凝结变酸的物质）

re·nounce /rɪ'naʊns/ *verb* (*formal*) **1 ~ sth** to state officially that you are no longer going to keep a title, position, etc. 声明放弃；宣布放弃 **SYN give sth↔up**: *to* ***renounce a claim/title/privilege/right*** 宣布放弃要求 / 头衔 / 特权 / 权利 **2 ~ sth** to state publicly that you no longer have a particular belief or that you will no longer behave in a particular way 宣布与…决裂；宣布摒弃：*to* ***renounce ideals/principles/beliefs, etc.*** 宣布放弃理想、原则、信仰等 ◇ *a joint declaration renouncing the use of violence* 声明放弃使用暴力的联合宣言 **3 ~ sb/sth** to state publicly that you no longer wish to have a connection with sb/sth because you disapprove of them 宣布断绝与…的关系 **SYN disown**: *He had renounced his former associates.* 他已经宣布与过去的伙伴拆伙。 ➲ SEE ALSO RENUNCIATION

reno·vate /'renəveɪt/ *verb* **~ sth** to repair and paint an old building, a piece of furniture, etc. so that it is in good condition again 修复；翻新；重新粉刷 ➲ COLLOCATIONS AT DECORATE ▶ **reno·va·tion** /ˌrenə'veɪʃn/ *noun* [U, C, usually pl.]: *buildings in need of renovation* 需要重新装修的大楼 ◇ *There will be extensive renovations to the hospital.* 这所医院将进行大规模的翻修。

re·nown /rɪ'naʊn/ *noun* [U] (*formal*) fame and respect because of sth you have done that people admire 名誉；声望：*He* ***won renown as*** *a fair judge.* 他赢得了公平裁判的荣誉。◇ *a pianist* ***of some/international/great*** *renown* 具有一定 / 国际 / 相当知名度的钢琴家

re·nowned /rɪ'naʊnd/ *adj.* famous and respected 有名的；闻名的；受尊敬的 **SYN celebrated, noted**: *a renowned author* 著名的作家 ◇ **~ as sth** *It is renowned as one of the region's best restaurants.* 这是本地区最好的饭店之一。◇ **~ for sth** *She is renowned for her patience.* 她的耐心是出了名的。

rent /rent/ *noun, verb* ➲ SEE ALSO REND

■ ***noun*** **1** [U, C] an amount of money that you regularly pay so that you can use a house, etc. 租金：*How much rent do you pay for this place?* 你租这个地方的租金是多少？◇ *The landlord has put the rent up again.* 房东又提

▼ **BRITISH/AMERICAN 英式 / 美式英语**

rent / hire / let

Verbs 动词

- You can **hire** something for a short period of time (*BrE only*), but **rent** something for a longer period. 短期租用可用 hire（仅用于英式英语），较长时间的租用则用 rent：*We can hire bikes for a day to explore the town.* 我们可租用自行车一天来游览这城镇。◇ *We don't own our TV, we rent it.* 我们没有自己的电视机，这是租的。
- In *NAmE*, **rent** is always used. It is sometimes now used in *BrE* instead of **hire**, too. 美式英语总是用 rent，现在英式英语有时也用 rent 代替 hire。
- The owners of a thing can **hire** it **out** for a short period (*BrE*). 物主短期租出某物可用 hire out（英式英语）：*Do you hire out bikes?* 你们出租自行车吗？ Or they can **rent** (**out**)/**let** (**out**) a building, etc. 出租房屋等可用 rent (out) / let (out)：*We rent out rooms in our house to students.* 我们把住宅里的房间出租给学生。
- Outside a building you could see 在建筑物外可看到：(*BrE*) *To let* 招租 ◇ (*especially NAmE*) *For rent* 招租
- To **hire** can also mean to employ somebody, especially in *NAmE*. * hire 亦含雇用之义，尤其在美式英语中：*We hired a new secretary.* 我们雇了一名新秘书。

➲ SEE ALSO LEASE *verb*

Nouns 名词

- The amount of money that you pay to rent something is **rent** or **rental** (more formal). When you hire something you pay a **hire charge** (*BrE*). 较长时间租用的租金为 rent 或 rental（较正式）。短期租借费用为 hire charge（英式英语）。 On a sign outside a shop you might see 在商店外的标牌上可看到：(*BrE*) *Bikes for hire* 出租自行车

➲ SEE ALSO LET, LEASE, HIRE *noun*

高房租了。◇ *a month's rent in advance* 预付的月租金 ◇ *a **high/low/fair rent*** 高的 / 低的 / 合理的租金 ◇ (*BrE*) *a rent book* (= used to record payments of rent) 租金登记簿 ➲ SYNONYMS AT RATE ➲ COLLOCATIONS AT HOUSE ➲ COMPARE HIRE *n.* (1) **2** [U, C] (*especially NAmE*) = RENTAL (1) **3** [C] (*formal*) a torn place in a piece of material or clothing 破裂处；裂口；撕裂

IDM **for rent** (*especially NAmE*) (especially on printed signs 尤用于告示) available to rent 出租；招租

■ ***verb*** **1** [T, I] to regularly pay money to sb so that you can use sth that they own, such as a house, some land, a machine, etc. 租用，租借（房屋、土地、机器等）：**~ (sth)** *to live in **rented accommodation/housing/property*** 住在租来的住所里 ◇ **~ sth from sb** *Who do you rent the land from?* 你从谁那里租用的土地？ **2** [T] to allow sb to use sth that you own such as a house or some land in exchange for regular payments 出租；将…租给：**~ sth (out) (to sb)** *He rents rooms in his house to students.* 他把家中的房间租给学生。◇ *The land is rented out to other farmers.* 这片土地租给别的农民了。◇ *She agreed to rent the room to me.* 她同意将这个房间租给我。◇ **~ sb sth** *She agreed to rent me the room.* 她同意租给我这个房间。 **3** [T] **~ sth** (*especially NAmE*) to pay money to sb so that you can use sth for a short period of time（短期）租用，租借：*We rented a car for the week and explored the area.* 我们租了一个星期的车考查这个地区。◇ *Shall we rent a movie this evening?* 我们今天晚上租电影看好吗？ ➲ COMPARE HIRE *v.* (1) **4** [I] (*NAmE*) to be available for sb to use if they pay a particular amount of money 以…出租；租金为：*The apartment rents for $500 a month.* 这套房间每月租金为 500 美元。

'rent-a- *combining form* (*informal, often humorous*) (in nouns and adjectives 构成名词和形容词) showing that the thing mentioned can be hired/rented 出租；可雇用：*rent-a-car* 租用汽车 ◇ *rent-a-crowd* 可雇用的人手

ren·tal /'rentl/ *noun* **1** (*also* **rent** *especially in NAmE*) [U, C, usually sing.] the amount of money that you pay to use sth for a particular period of time 租金：*Telephone charges include line rental.* 电话费包括线路租用费。 ➲ SYNONYMS AT RATE **2** [U] the act of renting sth or an arrangement to rent sth 出租；租赁；招租：*the world's largest car rental company* 世界最大的汽车租赁公司 ◇ *DVD rental* * DVD 出租 ◇ (*especially NAmE*) *a rental car* 供出租的汽车 ◇ *a minimum rental period of three months* 三个月的最低租用期 ➲ COMPARE HIRE *n.* (1) **3** [C] (*especially NAmE*) a house, car, or piece of equipment that you can rent 租用的房屋（或汽车、设备等）：*'Is this your own car?' 'No, it's a rental.'* "这是你自己的车吗？""不，是租来的。"

'rent boy *noun* (*BrE*) a young male PROSTITUTE 年轻的男妓

rent·ed /'rentɪd/ *adj.* that you pay rent for 租用的；租借的：*a rented studio* 租来的工作室

rent·er /'rentə(r)/ *noun* **1** a person who rents sth 承租人；租用人；租户：*house buyers and renters* 房屋的买主和租户 **2** (*NAmE*) a person or an organization that provides sth for people to rent 出租人；出租机构：*the nation's biggest automobile renter* 全国最大的汽车出租公司

,rent-'free *adj.* for which no rent is paid 免租金的；不收租金的：*rent-free housing* 不收租金的住房 ▶ **,rent-'free** *adv.*

ren·tier /'rɒntieɪ; *NAmE* 'rɑːntjeɪ/ *noun* (*specialist*) a person who lives from money earned from property and investments 靠房地产和投资生活的人；吃息族

re·nun·ci·ation /rɪ,nʌnsi'eɪʃn/ *noun* (*formal*) **1** [U, C] an act of stating publicly that you no longer believe sth or that you are giving sth up 声明摒弃；宣布放弃：*the renunciation of violence* 放弃使用暴力的声明 **2** [U] the act of rejecting physical pleasures, especially for religious reasons 弃绝物质享受；克己；禁欲 SYN **self-denial** ➲ SEE ALSO RENOUNCE

re·occur AW /,riːə'kɜː(r)/ *verb* (**-rr-**) [I] to happen again or a number of times 再次（或多次）发生；反复出现 SYN **recur**

re·of·fend /,riːə'fend/ *verb* [I] to commit a crime again 再犯罪；再犯法：*Without help, many released prisoners will reoffend.* 如果得不到帮助，很多获得释放的囚犯就会重蹈覆辙。 ▶ **re·of·fend·er** *noun*

re·open /,riː'əʊpən; *NAmE* -'oʊ-/ *verb* **1** [T, I] **~ (sth)** to open a shop/store, theatre, etc. again, or to be opened again, after being closed for a period of time 重新开业；重新开放（商店、剧场等）：*The school was reopened just two weeks after the fire.* 火灾之后仅两个星期，这所学校就重新开学了。◇ *The store will reopen at 9 a.m. on 2 January.* 商店将于元月 2 号上午 9 点重新开业。 **2** [T, I] **~ (sth)** to deal with or begin sth again after a period of time; to start again after a period of time 重新处理；再次开始；恢复：*to reopen a discussion* 重新开始讨论 ◇ *The police have decided to reopen the case.* 警方已经决定重新调查这个案子。◇ *Management have agreed to reopen talks with the union.* 资方已经同意和工会重新谈判。◇ *The trial reopened on 6 March.* 审判在 3 月 6 日再次进行。 ▶ **re·open·ing** *noun* [U, sing.]

IDM **re,open old 'wounds** to remind sb of sth unpleasant that happened or existed in the past 揭旧疮疤；揭老底

re·order /,riː'ɔːdə(r); *NAmE* -'ɔːrd-/ *verb* **1** [T, I] **~ (sth)** to ask sb to supply you with more of a product 再订购；追加订购：*Please quote this reference number when reordering stock.* 再次订货时请提供这个编号。 **2** [T] **~ sth** to change the order in which sth is arranged 重新布置；重新排列

re·organ·ize (*BrE also* **-ise**) /ri'ɔːɡənaɪz; *NAmE* -'ɔːrɡ-/ *verb* [T, I] **~ (sth)** to change the way in which sth is organized or done 重新组织；改组；整顿 ▶ **re·organ·iza·tion, -isa·tion** /ri,ɔːɡənaɪ'zeɪʃn; *NAmE* -,ɔːrɡənə'z-/ *noun* [U, C]: *the reorganization of the school system* 学校体制的整顿

re·ori·ent AW /,riː'ɔːrient/ *verb* **1** **~ sb/sth (to/towards/away from sb/sth)** to change the focus or direction of sb/sth 改变…的重点（或方向）：*Other governments may reorient their foreign policies away from the United States.* 其他政府可能调整他们的外交政策，不再以美国为重点。 **2** **~ yourself** to find your position again in relation to your surroundings 给（自己）重新定位 ▶ **re·orien·ta·tion** AW /,riː,ɔːriən'teɪʃn/ *noun* [U]

Rep. *abbr.* (in American politics 美国政治) **1** REPRESENTATIVE 众议院议员 **2** REPUBLICAN 共和党人；共和党党员

rep /rep/ *noun* (*informal*) **1** [C] = SALES REPRESENTATIVE, REPRESENTATIVE (2) **2** [C] a person who speaks officially for a group of people, especially at work 代表；发言人：*a union rep* 工会代表 **3** [U] (*informal*) the abbreviation for REPERTORY 保留剧目轮演（全写为 repertory）

re·pack·age /,riː'pækɪdʒ/ *verb* **1** **~ sth** to change the boxes, bags, etc. in which a product is sold 改变（产品）包装；重新包装 **2** **~ sth/sb** to present sth/sb in a new way 改变…的形象：*She earns more since she repackaged herself as a business consultant.* 自从把自己重新包装成商业顾问以来，她的收入增加了。

re·paid PAST TENSE, PAST PART. OF REPAY

re·pair /rɪ'peə(r); *NAmE* -'per/ *verb, noun*

■ ***verb*** **1** **~ sth** to restore sth that is broken, damaged or torn to good condition 修理；修补；修缮：*to repair a car/roof/road/television* 修理汽车 / 屋顶 / 道路 / 电视 ◇ *It's almost 15 years old. It isn't worth **having it repaired**.* 这东西差不多 15 年了。不值得送去修了。 **2** **~ sth** to say or do sth in order to improve a bad or unpleasant situation 补救；纠正；弥补 SYN **right**: *It was too late to repair the damage done to their relationship.* 太晚了，无法弥补他们的关系所遭受的创伤了。 ▶ **re·pair·er** *noun*：*TV repairers* 电视机修理工

PHR V **re'pair to...** (*formal* or *humorous*) to go to a particular place 去（某地）

■ ***noun*** [C, U] an act of repairing sth 修理；修补；修缮：*They agreed to pay the costs of any repairs.* 他们答应支付所有的修理费。◇ *I took my bike **in for repair**.* 我把自行车送去修了。◇ *The building was **in need of repair**.* 这座大楼

R

需要维修了。◇ *a TV repair shop* 电视机修配店 ◇ *The car was damaged* ***beyond repair*** (= it was too badly damaged to be repaired). 汽车损坏严重，无法修复。◇ *The hotel is currently* ***under repair*** (= being repaired). 这家酒店正在维修。◇ *The bridge will remain closed until essential* ***repair work*** *has been carried out.* 在基本修缮工作完成之前，这座桥暂时关闭。

IDM **in good, bad, etc. re'pair | in a good, bad, etc. state of re'pair** (*formal*) in good, etc. condition 状况良好（或不佳等）

re·pair·able /rɪˈpeərəbl; *NAmE* -ˈper-/ *adj.* [not usually before noun] that can be repaired 可修理；可修缮；可修补 **OPP** **irreparable**

re·pair·man /rɪˈpeəmæn; *NAmE* -ˈperm-/ *noun* (*pl.* **-men** /-men/) (*also* **re·pair·er** *especially in BrE*) a person whose job is to repair things 修理工：*a TV repairman* 电视机修理工

rep·ar·ation /ˌrepəˈreɪʃn/ *noun* (*formal*) **1** **reparations** [pl.] money that is paid by a country that has lost a war, for the damage, injuries, etc. that it has caused（战败国的）赔款 ➲ WORDFINDER NOTE AT PEACE **2** [U] the act of giving sth to sb or doing sth for them in order to show that you are sorry for suffering that you have caused 赔偿；弥补；补偿：*Offenders should be forced to* ***make reparation to*** *the community.* 应该强迫违法犯罪分子对社会作出补偿。

rep·ar·tee /ˌrepɑːˈtiː; *NAmE* -ɑːrˈtiː/ *noun* [U] clever and amusing comments and replies that are made quickly 机智而又巧妙的应对（或回答）

re·past /rɪˈpɑːst; *NAmE* -ˈpæst/ *noun* (*old-fashioned* or *formal*) a meal 餐；饭菜

re·pat·ri·ate /ˌriːˈpætrieɪt; *NAmE* -ˈpeɪt-/ *verb* **1** ~ **sb** (*formal*) to send or bring sb back to their own country 遣送回国；遣返：*The refugees were forcibly repatriated.* 难民被强制遣送回国。 **2** ~ **sth** (*business* 商) to send money or profits back to your own country 寄（钱）回国；将（利润）调回本国 ▶ **re·pat·ri·ation** /ˌriːˌpætriˈeɪʃn; *NAmE* -ˌpeɪt-/ *noun* [U, C]: *the repatriation of immigrants/profits* 遣返移民；调回利润 ◇ *a voluntary repatriation programme* 自愿遣返计划

repay /rɪˈpeɪ/ *verb* (**re·paid**, **re·paid** /rɪˈpeɪd/) **1** to pay back the money that you have borrowed from sb 归还；偿还；清偿：~ **sth** *to* ***repay a debt/loan/mortgage*** 偿还债务 / 贷款 / 按揭贷款 ◇ *I'll repay the money I owe them next week.* 我将在下个星期偿还欠他们的钱。◇ ~ **sth to sb** *The advance must be repaid to the publisher if the work is not completed on time.* 如果作品没有按时完成，预付款必须返还给出版商。◇ ~ **sb** *When are you going to repay them?* 你什么时候把钱还给他们？◇ ~ **sb sth** *I fully intend to repay them the money that they lent me.* 我非常想把他们借给我的钱还给他们。 **2** to give sth to sb or do sth for them in return for sth that they have done for you 酬报；报答 **SYN** **recompense**：~ **sb** (**for sth**) *How can I ever repay you for your generosity?* 你对我这样慷慨，我怎么才能报答你呢？◇ ~ **sth** (**with sth**) *Their trust was repaid with fierce loyalty.* 他们的信任获得的回报是忠心耿耿。 **3** ~ **sth** (*formal*) if sth **repays** your attention, interest, study, etc., it is worth spending time to look at it, etc. 值得：*The report repays careful reading.* 这份报告值得仔细阅读。

re·pay·able /rɪˈpeɪəbl/ *adj.* that can or must be paid back 可偿还的；必须偿还的；应回报的：*The loan is repayable in monthly instalments.* 这笔借款能以按月摊付的方式偿还。

re·pay·ment /rɪˈpeɪmənt/ *noun* **1** [U] the act of paying back money that you have borrowed from a bank, etc. 归还借款；偿还债务：*The loan is due for repayment by the end of the year.* 这笔借款要在年底还清。 **2** [C, usually pl.] a sum of money that you pay regularly to a bank, etc. until you have returned all the money that you owe 按期偿还的款项；分期偿还额：*We were unable to* ***meet*** (= pay) ***the repayments*** *on the loan.* 我们无法支付贷款的分期偿还额。◇ *mortgage repayments* 按揭贷款的偿还款项 ➲ SYNONYMS AT PAYMENT ➲ COLLOCATIONS AT FINANCE

re'payment mortgage *noun* (*BrE*) a type of MORTGAGE in which you pay regular sums of money to the bank, etc. until you have returned all the money and interest that you owe 固定偿还期按揭 ➲ COMPARE ENDOWMENT MORTGAGE

re·peal /rɪˈpiːl/ *verb* ~ **sth** if a government or other group or person with authority **repeals** a law, that law is no longer valid 废除，撤销，废止（法规） ▶ **re·peal** *noun* [U]

re·peat /rɪˈpiːt/ *verb, noun*

> **WORD FAMILY**
> **repeat** *verb, noun*
> **repeatable** *adj.* (≠ unrepeatable)
> **repeated** *adj.*
> **repeatedly** *adv.*
> **repetition** *noun*
> **repetitive** *adj.*
> **repetitious** *adj.*

■ ***verb***

• **SAY/WRITE AGAIN** 重复说 / 写 **1** [T] to say or write sth again or more than once 重复；重说；重写：~ **sth** *to repeat a question* 重复一遍问题 ◇ *I'm sorry—could you repeat that?* 对不起，你可以再说一遍吗？◇ *She kept repeating his name softly over and over again.* 她轻声地一遍又一遍地重复着他的名字。◇ *The opposition have been repeating their calls for the president's resignation.* 反对派一再要求总统辞职。◇ ~ **yourself** *Do say if I'm repeating myself* (= if I have already said this). 如果我在重复自己说过的话，请直言。◇ ~ **that…** *He's fond of repeating that the company's success is all down to him.* 他老爱说公司的成功全都归功于他。

• **DO AGAIN** 重做 **2** [T, I] ~ (**sth**) to do or produce sth again or more than once 重做；重新推出；重复：*to repeat a mistake/a process/an exercise* 重复一个错误 / 过程；反复练习 ◇ *The treatment should be repeated every two to three hours.* 这种治疗方法应该每隔两到三小时重复一次。◇ *They are hoping to repeat last year's victory.* 他们希望重复去年的胜利。◇ *These offers are unlikely to be repeated.* 这样的出价不大可能再有了。◇ *The programmes will be repeated next year.* 明年将继续开设这些课程。◇ ***to repeat the class/year/grade*** (= in a school, to take the class/year/grade again) 重修这门课；重读一年；留级 ◇ *Lift and lower the right leg 20 times. Repeat with the left leg.* 将右腿提放 20 次，换左腿重复同样的动作。

• **HAPPEN AGAIN** 再次发生 **3** [T, I] ~ (**sth/itself**) to happen more than once in the same way 重复发生；再次发生：*History has a strange way of repeating itself.* 历史会奇怪地重演。◇ *a repeating pattern/design* 重复出现的图案 / 设计

• **WHAT SB ELSE SAID** 他人的话 **4** [T] to tell sb sth that you have heard or been told by sb else 转述；转告：~ **sth to sb** *I don't want you to repeat a word of this to anyone.* 这些话你一个字也不要告诉别人。◇ ~ **sth** *The rumour has been widely repeated in the press.* 报界广泛转载了这一传闻。 **5** [T] to say sth that sb else has said, especially in order to learn it 复述，跟读（尤指为学习）：~ **sth** (**after sb**) *Listen and repeat each sentence after me.* 先听再跟着我朗读每个句子。◇ ~ **what…** *Can you repeat what I've just said word for word?* 你能一字不差地复述我刚才说过的话吗？◇ **+ speech** *'Are you really sure?' she repeated.* "你真的很肯定吗？" 她再次问道。

• **OF FOOD** 食物 **6** [I] ~ (**on sb**) (*BrE, informal*) if food **repeats**, you can taste it for some time after you have eaten it 留有余味：*Do you find that onions repeat on you?* 你是不是觉得吃了洋葱嘴里老有一股味儿？

• **FOR EMPHASIS** 强调 **7** [I, T] used to emphasize sth that you have already said （强调说过的话）再说一遍：*The claims are, I repeat, totally unfounded.* 我再说一遍，这些说法是毫无根据的。◇ ~ **sth** *I am not, repeat not, travelling in the same car as him!* 我不会，再说一遍，不会和他坐同一辆车的！

■ ***noun*** **1** a television or radio programme that has been broadcast before 重播的电视（或广播）节目：*'Is it a new series?' 'No, a repeat.'* "这是新播出的连续剧吗？" "不，是重播的。" **2** an event that is very similar to sth that happened before 重演的事物；重复的事件：*A repeat of the 1906 earthquake could kill up to 11 000 people.* 如果再次发生 1906 年的地震，可能会有多达 11 000 人死亡。◇ *She didn't want a* ***repeat performance*** *of what had happened the night before.* 她不想让前一天晚上的事重演。◇ (*business*

商) *a repeat order* (= for a further supply of the same goods) 续订货单 **3** (*music* 音) a passage that is repeated 重复段；反复部分

re·peat·able /rɪˈpiːtəbl/ *adj.* [not usually before noun] **1** (of a comment, etc. 评论等) (usually in negative sentences 通常用于否定句) polite and not offensive 有礼貌；不冒犯人：*His reply was not repeatable.* 他的回答不便重复。**2** that can be repeated 可重复 OPP **unrepeatable**

re·peated /rɪˈpiːtɪd/ *adj.* [only before noun] happening, said or done many times 重复的；反复发生的：*repeated absences from work* 一再旷工 ▶ **re·peat·ed·ly** *adv.*：*The victim had been stabbed repeatedly in the chest.* 受害者胸部多处被刺伤。

re·peat·er /rɪˈpiːtə(r)/ *noun* (*specialist*) a gun that you can fire several times without having to load it again 连发枪；转轮手枪

repel /rɪˈpel/ *verb* (**-ll-**) **1** [T] ~ **sb/sth** (*formal*) to successfully fight sb who is attacking you, your country, etc. and drive them away 击退；驱逐：*to* ***repel an attack/invasion/invader*** 击退进攻 / 入侵；驱逐入侵者 ◇ *Troops repelled an attempt to infiltrate the south of the island.* 部队挫败了对该岛南部的渗透企图。◇ (*figurative*) *The reptile's prickly skin repels nearly all of its predators.* 这种爬行动物浑身是刺，几乎所有的捕食者都退避三舍。**2** [T] ~ **sth** to drive, push or keep sth away 推开；赶走；驱除：*a cream that repels insects* 驱除昆虫的乳剂 ◇ *The fabric has been treated to repel water.* 这种织物进行过防水处理。**3** [T] ~ **sb** (not used in the progressive tenses 不用于进行时) to make sb feel horror or disgust 使恐惧；使厌恶 SYN **disgust, repulse**：*I was repelled by the smell.* 这种气味让我恶心。**4** [T, I] ~ (**sth**) (*specialist*) if one thing **repels** another, or if two things **repel** each other, an electrical or MAGNETIC force pushes them apart 排斥；相斥：*Like poles repel each other.* 同极相斥。OPP **attract** ⇨ SEE ALSO REPULSION, REPULSIVE

re·pel·lent /rɪˈpelənt/ *adj., noun*

■ *adj.* **1** ~ (**to sb**) (*formal*) very unpleasant; causing strong dislike 使人反感的；令人厌恶的 SYN **repulsive**：*Their political ideas are repellent to most people.* 他们的政治观点令大多数人反感。**2** (in compounds 构成复合词) not letting a particular substance, especially water, pass through it 防…的；隔绝…的：*water-repellent cloth* 防水布

■ *noun* [U, C] **1** a substance that is used for keeping insects away from you 驱虫剂：(*an*) *insect repellent* 驱虫剂 **2** a substance that is used on cloth, stone, etc. to prevent water from passing through it 防水剂：(*a*) *water repellent* 防水剂

re·pent /rɪˈpent/ *verb* [I, T] (*formal*) to feel and show that you are sorry for sth bad or wrong that you have done 后悔；悔过；忏悔：*God welcomes the sinner who repents.* 上帝欢迎悔过的罪人。◇ ~ **of sth** *She had repented of what she had done.* 她对自己所做的事深感懊悔。◇ ~ **sth** *He came to repent his hasty decision* (= wished he had not taken it). 他开始后悔自己的草率决定。⇨ WORDFINDER NOTE AT SORRY

re·pent·ance /rɪˈpentəns/ *noun* [U] ~ (**for sth**) (*formal*) the fact of showing that you are sorry for sth wrong that you have done 后悔；懊悔；悔过；忏悔 SYN **contrition, remorse**：*He shows no sign of repentance.* 他毫无悔意。

re·pent·ant /rɪˈpentənt/ *adj.* (*formal*) feeling or showing that you are sorry for sth wrong that you have done 后悔的；悔过的；表示悔改的 SYN **contrite, remorseful** OPP **unrepentant**

re·per·cus·sion /ˌriːpəˈkʌʃn; *NAmE* -pərˈk-/ *noun* [usually pl.] an indirect and usually bad result of an action or event that may happen some time afterwards（间接的）影响，反响，恶果 SYN **consequence**：*The collapse of the company will* ***have repercussions*** *for the whole industry.* 这家公司的垮台将会给整个行业造成间接的负面影响。⇨ SYNONYMS AT RESULT

rep·er·toire /ˈrepətwɑː(r); *NAmE* -pərt-/ *noun* **1** (*also formal* **rep·er·tory**) all the plays, songs, pieces of music, etc. that a performer knows and can perform（总称某人的）可表演项目：*a pianist with a wide repertoire* 能演奏很多曲子的钢琴师 **2** all the things that a person is able to do（某人的）全部才能，全部本领：*a young child's growing verbal repertoire* 小孩不断增长的语言表达能力

rep·er·tory /ˈrepətri; *NAmE* ˈrepərtɔːri/ *noun* **1** (*also informal* **rep**) [U] the type of work of a theatre company in which different plays are performed for short periods of time 保留剧目轮演：*an actor in repertory* 参加轮演剧目的演员 ◇ *a repertory company* 轮演剧目剧团 **2** [C] (*formal*) = REPERTOIRE (1)

repe·ti·tion /ˌrepəˈtɪʃn/ *noun* **1** [U, C] the fact of doing or saying the same thing many times 重复；重做；重说：*learning by repetition* 通过重复来学习 **2** [C] a thing that has been done or said before 重做的事；重说的话：*We do not want to see a repetition of last year's tragic events.* 我们不想看到去年的悲剧重演。

repe·ti·tious /ˌrepəˈtɪʃəs/ *adj.* (*often disapproving*) involving sth that is often repeated, in a way that becomes boring 重复的；一再的；重复乏味的：*a long and repetitious speech* 冗长重复的讲话 ▶ **repe·ti·tious·ly** *adv.* **repe·ti·tious·ness** *noun*

re·peti·tive /rɪˈpetətɪv/ *adj.* **1** saying or doing the same thing many times, so that it becomes boring 重复乏味的 SYN **monotonous**：*a repetitive task* 重复乏味的工作 **2** repeated many times 多次重复的：*a repetitive pattern of behaviour* 重复的行为模式 ▶ **re·peti·tive·ly** *adv.* **re·peti·tive·ness** *noun* [U]

re·phrase /ˌriːˈfreɪz/ *verb* ~ **sth** to say or write sth using different words in order to make the meaning clearer 换个说法说，改变词句（以使意思更清楚）

re·place /rɪˈpleɪs/ *verb* **1** ~ **sth/sb** to be used instead of sth/sb else; to do sth instead of sb/sth else 代替；取代 SYN **take over** (**from sth**)：*The new design will eventually replace all existing models.* 新的设计最终将会取代全部现有的型号。◇ *Teachers will never be replaced by computers in the classroom.* 课堂上电脑永远不会取代老师。**2** to remove sb/sth and put another person or thing in their place（用…）替换；（以…）接替：~ **sb/sth** *He will be difficult to replace when he leaves.* 他离开后，他的位置很难有人接替。◇ ~ **sb/sth with/by sb/sth** *It is not a good idea to miss meals and replace them with snacks.* 不吃正餐，改吃点心，这不是什么好主意。**3** ~ **sth** to change sth that is old, damaged, etc. for a similar thing that is newer or better 更换；更新：*All the old carpets need replacing.* 所有的旧地毯都需要更换。◇ *You'll be expected to replace any broken glasses.* 玻璃杯如有损坏，要负责赔偿。**4** ~ **sth** (**+ adv./prep.**) to put sth back in the place where it was before 把…放回原处：*I replaced the cup carefully in the saucer.* 我小心翼翼地将杯子放回茶碟。◇ *to replace the handset* (= after using the telephone). 放回电话听筒

re·place·able /rɪˈpleɪsəbl/ *adj.* that can be replaced 可替换的；可代替的 OPP **irreplaceable**

re·place·ment /rɪˈpleɪsmənt/ *noun* **1** [U] the act of replacing one thing with another, especially sth that is newer or better 替换；更换：*the replacement of worn car parts* 汽车上损坏零件的更换 ◇ *replacement windows* 新换的窗子 **2** [C] a thing that replaces sth, especially because the first thing is old, broken, etc. 替代品；替换物：*a hip replacement* 人工髋关节 **3** [C] ~ (**for sb**) a person who replaces another person in an organization, especially in their job（尤指工作中的）接替者，替代者：*We need to find a replacement for Sue.* 我们需要找一个替代休的人。

re·play *noun, verb*

■ *noun* /ˈriːpleɪ/ **1** (*sport* 体育) a game that is played again because neither side won in the previous game（由于未决出胜负而进行的）重赛 **2** the playing again of a short section of a film/movie, tape, etc. especially to look at or listen to sth more carefully（录像、录音等的）重放，重演，重播：*We watched a replay of the wedding on DVD.* 我

R

们看了重放的婚礼 DVD 录像。➲ SEE ALSO ACTION REPLAY **3** (*informal*) something that is repeated or happens in exactly the same way as it did before 重演的事物；重复出现的事物：*This election will not be a replay of the last one.* 这次选举将不会是上一次的重演。

■ *verb* /ˌriːˈpleɪ/ **1** [usually passive] **~ sth** to play a sports game again because neither team won the first game（因胜负未决）重赛 **2 ~ sth** to play again sth that has been recorded on tape, film, etc. 重新播放（录像、录音等）：*The police replayed footage of the accident over and over again.* 警察一遍又一遍地重放事故的片段。◇ (*figurative*) *He replayed the scene in his mind.* 他不断回想起当时的情景。

re·plen·ish /rɪˈplenɪʃ/ *verb* **~ sth (with sth)** (*formal*) to make sth full again by replacing what has been used 补充；重新装满 SYN **top sth↔up**：*to replenish food and water supplies* 补充食物和水 ◇ *Allow me to replenish your glass.* 让我再给您斟满。▶ **re·plen·ish·ment** *noun* [U]

re·plete /rɪˈpliːt/ *adj.* **1** [not before noun] **~ (with sth)** (*formal*) filled with sth; with a full supply of sth 充满；充足：*literature replete with drama and excitement* 充满紧张刺激情节的文学作品 **2** (*old-fashioned* or *formal*) very full of food 很饱；饱食

rep·lica /ˈreplɪkə/ *noun* a very good or exact copy of sth 复制品；仿制品：*a replica of the Eiffel Tower* 埃菲尔铁塔模型 ◇ *The weapon used in the raid was a replica.* 抢劫案中使用的武器是一件仿制品。◇ *replica guns* 仿制的枪支

rep·li·cate /ˈreplɪkeɪt/ *verb* **1** [T] **~ sth** (*formal*) to copy sth exactly 复制；（精确地）仿制 SYN **duplicate**：*Subsequent experiments failed to replicate these findings.* 后来的实验没有得出同样的结果。 **2** [T, I] **~ (itself)** (*specialist*) (of a virus or a MOLECULE 病毒或分子) to produce exact copies of itself 再造；再生；自我复制：*The drug prevents the virus from replicating itself.* 这种药能防止病毒复制。▶ **rep·lic·able** *adj.*：*The design is easily replicable.* 这种设计很容易仿制。 **rep·li·ca·tion** /ˌreplɪˈkeɪʃn/ *noun* [U, C]

reply 🔑 /rɪˈplaɪ/ *verb, noun*

■ *verb* (**re·plies**, **re·ply·ing**, **re·plied**, **re·plied**) **1** 🔑 [I, T] to say or write sth as an answer to sb/sth 回答；答复：**~ (to sb/sth) (with sth)** *to reply to a question/an advertisement* 回答问题；回应广告 ◇ *He never replied to any of my letters.* 他从来没给我回过信。◇ *She only replied with a smile.* 她只是报以微笑。◇ **+ speech** *'I won't let you down,' he replied confidently.* 他信心十足地答道："我不会让你失望的。" ◇ **~ that…** *The senator replied that he was not in a position to comment.* 参议员回答说他不宜发表评论。➲ NOTE AT ANSWER **2** [I] **~ (to sth) (with sth)** to do sth as a reaction to sth that sb has said or done 回应；作出反应：*The terrorists replied to the government's statement with more violence.* 恐怖分子以更多的暴力事件来回应政府的声明。

■ *noun* 🔑 [C, U] an act of replying to sth/sb in speech, writing or by some action 回答；答复：*We had over 100 replies to our advertisement.* 我们的广告收到了 100 多个回应。◇ *I asked her what her name was but she* ***made no reply***. 我问她叫什么名字，但她没有回答。◇ (*formal*) *I am writing* ***in reply to*** *your letter of 16 March.* * 3 月 16 日来函收悉，现答复如下。◇ (*BrE*) ***a reply-paid envelope*** (= on which you do not have to put a stamp because it has already been paid for) 邮资已付信封 ◇ (*BrE*) *Morocco scored four goals without reply to win the game.* 摩洛哥队在一球未失的情况下连入四球，赢得了这场比赛。➲ NOTE AT ANSWER

repo man /ˈriːpəʊ mæn; *NAmE* ˈriːpoʊ/ *noun* (*NAmE, informal*) a person whose job is to REPOSSESS (= take back) goods from people who still owe money for them and cannot pay（向拖欠货款者追回商品的）商品收回员

re·port 🔑 /rɪˈpɔːt; *NAmE* rɪˈpɔːrt/ *verb, noun*

■ *verb*

• **GIVE INFORMATION** 提供信息 **1** 🔑 [T, I] to give people information about sth that you have heard, seen, done, etc. 汇报；报告；通报：**~ sth (to sb)** *The crash happened seconds after the pilot reported engine trouble.* 飞行员报告发动机有故障后几秒钟飞机就坠毁了。◇ *Call me urgently if you have anything to report.* 如果有什么事要向我汇报，立即给我打电话。◇ **~ (on sth) (to sb)** *The committee will report on its research next month.* 委员会下个月将汇报他们的研究情况。◇ **~ (sb/sth) doing sth** *The neighbours reported seeing him leave the building around noon.* 邻居们反映说在中午时分看见他离开了大楼。◇ **~ sb/sth + adj.** *The doctor reported the patient fully recovered.* 医生说这位病人已经完全康复。◇ **~ sb/sth as sth/as doing sth** *The house was reported as being in excellent condition.* 报告说明这房子的状况极佳。◇ **be reported to be/have sth** *The house was reported to be in excellent condition.* 报告说明这房子的状况极佳。◇ **~ (that)…** *Employers reported that graduates were deficient in writing and problem-solving skills.* 雇主反映毕业生缺乏写作和解决问题的技能。◇ **~ what, how, etc.…** *She failed to report what had occurred.* 她对发生的事情没有报告。◇ **+ speech** *'The cabin's empty,' he reported.* "小屋是空的。" 他汇报说。

• **NEWS/STORY** 新闻；事件 **2** 🔑 [T, I] to present a written or spoken account of an event in a newspaper, on television, etc. 报道；公布；发表；宣布：**~ sth** *The stabbing was reported in the local press.* 当地的新闻媒体报道了持刀伤人事件。◇ **it is reported that…** *It was reported that several people had been arrested.* 据报道已有数人被捕。◇ **~ that…** *The TV news reported that several people had been arrested.* 据电视新闻报道，已有数人被捕。◇ **~ (on sth)** *She reports on royal stories for the BBC.* 她为英国广播公司做有关王室活动的报道。 **3** 🔑 **be reported** [T] used to show that sth has been stated, and you do not know if it is true or not（不知传言是否确凿）据说，传闻：**~ to do sth** *She is reported to earn over $10 million a year.* 据传她一年挣 1 000 多万美元。◇ **~ as doing sth** *The President is reported as saying that he needs a break.* 据传总统说他需要休息一下。◇ **it is reported that…** *It was reported that changes were being considered.* 有传言说改革措施正在酝酿之中。

• **CRIME/ACCIDENT, ETC.** 犯罪或事故等 **4** 🔑 [T] to tell a person in authority about a crime, an accident, an illness, etc. or about sth bad that sb has done 举报；告发：**~ sth (to sb)** *Have you reported the accident to the police yet?* 你将这次事故报警了吗？◇ *a decrease in the number of reported cases of AIDS* 艾滋病病例报告数量的减少 ◇ **~ sb (to sb) (for sth/for doing sth)** *He's already been reported twice for arriving late.* 他因为迟到已经两次被告发。◇ **~ sb/sth + adj.** *She has reported her daughter missing.* 女儿失踪，她已经向警方报案。

• **ARRIVE** 到达 **5** 🔑 [I] **~ (to sb/sth) (for sth)** to tell sb that you have arrived, for example for work or for a meeting with sb 报到：*You should report for duty at 9.30 a.m.* 你应该在上午 9:30 报到上班。◇ *All visitors must report to the reception desk on arrival.* 所有访客到达后务必在接待处报到。

PHR V **reˌport ˈback** to return to a place, especially in order to work again 回归；返回；（尤指）回到工作岗位：*Take an hour for lunch and report back at 2.* 花一个小时吃午饭，两点钟返回。 **reˌport ˈback (on sth) (to sb)** to give sb information about sth that they have asked you to find out about 汇报（所需信息）；反馈：*Find out as much as you can about him and report back to me.* 尽量查找有关他的资料，向我汇报。◇ *One person in the group should be prepared to report back to the class on your discussion.* 应由其中一名组员准备向全班汇报你们的讨论情况。◇ **report back that…** *They reported back that no laws had actually been broken.* 他们汇报说并没有真正发生违法的事。 **reˈport to sb** (not used in the progressive tenses 不用于进行时) (*business* 商) if you **report to** a particular manager in an organization that you work for, they are officially responsible for your work and tell you what to do 对…负责；隶属；从属

■ *noun*

• **OF NEWS** 新闻 **1** 🔑 **~ (on/of sth)** a written or spoken account of an event, especially one that is published or broadcast 报道：*Are these newspaper reports true?* 报纸上这些报道属实吗？◇ *a weather report* 天气预报 ➲ WORDFINDER NOTE AT JOURNALIST

• **INFORMATION** 信息 **2** 🔑 **~ (on sth)** a spoken or written description of sth containing information that sb needs to have 汇报；报告；记述：*a police/medical report* 警方的 / 医疗报告 ◇ *Can you give us a progress report?* 你可以给我们提供进度报告吗？

• **OFFICIAL STUDY** 研究 **3** ~ (**on sth**) an official document written by a group of people who have examined a particular situation or problem 调查报告：*The committee will publish their report on the health service in a few weeks.* 委员会将在几周内发表他们对公共医疗服务的调查报告。

• **STORY** 传说 **4** a story or piece of information that may or may not be true 传闻：*I don't believe these reports of UFO sightings.* 我不相信这些有关目击不明飞行物的传言。◇ *There are unconfirmed reports of a shooting in the capital.* 有未经证实的传言说在首都发生了枪击事件。

• **ON STUDENT'S WORK** 学生的学习 **5** (*BrE*) (*NAmE* **re'port card**) a written statement about a student's work at school, college, etc. 成绩报告单：*a school report* 学生成绩报告单 ◇ *to get a* ***good/bad report*** 成绩优异 / 欠佳

• **EMPLOYEE** 雇员 **6** (*BrE, business* 商) an employee whose work is the responsibility of a particular manager（某个主管的）下属：*a weekly meeting with my direct reports* 同我的直接下属一起开的周会

• **OF GUN** 枪炮 **7** the sound of an explosion or of a gun being fired 爆炸声；射击声 **SYN** **bang, blast**：*a loud report* 巨大的爆炸声

IDM **of bad/good re'port** (*formal*) talked about by people in a bad/good way 名声坏 / 好

▼**SYNONYMS** 同义词辨析

report

story • account • version

These are all words for a written or spoken account of events. 以上各词均指对所发生事情的记述、讲述。

report a written or spoken account of an event, especially one that is published or broadcast 尤指刊登或广播的报道：*Are these newspaper reports true?* 报纸上这些报道属实吗？

story an account, often spoken, of what happened to sb or of how sth happened; a report of events in a newspaper, magazine or news broadcast 常指对所发生事情的口头叙述、描述、（新闻）报道：*It was many years before the full story was made public.* 许多年之后，事情的全貌才公之于众。◇ *the front-page story* 头版报道

account a written or spoken description of sth that has happened 指对所发生事情的书面或口头描述、叙述、报告：*She gave the police a full account of the incident.* 她向警方详尽地叙述了所发生的事情。

REPORT OR ACCOUNT? 用 report 还是 account?

A **report** is always of recent events, especially news. An **account** may be of recent or past events. * report 总是指对最新事情的报道，尤指新闻报道。account 可指对最近的或过去的事情的叙述。

version a description of an event from the point of view of a particular person or group of people 指特定的人或群体对某事的描述、说法：*She gave us her version of what had happened that day.* 她从她的角度向我们描述了那天发生的事情。

PATTERNS

- a report/story **about** sth
- a **brief**/**short** report/story/account
- a **full** report/story/account/version
- a **news** report/story
- to **give** a(n) report/account/version

---

re·por·tage /rɪ'pɔːtɪdʒ; ˌrepɔː'tɑːʒ; *NAmE* rɪ'pɔːrt-; ˌrepɔːr't-/ *noun* [U] (*formal*) the reporting of news or the typical style in which this is done in newspapers, or on TV and radio 新闻报道；报道风格；报道文体

re·port·ed·ly /rɪ'pɔːtɪdli; *NAmE* -'pɔːrt-/ *adv.* according to what some people say 据说；据报道；据传闻：*The band have reportedly decided to split up.* 据说这个乐队已经决定解散。

reˌported 'question *noun* (*grammar* 语法) = INDIRECT QUESTION

reˌported 'speech (*also* **ˌindirect 'speech**) *noun* [U] (*grammar* 语法) a report of what sb has said that does not use their exact words 间接引语：*In reported speech, 'I'll come later' becomes 'He said he'd come later'.* 在间接引语中，I'll come later 变为 He said he'd come later。

re·port·er /rɪ'pɔːtə(r); *NAmE* -'pɔːrt-/ *noun* a person who collects and reports news for newspapers, radio or television 记者；通讯员：*a reporter from the New York Times*《纽约时报》的记者 ◇ *a crime reporter* 报道罪案的记者 ➲ COMPARE JOURNALIST ➲SEE ALSO CUB REPORTER

re·port·ing /rɪ'pɔːtɪŋ; *NAmE* -'pɔːrt-/ *noun* [U] the presenting of and writing about news on television and radio, and in newspapers 新闻报道：*accurate/balanced/objective reporting* 准确的 / 公正的 / 客观的新闻报道 ◇ (*BrE*) ***Reporting restrictions*** *on the trial have been lifted* (= it can now legally be reported). 对报道这次审讯的限制已经撤销。

re·pose /rɪ'pəʊz; *NAmE* rɪ'poʊz/ *noun, verb*

■ ***noun*** [U] (*literary*) a state of rest, sleep or feeling calm 休息；睡眠；平静；镇静

■ ***verb*** (*literary*) **1** [I] **+ adv./prep.** (of an object 物体) to be or be kept in a particular place 位于；被搁置在 **2** [I] **+ adv./prep.** (of a person 人) to lie or rest in a particular place 躺；休息

re·posi·tory /rɪ'pɒzətri; *NAmE* rɪ'pɑːzətɔːri/ *noun* (*pl.* **-ies**) (*formal*) **1** a place where sth is stored in large quantities 仓库；贮藏室；存放处 **2** a person or book that is full of information 学识渊博的人；智囊；知识宝典：*My father is a repository of family history.* 我的父亲对家族史无所不知。

re·pos·sess /ˌriːpə'zes/ *verb* [usually passive] **~ sth** to take back property or goods from sb who has arranged to buy them but who still owes money for them and cannot pay（因买者未如期付款而）收回（房地产、商品等）：(*BrE*) *First I lost my job, then my house was repossessed.* 我先是失去了工作，后来房子又被收回。 ➲ COLLOCATIONS AT HOUSE ➲COMPARE FORECLOSE (1)

re·pos·ses·sion /ˌriːpə'zeʃn/ *noun* **1** [U, C] the act of repossessing property, goods, etc.（财产、商品等的）收回：*families threatened with repossession* 受到房子将被收回威胁的家庭 ◇ *a repossession order* 物品收回令 **2** [C] a house, car, etc. that has been repossessed 被收回的房子（或汽车等）：*Auctions are the best place for buying repossessions.* 拍卖会是购买被收回商品的最佳地方。

rep·re·hen·sible /ˌreprɪ'hensəbl/ *adj.* (*formal*) morally wrong and deserving criticism（不道德而）应受指责的，应受谴责的 **SYN** **deplorable**

rep·re·sent /ˌreprɪ'zent/ *verb*

• **ACT/SPEAK FOR SB** 为某人做 / 说 **1** [often passive] **~ sb/sth** to be a member of a group of people and act or speak on their behalf at an event, a meeting, etc. 代表：*The competition attracted over 500 contestants representing 8 different countries.* 这次比赛吸引了代表 8 个不同国家的 500 多名参赛者。◇ *Local businesses are well represented on the committee* (= there are a lot of people from them on the committee). 委员会中有许多地方企业的代表。◇ *The President was represented at the ceremony by the Vice-President.* 副总统代表总统出席了这次庆典。 **2** **~ sb/sth** to act or speak officially for sb and defend their interests 作为…的代言人；维护…的利益：*The union represents over 200 000 teachers.* 工会代表着 20 余万名教师的利益。◇ *The association was formed to* ***represent the interests*** *of women artists.* 成立这个协会是为了维护女性艺术家的利益。◇ *Ms Dale is representing the defendant* (= is his/her lawyer) *in the case.* 在这个案件当中，戴尔女士为被告作辩护。

R

• **BE EQUAL TO** 等于 **3** 🔑 *linking verb* + **noun** (not used in the progressive tenses 不用于进行时) to be sth 等于；相当于；意味着 SYN **constitute**: *This contract represents 20% of the company's annual revenue.* 这份合约相当于公司 20% 的年收入。◇ *This decision represents a significant departure from previous policy.* 这个决定意味着在很大程度上脱离了原先的政策。

• **BE EXAMPLE OF** 成为例证 **4** 🔑 [no passive] ~ **sth** to be an example or expression of sth 成为…实例；成为典型；体现 SYN **be typical of**: *a project representing all that is good in the community* 体现着社区中一切美好形象的工程 ◇ *Those comments do not represent the views of us all.* 这些言论并不代表我们所有人的看法。

• **BE SYMBOL** 成为象征 **5** 🔑 ~ **sth** (not used in the progressive tenses 不用于进行时) to be a symbol of sth 作为…的象征；代表 SYN **symbolize**: *Each colour on the chart represents a different department.* 图表中的每一种颜色都代表一个不同的部门。◇ *Wind direction is represented by arrows.* 风向是用箭头表示的。

• **IN PICTURE** 图画 **6** 🔑 ~ **sb/sth (as sb/sth)** | ~ **sb/sth doing sth** (*formal*) to show sb/sth, especially in a picture 展示；描绘 SYN **depict**: *The carvings represent a hunting scene.* 这些雕刻作品描绘了一幅狩猎的场面。◇ *The results are represented in fig.3 below.* 结果如下面的图 3 所示。

• **DESCRIBE** 描述 **7** ~ **sb (as sth)** (*formal*) to present or describe sb/sth in a particular way, especially when this may not be fair （尤指不公平地）展现，描述，表现: *The king is represented as a villain in the play.* 剧中国王的形象是一个恶棍。◇ *The risks were represented as negligible.* 他们把风险说得微不足道。

• **MAKE FORMAL STATEMENT** 正式声明 **8** ~ **sth (to sb)** | ~ **that...** (*formal*) to make a formal statement to sb in authority to make your opinions known or to protest 正式提出（意见、抗议等）: *They represented their concerns to the authorities.* 他们向当局陈述了他们关心的问题。

re-present /ˌriː prɪˈzent/ *verb* ~ **sth** to give, show or send sth again, especially a cheque, bill, etc. that has not been paid（尤指未支付的支票、账单等）再给予，再呈上，再递上

rep·re·sen·ta·tion /ˌreprɪzenˈteɪʃn/ *noun* **1** [U, C] the act of presenting sb/sth in a particular way; something that shows or describes sth 表现；描述；描绘；表现形式 SYN **portrayal**: *the negative representation of single mothers in the media* 媒体对单身母亲的负面描述 ◇ *The snake swallowing its tail is a representation of infinity.* 蛇衔其尾表示无穷无尽。 **2** [U] the fact of having representatives who will speak or vote for you or on your behalf 有代理人；代表；维护；支持者: *The green movement lacks effective representation in Parliament.* 环境保护运动在议会中缺乏有力的支持者。 ◇ *The accused was not allowed legal representation.* 没有允许被告请律师。 ➲ SEE ALSO PROPORTIONAL REPRESENTATION **3 representations** [pl.] (*formal, especially BrE*) formal statements made to sb in authority, especially in order to make your opinions known or to protest 陈述；抗议: *We have **made representations to** the prime minister, but without success.* 我们同首相进行交涉，但没有效果。

rep·re·sen·ta·tion·al /ˌreprɪzenˈteɪʃnl/ *adj.* **1** (*specialist*) (especially of a style of art or painting 尤指艺术或绘画风格) trying to show things as they really are 具象派的 ➲ COMPARE ABSTRACT *adj.* (3) **2** involving the act of representing sb/sth 代表性的: *local representational democracy* 地方代议民主政体

rep·re·sen·ta·tive 🔑 /ˌreprɪˈzentətɪv/ *noun, adj.*

■ *noun* ~ **(of sb/sth) 1** 🔑 a person who has been chosen to speak or vote for sb else or on behalf of a group 代表: *a representative of the UN* 联合国代表 ◇ *our elected representatives in government* 政府中我们选举产生的代表 ◇ *a union representative* 工会代表 ◇ *The committee includes representatives from industry.* 这个委员会包括产业界的代表。 ➲ WORDFINDER NOTE AT UNION **2** 🔑 (*also informal* **rep**) a person who works for a company and travels around selling its products 销售代表；销售代理；代销人: *a sales representative* 销售代表 ◇ *She's our representative in France.* 她是我们公司驻法国的销售代表。 **3** 🔑 a person chosen to take the place of sb else 代表；代表他人者: *He was the Queen's representative at the ceremony.* 他代表女王出席了庆典。 **4** 🔑 a person who is typical of a particular group 典型人物；代表性人物: *The singer is regarded as a representative of the youth of her generation.* 这位歌手被看作是她那一代年轻人的典型代表。 **5 Representative** (*abbr.* **Rep.**) (in the US) a member of the House of Representatives, the Lower House of Congress; a member of the House of Representatives in the lower house of a state parliament （美国）众议院议员

■ *adj.* **1** 🔑 ~ **(of sb/sth)** typical of a particular group of people 典型的；有代表性的: *Is a questionnaire answered by 500 people **truly representative** of the population as a whole?* 由 500 人参加的问卷调查能真正代表所有民众吗？ **2** 🔑 [usually before noun] containing or including examples of all the different types of people or things in a large group 代表各类人（或事物）的: *a **representative sample** of teachers* 各类教师的代表 **3** 🔑 ~ **(of sth)** able to be used as a typical example of sth 可作为典型（或示例）的: *The painting is not representative of his work of the period.* 这幅画不是他在那个时期画作的代表作。 **4** (of a system of government, etc. 政治体制等) consisting of people who have been chosen to speak or vote on behalf of the rest of a group 由代表组成的；代议制的: *a representative democracy* 代议制民主政体 OPP **unrepresentative**

re·press /rɪˈpres/ *verb* **1** ~ **sth** to try not to have or show an emotion, a feeling, etc. 克制；压抑；抑制 SYN **control**: *to repress a smile* 忍住不笑 ◇ *He burst in, making no effort to repress his fury.* 他冲了进来，毫不掩饰自己的愤怒。 **2** [often passive] ~ **sb/sth** to use political and/or military force to control a group of people and restrict their freedom 压制；镇压 SYN **put down, suppress**

re·pressed /rɪˈprest/ *adj.* **1** (of a person 人) having emotions or desires that are not allowed to be expressed 压抑的；克制的 **2** (of emotions 情感) not expressed openly 受压抑的；被抑制的: *repressed anger* 被抑制的怒气

re·pres·sion /rɪˈpreʃn/ *noun* [U] **1** the act of using force to control a group of people and restrict their freedom 压制；镇压: *government repression* 政府的压制 **2** the act of controlling strong emotions and desires and not allowing them to be expressed so that they no longer seem to exist 抑制；克制；压抑: *sexual repression* 性压抑

re·pres·sive /rɪˈpresɪv/ *adj.* **1** (of a system of government 政治体制) controlling people by force and restricting their freedom 压制的；专制的；严厉的 SYN **dictatorial, tyrannical**: *a **repressive regime/measure/law*** 实行高压政策的政权；镇压措施；严厉的法律 **2** controlling emotions and desires and not allowing them to be expressed 压抑的；抑制的；克制的 ▸ **re·pres·sive·ly** *adv.* **re·pres·sive·ness** *noun* [U]

re·prieve /rɪˈpriːv/ *verb, noun*

■ *verb* [usually passive] (not usually used in the progressive tenses 通常不用于进行时) **1** ~ **sb** to officially cancel or delay a punishment for a prisoner who is CONDEMNED to death 撤销…的死刑；缓期执行…的死刑: *a reprieved murderer* 被判死刑而缓期执行的杀人犯 **2** ~ **sth** to officially cancel or delay plans to close sth or end sth 取消关闭；暂缓终止: *70 jobs have been reprieved until next April.* 有 70 个职位暂时保留到明年四月份。

■ *noun* [usually sing.] **1** an official order stopping a punishment, especially for a prisoner who is CONDEMNED to death 刑罚终止令；（尤指）死刑缓刑令 SYN **a stay of execution** **2** a delay before sth bad happens 延缓；缓解: *Campaigners have won a reprieve for the hospital threatened with closure.* 活动家们为这家受关闭威胁的医院赢得了喘息的机会。

rep·ri·mand /ˈreprɪmɑːnd; *NAmE* -mænd/ *verb* ~ **sb (for sth)** | + **speech** (*formal*) to tell sb officially that you do not approve of them or their actions 申斥；训斥；斥责 SYN **rebuke**: *The officers were severely reprimanded for their unprofessional behaviour.* 军官们因违反职业操守而受到了严厉的斥责。 ▸ **rep·ri·mand** *noun* [C, U]: *He received* *a severe reprimand for his behaviour.* 他的行为受到了谴责。

re·print *verb, noun*

■ ***verb*** /ˌriːˈprɪnt/ [usually passive] **~ sth** to print more copies of a book, an article, etc. with few or no changes 重印；再版

■ ***noun*** /ˈriːprɪnt/ **1** an act of printing more copies of a book because all the others have been sold 重印；再版 **2** a book that has been reprinted 重印本；再版本

re·prisal /rɪˈpraɪzl/ *noun* [C, U] a violent or aggressive act towards sb because of sth bad that they have done towards you 报复；报复行动 **SYN** **retaliation**: *They did not want to give evidence for fear of reprisals.* 他们因为害怕报复而不想作证。◇ *They shot ten hostages* ***in reprisal for*** *the assassination of their leader.* 他们的首领遭到暗杀。为了报复，他们枪杀了十名人质。 ➲ COLLOCATIONS AT WAR

re·prise /rɪˈpriːz/ *noun* [usually sing.] a repeated part of sth, especially a piece of music 重复部分；（尤指乐曲的）反复

repro /ˈriːprəʊ; *NAmE* -proʊ/ *adj., noun*

■ ***adj.*** (*informal*) copied, especially from a style that was originally made in the past（尤指按古典风格）复制的，仿制的：*Victorian repro furniture* 仿制的维多利亚式家具

■ ***noun*** **1** [C, U] something that is copied from a style that was originally made in the past 仿古物品 **2** [U] = REPROGRAPHICS

re·proach /rɪˈprəʊtʃ; *NAmE* -ˈproʊtʃ/ *noun, verb*

■ ***noun*** (*formal*) **1** [U] blame or criticism for sth you have done 责备；批评：*His voice was full of reproach.* 他的话完全是一种责备的语气。◇ *The captain's behaviour is* ***above/beyond reproach*** (= you cannot criticize it). 队长的行为无可厚非。 **2** [C] a word or remark expressing blame or criticism 责备的话语；批评的言辞：*He listened to his wife's bitter reproaches.* 他听着妻子严厉的责备。 **3** [U] a state of shame or loss of honour 羞耻；没面子；丢脸：*Her actions brought reproach upon herself.* 她的举动使她很丢面子。 **4** [sing.] **~ (to sb/sth)** a person or thing that brings shame on sb/sth（给…）带来羞辱的人（或事）；（使…）丢脸的人（或事） **SYN** **discredit**: *Such living conditions are a reproach to our society.* 这样的生活条件是我们这个社会的耻辱。

■ ***verb*** (*formal*) **1 ~ sb (for sth/for doing sth) | ~ sb (with sth/with doing sth) | ~ (sb) + speech** to blame or criticize sb for sth that they have done or not done, because you are disappointed in them 责备；指责；批评：*She was reproached by colleagues for leaking the story to the press.* 她因为将这件事透露给新闻媒体而受到同事的指责。 **2 ~ yourself (for sth/for doing sth) | ~ yourself (with sth)** to feel guilty about sth that you think you should have done in a different way 自责；（为…）感到内疚：*He reproached himself for not telling her the truth.* 他因为没有告诉她真相而自责。

re·proach·ful /rɪˈprəʊtʃfl; *NAmE* -ˈproʊtʃ-/ *adj.* expressing blame or criticism 表示责备（或批评）的：*a reproachful look* 责备的目光 ▶ **re·proach·ful·ly** /-fəli/ *adv.*

rep·ro·bate /ˈreprəbeɪt/ *noun* (*formal* or *humorous*) a person who behaves in a way that society thinks is immoral 堕落的人；不道德的人 ▶ **rep·ro·bate** *adj.* [only before noun]

re·pro·cess /riːˈprəʊses; *NAmE* riːˈprɑːses; -ˈproʊ-/ *verb* **~ sth** to treat waste material so that it can be used again 再加工（废品）：*All these countries reprocess nuclear fuel.* 这些国家均对核燃料进行再处理。

re·pro·duce 🔑 /ˌriːprəˈdjuːs; *NAmE* -ˈduːs/ *verb* **1** 🔑 [T] **~ sth** to make a copy of a picture, piece of text, etc. 复制：*It is illegal to reproduce these worksheets without permission from the publisher.* 未经出版者许可翻印这些习题是违法的。◇ *The photocopier reproduces colours very well.* 这台复印机复制的色彩效果很好。 **2** 🔑 [T] **~ sth** to produce sth again; to make sth happen again in the same way 再生产；再制造；使再次发生；再现：*The atmosphere of the novel is successfully reproduced in the movie.* 小说的氛围在电影中得到成功再现。 **3** 🔑 [I, T] if people, plants, animals, etc. **reproduce** or **reproduce themselves**, they produce young 繁殖；生育：*Most reptiles reproduce by laying eggs on land.* 大多数爬行动物在陆地产卵进行繁殖。◇ **~ itself** *cells reproducing themselves* (= making new ones) 自我繁殖的细胞 ▶ **re·pro·du·cible** /-əbl/ *adj.*

re·pro·duc·tion /ˌriːprəˈdʌkʃn/ *noun* **1** [U] the act or process of producing babies, young animals or plants 生殖；繁殖：*sexual reproduction* 有性生殖 **2** [U] the act or process of producing copies of a document, book, picture, etc. 复制；再版：*Use a black pen on white paper to ensure good reproduction.* 用白纸黑笔，以确保复制清晰。 **3** [U] the process of recording sounds onto tapes, CDs, DVDs, etc.（声音的）复制，录制：*Digital recording gives excellent sound reproduction.* 数字录音的声音效果极佳。 **4** [C] a thing that has been reproduced, especially a copy of a work of art（尤指艺术品的）复制品：*a catalogue with colour reproductions of the paintings for sale* 待售画作的彩色图样目录 ◇ *reproduction furniture* (= furniture made as a copy of an earlier style) 仿制的旧式家具

re·pro·duct·ive /ˌriːprəˈdʌktɪv/ *adj.* [only before noun] connected with reproducing babies, young animals or plants 生殖的；繁殖的：*reproductive organs* 生殖器官

repro·graph·ics /ˌriːprəˈgræfɪks/ (*also informal* **repro**) *noun* [U] (*specialist*) the science and practice of copying documents and pictures for publishing, etc. 复印术；复制术

re·proof /rɪˈpruːf/ *noun* (*formal*) **1** [U] blame or disapproval 责备；谴责；非难：*His words were a mixture of pity and reproof.* 他的话里既有同情也有责备。 **2** [C] a remark that expresses blame or disapproval 责备的话语；非难的言辞 **SYN** **rebuke**: *She received a mild reproof from the teacher.* 她受到了老师温和的责备。

re·prove /rɪˈpruːv/ *verb* **~ sb (for sth/for doing sth) | ~ (sb) + speech** (*formal*) to tell sb that you do not approve of sth that they have done 指责；责备；非难 **SYN** **rebuke**: *He reproved her for rushing away.* 他责备她不该匆匆离去。 ▶ **re·prov·ing** *adj.* [usually before noun]: *a reproving glance* 责备的一瞥 **re·prov·ing·ly** *adv.*

rep·tile /ˈreptaɪl; *NAmE also* -tl/ *noun* any animal that has cold blood and skin covered in SCALES, and that lays eggs. Snakes, CROCODILES and TORTOISES are all reptiles. 爬行动物 ➲ VISUAL VOCAB PAGE V13 ➲ COMPARE AMPHIBIAN ▶ **rep·til·ian** /repˈtɪliən/ *adj.*：*our reptilian ancestors* 我们像爬虫一样的祖先 ◇ (*figurative*) *He licked his lips in an unpleasantly reptilian way.* 他恶心地像爬虫般舔着嘴唇。

re·pub·lic /rɪˈpʌblɪk/ *noun* a country that is governed by a president and politicians elected by the people and where there is no king or queen 共和国；共和政体：*newly independent republics* 新独立的共和国 ◇ *the Republic of Ireland* 爱尔兰共和国 ➲ COMPARE MONARCHY (2)

re·pub·lic·an /rɪˈpʌblɪkən/ *noun, adj.*

■ ***noun*** **1** a person who supports a form of government with a president and politicians elected by the people and with no king or queen 拥护共和政体的人；共和主义者 ➲ COMPARE ROYALIST **2 Republican** (*abbr.* **R**, **Rep.**) a member or supporter of the Republican Party of the US（美国）共和党党员，共和党的支持者 ➲ COMPARE DEMOCRAT (2) **3 Republican** a person from Northern Ireland who believes that Northern Ireland should be part of the Republic of Ireland and not part of the United Kingdom 北爱尔兰共和主义者（认为北爱尔兰应脱离英国回归爱尔兰共和国） ➲ COMPARE LOYALIST (2)

■ ***adj.*** **1** connected with or like a republic; supporting the principles of a republic 共和国的；共和政体的；拥护共和政体的：*a republican government/movement* 共和政体 / 运动 **2** (*also* **Republican**) (*abbr.* **R**, **Rep.**) connected with the Republican Party in the US（美国）共和党的 **3** (*also* **Republican**) connected with or supporting the Republicans in Northern Ireland 北爱尔兰共和主义者的；支持北爱尔兰共和主义者的 ▶ **re·pub·lic·an·ism** (*also* **Re·pub·lic·an·ism**)

R

noun [U]: *a strong commitment to Republicanism* 对共和主义的强烈的信念

the Re'publican Party *noun* [sing.] one of the two main political parties in the US, usually considered to support conservative views, and to want to limit the power of central government（美国）共和党 ➲ COMPARE DEMOCRATIC PARTY

re·pudi·ate /rɪ'pju:dieɪt/ *verb* (*formal*) **1 ~ sth** to refuse to accept sth 拒绝；不接受；回绝 SYN **reject**: *to repudiate a suggestion* 拒绝一项建议 **2 ~ sth** to say officially and/or publicly that sth is not true（正式地）否认，驳斥 SYN **deny**: *to repudiate a report* 驳斥一份报告 **3 ~ sb** (*old-fashioned*) to refuse to be connected with sb any longer 拒绝与…往来；断绝同…的关系 SYN **disown**: *He repudiated his first wife and married her sister.* 他和第一个妻子离了婚，然后娶了她的妹妹。▶ **re·pudi·ation** /rɪˌpju:di'eɪʃn/ *noun* [U]

re·pudi·atory /rɪ'pju:diətri; *NAmE* -tɔ:ri/ *adj.* (*law* 律) relating to a situation in which sb refuses to do sth that they are legally required to do 拒绝履行法律义务的

re·pug·nance /rɪ'pʌgnəns/ *noun* [U] (*formal*) a strong feeling of dislike or disgust about sth 嫌恶；恶心；强烈的反感 SYN **repulsion**: *She was trying to overcome her physical repugnance for him.* 她努力克制对他非常强烈的反感。

re·pug·nant /rɪ'pʌgnənt/ *adj.* [not usually before noun] (*formal*) making you feel strong dislike or disgust 使十分嫌恶；使反感；不得人心 SYN **repulsive**: *We found his suggestion absolutely repugnant.* 我们觉得他的建议绝对不得人心。◇ **~ to sb** *The idea of eating meat was repugnant to her.* 一想到吃肉她就想吐。

re·pulse /rɪ'pʌls/ *verb* (*formal*) **1** [usually passive] **~ sb** to make sb feel disgust or strong dislike 使厌恶；使反感 SYN **repel**: *I was repulsed by the horrible smell.* 这种可怕的气味让我恶心。 **2 ~ sb/sth** to fight sb who is attacking you and drive them away 击退；打垮；驱逐 SYN **repel**: *to **repulse an attack/invasion/offensive*** 击退一次进攻 / 入侵 / 攻势 **3 ~ sb/sth** to refuse to accept sb's help, attempts to be friendly, etc. 拒绝接受；回绝 SYN **reject**: *Each time I tried to help I was repulsed.* 每次我想要帮忙都遭到了拒绝。◇ *She repulsed his advances.* 她拒绝了他的追求。

R

re·pul·sion /rɪ'pʌlʃn/ *noun* [U] **1** a feeling of very strong dislike of sth that you find extremely unpleasant 嫌恶感；强烈的反感；憎恶 **2** (*physics* 物) the force by which objects tend to push each other away 排斥力；斥力: *the forces of attraction and repulsion* 引力和斥力 ➲ SEE ALSO REPEL ➲ COMPARE ATTRACTION (4)

re·pul·sive /rɪ'pʌlsɪv/ *adj.* **1** causing a feeling of strong dislike; very unpleasant 令人厌恶的；令人反感的；十分讨厌的 SYN **disgusting**: *a repulsive sight/smell/habit* 令人厌恶的情景 / 气味 / 习惯 ◇ *What a repulsive man!* 这个人真讨厌！ ➲ SYNONYMS AT DISGUSTING **2** (*physics* 物) causing repulsion (= a force that pushes away) 引起排斥的；斥力的: *repulsive forces* 斥力 ▶ **re·pul·sive·ly** *adv.*: *repulsively ugly* 极其丑陋

re·pur·pose /ˌri:'pɜ:pəs; *NAmE* -'pɜ:rp-/ *verb* **~ sth** to change sth slightly in order to make it suitable for a new purpose（为适合新用途）对…稍加修改，略微改动

rep·ut·able /'repjətəbl/ *adj.* that people consider to be honest and to provide a good service 声誉好的；值得信赖的 SYN **respected**: *a reputable dealer/company/supplier* 可信赖的交易商 / 公司 / 供应商 ➲ COMPARE DISREPUTABLE

repu·ta·tion 🔑 /ˌrepju'teɪʃn/ *noun* [C, U] the opinion that people have about what sb/sth is like, based on what has happened in the past 名誉；名声: *to **earn/establish/build a reputation*** 赢得 / 确立 / 树立声誉 ◇ *to have **a good/bad reputation*** 有好 / 坏名声 ◇ **~ (as sth)** *She soon acquired a reputation as a first-class cook.* 她不久就获得了一级厨师的荣誉。◇ **~ (for sth/for doing sth)** *I'm aware of Mark's reputation for being late.* 我知道马克迟到是出了名的。◇ *to damage/ruin sb's reputation* 有损 / 毁坏某人的名声 ◇ *The weather in England is **living up to its reputation*** (= is exactly as expected). 英国的天气完全就如人们所说的那样。

re·pute /rɪ'pju:t/ *noun* [U] (*formal*) the opinion that people have of sb/sth 名誉；名声 SYN **reputation**: *She is a writer of international repute.* 她是一位享有国际声誉的作家。◇ *My parents were artists **of (some) repute*** (= having a very good reputation). 我的双亲是具有（一定）知名度的艺术家。

re·puted /rɪ'pju:tɪd/ *adj.* [not usually before noun] generally thought to be sth or to have done sth, although this is not certain 所谓；普遍认为；号称 SYN **rumoured**: **~ (to be sth)** *He is reputed to be the best heart surgeon in the country.* 他号称是这个国家最好的心脏外科医生。◇ **~ (to have done sth)** *The house is wrongly reputed to have been the poet's birthplace.* 这所房子被误以为是诗人的出生地。◇ *She sold her share of the company for a reputed £7 million.* 她的公司股份据说卖了 700 万英镑。▶ **re·puted·ly** *adv.*

re·quest 🔑 /rɪ'kwest/ *noun, verb*

■ ***noun*** **~ (for sth) | ~ (that...)** **1** 🔑 the action of asking for sth formally and politely（正式或礼貌的）要求，请求: *They made a request for further aid.* 他们要求再给一些援助。◇ *He was there **at the request of his manager/at his manager's request*** (= because his manager had asked him to go). 他按照经理的要求到了那里。◇ *The writer's name was withheld **by request*** (= because the writer asked for this to be done). 按照作者的要求，姓名不予公布。◇ *Catalogues are available **on request**.* 目录可以索取。**2** 🔑 a thing that you formally ask for 要求的事: *My request was granted.* 我的要求得到了满足。◇ *a radio request programme* (= a programme of music, songs, etc. that people have asked for) 电台点播节目

■ ***verb*** 🔑 (*formal*) to ask for sth or ask sb to do sth in a polite or formal way（礼貌或正式地）请求，要求: **~ sth (from sb)** *She requested permission to film at the White House.* 她申请准予在白宫拍摄。◇ *You can request a free copy of the leaflet.* 你可以索要一份免费的宣传单。◇ **~ sb to do sth** *You are requested not to smoke in the restaurant.* 请不要在餐馆里吸烟。◇ **~ that...** *She requested that no one be told of her decision until the next meeting.* 她要求下次开会前不要向任何人透露她的决定。◇ (*BrE also*) *She requested that no one should be told of her decision.* 她要求不要向任何人透露她的决定。◇ **+ speech** *'Please come with me,' he requested.* "请跟我来。"他要求道。

re'quest stop *noun* (*BrE*) a BUS STOP where buses stop only if sb signals to the driver that they want the bus to stop（公共汽车的）招呼站

re·quiem /'rekwiəm; -iem/ (*also* ˌ**requiem 'mass**) *noun* **1** a Christian ceremony for a person who has recently died, at which people say prayers for his or her soul（基督教）追思弥撒，安魂弥撒 **2** a piece of music for this ceremony 安魂曲；安魂弥撒曲

re·quire 🔑 AW /rɪ'kwaɪə(r)/ *verb* (not usually used in the progressive tenses 通常不用于进行时) (*formal*) **1** 🔑 to need sth; to depend on sb/sth 需要；依靠；依赖: **~ sth** *These pets require a lot of care and attention.* 这些宠物需要悉心照顾。◇ *This condition requires urgent treatment.* 这种情况得紧急处理。◇ *Do you require anything else?* (= in a shop/store, for example) 你还需要什么吗？◇ **~ sb/sth to do sth** *True marriage requires us to show trust and loyalty.* 真正的婚姻有赖于我们表现出信任与忠诚。◇ **~ that...** *The situation required that he be present.* 这种情形需要他在场。◇ (*BrE also*) *The situation required that he should be present.* 这种情形需要他在场。◇ **~ doing sth** *Lentils do not require soaking before cooking.* 小扁豆在烹饪前不必浸泡。**2** 🔑 [often passive] to make sb do or have sth, especially because it is necessary according to a particular law or set of rules 使做（某事）；使拥有（某物）；（尤指根据法规）规定: **~ sth** *The wearing of seat belts is required by law.* 法律规定必须系安全带。◇ *'Hamlet' is **required reading*** (= must be read) *for this course.* 《哈姆雷特》是这门课程的指定读物。◇ *Several students failed to reach* *the required standard.* 有几名学生没有达到规定的标准。◇ **~ sth of sb** *What exactly is required of a receptionist* (= what are they expected to do)? 接待员的职责到底是什么？◇ **~ sb to do sth** *All candidates will be required to take a short test.* 所有候选者都要参加一次小测验。◇ **~ that…** *We require that you comply with the following rules:…* 我们要求你遵守以下规则：… ➲SYNONYMS AT DEMAND

re·quire·ment 🔑 AW /rɪˈkwaɪəmənt; *NAmE* -ˈkwaɪərm-/ *noun* (*formal*) **1** 🔑 (*usually* **requirements**) [pl.] something that you need or want 所需的（或所要的）东西：*the basic requirements of life* 基本生活所需 ◇ *a software package to* ***meet your requirements*** 满足你需要的软件包 ◇ *Our immediate requirement is extra staff.* 我们亟须增加人手。◇ *These goods are* ***surplus to requirements*** (= more than we need). 这些货物超过了我们的需要。 **2** 🔑 something that you must have in order to do sth else 必要条件；必备的条件：*to* ***meet/fulfil/satisfy the requirements*** 符合／满足必备的条件 ◇ *What is the minimum entrance requirement for this course?* 这门课程的基本入学条件是什么？

requis·ite /ˈrekwɪzɪt/ *adj., noun*
▪***adj.*** [only before noun] (*formal*) necessary for a particular purpose 必需的；必备的；必不可少的：*She lacks the requisite experience for the job.* 她缺少做这份工作所必需的经验。
▪***noun*** (*formal*) something that you need for a particular purpose 必需的事物：*toilet requisites* (= soap, TOOTHPASTE, etc.) 洗漱用品 ◇ **~ for/of sth** *A university degree has become a requisite for entry into most professions.* 大学学位已经成为在大多数行业谋职的必要条件。 ➲COMPARE PREREQUISITE

requi·si·tion /ˌrekwɪˈzɪʃn/ *noun, verb*
▪***noun*** [C, U] a formal, official written request or demand for sth 正式要求；征用；需要：*the requisition of ships by the government* 政府对船只的征用 ◇ *a* ***requisition form/order*** 征用单；征用令
▪***verb*** **~ sth** to officially demand the use of a building, vehicle, etc., especially during a war or an emergency （尤指战时或紧急状态时）征用：*The school was requisitioned as a military hospital.* 学校被征用作为军用医院。

re·quite /rɪˈkwaɪt/ *verb* **~ sth** (*formal*) to give sth such as love, kindness, a favour, etc. in return for what sb has given you 回报，报以（友爱、善意等）：*requited love* 得到回报的爱 ➲COMPARE UNREQUITED

reroute /ˌriːˈruːt; *NAmE* -ˈraʊt/ *verb* **~ sth** to change the route that a road, vehicle, telephone call, etc. normally follows 改变…的路线；改变…的线路

rerun *noun, verb*
▪***noun*** /ˈriːrʌn/ **1** a television programme that is shown again 重播的电视节目：*reruns of old TV shows* 老电视节目的重播 **2** an event, such as a race or competition, that is held again 重新举行的事；重新赛跑；重赛 **3** something that is done in the same way as sth in the past 重演；再现：*We wanted to avoid a rerun of last year's disastrous trip.* 我们想避免去年那种糟糕的旅行再度出现。
▪***verb*** /ˌriːˈrʌn/ (**re·run·ning reran** /ˌriːˈræn/, **rerun**) **1 ~ sth** to show a film/movie, television programme, etc. again 重演；重播；重放；重映 **2 ~ sth** to do sth again in a similar way （以相同的方式）重做，再次进行：*to rerun an experiment* 重新做实验 **3 ~ sth** to run a race again 重新进行（赛跑等）

re·sale /ˈriːseɪl; ˌriːˈseɪl/ *noun* [U] the sale to another person of sth that you have bought 转卖；转售：*the resale value of a car* 汽车的转卖价格

re·sched·ule AW /ˌriːˈʃedjuːl; *NAmE* ˌriːˈskedʒuːl/ *verb* **1 ~ sth (for/to sth)** | **~ sth to do sth** to change the time at which sth has been arranged to happen, especially so that it takes place later 将…改期；修改…的时间表；重新安排：*The meeting has been rescheduled for next week.* 会议改期到下周举行。 **2 ~ sth** (*finance* 财) to arrange for sb to pay back money that they have borrowed at a later date than was originally agreed 推迟还款；延期还款 ▸**re·sched·ul·ing** *noun* [U, sing.]

re·scind /rɪˈsɪnd/ *verb* **~ sth** (*formal*) to officially state that a law, contract, decision, etc. is no longer valid 废除；取消；撤销 SYN **revoke**

re·scis·sion /rɪˈsɪʒn/ *noun* (*formal*) the act of cancelling or ending a law, an order, or an agreement 废除；取消；撤销

res·cue 🔑 /ˈreskjuː/ *verb, noun*
▪***verb*** 🔑 to save sb/sth from a dangerous or harmful situation 营救；援救；抢救：**~ sb/sth from sth/sb** *He rescued a child from drowning.* 他救起了一名落水儿童。◇ *The house was rescued from demolition.* 这所房子保住了，可以不拆。◇ *You rescued me from an embarrassing situation.* 我正感到尴尬，你为我解了围。◇ **~ sb/sth** *They were eventually rescued by helicopter.* 他们最后被直升机救走了。◇ **~ sb/sth + adj.** *She had despaired of ever being rescued alive.* 她那时对获救生还已经绝望了。 ➲SYNONYMS AT SAVE ▸**res·cuer** *noun*
▪***noun*** **1** 🔑 [U] the act of saving sb/sth from a dangerous or difficult situation; the fact of being saved 救援；营救；抢救；获救：*We had given up hope of rescue.* 我们那时已经放弃了获救的希望。◇ *A wealthy benefactor* ***came to their rescue*** *with a generous donation.* 一位富有的赞助人慷慨解囊挽救了他们。◇ *a* ***rescue attempt/operation*** 一次营救行动 ◇ *a* ***mountain rescue*** *team* 登山救援队 ◇ ***rescue workers/boats/helicopters*** 救援人员／船只／直升机 **2** 🔑 [C] an occasion when sb/sth is saved from a dangerous or difficult situation 营救行动：*Ten fishermen were saved in a daring sea rescue.* 在一次惊心动魄的海上营救行动中，十名渔民获救。

ˈrescue worker *noun* a person whose job is to try to save people from dangerous or difficult situations, especially after an accident or a disaster 救援人员；救护人员：*Rescue workers are working under very difficult conditions to find survivors from the blast.* 救援人员正在非常困难的条件下努力寻找爆炸的幸存者。

re·search 🔑 AW *noun, verb*
▪***noun*** 🔑 /rɪˈsɜːtʃ; ˈriːsɜːtʃ; *NAmE* -sɜːrtʃ/ [U] (*also* **re·searches** [pl.] *especially in BrE*) a careful study of a subject, especially in order to discover new facts or information about it 研究；调查；探索：***medical/historical/scientific, etc. research*** 医学、历史、科学等研究 ◇ ***to do/conduct/undertake research*** 做研究 ◇ **~ (into/on sth/sb)** *He has carried out extensive research into renewable energy sources.* 他对再生能源进行了广泛研究。◇ *Recent research on deaf children has produced some interesting findings about their speech.* 对失聪儿童的最新研究已经在言语能力方面取得了一些令人关注的结果。◇ *What have their researches shown?* 他们的研究证明了什么？◇ *a* ***research project/grant/student*** 研究项目／经费；研究生 ◇ *I've done some research to find out the cheapest way of travelling there.* 我查阅了一番，想找到去那里最省钱的方式。 ➲WORDFINDER NOTE AT SCIENCE ➲COLLOCATIONS AT SCIENTIFIC ➲SEE ALSO MARKET RESEARCH, OPERATIONAL RESEARCH
▪***verb*** 🔑 /rɪˈsɜːtʃ; *NAmE* -ˈsɜːrtʃ/ [I, T] to study sth carefully and try to discover new facts about it 研究；探讨；调查：**~ (into/in/on sth)** *They're researching into ways of improving people's diet.* 他们在研究如何改进人们的饮食。◇ **~ sth** *to research a problem/topic/market* 研究一个问题／课题／市场 ◇ *She's in New York researching her new book* (= finding facts and information to put in it). 她在纽约为她的新书搜集材料。◇ **~ how, what, etc.…** *We have to research how the product will actually be used.* 我们必须研究该产品的实际使用方法。 ▸**re·search·er** AW *noun*

reˌsearch and deˈvelopment *noun* [U] (*abbr.* **R & D**) (in industry, etc.) work that tries to find new products and processes or to improve existing ones 研究和开发

re·sect /rɪˈsekt/ *verb* **~ sth** (*medical* 医) to cut out part of an organ or a piece of TISSUE from the body 切除（部分器官或组织） ▸**re·sec·tion** /rɪˈsekʃn/ *noun* [U, C]

R

re·sell /ˌriːˈsel/ *verb* (**re·sold**, **re·sold** /ˌriːˈsəʊld; *NAmE* -ˈsoʊld/) ~ **sth** to sell sth that you have bought 转售；转卖：*He resells the goods at a profit.* 他转卖货品赢利。

re·sem·blance /rɪˈzembləns/ *noun* [C, U] the fact of being or looking similar to sb/sth 相似；相像 SYN **likeness**：*a striking/close/strong resemblance* 明显的 / 不小的 / 显著的相似之处 ◇ *family resemblances* 亲缘相似 ◇ ~ **to sb/sth** *She bears an uncanny resemblance to Dido.* 她长得酷似迪多。◇ *The movie* ***bears little resemblance to*** *the original novel.* 电影和原著相去甚远。◇ ~ **between A and B** *The resemblance between the two signatures was remarkable.* 两个签名的相似之处非常明显。

re·sem·ble /rɪˈzembl/ *verb* [no passive] (not used in the progressive tenses 不用于进行时) ~ **sb/sth** to look like or be similar to another person or thing 看起来像；显得像；像：*She closely resembles her sister.* 她和她姐姐很像。◇ *So many hotels resemble each other.* 许多酒店看上去都差不多。◇ *The plant resembles grass in appearance.* 这种植物的外形像草。

re·sent /rɪˈzent/ *verb* to feel bitter or angry about sth, especially because you feel it is unfair 愤恨；感到气愤；愤愤不平：~ **sth/sb** *I deeply resented her criticism.* 我对她的批评感到非常气愤。◇ ~ **doing sth** *He bitterly resents being treated like a child.* 他十分厌恶被别人当孩子对待。◇ ~ **sb doing sth** *She resented him making all the decisions.* 她讨厌什么事都要听他的。◇ (*formal*) *She resented his making all the decisions.* 她讨厌什么事都要听他的。

re·sent·ful /rɪˈzentfl/ *adj.* feeling bitter or angry about sth that you think is unfair 感到气愤的；憎恨的；愤慨的：*a resentful look* 充满怨恨的眼神 ◇ ~ **of/at/about sth** *They seemed to be resentful of our presence there.* 他们好像对我们在那里露面很生气。◇ *She was resentful at having been left out of the team.* 她对被运动队淘汰感到气愤。
▸ **re·sent·ful·ly** /-fəli/ *adv.*

re·sent·ment /rɪˈzentmənt/ *noun* [U, sing.] a feeling of anger or unhappiness about sth that you think is unfair 愤恨；怨恨：*to* ***feel/harbour/bear resentment towards/against*** *sb* 对某人感到 / 深怀 / 有怨恨 ◇ *She could not conceal the deep resentment she felt at the way she had been treated.* 受到那样的待遇，她无法掩藏内心强烈的愤恨。

re·ser·va·tion /ˌrezəˈveɪʃn; *NAmE* -zərˈv-/ *noun* **1** [C] an arrangement for a seat on a plane or train, a room in a hotel, etc. to be kept for you 预订；预约：*I'll call the restaurant and* ***make a reservation****.* 我要给餐厅打个电话预订座位。◇ *We have a reservation in the name of Grant.* 我们是以格兰特的名字预订的。➲ WORDFINDER NOTE AT HOTEL, RESTAURANT ➲ COLLOCATIONS AT RESTAURANT ➲ COMPARE BOOKING (1) **2** [C, U] a feeling of doubt about a plan or an idea 保留意见；疑惑 SYN **misgiving**：*I have serious* ***reservations*** *about his ability to do the job.* 我非常怀疑他有没有能力胜任这项工作。◇ *They support the measures* ***without reservation*** (= completely). 他们毫无保留地支持这些措施。 **3** (*also* **re·serve**) [C] an area of land in the US that is kept separate for Native Americans to live in（美国为美洲土著居民划出的）保留地，居留地 **4** [U] = RESERVATION POLICY ➲ SEE ALSO CENTRAL RESERVATION

reserˈvation policy (*also* **re·ser·va·tion**) *noun* [U] (in India) the policy of keeping a fixed number of jobs or places in schools, colleges, etc. for people who are members of SCHEDULED CASTES, SCHEDULED TRIBES or other BACKWARD CLASSES 预留政策（印度为表列种族、表列部族或落后种姓成员保留一定数量的工作岗位或入学名额等）

re·serve /rɪˈzɜːv; *NAmE* rɪˈzɜːrv/ *verb, noun*
■ *verb* **1** to ask for a seat, table, room, etc. to be available for you or sb else at a future time 预订，预约（座位、席位、房间等）SYN **book**：~ **sth for sb/sth** *I'd like to reserve a table for three for eight o'clock.* 我想预订八点钟供三人用餐的桌位。◇ ~ **sth** *I've reserved a room in the name of Jones.* 我以琼斯的名字预订了一个房间。➲ COMPARE BOOK *v.* (1) **2** to keep sth for sb/sth, so that it cannot be used by any other person or for any other reason 保留；预留：~ **sth for sb/sth** *These seats are reserved for special guests.* 这些座位是留给贵宾的。◇ ~ **sth** *I'd prefer to* ***reserve*** *(my)* ***judgement*** (= not make a decision) *until I know all the facts.* 在了解全部事实之前我不想发表意见。 **3** ~ **sth** to have or keep a particular power 拥有，保持，保留（某种权力）：*The management* ***reserves the right*** *to refuse admission.* 管理部门有权拒绝接收。◇ (*law* 律) ***All rights reserved*** (= nobody else can publish or copy this). 版权所有。
■ *noun*
• SUPPLY 补给 **1** [C, usually pl.] a supply of sth that is available to be used in the future or when it is needed 储备（量）；贮藏（量）：*large oil and gas reserves* 大量的石油和天然气贮藏量 ◇ *He discovered unexpected reserves of strength.* 他出乎意料地发现还有体力。◇ *reserve funds* 储备金
• PROTECTED LAND 受保护土地 **2** (*NAmE also* **pre·serve**) [C] a piece of land that is a protected area for animals, plants, etc.（动植物）保护区；自然保护区：*a wildlife reserve* 野生动植物保护区 ➲ SEE ALSO GAME RESERVE, NATURE RESERVE **3** [C] = RESERVATION (3)
• QUALITY/FEELING 品质；情感 **4** [U] the quality that sb has when they do not talk easily to other people about their ideas, feelings, etc. 内向；寡言少语；矜持 SYN **reticence**：*She found it difficult to make friends because of her natural reserve.* 她因天性矜持很难交到朋友。 **5** [U] (*formal*) a feeling that you do not want to accept or agree to sth, etc. until you are quite sure that it is all right to do so 谨慎；保留：*Any contract should be treated* ***with reserve*** *until it has been checked.* 任何契约在经过核实之前都应谨慎对待。◇ *She trusted him* ***without reserve*** (= completely). 她完全信任他。
• IN SPORT 体育运动 **6** [C] an extra player who plays in a team when one of the other players is injured or not available to play 替补队员；后备队员 **7 the reserves** [pl.] a team that is below the level of the main team 替补队；预备队；后备队
• MILITARY FORCE 军队 **8 the reserve** [sing.] (*also* **the reserves** [pl.]) an extra military force, etc. that is not part of a country's regular forces, but is available to be used when needed 预备役部队；后备部队：*the Army Reserve* 预备役部队 ◇ *the reserve police* 预备役警察
• PRICE 价格 **9** (*also* **reˈserve price**) [C] the lowest price that sb will accept for sth, especially sth that is sold at an AUCTION（尤指拍卖中的）底价，最低价
IDM **in reˈserve** available to be used in the future or when needed 储备；备用：*The money was being* ***kept in reserve*** *for their retirement.* 他们把钱存着以备退休后使用。◇ *200 police officers were* ***held in reserve****.* * 200 名警察随时待命。

re·served /rɪˈzɜːvd; *NAmE* rɪˈzɜːrvd/ *adj.* (of a person or their character 人或性格) slow or unwilling to show feelings or express opinions 内向的；寡言少语的；矜持的 SYN **shy** ➲ COMPARE UNRESERVED

re·serv·ist /rɪˈzɜːvɪst; *NAmE* -ˈzɜːrv-/ *noun* a soldier, etc. who is a member of the RESERVES (= a military force that can be used in an emergency) 预备役军人；后备军战士

res·er·voir /ˈrezəvwɑː(r); *NAmE* ˈrezərv-/ *noun* **1** a natural or artificial lake where water is stored before it is taken by pipes to houses, etc. 水库；蓄水池 **2** (*formal*) a large amount of sth that is available to be used（大量的）储备，储藏 **3** (*specialist*) a place in an engine or a machine where a liquid is kept before it is used 储液槽

reset /ˌriːˈset/ *verb* (**re·set·ting**, **reset**, **reset**) **1** ~ **sth** (**to sth**) | ~ **sth to do sth** to change a machine, an instrument or a control so that it gives a different time or number or is ready to use again 调整；重新设置：*You need to reset your watch to local time.* 你需要把表调整到当地时间。 **2** [often passive] ~ **sth** to place sth in the correct position again 重新安置；将…恢复原位：*to reset a broken bone* 重接断骨

re·set·tle /ˌriːˈsetl/ *verb* **1** [T, I] ~ (**sb**) to help people go and live in a new country or area; to go and live in a new country or area 帮助…定居他国（或别的地区）；

到他国（或别的地区）定居：*Many of the refugees were resettled in Britain and Canada.* 许多难民被安置到英国和加拿大。 **2** [T] ~ **sth** to start to use an area again as a place to live 使再次成为定居点：*The region was only resettled 200 years later.* 这一地区 200 年以后才重新有人居住。 **3** [I, T] ~ (**yourself**) to make yourself comfortable in a new position 重感舒适：*The birds flew around and then resettled on the pond.* 鸟儿飞来飞去，然后落在池塘边上。 ▸ **re·set·tle·ment** *noun* [U]: *the resettlement of refugees* 难民的重新安置 ◇ *a resettlement agency* 居民安置机构

re·shape /ˌriːˈʃeɪp/ *verb* ~ **sth** to change the shape or structure of sth 改变…的形状（或结构）；重塑；改组

re·shuf·fle /ˌriːˈʃʌfl/ (*also less frequent* **shuf·fle**) *verb* [T, I] ~ (**sth**) to change around the jobs that a group of people do, for example in a government 改组；进行岗位调整；更改职责配置：*The Prime Minister eventually decided against reshuffling the Cabinet.* 首相最终决定反对改组内阁。 ▸ **re·shuf·fle** /ˈriːʃʌfl/ *noun*：*a Cabinet reshuffle* 内阁改组

res·ide AW /rɪˈzaɪd/ *verb* [I] + **adv./prep.** (*formal*) to live in a particular place 居住在；定居于：*He returned to Britain in 1939, having resided abroad for many years.* 他在国外居住多年以后，于 1939 年回到了英国。

PHR V **reˈside in sb/sth** to be in sb/sth; to be caused by sth 在于；由…造成（或引起）：*The source of the problem resides in the fact that the currency is too strong.* 问题的根源在于货币过于坚挺。 **reˈside in/with sb/sth** (of a power, a right, etc. 权力、权利等) to belong to sb/sth 属于；隶属于 SYN **be vested in**：*The ultimate authority resides with the board of directors.* 最高权力属于董事会。

resi·dence AW /ˈrezɪdəns/ *noun* (*formal*) **1** [C] a house, especially a large or impressive one 住所；住房；（尤指）宅第，豪宅：*a desirable family residence for sale* (= for example, in an advertisement) 待售的理想家居 ◇ *10 Downing Street is the British Prime Minister's* ***official residence.*** 唐宁街 10 号是英国首相的官邸。 **2** [U] the state of living in a particular place 居住；定居：*They were not able to* ***take up residence*** *in their new home until the spring.* 他们到第二年春天才住进了新家。◇ *Please state your occupation and* ***place of residence.*** 请说明你的职业和住址。◇ *The flag flies when the Queen is* ***in residence.*** 女王驻跸在这里时有国旗飘扬。➲ SEE ALSO HALL OF RESIDENCE **3** (*also* **resi·dency**) [U] permission to live in a country that is not your own（在他国的）居住权，居留许可：*They have been denied residence in this country.* 这个国家不给他们居住资格。◇ *a residence permit* 居留许可证

IDM **in ˈresidence** having an official position in a particular place such as a college or university（在大学等处）有正式职位，常驻：*a writer in residence* 常驻作家

resi·dency /ˈrezɪdənsi/ *noun* (*pl.* **-ies**) (*formal*) **1** [U] = RESIDENCE (3)：*She has been granted permanent residency in Britain.* 她获准在英国永久居住。 **2** [U, C] the period of time that an artist, a writer or a musician spends working for a particular institution（艺术家、作家、音乐家为某机构工作的）驻留时间，驻留期 **3** [U] the state of living in a particular place 居住；定居：*a residency requirement for students* 要求学生住校 **4** [U, C] (*especially NAmE*) the period of time when a doctor working in a hospital receives special advanced training 高级专科住院医生实习期 **5** (*also* **resi·dence**) [C] the official house of sb such as an AMBASSADOR 官邸

resi·dent AW /ˈrezɪdənt/ *noun, adj.*

■ ***noun*** **1** a person who lives in a particular place or who has their home there 居民；住户：*a resident of the United States* 美国的居民 ◇ *There were confrontations between local residents and the police.* 当地居民和警察之间有过冲突。 **2** (*formal*) a person who is staying in a hotel（旅馆的）住宿者，旅客，房客：*The hotel restaurant is open to non-residents.* 旅店的餐馆对外开放。 **3** a doctor working in a hospital in the US who is receiving special advanced training（美国的）高级专科住院实习医生 ➲ COMPARE REGISTRAR (3)

■ ***adj.*** living in a particular place（在某地）居住的：*the town's resident population* (= not tourists or visitors) 镇上的居民 ◇ *to be resident abroad/in the US* 住在国外 / 美国 ◇ *Tom's our* ***resident expert*** (= our own expert) *on foreign movies.* 汤姆可是我们的外国电影专家。

ˌresident ˈalien *noun* (*NAmE, law* 律) a person from another country who has permission to stay in the US（获准在美国居留的）外籍居民，外侨

resi·den·tial AW /ˌrezɪˈdenʃl/ *adj.* [usually before noun] **1** (of an area of a town 城市中的地区) suitable for living in; consisting of houses rather than factories or offices 适合居住的；住宅的：*a quiet residential area* 安静的住宅区 ➲ WORDFINDER NOTE AT LOCATION **2** (of a job, a course, etc. 工作、课程等) requiring a person to live at a particular place; offering living accommodation 需要在某地居住的；提供住宿的：*a residential language course* 需要住校的语言课程 ◇ *a residential home for the elderly* 老人院 ◇ *residential care for children* 提供食宿的儿童福利院服务

ˈresidents' association *noun* a group of people who live in a particular area and join together to discuss the problems of that area 居民委员会；居民联合会

re·sidual /rɪˈzɪdjuəl; *NAmE* -dʒu-/ *adj.* [only before noun] (*formal*) remaining at the end of a process 剩余的；残留的 SYN **outstanding**：*There are still a few residual problems with the computer program.* 电脑程序还有一些残留问题。

re·sidu·ary /rɪˈzɪdjuəri; *NAmE* -dʒueri/ *adj.* **1** (*law* 律) remaining from the money and property left by a person who has died after all debts, gifts, etc. have been paid 剩余遗产的 **2** (*specialist*) remaining at the end of a process 剩余的；残留的

resi·due /ˈrezɪdjuː; *NAmE* -duː/ *noun* **1** a small amount of sth that remains at the end of a process 剩余物；残留物；残渣：*pesticide residues in fruit and vegetables* 残留在水果和蔬菜中的杀虫剂 **2** (*law* 律) the part of the money, property, etc. of a person who has died that remains after all the debts, gifts, etc. have been paid 剩余遗产：*The residue of the estate was divided equally among his children.* 剩余遗产被他的孩子平分了。

re·siduum /rɪˈzɪdjuəm/ *noun* (*pl.* **re·sidua** /-djuə/) (*specialist*) something that remains after a reaction or process has taken place（化学反应的）残基，残渣，残留物；（某种进程的）残体

re·sign /rɪˈzaɪn/ *verb* [I, T] to officially tell sb that you are leaving your job, an organization, etc. 辞职；辞去（某职务）：~ (**as sth**) *He resigned as manager after eight years.* 八年后，他辞去了经理的职务。◇ ~ (**from sth**) *Two members resigned from the board in protest.* 董事会的两名成员辞职以示抗议。◇ ~ **sth** *My father resigned his directorship last year.* 我父亲去年辞去了董事的职务。

PHR V **reˈsign yourself to sth** to accept sth unpleasant that cannot be changed or avoided 听任；只好接受；顺从：*She resigned herself to her fate.* 她只好听天由命了。◇ **resign yourself to doing sth** *We had to resign ourselves to making a loss on the sale.* 我们只好接受销售造成的亏损。

res·ig·na·tion /ˌrezɪɡˈneɪʃn/ *noun* **1** [U, C] the act of giving up your job or position; the occasion when you do this 辞职：*a letter of resignation* 辞职信 ◇ *There were calls for her resignation from the board of directors.* 有人要求她辞去董事会中的职务。◇ *Further resignations are expected.* 预计还会有人辞职。➲ COLLOCATIONS AT JOB **2** [C] a letter, for example to your employers, to say that you are giving up your job or position 辞职信；辞呈：*to* ***offer/hand in/tender your resignation*** 呈递 / 上交 / 提交辞职信 ◇ *We haven't received his resignation yet.* 我们还没有收到他的辞呈。 **3** [U] patient willingness to accept a difficult or unpleasant situation that you cannot change 顺从；听任：*They accepted their defeat with resignation.* 他们无可奈何地承认失败。

re·signed /rɪˈzaɪnd/ *adj.* being willing to calmly accept sth unpleasant or difficult that you cannot change 逆来顺受的；顺从的：*a resigned sigh* 无可奈何的叹息 ◇ ~ **to sth/doing sth** *He was resigned to never seeing his birthplace* again. 他认命了，甘愿永不再去他的出生地。▶ **re·sign·ed·ly** /-nɪdli/ *adv.* : *'I suppose you're right,' she said resignedly.* "看来你的话是对的。" 她无奈地说。

re·sil·i·ence /rɪ'zɪliəns/ (*also less frequent* **re·sili·ency** /-nsi/) *noun* [U] **1** the ability of people or things to feel better quickly after sth unpleasant, such as shock, injury, etc. 快速恢复的能力；适应力 **2** the ability of a substance to return to its original shape after it has been bent, stretched or pressed 还原能力；弹力

re·sili·ent /rɪ'zɪliənt/ *adj.* **1** able to feel better quickly after sth unpleasant such as shock, injury, etc. 可迅速恢复的；有适应力的： *He'll get over it—young people are amazingly resilient.* 他会克服的，年轻人的适应力惊人。 **2** (of a substance 物质) returning to its original shape after being bent, stretched, or pressed 有弹性（或弹力）的；能复原的 ▶ **re·sili·ent·ly** *adv.*

resin /'rezɪn; *NAmE* 'rezn/ *noun* [C, U] **1** a sticky substance that is produced by some trees and is used in making VARNISH, medicine, etc. 树脂 **2** an artificial substance similar to resin, used in making plastics 合成树脂 ▶ **res·in·ous** /'rezɪnəs; *NAmE* 'rezənəs/ *adj.* : *the resinous scent of pine trees* 松脂的香气

re·sist 🔑 /rɪ'zɪst/ *verb* **1** 🔑 [T, I] to refuse to accept sth and try to stop it from happening 抵制；阻挡 SYN **oppose**: ~ (**sth**) *to resist change* 抵制变革 ◇ *They are determined to resist pressure to change the law.* 他们决心顶住要求改革法律的压力。◇ ~ **doing sth** *The bank strongly resisted cutting interest rates.* 银行强烈反对降低利率。 **2** 🔑 [I, T] to fight back when attacked; to use force to stop sth from happening 反抗；回击；抵抗： *He tried to pin me down, but I resisted.* 他试图按住我，但我奋力反抗。◇ ~ **sth** *She was charged with **resisting arrest**.* 她被控拒捕。 **3** 🔑 [T, I] (usually in negative sentences 通常用于否定句) to stop yourself from having sth you like or doing sth you very much want to do 忍住；抵挡： ~ (**sth**) *I finished the cake. I couldn't resist it.* 我忍不住把整块蛋糕都吃了。◇ *I found the temptation to miss the class too hard to resist.* 我抵挡不住逃课的诱惑。◇ ~ **doing sth** *He couldn't resist showing off his new car.* 他忍不住炫耀起了他的新车。 ➲ MORE LIKE THIS 27, page R28 **4** 🔑 [T] ~ **sth** to not be harmed or damaged by sth 使不受…的伤害；抗（伤害）： *A healthy diet should help your body resist infection.* 健康饮食有助于身体抗感染。◇ *This new paint is designed to resist heat.* 这种新油漆具有耐热性。

re·sist·ance 🔑 /rɪ'zɪstəns/ *noun* **1** 🔑 [U, sing.] dislike of or opposition to a plan, an idea, etc.; refusal to obey 反对；抵制；抗拒： *As with all new ideas it met with resistance.* 和所有的新观念一样，它受到了抵制。◇ ~ **to sb/sth** *There has been a lot of resistance to this new law.* 这项新的法规已经遭到强烈抵制。◇ *Resistance to change has nearly destroyed the industry.* 对变革的抵制几乎毁了这个行业。 **2** 🔑 [U, sing.] the act of using force to oppose sb/sth 抵抗；反抗： *armed resistance* 武装反抗 ◇ *The defenders **put up a strong resistance**.* 保卫者顽强地抵抗。◇ ~ **to sb/sth** *The demonstrators **offered** little or no **resistance** to the police.* 示威者几乎没有对警察作任何反抗。 **3** 🔑 [U, sing.] ~ (**to sth**) the power not to be affected by sth 抗力；抵抗力： *AIDS lowers the body's resistance to infection.* 艾滋病降低了身体的抗感染能力。 **4** [U, sing.] ~ (**to sth**) a force that stops sth moving or makes it move more slowly 阻力： ***wind/air resistance*** (= in the design of planes or cars) 风阻；空气阻力 **5** [U, C] (*physics* 物) (*symb.* **R**) the opposition of a substance or device to the flow of an electrical current 电阻 ➲ COMPARE REACTANCE **6** (*often* **the Resistance**) [sing.+sing./pl. v.] a secret organization that resists the authorities, especially in a country that an enemy has control of（尤指敌占区的）秘密抵抗组织： *resistance fighters* 秘密抵抗战士 IDM ➲ SEE LINE *n.*

re·sist·ant /rɪ'zɪstənt/ *adj.* **1** ~ (**to sth**) not affected by sth; able to resist sth 抵抗的；有抵抗力的： *plants that are resistant to disease* 抗病植株 **2** ~ (**to sth**) opposing sth and trying to stop it happening 抵制的；阻止的： *Elderly people are not always resistant to change.* 上了年纪的人并不总是抵制变革。 **3 -resistant** (in adjectives 构成形容词) not damaged by the thing mentioned 抗…的；耐…的： *disease-resistant plants* 抗病植株 ◇ *fire-resistant materials* 耐火材料 ➲ SEE ALSO HEAT-RESISTANT, WATER-RESISTANT

re·sist·er /rɪ'zɪstə(r)/ *noun* a person who resists sb/sth 抵制者；抗拒者；反抗者

re·sist·ible /rɪ'zɪstəbl/ *adj.* that can be resisted 可抵制的；可抗拒的 OPP **irresistible**

re·sist·ive /rɪ'zɪstɪv/ *adj.* **1** able to survive or cope with the action or effect of sth 抗…的；耐…的 **2** (*physics* 物) relating to electrical resistance 电阻的 ▶ **re·sist·iv·ity** /ˌrɪzɪ'stɪvɪti/ *noun* [U, C]

re·sis·tor /rɪ'zɪstə(r)/ *noun* (*physics* 物) a device that has RESISTANCE to an electric current in a CIRCUIT 电阻器

resit /ˌriː'sɪt/ *verb* (**re·sit·ting**, **resat**, **resat** /ˌriː'sæt/) (*BrE*) (*also* **re·take** *BrE, NAmE*) [T, I] ~ (**sth**) to take an exam or a test again, usually after failing it the first time 重考；（通常指）补考 ➲ WORDFINDER NOTE AT EXAM ▶ **resit** /'riːsɪt/ (*also* **re·take**) *noun* : *Students are only allowed one resit.* 学生只有一次补考机会。

re·size /ˌriː'saɪz/ *verb* ~ **sth** to make sth bigger or smaller, especially an image on a computer screen 改变（尤指计算机图像等）的大小

re·skill /ˌriː'skɪl/ *verb* [I, T] ~ (**sb**) to learn new skills so that you can do a new job; to teach sb new skills（为新工作）学习新技能；教（某人）新技能

reso·lute /'rezəluːt/ *adj.* having or showing great determination 坚决的；有决心的 SYN **determined**: *resolute leadership* 坚定的领导 ◇ *He became even more resolute in his opposition to the plan.* 他更加坚决地反对这个计划。 OPP **irresolute** ▶ **reso·lute·ly** *adv.* : *They remain resolutely opposed to the idea.* 他们仍然坚决反对这种观点。 **reso·lute·ness** *noun* [U]

reso·lution AW /ˌrezə'luːʃn/ *noun* **1** [C] a formal statement of an opinion agreed on by a committee or a council, especially by means of a vote 决议；正式决定： ***to pass/adopt/carry a resolution*** 通过一项决议 **2** [U, sing.] the act of solving or settling a problem, disagreement, etc.（问题、分歧等的）解决，消除 SYN **settlement**: *The government is pressing for an early resolution of the dispute.* 政府正在不断敦促早日解决这起纠纷。 **3** [U] the quality of being resolute or determined 坚定；坚决；有决心 SYN **resolve**: *The reforms owe a great deal to the resolution of one man.* 这些改革主要归功于一个人的坚定决心。 **4** [C] ~ (**to do sth**) a firm decision to do or not to do sth 决心；决定： *She **made a resolution** to visit her relatives more often.* 她决定要多走走亲戚。◇ *Have you made any **New Year's resolutions*** (= for example, to give up smoking from 1 January)? 你有什么新年计划吗？ **5** [U, sing.] the power of a computer screen, printer, etc. to give a clear image, depending on the size of the dots that make up the image 清晰度；析像；分辨率： *high-resolution graphics* 高清晰度的图形

re·solve 🔑 AW /rɪ'zɒlv; *NAmE* rɪ'zɑːlv; rɪ'zɔːlv/ *verb, noun*

■ *verb* (*formal*) **1** 🔑 [T] ~ **sth/itself** to find an acceptable solution to a problem or difficulty 解决（问题或困难） SYN **settle**: ***to resolve an issue/a dispute/a conflict/a crisis*** 解决问题 / 争端 / 冲突 / 危机 ◇ *Both sides met in order to try to resolve their differences.* 双方会晤以努力解决分歧。 **2** [T, I] to make a firm decision to do sth 决心；决定： ~ **to do sth** *He resolved not to tell her the truth.* 他决定不告诉她真相。◇ ~ (**that**)... *She resolved (that) she would never see him again.* 她决心再也不见他了。◇ ~ **on sth/on doing sth** *We had resolved on making an early start.* 我们已经决定早点动身。 **3** [T] (of a committee, meeting, etc. 委员会、会议等) to reach a decision by means of a formal vote（经正式投票）作出决定，作出决议；表决： **it is resolved that...** *It was resolved that the matter be referred to a higher authority.* 经过表决，决定把这件事提交给上级主管部门。◇ ~ **that...** *They resolved that the matter be referred to a higher authority.* 他们经

R

过表决，决定把这件事提交给上级主管部门。◇ **~ to do sth** *The Supreme Council resolved to resume control over the national press.* 最高委员会作出决议恢复对国家新闻机构的控制。

PHR V **re'solve into sth | re'solve sth into sth** **1** to separate or to be separated into its parts（使）分解为：*to resolve a complex argument into its basic elements* 把一个复杂的论点分解成几个基本要点 **2** (of sth seen or heard at a distance 远处景物、响声等) to gradually turn into a different form when it is seen or heard more clearly 逐渐变为（另一种形式）；显现（为）：*The orange light resolved itself into four lanterns.* 橙色的光亮逐渐变成了四盏灯。 **3** to gradually become or be understood as sth 逐步变成；逐渐被理解为：*The discussion eventually resolved itself into two main issues.* 讨论后来集中在两大主要议题上。

■ ***noun*** [U] (*formal*) strong determination to achieve sth 决心；坚定的信念 SYN **resolution**: *The difficulties in her way merely strengthened her resolve.* 她所遇到的困难只是让她更加坚定。◇ **~ to do sth** *The government reiterated its resolve to uncover the truth.* 政府重申一定要查个水落石出。

re·solved /rɪˈzɒlvd; *NAmE* rɪˈzɑːlvd; rɪˈzɔːlvd/ *adj.* [not before noun] ~ (**to do sth**) (*formal*) determined 下定决心；坚定：*I was resolved not to see him.* 我决意不见他。

res·on·ance /ˈrezənəns/ *noun* **1** [U] (*formal*) (of sound 声音) the quality of being resonant 洪亮；响亮：*Her voice had a strange and thrilling resonance.* 她的声音洪亮，有一种奇特的震撼人心的效果。 **2** [C, U] (*specialist*) the sound or other VIBRATION produced in an object by sound or VIBRATIONS of a similar FREQUENCY from another object 共鸣；共振；谐振 **3** [U, C] (*formal*) (in a piece of writing, music, etc. 文章、乐曲等) the power to bring images, feelings, etc. into the mind of the person reading or listening; the images, etc. produced in this way 激发联想的力量；引起共鸣的力量；引起的联想（或共鸣）

res·on·ant /ˈrezənənt/ *adj.* **1** (*formal*) (of sound 声音) deep, clear and continuing for a long time 嘹亮的；响亮的；回响的；悠扬的：*a deep resonant voice* 深沉而响亮的声音 **2** (*specialist*) causing sounds to continue for a long time 共振的；谐振的；共鸣的 SYN **resounding**: *resonant frequencies* 谐振频率 **3** (*literary*) having the power to bring images, feelings, memories, etc. into your mind 引起联想的；产生共鸣的：*a poem filled with resonant imagery* 充满了让人浮想联翩的意象的诗歌 ▸ **res·on·ant·ly** *adv.*

res·on·ate /ˈrezəneɪt/ *verb* (*formal*) **1** [I] (of a voice, an instrument, etc. 嗓音、乐器等) to make a deep, clear sound that continues for a long time 产生共鸣；发出回响；回荡 **2** [I] (of a place 地方) to be filled with sound; to make a sound continue longer（使）回响，起回声 SYN **resound**: *a resonating chamber* 产生回音的房间 ◇ **~ with sth** *The room resonated with the chatter of 100 people.* 屋里充满了 100 人唧唧喳喳的声音。 **3** [I] ~ (**with sb/sth**) to remind sb of sth; to be similar to what sb thinks or believes 使产生联想；引起共鸣；和…的想法（或观念）类似：*These issues resonated with the voters.* 这些问题引起了投票者的共鸣。

PHR V **'resonate with sth** (*literary*) to be full of a particular quality or feeling 充满：*She makes a simple story resonate with complex themes and emotions.* 她使一部情节简单的小说充满了复杂的主题和情感。

res·on·ator /ˈrezəneɪtə(r)/ *noun* (*specialist*) a device for making sound louder and stronger, especially in a musical instrument 共振器；共鸣箱

re·sort 🔑 /rɪˈzɔːt; *NAmE* rɪˈzɔːrt/ *noun, verb*

■ ***noun*** **1** 🔑 [C] a place where a lot of people go on holiday/vacation 旅游胜地；度假胜地：***seaside/ski/mountain, etc. resorts*** 海滨、滑雪、山区等度假胜地 ◇ (*BrE*) *a popular **holiday resort*** 受欢迎的旅游胜地 ◇ *the resort town of Byron Bay* 度假小镇拜伦贝城 ➲ WORDFINDER NOTE AT TOURIST ➲ COLLOCATIONS AT TRAVEL **2** [U] **~ to sth** the act of using sth, especially sth bad or unpleasant, because nothing else is possible 诉诸；求助；采取 SYN **recourse**: *There are hopes that the conflict can be resolved **without resort** to violence.* 冲突有望不需要诉诸武力而得到解决。 **3** 🔑 **the first/last/final ~** the first or last course of action that you should or can take in a particular situation 应急措施；可首先（或最后）采取的手段：*Strike action should be regarded **as a last resort**, when all attempts to negotiate have failed.* 罢工应该是最后一着，在所有的谈判努力都告失败时才使用。◇ ***In the last resort*** (= in the end) *everyone must decide for themselves.* 最后人人都得自己作决定。

■ ***verb***

PHR V **re'sort to sth** 🔑 to make use of sth, especially sth bad, as a means of achieving sth, often because there is no other possible solution 诉诸；求助于；依靠 SYN **recourse**: *They felt obliged to resort to violence.* 他们觉得有必要诉诸暴力。◇ **resort to doing sth** *We may have to resort to using untrained staff.* 我们也许只能使用未受过训练的员工了。

re·sound /rɪˈzaʊnd/ *verb* (*formal*) **1** [I] ~ (**through sth**) (of a sound, voice, etc. 声音、嗓音等) to fill a place with sound 回响；回荡：*Laughter resounded through the house.* 笑声在屋里回荡。◇ (*figurative*) *The tragedy resounded around the world.* 这一惨案传遍了全世界。 **2** [I] ~ (**with/to sth**) (of a place 地方) to be filled with sound 回荡着声音；回响着声音：*The street resounded to the thud of marching feet.* 街道上回荡着行进步伐的铿锵声。

re·sound·ing /rɪˈzaʊndɪŋ/ *adj.* [only before noun] **1** very great 巨大的；令人瞩目的 SYN **emphatic**: ***a resounding victory/win/defeat*** 巨大的胜利 / 成功 / 失败 ◇ *The evening was **a resounding success**.* 晚会办得非常圆满。 **2** (of a sound 声音) very loud and continuing for a long time 响亮的；嘹亮的；回响的 SYN **resonant** ▸ **re·sound·ing·ly** *adv.*

re·source 🔑 AW /rɪˈsɔːs; -ˈzɔːs; *NAmE* ˈriːsɔːrs; rɪˈsɔːrs/ *noun, verb*

■ ***noun*** **1** 🔑 [C, usually pl.] a supply of sth that a country, an organization or a person has and can use, especially to increase their wealth 资源；财力：*the exploitation of minerals and other **natural resources*** 矿产和其他自然资源的开发 ◇ *We do not have the resources* (= money) *to update our computer software.* 我们没有钱来更新我们的电脑软件。◇ *We must make the most efficient use of the available financial resources.* 我们必须最有效地利用现有财力。◇ *We agreed to **pool our resources*** (= so that everyone gives sth). 我们同意把我们的资源集中起来。 ➲ COLLOCATIONS AT ENVIRONMENT ➲ SEE ALSO HUMAN RESOURCES **2** 🔑 [C] something that can be used to help achieve an aim, especially a book, equipment, etc. that provides information for teachers and students 有助于实现目标的东西；资料：*The database could be used as a teaching resource in colleges.* 该数据库可用作大学里的一种教学辅助工具。◇ *Time is your most valuable resource, especially in examinations.* 时间是你最宝贵的东西，尤其是在考试中。◇ *resource books for teachers* 教师参考书 **3 resources** [pl.] personal qualities such as courage and imagination that help you deal with difficult situations 勇气；才智；谋略：*He has no inner resources and hates being alone.* 他没有什么精神力量，因而害怕独处。

■ ***verb*** **~ sth** to provide sth with the money or equipment that is needed 向…提供资金（或设备）：*Schools in the area are still inadequately resourced.* 本地区的学校仍然没有足够的资金。

re·source·ful AW /rɪˈsɔːsfl; -ˈzɔːs-; *NAmE* -ˈsɔːrs-/ *adj.* (*approving*) good at finding ways of doing things and solving problems, etc. 机敏的；足智多谋的；随机应变的 SYN **enterprising** ▸ **re·source·ful·ly** /-fəli/ *adv.* **re·source·ful·ness** *noun* [U]

re·spawn /ˌriːˈspɔːn/ *verb* [I, T] ~ (**sb/sth**) if a character that has been killed in a video game **respawns** or is **respawned**, that character appears again in the game（电子游戏中的人物）重生，复活

re·spect 🔑 /rɪˈspekt/ *noun, verb*

■ ***noun*** **1** 🔑 [U, sing.] ~ (**for sb/sth**) a feeling of admiration for sb/sth because of their good qualities or achievements 尊敬；敬意；尊重：*I have the greatest respect for*

R

your brother. 我非常尊敬你的哥哥。◇ *A two-minute silence was held as a* ***mark of respect.*** 人们静默两分钟以示尊敬。◇ *A deep mutual respect and understanding developed between them.* 他们之间产生了深切的相互尊重和理解。◇ *It was very interesting. Respect!* (= used to praise sb) 这很有意思。了不起！ ➲ SEE ALSO SELF-RESPECT **OPP disrespect** **2** [U, sing.] ~ (**for sb/sth**) polite behaviour towards or care for sb/sth that you think is important 重视；尊重；维护：*to show a lack of respect for authority* 蔑视权威 ◇ *He has no respect for her feelings.* 他根本不尊重她的感情。◇ *Everyone has a right to be* ***treated with respect.*** 人人有权受到尊重。 **OPP disrespect** **3** [C] a particular aspect or detail of sth（事物的）方面，细节：***In this respect*** *we are very fortunate.* 在这方面，我们是很幸运的。◇ *There was one respect, however, in which they differed.* 然而，他们在一点上有分歧。

IDM in respect of sth (*formal* or *business* 商) **1** concerning 关于；就…而言：*A writ was served on the firm in respect of their unpaid bill.* 公司由于欠账而收到了传票。 **2** in payment for sth 作为…的报酬：*money received in respect of overtime worked* 得到的加班费 **with re'spect | with all due re'spect** (*formal*) used when you are going to disagree, usually quite strongly, with sb（通常在表示强烈不同意之前说）恕我直言：*With all due respect, the figures simply do not support you on this.* 恕我直言，这些数字根本不能支持你的观点。 **with respect to sth** (*formal* or *business* 商) concerning 关于；就…而言：*The two groups were similar with respect to income and status.* 这两组在收入和地位方面是相似的。 ➲ MORE AT RESPECT *n.*, PAY *v.*

■ *verb* **1** (not usually used in the progressive tenses 通常不用于进行时) to have a very good opinion of sb/sth; to admire sb/sth 尊敬；尊重；仰慕：**~ sb/sth** *I respect Jack's opinion on most subjects.* 在大多数事情上，我尊重杰克的意见。◇ *a much loved and* ***highly respected*** *teacher* 备受爱戴和尊敬的老师 ◇ **~ sb/sth for sth** *She had always been honest with me, and I respect her for that.* 她一直对我很诚实。我非常敬重她这一点。 **2** **~ sth** to be careful about sth; to make sure you do not do sth that sb would consider to be wrong 慎重对待；谨慎从事；尊重：*to respect other people's property* 不侵犯别人的财产 ◇ *She promised to respect our wishes.* 她保证尊重我们的愿望。◇ *He doesn't respect other people's right to privacy.* 他不尊重别人的隐私权。 **3** **~ sth** to agree not to break a law, principle, etc. 遵守；不损害；不违背：*The new leader has promised to respect the constitution.* 新的领导人承诺遵守宪法。

re·spect·abil·ity /rɪˌspektəˈbɪləti/ *noun* [U] the fact of being considered socially acceptable 体面；名望；得体

re·spect·able /rɪˈspektəbl/ *adj.* **1** considered by society to be acceptable, good or correct 体面的；得体的；值得尊敬的：*a highly respectable neighbourhood* 非常体面的街区 ◇ *a respectable married man* 正派的已婚男子 ◇ *Go and make yourself look respectable.* 去把自己弄得体面点儿。 **OPP disreputable** **2** fairly good; that there is not reason to be ashamed of 相当好的；不丢面子的 **SYN acceptable**：*a perfectly respectable result* 非常好的结果 ▶ **re·spect·ably** *adv.*：*respectably dressed* 穿得体面

re·spect·er /rɪˈspektə(r)/ *noun*

IDM be no respecter of 'persons to treat everyone in the same way, without being influenced by their importance, wealth, etc. 平等待人；一视同仁

re·spect·ful /rɪˈspektfl/ *adj.* showing or feeling respect 表示敬意的；尊敬的：*The onlookers stood at a respectful distance.* 旁观者站在一定的距离之外，以示尊敬。◇ *We were brought up to be respectful of authority.* 我们从小就学会了尊重权威。 **OPP disrespectful** ▶ **re·spect·ful·ly** /-fəli/ *adv.*：*He listened respectfully.* 他恭敬地听着。

re·spect·ing /rɪˈspektɪŋ/ *prep.* (*formal*) concerning 关于 **SYN with respect to sth**：*information respecting the child's whereabouts* 关于孩子下落的消息

re·spect·ive /rɪˈspektɪv/ *adj.* [only before noun] belonging or relating separately to each of the people or things already mentioned 分别的；各自的：*They are each recognized specialists in their respective fields.* 他们在各自的领域都被视为专家。◇ *the respective roles of men and women in society* 男女在社会中各自的角色

re·spect·ive·ly /rɪˈspektɪvli/ *adv.* in the same order as the people or things already mentioned 分别；各自；顺序为；依次为：*Julie and Mark, aged 17 and 19 respectively* 朱莉和马克，年龄分别为 17 岁和 19 岁

res·pir·ation /ˌrespəˈreɪʃn/ *noun* [U] (*formal*) the act of breathing 呼吸：*Blood pressure and respiration are also recorded.* 血压和呼吸也做了记录。 ➲ SEE ALSO ARTIFICIAL RESPIRATION

res·pir·ator /ˈrespəreɪtə(r)/ *noun* **1** a piece of equipment that makes it possible for sb to breathe over a long period when they are unable to do so naturally 人工呼吸器：*She was* ***put on a respirator.*** 给她戴上了人工呼吸器。 **2** a device worn over the nose and mouth to allow sb to breathe in a place where there is a lot of smoke, gas, etc. 防毒面具；口罩；面罩

re·spira·tory /rəˈspɪrətri; ˈrespərətri; *NAmE* ˈrespərətɔːri/ *adj.* connected with breathing 呼吸的：*the respiratory system* 呼吸系统 ◇ *respiratory diseases* 呼吸道疾病

re·spire /rɪˈspaɪə(r)/ *verb* [I] (*specialist*) to breathe 呼吸

res·pir·om·eter /ˌrespɪˈrɒmɪtə(r); *NAmE* -ˈrɑːm-/ *noun* (*medical* 医) a piece of equipment for measuring how much air sb's lungs will hold 肺活量计

res·pite /ˈrespaɪt; *NAmE* ˈrespɪt/ *noun* [sing., U] **1** ~ (**from sth**) a short break or escape from sth difficult or unpleasant 暂停；暂缓：*The drug brought a brief respite from the pain.* 药物暂时缓解了疼痛。◇ *There was no respite from the suffocating heat.* 闷热的天气根本没有缓解。◇ *She continued to work without respite.* 她连续工作，没有休息。◇ ***respite care*** (= temporary care arranged for old, mentally ill, etc. people so that the people who usually care for them can have a rest) 暂时托管（为老人或病人提供短期照料以使长期照顾者获得短暂休息） ➲ SYNONYMS AT REST **2** a short delay allowed before sth difficult or unpleasant must be done 短暂的延缓；喘息 **SYN reprieve**：*His creditors agreed to give him a temporary respite.* 他的债权人同意给他一个喘息的机会。

re·splen·dent /rɪˈsplendənt/ *adj.* ~ (**in sth**) (*formal* or *literary*) brightly coloured in an impressive way 辉煌的；灿烂的；华丽的：*He glimpsed Sonia, resplendent in a red dress.* 他瞥了索尼娅一眼，见她一身红衣，光彩照人。 ▶ **re·splen·dent·ly** *adv.*

re·spond **AW** /rɪˈspɒnd; *NAmE* rɪˈspɑːnd/ *verb* **1** [I, T] (*rather formal*) to give a spoken or written answer to sb/sth（口头或书面）回答，回应 **SYN reply**：*I asked him his name, but he didn't respond.* 我问他叫什么名字，可他没回答。◇ **~ (to sb/sth) (with sth)** *She never responded to my letter.* 她从来没给我回过信。◇ **+ speech** *'I'm not sure,' she responded.* "我不肯定。"她答道。◇ **~ that…** *When asked about the company's future, the director responded that he remained optimistic.* 问到公司的未来的时候，经理回答说他依然乐观。 ➲ NOTE AT ANSWER **2** [I] ~ (**to sth**) (**with sth/by doing sth**) to do sth as a reaction to sth that sb has said or done 作出反应；响应 **SYN react**：*How did they respond to the news?* 他们对这则消息有什么反应？◇ *The government responded by banning all future demonstrations.* 政府的反应是今后禁止一切示威活动。 **3** [I] ~ (**to sth/sb**) to react quickly or in the correct way to sth/sb 反应灵敏；作出正确反应：*The car responds very well to the controls.* 这辆汽车操纵自如。◇ *You can rely on him to respond to a challenge.* 你可以信赖他，他懂得应付挑战。 **4** [I] ~ (**to sth**) to improve as a result of a particular kind of treatment 有改进；见起色；显出效果：*The infection did not respond to the drugs.* 这些药物对感染没有起作用。

re·spond·ent **AW** /rɪˈspɒndənt; *NAmE* -ˈspɑːnd-/ *noun* **1** a person who answers questions, especially in a survey 回答问题的人；（尤指）调查对象：*60% of the respondents agreed with the suggestion.* 回复调查的人中 60% 同意这项建议。 **2** (*law* 律) a person who is accused of sth 被告

R

re·sponse 🔑 AW /rɪˈspɒns; *NAmE* rɪˈspɑːns/ *noun* **1** 🔑 [C, U] a spoken or written answer（口头的或书面的）回答，答复: *She made no response.* 她没作任何回答。◇ **~ to sb/sth** *In response to your enquiry…* 兹回复阁下询问… ◇ *I received an encouraging response to my advertisement.* 我的广告有了令人鼓舞的回应。 **2** 🔑 [C, U] a reaction to sth that has happened or been said 反应；响应: *The news provoked an angry response.* 这条消息引起了人们的愤怒。◇ *a positive response* 积极的反应 ◇ *I knocked on the door but there was no response.* 我敲了门，可是没有回应。◇ **~ (to sb/sth)** *The product was developed* **in response to** *customer demand.* 这种产品是为了满足顾客的需要而开发的。◇ *We sent out over 1 000 letters but the* **response rate** *has been low* (= few people replied). 我们寄出了 1 000 多封信，但回信寥寥。 **3** [C, usually pl.] **~ (to sb/sth)** a part of a church service that the people sing or speak as an answer to the part that the priest sings or speaks（礼拜仪式中的）答唱咏，启应经

resˈponse time *noun* the length of time that a person or system takes to react to sth 反应时间；回应时间: *The average response time to emergency calls was 9 minutes.* 紧急救助电话的平均回应时间是 9 分钟。

re·spon·si·bil·ity 🔑 /rɪˌspɒnsəˈbɪləti; *NAmE* -ˌspɑːn-/ *noun* (*pl.* **-ies**) **1** 🔑 [U, C] a duty to deal with or take care of sb/sth, so that you may be blamed if sth goes wrong 责任；负责: **~ (for sth)** *We are recruiting a sales manager with responsibility for the European market.* 我们正在招聘负责欧洲市场的销售经理。◇ **~ (for doing sth)** *They have responsibility for ensuring that the rules are enforced.* 他们有责任确保制度的执行。◇ **~ (to do sth)** *It is their responsibility to ensure that the rules are enforced.* 他们有责任确保制度的执行。◇ *parental rights and responsibilities* 父母的权利和义务 ◇ *to* **take/assume** *overall* **responsibility** *for personnel* 对人事部门全面负责 ◇ *I don't feel ready* **to take on** *new* **responsibilities**. 我觉得还没准备好承担新的责任。◇ *to be in a* **position of responsibility** 身居要位 ◇ *I did it* **on my own responsibility** (= without being told to and being willing to take the blame if it had gone wrong). 我做的这件事，由我自己负责。 **2** 🔑 [U] **~ (for sth)** blame for sth bad that has happened 事故责任: *The bank refuses to* **accept responsibility** *for the mistake.* 银行拒绝为这一错误承担责任。◇ *Nobody has* **claimed responsibility** *for the bombing.* 没有人声称对爆炸事件负责。 ➲ SEE ALSO DIMINISHED RESPONSIBILITY **3** 🔑 [U, C] a duty to help or take care of sb because of your job, position, etc. 职责；义务；任务: **~ (to/towards sb)** *She feels a strong* **sense of responsibility** *towards her employees.* 她对自己的雇员有很强的责任感。◇ **~ (to do sth)** *I think we have a* **moral responsibility** *to help these countries.* 我认为我们在道义上有责任帮助这些国家。

re·spon·sible 🔑 /rɪˈspɒnsəbl; *NAmE* -ˈspɑːn-/ *adj.*

• **HAVING JOB/DUTY** 有工作 / 职责 **1** 🔑 having the job or duty of doing sth or taking care of sb/sth, so that you may be blamed if sth goes wrong 有责任；负责；承担义务: **~ (for doing sth)** *Mike is responsible for designing the entire project.* 迈克负责设计全部工程。◇ **~ (for sb/sth)** *Even where parents no longer live together, they each continue to be responsible for their children.* 即使父母不再共同生活，他们也要分别对子女负责。

• **CAUSING STH** 引起某事 **2** 🔑 **~ (for sth)** being able to be blamed for sth 应受责备；有责任: *Who's responsible for this mess?* 是谁弄得这么乱？◇ *Everything will be done to bring those responsible to justice.* 将竭尽全力把罪魁祸首绳之以法。◇ *He is mentally ill and cannot* **be held responsible** *for his actions.* 他有精神病，不能对自己的行为负责。 **3** 🔑 **~ (for sth)** being the cause of sth 作为原因；成为起因: *Cigarette smoking is responsible for about 90% of deaths from lung cancer.* 因患肺癌而死亡者，约 90% 是吸烟所致。

• **TO SB IN AUTHORITY** 对主管者 **4** 🔑 **~ to sb/sth** having to report to sb/sth with authority or in a higher position and explain to them what you have done（向主管者或上级）承担责任: *The Council of Ministers is responsible to the Assembly.* 内阁须向议会负责。

• **RELIABLE** 可靠 **5** 🔑 (of people or their actions or behaviour 人或行为举止) that you can trust and rely on 可信任的；可信赖的；可靠的 SYN **conscientious**: *Clare has a mature and responsible attitude to work.* 克莱尔对待工作成熟而可信赖。 OPP **irresponsible**

• **JOB** 工作 **6** 🔑 [usually before noun] needing sb who can be trusted and relied on; involving important duties 责任重大的；需要可靠的人负责的: *a* **responsible job/position** 责任重大的工作 / 岗位

re·spon·sibly /rɪˈspɒnsəbli; *NAmE* -ˈspɑːn-/ *adv.* in a sensible way that shows you can be trusted 明事理地；认真负责地；可信赖地: *to act responsibly* 办事认真负责 OPP **irresponsibly**

re·spon·sive AW /rɪˈspɒnsɪv; *NAmE* -ˈspɑːn-/ *adj.* **1** [not usually before noun] **~ (to sb/sth)** reacting quickly and in a positive way 反应敏捷；反应积极: *Firms have to be responsive to consumer demand.* 公司必须对顾客的需求作出积极反应。◇ *a flu virus that is not responsive to treatment* 治疗无效的流感病毒 **2** **~ (to sb/sth)** reacting with interest or enthusiasm 反应热烈的；热情的 SYN **receptive**: *The club is responsive to new ideas.* 俱乐部对新的想法都表示欢迎。◇ *a responsive and enthusiastic audience* 反应热烈又热情的观众 **3** (*computing* 计) used to describe a website, etc. that changes to suit the kind of device you are using it on, for example by changing the size of the text or the way that items are arranged on the screen（网站等）响应式设计的，自适应的（可根据使用者的装置以适当的样式呈现内容） OPP **unresponsive** ▸ **re·spon·sive·ly** *adv.* **re·spon·sive·ness** AW *noun* [U]: *a lack of responsiveness to client needs* 对客户的需求反应冷淡

re·spray /ˌriːˈspreɪ/ *verb* **~ sth** to change the colour of sth, especially a car, by painting it with a spray 再喷漆；再喷涂 ▸ **re·spray** /ˈriːspreɪ/ *noun* [usually sing.]

rest 🔑 /rest/ *noun, verb*

▪ ***noun***

• **REMAINING PART/PEOPLE/THINGS** 剩余的部分 / 人 / 事物 **1** 🔑 [sing.] **the ~ (of sth)** the remaining part of sth 剩余部分；残留；其余: *I'm not doing this job for the rest of my life.* 我不会一辈子干这种工作。◇ *How would you like to spend the rest of the day?* 后半天你打算怎么过？◇ *Take what you want and throw the rest away.* 把你想要的拿走，其余的丢掉。 **2** 🔑 [pl.] **the ~ (of sth)** the remaining people or things; the others 其余的人；其他事物；其他: *Don't blame Alex. He's human, like the rest of us.* 不要责怪亚历克斯。他和我们大家一样，也是人。◇ *The first question was difficult, but the rest were pretty easy.* 第一个问题很难，但其余的都相当简单。

• **PERIOD OF RELAXING** 休息时间 **3** 🔑 [C, U] a period of relaxing, sleeping or doing nothing after a period of activity 休息时间；睡眠时间: *I had a good night's rest.* 我睡了一宿好觉。◇ *We stopped for a well-earned rest.* 我们停下来休息，也该休息一下了。◇ **~ (from sth)** *to* **have/take a rest** *from all your hard work* 放下繁重的工作，休息一下 ◇ *Try to* **get some rest**—*you have a busy day tomorrow.* 休息一下吧，你明天还要忙一天呢。◇ *There are no matches tomorrow, which is a* **rest day**, *but the tournament resumes on Monday.* 明天是休息日，没有比赛，但星期一继续比赛。

• **SUPPORT** 支撑物 **4** [C] (often in compounds 常构成复合词) an object that is used to support or hold sth 支撑物；支架；基座；托: *an armrest* (= for example on a seat or chair) 座椅扶手 ➲ VISUAL VOCAB PAGE V38

• **IN MUSIC** 音乐 **5** [C, U] a period of silence between notes; a sign that shows a rest between notes 休止；休止符 ➲ PICTURE AT MUSIC

IDM **and (all) the ˈrest (of it)** (*informal*) used at the end of a list to mean everything else that you might expect to be on the list（列举时用）诸如此类，等等: *He wants a big house and an expensive car and all the rest of it.* 他想要大房子、豪华汽车，如此等等。 **and the ˈrest** (*informal*) used to say that the actual amount or number of sth is much higher than sb has stated（比所说的）还要多；远不止此数: *'It cost 250 pounds…' 'And the rest, and the rest!'* "这要花 250 英镑…" "不止这些，不止！" **at ˈrest 1** (*specialist*) not moving 静止；不动: *At rest the insect looks like*

R

a dead leaf. 这种昆虫不动时看上去像一片枯叶。 **2** dead and therefore free from trouble or anxiety. People say 'at rest' to avoid saying 'dead'.（委婉说法，与 dead 同义）安息，长眠： *She now **lies at rest** in the churchyard.* 她现在长眠在教堂墓地里。 **come to 'rest** to stop moving 停止移动；不再移动：*The car crashed through the barrier and came to rest in a field.* 汽车闯过护栏，在一块田里停了下来。 ◇ *His eyes came to rest on Clara's face.* 他的目光停留在克拉拉的脸上。 **for the 'rest** (*BrE, formal*) apart from that; as far as other matters are concerned 除此之外；至于其他：*The book has some interesting passages about the author's childhood. For the rest, it is extremely dull.* 这本书中关于作者童年的一些章节倒还有意思。除此之外，便无聊至极。 **give it a 'rest** (*informal*) used to tell sb to stop talking about sth because they are annoying you 不要再提（恼人的事）了 **give sth a 'rest** (*informal*) to stop doing sth for a while 暂停；暂时不做 **lay sb to 'rest** to bury sb. People say 'to lay sb to rest' to avoid saying 'to bury' sb.（委婉说法，与 bury 同义）安葬：*George was laid to rest beside his parents.* 乔治被安葬在他父母墓旁。 **lay/put sth to 'rest** to stop sth by showing it is not true（通过揭穿假象）平息，使停止：*The announcement finally laid all the speculation about their future to rest.* 通告最终消除了一切有关他们的未来的推测。 **the rest is 'history** used when you are telling a story to say that you do not need to tell the end of it, because everyone knows it already 结局是尽人皆知的；结果如何不必赘述 ➲ MORE AT MIND *n.*, WICKED *n.*

▼ **SYNONYMS 同义词辨析**

rest

break • respite • time out • breathing space

These are all words for a short period of time spent relaxing. 以上各词均表示短暂的休息。

rest a period of relaxing, sleeping or doing nothing after a period of activity 指休息、睡眠： *We stopped for a well-earned rest.* 我们停下来作个应有的休息。

break a short period of time when you stop what you are doing and rest or eat 指间歇、休息： *Let's take a break.* 咱们休息一会儿吧。 NOTE In British English **break** is a period of time between lessons at school. The North American English word is **recess**. 在英式英语中，break 指课间休息。美式英语表示此义用 recess。

respite a short break from sth difficult or unpleasant 指从困境或不愉快、不舒适的状态中得到暂缓、暂停： *The drug brought a brief respite from the pain.* 药物暂时缓解了疼痛。

time out (*informal, especially NAmE*) time for resting or relaxing away from your usual work or studies 指暂停工作或学习的时间： *Take time out to relax by the pool.* 去游泳池边歇一歇吧。

breathing space a short rest in the middle of a period of mental or physical effort 指脑力或体力活动期间的短暂休息、喘息时间： *This delay gives the party a breathing space in which to sort out its policies.* 这一延误使该党有了喘息之机来厘定其政策。

PATTERNS

- (a) rest/break/respite/time out **from** sth
- to **have/take** (a) rest/break/time out
- to **give sb** (a) rest/break/respite/breathing space

■ *verb*

• **RELAX** 放松 **1** [I, T] to relax, sleep or do nothing after a period of activity or illness; to not use a part of your body for some time 休息；放松： *The doctor told me to rest.* 医生叫我休息。 ◇ *I can **rest easy** (= stop worrying) knowing that she's safely home.* 知道她安然无恙地回到家里，我就可以放心了。 ◇ (*figurative*) *He **won't rest** (= will never be satisfied) until he finds her.* 他非得找到她才会安心。 ◇ **~ sth** *Rest your eyes every half an hour.* 每过半小时让眼睛休息一下。 ➲ SEE ALSO RESTED

• **SUPPORT** 支撑 **2** [T, I] to support sth by putting it on or against sth; to be supported in this way（被）支撑；（使）倚靠；托： **~ sth + adv./prep.** *Rest your head on my shoulder.* 把头靠在我肩上。 ◇ *He rested his chin in his hands.* 他双手托着下巴。 ◇ **+ adv./prep.** *His chin rested on his hands.* 他双手托着下巴。 ◇ *Their bikes were resting against the wall.* 他们的自行车靠在墙上。

• **BE LEFT** 被搁置 **3** [I] if you let a matter **rest**, you stop discussing it or dealing with it 被搁置；中止： *The matter cannot rest there—I intend to sue.* 这件事不能就此了结，我打算提出诉讼。

• **BE BURIED** 被埋葬 **4** [I] **+ adv./prep.** to be buried. People say 'rest' to avoid saying 'be buried'.（委婉说法，与 be buried 同义）安息，长眠：*She rests beside her husband in the local cemetery.* 在当地的墓地里，她长眠在她丈夫的墓旁。 ◇ *May he **rest in peace**.* 愿他安息吧。 ➲ SEE ALSO RIP

IDM **rest as'sured (that...)** (*formal*) used to emphasize that what you say is true or will definitely happen（强调所言确凿无误）尽管放心： *You may rest assured that we will do all we can to find him.* 你就放心吧，我们会千方百计找到他。 **ˌrest your 'case 1 I rest my case** (*sometimes humorous*) used to say that you do not need to say any more about sth because you think that you have proved your point 我的论证到此为止（已经足够） **2** (*law* 律) used by lawyers in court to say that they have finished presenting their case（律师在法庭上）对案情陈述完毕： *The prosecution rests its case.* 控方对案情陈述完毕。 ➲ MORE AT EASY *adv.*, GOD, LAUREL

PHR V **'rest on/upon sb/sth 1** to depend or rely on sb/sth 依靠；依赖： *All our hopes now rest on you.* 现在所有的希望都寄托在你的身上。 **2** to look at sb/sth 凝视；凝望： *Her **eyes rested on** the piece of paper in my hand.* 她的目光落在我手里的一张纸上。 **'rest on sth** to be based on sth 基于；以…为基础： *The whole argument rests on a false assumption.* 全部论证都是基于一个错误的假设。 **'rest with sb (to do sth)** (*formal*) **if it rests with sb to do sth,** it is their responsibility to do it 是…的责任（或分内的事）： *It rests with management to justify their actions.* 管理部门应当为他们的行动说出个道理来。 ◇ *The final decision rests with the doctors.* 要由医生作出最后决定。

'rest area, 'rest stop *noun* (*NAmE*) an area beside an important road where people can stop their cars to rest, eat food, etc.（主干道旁的）停车休息区，休息站 ➲ COMPARE LAY-BY (1)

re·start /ˌriːˈstɑːt; *NAmE* -ˈstɑːrt/ *verb* [I, T] **~ (sth)** to start again, or to make sth start again, after it has stopped（使）重新开始：*to restart a game* 重新开始游戏 ◇ *The doctors struggled to restart his heart.* 医生竭力重新起搏他的心脏。 ▸ **re·start** /ˈriːstɑːt; *NAmE* ˈriːstɑːrt/ *noun*

re·state /ˌriːˈsteɪt/ *verb* **~ sth** (*formal*) to say sth again or in a different way, especially so that it is more clearly or strongly expressed 重申；重新表述 ▸ **re·state·ment** *noun* [U]

res·taur·ant /ˈrestrɒnt; *NAmE* -trɑːnt; -tərɑːnt/ *noun* a place where you can buy and eat a meal 餐馆；餐厅： *an Italian restaurant* 一家意大利餐馆 ◇ *We had a meal in a restaurant.* 我们在餐厅吃了顿饭。 ◇ *We went out to a restaurant to celebrate.* 我们到一家餐馆里庆祝了一番。 ◇ *a restaurant owner* 餐馆老板 ◇ *a self-service restaurant* 自助餐馆 ➲ COMPARE CAFE (1) ➲ **WORDFINDER NOTE** AT EAT

WORDFINDER 联想词： à la carte, course, cuisine, menu, order, reservation, service charge, speciality, waiter

'restaurant car *noun* (*BrE*) = DINING CAR

res·taura·teur /ˌrestərəˈtɜː(r)/ *noun* (*formal*) a person who owns and manages a restaurant 餐馆老板；餐厅经理

'rest cure *noun* a period spent resting or relaxing in order to improve your physical or mental health 休养疗法；静养法

rest·ed /ˈrestɪd/ *adj.* feeling healthy and full of energy because you have had a rest 休息后精力恢复（或精神振

作）的：*I awoke feeling rested and refreshed.* 我睡醒后感觉精力充沛，神清气爽。➲ SEE ALSO REST *v.* (1)

rest·ful /ˈrestfl/ *adj.* that makes you feel relaxed and peaceful 闲适宁静的；使人感到悠闲的 **SYN** **calm**：*a hotel with a restful atmosphere* 气氛闲适幽雅的旅馆

ˈ**rest home** *noun* a place where old or sick people are cared for 养老院；疗养院；休养所

ˈ**rest house** *noun* (in parts of Asia and Africa) a house or HUT that you can pay to stay in like a hotel room, especially in wild country（亚洲和非洲部分地区，尤指野外的）客栈，旅舍

ˈ**resting place** *noun* **1** a grave. People say 'resting place' to avoid saying 'grave'.（委婉说法，与 grave 同义）坟墓，安息处：*her **final/last resting place*** 她的长眠之处 **2** a place where you can rest 休息处

res·ti·tu·tion /ˌrestɪˈtjuːʃn; *NAmE* -ˈtuː-/ *noun* [U] ~ (**of sth**) (**to sb/sth**) **1** (*formal*) the act of giving back sth that was lost or stolen to its owner 归还（真正物主）；归还（赃物等）**SYN** **restoration** **2** (*law* 律) payment, usually money, for some harm or wrong that sb has suffered 赔偿；补偿；（通常指）赔款

rest·ive /ˈrestɪv/ *adj.* (*formal*) unable to stay still, or unwilling to be controlled, especially because you feel bored or not satisfied 难驾驭的；焦躁不安的；不耐烦的 ▸ **rest·ive·ness** *noun* [U]

▼ **COLLOCATIONS 词语搭配**

Restaurants 餐馆

Eating out 去餐馆吃饭

- **eat (lunch/dinner)/dine/meet** at/in a restaurant 在一家餐馆吃（午/晚）饭/进餐/碰面
- **go (out)/take sb (out)** for lunch/dinner/a meal 去/带某人去（外面）吃午饭/吃晚饭/用餐
- **have** a meal with sb 与某人一起吃饭
- **make/have** a reservation (in/under the name of Yamada)（以山田的名字）预订座位
- **reserve/**(*especially BrE*) **book** a table for six 预订一张坐六人的桌子
- **ask for/request** a table for two/a table by the window 要一张两人桌/靠窗的桌子

In the restaurant 在餐馆

- **wait** to be seated 等待就座
- **show sb** to their table 把某人引到桌旁
- **sit** in the corner/by the window/at the bar/at the counter 坐在角落/窗边/吧台边/柜台边
- **hand sb/give sb** the menu/wine list 把菜单/酒水单递给某人
- **open/read/study/peruse** the menu 打开/看/仔细看菜单
- the restaurant **has** a three-course set menu/a children's menu/an extensive wine list 这餐馆有一个三道菜的套餐/儿童菜单/丰富的酒水单
- **taste/sample/try** the wine 品尝葡萄酒
- the waiter **takes** your order 服务生帮你点餐
- **order/choose/have** the soup of the day/one of the specials/the house (*BrE*) speciality/(*especially NAmE*) specialty 点当日例汤/一道特色菜/餐馆特色菜
- **serve/finish** the first course/the starter/the main course/dessert/coffee 端上/吃完第一道菜/开胃菜/主菜/甜点；端上/喝完咖啡
- **complain about** the food/the service/your meal 抱怨食物/服务/饭菜不好
- **enjoy** your meal 享用饭菜

Paying 结账

- **pay/ask for** (*especially BrE*) the bill/(*NAmE*) the check 付账；要求结账
- **pay for/treat sb to** dinner/lunch/the meal 付晚饭/午饭/饭钱；请某人吃晚饭/午饭/饭
- service **is (not) included** 不含服务费
- **give sb/leave (sb)** a tip 给某人小费

rest·less /ˈrestləs/ *adj.* **1** unable to stay still or be happy where you are, because you are bored or need a change 坐立不安的；不耐烦的：*The audience was becoming restless.* 观众开始不耐烦了。◇ *After five years in the job, he was beginning to feel restless.* 这份工作干了五年以后，他开始厌烦了。 **2** without real rest or sleep 没有真正休息的；没有睡眠的 **SYN** **disturbed**：*a restless night* 不眠之夜 ▸ **rest·less·ly** *adv.*：*He moved restlessly from one foot to the other.* 他的两只脚不停地倒替着。 **rest·less·ness** *noun* [U]：*the restlessness of youth* 年轻人的躁动

re·stock /ˌriːˈstɒk; *NAmE* -ˈstɑːk/ *verb* [T, I] ~ (**sth**) (**with sth**) to fill sth with new or different things to replace those that have been used, sold, etc.; to get a new supply of sth 更新（旧物品）；补充（货源）；再补给

res·tor·ation **AW** /ˌrestəˈreɪʃn/ *noun* **1** [U, C] the work of repairing and cleaning an old building, a painting, etc. so that its condition is as good as it originally was 整修；修复：*The palace is closed **for restoration**.* 王宫因整修而停止开放。◇ *restoration work* 修复工作 **2** [U, C] ~ **of sth** the act of bringing back a system, a law, etc. that existed previously（规章制度等的）恢复：*the restoration of democracy/the monarchy* 民主制度/君主政体的恢复 **3** [U] ~ (**of sth**) the act of returning sth to its correct place, condition or owner 复原；复位；回归；归还：*the restoration of the Elgin marbles to Greece* 埃尔金大理石雕塑品之交还希腊 **4 the Restoration** [sing.] the time in Britain after 1660 when, following a period with no king or queen, Charles II became king 王政复辟时期（1660 年，英国经历了一段无王时期后，查理二世登基为王）：*Restoration comedy/poetry* (= written during and after this time) 王政复辟时期的喜剧/诗歌

re·stora·tive /rɪˈstɔːrətɪv/ *adj., noun*

■ ***adj.*** **1** (*formal*) making you feel strong and healthy again 恢复健康的；促使康复的：*the restorative power of fresh air* 新鲜空气的康复功效 **2** (*medical* 医) connected with treatment that repairs the body or a part of it 整容的；整形的：***restorative dentistry/surgery*** 整形牙科/外科

■ ***noun*** (*old-fashioned*) a thing that makes you feel better, stronger, etc. 有助于恢复健康的事物；滋补品

re·store **AW** /rɪˈstɔː(r)/ *verb* **1** ~ **sth** (**to sb**) to bring back a situation or feeling that existed before 恢复（某种情况或感受）：*The measures are intended to restore public confidence in the economy.* 这些举措旨在恢复公众对经济的信心。◇ ***Order was quickly restored** after the riots.* 暴乱过后秩序很快得到了恢复。◇ *Such kindness restores your faith in human nature* (= makes you believe most people are kind). 这样的善心使人又一次感到人性善良。◇ *The operation restored his sight* (= made him able to see again). 手术使他恢复了视力。 **2** ~ **sb/sth to sth** to bring sb/sth back to a former condition, place or position 使复原；使复位；使复职：*He is now fully restored to health.* 他现在完全恢复了健康。◇ *We hope to **restore** the garden **to its former glory*** (= make it as beautiful as it used to be). 我们想把这花园变得和过去一样美丽。 **3** ~ **sth** to repair a building, work of art, piece of furniture, etc. so that it looks as good as it did originally 修复；整修；使复原：*Her job is restoring old paintings.* 她的工作是修复旧画。 **4** ~ **sth** to bring a law, tradition, way of working, etc. back into use 重新采用（或实施）；恢复 **SYN** **reintroduce**：*to restore ancient traditions* 恢复古老的传统 ◇ *Some people argue that the death penalty should be restored.* 有些人主张恢复死刑。 **5** ~ **sth** (**to sb/sth**) (*formal*) to give sth that was lost or stolen back to sb 归还（失物、赃款等）：*The police have now restored the painting to its rightful owner.* 警察已经把这幅油画归还给了它的合法主人。

re·storer /rɪˈstɔːrə(r)/ *noun* a person whose job is to repair old buildings, works of art, etc. so that they look as they did when new 做修复工作的人

re·strain **AW** /rɪˈstreɪn/ *verb* **1** to stop sb/sth from doing sth, especially by using physical force（尤指用武力）制止，阻止，管制：~ **sb/sth** *The prisoner had to*

R

be restrained by the police. 警方只好强行制住囚犯。◇ He placed a restraining hand on her arm. 他拉住她的胳膊制止她。◇ ~ **sb/sth from sth/from doing sth** They have obtained an injunction restraining the company from selling the product. 他们已经得到阻止这家公司出售这一产品的禁销令。 **2** to stop yourself from feeling an emotion or doing sth that you would like to do 约束（自己）；控制（自己）；忍住：~ **sth** John managed to restrain his anger. 约翰努力压制住自己的怒气。◇ ~ **yourself** (**from sth/from doing sth**) She had to restrain herself from crying out in pain. 她只得忍住疼痛，不哭出来。 **3** ~ **sth** to stop sth that is growing or increasing from becoming too large 抑制；控制 SYN **keep under control**: The government is taking steps to restrain inflation. 政府正在采取措施控制通货膨胀。

re·strained AW /rɪˈstreɪnd/ adj. **1** showing calm control rather than emotion 克制的；有节制的：her restrained smile 她克制的微笑 **2** not too brightly coloured or decorated 不艳丽的；朴素的 SYN **discreet**: The costumes and lighting in the play were restrained. 这出戏的服装和灯光都很朴实。

reˈstraining order noun ~ (**against sb**) (especially NAmE) an official order given by a judge which demands that sth must or must not be done. A restraining order does not require a trial in court but only lasts for a limited period of time. 限制令 ➲COMPARE INJUNCTION (1)

re·straint AW /rɪˈstreɪnt/ noun **1** [C, usually pl.] ~ (**on sb/sth**) a rule, a fact, an idea, etc. that limits or controls what people can do 约束力；管制措施；制约因素：The government has imposed export restraints on some products. 政府对一些产品实行了出口控制。 ➲SYNONYMS AT LIMIT **2** [U] the act of controlling or limiting sth because it is necessary or sensible to do so 控制；限制：wage restraint 限制工资增长 **3** [U] the quality of behaving calmly and with control 克制；抑制；约束 SYN **self-control**: The police appealed to the crowd for restraint. 警方呼吁群众保持克制。◇ He **exercised** considerable **restraint** in ignoring the insults. 他表现出相当的克制，没去理会种种侮辱。 **4** [U] (formal) the use of physical force to control sb who is behaving in a violent way（武力）阻止，制止，制伏：the physical restraint of prisoners 对囚犯的人身限制 **5** [C] (formal) a type of SEAT BELT or safety device 座椅安全带；安全装置：Children must use an approved child restraint or adult seat belt. 儿童必须使用经过认可的儿童安全带或成人座椅安全带。

R

re·strict 🔑 AW /rɪˈstrɪkt/ verb **1** 🔑 to limit the size, amount or range of sth 限制，限定（数量、范围等）：~ **sth to sth** Speed is restricted to 30 mph in towns. 在城里车速不得超过每小时 30 英里。◇ We restrict the number of students per class to 10. 我们将每个班的学生人数限定为 10 人。◇ ~ **sth** Fog severely restricted visibility. 浓雾严重影响了能见度。◇ Having small children tends to restrict your freedom. 有了小孩往往会限制你的自由。 **2** 🔑 ~ **sth** to stop sb/sth from moving or acting freely 束缚；妨碍；阻碍 SYN **impede**: The long skirt restricted her movements. 长裙妨碍了她的行动。 **3** 🔑 ~ **sth** (**to sb**) to control sth with rules or laws（以法规）限制：Access to the club is restricted to members only. 俱乐部仅对会员开放。 **4** ~ **yourself/sb** (**to sth/to doing sth**) to allow yourself or sb to have only a limited amount of sth or to do only a particular kind of activity 约束；管束：I restrict myself to one cup of coffee a day. 我控制自己每天只喝一杯咖啡。

re·strict·ed 🔑 AW /rɪˈstrɪktɪd/ adj. **1** 🔑 limited or small in size or amount（大小或数量）有限的，很小的：a restricted space 有限的空间 ◇ a restricted range of foods 有限的食物种类 **2** 🔑 limited in what you are able to do（指能做的事）有限的，受限制的：In those days women led fairly restricted lives. 那时，妇女过着相当受限制的生活。◇ Her vision is restricted in one eye. 她只有一只眼睛有视力。 **3** 🔑 controlled by rules or laws 受（法规）制约的；受控制的；受约束的：to allow children only restricted access to the Internet 只允许儿童有限地接触互联网 ◇ (BrE) a restricted area (= controlled by laws about speed or parking)（车速或停车）限制区 ◇ The tournament is **restricted to** players under the age of 23. 这次比赛只允许 23 岁以下的选手参加。 **4** [usually before noun] (of a place 地方) only open to people with special permission, especially because it is secret or dangerous 不对公众开放的：to enter a restricted zone 进入禁区 **5** (BrE) officially secret and only available to people with special permission 保密的；限于内部传阅的 SYN **classified**: a restricted document 保密文件 OPP **unrestricted**

re·stric·tion 🔑 AW /rɪˈstrɪkʃn/ noun **1** 🔑 [C] a rule or law that limits what you can do or what can happen 限制规定；限制法规：**import/speed/travel, etc. restrictions** 进口、速度、旅行等限制 ◇ ~ **on sth** to **impose/place a restriction on sth** 对某事实行限制 ◇ The government has agreed to **lift restrictions** on press freedom. 政府已经同意撤销对新闻自由的限制。 ➲SYNONYMS AT LIMIT **2** [U] the act of limiting or controlling sb/sth 限制；约束：sports clothes that prevent any restriction of movement 宽松的运动服 **3** [C] a thing that limits the amount of freedom you have 制约因素：the restrictions of a prison 监狱的种种约束 ➲WORDFINDER NOTE AT FREEDOM

re·strict·ive AW /rɪˈstrɪktɪv/ adj. **1** preventing people from doing what they want 限制性的；约束的：restrictive laws 限制性法规 **2** (also **defining**) (grammar 语法) (of RELATIVE CLAUSES 关系从句) explaining which particular person or thing you are talking about rather than giving extra information about them. In 'The books which are on the table are mine', 'which are on the table' is a restrictive relative clause. 限制性的 ➲COMPARE NON-RESTRICTIVE ▶ **re·strict·ive·ly** AW adv.

reˌstrictive ˈpractices noun [pl.] (especially BrE, often disapproving) agreements or ways of working that limit the freedom of workers or employers in order to prevent competition or to protect people's jobs 限制竞争协议，限制竞争的行为（限制工人或雇主的自由，以防止竞争，保护就业）

re·string /ˌriːˈstrɪŋ/ verb (**restrung**, **restrung** /ˌriːˈstrʌŋ/) ~ **sth** to fit new strings on a musical instrument such as a GUITAR or VIOLIN, or on a sports RACKET 给（乐器或球拍）重新装弦

rest·room /ˈrestruːm; -rʊm/ noun (NAmE) a room with a toilet in a public place, such as a theatre or restaurant（公共场所的）盥洗室，洗手间；公共厕所

re·struc·ture AW /ˌriːˈstrʌktʃə(r)/ verb [T, I] ~ (**sth**) to organize sth such as a system or a company in a new and different way 调整结构；改组；重建 ▶ **re·struc·tur·ing** AW noun [U, C, usually sing.]

re·sult 🔑 /rɪˈzʌlt/ noun, verb

■**noun**

• **CAUSED BY STH** 由某事引起 **1** 🔑 [C, U] ~ (**of sth**) a thing that is caused or produced because of sth else 后果；结果：She died **as a result of** her injuries. 她因伤死亡。◇ The failure of the company was a direct result of bad management. 公司倒闭的直接原因是经营不善。◇ He made one big mistake, and, as a result, lost his job. 他犯了个大错，结果丢了工作。◇ The farm was flooded, **with the result that** most of the harvest was lost. 农场被淹，收成损失了一大半。◇ The **end result** (= the final one) of her hard work was a place at medical school. 她勤奋苦读，终于进了医学院。◇ This book is the result of 25 years of research. 这本书是 25 年研究的结晶。 ➲LANGUAGE BANK AT BECAUSE, CONSEQUENTLY

• **OF GAME/ELECTION** 比赛；选举 **2** 🔑 [C] ~ (**of sth**) the final score or the name of the winner in a sports event, competition, election, etc. 结果（包括比分、得票、获胜者或当选者名单等）：They will announce the result of the vote tonight. 今晚他们将宣布投票结果。◇ the election results 选举结果 ◇ the football results 足球比赛的结果 **3** [C, usually sing.] (BrE, informal) a victory or a success, especially in a game of football (SOCCER)（尤指足球比赛的）胜利，胜局：We badly need to **get a result** from this match. 这场比赛我们非赢不可。

• **OF EXAM** 考试 **4** 🔑 [C, usually pl.] (BrE) the mark/grade you get in an exam or in a number of exams 得分；成绩：

▼SYNONYMS 同义词辨析

result

consequence • outcome • repercussion

These are all words for a thing that is caused because of sth else. 以上各词均表示后果、结果。

result a thing that is caused or produced by sth else 指后果、结果： *She died as a result of her injuries.* 她因伤死亡。◇ *This book is the result of 25 years of research.* 这本书是 25 年研究的结晶。

consequence (*rather formal*) a result of sth that has happened, especially a bad result 尤指不好的结果、后果： *This decision could have serious consequences for the industry.* 这项决定可能对该行业造成严重后果。 NOTE **Consequences** is used most frequently to talk about possible negative results of an action. It is commonly used with such words as *adverse, dire, disastrous, fatal, harmful, negative, serious, tragic* and *unfortunate.* Even when there is no adjective, **consequences** often suggests negative results. * consequence 最常用以指某种行为可能产生的负面结果，常与 adverse、dire、disastrous、fatal、harmful、negative、serious、tragic、unfortunate 等词连用。即使没有形容词修饰，consequence 也常含负面结果之义。

outcome the result of an action or process 指行动或过程的结果、效果： *We are waiting to hear the final outcome of the negotiations.* 我们在等待谈判的最终结果。

RESULT OR OUTCOME? 用 result 还是 outcome?

Result is often used to talk about things that are caused directly by sth else. * result 常指由另一事物直接导致的结果： *Aggression is often the result of fear.* 好斗情绪通常是恐惧所致。 **Outcome** is more often used to talk about what happens at the end of a process when the exact relation of cause and effect is less clear. * outcome 较常指某一过程完结时的结果，此时，原因和结果之间的确切关系已不太明显： ~~*Aggression is often the outcome of fear.*~~ **Result** is often used after an event to talk about what happened. **Outcome** is often used before an action or process to talk about what is likely to happen. * result 通常是在事情过去之后谈及其结果，outcome 通常是在行动或过程之前谈及其可能产生的结果。

repercussion (*rather formal*) an indirect and usually bad result of an action or event that may happen some time afterwards 指一段时间后出现的间接的影响，通常指不良反响、恶果

PATTERNS

- to have consequences/repercussions **for** sb/sth
- **with** the result/consequence/outcome **that**...
- a(n)/the **possible** result/consequences/outcome/repercussions
- a(n)/the **likely**/**inevitable** result/consequences/outcome
- (a/an) **negative** results/consequences/outcome/repercussions
- **far-reaching**/**serious** results/consequences/repercussions
- to **have** a result/consequences/an outcome/repercussions

Have you had your results yet? 你知道考试成绩了吗？
• **OF TEST/RESEARCH** 测试；研究 **5** 🔑[C] ~ (**of sth**) the information that you get from a scientific test or piece of research 结果；成果： *the result of an experiment* 实验结果 ➲ WORDFINDER NOTE AT SCIENCE ➲ COLLOCATIONS AT SCIENTIFIC
• **SUCCESS** 成功 **6** 🔑 **results** [pl.] things that are achieved successfully 成功实现的事；成果；成效： *The project is beginning to show results.* 这项工程开始显出成效。◇ *a coach who knows how to get results from his players* 善于调动队员获取成功的教练
■ *verb* 🔑[I] ~ (**from sth**) to happen because of sth else that happened first （因…）发生；（随…）产生： *job losses resulting from changes in production* 生产革新造成的失业 ◇ *When water levels rise, flooding results.* 水位上升，就会发生洪水。◇ *It was a large explosion and the resulting damage was extensive.* 爆炸相当剧烈，造成的破坏范围很大。
PHR V **re'sult in sth** 🔑 to make sth happen 造成；导致 SYN **lead**[1]: *The cyclone has resulted in many thousands of deaths.* 气旋已经造成了成千上万的人死亡。◇ **result in sb/sth doing sth** *These policies resulted in many elderly people suffering hardship.* 这些政策使得许多老人饱受困苦。 ➲ LANGUAGE BANK AT CAUSE

re·sult·ant /rɪ'zʌltənt/ *adj.* [only before noun] (*formal*) caused by the thing that has just been mentioned 因而发生的；因此而产生的： *the growing economic crisis and resultant unemployment* 不断加剧的经济危机以及由此而产生的失业

re·sulta·tive /rɪ'zʌltətɪv/ *adj.* (*grammar* 语法) (of verbs, conjunctions or clauses 动词、连词或从句) expressing or relating to the result of an action 表示结果的；结果性的；结果格的

re·sume /rɪ'zjuːm; *NAmE* -'zuːm/ *verb* (*formal*) **1** [T, I] if you **resume** an activity, or if it **resumes**, it begins again or continues after an interruption 重新开始；（中断后）继续： ~ (**sth**) *to* **resume talks/negotiations** 重新进行会谈 / 谈判 ◇ *She resumed her career after an interval of six years.* 时隔六年之后她又开始了自己的职业生涯。◇ *The noise resumed, louder than before.* 噪声再起，比先前更大。◇ ~ **doing sth** *He got back in the car and resumed driving.* 他回到车上，继续开车。 **2** [T] ~ **your seat/place/position** to go back to the seat or place that you had before 回到（原来的座位、地方或位置）

ré·sumé /'rezjumeɪ; *NAmE* 'rezəmeɪ/ *noun* **1** ~ (**of sth**) a short summary or account of sth 摘要；概述；概要： *a brief résumé of events so far* 到目前为止事件的概述 **2** (*NAmE*) (*BrE* **cur·ricu·lum vitae**) a written record of your education and the jobs you have done, that you send when you are applying for a job （求职用的）履历，简历

re·sump·tion /rɪ'zʌmpʃn/ *noun* [sing., U] ~ (**of sth**) (*formal*) the act of beginning sth again after it has stopped 重新开始；继续进行；恢复： *We are hoping for an early resumption of peace talks.* 我们企盼着早日恢复和谈。

re·sup·ply /ˌriːsə'plaɪ/ *verb* ~ **sb** (**with sth**) to give sb new supplies of sth they need; to give sth to sb again in a different form 向…再供给（所需物品）；（以另一形式）重新提供 ▶ **re·supply** /'riːsəplaɪ/ *noun*

re·sur·face /ˌriː'sɜːfɪs; *NAmE* -'sɜːrf-/ *verb* **1** [I] to come to the surface again after being underwater or under the ground 再次浮出，再次露出（水面或地面）： *The submarine resurfaced.* 潜艇重新浮出水面。◇ (*figurative*) *All the old hostilities resurfaced when they met again.* 他们再次碰面时，过去的种种敌意又都冒了出来。 **2** [T] ~ **sth** to put a new surface on a road, path, etc. 重铺路面

re·sur·gence /rɪ'sɜːdʒəns; *NAmE* -'sɜːrdʒ-/ *noun* [sing., U] the return and growth of an activity that had stopped 复苏；复兴

re·sur·gent /rɪ'sɜːdʒənt; *NAmE* -'sɜːrdʒ-/ *adj.* [usually before noun] (*formal*) becoming stronger or more popular again 复兴的；恢复生机活力的；再度流行的

res·ur·rect /ˌrezə'rekt/ *verb* **1** ~ **sth** to bring back into use sth, such as a belief, a practice, etc., that had disappeared or been forgotten 重新应用；恢复使用；使复兴 SYN **revive** **2** ~ **sb** to bring a dead person back to life 起死回生；使复活 SYN **raise**

res·ur·rec·tion /ˌrezə'rekʃn/ *noun* **1 the Resurrection** [sing.] (in the Christian religion 基督教) the time when Jesus Christ returned to life again after his death; the time when all dead people will become alive again, when the world ends 耶稣复活；（世界末日）所有亡者复活 **2** [U, sing.] a new beginning for sth which is old or which had disappeared or become weak 复苏；复兴

re·sus·ci·tate /rɪ'sʌsɪteɪt/ *verb* ~ **sb/sth** to make sb start breathing again or become conscious again after

R

they have almost died 使苏醒；使恢复知觉 SYN **revive**: *He had a heart attack and all attempts to resuscitate him failed.* 他的心脏病发作，所有抢救他的努力都失败了。◇ (*figurative*) *efforts to resuscitate the economy* 重振经济的努力 ▸ **re·sus·ci·ta·tion** /rɪˌsʌsɪˈteɪʃn/ *noun* [U]: *frantic attempts at resuscitation* 拼命努力使人复苏 ➲ SEE ALSO MOUTH-TO-MOUTH RESUSCITATION

re·tail[1] /ˈriːteɪl/ *noun, adv., verb* ➲ SEE ALSO RETAIL[2]
■ *noun* [U] the selling of goods to the public, usually through shops/stores 零售: *The recommended retail price is £9.99.* 建议零售价为 9.99 英镑。◇ *department stores and other **retail outlets*** 百货商店和其他零售店 ◇ *the **retail trade*** 零售业 ➲ COMPARE WHOLESALE (1) ▸ **re·tail** *adv.*: *to buy/sell retail* (= in a shop/store) 零买；零卖
■ *verb* **1** [T] ~ **sth** to sell goods to the public, usually through shops/stores 零售: *The firm manufactures and retails its own range of sportswear.* 公司生产并零售自己的运动服装系列。 **2** [I] ~ **at/for sth** (*business* 商) to be sold at a particular price 以…价格销售: *The book retails at £14.95.* 这本书的零售价为 14.95 英镑。

re·tail[2] /rɪˈteɪl/ *verb* ~ **sth** (**to sb**) (*formal*) to tell people about sth, especially about a person's behaviour or private life 详说，述说（尤指别人的事情） SYN **recount**[1]: *She retailed the neighbours' activities with relish.* 她饶有兴趣地对邻居们的活动说三道四。 ➲ SEE ALSO RETAIL[1]

re·tail·er /ˈriːteɪlə(r)/ *noun* a person or business that sells goods to the public 零售商；零售店

re·tail·ing /ˈriːteɪlɪŋ/ *noun* [U] the business of selling goods to the public, usually through shops/stores 零售业: *career opportunities in retailing* 零售业的职业机会 ➲ COMPARE WHOLESALING

ˈretail park *noun* (*BrE*) an area containing a group of large shops/stores, located outside a town（城郊）零售商业区

ˌretail ˈprice index (*also* **ˈprice index**) *noun* [sing.] (*abbr.* **RPI**) (in Britain) a list of the prices of some ordinary goods and services which shows how much these prices change each month（英国）零售物价指数 ➲ SEE ALSO CONSUMER PRICE INDEX

R

ˌretail ˈtherapy *noun* [U] (*usually humorous*) the act of going shopping and buying things in order to make yourself feel more cheerful 购物疗法（对花钱买乐这一做法的戏称）: *I was ready for a little retail therapy.* 我准备去接受一下购物治疗。 ➲ **COLLOCATIONS AT SHOPPING**

re·tain 🔑 AW /rɪˈteɪn/ *verb* (*rather formal*) **1** 🔑 ~ **sth** to keep sth; to continue to have sth 保持；持有；保留；继续拥有 SYN **preserve**: *to retain your independence* 保持独立 ◇ *He struggled to retain control of the situation.* 他曾努力保持对局势的控制。◇ *The house retains much of its original charm.* 这所房子保留了许多原有的魅力。◇ *She retained her tennis title for the third year.* 她第三年保住了网球冠军的头衔。 **2** 🔑 ~ **sth** to continue to hold or contain sth 保持；继续容纳: *a soil that retains moisture* 保持水分的土壤 ◇ *This information is no longer retained within the computer's main memory.* 该数据已不再保留在计算机的主存储器中。◇ (*figurative*) *She has a good memory and finds it easy to retain facts.* 她记忆力好，很容易记住事情。 **3** ~ **sb/sth** (*law* 律) if a member of the public **retains** sb such as a lawyer, he or she pays money regularly or in advance so the lawyer, etc. will do work for him or her 聘请（律师等）: *a retaining fee* 给所委托律师的预付辩护费 ◇ *to retain the services of a lawyer* 聘定律师 ➲ SEE ALSO RETENTION, RETENTIVE

re·tain·er AW /rɪˈteɪnə(r)/ *noun* **1** a sum of money that is paid to sb to make sure they will be available to do work when they are needed（聘请律师等的）预付费用，保留金: *The agency will pay you a monthly retainer.* 这个机构将会每月付给你聘金。 **2** (*BrE*) a small amount of rent that you pay for a room, etc. when you are not there in order to keep it available for your use（为保留租房而付的）租房订金 **3** (*NAmE*) a device that keeps a person's teeth straight after they have had ORTHODONTIC treatment with BRACES（牙齿）固位体，保持器 **4** (*old-fashioned*) a servant, especially one who has been with a family for a long time（尤指服务多年的）仆人，家仆

re·tain·ing /rɪˈteɪnɪŋ/ *adj.* [only before noun] (*specialist*) intended to keep sth in the correct position 固定的；矫正的: *a **retaining wall*** (= one that keeps the earth or water behind it in position) 挡土墙；挡水墙

re·take *verb, noun*
■ *verb* /ˌriːˈteɪk/ (**re·took** /-ˈtʊk/, **re·taken** /-ˈteɪkən/) **1** ~ **sth** (especially of an army 尤指部队) to take control of sth such as a town again 收复（失地）；恢复控制: *Government forces moved in to retake the city.* 政府军开进城市，以恢复对它的控制。 ◇ (*figurative*) *Moore fought back to retake the lead later in the race.* 后来穆尔奋力反击，重新夺回了比赛中的领先地位。 **2** = RESIT
■ *noun* /ˈriːteɪk/ **1** the act of filming a scene in a film/movie again, because it was not right before 重拍（电影镜头） **2** = RESIT

re·tali·ate /rɪˈtælieɪt/ *verb* [I] to do sth harmful to sb because they have harmed you first 报复；反击；复仇 SYN **revenge**: ~ (**against sb/sth**) *to retaliate against an attack* 对攻击进行还击 ◇ ~ (**by doing sth/with sth**) *The boy hit his sister, who retaliated by kicking him.* 男孩打了他妹妹，妹妹则回敬了他一脚。 ▸ **re·tali·atory** /rɪˈtæliətri; *NAmE* -tɔːri/ *adj.*: *retaliatory action* 报复行动

re·tali·ation /rɪˌtæliˈeɪʃn/ *noun* [U] ~ (**against sb/sth**) (**for sth**) action that a person takes against sb who has harmed them in some way 报复 SYN **reprisal**: *retaliation against UN workers* 对联合国工作人员的报复 ◇ *The shooting may have been **in retaliation for** the arrest of the terrorist suspects.* 枪击事件可能是对逮捕嫌疑恐怖分子进行的报复行动。

re·tard *verb, noun*
■ *verb* /rɪˈtɑːd; *NAmE* rɪˈtɑːrd/ ~ **sth** (*formal*) to make the development or progress of sth slower 阻碍；减缓；使放慢速度 SYN **delay, slow**: *The progression of the disease can be retarded by early surgery.* 早期手术可以抑制病情的发展。 ▸ **re·tard·ation** /ˌriːtɑːˈdeɪʃn; *NAmE* ˌriːtɑːrˈd-/ *noun* [U]: *Many factors can lead to growth retardation in unborn babies.* 许多因素可以导致胎儿发育迟缓。
■ *noun* /ˈriːtɑːd; *NAmE* ˈriːtɑːrd/ (*taboo, slang*) an offensive way of describing sb who is not intelligent or who has not developed normally 迟钝的人；弱智

re·tard·ed /rɪˈtɑːdɪd; *NAmE* -ˈtɑːrd-/ *adj.* (*old-fashioned, offensive*) less developed mentally than is normal for a particular age 迟钝的；弱智的；智力发育迟缓的 SYN **backward**

retch /retʃ/ *verb* [I] to make sounds and movements as if you are VOMITING although you do not actually do so 干呕；干哕: *The smell made her retch.* 这气味让她恶心。

re·tell /ˌriːˈtel/ *verb* (**re·told**, **re·told** /ˌriːˈtəʊld; *NAmE* ˌriːˈtoʊld/) ~ **sth** to tell a story again, often in a different way（通常以不同的方式）复述，重新讲述

re·ten·tion AW /rɪˈtenʃn/ *noun* [U] (*formal*) **1** the action of keeping sth rather than losing it or stopping it 保持；维持；保留: *The company needs to improve its training and retention of staff.* 公司需要改进对员工的培训和留用工作。 **2** the action of keeping liquid, heat, etc. inside sth rather than letting it escape（液体、热量等的）保持，阻滞: *Eating too much salt can cause fluid retention.* 摄盐过多会导致体液潴留。 **3** the ability to remember things 记忆力；记性: *Visual material aids the retention of information.* 直观材料有助于加强记忆。 ➲ SEE ALSO RETAIN

re·ten·tive AW /rɪˈtentɪv/ *adj.* (of the memory 记忆力) able to store facts and remember things easily 有记性的；记忆力强的 ➲ SEE ALSO RETAIN

re·test /ˌriːˈtest/ *verb* ~ **sb/sth** to test sb/sth again 再测验；再测试；重新试验: *Subjects were retested one month later.* 受实验者一个月后再次接受测试。

re·think /ˌriːˈθɪŋk/ *verb* (**re·thought**, **re·thought** /-ˈθɔːt/) [T, I] ~ (**sth**) to think again about an idea, a course of action, etc., especially in order to change it 重新考虑: *to rethink a plan* 重新考虑一项计划 ▶ **re·think**/ˈriːθɪŋk/ (*also* **re·think·ing**) *noun* [sing.]: *a **radical rethink** of company policy* 对公司方针的彻底反思

reti·cent /ˈretɪsnt/ *adj.* (*formal*) unwilling to tell people about things 寡言少语; 不愿与人交谈; 有保留 SYN **reserved, uncommunicative**: *She was shy and reticent.* 她羞怯而寡言少语。◇ **~ about sth** *He was extremely reticent about his personal life.* 他对自己的私人生活讳莫如深。▶ **reti·cence**/-sns/ *noun* [U]

re·ticu·la·ted/rɪˈtɪkjuleɪtɪd/ *adj.* (*specialist*) built, arranged or marked like a net or network, with many small squares or sections 网状(结构)的; 网络状的

reti·cule/ˈretɪkjuːl/ *noun* (*old use* or *humorous*) a woman's small bag, usually made of cloth and with a string that can be pulled tight to close it (女用)收口手提包

ret·ina /ˈretɪnə; *NAmE* ˈretənə/ *noun* (*pl.* **ret·inas** or **ret·inae** /-niː/) a layer of TISSUE at the back of the eye that is sensitive to light and sends signals to the brain about what is seen 视网膜 ➲ VISUAL VOCAB PAGE V64 ▶ **ret·inal** /ˈretɪnl/ [usually before noun] *adj.*

ret·inue /ˈretɪnjuː; *NAmE* ˈretənuː/ *noun* [C+sing./pl. v.] a group of people who travel with an important person to provide help and support 随行人员; 扈从 SYN **entourage**

re·tire 🔑 /rɪˈtaɪə(r)/ *verb*

• **FROM JOB** 工作 **1** 🔑[I, T] to stop doing your job, especially because you have reached a particular age or because you are ill/sick; to tell sb they must stop doing their job (令)退职; (使)退休: **~ (from sth)** *She was forced to retire early from teaching because of ill health.* 她由于身体不好而被迫早早地从教学岗位上退休。◇ *The company's official retiring age is 65.* 公司正式的退休年龄为 65 岁。◇ **~ to sth** *My dream is to retire to a villa in France.* 我的梦想是退休后在法国住上一栋别墅。◇ **~ as sth** *He has no plans to retire as editor of the magazine.* 他还不打算从杂志主编的位子上退休。◇ **~ sb** *She was retired on medical grounds.* 她由于健康原因被安排退休了。 ➲ WORDFINDER NOTE AT EMPLOY, OLD

• **IN SPORT** 体育运动 **2** [I] to stop competing during a game, race, etc., usually because you are injured (因伤)退出(比赛等): **~ (from sth)** *She fell badly, spraining her ankle, and had to retire.* 她摔得很重,扭伤了脚踝,只好退出比赛。◇ **+ adj.** *He retired hurt in the first five minutes of the game.* 比赛才开始五分钟,他就因伤退场。

• **FROM/TO A PLACE** 地点 **3** [I] (*formal*) to leave a place, especially to go somewhere quieter or more private 离开(尤指去僻静处): *The jury retired to consider the evidence.* 陪审团退庭对证据进行评判。◇ **~ to sth** *After dinner he likes to retire to his study.* 晚饭后,他喜欢躲到书房里去。

• **OF ARMY** 军队 **4** [I] (*formal*) to move back from a battle in order to organize your soldiers in a different way 撤离,撤退(以进行休整)

• **GO TO BED** 睡觉 **5** [I] (*literary*) to go to bed 睡觉; 就寝: *I retired late that evening.* 那天晚上我睡得晚。

• **IN BASEBALL** 棒球 **6** [T] **~ sb** to make a player or team have to stop their turn at BATTING 使(击球员、击球方)出局: *He retired twelve batters in a row.* 他一连使十二个击球手出局。

re·tired 🔑 /rɪˈtaɪəd; *NAmE* rɪˈtaɪərd/ *adj.* having retired from work 已退休的; 已退职的: *a retired doctor* 退休医生 ◇ *Dad is retired now.* 爸爸现在已经退休了。

re·tir·ee /rɪˌtaɪəˈriː/ *noun* (*NAmE*) a person who has stopped working because of their age 退休人员; 退休者

re·tire·ment 🔑 /rɪˈtaɪəmənt; *NAmE* -ˈtaɪərm-/ *noun* **1** 🔑 [U, C] the fact of stopping work because you have reached a particular age; the time when you do this 退休; 退职; 退休年龄: *At 60, he was now approaching retirement.* 他 60 岁了,就要退休了。◇ *Susan is going to **take early retirement*** (= retire before the usual age). 苏珊要提前退休。◇ *retirement age* 退休年龄 ◇ *a retirement pension* 退休金 ➲ COLLOCATIONS AT JOB **2** 🔑 [U, sing.] the period of your life after you have stopped work at a particular age 退休生活: *to provide for retirement* 为退休生活做准备 ◇ *We all wish you a long and happy retirement.* 我们大家祝愿你的退休生活长久而幸福。◇ *Up to a third of one's life is now being spent **in retirement**.* 现在人们一生中能有三分之一的时间过退休生活。 ➲ COLLOCATIONS AT AGE **3** 🔑 [U] **~ (from sth)** the act of stopping a particular type of work, especially in sport, politics, etc. (尤指从体育、政治等方面的)退出,引退,退职: *He announced his retirement from football.* 他宣布退出足球运动。◇ *She **came out of retirement** to win two gold medals at the championships.* 她复出后在锦标赛上赢得了两枚金牌。

re'tirement home (*BrE also* ˌ**old 'people's home**) *noun* a place where old people live and are cared for 养老院; 敬老院

re'tirement plan *noun* (*NAmE*) = PENSION PLAN

re·tir·ing /rɪˈtaɪərɪŋ/ *adj.* preferring not to spend time with other people 不爱与人交往的 SYN **shy**: *a quiet, retiring man* 话少而又腼腆的男子

re·told PAST TENSE, PAST PART. OF RETELL

re·tool /ˌriːˈtuːl/ *verb* **1** [T, I] **~ (sth)** to replace or change the machines or equipment in a factory so that it can produce new or better goods 更换,重新装配(机器设备) **2** [T] **~ sth** (*NAmE, informal*) to organize sth in a new or different way 重新安排; 重组

re·tort/rɪˈtɔːt; *NAmE* rɪˈtɔːrt/ *verb, noun*

■ ***verb*** to reply quickly to a comment, in an angry, offended or humorous way (生气或幽默地)反驳,回嘴: **+ speech** *'Don't be ridiculous!' Pat retorted angrily.* "别荒唐了!"帕特生气地回答道。◇ **~ that...** *Sam retorted that it was my fault as much as his.* 萨姆反驳说我和他同样有错。

■ ***noun*** **1** a quick, angry or humorous reply (生气或幽默的)回应,反驳 SYN **rejoinder, riposte**: *She bit back* (= stopped herself from making) *a sharp retort.* 她克制住了自己,没有尖刻地反驳。 **2** a closed bottle with a long narrow bent SPOUT that is used in a laboratory for heating chemicals 曲颈甑; 曲颈瓶; 蒸馏器 ➲ VISUAL VOCAB PAGE V72

re·touch /ˌriːˈtʌtʃ/ *verb* **~ sth** to make small changes to a picture or photograph so that it looks better 修饰,修整(图片或照片等)

re·trace /rɪˈtreɪs/ *verb* **1** **~ sth** to go back along exactly the same path or route that you have come along 沿原路返回; 折回: *She turned around and began to **retrace her steps** towards the house.* 她转身沿原路向那栋房子走去。 **2** **~ sth** to make the same trip that sb else has made in the past 重走(别人走过的路线): *They are hoping to retrace the epic voyage of Christopher Columbus.* 他们期待着沿哥伦布的壮丽航程进行一次航行。 **3** **~ sth** to find out what sb has done or where they have been 追溯; 找出; 回顾: *Detectives are trying to retrace her movements on the night she disappeared.* 侦探们试图查出她失踪当晚的行踪。

re·tract /rɪˈtrækt/ *verb* **1** [T] **~ sth** (*formal*) to say that sth you have said earlier is not true or correct or that you did not mean it 撤销,收回(说过的话): *He made a false confession which he later retracted.* 他作了假供词,后来又翻供。◇ *They tried to persuade me to retract my words.* 他们试图说服我收回我的话。 **2** [T] **~ sth** (*formal*) to refuse to keep an agreement, a promise, etc. 撤回,收回(协议、承诺等): *to retract an offer* 撤销提议 **3** [I, T] (*specialist*) to move back into the main part of sth; to pull sth back into the main part of sth 缩回; 拉回: *The animal retracted into its shell.* 这只动物缩回到自己的壳里。◇ **~ sth** *The undercarriage was fully retracted.* 起落架被完全收起。

re·tract·able /rɪˈtræktəbl/ *adj.* that can be moved or pulled back into the main part of sth 可缩进的; 可拉回的: *a knife with a retractable blade* 弹簧刀

re·trac·tion /rɪˈtrækʃn/ *noun* (*formal*) **1** [C] a statement saying that sth you previously said or wrote is not true 撤销; 收回: *He demanded a full retraction of the allegations against him.* 他要求全部撤回针对他的无证指控。 **2** [U]

R

(*specialist*) the act of pulling sth back (= of retracting it) 收回；拉回：*the retraction of a cat's claws* 猫爪子的回缩

re·train /ˌriːˈtreɪn/ *verb* [I, T] to learn, or to teach sb, a new type of work, a new skill, etc.（接受）重新培养，再教育，再培训：**~ (sb) (as sth)** *She retrained as a teacher.* 她接受了教师再培训。◇ **~ sb to do sth** *Staff have been retrained to use the new technology.* 为使员工学会运用新技术，对他们进行了再培训。▶ **re·train·ing** *noun* [U]

re·tread /ˈriːtred/ *noun* **1** a tyre made by putting a new rubber surface on an old tyre 翻新的旧轮胎 **2** (*NAmE, disapproving*) a book, film/movie, song, etc. that contains ideas that have been used before（书籍、电影、歌曲等的）翻版

re·treat /rɪˈtriːt/ *verb, noun*

■ *verb*

• **FROM DANGER/DEFEAT** 遇险；失败 **1** [I] to move away from a place or an enemy because you are in danger or because you have been defeated 退却；撤退：*The army was forced to retreat after suffering heavy losses.* 部队因伤亡惨重被迫撤退。◇ *We retreated back down the mountain.* 我们从山上撤了下来。**OPP** **advance**

• **MOVE AWAY/BACK** 离开；退后 **2** [I] to move away or back 离开；离去；退去；后退 **SYN** **recede**：*He watched her retreating figure.* 他看着她的身影渐渐远去。◇ *The flood waters slowly retreated.* 洪水慢慢地消退了。

• **CHANGE DECISION** 改变决定 **3** [I] **+ adv./prep.** to change your mind about sth because of criticism or because a situation has become too difficult（由于批评或环境过于恶劣）改变主意，退缩 **SYN** **back off (from sth)**：*The government had retreated from its pledge to reduce class sizes.* 政府已经改变了缩小班级规模的承诺。

• **TO QUIET PLACE** 到僻静处 **4** [I] **(+ adv./prep.)** to escape to a place that is quieter or safer 隐退；逃避；躲避 **SYN** **retire**：*Bored with the conversation, she retreated to her bedroom.* 她厌倦了这样的交谈，躲进了自己的卧室。◇ (*figurative*) *He retreated into a world of fantasy.* 他遁入了幻想世界。

• **FINANCE** 金融 **5** [I] **+ noun** to lose value 跌价：*Share prices retreated 45p to 538p.* 这股票价格下跌 45 便士，降到了 538 便士。

■ *noun*

• **FROM DANGER/DEFEAT** 遇险；失败 **1** [C, usually sing., U] a movement away from a place or an enemy because of danger or defeat 撤退；退却：*Napoleon's retreat from Moscow* 拿破仑从莫斯科的撤退 ◇ *The army was* ***in full retreat*** (= retreating very quickly). 部队全线撤退。◇ ***to sound the retreat*** (= to give a loud signal for an army to move away) 发出撤退信号 ➲ COLLOCATIONS AT WAR

• **ESCAPE** 逃跑 **2** [C, usually sing., U] **~ (from/into sth)** an act of trying to escape from a particular situation to one that you think is safer or more pleasant 逃避；退避；躲避 **SYN** **escape**：*Is watching television a retreat from reality?* 看电视是对现实的一种逃避吗？

• **CHANGE OF DECISION** 改变决定 **3** [C, usually sing.] an act of changing a decision because of criticism or because a situation has become too difficult（由于批评或环境过于恶劣）改变决定，退缩：*The Senator made an embarrassing retreat from his earlier position.* 这位参议员很尴尬地改变了他早先的立场。

• **QUIET PLACE** 安静的地方 **4** [C] a quiet, private place that you go to in order to get away from your usual life 僻静处；隐居处：*a country retreat* 乡间隐居处 **5** [U, C] a period of time when sb stops their usual activities and goes to a quiet place for prayer and thought; an organized event when people can do this 静修期间（或活动）：*He went into retreat and tried to resolve the conflicts within himself.* 他去静修并试图调节自己内心的矛盾冲突。◇ *to go on a Buddhist retreat* 去参加佛教的静修 **IDM** SEE BEAT *v.*

re·trench /rɪˈtrentʃ/ *verb* **1** [I] (*formal*) (of a business, government, etc. 企业、政府等) to spend less money; to reduce costs 节约；紧缩开支 **2** [T] **~ sb** (*AustralE, NZE, SAfrE*) to tell sb that they cannot continue working for you 缩减（人员）➲ COLLOCATIONS AT UNEMPLOYMENT

▶ **re·trench·ment** *noun* [U, C]：*a period of retrenchment* 开支紧缩时期

re·trial /ˌriːˈtraɪəl; ˈriːtraɪəl/ *noun* [usually sing.] a new trial of a person whose criminal offence has already been judged once in court 复审；再审

ret·ri·bu·tion /ˌretrɪˈbjuːʃn/ *noun* [U] **~ (for sth)** (*formal*) severe punishment for sth seriously wrong that sb has done 严惩；惩罚；报应：*People are seeking retribution for the latest terrorist outrages.* 人们在设法对恐怖分子最近的暴行进行严惩。◇ *fear of divine retribution* (= punishment from God) 对上帝的惩罚的畏惧 ▶ **re·tribu·tive** /rɪˈtrɪbjətɪv/ *adj.* [usually before noun]：*retributive justice* 因果报应

re·trieval /rɪˈtriːvl/ *noun* [U] **1** (*formal*) the process of getting sth back, especially from a place where it should not be 取回；索回 **SYN** **recovery**：*The ship was buried, beyond retrieval, at the bottom of the sea.* 船已葬身海底，无法打捞。◇ (*figurative*) *By then the situation was* ***beyond retrieval*** (= impossible to put right). 到那时，局势已无法挽回。**2** (*computing* 计) the process of getting back information that is stored on a computer 数据检索：*methods of* ***information retrieval*** 数据检索方法

re·trieve /rɪˈtriːv/ *verb* **1** (*formal*) to bring or get sth back, especially from a place where it should not be 取回；索回 **SYN** **recover**：**~ sth from sb/sth** *She bent to retrieve her comb from the floor.* 她弯腰从地板上捡起她的梳子。◇ **~ sth** *The police have managed to retrieve some of the stolen money.* 警方已经追回了部分被盗钱款。**2** (*computing* 计) to find and get back data or information that has been stored in the memory of a computer 检索数据：**~ sth from sb/sth** *to retrieve information from the database* 从数据库检索资料 ◇ **~ sth** *The program allows you to retrieve items quickly by searching under a keyword.* 这个程序通过关键词进行搜索，能让你迅速获取数据项。➲ WORDFINDER NOTE AT PROGRAM **3** **~ sth** to make a bad situation better; to get back sth that was lost 扭转颓势；挽回；找回：*You can only* ***retrieve the situation*** *by apologizing.* 你只有道歉才能挽回这个局面。▶ **re·triev·able** /rɪˈtriːvəbl/ *adj.* **OPP** **irretrievable**

re·triever /rɪˈtriːvə(r)/ *noun* a large dog used in hunting to bring back birds that have been shot 寻回犬 ➲ SEE ALSO GOLDEN RETRIEVER

retro /ˈretrəʊ; *NAmE* -troʊ/ *adj.* using styles or fashions from the recent past（时装款式等）前不久刚流行过的，再度流行的，回归的：*the current Seventies retro trend* 当前回归七十年代的流行趋势

retro- /ˈretrəʊ; *NAmE* -troʊ/ *prefix* (in nouns, adjectives and adverbs 构成名词、形容词和副词) back or backwards 后；向后：*retrograde* 倒退的 ◇ *retrospectively* 回顾地 ➲ MORE LIKE THIS 6, page R25

retro·active /ˌretrəʊˈæktɪv; *NAmE* -troʊ-/ *adj.* (*formal*) = RETROSPECTIVE (2) ▶ **retro·active·ly** *adv.*：*The ruling should be applied retroactively.* 这一裁决应该具有追溯效力。

retro·fit /ˈretrəʊfɪt; *NAmE* -troʊ-/ *verb* (**-tt-**) **~ sth** to put a new piece of equipment into a machine that did not have it when it was built; to provide a machine with a new part, etc. 给机器设备装配（新部件）；翻新；改型：*Voice recorders were retrofitted into planes already in service.* 录音设备安在了正在服役的飞机上。◇ *They retrofitted the plane with improved seating.* 他们在飞机上安装了经过改良的座椅。▶ **retro·fit** *noun*

retro·flex /ˈretrəfleks/ *adj.* **1** (*medical* 医) (of a part of the body 身体部位) turned backwards 后屈的 **2** (*phonetics* 语音) (of a speech sound 语音) produced with the end of the tongue turned up against the hard PALATE 卷舌的

retro·grade /ˈretrəgreɪd/ *adj.* (*formal, disapproving*) (of an action 行为) making a situation worse or returning to how sth was in the past 倒退的；退化的；退步的：*The closure of the factory is* ***a retrograde step.*** 工厂的关闭是一大退步。

retro·gres·sive /ˌretrəˈgresɪv/ *adj.* (*formal, disapproving*) returning to old-fashioned ideas or methods instead of making progress 倒退的；退化的 **OPP** **progressive**

retro·spect /ˈretrəspekt/ *noun*
IDM **in retrospect** thinking about a past event or situation, often with a different opinion of it from the one you had at the time 回顾；回想；追溯往事：*In retrospect, I think that I was wrong.* 回首往事，我觉得当时我错了。◇ *The decision seems extremely odd, in retrospect.* 回想起来，这个决定显得极其荒谬。

retro·spec·tion /ˌretrəˈspekʃn/ *noun* [U] (*formal*) thinking about past events or situations 回顾；回忆

retro·spect·ive /ˌretrəˈspektɪv/ *adj., noun*
■ *adj.* **1** thinking about or connected with sth that happened in the past 回顾的；涉及以往的 **2** (*also less frequent, formal* **retro·active**) (of a new law or decision 新的法律或决定) intended to take effect from a particular date in the past rather than from the present date 有追溯效力的；溯及既往的：*retrospective legislation* 有溯及力的法律 ◇ *retrospective pay awards* 有追溯效力的加薪 ▸ **retro·spect·ive·ly** *adv.*：*She wrote retrospectively about her childhood.* 她追述了自己的童年生活。◇ *The new rule will be applied retrospectively.* 新的规定将具有溯及力。
■ *noun* a public exhibition of the work that an artist has done in the past, showing how his or her work has developed （艺术家作品）回顾展

retro·virus /ˈretrəʊvaɪrəs; *NAmE* ˈretroʊ-/ *noun* any of a group of viruses that includes HIV. Retroviruses multiply by making changes to DNA. 反转录病毒，逆转录病毒（如人类免疫缺损病毒）➲ SEE ALSO ANTIRETROVIRAL

retry /ˌriːˈtraɪ/ *verb* (**re·tries**, **re·try·ing**, **re·tried**, **re·tried**) **1** [T] ~ **sb/sth** to examine a person or case again in court 复审；重新审理 **2** [I] to make another attempt to do sth, especially on a computer（尤指在计算机上）重试

ret·sina /retˈsiːnə/ *noun* [U, C] a type of red or white wine from Greece that is given a special flavour with RESIN (1) 松香味希腊葡萄酒

re·turn 🔑 /rɪˈtɜːn; *NAmE* rɪˈtɜːrn/ *verb, noun*
■ *verb*
• **COME/GO BACK** 回来；回去 **1** 🔑 [I] to come or go back from one place to another 回来；回去；返回：*I waited a long time for him to return.* 我等他回来等了很长时间。◇ ~ (**to…**) (**from…**) *She's returning to Australia tomorrow after six months in Europe.* 她在欧洲逗留了六个月，明天要返回澳大利亚了。◇ *I returned from work to find the house empty.* 我下班回来，发现屋里空无一人。◇ *When did she return home from the trip?* 她是什么时候旅行回来的？
• **BRING/GIVE BACK** 拿回；归还 **2** 🔑 [T] to bring, give, put or send sth back to sb/sth 带回；送回；放回；退还：~ **sb/sth to sb/sth** *We had to return the hairdryer to the store because it was faulty.* 我们不得不将吹风机退回商店，因为它有残损。◇ *I must return some books to the library.* 我得把一些书还给图书馆。◇ ~ **sth** *Don't forget to return my pen!* 别忘了把钢笔还给我！◇ ~ **sb/sth + adj.** *I returned the letter unopened.* 我原封不动地将信退了回去。
• **OF FEELING/QUALITY** 感觉；特质 **3** 🔑 [I] to come back again 恢复；重现 SYN **reappear, resurface**: *The following day the pain returned.* 第二天又疼起来了。◇ *Her suspicions returned when things started going missing again.* 发现又有东西丢失的时候，她又怀疑起来。
• **TO PREVIOUS SUBJECT/ACTIVITY** 先前的话题 / 活动 **4** 🔑 [I] ~ (**to sth**) to start discussing a subject you were discussing earlier, or doing an activity you were doing earlier 重提；重新开始做：*He returns to this topic later in the report.* 他在报告中后来又提到这个话题。◇ *She looked up briefly then returned to her sewing.* 她抬头看了一眼，又接着做她的针线活儿。◇ *The doctor may allow her to **return to work** next week.* 医生也许会允许她下周回去上班。
• **TO PREVIOUS STATE** 先前的状态 **5** 🔑 [I] ~ **to sth** to go back to a previous state 恢复；回复：*Train services have **returned to normal** after the strike.* 罢工过后，列车运营已经恢复正常。
• **DO/GIVE THE SAME** 回报 **6** [T] ~ **sth** to do or give sth to sb because they have done or given the same to you first; to have the same feeling about sb that they have about you 回报；回应：*to return a favour/greeting/stare* 报恩；回应问候；回瞪一眼 ◇ *She phoned him several times but he was too busy to **return her call**.* 她给他打了几次电话，但他太忙，不能给她回电话。◇ *It's time we **returned their invitation*** (= invite them to sth as they invited us to sth first). 该我们回请他们了。◇ *He did not return her love.* 他没有回报她的爱。◇ *'You were both wonderful!' 'So were you!' we said, **returning the compliment**.* "你们俩太棒了！""你也一样啊！"我们也称赞道。◇ *to **return fire*** (= to shoot at sb who is shooting at you) 用枪炮还击
• **IN TENNIS** 网球 **7** [T] ~ **sth** to hit the ball back to your opponent during a game 回击；击回：*to return a service/shot* 击回发球 / 抽球
• **A VERDICT** 裁决 **8** [T] ~ **a verdict** to give a decision about sth in court 宣告（裁决）：*The jury returned a verdict of not guilty.* 陪审团宣告了无罪的判决。
• **ELECT POLITICIAN** 选政治人物 **9** [T, usually passive] ~ **sb** (**to sth**) | ~ **sb** (**as sth**) (*BrE*) to elect sb to a political position 选举；选出；推举
• **PROFIT/LOSS** 利润；损失 **10** [T] ~ **sth** (*business* 商) to give or produce a particular amount of money as a profit or loss 带来，产生（利润或损失）：*to return a high rate of interest* 有很高的利息回报 ◇ *Last year the company returned a loss of £157 million.* 去年，公司的亏损达 1.57 亿英镑。

▼ **SYNONYMS 同义词辨析**

return

come back • go back • get back • turn back

These words all mean to come or go back from one place to another. 以上各词均含回来、回去、返回之义。

return to come or go back from one place to another 指回来、回去、返回：*I waited a long time for him to return.* 我等他回来等了很长时间。 NOTE **Return** is slightly more formal than the other words in this group, and is used more often in writing or formal speech. * return 较本组其他的词稍正式，较常用于书面语或正式场合中。

come back to return 指回来、返回 NOTE **Come back** is usually used from the point of view of the person or place that sb returns to. * come back 通常指回到说话人处或所在的地方：*Come back and visit again soon!* 请早点儿再回来探访！

go back to return to the place you recently or originally came from or that you have been to before 指回去、返回 NOTE **Go back** is usually used from the point of view of the person who is returning. * go back 通常是从要返回者的角度来说：*Do you ever want to go back to China?* 你想过回中国去吗？

get back to arrive back somewhere, especially at your home or the place where you are staying 指返回、回去，尤指回家：*What time did you get back last night?* 你昨晚什么时候回家的？

turn back to return the way that you came, especially because sth stops you from continuing 指原路返回、往回走，尤指因某事阻止而不能继续前进：*The weather got so bad that we had to turn back.* 天气变得非常恶劣，我们不得不循原路折回。

PATTERNS
• to return/come back/go back/get back **to**/**from**/**with** sth
• to return/come back/go back/get back/turn back **again**
• to return/come back/go back/get back **home**/**to work**
• to return/come back/get back **safely**

■ *noun*
• **COMING BACK** 回来 **1** 🔑 [sing.] ~ (**to…**) (**from…**) the action of arriving in or coming back to a place that you were in before 回来；归来；返回：*He was met by his brother **on his return** from Italy.* 他从意大利回来的时候，是他弟弟去接他的。◇ *I saw the play on its return to Broadway.* 这部戏重回百老汇时我看过了。◇ *on the **return flight/journey**/*

R

trip 在返回的航班 / 旅程 / 路程上

• **GIVING/SENDING BACK** 归还；退回 **2** [U, sing.] the action of giving, putting or sending sth/sb back 归还；放回；退回： *We would appreciate the prompt return of books to the library.* 若能及时将图书归还给图书馆，我们将不胜感激。◇ *The judge ordered the return of the child to his mother.* 法官命令将孩子送回到他的母亲身边。◇ *Write your* ***return address*** (= the address that a reply should be sent to) *on the back of the envelope.* 请在信封的背面写明回信地址。

• **OF FEELING/STATE** 感觉；状况 **3** [sing.] ~ (**of sth**) the situation when a feeling or state that has not been experienced for some time starts again 重现；恢复 SYN **reappearance**: *the return of spring* 春之归来 ◇ *a return of my doubts* 我的疑心又起

• **TO PREVIOUS SITUATION/ACTIVITY** 先前的情况 / 活动 **4** [sing.] ~ **to sth** the action of going back to an activity or a situation that you used to do or be in 恢复；返回： *his return to power* 他的重新掌权 ◇ *They appealed for* ***a return to work*** (= after a strike). 他们呼吁复工。

• **PROFIT** 利益 **5** [U, C] the amount of profit that you get from sth 回报；收益；利润 SYN **earnings, yield**: *a high* ***rate of return*** *on capital* 资本的高回报率 ◇ *farmers seeking to improve returns from their crops* 寻求提高农作物利润的农民

• **OFFICIAL REPORT** 正式报告 **6** [C] an official report or statement that gives particular information to the government or another body 报告；陈述；申报： *census returns* 人口普查报告 ◇ *election returns* (= the number of votes for each candidate in an election) 选举结果报告 ➲ SEE ALSO TAX RETURN

• **TICKET** 票 **7** [C] (*BrE*) = RETURN TICKET： *'Brighton, please.' 'Single or return?'* "我要一张到布赖顿的票。" "单程的还是往返的？" ◇ *A return is cheaper than two singles.* 一张往返票比两张单程票便宜。◇ *the return fare to London* 到伦敦的往返票价 ➲ SEE ALSO DAY RETURN **8** [C] a ticket for the theatre or a sports game that was bought by sb but is given back to be sold again 退票

• **ON COMPUTER** 计算机 **9** [U] (*also* **re'turn key** [C]) the button that you press on a computer when you reach the end of an instruction, or to begin a new line 返回键；回车键；结束键： *To exit this option, press return.* 要退出这个选项，就按返回键。➲ WORDFINDER NOTE AT KEYBOARD

• **IN TENNIS** 网球 **10** [C] (in TENNIS and some other sports 网球和其他一些运动) the action of hitting the ball, etc. back to your opponent 击回球： *a powerful* ***return of serve*** 势大力沉的接发球

IDM **by re'turn (of 'post)** (*BrE*) using the next available post; as soon as possible 由下一班邮递；尽快： *Please reply by return of post.* 请即赐复。 **in re'turn (for sth)** **1** as a way of thanking sb or paying them for sth they have done 作为（对…的）回报： *Can I buy you lunch in return for your help?* 感谢你帮忙，我请你吃午饭好吗？ **2** as a response or reaction to sth 作为回应： *I asked her opinion, but she just asked me a question in return.* 我征求她的意见，她却只是反问了我一句。➲ MORE AT HAPPY, POINT *n.*, SALE

re·turn·able /rɪˈtɜːnəbl; *NAmE* -ˈtɜːrn-/ *adj.* **1** (*formal*) that can or must be given back after a period of time 可退还的；应归还的；必须交还的： *A returnable deposit is payable on arrival.* 抵达时应支付可退还押金。◇ *The application form is returnable not later than 7th June.* 申请表应不迟于 6 月 7 日交回。 **2** (of bottles and containers 瓶子和容器) that can be taken back to a shop/store in order to be used again 可退回的；可回收的 OPP **non-returnable**

re·turn·ee /rɪˌtɜːˈniː; *NAmE* rɪˌtɜːrˈniː/ *noun* [usually pl.] (*especially NAmE*) a person who returns to their own country, after living in another country 回国的人；归国者

re·turn·er /rɪˈtɜːnə(r); *NAmE* -ˈtɜːrn-/ *noun* (*BrE*) a person who goes back to work after not working for a long time 重返工作岗位者；再就业者

re'turning officer *noun* (*BrE*) an official in a particular area who is responsible for arranging an election and announcing the result 地方选举监察官

reˌturn 'match (*also* **reˌturn 'game**) *noun* (*especially BrE*) a second match or game between the same two players or teams（相同对手间的）第二回合比赛，再度交锋

reˌturn 'ticket (*also* **re·turn**) (*both BrE*) (*NAmE* ˌ**round-trip 'ticket**) *noun* a ticket for a journey to a place and back again 往返票

reˌturn 'visit *noun* a trip to a place that you have been to once before, or a trip to see sb who has already come to see you 重游；回访： *This hotel is worth a return visit.* 这家旅店值得再次光顾。◇ *The US president is* ***making a return visit*** *to Moscow.* 美国总统正在对莫斯科进行回访。

re·tweet /ˌriːˈtwiːt/ *verb* if you retweet a message written by another user on the Twitter SOCIAL NETWORKING service, the message can be seen by all of the people who regularly receive messages from you 转发（推特消息）；转推 ▸ **retweet** /ˈriːtwiːt/ *noun*

re·unify /ˌriːˈjuːnɪfaɪ/ *verb* (**re·uni·fies**, **re·uni·fy·ing**, **re·uni·fied**, **re·uni·fied**) [often passive] ~ **sth** to join together two or more regions or parts of a country so that they form a single political unit again 重新统一 ▸ **re·uni·fi·ca·tion** /ˌriːˌjuːnɪfɪˈkeɪʃn/ *noun* [U]: *the reunification of Germany* 德国的重新统一

re·union /ˌriːˈjuːniən/ *noun* **1** [C] a social occasion or party attended by a group of people who have not seen each other for a long time 重逢；团聚；聚会： *a family reunion* 家人团聚 ◇ *the school's annual reunion* 一年一度的校友联欢会 ◇ *a reunion of the class of '85* * 85 届同学聚会 **2** [C, U] ~ (**with sb**) | ~ (**between A and B**) the act of people coming together after they have been apart for some time 相聚；团圆： *an emotional reunion between mother and son* 母子团圆的激动场面 ◇ *Christmas is a time of reunion.* 圣诞节是团聚的日子。 **3** [U] the action of becoming a single group or organization again 重新结合；再度联合： *the reunion of the Church of England with the Church of Rome* 英格兰圣公会和天主教的再度联合

re·unite /ˌriːjuːˈnaɪt/ *verb* [T, I] **1** [usually passive] to bring two or more people together again after they have been separated for a long time; to come together again（使）重逢，再次相聚： ~ **A with/and B** *Last night she was reunited with her children.* 昨天晚上，她和她的子女团聚。◇ ~ (**sb**) *The family was reunited after the war.* 战争过后，一家人又相聚了。◇ *There have been rumours that the band will reunite for a world tour.* 有传言说这个乐队将再度聚集，作一次环球巡演。 **2** ~ (**sth**) to join together again separate areas or separate groups within an organization, a political party, etc.; to come together again（使）再结合，再联合： *As leader, his main aim is to reunite the party.* 作为领导，他的主要目标就是要使党内各派团结起来。

re·us·able /ˌriːˈjuːzəbl/ *adj.* that can be used again 可重复使用的；可再次使用的： *reusable plastic bottles* 可重复使用的塑料瓶

reuse /ˌriːˈjuːz/ *verb* ~ **sth** to use sth again 再次使用；重复使用： *Please reuse your envelopes.* 信封请重复利用。 ▸ **reuse** /ˌriːˈjuːs/ *noun* [U]

Rev. /rev/ (*BrE also* **Revd**) *abbr.* (used before a name) REVEREND（尊称神职人员）尊敬的，可敬的： *Rev. Jesse Jackson* 尊敬的杰西•杰克逊牧师

rev /rev/ *verb, noun*

■ ***verb*** (**-vv-**) [T, I] ~ (**sth**) (**up**) when you **rev** an engine or it **revs**, it runs quickly（使）快速运转： *The taxi driver revved up his engine.* 出租车司机把发动机发动起来。◇ *I could hear the car revving outside.* 我可以听到外面汽车发动的声音。

■ ***noun*** (*informal*) a complete turn of an engine, used when talking about an engine's speed（发动机的转速）一次旋转 SYN **revolution**: *4 000 revs per minute* 每分钟 4 000 转 ◇ *The needle on the rev counter soared.* 转数指针快速上升。➲ VISUAL VOCAB PAGE V56

re·value /ˌriːˈvæljuː/ *verb* **1** [T] ~ **sth** to estimate the value of sth again, especially giving it a higher value 重新评价，重新评估（尤指给予更高评价） **2** [T, I] ~ (**sth**) to increase the value of the money of a country when it is exchanged for the money of another country 提高（货币的）兑换价；使（货币）升值：*The yen is to be revalued.* 日元的兑换价将调高。 OPP **devalue** ▸ **re·valu·ation** /ˌriːvæljuˈeɪʃn/ *noun* [U, C, usually sing.]: *the revaluation of the pound* 英镑的升值

re·vamp /ˌriːˈvæmp/ *verb* ~ **sth** to make changes to the form of sth, usually to improve its appearance 改变；修改；（通常指）改进外观，翻新 ▸ **re·vamp** /ˈriːvæmp/ *noun* [sing.]

re·vanch·ism /rɪˈvæntʃɪzəm; -ˈvænʃ-/ *noun* [U] a policy of attacking sb who has attacked you, especially by a country in order to get back land（尤指国家为收复失地的）复仇主义

re·veal AW /rɪˈviːl/ *verb* **1** to make sth known to sb 揭示；显示；透露 SYN **disclose**：~ **sth** (**to sb**) *to reveal a secret* 泄露一条秘密 ◇ *Details of the murder were revealed by the local paper.* 地方报纸披露了谋杀的细节。◇ ~ (**that**)... *The report reveals (that) the company made a loss of £20 million last year.* 报告显示，公司去年亏损 2 000 万英镑。◇ **it is revealed that...** *It was revealed that important evidence had been suppressed.* 据透露，重要的证据被隐瞒了。◇ ~ **how, what, etc....** *Officers could not reveal how he died.* 警察们不能透露他的死因。◇ ~ **sb/sth to be/have sth** *Salted peanuts were recently revealed to be the nation's favourite snack.* 最近发现，咸味花生是该国最受人喜爱的小吃。 ➲ LANGUAGE BANK AT EVIDENCE **2** to show sth that previously could not be seen 显出；露出；展示 SYN **display**：~ **sth** *He laughed, revealing a line of white teeth.* 他笑了起来，露出一排洁白的牙齿。◇ *The door opened to reveal a cosy little room.* 房门打开，一间温暖舒适的小屋展现在眼前。◇ ~ **yourself** *She crouched in the dark, too frightened to reveal herself.* 她蜷缩在黑暗中，吓得不敢露面。 ➲ SEE ALSO REVELATION (1), (2), REVELATORY ➲ NOTE AT FAIL

reˌvealed reˈligion *noun* [U, C] religion that is based on a belief that God has shown himself 启示宗教，天启教（以神的启示为信仰基础）

re·veal·ing AW /rɪˈviːlɪŋ/ *adj.* **1** giving you interesting information that you did not know before 揭露真相的；发人深省的：*The document provided a revealing insight into the government's priorities.* 这份文件使人看出政府的轻重缓急是怎样安排的。◇ *The answers the children gave were extremely revealing.* 孩子们所给的答案极其发人深省。 **2** (of clothes 衣服) allowing more of sb's body to be seen than usual 暴露的；使身体过分裸露的：*a revealing blouse* 暴露的女式衬衫 ▸ **re·veal·ing·ly** *adv.* : *He spoke revealingly about his problems.* 他坦率地谈论他的问题。

re·veille /rɪˈvæli; *NAmE* ˈrevəli/ *noun* [U] a tune that is played to wake soldiers in the morning; the time when it is played（军队的）起床号，起床时间

revel /ˈrevl/ *verb, noun*

■ ***verb*** (**-ll-**, *US* **-l-**) [I] to spend time enjoying yourself in a noisy, enthusiastic way 狂欢作乐 SYN **make merry**

PHR V **ˈrevel in sth** to enjoy sth very much 陶醉于；着迷于；纵情于：*She was clearly revelling in all the attention.* 显而易见，她对大家的关注感到十分高兴。◇ **revel in doing sth** *Some people seem to revel in annoying others.* 有些人好像总是喜欢惹人烦。

■ ***noun*** [usually pl.] (*literary*) noisy celebrations 狂欢；喧闹的庆典

reve·la·tion AW /ˌrevəˈleɪʃn/ *noun* **1** [C] ~ (**about/concerning sth**) | ~ (**that...**) a fact that people are made aware of, especially one that has been secret and is surprising 被暴露的真相；被曝光的秘闻 SYN **disclosure**：*startling/sensational revelations about her private life* 对她的私生活令人吃惊的揭露 **2** [U] ~ (**of sth**) the act of making people aware of sth that has been secret 披露；揭露 SYN **disclosure**：*The company's financial problems followed the revelation of a major fraud scandal.* 重大的欺诈丑闻被揭露之后，公司随之出现了财政问题。 **3** [C, U] something that is considered to be a sign or message from God（上帝的）启示 ➲ COLLOCATIONS AT RELIGION ➲ SEE ALSO REVEAL

IDM **come as/be a revelation** (**to sb**) to be a completely new or surprising experience; to be different from what was expected 让人大开眼界；令人耳目一新；出乎意料

rev·ela·tory /ˌrevəˈleɪtəri; *NAmE* ˈrevələtɔːri/ *adj.* (*formal*) making people aware of sth that they did not know before 启发性的；启迪人的：*a revelatory insight* 有启发作用的见解 ➲ SEE ALSO REVEAL

rev·el·ler (*US* **rev·el·er**) /ˈrevələ(r)/ *noun* a person who is having fun in a noisy way, usually with a group of other people and often after drinking alcohol（醉酒）狂欢者

rev·el·ry /ˈrevlri/ *noun* [U] (*also* **rev·el·ries** [pl.]) noisy fun, usually involving a lot of eating and drinking 狂欢作乐 SYN **festivity, merrymaking**：*We could hear sounds of revelry from next door.* 我们能够听到隔壁纵饮狂欢的声音。◇ *New Year revelries* 新年狂欢

re·venge /rɪˈvendʒ/ *noun, verb*

■ ***noun*** [U] **1** something that you do in order to make sb suffer because they have made you suffer 报复；报仇：*He swore to **take** (**his**) **revenge on** his political enemies.* 他发誓要报复他的政敌。◇ *She is **seeking revenge for** the murder of her husband.* 丈夫遭到谋杀，她在寻找机会报仇。◇ *The bombing was **in revenge for** the assassination.* 爆炸事件是对暗杀行为的报复。◇ *an act of revenge* 报复行动 ◇ ***revenge attacks/killings*** 报复性的进攻 / 杀戮 **2** (*sport* 体育) the defeat of a person or team that defeated you in a previous game（曾经失败一方的）雪耻，打败对手：*The team wanted to get revenge for their defeat earlier in the season.* 球队想要为这个赛季早先的失败雪耻。

■ ***verb***

PHR V **reˈvenge yourself on sb | be reˈvenged on sb** (*literary*) to punish or hurt sb because they have made you suffer 报复；向（某人）报仇：*She vowed to be revenged on them all.* 她发誓一定要报复他们所有的人。 ➲ NOTE AT AVENGE

rev·enue AW /ˈrevənjuː; *NAmE* -nuː/ *noun* [U] (*also* **rev·enues** [pl.]) the money that a government receives from taxes or that an organization, etc. receives from its business 财政收入；税收收入；收益 SYN **receipt**：*a shortfall in tax revenue* 税收收入不足 ◇ *a slump in oil revenues* 石油收入的下跌 ◇ *The company's annual revenues rose by 30%.* 公司的年收入增加了 30%。 ➲ COLLOCATIONS AT BUSINESS ➲ SEE ALSO INLAND REVENUE

ˌRevenue and ˈCustoms *noun* = HM REVENUE AND CUSTOMS

re·verb /ˈriːvɜːb; rɪˈvɜːb; *NAmE* -vɜːrb/ *noun* [U] a sound effect that can be adjusted by electronic means to give music more or less of an ECHO 混响（效果）

re·ver·ber·ate /rɪˈvɜːbəreɪt; *NAmE* -ˈvɜːrb-/ *verb* **1** [I] (of a sound 声音) to be repeated several times as it is reflected off different surfaces 回响；回荡 SYN **echo**：*Her voice reverberated around the hall.* 她的声音在大厅里回荡。 **2** [I] ~ (**with/to sth**) (of a place 地方) to seem to shake because of a loud noise（由于强大的噪音）震颤，摇晃：*The hall reverberated with the sound of music and dancing.* 音乐和舞蹈的声音使得整个大厅似乎都在震颤。 **3** [I] (*formal*) to have a strong effect on people for a long time or over a large area 有长久深刻的影响；产生广泛影响：*Repercussions of the case continue to reverberate through the financial world.* 这件事持续影响着整个金融界。

re·ver·ber·ation /rɪˌvɜːbəˈreɪʃn; *NAmE* -ˌvɜːrb-/ *noun* **1** [C, usually pl., U] a loud noise that continues for some time after it has been produced because of the surfaces around it 回响；回声；反响 SYN **echo** **2** **reverberations** [pl.] the effects of sth that happens, especially unpleasant ones that spread among a large number of people 影响；（尤指）广泛的消极影响 SYN **repercussion**

R

re·vere /rɪˈvɪə(r); NAmE rɪˈvɪr/ *verb* [usually passive] ~ **sb (as sth)** (*formal*) to feel great respect or admiration for sb/sth 尊敬；崇敬 **SYN** **idolize**

rev·er·ence /ˈrevərəns/ *noun* [U] ~ (**for sb/sth**) (*formal*) a feeling of great respect or admiration for sb/sth 尊敬；崇敬：*The poem conveys his deep reverence for nature.* 这首诗表达了他对大自然的深深崇敬之情。

rev·er·end /ˈrevərənd/ *adj.* [only before noun] **Reverend** (*abbr.* **Rev.**) the title of a member of the clergy that is also sometimes used to talk to or about one（尊称神职人员）尊敬的，可敬的：*the Reverend Charles Dodgson* 尊敬的查尔斯・道奇森牧师 ◇ *Good morning, Reverend.* 早安，神父。➲ SEE ALSO RIGHT REVEREND

ˌReverend ˈMother *noun* a title of respect used when talking to or about a MOTHER SUPERIOR (= the head of a female religious community)（对女修道院院长的尊称）可敬的修女

rev·er·ent /ˈrevərənt/ *adj.* (*formal*) showing deep respect 充满敬意的；深表崇敬的 **SYN** **respectful** ▶ **rev·er·ent·ly** *adv.*

rev·er·en·tial /ˌrevəˈrenʃl/ *adj.* (*formal*) showing deep respect 充满敬意的；深表崇敬的：*His name was always mentioned in almost reverential tones.* 人们每次提起他的名字，语调中几乎总是充满了敬意。▶ **rev·er·en·tial·ly** /-ʃəli/ *adv.*：*She lowered her voice reverentially.* 她恭敬地放低了声音。

rev·erie /ˈrevəri/ *noun* [C, U] (*formal*) a state of thinking about pleasant things, almost as though you are dreaming 幻想；白日梦；梦想 **SYN** **daydream**：*She was jolted out of her reverie as the door opened.* 门一开就把她从幻想中惊醒。

re·vers /rɪˈvɪə(r); NAmE rɪˈvɪr/ *noun* (*pl.* **re·vers** /-ˈvɪəz; NAmE -ˈvɪrz/) (*specialist*) the edge of a coat, jacket, etc. that is turned back so that you see the opposite side of it, especially at the LAPEL（衣服的）翻边，翻口；（尤指）翻领

re·ver·sal **AW** /rɪˈvɜːsl; NAmE rɪˈvɜːrsl/ *noun* **1** [C, U] ~ (**of sth**) a change of sth so that it is the opposite of what it was 颠倒；彻底转变；反转；倒置：*a **complete/dramatic/sudden reversal** of policy* 政策的全面/剧烈/突然转变 ◇ *the reversal of a decision* 决定的撤销 ◇ *The government suffered a total **reversal of fortune(s)** last week.* 上星期，政府的命运发生了逆转。 **2** [C] a change from being successful to having problems or being defeated 倒退；逆转；退步；转胜为败：*the team's recent reversal* 球队最近的失败 ◇ *The company's financial problems were only a temporary reversal.* 公司的财务问题只是暂时的挫折。 **3** [C, U] an exchange of positions or functions between two or more people（位置或功能的）转换，交换：*It's a complete **role reversal/reversal of roles*** (= for example when a child cares for a parent). 这是彻底的角色转换。

re·verse 🔑 **AW** /rɪˈvɜːs; NAmE rɪˈvɜːrs/ *verb, noun, adj.*

■ *verb*

• **CHANGE TO OPPOSITE** 转化为对立面 **1** 🔑 [T] ~ **sth** to change sth completely so that it is the opposite of what it was before 颠倒；彻底转变；使完全相反：*to reverse a procedure/process/trend* 彻底改变程序/过程/趋势 ◇ *The government has failed to reverse the economic decline.* 政府未能扭转经济滑坡的趋势。 ◇ *It is sometimes possible to arrest or reverse the disease.* 有时可以阻止病情发展或使病情彻底好转。 **2** 🔑 [T] ~ **sth** to change a previous decision, law, etc. to the opposite one 撤销，废除（决定、法律等）**SYN** **revoke**：*The Court of Appeal reversed the decision.* 上诉法庭撤销了这项裁决。 **3** 🔑 [T] ~ **sth** to turn sth the opposite way around or change the order of sth around 使反转；使次序颠倒：*Writing is reversed in a mirror.* 镜子里的字是反的。◇ *You should reverse the order of these pages.* 你该把这几页的顺序颠倒过来。

• **EXCHANGE TWO THINGS** 交换 **4** 🔑 [T] ~ **sth** to exchange the positions or functions of two things 交换（位置或功能）：*It felt as if we had reversed our roles of parent and child.* 感觉我们就像家长和孩子交换了角色。◇ *She used to work for me, but our situations are now reversed.* 过去她为我工作，而现在我们的地位对调了。

• **YOURSELF** 自己 **5** [T] ~ **yourself** (**on sth**) (*NAmE*) to admit you were wrong or to stop having a particular position in an argument 承认错误；放弃（立场）：*He has reversed himself on a dozen issues.* 他已经不再坚持自己在一系列问题上的立场。

• **VEHICLE** 车辆 **6** 🔑 [I, T] (*especially BrE*) when a vehicle or its driver **reverses** or the driver **reverses** a vehicle, the vehicle goes backwards（使）倒退行驶；倒车：*He reversed around the corner.* 他倒车转过拐角。◇ *She reversed into a parking space.* 她将车倒着开进停车位。◇ *Caution! This truck is reversing.* 小心！卡车在倒车。◇ ~ **sth** *Now reverse the car.* 现在倒车。➲ COMPARE BACK *v.* (1)

• **TELEPHONE CALL** 打电话 **7** [T] ~ (**the**) **charges** (*BrE*) to make a telephone call that will be paid for by the person you are calling, not by you 打对方付费的电话：*I want to reverse the charges, please.* 劳驾，我想打一个由受话人付费的电话。➲ SEE ALSO COLLECT *adj.*

■ *noun*

• **OPPOSITE** 相反 **1** 🔑 **the reverse** [sing.] the opposite of what has just been mentioned 相反的情况（或事物）：*This problem is the reverse of the previous one.* 这个问题和上一个问题相反。◇ *Although I expected to enjoy living in the country, in fact **the reverse is true**.* 尽管我原以为会喜欢乡村生活，但实际情况正好相反。◇ *In the south, the reverse applies.* 在南方，情况相反。◇ *It wasn't easy to persuade her to come—**quite the reverse**.* 说服她过来不容易，实在太难了。

• **BACK** 后面 **2** 🔑 **the reverse** [sing.] the back of a coin, piece of material, piece of paper, etc. 后面；背面；反面

• **IN VEHICLE** 车辆 **3** 🔑 (*also* **reˌverse ˈgear**) [U] the machinery in a vehicle used to make it move backwards 倒挡：*Put the car **in/into reverse**.* 给汽车挂上倒挡。

• **LOSS/DEFEAT** 损失；失败 **4** [C] (*formal*) a loss or defeat; a change from success to failure 损失；失败；倒退 **SYN** **setback**：*Property values have suffered another reverse.* 房地产价值再次遭受损失。 ◇ *a damaging political reverse* 具有破坏性的政治倒退

IDM **in reˈverse** 🔑 in the opposite order or way 反向；相反 **SYN** **backwards**：*The secret number is my phone number in reverse.* 这个密码是我的电话号码的逆序排列。◇ *We did a similar trip to you, but in reverse.* 我们走了和你相似的旅程，但方向相反。 **go/put sth into reˈverse** to start to happen or to make sth happen in the opposite way（使）出现逆转，转化为对立面：*In 2008 economic growth went into reverse.* * 2008 年，经济增长发生了逆转。

■ *adj.* [only before noun]

• **OPPOSITE** 相反 **1** 🔑 opposite to what has been mentioned 相反的；反面的；反向的：*to travel in the reverse direction* 向相反方向行进 ◇ *The winners were announced **in reverse order*** (= the person in the lowest place was announced first). 获胜者是按逆序宣布的。◇ *The experiment had the reverse effect to what was intended.* 实验的结果与原来的意图相反。

• **BACK** 后面 **2** opposite to the front 背面的；反面的；后面的：*Iron the garment on the reverse side.* 这件衣服要从反面熨。

reˌverse-ˈcharge *adj.* a **reverse-charge** telephone call is paid for by the person who receives the call, not by the person who makes it（电话）由受话方付费的，对方付费的 ▶ **reˌverse-ˈcharge** *adv.*：*I didn't have any money so I had to call reverse-charge.* 我那时没钱，所以只好打对方付费电话。

reˌverse discrimiˈnation *noun* [U] (*disapproving*) the practice or policy of making sure that a particular number of jobs, etc. are given to people from groups that are often treated unfairly because of their race, sex, etc. 反向区别对待，反向歧视，逆向歧视（对因种族、性别等原因遭受歧视的群体在就业等方面给予特别照顾）**HELP** The term **reverse discrimination** is nearly always used in a disapproving way; to describe this policy in a way that is not necessarily disapproving use **positive discrimination** or **affirmative action**. * reverse discrimination 这个术语几

乎总是用于贬义；不一定含贬义的说法是 positive discrimination 或 affirmative action。

re,verse engi'neering *noun* [U] the copying of another company's product after examining it carefully to find out how it is made 逆向工程，倒序制造（研究另一家公司产品的制造后加以仿制）

re·vers·ible AW /rɪ'vɜːsəbl; *NAmE* -'vɜːrs-/ *adj.* **1** (of clothes, materials, etc. 衣服、材料等) that can be turned inside out and worn or used with either side showing 可翻转的；可两面穿的；正反两用的：*a reversible jacket* 可两面穿的夹克 **2** (of a process, an action or a disease 步骤、行动或疾病) that can be changed so that sth returns to its original state or situation 可逆的；可恢复原状的；可医治的：*Is the trend towards privatization reversible?* 私有化趋势可能逆转吗？◇ *reversible kidney failure* 可医治的肾衰竭 OPP **irreversible** ▸ **re·vers·ibil·ity** /rɪˌvɜːsə'bɪləti; *NAmE* -ˌvɜːrs-/ *noun* [U]

re'versing light (*BrE*) (*NAmE* **'backup light**) *noun* a white light at the back of a vehicle that comes on when the vehicle moves backwards 倒车灯

re·ver·sion /rɪ'vɜːʃn; *NAmE* rɪ'vɜːrʒn/ *noun* **1** [U, sing.] ~ (**to sth**) (*formal*) the act or process of returning to a former state or condition 倒退；回复；回归：*a reversion to traditional farming methods* 传统耕作方法的回归 **2** [U, C] (*law* 律) the return of land or property to sb（土地或财产的）归还，归属原主：*the reversion of Hong Kong to China* 香港回归中国

re·vert /rɪ'vɜːt; *NAmE* rɪ'vɜːrt/ *verb* [I] (+ **adv./prep.**) (*IndE, rather formal*) to reply 回复：*Excellent openings—kindly revert with your updated CV.* 绝佳招聘职位，请回信寄来您的最新简历。

PHR V **re'vert to sb/sth** (*law* 律) (of property, rights, etc. 财产、权利等) to return to the original owner again 归还；归属 ➲ SEE ALSO REVERSION **re'vert to sth** (*formal*) **1** to return to a former state; to start doing sth again that you used to do in the past 回复；恢复：*After her divorce she reverted to her maiden name.* 离婚以后，她重新用起娘家的姓氏。◇ *His manner seems to have reverted to normal.* 他的举止好像已经恢复了正常。◇ *Try not to revert to your old eating habits.* 尽力不要恢复你过去的饮食习惯。 **2** to return to an earlier topic or subject 重提，回到，恢复（先前的话题或主题）：*So, to revert to your earlier question…* 那么，回到你先前所提的问题… ◇ *The conversation kept reverting to the events of March 6th.* 谈话一再回到 3 月 6 日所发生的事件上来。

re·vet·ment /rɪ'vetmənt/ *noun* (*specialist*) stones or other material used to make a wall stronger, hold back a bank of earth, etc. 护岸工程；护坡

re·view 🔑 /rɪ'vjuː/ *noun, verb*

■ ***noun*** **1** 🔑 [U, C] an examination of sth, with the intention of changing it if necessary 评审，审查，检查，检讨（以进行必要的修改）：*the government's review of its education policy* 政府对其教育政策的检讨 ◇ *The case is* ***subject to judicial review.*** 这个案子必须接受司法审查。◇ *His parole application is* ***up for review*** *next week.* 他的假释申请下周审查。◇ *The terms of the contract are* ***under review.*** 合同条文正在审议。◇ ***a pay/salary review*** 薪酬审定 ◇ ***a review body/date/panel*** 评审机构 / 日期 / 小组 **2** 🔑 [C, U] a report in a newspaper or magazine, or on the Internet, television or radio, in which sb gives their opinion of a book, play, film/movie, etc.; the act of writing this kind of report（对图书、戏剧、电影等的）评介，评论：*a book review* 书评 ◇ *the reviews (page) in the papers* 报纸的评论版 ◇ ***good/bad/mixed/rave reviews*** *in the national press* 全国性报刊上良好的 / 不好的 / 毁誉参半的 / 高度赞誉的评论 ◇ *He submitted his latest novel for review.* 他提交了自己的最新小说供评论。➲ WORDFINDER NOTE AT NEWSPAPER ➲ COLLOCATIONS AT LITERATURE **3** [C] a report on a subject or on a series of events 报告；汇报；述评；回顾：*a review of customer complaints* 有关消费者投诉的汇报 ◇ *to publish a review of recent cancer research* 发表有关最近癌症研究的报告 **4** [C] (*formal*) a ceremony that involves an official INSPECTION of soldiers, etc. by an important visitor 阅兵式；检阅 **5** 🔑 [C] (*NAmE*) a lesson in which you look again at sth you have studied, especially in order to prepare for an exam（尤指为准备考试的）温习课，复习课

■ ***verb*** **1** 🔑 ~ **sth** to carefully examine or consider sth again, especially so that you can decide if it is necessary to make changes 复查；重新考虑 SYN **reassess**：*to review the evidence* 复查证据 ◇ *The government will review the situation later in the year.* 政府将在今年晚些时候对形势重新加以研究。➲ SYNONYMS AT EXAMINE **2** 🔑 ~ **sth** to think about past events, for example to try to understand why they happened 回顾；反思 SYN **take stock (of sth)**：*to review your failures and triumphs* 回顾自己的成功和失败 ◇ *She had been reviewing the previous week on her way home.* 她在回家的路上对前一个星期进行了回顾。 **3** 🔑 ~ **sth** to write a report of a book, play, film/movie, etc. in which you give your opinion of it 写（关于书籍、戏剧、电影等的）评论；评介：*The play was reviewed in the national newspapers.* 全国性报纸都对这部戏剧作了评论。 **4** ~ **sb/sth** to make an official INSPECTION of a group of soldiers, etc. in a military ceremony 检阅（部队） **5** 🔑 ~ **sth** (*especially NAmE*) to look again at sth you have studied, especially in order to prepare for an exam（尤指为准备考试而）温习，复习 **6** 🔑 ~ **sth** (*especially NAmE*) to check a piece of work to see if there are any mistakes 校阅；审核

re·view·er /rɪ'vjuːə(r)/ *noun* **1** a person who writes reviews of books, films/movies or plays 评论家；评论撰写者 **2** a person who examines or considers sth carefully, for example to see if any changes need to be made 检查者；审查者

re·vile /rɪ'vaɪl/ *verb* [usually passive] ~ **sb (for sth/for doing sth)** (*formal*) to criticize sb/sth in a way that shows how much you dislike them 辱骂；斥责

re·vise 🔑 AW /rɪ'vaɪz/ *verb* **1** 🔑 [T] ~ **sth** to change your opinions or plans, for example because of sth you have learned 改变，修改（意见或计划）：*I can see I will have to revise my opinions of his abilities now.* 我明白我现在不得不改变对他的能力的看法了。◇ *The government may need to revise its policy in the light of this report.* 政府可能需要根据这份报告改变其政策。 **2** 🔑 [T] ~ **sth** to change sth, such as a book or an estimate, in order to correct or improve it 修改，修订（书刊、估算等）：*a revised edition of a textbook* 课本的修订版 ◇ *I'll prepare a revised estimate for you.* 我将为你准备一份经过修正的评估报告。◇ *We may have to revise this figure upwards.* 我们也许要将这个数字往上调一调。 **3** 🔑 [I, T] (*BrE*) to prepare for an exam by looking again at work that you have done 复习；温习：*I spent the weekend revising for my exam.* 我花了整个周末复习备考。◇ *I can't come out tonight. I have to revise.* 我今晚不能出去。我得复习。◇ ~ **sth** *I'm revising Geography today.* 我今天复习地理。➲ WORDFINDER NOTE AT EXAM

re·vi·sion 🔑 AW /rɪ'vɪʒn/ *noun* **1** 🔑 [C] a change or set of changes to sth（一项、一轮等）修订，修改：*He made some minor revisions to the report before printing it out.* 把报告打印出来之前，他做了一些小的修改。 **2** 🔑 [U, C] the act of changing sth, or of examining sth with the intention of changing it 修订，修改（的进行）：*a system in need of revision* 需要更新的系统 ◇ *a revision of trading standards* 贸易标准的修改 **3** 🔑 [U] (*BrE*) the process of learning work for an exam 复习；温习：*Have you started your revision yet?* 你开始复习了吗？➲ COLLOCATIONS AT EDUCATION

re·vi·sion·ism /rɪ'vɪʒənɪzəm/ *noun* [U] (*politics* 政, *often disapproving*) ideas that are different from, and want to change, the main ideas or practices of a political system, especially MARXISM 修正主义 ▸ **re·vi·sion·ist** /-ʒənɪst/ *noun*：*bourgeois revisionists* 资产阶级修正主义者 **re·vi·sion·ist** /-ʒənɪst/ *adj.*：*revisionist historians* 修正主义历史学家

re·visit /ˌriː'vɪzɪt/ *verb* **1** ~ **sth** to visit a place again, especially after a long period of time 再访；重游 **2** ~ **sth** to return to an idea or a subject and discuss it again 重提；再次讨论：*It's an idea that may be worth revisiting at a later date.* 这个观点值得以后进一步探讨。

R

re·vit·al·ize (*BrE also* **-ise**) /ˌriːˈvaɪtəlaɪz/ *verb* **~ sth** to make sth stronger, more active or more healthy 使更强壮；使恢复生机（或健康）: *measures to revitalize the inner cities* 让内城区重焕活力的措施 ▶ **re·vit·al·iza·tion, -isa·tion** /ˌriːˌvaɪtəlaɪˈzeɪʃn; *NAmE* -ləˈz-/ *noun* [U]: *the revitalization of the steel industry* 钢铁工业的振兴

re·vival /rɪˈvaɪvl/ *noun* **1** [U, C] an improvement in the condition or strength of sth （状况或力量的）进步，振兴，复苏: *the revival of trade* 贸易振兴 ◇ *an economic revival* 经济复苏 ◇ *a* ***revival of interest*** *in folk music* 对民间音乐的兴趣的恢复 **2** [C, U] the process of sth becoming or being made popular or fashionable again 复兴；再流行: *a religious revival* 宗教的奋兴 ◇ *Jazz is enjoying a revival.* 爵士音乐再度盛行。 **3** [C] a new production of a play that has not been performed for some time（戏剧的）重演: *a revival of Peter Shaffer's 'Equus'* 彼得·谢弗的《马》的重演

re·vival·ism /rɪˈvaɪvəlɪzəm/ *noun* [U] **1** the process of creating interest in sth again, especially religion（尤指宗教的）奋兴运动 **2** the practice of using ideas, designs, etc. from the past 复兴；复古: *revivalism in architecture* 建筑的复古

re·vival·ist /rɪˈvaɪvəlɪst/ *noun* a person who tries to make sth popular again 推动复兴者；复兴运动倡导者 ▶ **re·vival·ist** *adj.*: *revivalist movements* 复兴运动 ◇ *a revivalist preacher* 宗教奋兴布道者

re·vive /rɪˈvaɪv/ *verb* **1** [I, T] to become, or to make sb/sth become, conscious or healthy and strong again（使）苏醒，复活: *The flowers soon revived in water.* 这些花见了水很快就活过来了。◇ *The economy is beginning to revive.* 经济开始复苏。◇ **~ sb/sth** *The paramedics couldn't revive her.* 护理人员无法使她苏醒。◇ *This movie is intended to revive her flagging career.* 这部电影意在使她渐趋衰败的事业再现辉煌。 **2** [T] **~ sth** to make sth start being used or done again 重新使用；使重做: *This quaint custom should be revived.* 应该恢复这一独特的风俗。◇ *She has been trying to revive the debate over equal pay.* 她一直在设法再次展开同工同酬的辩论。 **3** [T] **~ sth** to produce again a play, etc. that has not been performed for some time 重新上演: *This 1930s musical is being revived at the National Theatre.* 这部 20 世纪 30 年代的音乐剧正在国家剧院重新上演。 ➲ SEE ALSO REVIVAL

re·viv·ify /ˌriːˈvɪvɪfaɪ/ *verb* (**re·vivi·fies, re·vivi·fy·ing, re·vivi·fied, re·vivi·fied**) **~ sth** (*formal*) to give new life or health to sth 使获得新生；使复活；使再生；使恢复健康 SYN **revitalize**

revo·ca·tion /ˌrevəˈkeɪʃn/ *noun* [U, C] (*formal*) the act of cancelling a law, etc.（法律等的）撤销，废除: *the revocation of planning permission* 建筑许可的撤销

re·voke /rɪˈvəʊk; *NAmE* -ˈvoʊk/ *verb* **~ sth** (*formal*) to officially cancel sth so that it is no longer valid 取消；废除；使无效

re·volt /rɪˈvəʊlt; *NAmE* -ˈvoʊlt/ *noun, verb*

■ ***noun*** [C, U] a protest against authority, especially that of a government, often involving violence; the action of protesting against authority（尤指针对政府的）反抗，违抗；起义；叛乱 SYN **uprising**: *the Peasants' Revolt of 1381* * 1381 年的农民起义 ◇ *to* ***lead/stage a revolt*** 领导 / 发动起义 ◇ *The army quickly crushed the revolt.* 军队很快镇压了叛乱。◇ *the biggest back-bench revolt this government has ever seen* 本届政府所遭遇到的规模最大的一次普通下院议员的抗议 ◇ *Attempts to negotiate peace ended in armed revolt.* 和谈的努力最后以武装叛乱告终。◇ (*formal*) *The people rose* ***in revolt.*** 人民奋起反抗。 ➲ COLLOCATIONS AT WAR ➲ SEE ALSO REVOLUTION (1)

■ ***verb*** **1** [I] to take violent action against the people in power 反抗，反叛（当权者） SYN **rebel, rise**: *The peasants threatened to revolt.* 农民威胁说要造反。◇ **~ against sb/sth** *Finally the people revolted against the military dictatorship.* 人民最终起来反抗军事独裁。 **2** [I] **~ (against sth)** to behave in a way that is the opposite of what sb expects of you, especially in protest 叛逆；违抗 SYN **rebel**: *Teenagers often revolt against parental discipline.* 青少年常常不遵从父母的条条框框。 **3** [T] **~ sb** to make you feel horror or disgust 使惊骇；令人厌恶 SYN **disgust**: *All the violence in the movie revolted me.* 电影里的各种暴力场面令我非常震惊。◇ *The way he ate his food revolted me.* 他吃饭的样子让我感到恶心。 ➲ SEE ALSO REVULSION

re·volt·ing /rɪˈvəʊltɪŋ; *NAmE* -ˈvoʊlt-/ *adj.* extremely unpleasant 令人作呕的；极其讨厌的 SYN **disgusting**: *a revolting smell* 令人作呕的气味 ◇ *a revolting little man* 可恶的家伙 ➲ SYNONYMS AT DISGUSTING ▶ **re·volt·ing·ly** *adv.*: *revoltingly ugly* 丑得令人作呕

revo·lu·tion 🔑 AW /ˌrevəˈluːʃn/ *noun* **1** 🔑 [C, U] an attempt, by a large number of people, to change the government of a country, especially by violent action 革命: *a socialist revolution* 社会主义革命 ◇ *the outbreak of the French Revolution in 1789* * 1789 年法国大革命的爆发 ◇ *to start a revolution* 发动一场革命 ◇ *a country on the brink of revolution* 即将发生革命的国家 ➲ COLLOCATIONS AT POLITICS ➲ SEE ALSO COUNTER-REVOLUTION, REVOLT *n.* **2** 🔑 [C] a great change in conditions, ways of working, beliefs, etc. that affects large numbers of people 巨变；大变革: *a* ***cultural/social/scientific, etc. revolution*** 文化、社会、科学等的重大变革 ◇ **~ in sth** *A revolution in information technology is taking place.* 信息技术正在发生巨变。 ➲ SEE ALSO INDUSTRIAL REVOLUTION **3** [C, U] **~ (around/on sth)** a complete CIRCULAR movement around a point, especially of one planet around another（环绕中心点的）旋转；（尤指）天体运行: *the revolution of the earth around the sun* 地球环绕太阳的公转 ➲ SEE ALSO REVOLVE **4** (*also informal* **rev**) [C] a CIRCULAR movement made by sth fixed to a central point, for example in a car engine 旋转；绕轴旋转: *rotating at 300* ***revolutions per minute*** 以每分钟 300 转的速度旋转

revo·lu·tion·ary AW /ˌrevəˈluːʃənəri; *NAmE* -neri/ *adj., noun*

■ ***adj.*** **1** [usually before noun] connected with political revolution 革命的: *a revolutionary leader* 革命领袖 ◇ *revolutionary uprisings* 革命起义 **2** involving a great or complete change 革命性的；大变革的；巨变的: *a* ***revolutionary idea*** 革命性的想法 ◇ *a time of rapid and* ***revolutionary change*** 迅速剧烈变革的时期

■ ***noun*** (*pl.* **-ies**) a person who starts or supports a revolution, especially a political one （支持）改革者；（尤指）革命者，革命支持者: *socialist revolutionaries* 社会主义革命者

revo·lu·tion·ize AW (*BrE also* **-ise**) /ˌrevəˈluːʃənaɪz/ *verb* **~ sth** to completely change the way that sth is done 彻底改变；完全变革: *Aerial photography has revolutionized the study of archaeology.* 航空摄影已经给考古学研究带来了一场革命。

re·volve /rɪˈvɒlv; *NAmE* rɪˈvɑːlv; rɪˈvɔːlv/ *verb* [I] to go in a circle around a central point 旋转；环绕；转动: *The fan revolved slowly.* 电扇缓慢地转动着。◇ *The earth revolves on its axis.* 地球环绕自身的轴心转动。

PHR V **reˈvolve around/round sth** to move around sth in a circle 绕…旋转（或做圆周运动）: *The earth revolves around the sun.* 地球绕太阳公转。 **reˈvolve around/round sb/sth** to have sb/sth as the main interest or subject 围绕；以…为中心；将…作为主要兴趣（或主题）: *His whole life revolves around surfing.* 他一生都在做与冲浪相关的事。◇ *She thinks that the world revolves around her.* 她以为整个世界都以她为中心。◇ *The discussion revolved around the question of changing the club's name.* 讨论的中心问题是改变俱乐部的名称。

re·volver /rɪˈvɒlvə(r); *NAmE* -ˈvɑːl-; -ˈvɔːl-/ *noun* a small gun that has a container for bullets that turns around so that shots can be fired quickly without having to stop to put more bullets in 左轮手枪

re·volv·ing /rɪˈvɒlvɪŋ; *NAmE* -ˈvɔːl-; -ˈvɑːl-/ *adj.* [usually before noun] able to turn in a circle 旋转的: *a revolving chair* 转椅 ◇ *The theatre has a revolving stage.* 剧院有一个旋转舞台。

R

ˌ**revolving ˈdoor** *noun* **1** a type of door in an entrance to a large building that turns around in a circle as people go through it 旋转门 **2** used to talk about a place or an organization that people enter and then leave again very quickly 中转站（指人们进入后很快又离开的地方或机构）：*The company became a revolving-door workplace.* 这家公司成了工作的中转站。

revue /rɪˈvjuː/ *noun* [C, U] a show in a theatre, with songs, dances, jokes, short plays, etc., often about recent events 时事讽刺剧；活报剧

re·vul·sion /rɪˈvʌlʃn/ *noun* [U, sing.] ~ **(at/against/from sth)** (*formal*) a strong feeling of disgust or horror 嫌恶；恶心；惊恐 **SYN repugnance**: *She felt a deep sense of revulsion at the violence.* 她对这一暴行深恶痛绝。◇ *I started to feel a revulsion against their decadent lifestyle.* 我对他们那腐朽的生活方式开始感到厌恶。◇ *Most people viewed the bombings with revulsion.* 大多数人对爆炸事件表现出惊恐不安。⇨ SEE ALSO REVOLT *v.* (3)

re·ward /rɪˈwɔːd; *NAmE* rɪˈwɔːrd/ *noun, verb*

■ ***noun*** **1** [C, U] a thing that you are given because you have done sth good, worked hard, etc. 奖励；回报；报酬：*a financial reward* 经济奖励 ◇ ~ **(for sth/for doing sth)** *a reward for good behaviour* 优秀行为奖 ◇ *You deserve a reward for being so helpful.* 你帮了这么大的忙，理应受到奖励。◇ *Winning the match was* ***just reward*** *for the effort the team had made.* 赢得比赛的胜利是全队付出努力应得的回报。◇ *The company is now* ***reaping the rewards*** *of their investments.* 公司正在收获他们的投资回报。 **2** [C] an amount of money that is offered to sb for helping the police to find a criminal or for finding sth that is lost 赏格；悬赏金：*A £100 reward has been offered for the return of the necklace.* 已悬赏 100 英镑找寻项链。**IDM** SEE VIRTUE

■ ***verb*** [often passive] to give sth to sb because they have done sth good, worked hard, etc. 奖励；奖赏；给以报酬：~ **sb for sth** *She was rewarded for her efforts with a cash bonus.* 她因自己所作的努力而得到一笔奖金。◇ ~ **sb for doing sth** *He rewarded us handsomely* (= with a lot of money) *for helping him.* 对于我们的帮助，他大加酬谢。◇ ~ **sb with sth** *She started singing to the baby and was rewarded with a smile.* 她开始给孩子唱歌，孩子则报以微笑。◇ ~ **sb/sth** *Our patience was finally rewarded.* 我们的耐心最终得到了回报。

re·ward·ing /rɪˈwɔːdɪŋ; *NAmE* -ˈwɔːrd-/ *adj.* **1** (of an activity, etc. 活动等) worth doing; that makes you happy because you think it is useful or important 值得做的；有益的：*a rewarding experience/job* 有益的经历 / 工作 ⇨ SYNONYMS AT SATISFYING **2** producing a lot of money 报酬高的 **SYN profitable**: *Teaching is not very financially rewarding* (= is not very well paid). 教书不会有很高的报酬。**OPP unrewarding**

re·wind /ˌriːˈwaɪnd/ *verb* (**re·wound, re·wound** /-ˈwaʊnd/) [T, I] ~ **(sth)** to make sth such as a film or a recording go backwards 使（影片、录音、视频等）倒回；倒带

re·wire /ˌriːˈwaɪə(r)/ *verb* ~ **sth** to put new electrical wires into a building or piece of equipment 给（建筑物或设备）换新电线

re·word /ˌriːˈwɜːd; *NAmE* -ˈwɜːrd/ *verb* ~ **sth** to write sth again using different words in order to make it clearer or more acceptable 改写；修改措辞 ▶ **re·word·ing** *noun* [C, U]

re·work /ˌriːˈwɜːk; *NAmE* -ˈwɜːrk/ *verb* ~ **sth** to make changes to sth in order to improve it or make it more suitable 修改；重做；再加工 ▶ **re·work·ing** *noun* [C, U]: *The movie is a reworking of the Frankenstein story.* 这部电影是根据科学怪人的故事改编的。

re·writ·able /ˌriːˈraɪtəbl/ *adj.* (*computing* 计) able to be used again for different data 可重写的：*a rewritable CD* 可重写光盘

re·write /ˌriːˈraɪt/ *verb* (**re·wrote** /-ˈrəʊt; *NAmE* -ˈroʊt/, **re·writ·ten** /-ˈrɪtn/) ~ **sth** to write sth again in a different way, usually in order to improve it or because there is some new information 重写；改写：*I intend to rewrite the story for younger children.* 我想为年纪更小的孩子改写这篇故事。◇ *This essay will have to be completely rewritten.* 这篇文章得全部重写。◇ *an attempt to* ***rewrite history*** (= to present historical events in a way that shows or proves what you want them to) 改写历史的企图 ▶ **re·write** /ˈriːraɪt/ *noun*

Rex /reks/ *noun* [U] (*BrE, formal, from Latin*) a word meaning 'king', used, for example, in the titles of legal cases brought by the state when there is a king in Britain 国王（英国国王在位时用于政府诉讼案案目等）：*Rex v Jones* 国王诉琼斯案

RGN /ˌɑː dʒiː ˈen; *NAmE* ˌɑːr dʒiː ˈen/ *noun* (*BrE*) registered general nurse 注册全科护士

r.h. *abbr.* (in writing 书写形式) RIGHT HAND 右手

rhap·sod·ize (*BrE also* **-ise**) /ˈræpsədaɪz/ *verb* [I, T] ~ **(about/over sth)** | **+ speech** (*formal*) to talk or write with great enthusiasm about sth 热情地谈论（或写） **SYN be in, go into, etc. raptures (about/over sb/sth)**

rhap·sody /ˈræpsədi/ *noun* (*pl.* **-ies**) **1** (often in titles 常用于标题) a piece of music that is full of feeling and is not regular in form 狂想曲：*Liszt's Hungarian Rhapsodies* 李斯特的《匈牙利狂想曲》 **2** (*formal*) the expression of great enthusiasm or happiness in speech or writing （言语或文字的）狂热表达，充满欣喜的表达 ▶ **rhap·sodic** /ræpˈsɒdɪk; *NAmE* -ˈsɑːdɪk/ *adj.*

rhea /ˈriːə/ *noun* a large S American bird that does not fly 美洲鸵鸟

rheme /riːm/ *noun* (*linguistics* 语言) the part of a sentence or clause that adds new information to what the reader or audience already knows 表位，述位（提供新信息的句子成分） ⇨ COMPARE THEME *n.* (5)

rhe·nium /ˈriːniəm/ *noun* [U] (*symb.* **Re**) a chemical element. Rhenium is a rare silver-white metal that exists naturally in the ORES of MOLYBDENUM and some other metals. 铼

rhe·sus factor /ˈriːsəs fæktə(r)/ *noun* [sing.] (*medical* 医) a substance present in the red blood cells of around 85% of humans. Its presence (**rhesus positive**) or absence (**rhesus negative**) can be dangerous for babies when they are born and for people having BLOOD TRANSFUSIONS. * Rh 因子

rhe·sus monkey /ˈriːsəs mʌŋki/ *noun* a small S Asian MONKEY, often used in scientific experiments 恒河猴（一种南亚猕猴，常用于科学实验）

rhet·oric /ˈretərɪk/ *noun* [U] **1** (*formal, often disapproving*) speech or writing that is intended to influence people, but that is not completely honest or sincere 华而不实的言语；花言巧语：*the rhetoric of political slogans* 政治口号的虚华辞藻 ◇ *empty rhetoric* 空洞的花言巧语 **2** (*formal*) the skill of using language in speech or writing in a special way that influences or entertains people 修辞技巧；修辞 **SYN eloquence, oratory**

rhet·oric·al /rɪˈtɒrɪkl; *NAmE* -ˈtɔːr-/ *adj.* **1** (of a question 问题) asked only to make a statement or to produce an effect rather than to get an answer 反问的；反诘的：*'Don't you care what I do?' he asked, but it was a* ***rhetorical question***. "我做什么，难道你不关心吗？"他问道，可那是个反问。 **2** (*formal, often disapproving*) (of a speech or piece of writing 言语或文章) intended to influence people, but not completely honest or sincere 辞藻华丽的；虚夸的；花言巧语的 **3** (*formal*) connected with the art of RHETORIC 修辞的；修辞性的；带有修辞色彩的：*the use of rhetorical devices such as metaphor and irony* 诸如暗喻和反讽等修辞手法的运用 ▶ **rhet·oric·al·ly** /-kli/ *adv.*：*'Do you think I'm stupid?' she asked rhetorically.* "你以为我是傻瓜？"她反问道。◇ *a rhetorically structured essay* 讲究修辞结构的文章

rhet·or·ician /ˌretəˈrɪʃn/ *noun* (*specialist*) a person who is skilled in the art of formal rhetoric 修辞学家

rheu̦matic 'fever *noun* [U] a serious disease that causes fever with swelling and pain in the joints 风湿热

rheuma·tism /'ruːmətɪzəm/ *noun* [U] a disease that makes the muscles and joints painful, stiff and swollen 风湿（病） ▸ **rheum·at·ic** /ru'mætɪk/ *adj.*：*rheumatic pains* 风湿痛

rheuma·toid arth·ritis /ˌruːmətɔɪd ɑː'θraɪtɪs; *NAmE* ɑːr'θ-/ *noun* [U] (*medical* 医) a disease that gets worse over a period of time and causes painful swelling and permanent damage in the joints of the body, especially the fingers, wrists, feet and ankles 类风湿（性）关节炎

rheuma·tol·ogy /ˌruːmə'tɒlədʒi; *NAmE* -'tɑːl-/ *noun* [U] the study of the diseases of joints and muscles, such as RHEUMATISM and ARTHRITIS 风湿病学

rheumy /'ruːmi/ *adj.* (of the eyes 眼睛) containing a lot of water 充水的；充满黏液的

rhine·stone /'raɪnstəʊn; *NAmE* -stoʊn/ *noun* a clear stone that is intended to look like a diamond, used in cheap jewellery 莱茵石（用于仿钻石首饰）

rhin·itis /raɪ'naɪtɪs/ *noun* [U] (*medical* 医) a condition in which the inside of the nose becomes swollen and sore, caused by an infection or an ALLERGY 鼻炎（感染或过敏引起）

rhino /'raɪnəʊ; *NAmE* -noʊ/ *noun* (*pl.* **-os**) (*informal*) = RHINOCEROS：*black/white rhino* 黑 / 白犀牛 ◇ *rhino horn* 犀牛角

rhi·noceros /raɪ'nɒsərəs; *NAmE* -'nɑːs-/ *noun* (*pl.* **rhi·noceros** or **rhi·nocer·oses**) (*also informal* **rhino**) a large heavy animal with very thick skin and either one or two horns on its nose, that lives in Africa and Asia 犀，犀牛（栖于非洲和亚洲）

rhi·zome /'raɪzəʊm; *NAmE* -zoʊm/ *noun* (*specialist*) the thick STEM of some plants, such as IRIS and MINT, that grows along or under the ground and has roots and STEMS growing from it 根茎；根状茎

rho /rəʊ; *NAmE* roʊ/ *noun* the 17th letter of the Greek alphabet (Ρ, ρ) 希腊字母表的第 17 个字母

R

Rhodes scholar /ˌrəʊdz 'skɒlə(r); *NAmE* ˌroʊdz 'skɑːl-/ *noun* a student from the US, Germany or the Commonwealth who is given a SCHOLARSHIP to study in Britain at Oxford University from a fund that was started by Cecil Rhodes in 1902 获罗得斯奖学金的学生（罗得斯基金由塞西尔·罗得斯于 1902 年设立，为美国、德国或英联邦国家的学生提供到英国牛津大学学习的奖学金）

rho·dium /'rəʊdiəm; *NAmE* 'roʊ-/ *noun* [U] (*symb.* **Rh**) a chemical element. Rhodium is a hard silver-white metal that is usually found with PLATINUM. 铑

rhodo·den·dron /ˌrəʊdə'dendrən; *NAmE* ˌroʊ-/ *noun* a bush with large red, purple, pink or white flowers 杜鹃花

rhom·boid /'rɒmbɔɪd; *NAmE* 'rɑːm-/ *noun* (*geometry* 几何) a flat shape with four straight sides, with only the opposite sides and angles equal to each other 长菱形 ➲ PICTURE AT PARALLELOGRAM

rhom·bus /'rɒmbəs; *NAmE* 'rɑːm-/ *noun* (*geometry* 几何) a flat shape with four equal sides and four angles which are not 90° 菱形 ➲ PICTURE AT PARALLELOGRAM

rho·tic /'rəʊtɪk; *NAmE* 'roʊ-/ *adj.* (*phonetics* 语音) (of an accent 口音) pronouncing the /r/ after a vowel in words like *car*, *early*, etc. General American and Scottish accents are rhotic. * r 化的；r 类音的

rhu·barb /'ruːbɑːb; *NAmE* -bɑːrb/ *noun* [U] **1** the thick red STEMS of a garden plant, also called rhubarb, that are cooked and eaten as a fruit 大黄；大黄茎；馅饼菜：*rhubarb pie* 大黄馅饼 **2** a word that a group of actors repeat on stage to give the impression of a lot of people talking at the same time（演员们为了制造人声嘈杂的效果而重复说的词）

rhumba = RUMBA

rhyme /raɪm/ *noun, verb*

■ ***noun*** **1** [C] a word that has the same sound or ends with the same sound as another word 押韵词；同韵词：*Can you think of a rhyme for 'beauty'?* 你能想出和 beauty 押韵的词吗？ **2** [C] a short poem in which the last word in the line has the same sound as the last word in another line, especially the next one 押韵的短诗：*children's rhymes and stories* 儿歌和童话 ➲ SEE ALSO NURSERY RHYME **3** [U] the use of words in a poem or song that have the same sound, especially at the ends of lines 押韵；韵词的应用：*a poem written **in rhyme*** 押韵的诗 ◇ *the poet's use of rhyme* 诗人对韵的运用 ➲ WORDFINDER NOTE AT POETRY

IDM **there's no ˌrhyme or 'reason to/for sth | without ˌrhyme or 'reason** if there is **no rhyme or reason to sth** or it happens **without rhyme or reason**, it happens in a way that cannot be easily explained or understood 毫无道理；无规律可循；莫名其妙

■ ***verb*** **1** [I] ~ (**with sth**) if two words, syllables, etc. **rhyme**, or if one **rhymes** with the other, they have or end with the same sound （词或音节）押韵，和…同韵：*'Though' rhymes with 'low'.* * though 和 low 押韵。◇ *'Tough' and 'through' don't rhyme.* * tough 和 through 不押韵。◇ *rhyming couplets* 同韵偶句 **2** [T] ~ **sth** (**with sth**) to put words that sound the same together, for example when you are writing poetry 使押韵：*You can rhyme 'girl' with 'curl'.* 你可以用 girl 和 curl 押韵。 **3** [I] (of a poem 诗歌) to have lines that end with the same sound 押句尾韵：*I prefer poems that rhyme.* 我喜欢句尾押韵的诗。

'rhyming slang *noun* [U] a way of talking in which you use words or phrases that rhyme with the word you mean, instead of using that word. For example in COCKNEY rhyming slang 'apples and pears' means 'stairs'. 同韵俚语（以同韵的词或短语替代另一个词，如伦敦土话中用 apples and pears 代替 stairs）

rhythm 🔑 /'rɪðəm/ *noun* [U, C] **1** 🔑 a strong regular repeated pattern of sounds or movements 节奏；韵律；律动：*to dance to the rhythm of the music* 随着音乐的节奏跳舞 ◇ *music with **a fast/slow/steady rhythm*** 节奏快的 / 慢的 / 平稳的音乐 ◇ *jazz rhythms* 爵士乐的节奏 ◇ *He can't seem to play **in rhythm**.* 他的演奏好像不合节拍。◇ *The boat rocked up and down **in rhythm with** the sea.* 小船随着海浪起伏有致。◇ *the rhythm of her breathing* 她的呼吸节奏 ◇ *a dancer with a **natural sense of rhythm*** (= the ability to move in time to a fixed beat) 天生节奏感很强的舞蹈者 ➲ WORDFINDER NOTE AT SING **2** a regular pattern of changes or events 规则变化；规律；节律：*the rhythm of the seasons* 四季的更迭 ◇ ***biological/body rhythms*** 生物 / 人体节律 ➲ SEE ALSO BIORHYTHM

ˌrhythm and 'blues *noun* [U] (*abbr.* **R & B**) a type of music that is a mixture of BLUES and JAZZ and has a strong rhythm 节奏布鲁斯，节奏蓝调（由布鲁斯和爵士乐综合而成的节奏感很强的音乐）

ˌrhythm gui'tar *noun* [U] a GUITAR style that consists mainly of CHORDS played with a strong rhythm 节奏吉他 ➲ COMPARE LEAD GUITAR

rhyth·mic /'rɪðmɪk/ (*also less frequent* **rhyth·mic·al** /'rɪðmɪkl/) *adj.* having a regular pattern of sounds, movements or events 有节奏（或规律）的；节奏分明的：*music with a fast, rhythmic beat* 节奏快的音乐 ◇ *the rhythmic ticking of the clock* 时钟有节奏的滴答声 ▸ **rhyth·mic·al·ly** /-kli/ *adv.*

the 'rhythm method *noun* [sing.] a method of avoiding getting pregnant that involves a woman only having sex during the time of the month when she is unlikely to get pregnant 安全期避孕法

'rhythm section *noun* the part of a band that supplies the rhythm, usually consisting of drums, BASS[1], and sometimes piano （乐队的）节奏乐器组（通常由鼓、低音提琴，有时还有钢琴组成）

ria /'riːə/ *noun* (*specialist*) a long narrow area of water formed when a river valley floods 溺河（河谷被淹没形成的狭长水域）

rial (*also* **riyal**) /riːˈɑːl; ˈriːɑːl; *NAmE* riːˈɔːl/ *noun* **1** the unit of money in Iran and Oman 里亚尔（伊朗和阿曼的货币单位） **2 riyal** the unit of money in Saudi Arabia, Qatar and Yemen 里亚尔（沙特阿拉伯、卡塔尔和也门的货币单位）

rib /rɪb/ *noun, verb*

■ ***noun*** **1** [C] any of the curved bones that are connected to the SPINE and surround the chest 肋骨：***a broken/bruised/cracked rib*** 折断的／挫伤的／开裂的肋骨 ◇ ***Stop poking me in the ribs!*** 别捅我的腰！ ➲ VISUAL VOCAB PAGE V64 ➲ SEE ALSO RIBCAGE **2** [U, C] a piece of meat with one or more bones from the ribs of an animal 排骨 ➲ SEE ALSO SPARE RIB **3** [C] a curved piece of wood, metal or plastic that forms the frame of a boat, roof, etc. and makes it stronger（船或屋顶等的）肋拱，肋材 **4** [U, C] a way of knitting that produces a pattern of vertical lines in which some are higher than others （织物的）凸条花纹，罗纹：*a rib cotton sweater* 一件罗纹棉毛衫 IDM SEE DIG *v.*

■ ***verb*** **(-bb-) ~ sb (about/over sth)** (*old-fashioned, informal*) to laugh at sb and make jokes about them, but in a friendly way 嘲笑；逗弄；开（某人的）玩笑 SYN **tease**

rib·ald /ˈrɪbld; ˈraɪbɔːld/ *adj.* (of language or behaviour 言语或行为) referring to sex in a rude but humorous way 猥亵诙谐的

rib·ald·ry /ˈrɪbldri; ˈraɪb-/ *noun* [U] language or behaviour that refers to sex in a rude but humorous way 猥亵诙谐的言语（或行为）

ribbed /rɪbd/ *adj.* (especially of material for clothes 尤指衣料) having raised lines 有棱纹的：*a ribbed sweater* 有棱纹的毛衣

rib·bing /ˈrɪbɪŋ/ *noun* [U] **1** a pattern of raised lines in knitting or on a surface（织物或物体表面的）棱纹，凸条图案 **2** (*old-fashioned, informal*) the act of making fun of sb in a friendly way 开玩笑；取笑；逗弄 SYN **tease**

rib·bon /ˈrɪbən/ *noun* **1** [U, C] a narrow strip of material, used to tie things or for decoration（用于捆绑或装饰的）带子；丝带：*a present tied with yellow ribbon* 系着黄丝带的礼物 ◇ *lengths of velvet ribbon* 一段段天鹅绒带子 ◇ *She was wearing two blue silk ribbons in her hair.* 她的头发上系着两根蓝色丝带。 ➲ PICTURE AT ROPE **2** [C] something that is long and narrow in shape 带状物；狭长的东西：*The road was a ribbon of moonlight.* 这条路在月光下如同一条缎带。 **3** [C] a ribbon in special colours, or tied in a special way, that is given to sb as a prize or as a military honour, or that is worn by sb to show that they belong to a particular political party 绶带；勋带 ➲ COMPARE ROSETTE (1) **4** [C] a long strip of material containing ink that you put into TYPEWRITERS and some computer printers （打字机或打印机的）色带

IDM **cut/tear, etc. sth to ˈribbons** to cut/tear, etc. sth very badly （将某物）撕扯得粉碎，切成碎片

ˈribbon development *noun* [C, U] (*BrE, specialist*) houses that are built along a main road leading out of a village or town; the building of houses in this position 带状住宅区（村、镇沿公路延伸出的房屋）；带状房屋建设

ˈribbon lake *noun* (*specialist*) a long narrow lake 带状湖

rib·cage /ˈrɪbkeɪdʒ/ *noun* the structure of curved bones (called RIBS), that surrounds and protects the chest 胸廓 ➲ VISUAL VOCAB PAGE V64

ˈrib-eye (*also* **ˌrib-eye ˈsteak**) *noun* a piece of beef which is cut from outside the RIBS 牛里脊肉；里脊牛排

ribo·fla·vin /ˌraɪbəˈfleɪvɪn/ *noun* [U] a VITAMIN which is important for producing energy, found in milk, LIVER, eggs and green vegetables 核黄素；维生素 B_2

ˈrib-tickler *noun* (*informal*) a funny joke or story 笑话；惹人发笑的故事 ▶ **ˈrib-tickling** *adj.* ➲ MORE LIKE THIS 10, page R26

rice 🔑 /raɪs/ *noun* [U] short, narrow white or brown grain grown on wet land in hot countries as food; the plant that produces this grain 大米；稻米；稻：*a grain of rice* 一粒大米 ◇ ***boiled/steamed/fried rice*** 煮饭；蒸饭；炒饭 ◇ ***long-/short-grain rice*** 长粒／短粒稻米 ◇ ***brown rice*** (= without its outer covering removed) 糙米 ◇ ***rice paddies*** (= rice fields) 稻田 ➲ VISUAL VOCAB PAGE V35

ˈrice paper *noun* [U] a type of very thin paper made from tropical plants, used as a base for some types of cake 米纸（用热带植物制作的薄纸，用作糕饼垫底）

ˌrice ˈpudding *noun* [U, C] a DESSERT (= a sweet dish) made from rice cooked with milk and sugar 大米布丁

rich 🔑 /rɪtʃ/ *adj.* (**rich·er, rich·est**)
• **WITH A LOT OF MONEY** 钱多 **1** 🔑 having a lot of money or property 富有的；富裕的：*one of the richest women in the world* 世界上最富有的女人之一 ◇ *Nobody gets rich from writing nowadays.* 如今没有人能靠写作致富。◇ (*slang*) *to be* ***filthy/stinking*** (= extremely) ***rich*** 富得流油 OPP **poor** **2 the rich** *noun* [pl.] people who have a lot of

▼ **SYNONYMS 同义词辨析**

rich

wealthy • prosperous • affluent • well off • comfortable

These words all describe sb/sth that has a lot of money, property or valuable possessions. 以上各词均用以形容人富有或地方富饶。

rich (of a person) having a lot of money, property or valuable possessions; (of a country or city) producing a lot of wealth so that many of its people can live at a high standard 指（人）富有的、富裕的，（国家或城市）富庶的、富饶的

wealthy rich 指富有的、富饶的

RICH OR WEALTHY? 用 rich 还是 wealthy?

There is no real difference in meaning between these two words. Both are very frequent, but **rich** is more frequent and can be used in some fixed phrases where **wealthy** cannot. 上述两词在意义上无实质性区别。两词均很常用，不过 rich 更常用，并用于一些固定短语中，wealthy 则不能：~~*He's stinking/filthy wealthy.*~~ ◇ ~~*It's a favourite resort for the wealthy and famous.*~~

prosperous (*rather formal*) rich and successful 指繁荣的、成功的、兴旺的

affluent (*rather formal*) rich and with a good standard of living 指富裕的：*affluent Western countries* 富裕的西方国家

PROSPEROUS OR AFFLUENT? 用 prosperous 还是 affluent?

Both **prosperous** and **affluent** are used to talk about people and places. **Prosperous** is used much more than **affluent** to talk about times and periods. **Affluent** is often used to contrast rich people or societies with poor ones. Being **prosperous** is nearly always seen as a good thing. * prosperous 和 affluent 均用以指人和地方。prosperous 较 affluent 更常用以修饰时期或时代。affluent 常用于人或社会的贫富对比，prosperous 几乎总是被视为好事：*It's good to see you looking so prosperous.* 看到你成功的样子真是令人高兴。◇ ~~*It's good to see you looking so affluent.*~~

well off (often used in negative sentences) rich（常用于否定句中）指富裕、有钱：*His family is not very well off.* 他家境不太宽裕。NOTE The opposite of **well off** is **badly off**, but this is not very frequent; it is more common to say that sb is *not well off.* * well off 的反义词为 badly off，但不常用；指人不宽裕较常用 not well off。

comfortable having enough money to buy what you want without worrying about the cost 指富裕、宽裕：*They're not millionaires, but they're certainly very comfortable.* 他们不是百万富翁，但也很富裕。

PATTERNS

• a(n) rich/wealthy/prosperous/affluent/well-off **family**
• a rich/wealthy/prosperous/well-off **man/woman**
• a(n) rich/wealthy/prosperous/affluent **country/city**

R

money or property 富人；有钱人：*It's a favourite resort for the rich and famous.* 这是富人和名流最喜欢去度假的地方。 **OPP poor** ➲ MORE LIKE THIS 24, page R28 **3** (of a country 国家) producing a lot of wealth so that many of its people can live at a high standard 富庶的；富饶的：*the richest countries/economies/nations* 最富有的国家/经济体/国家 **OPP poor**

• FULL OF VARIETY 丰富多彩 **4** very interesting and full of variety 非常有趣的；丰富多彩的：*the region's rich history and culture* 这个地区丰富多彩的历史和文化 ◇ *She leads a rich and varied life.* 她过着丰富多彩的生活。

• CONTAINING/PROVIDING STH 含有；提供 **5** ~ **(in sth)** (often in compounds 常构成复合词) containing or providing a large supply of sth 大量含有（或提供）：*Oranges are rich in vitamin C.* 橘子含有丰富的维生素 C。◇ *The area is rich in wildlife.* 这个地区的野生动植物很多。◇ *His novels are a rich source of material for the movie industry.* 他的小说为电影业提供了大量素材。◇ *iron-rich rocks* 富含铁的岩石 **OPP poor**

• FOOD 食物 **6** containing a lot of fat, butter, eggs, etc. and making you feel full quickly 油腻的：*a rich creamy sauce* 味道很浓的奶油沙司 ◇ *a rich chocolate cake* 很油腻的巧克力蛋糕

• SOIL 土壤 **7** containing the substances that make it good for growing plants in 肥沃的；丰产的 **SYN fertile**：*a rich well-drained soil* 排水性能好的沃土 **OPP poor**

• COLOURS/SOUNDS 色彩；声音 **8** (of colours, sounds, smells and tastes 颜色、声音、气味和味道) strong or deep; very beautiful or pleasing 强烈的；深的；低沉的；美好的；宜人的：*rich dark reds* 浓重的深红色

• EXPENSIVE 昂贵 **9** (*literary*) expensive and beautiful 华丽而昂贵的 **SYN sumptuous**：*The rooms were decorated with rich fabrics.* 这些屋子装饰着华丽昂贵的织物。

• CRITICISM 批评 **10** (*informal, especially BrE*) used to say that a criticism sb makes is surprising and not reasonable, because they have the same fault (表示某人所作的批评是无稽之谈，因为他们本身也有同样的问题)：*Me? Lazy? That's rich, coming from you!* 我？懒？真可笑，你自己也一样！ ➲ COMPARE RICHNESS **IDM** SEE STRIKE *v.*

riches /ˈrɪtʃɪz/ *noun* [pl.] large amounts of money and valuable or beautiful possessions 财富；财产：*a career that brought him fame and riches* 使他名利双收的事业 ◇ *material riches* 物质财富 **IDM** SEE EMBARRASSMENT, RAG *n.*

rich·ly /ˈrɪtʃli/ *adv.* **1** in a beautiful and expensive manner 富丽堂皇地：*a richly decorated room* 装饰得富丽堂皇的房间 **2** used to express the fact that sth has a pleasant strong colour, taste or smell （色彩）鲜艳富丽地；（口味）醇美地；（气味）浓郁芬芳地：*a richly flavoured sauce* 味道很浓的调味汁 ◇ *The polished floor glowed richly.* 光洁无瑕的地板十分明亮。 **3** in a generous way 慷慨地；大方地：*She was richly rewarded for all her hard work.* 她一向勤劳苦干，得到了丰厚的回报。 **4** in a way that people think is right and good 恰如其分地；理所当然地；完全地 **SYN thoroughly**：*richly **deserved** success* 理应取得的成功 ◇ *richly earned respect* 理应受到的尊敬 **5** used to express the fact that the quality or thing mentioned is present in large amounts （表明品质突出或物质丰富）：*richly varied countryside* 各地情况迥异的乡村 ◇ *a richly atmospheric novel* 氛围渲染得很强烈的小说

rich·ness /ˈrɪtʃnəs/ *noun* [U] the state of being rich in sth, such as colour, minerals or interesting qualities 丰富；富饶；浓烈：*the richness and variety of marine life* 海洋生物的丰富多样 ➲ COMPARE WEALTH (3)

the Rich·ter scale /ˈrɪktə skeɪl; *NAmE* ˈrɪktər/ *noun* [sing.] a system for measuring how strong an EARTHQUAKE is 里氏震级，里克特震级（测量地震强度的标准）：*an earthquake measuring 7.3 on the Richter scale* 里氏 7.3 级的地震

ricin /ˈraɪsɪn/ *noun* [U] a very poisonous substance obtained from the seeds of the CASTOR OIL plant 蓖麻毒素；蓖麻毒蛋白

rick /rɪk/ *noun, verb*
▪ *noun* a large pile of HAY or STRAW that is built in a regular shape and covered to protect it from rain 干草堆；草垛
▪ *verb* ~ **sth** (*BrE*) to injure a part of your body by twisting it suddenly 扭伤 **SYN sprain**

rick·ets /ˈrɪkɪts/ *noun* [U] a disease of children caused by a lack of good food that makes the bones become soft and badly formed, especially in the legs 佝偻病

rick·ety /ˈrɪkəti/ *adj.* not strong or well made; likely to break 不结实的；不稳固的；易折断的：*a rickety chair* 摇摇晃晃的椅子

rick·shaw /ˈrɪkʃɔː/ *noun* a small light vehicle with two wheels used in some Asian countries to carry passengers. The rickshaw is pulled by sb walking or riding a bicycle. 人力车；黄包车

rico·chet /ˈrɪkəʃeɪ; *BrE also* -ʃet/ *verb, noun*
▪ *verb* (**rico·chet·ing** /ˈrɪkəʃeɪɪŋ/, **rico·cheted**, **rico·cheted** /ˈrɪkəʃeɪd/, *BrE also* **rico·chet·ting** /ˈrɪkəʃetɪŋ/, **rico·chet·ted**, **rico·chet·ted** /ˈrɪkəʃetɪd/) [I] **+ adv./prep.** (of a moving object 运动的物体) to hit a surface and come off it fast at a different angle 弹开；反弹出去：*The bullet ricocheted off a nearby wall.* 子弹从附近的一面墙上弹飞了。
▪ *noun* **1** [C] a ball, bullet or stone that ricochets 弹回的球（或子弹、石头）：*A woman protester was killed by a ricochet.* 一名女性抗议者被反弹的子弹击中身亡。 **2** [U] the action of ricocheting 弹回；反弹；弹开：*the ricochet of bricks and bottles off police riot shields* 砸在警察防暴盾牌上的砖块和瓶子弹回来

ric·tus /ˈrɪktəs/ *noun* (*formal*) a wide twisted or smiling mouth that does not look natural or relaxed 扭曲（或怪笑）的嘴；龇牙咧嘴

rid /rɪd/ *verb* (**rid·ding**, **rid**, **rid**)
IDM be ˈrid of sb/sth (*formal*) to be free of sb/sth that has been annoying you or that you do not want 摆脱：*She wanted to be rid of her parents and their authority.* 她想摆脱父母及其权威的束缚。◇ *I was glad to be rid of the car when I finally sold it.* 把车卖掉时，我很庆幸终于脱手了。◇ (*BrE*) *He was a nuisance and we're all **well rid of** him* (= we'll be much better without him). 他这人很讨厌，没有他我们都会舒服得多。 **get ˈrid of sb/sth** to make yourself free of sb/sth that is annoying you or that you do not want; to throw sth away 摆脱；丢弃；扔掉：*Try and get rid of your visitors before I get there.* 在我到达之前，想办法把你的客人打发走。◇ *The problem is getting rid of nuclear waste.* 问题是如何处理核废料。◇ *I can't get rid of this headache.* 我这头疼老是不好。◇ *We got rid of all the old furniture.* 我们扔掉了所有的旧家具。 ➲ MORE AT WANT *v.*
PHR V ˈrid sb/sth of sb/sth (*formal*) to remove sth that is causing a problem from a place, group, etc. 去除；清除：*Further measures will be taken to rid our streets of crime.* 将采取进一步的措施来防止街头犯罪。 **ˈrid yourself of sb/sth** (*formal*) to make yourself free from sb/sth that is annoying you or causing you a problem 摆脱；从…中解脱：*to rid yourself of guilt* 摆脱内疚 ◇ *He wanted to rid himself of the burden of the secret.* 他想把秘密说出来，让自己得到解脱。

rid·dance /ˈrɪdns/ *noun* [U]
IDM good ˈriddance (to sb/sth) an unkind way of saying that you are pleased that sb/sth has gone (不友善的话，表示很高兴某人或某物已离开)：*'Goodbye and good riddance!' she said to him angrily as he left.* 他离去时，她气愤地冲着他说："再见吧，早走早好！"

rid·den /ˈrɪdn/ *adj.* (usually in compounds 通常构成复合词) full of a particular unpleasant thing 充满（某种不良事物）的；满是…的：*a disease-ridden slum* 疾病流行的贫民窟 ◇ *a class-ridden society* 等级森严的社会 ◇ *She was guilt-ridden at the way she had treated him.* 她为过去曾那样对待他而深感内疚。◇ *She was ridden with guilt.* 她深感歉疚。 ➲ SEE ALSO RIDE *v.*

rid·dle /ˈrɪdl/ *noun, verb*
▪ *noun* **1** a question that is difficult to understand, and that has a surprising answer, that you ask sb as a game 谜；谜语：*Stop **talking in riddles*** (= saying things that

are confusing)—*say what you mean.* 别拐弯抹角了，有话直说。◇ *to solve the riddle of the Sphinx* 解开斯芬克斯之谜 **2** a mysterious event or situation that you cannot explain 神秘事件；无法解释的情况 SYN **mystery**: *the riddle of how the baby died* 婴儿死亡之谜

■ *verb* [usually passive] ~ **sb/sth** (**with sth**) to make a lot of holes in sb/sth 使布满窟窿: *The car was* ***riddled with bullets.*** 这辆车被子弹打得千疮百孔。

IDM **be 'riddled with sth** to be full of sth, especially sth bad or unpleasant 充满；充斥: *His body was riddled with cancer.* 恶性肿瘤遍布他的全身。◇ *Her typing was slow and riddled with mistakes.* 她打字很慢而且错误百出。

ride /raɪd/ *verb, noun*

■ *verb* (**rode** /rəʊd; *NAmE* roʊd/, **rid·den** /'rɪdn/)

• **HORSE** 马 **1** [I, T] to sit on a horse, etc. and control it as it moves 驾驭马匹；骑马: *I learnt to ride as a child.* 我小时候就学会了骑马。◇ **+ adv./prep.** *They rode along narrow country lanes.* 他们骑马走在狭窄的乡村小路上。◇ *He was riding on a large black horse.* 他骑在一匹高大的黑马上。◇ **~ sth** *She had never ridden a horse before.* 她以前从没骑过马。◇ *He's ridden six winners so far this year* (= in horse racing). 他今年到目前为止已六次在赛马中夺标。**2** **go riding** (*BrE*) (*NAmE* **go 'horseback riding**) [I] to spend time riding a horse for pleasure 骑马（消遣）: *How often do you go riding?* 你多长时间骑一次马？

• **BICYCLE/MOTORCYCLE** 自行车；摩托车 **3** [T, I] to sit on and control a bicycle, motorcycle, etc. 骑；驾驶: **~ sth** (**+ adv./prep.**) *The boys were riding their bikes around the streets.* 男孩子们骑着自行车在街上兜风。◇ *He rode a Harley Davidson.* 他骑着一辆哈雷摩托车。◇ (**+ adv./prep.**) *The ground there is too rough to ride over.* 那里地面高低不平，无法骑车。➲ WORDFINDER NOTE AT CYCLING

• **IN VEHICLE** 车辆 **4** [I, T] to travel in a vehicle, especially as a passenger 搭乘；乘坐: (**+ adv./prep.**) *I walked back while the others rode in the car.* 别人都乘车，而我是走回来的。◇ **~ sth** (**+ adv./prep.**) (*NAmE*) ***to ride the subway/an elevator, etc.*** 乘地铁、电梯等 ◇ *She rode the bus to school every day.* 她每天乘公共汽车去上学。

• **ON WATER/AIR** 在水面 / 空中 **5** [I, T] to float or be supported on water or air 漂浮；飘浮: (**+ adv./prep.**) *We watched the balloon riding high above the fields.* 我们看着气球高高地飘浮在田野上空。◇ **~ sth** *surfers riding the waves* 踏浪而行的冲浪者

• **GO THROUGH AREA** 穿越 **6** [T] ~ **sth** to go through or over an area on a horse, bicycle, etc.（骑马、自行车等）穿越，翻越: *We rode the mountain trails.* 我们骑着马走在山里的小路上。

• **CRITICIZE** 批评 **7** [T] ~ **sb** (*NAmE*) to criticize or TEASE sb in an annoying way 数落；嘲弄: *Why is everybody riding me today?* 怎么今天大家都拿我取笑？

IDM **be riding for a 'fall** to be doing sth that involves risks and that may end in disaster 做事莽撞；做招致风险的事 **be riding 'high** to be successful or very confident 获得成功；信心十足 **let sth 'ride** to decide to do nothing about a problem that you know you may have to deal with later 决定对…不立即采取行动 **ride the crest of sth** to enjoy great success or support because of a particular situation or event（因某种情况）处于鼎盛时期: *The band is riding the crest of its last tour.* 乐队正处于最近这次巡回演出后的顶峰状态。**ride 'herd on sb/sth** (*NAmE, informal*) to keep watch or control over sb/sth 监视；对某人 / 某物严加控制: *police riding herd on crowds of youths on the streets* 警方监视着街上成群结队的年轻人 **ride 'shotgun** (*NAmE, informal*) to ride in the front passenger seat of a car or truck 坐在车的前排座位上 **ride a/the wave of sth** to enjoy or be supported by the particular situation or quality mentioned 受益于某事；乘…之势: *Schools are riding a wave of renewed public interest.* 各校重新受益于公众的关注。➲ MORE AT WISH *n.*

PHR V **'ride on sth** (usually used in the progressive tenses 通常用于进行时) to depend on sth 依赖于；依靠: *My whole future is riding on this interview.* 我的未来全靠这次面试了。**,ride sth↔'out** to manage to survive a difficult situation or time without having to make great changes 安然渡过（难关）；经受得住 **,ride 'up** (of clothing 衣服) to move gradually upwards, out of position 慢慢向上移动；渐渐缩上去: *Short skirts tend to ride up when you sit down.* 坐下来的时候，短裙就会往上收。

■ *noun*

• **IN VEHICLE** 车辆 **1** a short journey in a vehicle, on a bicycle, etc.（乘车或骑车的）短途旅程: *a train ride through beautiful countryside* 乘火车穿越美丽乡村的旅程 ◇ *It's a ten-minute bus ride from here to town.* 从这里到镇上乘公共汽车要花十分钟。◇ *Steve* ***gave me a ride*** *on his motorbike.* 史蒂夫用摩托车捎了我一程。◇ ***We went for a ride*** *on our bikes.* 我们骑自行车出去兜了一圈。◇ *a bike ride* 骑自行车出行 **2** (*NAmE*) (*BrE, NAmE* **lift**) a free ride in a car, etc. to a place you want to get to 免费搭车；搭便车: *She hitched a ride to the station.* 她搭便车去车站。◇ *We managed to get a ride into town when we missed the bus.* 我们没赶上公共汽车，就设法搭了一辆便车去城里。**3** the kind of journey you make in a car, etc.（乘坐汽车等的）旅行: *a* ***smooth/comfortable/bumpy, etc. ride*** 舒适、颠簸等的旅行 ◇ (*figurative*) *The new legislation faces* ***a bumpy ride*** (= will meet with opposition and difficulties). 新的法规前路崎岖。

• **ON HORSE** 马 **4** a short journey on a horse, etc.（骑马等的）短途旅程: *a pony ride* 骑一会儿小马 ◇ *The kids had a ride on an elephant at the zoo.* 在动物园里，孩子们骑着大象走了一圈。◇ *He goes for a ride most mornings.* 他上午经常骑马出去兜一圈。

• **AT FUNFAIR** 游乐场 **5** a large machine at a FUNFAIR or AMUSEMENT PARK that you ride on for fun or excitement; an occasion when you go on one of these 供乘骑的游乐设施；乘坐（游乐设施）: *The rides are free.* 免费乘坐。◇ *a roller coaster ride* 坐一趟过山车

IDM **come/go along for the 'ride** (*informal*) to join in an activity for pleasure but without being seriously interested in it 随大溜；凑凑热闹；逢场作戏 **have a rough/an easy 'ride | give sb a rough/an easy 'ride** (*informal*) to experience/not experience difficulties when you are doing sth; to make things difficult/easy for sb（使）举步维艰（或一帆风顺）: *He will be given a rough ride at the party conference.* 在党员大会上他会很难过这一关。**take sb for a 'ride** (*informal*) to cheat or trick sb 欺骗；愚弄: *It's not a pleasant feeling to discover you've been taken for a ride by someone you trusted.* 发现被你信任的人骗了，心里很不是滋味。➲ MORE AT FREE *adj.*

'ride-off *noun* (*NAmE*) = JUMP-OFF

rider /'raɪdə(r)/ *noun* **1** a person who rides a horse, bicycle or motorcycle 骑手；骑马（或自行车、摩托车）的人: *Three riders* (= people riding horses) *were approaching.* 三个骑马的人越来越近。◇ *horses and their riders* 马匹及其骑手 ◇ *She's an experienced rider.* 她是位有经验的骑手。◇ *a motorcycle dispatch rider* 骑摩托车的通信员 ➲ VISUAL VOCAB PAGE V51 **2** ~ (**to sth**) an extra piece of information that is added to an official document 公文的附加材料；附文

ridge /rɪdʒ/ *noun, verb*

■ *noun* **1** a narrow area of high land along the top of a line of hills; a high pointed area near the top of a mountain 山脊；山脉: *walking along the ridge* 沿着山脊行走 ◇ *the north-east ridge of the Matterhorn* 马特峰的东北部 ➲ VISUAL VOCAB PAGE V5 **2** a raised line on the surface of sth; the point where two sloping surfaces join 隆起；脊；垄: *The ridges on the soles of my boots stopped me from slipping.* 我靴子底上有隆起的纹路，使我没有滑倒。◇ *the ridge of the roof* 屋脊 ➲ WORDFINDER NOTE AT MOUNTAIN ➲ VISUAL VOCAB PAGE V18 **3** [usually sing.] ~ (**of high pressure**) (*specialist*) a long narrow area of high pressure in the atmosphere（大气层的）高压脊 ➲ COMPARE TROUGH (3)

■ *verb* [usually passive] ~ **sth** to make narrow raised lines or areas on the surface of sth 使隆起；使形成脊状

ridged /rɪdʒd/ *adj.* (of an object or area 物体或地区) with raised lines on the surface 有隆凸线条的；有埂子的

'ridge tent (*BrE*) (*also* **'A-frame tent** *BrE, NAmE*) *noun* a tent which forms an upside-down V shape 三角帐篷 ➲ COMPARE DOME TENT, FRAME TENT

R

ridi·cule /ˈrɪdɪkjuːl/ *noun, verb*
■*noun* [U] unkind comments that make fun of sb/sth or make them look silly 嘲笑；奚落；讥笑 SYN **mockery**: *She is **an object of ridicule** in the tabloid newspapers.* 她是小报讥笑讽刺的对象。◇ *to **hold sb up to ridicule*** (= make fun of sb publicly) 公然取笑某人
■*verb* **~ sb/sth** to make sb/sth look silly by laughing at them or it in an unkind way 嘲笑；奚落；讥笑 SYN **make fun of sb/sth**

ri·dicu·lous /rɪˈdɪkjələs/ (*also* **ridic** /rɪˈdɪk/ *informal*) *adj.* very silly or unreasonable 愚蠢的；荒谬的；荒唐的 SYN **absurd, ludicrous**: *I look ridiculous in this hat.* 我戴这顶帽子看上去很可笑。◇ *Don't be ridiculous! You can't pay £50 for a T-shirt!* 别犯傻了！怎么能花 50 英镑买一件 T 恤衫！ ▸ **ri·dicu·lous·ly** *adv.*: *The meal was ridiculously expensive.* 这顿饭贵得离谱。 **ri·dicu·lous·ness** *noun* [U] IDM SEE SUBLIME *n.*

rid·ing /ˈraɪdɪŋ/ *noun* **1** (*BrE also* ˈ**horse riding**) (*NAmE also* ˈ**horseback riding**) [U] the sport or activity of riding horses 骑马：*I'm taking riding lessons.* 我在学习骑马。◇ *riding boots* 马靴 ◇ (*BrE*) *to **go riding*** 去骑马 ◇ (*NAmE*) *to **go horseback riding*** 去骑马 **2 Riding** one of the three former parts of the English county of Yorkshire called the **East Riding**, the **North Riding** and the **West Riding** 区（英格兰约克郡以前的东、西、北三个行政分区之一） ORIGIN From an Anglo-Saxon word meaning 'one third'. 源自盎格鲁 - 撒克逊单词，意为三分之一。

rife /raɪf/ *adj.* [not before noun] **1** if sth bad or unpleasant is **rife** in a place, it is very common there （坏事）盛行，普遍 SYN **widespread**: *It is a country where corruption is rife.* 这是个腐败成风的国家。◇ *Rumours are rife that he is going to resign.* 到处都在传，说他要辞职了。 **2 ~ (with sth)** full of sth bad or unpleasant 充斥，充满（坏事）：*Los Angeles is rife with gossip about the stars' private lives.* 洛杉矶盛传明星私生活的流言蜚语。

riff /rɪf/ *noun* a short repeated pattern of notes in popular music or JAZZ （流行音乐或爵士乐的）重复段

rif·fle /ˈrɪfl/ *verb* [I, T] to turn over papers or the pages of a book quickly and without reading them all 迅速翻动（纸张或书页） SYN **leaf**: **~ through sth** *He was riffling through the papers on his desk.* 他很快地翻着他桌上的文件。◇ **~ sth** *to riffle the pages of a book* 随意翻动书页

riff-raff /ˈrɪf ræf/ *noun* [U+sing./pl. v.] (*disapproving*) an insulting way of referring to people of low social class or people who are not considered socially acceptable 贱民；不三不四的下等人 ↻MORE LIKE THIS 11, page R26

rifle /ˈraɪfl/ *noun, verb*
■*noun* a gun with a long BARREL which you hold to your shoulder to fire 步枪；来复枪
■*verb* **1** [I, T] **~ (through) sth** to search quickly through sth in order to find or steal sth 快速搜寻；匆忙翻找：*She rifled through her clothes for something suitable to wear.* 她急匆匆地在衣服堆里找合适的衣服穿。 **2** [T] **~ sth** to steal sth from somewhere 偷窃；盗取：*His wallet had been rifled.* 他的钱包被偷了。 **3** [T] **~ sth + adv./prep.** to kick a ball very hard and straight in a game of football (SOCCER) 猛踢（足球）

rifle·man /ˈraɪflmən/ *noun* (*pl.* **-men** /-mən/) a soldier who carries a rifle （配备步枪的）步兵

ˈ**rifle range** *noun* **1** [C] a place where people practise shooting with rifles 步枪射击场 **2** [U] the distance that a bullet from a rifle will travel 步枪射程

rift /rɪft/ *noun* **1** a serious disagreement between people that stops their relationship from continuing 分裂；分歧；严重不和 SYN **breach, division**: *The rift within the party deepened.* 党内的分歧加深了。◇ *Efforts to **heal the rift** between the two countries have failed.* 弥合两国间分歧的各种努力都已失败。 ↻COLLOCATIONS AT INTERNATIONAL **2** a large crack or opening in the ground, rocks or clouds 断裂；裂缝；裂口

ˈ**rift valley** *noun* a valley with steep sides formed when two parallel cracks develop in the earth's surface and the land between them sinks 地堑；裂谷

rig /rɪɡ/ *verb, noun*
■*verb* (**-gg-**) [usually passive] **1 ~ sth** to arrange or influence sth in a dishonest way in order to get the result that you want （以不正当的手段）操纵，控制 SYN **fix**: *He said the election had been rigged.* 他说选举被人操纵了。◇ *to rig the market* (= to cause an artificial rise or fall in prices, in order to make a profit) 操纵市场 **2 ~ sth (with sth)** to provide a ship or boat with ropes, sails, etc.; to fit the sails, etc. in position （给船只）装帆，提供索具 **3 ~ sth (up) (with sth)** to fit equipment somewhere, sometimes secretly （秘密地）安装，装配：*The lights had been rigged (up) but not yet tested.* 灯已经装好了，但还没有经过测试。◇ *The car had been rigged with about 300 lbs of explosive.* 有人暗中在车上放了大约 300 磅炸药。
PHR V ˌ**rig sb/sth/yourself**↔ˈ**out (in/with sth)** [often passive] (*old-fashioned*) to provide sb/sth with a particular kind of clothes or equipment 给…提供（服装或设备）：*I was accepted for the job and rigged out in a uniform.* 我获得录用从事这份工作，并配发了制服。 ˌ**rig sth**↔ˈ**up** to make or to build sth quickly, using whatever materials are available （用现有的材料）匆匆做成，草草搭建：*We managed to rig up a shelter for the night.* 我们匆匆搭了个棚子过夜。
■*noun* **1** (especially in compounds 尤用于构成复合词) a large piece of equipment that is used for taking oil or gas from the ground or the bottom of the sea 钻机：*an oil rig* 石油钻机 **2** the way that the MASTS and sails on a boat, etc. are arranged 帆装（船桅和风帆等的安装模式） **3** (*NAmE, informal*) a large lorry/truck 大卡车；大货车 **4** equipment that is used for a special purpose 有专门用途的设备：*a CB radio rig* 民用波段无线电设备

rig·ging /ˈrɪɡɪŋ/ *noun* [U] **1** the ropes that support the MASTS and sails of a boat or ship （牵拉船桅和风帆的）绳索，索具 **2** the act of influencing sth in a dishonest way in order to get the result that you want 营私舞弊；操纵：*vote rigging* 操纵投票

right /raɪt/ *adj., adv., noun, verb, exclamation*
■*adj.*
• **MORALLY GOOD** 正当 **1** [not usually before noun] **~ (to do sth)** morally good or acceptable; correct according to law or a person's duty 正当；妥当：*You were quite right to criticize him.* 你批评他批评得很对。◇ *Is it ever right to kill?* 有没有什么情况下，杀人是对的？◇ *It seems **only right** to warn you of the risk.* 似乎应该警告你有风险。◇ *I hope we're doing **the right thing**.* 我希望我们这样做是妥当的。 OPP **wrong**
• **TRUE/CORRECT** 真实；正确 **2** true or correct as a fact 正确的；真正的；真实的：*Did you get the answer right?* 你回答得正确吗？◇ *'What's the **right time**?' '10.37.'* "现在的准确时间是几点？" "10 点 37 分。" ◇ *'David, isn't it?' 'Yes, **that's right**.'* "是戴维吗？" "对，没错。" ◇ (*informal*) *It was Monday you went to see Angie, right?* 你是星期一去看望安吉的，对不对？◇ *Let me **get this right*** (= understand correctly)—*you want us to do an extra ten hours' work for no extra pay?* 让我先搞清楚这一点，你想让我们加班十个小时而不给加班费，是不是？ OPP **wrong** ↻SYNONYMS AT TRUE
3 correct for a particular situation or thing, or for a particular person 适当的；正好的；恰当的：*Have you got **the right money*** (= the exact amount) *for the bus fare?* 你有数额刚好的零钱付公交车车费吗？◇ *Is this the right way to the beach?* 去海滩是走这条路吗？◇ *You're not holding it **the right way up**.* 你把它拿倒了。◇ *Are you sure you've got that on **the right way round**?* 你能肯定位置放对了吗？◇ *Next time we'll **get it right**.* 下次我们就不会错了。◇ *He's the right man for the job.* 他是这份工作的合适人选。◇ *I'm glad you split up. She wasn't right for you.* 我很高兴你们分手了。她不适合你。◇ *I was waiting for the right moment to ask him.* 我在等待时机问他这件事。◇ *She knows all **the right people*** (= important people, for example those who can help her career). 她认识所有那些关键人物。◇ *His success was down to being **in the right place at the right time*** (= being able to take opportunities when they came). 他的成功之处就在于把握住了时机。 OPP **wrong** **4**

[not before noun] correct in your opinion or judgement（意见或判断）准确，确切，恰当：~ (**about** sth) *She was right about Tom having no money.* 她认为汤姆没有钱，她的判断是对的。◇ ~ (**to do** sth) *You're right to be cautious.* 你保持谨慎是应当的。◇ *'It's not easy.' 'Yeah, you're right.'* "这不容易。""对，你说得没错。"◇ ~ (**in doing** sth) *Am I right in thinking we've met before?* 我们以前见过面，我说得对吗？ OPP **wrong**

- **NORMAL** 正常 **5** [not before noun] in a normal or good enough condition 正常；情况良好：*I don't feel quite right today* (= I feel ill/sick). 我今天感觉不太舒服。◇ *That sausage doesn't smell right.* 那香肠闻起来不对劲。◇ *Things aren't right between her parents.* 她父母的关系不太正常。◇ *If only I could have helped* **put** *matters* **right**. 要是我当时能帮着把错误纠正过来就好了。◇ *He's* **not quite right in the head** (= not mentally normal). 他精神不太正常。OPP **wrong**
- **NOT LEFT** 右面 **6** [only before noun] of, on or towards the side of the body that is towards the east when a person faces north 右边的：*my right eye* 我的右眼 ◇ *Keep on the right side of the road.* 靠马路的右边行走。◇ *Take a right turn at the intersection.* 在十字路口向右拐。 ➲ SEE ALSO RIGHT-WING OPP **left**
- **COMPLETE** 完全 **7** [only before noun] (*BrE, informal, especially disapproving*) used to emphasize sth bad（强调坏事）真正的，完全的：*You made a right mess of that!* 你把这件事完全给弄糟了！◇ *I felt a right idiot.* 我觉得自己就像个十足的白痴。 ➲ SEE ALSO ALL RIGHT *adj.* ➲ MORE LIKE THIS 20, page R27

▶ **right·ness** *noun* [U]: *the rightness* (= justice) *of their cause* 他们正义的事业 ◇ *the rightness of his decision* 他的正确决定

IDM ˌ**give your right ˈarm for sth/to do sth** (*informal*) used to say that sb is willing to give up a lot in order to have or do sth that they really want 为…情愿舍弃很多；不惜任何代价：*I'd have given my right arm to have been there with them.* 要是当时能跟他们一起去那儿，我宁愿放弃一切。 (**not**) **in your right ˈmind** (not) mentally normal 精神正常（或不正常） ➲ SYNONYMS AT MAD (**as**) **right as ˈrain** (*informal*) in excellent health or condition 十分健康；状况奇佳 **right eˈnough** (*informal*) certainly; in a way that cannot be denied 当然；无疑；不可否认：*You heard me right enough* (= so don't pretend that you did not). 你肯定听到我说了什么。 **right ˈon** (*informal*) used to express strong approval or encouragement（表示明确的赞同或鼓励）完全正确 ➲ SEE ALSO RIGHT-ON ˌ**right side ˈup** (*NAmE*) with the top part turned to the top; in the correct, normal position 正面朝上；位置正确；在正常位置：*I dropped my toast, but luckily it fell right side up.* 我把烤面包掉在地上，但幸好它正面朝上。 OPP **upside down** ˈ**she'll be right** (*AustralE, informal*) used to say that everything will be all right, even if there is a problem now 一切都会好的（即使现在有问题） ˌ**too ˈright** (*BrE, informal*) used to say that there is no doubt about sth 毫无疑问；一点不错；对极啦：*'We need to stick together.' 'Too right!'* "我们得团结一致。""对极啦！"◇ *'I'll have to do it again.' 'Too right you will.'* "我得再做一次。""你说得一点不错。" ➲ MORE AT BUTTON *n.*, FOOT *n.*, HEAD *n.*, HEART, IDEA, LEFT *adj.*, MIGHT *n.*, MR, NOTE *n.*, SIDE *n.*, TRACK *n.*

■ *adv.*

- **EXACTLY** 正好 **1** exactly; directly 正好；恰好；直接地：*Lee was standing* **right behind** *her.* 李就站在她身后。◇ *The wind was right in our faces.* 风迎面吹来。◇ *I'm* **right behind you** *on this one* (= I am supporting you). 在这件事情上，我完全支持你。◇ *The bus came right on time.* 公共汽车正好准时到达。
- **COMPLETELY** 完全 **2** all the way; completely 一直；径直；完全地：*The car spun right off the track.* 汽车完全开出了车道。◇ *I'm right out of ideas.* 我完全没了主意。◇ *She kept right on swimming until she reached the other side.* 她一直游到对岸。
- **IMMEDIATELY** 立即 **3** (*informal*) immediately; without delay 立即；马上；毫不耽搁：*I'll be right back.* 我马上就回来。◇ *I'll be right with you* (= I am coming very soon). 我这就过来。
- **CORRECTLY** 正确 **4** correctly 正确地；确切地：*You guessed right.* 你猜着了。 OPP **wrong**
- **SATISFACTORILY** 满意 **5** in the way that things should happen or are supposed to happen 顺利；正常：*Nothing's going right for me today.* 今天没有哪一件事让我顺心。 OPP **wrong**
- **NOT LEFT** 右面 **6** on or to the right side 在右边；向右边：*Turn right at the end of the street.* 在街的那头往右拐。 OPP **left**

IDM ˌ**right and ˈleft** everywhere 到处；处处：*She owes money right and left.* 她到处欠债。 **right aˈway/ˈoff** immediately; without delay 立即；马上；毫不耽搁：*I want it sent right away.* 马上把它发出去。◇ *I told him right off what I thought of him.* 我直截了当地告诉了他我对他的看法。 ˌ**right, left and ˈcentre** = LEFT, RIGHT AND CENTRE **right ˈnow 1** at this moment 此刻；此时此刻：*He's not in the office right now.* 他现在不在办公室。 **2**

▼SYNONYMS 同义词辨析

right

correct

Both these words describe a belief, opinion, decision or method that is suitable or the best one for a particular situation. 以上两词均指看法、意见、决定或方法等恰当、合适。

right if sb is right to do or think sth, that is a good thing to do or think in that situation 指正确的、妥当的、恰当的：*You're right to be cautious.* 你谨慎是应当的。◇ *You made the right decision.* 你的决定是正确的。◇ *'It's not easy.' 'Yes, you're right.'* "这不容易。""对，你说得没错。"

correct (of a method, belief, opinion or decision) right and suitable in a particular situation 指（方法、看法、意见或决定）正确的、恰当的、合适的：*What's the correct way to shut the machine down?* 这台机器应该怎么关？◇ *I don't think she's correct to say he's incompetent.* 我认为她说他无能是不对的。

RIGHT OR CORRECT? 用 right 还是 correct?

Correct is more formal than **right**. It is more often used for methods and **right** is more often used for beliefs, opinions and decisions. * correct 较 right 正式，较常修饰方法，right 则较常修饰看法、意见和决定。

PATTERNS

- right/correct **about** sb/sth
- right/correct **to do** sth
- right/correct **in thinking/believing/saying** sth
- the right/correct **decision/judgement/conclusion**
- the right/correct **way/method/approach**
- **absolutely/quite** right/correct

▼WHICH WORD? 词语辨析

right / rightly

- **Right** and **rightly** can both be used as adverbs. In the sense 'correctly' or 'in the right way', **right** is the usual adverb. It is only used after verbs. * right 和 rightly 均可用作副词。表示正确地、恰当地，则通常用副词 right；此词只用于动词之后：*He did it right.* 他做得对。◇ *Did I spell your name right?* 你的名字我拼得对不对？ **Rightly** cannot be used like this. In formal language **correctly** is used. 上述用法不能用 rightly，在正式用语中可用 correctly：*Is your name spelled correctly?* 你的名字拼正确了吗？
- The usual meaning of **rightly** is 'for a good reason' and it comes before an adjective. * rightly 的通常意义为理所当然地，用于形容词前：*They are rightly proud of their children.* 他们当然为他们的孩子而骄傲。 It can be used to mean 'correctly' before a verb or in particular phrases. 该词亦可表示正确地，用于动词前或某些短语中：*As you rightly say, we have a serious problem.* 你说得对，我们有严重困难。 In *NAmE* **rightly** is not at all common. 在美式英语中 rightly 一点也不常用。

🔑 immediately 立即；马上：*Do it right now!* 这件事马上做！ **right off the 'bat** (*informal, especially NAmE*) immediately; without delay 立即；马上；毫不耽搁：*We both liked each other right off the bat.* 我们俩一见如故。 **see sb 'right** (*informal*) to make sure that sb has all they need or want 确保（或负责）满足某人的一切需求：*You needn't worry about money—I'll see you right.* 你不必担心钱的问题，我会给你的。➲ MORE AT HIT *v.*, SERVE *v.*, STREET *n.*, WORD *n.*

■ ***noun***

• **STH MORALLY GOOD** 正当的事 **1** 🔑 [U, C] what is morally good or correct 正当；公正；正义；正确：*She doesn't understand the difference between right and wrong.* 她不能明辨是非。◇ *You **did right** to tell me about it.* 你把这件事告诉我，做得很对。◇ *They both had some right on their side.* 他们双方都有一定的道理。◇ *He wouldn't apologize. He knew he was **in the right*** (= had justice on his side). 他不肯道歉。他知道自己是有理的。◇ *It was difficult to establish **the rights and wrongs*** (= the true facts) *of the matter.* 很难确定这件事情的真相。**OPP** **wrong**

• **MORAL/LEGAL CLAIM** 正当 / 合法要求 **2** 🔑 [C, U] a moral or legal claim to have or get sth or to behave in a particular way 正当的要求；权利：**~ (to sth)** *Everyone has a right to a fair trial.* 每个人都有权获得公正的审判。◇ **~ (to do sth)** ***You have no right** to stop me from going in there.* 你无权阻止我进去。◇ ***What gives you the right** to do that?* 你有什么权利这样做？◇ *She **had every right** to be angry.* 她完全有理由生气。◇ *You're quite **within your rights** to ask for your money back.* 你完全有权要回你的钱。◇ ***By rights*** (= if justice were done) *half the money should be mine.* 按理说，应该有一半的钱归我。◇ *There is no right of appeal against the decision.* 关于这项判决，没有上诉权。◇ *Education is provided by the state **as of right*** (= everyone has a right to it). 受教育是国家赋予每一个人的权利。◇ *The property belongs to her **by right**.* 这份财产依法归她所有。◇ *They had fought hard for **equal rights**.* 他们为了获得平等权利已经进行了顽强的斗争。➲ SEE ALSO ANIMAL RIGHTS, CIVIL RIGHTS, HUMAN RIGHT

• **FOR BOOK/MOVIE, ETC.** 书籍或电影等 **3** 🔑 **rights** [pl.] the authority to perform, publish, film, etc. a particular work, event, etc. 版权；发行权：*He sold the rights for $2 million.* 他以 200 万美元的价格出售了版权。◇ *all rights reserved* (= protected or kept for the owners of the book, film/movie, etc.) 版权所有

• **NOT LEFT SIDE** 右面 **4** 🔑 **the/sb's right** [sing.] the right side or direction 右边；右方；右：*Take the first street **on the right**.* 走右手的第一条街。◇ *She seated me on her right.* 她让我坐在她的右边。**OPP** **left** **5** 🔑 [sing.] **the first, second, etc. ~** the first, second, etc. road on the right side 右边的（第一条、第二条等）路：*Take the first right, then the second left.* 在第一个路口向右拐，然后再在第二个路口向左拐。**OPP** **left** **6 a right** [sing.] a turn to the right 右拐；右转弯：*to make a right* 向右转弯 ◇ (*NAmE, informal*) *to hang a right* 右拐弯 **OPP** **left**

• **POLITICS** 政治 **7** 🔑 **the right**, **the Right** [sing.+sing./pl. v.] political groups that most strongly support the CAPITALIST system 右派组织（或政党）：*The Right in British politics is represented by the Conservative Party.* 英国政坛的右派是以保守党为代表的。**OPP** **left** ➲ COMPARE RIGHT WING (1) **8** 🔑 **the right** [sing.+sing./pl. v.] the part of a political party whose members are most conservative（政党内的）右派，右翼：*He's on the right of the Labour Party.* 他是工党内的右派成员。**OPP** **left**

• **IN BOXING** 拳击 **9** [C] a blow that is made with your right hand 右手拳 **OPP** **left**

IDM **bang to 'rights** (*BrE*) (*NAmE* **dead to 'rights**) (*informal*) with definite proof of having committed a crime, so that you cannot claim to be innocent 证据确凿；肯定无疑：*We've got you bang to rights handling stolen property.* 你在销赃时被我们抓了个正着。 **do 'right by sb** (*old-fashioned*) to treat sb fairly 公平对待 **in your own 'right** because of your personal qualifications or efforts, not because of your connection with sb else 凭自身的资格（或努力）：*She sings with a rock band, but she's also a jazz musician in her own right.* 她随一支摇滚乐队演唱，但她本身也是爵士乐手。 **put/set sb/sth to 'rights** to correct sb/sth; to put things in their right places or right order 纠正；改正；收拾；恢复秩序：*It took me ages to put things to rights after the workmen had left.* 工人们走后，我花了好长时间才收拾好。➲ MORE AT WORLD, WRONG *n.*

■ ***verb***

• **RETURN TO POSITION** 回复位置 **1 ~ sb/sth/yourself** to return sb/sth/yourself to the normal, vertical position 使回到正常位置；把…扶正；使…直立：*They learnt to right a capsized canoe.* 他们学会了将倾覆的独木舟翻过来。◇ *At last the plane **righted itself** and flew on.* 最后，飞机终于恢复了平稳，继续飞行。

• **CORRECT** 改正 **2 ~ sth** to correct sth that is wrong or not in its normal state 改正；纠正；使恢复正常：*Righting the economy will demand major cuts in expenditure.* 恢复经济需要大量削减开支。

IDM **right a 'wrong** to do sth to correct an unfair situation or sth bad that you have done 纠正错误；平反昭雪

■ ***exclamation*** (*BrE, informal*) **1** used to show that you accept a statement or an order（表示同意或遵从）是的，好的：*'You may find it hurts a little at first.' 'Right.'* "开始时，你会觉得有点疼。" "噢。" ◇ *'Barry's here.' 'Oh, right.'* "巴里在这儿。" "哦，太好了。" ◇ *'I'll have a whisky and soda.' **'Right you are**, sir.'* "我要一份威士忌加苏打。" "马上就送来，先生。" **2** used to get sb's attention to say that you are ready to do sth, or to tell them to do sth（引起注意，表示已做好准备或让别人做某事）嗨，喂：*Right! Let's get going.* 行了！我们走吧。 **3** used to check that sb agrees with you or has understood you（要确保对方同意或明白时说）对不：*So that's twenty of each sort, right?* 那么，每一种都是二十个，对不对？◇ *And I didn't think any more of it, right, but Mum says I should see a doctor.* 我本来不再想这事了，知道吗？可妈妈说我该看医生。 **4** (*ironic*) used to say that you do not believe sb or that you disagree with them（表示不相信或不同意）是吗，好哇：*'I won't be late tonight.' **'Yeah, right**.'* "今天晚上我不会晚的。" "是么，好哇。"

'right angle *noun* an angle of 90° 直角：*Place the table **at right angles/at a right angle** to the wall.* 将桌子跟墙垂直摆放。➲ PICTURE AT ANGLE, TRIANGLE ➲ COMPARE ACUTE ANGLE, OBTUSE ANGLE, REFLEX ANGLE

'right-angled *adj.* having or consisting of a right angle 直角的；有直角的

ˌright-angled 'triangle (*especially BrE*) (*NAmE usually* **ˌright 'triangle**) *noun* a triangle with a right angle 直角三角形 ➲ PICTURE AT TRIANGLE

ˌright 'brain *noun* [U, sing.] the right side of the human brain, that is thought to be used for creating new ideas and to be where emotions come from（人的）右脑（据信用于构思新思想和主管情感）➲ COMPARE LEFT BRAIN

ˌright-'click *verb* [T, I] **~ sth** | **~ (on sth)** to choose a particular function or item on a computer screen, etc., by pressing the button on a mouse that is on the right side 用鼠标右键点击；右击

right·eous /'raɪtʃəs/ *adj.* (*formal*) **1** morally right and good 公正的；正直的；正当的：*a righteous God* 公正的上帝 **2** that you think is morally acceptable or fair 正当的；公平合理的；正义的：***righteous anger/indignation, etc.*** 义愤等 ➲ SEE ALSO SELF-RIGHTEOUS ▶ **right·eous·ly** *adv.* **right·eous·ness** *noun* [U]

ˌright 'field *noun* [sing.] (in BASEBALL 棒球) the part of the field to the right of the BATTER 右外场（击球手右边的场地）

right·ful /'raɪtfl/ *adj.* [only before noun] (*formal*) that is correct, right or legal 正确的；公正的；合法的 **SYN** **proper**：*The stolen car was returned to its **rightful owner**.* 被盗的汽车还给了其合法的主人。▶ **right·ful·ly** /-fəli/ *adv.*：*She was only claiming what was rightfully hers.* 她只要求得到理应属于她的东西。

'right-hand *adj.* [only before noun] **1** on the right side of sth 右手的；右边的；右面的：*on the right-hand side of the road* 在路的右边 ◇ *the top right-hand corner of the screen* 屏幕的右上角 **2** intended for use by your right hand 右手的；供右手用的：*a right-hand glove* 右手的手套 OPP left-hand

ˌright-hand ˈdrive *adj.* (of a vehicle 车辆) with the driver's seat and STEERING WHEEL on the right side 右侧驾驶的 OPP **left-hand drive**

ˌright-ˈhanded *adj.* **1** a person who is **right-handed** uses their right hand for writing, using tools, etc. 惯用右手的 **2** a **right-handed** tool is designed to be used with the right hand 供右手使用的 OPP **left-handed** ▸ **ˌright-ˈhanded** *adv.*

ˌright-ˈhander *noun* **1** a person who uses their right hand for writing, using tools, etc. 惯用右手的人 **2** a hit with the right hand 右手的一击 OPP **left-hander**

ˌright-hand ˈman *noun* [sing.] a person who helps sb a lot and who they rely on, especially in an important job 左右手；得力助手：*the President's right-hand man* 总统的得力助手

ˌRight ˈHonourable *adj.* [only before noun] (*abbr.* **Rt Hon**) **1 the Right Honourable**... a title of respect used when talking to or about a person of high social rank, especially a lord （对上层社会人士，尤指对贵族的尊称）阁下 **2 the/my Right Honourable**... the title of respect used by Members of Parliament in Britain when talking to or about a senior Member of Parliament during a debate（英国议会成员对资深议员的尊称）阁下 ⊃ COMPARE HONOURABLE (6)

right·ist /ˈraɪtɪst/ *noun* a person who supports RIGHT-WING political parties and their ideas 右派人士；右翼分子 SYN **right-winger** OPP **leftist** ▸ **right·ist** *adj.*

right·ly /ˈraɪtli/ *adv.* **1** for a good reason 正当地；理由充分地 SYN **justifiably**: *The school was rightly proud of the excellent exam results.* 学校为这次出色的考试成绩感到骄傲，这是理所当然的。◇ *He was proud of his beautiful house, and **rightly so**.* 他为自己的漂亮房子感到骄傲，这是很自然的。◇ ***Quite rightly**, the environment is of great concern.* 当然，环境问题非常受关注。 **2** in a correct or accurate way 正确地；恰当地；精确地 SYN **correctly**: ***Rightly or wrongly**, many older people are afraid of violence in the streets.* 不管正不正当，反正许多年长者都害怕街头暴力。◇ *As she rightly pointed out, the illness can affect adults as well as children.* 她说得对，这种病不仅影响儿童，也会影响成年人。◇ *I **can't rightly say** what happened.* 我说不准到底发生了什么事。◇ ***I don't rightly know** where he's gone.* 我说不好他上哪儿去了。◇ ***If I remember rightly**, there's a train at six o'clock.* 如果我没记错的话，六点钟有一趟火车。 ⊃ NOTE AT RIGHT

ˌright-ˈminded (*also* **ˌright-ˈthinking**) *adj.* (of a person 人) having beliefs and opinions that most people approve of 有正义感的；正直的

right·most /ˈraɪtməʊst; *NAmE* -moʊst/ *adj.* [only before noun] furthest to the right 最右边的；最右面的

righto /ˈraɪtəʊ; *NAmE* -oʊ/ (*also* **righty-ho**) *exclamation* (*old-fashioned, BrE, informal*) used to show that you accept a statement or an order 好；行；对

ˌright of aˈbode *noun* [U] official permission that allows a person to live in a particular country 居留权

ˌright-of-ˈcentre *adj.* = CENTRE-RIGHT

ˌright of ˈway *noun* (*pl.* **rights of way**) **1** [U] (*especially BrE*) legal permission to go onto or through another person's land（进入或穿越他人土地的）通行权：*Private property—no right of way.* 私有房产，禁止穿行。 **2** [C] (*especially BrE*) a public path that goes through private land（穿越私有土地的）公用通道 **3** [U] the right to drive across or into a road before another vehicle（交通工具的）优先通行权：*I had right of way at the junction.* 我在这交叉路口有优先通行权。◇ *Whose right of way is it?* 这里谁有优先通行权？

ˌright-ˈon *adj.* (*BrE, informal, sometimes disapproving*) having political opinions or being aware of social issues that are fashionable and LEFT-WING 政见入时的；左倾的：*right-on middle-class intellectuals* 左倾的中产阶级知识分子

ˌRight ˈReverend *adj.* [only before noun] (*abbr.* **Rt Revd**) a title of respect used when talking about a BISHOP (= a senior priest)（尊称主教）尊敬的，可敬的

ˈrights issue *noun* (*business* 商) an offer to buy shares in a company at a cheaper price to people who already own some shares in it 认股权发行，有购股权的证券发行（公司以优惠价格向现有股东发售新股）

right·size /ˈraɪtsaɪz/ *verb* [I, T] ~ (**sth**) (*business* 商) to change the size of a company in order to reduce costs, especially by reducing the number of employees（通过裁员等）使公司规模适中，精简公司的规模

ˌright-ˈthinking *adj.* = RIGHT-MINDED

ˌright ˈtriangle *noun* (*NAmE*) = RIGHT-ANGLED TRIANGLE

right·ward /ˈraɪtwəd; *NAmE* -wərd/ (*also* **right·wards** /ˈraɪtwədz; *NAmE* -wərdz/ *especially in BrE*) *adj.* **1** on or to the right 在右侧的；向右的：*a rightward movement* 向右的移动 **2** towards more RIGHT-WING political ideas 右倾的：*a rightward shift in voting patterns* 选举格局的右倾化转变 ▸ **right·ward** (*also* **right·wards**) *adv.*

the ˌright ˈwing *noun* **1** [sing.+sing./pl. v.] the part of a political party whose members are least in favour of social change（政党中的）右翼，右派：*He is on the right wing of the party.* 他属于党内的右翼。 **2** [C, U] an attacking player or a position on the right side of the field in a sports game（体育比赛的）右边锋，右翼 OPP **left wing**

ˌright-ˈwing *adj.* strongly supporting the CAPITALIST system 右翼的；右派的：*right-wing policies* 右倾政策 OPP **left-wing**

ˌright-ˈwinger *noun* **1** a person on the right wing of a political party 右翼人士；右派成员：*She is a prominent Tory right-winger.* 她是保守党中赫赫有名的右派。 **2** a person who plays on the right side of the field in a sports game（体育比赛的）右边锋 OPP **left-winger**

righty-ho /ˈraɪti həʊ; *NAmE* hoʊ/ *exclamation* (*old-fashioned, BrE, informal*) = RIGHTO

rigid AW /ˈrɪdʒɪd/ *adj.* **1** (*often disapproving*) (of rules, methods, etc. 规则、方法等) very strict and difficult to change 死板的；僵硬的 SYN **inflexible**: *The curriculum was too narrow and too rigid.* 课程设置过于狭窄和死板。◇ *His rigid adherence to the rules made him unpopular.* 他对规则的刻板坚持使得他不受欢迎。 **2** (of a person 人) not willing to change their ideas or behaviour 固执的；僵化的；一成不变的 SYN **inflexible**: *rigid attitudes* 固执的态度 **3** (of an object or substance 物体或物质) stiff and difficult to move or bend 坚硬的；不弯曲的；僵直的：*a rigid support for the tent* 帐篷坚硬的支柱 ◇ *She sat upright, her body **rigid with fear**.* 她直挺挺地坐着，吓得浑身发僵。◇ (*figurative*) *I was **bored rigid*** (= extremely bored). 我觉得无聊极了。 ▸ **ri·gid·ity** AW /rɪˈdʒɪdəti/ *noun* [U, C]: *the rigidity of the law on this issue* 法律在这个问题上的僵化处理 ◇ *the rigidity of the metal bar* 金属栅栏的坚固性 **ri·gid·ly** AW *adv.*: *The speed limit must be rigidly enforced.* 必须严格执行限速规定。◇ *She stared rigidly ahead.* 她呆呆地盯着前方。

rig·mar·ole /ˈrɪgmərəʊl; *NAmE* -roʊl/ *noun* [U, sing.] **1** a long and complicated process that is annoying and seems unnecessary（不必要的）冗长复杂的手续：*I couldn't face the whole rigmarole of getting a work permit again.* 我无法再次面对获取工作许可证所需的各种冗长复杂的手续。 **2** a long and complicated story 冗长曲折的故事

rigor mor·tis /ˌrɪgə ˈmɔːtɪs; *NAmE* ˌrɪgər ˈmɔːrtɪs/ *noun* [U] the process by which the body becomes stiff after death 尸僵；死后强直

rig·or·ous /ˈrɪgərəs/ *adj.* **1** done carefully and with a lot of attention to detail 谨慎的；细致的；彻底的 SYN **thorough**: *a rigorous analysis* 细致的分析 **2** demanding that particular rules, processes, etc. are strictly followed 严格

R

的；严厉的 SYN strict: *The work failed to meet their rigorous standards.* 工作没有达到他们的严格标准。▶ **rig·or·ous·ly** *adv.*：*The country's press is rigorously controlled.* 这个国家的新闻出版事业受到严格控制。

rig·our (*especially US* **rigor**) /ˈrɪɡə(r)/ *noun* **1** [U] the fact of being careful and paying great attention to detail 谨慎；缜密；严谨：***academic/intellectual/scientific, etc. rigour*** 学术、思想、科学等方面的严谨 **2** [U] (*formal*) the fact of being strict or severe 严格；严厉 SYN **severity**: *This crime must be treated with the full rigour of the law.* 这一罪行必须严格依法审理。 **3 the rigours of sth** [pl.] the difficulties and unpleasant conditions of sth 艰苦；严酷：*The plants were unable to withstand the rigours of a harsh winter.* 这些植物经受不住严冬的考验。

ˈ**rig-out** *noun* (*BrE, informal, often disapproving*) a set of clothes worn together 一套衣服；一身装束：*Where are you going in that rig-out?* 你穿着那身打扮要去哪里？

the Rig Veda /ˌrɪɡ ˈveɪdə; ˈviːdə/ *noun* [sing.] the oldest and most important of the Vedas (= Hindu holy texts) 《梨俱吠陀》（印度教《吠陀》中最古老和最重要的一部）

rile /raɪl/ *verb* **~ sb | it riles sb that...** to annoy sb or make them angry 惹恼；激怒 SYN **anger**: *Nothing ever seemed to rile him.* 好像从来没有什么事让他烦恼。

IDM **be/get (all) ˌriled ˈup** (*informal, especially NAmE*) to be or get very annoyed 十分生气；恼火

Riley /ˈraɪli/ *noun* IDM SEE LIFE

rill /rɪl/ *noun* a shallow channel cut by water flowing over rock or soil 细沟

rim /rɪm/ *noun, verb*

■ *noun* **1** the edge of sth in the shape of a circle（圆形物体的）边沿：*He looked at them over the rim of his glass.* 他从杯口的上方看着他们。◇ *The rims of her eyes were red with crying.* 她的眼眶都哭红了。◇ *spectacles with gold rims* 金框眼镜 ➲ PICTURE AT EDGE **2** the metal edge of a wheel onto which the tyre is fixed 轮辋；轮圈 ➲ VISUAL VOCAB PAGE V55 **3 -rimmed** *adj.* having a particular type of rim 有…框（或边）的：*gold-rimmed spectacles* 金框眼镜 ◇ *red-rimmed eyes* (= for example, from crying) 眼眶红红的眼睛 ➲ SEE ALSO HORN-RIMMED

■ *verb* (**-mm-**) [often passive] **~ sth** (*formal*) to form an edge around sth 形成…的边沿；给…镶边

rime /raɪm/ *noun* [U] (*literary*) FROST 雾凇（颗粒状的霜晶）

rim·less /ˈrɪmləs/ *adj.* [only before noun] (of glasses 眼镜) having LENSES (= the transparent parts that you look through) that are not surrounded by frames 无框的

rind /raɪnd/ *noun* **1** [U] the thick outer layer of some types of fruit（某些水果的）厚皮，外壳：*lemon rind* 柠檬皮 ➲ COMPARE PEEL *n.* (1), SKIN *n.* (4), ZEST (3) **2** [U, C] the thick outer skin of some foods such as BACON and some types of cheese（熏肉和某些干酪等食物的）外皮

ring¹ 🔑 /rɪŋ/ *noun, verb* ➲ SEE ALSO RING²

■ *noun*

• **JEWELLERY** 首饰 **1** 🔑 [C] a piece of jewellery that you wear on your finger, consisting of a round band of gold, silver, etc., sometimes decorated with PRECIOUS STONES 戒指；指环：*a gold ring* 金戒指 ◇ *A diamond glittered on her* ***ring finger*** (= the finger next to the little finger, especially on the left hand). 一颗钻石在她的无名指上闪闪发光。➲ VISUAL VOCAB PAGE V70 ➲ SEE ALSO ENGAGEMENT RING, SIGNET RING, WEDDING RING

• **CIRCLE** 圆圈 **2** 🔑 [C] an object in the shape of a circle with a large hole in the middle 环状物；圈形的东西：*a key ring* 钥匙环 ◇ *curtain rings* 窗帘环 ◇ *onion rings* 洋葱圈 ➲ VISUAL VOCAB PAGE V52 **3** 🔑 [C] a round mark or shape 圆形标记；圆形：*She had dark rings around her eyes from lack of sleep.* 她因为缺觉，眼圈儿都黑了。◇ *The children sat on the floor in a ring.* 孩子们围成一圈，坐在地板上。

• **FOR PERFORMANCE/COMPETITION** 表演；比赛 **4** 🔑 [C] a confined area in which animals or people perform or compete, with seats around the outside for the audience 圆形表演场（或竞技场）：*a boxing ring* 拳击场 ◇ *a circus ring* 马戏场 ➲ SEE ALSO BULLRING

• **FOR COOKING** 烹饪 **5** [C] (*especially BrE*) a small flat place on a cooker/stove that is heated by gas or electricity and is used for cooking on 炉口；灶盘 SYN **burner**: *to turn off the gas ring* 关上煤气灶

• **GROUP OF PEOPLE** 人群 **6** [C] a group of people who are working together, especially in secret or illegally（尤指秘密的或非法的）团伙，帮派，集团：*a spy ring* 间谍网 ◇ *a drugs ring* 贩毒集团

IDM **run ˈrings around/round sb** (*informal*) to be much better at doing sth than sb else 做事远比某人好；遥遥领先 ➲ MORE AT HAT

■ *verb* (**ringed, ringed**)

• **SURROUND** 包围 **1** [often passive] **~ sb/sth (with sth)** to surround sb/sth 包围；环绕：*Thousands of demonstrators ringed the building.* 成千上万的示威者包围了大楼。

• **BIRD'S LEG** 鸟腿 **2 ~ sth** to put a metal ring around a bird's leg so that it can be easily identified in the future 给…戴上金属环（以便将来辨认）

• **DRAW CIRCLE** 画圆 **3 ~ sth** (*especially BrE*) to draw a circle around sth 绕…画圆；把…圈起来 SYN **circle**: *Ring the correct answer in pencil.* 用铅笔圈出正确答案。

rings 戒指；环

diamond ring 钻戒

key ring 钥匙环

boxing ring 拳击台

gas ring (*especially BrE*) / **burner** 煤气灶火圈

ring² 🔑 /rɪŋ/ *verb, noun* ➲ SEE ALSO RING¹

■ *verb* (**rang** /ræŋ/, **rung** /rʌŋ/)

• **TELEPHONE** 电话 **1** 🔑 (*BrE*) (*also* **call** *NAmE, BrE*) [T, I] to telephone sb/sth 给…打电话：**~ sb/sth up** *I'll ring you up later.* 我稍后再给你打电话。◇ *He rang up the police station.* 他给警察局打了电话。◇ **~ sb/sth** *When is the best time to ring New York?* 什么时间给纽约打电话最好？◇ **~ (up)** *David rang up while you were out.* 你不在的时候戴维打电话来了。◇ *He said he was ringing from London.* 他说他是从伦敦打来的。◇ *I'm ringing about your advertisement in the paper.* 我打电话来问一下你们在报纸上登的广告。◇ *She rang to say she'd be late.* 她打电话来说她要迟到。◇ **~ for sth** *Could you ring for a cab?* 你打电话叫辆出租车来好吗？➲ NOTE AT PHONE **2** 🔑 [I] (of a telephone 电话) to make a sound because sb is trying to telephone you 发出铃声：*Will you answer the telephone if it rings?* 电话铃响时你接一下好吗？

• **BELL** 铃；钟 **3** 🔑 [T, I] if you **ring** a bell or if a bell **rings**, it produces a sound（使）发出钟声，响起铃声：**~ (sth)** *Someone was ringing the doorbell.* 有人在按门铃。◇ *The church bells rang.* 教堂的钟声响了。◇ **~ for sb/sth** *Just ring for the nurse* (= attract the nurse's attention by ringing a bell) *if you need her.* 如果需要护士，按一下铃就行了。

• **WITH SOUND** 声响 **4** [I] **~ (with sth)** (*literary*) to be full of a sound; to fill a place with sound 回响；响彻 SYN **resound**: *The house rang with children's laughter.* 房子里回响着孩子们的笑声。◇ *Applause rang through the hall.* 掌声响彻整个大厅。

R

- **WITH QUALITY** 特性 **5** [I] ~ (**with sth**) to be full of a particular quality 充满：*His words rang with pride.* 他的话充满了骄傲。
- **OF EARS** 耳朵 **6** [I] to be uncomfortable and be unable to hear clearly, usually because you have heard a loud noise, etc. 嗡嗡作响：*The music was so loud it made my ears ring.* 音乐的声音太大了，震得我的耳朵嗡嗡响。

IDM **ring a 'bell** (*informal*) to sound familiar to you, as though you have heard it before 听起来耳熟：*His name rings a bell but I can't think where we met.* 他的名字听着很熟，但我想不起我们在哪里见过。 **ring the 'changes (with sth)** (*BrE*) to make changes to sth in order to have greater variety 使更多样化；变换花样：*Ring the changes with a new colour.* 用一种新的颜色来改变一下。 **ˌring in your 'ears/'head** to make you feel that you can still hear sth 在耳边回响：*His warning was still ringing in my ears.* 他的警告依然在我耳边回响。 **ˌring off the 'hook** (usually used in the progressive tenses 通常用于进行时) (of a telephone 电话) to ring many times 响声不断；铃声大作：*The phone has been ringing off the hook with offers of help.* 表示愿意提供援助的电话接连不断。 **ring 'true/'hollow/'false** to give the impression of being sincere/true or not sincere/true 给人以真实（或空洞、虚假）的印象：*It may seem a strange story but it rings true to me.* 这个故事也许显得离奇，但我却觉得很真实。 ➲ MORE AT ALARM *n.*

PHR V **ˌring a'round** = RING ROUND (SB/STH) **ˌring 'back | ˌring sb↔'back** (*BrE*) to telephone sb again, for example because they were not there when you called earlier, or to return a call they made to you （给某人）再打电话，回复电话：*He isn't here now—could you ring back later?* 他现在不在，你过会儿再打电话来好吗？ ◇ *I'll ask Simon to ring you back when he gets in.* 等西蒙来了，我让他给你回电话。 **ˌring 'in** (*BrE*) to telephone a television or radio show, or the place where you work 给电视（或电台）节目打电话；给自己的工作单位打电话 **ˌring 'in sth** to ring bells to celebrate sth, especially the new year 鸣钟欢庆（尤指新年） **ˌring 'off** (*BrE*) to put down the telephone because you have finished speaking 挂断电话：*He rang off before I could explain.* 我还没来得及解释他就挂了。 ➲ WORDFINDER NOTE AT CALL **ˌring 'out** to be heard loudly and clearly 清晰可闻；发出清脆的响声：*A number of shots rang out.* 这时听见几声清脆的枪声。 **ˌring 'round (sb/sth) | ˌring a'round (sb/sth)** (*BrE*) to telephone a number of people in order to organize sth or to get some information, etc. 电话通知，电话询问（各人）：*I rang round all the travel agents in the area.* 我打电话询问了那个地区所有的旅行社。 **ˌring 'through (to sb)** (*BrE*) to make a telephone call to sb, especially within the same building 打电话（给同一栋大楼内的人）：*Reception just rang through to say my visitor has arrived.* 接待处刚刚打电话来说我的客人到了。 **ˌring sth↔'up** to enter the cost of goods being bought in a shop/store on a CASH REGISTER by pressing the buttons; to make sales of a particular value 将（款额）输入现金出纳机；达到…销售额：*She rang up all the items on the till.* 她将各项款额都输入了现金出纳机。 ◇ *The company rang up sales of $166 million last year.* 公司去年的销售额为 1.66 亿美元。

■ ***noun***

- **OF BELL** 铃；钟 **1** [C] the sound that a bell makes; the act of ringing a bell 铃声；钟声；摇铃；敲钟：*There was a ring at the door.* 门铃响了。 ◇ *He gave a couple of loud rings on the doorbell.* 他使劲地按了几下门铃。
- **SOUND** 声响 **2** [sing.] a loud clear sound 清晰的响声：*the ring of horse's hooves on the cobblestones* 马蹄在鹅卵石上发出的清脆响声
- **QUALITY** 特性 **3** [sing.] ~ (**of sth**) a particular quality that words, sounds, etc. have （言语、声音等的）特性：*His explanation has a ring of truth about it.* 他的解释听上去真实可信。 ◇ *Her protestation of innocence **had a hollow ring to it*** (= did not sound sincere). 她自称无辜的辩白显得空洞乏力。 ◇ *The story had a **familiar ring** to it* (= as if I had heard it before). 这个故事听起来耳熟。

IDM **give sb a 'ring** (*BrE, informal*) to make a telephone call to sb 给某人打电话：*I'll give you a ring tomorrow.* 我明天给你打电话。 ➲ NOTE AT PHONE ➲ MORE AT BRASS

ring-a-ring o' roses /ˌrɪŋ ə rɪŋ ə ˈrəʊzɪz; *NAmE* ˈroʊzɪz/ (*BrE*) (*NAmE* **ˌring around the 'rosy**) *noun* [U] a singing game played by children, in which the players hold hands and dance in a circle, falling down at the end of the song 玫瑰花环（歌谣游戏，儿童手拉手围成一圈跳舞，歌曲唱完时倒下）

ring·back /ˈrɪŋbæk/ (*also* **Callback™**) *noun* [U, C] a telephone service that you can use if you call sb and their telephone is being used, so that your telephone will ring when the line is free; a call made using this service 回铃声（电话服务）；有回铃音的电话

'ring bearer *noun* (*NAmE*) a person, usually a boy, who carries the rings for the BRIDE and GROOM at a wedding （婚礼上的）捧戒指男孩，捧戒指者

'ring binder *noun* a file for holding papers, in which metal rings go through the edges of the pages, holding them in place 活页簿；活页夹 ➲ VISUAL VOCAB PAGE V71

'ring circuit (*also* **'ring main**) *noun* (*specialist*) an arrangement of wires which supply electricity to several different places in a room or building （房间或建筑物内的）环形电路

ringed /rɪŋd/ *adj.* [only before noun] **1** having a ring or rings on 戴戒指的：*a ringed finger* 戴着戒指的手指 **2** (especially of an animal or a bird 尤指动物或鸟) having a mark or marks like a ring on it 有环纹（或环斑）的：*a ringed plover* 胸部有带状纹的剑鸻

ringer /ˈrɪŋə(r)/ *noun* **1** = BELL-RINGER **2** (*NAmE*) a horse or person that takes part in a race illegally, for example by using a false name （以冒名顶替等手段）非法参赛的马（或人） **IDM** SEE DEAD *adj.*

ring·ette /rɪŋˈet/ *noun* [U] a Canadian game similar to ICE HOCKEY, played with a straight stick and rubber ring, especially by women 冰圈运动，冰上争圈（加拿大的一种类似冰球的运动，用直杆和橡皮圈，主要为女性参加）

'ring-fence *verb* (*BrE*) **1** ~ **sth** (*finance* 财) to protect a particular sum of money by putting restrictions on it so that it can only be used for a particular purpose 限制（资金的）用途 **2** ~ **sth** to protect sth by putting restrictions on it so that it can only be used by particular people or for a particular purpose 限制性地保护（以供专人专用）：*All employees can access the parts of the Intranet that are not ring-fenced.* 所有雇员都可进入内联网中无使用权限制的部分。 ▸ **'ring fence** *noun*：*The government has promised to put a ring fence around funding for education.* 政府已承诺教育资金保证用于教育。

'ring finger *noun* the finger next to the smallest one, especially on the left hand, on which a wedding ring is traditionally worn 无名指（尤指左手的，传统上用以戴结婚戒指） ➲ VISUAL VOCAB PAGE V64

ring·ing /ˈrɪŋɪŋ/ *adj.*, *noun*

■ ***adj.*** [only before noun] **1** (of a sound 声响) loud and clear 响亮的；清晰的 **2** (of a statement, etc. 陈述等) powerful and made with a lot of force 有力的；强劲的：*a ringing endorsement of her leadership* 对她的领导的有力支持

■ ***noun*** [sing., U] an act or a sound of ringing 嗡嗡作响；嗡嗡声：*There was an unpleasant ringing in my ears.* 我的耳朵里有一种烦人的嗡嗡声。

ring·lead·er /ˈrɪŋliːdə(r)/ *noun* (*disapproving*) a person who leads others in crime or in causing trouble 罪魁；头目；元凶

ring·let /ˈrɪŋlət/ *noun* [usually pl.] a long curl of hair hanging down from sb's head 垂下的长鬈发 ➲ VISUAL VOCAB PAGE V65

'ring main *noun* (*specialist*) **1** an arrangement of cables that allows electricity to be supplied to a series of places from either of two directions （电路的）环形干线 **2** = RING CIRCUIT **3** an arrangement of connected pipes that allows water, steam, etc. to enter and leave a system （管路的）环形主线

R

ring·mas·ter /ˈrɪŋmɑːstə(r); *NAmE* -mæs-/ *noun* a person in charge of a CIRCUS performance 马戏表演领班（或指挥）

ˈring pull (*BrE*) (*NAmE* **ˈpull tab**, **tab**) *noun* a small piece of metal with a ring attached which is pulled to open cans of food, drink, etc. （易拉罐等的）拉环；易拉环 ➲ VISUAL VOCAB PAGE V36

ˈring road (*BrE*) (*US* **ˈouter belt**) *noun* a road that is built around a city or town to reduce traffic in the centre 环路；环城路

ring·side /ˈrɪŋsaɪd/ *noun* [U] the area closest to the space in which a BOXING match or CIRCUS takes place （拳击场或马戏表演场等的）场边，台边区：*According to law, a doctor must be present at the ringside.* 按法律规定，场边必须有一名医生。◇ *a* ***ringside seat*** 靠近拳击台的观察席位

ring·tone /ˈrɪŋtəʊn; *NAmE* -toʊn/ *noun* the sound a telephone makes when sb is calling you. Ringtones are often short tunes, and the word is especially used to refer to the different sounds mobile/cell phones make when they ring. （尤指手机）铃声

ring·toss /ˈrɪŋtɒs; *NAmE* -tɔːs; -tɑːs/ (*NAmE*) (*BrE* **hoopla**) *noun* [U] a game in which players try to throw rings over objects in order to win them as prizes 投环套物

ring·worm /ˈrɪŋwɜːm; *NAmE* -wɜːrm/ *noun* [U] an infectious skin disease that produces small round red areas 癣

rink /rɪŋk/ *noun* **1** = ICE RINK **2** = SKATING RINK

rinky-dink /ˈrɪŋki dɪŋk/ *adj.* (*NAmE, informal*) of poor quality; cheap and/or old-fashioned 拙劣的；老旧廉价的：*a rinky-dink rhinestone necklace* 过时廉价的莱茵石项链 ◇ *a rinky-dink little town* 破破烂烂的小镇子

rinse /rɪns/ *verb, noun*

■ *verb* **1** ~ **sth** to wash sth with clean water only, not using soap （用清水）冲洗，洗涮：*Rinse the cooked pasta with boiling water.* 将煮过的意大利面在沸水里过一下。 **2** ~ **sth** to remove the soap from sth with clean water after washing it 冲掉…的皂液；漂洗；清洗 ➲ SYNONYMS AT CLEAN **3** ~ **sth + adv./prep.** to remove dirt, etc. from sth by washing it with clean water （用清水）冲掉，洗刷：*She rinsed the mud from her hands.* 她冲洗掉手上的泥浆。◇ *I wanted to rinse the taste out of my mouth.* 我想漱漱口，去掉嘴里的味道。➲ WORDFINDER NOTE AT LIQUID

PHR V **ˌrinse sth↔ˈout** to make sth clean, especially a container, by washing it with water 冲洗，洗刷干净（容器等）：*Rinse the cup out before use.* 使用前将杯子冲洗一下。

■ *noun* **1** [C] an act of rinsing sth 漂洗；冲洗；洗刷：*I gave the glass a rinse.* 我把杯子冲洗了一下。◇ *Fabric conditioner is added during the final rinse.* 在最后一遍漂洗时加入织物柔顺剂。 **2** [C, U] a liquid that you put on your hair when it is wet in order to change its colour 染发剂：*a blue rinse* 蓝色染发剂 **3** [C, U] a liquid used for cleaning the mouth and teeth 漱口液

riot /ˈraɪət/ *noun, verb*

■ *noun* **1** [C] a situation in which a group of people behave in a violent way in a public place, often as a protest 暴乱；骚乱：*One prison guard was killed when a riot broke out in the jail.* 一位狱警在监狱骚乱中丧生。◇ ***food/race riots*** 争抢食物的暴乱；种族骚乱 ➲ WORDFINDER NOTE AT PROTEST **2** [sing.] ~ **of sth** (*formal*) a collection of a lot of different types of the same thing 丰富多彩；品种繁多：*The garden was a* ***riot of colour***. 花园里色彩缤纷。 **3 a riot** [sing.] (*old-fashioned, informal*) a person or an event that is very amusing and enjoyable 非常有趣的人（或事）

IDM **run ˈriot 1** (of people 人) to behave in a way that is violent and/or not under control 撒野；恣意妄为 SYN **rampage**: *They let their kids run riot.* 他们听任自己的孩子撒野。 **2** if your imagination, a feeling, etc. **runs riot**, you allow it to develop and continue without trying to control it （指想象、情感等）任意发挥，奔放 **3** (of plants 植物) to grow and spread quickly 生长繁茂；疯长 ➲ MORE AT READ *v.*

■ *verb* [I] (of a crowd of people 人群) to behave in a violent way in a public place, often as a protest 发生骚乱；闹事 ▸ **riot·er** *noun*：*Rioters set fire to parked cars.* 暴徒放火焚烧停着的汽车。 **riot·ing** *noun* [U]: *Rioting broke out in the capital.* 首都爆发了骚乱事件。

ˈriot gear *noun* [U] the clothes and equipment used by the police when they are dealing with riots 防暴装备

riot·ous /ˈraɪətəs/ *adj.* [usually before noun] **1** (*formal* or *law* 律) noisy and/or violent, especially in a public place 骚乱的；暴乱的：*riotous behaviour* 暴乱行为 ◇ *The organizers of the march were charged with assault and* ***riotous assembly***. 游行组织者被控侵犯人身及暴乱集会。 **2** noisy, exciting and enjoyable in an uncontrolled way 狂欢的；纵情欢闹的 SYN **uproarious**: *a riotous party* 狂欢聚会 ◇ *riotous laughter* 放纵的笑声

riot·ous·ly /ˈraɪətəsli/ *adv.* extremely 极端；非常；极其：*riotously funny* 滑稽至极

ˈriot police *noun* [pl.] police who are trained to deal with people RIOTING 防暴警察

ˈriot shield (*also* **shield**) *noun* a piece of equipment made from strong plastic, used by the police to protect themselves from angry crowds 防暴盾牌

RIP (*also* **R.I.P.** *US, BrE*) /ˌɑːr aɪ ˈpiː/ *abbr.* rest in peace (often written on graves) 安息（通常书于墓碑）

rip /rɪp/ *verb, noun*

■ *verb* (**-pp-**) **1** [T, I] to tear sth or to become torn, often suddenly or violently （突然或猛烈地）撕破，裂开：~ **(sth)** *I ripped my jeans on the fence.* 我的牛仔裤在栅栏上划破了。◇ *The flags had been ripped in two.* 旗帜都被撕成了两半。◇ *I heard the tent rip.* 我听到了帐篷撕裂的声音。◇ ~ **sth + adj.** *She* ***ripped the letter open***. 她撕开那封信。 **2** [T] ~ **sth + adv./prep.** to remove sth quickly or violently, often by pulling it 猛地扯开；突然拉开：*He ripped off his tie.* 他一把拽掉领带。◇ *The carpet had been ripped from the stairs.* 地毯已经从楼梯上拖走了。 **3** [T] ~ **sth** (*computing* 计) to copy sound or video files from a website or CD on to a computer （从网站或光盘）撷取（音频或视频文件） **4** (*computing* 计) = RASTERIZE

IDM **let ˈrip (at sb)** (*informal*) to speak or do sth with great force, enthusiasm, etc. and without control 激动地说（或做）；忘乎所以地说（或做）：*When she gets angry with her boyfriend, she really lets rip at him.* 当她生男朋友气的时候，她真的对他破口大骂。◇ *The group let rip with a single from their new album.* 乐队充满激情地表演了他们新唱片中的一首单曲。 **let ˈrip | let sth ˈrip** (*informal*) **1** to go or allow sth such as a car to go as fast as possible （使）全速前进：*Once on the open road, he let rip.* 一上空旷的公路，他就全速行驶。◇ *Come on Steve—let her rip.* 来吧，史蒂夫，让车全速前进吧。 **2** to do sth or to allow sth to happen as fast as possible 尽快做；使尽快发生：*This would cause inflation to let rip again.* 这又将导致急剧的通货膨胀。 **rip sb/sth aˈpart/to ˈshreds/to ˈbits, etc.** to destroy sth; to criticize sb very strongly 摧毁；毁坏；猛烈抨击 ➲ MORE AT HEART, LIMB

PHR V **ˈrip at sth** to attack sth violently, usually by tearing or cutting it 猛烈撕扯；用力割 **ˌrip ˈinto sb (for/with sth)** to criticize sb and tell them that you are very angry with them 责备；斥责 **ˌrip ˈinto/ˈthrough sb/sth** to go very quickly and violently into or through sb/sth （快速而猛烈地）钻入，穿透：*A bullet ripped into his shoulder.* 一颗子弹穿透了他的肩头。 **ˌrip sb↔ˈoff** [usually passive] (*informal*) to cheat sb, by making them pay too much, by selling them sth of poor quality, etc. 敲诈；讹诈：*Tourists complain of being ripped off by local cab drivers.* 游客抱怨被当地的出租车司机敲了竹杠。➲ RELATED NOUN RIP-OFF (1) **ˌrip sth↔ˈoff** (*informal*) to steal sth 偷窃；盗取：*Thieves broke in and ripped off five computers.* 盗贼破门而入，偷走了五台电脑。 **ˌrip sth↔ˈup** to tear sth into small pieces 把某物撕碎：*He ripped up the letter and threw it in the fire.* 他把信撕碎，扔到火炉里。

■ *noun* [usually sing.] **1** a long tear in cloth, paper, etc. （织物、纸张等）撕开的大口子 **2** = RIP CURRENT

ri·par·ian /raɪˈpeəriən; *NAmE* -ˈper-/ *adj.* [usually before noun] **1** (*specialist*) growing in, living in, or relating to areas of wet land near to a river or stream 生长（或栖息）在河边湿地的；河边的 **2** (*law* 律) on, near or relating to the bank of a river 堤岸（上）的；堤岸近处的

rip·cord /ˈrɪpkɔːd; *NAmE* -kɔːrd/ *noun* the string that you pull to open a PARACHUTE（降落伞的）开伞索

ˌrip ˈcurrent (*also* **rip**) *noun* a strong current of water that flows away from the coast 离岸流；裂流

ripe /raɪp/ *adj.* (**riper**, **rip·est**) **1** (of fruit or crops 水果或庄稼) fully grown and ready to be eaten 成熟的 OPP **unripe** **2** (of cheese or wine 干酪或果酒) having a flavour that has fully developed 口味浓郁的；成熟的；醇美可口的 SYN **mature** **3** (of a smell 气味) strong and unpleasant 强烈的；难闻的 **4** ~ (**for sth**) ready or suitable for sth to happen 时机成熟的；适宜的：*This land is ripe for development.* 这片土地适宜开发。◇ *The conditions were ripe for social change.* 社会变革的时机已经成熟。◇ *Reforms were promised when **the time was ripe**.* 曾经作出承诺，时机一成熟就进行改革。▸ **ripe·ness** *noun* [U]

IDM **a/the ripe old age** (**of**...) an age that is considered to be very old（…的）高龄：*He lived to the ripe old age of 91.* 他活到了 91 岁的高龄。

ripen /ˈraɪpən/ *verb* [I, T] ~ (**sth**) to become ripe; to make sth ripe （使）成熟

ˈrip-off *noun* (*informal*) **1** [usually sing.] something that is not worth what you pay for it 索价过高（或物非所值）的东西：*$70 for a T-shirt! What a rip-off!* * 70 美元买一件 T 恤衫！太不值了！ **2** ~ (**of sth**) a copy of sth, especially one that is less expensive or not as good as the original thing 仿制品；冒牌货：*The single is a rip-off of a 70s hit.* 这首单曲是 70 年代的一首热门歌曲的翻版。

ri·poste /rɪˈpɒst; *NAmE* rɪˈpoʊst/ *noun* (*formal*) **1** a quick and clever reply, especially to criticism 机敏的回答；巧妙的反驳 SYN **retort**: *a witty riposte* 机智的回答 **2** a course of action that takes place in response to sth that has happened 反应；回应：*The US delivered an early riposte to the air attack.* 美国对空袭很快作出了反应。▸ **ri·poste** *verb* [T, I] (+ **speech**)

rip·per /ˈrɪpə(r)/ *noun* (*informal*) a person who is very good at SNOWBOARDING 滑雪板运动高手

rip·ping /ˈrɪpɪŋ/ *adj.* (*BrE, old-fashioned*) wonderful 极好的；美妙的

rip·ple /ˈrɪpl/ *noun, verb*

▪ ***noun*** **1** a small wave on the surface of a liquid, especially water in a lake, etc. 波纹；细浪；涟漪：*The air was so still that there was hardly a ripple on the pond's surface.* 空气静止不动，池塘的水面上几乎看不到波纹。 **2** a thing that looks or moves like a small wave（外观或运动）如波纹的东西：*ripples of sand* 沙滩上的波纹 **3** [usually sing.] ~ **of sth** a sound that gradually becomes louder and then quieter again 起伏的声音：***a ripple of applause/laughter*** 一阵阵的掌声 / 笑声 **4** [usually sing.] ~ **of sth** a feeling that gradually spreads through a person or group of people 逐渐扩散的感觉：*A ripple of fear passed through him.* 一股恐惧感传遍了他的全身。◇ *The announcement sent a ripple of excitement through the crowd.* 这件事一宣布就在人群里引起了一阵兴奋。

▪ ***verb*** **1** [I, T] to move or to make sth move in very small waves（使）如波浪般起伏：*The sea rippled and sparkled.* 大海波光粼粼。◇ *rippling muscles* 条条凸起的肌肉 ◇ ~ **sth** *The wind rippled the wheat in the fields.* 田野上的麦浪在风中起伏。 **2** [I] + **adv./prep.** (of a feeling, etc. 感觉等) to spread through a person or a group of people like a wave 扩散；涌起：*A gasp rippled through the crowd.* 人群中传出一片惊诧之声。

ˈripple effect *noun* a situation in which an event or action has an effect on sth, which then has an effect on sth else 连锁反应：*His resignation will have a ripple effect on the whole department.* 他的辞职将会在整个部门中引起连锁反应。

ˈrip-roaring *adj.* [only before noun] (*informal*) **1** noisy, exciting and/or full of activity 喧闹的；兴奋的；狂欢的：*a rip-roaring celebration* 欢乐的庆典 **2** ~ **drunk** extremely drunk 烂醉的 **3** ~ **success** a great success 巨大的（成功）

Rip Van Winkle /ˌrɪp væn ˈwɪŋkl/ *noun* a person who is surprised to find how much the world has changed over a period of time 对世界变化之大感到惊讶的人；李伯 ➲ MORE LIKE THIS 17, page R27 ORIGIN From the name of a character in a short story by the US writer Washington Irving. He sleeps for 20 years and wakes up to find that the world has completely changed. 源自美国作家华盛顿・欧文所著短篇小说中的人物瑞普・凡・温克尔，他沉睡 20 年后醒来，发现世间发生了天翻地覆的变化。

rise 🔑 /raɪz/ *noun, verb*

▪ ***noun***

• INCREASE 增加 **1** 🔑 [C] an increase in an amount, a number or a level（数量或水平的）增加，提高：*The industry is feeling the effects of recent price rises.* 这一行业已经感觉到了最近提价的影响。◇ ~ **in sth** *There has been **a sharp rise** in the number of people out of work.* 失业人数急剧增长。➲ LANGUAGE BANK AT INCREASE **2** 🔑 [C] (*BrE*) (*NAmE* **raise**) an increase in the money you are paid for the work you do 加薪；工资增长：*I'm going to ask for a rise.* 我打算要求加薪。◇ *He criticized the huge pay rises awarded to industry bosses.* 对于给企业老板大幅度加薪，他提出了批评。 ➲ WORDFINDER NOTE AT PAY

• IN POWER/IMPORTANCE 权力；重要性 **3** 🔑 [sing.] ~ (**of sb/sth**) the act of becoming more important, successful, powerful, etc.（重要性、优势、权力等的）增强：*the rise of fascism in Europe* 法西斯主义在欧洲的兴起 ◇ *the **rise and fall** of the British Empire* 英帝国的兴衰 ◇ *her meteoric **rise to power*** 她的迅速掌权

• UPWARD MOVEMENT 上升 **4** 🔑 [sing.] an upward movement 上升：*She watched the gentle **rise and fall** of his chest as he slept.* 她看着他睡着时微微起伏的胸膛。

• SLOPING LAND 斜坡 **5** [C] an area of land that slopes upwards 斜坡；小丘；小山 SYN **slope**: *The church was built at the top of a small rise.* 教堂建在一座小山顶上。➲ SEE ALSO HIGH-RISE

IDM **get a rise out of sb** to make sb react in an angry way by saying sth that you know will annoy them, especially as a joke 惹恼；故意激怒 **give ˈrise to sth** (*formal*) to cause sth to happen or exist 使发生（或存在）：*The novel's success gave rise to a number of sequels.* 这部小说的成功带来了一系列的续篇。

▪ ***verb*** (**rose** /rəʊz; *NAmE* roʊz/, **risen** /ˈrɪzn/)

• MOVE UPWARDS 上升 **1** 🔑 [I] (+ **adv./prep.**) to come or go upwards; to reach a higher level or position 上升；攀升；提高；达到较高水平（或位置）：*Smoke was rising from the chimney.* 烟从烟囱里升起。◇ *The river has risen (by) several metres.* 河水上升了好几米。

• GET UP 起身 **2** 🔑 [I] (+ **adv./prep.**) (*formal*) to get up from a lying, sitting or KNEELING position 起床；起立；站起来 SYN **get up**: *He was accustomed to rising* (= getting out of bed) *early.* 他习惯于早起。◇ *They rose from the table.* 他们从餐桌旁站起身。◇ *She rose to her feet.* 她站起身来。 ➲ SYNONYMS AT STAND

• OF SUN/MOON 太阳；月亮 **3** 🔑 [I] when the sun, moon, etc. **rises**, it appears above the HORIZON 升起：*The sun rises in the east.* 太阳从东方升起。OPP **set** ➲ WORDFINDER NOTE AT SUN

• END MEETING 结束会议 **4** [I] (*formal*) (of a group of people 一群人) to end a meeting 休会；闭会；散会 SYN **adjourn**: *The House* (= members of the House of Commons) *rose at 10 p.m.* 下议院于晚上 10 点钟散会。

• INCREASE 增加 **5** 🔑 [I] to increase in amount or number（数量）增加，增长，提高：*rising fuel bills* 不断增加的燃料费 ◇ *The price of gas rose.* 煤气价格上涨了。◇ *Gas **rose in price**.* 煤气涨价了。◇ *Unemployment rose (by) 3%.* 失业人数增长了 3%。◇ *Air pollution has risen above an acceptable level.* 空气污染已经超出了人们可接受的程度。➲ LANGUAGE BANK AT INCREASE

• BECOME POWERFUL/IMPORTANT 变得强大 / 重要 **6** 🔑 [I] (+ **adv./prep.**) to become more successful, important, powerful, etc. 变得更加成功（或重要、强大等）：*a rising young politician* 崭露头角的年轻政治家 ◇ *She rose to*

R

power in the 70s. 她于 20 世纪 70 年代掌握了大权。◇ *He rose to the rank of general.* 他升至将级军官。◇ *She* ***rose through the ranks*** *to become managing director.* 她从普通员工逐步晋升为总经理。

- **OF SOUND** 声响 **7** [I] if a sound **rises**, it becomes louder and higher 提高；增强：*Her voice rose angrily.* 她气得提高了嗓门。
- **OF WIND** 风 **8** [I] if the wind **rises**, it begins to blow more strongly 刮起来；刮得更猛 **SYN get up**
- **OF FEELING** 情感 **9** [I] (*formal*) if a feeling **rises** inside you, it begins and gets stronger 增强：*He felt anger rising inside him.* 他心里直冒火。◇ *Her* ***spirits rose*** (= she felt happier) *at the news.* 听到这个消息，她高兴起来。
- **OF YOUR COLOUR** 脸色 **10** [I] (*formal*) if your colour **rises**, your face becomes pink or red with embarrassment 脸红
- **OF HAIR** 毛发 **11** [I] if hair **rises**, it stands vertical instead of lying flat 竖起；立起来：*The hair on the back of my neck rose when I heard the scream.* 听到那尖叫声，我不禁毛骨悚然。
- **FIGHT** 战斗 **12** [I] **~ (up) (against sb/sth)** (*formal*) to begin to fight against your ruler or government or against a foreign army 起义；反抗；奋起 **SYN rebel**：*The peasants rose in revolt.* 农民起来造反了。◇ *He called on the people to rise up against the invaders.* 他号召民众起来反抗入侵者。➲ RELATED NOUN UPRISING
- **BECOME VISIBLE** 变得可见 **13** [I] (*formal*) to be or become visible above the surroundings 耸立；矗立；高出：*Mountains rose in the distance.* 远处山峦叠起。
- **OF LAND** 土地 **14** [I] if land **rises**, it slopes upwards 凸起；隆起：*The ground rose steeply all around.* 这块地方四周都是陡坡。
- **OF BEGINNING OF RIVER** 河源 **15** [I] **+ adv./prep.** a river **rises** where it begins to flow 起源；发源：*The Thames rises in the Cotswold hills.* 泰晤士河起源于科茨沃尔德丘陵。
- **OF BREAD/CAKES** 面包；蛋糕 **16** [I] when bread, cakes, etc. **rise**, they swell because of the action of YEAST or BAKING POWDER 发酵
- **OF DEAD PERSON** 死人 **17** [I] **~ (from sth)** to come to life again 复活；再生：*to rise from the dead* 复活 ◇ (*figurative*) *Can a new party* ***rise from the ashes*** *of the old one?* 在旧政党的灰烬中会诞生出一个新的政党吗？

▼ **WHICH WORD? 词语辨析**

rise / raise

Verbs 动词

- **Raise** is a verb that must have an object and **rise** is used without an object. When you **raise** something, you lift it to a higher position or increase it. 动词 raise 后必须接宾语，而 rise 不接宾语。raise 表示举起、提起、提升、增加：*He raised his head from the pillow.* 他从枕头上抬起头来。◇ *We were forced to raise the price.* 我们被迫提价。When people or things **rise**, they move from a lower to a higher position. 表示人或物从低处向高处上升用 rise：*She rose from the chair.* 她从椅子上站起来。◇ *The helicopter rose into the air.* 直升机升上了天空。**Rise** can also mean 'to increase in number or quantity'. * rise 亦表示数字上升或数量增加：*Costs are always rising.* 成本总是不断地增加。

Nouns 名词

- The noun **rise** means a movement upwards or an increase in an amount or quantity. 名词 rise 表示上升、升起、（数量的）增加：*a rise in interest rates* 利率的上升 In *BrE* it can also be used to mean an increase in pay. 在英式英语中亦可指工资的增加：*Should I ask my boss for a rise?* 我应要求老板增加工资吗？ In *NAmE* this is a **raise**. 在美式英语中此义用 raise 表示：*a three per cent pay raise* 百分之三的加薪 **Rise** can also mean the process of becoming more powerful or important. * rise 亦可表示地位提高：*his dramatic rise to power* 他的突然掌权

IDM ˌ**rise and 'shine** (*old-fashioned*) usually used in orders to tell sb to get out of bed and be active（通常用来催促起床）➲ MORE AT GORGE *n.*, HACKLES, HEIGHT

PHR V ˌ**rise a'bove sth** **1** to not be affected or limited by problems, insults, etc. 克服（障碍）；超越（限制）；战胜（困难）：*She had the courage and determination to rise above her physical disability.* 她有战胜自身残疾的勇气和决心。 **2** to be wise enough or morally good enough not to do sth wrong or not to think the same as other people 不为…所动；超脱：*I try to rise above prejudice.* 我尽力摆脱偏见。 **3** to be of a higher standard than other things of a similar kind 超群；出众；突出：*His work rarely rises above the mediocre.* 他工作平平，很少有突出的表现。'**rise to sth** **1** to show that you are able to deal with an unexpected situation, problem, etc. 能够处理，有能力处理（突发情况、问题等）：*Luckily, my mother* ***rose to the occasion.*** 幸好当时我母亲挺身而出。◇ *He was determined to* ***rise to the challenge.*** 他决心克服困难迎接挑战。 **2** to react when sb is deliberately trying to make you angry or get you interested in sth 上当；上钩；进圈套：*I refuse to rise to that sort of comment.* 我拒绝对那样的评论作出反应。◇ *As soon as I mentioned money he* ***rose to the bait.*** 我一提到钱，他就上钩了。

riser /ˈraɪzə(r)/ *noun* **1 early/late ~** a person who usually gets out of bed early/late in the morning（习惯于早或晚）起床的人 **2** (*specialist*) the vertical part between two steps in a set of stairs 立板（楼梯踏步板的竖直部分）➲ PICTURE AT STAIRCASE ➲ COMPARE TREAD *n.* (3)

ris·ible /ˈrɪzəbl/ *adj.* (*formal, disapproving*) deserving to be laughed at rather than taken seriously 可笑的；滑稽的 **SYN ludicrous, ridiculous**

ris·ing /ˈraɪzɪŋ/ *noun* a situation in which a group of people protest against, and try to get rid of, a government, a leader, etc. 起义；叛乱 **SYN revolt, uprising**

ˌ**rising 'damp** *noun* [U] (*BrE*) a condition in which water comes up from the ground into the walls of a building, causing damage 从地下渗入墙壁的潮气

'**rising sign** *noun* = ASCENDANT

risk /rɪsk/ *noun, verb*

■ ***noun*** **1** [C, U] the possibility of sth bad happening at some time in the future; a situation that could be dangerous or have a bad result 危险；风险：**~ (of sth/of doing sth)** *Smoking can increase the risk of developing heart disease.* 吸烟会增加得心脏病的危险。◇ *Patients should be made aware of the risks involved with this treatment.* 应该告诉病人这种治疗所涉及的风险。◇ **~ (that…)** *There is still a risk that the whole deal will fall through.* 整桩买卖化为泡影的风险仍然存在。◇ **~ (to sb/sth)** *The chemicals* ***pose little risk*** (= are not dangerous) *to human health.* 这些化学制品对人类健康没有什么危害。◇ ***a calculated risk*** (= one that you think is small compared with the possible benefits) 值得承担的风险 ◇ *Any business venture contains an* ***element of risk.*** 任何商业投资都包含一定的风险因素。◇ *We could probably trust her with the information but it's just not* ***worth the risk.*** 我们也许可以将这些资料托付给她，但实在不值得去担这样的风险。 **2** [C] **~ (to sth)** a person or thing that is likely to cause problems or danger at some time in the future 危险人物；会带来风险的事物：*The group was considered to be a risk to national security.* 这伙人被认为是威胁国家安全的危险分子。◇ *a major* ***health/fire risk*** 健康 / 火灾的一大隐患 **3** [C] **a good/bad/poor ~** a person or business that a bank or an insurance company is willing/unwilling to lend money or sell insurance to because they are likely/unlikely to pay back the money etc.（风险很小 / 很大的）借款人，保险对象：*With five previous claims, he's now a bad insurance risk.* 由于已有了五次索赔要求，他现在是一位风险很大的被保险人。➲ WORDFINDER NOTE AT INSURANCE, LOAN

IDM **at 'risk (from/of sth)** in danger of sth unpleasant or harmful happening 有危险；冒风险：*As with all diseases, certain groups will be more at risk than others.* 所有的疾病都是如此，一些群体比另一些群体更容易受到威胁。◇ *If we go to war, innocent lives will be* ***put at risk.*** 如果我们发动战争，无辜的生命就会受到威胁。**at the 'risk**

of doing sth used to introduce sth that may sound stupid or may offend sb（用以引出可能听上去愚蠢或冒犯人的话）冒着…的风险：*At the risk of showing my ignorance, how exactly does the Internet work?* 也许我难免显得无知，可互联网到底是怎么运作的呢？ **at risk to yourself/sb/sth** with the possibility of harming yourself/sb/sth 冒伤及…的危险：*He dived in to save the dog at considerable risk to his own life.* 他冒着相当大的生命危险跳到水里去救那只狗。 **do sth at your ˌown ˈrisk** to do sth even though you have been warned about the possible dangers and will have to take responsibility for anything bad that happens 自担风险；责任自负：*Persons swimming beyond this point do so at their own risk* (= on a notice). 游泳者越过此界限后果自负。◇ *Valuables are left at their owner's risk* (= on a notice). 贵重物品须看管，否则风险自负。 **run a ˈrisk (of sth/of doing sth)** to be in a situation in which sth bad could happen to you 冒风险；有…的危险：*People who are overweight run a risk of a heart attack or stroke.* 超重的人有犯心脏病和中风的危险。 **run the ˈrisk (of sth/of doing sth) | run ˈrisks** 🔑 to be or put yourself in a situation in which sth bad could happen to you 冒…的危险；冒险（做某事）：*We don't want to run the risk of losing their business.* 我们不想冒险失去他们的生意。◇ *Investment is all about running risks.* 投资就是要冒风险。 **take a ˈrisk | take ˈrisks** 🔑 to do sth even though you know that sth bad could happen as a result 冒险（做某事）：*That's a risk I'm not prepared to take.* 我不愿意去冒这个险。◇ *You have no right to take risks with other people's lives.* 你没有权利拿别人的生命去冒险。

■ ***verb*** **1** 🔑 **~ sth** to put sth valuable or important in a dangerous situation, in which it could be lost or damaged 面临危险；使处于危险境地：*He risked his life to save her.* 他冒着生命危险去救她。◇ *She was risking her own and her children's health.* 她在使自己和子女的健康遭受威胁。◇ *He risked all his money on a game of cards.* 他冒险把自己所有的钱都押在了一场纸牌游戏上。 **2** 🔑 to do sth that may mean that you get into a situation which is unpleasant or harmful for you 冒…的风险（或危险）：**~ sth** *There was no choice. If they stayed there, they risked death.* 他们别无选择。如果待在那儿，就面临死亡。◇ **~ (sb/sth) doing sth** *They knew they risked being arrested.* 他们知道自己冒着被捕的危险。 **3** 🔑 to do sth that you know is not really a good idea or may not succeed 冒险做；（明知结果而）大胆做：**~ sth** *He risked a glance at her furious face.* 他壮着胆子瞅了瞅她那张愤怒的脸。◇ *It was a difficult decision but we decided to risk it.* 这件事决心难下，但我们决定冒险一试。◇ **~ doing sth** *We've been advised not to risk travelling in these conditions.* 我们受到忠告，在这种条件下不要冒险出行。 ➲ MORE LIKE THIS 27, page R28

IDM **risk ˌlife and ˈlimb | risk your ˈneck** to risk being killed or injured in order to do sth 冒死；不惜受伤 ➲ MORE LIKE THIS 13, page R26

ˈrisk assessment *noun* [C, U] (*business* 商) the act of identifying possible risks, calculating how likely they are to happen and estimating what effects they might have, especially in the context of a company taking responsibility for the safety of its employees or members of the public 风险评估；（尤指公司中涉及员工或公众安全的）危险性评估：*The employer has an obligation to carry out a risk assessment.* 雇主有义务对危险作出评估。

ˈrisk-averse *adj.* not willing to do sth if it is possible that sth bad could happen as a result 不愿冒风险的：*We live in a risk-averse culture.* 我们生活在没有冒险精神的文化中。◇ *In business you cannot be innovative and risk-averse at the same time.* 经商不可能既要创新又不肯冒险。

ˈrisk-taking *noun* [U] the practice of doing things that involve risks in order to achieve sth 冒险；承担风险

risky /ˈrɪski/ *adj.* (**risk·ier**, **riski·est**) **HELP** You can also use **more risky** and **most risky**. 亦可用 more risky 和 most risky。 involving the possibility of sth bad happening 有危险（或风险）的 **SYN** **dangerous**：*Life as an aid worker can be a risky business* (= dangerous). 救援人员的工作会有危险。◇ *a risky investment* 有风险的投资 ◇ *It's far too risky to generalize from one set of results.* 仅根据一组结果进行概括是十分不可靠的。 ▸ **risk·ily** /-ɪli/ *adv.* **riski·ness** /-nəs/ *noun* [U]

ris·otto /rɪˈzɒtəʊ; *NAmE* rɪˈsɔːtoʊ; -ˈzɔː-/ *noun* (*pl.* **-os**) [C, U] an Italian dish of rice cooked with vegetables, meat, etc. 意大利肉汁烩饭

ris·qué /ˈrɪskeɪ; *NAmE* rɪˈskeɪ/ *adj.* a **risqué** performance, comment, joke, etc. is a little shocking, usually because it is about sex（表演、评论、笑话等）有伤风化的

ris·sole /ˈrɪsəʊl; *NAmE* -soʊl/ *noun* a small flat mass or ball of chopped meat that is fried. It is sometimes covered with BREADCRUMBS or, in the US, with PASTRY before it is cooked. 炸肉饼；炸肉丸

Rit·alin™ /ˈrɪtəlɪn/ *noun* a drug given to children who cannot keep quiet or still, to help them become calmer and concentrate better 利他林，立达宁，利他能（帮助多动儿童安静下来并集中注意力的药物）

rite /raɪt/ *noun* a ceremony performed by a particular group of people, often for religious purposes（宗教等的）仪式，典礼：*funeral rites* 丧葬仪式 ◇ *initiation rites* (= performed when a new member joins a secret society)（秘密团体的）入会仪式 ➲ COLLOCATIONS AT RELIGION ➲ SEE ALSO LAST RITES

ˌrite of ˈpassage *noun* a ceremony or an event that marks an important stage in sb's life（标志人生重要阶段的）通过仪式，重大事件

rit·ual /ˈrɪtʃuəl/ *noun, adj.*

■ ***noun*** [C, U] **1** a series of actions that are always performed in the same way, especially as part of a religious ceremony 程序；仪规；礼节；（尤指）宗教仪式：*religious rituals* 宗教仪式 ◇ *She objects to the ritual of organized religion.* 她反对有组织宗教的仪规。 ➲ COLLOCATIONS AT RELIGION **2** something that is done regularly and always in the same way 习惯；老规矩：*Sunday lunch with the in-laws has become something of a ritual.* 星期天和姻亲们共进午餐已经成了例行的公事。

■ ***adj.*** [only before noun] **1** done as part of a ritual or ceremony 仪式上的；庆典的：*ritual chanting* 礼仪上的圣咏演唱 **2** always done or said in the same way, especially when this is not sincere 习惯的；老套的；例行公事的：*ritual expressions of sympathy* 例行公事地表示同情 ▸ **rit·ual·ly** *adv.*：*The goat was ritually slaughtered.* 山羊按照仪式宰杀了。

ritu·al·is·tic /ˌrɪtʃuəˈlɪstɪk/ *adj.* [usually before noun] **1** connected with the rituals performed as part of a ceremony 仪式的：*a ritualistic act of worship* 崇拜仪式 **2** always done or said in the same way, especially when this is not sincere 老套的；例行公事的

ritu·al·ize (*BrE also* **-ise**) /ˈrɪtʃuəlaɪz/ *verb* [usually passive] **~ sth** (*formal*) to do sth in the same way or pattern every time 使仪式化；使程式化：*ritualized expressions of grief* 以例行的方式表达悲伤

ritzy /ˈrɪtsi/ *adj.* (*informal*) expensive and fashionable 昂贵时髦的；豪华的 **ORIGIN** From the **Ritz**, the name of several very comfortable and expensive hotels in London and other cities. 源自丽兹大酒店（the Ritz），该品牌的酒店以豪华著称，见于伦敦等大城市。

rival 🔑 /ˈraɪvl/ *noun, adj., verb*

■ ***noun*** 🔑 **~ (to sb/sth) (for sth)** a person, company or thing that competes with another in sport, business, etc. 竞争对手：*The two teams have always been rivals.* 这两个队一直是竞争对手。◇ *The Japanese are our biggest economic rivals.* 日本人是我们最大的经济竞争对手。◇ *This latest design has no rivals* (= it is easily the best design available). 这种最新款式独领风骚。

■ ***adj.*** 🔑 [only before noun] (of a person, company, thing, etc. 人、公司、事物等) competing with another person, company, thing, etc. 相互竞争的；对抗的：*a rival bid/claim/offer* 竞争投标；对立的权利要求；竞争的出价 ◇ *fighting between rival groups* 对立团体间的争斗 ◇ *He was shot by a member of a rival gang.* 他被敌对团伙的一名成员开枪击中。

■ ***verb*** (**-ll-**, *NAmE also* **-l-**) **~ sb/sth (for/in sth)** to be as good,

R

impressive, etc. as sb/sth else 与…相匹敌；比得上 SYN **compare**: *You will find scenery to rival anything you can see in the Alps.* 你看到的景色可与你在阿尔卑斯山所看到的景色相媲美。 ➲ SEE ALSO UNRIVALLED

ri·val·ry /ˈraɪvlri/ *noun* [C, U] (*pl.* **-ries**) a state in which two people, companies, etc. are competing for the same thing 竞争；竞赛；较量： ~ (**with sb/sth**) (**for sth**) *a fierce rivalry for world supremacy* 夺取世界霸权的激烈竞争 ◇ ~ (**between A and B**) (**for sth**) *There is a certain amount of friendly rivalry between the teams.* 两队间有某种程度上的友好较量。 ◇ *political rivalries* 政治对抗 ◇ *sibling rivalry* (= between brothers and sisters) 兄弟姐妹间的较劲

riven /ˈrɪvn/ *adj.* [not before noun] ~ (**by/with sth**) (*formal*) **1** (of a group of people 一群人) divided because of disagreements, especially in a violent way 分裂；四分五裂： *a party riven by internal disputes* 由于内部分歧而四分五裂的政党 **2** (of an object 物体) divided into two or more pieces 破裂；破碎

river /ˈrɪvə(r)/ *noun* **1** (*abbr.* **R.**) a natural flow of water that continues in a long line across land to the sea/ocean 河；江： *the River Thames* 泰晤士河 ◇ *the Hudson River* 哈得孙河 ◇ *on the banks of the river* (= the ground at the side of a river) 在河岸上 ◇ *to travel* **up/down river** (= in the opposite direction to/in the same direction as the way in which the river is flowing) 逆流而上；顺流而下 ◇ *the mouth of the river* (= where it enters the sea/ocean) 河口 ◇ *Can we swim* **in the river**? 我们可以下河游泳吗？ ◇ *a boat on the river* 河上的一条船 ◇ *They have a house on the river* (= beside it). 他们在河边有栋房子。 ➲ VISUAL VOCAB PAGES V3, V5

WORDFINDER 联想词: bend, course, current, dam, downstream, estuary, source, tributary, waterfall

2 ~ (**of sth**) a large amount of liquid that is flowing in a particular direction （液体）涌流： *Rivers of molten lava flowed down the mountain.* 大量的熔岩顺着山坡流下来。 IDM SEE SELL *v.*

river·bank /ˈrɪvəbæŋk; *NAmE* ˈrɪvər-/ *noun* the ground at the side of a river 河岸；河堤： *on the riverbank* 在河岸上 ➲ VISUAL VOCAB PAGE V3

ˈriver bed *noun* the area of ground over which a river usually flows 河床： *a dried-up river bed* 干涸的河床

ˈriver blindness *noun* [U] (*medical* 医) a tropical skin disease caused by a PARASITE of certain flies that breed in rivers, which can also cause a person to become blind 盘尾丝虫病，河盲症（由河中繁殖的苍蝇的寄生虫引起的热带皮肤病，可导致失明）

river·front /ˈrɪvəfrʌnt; *NAmE* -vərf-/ *noun* (*especially NAmE*) an area of land next to a river with buildings, shops/stores, restaurants, etc. on it 滨河地区

river·ine /ˈrɪvəraɪn/ *adj.* [usually before noun] (*specialist*) on, near, or relating to a river or the banks of a river 河流（上）的；河流附近的；河岸（上）的

river·side /ˈrɪvəsaɪd; *NAmE* -vərs-/ *noun* [sing.] the ground along either side of a river 河畔；河岸： *a riverside path* 滨河小道 ◇ *a walk by the riverside* 河边漫步

rivet /ˈrɪvɪt/ *noun, verb*

▪ ***noun*** a metal pin that is used to fasten two pieces of leather, metal, etc. together 铆钉

▪ ***verb*** [usually passive] **1** ~ **sb/sth** to hold sb's interest or attention so completely that they cannot look away or think of anything else 吸引住： *I was absolutely riveted by her story.* 我完全被她的故事吸引住了。 ◇ *My eyes were* **riveted on** *the figure lying in the road.* 我眼睛盯着躺在路上的人。 **2** ~ **sth** to fasten sth with rivets 铆接；（用铆钉）固定： *The steel plates were riveted together.* 钢板被固定在一起。

IDM **be riveted to the spot/ground** to be so shocked or frightened that you cannot move 吓呆了；呆若木鸡

rivet·ing /ˈrɪvɪtɪŋ/ *adj.* (*approving*) so interesting or exciting that it holds your attention completely 吸引人的；引人入胜的 SYN **engrossing**

rivi·era /ˌrɪviˈeərə; *NAmE* -ˈerə/ *noun* (*often* **Riviera**) an area by the sea that is warm and popular for holidays, especially the Mediterranean coast of France 海滨度假胜地（尤指法国的地中海海滨）： *the French Riviera* 法国的里维埃拉地区

rivu·let /ˈrɪvjələt/ *noun* (*formal*) a very small river; a small stream of water or other liquid 小河；小溪；溪流；细流

RM /ˌɑːr ˈem/ *abbr.* (in Britain) Royal Marine （英国）皇家海军陆战队 ➲ SEE ALSO MARINE *n.*

RN /ˌɑːr ˈen/ *noun* **1** REGISTERED NURSE 注册护士 **2** (in Britain) Royal Navy （英国）皇家海军

RNA /ˌɑːr en ˈeɪ/ *noun* [U] (*chemistry* 化) a chemical present in all living cells; like DNA it is a type of NUCLEIC ACID 核糖核酸

roach /rəʊtʃ; *NAmE* roʊtʃ/ *noun* **1** (*NAmE, informal*) = COCKROACH: *The apartments were infested with rats and roaches.* 公寓里面到处都是老鼠和蟑螂。 **2** (*pl.* **roach**) a small European FRESHWATER fish 拟鲤（见于欧洲的淡水小鱼） **3** (*slang*) the end part of a cigarette containing MARIJUANA 大麻卷烟的烟蒂

road /rəʊd; *NAmE* roʊd/ *noun* **1** a hard surface built for vehicles to travel on 路；道路；公路： *a* **main/major/minor road** 公路干线；大路；支路 ◇ *a* **country/mountain road** 乡村道路；山路 ◇ *They live just* **along/up/down the road** (= further on the same road). 他们就住在这条路前面不远的地方。 ◇ *The house is on a very busy road.* 房子位于一条交通非常繁忙的公路旁边。 ◇ *He was walking* **along the road** *when he was attacked.* 他正在路边散步，突然遭到袭击。 ◇ *It takes about five hours* **by road** (= driving). 开车大约要花五个小时。 ◇ *It would be better to transport the goods by rail rather than* **by road**. 用铁路运送这批货物会比用公路好。 ◇ *Take the first road on the left and then follow the signs.* 走左边的第一条路，然后循着路标走。 ◇ *We parked on a* **side road**. 我们把车停放在岔道上。 ◇ **road accidents/safety/users** 公路交通事故 / 安全；道路使用者 ➲ WORDFINDER NOTE AT CAR

WORDFINDER 联想词: bypass, carriageway, diversion, hard shoulder, lane, lay-by, motorway, roundabout, signpost

2 Road (*abbr.* **Rd**) used in names of roads, especially in towns（用于道路名称，尤指城镇的）路： *35 York Road* 约克路 35 号 **3** the way to achieving sth 途径；方法；路子： *to be* **on the road to** *recovery* 正在恢复之中 ◇ *We have discussed privatization, but we would prefer not to* **go down** *that particular* **road**. 我们已经讨论了私有化问题，但不想采用这种方法。

IDM **ˈany road** (*NEngE*) = ANYWAY **(further) along/down the ˈroad** at some time in the future 今后；在将来： *There are certain to be more job losses further down the road.* 往后肯定会有更多人失业。 **one for the ˈroad** (*informal*) a last alcoholic drink before you leave a party, etc. 告辞前喝的最后一杯酒 **on the ˈroad 1** travelling, especially for long distances or periods of time 在途中；（尤指）长途旅行中： *The band has been on the road for six months.* 那支乐队巡回演出已有六个月了。 **2** (of a car 汽车) in good condition so that it can be legally driven （状况良好）可行驶： *It will cost about £500 to get the car back on the road.* 要花大约 500 英镑才能让车子重新上路。 **3** moving from place to place, and having no permanent home 居无定所；漂泊： *Life on the road can be very hard.* 流浪生活会非常艰辛。 **the road to ˌhell is paved with good inˈtentions** (*saying*) it is not enough to intend to do good things; you must actually do them 黄泉路上徒有好意多；光说不练是不够的 ➲ MORE AT END *n.*, HIT *v.*, KICK, RUBBER, SHOW *n.*

road·block /ˈrəʊdblɒk; *NAmE* ˈroʊdblɑːk/ *noun* **1** a barrier put across the road by the police or army so that they can stop and search vehicles 路障 **2** (*NAmE*) something that stops a plan from going ahead 障碍

ˈroad fund licence (*also* **ˈtax disc**) *noun* (in Britain) a small circle of paper that was put on the window of a

▼ MORE ABOUT ... 补充说明

roads 路

Roads and streets 公路和街道

- In a town or city, **street** is the most general word for a road with houses and buildings on one or both sides. 在城镇，street 为最宽泛的用语，指街道： *a street map of London* 伦敦街道图 **Street** is not used for roads between towns, but streets in towns are often called **Road**. * street 不用以指城镇间的道路，而城镇里的街道常称作 Road： *Oxford Street* 牛津街 ◇ *Mile End Road* 迈尔恩德路 A **road map** of a country shows you the major routes between, around and through towns and cities. 一个国家的公路交通图（road map）标有连接、环绕和穿越各城镇的主要路线。
- Other words used in the names of streets include: **Circle**, **Court**, **Crescent**, **Drive**, **Hill** and **Way**. **Avenue** suggests a wide street lined with trees. A **lane** is a narrow street between buildings or, in *BrE*, a narrow country road. 其他可用于街道名称的词有 Circle、Court、Crescent、Drive、Hill 和 Way。avenue 指宽阔的林荫道，lane 指建筑物间的小巷、胡同，或在英式英语中指乡村小路。

The high street 市镇商业大街

- **High street** is used in *BrE*, especially as a name, for the main street of a town, where most shops, banks, etc. are. * high street 用于英式英语，尤作商店、银行等集中的市镇商业大街名： *the record store in the High Street* 商业大街的唱片商店 ◇ *high street shops* 市镇大街的商店 In *NAmE* **Main Street** is often used as a name for this street. 在美式英语中，此义常用 Main Street 表示。

Larger roads 较宽大的公路

- British and American English use different words for the roads that connect towns and cities. **Motorways**, (for example, the M57) in *BrE*, **freeways**, **highways** or **interstates**, (for example State Route 347, Interstate 94, the Long Island Expressway) in *NAmE*, are large divided roads built for long-distance traffic to avoid towns. 表示连接城镇的公路时，英式英语和美式英语的用词各异。motorway 用于英式英语（如 57 高速路），freeway、highway 或 interstate 用于美式英语（如 347 州道、94 州际公路、长岛高速公路），它们均指城外分道行驶的长途高速公路。
- A **ring road** (*BrE*) / an **outer belt** (*NAmE*) is built around a city or town to reduce traffic in the centre. This can also be called a **beltway** in *NAmE*, especially when it refers to the road around Washington D.C. A **bypass** passes around a town or city rather than through the centre. * ring road（英式英语）/ outer belt（美式英语）指为减少市中心的交通流量修建的环城公路。在美式英语中亦可叫做 beltway，不过该词通常指华盛顿市的环城公路。bypass 指不穿越市中心，绕过城市的旁道。

vehicle or on a motorcycle to show that the owner had paid the tax that allows them to use the vehicle on public roads （英国）路税付讫证（过去贴在机动车上，表示已缴税，可上路行驶）

'road hog *noun* (*informal, disapproving*) a person who drives in a dangerous way without thinking about the safety of other road users 莽撞的司机

road·hold·ing /'rəʊdhəʊldɪŋ; *NAmE* 'roʊdhoʊldɪŋ/ *noun* [U] the ability of a car to remain steady when it goes around a corner at a fast speed （汽车快速拐弯时的）稳定性能；抓地力

road·house /'rəʊdhaʊs; *NAmE* 'roʊd-/ *noun* (*old-fashioned, NAmE*) a restaurant or bar on a main road in the country （郊外公路干线上的）路边旅馆，路边餐馆

roadie /'rəʊdi; *NAmE* 'roʊdi/ *noun* (*informal*) a person who works with a band of musicians on tour, and helps move and set up their equipment （乐队巡回演出时的）随团杂务人员

road·kill /'rəʊdkɪl; *NAmE* 'roʊd-/ *noun* **1** [U] an animal, or animals, that have been killed by a car on the road 路杀动物（在公路上被车撞死的动物） **2** [C, U] the killing of an animal by a car hitting it on the road 路杀（汽车在公路上撞死动物）

'road map *noun* **1** a map that shows the roads of an area, especially one that is designed for a person who is driving a car （尤指为开车者设计的）公路交通图 **2** a set of instructions or suggestions about how to do sth or find out about sth 指南

'road movie *noun* a film/movie which is based on a journey made by the main character or characters （基于主角等旅行经历的）公路电影

'road pricing *noun* [U] the system of making drivers pay to use busy roads at certain times （繁忙路段的）道路收费制度

'road rage *noun* [U] a situation in which a driver becomes extremely angry or violent with the driver of another car because of the way they are driving 公路暴怒（司机之间因驾驶问题而大动肝火）

road·run·ner /'rəʊdrʌnə(r); *NAmE* 'roʊd-/ *noun* a N American bird of the CUCKOO family, that lives in desert areas and can run very fast 走鹃（杜鹃属，见于北美）

'road sense *noun* [U] the ability to behave in a safe way when driving, walking, etc. on roads 交通安全意识；道路安全意识

road·show /'rəʊdʃəʊ; *NAmE* 'roʊdʃoʊ/ *noun* a travelling show arranged by a radio or television programme, or by a magazine, company or political party （电台、电视台、杂志或公司组织的）巡回演出，巡回广播，路演；（政党的）巡回宣传

road·side /'rəʊdsaɪd; *NAmE* 'roʊd-/ *noun* [sing.] the edge of the road 路边；路旁： *We parked by the roadside.* 我们将车停放在路旁。◇ *a roadside cafe* 路边咖啡店

'road sign *noun* a sign near a road giving information or instructions to drivers 路标 ➲ VISUAL VOCAB PAGE V3

road·ster /'rəʊdstə(r); *NAmE* 'roʊd-/ *noun* (*old-fashioned*) a car with no roof and two seats 敞篷双座小汽车

'road tax *noun* [U] (in Britain) a tax that sb who owns a car must pay to drive on the roads （英国）公路税 ➲ WORDFINDER NOTE AT CAR

'road test *noun* **1** a test to see how a vehicle functions or what condition it is in （车辆的）道路试验 **2** (*NAmE*) = DRIVING TEST

'road-test *verb* **~ sth** to test a vehicle to see how it functions or what condition it is in 使（车辆）经受道路试验

'road train *noun* (*especially AustralE*) a large lorry/truck pulling one or more TRAILERS 公路列车（挂一节或多节拖车的大货车）

'road trip *noun* (*informal, especially NAmE*) a trip made in a car over a long distance 开车长途旅行；公路旅行

road·way /'rəʊdweɪ; *NAmE* 'roʊd-/ *noun* [C, U] a road or the part of a road used by vehicles 道路；车行道

road·works /'rəʊdwɜːks; *NAmE* 'roʊdwɜːrks/ *noun* [pl.] (*BrE*) (*NAmE* **road·work** [U]) repairs that are being done to the road; an area where these repairs are being done 道路修补；修补中的路段 ➲ WORDFINDER NOTE AT TRAFFIC

road·worthy /'rəʊdwɜːði; *NAmE* 'roʊdwɜːrði/ *adj.* (of a vehicle 车辆) in a safe condition to drive 适合行驶的；可安全行驶的 ▸ **road·worthi·ness** *noun* [U]

roam /rəʊm; *NAmE* roʊm/ *verb* **1** [I, T] to walk or travel around an area without any definite aim or direction 徜徉；闲逛；漫步 SYN **wander**: (+ **adv./prep.**) *The sheep are allowed to roam freely on this land.* 绵羊可以在这片地上自由走动。◇ **~ sth** *to roam the countryside/the streets, etc.* 在乡间、街上等闲逛 **2** [I, T] (of the eyes or hands 眼

R

睛或手) to move slowly over every part of sb/sth（缓慢地）扫遍，摸遍：~ (over sth/sb) *His gaze roamed over her.* 他聚精会神地上下打量她。◇ ~ sth/sb *Her eyes roamed the room.* 她将房间打量了一遍。

roam·ing /ˈrəʊmɪŋ; NAmE ˈroʊ-/ *noun* [U] using a mobile/cell phone by connecting to a different company's network, for example when you are in a different country（移动电话的）漫游：*international roaming charges* 国际漫游费用

roan /rəʊn; NAmE roʊn/ *noun* an animal, especially a horse, that has hair of two colours mixed together 毛色斑杂的动物（尤指马）：*a strawberry roan* (= with a mixture of brown and grey hair that looks pink) 一匹红毛杂色马 ▶ **roan** *adj.* [only before noun]

roar /rɔː(r)/ *verb, noun*

■ *verb* **1** [I] to make a very loud, deep sound 吼叫；咆哮：*We heard a lion roar.* 我们听见了狮子的吼声。◇ *The gun roared deafeningly.* 枪炮轰鸣声震耳欲聋。◇ *The engine roared to life* (= started noisily). 发动机隆隆启动。**2** [I, T] to shout sth very loudly 叫喊；大声地说：*The crowd roared.* 人群一片喧哗。◇ ~ **sth** (**out**) *The fans roared (out) their approval.* 崇拜者大声叫好。◇ + **speech** *'Stand back,' he roared.* "靠后站。" 他吼道。**3** [I] to laugh very loudly 放声大笑：*He looked so funny, we all roared.* 他看上去那么滑稽，我们都哈哈大笑。◇ ~ **with laughter** *It made them roar with laughter.* 这使他们大笑起来。**4** [I] + **adv./prep.** (of a vehicle or its rider/driver 车辆或驾驶者) to move very fast, making a lot of noise 呼啸而行；开得飞快：*She put her foot down and the car roared away.* 她踩下油门，车子呼啸而去。**5** [I] (of a fire 火) to burn brightly with a lot of flames, heat and noise 熊熊燃烧 IDM SEE VICTORY

■ *noun* **1** a loud deep sound made by an animal, especially a LION, or by sb's voice 咆哮；吼叫：*His speech was greeted by a roar of applause.* 他的讲话引来了雷鸣般的掌声。◇ *roars of laughter* 阵阵大笑 **2** a loud continuous noise made by the wind or sea, or by a machine（风或海的）呼啸声；（机器的）隆隆声：*I could barely hear above the roar of traffic.* 除了车辆的轰鸣声，我几乎什么也听不见。

R

roar·ing /ˈrɔːrɪŋ/ *adj.* [only before noun] **1** making a continuous loud deep noise 咆哮的；呼啸的；轰鸣的：*All we could hear was the sound of roaring water.* 我们只能听到汹涌澎湃的涛声。**2** (of a fire 火) burning with a lot of flames and heat 熊熊燃烧的

IDM **do a 'roaring trade (in sth)** (*informal*) to sell a lot of sth very quickly 生意兴隆；售出大量（某物）**ˌroaring 'drunk** extremely drunk and noisy 耍酒疯 **a ˌroaring suc'cess** (*informal*) a very great success 巨大的成功

the ˌroaring 'forties *noun* [pl.] an area of rough ocean between LATITUDES 40° and 50° south 咆哮西风带（南纬 40 至 50 度之间盛行西风的海域）

the ˌroaring 'twenties *noun* [pl.] the years from 1920 to 1929, considered as a time when people were confident and cheerful 兴旺的二十年代（指人们自信又快乐的 20 世纪 20 年代）

roast /rəʊst; NAmE roʊst/ *verb, noun, adj.*

■ *verb* **1** [T, I] ~ (**sth**) to cook food, especially meat, without liquid in an oven or over a fire; to be cooked in this way 烘，烤，焙（肉等）：*to roast a chicken* 烤一只鸡 ◇ *the smell of roasting meat* 烤肉的香味 ➲ COLLOCATIONS AT COOKING **2** [T, I] ~ (**sth**) to cook nuts, BEANS, etc. in order to dry them and turn them brown; to be cooked in this way 烘烤，焙，炒（坚果、豆子等）：*roasted chestnuts* 炒栗子 **3** [T] ~ **sb** (*informal* or *humorous*) to be very angry with sb; to criticize sb strongly（对某人）非常生气，严厉批评 **4** [I, T] ~ (**sth**) (*informal*) to become or to make sth become very hot in the sun or by a fire 暴晒；烘烤：*She could feel her skin beginning to roast.* 她能感觉到皮肤开始晒得发烫了。

■ *noun* **1** (*BrE also* **joint**) a large piece of meat that is cooked whole in the oven 烤肉：*the Sunday roast* 星期日烤肉大餐 **2** (*NAmE*) (often in compounds 常构成复合词) a party that takes place in sb's garden/yard at which food is cooked over an open fire 户外烧烤野餐：*a hot dog roast* 热狗烧烤野餐 **3** (*NAmE*) an event, especially a meal, at which people celebrate sb's life by telling funny stories about them 耍笑庆祝会（常为宴会，讲述主角的滑稽事）

■ *adj.* [only before noun] cooked in an oven or over a fire 烤的；焙的：*roast chicken* 烧鸡

roast·ing /ˈrəʊstɪŋ; NAmE ˈroʊ-/ *adj., noun*

■ *adj.* **1** [only before noun] used for roasting meat, vegetables, etc. 用于烤炙（或烘焙）的：*a roasting dish* 用于烘烤的盘子 **2** (*also* **ˌroasting 'hot**) so hot that you feel uncomfortable 燥热的；灼热的：*a roasting hot day* 酷热的一天

■ *noun* [U, sing.] (*slang*) an occasion when a woman has sex with more than one man（一女多男的）乱交

IDM **give sb/get a 'roasting** to criticize sb or be criticized in an angry way 严厉批评；受到严厉批评

rob 🔑 /rɒb; NAmE rɑːb/ *verb* (**-bb-**) ~ **sb/sth** (**of sth**) to steal money or property from a person or place 抢劫；掠夺；盗取：*to* **rob a bank** 抢劫银行 ◇ *The tomb had been robbed of its treasures.* 这座坟墓里的财宝早已被盗。➲ COLLOCATIONS AT CRIME

IDM **ˌrob sb 'blind** (*informal*) to cheat or trick sb so that they lose a lot of money 骗取某人大量钱财 **ˌrob the 'cradle** (*NAmE, informal*) to have a sexual relationship with a much younger person 老牛吃嫩草（指跟比自己年龄小很多的人发生性关系）**rob ˌPeter to pay 'Paul** (*saying*) to borrow money from one person to pay back what you owe to another person; to take money from one thing to use for sth else 借新债还旧账；拆东墙补西墙

PHR V **'rob sb/sth of sth** [often passive] to prevent sb having sth that they need or deserve 剥夺（某人所需或应得之物）SYN **deprive**：*A last-minute goal robbed the team of victory.* 最后一分钟的进球夺去了这支球队取胜的机会。◇ *He had been robbed of his dignity.* 他已失去了尊严。

rob·ber /ˈrɒbə(r); NAmE ˈrɑːb-/ *noun* a person who steals from a person or place, especially using violence or threats 强盗；盗贼；抢劫犯：*a bank robber* 银行抢劫犯

rob·bery /ˈrɒbəri; NAmE ˈrɑːb-/ *noun* [U, C] (*pl.* **-ies**) the crime of stealing money or goods from a bank, shop/store, person, etc., especially using violence or threats 盗窃；抢劫；掠夺：*armed robbery* (= using a gun, knife, etc.) 持械抢劫 ◇ *There has been a spate of robberies in the area recently.* 最近这一地区接连发生了多起抢劫案。➲ COLLOCATIONS AT CRIME ➲ COMPARE BURGLARY, THEFT IDM SEE DAYLIGHT, HIGHWAY

robe /rəʊb; NAmE roʊb/ *noun, verb*

■ *noun* **1** a long loose outer piece of clothing, especially one worn as a sign of rank or office at a special ceremony 袍服，礼袍（常于典礼中穿着以显示身份）：*coronation robes* 加冕礼袍 ◇ *cardinals in scarlet robes* 身披红袍的枢机主教 **2** = BATHROBE

■ *verb* [usually passive] ~ **sb/yourself** (**in sth**) (*formal*) to dress sb/yourself in long loose clothes or in the way mentioned（给某人）穿上礼袍：*a robed choir* 身着礼袍的唱诗班 ◇ *The priests were robed in black.* 各司祭都穿上了黑袍。

robin /ˈrɒbɪn; NAmE ˈrɑːb-/ *noun* **1** a small brown European bird with a red breast 欧亚鸲；欧洲知更鸟 **2** a grey American bird with a red breast, larger than a European robin 旅鸫，美洲知更鸟（毛灰色，胸部红色，比欧亚鸲大）➲ SEE ALSO ROUND ROBIN

ˌRobin 'Hood *noun* a person who takes or steals money from rich people and gives it to poor people 罗宾汉；劫富济贫者 ➲ MORE LIKE THIS 16, page R27 ORIGIN From the name of a character in traditional English stories who lived in a forest, robbing rich people and giving money to poor people. 源自英格兰民间传说中劫富济贫的绿林好汉罗宾汉。

robo·call /ˈrəʊbəʊkɔːl; NAmE ˈroʊboʊ-/ *noun* (*NAmE, informal, disapproving*) a phone call from a company that is trying to sell you sth, using an automatic DIALLING system to call your number and a recorded message

机器人电话（自动拨号播放录音信息的推销电话） MORE LIKE THIS 1, page R25

robot /ˈrəʊbɒt; *NAmE* ˈroʊbɑːt/ *noun* **1** a machine that can perform a complicated series of tasks automatically 机器人：*These cars are built by robots.* 这些汽车是由机器人制造的。 **2** (especially in stories) a machine that is made to look like a human and that can do some things that a human can do（尤指故事中的）机器人 **3** (*SAfrE*) a TRAFFIC LIGHT 交通信号灯：*Turn left at the first robot.* 在第一个交通信号灯处向左拐。

ro·bot·ic /rəʊˈbɒtɪk; *NAmE* roʊˈbɑːtɪk/ *adj.* **1** connected with robots 机器人的：*a robotic arm* 机械臂 **2** like a robot, making stiff movements, speaking without feeling or expression, etc. 像机器人的；呆板机械的

ro·bot·ics /rəʊˈbɒtɪks; *NAmE* roʊˈbɑːt-/ *noun* [U] the science of designing and operating ROBOTS 机器人科学（或技术）

ro·bust /rəʊˈbʌst; *NAmE* roʊ-/ *adj.* **1** strong and healthy 强健的；强壮的：*She was almost 90, but still very robust.* 她将近 90 岁了，但身体仍然十分强健。 **2** strong; able to survive being used a lot and not likely to break 结实的；耐用的；坚固的 SYN **sturdy**：*a robust piece of equipment* 经久耐用的设备 **3** (of a system or an organization 体制或机构) strong and not likely to fail or become weak 强劲的；富有活力的：*robust economic growth* 强劲的经济增长 **4** strong and full of determination; showing that you are sure about what you are doing or saying 坚定的；信心十足的 SYN **vigorous**：*It was a typically robust performance by the Foreign Secretary.* 这是外交大臣典型的有信心的表现。 ▶ **ro·bust·ly** *adv.*：*The furniture was robustly constructed.* 家具做得非常结实。 ◇ *They defended their policies robustly.* 他们坚定地捍卫自己的政策。 **ro·bust·ness** *noun* [U]

rock /rɒk; *NAmE* rɑːk/ *noun, verb*

■ ***noun***

• **HARD MATERIAL** 硬物 **1** [U, C] the hard solid material that forms part of the surface of the earth and some other planets 岩石：*They drilled through several layers of rock to reach the oil.* 他们钻透了几层岩石寻找石油。 ◇ *a cave with striking **rock formations*** (= shapes made naturally from rock) 有奇妙天然岩石造型的洞穴 ◇ *The tunnel was blasted out of solid rock.* 这条隧道是在坚固的岩石中炸出来的。 ◇ ***volcanic/igneous/sedimentary, etc. rocks*** 火山岩、火成岩、沉积岩等 **2** [C] a mass of rock standing above the earth's surface or in the sea/ocean 石山；礁石：*the Rock of Gibraltar* 直布罗陀山 ◇ *The ship crashed into the infamous Sker Point rocks and broke into three pieces.* 这艘船撞上了恶名远扬的斯戈尔尖岬暗礁群，断为三截。 VISUAL VOCAB PAGE V5 **3** [C] a large single piece of rock 巨石块；岩块：*They clambered over the rocks at the foot of the cliff.* 他们吃力地爬过了绝壁脚下的巨石。 ◇ *The sign said 'Danger: falling rocks'.* 警示牌上写着"危险：前有落石"。

• **STONE** 石头 **4** [C] (*NAmE*) a small stone 碎石；石子；小石块：*Protesters pelted the soldiers with rocks.* 抗议者向士兵投掷石块。

• **MUSIC** 音乐 **5** (*also* ˈ**rock music**) [U] a type of loud popular music, developed in the 1960s, with a strong beat played on electric GUITARS and drums 摇滚乐：*punk rock* 朋克摇滚乐 ◇ ***a rock band/star*** 摇滚乐队 / 明星

• **SWEET/CANDY** 糖果 **6** (*BrE*) [U] a type of hard sweet/candy made in long sticks, often sold in places where people go on holiday/vacation by the sea/ocean 棒棒糖：*a stick of Brighton rock* 一支布赖顿棒棒糖

• **JEWEL** 宝石 **7** [C, usually pl.] (*NAmE, informal*) a PRECIOUS STONE, especially a diamond 宝石；（尤指）钻石

• **PERSON** 人 **8** [C, usually sing.] a person who is emotionally strong and who you can rely on 可信赖的人；靠山：*He is my rock.* 他是我的主心骨。

IDM **(caught/stuck) between a ˌrock and a ˈhard place** in a situation where you have to choose between two things, both of which are unpleasant 进退两难；左右为难 **get your ˈrocks off** (*slang*) **1** to have an ORGASM 达到性高潮 **2** to do sth that you really enjoy 做自己真正喜欢的事；享受 **on the ˈrocks 1** a relationship or business that is **on the rocks** is having difficulties and is likely to fail soon（关系或生意）陷于困境，濒临崩溃：*Sue's marriage is on the rocks.* 休的婚姻触礁了。 **2** (of drinks 饮料) served with pieces of ice but no water 加冰块（但不加水）的：*Scotch on the rocks* 加冰块的苏格兰威士忌酒 MORE AT STEADY *adj.*

■ ***verb***

• **MOVE GENTLY** 轻轻移动 **1** [I, T] to move gently backwards and forwards or from side to side; to make sb/sth move in this way（使）轻轻摇晃，缓缓摆动：(**+ adv./prep.**) *The boat **rocked from side to side** in the waves.* 小船在波浪中摇荡。 ◇ *She was **rocking backwards and forwards** in her seat.* 她在座位上前摇后晃。 ◇ **~ sb/sth (+ adv./prep.)** *He rocked the baby gently in his arms.* 他抱着孩子轻轻摇晃。

• **SHOCK** 惊吓 **2** [T, often passive] **~ sb/sth** (*rather informal*) to shock sb/sth very much or make them afraid 惊吓；使震惊；使害怕：*The country was rocked by a series of political scandals.* 一连串的政治丑闻震惊全国。 ◇ *The news rocked the world.* 这则消息震惊了全世界。

• **SHAKE** 摇动 **3** [I, T] to shake or to make sth shake violently（使）剧烈摇摆，猛烈晃动：*The house rocked when the bomb exploded.* 炸弹爆炸时，房子都晃动了。 ◇ **~ sth** *The town was rocked by an earthquake.* 小镇受到地震的剧烈震动。 ◇ (*figurative*) *The scandal rocked the government* (= made the situation difficult for it). 丑闻使政府处境艰难。

• **DANCE** 舞蹈 **4** [I] (*old-fashioned*) to dance to rock music 随摇滚乐跳舞；跳摇滚

• **BE GOOD** 好 **5 sth rocks** [I] (*slang*) used to say that sth is very good 很好；棒极了：*Her new movie rocks!* 她的新电影棒极了！

• **FASHION** 时尚 **6** (*informal*) **~ sth** to wear sth or have a style of clothing, hair, etc. that makes you look attractive or confident 穿…服装，梳…发型（以彰显魅力）：*How to rock the retro look.* 如何装扮复古风。 ◇ *She rocked a red leather skirt at the award ceremony.* 她在颁奖典礼上穿了一条红色的皮裙，艳丽动人。

IDM **rock the ˈboat** (*informal*) to do sth that upsets a situation and causes problems 捣乱；惹麻烦：*She was told to keep her mouth shut and not rock the boat.* 有人叫她闭嘴，不要招惹是非。 MORE AT FOUNDATION

PHR V **rock ˈout** to perform or dance to rock music loudly and with a lot of energy 活力四射地表演摇滚乐；伴着摇滚乐曲劲舞

rocka·billy /ˈrɒkəbɪli; *NAmE* ˈrɑːk-/ *noun* [U] a type of American music that combines ROCK AND ROLL and country music 乡村摇滚乐（融合了摇滚乐和乡村音乐的美国音乐）

ˌrock and ˈroll (*also* **ˌrock ʼn' ˈroll**) *noun* [U] a type of music popular in the 1950s with a strong beat and simple tunes 摇滚乐

ˌrock ˈbottom *noun* [U] (*informal*) the lowest point or level that is possible 最低点；最低水平：*Prices hit rock bottom.* 价格降到了最低点。 ◇ *The marriage had reached rock bottom.* 婚姻已经走到了尽头。 ▶ **ˌrock-ˈbottom** *adj.*：*rock-bottom prices* 最低价格

ˈrock cake *noun* (*BrE*) a small cake that has a hard rough surface and contains dried fruit 岩皮饼；干果岩皮蛋糕

ˌrock ˈcandy *noun* [U] (*NAmE*) a type of hard sweet/candy made from sugar that is melted then allowed to form CRYSTALS 透明硬糖；冰糖

ˈrock climbing *noun* [U] the sport or activity of climbing steep rock surfaces 攀岩（运动）：*to go rock climbing* 去攀岩

ˈrock crystal *noun* [U] a pure clear form of QUARTZ (= a hard mineral) 水晶

rock·er /ˈrɒkə(r); *NAmE* ˈrɑːk-/ *noun* **1** one of the two curved pieces of wood on the bottom of a rocking chair（摇椅底部的）弧形摇杆 **2** (*especially NAmE*) = ROCKING CHAIR **3 Rocker** (*BrE*) a member of a group of young people in Britain, especially in the 1960s, who liked to wear leather jackets, ride motorcycles and listen to

R

ROCK AND ROLL music 摇滚青年（尤指 20 世纪 60 年代的某些英国青年，喜欢穿皮夹克、骑摩托车、听摇滚乐）➲ COMPARE MOD **4** a person who performs, dances to or enjoys rock music 摇滚乐表演者；跳摇滚舞的人；喜欢摇滚乐的人

IDM **be ˌoff your ˈrocker** (*informal*) to be crazy 发疯；疯狂

ˈrocker switch *noun* (*specialist*) a type of electrical switch often used, for example, for lights or electrical SOCKETS, where you press one end down to switch it on, and the other end down to switch it off again 翘板开关；摇杆开关

rock·ery /ˈrɒkəri; *NAmE* ˈrɑːk-/ *noun* (*pl.* **-ies**) (*also* **ˈrock garden**) a garden or part of a garden consisting of an arrangement of large stones with plants growing among them 假山花园；假山

rocket /ˈrɒkɪt; *NAmE* ˈrɑːkɪt/ *noun, verb*

■ *noun* **1** [C] a SPACECRAFT in the shape of a tube that is driven by a stream of gases let out behind it when fuel is burned inside 火箭：*a **space rocket*** 太空火箭 ◇ *The **rocket was launched** in 2007.* 这枚火箭发射于 2007 年。◇ *The idea **took off like a rocket*** (= it immediately became popular). 这种思想立即风靡一时。➲ WORDFINDER NOTE AT SPACE **2** [C] a MISSILE (= a weapon that travels through the air) that carries a bomb and is driven by a stream of burning gases 火箭武器；火箭（弹）：*a rocket attack* 火箭攻击 **3** [C] a FIREWORK that goes high into the air and then explodes with coloured lights 焰火；烟花 **4** [U] (*BrE*) (*NAmE* **aru·gula**) a plant with long green leaves that have a strong flavour and are eaten raw in salads 大蒜芥；芝麻菜；紫花南芥

IDM **to give sb a ˈrocket | to get a ˈrocket** (*BrE, informal*) to speak angrily to sb because they have done sth wrong; to be spoken to angrily for this reason（受到）痛骂，斥责

■ *verb* **1** [I] (+ **adv./prep.**) to increase very quickly and suddenly 快速增长；猛增 SYN **shoot up**：*rocketing prices* 飞涨的价格 ◇ *Unemployment has rocketed up again.* 失业人数再次猛增。◇ *The total has rocketed from 376 to 532.* 总数从 376 猛增到 532。 **2** [I] + **adv./prep.** to move very fast 迅速移动：*The car rocketed out of a side street.* 汽车从一条小路上嗖的一下开了出来。 **3** [I, T] to achieve or to make sb/sth achieve a successful position very quickly （使）迅速成功，迅速提高地位：~ **(sb/sth) to sth** *The band rocketed to stardom with their first single.* 这支乐队的第一首单曲使他们一举成名。 **4** [T] ~ **sth** to attack a place with rockets 用火箭弹攻击

ˈrocket-fuelled (*US* **ˈrocket-fueled**) *adj.* [only before noun] happening, moving or increasing very fast 急剧发生的；急速移动的；飞涨的：*There are already signs of rocket-fuelled growth.* 已经出现迅猛增长的迹象。

rock·et·ry /ˈrɒkɪtri; *NAmE* ˈrɑːk-/ *noun* [U] the area of science which deals with ROCKETS and with sending rockets into space; the use of rockets 火箭学；火箭技术

ˈrocket science *noun* [U]

IDM **it's not ˈrocket science** (*informal*) used to emphasize that sth is easy to do or understand 并非难事；不是很复杂 SYN **brain surgery**：*Go on, you can do it. It's not exactly rocket science, is it?* 继续干，你能做得到的。这并非难事，对吧？

ˈrock face *noun* a vertical surface of rock, especially on a mountain （尤指山体的）岩壁，崖面

rock·fall /ˈrɒkfɔːl; *NAmE* ˈrɑːk-/ *noun* the fact of rocks falling down; a pile of rocks that have fallen 岩崩；落石

ˈrock garden *noun* = ROCKERY

ˌrock-ˈhard *adj.* extremely hard or strong 极其坚硬的；极结实的

ˈrocking chair (*also* **rock·er** *especially in NAmE*) *noun* a chair with two curved pieces of wood under it that make it move backwards and forwards 摇椅 ➲ VISUAL VOCAB PAGE V22

ˈrocking horse *noun* a wooden horse for children that can be made to ROCK backwards and forwards（儿童游戏用的）木马 ➲ VISUAL VOCAB PAGE V41

ˈrock music *noun* = ROCK (5)

rock 'n' roll *noun* = ROCK AND ROLL

the Rock of Gibraltar /ˌrɒk əv dʒɪˈbrɔːltə(r); *NAmE* ˌrɑːk/ *noun* [sing.] a high CLIFF at the south-western edge of the Mediterranean Sea, near the town and port of Gibraltar. When people say that sth is like the Rock of Gibraltar, they mean it is very safe or solid. 直布罗陀巨岩，磐石山（位于地中海西南端直布罗陀港城附近的一处悬崖，象征十分安全或坚如磐石）：*When I invested my money with the company I was told it was as safe as the Rock of Gibraltar.* 我投资这家公司时，他们说它像直布罗陀巨岩一样可靠。

ˈrock pool (*BrE*) (*NAmE* **ˈtide pool**) *noun* a small amount of water that collects between the rocks by the sea/ocean（海边）岩石区潮水潭 ➲ VISUAL VOCAB PAGE V5

ˈrock salt *noun* [U] a kind of salt that comes from the ground 岩盐；石盐

ˌrock ˈsolid *adj.* **1** that you can trust not to change or to disappear 稳固的；坚实的；可信赖的：*The support for the party was rock solid.* 这一政党得到了坚定的支持。 **2** extremely hard and not likely to break 坚硬的；不会碎的

rocky /ˈrɒki; *NAmE* ˈrɑːki/ *adj.* (**rock·ier, rocki·est**) **1** made of rock; full of rocks 岩石的；多岩石的：*a rocky coastline* 岩石嶙峋的海岸线 ◇ *rocky soil* 多石的土壤 **2** difficult and not certain to continue or to be successful 困难的；难以维持的；不稳定的：*a rocky marriage* 不稳定的婚姻

ro·coco /rəˈkəʊkəʊ; *NAmE* rəˈkoʊkoʊ/ (*also* **Rococo**) *adj.* used to describe a style of ARCHITECTURE, furniture, etc. that has a lot of decoration, especially in the shape of curls; used to describe a style of literature or music that has a lot of detail and decoration. The rococo style was popular in the 18th century. 洛可可式的，过分修饰的（用以描述装饰精巧的建筑、家具等，以及描写细腻入微的文学、音乐风格。洛可可风格盛行于 18 世纪）

rod /rɒd; *NAmE* rɑːd/ *noun* **1** (often used in compounds 常用于构成复合词) a long straight piece of wood, metal or glass 杆；竿；棒 ➲ VISUAL VOCAB PAGES V22, V72 ➲ SEE ALSO LIGHTNING ROD (1) **2** = FISHING ROD：*fishing with rod and line* 用鱼竿钓鱼 ➲ WORDFINDER NOTE AT FISHING **3** (*also* **the rod**) (*old-fashioned*) a stick that is used for hitting people as a punishment （责打人用的）棍棒：*There used to be a saying: 'Spare the rod and spoil the child.'* 老话说："孩子不打不成器。" **4** (*NAmE, slang*) a small gun 手枪

IDM **make a rod for your own ˈback** to do sth that will cause problems for you in the future 自找麻烦；自讨苦吃 ➲ MORE AT BEAT *v.*, RULE *v.*

rode PAST TENSE OF RIDE

ro·dent /ˈrəʊdnt; *NAmE* ˈroʊ-/ *noun* any small animal that belongs to a group of animals with strong sharp front teeth. Mice, RATS and SQUIRRELS are all rodents. 啮齿动物 ➲ VISUAL VOCAB PAGE V12

rodeo /ˈrəʊdiəʊ; rəʊˈdeɪəʊ; *NAmE* ˈroʊdioʊ; roʊˈdeɪoʊ/ *noun* (*pl.* **-os**) a public competition, especially in the US, in which people show their skill at riding wild horses and catching CATTLE with ropes（尤指美国的）牛仔竞技比赛

roe /rəʊ; *NAmE* roʊ/ *noun* **1** [U, C] the mass of eggs inside a female fish (**hard roe**) or the SPERM of a male fish (**soft roe**), used as food 鱼子：*cod's roe* 鳕鱼子 **2** = ROE DEER

ˈroe deer *noun* (*pl.* **roe deer**) (*also* **roe**) a small European and Asian DEER 狍（一种产于欧亚的小鹿）

roent·gen /ˈrɜːntjən; ˈrɒnt-; -gən; *NAmE* ˈrentjən; ˈrʌnt-; -dʒən/ *noun* (*physics* 物) (*abbr.* **R**) a unit of RADIATION, used to measure the quantity of X-RAYS or GAMMA RAYS that have reached sb/sth 伦琴（辐射单位）

roent·gen·ium /ˌrɒntˈɡiːniəm; *NAmE* ˌrent-/ *noun* [U] (*symb.* **Rg**) a chemical element. Roentgenium is a RADIOACTIVE element that is produced artificially and has no known use. 轮（一种人工合成的放射性化学元素）

ROFL (*also* **ROTFL**) *abbr.* (*informal*) (especially in TEXT MESSAGES, emails, etc.) roll(ing) on the floor laughing (used to show that you find sth extremely funny) 笑得在地上打滚，笑翻（全写为 roll(ing) on the floor laughing，尤用于短信、电邮等）：*He did the funniest dance I've ever seen. ROFL.* 他跳的舞是我见过最滑稽的。笑翻了。➲ COMPARE LOL

roger /ˈrɒdʒə(r); *NAmE* ˈrɑːdʒ-/ *exclamation, verb*
■ ***exclamation*** people say **Roger!** in communication by radio to show that they have understood a message（用于无线电通信，表示已听懂信息）信息收到，明白
■ ***verb*** **~ sb** (*BrE, taboo, slang*) (of a man 男子) to have sex with sb 与某人性交

rogue /rəʊɡ; *NAmE* roʊɡ/ *noun, adj.*
■ ***noun*** **1** (*humorous*) a person who behaves badly, but in a harmless way 无赖；捣蛋鬼 SYN **scoundrel**: *He's a bit of a rogue, but very charming.* 他好捣蛋，但却很讨人喜欢。**2** (*old-fashioned*) a man who is dishonest and immoral 骗子；恶棍；流氓 SYN **rascal**: *a **rogues' gallery*** (= a collection of pictures of criminals) 案犯相片集
■ ***adj.*** [only before noun] **1** (of an animal 动物) living apart from the main group, and possibly dangerous 离群的 **2** behaving in a different way from other similar people or things, often causing damage 行为失常的；暴戾的：*a rogue gene* 变异基因 ◇ *a rogue police officer* 暴戾的警察 ➲ MORE LIKE THIS 20, page R27, 32, page R28

roguish /ˈrəʊɡɪʃ; *NAmE* ˈroʊ-/ *adj.* (*usually approving*) (of a person 人) pleasant and amusing but looking as if they might do sth wrong 调皮捣蛋的；顽皮的：*a roguish smile* 顽皮的微笑 ▶ **roguish·ly** *adv.*

Ro·hyp·nol™ /rəʊˈhɪpnɒl; *NAmE* roʊˈhɪpnɑːl/ *noun* [U] a drug that makes you want to sleep, and which can make you unable to remember what happens for a period after you take it 洛喜普诺，罗眠乐（强效安眠药，服后可致暂时失忆）

roil /rɔɪl/ **1** (*NAmE*) = RILE **2** [I, T] (*literary, formal*) (of a liquid, cloud, surface, etc.) to move quickly and violently in different directions; to make a liquid, cloud, surface, etc. move quickly and violently in different directions （使）动荡，翻腾；搅动：(*figurative*) *The collapse of the mortgage sector has roiled markets.* 按揭贷款业崩溃搅乱了市场。▶ **roiling** *adj.*：*the roiling sea* 波翻浪涌的大海

rois·ter·ing /ˈrɔɪstərɪŋ/ *adj.* (*old-fashioned*) having fun in a cheerful, noisy way 喧闹作乐的

roko /ˈrəʊkəʊ; *NAmE* ˈroʊkoʊ/ *noun* (*IndE*) a public meeting or march at which people show that they are protesting against or supporting sb/sth, especially one that involves blocking a railway or road（尤指阻断铁路或公路交通的）公众集会示威（或游行）：*Activists staged a rail roko to protest against the minister's decision.* 活动人士组织了阻断铁路集会，抗议部长的决定。

role 🔑 AW /rəʊl; *NAmE* roʊl/ *noun* **1** 🔑 the function or position that sb has or is expected to have in an organization, in society or in a relationship 职能；地位；角色：*the role of the teacher in the classroom* 教师在课堂上的作用 ◇ *She refused to take on the traditional woman's role.* 她拒绝承担传统妇女的角色。◇ *In many marriages there has been a complete **role reversal*** (= change of roles) *with the man staying at home and the woman going out to work.* 许多夫妻彻底交换了角色，男人待在家里而女人出外工作。**2** 🔑 an actor's part in a play, film/movie, etc.（演员的）角色：*It is one of the greatest roles she has played.* 这是她所扮演过的最重要的角色之一。◇ *Who is in the **leading role*** (= the most important one)? 谁扮演主角？➲ WORDFINDER NOTE AT ACTOR, PLAY ➲ COLLOCATIONS AT CINEMA **3** 🔑 the degree to which sb/sth is involved in a situation or an activity and the effect that they have on it 影响程度；作用：*the role of diet in preventing disease* 饮食在预防疾病中的作用 ◇ *The media play a **major role** in influencing people's opinions.* 媒体在影响舆论方面发挥着重要作用。◇ *a **key/vital role*** 关键 / 至关重要的作用

ˈrole model *noun* a person that you admire and try to copy 楷模；行为榜样

ˈrole-play *noun* a learning activity in which you behave in the way sb else would behave in a particular situation 角色扮演：*Role-play allows students to practise language in a safe situation.* 角色扮演可以使学生练习语言，说错了也没关系。▶ **ˈrole-play** *verb* [I, T] **~ (sth)**

ˈrole-playing game *noun* (*abbr.* **RPG**) a game in which players pretend to be imaginary characters who take part in adventures, especially in situations from FANTASY literature 角色扮演游戏（参加者假扮成幻想作品等中的虚构人物进行冒险）

rolls 卷

toilet roll (*BrE*)
roll of toilet paper
卫生纸卷

bread rolls
小圆面包

roll of tape
一卷胶带

roll 🔑 /rəʊl; *NAmE* roʊl/ *noun, verb*
■ ***noun***
• OF PAPER/CLOTH, ETC. 纸、织物等 **1** 🔑 [C] **~ (of sth)** a long piece of paper, cloth, film, etc. that has been wrapped around itself or a tube several times so that it forms the shape of a tube 卷；卷轴：*a roll of film* 一卷胶卷 ◇ *Wallpaper is sold in rolls.* 壁纸论卷销售。➲ VISUAL VOCAB PAGE V36 ➲ SEE ALSO TOILET ROLL
• OF SWEETS/CANDY 糖果 **2** 🔑 [C] **~ (of sth)** (*NAmE*) a paper tube wrapped around sweets/candy, etc. 一管：*a roll of mints* 一管薄荷糖 ➲ VISUAL VOCAB PAGE V36
• BREAD 面包 **3** 🔑 (*also* ˌbread ˈroll) [C] a small LOAF of bread for one person 小面包条；小圆面包：*Soup and a roll: £3.50* 汤和一小条面包：3.50 英镑 ◇ *a **chicken/cheese, etc. roll*** (= filled with chicken/cheese, etc.) 鸡肉卷、奶酪卷等 ➲ COMPARE BUN (2) ➲ SEE ALSO SAUSAGE ROLL, SPRING ROLL, SWISS ROLL
• OF BODY 身体 **4** [sing.] an act of rolling the body over and over 翻滚；打滚：*The kittens were enjoying a roll in the sunshine.* 那些小猫在阳光下嬉戏打滚。**5** [C] a physical exercise in which you roll your body on the ground, moving your back and legs over your head 滚翻；翻跟头：*a **forward/backward roll*** 前 / 后滚翻
• OF SHIP/PLANE 船只；飞机 **6** [U] the act of moving from side to side so that one side is higher than the other 摇晃；摇荡 ➲ COMPARE PITCH *n.* (8)
• OF FAT 脂肪 **7** [C] an area of too much fat on your body, especially around your waist 脂肪堆积的部位，肥胖的部位（尤指腰部）：*Rolls of fat hung over his belt.* 一堆肥肉坠在他的腰带上。
• LIST OF NAMES 名单 **8** [C] an official list of names 花名册；名单：*the **electoral roll*** (= a list of all the people who can vote in an election) 选民名册 ◇ *The chairman **called/took the roll*** (= called out the names on a list to check that everyone was present). 主席点了名。➲ SEE ALSO PAYROLL (1)
• SOUND 声音 **9** [C] **~ (of sth)** a deep continuous sound 隆隆声；持续的轰鸣声：*the distant roll of thunder* 远处隆隆的雷声 ◇ *a drum roll* 咚咚的鼓声
• OF DICE 骰子 **10** [C] an act of rolling a DICE 掷骰子：*The order of play is decided by the roll of a dice.* 比赛顺序是通过掷骰子决定的。

R

• **PHONETICS** 语音学 **11** = TRILL (3)

IDM **be on a 'roll** (*informal*) to be experiencing a period of success at what you are doing 连连获胜；连续交好运： *Don't stop me now—I'm on a roll!* 现在别阻止我，我正鸿运当头呢！ **a ˌroll in the 'hay** (*informal*) an act of having sex with sb 性交

■ ***verb***

• **TURN OVER** 翻转 **1** 🔑[I, T] to turn over and over and move in a particular direction; to make a round object do this （使）翻滚，滚动： **+ adv./prep.** *The ball rolled down the hill.* 球滚下了山。◇ *We watched the waves rolling onto the beach.* 我们望着波浪涌向海滩。◇ **~ sth + adv./prep.** *Delivery men were rolling barrels across the yard.* 送货人正把桶滚到院子另一边。 **2** 🔑[I, T] to turn over and over or round and round while remaining in the same place; to make sth do this （使）原地转圈，原地打转： **(+ adv./prep.)** *a dog rolling in the mud* 在泥浆里打滚的狗 ◇ *Her eyes rolled.* 她那双眼睛滴溜溜地转动。 ◇ **~ sth (+ adv./prep.)** *She* ***rolled her eyes*** *upwards* (= to show surprise or disapproval). 她翻了翻白眼。◇ *He was rolling a pencil between his fingers.* 他用手指捻动着铅笔。 **3** 🔑[I, T] **~ (sb/sth) over (onto sth) | ~ (sb/sth) (over) onto sth** to turn over to face a different direction; to make sb/sth do this （使）翻身，翻转： **~ over (onto sth)** *She rolled over to let the sun brown her back.* 她翻了个身，让太阳把她的背晒成古铜色。◇ **~ onto sth** *He rolled onto his back.* 他翻过身来仰面躺着。 ◇ **~ sb/sth (over) (onto sth)** *I rolled the baby over onto its stomach.* 我让婴儿翻过身去趴着。 ◇ *to* ***roll a dice/die*** (= in a game) 掷骰子 ◇ (*especially NAmE*) *She rolled her car in a 100 mph crash.* 她在时速 100 英里时翻了车。

• **MOVE (AS IF) ON WHEELS** 滚动 **4** 🔑[I, T] to move smoothly (on wheels or as if on wheels); to make sth do this （使）滚动： **(+ adv./prep.)** *The car began to roll back down the hill.* 汽车开始倒着往山下滑。◇ *The traffic rolled slowly forwards.* 车流缓缓地向前挪动。◇ *Mist was rolling in from the sea.* 薄雾从海上涌来。 ◇ **~ sth (+ adv./prep.)** *He rolled the trolley across the room.* 他推着手推车穿过房间。

• **MAKE BALL/TUBE** 做成球 / 管 **5** 🔑[T, I] **~ (sth) (up) (into sth)** to make sth/yourself into the shape of a ball or tube 使…成球状（或管状）： *I rolled the string into a ball.* 我把线绳儿绕成了一个球。◇ *We rolled up the carpet.* 我们把地毯卷了起来。◇ *a rolled-up newspaper* 卷成卷的报纸 ◇ *I always* ***roll my own*** (= make my own cigarettes). 我总是自己卷烟抽。◇ *The hedgehog rolled up into a ball.* 刺猬团成了一个球。 ➔ COMPARE UNROLL (1)

• **FOLD CLOTHING** 叠衣服 **6** 🔑[T] to fold the edge of a piece of clothing, etc. over and over on itself to make it shorter 把（衣服的边）卷起来： **~ sth up** *Roll up your sleeves.* 把你的袖子挽起来。◇ **~ sth + adv./prep.** *She rolled her jeans to her knees.* 她把牛仔裤卷到了膝盖处。 ➔ VISUAL VOCAB PAGE V66

• **MAKE STH FLAT** 使平坦 **7** [T] **~ sth (out)** to make sth flat by pushing sth heavy over it 使平坦；压平： *Roll the pastry on a floured surface.* 在撒了面粉的面板上将油酥面团擀平。

• **WRAP UP** 包裹 **8** [T] **~ sb/sth/yourself (up) in sth** to wrap or cover sb/sth/yourself in sth （用某物）包裹，覆盖： *Roll the meat in the breadcrumbs.* 用面包屑将肉裹起来。◇ *He rolled himself up in the blanket.* 他把自己裹在毯子里。

• **OF SHIP/PLANE/WALK** 船只；飞机；行走 **9** [I, T] **~ (sth) (+ adv./prep.)** to move or make sth move from side to side （使）摇摆，摇晃： *He walked with a rolling gait.* 他摇摇晃晃地走着。◇ *The ship was rolling heavily to and fro.* 轮船剧烈地颠簸着。 ➔ COMPARE PITCH *v.* (6)

• **MAKE SOUND** 发出声音 **10** [I, T] to make a long continuous sound 发出持续的声音： *rolling drums* 咚咚的鼓声 ◇ *Thunder rolled.* 雷声隆隆。◇ **~ sth** *to* ***roll your r's*** (= by letting your tongue VIBRATE with each 'r' sound) 发 r 的舌尖颤音

• **MACHINE** 机器 **11** [I, T] when a machine **rolls** or sb **rolls** it, it operates 启动；开动： *They had to repeat the scene because the cameras weren't rolling.* 他们只好重新拍摄这个镜头，因为摄影机没有启动。◇ **~ sth** *Roll the cameras!* 开拍！

IDM **be 'rolling in money/it** (*informal*) to have a lot of money 非常富有；财源滚滚；腰缠万贯 **let's 'roll** (*informal, especially NAmE*) used to suggest to a group of people that you should all start doing sth or going somewhere 咱们开始干吧；咱们动身吧 **rolled into 'one** combined in one person or thing 融为一体；集于一身： *Banks are several businesses rolled into one.* 银行集数种商业活动于一身。 **ˌrolling in the 'aisles** (*informal*) laughing a lot 大笑；笑声不断： *She soon had us rolling in the aisles.* 她很快就让我们笑个不停。 **a rolling 'stone gathers no 'moss** (*saying*) a person who moves from place to place, job to job, etc. does not have a lot of money, possessions or friends but is free from responsibilities 滚石不生苔，频迁不聚财 **'roll on…!** (*BrE, informal*) used to say that you want sth to happen or arrive soon …赶快到来吧： *Roll on Friday!* 星期五快来吧！ **roll up your 'sleeves** to prepare to work or fight 捋起袖子；准备动手；摩拳擦掌 **roll with the 'punches** to adapt yourself to a difficult situation 使自己适应艰苦环境 ➔ MORE AT BALL *n.*, GRAVE[1] *n.*, HEAD *n.*, READY *adj.*, TONGUE *n.*

PHR V **ˌroll a'round** (*BrE also* **ˌroll a'bout**) to be laughing so much that you can hardly control yourself 大笑不止 **ˌroll sth↔'back 1** to turn or force sth back or further away 击退；使后退： *to roll back the frontiers of space* 拓展太空领域 **2** (*NAmE*) to reduce prices, etc. 降低，削减（价格等）： *to roll back inflation* 降低通货膨胀 **ˌroll sth↔'down 1** to open sth by turning a handle 摇开；旋开： *He rolled down his car window and started shouting at them.* 他摇下车窗，朝他们大声喊起来。 **2** to make a rolled piece of clothing, etc. hang or lie flat 展开，铺开，摊开（卷状物）： *to roll down your sleeves* 捋下袖子 **ˌroll 'in** (*informal*) **1** to arrive in great numbers or amounts 大量涌入；滚滚而来： *Offers of help are still rolling in.* 仍然不断有人表示愿意提供援助。 **2** to arrive late at a place, without seeming worried or sorry 姗姗来迟： *Steve rolled in around lunchtime.* 到午饭时分，史蒂夫才慢吞吞地来了。 **ˌroll sth↔'out 1** to make sth flat by pushing sth over it 将…轧平： *Roll out the pastry.* 将油酥面团擀平。 ➔ VISUAL VOCAB PAGE V30 **2** to officially make a new product available or start a new political CAMPAIGN 正式推出（新产品）；开展（新的政治运动） **SYN** **launch**: *The new model is to be rolled out in July.* 这种新型号将在七月份推向市场。 ➔ RELATED NOUN ROLL-OUT **ˌroll 'over** (*informal*) to be easily defeated without even trying 不战自败；轻易认输： *We can't expect them to just roll over for us.* 我们不能指望他们会乖乖地向我们认输。 **ˌroll sb↔'over** (*BrE, informal*) to defeat sb easily 轻易打败某人： *They rolled us over in the replay.* 他们在重赛中轻而易举地战胜了我们。 **ˌroll sth↔'over** (*specialist*) to allow money that sb owes to be paid back at a later date 将（债务）转期；允许延期偿还（欠款）： *The bank refused to roll over the debt.* 银行拒不允许延期偿还借款。 ➔ RELATED NOUN ROLLOVER (1) **ˌroll 'up** (*informal*) to arrive 到达： *Bill finally rolled up two hours late.* 比尔最终迟到了两个小时。◇ *Roll up! Roll up!* (= used to invite people who are passing to form an audience) 快来看哪！快来看哪！ **ˌroll sth↔'up** to close sth by turning a handle （转动把手）关闭： *She rolled up all the windows.* 她摇上了所有的窗户。

roll·back /ˈrəʊlbæk; *NAmE* ˈroʊl-/ *noun* [sing., U] (*especially NAmE*) **1** a reduction in a price or in pay, to a past level （价格或工资等的）下跌，回落 **2** the act of changing a situation, law, etc. back to what it was before （情形、法律等的）回复，恢复

'roll bar *noun* a metal bar over the top of a car without a roof, used to make the car stronger and to protect passengers if the car turns over （敞篷汽车顶部起加固和保护作用的）翻车防护杆，防滚保护杆

'roll call *noun* [U, sing.] the reading of a list of names to a group of people to check who is there 点名： *Roll call will be at 7 a.m.* 早上 7 点钟点名。◇ *The guest list reads like a roll call of the nation's heroes.* 客人名单念起来就像是在列数民族英雄。

ˌrolled 'gold *noun* [U] gold in the form of a thin layer that is rolled onto sth to cover it 轧制金箔；包金

ˌrolled 'oats *noun* [pl.] OATS that have had their shells removed before being crushed, used especially for making PORRIDGE 燕麦片（尤用以做麦片粥）

roll·er /ˈrəʊlə(r); *NAmE* ˈroʊ-/ *noun* **1** a piece of wood, metal or plastic, shaped like a tube, that rolls over and over and is used in machines, for example to make sth flat, or to move sth 滚筒；滚轴：*the heavy steel rollers under the conveyor belt* 传送带下沉重的钢滚筒 **2** (often in compounds 常构成复合词) a machine or piece of equipment with a part shaped like a tube so that it rolls backwards and forwards. It may be used for making sth flat, crushing or spreading sth. 碾轧机；碾子：*Flatten the surface of the grass with a roller.* 用碾轧机把草轧平。◇ *a paint roller* 滚筒式油漆刷 ➲ VISUAL VOCAB PAGE V21 ➲ SEE ALSO STEAMROLLER *n.* **3** a piece of wood or metal, shaped like a tube, that is used for moving heavy objects 滚轴；滚柱：*We'll need to move the piano on rollers.* 我们需要用滚子来移动钢琴。 **4** a long, powerful wave in the sea/ocean 卷浪；巨浪：*Huge Atlantic rollers crashed onto the rocks.* 大西洋的巨浪冲击着岩石。 **5** a small plastic tube that hair is rolled around to give it curls 塑料发卷 SYN **curler**：*heated rollers* 经过加热的发卷 ◇ *Her hair was in rollers.* 她的头发用发卷卷着。➲ SEE ALSO HIGH ROLLER

roller·ball /ˈrəʊləbɔːl; *NAmE* ˈroʊlərb-/ *noun* **1** a type of BALLPOINT pen 宝珠笔；签字笔 **2** = TRACKBALL

Roll·er·blade™ /ˈrəʊləbleɪd; *NAmE* ˈroʊlərb-/ *noun* = IN-LINE SKATE ➲ VISUAL VOCAB PAGE V44 ▶ **Roll·er·blade** *verb* [I]

ˈ**roller blind** *noun* a covering for a window made of a roll of cloth that is fixed at the top of the window and can be pulled up and down 卷轴窗帘 ➲ VISUAL VOCAB PAGE V22

ˈ**roller coaster** *noun* **1** a track at a FAIRGROUND that goes up and down very steep slopes and that people ride on in a small train for fun and excitement（游乐场的）过山车，环滑车：*a roller-coaster ride* 乘坐过山车 **2** a situation that keeps changing very quickly 不断变化的局势：*The last few weeks have been a real roller coaster.* 过去的几个星期，形势真是变幻莫测。

ˈ**roller shoe** *noun* (*NAmE*) a sports shoe that has one or more wheels underneath it 滑轮鞋；暴走鞋

ˈ**roller skate** (*also* **skate**) *noun, verb*
■*noun* a type of boot with two pairs of small wheels attached to the bottom（四轮）旱冰鞋；滚轴溜冰鞋；轮式溜冰鞋：*a pair of roller skates* 一双旱冰鞋
■*verb* [I] to move over a hard surface wearing roller skates 滑旱冰；溜旱冰；滚轴溜冰 ▶ ˈ**roller skating** (*also* **skat·ing**) *noun* [U]

ˈ**roller towel** *noun* a long roll of towel, usually in a public toilet/bathroom, part of which hangs down for you to dry your hands on（公厕等处套在滚筒上的）环状擦手巾

rol·licking /ˈrɒlɪkɪŋ; *NAmE* ˈrɑːl-/ *adj., noun*
■*adj.* [only before noun] cheerful and often noisy 嬉闹的；喧闹嬉戏的 SYN **exuberant**：*a rollicking comedy* 喧闹的喜剧
■*noun* (*BrE, informal*) angry criticism for sth bad sb has done 申斥；斥责：*He gave us both a rollicking.* 他把我们俩训斥了一通。

roll·ing /ˈrəʊlɪŋ; *NAmE* ˈroʊ-/ *adj.* [only before noun] **1** (of hills or countryside 丘陵或乡村) having gentle slopes 起伏的 ➲ WORDFINDER NOTE AT LANDSCAPE **2** done in regular stages or at regular intervals over a period of time 规则的；周而复始的：*a rolling programme of reform* 逐步推进的改革计划

ˈ**rolling mill** *noun* a machine or factory that produces flat sheets of metal 轧（钢）机；轧（钢）厂

ˈ**rolling pin** *noun* a wooden or glass kitchen UTENSIL (= a tool) in the shape of a tube, used for rolling PASTRY flat 擀面杖 ➲ VISUAL VOCAB PAGES V27, V30

ˈ**rolling stock** *noun* [U] the engines, trains, etc. that are used on a railway/railroad（铁路上运行的）全部车辆（包括机车、车厢等）

roll·mop /ˈrəʊlmɒp; *NAmE* ˈroʊlmɑːp/ *noun* a piece of raw HERRING (= a type of fish) that is rolled up and preserved in VINEGAR, often sold in JARS 醋渍生鲱鱼卷（常瓶装出售）

ˌ**roll of** ˈ**honour** (*especially US* ˈ**honor roll**) *noun* [usually sing.] a list of people who are being praised officially for sth they have done 荣誉名册；光荣榜

ˈ**roll-on** *adj.* [only before noun] spread or put on the body using a ball that moves around in the top of a bottle or container 滚抹式的；走珠式的：*a roll-on deodorant* 走珠除臭剂 ▶ ˈ**roll-on** *noun*

ˌ**roll-**ˌ**on** ˌ**roll-**ˈ**off** *adj.* [usually before noun] (*abbr.* ˈ**ro-ro**) (*BrE*) (of a ship 轮船) designed so that cars can be driven straight on and off 滚装的；汽车可直接上下的：*a roll-on roll-off car ferry* 汽车可直接上下的渡船

ˈ**roll-out** *noun* an occasion when a company introduces or starts to use a new product 新产品发布会；新产品的推出

roll·over /ˈrəʊləʊvə(r); *NAmE* ˈroʊloʊvər/ *noun* **1** [U] (*specialist*) the act of allowing money that is owed to be paid at a later date 贷款展期；贷款延期偿还 **2** [U, C] (*BrE*) a prize of money in a competition or LOTTERY in a particular week, that is added to the prize given in the following week if nobody wins it（比赛或彩票奖金的）累积，滚动增加：*a rollover jackpot* 滚动增加的累积奖金 **3** [U] (*especially NAmE*) the turning over of a vehicle during an accident 翻车；倾翻

Rolls-Royce™ /ˌrəʊlz ˈrɔɪs; *NAmE* ˌroʊlz/ *noun* **1** (*also informal* **Rolls™**) a large, comfortable and expensive make of car made by a company in the UK 劳斯莱斯汽车（英国一种大型豪华轿车） **2 the ~ of sth** (*BrE*) something that is thought of as an example of the highest quality of a type of thing 同类中的极品；最优品：*This is the Rolls-Royce of canoes.* 这是独木舟中的极品。

ˌ**roll-top** ˈ**desk** *noun* a desk with a top that you roll back to open it 活动顶盖写字台；卷盖式办公桌

ˈ**roll-up** *noun* (*BrE, informal*) a cigarette that you make yourself with TOBACCO and special paper 手卷的纸烟

roly-poly /ˌrəʊli ˈpəʊli; *NAmE* ˌroʊli ˈpoʊli/ *adj., noun*
■*adj.* [only before noun] (*informal*) (of people 人) short, round and fat 矮胖的；圆胖的 SYN **plump**
■*noun* (*pl.* **-ies**) (*also* ˌ**roly-poly** ˈ**pudding**) [U, C] (*BrE*) a hot DESSERT (= a sweet dish) made from SUET PASTRY spread with jam and rolled up 果酱布丁卷（热甜食）

ROM /rɒm; *NAmE* rɑːm/ *noun* [U] the abbreviation for 'read-only memory' (computer memory that contains instructions or data that cannot be changed or removed) 只读存储器（全写为 read-only memory）➲ COMPARE CD-ROM

the Roma /ˈrəʊmə; *NAmE* ˈroʊmə/ *noun* [pl.] the ROMANI people 罗姆人：*the Roma population of eastern Europe* 东欧的罗姆人人口

ro·maine /rəʊˈmeɪn; *NAmE* roʊ-/ (*NAmE*) (*BrE also* **cos let·tuce**) *noun* [C, U] a type of LETTUCE with long crisp leaves 长叶莴苣；生菜

ro·maji /ˈrəʊmədʒi; *NAmE* ˈroʊ-/ *noun* [U] (*from Japanese*) a system of writing Japanese that uses the ROMAN ALPHABET（拼写日语的）罗马字系统

Roman /ˈrəʊmən; *NAmE* ˈroʊ-/ *adj., noun*
■*adj.* **1** connected with ancient Rome or the Roman Empire 古罗马的；古罗马帝国的：*a Roman road/temple/villa* 古罗马的公路 / 庙宇 / 别墅 ◇ *Roman Britain* 古罗马统治下的不列颠 **2** connected with the modern city of Rome 罗马的；罗马城的 **3** connected with the Roman Catholic Church 天主教的 **4 roman** roman type is ordinary printing type which does not lean forward 罗马体的；西文白正体的：*Definitions in this dictionary are printed in roman type.* 这本词典里的释义是用罗马体印刷的。➲ COMPARE ITALIC
■*noun* **1** [C] a member of the ancient Roman REPUBLIC or empire 古罗马人 **2** [C] a person from the modern city

R

of Rome（现代的）罗马人，罗马市民 **3 roman** [U] the ordinary style of printing that uses small letters that do not lean forward 罗马体；西文白正体 ➲ COMPARE ITALICS IDM SEE ROME

the ˌRoman ˈalphabet *noun* [sing.] the alphabet that is used in English and in most western European languages 罗马字母表

ˌRoman ˈCatholic (*also* **Cath·olic**) *noun* (*abbr.* **RC**) a member of the part of the Christian Church that has the POPE as its leader 天主教徒 ▶ **ˌRoman ˈCatholic** (*also* **Cath·olic**) *adj.* **ˌRoman Caˈtholicism** (*also* **Cath·oli·cism**) *noun* [U]

Ro·mance /rəʊˈmæns; ˈrəʊmæns; *NAmE* ˈroʊ-/ *adj.* [only before noun] **Romance** languages, such as French, Italian and Spanish, are languages that developed from Latin 罗曼语的（由拉丁语演变而成，如法语、意大利语、西班牙语等）

ro·mance /rəʊˈmæns; ˈrəʊmæns; *NAmE* ˈroʊ-/ *noun, verb*

■ *noun* **1** [C] an exciting, usually short, relationship between two people who are in love with each other（通常指短暂的）浪漫史，爱情关系，风流韵事：*a holiday romance* 假日浪漫史 ◇ *They had a* ***whirlwind romance****.* 他们之间有过一段短暂的风流韵事。 **2** [U] love or the feeling of being in love 恋爱；爱情：*Spring is here and romance is in the air.* 春天来了，到处洋溢着爱情的气息。◇ *How can you put the romance back into your marriage?* 怎样才能使你的婚姻再次充满绵绵爱意呢？ ➲ COLLOCATIONS AT MARRIAGE **3** [U] a feeling of excitement and adventure, especially connected to a particular place or activity 传奇色彩；浪漫氛围：*the romance of travel* 旅行奇趣 **4** [C] a story about a love affair 爱情故事：*She's a compulsive reader of romances.* 她热衷于阅读爱情故事。 **5** [C] a story of excitement and adventure, often set in the past 传奇故事：*medieval romances* 中世纪的传奇故事

■ *verb* **1** [I] to tell stories that are not true or to describe sth in a way that makes it seem more exciting or interesting than it really is 虚构（故事）；渲染 **2** [T] **~ sb** to have or to try to have a romantic relationship with sb 和（某人）谈情说爱；追求（某人）

Ro·man·esque /ˌrəʊməˈnesk; *NAmE* ˌroʊ-/ *adj.* used to describe a style of ARCHITECTURE that was popular in western Europe from the 10th to the 12th centuries and that had round ARCHES, thick walls and tall PILLARS 罗马式的，罗马风格的（指 10 到 12 世纪盛行于西欧的一种建筑风格，使用圆拱、厚墙、高柱子） ➲ SEE ALSO NORMAN (1)

Rom·ani (*also* **Rom·any**) /ˈrɒməni; ˈrəʊm-; *NAmE* ˈrɑːm-; ˈroʊm-/ *noun* (*pl.* **-ies**) **1** [C] a member of a race of people, originally from Asia, who traditionally travel around and live in CARAVANS 罗姆人（原生活在亚洲的民族，以四处漂泊、住大篷车为传统） ➲ SEE ALSO GYPSY (1), ROMA **2** [U] the language of Romani people 罗姆语 ▶ **Rom·ani** (*also* **Rom·any**) *adj.* [usually before noun]

ˌRoman ˈlaw *noun* the legal system of the ancient Romans, and the basis for CIVIL LAW in many countries 罗马法（古罗马法律，是很多国家制定民法的依据）

ˌRoman ˈnose *noun* a nose that curves out at the top 高鼻梁

ˌRoman ˈnumeral *noun* one of the letters used by the ancient Romans to represent numbers and still used today, in some situations. In this system I = 1, V = 5, X = 10, L = 50, C = 100, D = 500, M = 1 000 and these letters are used in combinations to form other numbers. 罗马数字：*Henry VIII* 亨利八世 ◇ *© BBC MMIX (2009)* * 2009 年英国广播公司版权 ➲ PICTURE AT IDEOGRAM ➲ COMPARE ARABIC NUMERAL

Romano- /rəˈmɑːnəʊ; *NAmE* -noʊ; roʊˈm-/ *combining form* (in nouns and adjectives 构成名词和形容词) Roman 罗马（的）：*Romano-British pottery* 罗马时代英国的陶器

ro·man·tic 🔑 /rəʊˈmæntɪk; *NAmE* roʊ-/ *adj., noun*

■ *adj.* **1** 🔑 connected or concerned with love or a sexual relationship 浪漫的；爱情的；情爱的：*a romantic candlelit dinner* 浪漫的烛光晚餐 ◇ *romantic stories/fiction/comedy* 言情故事 / 小说 / 喜剧 ◇ *I'm not interested in a romantic relationship.* 我对谈情说爱不感兴趣。 ➲ WORDFINDER NOTE AT LOVE **2** 🔑 (of people 人) showing feelings of love 多情的；表达爱情的：*Why don't you ever give me flowers? I wish you'd be more romantic.* 你为什么从来不给我送花？我真希望你能浪漫一点。 **3** 🔑 beautiful in a way that makes you think of love or feel strong emotions 浪漫的；富有情调的；美妙的：*romantic music* 富有情调的音乐 ◇ *romantic mountain scenery* 美妙的山区风光 **4** 🔑 having an attitude to life where imagination and the emotions are especially important; not looking at situations in a realistic way 富于幻想的；不切实际的：*a romantic view of life* 对于生活的不切实际的想法 ◇ *When I was younger, I had romantic ideas of becoming a writer.* 我年轻一些的时候幻想过要成为一名作家。 **5 Romantic** [usually before noun] used to describe literature, music or art, especially of the 19th century, that is concerned with strong feelings, imagination and a return to nature, rather than reason, order and INTELLECTUAL ideas 浪漫主义的，浪漫主义风格的（尤用以描述 19 世纪的文学、音乐或艺术，以情感强烈、想象和回归自然为特征）：*the Romantic movement* 浪漫主义运动 ◇ *Keats is one of the greatest Romantic poets.* 济慈是最伟大的浪漫主义诗人之一。▶ **ro·man·tic·al·ly** /-kli/ *adv.*：*to be romantically involved with sb* 与某人坠入情网 ◇ *Their names have been linked romantically.* 他们的名字因恋爱关系而连在一起。 ◇ *He talked romantically of the past and his youth.* 他情深意切地谈论着往昔和他的年少时光。

■ *noun* **1** a person who is emotional and has a lot of imagination, and who has ideas and hopes that may not be realistic 浪漫的人；耽于幻想的人：*an incurable romantic* 摆脱不了不切实际的幻想的人 ◇ *He was a romantic at heart and longed for adventure.* 他骨子里是一位浪漫的人，渴望历险。 **2 Romantic** a writer, a musician or an artist who writes, etc. in the style of Romanticism 浪漫主义作家（或音乐家、艺术家）

ro·man·ti·cism /rəʊˈmæntɪsɪzəm; *NAmE* roʊ-/ *noun* [U] **1** (*also* **Romanticism**) a style and movement in art, music and literature in the late 18th and early 19th century, in which strong feelings, imagination and a return to nature were more important than reason, order and INTELLECTUAL ideas 浪漫主义（18 世纪末 19 世纪初盛行于艺术、音乐及文学领域，以情感强烈、想象和回归自然为特征） ➲ COMPARE REALISM (3) **2** the quality of seeing people, events and situations as more exciting and interesting than they really are 浪漫精神；浪漫的态度 **3** strong feelings of love; the fact of showing emotion, affection, etc. 强烈的爱情；情感的表达

ro·man·ti·cize (*BrE also* **-ise**) /rəʊˈmæntɪsaɪz; *NAmE* roʊ-/ *verb* [T, I] **~ (sth)** to make sth seem more attractive or interesting than it really is 使浪漫化；使传奇化；使更加富有吸引力：*romanticizing the past* 把往日浪漫化 ◇ *a romanticized picture of parenthood* 一幅理想化的为人父母的情景

Rome /rəʊm; *NAmE* roʊm/ *noun*

IDM **Rome wasn't built in a ˈday** (*saying*) used to say that a complicated task will take a long time and needs patience 罗马不是一天建成的；复杂的工作不会一蹴而就 **when in ˈRome (do as the ˈRomans do)** (*saying*) used to say that when you are in a foreign country, or a situation you are not familiar with, you should behave in the way that the people around you behave 入乡随俗

romeo /ˈrəʊmiəʊ; *NAmE* ˈroʊmioʊ/ (*also* **Romeo**) *noun* (*pl.* **-os**) (*often humorous*) a young male lover or a man who has sex with a lot of women 年轻的男情人；风流放荡的男子 ORIGIN From the name of the young hero of Shakespeare's play *Romeo and Juliet.* 源自莎士比亚戏剧《罗密欧与朱丽叶》中的年轻男主人公的名字。

romp /rɒmp; *NAmE* rɑːmp; rɔːmp/ *verb, noun*

■ *verb* [I] (+ **adv./prep.**) to play in a happy and noisy way 嬉戏喧闹：*kids romping around in the snow* 在雪地里嬉戏

喧闹的孩子

IDM **romp home/to victory** to easily win a race or competition 轻易地取胜: *Their horse romped home in the 2 o'clock race.* 他们的马在两点钟的比赛中轻而易举地获得了胜利。◇ *The Dutch team romped to a 5–1 victory over Celtic.* 荷兰队以 5:1 轻松战胜了凯尔特队。

PHR V **ˌromp aˈway/aˈhead** (*BrE, informal*) to increase, make progress or win quickly and easily 快速增加; 进步神速; 轻易取胜 **ˌromp ˈthrough (sth)** (*BrE, informal*) to do sth easily and quickly 快速而轻易地做: *She romped through the exam questions.* 她很快就答完了试题。

■ ***noun*** (often used in newspapers 常用于报章) (*informal*) **1** [C] an enjoyable sexual experience that is not serious 风流韵事: *politicians involved in sex romps with call girls* 与电话应召女郎发生风流韵事的政治人物 **2** [C] an amusing book, play or film/movie that is full of action or adventure 妙趣横生的历险故事书（或戏剧、电影） **3** [sing.] an easy victory in a sports competition（体育竞赛中的）轻而易举的胜利: *They won in a 5–1 romp.* 他们以 5:1 轻松取胜。

romp·ers /ˈrɒmpəz; *NAmE* ˈrɑːmpərz; ˈrɔːm-/ *noun* [pl.] (*also* **ˈromper suit** [C]) (*old-fashioned*) a piece of clothing worn by a baby, that covers the body and legs（幼儿的）连衫裤

ron·davel /rɒnˈdɑːvl; *NAmE* rɑːn-/ *noun* (*SAfrE*) a round HUT with a pointed roof that is usually made from THATCH (= dried grass) 圆形尖顶（茅）屋

rondo /ˈrɒndəʊ; *NAmE* ˈrɑːndoʊ/ *noun* (*pl.* **-os**) a piece of music in which the main tune is repeated several times, sometimes forming part of a longer piece 回旋曲

roo /ruː/ *noun* (*informal*) = KANGAROO

rood screen /ˈruːd skriːn/ *noun* (*specialist*) a wooden or stone structure in some churches that divides the part near the ALTAR from the rest of the church（教堂内的）祭台屏风

roof /ruːf/ *noun, verb*

■ ***noun*** (*pl.* **roofs**) **1** the structure that covers or forms the top of a building or vehicle 顶部; 屋顶; 车顶: ***a flat/sloping roof*** 平顶; 斜顶 ◇ *a* ***thatched/slate, etc. roof*** 茅草、石板瓦等屋顶 ◇ *The corner of the classroom was damp where the roof had leaked.* 教室漏雨的一角是湿的。◇ *Tim climbed on to the garage roof.* 蒂姆爬到车库的房顶上。◇ *The roof of the car was not damaged in the accident.* 事故中，车顶没有遭到损坏。 ➲ SEE ALSO SUNROOF ➲ VISUAL VOCAB PAGE V18 **2** **-roofed** (in adjectives 构成形容词) having the type of roof mentioned 有…顶的: *flat-roofed buildings* 平顶的大楼 **3** the top of an underground space such as a tunnel or CAVE 洞顶; 隧道顶 **4** **~ of your mouth** the top of the inside of your mouth 口腔顶部; 腭部

IDM **go through the ˈroof** **1** (of prices, etc. 价格等) to rise or increase very quickly 飞涨; 激增 **2** (*also* **hit the ˈroof**) (*informal*) to become very angry 非常生气; 暴怒 **have a ˈroof over your head** to have somewhere to live 有栖身之所 **under one ˈroof** | **under the same ˈroof** in the same building or house 在同一座建筑中; 同在一个屋檐下: *There are various stores and restaurants all under one roof.* 在同一栋大楼里有各种商店和餐馆。◇ *I don't think I can live under the same roof as you any longer.* 我觉得我再也不能和你生活在同一个屋檐下了。**under your ˈroof** in your home 在家里: *I don't want her under my roof again.* 我再也不想让她到我家来了。 ➲ MORE AT HIT *v.*, RAISE *v.*

■ ***verb*** [often passive] to cover sth with a roof; to put a roof on a building 给…盖顶; 盖上屋顶: **~ sth (in/over)** *The shopping centre is not roofed over.* 购物中心是露天的。◇ **~ sth with/in sth** *Their cottage was roofed with green slate.* 他们的小房子盖的是绿瓦。

roof·er /ˈruːfə(r)/ *noun* a person whose job is to repair or build roofs 修理（或盖）屋顶的工人

ˈroof garden *noun* a garden on the flat roof of a building 屋顶花园

roof·ing /ˈruːfɪŋ/ *noun* [U] **1** material used for making or covering roofs 盖屋顶用的材料 **2** the process of building roofs 盖屋顶

ˈroof rack (*also* **ˈluggage rack** *especially in NAmE*) *noun* a metal frame fixed to the roof of a car and used for carrying bags, cases and other large objects 车顶行李架 ➲ PICTURE AT RACK

roof·top /ˈruːftɒp; *NAmE* -tɑːp/ *noun* the outside part of the roof of a building 屋顶外部; 外屋顶: *From the hill we looked out over the rooftops of Athens.* 我们从山上眺望雅典建筑的顶部。◇ *The prisoners staged a rooftop protest.* 囚犯在屋顶上举行了抗议活动。

IDM **ˌshout, etc. sth from the ˈrooftops** to talk about sth in a very public way 公开谈论: *He was in love and wanted to shout it from the rooftops.* 他要大声宣布，他恋爱了。

rooi·bos /ˈrɔɪbɒs; *NAmE* -bɔːs/ (*also* **redbush**) *noun* [U] (*SAfrE*) a type of bush grown in South Africa whose leaves are dried and used to make tea（南非）红叶茶树，洛依柏丝茶树: *rooibos tea* 南非红叶茶

rook /rʊk/ *noun* **1** a large black bird of the CROW family. Rooks build their nests in groups at the tops of trees. 秃鼻乌鸦 **2** = CASTLE (2)

rook·ery /ˈrʊkəri/ *noun* (*pl.* **-ies**) a group of trees with rooks' nests in them 秃鼻乌鸦群栖林地

rookie /ˈrʊki/ *noun* (*informal*) **1** (*especially NAmE*) a person who has just started a job or an activity and has very little experience 新手; 生手 **2** (*NAmE*) a member of a sports team in his or her first full year of playing that sport（第一年参加比赛的）新队员

room /ruːm; rʊm/ *noun, verb*

■ ***noun***

• **IN BUILDING** 建筑物 **1** [C] a part of a building that has its own walls, floor and ceiling and is usually used for a particular purpose 房间; 室: *He walked out of the room and slammed the door.* 他走出房间，猛地关上了房门。◇ *They were in* ***the next room*** *and we could hear every word they said.* 他们在隔壁房间里，我们可以听到他们说的每一句话。◇ *a* ***dining/living/sitting room*** 饭厅; 起居室 ◇ *They had to sit in the waiting room for an hour.* 他们不得不在候车室里等了一个小时。◇ *I think Simon is in his room* (= bedroom). 我看西蒙就在他自己的房间里。◇ *I don't want to watch television. I'll be in* ***the other room*** (= a different room). 我不想看电视。我到别的房间去吧。 **HELP** There are many compounds ending in **room**. You will find them at their place in the alphabet. 以 room 结尾的复合词很多，可在各字母中的适当位置查到。

• **-ROOMED/-ROOM** …室; …房间 **2** (in adjectives 构成形容词) having the number of rooms mentioned 有…室的; 有…个房间的: *a three-roomed/three-room apartment* 三室的套房

• **IN HOTEL** 旅馆 **3** [C] a bedroom in a hotel, etc. 客房: ***a double/single room*** 双人/单人客房 ◇ *I'd like to book a room with a view of the lake.* 我想预订一套可以看到湖面景色的客房。◇ *She lets out rooms to students.* 她把房间出租给学生。 ➲ COLLOCATIONS AT TRAVEL

• **PLACE TO LIVE** 居所 **4** **rooms** [pl.] (*old-fashioned, BrE*) a set of two or more rooms that you rent to live in（租用的）住所，寓所 **SYN** **lodging**: *They lived in rooms in Kensington.* 他们住在肯辛顿的出租房间。

• **SPACE** 空间 **5** [U] empty space that can be used for a particular purpose 空间; 余地: **~ (for sb/sth)** *Is there enough room for me in the car?* 车上还有空间让我坐吗? ◇ *There's room for one more at the table.* 这张桌子还有一个人的位置。◇ *Do you have room for a computer on your desk?* 你的写字台上还摆得下一台电脑吗? ◇ *Yes, there's* ***plenty of room.*** 是的，还很空呢。◇ *How can we* ***make room for*** *all the furniture?* 我们怎么腾得出地方放这些家具呢? ◇ *I'll move the table—it* ***takes up too much room.*** 我要挪动一下这张桌子，它太占地方了。◇ **~ (to do sth)** *Make sure you have plenty of room to sit comfortably.* 一

定要找个宽敞地儿坐得舒服一点。➲ SEE ALSO ELBOW ROOM, HEADROOM, HOUSEROOM, LEGROOM, STANDING ROOM

• **POSSIBILITY** 可能性 **6** [U] **~ for sth** the possibility of sth existing or happening; the opportunity to do sth 可能性；机会：*He had to be certain. There could be* ***no room for doubt.*** 他必须确定无误。不能有任何的疑惑。◇ *There's some* ***room for improvement*** *in your work* (= it is not as good as it could be). 你的工作还有改进的余地。◇ *It is important to give children room to think for themselves.* 给孩子机会让他们自己思考是很重要的。

• **PEOPLE** 人 **7** [sing.] all the people in a room 房间里所有的人：*The whole room burst into applause.* 屋里的人发出一片掌声。

IDM **no room to swing a 'cat** (*informal*) when sb says **there's no room to swing a cat**, they mean that a room is very small and that there is not enough space 没有活动的余地；连转身都很难 ➲ MORE AT ELEPHANT, MANOEUVRE *n.*, SMOKE *n.*

■ ***verb*** [I] **~ (with sb) | ~ (together)** (*NAmE*) to rent a room somewhere; to share a rented room or flat/apartment with sb 租房；合住：*She and Nancy roomed together at college.* 她和南希在大学里合住一处。

room·er /ˈruːmə(r); ˈrʊm-/ *noun* (*NAmE*) a person who rents a room in sb's house 租屋的房客

room·ful /ˈruːmfʊl; ˈrʊm-/ *noun* [sing.] a large number of people or things that are in a room 满屋子（东西或人）：*He announced his resignation to a roomful of reporters.* 他向满屋子的记者宣布他辞职了。

roomie /ˈruːmi; ˈrʊmi/ *noun* (*NAmE, informal*) = ROOMMATE

ˈ**rooming house** *noun* (*NAmE*) a building where rooms with furniture can be rented for living in（带家具的）出租公寓住房

roommate /ˈruːmmeɪt; ˈrʊm-/ *noun* (*also informal* **roomie**) **1** a person that you share a room with, especially at a college or university（尤指大学里的）室友，同住一室的人 **2** (*both NAmE*) (*BrE* **flat·mate**) a person who shares a flat/apartment with one or more others 合住公寓套间者；同住一屋的人

R

ˈ**room service** *noun* [U] a service provided in a hotel, by which guests can order food and drink to be brought to their rooms（旅馆）客房送餐服务：*He ordered coffee from room service.* 他让服务员送杯咖啡到他房里。➲ WORDFINDER NOTE AT HOTEL

ˈ**room temperature** *noun* [U] the normal temperature inside a building 室温；常温：*Serve the wine* ***at room temperature.*** 这种葡萄酒宜室温饮用。

roomy /ˈruːmi; ˈrʊmi/ *adj.* (**room·ier**, **roomi·est**) (*approving*) having a lot of space inside 宽敞的；宽大的 SYN **spacious**：*a surprisingly roomy car* 出奇宽敞的汽车 ▸ **roomi·ness** *noun* [U]

roost /ruːst/ *noun, verb*

■ ***noun*** a place where birds sleep（鸟类的）栖息处 IDM SEE RULE *v.*

■ ***verb*** [I] (of birds 鸟类) to rest or go to sleep somewhere 栖息 IDM SEE HOME *adv.*

roost·er /ˈruːstə(r)/ (*especially NAmE*) (*BrE also* **cock**) *noun* an adult male chicken 公鸡；雄鸡 ➲ COMPARE HEN (1)

root /ruːt/ *noun, verb*

■ ***noun***

• **OF PLANT** 植物 **1** [C] the part of a plant that grows under the ground and absorbs water and minerals that it sends to the rest of the plant 根；根茎：*deep spreading roots* 扎得很深的根 ◇ *I pulled the plant up* ***by*** (= including) ***the roots.*** 我把这棵植物连根拔起。◇ *Tree roots can cause damage to buildings.* 树根会给大楼造成损害。◇ ***root crops/vegetables*** (= plants whose roots you can eat, such as carrots) 根茎作物 / 蔬菜 ➲ COLLOCATIONS AT LIFE ➲ VISUAL VOCAB PAGES V10, V11 ➲ SEE ALSO GRASS ROOTS, TAPROOT

• **OF HAIR/TOOTH/NAIL** 头发；牙齿；指甲 **2** [C] the part of a hair, tooth, nail or tongue that attaches it to the rest of the body 根；根部：*hair that is blonde at the ends and dark at the roots* 发梢金黄而发根褐色的头发

• **MAIN CAUSE OF PROBLEM** 问题的主要原因 **3** [C, usually sing.] the main cause of sth, such as a problem or difficult situation 根源；起因：*Money, or love of money, is said to be the root of all evil.* 有人说钱和爱钱是万恶之源。◇ *We have to get to* ***the root of the problem.*** 我们必须找到问题的根源。◇ *What lies* ***at the root of*** *his troubles is a sense of insecurity.* 他的一切忧虑源于一种不安全感。◇ *What would you say was the* ***root cause*** *of the problem?* 你认为问题的根源是什么？

• **ORIGIN** 起源 **4** [C, usually pl.] the origin or basis of sth 起源；基础；根基：*Flamenco may have its roots in Arabic music.* 弗拉门科可能起源于阿拉伯音乐。

• **CONNECTION WITH PLACE** 与地方相关 **5** **roots** [pl.] the feelings or connections that you have with a place because you have lived there or your family came from there 根（指与出生地或原籍相关联的情感或联系）：*I'm proud of my Italian roots.* 我为我的意大利血统感到骄傲。◇ *After 20 years in America, I still feel my roots are in England.* 尽管在美国生活了 20 年，我还是觉得我的根在英格兰。

• **OF WORD** 单词 **6** [C] (*linguistics* 语言) the part of a word that has the main meaning and that its other forms are based on; a word that other words are formed from 词根：*'Walk' is the root of 'walks', 'walked', 'walking' and 'walker'.* * walk 是 walks、walked、walking 和 walker 的词根。

• **MATHEMATICS** 数学 **7** [C] a quantity which, when multiplied by itself a particular number of times, produces another quantity 方根；根 ➲ SEE ALSO CUBE ROOT, SQUARE ROOT

IDM **put down 'roots** **1** (of a plant 植物) to develop roots 生根 **2** to settle and live in one place 定居：*After ten years travelling the world, she felt it was time to put down roots somewhere.* 游历世界十年之后，她觉得该是找个地方定居的时候了。 ˌ**root and 'branch** thoroughly and completely 完全彻底：*The government set out to destroy the organization root and branch.* 政府着手完全彻底地摧毁这个组织。◇ *root-and-branch reforms* 全面彻底的改革 **take 'root** **1** (of a plant 植物) to develop roots 生根 **2** (of an idea 思想) to become accepted widely 植根；深入人心：*Fortunately, militarism failed to take root in Europe as a whole.* 幸运的是，军国主义没有能够深入整个欧洲。

■ ***verb***

• **OF PLANTS** 植物 **1** [I, T] **~ (sth)** to grow roots; to cause or encourage a plant to grow roots（使）生根

• **SEARCH** 寻找 **2** [I] to search for sth by moving things or turning things over 翻寻 SYN **rummage**：**~ (about/around) for sth** *pigs rooting for food* 拱土觅食的猪 ◇ *Who's been rooting around in my desk?* 谁乱翻我的书桌了？◇ **~ (through sth) (for sth)** *'It must be here somewhere,' she said, rooting through the suitcase.* "它一定就在这里的什么地方。" 她一边说一边翻着衣箱。

• **SEX** 性 **3** [I, T] **~ (sb)** (*AustralE, NZE, taboo, slang*) to have sex with sb（与某人）性交

PHR V ˈ**root for sb** [no passive] (usually used in the progressive tenses 通常用于进行时) (*informal*) to support or encourage sb in a sports competition or when they are in a difficult situation（体育比赛或遭遇困难时）给…助威，给…加油：*We're rooting for the Bulls.* 我们为公牛队加油。◇ *Good luck—I'm rooting for you!* 祝你好运，我支持你！

ˌ**root sth/sb**↔**'out** **1** to find the person or thing that is causing a problem and remove or get rid of them 找到并去除（祸根）；根除 **2** to find sb/sth after searching for a long time 终于发现（或找到） ˌ**root sb to 'sth** to make sb unable to move because of fear, shock, etc. 使（因害怕、惊吓等）呆住不动：*Embarrassment* ***rooted her to the spot.*** 她尴尬得呆住了。 ˌ**root sth**↔**'up** to dig or pull up a plant with its roots 连根挖起；连根拔起

ˈ**root beer** *noun* **1** [U, C] a sweet FIZZY drink (= with bubbles), that does not contain alcohol, made from GINGER and the roots of other plants. It is drunk especially in the US. 根汁汽水（用姜和其他植物的根制成，不含酒精，盛行于美国） **2** [C] a bottle, can or glass of root beer 一瓶（或听、杯）根汁饮料

ˈroot-bound *adj.* = POT-BOUND

ˈroot canal *noun* the space inside the root of a tooth（牙）根管

ˈroot directory *noun* (*computing* 计) a file that contains all the other files in a program, system, etc. 根目录

root·ed /ˈruːtɪd/ *adj.* **1** **~ in sth** developing from or being strongly influenced by sth 根源在于；由…产生：*His problems are deeply rooted in his childhood experiences.* 他的问题的祸根在于他童年的经历。 **2** fixed in one place; not moving or changing 固定在某地的；稳固的；根深蒂固的：*She was rooted to her chair.* 她坐在椅子上一动不动。◇ *Their life is rooted in Chicago now.* 他们在芝加哥定居了。◇ *Racism is still deeply rooted in our society.* 种族主义在我们的社会中仍然根深蒂固。 ➲ SEE ALSO DEEP-ROOTED **3** (*AustralE, slang*) extremely tired 疲惫不堪的；筋疲力尽的 **4** (*AustralE, slang*) too old or broken to use 老旧无用的；破得不能用的

IDM **rooted to the ˈspot** so frightened or shocked that you cannot move（惊吓得）呆住不动

root·er /ˈruːtə(r)/ *noun* (*NAmE, informal*) a person who supports a particular team or player（运动队或运动员的）支持者 SYN **supporter**

rootin'-tootin' /ˌruːtɪn ˈtuːtɪn/ *adj.* [only before noun] (*NAmE, informal*) enthusiastic, cheerful and lively 满腔热情的；热情奔放的

root·less /ˈruːtləs/ *adj.* having nowhere that you really think of as home, or as the place where you belong 无根的；没有归宿的；漂泊的：*She had had a rootless childhood moving from town to town.* 她小时候居无定所，在各地流浪。 ▸ **root·less·ness** *noun* [U]

rootsy /ˈruːtsi/ *adj.* (*informal*) (of music 音乐) belonging to a particular tradition, and not changed from the original style 维持特定风格的；正统的

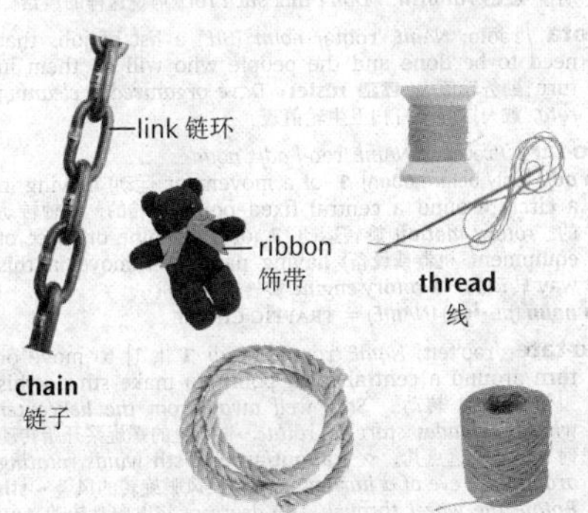

rope 🔑 /rəʊp; *NAmE* roʊp/ *noun, verb*

■ *noun* **1** 🔑 [C, U] very strong thick string made by twisting thinner strings, wires, etc. together 粗绳；线缆；绳索：*The rope broke and she fell 50 metres onto the rocks.* 绳索断了，她从 50 米的高空摔到了岩石上。◇ *We tied his hands together with rope.* 我们用绳子把他的手绑在一起。◇ *The anchor was attached to a length of rope.* 铁锚系在一段缆绳上。◇ *Coils of rope lay on the quayside.* 码头上放着一盘盘的绳子。 ➲ SEE ALSO JUMP ROPE, SKIPPING ROPE, TOW ROPE **2** **the ropes** [pl.] the fence made of rope that is around the edge of the area where a BOXING or WRESTLING match takes place（拳击或摔跤场四周的）围绳，圈绳 ➲ VISUAL VOCAB PAGE V52 **3** [C] a number of similar things attached together by a string or thread 串在一起的相似的东西：*a rope of pearls* 一串珍珠

IDM **give sb enough ˈrope** to allow sb freedom to do what they want, especially in the hope that they will make a mistake or look silly 放任自由，任其为所欲为（使其犯错误或出丑）：*The question was vague, giving the interviewee **enough rope to hang herself**.* 这个问题模棱两可，参加面试的人会胡乱发挥从而出错。 **on the ˈropes** (*informal*) very close to being defeated 濒于失败；即将失败 **show sb/know/learn the ˈropes** (*informal*) to show sb/know/learn how a particular job should be done 向某人演示 / 知道 / 学会如何做某事 ➲ MORE AT END *n.*, MONEY

■ *verb* **1** to tie one person or thing to another with a rope 用绳子捆（或绑、系）：**~ A and B together** *The thieves had roped the guard's feet together.* 窃贼把门卫的双脚捆在了一起。◇ **~ A to B** *I roped the goat to a post.* 我把山羊拴在一根柱子上。 **2** **~ sth** to tie sth with a rope so that it is held tightly and safely 用绳子系牢；捆紧：*I closed and roped the trunk.* 我把箱子盖上，用绳子捆结实。 **3** **~ sth** (*especially NAmE*) to catch an animal by throwing a circle of rope around it 用套索抓捕（动物）；套 SYN **lasso**

PHR V **ˌrope sb↔ˈin** | **ˌrope sb ˈinto sth** [usually passive] (*informal*) to persuade sb to join in an activity or to help to do sth, even when they do not want to 劝说某人加入；说服某人帮忙：**rope sb in to do sth** *Everyone was roped in to help with the show.* 每个人都被动员来为这次表演出力。◇ **rope sb into doing sth** *Ben was roped into making coffee for the whole team.* 本被请来为全队煮咖啡。 **ˌrope sth↔ˈoff** to separate an area from another one, using ropes, to stop people from entering it 用绳子围起（一片区域）：*Police roped off the street to investigate the accident.* 警察用绳子将街道圈起来调查事故。

ˌrope ˈladder *noun* a LADDER made of two long ropes connected by short pieces of wood or metal at regular intervals 绳梯

ropy (*also* **ropey**) /ˈrəʊpi; *NAmE* ˈroʊpi/ *adj.* (*BrE, informal*) **1** not in good condition; of bad quality 状况不佳的；质量差的；糟糕的：*We spent the night in a ropy old tent.* 我们在一个破旧的帐篷里过了一夜。 **2** feeling slightly ill/sick 感觉不适的；生小病的

ro-ro /ˈrəʊ rəʊ; *NAmE* ˈroʊ roʊ/ *abbr.* (*BrE*) ROLL-ON ROLL-OFF（轮船）轮渡式的，汽车可直接上下的

Rorschach test /ˈrɔːʃɑːk test; *NAmE* ˈrɔːrʃɑːk/ (*also* **ˈink-blot test**) *noun* (*psychology* 心) a test in which people have to say what different shapes made by ink make them think of 罗夏测验（受试者说出对各种墨迹的联想）；罗夏墨迹测验

rort /rɔːt; *NAmE* rɔːrt/ *noun* (*AustralE, NZE, informal*) a dishonest thing that sb does 欺诈；不诚实行为：*a tax rort* 逃税伎俩 ▸ **rort** *verb* [T, I]: **~ (sth)** *He was an expert at rorting the system* (= getting the best out of it for himself without actually doing anything illegal). 他善于钻制度的空子。

ros·ary /ˈrəʊzəri; *NAmE* ˈroʊ-/ *noun* (*pl.* **-ies**) **1** [C] a string of BEADS that are used by some Roman Catholics for counting prayers as they say them（天主教徒念经时用的）数珠，念珠 **2** **the Rosary** [sing.] the set of prayers said by Roman Catholics while counting rosary BEADS（天主教徒念的）玫瑰经

rose /rəʊz; *NAmE* roʊz/ *noun, adj.* ➲ SEE ALSO RISE *v.*

■ *noun* **1** [C] a flower with a sweet smell that grows on a bush with THORNS (= sharp points) on its STEMS 玫瑰（花）；蔷薇（花）：*a bunch of red roses* 一束红玫瑰花 ◇ *a rose bush/garden* 玫瑰丛；玫瑰园 ◇ *a climbing/rambling rose* 攀缘的 / 蔓生的蔷薇 ➲ VISUAL VOCAB PAGE V11 **2** (*also* **ˌrose ˈpink**) [U] a pink colour 粉红色 ➲ MORE LIKE THIS 15, page R26 **3** [C] a piece of metal or plastic with small holes in it that is attached to the end of a pipe or WATERING CAN so that the water comes out in a fine spray when you are watering plants（水管或喷壶的）莲蓬式喷嘴 **4** = CEILING ROSE

IDM **be coming up ˈroses** (*informal*) (of a situation 形势) to be developing in a successful way 顺利发展；蓬勃发展 **put ˈroses in sb's cheeks** (*BrE, informal*) to make sb look healthy 使双颊红润健康 **a ˌrose by any other ˌname would smell as ˈsweet** (*saying*) what is important is what

R

people or things are, not what they are called 玫瑰不叫玫瑰，依然芳香如故；名称并不是重要的东西 ➲ MORE AT BED *n.*, SMELL *v.*

■ ***adj.*** (*also* ˌ**rose ˈpink**) pink in colour 粉红色的

rosé /ˈrəʊzeɪ; *NAmE* roʊˈzeɪ/ *noun* [U, C] (*from French*) a light pink wine 玫瑰红葡萄酒；粉红葡萄酒：*a bottle of rosé* 一瓶玫瑰红葡萄酒 ◇ *an excellent rosé* 优质粉红葡萄酒 ➲ COMPARE RED WINE (1), WHITE WINE (1)

ros·eate /ˈrəʊziət; *NAmE* ˈroʊ-/ *adj.* [usually before noun] (*literary* or *specialist*) pink in colour 粉红色的；玫瑰色的

rose·bud /ˈrəʊzbʌd; *NAmE* ˈroʊz-/ *noun* the flower of a ROSE before it is open 玫瑰花蕾

ˈ**rose-coloured** (*especially US* ˈ**rose-colored**) *adj.* **1** pink in colour 粉红色的；玫瑰色的 **2** (*also* ˈ**rose-tinted**) used to describe an idea or a way of looking at a situation as being better or more positive than it really is（描述对形势的看法或观点过于乐观）：*a rose-tinted vision of the world* 对世界的理想化看法 ◇ *He tends to view the world* ***through rose-coloured spectacles.*** 他总是戴着玫瑰色的眼镜看世界。

ˈ**rose hip** *noun* = HIP (3)

rose·mary /ˈrəʊzməri; *NAmE* ˈroʊzmeri/ *noun* [U] a bush with small narrow leaves that smell sweet and are used in cooking as a HERB 迷迭香（灌木，叶子窄小，气味芬芳，可用于烹调）➲ VISUAL VOCAB PAGE V35

Rosetta Stone /rəʊˈzetə stəʊn; *NAmE* roʊˈzetə stoʊn/ *noun* [sing.] something, especially a discovery, that helps people to understand or find an explanation for a mystery or area of knowledge that not much was known about 有助于解释神秘事物（或未知领域）的事物；有启示作用的发现 ORIGIN From the name of an ancient stone with writing in three different languages on it that was found near Rosetta in Egypt in 1799. It has helped archaeologists to understand and translate many other ancient Egyptian texts. 源自 1799 年在埃及罗塞塔附近发现的刻有三种文字的古代罗塞塔石碑，考古学家由此解读了很多其他古埃及文本。

ros·ette /rəʊˈzet; *NAmE* roʊ-/ *noun* **1** a round decoration made of RIBBON that is worn by supporters of a political party or sports team, or to show that sb has won a prize 玫瑰形饰物（用缎带制成，政党或运动队的支持者所佩戴，亦作为获奖的标志）➲ PICTURE AT MEDAL **2** a thing that has the shape of a ROSE 玫瑰形的东西：*The leaves formed a dark green rosette.* 这些叶子聚在一起，像是一朵深绿色的玫瑰。

ˈ**rose water** *noun* [U] a liquid with a sweet smell made from ROSES, used as a PERFUME or in cooking 玫瑰香水（用作香水或烹调用）

ˌ**rose ˈwindow** *noun* a decorative round window in a church, often with coloured glass (= STAINED GLASS) in it 圆花窗（常有彩色玻璃）

rose·wood /ˈrəʊzwʊd; *NAmE* ˈroʊz-/ *noun* [U] the hard reddish-brown wood of a tropical tree, that has a pleasant smell and is used for making expensive furniture 黄檀木（产于热带，木质坚硬，气味芳香，用于制作贵重家具）

Rosh Hash·ana (*also* **Rosh Hash·anah**) /ˌrɒʃ həˈʃɑːnə; *NAmE* ˌrɑːʃ/ *noun* [U] the Jewish New Year festival, held in September 岁首节（犹太教历新年，在九月份）

rosin /ˈrɒzɪn; *NAmE* ˈrɑːzn/ *noun* [U] a substance that a player uses on the BOW² (3) of a musical instrument such as a VIOLIN so that it makes a better sound when it moves across the strings 松香 ▸ **rosin** *verb* ~ **sth**

ros·ter /ˈrɒstə(r); *NAmE* ˈrɑːs-; ˈrɔːs-/ *noun, verb*

■ ***noun*** **1** a list of people's names and the jobs that they have to do at a particular time 值勤名单 SYN **rota**: *a duty roster* 值勤表 **2** a list of the names of people who are available to do a job, play in a team, etc. 候选名单

■ ***verb*** ~ **sb (to do sth)** (*BrE*) to put sb's name on a roster 将（姓名）列入值勤名单：*The driver was rostered for Sunday.* 这名司机被安排在星期日值班。

ros·trum /ˈrɒstrəm; *NAmE* ˈrɑːs-; ˈrɔːs-/ *noun* (*pl.* **ros·trums** or **ros·tra** /-trə/) a small raised platform that a person stands on to make a speech, CONDUCT music, receive a prize, etc. 讲坛；指挥台；领奖台

rosy /ˈrəʊzi; *NAmE* ˈroʊzi/ *adj.* (**rosi·er, rosi·est**) **1** pink and pleasant in appearance 粉红色的；红润的：*She had rosy cheeks.* 她脸颊红润。**2** likely to be good or successful 美好的；乐观的 SYN **hopeful**: *The future is looking very rosy for our company.* 我们公司的前景一片光明。◇ *She* ***painted a rosy picture*** *of their life together in Italy* (= made it appear to be very good and perhaps better than it really was). 她把他们在意大利的共同生活描绘得非常美好。IDM SEE GARDEN *n.*

rot /rɒt; *NAmE* rɑːt/ *verb, noun*

■ ***verb*** (**-tt-**) [I, T] to decay, or make sth decay, naturally and gradually（使）腐烂，腐败变质 SYN **decompose**: *rotting leaves* 渐渐腐烂的叶子 ◇ ~ (**away**) *The window frame had rotted away completely.* 窗框已经完全烂掉了。◇ (*figurative*) *prisoners thrown in jail and* ***left to rot*** 投入大牢后就无人过问的囚犯 ◇ ~ **sth** *Too much sugar will rot your teeth.* 吃糖太多，就会出现蛀牙。➲ SEE ALSO ROTTEN *adj.* (1) ➲ MORE LIKE THIS 36, page R29

■ ***noun*** [U] **1** the process or state of decaying and falling apart 腐烂；腐败变质：*The wood must not get damp as rot can quickly result.* 木头不能受潮，否则很快就会烂掉。➲ SEE ALSO DRY ROT (1) **2 the rot** used to describe the fact that a situation is getting worse 形势恶化：***The rot set in*** *last year when they reorganized the department.* 去年他们重组这个部门时，衰败就开始了。◇ *The team should manage to* ***stop the rot*** *if they play well this week.* 如果球队本周比赛表现好，他们应该能够阻止形势的恶化。**3** (*old-fashioned, BrE*) nonsense; silly things that sb says 废话；胡说 SYN **rubbish**: *Don't talk such rot!* 别说这样的废话！

rota /ˈrəʊtə; *NAmE* ˈroʊtə/ *noun* (*BrE*) a list of jobs that need to be done and the people who will do them in turn 勤务轮值表 SYN **roster**: *Dave organized a cleaning rota.* 戴夫排好了打扫卫生轮值表。

ro·tary /ˈrəʊtəri; *NAmE* ˈroʊ-/ *adj., noun*

■ ***adj.*** [only before noun] **1** (of a movement 运动) moving in a circle around a central fixed point 旋转的；绕轴转动的：*rotary motion* 旋转运动 **2** (of a machine or piece of equipment 机器或设备) having parts that move in this way 转动的：*a rotary engine* 旋转式发动机

■ ***noun*** (*pl.* **-ies**) (*NAmE*) = TRAFFIC CIRCLE

ro·tate /rəʊˈteɪt; *NAmE* ˈroʊteɪt/ *verb* **1** [I, T] to move or turn around a central fixed point; to make sth do this（使）旋转，转动：*Stay well away from the helicopter when its blades start to rotate.* 直升机的螺旋桨开始转动时，尽量离远点儿。◇ ~ **about/around sth** *winds rotating around the eye of a hurricane* 绕飓风风眼旋转的风 ◇ ~ **sth** *Rotate the wheel through 180 degrees.* 将方向盘转动 180 度。**2** [I, T] if a job **rotates**, or if people **rotate** a job, they regularly change the job or regularly change who does the job（工作）由…轮值；（人员）轮换，轮值：(+ **adv./prep.**) *The EU presidency rotates among the members.* 欧盟主席一职由其成员国轮流担任。◇ *When I joined the company, I rotated around the different sections.* 我加入这个公司时，轮换过几个不同的部门。◇ ~ **sth** *We rotate the night shift so no one has to do it all the time.* 我们轮流值夜班，这样就不会有人总是夜班了。▸ **ro·tat·ing** *adj.* [only before noun]: *rotating parts* 旋转的部件 ◇ *a rotating presidency* 轮值主席之职

ro·ta·tion /rəʊˈteɪʃn; *NAmE* roʊ-/ *noun* **1** [U] the action of an object moving in a circle around a central fixed point 旋转；转动：*the daily rotation of the earth on its axis* 地球每天的自转 **2** [C] one complete movement in a circle around a fixed point（旋转的）一周，一圈：*This switch controls the number of rotations per minute.* 这个开关控制着每分钟的转数。**3** [U, C] the act of regularly changing the thing that is being used in a particular situation, or of changing the person who does a particular job 轮换；交替；换班：***crop rotation/the rotation of crops***

R

(= changing the crop that is grown on an area of land in order to protect the soil) 庄稼的轮作 ◇ *Wheat, maize and sugar beet are planted **in rotation**.* 小麦、玉米和甜菜是轮流种植的。 ◇ *The committee is chaired by all the members **in rotation**.* 委员会由所有成员轮流担任主席。 ▸ **ro·ta·tion·al** /-ʃənl/ *adj.* [only before noun]

Ro·ta·va·tor™ (*also* **Ro·to·va·tor**) /ˈrəʊtəveɪtə(r); *NAmE* ˈroʊ-/ *noun* (*BrE*) a machine with blades that turn and break up soil 罗塔瓦多旋耕机

ROTC /ˈrɒtsi; *NAmE* ˈrɑːt-/ *abbr.* (*US*) Reserve Officers' Training Corps (an organization for students in the US who are training to be military officers while they are studying) （美国在校学生的）预备役军官训练团

rote /rəʊt; *NAmE* roʊt/ *noun* [U] (often used as an adjective 常用作形容词) the process of learning sth by repeating it until you remember it rather than by understanding the meaning of it 死记硬背: *to learn **by rote*** 死记硬背地学习 ◇ *rote learning* 死记硬背的学习

ROTFL *abbr.* (*informal*) = ROFL

roti /ˈrəʊti; *NAmE* ˈroʊ-/ *noun* [U, C] **1** a type of S Asian bread that is cooked on a GRIDDLE （南亚）烙饼，烤饼 **2** (*IndE*) bread of any kind 面包

ro·tis·serie /rəʊˈtɪsəri; *NAmE* roʊ-/ *noun* (*from French*) a piece of equipment for cooking meat that turns it around on a long straight piece of metal (called a SPIT) 转架烤肉炉

rotor /ˈrəʊtə(r); *NAmE* ˈroʊ-/ *noun* a part of a machine that turns around a central point （机器的）转子，转动部件: *rotor blades on a helicopter* 直升机的旋翼桨叶 ⊃ VISUAL VOCAB PAGE V57

Ro·to·va·tor = ROTAVATOR™

rot·ten /ˈrɒtn; *NAmE* ˈrɑːtn/ *adj., adv.*

▪***adj.*** **1** (of food, wood, etc. 食物、树木等) that has decayed and cannot be eaten or used 腐烂的；腐败的；腐朽的: *the smell of rotten vegetables* 腐烂蔬菜的气味 ◇ *The fruit is starting to **go rotten**.* 水果已经开始腐烂变质了。 ◇ *rotten floorboards* 腐朽的木地板 **2** [usually before noun] (*informal*) very bad 非常糟糕的；恶劣的 SYN **terrible**: *I've had a rotten day!* 我这一天倒霉透了！ ◇ *What rotten luck!* 真倒霉！ ◇ *She's a rotten singer.* 她是个蹩脚的歌手。 **3** [usually before noun] (*informal*) dishonest 不诚实的；腐败的: *The organization is **rotten to the core**.* 这个组织腐败透顶。 **4** [not before noun] (*informal*) looking or feeling ill/sick 不舒服；不适: *She felt rotten.* 她感觉不舒服。 **5** [not before noun] (*informal*) feeling guilty about sth you have done 感到内疚（或惭愧）: *I feel rotten about leaving them behind.* 我丢下他们不管，感到很惭愧。 **6** [only before noun] (*informal*) used to emphasize that you are angry or upset about sth （强调非常生气或沮丧）倒霉的，破烂的: *You can keep your rotten money!* 你就留着你的臭钱吧！ ▸ **rot·ten·ness** *noun* [U]

IDM **a rotten ˈapple** one bad person who has a bad effect on others in a group 带来恶劣影响的人；害群之马

▪***adv.*** (*informal*) to a large degree; very much 很大程度上；非常: *She spoils the children rotten.* 她很溺爱孩子。 ◇ (*BrE*) *He fancies you (something) rotten.* 他非常迷恋你。

rot·ter /ˈrɒtə(r); *NAmE* ˈrɑːt-/ *noun* (*old-fashioned, BrE, informal*) a person who behaves badly towards other people 无赖；恶棍

Rott·weiler /ˈrɒtwaɪlə(r); -vaɪ-; *NAmE* ˈrɑːtwaɪ-; ˈrɔːtwaɪ-/ *noun* a large dog that can be very aggressive 罗威纳犬

ro·tund /rəʊˈtʌnd; *NAmE* roʊ-/ *adj.* (*formal* or *humorous*) having a fat round body 圆胖的；肥圆的 SYN **plump**: *the rotund figure of Mr Stevens* 史蒂文斯先生圆胖的体形 ▸ **ro·tund·ity** *noun* [U]

ro·tunda /rəʊˈtʌndə; *NAmE* roʊ-/ *noun* a round building or hall, especially one with a curved roof (= a DOME) 圆形建筑，圆形大厅（尤指带有圆顶的） ⊃ VISUAL VOCAB PAGE V14

rou·ble (*especially BrE*) (*NAmE usually* **ruble**) /ˈruːbl/ *noun* the unit of money in Russia 卢布（俄罗斯货币单位）

roué /ˈruːeɪ; *NAmE* ruːˈeɪ/ *noun* (*old-fashioned*) a man who drinks too much alcohol, uses illegal drugs, or is sexually immoral, especially a man who is fairly old （尤指上了年纪的）酒色之徒，瘾君子

rouge /ruːʒ/ *noun* [U] (*old-fashioned*) a red powder used by women for giving colour to their cheeks 胭脂 ▸ **rouge** *verb* ~ **sth**

rough 🔑 /rʌf/ *adj., noun, verb, adv.*

▪***adj.*** (**rough·er**, **rough·est**)

• NOT SMOOTH 不平滑 **1** 🔑 having a surface that is not even or regular 粗糙的；不平滑的；高低不平的: *rough ground* 高低不平的地面 ◇ *The skin on her hands was hard and rough.* 她手上的皮肤粗糙且没有弹性。 ◇ *Trim rough edges with a sharp knife.* 用锋利的刀将参差不齐的边切齐。 OPP **smooth**

• NOT EXACT 不确切 **2** 🔑 not exact; not including all details 不确切的；粗略的；大致的 SYN **approximate**: *a **rough calculation/estimate** of the cost* 对成本的粗略计算 / 估计 ◇ *I've got a **rough idea** of where I want to go.* 我大致知道我想去哪里了。 ◇ *There were about 20 people there, **at a rough guess**.* 那里约计有 20 人。 ◇ *a rough draft of a speech* 讲话草稿 ◇ *a rough sketch* 草图

• VIOLENT 粗暴 **3** 🔑 not gentle or careful; violent 粗暴的；粗野的；猛烈的: *This watch is not designed for rough treatment.* 这块手表不可猛烈震动。 ◇ *They complained of rough handling by the guards.* 他们投诉警卫对他们动粗。 ◇ *rough kids* 粗野的小孩 ◇ *Don't try any **rough stuff** with me!* 别想对我撒野！ **4** 🔑 where there is a lot of violence or crime 犯罪盛行的；充斥暴力的；危险的: *the roughest neighbourhood in the city* 市内最危险的街区 ⊃ WORDFINDER NOTE AT LOCATION

• SEA 海洋 **5** 🔑 having large and dangerous waves 汹涌的；风浪很大的: *It was too rough to sail that night.* 那天夜里风浪太大，无法行船。

• WEATHER 天气 **6** wild and with storms 恶劣的；有暴风雨的

• DIFFICULT 困难 **7** 🔑 difficult and unpleasant 艰难的；艰苦的 SYN **tough**: *He's had a really **rough time** recently* (= he's had a lot of problems). 他最近真是困难重重。 ◇ *We'll get someone in to do the rough work* (= the hard physical work). 我们会找个人来干这重活。

• NOT WELL 不舒服 **8** (*BrE*) not feeling well 不舒服的；不适的: *You look rough—are you OK?* 你看上去不太舒服，你没事吧？ ◇ *I had a rough night* (= I didn't sleep well). 我一夜没睡好觉。

• PLAIN/BASIC 简单；基本 **9** 🔑 simply made and not finished in every detail; plain or basic 粗糙的；不够精细的；朴实简单的: *rough wooden tables* 粗糙的木桌 ◇ *a rough track* 凹凸不平的小径 ◇ (*BrE*) *rough paper for making notes on* 做笔记的草稿纸

• NOT SMOOTH 令人不舒服 **10** not smooth or pleasant to taste, listen to, etc. 味道差的；涩的；刺耳的；令人难受的: *a rough wine/voice* 口感极差的葡萄酒；刺耳的声音 ▸ **rough·ness** *noun* [U] ⊃ SEE ALSO ROUGHLY (2)

IDM **a rough ˈdeal** the fact of being treated unfairly 不公平的待遇 **rough ˈedges** small parts of sth or of a person's character that are not yet as good as they should be 瑕疵；美中不足之处: *The ballet still had some rough edges.* 这段芭蕾舞还有不足之处。 ◇ *He had a few rough edges knocked off at school.* 他在学校改掉了一些坏毛病。 **the ˌrough end of the ˈpineapple** (*AustralE, informal*) a situation in which sb is treated badly or unfairly 受到不良（或不公平）对待的处境 ⊃ MORE AT RIDE *n.*

▪***noun***

• IN GOLF 高尔夫球 **1 the rough** [sing.] the part of a GOLF COURSE where the grass is long, making it more difficult to hit the ball （高尔夫球场的）长草区 ⊃ COMPARE FAIRWAY

• DRAWING/DESIGN 绘画；设计 **2** [C] (*specialist*) the first version of a drawing or design that has been done quickly and without much detail 草稿；草图

• VIOLENT PERSON 暴徒 **3** [C] (*old-fashioned, informal*) a violent person 暴徒；粗野的人: *a gang of roughs* 一帮暴徒

R

IDM in 'rough (*especially BrE*) if you write or draw sth **in rough**, you make a first version of it, not worrying too much about mistakes or details 粗略地；大致上 **take the ˌrough with the 'smooth** to accept the unpleasant or difficult things that happen in life as well as the good things 好事坏事都接受；既能享乐也能吃苦 ➲ MORE AT BIT

■ *verb*

IDM **'rough it** (*informal*) to live in a way that is not very comfortable for a short time 暂时过艰苦的生活；渡过暂时的难关：*We can sleep on the beach. I don't mind roughing it for a night or two.* 我们可以睡在海滩上，我不介意吃一两夜的苦。

PHR V **ˌrough sth↔'out** to draw or write sth without including all the details 画…的草图；草拟：*I've roughed out a few ideas.* 我已有几个初步设想。 **ˌrough sb↔'up** (*informal*) to hurt sb by hitting or kicking them 殴打；施以暴力：*He claimed that guards had roughed him up in prison.* 他声称看守们在监狱里殴打了他。

■ *adv.* using force or violence 粗鲁地；粗野地：*Do they always play this rough?* 他们比赛总是这么粗野吗？

IDM **live/sleep 'rough** (*BrE*) to live or sleep outdoors, usually because you have no home and no money 风餐露宿（通常因为无家可归或贫穷）：*young people sleeping rough on the streets* 露宿街头的年轻人

rough·age /'rʌfɪdʒ/ *noun* [U] the part of food that helps to keep a person healthy by keeping the BOWELS working and moving other food quickly through the body 食物中的粗纤维 SYN **fibre**

ˌrough-and-'ready *adj.* [usually before noun] **1** simple and prepared quickly but good enough for a particular situation 简单粗糙但可用的：*a rough-and-ready guide to the education system* 简略的教育制度指南 **2** (of a person 人) not very polite, educated or fashionable 粗犷的；粗鲁的；不拘小节的

ˌrough and 'tumble *noun* [U, sing.] **1** ~ (**of sth**) a situation in which people compete with each other and are aggressive in order to get what they want 激烈的竞争；混战：*the rough and tumble of politics* 政治上的混战 **2** noisy and slightly violent behaviour when children or animals are playing together（儿童或动物一起嬉戏时的）吵闹捣蛋行为

R

rough·cast /'rʌfkɑːst; *NAmE* -kæst/ *noun* [U] a type of PLASTER containing small stones that is used for covering the outside walls of buildings 粗灰泥 ▸ **rough-cast** *adj.*

'rough cut *noun* the first version of a film/movie, after the different scenes have been put together（影片的）初次剪辑版

'rough-cut *verb* ~ **sth** to cut sth quickly, without paying attention to the exact size 粗切（或剪、割等）

ˌrough 'diamond (*BrE*) (*NAmE* **ˌdiamond in the 'rough**) *noun* a person who has many good qualities even though they do not seem to be very polite, educated, etc. 外粗内秀的人

rough·en /'rʌfn/ *verb* [I, T] to become rough; to make sth rough 变粗糙；使粗糙：*His voice roughened with every word.* 他说话的声音越来越嘶哑。◇ ~ **sth** *Cold weather roughens your skin.* 天气寒冷，皮肤变得粗糙。

ˌrough-'hewn *adj.* [only before noun] **1** (of stone, wood, etc. 石头、木材等) cut in a way that leaves it with a rough surface 被砍凿得很粗糙的：*rough-hewn walls* 被弄得坑洼不平的墙壁 ◇ (*figurative*) *the rough-hewn features of his face* 他那饱经沧桑的脸 **2** (*formal*) (of a person or their behaviour 人或行为) not very polite or educated 粗鲁的；粗野的

rough·house /'rʌfhaʊs; -haʊz/ *verb* [I, T] ~ (**sb**) (*NAmE, informal*) to fight sb or play with sb roughly 打闹；玩闹：*Quit roughhousing, you two!* 你们两个别打打闹闹了！

rough·ing /'rʌfɪŋ/ *noun* [U] (in ICE HOCKEY and AMERICAN FOOTBALL 冰上曲棍球和美式足球) an illegal use of force, for which a PENALTY may be given（可能受罚的）粗野动作，犯规冲撞

ˌrough 'justice *noun* [U] **1** punishment that does not seem fair 不太公平的惩罚：*It was rough justice that they lost in the closing seconds of the game.* 他们在比赛的最后几秒钟落败，这不太公平。 **2** treatment that is fair but not official or expected 算得上公平的待遇：*There was a certain amount of rough justice in his downfall.* 他的垮台也算是大致公平。

rough·ly 🔑 /'rʌfli/ *adv.* **1** 🔑 approximately but not exactly 大约；大致；差不多：*Sales are up by roughly 10%.* 销售额上升了大约 10%。◇ *We live roughly halfway between here and the coast.* 我们住的地方大致在这里和海滨中间。◇ *They all left at roughly the same time.* 他们都是大约同一时间离开的。◇ ***Roughly speaking,*** *we receive about fifty letters a week on the subject.* 关于这个问题，粗略地说，我们每周收到大约五十封来信。 **2** 🔑 using force or not being careful and gentle 粗暴地；粗鲁地：*He pushed her roughly out of the way.* 他粗暴地把她推到一边。◇ *'What do you want?' she demanded roughly.* "你想怎么样？"她粗声粗气地问道。 **3** 🔑 in a way that does not leave a smooth surface 粗糙地；凹凸不平地：*roughly plastered walls* 灰泥抹得凹凸不平的墙壁

rough·neck /'rʌfnek/ *noun* (*informal*) **1** (*especially NAmE*) a man who is noisy, rude and aggressive 吵闹而粗鲁的人 **2** a man who works on an OIL RIG 石油钻井工；油井工人

rough·shod /'rʌfʃɒd; *NAmE* -ʃɑːd/ *adv.*

IDM **ride, etc. 'roughshod over sb** (*especially BrE*) (*US usually* **run 'roughshod over sb**) to treat sb badly and not worry about their feelings （对某人）为所欲为，横行霸道；任意蹂躏

roul·ette /ruː'let/ *noun* [U] a gambling game in which a ball is dropped onto a moving wheel that has holes with numbers on it. Players bet on which hole the ball will be in when the wheel stops. 轮盘赌 ➲ SEE ALSO RUSSIAN ROULETTE ➲ WORDFINDER NOTE AT GAMBLING

round 🔑 /raʊnd/ *adj., adv., prep., noun, verb*

■ *adj.* (**round·er**, **round·est**) **1** 🔑 shaped like a circle or a ball 圆形的；环形的；球形的：*a round plate* 圆盘子 ◇ *These glasses suit people with round faces.* 这款眼镜适合圆脸的人。◇ *The fruit are small and round.* 这种水果小而圆。◇ *Rugby isn't played with a round ball.* 橄榄球比赛用的不是圆球。◇ *the discovery that the world is round* 地球是圆的这一发现 ◇ *The child was watching it all with big round eyes* (= showing interest). 这孩子睁着又大又圆的眼睛看着这一切。◇ *a T-shirt with a round neck* 圆领 T 恤衫 ➲ SEE ALSO ROUND-EYED, ROUND-TABLE **2** 🔑 having a curved shape 弧形的；圆弧的：*the round green hills of Donegal* 多尼戈尔那些圆圆的绿山冈 ◇ *round brackets* (= in writing) 圆括号 ◇ *She had a small mouth and round pink cheeks.* 她的嘴小小的，圆脸蛋粉粉的。 **3** 🔑 [only before noun] a **round** figure or amount is one that is given as a whole number, usually one ending in 0 or 5 整数的；尾数是 0（或 5）的：*Make it a round figure—say forty dollars.* 凑个整数，就四十块钱吧。◇ *Two thousand is a nice round number—put that down.* 两千是个不错的整数，记下吧。◇ *Well,* ***in round figures*** (= not giving the exact figures) *we've spent twenty thousand so far.* 嗯，说个约数吧，我们至今花了有两万了。 ▸ **round·ness** *noun* [U]: *His face had lost its boyish roundness.* 他的脸已不是小时候那副圆圆的娃娃脸了。

■ *adv.* (*especially BrE*) (*NAmE usually* **around**) HELP For the special uses of **round** in phrasal verbs, look at the verb entries. For example, the meaning of **come round to sth** is given in the phrasal verb section of the entry for **come**. 关于 round 在短语动词中的特殊用法，见有关动词词条。如 come round to sth 在词条 come 的短语动词部分。 **1** 🔑 moving in a circle 旋转；环绕；兜圈子：*Everybody joins hands and dances round.* 大家手拉着手，围成一圈跳舞。◇ *How do you make the wheels go round?* 你是怎么让轮子转起来的？ ◇ *The children were spinning* ***round and round.*** 孩子们一个劲地转呀转。◇ (*figurative*) *The thought kept going round and round in her head.* 这个想法一直萦绕在她的心头。 **2** 🔑 measuring or marking the edge or outside of sth 周长；周围；绕一整圈：*a young tree* *measuring only 18 inches round* 周长只有 18 英寸的小树 ◇ *They've built a high fence* ***all round*** *to keep intruders out.* 他们在周围竖起了高高的篱笆，以防外人进入。 **3** on all sides of sb/sth 在周围；围绕： *A large crowd had gathered round to watch.* 一大群人聚在周围观看。 **4** at various places in an area 到处；四处： *People stood round waiting for something to happen.* 人们在各处站着，等待着发生什么事情。 **5** in a circle or curve to face another way or the opposite way 调转方向；转过来： *He turned the car round and drove back again.* 他调转车头，又开了回来。 ◇ *She looked round at the sound of his voice.* 听到他的声音，她扭头看了看。 **6** to the other side of sth 绕弯；迂回；向另一侧： *We walked round to the back of the house.* 我们绕到房子的后面。 ◇ *The road's blocked—you'll have to drive* ***the long way round.*** 这条路被堵了，你们得开车绕着走了。 **7** from one place, person, etc. to another 依次；挨个： *They've moved all the furniture round.* 他们把所有的家具搬动了一遍。 ◇ *He went round interviewing people about local traditions.* 他到处找人访谈，了解当地的传统。 ◇ *Pass the biscuits round.* 把饼干传给大家。 ◇ *Have we* ***enough cups to go round?*** 我们的杯子够大家用吗？ **8** (*informal*) to or at a particular place, especially where sb lives 到某地，在某地（尤指居住地）： *I'll be round in an hour.* 我过一个小时就到。 ◇ *We've invited the Frasers round this evening.* 我们已经邀请了弗雷泽一家今晚过来。 ➲ NOTE AT AROUND

IDM **,round a'bout 1** approximately 大约： *We're leaving round about ten.* 我们十点钟左右要离开。 ◇ *A new roof will cost round about £3 000.* 换新房顶大约要花 3 000 英镑。 **2** in the area near a place 在附近： *in Oxford and the villages round about* 在牛津及其附近的村庄 ➲ MORE AT TIME *n.*

■ ***prep.*** (*especially BrE*) (*NAmE usually* **around**) **1** in a circle 环绕；围绕： *the first woman to sail round the world* 第一位环球航行的女性 ◇ *The earth moves round the sun.* 地球绕着太阳转。 **2** on, to or from the other side of sth 绕过；在另一侧： *Our house is round the next bend.* 前面一拐弯就是我们家。 ◇ *There she is, coming round the corner.* 她来了，绕过拐角过来了。 ◇ *There must be* ***a way round*** *the problem.* 这个问题一定有办法解决。 **3** on all sides of sb/sth; surrounding sb/sth 在…周围；包围： *She put her arms round him.* 她张开双臂搂住他。 ◇ *He had a scarf round his neck.* 他脖子上围着围巾。 ◇ *They were all sitting round the table.* 他们围着桌子坐着。 **4** in or to many parts of sth 在…各处；到…各部分： *She looked all round the room.* 她将房间四下打量了一下。 **5** to fit in with particular people, ideas, etc. 适应；围绕（人、思想等）： *He has to organize his life round the kids.* 他不得不以孩子们为中心来安排自己的生活。 ➲ NOTE AT AROUND

IDM **,round 'here** near where you are now or where you live 在附近： *There are no decent schools round here.* 附近没有什么像样的学校。 ➲ MORE AT MILLSTONE

■ ***noun***

• **STAGE IN PROCESS** 进程 **1** a set of events which form part of a longer process 阶段；轮次： *the next round of peace talks* 下一轮和谈 ◇ *the final round of voting in the election* 选举的最后一轮投票

• **IN COMPETITIONS** 竞赛 **2** a stage in a competition or sports event 比赛阶段；轮次；局；场： *the qualifying rounds of the National Championships* 全国锦标赛的资格赛 ◇ *Anderson was knocked out of the tournament in the third round.* 安德森在锦标赛的第三轮被淘汰出局。 ➲ WORDFINDER NOTE AT COMPETITION **3** a stage in a BOXING or WRESTLING match（拳击或摔跤比赛的）回合： *The fight only lasted five rounds.* 比赛只持续了五个回合。 **4** a complete game of GOLF; a complete way around the course in some other sports, such as SHOWJUMPING（高尔夫球、马术场地障碍赛等的）一轮比赛，一局，一场： *We played a round of golf.* 我们打了一场高尔夫球。 ◇ *the first horse to jump a clear round* 干净利落地完成整套跳跃表演的第一匹马

• **REGULAR ACTIVITIES/ROUTE** 惯常的活动 / 路线 **5** a regular series of activities 一系列常规活动；惯常的活动： ***the daily round*** *of school life* 学校的日常生活 ◇ *Her life is one long round of parties and fun.* 她的生活就是没完没了的聚会娱乐。 **6** a regular route that sb takes when delivering or collecting sth; a regular series of visits that sb makes（收发信函等的）固定路线；照例要出去做的事情： *Dr Green was* ***on her*** *daily ward* ***rounds.*** 格林医生在进行每日一次的巡查病房。 ◇ (*BrE*) *a postman on his delivery round* 正在投递邮件的邮递员 ➲ SEE ALSO MILK ROUND (1), PAPER ROUND

• **DRINKS** 饮料 **7** a number of drinks bought by one person for all the others in a group（由一人给大家买的）一巡饮料： *a round of drinks* 一巡饮料 ◇ *It's my round* (= it is my turn to pay for the next set of drinks). 这一巡轮到我了。

• **BREAD** 面包 **8** (*BrE*) a whole slice of bread; SANDWICHES made from two whole slices of bread 一整片面包；（两整片面包做的）三明治： *Who's for another round of toast?* 谁还要烤面包片？ ◇ *two rounds of beef sandwiches* 两份牛肉三明治

• **CIRCLE** 圆 **9** a round object or piece of sth 圆形物体；圆块： *Cut the pastry into rounds.* 将油酥面团切成一个个圆块。

• **OF APPLAUSE/CHEERS** 掌声；欢呼声 **10 ~ of applause/cheers** a short period during which people show their approval of sb/sth by clapping, etc. 一阵： *There was a great round of applause when the dance ended.* 舞蹈结束的时候，爆发出了一阵热烈的掌声。

• **SHOT** 射击 **11** a single shot from a gun; a bullet for one shot 一次射击；一发子弹： *They fired several rounds at the crowd.* 他们朝人群开了几枪。 ◇ *We only have three rounds of ammunition left.* 我们只剩下三发子弹了。

• **SONG** 歌曲 **12** (*music* 音) a song for two or more voices in which each sings the same tune but starts at a different time 轮唱曲

IDM **do/go the 'rounds (of sth) 1** (*BrE*) (*NAmE* **make the 'rounds**) if news or a joke **does the rounds**, it is passed on quickly from one person to another 迅速传开；迅速流传 **2** (*BrE*) (*also* **make the 'rounds** *NAmE, BrE*) to go around from place to place, especially when looking for work or support for a political CAMPAIGN, etc. 到各处去，巡回（找工作或寻求对政治运动的支持等） **in the 'round 1** (of a work of art 艺术品) made so that it can be seen from all sides 圆雕的；可全方位观看的；立体的： *an opportunity to see Canova's work in the round* 观看卡诺瓦的圆雕艺术作品的机会 **2** (of a theatre or play 剧院或戏剧) with the people watching all around a central stage 舞台设在中央的

■ ***verb*** **1** [T] **~ sth** to go around a corner of a building, a bend in the road, etc. 绕行；绕过： *The boat rounded the tip of the island.* 小船绕过岛的尖端。 ◇ *We rounded the bend at high speed.* 我们高速驶过这段弯路。 **2** [T, I] **~ (sth)** to make sth into a round shape; to form into a round shape （使）成圆形；变圆： *She rounded her lips and whistled.* 她撮起嘴唇吹口哨。 ◇ *His eyes rounded with horror.* 他吓得两眼圆睁。 **3** [T] **~ sth (up/down) (to sth)** to increase or decrease a number to the next highest or lowest whole number（将数字调高或调低）使成为整数；把（数字）四舍五入

PHR V **,round sth↔'off (with sth) 1** (*NAmE also* **,round sth↔'out**) to finish an activity or complete sth in a good or suitable way 圆满结束；圆满完成： *She rounded off the tour with a concert at Carnegie Hall.* 她在卡内基音乐厅举行一场音乐会，以此圆满结束了她的巡回演出。 **2** to take the sharp or rough edges off sth 去除…的棱角；使…的边缘光滑： *You can round off the corners with sandpaper.* 你可以用砂纸把棱角打磨光滑。 **'round on sb** to suddenly speak angrily to sb and criticize or attack them 突然责骂（或指责） **SYN** **turn on**: *He rounded on journalists, calling them 'a pack of vultures'.* 他突然对记者大发雷霆，称他们是一帮乘人之危的家伙。 **,round sb/sth↔'up 1** to find and gather together people, animals or things 将…聚拢起来；使聚集： *I rounded up a few friends for a party.* 我找了几个朋友聚了聚。 ◇ *The cattle are rounded up in the evenings.* 到了晚上，牛都要圈起来。 **2** if police or soldiers **round up** a group of people, they find them and arrest or capture them 围捕；围剿 ➲ RELATED NOUN ROUND-UP (2)

round·about /'raʊndəbaʊt/ *noun, adj.*

■ ***noun*** (*BrE*) **1** (*NAmE* **'traffic circle, ro·tary**) a place where

R

two or more roads meet, forming a circle that all traffic must go around in the same direction（交通）环岛: *At the roundabout, take the second exit.* 到环岛后，走第二个出口。 ➲ SEE ALSO MINI-ROUNDABOUT ➲ **WORDFINDER NOTE** AT ROAD **2** (*NAmE* **ˈmerry-go-round**) a round platform for children to play on in a park, etc. that is pushed round while the children are sitting on it（游乐设施）旋转平台 **3** (*BrE*) = MERRY-GO-ROUND (1) **IDM** SEE SWING *n.*
■ ***adj.*** [usually before noun] not done or said using the shortest, simplest or most direct way possible 迂回的；间接的；兜圈子的: *It was a difficult and roundabout trip.* 这是一次艰难而曲折的旅行。◇ *He told us, in a very roundabout way, that he was thinking of leaving.* 他拐弯抹角地对我们说他想走了。

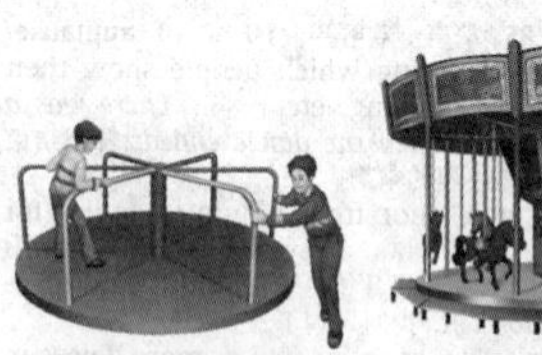

roundabout (*BrE*)
merry-go-round (*NAmE*)
旋转平台

merry-go-round / roundabout (*both BrE*)
carousel (*NAmE*)
旋转木马

ˈround bracket *noun* (*BrE*) = BRACKET (1)

round·ed ⚷ /ˈraʊndɪd/ *adj.* [usually before noun] **1** ⚷ having a round shape 圆形的: *a surface with rounded edges* 带圆边的面 ◇ *rounded shoulders* 曲背 **2** having a wide variety of qualities that combine to produce sth pleasant, complete and balanced 全面的；一应俱全的；完善的: *a smooth rounded taste* 舒爽醇厚的味道 ◇ *a fully rounded education* 非常全面的教育 **3** (*phonetics* 语音) (of a speech sound 语音) produced with the lips in a narrow round position 圆唇的 **OPP** **unrounded** ➲ SEE ALSO WELL ROUNDED

roundel /ˈraʊndl/ *noun* (*specialist*) a round design that is used as a decoration or to identify an aircraft 圆形图案（或标志）；（飞机的）圆形识别标志

round·ers /ˈraʊndəz; *NAmE* -ərz/ *noun* [U] a British game played especially in schools by two teams using a BAT and ball. Each player tries to hit the ball and then run around the four sides of a square before the other team can return the ball.（英国）圆场棒球 ➲ COMPARE BASEBALL (1)

ˌround-ˈeyed *adj.* with eyes that are fully open because of surprise, fear, etc.（因为吃惊、害怕等）两眼圆睁的

Round·head /ˈraʊndhed/ *noun* a person who supported Parliament against the King in the English Civil War (1642–49) 圆颅党人（1642 年至 1649 年英格兰内战期间支持议会反对国王）➲ COMPARE CAVALIER

round·house /ˈraʊndhaʊs/ *noun* a punch where the arm moves around in a wide curve 大弧度出拳；大抡拳

ˈroundhouse kick *noun* a move in KARATE and other MARTIAL ARTS, in which you turn on one foot as you make a high kick with the other（空手道等武术中的）回旋踢，旋踢

round·ing /ˈraʊndɪŋ/ *noun* [U] (*phonetics* 语音) the fact of producing a speech sound with the lips in a rounded position 发圆唇音；圆唇

round·ly /ˈraʊndli/ *adv.* strongly or by a large number of people 有力地；广泛地: *The report has been roundly criticized.* 这份报告受到了广泛的批评。◇ *They were roundly defeated* (= they lost by a large number of points). 他们一败涂地。

ˌround ˈrobin *noun* **1** (*sport* 体育) a competition in which every player or team plays every other player or team 循环赛 **2** a letter that has been signed by a large number of people who wish to express their opinions about sth 联名信（或意见书） **3** something that is made, written, etc. by several people who each add a part one after another 合作（或合写等）的东西；接龙创作: *a round robin story* 接龙故事 **4** a letter intended to be read by many people that is copied and sent to each one 大量复制传阅的信件

ˌround-ˈshouldered *adj.* with shoulders that are bent forward or sloping downwards 曲背的；溜肩膀

rounds·man /ˈraʊndzmən/ *noun* (*pl.* **-men** /-mən/) **1** (*NAmE* **ˈroute man**) a person who delivers things to people in a particular area（特定区域的）送货员 **2** (*NAmE*) the police officer in charge of a group of officers that is moving around an area（管区）巡警长 **3** (*AustralE*) a journalist who deals with a particular subject 专题记者

ˌround-ˈtable *adj.* [only before noun] (of discussions, meetings, etc. 讨论、会议等) at which everyone is equal and has the same rights 圆桌的；参与者权利均等的: *round-table talks* 圆桌会谈

ˌround-the-ˈclock (*also* **aˌround-the-ˈclock**) *adj.* [only before noun] lasting or happening all day and night 日夜不停的；持续一整天的: *round-the-clock nursing care* 全天的护理 ➲ SEE ALSO CLOCK *n.*

ˌround ˈtrip *noun* [C, U] a journey to a place and back again 来回旅行；往返旅程: *a 30-mile round trip to work* 上班往返 30 英里的路程 ◇ (*NAmE*) *It's 30 miles round trip to work.* 上班要走往返 30 英里的路程。 ▶ **ˌround-ˈtrip** *adj.* [only before noun] (*NAmE*) : *a round-trip ticket* 双程票 ➲ SEE ALSO RETURN TICKET

ˈround-up *noun* [usually sing.] **1** a summary of the most important points of a particular subject, especially the news（尤指新闻）概要，摘要: *We'll be back after the break with a round-up of today's other stories.* 休息之后我们会摘要报道今天其他的新闻。 **2** an act of bringing people or animals together in one place for a particular purpose 聚拢；驱集；聚集

round·worm /ˈraʊndwɜːm; *NAmE* -wɜːrm/ *noun* a small WORM that lives in the INTESTINES of pigs, humans and some other animals 线虫（动物）

rouse /raʊz/ *verb* **1** (*formal*) to wake sb up, especially when they are sleeping deeply 唤醒；使醒来: **~ sb from sleep/bed** *The telephone roused me from my sleep at 6 a.m.* 早晨 6 点钟，电话铃声就把我从睡梦中吵醒了。◇ **~ sb** *Nicky roused her with a gentle nudge.* 尼基用胳膊肘轻轻地将她推醒。 **2** to make sb want to start doing sth when they were not active or interested in doing it 使活跃起来；使产生兴趣: **~ sb/yourself (to sth)** *A lot of people were roused to action by the appeal.* 许多人响应号召行动起来。◇ **~ sb/yourself to do sth** *Richard couldn't rouse himself to say anything in reply.* 理查德没有兴趣回答。 **3 ~ sth** (*formal*) to make sb feel a particular emotion 激起（某种情感）: *to rouse sb's anger* 把某人惹火 ◇ *What* ***roused your suspicions*** (= what made you suspicious)? 你是怎么起疑心的？ **4** [usually passive] **~ sb** to make sb angry, excited or full of emotion 激怒；使激动: *Chris is not easily roused.* 克里斯不容易激动。➲ SEE ALSO AROUSE

rous·ing /ˈraʊzɪŋ/ *adj.* [usually before noun] **1** full of energy and enthusiasm 充满活力（或激情）的: *a rousing cheer* 热情的欢呼 ◇ *The team was given* ***a rousing reception*** *by the fans.* 球队受到了球迷的热烈欢迎。 **2** intended to make other people feel enthusiastic about sth 激励的；激动人心的: *a rousing speech* 使人振奋的讲话

roust /raʊst/ *verb* **~ sb (from sth)** (*NAmE*) to disturb sb or make them move from a place 打扰；扰乱；驱逐

roust·about /ˈraʊstəbaʊt/ *noun* (*especially NAmE*) a man with no special skills who does temporary work, for example on an OIL RIG or in a CIRCUS（石油钻井平台或马戏场等处的）杂工，非技术工

rout /raʊt/ *noun, verb*
■ *noun* [sing.] a situation in which sb is defeated easily and completely in a battle or competition 溃败；彻底失败
IDM **put sb to 'rout** (*literary*) to defeat sb easily and completely 彻底打败；使溃败
■ *verb* ~ sb to defeat sb completely in a competition, a battle, etc. 彻底击败；使溃败： *The Buffalo Bills routed the Atlanta Falcons 41–14.* 布法罗比尔队以 41:14 大胜亚特兰大猎鹰队。

route AW /ruːt; *NAmE also* raʊt/ *noun, verb*
■ *noun* **1** a way that you follow to get from one place to another 路线；路途： *Which is the best route to take?* 哪一条是最佳路线？ ◇ *Motorists are advised to find an alternative route.* 建议驾车者换一条路线。 ◇ *a coastal route* 沿海的路线 ◇ ~ (**from A to B**) *the quickest route from Florence to Rome* 从佛罗伦萨到罗马的最快捷的路线 ◇ *an escape route* 逃脱的路径 ➲ SEE ALSO EN ROUTE **2** a fixed way along which a bus, train, etc. regularly travels or goods are regularly sent（公共汽车和列车等的）常规路线，固定线路： *The house is not on a* ***bus route***. 这房子不在公交线上。 ◇ ***shipping routes*** 航运线路 ◇ *a* ***cycle route*** (= a path that is only for CYCLISTS) 自行车道 **3** ~ (**to sth**) a particular way of achieving sth 途径；渠道： *the route to success* 成功之路 **4** used before the number of a main road in the US（用于美国干线公路号码前）： *Route 66* * 66 号公路
■ *verb* (**rout·ing**, **route·ing**, **rout·ed**, **route·ed**) ~ **sb/sth** (+ **adv./prep.**) to send sb/sth by a particular route 按某路线发送： *Satellites route data all over the globe.* 卫星向全球各地传递信息。

Route 128 /ˌruːt ˌwʌn twentiˈeɪt/ *noun* (in the US) an area in Massachusetts where there are many companies connected with the computer and ELECTRONICS industries * 128 号公路高科技带（位于美国马萨诸塞州的计算机与电子工业区） ORIGIN From the name of an important road in the area. 源自该地区一条交通要道的名称。

'route man (*NAmE*) (*BrE* **rounds·man**) *noun* a person who delivers things to people in a particular area（特定区域的）送货员

'route march *noun* a long march for soldiers over a particular route, especially to improve their physical condition 长途行军（尤其为锻炼身体）；拉练

ˌroute 'one *noun* [U] (*BrE*) (in football (SOCCER) 足球) kicking the ball a long way towards your opponent's end, used as a direct way of attacking, rather than passing the ball between players 长传（直接）进攻

router[1] /ˈruːtə(r); *NAmE also* ˈraʊt-/ *noun* (*computing* 计) a device which sends data to the appropriate parts of a computer network 路由器（传送信息的专用网络设备） ➲ WORDFINDER NOTE AT COMPUTER ➲ VISUAL VOCAB PAGE V73

router[2] /ˈraʊtə(r)/ *noun* an electric tool which cuts shallow lines in surfaces 槽刨

rou·tine /ruːˈtiːn/ *noun, adj.*
■ *noun* **1** [C, U] the normal order and way in which you regularly do things 常规；正常顺序： *We are trying to get the baby into a routine for feeding and sleeping.* 我们试着让婴儿按时进食和睡觉。 ◇ *Make exercise a part of your* ***daily routine***. 让锻炼成为你日常生活的一部分。 ◇ *We clean and repair the machines* ***as a matter of routine***. 我们定期清洗和修理机器。 **2** [U] (*disapproving*) a situation in which life is boring because things are always done in the same way 生活乏味；无聊： *She needed a* ***break from routine***. 她需要摆脱一下刻板的生活。 **3** [C] a series of movements, jokes, etc. that are part of a performance（演出中的）一套动作，一系列笑话（等）： *a dance routine* 一套舞蹈动作 **4** [C] (*computing* 计) a list of instructions that enable a computer to perform a particular task 例程；例行程序
■ *adj.* [usually before noun] **1** done or happening as a normal part of a particular job, situation or process 常规的；例行公事的；日常的： ***routine enquiries/questions/tests*** 日常的询问；常规审问 / 检测 ◇ *The fault was discovered during a routine check.* 这个错误是在一次常规检查中发现的。 **2** not unusual or different in any way 平常的；正常的；毫不特别的： *He died of a heart attack during a routine operation.* 他在一次普通手术中死于心脏病。 **3** (*disapproving*) ordinary and boring 乏味的；平淡的 SYN **dull**, **humdrum**： *a routine job* 平淡乏味的工作 ◇ *This type of work rapidly becomes routine.* 这种工作很快就变得乏味无聊。 ▶ **rou·tine·ly** *adv.*： *Visitors are routinely checked as they enter the building.* 来访者在进入大楼时都要接受例行检查。

'routing number (*US*) (*BrE* **'sort code**) *noun* a number that is used to identify a particular bank（银行）识别代码

roux /ruː/ *noun* [C, U] (*pl.* **roux**) (*from French*) a mixture of fat and flour heated together until they form a mass, used for making sauces 油面酱（用脂肪和面粉混合煮至浓稠，用于制调味品）

rove /rəʊv; *NAmE* roʊv/ *verb* **1** [I, T] (*formal*) to travel from one place to another, often with no particular purpose 漫游；漂泊；流浪 SYN **roam**： + **adv./prep.** *A quarter of a million refugees roved around the country.* 这个国家有二十五万难民流离失所。 ◇ ~ **sth** *bands of thieves who roved the countryside* 在乡村流窜的盗贼团伙 **2** [I] (+ **adv./prep.**) if sb's eyes **rove**, the person keeps looking in different directions（眼睛）转来转去，环视，打量

rover /ˈrəʊvə(r); *NAmE* ˈroʊ-/ *noun* (*literary*) a person who likes to travel a lot rather than live in one place 漫游者；流浪者

rov·ing /ˈrəʊvɪŋ; *NAmE* ˈroʊ-/ *adj.* [usually before noun] travelling from one place to another and not staying anywhere permanently 流动的；漂泊的；漫游的；巡回的： *a roving reporter for ABC news* 美国广播公司的流动新闻记者 ◇ *Patrick's roving lifestyle takes him between London and Los Angeles.* 帕特里克漂泊不定的生活方式使他在伦敦和洛杉矶之间奔波。
IDM **have a roving 'eye** (*old-fashioned*) to always be looking for the chance to have a new sexual relationship 总是找机会寻花问柳；眼神不安分

row[1] /rəʊ; *NAmE* roʊ/ *noun, verb* ➲ SEE ALSO ROW[2]
■ *noun* **1** ~ (**of sb/sth**) a number of people standing or sitting next to each other in a line; a number of objects arranged in a line 一排；一列；一行： *a row of trees* 一行树木 ◇ *We sat* ***in a row*** *at the back of the room.* 我们在屋子的后面坐成一排。 ◇ *The vegetables were planted in neat rows.* 蔬菜种得整整齐齐。 **2** a line of seats in a cinema/movie theater, etc.（剧院、电影院等的）一排座位： *Let's sit in the back row.* 我们坐在最后一排吧。 ◇ *Our seats are five rows from the front.* 我们的座位在前面第五排。 **3** a complete line of STITCHES in knitting or CROCHET（编织中的）针行，一整行 ➲ VISUAL VOCAB PAGE V45 **4 Row** used in the name of some roads（用于某些道路名称）： *Manor Row* 庄园路 **5** [usually sing.] an act of ROWING a boat; the period of time spent doing this 划船（时间）： *We went for a row on the lake.* 我们去湖上划船了。 ➲ SEE ALSO DEATH ROW, SKID ROW
IDM **in a 'row** **1** if sth happens several times **in a row**, it happens in exactly the same way each time, and nothing different happens in the time between 连续几次地： *This is her third win in a row.* 这是她连续获得的第三次胜利。 **2** if sth happens for several days, etc. **in a row**, it happens on each of those days 接连几天（等）地： *Inflation has fallen for the third month in a row.* 通货膨胀率连续第三个月在下降。 ➲ MORE AT DUCK *n.*
■ *verb* **1** [I, T] to move a boat through water using OARS (= long wooden poles with flat ends) 划（船）： *We rowed around the island.* 我们绕着岛划船。 ◇ ~ **sth** *Grace rowed the boat out to sea again.* 格雷斯又划着船出海了。 **2** [T] ~ **sb** (+ **adv./prep.**) to take sb somewhere in a boat with OARS 划船送（某人）： *The fisherman rowed us back to the shore.* 渔夫划船将我们送回到岸上。
PHR V **ˌrow 'back** [I] to change an earlier statement, opinion or promise 改变原来的说法（或意见、承诺）： *The*

R

government is now trying to row back on its commitments. 政府现在试图收回先前的承诺。

row² /raʊ/ *noun, verb* ➲ SEE ALSO ROW¹

■ ***noun*** (*informal, especially BrE*) **1** [C] ~ (**about/over sth**) a serious disagreement between people, organizations, etc. about sth 严重分歧；纠纷：*A row has broken out over education.* 在教育问题上出现了严重分歧。 **2** [C] a noisy argument between two or more people 吵架；争吵 SYN **quarrel**: *She left him after a* ***blazing row.*** 大吵一场之后，她离他而去。◇ *family rows* 家庭里的争吵 ◇ *He* ***had a row with*** *his son.* 他跟儿子吵了一架。 **3** [sing.] a loud unpleasant noise 大的噪音 SYN **din, racket**: *Who's making that row?* 谁那么吵？

■ ***verb*** [I] (*BrE, informal*) to have a noisy argument 吵架；大声争辩：*Mike and Sue are always rowing.* 迈克和休总是吵架。◇ ~ (**with sb**) (**about sb/sth**) *She had rowed with her parents about her boyfriend.* 她和父母因为她的男朋友吵过架。

rowan /ˈrəʊən; ˈraʊən; *NAmE* ˈroʊən/ (*also* ˈ**rowan tree**, ˌ**mountain ˈash**) *noun* a small tree that has red BERRIES in the autumn/fall 花楸（树）；红果花楸；欧洲花楸

row·boat /ˈrəʊbəʊt; *NAmE* ˈroʊboʊt/ (*NAmE*) (*BrE* ˈ**rowing boat**) *noun* a small open boat that you move using OARS 划艇 ➲ VISUAL VOCAB PAGE V59

rowdy /ˈraʊdi/ *adj.* (**row·dier, row·di·est**) (of people 人) making a lot of noise or likely to cause trouble 吵闹的；惹是生非的；捣乱的 SYN **disorderly**: *a rowdy crowd at the pub* 酒吧里一群闹哄哄的家伙 ▸ **row·dily** *adv.* **row·di·ness** *noun* [U] **rowdy** *noun* (*pl.* **-ies**)：*rowdies and troublemakers* 吵闹的人和惹麻烦的人

rowdy·ism /ˈraʊdiɪzəm/ *noun* [U] behaviour that is noisy and causes trouble 吵闹行为；捣乱行为

rower /ˈrəʊə(r); *NAmE* ˈroʊ-/ *noun* a person who ROWS a boat 划船者

row house /ˈrəʊ haʊs; *NAmE* ˈroʊ/ (*also* ˈ**town house**) (*both NAmE*) (*BrE* ˌ**terraced ˈhouse**) *noun* a house that is one of a row of houses that are joined together on each side 联排式住宅 ➲ VISUAL VOCAB PAGE V16

row·ing /ˈrəʊɪŋ; *NAmE* ˈroʊɪŋ/ *noun* [U] the sport or activity of travelling in a boat using OARS 划船；划艇运动：*to go rowing* 去划船

ˈ**rowing boat** (*BrE*) (*NAmE* **row·boat**) *noun* a small open boat that you move using OARS 划艇 ➲ VISUAL VOCAB PAGE V59

ˈ**rowing machine** *noun* a piece of sports equipment on which you make the same movements as sb who is ROWING a boat 划船练习架；（陆上）划艇机 ➲ VISUAL VOCAB PAGE V46

row·lock /ˈrɒlək; ˈrəʊlɒk; *NAmE* ˈrɑːlək; ˈroʊlɑːk/ (*BrE*) (*NAmE* **oar·lock**) *noun* a device fixed to the side of a boat for holding an OAR （小船边缘的）桨架

royal 🔑 /ˈrɔɪəl/ *adj., noun*

■ ***adj.*** [only before noun] **1** 🔑 connected with or belonging to the king or queen of a country 国王的；女王的；皇家的；王室的：*the royal family* 王室 ◇ *the royal household* 王室 ➲ COMPARE REGAL ➲ WORDFINDER NOTE AT KING **2** (*abbr.* **R**) used in the names of organizations that serve or are supported by a king or queen（用于服务于国王或女王或受其赞助的组织名称）：*the Royal Navy* 英国皇家海军 ◇ *the Royal Society for the Protection of Birds* 皇家鸟类保护协会 **3** impressive; suitable for a king or queen 庄严的；盛大的；高贵的；适合国王（或女王）的 SYN **splendid**: *We were given a royal welcome.* 我们受到了盛大的欢迎。

■ ***noun*** [usually pl.] (*informal*) a member of a royal family 王室成员

the ˌRoyal Aˈcademy (*also* **the ˌRoyal Academy of ˈArts**) *noun* [sing.] a British organization whose members are famous artists. Its building in London contains an art school and space for exhibitions.（英国）皇家美术院（成员为著名艺术家，在伦敦设有艺术学校和展厅）

the ˌroyal asˈsent *noun* [sing.] (in Britain) the signature of an Act of Parliament by the king or queen so that it becomes law 御准（英国国王或女王对议会法案成为法例的批准）

ˌ**royal ˈblue** *adj.* deep bright blue 品蓝的；宝蓝的；藏蓝的 ▸ ˌ**royal ˈblue** *noun* [U] ➲ MORE LIKE THIS 15, page R26

ˌ**Royal Comˈmission** *noun* ~ (**on/into sth**) | ~ (**to do sth**) (in Britain) a group of people who are officially chosen to examine a particular law or subject and suggest any changes or new laws that should be introduced（英国）皇家委员会

ˌ**Royal ˈHighness** *noun* **His/Her/Your Royal Highness** a title of respect used when talking to or about a member of the royal family（用作王室成员的尊称）殿下：*Their Royal Highnesses, the Duke and Duchess of Kent* 肯特公爵和公爵夫人殿下

ˌ**royal ˈicing** *noun* [U] (*BrE*) a hard white covering for a fruit cake, made with sugar and the white part of eggs （水果蛋糕的）蛋白糖霜硬皮

roy·al·ist /ˈrɔɪəlɪst/ *noun* a person who believes that a country should have a king or queen 君主主义者；保皇主义者；保皇党人 SYN **monarchist** ➲ COMPARE REPUBLICAN *n.* (1) ▸ **roy·al·ist** *adj.*

ˌ**royal ˈjelly** *noun* [U] a substance that is produced by worker BEES and that is fed to a young queen bee 王浆；蜂王浆：*health food products containing royal jelly* 含蜂王浆的保健食品

roy·al·ly /ˈrɔɪəli/ *adv.* (*old-fashioned*) very well; in a very impressive way or to a great degree 非常好地；以盛情；极度

the ˌRoyal ˈMail *noun* (in Britain) the service that collects and delivers letters（英国）邮政

ˌ**royal ˈtennis** *noun* [U] (*AustralE*) = REAL TENNIS

roy·alty /ˈrɔɪəlti/ *noun* (*pl.* **-ies**) **1** [U] one or more members of a royal family 王室成员：*The gala evening was attended by royalty and politicians.* 王室成员和政坛要人参加了这个晚会。◇ *We were treated like royalty.* 我们受到了君王般的礼遇。 **2** [C, usually pl.] a sum of money that is paid to sb who has written a book, piece of music, etc. each time that it is sold or performed 版税：*All royalties from the album will go to charity.* 这张音乐专辑的全部版税收入将捐给慈善机构。◇ *She received £2 000* ***in royalties.*** 她得到了 2 000 英镑的版税。 **3** [C, usually pl.] a sum of money that is paid by an oil or mining company to the owner of the land that they are working on 矿区土地使用费（由采矿或石油公司等付给土地所有人）

ˌ**royal ˈwarrant** *noun* [usually sing.] a king's or queen's permission for a company to supply goods to them and to advertise this fact on the company's products, etc. 英廷供货许可证，王室御用许可证（公司向英国王室供应货物并可对此作产品广告）

the ˌroyal ˈwe *noun* [sing.] the use of 'we' instead of 'I' by a single person, as used traditionally by kings and queens in the past（旧时传统上国王或女王的自称，用 we 替代 I）

roz·zer /ˈrɒzə(r); *NAmE* ˈrɑːz-/ *noun* (*old-fashioned, BrE, informal*) a police officer 警察

RP /ˌɑː ˈpiː; *NAmE* ˌɑːr/ *noun* [U] the abbreviation for 'received pronunciation' (the standard form of British pronunciation, based on educated speech in southern England) 标准发音（全写为 received pronunciation，基于英格兰南部受教育阶层的发音）

RPG /ˌɑː piː ˈdʒiː; *NAmE* ˌɑːr/ *noun* = ROLE-PLAYING GAME

RPI /ˌɑː piː ˈaɪ; *NAmE* ˌɑːr/ *abbr.* RETAIL PRICE INDEX 零售物价指数

rpm /ˌɑː piː ˈem; *NAmE* ˌɑːr/ *abbr.* revolutions per minute (a measurement of the speed of an engine, a computer

HARD DRIVE, etc.) 每分钟转数（全写为 revolutions per minute）

RRP /ˌɑːr ɑː ˈpiː; *NAmE* ˌɑːr ɑːr/ *abbr.* recommended retail price 建议零售价格

RRSP /ˌɑːr ɑːr es ˈpiː/ *abbr.* (*CanE*) registered retirement savings plan (a special type of savings plan in which you can save money without paying taxes on it until you stop working when you are older) 注册退休储蓄计划（退休前免税的储蓄计划）

RSA /ˌɑːr es ˈeɪ/ *abbr.* (in the UK) Royal Society of Arts（英国）皇家艺术学会

RSI /ˌɑːr es ˈaɪ/ *noun* [U] the abbreviation for 'repetitive strain injury' or 'repetitive stress injury' (pain and swelling, especially in the arms and hands, caused by performing the same movement many times in a job or an activity) 反复应力性损伤，重复性劳损（全写为 repetitive strain injury 或 repetitive stress injury，由经常重复同一动作引起）

RSPCA /ˌɑːr es piː siː ˈeɪ/ *abbr.* (in the UK) Royal Society for the Prevention of Cruelty to Animals（英国）皇家防止虐待动物协会

RSS /ˌɑːr es ˈes/ *abbr.* (*computing* 计) Really Simple Syndication (a standard system for the distribution of information, especially news, from an Internet publisher to Internet users) 简易信息聚合（标准互联网信息传送系统，尤用于传送新闻）

RSVP (*BrE*) (*also* **R.S.V.P.** *US, BrE*) /ˌɑːr es viː ˈpiː/ *abbr.* (written on invitations) please reply (from French 'répondez s'il vous plaît') 敬请赐复（请柬用语，源自法语）

RT *abbr.* retweet (used when you want to show that a message that you put on the Twitter SOCIAL NETWORKING service was originally written by another person) 转推（全写为 retweet，用于所转发的消息前）: *RT @EddieSmith Great new menu at the Burger Shack www.theburgershack.com* 转推@埃迪・史密斯：汉堡小屋的美味新菜单 www.theburgershack.com

RTA /ˌɑː tiː ˈeɪ; *NAmE* ˌɑːr/ *abbr.* (*BrE*) road traffic accident 道路交通事故

RTF /ˌɑː tiː ˈef; *NAmE* ˌɑːr/ *abbr.* (*computing* 计) rich text format (a type of file containing data that can be used with different programs or systems) * RTF 格式，普通文本格式，富文本格式（可为不同的程序或系统兼容）: *an RTF file* * RTF 文件

Rt Hon *abbr.* (*BrE*) (in writing 书写形式) RIGHT HONOURABLE 阁下

Rt Revd (*also* **Rt. Rev.**) *abbr.* (*BrE*) (in writing 书写形式) RIGHT REVEREND（尊称主教）尊敬的，可敬的

rub 🔑 /rʌb/ *verb, noun*

■ *verb* (**-bb-**) **1** 🔑 [T, I] to move your hand, or sth such as a cloth, backwards and forwards over a surface while pressing firmly 擦；磨；搓: **~ sth** *She rubbed her chin thoughtfully.* 她若有所思地抚摩着下巴。◇ **~ sth/yourself with sth** *Rub the surface with sandpaper before painting.* 用砂纸打磨表面，然后再上油漆。◇ **~ sth/yourself against sth** *The cat rubbed itself against my legs.* 猫在我腿上蹭来蹭去。◇ **~ at sth** *I rubbed at the stain on the cloth.* 我擦了擦布上的污渍。◇ **~ against sth** *Animals had been rubbing against the trees.* 动物一直在这些树上蹭来蹭去。◇ **~ sth/yourself + adj.** *Rub the surface smooth.* 将表面擦光。 **2** 🔑 [T, I] to press two surfaces against each other and move them backwards and forwards; to be pressed together and move in this way （使）相互磨擦；搓: **~ sth (together)** *She rubbed her hands in delight.* 她高兴得直搓手。◇ **~ (together)** *It sounded like two pieces of wood rubbing together.* 听起来就像是两块木头在一起磨擦。 **3** 🔑 [I, T] (of a surface 表面) to move backwards and forwards many times against sth while pressing it, especially causing pain or damage 磨，摩擦（尤指引起疼痛或损害）: *The back of my shoe is rubbing.* 我的鞋后跟磨脚。◇ **~ on/against sth** *The wheel is rubbing on the mudguard.* 车轮蹭着挡泥板了。◇ **~ sth (+ adj.)** *The horse's neck was **rubbed raw** (= until the skin came off) where the rope had been.* 马脖子上套过缰绳的地方皮都给磨掉了。 **4** 🔑 [T] **~ sth + adv./prep.** to spread a liquid or other substance over a surface while pressing firmly 涂；抹；搽: *She rubbed the lotion into her skin.* 她把润肤液揉搓进皮肤里。 ➲ MORE LIKE THIS 36, page R29

IDM **rub sb's ˈnose in it** (*informal*) to keep reminding sb in an unkind way of their past mistakes 揭疮疤；不断恶意提起某人以往的过失 **rub ˈsalt into the wound | rub ˈsalt into sb's wounds** to make a difficult experience even more difficult for sb 在伤口上抹盐；使雪上加霜 **rub ˈshoulders with sb** (*NAmE also* **rub ˈelbows with sb**) to meet and spend time with a famous person, socially or as part of your job 与某名人接触（或交往） **rub sb up the wrong ˈway** (*BrE*) (*NAmE* **rub sb the wrong ˈway**) (*informal*) to make sb annoyed or angry, often without intending to, by doing or saying sth that offends them （无意中）惹人生气，触怒别人 ➲ MORE AT TWO

PHR V **ˌrub aˈlong (with sb/together)** (*BrE, informal*) (of two people 两个人) to live or work together in a friendly enough way 相处融洽；和谐共事 **ˌrub sb/yourself/sth↔ˈdown** to rub the skin of a person, horse, etc. hard with sth to make it clean and dry 将（人、马等）彻底擦干 **ˌrub sth↔ˈdown** to make sth smooth by rubbing it with a special material（用特别材料）将某物打磨光滑 **ˌrub it ˈin | ˌrub sth ˈin** [no passive] to keep reminding sb of sth they feel embarrassed about and want to forget 反复提及令人尴尬的事；触及痛处: *I know I was stupid; you don't have to rub it in.* 我知道我当时很愚蠢，你不必老提这件事。 **ˌrub ˈoff (on/onto sb)** (of personal qualities, behaviour, opinions, etc. 人的品质、行为、观点等) to become part of a person's character as a result of that person spending time with sb who has those qualities, etc. 感染；传给: *Her sense of fun has rubbed off on her children.* 她的幽默感已经传给了她的孩子。 **ˌrub sth↔ˈoff (sth) | ˌrub ˈoff** to remove sth or to be removed by rubbing （被）擦掉，抹掉: *She rubbed off the dead skin.* 她擦掉了死皮。◇ *The gold colouring had begun to rub off.* 金黄色已经开始剥落了。◇ (*BrE*) *If you write on the blackboard, rub it off at the end of the lesson.* 如果你在黑板上写字，下课时要擦掉。 **ˌrub sb↔ˈout** (*NAmE, slang*) to murder sb 干掉；做掉 **ˌrub sth↔ˈout** (*BrE*) (*also* **erase** *NAmE, BrE*) to remove the marks made by a pencil, etc., using a RUBBER/ERASER 用橡皮擦掉（字迹等）: *to rub out a mistake* 用橡皮擦掉错处

■ *noun* **1** [C, usually sing.] an act of rubbing a surface 擦；抹；搓；揉: *She gave her knee a quick rub.* 她很快地揉了揉膝盖。 **2 the rub** [sing.] (*formal* or *humorous*) a problem or difficulty 问题；困难: *The hotel is in the middle of nowhere and **there lies the rub**. We don't have a car.* 难就难在旅馆很偏远，我们又没有汽车。

rub·ber 🔑 /ˈrʌbə(r)/ *noun* **1** 🔑 [U] a strong substance that can be stretched and does not allow liquids to pass through it, used for making tyres, boots, etc. It is made from the liquid (= SAP) inside a tropical plant or is produced using chemicals. 橡胶: *a ball made of rubber* 皮球 ◇ *a rubber tree* 橡胶树 ➲ SEE ALSO FOAM RUBBER at FOAM *n.* (1), INDIA RUBBER **2** [C] (*BrE*) (*also* **eraser** *NAmE, BrE*) a small piece of rubber or a similar substance, used for removing pencil marks from paper; a piece of soft material used for removing CHALK marks from a BLACKBOARD 橡皮；黑板擦 ➲ VISUAL VOCAB PAGE V71 **3** [C] (*informal, especially NAmE*) = CONDOM **4** [C] (in some card games or sports) a competition consisting of a series of games or matches between the same teams or players （某些纸牌游戏或体育运动中相同的对手或队伍间）多轮决胜负的比赛

IDM **where the ˌrubber meets the ˈroad** (*NAmE*) the point at which sth is tested and you really find out whether it is successful or true 接受考验的时刻；检验成败的时刻；检验真伪的时刻: *Here's where the rubber meets the road: will consumers actually buy the product?* 检验成败的时刻到了：消费者真的会购买这种产品吗？ ➲ MORE AT BURN *v.* ▸ **rub·ber** *adj.* [usually before noun]: *a rubber ball* 皮球 ◇ *rubber gloves* 橡皮手套

ˌrubber ˈband (*BrE also* **eˌlastic ˈband**) *noun* a thin round piece of rubber used for holding things together 橡皮圈；橡皮筋 ➲ VISUAL VOCAB PAGE V71

ˌrubber ˈboot (*NAmE*) (*BrE* **wel·ling·ton**, **ˌwellington ˈboot**, *informal* **welly**) *noun* one of a pair of long rubber boots, usually reaching almost up to the knee, that you wear to stop your feet getting wet 及膝胶靴；威灵顿长筒靴 ➲ VISUAL VOCAB PAGE V69

ˌrubber ˈbullet *noun* a bullet made of rubber intended to injure but not to kill people, used by the army or police to control violent crowds 橡皮子弹（防暴用）

ˌrubber ˈdinghy (*also* **dinghy**) *noun* a small boat made of rubber that is filled with air, used especially for rescuing people from ships and planes 橡皮艇；橡皮筏

rub·ber·ized (*BrE also* **-ised**) /ˈrʌbəraɪzd/ *adj.* [only before noun] covered with rubber 橡胶包裹的；覆盖橡胶的：*rubberized cloth* 胶布

rub·ber·neck /ˈrʌbənek; *NAmE* -bərn-/ *verb* [I] (*informal, especially NAmE*) to turn to look at sth while you are driving past it（驾车时）扭头观望 ▸ **rub·ber·neck·er** *noun*

ˈrubber plant *noun* a plant with thick shiny green leaves, often grown indoors 橡胶植物（叶厚且有光泽，常种于室内）

ˌrubber ˈstamp *noun* **1** a small tool that you hold in your hand and use for printing the date, the name of an organization, etc. on a document 橡皮图章 ➲ VISUAL VOCAB PAGE V71 **2** (*disapproving*) a person or group that automatically gives approval to the actions or decisions of others 履行审批手续而没有实权的人（或机构）；橡皮图章：*Parliament is seen as a rubber stamp for decisions made elsewhere.* 议会被看作橡皮图章，只会批准他人的决定。

ˌrubber-ˈstamp *verb* **~ sth** (*often disapproving*) to give official approval to a law, plan, decision, etc., especially without considering it carefully（机械式）盖公章；（未经慎重考虑而）正式通过

rub·bery /ˈrʌbəri/ *adj.* **1** looking or feeling like rubber 似橡胶的；有弹性的：*The eggs were overcooked and rubbery.* 鸡蛋煮得太老了，像胶皮似的。 ➲ WORDFINDER NOTE AT CRISP **2** (of legs or knees 腿或膝盖) feeling weak and unable to support your weight 虚弱的；软弱无力的

rub·bing /ˈrʌbɪŋ/ *noun* a copy of writing or a design on a piece of stone or metal that is made by placing a piece of paper over it and rubbing with CHALK, a pencil, etc. 拓本 ➲ SEE ALSO BRASS RUBBING

ˈrubbing alcohol (*NAmE*) (*BrE* **ˌsurgical ˈspirit**) *noun* [U] a clear liquid, consisting mainly of alcohol, used for cleaning wounds, etc. 医用酒精；消毒用酒精

rub·bish 🔑 /ˈrʌbɪʃ/ *noun, verb*

▪ ***noun*** [U] **1** 🔑 (*especially BrE*) things that you throw away because you no longer want or need them 垃圾；废弃物：*a* ***rubbish bag/bin*** 垃圾袋；垃圾桶 ◇ *a* ***rubbish dump/heap/tip*** 垃圾场；垃圾堆；垃圾倾倒处 ◇ *The streets were littered with rubbish.* 街上到处都是垃圾。◇ ***garden/household rubbish*** 花园 / 生活垃圾 ➲ WORDFINDER NOTE AT WASTE ➲ COLLOCATIONS AT ENVIRONMENT ➲ SEE ALSO GARBAGE (1), TRASH *n.* (1) **2** 🔑 (*BrE, informal*) (also used as an adjective 也用作形容词) something that you think is of poor quality 劣质的东西：*I thought the play was rubbish!* 我觉得这部戏很差！◇ *Do we have to listen to this rubbish music?* 我们一定要听这样差劲的音乐吗？ **3** 🔑 (*BrE, informal*) comments, ideas, etc. that you think are stupid or wrong 废话；瞎说 SYN **nonsense**：*Rubbish! You're not fat.* 瞎说！你并不胖。◇ *You're talking a load of rubbish.* 你说的是一大堆废话。◇ *It's not rubbish—it's true!* 这不是瞎说，是真的！

▪ ***verb*** (*BrE, informal*) (*NAmE* **trash**) **~ sb/sth** to criticize sb/sth severely or treat them as though they are of no value 狠批；把…看得一文不值

▼ BRITISH/AMERICAN 英式 / 美式英语

rubbish / garbage / trash / refuse

- **Rubbish** is the usual word in *BrE* for the things that you throw away because you no longer want or need them. **Garbage** and **trash** are both used in *NAmE*. Inside the home, **garbage** tends to mean waste food and other wet material, while **trash** is paper, cardboard and dry material. 在英式英语中，rubbish 为常用词，指垃圾、废物。garbage 和 trash 均用于美式英语。生活垃圾中，garbage 多指废弃的食物和其他湿物质，而 trash 则指废弃的纸、硬纸板和干物质。
- In *BrE*, you put your **rubbish** in a **dustbin** in the street to be collected by the **dustmen**. In *NAmE*, your **garbage** and **trash** goes in a **garbage/trash can** in the street and is collected by **garbage men/collectors**. 在英式英语中，垃圾为 rubbish，街上的垃圾桶为 dustbin，清除垃圾的工人叫 dustman。在美式英语中，垃圾为 garbage 和 trash，街上的垃圾桶为 garbage/trash can，清除垃圾的工人叫 garbage man/collector。
- **Refuse** is a formal word and is used in both *BrE* and *NAmE*. **Refuse collector** is the formal word for a dustman or garbage collector. * refuse 为正式用语，用于英式英语和美式英语均可。refuse collector 为 dustman 或 garbage collector 的正式说法。

rub·bishy /ˈrʌbɪʃi/ *adj.* (*BrE, informal*) of very poor quality 质量低劣的；非常差劲的 SYN **trashy**：*rubbishy old films* 质量很差的老电影

rub·ble /ˈrʌbl/ *noun* [U] broken stones or bricks from a building or wall that has been destroyed or damaged 碎石；碎砖：*The bomb* ***reduced*** *the houses* ***to rubble.*** 炸弹把那片房子炸成了瓦砾。 ➲ WORDFINDER NOTE AT CONSTRUCTION

ˈrub-down *noun* **1** the act of rubbing sb/sth with a cloth or special material, for example to make a person dry or to make sth dry, clean or smooth 擦拭；揩；抹；打磨；磨光：*You may need to give the floor a rub-down with glasspaper.* 你可能得用玻璃砂纸打磨一下地板。 **2** (*NAmE*) the act of rubbing and pressing a person's body with the hands to reduce pain in the muscles and joints 按摩 SYN **massage**

Rube Goldberg /ˌruːb ˈɡəʊldbɜːɡ; *NAmE* ˈɡoʊldbɜːrɡ/ (*NAmE*) (*BrE* **Heath Rob·in·son**) *adj.* [only before noun] (*humorous*) (of machines and devices 机器和装置) having a very complicated design, especially when used to perform a very simple task; not practical 结构过于复杂的；不实用的

ru·bella /ruːˈbelə/ *noun* [U] (*medical* 医) = GERMAN MEASLES

Ru·ben·esque /ˌruːbəˈnesk/ *adj.* (of a woman 女人) having a round body with large breasts and hips 体形丰满的 ORIGIN From the name of the Flemish painter Peter Paul Rubens, who often painted women with large, fairly fat bodies. 源自佛兰德画家彼得・保罗・鲁本斯的名字，他常画高大丰满的女人。

Ru·bi·con /ˈruːbɪkən; *NAmE* -kɑːn/ **the Rubicon** *noun* [sing.] the point at which a decision has been taken which can no longer be changed 无法退回的界限；界线：*Today we* ***cross the Rubicon.*** *There is no going back.* 今天我们要破釜沉舟，背水一战了。 ORIGIN From the **Rubicon**, a stream which formed the border between Italy and Gaul. When Julius Caesar broke the law by crossing it with his army in 49BC, it led inevitably to war. 源自意大利和高卢的界河卢比孔河（Rubicon）。公元前 49 年，恺撒违规带兵越过卢比孔河，从而不可避免地引发了战争。

ru·bi·cund /ˈruːbɪkənd/ *adj.* (*literary*) (of a person's face 人的脸) having a healthy red colour 健康红润的 SYN **ruddy**

ru·bid·ium /rʊˈbɪdiəm/ *noun* [U] (*symb.* **Rb**) a chemical element. Rubidium is a rare soft silver-coloured metal that reacts strongly with water and burns when it is brought into contact with air. 铷

Rubik's Cube™ /'ru:bɪks kju:b/ *noun* a PUZZLE consisting of a plastic CUBE covered with coloured squares that you turn to make each side of the cube a different colour 魔方

ruble *noun* (*especially NAmE*) = ROUBLE

ru·bric /'ru:brɪk/ *noun* (*formal*) a title or set of instructions written in a book, an exam paper, etc.（书本或试卷等上的）标题，提示，说明

ruby /'ru:bi/ *noun* (*pl.* **-ies**) **1** [C, U] a dark red PRECIOUS STONE 红宝石：*a ruby ring* 红宝石戒指 **2** [U] a dark red colour 深红色 ▶ **ruby** *adj.* : *ruby lips* 深红色的嘴唇

ˌruby 'wedding (*BrE*) (*US* **ˌruby anni'versary**) (*also* **ˌruby 'wedding anniversary** *US, BrE*) *noun* the 40th anniversary of a wedding 红宝石婚（结婚 40 周年纪念）➲ COMPARE DIAMOND WEDDING, GOLDEN WEDDING, SILVER WEDDING

ruched /ru:ʃt/ *adj.* (of cloth, clothes, etc. 织物、衣服等) sewn so that they hang in folds 有褶边的；有褶饰的：*ruched curtains* 带褶边的窗帘

ruck /rʌk/ *noun, verb*

■ *noun* **1** [C] (in RUGBY 橄榄球) a group of players who gather round the ball when it is lying on the ground and push each other in order to get the ball 自由密集争球 **2** [sing.] a group of people standing closely together or fighting 拥在一起的人群；混乱打斗的人群 **3 the ruck** [sing.] (*disapproving*) ordinary people or events 普通人；寻常事：*She saw marriage to him as a way out of the ruck.* 她把同他结婚看作是出人头地的途径。

■ *verb* [I] (in RUGBY 橄榄球) to take part in a ruck (1) 进行自由密集争球

PHR V **ˌruck 'up | ˌruck sth↔'up** (of cloth 织物) to form untidy folds; to make sth do this（使）起皱褶：*Your dress is rucked up at the back.* 你的连衣裙后面起褶儿了。

ruck·sack /'rʌksæk/ (*BrE*) (*also* **back·pack** *NAmE, BrE*) *noun* a large bag, often supported on a light metal frame, carried on the back and used especially by people who go climbing or walking（尤指登山者或远足者使用的）背包，旅行包 ➲ VISUAL VOCAB PAGE V69

ruckus /'rʌkəs/ *noun* [sing.] (*informal, especially NAmE*) a situation in which there is a lot of noisy activity, confusion or argument 喧闹；骚动；争吵 SYN **commotion**

ruc·tions /'rʌkʃnz/ *noun* [pl.] (*especially BrE*) angry protests or arguments 愤怒的抗议；争吵：*There'll be ructions if her father ever finds out.* 一旦让她父亲发现了，就会发生争吵。

rud·der /'rʌdə(r)/ *noun* a piece of wood or metal at the back of a boat or an aircraft that is used for controlling its direction（船的）舵；（飞机的）方向舵 ➲ VISUAL VOCAB PAGE V57

rud·der·less /'rʌdələs; *NAmE* -dərl-/ *adj.* (*formal*) with nobody in control; not knowing what to do 无人管理的；无指导的；漫无目的的

ruddy /'rʌdi/ *adj., adv.*

■ *adj.* **1** (of a person's face 人的脸) looking red and healthy 红润健康的：*ruddy cheeks* 红润的面颊 ◇ *a ruddy complexion* 红润的脸色 **2** (*literary*) red in colour 红色的：*a ruddy sky* 红彤彤的天空 **3** [only before noun] (*BrE, informal*) a mild swear word that some people use to show that they are annoyed（表示生气）讨厌的，可恶的：*I can't get the ruddy car to start!* 我就是发动不了这破车！

■ *adv.* (*BrE, informal*) a mild swear word used by some people to emphasize what they are saying, especially when they are annoyed（加强语气，尤其生气时）非常，该死：*There was a ruddy great hole in the ceiling.* 天花板上有一个要命的大洞。

rude 🔑 /ru:d/ *adj.* (**ruder, rud·est**) **1** 🔑 having or showing a lack of respect for other people and their feelings 粗鲁的；无礼的；粗野的 SYN **impolite**：*a rude comment* 粗鲁的批评 ◇ **~ (to sb) (about sb/sth)** *The man was downright rude to us.* 这个家伙对我们无礼至极。◇ *Why are you so rude to your mother?* 你为什么对你的母亲这么没礼貌？◇ *She was very rude about my driving.* 她对我的开车方法横加指责。◇ **~ (to do sth)** *It's rude to speak when you're eating.* 吃东西的时候说话不礼貌。 **2** (*especially BrE*) (*NAmE usually* **crude**) connected with sex or the body in a way that people find offensive or embarrassing 猥亵的；下流的：*a rude gesture* 下流的手势 ◇ *Someone made a rude noise.* 有人发出了淫猥的噪音。◇ *The joke is too rude to repeat.* 这个笑话太下流，不宜重复。 **3** [only before noun] (*formal*) sudden, unpleasant and unexpected 突然的；突如其来的；猛烈的：*Those expecting good news will get a rude shock.* 那些等着听好消息的人会大吃一惊的。◇ *If the players think they can win this match easily, they are in for* ***a rude awakening.*** 如果选手们认为他们可以轻而易举地赢这场比赛，他们会遭到当头棒喝的。 **4** (*literary*) made in a simple, basic way 简单的；粗糙的；原始的 SYN **primitive**：*rude shacks* 简陋的小屋 ▶ **rude·ness** *noun* [U]：*She was critical to the point of rudeness.* 她挑剔得近乎无礼。

IDM **in rude 'health** (*old-fashioned, BrE*) looking or feeling very healthy 非常健康；十分健壮

▼ **SYNONYMS** 同义词辨析

rude

cheeky • insolent • disrespectful • impolite • impertinent • discourteous

These are all words for people showing a lack of respect for other people. 以上各词均指人粗鲁、无礼。

rude having or showing a lack of respect for other people and their feelings 指粗鲁的、无礼的、粗野的：*Why are you so rude to your mother?* 你为什么对你的母亲这么没礼貌？◇ *It's rude to speak when you're eating.* 吃东西时说话不礼貌。

cheeky (*BrE, informal*) (especially of children) rude in an amusing or an annoying way（尤指小孩子）厚脸皮的、鲁莽的、放肆的：*You cheeky monkey!* 你这厚脸皮的猴崽子！◇ *a cheeky grin* 厚颜无耻的龇牙一笑

insolent (*rather formal*) very rude, especially to sb who is older or more important（尤指对长者、重要人士）粗野的、无礼的、侮慢的 NOTE **Insolent** is used especially to talk about the behaviour of children towards adults.
* insolent 尤用于形容孩子对成年人的行为。

disrespectful (*rather formal*) showing a lack of respect for sb/sth 指不尊敬、无礼、轻蔑：*Some people said he had been disrespectful to the President in his last speech.* 有些人说他在最近一次讲话中对总统不尊重。

impolite (*rather formal*) not behaving in a pleasant way that follows the rules of society 指不礼貌、粗鲁：*Some people think it is impolite to ask someone's age.* 有些人认为询问别人的年龄是不礼貌的。NOTE **Impolite** is often used in the phrases *It seemed impolite* and *It would be impolite*. * impolite 常用于 it seemed impolite 和 it would be impolite 短语中。

impertinent (*rather formal*) not showing respect for sb who is older or more important 指（对长者或重要人士）粗鲁无礼、不尊敬 NOTE **Impertinent** is often used by people such as parents and teachers when they are telling children that they are angry with them for being rude. * impertinent 常用于父母、老师等对孩子的粗鲁行为表示气愤：*Don't be impertinent!* 不要粗鲁无礼！

discourteous (*formal*) having bad manners and not showing respect 指不礼貌、失礼、粗鲁：*He didn't wish to appear discourteous.* 他不想显得没礼貌。

PATTERNS

- rude/cheeky/disrespectful/impolite/discourteous **to sb**
- rude/impolite/impertinent **to do sth**

rude·ly 🔑 /'ru:dli/ *adv.* **1** 🔑 in a way that shows a lack of respect for other people and their feelings 粗鲁地；无礼地：*They brushed rudely past us.* 他们粗暴无礼地与我

R

们擦身而过。◇ *'What do you want?' she asked rudely.* "你要干什么？" 她粗鲁地问道。 **2** in a way that is sudden, unpleasant and unexpected 突然地；猛烈地；突如其来地： *I was rudely awakened by the phone ringing.* 我被突如其来的电话铃声吵醒了。

ru·di·men·tary /ˌruːdɪˈmentri/ *adj.* **1** (*formal*) dealing with only the most basic matters or ideas 基础的；基本的 **SYN** **basic**: *They were given only rudimentary training in the job.* 他们仅仅受过基本的职业训练。 **2** (*formal* or *specialist*) not highly or fully developed 未充分发展的；原始的 **SYN** **basic**: *Some dinosaurs had only rudimentary teeth.* 有些恐龙只有未充分长成的牙齿。

ru·di·ments /ˈruːdɪmənts/ *noun* [pl.] **the ~ (of sth)** (*formal*) the most basic or essential facts of a particular subject, skill, etc. 基础；基本原理（或技能） **SYN** **basics**

rue /ruː/ *verb* (**rue·ing**, **ruing**, **rued**, **rued**) **~ sth** (*old-fashioned* or *formal*) to feel bad about sth that happened or sth that you did because it had bad results 对…感到懊恼；懊悔 **SYN** **regret**: *He **rued the day** they had bought such a large house.* 他懊悔他们买了这样大的一所房子。

rue·ful /ˈruːfl/ *adj.* feeling or showing that you are sad or sorry 悲伤的；懊悔的；沮丧的： *a rueful smile* 惨然一笑 ▶ **rue·ful·ly** /ˈruːfəli/ *adv.* : *'So this is goodbye,' she said ruefully.* 她悲伤地说："那么，这就是告别了。"

ruff /rʌf/ *noun* **1** a ring of coloured or marked feathers or fur around the neck of a bird or an animal 翎颌（鸟兽的环形彩色项毛） **2** a wide stiff white COLLAR with many folds in it, worn especially in the 16th and 17th centuries 飞边（尤盛行于 16 和 17 世纪的白色轮状皱领）

ruf·fian /ˈrʌfiən/ *noun* (*old-fashioned*) a violent man, especially one who commits crimes 暴徒；恶棍 **SYN** **thug**

ruf·fle /ˈrʌfl/ *verb, noun*

■ ***verb*** **1** to disturb the smooth surface of sth, so that it is not even 弄皱；弄乱；使不平整： **~ sth** *She ruffled his hair affectionately.* 她情意绵绵地拨弄着他的头发。◇ **~ sth up** *The bird ruffled up its feathers.* 这只鸟竖起了羽毛。 **2** [often passive] **~ sb** to make sb annoyed, worried or upset 搅扰；激怒；使沮丧；使担心 **SYN** **fluster**: *She was obviously ruffled by his question.* 她显然被他的问题激怒了。◇ *He never **gets ruffled**, even under pressure.* 即使在压力之下，他也从不感到沮丧。

IDM **ruffle sb's/a few 'feathers** (*informal*) to annoy or upset sb or a group of people 激怒；骚扰；使不安： *The senator's speech ruffled a few feathers in the business world.* 这位参议员的讲话惹恼了一些商界人士。 ➲ MORE AT SMOOTH *v.*

■ ***noun*** [usually pl.] a strip of cloth that is sewn in folds and is used to decorate a piece of clothing at the neck or wrists（领口、袖口等的）褶饰，花边，荷叶边 **SYN** **frill**

ruf·fled /ˈrʌfld/ *adj.* decorated with ruffles 有褶饰边的 **SYN** **frilled**: *a ruffled blouse* 镶着皱裥的女式衬衫

rug /rʌɡ/ *noun* **1** a piece of thick material like a small carpet that is used for covering or decorating part of a floor 小地毯；垫子： *a hearth rug* (= in front of a FIREPLACE) 壁炉前的小地毯 ➲ VISUAL VOCAB PAGES V22, V24 **2** (*BrE*) a piece of thick warm material, like a BLANKET, that is used for wrapping around your legs to keep warm（盖腿的）厚毯子 **3** (*informal, especially NAmE*) = TOUPEE **IDM** SEE PULL *v.*, SWEEP *v.*

rugby /ˈrʌɡbi/ (*sometimes* **Rugby**) (*also* ˌ**rugby 'football**) *noun* [U] a game played by two teams of 13 or 15 players, using an OVAL ball which may be kicked or carried. Teams try to put the ball over the other team's line. 橄榄球运动 ➲ VISUAL VOCAB PAGE V47 **ORIGIN** Named after Rugby school, where the game was first played. 以第一次开展橄榄球运动的拉格比学校命名。

ˌ**Rugby 'League** *noun* [U] a form of rugby, with 13 players in a team 联盟橄榄球（每队 13 人）

ˌ**Rugby 'Union** (*also informal* **rug·ger** *especially in BrE*) *noun* [U] a form of rugby, with 15 players in a team 联合会橄榄球（每队 15 人）

rug·ged /ˈrʌɡɪd/ *adj.* **1** (of the landscape 地形) not level or smooth and having rocks rather than plants or trees 崎岖的；凹凸不平的；多岩石的： *rugged cliffs* 岩石突兀的悬崖绝壁 ◇ *They admired the rugged beauty of the coastline.* 他们对海岸线上岩石密布的美景赞叹不已。 ➲ WORDFINDER NOTE AT LANDSCAPE **2** [usually before noun] (*approving*) (of a man's face 男人的脸) having strong, attractive features 强健而富有魅力的；粗犷的 **3** [usually before noun] (of a person 人) determined to succeed in a difficult situation, even if this means using force or upsetting other people 坚强的；坚毅的： *a rugged individualist* 坚定的个人主义者 **4** (of equipment, clothing, etc. 设备、衣服等) strong and designed to be used in difficult conditions 结实的；耐用的： *A less rugged vehicle would never have made the trip.* 要不是这车结实，根本走不完这段路程。 ◇ *rugged outdoor clothing* 结实耐穿的户外服装 ➲ MORE LIKE THIS 22, page R27 ▶ **rug·ged·ly** *adv.*: *ruggedly handsome* 粗犷英俊 **rug·ged·ness** *noun* [U]

rug·ger /ˈrʌɡə(r)/ *noun* [U] (*informal, especially BrE*) = RUGBY UNION

'rugger-bugger *noun* (*BrE, informal*) an enthusiastic player or supporter of RUGBY, especially one who is noisy and aggressive 粗野狂热的橄榄球员（或球迷）

'rug rat *noun* (*NAmE, informal*) a child 小孩

ruin 🔑 /ˈruːɪn/ *verb, noun*

■ ***verb*** **1** 🔑 **~ sth** to damage sth so badly that it loses all its value, pleasure, etc.; to spoil sth 毁坏；破坏；糟蹋 **SYN** **wreck**: *The bad weather ruined our trip.* 天气恶劣，破坏了我们的旅行。 ◇ *That one mistake ruined his chances of getting the job.* 正是那个错误断送了他得到那份工作的机会。◇ *My new shoes **got ruined** in the mud.* 我的新鞋被泥浆给糟蹋了。 **2** 🔑 **~ sb/sth** to make sb/sth lose all their money, their position, etc. 使破产（或失去地位等）；毁灭： *If she loses the court case it will ruin her.* 如果败诉，她就完了。◇ *The country was ruined by the war.* 这个国家因战争而遭到严重破坏。

■ ***noun*** **1** 🔑 [U] the state or process of being destroyed or severely damaged 毁坏；破坏；毁灭： *A large number of churches **fell into ruin** after the revolution.* 革命过后，许多教堂都毁了。 **2** 🔑 [U] the fact of having no money, of having lost your job, position, etc. 破产；一无所有；失去工作（或地位等）： *The divorce ultimately led to his ruin.* 离婚最终使得他一贫如洗。◇ *The bank stepped in to save the company from **financial ruin**.* 银行的介入使这家公司免于破产。 **3** [sing.] something that causes a person, company, etc. to lose all their money, job, position, etc. 破产（或丢掉工作等）的根源；祸根 **SYN** **downfall**: *Gambling was his ruin.* 赌博毁了他。 **4** 🔑 [C] (*also* **ruins** [pl.]) the parts of a building that remain after it has been destroyed or severely damaged 残垣断壁；废墟： *The old mill is now little more than a ruin.* 老磨坊现在只剩下一点儿残垣断壁了。◇ *We visited the ruins of a Norman castle.* 我们参观了一座诺曼式城堡的遗迹。 ◇ (*figurative*) *He was determined to build a new life out of the ruins of his career.* 他决心从事业失败中爬起来，重新开始新的生活。

IDM **in 'ruins** destroyed or severely damaged 毁坏；严重受损；破败不堪： *Years of fighting have left the area in ruins.* 经年的战事已经使得这个地区满目疮痍。◇ *The scandal left his reputation in ruins.* 这件丑闻使他身败名裂。 ➲ MORE AT RACK *n.*

ruin·ation /ˌruːɪˈneɪʃn/ *noun* [U] (*formal*) the process of destroying sth/sb or being destroyed 毁灭；毁坏 **SYN** **destruction**: *Urban development has led to the ruination of vast areas of countryside.* 城市发展导致大片的乡村遭到毁坏。

ru·ined 🔑 /ˈruːɪnd/ *adj.* [only before noun] (of a building, town, etc. 建筑、城镇等) destroyed or severely damaged so that only parts remain 毁坏的；严重受损的： *a ruined castle* 破烂不堪的城堡

ruin·ous /ˈruːɪnəs/ *adj.* (*formal*) **1** costing a lot of money and more than you can afford 耗资巨大的；无法承担的：

ruinous legal fees 巨额法律费用 **2** causing serious problems or damage 破坏性的；导致严重问题的；灾难性的 **SYN devastating**: *The decision was to prove ruinous.* 后来证明这个决定造成了极大的损害。 **3** (*formal*) (of a town, building, etc. 城镇、建筑等) destroyed or severely damaged 破败的；严重受损的；已成废墟的：*a ruinous chapel* 已成废墟的小教堂 ◇ *The buildings were in a ruinous state.* 这些建筑破烂不堪。 ▶ **ruin·ous·ly** *adv.*：*ruinously expensive* 贵得无法承受

rule /ruːl/ *noun, verb*

■ *noun*

• **OF ACTIVITY/GAME** 活动；游戏 **1** [C] a statement of what may, must or must not be done in a particular situation or when playing a game 规则；规章；条例：*to* ***follow/obey/observe the rules*** 遵循 / 服从 / 遵守规则 ◇ *It's against* ***all rules and regulations.*** 这违背了所有的规章制度。 ◇ *to* ***break a rule*** (= not follow it) 违反规定 ◇ *This explains the rules under which the library operates.* 这份材料说明了图书馆的运作方式。 ◇ *Without* ***unwritten rules*** *civilized life would be impossible.* 没有不成文的规章，就不会有文明生活。 ➲ SEE ALSO GROUND RULE (1) ➲ **WORDFINDER NOTE** AT FREEDOM

• **ADVICE** 建议 **2** [C] a statement of what you are advised to do in a particular situation 建议；应做之事：*There are no* ***hard and fast rules*** *for planning healthy meals.* 在安排健康饮食方面，没有什么硬性规定。 ◇ *The first rule is to make eye contact with your interviewer.* 首先是眼睛要直视面试官。 ➲ SEE ALSO GOLDEN RULE

• **HABIT/NORMALLY TRUE** 习惯；常规 **3** [C, usually sing.] a habit; the normal state of things; what is true in most cases 习惯；常规；惯常的做法：*He makes it a rule never to borrow money.* 他的规矩是从不向人借钱。 ◇ *I go to bed early* ***as a rule.*** 我一贯睡得早。 ◇ *Cold winters here are* ***the exception rather than the rule*** (= are rare). 在这里，严寒的冬天并不多见。 ◇ ***As a general rule*** *vegetable oils are better for you than animal fats.* 一般来说，植物油比动物脂肪对人较有好处。

• **OF SYSTEM** 体系 **4** [C] a statement of what is possible according to a particular system, for example the grammar of a language 定律；规则：*the rules of grammar* 语法规则

• **GOVERNMENT/CONTROL** 统治；控制 **5** [U] the government of a country or control of a group of people by a particular person, group or system 统治；管理；支配；控制：***under civilian/military, etc. rule*** 在文官、军人等统治之下 ◇ ***majority rule*** (= government by the political party that most people have voted for) 获选票多数的政党组成政府的原则 ◇ *The 1972 act imposed* ***direct rule*** *from Westminster.* * 1972 年的法案强制实行了英国中央政府的直接统治。 ➲ SEE ALSO HOME RULE

• **MEASURING TOOL** 测量工具 **6** [C] a measuring instrument with a straight edge 尺；直尺 ➲ SEE ALSO SLIDE RULE

IDM **bend/stretch the 'rules** to change the rules to suit a particular person or situation 根据具体情况改变规则；通融 **play by sb's (own) 'rules** if sb **plays by their own rules** or makes other people **play by their rules**, they set the conditions for doing business or having a relationship 按某人定的规矩行事 **play by the 'rules** to deal fairly and honestly with people 按规则玩游戏；处事公正诚实；循规蹈矩 **the rules of the 'game** the standards of behaviour that most people accept or that actually operate in a particular area of life or business 游戏规则；大家共同遵守的行为标准 **the rule of 'law** the condition in which all members of society, including its rulers, accept the authority of the law 法治 **a rule of 'thumb** a practical method of doing or measuring sth, usually based on past experience rather than on exact measurement 实用的估算方法，经验工作法（常依据经验而非准确测量） **work to 'rule** to follow the rules of your job in a very strict way in order to cause delay, as a form of protest against your employer or your working conditions 按章工作；变相罢工 ➲ SEE ALSO WORK-TO-RULE ➲ MORE AT EXCEPTION

■ *verb*

• **GOVERN/CONTROL** 统治；控制 **1** [T, I] to control and have authority over a country, a group of people, etc. 控制；统治；支配：**~ sth** *At that time John ruled England.* 当时是约翰统治着英格兰。 ◇ (*figurative*) *Eighty million years ago, dinosaurs ruled the earth.* 八千万年前，地球是恐龙的天下。 ◇ **~ (over sb/sth)** *Charles I ruled for eleven years.* 查理一世统治了十一年。 ◇ *She once ruled over a vast empire.* 她曾统治过一个幅员辽阔的帝国。 ◇ (*figurative*) *After the revolution, anarchy ruled.* 革命以后，无政府主义大行其道。 **2** [T, often passive] **~ sth** (*often disapproving*) to be the main thing that influences and controls sb/sth 支配；控制；操纵：*The pursuit of money ruled his life.* 对金钱的追求支配着他的生活。 ◇ *We live in a society where we are ruled by the clock.* 我们生活在一个人人都围着时间转的社会。

• **GIVE OFFICIAL DECISION** 作出正式决定 **3** [I, T] to give an official decision about sth 决定；裁定；判决 **SYN pronounce**: **~ (on sth)** *The court will rule on the legality of the action.* 法庭将裁定此举是否合法。 ◇ **~ against/in favour of sb/sth** *The judge ruled against/in favour of the plaintiff.* 法官判原告败诉 / 胜诉。 ◇ **~ sb/sth + adj.** *The deal may be ruled illegal.* 这笔交易可能会被判定为非法。 ◇ **~ sb/sth to be/have sth** *The deal was ruled to be illegal.* 这笔交易被判定为非法。 ◇ **~ that...** *The court ruled that the women were unfairly dismissed.* 法院裁定这些妇女是被不公平地开除的。 ◇ **it is ruled that...** *It was ruled that the women had been unfairly dismissed.* 已经裁定这些妇女被开除是不公平的。

• **DRAW STRAIGHT LINE** 画直线 **4** [T] **~ sth** to draw a straight line using sth that has a firm straight edge 用直尺等画（线）；画（直线）：*Rule a line at the end of every piece of work.* 在每一篇作品的末尾画一条直线。

IDM **rule the 'roost** (*informal*) to be the most powerful member of a group 当头头；充当首领；主宰 **rule (sb/sth) with a rod of 'iron** to control a person or a group of people very severely 残酷统治；严厉控制 ➲ MORE AT COURT *n.*, DIVIDE *v.*, HEART

PHR V **,rule 'off | ,rule sth↔'off** to separate sth from the next section of writing by drawing a line underneath it 画线隔开 **,rule sb/sth↔'out 1** **rule sb/sth out (as sth)** to state that sth is not possible or that sb/sth is not suitable 把…排除在外；认为…不适合 **SYN exclude**: *Police have not ruled out the possibility that the man was murdered.* 警方尚未排除那个男子是被谋杀的可能性。 ◇ *The proposed solution was ruled out as too expensive.* 建议的解决方案被认为花钱太多而遭否决。 **2** to prevent sb from doing sth; to prevent sth from happening 阻止；防止…发生：*His age effectively ruled him out as a possible candidate.* 他的年岁使他根本不可能成为候选人。 **,rule sb 'out of sth** [usually passive] (in sport 体育运动) to state that a player, runner, etc. will not be able to take part in a sporting event; to prevent a player from taking part 声明某人不能参赛；阻止某人参赛：*He has been ruled out of the match with a knee injury.* 他因膝伤已经无缘参加这场比赛。

'rule book *noun* (*usually* **the rule book**) the set of rules that must be followed in a particular job, organization or game 规则（或规章）手册

ruled /ruːld/ *adj.* **ruled** paper has lines printed across it （纸张）有横格的，有平行线的

ruler /'ruːlə(r)/ *noun* **1** a person who rules or governs 统治者；支配者 **2** a straight strip of wood, plastic or metal, marked in centimetres or inches, used for measuring or for drawing straight lines 直尺 ➲ VISUAL VOCAB PAGE V72

rul·ing /'ruːlɪŋ/ *noun, adj.*

■ *noun* **~ (on sth)** an official decision made by sb in a position of authority, especially a judge 裁决；裁定；判决：*The court will make its ruling on the case next week.* 法庭下周将对本案作出裁决。

■ *adj.* [only before noun] having control over a particular group, country, etc. 统治的；支配的；占统治地位的：*the ruling party* 执政党

rum /rʌm/ *noun, adj.*

■ *noun* **1** [U, C] a strong alcoholic drink made from the juice of SUGAR CANE 朗姆酒（一种用甘蔗汁酿制的烈

R

性酒） **2** [C] a glass of rum 一杯朗姆酒

■ *adj.* [usually before noun] (*old-fashioned, BrE, informal*) strange 奇特的；古怪的 SYN **odd, peculiar**

rumba (*also* **rhumba**) /ˈrʌmbə/ *noun* a fast dance originally from Cuba; a piece of music for this dance 伦巴舞（源自古巴的一种快步舞）；伦巴舞曲

rum·ble /ˈrʌmbl/ *verb, noun*

■ *verb* **1** [I] to make a long deep sound or series of sounds 发出持续而低沉的声音；发出隆隆声：*The machine rumbled as it started up.* 机器轰鸣着发动起来。◇ *thunder rumbling in the distance* 远处隆隆的雷声 ◇ *I'm so hungry my* ***stomach's rumbling****.* 我饿得肚子咕咕叫了。 **2** [I] + **adv./prep.** to move slowly and heavily, making a rumbling sound 轰鸣着缓慢行进：*tanks rumbling through the streets* 隆隆地驶过街道的坦克 **3** [T] ~ **sb** (*BrE, informal*) to discover the truth about sb or what they are trying to hide 发现…的真相；看穿（阴谋）：*They knew they had been rumbled.* 他们知道自己已经被识破了。 **4** [I] (*NAmE, informal*) (of a GANG of young people 一伙年轻人) to fight against another GANG 打群架

PHR V **ˌrumble ˈon** (*especially BrE*) (of an argument, a disagreement, etc. 争论、分歧等) to continue slowly and steadily for a long time 缓慢而长久地持续；无休止地继续下去：*Discussions rumble on over the siting of the new airport.* 关于新机场的选址问题，讨论起来没完没了。

■ *noun* **1** [U, C] ~ (**of sth**) a long deep sound or series of sounds 持续而低沉的声音；隆隆声：*the rumble of thunder* 隆隆的雷声 ◇ *Inside, the noise of the traffic was reduced to a distant rumble.* 进到屋里，车辆的声音减弱了，就像是远处的隆隆声。◇ (*figurative*) *Although an agreement has been reached, rumbles of resentment can still be heard.* 尽管已有共识，但怨愤不满之声仍时有所闻。 **2** [C] (*NAmE, informal*) a fight in the street between two or more GANGS (= groups of young people) 打群架

ˈrumble strip *noun* (*informal*) a series of raised strips across a road or along its edge that make a loud noise when a vehicle drives over them in order to warn the driver to go slower or that he or she is too close to the edge of the road 齿纹震动带（路面的隆起带，车辆经过时发出很大响声，提醒司机减速或不要太靠近路边）

R

rum·bling /ˈrʌmblɪŋ/ *noun* **1** (also used as an adjective 也用作形容词) a long deep sound or series of sounds 低沉而持续的声音：*the rumblings of thunder* 隆隆的雷声 ◇ *a rumbling noise* 轰隆轰隆的声音 ◇ (*figurative*) *the rumblings of discontent* 啧有烦言 **2** [usually pl.] things that people are saying that may not be true 传言；传闻；谣传 SYN **rumour**：*There are rumblings that the election may have to be postponed.* 有传言说选举也许不得不延期。

rum·bus·tious /rʌmˈbʌstʃəs/ (*especially BrE*) (*NAmE usually* **ram·bunc·tious**) *adj.* [usually before noun] (*informal*) full of energy in a cheerful and noisy way 吵嚷的；喧闹的 SYN **boisterous**

ru·min·ant /ˈruːmɪnənt/ *noun* (*specialist*) any animal that brings back food from its stomach and chews it again. Cows and sheep are both ruminants. 反刍动物 ▸ **ru·min·ant** *adj.*：*ruminant animals* 反刍动物

ru·min·ate /ˈruːmɪneɪt/ *verb* [I, T] ~ (**on/over/about sth**) | + **speech** (*formal*) to think deeply about sth 沉思；认真思考 SYN **ponder** ▸ **ru·min·ation** /ˌruːmɪˈneɪʃn/ *noun* [C, U]

ru·mina·tive /ˈruːmɪnətɪv; *NAmE* -neɪtɪv/ *adj.* (*formal*) tending to think deeply and carefully about things 沉思的；冥思苦想的 SYN **pensive, thoughtful**：*in a ruminative mood* 陷于沉思 ▸ **ru·mina·tive·ly** *adv.*

rum·mage /ˈrʌmɪdʒ/ *verb, noun*

■ *verb* [I] + **adv./prep.** to move things around carelessly while searching for sth 翻寻；乱翻；搜寻：*She was rummaging around in her bag for her keys.* 她在自己的包里翻来翻去找钥匙。◇ *I rummaged through the contents of the box until I found the book I wanted.* 我把箱子都翻遍了才找到我要的书。

■ *noun* [sing.] the act of looking for sth among a group of other objects in a way that makes them untidy 翻寻；翻箱倒柜的寻找；搜寻：*Have a rummage around in the drawer and see if you can find a pen.* 翻翻抽屉，看能不能找到一支钢笔。

ˈrummage sale (*especially NAmE*) (*BrE also* **ˈjumble sale**) *noun* a sale of old or used clothes, etc. to make money for a church, school or other organization 旧杂物义卖（为教堂、学校或其他机构筹款）

rummy /ˈrʌmi/ *noun* [U] a simple card game in which players try to collect particular combinations of cards 拉米纸牌游戏（玩者要尽可能找出某种组合的牌）

ru·mour 🔑 (*especially US* **rumor**) /ˈruːmə(r)/ *noun, verb*

■ *noun* 🔑 [C, U] a piece of information, or a story, that people talk about, but that may not be true 谣言；传闻：*to* ***start/spread a rumour*** 制造 / 散布谣言 ◇ ~ (**of sth**) *There are widespread rumours of job losses.* 到处谣传要裁员。◇ ~ (**about sth**) *Some malicious rumours are circulating about his past.* 有人别有用心地散布谣言，说他过去如何如何。◇ ~ (**that...**) *I heard a rumour that they are getting married.* 我听到传闻，说他们要结婚了。◇ *Many of the stories are based on rumour.* 这些说法很多都是道听途说。◇ ***Rumour has it*** (= people say) *that he was murdered.* 有传言说他被杀害了。

■ *verb* **be rumoured** to be reported as a rumour and possibly not true 谣传；传说：**it is rumoured that...** ***It's widely rumoured that*** *she's getting promoted.* 到处都在传要提拔她了。◇ ~ **to be/have sth** *He was rumoured to be involved in the crime.* 有传言说他卷入了这桩罪行。 ▸ **ru·moured** *adj.* [only before noun]：*He denied his father's rumoured love affair.* 他否认谣传的他父亲的风流韵事。

rumour-monger (*especially US* **ru·mor·mon·ger**) /ˈruːmə mʌŋɡə(r); *NAmE* ˈruːmər/ *noun* a person who spreads rumours 散布谣言者

rump /rʌmp/ *noun* **1** [C] the round area of flesh at the top of the back legs of an animal that has four legs（兽类的）臀部 **2** [U] (*also* **ˌrump ˈsteak** [C, U]) a piece of good quality meat cut from the rump of a cow 臀肉牛排 **3** [C, usually sing.] (*humorous*) the part of the body that you sit on（人的）屁股蛋子 SYN **backside** **4** [sing.] (*BrE*) the small or unimportant part of a group or an organization that remains when most of its members have left（团体或组织的）无足轻重的残留部分

rum·ple /ˈrʌmpl/ *verb* ~ **sth** to make sth untidy or not smooth and neat 弄皱；弄乱：*She rumpled his hair playfully.* 她顽皮地弄乱他的头发。◇ *The bed was rumpled where he had slept.* 床上他睡过的地方有皱痕。

rum·pus /ˈrʌmpəs/ *noun* [usually sing.] (*informal*) a lot of noise that is made especially by people who are complaining about sth 喧闹；吵吵嚷嚷 SYN **commotion**：*to cause a rumpus* 引起骚动

ˈrumpus room *noun* (*NAmE, AustralE, NZE*) a room in a house for playing games in, sometimes in the BASEMENT 娱乐室（有时设在地下室）

rumpy pumpy /ˌrʌmpi ˈpʌmpi/ *noun* [U] (*BrE, informal, humorous*) the physical activity of sex 性行为

run 🔑 /rʌn/ *verb, noun*

■ *verb* (**running**, **ran** /ræn/, **run**)

• **MOVE FAST ON FOOT** 奔跑 **1** 🔑 [I] to move using your legs, going faster than when you walk 跑；奔跑：*Can you run as fast as Mike?* 你能和迈克跑得一样快吗？◇ *They turned and ran when they saw us coming.* 他们看见我们过来，转身就跑。◇ *She* ***came running*** *to meet us.* 她跑着来迎接我们。◇ *The dogs ran off as soon as we appeared.* 我们一露面狗就跑了。 HELP In spoken English **run** can be used with **and** plus another verb, instead of with **to** and the infinitive, especially to tell somebody to hurry and do something. 在口语中，run 可以和 and 加另一个动词连用，而不和 to 加动词不定式连用，尤用于叫某人赶快去做某事：*Run and get your swimsuits, kids.* 孩子们，快去拿你们的泳衣。◇ *I ran and knocked on the nearest door.* 我赶紧冲去敲紧邻的门。 **2** 🔑 [T] ~ **sth** to travel a particular distance by running 跑（某段距离）：*Who was the first person to run a mile* *in under four minutes?* 是谁第一个用了不到四分钟跑完一英里？ ➲ SEE ALSO MILE (4) **3** [I] (*sometimes* **go running**) to run as a sport 跑步；做跑步运动：*She used to run when she was at college.* 她上大学的时候经常跑步。◇ *I often go running before work.* 我常常在上班前跑步。

• **RACE** 赛跑比赛 **4** [I, T] to take part in a race 参加赛跑：**~ (in sth)** *He will be running in the 100 metres tonight.* 今晚他将参加 100 米赛跑。◇ *There are only five horses running in the first race.* 只有五匹马参加第一场比赛。◇ **~ sth** *to run the marathon* 参加马拉松比赛 ◇ *Holmes ran a fine race to take the gold medal.* 霍姆斯赛跑表现不错，获得了金牌。 ➲ SEE ALSO RUNNER (1) **5** [T, often passive] **~ sth** to make a race take place 开始（比赛）；使（比赛）开始：*The Derby will be run in spite of the bad weather.* 尽管天气恶劣，德比马赛仍将举行。

• **HURRY** 赶紧 **6** [I] **+ adv./prep.** to hurry from one place to another 迅速赶往；匆忙跑（到另一处）：*I've spent the whole day running around after the kids.* 我这一整天都跟在孩子们后面跑来跑去。 ➲ SEE ALSO RAT RUN

• **MANAGE** 管理 **7** [T] **~ sth** to be in charge of a business, etc. 管理；经营：*to run a hotel/store/language school* 经营一家旅店 / 商店 / 语言学校 ◇ *He has no idea how to run a business.* 他丝毫不懂企业管理。◇ *Stop trying to* ***run my life*** (= organize it) *for me.* 别老想操纵我的生活。◇ *The shareholders want more say in how the company is run.* 股东们想要在公司的经营管理上拥有更多的发言权。◇ *a badly run company* 经营不善的公司 ◇ *state-run industries* 国家经营的行业 ➲ SEE ALSO RUNNING *n.* (2)

• **PROVIDE** 提供 **8** [T] **~ sth** to make a service, course of study, etc. available to people 提供，开设（服务、课程等） **SYN** **organize**：*The college runs summer courses for foreign students.* 这所大学为外国学生开设暑期课程。

• **VEHICLE/MACHINE** 车辆；机器 **9** [T] **~ sth** (*BrE*) to own and use a vehicle or machine 拥有并使用（车辆或机器等）：*I can't afford to run a car on my salary.* 我的工资养不起汽车。 **10** [I, T] to operate or function; to make sth do this （使）运转，运行；操作：*Stan had the chainsaw running.* 斯坦开动了链锯。◇ (*figurative*) *Her life had always run smoothly before.* 她以前的生活一直很稳定。◇ **~ on sth** *Our van runs on* (= uses) *diesel.* 我们的货车用的是柴油。◇ **~ sth** *Could you run the engine for a moment?* 你来操作一会儿发动机好吗？

• **BUSES/TRAINS** 公共汽车；火车 **11** [I] (**+ adv./prep.**) to travel on a particular route （按某路线）行驶：*Buses to Oxford run every half hour.* 到牛津的汽车每半个小时发一趟。◇ *All the trains* ***are running late*** (= are leaving later than planned). 所有的列车都晚点了。 **12** [T] **~ sth (+ adv./prep.)** to make buses, trains, etc. travel on a particular route 使（按某一路线）行驶；使运行：*They run extra trains during the rush hour.* 他们在交通高峰时段加开了列车。

• **DRIVE SB** 开车送某人 **13** [T] **~ sb + adv./prep.** (*informal*) to drive sb to a place in a car 开车送：*Shall I run you home?* 我开车送你回家好吗？

• **MOVE SOMEWHERE** 移往某处 **14** [I] **+ adv./prep.** to move, especially quickly, in a particular direction（向某处）快速移动：*The car ran off the road into a ditch.* 汽车猛地开出路面，掉进沟里。◇ *A shiver ran down my spine.* 我猛然感到脊背发凉。◇ *The sledge ran smoothly over the frozen snow.* 雪橇在冻结的雪面上平稳地滑行。◇ *The old tramlines are still there but now no trams run on them.* 昔日的电车轨道还在，现在却没有电车在上面运行了。 **15** [T] **~ sth + adv./prep.** to move sth in a particular direction 移动（某物）：*She ran her fingers nervously through her hair.* 她紧张地用手指拨弄头发。◇ ***I ran my eyes over*** *the page.* 我匆匆地看了看这一页。

• **LEAD/STRETCH** 引导；伸展 **16** [I, T] to lead or stretch from one place to another; to make sth do this （使）导向；引导；（使）伸展，延伸：**+ adv./prep.** *He had a scar running down his left cheek.* 他左脸上竖着一道伤疤。◇ *The road runs parallel to the river.* 这条路和这条河是平行的。◇ **~ sth + adv./prep.** *We ran a cable from the lights to the stage.* 我们从电灯那里拉了一条电缆通到舞台。

• **CONTINUE FOR TIME** 持续 **17** [I] **~ (for sth)** to continue for a particular period of time without stopping 持续；延续：*Her last musical ran for six months on Broadway.* 她上一部音乐剧在百老汇连续上演了六个月。◇ *This debate will run and run!* 这场辩论会没完没了地继续下去！ **18** [I] **~ (for sth)** to operate or be valid for a particular period of time （在一段时间内）起作用，有效：*The permit runs for three months.* 许可证的有效期为三个月。◇ *The lease on my house only has a year left to run.* 我房子的租期只剩下一年了。

• **HAPPEN** 发生 **19** [I] (usually used in the progressive tenses 通常用于进行时) to happen at the time mentioned （在某时间）发生：**+ adv./prep.** *Programmes are* ***running*** *a few minutes* ***behind schedule*** *this evening.* 今晚播出的节目比预定的时间晚了几分钟。◇ *The murderer was given three life sentences, to run concurrently.* 这个杀人犯被判处三项无期徒刑，合并执行。

• **GUNS, DRUGS, ETC.** 枪支、毒品等 **20** [T] **~ sth (+ adv./prep.)** to bring or take sth into a country illegally and secretly 走私；非法携运；秘密携带 **SYN** **smuggle** ➲ SEE ALSO RUNNER (2)

• **OF STORY/ARGUMENT** 报道；论点 **21** [I, T] to have particular words, contents, etc. 包含（某种词语、内容等）：*Their argument ran something like this…* 他们的论点大致是这样的… ◇ **+ speech** *'Ten shot dead by gunmen,' ran the newspaper headline.* 报纸的标题为"枪手击毙十人"。

• **LIQUID** 液体 **22** [I] **+ adv./prep.** to flow 流淌；流动：*The tears ran down her cheeks.* 泪水顺着她的脸淌下来。◇ *Water was running all over the bathroom floor.* 浴室里水流满地。 **23** [T] to make liquid flow 使（液体）流动：**~ sth (into sth)** *She ran hot water into the bucket.* 她把热水注入桶里。◇ *to* ***run the hot tap*** (= to turn it so that water flows from it) 拧开热水龙头 ◇ **~ sth for sb** *I'll* ***run a bath*** *for you.* 我去给你放洗澡水。◇ **~ sb sth** *I'll* ***run you a bath.*** 我去给你放洗澡水。 **24** [I] to send out a liquid 输出，放出（液体）：*Who left the tap running?* 谁没关水龙头？◇ *Your nose is running* (= MUCUS is flowing from it). 你流鼻涕了。◇ *The smoke makes my eyes run.* 烟熏得我直流眼泪。 **25** [I] (usually used in the progressive tenses 通常用于进行时) **~ with sth** to be covered with a liquid 被（液体）覆盖；流满：*His face was running with sweat.* 他满脸是汗。◇ *The bathroom floor was running with water.* 浴室的地面上全是水。

• **OF COLOUR** 颜色 **26** [I] if the colour **runs** in a piece of clothing when it gets wet, it dissolves and may come out of the clothing into other things 掉色；退色

• **MELT** 熔化 **27** [I] (of a solid substance 固体) to melt 熔化：*The wax began to run.* 蜡开始熔化了。 ➲ SEE ALSO RUNNY

• **BE/BECOME** 是；成为 **28** [I] **+ adj.** to become different in a particular way, especially a bad way 变成，成为，变得（尤指不利的变化）：*The river* ***ran dry*** (= stopped flowing) *during the drought.* 这条河在干旱期间断流了。◇ *Supplies are* ***running low.*** 物资供应渐趋不足。◇ *We've* ***run short*** *of milk.* 我们牛奶不够了。◇ *You've got your rivals* ***running scared.*** 你已经使对手感到恐惧了。 **29** [I] **~ at sth** to be at or near a particular level 达到，接近（某程度）：*Inflation was running at 26%.* 通货膨胀达到了 26%。

• **OF NEWSPAPER/MAGAZINE** 报章杂志 **30** [T] **~ sth** to print and publish an item or a story 发表；刊登：*On advice from their lawyers they decided not to run the story.* 根据他们的律师的建议，他们决定不刊载这篇报道。

• **A TEST/CHECK** 测试；检验 **31** [T] **~ a test/check (on sth)** to do a test/check on sth （对…）进行（测试或检验）：*The doctors decided to run some more tests on the blood samples.* 医生决定对血样再进行一些化验。

• **IN ELECTION** 选举 **32** [I] to be a candidate in an election for a political position, especially in the US （尤指在美国）参加竞选：*Bush ran a second time in 2004.* * 2004 年，布什第二次参选。◇ **~ for sb/sth** *to run for president* 竞选总统 ◇ **~ in sth** *to run in the election* 参加竞选 ➲ COMPARE STAND *v.* (16)

• **OF TIGHTS/STOCKINGS** 裤袜；长袜 **33** [I] (*NAmE*) if TIGHTS or STOCKINGS **run**, a long thin hole appears in them 脱针；脱丝；抽丝 **SYN** **ladder**

IDM **HELP** Most idioms containing **run** are at the entries for the nouns and adjectives in the idioms, for example **run riot** is at **riot**. 大多数含 run 的习语，都可在该等习语中的名词及形容词相关词条找到，如 run riot 在词条 riot 下。 **come 'running** to be pleased to do what sb wants 赶

R

紧做某人喜欢的事；急于应某人的要求：*She knew she had only to call and he would come running.* 她知道只要打个电话，他就会高高兴兴地照办。 **'run for it** (often used in orders 常用于命令) to run in order to escape from sb/sth 逃跑 **,up and 'running** working fully and correctly 全面而准确地运行：*It will be a lot easier when we have the database up and running.* 等我们把数据库弄好以后，就省事多了。 ➲ MORE AT CLOSE[2] *adv.*, HIT *v.*

PHR V **'run across sb/sth** to meet sb or find sth by chance 偶然遇见（或看到）

,run 'after sb (*informal*) to try to have a romantic or sexual relationship with sb 追求 **SYN** **pursue**: *He's always running after younger women.* 他老是追年轻女子。 **,run 'after sb/sth** to run to try to catch sb/sth 追逐；追赶 **SYN** **pursue**

,run a'long (*old-fashioned, informal*) used in orders to tell sb, especially a child, to go away（尤用以命令儿童）走开

,run a'round with sb (*NAmE also* **'run with sb**) (*usually disapproving*) to spend a lot of time with sb 与（某人）厮混；互相往来：*She's always running around with older men.* 她老是跟年纪较大的男人来往。

'run at sb [no passive] to run towards sb to attack or as if to attack them 向某人冲去：*He ran at me with a knife.* 他拿着刀朝我冲过来。

,run a'way (from sb/...) to leave sb/a place suddenly; to escape from sb/a place 突然离开；逃离：*He ran away* ***from home*** *at the age of thirteen.* 他十三岁时离家出走。 ◇ *Looking at all the accusing faces, she felt a sudden urge to run away.* 看着一张张脸上那责备的神情，她突然想赶快溜走。 ➲ RELATED NOUN RUNAWAY **,run a'way from sth** to try to avoid sth because you are shy, lack confidence, etc. 避开；躲避；回避：*You can't just run away from the situation.* 这事你不能回避了事。 **,run a'way with you** if a feeling **runs away with you**, it gets out of your control 失去控制：*Her imagination tends to run away with her.* 她动辄想入非非。 **,run a'way/'off with sb | ,run a'way/'off (together)** to leave home, your husband, wife, etc. in order to have a relationship with another person 与某人私奔：*She ran away with her boss.* 她与老板私奔了。 ◇ *She and her boss ran away together.* 她和老板一起私奔了。 **,run a'way with sth 1** to win sth clearly or easily 轻而易举地赢得 **2** to believe sth that is not true 相信（不真实的东西）；误以为：*I don't want you to* ***run away with the impression*** *that all I do is have meetings all day.* 我不想让你误以为我整天的工作就是开会。

,run back 'over sth to discuss or consider sth again 再次讨论；重新考虑 **SYN** **review**: *I'll run back over the procedure once again.* 我将重新考虑这个程序。

,run sth 'by/'past sb (*informal*) to show sb sth or tell sb about an idea in order to see their reaction to it 给某人看，说给某人听（以观察其反应）

,run 'down 1 to lose power or stop working 耗尽能量；停止工作：*The battery has run down.* 电池没电了。 **2** to gradually stop functioning or become smaller in size or number 逐渐失去作用；萎缩；衰减：*British manufacturing industry has been running down for years.* 英国的制造业多年来一直在萎缩。 ➲ RELATED NOUN RUNDOWN (1) **,run sth↔'down 1** to make sth lose power or stop working 使耗尽能量；使停止工作：*If you leave your headlights on you'll soon run down the battery.* 如果你让车头灯一直亮着，很快就会把电池耗尽。 **2** to make sth gradually stop functioning or become smaller in size or number 使逐渐失去作用；使萎缩；使衰减：*The company is running down its sales force.* 公司正在削减销售人员。 ➲ RELATED NOUN RUNDOWN (1) **,run sb/sth↔'down 1** (of a vehicle or its driver 车辆或司机) to hit sb/sth and knock them/it to the ground 把…撞倒 **2** to criticize sb/sth in an unkind way 恶意批评；说…的坏话；贬低：*He's always running her down in front of other people.* 他总是在别人面前说她的坏话。 **3** to find sb/sth after a search（经过搜寻后）找到

,run sb↔'in (*old-fashioned, informal*) to arrest sb and take them to a police station 把某人扭送警察局 **,run sth↔'in** (*BrE*) (in the past) to prepare the engine of a new car for normal use by driving slowly and carefully（旧时）磨合运转，磨合驾驶：(*figurative*) *Whatever system you choose, it must be run in properly.* 不管你选择什么样的体系，都必须经过适当的磨合。

,run 'into sb (*informal*) to meet sb by chance 偶然遇见，碰到（某人）：*Guess who I ran into today!* 猜猜我今天碰见谁了！ **'run into sth 1** to enter an area of bad weather while travelling 途中遭遇（恶劣天气）：*We ran into thick fog on the way home.* 在回家的路上，我们遇上了大雾。 **2** to experience difficulties, etc. 遇到（困难等）：*Be careful not to run into debt.* 小心不要背上债务。 ◇ ***to run into danger/trouble/difficulties*** 遭遇危险 / 麻烦 / 困难 **3** to reach a particular level or amount 达到（某种水平或数量）：*Her income runs into six figures* (= is more than £100 000, $100 000, etc.). 她的收入达到了六位数。 **'run into sb/sth** to crash into sb/sth 撞上：*The bus went out of control and ran into a line of people.* 公共汽车失控，撞上了一排人。 **'run sth into sb/sth** to make a vehicle crash into sb/sth 开（车）撞上：*He ran his car into a tree.* 他开车撞上了一棵树。

,run 'off (*BrE*) (of a liquid 液体) to flow out of a container（从容器中）溢出，流出 **,run sth↔'off 1** to copy sth on a machine（用机器）复印，复制：*Could you run off twenty copies of the agenda?* 你给我复印二十份会议议程好吗？ **2** to cause a race to be run 举行，进行（赛跑等）：*The heats of the 200 metres will be run off tomorrow.* * 200 米预赛将在明天举行。 **3** to make a liquid flow out of a container 使溢出；使流出 **,run 'off with sb | ,run 'off (together)** = RUN AWAY/OFF WITH SB **,run 'off with sth** to steal sth and take it away 偷走：*The treasurer had run off with the club's funds.* 财务主管盗走了俱乐部的资金。

,run 'on to continue without stopping; to continue longer than is necessary or expected 持续；连续不断；拖延：*The meeting will finish promptly—I don't want it to run on.* 会议必须按时结束，我不想拖延下去。 **'run on sth** [no passive] if your thoughts, a discussion, etc. **run on** a subject, you think or talk a lot about that subject 以…为主题（或中心）；围绕

,run 'out 1 if a supply of sth **runs out**, it is used up or finished 用完；耗尽：*Time is running out for the trapped miners.* 被困矿工的时间不多了。 **2** if an agreement or a document **runs out**, it becomes no longer valid 过期；失效 **SYN** **expire** **,run 'out (of sth)** to use up or finish a supply of sth 用完，耗尽（供应品）：*We ran out of fuel.* 我们的燃料用光了。 ◇ *Could I have a cigarette? I seem to have run out.* 给我一支烟可以吗？我的烟好像抽完了。 **,run 'out on sb** (*informal*) to leave sb that you live with, especially when they need your help 弃某人而去；抛弃某人 **,run sb↔'out** [often passive] (in CRICKET 板球) to make a player stop BATTING by hitting the WICKET with the ball before the player has completed his or her run 将（正在跑的击球员）截杀出局

,run 'over if a container or its contents **run over**, the contents come over the edge of the container 溢出 **SYN** **overflow** **,run sb/sth↔'over** (of a vehicle or its driver 车辆或司机) to knock a person or an animal down and drive over their body or a part of it 撞倒并碾轧：*Two children were run over and killed.* 两名儿童被轧死了。 **,run 'over sth** to read through or practise sth quickly 快速通读（或练习）：*She ran over her notes before giving the lecture.* 讲课之前，她翻阅了一下自己的讲稿。

,run sth 'past sb = RUN STH BY/PAST SB：*Run that past me again.* 把那件事再说给我听听。

,run sb↔'through (*literary*) to kill sb by sticking a knife, SWORD, etc. through them（用刀、剑等）刺死 **,run 'through sth 1** to discuss, repeat or read sth quickly 匆匆讨论；快速阅读；很快地重复：*He ran through the names on the list.* 他快速浏览了一下名单。 ◇ *Could we run through your proposals once again?* 我们再简要讨论一下你的建议，好吗？ **2** [no passive] to pass quickly through sth 快速穿越；迅速传遍：*An angry murmur ran through the crowd.* 愤怒的抱怨声在人群中迅速蔓延。 ◇ *Thoughts of revenge kept running through his mind.* 报复的念头不断在他的脑子里闪过。 **3** [no passive] to be present in every part of sth 遍布：*A deep melancholy runs through her poetry.* 她的诗充满了深深的感伤。 **4** to perform, act or practise sth 表演；扮演；排练：*Can we run through Scene 3 again, please?* 请大家再来排练一下第 3 场好吗？ ➲ RELATED NOUN

RUN-THROUGH **5** to use up or spend money carelessly 挥霍：*She ran through the entire amount within two years.* 她不到两年就把所有的钱挥霍光了。

ˈrun to sth 1 to be of a particular size or amount 达到，有（某一规模或数量）：*The book runs to nearly 800 pages.* 这本书有近 800 页。 **2** (*especially BrE*) if you or your money will **not run to sth**, you do not have enough money for sth 有足够…的钱；足够…之用：*Our funds won't run to a trip abroad this year.* 今年我们没有足够的钱去国外旅行。

ˌrun sth↔ˈup 1 to allow a bill, debt, etc. to reach a large total 积欠（账款、债务等）；累积 **SYN** **accumulate**: *How had he managed to run up so many debts?* 他怎么欠了这么多债？ **2** to make a piece of clothing quickly, especially by sewing 赶制（衣服，尤指缝纫）：*to run up a blouse* 赶制一件女式衬衫 **3** to raise sth, especially a flag 竖起，升起（旗帜等） **ˌrun ˈup against sth** to experience a difficulty 遭遇（困难）：*The government is running up against considerable opposition to its tax reforms.* 政府的税务改革遇到了相当大的阻力。

ˈrun with sb = RUN AROUND WITH SB **ˈrun with sth** to accept or start to use a particular idea or method 采纳（某种想法、方法等）：*OK, let's run with Jan's suggestion.* 好，咱们就照简的建议干吧。

■ ***noun***

• **ON FOOT** 徒步 **1** [C] an act of running; a period of time spent running or the distance that sb runs 跑；跑步；跑步的时间（或距离）：*I go for a run every morning.* 我每天早晨都去跑步。◇ *a five-mile run* 跑上五英里 ◇ *Catching sight of her he* ***broke into a run*** (= started running). 他一看见她就跑了起来。◇ *I decided* ***to make a run for it*** (= to escape by running). 我决定逃跑。◇ *She took the stairs* ***at a run.*** 她跑着上了楼梯。➲ SEE ALSO FUN RUN

• **TRIP** 旅程 **2** [C] a trip by car, plane, boat, etc., especially a short one or one that is made regularly（尤指短程或定期、乘交通工具的）旅程，航程：*They took the car out for a run.* 他们开车出去旅行。➲ SEE ALSO MILK RUN, RAT RUN, SCHOOL RUN

• **OF SUCCESS/FAILURE** 成功；失败 **3** [C] a period of sth good or bad happening; a series of successes or failures 一段（幸运或倒霉的）时光；一系列（成功或失败）**SYN** **spell**: *a run of good/bad luck* 一连串好运 / 厄运 ◇ *Liverpool lost to Leeds, ending an unbeaten run of 18 games.* 利物浦队输给了利兹队，结束了连续 18 场不败的纪录。

• **OF PLAY/MOVIE** 戏剧；电影 **4** [C] a series of performances of a play or film/movie 连续上演（或放映）：*The show had a record-breaking run in the London theatre.* 这出戏在伦敦剧院连续上演，打破了演出纪录。

• **OF PRODUCT** 产品 **5** [C] the amount of a product that a company decides to make at one time 额定产量：*The first* ***print run*** *of 6 000 copies sold out.* 首印 6 000 册已全部售空。

• **MONEY** 钱 **6** [C, usually sing.] **~ on the dollar, pound, etc.** a situation when many people sell dollars, etc. and the value of the money falls 抛售（美元、英镑等） **7** [C, usually sing.] **~ on a bank** a situation when many people suddenly want to take their money out of a bank（到银行）挤提，挤兑

• **SUDDEN DEMAND** 急需 **8** [C, usually sing.] **~ on sth** a situation when many people suddenly want to buy sth 争购；抢购：*a run on the band's latest CD* 抢购这支乐队最新的激光唱片

• **WAY THINGS HAPPEN** 态势 **9** [sing.] **the ~ of sth** the way things usually happen; the way things seem to be happening on a particular occasion 态势；状况；趋势；动向：*In* ***the normal run of things*** *the only exercise he gets is climbing in and out of taxis.* 他平时的唯一运动就是上下出租车。◇ (*BrE*) *Wise scored in the 15th minute* ***against the run of play*** (= although the other team had seemed more likely to score). 怀斯在比赛进行到第 15 分钟的时候出人意料地得分。

• **IN SPORTS** 体育运动 **10** [C] a sloping track used in SKIING and some other sports（滑雪或其他运动中的）坡道，滑道：***a ski/toboggan, etc. run*** 滑雪道、雪橇滑道等 **11** [C] a point scored in the game of CRICKET or BASEBALL（板球或棒球中的）得分：*Our team won by four runs.* 我们队以四分的优势取胜。➲ SEE ALSO HOME RUN

• **IN ELECTION** 选举 **12** [sing.] (*NAmE*) an act of trying to get elected to public office 竞选：*He made an unsuccessful run for governor in 2008.* * 2008 年他竞选州长失败。

• **FOR ANIMALS/BIRDS** 畜；禽 **13** [C] (often in compounds 常构成复合词) a confined area in which animals or birds are kept as pets or on a farm 饲养场：*a chicken run* 养鸡场

• **IN MUSIC** 音乐 **14** [C] a series of notes sung or played quickly up or down the SCALE（顺着音阶的）急奏，急唱

• **IN CARD GAMES** 纸牌游戏 **15** [C] a series of cards held by one player 顺子

• **IN TIGHTS/STOCKINGS** 裤袜；长袜 **16** [C] (*NAmE*) = LADDER (3)

• **ILLNESS** 疾病 **17 the runs** [pl.] (*informal*) = DIARRHOEA ➲ SEE ALSO DRY RUN, DUMMY RUN, TRIAL RUN

IDM **the common, general, ordinary, usual run (of sth)** the average type of sth 普通类型：*He was very different from the general run of movie stars.* 他和一般的电影明星迥然不同。 **give sb/get/have the ˈrun of sth** to give sb/get/have permission to make full use of sth 允许某人充分使用；获准充分使用：*Her dogs have the run of the house.* 她的狗可以在家里自由活动。 **give sb a (good) run for their ˈmoney** to make sb try very hard, using all their skill and effort, in order to beat you in a game or competition 不让…轻易取胜；与…进行激烈竞争 **on the ˈrun 1** trying to avoid being captured 躲避：*He's on the run from the police.* 他在躲避警方的追捕。 **2** (*informal*) continuously active and moving around 忙碌；不停地奔波：*I've been on the run all day and I'm exhausted.* 我忙了一整天，累极了。◇ *Here are some quick recipes for when you're eating on the run* (= in a hurry). 这是一些快餐食谱，赶时间的话可以选。➲ MORE AT LONG *adj.*, SHORT *adj.*

run·about /ˈrʌnəbaʊt/ *noun* (*BrE, informal*) a small car, especially one used for short journeys（用于短途旅行的）小型汽车

run·around /ˈrʌnəraʊnd/ *noun*

IDM **give sb the ˈrunaround** (*informal*) to treat sb badly by not telling them the truth, or by not giving them the help or the information they need, and sending them somewhere else 隐瞒；搪塞；草草打发

run·away /ˈrʌnəweɪ/ *adj., noun*

■ ***adj.*** [only before noun] **1** (of a person 人) having left without telling anyone 逃跑的；出走的：*runaway children* 离家出走的儿童 **2** (of an animal or a vehicle 动物或车辆等) not under the control of its owner, rider or driver 失控的：*a runaway horse/car* 脱缰的马；失控的汽车 **3** happening very easily or quickly, and not able to be controlled 轻易的；迅速的；难以控制的：*a runaway winner/victory* 轻易获胜的人；轻而易举的胜利 ◇ *the* ***runaway success*** *of her first play* 她第一出戏的大获成功 ◇ *runaway inflation* 来势迅猛的通货膨胀

■ ***noun*** a person who has suddenly left or escaped from sb/sth, especially a child who has left home without telling anyone 逃跑者，逃避者，离家出走者（尤指儿童）：*teenage runaways living on the streets* 流落街头的离家出走的青少年

run·down /ˈrʌndaʊn/ *noun* [usually sing.] **1 ~ (in/of sth)** (*BrE*) a reduction in the amount, size or activity of sth, especially a business（尤指商业）削减，紧缩：*a rundown of transport services* 交通运输的缩减 **2 ~ (on/of sth)** an explanation or a description of sth 解释；描述：*I can give you a brief rundown on each of the applicants.* 我可以给你简单介绍一下每名申请人的情况。

ˌrun-ˈdown *adj.* **1** (of a building or place 建筑物或地方) in very bad condition; that has not been taken care of 破败的；失修的 **SYN** **neglected**: *run-down inner-city areas* 破败不堪的内城区 **2** (of a business, etc. 商业机构等) not as busy or as active as it used to be 衰败的；不景气的：*run-down transport services* 不景气的交通运输业 **3** [not before noun] (of a person 人) tired or slightly ill/sick, especially from working hard 疲惫；略感不适：*to be run-down* 疲惫不堪

R

rune /ruːn/ *noun* **1** one of the letters in an alphabet that people in northern Europe used in ancient times and cut into wood or stone 如尼字母（属于北欧古文字体系） **2** a symbol that has a mysterious or magic meaning 神秘的记号；有魔力的符号 ▶ **runic** /ˈruːnɪk/ *adj.*：*runic inscriptions* 用如尼文字刻的碑文

rung /rʌŋ/ *noun* one of the bars that forms a step in a LADDER（梯子的）横档，梯级：*He put his foot on the bottom rung to keep the ladder steady.* 他用脚踩住最底下的横档稳住梯子。◇ (*figurative*) *to get a foot on the bottom rung of the career ladder* 从事业阶梯的最低等级开始 ◇ *She was a few rungs above him on the social ladder.* 她的社会地位比他高了好几等。➲ VISUAL VOCAB PAGE V21 ➲ SEE ALSO RING² *v.*

ˈrun-in *noun* **1** ~ (**with sb**) (*informal*) an argument or a fight 争论；争吵；冲突：*The fiery player has had numerous run-ins with referees.* 这名脾气暴躁的队员曾和裁判员发生过无数次争吵。 **2** ~ (**to sth**) (*BrE*) = RUN-UP (1)

run·nel /ˈrʌnl/ *noun* (*formal* or *literary*) a small stream or channel 小溪；小河；细流

run·ner /ˈrʌnə(r)/ *noun* **1** a person or an animal that runs, especially one taking part in a race 奔跑的人，奔跑的动物（尤指参加速度比赛者）：*a long-distance/cross-country/marathon, etc. runner* 长跑、越野赛跑、马拉松等选手 ◇ *a list of runners* (= horses in a race) *and riders* 赛马和骑手名单 ➲ SEE ALSO FORERUNNER, FRONT RUNNER, ROADRUNNER **2** (especially in compounds 尤用于构成复合词) a person who takes goods illegally into or out of a place 走私者；偷运者：*a drug runner* 毒品走私分子 ➲ SEE ALSO GUNRUNNER **3** a strip of metal, plastic or wood that sth slides on or can move along on（金属、塑料或木制的）条状滑行装置：*the runners of a sledge* 雪橇的滑板 **4** a plant STEM that grows along the ground and puts down roots to form a new plant 纤匐枝 **5** a long narrow piece of cloth or carpet on a piece of furniture or on the floor 长条饰布；长条地毯 **6** a person in a company or an organization whose job is to take messages, documents, etc. from one place to another 送信人；信差 **7** (*CanE*) a shoe that is used for running or doing other sport in 跑鞋；运动鞋

IDM **do a ˈrunner** (*BrE, informal*) to leave or run away from somewhere in a hurry, especially to avoid paying a bill or receiving a punishment 匆忙逃离；逃跑

ˌrunner ˈbean (*also* **ˌstring ˈbean**) *noun* (*both BrE*) a type of BEAN which is a long flat green POD growing on a climbing plant also called a runner bean. The pods are cut up, cooked and eaten as a vegetable. 红花菜豆（植物）

ˌrunner-ˈup *noun* (*pl.* **runners-up**) a person or team that finishes second in a race or competition; a person or team that has not finished first but that wins a prize 第二名；亚军；非冠军的获奖者：*Winner: Kay Hall. Runner-up: Chris Platts.* 冠军：凯·霍尔。亚军：克里斯·普拉茨。◇ *They finished runners-up behind Sweden.* 他们紧随瑞典队之后，获得了第二名。◇ *The runners-up will all receive a £50 prize.* 没有拿到冠军的获奖者都将得到 50 英镑的奖金。➲ WORDFINDER NOTE AT COMPETITION

run·ning /ˈrʌnɪŋ/ *noun, adj.*

■ *noun* [U] **1** the action or sport of running 跑；跑步（运动）：*to go running* 去跑步 ◇ *running shoes* 跑鞋 **2** the activity of managing or operating sth 管理；操纵；操作：*the day-to-day running of a business* 企业的日常运营 ◇ *the running costs of a car* (= for example of fuel, repairs, insurance) 养车的费用 **3 -running** (in compounds 构成复合词) the activity of bringing sth such as drugs, guns, etc. into a country secretly and illegally 走私；偷运：*drug-running* 毒品走私

IDM **in/out of the ˈrunning** (**for sth**) (*informal*) having some/no chance of succeeding or achieving sth 有（或没有）成功的机会；能（或不能）获得 **make the ˈrunning** (*BrE, informal*) to set the speed at which sth is done; to take the lead in doing sth 领跑；带头；做榜样

■ *adj.* **1** used after a number and a noun such as 'year' 'day' or 'time', to say that sth has happened in the same way several times, without a change（置于数字和 year、day 或 time 等名词后，表示同样的事一再重复）连续：*She's won the championship three years running.* 她已连续三年获得冠军。◇ *It was the third day running that the train had been late.* 列车已经连续三天晚点了。◇ *No party has won an election four times running.* 没有一个政党在选举中连续四次获胜。 **2 running water** is water that is flowing somewhere or water that is supplied to a building and available to be used through taps/faucets（水）活的，流淌的，流动的：*I can hear the sound of running water.* 我听到流水的声音。◇ *a remote cottage without electricity or running water* 没有电和自来水的偏僻村舍 **3** [only before noun] lasting a long time; continuous 持久的；连续不断的 SYN **ongoing**：*For years he had fought a running battle with the authorities over the land.* 多年来，他为了那片土地同当局不断抗争。◇ *a running argument* 持久的争论 ◇ *His old raincoat became a running joke* (= people kept laughing at it). 他那件旧雨衣一直被人取笑。➲ SEE ALSO LONG-RUNNING **4 -running** (in compounds 构成复合词) running or flowing in the way mentioned …地流动的：*a fast-running river* 湍急的河流

IDM (**go and**) **take a running ˈjump** (*old-fashioned, informal*) used to tell sb in a rude way to go away 滚开；走开 ➲ MORE AT ORDER *n.*

ˈrunning back *noun* (in AMERICAN FOOTBALL 美式足球) an attacking player whose main job is to run forward carrying the ball （带球进攻的）跑卫

ˌrunning ˈcommentary *noun* a continuous description of an event, especially a sporting event, that sb gives as it happens （尤指对赛事的）现场评述，实况报道：*to give a running commentary on the game* 现场报道比赛实况

ˈrunning dog *noun* **1** (*disapproving*) a person who follows a political system or set of beliefs without questioning them 走狗（盲目遵从政治体制或信仰的人） **2** a dog which has been bred to run, especially for racing or for pulling a SLEDGE across snow（尤指比赛或拉雪橇的）跑狗；拖橇犬

ˌrunning ˈhead *noun* (*specialist*) a title or word printed at the top of each page of a book（书的）页首标题，眉题，天眉

ˈrunning mate *noun* [usually sing.] (*politics* 政) (in the US) a person who is chosen by the candidate in an election, especially that for president, to support them and to have the next highest political position if they win（美国）竞选伙伴，（尤指）副总统候选人：*The presidential nominee was advised to choose a woman as a running mate.* 有人建议总统候选人找一位女性竞选伙伴。➲ WORDFINDER NOTE AT CONGRESS

ˈrunning order *noun* [sing.] the order of the items in a television programme or a show; the order that members of a team will play in 播放顺序；上场顺序

ˌrunning reˈpairs *noun* [pl.] small things that you do to a piece of clothing, a vehicle, a machine, etc. to repair it or to keep it working 小修小补；修配

ˌrunning ˈsore *noun* a small area on the body that is infected and has liquid (called PUS) coming out of it 化脓处；脓疮

ˈrunning time *noun* the amount of time that a film/movie, a journey, etc. lasts（电影）片长；（旅程等的）持续时间

ˌrunning ˈtotal *noun* the total number or amount of things, money, etc. that changes as you add each new item 流水式总计；流水账总数

runny /ˈrʌni/ *adj.* (**run·nier**, **run·ni·est**) **1** (of your nose or eyes 鼻子或眼睛) producing a lot of liquid, for example when you have a cold 流鼻涕的；流眼泪的 **2** having more liquid than is usual; not solid 太稀的；水分过多的；软的：*runny honey* 水分过多的蜂蜜 ◇ *Omelettes should be runny in the middle.* 煎蛋卷包馅应该是软的。

ˈrun-off *noun* **1** [C] a second vote or competition that is held to find a winner because two people taking part in the first competition got the same result（对两名得票相同者的）决胜投票；（比赛打平后的）附加赛 **2** [U, C] rain, water or other liquid that runs off land into streams and rivers（雨、水或其他液体的）径流

ˌrun-of-the-ˈmill *adj.* (*often disapproving*) ordinary, with no special or interesting features 平凡的；普通的；乏味的

ˌrun-on ˈsentence *noun* two or more sentences or independent CLAUSES joined without the correct grammar 连写句，串句（不按正确语法连接的两个以上的句子或独立从句）

ˈrun-out *noun* (in CRICKET 板球) a situation in which a player fails to complete a RUN before an opposing player hits the STUMPS with the ball, and so is OUT（击球员的）被截杀出局

runt /rʌnt/ *noun* **1** the smallest, weakest animal of the young that are born from the same mother at the same time（一胎中）最弱小的动物：*the runt of the litter* 最弱小的幼崽 **2** (*informal, disapproving*) a rude way of referring to a small, weak or unimportant person 小矮个儿；小不点儿

ˈrun-through *noun* a practice for a performance of a play, show, etc. 排练；练习 **SYN** **rehearsal**

run·time /ˈrʌntaɪm/ *noun* (*computing* 计) **1** [U, C] the amount of time that a program takes to perform a task（程序所需的）运行时间 **2** [U, C] the time when a program is performing a task（程序应用中的）运行时，运行时间 **3** [C] a computer program that enables other computer programs to run inside it 运行系统，运行环境（为其他计算机程序提供运行平台）

ˈrun-up *noun* (*BrE*) **1** (*also less frequent* **ˈrun-in**) ~ **(to sth)** a period of time leading up to an important event; the preparation for this（重要事情的）前期；准备阶段；准备：*an increase in spending in the run-up to Christmas* 圣诞节前花费的增加 ◇ *during the run-up to the election* 在选举前的准备阶段 **2** the act of running or the distance you run, to gain speed before you jump a long distance, throw a ball, etc. 助跑；助跑距离

run·way /ˈrʌnweɪ/ *noun* **1** a long narrow strip of ground with a hard surface that an aircraft takes off from and lands on 飞机跑道 ➲ COLLOCATIONS AT TRAVEL **2** (*NAmE*) = CATWALK (1)

rupee /ruːˈpiː/ *noun* the unit of money in India, Pakistan and some other countries 卢比（印度、巴基斯坦等国的货币单位）

rup·ture /ˈrʌptʃə(r)/ *noun, verb*

■ ***noun*** [C, U] **1** (*medical* 医) an injury in which sth inside the body breaks apart or bursts（体内组织等的）断裂，破裂：*the rupture of a blood vessel* 血管破裂 **2** a situation when sth breaks or bursts 断裂；爆裂：*ruptures of oil and water pipelines* 石油和输水管道的爆裂 **3** (*informal*) a HERNIA of the ABDOMEN 疝气：*I nearly gave myself a rupture lifting that pile of books.* 提那一大堆书差点儿让我得了疝气。 **4** (*formal*) the ending of agreement or of good relations between people, countries, etc.（关系的）破裂，决裂；绝交：*a rupture in relations between the two countries* 两国关系的破裂 ◇ *Nothing could heal the rupture with his father.* 没有什么可以弥合他和父亲之间的裂痕。

■ ***verb*** **1** [T, I] ~ **(sth/yourself)** (*medical* 医) to burst or break apart sth inside the body; to be broken or burst apart（使体内组织等）断裂，裂开，破裂：*a ruptured appendix* 阑尾穿孔 ◇ *He ruptured himself* (= got a HERNIA) *trying to lift the piano.* 他试着搬动钢琴，发了疝气。 **2** [T, I] ~ **(sth)** (*formal*) to make sth such as a container or a pipe break or burst; to be broken or burst（使容器或管道等）断裂，破裂：*The impact ruptured both fuel tanks.* 冲撞使两个燃料箱都爆裂了。 ◇ *A pipe ruptured, leaking water all over the house.* 一根水管断裂，漏了满屋子的水。 **3** [T] ~ **sth** (*formal*) to make an agreement or good relations between people or countries end 使（友好关系）破裂；使绝交；毁掉（协议）：*the risk of rupturing North-South relations* 使南北关系破裂的危险

rural 🔑 /ˈrʊərəl; *NAmE* ˈrʊrəl/ *adj.* [usually before noun] connected with or like the countryside 乡村的；农村的；似农村的：*rural areas* 农村地区 ◇ *a rural economy* 农村经济 ◇ *rural America* 美国乡村 ◇ *a rural way of life* 乡村的生活方式 ➲ COMPARE URBAN (1) ➲ **WORDFINDER NOTE** AT LOCATION

ˌrural ˈdean *noun* = DEAN (2)

ˈrural route *noun* (*NAmE*) a route along which mail is delivered in rural areas 乡村邮递路线

Ruri·ta·nian /ˌrʊərɪˈteɪniən; *NAmE* ˌrʊrəˈt-/ *adj.* (especially of stories 尤指小说) full of romantic adventure 充满浪漫冒险的；浪漫国的 ➲ **MORE LIKE THIS** 17, page R27 **ORIGIN** From **Ruritania**, the name of an imaginary country in central Europe in stories by Anthony Hope. 源自安东尼·霍普所著小说中的虚构中欧国家鲁里坦尼亚王国。

ruse /ruːz/ *noun* a way of doing sth or of getting sth by cheating sb 诡计；骗术 **SYN** **trick**

rush 🔑 /rʌʃ/ *verb, noun*

■ ***verb***

• **MOVE FAST** 快速移动 **1** 🔑 [I, T] to move or to do sth with great speed, often too fast 迅速移动；急促：*We've got plenty of time; there's no need to rush.* 我们还有很多时间，用不着太急促。◇ *the sound of rushing water* 湍急的水声 ◇ **+ adv./prep.** *Don't rush off, I haven't finished.* 别急着走哇，我还没说完呢。◇ *I've been rushing around all day trying to get everything done.* 我一整天都四下忙活，想把所有的事都做完。◇ *People rushed to buy shares in the company.* 人们争着抢购该公司的股票。◇ **~ sth** *We had to rush our meal.* 我们只好匆匆忙忙地吃饭。

• **TAKE/SEND QUICKLY** 迅速带走 / 送出 **2** 🔑 [T] **~ sb/sth + adv./prep.** | **~ sb sth** to transport or send sb/sth somewhere with great speed 快速运输；速送：*Ambulances rushed the injured to the hospital.* 救护车迅速将伤者送往医院。◇ *Relief supplies were rushed in.* 救援物资很快就运来了。

• **DO STH TOO QUICKLY** 仓促行事 **3** 🔑 [I, T] to do sth or to make sb do sth without thinking about it carefully（使）仓促行事，匆忙行事，做事草率：**~ into sth/into doing sth** *We don't want to rush into having a baby.* 我们不急着要孩子。◇ **~ sb** *Don't rush me. I need time to think about it.* 别催我，我需要时间考虑一下。◇ **~ sb into sth/into doing sth** *I'm not going to be rushed into anything.* 我不会受人催促草率地做事。

• **ATTACK** 攻击 **4** [T] **~ sb/sth** to try to attack or capture sb/sth suddenly 突袭；突击抓捕：*A group of prisoners rushed an officer and managed to break out.* 一伙囚犯突然袭击狱警，越狱了。◇ *Fans rushed the stage after the concert.* 音乐会结束后乐迷一下子涌向舞台。

• **IN AMERICAN FOOTBALL** 美式足球 **5** [T] **~ sb** (*NAmE*) to run into sb who has the ball 突袭，冲向（持球人）**6** [I] (*NAmE*) to move forward and gain ground by carrying the ball and not passing it 带（球）奔跑；跑动带（球）

• **IN AMERICAN COLLEGES** 美国大学 **7** [T] **~ sb** (*NAmE*) to give a lot of attention to sb, especially to a student because you want them to join your FRATERNITY or SORORITY（为物色、招募目的）特别关注，非常关心：*He is being rushed by Sigma Nu.* * ΣN 联谊会正在拉拢他。 **IDM** SEE FOOL *n.*, FOOT *n.*

PHR V **ˌrush sth↔ˈout** to produce sth very quickly 仓促生产；赶制：*The editors rushed out an item on the crash for the late news.* 编辑们赶着将坠机事件编入晚间新闻报道中。 **ˌrush sth↔ˈthrough** | **ˌrush sth ˈthrough sth** to deal with official business very quickly by making the usual process shorter than usual 使快速通过；仓促处理：*to rush a bill through Parliament* 使议案在议会快速通过

■ ***noun***

• **FAST MOVEMENT** 迅速移动 **1** 🔑 [sing.] a sudden strong movement 猛烈移动；冲：*Shoppers **made a rush for** the exits.* 购物者冲向出口。◇ *She was trampled in the rush to get out.* 她在大伙儿往外冲的时候被人踩了。◇ *They listened to the rush of the sea below.* 他们听着下面汹涌澎湃的海浪声。◇ *The door blew open, letting in a rush of cold air.* 门

被风刮开了，一股冷风吹了进来。◇ *He had a **rush of blood to the head** (= suddenly lost control of himself) and punched the man.* 他一时冲动，挥拳打了那个男人。

- **HURRY** 匆忙 **2** [sing., U] a situation in which you are in a hurry and need to do things quickly 匆忙；仓促：*I can't stop—I'm **in a rush**.* 我不能停下来，我忙着呢。◇ ***What's the rush?*** 干吗这么急匆匆的？◇ *'I'll let you have the book back tomorrow.' '**There's no rush**.'* "我明天就把书还给你。" "不用着急。" ◇ *The words came out **in a rush**.* 那些话一股脑儿都出来了。◇ *a **rush job*** (= one that has been done quickly) 仓促做完的活儿
- **BUSY SITUATION** 忙碌 **3** [sing.] a situation in which people are very busy and there is a lot of activity 忙碌；繁忙：*The evening rush was just starting.* 繁忙的夜晚才刚开始。◇ *the Christmas rush* 圣诞节前的忙碌
- **OF FEELING** 感觉 **4** [sing.] ~ (**of sth**) a sudden strong emotion or sign of strong emotion 迸发的情绪；情绪迸发：*a sudden **rush of excitement/fear/anger*** 突然感到的兴奋 / 恐惧 / 愤怒 **5** [sing.] a sudden feeling of extreme pleasure or excitement 突如其来的极度愉悦（或兴奋）：*Parachuting will give you the rush of a lifetime.* 跳伞给你一生难求的刺激感觉。◇ *Users of the drug report experiencing a rush that lasts several minutes.* 服用这种药的人说有持续几分钟的亢奋感觉。
- **SUDDEN DEMAND** 急需 **6** [sing.] ~ (**on/for sth**) a sudden large demand for goods, etc. 大量急需；争相抢购：*There's been a rush on umbrellas this week.* 本周出现了抢购雨伞的现象。➲ SEE ALSO GOLD RUSH
- **PLANT** 植物 **7** [C, usually pl.] a tall plant like grass that grows near water. Its long thin STEMS can be dried and used for making BASKETS, the seats of chairs, etc. 灯芯草（干燥后可用于编制篮子、坐垫等）：*rush matting* 灯芯草编的席子
- **OF FILM/MOVIE** 电影 **8 rushes** [pl.] (*specialist*) the first prints of a film/movie before they have been EDITED 样片
- **IN AMERICAN FOOTBALL** 美式足球 **9** [C] an occasion when a player or players run towards a player on the other team who has the ball（向对方持球队员的）突袭：*There was a rush on the quarterback.* 对方球员冲向四分卫。 **10** [C] an occasion when a player runs forward with the ball 跑动带球：*Johnson carried the ball an average of 6 yards per rush.* 约翰逊跑动带球平均每次行进 6 码。
- **IN AMERICAN COLLEGES** 美国大学 **11** [sing.] (*NAmE*) the time when parties are held for students who want to join a FRATERNITY or SORORITY 学生联谊会纳新活动（时间）：*rush week* 学生联谊会纳新活动周 ◇ *a rush party* 学生纳新联谊会 IDM SEE BUM *n.*

rushed /rʌʃt/ *adj.* done too quickly or made to do sth too quickly 仓促而就的；草率的 SYN **hurried**: *It was a rushed decision made at the end of the meeting.* 那是会议结束时匆忙作出的决定。◇ *Let's start work on it now so we're not too rushed at the end.* 我们现在就开始干吧，免得最后太匆忙。IDM SEE FOOT *n.*

'rush hour *noun* [C, usually sing., U] the time, usually twice a day, when the roads are full of traffic and trains are crowded because people are travelling to or from work（上下班时的）交通高峰期：*the **morning/evening rush hour*** 早上的 / 傍晚的交通高峰期 ◇ *Don't travel **at rush hour/in the rush hour**.* 别在交通高峰期间出行。◇ *rush-hour traffic* 交通高峰期的车流 ➲ COLLOCATIONS AT DRIVING

rusk /rʌsk/ *noun* (*especially BrE*) a hard crisp biscuit for babies to eat（婴儿食用的）脆饼干

rus·set /ˈrʌsɪt/ *adj.* reddish-brown in colour 赤褐色的 ▸ **rus·set** *noun* [U]: *leaves of russet and gold* 赤褐色和金黄色的树叶

Rus·sian /ˈrʌʃn/ *adj., noun*
- ▪ *adj.* from or connected with Russia 俄罗斯的
- ▪ *noun* **1** [C] a person from Russia 俄罗斯人 **2** [U] the language of Russia 俄语

ˌRussian 'doll *noun* one of a set of hollow painted figures which fit inside each other 俄罗斯套娃

ˌRussian rou'lette *noun* [U] a dangerous game in which a person shoots at their own head with a gun that contains a bullet in only one of its chambers, so that the person does not know if the gun will fire or not 俄罗斯轮盘赌（危险游戏，参加者用装有一发子弹的转轮手枪对准自己头部射击）：(*figurative*) *The airline was accused of playing Russian roulette with passenger safety.* 这家航空公司被指责将乘客安全当儿戏。

Russo- /ˈrʌsəʊ; *NAmE* ˈrʌsoʊ/ *combining form* (in nouns and adjectives 构成名词和形容词) Russian 俄罗斯的：*Russo-Japanese relations* 俄日关系

rust /rʌst/ *noun, verb*
- ▪ ***noun*** [U] **1** a reddish-brown substance that is formed on some metals by the action of water and air 锈；铁锈：*pipes covered with rust* 生了锈的管子 ◇ *rust spots* 锈斑 ◇ *a rust-coloured dress* 赤褐色连衣裙 ➲ SEE ALSO RUSTY (1) **2** a plant disease that causes reddish-brown spots; the FUNGUS that causes this disease（植物的）锈病；锈菌
- ▪ ***verb*** [I, T] if metal **rusts** or sth **rusts** it, it becomes covered with rust（使）生锈 SYN **corrode**: *old rusting farming implements* 生锈的旧农具 ◇ *Brass doesn't rust.* 黄铜不生锈。◇ ~ **sth** *Water had got in and rusted the engine.* 发动机进水生锈了。 ▸ **rust·ed** *adj.*：*rusted iron* 生锈的铁 ➲ SEE ALSO RUSTY

PHR V **ˌrust a'way** to be gradually destroyed by rust 锈坏

'rust belt *noun* (*especially US*) a region that used to have a lot of industry, but that has now decreased in importance and wealth, especially parts of the northern US where there were many factories that have now closed 锈带（尤指美国北部衰败或萧条的工业区）

rus·tic /ˈrʌstɪk/ *adj., noun*
- ▪ ***adj.*** **1** (*approving*) typical of the country or of country people; simple 乡村（人）的；乡村（人）特色的；淳朴的：*an old cottage full of rustic charm* 充满了乡村魅力的旧农舍 **2** made very simply of rough wood 用粗糙木材做成的：*a rustic garden seat* 花园里的粗木座椅 ◇ *a rustic fence* 用粗糙木材搭成的栅栏 ▸ **rus·ti·city** /rʌˈstɪsəti/ *noun* [U]
- ▪ ***noun*** (*disapproving* or *humorous*) a person who lives in or comes from the country 乡下人；乡巴佬

rus·tle /ˈrʌsl/ *verb, noun*
- ▪ ***verb*** **1** [I, T] ~ (**sth**) if sth dry and light **rustles** or you **rustle it**, it makes a sound like paper, leaves, etc. moving or rubbing together（使）发出轻轻的摩擦声，发出沙沙声：*the sound of the trees rustling in the breeze* 树木在微风中发出的沙沙声 **2** [T] ~ **sth** to steal farm animals 偷窃（牲口）

PHR V **ˌrustle sth↔'up** (**for sb**) (*informal*) to make or find sth quickly for sb and without planning 很快制作；迅速找到；仓促凑成：*I'm sure I can rustle you up a sandwich.* 我保证能马上给你弄份三明治。◇ *She's trying to rustle up some funding for the project.* 她正设法尽快为这个项目筹集一些资金。

- ▪ ***noun*** [sing.] a light dry sound like leaves or pieces of paper moving or rubbing against each other 轻轻的摩擦声；沙沙声：*There was a rustle of paper as people turned the pages.* 人们翻动书页时发出沙沙的声响。◇ *I heard a faint rustle in the bushes.* 我听到树丛里发出一阵轻微的窸窣声。

rust·ler /ˈrʌslə(r)/ *noun* a person who steals farm animals 偷窃牲口的人

rust·ling /ˈrʌslɪŋ/ *noun* **1** [U, C] the sound of light, dry things moving together 瑟瑟声；沙沙声：*the soft rustling of leaves* 树叶柔和的沙沙声 **2** [U] the act of stealing farm animals 偷窃牲口

rust·proof /ˈrʌstpruːf/ *adj.* **rustproof** metal has had a substance put on it so that it will not RUST 防锈的；经过防锈处理的

rusty /ˈrʌsti/ *adj.* (**rust·ier, rusti·est**) **1** covered with RUST 生锈的：*rusty metal* 生锈的金属 ◇ *a rusty old car* 生了锈的旧汽车 **2** [not usually before noun] (*informal*) (of a sport, skill, etc. 体育运动、技能等) not as good as it used to be, because you have not been practising 荒疏；荒废；退步： *My tennis is very rusty these days.* 最近我的网球荒疏了。◇ *I haven't played the piano for ages—I may be a little rusty.* 我很久没有弹钢琴，可能会有点生疏。 ▸ **rusti·ness** *noun* [U]

rut /rʌt/ *noun* **1** [C] a deep track that a wheel makes in soft ground 车辙 **2** [C] a boring way of life that does not change 刻板乏味的生活： *I gave up my job because I felt I was* ***stuck in a rut.*** 我放弃了我的工作，因为我觉得那种生活呆板无聊。◇ *If you don't go out and meet new people, it's easy to* ***get into a rut.*** 如果你不出门结识新朋友，你的生活就容易变得刻板乏味。 **3** [U] (*also* **the rut**) the time of year when male animals, especially DEER, become sexually active（雄鹿等雄性动物的）发情期 ➲ SEE ALSO RUTTED, RUTTING

ru·ta·baga /ˌruːtəˈbeɪɡə/ (*NAmE*) (*BrE* **swede**) (*ScotE* **tur·nip**) *noun* [C, U] a large round yellow root vegetable 芜菁甘蓝；大头菜 ➲ VISUAL VOCAB PAGE V34

ru·the·nium /ruːˈθiːniəm/ *noun* [U] (*symb.* **Ru**) a chemical element. Ruthenium is a hard silver-white metal that breaks easily and is found in PLATINUM ORES. 钌

ruth·er·ford·ium /ˌrʌðəˈfɔːdiəm; *NAmE* ˌrʌðərˈfɔːrd-/ *noun* [U] (*symb.* **Rf**) a chemical element. Rutherfordium is RADIOACTIVE and does not exist in nature but is produced artificially when atoms COLLIDE (= crash into each other). 铲（放射性化学元素）

ruth·less /ˈruːθləs/ *adj.* (*disapproving*) (of people or their behaviour 人或行为) hard and cruel; determined to get what you want and not caring if you hurt other people 残酷无情的；残忍的： *a ruthless dictator* 残酷无情的独裁者 ◇ *The way she behaved towards him was utterly ruthless.* 她对待他真是无情至极。◇ *He has a ruthless determination to succeed.* 他有不获成功决不罢休的坚定决心。 ▸ **ruth·less·ly** *adv.* **ruth·less·ness** *noun* [U]

rut·ted /ˈrʌtɪd/ *adj.* (of a road or path 道路或小径) with deep tracks that have been made by wheels 有车辙的 ➲ SEE ALSO RUT (1)

rut·ting /ˈrʌtɪŋ/ *adj.* (of male animals, especially DEER 雄性动物，尤指鹿) in a time of sexual activity 处于发情期的： *rutting deer* 处于发情期的鹿 ◇ *the rutting season* 交配季节 ➲ SEE ALSO RUT (3)

RV /ˌɑː ˈviː; *NAmE* ˌɑːr/ (*NAmE*) (*BrE* **camp·er**, **ˈcamper van**) (*also* **motor·home** *NAmE*, *BrE*) *noun* a large vehicle designed for people to live and sleep in when they are travelling (the abbreviation for 'recreational vehicle') 野营车（供旅行时居住，全写为 recreational vehicle）

Rx /ˌɑːr ˈeks/ *noun* (*NAmE*) **1** the written abbreviation for a doctor's PRESCRIPTION 处方，药方（prescription 的缩写） **2** a solution to a problem 解决方法；办法： *There's no Rx for unemployment.* 失业问题无法解决。

-ry ➲ -ERY

rye /raɪ/ *noun* [U] a plant that looks like BARLEY but that produces larger grain, grown as food for animals and for making flour and WHISKY; the grain of this plant 黑麦；黑麦粒： *rye bread* 黑麦面包 ◇ *rye whisky* 黑麦威士忌酒 ➲ VISUAL VOCAB PAGE V35

rye·grass /ˈraɪɡrɑːs; *NAmE* -ɡræs/ *noun* [U] a type of grass which is grown as food for animals 黑麦草（可作动物饲料）

R

Ss

S /es/ *noun, abbr., symbol*

■ ***noun*** (*also* **s**) [C, U] (*pl.* **Ss**, **S's**, **s's** /ˈesɪz/) the 19th letter of the English alphabet 英语字母表的第 19 个字母：*'Snow' begins with (an) S/'S'.* * snow 一词以字母 s 开头。➲ SEE ALSO S-BEND

■ ***abbr.*** **1** (*pl.* **SS**) Saint 圣人；圣徒 **2** (especially for sizes of clothes) small （尤指服装的尺码）小号 **3** (*NAmE also* **So.**) south; southern 南方（的）；南部（的）：*S Yorkshire* 约克郡南部 **4** SIEMENS 西（门子）（电导单位）➲ SEE ALSO S AND H

■ ***symbol*** the symbol for ENTROPY 熵

-'s /s; z/ *suffix, short form*

■ ***suffix*** (added to nouns 加在名词后) **1** belonging to （表示所属关系）…的：*the woman's hat* 那个女人的帽子 ◇ *Peter's desk* 彼得的书桌 ◇ *children's clothes* 儿童服装 **2** used to refer to sb's home or, in British English, a particular shop （指某人的家，英式英语亦指某商店）…家，…店：*Shall we go to David's* (= David's house) *tonight?* 今晚我们去戴维家好吗？◇ (*BrE*) *I'll call in at the chemist's on my way home.* 我回家时顺便要去药房一趟。

■ ***short form*** (*informal*) **1** used after *he, she* or *it* and *where, what, who* or *how* to mean 'is' or 'has' （用于 he、she、it 和 where、what、who 以及 how 后，表示 is 或 has）：*She's still in the bath.* 她还在洗澡。◇ *What's he doing now?* 他现在在干什么呢？◇ *It's time to go now.* 该走了。◇ *Who's taken my pen?* 谁拿走了我的笔？◇ *Where's he gone?* 他上哪儿去了？◇ *It's gone wrong again.* 它又出毛病了。 **2** (used after *let* when making a suggestion that includes yourself and others 用于 let 后，建议自己和别人一起做某事) us 咱们；我们：*Let's go out for lunch.* 咱们出去吃午饭吧。

-s' *suffix* (forming the end of plural nouns 构成复数名词的后缀) belonging to （表示所属关系）…的：*the cats' tails* 这些猫的尾巴 ◇ *their wives' jobs* 他们妻子的工作

SA *abbr.* South Africa 南非

saag (*also* **sag**) /sæg; *BrE also* sɑːg/ *noun* [U] (*IndE*) = SPINACH

sab·bath /ˈsæbəθ/ (*often* **the Sabbath**) *noun* [sing.] (in Judaism and Christianity 犹太教和基督教) the holy day of the week that is used for resting and worshipping God. For Jews this day is Saturday and for Christians it is Sunday. 安息日（犹太教定为星期六，基督教定为星期日）：*to keep/break the Sabbath* (= to obey/not obey the religious rules for this day) 守 / 不守安息日

sab·bat·ic·al /səˈbætɪkl/ *noun* [C, U] a period of time when sb, especially a teacher at a university, is allowed to stop their normal work in order to study or travel （尤指供大学教师进行学术研究或旅游的）公休假，休假：*to take a year's sabbatical* 享受一年的公休假 ◇ *a* ***sabbatical term/year*** 休假学期 / 学年 ◇ *He's* ***on sabbatical.*** 他正休假。

saber (*NAmE*) = SABRE

sabji /ˈsʌbdʒiː/ = SABZI

sable /ˈseɪbl/ *noun* **1** [C] a small animal from northern Asia with dark yellowish-brown fur 紫貂；黑貂 **2** [U] the skin and fur of the sable, used for making expensive coats and artists' brushes 貂皮，貂毛（可制作名贵大衣或画笔）

sabo·tage /ˈsæbətɑːʒ/ *noun, verb*

■ ***noun*** [U] **1** the act of doing deliberate damage to equipment, transport, machines, etc. to prevent an enemy from using them, or to protest about sth （为防止敌人利用或表示抗议而对设备、交通等进行的）蓄意毁坏，人为破坏：*an act of* ***economic/military/industrial sabotage*** 经济 / 军事 / 工业破坏活动 ◇ *Police investigating the train derailment have not ruled out sabotage.* 警方调查火车出轨事件，没有排除人为破坏的可能。➲ WORDFINDER NOTE AT PROTEST **2** the act of deliberately spoiling sth in order to prevent it from being successful 故意妨碍；捣乱；刻意阻碍

■ ***verb*** **1** ~ **sth** to damage or destroy sth deliberately to prevent an enemy from using it or to protest about sth 蓄意破坏（以防止敌方利用或表示抗议）：*The main electricity supply had been sabotaged by the rebels.* 叛乱者破坏了供电干线。 **2** ~ **sth** to prevent sth from being successful or being achieved, especially deliberately 刻意阻碍；妨碍；捣乱：*Protesters failed to sabotage the peace talks.* 抗议者未能破坏和平谈判。◇ *The rise in interest rates sabotaged any chance of the firm's recovery.* 由于利率的提高，公司的复苏已无任何可能。

sabo·teur /ˌsæbəˈtɜː(r)/ *noun* a person who does deliberate damage to sth to prevent an enemy from using it, or to protest about sth （为防止敌方利用或为表示抗议的）蓄意破坏者：*Saboteurs blew up a small section of the track.* 有人蓄意炸毁了一小段铁路。◇ (*BrE*) ***hunt saboteurs*** (= people who try to stop people from hunting FOXES, etc.) 阻挠捕猎活动的人

sabre (*especially US* **saber**) /ˈseɪbə(r)/ *noun* **1** a heavy SWORD with a curved blade （弯刃）军刀，马刀 **2** a light SWORD with a thin blade used in the sport of FENCING （击剑运动用的）佩剑

ˈsabre-rattling (*especially US* **ˈsaber-rattling**) *noun* [U] the act of trying to frighten sb by threatening to use force 武力威胁；武力恫吓

sabre·tooth (*BrE*) (*US* **saber·tooth**) /ˈseɪbətuːθ; *NAmE* -bərt-/ (*BrE also* **ˌsabre-toothed ˈtiger**) (*US also* **ˌsaber-toothed ˈtiger**) *noun* a large animal of the cat family with two very long curved upper teeth, that lived thousands of years ago and is now EXTINCT 剑齿虎（有一对剑形犬牙的大型猫科动物，已灭绝）

sabzi /ˈsʌbziː/ (*also* **sabji**) *noun* [U, C] (*IndE*) vegetables, especially when cooked （尤指煮熟的）蔬菜；素菜

sac /sæk/ *noun* a part inside the body of a person, an animal or a plant, that is shaped like a bag, has thin skin around it, and contains liquid or air （人、动植物体内的）囊，液囊，气囊

sac·charin /ˈsækərɪn/ *noun* [U] a sweet chemical substance used instead of sugar, especially by people who are trying to lose weight 糖精

sac·char·ine (*also less frequent* **sac·char·in**) /ˈsækəriːn; -rɪn/ *adj.* (*disapproving*) (of people or things 人或物) too emotional in a way that seems exaggerated 情感过分强烈而显夸张的；故作多情的 **SYN** **sentimental**：*a saccharine smile* 甜蜜的笑容 ◇ *saccharine songs* 甜得发腻的歌

sacer·dotal /ˌsæsəˈdəʊtl; *NAmE* -sərˈdoʊtl/ *adj.* (*formal*) connected with a priest or priests 司祭的；司铎的

sa·chet /ˈsæʃeɪ; *NAmE* sæˈʃeɪ/ *noun* **1** (*BrE*) (*NAmE* **packet**) a closed plastic or paper package that contains a very small amount of liquid or a powder （密封的塑料或纸质）小袋：*a sachet of sauce/sugar/shampoo* 一小袋调味汁 / 糖 / 洗发剂 ➲ VISUAL VOCAB PAGE V36 **2** a small bag containing dried HERBS or flowers that you put with your clothes to make them smell pleasant （置于衣物中的）小香囊，小香袋

sack 🔑 /sæk/ *noun, verb*

■ ***noun*** **1** 🔑 [C] a large bag with no handles, made of strong rough material or strong paper or plastic, used for storing and carrying, for example flour, coal, etc. 麻布（或厚纸、塑料等）大袋 **2** 🔑 [C] (*NAmE*) a strong paper bag for carrying shopping （厚纸的）购物袋 **3** 🔑 [C] the contents of a sack 一满袋；一大袋东西：*They got through a sack of potatoes.* 他们把一麻袋土豆吃完了。◇ (*NAmE*) *two sacks of groceries* 两袋食品杂货 **4** 🔑 **the sack** [sing.] (*BrE, informal*) being told by your employer that you can no longer continue working for a company, etc., usually because of sth that you have done wrong 开除；解雇；炒鱿鱼：*He* ***got the sack*** *for swearing.* 他因说脏话而被开除。◇ *Her work was so poor that she was* ***given the sack.***

她工作干得很差，被炒了鱿鱼。◇ *Four hundred workers face the sack.* 四百名工人面临解雇的危险。 **5 the sack** [sing.] (*informal, especially NAmE*) a bed 床：*He caught them in the sack together.* 他撞见他们俩一起睡在床上。 **6** (*usually* **the sack**) [sing.] (*formal*) the act of stealing or destroying property in a captured town（在攻陷的城镇中的）抢劫，劫掠：*the sack of Rome* 对罗马城的洗劫 IDM SEE HIT *v.*

■ ***verb* 1** ~ **sb** (*informal, especially BrE*) to dismiss sb from a job 解雇；炒鱿鱼 SYN **fire**：*She was sacked for refusing to work on Sundays.* 她因拒绝在星期天上班被解雇了。➲ COLLOCATIONS AT UNEMPLOYMENT **2** ~ **sth** (of an army, etc., especially in the past) to destroy things and steal property in a town or building（尤指旧时军队等）破坏，劫掠：*Rome was sacked by the Goths in 410.* 罗马在 410 年遭到哥特人的洗劫。 **3** ~ **sb** (in AMERICAN FOOTBALL 美式足球) to knock down the QUARTERBACK 擒杀（四分卫）

PHR V **ˌsack ˈout** (*NAmE, informal*) to go to sleep or to bed 入睡；上床睡觉

sack·but /ˈsækbʌt/ *noun* a type of TROMBONE used in the RENAISSANCE period 拉推号，古长号（文艺复兴时期的长号）

sack·cloth /ˈsækklɒθ; *NAmE* -klɔːθ; -klɑːθ/ (*also* **sack·ing**) *noun* [U] a type of rough cloth made from JUTE, etc., used for making sacks 粗麻布；麻袋布

IDM **wear, put on, etc. ˌsackcloth and ˈashes** to behave in a way that shows that you are sorry for sth that you have done 忏悔；悔恨；后悔

sack·ful /ˈsækfʊl/ *noun* the amount contained in a sack 一大袋（的量）：*two sackfuls of flour* 两袋面粉

sack·ing /ˈsækɪŋ/ *noun* **1** [C] an act of sacking sb (= dismissing them from their job) 解雇 **2** [U] = SACKCLOTH

ˈsack race *noun* a race in which the competitors jump forward inside a sack 套袋赛跑，袋鼠跳（将双腿套在袋中跳跃前进）

sac·ra·ment /ˈsækrəmənt/ *noun* (in Christianity 基督教) **1** [C] an important religious ceremony such as marriage, BAPTISM or COMMUNION 圣事，圣礼（如婚配、圣洗或圣餐等） **2 the sacrament** [sing.] the bread and wine that are eaten and drunk during the service of COMMUNION 圣餐（包括面饼和葡萄酒）▶ **sac·ra·men·tal** /ˌsækrəˈmentl/ *adj.* [usually before noun]：*sacramental wine* 圣餐中的葡萄酒

sa·cred /ˈseɪkrɪd/ *adj.* **1** connected with God or a god; considered to be holy 上帝的；神的；神圣的：*a sacred image/shrine/temple* 圣像；圣地；圣殿 ◇ *sacred music* 圣乐 ◇ *Cows are sacred to Hindus.* 印度教徒认为牛是神圣的。 **2** very important and treated with great respect 受尊重的；受崇敬的 SYN **sacrosanct**：*Human life must always be sacred.* 人的生命在任何时候都必须得到尊重。◇ *For journalists* ***nothing is sacred*** (= they write about anything). 在记者眼里，没什么是不可诉诸笔端的。➲ MORE LIKE THIS 22, page R27 ▶ **sa·cred·ness** *noun* [U] ➲ SEE ALSO SANCTITY

ˌsacred ˈcow *noun* (*disapproving*) a custom, system, etc. that has existed for a long time and that many people think should not be questioned or criticized 不容置疑的习俗；批评不得的制度

sac·ri·fice /ˈsækrɪfaɪs/ *noun, verb*

■ ***noun* 1** [C, U] the fact of giving up sth important or valuable to you in order to get or do sth that seems more important; sth that you give up in this way 牺牲；舍弃：*The makers of the product assured us that there had been no sacrifice of quality.* 这一产品的制造商向我们保证说他们没有牺牲质量。◇ *Her parents* ***made sacrifices*** *so that she could have a good education.* 为了让她受良好的教育，她的父母作了很多牺牲。◇ *to make the* ***final/supreme sacrifice*** (= to die for your country, to save a friend, etc.) 牺牲生命 **2** [C, U] ~ (**to sb**) the act of offering sth to a god, especially an animal that has been killed in a special way; an animal, etc. that is offered in this way 祭献；祭祀；祭献的牲畜；祭品：*They offered sacrifices to the gods.* 他们向众神献上祭品。◇ *a human sacrifice* (= a person killed as a sacrifice) 用作祭品的人

■ ***verb* 1** [T] to give up sth that is important or valuable to you in order to get or do sth that seems more important for yourself or for another person 牺牲；献出：~ **sth for sb/sth** *She sacrificed everything for her children.* 她为子女牺牲了一切。◇ *The designers have sacrificed speed for fuel economy.* 设计者为节省燃料牺牲了速度。◇ ~ **sth** *Would you sacrifice a football game to go out with a girl?* 你愿意放弃一场足球赛，去跟一个女孩子约会吗？ **2** [T, I] ~ (**sb/sth**) to kill an animal or a person and offer it or them to a god, in order to please the god 以（人或动物）作祭献

sac·ri·fi·cial /ˌsækrɪˈfɪʃl/ *adj.* [usually before noun] offered as a sacrifice 用于祭献的：*a sacrificial lamb* 祭献的羔羊

sac·ri·lege /ˈsækrəlɪdʒ/ *noun* [U, sing.] an act of treating a holy thing or place without respect（对圣物或圣地的）亵渎；亵圣：(*figurative*) *It would be sacrilege to alter the composer's original markings.* 改动作曲家原有的符号是亵渎行为。➲ COLLOCATIONS AT RELIGION ▶ **sac·ri·le·gious** /ˌsækrəˈlɪdʒəs/ *adj.*

sac·ris·tan /ˈsækrɪstən/ *noun* a person whose job is to take care of the holy objects in a Christian church and to prepare the ALTAR for services（教堂的）圣器守司；管堂

sac·risty /ˈsækrɪsti/ *noun* (*pl.* **-ies**) a room in a church where a priest prepares for a service by putting on special clothes and where various objects used in worship are kept（教堂的）圣器室，祭衣间 SYN **vestry**

sacro·sanct /ˈsækrəʊsæŋkt; *NAmE* -kroʊ-/ *adj.* that is considered to be too important to change or question 神圣不容更改（或置疑）的 SYN **sacred**：*I'll work till late in the evening, but my weekends are sacrosanct.* 晚上加班我愿意，但周末休息没商量。

sac·rum /ˈseɪkrəm; ˈsæk-/ *noun* (*pl.* **sacra** /-krə/ *or* **sac·rums**) (*anatomy* 解) a bone in the lower back, between the two hip bones of the PELVIS 骶骨

SAD /sæd/ *abbr.* SEASONAL AFFECTIVE DISORDER 季节性情感障碍

sad /sæd/ *adj.* (**sad·der**, **sad·dest**)

• **UNHAPPY** 不快乐 **1** unhappy or showing unhappiness 悲哀的；难过的；显得悲哀的：~ (**to do sth**) *We are very sad to hear that you are leaving.* 听说你要走了，我们十分难过。◇ ~ (**that…**) *I was sad that she had to go.* 知道她得走了，我心里很难过。◇ ~ (**about sth**) *I felt terribly sad about it.* 我对此深感遗憾。◇ *She looked sad and tired.* 她看上去又伤心又疲惫。◇ *He gave a slight, sad smile.* 他露出一丝苦笑。◇ *The divorce left him* ***sadder and wiser*** (= having learned from the unpleasant experience). 离婚使他吃了苦头，但也学了乖。 **2** that makes you feel unhappy 令人悲哀的；让人难过的：*a sad story* 悲伤的故事 ◇ ~ (**to do sth**) ***It was sad to*** *see them go.* 看着他们离去，真让人难过。◇ ~ (**that…**) ***It is sad that*** *so many of his paintings have been lost.* 他的画作有很多已经失传了，真可惜。◇ *We had some sad news yesterday.* 昨天我们听到一些不幸的消息。◇ *He's a sad case—his wife died last year and he can't seem to manage without her.* 他是个不幸的人，去年死了老婆，而没她他好像就过不下去。◇ ***Sad to say*** (= unfortunately) *the house has now been demolished.* 可惜那座房子现在已经拆了。

• **UNACCEPTABLE** 让人无法接受 **3** unacceptable; deserving blame or criticism 让人无法接受的；该受责备（或批评）的 SYN **deplorable**：*a sad state of affairs* 糟糕的局面 ◇ ***It's a sad fact that*** *many of those killed were children.* 让人难以接受的是遇难者中很多是孩子。

• **BORING** 乏味 **4** (*informal*) boring or not fashionable 乏味的；过时的：*You sad old man.* 你这糟老头子。◇ *You'd have to be sad to wear a shirt like that.* 你穿着那样的衬衣会显得老气。

• **IN POOR CONDITION** 状况不佳 **5** in poor condition 状况不佳的：*The salad consisted of a few leaves of sad-looking lettuce.* 那道沙拉菜就是几片生菜的残叶。➲ SEE ALSO SADLY, SADNESS ➲ MORE LIKE THIS 35, page R29

S

sad·den /ˈsædn/ *verb* [often passive] (*formal*) to make sb sad 使悲伤；使伤心；使难过：**~ sb** *We were deeply saddened by the news of her death.* 听到她的死讯，我们深感悲伤。◇ **~ sb to do sth** *Fans were saddened to see the former champion play so badly.* 看到以前的冠军表现如此差劲，球迷感到难过。◇ **it saddens sb that…** *It saddened her that people could be so cruel.* 人竟能如此残忍，这让她痛心。

sad·dle /ˈsædl/ *noun, verb*
■ *noun* **1** a leather seat for a rider on a horse 马鞍：*She swung herself into the saddle.* 她飞身上马。 **2** a seat on a bicycle or motorcycle （自行车或摩托车的）车座 ➲ WORDFINDER NOTE AT CYCLING ➲ VISUAL VOCAB PAGE V55 **3** a piece of meat from the back of an animal （动物的）脊肉
IDM **in the ˈsaddle 1** in a position of authority and control 担任领导职务；掌权；在位 **2** riding a horse 骑马：*Three weeks after the accident he was back in the saddle.* 出事后三个星期，他就又骑上马了。
■ *verb* ~ sth to put a saddle on a horse 给（马）备鞍
PHR V **ˌsaddle ˈup | ˌsaddle sth↔ˈup** to put a saddle on a horse 给（马）备鞍 **ˈsaddle sb/yourself with sth** [often passive] to give sb/yourself an unpleasant responsibility, task, debt, etc. 使某人（或自己）肩负重担：*I've been saddled with organizing the conference.* 我被派担当组织会议的重任。◇ *The company was saddled with debts of £12 million.* 公司背着 1 200 万英镑的债务。

saddle·bag /ˈsædlbæg/ *noun* **1** one of a pair of bags put over the back of a horse 鞍囊；马褡裢 **2** a bag attached to the back of a bicycle or motorcycle saddle （挂在自行车或摩托车后座上的）挂包

ˈsaddle horse *noun* **1** a frame on which saddles are cleaned or stored 鞍具洗放架 **2** (*NAmE*) a horse which is used only for riding 骑用马

sad·dler /ˈsædlə(r)/ *noun* a person whose job is making, repairing and selling SADDLES and other leather goods 鞍匠；马具匠；马具商

sad·dlery /ˈsædləri/ *noun* [U] SADDLES and leather goods for horses; the art of making these 马具；马具制作工艺

ˈsaddle sore *adj.* feeling sore and stiff after riding a horse 鞍痛的（骑马后感觉胯疼腿僵）

ˈsaddle stitch *noun* a STITCH of thread or piece of wire put through the fold of a magazine, etc. to hold it together 骑马订（用于杂志等）

saddo /ˈsædəʊ; *NAmE* -doʊ/ *noun* (*pl.* **-os**) (*BrE, informal*) a person that you think is boring or not fashionable 乏味的人；老土：*a bunch of saddos who spend their lives playing computer games* 一群成天泡在电脑游戏里的无聊家伙

sadhu /ˈsɑːduː/ *noun* (*pl.* **-us**) a Hindu holy man, especially one who lives away from people and society 娑度（印度教圣人，尤指离群索居的隐士）

Sadie Haw·kins Day /ˌseɪdi ˈhɔːkɪnz deɪ/ *noun* (in the US) a day when there is a custom that women can invite men to a social event instead of waiting to be invited, especially to a **Sadie Hawkins Day** dance 萨迪·霍金斯节（美国节日，女士可主动邀请男士参加，尤指萨迪·霍金斯节舞会）

sad·ism /ˈseɪdɪzəm/ *noun* [U] **1** enjoyment from watching or making sb suffer 施虐癖，施虐狂；虐待狂：*There's a streak of sadism in his nature.* 他本性中有几分施虐倾向。 **2** a need to hurt sb in order to get sexual pleasure 性施虐狂 ➲ COMPARE MASOCHISM (1)

sad·ist /ˈseɪdɪst/ *noun* a person who gets pleasure, especially sexual pleasure, from hurting other people 施虐狂者；（尤指）性施虐狂者 ▸ **sad·is·tic** /səˈdɪstɪk/ *adj.*：*He took sadistic pleasure in taunting the boy.* 嘲讽这孩子让他感到施虐的快感。 **sad·is·tic·al·ly** /-kli/ *adv.*

sadly 🔑 /ˈsædli/ *adv.* **1** 🔑 unfortunately 令人遗憾；不幸地：*Sadly, after eight years of marriage they had grown apart.* 不幸的是，结婚八年后，他们的感情日渐淡薄了。 **2** 🔑 in a sad way 悲伤地；伤心地：*She shook her head sadly.* 她难过地摇摇头。 **3** 🔑 very much and in a way that makes you sad 极为；苦苦地：*She will be sadly missed.* 人们会很想她的。◇ *If you think I'm going to help you again, you're* **sadly** (= completely) **mistaken.** 你要是以为我还会再帮助你，那你就大错特错了。

sad·ness 🔑 /ˈsædnəs/ *noun* **1** 🔑 [U, sing.] the feeling of being sad 悲伤；悲痛；难过：*memories tinged with sadness* 略带悲伤的往事 ◇ *I felt a deep sadness.* 我感到深深的悲痛。 **2** [C, usually pl.] something which makes you sad 使人悲伤（或难过）的事：*our joys and sadnesses* 我们的欢乐和悲伤

sado·maso·chism /ˌseɪdəʊˈmæsəkɪzəm; *NAmE* -doʊ-/ *noun* [U] enjoyment from hurting sb and being hurt, especially during sexual activity 施虐受虐狂；（尤指）性施虐受虐狂 ▸ **sado·maso·chist** /ˌseɪdəʊˈmæsəkɪst; *NAmE* -doʊ-/ *noun* **sado·maso·chis·tic** /ˌseɪdəʊˌmæsəˈkɪstɪk; *NAmE* -doʊ-/ *adj.*

sae /ˌes eɪ ˈiː/ *noun* (*BrE*) the abbreviation for 'stamped addressed envelope' or 'self-addressed envelope' (an envelope on which you have written your name and address and usually put a stamp so that sb else can use it to send sth to you)（写上姓名地址且通常贴有邮票的）回邮信封（全写为 stamped addressed envelope 或 self-addressed envelope）：*Please enclose an sae for your test results.* 请附姓名地址邮资俱全的信封，以便邮递化验结果。 ➲ COMPARE SASE

sa·fari /səˈfɑːri/ *noun* [U, C] **1** a trip to see or hunt wild animals, especially in east or southern Africa （尤指在非洲东部或南部的）观赏（或捕猎）野兽的旅行；游猎：*to* ***be/go on safari*** 去游猎 ➲ WORDFINDER NOTE AT HUNT **2** (*EAfrE*) a journey; a period of time spent travelling or when you are not at home or work 长途旅行；旅游期间；外出期间：*I just got back from a month-long safari.* 我外出旅游了一个月刚刚回来。◇ *It arrived while I was on safari.* 这是在我外出期间送达的。 ➲ WORDFINDER NOTE AT JOURNEY

saˈfari park *noun* a park in which wild animals move around freely and are watched by visitors from their cars 野生动物园

saˈfari suit *noun* a light-coloured suit worn by men in hot weather, especially one with pockets on the front of the jacket 猎装（浅色男装，天热时穿，尤指前胸有衣袋的）

safe 🔑 /seɪf/ *adj., noun*
■ *adj.* (**safer, saf·est**)
• **PROTECTED** 受保护 **1** 🔑 [not before noun] protected from any danger or harm 处境（或情况）安全：*The children are quite safe here.* 孩子们在这里十分安全。◇ *She didn't* ***feel safe*** *on her own.* 她一个人待着，觉得不安全。◇ *Will the car be safe parked in the road?* 车停在马路上安全吗？◇ **~ (from sb/sth)** *They aimed to make the country safe from terrorist attacks.* 他们力图使国家免遭恐怖分子的袭击。◇ *Your secret is safe with me* (= I will not tell anyone else). 你的秘密不会从我这儿传出去。◇ *Here's your passport. Now* ***keep it safe.*** 这是你的护照。你可保管好了。 OPP unsafe
• **WITHOUT PHYSICAL DANGER** 对身体无害 **2** 🔑 not likely to lead to any physical harm or danger 不损害（或危害）健康的；安全的：**~ (for sb) (to do sth)** *Is the water here safe to drink?* 这儿的水能喝吗？◇ *The street is not safe for children to play in.* 孩子在大街上玩不安全。◇ *It is one of the safest cars in the world.* 这是世界上最安全的车型之一。◇ *We watched the explosion* ***from a safe distance.*** 我们在安全距离之外观看了爆破。◇ *Builders were called in* ***to make the building safe.*** 召来建筑工加固这栋大楼。 OPP unsafe
• **NOT HARMED/LOST** 没有受伤 / 丢失 **3** 🔑 not harmed, damaged, lost, etc. 未受伤害（或未遭损害、未丢失等）的：*We were glad she let us know she was safe.* 她告诉我们她平安无事，我们很高兴。◇ *The missing child was found* ***safe and well.*** 走失的孩子平平安安地找回来了。◇ *They turned up* ***safe and sound.*** 他们安然无恙地出现了。◇ *A reward was offered for the animal's* ***safe return.*** 悬赏要求将动物安全送还。

• PLACE 地方 **4** where sb/sth is not likely to be in danger or to be lost 无危险的；物品不会丢失的：*We all want to live in safer cities.* 我们都希望住在比较安全的城市里。◇ *Keep your passport in a safe place.* 把护照放到保险的地方。OPP **unsafe**

• WITHOUT RISK 无风险 **5** not involving much or any risk; not likely to be wrong or to upset sb 风险小的；无风险的；不大会错的；不致冒犯别人的：*a safe investment* 无风险的投资 ◇ *a safe subject for discussion* 没有忌讳的讨论题目 ◇ **~ (to do sth)** *It's safe to assume (that) there will always be a demand for new software.* 可以肯定地认为，人们对新的软件一直有需求。◇ *It would be safer to take more money with you in case of emergency.* 多带点钱保险些，以防急用。◇ (*disapproving*) *The show was well performed, but so safe and predictable.* 演出不错，只是太四平八稳，缺少新意。

• PERSON 人 **6** [usually before noun] doing an activity in a careful way 谨慎的；小心的 SYN **careful**: *a safe driver* 谨慎的司机

• LAW 法律 **7** based on good evidence 有确凿证据的：*a safe verdict* 确当的裁定 OPP **unsafe**

• APPROVING 赞同；满意 **8** (*BrE, informal*) used by young people to show that they approve of sb/sth (年轻人用语，表示赞同) 很好的，不错的，令人满意的：*I like him, he's safe.* 我喜欢他，他很不错。◇ *That kid's safe.* 那小家伙挺好的。 **9** (*BrE, informal*) used by young people as a way of accepting sth that is offered (年轻人用语，表示接受) 可以：*'You want some?' 'Yeah, safe.'* "你要一些吗？" "好的。" ⊃ SEE ALSO FAIL-SAFE

IDM **,better ,safe than 'sorry** (*saying*) used to say that it is wiser to be too careful than to act too quickly and do sth you may later wish you had not 宁可事先谨慎有余，不要事后追悔莫及 **in safe 'hands | in the safe hands of sb** being taken care of well by sb 在可靠的人手里；受到妥善照管：*I've left the kids in safe hands—with my parents.* 我把孩子托付给了靠得住的人，在我父母那儿。◇ *Their problem was in the safe hands of the experts.* 他们的问题交给行家处理了。 **on the 'safe side** being especially careful; taking no risks 谨慎为是；不冒险：*I took some extra cash just to be on the safe side.* 我多带了一些现金，以防万一。 **play (it) 'safe** to be careful; to avoid risks 谨慎行事；避免冒险 **(as) ,safe as 'houses** (*BrE*) very safe 非常安全 ⊃ MORE LIKE THIS 14, page R26 **safe in the knowledge that** confident because you know that sth is true or will happen 料定；确信：*She went out safe in the knowledge that she looked fabulous.* 她确信自己打扮得无可挑剔后才出门去。 **a safe pair of 'hands** (*especially BrE*) a person that you can trust to do a job well 靠得住的办事人 ⊃ MORE AT BET *n.*

■ ***noun*** a strong metal box or cupboard with a complicated lock, used for storing valuable things in, for example, money or jewellery 保险箱；保险柜

,safe 'conduct (*also* **,safe 'passage**) *noun* [U, C] official protection from being attacked, arrested, etc. when passing through an area; a document that promises this 安全通行权；安全通行证；通行许可证：*The guerrillas were promised safe conduct out of the country.* 游击队员得到承诺，可以安全离开这个国家。

'safe deposit box (*also* **'safety deposit box**) *noun* a metal box for storing valuable things, usually kept in a special room at a bank (银行的) 保管箱；保险箱

safe·guard /ˈseɪfɡɑːd; *NAmE* -ɡɑːrd/ *verb, noun*

■ ***verb*** [T, I] (*formal*) to protect sth/sb from loss, harm or damage; to keep sth/sb safe 保护；保障；捍卫：**~ sth** *to safeguard a person's interests* 维护某人的利益 ◇ *to safeguard jobs* 保住工作岗位 ◇ **~ sth/sb against/from sth** *The new card will safeguard the company against fraud.* 新卡将保护公司免遭诈骗。◇ **~ against sth** *The leaflet explains how to safeguard against dangers in the home.* 小册子告诉人们在家里如何防备各种危险。

■ ***noun*** **~ (against sth)** something that is designed to protect people from harm, risk or danger 安全设施；保护措施：*Stronger legal safeguards are needed to protect the consumer.* 需要有更有力的法律措施来保护消费者。

,safe 'haven *noun* a place where sb can go to be safe from danger or attack 安全的地方；避难所

'safe house *noun* a house used by people who are hiding, for example by criminals hiding from the police, or by people who are being protected by the police from other people who may wish to harm them (罪犯藏匿或警方保护人藏身等的) 藏身处，安全屋

,safe 'keeping *noun* [U] **1** the fact of sth being in a safe place where it will not be lost or damaged 妥善保管；存放在安全处：*She had put her watch in her pocket* ***for safe keeping.*** 为安全起见，她把手表放进了衣袋。 **2** the fact of sb/sth being taken care of by sb who can be trusted 安全照看；妥善照管：*The documents are* ***in the safe keeping*** *of our lawyers.* 那些文件由我们的律师妥善保管着。

safe·ly /ˈseɪfli/ *adv.* **1** without being harmed, damaged or lost 未受损伤（或损坏）；未丢失：*The plane landed safely.* 飞机安全降落。 **2** in a way that does not cause harm or that protects sb/sth from harm 安全地；无危害地：*The bomb has been safely disposed of.* 炸弹已安全处理。◇ *The money is safely locked in a drawer.* 钱锁在抽屉里，很稳当。 **3** without much possibility of being wrong 不大可能出错地；有把握地：*We can safely say that he will accept the job.* 我们可以有把握地说，他会接受这份工作。 **4** without any possibility of the situation changing 安稳地；安定地：*I thought the kids were safely tucked up in bed.* 我以为孩子们好好地在床上睡觉呢。 **5** without any problems being caused; with no risk 没问题地；毫无风险地：*These recommendations can safely be ignored.* 这些推荐信大可不必理会。

'safe mode *noun* [U] (*computing* 计) a way of starting a computer that makes it easier to find a problem without the risk of losing data (计算机启动的) 安全模式

,safe 'passage *noun* [U, C] = SAFE CONDUCT

the 'safe period *noun* [sing.] the time just before and during a woman's PERIOD when she is unlikely to become pregnant (女性经期前或来月经时不易怀孕的) 安全期

'safe room *noun* = PANIC ROOM

,safe 'seat *noun* (*BrE*) a CONSTITUENCY where a particular political party has a lot of support and is unlikely to be defeated in an election (在选举中) 稳操胜券的选区

,safe 'sex *noun* [U] sexual activity in which people try to protect themselves from AIDS and other sexual diseases, for example by using a CONDOM 安全性交（采取针对艾滋病和其他性病的预防措施）

safety /ˈseɪfti/ *noun* (*pl.* **-ies**) **1** [U] the state of being safe and protected from danger or harm 安全；平安：*a place where children can play* ***in safety*** 可以让儿童安全玩耍的地方 ◇ *The police are concerned for the safety of the 12-year-old boy who has been missing for three days.* 那个 12 岁的男孩失踪三天了，警方对他的安全感到担忧。◇ *He was kept in custody* ***for his own safety.*** 拘押他是为了他本人的安全。 **2** [U] the state of not being dangerous 安全性；无危险：*I'm worried about the safety of the treatment.* 我担心这种疗法是否安全。◇ *safety standards* 安全标准 ◇ *a local campaign to improve* ***road safety*** 当地改善道路安全状况的运动 ◇ *The airline has an excellent* ***safety record.*** 这家航空公司有极佳的安全记录。 **3** [U] a place where you are safe 安全处所：*I managed to swim* ***to safety.*** 我设法游到安全处。◇ *We watched the lions* ***from the safety of*** *the car.* 我们从车里看狮子，很安全。◇ *They reached safety seconds before the building was engulfed in flames.* 他们到达安全地几秒钟之后，那房子就成了一片火海。 **4** [C] (*NAmE*) = SAFETY CATCH **5** [C] (*NAmE*) (in AMERICAN FOOTBALL) a defending player who plays in a position far away from the other team (美式足球) 安全卫，中卫

IDM **,safety 'first** (*saying*) safety is the most important thing 安全第一 **there's ,safety in 'numbers** (*saying*) being in a group makes you safer and makes you feel more confident 人多保险

'safety belt *noun* = SEAT BELT

ˈsafety catch (*especially BrE*) (*NAmE usually* **safety**) *noun* a device that stops a gun from being fired or a machine from working by accident （枪、炮等的）保险机，保险栓；（机器设备的）安全掣子

ˈsafety curtain *noun* a curtain which can come down across the stage in a theatre, intended to stop a fire from spreading （剧场舞台的）防火帘，隔火帐，防火幕

ˈsafety deposit box *noun* = SAFE DEPOSIT BOX

ˈsafety glass *noun* [U] strong glass that does not break into sharp pieces 安全玻璃（碎片无尖锐棱角的高强度玻璃）

ˈsafety island *noun* (*US*) = TRAFFIC ISLAND

ˈsafety lamp *noun* a special lamp used by MINERS with a flame that does not cause underground gases to explode （矿工用的）安全灯；矿灯

ˈsafety match *noun* a type of match that will light only if it is rubbed against a specially prepared rough surface, often on the side of its box 安全火柴

ˈsafety measure *noun* something that you do in order to prevent sth bad or dangerous from happening 安全措施；预防措施

ˈsafety net *noun* **1** an arrangement that helps to prevent disaster if sth goes wrong （防备不测的）安全网；保障措施： *a financial safety net* 金融"安全网"◇ *people who have fallen through the safety net and ended up homeless on the streets* 未能享受保障措施终致流落街头的人 **2** a net placed underneath ACROBATS, etc. to catch them if they fall （保护杂技演员等的）安全网

ˈsafety pin *noun* a pin with a point bent back towards the head, that is covered when closed so that it cannot hurt you 安全别针 ➲ VISUAL VOCAB PAGE V68

ˈsafety razor *noun* a RAZOR with a cover over the blade to stop it from cutting the skin 安全剃刀；保险刀 ➲ COMPARE CUT-THROAT RAZOR

ˈsafety valve *noun* **1** a device that lets out steam or pressure in a machine when it becomes too great 安全阀 **2** a harmless way of letting out feelings of anger, excitement, etc. 疏导（情绪）的方法： *Exercise is a good safety valve for the tension that builds up at work.* 锻炼身体是排解工作压力的好办法。

saf·flower /ˈsæflaʊə(r)/ *noun* [C, U] a plant with orange flowers, whose seeds produce an oil which is used in cooking 红花（籽油可用于烹饪）

saf·fron /ˈsæfrən/ *noun* [U] **1** a bright yellow powder made from CROCUS flowers, used in cooking as a spice and to give colour to food 番红花粉（用作调味香料或食用色素）；藏红花；西红花 ➲ VISUAL VOCAB PAGE V35 **2** a bright orange-yellow colour 橘黄色 ▶ **saf·fron** *adj.*： *Buddhist monks in saffron robes* 身穿黄袍的和尚

sag[1] /sæg/ *verb* (**-gg-**) **1** [I] to hang or bend down in the middle, especially because of weight or pressure （尤指由于承重或受压）中间下垂，下凹： *a sagging roof* 凹陷的房顶 ◇ *The tent began to sag under the weight of the rain.* 雨水使得帐篷中间开始下坠。 ◇ *Your skin starts to sag as you get older.* 人老了，皮肤就会慢慢松弛。 **2** [I] to become weaker or fewer 减弱；减少： *Their share of the vote sagged badly at the last election.* 在上次选举中他们的得票数大幅下跌。 ▶ **sag** *noun* [U, C, usually sing.]： *Weight has caused the sag.* 承重导致下垂。 IDM SEE JAW *n.*

PHR V **ˌsag ˈoff | sag off sth** (*BrE, informal*) to stay away from school or work when you should be there, or leave before you should 逃学；旷课；旷工；早退： *We sagged off school and wrote the song.* 我们逃学写了那首歌。

sag[2] /sɑːg/ *noun* = SAAG

saga /ˈsɑːgə/ *noun* **1** a long traditional story about adventures and brave acts, especially one from Norway or Iceland 萨迦（尤指古代挪威或冰岛讲述冒险经历和英雄事迹的长篇故事） **2** a long story about events over a period of many years （讲述许多年间发生的事情的）长篇故事，长篇小说： *a family saga* 家世小说 **3** a long series of events or adventures and/or a report about them 一连串的事件（或经历）；一连串经历的讲述（或记述）： *The front page is devoted to the continuing saga of the hijack.* 头版是对劫持事件的连续报道。 ◇ (*humorous*) *the saga of how I missed the plane* 有关我如何误了飞机的一连串倒霉事儿

sa·ga·cious /səˈgeɪʃəs/ *adj.* (*formal*) showing good judgement and understanding 精明练达的；洞察事理的 SYN wise ▶ **sa·ga·city** /səˈgæsəti/ *noun* [U]

SAG-AFTRA /ˌsæg ˈæftrə/ *abbr.* (in the US) an organization that protects the interests of actors in films and television, formed from the Screen Actors Guild and the American Federation of Television and Radio Artists 美国演员工会和广播电视艺人联合会（由 the Screen Actors Guild and the American Federation of Television and Radio Artists 的首字母组合而成）

sage /seɪdʒ/ *noun, adj.*

■ ***noun*** **1** [U] a plant with flat, light green leaves that have a strong smell and are used in cooking as a HERB 鼠尾草（可用作调料） ➲ VISUAL VOCAB PAGE V35 **2** [C] (*formal*) a very wise person 哲人；智者；圣人

■ ***adj.*** (*literary*) wise, especially because you have a lot of experience 睿智的，贤明的（尤指因经验丰富） ▶ **sage·ly** *adv.*： *She nodded sagely.* 她点点头，一副洞悉一切的样子。

sage·brush /ˈseɪdʒbrʌʃ/ *noun* [U] a plant with leaves that smell sweet that grows in dry regions in the western US; an area of ground covered with sagebrush 灌木蒿；灌木蒿丛

saggy /ˈsægi/ *adj.* (**sag·gier, sag·gi·est**) (*informal*) no longer firm; hanging or sinking down in a way that is not attractive 松垂的；松弛耷拉的；下陷的

Sa·git·tar·ius /ˌsædʒɪˈteəriəs; *NAmE* -ˈter-/ *noun* **1** [U] the 9th sign of the ZODIAC, the ARCHER 黄道第九宫；人马宫；人马（星）座 **2** [sing.] a person born when the sun is in this sign, that is between 22 November and 20 December, approximately 属人马座的人（约出生于 11 月 22 日至 12 月 20 日） ▶ **Sa·git·tar·ian** *noun, adj.*

sago /ˈseɪgəʊ; *NAmE* -goʊ/ *noun* [U] hard white grains made from the soft inside of a type of PALM tree, often cooked with milk to make a DESSERT 西谷米，西米（由一种棕榈茎髓制成的白色硬粒状食物，常加牛奶制成甜点）： *sago pudding* 西米布丁

sa·guaro /səˈgwɑːrəʊ; *NAmE* -roʊ/ *noun* (*pl.* **-os**) a very large CACTUS that grows in the southern US and Mexico 萨瓜罗掌，巨山影掌（生长于美国南部和墨西哥的仙人掌）

sahib /sɑːb; ˈsɑːɪb/ *noun* used in India, especially in the past, to address a European man, especially one with some social or official status （印度旧时对欧洲男子的尊称）先生，老爷

said /sed/ **1** PAST TENSE, PAST PART. OF SAY **2** *adj.* [only before noun] (*formal* or *law* 律) = AFOREMENTIONED： *the said company* 上述公司

sail 🔑 /seɪl/ *verb, noun*

■ ***verb*** **1** 🔑 [I, T] (of a boat or ship or the people on it 船或船上的人) to travel on water using sails or an engine （船）航行；（人）乘船航行： (**+ adv./prep.**) *to sail into harbour* 驶入海港 ◇ *The dinghy sailed smoothly across the lake.* 小艇平稳地驶过湖面。 ◇ *The ferry sails from Newhaven to Dieppe.* 渡船行驶于纽黑文和迪耶普之间。 ◇ *one of the first people to sail around the world* 最早进行环球航行的人之一 ◇ **~ sth** *to sail the Atlantic* 在大西洋上航行 **2** 🔑 (*also* **go sailing**) [I, T] to control or travel on a boat with a sail, especially as a sport 驾驶（或乘坐）帆船航行（尤指作为体育运动）： *We spent the weekend sailing off the south coast.* 我们在南部海岸一带驾帆船度过了周末。 ◇ *Do you* **go sailing** *often?* 你常去驾帆船玩吗？ ◇ **~ sth** *She sails her own yacht.* 她驾驶自己的游艇。 **3** [I] (of a boat or ship or the people in it 船只或船上的人) to begin a journey on water 起航： *We sail at 2 p.m. tomorrow.* 我们明天下午两点起航。 ◇ **~ for sth** *He sailed for the West*

Indies from Portsmouth. 他从朴次茅斯起航，向西印度群岛进发。 **4** [I] **+ adv./prep.** to move quickly and smoothly in a particular direction; (of people) to move in a confident manner 掠；飘；浮游；（人）昂首而行，气宇轩昂地走：*clouds sailing across the sky* 飘过天空的云彩 ◇ *The ball sailed over the goalie's head.* 球从守门员头顶飞过。◇ *She sailed past, ignoring me completely.* 她翩然而过，看都不看我一眼。

IDM **sail close to the 'wind** to take a risk by doing sth that is dangerous or that may be illegal 冒风险（干危险或可能违法的事）

PHR V **,sail 'through (sth)** to pass an exam, a test, etc. without any difficulty 顺利通过（考试等）

■ ***noun*** **1** [C, U] a sheet of strong cloth which the wind blows against to make a boat or ship travel through the water 帆：*As the boat moved down the river the wind began to fill the sails.* 船顺河而下，风逐渐胀满了帆。◇ *a ship* ***under sail*** (= using sails) 张帆行驶的船 ◇ *in the days of sail* (= when ships all used sails) 在帆船时代 ◇ *She moved away like a ship* ***in full sail*** (= with all its sails spread out). 她一阵风似的走了。 **2** [sing.] a trip in a boat or ship 乘船航行：*We went for a sail.* 我们乘船兜了一趟风。◇ *a two-hour sail across the bay* 横渡海湾的两小时航程 **3** [C] a set of boards attached to the arm of a WINDMILL（风车的）翼板

IDM **set 'sail (from/for...)** (*formal*) to begin a trip by sea 起航；开航：*a liner setting sail from New York* 自纽约起航的邮轮 ◇ *We set sail (for France) at high tide.* 我们在涨潮时起航（前往法国）。➲ MORE AT TRIM *v.*, WIND[1] *n.*

sail·board /ˈseɪlbɔːd; *NAmE* -bɔːrd/ (*also* **board**) *noun* = WINDSURFER (1) ▶ **sail·board·er** *noun* **sail·board·ing** *noun* [U]

sail·boat /ˈseɪlbəʊt; *NAmE* -boʊt/ (*NAmE*) (*BrE* **sailing boat**) *noun* a boat with sails 帆船 ➲ VISUAL VOCAB PAGE V59

sail·cloth /ˈseɪlklɒθ; *NAmE* -klɔːθ; -klɑːθ/ *noun* [U] a type of strong cloth used for making sails 厚篷帆布

sail·ing /ˈseɪlɪŋ/ *noun* **1** [U] the sport or activity of travelling in a boat with sails 帆船运动；（乘帆船的）航行：*to go sailing* 去进行帆船运动 ◇ *a sailing club* 帆船俱乐部 **2** [C] one of the regular times that a ship leaves a port（从某港口开出的）航班：*There are six sailings a day.* 每天有六班船。 IDM SEE CLEAR *adj.*, PLAIN *adj.*

'sailing boat (*BrE*) (*NAmE* **sail·boat**) *noun* a boat with sails 帆船 ➲ VISUAL VOCAB PAGE V59

'sailing ship *noun* a ship with sails（大型）帆船

sail·maker /ˈseɪlmeɪkə(r)/ *noun* a person whose job is to make or repair sails 制帆工；修帆工 ▶ **sail·mak·ing** *noun* [U]

sail·or /ˈseɪlə(r)/ *noun* **1** a person who works on a ship as a member of the CREW 水手；海员 **2** a person who sails a boat 驾船人

IDM **a good/bad 'sailor** a person who rarely/often becomes sick at sea 很少 / 经常晕船的人

'sailor suit *noun* a suit for a child made in the style of an old-fashioned sailor's uniform（儿童的）水手装

saint /seɪnt; snt/ *noun* **1** (*abbr.* **S**, **St**) a person that the Christian Church recognizes as being very holy, because of the way they have lived or died（因其言行而被基督教会追封的）圣人，圣徒：*St John* 圣约翰 ◇ *St Valentine's Day* 圣瓦伦廷节（情人节）◇ *The children were all named after saints.* 这些孩子都取了圣徒的名字。 ➲ SEE ALSO PATRON SAINT, ST BERNARD **2** a very good, kind or patient person 圣人般的人（指特别善良、仁爱或有耐性的人）：*She's a saint to go on living with that man.* 能继续和那个男人一起生活，她简直是圣人。◇ *His behaviour would try* ***the patience of a saint.*** 他的行为就是再有修养的人也难以忍受。 ▶ **saint·hood** *noun* [U]

saint·ed /ˈseɪntɪd/ *adj.* [usually before noun] (*old-fashioned* or *humorous*) considered or officially stated to be a saint 被视为圣人的；被正式封为圣徒的：*And how is my sainted sister?* 我那大好人姐姐怎么样？

saint·ly /ˈseɪntli/ *adj.* like a SAINT; very holy and good 像圣人的；非常圣洁善良的：*to lead a saintly life* 过着圣洁的生活 ▶ **saint·li·ness** *noun* [U]

'saint's day *noun* (in the Christian Church) a day of the year when a particular SAINT is remembered and on which, in some countries, people who are named after that SAINT have celebrations（基督教）圣人庆节

saith /seθ/ (*old use*) = SAYS

sake[1] /seɪk/ *noun* ➲ SEE ALSO SAKE[2]

IDM **for Christ's, God's, goodness', heaven's, pity's, etc. 'sake** used to emphasize that it is important to do sth or when you are annoyed about sth（强调重要或表示恼火）看在上帝分上，天哪，行行好吧，千万：*Do be careful, for goodness' sake.* 千万要小心。◇ *Oh, for heaven's sake!* 哎哟，天哪！◇ *For pity's sake, help me!* 行行好，帮帮我吧！ HELP Some people find the use of **Christ**, **God** or **heaven** here offensive. 有人认为此处用 Christ、God 或 heaven 含冒犯意。 **for sth's sake** because of the interest or value sth has, not because of the advantages it may bring 为某事本身的缘故；鉴于事本身的价值：*I believe in education for its own sake.* 我相信教育本身就是有价值的。◇ *art for art's sake* 为艺术而艺术 **for the sake of sb/sth | for sb's/sth's sake** in order to help sb/sth or because you like sb/sth 为了某人（或某事）起见；因某人（或某事）的缘故：*They stayed together for the sake of the children.* 为了孩子，他们还待在一起。◇ *You can do it. Please, for my sake.* 这个你是能做的。求你了，就算为了我。◇ *I hope you're right, for all our sakes* (= because this is important for all of us). 我希望你没事，这对我们大家都好。 **for the sake of sth/of doing sth** in order to get or keep sth 为获得（或保持）某物：*The translation sacrifices naturalness for the sake of accuracy.* 这篇译文为求准确而牺牲了自然流畅。◇ *She gave up smoking for the sake of her health.* 为保持身体健康，她戒了烟。◇ *Don't get married* ***just for the sake of it.*** 不要为结婚而结婚。◇ *Let's suppose,* ***for the sake of argument*** (= in order to have a discussion), *that interest rates went up by 2%.* 为了便于讨论，假设利率提高了 2%。 ➲ MORE AT OLD

sake[2] (*also* **saki**) /ˈsɑːki/ *noun* [U, C] a Japanese alcoholic drink made from rice 日本清酒 ➲ SEE ALSO SAKE[1]

sa·laam /səˈlɑːm/ *verb* [I, T] ~ (**sb**) (in some Eastern countries) to say hello to sb in a formal way by bending forward from the waist and putting your right hand on your FOREHEAD 行额手礼（一些东方国家正式问候的方式，右手置额前鞠躬） ▶ **sa·laam** *noun*

sal·acious /səˈleɪʃəs/ *adj.* (*formal*) (of stories, pictures, etc. 故事、图画等) encouraging sexual desire or containing too much sexual detail 淫秽的；色情的 ▶ **sal·acious·ness** *noun* [U]

salad /ˈsæləd/ *noun* **1** [U, C] a mixture of raw vegetables such as LETTUCE, tomato and CUCUMBER, usually served with other food as part of a meal（生吃的）蔬菜色拉，蔬菜沙拉：*All main courses come with salad or vegetables.* 所有主菜都配有色拉或蔬菜。◇ *Is cold meat and salad OK for lunch?* 午饭吃冷肉和色拉行吗？◇ *a* ***side salad*** (= a small bowl of salad served with the main course of a meal) 配菜色拉（作为一道副菜）◇ *a* ***salad bowl*** (= a large bowl for serving salad in) 色拉碗 ➲ COLLOCATIONS AT COOKING ➲ SEE ALSO CAESAR SALAD, GREEN SALAD **2** [C, U] (in compounds 构成复合词) meat, fish, cheese, etc. served with salad（拌有肉、鱼、奶酪等的）混合色拉，混合沙拉：*a chicken salad* 鸡肉色拉 **3** [U, C] (in compounds 构成复合词) raw or cooked vegetables, etc. that are cut into small pieces, often mixed with MAYONNAISE and served cold with other food（或生或熟，多拌有蛋黄酱，与面食、豆类等一起食用的）蔬菜色拉，蔬菜沙拉：*potato salad* 土豆色拉 ◇ *a pasta salad* 意大利面食色拉 ➲ SEE ALSO FRUIT SALAD **4** [U] any green vegetable, especially LETTUCE, that is eaten raw in a salad 拌色拉的青菜（尤指生菜）：*salad plants* 色拉蔬菜

S

IDM **your ˈsalad days** (*old-fashioned*) the time when you are young and do not have much experience of life 年少不谙世事的岁月；涉世未深的青少年时代

ˈsalad cream *noun* [U] (*BrE*) a pale yellow sauce, similar to MAYONNAISE, sold in bottles and eaten on salads, in SANDWICHES, etc. 色拉酱；沙拉酱

ˈsalad dressing *noun* [U, C] = DRESSING (1)

sala·man·der /ˈsæləmændə(r)/ *noun* an animal like a LIZARD, with short legs and a long tail, that lives both on land and in water (= is an AMPHIBIAN) 蝾螈（两栖动物，形似蜥蜴） ➲ VISUAL VOCAB PAGE V13

sa·lami /səˈlɑːmi/ *noun* [U, C] (*pl.* **sa·lamis**) a type of large spicy SAUSAGE served cold in thin slices 萨拉米香肠（味浓，多切片冷食）

saˈlami slicing *noun* [U] (*informal*) the act of removing sth gradually by small amounts at a time 逐渐的除去

sal·ar·ied /ˈsælərid/ *adj.* **1** (of a person 人) receiving a salary 领薪水的：*a salaried employee* 领薪水的雇员 **2** (of a job 工作) for which a salary is paid 付给薪水的：*a salaried position* 付给薪水的职位

sal·ary /ˈsæləri/ *noun* (*pl.* **-ies**) money that employees receive for doing their job, especially professional employees or people working in an office, usually paid every month 薪金，薪水（尤指按月发放的）：*an annual salary of $40 000* * 4 万美元的年薪 ◇ *a 9% salary increase* 加薪 9% ◇ *She's* ***on a salary of*** *£24 000.* 她的薪金是 24 000 英镑。◇ (*BrE*) *He gets a* ***basic salary*** *plus commission.* 他领取基本薪金，外加佣金。◇ (*NAmE*) ***base salary*** 底薪 ➲ COMPARE WAGE *n.* ➲ SYNONYMS AT INCOME ➲ WORDFINDER NOTE AT PAY

sal·ary·man /ˈsælərimæn/ *noun* (*pl.* **-men** /-men/) (especially in Japan) a WHITE-COLLAR worker (= one who works in an office) （尤指日本的）白领阶层人员，白领

sal·but·am·ol /sælˈbjuːtəmɒl; *NAmE* -mɔːl; -mɑːl/ *noun* [U] a drug that is used in the treatment of medical conditions such as ASTHMA 沙丁胺醇，硫酸舒喘宁（哮喘等用）

sale /seɪl/ *noun* **1** [U, C] an act or the process of selling sth 出售；销售：*regulations governing the sale of alcoholic beverages* 含酒精饮料的销售管理条例 ◇ *I haven't* ***made a sale*** *all week.* 整整一个星期我什么也没卖出去。◇ *She gets 10% commission on each sale.* 每笔生意她得 10% 的佣金。**2** **sales** [pl.] the number of items sold 销售量：*Retail sales fell in November by 10%.* 十一月份零售量下降 10%。◇ *Export sales were up by 32% last year.* 去年出口销售量增长了 32%。◇ *the* ***sales figures*** *for May* 五月份的销售数字 ◇ *a* ***sales drive/campaign*** (= a special effort to sell more) 促销活动 ➲ COLLOCATIONS AT BUSINESS **3** **sales** [U] (*also* **ˈsales department** [C]) the part of a company that deals with selling its products 销售部：*a sales and marketing director* 市场销售部经理 ◇ *She works in sales/in the sales department.* 她在销售部工作。◇ *The Weldon Group has a 6 000 strong* ***sales force.*** 威尔登集团有 6 000 人的强大销售队伍。**4** [C] an occasion when a shop/store sells its goods at a lower price than usual 特价销售；廉价出售；大减价：*The sale starts next week.* 特价促销从下星期开始。◇ *the January sales* 元月大减价 ◇ *I bought a coat* ***in the sales.*** 我在大减价时买了一件外套。◇ *sale prices* 特价 **5** [C] an occasion when goods are sold, especially an AUCTION 销售活动；（尤指）拍卖：*a contemporary art sale* 当代艺术品拍卖会 ➲ SEE ALSO CAR BOOT SALE, GARAGE SALE, JUMBLE SALE ➲ WORDFINDER NOTE AT SHOP

IDM **for ˈsale** available to be bought, especially from the owner 待售；供出售（尤指从物主手里）：*I'm sorry, it's not for sale.* 抱歉，这个不卖。◇ *They've* ***put their house up for sale.*** 他们的房子现在出售。◇ *an increase in the number of stolen vehicles being* ***offered for sale*** 用于售卖的被盗车辆在数量上的增加 ◇ *a 'for sale' sign* "待售"标志 **on ˈsale** **1** available to be bought, especially in a shop/store （尤指在商店）出售，上市：*Tickets are on sale from the booking office.* 售票处正在售票。◇ *The new model* ***goes on sale*** *next month.* 新款下月上市。**2** (*especially NAmE, SAfrE*) being offered at a reduced price 折价销售；减价出售：*All video equipment is on sale today and tomorrow.* 所有录像设备今明两天降价出售。**(on) ˌsale or reˈturn** (*BrE*) (of goods 商品) supplied with the agreement that any item that is not sold can be sent back without having to be paid for 剩货包退（任何未售出的商品均可退给供货商）

sale·able /ˈseɪləbl/ *adj.* good enough to be sold; that sb will want to buy 适销的；有销路的：*a saleable product* 适销产品 ◇ *not in saleable condition* 不适合销售 **OPP** **unsaleable**

ˌsale of ˈwork *noun* (*pl.* **sales of work**) (*BrE*) a sale of things made by members of an organization, such as a church, often to make money for charity 自制物品义卖

sale·room /ˈseɪlruːm; -rʊm/ (*BrE*) (*NAmE* **sales·room**) *noun* a room where goods are sold at an AUCTION 拍卖场

ˈsales clerk (*also* **clerk**) (*both NAmE*) (*BrE* **ˈshop assistant, as·sist·ant**) *noun* a person whose job is to serve customers in a shop/store 店员；售货员

sales·girl /ˈseɪlzɡɜːl; *NAmE* -ɡɜːrl/ *noun* a girl or woman who works in a shop/store 女店员；女售货员

sales·man /ˈseɪlzmən/, **sales·woman** /ˈseɪlzwʊmən/ *noun* (*pl.* **-men** /-mən/, **-women** /-wɪmɪn/) a man or woman whose job is to sell goods, for example, in a shop/store 售货员；推销员：*a car salesman* 汽车推销员 ➲ NOTE AT GENDER ➲ MORE LIKE THIS 25, page R28

sales·man·ship /ˈseɪlzmənʃɪp/ *noun* [U] skill in persuading people to buy things 推销术；销售技巧

sales·per·son /ˈseɪlzpɜːsn; *NAmE* -pɜːrsn/ *noun* (*pl.* **-people**) a person whose job is to sell goods, for example, in a shop/store 售货员 ➲ MORE LIKE THIS 25, page R28

ˈsales representative (*also informal* **ˈsales rep, rep**) *noun* an employee of a company who travels around a particular area selling the company's goods to shops/stores, etc. 销售代表

sales·room /ˈseɪlzruːm; -rʊm/ (*NAmE*) (*BrE* **sale·room**) *noun* a room where goods are sold at an AUCTION 拍卖场

ˈsales slip *noun* (*NAmE*) = RECEIPT (1)

ˈsales talk *noun* [U] talk that tries to persuade sb to buy sth 推销商品的说辞

ˈsales tax *noun* [U, C] (in some countries) the part of the price you pay when you buy sth that goes to the government as tax 销售税（某些国家的税种，由消费者负担）

sales·woman *noun* ➲ SALESMAN

sali·cyl·ic acid /ˌsælɪˌsɪlɪk ˈæsɪd/ *noun* [U] a bitter chemical found in some plants, used in ASPIRIN (= a drug used for reducing pain and making your blood thinner) 水杨酸；邻羟基苯甲酸

sa·li·ent /ˈseɪliənt/ *adj.* [only before noun] most important or noticeable 最重要的；显著的；突出的：*She pointed out the* ***salient features*** *of the new design.* 她指出新设计的几个显著特征。◇ *He summarized the* ***salient points.*** 他对要点作了归纳。

sa·line /ˈseɪlaɪn; *NAmE* -liːn/ *adj., noun*

■ ***adj.*** [usually before noun] (*specialist*) containing salt 盐的；含盐的；咸的：*Wash the lenses in saline solution.* 用盐溶液清洗镜片。▸ **sal·in·ity** /səˈlɪnəti/ *noun* [U]：*to measure the salinity of the water* 测量水的盐度

■ ***noun*** [U] (*specialist*) a mixture of salt in water 盐水

Salis·bury steak /ˌsɔːlzbri ˈsteɪk/ *noun* (*NAmE*) finely chopped beef mixed with egg and onions made into a flat, round shape and cooked under or over a strong heat 索尔兹伯里牛肉饼（用碎牛肉和蛋、洋葱调制，大火煎烤而成）

sal·iva /səˈlaɪvə/ *noun* [U] the liquid that is produced in your mouth that helps you to swallow food 唾液

sal·iv·ary /sə'laɪvəri; 'sælɪvəri; *NAmE* 'sæləveri/ *adj.* (*specialist*) of or producing saliva 唾液的；产生唾液的

sali·vate /'sælɪveɪt/ *verb* [I] (*formal*) to produce more SALIVA in your mouth than usual, especially when you see or smell food （尤指看到或嗅到食物时）垂涎，流口水：(*figurative*) *He was salivating over the thought of the million dollars.* 想到那一百万美元，他垂涎欲滴。
▸ **sali·va·tion** /ˌsælɪ'veɪʃn/ *noun* [U]

sal·low /'sæləʊ; *NAmE* -loʊ/ *adj., noun*
▪ ***adj.*** (of a person's skin or face 人的皮肤或面色) having a slightly yellow colour that does not look healthy 灰黄的；蜡黄的 **SYN** **pasty**[2]
▪ ***noun*** a type of WILLOW tree that does not grow very tall 黄华柳

sally /'sæli/ *noun, verb*
▪ ***noun*** (*pl.* **sal·lies**) **1** a remark that is intended to entertain or amuse sb 俏皮话 **SYN** **witticism** **2** a sudden attack by an enemy 出击；突袭
▪ ***verb*** (**sal·lies**, **sally·ing**, **sal·lied**, **sal·lied**)
PHR V **ˌsally 'forth/'out** (*old-fashioned* or *literary*) to leave a place in a determined or enthusiastic way 毅然出发；兴冲冲地离开

sal·mon /'sæmən/ *noun* [C, U] (*pl.* **sal·mon**) a large fish with silver skin and pink flesh that is used for food. Salmon live in the sea but swim up rivers to lay their eggs. 鲑；大麻哈鱼：*a whole salmon* 一整条鲑鱼 ◇ *smoked salmon* 熏鲑鱼 ◇ *wild and farmed salmon* 野生和人工养殖的鲑鱼

sal·mon·ella /ˌsælmə'nelə/ *noun* [U] a type of bacteria that makes people sick if they eat infected food; an illness caused by this bacteria 沙门菌：*cases of salmonella poisoning* 沙门菌中毒病例 ◇ *an outbreak of salmonella* 沙门菌的爆发

ˌsalmon 'pink *adj.* orange-pink in colour, like the flesh of a salmon 鲑肉色的；橙红色的 ▸ **ˌsalmon 'pink** *noun* [U] ➲ MORE LIKE THIS 15, page R26

salon /'sælɒn; *NAmE* sə'lɑːn; sə'lɔːn/ *noun* **1** a shop/store that gives customers hair or beauty treatment or that sells expensive clothes 美发厅；美容院；高级服装店：*a beauty salon* 美容院 ◇ *a hairdressing salon* 美发厅 **2** (*old-fashioned*) a room in a large house used for entertaining guests （大宅中的）客厅，会客室 **3** (in the past) a regular meeting of writers, artists and other guests at the house of a famous or important person 沙龙（旧时作家、艺术家等在名流家中定期举行的聚会）：*a literary salon* 文艺沙龙

sal·oon /sə'luːn/ *noun* **1** (*also* **sa'loon car**) (*both BrE*) (*NAmE* **sedan**) a car with four doors and a BOOT/TRUNK (= space at the back for carrying things) which is separated from the part where the driver and passengers sit 小轿车；（三厢）四门轿车：*a five-seater family saloon* 五座家庭式轿车 ➲ VISUAL VOCAB PAGE V56 **2** (*also* **sa'loon bar**) (*both BrE*) = LOUNGE BAR **3** a bar where alcoholic drinks were sold in the western US and Canada in the past （旧时美国西部和加拿大的）酒吧，酒馆 **4** a large comfortable room on a ship, used by the passengers to sit and relax in （客轮上的）交谊厅

sal·op·ettes /ˌsælə'pets/ *noun* [pl.] a piece of clothing worn for SKIING or sailing, consisting of trousers/pants with a part that comes up over your shoulders （滑雪或帆船运动穿的）背带裤，工装裤

salsa /'sælsə; *NAmE* 'sɑːlsə/ *noun* **1** [U] a type of Latin American dance music 萨尔萨舞曲（一种拉丁美洲舞曲） **2** [C, U] a dance performed to this music 萨尔萨舞 **3** [U] a sauce eaten with Mexican food 辣番茄酱（常用于墨西哥食物）

sal·sify /'sælsəfi/ *noun* [U] (*BrE*) a plant with a long root that is cooked and eaten as a vegetable 蒜叶婆罗门参（可作蔬菜食用）

salt 🔑 /sɔːlt; *BrE also* sɒlt/ *noun, verb, adj.*
▪ ***noun*** **1** 🔑 [U] a white substance that is added to food to give it a better flavour or to preserve it. Salt is obtained from mines and is also found in sea water. It is sometimes called **common salt** to distinguish it from other chemical salts. 盐；食盐 **SYN** **sodium chloride**: *Pass the salt, please.* 请把盐递过来。◇ *a pinch of salt* (= a small amount of it) 一撮盐 ◇ *Season with salt and pepper.* 放盐和胡椒粉调味。◇ *sea salt* 海盐 ➲ SEE ALSO ROCK SALT **2** [C] (*chemistry* 化) a chemical formed from a metal and an acid 盐（金属和酸组成的化学物质）：*mineral salts* 矿盐 ➲ SEE ALSO EPSOM SALTS **3 salts** [pl.] a substance that looks or tastes like salt 形状（或味道）像盐的物质：*bath salts* (= used to give a pleasant smell to bath water) （放在洗澡水中使之芳香的）浴盐 ➲ SEE ALSO SMELLING SALTS
IDM **the salt of the 'earth** a very good and honest person that you can always depend on 世上的盐，地上的盐（指善良而诚实的人） ➲ MORE AT DOSE *n.*, PINCH *n.*, RUB *v.*, WORTH *adj.*
▪ ***verb*** **1** [usually passive] **~ sth** to put salt on or in food 在（食物）中放盐：*salted peanuts* 咸花生米 ◇ *a pan of boiling salted water* 一锅放了盐的开水 **2 ~ sth (down)** to preserve food with salt 用盐腌制（食物）：*salted fish* 咸鱼 **3 ~ sth** to put salt on roads to melt ice or snow 撒盐于…上（以使冰雪融化）
PHR V **ˌsalt sth↔a'way** to save sth for the future, secretly and usually dishonestly （通常指以欺瞒手段）秘密贮存：*She salted away the profits in foreign bank accounts.* 她把利润偷偷存在外国银行的账户上。
▪ ***adj.*** [only before noun] containing, tasting of or preserved with salt 含盐的；咸的；用盐腌制的：*salt water* 海水 ◇ *salt beef* 腌牛肉

ˌsalt-and-'pepper *adj.* = PEPPER-AND-SALT

salt·box /'sɔːltbɒks; *BrE also* 'sɒlt-; *NAmE* -bɑːks/ *noun* (*NAmE*) a house that has two floors at the front and one floor at the back, with a roof that slopes down between the two floors （坡顶）盐盒式房子

'salt cellar *noun* **1** (*BrE*) (*NAmE also* **'salt shaker**) a small container for salt, usually with one hole in the top, that is used at the table （餐桌用）小盐瓶 ➲ VISUAL VOCAB PAGE V23 **2** (*NAmE*) a small open dish containing salt 盐碟

'salt flats *noun* [pl.] a flat area of land, covered with a layer of salt 盐滩；盐坪

salt·ine /sɔːl'tiːn; sɒl-; *NAmE* sɔːl-/ (*also* **ˌsaltine 'cracker**) *noun* (*NAmE*) a thin dry biscuit with salt on top of it 苏打饼干；盐饼干

sal·tire /'sæltaɪə(r); 'sɔːl-/ (*also* **ˌsaltire 'cross**) *noun* **1** a cross in the shape of an X, especially on a COAT OF ARMS or a flag * X 形十字；（尤指盾徽或旗子上的） X 形十字图记 **2 the Saltire** the flag of Scotland, which is a white saltire on a blue background （蓝底白斜十字的）苏格兰旗，苏格兰圣安德鲁旗

'salt marsh (*also* **'salt meadow**) *noun* an area of open land near a coast that is regularly flooded by the sea 盐沼（在海岸附近，常遭海水淹灌）

'salt pan *noun* an area of low land where sea water has EVAPORATED to leave salt 盐磐，盐田，盐地（用蒸发法制取海盐的低地）

salt·petre (*US* **salt·peter**) /ˌsɔːlt'piːtə(r); *BrE also* ˌsɒlt-/ *noun* [U] a white powder used for preserving food and making matches and GUNPOWDER 硝石；钾硝；硝酸钾

'salt shaker *noun* (*NAmE*) = SALT CELLAR (1)

'salt truck (*US*) (*BrE* **grit·ter**) *noun* a large vehicle used for putting salt, sand or GRIT on the roads in winter when there is ice on them 铺沙机，撒盐车，撒沙车（在结冰的路面上使用）

'salt water *noun* [U] sea water; water containing salt 海水；咸水；盐水 ▸ **'salt·water** *adj.* [only before noun]: *saltwater fish* 咸水鱼 ➲ COMPARE FRESHWATER

S

salty /'sɔːlti; *BrE also* 'sɒlti/ *adj.* (**salt·ier, salti·est**) **1** containing or tasting of salt 含盐的；咸的： *salty food* 咸的食物 ◇ *salty sea air* 海边带咸味的空气 COMPARE SWEET *adj.* (1) **2** (*old-fashioned*) (of language or humour 语言或幽默) amusing and sometimes slightly rude 有趣的；逗笑的；有趣而略嫌粗俗的 ▶ **salti·ness** *noun* [U]: *She could taste the saltiness of her tears.* 她尝到了她眼泪的咸味。

sa·lu·bri·ous /sə'luːbriəs/ *adj.* (*formal*) (of a place 地方) pleasant to live in; clean and healthy 环境宜人的；清洁而有益健康的 OPP **insalubrious**

salu·tary /'sæljətri; *NAmE* -teri/ *adj.* having a good effect on sb/sth, though often seeming unpleasant 有益的（尽管往往让人不愉快）： *a* ***salutary lesson/experience/warning*** 有益的教训 / 经历 / 告诫 ◇ *The accident was a* ***salutary reminder*** *of the dangers of climbing.* 这次事故提醒人们注意登山的种种危险，倒也不无益处。

sa·lu·ta·tion /ˌsælju'teɪʃn/ *noun* **1** [C, U] (*formal*) something that you say to welcome or say hello to sb; the action of welcoming or saying hello to sb 招呼；致意；打招呼；致意的动作 **2** [C] (*specialist*) the words that are used in a letter to address the person you are writing to, for example 'Dear Sir'（信函中如 Dear Sir 之类的）称呼语

sa·lute /sə'luːt/ *verb, noun*

▪ ***verb*** **1** [I, T] to touch the side of your head with the fingers of your right hand to show respect, especially in the armed forces（尤指军队中）敬礼： *The sergeant stood to attention and saluted.* 中士立正敬礼。◇ **~ sb/sth** *to salute the flag/an officer* 向旗帜 / 长官敬礼 **2** [T] **~ sb/sth** (*formal*) to express respect and admiration for sb/sth 致敬；表示敬意 SYN **acknowledge**: *The players saluted the fans before leaving the field.* 球员在退场前向球迷致意。◇ *The president saluted the courage of those who had fought for their country.* 总统对那些为国战斗者的英勇精神表示敬意。

▪ ***noun*** **1** [C] the action of raising your right hand to the side of your head as a sign of respect, especially between soldiers and officers（尤指士兵和军官之间的）敬礼 **2** [C, U] a thing that you say or do to show your admiration or respect for sb/sth or to welcome sb 致敬；致意： *He raised his hat as a friendly salute.* 他举帽亲切致意。◇ *His first words were a salute to the people of South Africa.* 他开口首先向南非人民致敬。◇ *They all raised their glasses* ***in salute***. 他们都举杯致意。 **3** [C] an official occasion when guns are fired into the air to show respect for an important person 鸣礼炮；鸣炮致敬： *a 21-gun salute* 鸣炮 21 响的礼仪

sal·vage /'sælvɪdʒ/ *noun, verb*

▪ ***noun*** [U] **1** the act of saving things that have been, or are likely to be, damaged or lost, especially in a disaster or an accident（对财物等的）抢救： *the salvage of the wrecked tanker* 对失事油轮的打捞 ◇ *a* ***salvage company/operation/team*** 打捞公司；营救行动；抢救队 **2** the things that are saved from a disaster or an accident 抢救出的财物： *an exhibition of the salvage from the wreck* 沉船打捞物品展览

▪ ***verb*** **1** to save a badly damaged ship, etc. from being lost completely; to save parts or property from a damaged ship or from a fire, etc. 打捞；营救（失事船舶等）；抢救（失事船舶、火灾等中的财物）： **~ sth** *The wreck was salvaged by a team from the RAF.* 失事船只被英国皇家空军救援小组打捞起来了。 ◇ *The house was built using salvaged materials.* 这栋房子是用回收的废旧材料建成的。◇ **~ sth from sth** *We only managed to salvage two paintings from the fire.* 我们只从火灾中抢救出两幅画。 **2 ~ sth** to manage to rescue sth from a difficult situation; to stop a bad situation from being a complete failure 挽救；挽回： *What can I do to salvage my reputation?* (= get a good reputation again) 我怎样才能挽回我的名声呢？ ◇ *He wondered what he could do to salvage the situation.* 他不知道怎样才能挽救这个局面。◇ *United lost 5–2, salvaging a little pride with two late goals.* 联队以 2:5 失利，只靠后来两粒进球挽回了一点面子。

'salvage yard *noun* (*NAmE*) a place where old machines, cars, etc. are broken up so that the metal can be sold or used again （废旧机器、旧车等拆售的）废品回收场

sal·va·tion /sæl'veɪʃn/ *noun* [U] **1** (in Christianity 基督教) the state of being saved from the power of evil 得救；救恩；救世： *to pray for the salvation of the world* 为世人得救而祷告 **2** a way of protecting sb from danger, disaster, loss, etc.（危险、灾难、损失等的）避免方式，解救途径： *Group therapy classes have been his salvation.* 他一直靠参加集体治疗小组来调节心理。

the Sal,vation 'Army *noun* [sing.] a Christian organization whose members wear military uniforms and work to help poor people （基督教）救世军

salve *noun, verb*

▪ ***noun*** /sælv; *NAmE also* sæv/ [U, C] a substance that you put on a wound or sore skin to help it heal or to protect it 药膏；软膏；油膏 SEE ALSO LIPSALVE

▪ ***verb*** /sælv/ **~ your conscience** (*formal*) to do sth that makes you feel less guilty 使良心得到宽慰；减轻内疚感

sal·ver /'sælvə(r)/ *noun* a large plate, usually made of metal, on which drinks or food are served at a formal event 金属托盘（正式场合用于上饮料或食物）

salvo /'sælvəʊ; *NAmE* -voʊ/ *noun* (*pl.* **-os** or **-oes**) the act of firing several guns or dropping several bombs, etc. at the same time; a sudden attack 齐射；齐投；奇袭： *The first salvo exploded a short distance away.* 第一批投下的炸弹在不远处爆炸。◇ (*figurative*) *The newspaper article was* ***the opening salvo*** *in what proved to be a long battle.* 报上那篇文章是一场长期论战的开篇第一炮。

sal vola·tile /ˌsæl və'lætəli/ *noun* [U] a type of SMELLING SALTS 碳酸铵，挥发盐（一种嗅盐）

sal·war (*also* **shal·war**) /sʌl'wɑː(r)/ *noun* light loose trousers/pants that are tight around the ankles, sometimes worn by S Asian women （南亚）女式收口宽松裤： *a salwar kameez* (= a salwar worn with a KAMEEZ) 宽松裤克米兹套装

Sa·mar·itan /sə'mærɪtən/ *noun*

IDM **a ,good Sa'maritan** a person who gives help and sympathy to people who need it 善良的撒马利亚人；善人；乐善好施者 ORIGIN From the Bible story of a person from Samaria who helps an injured man that nobody else will help. 源自《圣经》，一个撒马利亚人向一个受伤但无人给予帮助的人伸出援助之手。

the Sa·mar·itans /ðə sə'mærɪtənz/ *noun* [pl.] a British charity that offers help to people who are worried, depressed, or in danger of killing themselves, by providing a phone number that they can ring in order to talk to somebody 撒马利亚会（英国慈善团体，为严重抑郁和想自杀的人提供热线电话谈心服务）

sa·mar·ium /sə'meəriəm; *NAmE* -'mer-/ *noun* [U] (*symb.* **Sm**) a chemical element. Samarium is a hard silver-white metal used in making strong MAGNETS. 钐

samba /'sæmbə/ *noun* a fast dance originally from Brazil; a piece of music for this dance 桑巴舞（源于巴西，节奏快）；桑巴舞曲

same /seɪm/ *adj., pron., adv.*

▪ ***adj.*** **1** exactly the one or ones referred to or mentioned; not different 同一的；相同的： *We have lived in the same house for twenty years.* 我们在同一座房子里住了二十年了。 ◇ *Our children go to the* ***same*** *school* ***as*** *theirs.* 我们的孩子和他们的孩子上同一所学校。◇ *She's still the* ***same*** *fun-loving person* ***that*** *I knew at college.* 她仍爱耍爱闹，还是上大学时的那副老样子。 ◇ *This one works in* ***exactly the same*** *way as the other.* 这个跟那个运转方法完全一样。 ◇ *They both said* ***much the same*** *thing.* 他们两人的话大致一样。◇ *He used* ***the very same*** (= exactly the same) *words.* 他用了完全相同的字眼儿。 ◇ *I resigned last Friday and left that same day.* 我上星期五辞了职，当天就离开了。 **2** exactly like the one or ones referred to or mentioned （与…）相同的，一模一样的： *I bought the*

S

same car as yours (= another car of that type). 我买了一辆车，和你那辆一模一样。◇ *She was wearing the **same** dress **that** I had on.* 她穿的连衣裙和我穿的一样。◇ *The same thing happened to me last week.* 上星期我也遇到了同样的事。

IDM HELP Most idioms containing **same** are at the entries for the nouns and verbs in the idioms, for example **be in the same boat** is at **boat**. 大多数含 same 的习语，都可在该等习语中的名词及动词相关词条找到，如 be in the same boat 在词条 boat 下。 **ˈsame old, ˈsame old** (*informal*) used to say that a situation has not changed at all 老样子；照旧不变：*'How's it going?' 'Oh, same old, same old.'* "情况怎么样？""哦，还是老样子。"

■ ***pron.* 1** **the ~ (as...)** the same thing or things (和…)同样的事物，相同的事物：*I would do the same again.* 我愿再做同样的事。◇ *I think the same as you do about this.* 在这件事上，我的想法和你一样。◇ *Just do the same as me* (= as I do). 跟着我做就行了。◇ *His latest movie is just **more of the same**—exotic locations, car chases and a final shoot-out.* 他的最新影片只不过是老一套，异国的场景、追车场面，最后一场枪战把对手干掉。◇ (*informal*) *'I'll have coffee.' 'Same for me, please* (= I will have one too).' "我喝咖啡。""我也来一杯。" **2** **the ~ (as...)** having the same number, colour, size, quality, etc. (数目、颜色、大小、质量等)相同，一样：*There are several brands and they're not all the same.* 有好几个品牌，不一样的。◇ *I'd like one the same as yours.* 我要一个和你一样的。**3** **the same** (*BrE*) the same person 同一个人：*'Was that George on the phone?' 'The same* (= yes, it was George).' "是跟乔治通的电话吗？""正是。"

IDM **ˌall/ˌjust the ˈsame** despite this 虽是这样；尽管如此 SYN **nevertheless**：*He's not very reliable, but I like him just the same.* 他不太可靠，但我还是喜欢他。◇ *'Will you stay for lunch?' 'No, but thanks all the same.'* "留下来吃午饭，好吗？""不了，多谢。"◇ *All the same, there's some truth in what she says.* 尽管如此，她说的还是有些道理的。 **be all the ˈsame to sb** to not be important to sb 对某人无关紧要（或无所谓）：*It's all the same to me whether we eat now or later.* 我们现在吃也行，过一会儿吃也行。我无所谓。 **ˌone and the ˈsame** the same person or thing 同一个人；同一事物：*It turns out that her aunt and my cousin are one and the same.* 原来她姑妈就是我表姐。 **(the) ˌsame aˈgain** (*informal*) used to ask sb to serve you the same drink as before 同样的（饮料）再来一份：*Same again, please!* 和刚才一样的，请再来一份！ **ˌsame ˈhere** (*informal*) (*also slang* **same**) used to say that sth is also true of you 我也一样；我也是：*'I can't wait to see it.' 'Same here.'* "我巴不得马上看到它。""我也一样。" **(the) ˌsame to ˈyou** (*informal*) (*also slang* **same**) used to answer a GREETING, an insult, etc. (回应问候、辱骂等)你也一样：*'Happy Christmas!' 'And the same to you!'* "圣诞快乐！""也祝您圣诞快乐！"◇ *'Get lost!' 'Same to you!'* "滚！""你也滚！"

■ ***adv.*** (*usually* **the same**) in the same way 同样：*We treat boys exactly **the same as** girls.* 男孩、女孩我们完全同等对待。◇ (*informal*) *He gave me five dollars, **same as usual**.* 和平时一样，他给了我五美元。

same·ness /ˈseɪmnəs/ *noun* [U] the quality of being the same; a lack of variety 相同性；同一性；千篇一律；单调：*She grew tired of the sameness of the food.* 饭菜单调，她都吃腻了。

ˈsame-sex *adj.* [only before noun] **1** of the same sex 同性别的：*The child's same-sex parent acts as a role model.* 孩子的同性家长是孩子效仿的榜样。**2** involving people of the same sex 涉及同性别的人的：*a same-sex relationship* 同性恋情

samey /ˈseɪmi/ *adj.* (*BrE, informal, disapproving*) not changing or different and therefore boring 千篇一律的；单调乏味的

sa·miti /ˈsæmɪti/ *noun* (*IndE*) a committee, a society or an association 委员会；协会；社团

sa·mosa /səˈməʊsə; *NAmE* -ˈmoʊ-/ *noun* a type of hot spicy S Asian food consisting of a triangle of thin crisp PASTRY filled with meat or vegetables and fried 萨莫萨三角炸饺（南亚食品）

samo·var /ˈsæməvɑː(r)/ *noun* a large container for heating water, used especially in Russia for making tea （尤指俄式）茶炊

samp /sæmp/ *noun* [U] (*SAfrE*) the inner parts of MAIZE (CORN) seeds that are crushed roughly; a type of PORRIDGE that is made from this 玉米糙；玉米糙粥

sam·pan /ˈsæmpæn/ *noun* a small boat with a flat bottom used along the coast and rivers of China 舢板

sam·ple /ˈsɑːmpl; *NAmE* ˈsæmpl/ *noun, verb*

■ ***noun* 1** a number of people or things taken from a larger group and used in tests to provide information about the group （抽查的）样本，样品：*The interviews were given to a **random sample** of students.* 随机抽选出部分学生进行了采访。◇ *The survey covers a **representative sample** of schools.* 调查覆盖了有代表性的一些学校。◇ *a sample survey* 抽样调查 **2** a small amount of a substance taken from a larger amount and tested in order to obtain information about the substance （化验的）取样，样本，样：*a blood sample* 血样 ◇ *Samples of the water contained pesticide.* 水样中含有杀虫剂。 ➲ WORDFINDER NOTE AT EXAMINE ➲ COLLOCATIONS AT SCIENTIFIC **3** a small amount or example of sth that can be looked at or tried to see what it is like （作为标准或代表的）样品，货样：*'I'd like to see a sample of your work,' said the manager.* "拿你作品的一个样本给我看看。"经理说。◇ *a free sample of shampoo* 免费试用的洗发剂 **4** (*specialist*) a piece of recorded music or sound that is used in a new piece of music （用于新乐曲中的）节录乐曲，选录乐曲（或声音）

■ ***verb* 1 ~ sth** to try a small amount of a particular food to see what it is like; to experience sth for a short time to see what it is like 尝；品尝；尝试；体验：*I sampled the delights of Greek cooking for the first time.* 我第一次品尝到希腊美食。 **2 ~ sb/sth** (*specialist*) to test, question, etc., part of sth or of a group of people in order to find out what the rest is like 抽样检验；取样；采样：*12% of the children sampled said they prefer cats to dogs.* 在被抽样调查的孩子中，12% 的人说他们喜欢猫胜过喜欢狗。 **3 ~ sth** (*specialist*) to record part of a piece of music, or a sound, in order to use it in a new piece of music 节录，选录（一段音乐或声音，用于新的乐曲中）

sam·pler /ˈsɑːmplə(r); *NAmE* ˈsæm-/ *noun* **1** a piece of cloth decorated with different STITCHES that people made in the past to show a person's skill at sewing （旧时的）刺绣样本 **2** a collection that shows typical examples of sth, especially pieces of music （尤指乐曲的）集锦，荟萃

sam·pling /ˈsɑːmplɪŋ; *NAmE* ˈsæm-/ *noun* [U] **1** the process of taking a sample 抽样；取样：*statistical sampling* 统计抽样 **2** (*specialist*) the process of copying and recording parts of a piece of music in an electronic form so that they can be used in a different piece of music （乐曲的）节录，选录

ˈsampling error *noun* (*statistics* 统计) a situation in which a set of results or figures does not show a true situation, because the group of people or things it was based on was not typical of a wider group 采样误差（所抽样本不具备代表性）

sam·urai /ˈsæmuraɪ/ *noun* (*pl.* **sam·urai**) (*from Japanese*) (in the past) a member of a powerful military class in Japan （旧时日本的）武士

sana·tor·ium /ˌsænəˈtɔːriəm/ (*NAmE also* **sani·tar·ium** /ˌsænəˈteəriəm; *NAmE* ˌsænəˈteriəm/) *noun* (*pl.* **-riums**, **-ria**) a place like a hospital where patients who have a lasting illness or who are getting better after an illness are treated 疗养院；休养所

sanc·tify /ˈsæŋktɪfaɪ/ *verb* (**sanc·ti·fies**, **sanc·ti·fied**, **sanc·ti·fy·ing**, **sanc·ti·fied**) [usually passive] (*formal*) **1 ~ sth** to make sth holy 使神圣化 **2 ~ sth** to make sth seem right or legal; to give official approval to sth 使正当化；

S

使合法化；批准；认可：*This was a practice sanctified by tradition.* 这是一种合乎传统的做法。▸ **sanc·ti·fi·ca·tion** /ˌsæŋktɪfɪˈkeɪʃn/ *noun* [U]

sanc·ti·mo·ni·ous /ˌsæŋktɪˈməʊniəs; *NAmE* -ˈmoʊ-/ *adj.* (*disapproving*) giving the impression that you feel you are better and more moral than other people 装作圣洁的；伪善的；道貌岸然的 **SYN** **self-righteous** ▸ **sanc·ti·mo·ni·ous·ly** *adv.* **sanc·ti·mo·ni·ous·ness** *noun* [U]

sanc·tion /ˈsæŋkʃn/ *noun, verb*

■ ***noun*** **1** [C, usually pl.] ~ (**against sb**) an official order that limits trade, contact, etc. with a particular country, in order to make it do sth, such as obeying international law 制裁：*Trade sanctions were imposed against any country that refused to sign the agreement.* 凡拒签该协议的国家均受到贸易制裁。◇ *The economic sanctions have been lifted.* 经济制裁业已取消。➲ **WORDFINDER NOTE** AT TRADE ➲ **COLLOCATIONS** AT INTERNATIONAL **2** [U] (*formal*) official permission or approval for an action or a change （正式）许可，批准 **SYN** **authorization**：*These changes will require the sanction of the court.* 这些变更须经法院认可。 **3** [C] ~ (**against sth**) a course of action that can be used, if necessary, to make people obey a law or behave in a particular way 制裁；约束；处罚 **SYN** **penalty**：*The ultimate sanction will be the closure of the restaurant.* 最严厉的处罚将是关闭这家餐馆。

■ ***verb*** **1** ~ **sth** (*formal*) to give permission for sth to take place 许可；准许；准予：*The government refused to sanction a further cut in interest rates.* 政府拒绝批准进一步降低利率。 **2** ~ **sb/sth** (*specialist*) to punish sb/sth; to impose a sanction (1) on sth 惩罚；实施制裁

sanc·tity /ˈsæŋktəti/ *noun* [U] **1** ~ (**of sth**) the state of being very important and worth protecting 神圣不可侵犯：*the **sanctity of marriage*** 婚姻之神圣 **2** the state of being holy 神圣性；圣洁性：*a life of sanctity, like that of St Francis* 圣方济各式的圣洁生活

sanc·tu·ary /ˈsæŋktʃuəri; *NAmE* -ueri/ *noun* (*pl.* **-ies**) **1** [C] an area where wild birds or animals are protected and encouraged to breed 鸟兽保护区；禁猎区 **SYN** **reserve**：*a **bird/wildlife sanctuary*** 鸟类 / 野生动物保护区 **2** [U] safety and protection, especially for people who are being chased or attacked 庇护；保护：*to take sanctuary in a place* 在某处避难 ◇ *The government offered sanctuary to 4 000 refugees.* 政府为 4 000 名难民提供了保护。◇ *She longed for the sanctuary of her own home.* 她渴望回到自己家中，不再担惊受怕。 **3** [C, usually sing.] a safe place, especially one where people who are being chased or attacked can stay and be protected 避难所；庇护所：*The church became a sanctuary for the refugees.* 教堂成为这些难民的庇护所。 **4** [C] a holy building or the part of it that is considered the most holy 圣所；圣殿

S

sanc·tum /ˈsæŋktəm/ *noun* [usually sing.] (*formal*) **1** a private room where sb can go and not be disturbed （不受干扰的）私室，密室：*She once allowed me into her **inner sanctum**.* 有一次她让我进入她的内室。 **2** a holy place 圣所

sand 🔑 /sænd/ *noun, verb*

■ ***noun*** **1** 🔑 [U] a substance that consists of very small fine grains of rock. Sand is found on beaches, in deserts, etc. 沙；沙子：*a **grain of sand*** 一粒沙子 ◇ *Concrete is a mixture of sand and cement.* 混凝土是沙和水泥的混合物。◇ *His hair was the colour of sand.* 他的头发呈沙褐色。◇ *The children were playing in the sand* (= for example, in a SANDPIT). 孩子们正在玩沙子。 ➲ **VISUAL VOCAB** PAGE V5 **2** 🔑 [U, C, usually pl.] a large area of sand on a beach 沙滩：*We went for a walk along the sand.* 我们去沙滩上散了散步。◇ *children playing on the sand* 在沙滩上玩耍的儿童 ◇ *miles of golden sands* 绵延数英里的金色沙滩 ➲ **SYNONYMS** AT COAST ➲ SEE ALSO SANDY (1) **IDM** SEE HEAD *n.*, SHIFT *v.*

■ ***verb*** ~ **sth** (**down**) to make sth smooth by rubbing it with sandpaper or using a sander （用砂纸或打磨机）打磨

san·dal /ˈsændl/ *noun* a type of light open shoe that is worn in warm weather. The top part consists of leather bands that attach the SOLE to your foot. 凉鞋 ➲ **VISUAL VOCAB** PAGE V69

san·dalled (*BrE*) (*US* **san·daled**) /ˈsændld/ *adj.* [only before noun] wearing sandals 穿凉鞋的：*sandalled feet* 穿着凉鞋的脚

san·dal·wood /ˈsændlwʊd/ *noun* [U] a type of oil with a sweet smell that is obtained from a hard tropical wood (also called sandalwood) and is used to make PERFUME 檀香油（提取自檀香木，用于制作香水）

sand·bag /ˈsændbæɡ/ *noun, verb*

■ ***noun*** a bag filled with sand used to build a wall as a protection against floods or explosions （用于防洪、防爆的）沙袋，沙包

■ ***verb*** (**-gg-**) **1** ~ **sth** to put sandbags in or around sth as protection against floods or explosions 在…堆沙袋；用沙袋封堵 **2** ~ **sb** (*informal, especially NAmE*) to attack sb by criticizing them strongly; to treat sb badly 猛烈抨击；粗暴对待

sand·bank /ˈsændbæŋk/ *noun* a raised area of sand in a river or the sea 沙洲；沙坝 ➲ **WORDFINDER NOTE** AT SEA ➲ **VISUAL VOCAB** PAGE V5

sand·bar /ˈsændbɑː(r)/ *noun* a long mass of sand at the point where a river meets the sea that is formed by the movement of the water （河口的）沙洲

sand·blast /ˈsændblɑːst; *NAmE* -blæst/ *verb* [often passive] ~ **sth** to clean, polish, decorate, etc. a surface by firing sand at it from a special machine 喷沙（用以清污、打磨或装饰物体表面）

sand·box /ˈsændbɒks; *NAmE* -bɑːks/ (*NAmE*) (*BrE* **sand·pit**) *noun* **1** an area in the ground or a shallow container, filled with sand for children to play in （供儿童玩的）沙坑 ➲ **VISUAL VOCAB** PAGE V41 **2** a test area on a computer system, where you can run software without affecting the hardware or other software 沙盒，沙箱（计算机系统测试区，在其中运行软件时不会影响到硬件或其他软件） **3** a video game style that allows players to explore the game freely, make changes to the way it looks, or establish their own rules 沙盒游戏（一种高自由度的电子游戏类型，玩家可自主探索游戏，改变其外观，或建立自己的规则）

sand·cas·tle /ˈsændkɑːsl; *NAmE* -kæsl/ *noun* a pile of sand made to look like a castle, usually by a child on a beach （通常指儿童在沙滩上堆成的）沙堡

ˈsand dune *noun* = DUNE

sand·er /ˈsændə(r)/ *noun* an electric tool with a rough surface used for making wood smooth 砂轮磨光机

s and h (*also* **s & h**) /ˌes ənd ˈeɪtʃ/ *abbr.* (*NAmE*) shipping and handling 运输与处理 ➲ COMPARE P. AND P.

ˈsand iron *noun* (*BrE*) = SAND WEDGE

S & L /ˌes ənd ˈel/ *abbr.* SAVINGS AND LOAN ASSOCIATION 房屋互助协会

sand·lot /ˈsændlɒt; *NAmE* -lɑːt/ *adj.* [only before noun] (*NAmE*) (of a sport 体育运动) played for enjoyment rather than as a job for money 非职业的；业余的

the sand·man /ˈsændmæn/ *noun* [sing.] an imaginary man who is said to help children get to sleep （传说中使小孩入睡的）睡魔

ˈsand mar·tin *noun* a bird like a small SWALLOW, that makes its nest in banks of sand 沙燕

sand·paper /ˈsændpeɪpə(r)/ *noun, verb*

■ ***noun*** [U] strong paper with a rough surface covered with sand or a similar substance, used for rubbing surfaces in order to make them smooth 砂纸

■ ***verb*** (*also* **sand**) ~ **sth** (**down**) to make sth smooth by rubbing it with sandpaper 用砂纸打磨

sand·piper /ˈsændpaɪpə(r)/ *noun* a small bird with long legs and a long beak that lives near rivers and lakes 鹬

sand·pit /ˈsændpɪt/ (*BrE*) (*NAmE* **sand·box**) *noun* an area in the ground or a shallow container, filled with sand for children to play in （供儿童玩的）沙坑 ➲ VISUAL VOCAB PAGE V41

sand·shoe /ˈsændʃuː/ *noun* (*ScotE, AustralE, NZE*) a PLIMSOLL (= a type of light cloth sports shoe with a rubber SOLE) 胶底帆布鞋；体操鞋

sand·stone /ˈsændstəʊn; *NAmE* -stoʊn/ *noun* [U] a type of stone that is formed of grains of sand tightly pressed together, used in building 砂岩

sand·storm /ˈsændstɔːm; *NAmE* -stɔːrm/ *noun* a storm in a desert in which sand is blown into the air by strong winds 沙暴

ˈsand trap (*also* **trap**) *noun* (*both especially NAmE*) = BUNKER (3)

ˈsand wedge (*BrE also* **ˈsand iron**) *noun* a GOLF CLUB used for hitting the ball out of sand 挖起杆（将高尔夫球从沙坑中打出）

sand·wich /ˈsænwɪtʃ; -wɪdʒ/ *noun, verb*

■ ***noun*** **1** (*also BrE, informal* **sar·nie**) two slices of bread, often spread with butter, with a layer of meat, cheese, etc. between them 夹心面包片；三明治：*a cheese sandwich* 奶酪三明治 ◇ *a **sandwich bar*** (= a place that sells sandwiches) 三明治柜台 ➲ SEE ALSO CLUB SANDWICH, OPEN SANDWICH **2** (*BrE*) (in compounds 构成复合词) a SPONGE CAKE consisting of two layers with jam and/or cream between them 夹心蛋糕

■ ***verb***

PHR V **ˈsandwich sb/sth between sb/sth** [usually passive] to fit sth/sb into a very small space between two other things or people, or between two times 把…夹（或插）在…中间：*I was sandwiched between two fat men on the bus.* 在公共汽车上，我被两个胖子挤在中间。 **ˌsandwich A and B toˈgether** (**with sth**) to put sth between two things to join them （用…）结合，粘合：*Sandwich the cakes together with cream.* 用奶油把两块蛋糕粘在一起。

ˈsandwich board *noun* a pair of boards with advertisements on them that sb wears at the front and back of their body as they walk around in public 夹板广告牌，三明治式广告牌（挂在胸前和后背的一副广告牌）

ˈsandwich course *noun* (*BrE*) a course of study which includes periods of study and periods of working in business or industry 工读交替制课程（部分时间上课，部分时间实习）

sandy /ˈsændi/ *adj.* (**sand·ier, sand·iest**) **1** covered with or containing sand 铺满沙子的；含沙的：*a sandy beach* 沙滩 ◇ *sandy soil* 沙质土壤 **2** (of hair 头发) having a light colour, between yellow and red 沙褐色的；浅棕色的 ➲ WORDFINDER NOTE AT BLONDE

sane /seɪn/ *adj.* (**saner, san·est**) **1** having a normal healthy mind; not mentally ill 精神健全的；神志正常的 **SYN** **sound**：*No sane person would do that.* 没有一个神志正常的人会做那样的事。 ◇ *Being able to get out of the city at the weekend **keeps me sane**.* 要不是能出城过过周末，我简直快憋疯了。 **2** sensible and reasonable 明智的；理智的；合乎情理的：*the sane way to solve the problem* 解决问题的明智方法 **OPP** **insane** ➲ SEE ALSO SANITY ▶ **sane·ly** *adv.*

sang PAST TENSE OF SING

san·geet /sʌnˈgiːt/ *noun* (*IndE*) a celebration held before a Hindu wedding ceremony for the woman who is getting married and her friends and relatives 桑吉派对（印度婚礼前为新娘及其亲友举办的庆祝活动）

sang·froid /sɒŋˈfrwɑː; *NAmE* sɑːŋ-/ *noun* [U] (*from French*) the ability to remain calm in a difficult or dangerous situation 镇定；沉着

sangh /sæŋ; *BrE also* sʌŋ/ *noun* (*IndE*) a group of people who meet together regularly because they have the same interest or aim; an association 联合会；协会：*The leader of the sangh appealed for peace.* 联合会领导人呼吁和平。

san·goma /sʌŋˈgəʊmə; sʌŋˈgɔːmə; *NAmE* -ˈgoʊ-/ *noun* (*SAfrE*) a person who is believed to have magic powers that can be used, for example, to find out why sb is ill/sick or protect sb from being harmed 巫师

san·gria /ˈsæŋgriə; sæŋˈgriːə/ *noun* [U, C] (*from Spanish*) an alcoholic drink made of red wine mixed with fruit, and sometimes with LEMONADE or BRANDY added 桑格里亚酒（红葡萄酒加水果和柠檬饮料或白兰地调制而成）

san·guin·ary /ˈsæŋgwɪnəri; *NAmE* -neri/ *adj.* (*formal*) involving or liking killing and blood （好）杀戮的；血腥的；嗜血成性的

san·guine /ˈsæŋgwɪn/ *adj.* ~ (**about sth**) (*formal*) cheerful and confident about the future 充满信心的；乐观的 **SYN** **optimistic**：*They are less sanguine about the company's long-term prospects.* 他们对公司的远景不那么乐观。 ◇ *He tends to **take a sanguine view** of the problems involved.* 他对涉及的问题持乐观态度。 ▶ **san·guine·ly** *adv.*

sani·tar·ium (*NAmE*) = SANATORIUM

sani·tary /ˈsænətri; *NAmE* -teri/ *adj.* **1** [only before noun] connected with keeping places clean and healthy to live in, especially by removing human waste 卫生的；环境卫生的；公共卫生的：*Overcrowding and **poor sanitary conditions** led to disease in the refugee camps.* 过度拥挤和恶劣的卫生状况导致难民营中出现疾病。 ◇ *The hut had no cooking or sanitary facilities.* 这间茅屋里没有厨具和卫生设施。 **2** clean; not likely to cause health problems 清洁的；卫生的 **SYN** **hygienic**：*The new houses were more sanitary than the old ones had been.* 新房子比老房子卫生。 **OPP** **insanitary**

ˈsanitary towel (*BrE*) (*NAmE* **ˈsanitary napkin**, *NAmE* **ˌsanitary ˈpad**) *noun* a thick piece of soft material that women wear outside their body to absorb the blood during their PERIOD 卫生巾；月经带 ➲ COMPARE TAMPON

sani·ta·tion /ˌsænɪˈteɪʃn/ *noun* [U] the equipment and systems that keep places clean, especially by removing human waste 卫生设备；卫生设施体系：*disease resulting from poor sanitation* 卫生条件差导致的疾病

sani·tize (*BrE also* **-ise**) /ˈsænɪtaɪz/ *verb* (*formal*) **1** ~ **sth** (*disapproving*) to remove the parts of sth that could be considered unpleasant 去除…中使人不快的内容；净化：*This sanitized account of his life does not mention his time in prison.* 这份生平记述对他的不光彩之处略而不表，没有提及他在监狱的日子。 **2** ~ **sth** to clean sth thoroughly using chemicals to remove bacteria （用化学制剂）消毒，使清洁 **SYN** **disinfect**

san·ity /ˈsænəti/ *noun* [U] **1** the state of having a normal healthy mind 精神健全；神志正常：*His behaviour was so strange that I began to doubt his sanity.* 他行为怪异，我有点怀疑他是否神智正常。 ◇ *to **keep/preserve your sanity*** 保持头脑清醒 **2** the state of being sensible and reasonable 明智；理智；通情达理：*After a series of road accidents the police pleaded for sanity among drivers.* 在发生一系列交通事故之后，警方提请驾驶员要审慎驾车。 **OPP** **insanity** ➲ SEE ALSO SANE

sank PAST TENSE OF SINK

sans /sænz/ *prep.* (*literary* or *humorous*) without 无；没有：*There were no potatoes so we had fish and chips sans the chips.* 那时没有土豆，所以我们吃了不带薯条的炸鱼薯条。

San·skrit /ˈsænskrɪt/ *noun* [U] an ancient language of India belonging to the Indo-European family, in which the Hindu holy texts are written and on which many modern languages are based 梵语（古印度语，属于印欧语系，用于印度教经文撰写，也是很多现代语言的基础）

sans serif (*also* **san·serif**) /ˌsæn ˈserɪf/ *noun* [U] (*specialist*) (in printing 印刷) a TYPEFACE in which the letters have no SERIF 无衬线字体

Santa Claus /ˈsæntə klɔːz/ (*also* **Santa**) (*BrE also* **ˌFather ˈChristmas**) *noun* an imaginary old man with red clothes

S

and a long white beard. Parents tell small children that he brings them presents at Christmas. 圣诞老人

sap /sæp/ *noun, verb*

■ ***noun*** **1** [U] the liquid in a plant or tree that carries food to all its parts（植物体内运送养分的）液，汁：*Maple syrup is made from sap extracted from the sugar maple tree.* 槭糖浆是用糖槭树中提取的树液制成的。 **2** [C] (*informal, especially NAmE*) a stupid person that you can easily trick, or treat unfairly 笨蛋；易上当的人

■ ***verb*** (**-pp-**) to make sth/sb weaker; to destroy sth gradually 使虚弱；削弱；逐渐破坏： **~ sth** *The hot sun sapped our energy.* 火辣辣的太阳烤得我们虚软无力。◇ **~ sb (of sth)** *Years of failure have sapped him of his confidence.* 连年失败使他逐渐丧失了自信。

sapi·ent /ˈseɪpiənt/ *adj.* (*literary*) having great intelligence or knowledge 睿智的；博学的 ▸ **sapi·ence** /-əns/ *noun* [U] **sapi·ent·ly** *adv.*

sap·ling /ˈsæplɪŋ/ *noun* a young tree 幼树

sapo·dilla /ˌsæpəˈdɪlə/ *noun* a large tropical American tree that produces a fruit that can be eaten and a substance used in CHEWING GUM 人心果（产于热带美洲，果实可食用，树胶可制口香糖）

sap·per /ˈsæpə(r)/ *noun* (*BrE*) a soldier whose job is to build or repair roads, bridges, etc. 工兵；工程兵

sap·phic /ˈsæfɪk/ *adj.* (*formal*) relating to LESBIANS 女同性恋的 ▸ **sap·phism** /ˈsæfɪzəm/ *noun* [U]

sap·phire /ˈsæfaɪə(r)/ *noun* **1** [C, U] a clear, bright blue PRECIOUS STONE 蓝宝石 **2** [U] a bright blue colour 宝蓝色；天蓝色 ▸ **sap·phire** *adj.*： *sapphire eyes* 宝蓝色的眼睛

sappy /ˈsæpi/ *adj.* (**sap·pier, sap·piest**) **1** (*NAmE, informal*) = SOPPY **2** (of plants 植物) full of SAP (= liquid) 汁液丰富的

sap·wood /ˈsæpwʊd/ *noun* [U] the soft younger outer layers of the wood of a tree, inside the BARK 边材，液材（处于树皮和心材之间）➲ COMPARE HEARTWOOD

Saran Wrap™ /səˈræn ræp/ *noun* [U] (*NAmE*) = PLASTIC WRAP

sar·casm /ˈsɑːkæzəm; *NAmE* ˈsɑːrk-/ *noun* [U] a way of using words that are the opposite of what you mean in order to be unpleasant to sb or to make fun of them 讽刺；嘲讽；挖苦：*'That will be useful,' she snapped with heavy sarcasm* (= she really thought it would not be useful at all). "还真有用啊。"她狠狠挖苦道。◇ *a hint/touch/trace of sarcasm in his voice* 他话语中的几分嘲讽

sar·cas·tic /sɑːˈkæstɪk; *NAmE* sɑːrˈk-/ (*also BrE, informal* **sarky**) *adj.* showing or expressing sarcasm 讽刺的；嘲讽的；挖苦的： *sarcastic comments* 冷嘲热讽的话 ◇ *a sarcastic manner* 嘲讽的态度 ◇ *'There's no need to be sarcastic,' she said.* "不必挖苦人嘛。"她说。 ▸ **sar·cas·tic·al·ly** /-kli/ *adv.*

sar·coma /sɑːˈkəʊmə; *NAmE* sɑːrˈkoʊmə/ *noun* (*medical* 医) a harmful (= MALIGNANT) lump (= a TUMOUR) that grows in certain parts of the body such as muscle or bone 肉瘤

sar·copha·gus /sɑːˈkɒfəgəs; *NAmE* sɑːrˈkɑːf-/ *noun* (*pl.* **sar·coph·agi** /sɑːˈkɒfəgaɪ; *NAmE* sɑːrˈkɑːf-/) a stone COFFIN (= box that a dead person is buried in), especially one that is decorated, used in ancient times（尤指古代有雕饰的）石棺

sar·dine /ˌsɑːˈdiːn; *NAmE* ˌsɑːrˈd-/ *noun* a small young sea fish (for example, a young PILCHARD) that is either eaten fresh or preserved in tins/cans 沙丁鱼

IDM **(packed, crammed, etc.) like sarˈdines** (*informal*) pressed tightly together in a way that is uncomfortable or unpleasant 拥挤不堪；挤得水泄不通

sar·don·ic /sɑːˈdɒnɪk; *NAmE* sɑːrˈdɑːnɪk/ *adj.* (*disapproving*) showing that you think that you are better than other people and do not take them seriously 轻慢的；轻蔑的；嘲弄的 SYN **mocking**： *a sardonic smile* 讪笑 ▸ **sar·don·ic·al·ly** /-kli/ *adv.*

sarge /sɑːdʒ; *NAmE* sɑːrdʒ/ *noun* (*informal*) used to talk to or about a SERGEANT 中士；巡佐；警佐

sari /ˈsɑːri/ *noun* a long piece of cloth that is wrapped around the body and worn as the main piece of clothing by women in S Asia 莎丽（南亚妇女裹在身上的长巾）

sarin /ˈsɑːrɪn/ *noun* [U] a type of poisonous gas used in chemical weapons 沙林（用于化学武器的一种毒气）

sarky /ˈsɑːki; *NAmE* ˈsɑːrki/ *adj.* (**sark·ier, sarki·est**) (*BrE, informal*) = SARCASTIC

sar·nie /ˈsɑːni; *NAmE* ˈsɑːrni/ *noun* (*BrE, informal*) = SANDWICH (1)

sar·ong /səˈrɒŋ; *NAmE* -ˈrɔːŋ; -ˈrɑːŋ/ *noun* a long piece of cloth wrapped around the body from the waist or the chest, worn by Malaysian and Indonesian men and women 莎笼（马来西亚人和印度尼西亚人裹在腰或胸以下的长条布，男女均穿）

sar·panch /ˈsɑːpʌntʃ; *NAmE* ˈsɑːrp-/ *noun* (in some S Asian countries) the head of a village（某些南亚国家的）村长

SARS /sɑːz; *NAmE* sɑːrz/ *noun* [U] the abbreviation for 'severe acute respiratory syndrome' (an illness that is easily spread from person to person, which affects the lungs and can sometimes cause death) 严重急性呼吸综合征（全写为 severe acute respiratory syndrome，通称传染性非典型肺炎，是可致命的传染病）： *No new SARS cases have been reported in the region.* 该区没有新增非典型肺炎病例。

sar·sa·par·illa /ˌsɑːspəˈrɪlə; ˌsɑːsəpə-; *NAmE* ˌsɑːrs-/ *noun* **1** [U] a dried substance that is used to flavour drinks and medicines, obtained from a plant also called sarsaparilla 洋菝葜干根（用于饮料和药的调味） **2** [U, C] a drink made with sarsaparilla 洋菝葜根汁饮料；沙士饮料

sar·tor·ial /sɑːˈtɔːriəl; *NAmE* sɑːrˈt-/ *adj.* [only before noun] (*formal*) relating to clothes, especially men's clothes, and the way they are made or worn 服装的；（尤指）男装的；衣着的 ▸ **sar·tor·ial·ly** /-riəli/ *adv.*

SAS /ˌes eɪ ˈes/ *abbr.* Special Air Service (a group of highly trained soldiers in Britain who are used on very secret or difficult military operations) 特种空军部队（英国一支用于秘密或艰巨军事行动的部队）

SASE *noun* (*NAmE*) the abbreviation used in writing for 'self-addressed stamped envelope' (an envelope on which you have written your name and address and put a stamp so that sb else can use it to send sth to you)（写上姓名地址并贴有邮票的）回邮信封（书写形式，全写为 self-addressed stamped envelope）➲ COMPARE SAE

sash /sæʃ/ *noun* **1** a long strip of cloth worn around the waist or over one shoulder, especially as part of a uniform（尤指制服的）腰带，肩带，饰带 **2** either of a pair of windows, one above the other, that are opened and closed by sliding them up and down inside the frame （垂直推拉窗任何一扇的）窗扇

sashay /ˈsæʃeɪ; *NAmE* sæˈʃeɪ/ *verb* [I] + **adv./prep.** to walk in a very confident but relaxed way, especially in order to be noticed 大摇大摆地走；神气地走

ˈsash cord *noun* a string or rope with a weight at one end attached to a sash window allowing it to stay open in any position （垂直推拉窗的）吊窗绳

sash·imi /ˈsæʃɪmi; *NAmE* sɑːˈʃiːmi/ *noun* [U, C] (*from Japanese*) a Japanese dish consisting of slices of raw fish, served with sauce 生鱼片（日本菜肴，蘸调味酱食用）

ˌsash ˈwindow *noun* a window that consists of two separate parts, one above the other that you open by sliding one of the parts up or down 垂直推拉窗 ➲ VISUAL VOCAB PAGE V18

Sas·quatch /ˈsæskwætʃ; -wɒtʃ; *NAmE* -wɑːtʃ/ *noun* = BIGFOOT

sass /sæs/ *noun, verb*

■ ***noun*** [U] (*informal, especially NAmE*) behaviour or talk that is rude and lacking respect 莽撞的行为；粗鲁的话

■ ***verb*** **~ sb** (*NAmE, informal*) to speak to sb in a rude way, without respect 对…粗鲁地（或恶声恶气地）说话；对…出言不逊：*Don't sass your mother!* 跟你母亲说话别大呼小叫的！

sas·sa·fras /ˈsæsəfræs/ *noun* a N American tree with pleasant-smelling leaves and BARK. Its leaves are sometimes used to make a type of tea. 檫树，微白檫树（产于北美，树叶和树皮味芳香，树叶有时用来泡茶）

Sas·sen·ach /ˈsæsənæk; -næx/ *noun* (*ScotE, disapproving* or *humorous*) an English person 英格兰人 ▸ **Sas·sen·ach** *adj.*

sassy /ˈsæsi/ *adj.* (**sas·sier**, **sas·si·est**) (*informal, especially NAmE*) **1** (*disapproving*) rude; showing a lack of respect 粗鲁的；无礼的 **2** (*approving*) fashionable and confident 时髦且自信的：*his sassy, streetwise daughter* 他那又时髦又精通都市生存之道的女儿

SAT *noun* **1 SAT™** /ˌes eɪ ˈtiː/ (in the US) the abbreviation for 'Scholastic Assessment Test' (a test taken by HIGH SCHOOL students who want to go to a college or university)（美国）学术能力评估测试（全写为 Scholastic Assessment Test，高中生升大学须通过的考试）：*to take the SAT* 参加学术能力评估测试 ◊ *I scored 1050 on the SAT.* 我在学术能力评估测试中得了 1 050 分。◊ *a SAT score* 学术能力评估测试成绩 **2** /sæt/ (in Britain) the abbreviation for 'Standard Assessment Task' (now officially called NCT)（英国）标准课业测评考试（全写为 Standard Assessment Task，现称为 NCT）

sat PAST TENSE, PAST PART. OF SIT

Satan /ˈseɪtn/ *noun* the DEVIL 撒旦；魔王

sa·tan·ic /səˈtænɪk; *NAmE also* seɪˈt-/ *adj.* **1** (*often* **Sa·tan·ic**) connected with the worship of the DEVIL 崇拜撒旦的：*satanic cults* 撒旦崇拜团体 ◊ *Not one incident of satanic abuse has actually been proved.* 没有一宗撒旦仪式虐待事件是得到过证实的。 **2** (*formal*) morally bad and evil 道德败坏的；邪恶的 **SYN** **demonic** ▸ **sa·tan·ic·al·ly** /-kli/ *adv.*

sa·tan·ism /ˈseɪtənɪzəm/ *noun* [U] the worship of Satan 撒旦崇拜 ▸ **sa·tan·ist** /ˈseɪtənɪst/ *noun*

satay /ˈsæteɪ; *NAmE* ˈsɑː-/ *noun* [U, C] a SE Asian dish consisting of meat or fish cooked on sticks and served with a sauce made with PEANUTS 沙茶酱烤肉，沙茶酱烤鱼（东南亚菜肴，蘸用花生做的酱食用）

satchel /ˈsætʃəl/ *noun* a bag with a long strap, that you hang over your shoulder or wear on your back, used especially for carrying school books 书包；肩背书包

sat·com (*also* **SATCOM**) /ˈsætkɒm; *NAmE* -kɑːm/ *noun* [U] satellite communications 卫星通信

sate /seɪt/ *verb* **~ sth** (*formal*) to satisfy a desire 满足（欲望）

sated /ˈseɪtɪd/ *adj.* [not usually before noun] **~ (with sth)** (*formal*) having had so much of sth that you do not need any more 餍足；餍腻：*sated with pleasure* 倦于享乐

sat·el·lite /ˈsætəlaɪt/ *noun* **1** an electronic device that is sent into space and moves around the earth or another planet. It is used for communicating by radio, television, etc. and for providing information. 人造卫星：*a* ***weather/communications satellite*** 气象 / 通信卫星 ◊ *The interview came live* ***by satellite*** *from Hollywood.* 采访是通过卫星从好莱坞现场传来的。◊ ***satellite television/TV*** (= broadcast using a satellite) 卫星电视 ◊ *a* ***satellite broadcast/channel/picture*** 卫星广播 / 频道 / 照片 ➲ WORDFINDER NOTE AT SPACE ➲ COLLOCATIONS AT TELEVISION **2** a natural object that moves around a larger natural object in space 卫星：*The moon is a satellite of earth.* 月球是地球的卫星。 **3** a town, a country or an organization that is controlled by and depends on another larger or more powerful one 卫星城；卫星国；外围组织：*satellite states* 卫星国

ˈsatellite dish *noun* a piece of equipment that receives signals from a satellite, used to enable people to watch satellite television 卫星电视碟形天线

ˈsatellite station *noun* **1** a company that broadcasts television programmes using a satellite 卫星电视台 **2** a place where special equipment is used to follow the movements of satellites and receive information from them 卫星地面站

sati (*also* **sut·tee**) /ˈsʌtiː; sʌˈtiː/ *noun* **1** [U] the former practice in Hinduism of a wife burning herself with the body of her dead husband 萨底，寡妇自焚殉夫（旧时印度教习俗） **2** [C] a wife who did this 自焚殉夫的寡妇

sa·ti·ate /ˈseɪʃieɪt/ *verb* [usually passive] **~ sb/sth** (*formal*) to give sb so much of sth that they do not feel they want any more 满足 ▸ **sa·ti·ation** /ˌseɪʃiˈeɪʃn/ *noun* [U]

sa·ti·ety /səˈtaɪəti/ *noun* [U] (*formal* or *specialist*) the state or feeling of being completely full of food, or of having had enough of sth 饱足；餍足；满足

satin /ˈsætɪn; *NAmE* ˈsætn/ *noun, adj.*

■ ***noun*** [U] a type of cloth with a smooth shiny surface 缎子：*a white satin ribbon* 白色缎带

■ ***adj.*** [only before noun] having the smooth shiny appearance of satin 缎子似的；平滑而有光泽的：*The paint has a satin finish.* 漆面像缎子一样光滑。

sat·iny /ˈsætɪni; *NAmE* ˈsætni/ *adj.* looking or feeling like satin 缎子似的；光滑的：*her satiny skin* 她那绸缎般光滑的皮肤

sat·ire /ˈsætaɪə(r)/ *noun* [U, C] a way of criticizing a person, an idea or an institution in which you use humour to show their faults or weaknesses; a piece of writing that uses this type of criticism 讽刺；讥讽；讽刺作品：***political/social satire*** 政治 / 社会讽刺作品 ◊ *a work full of* ***savage/biting satire*** 一部充满无情 / 辛辣讽刺的作品 ◊ *The novel is a stinging satire on American politics.* 这部小说是对美国政治的尖锐讽刺。

sa·tir·ic·al /səˈtɪrɪkl/ (*also less frequent* **sa·tir·ic** /səˈtɪrɪk/) *adj.* using satire to criticize sb/sth 讽刺的；讥讽的：*a satirical magazine* 讽刺杂志 ▸ **sa·tir·ic·al·ly** /-kli/ *adv.*

sat·ir·ist /ˈsætərɪst/ *noun* a person who writes or uses SATIRE 讽刺作家；惯于讽刺的人

sat·ir·ize (*BrE also* **-ise**) /ˈsætəraɪz/ *verb* **~ sb/sth** to use SATIRE to show the faults in a person, an organization, a system, etc. 讽刺；讥讽

sat·is·fac·tion 🔑 /ˌsætɪsˈfækʃn/ *noun* **1** [U, C] the good feeling that you have when you have achieved sth or when sth that you wanted to happen does happen; sth that gives you this feeling 满足；满意；欣慰；令人满意（或欣慰）的事：*to* ***gain/get/derive satisfaction*** *from sth* 从某事中得到满足感 ◊ *a* ***look/smile of satisfaction*** 心满意足的表情 / 笑容 ◊ *She looked back on her career* ***with great satisfaction.*** 回顾自己的事业，她深感欣慰。◊ *He* ***had the satisfaction of*** *seeing his book become a bestseller.* 看到自己的作品成了畅销书，他志得意满。◊ *She didn't want to* ***give him the satisfaction of*** *seeing her cry.* 她不愿当着他的面哭，让他幸灾乐祸。◊ *The company is trying to improve* ***customer satisfaction.*** 公司力图改进，让顾客更加满意。◊ *He was enjoying all the satisfactions of being a parent.* 他享受着做父亲所能得到的一切乐趣。➲ SEE ALSO DISSATISFACTION **2** [U] the act of FULFILLING a need or desire（需要或欲望的）满足，达到：*the satisfaction of sexual desires* 性欲的满足 ◊ *the satisfaction of your ambitions* 实现抱负 **3** [U] (*formal*) an acceptable way of

> **WORD FAMILY**
> **satisfaction** *noun* (≠ dissatisfaction)
> **satisfactory** *adj.* (≠ unsatisfactory)
> **satisfy** *verb*
> **satisfying** *adj.* (≠ unsatisfying)
> **satisfied** *adj.* (≠ dissatisfied) (≠ unsatisfied)

S

▼ SYNONYMS 同义词辨析

satisfaction

happiness • pride • contentment • fulfilment

These are all words for the good feeling that you have when you are happy or when you have achieved sth. 以上各词均指幸福、欣慰、满意的感觉和满足的心情。

satisfaction the good feeling that you have when you have achieved sth or when sth that you wanted to happen does happen 指取得成就、实现愿望时的满足、满意、欣慰： *He derived great satisfaction from knowing that his son was happy.* 得知儿子很幸福他深感欣慰。

happiness the good feeling that you have when you are happy 指幸福、快乐： *Money can't buy you happiness.* 金钱不能为你买到幸福。

pride a feeling of pleasure or satisfaction that you get when you or people who are connected with you have done sth well or own sth that other people admire 指自豪、骄傲、得意感： *The sight of her son graduating filled her with pride.* 儿子毕业的情景让她充满了自豪。

contentment (*rather formal*) a feeling of happiness or satisfaction with what you have 指对所拥有的一切感到满意、满足： *They found contentment in living a simple life.* 他们在简朴的生活中得到满足。

fulfilment a feeling of happiness or satisfaction with what you do or have done 指对所做的事感到满意、满足： *her search for personal fulfilment* 她对个人成就的追求

SATISFACTION, HAPPINESS, CONTENTMENT OR FULFILMENT? 用 satisfaction、happiness、contentment 还是 fulfilment?
You can feel **satisfaction** at achieving almost anything, small or large; you feel **fulfilment** when you do sth useful and enjoyable with your life. **Happiness** is the feeling you have when things give you pleasure and can be quite a lively feeling; **contentment** is a quieter feeling that you get when you have learned to find pleasure in things. 取得成就（无论大小）时的满足用 satisfaction；做了有益和令人愉快之事而感到满意时用 fulfilment；某些事情给人带来欢乐愉悦用 happiness；学会从事情中寻求快乐而内心平和的满足则用 contentment。

PATTERNS

- satisfaction/happiness/pride/contentment/fulfilment in sth
- **real** satisfaction/happiness/pride/contentment/fulfilment
- **true** satisfaction/happiness/contentment/fulfilment
- **great** satisfaction/happiness/pride
- **quiet** satisfaction/pride/contentment
- to **feel** satisfaction/happiness/pride/contentment
- to **bring sb** satisfaction/happiness/pride/contentment/fulfilment
- to **find** satisfaction/happiness/contentment/fulfilment

dealing with a complaint, a debt, an injury, etc. （抗议、投诉等的）妥善处理；（债务的）清偿；（伤害的）赔偿： *I complained to the manager but I didn't get any satisfaction.* 我向经理投诉，但问题丝毫没有得到解决。

IDM **to sb's satis'faction 1** if you do sth **to sb's satisfaction**, they are pleased with it 使某人满意： *The affair was settled to the complete satisfaction of the client.* 问题解决了，客户十分满意。 **2** if you prove sth **to sb's satisfaction**, they believe or accept it 使某人确信（或接受）： *Can you demonstrate to our satisfaction that your story is true?* 你能不能证实一下，让我们确信你说的是事实？

sat·is·fac·tory /ˌsætɪsˈfæktəri/ *adj.* good enough for a particular purpose 令人满意的；够好的；可以的 **SYN** **acceptable**: *a **satisfactory explanation/answer/solution/conclusion*** 令人满意的解释；站得住脚的回答；可行的解决办法；足以服人的结论 ◇ *The work is satisfactory but not outstanding.* 工作做得可以，但不出色。◇ *The existing law is not **entirely/wholly satisfactory**.* 现行法律并不十分完善。 **OPP** **unsatisfactory** ▶ **sat·is·fac·tor·ily** /-tərəli/ *adv.*: *Her disappearance has never been satisfactorily explained.* 她的失踪一直没有得到令人信服的解释。 ◇ *Our complaint was dealt with satisfactorily.* 我们的投诉得到了满意的处理。

sat·is·fied 🔑 /ˈsætɪsfaɪd/ *adj.* **1** 🔑 pleased because you have achieved sth or because sth that you wanted to happen has happened 满意的；满足的；欣慰的： *a satisfied smile* 满意的微笑 ◇ *a satisfied customer* 满意的顾客 ◇ **~ with sb/sth** *She's never satisfied with what she's got.* 她对自己的所得从不感到满足。 **OPP** **dissatisfied** ➲ SYNONYMS AT HAPPY **2** 🔑 **~ (that...)** | **~ (with sth)** believing or accepting that sth is true 确信的；信服的 **SYN** **convinced**: *I'm satisfied that they are telling the truth.* 我确信他们讲的是真话。 ➲ COMPARE UNSATISFIED

sat·isfy 🔑 /ˈsætɪsfaɪ/ *verb* (**sat·is·fies, sat·is·fy·ing, sat·is·fied, sat·is·fied**) **1** 🔑 **~ sb** (not used in the progressive tenses 不用于进行时) to make sb pleased by doing or giving them what they want 使满意；使满足： *Nothing satisfies him—he's always complaining.* 什么都难如他的意，他老在抱怨。 ◇ *The proposed plan will not satisfy everyone.* 拟议中的计划不会让所有人都满意。 **2** 🔑 **~ sth** to provide what is wanted, needed or asked for 满足（要求、需要等）： *The food wasn't enough to **satisfy his hunger**.* 这食物不足以让他解饿。◇ *to **satisfy sb's curiosity*** 满足某人的好奇心 ◇ *The education system must **satisfy the needs** of all children.* 教育体系必须满足所有儿童的需要。◇ *We cannot **satisfy demand** for the product.* 我们不能满足对该产品的需求。 ◇ *She failed to satisfy all the requirements for entry to the college.* 她没有达到进入那所学院的全部要求。 **3** 🔑 (not used in the progressive tenses 不用于进行时) (*formal*) to make sb certain sth is true or has been done 向…证实；使确信： **~ sb** *Her explanation did not satisfy the teacher.* 她的解释没有让老师信服。 ◇ **~ sb of sth** *People need to be satisfied of the need for a new system.* 需要使人们明白建立一个新体系的必要性。 ◇ **~ sb/yourself (that)...** *Once I had satisfied myself (that) it was the right decision, we went ahead.* 一旦我自己确信这个决定是正确的，我们便动手干了起来。

sat·is·fy·ing 🔑 /ˈsætɪsfaɪɪŋ/ *adj.* giving pleasure because it provides sth you need or want 令人满意（或满足）的： *a satisfying meal* 可口的饭菜 ◇ *a satisfying experience* 令人满意的经历 ◇ ***It's satisfying to** play a game really well.* 打一场出色的比赛是一件惬意的事。 ▶ **sat·is·fy·ing·ly** *adv.*

sat·nav (*also* **sat nav**) /ˈsætnæv/ *noun* [U, C] (*BrE*) the abbreviation for 'satellite navigation' (a computer system that uses information obtained from SATELLITES to guide the driver of a vehicle) 卫星导航（全写为 satellite navigation，利用接收到的卫星信息为驾车者导航的计算机系统）： *The drivers all have satnav in the van.* 司机都在货车里安装了卫星导航。 ➲ VISUAL VOCAB PAGE V56 ➲ COMPARE GPS

sat·sang /ˈsætsæŋ; *BrE also* ˈsʌtsʌŋ/ *noun* (*IndE*) a religious meeting where people read holy texts, think deeply about or talk about religious matters, etc. （印度教）灵修，读经会

sat·suma /sætˈsuːmə/ *noun* a type of small orange without seeds and with loose skin that comes off easily 萨摩蜜橘；无籽蜜橘

sat·ur·ate /ˈsætʃəreɪt/ *verb* **1** **~ sth** to make sth completely wet 使湿透；浸透 **SYN** **soak**: *The continuous rain had saturated the soil.* 连绵不断的雨把土地淋了个透。 **2** [often passive] **~ sth/sb (with/in sth)** to fill sth/sb completely with sth so that it is impossible or useless to add any more 使充满；使饱和： *The company had saturated the market for personal organizers* (= so that no new buyers could be found). 那家公司的产品已使电子记事簿市场饱和。

sat·ur·ated /ˈsætʃəreɪtɪd/ *adj.* **1** [not usually before noun] completely wet 湿透；浸透 **SYN** **soaked** ➲ SYNONYMS AT WET **2** [usually before noun] (*chemistry* 化) if a chemical SOLUTION (= a liquid with sth dissolved in it) is

saturated, it contains the greatest possible amount of the substance that has been dissolved in it（溶液）饱和的： *a saturated solution of sodium chloride* 氯化钠饱和溶液 ➲ WORDFINDER NOTE AT LIQUID **3** [usually before noun] (of colours 颜色) very strong 深的；浓的： *saturated reds* 深红色

ˌsaturated ˈfat *noun* [C, U] a type of fat found, for example, in butter, fried food and many types of meat, which encourages the harmful development of CHOLESTEROL 饱和脂肪（存在于黄油、煎炸食品和很多肉类中，能促使胆固醇增长，危害健康） ➲ SEE ALSO MONOUNSATURATED FAT, POLYUNSATURATED FAT, TRANS-FATTY ACID, UNSATURATED FAT

sat·ur·ation /ˌsætʃəˈreɪʃn/ *noun* [U] **1** (*often figurative*) the state or process that happens when no more of sth can be accepted or added because there is already too much of it or too many of them 饱和；饱和状态： *a business beset by price wars and **market saturation*** (= the fact that no new customers can be found) 一家受价格战和市场饱和困扰的企业 ◇ ***saturation bombing** of the city* (= covering the whole city) 对那座城市的全面轰炸 ◇ *There was **saturation coverage*** (= so much that it was impossible to avoid it or add to it) *of the event by the media.* 媒体对这一事件做了连篇累牍的报道。 **2** (*chemistry* 化) the degree to which sth is absorbed in sth else, expressed as a PERCENTAGE of the greatest possible 饱和度

▼SYNONYMS 同义词辨析

satisfying

rewarding • pleasing • gratifying • fulfilling

These words all describe an experience, activity or fact that gives you pleasure because it provides sth you need or want. 以上各词均形容经历、活动或现实令人满足或满意。

satisfying that gives you pleasure because it provides sth you need or want 指令人满意、满足： *It's satisfying to play a game really well.* 打一场出色的比赛是一件惬意的事。

rewarding (of an experience or activity) that makes you happy because you think it is useful or important; worth doing 指（经历或活动）有益的、有意义的、值得做的： *Nursing can be a very rewarding career.* 做护士可以是非常有意义的职业。

pleasing (*rather formal*) that gives you pleasure, especially to look at, hear or think about 尤指令看到、听到、想到的人高兴、满意： *It was a simple but pleasing design.* 这是一项简单但令人满意的设计。

gratifying (*formal*) that gives you pleasure, especially because it makes you feel that you have done well 指令人高兴，尤其对自己所做的事感到满意： *It is gratifying to see such good results.* 看到这么好的结果真令人欣慰。

fulfilling (of an experience or activity) that makes you happy, because it makes you feel your skills and talents are being used 指（经历或活动）使人感到有意义、欣慰、满足（因为自己的技能和才干得以发挥）： *I'm finding the work much more fulfilling now.* 我现在觉得这工作有意义多了。

SATISFYING, REWARDING OR FULFILLING? 用 satisfying、rewarding 还是 fulfilling?

Almost any experience, important or very brief, can be **satisfying. Rewarding** and **fulfilling** are used more for longer, more serious activities, such as jobs or careers. **Satisfying** and **fulfilling** are more about your personal satisfaction or happiness; **rewarding** is more about your sense of doing sth important and being useful to others. 几乎任何经历（重要的或短暂的）均可用 satisfying。rewarding 和 fulfilling 多指较长或较重要的活动有意义，如工作或职业。satisfying 和 fulfilling 多指带来个人的满足或幸福； rewarding 则多指所做之事重要的或对他人有益因而带给人满足感。

PATTERNS

- a satisfying/rewarding/gratifying/fulfilling **experience/feeling**
- (a) satisfying/rewarding/fulfilling **job/career/work**
- to **find sth** satisfying/rewarding/pleasing/gratifying

satuˈration point *noun* [U, sing.] **1** the stage at which no more of sth can be accepted or added because there is already too much of it or too many of them 饱和点；极限： *The market for computer games has reached saturation point.* 电脑游戏市场已达到饱和。 **2** (*chemistry* 化) the stage at which no more of a substance can be absorbed into a liquid or VAPOUR 饱和点

Sat·ur·day 🔑 /ˈsætədeɪ; -di; *NAmE* -tərd-/ *noun* [C, U] (*abbr.* **Sat.**) the day of the week after Friday and before Sunday 星期六 HELP To see how **Saturday** is used, look at the examples at **Monday**. * Saturday 的用法见词条 Monday 下的示例。 ORIGIN From the Old English for 'day of Saturn', translated from Latin *Saturni dies.* 源自古英语，原意为 day of Saturn（农神日），古英语则译自拉丁文 Saturni dies。

Sat·urn /ˈsætɜːn; -tən; *NAmE* -tɜːrn/ *noun* a large planet in the SOLAR SYSTEM that has rings around it and is 6th in order of distance from the sun 土星

Sat·ur·na·lia /ˌsætəˈneɪliə; *NAmE* -tərˈn-/ *noun* [U] an ancient Roman festival that took place in December, around the time that Christmas now takes place 萨图恩节，农神节（古罗马十二月份的节日，在如今圣诞节前后）

sat·ur·na·lian /ˌsætəˈneɪliən; *NAmE* -tərˈn-/ *adj.* **1** relating to Saturnalia 萨图恩节的；农神节的 **2** involving wild celebrations 狂欢的；热烈欢庆的

sat·ur·nine /ˈsætənaɪn; *NAmE* -tərn-/ *adj.* (*literary*) (of a person or their face 人或面部表情) looking serious and threatening 严肃而令人畏惧的；阴沉的

satyr /ˈsætə(r); *NAmE also* ˈseɪtər/ *noun* (in ancient Greek stories) a god of the woods, with a man's face and body and a GOAT'S legs and horns 萨堤尔（古希腊神话中半人半羊的森林之神）

sauce 🔑 /sɔːs/ *noun* **1** 🔑 [C, U] a thick liquid that is eaten with food to add flavour to it 调味汁；酱： ***tomato/cranberry/chilli, etc. sauce*** 番茄、越橘、辣椒等调味汁 ◇ *chicken in a white sauce* 白沙司鸡肉 ◇ *ice cream with a hot fudge sauce* 浇了热软糖汁的冰淇淋 ➲ SEE ALSO SOY SAUCE, TARTARE SAUCE, WHITE SAUCE **2** [U] (*old-fashioned, BrE, informal*) talk or behaviour that is annoying or lacking in respect 讨厌的话（或举动）；无礼的话（或举动） SYN **cheek**

IDM **what's ˌsauce for the ˈgoose is ˌsauce for the ˈgander** (*old-fashioned, saying*) what one person is allowed to do, another person must be allowed to do in a similar situation 适于此者亦应适于彼；应该一视同仁

ˈsauce boat *noun* a long low JUG used for serving or pouring sauce at a meal（船形）调味碟

sauce·pan /ˈsɔːspən; *NAmE* -pæn/ (*especially BrE*) (*NAmE usually* **pot**) *noun* a deep round metal pot with a lid and one long handle or two short handles, used for cooking things over heat（带盖，有一长柄或两耳的）深煮锅 ➲ VISUAL VOCAB PAGE V28

sau·cer /ˈsɔːsə(r)/ *noun* a small shallow round dish that a cup stands on; an object that is shaped like this 茶碟；茶托；碟状物： *cups and saucers* 茶杯和茶碟 ➲ VISUAL VOCAB PAGE V23 ➲ SEE ALSO FLYING SAUCER

saucy /ˈsɔːsi/ *adj.* (**sau·cier**, **sau·ci·est**) rude or referring to sex in a way that is amusing but not offensive 粗鲁的；粗俗的；不雅的；开色情玩笑的 SYN **cheeky**: *saucy jokes* 荤笑话 ◇ *a saucy smile* 无礼的一笑 ▸ **sau·cily** /-ɪli/ *adv.*

sauer·kraut /ˈsaʊəkraʊt; *NAmE* ˈsaʊərk-/ *noun* [U] (*from German*) CABBAGE (= a type of green vegetable) that is preserved in salt water and then cooked（酸）泡菜

S

sauna /ˈsɔːnə; ˈsaʊnə/ *noun* a period of time in which you sit or lie in a room (also called a sauna) which has been heated to a very high temperature. Some saunas involve the use of steam. 桑拿浴；蒸汽浴：*a hotel with a swimming pool and sauna* 带游泳池和桑拿浴室的旅馆 ◇ *to* ***have/take a sauna*** 洗桑拿浴

saun·ter /ˈsɔːntə(r)/ *verb* [I] **+ adv./prep.** to walk in a slow relaxed way 悠闲地走；漫步；闲逛 SYN **stroll**: *He sauntered by, looking as if he had all the time in the world.* 他悠闲地走过，仿佛时间对他来说是无穷无尽的。▶ **saun·ter** *noun* [sing.]: *This part of the route should be an easy saunter.* 这段路想必好走。

saur·ian /ˈsɔːriən/ *adj., noun* (*biology* 生)
■ ***adj.*** relating to LIZARDS 蜥蜴的
■ ***noun*** a large REPTILE, especially a DINOSAUR 大型爬行动物（尤指恐龙）

saus·age /ˈsɒsɪdʒ; *NAmE* ˈsɔːs-/ *noun* [C, U] a mixture of finely chopped meat, fat, bread, etc. in a long tube of skin, cooked and eaten whole or served cold in thin slices 香肠；腊肠：***beef/pork sausages*** 牛肉 / 猪肉香肠 ◇ *200g of garlic sausage* * 200 克蒜味香肠 ➲ SEE ALSO LIVER SAUSAGE
IDM **not a ˈsausage** (*old-fashioned, BrE, informal*) nothing at all 什么都没有

ˈsausage dog *noun* (*BrE, informal*) = DACHSHUND

ˈsausage meat *noun* [U] the mixture of finely chopped meat, fat, bread, etc. used for making sausages 香肠肉馅

ˌsausage ˈroll *noun* (*BrE*) a small tube of PASTRY filled with sausage meat and cooked 香肠卷（用油酥面皮卷上香肠肉馅烤制而成）

ˈsausage tree *noun* a large African tree that produces large grey fruit that hang downwards and have a similar shape to a sausage 香肠树，吊灯树，腊肠树（产于非洲，果实香肠状）

sauté /ˈsəʊteɪ; *NAmE* soʊˈteɪ/ *verb* (**sauté·ing, sautéed, sautéed** or **sauté·ing, sautéd, sautéd**) **~ sth** to fry food quickly in a little hot fat 嫩煎；炒 ▶ **sauté** *adj.* [only before noun]: *sauté potatoes* 煎土豆

sav·age /ˈsævɪdʒ/ *adj., noun, verb*
■ ***adj.*** **1** aggressive and violent; causing great harm 凶恶的；凶残的；损害严重的 SYN **brutal**: *savage dogs* 恶狗 ◇ *She had been badly hurt in what police described as 'a savage attack'.* 她遭受袭击而身受重伤，警方称这是一次"野蛮的袭击"。◇ *savage public spending cuts* 拼命削减公共开支 **2** involving very strong criticism 猛烈抨击的：*The article was a savage attack on the government's record.* 文章对政府的所作所为进行了猛烈的抨击。 **3** [only before noun] (*old-fashioned, taboo*) an offensive way of referring to groups of people or customs that are considered to be simple and not highly developed 蒙昧的；未开化的；野蛮的 SYN **primitive**: *a savage tribe* 野蛮部落 ▶ **sav·age·ly** *adv.*: *savagely attacked/criticized* 受到猛烈的攻击 / 批评 ◇ *'No!' he snarled savagely.* "不！"他恶狠狠地吼道。
■ ***noun*** **1** (*old-fashioned, taboo*) an offensive word for sb who belongs to a people that is simple and not developed 野蛮人；未开化的人：*the development of the human race from primitive savages* 人类走出蒙昧的演进过程 **2** a cruel and violent person 凶狠残暴的人：*He described the attack as the work of savages.* 他把这次袭击称为野蛮行径。
■ ***verb*** [usually passive] **1 ~ sb** (of an animal 动物) to attack sb violently, causing serious injury 凶狠地攻击（或伤害）；残害：*She was* ***savaged to death*** *by a bear.* 她遭熊袭击而丧命。 **2 ~ sb/sth** (*formal*) to criticize sb/sth severely 猛烈批评；激烈抨击：*Her latest novel has been savaged by the critics.* 她最近的一部小说受到评论家的猛烈批评。

sav·agery /ˈsævɪdʒri/ *noun* [U] behaviour that is very cruel and violent 残暴行为 SYN **violence**: *The police were shocked by the savagery of the attacks.* 警方对这些惨无人道的袭击感到震惊。

sa·van·nah (*also* **sa·vanna**) /səˈvænə/ *noun* [C, U] a wide flat open area of land, especially in Africa, that is covered with grass but has few trees 萨瓦纳（尤指非洲的稀树草原）➲ COMPARE VELD

sav·ant /ˈsævənt; *NAmE* sæˈvɑːnt/ *noun* (*formal*) **1** a person with great knowledge and ability 博学之士；学者；专家 **2** a person who is less intelligent than others but who has particular unusual abilities that other people do not have 独通一行的人；独开一窍的人

save 🔑 /seɪv/ *verb, noun, prep., conj.*
■ ***verb***
• **KEEP SAFE** 使安全 **1** 🔑 [T] to keep sb/sth safe from death, harm, loss, etc. 救；救助；挽救；拯救：**~ sb/sth** *to* ***save sb's life*** 救某人的命 ◇ *Doctors were unable to save her.* 医生未能把她救活。◇ *He's trying to save their marriage.* 他试图挽救他们的婚姻。◇ *She needs to win the next two games to save the match.* 只有下面的两场获胜，她才能挽回败局。◇ (*figurative*) *Thanks for doing that. You* ***saved my life*** (= helped me a lot). 谢谢你这么做。你帮了我大忙。◇ **~ sb/sth (from sth)** *to save a rare species (from extinction)* 拯救珍稀物种（免于灭绝）◇ **~ sb/sth from doing sth** *She saved a little girl from falling into the water.* 她救下一个眼看要落入水中的小女孩。
• **MONEY** 钱 **2** 🔑 [I, T] to keep money instead of spending it, especially in order to buy a particular thing 储蓄；攒钱：*I'm not very good at saving.* 我不大攒得住钱。◇ **~ (up) (for sth)** *I'm saving for a new bike.* 我正攒钱想买辆新自行车。◇ *We've been saving up to go to Australia.* 我们一直在攒钱，打算去澳大利亚。◇ **~ sth (up) (for sth)** *You should save a little each week.* 你应该每星期存一点钱。◇ *I've saved almost £100 so far.* 我至今已经攒了差不多 100 英镑了。
• **COLLECT STH** 收集 **3** [T] **~ sth** to collect sth because you like it or for a special purpose 收集；收藏：*I've been saving theatre programmes for years.* 我收藏剧院的节目单已有多年了。◇ *If you save ten tokens you can get a T-shirt.* 积十张礼品券便可得到一件 T 恤衫。
• **KEEP FOR FUTURE** 留存 **4** 🔑 [T] to keep sth to use or enjoy in the future 保留；保存：**~ sth (for sth/sb)** *He's saving his strength for the last part of the race.* 他保存体力，以便在比赛的最后阶段发力。◇ *We'll eat some now and save some for tomorrow.* 我们现在吃一些，留一些明天吃。◇ *Save some food for me.* 给我留点吃的。◇ **~ sb sth** *Save me some food.* 给我留点吃的。
• **NOT WASTE** 不浪费 **5** 🔑 [T, I] to avoid wasting sth or using more than necessary 节省；节约：**~ sth** *We'll take a cab to save time.* 我们坐出租车，好节省时间。◇ *Book early and save £50!* 及早订票，可省 50 英镑！◇ *We should try to save water.* 我们应设法节约用水。◇ **~ sth on sth** *The government is trying to save £1 million on defence.* 政府力图在国防开支上节约 100 万英镑。◇ **~ sb sth (on sth)** *If we go this way it will save us two hours on the trip.* 如果走这条路，可以缩短两小时的行程。◇ **~ on sth** *I save on fares by walking to work.* 我步行上班，可以省车钱。
• **AVOID STH BAD** 避免坏事 **6** 🔑 [T] to avoid doing sth difficult or unpleasant; to make sb able to avoid doing sth difficult or unpleasant 避免，免得（出现困难或不愉快的事）：**~ sb from doing sth** *The prize money saved her from having to find a job.* 这笔奖金使她不用非得找工作。◇ **~ sth** *She did it herself to save argument.* 她自己去做了，以免发生争论。◇ **~ sb sth** *Thanks for sending that letter for me—it saved me a trip.* 多谢你替我把那封信寄了，省得我跑一趟。◇ **~ doing sth** *He's grown a beard to save shaving.* 他留起了胡子，省得再刮脸。◇ **~ sb doing sth** *If you phone for an appointment, it'll save you waiting.* 如果电话预约，你就免得等了。
• **IN SPORT** 体育运动 **7** 🔑 [T, I] **~ (sth)** (in football (SOCCER), etc. 足球等) to prevent an opponent's shot from going in the goal 救球（阻碍对方得分）：*to save a penalty* 扑出一个点球 ◇ *The goalie saved Johnson's long-range shot.* 守门员扑出了约翰逊的远射。◇ (*BrE*) *The goalie saved brilliantly from Johnson's long-range shot.* 守门员漂亮地扑挡了约翰逊的远射。
• **COMPUTING** 计算机技术 **8** 🔑 [T, I] **~ (sth)** to make a computer keep work, for example by putting it on a disk 保存；存盘：*Save data frequently.* 资料要经常存盘。
IDM **not be able to do sth to ˌsave your ˈlife** (*informal*)

to be completely **unable to do sth** 完全干不了某事；死也做不了某事： *He can't interview people to save his life.* 要他的命，他也采访不了人。 **save sb's 'bacon/'neck** (*informal*) to rescue sb from a very difficult situation 解救某人摆脱困境 **save the 'day/situ'ation** to prevent failure or defeat, when this seems certain to happen 挽回败局；扭转局面： *Gerrard's late goal saved the day for Liverpool.* 杰拉德后来的进球为利物浦队挽回了败局。 **save (sb's) 'face** to avoid or help sb avoid embarrassment （使）保全面子： *She was fired, but she saved face by telling everyone she'd resigned.* 她被解雇了，但她爱面子，逢人便说是她辞职了。 **save your 'breath** (*informal*) used to tell sb that it is not worth wasting time and effort saying sth because it will not change anything 免费口舌： *Save your breath—you'll never persuade her.* 不用白费口舌了，你永远说服不了她。 **save your (own) 'skin/'hide/'neck** to try to avoid death, punishment, etc., especially by leaving others in an extremely difficult situation （尤指不惜置他人于困境而）保全自己的性命，使自己免受惩罚： *To save his own skin, he lied and blamed the accident on his friend.* 为了自保，他竟然说谎，把事故的责任推到朋友身上。

▪ ***noun*** (in football (SOCCER), etc. 足球等) an action by the GOALKEEPER that stops a goal being scored （守门员的）救球： *He made a spectacular save.* 他那扑救的动作令人叹为观止。

▪ ***prep.*** (*also* **save for**) (*old use* or *formal*) except sth 除了；除…外： *They knew nothing about her save her name.* 除名字外，他们对她一无所知。

▪ ***conj.*** (*old use* or *formal*) except 除了： *They found out nothing more save that she had borne a child.* 他们只查到她生过一个孩子，其他情况一无所知。

▼ **SYNONYMS 同义词辨析**

save

budget • economize • tighten your belt

These words all mean to spend less money. 以上各词均含存钱、节俭之义。

save to keep money instead of spending it, often in order to buy a particular thing 常指为了买某物而攒钱、储蓄： *I'm saving for a new car.* 我正攒钱想买辆新车。

budget to be careful about the amount of money you spend; to plan to spend an amount of money for a particular purpose 指谨慎花钱、把…编入预算： *If we budget carefully we'll be able to afford the trip.* 我们精打细算一点，就能够负担这次旅行。

economize to use less money, time, etc. than you normally use 指节省、节约、节俭

tighten your belt (*rather informal*) to spend less money because there is less available 指勒紧腰带省吃俭用： *With the price increases, we are all having to tighten our belts.* 由于物价上涨，我们都只好勒紧裤腰带了。

PATTERNS

- to save up/budget **for** sth
- to **have to** save/budget/economize/tighten our belts
- to **try to**/**manage to** save/budget/economize

▼ **SYNONYMS 同义词辨析**

save

rescue • bail out • redeem

These words all mean to prevent sb/sth from dying, losing sth, being harmed or embarrassed. 以上各词均含拯救、挽救、营救之义。

save to prevent sb/sth from dying, being harmed or destroyed or losing sth 指救、救助、挽救、拯救： *Doctors were unable to save him.* 医生未能把他救活。 ◇ *a campaign to save the panda from extinction* 一场拯救大熊猫免于灭绝的运动

rescue to save sb/sth from a dangerous or harmful situation 指营救、援救、抢救： *They were rescued by a passing cruise ship.* 他们被一艘经过的游轮救起。

bail sb out to rescue sb/sth from a difficult situation, especially by providing money 尤指资助某人脱离困境： *Don't expect me to bail you out if it all goes wrong.* 如果一切都搞砸了，就别指望我来解救你。

redeem (*formal, religion*) to save sb from the power of evil 指拯救、救赎： *He was a sinner, redeemed by the grace of God.* 他是一个罪人，承蒙上主的恩宠才获得救赎。 **NOTE** **Redeem** is also used in non-religious language in the phrase *redeem a situation*, which means to prevent a situation from being as bad as it might be. * redeem 亦用于非宗教语言中，如 redeem a situation 意为力挽狂澜。

PATTERNS

- to save/rescue/redeem sb/sth **from** sth
- to save/rescue/redeem a **situation**
- to save/redeem **sinners**/**mankind**
- to rescue sb/bail sb out **financially**

saver /ˈseɪvə(r)/ *noun* **1** a person who saves money and puts it in a bank, etc. for future use 储户；存户 **2** (*often in compounds* 常构成复合词) something that helps you spend less money or use less of the thing mentioned 有助于节省的事物： *a **money/time saver*** 省钱/省时的事物 ➲ SEE ALSO LIFESAVER

Savile Row /ˌsævl ˈrəʊ; *NAmE* ˈroʊ/ *noun* a street in London, England with many shops/stores that sell expensive clothes for men that are often specially made for each person 萨维尔街，裁缝街（英国伦敦的一条街道，聚集了售卖高档定制男装的店铺）： *He was wearing a Savile Row suit.* 他穿着在伦敦裁缝街定制的西装。

sav·ing /ˈseɪvɪŋ/ *noun* **1** [C] an amount of sth such as time or money that you do not need to use or spend 节省物；节省；节约： *Buy three and make a saving of 55p.* 买三件就能节省 55 便士。 ◇ *With the new boiler you can make big savings on fuel bills.* 用这种新锅炉，能省一大笔燃料开销。 **2** **savings** [pl.] money that you have saved, especially in a bank, etc. 储蓄金；存款： *He put all his savings into buying a boat.* 他用全部积蓄买了一条船。 ◇ *I opened a **savings account** at my local bank.* 我在本地银行开了一个储蓄账户。 ➲ COLLOCATIONS AT FINANCE **3** **-saving** (*in adjectives* 构成形容词) that prevents the waste of the thing mentioned or stops it from being necessary 节约的；节省…的： *energy-saving modifications* 节能改装 ◇ *labour-saving devices* 节省人力的装置 ◇ *space-saving fitted furniture* 节省空间的定做的家具 ➲ SEE ALSO FACE-SAVING

ˌsaving 'grace *noun* [usually sing.] the one good quality that a person or thing has that prevents them or it from being completely bad 仅有的优点；唯一可取之处

ˌsavings and 'loan association (*US*) (*BrE* **'building society**) *noun* (*abbr.* **S&L**) an organization like a bank that lends money to people who want to buy a house. People also save money with a building society. 房屋互助协会（提供住房贷款及储蓄服务）

sa·viour (*especially US* **sa·vior**) /ˈseɪvjə(r)/ *noun* **1** [usually sing.] a person who rescues sb/sth from a dangerous or difficult situation 救助者；拯救者；救星： *The new manager has been hailed as the saviour of the club.* 新任主教练被誉为俱乐部的救星。 **2** **the Saviour** [sing.] used in the Christian religion as another name for Jesus Christ 救主，救世主（耶稣基督）

'saviour sibling (*also* **savior sibling**) *noun* a child who is born through IVF in order to ensure that they have organs or cells that can be used to treat an older brother or sister with a serious medical condition 救命手足，兄姐救星（生下来是为了给患有重病的哥哥或姐姐提供器官或细胞移植的小孩，通过体外受精方式出生）

savoir faire /ˌsævwɑː ˈfeə(r); *NAmE* ˌsævwɑːr ˈfer/ *noun* [U] (*from French, approving*) the ability to behave in the appropriate way in social situations （应付裕如的）社交能力，处世能力

S

sa·vory (*NAmE*) = SAVOURY

sa·vour (*especially US* **savor**) /ˈseɪvə(r)/ *verb, noun*

■ ***verb*** **1** ~ **sth** to enjoy the full taste or flavour of sth, especially by eating or drinking it slowly 品味；细品；享用 SYN **relish**: *He ate his meal slowly, savouring every mouthful.* 他慢慢地吃着，细细地品味每一口美食。 **2** ~ **sth** to enjoy a feeling or an experience thoroughly 体会；体味；享受 SYN **relish**: *I wanted to savour every moment.* 我要细心品味，一刻也不错过。

PHR V **ˈsavour of sth** [no passive] (*formal*) to seem to have an amount of sth, especially sth bad 意味着；有点…，带有几分…（尤指坏事）： *His recent comments savour of hypocrisy.* 他最近那番评论显得有点虚伪。

■ ***noun*** [usually sing.] (*formal* or *literary*) a taste or smell, especially a pleasant one （尤指美好的）味道，气味，滋味: (*figurative*) *For Emma, life had lost its savour.* 对埃玛来说，生活已失去乐趣。

sa·voury (*especially US* **sa·vory**) /ˈseɪvəri/ *adj., noun*

■ ***adj.*** **1** having a taste that is salty, not sweet 咸味的；咸口的: *savoury snacks* 咸味点心 ➲ **WORDFINDER NOTE** AT TASTE **2** having a pleasant taste or smell 好吃的；好闻的；香的；美味的: *a savoury smell from the kitchen* 从厨房里传来的香味 ➲ SEE ALSO UNSAVOURY ➲ **MORE LIKE THIS** 23, page R27

■ ***noun*** [usually pl.] (*pl.* **-ies**) a small amount of a food with a salty taste, not a sweet one, often served at a party, etc. （在聚会等活动中常吃的）咸味小吃

savoy /səˈvɔɪ/ (*also* **saˌvoy ˈcabbage**) *noun* [U, C] a type of CABBAGE with leaves that are not smooth 皱叶甘蓝

savvy /ˈsævi/ *noun, adj.*

■ ***noun*** [U] (*informal*) practical knowledge or understanding of sth 实际知识；见识；了解: *political savvy* 政治见识

■ ***adj.*** (**sav·vier**, **sav·vi·est**) (*informal*) having practical knowledge and understanding of sth; having COMMON SENSE 有见识的；懂实际知识的；通情达理的: *savvy shoppers* 精明的购物者

saw /sɔː/ *noun, verb* ➲ SEE ALSO SEE *n.*

■ ***noun*** **1** (often in compounds 常构成复合词) a tool that has a long blade with sharp points (called TEETH) along one of its edges. A saw is moved backwards and forwards by hand or driven by electricity and is used for cutting wood or metal. 锯 ➲ SEE ALSO CHAINSAW, CIRCULAR SAW, FRETSAW, HACKSAW, HANDSAW, JIGSAW (3) **2** (*old-fashioned*) a short phrase or sentence that states a general truth about life or gives advice 谚语；格言

■ ***verb*** (**sawed**, **sawn** /sɔːn/) (*NAmE also* **sawed**, **sawed**) **1** [I, T] to use a saw to cut sth 锯: *The workmen sawed and hammered all day.* 工人整天又锯又锤。 ◇ **+ adv./prep.** *He accidentally sawed through a cable.* 他不小心锯断了电缆。 ◇ **~ sth (+ adv./prep.)** *She sawed the plank in half.* 她把木板锯成两截。 **2** [I, T] ~ (**away**) (**at sth**) | ~ **sth** to move sth backwards and forwards on sth as if using a saw 拉锯似的来回移动（某物）: *She sawed away at her violin.* 她不停地拉着小提琴。 ◇ *He was sawing energetically at a loaf of bread.* 他正用力切着一条面包。

PHR V **ˌsaw sth↔ˈdown** to cut sth and bring it to the ground using a saw 锯倒: *The tree had to be sawn down.* 这棵树只好锯倒。 **ˌsaw sth↔ˈoff** | **ˌsaw sth ˈoff sth** to remove sth by cutting it with a saw 锯掉；锯去: *We sawed the dead branches off the tree.* 我们锯掉了树上的枯枝。 **ˌsaw sth↔ˈup** (**into sth**) to cut sth into pieces with a saw 把…锯成（小块或碎片）: *We sawed the wood up into logs.* 我们把木头锯成很多块木材。

saw·dust /ˈsɔːdʌst/ *noun* [U] very small pieces of wood that fall as powder when wood is cut with a SAW 锯末

saw·horse /ˈsɔːhɔːs; *NAmE* -hɔːrs/ *noun* a wooden frame that supports wood that is being cut with a SAW 锯木架

sawm /saʊm; *NAmE* soʊm/ *noun* [U] the Muslim practice of not eating or drinking in the day during the ninth month of the Muslim year, called RAMADAN 斋戒（伊斯兰历九月里的日间禁饮食）

saw·mill /ˈsɔːmɪl/ *noun* a factory in which wood is cut into boards using machinery 锯木厂

ˌsawn-off ˈshotgun (*BrE*) (*NAmE* **ˌsawed-off ˈshotgun**) *noun* a SHOTGUN with part of its BARREL cut off 枪管锯短的猎枪

sax /sæks/ *noun* (*informal*) = SAXOPHONE

Saxon /ˈsæksn/ *noun* a member of a race of people once living in NW Germany, some of whom settled in Britain in the 5th and 6th centuries 撒克逊人（早期居住在今德国西北部，后其中一部分于 5、6 世纪定居在不列颠） ➲ SEE ALSO ANGLO-SAXON ► **Saxon** *adj.* : *Saxon churches/kings* 撒克逊教堂 / 国王

saxo·phone /ˈsæksəfəʊn; *NAmE* -foʊn/ (*also informal* **sax**) *noun* a metal musical instrument that you blow into, used especially in JAZZ 萨克斯管 ➲ **VISUAL VOCAB** PAGE V38

sax·opho·nist /sækˈsɒfənɪst; *NAmE* ˈsæksəfoʊnɪst/ *noun* a person who plays the saxophone 萨克斯管演奏者

say /seɪ/ *verb, noun, exclamation*

■ ***verb*** (**says** /sez/, **said**, **said** /sed/)

• **SPEAK** 说 **1** [I, T] to speak or tell sb sth, using words 说；讲；告诉: **+ speech** *'Hello!' she said.* "你好！"她说。 ◇ *'That was marvellous,' said Daniel.* "好极了。"丹尼尔说。 HELP In stories the subject often comes after **said**, **says** or **say** when it follows the actual words spoken, unless it is a pronoun. 在故事、小说中用于直接引语后面时，往往先出 said、says 或 say，再出主语，除非主语是代词。 ◇ **~ sth** *Be quiet, I have something to say.* 安静，我有话要说。 ◇ *I didn't believe a word she said.* 她说的话我一个字都不信。 ◇ *That's a terrible* ***thing to say.*** 这话说不得。 ◇ *He knew that if he wasn't back by midnight, his parents would* ***have something to say about it*** (= be angry). 他知道，要是他半夜还不回去，父母就会不高兴。 ◇ **~ sth to sb** *She said nothing to me about it.* 她没有跟我说过这件事。 ◇ **~ to sb/yourself + speech** ***I said to myself*** (= thought), *'That can't be right!'* 我心里想："这不对呀！" ◇ **~ (that)...** *He said (that) his name was Sam.* 他说他叫萨姆。 ◇ **it is said that...** *It is said that she lived to be over 100.* 据说她活了 100 多岁。 ◇ **~ (what, how, etc....)** *She finds it hard to say what she feels.* 她觉得心里的感受难以言述。 ◇ *'That's impossible!' '****So you say*** (= but I think you may be wrong).' "这不可能！" "不见得。" ◇ *'Why can't I go out now?' 'Because* ***I say so.****'* "为什么现在我不能出去？" "我说不行就不行。" ◇ *'What do you want it for?' '****I'd rather not say.****'* "你要这做什么？" "我还是不说的好。" ◇ **~ to do sth** *He said to meet him here.* 他说来这儿跟他见面。 ◇ **sb/sth is said to be/have sth** *He is said to have been a brilliant scholar.* 据说他曾是个了不起的学者。 ➲ **EXPRESS YOURSELF** AT INTERRUPT

• **REPEAT WORDS** 复述 **2** [T] **~ sth** to repeat words, phrases, etc. 念；朗诵；背诵: *to say a prayer* 祷告 ◇ *Try to say that line with more conviction.* 朗诵这一句时语气要更加坚定。

• **EXPRESS OPINION** 表达见解 **3** [T, I] to express an opinion on sth 表达，表述（见解）: **~ sth** ***Say what you like*** (= although you disagree) *about her, she's a fine singer.* 随你怎么说，反正她唱歌唱得很好。 ◇ ***I'll say this for them,*** *they're a very efficient company.* 我要为他们说句公道话，他们公司的效率的确很高。 ◇ *Anna thinks I'm lazy—****what do you say*** (= what is your opinion)? 安娜觉得我懒，你说呢？ ◇ **~ (that)...** ***I can't say I blame her*** *for resigning* (= I think she was right). 她辞职，我不能说她不对。 ◇ ***I say*** (= suggest) *we go without them.* 依我说，我们自己去，不带他们。 ◇ ***I wouldn't say*** *they were rich* (= in my opinion they are not rich). 要我说的话，他们并不富裕。 ◇ ***That's not to say*** *it's a bad movie* (= it is good but it is not without faults). 并不是说这部电影很糟糕。 ◇ **~ (what, how, etc....)** ***It's hard to say*** *what caused the accident.* 很难说造成事故的原因是什么。 ◇ *'When will it be finished?' '****I couldn't say*** (= I don't know).' "什么时候能完？" "不好说。"

• **GIVE EXAMPLE** 举例 **4** [T, no passive] to suggest or give sth as an example or a possibility 比方说；假设: **~ sth/sb** *You could learn the basics in,* ***let's say,*** *three months.* 比方说，三个月你就可以掌握基本知识。 ◇ *Let's take any writer, say* (= for example) *Dickens...* 我们随便举一个作家为例，比如说狄更斯… ◇ **~ (that)...** *Say you lose your job: what would you do then?* 假设你把工作丢了，那你怎么办呢？

• **SHOW THOUGHTS/FEELINGS** 表明思想 / 感情 **5** [T] **~ sth (to sb)** to make thoughts, feelings, etc. clear to sb by using words, looks, movements, etc. 表明，显示，表达（思想、感情）： *His angry glance **said it all**.* 他那愤愤的一瞥就道出了一切。◇ *That **says it all** really, doesn't it?* (= it shows clearly what is true) 这实际上就说明了一切，是不是？ ◇ *Just what is the artist trying to say in her work?* 这位艺术家究竟要在作品中表现什么呢？

• **GIVE WRITTEN INFORMATION** 标示 **6** [T, no passive] (of sth that is written or can be seen 书面材料或可见的东西) to give particular information or instructions 提供信息；指示： **+ speech** *The notice said 'Keep Out'.* 告示上写着"禁止入内"。◇ **~ sth** *The clock said three o'clock.* 时钟显示三点整。◇ **~ (that)...** *The instructions say (that) we should leave it to set for four hours.* 说明书上说我们应让它凝结四小时。◇ **~ where, why, etc....** *The book doesn't say where he was born.* 书上没说他是在哪儿出生的。◇ **~ to do sth** *The guidebook says to turn left.* 旅游指南上说应向左拐。

▼ WHICH WORD? 词语辨析

say / tell

• **Say** never has a person as the object. You **say something** or **say something to somebody**. **Say** is often used when you are giving somebody's exact words. * say 从不以人作宾语，可说 say something 或 say something to somebody。say 常与直接引语连用： *'Sit down,' she said.* "坐下。"她说。◇ *Anne said, 'I'm tired.'* 安妮说："我累了。"◇ *Anne said (that) she was tired.* 安妮说她累了。◇ *What did he say to you?* 他对你说了些什么？ You cannot use 'say about', but **say something about** is correct. 不能用 say about，但可说 say something about： *I want to say something/a few words/a little about my family.* 我想谈谈我的家庭。 **Say** can also be used with a clause when the person you are talking to is not mentioned. 没有指明说话对象时，say 亦可与从句连用： *She didn't say what she intended to do.* 她没说她想做什么。

• **Tell** usually has a person as the object and often has two objects. * tell 常带有两个宾语，其中一个通常是人： *Have you told him the news yet?* 你告诉他这消息了吗？ It is often used with 'that' clauses. 该词常与 that 从句连用： *Anne told me (that) she was tired.* 安妮对我说她累了。 **Tell** is usually used when somebody is giving facts or information, often with *what, where*, etc. * tell 通常在某人告知事实或提供信息时使用，常与 what、where 等词连用： *Can you tell me when the movie starts?* 你能告诉我电影什么时候开演吗？(BUT 但： *Can you give me some information about the school?* 你能给我讲讲这所学校的情况吗？) **Tell** is also used when you are giving somebody instructions. 发出指示时亦可用 tell： *The doctor told me to stay in bed.* 医生要我卧床休息。◇ *The doctor told me (that) I had to stay in bed.* 医生对我说我必须卧床休息。 OR 或： *The doctor said (that) I had to stay in bed.* 医生说我必须卧床休息。 NOT 不能说： ~~*The doctor said me to stay in bed.*~~

IDM **before you can say Jack 'Robinson** (*old-fashioned*) very quickly; in a very short time 转瞬间；一刹那；说时迟，那时快 **ˌgo without 'saying** to be very obvious or easy to predict 不用说；显而易见： *Of course I'll help you. That goes without saying.* 我当然会帮你。这还用说吗？ **have something, nothing, etc. to 'say for yourself** to be ready, unwilling, etc. to talk or give your views on sth 有话（或没什么等）要说： *She doesn't have much to say for herself* (= doesn't take part in conversation). 她没多少要说的。◇ *He had plenty to say for himself* (= he had a lot of opinions and was willing to talk). 他有一肚子的话要说。◇ *Late again—what have you got to say for yourself* (= what is your excuse)? 又迟到了，这回你有什么借口呢？ **ˌhaving 'said that** (*informal*) used to introduce an opinion that makes what you have just said seem less strong（用以缓和语气）虽然这么说，话虽如此： *I sometimes get worried in this job. Having said that, I enjoy doing it, it's a challenge.* 我有时会为这份工作而感到忧虑。话虽如此，我还是很喜欢干的，因为这是一个挑战。 **'I'll say!** (*old-fashioned, informal*) used for emphasis to say 'yes'（明确表示肯定）当然，没错： *'Does she see him often?' 'I'll say! Nearly every day.'* "她常去找他吗？""没错！差不多天天去。" **I 'must say** (*informal*) used to emphasize an opinion（强调所发表的意见）我必须说： *Well, I must say, that's the funniest thing I've heard all week.* 嘿，我要说，这是我整整一周听到的最好笑的事情。 **ˌI 'say** (*old-fashioned, BrE, informal*) **1** used to express surprise, shock, etc.（表示惊奇、震惊等）： *I say! What a huge cake!* 乖乖！多大的一个蛋糕啊！ **2** used to attract sb's attention or introduce a new subject of conversation（用以引起注意或引出新的话题）： *I say, can you lend me five pounds?* 我说，你能借我五英镑吗？ **it says a 'lot, very 'little, etc. for sb/sth** (*informal*) it shows a good/bad quality that sb/sth has 说明某人（或某事物）很好（或不怎么样等）： *It says a lot for her that she never lost her temper.* 她从没发过脾气，这说明她很有涵养。◇ *It didn't say much for their efficiency that the order arrived a week late.* 订货晚到了一个星期，可见他们的效率难以恭维。 **I ˌwouldn't say 'no (to sth)** (*informal*) used to say that you would like sth or to accept sth that is offered（表示想要或愿意接受某物）： *I wouldn't say no to a pizza.* 我倒是想来块比萨饼。◇ *'Tea, Brian?' 'I wouldn't say no.'* "要喝茶吗，布赖恩？""好哇。" **ˌleast 'said ˌsoonest 'mended** (*BrE, saying*) a bad situation will pass or be forgotten most quickly if nothing more is said about it 只要没人再说，事情就会过去 **the less/least said the 'better** the best thing to do is say as little as possible about sth 少说为妙 **ˌnever say 'die** (*saying*) do not stop hoping 别泄气；别气馁；不言放弃 **not say boo to a 'goose** (*BrE*) (*NAmE* **not say boo to 'anyone**) to be very shy or gentle 非常胆怯；十分温和： *He's so nervous he wouldn't say boo to a goose.* 他紧张得连大气都不敢喘。 **'not to say** used to introduce a stronger way of describing sth（引出语气更重的描述）即使不是…，虽不能说…： *a difficult, not to say impossible, task* 即便不是办不到，也是难办到的一项任务 **say 'cheese** used to ask sb to smile before you take their photograph（照相前请人微笑时）说"茄子"；笑一笑 **say 'no (to sth)** to refuse an offer, a suggestion, etc. 拒绝；谢绝： *If you don't invest in this, you're saying no to a potential fortune.* 你如果不在这上面投资，那是存心不想发财。 **ˌsay no 'more** (*informal*) used to say that you understand exactly what sb means or is trying to say, so it is unnecessary to say anything more 我早知道了；还用你说： *'They went to Paris together.' 'Say no more!'* "他们一起去了巴黎。""我早知道了！" **ˌsay your 'piece** to say exactly what you feel or think 说出心里话 **say 'what?** (*NAmE, informal*) used to express surprise at what sb has just said（表示惊奇）你说什么： *'He's getting married.' 'Say what?'* "他快结婚了。""你说什么？" **say 'when** used to ask sb to tell you when you should stop pouring a drink or serving food for them because they have enough（给饮料或食物时说）够了请说一声 **'that is to say** in other words 换句话说；也就是说： *three days from now, that is to say on Friday* 三天以后，也就是说星期五 **that's not 'saying much** used to say that sth is not very unusual or special 也没什么了不起；这说明不了什么： *She's a better player than me, but that's not saying much* (= because I am a very bad player). 她比我高明，但那也没什么了不起（因为我很差）。 **that 'said** used to introduce an opinion that makes what you have just said seem less strong（用以缓和语气）话虽如此 **there's no 'saying** used to say that it is impossible to predict what might happen 说不准；很难说： *There's no saying how he'll react.* 很难说他会有何种反应。 **there's something, not much, etc. to be said for sth/doing sth** there are/are not good reasons for doing sth, believing sth or agreeing with sth 有（或没有太多等）理由去做（或相信、同意）某事 **to ˌsay the 'least** without exaggerating at all 毫不夸张地说： *I was surprised, to say the least.* 毫不夸张地说，我感到吃惊。 **to say 'nothing of sth** used to introduce a further fact or thing in addition to those already mentioned 更不用说…；而且还 **SYN** **not to**

S

mention: *It was too expensive, to say nothing of the time it wasted.* 这太贵了，更不用说它浪费的时间了。**well 'said!** (*informal*) I agree completely 说得好；完全赞同：*'We must stand up for ourselves.' 'Well said, John.'* "我们必须自己起来保护自己。""说得好，约翰。" **,what do/would you 'say (to sth/doing sth)** (*informal*) would you like sth/to do sth? 你同意…吗；你看…好不好：*What do you say to eating out tonight?* 今晚到外边吃饭，怎么样？◇ *Let's go away for a weekend. What do you say?* 我们出去过周末，你说好不好？**what/whatever sb says, 'goes** (*informal, often humorous*) a particular person must be obeyed 凡是…说的，都得照办；无论…说什么，都能行得通：*Sarah wanted the kitchen painted green, and what she says, goes.* 萨拉想把厨房刷成绿色，而她说什么，就得照办。**what-ever you 'say** (*informal*) used to agree to sb's suggestion because you do not want to argue（因不想争论而同意）由你，随你 **when ,all is said and 'done** when everything is considered 说到底；毕竟；归根到底：*I know you're upset, but when all's said and done it isn't exactly a disaster.* 我知道你挺沮丧的，但说到底，事情并没什么大不了的。**who can 'say (...)?** used to say that nobody knows the answer to a question 谁知道（…）：*Who can say what will happen next year?* 谁能说得出明年会发生什么事？**who 'says (...)?** (*informal*) used to disagree with a statement or an opinion（表示不同意）谁说（…）：*Who says I can't do it?* 谁说我干不了这个？**who's to say (...)?** used to say that sth might happen or might have happened in a particular way, because nobody really knows（表示说不定某事会发生或本来会发生）谁说得准（…）：*Who's to say we would not have succeeded if we'd had more time?* 要是时间更充裕，没准儿我们就已成功了，谁说得准呢？**you can say 'that again** (*informal*) I agree with you completely 让你说对了；一点没错；正是这样：*'He's in a bad mood today.' 'You can say that again!'* "他今天情绪不好。""让你说对了！" **you can't say 'fairer (than 'that)** (*BrE, informal*) used to say that you think the offer you are making is reasonable or generous（出价时说）再公道不过了：*Look, I'll give you £100 for it. I can't say fairer than that.* 你看，我出 100 英镑买它，这再公道不过了。**you don't 'say!** (*informal, often ironic*) used to express surprise 我就知道；不会吧；不至于吧：*'They left without us.' 'You don't say!'* (= I'm not surprised) "他们撇下我们自个儿走了。""真的吗？" **you 'said it!** (*informal*) **1** (*BrE*) used to agree with sb when they say sth about themselves that you would not have been rude enough to say yourself（同意对方所作而碍于礼貌自己不便作出的评价）这话可是你说的：*'I know I'm not the world's greatest cook.' 'You said it!'* "我知道我的饭菜做得不是太好。""这话可是你说的！" **2** (*NAmE*) used to agree with sb's suggestion（同意对方的提议）正合我心意 ➲ MORE AT DARE *v.*, EASY *adv.*, ENOUGH *pron.*, GLAD, LET *v.*, MEAN *v.*, MIND *v.*, NEEDLESS, RECORD *n.*, SOON, SORRY *adj.*, SUFFICE, WORD *n.*

■ ***noun*** [sing., U] ~ (**in** sth) the right to influence sth by giving your opinion before a decision is made 决定权；发言权：*We had no say in the decision to sell the company.* 在决定出售公司的问题上，我们没有发言权。◇ *People want a greater say in local government.* 人们要求在当地的政务中有更大的发言权。◇ *The judge has the final say on the sentence.* 法官对判决有最后的决定权。

IDM **have your 'say** (*informal*) to have the opportunity to express yourself fully about sth 有机会充分发表意见：*She won't be happy until she's had her say.* 她要把话都说出来才舒畅。➲ SEE ALSO SAY YOUR PIECE at SAY *v.*

■ ***exclamation*** (*NAmE, informal*) **1** used for showing surprise or pleasure（表示惊讶或兴奋）嘿，啧啧：*Say, that's a nice haircut!* 啧啧，这个头发剪得很漂亮！**2** used for attracting sb's attention or for making a suggestion or comment（提请别人注意、提出建议或作出评论）喂，我说：*Say, how about going to a movie tonight?* 我说，今晚去看场电影怎么样？

say·ing /ˈseɪɪŋ/ *noun* a well-known phrase or statement that expresses sth about life that most people believe is wise and true 谚语；格言；警句：*'Accidents will happen', as the saying goes.* 常言道："意外事，总难免。"

'say-so *noun* [sing.] (*informal*) permission that sb gives to do sth 许可；准许：*Nothing could be done without her say-so.* 未经她准许，什么都不可以做。

IDM **on sb's 'say-so** based on a statement that sb makes without giving any proof 仅凭某人的空口白话；听信某人不实之词：*He hired and fired people on his partner's say-so.* 他雇谁辞谁全听他的合伙人的一句话。

'S-bend *noun* a bend in a road or pipe that is shaped like an S（道路或管道的）S 形弯

scab /skæb/ *noun* **1** [C] a hard dry covering that forms over a wound as it heals 痂 **2** [U] a skin disease of animals（动物）疥癣 **3** [U] a disease of plants, especially apples and potatoes, that causes a rough surface（植物）疮痂病，斑点病 **4** [C] (*informal, disapproving*) a worker who refuses to join a strike or takes the place of sb on strike 拒绝参加罢工的工人；顶替罢工者上班的工人；工贼 SYN **blackleg**

scab·bard /ˈskæbəd; *NAmE* -bərd/ *noun* a cover for a SWORD that is made of leather or metal（刀、剑的）鞘 SYN **sheath**

scab·by /ˈskæbi/ *adj.* covered in scabs 结痂的；有痂的

sca·bies /ˈskeɪbiːz/ *noun* [U] a skin disease that causes ITCHING and small red raised spots 疥疮

scab·rous /ˈskeɪbrəs; ˈskæb-/ *adj.* **1** (*formal*) offensive or shocking in a sexual way 猥亵的；淫秽的；有伤风化的 SYN **indecent** **2** (*specialist*) having a rough surface 表面粗糙的 SYN **scaly**：*scabrous skin* 粗糙的皮肤

scads /skædz/ *noun* [pl.] ~ (**of** sth) (*informal, especially NAmE*) large numbers or amounts of sth 大量；许多：*scads of $20 bills* 许多 20 美元的钞票

scaf·fold /ˈskæfəʊld; *NAmE* -foʊld/ *noun* **1** a platform used when EXECUTING criminals by cutting off their heads or hanging them from a rope 断头台；绞刑架 **2** a structure made of scaffolding, for workers to stand on when they are working on a building 脚手架；建筑架；鹰架

scaf·fold·ing /ˈskæfəldɪŋ/ *noun* [U] poles and boards that are joined together to make a structure for workers to stand on when they are working high up on the outside wall of a building 脚手架（组）；鹰架 ➲ WORDFINDER NOTE AT CONSTRUCTION

scal·able (*BrE* **scaleable**) /ˈskeɪləbl/ *adj.* **1** used to describe a computer, a network, software, etc. that can be adapted to meet greater needs in the future（计算机、网络、软件等）可扩展的，可升级的：*A business database needs to be scalable.* 商业数据库需要具备可以升级的条件。**2** designed to work on a large or small scale, according to needs 可改变大小的；可缩放的：*scalable graphics* 可变更大小的图形 ▶ **scal·abil·ity** *noun* [U]：*New database technology offers scalability for future growth.* 新的数据库技术为未来的发展提供了可扩展性。

sca·lar /ˈskeɪlə(r)/ *adj.* (*mathematics* 数) (of a quantity 量) having size but no direction 标量的；纯量的；无向量的 ▶ **sca·lar** *noun* ➲ COMPARE VECTOR (1)

scala·wag /ˈskæləwæg/ (*NAmE*) (*especially BrE* **scally·wag**) *noun* (*informal*) a person, especially a child, who behaves badly, but not in a serious way 调皮捣蛋的人，淘气鬼（尤指儿童）SYN **scamp**

scald /skɔːld/ *verb, noun*

■ ***verb*** ~ **sth/yourself** to burn yourself or part of your body with very hot liquid or steam 烫伤：*Be careful not to scald yourself with the steam.* 小心别让蒸汽把你烫着。◇ (*figurative*) *Tears scalded her eyes.* 她热泪盈眶。➲ SYNONYMS AT BURN ➲ COLLOCATIONS AT INJURY

■ ***noun*** an injury to the skin from very hot liquid or steam 烫伤

scald·ing /ˈskɔːldɪŋ/ *adj.* hot enough to SCALD 滚烫的；灼热的：*scalding water* 滚烫的水 ◇ (*figurative*) *Scalding tears poured down her face.* 滚烫的泪水从她脸上扑簌簌地流下来。▶ **scald·ing** *adv.*：*scalding hot* 灼热

scale 🔑 /skeɪl/ *noun, verb*

■ ***noun***

• SIZE 规模 **1** 🔑 [sing., U] the size or extent of sth, especially when compared with sth else（尤指与其他事物相比较时的）规模，范围，程度： *They entertain **on a large scale*** (= they hold expensive parties with a lot of guests). 他们大宴宾客。◇ *Here was corruption **on a grand scale**.* 这里的腐败现象曾十分严重。◇ *On a global scale, 77% of energy is created from fossil fuels.* 全球 77% 的能量产生自化石燃料。◇ *to achieve **economies of scale** in production* (= to produce many items so the cost of producing each one is reduced) 生产实现规模经济 ◇ **~ of sth** *It was impossible to comprehend **the full scale** of the disaster.* 这场灾难的深重程度当时还无法充分认识。◇ *It was not until morning that **the sheer scale** of the damage could be seen* (= how great it was). 直到早晨才看清了损害的严重程度。➲ SEE ALSO FULL-SCALE, LARGE-SCALE, SMALL-SCALE

• RANGE OF LEVELS 等级 **2** 🔑 [C] a range of levels or numbers used for measuring sth 等级；级别： *a five-point pay scale* 五分制工资等级 ◇ *to evaluate performance on a scale from 1 to 10* 按 1 到 10 级来评估业绩 ➲ SEE ALSO RICHTER SCALE, SLIDING SCALE, TIMESCALE **3** 🔑 [C, usually sing.] the set of all the different levels of sth, from the lowest to the highest 等级体系： ***At the other end of the scale**, life is a constant struggle to get enough to eat.* 对于处在社会最底层的人来说，生活就是为吃饱肚子而不断挣扎的过程。◇ *the social scale* 社会等级体系

• MARKS FOR MEASURING 衡量标度 **4** 🔑 [C] a series of marks at regular intervals on an instrument that is used for measuring 标度；刻度： *How much does it read on the scale?* 刻度显示的是多少？

• WEIGHING INSTRUMENT 衡器 **5** 🔑 **scales** [pl.] (*NAmE also* **scale**) an instrument for weighing people or things 秤；磅秤；天平： ***bathroom/kitchen/weighing scales*** 浴室秤；厨房用秤；秤 ◇ (*figurative*) *the scales of justice* (= represented as the two pans on a BALANCE (5)) 法律的天平 ➲ VISUAL VOCAB PAGE V25

• OF MAP/DIAGRAM/MODEL 地图；图表；模型 **6** 🔑 [C] the relation between the actual size of sth and its size on a map, diagram or model that represents it 比例；比例尺： *a scale of 1:25 000* * 1:25 000 的比例 ◇ ***a scale model/drawing*** 按比例缩放的模型 / 图画 ◇ *Both plans are drawn to the same scale.* 两张平面图是按同一比例绘制的。◇ *Is this diagram **to scale*** (= are all its parts the same size and shape in relation to each other as they are in the thing represented)? 这个示意图是按比例画的吗？➲ WORDFINDER NOTE AT MAP

• IN MUSIC 音乐 **7** [C] a series of musical notes moving upwards or downwards, with fixed intervals between each note, especially a series of eight starting on a particular note 音阶： *the scale of C major* * C 大调音阶 ◇ *to practise scales on the piano* 在钢琴上练习音阶 ➲ COMPARE KEY *n.* (5), OCTAVE

• OF FISH/REPTILE 鱼；爬行动物 **8** [C] any of the thin plates of hard material that cover the skin of many fish and REPTILES 鳞；鳞片

• IN WATER PIPES, ETC. 水管等 **9** (*BrE also* **fur**) [U] a hard greyish-white substance that is sometimes left inside water pipes and containers for heating water 水垢；水锈 ➲ SEE ALSO LIMESCALE

• ON TEETH 牙齿 **10** [U] a hard substance that forms on teeth, especially when they are not cleaned regularly 牙垢；牙石 ➲ COMPARE PLAQUE (2) IDM SEE TIP *v.*

■ ***verb***

• CLIMB 攀登 **1 ~ sth** (*formal*) to climb to the top of sth very high and steep 攀登；到达…顶点： *the first woman to scale the world's five highest peaks* 第一位登上世界五大高峰的女性 ◇ (*figurative*) *He has **scaled the heights** of his profession.* 他登上了他事业的顶峰。

• FISH 鱼 **2 ~ sth** to remove the small flat hard pieces of skin from a fish 去鳞

• TEETH 牙齿 **3 ~ sth** to remove TARTAR from the teeth by SCRAPING 刮除牙石： *The dentist scaled and polished my teeth.* 牙医为我刮除牙石，抛光了牙齿。

• CHANGE SIZE 改变大小 **4 ~ sth (from sth) (to sth)** (*specialist*) to change the size of sth 缩放： *Text can be scaled from 4 point to 108 point without any loss of quality.* 正文可以从 4 点调到 108 点，但印刷质量丝毫不会降低。

PHR V **ˌscale sth↔ˈdown** (*also* **ˌscale sth↔ˈback**) to reduce the number, size or extent of sth 减少（数量）；缩小（规模或范围）： *We are thinking of scaling down our training programmes next year.* 我们考虑在明年缩小培训的规模。◇ *The IMF has scaled back its growth forecasts for the next decade.* 国际货币基金组织已经调低了它对未来十年的增长预测。➲ SYNONYMS AT CUT **ˌscale sth↔ˈup** to increase the size or number of sth 增大，扩大（规模或数量）

scales 磅秤；比例；音阶；鳞

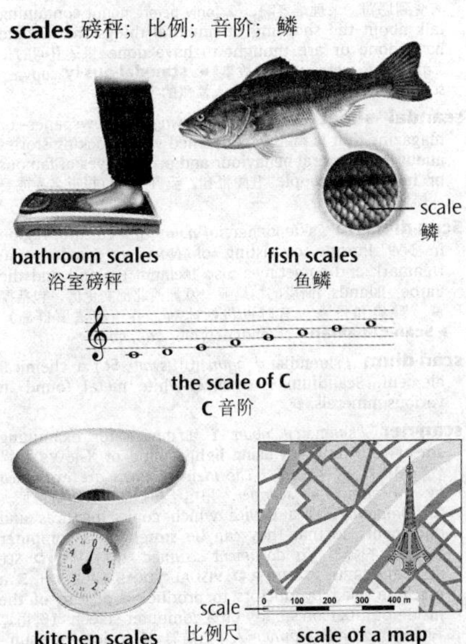

bathroom scales 浴室磅秤

fish scales 鱼鳞

the scale of C
C 音阶

kitchen scales 厨房用秤

scale of a map 地图的比例

sca·lene tri·angle /ˌskeɪliːn ˈtraɪæŋɡl/ *noun* (*geometry* 几何) a triangle whose sides are all of different lengths 不等边三角形；不规则三角形 ➲ PICTURE AT TRIANGLE

scal·lion /ˈskæliən/ *noun* (*NAmE, IrishE*) = GREEN ONION, SPRING ONION

scal·lop /ˈskɒləp; *NAmE* ˈskæləp/ *noun, verb*

■ ***noun* 1** a SHELLFISH that can be eaten, with two flat round shells that fit together 扇贝： *a scallop shell* 扇贝壳 **2** any one of a series of small curves cut on the edge of a piece of cloth, PASTRY, etc. for decoration（织物、糕点等的）扇形饰边；荷叶边

■ ***verb*** [usually passive] **~ sth** to decorate the edge of sth with small curves 给…加上扇形饰边： *a scalloped edge* 扇形边

scally /ˈskæli/ *noun* (*pl.* **-ies**) (*BrE, informal*) (used especially in Liverpool in NW England 尤用于英格兰西北部利物浦) a boy or young man who behaves badly or causes trouble 调皮捣蛋的男孩；行为不端（或滋事）的年轻男子

scally·wag /ˈskæliwæɡ/ (*BrE*) (*NAmE usually* **scala·wag**) *noun* (*informal*) a person, especially a child, who behaves badly, but not in a serious way 调皮捣蛋的人，淘气鬼（尤指儿童） SYN **scamp**

scalp /skælp/ *noun, verb*

■ ***noun* 1** the skin that covers the part of the head where the hair grows 头皮 **2** (in the past) the skin and hair that was removed from the head of a dead enemy by some Native American peoples as a sign of victory（旧时美洲土著从被杀的敌人头上剥下作为战利品的）带发头皮 **3** (*informal*) a symbol of the fact that sb has

S

been defeated or punished（表示某人已被打败或已受到惩罚的）标志：*They have claimed some impressive scalps in their bid for the championship.* 他们已在夺取冠军的征途上获得显著进展。

■ ***verb*** **1 ~ sb** to remove the skin and hair from the top of an enemy's head as a sign of victory（作为战利品，从被杀的敌人头上）剥下…的带发头皮 **2** (*NAmE*) (*BrE* **tout**) **~ sth** to sell tickets for a popular event illegally, at a price that is higher than the official price, especially outside a theatre, STADIUM, etc.（尤指在剧院、体育场等外以高价）倒卖门票，卖黑市票

scal·pel /ˈskælpəl/ *noun* a small sharp knife used by doctors in medical operations 解剖刀；手术刀 ➲ **WORDFINDER NOTE** AT OPERATION

scalp·er /ˈskælpə(r)/ (*NAmE*) (*BrE* **tout**, **ˈticket tout**) *noun* a person who buys tickets for concerts, sports events, etc. and then sells them to other people at a higher price（音乐会、体育比赛等以高价）倒卖门票者，票贩子：*ticket scalpers* 票贩子

scaly /ˈskeɪli/ *adj.* (**scali·er**, **scali·est**) (of skin 皮肤) covered with SCALES (8), or hard and dry, with small pieces that come off 有鳞屑的；有皮屑的

ˌscaly ˈanteater *noun* = PANGOLIN

scam /skæm/ *noun* (*informal*) a clever and dishonest plan for making money 欺诈；诈财骗局 ➲ **COLLOCATIONS** AT CRIME

scamp /skæmp/ *noun* (*old-fashioned*) a child who enjoys playing tricks and causing trouble 淘气鬼；捣乱鬼 **SYN** **scallywag**

scam·per /ˈskæmpə(r)/ *verb* [I] **+ adv./prep.** (especially of children or small animals 尤指儿童或小动物) to move quickly with short light steps 欢快地奔走；蹦蹦跳跳

scampi /ˈskæmpi/ *noun* [U+sing./pl. v.] (*BrE*) large PRAWNS (= a type of sea creature) covered with BREADCRUMBS or BATTER and fried 炸大虾：*scampi and chips* 炸大虾和炸薯条

scan /skæn/ *verb*, *noun*

■ ***verb*** (**-nn-**) **1** [T] to look at every part of sth carefully, especially because you are looking for a particular thing or person 细看；察看；审视；端详 **SYN** **scrutinize**：**~ sth for sth** *He scanned the horizon for any sign of land.* 他仔细眺望地平线，找寻陆地的踪影。◇ **~ sth** *She scanned his face anxiously.* 她急切地端详着他的脸。 **2** [T, I] to look quickly but not very carefully at a document, etc. 粗略地读；浏览；翻阅：**~ sth** (**for sth**) *I scanned the list quickly for my name.* 我很快浏览了一下名单，看有没有我的名字。◇ **~ through sth** (**for sth**) *She scanned through the newspaper over breakfast.* 她边吃早饭，边浏览报纸。 **3** [T] **~ sth** to get an image of an object, a part of sb's body, etc. on a computer by passing X-RAYS, ULTRASOUND waves or ELECTROMAGNETIC waves over it in a special machine（X射线、超声波、电磁波等）扫描：*Their brains are scanned so that researchers can monitor the progress of the disease.* 研究人员对他们的大脑加以扫描，以监视病情的发展。 **4** [T] **~ sth** (of a light, RADAR, etc. 光束、雷达等) to pass across an area 扫描；扫掠：*Concealed video cameras scan every part of the compound.* 几台暗藏的摄像机把院子里的每一个角落都拍了进去。 **5** [I, T] **~** (**sth**) (*computing* 计) (of a program 程序) to examine a computer program or document in order to look for a virus（为搜索病毒而）扫描（文件）：*This software is designed to scan all new files for viruses.* 这个软件是为扫描所有新文件的病毒而设计。 **6** [T] **~ sth** (*computing* 计) to pass light over a picture or document using a SCANNER in order to copy it and put it in the memory of a computer（用扫描设备）扫描（图像或文件）：*How do I scan a photo and attach it to an email?* 怎样把照片扫描并以附件形式加在电子邮件里呢？ **7** [I] (of poetry 诗歌) to have a regular rhythm according to fixed rules 符合韵律：*This line doesn't scan.* 这一行不合韵律。

PHR V **ˌscan sth ˈinto sth** | **ˌscan sth ˈin** (*computing* 计) to pass light over a picture or document using a SCANNER in order to copy it and put it in the memory of a computer 把…扫描进；扫描输入：*Text and pictures can be scanned into the computer.* 文字和图画可以扫描进计算机。

■ ***noun*** **1** [C] a medical test in which a machine produces a picture of the inside of a person's body on a computer screen after taking X-RAYS 扫描检查：*to have a brain scan* 做脑部扫描检查 ➲ **WORDFINDER NOTE** AT EXAMINE **2** [C] a medical test for pregnant women in which a machine uses ULTRASOUND to produce a picture of a baby inside its mother's body 胎儿扫描检查：*to have a scan* 做胎儿扫描检查 ➲ **WORDFINDER NOTE** AT PREGNANT **3** [sing.] the act of looking quickly through sth written or printed, usually in order to find sth 浏览；快速查阅

scan·dal /ˈskændl/ *noun* **1** [C, U] behaviour or an event that people think is morally or legally wrong and causes public feelings of shock or anger 丑行；使人震惊的丑事；丑闻：*a series of sex scandals* 一系列性丑闻 ◇ *to* ***cause/create a scandal*** 引发丑闻 ◇ ***The scandal broke*** (= became known to the public) *in May.* 这桩丑闻是在五月份曝光的。◇ *There has been* ***no hint of scandal*** *during his time in office.* 他在任期间没有任何丑闻。 **2** [U] talk or reports about the shocking or immoral things that people have done or are thought to have done 关于丑行的传言（或报道）；丑闻：*to spread scandal* 散布丑闻 ◇ *newspapers full of scandal* 充斥丑闻的报纸 **3** [sing.] **~** (**that…**) an action, attitude, etc. that you think is shocking and not at all acceptable 可耻的行为（或态度等）；不可原谅的行为（或态度等） **SYN** **disgrace**：***It is a scandal that*** *such a large town has no orchestra.* 这么大一座城市，竟然没有一支管弦乐队，真是说不过去。

scan·dal·ize (*BrE also* **-ise**) /ˈskændəlaɪz/ *verb* **~ sb** to do sth that people find very shocking（以出格行为）使震惊，使愤慨 **SYN** **outrage**：*She scandalized her family with her extravagant lifestyle.* 她奢侈的生活方式令家人侧目。

scan·dal·mon·ger /ˈskændlmʌŋɡə(r)/ *noun* (*disapproving*) a person who spreads stories about the shocking or immoral things that other people have done 散布丑闻者

scan·dal·ous /ˈskændələs/ *adj.* **1** shocking and unacceptable 可耻的；不可原谅的 **SYN** **disgraceful**：*a scandalous waste of money* 金钱的浪费触目惊心 ◇ **it is scandalous that…** *It is scandalous that he has not been punished.* 他没有受到惩罚，天理难容啊。 **2** [only before noun] containing talk about the shocking or immoral things that people have done or are thought to have done 讲述丑闻的：*scandalous stories* 丑闻故事 ► **scan·dal·ous·ly** *adv.*：*scandalously low pay* 低得令人愤慨的工资

ˈscandal sheet *noun* (*disapproving*) a newspaper or magazine that is mainly concerned with shocking stories about the immoral behaviour and private lives of famous or important people 丑闻报刊，流言小报（报道名人或要人绯闻或私生活等）

Scan·di·navia /ˌskændɪˈneɪviə/ *noun* [U] a cultural region in NW Europe consisting of Norway, Sweden and Denmark and sometimes also Iceland, Finland and the Faroe Islands 斯堪的纳维亚（欧洲西北部文化区，包括挪威、瑞典和丹麦，有时也包括冰岛、芬兰和法罗群岛）► **Scan·di·navian** /ˌskændɪˈneɪviən/ *adj.*, *noun*

scan·dium /ˈskændiəm/ *noun* [U] (*symb.* **Sc**) a chemical element. Scandium is a silver-white metal found in various minerals. 钪

scan·ner /ˈskænə(r)/ *noun* **1** a device for examining sth or recording sth using light, sound or X-RAYS 扫描仪；扫描器；扫描设备：*The identity cards are examined by an electronic scanner.* 用电子扫描器来检验身份证。 **2** (*computing* 计) a device which copies pictures and documents so that they can be stored on a computer 扫描仪；扫描器：*a document scanner* 文件扫描仪 ➲ SEE ALSO FLATBED SCANNER ➲ **VISUAL VOCAB** PAGE V71 **3** a machine used by doctors to produce a picture of the inside of a person's body on a computer screen（医用）扫描器：*a body scanner* 人体扫描器 **4** a piece of equipment for receiving and sending RADAR signals 扫掠天线；自动旋转雷达天线

scan·sion /ˈskænʃn/ *noun* [U] (*specialist*) the rhythm of a line of poetry （诗行的）韵律 ➲ WORDFINDER NOTE AT POETRY

scant /skænt/ *adj.* [only before noun] hardly any; not very much and not as much as there should be 一丁点的；微小的；不足的；欠缺的：*I paid scant attention to what she was saying.* 我没大注意她在说什么。◇ *The firefighters went back into the house with* **scant regard for** *their own safety.* 消防员奋不顾身地返回那座房子。

scanty /ˈskænti/ *adj.* (**scant·ier**, **scanti·est**) **1** too little in amount for what is needed 不足的；欠缺的；太少的：*Details of his life are scanty.* 关于他的生平，详细资料不多。 **2** (of clothes 衣服) very small and not covering much of your body 小而暴露身体的：*a scanty bikini* 遮不住多少身体的比基尼泳装 ▶ **scant·ily** *adv.*：*scantily dressed models* 衣着暴露的模特儿

-scape *combining form* (in nouns 构成名词) a view or scene of …景（色）：*landscape* 风景 ◇ *seascape* 海景 ◇ *moonscape* 月景

scape·goat /ˈskeɪpɡəʊt; *NAmE* -ɡoʊt/ *noun* a person who is blamed for sth bad that sb else has done or for some failure 替罪羊；代人受过者 SYN **fall guy**：*She felt she had been made a scapegoat for her boss's incompetence.* 她觉得，本是老板无能，但她却成了替罪羊。▶ **scape·goat** *verb* **~ sb/sth**

scap·ula /ˈskæpjʊlə/ *noun* (*pl.* **scapu·lae** /-liː/ or **scapu·las**) (*anatomy* 解) the SHOULDER BLADE 肩胛骨 ➲ VISUAL VOCAB PAGE V64

scar /skɑː(r)/ *noun, verb*

■ ***noun*** **1** a mark that is left on the skin after a wound has healed 伤疤；伤痕；瘢痕：*a scar on his cheek* 他脸上的伤疤 ◇ *Will the operation leave a scar?* 手术会不会留下疤痕？◇ *scar tissue* 瘢痕组织 **2** a permanent feeling of great sadness or mental pain that a person is left with after an unpleasant experience （精神上的）创伤；伤痕：*His years in prison have* **left** *deep scars.* 他在狱中的岁月给他留下了深深的创伤。 **3** something unpleasant or ugly that spoils the appearance or public image of sth 有损外观（或公共形象）的地方；污点；煞风景之处：*The town still bears the scars of war.* 城里依旧可见战争的疮痍。◇ *Racism has been a scar on the game.* 种族主义行为给这场赛事抹了黑。 **4** an area of a hill or CLIFF where there is exposed rock and no grass （小山或悬崖上的）裸岩

■ ***verb*** (**-rr-**) [often passive] **1 ~ sb/sth** (of a wound, etc. 伤口等) to leave a mark on the skin after it has healed 在…上结疤；给…留下瘢痕：*His face was badly scarred.* 他的脸上留下了明显的疤痕。 **2 ~ sb** (of an unpleasant experience 不愉快的经历) to leave sb with a feeling of sadness or mental pain 给…留下精神创伤：*The experience left her* **scarred for life**. 那段经历给她留下终生的创伤。 **3 ~ sth** to spoil the appearance of sth 损害…的外观：*The hills are scarred by quarries.* 采石场破坏了这些山的景观。◇ *battle-scarred buildings* 弹痕累累的建筑物

scarab /ˈskærəb/ (*also* **ˈscarab beetle**) *noun* a large black BEETLE (= an insect with a hard shell); a design showing a scarab beetle 金龟子；圣甲虫；甲虫形护符

scarce /skeəs; *NAmE* skers/ *adj., adv.*

■ ***adj.*** (**scar·cer**, **scar·cest**) if sth is **scarce**, there is not enough of it and it is only available in small quantities 缺乏的；不足的；稀少的：***scarce resources*** 稀缺资源 ◇ *Details of the accident are scarce.* 事故的详细情况了解不多。◇ *Food was becoming scarce.* 食物越来越紧缺。

IDM **ˌmake yourself ˈscarce** (*informal*) to leave somewhere and stay away for a time in order to avoid an unpleasant situation 躲开；回避；溜走

■ ***adv.*** (*literary*) only just; almost not 勉强；刚；几乎不；简直不：*I can scarce remember him.* 我几乎想不起他了。

scarce·ly /ˈskeəsli; *NAmE* ˈskers-/ *adv.* **1** only just; almost not 勉强；刚；几乎不；简直不：*I can scarcely believe it.* 我几乎不敢相信。◇ *We scarcely ever meet.* 我们难得见一面。◇ *Scarcely a week goes by without some new scandal in the papers.* 报上几乎周周都会登出新的丑闻。 **2** used to say that sth happens immediately after sth else happens （表示接连发生）刚一…就：*He had scarcely put the phone down when the doorbell rang.* 他刚放下电话，门铃就响了起来。◇ *Scarcely had the game started when it began to rain.* 比赛才开始就下起雨来了。 **3** used to suggest that sth is not at all reasonable or likely 实在不应该；根本不可能：*It was scarcely an occasion for laughter.* 笑得实在不是时候。◇ *She could scarcely complain, could she?* 她压根儿没什么好抱怨的，是不是？➲ NOTE AT HARDLY

scar·city /ˈskeəsəti; *NAmE* ˈskers-/ *noun* [U, C] (*pl.* **-ies**) if there is a **scarcity of** sth, there is not enough of it and it is difficult to obtain it 缺乏；不足；稀少 SYN **shortage**：*a time of scarcity* 物资短缺时期 ◇ *a scarcity of resources* 资源短缺

scare 🔑 /skeə(r); *NAmE* sker/ *verb, noun*

■ ***verb*** **1** 🔑 [T] to frighten sb 惊吓；使害怕；使恐惧：**~ sb** *You scared me.* 你吓了我一跳。◇ **it scares sb to do sth** *It scared me to think I was alone in the building.* 想到楼里只有我一个人，怪害怕的。➲ SYNONYMS AT FRIGHTEN **2** [I] to become frightened 受惊吓；害怕；恐惧：*He doesn't scare easily.* 他不轻易害怕。➲ SEE ALSO SCARY

IDM **scare the ˈshit out of sb | scare sb ˈshitless** (*taboo, slang*) to frighten sb very much 吓得某人屁滚尿流 ➲ MORE AT DAYLIGHTS, DEATH, LIFE

PHR V **ˌscare sb↔aˈway/ˈoff** 🔑 to make sb go away by frightening them 把…吓跑：*They managed to scare the bears away.* 他们设法把熊吓跑了。 **ˈscare sb into doing sth** to frighten sb in order to make them do sth 威胁，恐吓（某人做某事）：*Local businesses were scared into paying protection money.* 当地商家迫于威胁缴纳了保护费。 **ˌscare sb↔ˈoff** to make sb afraid of or nervous about doing sth, especially without intending to （尤指无意中）把人吓倒，使人害怕，使恐惧：*Rising prices are scaring customers off.* 不断上涨的价格把顾客吓跑了。 **ˌscare ˈup sth** (*NAmE, informal*) to find or make sth by using whatever is available （就现有材料）勉强凑合：*I'll see if I can scare up enough chairs for us all.* 我来看看能不能给大家凑够椅子。

■ ***noun*** **1** 🔑 [C] (used especially in newspapers 尤用于报章) a situation in which a lot of people are anxious or frightened about sth 恐慌；恐惧：***a bomb/health scare*** 炸弹 / 卫生恐慌 ◇ *recent scares about pesticides in food* 近来人们对含杀虫剂食物的恐慌 ◇ ***a scare story*** (= a news report that spreads more anxiety or fear about sth than is necessary) 引起恐慌的报道 ◇ *to cause a major scare* 引起严重恐慌 ◇ ***scare tactics*** (= ways of persuading people to do sth by frightening them) 恐吓战术 **2** 🔑 [sing.] a sudden feeling of fear 惊吓；惊恐：*You* **gave me a scare!** 你吓了我一跳！◇ *We've had quite a scare.* 我们吓得不轻。➲ SEE ALSO SCARY

scare·crow /ˈskeəkrəʊ; *NAmE* ˈskerkroʊ/ *noun* a figure made to look like a person, that is dressed in old clothes and put in a field to frighten birds away 稻草人

scared 🔑 /skeəd; *NAmE* skerd/ *adj.* frightened of sth or afraid that sth bad might happen 害怕；恐惧；畏惧；担心：**~ (of doing sth)** *She is scared of going out alone.* 她不敢一个人外出。◇ **~ (of sb/sth)** *He's scared of heights.* 他有恐高症。◇ **~ (to do sth)** *People are scared to use the buses late at night.* 人们害怕在深夜乘坐公共汽车。◇ **~ (that…)** *I'm scared (that) I'm going to fall.* 我担心自己快掉下去了。◇ *The thieves got scared and ran away.* 小偷害怕了，就跑了。◇ *a scared look* 惊恐的表情 ◇ *I was* **scared to death** (= very frightened). 我吓得要死。◇ *We were* **scared stiff** (= very frightened). 我们吓得呆若木鸡。➲ SYNONYMS AT AFRAID IDM SEE SHADOW *n.*, WIT, WITLESS

scaredy-cat /ˈskeədi kæt; *NAmE* ˈskerdi/ (*US also* **ˈfraidy cat**) *noun* (*informal, disapproving*) a children's word for a person who is easily frightened （儿童用语）胆小鬼

scare·mon·ger /ˈskeəmʌŋɡə(r); *NAmE* ˈskerm-/ *noun* (*disapproving*) a person who spreads stories deliberately to make people frightened or nervous 散布恐怖消息的人；制造恐慌的人；危言耸听的人 ▶ **scare·monger·ing** *noun* [U]

S

ˈ**scare quotes** *noun* [pl.] QUOTATION MARKS that a writer puts around a word or phrase to show that it is used in an unusual way, usually one that the writer does not agree with 着重引号（表示引号内的词或短语用法特别，通常为作者所不赞成）: *This pronouncement came from the organization's 'scientific' committee* (*the scare quotes are mine*). 这条声明来自该机构的“科学”委员会（着重引号为本人所加）。

scare·ware /ˈskeərweə(r); *NAmE* ˈskerwer/ *noun* [U] a type of computer program that tricks a user into buying and DOWNLOADING unnecessary software that could be dangerous for the computer 伪安全软件，恐吓性软件（诱使用户购买下载可能危害计算机的无用软件）

scarf /skɑːf; *NAmE* skɑːrf/ *noun, verb*

■ ***noun*** (*pl.* **scarves** /skɑːvz; *NAmE* skɑːrvz/ or *less frequent* **scarfs**) a piece of cloth that is worn around the neck, for example for warmth or decoration. Women also wear scarves over their shoulders or hair. 围巾；披巾；头巾: *a woollen/silk scarf* 羊毛/丝绸围巾 ➲ VISUAL VOCAB PAGE V70

■ ***verb*** (*NAmE*) (*BrE* **scoff**) [I, T] ~ (**sth**) (*informal*) to eat a lot of sth quickly 贪婪地吃；狼吞虎咽

scar·ify /ˈskærɪfaɪ; ˈskeə-; *NAmE* ˈsker-/ *verb* (**scari·fies, scari·fy·ing, scari·fied, scari·fied**) (*specialist*) **1** ~ **sth** to break up an area of grass, etc. and remove pieces of material from it that are not wanted 翻松（草地等） **2** ~ **sth** to make cuts in the surface of sth, especially skin 划破（尤指皮肤）

scar·let /ˈskɑːlət; *NAmE* ˈskɑːrlət/ *adj.* bright red in colour 猩红的；鲜红的: *scarlet berries* 鲜红的浆果 ◇ *She went scarlet with embarrassment.* 她窘得满脸通红。▶ **scar·let** *noun* [U]

ˌ**scarlet ˈfever** *noun* [U] a serious infectious disease that causes fever and red marks on the skin 猩红热

ˌ**scarlet ˈwoman** *noun* (*old-fashioned*) a woman who has sexual relationships with many different people 荡妇

scarp /skɑːp; *NAmE* skɑːrp/ *noun* (*specialist*) a very steep slope 陡坡；悬崖

scar·per /ˈskɑːpə(r); *NAmE* ˈskɑːrp-/ *verb* [I] (*BrE, informal*) to run away; to leave 逃跑；溜号: *The police arrived, so we scarpered.* 警察来了，于是我们就溜走了。

Scart /skɑːt; *NAmE* skɑːrt/ (*also* **SCART**) *noun* a device with 21 pins, used to connect video equipment to, for example, a television * Scart 连接器；21 针音视频信号连接器: *a Scart socket* * 21 针音视频信号线插孔

scarves PL. OF SCARF

scary /ˈskeəri; *NAmE* ˈskeri/ *adj.* (**scari·er, scari·est**) (*informal*) frightening 恐怖的；吓人的: *It was a really scary moment.* 那一刻真是吓人。◇ *a scary movie* 恐怖电影 ➲ SEE ALSO SCARE

scat /skæt/ *noun* [U] a style of JAZZ singing in which the voice is made to sound like a musical instrument 拟声唱法（模拟乐器的爵士乐歌唱方式）

scath·ing /ˈskeɪðɪŋ/ *adj.* criticizing sb or sth very severely in a way that shows no respect 严厉批评的；尖刻斥责的；粗暴抨击的 SYN **withering**: *a scathing attack on the new management* 针对新的管理层的猛烈抨击 ◇ ~ **about sb/sth** *He was scathing about the government's performance.* 他尖锐地批评了政府的表现。▶ **scath·ing·ly** *adv.*: *'Oh, she's just a kid,' he said scathingly.* “咳，她还是个孩子呢。”他尖刻地挖苦道。

scato·logic·al /ˌskætəˈlɒdʒɪkl; *NAmE* -ˈlɑːdʒ-/ *adj.* (*formal*) connected with human waste from the body in an unpleasant way 与粪便有关的: *scatological humour* 下作的幽默

scat·ter /ˈskætə(r)/ *verb, noun*

■ ***verb*** **1** [T] to throw or drop things in different directions so that they cover an area of ground 撒；撒播: ~ **sth** *They scattered his ashes at sea.* 他们把他的骨灰撒向大海。◇ ~ **sth on/over/around sth** *Scatter the grass seed over the lawn.* 把草籽撒到草坪上。◇ ~ **sth with sth** *Scatter the lawn with grass seed.* 在草坪上撒上草籽。 **2** [I, T] to move or to make people or animals move very quickly in different directions 散开；四散；使分散；驱散 SYN **disperse**: *At the first gunshot, the crowd scattered.* 枪声一响，人群便逃散了。◇ ~ **sb/sth** *The explosion scattered a flock of birds roosting in the trees.* 爆炸声把栖息在树丛中的鸟群惊散了。

■ ***noun*** [usually sing.] (*also* **scat·ter·ing** /ˈskætərɪŋ/ [sing.]) a small amount or number of things spread over an area 散落；三三两两；零零星星: *a scattering of houses* 稀稀落落的房屋

scat·ter·brain /ˈskætəbreɪn; *NAmE* -tərb-/ *noun* (*informal*) a person who is always losing or forgetting things and cannot think in an organized way 思想不集中的人；健忘的人 ▶ **scat·ter·brained** *adj.*

ˈ**scatter cushion** (*BrE*) (*NAmE* ˈ**throw pillow**) *noun* a small CUSHION that can be placed on furniture, on the floor, etc. for decoration 小靠垫；小装饰垫 ➲ VISUAL VOCAB PAGE V22

ˈ**scatter diagram** (*also* **scat·ter·gram** /ˈskætəgræm; *NAmE* -tərg-/) *noun* (*statistics* 统计) a diagram that shows the relationship between two VARIABLES by creating a pattern of dots （表示两变量关系的）点聚图，散布图

scat·tered /ˈskætəd; *NAmE* -tərd/ *adj.* spread far apart over a wide area or over a long period of time 分散的；零散的；疏落的: *a few scattered settlements* 几个分散的村落 ◇ *sunshine with scattered showers* 晴，间有零星阵雨 ◇ *Her family are scattered around the world.* 她的家人散居在世界各地。

scatter·gun /ˈskætəgʌn; *NAmE* -tərg-/ (*BrE*) (*NAmE usually* **scatter·shot** /ˈskætəʃɒt; *NAmE* -tərʃɑːt/) *adj.* [only before noun] referring to a way of doing or dealing with sth by considering many different possibilities, people, etc. in a way that is not well organized （处事）杂乱无章的，乱无头绪的，漫无边际的: *The scattergun approach to marketing means that the campaign is not targeted at particular individuals.* 促销活动采取渔翁撒网的方法，表示并非针对特定的人群。

scatty /ˈskæti/ *adj.* (**scat·tier, scat·ti·est**) (*BrE, informal*) tending to forget things and behave in a slightly silly way 健忘的；傻乎乎的

scav·enge /ˈskævɪndʒ/ *verb* **1** [T, I] (of a person, an animal or a bird 人、兽或鸟) to search through waste for things that can be used or eaten （从废弃物中）觅食；捡破烂；拾荒: ~ **sth** (**from sth**) *Much of their furniture was scavenged from other people's garbage.* 他们的家具许多都是从别人扔掉的东西中捡来的。◇ ~ (**through sth**) (**for sth**) *Dogs and foxes scavenged through the trash cans for something to eat.* 狗和狐狸从垃圾箱里寻找食物。 **2** [T, I] (of animals or birds 兽或鸟) to eat dead animals that have been killed by another animal, by a car, etc. 吃（动物尸体）: ~ **sth** *Crows scavenge carrion left on the roads.* 乌鸦吃弃在路上的腐肉。◇ ~ (**on sth**) *Some fish scavenge on dead fish in the wild.* 在大自然中，有的鱼以死鱼为食。

scav·en·ger /ˈskævɪndʒə(r)/ *noun* an animal, a bird or a person that scavenges 食腐肉的兽（或鸟）；捡破烂的人；拾荒者

ˈ**scavenger hunt** *noun* a game in which players have to find various objects 寻宝游戏（参加者必须找到各种物品）

scen·ario AW /səˈnɑːriəʊ; *NAmE* səˈnærioʊ/ *noun* (*pl.* **-os**) **1** a description of how things might happen in the future 设想；方案；预测: *Let me suggest a **possible scenario**.* 我来设想一种可能出现的情况。◇ *The **worst-case scenario*** (= the worst possible thing that could happen) *would be for the factory to be closed down.* 最坏的情况可能是工厂关闭。◇ *a **nightmare scenario*** 最坏的可能 **2** a written outline of what happens in a film/movie or play （电影或戏剧的）剧情梗概 SYN **synopsis** ➲ WORDFINDER NOTE AT FILM, PLOT

scene 🔑 /siːn/ *noun*

• PLACE 地点 **1** 🔑 [C, usually sing.] ~ (**of sth**) the place where sth happens, especially sth unpleasant （尤指不愉快事件发生的）地点，现场：*the scene of the accident/attack/crime* 事故 / 袭击 / 犯罪的现场 ◇ *Firefighters were on the scene immediately.* 消防队立刻赶到现场。➲ SYNONYMS AT PLACE

• EVENT 事件 **2** 🔑 [C] ~ (**of sth**) an event or a situation that you see, especially one of a particular type 事件；场面；情景：*The team's victory produced scenes of joy all over the country.* 球队的胜利使举国上下出现一派欢乐的场面。◇ *She witnessed some very distressing scenes.* 她目睹过一些令人非常痛苦的场面。

• IN MOVIE/PLAY, ETC. 电影、戏剧等 **3** 🔑 [C] a part of a film/movie, play or book in which the action happens in one place or is of one particular type 场面；片段；镜头：*The movie opens with a scene in a New York apartment.* 电影开头的一场戏发生在纽约一套公寓里。◇ ***love/sex scenes*** 爱情戏；床上戏 ◇ *I got very nervous before my big scene* (= the one where I have a very important part). 在演那场重头戏之前，我非常紧张。➲ WORDFINDER NOTE AT PLOT **4** 🔑 [C] one of the small sections that a play or an OPERA is divided into （戏剧或歌剧的）场：*Act I, Scene 2 of 'Macbeth'*《麦克白》第 1 幕第 2 场 ➲ WORDFINDER NOTE AT DRAMA, PLAY

• AREA OF ACTIVITY 活动领域 **5 the scene, the... scene** [sing.] (*informal*) a particular area of activity or way of life and the people who are part of it 活动领域；界；坛；圈子：*After years at the top, she just vanished from the scene.* 她在圈内雄踞首位许多年，突然销声匿迹了。◇ *the **club/dance/music, etc. scene*** 俱乐部圈子、舞坛、音乐界等 ◇ *A newcomer has appeared on the **fashion scene**.* 时装界出现了一位新人。

• VIEW 景象 **6** 🔑 [C] a view that you see 景象；景色；风光：*a delightful rural scene* 赏心悦目的乡村风光 ◇ *They went abroad for **a change of scene*** (= to see and experience new surroundings). 他们出国换换环境。➲ SYNONYMS AT VIEW

• PAINTING/PHOTOGRAPH 绘画；摄影 **7** 🔑 [C] a painting, drawing, or photograph of a place and the things that are happening there 表现…景色的绘画（或摄影）作品；以…风情为题材的绘画（或摄影）作品：*an exhibition of Parisian street scenes* 巴黎街景绘画作品展

• ARGUMENT 争吵 **8** [C, usually sing.] a loud, angry argument, especially one that happens in public and is embarrassing （尤指当众、有失体面的）争吵，吵闹：*She had **made a scene** in the middle of the party.* 她在聚会中间大闹了一场。◇ *'Please leave,' he said. 'I don't want a scene.'* "请你走吧，"他说，"我不希望发生争吵。" ➲ MORE LIKE THIS 20, page R27

IDM **behind the 'scenes 1** in the part of a theatre, etc. that the public does not usually see 在后台；在幕后：*The students were able to go behind the scenes to see how programmes are made.* 学生可以跑到后台，去看看节目是怎么制作出来的。**2** in a way that people in general are not aware of 秘密地；背地里；在幕后：*A lot of negotiating has been going on behind the scenes.* 广泛的谈判一直在秘密进行。◇ *behind-the-scenes work* 幕后工作 **not sb's 'scene** (*informal*) not the type of thing that sb likes or enjoys doing 不对某人的路子；不合某人的胃口 **set the 'scene (for sth) 1** to create a situation in which sth can easily happen or develop 为…做好准备（或铺平道路）：*His arrival set the scene for another argument.* 他这一来，又会引起一场争论。**2** to give sb the information and details they need in order to understand what comes next （向…）介绍背景，事先介绍情况：*The first part of the programme was just setting the scene.* 节目的第一部分不过是介绍背景而已。

scene-of-'crime *adj.* [only before noun] (*BrE*) relating to the part of the police service that examines the physical evidence of a crime that is present in the place where the crime was committed 犯罪现场的；作案现场的：*a scene-of-crime officer* 在作案现场取证的警察

scen·ery /ˈsiːnəri/ *noun* [U] **1** the natural features of an area, such as mountains, valleys, rivers and forests, when you are thinking about them being attractive to look at 风景；景色；风光：*The scenery is magnificent.* 景色壮丽。◇ *to enjoy the scenery* 欣赏风景 ➲ SYNONYMS AT COUNTRY **2** the painted background that is used to represent natural features or buildings on a theatre stage 舞台布景 ➲ WORDFINDER NOTE AT STAGE

scenic /ˈsiːnɪk/ *adj.* **1** [usually before noun] having beautiful natural scenery 风景优美的：*an area of scenic beauty* 风光秀丽的地区 ◇ *They took the **scenic route** back to the hotel.* 他们选了一条景色优美的路线回旅馆。◇ *a scenic drive* 驾车欣赏沿路景色 **2** [only before noun] connected with scenery in a theatre 舞台布景的：*scenic designs* 布景设计 ▶ **scen·ic·al·ly** /-kli/ *adv.*：*scenically attractive areas* 景色迷人的地区

scent /sent/ *noun, verb*

■ *noun* **1** [U, C] the pleasant smell that sth has 香味：*The air was filled with the scent of wild flowers.* 空气中弥漫着野花的芬芳。◇ *These flowers have no scent.* 这些花不香。**2** [U, C, usually sing.] the smell that a person or an animal leaves behind and that other animals such as dogs can follow （人的）气味，气息；（动物留下的）臭迹，遗臭 SYN **trail**：*The dogs must have lost her scent.* 狗准是闻不到她的气味了。**3** [U] (*especially BrE*) a liquid with a pleasant smell that you wear on your skin to make it smell nice 香水：*a bottle of scent* 一瓶香水 **4 ~ of sth** [sing.] the feeling that sth is present or is going to happen very soon 察觉；预感：*The scent of victory was in the air.* 胜利在望。

IDM **put/throw sb off the 'scent** to do sth to stop sb from finding you or discovering sth 使失去线索；摆脱追踪者；使迷失寻找方向 **on the 'scent (of sth)** close to discovering sth 已获得线索；已掌握蛛丝马迹

■ *verb* **1 ~ sth** to find sth by using the sense of smell 嗅出；闻到：*The dog scented a rabbit.* 狗嗅到了兔子的气息。**2 ~ sth** to begin to feel that sth exists or is about to happen 觉察出；预感到 SYN **sense**：*The press could scent a scandal.* 记者觉察出有桩丑闻。◇ *By then, the team was scenting victory.* 到那时，队员已经预感到即将获胜了。**3** [often passive] **~ sth (with sth)** to give sth a particular, pleasant smell 使具有香味：*Roses scented the night air.* 夜空中弥漫着玫瑰花香。

scent·ed /ˈsentɪd/ *adj.* having a strong pleasant smell 散发着浓香的；芬芳的

scent·less /ˈsentləs/ *adj.* without a smell 无气味的

scep·ter (*NAmE*) = SCEPTRE

scep·tic (*BrE*) (*NAmE* **skep·tic**) /ˈskeptɪk/ *noun* a person who usually doubts that claims or statements are true, especially those that other people believe in 惯持怀疑态度的人；怀疑论者 ➲ SEE ALSO EUROSCEPTIC

scep·tical (*BrE*) (*NAmE* **skep·tical**) /ˈskeptɪkl/ *adj.* ~ (**about/of sth**) having doubts that a claim or statement is true or that sth will happen 怀疑的：*I am sceptical about his chances of winning.* 我怀疑他取胜的可能性。◇ *The public remain sceptical of these claims.* 公众对这些说法仍持怀疑态度。◇ *She looked highly sceptical.* 她一脸深表怀疑的神色。▶ **scep·tic·al·ly** (*BrE*) (*NAmE* **skep·tic·al·ly**) /-kli/ *adv.*

scep·ti·cism (*BrE*) (*NAmE* **skep·ti·cism**) /ˈskeptɪsɪzəm/ *noun* [U, sing.] an attitude of doubting that claims or statements are true or that sth will happen 怀疑态度；怀疑主义：*Such claims should be regarded with a certain amount of scepticism.* 对这样的说法，大可不必全信。

sceptre (*US* **scep·ter**) /ˈseptə(r)/ *noun* a decorated ROD carried by a king or queen at ceremonies as a symbol of their power （象征王权的）节杖，权杖 ➲ COMPARE MACE (1), ORB (2)

schad·en·freude /ˈʃɑːdnfrɔɪdə/ *noun* [U] (*from German*) a feeling of pleasure at the bad things that happen to other people 幸灾乐祸

sched·ule 🔑 AW /ˈskedʒuːl; *BrE also* ˈʃed-; ˈʃedjuːl/ *noun, verb*

■ *noun* **1** 🔑 [C, U] a plan that lists all the work that you have to do and when you must do each thing 工作

S

计划；日程安排：*I have a hectic schedule for the next few days.* 我今后几天的日程紧得要命。◇ *We're working to a* ***tight schedule*** (= we have a lot of things to do in a short time). 我们的工作安排得很紧。◇ *Filming began* ***on schedule*** (= at the planned time). 拍摄如期开始。◇ *The new bridge has been finished two years* ***ahead of schedule***. 新桥提前两年落成。◇ *The tunnel project has already fallen* ***behind schedule***. 隧道工程已经晚了工期。**2** [C] (*NAmE*) = TIMETABLE (1)：*a train schedule* 列车时刻表 ◇ *Chinese will be on the school schedule from next year.* 从明年开始中文将排进学校的课程表。**3** [C] a list of the television and radio programmes that are on a particular channel and the times that they start （电视或广播）节目表：*The channel's schedules are filled with old films and repeats.* 这个频道安排的尽是老电影和重播节目。**4** [C] a written list of things, for example prices, rates or conditions（价格、收费或条款等的）一览表，明细表，清单：*tax schedules* 税率表 ➲ NOTE AT AGENDA

■ ***verb*** **1** [usually passive] to arrange for sth to happen at a particular time 安排；为…安排时间；预定：**~ sth (for sth)** *The meeting is scheduled for Friday afternoon.* 会议安排在星期五下午。◇ *One of the scheduled events is a talk on alternative medicine.* 安排的活动中有一项是关于替代疗法的讨论。◇ *We'll be stopping here for longer than scheduled.* 我们在这里停留的时间将比原定的久一点。◇ **~ sb/sth to do sth** *I'm scheduled to arrive in LA at 5 o'clock.* 我预计在 5 点钟抵达洛杉矶。**2 ~ sth (as sth)** (*formal*) to include sth in an official list of things 将…列入，收进（正式目录、清单等中）：*The substance has been scheduled as a poison.* 这种物质已被列为毒物。▶ **sched·uler** *noun*：*The President's schedulers allowed 90 minutes for TV interviews.* 为总统安排日程的官员留出了 90 分钟的电视采访时间。

ˌscheduled ˈcaste *noun* (in India) a CASTE (= division of society) that is listed in the Eighth Schedule of the Indian Constitution and recommended for special help in education and employment 表列种姓（列在印度宪法第八表的社会阶层，建议在教育和就业方面给予特别帮助）

ˈscheduled flight *noun* a plane service that leaves at a regular time each day or week （飞机）定期航班 ➲ COMPARE CHARTER FLIGHT

ˌscheduled ˈtribe *noun* (in India) a TRIBE that is listed in the Eighth Schedule of the Indian Constitution and recommended for special help in education and employment 表列部族（列在印度宪法第八表的部族，建议在教育和就业方面给予特别帮助）

S

schema /ˈskiːmə/ *noun* (*pl.* **sche·mas** or **sche·mata** /-mətə; skiːˈmɑːtə/) (*specialist*) an outline of a plan or theory （计划或理论的）提要，纲要

sche·mat·ic AW /skiːˈmætɪk/ *adj.* **1** in the form of a diagram that shows the main features or relationships but not the details 略图的；简表的：*a schematic diagram* 略图 **2** according to a fixed plan or pattern 严谨的；有章法的：*The play has a very schematic plot.* 这出戏的剧情非常严谨。▶ **sche·mat·ic·al·ly** AW /-kli/ *adv.*：*The process is shown schematically in figure 3.* 流程见示意图 3。

sche·ma·tize (*BrE also* **-ise**) /ˈskiːmətaɪz/ *verb* **~ sth** (*specialist*) to organize sth in a system 使系统化；使图式化：*schematized data* 图式化的资料

scheme AW /skiːm/ *noun, verb*

■ ***noun*** **1** (*BrE*) a plan or system for doing or organizing sth 计划；方案；体系；体制：*a training scheme* 培训方案 ◇ **~ (for doing sth)** *a local scheme for recycling newspapers* 当地的报纸回收计划 ◇ **~ (to do sth)** *to* ***introduce/operate*** *a scheme to improve links between schools and industry* 推行 / 实施加强学校和业界之间联系的方案 ◇ *Under the new scheme only successful schools will be given extra funding.* 在新体制下，只有办得好的学校才可获得额外经费。➲ SEE ALSO COLOUR SCHEME, PENSION SCHEME at PENSION PLAN **2** a plan for getting money or some other advantage for yourself, especially one that involves cheating other people 阴谋；诡计；计谋：*an elaborate scheme to avoid taxes* 周密的避税方案

IDM ▶ **the/sb's ˈscheme of things** the way things seem to be organized; the way sb wants everything to be organized 格局；心中的安排：*My personal problems are not really important in the* ***overall scheme of things***. 从全局来看，我个人的问题并非十分重要。◇ *I don't think marriage figures in his scheme of things.* 我想，婚姻在他的心目中是无足轻重的。

■ ***verb*** **1** [I, T] (*disapproving*) to make secret plans to do sth that will help yourself and possibly harm others 密谋；秘密策划；图谋 SYN **plot**：**~ (against sb)** *She seemed to feel that we were all scheming against her.* 她似乎觉得我们都在算计她。◇ **~ to do sth** *His colleagues, meanwhile, were busily scheming to get rid of him.* 与此同时，他的同事在加紧谋划除掉他。◇ **~ sth** *Her enemies were scheming her downfall.* 她的敌人正密谋把她搞垮。**2** [T] **~ sth** (*SAfrE, informal*) to think or form an opinion about sth 想；认为：*What do you scheme?* 你认为怎么样？◇ *'Do you think he'll come?' 'I scheme so.'* "你认为他会来吗？" "我想会来。"

schemer /ˈskiːmə(r)/ *noun* (*disapproving*) a person who plans secretly to do sth for their own advantage 搞阴谋的人；施诡计的人

schem·ing /ˈskiːmɪŋ/ *adj.* (*formal*) often planning secretly to do sth for your own advantage, especially by cheating other people 惯搞阴谋的；诡计多端的；狡诈的

the Schengen agreement /ˈʃeŋən əɡriːmənt/ *noun* an agreement between some European countries to remove controls at their borders so that, for example, people can move freely from one country to another without needing to show their passports 申根协议，申根协定（取消部分欧洲国家之间边境检查的协议）

scherzo /ˈskeətsəʊ; *NAmE* ˈskertsoʊ/ *noun* (*pl.* **-os**) (*from Italian*) a short, lively piece of music, that is often part of a longer piece 谐谑曲

schism /ˈskɪzəm; ˈsɪzəm/ *noun* [C, U] (*formal*) strong disagreement within an organization, especially a religious one, that makes its members divide into separate groups 分裂；宗派活动；（尤指）教会分裂 ▶ **schis·mat·ic** /skɪzˈmætɪk; sɪzˈmætɪk/ *adj.*

schist /ʃɪst/ *noun* [U] a type of rock formed of layers of different minerals, that breaks naturally into thin flat pieces 片岩

schiz·oid /ˈskɪtsɔɪd/ *adj.* (*specialist*) similar to or suffering from schizophrenia 精神分裂般的；类精神分裂症的；（患）精神分裂症的：*schizoid tendencies* 精神分裂倾向

schizo·phre·nia /ˌskɪtsəˈfriːniə/ *noun* [U] a mental illness in which a person becomes unable to link thought, emotion and behaviour, leading to WITHDRAWAL from reality and personal relationships 精神分裂症；早发性痴呆 ➲ WORDFINDER NOTE AT CONDITION

schizo·phren·ic /ˌskɪtsəˈfrenɪk/ *noun, adj.*

■ ***noun*** a person who suffers from schizophrenia 精神分裂症患者

■ ***adj.*** **1** suffering from schizophrenia 患精神分裂症的 **2** (*informal*) frequently changing your mind about sth or holding opinions about sth that seem to oppose each other 反复无常的；自相矛盾的

schlep (*also* **schlepp**) /ʃlep/ *verb* (**-pp-**) (*informal*) **1** [I] **+ adv./prep.** to go somewhere, especially if it is a slow, difficult journey, or you do not want to go （劳神耗时或不情愿地）去，赶往 **2** [T] **~ sth (+ adv./prep.)** to carry or pull sth heavy 搬，抬，拖，拉（重物）：*I'm not schlepping these suitcases all over town.* 我可不想提着这几个行李箱满城跑。ORIGIN From Yiddish *shlepn*, 'to drag'. 源自意第绪语 shlepn，意为"拖"。▶ **schlep** (*also* **schlepp**) *noun* [sing.]

schlock /ʃlɒk; *NAmE* ʃlɑːk/ *noun* [U] (*NAmE, informal*) things that are cheap and of poor quality 低档货；劣质便宜货 ▶ **schlocky** *adj.*：*a low-budget schlocky film* 低成本劣质影片

schmaltz /ʃmɔːlts/ *noun* [U] (*informal, disapproving*) the quality of being too SENTIMENTAL 过分感伤 ▸ **schmaltzy** *adj.* (**schmaltz·ier, schmaltzi·est**)

schmick /ʃmɪk/ *adj.* (*AustralE, informal*) fashionable, elegant or attractive 时髦的；优雅的；诱人的： *schmick clothes* 时髦衣服 ◇ *a schmick car* 漂亮的小汽车

schmo (*also* **shmo**) /ʃməʊ; *NAmE* ʃmoʊ/ *noun* (*pl.* **-oes**) (*NAmE, informal, disapproving*) a person who is stupid or foolish in an annoying way 笨蛋；傻瓜

schmooze /ʃmuːz/ *verb* [I, T] ~ (**with**) **sb** (*informal*) to talk in an informal and friendly way with sb, especially in order to gain an advantage by persuading people to like you and do what you want （尤指为利用某人而）闲谈，闲聊 SYN **chat** ▸ **schmooz·er** *noun*

schmuck /ʃmʌk/ *noun* (*informal, disapproving, especially NAmE*) a stupid person 傻瓜；笨蛋；蠢货： *He's such a schmuck!* 他真蠢！

schnapps /ʃnæps/ *noun* [U, C] (*from German*) a strong alcoholic drink made from grain （谷物酿制的）烈酒

schnau·zer /ˈʃnaʊzə(r)/ *noun* a dog with short rough hair which forms curls 髯狗；雪纳瑞犬

schnook /ʃnʊk/ *noun* (*NAmE, informal, disapproving*) a stupid or unimportant person 愚蠢的人；小人物

scholar /ˈskɒlə(r); *NAmE* ˈskɑːl-/ *noun* **1** a person who knows a lot about a particular subject because they have studied it in detail 学者： *a classical scholar* 研究拉丁文与希腊文的学者 ◇ *He was the most distinguished scholar in his field.* 他是这一领域成就最为卓著的学者。 **2** a student who has been given a scholarship to study at a school, college or university 奖学金获得者： *a Rhodes scholar* 罗德学者 **3** (*BrE, informal*) a clever person who works hard at school 聪颖勤奋的学生： *I was never much of a scholar.* 我从来不是那种用功的好学生。

schol·ar·ly /ˈskɒləli; *NAmE* ˈskɑːlərli/ *adj.* **1** (of a person 人) spending a lot of time studying and having a lot of knowledge about an academic subject 有学者素养的；有学问的 SYN **academic 2** connected with academic study 学术的；学术性的 SYN **academic**： *a scholarly journal* 学术期刊

schol·ar·ship /ˈskɒləʃɪp; *NAmE* ˈskɑːlərʃɪp/ *noun* **1** [C] an amount of money given to sb by an organization to help pay for their education 奖学金： *She won a scholarship to study at Stanford.* 她获得了奖学金，得以在斯坦福大学求学。 ◇ *He went to drama school on a scholarship.* 他靠奖学金上了戏剧学校。 **2** [U] the serious study of an academic subject and the knowledge and methods involved 学问；学术；学术研究 SYN **learning**： *a magnificent work of scholarship* 学术巨著

scho·las·tic /skəˈlæstɪk/ *adj.* [only before noun] (*formal*) **1** connected with schools and education 学校的；教育的；学业的： *scholastic achievements* 学业成绩 **2** connected with scholasticism 经院哲学的

scho·las·ti·cism /skəˈlæstɪsɪzəm/ *noun* [U] a system of philosophy, based on religious principles and writing, that was taught in universities in the Middle Ages 经院哲学

school 🔑 /skuːl/ *noun, verb*

■ *noun*

• **WHERE CHILDREN LEARN** 儿童学习的处所 **1** 🔑 [C] a place where children go to be educated （中、小）学校： *My brother and I went to the same school.* 我和我哥哥上的是同一所学校。 ◇ (*formal*) *Which school do they attend?* 他们上的是哪一所学校？ ◇ *I'm going to the school today to talk to Kim's teacher.* 今天我要去学校和金的老师谈一谈。 ◇ *We need more money for roads, hospitals and schools.* 我们需要更多的资金来修公路、建医院和办学校。 ◇ *school buildings* 校舍 **2** 🔑 [U] (used without *the* or *a* 不与 the 和 a 连用) the process of learning in a school; the time during your life when you go to a school 上学；上学阶段： (*BrE*) *to* ***start/leave school*** 入学；（结束义务教育）离开中学 ◇ (*NAmE*) *to* ***start/quit school*** 入学；（结束义务教育）离开中学 ◇ *Where did you go to school?* 你是在哪里上学的？ ◇ (*BrE*) *All my kids are still* ***at school.*** 我的孩子还都在上学。 ◇ (*NAmE*) *All my kids are still* ***in school.*** 我的孩子还都在上学。 ◇ (*NAmE*) *to* ***teach school*** (= teach in a school) 教书 ◇ *The transition from school to work can be difficult.* 从在学校念书到上班工作，这一转变有时候可真不容易。 ➲ COLLOCATIONS AT EDUCATION **3** 🔑 [U] (used without *the* or *a* 不与 the 和 a 连用) the time during the day when children are working in a school 上课（或上学）时间： *Shall I meet you after school today?* 今天放学后我去找你好吗？ ◇ *School begins at 9.* * 9 点开始上课。 ◇ *The kids are* ***at/in school*** *until 3.30.* 孩子们到 3:30 才放学。 ◇ ***after-school*** *activities* 课外活动

• **STUDENTS AND TEACHERS** 师生 **4** 🔑 **the school** [sing.] all the children or students and the teachers in a school 学校全体师生： *I had to stand up in front of the whole school.* 我只得在全校师生面前站起来。

• **FOR PARTICULAR SKILL** 培养专门技能 **5** 🔑 [C] (often in compounds 常构成复合词) a place where people go to learn a particular subject or skill 专业学校；专科学校： *a* ***drama/language/riding, etc. school*** 戏剧、语言、骑术等学校

• **COLLEGE/UNIVERSITY** 高等院校 **6** 🔑 [C, U] (*NAmE, informal*) a college or university; the time that you spend there 学院；大学；上大学时期： *famous schools like Yale and Harvard* 像耶鲁和哈佛这样的著名大学 ◇ *Where did you go to school?* 你是在哪里上的大学？ ➲ SEE ALSO GRADUATE SCHOOL **7** 🔑 [C] a department of a college or university that teaches a particular subject （高等院校的）学院，系： *the* ***business/medical/law school*** 商学院；医学院；法学院 ◇ *the School of Dentistry* 口腔医学系

• **OF WRITERS/ARTISTS** 作家；艺术家 **8** [C] a group of writers, artists, etc. whose style of work or opinions have been influenced by the same person or ideas 学派；流派： *the Dutch school of painting* 荷兰画派

• **OF FISH** 鱼 **9** [C] a large number of fish or other sea animals, swimming together 群： *a school of dolphins* 一群海豚 ➲ COMPARE SHOAL (1) HELP There are many compounds ending in **school**. You will find them at their place in the alphabet. 以 school 结尾的复合词很多，可在各字母中的适当位置查到。

IDM **school(s) of 'thought** a way of thinking that a number of people share 学派： *There are two schools of thought about how this illness should be treated.* 关于如何治疗这种疾病，有两派不同的意见。 ➲ MORE AT OLD

▼ **BRITISH/AMERICAN** 英式 / 美式英语

at / in school

• In *BrE* somebody who is attending school is **at school**. 在英式英语中，at school 表示上学： *I was at school with her sister.* 我和她妹妹过去在同一个学校读书。 In *NAmE* **in school** is used. 美式英语用 in school 表示： *I have a ten-year-old in school.* 我有个十岁的孩子在上学。 **In school** in *NAmE* can also mean 'attending a university'. 美式英语的 in school 亦可表示上大学。

▼ **GRAMMAR POINT** 语法说明

school

• When a **school** is being referred to as an institution, you do not need to use *the.* * school 指机构时，不需用定冠词 the： *When do the children finish school?* 孩子们什么时候毕业？ When you are talking about a particular building, *the* is used. 指校舍时要用定冠词 the： *I'll meet you outside the school.* 我在学校外面等你。 **Prison, jail, court,** and **church** work in the same way. * prison、jail、court 和 church 的用法相同： *Her husband spent three years in prison.* 她丈夫坐了三年牢。

➲ NOTE AT COLLEGE, HOSPITAL

■*verb*
• YOURSELF/ANIMAL 自己；动物 **1** (*formal*) to train sb/yourself/an animal to do sth 训练；使学会： **~ sb/sth/yourself (in sth)** *to school a horse* 驯马 ◇ *She had schooled herself in patience.* 她磨炼了自己的耐性。 ◇ **~ sb/sth/yourself to do sth** *I have schooled myself to remain calm under pressure.* 我练就一副在压力之下保持镇静的本领。
• CHILD 儿童 **2 ~ sb** (*formal*) to educate a child 教育；培养： *She should be schooled with her peers.* 她应当与她的同龄人一起接受教育。

ˈschool age *noun* [U] the age or period when a child normally attends school 学龄；学龄期： *children of school age* 学龄儿童 ◇ *school-age children* 学龄儿童

school·boy /ˈskuːlbɔɪ/ *noun* a boy who attends school （学校的）男生 ➲SYNONYMS AT STUDENT

school·child /ˈskuːltʃaɪld/ *noun* (*pl.* **school·chil·dren** /-tʃɪldrən/) (*also informal* **school·kid**) a child who attends school 学童；（中小学）学生 ➲SYNONYMS AT STUDENT

school·days /ˈskuːldeɪz/ *noun* [pl.] the period in your life when you go to school 学生时代： *She hadn't seen Laura since her schooldays.* 她自从离开学校就再没见过劳拉。

ˈschool district *noun* (in the US) an area that contains several schools that are governed together 学区（美国制度，区内学校统一管辖）

ˈschool friend (*also less frequent* **school·mate**) *noun* (*especially BrE*) a friend who attends or attended the same school as you 学友；同窗；校友： *She met up with some of her old* (= former) *school friends.* 她与几个老同学见面。

school·girl /ˈskuːlgɜːl; *NAmE* -gɜːrl/ *noun* a girl who attends school （学校的）女生 ➲SYNONYMS AT STUDENT

school·house /ˈskuːlhaʊs/ *noun* **1** a school building, especially a small one in a village in the past （尤指旧时乡村学校的）校舍 **2** a house for a teacher next to a small school （小型学校旁边的）教师住房

schoolie /ˈskuːli/ *noun* (*AustralE*) a school student at the end of his or her time at school 即将毕业的中学生

ˈSchoolies Week (*also* **Schoolies**) *noun* [U] (in Australia) a time in November or December each year when Year 12 (final-year) school students celebrate leaving school by having a holiday/vacation in a town with a beach 中学毕业庆祝周（每年十一月或十二月澳大利亚 12 年级学生在海滨城镇度假）

school·ing /ˈskuːlɪŋ/ *noun* [U] (*formal*) the education you receive at school 学校教育： *secondary schooling* 中等教育 ◇ *He had very little schooling.* 他没上过几天学。

school·kid /ˈskuːlkɪd/ *noun* (*informal*) = SCHOOLCHILD

ˌschool-ˈleaver *noun* (*BrE*) a person who has just left school, especially when they are looking for a job （尤指待业的）中学毕业生，应届生： *the problem of rising unemployment among school-leavers* 毕业生失业人数不断增长的问题

school·marm /ˈskuːlmɑːm; *NAmE* -mɑːrm/ *noun* (*disapproving, especially NAmE*) a woman who teaches in a school, especially one who is old-fashioned and strict （尤指古板而严厉的）女教师 ▸ **school·marm·ish** *adj.*

school·mas·ter /ˈskuːlmɑːstə(r); *NAmE* -mæs-/, **school·mis·tress** /ˈskuːlmɪstrəs/ *noun* (*old-fashioned, especially BrE*) a teacher in a school, especially a private school （尤指私立中小学的）教师 ➲COMPARE MASTER *n.* (5)

school·mate /ˈskuːlmeɪt/ *noun* (*especially BrE*) = SCHOOL FRIEND

school·room /ˈskuːlruːm; -rʊm/ *noun* (*old-fashioned*) a classroom 教室

the ˈschool run *noun* [sing.] (*BrE*) the journey that parents make to take their children to school or to bring them home again （父母）接送学童上学（或放学）的行程

school·teach·er /ˈskuːltiːtʃə(r)/ *noun* a person whose job is teaching in a school （中小学）教师

school·work /ˈskuːlwɜːk; *NAmE* -wɜːrk/ *noun* [U] work that students do at school or for school 学校作业；课堂作业；课外作业： *She is struggling to keep up with her schoolwork.* 她在努力完成作业。

school·yard /ˈskuːljɑːd; *NAmE* -jɑːrd/ *noun* (*NAmE*) an outdoor area of a school for children to play in 校园；（学校的）露天操场 ➲COMPARE PLAYGROUND (1)

schooner /ˈskuːnə(r)/ *noun* **1** a sailing ship with two or more MASTS (= posts that support the sails) （双桅或多桅）纵帆船 **2** a tall glass for SHERRY or beer 雪利酒杯；大啤酒杯

schtick, **schtuck**, **schtum**, **schtup** = SHTICK, SHTOOK, SHTUM, SHTUP

schwa (*also* **shwa**) /ʃwɑː/ *noun* (*phonetics* 语音) a vowel sound in parts of words that are not stressed, for example the 'a' in *about* or the 'e' in *moment*; the PHONETIC symbol for this, /ə/ 非重读央元音，弱央元音，混元音（如 about 中的 a 或 moment 中的 e 所发的音）；音标符号 /ə/

schwag /ʃwæg/ *noun* [U] (*especially NAmE, informal*) **1** products that are given away free, usually to help sell a product, service, etc. （为促销而免费送的）赠品： *I was given a lot of marketing schwag at the conference.* 我在会上收到了很多促销礼品。 **2** CANNABIS, usually of low quality （劣质）大麻

sci·at·ic /saɪˈætɪk/ *adj.* [only before noun] (*anatomy* 解) of the hip or of the nerve which goes from the PELVIS to the THIGH (= the **sciatic nerve**) 坐骨的；坐骨神经的

sci·at·ica /saɪˈætɪkə/ *noun* [U] pain in the back, hip and outer side of the leg, caused by pressure on the sciatic nerve 坐骨神经痛

sci·ence 🔑 /ˈsaɪəns/ *noun* **1** 🔑 [U] knowledge about the structure and behaviour of the natural and physical world, based on facts that you can prove, for example by experiments 科学；自然科学： *new developments in science and technology* 科学技术的新发展 ◇ *the advance of modern science* 现代科学的进展 ◇ *the laws of science* 科学定律 **2** 🔑 [U] the study of science 自然科学的学习与研究；理科： ***science students/teachers/courses*** 理科学生 / 教师 / 课程 **3** 🔑 [U, C] a particular branch of science 自然科学学科： *to study one of the sciences* 攻读一门自然科学 ➲ COMPARE ART *n.* (6), HUMANITY (4) **4** [sing.] a system for organizing the knowledge about a particular subject, especially one concerned with aspects of human behaviour or society （尤指人文、社会）学科，学： *a science of international politics* 国际政治学 ➲ SEE ALSO DOMESTIC SCIENCE, EARTH SCIENCE, LIFE SCIENCES, NATURAL SCIENCE, POLITICAL SCIENCE, ROCKET SCIENCE, SOCIAL SCIENCE IDM ➲ SEE BLIND *v.*

> **WORDFINDER** 联想词： analysis, evaluate, evidence, experiment, hypothesis, laboratory, research, result, study

ˈscience fair *noun* (*NAmE*) a competition in which students at a school compete to present the best science project （学校的）科学竞赛，科学展览

ˌscience ˈfiction (*also informal* **ˈsci-fi**) (*abbr.* **SF**) *noun* [U] a type of book, film/movie, etc. that is based on imagined scientific discoveries of the future, and often deals with space travel and life on other planets 科幻小说（或影片等）

ˈscience park *noun* an area where there are a lot of companies or organizations involved in scientific research and development 科技园区

sci·en·tif·ic 🔑 /ˌsaɪənˈtɪfɪk/ *adj.* [usually before noun] **1** 🔑 involving science; connected with science 科学（上）的；关于科学的： *a scientific discovery* 科学发现 ◇ *scientific knowledge* 科学知识 ◇ *sites of scientific interest* 引起科学界关注的地方 **2** (of a way of doing sth or thinking 做事或思想的方法) careful and logical 细致严谨的；科学的： *He took a very **scientific approach** to management.*

他采取了一种非常科学的管理方法。◇ *We need to be more scientific about this problem.* 在这个问题上我们需要更为严谨一些。 OPP **unscientific** ⊃ COMPARE NON-SCIENTIFIC ▸ **sci·en·tif·ic·al·ly** /-kli/ *adv.*

sci·en·tism /ˈsaɪəntɪzəm/ *noun* [U] **1** a way of thinking or expressing ideas that is considered to be typical of scientists 科学思维；科学方法；科学态度 **2** complete belief in scientific methods, or in the truth of scientific knowledge 科学至上主义；唯科学主义

sci·en·tist 🔑 /ˈsaɪəntɪst/ *noun* a person who studies one or more of the NATURAL SCIENCES (= for example, physics, chemistry and biology) 科学家：*a research scientist* 从事研究的科学家 ◇ *nuclear scientists* 核科学家 ◇ *scientists and engineers* 科学家和工程师 ◇ *the cartoon figure of the mad scientist working in his laboratory* 疯狂的科学家在实验室工作的卡通形象 ⊃ SEE ALSO COMPUTER SCIENTIST at COMPUTER SCIENCE, POLITICAL SCIENTIST, SOCIAL SCIENTIST

Sci·en·tol·ogy™ /ˌsaɪənˈtɒlədʒi; *NAmE* -ˈtɑːl-/ *noun* [U] a religious system based on getting knowledge of yourself and spiritual FULFILMENT through courses of study and training 科学论派（宗教修行体系，倡导通过学习和训练来获得自我认识和精神上的圆满）▸ **sci·en·tolo·gist** *noun*

sci-fi /ˈsaɪ faɪ/ *noun* [U] (*informal*) = SCIENCE FICTION

scimi·tar /ˈsɪmɪtə(r)/ *noun* a short curved SWORD with one sharp edge, used especially in Eastern countries （多为东方人所用的）短弯刀

scin·tilla /sɪnˈtɪlə/ *noun* [sing.] ~ (**of sth**) (*formal*) (usually in negative sentences 通常用于否定句) a very small amount of sth 一星半点；毫厘：*There is not a scintilla of truth in what she says.* 她的话没有半句可信。

scin·til·lat·ing /ˈsɪntɪleɪtɪŋ/ *adj.* very clever, amusing and interesting 幽默机智的；妙趣横生的：*a scintillating performance* 精彩的演出 ◇ *Statistics on unemployment levels hardly make for scintillating reading.* 失业统计数据读来不大会有趣味。

scion /ˈsaɪən/ *noun* **1** (*formal* or *literary*) a young member of a family, especially a famous or important one （尤指名门望族的）子弟 **2** (*specialist*) a piece of a plant, especially one cut to make a new plant 幼枝；（尤指）接穗

sci·rocco ⊃ SIROCCO

ˈscissor kick (*also* **ˈscissors kick**) *noun* **1** (in swimming 游泳) a strong kick with the legs moving in opposite directions 剪式打腿 **2** (in football (SOCCER) 足球) a kick made by jumping in the air so that you are almost parallel to the ground, with one leg raised and the other striking the ball 飞踢；侧钩

scis·sors 🔑 /ˈsɪzəz; *NAmE* ˈsɪzərz/ *noun* [pl.] a tool for cutting paper or cloth, that has two sharp blades with handles, joined together in the middle 剪刀：*a pair of scissors* 一把剪刀 ⊃ **VISUAL VOCAB** PAGES V21, V27 ⊃ SEE ALSO NAIL SCISSORS ⊃ **MORE LIKE THIS** 20, page R27 ▸ **scis·sor** *adj.* [only before noun]：*The legs move in a scissor action.* 两腿像剪刀似的运动。

sclera /ˈsklɪərə; *NAmE* ˈsklɪrə/ (*pl.* **-rae** /-riː/ or **-ras** /-rəz/) *noun* (*anatomy* 解) the white part of the eye 巩膜 ⊃ **VISUAL VOCAB** PAGE V64

scler·osis /skləˈrəʊsɪs; *NAmE* -ˈroʊ-/ *noun* [U] (*medical* 医) a condition in which soft TISSUE in the body becomes hard, in a way that is not normal 硬化；硬化症 ⊃ SEE ALSO MULTIPLE SCLEROSIS ▸ **scler·otic** /skləˈrɒtɪk; *NAmE* -ˈrɑːt-/ *adj.*

scoff /skɒf; *NAmE* skɔːf; skɑːf/ *verb* **1** [I, T] ~ (**at sb/sth**) | + **speech** to talk about sb/sth in a way that makes it clear that you think they are stupid or ridiculous 嘲笑；讥讽 SYN **mock**：*He scoffed at our amateurish attempts.* 他对我们不在行的尝试嗤之以鼻。◇ *Don't scoff—she's absolutely right.* 别嘲笑她，她绝对正确。 **2** (*BrE*) (*NAmE* **scarf**) [T] ~ (**sth**) (*informal*) to eat a lot of sth quickly 贪婪地吃；狼吞虎咽：*Who scoffed all the grapes?* 谁那么贪嘴，把葡萄全吃光了？

▼ **COLLOCATIONS** 词语搭配

Scientific research 科学研究

Theory 理论

- **formulate/advance** a theory/hypothesis 创立理论；提出假设
- **build/construct/create/develop** a simple/theoretical/mathematical model 创立一个简单/理论/数学模型
- **develop/establish/provide/use** a theoretical/conceptual framework 创立/建立/提供/使用理论/概念框架
- **advance/argue/develop** the thesis that… 提出/论证/详尽阐述…的论题
- **explore** an idea/a concept/a hypothesis 探讨一个想法/概念/假设
- **make** a prediction/an inference 预测；推断
- **base** a prediction/your calculations on sth 基于…做出预测/估算
- **investigate/evaluate/accept/challenge/reject** a theory/hypothesis/model 研究/评估/接受/质疑/拒绝接受一个理论/假设/模型

Experiment 实验

- **design** an experiment/a questionnaire/a study/a test 设计一项实验/问卷/研究/测试
- **do** research/an experiment/an analysis 做研究/实验/分析
- **make** observations/measurements/calculations 观察；测量；计算
- **carry out/conduct/perform** an experiment/a test/a longitudinal study/observations/clinical trials 进行实验/测试/纵向研究/观察/临床试验
- **run** an experiment/a simulation/clinical trials 进行实验/模拟/临床试验
- **repeat** an experiment/a test/an analysis 重做实验/测试/分析
- **replicate** a study/the results/the findings 做相同的研究；得出同样的结果/调查结果
- **observe/study/examine/investigate/assess** a pattern/a process/a behaviour/(*especially US*) a behavior 观察/研究/审查/调查/评估一种模式/一个过程/一种行为
- **fund/support** the research/project/study 资助/支持研究/项目/专题研究
- **seek/provide/get/secure** funding for research 寻求/提供/得到/争取到研究资金

Results 结果

- **collect/gather/extract** data/information 收集/提取数据/信息
- **yield** data/evidence/similar findings/the same results 得到数据/证据/类似调查结果/相同结果
- **analyse/examine** the data/soil samples/a specimen 分析/考查数据/土壤样本/样本
- **consider/compare/interpret** the results/findings 思考/比较/解释结果/调查结果
- **fit** the data/model 与数据/模型相符合
- **confirm/support/verify** a prediction/a hypothesis/the results/the findings 证实/支持/核实预测/假设/结果/调查结果
- **prove** a conjecture/hypothesis/theorem 证明猜测/假设/定理
- **draw/make/reach** the same conclusions 得出同样的结论
- **read/review** the records/literature 阅读/评论记录/文献
- **describe/report** an experiment/a study 描述/报告一项实验/研究
- **present/publish/summarize** the results/findings 提交/公布/总结结果/调查结果
- **present/publish/read/review/cite** a paper in a scientific journal 向科学杂志提交一篇论文；在科学杂志发表一篇论文；阅读/评论/引用科学杂志上的一篇论文

S

scoff·law /ˈskɒflɔː; *NAmE* ˈskɔːf-; ˈskɑːf-/ *noun* (*NAmE*, *informal*) a person who often breaks the law but in a way that is not very serious 无视法律的人

scold /skəʊld; *NAmE* skoʊld/ *verb* [T, I] **~ sb (for sth/for doing sth)** | **(+ speech)** (*formal*) to speak angrily to sb, especially a child, because they have done sth wrong 训斥，责骂（尤指孩子） **SYN rebuke**: *He scolded them for arriving late.* 他嫌他们迟到，训了他们一通。 ▶ **scold·ing** *noun* [usually sing.]: *I got a* **scolding** *from my mother.* 我挨了我妈一阵数落。

scoli·osis /ˌskəʊliˈəʊsɪs; ˌskɒl-; *NAmE* ˌskoʊliˈoʊsɪs/ *noun* [U] (*medical* 医) a condition in which the SPINE is curved in a way that is not normal 脊柱侧弯；脊柱侧凸

scone /skɒn; skəʊn; *NAmE* skɑːn; skoʊn/ *noun* a small round cake, sometimes with dried fruit in it and often eaten with butter, jam and cream spread on it 烤饼，司康饼（常抹黄油、果酱、奶油等，有时内夹干果）

scooch (*also* **scootch**) /skuːtʃ/ *verb* (*NAmE*, *informal*) **1** (*also* **scoot**) [I] **+ adv./prep.** to move a short distance, especially while sitting down（尤指坐下时）挪动位置：*She scooched over so that he could sit down next to her.* 她挪了一下，让他可以挨着她坐下。 **2** [I] **+ adv./prep.** to move or pass through a narrow space（从狭窄空间）挤过去：*I had to scooch between the wall and the sofa to reach the plug.* 我不得不从墙和沙发之间挤过去伸手够那个插头。

PHR V ˌ**scooch** ˈ**down** to put your body close to the ground by bending your legs under you 蹲下：*She scooched down behind a car so that he couldn't see her.* 她在汽车后面蹲下，这样他就看不到她了。

scoop /skuːp/ *noun*, *verb*

■***noun*** **1** [C] a tool like a large spoon with a deep bowl, used for picking up substances in powder form like flour, or for serving food like ice cream 勺；铲子：*Use an ice-cream scoop.* 用冰淇淋勺。 ➲ VISUAL VOCAB PAGE V27 **2** [C] the amount picked up by a scoop 一勺（的量）：*two scoops of mashed potato* 两勺土豆泥 **3** [C] a piece of important or exciting news that is printed in one newspaper before other newspapers know about it 抢先报道的新闻；独家新闻 **4 the scoop** [U] (*NAmE*, *informal*) the latest information about sb/sth, especially details that are not generally known（尤指详情鲜为人知的）最新消息：*I got the inside scoop on his new girlfriend.* 我得知有关他新女友的最新内幕消息。

■***verb*** **1** to move or lift sth with a scoop or sth like a scoop 用勺儿舀；用铲儿铲：**~ sth (+ adv./prep.)** *She scooped ice cream into their bowls.* 她用勺把冰淇淋舀到他们的碗里。 ◇ *First, scoop a hole in the soil.* 首先，在土里挖一个坑。 ◇ *Scoop out the melon flesh.* 用勺把瓜瓤挖出来。 ◇ **~ sth up (+ adv./prep.)** *He quickly scooped the money up from the desk.* 他一把把桌上的钱一把抓起来。 **2 ~ sb/sth (up) (+ adv./prep.)** to move or lift sb/sth with a quick continuous movement（敏捷地）抱起，拿起，捡起：*She scooped the child up in her arms.* 她一把抱起孩子。 **3 ~ sb/sth** to publish a story before all the other newspapers, television companies, etc. 抢先报道：*The paper had inside information and scooped all its rivals.* 这家报纸获得内部消息，抢在所有竞争对手之前发表了。 **4 ~ sth** (*informal*) to win sth, especially a large sum of money or a prize 获取，赢得（一大笔钱或丰厚的奖品）：*He scooped £10 000 on the lottery.* 他中彩得了 1 万英镑。

scooped /skuːpt/ (*also* **scoop**) *adj.* [only before noun] (of the neck of a woman's dress, etc. 连衣裙等的领子) cut low and round 低而圆的；深圆的：*a* **scooped neck/neckline** 深圆领；深领口

scoot /skuːt/ *verb* **1** [I] **(+ adv./prep.)** (*informal*) to go or leave somewhere in a hurry 疾行；匆匆离去：*I'd better scoot or I'll be late.* 我得快走，要不我该迟到了。 **2** (*NAmE*) = SCOOCH (1)

scootch *verb* = SCOOCH

scoot·er /ˈskuːtə(r)/ *noun* **1** (*BrE*) (*also* ˈ**motor scooter** *NAmE*, *BrE*) a light motorcycle, usually with small wheels and a curved metal cover at the front to protect the rider's legs 小型摩托车 ➲ VISUAL VOCAB PAGE V55 **2** a child's vehicle with two small wheels attached to a narrow board with a vertical handle. The rider holds the handle, puts one foot on the board and pushes against the ground with the other.（儿童）滑板车

scope AW /skəʊp; *NAmE* skoʊp/ *noun*, *verb*

■***noun*** [U] **1** the opportunity or ability to do or achieve sth（做或实现某事的）机会，能力 **SYN potential**: **~ (for sth)** *There's still plenty of scope for improvement.* 还有很大的改进余地。 ◇ *Her job offers very* **little scope** *for promotion.* 干着那样的工作，她几乎没有机会得到提拔。 ◇ **~ (for sb) (to do sth)** *The extra money will give us the scope to improve our facilities.* 有了这笔额外资金，我们就能把设备加以改进了。 ◇ *First try to do something that is* **within your scope**. 你先试着做一件自己力所能及的事。 **2** the range of things that a subject, an organization, an activity, etc. deals with（题目、组织、活动等的）范围：*Our powers are limited* **in scope**. 我们的权限不大。 ◇ *This subject lies* **beyond the scope of** *our investigation.* 这一问题超出了我们的调查范围。 ◇ *These issues were* **outside the scope** *of the article.* 这些问题不属本文论述范围。 **3 -scope** (in nouns 构成名词) an instrument for looking through or watching sth with …镜（观察仪器）：*microscope* 显微镜 ◇ *telescope* 望远镜

■***verb*** **1 ~ sth** (*informal*) to look at or examine sth thoroughly 仔细看；彻底检查：*His eyes scoped the room, trying to spot her in the crowd.* 他环顾房间四周，想在人群中找到她。 **2 ~ sth (out)** to examine sth carefully before you start work on it so that you know the size of the task（开始某项工作前）了解，查清，探明：*The information helped us scope the project.* 这些信息帮助我们在开展工作前了解该项目的情况。

PHR V ˌ**scope sth↔**ˈ**out** to look at sth carefully in order to see what it is like 端详；打量

scorch /skɔːtʃ; *NAmE* skɔːrtʃ/ *verb* **1** [T, I] **~ (sth)** | **~ sth + adj.** to burn and slightly damage a surface by making it too hot; to be slightly burned by heat（把…）烫坏，烧糊；烤焦（物体表面）：*I scorched my dress when I was ironing it.* 我把自己的连衣裙熨焦了。 ◇ *Don't stand so near the fire—your coat is scorching!* 别站得离火那么近，你的外衣都快烤焦了！ ➲ SYNONYMS AT BURN **2** [T, I] **~ (sth)** to become or to make sth become dry and brown, especially from the heat of the sun or from chemicals（使）枯黄，枯萎（尤指因暴晒或化学品的作用）：*scorched grass* 枯草 ◇ *The leaves will scorch if you water them in the sun.* 在太阳底下浇水，叶子会枯。 **3** [I] **+ adv./prep.** (*BrE*, *informal*) to move very fast 疾驰；飞驰：*The car scorched off down the road.* 汽车沿公路飞驰而去。

scorched ˈ**earth policy** *noun* (in a war) a policy of destroying anything in a particular area that may be useful to the enemy（战争中的）焦土政策

scorch·er /ˈskɔːtʃə(r); *NAmE* ˈskɔːrtʃ-/ *noun* (*informal*) **1** a very hot day 大热天 **2** (*BrE*) (used mainly in newspapers 主要用于报章) a very good stroke, shot, etc. in a sport 精彩的击球（或射门等）：*a scorcher of a free kick* 一记精准的任意球

scorch·ing /ˈskɔːtʃɪŋ; *NAmE* ˈskɔːrtʃ-/ *adj.* (*informal*) **1** very hot 酷热的 **SYN baking** **2** (*especially BrE*) used to emphasize how strong, powerful, etc. sth is 猛烈的；激烈的；有力的：*a scorching critique of the government's economic policy* 对政府经济政策的严厉批评

ˈ**scorch mark** *noun* a mark made on a surface by burning 焦痕

score 🔑 /skɔː(r)/ *noun*, *verb*

■***noun***

• **POINTS/GOALS, ETC.** 得分、进球等 **1** 🔑 [C] the number of points, goals, etc. scored by each player or team in a game or competition（游戏或比赛中的）得分，比分：*a* **high/low score** 高分；低分 ◇ *What's the score now?* 现在比分是多少？ ◇ *The final score was 4–3.* 最终的比分是 4:3。 ◇ *I'll* **keep (the) score**. 我来记分。 **2** 🔑 [C] (*especially NAmE*) the number of points sb gets for correct answers

S

in a test（考试中的）分数，成绩：*test scores* 考试分数 ◇ *an IQ score of 120* 智商 120 分 ◇ *a perfect score* 满分

• MUSIC 音乐 **3** [C] a written or printed version of a piece of music showing what each instrument is to play or what each voice is to sing 总谱：*an orchestral score* 管弦乐总谱 ◇ *the score of Verdi's 'Requiem'* 威尔第《安魂曲》的总谱 **4** [C] the music written for a film/movie or play（电影或戏剧的）配乐：*an award for best original score* 最佳原创配乐奖 ➲ WORDFINDER NOTE AT OPERA

• TWENTY 二十 **5** [C] (*pl.* **score**) a set or group of 20 or approximately 20 * 20 个；约 20 个：*Several cabs and a score of cars were parked outside.* 外边停着二十几辆汽车和几辆出租车。◇ *Doyle's success brought imitators* ***by the score*** (= very many). 多伊尔取得成功后，仿效者群起。◇ *the biblical age of three score years and ten* (= 70)《圣经》上所说的七十岁

• MANY 许多 **6** **scores** [pl.] very many 大量；很多：*There were scores of boxes and crates, all waiting to be checked and loaded.* 大批的箱子和板条箱等着检验后装运。

• CUT 刻痕 **7** [C] a cut in a surface, made with a sharp tool 刻痕；划痕；伤痕

• FACTS ABOUT SITUATION 真实情况 **8** **the score** [sing.] (*informal*) the real facts about the present situation 实情；真相：***What's the score?*** 情况怎么样？◇ *You don't have to lie to me. I* ***know the score.*** 你不必瞒我。我知道是怎么回事。

IDM **on 'that/'this score** as far as that/this is concerned 就那个（或这个）来说；在那个（或这个）问题上：*You don't have to worry on that score.* 那件事你不必担心。➲ MORE AT EVEN *v.*, SETTLE *v.*

■ *verb*

• GIVE/GET POINTS/GOALS 打分；得分 **1** [I, T] to win points, goals, etc. in a game or competition（在游戏或比赛中）得分：*Fraser scored again in the second half.* 弗雷泽在下半场时再次得分。◇ **~ sth** *to score a goal/try/touchdown/victory* 射门得分；带球触地得分；达阵得分；获胜 **2** [I] to keep a record of the points, goals, etc. won in a game or competition（在游戏或比赛中）记分：*Who's going to score?* 谁来记分呢？ **3** [T, I] to gain marks in a test or an exam（在考试中）得分：**~ sth** *She scored 98% in the French test.* 她法语考了 98 分。◇ **+ adv./prep.** *Girls usually score highly in language exams.* 在语言考试中，女生通常得高分。 **4** [T] **~ sth** to give sth/sb a particular number of points 评分；打分数：*The tests are scored by psychologists.* 测验由心理学家评分。◇ *Score each criterion on a scale of 1 to 5.* 按 1 到 5 分给每一种标准打分。◇ *a scoring system* 评分体系 **5** [T] **~ sth** to be worth a particular number of points 分值是；得…分：*Each correct answer will score two points.* 每答对一题得两分。

• SUCCEED 成功 **6** [T, I] to succeed; to have an advantage 获得胜利；取得优势：**~ (sth)** *The army continued to score successes in the south.* 军队在南方不断取得胜利。◇ *She's scored again with her latest blockbuster.* 她的新作大获成功，再次引起轰动。◇ **~ over sth** *Bicycles score over other forms of transport in towns.* 在城镇，自行车比其他交通工具更胜一筹。

• ARRANGE/WRITE MUSIC 谱曲；作曲 **7** [T, usually passive] to arrange a piece of music for one or more musical instruments or for voices 编总谱：**~ sth for sth** *The piece is scored for violin, viola and cello.* 这个乐谱是为小提琴、中提琴和大提琴演奏而编的。◇ **~ sth** *The director invited him to score the movie* (= write the music for it). 导演邀请他为电影配乐。

• CUT 刻痕 **8** [T] **~ sth** to make a cut or mark on a surface（在物体表面）划下痕迹，刻出记号：*Score the card first with a knife.* 先用刀在卡片上划出痕迹。

• HAVE SEX 发生性关系 **9** [I] **~ (with sb)** (*slang*) (especially of a man 尤指男人) to have sex with a new partner 和新伴侣发生性关系：*Did you score last night?* 你昨晚把她搞到手了吗？

• BUY DRUGS 买毒品 **10** [T, I] **~ (sth)** (*slang*) to buy or get illegal drugs 买（或搞到）毒品

IDM **,score a 'point/'points (off/against/over sb)** = SCORE OFF SB

PHR V **'score off sb** [no passive] (*especially BrE*) to show that you are better than sb, especially by making clever remarks, for example in an argument（尤指在辩论等活动中机灵地）驳倒，挫败：*He was always trying to score off his teachers.* 他老和老师抬杠。 **,score sth↔'out/'through** to draw a line or lines through sth 画掉；删去：*Her name had been scored out on the list.* 她的名字已从名单上画掉了。

score·board /ˈskɔːbɔːd; *NAmE* ˈskɔːrbɔːrd/ *noun* a large board on which the score in a game or competition is shown 记分牌

score·card /ˈskɔːkɑːd; *NAmE* ˈskɔːrkɑːrd/ *noun* a card or piece of paper that people watching or playing a game can use to write the score on, or on which the score can be officially recorded 记分卡

'score draw *noun* (*BrE*) the result of a football (SOCCER) match in which both teams score the same number of goals（足球比赛中双方入球数相等的）平局

score·less /ˈskɔːləs; *NAmE* ˈskɔːrləs/ *adj.* (of a game 体育比赛) without either team getting any points, goals, etc. 双方均未得分的；零比零的：*a scoreless draw* 零比零平局

score·line /ˈskɔːlaɪn; *NAmE* ˈskɔːrl-/ *noun* (*BrE*) (used mainly in newspapers 主要用于报章) the final score or result in a game, competition, etc.（体育比赛的）最终比分，最终结果：*a 2–1 scoreline* 最终比分 2:1 ◇ *The team did not play as badly as the scoreline suggests.* 这支球队的表现并不像最终比分所显示的那样糟糕。

scorer /ˈskɔːrə(r)/ *noun* **1** (in sports 体育运动) a player who scores points, goals, etc. 得分运动员；得分手：*United's top scorer* 联队的头号得分手 **2** a person who keeps a record of the points, goals, etc. scored in a game or competition（在游戏或比赛中的）记分人，记分员 **3** a **high/low ~** a person who gets a high/low number of points in a test or an exam（在测验或考试中）得高分者，得低分者

'score sheet *noun* (*BrE*) a piece of paper on which the score of a game can be officially recorded（比赛中的）记分单

IDM **get your name on the 'score sheet** (*informal*) (used in newspapers 用于报章) to score a goal, etc. 有一球（或一分）记入名下

scorn /skɔːn; *NAmE* skɔːrn/ *noun, verb*

■ *noun* [U] a strong feeling that sb/sth is stupid or not good enough, usually shown by the way you speak 轻蔑；鄙视 SYN **contempt**：*Her fellow teachers* ***greeted her proposal with scorn.*** 别的老师对她的提议不屑一顾。◇ **~ for sb/sth** *They had nothing but scorn for his political views.* 他们对他的政治观点只有鄙夷。

IDM **pour/heap 'scorn on sb/sth** to speak about sb/sth in a way that shows that you do not respect them or have a good opinion of them 嗤之以鼻；不屑一顾

■ *verb* **1** **~ sb/sth** to feel or show that you think sb/sth is stupid and you do not respect them or it 轻蔑；鄙视 SYN **dismiss**：*She scorned their views as old-fashioned.* 她对他们的观点嗤之以鼻，认为陈腐过时。 **2** (*formal*) to refuse to have or do sth because you are too proud 不屑于（接受或做）；轻蔑地拒绝：**~ sth** *to scorn an invitation* 轻蔑地回绝邀请 ◇ **~ to do sth** *She would have scorned to stoop to such tactics.* 她原本不屑于下作到使用那样的伎俩。 IDM SEE HELL

scorn·ful /ˈskɔːnfl; *NAmE* ˈskɔːrnfl/ *adj.* showing or feeling scorn 轻蔑的；鄙夷的 SYN **contemptuous**：*a scornful laugh* 轻蔑的冷笑 ◇ **~ of sth** *He was scornful of such 'female' activities as cooking.* 他看不起诸如做饭之类的"女人的"活儿。 ▸ **scorn·ful·ly** /-fəli/ *adv.*：*She laughed scornfully.* 她轻蔑地大笑。

Scor·pio /ˈskɔːpiəʊ; *NAmE* ˈskɔːrpioʊ/ *noun* **1** [U] the 8th sign of the ZODIAC, the SCORPION 黄道第八宫；天蝎宫；天蝎（星）座 **2** [C] (*pl.* **-os**) a person born when the sun is in this sign, that is between 23 October and 21 November, approximately 属天蝎座的人（约出生于 10 月 23 日至 11 月 21 日）

scor·pion /ˈskɔːpiən; *NAmE* ˈskɔːrp-/ *noun* a small creature like an insect with eight legs, two front CLAWS (= curved

S

and pointed arms) and a long tail that curves over its back and can give a poisonous sting. Scorpions live in hot countries. 蝎子 ➲ VISUAL VOCAB PAGE V13

Scot /skɒt; *NAmE* skɑːt/ *noun* **1** a person from Scotland 苏格兰人 **2 the Scots** [pl.] the people of Scotland （统称）苏格兰人 ➲ NOTE AT SCOTTISH

Scotch /skɒtʃ; *NAmE* skɑːtʃ/ *noun, adj.*
■ ***noun*** **1** [U] the type of WHISKY made in Scotland 苏格兰威士忌： *a bottle of Scotch* 一瓶苏格兰威士忌 **2** [C] a glass of Scotch 一杯苏格兰威士忌： *Do you want a Scotch?* 你要不要喝一杯苏格兰威士忌？
■ ***adj.*** of or connected with Scotland 苏格兰的 ➲ NOTE AT SCOTTISH

scotch /skɒtʃ; *NAmE* skɑːtʃ/ *verb* **~ sth** to stop sth from happening; to take action to end sth 阻止；挫败；平息；终止： *Plans for a merger have been scotched.* 合并计划停止实行。◇ *Rumours that he had fled the country were promptly scotched by his wife.* 他的妻子立刻驳斥了他已逃到国外的谣言。

ˌScotch ˈbonnet *noun* a type of very hot CHILLI 苏格兰帽红辣椒（极辣）

ˌScotch ˈbroth *noun* [U] (*BrE*) a thick soup containing vegetables and BARLEY (= a type of grain) 苏格兰浓汤（用蔬菜和大麦煮成）

ˌScotch ˈegg *noun* (*BrE*) a boiled egg covered with SAUSAGE MEAT and BREADCRUMBS, fried and eaten cold 苏格兰香肠蛋（鸡蛋煮熟后外裹香肠肉和面包屑，炸后作为冷餐食用）

ˈScotch tape™ (*NAmE*) (*BrE* **Sel·lo·tape™**, **ˈsticky tape**) *noun* [U] clear plastic tape that is sticky on one side, used for sticking things together 透明胶带；赛勒塔普胶黏带 ➲ VISUAL VOCAB PAGE V71

scot-ˈfree *adv.* (*informal*) without receiving the punishment you deserve 逃脱惩罚；逍遥法外： *They got off scot-free because of lack of evidence.* 由于证据不足，他们得以逍遥法外。 **ORIGIN** This idiom comes from the old English word 'scot' meaning 'tax'. People were scot-free if they didn't have to pay the tax. 本习语源自古英语 scot 一词，意为赋税。scot-free 表示无须纳税。

S

▼ **MORE ABOUT ...** 补充说明

describing things from Scotland 描述来自苏格兰的事物

- The adjective **Scottish** is the most general word used to describe the people and things of Scotland, while **Scots** is only used to describe its people, its law and especially its language. 形容词 Scottish 为含义最广的用语，形容来自苏格兰的人和物。Scots 仅用来表示苏格兰人、苏格兰法律，尤其是苏格兰语： *Scottish dancing* 苏格兰舞蹈 ◇ *the Scottish parliament* 苏格兰议会 ◇ *a well-known Scots poet* 著名的苏格兰诗人 ◇ *a slight Scots accent* 轻微的苏格兰口音
- The adjective **Scotch** is now mainly used in fixed expressions such as *Scotch whisky* and *Scotch broth* and sounds old-fashioned or insulting if it is used in any other way. 形容词 Scotch 现主要用于某些固定短语中，如 Scotch whisky（苏格兰威士忌）和 Scotch broth（苏格兰浓汤）。用于其他地方则显得过时或带有侮辱性。
- The noun **Scotch** means whisky, and the noun **Scots** refers to a language spoken in Scotland, closely related to English. A person who comes from Scotland is a **Scot**. 名词 Scotch 指苏格兰威士忌，而名词 Scots 指与英语密切相关的苏格兰语。苏格兰人用 Scot 表示： *The Scots won their match against England.* 苏格兰人在与英格兰人的比赛中获胜。

➲ NOTE AT BRITISH

Scot·land Yard /ˌskɒtlənd ˈjɑːd; *NAmE* ˌskɑːtlənd ˈjɑːrd/ *noun* [U+sing./pl. v.] (in Britain) the main office of the London police, especially the department that deals with serious crimes in London 伦敦警察厅（尤指其刑侦处）；苏格兰场： *Scotland Yard's anti-terrorist squad* 伦敦警察厅反恐小组 ◇ *Scotland Yard has/have been called in.* 已向伦敦警察厅报了案。

Scots /skɒts; *NAmE* skɑːts/ *adj., noun*
■ ***adj.*** of or connected with Scotland, and especially with the English language as spoken in Scotland or the Scots language 苏格兰的；（尤指）苏格兰英语的，苏格兰语的： *He spoke with a Scots accent.* 他说话带苏格兰口音。◇ *She comes from an old Scots family.* 她出生于一个古老的苏格兰家族。
■ ***noun*** [U] a language spoken in Scotland, closely related to English but with many differences 苏格兰英语

Scot·tie /ˈskɒti; *NAmE* ˈskɑːti/ *noun* (*informal*) = SCOTTISH TERRIER

Scot·tish /ˈskɒtɪʃ; *NAmE* ˈskɑːtɪʃ/ *adj.* of or connected with Scotland or its people 苏格兰的；苏格兰人的： *the Scottish Highlands* 苏格兰高地 ◇ *Scottish dancing* 苏格兰舞蹈

the ˌScottish ˈNational Party *noun* [sing.+sing./pl. v.] (*abbr.* **SNP**) a Scottish political party which wants Scotland to be an independent nation 苏格兰民族党（主张苏格兰独立）

the ˌScottish ˈParliament *noun* [sing.+sing./pl. v.] the parliament elected by the people of Scotland which has powers to make its own laws in areas such as education and health 苏格兰议会（由苏格兰人民选举产生，有权制定教育、卫生等法规）

ˌScottish ˈterrier (*also* **Scot·tie** *informal*) *noun* a small TERRIER (= type of dog) with rough hair and short legs 苏格兰㹴狗

scoun·drel /ˈskaʊndrəl/ *noun* (*old-fashioned*) a man who treats other people badly, especially by being dishonest or immoral 无赖；恶棍 **SYN** **rogue**

scour /ˈskaʊə(r)/ *verb* **1 ~ sth (for sb/sth)** to search a place or thing thoroughly in order to find sb/sth （彻底地）搜寻，搜查，翻找 **SYN** **comb**: *We scoured the area for somewhere to pitch our tent.* 我们四处查看，想找一个搭帐篷的地方。 **2 ~ sth (out)** to clean sth by rubbing its surface hard with rough material （用粗糙的物体）擦净，擦亮： *I had to scour out the pans.* 我得把这些锅擦干净。 **3 ~ sth (away/out) | ~ sth (from/out of sth)** to make a passage, hole, or mark in the ground, rocks, etc. as the result of movement, especially over a long period 冲刷成；冲刷出： *The water had raced down the slope and scoured out the bed of a stream.* 水顺着山坡流下来，冲刷出一条小河道。

scour·er /ˈskaʊərə(r)/ (*also* **ˈscouring pad**) *noun* a small ball of wire or stiff plastic used for cleaning pans （用以擦洗锅的）金属丝球，塑料丝球

scourge /skɜːdʒ; *NAmE* skɜːrdʒ/ *noun, verb*
■ ***noun*** **1** [usually sing.] **~ (of sb/sth)** (*formal*) a person or thing that causes trouble or suffering 祸害；祸根；灾害： ***the scourge of war/disease/poverty*** 战争 / 疾病 / 贫穷之苦 ◇ *Inflation was the scourge of the 1970s.* 通货膨胀曾是 20 世纪 70 年代的祸患。 **2** a WHIP used to punish people in the past （旧时用作刑具的）鞭子
■ ***verb*** **1** [usually passive] **~ sb** (*literary*) to cause trouble or suffering to sb 折磨；使受苦难；使痛苦： *He lay awake, scourged by his conscience.* 他备受良心的折磨，不能入睡。 **2 ~ sb** (*old use*) to hit sb with a scourge 鞭打；鞭笞 **SYN** **whip**

Scouse /skaʊs/ *noun* (*BrE, informal*) **1** (*also* **Scouser** /ˈskaʊsə(r)/) [C] a person from Liverpool in NW England （英格兰西北部的）利物浦人 **2** [U] a way of speaking, used by people from Liverpool 利物浦方言（或口音）
▸ **Scouse** *adj.*： *a Scouse accent* 利物浦口音

scout /skaʊt/ *noun, verb*
■ ***noun*** **1 the Scouts** [pl.] an organization (officially called the **Scout Association**) originally for boys, which trains

young people in practical skills and does a lot of activities with them, for example camping 童子军：*to join the Scouts* 参加童子军 **2** (*BrE*) a boy or girl who is a member of the Scouts 童子军成员：*Both my brothers were scouts.* 我的两个哥哥都当过童子军。◇ *a scout troop* 童子军中队 ➲ SEE ALSO BOY SCOUT, GUIDE *n.* (6) ➲ COMPARE BROWNIE (2), (3) **3** a person, an aircraft, etc. sent ahead to get information about the enemy's position, strength, etc. 侦察员；侦察机 ➲ WORDFINDER NOTE AT EXPLORE **4** = TALENT SCOUT

■*verb* **1** [T, I] to search an area or various areas in order to find or discover sth 侦察，搜寻（某处）：**~ sth (for sb/sth)** *They scouted the area for somewhere to stay the night.* 他们四处查看，想找个过夜的地方。◇ **~ (around) (for sb/sth)** *The kids were scouting around for wood for the fire.* 孩子们正在四处寻找柴火。◇ *a military scouting party* 军事侦察小分队 **2** [I, T] **~ (sb)** to look for sports players, actors, musicians, etc. who have special ability, so you can offer them work 物色（优秀运动员、演员、音乐家等）：*He scouts for Manchester United.* 他为曼彻斯特联队物色球员。

PHR V **,scout sth↔'out** to find out what an area is like or where sth is, by searching 搜索；侦察（地形）；勘察：*We went ahead to scout out the lie of the land.* 我们先一步出发，去侦察地形。

Scout·er /'skaʊtə(r)/ *noun* a person who is the leader of a group of scouts 童子军队长

scout·ing /'skaʊtɪŋ/ *noun* [U] the activities that boy and girl SCOUTS take part in; the Scout organization 童子军活动；童子军组织

scout·mas·ter /'skaʊtmɑːstə(r); *NAmE* -mæstər/ (*also* **'scout leader**) *noun* the adult in charge of a group of BOY SCOUTS 男童子军团长（由成年人担任）

scowl /skaʊl/ *verb, noun*

■*verb* [I] **~ (at sb/sth)** to look at sb/sth in an angry or annoyed way 怒视（某人或某物）SYN **glower** ➲ WORDFINDER NOTE AT EXPRESSION

■*noun* an angry look or expression 怒容；不悦的神色：*He looked up at me with a scowl.* 他脸色阴沉，抬眼看了看我。

SCQF /ˌes siː kjuː 'ef/ *noun* the abbreviation for 'Scottish Credit and Qualifications Framework' (all the exams and courses that Scottish students can take at different levels between the ages of approximately 15 and 18. These include National level exams and HIGHERS.) 苏格兰学分和学历体系（全写为 Scottish Credit and Qualifications Framework，苏格兰学生在约 15 至 18 岁可修的分级课程和考试，包括国家水平考试和高级证书考试）

Scrab·ble™ /'skræbl/ *noun* [U] a board game in which players try to make words from letters printed on small plastic blocks and connect them to words that have already been placed on the board 拼字游戏（用手中的字母组成新的单词，并和台面上已存在的单词接上）

scrab·ble /'skræbl/ *verb* [I] **~ (around/about) (for sth) | + adv./prep.** (*especially BrE*) to try to find or to do sth in a hurry or with difficulty, often by moving your hands or feet about quickly, without much control 忙乱地找；翻找；乱抓；乱动：*She scrabbled around in her bag for her glasses.* 她在包里翻来翻去找眼镜。◇ *He was scrabbling for a foothold on the steep slope.* 他在陡坡上挣扎着乱蹬，想找个落脚的地方。◇ *a sound like rats scrabbling on the other side of the wall* 墙那面一种像老鼠乱抓的声音

scrag·gly /'skrægli/ *adj.* (*NAmE, informal*) thin and growing in a way that is not even 稀疏凌乱的；散乱的：*a scraggly beard* 稀稀拉拉的胡子

scraggy /'skrægi/ *adj.* (**scrag·gier, scrag·gi·est**) (*disapproving*) (of people or animals 人或动物) very thin and not looking healthy 骨瘦如柴的；面黄肌瘦的 SYN **scrawny**：*a scraggy old cat* 一只瘦骨嶙峋的老猫

scram /skræm/ *verb* (**-mm-**) [I] (*old-fashioned, informal*) (usually used in orders 通常用于命令) to go away quickly 走开；滚：*Scram! I don't want you here.* 滚！不要待在我这儿。

scram·ble /'skræmbl/ *verb, noun*

■*verb*

• **WALK/CLIMB** 行走；攀爬 **1** [I] **+ adv./prep.** to move quickly, especially with difficulty, using your hands to help you （迅速而吃力地）爬，攀登 SYN **clamber**：*She managed to scramble over the wall.* 她手忙脚乱地翻过墙。◇ *He* ***scrambled to his feet*** *as we came in.* 我们进来时，他赶紧从地上爬起来。

• **PUSH/FIGHT** 推挤；争抢 **2** [I] to push, fight or compete with others in order to get or to reach sth 争抢；抢占；争夺：**~ for sth** *The audience scrambled for the exits.* 观众竞相朝出口拥去。◇ **~ to do sth** *Shoppers were scrambling to get the best bargains.* 顾客争先恐后地抢购最便宜的特价商品。

• **ACHIEVE STH WITH DIFFICULTY** 艰难地完成 **3** [T] to manage to achieve sth with difficulty, or in a hurry, without much control 艰难地（或仓促地）完成：**~ sth** *Cork scrambled a 1–0 win over Monaghan.* 科克队苦战莫纳亨队，以 1:0 获胜。◇ **~ sth + adv./prep.** *Rooney managed to scramble the ball into the net.* 鲁尼设法把球送进了网窝。

• **EGGS** 蛋 **4** [T, usually passive] **~ sth** to cook an egg by mixing the white and yellow parts together and heating them, sometimes with milk and butter 炒（蛋）：*scrambled eggs* 炒蛋

• **TELEPHONE/RADIO** 电话；无线电 **5** [T, often passive] **~ sth** to change the way that a telephone or radio message sounds so that only people with special equipment can understand it 扰码，倒频（改变电话或无线电信号，听众只有通过专门设备才能收听）：*scrambled satellite signals* 扰码卫星信号

• **CONFUSE THOUGHTS** 扰乱思维 **6** [T] **~ sth** to confuse sb's thoughts, ideas, etc. so that they have no order 扰乱（思维）：*Alcohol seemed to have scrambled his brain.* 酒精似乎扰乱了他的脑子。

• **AIRCRAFT** 飞机 **7** [T, I, usually passive] **~ (sth)** to order that planes, etc. should take off immediately in an emergency; to take off immediately in an emergency 命令（飞机等）紧急起飞；紧急起飞：*A helicopter was scrambled to help rescue three young climbers.* 直升机接到命令，紧急起飞前去营救三个登山的年轻人。◇ *They scrambled as soon as the call came through.* 命令刚一下达，他们便紧急起飞。

■*noun*

• **DIFFICULT WALK/CLIMB** 艰难行走 / 攀爬 **1** [sing.] a difficult walk or climb over rough ground, especially one in which you have to use your hands （尤指需要手脚并用的）艰难行走，爬，攀登

• **PUSH/FIGHT** 推挤；争抢 **2** [sing.] **~ (for sth)** a situation in which people push, fight or compete with each other in order to get or do sth 争抢；抢占；争夺 SYN **free-for-all**：*There was a mad scramble for the best seats.* 人们不顾一切地抢占最好的座位。

• **MOTORCYCLE RACE** 摩托车比赛 **3** [C] a race for motorcycles over rough ground 摩托车越野赛

scram·bler /'skræmblə(r)/ *noun* a device that changes radio or telephone signals or messages so that they cannot be understood by other people 扰码器

scram·bling /'skræmblɪŋ/ *noun* [U] (*BrE*) = MOTOCROSS

scrap /skræp/ *noun, verb*

■*noun* **1** [C] a small piece of sth, especially paper, cloth, etc. 碎片，小块（纸、布匹等）：*She scribbled his phone number on a scrap of paper.* 她把他的电话号码匆匆写在一张小纸片上。◇ (*figurative*) *scraps of information* 零星消息 ◇ (*figurative*) *She was just a scrap of a thing* (= small and thin). 她是个不起眼的小东西。 **2** [sing.] (usually with a negative 通常与否定式连用) a small amount of sth 丝毫；一丁点 SYN **bit**：*It won't make a* ***scrap of difference.*** 这不会有丝毫的差别。◇ *There's not a scrap of evidence to support his claim.* 没有丝毫证据支持他的说法。◇ *a barren landscape without a scrap of vegetation* 寸草不生的贫瘠地带 **3 scraps** [pl.] food left after a meal 残羹剩饭：*Give the scraps to the dog.* 把剩菜喂狗吧。 **4** [U] things that are not wanted or cannot be used for their original purpose,

S

but which have some value for the material they are made of 废料；废品：*We sold the car **for scrap*** (= so that any good parts can be used again). 我们把车当废品卖了。◇ ***scrap metal*** 废金属 ◇ ***a scrap dealer*** (= a person who buys and sells scrap) 废品商人 **5** [C] (*informal*) a short fight or disagreement 打架；争吵 SYN **squabble, scuffle**: *He was always getting into scraps at school.* 他在学校老跟人打架。➲ SEE ALSO SCRAPPY

■ *verb* (-pp-) **1** [T, often passive] **~ sth** to cancel or get rid of sth that is no longer practical or useful 废弃；取消；抛弃；报废：*They had been forced to scrap plans for a new school building.* 他们已被迫撤销了建筑新校舍的计划。◇ *The oldest of the aircraft were scrapped.* 最老的飞机报废了。**2** [I] (*informal*) to fight with sb 打架：*The bigger boys started scrapping.* 年龄较大的男孩打了起来。

scrap·book /'skræpbʊk/ *noun* a book with empty pages where you can stick pictures, newspaper articles, etc. 剪贴簿

scrape /skreɪp/ *verb, noun*

■ *verb*

• **REMOVE** 除去 **1** [T] to remove sth from a surface by moving sth sharp and hard like a knife across it 刮掉；削去：**~ sth (+ adv./prep.)** *She scraped the mud off her boots.* 她刮掉了靴子上的泥。◇ **~ sth + adj.** *The kids had scraped their plates clean.* 孩子们把自己的盘子刮得干干净净。

• **DAMAGE** 损坏 **2** [T] to rub sth by accident so that it gets damaged or hurt 擦坏；擦伤；刮坏；蹭破：**~ sth** *She fell and scraped her knee.* 她摔了一跤，把膝盖蹭破了。◇ **~ sth + adv./prep.** *I scraped the side of my car on the wall.* 我车的一侧被墙刮了。◇ *Sorry, I've scraped some paint off the car.* 抱歉，我把车刮掉了一块漆。◇ *The wire had scraped the skin from her fingers.* 她的手指头让金属丝刮掉了皮。

• **MAKE SOUND** 发出声音 **3** [I, T] to make an unpleasant noise by rubbing against a hard surface; to make sth do this （使）发出刺耳的刮擦声：**(+ adv./prep.)** *I could hear his pen scraping across the paper.* 我听得见他的钢笔在纸上沙沙地响。◇ *We could hear her scraping away at the violin.* 我们听得见她正一个劲儿吱吱呀呀地拉小提琴。◇ **~ sth (+ adv./prep.)** *Don't scrape your chairs on the floor.* 别把椅子在地板上蹭得嘎吱嘎吱响。

• **WIN WITH DIFFICULTY** 艰难获取 **4** [T, I] **~ (sth)** to manage to win or to get sth with difficulty 艰难取得；勉强获得：*The team scraped a narrow victory last year.* 这支队去年险胜。◇ (*BrE*) *I just scraped a pass in the exam.* 我考试勉强及格。◇ *They **scraped a living** by playing music on the streets.* 他们在街头演奏音乐，勉强维持生活。◇ *The government **scraped home** (= just won) by three votes.* 政府以三票的微弱优势勉强过关。

• **MAKE HOLE IN GROUND** 在地上挖坑 **5** [T] **~ sth (out)** to make a hole or hollow place in the ground 挖坑；挖洞：*He found a suitable place, scraped a hole and buried the bag in it.* 他找了个合适的地方，挖个坑，把包埋了进去。

• **PULL HAIR BACK** 朝后拢头发 **6** [T] **~ your hair back** to pull your hair tightly back, away from your face 把头发拢在后面：*Her hair was scraped back from her face in a ponytail.* 她的头发拢在后面，扎成一个马尾辫。

IDM **scrape (the bottom of) the 'barrel** (*disapproving*) to have to use whatever things or people you can get, because there is not much choice available （因别无选择）将就，凑合 ➲ MORE AT BOW[1] *v.*

PHR V **,scrape 'by (on sth)** to manage to live on the money you have, but with difficulty （靠…）勉强维持生计，糊口，艰难度日：*I can just scrape by on what my parents give me.* 我靠父母给的那点钱只能勉强度日。**,scrape 'in | ,scrape 'into sth** to manage to get a job, a position, a place at college, etc., but with difficulty 勉强获得（工作、职位、入学资格等）：*He scraped in with 180 votes.* 他以 180 票勉强当选。◇ *Our team just scraped into the semi-finals.* 我们这支队勉强挤入半决赛。**,scrape sth↔'out** to remove sth from inside sth else, using sth sharp or hard like a knife 挖出；掘出：*Scrape out the flesh of the melon with a spoon.* 用小勺挖出瓜瓤。**,scrape 'through | ,scrape 'through sth** to succeed in doing sth with difficulty, especially in passing an exam 艰难完成；勉强通过（考试）：*I might scrape through the exam if I'm lucky.* 要是走运的话，我也许能勉强及格。**,scrape sth↔to'gether/'up** to obtain or collect together sth, but with difficulty 勉强凑集；费力聚拢；艰难筹措：*We managed to scrape together eight volunteers.* 我们好不容易凑齐八名志愿者。

■ *noun*

• **ACTION/SOUND** 动作；声音 **1** [sing.] the action or unpleasant sound of one thing rubbing roughly against another 刮；铲；刮铲声；刮擦声：*the scrape of iron on stone* 铁摩擦石头发出的嚓嚓声

• **DAMAGE** 损坏 **2** [C] an injury or a mark caused by rubbing against sth rough 擦伤；擦痕：*She emerged from the overturned car with only a few scrapes and bruises.* 她从翻了的车里钻出来，只擦破一点皮，碰了几块瘀青。

• **DIFFICULT SITUATION** 困境 **3** [C] (*old-fashioned*) a difficult situation that you have caused yourself 自己造成的困境：*He was always getting into scrapes as a boy.* 他小时候老闯祸。

scraper /'skreɪpə(r)/ *noun* a tool used for scraping, for example for scraping mud from shoes or ice from a car 刮刀；刮削器

scrap·heap /'skræphiːp/ *noun* a pile of things, especially of metal, that are no longer wanted or useful 废物堆；（尤指）废金属堆

IDM **on the 'scrapheap** (*informal*) no longer wanted or considered useful 废弃的；丢弃的

scra·pie /'skreɪpi/ *noun* [U] a serious disease that affects the NERVOUS SYSTEM of sheep 痒病（损伤羊的神经系统的严重疾病）

scrap·ing /'skreɪpɪŋ/ *noun* [usually pl.] a small amount of sth produced by scratching a surface 刮屑；削片

'scrap paper *noun* [U] loose pieces of paper used for writing notes on （散的）便条纸

scrappy /'skræpi/ *adj.* (**scrap·pier, scrap·pi·est**) **1** consisting of individual sections, events, etc. that are not organized into a whole 散乱的；不连贯的；支离破碎的 SYN **bitty**: *a scrappy essay* 一篇内容凌乱的文章 **2** (*especially BrE*) not tidy and often of poor quality 不整洁的；粗陋的：*The note was written on a scrappy bit of paper.* 便条写在一片破纸上。➲ SEE ALSO SCRAP *n.*

scrap·yard /'skræpjɑːd; *NAmE* -jɑːrd/ (*BrE*) (*also* **junk·yard** *NAmE, BrE*) *noun* a place where old cars, machines, etc. are collected, so that parts of them, or the metal they are made of, can be sold to be used again （堆放旧汽车、旧机器等的）废品场

scratch /skrætʃ/ *verb, noun, adj.*

■ *verb*

• **RUB WITH YOUR NAILS** 用指甲挠 **1** [T, I] to rub your skin with your nails, usually because it is ITCHING 挠，搔（痒处）：**~ sth/yourself** *John yawned and scratched his chin.* 约翰打个哈欠，挠挠下巴。◇ *The dog scratched itself behind the ear.* 狗用爪子挠挠耳后。◇ **~ (at sth)** *Try not to scratch.* 尽量别挠。◇ *She scratched at the insect bites on her arm.* 她挠了挠胳膊上虫咬的包。

• **CUT SKIN** 划破皮肤 **2** [T, I] to cut or damage your skin slightly with sth sharp 划破，抓破，划伤，抓伤（皮肤）：**~ (sb/sth/yourself)** *I'd scratched my leg and it was bleeding.* 我把腿抓出了血。◇ *Does the cat scratch?* 这只猫抓人吗？◇ **~ sb/sth/yourself on sth** *She scratched herself on a nail.* 她被钉子划了一下。

• **DAMAGE SURFACE** 损坏表面 **3** [T] **~ sth** to damage the surface of sth, especially by accident, by making thin shallow marks on it （尤指意外地）擦破，划损，刮坏：*Be careful not to scratch the furniture.* 小心别刮坏家具。◇ *The car's paintwork is badly scratched.* 车的漆面划损得很厉害。

• **MAKE/REMOVE MARK** 造成 / 去除痕迹 **4** [T] **~ sth + adv./prep.** to make or remove a mark, etc. on sth deliberately, by rubbing it with sth hard or sharp 刮出（或刮去）痕迹；划下（或擦去）痕迹：*They scratched lines in the dirt to mark out a pitch.* 他们在泥地上划出一个球场。◇ *We scratched some of the dirt away.* 我们刮掉了一些脏东西。◇

(*figurative*) *You can scratch my name off the list.* 你可以把我的名字从名单上勾掉。

• **MAKE SOUND** 发出声音 **5** [I] (**+ adv./prep.**) to make an irritating noise by rubbing sth with sth sharp 刮（或擦、抓）出刺耳声：*His pen scratched away on the paper.* 他的笔在纸上沙沙地响。

• **A LIVING** 生计 **6** [T] **~ a living** to make enough money to live on, but with difficulty 勉强维持生活

• **CANCEL** 取消 **7** [T, I] to decide that sth cannot happen or sb/sth cannot take part in sth, before it starts 取消；撤销；退出：**~ sb/sth** *to scratch a rocket launch* 取消火箭发射计划 ◇ **~ sb/sth** (**from sth**) *The horse was scratched from the race because of injury.* 这匹马因伤被取消了比赛资格。◇ **~** (**from sth**) *She had scratched because of a knee injury.* 她因膝伤退出了比赛。

IDM **scratch your 'head** (**over sth**) to think hard in order to find an answer to sth 苦苦琢磨；苦思冥想；绞尽脑汁 **scratch the 'surface** (**of sth**) to deal with, understand, or find out about only a small part of a subject or problem 作肤浅的探讨；浅尝辄止；隔靴搔痒 **,you scratch 'my back and ,I'll scratch 'yours** (*saying*) used to say that if sb helps you, you will help them, even if this is unfair to others 礼尚往来；私相授受

PHR V **,scratch a'bout/a'round** (**for sth**) to search for sth, especially with difficulty （尤指艰难地）搜寻，查寻，查找 **,scratch sth↔'out** to remove a word, especially a name, from sth written, usually by putting a line through it 画掉，勾掉，删除（名字等）

■ ***noun***

• **MARK/CUT** 划痕；划伤 **1** [C] a mark, a cut or an injury made by scratching sb's skin or the surface of sth （皮肤或物体表面上的）划痕，划伤：*Her hands were covered in scratches from the brambles.* 她手上布满了荆棘划的口子。◇ *a scratch on the paintwork* 漆面上的一道划痕 ◇ *It's only **a scratch*** (= a very slight injury). 不过是轻微的划伤。◇ *He escaped **without a scratch*** (= was not hurt at all). 他毫发未损地逃了出去。

• **SOUND** 声音 **2** [sing.] the unpleasant sound of sth sharp or rough being rubbed against a surface 刮（或擦、抓）的刺耳声

• **WITH YOUR NAILS** 用指甲 **3** [sing.] the act of scratching a part of your body when it ITCHES 挠痒；搔痒：*Go on, have a good scratch!* 来吧，好好挠一挠！

IDM **from 'scratch 1** without any previous preparation or knowledge 从头开始；从零开始：*I learned German from scratch in six months.* 我从零学起，六个月学会了德语。**2** from the very beginning, not using any of the work done earlier 从头（做起）；从零开始：*They decided to dismantle the machine and start again from scratch.* 他们决定拆掉机器，从头再来。 **up to 'scratch** as good as sth/sb should be 达到要求；合乎标准 **SYN** **satisfactory**: *His work simply isn't up to scratch.* 他的工作根本达不到要求。◇ *It'll take months to bring the band up to scratch.* 得几个月工夫才能使乐队像个样子。

■ ***adj.*** (*BrE*) **1** put together in a hurry using whatever people or materials are available 仓促拼凑的：*a scratch team* 一支仓促组建的队伍 **2** (especially in GOLF 尤指高尔夫球) with no HANDICAP 无让杆的；无差点的：*a scratch player* 参加无让杆比赛的球手

'scratch card *noun* a card that you buy that has an area that you scratch off to find out if you have won some money or a prize 刮奖卡；刮刮卡

'scratch pad *noun* (*NAmE*) a small book of cheap paper for writing notes on 便笺簿

'scratch paper *noun* [U] (*NAmE*) cheap paper, or loose sheets of paper, for writing notes on 便条纸；草稿纸

scratchy /'skrætʃi/ *adj.* (**scratch·ier, scratchi·est**) **1** (of clothes or cloth 衣服或织物) rough and unpleasant to the touch 扎人的；粗糙刺激皮肤的 **SYN** **itchy** **2** (of a record, voice, etc. 录音、声音等) making a rough, unpleasant sound like sth being scratched across a surface 带沙沙的杂音的：*a scratchy recording of Mario Lanza* 一盘有杂音的马里奥·兰扎演唱录音 ◇ *a scratchy pen* 一支划纸的钢笔 **3** (of writing or drawings 字迹或图画) done without care 潦草的；粗制滥造的

scrawl /skrɔːl/ *verb, noun*

■ ***verb*** [T, I] to write sth in a careless untidy way, making it difficult to read 马马虎虎（或潦草）地写 **SYN** **scribble**: **~ sth** (**across/in/on/over sth**) *I tried to read his directions, scrawled on a piece of paper.* 我努力想弄明白他草草写在一片纸上的指示。◇ **~ across/in/on/over sth** *Someone had scrawled all over my notes.* 不知谁在我笔记上胡写乱画，弄得一塌糊涂。

■ ***noun*** a careless untidy way of writing; sth written in this way 不工整的字迹；潦草的笔迹；不工整的文字 **SYN** **scribble**: *Her signature was an illegible scrawl.* 她的签名潦草难辨。◇ *I can't be expected to read this scrawl!* 这种潦潦草草的东西我能看懂吗！ ◇ *The paper was covered in scrawls.* 满篇皆是潦草的文字。

scrawny /'skrɔːni/ *adj.* (**scrawn·ier, scrawni·est**) (*disapproving*) (of people or animals 人或动物) very thin in a way that is not attractive 干瘦的；瘦巴巴的 **SYN** **scraggy**

scream /skriːm/ *verb, noun*

■ ***verb*** **1** [I, T] to give a loud, high cry, because you are hurt, frightened, excited, etc. （因伤痛、害怕、激动等）尖叫 **SYN** **shriek**: *He covered her mouth to stop her from screaming.* 他捂上她的嘴，不让她叫出声来。◇ **~ in/with sth** *The kids were screaming with excitement.* 孩子们兴奋地喊叫着。◇ **~ out** (**in/with sth**) *People ran for the exits, screaming out in terror.* 人们惊恐万状，尖叫着奔向出口。◇ **~ yourself + adj.** *The baby was screaming itself hoarse.* 婴儿哭得嗓子都哑了。 **2** [T, I] to shout sth in a loud, high voice because of fear, anger, etc. （向某人或为某事）高声喊，大声叫 **SYN** **yell**: **+ speech** *'Help!' she screamed.* "救命啊！"她喊道。◇ **~** (**out**) (**for sth/sb**) *Someone was screaming for help.* 有人在喊救命。◇ **~ at sb** (**to do sth**) *He screamed at me to stop.* 他冲着我喊，要我停下来。◇ **~ sth** (**out**) (**at sb**) *She screamed abuse at him.* 她对他破口大骂。◇ **~** (**out**) **that...** *His sister screamed out that he was crazy.* 他姐姐大叫着说他昏了头。 ➲ SYNONYMS AT SHOUT **3** [I] to make a loud, high noise; to move fast, making this noise 发出大而尖的声音；呼啸而过 **SYN** **screech**: *Lights flashed and sirens screamed.* 灯光闪动，警报鸣叫。◇ **+ adv./prep.** *The powerboat screamed out to sea.* 汽艇呼啸着出海了。

IDM **scream blue 'murder** (*BrE*) (*NAmE* **scream bloody 'murder**) to scream loudly and for a long time, especially in order to protest about sth 不停地叫嚷（尤指叫屈、鸣不平）

PHR V **,scream 'out** (**for sth**) to be in need of attention in a very noticeable way 亟须；亟待 **SYN** **cry out**: *These books scream out to be included in a list of favourites.* 这几本书亟须列入最受读者喜爱的书目之中。

■ ***noun*** **1** [C] a loud high cry made by sb who is hurt, frightened, excited, etc.; a loud high noise 尖叫；尖锐刺耳的声音：*She let out a scream of pain.* 她疼得大叫一声。◇ *They ignored the baby's screams.* 他们对孩子的哭叫充耳不闻。◇ *He drove off with a scream of tyres.* 他驾车吱的一声开走了。**2** [sing.] (*old-fashioned, informal*) a person or thing that causes you to laugh 可笑的人（或物）：*He's a scream.* 他挺滑稽的。

scream·ing·ly /'skriːmɪŋli/ *adv.* extremely 极其；十足地：*It was screamingly obvious what we should do next.* 我们下一步该怎么做，再清楚不过了。

scree /skriː/ *noun* [U, C] an area of small loose stones, especially on a mountain, which may slide when you walk on them 碎石坡；岩屑堆 ➲ VISUAL VOCAB PAGE V5

screech /skriːtʃ/ *verb, noun*

■ ***verb*** **1** [I, T] to make a loud high unpleasant sound; to say sth using this sound 尖叫；发出尖锐刺耳的声音；尖声地说：*Monkeys were screeching in the trees.* 猴子在树上吱吱地叫着。◇ *The wind screeched in his ears.* 风呼呼地从他耳边吹过。◇ *screeching brakes* 尖锐的刹车声 ◇ *He screeched with pain.* 他疼得叫起来。◇ **+ speech** *'No, don't!' she screeched.* "不，不行！"她尖叫道。◇ **~** (**sth**) (**at sb**) *He screeched something at me.* 他冲我尖声嚷了一句什么。**2** [I] (**+ adv./prep.**) (of a vehicle 车辆) to make a loud high

S

unpleasant noise as it moves （行驶时）发出刺耳声：*The car **screeched to a halt** outside the hospital.* 汽车嘎地在医院外面停住。◇ *A police car screeched out of a side street.* 一辆警车咻的一声从一条小巷里驶了出来。

■ *noun* a loud high unpleasant cry or noise 刺耳的尖叫；尖锐刺耳的声音：*a **screech of brakes/tyres*** 制动器 / 轮胎吱的一声响 ◇ *She suddenly let out a screech.* 她猛地尖叫一声。

screed /skriːd/ *noun* a long piece of writing, especially one that is not very interesting 冗长的文章；长篇大论

screen /skriːn/ *noun, verb*

■ *noun*

• **OF TV/COMPUTER** 电视；计算机 **1** [C] the flat surface at the front of a television, computer, or other electronic device, on which you see pictures or information 屏幕；荧光屏；荧屏：*a computer screen* 计算机屏幕 ◇ *a monitor with a 21 inch screen* * 21 英寸屏幕的显示器 ◇ *They were staring at the television screen.* 当时他们正盯着电视屏幕。◇ *Move your cursor to the top of the screen.* 把你的光标移到屏幕顶端。◇ *the screen display* 屏幕显示 ◇ *Can you do a printout of this screen for me* (= of all the information on it)? 你能帮我把这一屏幕打印出来吗？ ➲ WORDFINDER NOTE AT COMPUTER ➲ VISUAL VOCAB PAGE V73 ➲ SEE ALSO ON-SCREEN **2** [C] the data or images shown on a computer screen （电脑屏幕上）一屏的内容；画面：*Press the F1 key to display a help screen.* 按 F1 键显示帮助画面。

• **FILMS/MOVIES/TV** 电影；电视 **3** [C] the large flat surface that films/movies or pictures are shown on 银幕：*a **cinema/movie screen*** 电影银幕 ◇ *an eight-screen cinema* 一家有八个放映厅的电影院 ◇ *The movie will be coming to your screens shortly.* 这部电影不久就会在你们那里上映。**4** (*often* **the screen**) [sing., U] films/movies or television in general （统称）电影，电视：*He has adapted the play for the screen.* 他把那部剧改编成了电影剧本。◇ *Some actors never watch themselves **on screen**.* 有的演员从来不看自己拍的戏。◇ *She was a star of **stage and screen*** (= plays and films/movies). 她是戏剧、电影两栖明星。◇ *a screen actor* 电影演员 ➲ SEE ALSO OFF-SCREEN, SILVER SCREEN, SMALL SCREEN

• **PIECE OF FURNITURE** 家具 **5** [C] a vertical piece of furniture or equipment that is fixed or that can be moved to divide a room or to keep one area hidden or separate 隔板；屏风；幕；帘：*The nurse put a screen around the bed.* 护士绕床拉了一道帘子。➲ SEE ALSO FIRE SCREEN

• **FOR HIDING/PROTECTING STH/SB** 用以掩藏 / 保护 **6** [C] ~ **(of sth)** something that prevents sb from seeing or being aware of sth, or that protects sb/sth 掩蔽物；掩护物；屏障；庇护：*We planted a screen of tall trees.* 我们种下一排大树作为屏障。◇ (*figurative*) *All the research was conducted behind a screen of secrecy.* 整个研究始终是秘密进行的。➲ SEE ALSO SMOKESCREEN, SUNSCREEN, WINDSCREEN

• **ON WINDOW/DOOR** 窗上；门上 **7** [C] (*especially NAmE*) a wire or plastic net that is held in a frame and fastened on a window, or a door, to let in air but keep out insects 纱窗；纱门：*screen doors* 纱门

• **IN CHURCH** 教堂里 **8** [C] a wood or stone structure in a church, that partly separates the main area from the ALTAR or CHOIR （拦在圣坛或唱诗班四周的木质或石砌）围屏 IDM SEE RADAR

■ *verb*

• **HIDE STH/SB** 遮蔽某物 / 某人 **1** ~ **sth/sb (from sth/sb)** to hide or protect sth/sb by placing sth in front of or around them 掩藏；遮蔽；保护 SYN **shield**：*Dark glasses screened his eyes from the sun.* 他戴了一副墨镜，保护眼睛不受阳光照射。

• **PROTECT SB** 保护某人 **2** ~ **sb from sb/sth** to protect sb from sth dangerous or unpleasant, especially to protect sb who has done sth illegal or dishonest 庇护；包庇；袒护 SYN **shield**

• **FOR DISEASE** 检查疾病 **3** [often passive] ~ **sb (for sth)** to examine people in order to find out if they have a particular disease or illness 筛查；检查：*Men over 55 should be regularly screened for prostate cancer.* * 55 岁以上的男性应定期做前列腺癌检查。

• **CHECK** 检查 **4** ~ **sb** (of a company, an organization, etc. 公司、组织等) to find out information about people who work or who want to work for you in order to make sure that they can be trusted 审查，调查（看是否可靠）：*Government employees may be screened by the security services.* 政府雇员可能要接受安全部门的审查。**5** ~ **sth** to check sth to see if it is suitable or if you want it 审查；筛选：*I use my voicemail to screen my phone calls.* 我用语音信箱筛选打来的电话。

• **SHOW FILM/MOVIE/PROGRAMME** 放映电影；播放节目 **6** [usually passive] ~ **sth** to show a film/movie, etc. in a cinema/movie theater or on television 放映（电影）；播放（电视节目）：*a list of films to be screened as part of the festival* 作为电影节部分内容拟放映的影片名单 ➲ COLLOCATIONS AT TELEVISION

PHR V ˌ**screen sth**↔**off** [often passive] to separate part of a room, etc. from the rest of it by putting a screen around it （用屏风等）隔开：*Beds can be screened off to give patients more privacy.* 可以用屏风把病床隔开，这样病人可以有更多的私密性。ˌ**screen sb**↔**out** to decide not to allow sb to join an organization, enter a country, etc. because you think they may cause trouble 遴选后剔除某人；不准某人入境 ˌ**screen sth**↔**out** to prevent sth harmful from entering or going through sth 遴选后剔除某物；遮挡某物穿透：*The ozone layer screens out dangerous rays from the sun.* 臭氧层能遮挡住来自太阳的有害射线。

ˈ**screen dump** *noun* a copy of what is on a computer screen at a particular time; the act of printing this out （计算机）屏幕转存，屏幕复制，屏幕打印

screener /ˈskriːnə(r)/ *noun* a person who checks people and their luggage at an airport （机场）安检员

screen·ing /ˈskriːnɪŋ/ *noun* **1** [C] the act of showing a film/movie or television programme （电影的）放映；（电视节目的）播放：*This will be the movie's first screening in this country.* 这将是这部电影首次在这个国家上映。**2** [U, C] the testing or examining of a large number of people or things for disease, faults, etc. 筛查：*breast cancer screening* 乳腺癌筛查

screen·play /ˈskriːnpleɪ/ *noun* the words that are written for a film/movie (= the SCRIPT), together with instructions for how it is to be acted and filmed 电影剧本 ➲ COLLOCATIONS AT CINEMA

ˈ**screen-print** *verb* [T, I] ~ **(sth)** to force ink or metal onto a surface through a screen of silk or artificial material to produce a picture 丝网印刷 ▸ ˈ**screen print** *noun*

ˈ**screen saver** *noun* a computer program that replaces a screen display on a computer with another, moving, display after a particular length of time, to stop the screen from being damaged 屏幕保护程序

screen·shot /ˈskriːnʃɒt; *NAmE* -ʃɑːt/ *noun* (*computing* 计) an image of the display on a screen, used when showing how a program works 屏幕截图，屏幕快照（用于展示程序运行方式）

ˈ**screen test** *noun* a test to see if sb is suitable to appear in a film/movie （挑选电影演员时）试镜头

screen·writer /ˈskriːnraɪtə(r)/ *noun* a person who writes SCREENPLAYS 电影剧本作家 ➲ COMPARE PLAYWRIGHT, SCRIPTWRITER

screw /skruː/ *noun, verb*

■ *noun* **1** [C] a thin pointed piece of metal like a nail with a raised SPIRAL line (called a THREAD) along it and a line or cross cut into its head. Screws are turned and pressed into wood, metal, etc. with a SCREWDRIVER in order to fasten two things together. 螺丝钉；螺丝：*One of the screws is loose.* 有一颗螺丝松了。◇ *Now tighten all the screws.* 现在把全部螺丝都拧紧。➲ COLLOCATIONS AT DECORATE ➲ VISUAL VOCAB PAGE V21 ➲ SEE ALSO CORKSCREW *n.* **2** [C] an act of turning a screw （对螺丝的）旋拧 **3** [sing.] (*taboo, slang*) an act of having sex 性交 **4** [sing.] (*taboo, slang*) a partner in sex 性交对象：*a good screw* 好的性交对象 **5** [C] a PROPELLER on a ship, a boat or an aircraft 螺旋桨 **6** [C] (*BrE, slang*) a prison officer 监狱看守；狱警

IDM **have a 'screw loose** to be slightly strange in your behaviour 举止略有异常；行为稍嫌古怪 **put the 'screws on (sb)** to force sb to do sth by frightening and threatening them 胁迫；威逼 ➲ MORE AT TURN *n.*

■ ***verb*** **1** [T] **~ sth + adv./prep.** to fasten one thing to another or make sth tight with a screw or screws 用螺丝固定（或拧牢）：*The bookcase is screwed to the wall.* 书架用螺丝固定在墙上了。◇ *You need to screw all the parts together.* 你得用螺丝把所有的零件固定在一起。◇ *Now screw down the lid.* 现在用螺丝将盖子固定好。➲ COMPARE UNSCREW **2** [T] to twist sth around in order to fasten it in place 旋紧；拧紧：**~ sth + adv./prep.** *She screwed the cap back on the jar.* 她又把广口瓶的盖子拧上。◇ **~ sth + adj.** *Screw the bolt tight.* 把螺栓拧紧。➲ COMPARE UNSCREW **3** [I] (**+ adv./prep.**) to be attached by screwing 拧上去：*The bulb should just screw into the socket.* 把灯泡拧到灯口上就行。◇ *The lid simply screws on.* 这盖子一拧就盖好了。**4** [T] to squeeze sth, especially a piece of paper, into a tight ball 把（纸等）揉成一团：**~ sth up (into sth)** *I screwed up the letter and threw it into the fire.* 我把那封信揉成一团，扔进了火里。◇ **~ sth (up) into sth** *Screw the foil into a little ball.* 把箔纸揉成小团。➲ SEE ALSO SCREWED-UP **5** [T] (*slang*) to cheat sb, especially by making them pay too much money for sth 诈骗（钱财等）：**~ sb** *We've been screwed.* 我们挨宰了。◇ **~ sb for sth** *How much did they screw you for* (= how much did you have to pay)? 他们坑了你多少钱？ **6** [I, T] **~ (sb)** (*taboo, slang*) to have sex with sb （和某人）性交

IDM **screw 'him, 'you, 'that, etc.** (*taboo, slang*) an offensive way of showing that you are annoyed or do not care about sb/sth 去他（或你）妈的；见他（或你、它）的鬼 **screw up your 'courage** to force yourself to be brave enough to do sth 鼓起勇气：*I finally screwed up my courage and went to the dentist.* 我终于鼓起勇气，去看了牙医。➲ MORE AT HEAD *n.*

PHR V **,screw a'round** (*taboo, slang*) to have sex with a lot of different people 乱搞；滥交 **,screw sth 'from/'out of sb** to force sb to give you sth 勒索；敲诈：*They screwed the money out of her by threats.* 他们威逼她交出了钱。**,screw 'up** (*slang*) to do sth badly or spoil sth 搞糟；搅乱；弄坏 **SYN** **mess up**：*You really screwed up there!* 你实在是搞了个一塌糊涂！➲ RELATED NOUN SCREW-UP **,screw sb↔'up** (*slang*) to upset or confuse sb so much that they are not able to deal with problems in their life 使烦恼得不能正常生活；使神经不正常：*Her father's death really screwed her up.* 父亲死后，她真是万念俱灰。➲ SEE ALSO SCREWED-UP **,screw sth↔'up** **1** to fasten sth with screws 用螺丝固定：*to screw up a crate* 用螺丝钉把板条箱钉好 **2** (*BrE*) to fasten sth by turning it 拧牢；旋紧：*I screwed up the jar and put it back on the shelf.* 我把瓶子拧上盖儿，放回搁架。**3** (*slang*) to do sth badly or spoil sth 搞糟；搅乱；弄坏：*Don't screw it up this time.* 这次可别搞砸了。➲ RELATED NOUN SCREW-UP **,screw your 'eyes/'face↔up** to contract the muscles of your eyes or face because the light is too strong, you are in pain, etc. （因光线太强或疼痛等）眯起眼睛，扭曲面部：*He took a sip of the medicine and screwed up his face.* 他喝了一小口药后做了个怪相。

screw·ball /'skruːbɔːl/ *noun* (*informal, especially NAmE*) a strange or crazy person 怪人；狂人

screw·cap /'skruːkæp/ *noun* a top for a container, especially a wine bottle, that screws onto it （尤指酒瓶的）螺旋盖，螺纹盖 ▶ **screw·cap** *adj.* [only before noun]: *screwcap bottles/wine* 带螺旋盖的瓶子；螺旋盖瓶装葡萄酒

screw·driver /'skruːdraɪvə(r)/ *noun* **1** a tool with a narrow blade that is specially shaped at the end, used for turning screws 螺丝刀；改锥 ➲ VISUAL VOCAB PAGE V21 **2** a COCKTAIL (= an alcoholic drink) made from VODKA and orange juice 伏特加橙汁鸡尾酒；螺丝刀（鸡尾酒）

,screwed-'up *adj.* **1** (*informal*) upset and anxious, especially because of sth bad that has happened to you in the past （因以前有过不幸遭遇）焦虑而紧张的：*an extremely screwed-up kid* 一个十分神经质的孩子 **2** (*especially BrE*) twisted into a ball 揉起来的；搓成一团的：*a screwed-up tissue* 揉成一团的纸巾 **3** if your face or eyes are **screwed-up**, the muscles are tight, because you are worried, in pain, etc., or because the light is too bright （因担忧、疼痛或光线太强等）面部扭曲，眯起眼睛，皱着眉头

'screw top *noun* a round cap or lid that can be screwed onto a bottle or jar （瓶子或罐子的）螺旋盖，螺纹盖 ➲ VISUAL VOCAB PAGE V36 ▶ **'screw-top** (*also* **'screw-topped**) *adj.* [only before noun]

'screw-up *noun* (*pl.* **screw-ups**) (*slang*) an occasion when you do sth badly or spoil sth 搞糟；弄砸；出错

screwy /'skruːi/ *adj.* (*informal*) strange or crazy 古怪的；荒诞的；疯狂的

scrib·ble /'skrɪbl/ *verb, noun*

■ ***verb*** **1** [T, I] to write sth quickly and carelessly, especially because you do not have much time 草草记下，匆匆书写（尤指因时间仓促） **SYN** **scrawl**：**~ sth** *He scribbled a note to his sister before leaving.* 临行前，他给妹妹草草写了一封短信。◇ **~ sth down** *She scribbled down her phone number and pushed it into his hand.* 她匆匆写下自己的电话号码，塞进他手里。◇ **~ (away)** *Throughout the interview the journalists scribbled away furiously.* 在整个采访过程中，记者忙不迭地记个不停。**2** [I] (**+ adv./prep.**) to draw marks that do not mean anything 胡写；乱画：*Someone had scribbled all over the table in crayon.* 不知谁用蜡笔胡写乱画，桌面上都涂满了。

■ ***noun*** **1** [U, sing.] careless and untidy writing 潦草的文字 **SYN** **scrawl**：*How do you expect me to read this scribble?* 这种写得歪歪扭扭的东西，让我怎么看？ **2** [C, usually pl.] marks or pictures that seem to have no meaning 胡写乱画的东西 **SYN** **scrawl**：*The page was covered with a mass of scribbles.* 那页纸上净是胡写乱画的东西。

scrib·bler /'skrɪblə(r)/ *noun* **1** (*disapproving* or *humorous*) a journalist, author or other writer 耍笔杆子的 **2** (*CanE*) a book with plain paper for writing in, especially for children at school （尤指供在校儿童用的）练习本，习字本

scribe /skraɪb/ *noun* a person who made copies of written documents before printing was invented （印刷术发明之前的）抄写员，抄书吏

scrim·mage /'skrɪmɪdʒ/ *noun* **1** a confused struggle or fight 混战；群架；你争我夺 **SYN** **scrum** **2** (in AMERICAN FOOTBALL 美式足球) a period of play that begins with the ball being placed on the ground 并列争球 **3** (*NAmE*) a practice game of AMERICAN FOOTBALL, BASKETBALL, etc. （美式足球、篮球等的）队内分组对抗赛，教学比赛

scrimp /skrɪmp/ *verb* [I] to spend very little money on the things that you need to live, especially so that you can save it to spend on sth else 省吃俭用，节衣缩食（尤指为了攒钱）：*They **scrimped and saved** to give the children a good education.* 他们省吃俭用，为的是攒钱让孩子受到良好的教育。

scrip /skrɪp/ *noun* (*business* 商) an extra share in a business, given out instead of a DIVIDEND （股息的）临时凭证；代价券

script /skrɪpt/ *noun, verb*

■ ***noun*** **1** [C] a written text of a play, film/movie, broadcast, talk, etc. 剧本；电影剧本；广播（或讲话等）稿：*That line isn't in the original script.* 原剧本中没有那句台词。**2** [U] writing done by hand 笔迹：*She admired his neat script.* 她欣赏他写的一手好字。➲ SEE ALSO MANUSCRIPT **3** [U, C] a set of letters in which a language is written （一种语言的）字母系统，字母表 **SYN** **alphabet**：*a document in Cyrillic script* 一份用西里尔字母书写的文件 **4** [C] (*BrE*) a candidate's written answer or answers in an exam 笔试答卷 **5** [U, C] (*computing* 计) a series of instructions for a computer, carried out in a particular order, for example when a link in a website is clicked 脚本（程序）（计算机的一系列指令）：*The bug was caused by an error in the script.* 这个故障是由脚本程序出错造成的。

■ ***verb*** [often passive] **~ sth** to write the script for a film/movie, play, etc. 为（电影或戏剧等）写剧本

script·ed /ˈskrɪptɪd/ *adj.* read from a script 照稿子念的：*a scripted talk* 照稿子念的讲话 OPP **unscripted**

scrip·tor·ium /skrɪpˈtɔːriəm/ *noun* (*pl.* **scrip·tor·iums** or **scrip·toria** /-ˈtɔːriə/) (*old use*) a room for writing in, especially in a MONASTERY （尤指修道院的）缮写室

scrip·ture /ˈskrɪptʃə(r)/ *noun* **1 Scripture** [U] (*also* **the Scriptures** [pl.]) the Bible 《圣经》 **2 scriptures** [pl.] the holy books of a particular religion （某宗教的）圣典，经文，经典：*Hindu scriptures* 印度教经文 ▶ **scrip·tural** /ˈskrɪptʃərəl/ *adj.*：*scriptural references* 《圣经》引文

script·writer /ˈskrɪptraɪtə(r)/ *noun* a person who writes the words for films/movies, television and radio plays （电影、电视剧、广播剧的）剧作家，编剧 ➲ COMPARE PLAYWRIGHT, SCREENWRITER

scrof·ula /ˈskrɒfjʊlə; *NAmE* ˈskrɔːf-/ *noun* [U] (especially in the past) a disease in which the GLANDS swelled, probably a form of TUBERCULOSIS 瘰疬；淋巴结核

scroll /skrəʊl; *NAmE* skroʊl/ *noun, verb*

■ *noun* **1** a long roll of paper for writing on （供书写的）长卷纸，卷轴 **2** a decoration cut in stone or wood with a curved shape like a roll of paper （石刻或木雕的）涡卷形装饰

■ *verb* [I, T] (*computing* 计) to move text on a computer screen up or down so that you can read different parts of it 滚屏；滚动：**+ adv./prep.** *Use the arrow keys to scroll through the list of files.* 用箭头键把文件目录滚动一遍。◇ *Scroll down to the bottom of the document.* 向下滚动到文件末尾。◇ **~ sth** *Use the arrow keys to scroll the list of files.* 用箭头键滚动文件目录。➲ WORDFINDER NOTE AT COMMAND

ˈscroll bar *noun* (*computing* 计) a strip at the edge of a computer screen that you use to scroll through a file with 滚动条 ➲ VISUAL VOCAB PAGE V74

Scrooge /skruːdʒ/ *noun* [usually sing.] (*informal, disapproving*) a person who is very unwilling to spend money 吝啬鬼；守财奴 ➲ MORE LIKE THIS 17, page R27 ORIGIN From **Ebenezer Scrooge**, a character in Charles Dickens' *A Christmas Carol* who is extremely mean. 源自狄更斯小说《圣诞颂歌》中一个极其吝啬的人物埃比尼泽・斯克鲁奇 (Ebenezer Scrooge)。

scrote /skrəʊt; *NAmE* skroʊt/ *noun* (*BrE, informal*) an insulting word for a man that you do not like or are angry with 混蛋（对男子的辱骂）

scro·tum /ˈskrəʊtəm; *NAmE* ˈskroʊ-/ *noun* (*pl.* **scro·tums** or **scrota** /ˈskrəʊtə; *NAmE* ˈskroʊ-/) the bag of skin that contains the TESTICLES in men and most male animals 阴囊

scrounge /skraʊndʒ/ *verb, noun*

■ *verb* [T, I] (*informal, disapproving*) to get sth from sb by asking them for it rather than by paying or working for it 白要；白拿 SYN **cadge**：**~ (sth) (off/from sb)** *He's always scrounging free meals off us.* 他老来我们家蹭饭吃。◇ **~ (for sth)** *What is she scrounging for this time?* 这次她又来要什么？▶ **scroun·ger** *noun*：*a campaign against welfare scroungers* 抵制领福利金而不工作的懒人的运动

■ *noun*

IDM **on the ˈscrounge** (*BrE, informal, disapproving*) trying to get sth by persuading sb to give it to you 讨要；索要

scrub /skrʌb/ *verb, noun*

■ *verb* (**-bb-**) **1** [T, I] to clean sth by rubbing it hard, perhaps with a brush and usually with soap and water 擦洗；刷洗：**~ sth/yourself** *I found him in the kitchen, scrubbing the floor.* 我发现他在厨房擦地板。◇ **~ sth/yourself down** *She scrubbed the counters down with bleach.* 她用漂白剂把柜台擦洗干净。◇ **~ (at sth)** *The woman scrubbed at her face with a tissue.* 那女人用纸巾擦脸。◇ **~ sth/yourself + adj.** *Scrub the vegetables clean.* 把蔬菜刷洗干净。**2** [T] **~ sth** (*informal*) to cancel sth that you have arranged to do 取消（原有安排）

PHR V **ˌscrub sth↔ˈoff | scrub sth ˈoff sth** to remove sth from the surface of an object by rubbing it hard with a brush, etc. （用刷子等）刷掉，擦掉：*This treatment involves scrubbing off the top layer of dead skin.* 这种治疗需要把死皮的表层除去。**ˌscrub sth↔ˈout** to clean the inside of sth by rubbing it hard with a brush and usually with soap and water （用刷子等）把某物从里到外擦洗干净 **ˌscrub ˈup** (of a doctor, nurse, etc. 医生、护士等) to wash your hands and arms before performing a medical operation （手术前）擦洗手和臂

■ *noun* **1** [sing.] an act of scrubbing sth 擦洗；刷洗：*I've given the floor a good scrub.* 我把地板彻底擦洗了一遍。**2** [U] small bushes and trees 灌木丛；矮树丛：*The bird disappeared into the scrub.* 鸟消失在矮树丛中。**3** (*also* **scrub·land**) [U] an area of dry land covered with small bushes and trees 硬叶灌丛带；低矮灌木丛林地 **4 scrubs** [pl.] (*specialist*) the special clothes worn by SURGEONS when they are doing medical operations 手术衣 ➲ WORDFINDER NOTE AT OPERATION

scrub·ber /ˈskrʌbə(r)/ *noun* **1** (*BrE, informal*) an offensive word for a PROSTITUTE or for a woman who has sex with a lot of men 婊子；淫荡女人 **2** a brush or other object that you use for cleaning things, for example pans （刷洗用的）刷子

ˈscrubbing brush (*BrE*) (*NAmE* **ˈscrub brush**) *noun* a stiff brush for cleaning floors and other surfaces （刷地板等的）硬毛刷，板刷

scrubby /ˈskrʌbi/ *adj.* **1** covered with small bushes and trees 长满灌木和矮树的；灌木丛生的：*a scrubby hillside* 灌木丛生的山坡 **2** (of trees 树) small and not fully developed 低矮的；矮小的：*scrubby vegetation* 灌木植被

scrub·land /ˈskrʌblənd/ *noun* [U] = SCRUB (3)

ˈscrub nurse (*NAmE*) (*BrE* **ˈtheatre nurse**) *noun* a nurse with special training, who helps during operations 手术室护士

ˈscrub room *noun* a place in a hospital next to an operating room/theatre, where doctors and nurses get ready for operations （手术室隔壁的）刷手间，术前消毒室

scruff /skrʌf/ *noun* (*BrE, informal*) a dirty or untidy person 邋遢的人

IDM **by the scruff of the/sb's ˈneck** roughly holding the back of an animal's or person's neck 揪着动物（或人）的脖颈儿：*She grabbed him by the scruff of the neck and threw him out.* 她一把抓住他的脖子，将他扔了出去。

scruffy /ˈskrʌfi/ *adj.* (**scruff·ier**, **scruffi·est**) (*informal*) dirty or untidy in appearance 外表不整洁的；邋遢的 SYN **shabby**：*He looked a little scruffy.* 他看着有点邋遢。◇ *scruffy pair of jeans* 脏兮兮的牛仔裤 ▶ **scruff·ily** *adv.* **scruffi·ness** *noun* [U]

scrum /skrʌm/ *noun* **1** (*also formal* **scrum·mage**) a part of a RUGBY game when players from both sides link themselves together in a group, with their heads down, and push against the other side. The ball is then thrown between them and each side tries to get it. （橄榄球的）并列争球 **2** the group of players who link themselves together in a scrum （橄榄球）并列争球的全体前锋 **3** (*especially BrE*) a crowd of people who are pushing each other 相互拥挤的人群：*There was a real scrum when the bus arrived.* 公共汽车到站时，人们一窝蜂都往上挤。

ˌscrum ˈhalf *noun* (in RUGBY 橄榄球) a player who puts the ball into the scrum 传锋

scrum·mage /ˈskrʌmɪdʒ/ *noun, verb*

■ *noun* (*formal*) = SCRUM (1)

■ *verb* (*also* **ˌscrum ˈdown**) [I] (*sport* 体育) to form a SCRUM during a game of RUGBY （橄榄球的）并列争球

scrummy /ˈskrʌmi/ *adj.* (**scrum·mier**, **scrum·mi·est**) (*BrE, informal*) tasting very good 味道极好的；美味的 SYN **delicious**：*a scrummy cake* 非常可口的蛋糕

scrump·tious /ˈskrʌmpʃəs/ *adj.* (*informal*) tasting very good 美味的；非常好吃的 SYN **delicious**

scrumpy /ˈskrʌmpi/ *noun* [U, C] (*BrE*) a type of strong CIDER (= an alcoholic drink made from apples), made especially in the west of England（尤指产于英格兰西部的）烈性苹果酒

scrunch /skrʌntʃ/ *verb* **1** [I] to make a loud sound like the one that is made when you walk on GRAVEL (= small stones) 发咔嚓咔嚓声；发出嘎吱声 **SYN** **crunch**: *The snow scrunched underfoot.* 雪在脚下发出嘎吱嘎吱的声音。 **2** [T] **~ sth (up)** to squeeze sth into a small round shape in your hands 把…揉成一团: *He scrunched up the note and threw it on the fire.* 他把便条揉成一团，扔进了火里。 **3** [T] **~ sth (up)** to make sth become smaller 使蜷缩；使收缩: *The hedgehog scrunched itself up into a ball.* 刺猬蜷成一个圆球。 **4** [T] **~ sth** to create a HAIRSTYLE with loose curls by squeezing the hair with the hands（用手揉捏头发）做松鬈发型 ▶ **scrunch** *noun* [sing.]: *the scrunch of tyres on the gravel* 轮胎碾在砾石上发出的咔嚓咔嚓声

ˌscrunch-ˈdry *verb* **~ sth** to create a HAIRSTYLE with loose curls by drying the hair while squeezing it with your hand 用手挤干（头发）使之松散鬈曲

scrunchy (*also* **scrunchie**) /ˈskrʌntʃi/ *noun* (*pl.* **-ies**) a RUBBER BAND covered in cloth used to fasten hair away from the face（包）布发箍，布发圈

scru·ple /ˈskruːpl/ *noun*, *verb*

■ ***noun*** [C, usually pl., U] a feeling that prevents you from doing sth that you think may be morally wrong（道德上的）顾忌，顾虑: *I overcame my moral scruples.* 我抛开了道德方面的顾虑。 ◇ *He **had no scruples about** spying on her.* 他肆无忌惮地暗中盯着她。 ◇ *She is totally **without scruple**.* 她完全无所顾忌。

■ ***verb*** [I] **not ~ to do sth** (*formal*) to be willing to do sth even if it might be wrong or immoral 无所顾忌地做；肆无忌惮地干

scru·pu·lous /ˈskruːpjələs/ *adj.* **1** careful about paying attention to every detail 仔细的；细致的；一丝不苟的 **SYN** **meticulous**: *You must be scrupulous about hygiene when you're preparing a baby's feed.* 给婴儿准备食物时，对卫生丝毫马虎不得。 ◇ *scrupulous attention to detail* 体察入微 **2 ~ (in sth/in doing sth)** careful to be honest and do what is right 审慎正直的；恪守道德规范的: *He was scrupulous in all his business dealings.* 他在所做的一切商业交易中都是清白的。 **OPP** **unscrupulous** ▶ **scru·pu·lous·ly** *adv.*: *Her house is scrupulously clean.* 她的家干干净净，纤尘不染。 ◇ *to be scrupulously honest* 极为诚实 **scru·pu·lous·ness** *noun* [U]

scru·tin·eer /ˌskruːtəˈnɪə(r); *NAmE* -ˈnɪr/ *noun* (*BrE*) a person who checks that an election or other vote is organized correctly and fairly 选举（或其他投票）监督员；监票人

scru·tin·ize (*BrE also* **-ise**) /ˈskruːtənaɪz/ *verb* **~ sb/sth** to look at or examine sb/sth carefully 仔细查看；认真检查；细致审查: *She leaned forward to scrutinize their faces.* 她探身向前，端详他们的面容。 ◇ *The statement was carefully scrutinized before publication.* 声明在发表前经过仔细审阅。

scru·tiny /ˈskruːtəni/ *noun* [U] (*formal*) careful and thorough examination 仔细检查；认真彻底的审查 **SYN** **inspection**: *Her argument doesn't really stand up to scrutiny.* 她的观点经不起认真推敲。 ◇ *Foreign policy has **come under close scrutiny** recently.* 近来，政府的外交政策受到了认真彻底的审查。 ◇ *The documents should be available for **public scrutiny**.* 这些文件须公之于世，交由公众审议。

scuba-diving /ˈskuːbə daɪvɪŋ/ (*also* **scuba**) *noun* [U] the sport or activity of swimming underwater using special breathing equipment consisting of a container of air which you carry on your back and a tube through which you breathe the air 戴水肺潜水: *to go scuba-diving* 进行戴水肺潜水 ➲ VISUAL VOCAB PAGE V44

scud /skʌd/ *verb* (**-dd-**) [I] **+ adv./prep.** (*literary*) (of clouds 云) to move quickly across the sky 飞掠；疾飞

scuff /skʌf/ *verb* **1 ~ sth (on sth)** to make a mark on the smooth surface of sth when you rub it against sth rough 磨损；磨坏: *I scuffed the heel of my shoe on the stonework.* 我的鞋跟被石头路磨坏了。 **2 ~ your feet, heels, etc.** to drag your feet along the ground as you walk 拖着脚走 ▶ **scuffed** *adj.*: *After only one day, his shoes were already scuffed and dirty.* 只一天，他的鞋就穿脏磨坏了。 **scuff** (*also* ˈ**scuff mark**) *noun*

scuf·fle /ˈskʌfl/ *noun*, *verb*

■ ***noun* ~ (with sb) | ~ (between A and B)** a short and not very violent fight or struggle（短暂而不太激烈的）肢体摩擦，冲突: ***Scuffles broke out** between police and demonstrators.* 警察和示威者之间发生了冲突。 ➲ SYNONYMS AT FIGHT

■ ***verb*** **1** [I] **~ (with sb)** (of two or more people 两人或多人之间) to fight or struggle with each other for a short time, in a way that is not very serious（短暂而不严重地）扭打，冲突，争斗: *She scuffled with photographers as she left her hotel.* 在离开所住的旅馆时，她和一些摄影记者发生了冲突。 **2** [I] **+ adv./prep.** to move quickly making a quiet rubbing noise 窸窸窣窣地疾行: *Some animal was scuffling in the bushes.* 有只动物在灌木丛中窸窸窣窣地穿行。

scuf·fling /ˈskʌflɪŋ/ *noun* [U] a low noise made by sth moving around（物体来回移动发出的）窸窸窣窣的响声: *He could hear whispering and scuffling on the other side of the door.* 他听见门那边的低语声和窸窸窣窣的走动声。

scull /skʌl/ *noun*, *verb*

■ ***noun*** **1** [C, usually pl.] one of a pair of small OARS used by a single person ROWING a boat, one in each hand（单人双桨船上的）短桨 **2 sculls** [pl.] a race between small light boats with pairs of sculls 双桨赛艇比赛: ***single/double sculls*** (= with one/two people in each boat) 单人 / 双人双桨赛艇比赛 **3** [C] a small light boat used in sculls races 双桨赛艇

■ ***verb*** [I] to ROW[1] a boat using sculls 用双桨划船

scull·er /ˈskʌlə(r)/ *noun* a person who ROWS[1] with sculls 划双桨者；双桨赛艇运动员

scull·ery /ˈskʌləri/ *noun* (*pl.* **-ies**) a small room next to the kitchen in an old house, originally used for washing dishes, etc. 洗涤室（老房子中设在厨房旁，洗涤餐具用）

scull·ing /ˈskʌlɪŋ/ *noun* [U] the sport of racing with SCULLS 双桨赛艇比赛

sculpt /skʌlpt/ *verb* [usually passive] **1** to make figures or objects by CARVING or shaping wood, stone, CLAY, metal, etc. 雕刻；雕塑: **~ sth (in sth)** *a display of animals sculpted in ice* 冰雕动物展 ◇ **~ sth (from/out of sth)** *The figures were sculpted from single blocks of marble.* 这些雕像都是用整块大理石雕成的。 ➲ COLLOCATIONS AT ART **2 ~ sth** to give sth a particular shape 使具有某种形状: *a coastline sculpted by the wind and sea* 在风和海水的作用下形成的海岸线

sculp·tor /ˈskʌlptə(r)/ *noun* a person who makes SCULPTURES 雕刻家；雕塑家

sculp·tress /ˈskʌlptrəs/ *noun* a woman who makes SCULPTURES 女雕刻家；女雕塑家 ➲ NOTE AT GENDER

sculp·ture /ˈskʌlptʃə(r)/ *noun* **1** [C, U] a work of art that is a solid figure or object made by CARVING or shaping wood, stone, CLAY, metal, etc. 雕像；雕塑品；雕刻品: *a marble sculpture of Venus* 维纳斯的大理石雕像 ◇ *He collects modern sculpture.* 他收藏现代雕塑。 ➲ COLLOCATIONS AT ART **2** [U] the art of making sculptures 雕刻术；雕塑术: *the techniques of sculpture in stone* 石雕技艺 ▶ **sculp·tural** /ˈskʌlptʃərəl/ *adj.*: *sculptural decoration* 雕饰

sculp·tured /ˈskʌlptʃəd; *NAmE* -tʃərd/ *adj.* [usually before noun] **1** (of figures or objects 人、物形象) CARVED or shaped from wood, stone, CLAY, metal, etc. 雕刻的；雕塑的 **2** (*approving*) (of part of the body 人体部位) having a clear and pleasing shape 线条清晰美观的: *sculptured cheekbones* 像雕塑般漂亮的颧骨

scum /skʌm/ *noun* **1** [U, sing.] a layer of bubbles or an unpleasant substance that forms on the surface of a liquid 浮沫；浮垢；浮渣：*Skim off any scum.* 撇净浮沫。◇ *stinking water covered by a thick green scum* 盖着厚厚一层绿色浮垢的臭水 **2** [U, pl.] (*informal*) an insulting word for people that you strongly disapprove of （骂人的话）渣滓，败类：*Don't waste your sympathy on scum like that.* 对这样的渣滓你没必要同情。◇ *Drug dealers are the* ***scum of the earth*** (= the worst people there are). 毒品贩子是社会渣滓。▶ **scummy** /ˈskʌmi/ *adj.*：*scummy water* 有浮垢的水 ◇ *scummy people dropping litter* 不讲公德、乱丢杂物的人

scum·bag /ˈskʌmbæg/ *noun* (*slang, offensive*) an unpleasant person 讨厌的人；卑鄙小人

scunge /skʌndʒ/ *noun* (*AustralE, NZE, informal*) **1** [U] dirt 污垢；尘土 **2** [C] an unpleasant person 讨厌的人 **3** [C] a person who does not like to spend money 吝啬鬼；抠门的人

scungy /ˈskʌndʒi/ *adj.* (**scun·gier**, **scun·gi·est**) (*AustralE, NZE, informal*) **1** dirty and unpleasant 肮脏的；污秽的 **2** not liking to spend money 吝啬的；抠门的

scup·per /ˈskʌpə(r)/ *verb* **~ sth** (*BrE, informal*) to cause sb/sth to fail 使泡汤；使成泡影 SYN **foil**：*The residents' protests scuppered his plans for developing the land.* 居民的抗议使他开发这片土地的计划泡了汤。

scur·ril·ous /ˈskʌrələs; *NAmE* ˈskɜːr-/ *adj.* (*formal*) very rude and insulting, and intended to damage sb's reputation 恶语毁谤的；用污言秽语谩骂的；辱骂的：*scurrilous rumours* 恶意中伤的谣言 ▶ **scur·ril·ous·ly** *adv.*

scurry /ˈskʌri; *NAmE* ˈskɜːri/ *verb* (**scur·ries**, **scurry·ing**, **scur·ried**, **scur·ried**) [I] + **adv./prep.** to run with quick short steps 碎步疾跑 SYN **scuttle**：*She said goodbye and scurried back to work.* 她说声再见，然后扭头跑回去干活了。◇ *Ants scurried around the pile of rotting food.* 蚂蚁围着那堆腐烂的食物跑来跑去。▶ **scurry** *noun* [sing.]

scurvy /ˈskɜːvi; *NAmE* ˈskɜːrvi/ *noun* [U] a disease caused by a lack of VITAMIN C from not eating enough fruit and vegetables 坏血病

scut·tle /ˈskʌtl/ *verb, noun*

■ *verb* **1** [I] + **adv./prep.** to run with quick short steps 碎步疾跑 SYN **scurry**：*She scuttled off when she heard the sound of his voice.* 听到他的说话声，她赶紧跑开了。◇ *He held his breath as a rat scuttled past.* 见一只老鼠跑过，他屏住了呼吸。**2** [T] **~ sth** to deliberately cause sth to fail （故意）破坏，阻止，阻挠 SYN **foil**：*Shareholders successfully scuttled the deal.* 股东成功地阻止了这桩交易。**3** [T] **~ sth** to sink a ship deliberately by making holes in the side or bottom of it 凿沉（船）

■ *noun* = COAL SCUTTLE

scuttle·butt /ˈskʌtlbʌt/ *noun* [U] (*NAmE, slang*) stories about other people's private lives, that may be unkind or not true 流言蜚语；谣言 SYN **gossip**

scuzzy /ˈskʌzi/ *adj.* (**scuzz·ier**, **scuz·zi·est**) (*informal, especially NAmE*) dirty and unpleasant 肮脏讨厌的；邋遢的

Scylla and Cha·ryb·dis /ˌsɪlə ənd kəˈrɪbdɪs; *NAmE also* tʃəˈr-/ *noun* used to refer to a situation in which an attempt to avoid one danger increases the risk from another danger 腹背受敌；进退两难 ➲ **MORE LIKE THIS** 16, page R27 ORIGIN From ancient Greek stories in which a female sea creature (called Scylla) tried to catch and eat sailors who passed between her cave and a whirlpool (called Charybdis). 源自古希腊神话，女海妖斯库拉 (Scylla) 试图抓住并吃掉从她的洞穴和卡律布狄斯漩涡 (Charybdis) 之间经过的水手。

scythe /saɪð/ *noun, verb*

■ *noun* a tool with a long handle and a slightly curved blade, used for cutting long grass, etc. 长柄大镰刀

■ *verb* [T, I] ~ (sth) to cut grass, etc. with a scythe 用长柄大镰刀割：*the scent of newly scythed grass* 新割下的草散发的清香

SD card /ˌes ˈdiː kɑːd; *NAmE* kɑːrd/ *noun* the abbreviation for 'secure digital card' (= a type of MEMORY CARD, used with digital cameras, mobile/cell phones, music players, etc.) 闪存卡，SD 卡（全写为 secure digital card，数码相机、手机、音乐播放器等所使用的内存卡）

SDHC card /ˌes diː eɪtʃ ˈsiː kɑːd; *NAmE* kɑːrd/ *noun* the abbreviation for 'secure digital high capacity card' (= a type of MEMORY CARD, that can store more data than an SD card) 大容量闪存卡，大容量 SD 卡（全写为 secure digital high capacity card，存储容量超过 SD 卡）

the SDLP /ˌes diː el ˈpiː/ *abbr.* (in Northern Ireland) Social Democratic and Labour Party (a political party of the left that is supported mainly by Catholics) 社会民主工党（北爱尔兰主要由天主教徒支持的左翼政党）

SE *abbr.* south-east; south-eastern 东南方（的）；东南部（的）：*SE Asia* 东南亚

sea 🔑 /siː/ *noun* **1** 🔑 (*often* **the sea**) [U] (*also literary* **seas** [pl.]) (*especially BrE*) the salt water that covers most of the earth's surface and surrounds its continents and islands 海；海洋：*to travel* ***by sea*** 海上旅行 ◇ *a cottage* ***by the sea*** 海滨小屋 ◇ *The waste was dumped* ***in the sea.*** 废物倒入海中。◇ *The wreck is lying at the bottom of the sea.* 沉船躺在海底。◇ *We left port and headed for* ***the open sea*** (= far away from land). 我们离开港口，向外海驶去。◇ *the cold seas of the Arctic* 北极地区寒冷的海洋 ◇ *a sea voyage* 海上航行 ◇ *a hotel room with sea view* 旅馆海景房 ➲ SEE ALSO HIGH SEAS, OCEAN

WORDFINDER 联想词：beach, **coast**, harbour, pier, sandbank, shoreline, surf, tide, wave

2 🔑 [C] (often **Sea**, especially as part of a name 常作 Sea，尤作名称的一部分) a large area of salt water that is part of an ocean or surrounded by land 海：*the North Sea* 北海 ◇ *the Caspian Sea* 里海 ➲ **VISUAL VOCAB** PAGE V5 **3** 🔑 [C] (*also* **seas** [pl.]) the movement of the waves of the sea 海面情况；海浪状况：*It was a calm sea.* 海上风平浪静。◇ *The sea was very rough.* 海上风急浪高。 **4** [sing.] **~ of sth** a large amount of sth that stretches over a wide area 大量；茫茫一片：*He looked down at the sea of smiling faces before him.* 他看着眼前这笑脸的海洋。

IDM **at ˈsea** **1** 🔑 on the sea, especially in a ship, or in the sea 在海上（尤指乘船）；在海里：*It happened on the second night at sea.* 事情发生在出海后的第二天夜里。◇ *They were* ***lost at sea.*** 他们在海上迷失了方向。 **2** confused and not knowing what to do 困惑；茫然；不知所措：*I'm* ***all at sea*** *with these new regulations.* 我全然不懂这些新的规章。 **go to ˈsea** to become a sailor 去当水手；当海员 **out to ˈsea** far away from land where the sea is deepest 向（或在）外海：*She fell overboard and was swept out to sea.* 她从船上落入水中，被海浪冲向外海。 **put (out) to ˈsea** to leave a port or HARBOUR by ship or boat 起航；出海 ➲ MORE AT DEVIL, FISH *n.*

▼ **BRITISH/AMERICAN 英式 / 美式英语**

sea / ocean

- In *BrE*, the usual word for the mass of salt water that covers most of the earth's surface is the **sea**. In *NAmE*, the usual word is the **ocean**. 在英式英语中，覆盖地球表面大部分地区的大片海水通常用 sea 表示。美式英语则通常用 ocean：*A swimmer drowned in the sea/ocean this morning.* 今天早上一名游泳者在海里淹死了。
- The names of particular areas of seas, however, are fixed. 然而，特定的海洋名称用 sea 或 ocean 是固定的：*the Mediterranean Sea* 地中海 ◇ *the Atlantic Ocean* 大西洋
- **Sea/ocean** are also used if you go to the coast on holiday/vacation. 到海滨度假亦可用 sea/ocean：*We're spending a week by the sea/at the ocean in June.* 我们六月份要在海滨度假一个星期。 In *NAmE* it is also common to say 美式英语亦常说：*We're going to the beach for vacation.* 我们要去海滨度假。

➲ NOTE AT COAST

ˌsea ˈair *noun* [U] air near the sea/ocean, thought to be good for the health 海边的空气：*a breath of sea air* 呼吸一下海边的空气

ˈsea anemone *noun* a simple, brightly coloured sea creature that sticks onto rocks and looks like a flower 海葵

the sea·bed /ˈsiːbed/ *noun* [sing.] the floor of the sea/ocean 海床；海底

sea·bird /ˈsiːbɜːd; *NAmE* -bɜːrd/ *noun* a bird that lives close to the sea, for example on CLIFFS or islands, and gets its food from it 海鸟 ➲ VISUAL VOCAB PAGE V12

sea·board /ˈsiːbɔːd; *NAmE* -bɔːrd/ *noun* the part of a country that is along its coast 沿海地区；海滨：*Australia's eastern seaboard* 澳大利亚东部沿海地区

sea·borg·ium /siːˈbɔːɡiəm; *NAmE* -ˈbɔːrɡ-/ *noun* [U] (*symb.* **Sg**) a RADIOACTIVE chemical element. Seaborgium is produced when atoms COLLIDE (= crash into each other). 𬭳（放射性化学元素）

sea·borne /ˈsiːbɔːn; *NAmE* -bɔːrn/ *adj.* [only before noun] carried in ships 海运的：*a seaborne invasion* 海上入侵

ˌsea ˈbreeze *noun* a wind blowing from the sea/ocean towards the land （从海洋吹向陆地的）海风

ˈsea change *noun* [usually sing.] a strong and noticeable change in a situation 大转变；巨变

ˌsea ˈcucumber *noun* an INVERTEBRATE animal that lives in the sea, with a thick body that is covered with lumps 海参

ˈsea dog *noun* (*informal*) a sailor who is old or who has a lot of experience 老水手；经验丰富的水手

sea·farer /ˈsiːfeərə(r); *NAmE* -fer-/ *noun* (*old-fashioned* or *formal*) a sailor 水手；海员

sea·far·ing /ˈsiːfeərɪŋ; *NAmE* -fer-/ *adj.* [only before noun] connected with work or travel on the sea/ocean 海上劳作（或航行）的：*a seafaring nation* 航海民族 ▸ **sea·far·ing** *noun* [U]

ˈsea fish *noun* (*pl.* **sea fish**) a fish that lives in the sea, rather than in rivers or lakes 海鱼

sea·food /ˈsiːfuːd/ *noun* [U] fish and sea creatures that can be eaten, especially SHELLFISH 海鲜，海味（尤指甲壳类）：*a seafood restaurant* 海鲜馆 ◇ *a seafood cocktail* 海鲜冷盘

ˈsea fret *noun* = FRET (2)

sea·front /ˈsiːfrʌnt/ (*often* **the seafront**) *noun* [sing.] the part of a town facing the sea/ocean （城镇的）滨海区，面海地区：*the grand houses along the seafront* 滨海区的豪宅

sea·going /ˈsiːɡəʊɪŋ; *NAmE* -ɡoʊ-/ *adj.* [only before noun] (of ships 船只) built for crossing the sea/ocean 远洋航行的

sea·grass /ˈsiːɡrɑːs; *NAmE* -ɡræs/ *noun* [U] a plant like grass that grows in or close to the sea 海草

ˌsea-ˈgreen *adj.* bluish-green in colour, like the sea （像海水似的）淡蓝绿色的；海绿色的 ▸ **ˌsea ˈgreen** *noun* [U] ➲ MORE LIKE THIS 15, page R26

sea·gull /ˈsiːɡʌl/ *noun* = GULL：*a flock of seagulls* 一群海鸥

seahorse /ˈsiːhɔːs; *NAmE* ˈsiːhɔːrs/ *noun* a small sea fish that swims in a vertical position and has a head that looks like the head of a horse 海马

seal 🔑 /siːl/ *verb, noun*

■ *verb*

• **CLOSE ENVELOPE** 封上信封 **1** 🔑 ~ **sth (up/down)** to close an envelope, etc. by sticking the edges of the opening together 封上（信封）：*Make sure you've signed the cheque before sealing the envelope.* 一定要在支票上签了名再封信封。◇ *a **sealed bid*** (= one that is kept in a sealed envelope and therefore remains secret until all other bids have been received) 密封（投）标

• **CLOSE CONTAINER** 密封容器 **2** 🔑 [often passive] ~ **sth (up)** (**with sth**) to close a container tightly or fill a crack, etc., especially so that air, liquid, etc. cannot get in or out 密封（容器）：*The organs are kept in sealed plastic bags.* 这些器官保存在密封塑料袋里。

• **COVER SURFACE** 覆盖表面 **3** [often passive] ~ **sth (with sth)** to cover the surface of sth with a substance in order to protect it 封盖…的表面：*The floors had been stripped and sealed with varnish.* 地板已清理干净，涂上了清漆。

• **MAKE STH DEFINITE** 确定 **4** ~ **sth** to make sth definite, so that it cannot be changed or argued about 确定；明确定下来；使成定局：*to seal a contract* 订立合同 ◇ *They drank a glass of wine to seal their new friendship.* 他们干了一杯，交成朋友。◇ *The discovery of new evidence **sealed his fate*** (= nothing could prevent what was going to happen to him). 新发现的证据决定了他的命运。

• **CLOSE BORDERS/EXITS** 关闭边界 / 出口 **5** ~ **sth** (of the police, army, etc. 警察、军队等) to prevent people from passing through a place 关闭；封闭；封锁：*Troops have sealed the borders between the countries.* 军队已关闭了两国边界。IDM SEE LIP, SIGN *v.*

PHR V **ˌseal sth↔ˈin** to prevent sth that is contained in sth else from escaping 把…封闭在里边 **ˈseal sth in sth** to put sth in an envelope, container, etc. and seal it 把…封闭在…里：*The body was sealed in a lead coffin.* 尸体安放在密闭的铅棺中。**ˌseal sth↔ˈoff** 🔑 (of the police, army 警察、军队) to prevent people from entering a particular area 封锁；封闭

■ *noun*

• **OFFICIAL MARK** 印章 **1** 🔑 [C] an official design or mark, stamped on a document to show that it is genuine and carries the authority of a particular person or organization 印章；图章；玺；印记：*The letter bore the president's seal.* 信上盖有总统的印章。

• **MAKING STH DEFINITE** 确认 **2** [sing.] a thing that makes sth definite 表示确认的事物；保证；信物：*The project has been given the government's **seal of approval*** (= official approval). 项目已由政府正式批准。◇ *I looked upon the gift as a seal on our friendship.* 我把你的礼物看作我们之间友谊的见证。

• **ON CONTAINERS** 容器 **3** 🔑 [C] a substance, strip of material, etc. used to fill a crack so that air, liquid, etc. cannot get in or out 密封垫（或带等）：*a jar with a rubber seal in the lid* 盖子上有密封垫的广口瓶 ◇ *Only drink bottled water and check the seal isn't broken.* 只喝瓶装水，并且要确保封口没有破损。

• **ON LETTERS/BOXES** 信件；盒子 **4** [C] a piece of WAX (= a soft substance produced by BEES), soft metal or paper that is placed across the opening of sth such as a letter or box and which has to be broken before the letter or box can be opened 封蜡；封铅；封条；火漆：*He broke the wax seal and unrolled the paper.* 他揭去封蜡，把纸卷展开。**5** [C] a piece of metal, a ring, etc. with a design on it, used for stamping a WAX or metal seal 封蜡模（印）；封铅模（印）

• **SEA ANIMAL** 海洋动物 **6** [C] a sea animal that eats fish and lives around coasts. There are many types of seal, some of which are hunted for their fur. 海豹：*a colony of seals* 一群海豹 ◇ *grey seals basking on the rocks* 在岩石上晒太阳的灰海豹

IDM **set the ˈseal on sth** (*formal*) to make sth definite or complete 使某事万无一失；使某事圆满：*Her election to the premiership set the seal on a remarkable political career.* 当选总理使她的政治生涯灿烂辉煌。**under ˈseal** (*formal*) (of a document 文件) in a sealed envelope that cannot be opened before a particular time 密封；加盖印信

ˈsea lane *noun* an official route at sea that is regularly used by ships 海上航路；海上航线

seal·ant /ˈsiːlənt/ (*also* **seal·er**) *noun* [U, C] a substance that is put onto a surface to stop air, water, etc. from entering or escaping from it 密封剂；密封胶；防渗漏剂

S

ˈsea legs *noun* [pl.] the ability to walk easily on a moving ship and not to feel sick at sea 在颠簸的船上行走自如且不晕船的本领：*It won't take you long to find your sea legs.* 不用多久你就会习惯船上生活。

seal·er /ˈsiːlə(r)/ *noun* **1** = SEALANT **2** a person who hunts SEALS 捕猎海豹者

ˈsea level *noun* [U] the average height of the sea/ocean, used as the basis for measuring the height of all places on land 海平面：*50 metres above sea level* 海拔 50 米

sea·lift /ˈsiːlɪft/ *noun* an operation to take people, soldiers, food, etc. to or from an area by ship, especially in an emergency （尤指紧急）海上运输，海上补给

seal·ing /ˈsiːlɪŋ/ *noun* [U] the activity of hunting SEALS 海豹捕猎

ˈsealing wax *noun* [U] a type of WAX that melts quickly when it is heated and becomes hard quickly when it cools, used in the past for sealing letters, etc. 封蜡；火漆

ˈsea lion *noun* a large SEAL (= a sea animal with thick fur, that eats fish and lives around the coast) that lives by the Pacific Ocean 海狮

seal·skin /ˈsiːlskɪn/ *noun* [U] the skin and fur of some types of SEAL, used for making clothes 海豹皮（用作衣料）

seam /siːm/ *noun* **1** a line along which two edges of cloth, etc. are joined or sewn together （缝合两块布等的）线缝，接缝：*a shoulder seam* 衣服肩膀上的接缝 ➲ WORDFINDER NOTE AT SEW **2** a thin layer of coal or other material, between layers of rock under the ground 矿层；煤层：*They struck a* **rich seam** *of iron ore.* 他们开出一个富铁矿层。◇ (*figurative*) *The book is a* **rich seam** *of information.* 这本书是一座丰富的知识宝库。**3** a line where two edges meet, for example the edges of wooden boards （合在一起的两块木板等之间的）接缝，缝隙，裂缝
IDM **be bursting/bulging at the ˈseams** (*informal*) to be very full, especially of people 人满为患；爆满 **be falling/coming apart at the ˈseams** (*informal*) to be going very badly wrong and likely to stop functioning completely 接近崩溃；快要散架：*She was falling apart at the seams, spending most of her time in tears.* 她成天泪汪汪的，都快垮了。➲ MORE AT FRAY *v.*

sea·man /ˈsiːmən/ *noun* (*pl.* **-men** /-mən/) a member of the navy or a sailor on a ship below the rank of an officer 水兵；水手；海员：*Seaman Bates* 《水手贝茨》◇ *a merchant seaman* 商船船员 ➲ SEE ALSO ABLE SEAMAN, ORDINARY SEAMAN

sea·man·ship /ˈsiːmənʃɪp/ *noun* [U] skill in sailing a boat or ship 航海技术；船艺

seamed /siːmd/ *adj.* **1** having a seam or seams 有（接）缝的：*seamed stockings* 有缝长袜 **2** (*literary*) covered with deep lines 布满皱纹的：*an old man with a brown seamed face* 棕色的脸上布满皱纹的老人

ˈsea mile *noun* = NAUTICAL MILE

seam·less /ˈsiːmləs/ *adj.* **1** without a SEAM 无（接）缝的：*a seamless garment* 无缝衣服 **2** with no spaces or pauses between one part and the next （两部分之间）无空隙的，不停顿的：*a seamless flow of talk* 连贯流畅的谈话 ▸ **seam·less·ly** *adv.*

seam·stress /ˈsiːmstrəs; ˈsem-/ *noun* (*old-fashioned*) a woman who can sew and make clothes or whose job is sewing and making clothes 会缝纫的女人；女裁缝

seamy /ˈsiːmi/ *adj.* (**seam·ier, seami·est**) unpleasant and immoral 污秽的；肮脏丑恶的 SYN **sordid**：*a seamy sex scandal* 龌龊的性丑闻 ◇ *the* **seamier side of life** 生活的阴暗面

se·ance /ˈseɪɒs; *NAmE* ˈseɪɑːns/ *noun* a meeting at which people try to make contact with and talk to the spirits of dead people 降神会（设法和亡灵说话）

sea·plane /ˈsiːpleɪn/ (*NAmE also* **hydro·plane**) *noun* a plane that can take off from and land on water 水上飞机 ➲ VISUAL VOCAB PAGE V58

sea·port /ˈsiːpɔːt; *NAmE* -pɔːrt/ *noun* a town with a HARBOUR used by large ships 海港城市：*the Baltic seaports* 波罗的海港口城市

ˈsea power *noun* **1** [U] the ability to control the seas with a strong navy 海上力量；海军实力 **2** [C] a country with a strong navy 海军强国

sear /sɪə(r); *NAmE* sɪr/ *verb* **1** [T] **~ sth** to burn the surface of sth in a way that is sudden and powerful 烧灼；灼伤；烤焦；轻煎：*The heat of the sun seared their faces.* 烈日把他们的脸都晒伤了。◇ *Sear the meat first* (= cook the outside of it quickly at a high temperature) *to retain its juices.* 先把肉稍煎一下以保存肉汁。**2** [I, T] (*formal*) to cause sb to feel sudden and great pain 使骤然感到剧痛：**+ adv./prep.** *The pain seared along her arm.* 她的胳膊一阵剧痛。◇ **~ sb** *Feelings of guilt seared him.* 他深感内疚。➲ SEE ALSO SEARING

search 🔑 /sɜːtʃ; *NAmE* sɜːrtʃ/ *noun, verb*
■ ***noun*** **1** 🔑 **~ (for sb/sth)** an attempt to find sb/sth, especially by looking carefully for them/it 搜索；搜寻；搜查；查找：*a long search for the murder weapon* 长时间搜寻杀人凶器 ◇ *Detectives carried out a thorough search of the building.* 侦探对那栋大楼进行了彻底的搜查。◇ *She went into the kitchen* **in search of** (= looking for) *a drink.* 她进了厨房，想找点喝的。◇ *The search for a cure goes on.* 人们还在继续探寻治疗方法。◇ ***The search is on*** (= has begun) *for someone to fill the post.* 已在物色一个人来担任这一职务。◇ *Eventually the search was called off.* 搜查最后被取消了。◇ *a* **search and rescue** *team* 搜救队 **2** 🔑 [C, U] (*computing* 计) an act or the activity of looking for information in a computer DATABASE or network 搜索；检索：*to do a search on the Internet* 在互联网上进行搜索 ◇ *Their main service, Internet search, is free to users.* 他们的主要服务，互联网搜索，供用户免费使用。
■ ***verb*** **1** 🔑 [I, T] to look carefully for sth/sb; to examine a particular place when looking for sb/sth 搜索；搜寻；搜查；查找：**~ (for sth/sb)** *She searched in vain for her passport.* 她翻找自己的护照，但没找着。◇ *Police searched for clues in the area.* 警察在那一地带查找线索。◇ **+ adv./prep.** *The customs officers searched through our bags.* 海关官员搜遍了我们的行李。◇ ***I've searched high and low*** *for those files.* 我为了找那些文件，四处都翻遍了。◇ **~ sth** *His house had clearly been searched and the book was missing.* 显然有人来搜过他的房子，那本书不见了。◇ **~ sth for sth/sb** *Police searched the area for clues.* 警察在那一地带查找线索。◇ *Firefighters searched the buildings for survivors.* 消防队员在建筑物中搜寻幸存者。◇ *searching the Web for interesting sites* 在网上寻找有趣的网站 **2** 🔑 [T] (especially of the police 尤指警察) to examine sb's clothes, their pockets, etc. in order to find sth that they may be hiding 搜查；搜身：**~ sb** *Visitors are regularly searched as they enter the building.* 参观者进入大楼时要接受例行的搜身检查。◇ **~ sb for sth** *The youths were arrested and searched for anything that would incriminate them.* 警察逮捕了那些年轻人，并进行搜身，看能不能找到可以认定他们有罪的物证。➲ SEE ALSO STRIP-SEARCH at STRIP SEARCH **3** 🔑 [I] **~ (for sth)** to think carefully about sth, especially in order to find the answer to a problem 思索，细想（问题答案等）：*He searched desperately for something to say.* 他搜肠刮肚，想找点话说。➲ SEE ALSO SOUL-SEARCHING
IDM **ˌsearch ˈme** (*informal*) used to emphasize that you do not know the answer to sb's question （强调不知道答案）我怎么知道：*'Why didn't she say anything?' 'Search me!'* "她怎么一声不吭？" "我怎么知道！"
PHR V **ˌsearch sth/sb↔ˈout** to look for sth/sb until you find them 找出；查到；搜寻到 SYN **track sb/sth↔down**：*Fighter pilots searched out and attacked enemy aircraft.* 战斗机驾驶员发现敌机后便进行攻击。

search·able /ˈsɜːtʃəbl; *NAmE* ˈsɜːrtʃ-/ *adj.* (of a computer DATABASE or network 计算机数据库或网络) having information organized in such a way that it can be searched for using a computer 可搜索的；可检索的：*a searchable database* 可检索数据库

ˈsearch engine *noun* a computer program that searches the Internet for information, especially by looking for documents containing a particular word or group of words （计算机）搜索引擎 ➲ WORDFINDER NOTE AT WEB

ˌsearch ˌengine optimiˈzation (*BrE also* **-iˈsation**) *noun* [U] (*abbr.* **SEO**) the process of making a website appear high on a list of results given by a search engine 搜索引擎优化（使网站在搜索结果列表中排名靠前）

search·er /ˈsɜːtʃə(r); *NAmE* ˈsɜːrtʃ-/ *noun* **1** a person who is trying to find sth/sb 搜索者；查找者 **2** (*computing* 计) a program that helps you find information in a computer DATABASE or network; a search engine 检索工具；搜索软件；搜索引擎

search·ing /ˈsɜːtʃɪŋ; *NAmE* ˈsɜːrtʃ-/ *adj.* [usually before noun] (of a look, a question, etc. 眼神、问题等) trying to find out the truth about sth; thorough and serious 深挖细究的；认真彻底的：*a* ***searching investigation/analysis/examination*** 认真彻底的调查 / 分析 / 检查 ◇ *He gave her a long* ***searching look.*** 他用探究的目光久久打量着她。◇ *The police asked him some* ***searching questions.*** 警方问了他一些深入的问题。▶ **search·ing·ly** *adv.*

search·light /ˈsɜːtʃlaɪt; *NAmE* ˈsɜːrtʃ-/ *noun* a powerful lamp that can be turned in any direction, used, for example, for finding people or vehicles at night 探照灯

ˈsearch party *noun* [C+sing./pl. v.] an organized group of people who are looking for a person or thing that is missing or lost 搜索队

ˈsearch warrant *noun* an official document that allows the police to search a building, for example to look for stolen property 搜查证；搜查令

sear·ing /ˈsɪərɪŋ; *NAmE* ˈsɪrɪŋ/ *adj.* [usually before noun] **1** so strong that it seems to burn you 灼人的；火辣辣的：*the searing heat of a tropical summer* 热带夏季灼人的热浪 ◇ *searing pain* 火辣辣的疼痛 **2** (of words or speech 文字或话语) powerful and critical 猛烈批评的：*a searing attack on the government* 对政府的猛烈抨击 ▶ **sear·ing·ly** *adv.* ➲ SEE ALSO SEAR

sea·scape /ˈsiːskeɪp/ *noun* a picture or view of the sea 海景；海景画 ➲ COMPARE TOWNSCAPE

ˈsea shanty *noun* (*BrE*) = SHANTY (2)

sea·shell /ˈsiːʃel/ *noun* the shell of a small creature that lives in the sea, often found empty when the creature has died 海贝壳

sea·shore /ˈsiːʃɔː(r)/ (*usually* **the seashore**) *noun* [usually sing.] the land along the edge of the sea or ocean, usually where there is sand and rocks 海岸；海滨 ➲ SYNONYMS AT COAST ➲ VISUAL VOCAB PAGE V5

sea·sick /ˈsiːsɪk/ *adj.* [not usually before noun] feeling ill/sick or wanting to VOMIT when you are travelling on a boat or ship 晕船：*to* ***be/feel/get seasick*** 晕船 ▶ **ˈsea·sick·ness** *noun* [U]

sea·side /ˈsiːsaɪd/ (*often* **the seaside**) *noun* [sing.] (*especially BrE*) an area that is by the sea, especially one where people go for a day or a holiday/vacation （尤指人们游玩、度假的）海边，海滨：*a trip to the seaside* 去海滨旅行 ◇ *a day* ***at/by the seaside*** 海滨一日 ➲ SYNONYMS AT COAST ▶ **sea·side** *adj.* [only before noun]: *a seaside resort* 海滨胜地 ◇ *a seaside vacation home* 海滨度假别墅

sea·son 🔑 /ˈsiːzn/ *noun, verb*
■ *noun* **1** 🔑 any of the four main periods of the year: spring, summer, autumn/fall and winter 季；季节：*the changing seasons* 四时更迭 **2** **the dry/rainy/wet ~** a period of the year in tropical countries when it is either very dry or it rains a lot （热带地区的）旱季，雨季 **3** 🔑 a period of time during a year when a particular activity happens or is done （一年中开展某项活动的）季节，旺季：*the* ***cricket/hunting/shooting, etc. season*** 板球赛季、狩猎季节等 ◇ *He scored his first goal of the season on Saturday.* 他在星期六的比赛中攻进了他在本赛季的第一个球。◇ *The female changes colour during the* ***breeding season.*** 在繁殖季节，雌性改变身上的颜色。◇ *The hotels are always full during* ***the peak season*** (= when most people are on holiday/vacation). 在旺季，这些旅馆总是客满。◇ (*BrE*) *the* ***holiday season*** 度假旺季 ◇ (*NAmE*) *the* ***tourist season*** 旅游旺季 ◇ (*NAmE*) *the* ***holiday season*** (= the time of Thanksgiving, Hanukkah, Christmas and New Year) 节假日期间（包括感恩节、犹太教修殿节、圣诞节和新年）◇ (*BrE*) *the* ***festive season*** (= Christmas and New Year) 圣诞节节期（即圣诞节和新年） ➲ SEE ALSO CLOSE SEASON, HIGH SEASON, LOW SEASON, OFF SEASON, SILLY SEASON **4** a period of time in which a play is shown in one place; a series of plays, films/movies or television programmes （一部戏剧在某地的）演出期，上演期；（戏剧、电影或电视节目的）一季，演播季：*The play opens for a second season in London next week.* 下周，这部剧将在伦敦开始第二轮演出。◇ *a season of films by Alfred Hitchcock* 希区柯克电影作品展 **5** a period of time during one year when a particular style of clothes, hair, etc. is popular and fashionable （一年中时装、发型等的）流行期：*This season's look is soft and romantic.* 这段时间的流行风格是柔和、浪漫。

IDM **in ˈseason** **1** (of fruit or vegetables 水果、蔬菜) easily available and ready to eat because it is the right time of year for them 当令的；在旺季的 **2** (of a female animal 雌性动物) ready to reproduce 处于发情期 **SYN** **on heat** **out of ˈseason** **1** (of fruit or vegetables 水果、蔬菜) not easily available because it is not the right time of year for them 不合时令的；在淡季的 **2** at the times of year when few people go on holiday/vacation 度假淡季；旅游淡季：*Hotels are cheaper out of season.* 在淡季，旅馆要便宜些。 **season's ˈgreetings** used at Christmas to wish sb an enjoyable holiday 圣诞快乐（圣诞节祝贺语）

■ *verb* [T, I] ~ (**sth**) (**with sth**) to add salt, pepper, etc. to food in order to give it more flavour 加调料调味；加作料：*Season the lamb with garlic.* 给羊肉加蒜调味。◇ *Add the mushrooms, and season to taste* (= add as much salt, pepper, etc. as you think is necessary). 加入蘑菇，并根据口味酌加调料。

sea·son·able /ˈsiːznəbl/ *adj.* usual or suitable for the time of year 当令的；应时的；合时令的：*seasonable temperatures* 合时令的气温 **OPP** **unseasonable**

sea·son·al /ˈsiːzənl/ *adj.* **1** happening or needed during a particular season; varying with the seasons 季节性的；随季节变化的：*seasonal workers brought in to cope with the Christmas period* 为应付圣诞节期间的业务而招聘的临时工 ◇ *seasonal variations in unemployment figures* 失业统计数字的季节性变化 ➲ WORDFINDER NOTE AT WORK **2** typical of or suitable for the time of year, especially Christmas 节令性的；适应节日需要的；（尤指）圣诞节的：*seasonal decorations* 圣诞节装饰品 **OPP** **unseasonal** ▶ **sea·son·al·ly** /-nəli/ *adv.*: *seasonally adjusted unemployment figures* (= not including the changes that always happen in different seasons) 不考虑季节因素的失业统计数字

ˌseasonal afˈfective disorder *noun* [U] (*abbr.* **SAD**) a medical condition in which a person feels sad and tired during late autumn/fall and winter when there is not much light from the sun 季节性情感障碍（秋冬两季因白昼缩短而易发作的抑郁症）

sea·son·al·ity /ˌsiːzəˈnæləti/ *noun* [U, sing.] (*specialist*) the fact of varying with the seasons 季节性：*a high degree of climatic seasonality* 明显的季节性气候变化

sea·soned /ˈsiːznd/ *adj.* **1** [usually before noun] (of a person 人) having a lot of experience of a particular activity 富有经验的；老于此道的：*a* ***seasoned campaigner/performer/traveller, etc.*** 经验丰富的社会运动家、表演者、旅行家等 **2** (of food 食物) with salt, pepper, etc. added to it 调好味的；加了作料的：*The sausage was very* ***highly seasoned.*** 这香肠调味很浓。**3** (of wood 木料) made suitable for use by being left outside 风干的，晾干的（可加工使用）

sea·son·ing /ˈsiːzənɪŋ/ *noun* [U, C] a substance used to add flavour to food, especially salt and pepper 调味品；作料

S

'season ticket *noun* a ticket that you can use many times within a particular period, for example on a regular train or bus journey, or for a series of games, and that costs less than paying separately each time 长期票（如火车通勤票、公交车月票、体育比赛套票等）: *an annual/a monthly/a weekly season ticket* 年票；月票；周票 ◇ *a season ticket holder* 持长期票的人

seat /siːt/ *noun, verb*

■*noun*

• PLACE TO SIT 可坐的地方 **1** a place where you can sit, for example a chair 座位，坐处（如椅子等）: *She sat back in her seat.* 她坐在座位上，朝后靠着。◇ *He put his shopping on the seat behind him.* 他把买的东西放在身后的座位上。◇ *Please* ***take a seat*** (= sit down). 请坐。◇ *Ladies and gentlemen, please* ***take your seats*** (= sit down). 各位来宾，请就座。◇ *a* ***window/corner seat*** (= one near a window/in a corner) 挨窗户 / 角落里的座位 ◇ *a* ***child seat*** (= for a child in a car)（汽车上的）儿童安全座椅 ◇ *Would you prefer a* ***window seat*** *or an* ***aisle seat****?* (= on a plane) 您想要靠窗的座位还是靠过道的座位？◇ *We used the branch of an old tree as a seat.* 我们坐在一棵老树的树杈上。◇ *We all filed back to our seats in silence.* 我们都默默无语，一个跟一个地回到座位上。➲ SYNONYMS AT SIT ➲ VISUAL VOCAB PAGE V56 ➲ SEE ALSO BACK SEAT, BUCKET SEAT, HOT SEAT, LOVE SEAT, PASSENGER SEAT

• -SEATER …座位 **2** (in nouns and adjectives 构成名词和形容词) with the number of seats mentioned 有…座位的；有…座的: (*BrE*) *a ten-seater minibus* 十座小公共汽车 ◇ *an all-seater stadium* (= in which nobody is allowed to stand) 全座席体育场

• PART OF CHAIR 椅子的一部分 **3** the part of a chair, etc. on which you actually sit（椅子等的）座部: *a steel chair with a plastic seat* 塑料座部的钢架椅子

• IN PLANE/TRAIN/THEATRE 飞机；火车；剧院 **4** a place where you pay to sit in a plane, train, theatre, etc. 座位: *to* ***book/reserve a seat*** (= for a concert, etc.) 预订一个座位 ◇ *There are no seats left on that flight.* 那次航班没座位了。

• OFFICIAL POSITION 职位 **5** an official position as a member of a parliament, council, committee, etc.（议会、理事会、委员会等的）席位: *a seat on the city council/in Parliament/in Congress* 市政会 / 议会 / 国会席位 ◇ *to* ***win/lose a seat*** (= in an election)（在选举中）赢得 / 失去一个席位 ◇ (*BrE*) *to* ***take your seat*** (= to begin your duties, especially in Parliament)（尤指在议会）就职 ◇ *The majority of seats on the board will be held by business representatives.* 理事会的多数席位将由工商界代表担任。➲ SEE ALSO SAFE SEAT

• TOWN/CITY 城镇；市 **6 ~ of sth** (*formal*) a place where people are involved in a particular activity, especially a city that has a university or the offices of a government（尤指大学或政府机关）所在地；中心: *Washington is the* ***seat of government*** *of the US.* 华盛顿是美国政府所在地。◇ *a university town renowned as a* ***seat of learning*** 有学术重镇之称的大学城

• COUNTRY HOUSE 乡村房舍 **7** (*also* ˌ**country 'seat**) (*both BrE*) a large house in the country, that belongs to a member of the upper class（上层社会人士的）乡村宅第: *the family seat in Norfolk* 在诺福克的祖宅

• PART OF BODY 身体部位 **8** (*especially formal*) the part of the body on which a person sits 臀部 SYN **buttock**

• PART OF TROUSERS/PANTS 裤子的一部分 **9** the part of a pair of trousers/pants that covers a person's seat（裤子的）后裆，臀部

IDM (**fly**) **by the seat of your 'pants** (*informal*) to act without careful thought and without a plan that you have made in advance, hoping that you will be lucky and be successful 临时凭感觉碰运气；凭经验瞎碰 SYN **wing it** **be in the 'driving seat** (*BrE*) (*NAmE* **be in the 'driver's seat**) to be the person in control of a situation 担任负责人；处于统领地位 ➲ MORE AT BACK SEAT, BUM *n.*, EDGE *n.*

■*verb*

• SIT DOWN 坐下 **1 ~ sb/yourself** (*formal*) to give sb a place to sit; to sit down in a place 向…提供座位；（使）就座；坐；落座: *Please wait to* ***be seated*** (= in a restaurant, etc.). 请等候安排入座。◇ *Please* ***be seated*** (= sit down). 请就座。◇ *He seated himself behind the desk.* 他在书桌后面坐下。➲ SYNONYMS AT SIT

• OF BUILDING/VEHICLE 建筑物；交通工具 **2 ~ sb** to have enough seats for a particular number of people 可坐…人；能容纳…人: *The aircraft seats 200 passengers.* 这架飞机能坐 200 名乘客。

'seat belt (*also* **'safety belt**) *noun* a belt that is attached to the seat in a car or a plane and that you fasten around yourself so that you are not thrown out of the seat if there is an accident（汽车或飞机上的）安全带: *Fasten your seat belts.* 系好安全带。➲ COLLOCATIONS AT DRIVING ➲ VISUAL VOCAB PAGE V56

seat·ing /ˈsiːtɪŋ/ *noun* [U] places to sit; seats 可坐的地方；座位: *The theatre has seating for about 500 people.* 这家剧院可坐 500 人左右。◇ *The room had a* ***seating capacity*** *of over 200.* 这个房间能容 200 多人就座。◇ *the* ***seating arrangements*** *for the conference* 会议的座位安排

seat·mate /ˈsiːtmeɪt/ *noun* a person that you sit next to when you are travelling, especially on a plane（尤指飞机上的）邻座乘客

'sea turtle *noun* (*NAmE*) = TURTLE (1)

'sea urchin (*also* **ur·chin**) *noun* a small sea creature with a round shell which is covered with SPIKES 海胆

ˌ**sea 'wall** *noun* a large strong wall built to stop the sea from flowing onto the land 海堤；防波堤

sea·ward /ˈsiːwəd; *NAmE* -wərd/ *adj.* towards the sea; in the direction of the sea 向海的；朝海的: *the seaward side of the coastal road* 海滨公路临海的一侧 ► **sea·ward** (*also* **sea·wards**) *adv.*: *Her gaze was fixed seawards.* 她凝望大海。

'sea water *noun* [U] water from the sea or ocean, that is salty 海水

sea·way /ˈsiːweɪ/ *noun* a passage from the sea through the land along which large ships can travel 海道（大型海轮可航行的通海河道）

sea·weed /ˈsiːwiːd/ *noun* [U, C] a plant that grows in the sea or ocean, or on rocks at the edge of the sea or ocean. There are many different types of seaweed, some of which are eaten as food. 海草；海藻

sea·worthy /ˈsiːwɜːði; *NAmE* -wɜːrði/ *adj.* (of a ship 船舶) in a suitable condition to sail 适宜航海的；能出海的 ► **sea·worthi·ness** *noun* [U]

se·ba·ceous /sɪˈbeɪʃəs/ *adj.* [usually before noun] (*biology* 生) producing a substance like oil in the body 分泌脂质的；皮脂腺的: *the sebaceous glands in the skin* 皮脂腺

seb·or·rhoea (*NAmE* **seb·or·rhea**) /ˌsebəˈrɪə; *NAmE* -ˈriːə/ *noun* [U] a medical condition of the skin in which an unusually large amount of SEBUM is produced by the SEBACEOUS GLANDS 皮脂溢出 ► **seb·or·rhoe·ic** (*NAmE* **seb·or·rhe·ic**) /ˌsebəˈriːɪk/ *adj.*

sebum /ˈsiːbəm/ *noun* [U] an oil-like substance produced by the SEBACEOUS GLANDS 皮脂

Sec. (*US also* **Secy.**) *abbr.* (in writing 书写形式) SECRETARY 秘书；助理；部长；大臣

sec /sek/ *noun* **a sec** [sing.] (*informal*) a very short time; a second 片刻；霎时: *Stay there. I'll be back* ***in a sec.*** 待着别走。我马上回来。◇ *Hang on* (= wait) *a sec.* 稍等一下。

sec. *abbr.* (in writing 书写形式) second(s) 秒

seca·teurs /ˌsekəˈtɜːz; *NAmE* -ˈtɜːrz/ *noun* [pl.] (*BrE*) a garden tool like a pair of strong scissors, used for cutting plant STEMS and small branches 整枝剪；修枝剪: *a pair of secateurs* 一把整枝剪

se·cede /sɪˈsiːd/ *verb* [I] **~ (from sth)** (*formal*) (of a state, country, etc. 州、邦、国家等) to officially leave an organization of states, countries, etc. and become independent 退出，脱离（组织等）: *The Republic of Panama seceded*

S

from Colombia in 1903. 巴拿马共和国于 1903 年脱离哥伦比亚。

se·ces·sion /sɪˈseʃn/ *noun* [U, C] ~ (**from sth**) the fact of an area or group becoming independent from the country or larger group that it belongs to （地区或集团从所属的国家或上级集团的）退出，脱离

se·ces·sion·ist /sɪˈseʃənɪst/ *adj.* [only before noun] supporting or connected with secession 赞成（或参与）脱离活动的；奉行分离主义的 ▶ **se·ces·sion·ist** *noun*： *a military campaign against the secessionists* 对分离主义者采取的军事行动

se·clude /sɪˈkluːd/ *verb* ~ **yourself/sb** (**from sb/sth**) (*formal*) to keep yourself/sb away from contact with other people （使）与…隔离，与…隔绝；（使）隐居，独处

se·cluded /sɪˈkluːdɪd/ *adj.* **1** (of a place 地方) quiet and private; not used or disturbed by other people 僻静的；清静的；不受打扰的： ***a secluded garden/beach/spot, etc.*** 僻静的花园、海滩、地点等 **2** without much contact with other people 隐居的；与世隔绝的 SYN **solitary**： *to lead a secluded life* 过隐居生活

se·clu·sion /sɪˈkluːʒn/ *noun* [U] the state of being private or of having little contact with other people 清静；隐居；与世隔绝： *the seclusion and peace of the island* 岛上的幽僻宁静

sec·ond¹ /ˈsekənd/ *det., ordinal number, adv., noun, verb* ➲ SEE ALSO SECOND²

■ ***det., ordinal number*** **1** happening or coming next after the first in a series of similar things or people; 2nd 第二（的）： *This is the second time it's happened.* 这已是第二次了。◇ *Italy scored a second goal just after half-time.* 下半场刚刚开始，意大利队便射入第二个球。◇ *the second of June/June 2nd* 六月二日 ◇ *He was the second to arrive.* 他是第二个到的。◇ *We have one child and are expecting our second in July.* 我们有一个孩子，第二个预期在七月出生。 **2** next in order of importance, size, quality, etc. to one other person or thing （重要性、规模、质量等）居第二位的： *Osaka is Japan's* ***second-largest*** *city.* 大阪是日本的第二大城市。◇ *Birmingham, the UK's second city* 伯明翰，英国的第二大城市 ◇ *The spreadsheet application is* ***second only to*** *word processing in terms of popularity.* 就受欢迎程度而言，电子制表软件仅次于文字处理软件。◇ *As a dancer, he is* ***second to none*** (= nobody is a better dancer than he is). 他的舞技不亚于任何人。 **3** [only before noun] another; in addition to one that you already own or use 另外的；外加的： *They have a second home in Tuscany.* 他们在托斯卡纳还有一个家。

■ ***adv.*** **1** after one other person or thing in order or importance 以第二名；以第二位： *She* ***came second*** *in the marathon.* 她在马拉松比赛中获得第二名。◇ *One of the smaller parties* ***came a close second*** (= nearly won). 其中一个较小的政党差一点就获胜了。◇ *I agreed to speak second.* 我同意第二个发言。◇ *He is a writer first and a scientist second.* 他首先是作家，然后才是科学家。◇ *I* ***came second (to) last*** (= the one before the last one) *in the race.* 我在赛跑中得了倒数第二。 **2** used to introduce the second of a list of points you want to make in a speech or piece of writing （用于列举）第二，其次 SYN **secondly**： *She did it first because she wanted to, and second because I asked her to.* 她做那件事，首先是因为她自己想做，其次是因为我要她做。 ➲ LANGUAGE BANK AT FIRST, PROCESS¹

■ ***noun*** **1** [C] (*symb.* ″) (*abbr.* **sec.**) a unit for measuring time. There are 60 seconds in one minute. 秒（时间单位）： *She can run 100 metres in just over 11 seconds.* 她跑 100 米只需 11 秒多一点。◇ ***For several seconds*** *he did not reply.* 一连几秒钟，他都没有回答。◇ *The light flashes* ***every 5 seconds.*** 灯光每 5 秒钟闪一次。◇ *The water flows at about 1.5 metres* ***per second.*** 水的流速约为每秒 1.5 米。 **2** [C] (*also informal* **sec**) a very short time 片刻；瞬间 SYN **moment**： *I'll be with you* ***in a second.*** 我马上就去你那儿。◇ *They had finished* ***in/within seconds.*** 他们一下子就做完了。 ➲ SEE ALSO SPLIT SECOND **3** [C] (*symb.* ″) a unit for measuring angles. There are 60 seconds in one minute. 秒（角度单位）： *1°6′10″* (= one degree, six minutes and ten seconds) * 1 度 6 分 10 秒 **4 seconds** [pl.] (*informal*) a second amount of the same food that you have just eaten 再来的一份食物： *Seconds, anybody?* 有谁需要再来一份吗？ **5** [C, usually pl.] an item that is sold at a lower price than usual because it is not perfect 次货；二等货；等外品 **6** (*also* ˌ**second ˈgear**) [U] one of four or five positions of the gears in a vehicle （车辆的）二挡： *When it's icy, move off* ***in second.*** 路面有冰时，起步挂二挡。 **7** [C] a level of university degree at British universities. An **upper second** is a good degree and a **lower second** is average. 二等学位（英国大学学位等级，upper second 为二等上，较好； lower second 为二等下，一般） ➲ COMPARE FIRST *n.* (6), THIRD *n.* (2) **8** [C] a person whose role is to help and support sb else, for example in a BOXING match or in a formal DUEL in the past （拳击比赛或旧时正式决斗的）助手 IDM ➤ SEE JUST *adv.*, WAIT *v.*

■ ***verb*** ~ **sth** to state officially at a meeting that you support another person's idea, suggestion, etc. so that it can be discussed and/or voted on 支持，赞成（主意、建议等）；附议： *Any proposal must be seconded by two other members of the committee.* 任何提案须有委员会其他两名委员附议。◇ (*informal*) *'Thank God that's finished.' 'I'll second that!'* (= I agree) "谢天谢地，总算结束了。" "可不是！" ➲ COMPARE PROPOSE (4) ➲ **WORDFINDER NOTE** AT DEBATE

se·cond² /sɪˈkɒnd; *NAmE* -ˈkɑːnd/ *verb* [usually passive] ~ **sb** (**from sth**) (**to sth**) (*especially BrE*) to send an employee to another department, office, etc. in order to do a different job for a short period of time 临时调派；短期调任： *Each year two teachers are seconded to industry for six months.* 每年有两名教师派到产业部门工作六个月。 ➲ SEE ALSO SECOND¹ ▶ **se·cond·ment** (*BrE*) *noun* [U, C]: *They met while she was* ***on secondment*** *from the Foreign Office.* 两人是在她从外交部调来短期任职时认识的。

sec·ond·ary /ˈsekəndri; *NAmE* -deri/ *adj.* **1** less important than sth else 次要的；从属的；辅助的： *That is just a* ***secondary consideration.*** 那只不过是次要的考虑因素。◇ *Experience is what matters—age is* ***of secondary importance.*** 重要的是经验，年龄是次要的。◇ ~ **to sth** *Raising animals was only secondary to other forms of farming.* 与其他农业生产相对而言，饲养牲畜只是副业。 **2** happening as a result of sth else 间接引发的；继发性的；次生的： *a secondary infection* 继发感染 ◇ *a secondary effect* 间接结果 ◇ *a secondary colour* (= made from mixing two primary colours) 次色 **3** [only before noun] connected with teaching children of 11–18 years 中等教育的；中学的： *secondary teachers* 中学教师 ◇ *the secondary curriculum* 中学课程 ➲ COMPARE ELEMENTARY (1), PRIMARY *adj.* (3), TERTIARY ▶ **sec·ond·ar·ily** /ˈsekəndrəli; *NAmE* ˌsekənˈderəli/ *adv.*： *Their clothing is primarily functional and only secondarily decorative.* 他们的衣服首重实用，其次才讲花式。

ˌ**secondary eduˈcation** *noun* [U] (*especially BrE*) education for children between the ages of 11 and 18 中等教育： *primary and secondary education* 小学和中学教育

ˈ**secondary industry** *noun* [U, C] (*economics* 经) the section of industry that uses RAW MATERIALS to make goods 第二产业（用原材料生产商品的产业） ➲ COMPARE PRIMARY INDUSTRY, TERTIARY INDUSTRY

ˌ**secondary ˈmodern** *noun* (in Britain until the 1970s) a school for young people between the ages of 11 and 16 who did not go to a GRAMMAR SCHOOL 现代中等学校（20 世纪 70 年代以前英国一种中学，招收未考入文法学校的 11 至 16 岁学生）

ˌ**secondary ˈpicketing** *noun* [U] (*BrE*) the act of preventing workers who are not involved in a strike from supplying goods to the company where the strike is held 二级纠察封锁（阻止未参加罢工的工人向公司供应货物）

ˈ**secondary school** *noun* a school for young people between the ages of 11 and 16 or 18 中等学校；中学 ➲ COMPARE HIGH SCHOOL, PRIMARY SCHOOL

S

ˈsecondary source *noun* a book or other source of information where the writer has taken the information from some other source and not collected it himself or herself 二手资料 ➲COMPARE PRIMARY SOURCE

ˌsecondary ˈstress *noun* [U, C] (*phonetics* 语音) the second strongest stress that is put on a syllable in a word or a phrase when it is spoken 次重音 ➲ COMPARE PRIMARY STRESS

ˌsecond ˈbest *adj.* **1** not as good as the best 次于最好的；第二好的：*The two teams seemed evenly matched but Arsenal came off **second best*** (= lost). 两支球队看似势均力敌，但阿森纳队最后还是输了。◇ *my second-best suit* 我的第二好的一套衣服 **2** not exactly what you want; not perfect 退而求其次的；将就的：*a second-best solution* 退而求其次的解决办法 ▶ **ˌsecond ˈbest** *noun* [U]: *Sometimes you have to **settle for*** (= be content with) ***second best.*** 有时候你只能退而求其次。

ˌsecond ˈchamber *noun* (*especially BrE*) = UPPER HOUSE

ˌsecond ˈclass *noun* [U] **1** a way of travelling on a train or ship that costs less and is less comfortable than FIRST CLASS. In Britain this is now usually called **standard class** （火车的）二等车厢；（船的）二等舱 **2** (in Britain) the class of mail that costs less and takes longer to arrive than FIRST CLASS 第二类邮件（在英国投递较第一类邮件慢，邮资也较低） **3** (in the US) the system of sending newspapers and magazines by mail 第二类邮件（美国报刊投递类别） **4** [U, sing.] the second highest standard of degree given by a British university, often divided into upper second class and lower second class 二等学位（英国大学学位等级）

ˌsecond-ˈclass *adj.* **1** (*disapproving*) (of a person 人) less important than other people 次要的；无足轻重的：*Older people should not be treated as **second-class citizens**.* 不应把老年人当二等公民对待。 **2** of a lower standard or quality than the best （质量、标准等）二流的，次等的：*a second-class education* 二流的教育 **3** [only before noun] connected with the less expensive way of travelling on a train, ship, etc. （车厢、船舱等）二等的：***second-class carriages/compartments/passengers*** 二等车厢 / 隔间 / 车厢乘客 **4** [only before noun] (in Britain) connected with letters, packages, etc. that you pay less to send and that are delivered less quickly 第二类的（英国邮件等级，投递较第一类慢，邮资也较低）：***second-class letters/stamps*** 第二类信件；第二类邮件所贴的邮票 **5** (in the US) connected with the system of sending newspapers and magazines by mail 第二类的（美国邮件等级，用于投递报刊） **6** [only before noun] used to describe a British university degree which is good but not of the highest class 二等的（英国大学学位）：*Applicants should have at least a second-class honours degree.* 申请者须有二等以上学位。 ▶ **ˌsecond ˈclass** *adv.*: *to send a letter second class* 按第二类邮件投递信件 ◇ *to travel second class* 乘二等舱出行

the ˌSecond ˈComing *noun* [sing.] a day in the future when Christians believe Jesus Christ will come back to earth 基督复临（基督徒相信耶稣基督将再度降临人间）

ˌsecond ˈcousin *noun* a child of a cousin of your mother or father 父母表兄弟（或姐妹）的孩子；父母堂兄弟（或姐妹）的孩子

ˌsecond-deˈgree *adj.* [only before noun] **1** **~ murder, assault, burglary, etc.** (*especially NAmE*) murder, etc. that is less serious than FIRST-DEGREE crimes 二级（谋杀、人身侵犯或入室盗窃等罪，严重程度低于一级） **2** **~ burns** burns of the second most serious of three kinds, causing BLISTERS but no permanent marks 二度（烧伤） ➲ COMPARE FIRST-DEGREE, THIRD-DEGREE

sec·ond·er /ˈsekəndə(r)/ *noun* a person who SECONDS a proposal, etc. (= supports it so that it can be discussed) 附议者；赞成者 ➲COMPARE PROPOSER

ˌsecond-geneˈration *adj.* **1** used to describe people who were born in the country they live in but whose parents came to live there from another country （移民后裔等）第二代的：*She was a second-generation Japanese-American.* 她是第二代日裔美国人。 **2** (of a product, technology, etc. 产品、技术等) at a more advanced stage of development than an earlier form 第二代的（更先进或改进了的）：*second-generation handheld computers* 第二代掌上电脑

ˌsecond-ˈguess *verb* **1** [T] **~ sb/sth** to guess what sb will do before they do it 猜测；预言：*It was impossible to second-guess the decision of the jury.* 陪审团的决定不可能预测。 **2** [T, I] **~ (sb/sth)** (*especially NAmE*) to criticize sb after a decision has been made; to criticize sth after it has happened 事后批评（或品评）；要事后聪明

ˈsecond hand *noun* the hand on some watches and clocks that shows seconds （钟表的）秒针 ➲ PICTURE AT CLOCK

ˌsecond-ˈhand *adj.* **1** not new; owned by sb else before 旧的；用过的；二手的：*a second-hand bookshop* (= for selling second-hand books) 旧书店 ◇ (*especially BrE*) *second-hand cars* 二手车 **2** (*often disapproving*) (of news, information, etc. 消息、信息等) learned from other people, not from your own experience 间接得来的；二手的：*second-hand opinions* 来自他人的观点 ▶ **ˌsecond-ˈhand** *adv.*: *I bought the camera second-hand.* 我买的这架照相机是二手货。◇ *I only heard about it second-hand.* 我只是听别人讲的。 ➲COMPARE FIRST-HAND

ˌsecond ˈhome *noun* **1** [C] a house or flat/apartment that sb owns as well as their main home and uses, for example, for holidays/vacations 别业；第二寓所；别墅 **2** [sing.] a place where sb lives and which they know as well as, and like as much as, their home 第二故乡；第二个家

ˌsecond in comˈmand *noun* a person who has the second highest rank in a group and takes charge when the leader is not there 副指挥官；二号人物

ˌsecond ˈlanguage *noun* a language that sb learns to speak well and that they use for work or at school, but that is not the language they learned first 第二语言：*ESL or English as a Second Language* * ESL —— 作为第二语言的英语

ˌsecond ˈlanguage acquisition *noun* [U] (*abbr.* **SLA**) (*linguistics* 语言) the learning of a second language 第二语言习得

ˌsecond lieuˈtenant *noun* an officer of lower rank in the army or the US AIR FORCE just below the rank of a LIEUTENANT 陆军少尉；（美国）空军少尉

sec·ond·ly /ˈsekəndli/ *adv.* used to introduce the second of a list of points you want to make in a speech or piece of writing （用于列举）第二，其次：*Firstly, it's expensive, and secondly, it's too slow.* 首先是价格贵，其次，速度太慢。

ˈsecond name *noun* (*especially BrE*) **1** a family name or surname 姓 **2** a second personal name 中间名：*His second name is Willem, after his grandfather.* 他的中间名是威廉，取自他祖父的名字。

ˌsecond ˈnature *noun* [U] **~ (to sb)** (**to do sth**) something that you do very easily and naturally, because it is part of your character or you have done it so many times 第二天性；习性

the ˌsecond ˈperson *noun* [sing.] (*grammar* 语法) the form of a pronoun or verb used when addressing sb 第二人称：*In the phrase 'you are', the verb 'are' is in the second person and the word 'you' is a second-person pronoun.* 在短语 you are 中，动词 are 是第二人称形式，而单词 you 是第二人称代词。 ➲ COMPARE FIRST PERSON, THIRD PERSON

ˌsecond-ˈrate *adj.* not very good or impressive 二流的；平庸的；普通的 SYN **mediocre**: *a second-rate player* 平庸的运动员

S

ˌ**second ˈsight** *noun* [U] the ability that some people seem to have to know or see what will happen in the future or what is happening in a different place 第二视觉（一些人似乎能预知或预见未来或别处发生的事的能力）

ˌ**second-ˈstring** *adj.* [only before noun] (*especially NAmE*) (usually of a player in a sports team 通常指运动队队员) only used occasionally where sb/sth else is not available 替补的：*a second-string quarterback* 替补四分卫 ▸ ˌ**second ˈstring** *noun*：*Wilson was a second string for New Zealand in last week's match.* 在上周的比赛中，威尔逊是新西兰队的替补队员。

ˌ**second ˈwind** *noun* [sing.] (*informal*) new energy that makes you able to continue with sth that had made you tired 恢复的精力；重振的精神；缓过劲来的状况

the ˌSecond ˌWorld ˈWar (*also* ˌ**World** ˌ**War ˈTwo**) *noun* [sing.] the second large international war, that was fought between 1939 and 1945 第二次世界大战（1939 至 1945 年）

se·crecy /ˈsiːkrəsi/ *noun* [U] the fact of making sure that nothing is known about sth; the state of being secret 保密；秘密：*the need for absolute secrecy in this matter* 在这件事情上绝对保密的必要性 ◇ *Everyone involved was* ***sworn to secrecy.*** 所有相关人员均被要求宣誓保密。◇ *The whole affair is still* ***shrouded in secrecy.*** 整个事件依旧秘而不宣。

se·cret 🔑 /ˈsiːkrət/ *adj., noun*

■ *adj.* **1** 🔑 known about by only a few people; kept hidden from others 秘密的；保密的；外人不得而知的：***secret information/meetings/talks*** 秘密信息 / 会议 / 会谈 ◇ **~ (from sb)** *He tried to* ***keep it secret*** *from his family.* 这件事他试图瞒着家里。◇ *Details of the proposals remain secret.* 提议的细节仍不得而知。◇ *a secret passage leading to the beach* 通往海滩的秘密通道 ➲ SEE ALSO TOP SECRET **2** 🔑 [only before noun] used to describe actions and behaviour that you do not tell other people about （指行为与习惯）暗中进行的，未公开的，隐秘的：*He's a secret drinker.* 他偷偷地喝酒。◇ *her secret fears* 她内心的担忧 ◇ *a secret room* 秘室 **3** [not usually before noun] **~ (about sth)** (of a person or their behaviour 人或行为) liking to have secrets that other people do not know about; showing this 诡秘；神秘 SYN **secretive**：*They were so secret about everything.* 他们无论对什么都那样神秘兮兮的。◇ *Jessica caught a secret smile flitting between the two of them.* 杰西卡看见他们俩诡秘地相视一笑。▸ **se·cret·ly** 🔑 *adv.*：*The police had secretly filmed the conversations.* 警察已秘密地把几次谈话拍摄下来。◇ *She was secretly pleased to see him.* 见到他，她心中窃喜。

■ *noun* **1** 🔑 [C] something that is known about by only a few people and not told to others 秘密；机密：*Can you* ***keep a secret?*** 你能保守秘密吗？◇ *The location of the ship is* ***a closely guarded secret.*** 那艘船的位置是高度机密。◇ *Shall we* ***let him in on*** (= tell him) ***the secret?*** 我们要不要把秘密透露给他？◇ *He* ***made no secret of*** *his ambition* (= he didn't try to hide it). 他并没有掩饰自己的雄心壮志。◇ *She was dismissed for revealing trade secrets.* 她因泄露商业机密被解雇。◇ ***official/State secrets*** 官方 / 国家机密 **2** 🔑 (*usually* **the secret**) [sing.] the best or only way to achieve sth; the way a particular person achieves sth 诀窍；秘诀：*Careful planning is the secret of success.* 仔细计划是成功的诀窍。◇ *She still looks so young. What's her secret?* 她看上去依旧那么年轻，她的保养秘诀是什么呢？ **3** [C, usually pl.] a thing that is not yet fully understood or that is difficult to understand 奥秘；奥妙：*the secrets of the universe* 宇宙的奥秘

IDM **in ˈsecret** 🔑 without other people knowing about it 秘密地；暗中：*The meeting was held in secret.* 会议是秘密召开的。➲ MORE AT GUILTY, OPEN *adj.*

ˌ**secret ˈagent** (*also* **agent**) *noun* a person who is used by a government to find out secret information about other countries or governments 特工人员；特务；间谍 SYN **spy**

sec·re·tar·ial /ˌsekrəˈteəriəl; *NAmE* -ˈter-/ *adj.* involving or connected with the work of a secretary 秘书的；文秘工作的：*secretarial work* 文秘工作

sec·re·tar·iat /ˌsekrəˈteəriət; -iæt; *NAmE* -ˈter-/ *noun* the department of a large international or political organization which is responsible for running it, especially the office of a SECRETARY GENERAL （大型国际组织、政治组织的）秘书处，书记处

sec·re·tary 🔑 /ˈsekrətri; *NAmE* -teri/ *noun* (*pl.* **-ies**) (*abbr.* **Sec.**) **1** 🔑 a person who works in an office, working for another person, dealing with letters and telephone calls, typing, keeping records, arranging meetings with people, etc. 秘书：*a* ***legal/medical secretary*** 法律 / 医务秘书 ◇ *Please contact my secretary to make an appointment.* 请和我的秘书联系，预约一个时间。➲ SEE ALSO PRIVATE SECRETARY **2** 🔑 an official of a club, society, etc. who deals with writing letters, keeping records, and making business arrangements （俱乐部、社团等的）干事，文书：*the membership secretary* 组织干事 ➲ WORDFINDER NOTE AT CLUB **3 Secretary** = SECRETARY OF STATE (1) ➲ SEE ALSO HOME SECRETARY, PERMANENT UNDERSECRETARY **4** 🔑 (*US*) the head of a government department, chosen by the President 政府部门首长；部长：*Secretary of the Treasury* 财政部长 **5** 🔑 (in Britain) an assistant of a government minister, an AMBASSADOR, etc. （英国的大臣、大使等的）助理 ➲ SEE ALSO UNDERSECRETARY

ˌ**secretary ˈgeneral** *noun* (*pl.* **secretaries general** or **secretary generals**) the person who is in charge of the department that deals with the running of a large international or political organization （大型国际或政治组织的）秘书长，总干事，总书记：*the former Secretary General of NATO* 北约前任秘书长

ˌ**Secretary of ˈState** *noun* **1** (*also* **Sec·re·tary**) (in Britain) the head of an important government department （英国）大臣：*the Secretary of State for Education* 教育大臣 ◇ *the Education Secretary* 教育大臣 ◇ *the Foreign Secretary* 外交大臣 **2** (in the US) the head of the government department that deals with foreign affairs （美国）国务卿

se·crete /sɪˈkriːt/ *verb* **1 ~ sth** (of part of the body or a plant 身体或植物器官) to produce a liquid substance 分泌：*Insulin is secreted by the pancreas.* 胰岛素是胰腺分泌的。**2 ~ sth (in sth)** (*formal*) to hide sth, especially sth small 隐藏，藏匿（小物件）：*The drugs were secreted in the lining of his case.* 毒品藏在他的皮箱内衬中。

se·cre·tion /sɪˈkriːʃn/ *noun* (*specialist*) **1** [U] the process by which liquid substances are produced by parts of the body or plants 分泌：*the secretion of bile by the liver* 肝脏分泌胆汁的过程 **2** [C, usually pl.] a liquid substance produced by parts of the body or plants 分泌物：*bodily secretions* 人体分泌物

se·cret·ive /ˈsiːkrətɪv/ *adj.* **~ (about sth)** tending or liking to hide your thoughts, feelings, actions, etc. from other people 惯于掩藏自己的；不外露的：*He's very secretive about his work.* 他对自己的工作讳莫如深。▸ **se·cret·ive·ly** *adv.* **se·cret·ive·ness** *noun* [U]

ˌ**secret poˈlice** *noun* [sing.+sing./pl. v.] a police force that works secretly to make sure that citizens behave as their government wants 秘密警察

ˌ**secret ˈservice** *noun* [usually sing.] a government department that is responsible for protecting its government's military and political secrets and for finding out the secrets of other governments （政府的）特工部门，特务机关

sect /sekt/ *noun* (*sometimes disapproving*) a small group of people who belong to a particular religion but who have some beliefs or practices which separate them from the rest of the group 派别；宗派

sect·ar·ian /sekˈteəriən; *NAmE* -ˈter-/ *adj.* [usually before noun] (*often disapproving*) connected with the differences that exist between groups of people who have different religious views （宗教）教派的，派性的：***sectarian attacks/violence*** 教派攻击 / 暴力活动 ◇ *attempts to break*

S

down the ***sectarian divide*** *in Northern Ireland* 旨在消除北爱尔兰的宗教派系分歧的努力

sect·ar·ian·ism /sek'teəriənɪzəm; *NAmE* -'ter-/ *noun* [U] (*often disapproving*) strong support for one particular religious or political group, especially when this leads to violence between different groups 宗派主义

sec·tion AW /'sekʃn/ *noun, verb*

■ ***noun***

- **PART/PIECE** 部分；部件 **1** [C] any of the parts into which sth is divided 部分；部门：*That section of the road is still closed.* 那段公路依旧封闭。◇ *The library has a large biology section.* 这个图书馆有大量的生物学藏书。◇ *the tail section of the plane* 飞机的尾部 **2** [C] a separate part of a structure from which the whole can be put together 部件；散件：*The shed comes in sections that you assemble yourself.* 棚屋以散件出售，需要自己组装。
- **OF DOCUMENT/BOOK** 文件；书籍 **3** [C] a separate part of a document, book, etc. 节；款；项；段；部分：*These issues will be discussed more fully in the next section.* 这些问题将在下一节中有更充分的讨论。◇*the sports section of the newspaper* 报纸的体育版
- **GROUP OF PEOPLE** 人的群体 **4** [C] a separate group within a larger group of people 阶层；界；组：*an issue that will affect large sections of the population* 涉及人口中广大阶层的问题 ◇ *the brass section of an orchestra* 管弦乐队的铜管乐器组 ➲ SEE ALSO RHYTHM SECTION
- **OF ORGANIZATION** 组织机构 **5** [C] a department in an organization, institution, etc. 部门；处；科；股；组 SYN **division**: *He's the director of the finance section.* 他是财务处处长。
- **DISTRICT** 地区 **6** [C] (*NAmE*) a district of a town, city or county 区；地区；地段：*the Dorchester section of Boston* 波士顿的多切斯特区
- **MEASUREMENT** 度量 **7** [C] (*NAmE*) a measure of land, equal to one square mile （土地单位）一平方英里
- **DIAGRAM** 图 **8** [C] a drawing or diagram of sth as it would look if it were cut from top to bottom or from one side to the other 剖面图；断面图：*The illustration shows a section through a leaf.* 图中所示为叶的剖面。◇ *The architect drew the house* ***in section.*** 建筑师绘制了房子的剖面图。➲ SEE ALSO CROSS SECTION
- **MEDICAL** 医疗 **9** [C, U] (*medical* 医) the act of cutting or separating sth in an operation 切开；切断：*The surgeon performed a section* (= made a cut) *on the vein.* 外科医生施行了静脉切开手术。➲ SEE ALSO CAESAREAN **10** [C] (*medical* 医, *biology* 生) a very thin flat piece cut from body TISSUE to be looked at under a MICROSCOPE （供显微镜下观察的）切片：*to examine a section from the kidney* 观察肾脏切片

■ ***verb***

- **MEDICAL/BIOLOGY** 医疗；生物学 **1** ~ **sth** (*medical* 医) to divide body TISSUE by cutting 切开；切断 **2** ~ **sth** (*biology* 生) to cut animal or plant TISSUE into thin slices in order to look at it under a MICROSCOPE 做（动物或植物组织的）切片
- **MENTAL PATIENT** 精神病人 **3** [often passive] ~ **sb** (*BrE*) to officially order a mentally ill person to go and receive treatment in a PSYCHIATRIC hospital, using a law that can force them to stay there until they are successfully treated （依法令精神病人）强制入院治疗

PHR V ˌ**section sth↔'off** to separate an area from a larger one 隔出；划出：*Parts of the town had been sectioned off.* 城市的部分地区被划了出去。

sec·tion·al /'sekʃənl/ *adj.* [usually before noun] **1** connected with one particular group within a community or an organization （社团或组织中）某群体的，某阶层的：*the sectional interests of managers and workers* 管理层和广大工人的不同利益 **2** made of separate sections 组合式的：*a sectional building* 组合式建筑 **3** connected with a CROSS SECTION of sth (= a surface or an image formed by cutting through sth from top to bottom) 剖面的；断面的：*a sectional drawing* 剖面图

ˌ**Section 'Eight** *noun* (*NAmE*) **1** [U] (in the past) a part of US army law that dealt with dismissing a soldier who was considered not suitable 美国陆军条例第八款（旧时据此开除被认为不适合当兵的军人的军籍） **2** [C] (*informal*) a soldier who has been dismissed from the US army because he is not mentally fit （由于心理不适而）遭开除军籍的军人

sec·tor AW /'sektə(r)/ *noun* **1** a part of an area of activity, especially of a country's economy （尤指一国经济的）部门，领域，行业：*the manufacturing sector* 制造业 ◇ *service-sector jobs* (= in hotels, restaurants, etc.) 服务性行业的工作 ➲ COLLOCATIONS AT ECONOMY ➲ SEE ALSO PRIVATE SECTOR, PUBLIC SECTOR, THIRD SECTOR **2** a part of a particular area, especially an area under military control （尤指军事管制的）区域，地带：*each sector of the war zone* 战区的每个军控地段 **3** (*geometry* 几何) a part of a circle lying between two straight lines drawn from the centre to the edge 扇形 ➲ PICTURE AT CIRCLE

secu·lar /'sekjələ(r)/ *adj.* **1** not connected with spiritual or religious matters 现世的；世俗的；非宗教的：*secular music* 世俗音乐 ◇ *Ours is a secular society.* 我们的社会是个世俗社会。**2** (of priests 司祭) living among ordinary people rather than in a religious community 教区的；在俗的

secu·lar·ism /'sekjələrɪzəm/ *noun* [U] (*specialist*) the belief that religion should not be involved in the organization of society, education, etc. 现世主义，世俗主义（认为社会结构和教育等应排除宗教的影响） ▸ **secu·lar·ist** /-lərɪst/ *adj.* [usually before noun]

secu·lar·iza·tion (*BrE also* **-isa·tion**) /ˌsekjələraɪ'zeɪʃn; *NAmE* -rə'z-/ *noun* [U] the process of removing the influence or power that religion has over sth 现世化；世俗化

secu·lar·ize (*BrE also* **-ise**) /'sekjələraɪz/ *verb* [often passive] ~ **sth** to make sth SECULAR; to remove sth from the control or influence of religion 使现世化；使世俗化；使脱离宗教控制：*a secularized society* 世俗化社会

se·cure AW /sɪ'kjʊə(r); *NAmE* sə'kjʊr/ *adj., verb*

■ ***adj.***

- **HAPPY/CONFIDENT** 满足；自信 **1** feeling happy and confident about yourself or a particular situation 安心的；有把握的：*At last they were able to* ***feel secure*** *about the future.* 他们终于觉得不必为将来而担忧了。◇ *She finished the match,* ***secure in the knowledge that*** *she was through to the next round.* 她打完比赛，知道自己已进入下一轮，心里踏实了。OPP **insecure**
- **CERTAIN/SAFE** 可靠；保险 **2** likely to continue or be successful for a long time 可靠的；牢靠的；稳固的 SYN **safe**: *a* ***secure job/income*** 稳定的工作 / 收入 ◇ *It's not a very secure way to make a living.* 以此谋生终非长久之计。◇ *The future of the company looks secure.* 看来公司未来不会有问题。OPP **insecure** **3** ~ **(against/from sth)** that cannot be affected or harmed by sth 安全的；稳妥的：*Information must be stored so that it is secure from accidental deletion.* 必须把资料保存起来，这样才不至于无意中删除。
- **BUILDING/DOOR/ROOM** 建筑物；门；房间 **4** guarded and/or made stronger so that it is difficult for people to enter or leave 严密把守的；牢固的；坚固的：*Check that all windows and doors have been made as secure as possible.* 看看是不是所有的门窗都关紧了。◇ *a secure unit for child offenders* 少年犯拘留病房 OPP **insecure**
- **FIRM** 牢固 **5** not likely to move, fall down, etc. 牢固的；稳固的；坚固的 SYN **stable**: *The aerial doesn't look very secure to me.* 我看这天线不太牢固。◇ *It was difficult to maintain a secure foothold on the ice.* 在冰上不容易站稳脚。◇ (*figurative*) *Our relationship was now on a more secure footing.* 现在，我们的关系有一个更为稳固的基础了。OPP **insecure**

▸ **se·cure·ly** AW *adv.* : *She locked the door securely behind her.* 她随手把门锁好。◇ *Make sure the ropes are securely fastened.* 务必把绳子拴牢。

■ ***verb*** (*formal*)

- **GET STH** 得到 **1** to obtain or achieve sth, especially when this means using a lot of effort （尤指经过努力）获得，取得，实现：~ **sth** *to secure a contract/deal* 订立合同；达

成协议 ◇ *The team managed to secure a place in the finals.* 球队拼得了决赛的一席之地。 ◇ *She secured 2 000 votes.* 她获得 2 000 票。 ◇ **~ sth for sb/sth/yourself** *He secured a place for himself at law school.* 他被法学院录取了。 ◇ **~ sb/sth/yourself sth** *He secured himself a place at law school.* 他被法学院录取了。
- **FASTEN FIRMLY** 牢靠地固定 **2 ~ sth (to sth)** to attach or fasten sth firmly 拴牢；扣紧；关严： *She secured the rope firmly to the back of the car.* 她把绳子牢牢地拴在车后面。
- **PROTECT FROM HARM** 使不受危害 **3** to protect sth so that it is safe and difficult to attack or damage 保护；保卫；使安全： **~ sth against sth** *to secure a property against intruders* 保护房产以免外人闯入 ◇ **~ sth** *The windows were secured with locks and bars.* 窗户已经插上栓，上了锁，都关好了。 ◇ (*figurative*) *a savings plan that will secure your child's future* 为您孩子的未来提供保障的储蓄计划
- **A LOAN** 借贷 **4 ~ sth** to legally agree to give sb property or goods that are worth the same amount as the money that you have borrowed from them, if you are unable to pay the money back 抵押： *a loan secured on the house* 以房子作抵押的贷款

se·cur·ity 🔑 AW /sɪˈkjʊərəti; *NAmE* səˈkjʊr-/ *noun* (*pl.* **-ies**)
- **PROTECTION** 保护 **1** 🔑 [U] the activities involved in protecting a country, building or person against attack, danger, etc. 保护措施；安全工作： ***national security*** (= the defence of a country) 国家安全 ◇ *airport security* 机场的安全措施 ◇ *They carried out* ***security checks*** *at the airport.* 他们在机场实行了安全检查。 ◇ *The visit took place amidst* ***tight security*** (= the use of many police officers). 访问是在戒备森严的情况下进行的。 ◇ *the* ***security forces/services*** (= the police, army, etc.) 安全部队 / 机构 ◇ ***a high/maximum security prison*** (= for dangerous criminals) 高度 / 最高级戒备的监狱 ➲ COLLOCATIONS AT INTERNATIONAL ➲ SEE ALSO HIGH-SECURITY **2** 🔑 [U+sing./pl. v.] the department of a large company or organization that deals with the protection of its buildings, equipment and staff 保卫部门；保安部门： *Security was/were called to the incident.* 保安人员被叫到事发现场。 **3** [U] a place at an airport where you go after your passport has been checked so that officials can find out if you are carrying illegal drugs or weapons 机场安检区： *My bag was emptied and searched when I went through security.* 通过安检时我的包被清空搜查。 ◇ *It took ages to clear security and reach the departure lounge.* 花了好长时间才通过安检到达候机室。 ➲ WORDFINDER NOTE AT AIRPORT **4** 🔑 [U] protection against sth bad that might happen in the future 担保；保证： *financial security* 财务担保 ◇ ***Job security*** (= the guarantee that you will keep your job) *is a thing of the past.* 稳定的工作是过去的事了。
- **FEELING HAPPY/SAFE** 感觉愉快 / 安全 **5** 🔑 [U] the state of feeling happy and safe from danger or worry 安全；平安： *the security of a loving family life* 安享天伦之乐 ◇ *She'd allowed herself to be lulled into* ***a false sense of security*** (= a feeling that she was safe when in fact she was in danger). 她不自觉地陷入了一种虚假的安全感之中。
- **FOR A LOAN** 贷款 **6** [U, C] a valuable item, such as a house, that you agree to give to sb if you are unable to pay back the money that you have borrowed from them 抵押品： *His home and business are being held* ***as security*** *for the loan.* 他是以房子和店铺为抵押得到这笔贷款的。
- **SHARES IN COMPANY** 公司股份 **7 securities** [pl.] (*finance* 财) documents proving that sb is the owner of shares, etc. in a particular company 证券 ➲ SEE ALSO SOCIAL SECURITY

seˈcurity blanket *noun* **1** (*BrE also* **ˈcomfort blanket**) a BLANKET or other object that a child holds in order to feel safe （儿童借以得到安全感的）安慰毯，安慰物 **2** something that provides protection against attack, danger, etc. 保护物；防护措施；安全保障： *A firewall provides an essential security blanket for your computer network.* 防火墙为计算机网络提供了基本安全保障。 **3** (*BrE*) official orders or measures that prevent people from knowing about, seeing, etc. sth 保密令；保密措施： *The government has thrown a security blanket around the talks.* 政府明令禁止泄露谈判内容。

the Seˈcurity Council (*also* **the ˌUN Seˈcurity Council**, **the ˌUnited Nations Seˈcurity Council**) *noun* [sing.] the part of the United Nations that tries to keep peace and order in the world, consisting of representatives of fifteen countries （联合国）安全理事会

seˈcurity guard *noun* a person whose job is to guard money, valuables, a building, etc. 保安人员

seˈcurity risk *noun* a person who cannot be given secret information because they are a danger to a particular country, organization, etc., especially because of their political beliefs （尤指因政治信仰而对国家、机构等安全构成威胁的）危险分子

Seˈcurity Service *noun* a government organization that protects a country and its secrets from enemies 国家安全机构

Secy. *abbr.* (*US*) = SEC.

sedan /sɪˈdæn/ (*NAmE*) (*BrE* **sa|loon, saˈloon car**) *noun* a car with four doors and a BOOT/TRUNK (= space at the back for carrying things) which is separated from the part where the driver and passengers sit 小轿车；（三厢四门）轿车 ➲ VISUAL VOCAB PAGE V56

seˌdan ˈchair *noun* a box containing a seat for one person, carried on poles by two people, used in the 17th and 18th centuries 轿子

sed·ate /sɪˈdeɪt/ *adj.*, *verb*
- ***adj.*** [usually before noun] **1** slow, calm and relaxed 镇定的；泰然的；不慌不忙的 SYN **unhurried**: *We followed the youngsters at a more sedate pace.* 我们跟在年轻人后面，步子稍慢一点。 **2** quiet, especially in a way that lacks excitement 宁静的；不热闹的： *a sedate country town* 宁静的乡间小镇 **3** (of a person 人) quiet and serious in a way that seems formal 庄重的；严肃的；不苟言笑的： *a sedate, sober man* 一个严肃审慎的人 ▸ **sed·ate·ly** *adv.*
- ***verb*** [often passive] **~ sb/sth** to give sb drugs in order to make them calm and/or to make them sleep 给…服镇静剂 SYN **tranquillize**: *Most of the patients are heavily sedated.* 多数病人服了大剂量镇静药。

sed·ation /sɪˈdeɪʃn/ *noun* [U] the act of giving sb drugs in order to make them calm or to make them sleep; the state that results from this 药物镇静；镇静状态： *The victim's wife was last night being kept* ***under sedation*** *in the local hospital.* 昨晚，受害人的妻子在当地医院用药后处于镇静状态。

seda·tive /ˈsedətɪv/ *noun* a drug that makes sb go to sleep or makes them feel calm and relaxed 镇静药 SYN **tranquillizer** ➲ WORDFINDER NOTE AT SLEEP ▸ **seda·tive** *adj.* [usually before noun]: *the sedative effect of the drug* 这药物的镇静效果

sed·en·tary /ˈsedntri; *NAmE* -teri/ *adj.* **1** (of work, activities, etc. 工作、活动等) in which you spend a lot of time sitting down 需要久坐的： ***a sedentary job/occupation/lifestyle*** 常久坐的工作 / 职业 / 生活方式 **2** (of people 人) spending a lot of time sitting down and not moving 惯于久坐不动的： *He became increasingly sedentary in later life.* 到晚年，他变得越来越不爱动了。 **3** (*specialist*) (of people or animals 人或动物) that stay and live in the same place or area 定居的；定栖的；不迁徙的： *Rhinos are largely sedentary animals.* 大致说来，犀牛是一种定栖动物。 ◇ *a sedentary population* 定居人口

Seder /ˈseɪdə(r)/ *noun* a Jewish CEREMONIAL service and dinner on the first night or first two nights of Passover 逾越节家宴（犹太教逾越节第一夜或第一第二两夜举行）

sedge /sedʒ/ *noun* [U] a plant like grass that grows in wet ground or near water 莎草；苔

sedi·ment /ˈsedɪmənt/ *noun* [U] **1** the solid material that settles at the bottom of a liquid 沉淀物 **2** (*geology* 地) sand, stones, mud, etc. carried by water or wind and left, for example, on the bottom of a lake, river, etc. 沉积物

S

sedi·ment·ary /ˌsedɪˈmentri/ *adj.* (*geology* 地) connected with or formed from the sand, stones, mud, etc. that settle at the bottom of lakes, etc. 沉积的；沉积形成的：*sedimentary rocks* 沉积岩

sedi·men·ta·tion /ˌsedɪmenˈteɪʃn/ *noun* [U] (*geology* 地) the process of depositing sediment 沉积（过程）

se·di·tion /sɪˈdɪʃn/ *noun* [U] (*formal*) the use of words or actions that are intended to encourage people to oppose a government 煽动叛乱的言论（或行动） SYN **insurrection** ▶ **se·di·tious** /sɪˈdɪʃəs/ *adj.*：*seditious activity* 煽动叛乱的活动

se·duce /sɪˈdjuːs; *NAmE* -ˈduːs/ *verb* **1** ~ **sb** to persuade sb to have sex with you, especially sb who is younger or who has less experience than you 诱奸 **2** ~ **sb (into sth/into doing sth)** to persuade sb to do sth that they would not usually agree to do by making it seem very attractive 诱骗；唆使 SYN **entice**: *The promise of huge profits seduced him into parting with his money.* 高额利润的许诺诱使他把钱交了出来。

se·du·cer /sɪˈdjuːsə(r); *NAmE* sɪˈduːsər/ *noun* a person who persuades sb to have sex with them 诱奸者

se·duc·tion /sɪˈdʌkʃn/ *noun* **1** [U, C] the act of persuading sb to have sex with you 诱奸：*Cleopatra's seduction of Caesar* 克里奥帕特拉对恺撒的引诱 **2** [C, usually pl., U] ~ **(of sth)** the qualities or features of sth that make it seem attractive 诱惑力；魅力；吸引力 SYN **enticement**: *Who could resist the seductions of the tropical island?* 谁能不为这个热带海岛的魅力而倾倒呢？

se·duc·tive /sɪˈdʌktɪv/ *adj.* **1** sexually attractive 诱人的；迷人的；有魅力的；性感的：*a seductive woman* 富有魅力的女人 ◇ *She used her most seductive voice.* 她运用了自己最有魅力的嗓音。**2** attractive in a way that makes you want to have or do sth 有吸引力的；令人神往的 SYN **tempting**: *The idea of retiring to the south of France is highly seductive.* 退休后到法国南方去，这个主意令人心驰神往。▶ **se·duc·tive·ly** *adv.* **se·duc·tive·ness** *noun* [U]

se·duc·tress /sɪˈdʌktrəs/ *noun* a woman who persuades sb to have sex with her 勾引男人的女人

sedu·lous /ˈsedjʊləs; *NAmE* ˈsedʒələs/ *adj.* (*formal*) showing great care and effort in your work 勤勉的；孜孜不倦的；勤奋的 SYN **diligent** ▶ **sedu·lous·ly** *adv.*

S

see /siː/ *verb, noun*

■ *verb* (**saw** /sɔː/, **seen** /siːn/)

• **USE EYES** 用眼 **1** [T, I] (not used in the progressive tenses 不用于进行时) to become aware of sb/sth by using your eyes 看见；见到；看出：~ **(sb/sth)** *She looked for him but couldn't see him in the crowd.* 她在人群里找来找去，但没看见他。◇ *The opera was the place to* ***see and be seen*** (= by other important or fashionable people). 歌剧院是个名流和时尚人士竞显丰采的地方。◇ ~ **(that)**... *He could see (that) she had been crying.* 他看得出她哭过。◇ ~ **what, how, etc.**... *Did you see what happened?* 你看见出什么事了吗？◇ ~ **sb/sth + adj.** *I hate to see you unhappy.* 我不愿见你不高兴。◇ ~ **sb/sth doing sth** *She was seen running away from the scene of the crime.* 有人看见她从犯罪现场跑开。◇ ~ **sb/sth do sth** *I saw you put the key in your pocket.* 我见你把钥匙放进了口袋里。◇ **sb/sth is seen to do sth** *He was seen to enter the building about the time the crime was committed.* 有人看见他在案发时间前后进入那栋建筑物。**2** [I] (not usually used in the progressive tenses 通常不用于进行时) to have or use the power of sight 看得见；看；有视力：*She will never see again* (= she has become blind). 她再也看不见东西了。◇ *On a clear day you* ***can see*** *for miles from here.* 在晴天，你从这儿能看出去很远。◇ ~ **to do sth** *It was getting dark and I* ***couldn't see*** *to read.* 天色黑下来，我看不成书了。

• **WATCH** 观看 **3** [T] (not usually used in the progressive tenses 通常不用于进行时) ~ **sth** to watch a game, television programme, performance, etc. 观看（比赛、电视节目、演出等）：*Did you see that programme on Brazil last night?* 昨晚你有没有看那个介绍巴西的节目？◇ *In the evening we went to see a movie.* 晚上，我们去看了一场电影。◇ *Fifty thousand people saw the match.* 有五万人观看了那场比赛。⊃ SYNONYMS AT LOOK

• **LOOK UP INFORMATION** 检索资料 **4** [T] (used in orders 用于祈使句) ~ **sth** to look at sth in order to find information 见；参见：*See page 158.* 参见第 158 页。

• **MEET BY CHANCE** 偶然遇见 **5** [T] ~ **sb** (not usually used in the progressive tenses 通常不用于进行时) to be near and recognize sb; to meet sb by chance 遇见；碰到；邂逅：*Guess who I saw at the party last night!* 你猜猜，昨天我在晚会上碰见谁了！

• **VISIT** 拜访 **6** [T] ~ **sb** to visit sb 拜访；看望；探视：*Come and see us again soon.* 早点再来看我们。

• **HAVE MEETING** 会见 **7** [T] ~ **sb (about sth)** to have a meeting with sb 会见；会晤：*You ought to see a doctor about that cough.* 你得找个大夫看看你的咳嗽。◇ *What is it you want to see me about?* 你找我有什么事？

• **SPEND TIME** 度过时间 **8** [T] (often used in the progressive tenses 常用于进行时) ~ **sb** to spend time with sb 与（某人）待在一起；交往：***Are you seeing anyone*** (= having a romantic relationship with anyone)? 你是不是跟什么人好上了？◇ *They've been* ***seeing a lot of each other*** (= spending a lot of time together) *recently.* 他们近来老泡在一起。

• **UNDERSTAND** 理解 **9** [I, T] (not usually used in the progressive tenses 通常不用于进行时) to understand sth 理解；明白；领会：*'It opens like this.' 'Oh,* ***I see****.'* "这样就打开了。" "哦，我明白了。" ◇ ~ **sth** *He didn't see the joke.* 他没听懂这则笑话。◇ *I don't think she* ***saw the point*** *of the story.* 我觉得她没有领会故事的中心意思。◇ *I can see both sides of the argument.* 争论双方的观点我都清楚。◇ *Make Lydia* ***see reason*** (= be sensible), *will you?* 你要让莉迪娅明白道理好不好？◇ ~ **(that)**... ***Can't you see*** *(that) he's taking advantage of you?* 他在利用你，难道你看不出来？◇ ***I don't see that it matters*** *what Josh thinks.* 乔希怎么想有什么要紧，我不明白。◇ ~ **what, why, etc.**... *'It's broken.' 'Oh yes,* ***I see what you mean****.'* "它破了。" "噢，我明白你的意思。" ◇ *'Can we go swimming?'* ***'I don't see why not*** (= yes, you can).*'* "我们可以去游泳吗？" "可以呀。" ◇ **be seen to do sth** *The government not only has to do something, it must* ***be seen to be doing something*** (= people must be aware that it is doing sth). 政府不仅必须采取措施，而且必须让人们知道它在采取措施。⊃ SYNONYMS AT UNDERSTAND

▼ **SYNONYMS 同义词辨析**

see

spot • catch • glimpse

These words all mean to become aware of sb/sth by using your eyes, especially suddenly or when it is not easy to see them/it. 以上各词均含看见、见到、看出之义，尤指突然发现或注意到。

see to become aware of sb/sth by using your eyes 指看见、见到、看出：*She looked for him but couldn't see him in the crowd.* 她在人群里找来找去，但没看见他。◇ *He could see (that) she had been crying.* 他看得出她哭过。

spot to see or notice sb/sth, especially suddenly or when they are not easy to see or notice 指看见、看出，尤指突然发现或注意到：*I've just spotted a mistake on the front cover.* 我刚才在封面上发现了一处错误。

catch to see or notice sth for a moment, but not clearly or completely 指瞥见、察觉：*She* ***caught sight*** *of a car in the distance.* 她瞥见远处有一辆车。◇ ***He caught a glimpse*** *of himself in the mirror.* 他看了一眼镜子中的自己。

glimpse (*literary*) to see sb/sth for a moment, but not clearly or completely 指瞥见、看一眼：*He'd glimpsed her through the window as he passed.* 他路过时透过窗户瞥见了她。

PATTERNS

- to see/spot **that/how/what/where/who...**
- to **suddenly** see/spot/catch/glimpse sb/sth

- HAVE OPINION 认为 **10** [T] **~ sth + adv./prep.** (not usually used in the progressive tenses 通常不用于进行时) to have an opinion of sth 认为；看待： *I see things differently now.* 现在，我看问题的方式不一样了。◇ *Try to see things from her point of view.* 设法从她那个角度去看问题。◇ *Lack of money is the main problem, **as I see it*** (= in my opinion). 依我看，主要问题是缺钱。◇ ***The way I see it**, you have three main problems.* 我认为你有三个主要问题。➲ SYNONYMS AT REGARD
- IMAGINE 想象 **11** [T] (not used in the progressive tenses 不用于进行时) to consider sth as a future possibility; to imagine sb/sth as sth 设想；想象： **~ sb/sth doing sth** *I can't see her changing her mind.* 我无法想象她会改变主意。◇ **~ sb/sth as sth** *His colleagues see him as a future director.* 他的同事认为他很可能是未来的负责人。➲ SYNONYMS AT IMAGINE
- FIND OUT 弄清 **12** [I, T] (not usually used in the progressive tenses 通常不用于进行时) to find out sth by looking, asking or waiting （通过查看、打听、等待）弄清，了解： *'Has the mail come yet?' 'I'll just go and see.'* "邮件来了没有？""我去看看。"◇ *'Is he going to get better?' 'I don't know, we'll just have to **wait and see**.'* "他会好起来吗？""不清楚，我们只能等着瞧了。"◇ *We'll have a great time, **you'll see**.* 你瞧着吧，我们会很开心的。◇ **~ what, how, etc.…** *Go and see what the kids are doing, will you?* 你去看看孩子们在干什么好不好？◇ *We'll have to **see how it goes**.* 我们得看看情况怎么样。◇ **~ (that)…** *I see (that) interest rates are going up again.* 我知道利率又在提高了。◇ **it is seen that…** *It can be seen that certain groups are more at risk than others.* 看得出，有的组风险大，有的组风险小。 **13** [I, T] (not usually used in the progressive tenses 通常不用于进行时) to find out or decide sth by thinking or considering 考虑；定夺： *'Will you be able to help us?' 'I don't know, I'll have to see.'* "你能帮助我们吗？""不好说，我得考虑一下。"◇ *'Can I go to the party?' '**We'll see** (= I'll decide later).'* "我能去参加聚会吗？""待会儿再看吧。"◇ **~ what, whether, etc.…** ***I'll see what I can do** to help.* 我考虑考虑，看我能帮上什么忙。
- MAKE SURE 确保 **14** [T] (not usually used in the progressive tenses 通常不用于进行时) **~ that…** to make sure that you do sth or that sth is done 确保；务必（做到）： *See that all the doors are locked before you leave.* 一定要把所有的门都锁好了再走。
- EXPERIENCE 经历 **15** [T] (not used in the progressive tenses 不用于进行时) **~ sth** to experience or suffer sth 经历；遭受： *He has seen a great deal in his long life.* 他在漫长的一生中经历了许多事情。◇ *I hope I never live to **see the day** when computers finally replace books.* 我可不愿意活到那一天，看着计算机最终取代书籍。◇ *It didn't surprise her—she **had seen it all before**.* 她没有大惊小怪，她以前全都见识过。
- WITNESS EVENT 见证事件 **16** [T] (not used in the progressive tenses 不用于进行时) **~ sth** to be the time when an event happens 为…发生的时间： *Next year sees the centenary of Mahler's death.* 明年是马勒逝世一百周年。 **17** [T] (not used in the progressive tenses 不用于进行时) **~ sth** to be the place where an event happens 为…发生的地点 SYN **witness**: *This stadium has seen many thrilling football games.* 在这座体育场里举办过许多激动人心的足球比赛。
- HELP 帮助 **18** [T] **~ sb + adv./prep.** to go with sb to help or protect them 送；护送： *I saw the old lady across* (= helped her cross) *the road.* 我护送老太太过马路。◇ *May I **see you home*** (= go with you as far as your house)? 我可不可以送你回家？◇ *My secretary will **see you out*** (= show you the way out of the building). 我的秘书会把你送出去。

IDM HELP Most idioms containing **see** are at the entries for the nouns and adjectives in the idioms, for example **not see the wood for the trees** is at **wood**. 大多数含 see 的习语，都可在该等习语中的名词及形容词相关词条找到，如 not see the wood for the trees 在词条 wood 下。 **for all (the world) to 'see** clearly visible; in a way that is clearly visible 明显；显而易见 **ˌlet me 'see/let's see** (*informal*) used when you are thinking or trying to remember sth 让我 / 咱们看看；让我 / 咱们想一想： *Now let me see—how old is she now?* 让我想一想，她现在多大了呢？ **see sth 'coming** to realize that there is going to be a problem before it happens 料到会有问题；意识到会出麻烦： *We should have seen it coming. There was no way he could keep going under all that pressure.* 我们本该料到的。承受着那么大的压力，他不可能坚持下去。 **ˌsee for your'self** to find out or look at sth yourself in order to be sure that what sb is saying is true 亲自看，亲自了解（以核实）： *If you don't believe me, go and see for yourself!* 要是不信我说的，你自己去看看！ **see sb/sth for what they 'are/it 'is** to realize that sb/sth is not as good, pleasant, etc. as they/it seem 看清某人（或事物）的真实状况（不是表面那样美好） **seeing that…** (*also informal* **seeing as (how)…**) because of the fact that… 鉴于；由于；因为： *Seeing that he's been off sick all week he's unlikely to come.* 他因病整整一周没有上班了，所以今天也不大可能来。 **'see you (a'round) | (I'll) be 'seeing you | ˌsee you 'later** (*informal*) goodbye 再见： *I'd better be going now. See you!* 现在我可该走了。再见！ **you 'see** (*informal*) used when you are explaining sth （作解释时说）你看，你知道，要知道： *You see, the thing is, we won't be finished before Friday.* 要知道，问题是星期五以前我们完不了事。

PHR V **'see about sth** to deal with sth 办理；照料；料理；安排： *I must see about* (= prepare) *lunch.* 我得做午饭了。◇ *He says he won't help, does he? Well, **we'll soon see about that*** (= I will demand that he does help). 他说他不帮忙，是不是？好，我们这就去找他。◇ **see about doing sth** *I'll have to see about getting that roof repaired.* 我得找人把房顶修一修。 **'see sth in sb/sth** to find sb/sth attractive or interesting 看上；看中；觉得…有趣： ***I don't know what she sees in him.*** 我不知道她看上他哪儿了。 **ˌsee sb↔'off 1** to go to a station, an airport, etc. to say goodbye to sb who is starting a journey 为…送行；送别 **2** (*BrE*) to force sb to leave a place, for example by chasing them 赶走，驱逐（某人）： *The dogs saw them off in no time.* 几条狗立刻把他们吓走了。 **3** (*BrE*) to defeat sb in a game, fight, etc. （在游戏、战斗等活动中）打败，击败： *The home team saw off the challengers by 68 points to 47.* 主队以 68:47 击败前来挑战的客队。 **ˌsee sb↔'out** (not used in the progressive tenses 不用于进行时) (*BrE*) to last longer than the rest of sb's life 寿命比某人长；看着某人故去： *I've had this coat for years, and I'm sure it will see me out.* 这件外衣我穿了好多年，我敢说它能穿一辈子。 **ˌsee sth↔'out** (not used in the progressive tenses 不用于进行时) (*BrE*) to reach the end or last until the end of sth 持续到…结束： *They had enough fuel to see the winter out.* 他们有足够的燃料过冬。◇ *He saw out his career in Italy.* 他在意大利一直工作到退休。 **ˌsee 'over sth** (*BrE*) to visit and look at a place carefully 察看（某处）： *We need to see over the house before we can make you an offer.* 我们需要好好看了房子以后才能给你开个价。 **ˌsee 'through sb/sth** (not used in the progressive tenses 不用于进行时) to realize the truth about sb/sth 看透；识破： *We saw through him from the start.* 一开始我们就识破他了。◇ *I can see through your little game* (= I am aware of the trick you are trying to play on me). 我看透了你的小把戏。 **ˌsee sth 'through** (not usually used in the progressive tenses 通常不用于进行时) to not give up doing a task, project, etc. until it is finished 把（任务、工程等）进行到底；坚持完成： *She's determined to see the job through.* 她决心完成这项工作。 **ˌsee sb 'through | ˌsee sb 'through sth** (not used in the progressive tenses 不用于进行时) to give help or support to sb for a particular period of time 帮助（或支持）某人度过： *Her courage and good humour saw her through.* 她靠着顽强的勇气和乐观的性格挺了过来。◇ *I only have $20 to see me through the week.* 我只有 20 美元来维持我这一周了。 **'see to sth** to deal with sth 办理；照管；料理： *Will you see to the arrangements for the next meeting?* 你来负责安排下次会议，好吗？◇ *Don't worry—**I'll see to it**.* 别担心，这事儿我来处理。◇ *We'll have to get that door seen to* (= repaired). 我们得找人把那扇门修一下。 **'see to it that…** to make sure that… 确保；务使： *Can you see to it that the email goes out this afternoon?* 你能确保今天下午把电邮发出去吗？

■ ***noun*** (*formal*) the district or office of a BISHOP or an ARCHBISHOP 主教（或大主教）教区；主教（或大主教）权限；牧座： *the Holy See* (= the office of the POPE) （罗马）宗座

S

seed /siːd/ *noun, verb*

■ ***noun***

• **OF PLANTS/FRUIT** 植物；果实 **1** [C, U] the small hard part produced by a plant, from which a new plant can grow 种子；籽：*a packet of wild flower seeds* 一包野花籽 ◇ *sesame seeds* 芝麻 ◇ ***Sow the seeds*** *outdoors in spring.* 春天把种子播在地里。◇ *These vegetables can be **grown from seed**.* 这些蔬菜可以撒籽栽种。◇ ***seed potatoes*** (= used for planting) 留种的土豆 ➲ COLLOCATIONS AT LIFE ➲ VISUAL VOCAB PAGES V10, V35 ➲ SEE ALSO BIRDSEED **2** [C] (*NAmE*) = PIP (1) ➲ VISUAL VOCAB PAGE V32

• **BEGINNING** 起源 **3** [C, usually pl.] ~ (**of sth**) the beginning of a feeling or a development which continues to grow 起源；起因；萌芽；开端：*the seeds of rebellion* 反叛的起因 ◇ *This **planted the seeds of** doubt in my mind.* 这件事在我心中播下了怀疑的种子。

• **IN TENNIS** 网球 **4** [C] (especially in TENNIS 尤指网球) one of the best players in a competition. The seeds are given a position in a list to try and make sure that they do not play each other in the early parts of the competition. 种子选手：*The top seed won comfortably.* 头号种子选手轻松获胜。◇ *the number one seed* 一号种子选手

• **OF A MAN** 男子 **5** [U] (*old-fashioned* or *humorous*) SEMEN 精液 **6** [U] (*literary*) all the people who are the children, grandchildren, etc. of one man （统称某人的）子孙，后裔，后代

IDM **go/run to 'seed 1** (especially of a vegetable plant 尤指蔬菜) to produce flowers and seeds as well as leaves 开花结籽 **2** to become much less attractive or good because of lack of attention 变得懒散颓废（或意志消沉）；衰败：*After his divorce, he let himself go to seed.* 离婚后，他自暴自弃。➲ MORE AT SOW[1]

■ ***verb***

• **OF A PLANT** 植物 **1** [I] to produce seeds 结籽 **2** [T] ~ **itself** to produce other plants using its own seeds （种子）繁殖

• **AREA OF GROUND** 土地 **3** [T, usually passive] ~ **sth** (**with sth**) to plant seeds in an area of ground 在…播种：*a newly seeded lawn* 新撒了草籽的草坪

• **IN TENNIS** 网球 **4** [T, usually passive] ~ **sb** to make sb a seed in a competition 确定（某人）为种子选手：*He has been seeded 14th at Wimbledon next week.* 他被确定为下周温布尔登网球赛的第 14 号种子选手。

seed·bed /ˈsiːdbed/ *noun* **1** an area of soil which has been specially prepared for planting seeds in 苗床 **2** [usually sing.] ~ (**of/for sth**) a place or situation in which sth can develop （某事物发展的）有利环境；温床

ˈseed cake *noun* [C, U] a cake containing CARAWAY seeds 籽香蛋糕；葛缕子籽糕饼

ˈseed corn *noun* [U] **1** the grain that is kept for planting the next year's crops 粮种 **2** people or things that will be successful or useful in the future 有远大前程的人（或事物）；日后有用的人（或事物）

seed·ed /ˈsiːdɪd/ *adj.* [usually before noun] **1** (especially of a TENNIS player 尤指网球运动员) given a number showing that they are one of the best players in a particular competition 确定为种子选手的：*a seeded player* 种子选手 **2** (of fruit 果实) with the seeds removed 去籽的；去核的：*seeded tomatoes* 去籽西红柿

seed·less /ˈsiːdləs/ *adj.* [usually before noun] (of fruit 果实) having no seeds 无籽的；无核的：*seedless grapes* 无籽葡萄

seed·ling /ˈsiːdlɪŋ/ *noun* a young plant that has grown from a seed 秧苗；籽苗；幼苗 ➲ VISUAL VOCAB PAGE V20

ˈseed money (*also* **ˈseed capital**) *noun* [U] money to start a new business, project, etc. 本钱；本金

ˈseed pearl *noun* a small PEARL 芥子珠（一种小颗粒珍珠，又称肌肉珍珠）

seeds·man /ˈsiːdzmən/ *noun* (*pl.* **-men** /-mən/) a person who grows and sells seeds 种农；种子商

seedy /ˈsiːdi/ *adj.* (**seed·ier, seedi·est**) (*disapproving*) dirty and unpleasant, possibly connected with immoral or illegal activities 肮脏的；污七八糟的；乌烟瘴气的；下流的：*a seedy bar* 污七八糟的酒吧 ◇ *the seedy world of prostitution* 乌烟瘴气的卖淫圈子 ◇ *a seedy-looking man* 一脸邪气的男人 ▶ **seedi·ness** *noun* [U]

ˌSeeing ˈEye dog™ *noun* (*NAmE*) = GUIDE DOG

seek AW /siːk/ *verb* (**sought, sought** /sɔːt/) (*formal*) **1** [T, I] to look for sth/sb 寻找：**~ sth/sb** *Drivers are advised to seek alternative routes.* 建议驾车者另寻其他路线。◇ **~ for sth/sb** (*BrE*) *They sought in vain for somewhere to shelter.* 他们怎么也找不到一个藏身的地方。**2** [T, I] ~ (**sth**) to try to obtain or achieve sth 寻求；谋求；争取：*to seek funding for a project* 为项目筹募资金 ◇ *Highly qualified secretary seeks employment.* (= in an advertisement) 优秀秘书求职（广告用语）◇ *We are currently seeking new ways of expanding our membership.* 目前，我们正探索发展会员的新途径。**3** [T] to ask sb for sth （向人）请求，寻求：**~ sth** *I think it's time we sought legal advice.* 我想我们现在该咨询一下律师了。◇ **~ sth from sb** *She managed to calm him down and seek help from a neighbour.* 她设法使他平静下来，然后向一位邻居求助。**4** [I] **~ to do sth** to try to do sth 试图；设法 SYN **attempt**：*They quickly sought to distance themselves from the protesters.* 他们迅速设法远离抗议者。**5 -seeking** (in adjectives and nouns 构成形容词和名词) looking for or trying to get the thing mentioned; the activity of doing this 寻求（或追求）…的；对…的寻求（或追求）：*attention-seeking behaviour* 为引起他人的注意而作出的行为 ◇ *Voluntary work can provide a framework for job-seeking.* 参与义务工作有助于奠定求职的基础。➲ SEE ALSO HEAT-SEEKING, HIDE-AND-SEEK, SELF-SEEKING

IDM **seek your ˈfortune** (*literary*) to try to find a way to become rich, especially by going to another place 外出寻找发财机会；外出闯荡；闯世界

PHR V **ˌseek sb/sth ˈout** to look for and find sb/sth, especially when this means using a lot of effort 挑选出；物色到

seek·er /ˈsiːkə(r)/ *noun* (often in compounds 常构成复合词) a person who is trying to find or get the thing mentioned 寻找者；寻求者；追求者；谋求者：***an attention/a publicity seeker*** 故意引人注意的人；追求出名的人 ◇ *seekers after the truth* 追求真理的人 ➲ SEE ALSO ASYLUM SEEKER, JOB SEEKER

seem /siːm/ *linking verb* **1** **~ (to sb) (to be) sth** (not used in the progressive tenses 不用于进行时) to give the impression of being or doing sth （给人印象）好像，似乎，看来 SYN **appear**：**+ adj.** *You seem happy.* 你好像挺高兴。◇ *Do whatever seems best to you.* 你觉得什么最好，就做什么。◇ **+ noun** *He seems a nice man.* 他看来是个好人。◇ **~ like sth** *It seemed like a good idea at the time.* 当时这主意好像不错。◇ **~ (as though…)** *It always seemed as though they would get married.* 他们一直仿佛是要结婚似的。◇ *'He'll be there, then?' 'So it seems* (= people say so).*'* "这么说，他要去那儿了？" "似乎是这样。" ◇ **it seems that…** *It seems that they know what they're doing.* 看来，他们知道自己在干什么。◇ **~ to do/be/have sth** *They seem to know what they're doing.* 看来，他们知道自己在干什么。**2** **~ to do/be/have sth** used to make what you say about your thoughts, feelings or actions less strong （用以缓和语气）感到好像，觉得似乎：*I seem to have left my book at home.* 我大概是把书忘在家里了。◇ *I can't seem to* (= I've tried, but I can't) *get started today.* 我怕是没法在今天开始了。**3** **it seems | it would seem** used to suggest that sth is true when you are not certain or when you want to be polite （表示不确切或客气）看来好像，似乎：**~ (that)…** *It would seem that we all agree.* 我们大家似乎都同意。◇ **+ adj.** *It seems only reasonable to ask students to buy a dictionary.* 要学生买一本词典似乎挺合情合理的。➲ LANGUAGE BANK AT IMPERSONAL, OPINION, PERHAPS

seem·ing /ˈsiːmɪŋ/ *adj.* [only before noun] (*formal*) appearing to be sth that may not be true 看似…（而实际未必）的；表面上的；貌似…的 SYN **apparent**：*a seeming impossibility* 表面看来不可能的事 ◇ *She handled the* *matter with seeming indifference.* 她看似漫不经心地处理了这件事。

seem·ing·ly /ˈsiːmɪŋli/ *adv.* **1** in a way that appears to be true but may in fact not be 看似；貌似；表面上：*a seemingly stupid question* 看似愚蠢的问题 ◇ *a* ***seemingly endless*** *journey* 似乎永远走不完的旅程 **2** (*formal*) according to what you have read or heard 据说；听说；看来 **SYN** **apparently**: *Seemingly, he borrowed the money from the bank.* 据说，他从银行贷出了那笔钱。

seem·ly /ˈsiːmli/ *adj.* (*old-fashioned* or *formal*) appropriate for a particular social situation 合适的；得体的；合乎礼仪的 **OPP** **unseemly**

seen PAST PART. OF SEE

seep /siːp/ *verb* [I] + **adv./prep.** (especially of liquids 尤指液体) to flow slowly and in small quantities through sth or into sth 渗；渗透 **SYN** **trickle**: *Blood was beginning to seep through the bandages.* 血开始从绷带渗出来。◇ *Water seeped from a crack in the pipe.* 水从管道的一个裂缝中渗出。◇ (*figurative*) *Gradually the pain seeped away.* 疼痛渐渐消失了。

seep·age /ˈsiːpɪdʒ/ *noun* [U, C, usually pl.] the process by which a liquid flows slowly and in small quantities through sth; the result of this process 渗；渗透；渗液：*Water gradually escapes by seepage through the ground.* 水逐渐从地上渗走了。◇ *oil seepages* 油渗

seer /sɪə(r); *NAmE* sɪr/ *noun* (*literary*) (especially in the past) a person who claims that they can see what is going to happen in the future（尤指旧时）预言家，先知 **SYN** **prophet**

seer·sucker /ˈsɪəsʌkə(r); *NAmE* ˈsɪrs-/ *noun* [U] a type of light cotton cloth with a pattern of raised lines and squares on its surface 绉条纹薄织物；泡泡纱

see-saw /ˈsiː sɔː/ *noun, verb*

■ ***noun*** **1** (*NAmE also* **ˈteeter-totter**) [C] a piece of equipment for children to play on consisting of a long flat piece of wood that is supported in the middle. A child sits at each end and makes the see-saw move up and down. 跷跷板 **2** [sing.] a situation in which things keep changing from one state to another and back again 拉锯局面（指来回往复，起伏不断）

■ ***verb*** [I] ~ (**from A to B**) to keep changing from one situation, opinion, emotion, etc. to another and back again（局势、意见、感情等）摇摆不定，不断反复，交替：*Her emotions see-sawed from anger to fear.* 她一会儿气，一会儿怕，情绪变来变去。◇ *Share prices see-sawed all day.* 整整一天，股票价格时涨时跌，不断变化。

seethe /siːð/ *verb* [I] **1** to be extremely angry about sth but try not to show other people how angry you are 强压怒火；生闷气 **SYN** **fume**: *She seethed silently in the corner.* 她在角落里默默地生闷气。◇ **~ with sth** *He marched off, seething with frustration.* 他大为失望，气呼呼地走开了。◇ **~ at sth** *Inwardly he was seething at this challenge to his authority.* 他因权威受到挑战而怒火中烧。**2** ~ (**with sth**) (*formal*) (of a place 地方) to be full of a lot of people or animals, especially when they are all moving around 充满，遍布，到处都是（人、动物）：*The resort is seething with tourists all year round.* 这处名胜一年四季游人如织。◇ *He became caught up in a* ***seething mass*** *of arms and legs.* 他被卷进了摩肩接踵的人群。**3** (*formal*) (of liquids 液体) to move around quickly and violently 翻滚；翻腾；涌动：*The grey ocean seethed beneath them.* 灰蒙蒙的大海在他们下面翻滚。

ˈsee-through *adj.* (of cloth 织物) very thin so that you can see through it 薄至透明的；可透视的：*a see-through blouse* 透明的女式衬衫

seg·ment *noun, verb*

■ ***noun*** /ˈsegmənt/ **1** a part of sth that is separate from the other parts or can be considered separately 部分；份；片；段：*She cleaned a small segment of the painting.* 她擦干净了这幅画的一小部分。◇ *Lines divided the area into segments.* 这一地区用线条分成了若干部分。**2** one of the sections of an orange, a lemon, etc.（柑橘、柠檬等的）瓣 ➲ VISUAL VOCAB PAGE V33 **3** (*geometry* 几何) a part of a circle separated from the rest by a single line 弓形；圆缺 ➲ PICTURE AT CIRCLE **4** (*phonetics* 语音) the smallest speech sound that a word can be divided into 音段

■ ***verb*** /segˈment/ [often passive] **~ sth** (*specialist*) to divide sth into different parts 分割；划分：*Market researchers often segment the population on the basis of age and social class.* 市场研究人员常常按年龄和社会阶层划分人口。◇ *The worm has a segmented body* (= with different sections joined together). 这条虫子的身体是分节的。

seg·men·tal /segˈmentl/ *adj.* (*phonetics* 语音) relating to the individual sounds that make up speech, as opposed to PROSODIC features such as stress and INTONATION 音段的

seg·men·ta·tion /ˌsegmenˈteɪʃn/ *noun* [U, C, usually pl.] (*specialist*) the act of dividing sth into different parts; one of these parts 分割；划分；分割成（或划分成）的部分

seg·re·gate /ˈsegrɪgeɪt/ *verb* (*formal*) **1 ~ sb** (**from sb**) to separate people of different races, religions or sexes and treat them in a different way 隔离并区别对待（不同种族、宗教或性别的人）：*a culture in which women are segregated from men* 妇女受到隔离歧视的文化 ◇ *a racially segregated community* 实行种族隔离的社会 ◇ *a segregated school* (= one for students of one race or religion only) 单一种族（或信仰）的学校 **OPP** **integrate** **2 ~ sth** (**from sth**) to keep one thing separate from another（使）分开，分离，隔离：*In all our restaurants, smoking and non-smoking areas are segregated from each other.* 在我们所有的餐馆中，吸烟区和非吸烟区都是分开的。

seg·re·ga·tion /ˌsegrɪˈgeɪʃn/ *noun* [U] (*formal*) **1** the act or policy of separating people of different races, religions or sexes and treating them in a different way（对不同种族、宗教或性别的人所采取的）隔离并区别对待，隔离政策：***racial/religious segregation*** 种族 / 宗教隔离 ◇ *segregation by age and sex* 按照年龄和性别而实施的隔离 ➲ COLLOCATIONS AT RACE **2** (*formal*) the act of separating people or things from a larger group 隔离（或分离）措施：*the segregation of smokers and non-smokers in restaurants* 把餐馆中的吸烟者与非吸烟者分隔开的做法

seg·re·ga·tion·ist /ˌsegrɪˈgeɪʃənɪst/ *adj.* supporting the separation of people according to their sex, race or religion（性别、种族、宗教）隔离主义的：*segregationist policies* 隔离主义政策 ▸ **seg·re·ga·tion·ist** *noun*

segue /ˈsegweɪ/ *verb* [I] + **adv./prep.** to move smoothly from one song, subject, place, etc. to another（顺利）转到，接入（另一首歌、话题、地方等）：*a spiritual that segued into a singalong chorus* 一首转为会众集体跟唱的灵歌 ◇ *He then segued into a discussion of atheism.* 然后他转入对无神论的论述。▸ **segue** *noun*

seine /seɪn/ (*also* **ˈseine net**) *noun* a type of fishing net which hangs down in the water and is pulled together at the ends to catch fish（捕鱼用）围网

seis·mic /ˈsaɪzmɪk/ *adj.* [only before noun] **1** connected with or caused by EARTHQUAKES 地震的；地震引起的：*seismic waves* 地震波 **2** having a very great effect; of very great size 影响深远的；重大的：*a* ***seismic shift*** *in the political process* 政治进程中的剧变

seis·mo·graph /ˈsaɪzməgrɑːf; *NAmE* -græf/ *noun* an instrument that measures and records information about EARTHQUAKES 地震仪；测震仪

seis·mol·ogy /saɪzˈmɒlədʒi; *NAmE* -ˈmɑːl-/ *noun* [U] the scientific study of EARTHQUAKES 地震学 ▸ **seis·mo·logic·al** /ˌsaɪzməˈlɒdʒɪkl; *NAmE* -ˈlɑːdʒ-/ *adj.*: *the National Seismological Institute* 国家地震研究所 **seis·molo·gist** /ˌsaɪzˈmɒlədʒɪst; *NAmE* -ˈmɑːl-/ *noun*

seize /siːz/ *verb* **1** to take sb/sth in your hand suddenly and using force 抓住；捉住；夺 **SYN** **grab**: **~ sth from sb** *She tried to seize the gun from him.* 她试图夺他的枪。◇ **~ sb/sth** *He seized her by the arm.* 他抓住她的胳膊。◇ *She* ***seized hold of*** *my hand.* 她抓住我的手。**2 ~ sth** (**from sb**) to take control of a place or situation, often suddenly

S

and violently （常指通过暴力突然）夺取，攻占，控制：*They seized the airport in a surprise attack.* 他们突袭攻占了机场。◇ *The army has **seized control of** the country.* 军队已经控制全国。◇ ***He seized power** in a military coup.* 他在军事政变中夺取了政权。**3 ~ sb** to arrest or capture sb 逮捕；捉拿；俘获：*The men were seized as they left the building.* 这些人在离开那栋房子时被抓获。**4 ~ sth** to take illegal or stolen goods away from sb 起获；没收；扣押：*A large quantity of drugs was seized during the raid.* 在这次突击行动中起获了大量毒品。**5 ~ a chance, an opportunity, the initiative, etc.** to be quick to make use of a chance, an opportunity, etc. 抓住，把握（机会、时机、主动等）**SYN grab**：*The party **seized** the initiative **with both hands*** (= quickly and with enthusiasm). 该党迅速掌握主动。**6 ~ sb** (of an emotion 情绪) to affect sb suddenly and deeply 突然侵袭；突然控制：*Panic seized her.* 她突然惊慌失措。◇ ***He was seized by** curiosity.* 他好奇心顿起。**7** = SEIZE UP (1)

PHR V **'seize on/upon sth** to suddenly show a lot of interest in sth, especially because you can use it to your advantage 利用；抓住（可利用的事物）**SYN pounce on/upon**：*The rumours were eagerly seized upon by the local press.* 当地报章迫不及待地对这些传闻加以炒作。**,seize 'up** (*NAmE also* **seize**) **1** (of the parts of a machine 机器部件) to stop moving or working correctly 停止运转；发生故障 **2** if a part of your body **seizes up**, you are unable to move it easily and it is often painful （身体）发僵

seiz·ure /'siːʒə(r)/ *noun* **1** [U, C] ~ (**of sth**) the use of legal authority to take sth from sb; an amount of sth that is taken in this way 起获；没收；起获的赃物；没收的财产：*The court ordered the seizure of his assets.* 法庭下令没收他的财产。◇ *the largest ever seizure of cocaine at a British port* 在英国口岸起获的历来数量最大的一批可卡因 **2** [U] ~ (**of sth**) the act of using force to take control of a country, town, etc. 夺取；占领；控制：*the army's seizure of power* 军队对政权的夺取 ◇ *the seizure of Burma by Japan in 1942* * 1942 年日军对缅甸的占领 **3** (*old-fashioned*) [C] a sudden attack of an illness, especially one that affects the brain （疾病，尤指脑病的）突然侵袭，发作

sel·dom /'seldəm/ *adv.* not often 不常；很少；难得 **SYN rarely**：*He had seldom seen a child with so much talent.* 有如此天赋的孩子他以往没见过几个。◇ *She **seldom, if ever,** goes to the theatre.* 她难得上剧院看场戏 —— 即便不能说从来不去。◇ *They seldom watch television these days.* 这些日子他们很少看电视。◇ (*literary*) *Seldom had he seen such beauty.* 他以前很少见过这样的美景。

se·lect 🔑 **AW** /sɪ'lekt/ *verb, adj.*

■ ***verb*** **1** 🔑 to choose sb/sth from a group of people or things, usually according to a system 选择；挑选；选拔：**~ sb/sth for sth** *He hasn't been selected for the team.* 他未能入选该队。◇ *All our hotels have been **carefully selected** for the excellent value they provide.* 我们的所有旅馆都是精心挑选的，最为合算。◇ **~ sb/sth as sth** *She was selected as the parliamentary candidate for Bath.* 她被选为巴斯选区的议员候选人。◇ **~ sb/sth** *a **randomly selected** sample of 23 schools* 随机抽选的 23 所学校作样本 ◇ *selected poems of T.S. Eliot* * T.S. 艾略特诗选 ◇ *This model is available at selected stores only.* 这种款式只在特定商店有售。◇ **~ sb/sth to do sth** *Six theatre companies have been selected to take part in this year's festival.* 已选定六个剧团参加今年的戏剧节。◇ **~ what, which, etc....** *Select what you want from the options available.* 从可选项中选择你想要的。➲ SYNONYMS AT CHOOSE **2 ~ sth** (*computing* 计) to mark sth on a computer screen; to choose sth, especially from a menu （在电脑屏幕上）选定；（从菜单中）选择，选取：*Select the text you want to format by holding down the left button on your mouse.* 按住鼠标左键选取你想要安排版式的文本。◇ *Select 'New Mail' from the 'Send' menu.* 从"发送"选单中选择"新邮件"。➲ WORDFINDER NOTE AT COMMAND

■ ***adj.*** **1** [only before noun] carefully chosen as the best out of a larger group of people or things 精选的；作为…精华的；优等的：*a select wine list* 名优葡萄酒目录 ◇ *Only a **select few*** (= a small number of people) *have been invited to the wedding.* 婚礼只邀请了几个至亲好友参加。**2** (of a society, club, place, etc. 社团、俱乐部、地方等) used by people who have a lot of money or a high social position 有钱、有社会地位的人使用的 **SYN exclusive**：*They live in a very select area.* 他们住在一个上层人士住宅区。◇ *a select club* 名流俱乐部

se,lect com'mittee *noun* (*BrE*) a small group of politicians or experts that have been chosen to examine a particular subject or problem 特别委员会（为研究某课题等而成立）

se·lect·ee /sɪ,lek'tiː/ *noun* **1** a person who is chosen for sth 选中的人；人选 **2** (*NAmE*) a person who is chosen to do MILITARY SERVICE 选征的士兵

se·lec·tion 🔑 **AW** /sɪ'lekʃn/ *noun* **1** 🔑 [U] the process of choosing sb/sth from a group of people or things, usually according to a system 选择；挑选；选拔：*The final team selection will be made tomorrow.* 明天将确定队伍的最后人选。◇ *the **random selection** of numbers* 号码的随机抽取 ◇ *selection criteria* 挑选标准 ◇ *the selection process* 选拔过程 **2** 🔑 [C] a number of people or things that have been chosen from a larger group 被挑选的人（或物）；被选中者；入选者：*A selection of readers' comments is published below.* 下面选登了部分读者的评论。➲ SYNONYMS AT CHOICE **3** 🔑 [C] a collection of things from which sth can be chosen 可供选择的事物 **SYN choice, range**：*The showroom has a **wide selection** of kitchens.* 展厅里有多种式样的厨房可供选择。➲ SEE ALSO NATURAL SELECTION

se·lec·tion·al /sɪ'lekʃənl/ *adj.* (*linguistics* 语言) used to describe the process by which each word limits what kind of words can be used with it in normal language （正规语言中单词对搭配词）选择的，限制的：*'Eat' has the selectional restriction that it must be followed by a kind of food, so 'I eat sky' is not possible.* * eat 一词之后限跟某种食物，所以不可能说 I eat sky。

se'lection committee *noun* a group of people who choose, for example, the members of a sports team （运动队队员等的）选拔委员会；遴选委员会

se·lect·ive **AW** /sɪ'lektɪv/ *adj.* **1** [usually before noun] affecting or concerned with only a small number of people or things from a larger group 选择性的；有选择的：*the selective breeding of cattle* 牛的选择性培育 ◇ *selective strike action* 有选择的罢工行动 **2 ~ (about/in sth)** tending to be careful about what or who you choose 认真挑选的；严格筛选的：*You will have to be selective about which information to include in the report.* 究竟要把哪些资料收入报告，你得仔细斟酌挑选。◇ *Their admissions policy is very selective.* 他们执行严格挑选的录取政策。◇ *a selective school* (= one that chooses which children to admit, especially according to ability) 择优录取学生的学校 ▶ **se·lect·ive·ly** **AW** *adv.*：*The product will be selectively marketed in the US* (= only in some areas). 这种产品将有选择地投放到美国某些地区的市场。**se·lect·iv·ity** /sə,lek'tɪvəti/ *noun* [U]：*Schools are tending towards greater selectivity.* 学校对新生的选拔有趋严之势。

se,lective 'service *noun* [U] (*NAmE*) a system in which people have to spend a period of time in the armed forces by law 义务兵役

se·lect·or **AW** /sɪ'lektə(r)/ *noun* **1** (*BrE*) a person who chooses the members of a particular sports team （运动队队员的）选拔人 **2** a device in an engine, a piece of machinery, etc. that allows you to choose a particular function 选择器；转换器

sel·en·ium /sə'liːniəm/ *noun* [U] (*symb.* **Se**) a chemical element. Selenium is a grey substance that is used in making electrical equipment and coloured glass. A lack of selenium in the human body can lead to illnesses such as DEPRESSION. 硒（化学元素，用于制造电气设备和有色玻璃，人体缺此元素可致抑郁等病）

self 🔑 /self/ *noun* (*pl.* **selves** /selvz/) **1** 🔑 [C, usually sing.] the type of person you are, especially the way you normally behave, look or feel （自己的）通常的行为方

S

式，本来面目，惯常心态：*You'll soon be feeling* ***your old self*** *again* (= feeling well or happy again). 你很快就会恢复原样的。◇ *He's not* ***his usual happy self*** *this morning.* 今天早上，他不像平素那样乐呵呵的。◇ *Only with a few people could she be* ***her real self*** (= show what she was really like rather than what she pretended to be). 只有和某几个人在一起时，她才能表现出真实的自我。◇ *his* ***private/professional self*** (= how he behaves at home/ work) 他在家里 / 上班时的样子 **2** [U] (*also* **the self** [sing.]) (*formal*) a person's personality or character that makes them different from other people 个性；自我：*Many people living in institutions have lost their sense of self* (= the feeling that they are individual people). 许多生活在福利院里的人已经失去了个性意识。◇ *the inner self* (= a person's emotional and spiritual character) 内心的思想感情 ◇ *a lack of confidence in the self* 缺乏自信 **3** [U] (*formal*) your own advantage or pleasure rather than that of other people 个人利益；一己的享乐；私心：*She didn't do it for any reason of self.* 她那样做绝不是出于私心。**4** [C] used to refer to a person （指一个人）自己，本人：*You didn't hurt your little self, did you?* 小家伙，你没伤着自己吧？◇ *We look forward to seeing Mrs Brown and* ***your good self*** *this evening.* 我们期盼今晚能见到布朗夫人和您本人。IDM SEE FORMER *adj.*

self- 🔑 /self/ *combining form* (in nouns and adjectives 构成名词和形容词) of, to or by yourself or itself 自身的；对自身；由自身：*self-control* 自我控制 ◇ *self-addressed* 写明回邮地址的 ◇ *self-taught* 自学的

ˌself-abˈsorbed *adj.* only concerned about or interested in yourself 只顾自己的；只关心自己的 ▶ **ˌself-abˈsorp·tion** *noun* [U]

ˌself-aˈbuse *noun* [U] **1** behaviour by which a person does harm to himself or herself 自我伤害；自残；自虐 **2** (*old-fashioned*) = MASTURBATION

ˌself-ˈaccess *noun* [U] a method of learning in which students choose their materials and use them to study on their own 自主学习法（由学生自选材料并自学）：*a* ***self-access centre/library*** 自主学习中心 / 图书馆

ˌself-actual·iˈza·tion *noun* [U] the fact of using your skills and abilities and achieving as much as you can possibly achieve 自我实现（利用自身技能取得尽可能大的成就）SYN **self-realization**

ˌself-adˈdressed *adj.* if an envelope is **self-addressed**, sb has written their own address on it （信封）写明回邮地址的

ˌself-adˈhesive *adj.* [usually before noun] covered on one side with a sticky substance so that it can be stuck to sth without the use of glue, etc. 自粘的：*self-adhesive tape* 自粘胶带

ˌself-anˈalysis *noun* [U] the study of your own character and behaviour, especially your reasons for doing things 自我分析（对自身性格和行为的分析，尤指做事的动机）

ˌself-apˈpoint·ed *adj.* [usually before noun] (*usually disapproving*) giving yourself a particular title, job, etc., especially without the agreement of other people 自封的；自己任命的

ˌself-apˈprais·al *noun* [U, C] an act or the process of judging your own work or achievements 自我评估（或评价）

ˌself-asˈsembly *adj.* (*BrE*) (of furniture 家具) bought in several parts that you have to put together yourself 自己组装的：*cheap self-assembly kitchen units* 便宜的自己组装的厨房设备 ▶ **ˌself-asˈsembly** *noun* [U]：*kitchen units for self-assembly* 需自己组装的厨房设备

ˌself-asˈsert·ive *adj.* very confident and not afraid to express your opinions 非常自信的；有主见的 ▶ **ˌself-asˈsertion**, **ˌself-asˈsert·ive·ness** *noun* [U]

ˌself-asˈsess·ment *noun* [U] **1** the process of judging your own progress, achievements, etc. 自我评估（或评价）**2** (*BrE*) a system of paying tax in which you calculate yourself how much you should pay 自行估税

ˌself-asˈsured *adj.* having a lot of confidence in yourself and your abilities 自信的；胸有成竹的 SYN **confident** ▶ **ˌself-asˈsurance** *noun* [U]

ˌself-aˈwareness *noun* [U] knowledge and understanding of your own character 自知；自明；自觉 ▶ **ˌself-aˈware** *adj.*

ˈself-build *noun* [U, C] (*BrE*) the building of homes by their owners; a home that is built in this way 自己建造住房；自己建造的住房：*self-build houses* 自建住宅

ˌself-ˈcatering *adj.* [usually before noun] (*BrE*) a **self-catering** holiday is one which provides you with accommodation and the equipment that is necessary to cook your own meals （度假方式）可自炊的，可下厨煮食的：*self-catering accommodation* 自炊式住宿 ➲ WORDFINDER NOTE AT HOLIDAY ▶ **ˌself-ˈcatering** *noun* [U] (*BrE*)：*All prices are based on a week's self-catering in shared accommodation.* 合伙住宿并自理膳食的全部费用按周计价。

ˌself-ˈcentred (*especially US* **ˌself-ˈcentered**) *adj.* (*disapproving*) tending to think only about yourself and not thinking about the needs or feelings of other people 自我中心的；只考虑自己的 ▶ **ˌself-ˈcentred·ness** (*especially US* **ˌself-ˈcentered·ness**) *noun* [U]

ˌself-conˈfessed *adj.* [only before noun] admitting that you are a particular type of person or have a particular problem, especially a bad one 自己承认的；自己坦白的：*a self-confessed thief* 自首的窃贼

ˌself-ˈconfident *adj.* having confidence in yourself and your abilities 自信的 SYN **self-assured, confident**：*a self-confident child* 自信的孩子 ◇ *a self-confident manner* 自信的态度 ▶ **ˌself-ˈconfidence** *noun* [U]：*He has no self-confidence.* 他毫无自信。

ˌself-congratu·ˈla·tion *noun* [U] (*usually disapproving*) a way of behaving that shows that you think you have done sth very well and are pleased with yourself 沾沾自喜；自鸣得意 ▶ **ˌself-conˈgratu·la·tory** *adj.*：*The winners gave themselves a self-congratulatory round of applause.* 这些获胜者得意地鼓掌，庆贺自己的胜利。

ˌself-ˈconscious *adj.* **1** ~ (**about sth**) nervous or embarrassed about your appearance or what other people think of you （因在意自己的外表或他人的看法）局促不安的，难为情的，不自然的：*He's always been self-conscious about being so short.* 他老为自己身材矮小而觉得难为情。**2** (*often disapproving*) done in a way that shows you are aware of the effect that is being produced 刻意的；有意而为的：*The humour of the play is self-conscious and contrived.* 这部剧的幽默是刻意而为的，而且牵强做作。OPP **unselfconscious** ▶ **ˌself-ˈconscious·ly** *adv.*：*She was self-consciously aware of his stare.* 她意识到他盯着她，感到不自在。**ˌself-ˈconscious·ness** *noun* [U]

ˌself-conˈtained *adj.* **1** not needing or depending on other people （指人）独立的，自立的：*Her father was a quiet self-contained man.* 她父亲生前是个好静而独立自主的人。**2** able to operate or exist without outside help or influence （指事物）自给的，独立的 SYN **independent**：*a self-contained community* 自给自足的社会 ◇ *Each chapter is self-contained and can be studied in isolation.* 每一章均自成一篇，可单独学习。**3** [usually before noun] (*BrE*) (of a flat/an apartment 公寓) having its own kitchen, bathroom and entrance 独门独户的；设施齐全的：*self-contained accommodation* 独门独户、设施齐全的住处

ˌself-contraˈdict·ory *adj.* containing two ideas or statements that cannot both be true 自相矛盾的 ▶ **ˌself-contra·ˈdic·tion** *noun* [U]

ˌself-conˈtrol *noun* [U] the ability to remain calm and not show your emotions even though you are feeling angry, excited, etc. 自制力；自我控制：*to* ***lose/regain your self-control*** 失去 / 恢复自制 ◇ *It took all his self-control not to shout at them.* 他强压怒火，没有冲他们叫嚷。▶ **ˌself-conˈtrolled** *adj.*

S

ˌself-corˈrect·ing *adj.* [usually before noun] that corrects or adjusts itself without outside help 自我纠正的；自动校正的；自我调节的：*The economic market is a self-correcting mechanism, that does not need regulation by government.* 经济市场是一种自我调节的机制，不需要政府调控。

ˌself-ˈcriticism *noun* [U] the process of looking at and judging your own faults or weaknesses 自我批评（或批判）▶ **ˌself-ˈcritical** *adj.*：*Don't be too self-critical.* 别太自责。

ˌself-deˈception *noun* [U] the act of making yourself believe sth that you know is not true 自我欺骗

ˌself-deˈfeat·ing *adj.* causing more problems and difficulties instead of solving them; not achieving what you wanted to achieve but having an opposite effect 事与愿违的；适得其反的；弄巧成拙的：*Paying children too much attention when they misbehave can be self-defeating.* 孩子有不良行为时，过分关注可能适得其反。

ˌself-deˈfence (*BrE*) (*NAmE* **ˌself-deˈfense**) *noun* [U] **1** something you say or do in order to protect yourself when you are being attacked, criticized, etc. 自卫；自我保护：*The man later told police that he was acting in self-defence.* 事后那人告诉警察，他当时是出于自卫。**2** the skill of being able to protect yourself from physical attack without using weapons 自卫术；防身术：*I'm taking classes in self-defence.* 我在上课学防身术。

ˌself-deˈlusion *noun* [U] the act of making yourself believe sth that you know is not true 自我欺骗

ˌself-deˈnial *noun* [U] the act of not having or doing the things you like, either because you do not have enough money, or for moral or religious reasons 克己；（宗教）弃绝自己 **SYN** **abstinence**

ˌself-ˈdeprecat·ing *adj.* done in a way that makes your own achievements or abilities seem unimportant 自我贬低的；自谦的：*He gave a self-deprecating shrug.* 他自谦地耸耸肩。▶ **ˌself-depreˈca·tion** *noun* [U]

ˌself-deˈstruct *verb* [I] (especially of a machine, etc. 尤指机器等) to destroy itself, usually by exploding 自毁；自爆：*This tape will self-destruct in 30 seconds.* 这盘磁带将在 30 秒后自毁。◇ (*figurative*) *In the last half hour of the movie the plot rapidly self-destructs.* 在电影的最后半个小时里，故事情节迅速了结。

ˌself-deˈstruc·tion *noun* [U] the act of doing things to deliberately harm yourself 自毁 ▶ **ˌself-deˈstruc·tive** *adj.*

ˌself-deˌtermiˈn·ation *noun* [U] (*formal*) **1** the right of a country or a region and its people to be independent and to choose their own government and political system （国家或地区及其人民的）自决权 **SYN** **independence** **2** the right or ability of a person to control their own FATE （个人）自主权，自主能力

ˌself-deˈvelop·ment *noun* [U] the process by which a person's character and abilities are developed （在性格、能力方面的）自我发展，自我提高：*Staff are encouraged to use the library for professional self-development.* 鼓励员工利用图书馆提高自己的专业水平。

ˌself-ˈdiscip·line *noun* [U] the ability to make yourself do sth, especially sth difficult or unpleasant 自律能力；自我约束能力：*It takes a lot of self-discipline to go jogging in winter.* 在冬天跑步是需要很大的自律力的。

ˌself-disˈcov·ery *noun* [U] the process of understanding more about yourself in order to make yourself happier 自我发现：*David left his boring job to go on a* ***journey of self-discovery.*** 戴维辞掉了他那份无聊的工作，开始了寻找自我之旅。

ˌself-ˈdoubt *noun* [U, C] the feeling that you are not good enough 自我怀疑

ˌself-ˈdrive *adj.* [only before noun] (*BrE*) **1** a **self-drive** car is one that you hire and drive yourself 租车人自行驾驶的 **2** a **self-drive** holiday is one on which you use your own car or a car you hire to travel to the holiday area 自驾（游）的

ˌself-ˈeducated *adj.* having learned things by reading books, etc. rather than at school or college 自我教育的；自学的；自修的

ˌself-efˈfacing *adj.* not wanting to attract attention to yourself or your abilities 谦逊的；不求闻达的 **SYN** **modest**：*He was a shy, self-effacing man.* 他是个腼腆谦逊的人。▶ **ˌself-efˈface·ment** *noun* [U]

ˌself-emˈployed *adj.* working for yourself and not employed by a company, etc. 个体经营的；单干的；自雇的：*a self-employed musician* 自己单干的乐师 ◇ *retirement plans for the self-employed* (= people who are self-employed) 个体经营者退休计划 ▶ **ˌself-emˈploy·ment** *noun* [U]

ˌself-eˈsteem *noun* [U] a feeling of being happy with your own character and abilities 自尊（心）**SYN** **self-worth**：*to have* ***high/low self-esteem*** 自尊心强 / 弱 ◇ *You need to build your self-esteem.* 你需要树立自尊心。

ˌself-ˈevident *adj.* obvious and needing no further proof or explanation 显而易见的；不言而喻的；明摆着的：*The dangers of such action are self-evident.* 这样的行动，其危险是明摆着的。◇ *a self-evident truth* 不证自明的真理 ▶ **ˌself-ˈevident·ly** *adv.*

ˌself-exˌamiˈn·ation *noun* [U] **1** the study of your own behaviour and beliefs to find out if they are right or wrong 自省；反省 **2** the act of checking your body for any signs of illness （对身体的）自我检查

ˌself-exˈplana·tory *adj.* easy to understand and not needing any more explanation 无须解释的；明白易晓的；一目了然的

ˌself-exˈpres·sion *noun* [U] the expression of your thoughts or feelings, especially through activities such as writing, painting, dancing, etc. 自我表现，自我表达（尤指通过写作、绘画、舞蹈等活动）：*You should encourage your child's attempts at self-expression.* 你应当鼓励孩子尝试表达自我。

ˌself-fulˈfil·ling *adj.* [usually before noun] a **self-fulfilling** PROPHECY is one that becomes true because people expect it to be true and behave in a way that will make it happen （预言等）自我应验的，自我实现的：*If you expect to fail, you will fail. It's a* ***self-fulfilling prophecy.*** 你如果预期失败，就会失败。这是一种自我应验的预测。

ˌself-fulˈfil·ment (*BrE*) (*also* **ˌself-fulˈfill·ment** *NAmE*) *noun* [U] the feeling of being happy and satisfied that you have everything you want or need 自我实现感；自我满足感

ˌself-ˈgovern·ment *noun* [U] the government or control of a country or an organization by its own people or members, not by others 自治 ▶ **ˌself-ˈgovern·ing** *adj.*

ˌself-ˈharm *noun* [U] the practice of deliberately injuring yourself, for example by cutting yourself, as a result of having serious emotional or mental problems （故意）自我伤害（常由情感、精神问题所致）▶ **ˌself-ˈharm** *verb* [I]：*As a teenager I was self-harming regularly.* 我十几岁时经常自残。

ˌself-ˈhelp *noun* [U] the act of relying on your own efforts and abilities in order to solve your problems, rather than depending on other people for help 自助；自立 ▶ **ˌself-ˈhelp** *adj.* [only before noun]：*a self-help discussion group for people suffering from depression* (= whose members help each other) 抑郁症患者自助讨论小组

selfie /ˈselfiː/ *noun* (*informal*) a photo of yourself that you take, typically with a SMARTPHONE or a WEBCAM, and usually put on a SOCIAL NETWORKING site 自拍照

ˌself-ˈimage *noun* the opinion or idea you have of yourself, especially of your appearance or abilities 自我形象；自我印象：*to have a* ***positive/negative self-image*** 有着正面的 / 负面的自我形象

ˌ**self-imˈport·ant** *adj.* (*disapproving*) thinking that you are more important than other people 自大的；妄自尊大的；自负的 **SYN** **arrogant** ▶ ˌ**self-imˈport·ance** *noun* [U] ˌ**self-imˈport·ant·ly** *adv.*

ˌ**self-imˈposed** *adj.* [usually before noun] a **self-imposed** task, duty, etc. is one that you force yourself to do rather than one that sb else forces you to do 自己强加的；自愿负担的；自己规定的

ˌ**self-imˈprove·ment** *noun* [U] the process by which a person improves their knowledge, status, character, etc. by their own efforts （在知识、地位、性格等方面的）自我改进，自我提高

ˌ**self-inˈduced** *adj.* (of illness, problems, etc. 疾病、问题等) caused by yourself 自己造成的： *self-induced vomiting* 自导呕吐

ˌ**self-inˈdulgent** *adj.* (*disapproving*) allowing yourself to have or do things that you like, especially when you do this too much or too often 放纵自己的；任性的 ▶ ˌ**self-inˈdulgence** *noun* [U]

ˌ**self-inˈflict·ed** *adj.* a **self-inflicted** injury, problem, etc. is one that you cause for yourself 自己造成的；加于自身的： *a self-inflicted wound* 自伤

ˌ**self-ˈinterest** *noun* [U] (*disapproving*) the fact of sb only considering their own interests and of not caring about things that would help other people 自私自利： *Not all of them were acting out of self-interest.* 他们当中，并非所有人的行动都是出于利己的目的。 ▶ ˌ**self-ˈinterest·ed** *adj.*

self·ish /ˈselfɪʃ/ *adj.* caring only about yourself rather than about other people 自私的： *selfish behaviour* 自私的行为 ◇ *Do you think I'm being selfish by not letting her go?* 你觉得我不让她走是自私吗？ ◇ *What a selfish thing to do!* 这样做，多么自私！ ◇ *It was selfish of him to leave all the work to you.* 他把所有的工作都推给你，真是自私。 **OPP** **unselfish, selfless** ▶ **self·ish·ly** *adv.*： *She looked forward, a little selfishly, to a weekend away from her family.* 她有点自私地盼着能够离家在外边度个周末。 **self·ish·ness** *noun* [U]

ˌ**self-ˈknowledge** *noun* [U] an understanding of yourself 自我了解；自知之明

self·less /ˈselfləs/ *adj.* thinking more about the needs, happiness, etc. of other people than about your own 无私的： *a life of selfless service to the community* 无私服务于社会的一生 **OPP** **selfish** ▶ **self·less·ly** *adv.* **self·less·ness** *noun* [U]

ˌ**self-ˈlove** *noun* [U] (*approving*) the feeling that your own happiness and wishes are important 自爱

ˌ**self-ˈmade** *adj.* [usually before noun] having become rich and successful through your own hard work rather than having had money given to you 靠自己奋斗成功的；白手起家的： *He was proud of the fact that he was a **self-made man**.* 他为自己白手起家而自豪。

ˌ**self-ˈmotivated** *adj.* if a person is **self-motivated**, they are capable of hard work and effort without the need for encouragement 自我激励的；自我勉励的；主动的 ▶ ˌ**self-motiˈva·tion** *noun* [U]

ˌ**self-mutiˈla·tion** *noun* [U] the act of wounding yourself, especially when this is a sign of mental illness 自残（尤指精神病征候）

ˌ**self-oˈpinion·ated** *adj.* (*disapproving*) believing that your own opinions are always right and refusing to listen to those of other people 刚愎自用的；固执己见的 **SYN** **opinionated**

ˌ**self-perˈpetu·at·ing** *adj.* continuing without any outside influence 自我持续的；自我继续的： *Revenge leads to a self-perpetuating cycle of violence.* 冤冤相报会导致永不休止的暴力。

ˌ**self-ˈpity** *noun* [U] (*often disapproving*) a feeling of pity for yourself, especially because of sth unpleasant or unfair that has happened to you 自怜： *She's not someone who likes to **wallow in self-pity**.* 她不是那种喜欢自怜的人。 ▶ ˌ**self-ˈpitying** *adj.*

ˌ**self-ˈportrait** *noun* a painting, etc. that you do of yourself 自画像

ˌ**self-posˈsessed** *adj.* able to remain calm and confident in a difficult situation 沉着的；镇定的；泰然自若的 ▶ ˌ**self-posˈses·sion** *noun* [U]： *He soon recovered his usual self-possession.* 他很快恢复了平时沉着冷静的样子。

ˌ**self-preserˈva·tion** *noun* [U] the fact of protecting yourself in a dangerous or difficult situation 自我保存；自我保护： *She was held back by some sense of self-preservation.* 一种自我保护意识使她没有贸然行动。

ˌ**self-proˈclaimed** *adj.* (*often disapproving*) giving yourself a particular title, job, etc. without the agreement or permission of other people 自称的；自命的

ˌ**self-proˈmotion** *noun* [U] (*disapproving*) the activity of making people notice you and your abilities, especially in a way that annoys other people 自我推销；自我吹嘘： *The article was a piece of blatant self-promotion.* 这篇文章是露骨的自我吹捧。

ˌ**self-raising ˈflour** (*US* ˈ**baking flour**, ˌ**self-rising ˈflour**) *noun* [U] flour that contains BAKING POWDER 自发面粉（含有发酵粉） ➲ COMPARE PLAIN FLOUR

ˌ**self-realiˈza·tion** *noun* [U] the fact of using your skills and abilities and achieving as much as you can possibly achieve 自我实现（利用自身技能取得尽可能大的成就） **SYN** **self-actualization**

self-referen·tial /ˌself refəˈrenʃl/ *adj.* (*specialist*) (of a work of literature 文学作品) referring to the fact of actually being a work of literature, or to the author, or to other works that the author has written 自我指涉的，自指的（即指向同一文学作品，或涉及作者或作者的其他作品）

ˌ**self-reˈgard** *noun* [U] a good opinion of yourself, which is considered bad if you have too little or too much 自尊；自我欣赏： *He suffers from a lack of self-regard.* 他缺乏自尊。 ▶ ˌ**self-reˈgard·ing** *adj.*： *His biography is nothing but self-regarding nonsense.* 他的传记只不过是自命不凡的一派胡言。

ˌ**self-ˈregulat·ing** *adj.* something that is **self-regulating** controls itself 自控的；自动调节的： *a self-regulating economy* 自我调节的经济 ▶ ˌ**self-reguˈla·tion** *noun* [U]

ˌ**self-reˈliant** *adj.* able to do or decide things by yourself, rather than depending on other people for help 自立的；自力更生的；自主的 **SYN** **independent** ▶ ˌ**self-reˈliance** *noun* [U]

ˌ**self-reˈspect** *noun* [U] a feeling of pride in yourself that what you do, say, etc. is right and good 自尊（心）

ˌ**self-reˈspect·ing** *adj.* [only before noun] (especially in negative sentences 尤用于否定句) having pride in yourself because you believe that what you do is right and good 有自尊心的： *No self-respecting journalist would ever work for that newspaper.* 凡有自尊心的记者都不会为那家报纸工作。

ˌ**self-reˈstraint** *noun* [U] the ability to stop yourself doing or saying sth that you want to because you know it is better not to 自我克制： *She **exercised** all her self-restraint and kept quiet.* 她好不容易才忍住没说话。

ˌ**self-ˈrighteous** *adj.* (*disapproving*) feeling or behaving as if what you say or do is always morally right, and other people are wrong 以正人君子自居的；自以为正直的 **SYN** **sanctimonious** ▶ ˌ**self-ˈrighteous·ly** *adv.* ˌ**self-ˈrighteous·ness** *noun* [U]

ˌ**self-rising ˈflour** (*also* ˈ**baking flour**) (*both US*) (*BrE* ˌ**self-raising ˈflour**) *noun* [U] flour that contains BAKING POWDER 自发面粉（含有发酵粉） ➲ COMPARE ALL-PURPOSE FLOUR

ˌ**self-ˈrule** *noun* [U] the governing of a country or an area by its own people 自治

S

,self-'sacrifice *noun* [U] (*approving*) the act of not allowing yourself to have or do sth in order to help other people 自我牺牲：*the courage and self-sacrifice of those who fought in the war* 投身战争的人的勇气和自我牺牲精神 ▶ **,self-'sacrifi·cing** *adj.*

self·same /'selfsem/ *adj.* [only before noun] **the, this, etc. selfsame...** used to emphasize that two people or things are the same（强调两者完全相同）同一的 SYN **identical**: *Jane had been wondering that selfsame thing.* 简也一直在为同一件事纳闷。

,self-'satisfied *adj.* (*disapproving*) too pleased with yourself or your own achievements 自鸣得意的；沾沾自喜的 SYN **smug**: *He had a self-satisfied smirk on his face.* 他脸上挂着得意扬扬的笑容。 ▶ **,self-satis'fac·tion** *noun* [U]: *a look of self-satisfaction* 沾沾自喜的神态

,self-'seeking *adj.* (*disapproving*) interested only in your own needs and interests rather than thinking about the needs of other people 追逐私利的 ▶ **,self-'seeking** *noun* [U]

,self-se'lection *noun* [U] a situation in which people decide for themselves to do sth rather than being chosen to do it 自行决定；自我选择 ▶ **,self-se'lect·ing** *adj.*：*a self-selecting group* 自荐小组 **,self-se'lected** *adj.*

,self-'service *adj.* [usually before noun] a **self-service** shop/store, restaurant, etc. is one in which customers serve themselves and then pay for the goods 自我服务的；（商店）自选的；（餐厅）自助的 ▶ **,self-'service** *noun* [U]: *The cafe provides quick self-service at low prices.* 那家小餐馆提供价格低廉、方便快捷的自助餐。

,self-'serving *adj.* (*disapproving*) interested only in gaining an advantage for yourself 只为个人打算的；一心谋私利的

,self-'starter *noun* (*approving*) a person who is able to work on their own and make their own decisions without needing anyone to tell them what to do 有主见的人；做事主动的人

,self-'storage *noun* [U] a service that provides a place where you can store things and a key so that you can get them when you need them 自助寄存；自助储物：*self-storage facilities/units* 自助寄存设备

,self-'study *noun* [U] the activity of learning about sth without a teacher to help you 自学；自修 ▶ **,self-'study** *adj.*：*self-study materials* 自学材料

,self-'styled *adj.* [only before noun] (*disapproving*) using a name or title that you have given yourself, especially when you do not have the right to do it 自封的；自诩的

,self-suf'ficient *adj.* ~ (**in sth**) able to do or produce everything that you need without the help of other people 自给自足的；自立的：*The country is totally self-sufficient in food production.* 在粮食生产上，这个国家完全做到了自给自足。 ▶ **,self-suf'ficiency** *noun* [U]

,self-sup'port·ing *adj.* having enough money to be able to operate without financial help from other people 资金自给的；经济独立的

,self-'taught *adj.* having learned sth by reading books, etc., rather than by sb teaching you 自学的；自修的：*a self-taught artist* 自学成才的艺术家

,self-'willed *adj.* (*disapproving*) determined to do what you want without caring about other people 任性的；固执的 SYN **headstrong**

,self-'worth *noun* [U] a feeling of confidence in yourself that you are a good and useful person 自我价值感 SYN **self-esteem**

selkie /'selki/ (*also* **silkie**) *noun* (in Scottish stories 苏格兰传说）an imaginary creature which sometimes looks like a human and sometimes looks like a SEAL 海豹人；海豹精

sell /sel/ *verb, noun*

■ *verb* (**sold, sold** /səʊld; *NAmE* soʊld/)

• **EXCHANGE FOR MONEY** 换取金钱 **1** [T, I] to give sth to sb in exchange for money 出让；转让：**~ sth (to sb) (for sth)** *I sold my car to James for £800.* 我把我的汽车转让给了詹姆斯，获得 800 英镑。◇ **~ sb sth (for sth)** *I sold James my car for £800.* 我以 800 英镑把我的汽车卖给了詹姆斯。◇ **~ (sth) (at sth)** *They sold the business* **at a profit/loss** (= they gained/lost money when they sold it). 他们把公司赢利 / 亏本让出。◇*We offered them a good price but they wouldn't sell.* 我们开了个好价钱，但他们不愿卖。

• **OFFER FOR SALE** 出售 **2** [T] **~ sth** to offer sth for people to buy 出售；卖售：*Most supermarkets sell a range of organic products.* 多数超级市场都经销一系列有机产品。◇ *Do you sell stamps?* 你这儿卖邮票吗？◇ *to sell insurance* 卖保险 ➲ COMPARE CROSS-SELLING

• **BE BOUGHT** 售出；销售 **3** [T, I] to be bought by people in the way or in the numbers mentioned; to be offered at the price mentioned 销售得…；卖出…；售价是…：**~ (sth)** *The magazine sells 300 000 copies a week.* 这本杂志一周售出 30 万册。◇ *The book sold well and was reprinted many times.* 这本书销路不错，重印了好多次。◇ *The new design just didn't sell* (= nobody bought it). 新款式无人问津。◇ **~ for/at sth** *The pens sell for just 50p each.* 这些钢笔每支只卖 50 便士。

• **PERSUADE** 推动；说服 **4** [I, T] to make people want to buy sth 促销；推销：*You may not like it but advertising sells.* 你也许不喜欢广告，但它能促销。◇ **~ sth** *It is quality not price that sells our products.* 我们的产品销路好，靠的是质量，而不是价格。 **5** [T] **~ sth/yourself (to sb)** to persuade sb that sth is a good idea, service, product, etc.; to persuade sb that you are the right person for a job, position, etc. 推荐；推销；自荐；自我推销：*Now we have to try and sell the idea to management.* 现在，我们必须设法说服管理层采纳这个意见。◇ *You really have to sell yourself at a job interview.* 应聘面试的时候，你真得推销你自己。

• **TAKE MONEY/REWARD** 收受钱财 / 报酬 **6** [T] **~ yourself (to sb)** (*disapproving*) to accept money or a reward from sb for doing sth that is against your principles 出卖自己；卖身 SYN **prostitute** ➲ SEE ALSO SALE ➲ MORE LIKE THIS 33, page R28

IDM **be 'sold on sth** (*informal*) to be very enthusiastic about sth 热衷于；对…极感兴趣 **sell your 'body** to have sex with sb in exchange for money 出卖肉体；卖淫 **sell sb down the 'river** (*informal*) to give poor or unfair treatment to sb you have promised to help 出卖（答应要帮助的人） ORIGIN From the custom of buying and selling slaves on the plantations on the Mississippi River in America. Slaves who caused trouble for their masters could be sold to plantation owners lower down the river, where conditions would be worse. 源自美国密西西比河沿岸种植园之间的奴隶买卖。惹麻烦的奴隶可能被主人卖到下游条件更为恶劣的种植园里。 **sell sb/yourself 'short** to not value sb/yourself highly enough and show this by the way you treat or present them/yourself 低估，轻视，小瞧（某人或自己） **sell your 'soul (to the devil)** to do anything, even sth bad or dishonest, in return for money, success or power 出卖灵魂（或良心） ➲ MORE AT HOT *adj.*, PUP

PHR V **,sell sth↔'off 1** to sell things cheaply because you want to get rid of them or because you need the money 甩卖；廉价出售 **2** to sell all or part of an industry, a company or land 出售，卖掉（产业、公司或土地）：*The Church sold off the land for housing.* 教会卖掉了那块地皮，用来盖房子了。 ➲ RELATED NOUN SELL-OFF

,sell sth↔'on to sell to sb else sth that you have bought not long before（买进后不久）转售，转让：*She managed the business for a year and then sold it on.* 这个企业她经营了一年，然后转手卖给了别人。 **,sell 'out | be ,sold 'out** (of tickets for a concert, sports game, etc. 音乐会、体育比赛等的票) to be all sold 售完：*The tickets sold out within hours.* 几小时内票就卖光了。◇ *This week's performances are completely sold out.* 本周的演出门票全部售完。 **,sell 'out (of sth) | be ,sold 'out (of sth)** to have sold all the available items, tickets, etc. 售空，卖光（某种商品、门票等）；脱销：*I'm sorry, we've sold out of bread.* 抱歉，我们的面包卖完了。◇ *We are already sold* *out for what should be a fantastic game.* 想来这场比赛一定精彩，我们的门票已经卖光了。 **ˌsell ˈout (to sb/sth)** **1** (*disapproving*) to change or give up your beliefs or principles 背叛信念；背弃原则： *He's a talented screenwriter who has sold out to TV soap operas.* 他是个有才华的电影编剧，却改行写起电视肥皂剧来了。 **2** to sell your business or a part of your business 出售（财产、企业等）： *The company eventually sold out to a multinational media group.* 公司最终卖给了一个跨国传媒集团。 ➲ RELATED NOUN SELL-OUT **ˌsell ˈup | ˌsell sth↔ˈup** (*especially BrE*) to sell your home, possessions, business, etc., usually because you are leaving the country or retiring 卖光（家当、企业等）

■ ***noun*** [sing.] (*informal*) something that is not as good as it seemed to be 让人失望的东西： *The band only played for about half an hour—it was a real sell.* 乐队仅仅演奏了大约半个小时，真让人失望。 ➲ SEE ALSO HARD SELL

ˈsell-by date (*BrE*) (*US* **ˈpull date**) *noun* the date printed on food packages, etc. after which the food must not be sold（食品等的）最迟销售日期，保质期： *This milk is past its sell-by date.* 这牛奶已经过了销售期限。◇ (*figurative*) *These policies are way past their sell-by date.* 这些政策早成老皇历了。

sell·er /ˈselə(r)/ *noun* **1** a person who sells sth 卖者；销售者；卖方： *a flower seller* 卖花人 ◇ *The law is intended to protect both the buyer and the seller.* 这项法律旨在保护买卖双方。 ➲ SEE ALSO BOOKSELLER ➲ COMPARE VENDOR **2 a good, poor, etc. ~** a product that has been sold in the amounts or way mentioned（畅销、滞销等的）商品： *This particular model is one of our biggest sellers.* 这种型号是我们销路最好的产品之一。 ➲ SEE ALSO BESTSELLER

IDM **a ˌseller's ˈmarket** a situation in which people selling sth have an advantage, because there is not a lot of a particular item for sale, and prices can be kept high 卖方市场

ˈselling point *noun* a feature of sth that makes people want to buy or use it 卖点（吸引顾客的产品特色）： *The price is obviously one of the main selling points.* 显然，价格低是一大卖点。 ◇ *Sales departments try to identify a product's USP or 'unique selling point'.* 销售部门试图确定一种产品的“独有卖点”。

ˈselling price *noun* the price at which sth is sold 销售价 ➲ COMPARE ASKING PRICE, COST PRICE

ˈsell-off *noun* **1** (*BrE*) the sale by the government of an industry or a service to individual people or private companies（国有企业的）出售 **2** (*NAmE, business* 商) the sale of a large number of STOCKS and SHARES, after which their value usually falls（证券）抛售

Sel·lo·tape™ /ˈseləteɪp/ *noun* (*also* **ˈsticky tape**) (*both BrE*) (*NAmE* **ˈScotch tape™**) [U] clear plastic tape that is sticky on one side, used for sticking things together 赛勒塔普胶粘带；透明胶带： *a roll of Sellotape* 一卷透明胶带 ◇ *The envelope was stuck down with Sellotape.* 信封是用透明胶带封口的。 ➲ VISUAL VOCAB PAGE V71

sel·lo·tape /ˈseləteɪp/ *verb* **~ sth (to sth)** (*BrE*) to join or stick things together with SELLOTAPE™ 用透明胶带粘贴： *We found a note sellotaped to the front door.* 我们看见正门上有一张用透明胶带贴的字条。

ˈsell-out *noun* [usually sing.] **1** a play, concert, etc. for which all the tickets have been sold 满座的演出（或比赛等）： *Next week's final looks like being a sell-out.* 看来下周的决赛将爆满。 ◇ *a sell-out tour* 场场爆满的巡回演出 **2** a situation in which sb is not loyal to a person or group who trusted them, by not doing sth that they promised to do, or by doing sth that they promised not to do 违反诺言；违背原则： *The workers see the deal as a union sell-out to management.* 工人认为这个协议是工会把他们出卖给了资方。

selt·zer /ˈseltsə(r)/ *noun* [U, C] FIZZY water (= with bubbles), usually containing minerals, used as a drink 塞尔兹（含汽）矿泉水

selv·edge (*also* **selv·age** *especially in NAmE*) /ˈselvɪdʒ/ *noun* an edge that is made on a piece of cloth, which stops the threads from coming apart (= stops it FRAYING)（布的）织边；布边

selves PL. OF SELF

se·man·tic /sɪˈmæntɪk/ *adj.* [usually before noun] (*linguistics* 语言) connected with the meaning of words and sentences 语义的 ▸ **se·man·tic·al·ly** /-kli/ *adv.* : *semantically related words* 语义上相关联的单词

seˌmantic ˈfield *noun* (*linguistics* 语言) a set of words with related meanings 语义场；语义域

se·man·tics /sɪˈmæntɪks/ *noun* [U] (*linguistics* 语言) **1** the study of the meanings of words and phrases 语义学 **2** the meaning of words, phrases or systems（单词、短语或其他符号系统的）含义 ➲ MORE LIKE THIS 29, page R28

sema·phore /ˈseməfɔː(r)/ *noun, verb*

■ ***noun*** [U] a system for sending signals in which you hold your arms or two flags in particular positions to represent different letters of the alphabet 信号标；旗语

■ ***verb*** [I, T] **~ (sth) | ~ that...** to send a message to sb by semaphore or a similar system of signals 打旗语；（用其他类似的信号系统）发信号

semb·lance /ˈsembləns/ *noun* [sing., U] **~ of sth** (*formal*) a situation in which sth seems to exist although this may not, in fact, be the case 表象；假象；外观；外貌： *The ceasefire brought about a semblance of peace.* 停火协定带来了表面的和平。 ◇ *Life at last returned to some semblance of normality.* 生活似乎终于恢复了正常。

semen /ˈsiːmən/ *noun* [U] the whitish liquid containing SPERM that is produced by the sex organs of men and male animals 精液

se·mes·ter /sɪˈmestə(r)/ *noun* one of the two periods that the school or college year is divided into 学期（一学年分两个学期）： *the **spring/fall semester*** 春季 / 秋季学期 ➲ SEE ALSO TERM *n.* (2) ➲ COMPARE TRIMESTER (2)

semi /ˈsemi/ *noun* (*pl.* **semis**) **1** (*BrE, informal*) a SEMI-DETACHED house (= one that is joined to another house by one shared wall) 半独立式住宅： *suburban semis* 郊区的半独立式住宅 **2** (*NAmE*) = SEMI-TRAILER **3** = SEMI-FINAL

semi- /ˈsemi/ *prefix* (in adjectives and nouns 构成形容词和名词) half; partly 半；部分： *semicircular* 半圆形的 ◇ *semi-final* 半决赛 ➲ MORE LIKE THIS 6, page R25

ˌsemi-ˈarid *adj.* (*specialist*) (of land or climate 土地或气候) dry; with little rain 半干旱的

ˌsemi-autoˈmat·ic *adj.* (of a gun 枪) able to load bullets automatically, and therefore very quickly, but not firing automatically 半自动的 ▸ **ˌsemi-autoˈmat·ic** *noun*

semi·breve /ˈsemibriːv/ (*BrE*) (*NAmE* **ˈwhole note**) *noun* (*music* 音) a note that lasts as long as four CROTCHETS/QUARTER NOTES 全音符 ➲ PICTURE AT MUSIC

semi·circle /ˈsemisɜːkl; *NAmE* -sɜːrkl/ *noun* **1** (*geometry* 几何) one half of a circle 半圆 ➲ PICTURE AT CIRCLE **2** the line that forms the edge of a semicircle 半圆弧线 **3** a thing, or a group of people or things, shaped like a semicircle 半圆形： *a semicircle of chairs* 摆成半圆形的椅子 ◇ *We sat in a semicircle round the fire.* 我们坐在炉火前，围成一个半圆形。 ▸ **semi·cir·cu·lar** /ˌsemiˈsɜːkjələ(r); *NAmE* -ˈsɜːrk-/ *adj.* : *a semicircular driveway* 半圆形车道

semi·colon /ˌsemiˈkəʊlən; *NAmE* ˈsemikoʊ-/ *noun* the mark (；) used to separate the parts of a complicated sentence or items in a detailed list, showing a pause that is longer than a comma but shorter than a full stop/period 分号 ➲ COMPARE COLON (1)

semi·con·duct·or /ˌsemikənˈdʌktə(r)/ *noun* (*specialist*) **1** a solid substance that CONDUCTS electricity in particular conditions, better than INSULATORS but not as well as CONDUCTORS 半导体 **2** a device containing a semiconductor used in ELECTRONICS 半导体装置

S

ˌsemi-deˈtached *adj.* (of a house 住宅) joined to another house by a wall on one side that is shared 半独立式的 ▸ **ˌsemi-deˈtached** *noun* (*BrE*) ⊃ VISUAL VOCAB PAGE V16 ⊃ COMPARE DETACHED (1) ⊃ SEE ALSO SEMI (1), TERRACED (1)

ˌsemi-ˈfinal (*also* **semi**) *noun* one of the two games or parts of a sports competition that are held to decide who will compete in the last part (the FINAL) 半决赛: *He's through to the semi-final of the men's singles.* 他已进入男子单打半决赛。 ▸ **ˌsemi-ˈfinalist** *noun*: *They are semi-finalists for the fourth year in succession.* 他们连续第四年打入半决赛。

semi·metal /ˈsemimetl/ *noun* (*BrE*) = METALLOID

sem·inal /ˈsemɪnl/ *adj.* **1** (*formal*) very important and having a strong influence on later developments （对以后的发展）影响深远的，有重大意义的: *a* ***seminal work/article/study*** 有巨大影响的著作 / 文章 / 研究 **2** [usually before noun] (*specialist*) of or containing SEMEN 精液的；含精液的: *seminal fluid* 精液

sem·inar /ˈsemɪnɑː(r)/ *noun* **1** a class at a university or college when a small group of students and a teacher discuss or study a particular topic （大学教师带领学生作专题讨论的）研讨课: *Teaching is by lectures and seminars.* 教学形式为讲座和研讨课。 ◇ *a graduate seminar* 研究生研讨课 ◇ *a seminar room* 研讨室 ⊃ WORDFINDER NOTE AT UNIVERSITY ⊃ COLLOCATIONS AT EDUCATION **2** a meeting for discussion or training 研讨会；培训会: *a one-day management seminar* 为期一天的管理研讨会

sem·in·ar·ian /ˌsemɪˈneəriən; *NAmE* -ˈner-/ *noun* a student in a seminary 神学院学生；修生

sem·in·ary /ˈsemɪnəri; *NAmE* -neri/ *noun* (*pl.* **-ies**) a college where priests, ministers or RABBIS are trained 神学院；修院

Sem·in·ole /ˈsemɪnəʊl; *NAmE* -oʊl/ *noun* (*pl.* **Sem·in·ole** or **Sem·in·oles**) a member of a Native American people, many of whom live in the US states of Oklahoma and Florida 塞米诺尔人（美洲土著，很多居于美国俄克拉何马州和佛罗里达州）

semi·ot·ics /ˌsemiˈɒtɪks; *NAmE* -ˈɑːtɪks/ *noun* [U] the study of signs and symbols and of their meaning and use 符号学 ⊃ MORE LIKE THIS 29, page R28 ▸ **semi·ot·ic** *adj.*: *semiotic analysis* 符号分析

ˌsemi-ˈprecious *adj.* [usually before noun] (of a JEWEL 珠宝) less valuable than the most valuable types of JEWELS 次贵重的；半宝石的

ˌsemi-proˈfes·sion·al *adj.* **semi-professional** musicians or sports players are paid for what they do, but do not do it as their main job （音乐家或运动员）半职业的 ▸ **ˌsemi-proˈfes·sion·al** *noun*

semi·quaver /ˈsemikweɪvə(r)/ (*BrE*) (*NAmE* **ˌsixˈteenth note**) *noun* (*music* 音) a note that lasts half as long as a QUAVER/EIGHTH NOTE 十六分音符 ⊃ PICTURE AT MUSIC

ˌsemi-ˈskilled *adj.* [usually before noun] (of workers 工人) having some special training or qualifications, but less than skilled people 半熟练的: *a semi-skilled machine operator* 半熟练机器操作员 ◇ *semi-skilled jobs* (= for people who have some special training) 半技术工作

ˌsemi-ˈskimmed *adj.* (*BrE*) (of milk 奶) that has had a lot of the fat removed 半脂的

Sem·ite /ˈsemaɪt/ *noun* a member of the peoples who speak Semitic languages, including Arabs and Jews 闪米特人（说闪米特语，包括阿拉伯人和犹太人）

Sem·it·ic /səˈmɪtɪk/ *adj.* **1** of or connected with the language group that includes Hebrew and Arabic 闪米特语族的，闪语的（包括希伯来语和阿拉伯语） **2** of or connected with the people who speak Semitic languages, especially Hebrew and Arabic 闪米特人（尤指操希伯来语和阿拉伯语的人）的；闪族的

semi·tone /ˈsemitəʊn; *NAmE* -toʊn/ (*BrE*) (*NAmE* **ˈhalf step, halftone**) *noun* (*music* 音) half a TONE on a musical SCALE, for example the INTERVAL between C and C♯ or between E and F 半音 ⊃ COMPARE STEP *n.* (10)

ˈsemi-trailer *noun* (*NAmE*) a TRAILER (1) that has wheels at the back and is supported at the front by the vehicle that is pulling it 半挂车；半拖车

ˌsemi-ˈtropic·al *adj.* = SUBTROPICAL

semi·vowel /ˈsemivaʊəl/ *noun* (*phonetics* 语音) a speech sound that sounds like a vowel but functions as a consonant, for example /w/ and /j/ in the English words *wet* and *yet* 半元音

semo·lina /ˌseməˈliːnə/ *noun* [U] **1** large hard grains of WHEAT used when crushed for making PASTA and sweet dishes 麦糁，粗面粉（用以制作意大利面食和甜食） **2** a sweet dish made from semolina and milk, eaten for DESSERT in Britain and for breakfast in the US 粗面粉布丁

sem·tex /ˈsemteks/ *noun* [U] a powerful EXPLOSIVE that is used for making bombs, often illegally 塞姆汀塑胶炸药（常用于非法制造炸弹）

Sen. *abbr.* SENATOR 参议员: *Sen. John K Nordqvist* 约翰 • K. 诺德奎斯特参议员

sen·ate 🔑 /ˈsenət/ *noun* (*usually* **the Senate**) **1** 🔑 [sing.] one of the two groups of elected politicians who make laws in some countries, for example in the US, Australia, Canada and France. The Senate is smaller than the other group but higher in rank. Many state parliaments in the US also have a Senate. 参议院（美国、澳大利亚、加拿大、法国等国家的两个立法机构之一；美国许多州议会也设有参议院）: *a member of the Senate* 参议员 ◇ *a Senate committee* 参议院委员会 ⊃ COMPARE CONGRESS (2), HOUSE OF REPRESENTATIVES ⊃ WORDFINDER NOTE AT CONGRESS ⊃ COLLOCATIONS AT POLITICS **2** [C, usually sing., U] (in some countries) the group of people who control a university （某些国家的）大学理事会，大学评议会: *the senate of Loughborough University* 拉夫伯勒大学评议会 **3** [sing.] (in ancient Rome) the most important council of the government; the building where the council met （古罗马的）元老院

sen·ator 🔑 /ˈsenətə(r)/ *noun* (*often* **Senator**) (*abbr.* **Sen.**) a member of a senate 参议员: *Senator McCarthy* 麦卡锡参议员 ◇ *She has served as a Democratic senator for North Carolina since 2009.* 自 2009 年以来，她一直是北卡罗来纳州的民主党参议员。 ▸ **sen·at·or·ial** /ˌsenəˈtɔːriəl/ *adj.* [only before noun]: *a senatorial candidate* 参议员候选人

send 🔑 /send/ *verb* (**sent, sent** /sent/)

- **BY MAIL/RADIO** 通过邮政 / 无线电 **1** 🔑 to make sth go or be taken to a place, especially by post/mail, email, radio, etc. 邮寄；发送: **~ sth** *to send a letter/package/cheque/fax/email* 寄信；寄包裹；寄支票；发传真；发电子邮件 ◇ *She sent the letter by airmail.* 她寄的是航空信。 ◇ (*BrE*) *to send sth by post* 邮寄某物 ◇ (*NAmE*) *to send sth by mail* 邮寄某物 ◇ **~ sth to sb** *A radio signal was sent to the spacecraft.* 向宇宙飞船发出了无线电信号。 ◇ *The CD player was faulty so we sent it back to the manufacturers.* 那台激光唱片机有毛病，因此我们把它送回了厂家。 ◇ *Have you sent a postcard to your mother yet?* 你给你母亲寄明信片了没有？ ◇ **~ sb sth** *Have you sent your mother a postcard yet?* 你给你母亲寄明信片了没有？ ◇ *I'll send you a text message.* 我会给你发一条短信。
- **MESSAGE** 信息 **2** 🔑 to tell sb sth by sending them a message 传达；转致；告知: **~ sth** *My parents* ***send their love.*** 我父母问您好。 ◇ **~ sth to sb** *What sort of message is that sending to young people?* 这给年轻人传达的是什么样的信息呢？ ◇ **~ sb sth** *He* ***sent me word*** *to come.* 他带话要我来。 ◇ **~ sth (that)**... *She* ***sent word*** *(that) she could not come.* 她带信儿说她来不了。 ◇ **~ to do sth** (*formal*) *She sent to say that she was coming home.* 她托人捎话说她要回家了。
- **SB SOMEWHERE** 让某人前往某处 **3** 🔑 to tell sb to go somewhere or to do sth; to arrange for sb to go somewhere 派遣；打发；安排去: **~ sb** *Ed couldn't make it so they*

S

sent me instead. 埃德去不了，所以他们就派我去了。◇ ~ sb + adv./prep. She sent the kids to bed early. 她早早打发孩子们上床睡觉。◇ to send sb to prison/boarding school 把某人关进监狱；安排某人上寄宿学校 ◇ ~ sb to do sth I've sent Tom to buy some milk. 我叫汤姆去买牛奶了。

• **MAKE STH MOVE QUICKLY** 使某物快速移动 **4** to make sth/sb move quickly or suddenly 使快速（或猛然）移动：**~ sth/sb doing sth** *Every step he took sent the pain shooting up his leg.* 他每走一步，疼痛就顺腿蹿上来。◇ *The punch sent him flying.* 那一拳打得他整个人抛了出去。◇ **~ sth/sb + adv./prep.** *The report sent share prices down a further 8p.* 这份报告一公布，股价又跌了 8 便士。

• **MAKE SB REACT** 使某人作出反应 **5** to make sb behave or react in a particular way 使作出（某种反应）；使表现出（某种行为）：**~ sb to sth** *Her music always sends me to sleep.* 她的音乐总使我进入梦乡。◇ **~ sb into sth** *Her account of the visit sent us into fits of laughter.* 她讲述参观的经过，我们听得一阵阵大笑。◇ **~ sb + adj.** *All the publicity nearly sent him crazy.* 成天生活在公众的注意之下让他差一点发疯了。➲ MORE LIKE THIS 33, page R28

IDM **send sb 'packing** (*informal*) to tell sb firmly or rudely to go away 叫某人卷铺盖走人；撵某人走 ➲ MORE AT COVENTRY, LOVE *n.*, THING

PHR V **,send a'way (to sb) (for sth)** = SEND OFF (FOR STH) **,send sb↔'down** (*BrE*) **1** (*informal*) to send sb to prison 判（某人）入狱 **2** (*old-fashioned*) to order a student to leave a university because of bad behaviour 开除；勒令退学 **'send for sb** 🔑 to ask or tell sb to come to you, especially in order to help you 请某人来（帮忙等）：*Send for a doctor, quickly!* 请个大夫来，快！ **'send for sth** 🔑 to ask sb to bring or deliver sth to you 让人带来（或送来）某物：*His son found him and sent for help.* 他儿子找到了他，然后向人求救。◇ *She sent for the latest sales figures.* 她要求把最新的销售统计数字给她送来。 **,send sb 'forth** (*old-fashioned* or *literary*) to send sb away from you to another place 派往；派遣 **,send 'forth sth** (*formal*) to produce a sound, signal, etc. so that other people can hear it, receive it, etc. 发出（声音、信号等）：*He opened his mouth and sent forth a stream of noise.* 他张开嘴，发出一连串声音。 **,send sb↔'in** to order sb to go to a place to deal with a difficult situation 派某人去（应付困难局面）：*Troops were sent in to restore order.* 部队被派去恢复秩序。 **,send sth↔'in** to send sth by post/mail to a place where it will be dealt with 寄去（处理）：*Have you sent in your application yet?* 你把申请书寄去了没有？ **,send 'off (for sth) | ,send a'way (to sb) (for sth)** to write to sb and ask them to send you sth by post/mail 邮购；函购；函索：*I've sent off for some books for my course.* 我已去函邮购一些上课用的书。 **,send sb↔'off** (*BrE*) (in a sports game 体育比赛) to order sb to leave the field because they have broken the rules of the game 罚某人下场：*Bale was sent off for a foul in the second half.* 贝尔在下半场因犯规被罚下场。 ➲ RELATED NOUN SENDING-OFF **,send sth↔'off** 🔑 to send sth to a place by post/mail 寄出；发出：*I'm sending the files off to my boss tomorrow.* 明天我要把这些档案给老板寄去。 **,send sth↔'on** **1** to send sth to a place so that it arrives before you get there 先期发运（或送达）：*We sent our furniture on by ship.* 我们提前把家具水运过去了。**2** to send a letter that has been sent to sb's old address to their new address 转寄，转投（信件） **SYN** **forward 3** to send sth from one place/person to another 转送；转递；转达：*They arranged for the information to be sent on to us.* 他们托人把信息转告我们。 **,send 'out for sth** to ask a restaurant or shop/store to deliver food to you at home or at work 请（某店）送来外卖食物：*Let's send out for a pizza.* 我们订一份外送比萨吧。 **,send sth↔'out** **1** to send sth to a lot of different people or places 分发；散发：*Have the invitations been sent out yet?* 请柬分发出去了没有？ **2** to produce sth, such as light, a signal, sound, etc. 发出（光、信号、声音等） **SYN** **emit** **,send sb/sth↔'up** (*informal*) to make people laugh at sb/sth by copying them/it in a funny way（通过滑稽模仿）取笑，讽刺，挖苦：*a TV programme that sends up politicians* 模仿取笑政治人物的电视节目 ➲ RELATED NOUN SEND-UP **,send sb↔'up** (*US, informal*) to send sb to prison 判（某人）入狱

send·er /ˈsendə(r)/ *noun* a person who sends sth 发送人；邮寄人：*If undelivered, please return to sender.* 若无法投递，请退还寄信人。

,sending-'off *noun* (*pl.* **sendings-off**) (*BrE*) (in football (SOCCER) 足球) a situation when a REFEREE tells a player to leave the field because they have broken the rules in a serious way（严重犯规）罚出场外

'send-off *noun* (*informal*) an occasion when people come together to say goodbye to sb who is leaving 送行；送别

'send-up *noun* (*informal*) an act of making sb/sth look silly by copying them in a funny way（为取笑的）滑稽模仿

Sen·eca /ˈsenəkə/ *noun* (*pl.* **Sen·eca** or **Sen·ecas**) a member of a Native American people, many of whom now live in the US states of New York and Ohio 塞内卡人（美洲土著，很多现居于美国纽约州和俄亥俄州）

sen·es·cence /sɪˈnesns/ *noun* [U] (*formal* or *specialist*) the process of becoming old and showing the effects of being old 衰老；老年化 ▶ **sen·es·cent** *adj.*

se·nile /ˈsiːnaɪl/ *adj.* behaving in a confused or strange way, and unable to remember things, because you are old 衰老的；年老糊涂的：*I think she's **going senile**.* 我想她是衰老了。➲ COLLOCATIONS AT AGE ▶ **se·nil·ity** /səˈnɪləti/ *noun* [U]：*an old man on the verge of senility* 渐显龙钟之态的老年人

,senile de'mentia *noun* [U] a serious mental DISORDER in old people that causes loss of memory, loss of control of the body, etc. 老年痴呆

se·nior 🔑 /ˈsiːniə(r)/ *adj.*, *noun*

■ ***adj.***

• **OF HIGH RANK** 级别高 **1** 🔑 **~ (to sb)** high in rank or status; higher in rank or status than others 级别（或地位）高的：*a **senior officer/manager/lecturer*** 高级军官 / 经理 / 讲师 ◇ *a **senior partner** in a law firm* 律师事务所的高级合伙人 ◇ *a **senior post/position*** 高级职位 ◇ *I have ten years' experience at senior management level.* 我有十年的高层管理经验。◇ (*BrE*) *Junior nurses usually work alongside more senior nurses.* 初级护士通常和较高级的护士一起工作。◇ *He is senior to me.* 他的职位比我高。◇ *The meeting should be chaired by the most senior person present.* 会议应由在座的职位最高的人主持。**OPP** **junior**

• **IN SPORT** 体育运动 **2** 🔑 [only before noun] for adults or people at a more advanced level 成人的；高级水平的：*to take part in senior competitions* 参加成人比赛 ◇ *He won the senior men's 400 metres.* 他获得男子甲组 400 米冠军。

• **FOR OLDER PEOPLE** 年长之人 **3** [only before noun] for SENIOR CITIZENS (= older people, especially those who have retired from work)（尤指已退休）年纪大的，老年的：*Get one third off rail fares with a senior railcard.* 持有老年火车通行优惠卡可减免三分之一车费。◇ *senior discounts/concessions* 老年折扣 / 优惠

• **FATHER** 父亲 **4** **Senior** (*abbr.* **Snr**, **Sr**) used after the name of a man who has the same name as his son, to avoid confusion（父子同名时，加在父亲的名字前）老，大 ➲ COMPARE JUNIOR *adj.* (3)

• **SCHOOL/COLLEGE** 中学；大学 **5** [only before noun] (*BrE*) (of a school or part of a school 学校或其中一部分) for children over the age of 11 or 13 中等的，中学的（招收 11 或 13 岁以上学生） **6** [only before noun] (*NAmE*) connected with the last year in HIGH SCHOOL or college（高中或大学）毕业年级的：*the senior prom* 毕业年级舞会

■ ***noun***

• **OLDER PERSON** 较年长的人 **1** 🔑 a person who is older than sb else 较…年长的人：*She was ten years his senior.* 她比他大十岁。◇ *My brother is my senior by two years.* 我哥哥比我大两岁。➲ COMPARE JUNIOR *n.* **2** (*especially NAmE*) = SENIOR CITIZEN

• **HIGHER RANK** 较高级别 **3** 🔑 a person who is higher in rank or status 级别（或地位）较高者；上级；上司：*She felt unappreciated both by her colleagues and her seniors.* 她觉得无论同事还是上司都不赏识她。

S

• IN SPORT 体育运动 **4** adults or people who have reached an advanced level 资深成人运动员；高水平运动员：*tennis coaching for juniors and seniors* 初、高级网球训练
• IN SCHOOL/COLLEGE 中学 / 大学里 **5** (*BrE*) a child at a senior school; an older child in a school 中学生；高年级学生 **6** (in the US and some other countries) a student in the last year at a HIGH SCHOOL or college （美国等若干国家高中和大学的）毕业班学生：*high school seniors* 高中毕业班学生 ➲ COMPARE SOPHOMORE

ˌsenior ˈcitizen (*also* **se·nior** *especially in NAmE*) *noun* an older person, especially sb who has retired from work. People often call sb a 'senior citizen' to avoid saying that they are old or using the expression 'old-age pensioner'. 资深公民，老年人（委婉说法，尤指退休者）

ˌsenior ˈcommon room *noun* (*abbr.* **SCR**) (*BrE*) a room used for social activities by teaching staff in a college or university （大学的）教师联谊活动室，教师交谊厅

ˌsenior ˈhigh school (*also* **ˌsenior ˈhigh**) *noun* (in the US) a school for young people between the ages of 14 and 18 （美国）高中 ➲ COMPARE JUNIOR HIGH SCHOOL

se·ni·or·ity /ˌsiːniˈɒrəti; *NAmE* -ˈɔːr-; -ˈɑːr-/ *noun* [U] **1** the fact of being older or of a higher rank than others 年长；级别高：*a position of seniority* 高级职位 **2** the rank that you have in a company because of the length of time you have worked there 资历：*a lawyer with five years' seniority* 有五年从业经验的律师 ◇ *Should promotion be based on merit or seniority?* 提拔一个人应当看业绩，还是看资历？

ˌsenior ˈmoment *noun* (*humorous*) an occasion when sb forgets sth, or does not think clearly (thought to be typical of what happens when people get older) 年长表现（幽默表达，指人失忆、忘事、糊涂的状况）：*It was an important meeting and a bad time to* ***have a senior moment***. 那是个重要会议，可不能犯糊涂。

sen·sa·tion /senˈseɪʃn/ *noun* **1** [C] a feeling that you get when sth affects your body 感觉；知觉：*a* ***tingling/burning, etc. sensation*** 刺痛、烧灼等的感觉 ◇ *I had a sensation of falling, as if in a dream.* 我有一种坠落的感觉，像在梦中似的。 **2** [U] the ability to feel through your sense of touch 感觉能力；知觉能力 SYN **feeling**: *She seemed to have lost all sensation in her arms.* 她的两条胳膊好像完全失去知觉了。 **3** [C, usually sing.] a general feeling or impression that is difficult to explain; an experience or a memory 直觉；莫名其妙的感觉；经历；回忆：*He had the eerie sensation of being watched.* 他不安地感到有人在监视他。 ◇ *When I arrived, I had the sensation that she had been expecting me.* 我到那儿后，感觉到她一直在等着我。 **4** [C, usually sing., U] very great surprise, excitement, or interest among a lot of people; the person or the thing that causes this surprise 轰动；哗然；引起轰动的人（或事物）：*News of his arrest* ***caused a sensation***. 他被捕的消息引起了轰动。 ◇ *The band became a sensation overnight.* 一夜之间，这支乐队名声大振。

sen·sa·tion·al /senˈseɪʃənl/ *adj.* **1** causing great surprise, excitement, or interest 轰动的；引起哗然的 SYN **thrilling**: *The result was a sensational 4–1 victory.* 比赛结果是轰动性的，以 4:1 狂胜对手。 **2** (*disapproving*) (of a newspaper, etc. 报章等) trying to get your interest by presenting facts or events as worse or more shocking than they really are 哗众取宠的；耸人听闻的 **3** (*informal*) extremely good; wonderful 极好的；绝妙的 SYN **fantastic**: *You look sensational in that dress!* 你穿这件连衣裙漂亮极了！
▶ **sen·sa·tion·al·ly** /-ʃənəli/ *adv.*：*They won sensationally against the top team.* 他们战胜了那支顶级球队，引起了轰动。 ◇ *The incident was sensationally reported in the press.* 报纸上对那一事件大肆渲染。 ◇ *He's sensationally good-looking!* 他长得太帅了！

sen·sa·tion·al·ism /senˈseɪʃənəlɪzəm/ *noun* [U] (*disapproving*) a way of getting people's interest by using shocking words or by presenting facts and events as worse or more shocking than they really are （指行文或报道）耸人听闻，哗众取宠 ▶ **sen·sa·tion·al·ist** /-ʃənəlɪst/ *adj.*：*sensationalist headlines* 耸人听闻的标题

sen·sa·tion·al·ize (*BrE also* **-ise**) /senˈseɪʃənəlaɪz/ *verb* **~ sth** (*disapproving*) to exaggerate a story so that it seems more exciting or shocking than it really is 故作耸人听闻地夸张；大肆渲染

sense /sens/ *noun, verb*
■ *noun*
• SIGHT/HEARING, ETC. 视觉、听觉等 **1** [C] one of the five powers (sight, hearing, smell, taste and touch) that your body uses to get information about the world around you 感觉官能（即视、听、嗅、味、触五觉）：*the five senses* 五种感觉官能 ◇ *Dogs have a keen* (= strong) ***sense of smell***. 狗的嗅觉很灵敏。 ◇ ***the sense organs*** (= eyes, ears, nose, etc.) 感觉器官 ◇ *I could hardly believe the evidence of my own senses* (= what I could see, hear, etc.). 我简直不敢相信自己的感觉。 ◇ *The mixture of sights, smells and sounds around her made her senses reel.* 四周的景象、气味和声音纷至沓来，使她晕头转向。 ➲ SEE ALSO SIXTH SENSE
• FEELING 感觉 **2** [C] a feeling about sth important （对重大事情的）感觉，意识：*He felt an overwhelming sense of loss.* 他感到非常失落。 ◇ ***a strong sense of purpose/identity/duty, etc.*** 强烈的目标感、很强的身份认同感、很强的责任感等 ◇ *Helmets can give cyclists* ***a false sense of security***. 头盔能给骑自行车的人一种虚假的安全感。 ◇ ***I had the sense that*** *he was worried about something.* 我感觉他有心事。
• UNDERSTANDING/JUDGEMENT 理解；判断 **3** [sing.] an understanding about sth; an ability to judge sth 理解力；判断力：*One of the most important things in a partner is* ***a sense of humour*** (= the ability to find things funny or make people laugh). 作为一个生活伴侣，最重要的素质之一是幽默感。 ◇ *He has a very good* ***sense of direction*** (= finds the way to a place easily). 他的方向感很强。 ◇ *She has lost all sense of direction in her life.* 她完全丧失了生活的方向。 ◇ *Always try to keep* ***a sense of proportion*** (= of the relative importance of different things). 对事情随时都要把握好孰轻孰重。 ◇ ***a sense of rhythm/timing*** 节奏感；时机感 ◇ *Alex doesn't have any* ***dress sense*** (= does not know which clothes look attractive). 亚历克斯对服装毫无鉴赏力。 ➲ SEE ALSO ROAD SENSE **4** [U] good understanding and judgement; knowledge of what is sensible or practical behaviour 见识；良好的判断；清醒的认识：*You should* ***have the sense to*** *take advice when it is offered.* 你要知道好歹，别人给你忠告，就该接受。 ◇ ***There's no sense in*** (= it is not sensible) *worrying about it now.* 现在大可不必为那件事忧虑。 ◇ *Can't you* ***talk sense*** (= say sth sensible)? 你就不能说点正经的？ ◇ *There's a lot of sense in what Mary says.* 玛丽说得很在理。 ➲ SEE ALSO COMMON SENSE, GOOD SENSE
• NORMAL STATE OF MIND 正常的精神状态 **5** **senses** [pl.] a normal state of mind; the ability to think clearly 健全的心智；清醒的思维能力；理智：*If she threatens to leave, it should* ***bring him to his senses***. 假如她威胁着要走，说不定他会清醒过来。 ◇ *He waited for Dora to* ***come to her senses*** *and return.* 他盼着多拉冷静下来后回来。 ◇ (*old-fashioned*) *Are you* ***out of your senses****? You'll be killed!* 你疯了吗？你会丢了性命的！ ◇ (*old-fashioned*) *Why does she want to marry him? She must have* ***taken leave of her senses***. 她怎么会要嫁给他呢？她准是脑子有毛病了。
• MEANING 意义 **6** [C] the meaning that a word or phrase has; a way of understanding sth 意义；含义；理解…的方式；看待…的角度：*The word 'love' is used in different senses by different people.* "爱"这个字不同的人用来表示不同的意思。 ◇ *education in its broadest sense* 最广泛意义上的教育 ◇ *He was a true friend,* ***in every sense of the word*** (= in every possible way). 无论从哪个角度讲，他都是个真正的朋友。 ◇ ***In a sense*** (= in one way) *it doesn't matter any more.* 从某种意义上说，这事已无关紧要了。 ◇ ***In some senses*** (= in one or more ways) *the criticisms were justified.* 在一定意义上，那些批评意见是有道理的。 ◇ (*formal*) ***In no sense*** *can the issue be said to be resolved.* 无论如何这个问题都不能说已经解决了。 ◇ *There is a sense in which we are all to blame for the tragedy.* 在某种意义上，对这个悲剧我们大家都有责任。 ➲ NOTE AT SENSIBLE
IDM **knock/talk some ˈsense into sb** to try and persuade sb to stop behaving in a stupid way, sometimes using

rough or violent methods 开导某人别干傻事；强使某人理智行事 **make 'sense 1** to have a meaning that you can easily understand 有道理；有意义；讲得通：*This sentence doesn't make sense.* 这个句子不通。**2** to be a sensible thing to do 是明智的；合乎情理：*It makes sense to buy the most up-to-date version.* 买最新的版本是明智的。◇ *There are strict medicals for pilots, which makes good sense.* 飞行员要接受严格的体检，这是很有道理的。**3** to be easy to understand or explain 表述清楚；易于理解；道理明显：*John wasn't making much sense on the phone.* 约翰在电话上说得不大清楚。◇ *Who would send me all these flowers? It makes no sense.* 谁会给我送这么多花呢？真不可思议。**make 'sense of sth** to understand sth that is difficult or has no clear meaning 理解，弄懂（不易理解的事物） **see 'sense** to start to be sensible or reasonable 变得明智起来；开始明白事理 **a sense of oc'casion** a feeling or understanding that an event is important or special 隆重的（或特别的）气氛：*Candles on the table gave the evening a sense of occasion.* 桌上点了一些蜡烛，使得那个晚上有一种特别的气氛。➲ MORE AT LEAVE *n.*

■ ***verb*** (not used in the progressive tenses 不用于进行时)

• **BECOME AWARE** 感觉 **1** to become aware of sth even though you cannot see it, hear it, etc. 感觉到；意识到；觉察出：**~ sth** *Sensing danger, they started to run.* 他们感到有危险，撒腿就跑。◇ **~ (that)...** *Lisa sensed that he did not believe her.* 莉萨意识到他不相信她。◇ *Thomas, she sensed, could convince anyone of anything.* 她觉得，托马斯能说服任何人相信任何事。◇ **~ sb/sth doing sth** *He sensed someone moving around behind him.* 他感觉有人在他后面走动。◇ **~ sb/sth do sth** *He sensed something move in the bushes.* 他察觉到灌木丛中有什么东西在动。◇ **~ how, what, etc....** *She could sense how nervous he was.* 她能感觉到他有多紧张。

• **OF MACHINE** 机器 **2 ~ sth** to discover and record sth 检测出：*equipment that senses the presence of toxic gases* 检测有毒气体的设备

sense·less /'sensləs/ *adj.* **1** (*disapproving*) having no meaning or purpose 无意义的；无目的的 **SYN pointless**：*senseless violence* 无谓的暴力 ◇ *His death was a senseless waste of life.* 他白浪费了性命，死得毫无意义。◇ *It's senseless to continue any further.* 再继续下去毫无意义。**2** [not before noun] unconscious 失去知觉：*He was beaten senseless.* 他被打昏了。◇ *She drank herself senseless.* 她喝得不省人事。**3** not using good judgement 不明智的；愚蠢的：*The police blamed senseless drivers who went too fast.* 警察责怪莽撞司机开快车。▶ **sense·less·ly** *adv.*

sens·ibil·ity /ˌsensə'bɪləti/ *noun* (*pl.* **-ies**) **1** [U, C] the ability to experience and understand deep feelings, especially in art and literature （尤指文艺方面的）感受能力，鉴赏力，敏感性：*a man of impeccable manners, charm and sensibility* 一个有魅力、懂感情、举止无可挑剔的男人 ◇ *artistic sensibility* 艺术鉴赏力 **2 sensibilities** [pl.] a person's feelings, especially when the person is easily offended or influenced by sth （尤指易受伤害或影响的）感情：*The article offended her religious sensibilities.* 那篇文章伤害了她的宗教感情。

sens·ible /'sensəbl/ *adj.* **1** (of people and their behaviour 人及其行为) able to make good judgements based on reason and experience rather than emotion; practical 明智的；理智的；合理的；切合实际的：*She's a sensible sort of person.* 她属于那种通情达理的人。◇ *I think that's a very sensible idea.* 我看这个主意很妥当。◇ *Say something sensible.* 说点正经的。◇ *I think **the sensible thing** would be to take a taxi home.* 我想还是坐出租车回家比较好。**2** (of clothes, etc. 服装等) useful rather than fashionable 朴素而实用的：*sensible shoes* 朴实而舒适的鞋 **3** (*formal* or *literary*) aware of sth 意识到；认识到：*I am sensible of the fact that mathematics is not a popular subject.* 我知道数学课不受欢迎。**OPP insensible**
HELP Use **silly** (sense 1) or **impractical** (senses 1 and 2) as the opposite for the other senses. 用 silly（第 1 义）或 impractical（第 1 及第 2 义）作为 sensible 义项 1 和 2 的反义词。➲ MORE LIKE THIS 23, page R27 ▶ **sens·ibly** /-əbli/ *adv.*：*to behave sensibly* 举止得体 ◇ *He decided, very sensibly, not to drive when he was so tired.* 他很累，所以决定不开车，这是很明智的。◇ *She's always very sensibly dressed.* 她的着装总是十分素雅得体。

▼ **WHICH WORD?** 词语辨析

sensible / sensitive

Sensible and **sensitive** are connected with two different meanings of sense. * sensible 和 sensitive 与 sense 的两个不同含义相联系。

• **Sensible** refers to your ability to make good judgements. * sensible 涉及判断：*She gave me some very sensible advice.* 她给了我一些非常合理的建议。◇ *It wasn't very sensible to go out on your own so late at night.* 这么晚一个人单独外出是不太明智的。

• **Sensitive** refers to how easily you react to things and how much you are aware of things or other people. * sensitive 涉及反应和洞察力：*a soap for sensitive skin* 敏感皮肤用的肥皂 ◇ *This movie may upset a sensitive child.* 这部影片可能使敏感的孩子感到难过。

sen·si·tive /'sensətɪv/ *adj.*

• **TO PEOPLE'S FEELINGS** 对他人的感情 **1** aware of and able to understand other people and their feelings 体贴的；体恤的；善解人意的：*a sensitive and caring man* 体贴的男人 ◇ **~ to sth** *She is very sensitive to other people's feelings.* 她很能体谅他人的感情。**OPP insensitive**

• **TO ART/MUSIC/LITERATURE** 对艺术／音乐／文学 **2** able to understand art, music and literature and to express yourself through them 感觉敏锐的；艺术感觉好的；有悟性的：*an actor's sensitive reading of the poem* 演员对那首诗富有表现力的朗诵 ◇ *a sensitive portrait* 栩栩如生的画像

• **EASILY UPSET** 容易生气 **3** easily offended or upset 易生气的；易被惹恼的；神经过敏的：*You're far too sensitive.* 你也太敏感了。◇ **~ about sth** *He's very sensitive about his weight.* 他很忌讳别人说他胖。◇ **~ to sth** *She's very sensitive to criticism.* 她一听批评就急。**OPP insensitive**

• **INFORMATION/SUBJECT** 信息；话题 **4** that you have to treat with great care because it may offend people or make them angry or embarrassed 须谨慎对待的；敏感的：*Health care is a politically sensitive issue.* 医疗卫生是一个政治敏感问题。

• **TO COLD/LIGHT/FOOD, ETC.** 对低温、光、食物等 **5** reacting quickly or more than usual to sth 敏感的；过敏的：*sensitive areas of the body* 身体的敏感区 ◇ **~ to sth** *My teeth are very sensitive to cold food.* 我的牙齿对冷食过敏。**OPP insensitive**

• **TO SMALL CHANGES** 对细微变化 **6 ~ (to sth)** able to measure very small changes 灵敏的：*a sensitive instrument* 灵敏的仪器 ◇ (*figurative*) *The Stock Exchange is very sensitive to political change.* 证券市场对政局变化非常敏感。**OPP insensitive**

▶ **sen·si·tive·ly** *adv.*：*She handled the matter sensitively.* 她谨慎细致地处理了那件事情。◇ *He writes sensitively.* 他文笔细腻。**IDM** SEE NERVE *n.*

sen·si·tiv·ity /ˌsensə'tɪvəti/ *noun* (*pl.* **-ies**)

• **TO PEOPLE'S FEELINGS** 对他人的感情 **1** [U] **~ (to sth)** the ability to understand other people's feelings 体贴；体恤；体察：*sensitivity to the needs of children* 体察孩子们的需要 ◇ *She pointed out with tact and sensitivity exactly where he had gone wrong.* 她明确指出了他的错误所在，既委婉又体贴。

• **TO ART/MUSIC/LITERATURE** 对艺术／音乐／文学 **2** [U] the ability to understand art, music and literature and to express yourself through them 敏锐的感觉；悟性：*She played with great sensitivity.* 她的表演很有悟性。

• **BEING EASILY UPSET** 容易生气 **3** [U, C, usually pl.] a tendency to be easily offended or upset by sth 容易生气；易被惹恼；敏感：*He's a mixture of anger and sensitivity.* 他气量小又太敏感。◇ *She was blind to the feelings and sensitivities of other people.* 她无视他人的情感和敏感之处。**OPP insensitivity**

• **OF INFORMATION/SUBJECT** 信息；话题 **4** [U] the fact of needing to be treated very carefully because it

S

may offend or upset people 敏感性：*Confidentiality is important because of the sensitivity of the information.* 这情报很敏感，务必保密。

• **TO FOOD/COLD/LIGHT, ETC.** 对食物、低温、光等 **5** [U, C, usually pl.] (*specialist*) the quality of reacting quickly or more than usual to sth 敏感性；过敏性：*food sensitivity* 食物过敏 ◇ *allergies and sensitivities* 过敏反应 ◇ *Some children develop a sensitivity to cow's milk.* 有的孩子对牛奶过敏。◇ *The eyes of some fish have a greater sensitivity to light than ours do.* 有些鱼的眼睛比人类的眼睛对光更敏感。

• **TO SMALL CHANGES** 对细微变化 **6** [U] the ability to measure very small changes 灵敏度：*the sensitivity of the test* 测试的灵敏度

sen·si·tize (*BrE also* **-ise**) /ˈsensətaɪz/ *verb* [usually passive] **1** ~ **sb/sth** (**to sth**) to make sb/sth more aware of sth, especially a problem or sth bad 使敏感（尤指对问题或不好的事）；使意识到：*People are becoming more sensitized to the dangers threatening the environment.* 人们越来越意识到危害环境的各种因素。 **2** ~ **sb/sth** (**to sth**) (*specialist*) to make sb/sth sensitive to physical or chemical changes, or to a particular substance 使对…过敏 ▶ **sen·si·tiza·tion, -isa·tion** /ˌsensətaɪˈzeɪʃn; *NAmE* -təˈz-/ *noun* [U]

sen·sor /ˈsensə(r)/ *noun* a device that can react to light, heat, pressure, etc. in order to make a machine, etc. do sth or show sth （探测光、热、压力等的）传感器，敏感元件：*security lights with an infrared sensor* (= that come on when a person is near them) 带红外线传感器的保安灯

sens·ory /ˈsensəri/ *adj.* [usually before noun] (*specialist*) connected with your physical senses 感觉的；感官的：*sensory organs* 感觉器官 ◇ *sensory deprivation* 感觉丧失

sens·ual /ˈsenʃuəl/ *adj.* **1** connected with your physical feelings; giving pleasure to your physical senses, especially sexual pleasure 感官的；肉欲的；愉悦感官的：*sensual pleasure* 感官之乐 **2** suggesting an interest in physical pleasure, especially sexual pleasure 喜欢感官享受的；耽于肉欲的：*sensual lips* 性感的嘴唇 ◇ *He was darkly sensual and mysterious.* 他耽于肉欲，而且让人捉摸不透。 ▶ **sen·su·al·ity** /ˌsenʃuˈæləti/ *noun* [U]：*the sensuality of his poetry* 他的诗专注于感官享受 **sen·su·al·ly** /-ʃuəli/ *adv.*

S

sen·su·ous /ˈsenʃuəs/ *adj.* **1** giving pleasure to your senses 愉悦感官的：*sensuous music* 悦耳的音乐 ◇ *I'm drawn to the poetic, sensuous qualities of her paintings.* 我喜欢她的画中那种充满诗意、赏心悦目的特性。 **2** suggesting an interest in sexual pleasure 肉感的；性感的：*his full sensuous lips* 他的丰满性感的嘴唇 ▶ **sen·su·ous·ly** *adv.* **sen·su·ous·ness** *noun* [U]

sent PAST TENSE, PAST PART. OF SEND

sen·tence 🔑 /ˈsentəns/ *noun, verb*

■ ***noun*** **1** 🔑 [C] (*grammar* 语法) a set of words expressing a statement, a question or an order, usually containing a subject and a verb. In written English sentences begin with a capital letter and end with a full stop/period (.), a question mark (?) or an exclamation mark/exclamation point (!). 句子 **2** 🔑 [C, U] the punishment given by a court 判决；宣判；判刑：*a **jail/prison sentence*** 判处监禁 ◇ *a **light/heavy sentence*** 轻判；重判 ◇ *to be **under sentence of death*** 被判处死刑 ◇ *The judge **passed sentence*** (= said what the punishment would be). 法官宣布了判决。◇ *The prisoner has **served*** (= completed) ***his sentence*** *and will be released tomorrow.* 犯人已服刑期满，明天将获释。➲ WORDFINDER NOTE AT PRISON ➲ COLLOCATIONS AT JUSTICE ➲ SEE ALSO DEATH SENTENCE, LIFE SENTENCE

■ ***verb*** [often passive] ~ **sb** (**to sth**) | ~ **sb to do sth** to say officially in court that sb is to receive a particular punishment 判决；宣判；判刑：*to be sentenced to death/life imprisonment/three years in prison* 被判死刑 / 终身监禁 / 三年徒刑

ˈ**sentence adverb** *noun* (*grammar* 语法) an adverb that expresses the speaker's attitude towards, or gives the subject of, the whole of the rest of the sentence 句副词：*In 'Luckily, I didn't tell anyone' and 'Financially, we have a serious problem', 'luckily' and 'financially' are sentence adverbs.* 在句子 Luckily, I didn't tell anyone 和 Financially, we have a serious problem 中，luckily 和 financially 是句副词。

sen·ten·cer /ˈsentənsə(r)/ *noun* (*formal*) a person who decides on the punishment for sb who is guilty of a crime 宣判人：*The judge was considered a tough sentencer.* 那位法官公认量刑严厉。

sen·ten·tious /senˈtenʃəs/ *adj.* (*formal, disapproving*) trying to sound important or intelligent, especially by expressing moral judgements 多格言警句的；（尤指）说教式的 ▶ **sen·ten·tious·ly** *adv.*

sen·tient /ˈsentiənt; ˈsenʃnt/ *adj.* [usually before noun] (*formal*) able to see or feel things through the senses 有感觉能力的；有知觉力的：*Man is a sentient being.* 人是有感觉的生物。

sen·ti·ment /ˈsentɪmənt/ *noun* **1** [C, U] (*formal*) a feeling or an opinion, especially one based on emotions （基于情感的）观点，看法；情绪：*the spread of nationalist sentiments* 民族主义情绪的传播 ◇ *This is a sentiment I wholeheartedly agree with.* 这种观点我完全赞同。◇ *Public sentiment is against any change to the law.* 公众的意见是反对对该法律作任何修改。 **2** [U] (*sometimes disapproving*) feelings of pity, romantic love, sadness, etc. which may be too strong or not appropriate （失之过度或不恰当的）伤感，柔情，哀伤：*There was no fatherly affection, no display of sentiment.* 没有温情脉脉的父爱流露。◇ *There is no room for sentiment in business.* 在生意场上心肠不能软。

sen·ti·men·tal /ˌsentɪˈmentl/ *adj.* **1** connected with your emotions, rather than reason 情感的（而非理性的）：*She kept the letters for sentimental reasons.* 她把那些信留作纪念。◇ *The ring wasn't worth very much but it had **great sentimental value**.* 那枚戒指值不了几个钱，但却极有情感价值。 **2** (*often disapproving*) producing emotions such as pity, romantic love or sadness, which may be too strong or not appropriate; feeling these emotions too much （失之过度或不恰当地）伤感的，充满柔情的；多愁善感的：*a slushy, sentimental love story* 庸俗缠绵的言情小说 ◇ *He's not the sort of man who gets **sentimental about** old friendships.* 他不是那种为旧日的友情唏嘘感伤的人。 OPP **unsentimental** ▶ **sen·ti·men·tal·ly** /-təli/ *adv.*

sen·ti·men·tal·ist /ˌsentɪˈmentəlɪst/ *noun* (*sometimes disapproving*) a person who is sentimental about things 好感伤者；多愁善感的人

sen·ti·men·tal·ity /ˌsentɪmenˈtæləti/ *noun* [U] (*disapproving*) the quality of being too sentimental 感伤情调；多愁善感

sen·ti·men·tal·ize (*BrE also* **-ise**) /ˌsentɪˈmentəlaɪz/ *verb* [T, I] ~ (**sth**) (*disapproving*) to present sth in an emotional way, emphasizing its good aspects and not mentioning its bad aspects 带着感情色彩描述好的方面：*Jackie was careful not to sentimentalize country life.* 杰基很注意，没有过分渲染乡村生活。

sen·ti·nel /ˈsentɪnl/ *noun* (*literary*) a soldier whose job is to guard sth 哨兵 SYN **sentry**：(*figurative*) *a tall round tower **standing sentinel** over the river* 镇守在河边的一座高高的圆塔

sen·try /ˈsentri/ *noun* (*pl.* **-ies**) a soldier whose job is to guard sth 哨兵：*to be on sentry duty* 放哨

ˈ**sentry box** *noun* a small shelter for a sentry to stand in 岗亭；哨岗

SEO /ˌes iː ˈəʊ; *NAmE* ˈoʊ/ *abbr.* = SEARCH ENGINE OPTIMIZATION

sepal /ˈsepl/ *noun* (*specialist*) a part of a flower, like a leaf, that lies under and supports the PETALS (= the delicate coloured parts that make up the head of the flower). Each flower has a ring of sepals called a CALYX. 萼片 ➲ VISUAL VOCAB PAGE V11

sep·ar·able /ˈsepərəbl/ *adj.* **1 ~ (from sth)** that can be separated from sth, or considered separately 可分开的；可分隔的；可分离的：*The moral question is not entirely separable from the financial one.* 道德问题和财政问题不能截然分开。 **2** (*grammar* 语法) (of a phrasal verb 短语动词) that can be used with the object going either between the verb and the PARTICLE or after the particle 可分的；可分离的；可分开的：*The phrasal verb 'tear up' is separable because you can say 'She tore the letter up' or 'She tore up the letter'.* * tear up 是可以分开的短语动词，因为既可以说 She tore the letter up，又可以说 She tore up the letter。 OPP **inseparable** ▶ **sep·ar·abil·ity** /ˌseprəˈbɪləti/ *noun* [U]

sep·ar·ate *adj., verb*

WORD FAMILY
separate *adj.*
separately *adv.*
separable *adj.* (≠ inseparable)
separate *verb*
separated *adj.*
separation *noun*

■ *adj.* /ˈseprət/ **1 ~ (from sth/sb)** forming a unit by itself; not joined to sth else 单独的；独立的；分开的：*separate bedrooms* 独立卧室 ◇ *Raw meat must be **kept separate** from cooked meat.* 生肉和熟肉必须分开存放。 ◇ *The school is housed in two separate buildings.* 学校设在两栋独立的楼房内。 **2** [usually before noun] different; not connected 不同的；不相关的：*It happened on three separate occasions.* 这事在三个不同的场合发生过。 ◇ *For the past three years they have been leading totally separate lives.* 三年来，他们完全是各过各的生活。 ▶ **sep·ar·ate·ness** *noun* [U]: *Japan's long-standing sense of separateness and uniqueness* 日本那种由来已久的自成一体、孑然独立的意识

IDM **go your separate ˈways 1** to end a relationship with sb 断绝往来；分道扬镳 **2** to go in a different direction from sb you have been travelling with 分路而行；分手 ➲ MORE AT COVER *n.*

■ *verb* /ˈsepəreɪt/ **1** [I, T] to divide into different parts or groups; to divide things into different parts or groups （使）分开，分离；分割；划分：*Stir the sauce constantly so that it does not separate.* 不停地搅动酱汁，免得出现分层。 ◇ **~ sth** *Separate the eggs* (= separate the YOLK from the white). 把蛋黄和蛋清分开。 ◇ **~ sth from/and sth** *It is impossible to separate belief from emotion.* 信仰和感情是分不开的。 ◇ **~ sth into sth** *Make a list of points and separate them into 'desirable' and 'essential'.* 列出各点，把它们分成"渴望拥有的"和"绝对必要的"两类。 **2** [I, T] to move apart; to make people or things move apart （使）分离，分散：*South America and Africa separated 200 million years ago.* 南美洲和非洲于 2 亿年前分离。 ◇ **~ from sth** *South America separated from Africa 200 million years ago.* * 2 亿年前南美洲和非洲分离。 ◇ **~ into sth** *We separated into several different search parties.* 我们分成几个搜索小组。 ◇ **~ sb/sth** *Police tried to separate the two men who were fighting.* 警察力图把两个打架的人分开。 ◇ *The war separated many families.* 这场战争使许多家庭离散。 ◇ **~ sb/sth from/and sb/sth** *Those suffering from infectious diseases were separated from the other patients.* 传染病患者同其他病人隔离开来。 **3** [T] to be between two people, areas, countries, etc. so that they are not touching or connected 隔开；阻隔：**~ sb/sth** *A thousand kilometres separates the two cities.* 两座城市相隔一千公里。 ◇ **~ sb/sth from/and sb** *A high wall separated our back yard from the playing field.* 我们的后院和运动场之间隔着一堵高墙。 **4** [I] to stop living together as a couple with your husband, wife or partner 分居：*They separated last year.* 他们于去年分居了。 ◇ **~ from sb** *He separated from his wife after 20 years of marriage.* 他和妻子在结婚 20 年后分居了。 ➲ COLLOCATIONS AT MARRIAGE **5** [T] **~ sb/sth (from sb/sth)** to make sb/sth different in some way from sb/sth else 区分；区别 SYN **divide**：*Politics is the only thing that separates us* (= that we disagree about). 我们之间唯一的分歧是政治观点。 ◇ *The judges found it impossible to separate the two contestants* (= they gave them equal scores). 裁判无法把两位参赛者分出高下。 ◇ *Only four points separate the top three teams.* 领先的三支队只相差四分。 IDM SEE MAN *n.*, SHEEP, WHEAT

PHR V **ˌseparate ˈout | ˌseparate sth↔ˈout** to divide into different parts; to divide sth into different parts 使某物分开；划分：*to separate out different meanings* 区分出不同的意思

sep·ar·ated /ˈsepəreɪtɪd/ *adj.* no longer living with your husband, wife or partner （和某人）分居的：*Her parents are separated but not divorced.* 她父母分居但没离婚。 ◇ **~ from sb** *He's been separated from his wife for a year.* 他和妻子分居一年了。 ➲ COLLOCATIONS AT MARRIAGE

sep·ar·ate·ly /ˈseprətli/ *adv.* **~ (from sb/sth)** as a separate person or thing; not together 单独地；分别地：*They were photographed separately and then as a group.* 他们先单独照相，然后合影。 ◇ *Last year's figures are shown separately.* 去年的数字分别列出。

sep·ar·ates /ˈseprəts/ *noun* [pl.] individual pieces of clothing, for example skirts, jackets, and trousers/pants, that are designed to be worn together in different combinations （可与其他不同衣服搭配穿的）单件衣服

ˈseparate school *noun* (*CanE*) a public school for Catholic children in some parts of Canada （加拿大一些地区为天主教儿童设立的）教会学校

sep·ar·ation /ˌsepəˈreɪʃn/ *noun* **1** [U, sing.] the act of separating people or things; the state of being separate 分离；分开；分割；隔离：**~ (from sb/sth)** *the state's eventual separation from the federation* 那个州最终与联邦的脱离 ◇ **~ (between A and B)** *the need for a clear separation between Church and State* 政教彻底分离的必要性 **2** [C] a period of time that people spend apart from each other 离别：*They were reunited after a separation of more than 20 years.* 他们离别 20 多年后重又聚首。 **3** [C] a decision that a husband and wife make to live apart while they are still legally married 分居：*a legal separation* 合法分居 ➲ COMPARE DIVORCE *n.* (1)

the ˌseparation of ˈpowers *noun* [sing.] the principle of the US Constitution that the political power of the government is divided between the President, Congress and the Supreme Court （美国宪法中行政、立法和司法的）三权分立制度 ➲ COMPARE CHECKS AND BALANCES

sep·ar·at·ist /ˈseprətɪst/ *noun* a member of a group of people within a country who want to separate from the rest of the country and form their own government 分离主义者；独立主义者：*Basque separatists* 巴斯克分裂主义者 ▶ **sep·ar·at·ism** /ˈseprətɪzəm/ *noun* [U] **sep·ar·at·ist** *adj.*：*a separatist movement* 分离主义运动

sep·ar·ator /ˈsepəreɪtə(r)/ *noun* a machine for separating things 分离器；分选机

Seph·ardi /seˈfɑːdi; *NAmE* -ˈfɑːrdi/ *noun* (*pl.* **Seph·ar·dim**) a Jew whose ANCESTORS came from Spain or N Africa 西班牙系犹太人（祖先居住在西班牙或北非） ➲ COMPARE ASHKENAZI ▶ **Seph·ar·dic** /-ɪk/ *adj.*

sepia /ˈsiːpiə/ *noun* [U] **1** a brown substance used in inks and paints and used in the past for printing photographs 乌贼墨颜料（或墨汁） **2** a reddish-brown colour 深褐色 ▶ **sepia** *adj.* [usually before noun]: ***sepia ink/prints/photographs*** 深褐色墨水 / 印刷品 / 照片

sepoy /ˈsiːpɔɪ/ *noun* **1** in the past, an Indian soldier serving under a British or European officer （旧时英国或欧洲长官手下的）印度兵 **2** (*IndE*) a soldier or police officer of the lowest rank 士兵；警员

sep·sis /ˈsepsɪs/ *noun* [U] (*medical* 医) an infection of part of the body in which PUS is produced 脓毒病；脓毒症

Sep·tem·ber /sepˈtembə(r)/ *noun* [U, C] (*abbr.* **Sept.**) the 9th month of the year, between August and October 九月 HELP To see how **September** is used, look at the examples at **April**. * September 的用法见词条 April 下的示例。

sep·tet /sepˈtet/ *noun* **1** [C+sing./pl. v.] a group of seven musicians or singers 七重奏乐团；七重唱组合 **2** [C] a piece of music for seven musicians or singers 七重奏（曲）；七重唱（曲）

S

sep·tic /ˈseptɪk/ *adj.* (of a wound or part of the body 伤口或身体部分) infected with harmful bacteria 感染病菌的；脓毒性的；腐败性的：*a septic finger* 被感染的手指 ◇ *A dirty cut may go septic.* 伤口不干净容易受感染。

septi·cae·mia (*BrE*) (*NAmE* **septi·ce·mia**) /ˌseptɪˈsiːmiə/ *noun* [U] (*medical* 医) infection of the blood by harmful bacteria 败血症 SYN **blood poisoning**

ˌseptic ˈtank *noun* a large container, usually underground, that holds human waste from toilets until the action of bacteria makes it liquid enough to be absorbed by the ground 化粪池

sep·tua·gen·ar·ian /ˌseptjuədʒəˈneəriən; *NAmE* ˌseptʃuədʒəˈneriən/ *noun* (*formal*) a person between 70 and 79 years old * 70 至 79 岁的人

sep·tum /ˈseptəm/ *noun* (*pl.* **septa** /ˈseptə/) (*anatomy* 解) a thin part that separates two hollow areas, for example the part of the nose between the NOSTRILS 隔膜；（动物）隔片，隔壁

se·pul·chral /səˈpʌlkrəl/ *adj.* (*literary*) looking or sounding sad and serious; making you think of death 阴沉的；阴森森的；死一般的 SYN **funereal**: *He spoke in sepulchral tones.* 他说话语气阴沉。

sep·ul·chre (*US* **sep·ul·cher**) /ˈseplkə(r)/ *noun* (*old use*) a place for a dead body, either cut in rock or built of stone（在岩石上凿出或用石头砌成的）坟墓，墓穴

se·quel /ˈsiːkwəl/ *noun* ~ (**to sth**) **1** a book, film/movie, play, etc. that continues the story of an earlier one（书、电影、戏剧等的）续篇，续集：*a sequel to the hit movie 'Madagascar'* 热门影片《马达加斯加》的续集 ➲ COMPARE PREQUEL **2** [usually sing.] something that happens after an earlier event or as a result of an earlier event 后续的事；随之而来的事；结果：*There was an interesting sequel to these events later in the year.* 这几件事发生以后，当年就出现了一种有趣的结果。

se·quence AW /ˈsiːkwəns/ *noun, verb*

■ *noun* **1** [C] a set of events, actions, numbers, etc. which have a particular order and which lead to a particular result 一系列；一连串：*He described* **the sequence of** *events leading up to the robbery.* 他描述了抢劫案发生前的一系列有关情况。**2** [C, U] the order that events, actions, etc. happen in or should happen in 顺序；次序：*The tasks had to be performed in a particular sequence.* 这些任务必须按一定次序去执行。◇ *Number the pages* **in sequence**. 按顺序标出页码。◇ *These pages are* **out of sequence**. 这几页排错了次序。**3** [C] a part of a film/movie that deals with one subject or topic or consists of one scene（电影中表现同一主题或场面的）一组镜头

■ *verb* **1** ~ **sth** (*specialist*) to arrange things into a sequence 按顺序排列 **2** ~ **sth** (*biology* 生) to identify the order in which a set of GENES or parts of MOLECULES are arranged 测定（整套基因或分子成分的）序列：*The human genome has now been sequenced.* 人体基因组的序列现已测定。▶ **se·quen·cing** *noun* [U]: *a gene sequencing project* 基因测序项目

the ˌsequence of ˈtenses *noun* [sing.] (*grammar* 语法) the rules according to which the tense of a SUBORDINATE CLAUSE depends on the tense of a main clause, so that, for example, '*I think that you* are *wrong*' becomes '*I thought that you* were *wrong*' in the past tense 时态的呼应，时态的一致（从句的时态受主句时态的制约）

se·quen·cer /ˈsiːkwənsə(r)/ *noun* an electronic instrument for recording and storing sounds so that they can be played later as part of a piece of music 音序器

se·quen·tial AW /sɪˈkwenʃl/ *adj.* (*formal*) following in order of time or place 按次序的；顺序的；序列的：*sequential data processing* 顺序数据处理 ▶ **se·quen·tial·ly** AW /-ʃəli/ *adv.*: *data stored sequentially on a computer* 顺序存储在计算机里的数据

se·ques·ter /sɪˈkwestə(r)/ *verb* (*law* 律) **1** = SEQUESTRATE **2** ~ **sb** to keep a JURY together in a place, in order to prevent them from talking to other people about a court case, or learning about it in the newspapers, on television, etc. 隔离（避免陪审团与公众接触）

se·ques·tered /sɪˈkwestəd; *NAmE* -tərd/ *adj.* [usually before noun] (*literary*) (of a place 地方) quiet and far away from people 僻静的；隐蔽幽静的

se·ques·trate /ˈsiːkwəstreɪt; *BrE also* sɪˈkwes-/ (*also* **se·ques·ter**) *verb* ~ **sth** (*law* 律) to take control of sb's property or ASSETS until a debt has been paid 强制管理，扣押（债务人资产） ▶ **se·ques·tra·tion** /ˌsiːkwəˈstreɪʃn/ *noun* [U, C]

se·quin /ˈsiːkwɪn/ *noun* a small round shiny disc sewn onto clothing as decoration（装饰衣服的）闪光小圆片 ▶ **se·quinned** (*NAmE* **se·quined**) /ˈsiːkwɪnd/ *adj.* [usually before noun] (*BrE*)

se·quoia /sɪˈkwɔɪə/ *noun* a very tall N American tree, a type of redwood 红杉

sera PL. OF SERUM

ser·aph /ˈserəf/ *noun* (*pl.* **ser·aph·im** /-fɪm/ or **ser·aphs**) an ANGEL of the highest rank 撒拉弗，色辣芬（基督教中级别最高的天使） ➲ COMPARE CHERUB (1)

ser·aph·ic /səˈræfɪk/ *adj.* (*literary*) **1** as beautiful, pure, etc. as an angel 天使般美丽（或纯洁等）的：*a seraphic child/nature* 天使般可爱的孩子 / 纯洁的本性 **2** extremely happy 无比快乐的：*a seraphic smile* 无比快乐的微笑

ser·en·ade /ˌserəˈneɪd/ *noun, verb*

■ *noun* **1** (in the past) a song or tune played or sung at night by a lover outside the window of the woman he loves（旧时男子在所爱慕的女子窗下演奏或歌唱的）小夜曲 **2** a gentle piece of music in several parts, usually for a small group of instruments（尤指供小型乐队演奏的）小夜曲

■ *verb* ~ **sb** to sing or play music to sb (as done in the past by a man singing under her window to the woman he loved)（对所爱慕的女子）唱小夜曲，奏小夜曲

ser·en·dip·ity /ˌserənˈdɪpəti/ *noun* [U] the fact of sth interesting or pleasant happening by chance 巧事；机缘凑巧 ▶ **ser·en·dip·it·ous** /-ˈdɪpətəs/ *adj.*: *serendipitous discoveries* 偶然的幸运发现

se·rene /səˈriːn/ *adj.* calm and peaceful 平静的；宁静的；安详的：*a lake, still and serene in the sunlight* 阳光下宁静安谧的湖水 ▶ **se·rene·ly** *adv.*: *serenely beautiful* 宁静而美丽 ◇ *She smiled serenely.* 她安详地微笑。**se·ren·ity** /səˈrenəti/ *noun* [U, sing.]: *The hotel offers a haven of peace and serenity away from the bustle of the city.* 那家旅馆远离闹市，是一个幽静安谧的好去处。

serf /sɜːf; *NAmE* sɜːrf/ *noun* (in the past) a person who was forced to live and work on land that belonged to a LANDOWNER whom they had to obey（旧时的）农奴

serf·dom /ˈsɜːfdəm; *NAmE* ˈsɜːrf-/ *noun* [U] the system under which crops were grown by serfs; the state of being a serf 农奴制；农奴身份：*the abolition of serfdom in Russia in 1861* * 1861 年农奴制在俄国的废除

serge /sɜːdʒ; *NAmE* sɜːrdʒ/ *noun* [U] a type of strong cloth made of wool, used for making clothes 哔叽：*a blue serge suit* 一套蓝色哔叽西服

ser·geant /ˈsɑːdʒənt; *NAmE* ˈsɑːrdʒ-/ *noun* (*abbr.* **Sergt, Sgt**) **1** a member of one of the middle ranks in the army and the AIR FORCE, below an officer 陆军（或空军）中士：*Sergeant Salter* 索尔特中士 ➲ SEE ALSO FLIGHT SERGEANT, STAFF SERGEANT **2** (in Britain) a police officer just below the rank of an INSPECTOR（英国警察）巡佐 **3** (in the US) a police officer just below the rank of a LIEUTENANT or CAPTAIN（美国警察）警佐 ➲ SEE ALSO SARGE

ˌsergeant ˈmajor *noun* (often used as a title 常用作头衔) **1** a soldier of middle rank in the British army who is responsible for helping the officer who organizes the affairs of a particular REGIMENT (= a large group of soldiers) 准尉副官（英国陆军中的团行政助理） **2** a soldier in

S

the US army of the highest rank of NON-COMMISSIONED OFFICERS 军士长（美国陆军中最高级军士）

ser·ial /ˈsɪəriəl; NAmE ˈsɪr-/ *noun, adj.*

■ ***noun*** a story on television or the radio, or in a magazine, that is broadcast or published in several separate parts 电视连续剧；广播连续剧；杂志连载小说

■ ***adj.*** **1** [usually before noun] (*specialist*) arranged in a series 顺序排列的；排成系列的：*tasks carried out in the same serial order* 按同样顺序完成的任务 **2** [only before noun] doing the same thing in the same way several times 连续的；多次的：*a serial rapist* 一个连续作案的强奸犯 **3** [only before noun] (of a story, etc. 小说等) broadcast or published in several separate parts 以连续剧形式播出的；连载的：*a novel in serial form* 一部连载小说 ▶ **ser·ial·ly** /-iəli/ *adv.*

seri·al·ize (*BrE also* **-ise**) /ˈsɪəriəlaɪz; NAmE ˈsɪr-/ *verb* **~ sth** to publish or broadcast sth in parts as a serial 连载；连播：*The novel was serialized on TV in six parts.* 这部小说分六集在电视上播出。 ▶ **seri·al·iza·tion, -isation** /ˌsɪəriəlaɪˈzeɪʃn; NAmE ˌsɪriələˈz-/ *noun* [C, U]：*a newspaper serialization of the book* 这部书在报上的连载

ˌ**serial ˈkiller** *noun* a person who murders several people one after the other in a similar way 连环杀手

ˌ**serial moˈnogamy** *noun* [U] the fact or custom of having more than one husband, wife or sexual partner in your life, but only one at a time 连续性单配偶生活，连续性一夫一妻制（指尽管一生有多个配偶或性伴，但同一时间只有一个配偶或性伴）

ˈ**serial number** *noun* a number put on a product, such as a camera, television, etc., in order to identify it 序列号；编号

ˈ**serial port** *noun* (*computing* 计) a point on a computer where you connect a device such as a mouse that sends or receives data one BIT at a time 串行端口

ser·ies 🔑 AW /ˈsɪəriːz; NAmE ˈsɪr-/ *noun* (*pl.* **ser·ies**) **1** 🔑 [C, usually sing.] **~ of sth** several events or things of a similar kind that happen one after the other 一系列；连续；接连：*The incident sparked off a whole **series of events** that nobody had foreseen.* 那一事件引发出一连串谁都没有料到的事。◇ *the latest in a series of articles on the nature of modern society* 论现代社会性质的一系列文章中最新的一篇 **2** 🔑 [C] a set of radio or television programmes that deal with the same subject or that have the same characters（广播或电视上题材或角色相同的）系列节目 ➲ COLLOCATIONS AT TELEVISION **3** [C] (*sport* 体育) a set of sports games played between the same two teams（两队之间的）系列比赛：*the **World Series*** (= in BASEBALL) 世界系列美国职业棒球锦标赛 ◇ *England have lost the **Test series*** (= of CRICKET matches) *against India.* 英格兰板球队在同印度队的系列比赛中落败。 **4** [U, C] (*specialist*) an electrical CIRCUIT in which the current passes through all the parts in the correct order 串联

serif /ˈserɪf/ *noun* a short line at the top or bottom of some styles of printed letters 衬线，截线（部分印刷体的西文字母顶端或底部的短线）：*a serif typeface* 衬线字体 ➲ COMPARE SANS SERIF

ser·ious 🔑 /ˈsɪəriəs; NAmE ˈsɪr-/ *adj.*

• **BAD** 不好 **1** 🔑 bad or dangerous 不好的；严重的；有危险的：*a **serious illness/problem/offence*** 严重的疾病 / 问题 / 罪行 ◇ *to cause **serious injury/damage*** 导致重伤；造成严重破坏 ◇ *They pose a serious threat to security.* 他们对安全构成严重威胁。◇ *The consequences could be serious.* 后果可能是严重的。

• **NEEDING THOUGHT** 需思考 **2** 🔑 needing to be thought about carefully; not only for pleasure 需认真思考的；严肃的：*a serious article* 一篇严肃的文章 ◇ *a serious newspaper* 一份严肃的报纸 ◇ *It's time to give serious consideration to this matter.* 到了认真考虑这一问题的时候了。

• **IMPORTANT** 重要 **3** 🔑 that must be treated as important 重要的；须重视的：*We need to get down to the serious business of working out costs.* 我们该认真地把成本算出来了。◇ *The team is a serious contender for the title this year.* 该队是今年不可轻视的夺标竞争者。

• **NOT SILLY** 理智 **4** 🔑 thinking about things in a careful and sensible way; not silly 严肃的；稳重的：***Be serious** for a moment; this is important.* 严肃点儿，这件事很重要。◇ *I'm afraid I'm not a very serious person.* 恐怕我不是一个非常严肃的人。

• **NOT JOKING** 不是开玩笑 **5** 🔑 sincere about sth; not joking or meant as a joke 当真的；认真的：*Believe me, I'm **deadly*** (= extremely) ***serious**.* 相信我，我绝对是当真的。◇ *Don't laugh, it's a serious suggestion.* 别笑，这是一项严肃的建议。◇ **~ (about doing sth)** *Is she serious about wanting to sell the house?* 她真想把房子卖掉吗？◇ **~ (about sb/sth)** *He's really serious about Penny and wants to get engaged.* 他对彭尼的确是认真的，他想跟她订婚。◇ (*informal*) ***You can't be serious!*** (= you must be joking) 你一定是在开玩笑吧！◇ *You think I did it? **Be serious!*** (= what you suggest is ridiculous) 你认为这是我干的？别开玩笑了！

• **LARGE AMOUNT** 大量 **6** (*informal*) used to emphasize that there is a large amount of sth（强调大量）：*You can earn serious money doing that.* 干那个，你能挣一大笔钱。◇ *I'm ready to do some serious eating* (= I am very hungry). 我饿得很，得好好吃一顿。

▼ **SYNONYMS** 同义词辨析

serious

grave • earnest • solemn

These words all describe sb who thinks and behaves carefully and sensibly, but often without much joy or laughter. 以上各词均形容人严肃、稳重、认真。

serious thinking about things in a careful and sensible way; not laughing about sth 指严肃的、稳重的、认真的：*He's not really a very serious person.* 他并不真是一个非常严肃的人。◇ ***Be serious for a moment; this is important.*** 严肃点儿，这件事很重要。

grave (*rather formal*) (of a person) serious in manner, as if sth sad, important, or worrying has just happened 指人严肃、庄严、沉重：*He looked very grave as he entered the room.* 他进屋时表情非常严肃。

earnest serious and sincere 指认真的、诚实的、真诚的：*The earnest young doctor answered all our questions.* 这个认真的年轻医生回答了我们所有的问题。

solemn looking or sounding very serious, without smiling; done or said in a very serious and sincere way 指表情严肃的、冷峻的、庄严的、郑重的：*Her expression grew solemn.* 她的表情显得严肃起来。◇ ***I made a solemn promise that I would return.*** 我郑重承诺过我会回来的。

PATTERNS

• a(n) serious/grave/earnest/solemn **expression/face**
• a serious/solemn **mood/atmosphere**

ser·ious·ly 🔑 /ˈsɪəriəsli; NAmE ˈsɪr-/ *adv.* **1** 🔑 in a serious way 严重地；严肃地；认真地：*to be **seriously ill/injured*** 重病；重伤 ◇ *You're not seriously expecting me to believe that?* 你不是真的以为我会相信那样的话吧？◇ *They are seriously concerned about security.* 他们非常关注安全问题。◇ *Smoking can seriously damage your health.* 吸烟会严重损害你的健康。 **2** 🔑 used at the beginning of a sentence to show a change from joking to being more serious（用于句首，表示转为谈正事）说正经的，说实在的：*Seriously though, it could be really dangerous.* 不过说实在的，这事说不好真的很危险。 **3** (*informal*) very; extremely 非常；极其：*They're seriously rich.* 他们极为富有。

IDM **take sb/sth ˈseriously** 🔑 to think that sb/sth is important and deserves your attention and respect 认真对待：*We take threats of this kind very seriously.* 我们对这类威胁非常重视。◇ *Why can't you ever take anything seriously?* 你怎么对什么都不当回事呢？

ser·ious·ness /ˈsɪəriəsnəs; NAmE ˈsɪr-/ *noun* [U, sing.] the state of being serious 严重；认真；严肃：*He spoke*

S

with a seriousness that was unusual in him. 他说话时神情少有地认真。

IDM **in all 'seriousness** very seriously; not as a joke 非常严肃地；认认真真地；说实在的

ser·mon /'sɜːmən; *NAmE* 'sɜːrmən/ *noun* **1** a talk on a moral or religious subject, usually given by a religious leader during a service 布道；讲道 ➲ SYNONYMS AT SPEECH ➲ COLLOCATIONS AT RELIGION **2** (*informal, usually disapproving*) moral advice that a person tries to give you in a long talk 冗长的说教

ser·mon·ize (*BrE also* **-ise**) /'sɜːmənaɪz; *NAmE* 'sɜːrm-/ *verb* [I] (*disapproving*) to give moral advice, especially when it is boring or not wanted （尤指让人厌烦地）说教，教训 SYN **moralize**

sero·tonin /ˌserə'təʊnɪn; *NAmE* -'toʊn-/ *noun* [U] a chemical in the brain that affects how messages are sent from the brain to the body, and also affects how a person feels * 5 羟色胺，血清素（神经递质，亦影响情绪等）

ser·pent /'sɜːpənt; *NAmE* 'sɜːrp-/ *noun* (*literary*) a snake, especially a large one 蛇；（尤指）大蛇

ser·pen·tine /'sɜːpəntaɪn; *NAmE* 'sɜːrpəntiːn/ *adj.* (*literary*) bending and twisting like a snake 弯弯曲曲的；蜿蜒的；盘旋的；迂回的 SYN **winding**: *the serpentine course of the river* 蜿蜒曲折的河道

ser·rated /sə'reɪtɪd/ *adj.* having a series of sharp points on the edge like a SAW 锯齿状的：*a knife with a **serrated edge*** 带锯齿刃的刀 ➲ VISUAL VOCAB PAGE V27

ser·ra·tion /se'reɪʃn/ *noun* a part on an edge or the blade of a knife that is sharp and pointed like a SAW 锯齿边；锯齿刃

ser·ried /'serid/ *adj.* [usually before noun] (*literary*) standing or arranged closely together in rows or lines （行列）密排的，密集的，靠拢的：*serried ranks of soldiers* 密集排列的士兵

serum /'sɪərəm; *NAmE* 'sɪrəm/ *noun* (*pl.* **sera** /'sɪərə; *NAmE* 'sɪrə/ or **ser·ums**) **1** [U] (*biology* 生) the thin liquid that remains from blood when the rest has CLOTTED 血清 **2** [U, C] (*medical* 医) serum taken from the blood of an animal and given to people to protect them from disease, poison, etc. 免疫血清：*snakebite serum* 抗蛇毒血清 **3** [U] any liquid like water in body TISSUE 浆液（体液的水样部分）

S

ser·vant /'sɜːvənt; *NAmE* 'sɜːrv-/ *noun* **1** a person who works in another person's house, and cooks, cleans, etc. for them 仆人；佣人：*a domestic servant* 家仆 ◇ *They treat their mother like a servant.* 他们像对待佣人一样对待自己的母亲。**2** a person who works for a company or an organization （公司或机构的）雇员，职员：*a public servant* 公务员 ➲ SEE ALSO CIVIL SERVANT **3** a person or thing that is controlled by sth 奴仆般受制（或献身）于…的人；服务于…的事物：*He was willing to make himself a servant of his art.* 他甘愿献身于自己的艺术。IDM SEE OBEDIENT

serve /sɜːv; *NAmE* sɜːrv/ *verb, noun*

■ *verb*

• **FOOD/DRINK** 食物；饮料 **1** [T, I] to give sb food or drink, for example at a restaurant or during a meal （给某人）提供；端上：**~ (sth)** *Breakfast is served between 7 and 10 a.m.* 早餐供应时间从上午 7 点到 10 点。◇ *Pour the sauce over the pasta and serve immediately.* 把酱汁浇在意大利面上就立刻上桌。◇ *Shall I serve?* 现在上菜好吗？◇ **~ sth with sth** *Serve the lamb with new potatoes and green beans.* 羊肉配新鲜土豆和青刀豆一起上。◇ **~ sth to sb** *They served a wonderful meal to more than fifty delegates.* 他们招待五十多位代表吃了一餐美味佳肴。◇ **~ sb with sth** *The delegates were served with a wonderful meal.* 代表们受到款待，吃了一餐美味佳肴。◇ **~ sb sth** *She served us a delicious lunch.* 她招待我们吃了一顿可口的午餐。◇ **~ sth + adj.** *The quiche can be served hot or cold.* 蛋奶馅饼热吃也行，冷吃也行。

2 [T] **~ sb/sth** (of an amount of food 食物的量) to be enough for sb/sth 够…吃（或用）：*This dish will serve four hungry people.* 这饭够四个饥饿的人吃。

• **CUSTOMERS** 顾客 **3** [T, I] **~ (sb)** (*especially BrE*) to help a customer or sell them sth in a shop/store 接待；服务：*Are you being served?* 有人接待您吗？◇ *She was serving behind the counter.* 她在柜台服务。

• **BE USEFUL** 有用 **4** [T] **~ sth/sb** to be useful to sb in achieving or satisfying sth 对…有用；能满足…的需要：*These experiments **serve** no useful **purpose**.* 这些实验没有任何实际意义。◇ *Most of their economic policies **serve the interests** of big business.* 他们的经济政策多半符合大企业的利益。◇ *How can we best **serve the needs** of future generations?* 我们怎样才最能满足后代子孙的需要？◇ *His linguistic ability **served him well** in his chosen profession.* 他的语言能力对他所选择的职业大有帮助。

• **PROVIDE STH** 提供 **5** [T] to provide an area or a group of people with a product or service （向某地或某群体）供应，提供：**~ sb/sth** *The centre will serve the whole community.* 这个中心将为整个社区提供服务。◇ **~ sb/sth with sth** *The town is well served with buses and major road links.* 这座城市乘坐公共汽车很方便，与干线公路的连接也很发达。

• **BE SUITABLE** 适合 **6** [I] **~ (as sth)** to be suitable for a particular use, especially when nothing else is available 可用作，可当…使（尤指别无选择时）：*The sofa will serve as a bed for a night or two.* 沙发可以当床凑合一两夜。

• **HAVE PARTICULAR RESULT** 产生某种结果 **7** [I, T] to have a particular effect or result 产生…的效果（或结果）：**~ as sth** *The judge said the punishment would serve as a warning to others.* 法官说这种惩罚将对其他人起到杀一儆百的作用。◇ **~ to do sth** *The attack was unsuccessful and **served only to** alert the enemy.* 进攻未奏效，反而使敌人警觉起来。

• **WORK** 工作 **8** [I, T] to work or perform duties for a person, an organization, a country, etc. （为…）工作，服务，履行义务，尽职责：**~ (as sth)** *He served as a captain in the army.* 他曾是一名陆军上尉。◇ **~ in/on/with sth** *She served in the medical corps.* 她在医务部队服过役。◇ **~ under/with sb** *He served under Tony Blair in the 1990s.* 他曾于 20 世纪 90 年代在托尼·布莱尔手下任职。◇ **~ sth** *I wanted to work somewhere where I could serve the community.* 我想找一个能够为公众服务的工作岗位。◇ **~ sb (as sth)** *He served the family faithfully for many years* (= as a servant). 他忠心耿耿，伺候这家人多年。**9** [T, I] to spend a period of time in a particular job or training for a job 任期为；担任（职务）时间达；培训期为：**~ sth** *He served a one-year apprenticeship.* 他做了一年的学徒。◇ **~ as sth** *She was elected to serve as secretary of the local party.* 她当选为地方党组织的书记。

• **TIME IN PRISON** 监禁时间 **10** [T] **~ sth** to spend a period of time in prison 服（刑）：*prisoners serving life sentences* 服无期徒刑的囚犯 ◇ *She is serving two years for theft.* 她因盗窃罪正在服两年徒刑。◇ *He has **served time*** (= been to prison) *before.* 他以前坐过牢。

• **OFFICIAL DOCUMENT** 正式文件 **11** [T] (*law* 律) to give or send sb an official document, especially one that orders them to appear in court 把…送达；向（某人）送交：**~ sth (on sb)** *to **serve a writ/summons** on sb* 把令状 / 传票送达某人 ◇ **~ sb with sth** *to serve sb with a writ/summons* 向某人送交令状 / 传票

• **IN SPORT** 体育运动 **12** [I, T] (in TENNIS, etc. 网球等) to start playing by throwing the ball into the air and hitting it 发（球）：*Who's serving?* 谁发球？◇ **~ sth** *She served an ace.* 她发球直接得分。

IDM **it serves sb 'right (for doing sth)** used to say that sth that has happened to sb is their own fault and they deserve it 咎由自取；罪有应得：*Left you, did she? It serves you right for being so selfish.* 她离开了你，是吗？那你活该，你太自私了。**serve your/its 'turn** (*BrE*) to be useful for a particular purpose or period of time （在某方面或某期间）发挥作用，派上用场；足以满足…的需要 **serve two 'masters** (usually used in negative sentences 通常用于否定句) to support two opposing parties, principles, etc. at the same time 侍奉二主（同时支持两个敌对的党派）；徘徊于两种对立原则之间 ➲ MORE AT FIRST *adv.*, MEMORY

PHR V **ˌserve sth↔'out 1** to continue doing sth, especially working or staying in prison, for a fixed period of time that has been set 干至期满；服满刑期：*He has three more years in prison before he's served out his sentence.* 他要在监狱里再待三年，才能服满刑期。◇ (*BrE*) *They didn't want me to serve out my notice.* 他们想不等我干到约定的离职时间就要我走。**2** (*BrE*) to share food or drink between a number of people 分发（食物或饮料）；（为众人）分餐：*I went around the guests serving out drinks.* 我四处走动给客人斟饮料。 ˌ**serve sth↔ˈup 1** to put food onto plates and give it to people 端上（食物）：*He served up a delicious meal.* 他端上一顿可口的饭菜。 **2** to give, offer or provide sth 给出；提供：*She served up the usual excuse.* 她给出的借口还是老一套。◇ *The teams served up some fantastic entertainment.* 这些队献上了精彩的表演。

■ ***noun*** (in TENNIS, etc. 网球等) the action of serving the ball to your opponent 发球

ser·ver /ˈsɜːvə(r); *NAmE* ˈsɜːrv-/ *noun* **1** (*computing* 计) a computer program that controls or supplies information to several computers connected in a network; the main computer on which this program is run 服务器 ➲ COLLOCATIONS AT EMAIL **2** (*sport* 体育) a player who is serving, for example in TENNIS 发球者 **3** [usually pl.] a kitchen UTENSIL (= tool) used for putting food onto sb's plate 上菜用具（往各人盘子里盛食物的叉、铲、勺等）：*salad servers* 分色拉用的叉匙 ➲ VISUAL VOCAB PAGE V23 **4** (*NAmE*) a person who serves food in a restaurant; a waiter or waitress （餐馆给顾客上菜的）侍者 **5** a person who helps a priest during a church service （教堂做礼拜时的）助祭，辅祭

serv·ery /ˈsɜːvəri; *NAmE* ˈsɜːrv-/ *noun* (*pl.* **-ies**) (*BrE*) part of a restaurant where you collect your food to take back to your table 取餐处（餐馆中供顾客端取食物的地方）

ser·vice 🔑 /ˈsɜːvɪs; *NAmE* ˈsɜːrv-/ *noun, verb*

■ ***noun***

• **PROVIDING STH** 提供 **1** 🔑 [C] a system that provides sth that the public needs, organized by the government or a private company 公共服务系统；公共事业：*the **ambulance/bus/telephone, etc. service*** 救护车、公共汽车、电话等服务系统 ◇ *The government aims to improve **public services**, especially education.* 政府致力于改善公共服务事业，尤其是教育。◇ ***Essential services*** (= the supply of water, gas, electricity) *will be maintained.* 生活必需的水、燃气、电将维持供应。➲ SEE ALSO EMERGENCY SERVICES, POSTAL SERVICE **2** 🔑 (*also* **Service**) [C] an organization or a company that provides sth for the public or does sth for the government 公共事业机构（或公司）：*the prison service* 监狱管理机构 ◇ *the BBC World Service* 英国广播公司对外广播 ➲ SEE ALSO CIVIL SERVICE, DIPLOMATIC SERVICE, FIRE SERVICE, HEALTH SERVICE, INTERNAL REVENUE SERVICE, NATIONAL HEALTH SERVICE, SECRET SERVICE, SECURITY SERVICE, SOCIAL SERVICES **3** 🔑 [C, U] a business whose work involves doing sth for customers but not producing goods; the work that such a business does 服务性企业（或行业、业务）：*financial services* 金融公司 ◇ *the development of new **goods and services*** 新的商品和服务领域的开发 ◇ *Smith's Catering Services* (= a company) *offers the best value.* 史密斯餐饮公司提供最超值的餐饮服务。◇ *We guarantee (an) excellent service.* 我们保证提供优质服务。◇ *the **service sector*** (= the part of the economy involved in this type of business) 服务业 ◇ *a service industry* 服务性行业

• **IN HOTEL/SHOP/RESTAURANT** 旅馆；商店；餐馆 **4** 🔑 [U] the serving of customers in hotels, restaurants, and shops/stores （对顾客的）接待，服务：*The food was good but the service was very slow.* 饭菜不错，但动作太慢。◇ *10% will be added to your bill for service.* 您付账时要另加 10% 的服务费。◇ *Our main concern is to provide quality **customer service**.* 我们最关心的是为顾客提供优质服务。➲ COLLOCATIONS AT RESTAURANT ➲ SEE ALSO ROOM SERVICE, SELF-SERVICE

• **WORK FOR ORGANIZATION** 为机构工作 **5** 🔑 [U] ~ (**to sth**) the work that sb does for an organization, etc., especially when it continues for a long time or is admired very much （尤指长期、受到敬重的）工作，效劳，服务：*She has just celebrated 25 years' service with the company.* 她刚庆祝了自己在公司任职 25 周年。◇ *The employees have good **conditions of service**.* 雇员有良好的工作条件。◇ *After retiring, she became involved in **voluntary service** in the local community.* 她在退休后投身于当地社区的志愿服务工作。➲ SEE ALSO JURY SERVICE at JURY DUTY

• **OF VEHICLE/MACHINE** 交通工具；机器 **6** [U] the use that you can get from a vehicle or machine; the state of being used 使用；使用状况：*That computer gave us very good service.* 我们那台计算机很好用。◇ *The ship will be taken out of service within two years.* 那艘船将在两年之内退役。**7** [C, U] an examination of a vehicle or machine followed by any work that is necessary to keep it operating well 检修；维护；维修；保养：*a service engineer* 维修技师 ◇ (*BrE*) *I had taken the car in for a service.* 我把车送去检修了。◇ (*NAmE*) *I had taken the car in for service.* 我把车送去检修了。➲ SEE ALSO AFTER-SALES SERVICE

• **SKILLS/HELP** 技艺；帮助 **8** [usually pl.] (*formal*) the particular skills or help that a person is able to offer （提供技术或帮助的）服务：~ (**of sb**) *You need the services of a good lawyer.* 你需要找一位好律师来帮助你。◇ ~ (**as sb/sth**) *He offered his services as a driver.* 他说他愿意开车。

• **ARMY/NAVY/AIR FORCE** 陆军；海军；空军 **9** [C, usually pl., U] the army, the navy and the AIR FORCE; the work done by people in them 海陆空三军；兵役：*Most of the boys went straight into **the services**.* 多数男生直接去服兵役了。◇ *He **saw service** in North Africa.* 他曾在北非服兵役。◇ *a service family* 军人家庭 ➲ SEE ALSO ACTIVE SERVICE, MILITARY SERVICE, NATIONAL SERVICE

• **RELIGIOUS CEREMONY** 宗教礼仪 **10** 🔑 [C] a religious ceremony 宗教礼仪；礼拜仪式：***morning/evening service*** 晨祷；晚祷 ◇ ***to hold/attend a service*** 举行 / 参加礼拜 ◇ ***a funeral/marriage/memorial, etc. service*** 丧葬、结婚、追思等宗教仪式 ➲ COLLOCATIONS AT RELIGION

• **BUS/TRAIN** 公共汽车；火车 **11** [C, usually sing.] a bus, train, etc. that goes regularly to a particular place at a particular time 班车；车次：*the cancellation of the 10.15 service to Glasgow* * 10 点 15 分开往格拉斯哥的车次取消

• **ON MOTORWAY** 高速公路 **12 services** [sing.+sing./pl. v.] (*BrE*) a place beside a MOTORWAY where you can stop for petrol, a meal, the toilets, etc. （可加油、用餐、上厕所等的）服务站：*motorway services* 高速公路服务站 ◇ *It's five miles to the next services.* 距下一个服务站还有五英里。➲ SEE ALSO SERVICE AREA, SERVICE STATION

• **IN TENNIS** 网球 **13** [C] an act of hitting the ball in order to start playing; the way that you hit it 发球；发球方式 SYN **serve**：*It's your service* (= your turn to start playing). 该你发球了。◇ *Her service has improved.* 她的发球有了提高。

• **SET OF PLATES, ETC.** 整套餐具等 **14** [C] a complete set of plates, dishes, etc. that match each other 整套餐具：*a tea service* (= cups, SAUCERS, a TEAPOT and plates, for serving tea) 一套茶具 ➲ SEE ALSO DINNER SERVICE

• **BEING SERVANT** 当仆人 **15** [U] (*old-fashioned*) the state or position of being a servant 仆人地位（或身份）：***to be in/go into service*** (= to be/become a servant) 做 / 去当佣人

• **OF OFFICIAL DOCUMENT** 正式文件 **16** [U] (*law* 律) the formal giving of an official document, etc. to sb 送达：*the service of a demand for payment* 缴款通知的送达

IDM **at the ˈservice of sb/sth | at sb's ˈservice** completely available for sb to use or to help sb 随时可供使用（或可以帮助）：*Health care must be at the service of all who need it.* 医疗保健机构必须为所有需要者提供服务。◇ (*formal or humorous*) *If you need anything, I am **at your service**.* 您要是需要什么，请尽管吩咐。 **be of ˈservice (to sb)** (*formal*) to be useful or helpful （对某人）有用，有帮助：*Can I be of service to anyone?* 有谁需要我帮忙吗？ **do sb a/no ˈservice** (*formal*) to do sth that is helpful/not helpful to sb 有助于（或无助于）某人：*She was doing herself no service by remaining silent.* 她老不吭气，这对她自己没好处。➲ MORE AT PRESS *v.*

■ ***verb***

• **VEHICLE/MACHINE** 交通工具；机器 **1** [usually passive] ~ **sth** to examine a vehicle or machine and repair it if necessary so that it continues to work correctly 检修；维护；维修；保养：*We need to have the car serviced.* 我们得把车送去检修一下了。

S

• PROVIDE STH 提供 **2** ~ **sth/sb** to provide people with sth they need, such as shops/stores, or a transport system 提供服务 SYN **serve**: *Botley is well serviced by a regular bus route into Oxford.* 从博特利到牛津有一条公交线路，按时发车，十分便利。◇ *This department services the international sales force* (= provides services for it). 这个部门向国际销售人员提供服务。

• PAY INTEREST 支付利息 **3** ~ **sth** (*specialist*) to pay interest on money that has been borrowed 支付（债务）利息：*The company can no longer* ***service its debts.*** 那家公司已无力支付债务利息。

ser·vice·able /ˈsɜːvɪsəbl; *NAmE* ˈsɜːrv-/ *adj.* suitable to be used 能用的：*The carpet is worn but still serviceable.* 地毯旧了，但还能用。

ˈservice area *noun* (*BrE*) a place on a MOTORWAY where you can stop and buy food, petrol, have a meal, go to the toilet, etc.（高速公路旁可停车用餐、加油、上厕所等的）服务区，服务站

ˈservice charge *noun* **1** an amount of money that is added to a bill, as an extra charge for a service （另加的）服务费：*That will be $50, plus a service charge of $2.50.* 您消费 50 美元，另加 2.50 美元的服务费。**2** (*BrE*) an amount of money that is added to a bill in a restaurant, for example 10% of the total, that goes to pay for the work of the staff（付给餐馆侍者的）小费，服务费 ➲ WORDFINDER NOTE AT RESTAURANT **3** an amount of money that is paid to the owner of an apartment building for services such as putting out rubbish/garbage, cleaning the stairs, etc.（付给房东的）服务费，清洁费

ˈservice club *noun* (*NAmE*) an organization whose members do things to help their local community 社区服务俱乐部

ˈservice industry *noun* [U, C] (*economics* 经) = TERTIARY INDUSTRY

ser·vice·man /ˈsɜːvɪsmən; *NAmE* ˈsɜːrv-/, **ser·vice·woman** /ˈsɜːvɪswʊmən; *NAmE* ˈsɜːrv-/ *noun* (*pl.* **-men** /-mən/, **-women** /-wɪmɪn/) a man or woman who is a member of the armed forces（男、女）军人 ➲ NOTE AT GENDER

ˈservice provider (*also* **ˈaccess provider**) *noun* a business company that provides a service to customers, especially one that connects customers to the Internet 服务供应商（尤指互联网服务供应商）：*an Internet service provider* 互联网服务供应商

ˈservice road (*NAmE also* **ˈfrontage road**) *noun* a side road that runs parallel to a main road, that you use to reach houses, shops/stores, etc. 辅路，支路（与主干公路平行，方便人们通往房屋、商店等）

ˈservice station *noun* **1** = GAS STATION, PETROL STATION **2** (*BrE*) an area and building beside a MOTORWAY where you can buy food and petrol, go to the toilet, etc.（高速公路旁可停车用餐、加油、上厕所等的）服务区，服务站：*a motorway service station* 高速公路服务站

ser·vicing /ˈsɜːvɪsɪŋ; *NAmE* ˈsɜːrv-/ *noun* [U] **1** the act of checking and repairing a vehicle, machine, etc. to keep it in good condition（车辆、机器等的）检修，维修，保养，维护：*Like any other type of equipment it requires regular servicing.* 它和其他类型的设备一样，也需要定期检修。**2** (*finance* 财) the act of paying interest on money that has been borrowed（债务的）利息支付：*debt servicing* 债务利息的支付

ser·vi·ette /ˌsɜːviˈet; *NAmE* ˌsɜːrv-/ *noun* (*BrE*) a piece of cloth or paper used at meals for protecting your clothes and cleaning your lips and fingers 餐巾；餐巾纸 SYN **napkin**

ser·vile /ˈsɜːvaɪl; *NAmE* ˈsɜːrvl; -vaɪl/ *adj.* (*disapproving*) wanting too much to please sb and obey them 奴性的；逢迎的；恭顺的 ▸ **ser·vil·ity** /sɜːˈvɪləti; *NAmE* sɜːrˈv-/ *noun* [U]

serv·ing /ˈsɜːvɪŋ; *NAmE* ˈsɜːrvɪŋ/ *noun* an amount of food for one person（供一个人吃的）一份食物：*This recipe will be enough for four servings.* 本食谱为四人量。

ser·vi·tor /ˈsɜːvɪtə(r); *NAmE* ˈsɜːrv-/ *noun* (*old use*) a male servant 男仆；男侍从

ser·vi·tude /ˈsɜːvɪtjuːd; *NAmE* ˈsɜːrvətuːd/ *noun* [U] (*formal*) the condition of being a SLAVE or being forced to obey another person 奴役（状况）；任人差遣（的状况）SYN **slavery**

servo /ˈsɜːvəʊ; *NAmE* ˈsɜːrvoʊ/ *noun* (*pl.* **-os**) (*specialist*) a part of a machine that controls a larger piece of machinery（机器的）伺服系统，随动系统

ses·ame /ˈsesəmi/ *noun* [U] a tropical plant grown for its seeds and their oil, which are used in cooking 芝麻；脂麻：*sesame seeds* 芝麻粒儿 ➲ SEE ALSO OPEN SESAME

ses·sion 🔑 /ˈseʃn/ *noun* **1** 🔑 [C] a period of time that is spent doing a particular activity 一场；一节；一段时间：*a* ***photo/recording/training, etc. session*** 拍照、录音、训练等时段 ◇ *The course is made up of 12 two-hour sessions.* 这门课总共上 12 次，每次两小时。➲ SEE ALSO JAM SESSION **2** 🔑 [C, U] a formal meeting or series of meetings of a court, a parliament, etc.; a period of time when such meetings are held（法庭的）开庭，开庭期；（议会等的）会议，会期：*a session of the UN General Assembly* 一届联合国大会 ◇ *The court is now* ***in session.*** 法庭现在正在开庭。◇ *The committee met* ***in closed session*** (= with nobody else present). 委员会举行了闭门会议。➲ SEE ALSO QUARTER SESSIONS **3** [C] a school or university year 学年 **4** [C] an occasion when people meet to play music, especially Irish music, in a pub/bar（酒吧里的）演奏会（尤指演奏爱尔兰音乐）

ˈsession musician *noun* a musician who is hired to play on recordings but is not a permanent member of a band（乐队为录音而雇用的）临时乐师

set 🔑 /set/ *verb, noun, adj.*

■ ***verb*** (**set·ting, set, set**)

• PUT/START 放置；开始 **1** 🔑 [T] ~ **sth/sb + adv./prep.** to put sth/sb in a particular place or position 放；置；使处于：*She set a tray down on the table.* 她把托盘放到桌上。◇ *They ate everything that was set in front of them.* 他们把放在面前的东西都吃光了。◇ *The house is set* (= located) *in fifty acres of parkland.* 房子四周是五十英亩开阔的绿地。**2** 🔑 [T] to cause sb/sth to be in a particular state; to start sth happening 使处于某种状况；使开始：~ **sb/sth + adv./prep.** *Her manner immediately* ***set*** *everyone* ***at their ease.*** 她的态度立刻使大家感到轻松了。◇ *He pulled the lever and* ***set*** *the machine* ***in motion.*** 他扳动操纵杆，启动了机器。◇ ~ **sb/sth + adj.** *The hijackers* ***set*** *the hostages* ***free.*** 劫机者释放了人质。◇ ~ **sb/sth doing sth** *Her remarks set me thinking.* 她的话引起了我的深思。

• PLAY/BOOK/MOVIE 戏剧；书；电影 **3** 🔑 [T, usually passive] ~ **sth + adv./prep.** to place the action of a play, novel or film/movie in a particular place, time, etc. 把故事情节安排在；以…为…设置背景：*The novel is set in London in the 1960s.* 这部小说以 20 世纪 60 年代的伦敦为背景。

• CLOCK/MACHINE 钟表；机器 **4** 🔑 [T] ~ **sth** (+ **adv./prep.**) to prepare or arrange sth so that it is ready for use or in position 设置；调整好；安排就绪：*She set the camera on automatic.* 她把照相机调到自动状态。◇ *I set my watch by* (= make it show the same time as) *the TV.* 我按电视对了手表。◇ *Set the alarm for 7 o'clock.* 把闹钟设在 7 点。

• TABLE 餐桌 **5** 🔑 [T] ~ **a/the table** (**for sb/sth**) to arrange knives, forks, etc. on a table for a meal 摆放餐具：*Could you set the table for dinner?* 你把餐具摆好，准备开饭，好吗？◇ *The table was set for six guests.* 桌上摆放了六位客人的餐具。

• JEWELLERY 珠宝 **6** [T, usually passive] to put a PRECIOUS STONE into a piece of jewellery 镶嵌：~ **A in B** *She had the sapphire set in a gold ring.* 她请人把蓝宝石镶嵌到一枚金戒指上。◇ ~ **B with A** *Her bracelet was set with emeralds.* 她的手镯上镶有绿宝石。

• ARRANGE 安排 **7** 🔑 [T] ~ **sth** to arrange or fix sth; to decide on sth 安排；确定；决定：*They haven't set a date for their wedding yet.* 他们还没有确定婚礼日期。◇

The government has set strict limits on public spending this year. 今年，政府对公共开支规定了严格的限额。

• **EXAMPLE/STANDARD, ETC.** 榜样、规范等 **8** [T] **~ sth** to fix sth so that others copy it or try to achieve it 树立；创立；开创：*This could **set a new fashion**.* 这或许会开创一种新时尚。◇ *They **set high standards** of customer service.* 他们制订了严格的客户服务标准。◇ *I am unwilling to **set a precedent**.* 我不想开先例。◇ *She **set a new world record** for the high jump.* 她创造了新的跳高世界纪录。◇ *I rely on you to **set a good example**.* 我指望你来树立一个好榜样。

• **WORK/TASK** 工作；任务 **9** [T] **~ sth (for sb) | ~ sb (to do sth)** to give sb a piece of work, a task, etc. 布置；分配；指派：**~ sth** *Who will be setting* (= writing the questions for) *the French exam?* 谁出法语试题？◇ **~ sth for sth** *What books have been set* (= are to be studied) *for the English course?* 英语课指定了要用哪些书？◇ **~ sth for sb/yourself** *She's set a difficult task for herself.* 她给自己安排了一项艰巨任务。◇ **~ sb/yourself sth** *She's set herself a difficult task.* 她给自己安排了一项艰巨任务。◇ **~ sb/yourself to do sth** *I've set myself to finish the job by the end of the month.* 我要求自己在月底以前完成这项工作。

• **BECOME FIRM** 凝固 **10** [I] to become firm or hard 凝固；凝结：*Leave the concrete to set for a few hours.* 让混凝土凝固几小时。◇ **+ adj.** *The glue had set hard.* 胶已经粘得很紧。

• **FACE** 脸 **11** [T, usually passive] **~ sth** to fix your face into a firm expression 使现出坚定的表情：*Her jaw was set in a determined manner.* 她下巴紧绷着，一副决不动摇的样子。

• **HAIR** 头发 **12** [T] **~ sth** to arrange sb's hair while it is wet so that it dries in a particular style 固定发型；做头发：*She had her hair washed and set.* 她去洗了头，做了发型。

• **BONE** 骨头 **13** [T, I] **~ (sth)** to put a broken bone into a fixed position and hold it there, so that it will heal; to heal in this way 把（断骨）复位；接（骨）：*The surgeon set her broken arm.* 医生给她接上了手臂上的断骨。

• **FOR PRINTING** 为印刷 **14** [T] **~ sth** (*specialist*) to use a machine or computer to arrange writing and images on pages in order to prepare a book, newspaper, etc. for printing 排版 ➲ SEE ALSO TYPESETTER

• **WORDS TO MUSIC** 为歌词谱曲 **15** [T] **~ sth (to sth)** to write music to go with words 为…谱曲；给…配乐：*Schubert set many poems to music.* 舒伯特为许多诗歌谱了曲。

• **OF SUN/MOON** 太阳；月亮 **16** [I] to go down below the HORIZON 落（下）：*We sat and watched the sun setting.* 我们坐着看太阳渐渐落下去。**OPP** **rise** ➲ SEE ALSO SUNSET *n.*

IDM **HELP** Idioms containing **set** are at the entries for the nouns and adjectives in the idioms, for example **set the pace** is at **pace** *n.* 含 set 的习语，都可在该等习语中的名词及形容词相关词条找到，如 set the pace 在词条 pace 的名词部分。

PHR V **'set about sb** (*BrE, old-fashioned, informal*) to attack sb 攻击；抨击 **'set about sth | ˌset about 'doing sth** [no passive] to start doing sth 开始做；着手做：*She set about the business of cleaning the house.* 她动手打扫起房子来。◇ *We need to set about finding a solution.* 我们得着手寻找一个解决办法。

set sb a'gainst sb to make sb oppose a friend, relative, etc. 使某人反对（朋友、亲人等）：*She accused her husband of setting the children against her.* 她指责丈夫唆使孩子们跟她作对。**set sth (off) against sth 1** to judge sth by comparing good or positive qualities with bad or negative ones 权衡利弊（或优缺点）：*Set against the benefits of the new technology, there is also a strong possibility that jobs will be lost.* 权衡利弊，新技术的确有种种好处，但也很可能使一些人失去工作。**2** (*finance* 财) to record sth as a business cost as a way of reducing the amount of tax you must pay 把…按营业成本记账以降低（税额）：*to set capital costs off against tax* 把资金成本按营业成本记账以减税

ˌset sb/sth a'part (from sb/sth) to make sb/sth different from or better than others 使与众不同；使突出；使优于…：*Her elegant style sets her apart from other journalists.* 她的高雅风格使她与其他记者截然不同。**ˌset sth↔a'part (for sth)** [usually passive] to keep sth for a special use or purpose 留出，拨出（专用）：*Two rooms were set apart for use as libraries.* 留出两个房间作为图书室。

ˌset sth↔a'side 1 to move sth to one side until you need it 把…放到一旁（或搁到一边）**2** to save or keep money or time for a particular purpose 省出，留出（钱或时间）：*She tries to set aside some money every month.* 她每个月都尽量存点钱。**3** to not consider sth, because other things are more important 暂时不考虑（或放一放）**SYN** **disregard**：*Let's set aside my personal feelings for now.* 目前咱们就不要顾及我的个人感情了。**4** (*law* 律) to state that a decision made by a court is not legally valid 撤销（法院的判决）；宣布无效：*The verdict was set aside by the Appeal Court.* 上诉法庭驳回了那个裁决。

ˌset sth/sb↔'back to delay the progress of sth/sb by a particular time 使推迟；耽误；使延误：*The bad weather set back the building programme by several weeks.* 天气恶劣，建筑计划延误了几个星期。➲ RELATED NOUN SETBACK **ˌset sb 'back sth** [no passive] (*informal*) to cost sb a particular amount of money 使花费；使破费：*The repairs could set you back over £200.* 这次修理大概得花你 200 多英镑。**ˌset sth 'back (from sth)** [usually passive] to place sth, especially a building, at a distance from sth 使（建筑物等）与…拉开距离：*The house is set well back from the road.* 这座房子离公路挺远。

ˌset sb↔'down (*BrE*) (of a bus or train, or its driver 公共汽车、火车或司机) to stop and allow sb to get off 让某人下车：*Passengers may be set down and picked up only at the official stops.* 乘客只有在正式车站方可上下车。**ˌset sth↔'down 1** to write sth down on paper in order to record it 写下；记下；登记 **2** to give sth as a rule, principle, etc. 制定，规定（规则、原则等）：*The standards were set down by the governing body.* 这些标准是由管理机构制定的。

ˌset 'forth (*literary*) to start a journey 出发；动身；启程 **ˌset sth↔'forth** (*formal*) to present sth or make it known 陈述；阐明 **SYN** **expound**：*The President set forth his views in a television broadcast.* 总统在电视讲话中阐述了自己的观点。

ˌset 'in (of rain, bad weather, infection, etc. 雨、恶劣天气、感染等) to begin and seem likely to continue 到来；开始：*The rain seemed to have set in for the day.* 这雨好像要下一天了。**ˌset sth 'in/'into sth** [usually passive] to fasten sth into a flat surface so that it does not stick out from it 把…装进…（或镶入…中）：*a plaque set into the wall* 嵌在墙上的牌匾

ˌset 'off to begin a journey 出发；动身；启程：*We set off for London just after ten.* 刚过十点，我们就动身上伦敦去了。**ˌset sth↔'off 1** to make a bomb, etc. explode 使（炸弹等）爆炸：*A gang of boys were setting off fireworks in the street.* 一帮男孩子正在街上放烟火。**2** to make an alarm start ringing 使（警报）响起；拉响（警报）：*Opening this door will set off the alarm.* 一开这道门，警铃就会响。**3** to start a process or series of events 引发；激起：*Panic on the stock market set off a wave of selling.* 股市恐慌引发了一轮抛售潮。**4** to make sth more noticeable or attractive by being placed near it 衬托；使显得更突出（或更漂亮）：*That blouse sets off the blue of her eyes.* 那件上衣衬托出了她的蓝眼睛。**ˌset sb 'off (doing sth)** to make sb start doing sth such as laughing, crying or talking 使某人笑（或哭、说等）起来

'set on/upon sb [usually passive] to attack sb suddenly 突然攻击；袭击：*I opened the gate, and was immediately set on by a large dog.* 我一开门，一条大狗就迎面扑来。**'set sb/sth on sb** to make a person or an animal attack sb suddenly 使突然攻击；使袭击：*The farmer threatened to set his dogs on us.* 农场主威胁要放出狗来咬我们。

ˌset 'out 1 to leave a place and begin a journey 出发；动身；启程：*They set out on the last stage of their journey.* 他们动身踏上最后一段行程。**2** to begin a job, task, etc. with a particular aim or goal （怀着目标）开始工作，展开任务：*She set out to break the world record.* 她一心努力要打破世界纪录。◇ *They succeeded in what they set out to do.* 他们实现了既定的目标。**ˌset sth↔'out 1** to arrange or display things 安排；摆放；陈列：*Her work is always very well set out.* 她总是把工作安排得很有条理。**2** to present ideas, facts, etc. in an organized way, in speech or writing （有条理地）陈述，阐明：*He set out his*

S

objections to the plan. 他陈述了他对这个计划的反对意见。◇ *She set out the reasons for her resignation in a long letter.* 她写了一封长信说明自己辞职的原因。

ˌset ˈto (*old-fashioned, informal*) to begin doing sth in a busy or determined way 起劲地干起来；毅然开始做

ˌset sb↔ˈup 1 to provide sb with the money that they need in order to do sth 资助，经济上扶植（某人）：*A bank loan helped to set him up in business.* 他靠一笔银行贷款做起了生意。 **2** (*informal*) to make sb healthier, stronger, more lively, etc. 使更健康（或强壮、活泼等）：*The break from work really set me up for the new year.* 放下工作稍事休息，的确使我更有精力在新的一年大干一场了。 **3** (*informal*) to trick sb, especially by making them appear guilty of sth 诬陷，冤枉（某人）；栽赃：*He denied the charges, saying the police had set him up.* 他否认那些指控，说警察冤枉他了。 ➲ RELATED NOUN SET-UP

ˌset sth↔ˈup 1 to build sth or put sth somewhere 建起；设立；设置：*The police set up roadblocks on routes out of the city.* 警察在城外的路上设置了路障。 **2** to make a piece of equipment or a machine ready for use 安装好，装配好，调试好（设备或机器）：*She set up her stereo in her bedroom.* 她把立体声音响装在了卧室里。 **3** to arrange for sth to happen 安排；策划：*I've set up a meeting for Friday.* 我已安排好在星期五开会。 **4** to create sth or start it 创建；建立；开办：*to set up a business* 开办公司 ◇ *A fund will be set up for the dead men's families.* 将为死者家属设立一项基金。 **5** to start a process or a series of events 引发；产生：*The slump on Wall Street set up a chain reaction in stock markets around the world.* 华尔街股价暴跌在全球股票市场上引起了连锁反应。 ➲ RELATED NOUN SET-UP **ˌset (yourself) ˈup (as sb)** to start running a business 立业；开始从事：*She took out a bank loan and set up on her own.* 她从银行贷了一笔款，自己干起来了。◇ *After leaving college, he set himself up as a freelance photographer.* 大学毕业后，他干起了自由摄影师。

■ ***noun***

• **GROUP** 一组 **1** [C] **~ (of sth)** a group of similar things that belong together in some way 一套，一副，一组（类似的东西）：*a set of six chairs* 六把成套的椅子 ◇ *a complete set of her novels* 一整套她的小说 ◇ *a set of false teeth* 一副假牙 ◇ *a new set of rules to learn* 要学的一套新规则 ◇ *You can borrow my keys—I have a spare set.* 你可以借用我的钥匙，我还有一套。 ➲ SEE ALSO TEA SET **2** [C] a group of objects used together, for example for playing a game 一套，一副，一组（配套使用的东西）：*a chess set* 一副国际象棋 **3** [C+sing./pl. v.] (*sometimes disapproving*) a group of people who have similar interests and spend a lot of time together socially 一伙（或一帮、一群）人；阶层；团伙：*the smart set* (= rich, fashionable people) 富裕时尚一族 ◇ *Dublin's literary set* 都柏林的文学圈子 ➲ SEE ALSO JET SET

• **TV/RADIO** 电视机；收音机 **4** [C] a piece of equipment for receiving television or radio signals 电视机；收音机

• **FOR PLAY/MOVIE** 戏剧；电影 **5** [C] the SCENERY used for a play, film/movie, etc. 布景：*We need volunteers to help build and paint the set.* 我们需要一些自愿帮忙搭建和粉刷布景的人。 **6** [C, U] a place where a play is performed or part of a film/movie is filmed 舞台；摄影场：*The cast must all be on (the) set by 7 in the morning.* 全体演员必须在早上 7 点钟到场。 ➲ WORDFINDER NOTE AT DRAMA, STAGE

• **IN SPORT** 体育运动 **7** [C] one section of a match in games such as TENNIS or VOLLEYBALL（网球的）盘；（排球比赛等的）局：*She won **in straight sets*** (= without losing a set). 她一盘未失，连连得胜。

• **MATHEMATICS** 数学 **8** [C] a group of things that have a shared quality 集；集合：*set theory* 集论

• **POP MUSIC** 流行音乐 **9** [C] a series of songs or pieces of music that a musician or group performs at a concert 一组歌曲（或乐曲）

• **CLASS** 班 **10** [C] (*BrE*) a group of school students with a similar ability in a particular subject（在某学科上能力相当的）一批学生：*She's in the top set for French.* 她的法语成绩名列前茅。

• **OF FACE/BODY** 脸；身体 **11** [sing.] **~ of sth** the way in which sb's face or body is fixed in a particular expression, especially one showing determination（尤指坚定的）姿势，姿态，神情：*She admired the firm set of his jaw.* 她喜欢他那副紧绷着下巴的刚毅神态。

• **HAIR** 头发 **12** [sing.] an act of arranging hair in a particular style while it is wet 头发的定型；做头发：***A shampoo and set** costs £15.* 洗头并做发型共 15 英镑。

• **BECOMING FIRM** 凝固 **13** [sing.] the state of becoming firm or solid 凝固；凝结

• **ANIMAL'S HOME** 兽穴 **14** [C] = SETT

• **PLANT** 植物 **15** [C] a young plant, SHOOT etc. for planting（供移植的）秧苗，插枝，球茎：*onion sets* 洋葱苗

■ ***adj.***

• **IN POSITION** 处于某位置 **1** in a particular position 位于（或处于）…的：*a house set in 40 acres of parkland* 一所坐落在一片 40 英亩开阔绿地上的房子 ◇ *He had close-set eyes.* 他的两眼靠得很近。

• **PLANNED** 安排好 **2** [usually before noun] planned or fixed 安排好的；确定的；固定的：*Each person was given set jobs to do.* 分配给每个人的工作都是预先确定好的。◇ *The school funds a set number of free places.* 学校资助固定数目的免费生。◇ *Mornings in our house always follow a set pattern.* 在我们家，每天早上的生活总是遵循一种固定的模式。 ➲ SEE ALSO SET BOOK

• **OPINIONS/IDEAS** 意见；观念 **3** not likely to change 固定的；顽固的；固执的：***set ideas/opinions/views** on how to teach* 不变的教学思想 / 主张 / 观点 ◇ *As people get older, they **get set in their ways**.* 随着年龄的增长，人就积习成性。

• **MEAL** 饭菜 **4** [only before noun] (of a meal in a restaurant 餐馆的饭菜) having a fixed price and a limited choice of dishes 套（餐）的：*a **set dinner/lunch/meal*** 一份晚餐 / 午餐套餐；一份套餐 ◇ *Shall we have the **set menu**?* 我们吃套餐好吗？

• **LIKELY/READY** 大概会；准备好 **5** likely to do sth; ready for sth or to do sth 有可能的；做好准备的：**~ for sth** *The team looks set for victory.* 看来这个队能赢。◇ **~ to do sth** *Interest rates look set to rise again.* 看样子利率又要提高了。◇ *Be set to leave by 10 o'clock.* 做好准备，最晚 10 点钟走。 ➲ LANGUAGE BANK AT EXPECT

• **FACE** 脸色 **6** [usually before noun] (of a person's expression 神情) fixed; not natural 呆板的；不自然的：*a set smile* 僵硬的笑容 ◇ *His face took on a set expression.* 他脸上现出凝滞的神态。

IDM **be (dead) set against sth/against doing sth** to be strongly opposed to sth 强烈反对（做）某事：*Why are you so dead set against the idea?* 你为什么那样死命地反对这个主意呢？ **be ˈset on sth/on doing sth** to want to do or have sth very much; to be determined to do sth 一心想做；决心做；十分想得到 ➲ MORE AT MARK *n.*

ˈset-aside *noun* [U] a system in which the government pays farmers not to use some of their land for growing crops; the land that the farmers are paid not to use 退耕补贴制度（由政府补贴，鼓励农民退耕部分耕地）；退耕地

set·back /ˈsetbæk/ *noun* a difficulty or problem that delays or prevents sth, or makes a situation worse 挫折；阻碍：*The team **suffered a major setback** when their best player was injured.* 最优秀的队员受了伤，使得这支队伍的实力大打折扣。◇ *The breakdown in talks represents a temporary setback in the peace process.* 谈判破裂意味着和平进程暂时受阻。

ˌset ˈbook (*also* **ˌset ˈtext**) *noun* (*both BrE*) a book that students must study for a particular exam（考试）指定课本，指定用书

seth /seɪt/ *noun* (*IndE*) **1** a MERCHANT (= a person who sells goods in large quantities) or BANKER (= a person with an important job in a bank) 商人；银行家 **2** a rich man 富人；有钱人 **3** a title added to a name to indicate high social status 塞斯（表示社会地位高的头衔）

ˌset ˈphrase *noun* a phrase that is always used in the same form 固定词组；成语：*Don't worry about the grammar, just learn this as a set phrase.* 别管语法，只要把这个作为固定词组来学习即可。

ˌset ˈpiece *noun* **1** a part of a play, film/movie, piece of music, etc. that has a well-known pattern or style, and is used to create a particular effect（戏剧、电影、音乐等中的）固定套路 **2** a move in a sports game that is well planned and practised（体育比赛的）攻防套路

ˌset ˈpoint *noun* (especially in TENNIS 尤指网球) a point that, if won by a player, will win them the SET (7) 盘点（再赢一分即赢得该盘）

ˈset square (*BrE*) (*NAmE* **tri·angle**) *noun* an instrument for drawing straight lines and angles, made from a flat piece of plastic or metal in the shape of a triangle with one angle of 90° 三角板；三角尺 ➲ VISUAL VOCAB PAGE V72

sett (*also* **set**) /set/ *noun* a hole in the ground where a BADGER lives 獾穴

set·tee /seˈtiː/ *noun* (*BrE*) a long comfortable seat with a back and arms, for two or more people to sit on 长沙发 SYN **sofa, couch**

set·ter /ˈsetə(r)/ *noun* **1** a large dog with long hair, sometimes used in hunting. There are several types of setter. 蹲伏猎狗，雪达犬（体大毛长，有几个品种） **2** (often in compounds 常构成复合词) a person who sets sth 制订者；规定者；安排者：*a quiz setter* 命题人 ➲ SEE ALSO JET-SETTER, PACESETTER, TRENDSETTER

set·ting /ˈsetɪŋ/ *noun* **1** a set of surroundings; the place at which sth happens 环境；背景：*a **rural/an ideal/a beautiful/an idyllic, etc. setting*** 乡村、理想、优美、田园等的环境 ◇ *It was **the perfect setting** for a wonderful Christmas.* 环境气氛无可挑剔，正是一个美好的圣诞节所需要的。➲ SYNONYMS AT ENVIRONMENT **2** the place and time at which the action of a play, novel, etc. takes place（戏剧、小说等的）情节背景：*short stories with a contemporary setting* 以当代生活为背景的短篇小说 **3** a position at which the controls on a machine can be set, to set the speed, height, temperature, etc.（机器上调节速度、高度、温度等的）挡，级，点：*The performance of the engine was tested at different settings.* 对引擎的性能在不同的挡上做了试验。 **4 settings** [pl.] the place on a computer or other electronic device where you can choose the way that it works or looks; the particular choices that you make（计算机或其他电子装置的）设置区，设定：*To change the size of the font, go to Settings.* 要更改字体的大小，请前往"设置"。 **5** (*music* 音) music written to go with a poem, etc.（为诗等谱的）曲：*Schubert's setting of a poem by Goethe* 舒伯特为歌德的一首诗谱的曲 **6** a piece of metal in which a PRECIOUS STONE is fixed to form a piece of jewellery（镶嵌宝石的）底座，底板，托板 **7** a complete set of equipment for eating with (knife, fork, spoon, glass, etc.) for one person, arranged on a table（摆在桌上供一人用的）一套餐具：*a place setting* 一个座位的整套餐具

set·tle 🔑 /ˈsetl/ *verb, noun*

■ ***verb***

• **END ARGUMENT** 结束纷争 **1** 🔑 [T, I] ~ (**sth**) to put an end to an argument or a disagreement 结束（争论、争端等）；解决（分歧、纠纷等）：*to **settle a dispute/an argument/a matter*** 解决争端 / 争论 / 事情 ◇ *It's time you **settled your differences** with your father.* 现在你该解决同你父亲之间的分歧了。◇ *There is pressure on the unions to settle.* 工会组织面临消除纷争的压力。◇ *The company has agreed to **settle out of court*** (= come to an agreement without going to court). 那家公司同意庭外和解。

• **DECIDE/ARRANGE** 决定；安排 **2** 🔑 [T, often passive] to decide or arrange sth finally（最终）决定，确定，安排好：**~ sth** *It's all settled—we're leaving on the nine o'clock plane.* 一切都定下来了，我们乘九点的航班走。◇ *Bob will be there? **That settles it**. I'm not coming.* 鲍勃会去吗？那好，我就不去了。◇ *He had to **settle his affairs*** (= arrange all his personal business) *in Paris before he could return home.* 他得把他在巴黎的事情处理好才能回家。◇ **it is settled that…** *It's been settled that we leave on the nine o'clock plane.* 已经定好我们乘坐九点的航班离开。

• **CHOOSE PERMANENT HOME** 选择永久住地 **3** 🔑 [I] **+ adv./prep.** to make a place your permanent home 定居：*She settled in Vienna after her father's death.* 父亲死后，她就在维也纳定居了。 **4** 🔑 [T, usually passive, I] **~ sth | + adv./prep.** (of a group of people 一批人) to make your permanent home in a country or an area as COLONISTS 殖民；作为移民在殖民地定居：*This region was settled by the Dutch in the nineteenth century.* 荷兰人于 19 世纪来到这一地区定居。➲ WORDFINDER NOTE AT EXPLORE

• **INTO COMFORTABLE POSITION/STATE** 进入舒适的位置 / 状态 **5** [I, T] to make yourself or sb else comfortable in a new position 使处于舒适的位置：**~ (back) (+ adv./prep.)** *Ellie settled back in her seat.* 埃利舒适地靠着椅背坐下。◇ **~ sb/yourself (+ adv./prep.)** *He settled himself comfortably in his usual chair.* 他在自己惯常坐的椅子上舒舒服服地坐下来。◇ *I settled her on the sofa and put a blanket over her.* 我把她放在沙发上安顿好，给她盖了一条毯子。 **6** [T] **~ sth + adv./prep.** to put sth carefully in a position so that it does not move 把…放好；安放：*She settled the blanket around her knees.* 她用毯子裹住膝盖。 **7** [I, T] to become or make sb/sth become calm or relaxed（使）平静下来，安静下来，定下心来：*The baby wouldn't settle.* 婴儿安静不下来。◇ **~ sb/sth** *I took a pill to help settle my nerves.* 我吃了一片药，好镇定一下神经。◇*This should settle your stomach.* 这样你的胃应该就不难受了。

• **COME TO REST** 停留 **8** [I] **~ (on/over sth)** to fall from above and come to rest on sth; to stay for some time on sth 降落；停留：*Dust had settled on everything.* 到处落满灰尘。◇ *Two birds settled on the fence.* 两只鸟落在篱笆上。◇ *I don't think the snow will settle* (= remain on the ground without melting). 我看这雪存不住。◇ *His gaze settled on her face.* 他的目光落在她脸上。

• **SINK DOWN** 沉降 **9** [I, T] **~ (sth)** to sink slowly down; to make sth do this（使）沉降，下陷，变得密实：*The contents of the package may have settled in transit.* 包裹里的东西可能在运输途中摇密实了。

• **PAY MONEY** 付钱 **10** [T, I] to pay the money that you owe 付清（欠款）；结算；结账：**~ sth** *Please settle your bill before leaving the hotel.* 请您先结账再离开旅馆。◇ *The insurance company is refusing to settle her claim.* 保险公司拒付她提出的索赔款项。◇ **~ (up) (with sb)** *Let me settle with you for the meal.* 我来把饭费付给你。◇ *I'll pay now—we can settle up later.* 现在我来付账，咱们以后再算。

IDM **settle a ˈscore/an acˈcount (with sb) | settle an old ˈscore** to hurt or punish sb who has harmed or cheated you in the past（和某人）算账，清算旧账；报复（某人）：*'Who would do such a thing?' 'Maybe someone with an old score to settle.'* "谁做得出这样的事呢？" "也许是结有宿怨的人吧。" ➲ MORE AT DUST *n.*

PHR V **ˌsettle ˈdown 1** 🔑 to get into a comfortable position, either sitting or lying 舒适地坐下（或躺下）：*I settled down with a book.* 我舒舒服服地坐下看书。 **2** 🔑 to start to have a quieter way of life, living in one place（在某地）定居下来，过安定的生活：*When are you going to get married and settle down?* 你打算什么时候成家，安定下来？ ➲ COLLOCATIONS AT AGE **ˌsettle ˈdown | ˌsettle sb↔ˈdown** 🔑 to become or make sb become calm, less excited, etc.（使某人）安静下来，平静下来：*It always takes the class a while to settle down at the start of the lesson.* 那个班一上课总得过一会儿才能安静下来。 **settle (down) to sth** to begin to give your attention to sth 开始认真对待；定下心来做：*They finally settled down to a discussion of the main issues.* 他们终于开始讨论一些主要问题了。◇ *He found it hard to settle to his work.* 他觉得定不下心来工作。 **ˈsettle for sth** to accept sth that is not exactly what you want but is the best that is available 勉强接受；将就：*In the end they had to settle for a draw.* 最后，他们只好接受平局的结果。◇ *I couldn't afford the house I really wanted, so I had to **settle for second best**.* 我真心想要的房子我买不起，所以只得退而求其次了。 **ˌsettle ˈin | ˌsettle ˈinto sth** to move into a new home, job, etc. and start to feel comfortable there 安顿下来；习惯于（新居）；适应（新工作）：*How are the kids settling into their new school?* 孩子们在新学校习惯了吗？ **ˈsettle on sth** to choose or make a decision about sth after thinking about it 选定；决定：*Have you settled on a name for the baby yet?* 你给孩子起好名字没有？ **ˈsettle sth on sb** (*law* 律) to formally arrange to give money or property to sb, especially in a WILL 转让（钱财）；（尤指在遗嘱中）赠与

S

■ *noun* an old-fashioned piece of furniture with a long wooden seat and a high back and arms, often also with a box for storing things under the seat 高背长椅（老式木家具，有扶手，座下多带柜）

set·tled /'setld/ *adj.* **1** not likely to change or move 不大可能变动的；稳定的：*settled weather* 持续不变的天气 ◇ *a settled way of life* 安定的生活方式 **2** comfortable and happy with your home, job, way of life, etc. 舒适自在的；（对住所、工作、生活方式等）习惯的 OPP **unsettled**

settle·ment /'setlmənt/ *noun* **1** [C] an official agreement that ends an argument between two people or groups （解决纷争的）协议：*to* ***negotiate a peace settlement*** 就和平协议进行谈判 ◇ *The management and unions have* ***reached a settlement*** *over new working conditions.* 资方和工会已就新的工作条件达成协议。◇ *an* ***out-of-court settlement*** (= money that is paid to sb or an agreement that is made to stop sb going to court) 庭外和解 **2** [U] the action of reaching an agreement 解决；处理：*the settlement of a dispute* 争端的解决 **3** [C] (*law* 律) the conditions, or a document stating the conditions, on which money or property is given to sb （关于钱财转让的）协议（书）：*a* ***divorce/marriage/property, etc. settlement*** 离婚、结婚、财产等协议 **4** [U] the action of paying back money that you owe （欠款的）支付，偿付，结算：*the settlement of a debt* 债务的偿还 ◇ *a cheque* ***in settlement*** *of a bill* 用于结账的支票 **5** [C] a place where people have come to live and make their homes, especially where few or no people lived before （尤指拓荒安家的）定居点：*signs of an Iron Age settlement* 铁器时代村落遗址 **6** [U] the process of people making their homes in a place 移民；殖民；开拓：*the settlement of the American West* 美国西部的开拓过程

'settlement house *noun* (*especially NAmE*) a public building in an area of a large city that has social problems, that provides social services such as advice and training to the people who live there 社区福利服务之家，街坊文教馆（为邻里提供多方面服务）

set·tler /'setlə(r)/ *noun* a person who goes to live in a new country or region 移民；殖民者：*white settlers in Africa* 非洲的白人移民

,set-'to *noun* [sing.] (*informal, especially BrE*) a small fight or an argument 打架；争吵

,set-,top 'box *noun* a device that changes a digital television signal into a form which can be seen on an ordinary television 机顶盒（数字电视转接装置，把数字电视信号转换成普通电视信号）

'set-up *noun* [usually sing.] (*informal*) **1** a way of organizing sth; a system 组织；机构；建制；体制：*I've only been here a couple of weeks and I don't really know the set-up.* 我刚来几个星期，对这里的组织情况不大了解。**2** a situation in which sb tricks you or makes it seem as if you have done sth wrong 陷害；栽赃：*He didn't steal the goods. It was a set-up.* 那些商品不是他偷的，这是栽赃。

sevak /'seɪvæk/ *noun* (*IndE*) **1** a male servant 男仆；男佣 **2** a male SOCIAL WORKER 男社会福利工作者；男社工

seven /'sevn/ *number* 7 七 HELP There are examples of how to use numbers at the entry for **five**. 数词用法示例见 five 条。

IDM **the seven-year 'itch** (*informal, humorous*) the desire for new sexual experience that is thought to be felt after seven years of marriage 七年之痒（婚后七年另觅新欢的欲望）➲ MORE AT SIX

the ,seven 'seas *noun* [pl.] all of the earth's oceans 世界所有海洋

the ,Seven 'Sisters *noun* [pl.] **1** the Pleiades, a group of seven stars 昴星团（七颗亮星）；七姊妹星团 **2** a group of seven traditional women's (or formerly women's) universities in the eastern US with high academic standards and a high social status 七姐妹学院（美国东部学业标准高、有声望的七所传统女子学院）

seven·teen /,sevn'tiːn/ *number* 17 十七 ▶ **seven·teenth** /,sevn'tiːnθ/ *ordinal number, noun* HELP There are examples of how to use ordinal numbers at the entry for **fifth**. 序数词用法示例见 fifth 条。

sev·enth /'sevnθ/ *ordinal number, noun*
■ *ordinal number* 7th 第七 HELP There are examples of how to use ordinal numbers at the entry for **fifth**. 序数词用法示例见 fifth 条。

IDM **in seventh 'heaven** extremely happy 身处七重天；极乐；极为幸福：*Now that he's been promoted he's in seventh heaven.* 他得到擢升，简直乐上天了。

■ *noun* each of seven equal parts of sth 七分之一

Seventh-Day Adventist /,sevnθ deɪ 'ædvəntɪst/ *noun* a member of a Christian religious group that believes that Christ will soon return to Earth 基督复临安息日会信徒

sev·enty /'sevnti/ **1** *number* 70 七十 **2** *noun* **the seventies** [pl.] numbers, years or temperatures from 70 to 79 七十几；七十年代 ▶ **sev·en·ti·eth** /'sevntiəθ/ *ordinal number, noun* HELP There are examples of how to use ordinal numbers at the entry for **fifth**. 序数词用法示例见 fifth 条。

IDM **in your 'seventies** between the ages of 70 and 79 * 70 多岁

sever /'sevə(r)/ *verb* (*formal*) **1** to cut sth into two pieces; to cut sth off sth 切开；割断；切下；割下：**~ sth** *to sever a rope* 割断绳子 ◇ *a severed artery* 切断的动脉 ◇ **~ sth from sth** *His hand was severed from his arm.* 他的手从胳膊上截断了。**2 ~ sth** to completely end a relationship or all communication with sb 断绝；中断 SYN **break off**：*The two countries have* ***severed*** *all diplomatic* ***links***. 两国断绝了一切外交关系。

sev·eral /'sevrəl/ *det., pron., adj.*
■ *det., pron.* more than two but not very many 几个；数个；一些：*Several letters arrived this morning.* 今天上午来了几封信。◇ *He's written several books about India.* 他写过几本关于印度的书。◇ *Several more people than usual came to the meeting.* 到会的人比平时多了几个。◇ *If you're looking for a photo of Alice you'll find several in here.* 你要是想找艾丽斯的照片的话，这儿有几张。◇ *Several of the paintings were destroyed in the fire.* 那些画有好几幅被大火烧毁了。
■ *adj.* (*formal*) separate 各自的；分别的：*They said goodbye and went their* ***several ways***. 他们道别后，便各自走了。

sev·er·al·ly /'sevrəli/ *adv.* (*formal* or *law* 律) separately 各自；分别：*Tenants are* ***jointly and severally*** *liable for payment of the rent.* 租金由承租人共同且分别承担。

sev·er·ance /'sevərəns/ *noun* [sing., U] (*formal*) **1** the act of ending a connection or relationship 断绝；中断：*the severance of diplomatic relations* 外交关系的断绝 **2** the act of ending sb's work contract 解雇；辞退：*employees given notice of severance* 接到解聘通知的雇员 ◇ ***severance pay/terms*** 解雇金；解雇条件

se·vere /sɪ'vɪə(r); *NAmE* -'vɪr/ *adj.* (**se·verer, se·ver·est**)
• **VERY BAD** 非常不好 **1** extremely bad or serious 极为恶劣的；十分严重的：*a severe handicap* 严重残疾 ◇ *His injuries are severe.* 他的伤很重。◇ *severe weather conditions* 恶劣的天气情况 ◇ *a severe winter* (= one during which the weather conditions are extremely bad) 严冬 ◇ *The party suffered severe losses during the last election.* 该党在上次选举中遭到惨败。◇ *a severe shortage of qualified staff* 合格员工的严重短缺
• **PUNISHMENT** 惩罚 **2** **~ (on/with sb)** punishing sb in an extreme way when they break a particular set of rules 严厉的；重的 SYN **harsh**：*The courts are becoming more severe on young offenders.* 法庭对青少年犯罪者的处罚趋于严厉。◇ ***a severe punishment/sentence*** 重罚；重判
• **NOT KIND** 不和善 **3** not kind or sympathetic and showing disapproval of sb/sth 严厉的；苛刻的 SYN **stern**：*a severe expression* 严厉的表情 ◇ *She was a severe woman who seldom smiled.* 她是个严肃的女人，脸上很少出现笑容。
• **VERY DIFFICULT** 非常困难 **4** extremely difficult and requiring a lot of skill or ability 艰难的；艰巨的；难度很大的 SYN **stiff**：*The marathon is a severe test of stamina.* 马拉松赛跑是对耐力的严峻考验。

S

• STYLE/APPEARANCE/CLOTHING 风格；外貌；衣着 **5** (*disapproving*) extremely plain and lacking any decoration 过于简朴的：*Modern furniture is a little too severe for my taste.* 现代家具有点过于简朴，我不大喜欢。◇ *Her hair was short and severe.* 她的头发不长，也没有花样。

▸ **se·vere·ly** adv.：*severely disabled* 严重残疾的 ◇ *areas severely affected by unemployment* 深受失业影响的地区 ◇ *Anyone breaking the law will be severely punished.* 违法者将受到严惩。◇ *a severely critical report* 一篇措辞严厉的批评报道 ◇ *Her hair was tied severely in a bun.* 她的头发简单地盘成了一个发髻。 **se·ver·ity** /sɪ'verəti/ noun [U]：*A prison sentence should match the severity of the crime.* 刑期长短要和罪行轻重一致。◇ *The chances of a full recovery will depend on the severity of her injuries.* 能否彻底康复取决于她受伤的严重程度。◇ *the severity of the problem* 问题的严重性 ◇ *He frowned with mock severity.* 他沉下脸来，装出一副严厉的样子。◇ *The elaborate facade contrasts strongly with the severity of the interior.* 精致的门面同室内的简朴形成强烈反差。

sev·ika /'seɪvɪkə/ noun (*IndE*) **1** a female servant 女仆；女佣 **2** a female SOCIAL WORKER 女社会福利工作者；女社工

Sev·ille orange /ˌsevɪl 'ɒrɪndʒ; *NAmE* 'ɔːr-; 'ɑːr-/ noun a type of bitter orange, used in making MARMALADE 酸橙（用于制酸果酱）

sew /səʊ; *NAmE* soʊ/ verb (**sewed**, **sewn** /səʊn; *NAmE* soʊn/ or **sewed**, **sewed**) **1** [I, T] to use a needle and thread to make STITCHES in cloth 缝；做针线活：*My mother taught me how to sew.* 我母亲教我做针线。◇ *to sew by hand/machine* 手工 / 机器缝制 ◇ ~ **sth** *to sew a seam* 缝接缝 **2** [T] to make, repair or attach sth using a needle and thread 缝制；缝补；缝上：~ **sth** *She sews all her own clothes.* 她所有的衣服都是自己缝的。◇ ~ **sth on** *Can you sew a button on for me?* 你能给我钉个扣子吗？◇ *Surgeons were able to sew the finger back on.* 外科医生把断指接上了。

WORDFINDER 联想词：baste, bind, embroidery, hem, lining, seam, stitch, tack, thread

PHR V ˌ**sew sth↔'up 1** to join or repair sth by sewing 缝合；缝补：*to sew up a seam* 缝上接缝 **2** [often passive] (*informal*) to arrange sth in an acceptable way 安排妥帖；办好；使万无一失：*It didn't take me long to sew up the deal.* 我没费多大工夫就把那桩生意做成了。◇ *They think they **have** the election **sewn up*** (= they think they are definitely going to win). 他们认为这次选举他们已万无一失。

sew·age /'suːɪdʒ; *BrE also* 'sjuː-/ noun [U] used water and waste substances that are produced by human bodies, that are carried away from houses and factories through special pipes (= SEWERS) （下水道的）污水，污物：*a ban on the dumping of raw sewage* (= that has not been treated with chemicals) *at sea* 禁止把未经处理的污水排入海中 ◇ *sewage disposal* 污水处理 ⊃ COMPARE WASTEWATER ⊃ WORDFINDER NOTE AT WASTE

'**sewage farm** noun (*BrE*) = SEWAGE WORKS

'**sewage plant** (*also* **sewage 'treatment plant**) noun (*especially NAmE*) = SEWAGE WORKS

'**sewage works** (*also* **sewage 'treatment works**, **sewage dis'posal works**) noun [C+sing./pl. v.] (*BrE*) a place where chemicals are used to clean sewage so that it can then be allowed to go into rivers, etc. or used to make MANURE 污水处理厂

sewer /'suːə(r); *BrE also* 'sjuː-/ noun an underground pipe that is used to carry sewage away from houses, factories, etc. 污水管；下水道；阴沟

sew·er·age /'suːərɪdʒ; *BrE also* 'sjuː-/ noun [U] the system by which sewage is carried away from houses, factories, etc. and is cleaned and made safe by adding chemicals to it 排水系统；污水处理

'**sewer grate** noun (*US*) = GRATE (2)

sew·ing /'səʊɪŋ; *NAmE* 'soʊ-/ noun [U] **1** the activity of making, repairing or decorating things made of cloth using a needle and thread 缝纫：*knitting and sewing* 编织和缝纫 ⊃ VISUAL VOCAB PAGE V45 **2** something that is being sewn 缝制中的衣物：*a pile of sewing* 一堆针线活儿

'**sewing machine** noun a machine that is used for sewing things that are made of cloth 缝纫机 ⊃ VISUAL VOCAB PAGE V45

sewn PAST PART. OF SEW

sex AW /seks/ noun, verb

■ noun **1** [U, C] the state of being male or female 性别 SYN **gender**：*How can you tell what sex a fish is?* 你怎样辨别一条鱼的雌雄？◇ *a process that allows couples to choose the sex of their baby* 使夫妇能选择婴儿性别的措施 ◇ *Please indicate your sex and date of birth below.* 请在下面写明你的性别和出生日期。◇ ***sex discrimination*** (= the act of treating men and women differently in an unfair way) 性别歧视 **2** [C] either of the two groups that people, animals and plants are divided into according to their function of producing young 男性；女性；雄性；雌性：*a member of **the opposite sex*** 一名异性成员 ◇ ***single-sex** schools* 单一性别学校 ⊃ SEE ALSO FAIR SEX **3** [U] physical activity between two people in which they touch each other's sexual organs, and which may include SEXUAL INTERCOURSE 性；性交；性行为；性活动：*It is illegal to **have sex** with a person under the age of 16.* 和 16 岁以下的未成年人发生性行为是违法的。◇ *gay sex* 同性恋性行为 ◇ *the **sex act*** 性行为 ◇ *a **sex attack*** 性侵犯 ◇ *a **sex shop*** (= one selling magazines, objects, etc. that are connected with sex) 性用品商店 ◇ ***sex education** in schools* 学校里的性教育 ◇ *These drugs may affect your **sex drive*** (= your interest in sex and the ability to have it). 这些药物可能影响你的性欲。⊃ SEE ALSO SAFE SEX, SEXUAL INTERCOURSE **4** **-sexed** (in adjectives 构成形容词) having the amount of sexual activity or desire mentioned 性行为…的；性欲…的：*a highly-sexed woman* 性欲旺盛的女人

■ verb ~ **sth** (*specialist*) to examine an animal in order to find out whether it is male or female 区分（动物）的性别

PHR V ˌ**sex sb↔'up** (*informal*) to make sb feel sexually excited 引起某人的性欲；勾引；挑逗 ˌ**sex sth↔'up** (*informal*) to make sth seem more exciting and interesting 提高某事物的魅力；使更吸引人：*The profession is trying to sex up its image.* 这个行业正在设法使自身形象更加吸引人。

sexa·gen·ar·ian /ˌseksədʒə'neəriən; *NAmE* -'ner-/ noun a person between 60 and 69 years old * 60 到 69 岁的人；六十几岁的人

'**sex appeal** noun [U] the quality of being attractive in a sexual way 性魅力；性感：*He exudes sex appeal.* 他浑身洋溢着性魅力。

'**sex change** noun [usually sing.] a medical operation in which parts of a person's body are changed so that they become like a person of the opposite sex 变性手术

'**sex chromosome** noun (*biology* 生) a CHROMOSOME that decides the sex of an animal or a plant 性染色体 ⊃ SEE ALSO X CHROMOSOME, Y CHROMOSOME

sex·ism AW /'seksɪzəm/ noun [U] the unfair treatment of people, especially women, because of their sex; the attitude that causes this （尤指对女性的）性别歧视，性别偏见：*legislation designed to combat sexism in the workplace* 旨在抵制工作场所的性别歧视的法规 ◇ *a study of sexism in language* 对语言中存在的性别歧视的研究

sex·ist /'seksɪst/ noun (*disapproving*) a person who treats other people, especially women, unfairly because of their sex or who makes offensive remarks about them 性别歧视者 ▸ **sex·ist** adj.：*a sexist attitude* 性别歧视的态度 ◇ *sexist language* 有性别歧视的语言

sex·less /'seksləs/ adj. **1** that is neither male nor female, or does not seem to be either male or female 无性（别）的：*a sexless figure* 无性别特征的体形 **2** in which there is no sexual desire or activity 性冷淡的；无性行为的

S

'sex life *noun* a person's sexual activities 性生活： *ways to improve your sex life* 改善性生活的办法

'sex maniac *noun* a person who wants to have sex more often than is normal and who thinks about it all the time 性欲狂者

'sex object *noun* a person considered only for their sexual attraction and not for their character or their intelligence 性（交）对象

'sex offender *noun* a person who has been found guilty of illegal sexual acts 性犯罪者

sex·ology /sek'sɒlədʒi; *NAmE* -'sɑːl-/ *noun* [U] the scientific study of human sexual behaviour 性学 ▶ **sex·olo·gist** /-dʒɪst/ *noun*

sex·pot /'sekspɒt; *NAmE* -pɑːt/ *noun* (*informal*) a person who is thought to be sexually attractive 性感的人

'sex symbol *noun* a famous person who is thought by many people to be sexually attractive 性感偶像

sext /sekst/ *verb* [I, T] to send sb sexual messages or photos showing naked people and sexual acts on a mobile/cell phone （用手机）发送色情信息（或照片）： **~ sb** ▶ **sext** *noun* **sexting** *noun* [U]

sex·tant /'sekstənt/ *noun* an instrument for measuring angles and distances, used to calculate the exact position of a ship or an aircraft 六分仪（用以计算船舶或飞机的准确位置）

sex·tet /seks'tet/ *noun* **1** [C+sing./pl. v.] a group of six musicians or singers who play or sing together 六重奏乐团；六重唱组合 **2** [C] a piece of music for six musicians or singers 六重奏（曲）；六重唱（曲）

sex·ton /'sekstən/ *noun* a person whose job is to take care of a church and its surroundings, ring the church bell, etc. 教堂司事（负责看管教堂及其周边设施、敲钟等）

sex·tu·plet /'sekstʊplət; sek'stjuːplət; -'stʌp-/ *noun* one of six children born at the same time to the same mother 六胞胎之一

'sex typing *noun* [U] **1** (*psychology* 心) the process of putting people into categories according to what people consider to be typical of each sex 按性别特征分类 **2** (*biology* 生) the process of finding out whether a person or other living thing is male or female, especially in difficult cases when special tests are necessary （尤指需要进行特别实验的）性别分型

sex·ual 🔑 AW /'sekʃuəl/ *adj.* **1** 🔑 [usually before noun] connected with the physical activity of sex 性行为的；性的： *sexual behaviour* 性行为 ◇ *They were not having a sexual relationship at the time.* 当时他们之间并不存在性关系。◇ *Her interest in him is purely sexual.* 她对他感兴趣纯粹是因为性的原因。 ◇ ***sexual orientation*** (= whether you are HETEROSEXUAL or HOMOSEXUAL) 性取向（指异性恋或同性恋） **2** [only before noun] connected with the process of producing young 生殖的；有性繁殖的： *the* ***sexual organs*** (= the PENIS, VAGINA, etc.) 生殖器官 ◇ *sexual reproduction* 有性繁殖 **3** [usually before noun] connected with the state of being male or female 性别的；性的： *sexual characteristics* 性别特征 ▶ **sex·ual·ly** 🔑 AW /'sekʃəli/ *adv.*： *sexually abused children* 受到性虐待的儿童 ◇ *She finds him sexually attractive.* 她觉得他富有性魅力。 ◇ *sexually explicit* 性方面露骨的 ◇ *Girls become sexually mature earlier than boys.* 女孩比男孩性成熟早。

,sexual 'harassment *noun* [U] comments about sex, physical contact, etc. usually happening at work, that a person finds annoying and offensive 性骚扰

,sexual 'intercourse (*also* **inter·course**) (*also formal* **co·itus**) *noun* [U] (*formal*) the physical activity of sex, usually describing the act of a man putting his PENIS inside a woman's VAGINA 性交；交媾

sexu·al·ity AW /,sekʃu'æləti/ *noun* [U] the feelings and activities connected with a person's sexual desires 性本能；性欲；性行为： ***male/female sexuality*** 男性 / 女性的性欲 ◇ *He was confused about his sexuality.* 他对自己的性向感到困惑。

sexu·al·ize (*BrE also* **-ise**) /'sekʃuəlaɪz/ *verb* **~ sb/sth** to make sb/sth seem sexually attractive 使性感 ▶ **sexu·al·iza·tion, -isa·tion** /,sekʃuəlaɪ'zeɪʃn; *NAmE* -lə'z-/ *noun* [U]

,sexually trans,mitted di'sease *noun* [C, U] (*abbr.* **STD**) any disease that is spread through sexual intercourse, such as SYPHILIS 性传播疾病

'sex worker *noun* a polite way of referring to a PROSTITUTE 性工作者（对以性行为换取金钱者的委婉说法）

sexy /'seksi/ *adj.* (**sex·ier, sexi·est**) **1** (of a person 人) sexually attractive 性感的： *the sexy lead singer* 性感的主唱 ◇ *She looked incredibly sexy in a black evening gown.* 她穿着黑色的晚礼服，显得性感极了。 **2** sexually exciting 引起性欲的；性感的： *sexy underwear* 性感的内衣 ◇ *a sexy look* 撩人的眼神 **3** (of a person 人) sexually excited 性欲发作的；性兴奋的： *The music and wine began to make him feel sexy.* 那音乐和酒逐渐使他性欲萌动。 **4** (*informal*) exciting and interesting 富有魅力的；迷人的；有吸引力的： *a sexy new range of software* 一系列很棒的新软件 ◇ *Accountancy just isn't sexy.* 会计工作实在乏味。 ▶ **sex·ily** *adv.* **sexi·ness** *noun* [U]

SF /,es 'ef/ *abbr.* SCIENCE FICTION 科幻小说（或影片等）

SFX /,es ef 'eks/ *abbr.* SPECIAL EFFECTS （电影或电视节目的）特技效果

SGML /,es dʒiː em 'el/ *abbr.* (*computing* 计) Standard Generalized Mark-up Language (a system used for marking text on a computer so that the text can be read on a different computer system or displayed in different forms) 标准通用置标语言

Sgt (*especially BrE*) (*also* **Sgt.** *NAmE, BrE*) *abbr.* SERGEANT 中士；巡佐；警佐： *Sgt Williams* 威廉斯中士

sh (*also* **shh**) /ʃ/ *exclamation* the way of writing the sound people make when they are telling sb to be quiet （用以让别人安静）嘘： *Sh! Keep your voice down!* 嘘！小声点儿！ ➲ MORE LIKE THIS 2, page R25

sha·bash /'ʃɑːbɑːʃ/ *exclamation* (*IndE*) used to tell sb that they have done well at sth 真棒；干得好

shabby /'ʃæbi/ *adj.* (**shab·bier, shab·bi·est**) **1** (of buildings, clothes, objects, etc. 建筑物、衣服、物品等) in poor condition because they have been used a lot 破旧的；破败的；破烂的 SYN **scruffy**： *She wore shabby old jeans and a T-shirt.* 她穿着一条破旧的牛仔裤和一件 T 恤衫。 **2** (of a person 人) badly dressed in clothes that have been worn a lot 衣着破旧的 SYN **scruffy**： *The old man was shabby and unkempt.* 老头蓬头垢面，衣衫褴褛。 **3** (of behaviour 行为) unfair or unreasonable 不公正的；不讲理的 SYN **shoddy**： *She tried to make up for her shabby treatment of him.* 她先前待他不好，这时候想弥补一下。 ▶ **shab·bily** /'ʃæbɪli/ *adv.*： *shabbily dressed* 衣衫褴褛 ◇ *I think you were very* ***shabbily treated.*** 要我说，你真是受大委屈了。 **shab·bi·ness** *noun* [U]

,shabby 'chic *adj.* using pieces of furniture, curtains, etc. that are informal and romantic in style, especially ones that seem old or worn; (of furniture, curtains, etc.) informal and romantic in style, and usually seeming old or worn （家居风格）浪漫怀旧的；（家具、窗帘等）做旧的，古朴浪漫的： *The rooms in the hotel are all shabby chic with beautiful old furniture and decor.* 这家旅馆的房间全是怀旧风格的，家具和装潢古朴典雅。 ▶ **,shabby 'chic** *noun* [U]

shack /ʃæk/ *noun, verb*

■ ***noun*** a small building, usually made of wood or metal, that has not been built well 简陋的小屋；棚屋

■ ***verb***

PHR V **,shack 'up with sb | be ,shacked 'up with sb** (*slang*) to start/be living with sb that you have a sexual relationship with, but that you are not married to

姘居；和（性伴侣）同居：*I hear he's shacked up with some woman.* 我听说他跟一个女人同居了。

shackle /ˈʃækl/ *verb* **1 ~ sb** to put shackles on sb 给（某人）戴镣铐：*The hostage had been shackled to a radiator.* 当时人质被铐在暖气片上。◊ *The prisoners were kept shackled during the trial.* 审判期间，犯人戴着镣铐。**2** [usually passive] **~ sb/sth** to prevent sb from behaving or speaking as they want 束缚；阻挠；成为…的羁绊

shackles /ˈʃæklz/ *noun* [pl.] **1** two metal rings joined together by a chain and placed around a prisoner's wrists or ankles to prevent them from escaping or moving easily 镣铐；手铐；脚镣 **2 ~ (of sth)** (*formal*) a particular state, set of conditions or circumstances, etc. that prevent you from saying or doing what you want 枷锁；桎梏；束缚：*a country struggling to free itself from the shackles of colonialism* 为摆脱殖民主义的枷锁而斗争的国家

shade 🔑 /ʃeɪd/ *noun, verb*

■ *noun*

• **OUT OF SUN** 背阴 **1** 🔑 [U] **~ (of sth)** an area that is dark and cool under or behind sth, for example a tree or building, because the sun's light does not get to it 阴凉处；背阴；（树）荫：*We sat down **in the shade of** the wall.* 我们在墙根的背阴处坐下。◊ *The temperature can reach 40°C **in the shade**.* 背阴处温度可达 40°C。◊ *The trees provide shade for the animals in the summer.* 夏天，这些树为动物提供乘凉的地方。➲ SEE ALSO SHADY

• **ON LAMP, ETC.** 灯等 **2** 🔑 [C] a thing that you use to prevent light from coming through or to make it less bright 灯罩：*I bought a new shade for the lamp.* 我给那盏灯买了一个新罩子。◊ *an eyeshade* 遮阳眼罩 ➲ SEE ALSO LAMPSHADE, SUNSHADE

• **ON WINDOW** 窗户 **3** [C] (*also* **'window shade**) (*both NAmE*) = BLIND (1) ➲ VISUAL VOCAB PAGE V22

• **OF COLOUR** 色彩 **4** 🔑 [C] **~ (of sth)** a particular form of a colour, that is, how dark or light it is 浓淡深浅；色度：*a **delicate/pale/rich/soft shade** of blue* 淡 / 浅 / 艳 / 柔和的蓝色 ➲ SYNONYMS AT COLOUR

• **IN PICTURE** 绘画 **5** [U] the dark areas in a picture, especially the use of these to produce variety 暗部；阴影部分：*The painting needs more **light and shade**.* 这幅画明暗层次不够。

▼ **WHICH WORD?** 词语辨析

shade / shadow

- **Shade** [U] is an area or a part of a place that is protected from the heat of the sun and so is darker and cooler. * shade（不可数名词）指阴凉处：*Let's sit in the shade for a while.* 咱们在阴凉处坐一会儿吧。
- A **shadow** [C] is the dark shape made when a light shines on a person or an object. * shadow（可数名词）指影子：*As the sun went down we cast long shadows on the lawn.* 太阳落山时我们在草坪上留下长长的影子。
- **Shadow** [U] is an area of darkness in which it is difficult to distinguish things easily. * shadow（不可数名词）指阴暗处、背光处：*Her face was in deep shadow.* 她的脸在阴暗处。

• **OF OPINION/FEELING** 看法；感觉 **6** [C, usually pl.] **~ of sth** a different kind or level of opinion, feeling, etc. 差别；不同：*politicians of all shades of opinion* 持各种政见的政治人物 ◊ *The word has many shades of meaning.* 这个词有很多层意思。

• **SLIGHTLY** 略微 **7 a shade** [sing.] a little; slightly 一点；略微 SYN **touch**：*He was feeling a shade disappointed.* 他略感失望。

• **FOR EYES** 眼睛 **8 shades** [pl.] (*informal*) = SUNGLASSES

• **GHOST** 鬼魂 **9** [C] (*literary*) the spirit of a dead person; a GHOST 阴魂；幽灵；鬼

IDM **put sb/sth in the 'shade** to be much better or more impressive than sb/sth 使（某人或事物）黯然失色；使相形见绌：*I tried hard but her work put mine in the shade.* 我费了很大力气，但她的成果让我相形见绌。**shades of sb/sth** (*informal*) used when you are referring to things that remind you of a particular person, thing or time（人物、事情、时间的）痕迹，影子，遗风：*short skirts and long boots—shades of the 1960s* 短裙和高筒靴 —— 20 世纪 60 年代的余韵

■ *verb*

• **FROM DIRECT LIGHT** 直射光线 **1** to prevent direct light from reaching sth 给…遮挡（光线）：**~ sb/sth** *The courtyard was shaded by high trees.* 庭院荫庇在大树下。◊ **~ sb/sth from/against sth** *She shaded her eyes against the sun.* 她遮住眼睛避免阳光直射。

• **LAMP** 灯 **2** [usually passive] **~ sth** to provide a screen for a lamp, light, etc. to make it less bright 加灯罩：*a shaded lamp* 有罩的灯

• **PART OF PICTURE** 图画的部分 **3** to make a part of a drawing, etc. darker, for example with an area of colour or with pencil lines 把…涂暗；画阴影：**~ sth** *What do the shaded areas on the map represent?* 地图上颜色深的部分代表什么？◊ **~ sth in** *I'm going to shade this part in.* 我要把这一部分画得再暗一些。

• **JUST WIN** 险胜 **4 ~ sth** (*BrE, informal*) to just win a contest 险胜

PHR V **,shade 'into sth** to change gradually into sth else, so that you cannot tell where one thing ends and the other thing begins（界线模糊地）渐变：*The scarlet of the wings shades into pink at the tips.* 猩红的翅膀到了翼端渐变成浅红。◊ *Distrust of foreigners can shade into racism.* 对外国人的不信任可能逐渐演变成种族主义。

shad·ing /ˈʃeɪdɪŋ/ *noun* **1** [U] the use of colour, pencil lines, etc. to give an impression of light and shade in a picture or to emphasize areas of a map, diagram, etc.（绘画的）明暗处理；（地图、图表等中）颜色浓淡强调某些部分的运用 **2 shadings** [pl.] slight differences that exist between different aspects of the same thing（同一事物不同层面之间的）细微差别

shadow 🔑 /ˈʃædəʊ; *NAmE* -doʊ/ *noun, verb, adj.*

■ *noun*

• **DARK SHAPE** 阴影 **1** 🔑 [C] the dark shape that sb/sth's form makes on a surface, for example on the ground, when they are between the light and the surface 阴影；影子：*The children were having fun, chasing each other's shadows.* 孩子们追逐着彼此的影子，玩得很开心。◊ *The ship's sail **cast a shadow** on the water.* 船帆在水面上投下一片影子。◊ *The shadows lengthened as the sun went down.* 随着太阳西下，影子越拉越长。◊ (*figurative*) *He didn't want to **cast a shadow on** (= spoil) their happiness.* 他不想给他们的幸福蒙上阴影。➲ PICTURE AT SHADE ➲ NOTE AT SHADE

• **DARKNESS** 黑暗 **2** 🔑 [U] (*also* **shadows** [pl.]) DARKNESS in a place or on sth, especially so that you cannot easily see who or what is there 昏暗处；背光处；阴暗处：*His face was deep **in shadow**, turned away from her.* 他扭过头去背着她，脸冲着暗处。◊ *I thought I saw a figure standing in the shadows.* 我好像看见阴暗处站着一个人。➲ NOTE AT SHADE

• **SMALL AMOUNT** 微量 **3** [sing.] **~ of sth** a very small amount of sth 少许；些微；一丁点 SYN **hint**：*A shadow of a smile touched his mouth.* 他嘴角透出一丝笑意。◊ *She knew **beyond a shadow of a doubt*** (= with no doubt at all) *that he was lying.* 她十分清楚他在说谎。

• **INFLUENCE** 影响 **4** [sing.] **~ of sb/sth** the strong (usually bad) influence of sb/sth （坏）影响：*The new leader wants to escape from the shadow of his predecessor.* 新任领导想要摆脱前任的影响。◇ *These people have been living for years **under the shadow** of fear.* 这些人多年来一直生活在恐惧的阴影中。

• **UNDER EYES** 眼睛下方 **5 shadows** [pl.] dark areas under sb's eyes, because they are tired, etc. 黑眼圈

• **SB THAT FOLLOWS SB** 跟随的人 **6** [C] a person or an animal that follows sb else all the time 形影不离的人（或动物）

• **STH NOT REAL** 虚幻事物 **7** [C] a thing that is not real or possible to obtain 虚幻的事物；不可能得到的东西：*You can't spend all your life **chasing shadows**.* 你不能一辈子追求虚无缥缈的东西。➲ SEE ALSO EYESHADOW, FIVE O'CLOCK SHADOW

IDM **be frightened/nervous/scared of your own 'shadow** to be very easily frightened; to be very nervous 非常胆小（或十分紧张） **in/under the 'shadow of 1** very close to 在…近旁：*The new market is in the shadow of the City Hall.* 新建的市场紧挨着市政厅。 **2** when you say that sb is **in/under the shadow of** another person, you mean that they do not receive as much attention as that person 被（某人的光彩）所掩盖 ➲ MORE AT FORMER *adj.*

■ ***verb***

• **FOLLOW AND WATCH** 跟踪监视 **1 ~ sb** to follow and watch sb closely and often secretly 跟踪；盯梢：*He was shadowed for a week by the secret police.* 他被秘密警察盯梢了一个星期。 **2 ~ sb** to be with sb who is doing a particular job, so that you can learn about it 跟随…实地学习（或参观）：*It is often helpful for teachers to shadow managers in industry.* 教师跟随业界的管理人员实地学习，常常会很有收获。

• **COVER WITH SHADOW** 投下阴影 **3 ~ sth** to cover sth with a shadow 在…上投下（或覆盖）阴影：*A wide-brimmed hat shadowed her face.* 一顶宽边帽把她的脸罩在阴影中。◇ *The bay was shadowed by magnificent cliffs.* 巍峨的悬崖把海湾笼罩在阴影里。➲ SEE ALSO OVERSHADOW

■ ***adj.*** [only before noun] (*BrE*, *politics* 政) used to refer to senior politicians of the main opposition party who would become government ministers if their party won the next election 影子内阁的：*the shadow Chancellor* 影子内阁的财政大臣 ◇ *the shadow Cabinet* 影子内阁

'shadow-box *verb* [I] to BOX with an imaginary opponent, especially for physical exercise or in order to train （尤指训练时与假想对手）做空拳攻防练习 ▶ **'shadow-boxing** *noun* [U]

shad·owy /ˈʃædəʊi; *NAmE* -doʊi/ *adj.* **1** dark and full of shadows 阴暗的；幽暗的；阴影中的；多阴的：*Someone was waiting in the shadowy doorway.* 有人守候在昏暗的门口。 **2** [usually before noun] difficult to see because there is not much light 昏暗的；朦胧的；模糊的：*Shadowy figures approached them out of the fog.* 从雾中模模糊糊出来几个人影，向他们走去。 **3** [usually before noun] that not much is known about 鲜为人知的；神秘莫测的：*the shadowy world of terrorism* 鲜为人知的恐怖主义世界

shady /ˈʃeɪdi/ *adj.* (**shadi·er, shadi·est**) **1** protected from direct light from the sun by trees, buildings, etc. 背阴的；阴凉的；多阴的：*a shady garden* 树影婆娑的花园 ◇ *We went to find somewhere cool and shady to have a drink.* 我们去找了一个阴凉的地方，喝了一杯。 **2** (of a tree, etc. 树等) providing shade from the sun 成荫的 **3** [usually before noun] (*informal*) seeming to be dishonest or illegal 可疑的；鬼祟的；非法的：*a shady businessman/deal* 行为可疑的商人；一宗有问题的交易

shaft /ʃɑːft; *NAmE* ʃæft/ *noun, verb*

■ ***noun*** **1** (often in compounds 常构成复合词) a long, narrow, usually vertical passage in a building or underground, used especially for a lift/elevator or as a way of allowing air in or out （电梯的）升降机井；通风井；竖井；井筒：*a **lift/elevator shaft*** 电梯井 ◇ *a mineshaft* 竖井 ◇ *a ventilation shaft* 通风井 **2** the long narrow part of an arrow, HAMMER, GOLF CLUB, etc. （箭、高尔夫球杆等的）杆；（锤等的）柄 **3** (often in compounds 常构成复合词) a metal bar that joins parts of a machine or an engine together, enabling power and movement to be passed from one part to another （机器的）轴 ➲ SEE ALSO CAMSHAFT, CRANKSHAFT **4** [usually pl.] either of the two poles at the front of a CARRIAGE or CART between which a horse is fastened in order to pull it （马车的）辕 **5 ~ of light, sunlight, etc.** (*literary*) a narrow strip of light 一束，一道（光、阳光等）：*A shaft of moonlight fell on the lake.* 一束月光照在湖面上。◇ (*figurative*) *a shaft of inspiration* 一道灵光 **6 ~ of pain, fear, etc.** (*literary*) a sudden strong feeling of pain, etc. that travels through your body 一阵（疼痛、害怕等）：*Shafts of fear ran through her as she heard footsteps behind her.* 她听见身后有脚步声，感到一阵毛骨悚然。 **7 ~ of sth** (*formal*) a clever remark that is intended to upset or annoy sb 讥讽；挖苦；尖酸的话：*a shaft of wit* 机智的调侃

IDM **give sb the 'shaft** (*NAmE, informal*) to treat sb unfairly 亏待，苛待（某人）

■ ***verb* ~ sb** (*informal*) to treat sb unfairly or cheat them 亏待；苛待；欺骗

shag /ʃæg/ *noun, verb, adj.*

■ ***noun*** **1** [U] a strong type of TOBACCO cut into long thin pieces 浓味烟丝；粗切烟丝 **2** [C] a large black bird with a long neck that lives near the sea 鸬鹚 **3** [C, usually sing.] (*BrE, taboo, slang*) an act of sex with sb 性交

■ ***verb*** (**-gg-**) [I, T] **~ (sb)** (*BrE, taboo, slang*) to have sex with sb 和…性交

■ ***adj.*** [only before noun] used to describe a carpet, etc., usually made of wool, that has long threads （地毯等）长绒的

shagged /ʃægd/ (*also* ˌ**shagged 'out**) *adj.* [not before noun] (*BrE, taboo, slang*) very tired 疲惫不堪；很累

shaggy /ˈʃægi/ *adj.* (**shag·gier, shag·gi·est**) **1** (of hair, fur, etc. 毛发、皮毛等) long and untidy 长而乱的；乱蓬蓬的：*a shaggy mane of hair* 一头蓬乱的长发 **2** having long untidy hair, fur, etc. 头发（或皮毛）蓬乱的：*a huge shaggy white dog* 皮毛乱蓬蓬的大白狗

shaggy-'dog story *noun* a very long joke with a silly or disappointing ending 冗长无趣的笑话

shah /ʃɑː/ *noun* the title of the kings of Iran in the past 沙（旧时伊朗国王的称号）

shaikh = SHEIKH

shake /ʃeɪk/ *verb, noun*

■ ***verb*** (**shook** /ʃʊk/, **shaken** /ˈʃeɪkən/)

• **OBJECT/BUILDING/PERSON** 物品；建筑物；人 **1** [I, T] to move or make sb/sth move with short quick movements from side to side or up and down 摇动；抖动；（使）颤动：*The whole house shakes when a train goes past.* 火车驶过时，整座房子都颤动起来。◇ **~ sb/sth** *Shake the bottle well before use.* 使用前摇匀瓶内物品。◇ *He shook her violently by the shoulders.* 他抓着她的肩膀使劲摇晃。◇ **~ sb/sth + adj.** *She shook her hair loose.* 她头一摇，头发就散开了。 **2** [T] **~ sth + adv./prep.** to move sth in a particular direction by shaking 摇（出）；抖（掉）：*She bent down to shake a pebble out of her shoe.* 她弯下腰，把鞋里的一粒石子抖出来。

• **YOUR HEAD** 头 **3** [T] **~ your head** to turn your head from side to side as a way of saying 'no' or to show sadness, disapproval, doubt, etc. 摇头：*She shook her head in disbelief.* 她摇摇头，不相信。

• **HANDS** 手 **4** [T] to take sb's hand and move it up and down as a way of saying hello or to show that you agree about sth （与某人）握手：**~ hands (with sb) (on sth)** *Do people in Italy shake hands when they meet?* 在意大利，人们见面时握手吗？◇ *They shook hands on the deal* (= to show that they had reached an agreement). 他们达成了协议，相互握手祝贺。◇ **~ sb's hand** *He shook my hand warmly.* 他热情地和我握手。◇ **~ sb by the hand** *Our host shook each of us warmly by the hand.* 主人热情地和我们每个人握手。

• **YOUR FIST** 拳头 **5** [T] **~ your fist (at sb)** to show that you are angry with sb; to threaten sb by shaking your FIST (= closed hand) 挥拳（威胁）

• **OF BODY** 身体 **6** [I] **~ (with sth)** to make short

quick movements that you cannot control, for example because you are cold or afraid 颤抖；发抖；战栗；哆嗦 SYN **tremble**: *He was shaking with fear.* 他吓得发抖。◇ *I was shaking like a leaf.* 我像树叶似的直哆嗦。◇ *Her hands had started to shake.* 她的手早已哆嗦起来。

- **OF VOICE** 声音 **7** [I] ~ (**with sth**) (of sb's voice 嗓音) to sound unsteady, usually because you are nervous, upset or angry 颤抖
- **SHOCK SB** 使震惊 **8** [T] (not used in the progressive tenses 不用于进行时) to shock or upset sb very much 使非常震惊（或烦恼）: **~ sb** *He was badly shaken by the news of her death.* 听到她的死讯，他大为震惊。◇ **~ sb up** *The accident really shook her up.* 出了事故，她烦透了。
- **BELIEF/IDEA** 信念；观点 **9** [T] ~ **sth** to make a belief or an idea less certain 动摇: *The incident had **shaken her faith** in him.* 这件事动摇了她对他的信心。◇ *This announcement is bound to **shake the confidence** of the industry.* 这个声明必将动摇这一行业的信心。
- **GET RID OF** 去除 **10** [T] to get rid of sth 去除；摆脱: **~ sth off** *I can't seem to shake off this cold.* 这场感冒我好像老好不了。◇ **~ sth** *He couldn't shake the feeling that there was something wrong.* 他总感觉有什么地方不对头。

IDM **shake in your 'shoes** (*informal*) to be very frightened or nervous 非常害怕（或紧张）；战战兢兢；心惊肉跳 **shake a 'leg** (*old-fashioned, informal*) used to tell sb to start to do sth or to hurry（用于催促）快点动手，行动快点 ➲ MORE AT FOUNDATION

PHR V **,shake 'down** (*informal*) to become familiar with a new situation and begin to work well in it 融入新环境；适应新工作 **,shake sb/sth↔'down** (*NAmE, informal*) **1** to search a person or place in a very thorough way 彻底搜查（某人、某地）➲ RELATED NOUN SHAKEDOWN **2** to threaten sb in order to get money from them 勒索；敲诈 **,shake sb↔'off** to get away from sb who is chasing or following you 摆脱，甩掉（某人）**'shake on sth** to shake hands in order to show that sth has been agreed 握手确认（达成共识）: *They shook on the deal.* 他们达成了协议，相互握手祝贺。◇ *Let's shake on it.* 让我们握手庆贺取得一致。**,shake sth↔'out** to open or spread sth by shaking, especially so that bits of dirt, dust, etc. come off it 抖开；将（某物）抖干净: *to shake out a duster* 把抹布抖干净 **,shake sb↔'up** to surprise sb and make them think about sth in a different way, become more active, etc. 震动；激励；使振作 **,shake sth↔'up** to make important changes in an organization, a profession, etc. in order to make it more efficient 彻底调整；重组（机构、行业等）➲ RELATED NOUN SHAKE-UP

■ *noun*

- **MOVEMENT** 动作 **1** [C, usually sing.] an act of shaking sth/sb 摇动；抖动；颤动: *Give the bottle a good shake before opening.* 打开瓶子前，先使劲摇一摇。◇ *He dismissed the idea with a firm shake of his head* (= turning it from side to side to mean 'no'). 他坚定地摇了摇头，否定了那个想法。◇ *She gave him a shake to wake him.* 她摇摇他，把他叫醒。➲ SEE ALSO HANDSHAKE
- **OF BODY** 身体 **2 the shakes** [pl.] (*informal*) a physical condition in which you cannot stop your body from shaking because of fear, illness, or because you have drunk too much alcohol 颤抖；战栗；哆嗦: *I always get the shakes before exams.* 考试前，我总是紧张得发抖。
- **DRINK** 饮料 **3** [C] = MILKSHAKE: *a strawberry shake* 一杯草莓奶昔

IDM **in two 'shakes | in a couple of 'shakes** (*informal*) very soon 立刻；马上 ➲ MORE AT FAIR *adj.*, GREAT *adj.*

shake·down /ˈʃeɪkdaʊn/ *noun* (*NAmE, informal*) **1** a situation in which sb tries to force sb else to give them money using violence, threats, etc. 勒索；敲诈 **2** a thorough search of sb/sth 彻底搜查: *a police shakedown of the area* 警方对这一地区的彻底搜查 **3** a test of a vehicle to see if there are any problems before it is used generally（交通工具的）试用，试航，试飞

shaken /ˈʃeɪkən/ (*also* **shaken 'up**) *adj.* [not usually before noun] shocked, upset or frightened by sth 震惊；烦恼；恐惧

'shake-out *noun* [usually sing.] **1** a situation in which people lose their jobs and less successful companies are forced to close because of competition and difficult economic conditions 经济衰退；经济萧条 **2** = SHAKE-UP

shaker /ˈʃeɪkə(r)/ *noun* **1** (often in compounds 常构成复合词) a container that is used for shaking things 摇动器；混合器；（盖上有孔的）作料瓶: *a salt shaker* 盐瓶 ◇ *a cocktail shaker* 鸡尾酒摇壶 ➲ VISUAL VOCAB PAGE V23 **2 Shaker** a member of a religious group in the US who live in a community in a very simple way and do not marry or have partners 震颤派教徒（美国教派，教徒禁欲独身，聚居一处，崇尚俭朴生活）IDM SEE MOVER

'shake-up (*also* **'shake-out**) *noun* ~ (**in/of sth**) a situation in which a lot of changes are made to a company, an organization, etc. in order to improve the way in which it works（机构的）重大调整，重组: *a management shake-up* 管理层的大调整

shak·ing /ˈʃeɪkɪŋ/ *noun* [sing., U] the act of shaking sth/sb or the fact of being shaken 摇动；抖动；颤动

shaky /ˈʃeɪki/ *adj.* (**shaki·er**, **shaki·est**) **1** shaking and feeling weak because you are ill/sick, emotional or old 颤抖的；颤巍巍的 SYN **unsteady**: *Her voice sounded shaky on the phone.* 电话里她的声音听着发颤。◇ *The old man was very shaky on his feet.* 老人站在那儿，颤巍巍的。**2** not firm or safe; not certain 不稳固的；不牢靠的；摇晃的；不确切的: *That ladder looks a little shaky.* 这梯子看来不大牢靠。◇ (*figurative*) *Her memories of the accident are a little shaky.* 那次事故她记不太清楚了。◇ (*figurative*) *The protesters are **on shaky ground*** (= it is not certain that their claims are valid). 抗议者未必站得住脚。**3** not seeming very successful; likely to fail 不大出色的；成问题的；可能失败的 SYN **uncertain**: *Business is looking shaky at the moment.* 从目前看，业务举步维艰。◇ *After a shaky start, they fought back to win 3–2.* 他们开局不顺，但最终以 3:2 反败为胜。▸ **shaki·ly** /-ɪli/ *adv.*: *'Get the doctor,' he whispered shakily.* "去请大夫。"他颤声低语说。

shale /ʃeɪl/ *noun* [U] a type of soft stone that splits easily into thin flat layers 页岩 ▸ **shaly** *adj.*

,shale 'gas *noun* [U] gas that is found in shale 页岩气: *the extraction of shale gas by fracking* 用水力压裂法开采页岩气

shall /ʃəl; *strong form* ʃæl/ *modal verb* (*negative* **shall not**, *short form* **shan't** /ʃɑːnt; *NAmE* ʃænt/, *pt* **should** /ʃʊd/, *negative* **should not**, *short form* **shouldn't** /ˈʃʊdnt/) (*especially BrE*) **1** (*becoming old-fashioned*) used with *I* and *we* for talking about or predicting the future（同 I

▼ **GRAMMAR POINT** 语法说明

shall / will

- In modern English the traditional difference between **shall** and **will** has almost disappeared, and **shall** is not used very much at all, especially in *NAmE*. **Shall** is now only used with *I* and *we*, and often sounds formal and old-fashioned. 在现代英语中，shall 和 will 的传统区别几乎不复存在。shall 基本上不怎么用，尤其在美式英语中。shall 目前只与 I 和 we 连用，且听起来常显得正式并过时。People are more likely to say 人们更可能说: *I'll* (= I will) *be late.* 我要迟到了。and 和: *'You'll* (= you will) *apologize immediately.' 'No I won't!'* "你赶快赔个不是。""不，我不！"
- In *BrE* **shall** is still used with *I* and *we* in questions or when you want to make a suggestion or an offer. 在英式英语中，shall 仍然与 I 和 we 连用，用于疑问句、提出建议或提供帮助: *What shall I wear to the party?* 我穿什么衣服去参加聚会呢？◇ *Shall we order some coffee?* 我们要些咖啡好吗？◇ *I'll drive, shall I?* 我来开车好吗？

➲ NOTE AT SHOULD

S

和 we 连用，表示将来）将要，将会：*This time next week I shall be in Scotland.* 下周这个时候我就在苏格兰了。◇ *We shan't be gone long.* 我们不会去很长时间的。◇ *I said that I should be pleased to help.* 我说过我乐意帮忙。**2** used in questions with *I* and *we* for making offers or suggestions or asking advice（在疑问句中同 I 和 we 连用，表示提出或征求意见）：*Shall I send you the book?* 我把书给你寄去，好不好？◇ *What shall we do this weekend?* 这个周末我们要做什么呢？◇ *Let's look at it again, shall we?* 我们再看一遍，好不好？**3** (*old-fashioned* or *formal*) used to show that you are determined, or to give an order or instruction（表示决心、命令或指示）必须，一定，应该：*He is determined that you shall succeed.* 他决心使你成功。◇ *Candidates shall remain in their seats until all the papers have been collected.* 考生必须留在座位上，等所有试卷收好以后方可离去。➲ NOTE AT MODAL

▼ EXPRESS YOURSELF 情景表达

Offering to do something 主动提出做某事

There are various ways of offering and accepting help. 表达提供和接受帮助有多种方式：

- ***Would you like me to help you with that?*** 你要我来帮你做这件事吗？
- ***Can I give you a hand?*** 要我帮一把吗？
- ***Can I help you with that?*** 要我帮你做这件事吗？
- ***Shall I carry that for you?*** (*BrE* or *formal, NAmE*) 我来帮你提着它好不好？
- ***Would it help if I spoke to Julie before you call her?*** 你给朱莉打电话之前我先跟她谈谈是否有帮助？
- ***Let me*** *take your bag.* 我帮你拿包吧。
- ***If there's anything I can do (to help), let me know.*** 要是我能帮上什么忙的话，请告诉我。

Responses 回应：

- ***That's very kind/nice/generous/thoughtful of you. Thank you.*** 你真是太好了 / 太慷慨了 / 太周到了。谢谢你。
- ***It's all right, thank you. I can manage/do it.*** 没事儿，谢谢你。我应付得了。
- ***Thanks. That would be very helpful.*** 谢谢，那会非常有用。

S

shal·lot /ʃəˈlɒt; *NAmE* -ˈlɑːt/ *noun* a vegetable like a small onion with a very strong taste 红葱头 ➲ VISUAL VOCAB PAGE V33

shal·low /ˈʃæləʊ; *NAmE* -loʊ/ *adj.* (**shal·low·er, shal·low·est**) **1** not having much distance between the top or surface and the bottom 浅的：*a shallow dish* 浅盘 ◇ *They were playing in **the shallow end*** (= of the swimming pool). 他们在游泳池的浅水区玩耍。◇ *These fish are found in shallow waters around the coast.* 这些鱼生长在海边浅水水域。OPP **deep** **2** (*disapproving*) (of a person, an idea, a comment, etc. 人、观点、评论等) not showing serious thought, feelings, etc. about sth 肤浅的；浅薄的 SYN **superficial** **3** **shallow breathing** involves taking in only a small amount of air each time（呼吸）浅的，弱的 ▸ **shal·low·ly** *adv.*: *He was breathing shallowly.* 他呼吸微弱。 **shal·low·ness** *noun* [U]

shal·lows /ˈʃæləʊz; *NAmE* -loʊz/ **the shallows** *noun* [pl.] a shallow place in a river or the sea（河海的）浅水处，浅滩

sha·lom /ʃəˈlɒm; *NAmE* -ˈloʊm/ *exclamation* a Hebrew word for 'hello' or 'goodbye' that means 'peace'（希伯来语，见面或告别时说）祝你平安

shalt /ʃælt/ *verb* **thou shalt** (*old use*) used to mean 'you shall', when talking to one person（义同 shall，用于第二人称单数）

shal·war = SALWAR

sham /ʃæm/ *noun, adj., verb*
■ ***noun*** (*disapproving*) **1** [sing.] a situation, feeling, system, etc. that is not as good or true as it seems to be 假象；假情假义；伪善；伪装：*The latest crime figures are a complete sham.* 最新的犯罪统计数字完全是捏造的。**2** [C, usually sing.] a person who pretends to be sth that they are not 假装…的人；冒充者；假冒者 **3** [U] behaviour, feelings, words, etc. that are intended to make sb/sth seem to be better than they really are 虚假的行为（或感情、言语等）；伪善：*Their promises turned out to be full of sham and hypocrisy.* 他们的许诺到头来全是空的、骗人的。
■ ***adj.*** [only before noun] (*usually disapproving*) not genuine but intended to seem real 虚假的；假装的 SYN **false**: *a sham marriage* 假结婚
■ ***verb*** (**-mm-**) [I, T] ~ (**sth**) | + **adj.** to pretend sth 假装；冒充：*Is he really sick or is he just shamming?* 他真病了，还是装的？

sha·man /ˈʃeɪmən; ˈʃɑːmən; ˈʃæmən/ *noun* a person in some religions and societies who is believed to be able to contact good and evil spirits and cure people of illnesses 萨满（据信能和善恶神灵沟通，能治病的人）▸ **sha·man·ic** /ʃəˈmænɪk/ *adj.*

shama·teur /ˈʃæmətə(r); -tʃə(r)/ *noun* (*disapproving*) a person who makes money playing a sport but is officially an AMATEUR（领取出场费的）冒牌业余运动员 ▸ **shama·teur·ism** /ˈʃæmətərɪzəm; -tʃər-/ *noun* [U]

shamba /ˈʃæmbə/ *noun* (*EAfrE*) a small farm or a field that is used for growing crops 小农场；农田

sham·ble /ˈʃæmbl/ *verb* [I] (+ **adv./prep.**) to walk in an awkward or lazy way, dragging your feet along the ground 拖着脚走；蹒跚

sham·bles /ˈʃæmblz/ *noun* [sing.] (*informal*) **1** a situation in which there is a lot of confusion 混乱局面；无序的场面；凌乱不堪；一片狼藉 SYN **mess**: *The press conference was a complete shambles.* 记者招待会一片混乱。◇ *What a shambles!* 好乱哪！◇ *The government **is in a shambles** over Europe.* 政府在欧洲问题上政策十分混乱。**2** a place which is dirty or untidy 肮脏（或凌乱）的地方 SYN **mess**: *The house was a shambles.* 那房子凌乱不堪。

sham·bol·ic /ʃæmˈbɒlɪk; *NAmE* -ˈbɑːl-/ *adj.* (*BrE, informal*) lacking order or organization 混乱的；没有次序的；乱七八糟的 SYN **chaotic, disorganized**

shame /ʃeɪm/ *noun, verb, exclamation*
■ ***noun*** **1** [U] the feelings of sadness, embarrassment and GUILT that you have when you know that sth you have done is wrong or stupid 羞耻；羞愧；惭愧：*His face burned with shame.* 他的脸因羞愧而发烫。◇ *She hung her head in shame.* 她羞愧地低下了头。◇ *He could not live with the shame of other people knowing the truth.* 别人知道了事情的真相，他羞得无地自容。◇ ***To my shame*** (= I feel shame that) *I refused to listen to her side of the story.* 使我感到惭愧的是，我拒绝听她对事情的解释。**2** [U] (*formal*) (only used in questions and negative sentences 仅用于疑问句和否定句) the ability to feel shame at sth you have done 羞耻心；羞愧感：*Have you no shame?* 你就不知道羞耻吗？**3** **a shame** [sing.] used to say that sth is a cause for feeling sad or disappointed 令人惋惜的事；让人遗憾的事 SYN **pity**: ***What a shame*** *they couldn't come.* 他们不能来了，真是遗憾。◇ ***It's a shame about*** *Tim, isn't it?* 蒂姆的事让人遗憾，你说是不是？◇ ***It's a shame that*** *she wasn't here to see it.* 真可惜，她没在这儿亲眼看看。◇ *It would be **a crying shame*** (= a great shame) *not to take them up on the offer.* 要是不接受他们的提议，将来后悔都来不及。**4** [U] the loss of respect that is caused when you do sth wrong or stupid 耻辱；丢脸：*There **is no shame in** wanting to be successful.* 有抱负不是什么丢脸的事。◇ (*formal*) *She felt that her failure would **bring shame on** her family.* 她觉得她的失败会使家人蒙羞。
IDM **put sb/sth to ˈshame** to be much better than sb/sth 大大胜过；使相形见绌；使自愧不如：*Their presentation put ours to shame.* 他们的演出使我们的相形见绌。 **ˈshame on you, him, etc.** (*informal*) used to say that sb should feel ashamed for sth they have said or done（责备时说）真丢脸，真不害臊 ➲ MORE AT NAME *v.*
■ ***verb*** **1** ~ **sb** to make sb feel ashamed 使羞愧（或惭愧）：

His generosity shamed them all. 他的大度使他们都感到羞愧。**2** ~ **sb** (*formal*) to make sb feel that they have lost honour or respect 使蒙受耻辱；使丢脸：*You have shamed your family.* 你使你的家庭蒙受了耻辱。

PHR V **'shame sb into doing sth** to persuade sb to do sth by making them feel ashamed not to do it 使某人羞愧而不得不做（某事）：*She shamed her father into promising more help.* 她使父亲感到过意不去，只好答应多给她些帮助。

■ ***exclamation*** (*SAfrE*) used to express sympathy, or to show that you like sb/sth （表示同情或喜爱）真可惜，太遗憾了，好极了，真棒：*Shame, she's so cute!* 哇，她简直是太漂亮了！

shame·faced /ˌʃeɪmˈfeɪst/ *adj.* feeling or looking ashamed because you have done sth bad or stupid 面带愧色的；羞惭的；惭愧的 **SYN** **sheepish**：*a shamefaced smile* 惭愧的笑容 ▸ **shame·faced·ly** /ˌʃeɪmˈfeɪstli; -ˈfeɪsɪdli/ *adv.*

shame·ful /ˈʃeɪmfl/ *adj.* that should make you feel ashamed 可耻的；丢脸的 **SYN** **disgraceful**：*shameful behaviour* 可耻的行为 ◇ *It was shameful the way she was treated.* 她竟然受到那样的对待，太不像话了。 ▸ **shame·ful·ly** /-fəli/ *adv.*

shame·less /ˈʃeɪmləs/ *adj.* (*disapproving*) not feeling ashamed of sth you have done, although other people think you should 无耻的；没廉耻的；不要脸的 **SYN** **unashamed** ▸ **shame·less·ly** *adv.* (*usually disapproving, sometimes approving*)：*The whole film is shamelessly romantic and glamorous.* 张扬的浪漫与华美贯穿整部电影。 **shame·less·ness** *noun* [U]

sha·mi·ana /ˌʃɑːmiˈɑːnə/ *noun* (*IndE*) a large tent used at social events （大型活动用的）大帐篷

sham·ing /ˈʃeɪmɪŋ/ *adj.* causing sb to feel ashamed 令人羞愧的：*a shaming defeat by a less experienced team* 令人羞愧地输给一支经验不如自己的队伍

sham·my /ˈʃæmi/ *noun* (*pl.* **-ies**) (*also* ˌ**shammy ˈleather**) [U, C] (*informal*) = CHAMOIS (2)

sham·poo /ʃæmˈpuː/ *noun, verb*

■ ***noun*** (*pl.* **-os**) **1** [C, U] a liquid soap that is used for washing your hair; a similar liquid used for cleaning carpets, furniture covers or a car 洗发水；洗发露；（洗地毯、家具罩套、汽车等的）洗涤剂：*a shampoo for greasy hair* 油性头发洗发剂 ◇ *carpet shampoo* 地毯洗涤剂 **2** [C, usually sing.] an act of washing your hair using shampoo 用洗发剂洗头发：*Rinse the hair thoroughly after each shampoo.* 每次用洗发剂洗发后都要彻底冲干净。 ◇ *a shampoo and set* (= an act of washing and styling sb's hair) 洗头发并做发型

■ ***verb*** (**sham·pooed**, **sham·pooed**) ~ **sth** to wash or clean hair, carpets, etc. with shampoo 用洗发剂洗（头发）；用洗涤剂洗（地毯等）

sham·rock /ˈʃæmrɒk; *NAmE* -rɑːk/ *noun* a small plant with three leaves on each STEM. The shamrock is the national symbol of Ireland. 三叶草（爱尔兰的国花）

shandy /ˈʃændi/ *noun* (*pl.* **-ies**) (*especially BrE*) **1** [U, C] a drink made by mixing beer with LEMONADE 香蒂啤酒（掺柠檬汁的啤酒） **2** [C] a glass or can of shandy 一杯（或一罐）香蒂啤酒：*Two shandies, please.* 请来两杯香蒂啤酒。

shang·hai /ˌʃæŋˈhaɪ/ *verb* (**shang·hai·ing** /-ˈhaɪɪŋ/, **shang·haied**, **shang·haied** /-ˈhaɪd/) ~ **sb** (**into doing sth**) (*old-fashioned, informal*) to trick or force sb into doing sth that they do not really want to do 诓骗；强迫

Shangri-La /ˌʃæŋgri ˈlɑː/ *noun* [sing.] a place that is extremely beautiful and where everything seems perfect, especially a place far away from modern life 香格里拉；（远离现代生活的）世外桃源 ➲ MORE LIKE THIS 17, page R27

ORIGIN From the name of an imaginary valley in Tibet in James Hilton's novel *Lost Horizon*, where people do not grow old. 源自詹姆斯・希尔顿的小说《消失的地平线》中虚构的西藏河谷香格里拉，那里的人青春永驻。

shank /ʃæŋk/ *noun* **1** the straight narrow part between the two ends of a tool or an object 长柄；杆 **2** the part of an animal's or a person's leg between the knee and ankle （动物或人的）胫，小腿 **3** the top part of the leg of an animal, cooked and eaten （动物的）大腿肉：*braised lamb shanks* 炖羊腿

IDM **(on) Shanks's ˈpony** (*BrE, informal*) walking, rather than travelling by car, bus, etc. 步行；徒步 **SYN** **on foot**

shan't /ʃɑːnt; *NAmE* ʃænt/ *short form* shall not 不会；不应该

shanti /ˈʃɑːnti/ *noun* [U] (*IndE*) (often used in religious songs or prayers) peace （常用于宗教歌曲或祷告）宁静，和平

shanty /ˈʃænti/ *noun* (*pl.* **-ies**) **1** a small house, built of pieces of wood, metal and cardboard, where very poor people live, especially on the edge of a big city 棚屋，简陋小屋（常搭建于城市边缘） **2** (*also* **ˈsea shanty**) (*US* **chanty**, **chantey**) a song that sailors traditionally used to sing while pulling ropes, etc. 水手号子（旧时水手边拉绳索等边唱的歌）

ˈshanty town *noun* an area in or near a town where poor people live in shanties 棚户区，贫民窟（在城镇中或近郊） ➲ WORDFINDER NOTE AT POOR

shape /ʃeɪp/ *noun, verb*

■ ***noun*** **1** [C, U] the form of the outer edges or surfaces of sth; an example of sth that has a particular form 形状；外形；样子；呈…形状的事物：*a rectangular shape* 长方形 ◇ *The pool was **in the shape of** a heart.* 游泳池呈心形。 ◇ *The island was originally circular **in shape**.* 这个岛原先为圆形。 ◇ *Squares, circles and triangles are types of shape.* 正方形、圆形和三角形是不同类型的形状。 ◇ *Candles come **in all shapes and sizes**.* 有各种形状和大小的蜡烛。 ◇ *You can recognize the fish by the shape of their fins.* 你可以根据鳍的形状来辨认这种鱼。 ◇ *This old T-shirt has completely lost its shape.* 这件旧 T 恤衫已经穿得完全走样了。 ◇ (*figurative*) *The government provides money **in the shape of*** (= consisting of) *grants and student loans.* 政府以助学金和学生贷款的形式提供资助。 **2** [C] a person or thing that is difficult to see clearly 模糊的影子 **SYN** **figure**：*Ghostly shapes moved around in the dark.* 有几个鬼一样的影子在黑暗中游荡。 **3** [U] the physical condition of sb/sth 状况；情况：*What sort of shape was the car in after the accident?* 这车出过事故以后状况如何？ ◇ *He's **in good shape** for a man of his age.* 作为那把年纪的人来说，他身体不错。 ◇ *I like to **keep in shape*** (= keep fit). 我喜欢健身。 **4** [U] the particular qualities or characteristics of sth 性质；特点：*Will new technology change the shape of broadcasting?* 新技术会改变广播的方式吗？

IDM **get (yourself) into ˈshape** to take exercise, eat healthy food, etc. in order to become physically fit 强身健体 **get/knock/lick sb into ˈshape** to train sb so that they do a particular job, task, etc. well 把某人培养成材（或训练出来） **get/knock/lick sth into ˈshape** to make sth more acceptable, organized or successful 把某事物整顿好；使某事物条理化（或更趋完善）：*I've got all the information together but it still needs knocking into shape.* 我把材料全都收集齐了，但还需要整理。 **give ˈshape to sth** (*formal*) to express or explain a particular idea, plan, etc. 表达，阐释（观点、计划等） **in ˈany (way,) shape or form** (*informal*) of any type 任何形式：*I don't approve of violence in any shape or form.* 我不赞成任何形式的暴力行为。 **out of ˈshape 1** not having the normal shape 变形的；走样的：*The wheel had been twisted out of shape.* 轮子已经扭曲变形了。 **2** (of a person 人) not in good physical condition 身体不好；不健康 **the ˌshape of ˌthings to ˈcome** the way things are likely to develop in the future 未来的状况 **take ˈshape** to develop and become more complete or organized 成形；有了模样 **throw shapes 1** (*BrE*) to dance 跳舞：*She spent the whole evening throwing shapes on the dance floor.* 她整晚都在舞池里跳舞。 **2** (*IrishE*) to behave in a way that makes you seem threatening, especially by standing as though you are ready to fight, without actually becoming violent 作势要打架；摆出气势汹汹的样子：(*figurative*) *The two main investors threw some shapes during the debate.* 两名主要投资人在辩论时剑拔弩张，火药味十足。 ◇ *I was worried he might get violent*

S

but he was just throwing shapes. 我担心他会动手，但他只是虚张声势。 ➲MORE AT BENT *adj.*

■*verb* **1** [T] to make sth into a particular shape 使成为…形状（或样子）；塑造： **~ A into B** *Shape the dough into a ball.* 把和好的面揉成一团。 ◇ **~ sth** *This tool is used for shaping wood.* 这个工具是用来加工木料的。 **2** [T] **~ sb/sth** to have an important influence on the way that sb/sth develops 决定…的形成；影响…的发展： *His ideas had been shaped by his experiences during the war.* 他的思想深受战时经历的影响。 ◇ *She had a leading role in shaping party policy.* 该党奉行何种政策，她起着主导作用。 **3** [I] **~ to do sth** to prepare to do sth, especially hit or kick sth 准备（做某动作）；摆好姿势： *She was shaping to hit her second shot.* 她正准备再一次击球。

IDM **'shape up or ship 'out** (*NAmE, informal*) used to tell sb that if they do not improve, work harder, etc. they will have to leave their job, position, etc. 不好好干就卷铺盖走人： *He finally faced up to his drug problem when his band told him to shape up or ship out.* 乐队警告他要么好好干，要么走人，这使他终于正视自己的吸毒问题。

PHR V **,shape 'up 1** to develop in a particular way, especially in a good way 进展（顺利）： *Our plans are shaping up nicely* (= showing signs that they will be successful). 我们的计划进行得很好。 **2** (*informal*) to improve your behaviour, work harder, etc. 改善（行为、工作等）： *If he doesn't shape up, he'll soon be out of a job.* 他要是不改好，很快就会丢饭碗的。

shaped /ʃeɪpt/ *adj.* having the type of shape mentioned 具有（或呈）…形状的： *a huge balloon* ***shaped like*** *a giant cow* 形似一头巨牛的大气球 ◇ *almond-shaped eyes* 杏眼 ◇ *an L-shaped room* * L 形房间 ➲SEE ALSO PEAR-SHAPED

shape·less /ˈʃeɪpləs/ *adj.* [usually before noun] (*often disapproving*) **1** not having any definite shape 无定形的；不成形的；样子不好看的： *a shapeless sweater* 样子难看的套头衫 **2** lacking clear organization 结构混乱的；条理不清的 SYN **unstructured**： *a shapeless and incoherent story* 结构混乱、情节不连贯的故事 ▶ **shape·less·ly** *adv.* **shape·less·ness** *noun* [U]

shape·ly /ˈʃeɪpli/ *adj.* (especially of a woman's body 尤指女子体形) having an attractive curved shape 有曲线美的；匀称的

S

'shape-shifter *noun* (in stories) a person or an animal that is able to change into other people, animals or things（传说中的）变形人，变形动物： *In the film he plays a shape-shifter, who takes the form of people's worst fears.* 他在影片中扮演一个变形人，以别人最恐惧的形象出现。 ▶ **'shape-shifting** *adj.*

shard /ʃɑːd; *NAmE* ʃɑːrd/ (*also* **sherd**) *noun* a piece of broken glass, metal, etc.（玻璃、金属等的）碎片： *shards of glass* 玻璃碎片

share /ʃeə(r); *NAmE* ʃer/ *verb, noun*

■*verb*

• **USE AT THE SAME TIME** 同时使用 **1** [T, I] **~ (sth) (with sb)** to have or use sth at the same time as sb else 共有；合用： *Sue shares a house with three other students.* 苏和另外三个学生合住一所房子。 ◇ *There isn't an empty table. Would you mind sharing?* 没有空桌子了。你愿不愿意和别人合用？

• **DIVIDE BETWEEN PEOPLE** 分给若干人 **2** [T] **~ sth (out) (among/between sb)** to divide sth between two or more people 分配；分摊： *We shared the pizza between the four of us.* 我们四个人把那份比萨饼分着吃了。 ➲SEE ALSO JOB-SHARING, POWER-SHARING

• **GIVE SOME OF YOURS** 把自己的分出一部分 **3** [T, I] **~ (sth) (with sb)** to give some of what you have to sb else; to let sb use sth that is yours 分享；共享： *Eli shared his chocolate with the other kids.* 伊莱把他的巧克力和其他孩子一起分着吃了。 ◇ *The conference is a good place to share information and exchange ideas.* 研讨会是互通信息、交流思想的好场所。 ◇ *John had no brothers or sisters and wasn't used to sharing.* 约翰没有兄弟姐妹，所以不习惯和他人分享东西。

• **FEELINGS/IDEAS/PROBLEMS** 感情；想法；问题 **4** [T, I] to have the same feelings, ideas, experiences, etc. as sb else 有同样的感情（或想法、经历等）： **~ sth** *They shared a common interest in botany.* 他们都对植物学感兴趣。 ◇ *a view that is widely shared* 一种得到广泛认同的观点 ◇ *shared values* 共同的价值观 ◇ **~ sth with sb** *People often share their political views with their parents.* 人常常跟自己的父母政治观点一致。 ◇ **~ in sth** *I didn't really share in her love of animals.* 我并不怎么像她那样喜欢动物。 **5** [T, I] to tell other people about your ideas, experiences and feelings 把自己的想法（或经历、感情）告诉（某人）： **~ sth** *Men often don't like to share their problems.* 男人往往不喜欢把自己的问题告诉他人。 ◇ *The two friends shared everything—they had no secrets.* 这两位朋友无话不谈，彼此之间毫无秘密。 ◇ *Please share this on Facebook and Twitter so we can get the word out.* 请把这个在脸书和推特上分享，好让更多人知道。 ◇ **~ (sth with sb)** *Would you like to share your experience with the rest of the group?* 你愿意把你的经验与组里其他人分享吗？ ◇ *The group listens while one person shares* (= tells other people about their experiences, feelings, etc.). 一个人在谈自己的情况时，小组的其他成员都听着。

• **BLAME/RESPONSIBILITY** 责任 **6** [I, T] to be equally involved in sth or responsible for sth 共同承担；分担： **~ in sth** *I try to get the kids to share in the housework.* 我尽量让孩子们分担家务活儿。 ◇ **~ sth (with sb)** *Both drivers shared the blame for the accident.* 事故责任由两个驾车人共同承担。

IDM **share and share a'like** (*saying*) used to say that everyone should share things equally and in a fair way 平均分享；平均分担 ➲MORE AT TROUBLE *n.*

■*noun*

• **PART/AMOUNT OF STH** 一部分；一定的量 **1** [C, usually sing.] **~ (of/in sth)** one part of sth that is divided between two or more people（在若干人之间分得的）一份： *How much was your share of the winnings?* 在赢的钱里你那份有多少？ ◇ *Next year we hope to have a bigger share of the market.* 明年我们希望获得更大的市场份额。 ◇ (*BrE*) *I'm looking for a* ***flat share*** (= a flat that is shared by two or more people who are not related). 我想找一套合租公寓。 ➲SEE ALSO MARKET SHARE, TIMESHARE **2** [sing.] the part that sb has in a particular activity that involves several people（在多人参加的活动中所占的）一份： *We all did our share.* 我们都尽力了。 ◇ **~ of sth** *Everyone must accept their share of the blame.* 每个人都必须承担自己那份责任。 **3** [sing.] **~ (of sth)** an amount of sth that is thought to be normal or acceptable for one person 正常的一份；可接受的一份： *I've had my share of luck in the past.* 以前，命运也不算亏待我。 ◇ *I've done my share of worrying for one day!* 就这一天而论，我操够了心！

• **IN BUSINESS** 企业 **4** [C] **~ (in sth)** any of the units of equal value into which a company is divided and sold to raise money. People who own shares receive part of the company's profits. 股份： *shares in British Telecom* 英国电信公司的股份 ◇ *a fall in* ***share prices*** 股票价格的跌落 ➲COMPARE STOCK *n.* (4) ➲SEE ALSO ORDINARY SHARE ➲WORDFINDER NOTE AT INVEST

• **FARM EQUIPMENT** 农具 **5** [C] (*NAmE*) = PLOUGHSHARE

IDM SEE CAKE *n.*, FAIR *adj.*, LION, PIE

-share *combining form* **1** (in nouns 构成名词) an arrangement to divide sth between two or more people, groups, etc. 分摊；分担： *a job-share* (= a job that is done by two people who each work for part of the week) 工作分担 ◇ (*BrE*) *a nanny share* (= an arrangement for sb to work for two families) 保姆（两家）共用 ➲SEE ALSO TIMESHARE **2** (in verbs 构成动词) using an arrangement to divide sth between two or more people, groups, etc. 共用；合用： (*especially BrE*) *We encourage people to carshare to reduce congestion on the roads.* 我们鼓励人们合伙用车以减少道路拥堵。 ◇ (*NAmE*) *to rideshare* 拼车

share·crop·per /ˈʃeəkrɒpə(r); *NAmE* ˈʃerkrɑːpər/ *noun* (*especially NAmE*) a farmer who gives part of his or her crop as rent to the owner of the land 佃农

share·hold·er /ˈʃeəhəʊldə(r); *NAmE* ˈʃerhoʊ-/ *noun* an owner of shares in a company or business 股东 ➲WORDFINDER NOTE AT COMPANY

share·hold·ing /ˈʃeəhəʊldɪŋ; *NAmE* ˈʃerhoʊ-/ *noun* the amount of a company or business that sb owns in the form of shares 持股；持股量

ˈ**share index** *noun* [usually sing.] a list that shows the current value of shares on the STOCK MARKET, based on the prices of shares of particular companies 股票价格指数

ˈ**share option** (*BrE*) (*NAmE* ˈ**stock option**) *noun* a right given to employees to buy shares in their company at a fixed price 股票期权，认股选择权（让员工可按固定价格购买所属公司的股票）

ˈ**share-out** *noun* [usually sing.] (*BrE*) an act of dividing sth between two or more people; the amount of sth that one person receives when it is divided 分配；分配额；份额

share·ware /ˈʃeəweə(r); *NAmE* ˈʃerwer/ *noun* [U] (*computing* 计) computer software (= programs, etc.) that is available free for a user to test, after which they must pay if they wish to continue using it 共享软件（供买前试用）➲ COMPARE FREEWARE

sha·ria (*also* **sha·riah**) /ʃəˈriːə/ *noun* [U] the system of religious laws that Muslims follow 舍利阿；伊斯兰教教法

shark /ʃɑːk; *NAmE* ʃɑːrk/ *noun* **1** a large sea fish with very sharp teeth and a pointed FIN on its back. There are several types of shark, some of which can attack people swimming. 鲨鱼 **2** (*informal, disapproving*) a person who is dishonest in business, especially sb who gives bad advice and gets people to pay too much for sth 坑蒙拐骗的人；诈骗者 ➲ SEE ALSO LOAN SHARK

sharp 🔑 /ʃɑːp; *NAmE* ʃɑːrp/ *adj., adv., noun*

■ *adj.* (**sharp·er**, **sharp·est**)

• **EDGE/POINT** 锋；尖 **1** 🔑 having a fine edge or point, especially of sth that can cut or make a hole in sth 锋利的；锐利的；尖的：*a sharp knife* 锋利的刀 ◇ *sharp teeth* 锋利的牙齿 OPP **blunt**

• **RISE/DROP/CHANGE** 升；降；变化 **2** 🔑 [usually before noun] sudden and rapid, especially of a change in sth（变化）急剧的，骤然的：*a sharp drop in prices* 价格的骤降 ◇ *a sharp rise in crime* 犯罪率的急剧上升 ◇ *a sharp increase in unemployment* 失业人数的剧增 ◇ *He heard a* ***sharp intake of breath.*** 他听到猛地倒吸一口气的声音。◇ *We need to give young criminals a* ***short, sharp shock*** (= a punishment that is very unpleasant for a short time). 对青少年罪犯我们需要给以短暂但严厉的惩处。

• **CLEAR/DEFINITE** 清楚；明确 **3** 🔑 [usually before noun] clear and definite清楚明确的；清晰的；鲜明的：*a sharp outline* 清晰的轮廓 ◇ *The photograph is not very sharp* (= there are no clear contrasts between areas of light and shade). 这张照片不是很清晰。◇ *She drew a* ***sharp distinction*** *between domestic and international politics.* 她将国内政治和国际政治截然分开。◇ *In* ***sharp contrast*** *to her mood, the clouds were breaking up to reveal a blue sky.* 乌云渐渐散开，露出了蓝天，这和她的情绪形成了鲜明的对照。◇ *The issue must be brought into sharper focus.* 必须更集中关注这个问题。

• **MIND/EYES** 头脑；眼睛 **4** 🔑 (of people or their minds, eyes, etc. 人或人的头脑、眼睛等) quick to notice or understand things or to react 敏锐的；灵敏的；敏捷的：*to have sharp eyes* 有敏锐的眼睛 ◇ *a girl of sharp intelligence* 聪颖的女孩 ◇ *a sharp sense of humour* 很强的幽默感 ◇ *He kept a sharp lookout for any strangers.* 他警惕地守望着，不放过任何一个陌生人。◇ *It was very sharp of you to see that!* 你能看到这一点，很有洞察力！

• **CRITICAL** 批评性 **5** 🔑 (of a person or what they say 人或言语) critical or severe 尖锐的；严厉的：*sharp criticism* 尖锐的批评 ◇ *Emma has a* ***sharp tongue*** (= she often speaks in an unpleasant or unkind way). 埃玛说话尖刻。◇ **~ with sb** *He was very sharp with me when I was late.* 我迟到了，让他狠狠训了一通。

• **SOUNDS** 声音 **6** 🔑 [usually before noun] loud, sudden and often high in tone 突然而响亮的：*She read out the list in sharp, clipped tones.* 她清脆快速地宣读了名单。◇ *There was a sharp knock on the door.* 敲门声大作。

• **FEELING** 感觉 **7** 🔑 (of a physical feeling or an emotion 感觉或感情) very strong and sudden, often like being cut or wounded（常指受伤似的）剧烈的，猛烈的 SYN **intense**: *He winced as a sharp pain shot through his leg.* 腿上一阵剧痛，疼得他龇牙咧嘴。◇ *Polly felt a sharp pang of jealousy.* 波利感到一阵强烈的嫉妒。

• **CURVES** 弯儿 **8** 🔑 changing direction suddenly （方向）急转的：*a sharp bend in the road* 公路上的急转弯 ◇ *a sharp turn to the left* 向左的急转

• **FLAVOUR/SMELL** 味道；气味 **9** 🔑 strong and slightly bitter 强烈略苦的；辛辣的；刺鼻的：*The cheese has a distinctively sharp taste.* 这奶酪味道很冲。➲ SYNONYMS AT BITTER

• **FROST/WIND** 霜；风 **10** 🔑 used to describe a very cold or very severe FROST or wind 严寒的；凛冽的 ➲ SEE ALSO RAZOR-SHARP

• **CLEVER AND DISHONEST** 狡诈 **11** (*disapproving*) (of a person or their way of doing business 人或做事方式) clever but possibly dishonest 狡猾的；诡诈的：*His lawyer's a* ***sharp operator.*** 他的律师是个老狐狸。◇ *The firm had to face some* ***sharp practice*** *from competing companies.* 公司不得不面对竞争对手们的小动作。

• **CLOTHES** 衣服 **12** [usually before noun] (of clothes or the way sb dresses 衣服或衣着风格) fashionable and new 时髦的；入时的：*The consultants were a group of men in* ***sharp suits.*** 顾问都是些衣着入时的男人。◇ *Todd is a* ***sharp dresser.*** 托德衣着时髦。

• **FACE/FEATURES** 脸；相貌 **13** not full or round in shape 瘦削的；不丰满的：*a man with a thin face and sharp features* (= a pointed nose and chin) 脸瘦而棱角分明的男人

• **IN MUSIC** 音乐 **14** used after the name of a note to mean a note a SEMITONE/HALF STEP higher 升半音的：*the Piano Sonata in C sharp minor* 升 C 小调钢琴奏鸣曲 ➲ PICTURE AT MUSIC OPP **flat** ➲ COMPARE NATURAL *adj.* (9) **15** above the correct PITCH (= how high or low a note sounds) 偏高音的：*That note sounded sharp.* 这个音听着偏高。OPP **flat**

▸ **sharp·ness** *noun* [U, sing.]: *There was a sudden sharpness in her voice.* 她的嗓音突然抬高了。

IDM **look ˈsharp** (*BrE, informal*) used in orders to tell sb to be quick or to hurry 赶快；赶紧：*You'd better look sharp or you'll be late.* 你得快点，不然就迟到了。**not the sharpest knife in the ˈdrawer | not the sharpest tool in the ˈbox** (*informal, humorous*) not intelligent 不聪明；迟钝：*He's not exactly the sharpest knife in the drawer, is he?* 他的脑子不灵活，是不是？**the ˈsharp end (of sth)** (*BrE, informal*) the place or position of greatest difficulty or responsibility 最为困难（或责任极其重大）的地方（或职位）：*He started work at the sharp end of the business, as a salesman.* 他从这一行最为棘手的工作做起，当了推销员。

■ *adv.*

• **EXACTLY** 准确地 **1** used after an expression for a time of day to mean 'exactly'（用于表时间的词语后，表示准时）…整：*Please be here at seven o'clock sharp.* 请七点整到这里。

• **LEFT/RIGHT** 左；右 **2** (*BrE*) **~ left/right** turning suddenly to the left or right 向左 / 向右急转

• **MUSIC** 音乐 **3** (*comparative* **sharp·er**, *no superlative*) above the correct PITCH (= how high or low a note sounds) 偏高音地 OPP **flat**

■ *noun* **1** (*music* 音) a note played a SEMITONE/HALF STEP higher than the note that is named. The written symbol is (♯) 升半音；升号：*It's a difficult piece to play, full of sharps and flats.* 这支乐曲不好演奏，到处是升降记号。OPP **flat** ➲ COMPARE NATURAL *n.* (2) **2 sharps** [pl.] (*medical* 医) things with a sharp edge or point, such as needles and SYRINGES 锐利的东西（如针、注射器等）：*the safe disposal of sharps* 对有利刃或尖刺的东西的安全处置

sharp·en /ˈʃɑːpən; *NAmE* ˈʃɑːrpən/ *verb* **1** [T, I] **~ (sth)** to make sth sharper; to become sharper（使）变得锋利，变得清晰：*This knife needs sharpening.* 这把刀需要磨了。◇ *The outline of the trees sharpened as it grew lighter.* 随着天色转亮，树的轮廓变得清晰了。**2** [I, T] **~ (sth)** if a sense or feeling **sharpens** or sth **sharpens** it, it becomes stronger and/or clearer（使感觉或感情）加强，加重，变得更明显：*The sea air sharpened our appetites.* 海上的空

S

气增进了我们的食欲。 **3** [T] **~ sth** to make a disagreement between people, or an issue on which people disagree, clearer and more likely to produce a result 使尖锐；使明朗： *There is a need to sharpen the focus of the discussion.* 有必要使讨论的焦点更加集中。 **4** [I, T] to become or make sth better, more skilful, more effective, etc. than before （使）提高，改善 SYN **improve**: **~ (up)** *He needs to sharpen up before the Olympic trials.* 在奥运会选拔赛之前，他需要进一步磨砺自己。 ◇ **~ sth (up)** *She's doing a course to sharpen her business skills.* 她正进修，以提高自己的业务技能。 **5** [I, T] **~ (sth)** if your voice **sharpens** or sth **sharpens** it, it becomes high and loud in an unpleasant way （使声音）变得尖锐，变得刺耳

sharp·en·er /ˈʃɑːpnə(r); *NAmE* ˈʃɑːrp-/ *noun* (usually in compounds 通常构成复合词) a tool or machine that makes things sharp 磨具；削具： *a pencil sharpener* 卷笔刀 ◇ *a knife sharpener* 磨刀石 ➲ VISUAL VOCAB PAGE V71

ˌsharp-ˈeyed *adj.* able to see very well and quick to notice things 眼尖的；目光敏锐的 SYN **observant**: *A sharp-eyed reader spotted the mistake in yesterday's paper.* 一个眼尖的读者发现了昨天报纸上的错误。

sharp·ish /ˈʃɑːpɪʃ; *NAmE* ˈʃɑːrpɪʃ/ *adv.* (*BrE, informal*) quickly; in a short time 迅速；不久；马上

sharp·ly /ˈʃɑːpli; *NAmE* ˈʃɑːrpli/ *adv.* **1** in a critical, rough or severe way 尖刻地；严厉地；猛烈地： *The report was sharply critical of the police.* 报道猛烈地抨击了警方。 ◇ *'Is there a problem?' he asked sharply.* "有问题吗？"他厉声喝问。 **2** suddenly and by a large amount 急剧地；突然大幅度地： *Profits fell sharply following the takeover.* 接管后，利润突然大幅度降低。 ◇ *The road fell sharply to the sea.* 公路陡然下坡，通向大海。 **3** in a way that clearly shows the differences between two things 鲜明地；明显地： *Their experiences contrast sharply with those of other children.* 他们的经历和其他孩子的经历形成鲜明的对比。 **4** quickly and suddenly or loudly 迅疾而突然地；急促而大声地： *She moved sharply across the room to block his exit.* 她疾步冲到门口，挡住他的去路。 ◇ *He rapped sharply on the window.* 他猛敲窗户。 **5** used to emphasize that sth has a sharp point or edge （用以强调物体尖锐或锋利）： *sharply pointed* 尖尖的

ˈsharp sharp (*also* **sharp**) *exclamation* (*SAfrE*) (*informal*) **1** used to express approval or agreement （表示赞许）对，好 **2** used as a greeting when people meet or part （表示问候或道别）你好，再见

sharp·shoot·er /ˈʃɑːpʃuːtə(r); *NAmE* ˈʃɑːrp-/ *noun* a person who is skilled at shooting a gun 神枪手；神射手

shat PAST TENSE, PAST PART. OF SHIT

shat·ter /ˈʃætə(r)/ *verb* **1** [I, T] to suddenly break into small pieces; to make sth suddenly break into small pieces （使）破碎，碎裂： **~ (into sth)** *He dropped the vase and it shattered into pieces on the floor.* 他失手把花瓶掉到地板上摔碎了。 ◇ *the sound of shattering glass* 玻璃破碎的声音 ◇ **~ sth (into sth)** *The explosion shattered all the windows in the building.* 大楼所有的玻璃都在爆炸中震碎了。 **2** [T, I] to destroy sth completely, especially sb's feelings, hopes or beliefs; to be destroyed in this way （使感情、希望或信念等）粉碎，破灭；被粉碎；被破坏： **~ sth (into sth)** *Anna's self-confidence had been completely shattered.* 安娜的自信心彻底崩溃了。 ◇ *Her experience of divorce shattered her illusions about love.* 她的离婚经历使她对爱情的幻想破灭了。 ◇ **~ (into sth)** *My whole world shattered into a million pieces.* 我的整个世界全塌了。 **3** [T] **~ sb** to make sb feel extremely shocked and upset 使极为惊愕难过；给予极大打击： *The unexpected death of their son shattered them.* 儿子的意外死亡给他们带来沉重的打击。

shat·tered /ˈʃætəd; *NAmE* -tərd/ *adj.* **1** very shocked and upset 非常惊愕难过的；遭受极大打击的： *The experience left her feeling absolutely shattered.* 她在这次经历之后，感到彻底垮了。 **2** (*BrE, informal*) very tired 筋疲力尽的 SYN **exhausted**

shat·ter·ing /ˈʃætərɪŋ/ *adj.* **1** very shocking and upsetting 令人非常惊愕难过的；给人以极大打击的： *a shattering experience* 令人痛苦不堪的经历 ◇ *The news of his death came as a shattering blow.* 他的死讯让人惊愕不已。 **2** very loud 非常响亮的 SYN **deafening** ▶ **shat·ter·ing·ly** *adv.*

ˈshatter-proof *adj.* designed not to SHATTER 防碎的；不碎的： *shatter-proof glass* 防碎玻璃

shauri /ˈʃaʊriː/ *noun* (*EAfrE*) something that needs to be discussed or decided; something that causes a problem 需要讨论（或决定）的事；麻烦事；问题

shave /ʃeɪv/ *verb, noun*

■ ***verb*** **1** [I, T] to cut hair from the skin, especially the face, using a RAZOR 剃（须发）；（尤指）刮脸： *Mike cut himself shaving.* 迈克刮胡子时把脸划破了。 ◇ **~ sb/sth/yourself** *The nurse washed and shaved him.* 护士给他洗了脸，刮了胡子。 ◇ *a shaved head* 剃光的头 ➲ VISUAL VOCAB PAGE V65 ➲ SEE ALSO SHAVEN **2** [T] **~ sth** to cut a small amount off a price, etc. （少量地）削减，调低，降价： *The firm had shaved profit margins.* 公司调低了利润率。

PHR V **ˌshave sth↔ˈoff** | **ˌshave sth ˈoff sth** **1** to remove a beard or MOUSTACHE by shaving 剃掉，刮去（胡须）： *Charles decided to shave off his beard.* 查尔斯决定刮掉胡子。 **2** to cut very thin pieces from the surface of wood, etc. 削掉；刨去；切掉： *I had to shave a few millimetres off the door to make it shut.* 我把门刨去了几毫米才能关上。 **3** to reduce a number by a very small amount （微量地）减少，缩小： *He shaved a tenth of a second off the world record.* 他把世界纪录缩短了十分之一秒。

■ ***noun*** an act of shaving 修面；刮脸；剃须： *I need a shave.* 我需要刮胡子了。 ◇ *to have a shave* 刮脸 IDM SEE CLOSE² *adj.*

shaven /ˈʃeɪvn/ *adj.* with all the hair shaved off 剃光的；刮干净的： *a shaven head* 剃光的头 ➲ SEE ALSO CLEAN-SHAVEN ➲ COMPARE UNSHAVEN ➲ VISUAL VOCAB PAGE V65

shaver /ˈʃeɪvə(r)/ (*also* **eˌlectric ˈrazor**) *noun* an electric tool for shaving 电动剃须刀 ➲ VISUAL VOCAB PAGE V25 ➲ COMPARE RAZOR

ˈshaving cream, **ˈshaving foam** *noun* [U] special cream or FOAM for spreading over the face with a **shaving brush** before shaving 剃须膏；修面霜

shav·ings /ˈʃeɪvɪŋz/ *noun* [pl.] thin pieces cut from a piece of wood, etc. using a sharp tool, especially a PLANE （刨等削下的）削片；刨花

Sha·vu·oth /ʃəˈvuːəs; ʃaˈvʊɒt; *NAmE* ʃəˈvuːoʊt; -oʊθ/ (*also* **ˌFeast of ˈWeeks**, **Pente·cost**) *noun* [U] a Jewish festival that takes place 50 days after the second day of Passover 七七节，五旬节（犹太人节日，在逾越节次日之后第 50 天）

shawl /ʃɔːl/ *noun* a large piece of cloth worn by a woman around the shoulders or head, or wrapped around a baby （女用）披巾，披肩；襁褓

Shaw·nee /ˈʃɔːniː/ *noun* (*pl.* **Shaw·nee** or **Shaw·nees**) a member of a Native American people, many of whom now live in the US state of Oklahoma 肖尼人（美洲土著，很多现居于美国俄克拉何马州）

she /ʃi; *strong form* ʃiː/ *pron., noun*

■ ***pron.*** (used as the subject of a verb 用作动词的主语) a female person or animal that has already been mentioned or is easily identified 她；（指雌性动物）它： *'What does your sister do?' 'She's a dentist.'* "你姐姐做什么工作？""她是牙科医生。" ◇ *Doesn't she* (= the woman we are looking at) *look like Sue?* 她看上去不是很像休吗？ ➲ COMPARE HER *pron.* ➲ NOTE AT GENDER

■ ***noun*** **1** [sing.] (*informal*) a female 女性；雌性： *What a sweet little dog. Is it a he or a she?* 多可爱的小狗啊！是公的，还是母的？ **2** **she-** (in compound nouns 构成复合名词) a female animal 雌性动物： *a she-wolf* 母狼

s/he *pron.* used in writing by some people when the subject of the verb could be either female (she) or male (he) 他 / 她（主语既可为女性又可为男性时可用于书面）： *If a student does not attend all the classes, s/he will not* *be allowed to take the exam.* 如果学生缺课，他 / 她就不能参加考试。

shea butter /ˈʃiː bʌtə(r); *BrE also* ˈʃiːə; *NAmE also* ˈʃeɪ/ *noun* [U] a type of fat obtained from the nuts of the **shea tree**, used in foods and COSMETICS 乳木果油（从乳果木的果实中提取的油脂，用于食品和化妆品）

sheaf /ʃiːf/ *noun* (*pl.* **sheaves** /ʃiːvz/) **1** a number of pieces of paper tied or held together 一叠，一沓，一扎（纸） **2** a bunch of WHEAT tied together after being cut（收割的）小麦捆

shear /ʃɪə(r); *NAmE* ʃɪr/ *verb* (**sheared**, **shorn** /ʃɔːn; *NAmE* ʃɔːrn/ or **sheared**, **sheared**) **1** [T] **~ sth** to cut the wool off a sheep 给（羊）剪（羊毛）：*It was time for the sheep to be shorn.* 是剪羊毛的时节了。◇ *sheep shearing* 剪羊毛 **2** [T] **~ sth** (*formal*) to cut off sb's hair 剪（头发）：*shorn hair* 剪得很短的头发 **3** [I, T] **~ (sth) (off)** (*specialist*) (especially of metal 尤指金属) to break under pressure; to cut through sth and make it break 切断；剪切；断：*The bolts holding the wheel in place sheared off.* 固定这个轮子的几个螺栓断了。

PHR V **be ˈshorn of sth** (*literary*) to have sth important taken away from you 被剥夺；被褫夺：*Shorn of his power, the deposed king went into exile.* 权力被褫夺后，遭废黜的国王流亡国外。

shears /ʃɪəz; *NAmE* ʃɪrz/ *noun* [pl.] a garden tool like a very large pair of scissors, used for cutting bushes and HEDGES 大剪刀（用来修剪灌木、树篱等）：*a pair of garden shears* 一把园艺剪 ➲ SEE ALSO PINKING SHEARS

shear·water /ˈʃɪəwɔːtə(r); *NAmE* ˈʃɪr-/ *noun* a bird with long wings that often flies low over the sea 剪水鹱（常沿海浪波谷滑翔）

sheath /ʃiːθ/ *noun* (*pl.* **sheaths** /ʃiːðz/) **1** a cover that fits closely over the blade of a knife or other sharp weapon or tool（刀、剑等的）鞘；（工具的）套 ➲ PICTURE AT SWORD **2** any covering that fits closely over sth for protection 护套；护层；护皮：*the sheath around an electric cable* 电线护皮 **3** (*BrE*) = CONDOM (1) **4** a woman's dress that fits the body closely 紧身连衣裙

sheathe /ʃiːð/ *verb* **1** **~ sth** (*literary*) to put a knife or SWORD into a sheath 把（刀或剑）插入鞘中 **2** [usually passive] **~ sth (in/with sth)** to cover sth in a material, especially in order to protect it 给某物加护套（或护层、护皮）

ˈsheath knife *noun* a short knife with a SHEATH (= cover) 带鞘的短刀；鞘刀

sheaves PL. OF SHEAF

she·bang /ʃɪˈbæŋ/ *noun*

IDM **the whole sheˈbang** (*informal*) the whole thing; everything 整个事情；这一切

she·been /ʃɪˈbiːn/ *noun* (*informal*) (especially in Ireland, Scotland and South Africa) a place where alcoholic drinks are sold, usually illegally（尤指爱尔兰、苏格兰和南非的）无执照酒馆，非法售酒处

shed /ʃed/ *noun, verb*

■ ***noun*** (often in compounds 常构成复合词) **1** a small simple building, usually built of wood or metal, used for keeping things in 简易房，棚（用于贮藏物品）：*a bicycle shed* 自行车棚 ◇ (*BrE*) *a garden shed* 园艺工具棚 ➲ VISUAL VOCAB PAGE V20 **2** (*BrE*) a large industrial building, used for working in or keeping equipment（工业上用于生产或存放设备的）厂房，工棚，库房：*an engine shed* 机车库 **3** (*AustralE, NZE*) a building with open sides where the wool is cut off sheep (= they are SHEARED) or where cows are MILKED 剪羊毛棚；挤奶棚 ➲ SEE ALSO COWSHED, POTTING SHED, WOODSHED

■ ***verb*** (**shed·ding**, **shed**, **shed**)

• **GET RID OF** 去除 **1** **~ sth** (often used in newspapers 常用于报章) to get rid of sth that is no longer wanted 去除；摆脱：*The factory is shedding a large number of jobs.* 这家工厂正大批裁员。◇ *a quick way to shed unwanted pounds* (= extra weight or fat on your body) 快速减肥的方法 ◇ *Museums have been trying hard to shed their stuffy image.* 博物馆一直在努力改变自己沉闷的形象。

• **DROP** 使落下 **2** **~ sth** (*formal*) to let sth fall; to drop sth 使落下；使掉下：*Luke shed his clothes onto the floor.* 卢克把衣服脱在地板上。◇ *A duck's feathers shed water immediately.* 鸭子的羽毛不沾水。 **3** **~ sth** (*BrE*) (of a vehicle 车辆) to lose or drop what it is carrying 掉落（货物）：*The traffic jam was caused by a lorry* ***shedding its load.*** 交通堵塞是因为一辆卡车掉下了货物。

• **SKIN/LEAVES** 皮；叶 **4** **~ sth** if an animal **sheds** its skin, or a plant **sheds** leaves, it loses them naturally 蜕；落

• **LIGHT** 光 **5** **~ sth (on/over sb/sth)** to send light over sth; to let light fall somewhere 散发出光；把光照到（或洒在）…上：*The candles shed a soft glow on her face.* 蜡烛在她的脸上映着一层柔光。

• **TEARS** 眼泪 **6** **~ tears** (*formal* or *literary*) to cry 哭；流泪：*She shed no tears when she heard he was dead.* 她听到他的死讯时没流一滴眼泪。

• **BLOOD** 血 **7** **~ blood** (*formal*) to kill or injure people, especially in a war（尤指在战争中）造成伤亡；使流血 ➲ SEE ALSO BLOODSHED IDM SEE LIGHT *n.*

she'd /ʃiːd/ *short form* **1** she had **2** she would

ˈshe-devil *noun* a very cruel woman 狠毒的女人；女恶魔

shed·load /ˈʃedləʊd; *NAmE* -loʊd/ *noun* **~ (of sth)** (*BrE, informal*) a large amount of sth, especially money 大量（金钱等）；许多：*The project cost a shedload of money.* 这个项目花费了一大笔钱。◇ *This should save you shedloads.* 这应该可以帮你省下许多钱。

sheen /ʃiːn/ *noun* [sing., U] a soft smooth shiny quality 光泽；光辉；光彩 SYN **shine**: *hair with a healthy sheen* 闪着健康光泽的头发

sheep 🔑 /ʃiːp/ *noun* (*pl.* **sheep**) an animal with a thick coat, kept on farms for its meat (called MUTTON OR LAMB) or its wool 羊；绵羊：*a flock of sheep* 一群羊 ◇ *Sheep were grazing in the fields.* 羊在野地里吃草。➲ COMPARE EWE, LAMB *n.*, RAM *n.* (1) ➲ SEE ALSO BLACK SHEEP

IDM **like ˈsheep** (*disapproving*) if people behave **like sheep**, they all do what the others are doing, without thinking for themselves 盲从 **sort out/separate the ˌsheep from the ˈgoats** to distinguish people who are good at sth, intelligent, etc. from those who are not 区分能手与常人；分清智者和庸人 ➲ MORE AT COUNT *v.*, WELL *adv.*, WOLF *n.*

ˈsheep dip *noun* [U, C] a liquid which is used to kill insects, etc. in a sheep's coat; the container in which sheep are put to treat them with this 浴羊药液（用以浸杀羊毛中的寄生虫等）；（盛有药液的）浴羊槽

sheep·dog /ˈʃiːpdɒg; *NAmE* -dɔːg; -dɑːg/ *noun* **1** a dog that is trained to help control sheep on a farm 牧羊犬 **2** (*BrE*) a dog of a breed that is often used for controlling sheep, especially a COLLIE 牧羊犬；柯利牧羊犬 ➲ SEE ALSO OLD ENGLISH SHEEPDOG

sheep·fold /ˈʃiːpfəʊld; *NAmE* -foʊld/ *noun* an area in a field surrounded by a fence or wall where sheep are kept for safety 羊圈；羊栏

sheep·herd·er /ˈʃiːphɜːdə(r); *NAmE* -hɜːrd-/ *noun* (*NAmE*) = SHEPHERD

sheep·ish /ˈʃiːpɪʃ/ *adj.* looking or feeling embarrassed because you have done sth silly or wrong 窘迫的；难为情的；不好意思的 SYN **shamefaced**: *Mary gave her a sheepish grin.* 玛丽难为情地冲她咧嘴一笑。▶ **sheep·ish·ly** *adv.*

sheep·skin /ˈʃiːpskɪn/ *noun* [U, C] the skin of a sheep with the wool still on it 带毛绵羊皮：*a* ***sheepskin coat/rug*** 羊皮袄；羊皮毯

sheer /ʃɪə(r); *NAmE* ʃɪr/ *adj., adv., verb*

■ ***adj.*** **1** [only before noun] used to emphasize the size, degree or amount of sth（用来强调事物的大小、程度或数量）：*The area is under threat from the sheer number of tourists using it.* 这一地区由于游客人数太多而面临威胁。◇ *We were impressed by the sheer size of the cathedral.*

S

大教堂的宏大规模给我们留下了深刻的印象。**2** [only before noun] complete and not mixed with anything else 完全的；纯粹的；十足的 SYN **utter**: *The concert was sheer delight.* 这场音乐会是一次十足的享受。◇ *I only agreed out of sheer desperation.* 我一时情急才同意的。➲ MORE LIKE THIS 32, page R28 **3** very steep 陡峭的：*sheer cliffs/slopes* 悬崖峭壁；陡坡 ◇ *Outside there was a sheer drop down to the sea below.* 外面是一道陡坡，直插大海。**4** (of cloth, etc. 织物等) thin, light and almost transparent 又薄又轻几乎透明的：*sheer nylon* 透明尼龙

■ ***adv.*** straight up or down 垂直地；陡峭地：*The cliffs rise sheer from the beach.* 悬崖从海滩上拔地而起。◇ *The ground dropped sheer away at our feet.* 在我们脚下，地势陡降。

■ ***verb***

PHR V **ˌsheer aˈway/ˈoff (from sth)** to change direction suddenly, especially in order to avoid hitting sth 急转，急拐（避开某物）：(*figurative*) *Her mind sheered away from images she did not wish to dwell on.* 她有意不去想那些她不愿多想的事情。

sheet /ʃiːt/ *noun*

• **ON BED** 床上 **1** a large piece of thin cloth used on a bed to lie on or lie under 床单；被单：*Have you **changed the sheets** (= put clean sheets on the bed)?* 被单你换了吗？◇ *He slid between the sheets and closed his eyes.* 他钻进被子里，闭上了眼睛。➲ VISUAL VOCAB PAGE V24 ➲ SEE ALSO DUST SHEET

• **OF PAPER** 纸 **2** a piece of paper for writing or printing on, etc. usually in a standard size 一张（通常指标准尺寸的纸）：*a **clean/blank sheet of paper*** (= with no writing on it) 一张白纸 ◇ *Pick up one of our free information sheets at reception.* 请在接待处拿一份我们的免费资料。

• **FLAT THIN PIECE** 片 **3** a flat thin piece of any material, normally square or RECTANGULAR 薄片，薄板（多指正方形或长方形的）：*a **sheet of glass/steel*** 一块玻璃；一张钢板 ◇ ***sheet metal*** (= metal that has been made into thin sheets) 金属板 ◇ *Place the dough on a **baking sheet*** (= for cooking sth in an oven). 把面团放在烤板上。

• **WIDE FLAT AREA** 大片 **4** a wide flat area of sth, covering the surface of sth else 一大片（覆盖物）：*The road was covered with a sheet of ice.* 路面结了一层冰。

• **OF FIRE/WATER** 火；水 **5** a large moving mass of fire or water 一大片，一大堆，一大摊（移动的火或水）：*a sheet of flame* 一片火海 ◇ *The rain was coming down **in sheets*** (= very heavily). 大雨倾盆而下。

• **ON SAIL** 帆上 **6** (*specialist*) a rope or chain fastened to the lower corner of a sail to hold it and to control the angle of the sail 帆脚索；拉帆绳 HELP There are other compounds ending **sheet**. You will find them at their place in the alphabet. 其他以 sheet 结尾的复合词，可在各字母中的适当位置查到。IDM SEE CLEAN *adj.*

ˈsheet anchor *noun* a person or thing that you can depend on in a difficult situation（困难时的）靠山，指望，对策

sheet·ing /ˈʃiːtɪŋ/ *noun* [U] **1** metal, plastic, etc. made into flat thin pieces 薄片；压片；薄膜：***metal/plastic/polythene sheeting*** 金属薄片；塑料 / 聚乙烯薄膜 **2** cloth used for making sheets for beds 床单布；被单布

ˌsheet ˈlightning *noun* [U] LIGHTNING that appears as a broad area of light in the sky 片状闪电 ➲ COMPARE FORKED LIGHTNING

ˈsheet music *noun* [U] printed music as opposed to recorded music; printed music published on separate sheets of paper that are not fastened together to form a book 活页乐谱（与录音音乐相对）

sheikh /ʃeɪk; ʃiːk/ (*also* **shaikh** /ʃeɪk/) *noun* **1** an Arab prince or leader; the head of an Arab family, village, etc. 谢赫，筛海（阿拉伯的亲王、酋长、首领、族长、村长等）**2** a leader in a Muslim community or organization（穆斯林共同体或组织的）长老

sheikh·dom /ˈʃeɪkdəm; ˈʃiːk-/ *noun* an area of land ruled by a sheikh （阿拉伯）酋长统辖的领土，酋长国

sheila /ˈʃiːlə/ *noun* (*AustralE, NZE, slang*) a girl or young woman 小妞；少女；年轻女子

shekel /ˈʃekl/ *noun* **1** the unit of money in Israel 谢克尔（以色列货币单位）**2** an ancient silver coin used by the Jews 谢克尔（古代犹太人用的银币）

shel·duck /ˈʃeldʌk/ *noun* (*pl.* **shel·duck** or **shelducks**) a type of wild DUCK that lives on or near the coast 翘鼻麻鸭；花凫

shelf /ʃelf/ *noun* (*pl.* **shelves** /ʃelvz/) **1** a flat board, made of wood, metal, glass, etc., fixed to the wall or forming part of a cupboard/closet, BOOKCASE, etc., for things to be placed on （固定在墙上的或橱柜、书架等的）架子，搁板：*I helped him put up some shelves in his bedroom.* 我帮他在卧室里装了几个搁架。◇ *The book I wanted was on the top shelf.* 我想要的那本书在书架的最上层。◇ ***supermarket/library shelves*** 超市的货架；图书馆的书架 ◇ *empty shelves* 空搁板 ➲ COLLOCATIONS AT DECORATE, SHOPPING ➲ VISUAL VOCAB PAGES V22, V26 **2** (*geology* 地) a thing shaped like a shelf, especially a piece of rock sticking out from a CLIFF or from the edge of a mass of land under the sea （悬崖上或海底）突出的岩石；陆架；陆棚：*the continental shelf* 大陆架 ➲ SEE ALSO SHELVE

IDM **on the ˈshelf** (*informal*) **1** not wanted by anyone; not used （无用而）闲置的；搁置的 **2** (*old-fashioned*) (especially of women 尤指女人) considered to be too old to get married 年龄大得嫁不出去的 **off the ˈshelf** that can be bought immediately and does not have to be specially designed or ordered 现成有售的；不用定制的：*I bought this package off the shelf.* 我买的这一盒是现货。◇ *off-the-shelf software packages* 现成软件包 ➲ COMPARE OFF THE PEG at PEG *n.*

ˈshelf life *noun* [usually sing.] the length of time that food, etc. can be kept before it is too old to be sold （食品等的）货架期，保存期

ˈshelf-stacker *noun* a person whose job is to fill shelves with goods to be sold, especially in a supermarket （尤指超市的）货物上架员，上货员

shell /ʃel/ *noun, verb*

■ ***noun*** **1** [C, U] the hard outer part of eggs, nuts, some seeds and some animals （蛋、坚果、某些种子和某些动物的）壳：*We collected shells on the beach.* 我们在海滩拾贝壳。◇ *snail shells* 蜗牛壳 ◇ *walnut shells* 核桃壳 ◇ *earrings made out of coconut shell* 用椰子壳做的耳坠 ➲ PICTURE AT SHELLFISH ➲ VISUAL VOCAB PAGES V13, V33, V35 ➲ SEE ALSO EGGSHELL, NUTSHELL, SEASHELL, TORTOISESHELL **2** [C] any object that looks like the shell of a SNAIL or sea creature 壳状物：*pasta shells* 贝壳形意大利面 **3** [C] a metal case filled with EXPLOSIVE, to be fired from a large gun 炮弹 **4** (*NAmE*) = CARTRIDGE (1) **5** [C] the walls or outer structure of sth, for example, an empty building or ship after a fire or a bomb attack （房屋或船舶等的）骨架，框架，壳体：*The house was now a shell gutted by flames.* 房子烧得只剩个空骨架了。◇ (*figurative*) *My life has been an empty shell since he died.* 他死后，我的生活就成了一个徒有其表的空壳子。**6** [C] any structure that forms a hard outer frame （任何物体的）外壳，壳体：*the body shell of a car* 车身外壳 **7** [sing.] the outer layer of sb's personality; how they seem to be or feel （人的）表面性格，表面人格，表面感情，外表：*She had developed a shell of indifference.* 她养成一副冷漠的外表。

IDM **come out of your ˈshell** to become less shy and more confident when talking to other people （和人交谈时）放大胆子，不缩手缩脚 **to go, retreat, etc. into your ˈshell** to become shyer and avoid talking to other people 变得羞怯（或内向、孤僻）

■ ***verb*** **1** [T, I] ~ (**sth**) to fire shells at sth 炮击：*They shelled the city all night.* 他们整夜炮轰那座城市。◇ *Just as they were leaving, the rebels started shelling.* 他们正要撤离，叛军开始了炮击。**2** [T] ~ **sth** to remove the shell or covering from nuts, PEAS, etc. 给…去壳

PHR V ˌ**shell** ˈ**out** (**for sth**) | ˌ**shell sth**↔ˈ**out** (**for sth**) (*informal*) to pay a lot of money for sth 付（一大笔钱） **SYN** **fork out** (**for sth**): *The band shelled out $100 000 for a mobile recording studio.* 乐队花了 10 万美元购置一间移动录音室。

she'll /ʃiːl/ *short form* she will

shel·lac /ʃəˈlæk; ˈʃelæk/ *noun, verb*
■ ***noun*** [U] a natural substance used in making varnish to protect surfaces and make them hard 虫胶；紫（胶虫）胶
■ ***verb*** (**-ck-**) **1 ~ sth** to cover sth with shellac 以虫胶清漆覆盖；用虫胶清漆涂刷 **2** [usually passive] **~ sb** (*NAmE, informal*) to defeat sb very easily 轻易击败：*The Republicans got shellacked in the elections.* 共和党在选举中一败涂地。

shell·fire /ˈʃelfaɪə(r)/ *noun* [U] attacks or explosions caused by SHELLS being fired from large guns 炮火；炮击

shellfish 水生有壳动物

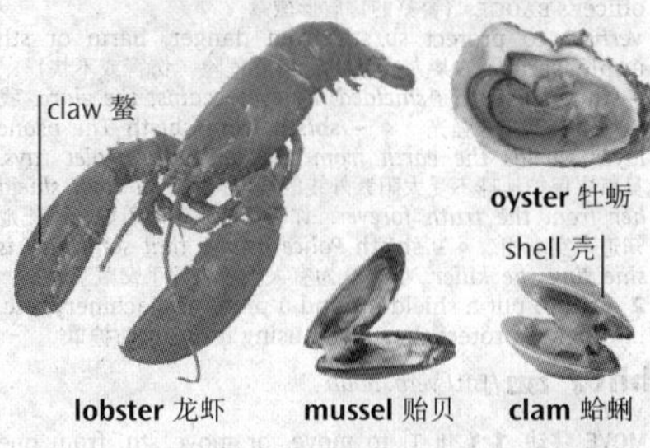

shell·fish /ˈʃelfɪʃ/ *noun* (*pl.* **shell·fish**) a creature with a shell, that lives in water, especially one of the types that can be eaten. OYSTERS and CRABS are both shellfish. （尤指可以吃的）水生有壳动物 ➲ COMPARE CRUSTACEAN, MOLLUSC

ˈ**shell game** *noun* (*NAmE*) **1 the** ˈ**shell game** a game in which three cups are moved around, and players must guess which is the one with a small object underneath 果壳猜测游戏（移动三个杯子，参加者须猜测哪个杯子扣着小物体） **2** an act by an organization or a politician that tricks people in a clever way （机构或政客的）骗局，骗术

shell·ing /ˈʃelɪŋ/ *noun* [U] the firing of SHELLS from large guns 炮击：*We suffered weeks of heavy shelling.* 我们遭受了几星期的密集炮击。

ˈ**shell shock** *noun* [U] a mental illness that can affect soldiers who have been in battle for a long time 弹震症，战斗疲劳症（长期作战引起的精神疾患）

ˈ**shell-shocked** *adj.* **1** shocked, confused or anxious because of a difficult situation, and unable to think or act normally （因困境而）吓昏了头的，糊涂得不知所措的，焦虑得无法应对的 **2** suffering from shell shock 患弹震症的

ˈ**shell suit** *noun* (*BrE*) a loose pair of trousers/pants and matching jacket worn as informal clothes. Shell suits are made of a light, slightly shiny, material and are often brightly coloured. 休闲装；休闲服 ➲ COMPARE TRACKSUIT

shel·ter 🔑 /ˈʃeltə(r)/ *noun, verb*
■ ***noun*** **1** 🔑 [U] the fact of having a place to live or stay, considered as a basic human need 居所；住处：*Human beings need food, clothing and shelter.* 人类有衣、食、住的需求。 **2** 🔑 [U] **~ (from sth)** protection from rain, danger or attack 遮蔽，庇护，避难（避雨、躲避危险或攻击）：*to take shelter from the storm* 躲避暴风雨 ◇ *The fox was running for the shelter of the trees.* 狐狸朝树丛跑，想要躲藏起来。 ◇ *People were desperately seeking shelter from the gunfire.* 人们拼命地找地方躲避炮火。 **3** 🔑 [C] (often in compounds 常构成复合词) a structure built to give protection, especially from the weather or from attack （尤指用以躲避风雨或攻击的）遮蔽物，庇护处，避难处：*They built a rough shelter from old pieces of wood.* 他们用旧木条搭了一个简陋的窝棚。 ◇ *an air-raid shelter* 防空洞 ➲ SEE ALSO BUS SHELTER **4** [C] a building, usually owned by a charity, that provides a place to stay for people without a home, or protection for people or animals who have been badly treated （无家可归者或受虐待者的）收容所，庇护所：*a night shelter for the homeless* 无家可归者夜间收容所 ◇ *an animal shelter* 动物收容处 ➲ SEE ALSO HOSTEL
■ ***verb*** **1** 🔑 [T] to give sb/sth a place where they are protected from the weather or from danger; to protect sb/sth 保护；掩蔽：**~ sb/sth from sb/sth** *Trees shelter the house from the wind.* 树给房子挡住了风。 ◇ **~ sb/sth** *helping the poor and sheltering the homeless* 帮助贫穷者，庇护无家可归者 ◇ *Perhaps I sheltered my daughter too much* (= protected her too much from unpleasant or difficult experiences). 也许我对女儿保护过度了。 **2** 🔑 [I] **~ (from sth)** to stay in a place that protects you from the weather or from danger 躲避（风雨或危险）：*We sheltered from the rain in a doorway.* 我们在一处门廊里避雨。 ➲ WORDFINDER NOTE AT RAIN

shel·tered /ˈʃeltəd; *NAmE* -tərd/ *adj.* **1** (of a place 地方) protected from bad weather 有遮蔽物（不受恶劣天气侵袭）的：*a sheltered beach* 有天然屏障的海滩 **2** (*sometimes disapproving*) protected from the more unpleasant aspects or difficulties of life 受庇护的；受到保护的：*She had a very sheltered childhood.* 她有过一个备受呵护的童年。 ◇ *They both lead very sheltered lives.* 他们两人都过着呵护备至的生活。 **3** [only before noun] (*BrE*) (of houses, flats/apartments, etc. 房舍、公寓等) designed for people, especially old people, who can still live fairly independent lives, but with staff available to help them if necessary 为需要者（尤指老年人）提供照顾的：***sheltered accommodation/housing*** 福利院的住宿 ◇ ***a sheltered workshop*** *for the blind* 盲人福利工场

shelve /ʃelv/ *verb* **1** [T] **~ sth** to decide not to continue with a plan, either for a short time or permanently 搁置，停止（计划） **SYN** **put on ice**: *The government has shelved the idea until at least next year.* 政府决定把这个想法先放一放，至少推迟到明年再说。 **2** [T] **~ sth** to put books, etc. on a shelf 把…放在架子（或搁板）上 **3** [I] (**+ adv./prep.**) (of land 陆地) to slope downwards 倾斜；成斜坡：*The beach shelved gently down to the water.* 海滩缓缓地向下没入水中。

shelves PL. OF SHELF

shelv·ing /ˈʃelvɪŋ/ *noun* [U] shelves; material for making shelves 架子；搁板；做架子的材料：*wooden shelving* 木搁板

ˈ**she-male** *noun* (*informal*) a TRANSSEXUAL, especially one who works as a PROSTITUTE （尤指卖淫的）变性人

she·nani·gans /ʃɪˈnænɪɡənz/ *noun* [pl.] (*informal*) secret or dishonest activities that people find interesting or amusing 诡计；恶作剧；耍手腕；鬼把戏

Sheng /ʃeŋ/ *noun* [U] (in Kenya) a simple form of language that includes words from English, Kiswahili and other African languages, used especially between young people in cities 盛语（肯尼亚的一种简单的语言，包括英语、斯瓦希里语等非洲语言的词汇，尤在城市青年之间使用）

shep·herd /ˈʃepəd; *NAmE* -ərd/ *noun, verb*
■ ***noun*** (*NAmE also* **sheep·herd·er**) a person whose job is to take care of sheep 牧羊人；羊倌
■ ***verb*** **~ sb + adv./prep.** to guide sb or a group of people somewhere, making sure they go where you want them to go 带领；引；护送

shep·herd·ess /ˌʃepəˈdes; ˈʃepədəs; *NAmE* ˌʃepərˈdes; ˈʃepərdəs/ *noun* (*old-fashioned*) a woman who takes care of sheep 女牧羊人；牧羊女

ˌ**shepherd's** ˈ**pie** (*also* ˌ**cottage** ˈ**pie**) *noun* [C, U] (*especially BrE*) a dish of MINCED (= finely chopped) meat covered with a layer of MASHED potato 肉馅土豆泥饼；肉馅薯饼

S

sher·bet /ˈʃɜːbət; *NAmE* ˈʃɜːrbət/ *noun* **1** [U] (*BrE*) a powder that tastes of fruit and FIZZES when you put it in your mouth, eaten as a sweet/candy 果味汽水粉糖 **2** [C, U] (*NAmE, becoming old-fashioned*) = SORBET

sherd /ʃɜːd; *NAmE* ʃɜːrd/ *noun* = SHARD

sher·iff /ˈʃerɪf/ *noun* **1** (in the US) an elected officer responsible for keeping law and order in a county or town 县治安官，城镇治安官（美国民选地方官员） **2** (*often* **High Sheriff**) (in England and Wales) an officer representing the king or queen in counties, and some cities, who performs some legal duties and attends ceremonies 郡督（英格兰和威尔士官员，为英王在各郡和部分城市的代表） **3** (in Scotland) a judge（苏格兰）法官 **4** (in Canada) an official who works in a court preparing court cases（加拿大法院准备诉讼案件的）执行员

ˈ**sheriff court** *noun* a lower court in Scotland（苏格兰的）郡法院

Sher·lock /ˈʃɜːlɒk; *NAmE* ˈʃɜːrlɑːk/ (*also* **Sherlock Holmes** /ˈʃɜːlɒk həʊmz; *NAmE* hoʊmz/) *noun* (*informal, sometimes ironic*) a person who tries to find an explanation for a crime or sth mysterious or who shows that they understand sth quickly, especially sth that is not obvious（自命）福尔摩斯；（自命）有侦探头脑的人：*Oh, well done, Sherlock. Did you figure that out all by yourself?* 喔，干得好，大侦探。全是你自己推断出来的吗？ ➲ MORE LIKE THIS 17, page R27 **ORIGIN** From Sherlock Holmes, a very clever detective in stories by Arthur Conan Doyle, published in the late 19th and early 20th centuries. 源自阿瑟•柯南•道尔于 19 世纪末 20 世纪初发表的一系列小说中一位十分机智的侦探夏洛克•福尔摩斯。

Sherpa /ˈʃɜːpə; *NAmE* ˈʃɜːrpə/ *noun* a member of a Himalayan people, who often guide people in the mountains, sometimes carrying their bags, etc. 夏尔巴人（居住在喜马拉雅山脉的一个部族，常作登山向导或搬运工等）

sherry /ˈʃeri/ *noun* (*pl.* **-ies**) **1** [U, C] a strong yellow or brown wine, originally from southern Spain. It is often drunk before meals. 雪利酒（烈性葡萄酒，原产自西班牙南部）：***sweet/dry sherry*** 甜 / 无甜味的雪利酒 ◇ ***cream sherry*** (= a type of very sweet sherry) 浓甜雪利酒 ◇ *fine quality sherries* 优质雪利酒 ◇ ***a sherry glass*** (= a type of small narrow wine glass) 雪利酒杯（一种细小玻璃酒杯） **2** [C] a glass of sherry 一杯雪利酒：*I'll have a sherry.* 我要一杯雪利酒。

sher·wani /ʃɜːˈwɑːni; *NAmE* ʃɜːrˈw-/ *noun* a knee-length coat with buttons up to the neck, sometimes worn by men from S Asia（南亚男装）高领及膝外套

she's *short form* **1** /ʃiːz; ʃiz/ she is **2** /ʃiːz/ she has

Shetland pony /ˌʃetlənd ˈpəʊni; *NAmE* ˈpoʊni/ *noun* a very small, strong horse with a rough coat 设得兰矮种马

shh = SH

Shia (*also* **Shi'a**) /ˈʃɪə/ *noun* (*pl.* **Shia** or **Shias**) **1** [U] one of the two main branches of the Islamic religion 什叶派（伊斯兰教的两大派别之一） ➲ COMPARE SUNNI (1) **2** [C] (*also* **Shi·ite, Shi'ite**) a member of the Shia branch of Islam 什叶派穆斯林

shi·atsu /ʃiˈætsuː/ *noun* [U] (*from Japanese*) = ACUPRESSURE

shib·bo·leth /ˈʃɪbəleθ/ *noun* (*formal*) **1** an old idea, principle or phrase that is no longer accepted by many people as important or appropriate to modern life 过时的观点；陈旧的原则；陈词滥调 **2** a custom, word, etc. that distinguishes one group of people from another 某群体特有的习惯（或用语等） **ORIGIN** From a Hebrew word meaning 'ear of corn'. In the Bible story, Jephthah, the leader of the Gileadites, was able to use it as a test to tell which were his own men, because others found the 'sh' sound difficult to pronounce. 源自希伯来语，意为"谷穗"。据《圣经》记载，基列人首领耶弗他能用这一词语来分辨谁是自己人，因为异族人难以发准 sh 音。

shied PAST TENSE, PAST PART. OF SHY

shield /ʃiːld/ *noun, verb*

■ ***noun*** **1** a large piece of metal or leather carried by soldiers in the past to protect the body when fighting 盾（牌） **2** = RIOT SHIELD **3** a person or thing used to protect sb/sth, especially by forming a barrier 保护人；保护物；掩护物；屏障：*The gunman used the hostages as **a human shield**.* 持枪歹徒用人质作人体盾牌。◇ *Water is not an effective shield against the sun's more harmful rays.* 水不能有效阻挡太阳中更有害的射线。◇ *She hid her true feelings behind a shield of cold indifference.* 她把自己的真实感情掩藏在一副冷漠的外表后面。 **4** a plate or screen that protects a machine or the person using it from damage or injury（保护机器和操作者的）护罩，防护屏，挡板 **5** an object in the shape of a shield, given as a prize in a sports competition, etc. 盾形奖牌 ➲ PICTURE AT MEDAL **6** a drawing or model of a shield showing a COAT OF ARMS 盾形纹徽；盾形徽章 **7** (*NAmE*) a police officer's BADGE（警察的）盾形徽章

■ ***verb*** **1** to protect sb/sth from danger, harm or sth unpleasant 保护某人或某物（免遭危险、伤害或不快）：**~ sth against sth** *I shielded my eyes against the glare.* 我挡住眼睛以避开强光。◇ **~ sb/sth from sb/sth** *The ozone layer shields the earth from the sun's ultraviolet rays.* 臭氧层保护地球不受太阳紫外线的辐射。◇ *You can't shield her from the truth forever.* 你不可能永远瞒着她，不让她知道事实真相。◇ **~ sb/sth** *Police believe that somebody is shielding the killer.* 警方认为有人把杀人凶手窝藏了起来。 **2 ~ sth** to put a shield around a piece of machinery, etc. in order to protect the person using it 给…加防护罩

shift 🔑 **AW** /ʃɪft/ *verb, noun*

■ ***verb***

• **MOVE** 移动 **1** 🔑 [I, T] to move, or move sth, from one position or place to another 转移；挪动：*Lydia shifted uncomfortably in her chair.* 莉迪亚在椅子上不安地动来动去。◇ **~ (from…) (to…)** *The action of the novel shifts from Paris to London.* 小说情节从巴黎移到了伦敦。◇ **~ sth** *Could you help me shift some furniture?* 你能帮我挪几件家具吗？◇ **~ sth (from…) (to…)** *He shifted his gaze from the child to her.* 他把目光从孩子身上移到她身上。◇ *She shifted her weight from one foot to the other.* 她把身体的重量从一只脚换到另一只脚上。 **2** [I, T] **~ (yourself)** (*BrE, informal*) to move quickly 赶快；快速移动 **SYN** **hurry**

• **SITUATION/OPINION/POLICY** 情况；意见；政策 **3** 🔑 [I] (of a situation, an opinion, a policy etc. 情况、意见、政策等) to change from one state, position, etc. to another 改变；转向：*Public attitudes towards marriage have shifted over the past 50 years.* * 50 年来，公众对婚姻的态度已经改变。◇ **~ (from…) (to/towards/toward…)** *The balance of power shifted away from workers towards employers.* 强势的一方从工人转为雇主。 **4** [T] to change your opinion of or attitude towards sth, or change the way that you do sth 改变观点（或态度、做事方式等）：**~ sth** *We need to shift the focus of this debate.* 我们需要转换一下辩论的焦点。◇ **~ sth (from…) (to/towards/toward…)** *The new policy shifted the emphasis away from fighting inflation.* 新政策不再把重点放在抑制通货膨胀上。

• **RESPONSIBILITY** 责任 **5** [T] **~ responsibility/blame (for sth) (onto sb)** to make sb else responsible for sth you should do or sth bad that you have done 推卸，转嫁（责任）：*He tried to shift the blame for his mistakes onto his colleagues.* 他自己犯了错误，却试图把责任推给同事。

• **REMOVE MARK** 去除污迹 **6** [T] **~ sth** to remove sth such as a dirty mark 去除（污迹等） **SYN** **get rid of sb/sth**：*a detergent that shifts even the most stubborn stains* 能去除极顽固的污渍的洗涤剂

• **SELL GOODS** 销售商品 **7** [T] **~ sth** to sell goods, especially goods that are difficult to sell 销售，出售（尤指销路不好的商品）：*They cut prices drastically to try and shift stock.* 他们大幅度降价，试图销出存货。

• **IN VEHICLE** 车辆 **8** [I] (*NAmE*) to change the gears when you are driving a vehicle 换（挡）：*to shift into second gear* 换成二挡

IDM **shift your ˈground** (*usually disapproving*) to change your opinion about a subject, especially during a discussion（尤指讨论时）改变立场 **(the) ˌshifting ˈsands (of sth)** used to describe a situation that changes so often that it is difficult to understand or deal with it 变幻莫测；变化无常

PHR V **ˌshift for yourˈself** (*BrE*) to do things without help from other people 独立设法应付；独立谋生；自立：*You're going to have to shift for yourself from now on.* 从今以以后，你就得独自谋生了。

▪ ***noun***

• **CHANGE** 改变 **1** [C] ~ (**in sth**) a change in position or direction 改变；转移；转换；变换：*a dramatic shift in public opinion* 公众舆论的急剧变化 ◇ *a shift of emphasis* 重点的转移 ➲ SEE ALSO PARADIGM SHIFT

• **PERIOD OF WORK** 工作时间 **2** [C] a period of time worked by a group of workers who start work as another group finishes 班；轮班；轮班工作时间：*to be on the* ***day/night shift*** *at the factory* 在工厂上日班 / 夜班 ◇ *to work an eight-hour shift* 按每班八小时轮班工作 ◇ *working in shifts* 轮班工作 ◇ ***shift workers/work*** 轮班工作的工人；轮班作业 ➲ COLLOCATIONS AT JOB ➲ SEE ALSO SWING SHIFT **3** [C+ sing./pl. v.] the workers who work a particular shift 轮班职工：*The night shift has/have just come off duty.* 上夜班的刚刚下班。➲ **WORDFINDER NOTE** AT FACTORY

• **ON COMPUTER** 计算机 **4** [U] (*also* **shift key** [sing.]) the system on a computer keyboard or TYPEWRITER that allows capital letters or a different set of characters to be typed; the key that operates this system（计算机键盘或打字机上的）转换（键），换挡（键）➲ **WORDFINDER NOTE** AT KEYBOARD

• **CLOTHING** 服装 **5** [C] a woman's simple straight dress 直筒式连衣裙 **6** [C] a simple straight piece of clothing worn by women in the past as underwear（旧时妇女穿的）直筒式内衣

shift·er /ˈʃɪftə(r)/ *noun* (*especially NAmE*) the GEARBOX of a vehicle or the set of gears on a bicycle（汽车的）变速箱，齿轮箱；（自行车的）传动装置

ˌshifting ˌcultiˈvation *noun* [U] (*specialist*) a way of farming in some tropical countries in which farmers use an area of land until it cannot be used for growing plants any more, then move to a new area of land（某些热带国家的）移耕农业，迁徙耕作，游耕

shift·less /ˈʃɪftləs/ *adj.* (*disapproving*) lazy and having no ambition to succeed in life 没志气的；不思上进的；混日子的

shifty /ˈʃɪfti/ *adj.* (**shift·ier, shifti·est**) (*informal*) seeming to be dishonest; looking guilty about sth 看着不可靠的；贼眉鼠眼的；显得心里有鬼的 SYN **furtive**：*shifty eyes* 贼溜溜的眼睛 ◇ *to look shifty* 显得贼头贼脑的 ▸ **shift·ily** /-ɪli/ *adv.*

shii·take (*also* **shi·take**) /ʃɪˈtɑːki; ʃiː-/ (*also* **ˌshiitake ˈmushroom**) *noun* (*from Japanese*) a type of Japanese or Chinese MUSHROOM 香菇；香蕈

Shi·ite (*also* **Shi'ite**) /ˈʃiːaɪt/ *noun* a member of the Shia branch of Islam（伊斯兰教的）什叶派穆斯林 ➲ COMPARE SUNNI (2) ▸ **Shi·ite** (*also* **Shi'ite**) *adj.* [usually before noun]

shil·ling /ˈʃɪlɪŋ/ *noun* **1** a British coin in use until 1971, worth 12 old pence. There were 20 shillings in one pound. 先令（英国 1971 年以前货币单位，一先令值 12 旧便士，20 先令合一英镑）**2** the unit of money in Kenya, Uganda, Tanzania and Somalia 先令（肯尼亚、乌干达、坦桑尼亚和索马里货币单位）

shilly-shally /ˈʃɪli ʃæli/ *verb* (**shilly-shallies, shilly-shally·ing, shilly-shallied, shilly-shallied**) [I] (*informal, disapproving*) to take a long time to do sth, especially to make a decision 犹豫；踌躇 SYN **dither**：*Stop shilly-shallying and make up your mind.* 别犹豫了，拿主意吧。➲ **MORE LIKE THIS** 11, page R26

shim /ʃɪm/ *noun* (*NAmE*) a thin piece of wood, rubber, metal, etc. which is thicker at one end than the other, that you use to fill a space between two things that do not fit well together（木、橡胶、金属等）楔子，垫片，填隙片

shim·mer /ˈʃɪmə(r)/ *verb, noun*

▪ ***verb*** [I] to shine with a soft light that seems to move slightly 发出微弱的闪光；闪烁：*The sea was shimmering in the sunlight.* 阳光下海水波光闪烁。➲ SYNONYMS AT SHINE

▪ ***noun*** [U, sing.] a shining light that seems to move slightly 闪烁的光：*a shimmer of moonlight in the dark sky* 黑暗的夜空中忽明忽暗的月光

shimmy /ˈʃɪmi/ *verb* (**shim·mies, shimmy·ing, shim·mied, shim·mied**) [I] **+ adv./prep.** to dance or move in a way that involves shaking your hips and shoulders（抖动着肩膀和臀部）跳希米舞；一扭一摆地走

shin /ʃɪn/ *noun, verb*

▪ ***noun*** the front part of the leg below the knee 胫；胫部 ➲ VISUAL VOCAB PAGE V64

▪ ***verb*** (**-nn-**) (*BrE*) (*NAmE* **shinny**)

PHR V **ˈshin/ˈshinny up/down sth** (*informal*) to climb up or down sth quickly, using your hands and legs 爬：*He shinned down the drainpipe and ran off.* 他顺着排水管爬下去跑了。

ˈshin bone *noun* the front and larger bone of the two bones in the lower part of the leg between the knee and the ankle 胫骨 SYN **tibia** ➲ **VISUAL VOCAB** PAGE V64

shin·dig /ˈʃɪndɪɡ/ *noun* (*informal*) a big noisy party 盛大而喧闹的聚会；盛大舞会

shine /ʃaɪn/ *verb, noun*

▪ ***verb*** (**shone, shone** /ʃɒn; *NAmE* ʃoʊn/) HELP In sense 2 in *NAmE* **shined** can also be used for the past tense and past participle. In sense 3 **shined** is used for the past tense and past participle. 作第 2 义时，在美式英语中过去式和过去分词也可用 shined；作第 3 义时过去式和过去分词用 shined。**1** [I] to produce or reflect light; to be bright 发光；反光；照耀：*The sun shone brightly in a cloudless sky.* 太阳在无云的天空中明亮地照耀着。◇ *The dark polished wood shone like glass.* 抛光后的深色木料像玻璃一样熠熠闪光。◇ (*figurative*) *Her eyes were shining with excitement.* 她兴奋得两眼放光。◇ *Excitement was shining in her eyes.* 她眼里闪着兴奋的光芒。➲ **SYNONYMS** ON NEXT PAGE **2** (*NAmE also* **shined, shined**) [T] ~ **sth** (**+ adv./prep.**) to aim or point the light of a lamp, etc. in a particular direction 把…照向；使…光投向：*He shone the flashlight around the cellar.* 他用手电筒往地窖各处照了照。◇ (*figurative*) *Campaigners are shining a spotlight on the world's diminishing natural resources.* 从事这场运动的人要使公众注意到世界上的自然资源日益减少。**3** (**shined, shined**) [T] ~ **sth** to polish sth; to make sth smooth and bright 擦亮；擦光：*He shined shoes and sold newspapers to make money.* 他靠擦鞋、卖报挣钱。**4** [I] to be very good at sth 出色；出类拔萃：*He failed to shine academically but he was very good at sports.* 他学业不怎么样，但体育却棒极了。◇ *She has set a* ***shining example*** *of loyal service over four decades.* 四十年间，她树立了一个忠诚服务的光辉榜样。➲ SEE ALSO SHINY IDM SEE HAY, KNIGHT *n.*, RISE *v.*

PHR V **ˌshine ˈthrough** (**sth**) (of a quality 某种品质) to be easy to see or notice 显现出来；很明显：*Her old professional skills shone through.* 她在行的专业技巧顿时显现无遗。

▪ ***noun*** [sing.] the bright quality that sth has when light is reflected on it 光亮；光泽：*a shampoo that gives your hair body and shine* 一种能使头发浓密发亮的洗发剂

IDM **take a ˈshine to sb/sth** (*informal*) to begin to like sb very much as soon as you see or meet them 一眼就看上；一见钟情 **take the ˈshine off sth** (*informal*) to make sth seem much less good than it did at first 使…黯然失色 ➲ MORE AT RAIN *n.*

shiner /ˈʃaɪnə(r)/ *noun* (*informal*) an area of dark skin that can form around sb's eye when they receive a blow to it（被打成的）青肿眼眶 SYN **black eye**

shin·gle /ˈʃɪŋɡl/ *noun* **1** [U] a mass of small smooth stones on a beach or at the side of a river（海滨或河边的）卵石滩：*a shingle beach* 卵石海滩 ➲ **VISUAL VOCAB** PAGE V5 **2** [C, U] a small flat piece of wood that is used to cover a wall or roof of a building 墙面板；木瓦；屋顶板 **3** [C] (*NAmE*) a board with a sign on it, in front of a doctor's or lawyer's office（诊所或律师事务所挂的）招牌：*He hung*

S

out his own shingle (= started a business as a doctor or lawyer). 他独自挂牌开业了。

shin·gled /ˈʃɪŋɡld/ *adj.* (of a roof, building, etc. 房顶、建筑物等) covered with shingles 盖木瓦的

shin·gles /ˈʃɪŋɡlz/ *noun* [U] (*medical* 医) a disease that affects the nerves and produces a band of painful spots on the skin 带状疱疹

▼ **SYNONYMS 同义词辨析**

shine

gleam • glow • sparkle • glisten • shimmer • glitter • twinkle • glint

These words all mean to produce or reflect light. 以上各词均含发光、反光之义。

shine to produce or reflect light, especially brightly 指发光、反光、照耀： *The sun was shining and the sky was blue.* 阳光灿烂，天空一片蓝。

gleam to shine with a clear bright or pale light, especially a reflected light 指闪烁、隐约闪光、微光反射： *Moonlight gleamed on the water.* 月光照在水面上泛起粼粼波光。

glow (often of sth hot or warm) to produce a dull steady light 常指热的物体发出微弱而稳定的光： *The end of his cigarette glowed red.* 他的烟头发着微弱的红光。

sparkle to shine brightly with small flashes of light 指闪烁、闪耀： *The diamonds sparkled in the light.* 钻石在灯光下闪闪发亮。

glisten (of sth wet) to shine 指湿物闪光、闪亮： *The road glistened wet after the rain.* 雨后的道路润泽闪亮。

shimmer to shine with a soft light that seems to shake slightly 指发出微弱的闪光、闪烁： *Everything seemed to shimmer in the heat.* 在高温下所有的东西都好像在闪光。

glitter to shine brightly with small flashes of reflected light 指闪亮、闪耀： *The ceiling of the cathedral glittered with gold.* 大教堂的天花板金光闪闪。

SPARKLE OR GLITTER? 用 sparkle 还是 glitter?

There is very little difference in meaning between these two words. **Glitter** can sometimes suggest a lack of depth, but this is more frequent in the figurative use of **glitter** as a noun. 以上两词在意义上几乎没有差别。glitter 有时暗指缺乏深度，但这较常在 glitter 作名词时作比喻义用： *the superficial glitter of show business* 表面上光彩迷人的演艺业 **Sparkle** is also often used to talk about light reflected off a surface, but things that produce light can also sparkle. * sparkle 亦常用以指物体表面反光，但物体发出亮光也可用 sparkle： *Stars sparkled in the sky.* 星星在天空中闪烁。

twinkle to shine with a light that changes rapidly from bright to faint to bright again 指一明一暗地闪耀、闪烁： *Stars twinkled in the sky.* 星星在天空中闪烁。

glint to give small bright flashes of reflected light 指微微闪光、闪亮、反光： *The blade of the knife glinted in the darkness.* 刀刃在黑暗中亮了亮。

PATTERNS

- to shine/gleam/sparkle/glisten/shimmer/glitter/glint **on** sth
- to shine/gleam/glow/sparkle/glisten/shimmer/glitter/twinkle/glint **with** sth
- to shine/gleam/sparkle/glisten/shimmer/glitter/glint **in the sunlight**
- to shine/gleam/glisten/shimmer/glitter/glint **in the moonlight**
- the **stars** shine/sparkle/glitter/twinkle
- sb's **eyes** shine/gleam/glow/sparkle/glisten/glitter/twinkle/glint
- to shine/gleam/glow/glitter **brightly**
- to shine/gleam/glow/shimmer **softly**

shin·gly /ˈʃɪŋɡli/ *adj.* (of a beach 海滩) covered in shingle 遍布卵石的

ˈshin guard (*BrE also* **ˈshin pad**) *noun* a piece of thick material that is used to protect the lower front part of the leg when playing sports 护胫，护腿板（体育运动时戴）

shinny /ˈʃɪni/ *verb, noun*

■ ***verb*** (**shin·nies**, **shinny·ing**, **shin·nied**, **shin·nied**) (*NAmE*) (*BrE* **shin**)

PHR V **ˈshin/ˈshinny up/down sth** (*informal*) to climb up or down sth quickly, using your hands and legs 爬

■ ***noun*** (*also* **ˈshinny hockey**) [U] an informal form of ICE HOCKEY, played especially by children （尤指儿童玩的）简化冰上曲棍球运动

ˈshin splints *noun* [pl.] sharp pain in the front parts of the lower legs caused by too much exercise, especially on a hard surface 外胫炎（因运动过量引起的胫部疼痛）

Shinto /ˈʃɪntəʊ; *NAmE* -toʊ/ (*also* **Shin·to·ism** /ˈʃɪntəʊɪzəm; *NAmE* -toʊ-/) *noun* [U] a Japanese religion whose practices include the worship of ANCESTORS and a belief in nature spirits （日本）神道教

shinty /ˈʃɪnti/ *noun* [U] a Scottish game similar to HOCKEY, played with curved sticks by teams of twelve players 简化曲棍球（苏格兰运动，每队 12 人）

shiny 🔑 /ˈʃaɪni/ *adj.* (**shini·er**, **shini·est**) smooth and bright; reflecting the light 光亮的；锃亮的；反光的；有光泽的： *shiny black hair* 有光泽的黑发

IDM **shiny new** (*approving*) very new and attractive 新颖的；新奇的；新异的： *shiny new stuff/software* 新奇的玩意儿 / 软件

ship 🔑 /ʃɪp/ *noun, verb*

■ ***noun*** 🔑 a large boat that carries people or goods by sea （大）船；舰： *There are two restaurants **on board ship**.* 船上有两个餐厅。 ◇ *a **sailing/cargo/cruise ship*** 帆船；货船；邮轮 ◇ *a **ship's captain/crew/company/cook*** 船长；全体船员；随船厨师 ◇ *Raw materials and labour come **by ship**, rail or road.* 原料和工人经水上、铁路和公路运送而来。 ➲ COLLOCATIONS AT TRAVEL ➲ VISUAL VOCAB PAGE V59 ➲ SEE ALSO AIRSHIP, FLAGSHIP, LIGHTSHIP IDM SEE JUMP *v.*, SINK *v.*, SPOIL *v.*, TIGHT *adj.*

■ ***verb*** (**-pp-**) **1** [T] **~ sb/sth + adv./prep.** to send or transport sb/sth by ship or by another means of transport 船运；运输；运送： *The company ships its goods all over the world.* 公司把货物运往世界各地。 ◇ *He was arrested and shipped back to the UK for trial.* 他被捕后被押解回英国接受审判。 **2** [I, T] to be available to be bought; to make sth available to be bought 上市；把…推向市场： *The software is due to ship next month.* 这个软件定于下月上市。 ◇ **~ sth** *The company continues to ship more computer systems than its rivals.* 这家公司继续比竞争对手推出更多的计算机系统。 **3** [T] **~ water** (of a boat, etc. 船等) to have water coming in over the sides 舷侧进水 IDM SEE SHAPE *v.*

PHR V **ˌship sb ↔ˈoff** (*disapproving*) to send sb to a place where they will stay 送走；遣送： *The children were shipped off to a boarding school at an early age.* 孩子们在幼年时就被送到了一所寄宿学校。

-ship *suffix* (in nouns 构成名词) **1** the state or quality of 状态；性质；品质： *ownership* 所有权 ◇ *friendship* 友谊 **2** the status or office of 地位；资格；职位： *citizenship* 公民资格 ◇ *professorship* 教授职位 **3** skill or ability as 技艺；技能： *musicianship* 音乐技艺 **4** the group of 集体： *membership* 全体成员 ➲ MORE LIKE THIS 7, page R25

ship·board /ˈʃɪpbɔːd; *NAmE* -bɔːrd/ *adj.* [only before noun] happening on a ship 船上发生的： *shipboard romances* 船上恋情

ship·build·er /ˈʃɪpbɪldə(r)/ *noun* a person or company that builds ships 造船工人；造船公司 ▶ **ship·build·ing** *noun* [U]: *the shipbuilding industry* 造船工业

ship·load /ˈʃɪpləʊd; *NAmE* -loʊd/ *noun* as many goods or passengers as a ship can carry 船只运载量

ship·mate /ˈʃɪpmeɪt/ *noun* sailors who are **shipmates** are sailing on the same ship as each other 同船船员

ship·ment /ˈʃɪpmənt/ *noun* **1** [U] the process of sending goods from one place to another 运输；运送；装运：*The goods are ready for shipment.* 货物备妥待运。◇ *the illegal shipment of arms* 非法的军火运输 ◇ *shipment costs* 运费 **2** [C] a load of goods that are sent from one place to another 运输的货物：*arms shipments* 运送的几批军火 ◇ *a shipment of arms* 运送的一批军火

ship·owner /ˈʃɪpəʊnə(r); *NAmE* -oʊn-/ *noun* a person or company that owns a ship or ships 船主；船东

ship·per /ˈʃɪpə(r)/ *noun* a person or company that arranges for goods to be sent from one place to another, especially by ship （船运货物的）托运人，发货人

ship·ping /ˈʃɪpɪŋ/ *noun* [U] **1** ships in general or considered as a group 船舶：*The canal is open to shipping.* 运河可以通航了。◇ *international* ***shipping lanes*** (= routes for ships) 国际海上航道 **2** the activity of carrying people or goods from one place to another by ship 航运；海运：*a shipping company* 船运公司 ◇ *She arranged for the shipping of her furniture to England.* 她正安排将家具海运到英格兰。 ➲ WORDFINDER NOTE AT INDUSTRY

ˈshipping forecast (*BrE*) (*US* **the ˈshipping news** [U]) *noun* a radio broadcast giving a report for ships on the weather conditions at sea 海上天气预报

ˈship's chandler *noun* = CHANDLER

ship·shape /ˈʃɪpʃeɪp/ *adj.* [not usually before noun] clean and neat; in good condition and ready to use 整洁；井井有条；良好可用

ˌship-to-ˈshore *adj.* [only before noun] providing communication between people on a ship and people on land （指通讯）由船至岸的：*a ship-to-shore radio* 由船至岸无线电设备

ship·wreck /ˈʃɪprek/ *noun, verb*

■ ***noun*** **1** [U, C] the loss or destruction of a ship at sea because of a storm or because it hits rocks, etc. 船舶失事；海难：*They narrowly escaped shipwreck in a storm in the North Sea.* 他们在北海遇到风暴，船险些失事。**2** [C] a ship that has been lost or destroyed at sea 失事的船；沉船：*The contents of shipwrecks belong to the state.* 一切沉船中的物品均属国家所有。

■ ***verb*** **be shipwrecked** to be left somewhere after the ship that you have been sailing in has been lost or destroyed at sea 遭遇海难；船只失事 ► **ship·wrecked** *adj.*：*a shipwrecked sailor* 遭遇海难的水手

ship·yard /ˈʃɪpjɑːd; *NAmE* -jɑːrd/ *noun* a place where ships are built or repaired 船坞；造船厂；修船厂：*hipyard workers* 船坞工人

shire /ˈʃaɪə(r); ʃə(r)/ *noun* (*BrE*) **1** [C] (*old use*) a county (now used in the names of some counties in Britain, for example *Hampshire, Yorkshire*) 郡（现在用于英国部分郡名，如 Hampshire、Yorkshire） **2 the Shires** (*also* **the Shire Counties**) [pl.] counties in central England that are in country areas 英格兰中部诸郡

ˈshire horse *noun* a large powerful horse, used for pulling loads 中部大挽马；夏尔马

shirk /ʃɜːk; *NAmE* ʃɜːrk/ *verb* [I, T] to avoid doing sth you should do, especially because you are too lazy 逃避（工作）；躲懒：*Discipline in the company was strict and no one shirked.* 公司有严格的纪律，没有人偷懒。◇ **~ from sth/doing sth** *A determined burglar will not shirk from breaking a window to gain entry.* 一个决计要下手的窃贼会不惜破窗而入。◇ **~ sth/doing sth** *She never shirked her responsibilities.* 她从不逃避自己的职责。 ► **shirk·er** *noun*

shirt 🔑 /ʃɜːt; *NAmE* ʃɜːrt/ *noun* a piece of clothing (usually for men), worn on the upper part of the body, made of light cloth, with sleeves and usually with a COLLAR and buttons down the front （尤指男式的）衬衫：*to wear a shirt and tie* 穿衬衫，打领带 ◇ *a short-sleeved shirt* 短袖衬衫 ◇ *a football shirt* 足球衫 ➲ VISUAL VOCAB PAGE V68 ➲ SEE ALSO NIGHTSHIRT, POLO SHIRT, STUFFED SHIRT, SWEATSHIRT, T-SHIRT

IDM **keep your ˈshirt on** (*informal*) used to tell sb not to get angry 别生气；保持冷静：*Keep your shirt on! It was only a joke.* 别生气！开个玩笑而已。 **put your ˈshirt on sb/sth** (*BrE, informal*) to bet all your money on sb/sth 把所有的钱全押在…上 **the ˌshirt off sb's ˈback** anything that sb has, including the things they really need themselves, that sb else takes from them or they are willing to give （别人拿走或自愿送掉的）全部家当

ˈshirt front *noun* the front part of a shirt, especially the stiff front part of a formal white shirt 衬衫的前襟（尤指礼服白衬衫前面硬挺的部分）

shirt·sleeve /ˈʃɜːtsliːv; *NAmE* ˈʃɜːrt-/ *noun* [usually pl.] a sleeve of a shirt 衬衫的袖子

IDM **in (your) ˈshirtsleeves** wearing a shirt without a jacket, etc. on top of it 只穿衬衫（未穿外衣）

ˈshirt tail *noun* the part of a shirt that is below the waist and is usually inside your trousers/pants 衬衫的下摆

shirty /ˈʃɜːti; *NAmE* ˈʃɜːrti/ *adj.* **~ (with sb)** (*BrE, informal*) angry or annoyed with sb about sth, and acting in a rude way 生气；动怒；发脾气

shish kebab /ˈʃɪʃ kɪbæb/ *noun* (*especially NAmE*) = KEBAB

shit /ʃɪt/ *exclamation, noun, verb, adj.*

■ ***exclamation*** (*taboo, slang*) a swear word that many people find offensive, used to show that you are angry or annoyed （表示气愤或恼怒）：*Shit! I've lost my keys!* 他妈的！我把钥匙丢了！ HELP Less offensive exclamations to use are **damn**, or **darn it** (*especially NAmE*), and **blast** or **bother** (*BrE*). 冒犯程度比 shit 低一些的说法有 damn 或 darn it（尤用于美式英语）以及英式英语的 blast 或 bother。

■ ***noun*** (*taboo, slang*) **1** [U] solid waste matter from the BOWELS 屎；粪便 SYN **excrement**：*a pile of dog shit on the path* 小路上的一堆狗屎 HELP A more polite way to express this example would be 'a pile of dog poo/poop'. 较文雅的说法是 a pile of dog poo/poop。**2** [sing.] an act of emptying solid waste matter from the BOWELS 拉屎：*to have/take a shit* 拉屎 **3** [U] stupid remarks or writing; nonsense 胡扯；废话；狗屁：*You're talking shit!* 你在瞎扯淡！◇ *She's so full of shit.* 她满嘴废话。 ➲ SEE ALSO BULLSHIT *n.* **4** [C] (*disapproving*) an unpleasant person who treats other people badly 可鄙的人；讨厌家伙：*He's an arrogant little shit.* 他是个傲慢的卑鄙小人。**5** [U] criticism or unfair treatment 责骂；欺侮：*I'm not going to take any shit from them.* 我可不受他们的气。

IDM **beat, kick, etc. the ˈshit out of sb** to attack sb violently so that you injure them 把某人打得屁滚尿流；揍扁 **in the ˈshit | in ˌdeep ˈshit** in trouble 遇到麻烦：*I'll be in the shit if I don't get this work finished today.* 要是今天不把这活儿做完，那我就惨了。 **like ˈshit** really bad, ill/sick etc.; really badly 糟透；十分差劲：*I woke up feeling like shit.* 我醒来感觉很不舒服。◇ *We get treated like shit in this job.* 我们这个活儿真不是人干的。 **no ˈshit!** (*often ironic*) used to show that you are surprised, impressed, etc. or that you are pretending to be （表示或假装惊讶等） **not give a ˈshit (about sb/sth)** to not care at all about sb/sth 一点不在乎；毫不关心：*He doesn't give a shit about anybody else.* 别人他谁都不放在心上。 **shit ˈhappens** used to express the idea that we must accept that bad things often happen without reason 天有不测风云；坏事难免会发生 **when the ˌshit hits the ˈfan** when sb in authority finds out about sth bad or wrong that sb has done 做了坏事（或错事）被发现：*When the shit hits the fan, I don't want to be here.* 事情一旦败露，我就不想待在这儿了。 ➲ MORE AT BUG *v.*, CROCK, SCARE *v.*

■ ***verb*** (**shit·ting, shit, shit**) (*taboo, slang*) HELP **shat** /ʃæt/ and, in *BrE*, **shit·ted** are also used for the past tense and past participle. 过去式和过去分词也用 shat，英式英语还用 shitted。 **1** [I, T] **~ (sth)** to empty solid waste matter from the BOWELS 拉屎 HELP A more polite way of expressing this is 'to go to the toilet/lavatory' (*BrE*), 'to go to the bathroom' (*NAmE*) or 'to go'. A more formal expression is 'to empty the bowels'. 较文雅的说法是 to go to the toilet/lavatory（英式英语）、to go to the bathroom（美式英语）或 to go。更正式的说法是 to empty the bowels。**2** [T] **~ yourself** to

S

empty solid waste matter from the BOWELS by accident 意外地拉屎 **3** [T] **~ yourself** to be very frightened 非常害怕
■ ***adj.*** (*taboo, slang, especially BrE*) very bad 非常糟糕：*You're shit and you know you are!* 你狗屁不是！知道吧，狗屁不是！◇ *They're a shit team.* 他们那支队臭得很。

shi·take *noun* = SHIITAKE

shite /ʃaɪt/ *exclamation, noun* [U] (*BrE, taboo, slang*) another word for SHIT （shit 的变体）屎，粪便

ˈshit-faced *adj.* (*taboo, slang*) very drunk 喝得脸色煞白的；烂醉如泥的

shit·hole /ˈʃɪthəʊl; *NAmE* -hoʊl/ *noun* (*taboo, slang*) a very dirty or unpleasant place 极其肮脏的地方；令人厌恶的地方

ˈshit-hot *adj.* (*taboo, slang*) extremely good at sth 十分精通的；驾轻就熟的：*a shit-hot lawyer* 精明的律师

shit·house /ˈʃɪthaʊs/ *noun* (*taboo, slang*) a toilet/bathroom 厕所；卫生间

shit·less /ˈʃɪtləs/ *adj.* (*taboo, slang*) IDM SEE SCARE *v.*

ˌshit-ˈscared *adj.* [not before noun] (*taboo, slang*) very frightened 吓破胆；吓得屁滚尿流

ˈshit stirrer *noun* (*BrE, taboo, slang*) a person who tries to make situations in which people disagree even worse 搅屎棍；遇事生风的人 ▶ **ˈshit stirring** *noun* [U]

shitty /ˈʃɪti/ *adj.* (*taboo, slang*) **1** unpleasant; very bad 令人厌恶的；非常糟糕的 **2** unfair or unkind 不公平的；不厚道的；卑劣的：*What a shitty way to treat a friend!* 这样对待一个朋友，真做得出来！

shiver /ˈʃɪvə(r)/ *verb, noun*
■ ***verb*** [I] (of a person 人) to shake slightly because you are cold, frightened, excited, etc. 颤抖，哆嗦（因寒冷、恐惧、激动等）：*Don't stand outside shivering—come inside and get warm!* 别站在外面冻得打哆嗦了，进来暖暖身子吧！◇ *He shivered at the thought of the cold, dark sea.* 那寒冷黑暗的大海，他想想都吓得发抖。◇ **~ with sth** *to shiver* ***with cold/excitement/pleasure, etc.*** 冷得发抖、激动得发抖、高兴得发抖等
■ ***noun*** **1** [C] a sudden shaking movement of your body because you are cold, frightened, excited, etc. 颤抖，哆嗦（因寒冷、恐惧、激动等）：*The sound of his voice* ***sent shivers down her spine.*** 一听见他的说话声，她就背上一阵阵发冷。◇ *He felt a cold shiver of fear run through him.* 他吓得打了一个寒战。**2 the shivers** [pl.] shaking movements of your body because of fear or a high temperature 寒战，寒噤（因恐惧或发高烧）：*I don't like him. He* ***gives me the shivers.*** 我不喜欢他，一见他我就不寒而栗。◇ *Symptoms include headaches, vomiting and the shivers.* 症状包括头痛、呕吐和打寒噤。

shiv·ery /ˈʃɪvəri/ *adj.* shaking with cold, fear, illness, etc. 颤抖的，战栗的，哆嗦的（因寒冷、恐惧、患病等）

shmo = SCHMO

shoal /ʃəʊl; *NAmE* ʃoʊl/ *noun* **1** a large number of fish swimming together as a group 鱼群 ➲ COMPARE SCHOOL *n.* (9) **2** a small hill of sand just below the surface of the sea 浅滩；水下沙洲

shock 🔑 /ʃɒk; *NAmE* ʃɑːk/ *noun, verb*
■ ***noun***
• **SURPRISE** 震惊 **1** 🔑 [C, usually sing., U] a strong feeling of surprise as a result of sth happening, especially sth unpleasant; the event that causes this feeling 震惊；惊愕；令人震惊的事：*The news of my promotion* ***came as a shock.*** 我获晋升的消息着实让我一惊。◇ *He's still* ***in a state of shock.*** 他至今还惊魂未定。◇ *I got a terrible shock the other day.* 前两天，可把我吓坏了。◇ *She still hadn't got over the shock of seeing him again.* 竟然又见到了他，她到现在还惊愕不已。◇ (*informal*) *If you think the job will be easy,* ***you're in for a shock.*** 如果你以为这项工作容易，那你就会大吃一惊。◇ *Losing in the first round was* ***a shock to the system*** (= it was more of a shock because it was not expected). 首轮失利让人大为震惊。◇ *The team suffered a shock defeat in the first round.* 球队首轮失利，十分意外。➲ SEE ALSO CULTURE SHOCK
• **MEDICAL** 医学上 **2** 🔑 [U] a serious medical condition, usually the result of injury in which a person has lost a lot of blood and they are extremely weak 休克：*She was taken to hospital* ***suffering from shock.*** 她因休克被送到医院。◇ *He isn't seriously injured but he is* ***in*** (***a state of***) ***shock.*** 他伤得不重，但处于休克状态。➲ SEE ALSO SHELL SHOCK, TOXIC SHOCK SYNDROME
• **VIOLENT SHAKING** 剧烈震动 **3** 🔑 [C, U] a violent shaking movement that is caused by an explosion, EARTHQUAKE, etc. （由爆炸、地震等引起的）剧烈震动，剧烈震荡：*The shock of the explosion could be felt up to six miles away.* 爆炸引起的剧烈震荡在六英里之外都能感觉到。◇ *The bumper absorbs shock on impact.* 遇到撞击时保险杠能减轻震动。
• **FROM ELECTRICITY** 电 **4** 🔑 [C] = ELECTRIC SHOCK：*Don't touch that wire or you'll* ***get a shock.*** 别碰那根电线，不然会触电的。
• **OF HAIR** 头发 **5** a thick mass of hair on a person's head 浓密的一堆（头发）

IDM **ˌshock ˈhorror** (*BrE, informal, often humorous*) used when you pretend to be shocked by sth that is not really very serious or surprising 好恐怖哦（假装震惊时说）➲ SEE ALSO SHOCK-HORROR

■ ***verb***
• **SURPRISE AND UPSET** 震惊 **1** 🔑 [T, often passive] to surprise and upset sb 使震惊；使惊愕：**~ sb** *It shocks you when something like that happens.* 发生这样的事情，使人觉得难以置信。◇ *We were all shocked at the news of his death.* 听到他的死讯，我们都感到震惊。◇ **~ sb that…** *Neighbours were shocked that such an attack could happen in their area.* 竟有这样的暴力行为发生在这一地区，邻居们大为惊骇。◇ **~ sb to do sth** ***I was shocked to*** *hear that he had resigned.* 听到他辞职的消息，我深感意外。
• **OFFEND/DISGUST** 使气愤／厌恶 **2** 🔑 [I, T] (of bad language, immoral behaviour, etc. 脏话、不道德行为等) to make sb feel offended or disgusted 使气愤；使厌恶：*These*

▼ **SYNONYMS 同义词辨析**

shock

appal • horrify • disgust • sicken • repel

These words all mean to surprise and upset sb very much. 以上各词均含使人震惊、惊愕之义。

shock [often passive] to surprise sb, usually in a way that upsets them 指使震惊、使惊愕：*We were all shocked at the news of his death.* 听到他的死讯，我们都感到震惊。

appal/appall to shock and upset sb very much 指使大为震惊、使惊骇：*The brutality of the crime has appalled the public.* 罪行之残暴使公众大为震惊。

horrify to make sb feel extremely shocked, upset or frightened 指使惊吓、使惊恐、恐吓：*The whole country was horrified by the killings.* 全国都对这些凶杀案感到大为震惊。

disgust to make sb feel shocked and almost ill because sth is so unpleasant 指使作呕、使厌恶、使反感：*The level of violence in the movie really disgusted me.* 影片中的暴力程度实在让我反感。

sicken (*BrE*) to make sb feel very shocked, angry and almost ill because sth is so unpleasant 指使大为震惊、使愤怒、使作呕：*The public is becoming sickened by these images of violence and death.* 公众看到这些充满暴力和死亡的画面大为震惊。

repel [often passive] (*rather formal*) to make sb feel rather disgusted 指使恶心、使厌恶：*I was repelled by the smell of drink on his breath.* 他满口酒气，让我恶心。

PATTERNS
- shocked/appalled/horrified/disgusted **at** sb/sth
- to shock/appal/horrify/disgust sb **that**…
- to shock/appal/horrify/disgust/sicken sb **to think/see/hear**…
- **sb's behaviour** shocks/appals sb
- **violence/an idea** shocks/appals/horrifies/disgusts sb

movies deliberately set out to shock. 这些电影存心让人恶心。◇ ~ sb (to do sth) *She enjoys shocking people by saying outrageous things.* 她喜欢故意说些不堪入耳的话让人讨厌。
▸ **shocked** adj. : *For a few minutes we stood in shocked silence.* 一时间，我们站在那儿惊讶得说不出话来。

ˈshock absorber *noun* a device that is fitted to each wheel of a vehicle in order to reduce the effects of travelling over rough ground, so that passengers can be more comfortable 减振器

shock·er /ˈʃɒkə(r); *NAmE* ˈʃɑːk-/ *noun* (*informal*) **1** a film/movie, piece of news or person that shocks you 令人震惊的电影（或新闻、人）**2** something that is of very low quality 质量低劣的东西

ˈshock-headed (*also* **ˈshock-haired**) *adj.* (of people 人) having a lot of thick untidy hair 头发浓密蓬乱的

ˈshock-horror *adj.* intending to make people very shocked or very angry 意欲令人震惊（或愤怒）的；令人发指的：*a shock-horror advertising campaign* 一次引起公愤的广告活动 ➲ SEE ALSO SHOCK HORROR at SHOCK *n.*

shock·ing /ˈʃɒkɪŋ; *NAmE* ˈʃɑːk-/ *adj.* **1** that offends or upsets people; that is morally wrong 令人气愤的；惹人憎恶的；不道德的：*shocking behaviour* 骇人听闻的行为 ◇ *shocking news* 令人震惊的消息 ◇ *It is shocking that they involved children in the crime.* 令人发指的是，他们教唆儿童参与犯罪活动。◇ *a shocking waste of money* 令人咋舌的挥霍行为 **2** (*informal, especially BrE*) very bad 非常糟糕的：*The house was left in a shocking state.* 那座房子破败得不成样子了。 ▸ **shock·ing·ly** *adv.* : *a shockingly high mortality rate* 高得惊人的死亡率

ˌshocking ˈpink *adj.* very bright pink in colour 艳粉红色的 ▸ **ˌshocking ˈpink** *noun* [U] ➲ **MORE LIKE THIS** 15, page R26

ˈshock jock *noun* (*informal, especially NAmE*) a DISC JOCKEY on a radio show who deliberately expresses opinions or uses language that many people find offensive 惊世骇俗的唱片节目主持人

shock·proof /ˈʃɒkpruːf; *NAmE* ˈʃɑːk-/ *adj.* made so that it cannot be damaged if it is dropped or hit 防震的：*My watch is shockproof and waterproof.* 我的手表防震防水。

ˈshock tactics *noun* [pl.] actions that are done to deliberately shock people in order to persuade them to do sth or to react in a particular way 震惊战术，耸动视听术（有意让人震惊，以说服他人做某事或做出某种反应的策略）

ˈshock therapy (*also* **ˈshock treatment**) *noun* [U] a way of treating mental illness by giving ELECTRIC SHOCKS or a drug that has a similar effect 休克疗法（通过电击或有类似电击作用的药物来治疗精神病）

ˈshock troops *noun* [pl.] soldiers who are specially trained to make sudden attacks on the enemy 突击部队

ˈshock wave *noun* **1** a movement of very high air pressure that is caused by an explosion, EARTHQUAKE, etc. （爆炸、地震等引起的）冲击波 **2 shock waves** [pl.] feelings of shock that people experience when sth bad happens suddenly 震惊；震荡：*The murder sent shock waves through the whole community.* 凶杀案震惊了整个社区。

shod /ʃɒd; *NAmE* ʃɑːd/ *adj.* (*literary*) wearing shoes of the type mentioned 穿着…鞋的：*She turned on her elegantly shod heel.* 她突然转身，脚上穿着雅致的皮鞋。➲ SEE ALSO SHOE *v.*

shoddy /ˈʃɒdi; *NAmE* ˈʃɑːdi/ *adj.* (**shod·dier, shod·di·est**) **1** (of goods, work, etc. 商品、工作等) made or done badly and with not enough care 做工粗糙的；粗制滥造的；劣质的 SYN **second-rate**：*shoddy goods* 劣质商品 ◇ *shoddy workmanship* 粗糙的做工 **2** dishonest or unfair 奸诈的；卑鄙的：*shoddy treatment* 不好的对待 ▸ **shod·dily** *adv.* **shod·di·ness** *noun* [U]

shoe /ʃuː/ *noun, verb*
■ ***noun*** **1** one of a pair of outer coverings for your feet, usually made of leather or plastic 鞋：*a pair of shoes* 一双鞋 ◇ *He took his shoes and socks off.* 他脱掉鞋袜。◇ *What's your shoe size?* 你穿多大的鞋？◇ *a shoe brush* 鞋刷 ◇ *shoe polish* 鞋油 ➲ **VISUAL VOCAB** PAGE V69 ➲ SEE ALSO SNOWSHOE **2** = HORSESHOE
IDM **be in sb's shoes | put yourself in sb's shoes** to be in, or imagine that you are in, another person's situation, especially when it is an unpleasant or difficult one 处于某人的境地；设身处地：*I wouldn't like to be in your shoes when they find out about it.* 等他们弄清事情真相的时候，你的日子就很不好过了。 **if ˌI were in ˈyour shoes** used to introduce a piece of advice you are giving to sb （引出建议）要是我处在你的境地，换了我是你的话：*If I were in your shoes, I'd resign immediately.* 要是我处在你的地位，我就立刻辞职。 **if the shoe fits (, wear it)** (*NAmE*) (*BrE* **if the cap fits (, wear it)**) if you feel that a remark applies to you, you should accept it and take it as a warning or criticism 有则改之 **the shoe is on the other ˈfoot** (*NAmE*) (*BrE* **the boot is on the other ˈfoot**) used to say that a situation has changed so that sb now has power or authority over the person who used to have power or authority over them 情况正好相反；宾主易位 ➲ MORE AT FILL *v.*, SHAKE *v.*, STEP *v.*
■ ***verb*** (**shoe·ing, shod, shod** /ʃɒd; *NAmE* ʃɑːd/) **~ sth** to put one or more HORSESHOES on a horse 给（马）钉蹄铁：*The horses were sent to the blacksmith to be shod.* 马送到铁匠那儿钉马掌去了。

shoe·box /ˈʃuːbɒks; *NAmE* -bɑːks/ *noun* **1** a box in which you take a pair of new shoes home from a shop 鞋盒 **2** (*disapproving*) a very small house with a square shape and no interesting features, especially one that is very similar to all the ones around it （尤指千篇一律的）小平房，鞋盒式住房

shoe·horn /ˈʃuːhɔːn; *NAmE* -hɔːrn/ *noun, verb*
■ ***noun*** a curved piece of plastic or metal, used to help your heel slide into a shoe 鞋拔
■ ***verb*** **~ sth + adv./prep.** to succeed in putting sth into a small space or a place where it does not fit very easily 把…硬塞进：*They managed to shoehorn the material onto just one CD.* 他们设法把材料全部塞进一张光盘。

shoe·lace /ˈʃuːleɪs/ (*also* **lace**) (*NAmE also* **shoe·string**) *noun* a long thin piece of material like string that goes through the holes on a shoe and is used to fasten it 鞋带：*a pair of shoelaces* 一副鞋带 ◇ *to **tie/untie** your **shoelaces*** 系 / 解鞋带 ◇ *Your shoelace is undone.* 你的鞋带松开了。 ➲ **VISUAL VOCAB** PAGE V69

shoe·maker /ˈʃuːmeɪkə(r)/ *noun* a person whose job is making shoes and boots 鞋匠；制鞋工人 ➲ COMPARE COBBLER (2) ▸ **shoe·mak·ing** *noun* [U]

shoe·shine /ˈʃuːʃaɪn/ *noun* [U] (*especially NAmE*) the activity of cleaning people's shoes for money 擦鞋（生意）：*a shoeshine stand on West 32nd Street* 西 32 街上的一家擦鞋摊

shoe·string /ˈʃuːstrɪŋ/ *noun, adj.*
■ ***noun*** (*NAmE*) = SHOELACE
IDM **on a ˈshoestring** (*informal*) using very little money 以极少的钱：*In the early years, the business was run on a shoestring.* 早年，这家店铺是小本经营的。
■ ***adj.*** [only before noun] (*informal*) that uses very little money 用钱极少的：*The club exists on a shoestring budget.* 这家俱乐部靠一点小钱艰难度日。

ˌshoestring poˈtatoes *noun* [pl.] (*NAmE*) potatoes cut into long thin strips and fried in oil 炸薯条

ˈshoe tree *noun* an object shaped like a shoe that you put inside a shoe when you are not wearing it to help the shoe keep its shape 鞋楦

sho·gun /ˈʃəʊɡən; *NAmE* ˈʃoʊ-/ *noun* (in the past) a Japanese military leader （旧时的）日本将军

shojo /ˈʃəʊdʒəʊ; *NAmE* ˈʃoʊdʒoʊ/ *noun* [C, U] (*pl.* **shojo**) a Japanese form of COMIC STRIP for girls that is usually about personal and romantic relationships （日本）少女漫画（通常以个人情爱为题材）

S

Shona /ˈʃəʊnə; *NAmE* ˈʃoʊ-/ *noun* [U] a language spoken by the Shona peoples of southern Africa, used in Zimbabwe and other parts of southern Africa 绍纳语（非洲南部绍纳人讲的方言，用于津巴布韦等地区）

shone PAST TENSE, PAST PART. OF SHINE

sho·nen /ˈʃəʊnən; *NAmE* ˈʃoʊ-/ *noun* [C, U] (*pl.* **shonen**) a Japanese form of COMIC STRIP for boys that usually has a lot of exciting action and adventure （日本）少年漫画（通常以刺激的打斗和冒险为题材）: *The comic is one of Japan's top-selling shonen.* 这本漫画是日本最畅销的少年漫画之一。

shonky /ˈʃɒŋki; *NAmE* ˈʃɔːŋ-; ˈʃɑːŋ-/ *adj.* (**shonk·ier, shonki·est**) (*AustralE, NZE, informal*) not honest or legal 不诚实的；不合法的

shoo /ʃuː/ *verb, exclamation*

■ ***verb*** (**shoo·ing, shooed, shooed**) **~ sb/sth (+ adv./prep.)** to make sb/sth go away or to another place, especially by saying 'shoo' and waving your arms and hands（尤指发出嘘声并挥手）赶走，轰走: *He shooed the dog out of the kitchen.* 他嘘嘘地把狗赶出了厨房。

■ ***exclamation*** used to tell a child or an animal to go away（表示赶小孩或动物走的声音）嘘，去

shoo·fly pie /ˌʃuːflaɪ ˈpaɪ/ *noun* [C, U] (*NAmE*) an open PIE filled with brown sugar and TREACLE/MOLASSES 开口糖馅饼（用红糖和糖浆填充） **ORIGIN** From the need to say *shoo!* to the flies that the sugar attracts. 用嘘声 (shoo!) 驱赶糖蜜招引的苍蝇，故名。

ˈshoo-in *noun* **~ (for sth) | ~ (to do sth)** (*NAmE, informal*) a person or team that will win easily 稳操胜券的人（或队）

shook PAST TENSE, PAST PART. OF SHAKE

shoot /ʃuːt/ *verb, noun, exclamation*

■ ***verb*** (**shot, shot** /ʃɒt; *NAmE* ʃɑːt/)

• **WEAPON** 武器 **1** [I, T] to fire a gun or other weapon; to fire sth from a weapon 开（枪或其他武器）；射击；发射: *Don't shoot—I surrender.* 别开枪，我投降。◇ **~ (sth) (at sb/sth)** *troops shooting at the enemy* 向敌人射击的部队 ◇ *The police rarely* ***shoot to kill*** (= try to kill the people they shoot at). 一般来说，警察开枪不是要打死人。◇ **~ sth (from sth)** *He shot an arrow from his bow.* 他张弓射了一箭。◇ *They shot the lock off* (= removed it by shooting). 他们开枪把锁打掉。➲ COLLOCATIONS AT WAR **2** [T] to kill or wound a person or an animal with a bullet, etc. 射杀；射伤: **~ sb/sth/yourself** *A man was shot in the leg.* 一个人被射中腿部。◇ *He shot himself during a fit of depression.* 他一时心灰意冷，开枪自杀了。◇ *The guards were ordered to* ***shoot on sight*** *anyone trying to escape.* 卫兵接到命令，看见有谁企图逃跑就立即开枪。◇ **~ sb/sth + adj.** *Three people were* ***shot dead*** *during the robbery.* 抢劫过程中有三人被开枪打死。**3** [T, I] **~ (sth)** (of a gun or other weapon 枪或其他武器) to fire bullets, etc. 发射（子弹等）: *This is just a toy gun—it doesn't shoot real bullets.* 这只是一支玩具枪，不能射真子弹。

• **FOR SPORT** 体育运动 **4** [T, I] **~ (sth)** to hunt and kill birds and animals with a gun as a sport 打猎；狩猎；打（猎物）；猎杀: *to shoot pheasants* 打野鸡 ◇ *They go* ***shooting*** *in Scotland.* 他们上苏格兰去打猎。

• **MOVE QUICKLY** 快速移动 **5** [I, T] to move suddenly or quickly in one direction; to make sb/sth move in this way（使朝某方向）冲，奔，飞驰: **+ adv./prep.** *A plane shot across the sky.* 飞机掠过天空。◇ *His hand shot out to grab her.* 他猛地伸出手去抓她。◇ *Flames were shooting up through the roof.* 火不断从房顶蹿上来。◇ (*figurative*) *The band's last single shot straight to number one in the charts.* 这支乐队的最新单曲一推出便飙上排行榜的首位。◇ **~ sth + adv./prep.** *He shot out his hand to grab her.* 他猛地伸出手去抓她。

• **OF PAIN** 疼痛 **6** [I] to move suddenly and quickly and be very sharp 剧痛跳窜: *a shooting pain in the back* 背部的一阵剧痛 ◇ **+ adv./prep.** *The pain shot up her arm.* 疼痛顺着她的胳膊窜了上来。

• **DIRECT AT SB** 朝向某人 **7** [T, no passive] to direct sth at sb suddenly or quickly 突然把…投向: **~ sth at sb** *Journalists were shooting questions at the candidates.* 记者纷纷向几位候选人发问。◇ *She shot an angry glance at him.* 她很生气，瞪了他一眼。◇ **~ sb sth** *She shot him an angry glance.* 她很生气，瞪了他一眼。

• **FILM/PHOTOGRAPH** 电影；照片 **8** [I, T] to make a film/movie or photograph of sth 拍摄；摄影: *Cameras ready? OK, shoot!* 摄影机准备好了吗？好，开拍！◇ **~ sth (+ adv./prep.)** *Where was the movie shot?* 那部电影是在哪儿拍的？◇ *The movie was shot in black and white.* 那部电影以黑白片拍摄。

• **IN SPORTS** 体育运动 **9** [I, T] (in football (SOCCER), HOCKEY, etc. 足球、曲棍球等) to try to kick, hit or throw the ball into a goal or to score a point 射门；投篮: **~ (at sth)** *He should have shot instead of passing.* 他本该射门，不该传球。◇ (*especially NAmE*) **~ sth** *After school we'd be on the driveway* ***shooting baskets*** (= playing BASKETBALL). 放学后，我们就在车行道上打篮球。**10** [T] **~ sth** (*informal*) (in GOLF 高尔夫球) to make a particular score in a complete ROUND or competition（在整场比赛中）击出…杆: *She shot a 75 in the first round.* 她在第一轮比赛中击出 75 杆。

• **PLAY GAME** 玩游戏 **11** [T] **~ sth** (*especially NAmE*) to play particular games 玩，打（某种游戏）: *to shoot pool* 打普尔

IDM **be/get ˈshot of sb/sth** (*BrE, informal*) to get rid of sb/sth so you no longer have the problems they cause 摆脱；处理: *I'll be glad to get shot of this car.* 我很想卖掉这辆车。 **have shot your ˈbolt** (*informal*) to have used all your power, money or supplies 竭尽全力；倾其所有 **be like shooting ˌfish in a ˈbarrel** (*informal*) used to emphasize how easy it is to do sth 易如反掌；探囊取物；手到擒来: *What do you mean you can't do it? It'll be like shooting fish in a barrel!* 你说干不了是什么意思？这不是小事一桩嘛！ **shoot the ˈbreeze/ˈbull** (*NAmE, informal*) to have a conversation in an informal way 聊天；闲聊 **SYN** **chat**: *We sat around in the bar, shooting the breeze.* 我们闲坐在酒吧里聊天。 **ˌshoot from the ˈhip** to react quickly without thinking carefully first 轻率应对；鲁莽行事；仓促反应 **ˌshoot yourself in the ˈfoot** (*informal*) to do or say sth that will cause you a lot of trouble or harm, especially when you are trying to get an advantage for yourself 搬起石头砸自己的脚 **ˌshoot it ˈout (with sb)** (*informal*) to fight against sb with guns, especially until one side is killed or defeated 开枪拼个你死我活；（和…）决一死战: *The gang decided to shoot it out with the police.* 那伙匪徒决定开枪和警察死拼。➲ RELATED NOUN SHOOT-OUT **shoot the ˈmessenger** to blame the person who gives the news that sth bad has happened, instead of the person who is really responsible 拿报信人出气（而非责备问题的责任人）: *Don't shoot the messenger!* 别错怪好人！ **ˌshoot your ˈmouth off (about sth)** (*informal*) **1** to talk with too much pride about sth 吹嘘；大吹大擂 **2** to talk about sth that is private or secret 张扬；信口乱讲（涉及隐私或秘密的事） **shoot the ˈrapids** to go in a boat over part of a river where the water flows very fast 急流划艇

PHR V **ˌshoot sb/sth↔ˈdown 1** to make sb/sth fall to the ground by shooting them/it 射倒；击毙；击落: *Several planes were shot down by enemy fire.* 几架飞机被敌人的炮火击落。 **2** to be very critical of sb's ideas, opinions, etc. 批驳，驳倒，彻底推翻（观点、意见等）: *His latest theory has been* ***shot down in flames.*** 他的最新理论被彻底推翻了。 **ˈshoot for sth** (*NAmE, informal*) to try to achieve or get sth, especially sth difficult 力争达到；努力获取: *We've been shooting for a pay raise for months.* 几个月来，我们一直在争取加薪。 **ˌshoot ˈoff** (*informal*) to leave very quickly 迅速离去 **SYN** **dash**: *I had to shoot off at the end of the meeting.* 我不得不一散会就跑。 **ˌshoot sth ˈoff** (*NAmE*) to light FIREWORKS and make them go off 燃放（烟花） **SYN** **let off, set off** **ˌshoot ˈthrough** (*AustralE, NZE, informal*) to leave, especially in order to avoid sb/sth 离去；躲避: *I was only five when my Dad shot through.* 我父亲出走时我才五岁。 **ˌshoot ˈup 1** to grow very quickly 迅速长高；蹿个儿: *Their kids have shot up since I last saw them.* 自我上次见了以后，他们家几个孩子一下子长高了。**2** to rise suddenly by a large amount 陡增；猛涨；迅速上升: *Ticket prices* *shot up last year.* 去年票价猛涨。 ➲ LANGUAGE BANK AT INCREASE **3** (*slang*) to INJECT an illegal drug directly into your blood 注射（毒品） ˌ**shoot sth↔ˈup 1** to cause great damage to sth by shooting 开枪打坏；击毁 **2** [no passive] (*slang*) to INJECT an illegal drug directly into your blood 注射（毒品）

■ *noun*

• **PLANT** 植物 **1** the part that grows up from the ground when a plant starts to grow; a new part that grows on plants or trees 幼苗；嫩芽；新枝：*new green shoots* 绿色的新芽 ◇ *bamboo shoots* 竹笋 ➲ VISUAL VOCAB PAGE V11

• **FILM/PHOTOGRAPHS** 电影；照片 **2** an occasion when sb takes professional photographs for a particular purpose or makes a film/movie 拍摄；摄影：*a fashion shoot* 时装摄影 ➲ SEE ALSO PHOTO SHOOT

• **FOR SPORT** 体育运动 **3** (*especially BrE*) an occasion when a group of people hunt and shoot animals or birds for sport; the land where this happens 狩猎；狩猎场

■ *exclamation* **1** (*NAmE*) used to show that you are annoyed when you do sth stupid or when sth goes wrong (to avoid saying 'shit')（做了蠢事或事情出了差错感到懊恼，避免说 shit）：*Shoot! I've forgotten my book!* 倒霉！我忘了带书！ **2** (*especially NAmE*) used to tell sb to say what they want to say（让某人把话说出来）说吧，请讲：*You want to tell me something? OK, shoot!* 你有话要告诉我？那好，说吧！

ˈ**shoot-'em-up** *adj.* (*informal*) a **shoot-'em-up** computer game, etc. is one involving a lot of violence with guns（电脑游戏等）充满枪战暴力的

shoot·er /ˈʃuːtə(r)/ *noun* **1** a person or weapon that shoots 射手；射击武器 ➲ SEE ALSO PEA-SHOOTER, SHARP-SHOOTER, SIX-SHOOTER, TROUBLESHOOTER **2** (*informal*) a gun 枪 **3** (*NAmE*) (used especially in news reports 尤用于新闻报道) a person who uses a gun to kill people（开枪杀人的）枪手，凶犯

shoot·ing 🔑 /ˈʃuːtɪŋ/ *noun* **1** 🔑 [C] a situation in which a person is shot with a gun 枪击；枪杀：*Terrorist groups claimed responsibility for the shootings and bomb attacks.* 恐怖主义组织声称对这几起枪击和爆炸事件负责。◇ *a serious shooting incident* 一起重大的枪击事件 **2** [U] the sport of shooting animals and birds with guns 狩猎：*grouse shooting* 猎松鸡 **3** 🔑 [U] the process of filming a film/movie （电影的）拍摄：*Shooting began early this year.* 拍摄于今年初开始。

ˈ**shooting gallery** *noun* **1** a place where people shoot guns at objects for practice or to win prizes 射击场；打靶场 **2** (*especially NAmE*) a place where people go to take drugs 吸毒场所；注射毒品场所

ˈ**shooting match** *noun* an occasion when people or groups fight or attack each other 打架；斗殴

IDM **the whole ˈshooting match** (*BrE, informal*) everything, or a situation which includes everything 所有东西；全部物品；整个

ˌ**shooting ˈstar** (*also* ˌ**falling ˈstar**) *noun* a small METEOR (= a piece of rock in outer space) that travels very fast and burns with a bright light as it enters the earth's atmosphere 流星

ˈ**shooting stick** *noun* a pointed stick that has a handle at the top which opens out to make a simple seat 折叠座手杖（尖头，上端的手柄可打开成为坐凳）

ˈ**shoot-out** *noun* a fight that is fought with guns until one side is killed or defeated 你死我活的枪战 ➲ SEE ALSO PENALTY SHOOT-OUT

shop 🔑 /ʃɒp; *NAmE* ʃɑːp/ *noun, verb*

■ *noun*

• **WHERE YOU BUY STH** 买东西的地方 **1** 🔑 [C] (*especially BrE*) a building or part of a building where you can buy goods or services 商店；店铺：*a shoe shop* 鞋店 ◇ *There's a little gift shop around the corner.* 在街角附近有一家小礼品店。◇ (*BrE*) *a butcher's shop* 肉铺 ◇ (*NAmE*) *a butcher shop* 肉铺 ◇ (*BrE*) *I'm just going down **to the shops**. Can I get you anything?* 我要上街去。你有要买的吗？ ➲ COLLOCATIONS AT SHOPPING ➲ VISUAL VOCAB PAGE V3 ➲ SEE ALSO BAKESHOP, COFFEE SHOP, CORNER SHOP, FACTORY SHOP

WORDFINDER 联想词：assistant, **buy**, counter, display, fitting room, promotion, sale, **store**, till

• **FOR MAKING/REPAIRING THINGS** 制造 / 修理东西 **2** (*also* **work·shop**) [C] (especially in compounds 尤用于构成复合词) a place where things are made or repaired, especially part of a factory where a particular type of work is done 工厂；工场；作坊；（尤指）车间：*a repair shop* 修理厂 ◇ *a paint shop* (= where cars are painted) 喷漆车间 ➲ SEE ALSO BODY SHOP

• **SHOPPING** 购物 **3** [sing.] (*BrE, informal*) an act of going shopping, especially for food and other items needed in the house 购物；采买：*I **do a** weekly **shop** at the supermarket.* 我一周上超市一次。

• **SCHOOL SUBJECT** 学校科目 **4** (*also* **ˈshop class**) [U] (*both NAmE*) = INDUSTRIAL ARTS

• **ROOM FOR TOOLS** 放工具的房间 **5** (*also* **work·shop**) [C] (*NAmE*) a room in a house where tools are kept for making repairs to the house, building things out of wood, etc. 工具贮藏室

IDM **all ˈover the shop** (*BrE, informal*) = ALL OVER THE PLACE ˌ**set up ˈshop** to start a business 开业；开张 ➲ MORE AT BULL, HIT *v.*, MIND *v.*, SHUT *v.*, TALK *v.*

■ *verb* (**-pp-**)

• **BUY** 购买 **1** 🔑 [I] ~ (**for sth**) to buy things in shops/stores 去商店买；在商店购物：*to shop for food* 去商店买食物 ◇ *He likes to shop at the local market.* 他喜欢到本地市场买东西。◇ *She was determined to go out and **shop till she dropped**.* 她决意要外出购物，直到累得站不住才罢休。 **2** 🔑 **go shopping** [I] to spend time going to shops/stores and looking for things to buy 逛商店：*There should be plenty of time to go shopping before we leave New York.* 我们离开纽约前应该还有充足的时间去逛商店。◇ *'Where's Mum?' 'She went shopping.'* "妈妈呢？" "买东西去了。"

• **TELL POLICE ABOUT SB** 向警察告发 **3** [T] ~ **sb** (**to sb**) (*BrE, informal*) to give information to sb, especially to the police, about sb who has committed a crime （向警察等）告发：*He didn't expect his own mother to shop him to the police.* 他没想到自己的母亲会向警方告发他。

PHR V ˌ**shop aˈround** (**for sth**) to compare the quality or prices of goods or services that are offered by different shops/stores, companies, etc. so that you can choose the best 货比三家而后买；比较选购：*Shop around for the best deal.* 要货比三家，买最合算的。

shop·aho·lic /ˌʃɒpəˈhɒlɪk; *NAmE* ˌʃɑːpəˈhɔːlɪk; -ˈhɑːl-/ *noun* (*informal*) a person who enjoys shopping very much and spends too much time or money doing it 购物狂 ▶ **shop·aho·lic** *adj.*

ˈ**shop assistant** (*also* **as·sist·ant**) (*both BrE*) (*NAmE* **ˈsales clerk**, **clerk**) *noun* a person whose job is to serve customers in a shop/store 店员；售货员

ˈ**shop-bought** (*BrE*) (*NAmE* **store-bought**) *adj.* [only before noun] bought from a shop/store and not made at home 从商店买的（而非家里做的）：*shop-bought cakes* 从商店买的糕点

shop·fit·ting /ˈʃɒpfɪtɪŋ; *NAmE* ˈʃɑːp-/ *noun* [U] the business of putting equipment and furniture into shops/stores 店铺装潢（业） ▶ **shop·fit·ter** *noun*

ˌ**shop ˈfloor** *noun* [sing.] **1** the area in a factory where the goods are made by the workers （工厂的）生产区：*to work on the shop floor* 在生产区工作 **2** the workers in a factory, not the managers 工厂工人（非管理人员） ➲ WORDFINDER NOTE AT FACTORY

shop·front /ˈʃɒpfrʌnt; *NAmE* ˈʃɑːp-/ (*BrE*) (*NAmE* **store-front**) *noun* the outside of a shop/store that faces the street 商店门面；店面

shop·house /ˈʃɒphaʊs; *NAmE* ˈʃɑːp-/ *noun* (in SE Asia) a shop that opens onto the street and is used as the owner's home 店屋（东南亚兼作住房的门面房）

S

shop·keep·er /ˈʃɒpkiːpə(r); *NAmE* ˈʃɑːp-/ (*also* **store·keep·er** *especially in NAmE*) *noun* a person who owns or manages a shop/store, usually a small one （通常指小商店的）店主

shop·lift·ing /ˈʃɒplɪftɪŋ; *NAmE* ˈʃɑːp-/ *noun* [U] the crime of stealing goods from a shop/store by deliberately leaving without paying for them 商店行窃（罪） ⇨ COLLOCATIONS AT SHOPPING ▶ **shop·lift** *verb* [I, T] ~ (sth) **shop·lift·er** *noun* : *Shoplifters will be prosecuted.* 在本店行窃者将被起诉。

shop·lot /ˈʃɒplɒt; *NAmE* ˈʃɑːplɑːt/ *noun* (*SEAsianE*) the amount of space that a shop/store fills 商店占地面积

shop·per /ˈʃɒpə(r); *NAmE* ˈʃɑːp-/ *noun* a person who buys goods from shops/stores 购物者；（商店的）顾客：*The streets were full of Christmas shoppers.* 街上挤满了为圣诞节采购的人。 ⇨ SEE ALSO MYSTERY SHOPPER, PERSONAL SHOPPER

shop·ping ⚿ /ˈʃɒpɪŋ; *NAmE* ˈʃɑːp-/ *noun* [U] **1** ⚿ the activity of going to shops/stores and buying things 购物：*to go **shopping*** 去购物 ◇ (*BrE*) *When shall I do the shopping?* 我什么时候去买东西呢？ ◇ (*BrE*) *We do our shopping on Saturdays.* 我们星期六购物。 ◇ *a shopping basket* 购物篮 ◇ *a shopping trolley* 购物手推车 ◇ (*NAmE*) *a shopping cart* 购物手推车 ⇨ SEE ALSO WINDOW-SHOPPING **2** ⚿ (*especially BrE*) the things that you have bought from shops/stores 从商店采买的东西：*to put the shopping in the car* 把买好的东西放进汽车

ˈshopping arcade *noun* = ARCADE (3)

ˈshopping bag *noun* **1** a large, strong bag made of cloth, plastic, etc. used for carrying your shopping 购物袋 ⇨ VISUAL VOCAB PAGE V36 **2** (*NAmE*) (*BrE* **ˈcarrier bag**, **car·rier**) a paper or plastic bag for carrying shopping （纸或塑料的）购物袋，手提袋

ˈshopping cart 1 (*NAmE*) a large basket on wheels into which you put the things that you want to buy as you push it round a store 购物车；购物手推车 **2** (*especially NAmE* **cart**) (*BrE usually* **basket**) a facility on a website that records the items that you select to buy （购物网站上的）购物车，购物篮

ˈshopping centre (*BrE*) (*NAmE* **ˈshopping center**) *noun* a group of shops/stores built together, sometimes under one roof 购物中心（集中一批商店，有时在同一建筑物内） ⇨ VISUAL VOCAB PAGE V3

ˈshopping list *noun* a list that you make of all the things that you need to buy when you go shopping 购物单；采购单：(*figurative*) *The union presented a shopping list of demands to the management.* 工会向资方提交了一份写明各项要求的清单。

ˈshopping mall *noun* (*especially NAmE*) = MALL

ˈshop-soiled (*BrE*) (*NAmE* **shop·worn**) *adj.* (of goods 商品) dirty or not in perfect condition because they have been in a shop/store for a long time 在商店摆放旧了的：*a sale of shop-soiled goods at half price* 半价促销商店陈货

ˌshop ˈsteward *noun* (*especially BrE*) a person who is elected by members of a trade/labor union in a factory or company to represent them in meetings with managers 工会谈判代表

ˈshop talk *noun* [U] talk about your work or your business 有关工作（或公事）的谈话

ˌshop ˈwindow (*BrE*) (*NAmE* **ˌstore ˈwindow**) (*also* **window**) *noun* the glass at the front of a shop/store and the area behind it where goods are shown to the public 商店橱窗

shop·worn /ˈʃɒpwɔːn; *NAmE* ˈʃɑːpwɔːrn/ (*NAmE*) (*BrE* **ˈshop-soiled**) *adj.* (of goods 商品) dirty or not in perfect condition because they have been in a shop/store for a long time 在商店摆放旧了的：(*figurative*) *a shopworn argument* (= that is no longer new or useful) 陈旧的论点

▼ **COLLOCATIONS** 词语搭配

Shopping 购物

Shopping 购物

- **go/go out/be out** shopping 去 / 外出 / 在外购物
- **go to** (*especially BrE*) the shops/(*especially NAmE*) a store/(*especially NAmE*) the mall 去商店 / 商场
- **do** (*BrE*) the shopping/(*especially NAmE*) the grocery shopping/a bit of window-shopping 购物；购买食品杂货；逛街浏览一下商店橱窗
- (*NAmE, informal*) **hit/hang out at** the mall 去逛商场；在商场闲逛
- **try on** clothes/shoes 试穿衣服 / 鞋
- **indulge in** some retail therapy 沉迷于购物疗法（疯狂购物以抚慰心灵）
- **go on** a spending spree 痛痛快快地花一通钱
- **cut/cut back on/reduce** your spending 减少花销
- **be/get caught** shoplifting 在商店行窃被当场逮住
- **donate sth to/take sth to/find sth in** (*BrE*) a charity shop/(*NAmE*) a thrift store 把某物捐赠给 / 拿到慈善商店；在慈善商店发现某物
- **buy/sell/find sth at** (*BrE*) a car boot sale/(*BrE*) a jumble sale/a garage sale/(*NAmE*) a yard sale 在后备箱旧货市场 / 旧杂物义卖 / 车库里进行的旧物销售 / 庭院拍卖会购买 / 出售 / 找到某物
- **find/get/pick up** a bargain 找到 / 买到便宜货

At the shop/store 在商店

- **load/push/wheel** (*BrE*) a trolley/(*NAmE*) a cart 往手推车里装东西；推手推车
- **stand in/wait in** (*BrE*) the checkout queue/(*NAmE*) the checkout line 排队付款
- (*NAmE*) **stand in line**/ (*BrE*) **queue** at the checkout 在付款处排队
- **bag** (*especially NAmE*) (your) groceries 把食品杂货装进袋子
- **pack** (**away**) (*especially BrE*) your shopping 将所购之物打包
- **stack/stock/restock** the shelves at a store (with sth) （把某物）放上 / 补齐放上商店的货架
- **be** (**found**) **on/appear on** supermarket/shop/store shelves 在超市 / 商店有售
- **be in/have in/be out of/run out of** stock 有货；脱销
- **deal with/help/serve** customers 应付 / 帮助 / 服务顾客
- **run** a special promotion 搞特别促销活动
- **be on** special offer 正在搞特价优惠

Buying goods 买商品

- **make/complete** a purchase 采购
- **buy/purchase sth** online/by mail order 网购；邮购
- **make/place/take** an order for sth 订购某物
- **buy/order sth** in bulk/in advance 大批 / 提前购买 / 订购某物
- **accept/take** credit cards 接受信用卡
- **pay** (in) cash/by (credit/debit) card/(*BrE*) with a gift voucher/(*NAmE*) with a gift certificate 用现金 / （信用 / 借记）卡 / 礼券支付
- **enter** your PIN number 输入你的个人识别密码
- **ask for/get/obtain** a receipt 索要 / 拿到收据
- **return/exchange** an item/a product 退还 / 更换商品 / 产品
- **be entitled to/ask for/demand** a refund 有资格要求 / 要求退款
- **compare** prices 对比价格
- **offer** (sb)/**give** (sb)/**get/receive** a 30% discount 给（某人）/ 得到 30% 的折扣

shore /ʃɔː(r)/ *noun, verb*

■ ***noun*** **1** [C, U] the land along the edge of the sea or ocean, a lake or another large area of water（海洋、湖泊等大水域的）岸，滨：*a rocky/sandy shore* 岩岸；沙岸 ◇ *to swim from the boat* ***to the shore*** 下船游上岸 ◇ *a house on the shores of the lake* 湖畔的房子 ◇ *The ship was anchored* ***off shore****.* 船停泊在离岸不远的地方。 ➲ WORDFINDER NOTE AT COAST **2 shores** [pl.] (*especially literary*) a country, especially one with a coast 国家（尤指濒海国家）：*foreign shores* 外国 ◇ *What brings you to these shores?* 是什么把你带到这个国家来的？

■ ***verb***

PHR V ˌ**shore sth**↔ˈ**up 1** to support part of a building or other large structure by placing large pieces of wood or metal against or under it so that it does not fall down 用撑柱支撑 **2** to help to support sth that is weak or going to fail 支撑；稳住

shore·line /ˈʃɔːlaɪn; *NAmE* ˈʃɔːrl-/ *noun* [usually sing.] the edge of the sea, the ocean or a lake 海（或湖）滨线；海（或湖）岸线：*a rocky shoreline* 岩质海岸线 ◇ *The road follows the shoreline for a few miles.* 公路沿海岸线逶迤而行几英里。 ➲ WORDFINDER NOTE AT SEA

shorn PAST PART. OF SHEAR

short 🔑 /ʃɔːt; *NAmE* ʃɔːrt/ *adj., adv., noun, verb*

■ ***adj.*** (**short·er, short·est**)

• LENGTH/DISTANCE 长度；距离 **1** measuring or covering a small length or distance, or a smaller length or distance than usual 短的：*He had short curly hair.* 他有一头短鬈发。◇ *a short walk* 短距离步行 ◇ *a short skirt* 短裙 OPP long

• HEIGHT 高度 **2** (of a person 人) small in height 个子矮的：*She was short and dumpy.* 她又矮又胖。 OPP tall

• TIME 时间 **3** lasting or taking a small amount of time or less time than usual 短的；短期的；短暂的：*I'm going to France for a short break.* 我打算去法国度个短假。◇ *Which is the shortest day of the year?* 一年中哪一天最短？◇ *a short book* (= taking a short time to read, because it does not have many pages) 一本小书 ◇ *She has a very* ***short memory*** (= remembers only things that have happened recently). 她的记性很差。◇ (*informal*) ***Life's too short*** *to sit around moping.* 人生苦短，不能整天坐在那儿自寻烦恼。◇ *It was all over in a relatively* ***short space of time****.* 不一会儿工夫就完全结束了。 OPP long **4** [only before noun] (of a period of time 一段时间) seeming to have passed very quickly 短短的：*Just two short years ago he was the best player in the country.* 短短两年前，他还是全国最优秀的运动员。 OPP long

• NOT ENOUGH 不足 **5** [not before noun] ~ (**of sth**) not having enough of sth; lacking sth 不足；短缺：*I'm afraid I'm a little short* (= of money) *this month.* 这个月我恐怕手头有点紧。◇ *She is not short of excuses when things go wrong.* 事情出了差错，她老有借口。 **6 ~ on sth** (*informal*) lacking or not having enough of a particular quality 缺乏，缺少（某种品质）：*He was a big strapping guy but short on brains.* 他五大三粗，但头脑简单。 **7** [not before noun] not easily available; not supplying as much as you need 紧俏；紧缺：*Money was short at that time.* 那时候，钱紧缺。 **8** [not before noun] ~ (**of sth**) less than the number, amount or distance mentioned or needed 少于；缺少；未达到：*Her last throw was only three centimetres short of the world record.* 她的最后一掷距世界纪录只差三厘米。◇ *The team was five players short.* 球队还缺五名球员。◇ *She was just short of her 90th birthday when she died.* 她去世时就快过 90 岁生日了。

• OF BREATH 呼吸 **9 ~ of breath** having difficulty breathing, for example because of illness （呼吸）短促，困难；（气）急

• NAME/WORD 名称；单词 **10 ~ for sth** being a shorter form of a name or word 简略的；缩写的：*Call me Jo—it's short for Joanna.* 叫我乔好了，这是乔安娜的简称。◇ *file transfer protocol or FTP for short* * file transfer protocol（文件传输协议）或简称 FTP

• RUDE 无礼 **11** [not before noun] ~ (**with sb**) (of a person 人) speaking to sb using few words in a way that seems rude 简单粗暴；简慢无礼：*I'm sorry I was short with you earlier—I had other things on my mind.* 对不起，我刚才怠慢你了，我脑子里在想别的事。

• VOWEL 元音 **12** (*phonetics* 语音) a **short** vowel is pronounced for a shorter time than other vowels 短音的：*Compare the short vowel in 'full' and the long vowel in 'fool'.* 比较 full 中的短元音和 fool 中的长元音。 OPP long ➲ SEE ALSO SHORTLY

▸ **short·ness** *noun* [U]: *She suffered from shortness of breath.* 她患有气急的毛病。

IDM **a ˌbrick short of a ˈload, two ˌsandwiches short of a ˈpicnic, etc.** (*informal*) (of a person 人) stupid; not very intelligent 冒傻气的；不大聪明的 **get the short end of the ˈstick** (*NAmE*) (*BrE* **ˌdraw the short ˈstraw**) to be the person in a group who is chosen or forced to perform an unpleasant duty or task 抽到倒霉签；被派做苦差事 **give sb/sth/get short ˈshrift** to give sb/get little attention or sympathy 不重视（或同情）；不受重视（或同情） **have/be on a short ˈfuse** to have a tendency to get angry quickly and easily 动辄发火；性情暴躁；脾气不好：*You may find your temper on a short fuse when confronting your teenager.* 对付十几岁的半大孩子，你可能动不动就会生气。 **in ˌshort ˈorder** quickly and without trouble 麻利；简单省事 **in the ˈshort run** concerning the immediate future 从短期来看；眼下：*In the short run, unemployment may fall.* 从短期来看，失业率可能降低。 **in ˌshort supˈply** not existing in large enough quantities to satisfy demand 不充裕；短缺；紧缺：*Basic foodstuffs were in short supply.* 基本食物紧缺。◇ *Sunshine will be in short supply for the west coast.* 西海岸将不会有充足的阳光。 **little/nothing short of ˈsth** used when you are saying that sth is almost true, or is equal to sth 可以说是；无异于；近乎：*Last year's figures were little short of disastrous.* 去年的数字简直是灾难。◇ *The transformation has been nothing short of a miracle.* 这种转化堪称奇迹。 **make short ˈwork of sth/sb** to defeat, deal with sth/sb quickly 干净利落地打败（或处理）；三下五除二就打垮（或解决）：*Liverpool made short work of the opposition* (= in a football/SOCCER game). 利物浦队干净利落地击败了对手。◇ *He made short work of his lunch* (= ate it quickly). 他三下两下吃完午饭。 **ˌshort and ˈsweet** (*informal*) pleasant but not lasting a long time 短暂而美好；简明扼要；紧凑：*We haven't much time so I'll keep it short and sweet.* 我们时间不多，我就长话短说吧。 ➲ MORE LIKE THIS 13, page R26 ➲ MORE AT LIFE, LONG *adj.*, MEASURE *n.*, NOTICE *n.*, TERM *n.*, THICK *adj.*

■ ***adv.*** (**short·er, short·est**) **1** if you **go short of** or **run short of** sth, you do not have enough of it 缺少；不足：*I'd never let you go short of anything.* 我什么都不会让你缺的。◇ *Mothers regularly go short of food to ensure their children have enough.* 为了保证自己的孩子吃饱饭，做母亲的经常忍饥挨饿。◇ *They had* ***run short of*** (= used most of their supply of) *fuel.* 他们燃料不够用了。 **2** not as far as you need or expect 未达到；不及：*All too often you pitch the ball short.* 你投球老是距离不够。 **3** before the time expected or arranged; before the natural time 中间（打断）；过早地（终止）：*a career tragically* ***cut short*** *by illness* 因病不幸中断的事业 ◇ *I'm afraid I'm going to have to* ***stop*** *you* ***short*** *there, as time is running out.* 时间快到了，恐怕我得就此打断你了。

IDM **be caught ˈshort** (*BrE also* **be taken ˈshort**) **1** (*BrE, informal*) to suddenly feel an urgent need to go to the toilet/bathroom 突然感觉要上厕所；内急 **2** to be put at a disadvantage 被置于不利地位 **come ˈshort** (*SAfrE, informal*) to have an accident; to get into trouble 出事故；遇到麻烦 **fall ˈshort of sth** to fail to reach the standard that you expected or need 未达到；不符合：*The hotel fell far short of their expectations.* 旅馆远没有他们预期的那么好。 **short of (doing) sth** without sth; without doing sth; unless sth happens 没有；如果不；除非：*Short of a miracle, we're certain to lose.* 除非发生奇迹，否则我们输定了。◇ *Short of asking her to leave* (= and we don't want to do that) *there's not a lot we can do about the situation.* 要是不请她走，我们也就没有多少办法应付这种局面了。 **pull, bring, etc. sb up ˈshort** to make sb suddenly stop what they are doing 使某人突然停止：*I was brought up short by a terrible thought.* 一个可怕的念头闪

S

过，我一下子愣住了。 ➲MORE AT SELL *v.*, STOP *v.*

■**noun** (*informal*) ➲SEE ALSO SHORTS **1** (*BrE*) a small strong alcoholic drink, for example of WHISKY 少量烈酒 **2** a short film/movie, especially one that is shown before the main film （尤指在正片前放映的）电影短片 **3** (*informal*) = SHORT CIRCUIT

IDM **in 'short** in a few words 总之；简言之：*His novels belong to a great but vanished age. They are, in short, old-fashioned.* 他的小说属于一个辉煌但已逝去的时代。一句话，已经过时了。 ➲MORE AT LONG *adj.*

■**verb** [I, T] **~ (sth) (out)** (*informal*) = SHORT-CIRCUIT

short·age /ˈʃɔːtɪdʒ; *NAmE* ˈʃɔːrt-/ *noun* [C, U] a situation when there is not enough of the people or things that are needed 不足；缺少；短缺：*food/housing/water shortages* 食物 / 住房 / 用水短缺 ◇ *a shortage of funds* 资金不足 ◇ *There is no shortage of* (= there are plenty of) *things to do in the town.* 城里不愁找不到活儿干。

'short-arse (*BrE*) (*US* **'short-ass**) *noun* (*slang, disapproving*) a person who is not very tall 矮子；矬子

short ˌback and 'sides *noun* [sing.] (*BrE, old-fashioned*) a way of cutting a man's hair so that the hair is very short at the sides and the back of the head 盖式发型（脑后和两侧均剪得很短的男式发型）

short·bread /ˈʃɔːtbred; *NAmE* ˈʃɔːrt-/ (*BrE also* **short·cake**) *noun* [U] a rich crisp biscuit/cookie made with flour, sugar and a lot of butter 黄油甜酥饼干

short·cake /ˈʃɔːtkeɪk; *NAmE* ˈʃɔːrt-/ *noun* [U] **1** (*BrE*) = SHORTBREAD **2** a cake with a PASTRY base and cream and fruit on top 水果奶油酥饼：*strawberry shortcake* 草莓酥饼

ˌshort-'change *verb* [often passive] **1 ~ sb** to give back less than the correct amount of money to sb who has paid for sth with more than the exact price 少找给（某人）零钱：*I think I've been short-changed at the bar.* 我觉得酒吧没给我找够零钱。 ➲WORDFINDER NOTE AT BUY **2 ~ sb** to treat sb unfairly by not giving them what they have earned or deserve 亏待；克扣

ˌshort 'circuit (*also informal* **short**) *noun* a failure in an electrical CIRCUIT, when electricity travels along the wrong route because of damaged wires or a fault in the connections between the wires 短路

S

ˌshort-'circuit (*also informal* **short**) *verb* **1** [I, T] **~ (sth)** to have a short circuit; to make sth have a short circuit （使）短路：*The wires had short-circuited and burnt out.* 电线短路，烧坏了。 **2** [T] **~ sth** to succeed in doing sth more quickly than usual, without going through all the usual processes （做事）抄近路，走捷径

short·com·ing /ˈʃɔːtkʌmɪŋ; *NAmE* ˈʃɔːrt-/ *noun* [usually pl.] a fault in sb's character, a plan, a system, etc. 缺点；短处 SYN **defect**

short·crust pastry /ˌʃɔːtkrʌst ˈpeɪstri; *NAmE* ˌʃɔːrt-/ *noun* [U] a type of PASTRY that CRUMBLES easily, used for making PIES, etc. 酥皮面团

shortcut /ˈʃɔːtkʌt; *NAmE* ˈʃɔːrt-/ *noun* **1** a quicker or shorter way of getting to a place 近路；捷径：*You can take a shortcut across the field.* 你可以抄近道从田里穿过去。 **2** a way of doing sth that is quicker than the usual way （做某事的）快捷办法，捷径：*There are no shortcuts to economic recovery.* 经济复苏没有捷径可走。

short·en /ˈʃɔːtn; *NAmE* ˈʃɔːrtn/ *verb* [T, I] to make sth shorter; to become shorter （使）变短，缩短：**~ (sth)** *Injury problems could shorten his career.* 受伤的问题有可能缩短他的职业生涯。 ◇ *a shortened version of the game* 简化了的比赛 ◇ *In November the temperatures drop and the days shorten.* 十一月气温下降，白天变短。 ◇ **~ sth to sth** *Her name's Katherine, generally shortened to Kay.* 她名叫凯瑟琳，通常简称凯。 OPP **lengthen**

short·en·ing /ˈʃɔːtnɪŋ; *NAmE* ˈʃɔːrt-/ *noun* [U] fat that is used for making PASTRY （制作油酥点心用的）起酥油

short·fall /ˈʃɔːtfɔːl; *NAmE* ˈʃɔːrt-/ *noun* **~ (in sth)** if there is **a shortfall in** sth, there is less of it than you need or expect 缺口；差额；亏空 SYN **deficit**

short·hair /ˈʃɔːtheə(r); *NAmE* ˈʃɔːrther/ *noun* a breed of cat with short hair 短毛猫 ➲COMPARE LONGHAIR

short·hand /ˈʃɔːthænd; *NAmE* ˈʃɔːrt-/ *noun* **1** (*NAmE also* **sten·og·raphy**) [U] a quick way of writing using special signs or abbreviations, used especially to record what sb is saying 速记（法）：*typing and shorthand* 打字和速记 ◇ *to take sth down* **in shorthand** 用速记记录某事 ◇ *a shorthand typist* 速记打字员 **2** [U, C, usually sing.] **~ (for sth)** a shorter way of saying or referring to sth, which may not be as accurate as the more complicated way of saying it （对某事）简略的表达方式

ˌshort-'handed *adj.* [not usually before noun] not having as many workers or people who can help as you need 人手不足 SYN **short-staffed**

ˌshort-haul *adj.* [only before noun] that involves transporting people or goods over short distances, especially by plane （尤指空运）短途运输的 OPP **long-haul**

short·horn /ˈʃɔːthɔːn; *NAmE* ˈʃɔːrthɔːrn/ *noun* a breed of cow with short horns 短角牛

shortie = SHORTY

short·list /ˈʃɔːtlɪst; *NAmE* ˈʃɔːrt-/ *noun, verb*

■**noun** [usually sing.] a small number of candidates for a job, etc., who have been chosen from all the people who applied 入围名单：*to draw up a shortlist* 拟就入围名单 ◇ *a shortlist for a literary prize* 一项文学奖的入围名单 ◇ *She is on my* **shortlist** *of great singers.* 她是我心目中的优秀歌唱家之一。 ➲WORDFINDER NOTE AT APPLY

■**verb** [usually passive] **~ sb/sth (for sth)** (*BrE*) to put sb/sth on a shortlist for a job, prize, etc. 把…列入入围名单：*Candidates who are shortlisted for interview will be contacted by the end of the week.* 入围参加面试的求职者将在周末以前得到通知。

ˌshort-'lived *adj.* lasting only for a short time 短暂的

short·ly 🔑 /ˈʃɔːtli; *NAmE* ˈʃɔːrt-/ *adv.* **1** 🔑 a short time; not long 不多时；不久：*She arrived shortly after us.* 我们刚到不多会儿她就到了。 ◇ *I saw him shortly before he died.* 在他去世前不久我还见过他一面。 **2** 🔑 soon 立刻；马上：*I'll be ready shortly.* 我马上就准备好了。 **3** in an angry and impatient way 没好气地；不耐烦地 SYN **sharply**

ˌshort-order 'cook *noun* a person who works in a restaurant cooking food that can be prepared quickly 快餐厨师

ˌshort-'range *adj.* [usually before noun] **1** (of weapons 武器) designed to travel only over short distances 短程的；近程的：*short-range missiles* 短程导弹 **2** (of plans, etc. 计划等) connected with a short period of time in the future 短期的；近期的：*a short-range weather forecast* 短期天气预报 ➲COMPARE LONG-RANGE

shorts /ʃɔːts; *NAmE* ʃɔːrts/ *noun* [pl.] **1** short trousers/pants that end above or at the knee 短裤：*a pair of tennis shorts* 一条网球短裤 ◇ *He was wearing a T-shirt and shorts.* 他穿着 T 恤衫和短裤。 ➲VISUAL VOCAB PAGE V68 **2** (*NAmE*) = BOXER SHORTS

ˌshort-'sighted *adj.* **1** (*especially BrE*) (*NAmE usually* **near-sighted**) able to see things clearly only if they are very close to you 近视的 OPP **long-sighted** **2** not thinking carefully about the possible effects of sth or what might happen in the future 目光短浅的；无远见的：*a short-sighted policy* 目光短浅的政策 ▸**ˌshort 'sight** (*also* **ˌshort-'sighted·ness**) *noun* [U]: *She suffered from short sight.* 她眼睛近视。 ◇ *Many people accused the government of short-sightedness.* 很多人谴责政府目光短浅。 **ˌshort-'sighted·ly** *adv.*

ˌshort-'staffed *adj.* [not usually before noun] having fewer members of staff than you need or usually have 人员配备不足；人手短缺 SYN **short-handed** ➲SEE ALSO UNDERSTAFFED

ˌshort-ˈstay *adj.* [only before noun] (*BrE*) (of a place 地方) where you only stay for a short time 临时停留的；暂住的：*a short-stay car park* 短时停车场

ˌshort ˈstory *noun* a story, usually about imaginary characters and events, that is short enough to be read from beginning to end without stopping 短篇小说

ˌshort ˈtemper *noun* [sing.] a tendency to become angry very quickly and easily 暴躁脾气 ▸ **ˌshort-ˈtempered** *adj.*

ˌshort-ˈterm *adj.* [usually before noun] lasting a short time; designed only for a short period of time in the future 短期的；近期的：*a short-term loan* 短期贷款 ◇ *to find work on a short-term contract* 找一份短期合同工作 ◇ *short-term plans* 近期计划 ◇ *a short-term solution to the problem* 解决这个问题的短期措施 ◇ *His **short-term memory*** (= the ability to remember things that happened a short time ago) *is failing.* 他的短时记忆越来越差了。➲ COMPARE LONG-TERM

ˌshort-ˈtermism *noun* [U] a way of thinking or planning that is concerned with the advantages or profits you could have now, rather than the effects in the future 只注重短期效益的思维方式

ˌshort ˈtime *noun* [U] (*BrE*) if workers are put on **short time**, they work for fewer hours than usual, because there is not enough work to do or not enough money to pay them 短工时；开工不足

ˌshort ˈwave *noun* [C, U] (*abbr.* **SW**) a radio wave that has a FREQUENCY between 3 and 30 MEGAHERTZ （无线电）短波 ➲ COMPARE LONG WAVE, MEDIUM WAVE

shorty (*also* **shortie**) /ˈʃɔːti; *NAmE* ˈʃɔːrti/ *noun* (*pl.* **-ies**) (*informal*) a person who is shorter than average 矮子

Sho·shone /ʃəʊˈʃəʊni; *NAmE* ʃoʊˈʃoʊni/ *noun* (*pl.* **Sho·shone** or **Sho·shones**) a member of a Native American people many of whom now live in the US state of Wyoming 肖肖尼人（美洲土著，很多现居于美国怀俄明州）

shot 🔑 /ʃɒt; *NAmE* ʃɑːt/ *noun, adj.* ➲ SEE ALSO SHOOT *v.*

■ ***noun***

• **WITH GUN** 用枪炮 **1** 🔑 [C] **~ (at sb/sth)** the act of firing a gun; the sound this makes 射击；开枪（或炮）；枪（或炮）声：*The man fired several shots from his pistol.* 那个男人用手枪开了几枪。◇ *Someone **took a shot at** the car.* 有人朝轿车开了一枪。◇ *We heard some shots in the distance.* 我们听见远处有几声枪响。➲ SEE ALSO GUNSHOT, POTSHOT **2** [C] **a good, bad, etc. ~** a person who shoots a gun in a particular way (well, badly, etc.) 优秀（或不高明等的）射手，枪手，炮手

• **BULLETS** 子弹 **3** (*also* **ˌlead ˈshot**) [U] a large number of small metal balls that you fire together from a SHOTGUN 铅沙弹 ➲ SEE ALSO BUCKSHOT **4** [C] (*pl.* **shot**) a large stone or metal ball that was shot from a CANNON or large gun in the past （旧时用大炮发射的石质或金属的）弹丸

• **REMARK/ACTION** 言语；行动 **5** [C] a remark or an action that is usually one of a series, and is aimed against sb/sth that you are arguing or competing with （针对对手、多为一系列之一的）一席话，一击：*This statement was **the opening shot** in the argument.* 这番话打响了争论的第一炮。◇ *The supermarket **fired the first shot** in a price war today.* 今天，这家超市打响了价格战的头一炮。

• **ATTEMPT** 尝试 **6** [C, usually sing.] **~ (at sth/at doing sth)** (*informal*) the act of trying to do or achieve sth 尝试；努力：*The team are looking good for a shot at the title.* 看来这个队力争夺冠的势头不错。◇ *I've never produced a play before but I'll **have a shot at** it.* 我从来没有制作过一出戏剧，不过我要尝试一下。◇ *I'm willing to **give it a shot**.* 我愿意试试。◇ *Just **give it your best shot*** (= try as hard as you can) *and you'll be fine.* 只要尽自己最大努力，你就会有好的结果。

• **IN SPORT** 体育运动 **7** 🔑 [C] the action of hitting, kicking or throwing the ball in order to score a point or goal in a game 击球；射门；投篮：*Taylor scored with a low shot into the corner of the net.* 泰勒一脚低射，把球射入网角。◇ *Good shot!* 好球！ **8** (*often* **the shot**) [sing.] the heavy ball that is used in the sports competition called SHOT-PUT 铅球

• **PHOTOGRAPH** 照片 **9** [C] a photograph 照片：*I got some good shots of people at the party.* 我给参加聚会的人拍了几张精彩的照片。➲ SEE ALSO MUGSHOT, SNAPSHOT ➲ SYNONYMS AT PHOTOGRAPH

• **SCENE IN FILM/MOVIE** 电影中的镜头 **10** [C] a scene in a film/movie that is filmed continuously by one camera （电影中的）镜头：*the opening shot of a character walking across a desert* 影片开头呈现一个人穿越沙漠的镜头

• **DRUG** 药物 **11** [C] (*informal, especially NAmE*) a small amount of a drug that is put into your body using a SYRINGE 注射 **SYN** **injection**：*a flu shot* (= to protect you against flu) 打预防流感的针 ◇ *a shot of morphine* 打一针吗啡

• **DRINK** 饮料 **12** [C] (*informal*) a small amount of a drink, especially a strong alcoholic one 少量饮料；（尤指）少量烈酒：*a shot of whisky* 一点威士忌

• **OF SPACECRAFT** 航天器 **13** [C] an occasion when a SPACECRAFT is sent into space 发射：*The space shot was shown live on television.* 此次太空发射在电视上做了实况转播。

• **HORSE/DOG IN RACE** 比赛中的马/狗 **14** [sing.] (used with numbers 与数字连用) a horse, dog, etc. that has the particular chance of winning a race that is mentioned 有…获胜可能的马（或狗）：*The horse is a 10–1 shot.* 这匹马的获胜率为 10:1。**HELP** You will find other compounds ending in **shot** at their place in the alphabet. 其他以 shot 结尾的复合词可在各字母中的适当位置查到。

IDM **like a ˈshot** (*informal*) very quickly and without hesitating 立刻；飞快地；毫不犹豫：*If I had the chance to go there, I'd go like a shot.* 要是我有机会去那儿，我会毫不犹豫就去的。 **a shot across the/sb's ˈbows** something that you say or do as a warning to sb about what might happen if they do not change, etc. （若不改变就会有某种后果的）警告 **a shot in the ˈarm** something that gives sb/sth the help or encouragement they need 鼓舞的力量；令人振奋的事情；强心针 ➲ MORE AT BIG *adj.*, CALL *v.*, DARK *n.*, LONG *adj.*, PARTING *adj.*

■ ***adj.*** **1 ~ (with sth)** (of cloth, hair, etc. 织物、毛发等) having another colour showing through or mixed with the main colour 杂色的；闪色的：*shot silk* 闪光绸 **2** [not before noun] (*informal*) in a very bad condition; destroyed 破烂不堪；筋疲力尽；毁坏：*The brakes on this car are shot.* 这辆车上的刹车完全失灵了。◇ *I'm shot—I'm too old for this job.* 我一点力气都没有了，我这岁数干不动这活儿了。◇ *After the accident his nerves were **shot to pieces**.* 经历了那场事故，他的神经脆弱到了极点。

IDM **be/get ˈshot of sb/sth** (*BrE, informal*) to get rid of sb/sth so you no longer have the problems they cause 摆脱；解决；处理 **shot through with sth** containing a lot of a particular colour, quality or feature 布满，充满，富有（某种颜色、品质或特征）：*a voice shot through with emotion* 富有感情的声音

shot·gun /ˈʃɒtɡʌn; *NAmE* ˈʃɑːt-/ *noun* a long gun that fires a lot of small metal bullets (called SHOT) and is used especially for shooting birds or animals 猎枪；霰弹枪 ➲ SEE ALSO SAWN-OFF SHOTGUN **IDM** SEE RIDE *v.*

ˌshotgun ˈwedding (*also* **ˌshotgun ˈmarriage**) *noun* (*old-fashioned, informal*) a wedding that has to take place quickly because the woman is pregnant （因女方怀孕而仓促举行的）闪电式结婚

shot·making /ˈʃɒtmeɪkɪŋ; *NAmE* ˈʃɑːt-/ *noun* [U] (in GOLF, TENNIS, etc. 高尔夫球、网球等) a way of playing in which a player takes risks in order to win more points （冒险）准确击球

Shoto·kan /ʃəʊˈtəʊkæn; *NAmE* ʃoʊˈtoʊ-/ *noun* [U] (*from Japanese*) a popular form of KARATE 松涛馆（空手道的一个流派）

the ˈshot-put *noun* [sing.] (*also* **ˈshot-putting**, **ˌputting the ˈshot**) the event or sport of throwing a heavy metal ball (called a SHOT) as far as possible 推铅球

should 🔑 /ʃəd; *strong form* ʃʊd/ *modal verb* (*negative* **should not**, *short form* **shouldn't** /ˈʃʊdnt/) **1** 🔑 used to show what is right, appropriate, etc., especially when

S

criticizing sb's actions（尤用于纠正别人）应该，应当：*You shouldn't drink and drive.* 你不该酒后驾车。◇ *He should have been more careful.* 他应当更小心点儿才是。◇ *A present for me? You **shouldn't have!*** (= used to thank sb politely) 给我的礼物？您太客气了！ **2** 🔑 used for giving or asking for advice（提出或征询建议）该，可以：*You should stop worrying about it.* 你该不用再为此事担忧了。◇ *Should I call him and apologize?* 我是不是应该打电话向他道歉？◇ ***I should** wait a little longer, **if I were you**.* 假如我是你的话，我会再等一会儿。◇ (*ironic*) *'She doesn't think she'll get a job.' 'She should worry, with all her qualifications* (= she does not need to worry).*'* "她担心找不到工作。""她那么好的条件，还担心什么呀。" **3** 🔑 used to say that you expect sth is true or will happen（表示预期）应该会，可能：*We should arrive before dark.* 我们天黑以前应该能赶到。◇ *I should have finished the book by Friday.* 到星期五我应该能读完那本书。◇ *The roads should be less crowded today.* 今天路上该不那么拥挤了吧。 **4** 🔑 used to say that sth that was expected has not happened（表示与预期相反）本应，本当：*It should be snowing now, according to the weather forecast.* 按天气预报，现在该下雪才是。◇ *The bus should have arrived ten minutes ago.* 公共汽车十分钟以前就该到了。 **5** (*BrE, formal*) used after *I* or *we* instead of *would* for describing what you would do if sth else happened first（与 I 或 we 连用代替 would，表示虚拟结果）就将：*If I were asked to work on Sundays, I should resign.* 要是叫我星期天加班，我就辞职不干了。 **6** (*formal*) used to refer to a possible event or situation（表示可能）假如，万一：*If you should change your mind, do let me know.* 假如你改变主意的话，一定要告诉我。◇ *In case you should need any help, here's my number.* 万一你需要帮助的话，这是我的电话号码。◇ *Should anyone call* (= if anyone calls)*, please tell them I'm busy.* 如果有人打电话来，请告诉他我正忙着。 **7** 🔑 used as the past form of *shall* when reporting what sb has said（在间接引语中用作 shall 的过去时）：*He asked me what time he should come.* (= His words were: 'What time shall I come?') 他问我他应该什么时候来。◇ (*BrE, formal*) *I said* (*that*) *I should be glad to help.* 我说我乐意帮忙。 **8** 🔑 (*BrE*) used after *that* when sth is suggested or arranged（用于 that 引导的、表示建议或安排的从句中）：*She recommended that I should take some time off.* 她建议我应该休息一段时间。◇ *In order that training should be effective it must be planned systematically.* 为使培训有成效，必须有系统的计划。 HELP In both *NAmE* and *BrE* this idea can be expressed without 'should'. 在美式英语和英式英语中，表达这一意思均可省掉 should：*She recommended that I take some time off.* 她建议我应该休息一段时间。◇ *In order that training be effective…* 为使培训有成效… **9** used after *that* after many adjectives that describe feelings（用于许多表示感情的形容词后的 that 从句中）：*I'm anxious that we should allow plenty of time.* 我殷切希望我们能留出充裕的时间。◇ *I find it astonishing that he should be so rude to you.* 他竟然对你这样无礼，真叫我吃惊。 **10** (*BrE, formal*) used with *I* and *we* in polite requests（与 I 和 we 连用，表示客气地请求）：*I should like to call my lawyer.* 我希望给我的律师打个电话。◇ *We should be grateful for your help.* 对您的帮助我们会非常感激。 **11** 🔑 used with *I* and *we* to give opinions that you are not certain about（与 I 和 we 连用，表示没有把握）：*I should imagine it will take about three hours.* 我想得用差不多三个小时吧。◇ *'Is this enough food for everyone?' '**I should think so.**'* "这些食物够所有人吃吗？""我觉得够了吧。"◇ *'Will it matter?' '**I shouldn't think so.**'* "这有关系吗？""我觉得没有吧。" **12** used for expressing strong agreement（表示十分赞同）：*'I know it's expensive but it will last for years.' '**I should hope so too!**'* "我知道价钱贵，但能用好多年。""我也是这么想的！"◇ *'Nobody will oppose it.' '**I should think not!**'* "谁也不会反对的。""我想也是！" **13 why, how, who, what ~ sb/sth do** used to refuse sth or to show that you are annoyed at a request; used to express surprise about an event or a situation（表示拒绝、恼怒或惊奇）：*Why should I help him? He's never done anything for me.* 我干吗要帮他呢？他从来没为我做过什么。◇ *How should I know where you've left your bag?* 我怎么知道你把包丢在哪儿了？◇ *I got on the bus and who should be sitting in front of me but Tony!* 我上了公共汽车，没想到坐在我前面的竟然是托尼！ **14** used to tell sb that sth would amuse or surprise them if they saw or experienced it（表示假如对方看见或经历某事物，一定会感兴趣或吃惊）真该，真应当：*You should have seen her face when she found out!* 你真该看看她发现事情真相时脸上的表情！ ➲ NOTE AT MODAL

▼ **GRAMMAR POINT** 语法说明

should / ought / had better

- **Should** and **ought to** are both used to say that something is the best thing or the right thing to do, but **should** is much more common. * should 和 ought to 均用以表示应该做某事，不过 should 常用得多：*You should take the baby to the doctor's.* 你应该把这婴儿带去看看医生。◇ *I ought to give up smoking.* 我应该戒烟。 In questions, **should** is usually used instead of **ought to**. 在疑问句中，通常用 should 而不是 ought to：*Should we call the doctor?* 我们叫医生来好吗？
- **Had better** can also be used to say what is the best thing to do in a situation that is happening now. * had better 亦可用以表示在目前状况下最好做某事：*We'd better hurry or we'll miss the train.* 我们最好快点，否则就赶不上火车了。
- You form the past by using **should have** or **ought to have**. 过去时用 should have 或 ought to have 构成：*She should have asked for some help.* 她本应该请求帮助的。◇ *You ought to have been more careful.* 你本应该更小心一点的。
- The forms **should not** or **shouldn't** (and **ought not to** or **oughtn't to**, which are rare in *NAmE* and formal in *BrE*) are used to say that something is a bad idea or the wrong thing to do. * should not 或 shouldn't（以及在美式英语中很少见，在英式英语中为正式用法的 ought not to 或 oughtn't to）表示不应该：*You shouldn't drive so fast.* 你不应该把车开得这么快。
- The forms **should not have** or **shouldn't have** and, much less frequently, **ought not to have** or **oughtn't to have** are used to talk about the past. * should not have 或 shouldn't have 以及很少用的 ought not to have 或 oughtn't to have 均用于指过去：*I'm sorry, I shouldn't have lost my temper.* 对不起，我不该发脾气。

▼ **GRAMMAR POINT** 语法说明

should / would

- In modern English, the traditional difference between **should** and **would** in reported sentences, conditions, requests, etc. has disappeared and **should** is not used very much at all. In spoken English the short form **'d** is usually used. 在现代英语中，should 和 would 在间接引述中、在表示条件、请求等句子中的传统区别已不复存在；should 基本上不怎么用。在口语中常用简约式 'd 表示：*I said I'd* (*I would*) *be late.* 我说我要迟到了。◇ *He'd* (*he would*) *have liked to have been an actor.* 他本来想当演员。◇ *I'd* (*I would*) *really prefer tea.* 我倒是更喜欢喝茶。
- The main use of **should** now is to tell somebody what they ought to do, to give advice, or to add emphasis. 现在 should 主要用于告诉某人应该做什么、给予忠告或加强语气：*We should really go and visit them soon.* 我们的确应该马上去看看他们。◇ *You should have seen it!* 你应该看见的！

shoul·der 🔑 /ˈʃəʊldə(r); *NAmE* ˈʃoʊ-/ *noun, verb*

■ ***noun***

- **PART OF BODY** 身体部位 **1** 🔑 [C] either of the two parts of the body between the top of each arm and the neck 肩；肩胛：*He slung the bag over his shoulder.* 他把包一甩，挎在肩上。◇ *She tapped him on the shoulder.* 她拍了拍他的肩膀。◇ *He looked back over his shoulder.* 他扭头朝

S

后看。◇ *She **shrugged her shoulders** (= showing that she didn't know or care).* 她耸了耸肩。◇ *an **off-the-shoulder** dress* 露肩连衣裙 ◇ *He carried the child on his shoulders.* 他把孩子扛在肩上。➲ COLLOCATIONS AT PHYSICAL ➲ VISUAL VOCAB PAGE V64

- **-SHOULDERED** 肩膀… **2** (in adjectives 构成形容词) having the type of shoulders mentioned …肩膀的: *broad-shouldered* 宽肩的 ➲ SEE ALSO ROUND-SHOULDERED
- **CLOTHING** 衣服 **3** 🔑 [C] the part of a piece of clothing that covers the shoulder（衣服的）肩部: *a jacket with padded shoulders* 带垫肩的夹克
- **MEAT** 肉 **4** [U, C] ~ (**of sth**) meat from the top part of one of the front legs of an animal that has four legs 前腿连肩肉
- **OF MOUNTAIN/BOTTLE, ETC.** 山、瓶子等 **5** [C] ~ (**of sth**) a part of sth, such as a bottle or mountain, that is shaped like a shoulder 山肩；瓶肩: *The village lay just around the shoulder of the hill.* 村子恰好坐落在山肩处。
- **SIDE OF ROAD** 公路边 **6** [C] (*NAmE*) an area of ground at the side of a road where vehicles can stop in an emergency 路肩（公路两侧供车辆紧急停靠的地带）: *No shoulder for next 5 miles.* 前方 5 英里之内没有路肩。➲ SEE ALSO HARD SHOULDER, SOFT SHOULDER

IDM **be looking over your 'shoulder** to be anxious and have the feeling that sb is going to do sth unpleasant or harmful to you 惴惴不安；小心提防 **on sb's shoulders** if blame, GUILT, etc. is **on sb's shoulders**, they must take responsibility for it 由某人承担 **put your shoulder to the 'wheel** to start working very hard at a particular task 着手大干起来；全力以赴 **a shoulder to 'cry on** used to describe a person who listens to your problems and gives you sympathy 倾诉的对象 **,shoulder to 'shoulder (with sb)** **1** physically close to sb 肩并肩地；紧挨着 **2** as one group that has the same aims, opinions, etc. 并肩；齐心协力 ➲ MORE AT CHIP *n.*, COLD *adj.*, HEAD *n.*, OLD, RUB *v.*, STRAIGHT *adv.*

■ ***verb***

- **ACCEPT RESPONSIBILITY** 承担责任 **1** [T] ~ **sth** to accept the responsibility for sth 承担；担负: *to **shoulder the responsibility/blame for sth*** 对某事承担责任 / 过失 ◇ *women who shoulder the double burden of childcare and full-time work* 既抚养孩子又做全职工作、承担着双重负担的妇女
- **PUSH WITH SHOULDER** 用肩推 **2** [T, I] to push forward with your shoulder in order to get somewhere 挤；闯: ~ **your way + adv./prep.** *He shouldered his way through the crowd and went after her.* 他侧身从人群中挤了过去，跟在她后面。◇ **+ adv./prep.** *She shouldered past a woman with a screaming baby.* 她从一个怀抱啼哭婴儿的女人身边挤了过去。**3** [T] ~ **sb/sth + adv./prep.** to push sb/sth out of your way with your shoulder（用肩膀）推开，顶开: *He shouldered the man aside.* 他一膀子把那男人撞到了一旁。
- **CARRY ON SHOULDER** 肩负 **4** [T] ~ **sth** to carry sth on your shoulder 背；扛；挑；担: *She shouldered her bag and set off home.* 她扛起包朝家走去。

'shoulder bag *noun* a bag, especially a HANDBAG, that is carried over the shoulder with a long narrow piece of leather, etc.（小）挎包 ➲ VISUAL VOCAB PAGE V69

'shoulder blade *noun* either of the two large flat bones at the top of the back 肩胛骨 **SYN** **scapula** ➲ VISUAL VOCAB PAGE V64

,shoulder-'high *adj., adv.* as high as a person's shoulders 齐肩高的（地）: *a shoulder-high wall* 一堵齐肩高的墙 ◇ *They carried him shoulder-high through the crowd.* 他们把他抬在肩头，穿过人群。

'shoulder-length *adj.* (especially of hair 尤指头发) long enough to reach your shoulders 齐肩的 ➲ VISUAL VOCAB PAGE V65

'shoulder pad *noun* [usually pl.] **1** a small piece of thick cloth that is sewn into the shoulder of a dress, jacket, etc. to make a person's shoulders look bigger（衣服）垫肩 **2** a piece of hard plastic that people wear under their shirts to protect their shoulders when playing AMERICAN FOOTBALL, ICE HOCKEY, etc.（美式足球、冰球等运动衣内的）护肩 ➲ VISUAL VOCAB PAGE V48

'shoulder strap *noun* **1** a strip of cloth on a dress or other piece of clothing that goes over your shoulder from the front to the back（衣服）肩带 **2** a long strip of cloth, leather, etc. that is attached to a bag so that you can carry it over your shoulder（背包）背带

'shoulder surfing *noun* [U] (*informal*) the practice of watching a person who is getting money from a machine, filling out a form, etc., in order to find out their personal information 肩窥（窥视他人从提款机取款、填表等以了解其个人信息的做法）

shout 🔑 /ʃaʊt/ *verb, noun*

■ ***verb*** **1** 🔑 [I, T] to say sth in a loud voice; to speak loudly/angrily to sb 大声说；叫；嚷；斥责；怒骂: *Stop shouting and listen!* 别嚷了，听着！◇ ~ **for sth** *I shouted for help but nobody came.* 我大声呼救，但没人来。◇ ~ **at sb** *Then he started shouting and swearing at her.* 这时，他冲着她又叫又骂起来。◇ ~ **at sb to do sth** *She shouted at him to shut the gate.* 她大声吆喝他把大门关上。◇ ~ **sth (at/to sb)** *to shout abuse/encouragement/orders* 高声辱骂 / 鼓励 / 命令 ◇ ~ **that...** *He shouted that he couldn't swim.* 他大叫他不会游泳。◇ ~ **yourself + adj.** *She shouted herself hoarse, cheering on the team.* 她为运动队加油，嗓子都喊哑了。◇ **+ speech** *'Run!' he shouted.* "跑！"他大喊一声。 **2** 🔑 [I]

▼ **SYNONYMS** 同义词辨析

shout

yell • cry • scream • cheer • bellow • raise your voice

These words all mean to say sth in a very loud voice. 以上各词均指大声说出、叫嚷。

shout to say sth in a loud voice; to speak loudly and often angrily to sb 指大声说、叫、嚷、斥责、怒骂: *Stop shouting and listen!* 别嚷了，听着！◇ *'Run!' he shouted.* "跑！"他大喊一声。

yell to shout loudly, for example because you are angry, excited, frightened or in pain 指（因气愤、激动、害怕或痛苦而）叫喊、大喊、吼叫: *She yelled at the boy to get down from the wall.* 她冲小孩大喊，让他从墙上下来。

cry (*rather formal* or *literary*) to shout loudly 指喊叫、呼喊、呼叫: *She ran over to the window and cried for help.* 她跑到窗口呼喊救命。

scream to shout sth in a loud high voice because you are afraid, angry or excited 指（因害怕、气愤或激动而）尖叫、大叫: *He screamed at me to stop.* 他冲着我大叫，要我停下来。

cheer (especially of a crowd of people) to shout loudly to show support or praise for sb, or to give them encouragement（尤指一群人）欢呼、喝彩、加油: *We all cheered as the team came onto the field.* 球队入场时我们都欢呼起来。

bellow to shout in a loud deep voice, especially because you are angry 指大声吼叫，尤指怒吼: *'Quiet!' the teacher bellowed.* "安静！"老师大吼道。

raise your voice to speak loudly to sb, especially because you are angry（尤指因气愤而）提高嗓门、大声说话: *She never once raised her voice to us.* 她从未对我们提高嗓门说话。

PATTERNS

- to shout/yell/cry/raise your voice **to** sb
- to shout/yell/scream/bellow **at** sb
- to shout/yell/cry out/scream/bellow **in** pain/anguish/rage, etc.
- to shout/cry out/scream **for** joy/excitement/delight, etc.
- to shout/yell/cry out/scream **with** excitement/triumph, etc.
- to shout/yell/scream/bellow at sb **to do sth**
- to shout/yell/scream **abuse**
- to shout/yell/cry/scream **for help**

S

~ (**out**) to make a loud noise 呼叫；喊叫：*She shouted out in pain when she tried to move her leg.* 她想动动腿，结果疼得大叫起来。**3** [I, T] (*AustralE, NZE*) to buy drinks or food for sb in a bar, restaurant, etc.（在酒吧、餐厅等）请人喝饮料（或吃东西）：*I'll shout—what are you drinking?* 我请客，你想喝什么？◇ ~ (**sb**) **sth** *Who's going to shout me a drink?* 谁要请我喝一杯？

PHR V **ˌshout sb↔ˈdown** to shout so that sb who is speaking cannot be heard 用喊叫声盖过某人的讲话：*The speaker was shouted down by a group of protesters.* 一群抗议者大叫大嚷，盖过了讲话人的声音。**ˌshout sth↔ˈout** to say sth in a loud voice so that it can be clearly heard 大声说出：*Don't shout out all the answers.* 别把所有的答案都大声说出来。◇ **+ speech** *'I'm over here!' I shouted out.* "我在这边！"我大声喊道。

■ ***noun*** **1** a loud cry of anger, fear, excitement, etc.（愤怒、害怕、激动等的）呼喊，喊叫声：*angry shouts* 愤怒的叫喊 ◇ *a shout of anger* 一声怒吼 ◇ *I heard her warning shout too late.* 我听到她的大声警告，但已经太晚了。**2** (*BrE, informal*) a person's turn to buy drinks 轮到某人请客（喝饮料）：*What are you drinking? It's my shout.* 你喝什么？该我请客了。

IDM **be ˌin with a ˈshout (of sth/of doing sth)** (*informal*) to have a good chance of winning sth or of achieving sth 成功在望 **give sb a ˈshout** (*informal*) to tell sb sth 告诉某人：*Give me a shout when you're ready.* 准备好了告诉我一声。

shout·ing /ˈʃaʊtɪŋ/ *noun* [U] loud cries from a number of people（多人的）叫喊，叫嚷：*Didn't you hear all the shouting?* 你难道没有听到那一片叫喊声？

IDM **be all over bar the ˈshouting** (*BrE*) (of an activity or a competition 活动或比赛) to be almost finished or decided, so that there is no doubt about the final result 基本大功告成；大局已定；胜负已分明 **within ˈshouting distance** (*especially NAmE*) (*BrE also* **within ˈspitting distance (of sth)**) (*informal*) very close 很近

ˈshouting match *noun* an argument or a disagreement when people shout loudly at each other 高声的争论

ˈshout-out *noun* (*informal*) a public expression of thanks or welcome 公开道谢；当众问候：*This is a shout-out to all our sponsors and advertisers.* 这是对我们所有赞助方和广告商的公开致谢。

shouty /ˈʃaʊti/ *adj.* (*informal*) doing or involving a lot of shouting 大喊大叫的；吵吵嚷嚷的：*a shouty conversation on the stairs* 楼梯上的高声谈话

shove /ʃʌv/ *verb, noun*

■ ***verb*** **1** [I, T] to push sb/sth in a rough way 猛推；乱挤；推撞：*The crowd was* ***pushing and shoving*** *to get a better view.* 人们挤来挤去，想看得清楚点儿。◇ **+ adv./prep.** *The door wouldn't open no matter how hard she shoved.* 她怎么使劲推，门都推不开。◇ ~ **sb/sth (+ adv./prep.)** *He shoved her down the stairs.* 他把她推下楼梯。**2** [T] ~ **sth (+ adv./prep.)** (*informal*) to put sth somewhere roughly or carelessly 乱放；随便放；胡乱丢；随手扔：*She shoved the book into her bag and hurried off.* 她把书胡乱塞进包里就急急忙忙走了。◇ *He came over and shoved a piece of paper into my hand.* 他走过来往我手里塞了一张纸条。◇ *Shove your suitcase under the bed.* 把你的手提箱塞到床底下吧。

IDM **ˈshove it** (*informal, especially NAmE*) used to say rudely that you will not accept or do sth（粗鲁地表示不接受或不做某事）去他的，没门儿，去他妈的：*'The boss wants that report now.' 'Yeah? Tell him he can shove it.'* "老板现在要那份报告。""是吗？你告诉他没门儿。"

PHR V **ˌshove ˈoff** (*BrE, informal*) used to tell sb rudely to go away 滚；滚开 **ˌshove ˈup** (*BrE, informal*) to move in order to make a space for sb to sit down beside you 挪出空位：*Shove up! Jan wants to sit down.* 挪一挪！简要坐下来。

■ ***noun*** [usually sing.] a strong push 猛推：*You have to* ***give*** *the door* ***a shove*** *or it won't close.* 这门你得猛推一下，否则关不上。IDM SEE PUSH *n.*

shovel /ˈʃʌvl/ *noun, verb*

■ ***noun*** **1** a tool with a long handle and a broad blade with curved edges, used for moving earth, snow, sand, etc. 铲；铁铲：*workmen with picks and shovels* 手拿镐铲的工人 ◇ (*NAmE*) *The children took their* ***pails and shovels*** *to the beach.* 孩子们带着桶和铲子到海滩上去了。➲ VISUAL VOCAB PAGE V20 ➲ COMPARE SPADE (1) **2** the part of a large machine or vehicle that digs or moves earth（推土机、挖土机等的）铲，铲形部分

■ ***verb*** (**-ll-**, *US* **-l-**) ~ **sth (+ adv./prep.)** to lift and move earth, stones, coal, etc. with a shovel 铲；铲起：*A gang of workmen were shovelling rubble onto a truck.* 一帮工人正用铁锹往卡车上装碎石。◇ *They went out in freezing conditions to shovel snow.* 他们冒着严寒出去铲雪。◇ (*NAmE*) *to* ***shovel the sidewalk/driveway*** (= to remove snow) 铲除人行道 / 车行道上的积雪 ◇ (*figurative*) *He sat at the table, shovelling food into his mouth.* 他坐在桌前，一个劲地往嘴里塞吃的。

shovel·ful /ˈʃʌvlfʊl/ *noun* the amount that a shovel can hold 一铲（的量）

ˈshovel-ready *adj.* (of a construction project) at the stage where workers can be employed and building begun（建筑工程）准备就绪的，可马上动工的

show /ʃəʊ; *NAmE* ʃoʊ/ *verb, noun*

■ ***verb*** (**showed, shown** /ʃəʊn; *NAmE* ʃoʊn/, **showed**) HELP The form **showed** is rare as a past participle. * showed 用作过去分词很罕见。

• **MAKE CLEAR** 表明 **1** [T] to make sth clear; to prove sth 表明；证明：~ (**that**)... *The figures clearly show that her claims are false.* 这些数字清楚地表明，她的说法是错误的。◇ ~ **sb that...** *Market research has shown us that people want quality, not just low prices.* 市场研究告诉我们，人们需要的是高质量，而不仅仅是低价格。◇ ~ **sth** *a report showing the company's current situation* 表明公司当前状况的一份报告 ◇ ~ **sb/sth to be/have sth** *His new book shows him to be a first-rate storyteller.* 他的新著表明他讲故事的本领是一流的。◇ ~ (**sb**) **how, what, etc....** *This shows how people are influenced by TV advertisements.* 这表明电视广告对人们的影响有多大。➲ LANGUAGE BANK AT ILLUSTRATE

• **LET SB SEE STH** 给人看 **2** [T] to let sb see sth 给…看；出示；展示：~ **sth** *You have to show your ticket as you go in.* 进场必须出示门票。◇ ~ **sth to sb** *If there's a letter from France please show it to me.* 如有法国来的信，请拿给我看看。◇ *Have you shown your work to anyone?* 你有没有把你做的活儿给谁看过？◇ ~ **sb sth** *Have you shown anyone your work?* 你有没有给谁看过你做的活儿？

• **TEACH** 教 **3** [T] to help sb to do sth by letting them watch you do it or by explaining it（通过示范）教，解说；演示：~ **sth to sb** *She showed the technique to her students.* 她向学生演示了那个技巧。◇ ~ **sb sth** *She showed her students the technique.* 她向学生演示了那个技巧。◇ *Can you show me how to do it?* 你能教我怎么做吗？

• **POINT** 指 **4** [T] ~ **sb sth** to point to sth so that sb can see where or what it is 指给某人看；指出：*He showed me our location on the map.* 他在地图上给我指出我们所处的位置。◇ ~ **sb which, what, etc....** *Show me which picture you drew.* 指给我看哪张画是你画的。

• **GUIDE** 引导 **5** [T] to lead or guide sb to a place 引；带；领：~ **sb + adv./prep.** *The attendant showed us to our seats.* 服务员把我们带到我们的座位。◇ *We were shown into the waiting room.* 我们被领进等候室。◇ ~ **sb sth** *I'll go first and* ***show you the way.*** 我先走，给你带路。➲ SYNONYMS AT TAKE

• **QUALITY/BEHAVIOUR/FEELING** 品质；行为；感情 **6** [T] to make it clear that you have a particular quality 表现；体现：~ **sth** *to show great courage* 表现出极大的勇气 ◇ ~ **yourself + adj.** *She had shown herself unable to deal with money.* 她所做的事已表明她不善理财。◇ ~ **yourself to be/have sth** *He has shown himself to be ready to make compromises.* 他表现出自己愿意妥协。◇ ~ **that...** *He has shown that he is ready to make compromises.* 他表现出愿意妥协。**7** [T] to behave in a particular way towards sb（对某人）表现出；对待；表示：~ **sth (for/to sb)** *They showed no respect for their parents.* 他们毫不尊敬自己的父母。◇ ~ **sb sth** *They showed their parents no respect.* 他

们毫不尊敬自己的父母。 **8** [I, T] if a feeling or quality **shows**, or if you **show** it, people can see it 显示出；流露出： *Fear showed in his eyes.* 他眼里显出了害怕的神色。 ◇ *She tried not to let her disappointment show.* 她极力掩饰自己的失望情绪。 ◇ *She's nearly forty now. **And it shows*** (= it's obvious). 她年近四十，一望便知。 ◇ **~ sth** *Her expression showed her disappointment.* 从她的表情可以看出她很失望。 ◇ *James began to **show signs of** impatience.* 詹姆斯开始显得不耐烦。 ◇ **~ how, what, etc....** *She tried not to show how disappointed she was.* 她极力掩饰她是多么失望。

- **BE VISIBLE** 看得见 **9** [I, T] if sth **shows**, people can see it. If sth **shows** a mark, dirt, etc., the mark can be seen. 露出；显出： *She had a warm woollen hat and scarf on that left only her eyes and nose showing.* 她戴着保暖呢帽和围巾，只露出了眼睛和鼻子。 ◇ **~ sth** *Their new white carpet showed every mark.* 他们新铺的白地毯有一点脏都看得出。
- **INFORMATION** 信息 **10** [T] (not usually used in the progressive tenses 通常不用于进行时) **~ sth** to give particular information, or a time or measurement 标示，表明（信息、时间、计量）： *The map shows the principal towns and rivers.* 这张地图标出了主要城镇和河流。 ◇ *The clock showed midnight.* 时钟显示已是午夜。 ◇ *The end-of-year accounts show a loss.* 年终账面显示出现了亏损。
- **OF PICTURE/PHOTOGRAPH** 图画；照片 **11** [T] **~ sth** | **~ sb/sth (as sth)** | **~ sb/sth doing sth** to be of sb/sth; to represent sb/sth 描绘，描述，表现（为）： *She had objected to a photo showing her in a bikini.* 她曾反对给自己拍穿比基尼泳装的照片。
- **FOR PUBLIC TO SEE** 让公众看 **12** [I, T] to be or make sth available for the public to see 展览；陈列；上映；演出： *The movie is now showing at all major movie theaters.* 这部影片目前正在各大影院上映。 ◇ **~ sth** *The movie is being shown now.* 这部影片目前正在上映。 ◇ *She plans to show her paintings early next year.* 她计划明年初展出自己的绘画作品。
- **PROVE** 证明 **13** [T, no passive] (*informal*) to prove that you can do sth or are sth 证明；表明： **~ sb (sth)** *They think I can't do it, but I'll show them!* 他们以为我做不了，我却要做给他们看看！ ◇ **~ yourself to be/have sth** *He has shown himself to be a caring father.* 他已经证明了自己是个有爱心的父亲。
- **ARRIVE** 到来 **14** [I] (*informal, especially NAmE*) to arrive where you have arranged to meet sb or do sth 如约赶到；出现；露面： *I waited an hour but he didn't show.* 我等了一个小时，可他一直没露面。 ➲ SEE ALSO SHOW UP
- **ANIMAL** 动物 **15** [T] **~ sth** to enter an animal in a competition 替（动物）报名参加比赛 ➲ **MORE LIKE THIS** 33, page R28

IDM **it goes to 'show** used to say that sth proves sth 证明；表明： *It just goes to show what you can do when you really try.* 这就表明，当你真下功夫时能做成什么事。 **show sb the 'door** to ask sb to leave, because they are no longer welcome 要某人离开；下逐客令 **show your 'face** to appear among your friends or in public 露面；公开见人： *She stayed at home, afraid to show her face.* 她待在家里，不敢露面。 **show your 'hand/'cards** (*NAmE also* **tip your 'hand**) to make your plans or intentions known 摊牌；让对手摸着底细；公开自己的意图 **show sb who's 'boss** to make it clear to sb that you have more power and authority than they have 让某人知道谁说了算 **show the 'way** to do sth first so that other people can follow 示范 **show 'willing** (*BrE*) to show that you are ready to help, work hard, etc. if necessary 表示愿意；有乐于…的意思 **(have) something, nothing, etc. to 'show for sth** (to have) something, nothing, etc. as a result of sth 在…方面有（或没有等）成绩；在…方面有（或没有等）结果： *All those years of hard work, and nothing to show for it!* 苦干这么多年，却毫无成绩可言！ ➲ MORE AT FLAG *n.*, PACE[1] *n.*, ROPE *n.*

PHR V **ˌshow sb a'round/'round (sth)** to be a guide for sb when they visit a place for the first time to show them what is interesting 领（某人）参观；带（某人）巡视： *We were shown around the school by one of the students.* 我们由其中一名学生领着参观了学校。 ◇ *Has anyone shown you round yet?* 有没有人带你四处走走？ **ˌshow 'off** (*informal, disapproving*) to try to impress others by talking about your abilities, possessions, etc. 炫耀自己；卖弄自己： *He's just showing off because that girl he likes is here.* 他不过是在表现自己，因为他喜欢的那个姑娘在场。 ➲ RELATED NOUN SHOW-OFF **ˌshow sb/sth↔'off** to show people sb/sth that you are proud of 炫耀；卖弄；显示： *She wanted to show off her new husband at the party.* 她想在聚会上炫耀自己的新婚丈夫。 ◇ **show off how, what, etc....** *He likes to show off how well he speaks French.* 他喜欢向人展示他法语讲得有多好。 **ˌshow sth↔'off** (of clothing 服装) to make sb look attractive, by showing their best features 使显得漂亮；使夺目；衬托： *a dress that shows off her figure* 衬托出她优美身材的连衣裙 **ˌshow 'through** | **ˌshow 'through sth** to be able to be seen behind or under sth else （从某物）透出；（从某事）显露： *The writing on the other side of the page shows through.* 写在纸背面的字透了过来。 ◇ (*figurative*) *When he spoke, his bitterness showed through.* 他说话时流露出内心的辛酸。 ◇ *Veins showed through her pale skin.* 她苍白的皮肤下一条条血管清晰可见。 **ˌshow 'up** (*informal*) to arrive where you have arranged to meet sb or do sth 如约赶到；出现；露面： *It was getting late when she finally showed up.* 天色已晚，她终于赶到了。 **ˌshow 'up** | **ˌshow sth↔'up** to become visible; to make sth become visible （使）看得见，变得明显，显现出来： *a broken bone showed up on the X-ray* * X 光照片上显示出的一根断骨 ◇ *The harsh light showed up the lines on her face.* 在耀眼的光线下，她脸上的皱纹清晰可见。 **ˌshow sb↔'up 1** (*BrE, informal*) to make sb feel embarrassed by behaving badly （因举止不妥而）使人难堪，使人尴尬，使人丢脸： *He showed me up by snoring during the concert.* 他在音乐会上呼呼大睡，真给我丢脸。 **2** to make sb feel embarrassed by doing sth better than them （做得比别人好而）使人难堪，使人尴尬，使人丢脸

■ ***noun***

- **ENTERTAINMENT** 娱乐 **1** [C] a theatre performance, especially one that includes singing and dancing 演出；歌舞表演： *to go to a show* 去看演出 ◇ *a one-woman/-man show* 女 / 男演员单人表演 ◇ *to put on/stage a show* 上演 / 演出节目 ◇ *She's the **star of the show**!* 她是这台演出的明星！ ➲ SEE ALSO FLOOR SHOW, ROADSHOW **2** [C] a programme on television or the radio （电视或广播）节目： *to **host a show*** 主持节目 ◇ *a **TV/radio show*** 电视 / 广播节目 ◇ *a **quiz show*** 知识问答节目 ➲ **COLLOCATIONS** AT TELEVISION ➲ SEE ALSO CHAT SHOW, GAME SHOW, ROADSHOW, TALK SHOW **3** [C] (*NAmE, informal*) a concert, especially of rock music （尤指摇滚）音乐会
- **OF COLLECTION OF THINGS** 收藏品 **4** [C, U] an occasion when a collection of things are brought together for people to look at 展览；展览会： *an agricultural show* 农业展览会 ◇ *The latest computers will be **on show** at the exhibition.* 最新型的计算机将在展览会上展出。 ➲ SEE ALSO FASHION SHOW, PEEP SHOW
- **OF FEELING** 感受 **5** [C] an action or a way of behaving that shows how you feel （体现内心感受的）动作，行为，样子 **SYN** **display**： *a show of emotion* 激动的样子 ◇ *a show of support* 表示支持 ◇ ***a show of force/strength** by the army* 军队显示的武力 / 实力
- **INSINCERE ACT** 不真诚的行为 **6** [U, sing.] something that is done only to give a good impression, but is not sincere 装出的样子；虚假的外观；假象： *He may seem charming, but it's all show!* 他看起来可能很有魅力，但那都是表面的！ ◇ *She pretends to be interested in opera, but it's only **for show**.* 她做出一副对歌剧感兴趣的样子，但这不过是装门面而已。 ◇ *He **made a great show of** affection, but I knew he didn't mean it.* 他大表爱慕之情，但我知道他不是真心的。
- **COLOURFUL SIGHT** 色彩缤纷的景象 **7** [C, U] a brightly coloured or pleasing sight 色彩缤纷的景象 **SYN** **display**： *a lovely show of spring flowers* 春天百花争艳的美景
- **EVENT/SITUATION** 事情；场面 **8** [sing.] (*informal*) an event, a business or a situation where sth is being done or organized 事情；机构；场面： *She runs the whole show.* 整个这一摊儿都由她管。 ◇ *I won't interfere—it's your show.* 我不会插手，这归你管。
- **GOOD/POOR SHOW** 好的 / 不好的表现 **9** [C, usually sing.] (*informal, especially BrE*) something that is done in a

S

particular way 表现：*The team **put on a good show** in the competition.* 这支队伍在比赛中有上佳表现。◇ *It's a poor show if he forgets your birthday.* 要是他忘了你的生日，那可太差劲了。

IDM **for 'show** intended to be seen but not used 供展览的；装门面的；中看不中用的：*These items are just for show—they're not for sale.* 这些物品仅供展览，不卖。**get the ˌshow on the 'road** (*informal*) to start an activity or a journey 开始；出发：*Let's get this show on the road!* 咱们这就开始吧！(**jolly**) **good 'show!** (*old-fashioned, BrE, informal*) used to show you like sth or to say that sb has done sth well（喝彩）好，真棒 **a show of 'hands** a group of people each raising a hand to vote for or against sth 举手表决 ➲ MORE AT DOG *n.*, STEAL *v.*

ˌshow-and-'tell *noun* [U] an activity in which children have to bring sth to show their class and talk about it to them 展示和讲述（学生自带物品到课堂讲述的活动）

show·boat /ˈʃəʊbəʊt; *NAmE* ˈʃoʊboʊt/ *verb, noun*

▪ **verb** [I] (*informal, often disapproving*) to behave in a way that tries to show people how clever, skilful, etc. you are 卖弄；炫耀 ▸ **show·boat·ing** *noun* [U]

▪ **noun** (*NAmE*) a boat on which musical shows are performed 演艺船

'show business (*also informal* **show·biz** /ˈʃəʊbɪz; *NAmE* ˈʃoʊ-/) *noun* [U] the business of providing public entertainment, for example in the theatre, in films/movies or in television 娱乐行业；娱乐界；演艺界：*to **be in show business*** 从事演艺工作 ◇ *show-business **people/stars*** 演艺界人士 / 明星 ◇ *That's showbiz!* 这就是娱乐界！

show·case /ˈʃəʊkeɪs; *NAmE* ˈʃoʊ-/ *noun* **1** [usually sing.] ~ (**for sb/sth**) an event that presents sb's abilities or the good qualities of sth in an attractive way 展示（本领、才华或优良品质）的场合：*The festival was a showcase for young musicians.* 音乐节是青年音乐家展现才华的场合。**2** a box with a glass top or sides that is used for showing objects in a shop/store, museum, etc.（商店或博物馆等的）玻璃柜台，玻璃陈列柜 ▸ **show·case** *verb*：**~ sth** *Jack found a film role that showcased all his talents.* 杰克找到了充分展示他才华的电影角色。

show·down /ˈʃəʊdaʊn; *NAmE* ˈʃoʊ-/ *noun* [usually sing.] an argument, a fight or a test that will settle a disagreement that has lasted for a long time 决出胜负的较量；最后的决战：*Management are facing a showdown with union members today.* 今天资方准备和工会成员摊牌。◇ *Fans gathered outside the stadium for the final showdown* (= the game that will decide the winner of the competition). 球迷聚集在体育场外等着看最后的决赛。

shower 🔑 /ˈʃaʊə(r)/ *noun, verb*

▪ **noun** **1** 🔑 a piece of equipment producing a spray of water that you stand under to wash yourself; the small room or part of a room that contains a shower 淋浴器；淋浴间：*a hotel room with bath and shower* 配备有浴缸和淋浴器的旅馆客房 ◇ *He's **in the shower**.* 他在淋浴间冲澡。◇ *a shower cubicle* 淋浴间 ➲ VISUAL VOCAB PAGE V25 **2** 🔑 the act of washing yourself with a shower 淋浴：(*especially BrE*) *to **have a shower*** 洗淋浴 ◇ (*especially NAmE*) *to **take a shower*** 洗淋浴 ◇ *shower gel* 沐浴乳 **3** 🔑 a short period of rain or snow 阵雨；阵雪：*scattered showers* 零星小雨 ◇ *April showers* 四月的阵雨 ◇ *We were caught in a heavy shower.* 我们遇上一阵大雨。◇ *snow showers* 阵雪 ◇ *wintry showers* (= of snow) 寒冬的阵雪 ➲ WORDFINDER NOTE AT RAIN **4** a large number of things that arrive or fall together 一大批；一阵；一连串：*a shower of leaves* 纷纷落下的叶子 ◇ *a shower of sparks from the fire* 火中迸发的一串火星 ◇ *a shower of kisses* 一阵亲吻 **5** (*NAmE*) a party at which you give presents to a woman who is getting married or having a baby 送礼聚会（为即将结婚或分娩的妇女举行）：*a **bridal/baby shower*** 为准新娘 / 为准妈妈举行的送礼聚会

▪ **verb** **1** [I] to wash yourself under a shower （洗）淋浴：*She showered and dressed and went downstairs.* 她冲了澡，穿上衣服下楼去了。**2** [I] ~ (**down**) **on sb/sth** | **~ down** to fall onto sb/sth, especially in a lot of small pieces 洒落；纷纷降落：*Volcanic ash showered down on the town after the eruption.* 火山喷发后，小城落了一层火山灰。**3** [T] **~ sb with sth** to drop a lot of small things onto sb 抛撒；使纷纷降落：*The bride and groom were showered with rice as they left the church.* 新郎和新娘走出教堂时，人们朝他们抛撒大米。◇ *The roof collapsed, showering us with dust and debris.* 屋顶塌了下来，灰尘、碎片纷纷落在我们身上。**4** [T] to give sb a lot of sth 大量地给：**~ sb with sth** *He showered her with gifts.* 他送给她许多礼物。◇ **~ sth on sb** *He showered gifts on her.* 他送给她许多礼物。

show·ery /ˈʃaʊəri/ *adj.* (of the weather 天气) with frequent showers of rain 下阵雨的；多阵雨的：*a showery day* 阵雨天

show·girl /ˈʃəʊɡɜːl; *NAmE* ˈʃoʊɡɜːrl/ *noun* a female performer who sings and dances in a musical show 歌舞女演员

show·ground /ˈʃəʊɡraʊnd; *NAmE* ˈʃoʊ-/ *noun* a large outdoor area where FAIRS, farm shows, etc. take place（室外）展览场地

'show house (*also* **'show home**) (*both BrE*) (*NAmE* **'model home**) *noun* a house in a group of new houses that has been painted and filled with furniture, so that people who might want to buy one of the houses can see what they will be like 样品房，样板间（供购买房子的顾客参观）

show·ing /ˈʃəʊɪŋ; *NAmE* ˈʃoʊ-/ *noun* **1** an act of showing a film/movie 放映：*There are three showings a day.* 一天放映三场。**2** [usually sing.] evidence of how well or how badly sb/sth is performing 表现：*the **strong/poor showing** of the Green Party in the election* 绿党在这次选举中的强劲 / 不佳表现 ◇ *On* (= judging by) *last week's showing, the team is unlikely to win today.* 从上星期的表现来看，这支队伍今天不大可能获胜。

show·jump·ing /ˈʃəʊdʒʌmpɪŋ; *NAmE* ˈʃoʊ-/ *noun* [U] the sport of riding a horse and jumping over a set of fences as quickly as possible（马术项目）超越障碍比赛 ➲ VISUAL VOCAB PAGE V51

show·man /ˈʃəʊmən; *NAmE* ˈʃoʊ-/ *noun* (*pl.* **-men** /-mən/) **1** a person who does things in an entertaining way and is good at getting people's attention 善于引起公众注意的人；喜欢出风头的人 **2** a person who organizes public entertainments, especially at FAIRGROUNDS（尤指露天游乐场的）演出主持人，演出经理人

show·man·ship /ˈʃəʊmənʃɪp; *NAmE* ˈʃoʊ-/ *noun* [U] skill in doing things in an entertaining way and getting a lot of attention 主持演出的技巧；演艺艺术；善于表演的技能

shown PAST PART. OF SHOW

'show-off *noun* (*informal, disapproving*) a person who tries to impress other people by showing how good he or she is at doing sth 爱炫耀的人；喜欢卖弄的人

show·piece /ˈʃəʊpiːs; *NAmE* ˈʃoʊ-/ *noun* an excellent example of sth that people are meant to see and admire（供展示用的）优质样品

show·place /ˈʃəʊpleɪs; *NAmE* ˈʃoʊ-/ *noun* a place of great beauty, historical interest, etc. that is open to the public 风景名胜；古迹名胜；游览胜地

show·room /ˈʃəʊruːm; -rʊm; *NAmE* ˈʃoʊ-/ *noun* a large shop/store in which goods for sale, especially cars and electrical goods, are displayed 商品陈列室；展销厅：*a car showroom* 汽车展销厅

'show-stopper *noun* (*informal*) a performance that is very impressive and receives a lot of APPLAUSE from the audience 受到阵阵鼓掌喝彩的节目 ▸ **'show-stopping** *adj.* [only before noun]：*a show-stopping performance* 受到阵阵鼓掌喝彩的节目

show·time /ˈʃəʊtaɪm; *NAmE* ˈʃoʊ-/ *noun* [U] the time that a theatre performance will begin 开演时间：*It's five minutes to showtime and the theatre is packed.* 离演出开始还有五分钟，剧场里已座无虚席。◇ (*figurative, NAmE*) *Everybody ready? It's showtime!* 大家都准备好了吗？演出开始！

ˈ**show trial** *noun* an unfair trial of sb in court, organized by a government for political reasons, not in order to find out the truth （出于政治目的）摆样子的审判，走过场的审讯

showy /ˈʃəʊi; *NAmE* ˈʃoʊi/ *adj.* (*often disapproving*) so brightly coloured, large or exaggerated that it attracts a lot of attention 显眼的；艳丽的；花哨的 SYN **ostentatious**: *showy flowers* 艳丽的花朵 ▶ **show·ily** /-ɪli/ *adv.* **showi·ness** *noun* [U]

shrank PAST TENSE OF SHRINK

shrap·nel /ˈʃræpnəl/ *noun* [U] small pieces of metal that are thrown up and away from an exploding bomb 飞溅的弹片

shred /ʃred/ *verb, noun*

■ ***verb*** (**-dd-**) ~ **sth** to cut or tear sth into small pieces 切碎；撕碎：*Serve the fish on a bed of shredded lettuce.* 先铺一层碎生菜叶，再把鱼放上，就可以上桌了。◇ *He was accused of shredding documents relating to the case* (= putting them in a SHREDDER). 他被指控把与案件有关的文件用碎纸机销毁了。➲ MORE LIKE THIS 36, page R29

■ ***noun*** **1** [usually pl.] a small thin piece that has been torn or cut from sth （撕或切的）细条，碎片 SYN **scrap**: *shreds of paper* 碎纸片 ◇ *His jacket had been* ***torn to shreds*** *by the barbed wire.* 他的夹克被铁丝网挂得稀烂。 **2** [usually sing.] ~ **of sth** (used especially in negative sentences 尤用于否定句) a very small amount of sth 极少量；些许；一丁点：*There is* ***not a shred of evidence*** *to support his claim.* 没有丝毫证据支持他的说法。

IDM **in ˈshreds 1** very badly damaged 损害严重 SYN **in tatters**: *Her nerves were in shreds.* 她的神经崩溃了。◇ *The country's economy is in shreds.* 国家经济已是百孔千疮。 **2** torn in many places 破破烂烂的：*The document was in shreds on the floor.* 那份文件在地上，已经破烂不堪。 **pick/pull/tear sb/sth to ˈpieces/ˈshreds** (*informal*) to criticize sb, or their work or ideas, very severely 把某人（或其作品、观点等）批驳得体无完肤

shred·der /ˈʃredə(r)/ *noun* a machine that tears sth into small pieces, especially paper, so that nobody can read what was printed on it 切碎机；（尤指）碎纸机

shrew /ʃruː/ *noun* **1** a small animal like a mouse with a long nose 鼩鼱（形似鼠，吻长） **2** (*old-fashioned*) a bad-tempered unpleasant woman 泼妇；悍妇

shrewd /ʃruːd/ *adj.* (**shrewd·er**, **shrewd·est**) **1** clever at understanding and making judgements about a situation 精明的；敏锐的；有眼光的；精于盘算的 SYN **astute**: *a shrewd businessman* 精明的商人 ◇ *She is a shrewd judge of character.* 她看人看得很准。 **2** showing good judgement and likely to be right 判断得准的；高明的：*a shrewd move* 高招 ◇ *I* ***have a shrewd idea*** *who the mystery caller was.* 这个神秘的来访者是谁，我能猜个八九不离十。 ▶ **shrewd·ly** *adv.* **shrewd·ness** *noun* [U]

shrew·ish /ˈʃruːɪʃ/ *adj.* (*old-fashioned*) (of women 女人) bad-tempered and always arguing 脾气坏且爱争吵的

Shri (*also* **Sri**) /ʃriː; sriː/ *noun* (*IndE*) **1** a title used before the names of gods or holy books, showing respect （用于神的姓名或宗教典籍前，表示尊敬）神，圣 **2** a title of respect for a man （对男子的尊称）先生

shriek /ʃriːk/ *verb, noun*

■ ***verb*** **1** [I] to give a loud high shout, for example when you are excited, frightened or in pain 尖叫 SYN **scream**: ~ (**in sth**) *She shrieked in fright.* 她吓得尖叫起来。◇ ~ **with sth** *The audience was shrieking with laughter.* 观众放声大笑。◇ ~ **at sb** (*figurative*) *The answer shrieked at her* (= was very obvious). 答案就明摆在她面前。 **2** [T] to say sth in a loud, high voice 尖声说 SYN **scream**: ~ **sth** (**at sb**) *She was shrieking abuse at them as they carried her off.* 他们把她抬走的时候，她冲着他们尖声叫骂。◇ + **speech** *'Look out!' he shrieked.* "小心！"他尖叫道。

■ ***noun*** a loud high shout, for example one that you make when you are excited, frightened or in pain 尖叫：*She let out a piercing shriek.* 她发出一声刺耳的尖叫。◇ *a shriek of delight* 兴奋的叫声

shrift /ʃrɪft/ *noun* IDM SEE SHORT *adj.*

shrike /ʃraɪk/ *noun* a bird with a strong beak, that catches small birds and insects and sticks them on THORNS 伯劳（鸟，喙强有力，扑捉到小鸟和昆虫后将其挂在荆棘上）

shrill /ʃrɪl/ *adj., verb*

■ ***adj.*** (**shrill·er**, **shrill·est**) **1** (of sounds or voices 声音或嗓音) very high and loud, in an unpleasant way 刺耳的；尖声的；尖厉的 SYN **piercing**: *a shrill voice* 刺耳的嗓音 **2** loud and determined but often unreasonable 闹着非要…不可的；不依不饶的：*shrill demands/protests* 坚持要求；拼命抗议 ▶ **shrilly** /ˈʃrɪlli/ *adv.* **shrill·ness** *noun* [U]

■ ***verb*** **1** [I] to make an unpleasant high loud sound 发出刺耳的声音；尖叫：*Behind him, the telephone shrilled.* 在他身后，电话铃声刺耳地响了起来。 **2** [T] + **speech** to say sth in a loud, high voice 尖声说 SYN **shriek**: *'Wait for me!' she shrilled.* "等等我！"她尖声叫道。

Shri·mati (*also* **Sri·mati**) /ˈʃriːmʌti; ˈsriː-/ *noun* (*IndE*) a title of respect or affection for a woman （对女子的敬称或爱称）女士，夫人：*Shrimati Sonya Gandhi* 索尼娅・甘地夫人

shrimp /ʃrɪmp/ *noun* (*pl.* **shrimps** or **shrimp**) **1** a small SHELLFISH that can be eaten, like a PRAWN but smaller. Shrimps turn pink when cooked. 虾；小虾 **2** (*NAmE*) = PRAWN: *grilled shrimp* 烤虾

shrimp·ing /ˈʃrɪmpɪŋ/ *noun* [U] the activity of catching shrimps 捕小虾：*a shrimping net* 捕虾网 ▶ **shrimp·er** *noun* (*especially NAmE*): *shrimpers and fishermen in the Gulf of Mexico* 墨西哥湾捕鱼虾的渔民

shrine /ʃraɪn/ *noun* **1** a place where people come to worship because it is connected with a holy person or event 圣地；圣祠；神庙；神龛：~ (**to sb/sth**) *a shrine to the Virgin Mary* 敬奉圣母马利亚的朝圣地 ◇ ~ (**of sb/sth**) *to visit the shrine of Mecca* 前往圣地麦加朝拜 **2** ~ (**for sb**) | ~ (**to sb/sth**) a place that people visit because it is connected with sb/sth that is important to them 具有重要意义的地方：*Wimbledon is a shrine for all lovers of tennis.* 温布尔登是所有网球爱好者的圣地。

shrink /ʃrɪŋk/ *verb, noun*

■ ***verb*** (**shrank** /ʃræŋk/, **shrunk** /ʃrʌŋk/ or **shrunk**, **shrunk**) **1** [I, T] ~ (**sth**) to become smaller, especially when washed in water that is too hot; to make clothes, cloth, etc. smaller in this way （使）缩水，收缩，缩小，皱缩：*My sweater shrank in the wash.* 我的毛衣缩水了。 **2** [I, T] to become or to make sth smaller in size or amount （使）缩小，收缩，减少：*The tumour had shrunk to the size of a pea.* 肿瘤已缩小到豌豆大小。◇ *The market for their products is shrinking.* 市场对他们产品的需求在减少。◇ ~ **sth** *There was a movie called 'Honey, I Shrunk the Kids'.* 有部电影名叫《亲爱的，我把孩子缩小了》。◇ *Television in a sense has shrunk the world.* 从某种意义上说，电视把世界缩小了。 ➲ SEE ALSO SHRUNKEN **3** [I] + **adv./prep.** to move back or away from sth because you are frightened or shocked 退缩；畏缩 SYN **cower**: *He shrank back against the wall as he heard them approaching.* 听见他们朝这边来，他退到墙根。

IDM **a ˌshrinking ˈviolet** (*humorous*) a way of describing a very shy person （指羞怯的人）

PHR V ˈ**shrink from sth** to be unwilling to do sth that is difficult or unpleasant 畏避，回避（困难等）：*We made it clear to them that we would not shrink from confrontation.* 我们向他们清楚地表明，我们不会畏避交锋。◇ **shrink from doing sth** *They did not shrink from doing what was right.* 只要做得对，他们就无所畏惧。

■ ***noun*** (*slang, humorous*) a PSYCHIATRIST or PSYCHOLOGIST 精神病学家；心理学家

shrink·age /ˈʃrɪŋkɪdʒ/ *noun* [U] the process of becoming smaller in size; the amount by which sth becomes smaller 缩小；收缩；收缩量；收缩程度：*the shrinkage of heavy industry* 重工业的萎缩 ◇ *She bought a slightly larger size to allow for shrinkage.* 她买了一件尺码稍大的以防缩水。

S

ˈshrink-wrapped *adj.* wrapped tightly in a thin plastic covering 用收缩塑料薄膜包装的

shrivel /ˈʃrɪvl/ *verb* (-ll-, *US* -l-) [I, T] to become or make sth dry and WRINKLED as a result of heat, cold or being old （使）枯萎，干枯，皱缩： ~ (**up**) *The leaves on the plant had shrivelled up from lack of water.* 因为缺水，植物的叶子已经枯萎了。◇ ~ **sth** (**up**) *The hot weather had shrivelled the grapes in every vineyard.* 天气炎热，各家葡萄园的葡萄都蔫了。▶ **shriv·elled** *adj.*：*a shrivelled old man* 一个干巴老头

shroom /ʃruːm; ʃrʊm/ (*informal, especially NAmE*) (*also* **magic mushroom** *BrE* or *becoming old-fashioned, NAmE*) *noun* a type of MUSHROOM that has an effect like some drugs and that may make people who eat it HALLUCINATE (= see things that are not there) 致幻蘑菇 ▶ **shroom** *verb* [I]: *Joe was shrooming last night and has a killer headache today.* 乔昨晚吃了致幻蘑菇，今天头痛欲裂。

shroud /ʃraʊd/ *noun, verb*

■ ***noun* 1** a piece of cloth that a dead person's body is wrapped in before it is buried 裹尸布；寿衣 **2** ~ **of sth** (*literary*) a thing that covers, surrounds or hides sth 覆盖物；遮蔽物：*The organization is cloaked in a shroud of secrecy.* 这个组织笼罩着一种诡秘的气氛。◇ *a shroud of smoke* 一片烟雾

■ ***verb*** [usually passive] **1** ~ **sth in sth** (of DARKNESS, clouds, cloth, etc. 黑暗、云、织物等) to cover or hide sth 覆盖；隐藏；遮蔽：*The city was shrouded in mist.* 城市笼罩在雾霭之中。**2** ~ **sth in sth** to hide information or keep it secret and mysterious 隐瞒；保密：*His family background is shrouded in mystery.* 他的家庭背景蒙上了神秘的色彩。

ˈshroud-waving *noun* [U] (*BrE*) (*informal*) the practice of warning about the bad effect on medical care if more money is not provided by the government to pay for more doctors, hospitals, etc. 挥裹尸布示警（告诫政府不增加投入会对医疗保健产生严重影响）

Shrove Tuesday /ˌʃrəʊv ˈtjuːzdeɪ; -di; *NAmE* ˌʃroʊv ˈtuːz-/ *noun* [U, C] (in the Christian Church) the day before the beginning of Lent 忏悔日（基督教大斋期的前一天）➲ COMPARE MARDI GRAS, PANCAKE DAY ➲ SEE ALSO ASH WEDNESDAY

S

shrub /ʃrʌb/ *noun* a large plant that is smaller than a tree and that has several STEMS of wood coming from the ground 灌木 **SYN** **bush**

shrub·bery /ˈʃrʌbəri/ *noun* [C, U] (*pl.* **-ies**) an area planted with shrubs 灌木丛

shrubby /ˈʃrʌbi/ *adj.* (of plants 植物) like a SHRUB 像灌木的；灌木状的

shrug /ʃrʌɡ/ *verb, noun*

■ ***verb*** (-gg-) [I, T, no passive] to raise your shoulders and then drop them to show that you do not know or care about sth 耸肩（表示不知道或不在乎）：*Sam shrugged and said nothing.* 萨姆耸耸肩膀，什么也没说。◇ ~ **sth** *'I don't know,' Anna replied, shrugging her shoulders.* "我不知道。"安娜耸耸肩膀，应了一句。

■ ***noun* 1** [usually sing.] an act of raising your shoulders and then dropping them to show that you do not know or care about sth 耸肩（表示不知道或不在乎）：*Andy gave a shrug. 'It doesn't matter.'* 安迪耸耸肩："这没关系。" **2** [C] a very short knitted piece of clothing that is open at the front and usually has sleeves made from the same piece as the back and front 带袖短披肩

PHR V **ˌshrug sth ˈoff/aˈside** to treat sth as if it is not important 不把…当回事；对…满不在乎；对…不予理睬 **SYN** **dismiss**: *Shrugging off her injury, she played on.* 她不顾自己受了伤，继续进行比赛。◇ *He shrugged aside suggestions that he resign.* 对于让他辞职的建议，他根本不予理会。**ˌshrug sb/sth ˈoff/aˈway** to push sb/sth back or away with your shoulders 甩开；摆脱；抖落：*Kevin shrugged off his jacket.* 凯文肩膀一抖，脱掉了夹克。◇ *She shrugged him away angrily.* 她生气地甩开他。

shrunk PAST TENSE, PAST PART. OF SHRINK

shrunk·en /ˈʃrʌŋkən/ *adj.* [usually before noun] that has become smaller (and less attractive) 皱缩的；干枯的 **SYN** **wizened**：*a shrunken old woman* 干瘪的老妇人

shtetl /ˈʃtetl/ *noun* a small Jewish town or village in eastern Europe in the past （东欧旧时的）犹太小镇（或小村）

shtick (*also* **schtick**) /ʃtɪk/ *noun* [U, sing.] (*especially NAmE*) **1** a style of humour that is typical of a particular performer （独特的）幽默风格；（某演员的）表演手法 **2** a particular ability that sb has 特长；擅长的本领

shtook (*also* **schtuck**) /ʃtʊk/ *noun* [U]

IDM **be in ˈshtook** (*BrE, informal*) to be in serious trouble 遇到大麻烦；陷入严重困境

shtum (*also* **schtum**) /ʃtʊm/ *noun* [U]

IDM **keep/stay ˈshtum** (*BrE, informal*) to not speak 保持沉默：*Police have appealed for witnesses, but it seems the locals are keeping shtum.* 警方已呼吁目击者出来作证，但看来当地人都三缄其口。

shtup (*also* **schtup**) /ʃtʊp/ *verb* (-pp-) ~ **sb** (*NAmE, slang*) to have sex with sb （与某人）发生性关系

shuck /ʃʌk/ *noun, verb*

■ ***noun*** (*NAmE*) the outer covering of a nut, plant, etc. or an OYSTER or a CLAM （坚果或牡蛎、蛤等的）壳；（植物的）荚，外皮

■ ***verb*** ~ **sth** (*NAmE*) to remove the shell or covering of nuts, SHELLFISH, etc. 剥…的壳（或荚）；去…的外皮

shucks /ʃʌks/ *exclamation* (*old-fashioned, NAmE, informal*) used to express embarrassment or disappointment （表示窘迫或失望）

shud·der /ˈʃʌdə(r)/ *verb, noun*

■ ***verb* 1** [I] to shake because you are cold or frightened, or because of a strong feeling （因寒冷、害怕或激动而）发抖，打颤，战栗：*Just thinking about the accident makes me shudder.* 只要一想起那场事故，我就发抖。◇ ~ **with sth** *Alone in the car, she shuddered with fear.* 她一个人待在车里，害怕得直哆嗦。◇ ~ **at sth** *I shuddered at the thought of all the trouble I'd caused.* 一想到我闯的祸，就不寒而栗。◇ ~ **to do sth** *I shudder to think how much this is all going to cost* (= I don't want to think about it because it is too unpleasant). 想想这一切得花多少钱，我就发怵。**2** [I] (of a vehicle, machine, etc. 交通工具、机器等) to shake very hard 强烈震动；剧烈抖动：*The bus shuddered to a halt.* 公共汽车剧烈地晃动着停了下来。

■ ***noun*** [usually sing.] **1** a shaking movement you make because you are cold, frightened or disgusted （因寒冷、害怕或反感等引起的）发抖，打颤，战栗：*a shudder of fear* 害怕的颤抖 ◇ *She gave an involuntary shudder.* 她不由自主地抖了一下。**2** a strong shaking movement 强烈的震动；剧烈的抖动：*The elevator rose with a shudder.* 电梯猛震一下，升上去了。

shuf·fle /ˈʃʌfl/ *verb, noun*

■ ***verb* 1** [I] + **adv./prep.** to walk slowly without lifting your feet completely off the ground. 拖着脚走：*He shuffled across the room to the window.* 他拖着脚走到房间那头的窗户跟前。◇ *The line shuffled forward a little.* 队列往前挪了挪。**2** [T, I] ~ (**sth**) to move from one foot to another; to move your feet in an awkward or embarrassed way （笨拙或尴尬地）把脚动来动去；坐立不安：*Jenny shuffled her feet and blushed with shame.* 珍妮来回倒换着脚，羞愧得脸红了。**3** [T, I] ~ (**sth**) to mix cards up in a PACK/DECK of PLAYING CARDS before playing a game 洗（牌）：*Shuffle the cards and deal out seven to each player.* 洗洗牌，然后给每人发七张。➲ WORDFINDER NOTE AT CARD **4** [T] ~ **sth** to move paper or things into different positions or a different order 把（纸张等）变换位置，打乱次序：*I shuffled the documents on my desk.* 我胡乱翻动桌上的文件。

■ ***noun*** [usually sing.] **1** a slow walk in which you take small steps and do not lift your feet completely off the ground 拖着脚走 **2** the act of mixing cards before a card game 洗牌：*Give the cards a good shuffle.* 把牌好好洗一洗。**3** a type of dancing in which you take small steps and do not lift your feet completely off the ground 曳步舞 **4** = RESHUFFLE

IDM **lose sb/sth in the 'shuffle** [usually passive] (*NAmE*) to not notice sb/sth or pay attention to sb/sth because of a confusing situation 在混乱中没有注意到；忽略；遗失：*Middle children tend to get lost in the shuffle.* 排行居中的子女往往得不到充分的关注。**on 'shuffle** (of pieces of music stored on a music player, such as an MP3 player 播放器中的音乐) not in any special order 随机播放：*I put the iPod on shuffle and hit play.* 我把 iPod 设置成随机播放，然后按播放键。

shuf·fle·board /ˈʃʌflbɔːd; *NAmE* -bɔːrd/ *noun* [U] a game in which players use long sticks to push discs towards spaces with numbers on a board 推移板游戏（用推杆将圆盘推至推移板上的不同得分区）

shufti /ˈʃʊfti/ *noun* [sing.]

IDM **have a shufti (at sth)** (*BrE, informal*) to have a quick look at sth （对…）扫一眼；瞥

shun /ʃʌn/ *verb* (**-nn-**) **~ sb/sth** to avoid sb/sth 避开；回避；避免：*She was shunned by her family when she remarried.* 她再婚后家里人都躲着她。◇ *an actor who shuns publicity* 一个避免引起公众注意的演员

shunt /ʃʌnt/ *verb, noun*

■ *verb* **1 ~ sth** to move a train or a coach/car of a train from one track to another 使（火车或火车车厢）转轨 **2 ~ sb/sth + adv./prep.** (*usually disapproving*) to move sb/sth to a different place, especially a less important one 调往，转至（次要的地方）：*John was shunted sideways to a job in sales.* 约翰被平级调动到销售部门的一个岗位上。

■ *noun* **1** (*BrE, informal*) a road accident in which one vehicle crashes into the back of another 车辆追尾事故 **2** (*medical* 医) a small tube put in your body in a medical operation to allow the blood or other FLUID to flow from one place to another 分流管

shush /ʃʊʃ/ *exclamation, verb*

■ *exclamation* used to tell sb to be quiet （要某人安静）嘘

■ *verb* **~ sb** to tell sb to be quiet, especially by saying 'shush', or by putting your finger against your lips （尤指通过"嘘"声或把手指竖在嘴唇上）要某人安静，嘘：*Lyn shushed the children.* 林恩"嘘"了一声，让孩子们安静下来。

shut /ʃʌt/ *verb, adj.*

■ *verb* (**shut·ting, shut, shut**) **1** [T, I] **~ (sth)** to make sth close; to become closed 关闭；关上；合上：*Philip went into his room and shut the door behind him.* 菲利普进了自己的房间，随手把门关上。◇ *I can't shut my suitcase—it's too full.* 我的手提箱合不上，装得太满了。◇ *She shut her eyes and fell asleep immediately.* 她闭上眼，立刻就睡着了。◇ *He shut his book and looked up.* 他合上书，抬起头来。◇ *The window won't shut.* 这窗子关不上。◇ *The doors open and shut automatically.* 这些门都是自动开关的。**2** [I, T] **~ (sth)** (*BrE*) when a shop/store, restaurant, etc. **shuts** or when sb **shuts** it, it stops being open for business and you cannot go into it （使）停止营业，关门，打烊：*The bank shuts at 4.* 那家银行 4 点钟关门。➲ NOTE AT CLOSE[1]

IDM **shut your 'mouth/'face!** (*slang*) a rude way of telling sb to be quiet or stop talking （粗暴地要某人停止说话）住口，闭嘴 **shut up 'shop** (*BrE, informal*) to close a business permanently or to stop working for the day 停业；关张；倒闭；打烊 ➲ MORE AT DOOR, EAR, EYE *n.*, MOUTH *n.*

PHR V **ˌshut sb/sth↔a'way** to put sb/sth in a place where other people cannot see or find them 把…藏起来；隔离；禁闭 **ˌshut yourself a'way** to go somewhere where you will be completely alone 独自躲起来；隐藏 **ˌshut 'down** (of a factory, shop/store, etc. or a machine 工厂、商店或机器等) to stop opening for business; to stop working 关张；停业；倒闭；关闭；停止运转 ➲ RELATED NOUN SHUTDOWN **ˌshut sth↔'down** to stop a factory, shop/store, etc. from opening for business; to stop a machine from working （使）关张，停业，倒闭，关闭，停止运转：*The computer system will be shut down over the weekend.* 计算机系统周末关闭。➲ RELATED NOUN SHUTDOWN **ˌshut sb/yourself 'in (sth)** to put sb in a room and keep them there; to go to a room and stay there 把某人（或自己）关在房间里；把…关起来：*She shut the dog in the shed while she prepared the barbecue.* 她准备户外烧烤时把狗关在棚里。**'shut sth in sth** to trap sth by closing a door, lid, etc. on it 把某物卡在…里（或夹在…中）：*Sam shut his finger in the car door.* 萨姆给车门夹住了手指。**ˌshut 'off** (of a machine, tool, etc. 机器、工具等) to stop working 关闭；关上；停止运转：*The engines shut off automatically in an emergency.* 遇到紧急情况发动机便自动停止工作。**ˌshut sth↔'off 1** to stop a machine, tool, etc. from working 关闭机器（或工具等）；使机器（或工具等）停止运转 **2** to stop a supply of gas, water, etc. from flowing or reaching a place 切断煤气（或水等）的供应；停止供应煤气（或水等）：*A valve immediately shuts off the gas when the lid is closed.* 当盖子合上时，立刻会有一个阀门切断煤气。**ˌshut yourself 'off (from sth)** to avoid seeing people or having contact with anyone 躲开；不接触：*Martin shut himself off from the world to write his book.* 马丁不与外界接触，专心写他的书。**ˌshut sb/sth 'off from sth** to separate sb/sth from sth 使与…隔离（或隔绝）：*Bosnia is shut off from the Adriatic by the mountains.* 波斯尼亚和亚得里亚海之间有群山相隔。**ˌshut sb/sth↔'out (of sth) 1** to prevent sb/sth from entering a place 使…不能进入；挡住；遮住：*Mum, Ben keeps shutting me out of the bedroom!* 妈，本老不让我进卧室！◇ *sunglasses that shut out 99% of the sun's harmful rays* 能遮挡 99% 的太阳有害射线的太阳镜 **2** to not allow a person to share or be part of your thoughts; to stop yourself from having particular feelings 把某人排除在…外；不把…告诉某人；克制某种感情：*I wanted to shut John out of my life for ever.* 我想永远不让约翰走进我的生活。◇ *She learned to shut out her angry feelings.* 她学会了克制自己的愤怒。◇ *If you shut me out, how can I help you?* 如果你什么也不告诉我，我怎么帮你呢？**ˌshut 'up** (*informal*) to stop talking (often used as an order as a rude way of telling sb to stop talking) （常用来粗暴地让某人停止说话）住口，闭嘴：*Just shut up and listen!* 住口，听着！◇ *Will you tell Mike to shut up?* 你让迈克闭嘴好不好？◇ *When they'd finally shut up, I started again.* 等他们最终住了嘴，我又重新开始讲。**ˌshut sb 'up** to make sb stop talking 使某人住口；让某人闭嘴 **SYN** **silence**：*She kicked Anne under the table to shut her up.* 她在桌子底下踢了安妮一脚，让她住嘴。**ˌshut sth↔'up** to close a room, house, etc. 关上（房屋等）**ˌshut sb/sth 'up (in sth)** to keep sb/sth in a place and prevent them from going anywhere 把…关（或藏）起来；把…关（或藏）在

■ *adj.* [not before noun] **1** not open 关闭；合拢 **SYN** **closed**：*The door was shut.* 门关着。◇ *She slammed the door shut.* 她哐的一声把门关上了。◇ *Keep your eyes shut.* 别睁开眼睛。**2** (*BrE*) not open for business 停业；关门 **SYN** **closed**：*Unfortunately the bank is shut now.* 不凑巧，银行现在不营业。

shut·down /ˈʃʌtdaʊn/ *noun* the act of closing a factory or business or stopping a large machine from working, either temporarily or permanently 停业；停工；关闭；倒闭；停止运转：*factory shutdowns* 工厂的倒闭 ◇ *the nuclear reactor's emergency shutdown procedures* 核反应堆的紧急关闭程序

'shut-eye *noun* [U] (*informal*) sleep 睡眠

'shut-in *noun* (*NAmE*) a person who cannot leave their home very easily because they are ill/sick or disabled 因病（或残疾）外出困难的人；卧病在家的人

shut·out /ˈʃʌtaʊt/ *noun* (*NAmE*) a game in which one team prevents the other from scoring 完胜（比赛中不让对手得分）

shut·ter /ˈʃʌtə(r)/ *noun* **1** [usually pl.] one of a pair of wooden or metal covers that can be closed over the outside of a window to keep out light or protect the windows from damage 活动护窗；百叶窗：*to open/close the shutters* 打开 / 关上护窗 ◇ (*BrE, figurative*) *More than 70 000 shopkeepers have been forced to put up the shutters* (= close down their businesses) *in the past year.* 去年，有

S

7 万多家商店被迫关了门。 ➲ VISUAL VOCAB PAGES V18, V22 **2** the part of a camera that opens to allow light to pass through the LENS when you take a photograph（照相机的）快门

IDM ˌ**bring/ˌput down the ˈshutters** to stop letting sb know what your thoughts or feelings are; to stop letting yourself think about sth 掩藏自己的思想感情；锁上心扉；不再想某件事

shut·ter·bug /ˈʃʌtəbʌg; *NAmE* ˈʃʌtər-/ *noun* (*NAmE, informal*) a person who likes to take a lot of photographs 摄影迷；摄影爱好者

shut·tered /ˈʃʌtəd; *NAmE* -tərd/ *adj.* with the shutters closed; with shutters fitted 关上（或装有）护窗的

ˈ**shutter speed** *noun* the length of time that a camera's SHUTTER remains open（照相机的）快门速度

shut·tle /ˈʃʌtl/ *noun, verb*

■ ***noun*** **1** a plane, bus or train that travels regularly between two places 来往于两地之间的航班（或班车、火车）：*a shuttle service between London and Edinburgh* 往返于伦敦和爱丁堡之间的航班 **2** = SPACE SHUTTLE **3** a pointed tool used in making cloth to pull a thread backwards and forwards over the other threads that pass along the length of the cloth 梭；梭子 **4 the Shuttle** [sing.] a train service that takes cars and their passengers through the Channel Tunnel between England and France（英法之间英吉利海峡隧道的）穿梭火车

■ ***verb*** **1** [I] ~ (**between A and B**) to travel between two places frequently 频繁往来（于甲地和乙地之间）：*Her childhood was spent shuttling between her mother and father.* 她的童年是在父母之间穿梭往来中度过的。**2** [T] ~ **sb** (+ **adv./prep.**) to carry people between two places that are close, making regular journeys between the two places（在较近的两地之间定时）往返运送：*A bus shuttles passengers back and forth from the station to the terminal.* 一辆公共汽车在火车站和航站楼之间往返运送旅客。

shuttle·cock /ˈʃʌtlkɒk; *NAmE* -kɑːk/ (*NAmE also* **bird·ie**) *noun* the object that players hit backwards and forwards in the game of BADMINTON 羽毛球 ➲ VISUAL VOCAB PAGE V48

ˌ**shuttle diˈplomacy** *noun* [U] international talks in which people travel between two or more countries in order to talk to the different governments involved 穿梭外交

shut·tler /ˈʃʌtlə(r)/ *noun* (*IndE*) a person who plays BADMINTON 羽毛球运动员

shwa *noun* = SCHWA

shy 🔑 /ʃaɪ/ *adj., verb*

■ ***adj.*** (**shyer**, **shy·est**) **1** 🔑 (of people 人) nervous or embarrassed about meeting and speaking to other people 羞怯的；腼腆的；怕生的 SYN **timid**：*a quiet, shy man* 不大说话、腼腆的人 ◇ *Don't be shy—come and say hello.* 别害羞，过来问个好。◇ *She was too shy to ask anyone for help.* 她太腼腆，不愿向任何人求助。◇ *As a teenager I was **painfully shy**.* 我十几岁的时候腼腆得很。◇ *She's very shy with adults.* 她在大人面前很拘束。**2** 🔑 showing that sb is nervous or embarrassed about meeting and speaking to other people 显得腼腆的；看着羞怯的：*a shy smile* 腼腆的微笑 **3** (of animals 动物) easily frightened and not willing to come near people 怕人的；易受惊的；胆小的：*The panda is a shy creature.* 熊猫是一种胆小的动物。**4** [not before noun] ~ **of/about** (**doing**) **sth** afraid of doing sth or being involved in sth 害怕（做）；对（做）…心怀顾忌：*The band has never been shy of publicity.* 这支乐队一向不惮招摇。◇ *He disliked her and had never been shy of saying so.* 他不喜欢她，而且从来不忌讳说出来。**5** [not before noun] ~ (**of sth**) (*informal, especially NAmE*) lacking the amount that is needed 欠缺；不足；未达到；不够：*He died before Christmas, only a month shy of his 90th birthday.* 他在圣诞节前去世了，仅差一个月就满 90 岁。◇ *We are still two players shy (of a full team).* 我们还缺两名队员（凑成一支队）。**6 -shy** (in compounds 构成复合词) avoiding or not liking the thing mentioned 躲避（或不喜欢）…的：*camera-shy* (= not liking to be photographed) 不爱照相 ◇ *He's always been work-shy.* 他总是躲避工作。
▸ **shyly** *adv.* **shy·ness** *noun* [U] IDM SEE FIGHT *v.*, ONCE *adv.*

■ ***verb*** (**shies**, **shy·ing**, **shied**, **shied** /ʃaɪd/) [I] ~ (**at sth**) (especially of a horse 尤指马) to turn away with a sudden movement because it is afraid or surprised 被吓退；被惊走：*My horse shied at the unfamiliar noise.* 这陌生的声音把我的马惊跑了。➲ SEE ALSO COCONUT SHY

PHR V ˌ**shy aˈway** (**from sth**) to avoid doing sth because you are nervous or frightened 畏避；回避；躲避；避免做：*Hugh never shied away from his responsibilities.* 该自己承担的责任，休从不回避。◇ *The newspapers have shied away from investigating the story.* 各家报纸纷纷退避，不敢调查详情。

shy·ster /ˈʃaɪstə(r)/ *noun* (*informal, especially NAmE*) a dishonest person, especially a lawyer 不择手段的人；卑鄙小人；（尤指）奸诈的律师

SI /ˌes ˈaɪ/ *abbr.* International System (used to describe units of measurement; from French 'Système International') 国际单位制（源自法语 Système International）：*SI units* 国际单位

Siamese cat /ˌsaɪəmiːz ˈkæt/ (*also* **Siam·ese**) *noun* a cat with short pale fur and a brown face, ears, tail and feet 暹罗猫

ˌ**Siamese ˈtwin** *noun* = CONJOINED TWIN

sib /sɪb/ *noun* (*biology* 生) a brother or sister 胞亲

sibi·lant /ˈsɪbɪlənt/ *adj., noun*

■ ***adj.*** (*formal* or *literary*) making a 's' or 'sh' sound 发咝咝声的：*the sibilant sound of whispering* 窃窃私语声

■ ***noun*** (*phonetics* 语音) a sibilant sound made in speech, such as /s/ and /z/ in the English words *sip* and *zip* 咝音；咝擦音

sib·ling /ˈsɪblɪŋ/ *noun* (*formal* or *specialist*) a brother or sister 兄；弟；姐；妹：*squabbles between siblings* 兄弟姐妹间的口角 ◇ ***sibling rivalry*** (= competition between brothers and sisters) 兄弟姐妹间的竞争

sibyl /ˈsɪbl/ *noun* **1** in ancient times, a woman who was thought to be able to communicate messages from a god 西比尔，西比拉（传说中能传达神谕的女子） **2** (*literary*) a woman who can predict the future 女预言家

sic /sɪk; siːk/ *adv., verb*

■ ***adv.*** (*from Latin*) written after a word that you have copied from somewhere, to show that you know that the word is wrongly spelled or wrong in some other way（注于引文后，表示原文存在拼写等错误）原文如此：*In the letter to parents it said: 'The school is proud of it's* [sic] *record of excellence'.* 在致家长的信中写道："The school is proud of it's（原文如此）record of excellence"。

■ ***verb*** (**-cc-**) ~ **sb** (*NAmE, informal*) to attack sb 攻击：*Sic him, Duke!* (= said to a dog) 杜克，咬他！（对狗说）

PHR V ˈ**sic sth on sb** (*NAmE, informal*) to tell a dog to attack sb 放狗去咬某人

sick 🔑 /sɪk/ *adj., noun, verb*

■ ***adj.***

• **ILL** 患病 **1** 🔑 physically or mentally ill（身体或精神）生病的，有病的：*a sick child* 生病的孩子 ◇ *Her mother's very sick.* 她母亲病得很厉害。◇ *Peter has **been off sick*** (= away from work because he is ill) *for two weeks.* 彼得因病两周没上班了。◇ *Emma has just **called in sick*** (= telephoned to say she will not be coming to work because she is ill). 埃玛刚才打电话来请病假了。◇ (*BrE*) *Britain's workers **went sick*** (= did not go to work because they were ill) *for a record number of days last year.* 去年英国工人的病假天数创下了纪录。◇ (*NAmE*) *I can't afford to **get sick*** (= become ill). 我病不起。➲ COLLOCATIONS AT ILL

• **WANTING TO VOMIT** 想呕吐 **2** 🔑 [not usually before noun] feeling that you want to VOMIT 想呕吐；恶心：*Mum, I **feel sick**!* 妈，我想吐！◇ *If you eat any more cake you'll **make yourself sick**.* 你要是再吃蛋糕，就该吐了。◇ *a sick feeling in your stomach* 反胃的感觉

S

• **-SICK** 不适 **3** (in compounds 构成复合词) feeling sick as a result of travelling on a ship, plane, etc. 晕船；晕机；晕车：*seasick* 晕船 ◇ *airsick* 晕机 ◇ *carsick* 晕车 ◇ *travel-sick* 旅行晕眩的

• **BORED** 厌倦 **4** (*informal*) bored with or annoyed about sth that has been happening for a long time, and wanting it to stop （对…）厌倦的，厌烦的，厌恶的：**~ of sb/sth** *I'm sick of the way you've treated me.* 你对待我的那一套我都厌倦了。◇ *I'm **sick and tired of** your moaning.* 你的牢骚我都听腻了。◇ *I'm **sick to death of** all of you!* 你们全都烦死人了！◇ **~ of doing sth** *We're sick of waiting around like this.* 这么等来等去，我们感到很腻味。

• **CRUEL/STRANGE** 残酷；古怪 **5** (*informal*) (especially of humour 尤指幽默) dealing with suffering, disease or death in a cruel way that some people think is offensive 令人毛骨悚然的；可怕的；残酷的：*a sick joke* 令人反感的笑话 ◇ *That's really sick.* 那真够吓人的。**6** (*informal*) getting enjoyment from doing strange or cruel things 变态的；病态的：*a sick mind* 变态的心理 ◇ *People think I'm sick for having a rat as a pet.* 人们认为我养只耗子当宠物是变态。◇ *We live in a sick society.* 我们生活在一个病态的社会里。

• **GOOD** 好 **7** (*slang*) very good, enjoyable, etc. 非常棒；极好玩：*I love that song—it's sick!* 我非常喜欢那首歌，它棒极了！➲ SEE ALSO HOMESICK, LOVESICK

IDM **be ˈsick** (*especially BrE*) to bring food from your stomach back out through your mouth 呕吐 **SYN** **vomit**: *I was sick three times in the night.* 夜里我吐了三次。◇ *She had been **violently sick**.* 她一直吐得很厉害。 **be worried ˈsick; be ˈsick with worry** to be extremely worried 极度担心；担心得要命：*Where have you been? I've been worried sick about you.* 你上哪儿去了？把我急死了。 **fall ˈsick** (*also old-fashioned* **take ˈsick**) (*formal*) to become ill/sick 患病；生病 **make sb ˈsick** to make sb angry or disgusted 使厌恶；使反感：*His hypocrisy makes me sick.* 他的虚伪让我恶心。 **(as) sick as a ˈdog** (*informal*) feeling very ill/sick; VOMITING a lot 病得很重；呕吐得厉害 **(as) sick as a ˈparrot** (*BrE, humorous*) very disappointed 大失所望 **sick at ˈheart** (*formal*) very unhappy or disappointed 十分不快；非常失望 **sick to your ˈstomach 1** feeling very angry or worried 非常生气；非常担心：*Nora turned sick to her stomach on hearing this news.* 听了这个消息，诺拉变得忧心忡忡。**2** (*NAmE*) feeling that you want to VOMIT 想呕吐；恶心

■ ***noun***

• **VOMIT** 呕吐 **1** [U] (*BrE, informal*) food that you bring back up from your stomach through your mouth 呕吐物 **SYN** **vomit**

• **ILL PEOPLE** 病人 **2 the sick** [pl.] people who are ill/sick 病人：*All the sick and wounded were evacuated.* 所有伤病人员都给撤离了。➲ MORE LIKE THIS 24, page R28

■ ***verb***

PHR V **ˌsick sth↔ˈup** (*BrE, informal*) to bring sth up from the stomach back out through your mouth 吐出 **SYN** **vomit**

ˈsick bag *noun* a paper bag on a boat or plane into which you can VOMIT （船或飞机上的）呕吐用袋，卫生袋

sick·bay /ˈsɪkbeɪ/ *noun* a room or rooms, for example on a ship or in a school, with beds for people who are ill/sick （船上或学校等的）病室，保健室

sick·bed /ˈsɪkbed/ *noun* [sing.] the bed on which a person who is ill/sick is lying 病床：*The President left his sickbed to attend the ceremony.* 总统带病去出席那个仪式。

ˌsick ˈbuilding syndrome *noun* [U] a condition that affects people who work in large offices, making them feel tired and causing headaches, sore eyes and breathing problems, thought to be caused by, for example, the lack of fresh air or by chemicals in the air 病态建筑综合征，病态大楼症候群（办公大楼中因新鲜空气缺乏等原因而引起的疲倦、头疼、眼睛疼痛、呼吸困难等症状）

sick·en /ˈsɪkən/ *verb* (*BrE*) **1** [T] **~ sb** to make sb feel very shocked and angry 使大为震惊；使愤怒 **SYN** **disgust** **2** [I] to become ill/sick 患病；生病：(*old-fashioned*) *The baby sickened and died before his first birthday.* 婴儿没过周岁就病死了。◇ (*BrE*) *Faye hasn't eaten all day—she must **be sickening for something**.* 费伊一天没吃饭了，她一定是哪儿不舒服了。

sick·en·ing /ˈsɪkənɪŋ/ *adj.* **1** making you feel disgusted or shocked 让人厌恶的；令人作呕的；令人震惊的 **SYN** **repulsive**: *the sickening stench of burnt flesh* 肉燃烧所发出的令人作呕的恶臭 **2** making you afraid that sb has been badly hurt or that sth has been broken 给人以不祥感觉的；让人觉得不妙的：*Her head hit the ground with a sickening thud.* 她的头撞在地上，那声闷响让人揪心。**3** (*informal*) making you feel jealous or annoyed 令人忌妒的；让人烦恼的：*'She's off to the Bahamas for a month.' 'How sickening!'* "她去巴哈马群岛了，要待一个月。""多让人忌妒哇！" ▸ **sick·en·ing·ly** *adv.*

sickie /ˈsɪki/ *noun* (*BrE, informal*) a day when you say that you are ill/sick and cannot go to work when it is not really true 称病缺勤；假病假：*to pull/throw/chuck a sickie* 装病请假

sickle /ˈsɪkl/ *noun* a tool with a curved blade and a short handle, used for cutting grass, etc. 镰刀 ➲ SEE ALSO HAMMER AND SICKLE

ˈsick leave *noun* [U] permission to be away from work because of illness; the period of time spent away from work 病假；病假期：*to be on sick leave* 休病假

ˌsickle-cell aˈnaemia (*also* **ˈsickle-cell disease**) *noun* [U] a serious form of ANAEMIA (= a disease of the blood) that is found mostly in people of African family origins, and which is passed down from parents to children 镰状细胞贫血（多见于非裔的遗传病）

sick·ly /ˈsɪkli/ *adj.* (**sick·lier**, **sick·li·est**) **1** often ill/sick 常生病的；多病的；爱闹病的：*He was a sickly child.* 他是个爱闹病的孩子。**2** not looking healthy and strong 不健壮的；体弱的；有病容的 **SYN** **frail**: *She looked pale and sickly.* 她面色苍白，病恹恹的。◇ *sickly plants* 长势差的植物 **3** that makes you feel sick, especially because it is too sweet or full of false emotion （尤指太甜或充斥着虚情假意）令人生厌的，让人恶心的：*a sickly sweet smell* 香得发腻的气味 ◇ *She gave me a sickly smile.* 她朝我递来一脸假笑。**4** (of colours 颜色) unpleasant to look at 难看的；看着不舒服的：*a sickly green colour* 一种难看的绿色

sick·ness /ˈsɪknəs/ *noun* **1** [U] illness; bad health 疾病；不健康：*She's been off work because of sickness.* 她因病没有上班。◇ *insurance against sickness and unemployment* 疾病和失业保险 ➲ SYNONYMS AT ILLNESS **2** [U, C, usually sing.] a particular type of illness or disease …病；…症：***altitude/travel/radiation, etc. sickness*** 高原病、旅行眩晕、辐射病等 ➲ SEE ALSO SLEEPING SICKNESS **3** [U] (*especially BrE*) the feeling that you are likely to VOMIT (= bring food back up from the stomach to the mouth); the fact of VOMITING 恶心；呕吐 **SYN** **nausea**: *symptoms include sickness and diarrhoea* 症状包括呕吐和腹泻 ◇ *The sickness passed off after a while.* 过了一会儿，就不觉得恶心了。➲ SEE ALSO MORNING SICKNESS **4** [sing.] a feeling of great sadness, disappointment or disgust 悲伤；失望；厌恶；反感

ˈsickness benefit *noun* [U] (*BrE*) money paid by the government to people who are away from work because of illness 疾病补助金（由政府发放给因病不能上班的职工）➲ COMPARE SICK PAY

sicko /ˈsɪkəʊ; *NAmE* -koʊ/ *noun* (*pl.* **-os**) (*informal, especially NAmE*) a person who gets enjoyment from doing strange and cruel things 从病态行为取乐的人；（精神）变态者：*child molesters and other sickos* 对儿童进行性骚扰者及其他变态狂

sick·out /ˈsɪkaʊt/ *noun* (*NAmE*) a strike in which all the workers at a company say they are sick and stay at home 集体称病罢工

ˈsick pay *noun* [U] pay given to an employee who is away from work because of illness 病假工资 ➲ COMPARE SICKNESS BENEFIT

S

sick·room /ˈsɪkruːm; -rʊm/ *noun* a room in which a person who is ill/sick is lying in bed 病房；病室

side 🔑 /saɪd/ *noun, verb*

■ ***noun***

• **LEFT/RIGHT** 左；右 **1** 🔑 [C, usually sing.] either of the two halves of a surface, an object or an area that is divided by an imaginary central line（由想象的中线分出的）一边，一侧：*They drive on the left-hand side of the road in Japan.* 在日本驾车靠左行。◇ *the right side of the brain* 脑的右半部 ◇ *satellite links to the other side of the world* 与世界的另一边卫星连线 ◇ *She was on the far side of the room.* 她在房间的那一边。◇ *They crossed from one side of London to the other.* 他们从伦敦的这一头到了另一头。◇ *Keep on your side of the bed!* 你还是睡你那边吧！**2** 🔑 [C, usually sing.] a position or an area to the left or right of sth（事物左方或右方的）一旁，一边，一侧：*There is a large window **on either side of** the front door.* 前门两侧各有一个大窗户。◇ *He crossed the bridge to **the other side** of the river.* 他过桥到了河对岸。◇ *people on both sides of the Atlantic* 大西洋两岸的人 ◇ *She tilted her head **to one side**.* 她把头歪到一边。

• **NOT TOP OR BOTTOM** 侧面 **3** 🔑 [C] one of the flat surfaces of sth that is not the top or bottom, front or back 侧面：*Write your name on the side of the box.* 把你的姓名写在盒子的侧面。◇ *There's a scratch on the side of my car.* 我的汽车侧面有一道划痕。◇ *The kitchen door is at the side of the house.* 厨房门开在房子的侧面。◇ *a **side door/entrance/window*** 侧门；侧边入口；侧窗 ◇ *Now lay the jar on its side.* 现在把广口瓶侧着放倒。**4** 🔑 [C] the vertical or sloping surface around sth, but not the top or bottom of it 斜面；垂直面：*A path went up the side of the hill.* 沿着山坡往上有一条小路。◇ *Brush the sides of the tin with butter.* 在烤模的四周刷上黄油。➲ SEE ALSO HILLSIDE, MOUNTAINSIDE

• **EDGE** 边缘 **5** 🔑 [C] a part or an area of sth near the edge and away from the middle 边缘；边：*She sat on the side of the bed.* 她坐在床边。◇ *A van was parked at the side of the road.* 路边停着一辆面包车。◇ *the south side of the lake* 湖的南侧 ➲ SEE ALSO BEDSIDE, FIRESIDE, RINGSIDE, RIVERSIDE, ROADSIDE, SEASIDE

• **OF BODY** 身体 **6** 🔑 [C, usually sing.] either the right or left part of a person's body, from the ARMPIT (= where the arm joins the body) to the hip 侧面；胁：*She has a pain down her right side.* 她身子右边疼。◇ *He was lying on his side.* 他侧卧着。

• **NEAR TO SB/STH** 某人 / 某物的近旁 **7** 🔑 [sing.] a place or position very near to sb/sth 近旁；旁边；身边：*Keep close to my side.* 紧挨着我，别走开。◇ *Her husband stood at her side.* 她丈夫站在她身边。

• **OF STH FLAT AND THIN** 平而薄的东西 **8** 🔑 [C] either of two surfaces of sth flat and thin, such as paper or cloth 一面：*Write on one side of the paper only.* 只在纸的一面写。◇ *Fry the steaks for two minutes on each side.* 牛排两面各煎两分钟。

• **PAGE** 页 **9** [C] the amount of writing needed to fill one side of a sheet of paper 一面纸的文字：*He told us not to write more than three sides.* 他告诉我们写字不要超过三面纸。

• **MATHEMATICS** 数学 **10** 🔑 [C] any of the flat surfaces of a solid object（立体的）面：*A cube has six sides.* 立方体有六面。**11** 🔑 [C] any of the lines that form a flat shape such as a square or triangle（平面图形的）边：*a shape with five sides* 五边形 ◇ *The farm buildings form three sides of a square.* 这几栋农舍构成一个正方形的三个边。➲ PICTURE AT POLYGON

• **-SIDED** 有…面（或边）**12** used in adjectives to state the number or type of sides（构成形容词）有…面（或边）的：*a six-sided object* 六面体 ◇ *a glass-sided container* 玻璃面的容器

• **IN WAR/ARGUMENT** 战争；争论 **13** 🔑 [C] one of the two or more people or groups taking part in an argument, war, etc. 一方；一派：*We have finally reached an agreement acceptable to all sides.* 我们最终达成一项各方都能接受的协议。◇ *At some point during the war he seems to have **changed sides**.* 战争期间，他好像在某个时候曾经转投对方营垒。◇ *to be **on the winning/losing side*** 在获胜 / 失败一方 **14** 🔑 [C] one of the opinions, attitudes or positions held by sb in an argument, a business arrangement, etc. 一方的意见（或态度、立场）：*We heard both **sides of the argument**.* 我们听过了辩论双方的意见。◇ *I just want you to hear **my side of the story** first.* 我只想要你先听听我的说法。◇ *Will you **keep your side of the bargain**?* 你那一方能不能遵守协议？

• **ASPECT** 方面 **15** 🔑 [C] a particular aspect of sth, especially a situation or a person's character 方面：*These poems reveal her gentle side.* 这些诗显示出她温柔的一面。◇ *This is a side of Alan that I never knew existed.* 我以前从来不知道艾伦还有这样的一面。◇ *It's good you can see **the funny side** of the situation.* 你能看到情况可笑的一面，这很好。◇ *I'll take care of that side of things.* 那方面的事情由我来处理。

• **FEELING THAT YOU ARE BETTER** 优越感 **16** [U] (*BrE, informal*) a feeling that you are better than other people 优越感；架子：*There was **no side** to him at all.* 他一点架子也没有。

• **SPORTS TEAM** 运动队 **17** [C] a sports team 运动队：*The French have a very strong side.* 法国队非常强大。◇ *We were **on the winning/losing side**.* 我们支持获胜 / 失利的一方。

• **OF FAMILY** 亲属 **18** [C] the part of your family that people belong to who are related either to your mother or to your father 母系；父系；血统：*a cousin on my father's side* (= a child of my father's brother or sister) 我父亲那边的表亲

• **FOOD** 食物 **19** (*NAmE, informal*) = SIDE DISH：*Your dinner comes with a choice of two sides.* 您的正餐有两道配菜可供选择。

• **MEAT** 肉 **20** [C] **a ~ of beef/bacon, etc.** one of the two halves of an animal that has been killed for meat 一扇（牛肉 / 熏猪肉等）

• **TV CHANNEL** 电视频道 **21** [C] (*old-fashioned, BrE, informal*) a television channel 电视频道：*What's on the other side?* 另一个频道上演什么？

IDM **come down on ˈone side of the fence or the ˈother** to choose between two possible choices 二者择其一；支持两方中的一方 **from ˌside to ˈside** 🔑 moving to the left and then to the right and then back again 左右来回（摇摆）：*He shook his head slowly from side to side.* 他慢慢地摇了摇头。◇ *The ship rolled from side to side.* 船左右摇晃。**get on the right/wrong ˈside of sb** to make sb pleased with you/annoyed with you 讨得某人的欢心；惹得某人恼怒 **have sth on your ˈside** to have sth as an advantage that will make it more likely that you will achieve sth 有…的优势 **let the ˈside down** (*especially BrE*) to fail to give your friends, family, etc. the help and support they expect, or to behave in a way that makes them disappointed 使自己人失望；未能帮助（或支持）自己的一方 **not leave sb's ˈside** to stay with sb, especially in order to take care of them（尤指为了照顾）不离某人左右 **on/from all ˈsides | on/from every ˈside** in or from all directions; everywhere 从四面八方；到处：*We realized we were surrounded on all sides.* 我们意识到我们被包围了。◇ *Disaster threatens on every side.* 灾祸四伏。**on the ˈbig, ˈsmall, ˈhigh, etc. side** (*informal*) slightly too big, small, high, etc. 稍偏大（或小、高等）：*These shoes are a little on the tight side.* 这双鞋略有点紧。**on the other side of the ˈfence** in a situation that is different from the one that you are in 与自己所处情况不同的一面；事物的另一面 **on the ˌright/ˌwrong side of ˈ40, ˈ50, etc.** (*informal*) younger or older than 40, 50, etc. years of age 不到 / 已过 40 岁（或 50 岁等）**on the ˈside** (*informal*) **1** in addition to your main job 作为副业；兼职；在正事之外：*a mechanic who buys and sells cars on the side* 兼做汽车买卖的机修工 **2** secretly or illegally 秘密地；偷偷摸摸地；非法地：*He's married but he has a girlfriend on the side.* 他有妻室，但暗地里还有一个女友。**3** (*especially NAmE*) (of food in a restaurant 餐馆的食物) served at the same time as the main part of the meal, but on a separate plate 作为配菜 **on/to one ˈside 1** out of your way 在（或到）一边；在（或到）一旁：*I left my bags on one side.* 我把几个包丢在一边。**2** to be dealt with later 搁置；暂不处理：*I put his complaint to one side until I* *had more time.* 我把他的投诉放到一边，等时间充裕些再处理。◇ *Leaving that to one side for a moment, are there any other questions?* 把这个先放一放，还有没有别的问题？**be on sb's side** to support and agree with sb 站在某人一边；和某人观点一致：*I'm definitely on your side in this.* 在这个问题上，我毫不含糊地站在你这一边。◇ *Whose side are you on anyway?* 你到底赞成谁的观点呢？**the other side of the 'coin** the aspect of a situation that is the opposite of or contrasts with the one you have been talking about 事情的另一面 **,side by 'side 1** close together and facing in the same direction 并排；并肩地：*There were two children ahead, walking side by side.* 前面有两个孩子肩并肩走着。**2** together, without any difficulties 并行不悖；相安无事：*We have been using both systems, side by side, for two years.* 两年来，两套系统我们一直同时使用，互不影响。◇ *The two communities exist happily side by side.* 两个群体和睦共处，相安无事。**take 'sides** to express support for sb in a disagreement 表示支持一方；表明立场：*She didn't think it was wise to take sides in their argument.* 对于他们的辩论，她觉得向着谁都不明智。**take/draw sb to one 'side** to speak to sb in private, especially in order to warn or tell them about sth 把某人拉到一边（悄悄说话）**this side of...** before a particular time, event, age, etc. 在…之前：*They aren't likely to arrive this side of midnight.* 午夜之前他们不大可能赶到。➲ MORE AT BED *n.*, BIT, BRIGHT *adj.*, CREDIT *n.*, DISTAFF, ERR, GRASS *n.*, KNOW *v.*, LAUGH *v.*, RIGHT *adj.*, SAFE *adj.*, SPLIT *v.*, THORN, TIME *n.*, TWO, WRONG *adj.*

■ ***verb***

PHR V **'side with sb (against sb/sth)** to support one person or group in an argument against sb else 支持某人（反对…）；和某人站在一起（反对…）：*The kids always sided with their mother against me.* 孩子们总是和妈妈站在一边，跟我唱对台戏。

side·bar /ˈsaɪdbɑː(r)/ *noun* **1** a short article in a newspaper or magazine that is printed next to a main article, and gives extra information（报纸或杂志的）花絮报道 **2** a narrow area on the side of a computer screen or a WEB PAGE that is separate from the main part of the page（电脑屏幕或网页的）侧边栏，边注栏 **3** (*especially NAmE*) an issue, event, action, etc. that is less important than the main one 次要问题（或事件、行动等）：*The promoter provided free concerts as a sidebar to the festival.* 筹办单位举办免费音乐会为节日助兴。**4** (*also* **,sidebar 'conference**) (*US*) (in a court of law) a discussion between the judge and the lawyers that the JURY cannot hear（法庭上）旁厅会议（法官和律师之间避开陪审团的小会）

side·board /ˈsaɪdbɔːd; *NAmE* -bɔːrd/ (*NAmE also* **buf·fet**) *noun* **1** a piece of furniture in a DINING ROOM for putting food on before it is served, with drawers for storing knives, forks, etc. 餐具柜 ➲ VISUAL VOCAB PAGE V23 **2** = SIDEBURN

side·burn /ˈsaɪdbɜːn; *NAmE* -bɜːrn/ (*BrE also* **side·board**) *noun* [usually pl.] hair that grows down the sides of a man's face in front of his ears（男子的）鬓角 ➲ VISUAL VOCAB PAGE V65

side·car /ˈsaɪdkɑː(r)/ *noun* a small vehicle attached to the side of a motorcycle in which a passenger can ride（摩托车的）跨斗，边车

'side dish (*NAmE*, *informal* **side**) *noun* a small amount of food, for example a salad, served with the main course of a meal（随同主菜一起上的）配菜 **SYN** **side order**

'side effect *noun* [usually pl.] **1** an extra and usually bad effect that a drug has on you, as well as curing illness or pain（药物的）副作用 **2** an unexpected result of a situation or course of action that happens as well as the result you were aiming for 意外的连带后果

'side-foot *verb* **~ sth** to kick a ball with the inside part of your foot 用脚内侧踢，侧脚踢（球）

'side issue *noun* an issue that is less important than the main issue, and may take attention away from it 次要问题

side·kick /ˈsaɪdkɪk/ *noun* (*informal*) a person who helps another more important or more intelligent person 助手；副手：*Batman and his young sidekick Robin* 蝙蝠侠和他的年轻助手罗宾

side·light /ˈsaɪdlaɪt/ *noun* **1 ~ (on sb/sth)** a piece of information, usually given by accident or in connection with another subject, that helps you to understand sb/sth 意外线索；侧面了解的情况；间接消息 **2** (*BrE*) either of a pair of small lights at the front of a vehicle（车辆前面的）侧灯

side·line /ˈsaɪdlaɪn/ *noun, verb*

■ ***noun*** **1** [C] an activity that you do as well as your main job in order to earn extra money 兼职；副业；兼营业务 **2** **sidelines** [pl.] the lines along the two long sides of a sports field, TENNIS COURT, etc. that mark the outer edges; the area just outside these（球场等的）边线，两侧场外区域：*The coach stood on the sidelines yelling instructions to the players.* 教练站在场外，大声指挥运动员。

IDM **on/from the 'sidelines** watching sth but not actually involved in it 从旁观者的角度；置身局外：*He was content to watch from the sidelines as his wife built up a successful business empire.* 他满足于站在一旁，看妻子一步步地建立起一个成功的商业帝国。

■ ***verb*** [usually passive] **1 ~ sb** to prevent sb from playing in a team, especially because of an injury 使退出比赛，使下场（尤指由于受伤）：*The player has been sidelined by a knee injury.* 这名队员因膝部受伤而下场。**2 ~ sb** to prevent sb from having an important part in sth that other people are doing 把…排除在核心之外；使靠边：*The vice-president is increasingly being sidelined.* 副总统被日益排挤到权力中心之外。

side·long /ˈsaɪdlɒŋ; *NAmE* -lɔːŋ/ *adj.* [only before noun] (of a look 目光) out of the corner of your eye, especially in a way that is secret or disapproving 侧眼偷看的；斜着眼看的；睨视的：*She cast **a sidelong glance** at Eric to see if he had noticed her blunder.* 她偷偷斜扫了埃里克一眼，看他有没有留意到她的错误。▶ **side·long** *adv.*：*She looked sidelong at him.* 她斜眼看他。

,side-'on *adv.* (*BrE*) coming from the side rather than from the front or back 从侧面；侧向：*The car hit us side-on.* 那辆车从侧面撞了我们。

'side order *noun* a small amount of food ordered in a restaurant to go with the main dish, but served separately（主菜之外）另点的配菜 **SYN** **side dish**：*a side order of fries* 另点的一份炸薯条

'side plate *noun* a small plate used for bread or other food that goes with a meal 面包盘；小吃盘 ➲ VISUAL VOCAB PAGE V23

sid·er·eal /saɪˈdɪəriəl; *NAmE* -ˈdɪr-/ *adj.* (*astronomy* 天) related to the stars that are far away, not the sun or planets 恒星的

'side road *noun* a smaller and less important road leading off a main road 支线；叉道；旁路

'side-saddle *adv.* if you ride a horse **side-saddle**, you ride with both your legs on the same side of the horse 在横鞍上；侧骑

'side salad *noun* a salad served with the main course of a meal 配菜色拉

side·show /ˈsaɪdʃəʊ; *NAmE* -ʃoʊ/ *noun* **1** a separate small show or attraction at a FAIR or CIRCUS where you pay to see a performance or take part in a game（游园会或马戏中穿插的）小节目，杂耍 **2** an activity or event that is much less important than the main activity or event 次要活动；附带事件

'side-splitting *adj.* (*informal*) extremely funny; making people laugh a lot 滑稽透顶的；令人捧腹的：*side-splitting anecdotes* 滑稽可笑的奇闻逸事 ➲ MORE LIKE THIS 10, page

S

R26 ▶ **'side-splittingly** *adv.*： *side-splittingly funny* 极其滑稽可笑的

side·step /'saɪdstep/ *verb* (**-pp-**) **1** [T] **~ sth** to avoid answering a question or dealing with a problem 回避，规避（问题等）：*Did you notice how she neatly sidestepped the question?* 你有没有注意到她多么巧妙地回避了那个问题？ **2** [T, I] **~ (sth)** to avoid sth, for example being hit, by stepping to one side 横跨一步躲过；侧移一步闪过：*He cleverly sidestepped the tackle.* 他巧妙地一晃，绕过阻截队员。

'side street *noun* a less important street leading off a road in a town 小路；小街

side·swipe /'saɪdswaɪp/ *noun* **1** (*NAmE*) a hit from the side 擦边撞击；侧撞；擦撞：*a sideswipe by a truck* 卡车的擦撞 **2** **~ (at sb/sth)** (*informal*) a critical comment made about sb/sth while you are talking about sb/sth completely different 借机抨击；借题发挥的批评：*It was a good speech, but he couldn't resist taking a sideswipe at his opponent.* 他的讲话不错，可他还是忍不住借机把对手抨击了一番。 ▶ **side·swipe** *verb* **~ sb/sth** (*NAmE*)： *The bus sideswiped two parked cars.* 公共汽车擦边撞上了两辆停在那儿的汽车。

side·track /'saɪdtræk/ *verb* [usually passive] **~ sb (into doing sth)** to make sb start to talk about or do sth that is different from the main thing that they are supposed to be talking about or doing 使转变话题；使转移目标 SYN **distract**: *I was supposed to be writing a letter but I'm afraid I got sidetracked.* 我本来应该在写信，但后来恐怕是分心干别的去了。

'side view *noun* a view of sth from the side 侧景；侧视图；侧面图：*The picture shows a side view of the house.* 这张图是房子的侧面。

side·walk /'saɪdwɔːk/ (*NAmE*) (*BrE* **pave·ment**) *noun* a flat part at the side of a road for people to walk on（马路边的）人行道 ⊃VISUAL VOCAB PAGE V3

'sidewalk artist (*NAmE*) (*BrE* **'pavement artist**) *noun* an artist who draws pictures in CHALK on the PAVEMENT/SIDEWALK, hoping to get money from people who pass 街头画家，马路画家（在人行道上用粉笔作画讨钱）

S

side·ward /'saɪdwəd; *NAmE* -wərd/ *adj.* to, towards or from the side（向）一侧的；（向）一边的：*a sideward glance* 斜视的一眼 ▶ **side·ward** (*also* **side·wards**) *adv.*： *He was blown sidewards by the wind.* 他被风吹到旁边。

side·ways 🔑 /'saɪdweɪz/ *adv.* **1** 🔑 to, towards or from the side 往（或向、从）一侧：*He looked sideways at her.* 他斜着眼看她。◇ *The truck skidded sideways across the road.* 卡车横着滑到公路另一侧。◇ *He has been moved sideways* (= moved to another job at the same level as before, not higher or lower). 他平级调动工作了。 **2** 🔑 with one side facing forwards 侧着；侧面朝前：*She sat sideways on the chair.* 她侧坐在椅子上。 ▶ **side·ways** 🔑 *adj.*： *She slid him a sideways glance.* 她斜眼看了他一下。◇ *a sideways move* 侧移 IDM SEE KNOCK *v.*

'side whiskers *noun* [pl.] hair growing on the sides of a man's face down to, but not on, the chin（男子的）络腮胡子，连鬓胡子

side·wind·er /'saɪdwaɪndə(r)/ *noun* a poisonous N American snake that moves sideways across the desert by throwing its body in an S shape 侧进蛇，角响尾蛇（北美沙漠地带毒蛇）

sid·ing /'saɪdɪŋ/ *noun* **1** a short track beside a main railway/railroad line, where trains can stand when they are not being used（火车停靠的）站线 **2** (*NAmE*) material used to cover and protect the outside walls of buildings 壁板；墙板；挡板

sidle /'saɪdl/ *verb* [I] **+ adv./prep.** to walk somewhere in a shy or uncertain way as if you do not want to be noticed 犹犹豫豫地走；羞怯地走；悄悄地走：*She sidled up to me and whispered something in my ear.* 她悄悄走上前来，对我耳语了几句。

SIDS /ˌes aɪ diː 'es; sɪdz/ *noun* [U] the abbreviation for 'sudden infant death syndrome' (the sudden death while sleeping of a baby which appears to be healthy) 婴儿猝死综合征 SYN **cot death**

siege /siːdʒ/ *noun* **1** a military operation in which an army tries to capture a town by surrounding it and stopping the supply of food, etc. to the people inside（军队对城镇的）围困，包围，围攻，封锁：*the siege of Troy* 特洛伊之围 ◇ *The siege was finally lifted* (= ended) *after six months.* 六个月后封锁最终解除了。◇ *The police placed the city centre under a virtual* ***state of siege*** (= it was hard to get in or out). 警方可说是已封锁了市中心。 **2** a situation in which the police surround a building where people are living or hiding, in order to make them come out（警察对建筑物的）包围，封锁 ⊃SEE ALSO BESIEGE

IDM **under 'siege** **1** surrounded by an army or the police in a siege 被包围；被围困；被封锁 **2** being criticized all the time or put under pressure by problems, questions, etc. 一再遭到批评的；受…困扰的 **lay 'siege to sth** **1** to begin a siege of a town, building, etc. 围困，围攻（城镇、建筑物等） **2** to surround a building, especially in order to speak to or question the person or people living or working there 包围（某建筑物，旨在和里面的人对话或质询）

'siege mentality *noun* [sing., U] a feeling that you are surrounded by enemies and must protect yourself 受围心态（感觉周围都是敌人因而必须自卫）

sie·mens /'siːmənz/ *noun* (*abbr.* **S**) (*physics* 物) the standard unit for measuring how well an object CONDUCTS electricity 西（门子）（电导单位）

si·enna /si'enə/ *noun* [U] a type of dark yellow or red CLAY used for giving colour to paints, etc.（富铁）黄土，褐土（用作颜料）

si·erra /si'erə/ *noun* (especially in place names 尤用于地名) a long range of steep mountains with sharp points, especially in Spain and America（尤指西班牙和美洲的）锯齿状山脉：*the Sierra Nevada* 内华达山脉

si·esta /si'estə/ *noun* a rest or sleep taken in the early afternoon, especially in hot countries（尤指在气候炎热的国家的）午睡，午休：*to* ***have/take a siesta*** 睡午觉 ⊃COMPARE NAP *n.* (1)

sieve /sɪv/ *noun, verb*

■ ***noun*** a tool for separating solids from liquids or larger solids from smaller solids, made of a wire or plastic net attached to a ring. The liquid or small pieces pass through the net but the larger pieces do not. 滤器；筛子；笊篱；漏勺 ⊃VISUAL VOCAB PAGE V27

IDM **have a memory/mind like a 'sieve** (*informal*) to have a very bad memory; to forget things easily 记性差；健忘

■ ***verb*** **~ sth** to put sth through a sieve 筛；过筛；滤

sie·vert /'siːvət; *NAmE* -vərt/ *noun* (*abbr.* **Sv**) (*physics* 物) a unit for measuring the effect of RADIATION 希沃特（辐射效果单位，简称希）

sift /sɪft/ *verb* **1** [T] **~ sth** to put flour or some other fine substance through a SIEVE/SIFTER 筛（面粉或颗粒较细的物质）：*Sift the flour into a bowl.* 把面粉筛到碗里。 **2** [T, I] to examine sth very carefully in order to decide what is important or useful or to find sth important 细查；详审： **~ sth** *We will sift every scrap of evidence.* 我们将细查每一点证据。◇ **~ through sth** *Crash investigators have been sifting through the wreckage of the aircraft.* 调查坠机事件的专家一直在仔细检查飞机残骸。 **3** [T] **~ sth (out) from sth** to separate sth from a group of things 区分；挑选；精选：*She looked quickly through the papers, sifting out from the pile anything that looked interesting.* 她很快地翻了一下那摞文件，把所有看着有趣的东西都拣了出来。

PHR V **ˌsift sth↔'out** **1** to remove sth that you do not want from a substance by putting it through a SIEVE 筛除；筛去：*Put the flour through a sieve to sift out the lumps.* 把面粉过筛，除去面块。 **2** to separate sth, usually sth you do not want, from a group of things 剔除；淘

汰: *We need to sift out the applications that have no chance of succeeding.* 我们需要剔出那些成功无望的申请。

sift·er /ˈsɪftə(r)/ *noun* **1** (*NAmE*) a small SIEVE used for sifting flour（面粉）筛子；罗 ➲ VISUAL VOCAB PAGE V27 **2** a container with a lot of small holes in the top, used for shaking flour or sugar onto things 撒…瓶（盖上有许多小孔，用于撒面粉等粉状物或糖）：*a sugar sifter* 撒糖瓶

sigh /saɪ/ *verb, noun*

■ *verb* **1** [I] to take and then let out a long deep breath that can be heard, to show that you are disappointed, sad, tired, etc. 叹气；叹息：*He* ***sighed deeply*** *at the thought.* 想到这里，他深深叹了口气。◇ **~ with sth** *She* ***sighed with relief*** *that it was all over.* 事情总算全都过去了，她轻松地舒了一口气。**2** [T] **+ speech** to say sth with a sigh 叹着气说；叹息道：*'Oh well, better luck next time,' she sighed.* "唉，就这样了，但愿下一次运气好些。" 她叹息道。**3** [I] (*literary*) (especially of the wind 尤指风) to make a long sound like a sigh 悲鸣

■ *noun* an act or the sound of sighing 叹气；叹息：***to give/heave/let out a sigh*** 发出叹息 ◇ *a deep sigh* 深深的叹息 ◇ *'I'll wait,' he said with a sigh.* "我就等呗。" 他叹口气说。◇ *We all* ***breathed a sigh of relief*** *when it was over.* 事情过去了，我们大家都松了一口气。

sight 🔑 /saɪt/ *noun, verb*

■ ***noun***

• **ABILITY TO SEE** 视力 **1** 🔑 [U] the ability to see 视力；视觉 **SYN** **eyesight**: *to lose your sight* (= to become blind) 失明 ◇ *She has very good sight.* 她的视力很好。◇ *The disease has affected her sight.* 这种病影响了她的视力。◇ *He has very little sight in his right eye.* 他右眼视力极弱。

• **ACT OF SEEING** 看见 **2** 🔑 [U] **~ of sb/sth** the act of seeing sb/sth 看见：*After ten days at sea, we had our first sight of land.* 我们在海上航行十天之后，首次看见陆地。◇ *I have been known to faint* ***at the sight of*** *blood.* 大家都知道，我看到血就会昏倒。◇ *The soldiers were given orders to shoot* ***on sight*** (= as soon as they saw sb). 士兵得到命令，见人就射击。◇ *She* ***caught sight*** *of a car in the distance.* 她看见远处有一辆汽车。

• **HOW FAR YOU CAN SEE** 视野 **3** 🔑 [U] the area or distance within which sb can see or sth can be seen 视力范围；视野：*There was no one* ***in sight***. 一个人也看不见。◇ *At last we* ***came in sight of*** *a few houses.* 最后，我们看到了几座房屋。◇ *A bicycle came into sight on the main road.* 大路上出现了一辆自行车。◇ *The end is* ***in sight*** (= will happen soon). 结局已现端倪。◇ *Leave any valuables in your car* ***out of sight.*** 把贵重物品留在车里看不见的地方。◇ ***Keep out of sight*** (= stay where you cannot be seen). 不要露面。◇ *She never lets her daughter* ***out of her sight*** (= always keeps her where she can see her). 她从来不让女儿走出她的视线。◇ *Get out of my sight!* (= Go away!) 滚开！◇ *The boat disappeared* ***from sight.*** 那艘船从视野中消失了。◇ *The house was* ***hidden from sight*** *behind some trees.* 房子藏在树林后面。◇ *He had placed himself directly in my* ***line of sight.*** 当时他恰好出现在我的视线中。

• **WHAT YOU CAN SEE** 看见的事物 **4** 🔑 [C] a thing that you see or can see 看见（或看得见）的事物；景象；情景：*It's a spectacular sight as the flamingos lift into the air.* 一群红鹳飞向空中，景象十分壮观。◇ *The museum attempts to recreate* ***the sights and sounds of*** *wartime Britain.* 博物馆试图再现战时英国的情景。◇ *He was a* ***sorry sight,*** *soaked to the skin and shivering.* 他浑身湿透，打着寒战，一副凄惨的样子。◇ *The bird is now a rare sight in this country.* 如今在这个国家，这种鸟已罕见了。➲ SYNONYMS AT VIEW

• **INTERESTING PLACES** 好玩的地方 **5** 🔑 **sights** [pl.] the interesting places, especially in a town or city, that are often visited by tourists 名胜；风景：*We're going to Paris for the weekend to* ***see the sights.*** 我们打算去巴黎过周末，参观那里的名胜。

• **RIDICULOUS/UNTIDY PERSON** 可笑的 / 邋遢的人 **6 a sight** [sing.] (*informal, especially BrE*) a person or thing that looks ridiculous, untidy, unpleasant, etc. 滑稽可笑（或邋遢、脏乱、讨厌）的人（或物）：*She looks a sight in that hat!* 她戴着那顶帽子，样子够滑稽的！

• **ON GUN/TELESCOPE** 枪炮；望远镜 **7** [C, usually pl.] a device that you look through to aim a gun, etc. or to look at sth through a TELESCOPE, etc. 瞄准器；观测器：*He had the deer* ***in his sights*** *now.* 他现在瞄准了那头鹿。◇ (*figurative*) *Even as a young actress, she always had Hollywood firmly in her sights* (= as her final goal). 她还是年轻演员的时候，就瞄准了好莱坞。

▼ **SYNONYMS** 同义词辨析

sight

view • **vision**

These are all words for the area or distance that you can see from a particular position. 以上各词均指视力范围、视野。

sight the area or distance that you can see from a particular position 指视力范围、视野：*He looked up the street, but there was no one in sight.* 他朝街上望去，一个人也没看见。◇ *Leave any valuables in your car out of sight.* 把贵重物品留在车里看不见的地方。

view (*rather formal*) the area or distance that you can see from a particular position 指视力范围、视野：*The lake soon came into view.* 那湖很快便映入眼帘。

vision the area that you can see from a particular position 指视野：*The couple moved outside her field of vision* (= total area you can see from a particular position). 这对夫妇离开了她的视野。

SIGHT, VIEW OR VISION? 用 sight、view 还是 vision?

View is more literary than **sight** or **vision**. It is the only word for talking about how well you can see. * view 较 sight 和 vision 书面化，是其中唯一指视野清晰程度的词：~~*I didn't have a good sight/vision of the stage.*~~

Vision must always be used with a possessive pronoun. * vision 总是与物主代词连用：*my/his/her etc.* (*field of*) *vision* 我 / 他 / 她…的视野 It is not used with the prepositions *in, into* and *out of* that are very frequent with **sight** and **view**. * vision 不与介词 in、into 和 out of 连用，但 sight 和 view 常与这些介词连用：~~*There was nobody in vision.*~~ ◇ ~~*A tall figure came into vision.*~~

PATTERNS

- **in/out of** sight/view
- **in/within** sight/view **of** sth
- to **come into/disappear from** sight/view/sb's vision
- to **come in** sight/view **of** sb/sth
- to **block** sb's view/vision
- sb's **line of** sight/vision
- sb's **field of** view/vision

IDM **at first ˈsight 1** 🔑 when you first begin to consider sth 乍一看；初看时：*At first sight, it may look like a generous offer, but always read the small print.* 乍一看，对方给出的条件好像很优厚，但任何时候都不要小看那些小号字印刷的附加条款。**2** 🔑 when you see sb/sth for the first time 初次见到：*It was* ***love at first sight*** (= we fell in love the first time we saw each other). 我们一见钟情。**hate, be sick of, etc. the ˈsight of sb/sth** (*informal*) to hate, etc. sb/sth very much 十分厌恶；讨厌：*I can't stand the sight of him!* 我看见他就烦！**in the sight of sb/in sb's sight** (*formal*) in sb's opinion 从某人的观点来看；在某人看来：*We are all equal in the sight of God.* 在上帝眼里我们都是平等的。**lose ˈsight of sb/sth 1** to become no longer able to see sb/sth 再也见不着：*They finally lost sight of land.* 他们终于看不见陆地了。**2** to stop considering sth; to forget sth 忽略；忘记：*We must not lose sight of our original aim.* 我们决不能忘记我们最初的目标。**ˌout of ˈsight, ˌout of ˈmind** (*saying*) used to say sb will quickly be forgotten when they are no longer with you 眼不见，心不想 **raise/lower your ˈsights** to expect more/less from a situation 提高 / 降低要求；眼光变高 / 变低 **set your sights on sth/on doing sth** to decide that you want sth and to try very hard to get it 以…为奋斗目标；决心做到：*She's set her sights on getting into Harvard.* 她决心要上哈佛大学。**a (damn, etc.) sight better, etc.** | **a (damn, etc.) sight too good, etc.** (*informal*) very much better;

S

much too good, etc.（好）得多；非常（好）：*She's done a darn sight better than I have.* 她干得比我强多了。◇ *It's worth a damn sight more than I thought.* 它的价值比我原先想的高多了。**a ˌsight for sore ˈeyes** (*informal*) a person or thing that you are pleased to see; something that is very pleasant to look at 喜欢见到的人（或物） **sight unˈseen** if you buy sth **sight unseen**, you do not have an opportunity to see it before you buy it 在未见过的情况下；事先未经检查 ➲ MORE AT HEAVE *v.*, KNOW *v.*, NOWHERE, PRETTY *adj.*

■ ***verb*** ~ sth (*formal*) to suddenly see sth, especially sth you have been looking for 看到，发现（期待的事物）：*After twelve days at sea, they sighted land.* 在海上航行十二天后他们看到了陆地。

sight·ed /ˈsaɪtɪd/ *adj.* **1** able to see; not blind 看得见的；有视力的：*the blind parents of sighted children* 有正常视力的孩子的盲人父母 **2 -sighted** (in compounds 构成复合词) able to see in the way mentioned 有…视力的；视力…的：*partially sighted* 弱视的 ◇ *short-sighted* 近视的 ◇ *long-sighted* 远视的

sight·ing /ˈsaɪtɪŋ/ *noun* an occasion when sb sees sb/sth, especially sth unusual or sth that lasts for only a short time 看见，目睹（不寻常或短暂出现的事物）：*a reported sighting of the Loch Ness monster* 据报道有人看见尼斯湖水怪

sight·less /ˈsaɪtləs/ *adj.* (*literary*) unable to see 看不见的；盲的 **SYN** **blind**：*The statue stared down at them with sightless eyes.* 雕像用一双盲眼俯视着他们。

ˈsight-line *noun* = LINE OF SIGHT

ˈsight-read *verb* [I, T] ~ (**sth**) to play or sing written music when you see it for the first time, without practising it first 视奏，视唱（事先没有练习，直接看着乐谱演奏或演唱） ▶ **ˈsight-reader** *noun* **ˈsight-reading** *noun* [U]

sight·see·ing /ˈsaɪtsiːɪŋ/ *noun* [U] the activity of visiting interesting buildings and places as a tourist 观光；游览：*to go sightseeing* 去观光 ◇ *Did you have a chance to* ***do any sightseeing****?* 你有没有出去游览的机会？◇ *a sightseeing tour of the city* 游览那座城市 ➲ **WORDFINDER NOTE** AT TOURIST ➲ **COLLOCATIONS** AT TRAVEL ▶ **sight·see** *verb* [I] (only used in the progressive tenses 仅用于进行时) **sight·seer** *noun* **SYN** **tourist**：*Oxford attracts large numbers of sightseers.* 牛津吸引着大量观光客。

S

sigma /ˈsɪɡmə/ *noun* the 18th letter of the Greek alphabet (Σ, σ) 希腊字母表的第 18 个字母

sign /saɪn/ *noun, verb*

■ ***noun***

• **SHOWING STH** 显示 **1** [C, U] an event, an action, a fact, etc. that shows that sth exists, is happening or may happen in the future 迹象；征兆；预兆 **SYN** **indication**：~ (**of sth/sb**) *Headaches may be a sign of stress.* 头痛可能是紧张的迹象。◇ *There is no sign of John anywhere.* 哪儿都没有约翰的影子。◇ *Call the police at the first sign of trouble.* 一有闹事的苗头就叫警察。◇ *There was no* ***sign of life*** *in the house* (= there seemed to be nobody there). 那座房子没有一点住人的迹象。◇ *Her work is* ***showing some signs of*** *improvement.* 她的工作出现了一些改进的迹象。◇ ~ (**of doing sth**) *The gloomy weather* ***shows no sign of*** *improving.* 阴沉的天气没有丝毫转晴的迹象。◇ *The fact that he didn't say 'no' immediately is a* ***good sign****.* 他没有马上拒绝，这是好征兆。◇ ~ (**that...**) *If an interview is too easy, it's* ***a sure sign that*** *you haven't got the job.* 如果面试太简单，那必定表示你没得到那份工作。◇ *If I had noticed the* ***warning signs****, none of this would have happened.* 要是我当时注意到了那些危险苗头，这种事就一桩也不会发生。

• **FOR INFORMATION/WARNING** 提供信息；用以提醒 **2** [C] a piece of paper, wood or metal that has writing or a picture on it that gives you information, instructions, a warning, etc. 招牌；标牌；指示牌；标志：*a* ***road/traffic sign*** 道路 / 交通标志 ◇ *a* ***shop/pub sign*** 商店 / 酒吧招牌 ◇ *The sign on the wall said 'Now wash your hands'.* 墙上的牌子上写着"请洗手"。◇ ***Follow the signs*** *for the city centre.* 照标牌的指示到市中心。

• **MOVEMENT/SOUND** 动作；声音 **3** [C] a movement or sound that you make to tell sb sth 示意的动作（或声音）；手势：*He* ***gave a thumbs-up sign****.* 他竖起了大拇指表示赞同。◇ *She nodded as a sign for us to sit down.* 她点头示意我们坐下。➲ SEE ALSO V-SIGN

• **SYMBOL** 符号 **4** [C] a mark used to represent sth, especially in mathematics 符号；记号：*a plus/minus sign* (= +/–) 加号；减号 ◇ *a dollar/pound sign* (= $/£) 美元 / 英镑的符号

• **STAR SIGN** 星座 **5** [C] (*informal*) = STAR SIGN：*What sign are you?* 你是什么星座？

IDM **a ˌsign of the ˈtimes** something that you feel shows what things are like now, especially how bad they are 时代特征（含贬义）

■ ***verb***

• **YOUR NAME** 姓名 **1** [I, T] to write your name on a

▼ **SYNONYMS** 同义词辨析

sign

indication • symptom • symbol • indicator • signal

These are all words for an event, action or fact that shows that sth exists, is happening or may happen in the future. 以上各词均指迹象、征兆、预兆。

sign an event, action or fact that shows that sth exists, is happening or may happen in the future 指迹象、征兆、预兆：*Headaches may be a sign of stress.* 头痛可能是紧张的迹象。

indication (*rather formal*) a remark or sign that shows that sth is happening or what sb is thinking or feeling 指标示、象征：*They gave no* ***indication as to*** *how the work should be done.* 他们根本没说明这项工作该怎样做。

SIGN OR INDICATION? 用 sign 还是 indication?

An **indication** often comes in the form of sth that sb says; a **sign** is usually sth that happens or sth that sb does.
* indication 常指通过某人说的话表明，sign 通常为发生的事或某人所做的事。

symptom a change in your body or mind that shows that you are not healthy; a sign that sth exists, especially sth bad 指症状、征候、征兆：*Symptoms include a sore throat.* 症状包括嗓子疼。◇ *The rise in inflation was just one symptom of the poor state of the economy.* 通胀上升不过是经济不景气的一个征候。

symbol a person, object or event that represents a more general quality or situation 指象征：*The dove is a universal symbol of peace.* 鸽子普遍象征着和平。

indicator (*rather formal*) a sign that shows you what sth is like or how a situation is changing 指指示信号、标志、迹象：*the economic indicators* 经济指标

signal an event, action or fact that shows that sth exists, is happening or may happen in the future 指标志、预示、信号：*Chest pains can be a warning signal of heart problems.* 胸部疼痛可能是心脏病的报警信号。

SIGN OR SIGNAL? 用 sign 还是 signal?

Signal is often used to talk about an event, action or fact that suggests to sb that they should do sth. **Sign** is not usually used in this way. * signal 常用以指应该采取行动的暗号、信号；sign 通常不用于此义：~~*Reducing prison sentences would send the wrong signs to criminals.*~~

PATTERNS

- a(n) sign/indication/symptom/symbol/indicator/signal **of** sth
- a(n) sign/indication/symptom/indicator/signal **that**...
- a **clear** sign/indication/symptom/symbol/indicator/signal
- an **obvious** sign/indication/symptom/symbol/indicator
- an **early** sign/indication/symptom/indicator/signal
- an **outward** sign/indication/symbol
- **to give** a(n) sign/indication/signal

document, letter, etc. to show that you have written it, that you agree with what it says, or that it is genuine 签（名）；署（名）；签字；签署：*Sign here, please.* 请在这里签名。◇ **~ sth** *Sign your name here, please.* 请在这里签名。◇ *You haven't signed the letter.* 这封信您还没有署名。◇ *to sign a cheque* 在支票上签字 ◇ *The treaty was signed on 24 March.* 条约是3月24日签订的。◇ *The player was signing autographs for a group of fans.* 这名队员正在为一群球迷签名。◇ **~ yourself + noun** *He signed himself 'Jimmy'.* 他署名"吉米"。

• **CONTRACT** 合同 **2** [T, I] to arrange for sb, for example a sports player or musician, to sign a contract agreeing to work for your company; to sign a contract agreeing to work for a company 和…签约（达成雇佣关系）：**~ sb** *United have just signed a new goalie.* 联队最近和一名新守门员签约。◇ **~ for sth** *He signed for United yesterday.* 昨天他和联队签了约。◇ **~ with sth** *The band signed with Virgin Records.* 乐队同维京唱片公司签了约。

• **MAKE MOVEMENT/SOUND** 做出动作；发出声音 **3** [I, T] **~ (to/for sb) (to do sth)** | **~ that...** to make a request or tell sb to do sth by using a sign, especially a hand movement 示意；打手势 **SYN** **signal**: *The hotel manager signed to the porter to pick up my case.* 旅馆经理示意行李员替我拿箱子。

• **FOR DEAF PERSON** 对聋人 **4** [I, T] to use sign language to communicate with sb 打手语：*She learnt to sign to help her deaf child.* 为帮助她耳聋的孩子，她学会了手语。◇ **~ sth** *An increasing number of plays are now being signed.* 现在越来越多的戏剧配上了手语。▶ **sign·er** *noun*：*the signers of the petition* 在请愿书上签名的人 ◇ *signers communicating information to deaf people* 向聋人传递信息的手语译员

IDM **ˌsigned and ˈsealed** | **ˌsigned, ˌsealed and deˈlivered** definite, because all the legal documents have been signed 签名盖章完毕的；铁定的；成定局的 ➲ MORE LIKE THIS 13, page R26 **sign on the dotted ˈline** (*informal*) to sign a document to show that you have agreed to buy sth or do sth 在签字处签上姓名（表示同意）；签名同意：*Just sign on the dotted line and the car is yours.* 只要在虚线上签名，这车就归你了。➲ MORE AT PLEDGE *n.*

PHR V **ˌsign sth↔aˈway** to lose your rights or property by signing a document 签字放弃，签字让与（权利或财产）**ˈsign for sth** to sign a document to show that you have received sth 签收 **ˌsign ˈin/ˈout** | **ˌsign sb↔ˈin/ˈout** to write your/sb's name when you arrive at or leave an office, a club, etc. 签到/签退；替某人签到/签退：*All visitors must sign in on arrival.* 来客均须签到。◇ *You must sign guests out when they leave the club.* 客人离开俱乐部时，你必须为他们签退。**ˌsign ˈoff 1** (*BrE*) to end a letter 结束写信 **SYN** **finish**: *She signed off with 'Yours, Janet'.* 她在信末写上"你的珍妮特"。**2** to end a broadcast by saying goodbye or playing a piece of music（以说再见或播放音乐的形式）结束广播 **ˌsign sth↔ˈoff** to give your formal approval to sth, by signing your name 签字认可；签名赞同 **ˌsign ˈoff on sth** (*NAmE, informal*) to express your approval of sth formally and definitely 批准：*The President hasn't signed off on this report.* 这份报告总统尚未批准。**ˌsign ˈon** (*BrE, informal*) to sign a form stating that you are an unemployed person so that you can receive payment from the government 办理失业登记（以领取失业救济金）**ˌsign ˈon/ˈup** | **ˌsign sb↔ˈon/ˈup** to sign a form or contract which says that you agree to do a job or become a soldier; to persuade sb to sign a form or contract like this（使）签约受雇（或入伍）**SYN** **enlist**: *He signed on for five years in the army.* 他签了在部队服役五年的合同。◇ *The company has signed up three top models for the fashion show.* 为时装表演，公司签约聘了三名顶尖模特儿。**ˌsign sth↔ˈover (to sb)** to give your rights or property to sb else by signing a document 签字转让（权利或财产）：*She has signed the house over to her daughter.* 她签署了转让手续，把房子过到女儿名下。**ˌsign ˈup (for sth)** to arrange to do a course of study by adding your name to the list of people doing it 报名（参加课程）**ˌsign ˈup to sth 1** (*BrE*) to commit yourself to a project or course of action, especially one that you have agreed with a group of other people, countries or organizations 签署同意；签订：*How many countries have signed up to the Kyoto protocol on climate change?* 有多少个国家签订了关于气候变化的《京都议定书》？ **2** **sign up to do sth** to agree to take part in sth 同意参与：*We have about 100 people signed up to help so far.* 到目前为止我们有大约100人同意提供帮助。

sign·age /ˈsaɪnɪdʒ/ *noun* [U] (*specialist*) signs, especially ones that give instructions or directions to the public（统称）标志，标识，标记

sig·nal 🔑 /ˈsɪɡnəl/ *noun, verb, adj.*

■ ***noun*** **1** 🔑 a movement or sound that you make to give sb information, instructions, a warning, etc. 信号；暗号 **SYN** **sign**: *a **danger/warning/distress, etc. signal*** 危险、警告、求救等信号 ◇ *At an agreed signal they left the room.* 收到约定的信号后，他们离开了房间。◇ *The siren was a signal for everyone to leave the building.* 警报器一响，就是要所有人离开大楼。◇ *When I **give the signal**, run!* 我一发信号，你就跑！◇ (*NAmE*) *All I get is a **busy signal** when I dial his number* (= his phone is being used). 我什么时候拨他的电话听到的都是忙音。◇ ***hand signals*** (= movements that CYCLISTS and drivers make with their hands to tell other people that they are going to stop, turn, etc.)（骑车人和驾车人的）示意手势 ➲ SEE ALSO TURN SIGNAL **2** 🔑 an event, an action, a fact, etc. that shows that sth exists or is likely to happen 标志；预示；信号 **SYN** **indication**: *The rise in inflation is a **clear signal** that the government's policies are not working.* 通货膨胀率的上升清楚地表明，政府的政策不起作用。◇ *Chest pains can be a **warning signal** of heart problems.* 胸部疼痛可能是心脏病的先兆。◇ *Reducing prison sentences would **send the wrong signals** to criminals.* 减刑会向犯罪分子发出错误的信号。➲ SYNONYMS AT SIGN **3** 🔑 a piece of equipment that uses different coloured lights to tell drivers to go slower, stop, etc., used especially on railways/railroads and roads（尤指铁路和公路上的）指示灯，信号灯，红绿灯：*traffic signals* 交通信号灯 ◇ *a stop signal* 停车信号 **4** 🔑 a series of electrical waves that carry sounds, pictures or messages, for example to a radio, television or mobile/cell phone（传输声音、图像或其他信息的电波）信号：*TV signals* 电视信号 ◇ *a high-frequency signal* 高频信号 ◇ *a radar signal* 雷达信号 ◇ *to **detect/pick up signals*** 探测到/收到信号 ◇ *to **emit a signal*** 发射信号 ◇ *I couldn't **get a signal** on my cell phone.* 我的手机接收不到信号了。

■ ***verb*** (**-ll-**, *US* **-l-**) **1** 🔑 [I, T] to make a movement or sound to give sb a message, an order, etc. 发信号；发暗号；示意：*Don't fire until I signal.* 等我发出信号后再开枪。◇ *Did you signal before you turned right?* 右转弯前你示意了吗？◇ **~ (to sb) (for sth)** *He signalled to the waiter for the bill.* 他示意服务员结账。◇ **~ to/for sb to do sth** *He signalled to us to join him.* 他示意要我们去他那儿。◇ **~ sb to do sth** *She signalled him to follow.* 她示意他跟她走。◇ **~ sth** *The referee signalled a foul.* 裁判鸣哨示意犯规。◇ **~ (that)...** *She signalled (that) it was time to leave.* 她示意该走了。◇ **~ which, what, etc....** *You must signal which way you are going to turn.* 你要朝哪个方向转，必须发出信号。**2** [T] **~ sth** to be a sign that sth exists or is likely to happen 标志；表明；预示 **SYN** **indicate**: *This announcement signalled a clear change of policy.* 这个声明显示政策有明显的改变。◇ *The scandal surely signals the end of his political career.* 毫无疑问，这桩丑闻预示他的政治生涯就此结束。**3** [T] to do sth to make your feelings or opinions known 表达；表示；显示：**~ sth** *He signalled his discontent by refusing to vote.* 他拒绝投票以示不满。◇ **~ (that)...** *She has signalled (that) she is willing to stand as a candidate.* 她表示愿意作为候选人参加竞选。➲ MORE LIKE THIS 36, page R29

■ ***adj.*** [only before noun] (*formal*) important and noticeable 重大的；显要的：*a signal honour* 极大的荣誉 ▶ **sig·nal·ly** /-nəli/ *adv.*：*They have signally failed to keep their election promises.* 他们显然没有履行自己的竞选承诺。

ˈsignal box *noun* (*BrE*) a building beside a railway/railroad from which rail signals are operated（铁路上的）信号房

sig·nal·ler (*US* **sig·nal·er**) /ˈsɪɡnələ(r)/ *noun* = SIGNALMAN

S

sig·nal·man /ˈsɪɡnəlmən/ *noun* (*pl.* **-men** /-mən/) (*also* **sig·nal·ler**) **1** a person whose job is operating signals on a railway（铁路上的）信号员，信号工 **2** a person trained to give and receive signals in the army or navy（军队的）信号兵，通信兵

ˌ**signal-to-ˈnoise ratio** *noun* **1** (*specialist*) the strength of an electronic signal that you want to receive, compared to the strength of the signals that you do not want 信噪比；信号噪声比 **2** a measure of how much useful information you receive, compared to information which is not useful 讯息对杂讯比；讯杂比

sig·na·tory /ˈsɪɡnətri; *NAmE* -tɔːri/ *noun* (*pl.* **-ies**) ~ (**to/of sth**) (*formal*) a person, a country or an organization that has signed an official agreement（协议的）签署者，签署方，签署国：*a signatory of the Declaration of Independence*《独立宣言》的签署者 ◇ *Many countries are signatories to/of the Berne Convention.* 很多国家都是《伯尔尼公约》的签署国。

sig·na·ture /ˈsɪɡnətʃə(r)/ *noun* **1** [C] your name as you usually write it, for example at the end of a letter 签名；署名：*Someone had forged her signature on the cheque.* 有人在支票上伪造了她的签名。◇ *They collected 10 000 signatures for their petition.* 他们在请愿书上征集了1万人的签名。◇ *He was attacked for having* ***put his signature to*** *the deal.* 他因在协议上签了字而受到攻击。**2** [U] (*formal*) the act of signing sth 签名；署名；签字；签署：*Two copies of the contract will be sent to you for signature.* 合同一式两份，将送交您签署。**3** [C, usually sing.] a particular quality that makes sth different from other similar things and makes it easy to recognize 明显特征；鲜明特色；识别标志：*Bright colours are his signature.* 他总爱用亮丽的色彩。➲ SEE ALSO DIGITAL SIGNATURE, KEY SIGNATURE, TIME SIGNATURE

ˈ**signature tune** *noun* (*BrE*) a short tune played at the beginning and end of a particular television or radio programme, or one that is connected with a particular performer（电视、广播节目的或某主持人主持节目时播放的）信号曲，开始曲，结束曲 ➲ COMPARE THEME MUSIC

sign·board /ˈsaɪnbɔːd; *NAmE* -bɔːrd/ *noun* a piece of wood that has some information on it, such as a name, and is displayed outside a shop/store, hotel, etc.（商店、旅馆等的）招牌，告示牌，广告牌

sig·net ring /ˈsɪɡnət rɪŋ/ *noun* a ring with a design cut into it, that you wear on your finger 图章戒指 ➲ VISUAL VOCAB PAGE V70

sig·nifi·cance AW /sɪɡˈnɪfɪkəns/ *noun* [U, C] **1** the importance of sth, especially when this has an effect on what happens in the future（尤指对将来有影响的）重要性，意义：*a decision of major political significance* 具有重大政治意义的决定 ◇ *The new drug has great significance for the treatment of the disease.* 这种新药对于这种病的治疗有重大的意义。◇ *They discussed the* ***statistical significance*** *of the results.* 他们讨论了这些结果在统计学上的意义。**2** the meaning of sth 意思；含义：*She couldn't grasp the full significance of what he had said.* 她未能充分领会他那番话的意思。◇ *Do these symbols have any particular significance?* 这些符号有什么特别的含义吗？ ➲ COMPARE INSIGNIFICANCE at INSIGNIFICANT

sig·nifi·cant AW /sɪɡˈnɪfɪkənt/ *adj.* **1** large or important enough to have an effect or to be noticed 有重大意义的；显著的：*a highly significant discovery* 有重大意义的发现 ◇ *The results of the experiment are not* ***statistically significant.*** 从统计学的观点看，实验结果意义不明显。◇ *There are no significant differences between the two groups of students.* 这两组学生没有明显差别。◇ *Your work has shown a significant improvement.* 你的工作有了显著改进。◇ ***It is significant that*** *girls generally do better in examinations than boys.* 很明显，女生的考试成绩一般比男生的好。➲ COMPARE INSIGNIFICANT **2** having a particular meaning 有某种意义的：*It is significant that he changed his will only days before his death.* 他在临终前几天修改遗嘱，这很能说明问题。**3** [usually before noun] having a special or secret meaning that is not understood by everyone 别有含义的；意味深长的 SYN **meaningful**：*a* ***significant look/smile*** 意味深长的眼神/微笑

sig·nifi·cant·ly AW /sɪɡˈnɪfɪkəntli/ *adv.* **1** in a way that is large or important enough to have an effect on sth or to be noticed 有重大意义地；显著地；明显地：*The two sets of figures are not significantly different.* 这两组数字没有明显的差别。◇ *Profits have increased significantly over the past few years.* 几年来，利润大幅度提高了。**2** in a way that has a particular meaning 有某种意义：*Significantly, he did not deny that there might be an election.* 值得注意的是，他没有否认可能举行选举。**3** in a way that has a special or secret meaning 别有含义地；意味深长地：*She paused significantly before she answered.* 她在回答之前意味深长地停顿了一下。

sigˌnificant ˈother *noun* (*often humorous*) your husband, wife, partner or sb that you have a special relationship with 有特殊关系的那一位（如配偶、情人、恋人）

sig·ni·fi·ca·tion /ˌsɪɡnɪfɪˈkeɪʃn/ *noun* (*formal* or *linguistics* 语言) [U, C] the exact meaning of sth, especially a word or phrase（尤指词或短语的）含义，意思，意义

sig·ni·fied /ˈsɪɡnɪfaɪd/ *noun* (*linguistics* 语言) the meaning expressed by a LINGUISTIC sign, rather than its form 所指（语言符号的意义）➲ COMPARE SIGNIFIER

sig·ni·fier /ˈsɪɡnɪfaɪə(r)/ *noun* (*linguistics* 语言) the form of a LINGUISTIC sign, for example its sound or its printed form, rather than the meaning it expresses 能指（语言符号的形式）➲ COMPARE SIGNIFIED

sig·nify AW /ˈsɪɡnɪfaɪ/ *verb* (**sig·ni·fies**, **sig·ni·fy·ing**, **sig·ni·fied**, **sig·ni·fied**) (*formal*) **1** [T] to be a sign of sth 表示；说明；预示 SYN **mean**：~ **sth** *This decision signified a radical change in their policies.* 这个决定表明了他们的政策发生了根本的变化。◇ ~ **that…** *This mark signifies that the products conform to an approved standard.* 这个标志说明这些产品符合指定的标准。◇ *The white belt signifies that he's an absolute beginner.* 白腰带表示他完全是个新手。**2** [T] to do sth to make your feelings, intentions, etc. known 表达，表示，显示（感情、意愿等）：~ **sth** *She signified her approval with a smile.* 她笑了笑表示赞同。◇ ~ **that…** *He nodded to signify that he agreed.* 他点头表示同意。**3** [I] (usually used in questions or negative sentences 通常用于疑问句或否定句) to be important or to matter 具有重要性；要紧：*His presence no longer signified.* 他在不在场已不重要。

sign·ing /ˈsaɪnɪŋ/ *noun* **1** [U] the act of writing your name at the end of an official document to show that you accept it 签署；签字：*the signing of the Treaty of Rome*《罗马条约》的签署 **2** [C] (*BrE*) a person who has just signed a contract to join a particular sports team or record or film company（运动队、唱片公司或电影公司的）签约受聘者，签约受雇者 **3** [U] the act of making an official contract that arranges for sb to join a sports team or a record or film company 签约聘用，签约雇用（安排某人加入运动队、唱片公司或电影公司）**4** [U] the act of using sign language 手势语的使用：*the use of signing in classrooms* 手势语在课堂上的使用

ˈ**sign language** *noun* [U, C] a system of communicating with people who cannot hear, by using hand movements rather than spoken words 手势语

sign·post /ˈsaɪnpəʊst; *NAmE* -poʊst/ *noun, verb*

■ ***noun*** a sign at the side of a road giving information about the direction and distance of places 路标：*Follow the signposts to the superstore.* 跟着路标走就能到超市。◇ (*figurative*) *The chapter headings are useful signposts to the content of the book.* 章节标题有助于了解书的内容。➲ WORDFINDER NOTE AT ROAD ➲ VISUAL VOCAB PAGE V3

■ ***verb*** (*BrE*) **1** [usually passive] ~ **sth** to mark a road, place, etc. with signposts 设置路标：*The route is well signposted.* 这条路线路标设置完善。**2** ~ **sth** to show clearly the way that an argument, a speech, etc. will develop 介绍（论证、讲话等的）要点：*You need to signpost for the reader*

S

the various points you are going to make. 你需要向读者介绍你将阐述的各个论点。▶ **sign·post·ing** *noun* [U]

sign·writer /ˈsaɪnraɪtə(r)/ (*also* **ˈsign painter**) *noun* a person who paints signs and advertisements for shops/stores and businesses 画招牌者；画广告者 ▶ **ˈsign·writ·ing** *noun* [U]

Sikh /siːk/ *noun* a member of a religion (called **Sikhism**) that developed in Punjab in the late 15th century and is based on a belief that there is only one God 锡克教教徒（锡克教在 15 世纪晚期产生于旁遮普地区，相信一神论）▶ **Sikh** *adj.*

sil·age /ˈsaɪlɪdʒ/ *noun* [U] grass or other green crops that are stored without being dried and are used to feed farm animals in winter 青贮饲料

si·lence /ˈsaɪləns/ *noun, verb, exclamation*
■ *noun* **1** [U] a complete lack of noise or sound 寂静；无声 SYN **quiet**: *Their footsteps echoed in the silence.* 他们的脚步声在一片寂静中回荡着。◇ *A scream broke the silence of the night.* 一声尖叫划破了寂静的夜晚。◇ *I need **absolute silence** when I'm working.* 我工作时需要绝对的安静。 **2** [C, U] a situation when nobody is speaking 沉默；缄默；默不作声：*an **embarrassed/awkward silence*** 难堪 / 尴尬的沉默 ◇ *a moment's stunned silence* 一时惊愕得说不出话来 ◇ *I got used to his long silences.* 我已习惯了他半天不说话的样子。◇ *They finished their meal **in total silence**.* 他们默不作声地吃完饭。◇ *She lapsed into silence again.* 她又沉默下来。◇ *There was a **deafening silence*** (= one that is very noticeable). 四下里静得刺耳。◇ *a two-minute silence in honour of those who had died* 为死去的人默哀两分钟 **3** [U, sing.] a situation in which sb refuses to talk about sth or to answer questions 缄默；缄口不谈；拒绝回答：*She **broke her public silence** in a TV interview.* 她接受了一次电视采访，就此结束了她不在公开场合说话的状态。◇ ~ (**on sth**) *The company's silence on the subject has been taken as an admission of guilt.* 公司在这个问题上保持沉默被当作是承认有罪。◇ *the **right to silence*** (= the legal right not to say anything when you are arrested) 沉默权 ◇ *There is **a conspiracy of silence** about what is happening* (= everyone has agreed not to discuss it). 对于发生的事情，大家一致保持缄默。**4** [U] a situation in which people do not communicate with each other by letter or telephone 互相不通音信的情形；无书信（或电话）联系：*The phone call came after months of silence.* 几个月没有音信之后，打来了一个电话。
IDM **ˌsilence is ˈgolden** (*saying*) it is often best not to say anything 沉默是金 ➔ MORE AT HEAVY *adj.*, PREGNANT
■ *verb* **1** ~ **sb/sth** to make sb/sth stop speaking or making a noise 使安静；使不说话：*She silenced him with a glare.* 她瞪了他一眼，他就不作声了。◇ *Our bombs silenced the enemy's guns* (= they destroyed them). 我们的轰炸把敌人的炮火打哑了。**2** ~ **sb/sth** to make sb stop expressing opinions that are opposed to yours 压制，使不再发表（反对意见）：*All protest had been silenced.* 一切反对的声音都被压了下去。◇ *Her recent achievements have silenced her critics.* 她近来取得的成果让那些批评她的人无话可说了。
■ *exclamation* (*formal*) used to tell people to be quiet（用以让人们安静）安静，静下来：*Silence in court!* 法庭内保持肃静！

si·len·cer /ˈsaɪlənsə(r)/ *noun* **1** (*BrE*) (*NAmE* **muf·fler**) a device that is fixed to the EXHAUST of a vehicle in order to reduce the amount of noise that the engine makes（发动机的）消声器 ➔ VISUAL VOCAB PAGE V55 **2** a device that is fixed to the end of a gun in order to reduce the amount of noise that it makes when it is fired（枪支的）消音器

si·lent /ˈsaɪlənt/ *adj.* **1** (of a person 人) not speaking 不说话的；沉默的：*to **remain/stay/keep silent*** 保持沉默 ◇ *They huddled together in silent groups.* 他们一群群地围在一起，默不作声。◇ *As the curtain rose, the audience **fell silent**.* 幕启时，观众安静下来。◇ *He gave me **the silent treatment*** (= did not speak to me because he was angry). 他对我不予理睬。**2** [only before noun] (especially of a man 尤指男人) not talking very much 很少说话的；不爱说话的；少言寡语的 SYN **quiet**: *He's the **strong silent** type.* 他是那种强悍而沉默寡言的人。 **3** where there is little or no sound; making little or no sound 无声的；安静的；不喧闹的 SYN **quiet**: *At last the traffic **fell silent**.* 车辆的喧嚣终于消逝了。◇ *The streets were silent and deserted.* 大街小巷寂无一人。**4** [only before noun] not expressed with words or sound 不用言语表达的；无声的：*a **silent prayer/protest*** 默祷；无声的抗议 ◇ *They nodded in **silent agreement**.* 他们默默地点头表示同意。**5** ~ (**on/about sth**) not giving information about sth; refusing to speak about sth 不提供情况的；未谈及的；拒绝讲的：*The report is strangely silent on this issue.* 很奇怪，报告对这个问题避而不谈。◇ *the right to **remain silent*** (= the legal right not to say anything when you are arrested) 沉默权 **6** [only before noun] (of old films/movies 过去的电影) with pictures but no sound 无声的；无声电影的：*a **silent film/movie*** 无声电影 ◇ *stars of the **silent screen*** 无声电影时代的明星 **7** (of a letter in a word 单词中的字母) written but not pronounced 不发音的：*The 'b' in 'lamb' is silent.* * lamb 中的 b 不发音。

si·lent·ly /ˈsaɪləntli/ *adv.* **1** without speaking 默默地；不说话地：*They marched silently through the streets.* 队伍无声地穿过街道。**2** without making any or much sound 悄悄地；静静地 SYN **quietly**: *She crept silently out of the room.* 她悄悄溜出房间。**3** without using words or sounds to express sth 无声地；默默地；不用言语表达地：*She prayed silently.* 她默默地祷告。◇ *He silently agreed with much of what she had said.* 对于她所讲的，有很多他暗自赞同。
IDM **sit/stand ˌsilently ˈby** to do or say nothing to help sb or deal with a difficult situation 袖手旁观；坐视

the ˌsilent maˈjority *noun* [sing.+sing./pl. v.] the large number of people in a country who think the same as each other, but do not express their views publicly 沉默的大多数（不公开表达自己意见的广大民众）

ˌsilent ˈpartner (*NAmE*) (*BrE* **ˌsleeping ˈpartner**) *noun* a person who has put money into a business company but who is not actually involved in running it 隐名合伙人，隐名股东（在企业中有股份但不参与经营）

sil·hou·ette /ˌsɪluˈet/ *noun, verb*
■ *noun* **1** [C, U] the dark outline or shape of a person or an object that you see against a light background（浅色背景衬托出的）暗色轮廓：*the silhouette of chimneys and towers* 烟囱和塔楼的轮廓 ◇ *The mountains stood out **in silhouette**.* 群山的轮廓衬托了出来。**2** [C] the shape of a person's body or of an object（人的）体形；（事物的）形状：*The dress is fitted to give you a flattering silhouette.* 穿这件连衣裙，你显得更有身段了。**3** [C] a picture that shows sb/sth as a black shape against a light background, especially one that shows the side view of a person's face 剪影；（尤指人脸的）侧影
■ *verb* [usually passive] ~ **sb/sth** (**against sth**) to make sth appear as a silhouette 使呈现暗色轮廓：*A figure stood in the doorway, silhouetted against the light.* 门口站着一个人，屋里的亮光映衬出他的轮廓。

sil·ica /ˈsɪlɪkə/ *noun* [U] (*symb.* SiO_2) a chemical containing silicon found in sand and in rocks such as QUARTZ, used in making glass and CEMENT 二氧化硅

ˈsilica gel *noun* [U] a substance made from silica in the form of grains, which keeps things dry by absorbing water 硅胶（颗粒状干燥剂）

sili·cate /ˈsɪlɪkeɪt/ *noun* [C, U] **1** (*chemistry* 化) any COMPOUND containing SILICON and OXYGEN 硅酸盐：*aluminium silicate* 硅酸铝 **2** a mineral that contains silica. There are many different silicates and they form a large part of the earth's CRUST. 硅酸盐矿物

sil·icon /ˈsɪlɪkən/ *noun* [U] (*symb.* **Si**) a chemical element. Silicon exists as a grey solid or as a brown powder and is found in rocks and sand. It is used in making glass and TRANSISTORS. 硅

ˌsilicon ˈchip *noun* a very small piece of silicon used to carry a complicated electronic CIRCUIT 硅片

S

sili·cone /ˈsɪlɪkəʊn; *NAmE* -koʊn/ *noun* [U] a chemical containing silicon. There are several different types of silicone, used to make paint, artificial rubber, VARNISH, etc. 硅酮；聚硅氧烷：*a silicone breast implant* 硅酮乳房假体

ˌSilicon ˈValley *noun* [U] the area in California where there are many companies connected with the computer and ELECTRONICS industries, sometimes used to refer to any area where there are a lot of computer companies 硅谷（美国加利福尼亚州一处计算机和电子公司聚集地，有时用以指任何计算机公司聚集地） ➲ MORE LIKE THIS 19, page R27

sili·cosis /ˌsɪlɪˈkəʊsɪs; *NAmE* -ˈkoʊ-/ *noun* [U] (*medical* 医) a serious lung disease caused by breathing in dust containing SILICA 硅沉着病，硅肺病，硅肺（长期吸入二氧化硅造成的肺部疾病）

silk /sɪlk/ *noun* **1** [U] fine soft thread produced by SILKWORMS （蚕）丝 **2** [U] a type of fine smooth cloth made from silk thread 丝织物；丝绸：*a silk blouse* 女式丝绸衬衫 ◊ *silk stockings* 长筒丝袜 ◊ *made of pure silk* 纯丝做的 ◊ *Her skin was **as smooth as silk**.* 她的皮肤像丝绸一样光滑。➲ SEE ALSO WATERED SILK **3** [U] silk thread used for sewing（用于缝纫的）丝线 **4 silks** [pl.] clothes made of silk, especially the coloured shirts worn by people riding horses in a race (= JOCKEYS) 丝绸衣服（尤指骑师在赛马时穿的彩色赛马衫） **5** [C] (*BrE, law* 律) a type of lawyer who represents the government (= a KING'S COUNSEL/QUEEN'S COUNSEL) 皇家大律师；王室法律顾问：*to take silk* (= to become this type of lawyer) 担任皇家大律师
IDM **make a silk ˌpurse out of a sow's ˈear** to succeed in making sth good out of material that does not seem very good at all 用劣材制精品；化腐朽为神奇

silk·en /ˈsɪlkən/ *adj.* (*literary*) **1** [usually before noun] soft, smooth and shiny like silk 丝绸一样的；柔软光洁的：*silken hair* 柔软光滑的头发 **2** [usually before noun] smooth and gentle 柔和的；温和的；轻柔的：*her silken voice* 她那柔和的嗓音 **3** [only before noun] made of silk 丝制的；丝质的；丝绸的：*silken ribbons* 丝带

silkie /ˈsɪlki/ *noun* = SELKIE

ˈsilk screen *noun* **1** [U] a method of printing in which ink is forced through a design cut in a piece of fine cloth 丝网印刷：*silk-screen prints* 丝网印刷的图案 **2** [C] a picture, etc. produced by this method 丝网印刷画；丝网印刷品：*Warhol's silk screen of Marilyn Monroe* 沃霍尔所作的玛丽莲·梦露丝网印刷画 ▸ **ˈsilk-screen** *verb* ~ sth

silk·worm /ˈsɪlkwɜːm; *NAmE* -wɜːrm/ *noun* a CATERPILLAR (= a small creature like a WORM with legs) that produces silk thread 蚕

silky /ˈsɪlki/ *adj.* (**silk·ier, silki·est**) **1** soft, smooth and shiny like silk 丝绸一样的；柔软光洁的：*silky fur* 像丝绸一样的毛皮 **2** [usually before noun] smooth and gentle 柔和的；温和的；轻柔的：*He spoke in a silky tone.* 他说话柔声细语的。**3** made of silk or cloth that looks like silk 丝（或像丝的织物）制的；丝绸（或像丝绸的织物）的：*a silky dress* 丝质连衣裙 ▸ **silk·ily** *adv.*：*'How have I changed?' he asked silkily.* "我变得怎么样了？"他柔声问道。 **silki·ness** *noun* [U] **silky** *adv.*：*The leaves are grey and silky smooth.* 叶子呈灰色，平整光洁。

sill /sɪl/ *noun* **1** = WINDOWSILL **2** a piece of metal that forms part of the frame of a vehicle below the doors （车体的）门槛

silly /ˈsɪli/ *adj., noun*
■ *adj.* (**sil·lier, sil·li·est**) **1** showing a lack of thought, understanding or judgement 愚蠢的；不明事理的；没头脑的；傻的 SYN **foolish**：*a silly idea* 愚蠢的想法 ◊ *That was **a silly thing to do**!* 那事做得蠢！◊ *Her work is full of silly mistakes.* 她满篇都是愚蠢的错误。◊ *'I can walk home.' 'Don't be silly—it's much too far!'* "我可以走回家去。""别犯傻了，远得很哪！"◊ *You silly boy!* 你这傻小子！**2** stupid or embarrassing, especially in a way that is more typical of a child than an adult（尤指像小孩一样）可笑的，荒唐的，冒傻气的 SYN **ridiculous**：*a silly sense of humour* 可笑的幽默感 ◊ *a silly game* 可笑的游戏 ◊ *I feel silly in these clothes.* 穿上这些衣服，我觉得很可笑。◊ *She had a silly grin on her face.* 她一脸憨笑。◊ (*especially BrE*) *I got it for a silly price* (= very cheap). 我买它差不多没花钱。**3** not practical or serious 不实用的；闹着玩的：*We had to wear these silly little hats.* 我们不得不戴这些傻里傻气的小帽子。◊ *Why worry about a silly thing like that?* 干吗为那种无谓的事发愁啊？ ▸ **sil·li·ness** *noun* [U]
IDM **ˌdrink, ˌlaugh, ˌshout, etc. yourself ˈsilly** (*informal*) to drink, laugh, shout, etc. so much that you cannot behave in a sensible way 喝（或笑、叫等）得傻里傻气的 **play ˈsilly buggers** (*BrE, informal*) to behave in a stupid and annoying way 胡闹；顽皮；做怪样子 ➲ MORE AT GAME *n.*
■ *noun* (*BrE also* **ˌsilly ˈbilly**) [sing.] (*informal*) often used when speaking to children to say that they are not behaving in a sensible way（常用于向孩子指出其愚蠢行为）傻孩子，淘气鬼：*No, silly, those aren't your shoes!* 不对，傻孩子，那不是你的鞋！

the ˈsilly season *noun* [sing.] (*BrE*) the time, usually in the summer, when newspapers are full of unimportant stories because there is little serious news 无聊季节（通常为夏季，因没有重大新闻，报上充斥着无聊内容）

silo /ˈsaɪləʊ; *NAmE* -loʊ/ *noun* (*pl.* **-os**) **1** a tall tower on a farm used for storing grain, etc. 筒仓 ➲ VISUAL VOCAB PAGE V3 **2** an underground place where nuclear weapons or dangerous substances are kept（核武器的）发射井；（危险物品的）地下贮藏库 **3** an underground place where SILAGE is made and stored 青贮窖 **4** a system, process, department, etc. that operates separately or is thought of as separate from others 独立运行的系统（或流程、部门等）：*Some departments have become silos and no longer communicate regularly with one another.* 一些部门已各自为政，不再定期相互沟通。◊ *In some countries, the economy and foreign policy are considered in separate silos.* 在一些国家，经济和外交政策被视为相互独立的范畴。

silt /sɪlt/ *noun, verb*
■ *noun* [U] sand, mud, etc. that is carried by flowing water and is left at the mouth of a river or in a HARBOUR（沉积在河口或港口的）泥沙，淤泥，粉砂 ▸ **silty** *adj.*：*silty soils* 粉砂土
■ *verb*
PHR V **ˌsilt sth↔ˈup** | **ˌsilt ˈup** to block sth with silt; to become blocked with silt（使）淤塞：*Sand has silted up the river delta.* 泥沙把这条河的三角洲淤塞了。◊ *The harbour has now silted up.* 港口现已淤塞。

sil·ver /ˈsɪlvə(r)/ *noun, adj., verb*
■ *noun* **1** [U] (*symb.* **Ag**) a chemical element. Silver is a greyish-white PRECIOUS METAL used for making coins, jewellery, decorative objects, etc. 银：*a silver chain* 银链 ◊ *made of **solid silver*** 纯银制造 ◊ *a silver mine* 银矿 **2** [U] coins that are made of silver or a metal that looks like silver 银币（银或似银金属制成的硬币）：*I need £2 in silver for the parking meter.* 我需要在停车收费器里投 2 英镑银币。**3** [U] dishes, decorative objects, etc. that are made of silver 银器：*They've had to sell the family silver to pay the bills.* 他们不得已卖掉家传的银器去支付账单。**4** [U] a shiny greyish-white colour 银色；银白色；银灰色 ➲ SEE ALSO SILVERY **5** [U, C] = SILVER MEDAL：*She won silver in last year's championships.* 她在去年的锦标赛上获得银牌。◊ *The team won two silvers and a bronze.* 这个运动队获得两枚银牌和一枚铜牌。
IDM **on a silver ˈplatter** if you are given sth **on a silver platter**, you do not have to do much to get it 无须费劲；唾手可得：*These rich kids expect to have it all handed to them on a silver platter.* 这些富家子弟指望一切都有人拱手送上。➲ MORE AT BORN *v.*, CLOUD *n.*, CROSS *v.*
■ *adj.* shiny greyish-white in colour 银色的；银白色的；银灰色的：*a silver car* 银灰色汽车 ◊ *silver hair* 银发 ➲ SEE ALSO SILVERY
■ *verb* **1** [usually passive] ~ **sth** to cover the surface of sth with a thin layer of silver or sth that looks like silver 给…镀（或包）银；给…镀（或包）似银的物质 **2** ~ **sth** (*especially literary*) to make sth become bright like silver

使具有银色光泽；使变成银色：*Moonlight was silvering the countryside.* 月光下的乡村泛着银光。

ˌsilver anniˈversary *noun* (*especially US*) **1** (*also* **ˌsilver ˈwedding anniversary** *BrE, NAmE*) (*BrE* **ˌsilver ˈwedding**) the 25th anniversary of a wedding 银婚（结婚 25 周年纪念） **2** (*BrE* **ˌsilver ˈjubilee**) the 25th anniversary of an important event; a celebration of sth that began 25 years ago * 25 周年；25 周年纪念

silver·back /ˈsɪlvəbæk; *NAmE* -vərb-/ *noun* a male adult GORILLA with white or silver hair across its back 银背大猩猩（背部有白色或银白色毛的雄性成年大猩猩）

ˌsilver ˈband *noun* (*BrE*) a BRASS BAND which uses silver-coloured instruments 银管乐队（使用银色乐器的铜管乐队）

ˌsilver ˈbirch *noun* [C, U] a tree with smooth, very pale grey or white BARK and thin branches, that grows in northern countries 欧洲桦；银桦

sil·ver·fish /ˈsɪlvəfɪʃ; *NAmE* -vərf-/ *noun* (*pl.* **sil·ver·fish**) a small silver insect without wings that lives in houses and that can cause damage to materials such as cloth and paper 蠹鱼，衣鱼（蛀食织物、纸张等的小虫）

ˌsilver ˈfoil *noun* [U] (*BrE*) = FOIL (1)

ˌsilver ˈjubilee (*BrE*) (*US* **ˌsilver anniˈversary**) *noun* [usually sing.] the 25th anniversary of an important event; a celebration of sth that began 25 years ago * 25 周年；25 周年纪念：*the silver jubilee of the Queen's accession* 女王登基 25 周年大庆 ◇ *The college celebrated its silver jubilee last year.* 这所学院去年举行了建院 25 周年庆祝活动。➲ COMPARE DIAMOND JUBILEE, GOLDEN JUBILEE

ˌsilver ˈmedal *noun* [C] (*also* **sil·ver** [U, C]) a MEDAL that is given to the person or the team that wins the second prize in a race or competition 银质奖章；银牌：*an Olympic silver medal winner* 获奥运会银牌的运动员 ➲ COMPARE BRONZE MEDAL, GOLD MEDAL ▸ **ˌsilver ˈmedallist** (*BrE*) (*NAmE* **ˌsilver ˈmedalist**) *noun*：*He's an Olympic silver medallist.* 他是奥运会银牌得主。

ˌsilver ˈpaper *noun* [U] (*BrE*) very thin, shiny sheets of ALUMINIUM/ALUMINUM that are used for wrapping chocolate, etc.（包巧克力等的）锡纸

ˌsilver ˈplate *noun* [U] metal that is covered with a thin layer of silver; objects that are made of this metal 镀（或包）银金属；镀（或包）银金属器皿 ▸ **ˌsilver-ˈplated** *adj.*

the ˌsilver ˈscreen *noun* [sing.] (*old-fashioned*) the film/movie industry 电影业

ˌsilver ˈservice *noun* [U] a style of serving food at formal meals in which the person serving uses a silver fork and spoon 银级服务（正式用餐时侍者用银叉和银勺上菜）

sil·ver·smith /ˈsɪlvəsmɪθ; *NAmE* -vərs-/ *noun* a person who makes, repairs or sells articles made of silver 银匠；银器商

ˌsilver ˈsurfer *noun* (*informal*) an old person who spends a lot of time using the Internet 银发网民（指经常上互联网的老年人）

sil·ver·tail /ˈsɪlvəteɪl; *NAmE* ˈsɪlvər-/ *noun* (*AustralE, informal*) a famous or socially important person 名人；要人；有社会地位的人

ˌsilver ˈtongue *noun* (*formal*) great skill at persuading people to do or to believe what you say 口才；辩才 ▸ **ˌsilver-ˈtongued** *adj.*

sil·ver·ware /ˈsɪlvəweə(r); *NAmE* -vərwer/ *noun* [U] **1** objects that are made of or covered with silver, especially knives, forks, dishes, etc. that are used for eating and serving food 银器，镀银器皿（尤指餐具）：*a piece of silverware* 一件银器 **2** (*also* **flat·ware**) (*both NAmE*) (*also* **cut·lery** *especially in BrE*) knives, forks and spoons, used for eating and serving food 餐具（刀、叉和匙）**3** (*BrE, informal*) a silver cup that you win in a sports competition（体育比赛中的）银杯 **SYN** **trophy**

ˌsilver ˈwedding (*BrE*) (*US* **ˌsilver anniˈversary**) (*also* **ˌsilver ˈwedding anniversary** *US, BrE*) *noun* the 25th anniversary of a wedding 银婚（结婚 25 周年纪念）：*They celebrated their silver wedding in May.* 他们于五月份庆祝了银婚纪念日。➲ COMPARE DIAMOND WEDDING, GOLDEN WEDDING, RUBY WEDDING

sil·very /ˈsɪlvəri/ *adj.* [usually before noun] **1** shiny like silver; having the colour of silver 闪着银光的；银色的：*silvery light* 银光 ◇ *a silvery grey colour* 银灰色 **2** (*literary*) (especially of a voice 尤指嗓音) having a pleasant musical sound 银铃般的；悦耳的

sim /sɪm/ *noun* (*informal*) a computer or video game that SIMULATES (= artificially creates the feeling of experiencing) an activity such as flying an aircraft or playing a sport 模拟电脑（或电子）游戏；仿真游戏

ˈSIM card *noun* the abbreviation for 'subscriber identification module' (a plastic card inside a mobile/cell phone that stores information to identify the phone and the person using it) 用户识别模块，SIM 卡（全写为 subscriber identification module，移动电话内存储的识别手机和用户信息的塑料卡）➲ COLLOCATIONS AT PHONE

sim·ian /ˈsɪmiən/ *adj.* (*specialist*) like a MONKEY or an ape; connected with monkeys or apes 像猿（或猴）的；猿（或猴）的

simi·lar 🔑 **AW** /ˈsɪmələ(r)/ *adj.* like sb/sth but not exactly the same 相像的；相仿的；类似的：*We have very similar interests.* 我们兴趣相仿。◇ **~ (to sb/sth)** *My teaching style is similar to that of most other teachers.* 我的教学风格和多数教师相似。◇ **~ (in sth)** *The two houses are similar in size.* 两座房子大小差不多。◇ *The brothers look very similar.* 弟兄几个长得很像。◇ *All our patients have broadly similar problems.* 我们所有的病人问题大致相似。**OPP** **different, dissimilar**

simi·lar·ity **AW** /ˌsɪməˈlærəti/ *noun* (*pl.* **-ies**) **1** [U, sing.] the state of being like sb/sth but not exactly the same 相似性；相仿性；类似性 **SYN** **resemblance**：**~ (between A and B)** *The report highlights the similarity between the two groups.* 这份报告强调两组之间的相似性。◇ **~ (to sb/sth)** *She bears a* ***striking similarity*** *to her mother.* 她跟她母亲十分相像。◇ **~ (in sth)** *There is some similarity in the way they sing.* 他们的演唱风格有点像。◇ *They are both doctors but that is where the similarity ends.* 两人都是医生，但他们的相似之处仅此而已。**2** [C] a feature that things or people have that makes them like each other 相似处；相似点；类似的地方 **SYN** **resemblance**：*a study of the similarities and differences between the two countries* 对这两个国家的异同点的研究 ◇ **~ in/of sth** *similarities in/of style* 风格上的相似之处 ◇ **~ to/with sb/sth** *The karate bout has many similarities to a boxing match.* 空手道比赛和拳击比赛有许多类似的地方。**OPP** **difference, dissimilarity** ➲ LANGUAGE BANK ON NEXT PAGE

simi·lar·ly 🔑 **AW** /ˈsɪmələli; *NAmE* -lərli/ *adv.* **1** 🔑 in almost the same way 相似地；类似地；差不多地：*Husband and wife were similarly successful in their chosen careers.* 夫妇俩在各自所选择的事业上都很成功。**2** 🔑 used to say that two facts, actions, statements, etc. are like each other 同样；也：*The United States won most of the track and field events. Similarly, in swimming, the top three places went to Americans.* 美国队赢得了田径比赛大多数项目的胜利。同样，在游泳方面，美国人也囊括了前三名。➲ LANGUAGE BANK ON NEXT PAGE

sim·ile /ˈsɪməli/ *noun* [C, U] (*specialist*) a word or phrase that compares sth to sth else, using the words *like* or *as*, for example *a face like a mask* or *as white as snow*; the use of such words and phrases 明喻；明喻的运用 ➲ COMPARE METAPHOR

si·mili·tude /sɪˈmɪlɪtjuːd; *NAmE* -tuːd/ *noun* [U] (*formal*) **~ (between A and B)** | **~ (to sb/sth)** the state of being similar to sth 相似；类似；相仿：*the similitude between humans and gorillas* 人类和大猩猩的相像

S

▼ LANGUAGE BANK 用语库

similarly

Making comparisons 进行比较

- *This chart **provides a comparison of** the ways that teenage boys and girls in the UK spend their free time.* 这个图表对英国十几岁的男生和女生打发空闲时间的方式进行了对比。
- *In many cases, the results for boys and girls are virtually **the same/identical**.* 在许多情况下，对男女生的调查结果实际上是相同的。
- *In many cases, the results for boys are virtually **the same as/identical to** the results for girls.* 在许多情况下，对男生的调查结果实际上和对女生的调查结果是相同的。
- ***Both** boys **and** girls spend the bulk of their free time with friends.* 男生和女生的大部分空闲时间都和朋友一起度过。
- *Most of the boys do more than two hours of sport a week, **as do** many of the girls.* 大多数男生每周会做两个多小时的运动，这和许多女生是一样的。
- ***Like** many of the girls, most of the boys spend a large part of their free time using the Internet.* 像许多女孩子一样，大多数男孩子也把大量空闲时间花在上网。
- *The girls particularly enjoy using social networking websites. **Similarly**, nearly all the boys said they spent at least two to three hours a week on these sites.* 女生们特别喜欢上社交网站。同样，几乎所有男生都说他们每周在这些网站上花的时间至少有两到三个小时。

➲ LANGUAGE BANK AT CONTRAST, ILLUSTRATE, PROPORTION, SURPRISING

sim·mer /ˈsɪmə(r)/ *verb, noun*

■ ***verb*** **1** [T, I] ~ (**sth**) to cook sth by keeping it almost at boiling point; to be cooked in this way 用文火炖；煨：*Simmer the sauce gently for 10 minutes.* 把调味汁用文火炖 10 分钟。◇ *Leave the soup to simmer.* 让汤煨着。➲ COLLOCATIONS AT COOKING **2** [I] ~ (**with sth**) to be filled with a strong feeling, especially anger, which you have difficulty controlling 充满（难以控制的感情，尤指愤怒）**SYN** **seethe**: *She was still simmering with resentment.* 她依旧憋着一肚子的怨恨。◇ *Anger simmered inside him.* 他心里郁结着怒火。**3** [I] (of an argument, a disagreement, etc. 争论、分歧等) to develop for a period of time without any real anger or violence being shown 即将爆发；酝酿：*This argument has been simmering for months.* 这场争论已酝酿了几个月了。

PHR V ˌ**simmer ˈdown** (*informal*) to become calm after a period of anger or excitement 平息下来；平静下来：*I left him alone until he simmered down.* 等他平静下来之后我才去找他。

■ ***noun*** [sing.] the state when sth is almost boiling 即将沸腾状态；文火炖；小火煨：*Bring the sauce to a simmer and cook for 5 minutes.* 改用文火，把调味汁炖 5 分钟。

sim·nel cake /ˈsɪmnəl keɪk/ *noun* [C, U] a type of cake made with dried fruit, traditionally eaten in Britain at Easter（英国人在复活节吃的）果脯蛋糕

Simon says /ˌsaɪmən ˈsez/ *noun* [U] a children's game in which players should only do what a person says if he/she says 'Simon says…' at the beginning of the instruction 得令游戏（儿童游戏，有人在发指令开始时说"西蒙说"，参加者才能照做）

sim·pat·ico /sɪmˈpætɪkəʊ; *NAmE* -koʊ/ *adj.* (*informal, from Spanish*) **1** (of a person 人) pleasant; easy to like 和善的；讨人喜欢的 **2** (of a person 人) with similar interests and ideas to yours 志趣相投的 **SYN** **compatible**

sim·per /ˈsɪmpə(r)/ *verb* [I, T] to smile in a silly and annoying way 矫揉造作地笑；扭捏作态地笑：*a silly simpering girl* 扭捏作态、嘻嘻傻笑的女孩子 ◇ **+ speech** *'You're such a darling,' she simpered.* "你可真讨人喜欢。" 她卖弄风情地笑着说。 ▶ **sim·per** *noun* [sing.] **sim·per·ing·ly** /ˈsɪmpərɪŋli/ *adv.*

sim·ple 🔑 /ˈsɪmpl/ *adj.* (**sim·pler**, **sim·plest**) **HELP** You can also use **more simple** and **most simple**. 亦可用 more simple 和 most simple。

- **EASY** 容易 **1** 🔑 not complicated; easy to understand or do 易于理解的；易做的；简单的 **SYN** **easy**: *a simple solution* 简单的解决办法 ◇ *The answer is really quite simple.* 实际上答案相当简单。◇ *This machine is very simple to use.* 这台机器操作非常简单。◇ *We lost because we played badly. It's **as simple as that**.* 我们输了是因为我们打得不好。原因就这么简单。◇ *Give the necessary information but **keep it simple**.* 说说基本情况，简单一点。
- **BASIC/PLAIN** 基本；朴素 **2** 🔑 basic or plain without anything extra or unnecessary 朴素的；简朴的；不加装饰的：*simple but elegant clothes* 素雅的衣服 ◇ *We had a simple meal of soup and bread.* 我们喝汤，吃面包，吃了顿简餐。◇ *The accommodation is simple but spacious.* 住处简朴但宽敞。**OPP** **fancy**
- **FOR EMPHASIS** 强调 **3** used before a noun to emphasize that it is exactly that and nothing else（用在名词前表示强调）纯粹的，完全的，不折不扣的：*Nobody wanted to believe the simple truth.* 谁也不愿意相信这明显的事实。◇ *It was a matter of simple survival.* 这完全是能不能生存的问题。◇ *It's nothing to worry about—just a simple headache.* 不用担心，只是有点儿头痛。◇ *I had to do it **for the simple reason that*** (= because) *I couldn't trust anyone else.* 我只能这么做，纯粹是因为我信不过任何人。➲ SYNONYMS AT PLAIN
- **WITH FEW PARTS** 部位少 **4** 🔑 [usually before noun] consisting of only a few parts; not complicated in structure 部位少的；结构简单的：*simple forms of life, for example amoebas* 如变形虫之类的简单生命形式 ◇ *a simple machine* 结构简单的机器 ◇ (*grammar* 语法) *a **simple sentence*** (= one with only one verb) 简单句
- **ORDINARY** 普通 **5** 🔑 [only before noun] (of a person 人) ordinary; not special 普通的；一般的；平凡的：*I'm a simple country girl.* 我是一个普普通通的乡村姑娘。
- **NOT INTELLIGENT** 智力低下 **6** [not usually before noun] (of a person 人) not very intelligent; not mentally normal 智力低下；迟钝；笨：*He's not mad—just a little simple.* 他不是疯，只是智力稍低。
- **GRAMMAR** 语法 **7** used to describe the present or past tense of a verb that is formed without using an auxiliary verb, as in *She loves him* (= the simple present tense) or *He arrived late* (= the simple past tense)（无须用助动词构成的动词时态）简单的，一般的 ➲ SEE ALSO SIMPLY **IDM** SEE PURE

ˌ**simple ˈfracture** *noun* an injury when a bone in your body is broken but does not come through the skin 单纯骨折；无创骨折 ➲ COMPARE COMPOUND FRACTURE

ˌ**simple ˈinterest** *noun* [U] (*finance* 财) interest that is paid only on the original amount of money that you invested, and not on any interest that it has earned 单利 ➲ COMPARE COMPOUND INTEREST

ˌ**simple-ˈminded** *adj.* (*disapproving*) not intelligent; not able to understand how complicated things are 智力低下的；愚蠢的；头脑简单的：*a simple-minded person* 头脑简单的人 ◇ *a simple-minded approach* 笨方法

simple·ton /ˈsɪmpltən/ *noun* (*old-fashioned*) a person who is not very intelligent and can be tricked easily 傻瓜；易上当受骗的人

sim·plex /ˈsɪmpleks/ *noun* (*linguistics* 语言) a simple word that is not made of other words 简单词；单纯词 ➲ COMPARE COMPOUND *n.* (3)

sim·pli·city /sɪmˈplɪsəti/ *noun* (*pl.* **-ies**) **1** [U] the quality of being easy to understand or use 简单（性）；容易（性）：*the relative simplicity of the new PC* 新型个人电脑的相对简易 ◇ ***For the sake of simplicity**, let's divide the discussion into two parts.* 为了方便起见，我们把讨论分成两部分。**2** [U] (*approving*) the quality of being natural and plain 质朴；淳朴：*the simplicity of the architecture* 建筑风格的质朴 ◇ *the simplicity of country living* 乡村生活的淳朴 **3** [C, usually pl.] an aspect of sth that is easy, natural or plain 简单（或质朴、朴素）之处：*the simplicities of our* *old way of life* 我们过去的生活方式的种种简朴之处

IDM **be sim,plicity it'self** to be very easy or plain 非常简单；非常朴素

sim·pli·fi·ca·tion /ˌsɪmplɪfɪ'keɪʃn/ *noun* **1** [U, sing.] the process of making sth easier to do or understand 简化：*Complaints have led to (a) simplification of the rules.* 因为人们的抱怨，规则简化了。**2** [C] the thing that results when you make a problem, statement, system, etc. easier to understand or do 简化的事物：*A number of simplifications have been made to the taxation system.* 税收制度已经历过多次简化。➲ COMPARE OVERSIMPLIFICATION at OVERSIMPLIFY

sim·plify /'sɪmplɪfaɪ/ *verb* (**sim·pli·fies**, **sim·pli·fy·ing**, **sim·pli·fied**, **sim·pli·fied**) **~ sth** to make sth easier to do or understand 使简化；使简易：*The application forms have now been simplified.* 申请表格现已简化了。◇ *I hope his appointment will* ***simplify matters***. 我希望他任命以后事情会好办一些。◇ *a simplified version of the story for young children* 供幼儿阅读的故事简写本

sim·plis·tic /sɪm'plɪstɪk/ *adj.* (*disapproving*) making a problem, situation, etc. seem less difficult or complicated than it really is（把问题、局面等）过分简单化的 ▶ **sim·plis·tic·al·ly** /-kli/ *adv.*

sim·ply 🔑 /'sɪmpli/ *adv.* **1** 🔑 used to emphasize how easy or basic sth is （强调简单）仅仅，只，不过 SYN **just**：*Simply add hot water and stir.* 只需加上热水搅动就行。◇ *The runway is simply a strip of grass.* 所谓跑道不过是一长条草地而已。◇ *Fame is often* ***simply a matter of*** *being in the right place at the right time.* 成名常常是身在其位，恰逢其时，仅此而已。◇ *You can enjoy all the water sports, or simply lie on the beach.* 你可以进行所有的水上运动，或只是躺在沙滩上。**2** used to emphasize a statement （强调某说法）确实，简直 SYN **absolutely**：*You simply must see the play.* 那出戏你真得看看。◇ *The view is simply wonderful!* 景色美极了！◇ *That is simply not true!* 那根本不是真的！◇ *I haven't seen her for simply ages.* 我真是好久没见她了。**3** 🔑 in a way that is easy to understand 简单地：*The book explains grammar simply and clearly.* 这本书对语法解释得简明扼要。◇ *Anyway,* ***to put it simply***, *we still owe them £2 000.* 反正简单地说，我们还欠他们 2 000 英镑。**4** 🔑 in a way that is natural and plain 简朴地；朴素地：*The rooms are simply furnished.* 房间都陈设简朴。◇ *They live simply* (= they do not spend much money). 他们生活简朴。**5** used to introduce a summary or an explanation of sth that you have just said or done（引出概括或解释）不过，只是：*I don't want to be rude,* ***it's simply that*** *we have to be careful who we give this information to.* 我不是有意无礼，只不过这份资料给谁我们必须很慎重。

sim·sim /'sɪmsɪm/ *noun* [U] an E African word for SESAME (= a type of plant whose seeds and their oil are used in cooking)（东非用语）芝麻

simu·lac·rum /ˌsɪmju'leɪkrəm/ *noun* (*pl.* **simu·lacra** /-krə/) (*formal*) something that looks like sb/sth else or that is made to look like sb/sth else 假象；模拟物；幻影 SYN **copy**

simu·late AW /'sɪmjuleɪt/ *verb* **1 ~ sth** to pretend that you have a particular feeling 假装；冒充；装作 SYN **feign**：*I tried to simulate surprise at the news.* 听到这个消息后，我竭力装出一副吃惊的样子。**2 ~ sth** to create particular conditions that exist in real life using computers, models, etc., usually for study or training purposes（用计算机或模型等）模拟：*Computer software can be used to simulate conditions on the seabed.* 计算机软件可用于模拟海底状况。**3 ~ sth** to be made to look like sth else 模仿；冒充：*a gas heater that simulates a coal fire* 模仿煤炉的煤气暖炉

simu·lated AW /'sɪmjuleɪtɪd/ *adj.* [only before noun] not real, but made to look, feel, etc. like the real thing 假装的；仿造的；模拟的：*simulated leather* 人造革 ◇ *'How wonderful!' she said with simulated enthusiasm.* "多棒啊！"她装出一副兴致勃勃的样子说道。◇ *The experiments were carried out under simulated examination conditions.* 试验是在模拟的情况下进行的。

simu·la·tion AW /ˌsɪmju'leɪʃn/ *noun* **1** [C, U] a situation in which a particular set of conditions is created artificially in order to study or experience sth that could exist in reality 模拟；仿真：*a computer simulation of how the planet functions* 行星活动方式的计算机模拟图像 ◇ *a simulation model* 仿真模型 **2** [U] the act of pretending that sth is real when it is not 假装；冒充：*the simulation of genuine concern* 假装真诚关心

simu·la·tor /'sɪmjuleɪtə(r)/ *noun* a piece of equipment that artificially creates a particular set of conditions in order to train sb to deal with a situation that they may experience in reality 模拟装置：*a flight simulator* 飞行模拟器

sim·ul·cast /'sɪmlkɑːst; *NAmE* 'sɪmlkæst; *also* 'saɪm-/ *noun* a programme, often recording a live event, that is broadcast on two or more television channels, radio channels, Internet sites, etc., or using two or more of these types of medium at the same time（电视、广播频道、网站等）同步播送节目，同步直播；多媒体同步直播：*You can either watch live coverage of the event on television or listen to the radio simulcast.* 可在电视上收看这一活动的现场直播，或收听电台的同播。▶ **sim·ul·cast** *verb* (**sim·ul·cast**, **sim·ul·cast**) **~ sth**：*The show will be simulcast on television and the Internet.* 演出将在电视和互联网同步直播。➲ MORE LIKE THIS 1, page R25

sim·ul·tan·eous /ˌsɪml'teɪniəs; *NAmE* ˌsaɪml-/ *adj.* happening or done at the same time as sth else 同时发生（或进行）的；同步的：*There were several simultaneous attacks by the rebels.* 反叛者同时发动了几起攻击。◇ ***simultaneous translation/interpreting*** 同声传译 ▶ **sim·ul·tan·eity** /ˌsɪmltə'neɪəti; *NAmE* ˌsaɪmltə'niːəti/ *noun* [U] **sim·ul·tan·eous·ly** *adv.*：*The game will be broadcast simultaneously on TV and radio.* 比赛将同时在电视和电台转播。➲ LANGUAGE BANK AT PROCESS[1]

ˌsimulˌtaneous eˈquations *noun* [pl.] (*mathematics* 数) EQUATIONS involving two or more unknown quantities that have the same values in each equation 解线性方程；联立方程

SIN /ˌes aɪ 'en/ *abbr.* (*CanE*) SOCIAL INSURANCE NUMBER（加拿大）社会保险号码

sin /sɪn/ *noun, verb, abbr.*

■ ***noun*** **1** [C] an offence against God or against a religious or moral law 罪，罪恶，罪过（对神的冒犯或对宗教戒律、道德规范的违犯）：*to commit a sin* 犯罪 ◇ *Confess your sins to God and he will forgive you.* 向上帝忏悔，上帝就会宽恕你。◇ *The Bible says that stealing is a sin.*《圣经》上说偷盗有罪。➲ COLLOCATIONS AT RELIGION ➲ SEE ALSO MORTAL SIN, ORIGINAL SIN **2** [U] the act of breaking a religious or moral law 罪行，犯罪（违犯宗教戒律、道德规范的行为）：*a life of sin* 罪过的一生 **3** [C, usually sing.] (*informal*) an action that people strongly disapprove of 过错；过失；恶行：*It's a sin to waste taxpayers' money like that.* 这样挥霍纳税人的钱太不应该。➲ SEE ALSO SINFUL, SINNER

IDM **be/do sth for your sins** (*informal, humorous, especially BrE*) used to say that sth that sb does is like a punishment（表示所做的事无异于惩罚）自作自受，活该：*She works with us in Accounts, for her sins!* 她跟我们一样也在财务室做事，活该如此！ **(as) miserable/ugly as 'sin** (*informal*) used to emphasize that sb is very unhappy or ugly 可怜得 / 难看得要命 ➲ MORE LIKE THIS 14, page R26 ➲ MORE AT LIVE[1], MULTITUDE

■ ***verb*** (**-nn-**) [I] to break a religious or moral law 犯戒律；犯过失：*Forgive me, Lord, for I have sinned.* 主啊，宽恕我吧，我犯了罪。◇ **~ against sb/sth** *He was more sinned against than sinning* (= although he did wrong, other people treated him even worse). 他过错无多而报应太重。

■ ***abbr.*** (*mathematics* 数) SINE 正弦

'sin bin *noun* (*informal*) (in some sports, for example ICE HOCKEY 冰球等体育运动) a place away from the playing

S

area where the REFEREE sends a player who has broken the rules 被罚下场的球员座位；受罚席

since /sɪns/ *prep., conj., adv.*

■ ***prep.*** **1** (used with the present perfect or past perfect tense 与现在完成时或过去完成时连用) from a time in the past until a later past time, or until now 自…以后；从…以来：*She's been off work since Tuesday.* 星期二以来她一直没上班。◇ *We've lived here since 2006.* 从2006年开始我们便住在这里。◇ *I haven't eaten since breakfast.* 早饭以后我还没吃过东西呢。◇ *He's been working in a bank since leaving school.* 他中学毕业以后一直在一家银行工作。◇ *Since the party she had only spoken to him once.* 那次聚会以后，她只和他说过一次话。◇ *'They've split up.' '**Since when?**'* "他们分手了。" "什么时候的事儿？" ◇ *That was years ago. I've changed jobs **since then**.* 那是多年以前的事了。自那以来我已经换过几个工作了。HELP Use **for**, not **since**, with a period of time. 指一段时间用for，不用since：*I've been learning English for five years.* 我学英语已经五年了。◇ ~~*I've been learning English since five years.*~~ **2 ~ when?** used when you are showing that you are angry about sth（表示气愤）何曾，什么时候：*Since when did he ever listen to me?* 他什么时候听过我的话？

■ ***conj.*** **1** (used with the present perfect, past perfect or simple present tense in the main clause 与用现在完成时、过去完成时或一般现在时的主句连用) from an event in the past until a later past event, or until now 从…以后；自…以来：*Cath hasn't phoned since she went to Berlin.* 卡思自从去了柏林还没有打来过电话。◇ *It was the first time I'd had visitors since I'd moved to London.* 那是我搬到伦敦以后第一次有人来看我。◇ *It's twenty years since I've seen her.* 我已经二十年没见她了。◇ *How long is it since we last went to the theatre?* 我们多久没去看戏了？◇ *She had been worrying **ever since** the letter arrived.* 自从接到那封信后她就一直焦虑不安。**2** because; as 因为；由于；既然：*We thought that, since we were in the area, we'd stop by and see them.* 我们想，既然到了这个地方，就该顺便去看看他们。

■ ***adv.*** (used with the present perfect or past perfect tense 与现在完成时或过去完成时连用) **1** from a time in the past until a later past time, or until now 自…以后；从…以来：*He left home two weeks ago and we haven't heard from him since.* 他两周前离家外出，我们至今还没有他的音信。◇ *The original building has **long since** (= long before now) been demolished.* 原来的建筑老早就拆了。**2** at a time after a particular time in the past 此后；后来：*We were divorced two years ago and she has since remarried.* 我们两年前离了婚，之后她又再婚了。

sin·cere /sɪnˈsɪə(r); *NAmE* -ˈsɪr/ *adj.* (*superlative* **sin·cerest**, *no comparative*) **1** (of feelings, beliefs or behaviour 感情、信念或行为) showing what you really think or feel 真诚的；诚挚的；诚恳的 SYN **genuine**：*a sincere attempt to resolve the problem* 解决这一问题的认真尝试 ◇ *sincere regret* 真诚的悔恨 ◇ *Please accept our sincere thanks.* 请接受我们诚挚的谢意。◇ *a sincere apology* 诚恳的道歉 **2** (of a person 人) saying only what you really think or feel 诚实的；坦率的 SYN **honest**：*He seemed sincere enough when he said he wanted to help.* 他表示愿意帮忙，样子很真诚。◇ **~ in sth** *She is never completely sincere in what she says about people.* 她谈论别人，一向不尽坦诚。OPP **insincere** ▶ **sin·cer·ity** /sɪnˈserəti/ *noun* [U]：*She spoke with total sincerity.* 她讲的是由衷之言。◇ *I can say **in all sincerity** that I knew nothing of these plans.* 我可以十分坦诚地说，这些计划我一无所知。

sin·cere·ly /sɪnˈsɪəli; *NAmE* -ˈsɪrli/ *adv.* in a way that shows what you really feel or think about sb/sth 真诚地；诚实地：*I sincerely believe that this is the right decision.* 我由衷地认为这个决定是正确的。◇ *'I won't let you down.' 'I sincerely hope not.'* "我不会让你失望的。" "但愿如此。"

IDM **Yours sincerely** (*NAmE* **Sincerely (yours)**) (*formal*) used at the end of a formal letter before you sign your name, when you have addressed sb by their name（正式信函署名前的套语，只用于以收信人姓名相称呼的信函）

Sindhi /ˈsɪndi/ *noun* [U] a language spoken in Sind in Pakistan and in western India 信德语（通行于巴基斯坦信德省和印度西部）

sine /saɪn/ *noun* (*abbr.* **sin**) (*mathematics* 数) the RATIO of the length of the side opposite one of the angles in a RIGHT-ANGLED triangle that are less than 90° to the length of the longest side 正弦 ➲ COMPARE COSINE, TANGENT

sine·cure /ˈsɪnɪkjʊə(r); ˈsaɪn-; *NAmE* -kjʊr/ *noun* (*formal*) a job that you are paid for even though it involves little or no work 闲职；挂名职位

sine die /ˌsaɪni ˈdaɪiː; ˌsɪneɪ ˈdiːeɪ/ *adv.* (*from Latin, formal, law* 律) without a future date being arranged 无限期地：*The case was adjourned sine die.* 此案无限期延迟审理。

sine qua non /ˌsɪneɪ kwɑː ˈnəʊn; *NAmE* ˈnoʊn/ *noun* [sing.] **~ (of/for sth)** (*from Latin, formal*) something that is essential before you can achieve sth else 必要条件

sinew /ˈsɪnjuː/ *noun* **1** [C, U] a strong band of TISSUE in the body that joins a muscle to a bone 肌腱 **2** [usually pl.] (*literary*) a source of strength or power 力量的来源；关键环节；要害之处 IDM SEE STRAIN *v.*

sinewy /ˈsɪnjuːi/ *adj.* (of a person or an animal 人或动物) having a thin body and strong muscles 肌肉发达的；矫健的；强健的 SYN **wiry**

sin·ful /ˈsɪnfl/ *adj.* (*formal*) morally wrong or evil 不道德的；邪恶的 SYN **immoral**：*sinful thoughts* 邪恶的想法 ◇ *It is sinful to lie.* 说谎是不道德的。◇ (*informal*) *It's sinful to waste good food!* 浪费好好的食物是有罪的！▶ **sin·ful·ly** /-fəli/ *adv.* **sin·ful·ness** *noun* [U]

sing /sɪŋ/ *verb* (**sang** /sæŋ/, **sung** /sʌŋ/) **1** [I, T] to make musical sounds with your voice in the form of a song or tune 唱（歌）；演唱：*She usually sings in the shower.* 她常常边冲澡边唱歌。◇ *I just can't sing in tune!* 我一唱就走调！◇ **~ to sb** *He was singing softly to the baby.* 他对宝宝轻声哼着歌。◇ **~ sth to sb** *Will you sing a song to us?* 你给我们唱支歌好吗？◇ **~ sb sth** *Will you sing us a song?* 你给我们唱支歌好吗？◇ **~ sth** *Now I'd like to sing a song by the Beatles.* 现在我来唱一首披头士乐队的歌。◇ **~ sb to sleep** *She **sang the baby to sleep*** (= sang until the baby went to sleep). 她哼着歌把宝宝哄睡了。➲ COLLOCATIONS AT MUSIC ➲ MORE LIKE THIS 33, page R28

WORDFINDER 联想词：beat, harmony, melody, **music**, note, rhythm, tempo, tone, vocal

2 [I] (of birds 鸟) to make high musical sounds 鸣；啼；啼啭：*The birds were singing outside my window.* 鸟儿在我窗外啼啭。**3** [I] (+ **adv./prep.**) to make a high ringing sound like a whistle 鸣鸣作响；发嗖嗖声：*Bullets sang past my ears.* 子弹嗖嗖地从我耳边飞过。▶ **sing** *noun* [sing.]：*Let's have a sing.* 我们唱支歌吧。

IDM **sing a different ˈtune** to change your opinion about sb/sth or your attitude towards sb/sth 改变观点（或态度）；改弦易辙 **sing from the same ˈhymn/ˈsong sheet** (*BrE, informal*) to show that you are in agreement with each other by saying the same things in public 唱同一调子（在公开场合口径一致）➲ MORE AT FAT *adj.*

PHR V **ˌsing aˈlong (with sb/sth)** | **ˌsing aˈlong (to sth)** to sing together with sb who is already singing or while a record, radio, or musical instrument is playing 随着（某人、唱片等）唱：*Do sing along if you know the words.* 要是知道歌词，你就跟着唱吧。➲ RELATED NOUN SINGALONG **ˈsing of sth** (*old-fashioned* or *formal*) to mention sth in a song or a poem, especially to praise it（用诗歌）讲述，歌颂，赞美 **ˌsing ˈout** to sing or say sth clearly and loudly 叫出；唱出：*A voice suddenly sang out above the rest.* 在一片嘈杂声中突然传出一个人的声音。**ˌsing ˈup** (*BrE*) (*NAmE* **ˌsing ˈout**) to sing more loudly 更大声地唱；放开嗓门唱：*Sing up, let's hear you.* 大声唱，我们听不见。

sing·along /ˈsɪŋəlɒŋ; *NAmE* -lɔːŋ; -lɑːŋ/ (*BrE also* **ˈsing-song**) *noun* an informal occasion at which people sing songs together 众人自娱歌唱会

singe /sɪndʒ/ *verb* (**singe·ing**, **singed**, **singed**) [T, I] **~ (sth)** to burn the surface of sth slightly, usually by mistake;

to be burnt in this way（尤指不小心）烤焦，烫煳：*He singed his hair as he tried to light his cigarette.* 他点烟时把头发给燎了。◇ *the smell of singeing fur* 毛皮烧焦的气味 ➲ SYNONYMS AT BURN

sing·er /ˈsɪŋə(r)/ *noun* a person who sings, or whose job is singing, especially in public 唱歌的人；歌唱家；歌手：*She's a wonderful singer.* 她唱歌唱得非常好。◇ *an opera singer* 歌剧演员

sing·ing /ˈsɪŋɪŋ/ *noun* [U] the activity of making musical sounds with your voice 唱歌；歌唱：*the beautiful singing of birds* 鸟儿动听的歌唱 ◇ *choral singing* 合唱 ◇ *There was singing and dancing all night.* 通宵唱歌跳舞。◇ *a singing teacher* 声乐教师 ◇ *She has a beautiful singing voice.* 她有一副唱歌的好嗓子。

sin·gle /ˈsɪŋgl/ *adj., noun, verb*

■ *adj.*

• **ONE** 一个 **1** [only before noun] only one 仅有一个的；单一的；单个的：*He sent her a single red rose.* 他送给她一枝红玫瑰。◇ *a **single-sex school*** (= for boys only or for girls only) 男子（或女子）学校 ◇ *All these jobs can now be done by one single machine.* 所有这些工作现在只用一台机器就可以完成。◇ *I couldn't understand a single word she said!* 她讲的东西我一个字都听不懂！◇ *the European **single currency**, the euro* 欧洲单一货币欧元 ◇ (*BrE*) *a **single honours** degree* (= for which you study only one subject) 单科荣誉学位

• **FOR EMPHASIS** 强调 **2** [only before noun] used to emphasize that you are referring to one particular person or thing on its own（特指某人或事物）：*Unemployment is the single most important factor in the growing crime rates.* 失业是犯罪率日益上升最重要的一个因素。◇ *We eat rice **every single day**.* 我们天天吃米饭。

• **NOT MARRIED** 未婚 **3** (of a person 人) not married or having a romantic relationship with sb 单身的；未婚的；无伴侣的：*The apartments are ideal for single people living alone.* 这些公寓供单身者独自居住最为理想。◇ *Are you still single?* 你还是单身吗？ ➲ SEE ALSO SINGLE PARENT

• **FOR ONE PERSON** 供一个人使用 **4** [only before noun] intended to be used by only one person 单人的：*a **single bed/room*** 单人床 / 房间 ➲ VISUAL VOCAB PAGE V24 ➲ COMPARE DOUBLE *adj.* (3)

• **TICKET** 票 **5** [only before noun] (*BrE*) (*also* **one-way** *NAmE, BrE*) a **single** ticket, etc. can be used for travelling to a place but not back again 单程的：*a single ticket* 单程票 ◇ *How much is the single fare to Glasgow?* 去格拉斯哥的单程票多少钱？ ➲ COMPARE RETURN *n.* (7) IDM SEE FILE *n.*, GLANCE *n.*

■ *noun*

• **TICKET** 票 **1** [C] (*BrE*) a ticket that allows you to travel to a place but not back again 单程票：*How much is a single to York?* 去约克的单程票多少钱？ ➲ COMPARE RETURN *n.* (7)

• **MUSIC** 音乐 **2** [C] a piece of recorded music, usually popular music, that consists of one song; a CD that a single is recorded on 单曲（常指流行音乐）；单曲激光唱片：*The band releases its new single next week.* 这支乐队将于下周发行新的单曲唱片。 ➲ COMPARE ALBUM (2)

• **ROOM** 房间 **3** [C] a room in a hotel, etc. for one person（旅馆等的）单人房间 ➲ COMPARE DOUBLE *n.* (5)

• **MONEY** 钱 **4** [C] (*NAmE*) a bill/note that is worth one dollar 一美元纸币 ➲ COMPARE DOUBLE *n.*

• **UNMARRIED PEOPLE** 未婚者 **5 singles** [pl.] people who are not married and do not have a romantic relationship with sb else 单身者；无伴侣者：*They organize parties for singles.* 他们为单身者组织聚会。◇ *a **singles bar/club*** 单身酒吧 / 俱乐部

• **IN SPORT** 体育运动 **6 singles** [U+sing./pl. v.] (especially in TENNIS 尤指网球) a game when only one player plays against one other; a series of two or more of these games 单打（比赛）：*the women's singles champion* 女子单打冠军 ◇ *the first round of the men's singles* 男子单打第一轮 ◇ *a singles match* 单打比赛 ◇ *She's won three singles titles this year.* 她今年获得三个单打冠军。 ➲ COMPARE DOUBLE *n.* **7** [C] (in CRICKET 板球) a hit from which a player scores one RUN (= point) 一分打 **8** [C] (in BASEBALL 棒球) a hit that only allows the player to run to FIRST BASE 一垒打

■ *verb*

PHR V ˌ**single sb/sth**↔ˈ**out** (**for sth/as sb/sth**) to choose sb/sth from a group for special attention 单独挑出：*She was singled out for criticism.* 她被单挑出来进行批评。◇ *He was singled out as the outstanding performer of the games.* 他被评选为这次运动会表现最出色的运动员。

ˌ**single ˈbed** (*NAmE also* ˌ**twin ˈbed**) *noun* a bed big enough for one person 单人床 ➲ VISUAL VOCAB PAGE V24

ˌ**single-ˈbreast·ed** *adj.* (of a jacket or coat 上衣) having only one row of buttons that fasten in the middle 单排扣的 ➲ COMPARE DOUBLE-BREASTED

ˌ**single ˈcombat** *noun* [U] fighting between two people, usually with weapons 一对一的搏斗（通常用武器）

ˌ**single ˈcream** *noun* [U] (*BrE*) thin cream which is used in cooking and for pouring over food 稀奶油 ➲ COMPARE DOUBLE CREAM

ˌ**single-ˈdecker** *noun* a bus with only one level 单层公共汽车 ➲ VISUAL VOCAB PAGE V62 ➲ COMPARE DOUBLE-DECKER (1)

ˌ**single ˈfigures** *noun* [pl.] a number that is less than ten 个位数；一位数：*Inflation is down to single figures.* 通货膨胀率降到一位数了。◇ *The number of people who fail each year is now **in single figures**.* 每年考试不及格的学生现在不足十人。

ˌ**single-ˈhanded** *adv.* on your own with nobody helping you 独自；单枪匹马地；独立 SYN **alone**：*to sail around the world single-handed* 单人环球航行 ▶ ˌ**single-ˈhanded** *adj.*：*a single-handed voyage* 单人航行 ˌ**single-ˈhanded·ly** *adv.*

ˌ**single ˈmarket** *noun* [usually sing.] (*economics* 经) a group of countries that have few or no restrictions on the movement of goods, money and people between the members of the group 单一市场（由若干国家构成，成员国之间对于相互间的商品交易、货币流通及人员往来限制极少或没有限制）

ˌ**single-ˈminded** *adj.* only thinking about one particular aim or goal because you are determined to achieve sth 一心一意的；专心致志的：*the single-minded pursuit of power* 一心追逐权力 ◇ *She is very single-minded about her career.* 她一心专注于自己的事业。 ▶ ˌ**single-ˈminded·ly** *adv.* ˌ**single-ˈminded·ness** *noun* [U]

single·ness /ˈsɪŋglnəs/ *noun* [U] **1 ~ of purpose** the ability to think about one particular aim or goal because you are determined to succeed（目标）专一 **2** the state of not being married or having a partner 单身；单身生活

ˌ**single ˈparent** *noun* a person who takes care of their child or children without a husband, wife or partner 单亲：*a single-parent family* 单亲家庭

sing·let /ˈsɪŋglət/ *noun* (*BrE*) a piece of clothing without sleeves, worn under or instead of a shirt; a similar piece of clothing worn by runners, etc. 背心；无袖汗衫；运动背心 ➲ COMPARE VEST *n.* (1)

single·ton /ˈsɪŋgltən/ *noun* **1** a single item of the kind that you are talking about（所提及的）单项物，单个的人 **2** a person who is not married or in a romantic relationship 单身男子（或女子） **3** a person or an animal that is not a twin, etc.（非孪生的）单生儿，单生幼畜

ˌ**single transˌferable ˈvote** *noun* [sing.] (*politics* 政) a system for electing representatives in which a person's vote can be given to their second or third choice if their first choice is defeated, or if their first choice wins with more votes than they need 单一可转移投票制，单记可让渡投票制（所选的第一位候选人失败或所得票数已经超过必要数额，选票可转给所选的第二或第三候选人）

ˌ**single-ˈuse** *adj.* [only before noun] made to be used once only 供一次使用的：*disposable single-use cameras* 一次性相机

S

sin·gly /ˈsɪŋɡli/ *adv.* alone; one at a time 单个地；单独地；一个一个地 SYN **individually**: *The stamps are available singly or in books of ten.* 邮票有单枚的，也有十枚一册的。◇ *Guests arrived singly or in groups.* 客人有单个来的，也有三三两两一起到的。

ˈ**sing-song** *noun, adj.*
■ ***noun*** **1** [C] (*BrE*) = SINGALONG **2** [sing.] a way of speaking in which a person's voice keeps rising and falling 声音起伏的说话腔调
■ ***adj.*** [only before noun] a **sing-song** voice keeps rising and falling 说话音调起伏的

sin·gu·lar /ˈsɪŋɡjələ(r)/ *noun, adj.*
■ ***noun*** [sing.] (*grammar* 语法) a form of a noun or verb that refers to one person or thing 单数；单数形式：*The singular of 'bacteria' is 'bacterium'.* * bacteria 的单数形式是 bacterium。◇ *The verb should be* ***in the singular.*** 这个动词应当用单数形式。➲ COMPARE PLURAL *n.* ➲ **WORDFINDER NOTE AT GRAMMAR**
■ ***adj.*** **1** (*grammar* 语法) connected with or having the singular form 单数的；单数形式的：*a* ***singular noun/verb/ending*** 单数名词 / 动词 / 词尾 **2** (*formal*) very great or obvious 非凡的；突出的；显著的 SYN **outstanding**: *landscape of singular beauty* 无比优美的风景 **3** (*literary*) unusual; strange 奇特的；奇怪的；异常的 SYN **eccentric**: *a singular style of dress* 奇特的服装款式

sin·gu·lar·ity /ˌsɪŋɡjuˈlærəti/ *noun* [U] (*formal*) the quality of sth that makes it unusual or strange 奇特；奇怪；异常

sin·gu·lar·ly /ˈsɪŋɡjələli; *NAmE* -lərli/ *adv.* (*formal*) very; in an unusual way 非常；特别；异常地：*singularly beautiful* 特别漂亮 ◇ *He chose a singularly inappropriate moment to make his request.* 他选在一个极其不恰当的时刻提出要求。

Sin·hal·ese /ˌsɪnhəˈliːz; ˌsɪnə-/ *noun* (*pl.* **Sin·hal·ese**) **1** [C] a member of a race of people living in Sri Lanka 僧伽罗人（居住在斯里兰卡）**2** [U] the language of the Sinhalese 僧伽罗语 ▸ **Sin·hal·ese** *adj.*

sin·is·ter /ˈsɪnɪstə(r)/ *adj.* seeming evil or dangerous; making you think sth bad will happen 邪恶的；险恶的；不祥的；有凶兆的：*There was something cold and sinister about him.* 他给人一种冷酷阴险的感觉。◇ *There is another, more sinister, possibility.* 还有另一种更糟糕的可能。

S

sink /sɪŋk/ *verb, noun, adj.*
■ ***verb*** (**sank** /sæŋk/, **sunk** /sʌŋk/, *less frequent* **sunk, sunk**)
• **IN WATER/MUD, ETC.** 在水 / 泥等里 **1** [I] to go down below the surface or towards the bottom of a liquid or soft substance 下沉；下陷；沉没：*The ship sank to the bottom of the sea.* 船沉入海底。◇ *We're sinking!* 我们正在下沉！◇ *The wheels started to sink into the mud.* 车轮渐渐陷进泥里。◇ *to* ***sink like a stone*** 立即沉没
• **BOAT** 船只 **2** [T] **~ sth** to damage a boat or ship so that it goes below the surface of the sea, etc. 使下沉；使沉没：*a battleship sunk by a torpedo* 被鱼雷击沉的战列舰
• **FALL/SIT DOWN** 倒下；坐下 **3** [I] **+ adv./prep.** (of a person 人) to move downwards, especially by falling or sitting down 倒下；坐下 SYN **collapse**: *I sank into an armchair.* 我坐到扶手椅上。◇ *She* ***sank back*** *into her seat, exhausted.* 她筋疲力尽，又坐回椅子上。◇ *The old man had* ***sunk to his knees.*** 老头跪在了地上。
• **MOVE DOWNWARDS** 下降 **4** [I] (of an object 物体) to move slowly downwards 下沉；下陷；沉降：*The sun was sinking in the west.* 太阳西下。◇ *The foundations of the building are starting to sink.* 楼房的地基开始下陷。
• **BECOME WEAKER** 减弱 **5** [I] to decrease in amount, volume, strength, etc. 降低；减少；减弱：*The pound has sunk to its lowest recorded level against the dollar.* 英镑对美元的比价降到了有记录以来最低水平。◇ *He is clearly* ***sinking fast*** (= getting weaker quickly and will soon die). 很明显，他的身体在急剧衰弱。
• **OF VOICE** 声音 **6** [I] to become quieter 变低；变小 SYN **fade**: *Her voice sank to a whisper.* 她的声音变成了耳语。
• **DIG IN GROUND** 在地上挖掘 **7** [T] **~ sth** to make a deep hole in the ground 挖，掘（深坑、深洞）SYN **drill**: *to sink a well/shaft/mine* 掘水井 / 竖井 / 矿井 **8** [T] **~ sth (+ adv./prep.)** to place sth in the ground by digging 埋入；打下：*to sink a post into the ground* 在地下埋入一根杆子 ➲ SEE ALSO SUNKEN
• **PREVENT SUCCESS** 使不成功 **9** [T] **~ sth/sb** (*informal*) to prevent sb or sb's plans from succeeding 使失败；使受挫；阻挠：*I think I've just sunk my chances of getting the job.* 我想，我刚刚葬送了得到那份工作的机会。◇ *If the car breaks down, we'll* ***be sunk*** (= have serious problems). 要是车坏了，咱们可就惨了。
• **BALL** 球 **10** [T] **~ sth** to hit a ball into a hole in GOLF or SNOOKER（高尔夫球）击球入洞；（斯诺克）击球入袋：*He sank a 12-foot putt to win the match.* 他以一记 12 英尺的轻击入洞赢了比赛。
• **ALCOHOL** 酒 **11** [T] **~ sth** (*BrE, informal*) to drink sth quickly, especially a large amount of alcohol 猛喝；灌
IDM **be ˈsunk in sth** to be in a state of unhappiness or deep thought 陷入不快（或沉思）中：*She just sat there, sunk in thought.* 她只一味地坐在那儿，陷入了沉思。**(like rats) deserting/leaving a sinking ˈship** (*humorous, disapproving*) used to talk about people who leave an organization, a company, etc. that is having difficulties, without caring about the people who are left（比喻只顾自己而离开处于困境中的机构等）（像）逃离沉船（的老鼠）**sink your ˈdifferences** to agree to forget about your disagreements 摒弃分歧；搁置歧见 **a/that ˈsinking feeling** (*informal*) an unpleasant feeling that you get when you realize that sth bad has happened or is going to happen 不祥的感觉；沮丧之情 **ˌsink or ˈswim** to be in a situation where you will either succeed by your own efforts or fail completely 不自救，必沉沦；自己努力，以求生存：*The new students were just left to sink or swim.* 学校完全让新生自生自灭。**ˌsink so ˈlow | sink to sth** to have such low moral standards that you do sth very bad 堕落到这种地步；沉沦到某种程度：*Stealing from your friends? How could you sink so low?* 偷到你的朋友头上了？你怎么能堕落到这种地步呢？◇ *I can't believe that anyone would sink to such depths.* 我无法相信竟然有人能堕落到这种程度。➲ MORE AT HEART
PHR V **ˌsink ˈin | ˌsink ˈinto sth 1** (of words, an event, etc. 话语、事情等) to be fully understood or realized 被完全理解；被充分意识到：*He paused to allow his words to sink in.* 他停了一下，好让人充分领会他的意思。◇ *The full scale of the disaster has yet to sink in.* 人们还没有完全意识到这场灾难的严重程度。**2** (of liquids 液体) to go down into another substance through the surface 渗透；渗入：*The rain sank into the dry ground.* 雨水渗进了干地里。**ˈsink into sth** to go gradually into a less active, happy or pleasant state 渐渐进入（消极、不快等的）状态：*She sank into a deep sleep.* 她沉沉地睡去。◇ *He sank deeper into depression.* 他越来越消沉。**ˌsink ˈinto sth | ˌsink sth ˈinto sth** to go, or to make sth sharp go, deep into sth solid （把某物）插入：*The dog sank its teeth into my leg* (= bit it). 狗狠咬了我的腿。◇ *I felt her nails sink into my wrist.* 我感觉她的指甲抠进了我的手腕里。**ˌsink sth ˈinto sth** to spend a lot of money on a business or an activity, for example in order to make money from it in the future 把资金投入企业（或活动）：*We sank all our savings into the venture.* 我们把所有的积蓄都投进了那家企业。
■ ***noun*** **1** a large open container in a kitchen that has taps/faucets to supply water and that you use for washing dishes in（厨房里的）洗涤池，洗碗槽：*Don't just leave your dirty plates in the sink!* 别把脏盘子往洗碗槽里一放就不管了！◇ *I felt chained to the kitchen sink* (= I had to spend all my time doing jobs in the house). 我觉得就像拴在了灶台上一样。➲ PICTURE AT PLUG ➲ **VISUAL VOCAB PAGE V26 2** (*especially NAmE*) = WASHBASIN IDM SEE KITCHEN
■ ***adj.*** [only before noun] (*BrE*) located in a poor area where social conditions are bad 位于贫穷地区的；贫民窟的：*the misery of life in* ***sink estates*** 贫民窟里的悲惨生活 ◇ *a* ***sink school*** 贫困地区的学校

sink·er /ˈsɪŋkə(r)/ *noun* a weight that is attached to a FISHING LINE or net to keep it under the water（钓丝或渔网上的）沉子，铅锤，坠子 IDM SEE HOOK *n.*

sink·hole /ˈsɪŋkhəʊl; *NAmE* -hoʊl/ (*also* ˈ**swallow hole**) *noun* (*geology* 地) a large hole in the ground that a river flows into, created over a long period of time by water that has fallen as rain 落水洞（在地下，雨水长期渗落形成）

sin·ner /ˈsɪnə(r)/ *noun* (*formal*) a person who has committed a SIN or SINS (= broken God's law) 罪人

Sinn Fein /ˌʃɪn ˈfeɪn/ *noun* [U+sing./pl. v.] an Irish political party that wants Northern Ireland and the Republic of Ireland to become one country 新芬党（爱尔兰政党，主张北爱尔兰和爱尔兰共和国统一）

Sino- /ˈsaɪnəʊ; *NAmE* -noʊ/ *combining form* (in nouns and adjectives 构成名词和形容词) Chinese 中国的；中国人（的）：*Sino-Japanese relations* 中日关系

sinu·ous /ˈsɪnjuəs/ *adj.* (*literary*) turning while moving, in an elegant way; having many curves 弯曲有致的；蜿蜒的：*a sinuous movement* 婀娜多姿的动作 ◇ *the sinuous grace of a cat* 猫的灵活优美 ◇ *the sinuous course of the river* 弯弯曲曲的河道 ▸ **sinu·ous·ly** *adv.*

si·nus /ˈsaɪnəs/ *noun* any of the hollow spaces in the bones of the head that are connected to the inside of the nose 窦；窦道：*blocked sinuses* 窦性传导阻滞

si·nus·itis /ˌsaɪnəˈsaɪtɪs/ *noun* [U] the painful swelling of the sinuses 鼻窦炎

-sion ➲ -ION

Sioux /suː/ *noun* (*pl.* **Sioux**) a member of a Native American people from the northern central region of the U.S. 苏人（美国中北部地区的美洲土著）

sip /sɪp/ *verb, noun*

■ ***verb*** (**-pp-**) [I, T] to drink sth, taking a very small amount each time 小口喝；抿：**~ (at sth)** *She sat there, sipping at her tea.* 她坐在那儿抿着茶。◇ **~ sth** *He slowly sipped his wine.* 他慢酌浅饮。

■ ***noun*** a very small amount of a drink that you take into your mouth 一小口（饮料）：*to* ***have/take a sip*** *of water* 喝一小口水

si·phon (*also* **sy·phon**) /ˈsaɪfn/ *noun, verb*

■ ***noun*** a tube that is used to move liquid from one container down into another, lower container 虹吸管

■ ***verb*** **1 ~ sth (+ adv./prep.)** to move a liquid from one container to another, using a siphon 用虹吸管吸（或抽）：*I siphoned the gasoline out of the car into a can.* 我用虹吸管把汽车里的汽油抽到桶里。◇ *The waste liquid needs to be siphoned off.* 需要把废液抽走。**2 ~ sth (+ adv./prep.)** (*informal*) to remove money from one place and move it to another, especially dishonestly or illegally（尤指私自或非法）抽走，转移（钱）**SYN** **divert**：*She has been accused of* ***siphoning off*** *thousands of pounds from the company into her own bank account.* 她被指控把公司的几千英镑转移到了自己的账户里。

sippy cup /ˈsɪpi kʌp/ *noun* (*NAmE, informal*) **1** a cup with a lid that has holes in it so that a baby can suck liquid from it（幼儿用）鸭嘴杯 **2** (*especially NAmE*) a cardboard or plastic cup with a lid with a hole in it, that is used when you buy a drink to take away and drink somewhere else 外卖饮料杯（有盖，盖上有孔）

sir 🔑 /sɜː(r); sə(r)/ *noun* **1** 🔑 used as a polite way of addressing a man whose name you do not know, for example in a shop/store or restaurant, or to show respect（对不认识的男性的称呼或对男性的尊称）先生：*Good morning, sir. Can I help you?* 早上好，先生。您要点什么？◇ *Are you ready to order, sir?* 先生，可以点菜了吗？◇ *'Report to me tomorrow, corporal!' 'Yes, sir!'* “下士，明天来向我报告！”“是，长官！”◇ *'Thank you very much.' 'You're welcome, sir. Have a nice day.'* “多谢。”“不客气，先生。祝您愉快。” ➲ COMPARE MA'AM (1) ➲ SEE ALSO MADAM (1) **2** 🔑 **Dear Sir/Sirs** used at the beginning of a formal business letter when you do not know the name of the man or people that you are dealing with（正式信函中对不知其名的男性收信人的称呼）先生，阁下：*Dear Sir/Sirs* 亲爱的先生/诸位先生 ◇ *Dear Sir or Madam* 亲爱的先生或女士 **3** 🔑 **Sir** a title that is used before the first name of a man who has received one of the highest British honours (= a KNIGHT), or before the first name of a BARONET（贵族头衔，用于爵士或准男爵的名字或姓名前面）爵士：*Sir Paul McCartney* 保罗·麦卡特尼爵士 ◇ *Thank you, Sir Paul.* 谢谢，保罗爵士。➲ COMPARE LADY (6) **4** (*BrE*) used as a form of address by children in school to a male teacher（中小学生对男教师的称呼）先生，老师：*Please, sir, can I open a window?* 老师，请允许我打开一扇窗户好吗？ ➲ COMPARE MISS *n.* (4)

IDM ˌ**no ˈsir!** | ˌ**no siˈree!** (*informal, especially NAmE*) certainly not 决不：*We will never allow that to happen! No sir!* 我们决不会允许那样的事情发生！决不会！ˌ**yes ˈsir!** | ˌ**yes siˈree!** (*informal, especially NAmE*) used to emphasize that sth is true（强调所言不虚）的确：*That's a fine car you have. Yes sir!* 你这辆车真好。的确好！

sire /ˈsaɪə(r)/ *noun, verb*

■ ***noun*** **1** (*specialist*) the male parent of an animal, especially a horse 雄性种畜；（尤指）公种马 ➲ COMPARE DAM *n.* (2) **2** (*old use*) a word that people used when they addressed a king（旧时对国王的称呼）陛下

■ ***verb*** **1 ~ sth** to be the male parent of an animal, especially a horse（种马等雄性动物）生殖，繁殖 **2 ~ sth** (*old-fashioned* or *humorous*) to become the father of a child 成为父亲

siree (*also* **sir·ree**) /səˈriː/ *exclamation* (*NAmE, informal*) used for emphasis, especially after 'yes' or 'no'（加强语气，尤在 yes 或 no 之后）：*He's not going to do it, no siree.* 他不会干这事的，绝对不会。

siren /ˈsaɪrən/ *noun* **1** a device that makes a long loud sound as a signal or warning 汽笛；警报器；警笛：*an air-raid siren* 空袭警报器 ◇ *A police car raced past with its siren wailing.* 一辆警车鸣着警报器飞驰而过。**2** (in ancient Greek stories) any of a group of sea creatures that were part woman and part bird, or part woman and part fish, whose beautiful singing made sailors sail towards them into rocks or dangerous waters 塞壬（古希腊神话中半人半鸟或半人半鱼的女海妖，以美妙歌声诱使水手驶向礁石或进入危险水域）**3** a woman who is very attractive or beautiful but also dangerous 妖冶而危险的女人；性感妖女 **4 ~ voices/song/call** (*literary*) the TEMPTATION to do sth that seems very attractive but that will have bad results 危险的诱惑：*The government must resist the siren voices calling for tax cuts.* 政府万万不可听信那些鼓吹减税的动听言辞。

sir·loin /ˈsɜːlɔɪn; *NAmE* ˈsɜːrl-/ (*also* ˌ**sirloin ˈsteak**) *noun* [U, C] good quality beef that is cut from a cow's back 牛里脊肉；牛上腰肉

si·rocco (*also* **sci·rocco**) /sɪˈrɒkəʊ; *NAmE* sɪˈrɑːkoʊ/ *noun* (*pl.* **-os**) a hot wind that blows from Africa into southern Europe 西洛可风（从非洲吹到欧洲南部的热风）

sis /sɪs/ *noun* (*informal*) sister (used when you are speaking to her)（用于直接称呼）姐姐，妹妹

sisal /ˈsaɪsl/ *noun* [U] strong FIBRES made from the leaves of a tropical plant also called sisal, used for making rope, floor coverings, etc. 西沙尔麻，剑麻（用同名热带植物制成的纤维，用于制绳、织地毯等）

sissy (*BrE also* **cissy**) /ˈsɪsi/ *noun* (*pl.* **-ies**) (*informal, disapproving*) a boy that other men or boys laugh at because they think he is weak or frightened, or only interested in the sort of things girls like 柔弱（或怯懦）的男孩；女孩子气的男孩 **SYN** **wimp** ▸ **sissy** *adj.*

sis·ter 🔑 /ˈsɪstə(r)/ *noun* **1** 🔑 a girl or woman who has the same mother and father as another person 姐姐；妹妹：*She's my sister.* 她是我姐姐。◇ *an* ***older/younger sister*** 姐姐；妹妹 ◇ (*informal*) *a* ***big/little/kid sister*** 大姐；小妹；年幼的妹妹 ◇ *We're sisters.* 我们是姐妹。◇ *Do you have any* ***brothers or sisters****?* 你有兄弟姐妹吗？◇ *My best friend has been like a sister to me* (= very close). 我最要好的一个朋友和我亲如姐妹。➲ SEE ALSO HALF-SISTER, STEPSISTER **2** used for talking to or about other members of a women's organization or other women who have the same ideas, purpose, etc. as yourself（称志同道合者）姐妹：*They supported their sisters in the dispute.* 在争论中，她们支持自己的姐妹。**3 Sister** (*BrE*) a senior female nurse who is in charge of a hospital WARD 护士长 ➲ SEE ALSO CHARGE NURSE **4 Sister** a female member of a religious group, especially a NUN 女教友；（尤指）修女：*Sister Mary* 修女玛丽 ◇ *the Sisters of Charity* 仁爱修女会 **5** (in the US) a member of a SORORITY (= a club for a group of female students at a college or university)（美国大学）女生联谊会会员 **6** (*NAmE, informal*) used by black people as a form of address for a black woman（黑人的互相称谓）大姐 **7** (usually used as an adjective 通常用作形容词) a thing that belongs to the same type or group as sth else 同类型的；同一批的；如同姐妹的：*our sister company in Italy* 我们在意大利的姊妹公司 ◇ *a sister ship* 同一类型的船

sis·ter·hood /ˈsɪstəhʊd; *NAmE* -tərh-/ *noun* **1** [U] the close loyal relationship between women who share ideas and aims（志同道合者之间的）姐妹情谊 **2** [C+sing./pl. v.] a group of women who live in a community together, especially a religious one 妇女团体；修女会

ˈsister-in-law *noun* (*pl.* **sisters-in-law**) the sister of your husband or wife; your brother's wife; the wife of your husband or wife's brother 配偶的姐姐（或妹妹）；嫂子；弟媳；配偶的嫂子（或弟媳）➲ COMPARE BROTHER-IN-LAW

sis·ter·ly /ˈsɪstəli; *NAmE* -tərli/ *adj.* typical of or like a sister 姐妹的；姐妹般的：*She gave him a sisterly kiss.* 她像姐姐一样亲了他一下。

Sisy·phean /ˌsɪsɪˈfiːən/ *adj.* (of a task 任务) impossible to complete 不可能完成的；永无休止的 **ORIGIN** From the Greek myth in which **Sisyphus** was punished for the bad things he had done in his life with the never-ending task of rolling a large stone to the top of a hill, from which it always rolled down again. 源自希腊神话，西绪福斯（Sisyphus）因前生罪恶受惩罚，无休止地将一块巨石滚到山顶，而巨石总是一再滚落。

sit /sɪt/ *verb* (**sit·ting**, **sat**, **sat** /sæt/)

- **ON CHAIR, ETC.** 在椅子等上面 **1** [I] to rest your weight on your bottom with your back vertical, for example on/in a chair 坐：*She sat and stared at the letter in front of her.* 她坐在那儿，凝视着面前的那封信。◇ **+ adv./prep.** *May I sit here?* 我可以坐在这儿吗？◇ *Just sit still!* 坐着别动！◇ *He went and sat beside her.* 他走过去坐在她身边。◇ *She was sitting at her desk.* 她坐在书桌前。◇ **~ doing sth** *We sat talking for hours.* 我们坐着谈了好几个小时。➲ SEE ALSO SIT DOWN **2** [T] **~ sb + adv./prep.** to put sb in a sitting position 使坐；使就座：*He lifted the child and sat her on the wall.* 他抱起孩子，让她坐在墙头上。
- **OF THINGS** 事物 **3** [I] to be in a particular place 处在；坐落在；被放在：**+ adv./prep.** *A large bus was sitting outside.* 外面停着一辆大巴士。◇ *The pot was sitting in a pool of water.* 罐子放在水里。◇ *The jacket sat beautifully on her shoulders* (= fitted well). 那件夹克穿在她身上很合身。◇ **+ adj.** *The box sat unopened on the shelf.* 盒子搁在架子上，没有打开。
- **HAVE OFFICIAL POSITION** 担任职务 **4** [I] to have an official position as sth or as a member of sth（在…中）任职；任（…的）代表；担任：**~ as sth** *He was sitting as a temporary judge.* 由他担任临时法官。◇ *They both sat as MPs in the House of Commons.* 他们两人都曾是下院议员。◇ **~ in/on sth** *She sat on a number of committees.* 她在几个委员会里任职。◇ **~ for sth** *For years he sat for Henley* (= was the MP for that CONSTITUENCY). 他多年担任代表亨利选区的议会议员。
- **OF PARLIAMENT, ETC.** 议会等 **5** [I] (of a parliament, committee, court of law, etc. 议会、委员会、法庭等) to meet in order to do official business 开会；开庭：*Parliament sits for less than six months of the year.* 议会一年的开会时间不足六个月。
- **EXAM** 考试 **6** [T, I] (*rather formal*) to do an exam 参加考试；应试：(*BrE*) **~ sth** *Candidates will sit the examinations in June.* 考生将在六月参加考试。◇ *Most of the students sit at least 5 GCSEs.* 大多数学生至少参加 5 门普通中等教育证书考试。◇ (*especially NAmE*) **~ for sth** *He was about to sit for his entrance exam.* 当时他正要参加入学考试。
- **OF BIRD** 鸟 **7** [I] (**+ adv./prep.**) to rest on a branch, etc. or to stay on a nest to keep the eggs warm 停落；栖；孵（卵）
- **OF DOG** 狗 **8** [I] to sit on its bottom with its front legs straight 蹲；坐：*Rover! Sit!* 罗弗！蹲下！
- **TAKE CARE OF CHILDREN** 照看小孩 **9** [I] **~ (for sb)** = BABYSIT：*Who's sitting for you?* 谁给你看着孩子呢？➲ SEE ALSO HOUSE-SIT

IDM **be ˌsitting ˈpretty** (*informal*) to be in a good situation, especially when others are not（尤指在他人处境不好时）处境好 **sit at sb's ˈfeet** to admire sb very much, especially a teacher or sb from whom you try to learn 崇拜；拜倒在某人脚下 **sit comfortably, easily, well, etc. (with sth)** to seem right, natural, suitable, etc. in a particular place or situation（在某位置或某场合）显得合适，显得自然，如鱼得水：*His views did not sit comfortably with the management line.* 他的意见和管理部门的方针不大吻合。**sit in ˈjudgement (on/over/upon sb)** to decide whether sb's behaviour is right or wrong, especially when you have no right to do this 褒贬（某人）；（对某人）妄加评判：*How dare you sit in judgement on me?* 你怎么敢对我妄加评论？ **sit on the ˈfence** to avoid becoming involved in deciding or influencing sth 骑墙；持观望态度：*He tends to sit on the fence at meetings.* 开会时他往往持观望态度。**ˌsit ˈtight 1** to stay where you are rather than moving away or changing position 待着不动；守在原地：*We sat tight and waited to be rescued.* 我们守在原地，等待救援。**2** to stay in the same situation,

---

▼ SYNONYMS 同义词辨析

sit

sit down • be seated • take a seat • perch

These words all mean to rest your weight on your bottom with your back upright, for example on a chair. 以上各词均含坐下之义。

sit to rest your weight on your bottom with your back upright, for example on a chair 指坐：*May I sit here?* 我可以坐在这儿吗？◇ *Sit still, will you!* 坐着别动！**NOTE** **Sit** is usually used with an adverb or prepositional phrase to show where or how sb sits, but sometimes another phrase or clause is used to show what sb does while they are sitting. * sit 通常与副词或介词短语连用，表示坐的地方或方式，但有时也与另一短语或从句连用，表明坐着时在做某事：*We sat talking for hours.* 我们坐着谈了好几个小时。

sit down/sit yourself down to move from a standing position to a sitting position 指坐下、就座：*Please sit down.* 请坐。◇ *Come in and sit yourselves down.* 都进来坐下。

be seated (*formal*) to be sitting 指坐着：*She was seated at the head of the table.* 她坐在桌子的上座。**NOTE** **Be seated** is often used as a formal way of inviting sb to sit down. * be seated 常为请人就座的正式表达方式：*Please be seated.* 请就座。

take a seat to sit down 指坐下、就座 **NOTE** **Take a seat** is used especially as a polite way of inviting sb to sit down. * take a seat 尤作请人就座的礼貌用语：*Please take a seat.* 请坐。

perch (*rather informal*) to sit on sth, especially on the edge of sth 指坐在…上，尤指坐在…边沿：*She perched herself on the edge of the bed.* 她坐在床沿上。**NOTE** **Perch** is always used with an adverb or prepositional phrase to show where sb is perching. * perch 总是与副词或介词短语连用表示坐的地方。

PATTERNS

- to sit/sit down/be seated/take a seat/perch **on** sth
- to sit/sit down/be seated/take a seat **in** sth

without changing your mind or taking any action 静观事态变化；不轻举妄动：*Shareholders are being advised to sit tight until the crisis passes.* 股东们得到的忠告是，静待危机过去。➲ MORE AT BOLT *adv.*, LAUREL, SILENTLY

PHR V **,sit a'bout/a'round** (*often disapproving*) to spend time doing nothing very useful 无所事事地消磨时间；闲坐：*I'm far too busy to sit around here.* 我忙得不可开交，没空在这儿闲坐。◇ **sit about/around doing sth** *He just sits around watching TV.* 他整天闲坐着看电视。**,sit 'back 1** to sit on sth, usually a chair, in a relaxed position 舒舒服服地坐好：*He sat back in his chair and started to read.* 他安稳地坐在椅子上，读起书来。**2** to relax, especially by not getting too involved in or anxious about sth 袖手旁观（尤指不积极参与或不挂念某事）：*She's not the kind of person who can sit back and let others do all the work.* 她不是那种自己歇着、什么活儿都让别人干的人。**,sit 'by** to take no action to stop sth bad or wrong from happening 坐视不管；无动于衷：*We cannot just sit by and watch this tragedy happen.* 我们不能坐视这样的悲剧发生。**,sit 'down | ,sit yourself 'down** 🔑 to move from a standing position to a sitting position 坐下；就座：*Please sit down.* 请坐。◇ *He sat down on the bed.* 他在床边坐下。◇ *They sat down to consider the problem.* 他们坐下来考虑这一问题。◇ *Come in and sit yourselves down.* 都进来坐下。**,sit 'down and do sth** to give sth time and attention in order to try to solve a problem or achieve sth 坐下来认真做某事：*This is something that we should sit down and discuss as a team.* 这件事我们应当坐下来一起认真讨论一下。**'sit for sb/sth** [no passive] to be a model for an artist or a photographer 为…做模特：*to sit for your portrait* 摆好姿势让画家画肖像 ◇ *She sat for Augustus John.* 她为奥古斯塔斯·约翰当过模特。**,sit 'in for sb** to do sb's job or perform their duties while they are away, sick, etc. 顶班；代某人履行职责 SYN **stand in** (**for sb**) **,sit 'in on sth** to attend a meeting, class, etc. in order to listen to or learn from it rather than to take an active part 列席（会议）；旁听（课）**'sit on sth** (*informal*) to have received a letter, report, etc. from sb and then not replied or taken any action concerning it 拖延；积压；搁置：*They have been sitting on my application for a month now.* 他们压着我的申请不办有一个月了。**,sit sth↔'out 1** to stay in a place and wait for sth unpleasant or boring to finish 耐心等到结束；熬到结束：*We sat out the storm in a cafe.* 我们坐在一家咖啡馆里，一直等到暴风雨过去。**2** to not take part in a dance, game or other activity 坐在一旁（不参加跳舞、游戏等活动）**'sit through sth** to stay until the end of a performance, speech, meeting, etc. that you think is boring or too long 坐到（表演、演讲、会议等）结束：*We had to sit through nearly two hours of speeches.* 我们不得不耐着性子听完将近两个小时的讲话。**,sit 'up 1** to be or move yourself into a sitting position, rather than lying down or leaning back 坐起来；坐直：*Sit up straight—don't slouch.* 坐直了，别无精打采的。**2** to not go to bed until later than usual 熬夜；迟睡：*We sat up half the night, talking.* 我们谈到了半夜才睡。**,sit 'up (and do sth)** (*informal*) to start to pay careful attention to what is happening, being said, etc. 关注起来；警觉起来：*The proposal had made his clients* ***sit up and take notice.*** 这项建议引起了他的主顾们的关注。**,sit sb 'up** to move sb into a sitting position after they have been lying down 使坐起来

▼ **GRAMMAR POINT** 语法说明

sit

- You can use *on*, *in* and *at* with **sit**. You **sit on** a chair, a step, the edge of the table, etc. You **sit in** an armchair. If you are **sitting at** a table, desk, etc. you are sitting in a chair close to it, usually so that you can eat a meal, do some work, etc. * sit 可与 on、in 和 at 连用：坐在椅子上、台阶上、桌子边上等用 sit on；坐在扶手椅上用 sit in；坐在桌子、书桌等旁吃饭、工作等用 sit at。

sitar /sɪ'tɑː(r); 'sɪtɑː(r)/ *noun* a musical instrument from S Asia like a GUITAR, with a long neck and two sets of metal strings 西塔尔（源自南亚形似吉他的弦乐器）➲ VISUAL VOCAB PAGE V40

sit·com /'sɪtkɒm; *NAmE* -kɑːm/ (*also formal* **,situation 'comedy**) *noun* [C, U] a regular programme on television that shows the same characters in different amusing situations 情景喜剧 ➲ WORDFINDER NOTE AT PROGRAMME ➲ MORE LIKE THIS 1, page R25

'sit-down *noun* [sing.] (*BrE, informal*) a rest while sitting in a chair 坐下休息：*I need a cup of tea and a sit-down.* 我需要坐下来，喝杯茶，休息一下。▶ **'sit-down** *adj.* [only before noun]: *a sit-down protest* (= in which people sit down to block a road or the entrance to a building until people listen to their demands) 静坐抗议 ◇ *a sit-down meal for 50 wedding guests* (= served to people sitting at tables) 为 50 位参加婚礼的客人摆的坐式宴席

site 🔑 AW /saɪt/ *noun, verb*

■ ***noun*** **1** 🔑 a place where a building, town, etc. was, is or will be located（建筑物、城镇等的）地点，位置，建筑工地：*the site of a sixteenth century abbey* 一座十六世纪的修道院的旧址 ◇ *to work on a* ***building/construction site*** 在建筑工地工作 ◇ *A site has been chosen for the new school.* 已为新学校选了校址。◇ *All the materials are* ***on site*** *so that work can start immediately.* 所有材料都已运抵工地，可以立即开工。➲ SYNONYMS AT PLACE ➲ WORDFINDER NOTE AT CONSTRUCTION **2** 🔑 a place where sth has happened or that is used for sth 现场；发生地；场所：*the site of the battle* 战场 ◇ *an archaeological site* 考古现场 ◇ ***a camping/caravan site*** 营地；旅行拖车停车点 **3** 🔑 (*computing* 计) a place on the Internet where a company, an organization, a university, etc. puts information 站点；网站 ➲ COLLOCATIONS AT EMAIL ➲ SEE ALSO MIRROR SITE, WEBSITE

■ ***verb*** [often passive] **~ sth + adv./prep.** to build or place sth in a particular position 使坐落在；为…选址：*There was a meeting to discuss the siting of the new school.* 已开会讨论了新学校的选址。◇ *The castle is magnificently sited high up on a cliff.* 城堡坐落在高高的悬崖，十分壮观。

'sit-in *noun* a protest in which a group of workers, students, etc. refuse to leave their factory, college, etc. until people listen to their demands（建筑物内的）静坐罢工，静坐示威：*to* ***hold/stage a sit-in*** 举行静坐示威

sit·ter /'sɪtə(r)/ *noun* **1** a person who sits or stands somewhere so that sb can paint a picture of them or photograph them 摆姿势让人画像（或拍照）的人 **2** (*especially NAmE*) = BABYSITTER **3** (*BrE, informal*) (in football (SOCCER) 足球) an easy chance to score a goal 得分良机

sit·ting /'sɪtɪŋ/ *noun* **1** a period of time during which a court or a parliament deals with its business（法院或议会的）开会，会议，开庭（期间）**2** a time when a meal is served in a hotel, etc. to a number of people at the same time （旅馆等分段安排客人用餐的）一轮，一次：*A hundred people can be served* ***at one sitting*** (= at the same time). 可同时供一百人就餐。**3** a period of time that a person spends sitting and doing an activity 一次（坐着活动的时间）：*I read the book* ***in one sitting.*** 我坐下来一口气就把那本书看完了。**4** a period of time when sb sits or stands to have their picture painted or be photographed（摆姿势让人画像或拍照的）一次（时间）

,sitting 'duck (*also* **,sitting 'target**) *noun* a person or thing that is easy to attack 易受攻击者；易被击中的目标

'sitting room *noun* = LIVING ROOM

,sitting 'tenant *noun* (*BrE*) a person who is living in a rented house or flat and who has the legal right to stay there （房屋或公寓有合法权利的）现有房客，现租户

situ ➲ IN SITU

situ·ate /'sɪtʃueɪt/ *verb* (*formal*) **1 ~ sth + adv./prep.** to build or place sth in a particular position 使位于；使坐落于 **2 ~ sth + adv./prep.** to consider how an idea, event, etc. is related to other things that influence your view of it 将…置于；使联系：*Let me try and situate the events in*

S

their historical context. 我尽量把这些事件与其历史背景联系起来。

situ·ated /ˈsɪtʃueɪtɪd/ *adj.* [not before noun] (*formal*) **1** in a particular place or position 位于；坐落在：*My bedroom was situated on the top floor of the house.* 我的卧室在房子的顶层。◇ *The hotel is **beautifully situated** in a quiet spot near the river.* 旅馆环境优美，坐落在河边一个僻静的地方。◇ *All the best theatres and restaurants are situated within a few minutes' walk of each other.* 所有最好的剧院和饭店相隔只有几分钟的路程。**2** (of a person, an organization, etc. 人、组织等) in a particular situation or in particular circumstances 处于…状况；处境…：*Small businesses are well situated to benefit from the single market.* 小企业所处的形势有利于从单一市场中受益。

situ·ation /ˌsɪtʃuˈeɪʃn/ *noun* **1** all the circumstances and things that are happening at a particular time and in a particular place 情况；状况；形势；局面：*to be **in a difficult situation*** 处境困难 ◇ *You could get into **a situation where** you have to decide immediately.* 你可能遇上一种情况，使你不得不立刻作出决定。◇ *We have all been in similar embarrassing situations.* 我们都遇到过类似的尴尬局面。◇ *the present **economic/financial/political, etc. situation*** 目前的经济、财政、政治等形势 ◇ *He could see no way out of the situation.* 他找不到摆脱困境的出路。◇ *In your situation, I would look for another job.* 假如我是你的话，我会另找工作。◇ *What we have here is a crisis situation.* 我们在这里所面临的是一个危机局面。◇ *I'm in a **no-win situation*** (= whatever I do will be bad for me). 我处在一种注定要失败的境地。**2** (*formal*) the kind of area or surroundings that a building or town has（建筑物或城镇的）地理位置，环境特点：*The town is in a delightful situation in a wide green valley.* 小城坐落在一个宽阔而草木苍翠的河谷中，环境宜人。**3** (*old-fashioned* or *formal*) a job 职业；工作岗位：***Situations Vacant*** (= the title of the section in a newspaper where jobs are advertised) 招聘（报章中的招聘广告栏）IDM SEE SAVE *v.* ▶ **situ·ation·al** /ˌsɪtʃuˈeɪʃənl/ *adj.*

ˌsituation ˈcomedy *noun* [C, U] (*formal*) = SITCOM

ˈsit-up (*also* **crunch**) *noun* an exercise for making your stomach muscles strong, in which you lie on your back on the floor and raise the top part of your body to a sitting position 仰卧起坐 ⇨VISUAL VOCAB PAGE V46

six /sɪks/ *number* 6 六 HELP There are examples of how to use numbers at the entry for **five**. 数词用法示例见 five 条。

IDM **at ˌsixes and ˈsevens** (*informal*) in confusion; not well organized 乱七八糟；凌乱 **be ˌsix feet ˈunder** (*informal*) to be dead and in a grave 入土；在九泉之下 **hit/knock sb for ˈsix** (*BrE*) to affect sb very deeply 极大地影响某人 **it's six of ˌone and half a dozen of the ˈother** (*saying*) used to say that there is not much real difference between two possible choices 半斤八两；不相上下

the ˌSix ˈCounties *noun* [pl.] a way of referring to Northern Ireland, used especially by people who want the whole of Ireland to be one country 北爱尔兰六郡（尤指希望爱尔兰统一的人对北爱尔兰的一种提法）

sixer /ˈsɪksə(r)/ *noun* (*especially IndE*) (in cricket) a hit that scores six points（板球）六分打，六分球

ˌsix-ˈfigure *adj.* [only before noun] used to describe a number that is 100 000 or more 六位数的：*a six-figure salary* 六位数的薪金

six·fold /ˈsɪksfəʊld; *NAmE* -foʊld/ *adj., adv.* ⇨-FOLD

ˈsix-gun *noun* = SIX-SHOOTER

ˈsix-pack *noun* **1** a set of six bottles or cans sold together, especially of beer（尤指啤酒）六瓶装，六罐装 **2** (*informal*) stomach muscles that are very strong and that you can see clearly across sb's stomach 块块隆起的腹肌

▼ **SYNONYMS 同义词辨析**

situation

circumstances • position • conditions • things • the case • state of affairs

These are all words for the conditions and facts that are connected with and affect the way things are. 以上各词均指情况、状况。

situation all the things that are happening at a particular time and in a particular place 指情况、状况、形势、局面：*the present economic situation* 目前的经济形势

circumstances the facts that are connected with and affect a situation, an event or an action; the conditions of a person's life, especially the money they have 指条件、环境、状况、境况，（尤指）经济状况：*The ship sank in mysterious circumstances.* 那艘船神秘地沉没了。

position the situation that sb is in, especially when it affects what they can and cannot do 指处境、地位、状况：*She felt she was in a position of power.* 她觉得她自己有权力。

conditions the circumstances in which people live, work or do things; the physical situation that affects how sth happens 指居住、工作或做事情的环境、境况、条件，影响某事发生的物质环境、状态、条件：*We were forced to work outside in freezing conditions.* 我们被迫在户外天寒地冻的环境下工作。

CIRCUMSTANCES OR CONDITIONS? 用 circumstances 还是 conditions?

Circumstances refers to sb's financial situation; **conditions** are things such as the quality and amount of food or shelter they have. The **circumstances** that affect an event are the facts surrounding it; the **conditions** that affect it are usually physical ones, such as the weather. * circumstances 指人的经济状况；conditions 指人的食宿等状况。circumstances 指影响某事的周边环境；conditions 通常指影响某事的物质环境，如天气。

things (*rather informal*) the general situation, as it affects sb 指形势、局面、情况、事态：*Hi, Jane! **How are things?*** 喂，简，近来怎么样？◇ *Think things over before you decide.* 先把情况考虑周全再作决定。

the case the true situation 指实情、事实：*If that is the case* (= if the situation described is true), *we need more staff.* 如果真是那样，我们就需要更多的员工了。

state of affairs a situation 指事态、情况、形势：*How did this unhappy state of affairs come about?* 这种不幸的情况是怎么发生的呢？

SITUATION OR STATE OF AFFAIRS? 用 situation 还是 state of affairs?

State of affairs is mostly used with *this*. It is also used with adjectives describing how good or bad a situation is, such as *happy, sorry, shocking, sad* and *unhappy*, as well as those relating to time, such as *present* and *current*. **Situation** is much more frequent and is used in a wider variety of contexts. * state of affairs 多与 this 连用，亦与表示形势好坏的形容词（如 happy、sorry、shocking、sad 和 unhappy）以及与时间有关的形容词（如 present 和 current）连用。situation 常用得多，且用于更广泛的语境中。

PATTERNS

- **in** (a) particular situation/circumstances/position/state of affairs
- the/sb's **economic/financial/social** situation/circumstances/position/conditions
- (a/an) **happy/unhappy** situation/circumstances/position/state of affairs
- to **look at/review** the situation/circumstances/conditions/things

six·pence /ˈsɪkspəns/ *noun* a British coin in use until 1971, worth six old pence 六便士硬币（英国 1971 年以前使用）

ˈsix-shooter (*also* **ˈsix-gun**) *noun* (*especially NAmE*) a small gun that holds six bullets 六发左轮手枪

six·teen 🔑 /ˌsɪksˈtiːn/ *number* 16 十六 ▸ **six·teenth** /ˌsɪksˈtiːnθ/ *ordinal number, noun* HELP There are examples of how to use ordinal numbers at the entry for **fifth**. 序数词用法示例见 fifth 条。

ˌsixˈteenth note (*NAmE*) (*BrE* **semi·quaver**) *noun* (*music* 音) a note that lasts half as long as a QUAVER/EIGHTH NOTE 十六分音符 ➲ PICTURE AT MUSIC

sixth 🔑 /sɪksθ/ *ordinal number, noun*

■ ***ordinal number*** 🔑 6th 第六 HELP There are examples of how to use ordinal numbers at the entry for **fifth**. 序数词用法示例见 fifth 条。

■ ***noun*** 🔑 each of six equal parts of sth 六分之一

ˈsixth form *noun* [usually sing.] (*BrE*) the two final years at school for students between the ages of 16 and 18 who are preparing to take A LEVELS (= advanced level exams) 第六学级（英国中等学校的最后两年，学生年龄在 16 至 18 岁之间，准备参加高级证书考试）: *Sue is in the sixth form now.* 休正在读中学最后两年。

ˌsixth-form ˈcollege *noun* (in Britain) a school for students over the age of 16（英国）第六学级学院

ˈsixth-former *noun* (*BrE*) a student who is in the sixth form at school 第六学级学生

ˌsixth ˈsense *noun* [sing.] a special ability to know sth without using any of the five senses that include sight, touch, etc. 第六感觉；直觉：*My sixth sense told me to stay here and wait.* 直觉告诉我应该待在这儿等着。

sixty 🔑 /ˈsɪksti/ **1** 🔑 *number* 60 六十 **2** *noun* **the sixties** [pl.] numbers, years or temperatures from 60 to 69 六十几；六十年代 ▸ **six·ti·eth** 🔑 /ˈsɪkstiəθ/ *ordinal number, noun* HELP There are examples of how to use ordinal numbers at the entry for **fifth**. 序数词用法示例见 fifth 条。

IDM **in your ˈsixties** between the ages of 60 and 69 * 60 多岁

the ˌsixty-four ˌthousand ˌdollar ˈquestion *noun* (*informal*) the thing that people most want to know, or that is most important 最想知道（或最重要）的事情；关键问题 ORIGIN From the name of a US television show which gave prizes of money to people who answered questions correctly. The correct answer to the last question was worth $64 000. 源自美国有奖竞答电视节目名称，答对最后一题的奖金为 64 000 美元。

size 🔑 /saɪz/ *noun, verb*

■ ***noun***

• **HOW LARGE/SMALL** 大小 **1** 🔑 [U, C] how large or small a person or thing is 大小：*an area **the size of*** (= the same size as) *Wales* 一个面积相当于威尔士的地区 ◇ *They complained about the size of their gas bill.* 他们抱怨煤气费用太高。◇ *Dogs come **in all shapes and sizes**.* 狗有大有小，模样也各不相同。◇ *The facilities are excellent for a town that size.* 对于如此规模的一个城镇来说，其市政设施堪称一流。◇ *The kitchen is **a good size*** (= not small). 这厨房够大的。◇ *It's similar **in size** to a tomato.* 大小和西红柿差不多。**2** 🔑 [U] the large amount or extent of sth 大量；大规模：*You should have seen the size of their house!* 你真该看看他们的房子有多大！◇ *We were shocked at the size of his debts.* 他欠债之多让我们震惊。

• **OF CLOTHES/SHOES/GOODS** 服装；鞋；商品 **3** 🔑 [C, U] one of a number of standard measurements in which clothes, shoes and other goods are made and sold 尺码；号：*The jacket was the wrong size.* 这件夹克尺码不对。◇ *It's not my size.* 这个号我不能穿。◇ *They didn't have the jacket **in my size**.* 那款夹克没有我穿的尺码。◇ *She's a size 12 in clothes.* 她穿 12 号的衣服。◇ *The hats are made in three sizes: small, medium and large.* 这些帽子分小、中、大三个尺码。◇ *I need a bigger/smaller size.* 我需要一件尺码稍大 / 稍小的。◇ *What size do you take?* 你穿多大号的？◇ *She takes (a) size 5 in shoes.* 她穿 5 号鞋。◇ *Do you have these shoes in (a) size 5?* 这款鞋有 5 号的吗？◇ *Try this one **for size*** (= to see if it is the correct size). 试试这件，看尺码合适不合适。◇ *The glass can be **cut to size*** (= cut to the exact measurements) *for you.* 玻璃可以切割成你要的尺寸。HELP To ask about the size of something, you usually say: *How big?* You use: *What size?* to ask about something that is produced in fixed measurements. 问某物的大小，通常说 How big。What size 则用来询问制成品的固定尺寸。

• **-SIZED/-SIZE** …大小 **4** (in adjectives 构成形容词) having the size mentioned …大小的；…规模的：*a medium-sized house* 中等大小的房子 ◇ *Cut it into bite-size pieces.* 把它切成能一口吃下去的小块。➲ SEE ALSO KING-SIZE, MAN-SIZED, PINT-SIZED, QUEEN-SIZE

• **STICKY SUBSTANCE** 胶料 **5** [U] a sticky substance that is used for making material stiff or for preparing walls for WALLPAPER（使织物等坚挺的）胶料，浆料；（贴壁纸用的）涂料

IDM **cut sb down to ˈsize** to show sb that they are not as important as they think they are 使某人有自知之明；让某人知道自己是谁 **that's about the ˈsize of it** (*informal*) that's how the situation seems to be 情况大致就是这样：*'So they won't pay up?' 'That's about the size of it.'* "这么说他们不打算还清欠款？" "基本是这样。"

■ ***verb***

• **GIVE SIZE** 测量大小 **1** [usually passive] **~ sth** to mark the size of sth; to give a size to sth 标定…的大小；确定…的尺寸：*The screws are sized in millimetres.* 这些螺丝是用毫米标定大小的。

• **CHANGE SIZE** 改变大小 **2** [usually passive] **~ sth** to change the size of sth 改变…的大小：*The fonts can be sized according to what effect you want.* 可根据你想要的效果改变字号。

• **MAKE STICKY** 使胶黏 **3** **~ sth** to cover sth with a sticky substance called SIZE 上胶料；上浆；上涂料

PHR V **ˌsize sb/sth ↔ˈup** (*informal*) to form a judgement or an opinion about sb/sth 估量；判断 SYN **sum up**: *She knew that he was looking at her, sizing her up.* 她知道他在盯着她看，打量她。◇ *He sized up the situation very quickly.* 他很快对形势作出了判断。

size·able (*also* **siz·able**) /ˈsaɪzəbl/ *adj.* fairly large 相当大的 SYN **considerable**: *The town has a sizeable Sikh population.* 城里有为数众多的锡克教教徒。

ˌsize ˈzero *noun* [U, C] (in the US) the smallest size for women's clothes, used to describe women who are extremely thin 零号（在美国指女服的最小号，用以描述极瘦女子）：*size zero models and celebrities* 瘦极了的模特儿和名人 ◇ *She is a size zero.* 她瘦得不能再瘦。

siz·zle /ˈsɪzl/ *verb* [I] **1** to make the sound of food frying in hot oil 发出（油煎食物的）嗞嗞声：*sizzling sausages* 煎得嗞嗞作响的香肠 **2** to be very exciting, especially in a sexual way 撩拨人心；性感火辣：*The screen sizzles whenever she appears on it.* 她每次现身荧屏都性感撩人。▸ **siz·zle** *noun* [sing., U]

siz·zling /ˈsɪzlɪŋ/ *adj.* **1** very hot 酷热的：*sizzling summer temperatures* 夏日灼人的高温 **2** very exciting 热烈的；激情迸发的：*a sizzling love affair* 热烈的风流韵事

sjam·bok /ˈʃæmbɒk; *NAmE* -bɑːk/ *noun* (*SAfrE*) a long, stiff WHIP made of leather 粗长皮鞭

ska /skɑː/ *noun* [U] a type of fast popular music with strong rhythms, developed in Jamaica in the 1960s and that developed into REGGAE 斯卡（20 世纪 60 年代兴起于牙买加的一种节奏强而快的流行音乐，后来发展成雷盖音乐）

skank /skæŋk/ *noun* (*informal, especially NAmE*) an unpleasant person 缺德的人；讨厌鬼

skanky /ˈskæŋki/ *adj.* (*informal, especially NAmE*) very unpleasant 令人反感的；令人讨厌的

skate /skeɪt/ *verb, noun*

■ ***verb*** **1** [I, T] to move on skates (usually referring to ICE SKATING, if no other information is given)（通常指）滑冰，溜冰：*Can you skate?* 你会滑冰吗？◇ *It was so cold*

S

that we were able to **go skating** on the lake. 天气极冷，我们能到湖上去滑冰了。◇ ~ **sth** *He skated an exciting programme at the American Championships.* 他在美国锦标赛上滑出一组扣人心弦的动作。**2** [I] to ride on a SKATEBOARD 滑（滑板）IDM SEE THIN *adj.*

PHR V ˌ**skate ˈover sth** to avoid talking about or considering a difficult subject 回避；避免涉及：*He politely skated over the issue.* 他礼貌地避开了那个问题。

■ ***noun*** **1** = ICE SKATE, ROLLER SKATE: *a pair of skates* 一双冰鞋 ➲ VISUAL VOCAB PAGE V48 **2** (*pl.* **skate** or **skates**) a large flat sea fish that can be eaten 鳐（扁体鱼，可食用）

IDM **get/put your ˈskates on** (*BrE, informal*) used to tell sb to hurry 赶紧；赶快：*Get your skates on or you'll miss the bus.* 快点，要不你就赶不上公共汽车了。

skate·board /ˈskeɪtbɔːd; *NAmE* -bɔːrd/ *noun* a short narrow board with small wheels at each end, which you stand on and ride as a sport 滑板：*a **skateboard park/ramp*** 滑板场 / 坡道 ▶ **skate·board** *verb* [I] **skate·board·er** *noun* **skate·board·ing** *noun* [U]: *a skateboarding magazine* 滑板运动杂志 ➲ VISUAL VOCAB PAGE V44

skate·park /ˈskeɪtpɑːk; *NAmE* -pɑːrk/ *noun* an area built for people to use SKATEBOARDS, with slopes, curves, etc. 滑板运动场（有斜坡、曲面等）

skater /ˈskeɪtə(r)/ *noun* **1** a person who skates for pleasure or as a sport 滑冰者；溜冰者；滑冰运动员：*a **figure/speed skater*** 花样滑冰 / 速滑运动员 ➲ SEE ALSO ICE SKATER at ICE-SKATE **2** = SKATEBOARDER: *Extreme skaters perform jumps, spins, flips, etc.* 极限滑板运动员能做跳跃、旋转、空翻等动作。

ˈ**skate shoe** (*especially BrE*) (*also* **Heely™** *especially in BrE, NAmE* ˈ**roller shoe**) *noun* a sports shoe that has one or more wheels underneath it 暴走鞋；飞行鞋；滑轮运动鞋

skat·ing /ˈskeɪtɪŋ/ *noun* [U] **1** (*also* ˈ**ice skating**) the sport or activity of moving on ice on SKATES 滑冰；溜冰：*to go skating* 去滑冰 ➲ SEE ALSO FIGURE-SKATING, SPEED SKATING **2** = ROLLER SKATE IDM SEE THIN *adj.*

ˈ**skating rink** (*also* **rink**) *noun* **1** = ICE RINK ➲ VISUAL VOCAB PAGE V44 **2** an area or a building where you can ROLLER SKATE 旱冰场；旱冰馆

ske·dad·dle /skɪˈdædl/ *verb* [I] (*informal, humorous*) to move away or leave a place quickly, especially in order to avoid sb 匆忙离去，溜走（尤指为了躲避某人）

skeet·er /ˈskiːtə(r)/ *noun* (*NAmE, informal, humorous*) = MOSQUITO

skeet shooting /ˈskiːt ʃuːtɪŋ/ (*NAmE*) (*BrE* ˌ**clay ˈpigeon shooting**) *noun* a sport in which a disc of baked clay (called a **clay pigeon**) is thrown into the air for people to shoot at 泥鸽飞靶射击运动

skein /skeɪn/ *noun* a long piece of wool, thread, or YARN that is loosely tied together 一束，一绞（毛线、线或纱）

skel·etal /ˈskelətl/ *adj.* **1** (*specialist*) connected with the skeleton of a person or an animal 骨骼的 **2** looking like a skeleton 骨瘦如柴的：*skeletal figures dressed in rags* 衣衫褴褛、骨瘦如柴的人 **3** that exists only in a basic form, as an outline 梗概的；提纲性的；提要性的；轮廓的：*He has written only a skeletal plot for the book so far.* 那本书他目前只写了一个情节梗概。

skel·eton /ˈskelɪtn/ *noun* **1** [C] the structure of bones that supports the body of a person or an animal; a model of this structure 骨骼；骨架；骨骼标本：*The human skeleton consists of 206 bones.* 人的骨骼由 206 块骨头组成。◇ *a dinosaur skeleton* 恐龙骨架 ➲ VISUAL VOCAB PAGE V64 **2** [C] (*informal*) a very thin person or animal 骨瘦如柴的人（或动物）**3** [C, usually sing.] the main structure that supports a building, etc.（建筑物等的）骨架，框架 SYN **framework**: *Only the concrete skeleton of the factory remained.* 厂房只剩下混凝土骨架了。**4** [C, usually sing.] the basic outline of a plan, piece of writing, etc. to which more details can be added later 梗概；提纲；提要；轮廓：*Examples were used to flesh out the skeleton of the argument.* 通过例证使干巴巴的论点充实起来。**5** [C] ~ **staff, crew, etc.** the smallest number of people, etc. that you need to do sth（维持运转所需的）最少人员，基干人员：*There will only be a skeleton staff on duty over the holiday.* 假期将只留必需的少数职员值班。◇ *We managed to operate a skeleton bus service during the strike.* 罢工期间，我们设法保持最起码的公共汽车营运。**6** [C] (*sport* 体育) a type of SLEDGE/SLED (= a vehicle for sliding over ice) for racing, used by one person lying on their front with their feet pointing backwards（一种单人比赛用的）俯式冰橇，骨架雪车 **7** [U] the sport or event of racing down a special track of ice on a skeleton 俯式冰橇运动：*Canada won gold and silver in the skeleton.* 加拿大选手在俯式冰橇项目中包揽金银牌。

IDM **a skeleton in the ˈcupboard** (*BrE*) (*also* **a skeleton in the ˈcloset** *NAmE, BrE*) (*informal*) something shocking, embarrassing, etc. that has happened to you or your family in the past that you want to keep secret 隐衷；不可外扬的家丑

ˈ**skeleton key** *noun* a key that will open several different locks 万能钥匙

skelm /skelm/ *noun* (*SAfrE*) a person that you believe is a criminal or that you do not trust 地痞；流氓；无赖；不可信任的人

skep·tic (*NAmE*) (*BrE* **scep·tic**) /ˈskeptɪk/ *noun* a person who usually doubts that claims or statements are true, especially those that other people believe in 惯持怀疑态度的人；怀疑论者

skep·tical (*NAmE*) (*BrE* **scep·tical**) /ˈskeptɪkl/ *adj.* ~ (**about/of sth**) having doubts that a claim or statement is true or that sth will happen 怀疑的：*I am skeptical about his chances of winning.* 我怀疑他取胜的可能性。◇ *The public remain skeptical of these claims.* 公众对这些说法仍持怀疑态度。◇ *She looked highly skeptical.* 她一脸深表怀疑的神色。▶ **skep·tic·al·ly** (*NAmE*) (*BrE* **scep·tic·al·ly**) /-kli/ *adv.*

skep·ti·cism (*NAmE*) (*BrE* **scep·ti·cism**) /ˈskeptɪsɪzəm/ *noun* [U, sing.] an attitude of doubting that claims or statements are true or that sth will happen 怀疑态度；怀疑主义：*Such claims should be regarded with a certain amount of skepticism.* 对这样的说法，大可不必全信。

sketch /sketʃ/ *noun, verb*

■ ***noun*** **1** a simple picture that is drawn quickly and does not have many details 素描；速写；草图：*The artist is making sketches for his next painting.* 画家正为他的下一幅作品画素描。◇ *She drew a **sketch map** of the area to show us the way.* 她画了一幅这个地区的略图，用来给我们指路。➲ SYNONYMS AT PICTURE ➲ COLLOCATIONS AT ART **2** a short funny scene on television, in the theatre, etc. 幽默短剧；小品：*The drama group did a sketch about a couple buying a new car.* 剧社上演了一出夫妻二人买新车的短剧。➲ WORDFINDER NOTE AT COMEDY **3** a short report or story that gives only basic details about sth 简报；速写；概述：*a biographical sketch of the Prime Minister* 首相生平简介

■ ***verb*** **1** [T, I] ~ (**sb/sth**) to make a quick drawing of sb/sth 画素描；画速写：*He quickly sketched the view from the window.* 他很快勾勒出了窗外的风景。**2** [T] ~ **sth** (**out**) to give a general description of sth, giving only the basic facts 概述；简述 SYN **outline**: *She sketched out her plan for tackling the problem.* 她简要叙述了解决问题的计划。

PHR V ˌ**sketch sth↔ˈin** to give more information or details about sth 补充说明；给…补充细节

sketch·book /ˈsketʃbʊk/ (*also* ˈ**sketch pad**) *noun* a book of sheets of paper for drawing on 素描簿；速写册；写生本

sketchy /ˈsketʃi/ *adj.* (**sketch·ier, sketch·iest**) not complete or detailed and therefore not very useful 粗略的；概略的；不完备的 SYN **rough**: *He gave us a very sketchy account of his visit.* 他跟我们非常粗略地讲了他参观的情况。◇ *sketchy notes* 简略的笔记 ▶ **sketch·ily** *adv.* **sketchi·ness** *noun* [U]

skew /skjuː/ *verb* **1** [T] ~ **sth** to change or influence sth with the result that it is not accurate, fair, normal, etc. 歪曲；曲解；使不公允；影响…的准确性：*to skew the statistics* 影响统计数字的准确性 **2** [I] + **adv./prep.** (*BrE*) to move or lie at an angle, especially in a position that is not normal 偏离；歪斜：*The ball skewed off at a right angle.* 球呈直角偏离弹了出去。

skew·bald /ˈskjuːbɔːld/ *adj.* (of a horse 马) with areas on it of white and another colour, usually not black 白花斑的（通常不带黑色）➲ COMPARE PIEBALD ▶ **skew·bald** *noun*: *He was riding a skewbald.* 他骑着一匹白花斑马。

skewed /skjuːd/ *adj.* **1** (of information 信息) not accurate or correct 歪曲的；有偏颇的；不准确的 SYN **distort**: *skewed statistics* 不准确的统计 **2** ~ (**towards sb/sth**) directed towards a particular group, place, etc. in a way that may not be accurate or fair 偏向（或偏重）…的：*The book is heavily skewed towards American readers.* 这本书严重倾向于美国读者。**3** not straight or level 偏的；斜的；歪的：*The car had ended up skewed across the road.* 汽车最终斜着停在公路上。➲ SEE ALSO ASKEW

skew·er /ˈskjuːə(r)/ *noun, verb*

■ ***noun*** a long thin pointed piece of metal or wood that is pushed through pieces of meat, vegetables, etc. to hold them together while they are cooking, or used to test whether sth is completely cooked（烹饪用）扦子，串肉扦

■ ***verb*** ~ **sth** to push a skewer or other thin pointed object through sth 用扦子串住

ˌskew-ˈwhiff *adj.* (*BrE, informal*) not straight 偏的；斜的；歪的

ski /skiː/ *noun, adj., verb*

■ ***noun*** (*pl.* **skis**) **1** one of a pair of long narrow pieces of wood, metal or plastic that you attach to boots so that you can move smoothly over snow 滑雪板：*a pair of skis* 一副滑雪板 ➲ VISUAL VOCAB PAGES V52, V58 **2** = WATERSKI

■ ***adj.*** [only before noun] connected with the sport of skiing 滑雪的：*ski boots* 滑雪靴 ◇ *the ski slopes* 滑雪坡

■ ***verb*** (**ski·ing, skied, skied**) **1** [I] (+ **adv./prep.**) to move over snow on skis, especially as a sport 滑雪（运动）**2** **go skiing** [I] to spend time skiing for pleasure 滑雪（作为娱乐）：*We went skiing in France in March.* 三月份我们去法国滑雪了。➲ SEE ALSO SKIING, WATERSKI *v.*

skid /skɪd/ *verb, noun*

■ ***verb*** (**-dd-**) [I] (usually of a vehicle 通常指车辆) to slide sideways or forwards in an uncontrolled way 侧滑；打滑；滑行：*The car skidded on the ice and went straight into the wall.* 汽车在冰上打滑，径直撞到了墙上。◇ *The taxi* ***skidded to a halt*** *just in time.* 出租车滑行了一段路后，及时停了下来。◇ *Her foot skidded on the wet floor and she fell heavily.* 她一只脚在湿地板上一滑，重重地摔了一跤。➲ MORE LIKE THIS 36, page R29

■ ***noun*** **1** the movement of a vehicle when it suddenly slides sideways in an uncontrolled way 侧滑；打滑；突然向一侧滑行：*The motorbike* ***went into a skid.*** 摩托车朝一侧滑了出去。◇ *The* ***skid marks*** *on the road showed how fast the car had been travelling.* 公路上留下的滑行痕迹说明这辆车当时开得有多快。**2** a part that is underneath some aircraft, beside the wheels, and is used for landing（飞机的）起落橇，滑橇：*the skids of a helicopter* 直升机的起落橇 ➲ VISUAL VOCAB PAGE V58

IDM **put the ˈskids under sb/sth** (*informal*) to stop sb/sth from being successful or making progress 使失败；使走下坡路 **be on the ˈskids** (*informal*) to be in a bad situation that will get worse 逐渐衰落；走下坡路

skid·pan /ˈskɪdpæn/ *noun* an area with a surface that is especially prepared so that drivers can practise controlling skids（供驾车者练习控制车辆打滑的）转向试验场

ˌskid ˈrow *noun* [U] (*informal, especially NAmE*) used to describe the poorest part of a town, the sort of place where people who have no home or job and who drink too much alcohol live（城市中流浪、失业、酗酒的人聚居的）贫民区，穷街陋巷：*to be on skid row* 住在贫民区

skier /ˈskiːə(r)/ *noun* a person who skis 滑雪者

skies PL. OF SKY

skiff /skɪf/ *noun* a small light boat for ROWING or sailing, usually for one person（通常指单人的）小划艇，小帆船

skif·fle /ˈskɪfl/ *noun* a type of music popular in the 1950s, that was a mixture of JAZZ and FOLK MUSIC 即兴摇滚乐（流行于 20 世纪 50 年代，结合了爵士乐和民间音乐）

ski·ing /ˈskiːɪŋ/ *noun* [U] the sport or activity of moving over snow on skis 滑雪（运动）：*to* ***go skiing*** 去滑雪 ◇ ***downhill/cross-country skiing*** 速降 / 越野滑雪 ◇ ***a skiing holiday/instructor/lesson/vacation*** 滑雪假日 / 教练 / 课 / 假期

ski·joring /ˈskiːdʒɔːrɪŋ; ˌskiːˈdʒɔːr-/ *noun* [U] the activity of being pulled over snow or ice on skis, by a horse or dog 乘马（或狗）拉雪橇

ˈski jump *noun* a very steep artificial slope that ends suddenly and that is covered with snow. People ski down the slope, jump off the end and see how far they can travel through the air before landing. 跳台滑雪 ▶ **ˈski jumper** *noun* **ˈski jumping** *noun* [U]: *Is ski jumping an Olympic sport?* 跳台滑雪是奥运会项目吗？◇ *the Swiss ski-jumping team* 瑞士跳台滑雪队

skil·ful (*especially US* **skill·ful**) /ˈskɪlfl/ *adj.* **1** (of a person 人) good at doing sth, especially sth that needs a particular ability or special training 技术好的；功夫深的；熟练的 SYN **accomplished**: *a skilful player/performer/teacher* 技术好的运动员；功夫深的表演者；会教学的老师 **2** made or done very well 制作精良的；处理巧妙的 SYN **professional**: *Thanks to her skilful handling of the affair, the problem was averted.* 多亏她对事情处理得巧妙，才避免了麻烦。▶ **skil·ful·ly** /-fəli/ *adv.*

ˈski lift *noun* a machine for taking SKIERS up a slope so that they can then ski down（运送滑雪者上坡的）上山吊椅

skill /skɪl/ *noun* **1** [U] the ability to do sth well 技巧；技艺：*The job requires skill and an eye for detail.* 这项工作需要技巧和敏锐的眼光。◇ ~ **in/at sth/doing sth** *What made him remarkable as a photographer was his skill in capturing the moment.* 他捕捉瞬间画面的能力使他成为一名不同凡响的摄影师。**2** [C] a particular ability or type of ability 技术；技能：*We need people with practical skills like carpentry.* 我们需要有木工等实用技术的人。◇ *management skills* 管理能力

skilled /skɪld/ *adj.* **1** having enough ability, experience and knowledge to be able to do sth well 有技能的；熟练的：*a skilled engineer/negotiator/craftsman* 高明的工程师；老练的谈判者；技术熟练的工匠 ◇ *a shortage of* ***skilled labour*** (= people who have had training in a skill) 缺乏技术工人 ◇ ~ **in/at sth/doing sth** *She is* ***highly skilled*** *at dealing with difficult customers.* 应付难缠的顾客她很有一套。**2** (of a job 工作) needing special abilities or training 需要专门技术的 SYN **expert**: *Furniture-making is very skilled work.* 做家具是技术性很强的活儿。OPP **unskilled** ➲ WORDFINDER NOTE AT WORK

skil·let /ˈskɪlɪt/ *noun* (*NAmE*) = FRYING PAN

skill·ful (*NAmE*) = SKILFUL

ˈskill set *noun* a person's range of skills or abilities（某人）一应技能综合

skim /skɪm/ *verb* (**-mm-**) **1** [T] to remove fat, cream, etc. from the surface of a liquid 撇去（液体上的油脂或乳脂等）：~ **sth off/from sth** *Skim the scum off the jam and let it cool.* 撇去果酱上的浮沫，让它冷却。◇ ~ **sth** *Skim the jam and let it cool.* 撇去果酱上的浮沫，让它冷却。**2** [I, T, no passive] to move quickly and lightly over a surface, not touching it or only touching it occasionally; to make sth do this（使）掠过，擦过，滑过：~ **along/over, etc. sth** *We watched the birds skimming over the lake.* 我们看着鸟儿贴着湖面飞过。◇ ~ **sth** *The speedboat took off, skimming the waves.* 快艇擦着波浪飞驰而去。◇ (*figurative*) *This report has barely* ***skimmed the surface*** *of the subject.* 报告对这个问题谈得很肤浅。◇ ~ **sth across, over, etc. sth** (*BrE*) *Small boys were skimming stones across the water.* 几个小男孩用石块打水漂。➲ SEE ALSO SKIP *v.* (7) **3** [I, T] to read sth

S

quickly in order to find a particular point or the main points 浏览；略读：~ **through/over sth** *He skimmed through the article trying to find his name.* 他浏览文章寻找自己的名字。◇ ~ **sth** *I always skim the financial section of the newspaper.* 我总要浏览一下报纸上的财经版。**4** [T] ~ **sth** (**from sth**) (*informal*) to steal small amounts of money frequently over a period of time 惯偷（小数额的钱）**5** [I, T] ~ (**sth**) to illegally copy electronic information from a credit card in order to use it without the owner's permission 盗用（信用卡电子信息）

PHR V ˌ**skim sth/sb**↔ˈ**off** to take for yourself the best part of sth, often in an unfair way 攫取（最好的部分）；捞取（精华部分）

ˌ**skimmed** ˈ**milk** (*BrE*) (*also* ˌ**skim** ˈ**milk** *NAmE*, *BrE*) *noun* [U] milk that contains less fat than normal because the cream has been removed from it 脱脂奶

skimp /skɪmp/ *verb* [I] ~ (**on sth**) to try to spend less time, money, etc. on sth than is really needed 节省，吝惜（时间、钱等）：*Older people should not skimp on food or heating.* 老人吃饭和取暖不应吝惜。

skimpy /ˈskɪmpi/ *adj.* (**skimp·ier**, **skimpi·est**) **1** (of clothes 衣服) very small and not covering much of your body 小而暴露的：*a skimpy dress* 短而暴露的连衣裙 **2** (*disapproving*) not large enough in amount or size（数量或大小）不足的，不够的：*a skimpy meal* 吃不饱的一顿饭 ◇ *They provided only skimpy details.* 他们提供的细节不充分。

skin /skɪn/ *noun, verb*

▪ *noun*

• **ON BODY** 身体 **1** [U, C] the layer of TISSUE that covers the body 皮；皮肤：*to have* ***dark/fair/olive, etc. skin*** 皮肤黝黑、白皙、浅褐色等 ◇ *The snake sheds its skin once a year.* 蛇一年蜕一次皮。◇ *cosmetics for sensitive skins* 过敏性皮肤适用的化妆品 ◇ *skin cancer* 皮肤癌 ⊃ COLLOCATIONS AT PHYSICAL ⊃ SEE ALSO FORESKIN, REDSKIN

• **-SKINNED** 有…皮肤 **2** (in adjectives 构成形容词) having the type of skin mentioned …皮肤的：*dark-skinned* 深色皮肤的 ◇ *fair-skinned* 白皙皮肤的 ⊃ SEE ALSO THICK-SKINNED, THIN-SKINNED ⊃ MORE LIKE THIS 8, page R25

• **OF DEAD ANIMAL** 死兽 **3** [C, U] (often in compounds 常构成复合词) the skin of a dead animal with or without its fur, used for making leather, etc.（兽）皮；毛皮；皮张：*The skins are removed and laid out to dry.* 皮剥下来，摊开晾干。◇ *a tiger skin rug* 虎皮毯

• **OF FRUIT/VEGETABLES** 水果；蔬菜 **4** [C, U] the outer layer of some fruits and vegetables（某些果实和蔬菜的）皮，壳：*Remove the skins by soaking the tomatoes in hot water.* 把西红柿放在热水里烫一下去皮。⊃ VISUAL VOCAB PAGE V33 ⊃ SEE ALSO BANANA SKIN ⊃ COMPARE PEEL *n.* (1), RIND (1), ZEST (3)

• **OF SAUSAGE** 香肠 **5** [C, U] the thin outer layer of a SAUSAGE 外皮；肠衣：*Prick the skins before grilling.* 烤前先在肠衣上扎孔。

• **ON LIQUIDS** 液体 **6** [C, U] the thin layer that forms on the surface of some liquids, especially when they become cold after being heated（尤指加热冷却后形成的）薄层，皮：*A skin had formed on the top of the milk.* 奶上结了一层奶皮。

• **OUTSIDE LAYER** 外壳 **7** [C] a layer that covers the outside of sth 外壳；外层：*the outer skin of the earth* 地壳 ◇ *the metal skin of the aircraft* 飞机的金属外壳 **8** [C] a special cover for any small electronic device that you can carry with you so that you can listen to music（便携式电子音乐播放器的）护套，保护壳：*You can create your own custom skin for your iPod.* 你可以为你的 iPod 制作个性化护套。

• **IN A COMPUTER PROGRAM** 计算机程序 **9** [C] (*computing* 计) the INTERFACE of a computer program (= the way a computer program presents information on screen), that the user can change to suit their particular preferences 皮肤（电脑程序的用户界面，可按个人喜好变换）

IDM **by the** ˌ**skin of your** ˈ**teeth** (*informal*) if you do sth **by the skin of your teeth**, you only just manage to do it 刚好；勉强 **get under sb's** ˈ**skin** (*informal*) to annoy sb 惹某人生气（或恼火）：*Don't let him get under your skin.* 别让他惹你生气。**have got sb under your** ˈ**skin** (*informal*) to be extremely attracted to sb 极其迷恋；被某人深深打动 **it's no skin off** ˈ**my,** ˈ**your,** ˈ**his, etc. nose** (*informal*) used to say that sb is not upset or annoyed about sth because it does not affect them in a bad way（指某人没有受到不良影响）这不关某人的事，这跟某人没关系 **make your** ˈ**skin crawl** to make you feel afraid or full of disgust 使人毛骨悚然；让人起鸡皮疙瘩 (**nothing but/all/only**) **skin and** ˈ**bone** (*informal*) extremely thin in a way that is not attractive or healthy 瘦得皮包骨；瘦骨嶙峋 ⊃ MORE AT JUMP *v.*, SAVE *v.*, THICK *adj.*, THIN *adj.*

▪ *verb* (**-nn-**)

• **ANIMAL/FRUIT/VEGETABLE** 动物；水果；蔬菜 **1** ~ **sth** to take the skin off an animal, a fruit or a vegetable 剥皮；扒皮；削皮：*You'll need four ripe tomatoes, skinned and chopped.* 需要四个成熟了的西红柿，去皮切碎。

• **PART OF BODY** 身体部位 **2** ~ **sth** to rub the skin off part of your body by accident 擦破（身体某部位的）皮肤：*He skinned his knees climbing down the tree.* 他从树上爬下来时把膝盖蹭破了。**3** (*computing* 计) ~ **sth** to change the way that a computer program presents information on the screen to suit your particular needs 换皮肤（指更改用户界面） **IDM** SEE EYE *n.*, WAY *n.*

PHR V ˌ**skin** ˈ**up** (*BrE, informal*) to make a cigarette containing MARIJUANA 用大麻做纸烟

skin·care /ˈskɪnkeə(r); *NAmE* -ker/ *noun* [U] the use of creams and special products to look after your skin 皮肤护理；护肤

ˌ**skin-**ˈ**deep** *adj.* [not usually before noun] (of a feeling or an attitude 感情或态度) not as important or strongly felt as it appears to be 不深刻；肤浅 **SYN** **superficial** **IDM** SEE BEAUTY

skin·der (*also* **skin·ner**) /ˈskɪnə(r)/ *noun, verb* (*SAfrE*) (*informal*)

▪ *noun* [U] conversation about other people's private lives, often including details which may not be true（涉及他人隐私的）八卦闲聊，闲言碎语：*They talk a lot of skinder.* 他们好讲八卦。

▪ *verb* [I] to talk about other people's private lives, often including details which may not be true 说闲话；讲八卦：*He loves to skinder.* 他喜欢说别人闲话。◇ *She wondered what they were skindering about.* 她想知道他们在聊什么八卦。

ˈ**skin-diving** *noun* [U] the sport or activity of swimming underwater with simple breathing equipment but without a special suit for protection 自由潜水（只用简单呼吸设备）：*to go skin-diving* 去自由潜泳 ▸ ˈ**skin-diver** *noun*

skin·flint /ˈskɪnflɪnt/ *noun* (*informal, disapproving*) a person who does not like spending money 吝啬鬼；铁公鸡 **SYN** **miser**

skin·ful /ˈskɪnfʊl/ *noun* [usually sing.] (*BrE, slang*) a large quantity of alcohol to drink, enough to make you very drunk 足以喝醉的量

ˈ**skin graft** *noun* a medical operation in which healthy skin is taken from one part of sb's body and placed over another part to replace skin that has been burned or damaged; a piece of skin that is moved in this way 植皮；皮肤移植；皮移植片

skin·head /ˈskɪnhed/ *noun* a young person with very short hair, especially one who is violent, aggressive and RACIST 光头仔（尤指暴虐、好斗的青年种族主义者）

skink /skɪŋk/ *noun* a LIZARD with short legs or with no legs 石龙子（蜥蜴，肢体不发达或完全退化）

skin·ner *noun, verb* (*SAfrE, informal*) = SKINDER

skinny /ˈskɪni/ *adj., noun*

▪ *adj.* (**skin·nier**, **skin·ni·est**) **1** (*informal, usually disapproving*) very thin, especially in a way that you find unpleasant or ugly 极瘦的；干瘦的；皮包骨的：*skinny legs* 干瘦的腿 **2** (of clothes 衣服) designed to fit closely to the body 紧身的：*a skinny sweater* 紧身套头衫 **3** (*NAmE, informal*) low in fat 低脂肪的：*a skinny latte* 脱脂拿铁咖啡

▪ *noun* [U] **the** ~ (**on sb/sth**) (*NAmE, informal*) information

S

about sb/sth, especially details that are not generally known（不公开的）信息；内幕消息：*This book gives you the skinny on Hollywood.* 这本书披露了好莱坞的内幕。

ˈ**skinny-dipping** *noun* [U] (*informal*) swimming without any clothes on 裸泳

skint /skɪnt/ *adj.* [not usually before noun] (*BrE, informal*) having no money 没钱；不名一文

skin·tight /ˌskɪnˈtaɪt/ *adj.* (of clothes 衣服) fitting very closely to the body 紧身的

skip /skɪp/ *verb, noun*

■ ***verb*** (-pp-)

• **MOVE WITH JUMPS** 蹦蹦跳跳地走 **1** [I] (+ **adv./prep.**) to move forwards lightly and quickly making a little jump with each step 蹦蹦跳跳地走：*She skipped happily along beside me.* 她连蹦带跳，高高兴兴地跟着我走。

• **JUMP OVER ROPE** 跳绳 **2** [I] (*BrE*) (*NAmE* ˌ**jump** ˈ**rope**, ˌ**skip** ˈ**rope**) [T] to jump over a rope which is held at both ends by yourself or by two other people and is passed again and again over your head and under your feet 跳绳：*The girls were skipping in the playground.* 姑娘们在操场上跳绳。◇ *She likes to skip rope as a warm-up.* 她喜欢以跳绳来热身。

• **NOT DO STH** 不做某事 **3** [T] ~ **sth** to not do sth that you usually do or should do 不做（应做的事等）；不参加：*I often skip breakfast altogether.* 我常常干脆不吃早饭。◇ (*especially NAmE*) *She decided to* **skip class** *that afternoon.* 她决定那天下午逃课。**4** [T, I] to leave out sth that would normally be the next thing that you would do, read, etc. 跳过（正常的步骤等）；略过；漏过：~ **sth** *You can skip the next chapter if you have covered the topic in class.* 下一章，你要是在课堂上已经讲到了，就可以跳过。◇ ~ **over sth** *I skipped over the last part of the book.* 那本书的最后一部分我略过没读。◇ ~ **to sth** *I suggest we skip to the last item on the agenda.* 我建议我们跳到议程的最后一项。

• **CHANGE QUICKLY** 快速转换 **5** [I] + **adv./prep.** to move from one place to another or from one subject to another very quickly 快速转移；骤然转换（话题）：*She kept skipping from one topic of conversation to another.* 她一再转换谈话的话题。

• **LEAVE SECRETLY** 秘密离去 **6** [T] ~ **sth** to leave a place secretly or suddenly 悄悄溜走；突然离开：*The bombers skipped the country shortly after the blast.* 爆炸后不久，放置炸弹的人就逃离了这个国家。

• **STONES** 石块 **7** (*BrE also* **skim**) [T] ~ **sth** (**across, over, etc. sth**) to make a flat stone jump across the surface of water 打水漂：*The boys were skipping stones across the pond.* 那几个男孩子用石块往水塘里打水漂。

IDM ˈ**skip it** (*informal*) used to tell sb rudely that you do not want to talk about sth or repeat what you have said（粗暴地表示不想谈论或重复说）别提这事儿，不说这个了：*'What were you saying?' 'Oh, skip it!'* "你刚才说什么来着？""噢，不提了！"

PHR V ˌ**skip** ˈ**off/**ˈ**out** to leave secretly or suddenly 溜走；突然离去 ˌ**skip** ˈ**out on sb** (*NAmE*) to leave sb, especially when they need you（尤指不顾某人而）离开，溜走

■ ***noun***

• **MOVEMENT** 动作 **1** a skipping movement 蹦跳：*She gave a skip and a jump and was off down the street.* 她一蹦一跳就顺着马路跑了。

• **CONTAINER FOR WASTE** 废料箱 **2** (*BrE*) (*NAmE* **Dumpster™**) a large open container for putting old bricks, rubbish/garbage, etc. in. The skip is then loaded on a lorry/truck and taken away. 废料桶（装工地废料、垃圾等，由卡车拖走）

ˈ**ski pants** *noun* [pl.] **1** trousers/pants worn for skiing 滑雪裤 **2** narrow trousers/pants made from a type of cloth that stretches and with a part that goes under the foot 健美裤；踩脚裤

ˈ**ski-plane** *noun* a plane with two parts like skis fixed to the bottom so that it can land on snow or ice 滑橇起落架飞机；雪上飞机 ➲ VISUAL VOCAB PAGE V58

ˈ**ski pole** (*BrE also* ˈ**ski stick**) *noun* a stick used to push yourself forward while skiing 滑雪杖；滑雪杆

skip·per /ˈskɪpə(r)/ *noun, verb*

■ ***noun*** **1** the captain of a small ship or fishing boat（小船或渔船的）船长 **2** (*informal, especially BrE*) the captain of a sports team（运动队的）队长

■ ***verb*** ~ **sth** to be the captain of a boat, sports team, etc. 当船长（或运动队队长等）：*to skipper a yacht* 当帆船船长 ◇ (*especially BrE*) *He skippered the team to victory.* 他率领队伍取得了胜利。

ˈ**skipping rope** (*BrE*) (*NAmE* ˈ**jump rope**) *noun* a piece of rope, usually with a handle at each end, that you hold, turn over your head and then jump over, for fun or to keep fit 跳绳 ➲ VISUAL VOCAB PAGE V41

skir·mish /ˈskɜːmɪʃ; *NAmE* ˈskɜːrmɪʃ/ *noun, verb*

■ ***noun*** **1** a short fight between small groups of soldiers, etc., especially one that is not planned 小规模战斗；小冲突；（尤指）遭遇战 **2** a short argument, especially between political opponents（尤指政治上对立双方的）小争执，小争论

■ ***verb*** [I] to take part in a short fight or argument 发生小规模战斗（或冲突、争执）▶ **skir·mish·er** *noun* **skir·mish·ing** *noun* [U]: *There are reports of skirmishing along the border.* 有报道称在边界一带发生了小规模冲突。

skirt 🔑 /skɜːt; *NAmE* skɜːrt/ *noun, verb*

■ ***noun*** **1** 🔑 [C] a piece of clothing for a woman or girl that hangs from the waist 女裙；裙子：***a long/short/straight/pleated, etc. skirt*** 长裙、短裙、直筒裙、百褶裙等 ➲ VISUAL VOCAB PAGE V66 **2** [C] (*also* **skirts** [pl.]) the part of a dress, coat, etc. that hangs below the waist（连衣裙、外衣等的）下摆 **3** [C] an outer covering or part used to protect the base of a vehicle or machine（车辆或机器基座的）挡板，裙板：*the rubber skirt around the bottom of a hovercraft* 气垫船底部四周的橡胶挡板 ➲ VISUAL VOCAB PAGE V59

■ ***verb*** **1** [T, I] to be or go around the edge of sth 环绕…的四周；位于…的边缘；沿…的边缘走：~ **sth** *They followed the road that skirted the lake.* 他们顺着湖边公路走。◇ ~ **around/round sth** *I skirted around the field and crossed the bridge.* 我沿着田边走，又绕过了那座桥。**2** [T, I] to avoid talking about a subject, especially because it is difficult or embarrassing 绕开，回避（话题）：~ **sth** *He carefully skirted the issue of where they would live.* 他小心地避开了他们将住在何处这个问题。◇ ~ **around/round sth** *She tactfully skirted around the subject of money.* 她巧妙地避口不提钱的事。

ˈ**skirting board** (*also* **skirt·ing**) (*both BrE*) (*NAmE* **base·board**) *noun* [C, U] a narrow piece of wood that is fixed along the bottom of the walls in a house 踢脚板；壁脚板

ˈ**ski run** (*also* **run**) *noun* a track that is marked on a slope that you ski down 滑雪道；滑雪坡

skit /skɪt/ *noun* ~ (**on sth**) a short piece of humorous writing or a performance that makes fun of sb/sth by copying them 幽默短文，滑稽短剧，幽默讽刺小品（常用模仿手法）：*a skit on daytime TV programmes* 戏评日间电视节目的幽默短文

ˈ**ski tow** *noun* **1** a machine which pulls you up the mountain on your skis（运送滑雪者上坡的）电缆车，上山吊椅 **2** a rope which pulls you when you are WATERSKIING（水橇运动的）拖绳

skit·ter /ˈskɪtə(r)/ *verb* [I] + **adv./prep.** to run or move very quickly and lightly 轻捷地跑；轻快地动

skit·tish /ˈskɪtɪʃ/ *adj.* **1** (of horses 马) easily excited or frightened and therefore difficult to control 易惊而难以驾驭的 **2** (of people 人) not very serious and with ideas and feelings that keep changing 轻浮的；易变的；反复无常的 **3** (*especially NAmE, business* 商) likely to change suddenly 说变就变的；变幻莫测的：*skittish financial markets* 变幻莫测的金融市场 ▶ **skit·tish·ly** *adv.* **skit·tish·ness** *noun* [U]

skit·tle /ˈskɪtl/ *noun* **1** [C] (in Britain) a wooden or plastic object used in the game of skittles（英国滚球撞柱游戏的）木柱，塑料柱 **2 skittles** [U] (in Britain) a game in which players roll a ball at nine skittles and try to knock

S

over as many of them as possible（英国）滚球撞柱游戏 ➲ COMPARE TENPIN BOWLING

skive /skaɪv/ *verb* [I, T] (*BrE, informal*) to avoid work or school by staying away or leaving early 躲避（工作）；逃（学）**SYN** **bunk off**: *'Where's Tom?' 'Skiving as usual.'* "汤姆去哪了？""和往常一样，溜了。" ◇ **~ off** *She always skives off early on Fridays.* 每到星期五，她总是早早就溜了。◇ **~ sth** *I skived the last lecture.* 最后一节课我溜了。

▶ **skiver** *noun*

skivvy /ˈskɪvi/ *noun, verb*

■ *noun* (*pl.* **-ies**) **1** [C] (*BrE, informal*) a servant, usually female, who does all the dirty or boring jobs in a house 仆人，佣人（通常指干粗活、脏活的女佣）: *He treats his wife like a skivvy.* 他待妻子就跟对奴仆似的。**2 Skiv·vies™** [pl.] (*NAmE, informal*) underwear, especially men's underwear（尤指男式）内衣

■ *verb* (**skiv·vies**, **skivvy·ing**, **skiv·vied**, **skiv·vied**) [I] (*BrE, informal*) to do dirty or boring jobs 干粗活；干脏活；做佣人的活

skolly /ˈskɒli; *NAmE* ˈskɑːli/ *noun* (*pl.* **-ies**) (*SAfrE, informal*) a young person who commits crimes or behaves badly 恶少；小流氓

skua /ˈskjuːə/ *noun* a large brownish bird that lives near the sea. It eats fish, which it sometimes takes from other birds. 贼鸥（褐色掠食性海鸟）

skul·dug·gery (*also* **skull·dug·gery**) /skʌlˈdʌɡəri/ *noun* [U] (*old-fashioned* or *humorous*) dishonest behaviour or activities 阴谋诡计；花招；欺骗

skulk /skʌlk/ *verb* [I] **+ adv./prep.** (*disapproving*) to hide or move around secretly, especially when you are planning sth bad 潜伏；偷偷摸摸地走动；鬼鬼祟祟地活动: *There was someone skulking behind the bushes.* 有人藏在灌木后面。

skull /skʌl/ *noun* **1** the bone structure that forms the head and surrounds and protects the brain 颅骨；头（盖）骨 **SYN** **cranium**: *a fractured skull* 破裂的颅骨 ➲ VISUAL VOCAB PAGE V64 **2** (*informal*) the head or the brain 脑袋；脑子；脑瓜: *Her skull was crammed with too many thoughts.* 她脑瓜子里想法太多。◇ (*informal*) *When will he* ***get it into his thick skull*** *that I never want to see him again!* 那笨头笨脑的家伙什么时候才能明白我再也不想见他了！

S

ˌskull and ˈcrossbones *noun* [sing.] a picture of a human skull above two crossed bones, used in the past on the flags of PIRATE ships, and now used as a warning on containers with dangerous substances inside 骷髅旗，骷髅画（旧时画在海盗旗上，现在作为警示印在危险物品的容器上）

skull·cap /ˈskʌlkæp/ *noun* a small round cap worn on top of the head, especially by male Jews and Catholic BISHOPS, CARDINALS, etc.（多为犹太男子所戴的）无檐小圆帽，无檐便帽；（天主教主教、枢机主教等所戴的）主教帽 ➲ SEE ALSO YARMULKE

skull·dug·gery = SKULDUGGERY

skunk /skʌŋk/ (*NAmE also* **pole·cat**) *noun* **1** [C] a small black and white N American animal that can produce a strong unpleasant smell to defend itself when it is attacked 北美臭鼬 **2** [U] (*slang*) = SKUNKWEED **IDM** SEE DRUNK *adj.*

skunk·weed /ˈskʌŋkwiːd/ (*also slang* **skunk**) *noun* [U] a strong type of CANNABIS 强效大麻

skunk·works /ˈskʌŋkwɜːkz; *NAmE* -wɜːrkz/ *noun* (*pl.* **skunk·works**) (*NAmE, informal*) a small laboratory or department of a large company used for doing new scientific research or developing new products（大公司从事科研和新产品开发的）实验室，科研部门，研发部门

sky 🔑 /skaɪ/ *noun, verb*

■ *noun* 🔑 [C, U] (*pl.* **skies**) the space above the earth that you can see when you look up, where clouds and the sun, moon and stars appear 天；天空 **HELP** You usually say **the sky**. When **sky** is used with an adjective, use **a... sky**. You can also use the plural form **skies**, especially when you are thinking about the great extent of the sky. 通常说 the sky。与形容词连用时说 a ... sky。也可以用复数形式 skies，尤其指天空辽阔无边: *What's that in the sky?* 天上那个东西是什么？◇ *The sky suddenly went dark and it started to rain.* 天空骤然转暗，随即下起雨来。◇ *the night sky* 夜空 ◇ *a cloudless sky* 无云的天空 ◇ *cloudless skies* 无云的天空 ◇ *a land of blue skies and sunshine* 一个蓝天丽日的国度 ◇ *The skies above London were ablaze with a spectacular firework display.* 伦敦上空礼花绽放，景象壮观。➲ COLLOCATIONS AT WEATHER

IDM **the sky's the ˈlimit** (*informal*) there is no limit to what sb can achieve, earn, do, etc. 无穷尽；什么都可能；不可限量: *With a talent like his, the sky's the limit.* 以他的禀赋，前途不可限量。➲ MORE AT GREAT *adj.*, PIE, PRAISE *v.*

■ *verb* (**skies**, **sky·ing**, **skied**, **skied**) **~ sth** to hit a ball very high into the air 把（球）击向高空: *She skied her tee shot.* 她开球那一杆打了一个高空球。

ˌsky-ˈblue *adj.* bright blue in colour, like the sky on a clear day 天蓝色的；蔚蓝色的 ▶ **ˌsky ˈblue** *noun* [U] ➲ MORE LIKE THIS 15, page R26

sky·box /ˈskaɪbɒks; *NAmE* -bɑːks/ *noun* (*NAmE*) an area of expensive seats, separated from other areas, high up in a sports ground（体育场的）贵宾看台

sky·cap /ˈskaɪkæp/ *noun* (*NAmE*) a person whose job is to carry people's bags at an airport 机场行李工

sky·div·ing /ˈskaɪdaɪvɪŋ/ *noun* [U] a sport in which you jump from a plane and fall for as long as you safely can before opening your PARACHUTE 延缓张伞跳伞运动；特技跳伞运动: *to go skydiving* 进行特技跳伞 ➲ VISUAL VOCAB PAGE V54 ▶ **sky·diver** *noun*

ˌsky-ˈhigh *adj.* very high; too high 极高的；太高的: *His confidence is still sky-high.* 他依旧信心十足。◇ *sky-high interest rates* 极高的利率 ▶ **ˌsky-ˈhigh** *adv.*: *After the election, prices went sky-high.* 选举后，物价飞涨。

sky·lark /ˈskaɪlɑːk; *NAmE* -lɑːrk/ *noun* a small bird that sings while it flies high up in the sky 云雀

sky·light /ˈskaɪlaɪt/ *noun* a small window in a roof（房顶的）天窗 ➲ VISUAL VOCAB PAGE V18

sky·line /ˈskaɪlaɪn/ *noun* the outline of buildings, trees, hills, etc. seen against the sky（建筑物、树、山等在天空映衬下的）轮廓线；天际线: *the New York skyline* 纽约的空中轮廓线

ˈsky marshal *noun* = AIR MARSHAL (2)

Skype™ /skaɪp/ *noun, verb*

■ *noun* [U] a telephone system that works by direct communication between users' computers on the Internet, without the need for a central SERVER * Skype 网络通话系统: *Broadcasters are using Skype for interviews.* 电视台用 Skype 进行采访。➲ SEE ALSO VoIP

■ *verb* [T, I] to speak (with sb) using Skype 用 Skype 通话: **~ sb** *I'll Skype you later.* 回头我用 Skype 打给你。◇ **~ (with sb)** *She Skypes with her grandchildren.* 她用 Skype 跟孙子们通话。

sky·rocket /ˈskaɪrɒkɪt; *NAmE* -rɑːk-/ *verb* [I] (of prices, etc. 价格等) to rise quickly to a very high level 飞涨；猛涨

sky·scraper /ˈskaɪskreɪpə(r)/ *noun* a very tall building in a city 摩天大楼 ➲ VISUAL VOCAB PAGES V3, V15

ˈsky surfing *noun* [U] the sport of jumping from a plane and travelling through the air on a board before landing with a PARACHUTE 空中滑板运动；空中滑翔

sky·wards /ˈskaɪwədz; *NAmE* -wərdz/ (*also* **sky·ward**) *adv.* towards the sky; up into the sky 向天空；朝天空: *She pointed skywards.* 她指向天空。◇ *The rocket soared skywards.* 火箭呼啸着朝天上飞去。

SLA /ˌes el ˈeɪ/ *abbr.* (*linguistics* 语言) SECOND LANGUAGE ACQUISITION 第二语言习得

slab /slæb/ *noun* **1** a thick flat piece of stone, wood or other hard material （石、木等坚硬物质的）厚板：*a slab of marble/concrete* 大理石板；混凝土板 ◇ *The road was paved with smooth **stone slabs**.* 道路用平整的石板铺成。◇ ***paving slabs*** 铺路石板 ◇ *a dead body **on the slab*** (= on a table in a MORTUARY) 停尸桌上的尸体 **2** a thick, flat slice or piece of sth 厚片；厚块：*a slab of chocolate* 一大块巧克力 ◇ *slabs of meat* 切成厚片的肉

slack /slæk/ *adj., noun, verb*

■***adj.*** (**slack·er**, **slack·est**) **1** not stretched tight 不紧的；松弛的 SYN **loose**：*She was staring into space, her mouth slack.* 她双唇微张，失神地望着前方。◇ *The rope suddenly went slack.* 绳子突然松了。◇ *slack muscles* 松弛的肌肉 **2** (of business 生意) not having many customers or sales; not busy 萧条的；冷清的；清淡的：*a slack period* 萧条期 **3** (*disapproving*) not putting enough care, attention or energy into sth and so not doing it well enough 懈怠的；不用心的；敷衍了事的；吊儿郎当的：*He's been very slack in his work lately.* 近来他工作很不认真。◇ *Discipline in the classroom is very slack.* 班里纪律十分松懈。▶ **slack·ly** *adv.*：*Her arms hung slackly by her sides.* 她的双手无力地垂放在身体的两侧。 **slack·ness** *noun* [U]

■***noun*** [U] ➲ SEE ALSO SLACKS **1** the part of a rope, etc. that is hanging loosely（绳索的）松弛部分：*There's too much slack in the tow rope.* 拖缆太松。**2** people, money or space that should be used more fully in an organization （组织中人员、资金或地方的）富余部分，闲置部分：*There's very little slack in the budget.* 预算中没有多少剩余款项。**3** very small pieces of coal 煤屑；煤末

IDM **cut sb some 'slack** (*informal*) to be less critical of sb or less strict with them 不过于挑剔某人；对某人宽容些：*Hey, cut him some slack! He's doing his best!* 嗨，别对他那么吹毛求疵！他已经尽全力了！ **take up the 'slack 1** to improve the way money or people are used in an organization 提高（资金或人员使用的）效率 **2** to pull on a rope, etc. until it is tight 收紧松弛的绳索

■***verb*** [I] to work less hard than you usually do or should do 懈怠；怠惰；偷懒

PHR V ˌ**slack 'off** (**on sth**) to do sth more slowly or with less energy than before 松懈；放松；懈怠

slack·en /'slækən/ *verb* **1** [I, T] to gradually become, or to make sth become, slower, less active, etc. （使）放慢，减缓，萧条 SYN **relax**：**~ (off)** *We've been really busy, but things are starting to slacken off now.* 近来我们的确很忙，不过现在情况开始有所缓解了。◇ **~ sth** *She slackened her pace a little* (= walked a little more slowly). 她略微放慢脚步。**2** [I, T] to become, or to make sth become, less tight （使）变得松弛 SYN **loosen**：*His grip slackened and she pulled away from him.* 他抓得不那么紧了，她顺势挣脱开来。◇ **~ sth** *He slackened the ropes slightly.* 他把绳子稍稍放松一些。

slack·er /'slækə(r)/ *noun* (*informal, disapproving*) a person who is lazy and avoids work 偷懒的人；怠惰的人

slack·lin·ing /'slæklamıŋ/ *noun* [U] the activity or sport of balancing on a rope or a strong strip of cloth that is fixed above the ground but not stretched tightly 走软绳运动（在软绳或布带上行走并保持平衡）

slacks /slæks/ *noun* [pl.] (*old-fashioned* or *NAmE, formal*) trousers/pants for men or women, that are not part of a suit 便裤；宽松的长裤：*a pair of slacks* 一条便裤

slag /slæg/ *noun, verb*

■***noun*** **1** [U] the waste material that remains after metal has been removed from rock 矿渣；熔渣；炉渣 **2** [C] (*BrE, slang*) an offensive word for a woman, used to suggest that she has a lot of sexual partners 荡妇；破鞋

■***verb*** (**-gg-**)

PHR V ˌ**slag sb↔'off** (*BrE, slang*) to say cruel or critical things about sb 臭骂；贬损；辱骂：*I hate the way he's always slagging off his colleagues.* 他老损他的同事，我看不惯。

slag·ging /'slægıŋ/ (*also* ˌ**slagging-'off**) *noun* (*informal*) the act of speaking to or about sb in a critical and insulting way 贬损；辱骂：*He got a slagging from bloggers about his recent comments.* 他因他新近的评论遭到博客作者的辱骂。

'slag heap *noun* a large pile of slag from a mine 熔渣堆

slain PAST PART. OF SLAY

slake /sleık/ *verb* (*literary*) **1 ~ your thirst** to drink so that you no longer feel thirsty 缓和（口渴）；解（渴） SYN **quench 2 ~ sth** to satisfy a desire 满足（欲望）

sla·lom /'slɑːləm/ *noun* a race for people on SKIS or in CANOES along a winding course marked by poles （滑雪）回转赛；（皮划艇）激流回旋，障碍回旋

slam /slæm/ *verb, noun*

■***verb*** (**-mm-**) **1** [I, T] to shut, or to make sth shut, with a lot of force, making a loud noise （使…）砰地关上 SYN **bang**：*I heard the door slam behind him.* 我听见他砰地把身后的门关上。◇ **+ adj.** *A window slammed shut in the wind.* 风吹得一扇窗户哐地关上了。◇ **~ sth** *He stormed out of the house, slamming the door as he left.* 他怒气冲冲地从房子里出来，把门砰地关上。◇ **~ sth + adj.** *She slammed the lid shut.* 她砰的一声盖上盖子。◇ **+ adv./prep.** *She slammed out of the room* (= went out and slammed the door behind her). 她随手砰的一声关上门出去了。**2** [T] **~ sth + adv./prep.** to put, push or throw sth into a particular place or position with a lot of force 用力一放；使劲一推；猛劲一摔：*She slammed down the phone angrily.* 她气呼呼地啪的一声挂上电话。◇ *He slammed on the brakes* (= stopped the car very suddenly). 他猛地刹住汽车。**3** [T] **~ sb/sth** (used especially in newspapers 尤用于报章) to criticize sb/sth very strongly 猛烈抨击 IDM SEE DOOR

PHR V ˌ**slam 'into/a'gainst sb/sth** | ˌ**slam sth 'into/a'gainst sb/sth** to crash into sth with a lot of force; to make sth crash into sth with a lot of force （使）重重地撞上 ➲ SYNONYMS AT CRASH

■***noun*** [usually sing.] an act of slamming sth; the noise of sth being slammed 猛关（或推、摔、撞等）；猛摔（或撞等）的声音：*She gave the door a good hard slam.* 她使劲一推，门砰的一声关上了。➲ SEE ALSO GRAND SLAM

'slam dunk *noun* **1** (in BASKETBALL 篮球) the act of jumping up and putting the ball through the net with a lot of force 强力灌篮；扣篮 **2** (*NAmE, informal*) something that is certain to be successful 必定成功的事；稳操胜券的事：*Politically, this issue is a slam dunk for the party.* 在政治上，这个议题是这个党的一张胜券。

'slam-dunk *verb* **~ sth** (in BASKETBALL 篮球) to jump up and put the ball through the net with a lot of force 扣篮

slam·mer /'slæmə(r)/ *noun* **1 the slammer** [sing.] (*slang*) prison 监狱 **2** [C] (*also* **teˌquila 'slammer**) an alcoholic drink made by mixing TEQUILA and LEMONADE, which is drunk quickly after covering the glass and hitting it on the table to make the drink fill with bubbles 龙舌兰鸡尾酒（加柠檬汽水等）

slan·der /'slɑːndə(r); *NAmE* 'slæn-/ *noun, verb*

■***noun*** [C, U] a false spoken statement intended to damage the good opinion people have of sb; the legal offence of making this kind of statement 口头诽谤；口头诽谤罪：*a vicious slander on the company's good name* 对那家公司良好声誉的恶意诽谤 ◇ *He's suing them for slander.* 他控告他们口头诽谤。➲ COMPARE LIBEL *n.* ▶ **slan·der·ous** /-dərəs/ *adj.*：*a slanderous remark* 诽谤性话语

■***verb*** **~ sb/sth** to make a false spoken statement about sb that is intended to damage the good opinion that people have of them 口头诽谤；诋毁；中伤：*He angrily accused the investigators of slandering both him and his family.* 他气愤地指责调查者诋毁他和他的家人。➲ COMPARE LIBEL *v.*

slang /slæŋ/ *noun* [U] very informal words and expressions that are more common in spoken language, especially used by a particular group of people, for example, children, criminals, soldiers, etc. 俚语：*teenage slang* 青少年俚语 ◇ *a **slang word/expression/term*** 俚语 ➲ SEE ALSO RHYMING SLANG

'slanging match *noun* (*BrE, informal*) an angry argument in which people insult each other 互相谩骂

S

slangy /ˈslæŋi/ *adj.* (**slang·ier**, **slangi·est**) containing a lot of slang 充满俚语的：*a slangy style* 大量使用俚语的文体

slant /slɑːnt; *NAmE* slænt/ *verb, noun*

■ *verb* **1** [I, T] to slope or to make sth slope in a particular direction or at a particular angle（使）倾斜，歪斜：**+ adv./prep.** (*literary*) *The sun slanted through the window.* 太阳斜照进窗户。◇ **~ sth + adv./prep.** *Slant your skis a little more to the left.* 把滑雪板略微向左斜一点。**2** [T] **~ sth (+ adv./prep.)** (*sometimes disapproving*) to present information based on a particular way of thinking, especially in an unfair way 有倾向性地陈述；有偏向地报道：*The findings of the report had been slanted in favour of the manufacturers.* 报告中的调查结果偏袒制造商。

■ *noun* **1** a sloping position 倾斜；歪斜；斜线；斜面：*The sofa faced the fire* ***at a slant.*** 沙发斜对着壁炉。◇ *Cut the flower stems* ***on the slant.*** 把花茎斜着切断。**2 ~ (on sth/sb)** a way of thinking about sth, especially one that shows support for a particular opinion or side in a disagreement（有倾向性的）观点，态度：*She put a* ***new slant*** *on the play.* 她对那出戏提出了一种新的见解。

slant·ed /ˈslɑːntɪd; *NAmE* ˈslæntɪd/ *adj.* **1** sloping in one direction 倾斜的；歪斜的：*She had slanted brown eyes.* 她有一双棕色的丹凤眼。**2 ~ (towards sb/sth)** tending to be in favour of one person or thing in a way that may be unfair to others 有倾向性的；有偏向性的：*a biased and slanted view of events* 对事件有失公正、带倾向性的观点

slant·ing /ˈslɑːntɪŋ; *NAmE* ˈslæntɪŋ/ *adj.* not straight or level; sloping 不直的；不平的；斜的；歪的：*slanting eyes/handwriting/rain* 斜眼；歪斜的字迹；斜落的雨

slap /slæp/ *verb, noun, adv.*

■ *verb* (**-pp-**) **1** [T] **~ sb/sth (+ adv./prep.)** to hit sb/sth with the flat part of your hand（用手掌）打，拍，掴 SYN **smack**: *She slapped his face hard.* 她狠狠给了他一个耳光。◇ *She slapped him hard across the face.* 她狠狠给了他一个耳光。◇ *'Congratulations!' he said, slapping me on the back.* "祝贺你！"他拍着我的背说。**2** [T] **~ sth + adv./prep.** to put sth on a surface in a quick, careless and often noisy way, especially because you are angry（尤指生气地）啪的一声放下，随意扔放：*He slapped the newspaper down on the desk.* 他啪的一声把报纸摔在桌上。◇ *She slapped a $10 bill into my hand.* 她啪地把一张 10 美元钞票放在我手里。**3** [I] **+ adv./prep.** to hit against sth with the noise of sb being slapped 啪地击打（或撞上）：*The water slapped against the side of the boat.* 水拍击船舷。➲ SEE ALSO HAPPY SLAPPING

PHR V **ˌslap sb aˈbout/aˈround** (*informal*) to hit sb regularly or often 常常打，动辄殴打（某人）：*Her ex-husband used to slap her around.* 她的前夫过去动不动就打她。**ˌslap sb/sth↔ˈdown** (*informal*) to criticize sb in an unfair way, often in public, so that they feel embarrassed or less confident 训斥；申斥；公开指责 **ˈslap sth on sb/sth** (*informal*) to order, especially in a sudden or an unfair way, that sth must happen or sb must do sth 强制实行；强迫某人做：*The company slapped a ban on using email on the staff.* 公司对员工使用电子邮件发出禁令。**ˌslap sth ˈon sth** (*informal*) to increase the price of sth suddenly 忽然提价：*They've slapped 50p on the price of a pack of cigarettes.* 他们把一包香烟的价格一下子提高了 50 便士。**ˌslap sth ˈon sth | ˌslap sth↔ˈon** to spread sth on a surface in a quick, careless way（在…上）胡乱涂抹，随意涂抹：*Just slap some paint on the walls and it'll look fine.* 在墙上随便刷点漆，就看着漂亮了。◇ *I'd better slap some make-up on before I go out.* 我出门之前最好是简单化化妆。

■ *noun* **1** [C] the action of hitting sb/sth with the flat part of your hand（用手掌）打，拍，掴：*She gave him a slap across the face.* 她打了他一个耳光。◇ *He gave me a hearty slap on the back.* 他热情地在我背上拍了一下。**2** [sing.] the noise made by hitting sb/sth with the flat part of your hand; a similar noise made by sth else 拍打声；类似拍打的声音：*the gentle slap of water against the shore* 水轻轻的拍岸声 **3** [U] (*BrE, informal*) = MAKE-UP (1)

IDM **slap and ˈtickle** (*old-fashioned, BrE, informal*) enthusiastic kissing and CUDDLING between lovers（情人之间的）拥抱亲吻 **a slap in the ˈface** an action that seems to be intended as a deliberate insult to sb 一记耳光；侮辱；打击 **a slap on the ˈwrist** (*informal*) a warning or mild punishment 警告；轻微的惩罚

■ *adv.* (*also* **ˌslap ˈbang**) (*informal*) **1** straight, and with great force 猛然；径直：*Storming out of her room, she went slap into Luke.* 她怒气冲冲地冲出房间，迎面和卢克撞了个满怀。**2** exactly 恰好；正好：*Their apartment is slap bang in the middle of town.* 他们住的公寓恰巧在全城的中心。

slap·dash /ˈslæpdæʃ/ *adj.* done, or doing sth, too quickly and carelessly 仓促马虎的；毛躁的；潦草的：*She has a very slapdash approach to keeping accounts.* 她记账十分潦草马虎。◇ *a slapdash piece of writing* 一篇粗制滥造的文章

ˌslap-ˈhappy *adj.* (*informal*) **1** cheerful, but careless about things that should be taken seriously 嘻嘻哈哈的；什么都不放在心上的；大大咧咧的：*a slap-happy approach to life* 大大咧咧的生活态度 **2** (*especially NAmE*) = PUNCH-DRUNK

slap·head /ˈslæphed/ *noun* (*BrE, informal*) an unkind way of referring to a man with little or no hair on his head 稀发佬；秃子

slap·per /ˈslæpə(r)/ *noun* (*BrE, slang*) an offensive word for a woman, used to suggest that she has a lot of sexual partners 荡妇；淫妇

slap·stick /ˈslæpstɪk/ *noun* [U] the type of humour that is based on simple actions, for example people hitting each other, falling down, etc. 打闹剧；粗俗滑稽剧 ➲ WORDFINDER NOTE AT COMEDY

ˈslap-up *adj.* [only before noun] (*BrE, informal*) (of a meal 饭菜) large and very good 丰盛高档的

slash /slæʃ/ *verb, noun*

■ *verb* **1 ~ sth** to make a long cut with a sharp object, especially in a violent way（用利器）砍，劈 SYN **slit**: *Someone had slashed the tyres on my car.* 有人把我的汽车轮胎割破了。◇ *She tried to kill herself by slashing her wrists.* 她试图割腕自杀。◇ *We had to* ***slash our way*** *through the undergrowth with sticks.* 我们挥舞着木棍一路劈砍，才在密林里开出一条路，穿了过去。**2** [often passive] **~ sth** (*informal*) (often used in newspapers 常用于报章) to reduce sth by a large amount 大幅度削减；大大降低：*to* ***slash costs/prices/fares, etc.*** 大幅度降低成本、价格、车费等 ◇ *The workforce has been slashed by half.* 职工人数裁减了一半。➲ SYNONYMS AT CUT

PHR V **ˈslash at sb/sth (with sth)** to attack sb violently with a knife, etc.（用刀等）猛砍，砍击

■ *noun* **1** [C] a sharp movement made with a knife, etc. in order to cut sb/sth（用刀等的）砍，劈 **2** [C] a long narrow wound or cut（长而窄的）伤口，切口，砍痕：*a slash across his right cheek* 他右脸上的一道刀伤 ◇ (*figurative*) *Her mouth was a slash of red lipstick.* 她的嘴就是口红抹出的一道缝。**3** [C] (*BrE also* **ob·lique**) the symbol (/) used to show alternatives, as in *lunch and/or dinner* and *4/5 people* and to write FRACTIONS, as in ¾ 斜杠；斜线号 ➲ SEE ALSO BACKSLASH, FORWARD SLASH ➲ WORDFINDER NOTE AT KEYBOARD **4 a slash** [sing.] (*BrE, slang*) an act of URINATING 撒尿：*He's just nipped out to have a slash.* 他刚才急急忙忙跑出去撒了一泡尿。

ˌslash-and-ˈburn *adj.* **1** relating to a method of farming in which existing plants, crops, etc. are cut down and burned before new seeds are planted 刀耕火种的；烧垦的：*slash-and-burn agriculture* 刀耕火种农业 **2** aggressive and causing a lot of harm or damage 好斗的；残忍的

slash·er /ˈslæʃə(r)/ (*also* **ˈslasher film**, **ˈslasher movie**) *noun* a frightening film/movie, in which an unknown person kills a lot of people 杀人狂电影

slat /slæt/ *noun* **1** one of a series of thin flat pieces of wood, metal or plastic, used in furniture, fences, etc.（家具、栅栏等上的）板条，窄条，横档 ➲ VISUAL VOCAB PAGE V22 **2** (*specialist*) a part of the wing of an aircraft, on the front of the wing, that can be moved up or down to control upward or downward movement 前缘缝翼

S

（机翼前缘的一部分，可使其上下移动来控制飞机的升降）
➲VISUAL VOCAB PAGE V57

slate /sleɪt/ *noun, verb*

■***noun*** **1** [U] a type of dark grey stone that splits easily into thin flat layers 板岩；石板：*a slate quarry* 板岩采石场 ◇ *The sea was the colour of slate.* 大海的颜色像石板。**2** [C] a small thin piece of slate, used for covering roofs（盖房顶的）石板瓦：*A loose slate had fallen from the roof.* 一块松动的石板瓦从房顶上掉了下来。**3** [C] (*NAmE*) a list of the candidates in an election（选举中的）候选人名单：*a slate of candidates* 候选人名单 ◇ *the Democratic slate* 民主党候选人名单 **4** [C] a small sheet of slate in a wooden frame, used in the past in schools for children to write on（旧时学生用以写字的）石板 **5** [C] a small computer that is easy to carry, that has a screen that you can write on with an electronic pen but no physical keyboard; a TABLET PC™ 触控式电脑；平板电脑 **IDM** SEE CLEAN *adj.*, WIPE *v.*

■***verb*** **1 ~ sb/sth (for sth)** (*BrE*) to criticize sb/sth, especially in a newspaper（尤指在报纸上）批评，抨击：*to slate a book/play/writer* 批评一部书 / 一出戏 / 一位作家 **2** [usually passive] to plan that sth will happen at a particular time in the future 预定；计划；安排：**~ sth for sth** *The houses were first slated for demolition five years ago.* 这些房子在五年前就确定要拆除了。◇ **~ sth to do sth** *The new store is slated to open in spring.* 新商店预计春天开业。**3** [usually passive] (*informal, especially NAmE*) to suggest or choose sb for a job, position, etc. 推举；选定：**~ sb for sth** *I was told that I was being slated for promotion.* 我听说，我被定为提升的人选。◇ **~ sb to do sth** *He is slated to play the lead in the new musical.* 他获选在新的音乐剧中担任主角。

slated /ˈsleɪtɪd/ *adj.* covered with pieces of SLATE 盖石板瓦的：*a slated roof* 石板瓦房顶

ˌslate-ˈgrey *adj.* bluish-grey in colour, like slate 石板灰的；蓝灰色的 ➲MORE LIKE THIS 15, page R26

slather /ˈslæðə(r)/ *verb*

PHR V **ˈslather sth on/over sth | ˈslather with/in sth | ˌslather sth↔ˈon** to cover sth with a thick layer of a substance（在…上）厚厚涂抹：*hot dogs slathered with mustard* 抹了厚厚一层芥末的热狗

slat·ted /ˈslætɪd/ *adj.* [usually before noun] made of slats (= thin pieces of wood) 用板条做的：*slatted blinds* 百叶窗

slat·tern /ˈslætən; *NAmE* -tərn/ *noun* (*old-fashioned*) a dirty untidy woman 邋遢的女人 ▶ **slat·tern·ly** *adj.*: *a slatternly girl* 邋里邋遢的女孩子

slaty (*also* **slatey**) /ˈsleɪti/ *adj.* **1** having a dark grey colour 深灰色的；石板色的：*a slaty sky* 灰暗的天空 **2** containing SLATE; like SLATE 含板岩的；石板似的：*slaty rock* 板岩

slaugh·ter /ˈslɔːtə(r)/ *noun, verb*

■***noun*** [U] **1** the killing of animals for their meat 屠宰；宰杀：*cows taken for slaughter* 待宰奶牛 **2** the cruel killing of large numbers of people at one time, especially in a war（尤指战争中的）屠杀，杀戮 **SYN** **massacre**: *the wholesale slaughter of innocent people* 对无辜民众的大规模杀戮 **IDM** SEE LAMB *n.*

■***verb*** **1 ~ sth** to kill an animal, usually for its meat 屠宰；宰杀 **SYN** **butcher** **2 ~ sb/sth** to kill a large number of people or animals violently 屠杀；杀戮 **SYN** **massacre**: *Men, women and children were slaughtered and villages destroyed.* 村庄被毁，男人、女人和儿童惨遭杀戮。**3 ~ sb/sth** (*informal*) to defeat sb/sth by a large number of points in a sports game, competition, etc.（在体育比赛等竞赛中）大比分击败，使惨败：*We were slaughtered 10–1 by the home team.* 我们以 1:10 惨败给主队。

slaugh·ter·house /ˈslɔːtəhaʊs; *NAmE* -tərh-/ *noun* (*BrE also* **ab·at·toir**) a building where animals are killed for food 屠宰场

Slav /slɑːv/ *noun* a member of any of the races of people of central and eastern Europe who speak Slavic languages 斯拉夫人

slave /sleɪv/ *noun, verb*

■***noun*** **1** a person who is owned by another person and is forced to work for them 奴隶：*She treated her daughter like a slave.* 她对待女儿像对待奴隶一样。➲ WORDFINDER NOTE AT FREEDOM **2** a person who is so strongly influenced by sth that they cannot live without it, or cannot make their own decisions 完全受（某事物）控制的人；完全依赖（某事物）的人：**~ of sth** *We are slaves of the motor car.* 我们离不了汽车。◇ **~ to sth** *Sue's a slave to fashion.* 休是个拼命赶时髦的人。**3** (*specialist*) a device that is directly controlled by another one 从动装置

■***verb*** [I] **~ (away) (at sth)** to work very hard 苦干；辛勤地工作：*I've been slaving away all day trying to get this work finished.* 我整天苦干，想把这项工作赶完。◇ *I haven't got time to spend hours **slaving over a hot stove*** (= doing a lot of cooking). 我没时间老围着灶台转。

ˈslave-driver *noun* (*disapproving*) a person who makes people work extremely hard 残酷的监工；逼迫他人拼命干活儿的人 **SYN** **tyrant**

ˌslave ˈlabour (*especially US* **ˌslave ˈlabor**) *noun* [U] **1** work that is done by slaves; the slaves who do the work 奴隶劳动；干苦役的奴隶：*Huge palaces were built by slave labour.* 宏伟的宫殿是奴隶建成的。**2** (*informal*) work that is very hard and very badly paid 繁重而报酬很低的工作：*I left because the job was just slave labour.* 我之所以离开是因为那工作简直是奴隶干的。

slaver[1] /ˈslævə(r)/ *verb* [I] (usually of an animal 通常指动物) to let SALIVA (= the liquid produced in the mouth) run out of the mouth, especially when hungry or excited（尤指因饥饿或兴奋）流口水，垂涎：*slavering dogs* 淌着口水的狗

slaver[2] /ˈsleɪvə(r)/ *noun* **1** (in the past) a person who bought and sold SLAVES（旧时）奴隶贩子 **2** a ship that was used in the past for carrying SLAVES（旧时）贩运奴隶的船

slav·ery /ˈsleɪvəri/ *noun* [U] **1** the state of being a SLAVE 奴隶身份：*to **be sold into slavery*** 被卖为奴 **2** the practice of having SLAVES 奴隶制；蓄奴：*the abolition of slavery* 奴隶制的废除 **OPP** **freedom**

ˈslave trade *noun* [sing.] the buying and selling of people as SLAVES, especially in the 17th–19th centuries（尤指 17–19 世纪的）奴隶买卖

Slav·ic /ˈslɑːvɪk/ (*also* **Slav·on·ic**) *adj.* of or connected with Slavs or their languages, which include Russian, Polish, Czech and a number of other languages 斯拉夫人的；斯拉夫语的

slav·ish /ˈsleɪvɪʃ/ *adj.* (*disapproving*) following or copying sb/sth exactly without having any original thought at all 无独创性的；盲从的；照搬的：*a slavish adherence to the rules* 墨守成规 ▶ **slav·ish·ly** *adv.*

Sla·von·ic /sləˈvɒnɪk; *NAmE* -ˈvɑːn-/ *adj.* = SLAVIC

slay /sleɪ/ *verb* (**slew** /sluː/, **slain** /sleɪn/) **1 ~ sb/sth** (*old-fashioned* or *literary*) to kill sb/sth in a war or a fight（在战争或搏斗中）杀，杀死：*St George slew the dragon.* 圣乔治杀死了那条龙。**2 ~ sb** (*especially NAmE*) (used especially in newspapers 尤用于报章) to murder sb 杀害；残害；谋杀：*Two passengers were slain by the hijackers.* 两名乘客遭劫机者杀害。**3 ~ sb** (*old-fashioned, informal, especially NAmE*) to have a strong effect on sb, especially to make them laugh （尤指借着使人发笑而）深深打动，迷住：*Those old movies still slay me!* 那些老影片依旧让我着迷！ ▶ **slay·ing** *noun* (*especially NAmE*)：*the drug-related slayings of five people* 那宗和毒品有关的五人被杀的案子

sleaze /sliːz/ *noun* **1** [U] dishonest or illegal behaviour, especially by politicians or business people（尤指政客或商人的）舞弊，欺诈，违法行为：*allegations of sleaze* 关于舞弊的指控 ◇ *The candidate was seriously damaged by the sleaze factor.* 那位候选人的形象因丑闻而受到严重损害。**2** [U] behaviour or conditions that are unpleasant and not socially acceptable, especially because sex is involved（尤指涉及性的）污秽，肮脏，乌烟瘴气：*the sleaze of a town that was once a naval base* 一度是海军基地的小城里

S

那乌烟瘴气的社会氛围 **3** [C] (*also* **sleaze·bag** /ˈsliːzbæg/, **sleaze·ball** /ˈsliːzbɔːl/ *especially in NAmE*) a dishonest or immoral person 奸徒；卑鄙的人；下流坯

sleazy /ˈsliːzi/ *adj.* (**sleaz·ier**, **sleazi·est**) (*informal*) **1** (of a place 地方) dirty, unpleasant and not socially acceptable, especially because sex is involved（尤指涉及性）肮脏的，污秽的，乌烟瘴气的，藏污纳垢的 **SYN** **disreputable**: *a sleazy bar* 乌烟瘴气的酒吧 **2** (of people 人) immoral and unpleasant 不正派的；道德败坏的；堕落的；卑鄙的：*a sleazy reporter* 不正派的记者 ▸ **sleazi·ness** *noun* [U]

sleb /sleb/ *noun* (*informal*) = CELEBRITY (1)

sled /sled/ *noun, verb* (**-dd-**) (*especially NAmE*) = SLEDGE ▸ **sled·ding** /ˈsledɪŋ/ *noun* [U]

sledge (*BrE*) (*also* **sled** *NAmE, BrE*)
雪橇

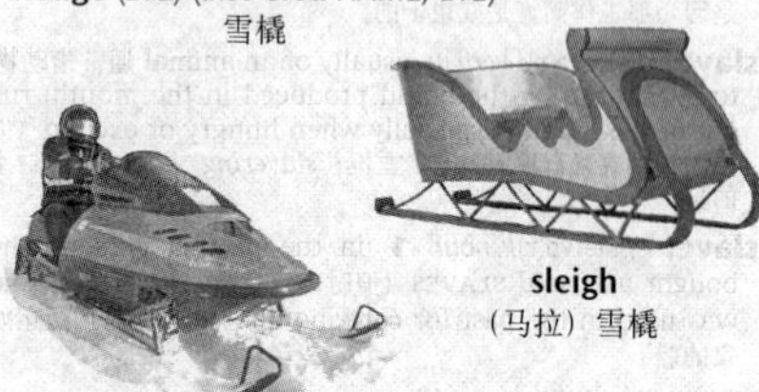

sleigh
（马拉）雪橇

snowmobile 机动雪橇

sledge /sledʒ/ (*BrE*) (*also* **sled** *NAmE, BrE*) *noun, verb*

■ ***noun*** a vehicle for travelling over snow and ice, with long narrow strips of wood or metal instead of wheels. Larger sledges are pulled by horses or dogs and smaller ones are used for going down hills as a sport or for pleasure. 雪橇 ➲ COMPARE SLEIGH, TOBOGGAN *n.*

■ ***verb*** [I] to ride on a sledge/sled 乘雪橇：*We were hoping we could go sledging.* 我们本来希望能去乘雪橇。

sledge·ham·mer /ˈsledʒhæmə(r)/ *noun* a large heavy hammer with a long handle（有长柄的）大锤

IDM **use a ˌsledgehammer to crack a ˈnut** to use more force than is necessary 抡着大锤砸核桃；杀鸡用牛刀

sledg·ing /ˈsledʒɪŋ/ *noun* [U] **1** (*BrE*) (*NAmE* **sledding**) the activity of riding on a sledge 滑雪橇：*to go sledging* 去滑雪橇 **2** (in CRICKET) insults to players in the opposing team in order to destroy their concentration（板球运动中为分散对手注意力的）辱骂 ➲ COMPARE TRASH TALK

sleek /sliːk/ *adj., verb*

■ ***adj.*** (**sleek·er**, **sleek·est**) **1** (*approving*) smooth and shiny 光滑的；光亮的 **SYN** **glossy**: *sleek black hair* 乌黑油亮的头发 ◇ *the sleek dark head of a seal* 黑乎乎、油光光的海豹脑袋 **2** (*approving*) having an elegant smooth shape 线条流畅的；造型优美的：*a sleek yacht* 造型优美的游艇 ◇ *the sleek lines of the new car* 新车流畅的线条 **3** (*often disapproving*) (of a person 人) looking rich, and dressed in elegant and expensive clothes 阔气的；衣冠楚楚的；时髦的：*a sleek and ambitious politician* 衣冠楚楚、野心勃勃的政客 ▸ **sleek·ly** *adv.* **sleek·ness** *noun* [U]

■ ***verb*** ~ sth (**back/down**) to make sth, especially hair, smooth and shiny 使（头发等）发油光；使平整光亮：*His glossy hair was sleeked back over his ears.* 他那油亮的头发平平整整地梳向耳后。

sleep 🔑 /sliːp/ *verb, noun*

■ ***verb*** (**slept**, **slept** /slept/) **1** 🔑 [I] (+ **adv./prep.**) to rest with your eyes closed and your mind and body not active 睡；睡觉；入睡：*to sleep well/deeply/soundly/badly* 睡得好；沉睡；酣睡；睡得不好 ◇ *I couldn't sleep because of the noise.* 嘈杂声吵得我睡不着。◇ *I had to sleep on the sofa.* 我只得睡在沙发上。◇ *He slept solidly for ten hours.* 他整整睡了十个小时。◇ *I slept at my sister's house last night* (= stayed the night there). 昨晚我住在妹妹家了。◇ *We both slept right through* (= were not woken up by) *the storm.* 我们两人睡得很沉，浑然不知有暴风雨。◇ *She only sleeps for four hours a night.* 她每天晚上只睡四个小时。◇ *We sometimes sleep late at the weekends* (= until late in the morning). 周末我们有时候睡懒觉。◇ *I put the sleeping baby down gently.* 我把睡着的宝宝轻轻放下。◇ *What are our sleeping arrangements here* (= where shall we sleep)? 我们在这儿睡觉是怎么安排的？

WORDFINDER 联想词：doze, dream, drowsy, insomnia, oversleep, REM, sedative, soporific, tired

HELP It is more common to say that somebody **is asleep** than to say that somebody **is sleeping**. **Sleep** can only be used in the passive with a preposition such as **in** or **on**. * somebody is asleep 比 somebody is sleeping 更常见。sleep 只有和 in 或 on 等介词连用时才可以用被动语态：*It was clear her bed hadn't been slept in.* 她的床明显没有睡过的痕迹。**2** [T, no passive] ~ **sb** to have enough beds for a particular number of people 可供…人睡觉；可供…人住宿：*The apartment sleeps six.* 这套公寓能睡六个人。◇ *The hotel sleeps 120 guests.* 这家旅馆可供 120 位客人住宿。

IDM **let sleeping dogs ˈlie** (*saying*) to avoid mentioning a subject or sth that happened in the past, in order to avoid any problems or arguments 过去的事就不要再提了；不要没事找事 **sleep like a ˈlog/ˈbaby** (*informal*) to sleep very well 沉睡；酣睡 **sleep ˈtight** (*informal*) used especially to children before they go to bed to say that you hope they sleep well（尤用以打发孩子睡觉）睡个好觉：*Goodnight, sleep tight!* 晚安，睡个好觉！➲ MORE AT ROUGH *adv.*, WINK *n.*

PHR V **ˌsleep aˈround** (*informal, disapproving*) to have sex with a lot of different people 到处跟人睡觉；乱搞男女关系 **ˌsleep ˈin** to sleep until after the time you usually get up in the morning 迟起；睡过头；睡懒觉 **ˌsleep sth**↔

▼ SYNONYMS 同义词辨析

sleep

doze • nap • snooze

These words all mean to rest with your eyes closed and your mind and body not active. 以上各词均含睡觉、入睡之义。

sleep to rest with your eyes shut and your mind and body not active 指睡、睡觉、入睡：*Did you sleep well?* 你睡得好吗？◇ *I couldn't sleep last night.* 我昨天晚上睡不着。**NOTE** It is more usual to say that sb is **asleep** than that they are **sleeping**; but if you use an adverb to say how they are sleeping, use **sleeping**. 表示在睡觉，asleep 较 sleeping 常用，但如果用副词表示睡的状态就用 sleeping：*'What's Ashley doing?' 'Sh! She's asleep.'* "阿什利在干什么？""嘘，她在睡觉。" ◇ *The baby was sleeping peacefully.* 婴儿睡得很安稳。◇ ~~*The baby was asleep peacefully.*~~

doze to sleep lightly, waking up easily, often when you are not in bed 指打瞌睡、打盹儿，通常不是躺在床上：*He was dozing in front of the TV.* 他在电视机前打瞌睡。

nap to sleep for a short time, especially during the day. 尤指日间的小睡、打盹儿

snooze (*informal*) to sleep lightly for a short time, especially during the day and usually not in bed 尤指日间的小睡、打盹儿，通常不是躺在床上：*My brother was snoozing on the sofa.* 我弟弟正在沙发上打盹儿。

PATTERNS

- to sleep/doze **lightly/fitfully**
- to doze/snooze **gently**

S

ˈ**off** to get better after sth, especially drinking too much alcohol, by sleeping 靠睡觉来消除；睡一觉熬过酒劲：*Let's leave him to **sleep it off**.* 咱们让他睡吧，一觉醒来就没事了。ˈ**sleep on sth** (*informal*) to delay making a decision about sth until the next day, so that you have time to think about it 把…留待第二天决定；把…拖延到第二天再说：*Could I sleep on it and let you know tomorrow?* 能不能让我晚上考虑考虑，明天答复你？ ˌ**sleep ˈover** to stay the night at sb else's home 在别人家里过夜：*It's very late now—why don't you sleep over?* 现在已经很晚了，为什么不就睡这儿呢？ ◇ *Can I sleep over at my friend's house?* 我能不能在我朋友家过夜？ ➲ RELATED NOUN SLEEPOVER ˈ**sleep together** | ˈ**sleep with sb** (*informal*) to have sex with sb, especially sb you are not married to 和某人（尤指非配偶）发生性关系：*I know he's going out with her, but I don't think they're sleeping together.* 我知道他跟她在谈恋爱，不过我想他们还不至于上床吧。◇ *Everyone knows she sleeps with the boss.* 人人知道她跟老板睡觉。

■ ***noun* 1** 🔑 [U] the natural state of rest in which your eyes are closed, your body is not active, and your mind is not conscious 睡觉；睡眠：*I need to **get some sleep**.* 我得睡一会儿。◇ *I didn't **get much sleep** last night.* 昨晚我没睡好。◇ *Can you give me something to help me **get to sleep** (= start sleeping)?* 你能不能给我点能让我入睡的东西？ ◇ ***Go to sleep**—it's late.* 快睡吧，不早了。◇ *He cried out **in his sleep**.* 他在睡梦中大叫。◇ *Anxiety can be caused by **lack of sleep**.* 睡眠不足可能导致焦虑。◇ *His talk nearly **sent me to sleep** (= it was boring).* 他的讲话差点让我睡着了。◇ *Try to go **back to sleep**.* 再继续睡吧。 **2** 🔑 [sing.] a period of sleep 睡眠时间；一觉：*Did you have a good sleep?* 睡得好吗？ ◇ *Ros fell into a deep sleep.* 罗斯睡着了，睡得很沉。◇ *I'll feel better after a **good night's sleep** (= a night when I sleep well).* 好好睡一晚，我就会觉得好些了。**3** [U] (*informal*) the substance that sometimes forms in the corners of your eyes after you have been sleeping 眼屎

IDM **be able to do sth in your ˈsleep** (*informal*) to be able to do sth very easily because you have done it many times before 闭着眼睛也能做 ˌ**go to ˈsleep** (*informal*) if part of your body **goes to sleep**, you lose the sense of feeling in it, usually because it has been in the same position for too long（身体某部位）麻木，发麻 **not lose ˈsleep/lose no ˈsleep over sth** to not worry much about sth 不大为某事操心：*It's not worth losing sleep over.* 那件事不值得焦虑。**put sb to ˈsleep** (*informal*) to make sb unconscious before an operation by using drugs (called an ANAESTHETIC)（用药物）麻醉 **put sth to ˈsleep** to kill a sick or injured animal by giving it drugs so that it dies without pain. People say 'put to sleep' to avoid saying 'kill'.（用药物）使长眠，无痛苦地杀死（生病或受伤的动物） ➲ MORE AT WINK *n.*

sleep·er /ˈsliːpə(r)/ *noun* **1** (used with an adjective 与形容词连用) a person who sleeps in a particular way 睡得…的人：*a **heavy/light/sound sleeper*** 睡得很沉 / 轻 / 香的人 **2** a person who is asleep 睡觉者；睡眠者：*Only the snores of the sleepers broke the silence of the house.* 只有睡觉的人发出的鼾声打破了屋内的寂静。**3** a night train with beds for passengers on it 卧铺列车：*the London–Edinburgh sleeper* 伦敦到爱丁堡的卧铺列车 **4** = SLEEPING CAR **5** (*BrE*) (*NAmE* **tie**) one of the heavy pieces of wood or concrete on which the rails on a railway/railroad track are laid（铁路）枕木，轨枕 ➲ VISUAL VOCAB PAGE V63 **6** (*informal, especially NAmE*) a film/movie, play or book that for a long time is not very successful and then is suddenly a success（出人意外地成功的）冷门电影（或戏剧、著作等） **7** (*also* ˌ**sleeper ˈagent**) a SPY who is sent to live in a country as a normal citizen and is not used until much later 休眠间谍（暂时不从事间谍活动） **8** (*BrE*) a ring or piece of metal that you wear in an ear that has been PIERCED (= had a hole made in it) to keep the hole from closing（为保持耳环孔不闭合而戴的）耳环，耳钉

ˈ**sleeping bag** *noun* a thick warm bag that you use for sleeping in, for example when you are camping 睡袋 ➲ VISUAL VOCAB PAGE V24

ˌ**Sleeping ˈBeauty** *noun* used to refer to sb who has been asleep for a long time 睡了很长时间的人：*OK, Sleeping Beauty, time to get up.* 好啦，睡美人，该起床了。 ➲ MORE LIKE THIS 16, page R27 **ORIGIN** From the European fairy tale about a beautiful girl who sleeps for a hundred years and is woken up when a prince kisses her. 源自欧洲童话，沉睡百年的美丽少女被王子的亲吻唤醒。

ˈ**sleeping car** (*also* **sleep·er**) *noun* a coach/car on a train with beds for people to sleep in 卧铺车厢

ˌ**sleeping ˈpartner** (*BrE*) (*NAmE* ˌ**silent ˈpartner**) *noun* a person who has put money into a business company but who is not actually involved in running it 隐名合伙人，隐名股东（在企业中有股份但不参与经营）

ˈ**sleeping pill** (*BrE also* ˈ**sleeping tablet**) *noun* a pill containing a drug that helps you to sleep 安眠药 ➲ MORE LIKE THIS 9, page R26

ˌ**sleeping poˈliceman** *noun* (*BrE, informal*) = SPEED HUMP

ˈ**sleeping sickness** *noun* [U] a tropical disease carried by the TSETSE FLY that causes a feeling of wanting to go to sleep and usually causes death 非洲锥虫病；睡眠病（由采采蝇传播的热带疾病，患者嗜睡，通常导致死亡）

sleep·less /ˈsliːpləs/ *adj.* **1** [only before noun] without sleep 没有睡觉的；不眠的：*I've had a few **sleepless nights** recently.* 最近我有好几个晚上没睡觉。**2** [not before noun] not able to sleep 睡不着；失眠：*She lay sleepless until dawn.* 她躺在那儿，直到天亮才睡着。▶ **sleep·less·ly** *adv.* **sleep·less·ness** *noun* [U] **SYN** **insomnia**：*to suffer from sleeplessness* 受失眠之苦

sleep·over /ˈsliːpəʊvə(r); *NAmE* -oʊ-/ (*NAmE also* ˈ**slumber party**) *noun* a party for children or young people when a group of them spend the night at one house（儿童或年轻人在某人家玩乐并过夜的）聚会

sleep·walk /ˈsliːpwɔːk/ *verb* [I] to walk around while you are asleep 梦游 ▶ **sleep·walk·er** (*also formal* **som·nam·bu·list**) *noun*

sleepy /ˈsliːpi/ *adj.* (**sleep·ier, sleepi·est**) **1** needing sleep; ready to go to sleep 困倦的；瞌睡的 **SYN** **drowsy**：*a sleepy child* 打瞌睡的孩子 ◇ *He had begun to feel sleepy.* 他开始觉得困了。◇ *The heat and the wine made her sleepy.* 周围暖洋洋的，又喝了酒，她感觉昏昏欲睡。 **2** (of places 地方) quiet and where nothing much happens 安静的；冷清的；不热闹的：*a sleepy little town* 宁静的小城 ▶ **sleep·ily** /-ɪli/ *adv.*：*She yawned sleepily.* 她困得打着哈欠。 **sleepi·ness** *noun* [U]

sleepy·head /ˈsliːpihed/ *noun* (*informal*) a way of addressing sb who is not completely awake（称呼没睡醒的人）懒鬼，瞌睡虫：*Come on sleepyhead—time to get up.* 快点吧，懒鬼，该起床了。

sleet /sliːt/ *noun, verb*

■ ***noun*** [U] a mixture of rain and snow 雨夹雪 ➲ WORDFINDER NOTE AT SNOW

■ ***verb*** [I] when **it is sleeting**, a mixture of rain and snow is falling from the sky 下雨夹雪

sleeve 🔑 /sliːv/ *noun* **1** 🔑 a part of a piece of clothing that covers all or part of your arm 袖子：*a dress with short/long sleeves* 短袖 / 长袖连衣裙 ◇ *Dan rolled up his sleeves and washed his hands.* 丹挽起袖子洗了洗手。 ➲ VISUAL VOCAB PAGES V66, V68 ➲ SEE ALSO SHIRTSLEEVE **2** **-sleeved** (in adjectives 构成形容词) having sleeves of the type mentioned 有…袖子的：*a short-sleeved shirt* 短袖衬衫 ➲ VISUAL VOCAB PAGE V66 **3** (*also* **jacket** *especially in NAmE*) a stiff paper or cardboard envelope for a record 唱片套：*a colourful sleeve design* 色彩斑斓的唱片套设计 **4** a tube that covers a part of a machine to protect it（机器的）套筒，套管 ▶ **sleeve·less** /ˈsliːvləs/ *adj.*：*a sleeveless dress* 无袖连衣裙 ➲ VISUAL VOCAB PAGE V66

IDM **have/keep sth up your ˈsleeve** to keep a plan or an idea secret until you need to use it 有锦囊妙计；胸中自有主张 ➲ MORE AT ACE *n.*, CARD *n.*, LAUGH *v.*, ROLL *v.*, TRICK *n.*, WEAR *v.*

ˈ**sleeve note** *noun* (*BrE*) = LINER NOTE

S

sleigh /sleɪ/ *noun* a SLEDGE (= a vehicle that slides over snow), especially one pulled by horses（尤指马拉的）雪橇：*a sleigh ride* 乘雪橇 ➲ PICTURE AT SLEDGE ➲ MORE LIKE THIS 20, page R27

sleight of hand /ˌslaɪt əv ˈhænd/ *noun* [U] **1** (*also formal* **le·ger·de·main**) skilful movements of your hand that other people cannot see（隐蔽的）敏捷手法，灵巧手法：*The trick is done simply by sleight of hand.* 变这个戏法全凭手法敏捷。**2** the fact of tricking people in a clever way 把戏；花招：*Last year's profits were more the result of financial sleight of hand than genuine growth.* 去年的赢利更多是因为财务手法，而不是真正的增长。

slen·der /ˈslendə(r)/ *adj.* (**slen·derer**, **slen·derest**) HELP You can also use **more slender** and **most slender**. 亦可用 more slender 和 most slender。**1** (*approving*) (of people or their bodies 人或人体) thin in an attractive or elegant way 苗条的；纤细的 SYN **slim**：*her slender figure* 她苗条的身材 ◇ *long, slender fingers* 修长纤细的手指 **2** thin or narrow 细的；窄的：*a glass with a slender stem* 高脚酒杯 **3** small in amount or size and hardly enough 微薄的；不足的：*to win by a* ***slender margin/majority*** 以微弱优势 / 多数获胜 ◇ *people of* ***slender means*** (= with little money) 穷人 ◇ *Australia held a slender 1–0 lead at half-time.* 澳大利亚队在上半场结束时以 1:0 的微弱优势领先。▶ **slen·der·ness** *noun* [U]

slept PAST TENSE, PAST PART. OF SLEEP

sleuth /sluːθ/ *noun* (*old-fashioned* or *humorous*) a person who investigates crimes 侦探 SYN **detective**：*an amateur sleuth* 业余侦探

sleuth·ing /ˈsluːθɪŋ/ *noun* [U] the act of investigating a crime or mysterious event 侦查，调查（犯罪案件或神秘事件）：*to do some private sleuthing* 进行私人侦查

slew /sluː/ *verb, noun* ➲ SEE ALSO SLAY

■ ***verb*** [I, T] (especially of a vehicle 尤指车辆) to turn or slide suddenly in another direction; to make a vehicle do this（使）突然转向，急转：**+ adv./prep.** *The car skidded and slewed sideways.* 汽车打滑，向一侧偏去。◇ **~ sth + adv./prep.** *He slewed the motorbike over as they hit the freeway.* 他们冲到高速公路时，他赶紧把摩托车调转方向。

■ ***noun*** [sing.] **~ of sth** (*informal, especially NAmE*) a large number or amount of sth 大量；许多

S

slice /slaɪs/ *noun, verb*

■ ***noun*** **1** a thin flat piece of food that has been cut off a larger piece（切下的食物）薄片，片：*a slice of bread* 一片面包 ◇ *Cut the meat into thin slices.* 把肉切成薄片。**2** (*informal*) a part or share of sth 部分；份额：*Our firm is well placed to grab a large slice of the market.* 我们公司处境有利，足以获得巨大的市场份额。**3** a kitchen UTENSIL (= tool) that you use to lift and serve pieces of food 锅铲；（餐桌用）小铲：*a fish slice* 煎鱼铲 ◇ *a cake slice* 蛋糕铲 ➲ VISUAL VOCAB PAGE V27 **4** (*sport* 体育) (in GOLF, TENNIS, etc. 高尔夫球、网球等) a stroke that makes the ball spin to one side rather than going straight ahead 削球；侧旋球；斜切打

IDM **a ˌslice of ˈlife** a film/movie, play or book that gives a very realistic view of ordinary life 反映现实生活的电影（或戏剧、书）➲ MORE AT ACTION *n.*, CAKE *n.*, PIE

■ ***verb*** **1** [T] **~ sth (up)** to cut sth into slices 把…切成（薄）片：*to slice (up) onions* 把洋葱切成片 ◇ *Slice the cucumber thinly.* 把黄瓜切成薄薄的片。◇ *a sliced loaf* 切片面包 ➲ COLLOCATIONS AT COOKING ➲ VISUAL VOCAB PAGE V30 ➲ SEE ALSO SALAMI SLICING **2** [I] to cut sth easily with or as if with a sharp blade 切；割；划：**+ adv./prep.** *He accidentally* ***sliced through*** *his finger.* 他不小心把指头割破了。◇ *A piece of glass sliced into his shoulder.* 一块玻璃划破他的肩膀。◇ (*figurative*) *Her speech sliced through all the confusion surrounding the situation.* 她一席话把整个事态的一切纷扰剖析得清清楚楚。◇ **~ sth (+ adj.)** *The knife sliced his jacket.* 那把刀划破了他的上衣。◇ *He sliced the fruit open.* 他把水果切开了。◇ (*figurative*) *The ship sliced the water.* 船破浪前进。**3** [T] **~ sth** (*sport* 体育) to hit a ball so that it spins and does not move in the expected direction 削（球）；斜切打：*He managed to slice a shot over the net.* 他设法把球斜切过网。**4** [T] **~ sth** (in GOLF 高尔夫球) to hit the ball so that it flies away in a curve, when you do not mean to（无意中）打出弧线球 **5** [T] **~ sth** (*NAmE, informal*) to reduce sth by a large amount 大幅度削减；大量降低：*The new tax has sliced annual bonuses by 30 percent.* 由于征收新税，年度红利减少了 30%。

IDM **ˌslice and ˈdice (sth)** (*computing* 计) to divide information into small parts in order to study it more closely or to see it in different ways 切割，分割（信息）：*The software lets you slice and dice the data and display it in different formats.* 这软件使你能够对数据进行切割，以不同的格式显示出来。➲ MORE LIKE THIS 12, page R26 ➲ MORE AT WAY *n.*

PHR V **ˌslice sth ↔off/aˈway | ˌslice sth ˈoff sth** to cut sth from a larger piece 切下；割下：*Slice a piece off.* 切下一片。◇ (*figurative*) *He sliced two seconds off the world record.* 他把世界纪录缩短了两秒。

ˌsliced ˈbread *noun* [U] bread that is sold already cut into slices 切片面包：*a loaf of sliced bread* 一条切片面包

IDM **the best thing since sliced ˈbread** (*informal*) if you say that sth is **the best thing since sliced bread**, you think it is extremely good, interesting, etc. 极好（或极有意思等）的事物

slick /slɪk/ *adj., noun, verb*

■ ***adj.*** (**slick·er**, **slick·est**) **1** (*sometimes disapproving*) done or made in a way that is clever and efficient but often does not seem to be sincere or lacks important ideas 华而不实的；虚有其表的；取巧的：*a slick advertising campaign* 华而不实的广告攻势 ◇ *a slick performance* 表面热闹但内容贫乏的演出 **2** (*sometimes disapproving*) speaking very easily and smoothly but in a way that does not seem sincere 花言巧语的；能说会道的；油滑的 SYN **glib**：*slick TV presenters* 伶牙俐齿的电视节目主持人 ◇ *a slick salesman* 花言巧语的推销员 **3** done quickly and smoothly 娴熟的；灵巧的；流畅的 SYN **skilful**：*The crowd enjoyed the team's slick passing.* 观众欣赏了这支球队娴熟的传接配合。◇ *a slick gear change* 平滑的换挡 **4** smooth and difficult to hold or move on 滑的；滑溜溜的 SYN **slippery**：*The roads were slick with rain.* 下雨路滑。▶ **slick·ly** *adv.*：*The magazine is slickly produced.* 这份杂志办得华而不实。**slick·ness** *noun* [U]

■ ***noun*** **1** (*also* **ˈoil slick**) an area of oil that is floating on the surface of the sea（海上）浮油，浮油膜 **2** a small area of sth wet and shiny 一小片湿而亮的地方：*a slick of sweat* 涔涔的汗水

■ ***verb*** [usually passive] **~ sth + adv./prep.** to make hair very flat and smooth by putting oil, water, etc. on it 使（头发）平整光溜：*His hair was* ***slicked back/down*** *with gel.* 他的头发用了发胶，朝后 / 朝下梳得平平整整的。

slick·er /ˈslɪkə(r)/ *noun* (*NAmE*) a long loose coat that keeps you dry in the rain（长而宽松的）雨衣 ➲ SEE ALSO CITY SLICKER

slide /slaɪd/ *verb, noun*

■ ***verb*** (**slid**, **slid** /slɪd/)

• **MOVE SMOOTHLY/QUIETLY** 滑行；悄悄地移动 **1** [I, T] to move easily over a smooth or wet surface; to make sth move in this way（使）滑行，滑动：(**+ adv./prep.**) *We slid down the grassy slope.* 我们从草坡上滑了下来。◇ *The drawers slide in and out easily.* 这几个抽屉好推好拉。◇ **~ sth + adv./prep.** *She slid her hand along the rail.* 她把手搭在栏杆上滑动着。◇ **~ (sth) + adj.** *The automatic doors slid open.* 自动门慢慢开了。**2** [I, T] to move quickly and quietly, for example in order not to be noticed; to make sth move in this way（使）快捷而悄声地移动 SYN **slip**：**+ adv./prep.** *He slid into bed.* 他不声不响地钻进被子。◇ *She slid out while no one was looking.* 她趁着没人看见溜了出去。◇ **~ sth + adv./prep.** *The man slid the money quickly into his pocket.* 那人很快把钱塞进自己的口袋。

• **BECOME LOWER/WORSE** 降低；衰落 **3** [I] **~ (from...) (to...)** to become gradually lower or of less value 逐渐降低；贬值：*Shares slid to a 10-year low.* 股价跌到了 10 年来的最低点。**4** [I] **~ (down/into/towards sth)** to move gradually into a worse situation 衰落（成）；逐渐陷入；逐渐衰退（到）：*The industry has slid into decline.* 这个行业已成衰

退之势。◇ *They were sliding towards bankruptcy.* 他们正逐渐濒临破产。◇ *He got depressed and began to* ***let things slide*** (= failed to give things the attention they needed). 他意气消沉，得过且过。

■***noun***

• **BECOMING LOWER/WORSE** 降低；衰落 **1** [C, usually sing.] a change to a lower or worse condition 降低；跌落；衰落：*a downward slide in the price of oil* 石油价格的下跌 ◇ *the team's slide down the table* 球队排名的下降 ◇ *talks to prevent* ***a slide into*** *civil war* 旨在避免陷入内战的谈判 ◇ *The economy is* ***on the slide*** (= getting worse). 经济日益衰退。

• **ON ICE** 在冰上 **2** [sing.] a long, smooth movement on ice or a smooth surface（在冰上或光滑表面上的）滑行，滑动 **SYN** **skid**: *Her car went into a slide.* 她的车打起滑来。

• **FOR CHILDREN** 儿童 **3** [C] a structure with a steep slope that children use for sliding down 滑梯：*to go down the slide* 溜滑梯 ➲VISUAL VOCAB PAGE V41

• **FALL OF ROCK** 山岩崩塌 **4** [C] a sudden fall of a large amount of rock or earth down a hill 山崩；岩崩；土崩；崩塌 **SYN** **landslide**: *I was afraid of starting a slide of loose stones.* 我当时担心会引起松散石块崩塌。

• **PHOTOGRAPH** 照片 **5** [C] a small piece of film held in a frame that can be shown on a screen when you shine a light through it 幻灯片 **SYN** **transparency**: *a talk with colour slides* 辅以彩色幻灯片的讲话

• **COMPUTERS** 计算机 **6** [C] one page of an electronic presentation, that may contain text and images, that is usually viewed on a computer screen or projected onto a larger screen 投影片： *I'm still working on the slides for my presentation.* 我还在准备演示用的投影片。

• **FOR MICROSCOPE** 显微镜 **7** [C] a small piece of glass that sth is placed on so that it can be looked at under a MICROSCOPE 载玻片 ➲VISUAL VOCAB PAGE V72

• **PART OF MUSICAL INSTRUMENT** 乐器部件 **8** [C] a part of a musical instrument or other device that slides backwards and forwards（乐器上的）拉管，滑管，滑动装置 ➲VISUAL VOCAB PAGE V37

• **FOR HAIR** 头发 **9** [C] (*BrE*) = HAIRSLIDE

'slide projector *noun* a piece of equipment for displaying SLIDES (= small pieces of film held in frames) on a screen 幻灯机 ➲COMPARE DATA PROJECTOR, OVERHEAD PROJECTOR

sli·der /'slaɪdə(r)/ *noun* **1** a device for controlling sth such as the volume of a radio, which you slide up and down or from side to side（控制收音机音量等的）滑杆，滑动器 **2** (*computing* 计) an ICON that you can slide up and down or from side to side with the mouse 浮动块；滑动条；滑块 **3** a FRESHWATER TURTLE from N America 红腹彩龟（北美淡水龟）

'slide rule *noun* a long narrow instrument like a ruler, with a middle part that slides backwards and forwards, used for calculating numbers 计算尺；滑尺

'slide show (*also* **slide·show**) *noun* **1** a number of slides (= small pieces of film held in frames) shown to an audience using a SLIDE PROJECTOR, often during a lecture（常指讲演中的）幻灯片放映 **2** (*computing* 计) a piece of software that shows a number of images on a computer screen in a particular order 幻灯片放映软件；幻灯片放映软体：*a slideshow presentation* 幻灯片演示

,sliding 'door *noun* a door that slides across an opening rather than swinging away from it 滑门；推拉门

,sliding 'scale *noun* a system in which the rate at which sth is paid varies according to particular conditions 浮动费率制（根据情况上下浮动费率的交纳制度）：*Fees are calculated* ***on a sliding scale*** *according to income* (= richer people pay more). 按浮动费率制根据收入高低计算收费。

slight /slaɪt/ *adj., noun, verb*

■***adj.*** (**slight·er, slight·est**) **1** very small in degree 轻微的；略微的：*a slight increase/change/delay/difference* 略微的增长/变化/拖延/差异 ◇ *I woke up with a slight headache.* 我醒来时有点头痛。◇ *The damage was slight.* 损失很小。◇ *She takes offence at the slightest thing* (= is very easily offended). 她动辄生气。◇ *There was* ***not the slightest*** *hint of trouble.* 当时看不出丝毫会出现麻烦的迹象。 **2** small and thin in size 细小的；纤细的；瘦小的：*a slight woman* 瘦小的女子 **3** (*formal*) not deserving serious attention 无须重视的；不足道的：*This is a very slight novel.* 这是一部颇不足道的小说。

IDM **not in the 'slightest** not at all 一点也不；毫不；根本没有：*He didn't seem to mind in the slightest.* 他好像一点都不在乎。

■***noun*** ~ (**on sb/sth**) an act or a remark that criticizes sth or offends sb 侮慢；冷落；轻视 **SYN** **insult**: *Nick took her comment as a slight on his abilities as a manager.* 尼克觉得，她的话是藐视他当经理的能力。

■***verb*** [usually passive] ~ **sb** to treat sb rudely or without respect 侮慢；冷落；轻视 **SYN** **insult**: *She* ***felt slighted*** *because she hadn't been invited.* 她没有受到邀请，觉得受了冷落。 ▶ **slight·ing** *adj.* [only before noun]: *slighting remarks* 不敬的话语

slight·ly /'slaɪtli/ *adv.* **1** a little 略微；稍微：*a slightly different version* 略有不同的说法 ◇ *We took a slightly more direct route.* 我们选择了一条略近的路线。◇ *I knew her slightly.* 我对她略知一二。◇ *'Are you worried?' 'Only slightly.'* "你担心吗？""稍微有点。" **2** a **slightly built** person is small and thin 身材瘦小的

slim /slɪm/ *adj., verb, noun*

■***adj.*** (**slim·mer, slim·mest**) **1** (*approving*) (of a person 人) thin, in a way that is attractive 苗条的；纤细的：*a slim figure/body/waist* 苗条的体形/身材；纤细的腰肢 ◇ *She was tall and slim.* 她是个瘦高个儿。◇ *How do you manage to stay so slim?* 你是怎样把身材保持得这么苗条的？◇ (*figurative*) *Many companies are a lot slimmer than they used to be* (= have fewer workers). 许多公司的员工比过去少多了。➲SEE ALSO SLIMMER, SLIMMING **2** thinner than usual 单薄的：*a* ***slim volume*** *of poetry* 一本薄薄的诗集 **3** not as big as you would like or expect 微薄的；不足的；少的；小的 **SYN** **small**: *a* ***slim chance*** *of success* 成功的可能性不大 ◇ *The party was returned to power with a* ***slim majority.*** 该党以微弱多数重新上台。▶ **slim·ness** *noun* [U]

■***verb*** (**-mm-**) [I] (*BrE*) (usually used in the progressive tenses 通常用于进行时) to try to become thinner, for example by eating less（靠节食等）变苗条，减肥 **SYN** **diet**: *You can still eat breakfast when you are slimming.* 你减肥也可以吃早饭嘛！ ➲COLLOCATIONS AT DIET

PHR V **,slim 'down** to become thinner, for example as a result of eating less（靠节食等）变苗条，减肥 **,slim 'down** | **,slim sth↔'down** to make a company or an organization smaller, by reducing the number of jobs in it; to be made smaller in this way 精简（机构）；裁减（人员）；减少（岗位）：*They're restructuring and slimming down the workforce.* 他们正对职工加以重组和裁减。◇ *The industry may have to slim down even further.* 这个行业可能还得进一步压缩。◇ *the new, slimmed-down company* 精简人员后的新公司 ➲SEE ALSO SLIMMING

■***noun*** [U] an African word for AIDS（非洲用语）艾滋病

slime /slaɪm/ *noun* [U] any unpleasant thick liquid substance 污浊的泥浆；（恶心的）黏液：*The pond was full of mud and green slime.* 池子里满是淤泥和绿色的污水。➲SEE ALSO SLIMY

slime·ball /'slaɪmbɔːl/ (*also* **slime·bag** /'slaɪmbæg/) *noun* (*informal*) an unpleasant or disgusting person 令人反感的人；卑劣的人；浑球

slim·line /'slɪmlaɪn/ *adj.* [only before noun] **1** smaller or thinner in design than usual 式样小巧的；薄型的：*a slimline phone* 小巧的电话 **2** (*BrE*) (of a drink 饮料) containing very little sugar 低糖的：*slimline tonic water* 低糖奎宁水

slim·mer /'slɪmə(r)/ *noun* (*BrE*) a person who is trying to lose weight 减肥者；减轻体重者：*a calorie-controlled diet for slimmers* 控制热量的减肥食谱 ➲SEE ALSO SLIM *v.*

slim·ming /'slɪmɪŋ/ *noun* [U] (*BrE*) the practice of trying to lose weight 减肥；减轻体重：*a slimming club* 减肥俱乐部 ➲SEE ALSO SLIM *v.*

slimy /'slaɪmi/ *adj.* (**slimi·er, slimi·est**) **1** like or covered with SLIME 似泥浆的；粘有黏液的：*thick slimy mud* 黏稠

S

的污泥 ◇ *The walls were black, cold and slimy.* 墙又黑又冷，上面满是黏湿的污迹。**2** (*informal, disapproving*) (of a person or their manner 人或行为方式、态度) polite and extremely friendly in a way that is not sincere or honest 谄媚的；讨好的；假惺惺的

sling /slɪŋ/ *verb, noun*

▪ ***verb*** (**slung, slung** /slʌŋ/) **1** (*informal, especially BrE*) to throw sth somewhere in a careless way (随便地) 扔，丢 SYN **chuck**: **~ sth + adv./prep.** *Don't just sling your clothes on the floor.* 不要把衣服往地板上一扔就不管了。◇ **~ sb sth** *Sling me an apple, will you?* 扔个苹果给我，好吗？➲ SEE ALSO MUD-SLINGING **2** [often passive] **~ sth + adv./prep.** to put sth somewhere where it hangs loosely 挂；吊：*Her bag was slung over her shoulder.* 她将包挎在肩上。◇ *We slung a hammock between two trees.* 我们在两棵树之间挂了一张吊床。**3** [often passive] **~ sb + adv./prep.** (*informal*) to put sb somewhere by force; to make sb leave somewhere 遣送；押往；撵走；驱逐：*They were slung out of the club for fighting.* 他们因打架被赶出了俱乐部。

IDM **sling your 'hook** (*BrE, informal*) (used especially in orders 尤用于命令) to go away 走开；滚蛋

PHR V **ˌsling 'off at sb** (*AustralE, NZE, informal*) to laugh at sb in an unkind way 嘲笑；讥笑

▪ ***noun*** **1** a band of cloth that is tied around a person's neck and used to support a broken or injured arm (悬吊受伤手臂的) 悬带，吊腕带：*He had his arm* ***in a sling.*** 他用悬带吊着胳膊。**2** a device consisting of a band, ropes, etc. for holding and lifting heavy objects (悬挂或起吊重物的) 吊索，吊链，吊带：*The engine was lifted in a sling of steel rope.* 引擎用钢丝吊索吊了起来。**3** a device like a bag for carrying a baby on your back or in front of you (用以背婴儿的) 吊兜 **4** (in the past) a simple weapon made from a band of leather, etc., used for throwing stones 投石器 (旧时武器) SYN **catapult**

sling·back /ˈslɪŋbæk/ *noun* a woman's shoe that is open at the back with a narrow piece of leather, etc. around the heel 露跟女鞋 (后帮为窄带) ➲ VISUAL VOCAB PAGE V69

sling·shot /ˈslɪŋʃɒt; *NAmE* -ʃɑːt/ (*NAmE*) (*BrE* **cata·pult**) *noun* a stick shaped like a Y with a rubber band attached to it, used by children for shooting stones 弹弓 ➲ PICTURE AT CATAPULT

slink /slɪŋk/ *verb* (**slunk, slunk** /slʌŋk/) [I] **+ adv./prep.** to move somewhere very quietly and slowly, especially because you are ashamed or do not want to be seen 偷偷摸摸地走；躲躲闪闪地走；溜 SYN **creep**: *John was trying to slink into the house by the back door.* 约翰想从后门溜进房子里。◇ *The dog howled and slunk away.* 那狗凄厉地叫着逃走了。

slinky /ˈslɪŋki/ *adj.* (**slink·ier, slinki·est**) **1** (of a woman's clothes 女式服装) fitting closely to the body in a sexually attractive way 紧身而性感的；身体线条毕现的 **2** (of movement or sound 动作或声音) smooth and slow, often in a way that is sexually attractive 袅娜的；婀娜多姿的；柔媚的；柔美的

slip 🔑 /slɪp/ *verb, noun*

▪ ***verb*** (**-pp-**)

• **SLIDE/FALL** 滑；倒 **1** 🔑 [I] **~ (over)** to slide a short distance by accident so that you fall or nearly fall 滑倒；滑跌：*She slipped over on the ice and broke her leg.* 她在冰上滑倒把腿摔断了。◇ *As I ran up the stairs, my foot slipped and I fell.* 我跑上楼梯时失脚摔倒了。

• **OUT OF POSITION** 脱离位置 **2** 🔑 [I] (**+ adv./prep.**) to slide out of position or out of your hand 滑落；滑离；脱落：*His hat had slipped over one eye.* 他的帽子滑下来遮住了一只眼睛。◇ *The fish slipped out of my hand.* 鱼从我手里溜掉了。◇ *The child* ***slipped from his grasp*** *and ran off.* 他一把没抓牢，让那孩子跑掉了。◇ (*figurative*) *She was careful not to let her control slip.* 她小心翼翼，不让自己失控。

• **GO/PUT QUICKLY** 快速地走 / 放置 **3** 🔑 [I] **+ adv./prep.** to go somewhere quickly and quietly, especially without being noticed 悄悄疾行；溜 SYN **creep**: *She slipped out of the house before the others were awake.* 她趁别人还没醒，溜出了房子。◇ *The ship slipped into the harbour at night.* 船在夜间悄然进港。◇ (*figurative*) *She knew that time was slipping away.* 她知道时间在飞逝。**4** 🔑 [T] to put sth somewhere quickly, quietly or secretly 迅速放置；悄悄塞；偷偷放：**~ sth + adv./prep.** *Anna slipped her hand into his.* 安娜悄悄把手伸过去，让他握住。◇ *I managed to slip a few jokes into my speech.* 我设法在讲话中穿插了几个笑话。◇ *I managed to* ***slip in*** *a few jokes.* 我设法穿插了几个笑话。◇ **~ sth to sb** *They'd slipped some money to the guards.* 他们悄悄塞给卫兵一些钱。◇ **~ sb sth** *They'd slipped the guards some money.* 他们悄悄塞给卫兵一些钱。

• **BECOME WORSE** 变差 **5** 🔑 [I] to fall to a lower level; to become worse 下降；退步；变差：*His popularity has slipped recently.* 近来他已不如过去那样受欢迎。◇ *That's three times she's beaten me—****I must be slipping!*** 她已经赢了我三回了，我一定是退步了！

• **INTO DIFFICULT SITUATION** 陷入困境 **6** [I] **+ adv./prep.** to pass into a particular state or situation, especially a difficult or unpleasant one 陷入，进入 (困难或不愉快的处境)：*He began to* ***slip into*** *debt.* 他开始欠债了。◇ *The patient had* ***slipped into*** *a coma.* 病人陷入昏迷状态。◇ *We seem to have slipped behind schedule.* 我们好像已经赶不上日程安排了。

• **CLOTHES ON/OFF** 穿 / 脱衣服 **7** [I, T] to put clothes on or to take them off quickly and easily (迅速且容易地) 穿上，脱下：**+ adv./prep.** *to* ***slip into/out of a dress*** 麻利地穿上 / 脱掉连衣裙 ◇ **~ sth + adv./prep.** *to* ***slip your shoes on/off*** 蹬上 / 脱了鞋◇ *He slipped a coat over his sweatshirt.* 他将一件外衣披在长袖套衫上。

• **GET FREE** 摆脱 **8** [T] to get free; to make sth/sb/yourself free from sth 摆脱；挣脱；松开；放走：**~ sth** *The ship had slipped its moorings in the night.* 那艘船在夜间漂离了停泊处。◇ **~ (sth) + adj.** *The animal had* ***slipped free*** *and escaped.* 那头动物挣脱逃跑了。

IDM **let 'slip sth** to give sb information that is supposed to be secret 泄露；无意中说出：*I happened to* ***let it slip*** *that he had given me £1 000 for the car.* 我一不小心说出了他花 1 000 英镑买走我那辆车的事。◇ *She tried not to let slip what she knew.* 她尽量不把她所知道的事泄露出去。**let sth 'slip (through your fingers)** to miss or fail to use an opportunity 错过 (机会)；失去 (机会)：*Don't let the chance to work abroad slip through your fingers.* 这个出国工作的机会你可不要错过。**slip your 'mind** if sth **slips your mind**, you forget it or forget to do it 被遗忘 **ˌslip one 'over on sb** (*informal*) to trick sb 欺骗；愚弄 **slip through the 'net** when sb/sth **slips through the net**, an organization or a system fails to find them and deal with them 漏网；被漏掉：*We tried to contact all former students, but one or two slipped through the net.* 我们试图同所有的校友取得联系，但有一两个未能找到。➲ MORE AT GEAR *n.*, TONGUE *n.*

PHR V **ˌslip a'way** to stop existing; to disappear or die 消失；消亡；死去：*Their support gradually slipped away.* 他们逐渐失去支持。**ˌslip 'out** when sth **slips out**, you say it without really intending to 无意中说出 (或泄露)：*I'm sorry I said that. It just slipped out.* 抱歉，我说了这样的话。这不过是无意中说出口的。**ˌslip 'up** (*informal*) to make a careless mistake 疏忽；不小心出差错：*We can't afford to slip up.* 我们疏忽不得。➲ RELATED NOUN SLIP-UP

▪ ***noun***

• **SMALL MISTAKE** 差错 **1** a small mistake, usually made by being careless or not paying attention 差错；疏漏；纰漏：*He recited the whole poem without making a single slip.* 他一字不差地背诵了全诗。➲ SEE ALSO FREUDIAN SLIP ➲ SYNONYMS AT MISTAKE

• **PIECE OF PAPER** 纸 **2** a small piece of paper, especially one for writing on or with sth printed on it 纸条；便条；小纸片：*I wrote it down on a slip of paper.* 我把它记在一张纸条上。◇ *a betting slip* 赌注单 ➲ SEE ALSO PAYSLIP

• **ACT OF SLIPPING** 滑跌 **3** an act of slipping 滑跌；滑倒；失脚：*One slip and you could fall to your death.* 一失脚，你就会摔死。

• **CLOTHING** 衣服 **4** a piece of women's underwear like a thin dress or skirt, worn under a dress 衬裙

• **IN CRICKET** 板球 **5** a player who stands behind and to one side of the BATSMAN and tries to catch the ball; the position on the field where this player stands (击球员后侧

S

的）守场员；守场员所站的位置

IDM **give sb the 'slip** (*informal*) to escape or get away from sb who is following or chasing you 摆脱某人的追踪；甩掉跟踪者 **a 'slip of a boy, girl, etc.** (*old-fashioned*) a small or thin, usually young, person 小男孩（或女孩等）；瘦男孩（或女孩等） **a slip of the 'pen/'tongue** a small mistake in sth that you write or say 笔误；口误：*Did I call you Richard? Sorry, Robert, just a slip of the tongue.* 我刚才是不是叫你理查德了？对不起，罗伯特，我是一时口误。 **there's ˌmany a 'slip 'twixt ˌcup and 'lip** (*saying*) nothing is completely certain until it really happens because things can easily go wrong 到嘴的鸭子也会飞走（指没有十拿九稳的事）

slipcase /ˈslɪpkeɪs/ *noun* a stiff cover that a book or other object fits into（书等的）硬套，盒

slipcover /ˈslɪpkʌvə(r)/ (*NAmE*) (*BrE* **ˌloose 'cover**) *noun* a cover for a chair, etc. that you can take off, for example to wash it（椅子等的）活套，活罩

'slip knot *noun* a knot that can slide easily along the rope, etc. on which it is tied, in order to make the LOOP or rope tighter or looser 活结；滑结

'slip-on *noun* a shoe that you can slide your feet into without having to tie LACES 无带（或无扣）便鞋：*a pair of slip-ons* 一双无带便鞋 ◇ *slip-on shoes* 无带便鞋

slip·page /ˈslɪpɪdʒ/ *noun* [U, C, usually sing.] **1** failure to achieve an aim or complete a task by a particular date 延误；逾期 **2** a slight or gradual fall in the amount, value, etc. of sth（微弱或逐渐的）下降，降低，贬值

ˌslipped 'disc *noun* a painful condition caused when one of the discs between the bones of the SPINE in a person's back moves out of place 椎间盘突出；滑出椎间盘

slip·per /ˈslɪpə(r)/ *noun* a loose soft shoe that you wear in the house（室内）便鞋，拖鞋：*a pair of slippers* 一双拖鞋 ➲ VISUAL VOCAB PAGE V69 ➲ SEE ALSO CARPET SLIPPER

slip·pered /ˈslɪpəd; *NAmE* -pərd/ *adj.* wearing slippers 穿拖鞋的；穿便鞋的：*slippered feet* 穿着拖鞋的双脚

slip·pery /ˈslɪpəri/ *adj.* **1** (*also informal* **slippy**) difficult to hold or to stand or move on, because it is smooth, wet or polished 滑的；滑得抓不住（或站不稳、难以行走）的：*slippery like a fish* 滑得像条鱼似的 ◇ *In places the path can be wet and slippery.* 这条小径有些路段又湿又滑。◇ *His hand was slippery with sweat.* 他的手汗津津的。 **2** (*informal*) (of a person 人) that you cannot trust 油滑的；滑头滑脑的；靠不住的：*Don't believe what he says—he's a slippery customer* (= person). 你可别信他说的话，他是个滑头的家伙。 **3** (*informal*) (of a situation, subject, problem, etc. 情况、课题、问题等) difficult to deal with and that you have to think about carefully 难以应对的；棘手的：*Freedom is a slippery concept* (= because its meaning changes according to your point of view). 自由是一个难以明确的概念。

IDM **the/a slippery 'slope** a course of action that is difficult to stop once it has begun, and can lead to serious problems or disaster 使人滑向深渊的斜坡；危险的境地

slippy /ˈslɪpi/ *adj.* (**slip·pier**, **slip·piest**) (*informal*) = SLIPPERY

'slip road (*BrE*) (*NAmE* **ramp**) *noun* a road used for driving onto or off a major road such as a MOTORWAY or INTERSTATE（进出高速公路等的）匝道，引路，支路 ➲ COMPARE ACCESS ROAD

slip·shod /ˈslɪpʃɒd; *NAmE* -ʃɑːd/ *adj.* done without care; doing things without care 马虎的；敷衍了事的 SYN **careless**

slip·stream /ˈslɪpstriːm/ *noun* [sing.] the stream of air behind a vehicle that is moving very fast（高速行驶的交通工具后面的）滑流，低压气穴

'slip-up *noun* (*informal*) a careless mistake 疏漏；差错

slip·way /ˈslɪpweɪ/ *noun* a sloping track leading down to water, on which ships are built or pulled up out of the water for repairs, or from which they are launched（造船或修船的）船台，滑台，滑道

slit /slɪt/ *noun, verb*

■ ***noun*** a long narrow cut or opening 狭长的切口；长而窄的口子；狭缝；裂缝：*a long skirt with a slit up the side* 侧开衩的长裙 ◇ *His eyes narrowed into slits.* 他的眼睛眯成两道缝。

■ ***verb*** (**slit·ting**, **slit**, **slit**) to make a long narrow cut or opening in sth 在…上开狭长口子；切开；划破：**~ sth** *Slit the roll with a sharp knife.* 用快刀把面包切开。 ◇ *The child's throat had been slit.* 那孩子的喉咙被人割破了。◇ *Her skirt was slit at both sides* (= designed with an opening at the bottom on each side). 她的裙子两边都开了衩。 ◇ **~ sth + adj.** *He slit open the envelope and took out the letter.* 他拆开信封，抽出信来。

'slit-eyed *adj.* having narrow eyes (often used in an offensive way to refer to people from E Asia) 细长眼的（常用以描述东亚人，含冒犯意）

slither /ˈslɪðə(r)/ *verb* **1** [I] **+ adv./prep.** to move somewhere in a smooth, controlled way, often close to the ground 滑行；蛇行；爬行 SYN **glide**: *The snake slithered away as we approached.* 我们一走近，蛇就爬走了。 **2 + adv./prep.** to move somewhere without much control, for example because the ground is steep or wet（因地面陡峭或湿滑等）跌跌撞撞地溜行，踉踉跄跄地走 SYN **slide**: *We slithered down the slope to the road.* 我们跌跌撞撞地顺着坡跑到了公路上。◇ *They were slithering around on the ice.* 他们在冰上踉踉跄跄地滑行。

slith·ery /ˈslɪðəri/ *adj.* difficult to hold or stand on because it is wet or smooth; moving in a slithering way 滑溜溜的；滑行的；跌跌撞撞地滑行的

slitty-eyed /ˌslɪti ˈaɪd/ *adj.* (*offensive*) having narrow eyes (often used in an offensive way to refer to people from E Asia) 细长眼的（常用以描述东亚人，含冒犯意）

sliver /ˈslɪvə(r)/ *noun* a small or thin piece of sth that is cut or broken off from a larger piece（切下或碎裂的）小块，薄片：*slivers of glass* 玻璃碎片 ◇ (*figurative*) *A sliver of light showed under the door.* 门底下现出一丝亮光。

slob /slɒb; *NAmE* slɑːb/ *noun, verb*

■ ***noun*** (*informal, disapproving*) a person who is lazy and dirty or untidy 懒惰而邋遢的人：*Get out of bed, you fat slob!* 起床吧，你这个胖懒虫！

■ ***verb*** (**-bb-**)

PHR V **ˌslob a'round/'out** (*BrE, informal*) to spend time being lazy and doing nothing 游手好闲；无所事事

slob·ber /ˈslɒbə(r); *NAmE* ˈslɑːb-/ *verb* [I] to let SALIVA come out of your mouth 流涎；流口水 SYN **dribble**

PHR V **'slobber over sb/sth** (*informal, disapproving*) to show how much you like or want sb/sth without any pride or control 对…垂涎欲滴；毫不掩饰地表示喜爱

sloe /sləʊ; *NAmE* sloʊ/ *noun* a bitter wild fruit like a small PLUM that grows on a bush called a BLACKTHORN 黑刺李（果）

ˌsloe 'eyes *noun* [pl.] attractive, dark eyes, usually ones that are long and thin（通常指细长的）迷人黑眼睛 ▸ **ˌsloe-'eyed** *adj.*

ˌsloe 'gin *noun* [U, C] a strong alcoholic drink made by leaving sloes in GIN so that the gin has the flavour and the colour of the sloes 黑刺李杜松子酒

slog /slɒg; *NAmE* slɑːg/ *verb, noun*

■ ***verb*** (**-gg-**) (*informal*) **1** [I, T] to work hard and steadily at sth, especially sth that takes a long time and is boring or difficult 埋头苦干；坚持不懈地做： **~ (away) (at sth)** *He's been slogging away at that piece of music for weeks.* 他苦练那段乐曲已有好几个星期了。◇ **~ (through sth)** *The teacher made us slog through long lists of vocabulary.* 老师让我们下苦功记住一些长长的词汇表。 ◇ **~ your way through sth** *She slogged her way through four piles of ironing.* 她辛辛苦苦一连熨了四堆衣服。 **2** [I, T] to walk or travel somewhere steadily, with great effort or difficulty 顽强地走；奋力前行；艰难行进： **+ adv./prep.** *I've been*

S

slogging around the streets of London all day. 整整一天，我一直在伦敦街头走来走去。◇ **~ your way through sth** *He started to slog his way through the undergrowth.* 他踏上了穿越下木层的艰难征程。**3** [T, I] ~ **(sth)** (+ **adv./prep.**) to hit a ball very hard but often without skill 猛击，笨拙地猛击（球）

IDM ˌ**slog it ˈout** (*BrE, informal*) to fight or compete in order to prove who is the strongest, the best, etc. 决出胜负；决一雌雄 ➲ MORE AT GUT *n.*

■ ***noun*** [U, C, usually sing.] a period of hard work or effort 一段时间的艰苦工作（或努力）：*Writing the book took ten months of hard slog.* 这本书是苦熬十个月写出来的。◇ *It was a long slog to the top of the mountain.* 到山顶的路漫长而艰难。

slo·gan /ˈsləʊɡən; *NAmE* ˈsloʊ-/ (*also NAmE, informal* ˈ**tag line**) *noun* a word or phrase that is easy to remember, used for example by a political party or in advertising to attract people's attention or to suggest an idea quickly 标语；口号：*an* ***advertising slogan*** 广告口号 ◇ *a* ***campaign slogan*** 竞选口号 ◇ *The crowd began chanting anti-government* ***slogans***. 人群开始反复高呼反政府口号。

slo·gan·eer·ing /ˌsləʊɡəˈnɪərɪŋ; *NAmE* ˌsloʊɡəˈnɪrɪŋ/ *noun* [U] (*disapproving*) the use of slogans in advertisements, by politicians, etc. 标语口号的使用

slo-mo /ˈsləʊ məʊ; *NAmE* ˈsloʊ moʊ/ *noun* [U] (*informal*) = SLOW MOTION

sloop /sluːp/ *noun* a small sailing ship with one MAST (= a post to support the sails) 单桅帆船

slop /slɒp; *NAmE* slɑːp/ *verb, noun*

■ ***verb*** (**-pp-**) **1** [I] **+ adv./prep.** (of a liquid 液体) to move around in a container, often so that some liquid comes out over the edge 晃荡；（常指）溢出，溅出：*Water was slopping around in the bottom of the boat.* 船底有水在晃荡。◇ *As he put the glass down the beer slopped over onto the table.* 他放下杯子时，啤酒撒到了桌子上。**2** [T] ~ **sth** (+ **adv./prep.**) to make liquid or food come out of a container in an untidy way 倒出；使泼出；使溅洒 SYN **spill**：*He got out of the bath, slopping water over the sides.* 他从浴缸里出来，水也跟着溅洒了出来。◇ *She slopped some beans onto a plate.* 她往盘子里倒了一些豆子。

PHR V ˌ**slop aˈbout/aˈround** (*BrE, informal*) **1** to spend time relaxing or being lazy 休息；放松；偷懒：*He used to slop around all day in his pyjamas.* 以前，他时常整天穿着睡衣闲逛。**2** to move around in water, mud. etc.（在水、泥等里）蹚来蹚去，走动 ˌ**slop ˈout** (*BrE*) when prisoners **slop out**, they empty the containers that they use as toilets（囚犯）倒便桶

■ ***noun*** [U] (*also* **slops** [pl.]) **1** waste food, sometimes fed to animals 泔水；（倒掉的）剩饭菜 **2** liquid or partly liquid waste, for example URINE or dirty water from baths 污水；脏水：*a slop bucket* 污水桶

slope 🔑 /sləʊp; *NAmE* sloʊp/ *noun, verb*

■ ***noun*** **1** 🔑 [C] a surface or piece of land that slopes (= is higher at one end than the other) 斜坡；坡地 SYN **incline**：*a grassy slope* 长满草的斜坡 ◇ *The town is built* ***on a slope***. 这座城建在斜坡上。**2** 🔑 [C, usually pl.] an area of land that is part of a mountain or hill 山坡：*the eastern slopes of the Andes* 安第斯山脉东坡 ◇ *ski slopes* 滑雪斜坡 ◇ *He spends all winter* ***on the slopes*** (= SKIING). 整个冬天他都在山坡上滑雪。➲ WORDFINDER NOTE AT MOUNTAIN ➲ VISUAL VOCAB PAGE V5 **3** 🔑 [sing., U] the amount by which sth slopes 斜度；坡度：*a* ***gentle/steep slope*** 缓坡；陡坡 ◇ *a slope of 45 degrees* * 45 度的坡度 ◇ *the angle of slope* 倾角 IDM SEE SLIPPERY

■ ***verb*** **1** 🔑 [I] (+ **adv./prep.**) (of a horizontal surface 水平面) to be at an angle so that it is higher at one end than the other 倾斜；有坡度：*The garden slopes away towards the river.* 花园向河边倾斜下去。◇ *sloping shoulders* 斜肩 **2** 🔑 [I] (+ **adv./prep.**) (of sth vertical 垂直物) to be at an angle rather than being straight or vertical 倾斜：*His handwriting slopes backwards.* 他写的字向后斜。◇ *It was a very old house with sloping walls.* 这房子已经很旧，墙都歪了。**3** [I] **+ adv./prep.** (*BrE, informal*) to go somewhere quietly, especially in order to avoid sth/sb 悄悄地走；潜行；溜 SYN **slink**：*They got bored waiting for him and* ***sloped off***. 他们等他等得不耐烦，就悄悄走了。

sloppy /ˈslɒpi; *NAmE* ˈslɑːpi/ *adj.* (**slop·pier, slop·pi·est**) **1** that shows a lack of care, thought or effort 马虎的；凌乱的；草率的：*sloppy thinking* 不认真的思考 ◇ *Your work is sloppy.* 你的工作做得不认真。◇ *a sloppy worker* 干活马虎的人 **2** (of clothes 衣服) loose and without much shape 肥大而难看的 SYN **baggy**：*a sloppy T-shirt* 宽大松垮的 T 恤衫 **3** (*informal, especially BrE*) romantic in a silly or embarrassing way 庸俗伤感的：*a sloppy love story* 庸俗伤感的爱情故事 **4** containing too much liquid 太稀的：*Don't make the mixture too sloppy.* 别调得太稀。◇ (*informal*) *She gave him a big sloppy kiss.* 她张开湿乎乎的嘴唇狠狠地亲了他一口。▶ **slop·pily** /-ɪli/ *adv.*：*a sloppily run department* 管理松懈的部门 **slop·pi·ness** *noun* [U]：*There is no excuse for sloppiness in your work.* 你在工作中敷衍了事，这无论如何说不过去。

sloppy joe /ˌslɒpi ˈdʒəʊ; *NAmE* ˌslɑːpi ˈdʒoʊ/ *noun* (*NAmE*) finely chopped meat served in a spicy tomato sauce inside a BUN (= bread roll)（涂在面包卷里的）茄汁肉末酱

slosh /slɒʃ; *NAmE* slɑːʃ/ *verb* (*informal*) **1** [I] **+ adv./prep.** (of liquid 液体) to move around making a lot of noise or coming out over the edge of sth 哗啦哗啦地晃荡；撒出；溅出：*The water was sloshing around under our feet.* 水在我们脚下哗啦哗啦地流动。◇ *Some of the paint sloshed out of the can.* 桶里撒出了一些油漆。**2** [T] ~ **sth + adv./prep.** to make liquid move in a noisy way; to use liquid carelessly 使（液体）哗啦哗啦地摇荡；搅动（液体）；连倒带撒：*The children were sloshing water everywhere.* 孩子们把水撒得四处都是。◇ *She sloshed coffee into the mugs.* 她连倒带撒地把咖啡倒进那些杯子里。**3** [I] **+ adv./prep.** to walk noisily in water or mud（在水或泥里）扑哧扑哧地走：*We all sloshed around in the puddles.* 我们都噗噗地踩着一摊摊的积水。

PHR V ˌ**slosh aˈbout/aˈround** (*BrE, informal*) (especially of money 尤指钱) to be available or present in large quantities 可大量获得；大量存在

sloshed /slɒʃt; *NAmE* slɑːʃt/ *adj.* (*informal*) drunk 喝醉的

slot /slɒt; *NAmE* slɑːt/ *noun, verb*

■ ***noun*** **1** a long narrow opening, into which you put or fit sth（投放或插入东西的）窄缝，扁口：*to put some coins in the slot* 往投币口中塞几个硬币 **2** a position, a time or an opportunity for sb/sth, for example in a list, a programme of events or a series of broadcasts（名单、日程安排或广播节目表中的）位置，时间，机会：*He has a regular slot on the late-night programme.* 他在深夜节目中有一档固定栏目。◇ *Their album has occupied the Number One slot for the past six weeks.* 他们的唱片在最近六周占据排行榜首位。◇ *the airport's take-off and landing slots* 机场的起飞降落时间表

■ ***verb*** (**-tt-**) [T, I] to put sth into a space that is available or designed for it; to fit into such a space 投放；插入；（被）塞进；（被）装入：**~ sth + adv./prep.** *He slotted a disk into the drive.* 他把光盘放入驱动器中。◇ *The bed comes in sections which can be quickly* ***slotted together***. 这种床以散件套装出售，可以快速组装起来。◇ **+ adv./prep.** *The dishwasher slots neatly between the cupboards.* 洗碗机刚好可以放在两个碗橱之间。IDM SEE PLACE *n.*

PHR V ˌ**slot sb/sth↔ˈin** to manage to find a position, a time or an opportunity for sb/sth 为…安排时间（或提供机会）；安置：*I can slot you in between 3 and 4.* 我可以把你插到第 3 和第 4 之间。◇ *We slotted in some extra lessons before the exam.* 我们在考试前加了几节课。

sloth /sləʊθ; *NAmE* sloʊθ/ *noun* **1** [C] an animal that lives in trees in tropical parts of America and moves very slowly 树懒（美洲热带动物，行动缓慢）**2** [U] (*formal*) the bad habit of being lazy and unwilling to work 懒散；怠惰

sloth·ful /ˈsləʊθfl; *NAmE* ˈsloʊθfl/ *adj.* (*formal*) lazy 懒散的；怠惰的

ˈ**slot machine** *noun* **1** (*BrE*) a machine with an opening for coins, used for selling things such as cigarettes and bars of chocolate 投币自动售货机 **2** (*especially NAmE*) (*also* ˌ**one-armed 'bandit** *NAmE, BrE*) (*BrE also* **'fruit machine**) a gambling machine that you put coins into and that gives money back if particular pictures appear together on the screen 吃角子老虎赌博机；老虎机

slot·ted /'slɒtɪd; *NAmE* 'slɑːt-/ *adj.* [usually before noun] (*specialist*) **1** having a SLOT or SLOTS in it 开槽的；有窄缝的；带扁口的 **2** (of a screw 螺丝钉) having a SLOT in it rather than a cross shape 槽头的，一字形槽口的（非十字形的） ➲ COMPARE PHILLIPS

ˌ**slotted 'spoon** *noun* a large spoon with holes in it 大漏勺；笊篱

slouch /slaʊtʃ/ *verb, noun*

■ ***verb*** [I] (+ **adv./prep.**) to stand, sit or move in a lazy way, often with your shoulders and head bent forward 没精打采地站（或坐、走）；低头垂肩地站（或坐、走）：*Sit up straight. Don't slouch.* 挺起胸坐直，别歪歪斜斜的。

■ ***noun*** [usually sing.] a way of standing or sitting in which your shoulders are not straight, so that you look tired or lazy 没精打采地站（或坐）的姿态

IDM **be no 'slouch** (*informal*) to be very good at sth or quick to do sth 擅长于；干得麻利：*She's no slouch on the guitar.* 她是弹吉他的好手。

slouchy /'slaʊtʃi/ *adj.* (**slouch·ier**, **slouchi·est**) **1** (*disapproving*) holding your body in a lazy way, often with your shoulders and head bent forward 懒散的；垂肩弓背的；佝偻的：*his slouchy posture* 他那懒散疲沓的姿势 **2** (*approving*) (of clothes 衣服) without a firm outline; not stiff 松沓沓的；软搭搭的：*The slouchy suede boots look great with slim pants.* 这双软帮绒面革靴子配紧身裤看上去很棒。

slough[1] /slʌf/ *verb* to lose a layer of dead skin, etc. 蜕（皮）；使脱落：**~ sth** *a snake sloughing its skin* 正在蜕皮的蛇 ◇ **~ sth off** *Slough off dead skin cells by using a facial scrub.* 用面部磨砂膏去除死皮。

PHR V ˌ**slough sth↔'off** (*formal*) to get rid of sth that you no longer want 摒弃；抛弃；摆脱：*Responsibilities are not sloughed off so easily.* 责任不是那么容易推卸的。

slough[2] /slaʊ; *NAmE* sluː/ *noun* (*literary*) **1** [sing.] **~ of misery, despair, etc.** a state of sadness with no hope 苦难的深渊；绝望的境地 **2** [C] a very soft wet area of land 泥沼；泥淖；沼泽

slov·en·ly /'slʌvnli/ *adj.* careless, untidy or dirty in appearance or habits 邋遢的；衣冠不整的；凌乱的；马虎的：*He grew lazy and slovenly in his habits.* 他养成了懒散邋遢的习惯。▶ **slov·en·li·ness** *noun* [U]

slow 🔑 /sləʊ; *NAmE* sloʊ/ *adj., adv., verb*

■ ***adj.*** (**slow·er**, **slow·est**)

• **NOT FAST** 速度低 **1** 🔑 not moving, acting or done quickly; taking a long time; not fast 缓慢的；迟缓的；耗时的；慢的：*a slow driver* 开车慢的人 ◇ *Progress was slower than expected.* 进展比预计的缓慢。◇ *The country is experiencing slow but steady economic growth.* 国家经济正在缓慢但稳步地增长。◇ *Collecting data is a* ***painfully slow*** *process.* 收集材料的过程慢得让人难受。◇ *a slow, lingering death* 缓慢而拖延时日的死亡 ◇ *Oh you're so slow; come on, hurry up!* 哎哟，你可真慢；加把劲，快点！ ◇ *The slow movement opens with a cello solo.* 慢乐章开头是一段大提琴独奏。◇ *She gave a slow smile.* 她慢慢地笑了笑。**2** 🔑 not going or allowing you to go at a fast speed 慢速的；低速的：*I missed the fast train and had to get the slow one* (= the one that stops at all the stations). 我误了快车，只得坐慢车。

• **WITH DELAY** 拖延 **3** 🔑 hesitating to do sth or not doing sth immediately 迟迟不…；不乐意；慢吞吞的：**~ to do sth** *She wasn't slow to realize what was going on.* 她很快意识到出了什么事。◇ **~ in doing sth** *His poetry was slow in achieving recognition.* 他的诗迟迟得不到赏识。◇ **~ doing sth** *They were very slow paying me.* 他们迟迟不付钱给我。

• **NOT CLEVER** 不聪明 **4** 🔑 not quick to learn; finding things hard to understand 迟钝的；笨的；理解力差的：*He's the slowest in the class.* 他是班里最迟钝的。

• **NOT BUSY** 不忙碌 **5** not very busy; containing little action 不忙碌的；清淡的；冷清的 **SYN** **sluggish**：*Sales are slow* (= not many goods are being sold). 销售不旺。

• **WATCH/CLOCK** 表；钟 **6** [not before noun] showing a time earlier than the correct time 慢：*My watch is five minutes slow* (= it shows 1.45 when it is 1.50). 我的手表慢五分钟。

• **IN PHOTOGRAPHY** 摄影 **7 slow** film is not very sensitive to light（胶片）曝光慢的

▶ **slow·ness** *noun* [U]: *There was impatience over the slowness of reform.* 人们对改革的缓慢进程缺乏耐心。

IDM **do a slow 'burn** (*NAmE, informal*) to slowly get angry 慢慢生起气来 ➲ MORE AT MARK *n.*, UPTAKE

■ ***adv.*** (**slow·er**, **slow·est**) (used especially in the comparative and superlative forms, or in compounds 尤用于比较级、最高级形式或构成复合词) at a slow speed 慢速地；缓慢地 **SYN** **slowly**：*Could you go a little slower?* 你能走慢点吗？◇ *slow-drying paint* 慢干漆 ◇ *slow-moving traffic* 缓慢行进的车辆 ◇ (*NAmE*) *Drive slow!* 慢驶！

IDM **go 'slow (on sth)** to show less enthusiasm for achieving sth（对某事）热情减退：*The government is going slow on tax reforms.* 政府对于税务改革渐渐失去了热情。➲ SEE ALSO GO-SLOW

▼ **WHICH WORD?** 词语辨析

slow / slowly

• **Slowly** is the usual adverb from the adjective **slow**. **Slow** is sometimes used as an adverb in informal language, on road signs, etc. It can also be used to form compounds. * slowly 是常用副词，源自形容词 slow。有时，slow 作为非正式用语或在路标等中也用作副词，亦可用以构成复合词：*Slow. Major road ahead.* 慢行。前方干道。◇ *a slow-acting drug* 药效慢的药 ◇ ~~*They walk very slow.*~~ In the comparative both **slower** and **more slowly** are used. 比较级作 slower 和 more slowly 均可：*Can you speak slower/more slowly?* 你说慢点行吗？

■ ***verb*** [I, T] to go or to make sth/sb go at a slower speed or be less active（使）放慢速度，减缓，松劲：*Economic growth has slowed a little.* 经济增长稍有减缓。◇ *The bus* ***slowed to a halt.*** 公共汽车减速停了下来。◇ **~ down/up** *The car slowed down as it approached the junction.* 汽车在驶近交叉路口时放慢了速度。◇ *The game slowed up little in the second half.* 比赛节奏在下半场几乎没有减慢。◇ *You must slow down* (= work less hard) *or you'll make yourself ill.* 你得松松劲，不然会累病的。◇ **~ sth/sb down/up** *The ice on the roads was slowing us down.* 公路上有冰，减缓了我们的速度。◇ **~ sth/sb** *We hope to slow the spread of the disease.* 我们希望能够减缓疾病的传播速度。➲ SEE ALSO SLOWDOWN

S

slow·coach /'sləʊkəʊtʃ; *NAmE* 'sloʊkoʊtʃ/ (*BrE*) (*NAmE* **'slow·poke**) *noun* (*informal*) a person who moves, acts or works too slowly 动作迟缓的人

'slow cooker *noun* an electric pot used for cooking meat and vegetables slowly in liquid 电焖烧锅；电炖锅

slow·down /'sləʊdaʊn; *NAmE* 'sloʊ-/ *noun* **1** a reduction in speed or activity 减速；减缓：*a slowdown in economic growth* 经济增长的减缓 **2** (*NAmE*) (*BrE* ˌ**go-'slow**) a protest that workers make by doing their work more slowly than usual 怠工 ➲ COMPARE WORK-TO-RULE

ˌ**slow 'food** *noun* [U] traditional food and ways of producing, cooking and eating it 慢餐，慢食（指传统食品及其生产、烹饪和食用）➲ COMPARE FAST FOOD

'slow lane *noun* [sing.] the part of a major road such as a MOTORWAY or INTERSTATE where vehicles drive slowest 慢车道

IDM **in the 'slow lane** not making progress as fast as other people, countries, companies, etc. 在慢车道上；被甩在后面；落后

slow·ly /ˈsləʊli; NAmE ˈsloʊli/ *adv.* at a slow speed; not quickly 慢速地；缓慢地；迟缓地：*to move slowly* 慢慢移动 ◇ *Please could you speak more slowly?* 请您说慢一点好不好？◇ *The boat chugged slowly along.* 船突突地缓慢前进。◇ *He found that life moved slowly in the countryside.* 他发现乡村的生活节奏慢。◇ *Don't rush into a decision. Take it slowly.* 不要急于作决定。慢慢来。◇ *Slowly things began to improve.* 慢慢地，情况开始好转了。➲ NOTE AT SLOW

IDM ˌ**slowly but ˈsurely** making slow but definite progress 缓慢但扎实地；稳扎稳打地：*We'll get there slowly but surely.* 我们虽慢，但准能赶到那儿。

ˌ**slow ˈmotion** *noun* [U] (in a film/movie or on television 电影或电视) the method of showing action at a much slower speed than it happened in real life 慢动作：*Some scenes were filmed* ***in slow motion***. 几组镜头被拍成了慢动作。◇ *a slow-motion replay* 慢动作重放

slow·poke /ˈsləʊpəʊk; NAmE ˈsloʊpoʊk/ (*NAmE*) (*BrE* **slow·coach**) *noun* (*informal*) a person who moves, acts or works too slowly 动作迟缓的人

ˈ**slow-witted** *adj.* not able to think quickly; slow to learn or understand things 脑子反应慢的；头脑迟钝的 OPP **quick-witted**

ˈ**slow-worm** (*also* **blind·worm**) *noun* a small European REPTILE with no legs, like a snake 慢缺肢蜥，盲蛇蜥（无腿爬行动物，生活在欧洲）

SLR /ˌes el ˈɑː(r)/ *abbr.* single-lens reflex (used to describe a camera in which there is only one LENS which both forms the image on the film and provides the image in the VIEWFINDER)（照相机）单镜头反光式，单反

slub /slʌb/ *noun* a lump or thick place in wool or thread（毛线或线的）粗节，糙粒 ▶ **slubbed** /slʌbd/ *adj.*

sludge /slʌdʒ/ *noun* [U] **1** thick, soft, wet mud or a substance that looks like it 烂泥；淤泥；烂泥状沉积物 SYN **slime**：*There was some sludge at the bottom of the tank.* 油箱底有油泥。**2** industrial or human waste that has been treated 工业淤泥；工业污泥；生活污物：*industrial sludge* 工业淤泥 ◇ *the use of sewage sludge as a fertilizer on farm land* 把下水道污泥用作农田肥料的做法

slug /slʌɡ/ *noun, verb*

■ *noun* **1** a small soft creature, like a SNAIL without a shell, that moves very slowly and often eats garden plants 缓步虫；蛞蝓 ➲ VISUAL VOCAB PAGE V13 **2** (*informal*) a small amount of a strong alcoholic drink 少量，一小杯（烈性酒）：*He took another slug of whisky.* 他又喝了一点威士忌。**3** (*informal, especially NAmE*) a bullet 子弹 **4** (*NAmE, informal*) a piece of metal shaped like a coin used to get things from machines, etc., sometimes illegally 硬币形金属片，假硬币（有时用以从自动售货机中骗取东西）

■ *verb* (**-gg-**) **1** ~ **sb** (*informal*) to hit sb hard, especially with your closed hand 用力打；狠揍 **2** ~ **sth** (in BASEBALL 棒球) to hit the ball hard 猛击（球）

IDM ˌ**slug it ˈout** to fight or compete until it is clear who has won 决出胜负；一决雌雄

slug·fest /ˈslʌɡfest/ *noun* (*informal, especially NAmE*) an angry argument in which people insult each other 争吵；对骂：*The battle between the two Democrats is turning into a nasty little slugfest.* 两个民主党人之间的斗争正演化成一场令人厌恶的对骂。

slug·gard /ˈslʌɡəd; NAmE -ɡərd/ *noun* (*formal*) a slow, lazy person 懒惰的人；懒散的人 ▶ **slug·gard·ly** *adj.*

slug·ger /ˈslʌɡə(r)/ *noun* (*NAmE, informal*) **1** (in BASEBALL 棒球) a player who hits the ball, especially one who hits it very hard and for long distances 击球手；（尤指）击球强手；强打；强棒 **2** (*approving*) used when speaking to or about sb, especially a young boy, who tries really hard at sth, and that you feel affection for 猛人（尤指男孩）：*Hang in there, slugger. You can do it!* 坚持，拼命三郎。你行的！

slug·gish /ˈslʌɡɪʃ/ *adj.* moving, reacting or working more slowly than normal and in a way that seems lazy 缓慢的；迟缓的；懒洋洋的：*sluggish traffic* 缓缓移动的车流 ◇ *a sluggish economy* 经济停滞 ◇ *the sluggish black waters of the canal* 运河里缓慢流动的黑乎乎的河水 ◇ *He felt very heavy and sluggish after the meal.* 饭后他感觉身子很沉，不想动。▶ **slug·gish·ly** *adv.* **slug·gish·ness** *noun* [U]

sluice /sluːs/ *noun, verb*

■ *noun* (*also* ˈ**sluice gate**) a sliding gate or other device for controlling the flow of water out of or into a CANAL, etc. 水闸；闸门

■ *verb* **1** [T] ~ **sth** (**down/out**) | ~ **sth** (**with sth**) to wash sth with a stream of water 冲洗：*The ship's crew was sluicing down the deck.* 船员们正在冲洗甲板。**2** [I] + **adv./prep.** (of water 水) to flow somewhere in large quantities（大量地）流，泻

slum /slʌm/ *noun, verb*

■ *noun* an area of a city that is very poor and where the houses are dirty and in bad condition 贫民窟；棚屋区：*a slum area* 贫民区 ◇ ***city/urban slums*** 城市贫民窟 ◇ *She was brought up in the slums of Leeds.* 她是在利兹的贫民区长大的。➲ WORDFINDER NOTE AT CITY

■ *verb* (**-mm-**) [I] (*usually* **be slumming**) (*informal*) to spend time in places or conditions that are much worse than those you are used to（短期）去贫穷地方体验生活，过简朴生活：*There are plenty of ways you can cut costs on your trip without slumming.* 在旅行中，有许多办法既可以减少开销又不至于让自己过得太苦。

IDM ˈ**slum it** (*often humorous*) to accept conditions that are worse than those you are used to 将就着过简朴生活；过穷日子：*Several businessmen had to slum it in economy class.* 几个商人只好将就着坐在经济舱里。

slum·ber /ˈslʌmbə(r)/ *noun, verb*

■ *noun* [U, C, usually pl.] (*literary*) sleep; a time when sb is asleep 睡眠：*She fell into a deep and peaceful slumber.* 她睡着了，睡得又沉又香。

■ *verb* [I] (*literary*) to sleep 睡；睡眠

ˈ**slumber party** *noun* (*NAmE*) = SLEEPOVER

slum·lord /ˈslʌmlɔːd; NAmE -lɔːrd/ *noun* (*NAmE, informal*) a person who owns houses or flats/apartments in a poor area and who charges very high rent for them even though they are in bad condition（收取高额租金的）贫民窟房东

slump /slʌmp/ *verb, noun*

■ *verb* **1** [I] to fall in price, value, number, etc., suddenly and by a large amount（价格、价值、数量等）骤降，猛跌，锐减 SYN **drop**：*Sales have slumped this year.* 今年销售量锐减。◇ ~ **by sth** *Profits slumped by over 50%.* 利润突降 50% 以上。◇ ~ (**from sth**) (**to sth**) *The paper's circulation has slumped to 90 000.* 此报纸的发行量骤减至 9 万份。➲ WORDFINDER NOTE AT TREND **2** [I] + **adv./prep.** to sit or fall down heavily 重重地坐下（或倒下）：*The old man slumped down in his chair.* 老先生一屁股跌坐到椅子上。◇ *She slumped to her knees.* 她扑通一声跪倒在地。

■ *noun* **1** ~ (**in sth**) a sudden fall in sales, prices, the value of sth, etc.（销售量、价格、价值等的）骤降，猛跌，锐减 SYN **decline**：*a slump in profits* 利润锐减 **2** a period when a country's economy or a business is doing very badly 萧条期；衰退：*the slump of the 1930s* * 20 世纪 30 年代的大萧条 ◇ *The toy industry is in a slump.* 玩具业现在不景气。➲ COMPARE BOOM *n.* (1)

slumped /slʌmpt/ *adj.* [not usually before noun] ~ (**against/over sth**) sitting with your body leaning forward, for example because you are asleep or unconscious（因睡着或昏迷等）弯着身子坐，伏：*The driver was slumped exhausted over the wheel.* 司机伏在方向盘上，疲惫不堪。

slung PAST TENSE, PAST PART. OF SLING

slunk PAST TENSE, PAST PART. OF SLINK

slur /slɜː(r)/ *verb, noun*

■ *verb* (**-rr-**) **1** ~ **sth** | + **speech** to pronounce words in a way that is not clear so that they run into each other, usually because you are drunk or tired 含混不清地说话（通常因醉酒或疲劳）：*She had drunk too much and her* *speech was slurred.* 她喝得太多了，话都说不利索了。**2** ~ **sth** (*music* 音) to play or sing a group of two or more musical notes so that each one runs smoothly into the next 连奏；连唱 **3** ~ **sb/sth** to harm sb's reputation by making unfair or false statements about them 诽谤；诋毁；污辱

■ ***noun*** **1** ~ (**on sb/sth**) an unfair remark about sb/sth that may damage other people's opinion of them 诽谤；诋毁；污辱 **SYN insult**: *She had dared to* ***cast a slur*** *on his character.* 她竟敢对他的人品加以诋毁。◇ (*especially NAmE*) *The crowd started throwing bottles and shouting* ***racial slurs.*** 人群开始扔瓶子，并高声地进行种族污辱。**2** (*music* 音) a curved sign used to show that two or more notes are to be played smoothly and without a break 连音线

slurp /slɜːp; *NAmE* slɜːrp/ *verb* (*informal*) **1** [T, I] to make a loud noise while you are drinking sth（喝东西时）发出啧啧的声音：~ **sth** *He was slurping his tea.* 他正咂着嘴喝茶。◇ ~ (**from sth**) *She slurped noisily from her cup.* 她端着杯子，啧啧作响地喝着。**2** [I] to make a noise like this 啧啧地响：*The water slurped in the tank.* 水在箱里嘶嘶地响。▸ **slurp** *noun* [usually sing.]: *She took a slurp from her mug.* 她啧地从杯子里喝了一口。

slurry /ˈslʌri; *NAmE* ˈslɜːri/ *noun* [U] a thick liquid consisting of water mixed with animal waste, CLAY, coal dust or CEMENT（由水和动物粪便、土、煤末或水泥等分别混合而成的）粪浆，泥浆，浆料

slush /slʌʃ/ *noun* [U] **1** partly melted snow that is usually dirty 融雪；雪泥：*In the city the clean white snow had turned to grey slush.* 在城市里，洁白的雪已化为灰色的雪泥。➲ WORDFINDER NOTE AT SNOW **2** (*informal, disapproving*) stories, films/movies or feelings that are considered to be silly and without value because they are too emotional and romantic 矫揉造作的言情小说（或电影）；庸俗的言情 ▸ **slushy** *adj.*：*slushy pavements* 雪泥覆盖的人行道 ◇ *slushy romantic fiction* 矫揉造作的言情小说

ˈslush fund *noun* (*disapproving*) a sum of money kept for illegal purposes, especially in politics（尤指用于政治目的的）非法基金

slut /slʌt/ *noun* (*disapproving, offensive*) **1** a woman who has many sexual partners 荡妇；淫妇 **2** a woman who is very untidy or lazy 邋遢女人；懒婆娘 ▸ **slut·tish** *adj.*

sly /slaɪ/ *adj.* **1** (*disapproving*) acting or done in a secret or dishonest way, often intending to trick people 诡诈的；狡诈的 **SYN cunning**: *a sly political move* 诡诈的政治手段 ◇ (*humorous*) *You sly old devil! How long have you known?* 你这个老滑头！你知道有多久了？ **2** [usually before noun] suggesting that you know sth secret that other people do not know 诡秘的（表示自己知道别人不知道的秘密）**SYN knowing**: *a sly smile/grin/look/glance, etc.* 诡秘的微笑、咧嘴一笑、神色、一瞥等 ▸ **slyly** *adv.*：*He glanced at her slyly.* 他诡秘地朝她瞥了一眼。**sly·ness** *noun* [U]

IDM on the ˈsly secretly; not wanting other people to discover what you are doing 秘密地；偷偷地；背地里：*He has to visit them on the sly.* 他只得偷偷地去看望他们。

smack /smæk/ *verb, noun, adv.*

■ ***verb*** **1** [T] ~ **sb/sth** (*especially BrE*) to hit sb with your open hand, especially as a punishment 用巴掌打；掴：*I think it's wrong to smack children.* 我觉得打孩子不对。➲ COMPARE SPANK **2** [T] ~ **sth + adv./prep.** to put sth somewhere with a lot of force so that it makes a loud noise 啪的一声使劲放（或扔、甩等）**SYN bang**: *She smacked her hand down on to the table.* 她啪地一拍桌子。◇ *He smacked a fist into the palm of his hand.* 他用拳头啪地猛击一下手掌。**3** [I] **+ adv./prep.** to hit against sth with a lot of force 使劲碰（或撞）**SYN crash**: *Two players accidentally smacked into each other.* 两名运动员不巧撞在了一起。

IDM SEE LIP

PHR V ˈsmack of sth to seem to contain or involve a particular unpleasant quality 有…味道；带有…意味：*Her behaviour smacks of hypocrisy.* 她的行为有点虚伪。◇ *Today's announcement smacks of a government cover-up.* 今天的声明颇有政府想掩盖事实的味道。**ˌsmack sb↔ˈup** (*BrE, informal*) to hit sb hard with your hand, many times（多次）用手狠打，猛揍

■ ***noun*** **1** [C] (*especially BrE*) a sharp hit given with your open hand, especially to a child as a punishment 打巴掌，掴（尤指对小孩的惩戒）：*You'll get a smack on your backside if you're not careful.* 要是不小心，就打你的屁股。**2** [C] (*informal*) a hard hit given with a closed hand（打出的）一拳 **SYN punch**: *a smack on the jaw* 在下巴上打了一拳 **3** [C, usually sing.] a short loud sound 啪的一声；砰的一声：*She closed the ledger with a smack.* 她啪的一声合上了账簿。**4** [C] (*informal*) a loud kiss 出声的吻；响吻：*a smack on the lips/cheek* 在嘴上 / 脸上响亮地亲一下 **5** [U] (*slang*) the drug HEROIN 海洛因；白面儿：*smack addicts* 吸白粉成瘾的人 **6** [C] (*BrE*) a small fishing boat 小渔船

■ ***adv.*** (*informal*) **1** (*NAmE also* **ˈsmack-dab**) exactly or directly in a place 恰好；直接；不偏不倚地：*It landed* ***smack in the middle*** *of the carpet.* 它正好落在地毯中央。**2** with sudden, violent force, often making a loud noise 猛地；猛然作声地：*The car drove smack into a brick wall.* 汽车嗵的一声撞上了砖墙。

smack·er /ˈsmækə(r)/ *noun* **1** (*informal*) a loud kiss 出声的吻；响吻 **2** (*slang*) a British pound or US dollar * 1 英镑；1 美元

smack·ing /ˈsmækɪŋ/ *noun* [sing., U] (*especially BrE*) an act of hitting sb, especially a child, several times with your open hand, as a punishment（打）一个巴掌；（用巴掌）一顿揍：*He gave both of the children a good smacking.* 他把两个孩子都狠揍了一顿。◇ *We don't approve of smacking.* 我们不赞成打孩子。

small 🔑 /smɔːl/ *adj., adv., noun*

■ ***adj.*** (**small·er, small·est**)

• **NOT LARGE** 小 **1** 🔑 not large in size, number, degree, amount, etc.（尺寸、数量、程度等）小的：*a small house/town/car/man* 小房子；小镇；小型汽车；小个子男人 ◇ *A much smaller number of students passed than I had expected.* 通过考试的学生比我预计的少得多。◇ *They're having a relatively small wedding.* 他们准备办个相对小型的婚礼。◇ *That dress is too small for you.* 那件连衣裙你穿太小。◇ *'I don't agree,' he said in a small* (= quiet) *voice.* "我不同意。"他小声说。**2** 🔑 (*abbr.* **S**) used to describe one size in a range of sizes of clothes, food, products used in the house, etc.（服装、食品、家庭用品等）小号的，小型的：*small, medium, large* 小号、中号、大号 ◇ *This is too big—have you got a small one?* 这个太大了，有没有小的？ **3** 🔑 not as big as sth else of the same kind（同类事物中）小的：*the small intestine* 小肠

• **YOUNG** 年幼 **4** 🔑 young 年幼的；幼小的：*They have three small children.* 他们有三个年幼的孩子。◇ *We travelled around a lot when I was small.* 我小的时候，我们时常四处旅行。◇ *As a small boy he had spent most of his time with his grandparents.* 他幼年时多半时间是跟爷爷奶奶在一起。

• **NOT IMPORTANT** 不重要 **5** 🔑 slight; not important 些微的；不重要的：*I made only a few small changes to the report.* 我对报告只做了几处小改动。◇ *She noticed several small errors in his work.* 她注意到他作业中有几处小错。◇ *Everything had been planned down to the smallest detail.* 一切都已做了细致入微的安排。◇ *It was* ***no small*** *achievement getting her to agree to the deal.* 能让她同意那笔交易可是个不小的成就。

• **BUSINESS** 企业 **6** 🔑 [usually before noun] not doing business on a very large scale 小规模的：*a small farmer* 小农场主 ◇ *The government is planning to give more help to small businesses.* 政府正计划给予小企业更多帮助。

• **LETTERS** 字母 **7** [usually before noun] not written or printed as capitals 小写的：*Should I write 'god'* ***with a small 'g'*** *or a capital?* * god 里面的字母 g，我该写成小写还是大写？◇ *She's a socialist* ***with a small 's'*** (= she has socialist ideas but is not a member of a socialist party). 她信仰社会主义，但不是社会党人。

• **NOT MUCH** 少 **8** [only before noun] (used with uncountable nouns 与不可数名词连用) little; not much 极少的；不多的：*The government has small cause for optimism.* 几乎没有什么可以使政府感到乐观的。◇ *They have small hope of succeeding.* 他们成功的希望不大。

▸ **small·ness** *noun* [U]

S

IDM **be grateful/thankful for small 'mercies** to be happy that a situation that is bad is not as bad as it could have been 为情况不太坏而庆幸：*Well, at least you weren't hurt. I suppose we should be grateful for small mercies.* 好啦，至少你没受伤。我想这就该让我们知足了。**it's a ˌsmall 'world** (*saying*) used to express your surprise when you meet sb you know in an unexpected place, or when you are talking to sb and find out that you both know the same person（意外遇见某人或发现对方也认识某人时表示惊讶）世界真小 **look/feel 'small** to look or feel stupid, weak, ashamed, etc. 显得（或感觉）矮人一截；愧不如人 ➲ MORE AT BIG *adj.*, GREAT *adj.*, HOUR, STILL *adj.*, SWEAT *v.*, WAY *n.*, WONDER *n.*

■ ***adv.*** (**small·er, small·est**) **1** into small pieces 成为小块：*Chop the cabbage up small.* 把卷心菜剁碎。**2** in a small size 小小地：*You can fit it all in if you write very small.* 你字写小点，就可以全部填进去。

■ ***noun*** **1 the ~ of the/sb's back** [sing.] the lower part of the back where it curves in 后腰 ➲ VISUAL VOCAB PAGE V64 **2 smalls** [pl.] (*old-fashioned, BrE, informal*) small items of clothing, especially underwear 小件衣服（尤指内衣）

'small ads *noun* [pl.] (*BrE, informal*) = CLASSIFIED ADVERTISEMENTS

'small arms *noun* [pl.] small light weapons that you can carry in your hands 轻武器

ˌsmall 'beer (*BrE*) (*NAmE* **ˌsmall po'tatoes**) *noun* [U] (*informal*) a person or thing that has no great importance or value, especially when compared with sb/sth else（相比较之下）无足轻重的人（或事物）

'small-bore *adj.* **1** a **small-bore** gun is narrow inside（枪）小口径的 **2** (*informal, especially NAmE*) not important 无足轻重的；微不足道的：*small-bore issues* 无关紧要的问题

ˌsmall 'capitals (*also* **ˌsmall 'caps**) *noun* [pl.] (*specialist*) capital letters which are the same height as LOWER-CASE letters 小大写字母（与小写字母同等高度的大写字母）

ˌsmall 'change *noun* [U] **1** coins of low value 小面值硬币；零钱：*Have you got any small change for the phone?* 你有没有打电话的零钱？**2** something that is of little value when compared with sth else（相比较之下）没有什么价值的东西

ˌsmall 'claims court *noun* a local court which deals with cases involving small amounts of money 小额索赔（地方）法院

ˌsmall 'fortune *noun* [usually sing.] (*informal*) a lot of money 一大笔钱：*That holiday cost me a small fortune.* 那次度假花了我一大笔钱。

'small fry *noun* [U+sing./pl. v.] (*informal*) people or things that are considered unimportant compared to sb/sth else （相比较之下）不重要的人（或事物）：*That's small fry to her.* 对她来说，那不值一提。◇ *People like us are small fry to such a large business.* 对于这样一家大公司来说，我们这样的人不过是小鱼小虾。

small·hold·er /'smɔːlhəʊldə(r); *NAmE* -hoʊ-/ *noun* (*BrE*) a person who owns or rents a small piece of land for farming 小农场主；小农业经营者

small·hold·ing /'smɔːlhəʊldɪŋ; *NAmE* -hoʊ-/ *noun* a small piece of land used for farming 一小块耕地

small·ish /'smɔːlɪʃ/ *adj.* fairly small 相当小的；颇小的：*a smallish town* 相当小的城镇

ˌsmall-'minded *adj.* (*disapproving*) having fixed opinions and ways of doing things and not willing to change them or consider other people's opinions or feelings; interested in small problems and details and not in things which are really important 狭隘的；固执己见的；心胸狭窄的；目光短浅的 SYN **intolerant, petty** ▸ **ˌsmall-'minded·ness** *noun* [U]

ˌsmall po'tatoes (*NAmE*) (*BrE* **ˌsmall 'beer**) *noun* [U] (*informal*) a person or thing that has no great importance or value, especially when compared with sb/sth else（尤指相比较之下）无足轻重的人（或事物）

small·pox /'smɔːlpɒks; *NAmE* -pɑːks/ *noun* [U] a serious infectious disease (now extremely rare) that causes fever, leaves permanent marks on the skin and often causes death 天花

the ˌsmall 'print (*BrE*) (*NAmE* **the ˌfine 'print**) *noun* [U] the important details of an agreement or a legal document that are usually printed in small type and are therefore easy to miss（合同或法律文件等中易被忽略但很重要的）小字号的附加条款：*Read all the small print before signing.* 把小字号的附加条款全部看过以后再签字。

ˌsmall-'scale *adj.* **1** (of an organization, activity, etc. 组织、活动等) not large in size or extent; limited in what it does 小型的；小范围的；小规模的：*small-scale farming* 小规模农业 ◇ *a small-scale study of couples in second marriages* 对再婚夫妇的小范围研究 **2** (of maps, drawings, etc. 地图、图样等) drawn to a small scale so that not many details are shown 按小比例绘制的；小比例尺的 OPP **large-scale**

the ˌsmall 'screen *noun* [sing.] television (when contrasted with cinema) 电视（与电影相对而言）：*This will be the film's first showing on the small screen.* 这将是这部电影首次在电视上播放。◇ *his first small-screen role* 他的第一个电视剧角色

'small talk *noun* [U] polite conversation about ordinary or unimportant subjects, especially at social occasions 寒暄；闲谈；聊天

'small-time *adj.* [only before noun] (*informal, disapproving*) (often of criminals 常指罪犯) not very important or successful 不太重要的；不高明的 SYN **petty**：*a small-time crook* 手段不高明的骗子 ➲ COMPARE BIG TIME

'small-town *adj.* [only before noun] **1** (*disapproving*) not showing much interest in new ideas or what is happening outside your own environment 乡镇气的；保守狭隘的；落后闭塞的 SYN **narrow-minded**：*small-town values* 保守狭隘的价值观 **2** connected with a small town 小城镇的：*small-town America* (= people who live in small towns in America) 小城镇美国人

smarmy /'smɑːmi; *NAmE* 'smɑːrmi/ *adj.* (**smarm·ier, smarmi·est**) (*informal, disapproving*) too polite in a way that is not sincere 过分殷勤的；谄媚的 SYN **smooth**：*a smarmy salesman* 逢迎讨好的推销员

smart 🔑 /smɑːt; *NAmE* smɑːrt/ *adj.*, *verb*

■ ***adj.*** (**smart·er, smart·est**)

• **CLEAN/NEAT** 整洁 **1** 🔑 (of people 人) looking clean and neat; well dressed in fashionable and/or formal clothes 衣冠楚楚的；衣着讲究的：*You look very smart in that suit.* 你穿上那套衣服显得很精神。**2** 🔑 (of clothes, etc. 衣服等) clean, neat and looking new and attractive 整洁而漂亮的；光鲜的：*They were wearing their smartest clothes.* 他们都穿了最讲究的衣服。

• **INTELLIGENT** 聪明 **3** 🔑 (*especially NAmE*) intelligent 聪明的；机敏的；精明的：*She's smarter than her brother.* 她比她哥哥聪明。◇ *That was a* ***smart*** *career* ***move.*** 那是个人事业发展上的一着妙棋。◇ *OK, I admit it was not the smartest thing I ever did* (= it was a stupid thing to do). 好吧，我承认那件事我办得很不漂亮。➲ SYNONYMS AT INTELLIGENT

• **FASHIONABLE** 时髦 **4** connected with fashionable rich people 时髦人物的；高档的：*smart restaurants* 高档餐馆 ◇ *She mixes with* ***the smart set.*** 她跟那帮时髦人物交往。

• **QUICK** 快速 **5** (of a movement, etc. 动作等) quick and usually done with force 快速的；敏捷的；迅速而有力的 SYN **brisk**：*He was struck with a smart crack on the head.* 他头上突然被猛击了一下。◇ *We set off at a smart pace.* 我们快步出发了。

• **COMPUTER-CONTROLLED** 计算机控制 **6** (of a device, especially a weapon/bomb 尤指武器、炸弹等装置) controlled by a computer, so that it appears to act in an intelligent way 智能的：*smart bombs* 制导炸弹 ◇ *This smart washing machine will dispense an optimal amount of water for the load.* 这台智能洗衣机会根据衣物多少适当安排进水量。

S

▸ **smart·ly** *adv.*: *smartly dressed* 衣着光鲜 ◇ *He ran off pretty smartly* (= quickly and suddenly). 他一下子跑掉了。 **smart·ness** *noun* [U]

■ *verb* **1** [I] ~ (**from sth**) to feel a sharp stinging pain in a part of your body 感到剧烈刺痛: *His eyes were smarting from the smoke.* 他给烟熏得两眼生疼。 **2** [I] ~ (**from/over sth**) to feel upset about a criticism, failure, etc.（因批评、失败等）难过，烦恼: *They are still smarting from the 4–0 defeat last week.* 他们仍为上星期 0:4 惨败而难过。 ➲ SEE ALSO SMARTS

smart alec (*BrE*) (*NAmE usually* **smart aleck**) /ˈsmɑːt ælɪk; *NAmE* ˈsmɑːrt/ (*also* **ˈsmarty-pants**) (*BrE also* **ˈsmart-arse**) (*NAmE also* **ˈsmart-ass**) *noun* (*informal, disapproving*) a person who thinks they are very clever and likes to show people this in an annoying way 自诩聪明的人；好逞能的人

ˈsmart bomb *noun* a weapon controlled by an electronic device that is intended to cause damage to the target while avoiding damage to other people, buildings, etc. that are in the area （直中目标不伤其他的）制导炸弹，灵巧炸弹

ˈsmart card *noun* a small plastic card on which information is stored in electronic form 智能卡；灵通卡；高级磁卡 ➲ SEE ALSO CHIP CARD

smart·en /ˈsmɑːtn; *NAmE* ˈsmɑːrtn/ *verb*

PHR V **ˌsmarten sb/sth↔ˈup** | **ˌsmarten (yourself) ˈup** (*especially BrE*) to make yourself, another person or a place look neater or more attractive（使）整洁起来，变得光鲜亮丽: *The hotel has been smartened up by the new owners.* 新主人把旅馆修葺一新。

smart·ish /ˈsmɑːtɪʃ; *NAmE* ˈsmɑːrt-/ *adj., adv.* (*informal, especially BrE*) quick; quickly 很快的（地）；迅速的（地）: *We set off at a smartish pace.* 我们快步出发了。◇ *You'd better move smartish.* 你最好快一些。

the ˈsmart money *noun* [U] **1** money that is invested or bet by people who have expert knowledge 行家的投资（或赌注）；明智的投资（或赌注）: *It seems the smart money is no longer in insurance* (= is no longer being invested in insurance companies). 似乎专业投资不再投向保险业。◇ *The smart money is on him for the best actor award.* 内行认为他将获最佳演员奖。 **2** people who have expert knowledge of sth 有专业知识的人；知情者；行家: *The smart money says that he's likely to withdraw from the leadership campaign.* 据知情者说，他很可能退出领导人竞选。

smart·phone /ˈsmɑːtfəʊn; *NAmE* ˈsmɑːrtfoʊn/ *noun* a mobile/cell phone that also has some of the functions of a computer, for example the facility to use APPS and the Internet 智能手机 ➲ VISUAL VOCAB PAGE V73 ➲ COMPARE FEATURE PHONE

smarts /smɑːts; *NAmE* smɑːrts/ *noun* [U] (*NAmE, informal*) intelligence 智慧；聪明才智: *She made it to the top on her smarts.* 她靠自己的聪明才智获得成功。

ˈsmarty-pants *noun* = SMART ALEC

smash 🔑 /smæʃ/ *verb, noun*

■ *verb*

• **BREAK** 打碎 **1** 🔑 [T, I] ~ (**sth**) to break sth, or to be broken, violently and noisily into many pieces（哗啦一声）打碎，打破，破碎: *Several windows had been smashed.* 几扇窗户噼里啪啦打碎了。◇ *He smashed the radio to pieces.* 他啪的一声把收音机摔得稀巴烂。◇ *The glass bowl smashed into a thousand pieces.* 玻璃碗咣的一声摔了个粉碎。

• **HIT VERY HARD** 猛烈撞击 **2** 🔑 [I, T] to move with a lot of force against sth solid; to make sth do this（使）猛烈撞击，猛烈碰撞: **+ adv./prep.** *the sound of waves smashing against the rocks* 浪涛猛烈撞击礁石的声音 ◇ *The car smashed into a tree.* 汽车猛地撞到了树上。 ◇ **~ sth + adv./prep.** *Mark smashed his fist down on the desk.* 马克狠狠地把拳头砸在桌上。 ➲ SYNONYMS AT CRASH **3** 🔑 [T, I] to hit sth very hard and break it, in order to get through it（用力）撞开，击穿，闯过: **~ sth + adv./prep.** *They had to smash holes in the ice.* 他们只好奋力在冰上凿洞。◇ *The elephant smashed its way through the trees.* 大象横冲直撞，闯过树丛。◇ **~ sth + adj.** *We had to smash the door open.* 我们只得用力把门撞开。◇ **+ adv./prep.** *They had smashed through a glass door to get in.* 他们砸破一道玻璃门进去了。 **4** [T] **~ sth/sb** (**+ adv./prep.**) to hit sth/sb very hard 猛击 SYN **slam**: *He smashed the ball into the goal.* 他一记劲射，球进了。

• **DESTROY/DEFEAT** 捣毁；打败 **5** [T] **~ sth/sb** to destroy, defeat or put an end to sth/sb 捣毁；打败；粉碎；使结束: *Police say they have smashed a major drugs ring.* 警方说他们摧毁了一个大贩毒集团。 ◇ *She has smashed the world record* (= broken it by a large amount). 她大破世界纪录。

• **CRASH VEHICLE** 撞车 **6** [T] **~ sth** (**up**) to crash a vehicle 撞毁（车辆）: *He's smashed (up) his new car.* 他把自己的新车撞毁了。 ➲ SYNONYMS AT CRASH

• **IN TENNIS, ETC.** 网球等 **7** [T] **~ sth** to hit a high ball downwards and very hard over the net 扣杀

PHR V **ˌsmash sth↔ˈdown** to make sth fall down by hitting it hard and breaking it（用力）击倒，打翻: *The police had to smash the door down.* 警察不得不破门而入。 **ˌsmash sth↔ˈin** to make a hole in sth by hitting it with a lot of force（用力）打破，撞坏: *Vandals had smashed the door in.* 破坏分子把门撞破了。◇ (*informal*) *I wanted to **smash his face in*** (= hit him hard in the face). 当时我真想把他的脸打瘪。 **ˌsmash sth↔ˈup** to destroy sth deliberately（蓄意）捣毁，破坏: *Youths had broken into the bar and smashed the place up.* 一群年轻人闯进酒吧，把里面砸了个乱七八糟。

■ *noun*

• **ACT OF BREAKING** 破碎；打碎 **1** 🔑 [sing.] an act of breaking sth noisily into pieces; the sound this makes 破碎；打碎；破碎（或打碎）的哗啦声: *The cup hit the floor with a smash.* 杯子掉到地上哗啦一声摔碎了。

• **VEHICLE CRASH** 撞车 **2** [C] (*BrE*) an accident in which a vehicle hits another vehicle 撞车: *a car smash* 撞车事故

• **IN TENNIS, ETC.** 网球等 **3** [C] a way of hitting the ball downwards and very hard 高压球；扣球

• **SONG/MOVIE/PLAY** 歌曲；电影；戏剧 **4** (*also* **ˌsmash ˈhit**) [C] a song, film/movie or play that is very popular 十分走红的歌曲（或电影、戏剧）: *her latest chart smash* 她的最新一首十分走红的上榜歌曲

ˌsmash-and-ˈgrab *adj.* [only before noun] (*BrE*) relating to the act of stealing from a shop/store by breaking a window and taking the goods you can see or reach easily 砸橱窗抢劫的: *a smash-and-grab raid* 砸橱窗抢劫

smashed /smæʃt/ *adj.* [not before noun] (*slang*) very drunk 大醉

smash·er /ˈsmæʃə(r)/ *noun* (*old-fashioned, BrE, informal*) a very good or attractive person or thing 很好的人；很漂亮的人；十分讨人喜欢的人（或事物）

smash·ing /ˈsmæʃɪŋ/ *adj.* (*old-fashioned, informal*) very good or enjoyable 非常好的；十分愉快的 SYN **great**: *We had a smashing time.* 我们过得非常愉快。

ˈsmash-up *noun* (*informal*) a crash in which vehicles are very badly damaged 严重撞车事故

smat·ter·ing /ˈsmætərɪŋ/ *noun* [sing.] ~ (**of sth**) a small amount of sth, especially knowledge of a language （尤指对语言）略知，浅知: *He only has a smattering of French.* 他只懂一点法语。

smear /smɪə(r); *NAmE* smɪr/ *verb, noun*

■ *verb* **1** [T] to spread an OILY or soft substance over a surface in a rough or careless way（用油性或稀软物质）胡乱涂抹 SYN **daub**: **~ sth on/over sth** *The children had smeared mud on the walls.* 那几个孩子往墙上抹了泥巴。◇ **~ sth with sth** *The children had smeared the walls with mud.* 那几个孩子往墙上抹了泥巴。 **2** [T] **~ sth** to make sth dirty or GREASY 弄脏；弄上油污: *His glasses were smeared.* 他的眼镜脏了。◇ *smeared windows* 脏了的窗户 **3** [T] **~ sb/sth** to damage sb's reputation by saying unpleasant things about them that are not true 诽谤；诋毁 SYN **slander**: *The story was an attempt to smear the party leader.* 这篇报道是企图玷污该党领袖的声誉。 **4** [T, I]

S

~ (sth) to rub writing, a drawing, etc. so that it is no longer clear; to become not clear in this way 把（字迹、图画等）蹭得模糊不清；变得模糊不清 SYN **smudge**: *The last few words of the letter were smeared.* 信的最后几个字蹭得看不清了。

■ ***noun*** **1** an OILY or dirty mark 污迹；污渍；污点：*a smear of jam* 果酱渍 ➲ SYNONYMS AT MARK **2** a story that is not true about sb that is intended to damage their reputation, especially in politics（尤指政治上的）抹黑，丑化：*He was a victim of a* ***smear campaign.*** 他受到对方的毁谤攻击。**3** (*BrE*) = SMEAR TEST

ˈsmear test (*also* **smear**, **ˌcervical ˈsmear**) (*all BrE*) (*NAmE* **ˈPap smear**) *noun* a medical test in which a very small amount of TISSUE from a woman's CERVIX is removed and examined for cancer cells 宫颈刮片检查（从妇女子宫颈取少许组织，以检查是否有癌细胞）

smell /smel/ *verb, noun*

■ ***verb*** (**smelled**, **smelled**) (*BrE also* **smelt**, **smelt** /smelt/) **1** [I] to have a particular smell 有（或发出）…气味：**+ adj.** *The room smelt damp.* 屋子里有潮气。◇ *Dinner smells good.* 饭菜闻起来很香啊。◇ *a bunch of sweet-smelling flowers* 一束散发着馨香的花 ◇ **~ of sth** *His breath smelt of garlic.* 他嘴里有蒜味。◇ **~ like sth** *What does the perfume smell like?* 这种香水闻起来怎么样？ **2** [T, no passive] (not used in the progressive tenses; often with *can* or *could* 不用于进行时；常与 can 或 could 连用) to notice or recognize a particular smell 闻到，嗅到（气味）：**~ sth** *He said he could smell gas when he entered the room.* 他一进屋就说闻到了煤气味。◇ *The dog had smelt a rabbit.* 狗嗅到了兔子的气味。◇ *I could smell alcohol on his breath.* 我闻到他呼吸气中有酒味。◇ **~ sth doing sth** *Can you smell something burning?* 你有没有闻到什么东西烧焦了？ ◇ **~ (that)...** *I could smell that something was burning.* 我闻得到有什么东西烧焦了。 **3** [I] (not used in the progressive tenses; often with *can* or *could* 不用于进行时，常与 can 或 could 连用) to be able to notice and recognize smells 能闻到气味；能嗅到气味：*I can't smell because I've got a bad cold.* 我患了重感冒闻不到气味。 **4** [T] **~ sth** (not usually used in the passive 通常不用于被动语态) to put your nose near sth and breathe in so that you can discover or identify its smell 闻，嗅（气味） SYN **sniff**: *Smell this and tell me what you think it is.* 你闻一下这个，然后告诉我你觉得是什么。◇ *I bent down to smell the flowers.* 我弯下腰闻花香。 **5** [I] (not used in the progressive tenses 不用于进行时) to have an unpleasant smell 有难闻的气味；散发着臭气：*The drains smell.* 下水道散发着臭气。◇ *It smells in here.* 这儿有一股难闻的气味。◇ *He hadn't washed for days and was beginning to smell.* 他好久没洗澡了，身上都有味儿了。 **6** [T, no passive] **~ sth** to feel that sth exists or is going to happen 觉察出；感觉到：*He smelt danger.* 他意识到了危险。◇ *I can smell trouble.* 我感觉会有麻烦。

IDM **come up/out of sth smelling of ˈroses** (*informal*) to still have a good reputation, even though you have been involved in sth that might have given people a bad opinion of you 虽卷入…而好名声依旧；事后于名誉无损 **ˌsmell a ˈrat** (*informal*) to suspect that sth is wrong about a situation 怀疑事情不妙；感觉情况不对 ➲ MORE AT ROSE *n.*, WAKE *v.*

PHR V **ˌsmell sb/sth↔ˈout 1** to be aware of fear, danger, trouble, etc. in a situation 觉察到，意识到（坏事、危险、麻烦等）：*He could always smell out fear.* 别人有什么恐惧，他总能觉察到。 **2** to find sth by smelling 嗅出；闻出：*dogs trained to smell out drugs* 受过训练的缉毒犬

■ ***noun*** **1** [C, U] the quality of sth that people and animals sense through their noses 气味：*a faint/strong smell of garlic* 淡淡的/浓重的蒜味 ◇ ***a sweet/fresh/musty smell*** 香甜的/新鲜的/发霉的气味 ◇ *There was a smell of burning in the air.* 空气中有一股烧东西的焦煳味。◇ *The smells from the kitchen filled the room.* 满屋子都是从厨房飘来的气味。 **2** [sing.] an unpleasant smell 难闻的气味；臭味：*What's that smell?* 这是一股什么臭味？ ◇ *Yuk! What a smell!* 哎哟！多难闻的气味！ **3** [U] the ability to sense things with the nose 嗅觉：*Dogs have a very good* ***sense of smell.*** 狗的嗅觉非常灵敏。◇ *Taste and smell are closely connected.* 味觉和嗅觉有密切的联系。 **4** [C] the act of smelling sth 嗅；闻 SYN **sniff**: *He took one smell of the liquid and his eyes began to water.* 他闻了一下那种液体，就流起泪来了。 IDM SEE SWEET *adj.*

▼ VOCABULARY BUILDING 词汇扩充

Smells 气味

Describing smells 描述气味

These adjectives describe pleasant smells 下列形容词描述令人愉悦的气味：

- **scented** candles 香烛
- **aromatic** oils 芳香油
- **fragrant** perfume 芬芳的香水
- **sweet-smelling** flowers 芳香扑鼻的花

To describe unpleasant smells you can use 描述令人不快的气味可以说：

- **smelly** cheese 有难闻气味的奶酪
- **stinking** fish 发臭的鱼
- **musty** old books 发霉的旧书
- **acrid** smoke 呛人的烟

Types of smell 各种气味

Pleasant smells 令人愉悦的气味：

- the rich **aroma** of fresh coffee 新鲜咖啡醇厚的香味
- a herb with a delicate **fragrance** 散发淡雅香气的芳草
- a rose's sweet **perfume** 玫瑰的芳香
- the **scent** of wild flowers 野花的芬芳

Unpleasant smells 难闻的气味：

- nasty household **odours** 家里难闻的气味
- the **stench** of rotting meat 腐肉的恶臭
- the **stink** of stale sweat 汗臭味
- the **reek** of beer and tobacco 啤酒和烟草的强烈臭味

ˈsmelling salts *noun* [pl.] a chemical with a very strong smell, kept in a small bottle, used especially in the past for putting under the nose of a person who has become unconscious 嗅盐（有刺鼻的气味，旧时用作苏醒剂）

smelly /ˈsmeli/ *adj.* (**smell·ier**, **smelli·est**) (*informal*) having an unpleasant smell 有难闻气味的；有臭味的：*smelly feet* 臭脚

smelt /smelt/ *verb* **~ sth** to heat and melt ORE (= rock that contains metal) in order to obtain the metal it contains 熔炼；提炼（金属）：*a method of smelting iron* 一种炼铁方法 ➲ SEE ALSO SMELL *v.*

smelt·er /ˈsmeltə(r)/ *noun* a piece of equipment for smelting metal 熔炉

smidgen (*also* **smidg·eon**, **smid·gin**) /ˈsmɪdʒən/ *noun* [sing.] **~ (of sth)** (*informal*) a small piece or amount of sth 少量；一点点：*'Sugar?' 'Just a smidgen.'* "放糖吗？""只放一点。"

smile /smaɪl/ *verb, noun*

■ ***verb*** **1** [I] to make a smile appear on your face 微笑；笑：*to smile sweetly/faintly/broadly, etc.* 嫣然一笑、淡然一笑、咧嘴一笑等 ◇ *He smiled with relief.* 他宽慰地笑了。◇ *He never seems to smile.* 他好像从来都不笑。◇ **~ at sb/sth** *She smiled at him and he* ***smiled back.*** 她冲他笑笑，他也冲她笑笑。◇ *I had to smile at* (= was amused by) *his optimism.* 对他的乐观态度，我只好一笑置之。 **2** [T] to say or express sth with a smile 微笑着说；微笑地表示：**~ sth** *She smiled her thanks.* 她笑了笑表示感谢。◇ **+ speech** *'Perfect,' he smiled.* "好极了。"他微笑着说。 **3** [T, no passive] **~ sth** to give a smile of a particular type 现出（某种）笑容：*to smile a small smile* 微微一笑 ◇ *She smiled a smile of dry amusement.* 她心里觉得很滑稽，但只是含蓄地微微一笑。 IDM SEE EAR

PHR V **ˈsmile on sb/sth** (*formal*) if luck, etc. **smiles on** you, you are lucky or successful 有利于；垂青；带来好运

■ ***noun*** the expression that you have on your face when you are happy, amused, etc. in which the corners of your mouth turn upwards 微笑；笑容：*'Oh, hello,' he said, **with a smile**.* "嗨，你好。"他微笑着说。◇ *She **gave a** wry **smile**.* 她苦笑一下。◇ *He had a big smile on his face.* 他笑容满面。◇ *I'm going to **wipe that smile off your face*** (= make you stop thinking this is funny). 我会让你笑不出来的。

IDM **all 'smiles** looking very happy, especially soon after you have been looking worried or sad（尤指愁眉苦脸或悲伤之后）一脸笑意，喜滋滋的：*Twelve hours later she was all smiles again.* 十二小时之后，她又喜笑颜开了。

smiley /'smaɪli/ *noun* **1** a simple picture of a smiling face that is drawn as a circle with two eyes and a curved mouth 笑脸图（用 ☺ 表示）**2** a simple picture or series of keyboard symbols :-) that represents a smiling face. The symbols are used, for example, in email or text messages to show that the person sending the message is pleased or joking. 微笑符（例如用 :-) 表示）

smil·ing·ly /'smaɪlɪŋli/ *adv.* with a smile or smiles 微笑着

smirk /smɜːk; *NAmE* smɜːrk/ *verb* [I] to smile in a silly or unpleasant way that shows that you are pleased with yourself, know sth that other people do not know, etc. 自鸣得意地笑；傻笑：*It was hard not to smirk.* 让人忍俊不禁。◇ *He smirked unpleasantly when we told him the bad news.* 我们把坏消息告诉他时，他脸上现出一丝奸笑。➲ WORDFINDER NOTE AT EXPRESSION ▶ **smirk** *noun*: *She had a self-satisfied smirk on her face.* 她满脸扬扬得意的样子。

smite /smaɪt/ *verb* (**smote** /sməʊt; *NAmE* smoʊt/, **smit·ten** /'smɪtn/) (*old use* or *literary*) **1** ~ **sb/sth** to hit sb/sth hard; to attack or punish sb 重打；猛击；攻击；惩罚 **2** ~ **sb** to have a great effect on sb, especially an unpleasant or serious one 使深感（不安、不快等）；深深影响 ➲ SEE ALSO SMITTEN

smith /smɪθ/ *noun* = BLACKSMITH ➲ SEE ALSO GOLDSMITH, GUNSMITH, LOCKSMITH, SILVERSMITH

smith·er·eens /ˌsmɪðə'riːnz/ *noun* [pl.]

IDM **smash, blow, etc. sth to smithe'reens** (*informal*) to destroy sth completely by breaking it into small pieces 把某物砸（或打等）得粉碎

smithy /'smɪði; *NAmE* -θi/ *noun* (*pl.* **-ies**) a place where a BLACKSMITH works 铁匠铺

smit·ten /'smɪtn/ *adj.* [not usually before noun] **1** ~ (**with/by sb/sth**) (*especially humorous*) suddenly feeling that you are in love with sb 突然爱上；一下子爱上：*From the moment they met, he was completely smitten by her.* 从一见面的那一刻起，他就完全被她迷住了。**2** ~ **with/by sth** severely affected by a feeling, disease, etc. 痛感；备受…的煎熬 ➲ SEE ALSO SMITE

smock /smɒk; *NAmE* smɑːk/ *noun* **1** a loose comfortable piece of clothing like a long shirt, worn especially by women（多为女性穿的）宽松式衬衫 **2** a long loose piece of clothing worn over other clothes to protect them from dirt, etc. 罩衣；工作服：*an artist's smock* 画家的罩衫

smock·ing /'smɒkɪŋ; *NAmE* 'smɑːk-/ *noun* [U] decoration on clothing consisting of very small tight folds which are sewn together（衣服的）褶裥，缩褶

smog /smɒg; *NAmE* smɑːg/ *noun* [U, C] a form of air pollution that is or looks like a mixture of smoke and FOG, especially in cities 烟雾（烟与雾混合的空气污染物，尤见于城市）：*attempts to reduce smog caused by traffic fumes* 旨在降低车辆尾气造成的烟雾的措施 ➲ VISUAL VOCAB PAGE V7 ➲ MORE LIKE THIS 1, page R25 ▶ **smoggy** *adj.*

smoke /sməʊk; *NAmE* smoʊk/ *noun, verb*

■ ***noun*** **1** [U] the grey, white or black gas that is produced by sth burning 烟：*cigarette smoke* 香烟产生的烟 ◇ *Clouds of thick black smoke billowed from the car's exhaust.* 从汽车排气管冒出一股股黑色浓烟。**2** [C, usually sing.] (*informal*) an act of smoking a cigarette 吸烟；抽烟：*Are you coming outside for a smoke?* 你是不是出来抽支烟？ **3 the Smoke** [sing.] (*BrE, informal*) = BIG SMOKE

IDM **go up in 'smoke 1** to be completely burnt 被烧毁；被烧光：*The whole house went up in smoke.* 整座房子被烧毁了。**2** if your plans, hopes, etc. **go up in smoke**, they fail completely 告吹；成泡影；破灭 (**there is**) **no smoke without 'fire** (*BrE*) (*NAmE* **where there's smoke, there's 'fire**) (*saying*) if sth bad is being said about sb/sth, it usually has some truth in it 无火不生烟；无风不起浪 **a smoke-filled 'room** (*disapproving*) a decision that people describe as being made in **a smoke-filled room** is made by a small group of people at a private meeting, rather than in an open and DEMOCRATIC way（少数人密谋决策的）密室 ➲ MORE AT BLOW *v.*

■ ***verb*** **1** [T, I] ~ (**sth**) to suck smoke from a cigarette, pipe, etc. into your mouth and let it out again 吸（烟）；抽（烟）：*He was smoking a large cigar.* 他正抽着一支大雪茄。◇ *How many cigarettes do you smoke a day?* 你一天抽几支香烟？◇ *Do you mind if I smoke?* 我抽烟你介意吗？ **2** [I] to use cigarettes, etc. in this way as a habit（习惯性）吸烟，抽烟：*Do you smoke?* 你抽烟吗？◇ *She smokes heavily.* 她的烟瘾大。➲ SEE ALSO CHAIN-SMOKE **3** [I] to produce smoke 冒烟：*smoking factory chimneys* 冒着烟的工厂烟囱 ◇ *the smoking remains of burnt-out cars* 烧毁的车辆还在冒烟的残骸 **4** [T, usually passive] ~ **sth** to preserve meat or fish by hanging it in smoke from wood fires to give it a special taste 熏制（肉或鱼）：*smoked salmon* 熏鲑鱼

PHR V **ˌsmoke sb/sth↔'out 1** to force sb/sth to come out of a place by filling it with smoke 用烟熏出来：*to smoke out wasps from a nest* 把黄蜂从窝里熏出来 **2** to take action to discover where sb is hiding or to make a secret publicly known 查清（某人藏匿处）；揭露（秘密）：*The police are determined to smoke out the leaders of the gang.* 警方决心查出犯罪团伙头目的藏匿处。

'smoke alarm (*also* **'smoke detector**) *noun* a device that makes a loud noise if smoke is in the air to warn you of a fire 烟雾报警器（用于预防火灾）

'smoke bomb *noun* a bomb that produces clouds of smoke when it explodes 烟幕弹

ˌsmoked 'glass *noun* [U] glass that has been deliberately made dark by smoke（通过烟熏处理的）烟色玻璃

'smoke-free *adj.* free from cigarette smoke; where smoking is not allowed 无人吸烟的；禁止吸烟的：*a smoke-free working environment* 无烟工作环境

smoke·less /'sməʊkləs; *NAmE* 'smoʊk-/ *adj.* [usually before noun] **1** able to burn without producing smoke（燃烧时）不产生烟的，无烟的：*smokeless fuels* 无烟燃料 **2** free from smoke 不冒烟的；无烟的：*a smokeless zone* (= where smoke from factories or houses is not allowed) 无烟区（禁止工厂或家庭使用有烟燃料的地区）

smoker /'sməʊkə(r); *NAmE* 'smoʊk-/ *noun* a person who smokes TOBACCO regularly 吸烟者：*a **heavy smoker*** (= sb who smokes a lot) 烟瘾大的人 ◇ ***a smoker's cough*** 吸烟过多引起的咳嗽 ◇ ***a cigarette/cigar/pipe smoker*** 抽香烟／雪茄／烟斗的人 OPP **non-smoker**

smoke·screen /'sməʊkskriːn; *NAmE* 'smoʊk-/ *noun* **1** something that you do or say in order to hide what you are really doing or intending 烟幕（用以掩盖真相的言行）；障眼法 **2** a cloud of smoke used to hide soldiers, ships, etc. during a battle（战斗中用以掩蔽士兵、舰船等的）烟幕

'smoke shop *noun* (*NAmE*) a shop/store selling cigarettes, TOBACCO, etc. 烟草商店；烟行

'smoke signal *noun* [usually pl.] **1** a signal that is sent to sb who is far away, using smoke 烟雾信号 **2** a sign of what sb is thinking or doing（思想或行动的）标记，迹象

smoke·stack /'sməʊkstæk; *NAmE* 'smoʊk-/ *noun* (*especially NAmE*) **1** a tall CHIMNEY that takes away smoke from factories（工厂的）大烟囱 **2** (*also* **fun·nel**) a metal CHIMNEY, for example on a ship or an engine, through which smoke comes out（轮船或火车头上的）外烟筒

S

Smokey Bear /ˌsməʊki ˈbeə(r); *NAmE* ˌsmoʊki ˈber/ (*also* **ˌSmokey the ˈBear**, **ˈSmokey**) *noun* **1** the symbol used by the US Forest Service on signs and advertising about preventing forest fires 防火护林熊（美国林业局用于森林防火标志和广告的标记） **2** (*informal*) (in the US) a member of the police force that is responsible for the highway （美国）高速公路巡逻警

smok·ing /ˈsməʊkɪŋ; *NAmE* ˈsmoʊk-/ *noun* [U] the activity or habit of smoking cigarettes, etc. 吸烟；抽烟：*No Smoking* (= for example, on a notice) 禁止吸烟 ◇ *Would you like smoking or non-smoking?* (= for example, in a restaurant) 你喜欢在吸烟区还是非吸烟区？ ◇ *He's trying to* ***give up smoking***. 他正设法戒烟。➲ COMPARE NON-SMOKING

ˈsmoking ceremony *noun* (*AustralE*) (in Aboriginal culture) a ceremony in which smoke is used for RITUAL purposes, especially after death（澳大利亚土著文化中尤在人死后举行的）起烟仪式

ˌsmoking ˈgun *noun* [sing.] (*informal*) something that seems to prove that sb has done sth wrong or illegal 犯错（或犯法的）证据：*This memo could be the smoking gun that investigators have been looking for.* 这份备忘录可能是调查人员一直在寻找的证据。

ˈsmoking jacket *noun* a man's comfortable jacket worn in the past, often made of VELVET 吸烟服（旧时男人穿的宽松便服，多用丝绒做成）

smoko /ˈsməʊkəʊ; *NAmE* ˈsmoʊkoʊ/ *noun* (*pl.* **-os**) (*AustralE, NZE, informal*) a rest from work, for example to smoke a cigarette（抽烟等）工间休息

smoky /ˈsməʊki; *NAmE* ˈsmoʊki/ *adj.* (**smoki·er**, **smoki·est**) **1** full of smoke 烟雾弥漫的：*a smoky atmosphere* 烟雾弥漫的空气 ◇ *a smoky pub* 烟雾腾腾的酒吧 **2** producing a lot of smoke 多烟的；冒出大量烟的：*a smoky fire* 冒着浓烟的火 **3** tasting or smelling like smoke 有烟熏味的：*a smoky flavour* 烟熏味 **4** having the colour or appearance of smoke 烟灰色的；似烟的：*smoky blue glass* 灰蓝色玻璃 OPP clear

smol·der (*NAmE*) = SMOULDER

smooch /smuːtʃ/ *verb* [I] (*informal*) to kiss and hold sb closely, especially when you are dancing slowly（尤指慢舞时）接吻拥抱

smoodge /smuːdʒ/ *verb* [I] ~ (**to sb**) (*AustralE, NZE, informal*) to behave in a friendly way towards sb because you want them to give you sth or do sth for you（和某人）套近乎；讨好 ▸ **smoodge** *noun* [U]: *What's wrong with a bit of smoodge between friends?* 朋友之间互相恭维一下有什么不妥？

smooth /smuːð/ *adj., verb*

■ *adj.* (**smooth·er**, **smooth·est**)

• **FLAT/EVEN** 平整；平滑 **1** completely flat and even, without any lumps, holes or rough areas 平整的；平坦的；平滑的；光滑的：*a lotion to make your skin feel soft and smooth* 能使皮肤柔软光滑的护肤液 ◇ *The water was as smooth as glass.* 水平如镜。◇ *a paint that gives a smooth, silky finish* 使表面如丝般光滑的油漆 ◇ *Over the years, the stone steps had worn smooth.* 日久天长，石阶已经磨得光溜溜的。OPP **rough**

• **WITHOUT LUMPS** 无结块 **2** (of a liquid mixture 液体混合物) without any lumps 无结块的；混合均匀的：*Mix the flour with the milk to form a smooth paste.* 把面粉和牛奶和成均匀的面糊。

• **WITHOUT PROBLEMS** 顺利 **3** happening or continuing without any problems 顺利的；平稳的：*They are introducing new measures to ensure the smooth running of the business.* 他们正采取新措施，以确保公司平稳运转。◇ *They could not ensure a smooth transfer of political power.* 他们无法保证政权的顺利交接。

• **MOVEMENT** 运动 **4** even and regular, without sudden stops and starts 平稳的；连续而流畅的：*The car's improved suspension gives you a smoother ride.* 汽车悬挂经过改进，乘坐起来更平稳。◇ *The plane made a smooth landing.* 飞机平稳降落。◇ *She swung herself over the gate in one smooth movement.* 她从栅栏门上一跃而过。

• **MAN** 人 **5** (*often disapproving*) (of people, especially men, and their behaviour 人，尤指男人及行为) very polite and pleasant, but in a way that is often not very sincere 圆通的；八面玲珑的 SYN **smarmy**: *I don't like him. He's far too smooth for me.* 我不喜欢他。我觉得他太圆滑。◇ *He's something of a* ***smooth operator***. 可以说，他是一个八面玲珑的滑头。

• **DRINK/TASTE** 饮料；味道 **6** pleasant and not bitter 醇和的；香醇的：*This coffee has a smooth, rich taste.* 这种咖啡味道醇厚。

• **VOICE/MUSIC** 嗓音；音乐 **7** nice to hear, and without any rough or unpleasant sounds 悦耳的；圆润的

▸ **smooth·ness** *noun* [U]: *the smoothness of her skin* 她的皮肤细腻光滑 ◇ *They admired the smoothness and efficiency with which the business was run.* 他们钦佩这家公司协调高效的管理方式。IDM SEE ROUGH *n.*

■ *verb* **1** to make sth smooth 使平整；使平坦；使平滑；使光滑：**~ sth (back/down/out)** *He smoothed his hair back.* 他朝后捋了捋头发。◇ *She was smoothing out the creases in her skirt.* 她正设法弄平裙子上的皱褶。◇ **~ sth + adj.** *He took the letter and smoothed it flat on the table.* 他接过信，在桌上展平。**2 ~ sth on/into/over sth** to put a layer of a soft substance over a surface（将软物质）均匀涂抹于：*Smooth the icing over the top of the cake.* 在蛋糕顶上均匀地铺一层糖霜。

IDM **smooth the ˈpath/ˈway** to make it easier for sb/sth to develop or make progress 铺平道路：*These negotiations are intended to smooth the path to a peace treaty.* 这些谈判目的在于为签订和平条约铺平道路。**smooth (sb's) ruffled ˈfeathers** to make sb feel less angry or offended 使息怒；劝解

PHR V **ˌsmooth sth↔aˈway/ˈout** to make problems or difficulties disappear 消除（问题）；克服（困难） **ˌsmooth sth↔ˈover** to make problems or difficulties seem less important or serious, especially by talking to people 缓和；调解；斡旋：*She spoke to both sides in the dispute in an attempt to smooth things over.* 她和争执双方谈话，试图进行调解。

smoothie /ˈsmuːði/ *noun* **1** (*informal*) a man who dresses well and talks very politely and confidently but who is often not honest or sincere 体面而圆通的男人；八面玲珑的男人 **2** a drink made of fruit or fruit juice mixed with milk or ice cream 水果沙冰；鲜果奶昔

smooth·ly /ˈsmuːðli/ *adv.* **1** in an even way, without suddenly stopping and starting again 平稳地；连续而流畅地：*Traffic is now flowing smoothly again.* 现在，交通又畅通了。◇ *The engine was running smoothly.* 发动机在平稳运转。**2** without problems or difficulties 顺利地：*The interview* ***went smoothly***. 面谈进展顺利。**3** in a calm or confident way 平静地；自信地：*'Would you like to come this way?' he said smoothly.* "你上这边来好吗？"他平静地说。**4** in a way that produces a smooth surface or mixture 平整地；平滑地；均匀地：*The colours blend smoothly together.* 这些颜色可以均匀地配在一起。

ˌsmooth ˈmuscle *noun* [U] (*anatomy* 解) the type of muscle found in the organs inside the body, that is not under conscious control 平滑肌

ˌsmooth-ˈtalking *adj.* (*usually disapproving*) talking very politely and confidently, especially to persuade sb to do sth, but in a way that may not be honest or sincere 花言巧语的；巧舌如簧的

s'more /smɔː(r)/ *noun* (*NAmE*) a cooked MARSHMALLOW eaten with chocolate between two GRAHAM CRACKERS (= a type of cookie) that is traditionally cooked over a fire when camping 棉花糖巧克力夹心饼（用两块全麦饼干夹棉花软糖和巧克力制作而成）

smor·gas·bord /ˈsmɔːɡəsbɔːd; *NAmE* ˈsmɔːrɡəsbɔːrd/ *noun* [U, sing.] (*from Swedish*) a meal at which you serve yourself from a large range of hot and cold dishes 自助餐

smote PAST TENSE OF SMITE

smother /ˈsmʌðə(r)/ *verb* **1 ~ sb (with sth)** to kill sb by covering their face so that they cannot breathe 捂死；闷死 **SYN** **suffocate**: *He smothered the baby with a pillow.* 他用枕头把婴儿闷死了。**2 ~ sth/sb with/in sth** to cover sth/sb thickly or with too much of sth（用某物）厚厚地覆盖：*a rich dessert smothered in cream* 涂了厚厚一层奶油的多脂甜点 ◇ *She smothered him with kisses.* 她劈头盖脑给他一通狂吻。**3 ~ sth** to prevent sth from developing or being expressed 抑制；扼杀；忍住 **SYN** **stifle**: *to smother a yawn/giggle/grin* 把哈欠忍了回去；憋住不笑出声来；刚想咧嘴笑又收了回去 ◇ *The voices of the opposition were effectively smothered.* 反对党的声音被有效地压制了下去。**4 ~ sb** to give sb too much love or protection so that they feel restricted（因溺爱等）使…觉得压抑：*Her husband was very loving, but she felt smothered.* 丈夫对她百般宠爱，但这让她觉得不自在。**5 ~ sth** to make a fire stop burning by covering it with sth 把（火）闷熄：*He tried to smother the flames with a blanket.* 他试图用毯子把火扑灭。

smoul·der (*especially US* **smol·der**) /ˈsməʊldə(r); *NAmE* ˈsmoʊ-/ *verb* **1** [I] to burn slowly without a flame（无明火地）阴燃，闷燃：*The bonfire was still smouldering the next day.* 到了第二天，篝火还在闷燃。◇ *a smouldering cigarette* 慢慢燃烧的香烟 ◇ (*figurative*) *The feud smouldered on for years.* 这场冤仇积结了多年。**2** [I] (*formal*) to be filled with a strong emotion that you do not fully express（感情）郁积，压在心头 **SYN** **burn**: **~ (with sth)** *His eyes smouldered with anger.* 他眼里冒着强压的怒火。◇ **~ (in sth)** *Anger smouldered in his eyes.* 强压的怒火在他眼里燃烧。

SMS /ˌes em ˈes/ *noun, verb*

■ ***noun*** **1** [U] the abbreviation for 'short message service' (a system for sending short written messages from one mobile/cell phone to another)（手机的）短信服务（全写为 short message service）**2** [C] a message sent by SMS（手机）短信，短消息 **SYN** **text, text message**: *I'm trying to send an SMS.* 我正想发短信。➲ COLLOCATIONS AT PHONE ➲ COMPARE EMS

■ ***verb*** [T, I] **~ (sb)** to send a message to sb by SMS（用手机）发短信 **SYN** **text, text message**: *He SMSed me every day.* 他曾每天给我发短信。◇ *If you have any comments, just email or SMS.* 假如你有任何意见，可发电子邮件或短信。◇ *She spends her time chatting and SMSing.* 她通过聊天和发短信消磨时间。

smudge /smʌdʒ/ *noun, verb*

■ ***noun*** a dirty mark with no clear shape（模糊的）污迹，污痕 **SYN** **smear**: *a smudge of lipstick on a cup* 留在杯子上的口红印

■ ***verb*** **1** [T, I] **~ (sth)** to touch or rub sth, especially wet ink or paint, so that it is no longer clear; to become not clear in this way 把…擦模糊（或弄得看不清楚）；变模糊：*He had smudged his signature with his sleeve.* 他用袖子把自己的签字擦得看不清了。◇ *Tears had smudged her mascara.* 她的睫毛膏被泪水弄糊了。◇ *Her lipstick had smudged.* 她的口红模糊了。**2** [T] **~ sth** to make a dirty mark on a surface 弄脏；留下污迹 **SYN** **smear**: *The mirror was smudged with fingerprints.* 镜子上有脏手印。

smudgy /ˈsmʌdʒi/ *adj.* **1** with dirty marks on 有脏痕的；有污迹的 **2** (of a picture, writing, etc. 图画、字迹等) with edges that are not clear 模糊不清的 **SYN** **blurred**

smug /smʌɡ/ *adj.* (*disapproving*) looking or feeling too pleased about sth you have done or achieved 沾沾自喜的；自鸣得意的 **SYN** **complacent**: ***a smug expression/smile/face, etc.*** 沾沾自喜的表情、笑容、面容等 ◇ *What are you looking so smug about?* 你怎么这样一副神气活现的样子？ ▶ **smug·ly** *adv.* **smug·ness** *noun* [U]

smug·gle /ˈsmʌɡl/ *verb* **~ sth/sb (+ adv./prep.)** to take, send or bring goods or people secretly and illegally into or out of a country, etc. 走私；私运；偷运：*They were caught smuggling diamonds into the country.* 他们走私钻石入境时被发现了。◇ *He managed to smuggle a gun into the prison.* 他设法把一支枪偷偷送进了监狱。◇ *smuggled drugs* 走私的毒品 ➲ COLLOCATIONS AT CRIME

smug·gler /ˈsmʌɡlə(r)/ *noun* a person who takes goods into or out of a country illegally 走私者

smug·gling /ˈsmʌɡlɪŋ/ *noun* [U] the crime of taking, sending or bringing goods secretly and illegally into or out of a country 走私（罪）：*drug smuggling* 毒品走私

smut /smʌt/ *noun* **1** [U] (*informal*) stories, pictures or comments about sex that deal with it in a way that some people find offensive 淫秽小说（或图片、言语）**2** [U, C] dirt, ASH, etc. that causes a black mark on sth; a black mark made by this（黑色）污物，灰垢，污迹，污点

smutty /ˈsmʌti/ *adj.* [usually before noun] (*informal*) (of stories, pictures and comments 小说、图片和言语) dealing with sex in a way that some people find offensive 淫秽的；下流的；猥亵的：*smutty jokes* 下流笑话

snack /snæk/ *noun, verb*

■ ***noun*** **1** (*informal*) a small meal or amount of food, usually eaten in a hurry 点心；小吃；快餐：*a mid-morning snack* 上午十点左右吃的点心 ◇ *I only have time for a snack at lunchtime.* 中午，我的时间只够吃点心。◇ *Do you serve bar snacks?* 你这儿卖不卖快餐？ ◇ *a snack lunch* 快餐午饭 **2** (*AustralE, informal*) a thing that is easy to do 易办到的事；"小菜一碟"：*It'll be a snack.* 这不过是小事一桩。

■ ***verb*** [I] **~ on sth** to eat snacks between or instead of main meals 吃点心（或快餐、小吃）：*It's healthier to snack on fruit rather than chocolate.* 作为点心，水果比巧克力更有益于健康。

ˈsnack bar *noun* a place where you can buy a small quick meal, such as a SANDWICH 快餐柜台；快餐部；小吃部；点心铺

snaf·fle /ˈsnæfl/ *verb* **~ sth** (*BrE, informal*) to take sth quickly for yourself, especially before anyone else has had the time or opportunity（尤指抢先）攫取，偷窃

snafu /snæˈfuː/ *noun* [sing.] (*NAmE, informal*) a situation in which nothing happens as planned（一切均未按计划发生的）混乱局面：*It was another bureaucratic snafu.* 又让官僚主义搞成了一团糟。

snag /snæɡ/ *noun, verb*

■ ***noun*** **1** (*informal*) a problem or difficulty, especially one that is small, hidden or unexpected（尤指潜在的、意外的、不严重的）问题，困难，障碍，麻烦 **SYN** **difficulty**: *There is just one small snag—where is the money coming from?* 只有一个小问题：钱从哪儿来？ ◇ *Let me know if you run into any snags.* 要是遇到什么麻烦就告诉我。**2** an object or a part of an object that is rough or sharp and may cut sth 突出物；尖齿；尖角；尖刺 **3** (*AustralE, NZE, informal*) a SAUSAGE 香肠

■ ***verb*** **(-gg-)** **1** [T, I] to catch or tear sth on sth rough or sharp; to become caught or torn in this way（在带尖的东西上）钩住，挂破，被钩住，被挂破：**~ sth on/in sth** *I snagged my sweater on the wire fence.* 我的毛衣被铁丝网栅栏钩住了。◇ **~ sth** *The fence snagged my sweater.* 栅栏把我的毛衣挂住了。◇ **~ (on/in sth)** *The nets snagged on some rocks.* 渔网缠在礁石上了。**2** [T] **~ sth (from sb)** (*NAmE, informal*) to succeed in getting sth quickly, often before other people 抓住；抢先获得：*I snagged a ride from Joe.* 我截住乔的车搭了一段路。

snag·gle /ˈsnæɡl/ *noun, verb*

■ ***noun*** an untidy or confused collection of things 繁杂（或混乱）的事物：*a snaggle of restrictions* 杂乱无章的种种限制

■ ***verb*** [I] to become twisted, untidy or confused 缠结在一起；变凌乱；变混乱：*My hair snaggles when I wash it.* 我的头发一洗就打结。

ˈsnaggle-tooth *noun* (*informal*) a tooth which sticks out or is a strange shape 龅牙；歪牙 ▶ **ˈsnaggle-toothed** *adj.*

snail /sneɪl/ *noun* a small soft creature with a hard round shell on its back, that moves very slowly and often eats garden plants. Some types of snail can be eaten. 蜗牛 ➲ VISUAL VOCAB PAGE V13

IDM **at a ˈsnail's pace** very slowly 非常缓慢

S

ˈsnail mail *noun* [U] (*informal*, *humorous*) used especially by people who use email to describe the system of sending letters by ordinary mail 慢速邮递（电邮使用者用以指普通邮寄）

snake /sneɪk/ *noun*, *verb*
■ ***noun*** a REPTILE with a very long thin body and no legs. There are many types of snake, some of which are poisonous. 蛇：*a snake coiled up in the grass* 盘在草丛里的一条蛇 ◊ *Venomous snakes spit and hiss when they are cornered.* 毒蛇在无法逃脱时会发出愤怒的呼呼嗞嗞的声音。
IDM **a ˌsnake (in the ˈgrass)** (*disapproving*) a person who pretends to be your friend but who cannot be trusted 阴险的人；潜伏的敌人；虚假的人
■ ***verb*** [I, T] to move like a snake, in long twisting curves; to go in a particular direction in long twisting curves 曲折前行；蛇行；蜿蜒伸展 SYN **meander**: **+ adv./prep.** *The road snaked away into the distance.* 公路蜿蜒伸向远方。◊ **~ its way + adv./prep.** *The procession snaked its way through narrow streets.* 队伍沿着狭窄的街道曲折穿行。

snake·bite /ˈsneɪkbaɪt/ *noun* [C, U] **1** a wound that you get when a poisonous snake bites you 毒蛇咬伤 **2** an alcoholic drink made of equal parts of beer and CIDER "蛇之吻"鸡尾酒（啤酒加苹果酒各半调制而成）

Snake·board™ /ˈsneɪkbɔːd; *NAmE* -bɔːrd/ *noun* ➲ STREETBOARD

ˈsnake charmer *noun* an entertainer who seems to be able to control snakes and make them move by playing music to them 耍蛇人；弄蛇人

ˈsnake eyes *noun* [pl.] (*informal*) a result in a game when you throw two dice and both show one dot 蛇眼（掷出的两枚骰子均为一点）

ˈsnake oil *noun* [U] (*informal*, *especially NAmE*) something, for example medicine, that sb tries to sell you, but that is not effective or useful 推销者的所谓"万应灵药"；狗皮膏药（毫无用处或效果的推销品）：*a snake-oil salesman* 劣质品推销员

ˈsnake pit *noun* **1** a hole in the ground in which snakes are kept 蛇洞；蛇坑 **2** a place which is extremely unpleasant or dangerous 蛇窝（令人反感或极其危险的地方）

S

ˌsnakes and ˈladders (*BrE*) *noun* [U] a children's game played on a special board with pictures of snakes and LADDERS on it. Players move their pieces up the ladders to go forward and down the snakes to go back. 蛇梯棋（棋子顺梯子图案前进，顺着蛇图案后退）➲ SEE ALSO CHUTES AND LADDERS™ ➲ VISUAL VOCAB PAGE V42

snake·skin /ˈsneɪkskɪn/ *noun* [U] the skin of a snake, used for making expensive shoes, bags, etc. 蛇皮（用于制作名贵的鞋、包等）

snaky /ˈsneɪki/ *adj.* (*AustralE*, *NZE*, *informal*) angry 生气的；发怒的：*What are you snaky about?* 你为啥发火？

snap /snæp/ *verb*, *noun*, *adj.*, *exclamation*
■ ***verb*** (-pp-)
• **BREAK** 断开 **1** [T, I] to break sth suddenly with a sharp noise; to be broken in this way（使咔嚓）断裂，绷断：**~ sth** *The wind had snapped the tree in two.* 风把树咔嚓一声刮断了。◊ **~ sth off (sth)** *He snapped a twig off a bush.* 他啪地从灌木上折下一小枝。◊ **~ (off)** *Suddenly, the rope snapped.* 突然，绳子啪地绷断了。◊ *The branch she was standing on must have snapped off.* 她当时踩的树枝一定是突然折断了。
• **OPEN/CLOSE/MOVE INTO POSITION** 打开；关上；进入适当位置 **2** [I, T] to move, or to move sth, into a particular position quickly, especially with a sudden sharp noise（使啪地）打开，关上，移到某位置：**+ adj.** *The lid snapped shut.* 盖子啪地合上了。◊ *His eyes snapped open.* 他两眼唰地睁开了。◊ **+ adv./prep.** *He snapped to attention and saluted.* 他啪的一下立正敬礼。◊ **~ sth + adj.** *She snapped the bag shut.* 她啪的一声把包合上了。
• **SPEAK IMPATIENTLY** 不耐烦地说 **3** [T, I] to speak or say sth in an impatient, usually angry, voice 厉声说；怒气冲冲地说；不耐烦地说：**+ speech** *'Don't just stand there,' she snapped.* "别光站在那儿。"她生气地说。◊ **~ (at sb)** *I was tempted to snap back angrily at him.* 我真想没好气地顶他几句。◊ **~ sth** *He snapped a reply.* 他气冲冲地回了一句。
• **OF ANIMAL** 动物 **4** [I] **~ (at sb/sth)** to try to bite sb/sth 咬 SYN **nip**: *The dogs snarled and snapped at our heels.* 几条狗边叫边向着我们的脚后跟咬来。
• **TAKE PHOTOGRAPH** 拍照 **5** [T, I] (*informal*) to take a photograph 拍照；摄影：**~ sth** *A passing tourist snapped the incident.* 一个过路的游客把这件事拍了下来。◊ **~ (away)** *She seemed oblivious to the crowds of photographers snapping away.* 成群的摄影者不停地拍照，她好像浑然不觉。
• **LOSE CONTROL** 失去控制 **6** [I] to suddenly be unable to control your feelings any longer because the situation has become too difficult 突然失去自制力；一下子无法自持：*My patience finally snapped.* 我终于忍不住了。◊ *When he said that, something snapped inside her.* 听他说到这里，她内心的感情一下子翻腾起来。◊ *And that did it. I snapped.* 就这一下，我再也承受不住了。
• **FASTEN CLOTHING** 扣衣服 **7** [I, T] **~ (sth)** (*NAmE*) to fasten a piece of clothing with a snap 用子母扣扣，用揿扣扣（衣服）
IDM **snap your ˈfingers** to make a sharp noise by moving your second or third finger quickly against your thumb, to attract sb's attention, or to mark the beat of music, for example 打榧子，弹指头（捻拇指作响）**ˌsnap ˈout of it/sth | ˌsnap sb ˈout of it/sth** [no passive] (*informal*) to make an effort to stop feeling unhappy or depressed; to help sb to stop feeling unhappy（使）抛掉不愉快情绪，摆脱郁闷心境：*You've been depressed for weeks. It's time you snapped out of it.* 你情绪低落好几周了。现在该振作起来了。**ˌsnap ˈto it** (*informal*) used, especially in orders, to tell sb to start working harder or more quickly（尤用于催促）加把劲，赶快 ➲ MORE AT HEAD *n.*
PHR V **ˌsnap sth↔ˈout** to say sth in a sharp unpleasant way 厉声说出：*The sergeant snapped out an order.* 中士厉声下达命令。**ˌsnap sth↔ˈup** (*informal*) to buy or obtain sth quickly because it is cheap or you want it very much 抢购；抢先弄到手：*All the best bargains were snapped up within hours.* 所有最划得来的便宜货几小时之内就被抢购一空了。◊ (*figurative*) *She's been snapped up by Hollywood to star in two major movies.* 好莱坞抢先邀请她在两部大片中担当主角。
■ ***noun***
• **SHARP NOISE** 尖厉的声音 **1** [C] a sudden sharp noise, especially one made by sth closing or breaking（尤指关上或断裂的声音）啪嗒声，咔嚓声：*She closed her purse with a snap.* 她啪嗒一声合上了钱包。◊ *the snap of a twig* 小树枝折断的咔嚓声
• **PHOTOGRAPH** 照片 **2** (*also* **snap·shot**) [C] a photograph, especially one taken quickly（尤指抢拍的）照片：*holiday snaps* 假日拍的照片
• **CARD GAME** 扑克牌游戏 **3 Snap** [U] a card game in which players take turns to put cards down and try to be the first to call out 'snap' when two similar cards are put down together "对儿"牌游戏（游戏者轮流下牌，出现相同的牌时要抢先喊"对儿"）
• **FASTENER** 扣子 **4** (*NAmE*) (*BrE* **ˈpress stud**, **pop·per**) a type of button used for fastening clothes, consisting of two metal or plastic sections that can be pressed together 揿扣；子母扣 ➲ VISUAL VOCAB PAGE V68 ➲ SEE ALSO BRANDY SNAP, COLD SNAP
IDM **be a ˈsnap** (*NAmE*, *informal*) to be very easy to do 十分容易（做）：*This job's a snap.* 这活儿不过是小菜一碟。
■ ***adj.*** [only before noun] made or done quickly and without careful thought or preparation 匆忙的；仓促的：*It was a **snap decision**.* 那是个仓促的决定。◊ *They held a **snap election**.* 他们临时举行了选举。
■ ***exclamation*** **1** you say **snap!** in the card game called 'Snap' when two cards that are the same are put down（在"对儿"牌游戏中出现同样的牌时喊的）对儿 **2** (*BrE*, *informal*) people say **snap!** to show that they are surprised when two things are the same（对于两件相同事物表示惊讶）真巧：*Snap! I've just bought that CD too!* 真是巧了！我也刚买了那张光盘！

snap·dragon /ˈsnæpdræɡən/ *noun* a small garden plant with red, white, yellow or pink flowers that open and shut like a mouth when squeezed 啮龙花，金鱼草（庭园植物，花的口部呈唇形，裂片闭合）

snap·per /ˈsnæpə(r)/ *noun* **1** [C, U] a fish that lives in warm seas and is used for food 啮鱼（食用鱼，盛产于热带海域） **2** [C] (*informal*, *BrE*) a photographer, especially one who takes pictures of famous people for newspapers and magazines（尤指为报章杂志拍摄名人照片的）摄影者

snappy /ˈsnæpi/ *adj.* (**snap·pier**, **snap·pi·est**) **1** (of a remark, title, etc. 言语、标题等) clever or amusing and short 精练的；简洁的：*a snappy slogan* 精练的口号 ◇ *a snappy answer* 简洁的回答 **2** [usually before noun] (*informal*) attractive and fashionable 漂亮入时的：*a snappy outfit* 漂亮的套装 ◇ *She's a **snappy dresser**.* 她衣着入时。**3** (of people or their behaviour 人或行为) tending to speak to people in a bad-tempered, impatient way 烦躁的；没好气的 **4** lively; quick 活泼的；敏捷的：*a snappy tune* 活泼的曲调 ▶ **snap·pily** *adv.*: *He summarized the speech snappily.* 他对讲话做了精练的概括。◇ *snappily dressed* 衣着入时的 ◇ *'What?' she asked snappily.* "什么？" 她不耐烦地问。**snap·pi·ness** *noun* [U]

IDM **ˌmake it ˈsnappy** (*informal*) used to tell sb to do sth quickly or to hurry（用于催促）赶紧，快点

snap·shot /ˈsnæpʃɒt; *NAmE* -ʃɑːt/ *noun* **1** = SNAP: *snapshots of the children* 孩子们的照片 ➲ SYNONYMS AT PHOTOGRAPH **2** [usually sing.] a short description or a small amount of information that gives you an idea of what sth is like 简介；简要说明

snare /sneə(r); *NAmE* sner/ *noun*, *verb*

■ ***noun*** **1** a device used for catching small animals and birds, especially one that holds their leg so that they cannot escape（捕鸟、兽的）陷阱，罗网，套子 SYN **trap** **2** (*formal*) a situation which seems attractive but is unpleasant and difficult to escape from 陷阱；圈套；骗局 **3** the metal strings that are stretched across the bottom of a snare drum（绷在小鼓下鼓皮的）响弦

■ ***verb*** **~ sth/sb** to catch sth, especially an animal, in a snare 设陷阱（或罗网、套子）捕捉 SYN **trap**: *to snare a rabbit* 套兔子 ◇ (*figurative*) *Her one thought was to snare a rich husband.* 她一心要攀住一个有钱的丈夫。◇ (*figurative*) *He found himself snared in a web of intrigue.* 他发现自己中了圈套。

ˈsnare drum *noun* a small drum with metal strings across one side that make a continuous sound when the drum is hit 小鼓（一面绷有金属响弦） ➲ VISUAL VOCAB PAGE V37

snarf /snɑːf; *NAmE* snɑːrf/ *verb* **~ sth** (*informal*, *especially NAmE*) to eat or drink sth very quickly or in a way that people think is GREEDY 很快地吃（或喝）；贪婪地吃（或喝）：*The kids snarfed up all the cookies.* 孩子们一顿狼吞虎咽，把曲奇饼全吃光了。

snark /snɑːk; *NAmE* snɑːrk/ *verb*, *noun* (*NAmE*, *informal*)

■ ***verb*** [I] **~ (at/about/on sb/sth)** to criticize sb/sth in an indirect and very unkind way 讥讽；暗讽；挖苦：*There's plenty to snark about in the article.* 这篇文章中大有可引人讥讽之处。

■ ***noun*** [U, C] very critical comments, made in an indirect way; a comment of this type 讥讽；暗讽；挖苦

snarky /ˈsnɑːki; *NAmE* ˈsnɑːrki/ *adj.* (*NAmE*, *informal*) criticizing sb in an unkind way 尖锐批评的；讽刺挖苦的：*a snarky remark* 尖刻的指责

snarl /snɑːl; *NAmE* snɑːrl/ *verb*, *noun*

■ ***verb*** **1** [I] **~ (at sb/sth)** (of dogs, etc. 狗等) to show the teeth and make a deep angry noise in the throat 龇牙低吼：*The dog snarled at us.* 狗朝我们低声吼叫。**2** [T] to speak in an angry or bad-tempered way 咆哮着说；不耐烦地说：**+ speech (at sb)** *'Get out of here!' he snarled.* "滚开！" 他吼道。◇ **~ sth (at sb)** *She snarled abuse at anyone who happened to walk past.* 谁碰巧走过，她就冲谁叫骂。

PHR V **ˌsnarl ˈup | ˌsnarl sth↔ˈup** **1** to involve sb/sth in a situation that stops their movement or progress; to become involved in a situation like this 阻塞；妨碍（某事物）：*The accident snarled up the traffic all day.* 这次事故使交通堵塞了整整一天。**2** to become caught or twisted; to make sth do this（使）缠结：*The sheets kept getting snarled up.* 床单老缠到一起。➲ RELATED NOUN SNARL-UP

■ ***noun*** **1** [usually sing.] a deep sound that an animal makes when it is angry and shows its teeth（动物的）龇牙低吼：*The dog bared its teeth in a snarl.* 那条狗龇着牙低声吼叫。**2** [usually sing.] an act of speaking in an angry or bad-tempered way; the sound you make when you are angry, in pain, etc. 愤怒叫嚷（声）；咆哮（声）；疼痛叫声：*a snarl of hate* 充满仇恨的吼声 **3** = SNARL-UP: *rush-hour traffic snarls* 高峰时间的交通阻塞 **4** (*informal*) something that has become twisted in an untidy way 缠结物；蓬乱的事物：*She used conditioner to remove the snarls from her hair.* 她用护发剂梳顺了头发。

ˈsnarl-up (*also* **snarl**) *noun* (*BrE*, *informal*) a situation in which traffic is unable to move 交通阻塞 SYN **jam**

snatch /snætʃ/ *verb*, *noun*

■ ***verb*** **1** [T, I] to take sth quickly and often rudely or roughly 一把抓起；一下夺过 SYN **grab**: **~ sth (+ adv./prep.)** *She managed to snatch the gun from his hand.* 她设法从他手里夺过了枪。◇ *Gordon snatched up his jacket and left the room.* 戈登一把抓起上衣，出了房间。◇ **(+ adv./prep.)** *Hey, you kids! Don't all snatch!* 嗨，孩子们！别抢啊！**2** [T] **~ sb/sth (from sb/sth)** to take sb/sth away from a person or place, especially by force; to steal sth 夺去；抢走；偷窃 SYN **steal**: *The raiders snatched $100 from the cash register.* 劫匪从现金出纳机里抢走了 100 美元。◇ *The baby was snatched from its parents' car.* 婴儿是从父母的车上被抢走的。**3** [T] **~ sth** to take or get sth quickly, especially because you do not have much time 抓紧时间做；乘机获得：*I managed to snatch an hour's sleep.* 我偷空儿睡了一小时的觉。◇ *The team snatched a dramatic victory in the last minute of the game.* 该队在比赛的最后一分钟戏剧性地获胜。

IDM **snatch ˌvictory from the jaws of deˈfeat** to win sth even though it seemed up until the last moment that you would lose 在最后一刻反败为胜 HELP The idiom is often reversed for humorous effect to show that a person or team were expected to win, but then lost at the last moment, snatching defeat from the jaws of victory. 这个习语常反用以表示幽默：snatch defeat from the jaws of victory，指原本胜算很大，但在最后一刻落败。

PHR V **ˈsnatch at sth** **1** to try to take hold of sth with your hands 伸手抓；试图夺：*He snatched at the steering wheel but I pushed him away.* 他伸手来抓方向盘，但我把他推开了。**2** to take an opportunity to do sth 抓住机会：*We snatched at every moment we could be together.* 一有时间，我们就待在一起。

■ ***noun*** **1** a very small part of a conversation or some music that you hear（听到的）只言片语，音乐片段 SYN **snippet**: *a snatch of music* 音乐片段 ◇ *I only caught snatches of the conversation.* 我只听到谈话的只言片语。**2** an act of moving your hand very quickly to take or steal sth 抓；夺；抢夺；偷窃：*a bag snatch* 抢夺手提包 ◇ *to **make a snatch** at sth* 抢夺某物 **3** (*taboo*, *slang*) an offensive word for a woman's outer sex organs（女性的）阴部

IDM **in ˈsnatches** for short periods rather than continuously 断断续续地：*Sleep came to him in brief snatches.* 他时睡时醒。

snatch·er /ˈsnætʃə(r)/ *noun* (often in compounds 常构成复合词) a person who takes sth quickly with their hand and steals it 抢劫者：*a purse snatcher* 抢钱包的贼

ˈsnatch squad *noun* [C+sing./pl. v.] a group of police officers or soldiers whose job is to remove people from a crowd who are considered to be causing trouble（驱逐领头闹事者的）搜捕队，防暴部队

snazzy /ˈsnæzi/ *adj.* (**snaz·zier**, **snaz·zi·est**) (*informal*) (of clothes, cars, etc. 服装、汽车等) fashionable, bright and modern, and attracting your attention 漂亮而时髦的；吸引人的 SYN **jazzy**, **smart**: *a snazzy tie* 漂亮的领带

sneak /sniːk/ *verb*, *noun*, *adj.*

■ ***verb*** HELP The usual past form is **sneaked**, but **snuck** /snʌk/ is now very common in informal speech in *NAmE* and some people use it in *BrE* too. However, many people think that it

S

is not correct and it should not be used in formal writing. 过去式通常为 sneaked，但在美式英语非正式的口语中，现在普遍用 snuck，在英式英语中也有人用 snuck。不过，许多人认为这不正确，不应在正式书面语中使用。**1** [I] **+ adv./prep.** to go somewhere secretly, trying to avoid being seen 偷偷地走；溜 SYN **creep**: *I sneaked up the stairs.* 我蹑手蹑脚地上了楼。**2** [T] to do sth or take sb/sth somewhere secretly, often without permission 偷偷地做；偷带；偷拿：**~ sth** *We sneaked a look at her diary.* 我们偷偷看了一眼她的日记。◇ *If the gate is open, you can **sneak a peek** at the gardens.* 如果大门开着，你可以偷瞥一眼花园。◇ **~ sth to sb** *I managed to sneak a note to him.* 我设法偷偷给他递了张条子。◇ **~ sb sth** *I managed to sneak him a note.* 我设法偷偷给他递了张条子。**3** [T] **~ sth** (*informal*) to secretly take sth small or unimportant 偷走（不重要的或小的东西）SYN **pinch**: *I sneaked a cake when they were out of the room.* 趁他们不在屋里，我偷拿了一块蛋糕。**4** [I] **~ (on sb) (to sb)** (*old-fashioned, BrE, disapproving*) to tell an adult that another child has done sth wrong, especially in order to cause trouble（儿童向成人）打小报告，告状 SYN **snitch**: *Did you sneak on me to the teacher?* 你有没有向老师告我的状？

PHR V **ˌsneak ˈup (on sb/sth)** to move towards sb very quietly so that they do not see or hear you until you reach them 偷偷走近：*He sneaked up on his sister and shouted 'Boo!'.* 他偷偷溜到妹妹身边，然后大喊一声"嘿！"

■ ***noun*** (*old-fashioned, disapproving*) a person, especially a child, who tells sb about sth wrong that another person has done 打小报告的人，告状者（尤指儿童）SYN **snitch**

■ ***adj.*** [only before noun] done without any warning 突然的；出其不意的：*a sneak attack* 偷袭

sneak·er /ˈsniːkə(r)/ (*NAmE*) (*BrE* **train·er**, **ˈtraining shoe**) *noun* [usually pl.] a shoe that you wear for sports or as informal clothing 运动鞋；便鞋：*He wore old jeans and a pair of sneakers.* 他穿一条旧牛仔裤，脚蹬运动鞋。➲ VISUAL VOCAB PAGE V69

sneak·ing /ˈsniːkɪŋ/ *adj.* [only before noun] if you have a **sneaking** feeling for sb or about sth, you do not want to admit it to other people, because you feel embarrassed, or you are not sure that this feeling is right（指不愿公开的感觉）暗中的，私下的：*She had always had a sneaking affection for him.* 以前她一直暗暗倾心于他。◇ *I have a sneaking suspicion that she knows more than she's telling us.* 我私下怀疑，她还知道一些情况没有告诉我们。

ˌsneak ˈpreview *noun* an opportunity to see sth before it is officially shown to the public（公开放映前的）预映，试映

ˈsneak thief *noun* a person who steals things without using force or breaking doors or windows（偷而不抢的）小偷

sneaky /ˈsniːki/ *adj.* (**sneak·ier**, **sneaki·est**) (*informal*) behaving in a secret and sometimes dishonest or unpleasant way 悄悄的；偷偷摸摸的；鬼鬼祟祟的 SYN **crafty**: *That was a sneaky trick!* 这种把戏可不够光明正大！▶ **sneak·ily** /-ɪli/ *adv.*

sneer /snɪə(r); *NAmE* snɪr/ *verb, noun*

■ ***verb*** [I, T] to show that you have no respect for sb by the expression on your face or by the way you speak 嘲笑；讥讽；嗤笑 SYN **mock**: **~ (at sb/sth)** *He sneered at people who liked pop music.* 他嘲笑喜欢流行音乐的人。◇ *a sneering comment* 讥讽的话 ◇ **+ speech** *'You? A writer?' she sneered.* "你？是作家？"她不屑地说。➲ WORDFINDER NOTE AT EXPRESSION ▶ **sneer·ing·ly** /ˈsnɪərɪŋli; *NAmE* ˈsnɪr-/ *adv.*

■ ***noun*** [usually sing.] an unpleasant look, smile or comment that shows you do not respect sb/sth 嘲笑；讥讽：*A faint sneer of satisfaction crossed her face.* 她的脸上掠过一丝得意的冷笑。

sneeze /sniːz/ *verb, noun*

■ ***verb*** [I] to have air come suddenly and noisily out through your nose and mouth in a way that you cannot control, for example because you have a cold 打喷嚏：*I've been sneezing all morning.* 我一上午老是打喷嚏。

IDM **not to be ˈsneezed at** (*informal*) good enough to be accepted or considered seriously 值得认真对待；不可轻视：*In those days, $20 was not a sum to be sneezed at.* 那时候，20 美元可不能不当回事。

■ ***noun*** the act of sneezing or the noise you make when you sneeze 喷嚏；喷嚏声：*coughs and sneezes* 咳嗽和喷嚏 ◇ *She gave a violent sneeze.* 她打了个大喷嚏。

snicker /ˈsnɪkə(r)/ *verb* (*especially NAmE*) (*also especially BrE* **snig·ger**) [I] **~ (at sb/sth)** to laugh in a quiet unpleasant way, especially at sth rude or at sb's problems or mistakes 窃笑；暗笑 SYN **titter** ▶ **snicker** *noun*

snide /snaɪd/ *adj.* (*informal*) criticizing sb/sth in an unkind and indirect way 讽刺的；挖苦的：***snide comments/remarks*** 挖苦的议论 / 话语 ▶ **snide·ly** *adv.*

sniff /snɪf/ *verb, noun*

■ ***verb*** **1** [I] to breathe air in through your nose in a way that makes a sound, especially when you are crying, have a cold, etc. 抽鼻子（尤指哭泣、患感冒等时出声地用鼻子吸气）：*We all had colds and couldn't stop sniffing and sneezing.* 我们都感冒了，一个劲地抽鼻子，打喷嚏。**2** [T, I] to breathe air in through the nose in order to discover or enjoy the smell of sth（吸着气）嗅，闻 SYN **smell**: **~ sth** *sniffing the fresh morning air* 吸着早晨的新鲜空气 ◇ *to sniff glue* 吸胶毒 ◇ **~ (at sth)** *The dog sniffed at my shoes.* 那条狗嗅我的鞋。➲ SEE ALSO GLUE-SNIFFING **3** [T, I] **+ speech | ~ (sth)** to say sth in a complaining or disapproving way 抱怨；不以为然地说：*'It's hardly what I'd call elegant,' she sniffed.* "要我说，这很难称得上雅致。"她不以为然地说。

IDM **not to be ˈsniffed at** (*informal*) good enough to be accepted or considered seriously 值得认真对待；不可轻视：*In those days, $20 was not a sum to be sniffed at.* 那时候，20 美元可不能不当回事。

PHR V **ˌsniff aˈround/ˈround** (*informal*) to try to find out information about sb/sth, especially secret information 探查，打探，访查（秘密信息）：*We don't want journalists sniffing around.* 我们不想要记者四处打探。**ˈsniff around/round sb** [no passive] (*especially BrE*) to try to get sb as a lover, employee, etc. 追求，寻求聘用（某人）：*Hollywood agents have been sniffing around him.* 一些好莱坞的经纪人一直追着想签下他。**ˈsniff at sth** to show no interest in or respect for sth 对…嗤之以鼻（或不屑一顾）**ˌsniff sb/sth↔ˈout 1** to discover or find sb/sth by using your sense of smell 嗅出：*The dogs are trained to sniff out drugs.* 这些狗经过训练来嗅查毒品。**2** (*informal*) to discover or find sb/sth by looking 看出；觉察出：*Journalists are good at sniffing out a scandal.* 记者善于发现丑闻。

■ ***noun*** **1** [C] an act or the sound of sniffing 吸气（声）；抽鼻子（声）；嗅；闻：*She took a deep sniff of the perfume.* 她使劲闻了闻香水。◇ *My mother gave a sniff of disapproval.* 我母亲哼了一声，表示不同意。◇ *His sobs soon turned to sniffs.* 不多时，他的呜咽变成了啜泣。**2** [sing.] **~ of sth** an idea of what sth is like or that sth is going to happen 感觉；察觉：*The sniff of power went to his head.* 权力在望的感觉使他得意忘形。◇ *They make threats but back down at the first sniff of trouble.* 他们起先气势汹汹，但一看情形不妙立刻软了下来。**3** [sing.] **~ of sth** a small chance of sth 微小的可能性：*She didn't get even a sniff at a medal.* 她根本不可能拿到奖牌。

IDM **have a (good) ˌsniff aˈround** to examine a place carefully 仔细检查（某处）

ˈsniffer dog *noun* (*informal, especially BrE*) a dog that is trained to find drugs or EXPLOSIVES by smell（训练来嗅查毒品或炸药的）嗅探犬

snif·fle /ˈsnɪfl/ *verb, noun*

■ ***verb*** [I, T] (**+ speech**) to sniff or keep sniffing, especially because you are crying or have a cold（尤指因哭泣或患感冒）抽鼻子

■ ***noun*** an act or the sound of sniffling 抽鼻子（声）：*After a while, her sniffles died away.* 过了一会儿，她抽鼻子的声音逐渐平息了。

IDM **get, have, etc. the ˈsniffles** (*informal*) to get, have, etc. a slight cold 患轻感冒

S

sniffy /ˈsnɪfi/ *adj.* ~ (**about sth**) (*informal*) not approving of sth/sb because you think they are not good enough for you（对…）轻视，不屑一顾

snif·ter /ˈsnɪftə(r)/ *noun* **1** (*especially NAmE*) a large glass used for drinking BRANDY 白兰地酒杯 **2** (*old-fashioned, BrE, informal*) a small amount of a strong alcoholic drink 少量烈酒

snig·ger /ˈsnɪɡə(r)/ *verb, noun*

■ ***verb*** (*especially BrE*) (*also* **snicker** *NAmE, BrE*) [I, T] ~ (**at sb/sth**) | + **speech** to laugh in a quiet unpleasant way, especially at sth rude or at sb's problems or mistakes 窃笑；暗笑 SYN **titter**：*What are you sniggering at?* 你偷偷笑什么呢？

■ ***noun*** (*especially BrE*) (*also* **snicker** *NAmE, BrE*) a quiet unpleasant laugh, especially at sth rude or at sb's problems or mistakes 窃笑；暗笑 SYN **titter**

snip /snɪp/ *verb, noun*

■ ***verb*** (**-pp-**) [T, I] to cut sth with scissors using short quick strokes （用剪刀快速）剪，剪断，剪开：~ **sth** *Snip a tiny hole in the paper.* 在纸上剪一个小孔。◇ ~ (**at/through sth**) *She snipped at the loose threads hanging down.* 她把垂下来的线头剪掉。

PHR V ˌ**snip sth↔ˈoff** to remove sth by cutting it with scissors in short quick strokes（快速）剪去，剪掉

■ ***noun*** **1** [C] an act of cutting sth with scissors; the sound that this makes 剪；剪东西的咔嚓声：*Make a series of small snips along the edge of the fabric.* 顺着布边细碎地剪。◇ *Snip, snip, went the scissors.* 剪刀咔嚓咔嚓地剪着。**2 snips** [pl.] a tool like large scissors, used for cutting metal（剪金属用的）平头剪 **3 a snip** [sing.] (*BrE, informal*) a thing that is cheap and good value 价廉物美的东西；便宜货 SYN **bargain**：*It's a snip at only £25.* 这个只卖 25 英镑，真是便宜。

snipe /snaɪp/ *verb, noun*

■ ***verb*** **1** [I] ~ (**at sb/sth**) to shoot at sb from a hiding place, usually from a distance 狙击；打冷枪：*Gunmen continued to snipe at people leaving their homes to find food.* 枪手不断伏击外出找寻食物的人。**2** [I] ~ (**at sb/sth**) to criticize sb in an unpleasant way 冷言冷语地指摘；抨击 ▶ **snip·ing** *noun* [U]：*Aid workers remain in the area despite continuous sniping.* 尽管冷枪不断，但救援人员仍然留在这一地区。

■ ***noun*** (*pl.* **snipe**) a bird with a long straight beak that lives on wet ground 沙锥（喙长直，生活在潮湿地区）

sniper /ˈsnaɪpə(r)/ *noun* a person who shoots at sb from a hidden position 狙击手

snip·pet /ˈsnɪpɪt/ *noun* **1** a small piece of information or news 一小条（消息）；一则（新闻）：*Have you got any interesting snippets for me?* 你有没有什么有趣的消息告诉我？◇ *a snippet of information* 一点消息 **2** a short piece of a conversation, piece of music, etc. 一小段（谈话、音乐等）SYN **snatch, extract**

snippy /ˈsnɪpi/ *adj.* (*NAmE, informal*) rude; not showing respect 粗野无礼的；盛气凌人的

snit /snɪt/ *noun*

IDM **be in a ˈsnit** (*NAmE*) to be bad-tempered and refuse to speak to anybody for a time because you are angry about sth 气恼；生闷气

snitch /snɪtʃ/ *verb* [I] ~ (**on sb**) (**to sb**) (*informal, disapproving*) to tell a parent, teacher, etc. about sth wrong that another child has done（向家长、教师等）告发，告密，告状 SYN **sneak**：*Johnnie snitched on me to his mom.* 约翰尼在他妈妈那儿告了我的状。▶ **snitch** *noun*：*You little snitch! I'll never tell you anything again!* 你这家伙就爱告密！以后我什么话都不跟你说了！

snivel /ˈsnɪvl/ *verb* (**-ll-**, *US* **-l-**) [I] to cry and complain in a way that people think is annoying（令人讨厌地）哭诉 SYN **whine**

sniv·el·ling (*especially US* **sniv·el·ing**) /ˈsnɪvlɪŋ/ *adj.* [only before noun] (*disapproving*) tending to cry or complain a lot in a way that annoys people 哭哭啼啼的；爱哭诉的：*a snivelling little brat* 爱哭闹的小淘气

snob /snɒb; *NAmE* snɑːb/ *noun* (*disapproving*) **1** a person who admires people in the higher social classes too much and has no respect for people in the lower social classes 势利小人；谄上欺下的人：*She's such a snob!* 她就是那么一个势利的人！**2** a person who thinks they are much better than other people because they are intelligent or like things that many people do not like 自以为优越的人；自命高雅的人：*an* ***intellectual snob*** 自命知识渊博的人 ◇ *a* ***food/wine, etc. snob*** 自命精于品味美食、葡萄酒等的人 ◇ *There is a* ***snob value*** *in driving the latest model.* 开最新款式的车能满足一种庸俗的虚荣心。

snob·bery /ˈsnɒbəri; *NAmE* ˈsnɑːb-/ *noun* [U] (*disapproving*) the attitudes and behaviour of people who are snobs 势利态度（或行为）；自以为优越的态度（或行为）：*intellectual snobbery* 智力上的自我优越感 ➲ SEE ALSO INVERTED SNOBBERY

snob·bish /ˈsnɒbɪʃ; *NAmE* ˈsnɑːb-/ (*also informal* **snobby** /ˈsnɒbi; *NAmE* ˈsnɑːbi/) *adj.* (*disapproving*) thinking that having a high social class is very important; feeling that you are better than other people because you are more intelligent or like things that many people do not like 势利的；自命不凡的 ▶ **snob·bish·ness** *noun* [U]

snog /snɒɡ; *NAmE* snɑːɡ/ *verb* (**-gg-**) [I, T] (*BrE, informal*) (of two people 两个人) to kiss each other, especially for a long time（尤指长时间地）接吻：*They were snogging on the sofa.* 他们正在沙发上接吻。◇ ~ **sb** *I caught him snogging my friend.* 我撞见他正在吻我的朋友。▶ **snog** *noun* [sing.]

snood /snuːd/ *noun* a net or bag worn over the hair at the back of a woman's head for decoration（女用）束发网

snook /snuːk/ *noun* IDM SEE COCK *v.*

snook·er /ˈsnuːkə(r)/ *noun, verb*

■ ***noun*** **1** [U] a game for two people played on a long table covered with green cloth. Players use CUES (= long sticks) to hit a white ball against other balls (15 red and 6 of other colours) in order to get the coloured balls into pockets at the edge of the table, in a particular set order. 斯诺克（供两人打的落袋台球，打球人用球杆击打白色母球，按一定顺序撞 15 个红球和 6 个彩球入袋）：*to* ***play snooker*** 打斯诺克 ◇ *a* ***game of snooker*** 斯诺克比赛 ◇ *a* ***snooker hall/player/table, etc.*** 斯诺克厅、斯诺克运动员、斯诺克球桌等 ➲ COMPARE BILLIARDS, POOL *n.* (6) **2** [C] a position in snooker in which one player has made it very difficult for the opponent to play a shot within the rules（斯诺克比赛中的）障碍球

■ ***verb*** [usually passive] **1** ~ **sb** (in the game of snooker 斯诺克比赛) to have your opponent in a snooker *n.* (2) 设障碍球 **2** ~ **sb/sth** (*BrE, informal*) to make it impossible for sb to do sth, especially sth they want to do 阻挠；使落空：*Any plans I'd had for the weekend were by now well and truly snookered.* 我原先设想的各项周末计划，这时候就彻底落空了。**3** ~ **sb** (*NAmE, informal*) to cheat or trick sb 欺骗；使上当

snoop /snuːp/ *verb, noun*

■ ***verb*** [I] (*informal, disapproving*) to find out private things about sb, especially by looking secretly around a place 窥探；打探；探听：~ (**around/round sth**) *Someone's been snooping around my apartment.* 有个人一直在我住所周围窥探。◇ ~ (**on sb**) *journalists snooping on politicians* 跟踪政治人物的记者

■ ***noun*** **1** (*also* **snoop·er**) a person who looks around a place secretly to find out private things about sb 窥探者；打探他人私事的人 **2** [sing.] a secret look around a place 窥探：*He had a snoop around her office.* 他在她的办公室周围窥探一番。

snoot /snuːt/ *noun* (*NAmE, informal*) **1** a person's nose（人的）鼻子 **2** (*disapproving*) a person who treats other people as if they are not as good or as important as them 鼻子朝天的人（瞧不起别人）；势利眼

S

snooty /ˈsnuːti/ (*also informal* **snotty**) *adj.* (**snoot·ier, snooti·est**) (*disapproving*) treating people as if they are not as good or as important as you 傲慢的；目中无人的 SYN **snobbish** ▸ **snoot·ily** *adv.* **snooti·ness** *noun* [U]

snooze /snuːz/ *verb* [I] (*informal*) to have a short light sleep, especially during the day and usually not in bed （尤指在白天）小睡，打盹：*My brother was snoozing on the sofa.* 我弟弟正在沙发上打盹。➲ SYNONYMS AT SLEEP ▸ **snooze** *noun* [sing.]: *I often have a snooze after lunch.* 我常在午饭后睡个小觉。

ˈsnooze button *noun* a button on a CLOCK RADIO which you press when you wake up, so that you can sleep a little longer and be woken up again after a short time （收音机闹钟的）小睡催醒按钮

snore /snɔː(r)/ *verb, noun*
■ *verb* [I] to breathe noisily through your nose and mouth while you are asleep 打鼾；打呼噜：*I could hear Paul snoring in the next room.* 我听得见保罗在隔壁房间里打呼噜。▸ **snorer** *noun* **snor·ing** *noun* [U]: *loud snoring* 响亮的鼾声
■ *noun* noisy breathing while you are asleep 呼噜声；鼾声：*She lay awake listening to his snores.* 她没睡着，躺在那儿听他打呼噜。

snor·kel /ˈsnɔːkl; *NAmE* ˈsnɔːrkl/ *noun* a tube that you can breathe air through when you are swimming under the surface of the water （浮潜用的）呼吸管 ➲ VISUAL VOCAB PAGE V44 ▸ **snor·kel** *verb* (-**ll**-, *especially US* -**l**-) [I]

snor·kel·ling (*especially US* **snor·kel·ing**) /ˈsnɔːkəlɪŋ; *NAmE* ˈsnɔːrk-/ *noun* [U] the sport or activity of swimming underwater with a snorkel 带呼吸管潜水；浮潜：*to go snorkelling* 去浮潜 ➲ VISUAL VOCAB PAGE V44

snort /snɔːt; *NAmE* snɔːrt/ *verb, noun*
■ *verb* **1** [I, T] to make a loud sound by breathing air out noisily through your nose, especially to show that you are angry or amused （表示气愤或被逗乐）喷鼻息，哼：*The horse snorted and tossed its head.* 马打了个响鼻儿，晃晃脑袋。◇ ~ **with sth** *to snort with laughter* 扑哧一声笑了 ◇ ~ **in sth** *She snorted in disgust.* 她厌恶地哼了一声。◇ + **speech** *'You!' he snorted contemptuously.* "你！"他轻蔑地哼了一声。**2** [T] ~ **sth** to take drugs by breathing them in through the nose 用鼻子吸（毒品）：*to snort cocaine* 吸可卡因
■ *noun* **1** a loud sound that you make by breathing air out noisily through your nose, especially to show that you are angry or amused （尤指表示气愤或被逗乐的）喷鼻息，哼：*to give a snort* 哼了一声 ◇ *a snort of disgust* 厌恶的哼声 ◇ *I could hear the snort and stamp of a horse.* 我能听见马打响鼻儿、跺蹄子的声音。**2** a small amount of a drug that is breathed in through the nose; an act of taking a drug in this way （用鼻子吸入的）毒品；用鼻子吸毒：*to take a snort of cocaine* 吸一下可卡因

snot /snɒt; *NAmE* snɑːt/ *noun* [U] (*informal*) a word that some people find offensive, used to describe the liquid substance (= MUCUS) that is produced in the nose 鼻涕（有人认为是粗俗用语）

snotty /ˈsnɒti; *NAmE* ˈsnɑːti/ *adj.* (**snot·tier, snot·ti·est**) (*also* ˌ**snotty-ˈnosed**) (*informal*) **1** = SNOOTY **2** full of or covered in snot 流鼻涕的；满是鼻涕的：*a snotty nose* 流着鼻涕的鼻子 ◇ *snotty kids* 淌着鼻涕的小孩

snout /snaʊt/ *noun* **1** the long nose and area around the mouth of some types of animal, such as a pig （猪等动物的）口鼻部，吻 ➲ VISUAL VOCAB PAGE V12 ➲ COMPARE MUZZLE *n.* (1) **2** (*informal, humorous*) a person's nose （人的）鼻子 **3** a part of sth that sticks out at the front 吻状突出物：*the snout of a pistol* 手枪枪管

snow 🔑 /snəʊ; *NAmE* snoʊ/ *noun, verb*
■ *noun* **1** 🔑 [U] small soft white pieces (called FLAKES) of frozen water that fall from the sky in cold weather; this substance when it is lying on the ground 雪；雪花；积雪：*Snow was falling heavily.* 正下着大雪。◇ *We had snow in May this year.* 今年五月我们这儿下了雪。◇ *The snow was beginning to melt.* 积雪开始融化了。◇ *Children were playing in the snow.* 孩子们正在雪地里玩。◇ *20 cm of snow were expected today.* 原来预计今天下 20 厘米厚的雪。◇ *The snow didn't settle* (= stay on the ground). 雪没积起来。◇ *Her skin was* **as white as snow**. 她的皮肤雪白。➲ COLLOCATIONS AT WEATHER ➲ VISUAL VOCAB PAGE V5

> **WORDFINDER** 联想词： avalanche, blizzard, drift, flurry, hail, icicle, sleet, slush, thaw

2 snows [pl.] (*literary*) an amount of snow that falls in one particular place or at one particular time （某地或某时的）降雪量；一场雪：*the first snows of winter* 冬天的头几场雪 ◇ *the snows of Kilimanjaro* 乞力马扎罗山的积雪

IDM **as clean, pure, etc. as the driven ˈsnow** extremely clean, pure, etc. 冰清玉洁；纯洁无瑕
■ *verb* **1** 🔑 [I] when **it snows**, snow falls from the sky 下雪：*It's been snowing heavily all day.* 大雪下了一整天。**2** [T] ~ **sb** (*NAmE, informal*) to impress sb a lot by the things you say, especially if these are not true or not sincere （用花言巧语）蒙，唬：*He really snowed me with all his talk of buying a Porsche.* 他嘴上老说要买一辆保时捷，还真把我唬住了。

IDM **be snowed ˈin/ˈup** to be unable to leave a place because of heavy snow 被雪困住 **be snowed ˈunder (with sth)** to have more things, especially work, than you feel able to deal with （事情太多而）应接不暇，忙得不可开交：*I'd love to come but I'm completely snowed under at the moment.* 我很想来，但眼下实在是忙得没工夫。 **be snowed ˈup** (especially of a road 尤指道路) to be blocked with snow 被雪封住

snow·ball /ˈsnəʊbɔːl; *NAmE* ˈsnoʊ-/ *noun, verb*
■ *noun* **1** [C] a ball that you make out of snow to throw at sb/sth in a game 雪球：*a snowball fight* 雪仗 **2** [sing.] (often used as an adjective 常用作形容词) a situation that develops more and more quickly as it continues 滚雪球般发展的情形：*All this publicity has had a* **snowball effect** *on the sales of their latest album.* 所有这些宣传对他们最新唱片的销售产生了一种滚雪球效应。**3** [C] a drink that is a mixture of LEMONADE and a LIQUEUR (= a strong sweet alcoholic drink) made with eggs 雪球鸡尾酒（含白兰地蛋酒和柠檬汽水）

IDM **not have a ˌsnowball's chance in ˈhell** (*informal*) to have no chance at all 根本不可能；毫无机会
■ *verb* [I] if a problem, a plan, an activity, etc. **snowballs**, it quickly becomes much bigger, more serious, more important, etc. 滚雪球般迅速增大（或趋于严重、变得重要等）

the ˈSnow Belt *noun* [sing.] (*informal*) the northern and north-eastern states of the US where the winters are very cold 多雪地带（美国北部和东北部的州）

snow·bird /ˈsnəʊbɜːd; *NAmE* ˈsnoʊbɜːrd/ *noun* (*NAmE, informal*) a person who spends the winter in a warmer climate, especially an old person from the north of the US, or from Canada, who spends the winter in the south 到温暖地带过冬的人；（尤指美国北方或加拿大到南方过冬的）候鸟老人

ˈsnow-blind *adj.* unable to see because of the light reflected from a large area of snow 雪盲的 ▸ **ˈsnow-blindness** *noun* [U]

snow·blow·er /ˈsnəʊbləʊə(r); *NAmE* ˈsnoʊbloʊər/ *noun* a machine that removes snow from roads or paths by blowing it to one side 吹雪机

snow·board /ˈsnəʊbɔːd; *NAmE* ˈsnoʊbɔːrd/ *noun* a long wide board that a person stands on to move over snow in the sport of snowboarding 滑雪板 ➲ VISUAL VOCAB PAGE V53

snow·board·ing /ˈsnəʊbɔːdɪŋ; *NAmE* ˈsnoʊbɔːrd-/ *noun* [U] the sport of moving over snow on a snowboard 单板滑雪；滑雪板运动：*to go snowboarding* 进行滑雪板运动 ◇ *Snowboarding is now an Olympic sport.* 单板滑雪现在是奥运会比赛项目。▸ **snow·board·er** *noun* ➲ VISUAL VOCAB PAGE V53

S

snow·bound /ˈsnəʊbaʊnd; *NAmE* ˈsnoʊ-/ *adj.* **1** (of a person or vehicle 人或车辆) trapped in a particular place and unable to move because a lot of snow has fallen 被雪困住的 **2** (of a road or building 道路或建筑物) that you cannot use or reach because a lot of snow has fallen 被雪封住的

ˈsnow cannon (*BrE*) (*also* **ˈsnow gun** *US, BrE*) *noun* a machine which makes artificial snow and blows it onto SKI slopes 造雪机，喷雪炮（给滑雪道人工喷雪）

ˈsnow-capped *adj.* (*literary*) (of mountains and hills 山) covered with snow on top 顶部被雪覆盖的

ˈsnow chains *noun* [pl.] chains that are put on the wheels of a car so that it can drive over snow 雪地防滑链（汽车在雪地上行驶时用）

snow·clone /ˈsnəʊkləʊn; *NAmE* ˈsnoʊkloʊn/ *noun* a well-known phrase such as a quotation or proverb that has been changed in different ways by many speakers and/or writers, for example 'When in Buenos Aires' and 'When in Copenhagen', adapted from the proverb 'When in Rome (do as the Romans do).' 雪克隆，名言名句改编（为人熟知的名言或谚语等通过替换原文的某些词语而创造出新用法，如 When in Rome (do as the Romans do) 改成 When in Buenos Aires 或 When in Copenhagen 等）

ˈsnow-covered (*also literary* **ˈsnow-clad**) *adj.* [usually before noun] covered with snow 被雪覆盖的：*snow-covered fields* 白雪覆盖的田野

snow·drift /ˈsnəʊdrɪft; *NAmE* ˈsnoʊ-/ *noun* a deep pile of snow that has been blown together by the wind（风吹成的）雪堆

snow·drop /ˈsnəʊdrɒp; *NAmE* ˈsnoʊdrɑːp/ *noun* a small white flower that appears in early spring 雪花莲（早春开白花）

snow·fall /ˈsnəʊfɔːl; *NAmE* ˈsnoʊ-/ *noun* [C, U] an occasion when snow falls; the amount of snow that falls in a particular place in a period of time 下雪；降雪（量）：*a **heavy/light snowfall*** 大雪；小雪 ◇ *an area of low snowfall* 降雪量少的地区 ◇ *What is the average annual snowfall for this state?* 这个国家的年平均降雪量是多少？

snow·field /ˈsnəʊfiːld; *NAmE* ˈsnoʊ-/ *noun* a large area that is always covered with snow, for example in the mountains 雪原（终年积雪的地区）

snow·flake /ˈsnəʊfleɪk; *NAmE* ˈsnoʊ-/ *noun* a small soft piece of frozen water that falls from the sky as snow 雪花；雪片

ˈsnow gun (*BrE also* **ˈsnow cannon**) *noun* a machine which makes artificial snow and blows it onto SKI slopes 造雪机，喷雪炮（给滑雪道人工喷雪）

ˈsnow job *noun* (*NAmE, informal*) an attempt to trick sb or to persuade them to support sth by telling them things that are not true, or by praising them too much 花言巧语的劝说；诱骗

the snow·line /ˈsnəʊlaɪn; *NAmE* ˈsnoʊ-/ *noun* [sing.] the level on mountains above which snow never melts completely 雪线 ➲ VISUAL VOCAB PAGE V5

snow·man /ˈsnəʊmæn; *NAmE* ˈsnoʊ-/ *noun* (*pl.* **-men** /-men/) a figure like a man that people, especially children, make out of snow for fun（用雪堆成的）雪人

snow·mobile /ˈsnəʊməbiːl; *NAmE* ˈsnoʊmoʊ-/ (*also* **ski-mobile**) *noun* a vehicle that can move over snow and ice easily 机动雪橇；雪地机动车 ➲ PICTURE AT SLEDGE

ˈsnow pea (*NAmE*) (*BrE* **mange·tout**) *noun* [usually pl.] a type of very small PEA that grows in long, flat green PODS that are cooked and eaten whole 荷兰豆

snow·plough (*NAmE* **snow·plow**) /ˈsnəʊplaʊ; *NAmE* ˈsnoʊ-/ *noun, verb*

- *noun* a vehicle or machine for cleaning snow from roads or railways 雪犁，扫雪机（用以清除公路或铁路上的积雪）
- *verb* [I] to bring the two points of your SKIS together, in order to go slower or stop（滑雪时）犁式制动，犁式滑降

snow·shoe /ˈsnəʊʃuː; *NAmE* ˈsnoʊ-/ *noun* one of a pair of flat frames that you attach to the bottom of your shoes so that you can walk on deep snow without sinking in 雪鞋（平面框式结构，可固定在鞋底，在深雪中行走时穿）

snow·slide /ˈsnəʊslaɪd; *NAmE* ˈsnoʊ-/ *noun* (*NAmE*) = AVALANCHE

snow·storm /ˈsnəʊstɔːm; *NAmE* ˈsnoʊstɔːrm/ *noun* a very heavy fall of snow, usually with a strong wind 雪暴；暴风雪

ˌsnow-ˈwhite *adj.* pure white in colour 雪白的：*snow-white sheets* 雪白的床单 ➲ MORE LIKE THIS 15, page R26

snowy /ˈsnəʊi; *NAmE* ˈsnoʊi/ *adj.* (**snow·ier, snowi·est**) **1** [usually before noun] covered with snow 被雪覆盖的：*snowy fields* 白雪覆盖的田野 **2** (of a period of time 一段时间) when a lot of snow falls 下雪多的：*a snowy weekend* 大雪纷飞的周末 **3** (*literary*) very white, like new snow 雪白的：*snowy hair* 白发

SNP /ˌes en ˈpiː/ *abbr.* SCOTTISH NATIONAL PARTY 苏格兰民族党

Snr *abbr.* = SR

snub /snʌb/ *verb, noun*

- *verb* (**-bb-**) **1** ~ **sb** to insult sb, especially by ignoring them when you meet 冷落；怠慢 SYN **cold-shoulder**: *I tried to be friendly, but she snubbed me completely.* 我尽量和气，但她根本不答理我。**2** ~ **sth** to refuse to attend or accept sth, for example as a protest 拒不出席；拒不接受；抵制 SYN **boycott**: *All the country's leading players snubbed the tournament.* 全国的顶尖运动员都抵制那次比赛。
- *noun* ~ (**to sb**) an action or a comment that is deliberately rude in order to show sb that you do not like or respect them 冷落；怠慢的言辞（或行为）SYN **insult**: *Her refusal to attend the dinner is being seen as a deliberate snub to the President.* 在人们看来，她拒不出席宴会是有意让总统难堪。
- *adj.* [only before noun] (of a nose 鼻子) short, flat and turned up at the end 短平而上翘的 ▸ **ˌsnub-ˈnosed** *adj.*: *a snub-nosed child* 鼻子短平且上翘的孩子 ◇ *a snub-nosed revolver* (= with a short BARREL) 短管左轮手枪

snuck PAST TENSE, PAST PART. OF SNEAK

snuff /snʌf/ *verb, noun*

- *verb* **1** [T] ~ **sth** (**out**) to stop a small flame from burning, especially by pressing it between your fingers or covering it with sth 掐灭，闷熄，熄灭（小火苗）SYN **extinguish** **2** [I, T] ~ (**sth**) (of an animal 动物) to smell sth by breathing in noisily through the nose 出声地嗅：*The dogs were snuffing gently at my feet.* 几只狗轻轻地嗅着我的脚。

IDM **ˈsnuff it** (*BrE, slang, humorous*) to die 死

PHR V **ˌsnuff sth↔ˈout** to stop or destroy sth completely 扼杀；消灭：*An innocent child's life has been snuffed out by this senseless shooting.* 这胡乱一枪就要了一个无辜孩子的命。

- *noun* [U] TOBACCO in the form of a powder that people take by breathing it into their noses 鼻烟

IDM **ˌup to ˈsnuff** (*NAmE*) (*BrE* **ˌup to the ˈmark**) as good as it/they should be 达到要求；符合标准 SYN **up to scratch**

snuff·box /ˈsnʌfbɒks; *NAmE* -bɑːks/ *noun* a small, usually decorated, box for holding snuff 鼻烟盒

snuf·fle /ˈsnʌfl/ *verb, noun*

- *verb* **1** [I, T] (+ **speech**) to breathe noisily because you have a cold or you are crying（因感冒或哭泣）鼻子呼哧出声，抽鼻子 SYN **sniff**: *I could hear the child snuffling in her sleep.* 我听见这女孩睡着了还在抽鼻子。**2** [I] ~ (**about/around**) if an animal **snuffles**, it breathes noisily through its nose, especially while it is smelling sth 哧哧地嗅
- *noun* (*also less frequent* **snuf·fling**) an act or the sound of snuffling 抽鼻子（声）；嗅；嗅东西时发出的呼哧声：*The*

S

silence was broken only by the snuffles of the dogs. 除了不时听见狗喘气的声音，四下里一片寂静。◇ His breath came in snuffles. 他呼哧呼哧地呼吸着。

IDM **get, have, etc. the 'snuffles** (*informal*) to get/have a cold 患感冒

'snuff movie *noun* a film/movie that shows a real murder, intended as entertainment 谋杀实况影片

snug /snʌg/ *adj., noun*

■ *adj.* **1** warm, comfortable and protected, especially from the cold 温暖舒适的；保暖的 SYN **cosy**: *a snug little house* 温暖舒适的小房子 ◇ *I spent the afternoon snug and warm in bed.* 我在床上躺了一下午，又暖和又舒服。**2** fitting sb/sth closely 贴身的；紧身的；严密的；严实的: *The elastic at the waist gives a nice snug fit.* 腰间的松紧带使衣服正好紧紧贴在身上。 ▶ **snug·ly** *adv.*: *I left the children tucked up snugly in bed.* 我给孩子们掖好被子，让他们暖暖乎乎地入睡。◇ *The lid should fit snugly.* 盖子要盖紧。 **snug·ness** *noun* [U]

■ *noun* (*BrE*) a small comfortable room in a pub, with seats for only a few people（酒吧里的）包间，雅座

snug·gle /'snʌgl/ *verb* [I, T] to get into, or to put sb/sth into, a warm comfortable position, especially close to sb（使）依偎，紧贴，蜷伏: **+ adv./prep.** *The child* ***snuggled up*** *to her mother.* 孩子依偎着她的母亲。◇ *He* ***snuggled down*** *under the bedclothes.* 他躺下以后盖上被子，很舒服。◇ *She snuggled closer.* 她把身子蜷得更紧些。◇ **~ sth + adv./prep.** *He snuggled his head onto her shoulder.* 他把头倚在她肩上。

So. *abbr.* (*NAmE*) south; southern 南方（的）；南部（的）

so /səʊ; *NAmE* soʊ/ *adv., conj., noun*

■ *adv.* **1** to such a great degree（表示程度）这么，这样，那么，那样，如此: *Don't look so angry.* 别那样怒气冲冲的。◇ *There's no need to worry so.* 没必要这样着急。◇ **~... (that)...** *She spoke so quietly (that) I could hardly hear her.* 她说话轻得我几乎听不见。◇ **~... as to do sth** *I'm not so stupid as to believe that.* 我还不至于傻得连那样的话都相信。◇ (*formal, especially BrE*) ***Would you be so kind as to*** *lock the door when you leave?* 请您离开时把门锁上好吗？**2** very; extremely 很；极: *I'm so glad to see you.* 见到你真高兴。◇ *We have so much to do.* 我们有很多事要做。◇ *Their attitude is* ***so very*** *English.* 他们的态度是十足的英国人的态度。◇ *The article was* ***just so much*** (= nothing but) *nonsense.* 那篇文章纯粹是胡说八道。◇ (*BrE*) *He sat there* ***ever so*** *quietly.* 他静悄悄地坐在那儿。◇ (*BrE*) *I do love it so.* 我实在是太喜欢它了。**3** **not ~... (as...)** (used in comparisons 用于比较) not to the same degree 不如…（这么…）；不像…（那样…）: *I haven't enjoyed myself so much for a long time.* 我好长时间没有这么快活了。◇ *It wasn't so good as last time.* 这次不如上次好。◇ *It's not so easy as you'd think.* 不像你想的那么容易。◇ *He was not so quick a learner as his brother.* 他学东西不像他哥哥那么快。◇ *It's* ***not so much*** *a hobby* ***as*** *a career* (= more like a career than a hobby). 这与其说是爱好，不如说是职业。◇ (*disapproving*) *Off she went* ***without so much as*** (= without even) *a 'goodbye'.* 她连声"再见"都没说就走了。**4** used to show the size, amount or number of sth（表示大小或数量）这么，那么: *The fish was about so big* (= said when using your hands to show the size). 那条鱼差不多有这么长。◇ *There are* ***only so many*** (= only a limited number of) *hours in a day.* 一天不过这么几个小时。**5** used to refer back to sth that has already been mentioned（指刚说过的事物）这样，如此: *'Is he coming?' 'I hope so.'* "他来吗？""我希望他来。"◇ *'Did they mind?' '****I don't think so****.'* "他们有没有介意？""我想没有。"◇ *If she notices, she never* ***says so****.* 就算她留意到，她也从来不说。◇ *I might be away next week.* ***If so****, I won't be able to see you.* 下星期我可能外出。要是那样，我就见不到你了。◇ *We are very busy—****so much so that*** *we won't be able to take time off this year.* 我们很忙，忙得今年都没时间休假了。◇ *Programs are expensive, and* ***even more so*** *if you have to keep altering them.* 买软件很贵，要是老得更换，那就更贵了。◇ *I hear that you're a writer—****is that so*** (= is that true)? 听说你是作家，是吗？◇ *He thinks I dislike him but that just isn't so.* 他以为我讨厌他，其实不是那么回事。◇ *George is going to help me, or* ***so he says*** (= that is what he says). 乔治会帮我，他是这么说的。◇ *They asked me to call them and I* ***did so*** (= I called). 他们要我叫他们，于是我就叫了。**6** also 也: *Times have changed and* ***so have I****.* 时代变了，我也变了。◇ *'I prefer the first version.' '****So do we****.'* "我喜欢第一稿。""我们也是。" HELP You cannot use **so** with negative verbs. Use **neither** or **either**. * so 不与动词的否定式连用。否定中用 neither 或 either: *'I'm not hungry.' '****Neither am I/I'm not*** *very hungry* ***either****.'* "我不饿。""我也不太饿。" **7** used to agree that sth is true, especially when you are surprised（尤指感到惊讶时表示同意）的确如此: *'You were there, too.' '****So I was****—I'd forgotten.'* "当时你也在那儿。""是啊，我给忘了。"◇ *'There's another one.' '****So there is****.'* "还有一个。""可不是吗。" **8** (*informal*) used, often with a negative, before adjectives and noun phrases to emphasize sth that you are saying（常与否定词连用，置于形容词和名词短语前以加强语气）: *He is* ***so not*** *the right person for you.* 他这个人绝对不适合你。◇ *That is* ***so not*** *cool.* 那实在不怎么样。**9** (*informal*) used, especially by children, to say that what sb says is not the case and the opposite is true（儿童常用以反驳对方）偏偏，就: *'You're not telling the truth, are you?' 'I am, so!'* "你说的不是实话，对不对？""就是实话，就是！" **10** used when you are showing sb how to do sth or telling them how sth happened（演示或描述事由）这样: *Stand with your arms out, so.* 两臂伸开站着，像这样。◇ (*literary*) ***So it was that*** *he finally returned home.* 就这样，他终于回到了家。

IDM **and 'so forth | and 'so on (and 'so forth)** used at the end of a list to show that it continues in the same way …等等；诸如此类: *We discussed everything—when to go, what to see and so on.* 我们什么都商量过了，什么时候走、看什么等等。 **... or so** used after a number, an amount, etc. to show that it is not exact …左右；…上下: *There were twenty or so* (= about twenty) *people there.* 那儿有差不多二十个人。◇ *We stayed for an hour or so.* 我们待了一个小时左右。**so as to do sth** with the intention of doing sth 为了做某事；以便做某事: *We went early so as to get good seats.* 为了占到好座位，我们早早就去了。**so 'be it** (*formal*) used to show that you accept sth and will not try to change it or cannot change it（表示完全接受）就那样好了: *If he doesn't want to be involved, then so be it.* 要是他不想参与，那就随他的便好了。**,so much for 'sth 1** used to show that you have finished talking about sth（表示就某事讲完了）关于…就讲这么多，…到此为止: *So much for the situation in Germany. Now we turn our attention to France.* 德国的形势就讲到这里。现在我们来看看法国的情况。**2** (*informal*) used to suggest that sth has not been successful or useful（表示行不通或没用）作罢好了，快别提了: *So much for that idea!* 快别提那个主意了！**so... that** (*formal*) in such a way that 这样…为的是；如此…以至: *The programme has been so organized that none of the talks overlap.* 日程做了精心安排，以使每一讲都没有重复内容。**(all) the 'more so because...** used to give an important extra reason why sth is true（表示另外的重要原因）尤其因为: *His achievement is remarkable; all the more so because he had no help at all.* 他的成就非同一般，而由于他没有得到过任何帮助，更显不凡。

■ *conj.* **1** used to show the reason for sth（表示因果关系）因此，所以: *It was still painful so I went to see a doctor.* 那地方还疼，因此我去看了医生。 **2** **~ (that...)** used to show the result of sth（引出结果）因此，所以: *Nothing more was heard from him so that we began to wonder if he was dead.* 此后再没收到他的消息，于是我们开始怀疑他是不是死了。**3** **~ (that...)** used to show the purpose of sth（表示目的）为了，以便: *But I gave you a map so you wouldn't get lost!* 但我怕你迷路，给过你一张地图！◇ *She worked hard so that everything would be ready in time.* 她努力工作，为的是及时做好各项准备。**4** used to introduce the next part of a story（引出下文）: *So after shouting and screaming for an hour she walked out in tears.* 就这样，又嚷又叫了一个小时后，她流着泪走了出来。**5** (*informal*) used to show that you think sth is not important, especially after sb has criticized you for it（认为某事无关紧要，尤用于反驳他人的指责时）: *So I*

S

had a couple of drinks on the way home. What's wrong with that? 我不过是在回家的路上喝了两杯。这怎么啦？◇ 'You've been smoking again.' 'So?' "你近来又抽烟了。" "抽又怎么啦？" **6** (*informal*) used to introduce a comment or a question（引出评论或问题）：*So, let's see. What do we need to take?* 那么，大家想想，我们需要带什么？◇ *So, what have you been doing today?* 那你今天都干什么了？ **7** (*informal*) used when you are making a final statement（引出结束语）：*So, that's it for today.* 好，今天就讲到这里。**8** (*informal*) used in questions to refer to sth that has just been said（在问句中代指刚谈论的事）：*So there's nothing we can do about it?* 这么说，我们一点办法都没有了？◇ *'I've just got back from a trip to Rome.' 'So, how was it?'* "我去了一趟罗马，刚回来。" "是吗？怎么样？" **9** used when stating that two events, situations, etc. are similar（指出两种情况等相类似）：***Just as** large companies are having to cut back, **so** small businesses are being forced to close.* 大公司不得不紧缩，小企业则被迫关闭。

IDM **so 'what?** (*informal*) used to show that you think sth is not important, especially after sb has criticized you for it（认为某事无关紧要，尤用于反驳他人的指责时）：*'He's fifteen years younger than you!' 'So what?'* "他比你小十五岁呢！" "那又怎么啦？" ◇ *So what if nobody else agrees with me?* 就算没有一个人赞成我的意见，那又怎么样？

■ ***noun*** = SOH

soak /səʊk; *NAmE* soʊk/ *verb, noun*

■ ***verb*** **1** [T, I] to put sth in liquid for a time so that it becomes completely wet; to become completely wet in this way 浸泡；浸湿；浸透；湿透：**~ sth (in sth)** *I usually soak the beans overnight.* 我通常把豆子泡一夜。◇ *If you soak the tablecloth before you wash it, the stains should come out.* 先把桌布浸一浸再洗，污迹就能去掉。◇ **~ (in sth)** *Leave the apricots **to soak** for 20 minutes.* 把杏子浸泡 20 分钟。◇ *I'm going to go and soak in the bath.* 我要去泡个澡。**2** [T] **~ sb/sth** to make sb/sth completely wet 使湿透；把…浸湿 SYN **drench**: *A sudden shower of rain soaked the spectators.* 突如其来的一阵雨把观众淋了个透。**3** [T] **~ sb** (*informal*) to obtain a lot of money from sb by making them pay very high taxes or prices 向（某人）敲竹杠；宰（某人）；向（某人）征收重税：*He was accused of soaking his clients.* 他被指控向客户敲竹杠。

PHR V **'soak into/through sth | soak 'in** (of a liquid 液体) to enter or pass through sth 渗入；渗透：*Blood had soaked through the bandage.* 血透过绷带渗了出来。**,soak sth↔'off/'out** to remove sth by leaving it in water 把…泡掉 **,soak sth↔'up 1** to take in or absorb liquid 吸收，吸掉（液体）：*Use a cloth to soak up some of the excess water.* 用布把多余的水吸去。**2** to absorb sth into your senses, your body or your mind（通过感官、身心）吸取，摄取：*We were just sitting soaking up the atmosphere.* 我们就坐在那儿感受着那里的气氛。

■ ***noun*** (*also* **soak·ing**) [sing.] **1** an act of leaving sth in a liquid for a period of time; an act of making sb/sth wet 浸泡；浸渍；湿透：*Give the shirt a good soak before you wash it.* 把衬衫好好泡一泡再洗。**2** (*informal*) a period of time spent in a bath 洗澡；泡澡

soaked /səʊkt; *NAmE* soʊkt/ *adj.* **1** [not usually before noun] **~ (with sth)** very wet 湿透 SYN **drench**: *He woke up soaked with sweat.* 他醒了，浑身大汗淋漓。◇ *You're **soaked through**!* (= completely wet) 你都湿透了！◇ *They were **soaked to the skin**.* 他们浑身湿透。◇ *You'll **get soaked** if you go out in this rain.* 冒这样的雨出去，你会成落汤鸡的。◇ *Your clothes are soaked!* 你的衣服全都湿透了！ ➲ SYNONYMS AT WET **2 -soaked** used with nouns to form adjectives describing sth that is made completely wet with the thing mentioned（和名词组成形容词）浸透了…的，被…浸湿的：*a blood-soaked cloth* 一块浸透了鲜血的布 ◇ *rain-soaked clothing* 雨水淋透的衣服

soak·ing /'səʊkɪŋ; *NAmE* 'soʊ-/ (*also* **,soaking 'wet**) *adj.* completely wet 湿透的；湿淋淋的 SYN **sopping**: *That coat is soaking—take it off.* 那件上衣都湿透了，脱下来吧。◇ *We arrived home soaking wet.* 我们回到家时，浑身湿淋淋的。

so-and-so /'səʊ ən səʊ; *NAmE* 'soʊ ən soʊ/ *noun* (*pl.* **so-and-sos**) (*informal*) **1** [usually sing.] used to refer to a person, thing, etc. when you do not know their name or when you are talking in a general way（指叫不上名字的人、物，或泛指）某某人（或事物）：*What would you say to Mrs So-and-so who has called to complain about a noisy neighbour?* 要是哪位太太嫌邻居太吵闹，打电话投诉，你怎么跟她说？**2** an annoying or unpleasant person. People sometimes say **so-and-so** to avoid using an offensive word. 恼人的家伙；讨厌鬼：*He's an ungrateful so-and-so.* 他是个忘恩负义的家伙。

soap /səʊp; *NAmE* soʊp/ *noun, verb*

■ ***noun*** **1** [U, C] a substance that you use with water for washing your body 肥皂：*soap and water* 肥皂和水 ◇ ***a bar/piece of soap*** 一块肥皂 ◇ *soap bubbles* 肥皂泡 **2** [C] (*informal*) = SOAP OPERA: *soaps on TV* 电视上播出的肥皂剧 ◇ *She's a US soap star.* 她是美国肥皂剧明星。

■ ***verb*** **~ yourself/sb/sth** to rub yourself/sb/sth with soap 抹肥皂；用肥皂擦洗 ➲ SEE ALSO SOFT-SOAP

soap·box /'səʊpbɒks; *NAmE* 'soʊpbɑːks/ *noun* a small temporary platform that sb stands on to make a speech in a public place, usually outdoors（多指户外的）临时演讲台

IDM **get/be on your 'soapbox** (*informal*) to express the strong opinions that you have about a particular subject 发表激烈的意见

'soap flakes *noun* [pl.] very small thin pieces of soap that are sold in boxes, used for washing clothes by hand 肥皂片（手洗衣物用）

'soap opera (*also informal* **soap**) *noun* [C, U] a story about the lives and problems of a group of people which is broadcast every day or several times a week on television or radio 肥皂剧 ➲ COLLOCATIONS AT TELEVISION

'soap powder *noun* [U, C] (*BrE*) a powder made from soap and other substances that you use for washing your clothes, especially in a machine 洗衣粉；肥皂粉

soap·stone /'səʊpstəʊn; *NAmE* 'soʊpstoʊn/ *noun* [U] a type of soft stone that feels like soap, used in making decorative objects 皂石（质软，用作装饰材料）

soap·suds /'səʊpsʌdz; *NAmE* 'soʊp-/ *noun* [pl.] = SUDS

soapy /'səʊpi; *NAmE* 'soʊpi/ *adj.* [usually before noun] **1** full of soap; covered with soap 满是肥皂的；涂满肥皂的 **2** tasting or feeling like soap 有肥皂味的；摸着像肥皂的

soar /sɔː(r)/ *verb* **1** [I] if the value, amount or level of sth **soars**, it rises very quickly 急升；猛增 SYN **rocket**: ***soaring costs/prices/temperatures*** 猛增的成本；飞涨的物价；骤升的温度 ◇ *Unemployment has soared to 18%.* 失业率猛升到了 18%。**2** [I] **~ (up) (into sth)** to rise quickly and smoothly up into the air 升空；升腾：*The rocket soared (up) into the air.* 火箭升空。◇ (*figurative*) *Her spirits soared* (= she became very happy and excited). 她情绪高涨。**3** [I] to fly very high in the air or remain high in the air 高飞；翱翔：*an eagle soaring high above the cliffs* 在山崖上空高高翱翔的鹰 **4** [I] to be very high or tall 高耸；耸立：*soaring mountains* 屹立的群山 ◇ *The building soared above us.* 在我们眼前，那座大楼巍然高耸。**5** [I] when music **soars**, it becomes higher or louder（音乐）升高，增强：*soaring strings* 激昂的弦乐

soar·away /'sɔːrəweɪ/ *adj.* [only before noun] (*BrE*) (especially of success 尤指成功) very great; growing very quickly 巨大的；迅速获得的

SOB /,es əʊ 'biː; *NAmE* ,es oʊ 'biː/ *noun* (*slang, especially NAmE*) = SON OF A BITCH

sob /sɒb; *NAmE* sɑːb/ *verb, noun*

■ ***verb*** **(-bb-) 1** [I] to cry noisily, taking sudden, sharp breaths 抽噎；啜泣；呜咽：*I heard a child sobbing loudly.* 我听见有个孩子在呜呜地哭。◇ *He started to sob uncontrollably.* 他不由自主地抽噎起来。**2** [T] to say sth while you are crying 哭诉；泣诉；抽噎着说：**+ speech** *'I hate him,' she sobbed.* "我恨他。" 她抽噎着说。◇ **~ sth (out)** *He sobbed out his troubles.* 他哭着述说了自己的烦恼。➲ MORE LIKE THIS 36, page R29

S

IDM **sob your 'heart out** to cry noisily for a long time because you are very sad 悲切地哭泣；很伤心地哭泣

■ ***noun*** an act or the sound of sobbing 抽噎（声）；啜泣（声）；呜咽（声）：*He gave a deep sob.* 他发出一声低沉的抽噎声。◇ *Her body was racked* (= shaken) *with sobs.* 她哭得身子一抽一抽的。

sober /ˈsəʊbə(r); NAmE ˈsoʊ-/ *adj., verb*

■ ***adj.*** **1** [not usually before noun] not drunk (= not affected by alcohol) 未醉：*I promised him that I'd stay sober tonight.* 我答应过他，今晚我不会喝醉。◇ *He was **as sober as a judge*** (= completely sober). 他一点没醉。 **2** (of people and their behaviour 人及其行为) serious and sensible 持重的；冷静的：*a sober assessment of the situation* 对形势的冷静估计 ◇ *He is honest, sober and hard-working.* 他诚实、稳重、勤奋。◇ ***On sober reflection*** (= after some serious thought), *I don't think I really need a car after all.* 冷静地想了想以后，我觉得我其实并不需要车。 **3** (of colours or clothes 颜色或服装) plain and not bright 素净的；淡素的：*a sober grey suit* 一套素净的灰西装 ▶ **sober·ly** *adv.* IDM SEE STONE COLD

■ ***verb*** [T, I] ~ (**sb**) to make sb behave or think in a more serious and sensible way; to become more serious and sensible（使）变得持重，变得冷静：*The bad news sobered us for a while.* 坏消息使我们冷静了一会儿。◇ *He suddenly sobered.* 他突然严肃起来。

PHR V **ˌsober ˈup | ˌsober sb ˈup** to become or to make sb no longer drunk（使）醒酒：*Stay here with us until you've sobered up.* 你就待在我们这儿，等酒醒了再走。

sober·ing /ˈsəʊbərɪŋ; NAmE ˈsoʊ-/ *adj.* making you feel serious and think carefully 令人警醒的；使人冷静的：*a **sobering effect/experience/thought, etc.*** 令人警醒的效果、经历、思想等 ◇ ***It is sobering** to realize that this is not a new problem.* 意识到这并不是新问题，就会使人冷静下来。

so·bri·ety /səˈbraɪəti/ *noun* [U] (*formal*) **1** the state of being sober (= not being drunk) 未醉 OPP **insobriety** **2** the fact of being sensible and serious 持重；冷静

so·bri·quet /ˈsəʊbrɪkeɪ; NAmE ˈsoʊ-/ (*also* **sou·bri·quet**) *noun* (*formal*) an informal name or title that you give sb/sth 绰号；外号 SYN **nickname**

ˈsob story *noun* (*informal, disapproving*) a story that sb tells you just to make you feel sorry for them, especially one that does not have that effect or is not true（目的在于引起同情或怜悯的）伤感故事

Soc. *abbr.* (in writing 书写形式) SOCIETY 协会；学会：*Royal Geographical Soc.* 皇家地理学会

soca /ˈsəʊkə; NAmE ˈsoʊ-/ *noun* [U] a type of dance music, originally from the Caribbean, which mixes SOUL and CALYPSO 索卡乐，灵卡乐（源于加勒比海的舞曲，融合了灵乐和卡利普索民歌）

ˌso-ˈcalled AW *adj.* **1** [only before noun] used to show that you do not think that the word or phrase that is being used to describe sb/sth is appropriate（表示不认同）所谓的：*the opinion of a so-called 'expert'* 一个所谓的"专家"的意见 ◇ *How have these so-called improvements helped the local community?* 这些所谓的进步对当地社会有什么帮助呢？ **2** [usually before noun] used to introduce the word that people usually use to describe sth（引出约定俗成的称谓）人称…的，号称…的：*artists from the so-called 'School of London'* 号称"伦敦派"的一群艺术家

soc·cer /ˈsɒkə(r); NAmE ˈsɑːk-/ (*BrE also* **foot·ball**) (*BrE also, formal* **Asˌsociation ˈfootball**) (*also BrE, informal* **footy, footie**) *noun* [U] a game played by two teams of 11 players, using a round ball which players kick up and down the playing field. Teams try to kick the ball into the other team's goal. 足球运动：*soccer players* 足球运动员 ◇ *a **soccer pitch/team/match*** 足球场；足球队；足球比赛 ➲ VISUAL VOCAB PAGE V48

ˈsoccer mom *noun* (*NAmE, informal*) a mother who spends a lot of time taking her children to activities such as sports and music lessons, used as a way of referring to a typical mother from the MIDDLE CLASSES 足球妈妈（花许多时间带孩子参加体育活动、音乐课等的母亲，尤指典型的中产阶级母亲）

so·ci·able /ˈsəʊʃəbl; NAmE ˈsoʊ-/ (*also less frequent* **so·cial**) *adj.* (of people 人) enjoying spending time with other people 好交际的；合群的；友好的 SYN **gregarious**：*She's a sociable child who'll talk to anyone.* 她是个合群的孩子，跟谁都有话说。◇ *I'm not feeling very sociable this evening.* 今晚我不大想跟人应酬。◇ *We had a very sociable weekend* (= we did a lot of things with other people). 我们大伙过了一个十分热闹的周末。➲ COMPARE ANTISOCIAL OPP **unsociable** ▶ **so·ci·abil·ity** /ˌsəʊʃəˈbɪləti; NAmE ˌsoʊ-/ *noun* [U] **so·ci·ably** *adv.*

so·cial 🔑 /ˈsəʊʃl; NAmE ˈsoʊʃl/ *adj., noun*

■ ***adj.***

• CONNECTED WITH SOCIETY 社会 **1** 🔑 [only before noun] connected with society and the way it is organized 社会的：*social issues/problems/reforms* 社会议题 / 问题 / 改革 ◇ *a call for social and economic change* 进行社会和经济变革的要求 **2** 🔑 [only before noun] connected with your position in society 社会上的；社会地位的：***social class/background*** 社会阶层 / 背景 ◇ *social advancement* (= improving your position in society) 社会地位的提高

• ACTIVITIES WITH OTHERS 社交活动 **3** 🔑 [only before noun] connected with activities in which people meet each other for pleasure 社交的；交际的；联谊的：*a busy **social life*** 繁忙的社交生活 ◇ *Team sports help to develop a child's **social skills*** (= the ability to talk easily to other people and do things in a group). 集体体育运动有助于培养孩子的交际能力。◇ *Social events and training days are arranged for all the staff.* 为所有员工安排联谊活动和培训。◇ *Join a social club to make new friends.* 加入一个社交俱乐部，好交一些新朋友。

• ANIMALS 动物 **4** [only before noun] (*specialist*) living naturally in groups, rather than alone 群居的

• FRIENDLY 友好 **5** = SOCIABLE

▶ **so·cial·ly** 🔑 /-ʃəli/ *adv.*: *The reforms will bring benefits, socially and politically.* 这些改革措施在社会领域和政治领域均会带来益处。◇ *This type of behaviour is no longer socially acceptable.* 这种行为已不为社会所接受。◇ *a socially disadvantaged family* (= one that is poor and from a low social class) 社会地位低下的家庭 ◇ *We meet at work, but never socially.* 我们上班常见面，但在社交场合从未碰见过。◇ *Carnivores are usually socially complex mammals.* 在哺乳动物中，食肉动物通常有着复杂的社会关系。

■ ***noun*** **1** [C] (*old-fashioned*) a party that is organized by a group or club 联谊会；联欢会 **2 the social** [U] (*BrE, informal*) = SOCIAL SECURITY: *We're living on the social now.* 我们现在靠社会保障金维持生活。

ˌsocial ˈbookmarking *noun* [U] (*computing* 计) a way of BOOKMARKING (= storing and labelling) the addresses of pages on the Internet, using a special service that enables you to make them available to other Internet users 社交书签，网页书签，网摘（可将收藏的网址在互联网上与人分享）

ˌsocial ˈclimber *noun* (*disapproving*) a person who tries to improve their position in society by becoming friendly with people who belong to a higher social class 攀附权贵借以挤入上流社会的人；趋炎附势向上爬的人

ˌsocial ˈconscience *noun* [sing., U] the state of being aware of the problems that affect a lot of people in society, such as being poor or having no home, and wanting to do sth to help these people 社会良知；社会责任感

ˌsocial ˈcontract (*also* **ˌsocial ˈcompact**) *noun* [sing.] an agreement among citizens to behave in a way that benefits everybody 社会契约，民约（以公益约束行为）

ˌsocial deˈmocracy *noun* [U, C] a political system that combines the principles of SOCIALISM with the greater personal freedom of DEMOCRACY; a country that has this political system of government 社会民主主义；社会民主主义国家 ▶ **ˌsocial ˈdemocrat** *noun* **ˌsocial demoˈcratic** *adj.* [only before noun]

ˌsocial engiˈneering *noun* [U] the attempt to change society and to deal with social problems according to particular political beliefs, for example by changing the law 社会工程（根据政治信念改造社会）

ˌ**social fund** *noun* [usually sing.] a sum of money that can be used to help people who have financial, family or other social problems 社会基金（向困难者提供资助）

ˌ**social 'gaming** *noun* [U] the activity of playing computer games that are run through a SOCIAL NETWORKING website 社交网络游戏 ▸ ˌ**social 'gamer** *noun*

ˌ**social 'housing** *noun* [U] (in Britain) houses or flats/apartments that are provided by a local council or another organization for people to buy or rent at a low price 社会福利住房（英国由地方政府或其他机构提供的低价或低租金住房）

ˌ**Social In'surance number** *noun* (*abbr.* **SIN**) a number that the Canadian government uses to identify you, and that you use when you fill out official forms, apply for a job, etc.（加拿大政府用于识别身份等的）社会保险号码

so·cial·ism /'səʊʃəlɪzəm; *NAmE* 'soʊ-/ *noun* [U] a set of political and economic theories based on the belief that everyone has an equal right to a share of a country's wealth and that the government should own and control the main industries 社会主义 ➲ COMPARE CAPITALISM, COMMUNISM, SOCIAL DEMOCRACY ➲ **WORDFINDER NOTE** AT SYSTEM

so·cial·ist /'səʊʃəlɪst; *NAmE* 'soʊ-/ *noun* a person who believes in or supports socialism; a member of a political party that believes in socialism 社会主义者；社会党党员 ▸ **so·cial·ist** *adj.* [usually before noun]: *a socialist country* 社会主义国家 ◇ *socialist beliefs* 社会主义信仰 ◇ *the ruling Socialist Party* 执政的社会党

so·cial·is·tic /ˌsəʊʃə'lɪstɪk; *NAmE* ˌsoʊ-/ *adj.* [usually before noun] (*often disapproving*) having some of the features of socialism 有社会主义倾向的；有一定社会主义特点的

ˌ**socialist 'realism** *noun* [U] a theory that was put into practice in some COMMUNIST countries, especially in the Soviet Union under Stalin, that art, music and literature should be used to show people the principles of a SOCIALIST society and encourage them to support it 社会主义现实主义（尤指斯大林领导时期的苏联等一些共产党国家实践的理论，即艺术、音乐和文学应要表现和引导受众支持社会主义）

so·cial·ite /'səʊʃəlaɪt; *NAmE* 'soʊ-/ *noun* (*sometimes disapproving*) a person who goes to a lot of fashionable parties and is often written about in the newspapers, etc. 时尚界名人；社交名流

so·cial·iza·tion (*BrE also* **-isa·tion**) /ˌsəʊʃəlaɪ'zeɪʃn; *NAmE* ˌsoʊʃələ'z-/ *noun* [U] (*formal*) the process by which sb, especially a child, learns to behave in a way that is acceptable in their society 适应社会的过程；社会化

so·cial·ize (*BrE also* **-ise**) /'səʊʃəlaɪz; *NAmE* 'soʊ-/ *verb* **1** [I] ~ (**with sb**) to meet and spend time with people in a friendly way, in order to enjoy yourself（和他人）交往，交际 **SYN** **mix**: *I enjoy socializing with the other students.* 我喜欢和同学来往。◇ *Maybe you should socialize more.* 也许你应该多和人交往。**2** [T, often passive] ~ **sb** (**to do sth**) (*formal*) to teach people to behave in ways that are acceptable to their society 使适应社会: *The family has the important function of socializing children.* 家庭有教孩子适应社会的重要作用。**3** [T, usually passive] ~ **sth** to organize sth according to the principles of SOCIALISM 使社会主义化；按社会主义原则行事

ˌ**socialized 'medicine** *noun* [U] (*US*) medical and hospital care provided by the government for everyone by paying for it with public money 公费医疗制度

ˌ**social 'media** *noun* [U, pl.] websites and software programs used for SOCIAL NETWORKING 网络社交媒体: *social media sites such as Facebook and Twitter* 诸如脸书和推特之类的社交网站 ➲ **WORDFINDER NOTE** AT WEBSITE

ˌ**social 'network** *noun* **1** a SOCIAL NETWORKING site or application through which users can communicate with each other by adding information, messages, images, etc. 社交网站；社交网站应用程序 **2** a network of social connections and personal relationships between people 社会关系网；人脉: *People in the region usually have a broad social network.* 这地区的人通常都人脉很广。

ˌ**social 'networking** *noun* [U] communication with people who share your interests using a website or other service on the Internet 网络社交；社交网络活动: *a social networking site* 社交网站 ➲ **COLLOCATIONS** AT EMAIL

ˌ**social psy'chology** *noun* [U] the study of people's behaviour, attitudes, etc. in society 社会心理学 ▸ ˌ**social psy'chologist** *noun*

ˌ**social 'science** *noun* **1** [U] (*also* ˌ**social 'studies**) the study of people in society 社会科学 **2** [C] a particular subject connected with the study of people in society, for example geography, ECONOMICS or SOCIOLOGY 社会科学学科

ˌ**social 'scientist** *noun* a person who studies social science 社会科学家

ˌ**social 'secretary** *noun* the person who organizes social activities for an organization or for another person 社交秘书（负责为机构或个人组织社交活动）

ˌ**social se'curity** *noun* [U] **1** (*BrE*) (*also* **wel·fare** *NAmE, BrE*) money that the government pays regularly to people who are poor, unemployed, sick, etc. 社会保障金（政府定期向贫穷、失业、患病等人发放）: *to live on social security* 靠社会保障金生活 ◇ *social security payments* 社会保障金支付款项 **2 Social Security** (in the US) a system in which people pay money regularly to the government when they are working and receive payments from the government when they are unable to work, especially when they are sick or too old to work（美国）社会保障制度 ➲ COMPARE NATIONAL INSURANCE

ˌ**Social Se'curity number** *noun* (*abbr.* **SSN**) (in the US) an official identity number that everyone is given when they are born 社会保障号码（美国人出生时得到的正式身份号码）

ˌ**social 'services** *noun* [pl.] a system that is organized by the local government to help people who have financial or family problems; the department or the people who provide this help 社会福利制度（由当地政府组织，向困难者提供帮助的制度）；社会福利部门；社会福利工作人员: *a leaflet on the range of social services available* 宣传现有社会福利范围的传单 ◇ *the local social services department* 当地的社会福利部门

ˌ**social 'software** *noun* [U] computer software that enables users to communicate and share data 社交软件

ˌ**social 'studies** *noun* [pl.] = SOCIAL SCIENCE (1)

'**social work** *noun* [U] paid work that involves giving help and advice to people living in the community who have financial or family problems 社会福利工作

'**social worker** *noun* a person whose job is social work 社会福利工作者

so·ci·etal /sə'saɪətl/ *adj.* [only before noun] (*specialist*) connected with society and the way it is organized 社会的；关于社会的

so·ci·ety 🔑 /sə'saɪəti/ *noun* (*pl.* **-ies**) **1** 🔑 [U] people in general, living together in communities 社会（以群体形式生活在一起的人的总称）: *policies that will benefit society as a whole* 将有利于整个社会的政策 ◇ *Racism exists at all levels of society.* 种族主义存在于社会各阶层。◇ *They carried out research into the roles of men and women in today's society* 他们就男人和女人在当今社会中所扮演的角色展开研究。➲ **WORDFINDER NOTE** AT EQUAL

WORDFINDER 联想词: civil rights, class, conform, convention, culture, custom, elite, equality, outsider

2 🔑 [C, U] a particular community of people who share the same customs, laws, etc. 社会（共同遵守一定的习俗、法律等的特定群体）: *modern industrial societies* 现代

工业社会◇ *demand created by a consumer society* 消费型社会所产生的需求 ◇ *Can Britain ever be a classless society?* 英国能否有朝一日成为一个无阶级社会？ ◇ *They were discussing the problems of Western society.* 当时他们正在讨论西方社会的问题。**3** [C] (*abbr.* **Soc.**) (especially in names 尤用于名称) a group of people who join together for a particular purpose 社团；协会；学会：*a member of the drama society* 剧社成员 ◇ *the American Society of Newspaper Editors* 美国报纸主编协会 ➲ WORDFINDER NOTE AT CLUB ➲ SEE ALSO BUILDING SOCIETY, FRIENDLY SOCIETY **4** [U] the group of people in a country who are fashionable, rich and powerful 上流社会：*Their daughter married into* ***high society***. 他们的女儿嫁到了上层人家。◇ *a society wedding* 上层社会的婚礼 **5** [U] (*formal*) the state of being with other people 相伴；交往 SYN **company**: *He was a solitary man who avoided the society of others.* 他是个孤僻的人，不愿和人交往。

socio- /ˈsəʊsiəʊ; *NAmE* ˈsoʊsioʊ/ *combining form* (in nouns, adjectives and adverbs 构成名词、形容词和副词) connected with society or the study of society 社会的；社会学的：*socio-economic* 社会与经济的 ◇ *sociolinguistics* 社会语言学

so·cio·cul·tural /ˌsəʊsiəʊˈkʌltʃərəl; *NAmE* ˌsoʊsioʊ-/ *adj.* relating to society and culture 社会与文化的

ˌsocio-ˌecoˈnomic *adj.* relating to society and economics 社会与经济的；社经的：*people from different socio-economic backgrounds* 有不同社会与经济背景的人

socio·lect /ˈsəʊsiəʊlekt; *NAmE* ˈsoʊsioʊ-/ *noun* (*linguistics* 语言) a variety of a language that the members of a particular social class or social group speak 社会方言（某社会阶层或群体使用的一种语言变体）

socio·lin·guis·tics /ˌsəʊsiəʊlɪŋˈɡwɪstɪks; *NAmE* ˌsoʊsioʊ-/ *noun* [U] the study of the way language is affected by differences in social class, region, sex, etc. 社会语言学 ▶ **socio·lin·guis·tic** /ˌsəʊsiəʊlɪŋˈɡwɪstɪk; *NAmE* ˌsoʊsioʊ-/ *adj.*

soci·olo·gist /ˌsəʊsiˈɒlədʒɪst; *NAmE* ˌsoʊsiˈɑːl-/ *noun* a person who studies sociology 社会学家

soci·ology /ˌsəʊsiˈɒlədʒi; *NAmE* ˌsoʊsiˈɑːl-/ *noun* [U] the scientific study of the nature and development of society and social behaviour 社会学 ▶ **socio·logic·al** /ˌsəʊsiəˈlɒdʒɪkl; *NAmE* ˌsoʊsiəˈlɑːdʒ-/ *adj.*: *sociological theories* 社会学理论 **socio·logic·al·ly** /-kli/ *adv.*

socio·path /ˈsəʊsiəʊpæθ; *NAmE* ˈsoʊsioʊ-/ *noun* a person who has a mental illness and who behaves in an aggressive or dangerous way towards other people（因心理障碍而有攻击或伤害他人行为的）反社会者

socio·politic·al /ˌsəʊsiəʊpəˈlɪtɪkl; *NAmE* ˌsoʊsioʊ-/ *adj.* relating to society and politics 社会与政治的

sock /sɒk; *NAmE* sɑːk/ *noun, verb*

■ ***noun*** **1** a piece of clothing that is worn over the foot, ankle and lower part of the leg, especially inside a shoe 短袜：*a pair of socks* 一双短袜 **2** (*informal*) a strong blow, especially with the FIST（尤指用拳头）猛击，重击：*He gave him a sock on the jaw.* 他朝他的下巴猛击了一拳。

IDM **blow/knock sb's ˈsocks off** (*informal*) to surprise or impress sb very much 使某人万分惊愕；给某人留下深刻印象 **put a ˈsock in it** (*old-fashioned, BrE, informal*) used to tell sb to stop talking or making a noise（让某人安静）住嘴，别出声 ➲ MORE AT PULL *v.*

■ ***verb*** ~ **sb** (*informal*) to hit sb hard 猛击；狠打：*She got angry and socked him in the mouth.* 她生气了，朝他嘴巴一拳挥过去。◇ (*figurative*) *The banks are socking customers with higher charges.* 银行提高手续费，损害了客户的利益。

IDM **ˈsock it to sb** (*informal* or *humorous*) to do sth or tell sb sth in a strong and effective way 直截了当地做某事；强硬地对某人说某事：*Go in there and sock it to 'em!* 你进去，直截了当地告诉他们！

PHR V **ˌsock sth↔aˈway** (*NAmE*) to save money 储存（钱）；积攒（钱）

socket /ˈsɒkɪt; *NAmE* ˈsɑːkɪt/ *noun* **1** (*BrE also* **ˈpower point**) (*NAmE also* **out·let**, **re·cep·tacle**) a device in a wall that you put a plug into in order to connect electrical equipment to the power supply of a building（电源）插座：*a wall socket* 墙壁插座 ➲ PICTURE AT PLUG **2** a device on a piece of electrical equipment that you can fix a plug, a light BULB, etc. into（电器上的）插口，插孔，管座：*an aerial socket on the television* 电视机上的天线插孔 **3** a curved hollow space in the surface of sth that another part fits into or moves around in 托座；孔穴；窝；槽；臼：*His eyes bulged in their sockets.* 他的两眼从眼窝里鼓出来。

ˈsock puppet *noun* **1** a type of PUPPET (1), made from a sock, that you put over your hand 袜子手偶 **2** a person whose actions are controlled by another 傀儡：*He accused the politician of being a capitalist sock puppet.* 他谴责那个政客是资本主义的傀儡。**3** a false online identity, usually created by a person or group in order to promote their own opinions 马甲（在网络上的虚假身份）：*He created sock puppets to write positive comments about his blog posts.* 他创建了几个马甲号，给自己的博客帖子写好评。▶ **ˈsock puppetry** *noun* [U]

sod /sɒd; *NAmE* sɑːd/ *noun, verb*

■ ***noun*** **1** (*BrE, taboo, slang*) used to refer to a person, especially a man, that you are annoyed with or think is unpleasant（指讨厌的人，尤指男人）讨厌鬼：*You stupid sod!* 你这个讨厌的蠢货！**2** (*BrE, taboo, slang*) used with an adjective to refer to a person, especially a man（与形容词连用，指人，尤指男人）家伙：*The poor old sod got the sack yesterday.* 那位可怜的老兄昨天给解雇了。◇ *You lucky sod!* 你小子好福气呀！HELP You can use words like **man**, **boy**, **devil** or **thing** instead. 也可用 man、boy、devil 或 thing 等词代替。**3** (*BrE, taboo, slang*) a thing that is difficult or causes problems 难办的事；惹麻烦的事：*It was a real sod of a job.* 这活儿真是棘手。**4** [usually sing.] (*formal* or *literary*) a layer of earth with grass growing on it; a piece of this that has been removed 长草的土层；（移植的）草皮：*under the sod* (= in your grave) 入土

■ ***verb*** (**-dd-**) ~ **sth** (*BrE, taboo, slang*) (only used in orders 仅用于命令) a swear word that many people find offensive, used when sb is annoyed about sth or to show that they do not care about sth（表示烦恼或不在乎）去他妈的：*Sod this car! It's always breaking down.* 这辆车他妈的老出毛病。◇ *Oh, sod it! I'm not doing any more.* 哼，去他妈的！我不干了。IDM SEE LARK *n.*

PHR V **ˌsod ˈoff** (*BrE, taboo, slang*) (usually used in orders 通常用于命令) to go away 滚；滚蛋：*Sod off, the pair of you!* 你们俩，都给我滚！

soda /ˈsəʊdə; *NAmE* ˈsoʊdə/ *noun* **1** [U, C] = SODA WATER: *a Scotch and soda* 一杯加汽水的苏格兰威士忌 **2** (*also old-fashioned* **ˈsoda pop**) (*both NAmE*) [U, C] a sweet FIZZY drink (= a drink with bubbles) made with soda water, fruit flavour and sometimes ice cream 苏打汽水（加果味，有时加入冰淇淋）：*He had an ice-cream soda.* 他喝了一杯冰淇淋果味汽水。**3** [U] a chemical substance in common use that is a COMPOUND of SODIUM 苏打；纯碱；无水碳酸钠：***baking/washing soda*** 小苏打；洗涤碱 ➲ SEE ALSO CAUSTIC SODA, SODIUM BICARBONATE, SODIUM CARBONATE

ˈsoda bread *noun* [U] bread that rises because of SODIUM BICARBONATE that is added instead of YEAST (popular in Ireland) 苏打面包（爱尔兰人常吃）

ˈsoda fountain *noun* (*NAmE*) **1** (*BrE* **ˈsoda siphon**) a bottle containing soda water or another drink, with a device that you press to pour the drink and put bubbles into it （压杆式）苏打水瓶，汽水瓶 **2** (*old-fashioned*) a type of bar where you can buy sodas to drink, ICE CREAMS, etc. 冷饮柜台；冷饮部

ˌsod ˈall *noun* [U] (*BrE, taboo, slang*) a phrase that some people find offensive, used to mean 'none at all' or 'nothing at all' 他妈的一个也没有

ˈsoda pop *noun* (*old-fashioned*) = SODA (2)

ˈsoda siphon (*BrE*) (*NAmE* **ˈsoda fountain**) *noun* a bottle containing soda water or another drink, with a device that you press to pour the drink and put bubbles into it （压杆式）苏打水瓶，汽水瓶

'soda water (*also* **soda**) *noun* **1** [U, C] FIZZY water (= water with bubbles) used as a drink on its own or to mix with alcoholic drinks or fruit juice (originally made with SODIUM BICARBONATE) 汽水；苏打水 **2** [C] a glass of soda water 一杯汽水

sod·den /'sɒdn; *NAmE* 'sɑːdn/ *adj.* **1** extremely wet 湿透的；湿漉漉的 SYN **soaked**: *sodden grass* 湿漉漉的草 **2 -sodden** extremely wet with the thing mentioned 被…湿透的；浸透…的；饱含…的：*a rain-sodden jacket* 雨水淋透的夹克

sod·ding /'sɒdɪŋ; *NAmE* 'sɑːd-/ *adj.* [only before noun] (*BrE, taboo, slang*) a swear word that many people find offensive, used to emphasize a comment or an angry statement（用以加强语气）：*I couldn't understand a sodding thing!* 我他妈的一点儿都搞不懂！

so·dium /'səʊdiəm; *NAmE* 'soʊ-/ *noun* [U] (*symb.* **Na**) a chemical element. Sodium is a soft silver-white metal that is found naturally only in COMPOUNDS, such as salt. 钠

ˌsodium biˈcarbonate (*also* **biˌcarbonate of ˈsoda**, **ˈbaking soda**) (*also informal* **bi·carb**) *noun* [U] (*symb.* $NaHCO_3$) a chemical in the form of a white powder that dissolves and is used in baking to make cakes, etc. rise and become light, and in making FIZZY drinks and some medicines 碳酸氢钠；小苏打

ˌsodium ˈcarbonate (*also* **ˈwashing soda**) *noun* [U] (*symb.* Na_2CO_3) a chemical in the form of white CRYSTALS or powder that dissolves and is used in making glass, soap and paper, and for making water soft 碳酸钠

ˌsodium ˈchloride *noun* [U] (*symb.* **NaCl**) common salt (a chemical made up of SODIUM and CHLORINE) 氯化钠；食盐

Sodom and Gom·or·rah /ˌsɒdəm ən gəˈmɒrə; *NAmE* ˌsɑːdəm ən gəˈmɔːrə/ *noun* a place that is full of people behaving in a sexually immoral way 淫荡的地方；罪恶之城：*The village had a reputation as a latter-day Sodom and Gomorrah.* 这个村子曾经被称为现代版的邪恶之城。ORIGIN From the names of two cities in the Bible which were destroyed by God to punish the people for their sexually immoral behaviour. 源自《圣经》中两座城所多玛和蛾摩拉的名称，上帝为惩罚市民的淫荡行为而将其毁灭。

sod·om·ite /'sɒdəmaɪt; *NAmE* 'sɑːd-/ *noun* (*old-fashioned, formal*) a person who practises sodomy 鸡奸者

sod·om·ize (*BrE also* **-ise**) /'sɒdəmaɪz; *NAmE* 'sɑːd-/ *verb* ~ **sb** (*disapproving*) to have ANAL sex with sb 鸡奸

sod·omy /'sɒdəmi; *NAmE* 'sɑːd-/ *noun* [U] a sexual act in which a man puts his PENIS in sb's, especially another man's, ANUS 鸡奸

ˌSod's ˈLaw *noun* [U] (*BrE, humorous*) the tendency for things to happen in just the way that you do not want, and in a way that is not useful 事与愿违的倾向，造物弄人法则（指发生的事情常和人的愿望恰恰相反）：*We always play better when we are not being recorded—but that's Sod's Law, isn't it?* 我们总是不录音的时候演奏得好些，真是应了那句老话，越想做好就越做不好，是不是？◇ *It was Sod's Law—the only day he could manage was the day I couldn't miss work.* 真是天不遂人愿，他只有那天抽得出时间，偏偏我上班离不开。

sofa /'səʊfə; *NAmE* 'soʊfə/ *noun* a long comfortable seat with a back and arms, for two or more people to sit on 长沙发 SYN **settee, couch** ➲ VISUAL VOCAB PAGE V22

'sofa bed *noun* a sofa that can be folded out to form a bed（可打开变成床的）两用沙发，沙发床 ➲ VISUAL VOCAB PAGE V24

soft /sɒft; *NAmE* sɔːft/ *adj.* (**soft·er, soft·est**)
• **NOT HARD** 不硬 **1** changing shape easily when pressed; not stiff or firm 软的；柔软的：*soft margarine* 软人造黄油 ◇ *soft feather pillows* 柔软的羽毛枕头 ◇ *The grass was soft and springy.* 草柔软而有弹性。**2** less hard than average 硬度较低的；较软的：*soft rocks such as limestone* 诸如石灰岩之类的软岩 ◇ *soft cheeses* 软奶酪 OPP **hard**
• **NOT ROUGH** 不粗糙 **3** smooth and pleasant to touch 柔滑的；细滑的；细腻的：*soft skin* 柔滑的皮肤 OPP **rough**
• **WITHOUT ANGLES/EDGES** 无棱角 **4** not having sharp angles or hard edges 无棱角的；轮廓不鲜明的；线条柔和的：*This season's fashions focus on warm tones and soft lines.* 本季时装主要流行暖色调和柔和线条。◇ *The moon's pale light cast soft shadows.* 淡淡的月光投下柔和的暗影。
• **LIGHT/COLOURS** 光线；色彩 **5** [usually before noun] not too bright, in a way that is pleasant and relaxing to the eyes 柔和的；悦目的：*a soft pink* 柔和的粉红色 ◇ *the soft glow of candlelight* 柔和的烛光 OPP **harsh**
• **RAIN/WIND** 风雨 **6** not strong or violent 不强烈的；小的；和缓的 SYN **light**: *A soft breeze rustled the trees.* 微风吹拂，树叶飒飒作响。
• **SOUNDS** 声音 **7** not loud, and usually pleasant and gentle 轻的；轻柔的；柔和悦耳的 SYN **quiet**: *soft background music* 轻柔的背景音乐 ◇ *a soft voice* 柔和悦耳的嗓音
• **SYMPATHETIC** 同情 **8** kind and sympathetic; easily affected by other people's suffering 有同情心的；仁厚的；心肠软的：*Julia's soft heart was touched by his grief.* 朱莉娅心肠软，见他悲伤动了恻隐之心。OPP **hard**
• **NOT STRICT** 不严厉 **9** (*usually disapproving*) not strict or severe; not strict or severe enough 不（够）严厉的；态度偏软的；（对…）心慈手软的 SYN **lenient**: ~ **(on sb/sth)** *The government is not becoming soft on crime.* 政府对犯罪行为并非日渐手软。◇ ~ **(with sb)** *If you're too soft with these kids they'll never respect you.* 你要是太迁就这些孩子，他们永远不会尊敬你。OPP **tough**
• **CRAZY** 失去理智 **10** (*informal, disapproving*) stupid or crazy 愚蠢的；没头脑的；脑子发昏的：*He must be going* ***soft in the head.*** 他准是脑子出毛病了。
• **NOT BRAVE/TOUGH ENOUGH** 不够勇敢 / 顽强 **11** (*informal, disapproving*) not brave enough; wanting to be safe and comfortable 畏首畏尾的；不够泼辣的；但求安稳的：*Stay in a hotel? Don't be so soft. I want to camp out under the stars.* 住旅馆？别那么贪图安逸了。我想顶着星星露天宿营。
• **TOO EASY** 太容易 **12** (*disapproving*) not involving much work; too easy and comfortable 轻松的；安逸的：*They had got too used to the soft life at home.* 他们实在是过惯了家里的安逸生活。OPP **hard**
• **WATER** 水 **13** not containing mineral salts and therefore good for washing 软性的（无矿盐因而适用于洗涤）：*You won't need much soap—the water here is very soft.* 你不必多用肥皂，这儿的水很软。OPP **hard**
• **CONSONANTS** 辅音 **14** (*phonetics* 语音) not sounding hard, for example 'c' in *city* and 'g' in *general* 发软音的（如 city 中 c 字母和 general 中 g 字母的发音）OPP **hard** ▸ **soft·ness** *noun* [U, sing.]: *the softness of her skin* 她皮肤的柔滑 ◇ *the softness of the water* 水的软性 ➲ SEE ALSO SOFTLY

IDM **have a soft 'spot for sb/sth** (*also IndE* **have a soft corner for sb/sth**) (*informal*) to like sb/sth 喜欢某人（或某物）：*She's always had a soft spot for you.* 她一直喜欢你。➲ MORE AT OPTION *n.*, TOUCH *n.*

soft·ball /'sɒftbɔːl; *NAmE* 'sɔːft-/ *noun* **1** [U] a game similar to BASEBALL but played on a smaller field with a larger, softer ball 垒球运动 **2** [C] the ball used in softball 垒球

ˌsoft-'boiled *adj.* (of eggs 蛋) boiled for a short time so that the YOLK is still soft or liquid 煮得嫩的 ➲ COMPARE HARD-BOILED (1)

ˌsoft 'centre *noun* (*BrE*) **1** [usually pl.] a chocolate with a soft mixture inside 软夹心巧克力 **2** if sb has a **soft centre**, they are not really as severe as they seem（表面严厉）心肠软；外刚内柔 ▸ **ˌsoft-'centred** *adj.*

'soft-core *adj.* [usually before noun] showing or describing sexual activity without being too detailed or shocking 软性色情的；（性描写等）隐晦的，含蓄的 ➲ COMPARE HARD-CORE

ˌsoft 'drink *noun* a cold drink that does not contain alcohol 软饮料（不含酒精）➲ COMPARE HARD *adj.* (11)

ˌsoft ˈdrug *noun* an illegal drug, such as CANNABIS, that some people take for pleasure, that is not considered very harmful or likely to cause ADDICTION 软毒品（危害不很大或不易成瘾，如大麻） ➲ COMPARE HARD DRUG

soft·en /ˈsɒfn; *NAmE* ˈsɔːfn/ *verb* **1** [I, T] to become, or to make sth softer（使）变软，软化：*Fry the onions until they soften.* 把洋葱炒软。◇ **~ sth** *a lotion to soften the skin* 润肤露 ◇ *Linseed oil will soften stiff leather.* 亚麻籽油可软化僵硬的皮革。**2** [I, T] **~ (sth)** to become or to make sth less bright, rough or strong（使）柔和，和缓：*Trees soften the outline of the house.* 树木使房子的轮廓显得柔和。**3** [I, T] to become or to make sb/sth more sympathetic and less severe or critical（使）态度缓和，变温和，变宽厚：*She felt herself softening towards him.* 她感觉自己对他逐渐温和起来。◇ *His face softened as he looked at his son.* 他看着儿子，紧绷的面孔松弛下来。◇ **~ sb/sth** *She softened her tone a little.* 她稍稍缓和了一下语气。**4** [T] **~ sth** to reduce the force or the unpleasant effects of sth 减轻；减缓；削弱 SYN **cushion**：*Airbags are designed to soften the impact of a car crash.* 气囊用来减轻汽车碰撞的冲击力。IDM SEE BLOW *n.* ➲ MORE LIKE THIS 20, page R27

PHR V **ˌsoften sb↔ˈup** (*informal*) **1** to try to persuade sb to do sth for you by being very nice to them before you ask them 打动；诱导；拉拢：*Potential customers are softened up with free gifts before the sales talk.* 谈生意之前，先送给潜在的客户一些赠品，以联络感情。**2** to make an enemy weaker and easier to attack 削弱，瓦解（敌人力量）

soft·en·er /ˈsɒfnə(r); *NAmE* ˈsɔːf-/ *noun* **1** [C] a device that is used with chemicals to make hard water soft（硬水）软化器：*a water softener* 硬水软化器 **2** [U, C] a substance that you add when washing clothes to make them feel soft（衣物的）柔顺剂

ˌsoft ˈerror *noun* (*computing* 计) an error or fault that makes a program or OPERATING SYSTEM stop working, but that can often be corrected by switching the computer off then on again 软差错（可通过关机重启纠正）

ˌsoft ˈfocus *noun* [U] a method of producing a photograph so that the edges of the image are not clear, in order to make it look more romantic and attractive 柔焦，软聚焦（摄影技巧）

ˌsoft ˈfruit *noun* [C, U] small fruits without large seeds or hard skin, such as STRAWBERRIES or CURRANTS 无核小果（如草莓或醋栗）

ˌsoft ˈfurnishings *noun* [pl.] (*BrE*) CUSHIONS, curtains and other things made from cloth that are found in a house 室内织物陈设（如靠垫、窗帘等）

ˈsoft goods *noun* [pl.] **1** things that are made of cloth, such as clothes and curtains 纺织品，布制品（如服装、窗帘等）**2** (*business* 商) any type of cloth 布料 SYN **textile**

ˌsoft-ˈhearted *adj.* kind, sympathetic and emotional 有同情心的；心肠软的；热心肠的 SYN **kind-hearted** OPP **hard-hearted**

softie (*also* **softy**) /ˈsɒfti; *NAmE* ˈsɔːfti/ *noun* (*pl.* **-ies**) (*informal*) a kind, sympathetic or emotional person 有同情心的人；心肠软的人；热心肠的人：*There's no need to be afraid of him—he's a big softie.* 没必要害怕他，他心特好。

soft·ly /ˈsɒftli; *NAmE* ˈsɔːftli/ *adv.* in a soft way 轻轻地；轻柔地；温和地；柔和地：*She closed the door softly behind her.* 她随手轻轻关上门。◇ *'I missed you,' he said softly.* "我想你了。"他柔声说道。◇ *The room was softly lit by a lamp.* 屋里点着一盏灯，光线很柔和。◇ *a softly tailored suit* 一套裁剪线条很柔和的西装

ˌsoftly-ˈsoftly *adj.* (*BrE, informal*) (of a way of doing sth 做事方式) careful and patient, with no sudden actions 细致耐心的：*The police used a* ***softly-softly approach*** *with him.* 警方对他采取了耐心细致的方法。

ˌsoftly-ˈspoken *adj.* = SOFT-SPOKEN

ˈsoft pedal *noun* (*music* 音) a PEDAL on a piano that is pressed to make the sound quieter（钢琴的）弱音踏板

ˌsoft-ˈpedal *verb* (**-ll-**, *US* **-l-**) [T, I] **~ (on) sth** (*informal*) to treat sth as less serious or important than it really is 低调处理；降低…的调门；对…轻描淡写：*Television has been accused of soft-pedalling bad news.* 有人指责电视对坏消息轻描淡写。

ˌsoft ˈporn *noun* [U] films/movies, books, pictures, etc. that show or describe sexual activity in a way that is sexually exciting but not in a very detailed or violent way 软色情作品（指非赤裸裸描写性行为的电影、书籍、图画等）➲ COMPARE HARD PORN

ˌsoft ˈsell *noun* [sing.] a method of selling that involves persuading sb to buy sth rather than using pressure or aggressive methods 软推销；劝诱推销 ➲ COMPARE HARD SELL

ˈsoft-shoe *noun, verb*

- ***noun*** [U] a type of dance like TAP, performed with soft shoes which do not make a noise 软鞋踢踏舞：*a soft-shoe shuffle* 软鞋曳步舞
- ***verb*** **1** [I] to perform a soft-shoe dance 跳软鞋踢踏舞 **2** [I] **+ adv./prep.** to move somewhere very quietly, without attracting attention 蹑手蹑脚地走；悄悄地移动

ˌsoft ˈshoulder *noun* (*NAmE*) a strip of ground with a soft surface at the edge of a road（公路边未铺砌的）软质路肩 ➲ COMPARE VERGE *n.*

ˌsoft ˈskills *noun* [pl.] personal qualities that enable you to communicate well with other people 软能力；软技能；人际交往能力：*Candidates should demonstrate soft skills, such as team work, enthusiasm and emotional intelligence.* 申请人应展现自己的软能力，比如团队协作、热情和情商。

ˌsoft-ˈsoap *verb* **~ sb** (*informal*) to say nice things to sb in order to persuade them to do sth（为让某人做某事）说好听的，奉承，灌迷魂汤；劝诱 ▶ **ˌsoft ˈsoap** *noun* [U]

ˌsoft-ˈspoken (*also less frequent* **ˌsoftly-ˈspoken**) *adj.* having a gentle and quiet voice 低声细气的

ˌsoft ˈtarget *noun* a person or thing that it is very easy to attack 易受攻击的人（或事物）；软目标

ˌsoft ˈtissue *noun* [U, C] (*anatomy* 解) the parts of the body that are not bone, for example the skin and muscles（皮肤、肌肉等）软组织

ˈsoft-top *noun* a type of car that has a soft roof that can be folded down or removed; the roof of such a car 软顶篷汽车；（汽车的）软顶篷 ➲ SEE ALSO CONVERTIBLE *n.*

ˌsoft ˈtoy (*BrE*) (*also* **ˌstuffed ˈanimal** *NAmE, BrE*) *noun* a toy in the shape of an animal, made of cloth and filled with a soft substance（动物造型的）软体玩具，布绒玩具 ➲ VISUAL VOCAB PAGE V41

soft·ware /ˈsɒftweə(r); *NAmE* ˈsɔːftwer/ *noun* [U] the programs, etc. used to operate a computer 软件：***application/system software*** 应用 / 系统软件 ◇ ***design/educational/music-sharing, etc. software*** 设计、教育、音乐共享等软件 ◇ *to* ***install/run a piece of software*** 安装 / 运行一个软件 ◇ *Will the software run on my machine?* 这个软件在我的机器上能用吗？ ➲ COMPARE HARDWARE (1) ➲ WORDFINDER NOTE AT PROGRAM ➲ MORE LIKE THIS 28, page R28

> **WORDFINDER** 联想词：animation, application, authoring, beta version, configure, demo, install, interactive, spreadsheet

ˈsoftware engineer *noun* a person who writes computer programs 软件工程师

ˈsoftware package *noun* (*computing* 计) = PACKAGE (4)

soft·wood /ˈsɒftwʊd; *NAmE* ˈsɔːft-/ *noun* [U, C] wood from trees such as PINE, that is cheap to produce and can be cut easily 软质木，软木（如松木） ➲ COMPARE HARDWOOD

softy = SOFTIE

soggy /ˈsɒgi; *NAmE* ˈsɑːgi/ *adj.* (**sog·gier**, **sog·gi·est**) wet and soft, usually in a way that is unpleasant 湿而软的；

潮湿的；受潮的：*We squelched over the soggy ground.* 我们咕叽咕叽地走过泥泞的土地。◇ *soggy bread* 受潮的面包

soh (*also* **so**) /səʊ; *NAmE* soʊ/ (*also* **sol**) *noun* (*music* 音) the fifth note of a MAJOR SCALE 大调音阶的第 5 音

soi-disant /ˌswɑː diːˈzɒ̃; *NAmE* -ˈzɑ̃ː/ *adj.* [only before noun] (*from French*) used to show sb's description of himself/herself, usually when you do not agree with it 自诩的；自称的；自命的：*a soi-disant novelist* 自封的小说家

soi·gnée /ˈswɑːnjeɪ; *NAmE* swɑːnˈjeɪ/ *adj.* (*from French, formal*) (of a woman 女性) elegant; carefully and neatly dressed 优雅的；衣着讲究的；穿戴整洁的

soil /sɔɪl/ *noun, verb*

■ ***noun*** [U, C] **1** the top layer of the earth in which plants, trees, etc. grow 土壤：***poor/dry/acid/sandy/fertile, etc. soil*** 贫瘠、干旱、酸性、沙质、肥沃等的土壤 ◇ *the study of rocks and soils* 对岩石和土壤的研究 ◇ *soil erosion* 土壤侵蚀 **2** (*literary*) a country; an area of land 国土；领土；土地：*It was the first time I had set foot on African soil.* 那是我第一次踏足非洲大地。

▼ SYNONYMS 同义词辨析

soil

mud • dust • clay • land • earth • dirt • ground

These are all words for the top layer of the earth in which plants grow. 以上各词均指土壤。

soil the top layer of the earth in which plants grow 指土壤：*Plant the seedlings in damp soil.* 把幼苗种在湿润的土壤里。

mud wet soil that is soft and sticky 指泥、淤泥、泥浆：*The car wheels got stuck in the mud.* 汽车轮子陷到泥里去了。

dust a fine powder that consists of very small pieces of rock, earth, etc. 指沙石、沙土、尘土：*A cloud of dust rose as the truck set off.* 卡车起动时扬起一片灰尘。

clay a type of heavy sticky soil that becomes hard when it is baked and is used to make things such as pots and bricks 指黏土、陶土：*The tiles are made of clay.* 这些砖是用陶土制成的。

land an area of ground, especially of a particular type 尤指某种类型的地带、土地：*an area of rich, fertile land* 土地富饶肥沃的地域

earth the substance that plants grow in 指土、泥、泥土 NOTE **Earth** is often used about the soil found in gardens or used for gardening. * earth 常用以指花园里或种花用的泥土：*She put some earth into the pot.* 她在花盆里放了一些泥土。

dirt (*especially NAmE*) soil, especially loose soil 指泥土，尤指松土、散土：*Pack the dirt firmly around the plants.* 将植物周围的土培实。

ground an area of soil 指土地：*The car got stuck in the muddy ground.* 汽车陷到泥地里了。◇ *They drove across miles of rough, stony ground.* 他们驶过数英里崎岖不平、多石的土地。NOTE **Ground** is not used for loose soil. * ground 不用以指松土、散土：~~*a handful of dry ground*~~

PATTERNS

- **good/rich** soil/land/earth
- **fertile/infertile** soil/land/ground
- to **dig** the soil/mud/clay/land/earth/ground
- to **cultivate** the soil/land/ground

■ ***verb*** [often passive] **~ sth** (*formal*) to make sth dirty 弄脏：*soiled linen* 脏了的日用织品 ◇ (*figurative*) *I don't want you **soiling your hands** with this sort of work* (= doing sth unpleasant or wrong). 我不希望你干这种事，免得脏了你的手。➲ SEE ALSO SHOP-SOILED

ˈsoil science *noun* [U] the study of soil, for example the study of its structure or characteristics 土壤学（研究土壤结构或特性等）

soirée /ˈswɑːreɪ; *NAmE* swɑːˈreɪ/ *noun* (*from French, formal*) a formal party in the evening, especially at sb's home （尤指在家里举行的）社交晚会

so·journ /ˈsɒdʒən; *NAmE* ˈsoʊdʒɜːrn/ *noun* (*literary*) a temporary stay in a place away from your home 逗留；暂住；旅居 ▶ **so·journ** *verb* [I] **+ adv./prep.**

sol /sɒl; *NAmE* soʊl/ *noun* = SOH

sol·ace /ˈsɒləs; *NAmE* ˈsɑːləs/ *noun* [U, sing.] (*formal*) a feeling of emotional comfort when you are sad or disappointed; a person or thing that makes you feel better or happier when you are sad or disappointed 安慰；慰藉；给以安慰的人（或事物）SYN **comfort**：*He sought solace in the whisky bottle.* 他借酒浇愁。◇ *She turned to Rob for solace.* 她去罗布那儿寻求慰藉。◇ *His grandchildren were a solace in his old age.* 他晚年从孙儿们身上得到安慰。▶ **so·lace** *verb* **~ sb** (*literary*)：*She smiled, as though solaced by the memory.* 她笑了，仿佛在往事的回忆中得到了安慰。

solar /ˈsəʊlə(r); *NAmE* ˈsoʊ-/ *adj.* [only before noun] **1** of or connected with the sun 太阳的：*solar radiation* 太阳辐射 ◇ *the solar cycle* 太阳活动周 ➲ WORDFINDER NOTE AT SUN **2** using the sun's energy 太阳能的：***solar power/heating*** 太阳能；太阳能加热 ➲ WORDFINDER NOTE AT ENERGY ➲ COLLOCATIONS AT ENVIRONMENT ➲ VISUAL VOCAB PAGE V9

ˌsolar ˈcell *noun* a device that converts light and heat energy from the sun into electricity 太阳能电池

ˈsolar cooker *noun* (*IndE*) a container for cooking food that uses heat from the sun 太阳能灶具

ˌsolar ˈfarm *noun* an area of land on which there are a lot of solar panels for producing electricity 太阳能电场；太阳能电站

sol·ar·ium /səˈleəriəm; *NAmE* -ˈler-/ *noun* a room whose walls are mainly made of glass, or which has special lamps, where people go to get a SUNTAN (= make their skin go brown) using light from the sun or artificial light 日光浴室；日光室

ˌsolar ˈpanel *noun* a piece of equipment on a roof that uses light and heat energy from the sun to produce hot water and electricity 太阳能电池板 ➲ VISUAL VOCAB PAGE V9

solar plexus /ˌsəʊlə ˈpleksəs; *NAmE* ˌsoʊlər/ *noun* [sing.] **1** (*anatomy* 解) a system of nerves at the base of the stomach 腹腔神经丛 **2** (*informal*) the part of the body at the top of the stomach, below the RIBS 心口：*a painful punch in the solar plexus* 胸口上挨的很疼的一拳

ˈsolar system *noun* **1 the solar system** [sing.] the sun and all the planets that move around it 太阳系 **2** [C] any group of planets that all move around the same star 类太阳系

ˌsolar ˈyear *noun* the time it takes the earth to go around the sun once, approximately 365¼ days 太阳年

sold PAST TENSE, PAST PART. OF SELL

sol·der /ˈsəʊldə(r); ˈsɒldə(r); *NAmE* ˈsɑːdər/ *noun, verb*

■ ***noun*** [U] a mixture of metals that is heated and melted and then used to join metals, wires, etc. together 焊料；焊锡

■ ***verb*** **~ sth (to/onto sth)** | **~ (A and B together)** to join pieces of metal or wire with solder 焊接；焊合

ˈsoldering iron *noun* a tool that is heated and used for joining metals and wires by soldering them 烙铁

sol·dier /ˈsəʊldʒə(r); *NAmE* ˈsoʊl-/ *noun, verb*

■ ***noun*** a member of an army, especially one who is not an officer 军人；（尤指）士兵：*soldiers in uniform* 穿军装的士兵 ◇ *soldiers on duty* 值勤的士兵 ➲ SEE ALSO FOOT SOLDIER (1)

■ ***verb***

PHR V **ˌsoldier ˈon** to continue with what you are doing

S

or trying to achieve, especially when this is difficult or unpleasant 坚持；硬挺着

sol·dier·ing /'səʊldʒərɪŋ; *NAmE* 'soʊl-/ *noun* [U] the life or activity of being a soldier 军旅生活；行伍生涯；当兵

sol·dier·ly /'səʊldʒəli; *NAmE* 'soʊldʒərli/ *adj.* typical of a good soldier 有军人气质的；英武的

ˌsoldier of 'fortune *noun* a person who fights for any country or person who will pay them 雇佣兵 **SYN** **mercenary**

sol·diery /'səʊldʒəri; *NAmE* 'soʊl-/ *noun* [U+sing./pl. v.] (*old-fashioned*) a group of soldiers, especially of a particular kind（尤指某种类型的）军队，队伍

ˌsold 'out *adj.* **1** if a concert, match, etc. is **sold out**, there are no more tickets available for it（音乐会、比赛等）票已售完的，满场的，满座的 **2** if a shop/store is **sold out** of a product, it has no more of it left to sell（商品）销售一空的

sole **AW** /səʊl; *NAmE* soʊl/ *adj., noun, verb*

■ ***adj.*** [only before noun] **1** only; single 仅有的；唯一的：*the **sole surviving** member of the family* 那一家唯一在世的成员 ◇ *My **sole reason** for coming here was to see you.* 我到这儿唯一的原因就是来看你。◇ *This is the sole means of access to the building.* 这是这栋建筑物唯一的入口。**2** belonging to one person or group; not shared 独占的；专有的；全权处理的：*She has **sole responsibility** for the project.* 那个项目由她一人负责。◇ ***the sole owner*** 拥有全部产权的物主

■ ***noun*** **1** [C] the bottom surface of the foot 脚掌；脚底（板）：*The hot sand burned the **soles of their feet**.* 灼热的沙地使他们的脚掌感到火辣辣的。 ➲ VISUAL VOCAB PAGE V64 **2** [C] the bottom part of a shoe or sock, not including the heel 鞋底；袜底：*leather soles* 皮质鞋底 ➲ VISUAL VOCAB PAGE V69 ➲ COMPARE HEEL *n.* (2), (3) **3 -soled** (in adjectives 构成形容词) having the type of soles mentioned 有…底的：*rubber-soled shoes* 胶底鞋 **4** [U, C] (*pl.* **sole**) a flat sea fish that is used for food 鳎（可食用比目鱼）

■ ***verb*** [usually passive] **~ sth** to repair a shoe by replacing the sole 给（鞋）换底

sol·ecism /'sɒlɪsɪzəm; *NAmE* 'sɑːl-/ *noun* (*formal*) **1** a mistake in the use of language in speech or writing 语言错误；语病 **2** an example of bad manners or unacceptable behaviour 失礼；粗俗的举止（或话语）

S

sole·ly **AW** /'səʊlli; *NAmE* 'soʊlli/ *adv.* only; not involving sb/sth else 仅；只；唯；单独地：*She was motivated solely by self-interest.* 她完全是出于私利。◇ *Selection is based solely on merit.* 选拔唯贤。◇ *He became solely responsible for the firm.* 他成了公司唯一的负责人。

sol·emn /'sɒləm; *NAmE* 'sɑːləm/ *adj.* **1** (of a person 人) not happy or smiling 冷峻的；表情严肃的 **SYN** **serious**：*Her face grew solemn.* 她的脸显得严肃起来。◇ *a solemn expression* 冷峻的表情 **OPP** **cheerful** **2** done, said, etc. in a very serious and sincere way 庄严的；严正的；郑重的：*a **solemn oath/undertaking/vow, etc.*** 庄严的誓言、郑重的承诺、严肃的誓约等 **3** (of a religious ceremony or formal occasion 宗教仪式或正式场合) performed in a serious way 庄严的；隆重的：*a solemn ritual* 隆重的仪式 ➲ MORE LIKE THIS 20, page R27 ▶ **sol·emn·ly** *adv.*：*He nodded solemnly.* 他郑重地点了点头。◇ *She solemnly promised not to say a word to anyone about it.* 她郑重承诺不向任何人透露一个字。◇ *The choir walked solemnly past.* 唱诗班庄严地走过。

so·lem·nity /sə'lemnəti/ *noun* **1** [U] the quality of being solemn 庄严；庄重；严肃；郑重：*He was smiling, but his eyes retained a look of solemnity.* 他脸上挂着笑容，但眼神依旧严肃。◇ *He was buried with great pomp and solemnity.* 他的葬礼盛大而隆重。**2** **solemnities** [pl.] (*formal*) formal things that people do at a serious event or occasion（重大场合的）礼仪，仪式：*to observe the solemnities of the occasion* 遵守这一盛典的礼仪

sol·em·nize (*BrE also* **-ise**) /'sɒləmnaɪz; *NAmE* 'sɑːl-/ *verb* **~ sth** (*formal*) to perform a religious ceremony, especially a marriage 举行（宗教仪式，尤指婚礼）

so·len·oid /'sɒlənɔɪd; 'səʊl-; *NAmE* 'sɑːl-; 'soʊl-/ *noun* (*physics* 物) a piece of wire, wound into circles, which acts as a MAGNET when carrying an electric current 螺线管（通电时产生磁场）

ˌsol-'fa *noun* (*also* **ˌtonic ˌsol-'fa**) (*music* 音) a system of naming the notes of the SCALE, used in teaching singing（歌唱教学的）首调唱名法

so·licit /sə'lɪsɪt/ *verb* **1** [T, I] (*formal*) to ask sb for sth, such as support, money or information; to try to get sth or persuade sb to do sth 索求，请求…给予（援助、钱或信息）；征求；筹集：**~ sth (from sb)** *They were planning to solicit funds from a number of organizations.* 他们正计划向一些机构募集资金。◇ **~ sb (for sth)** *Historians and critics are solicited for their opinions.* 向历史学家和批评家征求了意见。◇ **~ (for sth)** *to solicit for money* 筹款 ◇ **~ sb to do sth** *Volunteers are being solicited to assist with the project.* 正在征求志愿者来协助该项目。**2** [I, T] **~ (sb)** (of a PROSTITUTE 妓女) to offer to have sex with people in return for money 招徕（嫖客）；拉（客）：*Prostitutes solicited openly in the streets.* 妓女公然在街上拉客。◇ *the crime of soliciting* 拉客卖淫罪 ▶ **so·lici·ta·tion** /səˌlɪsɪ'teɪʃn/ *noun* [U, C] (*especially NAmE*)：*the solicitation of money for election funds* 竞选资金筹集活动

so·lici·tor /sə'lɪsɪtə(r)/ *noun* **1** (*BrE*) a lawyer who prepares legal documents, for example for the sale of land or buildings, advises people on legal matters, and can speak for them in some courts of law 事务律师，诉状律师（代拟法律文书、提供法律咨询等的一般辩护律师） ➲ NOTE AT LAWYER **2** (*NAmE*) a person whose job is to visit or telephone people and try to sell them sth 推销员 **3** (*NAmE*) the most senior legal officer of a city, town or government department（城镇或政府部门负责法律事务的）法务官

soˌlicitor 'general *noun* (*pl.* **solicitors general**) a senior legal officer in Britain or the US, next in rank below the ATTORNEY GENERAL（英国）副检察长；（美国）司法部副部长

so·lici·tous /sə'lɪsɪtəs/ *adj.* (*formal*) being very concerned for sb and wanting to make sure that they are comfortable, well or happy 操心的；关怀的；关切的 **SYN** **attentive** ▶ **so·lici·tous·ly** *adv.* (*formal*)

so·lici·tude /sə'lɪsɪtjuːd; *NAmE* -tuːd/ *noun* [U] **~ (for sb/sth)** (*formal*) anxious care for sb's comfort, health or happiness 牵挂；关怀；关切：*I was touched by his solicitude for the boy.* 他对孩子的关怀让我感动。

solids 立体

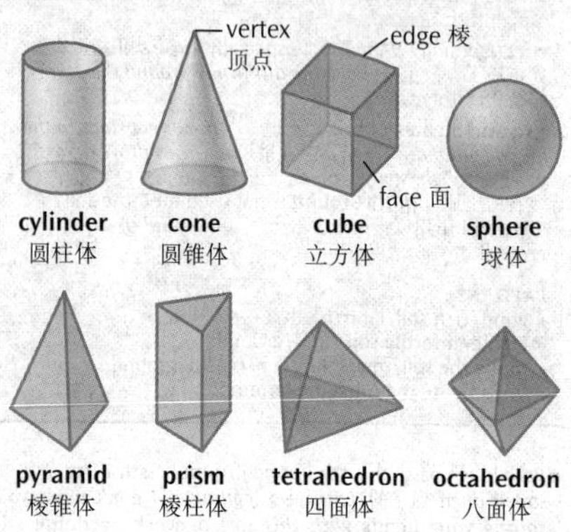

solid 🔑 /'sɒlɪd; *NAmE* 'sɑːl-/ *adj., noun*

■ ***adj.***

• **NOT LIQUID/GAS** 非液体 / 气体 **1** 🔑 hard or firm; not in the form of a liquid or gas 固体的；坚硬的：*The planet*

Jupiter may have no solid surface at all. 木星表面可能根本就不是固体的。◇ *The boat bumped against a solid object.* 船撞到了硬物。◇ *She had refused all solid food.* 所有的固体食物她都不肯吃。◇ *It was so cold that the stream had* ***frozen solid***. 天气很冷，小河冻得结成冰了。◇ *The boiler uses* ***solid fuel***. 这个锅炉烧固体燃料。

- **WITHOUT HOLES OR SPACES** 无空隙 **2** having no holes or spaces inside; not hollow 无空隙的；非中空的；实心的：*They were drilling through solid rock.* 他们正在把实心岩钻通。◇ *The stores are* ***packed solid*** (= very full and crowded) *at this time of year.* 每年一到这个时候，商店总是挤得水泄不通。
- **STRONG** 结实 **3** strong and made well 结实的；坚固的；牢固的：*These chains seem fairly solid.* 这些链子看着挺结实。
- **RELIABLE** 可靠 **4** that you can rely on; having a strong basis 可靠的；可信赖的；坚实的：*As yet, they have no solid evidence.* 他们至今没有任何可靠的证据。◇ *This provided a solid foundation for their marriage.* 这为他们的婚姻提供了坚实的基础。◇ *The Irish team were* ***solid as a rock*** *in defence.* 爱尔兰队的防守坚如磐石。
- **GOOD BUT NOT SPECIAL** 不错 **5** definitely good and steady but perhaps not excellent or special 相当不错（但谈不上出色或独特）的：*2008 was a year of solid achievement.* * 2008 年是颇有成绩的一年。◇ *He's a solid player.* 他是个相当不错的运动员。
- **MATERIAL** 材料 **6** [only before noun] made completely of the material mentioned (that is, the material is not only on the surface) 纯质的；纯…的；全…的：*a solid gold bracelet* 纯金手镯
- **PERIOD OF TIME** 一段时间 **7** (*informal*) without a pause; continuous 连续的；不间断的；整整的：*The essay represents a solid week's work.* 这篇文章是用整整一星期写出来的。◇ *It rained for two hours solid this afternoon.* 今天下午连着下了两个小时的雨。
- **COLOUR** 色彩 **8** of the colour mentioned and no other colour 纯色的；单色的：*One cat is black and white, the other solid black.* 一只猫是黑白花色的，另一只猫是纯黑色的。
- **SHAPE** 形状 **9** (*geometry* 几何) a shape that is **solid** has length, width and height and is not flat 立体的；立方的：*A cube is a solid figure.* 立方体是一种立体图形。
- **IN AGREEMENT** 一致 **10** in complete agreement; agreed on by everyone 一致的；意见统一的：*The strike was solid, supported by all the members.* 这次罢工是统一行动，得到所有成员的支持。➲ SEE ALSO ROCK SOLID

■ ***noun***

- **NOT LIQUID/GAS** 非液体 / 气体 **1** a substance or an object that is solid, not a liquid or a gas 固体：*liquids and solids* 液体与固体 ◇ *The baby is not yet on solids* (= eating solid food). 婴儿还不能吃固体食物。
- **SHAPE** 形状 **2** (*geometry* 几何) a shape which has length, width and height, such as a CUBE 立体图形

sol·i·dar·ity /ˌsɒlɪˈdærəti; *NAmE* ˌsɑːl-/ *noun* [U] support by one person or group of people for another because they share feelings, opinions, aims, etc. 团结；齐心协力；同心同德；相互支持：*community solidarity* 社区团结 ◇ **~ with sb** *to express/show solidarity with sb* 表示 / 表明支持某人 ◇ *Demonstrations were held as* ***a gesture of solidarity*** *with the hunger strikers.* 人们举行示威游行，以表示对绝食抗议者的支持。

so·lid·ify /səˈlɪdɪfaɪ/ *verb* (**so·lidi·fies**, **so·lidi·fy·ing**, **so·lidi·fied**, **so·lidi·fied**) **1** [I, T] **~ (into sth)** | **~ (sth)** to become solid; to make sth solid（使）凝固，变硬，变得结实：*The mixture will solidify into toffee.* 这种混合物凝固后就成了太妃糖。◇ *solidified lava* 固结熔岩 **2** [I, T] (*formal*) (of ideas, etc. 观念等) to become or to make sth become more definite and less likely to change（使）变得坚定，变得稳固，巩固：**~ (into sth)** *Vague objections to the system solidified into firm opposition.* 先前对这一制度不大明朗的反对演变成了坚决的抵制。◇ **~ sth** *They solidified their position as Britain's top band.* 他们巩固了自己作为英国顶尖乐队的地位。▸ **so·lidi·fi·ca·tion** /səˌlɪdɪfɪˈkeɪʃn/ *noun* [U]

so·lid·ity /səˈlɪdəti/ *noun* [U] the quality or state of being solid 固态；坚固性；可靠性：*the strength and solidity of Romanesque architecture* 罗马式建筑坚固结实的特性 ◇ *Her writings have extraordinary depth and solidity.* 她写的东西立意极深，内容特别充实。◇ *the solidity of his support for his staff* 他对自己的工作班子的有力支持

sol·id·ly /ˈsɒlɪdli; *NAmE* ˈsɑːl-/ *adv.* **1** in a firm and strong way 坚固地；结实地；牢固地：*a large, solidly-built house* 建造得坚固的大房子 ◇ *He stood solidly in my path.* 他把我的路挡得死死的。**2** continuously; without stopping 连续地；不间断地；整整地：*It rained solidly for three hours.* 雨下了整整三个小时。 **3** agreeing with or supporting sb/sth completely 一致地；完全支持：*The state is solidly Republican.* 这个州是共和党的天下。

ˌsolid-ˈstate *adj.* (*specialist*) using or containing solid SEMICONDUCTORS 固态半导体的；固体的：*a solid-state radio* 固态半导体收音机

so·lilo·quy /səˈlɪləkwi/ *noun* [C, U] (*pl.* **-ies**) a speech in a play in which a character, who is alone on the stage, speaks his or her thoughts; the act of speaking thoughts in this way 独白（的台词）；独白：*Hamlet's famous soliloquy, 'To be or not to be…'* 哈姆雷特那段"生存还是毁灭…"的著名独白 ◇ *the playwright's use of soliloquy* 这位剧作家对于独白的运用 ➲ COMPARE MONOLOGUE ➲ **WORDFINDER NOTE** AT DRAMA ▸ **so·lilo·quize**, **-ise** /səˈlɪləkwaɪz/ *verb* [I]

sol·ip·sism /ˈsɒlɪpsɪzəm; *NAmE* ˈsɑːl-/ *noun* [U] (*philosophy* 哲) the theory that only the SELF exists or can be known 唯我论 ▸ **sol·ip·sis·tic** /ˌsɒlɪpˈsɪstɪk; *NAmE* ˌsɑːl-/ *adj.*

soli·taire /ˌsɒlɪˈteə(r); *NAmE* ˈsɑːləter/ *noun* **1** [U] (*BrE*) a game for one person in which you remove pieces from their places on a special board after moving other pieces over them. The aim is to finish with only one piece left on the board. 单人跳棋 **2** (*NAmE*) (*BrE* **pa·tience**) [U] a card game for only one player 单人纸牌游戏 **3** [C] a single PRECIOUS STONE; a piece of jewellery with a single precious stone in it 独粒宝石；独粒宝石首饰

soli·tary /ˈsɒlətri; *NAmE* ˈsɑːləteri/ *adj., noun*

■ ***adj.*** **1** [usually before noun] done alone; without other people 独自的；单独的：*She enjoys long solitary walks.* 她喜欢独自长距离散步。◇ *He led a solitary life.* 他过着独居生活。**2** (of a person or an animal 人或动物) enjoying being alone; frequently spending time alone 喜欢（或惯于）独处的：*He was a solitary child.* 他是一个孤僻的孩子。◇ *Tigers are solitary animals.* 虎是独居动物。**3** (of a person, thing or place 人、物或处所) alone, with no other people or things around 单个的；孤单的；孤零零的 SYN **single**：*a solitary farm* 孤然孑立的农场 ◇ *A solitary light burned dimly in the hall.* 大厅里点着一盏孤灯，发出昏暗的光。 **4** [usually before noun] (especially in negative sentences and questions 尤用于否定句和疑问句) only one 唯一的；仅有的 SYN **single**：*There was not a solitary shred of evidence* (= none at all). 一丁点证据都没有。 ▸ **soli·tari·ness** *noun* [U]

■ ***noun*** (*pl.* **-ies**) **1** [U] (*informal*) = SOLITARY CONFINEMENT **2** [C] (*formal*) a person who chooses to live alone 独居者

ˌsolitary conˈfinement (*also informal* **soli·tary**) *noun* [U] a punishment in which a prisoner is kept alone in a separate cell 单独监禁；单独禁闭：*to be in solitary confinement* 被单独监禁

soli·tude /ˈsɒlɪtjuːd; *NAmE* ˈsɑːlətuːd/ *noun* [U] the state of being alone, especially when you find this pleasant 独处；独居 SYN **privacy**：*She longed for peace and solitude.* 她渴望安宁，渴望独享清静。

solo /ˈsəʊləʊ; *NAmE* ˈsoʊloʊ/ *adj., noun*

■ ***adj.*** [only before noun] **1** done by one person alone, without anyone helping them 独自的；单独的：*his first solo flight* 他的首次单飞 ◇ *a solo effort* 一人之力 **2** connected with or played as a musical solo 独唱的；独奏的：*a solo artist* (= for example a singer who sings on their own, not as part of a group) 独唱歌手 ◇ *a piece for solo violin* 小提琴独奏曲 ▸ **solo** *adv.*：*She wanted to fly solo across the Atlantic.* 她想独自一人驾机飞越大西洋。◇ *After three years with the band he decided to* ***go solo***. 在那支乐队里三年之后，他决定单飞。

S

■ ***noun*** (*pl.* **-os**) **1** a piece of music, dance or entertainment performed by only one person 独唱；独奏；独舞；单人表演：*a guitar solo* 吉他独奏 ➲ COMPARE DUET **2** a flight in which the pilot flies alone without an INSTRUCTOR (= teacher) 单飞

solo·ist /ˈsəʊləʊɪst; *NAmE* ˈsoʊloʊ-/ *noun* a person who plays an instrument or performs alone 独奏者；独唱者；单独表演者 ➲ **WORDFINDER NOTE** AT CONCERT

Solo·mon /ˈsɒləmən; *NAmE* ˈsɑːl-/ *noun* used to talk about a very wise person 智者；智慧超群的人：*In this job you need to exhibit the wisdom of Solomon.* 做这份工作需要表现出所罗门王一样的才智。**ORIGIN** From Solomon in the Bible, a king of Israel who was famous for being wise. 源自《圣经》中以智慧著称的以色列王所罗门。

sol·stice /ˈsɒlstɪs; *NAmE* ˈsɑːlstəs/ *noun* either of the two times of the year at which the sun reaches its highest or lowest point in the sky at midday, marked by the longest and shortest days 至（点）；（夏或冬）至：*the **summer/ winter solstice*** 夏至；冬至 ➲ **WORDFINDER NOTE** AT SUN

sol·uble /ˈsɒljəbl; *NAmE* ˈsɑːl-/ *adj.* **1 ~ (in sth)** that can be dissolved in a liquid 可溶的：*soluble aspirin* 可溶性阿司匹林 ◇ *Glucose is soluble in water.* 葡萄糖可溶于水。**2** (*formal*) (of a problem 问题) that can be solved 可解决的；可解的 **OPP** **insoluble** ▸ **solu·bil·ity** /ˌsɒljuˈbɪləti; *NAmE* ˌsɑːl-/ *noun* [U]

so·lu·tion 🔑 /səˈluːʃn/ *noun* **1** 🔑 [C] **~ (to sth)** a way of solving a problem or dealing with a difficult situation 解决办法；处理手段 **SYN** **answer**：*Attempts to **find a solution** have failed.* 试图找到解决办法的种种努力全都失败了。◇ *There's no simple solution to this problem.* 这个问题没有简单的解决办法。◇ *Do you have a better solution?* 你有更好的解决办法吗？ **2** 🔑 [C] **~ (to sth)** an answer to a PUZZLE or to a problem in mathematics 答案；解；谜底：*The solution to last week's quiz is on page 81.* 上星期测验的答案在第 81 页。**3** 🔑 [C, U] a liquid in which sth is dissolved 溶液：*an alkaline solution* 碱溶液 ◇ *saline solution* 盐溶液 ➲ **WORDFINDER NOTE** AT CHEMISTRY **4** [U] the process of dissolving a solid or gas in a liquid 溶解（过程）：*the solution of glucose in water* 葡萄糖在水中的溶解

solve 🔑 /sɒlv; *NAmE* sɑːlv; sɔːlv/ *verb* **1** 🔑 **~ sth** to find a way of dealing with a problem or difficult situation 解决；处理：*Attempts are being made to solve the problem of waste disposal.* 正在想办法解决废物处理的问题。**2** 🔑 **~ sth** to find the correct answer or explanation for sth 解答；破解：*to **solve an equation/a puzzle/a riddle*** 解方程；解难题；解谜 ◇ *to **solve a crime/mystery*** 破案；解开奥秘 ▸ **solv·able** *adj.*：*These problems are all solvable.* 这些问题都是可以解决的。

solv·ency /ˈsɒlvənsi; *NAmE* ˈsɑːl-/ *noun* [U] the state of not being in debt (= not owing money) 无债务；不负债

solv·ent /ˈsɒlvənt; *NAmE* ˈsɑːl-/ *noun, adj.*

■ ***noun*** [U, C] a substance, especially a liquid, that can dissolve another substance 溶剂；溶媒

■ ***adj.*** **1** [not usually before noun] having enough money to pay your debts; not in debt 有偿付能力；无债务 **OPP** **insolvent** **2** (*specialist*) able to dissolve another substance, or be dissolved in another substance 有溶解力的；可溶解的：*Lead is more solvent in acidic water.* 铅在酸性水中更易溶解。

ˈ**solvent abuse** *noun* [U] the practice of breathing in gases from glue or similar substances in order to produce a state of excitement 溶媒滥用，挥发性溶剂使用（如嗅吸胶毒以产生兴奋感）➲ SEE ALSO GLUE-SNIFFING

solv·er /ˈsɒlvə(r); *NAmE* ˈsɑːl-; ˈsɔːl-/ *noun* a person who finds an answer to a problem or a difficult situation（问题的）解决者；（困难局面的）处理者：*She's a good **problem solver**.* 她是解决问题的高手。

sombre (*BrE*) (*US* **som·ber**) /ˈsɒmbə(r); *NAmE* ˈsɑːm-/ *adj.* **1** dark in colour; dull 昏暗的；阴沉的；暗淡的 **SYN** **drab**：*dressed in sombre shades of grey and black* 穿着灰色和黑色的暗色调衣服 **2** sad and serious 阴郁的；沮丧的 **SYN** **melancholy**：*Paul was in a **sombre mood**.* 保罗当时心情忧郁。◇ *The year ended on a sombre note.* 那一年在沉闷的气氛中结束了。▸ **sombre·ly** (*BrE*) (*US* **som·berly**) *adv.* **sombre·ness** (*BrE*) (*US* **somber·ness**) *noun* [U]

som·brero /sɒmˈbreərəʊ; *NAmE* sɑːmˈbreroʊ/ *noun* (*pl.* **-os**) a Mexican hat for men that is tall with a very wide BRIM, turned up at the edges（墨西哥）阔边帽 ➲ **VISUAL VOCAB PAGE V70**

some 🔑 *det., pron., adv.*

■ ***det.*** /səm; *strong form* sʌm/ **1** 🔑 used with uncountable nouns or plural countable nouns to mean 'an amount of' or 'a number of', when the amount or number is not given（与不可数名词或复数可数名词连用）一些，若干：*There's still some wine in the bottle.* 瓶子里还有些葡萄酒。◇ *Have some more vegetables.* 再吃点蔬菜吧。**HELP** In negative sentences and questions **any** is usually used instead of 'some'. 在否定句和疑问句中，通常用 any，而不用 some：*I don't want any more vegetables.* 我不想要更多蔬菜了。◇ *Is there any wine left?* 还有剩下的葡萄酒吗？However, **some** is used in questions that expect a positive reply. 但在预料会得到肯定回答的疑问句中仍用 some：*Would you like some milk in your coffee?* 你的咖啡要加牛奶吗？ ◇ *Didn't you borrow some books of mine?* 你不是向我借了几本书吗？ **2** 🔑 /sʌm/ used to refer to certain members of a group or certain types of a thing, but not all of them（指群体中的某些成员或事物的某些类型）某些，部分，有的：*Some people find this more difficult than others.* 这件事有人觉得难，有人觉得不难。◇ *I like some modern music* (= but not all of it). 有些现代音乐我喜欢。**3** 🔑 /sʌm/ a large number or amount of sth 好些；不少的；相当多的：*It was with some surprise that I heard the news.* 听到这个消息我吃惊不小。◇ *We've known each other for some years now.* 我们俩认识有些年头了。◇ *We're going to be working together for **some time*** (= a long time). 我们要在一起工作相当一段时间。**4** 🔑 /sʌm/ a small amount or number of sth 少量的；不多的：*There is some hope that things will improve.* 情况好转还是有希望的。**5** 🔑 used with singular nouns to refer to a person, place, thing or time that is not known or not identified（与单数名词连用，表示未知或未确指的人、地、事物或时间）某个：*There must be some mistake.* 一定是出了什么差错。◇ *He's in **some kind of** trouble.* 他遇到了什么麻烦。◇ *She won a competition in **some** newspaper **or other**.* 她在某报举办的竞赛中得了奖。◇ *I'll see you again some time, I'm sure.* 我敢肯定，什么时候我们还会再见面的。**6** /sʌm/ (*informal, sometimes ironic*) used to express a positive or negative opinion aboutsb/sth（表达褒贬意见时用）真可谓，算不上：*That was some party!* 那才叫晚会！◇ *Some expert you are! You know even less than me.* 你也算专家！你还不如我呢。

■ ***pron.*** /sʌm/ **~ (of sb/sth)** **1** 🔑 used to refer to an amount of sth or a number of people or things when the amount or number is not given（数量不确切时用）有些人，有些事物：*Some disapprove of the idea.* 有些人不赞成这个主意。◇ *You'll find some in the drawer.* 你会在抽屉里找到一些。◇ *Here are some of our suggestions.* 这是我们的一些建议。**HELP** In negative sentences and questions **any** is usually used instead of 'some'. 在否定句和疑问句中，通常用 any，而不用 some：*I don't want any.* 我不想要。◇ *Do you have any of the larger ones?* 有没有尺码大一点的？However, **some** is used in questions that expect a positive reply. 但在预料会得到肯定回答的疑问句中仍用 some：*Would you like some?* 你要来一点儿吗？◇ *Weren't you looking for some of those?* 你当时是不是在找那一种的？ **2** 🔑 a part of the whole number or amount being considered 部分；有的；有些；若干：*All these students are good, but some work harder than others.* 这些学生全都不错，但有的很用功，有的没那么用功。◇ *Some of the music was weird.* 这音乐有些地方有点怪。

IDM **... and ˈthen some** (*informal*) and a lot more than that 远不止这些；此外还有不少：*We got our money's worth and then some.* 我们的钱花得值，太值了。

■ ***adv.*** /sʌm/ **1** used before numbers to mean 'approximately'（用于数词前，意同 approximately）大约，差不多：*Some thirty people attended the funeral.* 大约有三十人参加了葬礼。**2** (*NAmE, informal*) to some degree 稍微；有

点：*He needs feeding up some.* 他需要多吃些东西补一补。◇ *'Are you finding the work any easier?' 'Some.'* "你是不是觉得工作顺手一些了？""是顺手一些了。"

-some *suffix* **1** (in adjectives 构成形容词) producing; likely to 引起（或易于）…的：*fearsome* 可怕的 ◇ *quarrelsome* 爱争吵的 **2** (in nouns 构成名词) a group of the number mentioned …人（或…个）一组：*a foursome* 四人组合

some·body /'sʌmbədi/ *pron.* = SOMEONE：*Somebody should have told me.* 应该有人告诉我才是。◇ *She thinks she's really somebody in that car.* 她以为，坐上那辆车，她就真成个人物了。**OPP nobody**

'some day (*also* **someday**) *adv.* at some time in the future 总有一天；有朝一日；将来：*Some day he'll be famous.* 总有一天他会成名的。

some·how /'sʌmhaʊ/ *adv.* **1** (*also NAmE, informal* **some·way, some·ways**) in a way that is not known or certain 以某种方式（或方法）：*We must stop him from seeing her somehow.* 不管怎么着，我们都不能让他见到她。◇ ***Somehow or other** I must get a new job.* 我必须想方设法找份新工作。**2** for a reason that you do not know or understand 由于某种未知的原因；不知为什么；不知怎么地：*Somehow, I don't feel I can trust him.* 不知为什么，我觉得不能信任他。◇ *She looked different somehow.* 不知怎么地，她看上去变了。

some·one /'sʌmwʌn/ (*also* **some·body**) *pron.* **1** a person who is not known or mentioned by name 某人：*There's someone at the door.* 门口有个人。◇ *Someone's left their bag behind.* 有人把包落下了。◇ *It's time for someone new* (= a new person) *to take over.* 现在该换个新人来干了。◇ *It couldn't have been me—it must have been **someone else*** (= a different person). 那不可能是我，准是别人。◇ *Should we call a doctor **or someone**?* 我们要不要请个大夫什么的？ **HELP** The difference between **someone** and **anyone** is the same as the difference between **some** and **any**. Look at the notes there. * someone 和 anyone 的区别与 some 和 any 的区别相同。参看该两词条下的注解。**2** an important person 重要人物：*He was a small-time lawyer keen to **be someone**.* 他是个没有什么名堂却总想出人头地的律师。➲ COMPARE NOBODY *pron.*

some·place /'sʌmpleɪs/ *adv., pron.* (*NAmE*) = SOMEWHERE：*It has to go someplace.* 它一定是搁在什么地方了。◇ *Can't you do that **someplace else**?* 那件事你就不能换个地方干吗？◇ *We need to find **someplace to live**.* 我们需要找个住的地方。

som·er·sault /'sʌməsɔːlt; *NAmE* -mərs-/ *noun, verb*

■ ***noun*** a movement in which sb turns over completely, with their feet over their head, on the ground or in the air 翻滚；空翻；筋斗：*to **do/turn a somersault*** 做翻滚动作 ◇ *He turned back somersaults.* 他做了几个后空翻。◇ (*figurative*) *Her heart did a complete somersault when she saw him.* 她见到他，心里咯噔了一下。

■ ***verb*** [I] (**+ adv./prep.**) to turn over completely in the air 做翻滚；做空翻：*The car hit the kerb and somersaulted into the air.* 汽车撞到马路牙子上，腾空翻了出去。

some·thing /'sʌmθɪŋ/ *pron., adv.*

■ ***pron.*** **1** a thing that is not known or mentioned by name 某事；某物：*We stopped for something to eat.* 我们停下来吃点儿东西。◇ *Give me **something to do**.* 给我点活儿干吧。◇ *There's something wrong with the TV.* 电视出毛病了。◇ ***There's something about** this place that frightens me.* 这个地方有点儿让我害怕。◇ *Don't just stand there. **Do something!*** 别在那儿干站着，做点儿什么吧！◇ *His name is Alan something* (= I don't know his other name). 他的名字叫艾伦什么的。◇ *She's a professor of **something or other*** (= I'm not sure what) *at Leeds.* 她是利兹大学某个学科的教授。◇ *He's **something in*** (= has a job connected with) *television.* 他是搞电视的。◇ *The car hit a tree **or something**.* 汽车撞上了树或别的什么东西。◇ *I could just eat **a little something**.* 我只能吃一点点东西。 **HELP** The difference between **something** and **anything** is the same as the difference between **some** and **any**. Look at the notes there. * something 和 anything 的区别与 some 和 any 的区别相同。参看该两词条下的注解。**2** (*informal*) a thing that is thought to be important or worth taking notice of 被认为重要（或值得注意）的事物：*There's **something in*** (= some truth or some fact or opinion worth considering in) *what he says.* 他的话不无道理。◇ *It's **quite something*** (= a thing that you should feel happy about) *to have a job at all these days.* 如今能有份工作就该知足了。◇ *'We should finish by tomorrow.' '**That's something*** (= a good thing), *anyway.'* "我们明天应该就能结束了。""那也好哇。" **3** (*informal*) used to show that a description or an amount, etc. is not exact（表示不确切的描述或数量）大致，左右：*She called at **something after** ten o'clock.* 她十点多钟来过电话。◇ *a new comedy aimed at **thirty-somethings*** (= people between thirty and forty years old) 一部以三十几岁的人为主要观众的新喜剧 ◇ *It tastes **something like** melon.* 这吃起来有点儿像甜瓜。◇ *They pay six pounds an hour. **Something like that**.* 他们按每小时六英镑付费，大致如此。◇ *She found herself **something of a*** (= to some degree a) *celebrity.* 她发现自己差不多成名人了。◇ *The programme's **something to do with*** (= in some way about) *the environment.* 这是一个跟环境有关的节目。◇ *He gave her a wry look, **something between** amusement and regret.* 他用颇耐玩味的目光看她一眼，说不清是开心，还是怅惋。

IDM **'make something of yourself** to be successful in life 有所成就；获得成功 **something 'else 1** a different thing; another thing 另外一件事；别的东西：*He said something else that I thought was interesting.* 他讲的另外一件事我觉得挺有意思的。**2** (*informal*) a person, a thing or an event that is much better than others of a similar type 出色的人（或事物）：*I've seen some fine players, but she's something else.* 优秀运动员我见过不少，但她出类拔萃。

■ ***adv.*** (*non-standard*) used with an adjective to emphasize a statement（与形容词连用）很，非常：*She was swearing something terrible.* 她骂得很难听。

some·time /'sʌmtaɪm/ *adv., adj.*

■ ***adv.*** (*also* **'some time**) at a time that you do not know exactly or has not yet been decided 在某时（不确切或尚未决定）：*I saw him sometime last summer.* 我去年夏天什么时候见过他。◇ *We must get together sometime.* 我们一定要找个时间聚一下。

■ ***adj.*** [only before noun] (*formal*) **1** used to refer to what sb used to be（指某人曾经是…）从前的，一度的：*Thomas Atkins, sometime vicar of this parish* 本教区先前的牧师托马斯·阿特金斯 **2** (*NAmE*) used to refer to what sb does occasionally 间或的；偶尔的：*a sometime contributor to this magazine* 一位偶尔给本刊投稿的作者

some·times /'sʌmtaɪmz/ *adv.* occasionally rather than all of the time 有时；间或：*Sometimes I go by car.* 有时我坐车去。◇ *He sometimes writes to me.* 他偶尔给我写封信。◇ *I like to be on my own sometimes.* 有时候我喜欢一个人待着。

some·way /'sʌmweɪ/ (*also* **someways** /'sʌmweɪz/) *adv.* (*NAmE, informal*) = SOMEHOW (1)

some·what **AW** /'sʌmwɒt; *NAmE* -wʌt/ *adv.* to some degree 有点；有几分；稍微 **SYN** **rather**：*I was somewhat surprised to see him.* 见到他我有点诧异。◇ *The situation has changed somewhat since we last met.* 自我们上次见面以来情况有些变化。◇ *What happened to them remains **somewhat of** a mystery.* 他们到底出了什么事，到现在仍可以说是个谜。

some·where /'sʌmweə(r); *NAmE* -wer/ (*NAmE also* **some·place**) *adv.* in, at or to a place that you do not know or do not mention by name 在某处；到某处：*I've seen him somewhere before.* 我以前在哪儿见过他。◇ *Can we go somewhere warm?* 我们能不能去个暖和的地方？◇ *I've already looked there—it must be **somewhere else**.* 我已经去那儿看过了，肯定是在别处。◇ *He went to school in York **or somewhere*** (= I'm not sure where). 他是在约克还是什么地方上的学。◇ *They live **somewhere or other** in France.* 他们住在法国的一个什么地方。**HELP** The difference between **somewhere** and **anywhere** is the same as the difference between **some** and **any**. Look at the notes there.

S

* somewhere 和 anywhere 的区别与 some 和 any 的区别相同。参看该两词条下的注解。 ▶ **some·where** (*NAmE also* **some·place**) *pron.*: *We need to find* **somewhere to** (= a place to) *live.* 我们需要找个住处。◇ *I know somewhere we can go.* 我知道有个地方我们可以去。

IDM **'get somewhere** (*informal*) to make progress in what you are doing 有进展 **somewhere around, between, etc. sth** approximately the number or amount mentioned 大约…；…左右: *It cost somewhere around two thousand dollars.* 买下来要花大约两千美元。

som·mer /'sɒmə; *NAmE* 'sɑːmə/ *adv.* (*SAfrE, informal*) just; simply 只是；仅仅: *He sommer hit me without saying anything.* 他一句话不说就打我。

som·nam·bu·list /sɒm'næmbjəlɪst; *NAmE* sɑːm-/ *noun* (*formal*) = SLEEPWALKER ▶ **som·nam·bu·lism** /-lɪzəm/ *noun* [U]

som·no·lent /'sɒmnələnt; *NAmE* 'sɑːm-/ *adj.* (*formal*) **1** almost asleep 瞌睡的；困倦的；睡意蒙眬的: *a somnolent cat* 打瞌睡的猫 ◇ (*figurative*) *a somnolent town* 安谧的小城 **2** making you feel tired 催眠的；使人昏昏欲睡的: *a somnolent Sunday afternoon* 使人昏昏欲睡的星期天下午 ▶ **som·no·lence** *noun* [U]

son /sʌn/ *noun* **1** [C] a person's male child 儿子: *We have two sons and a daughter.* 我们有两个儿子，一个女儿。◇ *They have three grown-up sons.* 他们有三个成年的儿子。◇ *He's the son of an Oxford professor.* 他是牛津大学一位教授的儿子。◇ *Maine & Sons, Grocers* (= the name of a company on a sign) 梅因父子杂货店 ➲ COLLOCATIONS AT CHILD **2** [sing.] (*informal*) a friendly form of address that is used by an older man to a young man or boy (年长者对年轻男子或男孩的爱称) 孩子: *Well, son, how can I help you?* 那么，孩子，我能为你做点什么呢？ **3** [C] (*literary*) a man who belongs to a particular place or country, etc. (某个地方、国家等的) 男性成员，子孙: *one of France's most famous sons* 法国最著名的人士之一 **4 my son** (*formal*) used by a priest to address a boy or man (司铎对男子或男孩的称呼) 孩子 **5 the Son** [sing.] Jesus Christ as the second member of the TRINITY 圣子 (耶稣基督): *the Father, the Son and the Holy Spirit* 圣父、圣子和圣灵 IDM SEE FATHER *n.*, FAVOURITE *adj.*, PRODIGAL

sonar /'səʊnɑː(r); *NAmE* 'soʊ-/ *noun* [U] equipment or a system for finding objects underwater using sound waves 声呐 (利用声波探测水下物体的装置或系统) ➲ COMPARE RADAR

son·ata /sə'nɑːtə/ *noun* a piece of music for one instrument or for one instrument and a piano, usually divided into three or four parts 奏鸣曲

son et lu·mi·ère /ˌsɒn eɪ 'luːmjeə(r); *NAmE* ˌsɔːn eɪ luːm'jer/ *noun* [U] (*from French*) a performance held at night at a famous place that tells its history with special lights and sound 声光表演 (在名胜地点举行，借助声光效果，介绍该地掌故)

song /sɒŋ; *NAmE* sɔːŋ/ *noun* **1** [C] a short piece of music with words that you sing 歌；歌曲: *a folk/love/pop, etc.* **song** 民歌、情歌、流行歌曲等 ◇ *We sang a song together.* 我们一起唱了一首歌。➲ COLLOCATIONS AT MUSIC ➲ SEE ALSO SWANSONG **2** [U] songs in general; music for singing (统称) 歌曲；歌唱；声乐: *The story is told through song and dance.* 故事是通过歌舞的形式来表现的。◇ *Suddenly he* **burst into song** (= started to sing). 突然间，他放声唱了起来。➲ SEE ALSO PLAINSONG **3** [U, C] the musical sounds that birds make (鸟的) 鸣啭，啼啭: *the song of the blackbird* 黑鹂的鸣啭

IDM **for a 'song** (*informal*) very cheaply; at a low price 非常便宜；以低价 **a song and 'dance (about sth)** **1** (*BrE, informal, disapproving*) if you make a **song and dance** about sth, you complain or talk about it too much when this is not necessary 小题大做的抱怨；无谓的吵闹；胡搅蛮缠 **2** [C] (*NAmE, informal*) a long explanation about sth, or excuse for sth 冗长的解释；絮叨的托辞 **on 'song** (*informal*) working or performing well 性能良好；运转顺畅 ➲ MORE AT SING

song·bird /'sɒŋbɜːd; *NAmE* 'sɔːŋbɜːrd/ *noun* a bird that has a musical call, for example a BLACKBIRD or THRUSH 鸣禽

song·book /'sɒŋbʊk; *NAmE* 'sɔːŋ-/ *noun* a book containing the music and words of different songs 歌曲集；歌本

song·smith /'sɒŋsmɪθ; *NAmE* 'sɔːŋ-/ *noun* (*informal*) a person who writes popular songs 写流行歌曲的人

song·ster /'sɒŋstə(r); *NAmE* 'sɔːŋ-/ *noun* (*old-fashioned*) **1** a word sometimes used in newspapers to mean 'singer' (报章上有时用以表示 singer) 歌手，歌唱家 **2** a SONGBIRD 鸣禽

song·stress /'sɒŋstrəs; *NAmE* 'sɔːŋ-/ *noun* a word sometimes used in newspapers to mean 'a woman singer' (报章上有时用以表示 woman singer) 女歌手，女歌唱家

song·writer /'sɒŋraɪtə(r); *NAmE* 'sɔːŋ-/ *noun* a person who writes the words and usually also the music for songs 歌词作者；歌曲的词曲作者: *singer-songwriter Paul Simon* 歌手兼词曲作者保罗·西蒙

song·writ·ing /'sɒŋraɪtɪŋ; *NAmE* 'sɔːŋ-/ *noun* [U] the process of writing songs 歌曲创作

sonic /'sɒnɪk; *NAmE* 'sɑːnɪk/ *adj.* (*specialist*) connected with sound or the speed of sound 声音的；声速的: *sonic waves* 声波

ˌsonic 'boom *noun* the EXPLOSIVE sound that is made when an aircraft travels faster than the speed of sound 声爆；音爆 (飞机超声速飞行时发出的巨大声响)；声震

'son-in-law *noun* (*pl.* **sons-in-law**) the husband of your daughter 女婿 ➲ COMPARE DAUGHTER-IN-LAW

son·net /'sɒnɪt; *NAmE* 'sɑːnɪt/ *noun* a poem that has 14 lines, each containing 10 syllables, and a fixed pattern of RHYME 十四行诗；商籁体: *Shakespeare's sonnets* 莎士比亚的十四行诗

sonny /'sʌni/ *noun* [sing.] (*old-fashioned*) a word used by an older person to address a young man or boy (年长者对年轻男子或男孩的称呼) 孩子

ˌson of a 'bitch *noun* (*pl.* **sons of bitches**) (*also* **SOB** *especially in NAmE*) (*taboo, slang*) an offensive word for a person that you think is bad or very unpleasant 狗娘养的；王八蛋；浑蛋: *I'll kill that son of a bitch when I get my hands on him!* 我要是逮住那个狗崽子，非要了他的狗命不可！

ˌson of a 'gun *noun* (*pl.* **sons of guns**) (*NAmE, informal*) **1** a person or thing that you are annoyed with 龟孙子；破烂货: *My car's at the shop—the son of a gun broke down again.* 我的车在修理厂呢，这破玩意儿又坏了。**2** used to express the fact that you are surprised or annoyed (表示惊讶或气恼) 好家伙，他妈的: *Well, son of a gun—and I thought the old guy couldn't dance!* 嘿，好家伙，我还以为那老家伙不会跳舞呢！**3** (*old-fashioned*) used by a man to address or talk about a male friend that he admires and likes (男性称呼或谈论所钦佩或喜欢的男性朋友) 哥们儿: *Frank, you old son of a gun—I haven't seen you for months.* 弗兰克，老哥们儿，好几个月没见你了。

son·or·ous /'sɒnərəs; *NAmE* 'sɑːn-/ *adj.* (*formal*) having a pleasant full deep sound 雄浑的；浑厚的: *a sonorous voice* 浑厚的嗓音 ▶ **son·or·ity** /sə'nɒrəti; *NAmE* -'nɔːr-/ *noun* [U, C]: *the rich sonority of the bass* 男低音饱满浑厚的音色 **son·or·ous·ly** *adv.*

sook /sʊk; sʊk/ *noun* (*informal, AustralE, NZE, CanE*) **1** a person who is not brave 胆小鬼；懦夫 SYN **coward**, **crybaby** **2** a young cow that has been fed from a bottle, not by its mother 用奶瓶喂养的小牛

soon /suːn/ *adv.* (**soon·er**, **soon·est**) **1** in a short time from now; a short time after sth else has happened 很快；马上；不久: *We'll be home soon./We'll soon be home.* 我们很快就要到家了。◇ *She sold the house soon after her husband died.* 丈夫去世后不久，她就把房子卖了。◇ *I soon realized the mistake.* 我很快意识到犯了错误。

◇ *It soon became clear that the programme was a failure.* 没多久便清楚地看出，这个节目不受欢迎。◇ ***See you soon!*** 再见！**2** early; quickly 早；快：*How soon can you get here?* 你多快能赶到这儿？◇ *We'll deliver the goods **as soon as** we can.* 我们将尽快交货。◇ *Please send it **as soon as possible**.* 请尽快把它寄出去。◇ *Next Monday is **the soonest** we can deliver.* 我们交货最早要到下星期一。◇ *They arrived home sooner than expected.* 他们很快就到家了，比预料的要早。◇ ***The sooner** we set off, **the sooner** we will arrive.* 我们走得越早就到得越早。◇ *The note said, 'Call Bill soonest'* (= as soon as possible). 纸条上写着："尽快给比尔打电话"。◇ ***All too soon** the party was over.* 转眼之间，聚会就结束了。➲ SEE ALSO ASAP

IDM **no sooner said than 'done** used to say that sth was, or will be, done immediately 说干就干 **no sooner… than…** used to say that sth happens immediately after sth else 一…就；刚…就：*No sooner had she said it than she burst into tears.* 她刚一说完，泪水便夺眶而出。➲ NOTE AT HARDLY **the ˌsooner the 'better** very soon; as soon as possible 尽早；越快越好：*'When shall I tell him?' 'The sooner the better.'* "我什么时候告诉他呢？""越快越好。" **ˌsooner or 'later** at some time in the future, even if you are not sure exactly when 迟早；早晚有一天：*Sooner or later you will have to make a decision.* 你早晚得拿个主意。**ˌsooner rather than 'later** after a short time rather than after a long time 赶早不赶晚；及早：*We urged them to sort out the problem sooner rather than later.* 我们敦促他们及早解决那个问题。**I, etc. would sooner do sth (than sth else)** to prefer to do sth (than do sth else) 宁愿做某事（而不愿做另一件事）：*She'd sooner share a house with other students than live at home with her parents.* 她宁可和其他学生合住，也不愿跟父母住在家里。➲ MORE AT ANY TIME, JUST *adv.*, SAY *v.*

soot /sʊt/ *noun* [U] black powder that is produced when wood, coal, etc. is burnt 煤烟子；油烟 ➲ SEE ALSO SOOTY

soothe /suːð/ *verb* **1 ~ sb** to make sb who is anxious, upset, etc. feel calmer 安慰；抚慰；劝慰 **SYN** **calm**：*The music soothed her for a while.* 音乐让她稍微安静了一会儿。**2 ~ sth** to make a TENSE or painful part of your body feel more comfortable 减轻，缓解，缓和（身体某部位的紧张或疼痛） **SYN** **relieve**：*This should soothe the pain.* 这个应该能缓解疼痛。◇ *Take a warm bath to soothe tense, tired muscles.* 洗个热水澡，让紧张疲劳的肌肉放松一下。▶ **sooth·ing** *adj.*：*a soothing voice/lotion* 让人感到安慰的嗓音；镇痛液 **sooth·ing·ly** *adv.*：*'There's no need to worry,' he said soothingly.* "不必担忧。"他宽慰道。

PHR V **'soothe sth↔away** to remove a pain or an unpleasant feeling 解除；消除；消释

sooth·er /ˈsuːðə(r)/ *noun* (*CanE*) a specially shaped rubber or plastic object for a baby to suck 安抚奶嘴 **SYN** **dummy**

sooth·say·er /ˈsuːθseɪə(r)/ *noun* (*old use*) a person who is believed to be able to tell what will happen in the future 占卜者；预言者

sooty /ˈsʊti/ *adj.* **1** covered with SOOT 沾满煤烟子的 **2** of the colour of SOOT 煤烟子一样黑的；炭黑色的

sop /sɒp; *NAmE* sɑːp/ *noun* [usually sing.] **~ (to sb/sth)** a small, not very important, thing that is offered to sb who is angry or disappointed in order to make them feel better（为缓和某人愤怒或失望情绪而赠与的）小东西

soph·ist /ˈsɒfɪst; *NAmE* ˈsɑːf-/ *noun* **1** a teacher of philosophy in ancient Greece, especially one with an attitude of doubting that statements are true（古希腊的）哲学教师；（尤指怀质疑态度的）哲人，智者 **2** a person who uses clever but wrong arguments 诡辩者；诡辩家

so·phis·ti·cate /səˈfɪstɪkeɪt/ *noun* (*formal*) a sophisticated person 老于世故的人；见多识广的人

so·phis·ti·cated /səˈfɪstɪkeɪtɪd/ *adj.* **1** having a lot of experience of the world and knowing about fashion, culture and other things that people think are socially important 见多识广的；老练的；见过世面的：*the sophisticated pleasures of city life* 城市生活中五花八门的享乐 ◇ *Mark is a smart and sophisticated young man.* 马克是一个聪明老成的年轻人。➲ COMPARE NAIVE (2) **2** (of a machine, system, etc. 机器、体系等) clever and complicated in the way that it works or is presented 复杂巧妙的；先进的；精密的：*highly sophisticated computer systems* 十分先进的计算机系统 ◇ *Medical techniques are becoming more sophisticated all the time.* 医疗技术日益复杂精妙。**3** (of a person 人) able to understand difficult or complicated ideas 水平高的；在行的：*a sophisticated audience* 有鉴赏力的观众 **OPP** **unsophisticated**

so·phis·ti·ca·tion /səˌfɪstɪˈkeɪʃn/ *noun* [U] the quality of being sophisticated 世故；复杂巧妙；高水平

soph·is·try /ˈsɒfɪstri; *NAmE* ˈsɑːf-/ *noun* (*pl.* **-ies**) (*formal*) **1** [U] the use of clever arguments to persuade people that sth is true when it is really false 诡辩术 **2** [C] a reason or an explanation that tries to show that sth is true when it is really false 诡辩

sopho·more /ˈsɒfəmɔː(r); *NAmE* ˈsɑːf-/ *noun* (*US*) **1** a student in the second year of a course of study at a college or university（大学）二年级学生 **2** a HIGH SCHOOL student in the 10th grade（高中）二年级学生 ➲ COMPARE FRESHMAN, JUNIOR *n.* (4), SENIOR *n.* (6)

sop·or·if·ic /ˌsɒpəˈrɪfɪk; *NAmE* ˌsɑːp-/ *adj.* (*formal*) making you want to go to sleep 催眠的；让人瞌睡的：*the soporific effect of the sun* 太阳让人昏昏欲睡的作用 ➲ WORDFINDER NOTE AT SLEEP

sop·ping /ˈsɒpɪŋ; *NAmE* ˈsɑːp-/ (*also* **ˌsopping 'wet**) *adj.* (*informal*) very wet 湿透的 **SYN** **soaking**

soppy /ˈsɒpi; *NAmE* ˈsɑːpi/ (*especially BrE*) (**sop·pier, sop·pi·est**) (*NAmE usually* **sappy**) *adj.* (*informal*) silly and SENTIMENTAL; full of unnecessary emotion 一味情意缠绵的；感情过于丰富的；多愁善感的：*soppy love songs* 缠绵的情歌

sop·rano /səˈprɑːnəʊ; *NAmE* səˈprɑːnoʊ; -ˈpræn-/ *noun, adj.*
■ ***noun*** (*pl.* **-os** /-nəʊz; *NAmE* -noʊz/) a singing voice with the highest range for a woman or boy; a singer with a soprano voice 女高音声部；女高音歌手 ➲ COMPARE ALTO *n.* (1), MEZZO-SOPRANO, TREBLE *n.* (2)
■ ***adj.*** [only before noun] (of a musical instrument 乐器) with the highest range of notes in its group 高音的：*a soprano saxophone* 高音萨克斯管 ➲ COMPARE ALTO *adj.*, BASS[1] *adj.*, TENOR *adj.*

soˌprano re'corder (*NAmE*) (*BrE* **ˌdescant re'corder**) *noun* (*music* 音) the most common size of RECORDER (= a musical instrument in the shape of a pipe that you blow into), with a high range of notes 高音竖笛

sor·bet /ˈsɔːbeɪ; *NAmE* ˈsɔːrbət/ (*BrE also* **'water ice**) *noun* [C, U] a sweet frozen food made from sugar, water and fruit juice, often eaten as a DESSERT 雪糕；冰糕

sor·cer·er /ˈsɔːsərə(r); *NAmE* ˈsɔːrs-/ *noun* (in stories) a man with magic powers, who is helped by evil spirits（故事中的）术士，男巫，巫师

sor·cer·ess /ˈsɔːsərəs; *NAmE* ˈsɔːrs-/ *noun* (in stories) a woman with magic powers, who is helped by evil spirits（故事中的）女术士，女巫，巫婆

sor·cery /ˈsɔːsəri; *NAmE* ˈsɔːrs-/ *noun* [U] magic that uses evil spirits 法道；巫术 **SYN** **black magic**

sor·did /ˈsɔːdɪd; *NAmE* ˈsɔːrdɪd/ *adj.* **1** immoral or dishonest 卑鄙的；丑恶的；无耻的：*It was a shock to discover the truth about his sordid past.* 他以往的丑行被发现时，人们感到震惊。◇ *I didn't want to hear **the sordid details** of their relationship.* 我不想听他们之间的那些龌龊细节。**2** very dirty and unpleasant 肮脏的；污秽的 **SYN** **squalid**：*people living in sordid conditions* 生活环境肮脏不堪的人

sore /sɔː(r)/ *adj., noun*
■ ***adj.*** **1** if a part of your body is **sore**, it is painful, and often red, especially because of infection or because a muscle has been used too much（发炎）疼痛的；酸痛的：*to have a sore throat* 嗓子疼 ◇ *His feet were sore after the walk.* 他走路把脚都走疼了。◇ *My stomach is still sore* (= painful) *after the operation.* 手术后，我的胃还在疼。➲

S

WORDFINDER NOTE AT HURT ➲ SYNONYMS AT PAINFUL **2** [not before noun] ~ (**at sb/about sth**) (*informal, especially NAmE*) upset and angry, especially because you have been treated unfairly 气恼；愤慨；愤愤不平 **SYN annoyed** ▸ **sore·ness** *noun* [U]: *an ointment to reduce soreness and swelling* 止痛消肿软膏

IDM **a ˌsore ˈpoint** a subject that makes you feel angry or upset when it is mentioned 心病；疼处；伤心事：*It's a sore point with Sue's parents that the children have not been baptized yet.* 孩子们至今未受洗礼，这是休的父母的一块心病。**stand/stick out like a sore ˈthumb** to be very noticeable in an unpleasant way 招眼；扎眼 ➲ MORE AT BEAR *n.*, SIGHT *n.*

■ ***noun*** a painful, often red, place on your body where there is a wound or an infection 痛处；伤处；疮 **SYN wound**[1]: *open sores* 开放性溃疡 ➲ SEE ALSO BEDSORE, CANKER SORE, COLD SORE

sore·ly /ˈsɔːli; *NAmE* ˈsɔːrli/ *adv.* seriously; very much 严重地；非常：*I was **sorely tempted** to complain, but I didn't.* 我极想发牢骚，但还是没开口。◇ *If you don't come to the reunion you'll be **sorely missed**.* 你要是不来参加团聚，大家会非常想念你的。

sor·ghum /ˈsɔːɡəm; *NAmE* ˈsɔːrɡəm/ *noun* [U] very small grain grown as food in tropical countries; the plant that produces this grain 高粱；高粱米

sor·or·ity /səˈrɒrəti; *NAmE* -ˈrɔːr-; -ˈrɑːr-/ *noun* (*pl.* **-ies**) (*NAmE*) a club for a group of women students at an American college or university（美国大学里的）女生联谊会 ➲ COMPARE FRATERNITY (2)

sor·rel /ˈsɒrəl; *NAmE* ˈsɔːr-/ *noun* [U] a plant with leaves that taste bitter and are used in salads or in making soup or sauces 酸模，酸叶草（叶子味苦，可用于做色拉、汤或酱汁）

sor·row /ˈsɒrəʊ; *NAmE* ˈsɑːroʊ/ *noun, verb*

■ ***noun* 1** [U] ~ (**at/for/over sth**) (*rather formal*) a feeling of great sadness because sth very bad has happened 悲伤；悲痛；悲哀 **SYN grief**: *He expressed his sorrow at the news of her death.* 听到她的死讯，他表示哀伤。◇ *They said that the decision was made **more in sorrow than in anger**.* 他们说作出这个决定，与其说是出于气愤，不如说是出于悲伤。 **2** [C] a very sad event or situation 伤心事；悲伤事；不幸：*the joys and sorrows of childhood* 童年的欢乐和悲伤

■ ***verb*** [I] (*literary*) to feel or express great sadness 感到（或表示）悲伤：*the sorrowing relatives* 悲伤的亲属

sor·row·ful /ˈsɒrəʊfl; *NAmE* ˈsɑːroʊ-/ *adj.* (*literary*) very sad 悲伤的；悲痛的；悲哀的：*her sorrowful eyes* 她悲伤的双眼 ▸ **sor·row·ful·ly** /-fəli/ *adv.*

sorry /ˈsɒri; *NAmE* ˈsɑːri; ˈsɔːri/ *adj., exclamation*

■ ***adj.*** (**sor·rier, sor·ri·est**) **HELP** You can also use **more sorry** and **most sorry**. 亦可用 more sorry 和 most sorry。 **1** [not before noun] feeling sad and sympathetic 难过；惋惜；同情：~ (**that**)… *I'm sorry that your husband lost his job.* 你丈夫把工作丢了，我很惋惜。◇ ~ (**to see, hear, etc.**) *We're sorry to hear that your father's in hospital again.* 听说你父亲又住院了，我们心里都不好受。◇ ~ (**about sth**) *No one is sorrier than I am about what happened.* 发生了这样的事，我比谁都难过。➲ EXPRESS YOURSELF AT SYMPATHY **2** [not before noun] feeling sad and ashamed about sth that has been done 歉疚；惭愧；过意不去：~ (**about sth**) *We're very sorry about the damage to your car.* 损坏了你的车，我们真是过意不去。◇ ~ (**for sth/doing sth**) *He says he's really sorry for taking the car without asking.* 他没打招呼就用了车，他说他为此感到非常抱歉。◇ ~ (**that**)… *She was sorry that she'd lost her temper.* 她为自己发了脾气而感到愧疚。◇ *If you **say you're sorry** we'll forgive you.* 你要是道歉，我们就原谅你。

> **WORDFINDER** 联想词：amends, apologize, ashamed, embarrassed, forgive, regret, remorse, repent, sympathy

3 [not before noun] feeling disappointed about sth and wishing you had done sth different or had not done sth 后悔；遗憾；不忍：~ (**that**)… *She was sorry that she'd lost contact with Mary.* 她懊悔跟玛丽失去了联系。◇ *You'll be sorry if I catch you!* 要是让我抓着，你会后悔的！◇ ~ **to do sth** *I was genuinely sorry to be leaving college.* 大学毕业时，我打心底里舍不得离去。 **4** [only before noun] very sad or bad, especially making you feel pity or disapproval 悲惨的；破败的；可怜的：*The business is in a **sorry state**.* 公司境况真是糟糕。◇ *They were a **sorry sight** when they eventually got off the boat.* 他们最终从船上下来，一副惨兮兮的样子。

> **▼ EXPRESS YOURSELF 情景表达**
>
> **Apologizing 道歉**
>
> When you have caused a problem for somebody, they are less likely to be very angry if you can make a polite apology. 给别人造成麻烦时礼貌地道歉，对方会比较不那么生气：
>
> - ***I'm so/terribly/very sorry** I'm late.* 非常抱歉，我迟到了。
> - ***I do apologize.** I'll get you another cup.* 很抱歉，我再给您拿一杯。
> - ***I must apologize** for keeping you waiting.* (*BrE*) 很抱歉让您久等了。
> - ***We would like to apologize** on behalf of the management.* 我们谨代表管理层致歉。
> - ***We would like to offer/Please accept our apologies** for the inconvenience.* 给您带来了不便，我们谨表歉意 / 请接受我们的歉意。
>
> Responses 回应：
>
> - ***That's all right/OK.*** 没关系。
> - ***No problem.*** 不打紧。
> - ***Don't worry about it.*** 别放在心上。
> - ***It's fine, really.*** 没事儿，真的。

IDM **be/feel sorry for sb** to feel pity or sympathy for sb 怜悯；同情：*He decided to help Jan as he felt sorry for her.* 他同情简的遭遇，决定帮助她。**feel sorry for yourself** (*informal, disapproving*) to feel unhappy; to pity yourself 感觉不幸；自我怜悯：*Stop feeling sorry for yourself and think about other people for a change.* 别老觉得自己委屈了，也替别人想一想吧。**I'm sorry 1** used when you are apologizing for sth（道歉时用）很抱歉，请原谅：*I'm sorry, I forgot.* 对不起，我忘了。◇ *Oh, I'm sorry. Have I taken the one you wanted?* 哟，对不起。我是不是拿了你想要的那个？◇ *I'm sorry. I can't make it tomorrow.* 很抱歉。我明天不行。**2** used for disagreeing with sb or politely saying 'no'（表示不同意或委婉地拒绝）对不起：*I'm sorry, I don't agree.* 对不起，我不同意。◇ *I'm sorry, I'd rather you didn't go.* 恕我直言，我看你还是不去为好。**3** used for introducing bad news（引出坏消息）很遗憾：*I'm sorry to have to tell you you've failed.* 我只能遗憾地告诉你，你不及格。**I'm ˈsorry to say** used for saying that sth is disappointing（表示某事令人失望）我遗憾地说：*He didn't accept the job, I'm sorry to say.* 我很遗憾，他不接受那项工作。➲ MORE AT SAFE *adj.*

■ ***exclamation* 1** used when you are APOLOGIZING for sth（道歉时用）很抱歉，请原谅：*Sorry I'm late!* 对不起，我来晚了！◇ *Did I stand on your foot? Sorry!* 我是不是踩你脚了？抱歉！◇ *Sorry to bother you, but could I speak to you for a moment?* 不好意思打搅你，我能不能跟你说几句话？◇ *Sorry, we don't allow dogs in the house.* 对不起，我们是不让狗进屋的。◇ *He didn't even **say sorry**.* 他连句道歉的话也没有说。 **2** (*especially BrE*) used for asking sb to repeat sth that you have not heard clearly（请某人重复你没听清楚的话）你说什么，请再说一遍：*Sorry? Could you repeat the question?* 你说什么？能不能把你的问题再说一遍？ **3** used for correcting yourself when you have said sth wrong（纠正自己说错的话）不对，应该是：*Take the first turning, sorry, the third turning on the right.* 到第一个，不，到第三个路口往右拐。

sort /sɔːt; *NAmE* sɔːrt/ *noun, verb*

■ ***noun* 1** [C] a group or type of people or things that are similar in a particular way 种类；类别；品种 **SYN kind**: *'What **sort of** music do you like?' 'Oh, **all sorts**.'*

S

"你喜欢哪一类音乐?""噢，哪一类都喜欢。" ◇ *This sort of problem is quite common./These sorts of problems are quite common.* 这类问题相当普遍。/这几类问题相当普遍。◇ *He's the sort of person who only cares about money.* 他这种人一心只想着钱。◇ *For dessert there's a fruit pie **of some sort*** (= you are not sure what kind). 甜点是一种水果派。◇ *Most people went on training courses **of one sort or another*** (= of various types) *last year.* 多数人去年都上过这样那样的培训班。◇ (*informal*) *There were snacks—peanuts, olives, **that sort of thing**.* 有各种小吃，花生米、橄榄什么的。◇ (*informal*) *There are **all sorts of** activities* (= many different ones) *for kids at the campsite.* 在营地有为孩子们组织的各种各样的活动。◇ (*informal*) ***What sort of** price did you want to pay?* (= approximately how much) 你想出什么样的价? ◇ (*informal*) ***What sort of** time do you call this?* (= I'm very angry that you have come so late.) 你看看这都什么时候了? ➲ NOTE AT KIND **2** [C, usually sing.] (*informal, especially BrE*) a particular type of person 某一种（或某一类）人: *My brother would never cheat on his wife; he's not that sort.* 我哥哥永远不会背着妻子在外面拈花惹草，他不是那种人。**3** (*computing* 计) [sing.] the process of putting data in a particular order 排序; 分类: *to do a sort* 进行排序

IDM **it takes all sorts (to make a world)** (*saying*) used to say that you think sb's behaviour is very strange or unusual but that everyone is different and likes different things （认为某人行为怪诞或不寻常时说）世界之大无奇不有，林子大了什么鸟都有 **of 'sorts** (*informal*) used when you are saying that sth is not a good example of a particular type of thing（表示某事物不够好）勉强算的，凑合的: *He offered us an apology of sorts.* 他给我们勉强道了个歉。**out of 'sorts** (*especially BrE*) ill/sick or upset 身体不适; 心情烦恼: *She was tired and out of sorts by the time she arrived home.* 她回到家里，又累又烦。**sort of** (*also* **sorta**) (*informal*) 🔑 to some extent but in a way that you cannot easily describe 有几分; 有那么一点: *She sort of pretends that she doesn't really care.* 她摆出一副并不真正在乎的样子。◇ *'Do you understand?' 'Sort of.'* "你懂了吗?""有点懂了。" **a sort of sth** 🔑 (*informal*) used for describing sth in a not very exact way（表示不十分准确）近似于某物，有点像是某物: *I had a sort of feeling that he wouldn't come.* 我隐约觉得他不会来。◇ *They're a sort of greenish-blue colour.* 它们的颜色近乎带点绿的蓝色。➲ MORE AT KIND *n.*

■ ***verb*** **1** 🔑 to arrange things in groups or in a particular order according to their type, etc.; to separate things of one type from others 整理; 把…分类: **~ sth** *sorting the mail* 分理信件 ◇ **~ sth into sth** *The computer sorts the words into alphabetical order.* 计算机按字母顺序排列这些单词。◇ *Rubbish can easily be separated and sorted into plastics, glass and paper.* 垃圾很容易分开，可归入塑料、玻璃和纸三类。◇ **~ sth from sth** *Women and children sorted the ore from the rock.* 妇女和孩子把矿石从岩石中分拣出来。➲ SEE ALSO SORT STH↔OUT at SORT **2** 🔑 [often passive] **~ sth** (*informal, especially BrE*) to deal with a problem successfully or organize sth/sb properly 妥善处理; 安排妥当: *I'm really busy—can you sort it?* 我真的很忙，你能处理一下吗? ➲ COMPARE SORTED **IDM** SEE MAN *n.*, SHEEP, WHEAT

PHR V **,sort itself 'out** (of a problem 问题) to stop being a problem without anyone having to take action 自行化解: *It will all sort itself out in the end.* 问题最后都会自行解决。**,sort sth↔'out 1** 🔑 (*informal*) to organize the contents of sth; to tidy sth 理顺; 整理: *The cupboards need sorting out.* 柜橱该整理一下了。**2** to organize sth successfully 把…安排好: *If you're going to the bus station, can you sort out the tickets for tomorrow?* 你要去汽车站的话，能不能把明天的车票买好? **,sort sth↔'out (from sth)** to separate sth from a larger group（从…中）区分出来，辨别出来: *Could you sort out the toys that can be thrown away?* 你把可以扔掉的玩具挑出来，好吗? ➲ RELATED NOUN SORT-OUT **,sort sth/sb/yourself 'out** 🔑 (*especially BrE*) to deal with sb's/your own problems successfully 妥善处理某人（或自己）的问题: *If you can wait a moment, I'll sort it all out for you.* 要是你能等一会儿，我就可以把什么都给你弄好。◇ *You load up the car and I'll sort the kids out.* 你装车，我把孩子们安顿好。**,sort sb↔'out** (*BrE, informal*) to deal with sb who is causing trouble, etc. especially by punishing or attacking them 整治，惩罚，收拾（某人）: *Wait till I get my hands on him—I'll soon sort him out!* 等他落到我手里，我立马就收拾他! **'sort through sth (for sth)** to look through a number of things, either in order to find sth or to put them in order 翻查; 归整: *I sorted through my paperwork.* 我把文件纸张都归整好了。◇ *She sorted through her suitcase for something to wear.* 她翻遍行李箱找件衣服穿。

'sort code (*BrE*) (*US* **'routing number**) *noun* a number that is used to identify a particular bank（银行）识别代码

sorted /'sɔːtɪd; *NAmE* 'sɔːrt-/ *adj.* [not before noun] (*BrE, informal*) completed, solved or organized 完成的; 已解决的; 整理好的: *Don't worry. We'll soon have this sorted.* 别担心，我们马上把这弄好。◇ *It's our problem. We'll **get it sorted**.* 这是我们的问题，我们来处理。◇ *It's all sorted.* 全都弄好了。◇ *It's time you **got yourself sorted**.* 现在你该把自己的事好好安排一下了。➲ COMPARE SORT *v.* (2)

sor·tie /'sɔːti; *NAmE* 'sɔːrti/ *noun* **1** a flight that is made by an aircraft during military operations; an attack made by soldiers（在军事行动中飞机的）出动架次;（军队的）出击 **SYN** **raid** **2** a short trip away from your home or the place where you are（短暂）外出，出门 **SYN** **foray** **3 ~ into sth** an effort that you make to do or join sth new 尝试参与; 一试身手 **SYN** **foray**: *His first sortie into politics was unsuccessful.* 他初涉政坛并不成功。

'sorting office *noun* (*BrE*) a place where mail is sorted before being delivered 邮件分拣室

'sort-out *noun* (*BrE, informal*) an act of arranging or organizing the contents of sth in a tidy or neat way and removing things you do not want 整理; 清理

SOS /,es əʊ 'es; *NAmE* oʊ/ *noun* [sing.] **1** a signal or message that a ship or plane sends when it needs urgent help（船舶或飞机发出的）紧急呼救信号: *to send an SOS* 发出紧急呼救信号 ◇ *an SOS message* 紧急呼救信号 **2** an urgent request for help 紧急求助的请求: *We've received an SOS from the area asking for food parcels.* 我们收到来自那一地区的紧急求援信息，他们急需食物包。➲ SEE ALSO MAYDAY

sosa·tie /sə'sɑːti/ *noun* (*SAfrE*) small pieces of meat or vegetables that are cooked on a stick, usually over an open fire 烤肉串; 烤蔬菜串 **SYN** **kebab**

,so-'so *adj.* (*informal*) not particularly good or bad; average 一般的; 普通的; 中等的; 不好也不差的: *'How are you feeling today?' 'So-so.'* "你今天感觉怎么样?""还可以。" ▸ **,so-'so** *adv.*: *I only did so-so in the exam.* 我在考试中考得一般。

sotto voce /,sɒtəʊ 'vəʊtʃi; *NAmE* ,sɑːtoʊ 'voʊ-/ *adv.* (*from Italian, formal*) in a quiet voice so that not everyone can hear 小声地; 轻声地 ▸ **sotto voce** *adj.*

sou /suː/ *noun* [sing.] (*old-fashioned, BrE, informal*) if you do not have a **sou**, you have no money at all 一点钱; 一文钱

sou·bri·quet /'suːbrɪkeɪ/ *noun* = SOBRIQUET

souf·flé /'suːfleɪ; *NAmE* suː'fleɪ/ *noun* [C, U] a dish made from egg whites, milk and flour mixed together to make it light, flavoured with cheese, fruit, etc. and baked until it rises 蛋奶酥: *a cheese soufflé* 奶酪蛋奶酥

sough /saʊ; sʌf/ *verb* [I] (*literary*) (especially of the wind 尤指风) to make a soft whistling sound 作沙沙声; 作飒飒声

sought **AW** PAST TENSE, PAST PART. OF SEEK

'sought after *adj.* wanted by many people, because it is of very good quality or difficult to get or to find 争相获得的; 吃香的; 广受欢迎的: *This design is the most sought after.* 这款设计最受欢迎。◇ *a much sought-after actress* 非常走红的女演员

souk /suːk/ *noun* a market in an Arab country（阿拉伯国家的）露天市场

S

soul 🔑 /səʊl; *NAmE* soʊl/ *noun*
• SPIRIT OF PERSON 人的灵魂 **1** 🔑[C] the spiritual part of a person, believed to exist after death 灵魂: *He believed his immortal soul was in peril.* 他认为他不死的灵魂有堕入地狱的危险。◇ *The howling wind sounded like the wailing of lost souls* (= the spirits of dead people who are not in heaven). 怒吼的风如同堕入地狱的灵魂在哀声恸哭。➲ COLLOCATIONS AT RELIGION
• INNER CHARACTER 内在个性 **2** 🔑[C] a person's inner character, containing their true thoughts and feelings 心性；内心；心灵: *There was a feeling of restlessness deep in her soul.* 她内心深处感到焦躁不安。
• SPIRITUAL/MORAL/ARTISTIC QUALITIES 精神 / 道德 / 艺术品质 **3** 🔑[sing.] the spiritual and moral qualities of humans in general（人类整体的）精神世界（包括精神品质和道德品质）SYN **psyche**: *the dark side of the human soul* 人类精神世界中阴暗的一面 **4** [U, C] strong and good human feeling, especially that gives a work of art its quality or enables sb to recognize and enjoy that quality 真挚情感；高尚情操；气魄: *It was a very polished performance, but it lacked soul.* 这场演出技艺很精湛，但缺少真挚的情感。**5** [sing.] **the ~ of sth** a perfect example of a good quality 典范；化身: *He is the soul of discretion.* 他是谨慎的典范。
• PERSON 人 **6** [C] (*becoming old-fashioned*) a person of a particular type 某种人: *She's lost all her money, poor soul.* 可怜的人，她的钱全没了。◇ *You're a brave soul.* 你真勇敢。**7** [C] (especially in negative sentences 尤用于否定句) a person 人: *There wasn't a soul in sight* (= nobody was in sight). 连个人影都不见。◇ *Don't tell a soul* (= do not tell anyone). 谁也别告诉。◇ (*literary*) *a village of 300 souls* (= with 300 people living there) 一个 300 人的村子
• MUSIC 音乐 **8** (*also* ˈ**soul music**) [U] a type of music that expresses strong emotions, made popular by African American musicians 灵乐，灵歌，灵魂音乐（感情强烈，源于非裔美国人的音乐）: *a soul singer* 灵乐歌手
IDM **good for the ˈsoul** (*humorous*) good for you, even if it seems unpleasant 其实有好处: *'Want a ride?' 'No thanks. Walking is good for the soul.'* "搭车吗？" "不，谢谢。步行有步行的好处。" ➲ MORE AT BARE *v.*, BODY, GOD, HEART, LIFE, SELL *v.*

ˈ**soul-destroy·ing** *adj.* (of a job or task 工作或任务) very dull and boring, because it has to be repeated many times or because there will never be any improvement 单调枯燥的；消磨精神的

ˈ**soul food** *noun* [U] the type of food that was traditionally eaten by black people in the southern US 美国南方黑人的传统食物

soul·ful /ˈsəʊlfl; *NAmE* ˈsoʊlfl/ *adj.* expressing deep feelings, especially feelings of sadness or love 深情的；（尤指）凄婉的，脉脉含情的: *soulful eyes* 深情的眼睛 ◇ *a soulful song* 一首凄婉的歌 ▶ **soul·ful·ly** /-fəli/ *adv.* **soul·ful·ness** *noun* [U]

soul·less /ˈsəʊlləs; *NAmE* ˈsoʊl-/ *adj.* **1** (of things and places 事物或处所) lacking any attractive or interesting qualities that make people feel happy 没有生气的；呆板的；乏味的 SYN **depressing**: *They live in soulless concrete blocks.* 他们住在了无生气的混凝土楼房里。**2** (of a person 人) lacking the ability to feel emotions 不懂感情的；淡漠的

soul·mate /ˈsəʊlmeɪt; *NAmE* ˈsoʊlmeɪt/ *noun* a person that you have a special friendship with because you understand each other's feelings and interests 知心朋友；知己

ˈ**soul music** *noun* [U] = SOUL (8)

ˈ**soul-searching** *noun* [U] the careful examination of your thoughts and feelings, for example in order to reach the correct decision or solution to sth 反省；内省

sound 🔑 /saʊnd/ *noun, verb, adj., adv.*
■ *noun*
• STH YOU HEAR 声音 **1** 🔑[C] something that you can hear 声音；响声 SYN **noise**: *a* ***high/low sound*** 高的 / 低的声音 ◇ *a* ***clicking/buzzing/scratching, etc. sound*** 咔嗒咔嗒、嗡嗡、嚓嚓等的声音 ◇ *the different sounds and smells of the forest* 森林里的各种声音、各种气息 ◇ *She heard the sound of footsteps outside.* 她听见外面有脚步声。◇ *He crept into the house trying not to* ***make a sound***. 他蹑手蹑脚地溜进房子里，尽量不弄出一点声响。**2** 🔑[U] continuous rapid movements (called VIBRATIONS) that travel through air or water and can be heard when they reach a person's or an animal's ear 声；声响: *Sound travels more slowly than light.* 声比光传播得慢。➲ NOTE AT NOISE
• FROM TELEVISION/RADIO 电视；收音机 **3** 🔑[U] what you can hear coming from a television, radio, etc., or as part of a film/movie 声音；音响: *Could you* ***turn the sound up/down***? 你能把音量调大 / 调小一些吗？◇ *The* ***sound quality*** *of the tapes was excellent.* 磁带的音响效果极佳。
• OF MUSICIANS 音乐家 **4** [C, U] the effect that is produced by the music of a particular singer or group of musicians 嗓音；音乐风格: *I like their sound.* 我喜欢他们的音乐风格。
• IMPRESSION 印象 **5** [sing.] **the ~ of sth** the idea or impression that you get of sb/sth from what sb says or what you read 印象；感觉: *They had a wonderful time by* ***the sound of it***. 听起来他们好像过得很愉快。◇ ***From the sound of things*** *you were lucky to find him.* 看起来你能找到他真是幸运。◇ *They're consulting a lawyer? I* ***don't like the sound of that***. 他们正向一位律师咨询？这消息不大好哇。
• WATER 水域 **6** [C] (often in place names 常用于地名) a narrow passage of water that joins two larger areas of water 海峡；海湾 SYN **strait**
IDM **like, etc. the sound of your own ˈvoice** (*disapproving*) to like talking a lot or too much, usually without wanting to listen to other people 爱啰嗦；喜欢说个没完 **within (the) sound of sth** (*BrE*) near enough to be able to hear sth 在听得见…的范围内: *a house within sound of the sea* 听得见海浪声的房子
■ *verb* (not usually used in the progressive tenses 通常不用于进行时)
• GIVE IMPRESSION 给以印象 **1** 🔑 *linking verb* to give a particular impression when heard or read about 听起来好像；让人听着好像: **+ adj.** *His voice sounded strange on the phone.* 他的声音在电话里听着挺怪的。◇ *She didn't sound surprised when I told her the news.* 我把消息告诉她时，她好像并不感到惊讶。◇ *His explanation sounds reasonable to me.* 他的解释我听着有道理。◇ *Leo* ***made it sound*** *so easy. But it wasn't.* 利奥把这事说得好像挺简单，但其实不是那么回事。◇ **+ noun** *She sounds just the person we need for the job.* 看来她正是我们要找的干这份工作的人。◇ **~ like sb/sth** *You sounded just like your father when you said that.* 你说这话，听着跟你父亲一模一样。◇ **~ as if/as though…** *I hope I don't sound as if/as though I'm criticizing you.* 我希望不要听起来好像我在批评你。HELP In spoken English people often use **like** instead of **as if** or **as though**, especially in *NAmE*, but this is not considered correct in written *BrE*. 英语口语中，尤其是美式英语，常用 like 代替 as if 或 as though；书面英式英语中，此用法被视为不正确。
• -SOUNDING 听起来… **2** (in adjectives 构成形容词) giving the impression of having a particular sound 听起来…的: *an Italian-sounding name* 听着像意大利人的名字 ◇ *fine-sounding words* 听上去华而不实的话语
• PRODUCE SOUND 发出声音 **3** [I, T] to produce a sound; to make sth such as a musical instrument produce a sound（使）发出声音，响: *The bell sounded for the end of the class.* 下课铃响了。◇ (*BrE*) **~ sth** *Passing motorists sounded their horns in support.* 开车路过的人按响喇叭表示支持。
• GIVE WARNING/SIGNAL 发出警报 / 信号 **4** 🔑[T] **~ sth** to give a signal such as a warning by making a sound 鸣警报；拉响警报；发出警报: *When I saw the smoke, I tried to* ***sound the alarm***. 看到烟后，我就设法发出警报。◇ (*figurative*) *Scientists have* ***sounded a note of caution*** *on the technique.* 科学家已告诫人类慎重对待这项技术。◇ *Leaving him out of the team may* ***sound the death knell*** *for our chances of winning* (= signal the end of our chances). 不让他参加比赛，也许就意味着我们全无获胜的可能了。
• PRONOUNCE 发音 **5** [T] **~ sth** (*specialist*) to pronounce sth 发（音）: *You don't sound the 'b' in the word 'comb'.* 说 comb 时字母 b 不发音。

• **MEASURE DEPTH** 测量深度 **6** [T, I] ~ (**sth**) (*specialist*) to measure the depth of the sea or a lake by using a line with a weight attached, or an electronic instrument 测（海或湖的）深度

IDM (**it**) ˌ**sounds like a plan to** ˈ**me** (*especially NAmE*) used to agree to a suggestion that you think is good（这）听起来真是不错 ➲ MORE AT NOTE *n.*, SUSPICIOUSLY

PHR V ˌ**sound** ˈ**off** (**about sth**) (*informal, disapproving*) to express your opinions loudly or in an aggressive way 高谈阔论；夸夸其谈 ˌ**sound sb**↔ˈ**out** (**about/on sth**) | ˌ**sound sth**↔ˈ**out** to try to find out from sb what they think about sth, often in an indirect way 试探某人（对某事）的看法；探口风：*I wanted to sound him out about a job.* 我想就一项工作探探他的口风。◇ *They decided to sound out her interest in the project.* 他们决定试探一下她对那个项目的兴趣。

■ ***adj.*** (**sound·er, sound·est**)

• **RELIABLE** 可靠 **1** sensible; that you can rely on and that will probably give good results 明智的；合理的；正确的；可靠的：*a person of sound judgement* 判断力强的人 ◇ *He gave me some very sound advice.* 他给了我一些非常合理的忠告。◇ *This gives the design team a sound basis for their work.* 这为设计组开展工作提供了坚实的基础。◇ *The proposal makes sound commercial sense.* 这项建议从营利的角度看是完全合情合理的。◇ *Their policies are environmentally sound.* 他们的政策对环境没有不利的影响。 **OPP** unsound

• **THOROUGH** 透彻 **2** [only before noun] good and thorough 透彻的；完备的；全面的：*a sound knowledge/understanding of sth* 对某事透彻的了解 / 理解 ◇ *He has **a sound grasp of** the issues.* 他对这些问题掌握得很全面。

• **NOT DAMAGED/HURT** 无损伤；未受伤 **3** in good condition; not damaged, hurt, etc. 完好的；健康的；无损伤的；未受伤的：*We arrived home **safe and sound**.* 我们安然无恙地到了家。◇ *to be **of sound mind*** (= not mentally ill) 神志健全 ◇ *The house needs attention but the roof is sound.* 房子需要修葺，不过屋顶还完好无损。 **OPP** unsound

• **SLEEP** 睡眠 **4** [usually before noun] deep and peaceful 酣畅的；香甜的：*to have a sound night's sleep* 一夜酣睡 ◇ *to be **a sound sleeper*** 睡得很沉的人

• **GOOD, BUT NOT EXCELLENT** 良好 **5** good and accurate, but not excellent 不错的；实实在在的：*a sound piece of writing* 一篇不错的文章 ◇ *a sound tennis player* 颇具实力的网球运动员

• **PHYSICAL PUNISHMENT** 体罚 **6** severe 严厉的；重的：*to give sb a sound beating* 痛打某人一顿
▶ **sound·ness** *noun* [U]: *soundness of judgement* 判断力强 ◇ *financial soundness* 良好的财政状况 ◇ *the soundness of the building's foundations* 建筑物地基的坚固 ➲ SEE ALSO SOUNDLY

IDM (**as**) **sound as a** ˈ**bell** (*informal*) in perfect condition 状况极佳；十分健康 ➲ MORE LIKE THIS 14, page R26

■ ***adv.*** ~ **asleep** very deeply asleep 酣（睡）；（睡得）沉

sound·alike /ˈsaʊndəlaɪk/ *noun* a person who sounds very similar to sb who is famous 声音很像名人的人

the ˈ**sound barrier** *noun* [sing.] the point at which an aircraft's speed is the same as the speed of sound, causing reduced control, a very loud noise (called a SONIC BOOM) and various other effects 声障；音障：*to break the sound barrier* (= to travel faster than the speed of sound) 突破声障（即速度超过声速）

ˈ**sound bite** *noun* a short phrase or sentence taken from a longer speech, especially a speech made by a politician, that is considered to be particularly effective or appropriate（来自政治家讲话等的）摘引精句，名言

ˈ**sound card** *noun* (*computing* 计) a device that can be put into a computer to allow the use of sound with MULTIMEDIA software 声卡

sound·check /ˈsaʊndtʃek/ *noun* a process of checking that the equipment used for recording music, or for playing music at a concert, is working correctly and producing sound of a good quality（对录音或音响设备的）校音

ˈ**sound effect** *noun* [usually pl.] a sound that is made artificially, for example the sound of the wind or a battle, and used in a film/movie, play, computer game, etc. to make it more realistic 音效 ➲ WORDFINDER NOTE AT FILM

ˈ**sound engineer** *noun* a person who works in a recording or broadcasting studio and whose job is to control the levels and balance of sound 音响师

sound·ing /ˈsaʊndɪŋ/ *noun* **1 soundings** [pl.] careful questions that are asked in order to find out people's opinions about sth 意见调查；征询意见：*They will **take soundings** among party members.* 他们将在党员中间征询意见。◇ *What do your soundings show?* 你的调查结果如何？ **2** [C] a measurement that is made to find out how deep water is 水深测量：*They **took soundings** along the canal.* 他们沿运河测量了水深。

ˈ**sounding board** *noun* a person or group of people that you discuss your ideas with before you make them known or reach a decision 决策咨询人（或班子）

sound·less /ˈsaʊndləs/ *adj.* without making any sound; silent 无声的；寂静的：*Her lips parted in a soundless scream.* 她张开嘴想喊，但喊不出声来。 ▶ **sound·less·ly** *adv.*

sound·ly /ˈsaʊndli/ *adv.* **1** if you sleep **soundly**, you sleep very well and very deeply 酣（睡）；（睡得）沉 **2** in a way that is sensible or can be relied on 明智地；可靠地：*a soundly based conclusion* 有充分依据的结论 **3** completely and thoroughly 完全彻底地：*The team was soundly defeated.* 该队一败涂地。**4** strongly; firmly 坚固地；牢固地：*These houses are soundly built.* 这些房子盖得结实。**5** very well, but not in an excellent way 不错地；很好但并非优异地：*He played soundly.* 他在比赛中表现还不错。**6** (of physical punishment 体罚) severely 严厉地：*He was soundly beaten by his mother.* 他被母亲狠揍了一顿。

sound·proof /ˈsaʊndpruːf/ (*also* **sound·proofed**) *adj.* made so that sound cannot pass through it or into it 隔声的：*a soundproof room* 隔声室 ▶ **sound·proof** *verb* ~ **sth**

ˈ**sound stage** *noun* a platform or a special area where sound can be recorded, for example for a film/movie（电影制作等的）录音平台，录音场

ˈ**sound system** *noun* equipment for playing recorded or live music and for making it louder 音响系统

sound·track /ˈsaʊndtræk/ *noun* **1** all the music, speech and sounds that are recorded for a film/movie（电影的）声迹，声带：*The soundtrack of 'Casablanca' took weeks to edit.*《卡萨布兰卡》的声带花了好几个星期才剪辑好。**2** some of the music, and sometimes some speech, from a film/movie or musical that is released on CD, the Internet, etc. for people to buy 电影（或音乐剧）原声音乐（或配音、对白）：*I've just bought the soundtrack of the latest Miyazaki movie.* 我刚买了宫崎骏最新电影的原声唱片。➲ COLLOCATIONS AT CINEMA

ˈ**sound wave** *noun* a VIBRATION in the air, in water, etc. that we hear as sound 声波

soup /suːp/ *noun, verb*

■ ***noun*** [U, C] a liquid food made by boiling meat, vegetables, etc. in water, often eaten as the first course of a meal 汤；羹：*a bowl of soup* 一碗汤 ◇ *chicken soup* 鸡汤 ◇ (*BrE*) ***tinned/packet soups*** 罐装汤；袋装汤 ◇ (*NAmE*) ***canned/packaged soups*** 罐装汤；袋装汤 ◇ ***a soup spoon/plate*** 汤匙；汤盘 ➲ VISUAL VOCAB PAGE V23

IDM **from** ˌ**soup to** ˈ**nuts** (*NAmE, informal*) from beginning to end 从头到尾；完全；全部：*She told me the whole story from soup to nuts.* 她把事情的来龙去脉都告诉了我。
in the ˈ**soup** (*informal*) in trouble 遇到麻烦：*We're all in the soup now.* 我们这下遇到麻烦了。

■ ***verb***

PHR V ˌ**soup sth**↔ˈ**up** (*informal*) to make changes to sth such as a car or computer, so that it is more powerful or exciting than before 通过改装（汽车、计算机等）增强功能

soup·çon /ˈsuːpsɒn; *NAmE* -sɑːn/ *noun* [sing.] (*from French, sometimes humorous*) a very small amount 微量；一丁点

ˈsoup kitchen *noun* a place where people who have no money can get soup and other food free 施食处（为穷人免费提供食物）

soupy /ˈsuːpi/ *adj.* **1** similar to soup 汤似的；羹一般的：*a soupy stew* 像汤一样的炖菜 **2** (of the air 空气) very damp and unpleasant 潮湿难忍的；阴湿的 **3** (*informal*) emotional in a way that is exaggerated and embarrassing 过于伤感的；太多愁善感的

sour /ˈsaʊə(r)/ *adj., verb*

■ ***adj.*** **1** having a taste like that of a lemon or of fruit that is not ready to eat 酸的；有酸味的：*sour apples* 酸苹果 ◇ *a sour flavour* 酸味 **OPP sweet** ➲ SEE ALSO SWEET-AND-SOUR ➲ SYNONYMS AT BITTER ➲ WORDFINDER NOTE AT TASTE **2** (especially of milk 尤指牛奶) having an unpleasant taste or smell because it is not fresh 酸腐的；馊的：*to turn/go sour* 馊了 ➲ SYNONYMS AT BITTER **3** (of people 人) not cheerful; bad-tempered and unpleasant 阴郁的；闷闷不乐的；没好气的：*a sour and disillusioned woman* 郁郁寡欢、幻想破灭的女人 ◇ *a sour face* 阴郁的脸色 ◇ *The meeting ended on a **sour note** with several people walking out.* 几个人退席，会议不欢而散。▶ **sour·ly** *adv.*: *'Who asked you?' he said sourly.* "谁问你了？"他没好气地说。**sour·ness** *noun* [U]

IDM go/turn ˈsour to stop being pleasant or working properly 变坏；恶化；出毛病：*Their relationship soon went sour.* 他们的关系很快有了嫌隙。**sour ˈgrapes** (*saying*) used to show that you think sb is jealous and is pretending that sth is not important 酸葡萄（表示某人表面贬低某事物，实则是嫉妒）：*He said he didn't want the job anyway, but that's just sour grapes.* 他说他其实并不想干这份工作，这不过是吃不着葡萄就说葡萄酸而已。

■ ***verb*** **1** [I, T] (of relationships, attitudes, people, etc. 关系、态度、人等) to change so that they become less pleasant or friendly than before; to make sth do this （使）变坏，恶化：*The atmosphere at the house soured.* 屋子里的气氛不对了。◇ **~ sth** *The disagreement over trade tariffs has soured relations between the two countries.* 贸易关税上的分歧导致两国关系恶化。**2** [I, T] **~ (sth)** if milk **sours** or if sth **sours** it, it becomes sour and has an unpleasant taste or smell（牛奶等）变味，酸腐；使变酸腐

source **AW** /sɔːs; *NAmE* sɔːrs/ *noun, verb*

■ ***noun*** **1** a place, person or thing that you get sth from 来源；出处：*renewable **energy sources*** 可再生能源 ◇ *Your local library will be a useful **source of information**.* 你们当地的图书馆将是很有用的资料来源。◇ *What is their main source of income?* 他们的主要收入来源是什么？**2** [usually pl.] a person, book or document that provides information, especially for study, a piece of written work or news 信息来源；原始资料：*He refused to name his sources.* 他拒绝说出消息的来源。◇ *Government sources indicated yesterday that cuts may have to be made.* 政府方面昨天透露，削减可能势在必行。◇ *source material* 原始资料 ◇ *Historians use a wide range of **primary and secondary sources** for their research.* 历史学家在研究中使用大量的原始资料和二手资料。**3** a person or thing that causes sth, especially a problem 起源；根源；原因：*a source of violence* 暴力的根源 ◇ *a source of confusion* 困惑的缘由 **4** the place where a river or stream starts 源头；发源地：*the source of the Nile* 尼罗河的发源地 ➲ WORDFINDER NOTE AT RIVER ➲ VISUAL VOCAB PAGE V5

IDM at ˈsource at the place or the point that sth comes from or begins 在源头；从一开始：*Is your salary taxed at source* (= by your employer)*?* 你领的是税后工资吗？

■ ***verb*** [often passive] **~ sth (from...)** (*business* 商) to get sth from a particular place （从…）获得：*We source all the meat sold in our stores from British farms.* 我们商店里卖的肉均从英国农场购进。➲ SEE ALSO OUTSOURCE

source·book /ˈsɔːsbʊk; *NAmE* ˈsɔːrs-/ *noun* a collection of texts on a particular subject, used especially as an introduction to the subject（有关某专题的）原始资料集，绪论资料集

ˈsource code *noun* [U] (*computing* 计) a computer program written in text form that must be translated into another form, such as MACHINE CODE, before it can run on a computer 源（代）码

ˌsour ˈcream (*BrE also* **ˌsoured ˈcream**) *noun* [U] cream that has been made sour by adding bacteria to it, used in cooking 酸奶油（烹饪用）

sour·dough /ˈsaʊədəʊ; *NAmE* ˈsaʊərdoʊ/ *noun* [U] DOUGH (= a mixture of flour, fat and water) that is left to FERMENT so that it has a sour taste, used for making bread; bread made with this DOUGH 酸面团；发面面包

ˈsour-faced *adj.* [usually before noun] (of a person 人) having a bad-tempered or unpleasant expression 脸色阴沉的；显得不高兴的

sour·puss /ˈsaʊəpʊs; *NAmE* ˈsaʊərpʊs/ *noun* (*informal*) a person who is not cheerful or pleasant 阴郁的人；整天绷着脸的人；性情乖戾的人

sousa·phone /ˈsuːzəfəʊn; *NAmE* -foʊn/ *noun* a BRASS instrument like a TUBA, used in marching bands in the US 苏萨大号，苏泽大号（美国行进乐队用）

souse /saʊs/ *verb* **~ sth/sb** [usually passive] to SOAK sth/sb completely in a liquid 把…浸透；使湿透；腌

soused /saʊst/ *adj.* **1** [only before noun] (of fish 鱼) preserved in salt water and VINEGAR 腌制的：*soused herring* 腌鲱鱼 **2** (*old-fashioned, informal*) drunk 喝醉的

south /saʊθ/ *noun, adj., adv.*

■ ***noun*** [U, sing.] (*abbr.* **S**, **So.**) **1** (*usually* **the south**) the direction that is on your right when you watch the sun rise; one of the four main points of the COMPASS 南；南方：*Which way is south?* 哪边是南？◇ *warmer weather coming from the south* 从南方来的渐暖天气 ◇ *He lives **to the south of*** (= further south than) *the city.* 他住在城外南边。➲ PICTURE AT COMPASS ➲ COMPARE EAST *n.*, NORTH *n.*, WEST *n.* **2** **the south, the South** the southern part of a country, a region or the world 南方；南部：*birds flying to the south for the winter* 飞往南方过冬的鸟 ◇ *They bought a villa in the South of France.* 他们在法国南部买了一座别墅。◇ *Houses are less expensive in the North than in the South* (= of England). （英格兰）北方的房子比南方便宜。**3 the South** the southern states of the US 美国南方各州；美国南方 ➲ SEE ALSO DEEP SOUTH **4 the South** the poorer countries in the southern half of the world（南半球的）发展中国家

■ ***adj.*** (*abbr.* **S**, **So.**) [only before noun] **1** in or towards the south 南方的；向南的；南部的：*South Wales* 南威尔士 ◇ *They live on the south coast.* 他们住在南海岸。**2** **a south wind** blows from the south 南风的；南方吹来的 ➲ COMPARE SOUTHERLY *adj.*

■ ***adv.*** **1** towards the south 向南；朝南：*This room faces south.* 这间房朝南。**2** **~ of sth** nearer to the south than sth …以南；在…之南：*They live ten miles south of Bristol.* 他们居住在布里斯托尔以南十英里的地方。**3** **~ of sth** (*informal, NAmE* or *finance* 财) less or lower than sth 少于；低于：*The drug is achieving revenues just south of $1 billion per quarter.* 药品每个季度的收益仅略低于 10 亿美元。**OPP north**

IDM down ˈsouth (*informal*) to or in the south, especially of England（尤指英格兰）往南方，在南方：*They've gone to live down south.* 他们到南方去住了。

ˌSouth Aˈmerica *noun* [U] the continent which is to the south of Central America and N America 南美洲 ➲ COMPARE LATIN AMERICA

south·bound /ˈsaʊθbaʊnd/ *adj.* travelling or leading towards the south 南行的；向南的：*southbound traffic* 南行的车辆 ◇ *the southbound carriageway of the motorway* 高速公路的南向车行道

the ˌSouth-ˈEast *noun* (*BrE*) the south-eastern part of England which is the richest part of the country and has the highest population 英格兰东南部（英国最富有、人口最多的地区）

ˌsouth-ˈeast *noun* (*usually* **the south-east**) [sing.] (*abbr.* **SE**) the direction or region at an equal distance between south and east 东南；东南方；东南地区 ➲ PICTURE AT COMPASS ▶ ˌ**south-ˈeast** *adv., adj.*

ˌ**south-ˈeaster·ly** *adj.* **1** [only before noun] in or towards the south-east 东南方的；向东南的；东南部的 **2** [usually before noun] (of winds 风) blowing from the south-east 从东南吹来的

ˌ**south-ˈeastern** *adj.* [only before noun] (*abbr.* **SE**) connected with the south-east 东南的；东南方向的

ˌ**south-ˈeastwards** (*also* ˌ**south-ˈeastward**) *adv.* towards the south-east 向东南；朝东南 ▶ ˌ**south-ˈeastward** *adj.*

south·er·ly /ˈsʌðəli; *NAmE* -ərli/ *adj., noun*

■ ***adj.*** **1** [only before noun] in or towards the south 南方的；向南的；南部的：*travelling in a southerly direction* 朝南行进 **2** [usually before noun] (of winds 风) blowing from the south 从南方吹来的：*a warm southerly breeze* 从南边吹来的和煦微风 ➲ COMPARE SOUTH *adj.*

■ ***noun*** (*pl.* **-ies**) a wind that blows from the south 南风

south·ern (*also* **Southern**) /ˈsʌðən; *NAmE* -ərn/ *adj.* (*abbr.* **S**) [usually before noun] located in the south or facing south; connected with or typical of the south part of the world or a region 南方的；向南的；南部的：*the southern slopes of the mountains* 山的南坡 ◇ *southern Spain* 西班牙南部 ◇ *a southern accent* 南方口音

ˌ**southern ˈbelle** *noun* (*old-fashioned, NAmE*) a young attractive woman from the southern US（美国）南方美女

the ˌ**Southern ˈCone** *noun* [sing.] the region of S America which consists of Brazil, Paraguay, Uruguay, Argentina and Chile 南锥地区（南美洲的巴西、巴拉圭、乌拉圭、阿根廷和智利）

the ˌ**Southern ˈCross** *noun* [sing.] a group of stars in the shape of a cross that can be seen from the southern HEMISPHERE 南十字（星）座

south·ern·er /ˈsʌðənə(r); *NAmE* -ərn-/ *noun* a person who comes from or lives in the southern part of a country 南方人

the ˌ**Southern ˈLights** *noun* [pl.] (*also* **aur·ora aus·tra·lis**) bands of coloured light that are sometimes seen in the sky at night in the most southern countries of the world 南极光

south·ern·most /ˈsʌðənməʊst; *NAmE* -ərnmoʊst/ *adj.* [usually before noun] furthest south 最南的；最南端的；最南部的：*the southernmost part of the island* 岛的最南端

south·paw /ˈsaʊθpɔː/ *noun* (*informal, especially NAmE*) a person who prefers to use their left hand rather than their right, especially in a sport such as BOXING（尤指拳击等运动中）惯用左手的人，左撇子

the ˌ**South ˈPole** *noun* [sing.] the point of the earth that is furthest south 南极

ˌ**south-south-ˈeast** *noun* [sing.] (*abbr.* **SSE**) the direction at an equal distance between south and south-east 南东南；南东南方 ▶ ˌ**south-south-ˈeast** *adv.*

ˌ**south-south-ˈwest** *noun* [sing.] (*abbr.* **SSW**) the direction at an equal distance between south and south-west 南西南；南西南方 ▶ ˌ**south-south-ˈwest** *adv.*

south·wards /ˈsaʊθwədz; *NAmE* -wərdz/ (*also* **south·ward**) *adv.* towards the south 向南；朝南：*to turn southwards* 转向南 ▶ **south·ward** *adj.*：*in a southward direction* 向南

ˌ**south-ˈwest** *noun* (*usually* **the south-west**) [sing.] (*abbr.* **SW**) the direction or region at an equal distance between south and west 西南；西南方；西南地区 ➲ PICTURE AT COMPASS ▶ ˌ**south-ˈwest** *adv., adj.*

ˌ**south-ˈwester·ly** *adj.* **1** [only before noun] in or towards the south-west 西南方的；向西南的；西南部的 **2** [usually before noun] (of winds 风) blowing from the south-west 从西南吹来的

ˌ**south-ˈwestern** *adj.* [only before noun] (*abbr.* **SW**) connected with the south-west 西南的；西南方向的

ˌ**south-ˈwestwards** (*also* ˌ**south-ˈwestward**) *adv.* towards the south-west 向西南；朝西南 ▶ ˌ**south-ˈwestward** *adj.*

sou·venir /ˌsuːvəˈnɪə(r); *NAmE* -ˈnɪr; ˈsuːvənɪr/ *noun* a thing that you buy and/or keep to remind yourself of a place, an occasion or a holiday/vacation; something that you bring back for other people when you have been on holiday/vacation 纪念物；纪念品；（度假时买回来送人的）礼物 **SYN** **memento**：*I bought the ring **as a souvenir of** Greece.* 我买了一枚戒指，留作对希腊的纪念。◇ *a **souvenir shop*** 纪念品商店 ➲ COLLOCATIONS AT TRAVEL

souv·la·ki /suːˈvlæki/ *noun* [U, C] a Greek dish consisting of pieces of meat cooked on sticks（希腊）烤肉串

sou'·wester /ˌsaʊˈwestə(r)/ *noun* **1** a hat made of shiny material that keeps out the rain, with a long wide piece at the back to protect the neck 防雨帽（后檐宽长可护颈）➲ VISUAL VOCAB PAGE V70 **2** a strong wind or storm coming from the south-west 西南强风；西南风暴

sov·er·eign /ˈsɒvrɪn; *NAmE* ˈsɑːvrən/ *noun, adj.*

■ ***noun*** **1** (*formal*) a king or queen 君主；元首 **2** an old British gold coin worth one pound 金镑（旧时英国金币，面值一英镑）

■ ***adj.*** (*formal*) **1** [only before noun] (of a country or state 国家) free to govern itself; completely independent 有主权的；完全独立的 **SYN** **autonomous** **2** having complete power or the greatest power in the country 掌握全部权力的；有至高无上的权力的：*a sovereign ruler* 最高统治者

the ˌ**Sovereign ˈGrant** *noun* [sing.] a sum of money given to the British royal family each year by Parliament for their work and their properties. This replaced the Civil List. 君主拨款（英国议会每年提供，取代王室年俸）

sov·er·eign·ty /ˈsɒvrənti; *NAmE* ˈsɑːv-/ *noun* [U] (*formal*) **1** ~ (**over sth**) complete power to govern a country 主权；最高统治权；最高权威：*The country claimed sovereignty over the island.* 那个国家声称对该岛拥有主权。◇ *the sovereignty of Parliament* 议会的最高权威 ◇ (*figurative*) *the idea of consumer sovereignty* 消费者至上的观念 **2** the state of being a country with freedom to govern itself 独立自主：*The declaration proclaimed the **full sovereignty** of the republic.* 这份宣言宣告这个共和国完全独立自主。➲ COLLOCATIONS AT INTERNATIONAL

So·viet /ˈsəʊviət; ˈsɒv-; *NAmE* ˈsoʊviet; ˈsɑːv-/ *adj.* [usually before noun] connected with the former USSR 苏联的

so·viet /ˈsəʊviət; ˈsɒv-; *NAmE* ˈsoʊviet; ˈsɑːv-/ *noun* **1** [C] an elected local, district or national council in the former USSR 苏维埃（苏联的各级代表会议）**2** **the Soviets** [pl.] (*especially NAmE*) the people of the former USSR 苏联人

sow[1] /səʊ; *NAmE* soʊ/ *verb* ➲ SEE ALSO SOW[2] (**sowed, sown** /səʊn; *NAmE* soʊn/, **sowed, sowed**) **1** [T, I] to plant or spread seeds in or on the ground 播种；种：~ (**sth**) *Sow the seeds in rows.* 一垄一垄地播种。◇ *Water well after sowing.* 播种后要浇足水。◇ ~ **sth with sth** *The fields around had been sown with wheat.* 周围的地里种上了小麦。➲ COLLOCATIONS AT FARMING **2** [T] ~ **sth** (**in sth**) to introduce or spread feelings or ideas, especially ones that cause trouble 灌输；激起；散布；煽动：*to sow doubt in sb's mind* 使某人心怀疑虑 ◇ *to sow confusion* 制造混乱

IDM **sow the seeds of sth** to start the process that leads to a particular situation or result 成为…的肇端；播下…的种子 **sow** (**your**) **wild ˈoats** (of young men 青年男子) to go through a period of wild behaviour while young, especially having a lot of romantic or sexual relationships 过放荡不羁的生活 ➲ MORE AT REAP

sow[2] /saʊ/ *noun* a female pig 母猪 ➲ COMPARE BOAR, HOG *n.* ➲ SEE ALSO SOW[1] **IDM** SEE SILK

sower /ˈsəʊə(r); *NAmE* ˈsoʊ-/ *noun* a person or machine that puts seeds in the ground 播种者；播种机

soya /ˈsɔɪə/ (*BrE*) (*NAmE* **soy** /sɔɪ/) *noun* [U] the plant on which soya beans grow; the food obtained from soya beans 大豆（作物）；大豆食物：*a soya crop* 大豆作物 ◇ *soya flour* 豆面

S

'soya bean (*BrE*) (*NAmE* **soy·bean** /'sɔɪbiːn/) *noun* a type of BEAN, originally from SE Asia, that is used instead of meat or animal PROTEIN in some types of food 大豆

'soya milk *noun* [U] a liquid made from soya beans, used instead of milk 豆浆

soy sauce /ˌsɔɪ 'sɔːs/ (*also* **ˌsoya 'sauce**) *noun* [U] a thin dark brown sauce that is made from soya beans and has a salty taste, used in Chinese and Japanese cooking 酱油

soz /sɒz; *NAmE* sɑːz/ *exclamation* (*BrE, informal*) (especially in TEXT MESSAGES, emails, etc. 尤用于短信、电邮等) sorry 对不起；抱歉：*Soz, I forgot.* 对不起，我忘了。

soz·zled /'sɒzld; *NAmE* 'sɑːzld/ *adj.* (*BrE, slang*) very drunk 大醉的；烂醉的

spa /spɑː/ *noun* **1** a place where water with minerals in it, which is considered to be good for your health, comes up naturally out of the ground; the name given to a town that has such a place and where there are, or were, places where people could drink the water 矿泉疗养地；矿泉城：*Leamington Spa* 利明顿矿泉城 ◇ *a spa town* 有矿泉的城镇 ◇ *spa waters* 矿泉水 **2** a place where people can relax and improve their health, with, for example, a swimming pool 休闲健身中心：*a superb **health spa** which includes sauna, Turkish bath and fitness rooms* 内设桑拿浴室、土耳其浴室和健身房的第一流的休闲健身中心 **3** (*especially NAmE*) = JACUZZI™

space 🔑 /speɪs/ *noun, verb*

■ ***noun***

• **EMPTY AREA** 空间 **1** 🔑 [U] an amount of an area or of a place that is empty or that is available for use（可利用的）空地，空间 **SYN** **room**：*floor/office/shelf, etc.* ***space*** 楼面面积、办公室里的空间、搁架上的空当等 ◇ *We must make good use of the available space.* 我们必须充分利用现有空间。◇ *That desk **takes up** too much **space**.* 那张桌子占的地方太大。◇ *There is very little **storage space** in the department.* 这个部门存放东西的地方很小。◇ *Can we **make space** for an extra chair?* 我们能不能腾个空再放一把椅子？◇ *How much **disk space** will it take up?* (= on a computer) 这会占用多少磁盘空间？ **2** 🔑 [C] an area or a place that is empty 空；空隙；空子；空当：*a large/small/narrow/wide space* 大/小/窄/宽的空当 ◇ *a space two metres by three metres* 长三米宽两米的空间 ◇ *a **parking space*** 停车的空地 ◇ *crowded together in a confined space* 一起挤在狭小的空间 ◇ *I'll clear a space for your books.* 我来腾出一块地方好放你的书。◇ *Put it in the space between the table and the wall.* 桌子和墙中间有个空，把它放那儿去。**3** 🔑 [U] the quality of being large and empty, allowing you to move freely 宽敞；空旷；开阔 **SYN** **spaciousness**：*The room has been furnished and decorated to give a feeling of space.* 经过装潢和布置，这间屋子给人一种宽敞的感觉。**4** 🔑 [C, U] a large area of land that has no buildings on it（无建筑物的）大片空地，开阔地：*the **wide open spaces** of the Canadian prairies* 加拿大一片片广袤的草原 ◇ *It's a city with fine buildings and plenty of **open space**.* 这座城市既有漂亮的建筑又有开阔的空地。➲ SYNONYMS AT LAND **5** [C] a place, especially a room or a building, that can be used for a particular purpose（某用途的）场所，场地：*The venue is a great space for music.* 这地方是开音乐会的绝佳场所。

• **OUTSIDE EARTH'S ATMOSPHERE** 地球大气以外 **6** 🔑 (*also* **ˌouter 'space**) [U] the area outside the earth's atmosphere where all the other planets and stars are 外层空间；太空：*the first woman in space* 第一位进入太空的女性 ◇ *the possibility of visitors from **outer space*** 出现外层空间来客的可能性 ◇ *a space flight/mission* 太空飞行；太空飞行任务 ➲ WORDFINDER NOTE AT UNIVERSE

> **WORDFINDER** 联想词： astronaut, countdown, dock, launch, mission, orbit, rocket, satellite, weightless

• **PERIOD OF TIME** 一段时间 **7** [C, usually sing.] a period of time 一段时间；期间：*Forty-four people died **in the space of** five days.* 五天里死了四十四个人。◇ *They had achieved a lot **in a short space of time**.* 他们在短时间内取得了很大的成绩。◇ *Leave a space of two weeks between appointments.* 每次约见要间隔两个星期。

• **IN WRITING/PRINTING** 书写；印刷 **8** [U, C] the part of a line, page or document that is empty 空白；空行；空格：*Don't waste space by leaving a wide margin.* 页边不要留太宽浪费版面。◇ *There was not enough space to print all the letters we received.* 版面有限，无法悉数刊载我们收到的所有来信。◇ *Leave a space after the comma.* 逗号后面要留一个空格。

• **FREEDOM** 自由 **9** [U] the freedom and the time to think or do what you want to 自我支配的自由；属于自己的空间：*She was upset and **needed space**.* 她心境不佳，需要一片自己的天地。◇ *You have to **give** teenagers plenty of **space**.* 必须给青少年充足的自由空间。➲ SEE ALSO BREATHING SPACE

• **WHERE THINGS EXIST/MOVE** 空间 **10** [U] the whole area in which all things exist and move 空间：*It is quite possible that space and time are finite.* 很有可能空间和时间是有限的。

IDM **look/stare/gaze into 'space** to look straight in front of you without looking at a particular thing, usually because you are thinking about sth 若有所思地望着前方；出神地凝视前方 ➲ MORE AT PLACE *n.*, WASTE *n.*, WATCH *v.*

■ ***verb*** [often passive] **~ sth (+ adv./prep.)** to arrange things so that they have regular spaces between them 以一定间隔排列：***evenly spaced** plants* 间隔均匀的秧苗 ◇ *a row of **closely spaced** dots* 一行排列紧密的小点 ◇ *Space the posts about a metre apart.* 这些杆子之间要间隔一米左右。

PHR V **ˌspace 'out** (*informal, especially NAmE*) to take no notice of what is happening around you, especially as a result of taking drugs 精神恍惚，神志迷糊（常因吸毒）➲ SEE ALSO SPACED OUT **ˌspace sth↔'out** to arrange things with a wide space between them 使拉开间距；使隔开：*The houses are spaced out in this area of town.* 在城市的这一地区，房屋坐落稀疏。

'space-age *adj.* [usually before noun] (*informal*) (especially of design or technology 尤指样式或技术) very modern and advanced 太空时代的；非常先进的：*a space-age kitchen* 太空时代的厨房

'space bar *noun* a bar on the keyboard of a computer or TYPEWRITER that you press to make spaces between words（计算机或打字机的）空格键 ➲ WORDFINDER NOTE AT KEYBOARD ➲ VISUAL VOCAB PAGE V73

'space cadet *noun* (*slang*) a person who behaves strangely and often forgets things, as though he or she is using drugs 行为异常的人；精神恍惚的人

space·craft /'speɪskrɑːft; *NAmE* -kræft/ *noun* (*pl.* **space·craft**) a vehicle that travels in space 航天（飞行）器；宇宙飞船；太空船

ˌspaced 'out (*also* **spacey**) *adj.* (*informal*) not completely conscious of what is happening around you, often because of taking drugs 精神恍惚的，神志迷糊的（常指因吸食毒品）

'space heater *noun* (*NAmE*) an electric device for heating a room 小型取暖器

space·man /'speɪsmæn/ *noun* (*pl.* **-men** /-men/) **1** (*informal*) a man who travels into space; an ASTRONAUT 宇航员；航天员 **2** (in stories) a creature that visits the earth from another planet（小说中的）外星人 **SYN** **alien** ➲ SEE ALSO SPACEWOMAN

'space probe *noun* = PROBE (2)

the 'space race *noun* competition between the US and the Soviet Union in the 1950s and 60s to be the first to explore space 太空竞赛（20 世纪 50 和 60 年代美国和苏联之间为取得宇宙探索领先地位而进行的竞争）

space·ship /'speɪsʃɪp/ *noun* a vehicle that travels in space, carrying people（航天）飞船

'space shuttle (*also* **shuttle**) *noun* a SPACECRAFT designed to be used, for example, for travelling between the earth and a space station 航天飞机

'space station *noun* a large structure that is sent into space and remains above the earth as a base for people working and travelling in space 太空站；航天站；空间站

space·suit /ˈspeɪssuːt; *BrE also* -sjuːt/ *noun* a special suit that covers the whole body and has a supply of air, allowing sb to survive and move around in space 航天服；宇航服

ˈspace-time *noun* [U] (*physics* 物) the universe considered as a CONTINUUM with four measurements—length, width, depth and time—inside which any event or physical object is located 时空（一体）

space·walk /ˈspeɪswɔːk/ *noun* a period of time that an ASTRONAUT spends in space outside a SPACECRAFT 太空行走（宇航员在宇宙飞船外的活动）

space·woman /ˈspeɪswʊmən/ *noun* (*pl.* **-women** /-wɪmɪn/) a woman who travels into space 女宇航员

spacey /ˈspeɪsi/ *adj.* = SPACED OUT

spa·cial = SPATIAL

spa·cing /ˈspeɪsɪŋ/ *noun* [U] **1** the amount of space that is left between things, especially between the words or lines printed on a page（空间）间隔；（尤指）字距，行距：***single/double spacing*** (= with one or two lines left between lines of type) 单倍 / 双倍行距 **2** the amount of time that is left between things happening（时间）间隔

spa·cious /ˈspeɪʃəs/ *adj.* (*approving*) (of a room or building 房间或建筑物) large and with plenty of space for people to move around in 宽敞的 SYN **roomy** ▶ **spa·cious·ly** *adv.* **spa·cious·ness** *noun* [U]: *White walls can give a feeling of spaciousness.* 白墙能给人一种宽敞的感觉。

spade /speɪd/ *noun* **1** [C] a garden tool with a broad metal blade and a long handle, used for digging 锹；铲：*Turn the soil over with a spade.* 用锹把地翻一遍。◇ (*BrE*) *The children took their* ***buckets and spades*** *to the beach.* 孩子们带上自己的桶和铲子到海滩去了。➲ VISUAL VOCAB PAGE V20 ➲ COMPARE SHOVEL *n.* (1) **2 spades** [pl., U] one of the four sets of cards (called SUITS) in a PACK/DECK of cards. The cards have a black design shaped like pointed leaves with short STEMS.（纸牌中的）黑桃：*the five/queen/ace of spades* 黑桃五 / 王后 / A ➲ VISUAL VOCAB PAGE V42 **3** [C] a card from the set of spades 黑桃牌：*You must play a spade if you have one.* 你如果有黑桃牌，就必须打出来。**4** [C] (*taboo, slang*) an offensive word for a black person 黑人；黑鬼

IDM **in ˈspades** (*informal*) in large amounts or to a great degree 大量；非常：*He'd got his revenge now, and in spades.* 现在他报了仇，痛快淋漓地报了仇。➲ MORE AT CALL *v.*

spade·work /ˈspeɪdwɜːk; *NAmE* -wɜːrk/ *noun* [U] the hard work that has to be done in order to prepare for sth 艰苦的前期准备工作

spa·ghetti /spəˈɡeti/ *noun* [U] PASTA in the shape of long thin pieces that look like string when they are cooked 意大利细面条

spa·ghetti bol·ognese (*also* **spa·ghetti bol·ognaise**) /spəˌɡeti ˌbɒləˈneɪz; *NAmE* ˌboʊlənˈjeɪz/ *noun* [U, C] a dish of spaghetti with a sauce of meat, tomatoes, etc. 意大利波伦亚面条（用肉、番茄等做浇头）

spaˌghetti ˈwestern *noun* a film/movie about COWBOYS, made in Europe by Italian companies（意大利公司在欧洲制作的）意大利式西部片

spake /speɪk/ (*old use*) PAST TENSE OF SPEAK

spam /spæm/ *noun, verb*

■ ***verb*** [T] (-**mm**-) to send the same message to large numbers of Internet users who have not requested the information 滥发（电子信息）：*The criminal gang were spamming phishing emails.* 这一犯罪团伙当时正在滥发网络钓鱼邮件。◇ *Some idiot has been spamming my blog with comments.* 某个白痴一直在我的博客刷屏。

■ ***noun*** [U] **1 Spam™** finely chopped cooked meat that has been pressed together in a container, usually sold in cans and served cold in slices（斯帕姆）午餐肉 **2** (*informal*) advertising material sent by email to people who have not asked for it 滥发的电邮；垃圾电邮 ➲ COLLOCATIONS AT EMAIL ➲ COMPARE JUNK MAIL, SPIM

spam·ming /ˈspæmɪŋ/ *noun* [U] (*informal*) the practice of sending mail, especially advertising material, through the Internet to a large number of people who have not asked for it 大量发出垃圾电邮 ▶ **spam·mer** /ˈspæmə(r)/ *noun*

span /spæn/ *noun, verb, adj.*

■ ***noun*** **1** the length of time that sth lasts or is able to continue 持续时间：*I worked with him over a span of six years.* 我和他共事达六年之久。◇ *The project must be completed within a specific* ***time span***. 这项工程必须在规定期限内完成。◇ *Small children have a short* ***attention span***. 幼儿注意力持续时间短。➲ SEE ALSO LIFESPAN **2 ~ (of sth)** a range or variety of sth 范围；包括的种类：*Managers have a* ***wide span of*** *control.* 经理的职权范围很大。◇ *These forests cover a broad span of latitudes.* 这些森林绵延在多个纬度上。**3** the part of a bridge or an ARCH between one vertical support and another（桥或拱的）跨径，跨度，跨距：*The bridge crosses the river in a single span.* 河上的桥为单跨桥。**4** the width of sth from one side to the other 宽度；翼展：*The kite has a span of 1.5 metres.* 风筝宽 1.5 米。➲ SEE ALSO WINGSPAN

■ ***verb*** (-**nn**-) **1 ~ sth** to last all through a period of time or to cover the whole of it 持续；贯穿：*His acting career spanned 55 years.* 他的演艺生涯长达 55 年。◇ *Family photos spanning five generations were stolen.* 一家五代人的照片失窃了。**2 ~ sth** to include a large area or a lot of things 包括（广大地区）；涵盖（多项内容）：*The operation, which spanned nine countries, resulted in 200 arrests.* 这次行动涉及九个国家，逮捕了 200 人。**3 ~ sth** to stretch right across sth, from one side to the other 横跨；跨越 SYN **cross**: *a series of bridges spanning the river* 架在河上的一系列桥梁

■ ***adj.*** IDM SEE SPICK

span·dex /ˈspændeks/ *noun* = LYCRA™

span·gle /ˈspæŋɡl/ *verb, noun*

■ ***verb*** [usually passive] **~ sth (with sth)** to cover or to decorate sth with small pieces of sth shiny 用闪光片布满（或装饰）➲ SEE ALSO STAR-SPANGLED BANNER

■ ***noun*** a small piece of shiny metal or plastic used to decorate clothes（装饰服装的）闪光金属片，闪光塑料片 SYN **sequin**

Spang·lish /ˈspæŋɡlɪʃ/ *noun* [U] (*informal*) language which is a mixture of Spanish and English, especially a type of Spanish that includes many English words 西英混合语（尤指包含很多英语词的西班牙语）

span·iel /ˈspænjəl/ *noun* a dog with large soft ears that hang down. There are several types of spaniel. 猎，西班牙猎狗（大耳下垂，品种甚多）

Span·ish /ˈspænɪʃ/ *adj., noun*

■ ***adj.*** from or connected with Spain 西班牙的

■ ***noun*** [U] the language of Spain, Mexico and most countries in Central and S America 西班牙语（通用于西班牙、墨西哥以及中、南美洲多数国家）

ˌSpanish ˈfly *noun* (*pl.* **Spanish flies**) **1** [C] a bright green insect that has a strong smell and produces a harmful substance 西班牙绿芫菁 **2** [U] a poisonous mixture made from the crushed bodies of these insects, that is said to give people a strong desire to have sex 西班牙绿芫菁混合剂（有毒性，据信可催情）

the ˌSpanish Inquiˈsition *noun* [sing.] **1** the organization set up by the Roman Catholic Church in Spain in the 15th century to punish people who opposed its beliefs, known for its cruel and severe methods 西班牙异端裁判所（15 世纪设立于西班牙的天主教会组织，因残酷迫害异教而闻名）**2** (*often humorous*) used to say that you do not like the fact that sb is questioning you a lot about sth（表示不满）逼问，追问：*What is this? The Spanish Inquisition?* 这是怎么回事？严刑逼供吗？

S

ˌ**Spanish ˈmoss** *noun* [U] a tropical American plant that has long thin grey leaves and that grows over trees 铁兰；西班牙藓

spank /spæŋk/ *verb* **~ sb/sth** to hit sb, especially a child, several times on their bottom as a punishment 打（小孩的）屁股 ➲ COMPARE SMACK *v.* (1) ▶ **spank** *noun*

spank·ing /ˈspæŋkɪŋ/ *noun, adv., adj.*
■ ***noun*** [C, U] a series of hits on the bottom, given to sb, especially a child, as a punishment 打屁股（尤指打小孩）: *to give sb a spanking* 打某人屁股 ◊ *I don't agree with spanking.* 我不赞成打屁股。
■ ***adv.*** (*informal*) when you say that sth is **spanking** new, etc. you are emphasizing that it is very new, etc. 非常；十足
■ ***adj.*** [only before noun] (*informal*) very fast, good or impressive 飞快的；了不起的；令人赞叹的: *The horse set off at a spanking pace.* 那匹马一溜烟飞奔而去。

span·ner /ˈspænə(r)/ (*BrE*) (*also* **wrench** *NAmE, BrE*) *noun* a metal tool with a specially shaped end for holding and turning NUTS and BOLTS (= small metal rings and pins that hold things together) 扳手；扳子；扳钳 ➲ VISUAL VOCAB PAGE V21 ➲ COMPARE ADJUSTABLE SPANNER
IDM **(throw) a ˈspanner in the works** (*BrE*) (*NAmE* **(throw) a (ˈmonkey) ˈwrench in the works**) (to cause) a delay or problem with sth that sb is planning or doing 干扰；出难题；从中捣乱

spar /spɑː(r)/ *verb, noun*
■ ***verb*** (**-rr-**) **1** [I] **~ (with sb)** to make the movements used in BOXING, either in training or to test the speed of your opponent's reaction 练习拳击；虚晃一拳 **2** [I] **~ (with sb)** to argue with sb, usually in a friendly way（多指在友好气氛中）辩论，争论
■ ***noun*** **1** a strong pole used to support the sails, etc. on a ship（船上用作桅杆等的）圆材 **2** a structure that supports the wing of an aircraft（飞机的）翼梁

spare 🔑 /speə(r); *NAmE* sper/ *adj., verb, noun*
■ ***adj.***
• NOT USED/NEEDED 用不着 **1** 🔑 [usually before noun] that is not being used or is not needed at the present time 不用的；闲置的: *We've got a spare bedroom, if you'd like to stay.* 要是愿意你就住下，我们空着一间卧室。◊ *I'm afraid I haven't got any* ***spare cash.*** 恐怕我手头没有多余的现金。◊ *Are there any tickets* ***going spare*** (= are there any available, not being used by sb else)? 有多余的票吗？
• EXTRA 外加 **2** 🔑 [only before noun] kept in case you need to replace the one you usually use; extra 备用的；外加的: *a spare key/tyre* 备用钥匙 / 轮胎 ◊ *Take some spare clothes in case you get wet.* 多带几件衣服，以备身上弄湿了好穿。
• TIME 时间 **3** 🔑 available to do what you want with rather than work 空闲的；空余的: *He's studying music in his* ***spare time.*** 他在空闲时间学音乐。◊ *I haven't had a spare moment this morning.* 我一上午一会儿也没闲着。
• PERSON 人 **4** thin, and usually quite tall 瘦的；瘦高的
IDM **go ˈspare** (*BrE, informal*) to become very angry or upset 气急败坏；焦虑万分
■ ***verb***
• TIME/MONEY/ROOM/THOUGHT, ETC. 时间、钱、房间、心思等 **1** to make sth such as time or money available to sb or for sth, especially when it requires an effort for you to do this 抽出；拨出；留出；匀出: **~ sth/sb** *I'd love to have a break, but I can't spare the time just now.* 我是想休息一下，可眼下找不出时间。◊ *Could you spare one of your staff to help us out?* 你能不能从你手下抽一个人过来帮帮我们？◊ **~ sth/sb for sb/sth** *We can only spare one room for you.* 我们只能给你腾出一个房间。◊ *You should* ***spare a thought for*** (= think about) *the person who cleans up after you.* 你应该为随后打扫的人着想啊。◊ **~ sb sth** *Surely you can spare me a few minutes?* 你应该能为我空出几分钟时间吧？
• SAVE SB PAIN/TROUBLE 免得痛苦 / 麻烦 **2** to save sb/yourself from having to go through an unpleasant experience 省得；免去: **~ sb/yourself sth** *He wanted to spare his mother any anxiety.* 他不想让母亲有丝毫的担忧。◊ *Please* ***spare me*** (= do not tell me) ***the gruesome details.*** 那些让人毛骨悚然的细节就请你不要讲了。◊ *You could have spared yourself an unnecessary trip by phoning in advance.* 你要是先打个电话就用不着跑这一趟了。◊ **~ sb/yourself from sth** *She was spared from the ordeal of appearing in court.* 她无须出庭受折磨了。
• NOT HARM/DAMAGE 不伤害；不损坏 **3** [usually passive] **~ sb/sth (from sth)** (*formal*) to allow sb/sth to escape harm, damage or death, especially when others do not escape it 饶恕；赦免；放过；使逃脱: **~ sb/sth (from sth)** *They killed the men but spared the children.* 他们杀死了大人，但放过了孩子。◊ *During the bombing only one house was spared* (= was not hit by a bomb). 在轰炸中，只有一座房子幸免。◊ **~ sb/sth sth** *Hong Kong was spared a direct hit, but the storm still brought heavy rains and powerful winds.* 香港虽然未遭正面吹袭，但风暴还是带来了大雨和强风。
• NO EFFORT/EXPENSE, ETC. 尽力、破费等 **4 ~ no effort, expense, etc.** to do everything possible to achieve sth or to do sth well without trying to limit the time or money involved 不吝惜（时间、金钱）: *He spared no effort to make her happy again.* 为使她重新快乐起来，他想尽了办法。◊ ***No expense was spared*** *in furnishing the new office.* 装潢新办公室不惜工本。
• WORK HARD 努力工作 **5 not ~ yourself** to work as hard as possible 不遗余力
IDM **spare sb's ˈblushes** (*BrE*) to save sb from an embarrassing situation 不让某人难堪；免得某人丢面子 **spare sb's ˈfeelings** to be careful not to do or say anything that might upset sb 不惹某人难受；避免触及某人的痛处 **to ˈspare** if you have time, money, etc. **to spare**, you have more than you need 多余；富余: *I've got absolutely no money to spare this month.* 我这个月一点儿富余钱都没有。◊ *We arrived at the airport with five minutes to spare.* 我们赶到机场时还剩五分钟。
■ ***noun*** **1** 🔑 an extra thing that you keep in case you need to replace the one you usually use (used especially about a tyre of a car) 备用品；备用轮胎: *to get the spare out of the boot/trunk* 从汽车行李箱中取出备用轮胎 ◊ *I've lost my key and I haven't got a spare.* 我把钥匙丢了，还没有备用的。**2 spares** [pl.] (*especially BrE*) = SPARE PART: *It can be difficult to get spares for some older makes of car.* 有些旧型号汽车可能不好买配件。

ˌ**spare ˈpart** *noun* [usually pl.] a new part that you buy to replace an old or broken part of a car, machine, etc. 备件；配件；零件

ˌ**spare ˈrib** *noun* a RIB of PORK (= meat from a pig) with most of the meat cut off 猪排骨: *barbecued spare ribs* 烤排骨

ˌ**spare ˈtyre** (*BrE*) (*NAmE* ˌ**spare ˈtire**) *noun* **1** an extra wheel for a car 备用轮胎 **2** (*humorous*) a large roll of fat around sb's waist 肥胖的腰

spar·ing /ˈspeərɪŋ; *NAmE* ˈsper-/ *adj.* careful to use or give only a little of sth 慎用；俭省的；吝惜的: *Doctors now advise only* ***sparing use of*** *such creams.* 现在大夫建议，这种乳霜要慎用。◊ **~ with sth** *He was always sparing with his praise.* 他从不轻易说赞扬话。▶ **spar·ing·ly** *adv.*: *Use the cream very sparingly.* 这种乳霜要尽可能少用。

spark /spɑːk; *NAmE* spɑːrk/ *noun, verb*
■ ***noun*** **1** [C] a very small burning piece of material that is produced by sth that is burning or by hitting two hard substances together 火花；火星: *A shower of sparks flew up the chimney.* 烟囱里飞出无数火星。**2** [C] a small flash of light produced by an electric current 电火花: *sparks from a faulty light switch* 漏电的电灯开关发出的火花 ◊ *A spark ignites the fuel in a car engine.* 汽车发动机中的燃料由火花点燃。**3** [C, usually sing.] **~ of sth** a small amount of a particular quality or feeling（指品质或感情）一星，丝毫，一丁点 SYN **glimmer**: *a spark of hope* 一线希望 **4** [U, sing.] a special quality of energy, intelligence or enthusiasm that makes sb very clever, amusing, etc. 生气；活力；才华；热情: *As a writer he seemed to lack creative spark.* 作为作家，他似乎缺少创作激情。**5** [C] an action or event that causes sth important to develop, especially trouble or violence 诱因；导火线: *the sparks of revolution*

革命的导火线 **6** [C, usually pl.] feelings of anger or excitement between people 愤怒的情感；激烈的情绪：*Sparks flew at the meeting* (= there was a lot of argument). 会上争论激烈，火星四溅。 IDM SEE BRIGHT *adj.*

■ *verb* **1** [T] to cause sth to start or develop, especially suddenly 引发；触发：**~ sth** *The proposal would spark a storm of protest around the country.* 这一提案将引发全国性的抗议浪潮。◇ *Winds brought down power lines, sparking a fire.* 大风刮断电线，引起了火灾。◇ **~ sth off** *The riots were sparked off by the arrest of a local leader.* 骚乱是因逮捕一名当地领导人而触发的。**2** [I] to produce small flashes of fire or electricity 冒火花；飞火星；产生电火花：*a sparking, crackling fire* 噼啪直响、火星飞迸的火 ◇ (*figurative*) *The game suddenly sparked to life.* 比赛突然变得激烈起来。

PHR V ˌ**spark 'up sth** to begin a conversation, an argument, a friendship, etc., often suddenly 激起，突然引发（交谈、争论、友谊等）：*I tried to spark up a conversation with her.* 我设法跟她攀谈起来。

spar·kle /'spɑːkl; *NAmE* 'spɑːrkl/ *verb, noun*

■ *verb* **1** [I] **~ (with sth)** to shine brightly with small flashes of light 闪烁；闪耀：*sparkling eyes* 炯炯有神的眼睛 ◇ *Her jewellery sparkled in the candlelight.* 烛光下，她的首饰光彩熠熠。 ➲ SYNONYMS AT SHINE **2** [I] **~ (with sth)** to be full of life, enthusiasm or humour 生气勃勃；热情奔放；神采飞扬：*He always sparkles at parties.* 在各种聚会上，他总是光芒四射。

■ *noun* [C, U] **1** a series of flashes of light produced by light hitting a shiny surface 闪烁（或闪耀）的光：*the sparkle of glass* 玻璃闪耀的亮光 ◇ (*figurative*) *There was a sparkle of excitement in her eyes.* 她眼里闪耀着激动的光芒。**2** the quality of being lively and original 生动新颖；亮点：*The performance lacked sparkle.* 这场演出缺少亮点。

spark·ler /'spɑːklə(r); *NAmE* 'spɑːrk-/ *noun* a type of small FIREWORK that you hold in your hand and light. It burns with many bright SPARKS. 烟花棒

spark·ling /'spɑːklɪŋ; *NAmE* 'spɑːrk-/ *adj.* **1** (*also less frequent, informal* **sparkly** /'spɑːkli; *NAmE* 'spɑːrkli/) shining and flashing with light 闪烁的；闪耀的：*the calm and sparkling waters of the lake* 平静的波光粼粼的湖水 ◇ *sparkling blue eyes* 亮晶晶的蓝眼睛 **2** (of drinks 饮料) containing bubbles of gas 起泡的 SYN **fizzy**：*a sparkling wine* 汽酒 ◇ *sparkling mineral water* 矿泉汽水 **3** interesting and amusing 妙趣横生的：*a sparkling conversation/personality* 妙趣横生的谈话；风趣的人 **4** excellent; of very good quality 出色的；上乘的 SYN **brilliant**：*The champion was **in sparkling form**.* 夺冠者状态极佳。

'spark plug (*also* **plug**) (*BrE also* **'sparking plug**) *noun* a part in a car engine that produces a SPARK (= a flash of electricity) which makes the fuel burn and starts the engine 火花塞

sparky /'spɑːki; *NAmE* 'spɑːrki/ *adj.* (*BrE, informal*) full of life; interesting and amusing 生气勃勃的；充满活力的；有意思的：*a sparky personality* 活泼的性格

'sparring partner *noun* **1** a person that you regularly have friendly arguments or discussions with 切磋问题的对手 **2** (in BOXING 拳击运动) a person that a BOXER regularly practises with 陪练员

spar·row /'spærəʊ; *NAmE* -roʊ/ *noun* a small brown and grey bird, common in many parts of the world 麻雀

spar·row·hawk /'spærəʊhɔːk; *NAmE* -roʊ-/ *noun* a small BIRD OF PREY (= a bird that kills other creatures for food) of the HAWK family 雀鹰

sparse /spɑːs; *NAmE* spɑːrs/ *adj.* (**sparser**, **spars·est**) only present in small amounts or numbers and often spread over a large area 稀少的；稀疏的；零落的：*the sparse population of the islands* 那些岛上零星的人口 ◇ *Vegetation becomes sparse higher up the mountains.* 山上越高的地方植物越稀少。◇ *The information available on the subject is sparse.* 这个题目资料匮乏。▶ **sparse·ly** *adv.*: *a sparsely populated area* 人口稀少的地区 **sparse·ness** *noun* [U]

spar·tan /'spɑːtn; *NAmE* 'spɑːrtn/ *adj.* (of conditions 生活条件) simple or severe; lacking anything that makes life easier or more pleasant 斯巴达式的；简朴的；清苦的

ORIGIN From **Sparta**, a powerful city in ancient Greece, where the people were not interested in comfort or luxury. 源自斯巴达（Sparta），古希腊的强大城邦。斯巴达人不追求舒适奢华。 OPP **luxurious**

spasm /'spæzəm/ *noun* **1** [C, U] a sudden and often painful contracting of a muscle, which you cannot control 痉挛；抽搐：*a muscle spasm* 肌肉痉挛 ◇ *The injection sent his leg **into spasm**.* 一针打下去，他的腿就痉挛了。**2** [C] **~ (of sth)** a sudden strong feeling or reaction that lasts for a short time（感情或反应）一阵阵发作，阵发：*a spasm of anxiety/anger/coughing/pain, etc.* 突然一阵焦虑、愤怒、咳嗽、疼痛等

spas·mod·ic /spæz'mɒdɪk; *NAmE* -'mɑːd-/ *adj.* **1** happening suddenly for short periods of time; not regular or continuous 一阵阵的；阵发性的；断断续续的：*There was spasmodic fighting in the area yesterday.* 昨天，那一地区发生过零星的战斗。**2** (*specialist*) caused by your muscles becoming tight in a way that you cannot control 痉挛（性）的：*spasmodic movements* 痉挛性动作 ▶ **spas·mod·ic·al·ly** /-kli/ *adv.*

spas·tic /'spæstɪk/ *adj.* **1** (*medical* 医 or *old-fashioned*) having or caused by CEREBRAL PALSY, an illness which makes it difficult for sb to control their muscles and movements. Using this word is now often considered offensive. 痉挛性的；痉挛性麻痹的（此词现常被认为有冒犯意）：*spastic children* 痉挛性麻痹症患儿 ◇ *spastic reactions* 痉挛性麻痹症反应 **2** (*informal*) an offensive word, sometimes used by children to mean 'stupid'（有时儿童用以骂人愚蠢）笨拙的，无能的 ▶ **spas·tic** *noun*

spat /spæt/ *noun* **1** (*informal*) a short argument or disagreement about sth unimportant 小争吵；小别扭；口角 **2** [usually pl.] a cloth covering for the ankle that was worn in the past by men over the shoe and fastened with buttons at the side（旧时男子用的）鞋罩 ➲ SEE ALSO SPIT *v.*

spate /speɪt/ *noun* [usually sing.] **~ of sth** a large number of things, which are usually unpleasant, that happen suddenly within a short period of time 一连串，接二连三（通常指不愉快的事物）：*The bombing was the latest in a spate of terrorist attacks.* 这次炸弹爆炸事件是一连串恐怖主义袭击中最近的一起。

IDM **in (full) 'spate** (*especially BrE*) (of a river 河流) containing more water and flowing more strongly than usual 暴涨；发洪水：*After heavy rain, the river was in spate.* 大雨过后，河水暴涨。◇ (*figurative*) *Celia was **in full spate*** (= completely involved in talking and not likely to stop or able to be interrupted). 西莉亚口若悬河，滔滔不绝。

spa·tial (*also* **spa·cial**) /'speɪʃl/ *adj.* (*formal* or *specialist*) relating to space and the position, size, shape, etc. of things in it 空间的：*changes taking place in the spatial distribution of the population* 人口的地域分布所发生的变化 ◇ *the development of a child's spatial awareness* (= the ability to judge the positions and sizes of objects) 孩子空间意识的形成 ▶ **spa·tial·ly** /-ʃəli/ *adv.*

spat·ter /'spætə(r)/ *verb, noun*

■ *verb* **1** [T] to cover sb/sth with drops of liquid, dirt, etc., especially by accident 溅；洒 SYN **splash**：**~ sb/sth** *blood-spattered walls* 血染的墙壁 ◇ **~ sb/sth with sth** *As the bus passed, it spattered us with mud.* 公共汽车开过时溅了我们一身泥。◇ **~ sth on/over sb/sth** *Oil was spattered on the floor.* 地板上落满了油点。**2** [I] **+ adv./prep.** (of liquid 液体) to fall on a surface in drops, often noisily 洒落；滴滴答答地落下：*We heard the rain spattering on the roof.* 我们听见雨点噼里啪啦地打在房顶上。

■ *noun* (*also* **spat·ter·ing**) [sing.] **~ (of sth)** a number of drops of a liquid or small amounts of sth that hit a surface; the noise this makes 洒；溅；滴答声；飞溅声：*a spatter of rain against the window* 雨点打在窗户上的噼啪声 ◇ *a spattering of blood* 点点血迹 ◇ (*figurative*) *a spatter of applause* 稀稀落落的掌声

S

spat·ula /ˈspætʃələ/ *noun* **1** a tool with a broad flat blade used for mixing and spreading things, especially in cooking and painting（烹饪、油漆等活动中用以调拌或涂敷的）铲，刮勺，抹刀，刮刀 ➲ VISUAL VOCAB PAGES V27, V28, V72 **2** (*especially NAmE*) (*BrE usually* ˈ**fish slice**) a kitchen UTENSIL that has a broad flat blade with narrow holes in it, attached to a long handle, used for turning and lifting food when cooking 煎鱼锅铲，漏铲（铲面有细长孔）➲ VISUAL VOCAB PAGE V27 **3** (*BrE*) (*NAmE* ˈ**tongue depressor**) a thin flat instrument that doctors use for pressing the tongue down when they are examining sb's throat 压舌板

spawn /spɔːn/ *verb, noun*
■ ***verb*** **1** [I, T] **~ (sth)** (of fish, FROGS, etc. 鱼、蛙等) to lay eggs 产卵 **2** [T] **~ sth** (*often disapproving*) to cause sth to develop or be produced 引发；引起；导致；造成：*The band's album spawned a string of hit singles.* 这支乐队的专辑带出一连串走红的单曲。
■ ***noun*** [U] a soft substance containing the eggs of fish, FROGS etc.（鱼、蛙等的）卵 ➲ SEE ALSO FROGSPAWN

spay /speɪ/ *verb* **~ sth** (*specialist*) to remove the OVARIES of a female animal, to prevent it from breeding 切除雌兽的卵巢；骟（雌兽）：*Have you had your cat spayed?* 你的母猫骟了没有？

spaza /ˈspɑːzə/ *noun* (*SAfrE*) a small shop/store that sb operates from their home, selling food, drinks, cigarettes, etc. to local people, especially in a TOWNSHIP（尤指黑人城镇的）家庭杂货店，街头小店

speak 🔑 /spiːk/ *verb* (**spoke** /spəʊk; *NAmE* spoʊk/, **spoken** /ˈspəʊkən; *NAmE* ˈspoʊ-/)

> **WORD FAMILY**
> **speak** *verb*
> **speaker** *noun*
> **speech** *noun*
> **spoken** *adj.* (≠ unspoken)

• **HAVE CONVERSATION** 交谈 **1** 🔑 [I] to talk to sb about sth; to have a conversation with sb 谈；谈话；交谈：**~ (to sb) (about sth/sb)** *I've spoken to the manager about it.* 那件事我已经和经理谈过了。◇ *The President refused to speak to the waiting journalists.* 总统拒绝同等候的记者讲话。◇ *'Can I speak to Susan?' 'Speaking.'* (= at the beginning of a telephone conversation) "请让苏珊接电话好吗？""我就是。" ◇ *'Do you know him?' 'Not to speak to.'* (= only by sight) "你认识他吗？""见过但没说过话。" ◇ *I saw her in the street but we didn't speak.* 我在街上看见她了，但我们没有谈话。◇ (*especially NAmE*) **~ (with sb) (about sth/sb)** *Can I speak with you for a minute?* 我能跟你谈一会儿吗？ ➲ SYNONYMS AT TALK

• **USE VOICE** 说话 **2** 🔑 [I] to use your voice to say sth 说话；讲话：*He can't speak because of a throat infection.* 他嗓子发炎不能说话。◇ *Please speak more slowly.* 请讲慢点。◇ *Without speaking, she stood up and went out.* 她没有说话，站起身来走了出去。◇ *He speaks with a strange accent.* 他说话的口音很特别。◇ *She has a beautiful speaking voice.* 她说话的音色很美。

• **MENTION/DESCRIBE** 提起；讲述 **3** 🔑 [I] **~ of/about sth/sb** to mention or describe sth/sb 提起；讲述：*She still speaks about him with great affection.* 说起他来她依旧一往情深。◇ *Witnesses spoke of a great ball of flame.* 目击者都谈到有个大火球。◇ *Speaking of travelling,* (= referring back to a subject just mentioned) *are you going anywhere exciting this year?* 说到旅游，你今年要去什么好玩的地方吗？ ➲ SYNONYMS AT MENTION

• **A LANGUAGE** 语言 **4** 🔑 [T] (not used in the progressive tenses 不用于进行时) **~ sth** to be able to use a particular language 会说，会讲（某种语言）：*to speak several languages* 会讲几种语言 ◇ *to speak a little Urdu* 会说一点乌尔都语 ◇ *Do you speak English?* 你会说英语吗？ **5** 🔑 [T, I] to use a particular language to express yourself 用（某种语言）说话：**~ sth** *What language is it they're speaking?* 他们讲的是什么语？ ◇ **~ in sth** *Would you prefer it if we spoke in German?* 我们用德语讲好吗？

• **-SPEAKING** 讲…语 **6** (in adjectives 构成形容词) speaking the language mentioned 讲…语的：*French-speaking Canada* 加拿大法语区 ◇ *non-English-speaking students* 不会讲英语的学生

• **MAKE SPEECH** 发表讲话 **7** 🔑 [I] (**+ adv./prep.**) to make a speech to an audience 发言；演说；演讲：*to speak in public* 公开演讲 ◇ *to speak on the radio* 在电台上讲话 ◇ *to speak at a conference* 在会上发言 ◇ *Professor Wilson was invited to speak about the results of his research.* 威尔逊教授获邀就自己的研究成果发言。◇ *She **spoke in favour of** the new tax.* 她发表演说，支持新税。◇ *He has a number of **speaking engagements** this week.* 他这个星期安排了几次演讲。➲ WORDFINDER NOTE AT DEBATE

• **SAY/STATE** 说；讲述 **8** [T] **~ sth** to say or state sth 说；讲述：*She was clearly **speaking the truth**.* 她讲的显然是实情。◇ *He spoke the final words of the play.* 剧中最后的台词是他说的。

IDM **be on ˈspeaking terms (with sb)** | **be ˈspeaking (to sb)** to be willing to be polite or friendly towards sb, especially after an argument（与某人）和好如初，和睦相处：*She's not been on speaking terms with her uncle for years.* 多年来她跟她叔叔一直不说话。◇ *Are they speaking to each other again yet?* 他们俩和好了没有？ ˈ**generally,** ˈ**broadly,** ˈ**roughly,** ˈ**relatively, etc. speaking** used to show that what you are saying is true in a general, etc. way 总的、一般、粗略、相对等说来：*Generally speaking, the more you pay, the more you get.* 一般来说，花钱多，买的东西就多。◇ *There are, broadly speaking, two ways of doing this.* 大致说来，做这件事有两种方法。 ◇ *Personally speaking, I've always preferred Italian food.* 就我个人来讲，我总是偏爱意大利菜。➲ LANGUAGE BANK AT GENERALLY **no…/nothing to ˈspeak of** such a small amount that it is not worth mentioning 不值一提；微不足道：*They've got no friends to speak of.* 他们没一个像样的朋友。◇ *She's saved a little money but nothing to speak of.* 她攒了一点钱，不过数目不值一提。ˌ**so to ˈspeak** used to emphasize that you are expressing sth in an unusual or amusing way 可以说；可谓：*They were all very similar. All cut from the same cloth, so to speak.* 他们都十分相像。可以说就跟一块布上剪下来似的。**speak for itˈself/themˈselves** to be so easy to see and understand that you do not need to say anything else about it/them 不言而喻；有目共睹：*Her success speaks for itself.* 她的成功有目共睹。**speak for myˈself/herˈself/himˈself, etc.** to express what you think or want yourself, rather than sb else doing it for you 自己说（而非让别人替自己说）：*I'm quite capable of speaking for myself, thank you!* 我自己会说，谢谢了！ **speak for yourˈself** (*informal*) used to tell sb that a general statement they have just made is not true of you（告诉某人不要以为自己的概括性意见适用于大家）只说你自己，那是你：*'We didn't play very well.' 'Speak for yourself!'* (= I think that I played well.) "我们打得不太好。""是说你自己吧！" **speaking as sth** used to say that you are the type of person mentioned and are expressing your opinion from that point of view（表示从某种角度看问题）作为…来说：*Speaking as a parent, I'm very concerned about standards in education.* 作为家长，我十分关注教育的水准。**speak your ˈmind** to say exactly what you think, in a very direct way 说心里话；说实在的；坦率地说 ˌ**speak out of ˈturn** to say sth when you should not, for example because it is not the right time or you are not the right person to say it 说话不合时宜（或不合身份） **speak ˈvolumes (about/for sth/sb)** to tell you a lot about sth/sb, without the need for words 充分说明；清楚表明 **speak ˈwell/ˈill of sb** (*formal*) to say good or bad things about sb 称赞（或贬损）某人；说某人的好话（或坏话）➲ MORE AT ACTION *n.*, DEVIL, FACT, ILL *adv.*, LANGUAGE, MANNER, STRICTLY, TURN *n.*

PHR V ˈ**speak for sb** to state the views or wishes of a person or a group; to act as a representative for sb 代（或代表）某人讲话 ˈ**speak of sth** (*formal*) to be evidence that sth exists or is present 表明；说明：*Everything here speaks of perfect good taste.* 这里的一切都体现出极为高雅的情趣。ˌ**speak ˈout (against sth)** 🔑 to state your opinions publicly, especially in opposition to sth and in a way that takes courage 挺身（反对某事物）；公开站出来（反对）➲ SEE ALSO OUTSPOKEN ˈ**speak to sb (about sth)** (*informal*) to talk to sb in a serious way about sth wrong they have done, to try to stop them doing it again（为某事）数说某人 ˈ**speak to sb/sth** to attract or interest sb/sth 吸引；使感兴趣：*The story spoke to him directly.* 这个故事立刻吸引了他。◇ *It's a design that speaks to the senses.* 这是一个诉诸感官的设计。**'speak to sth 1** to discuss or comment on a topic, problem or situation 讨论；评论：*The show wants to speak to real issues affecting young people.* 这档节目想要讨论深切影响年轻人的问题。**2** to be evidence that sth exists or is true 证实；说明：*The number of cleaning firms **speaks to the fact that** cleaning is considered an important service.* 保洁被视为一项重要的服务，保洁公司的数量证明了这个事实。**,speak 'up** usually used in orders to tell sb to speak more loudly 大声点说：*Please speak up—we can't hear you at the back.* 请大声点讲，我们在后面听不见。**,speak 'up (for sb/sth)** to say what you think clearly and freely, especially in order to support or defend sb/sth 明确表态；（尤指为…）说好话，辩护

-speak /spiːk/ *combining form* (in nouns 构成名词) (*informal, often disapproving*) the language used by a particular group of people, especially when it is difficult for other people to understand or they find it annoying（尤指令他人费解或厌烦的）圈中行话，用语：*management-speak* 管理层用语 ◇ *Visitors to websites don't want to read marketing-speak.* 网页浏览者不想看推销语言。

speak·easy /ˈspiːkiːzi/ *noun* (*pl.* **-ies**) **1** a place in the US where people could buy alcohol illegally, at the time in the 1920s and 1930s when it was illegal to make or sell alcohol（美国 20 世纪 20、30 年代禁酒期间）非法经营的酒店 **2** a bar like this today that operates legally but secretly 合法但秘密经营的酒吧

speak·er /ˈspiːkə(r)/ *noun* **1** a person who gives a talk or makes a speech 发言者；演讲者：*He was a **guest speaker** at the conference.* 他是会议的特邀演讲人。◇ *She was a brilliant **public speaker**.* 她很擅长在公开场合演讲。➲ WORDFINDER NOTE AT CONFERENCE **2** a person who is or was speaking 说话者：*I looked around to see who the speaker was.* 我四下环顾看说话的是谁。**3** a person who speaks a particular language 讲（某种语言）的人：*Chinese speakers* 讲汉语的人 ◇ *a **native speaker** of English* 以英语为母语的人 **4** **(the) Speaker** the title of the person whose job is to control the discussions in a parliament（议会的）议长：*the Speaker of the House of Commons/Representatives* 英国下议院 / 美国众议院议长 **5** the part of a radio, computer or piece of musical equipment that the sound comes out of 扬声器；喇叭 ➲ SEE ALSO LOUDSPEAKER

▼ **SYNONYMS 同义词辨析**

speaker

communicator • gossip • talker

These are all words for a person who talks or who is talking, especially in a particular way. 以上各词均指说话者，尤指以某种方式说话的人。

speaker a person who is or was speaking; a person who speaks a particular language 指发言者、讲某种语言的人：*I looked around to see who the speaker was.* 我四下环顾看说话的是谁。◇ *a fluent Arabic speaker* 阿拉伯语讲得流利的人

communicator (*rather formal*) a person who is able to describe their ideas and feelings clearly to others 指交际者、交流者：*The ideal candidate will be an effective communicator.* 理想的候选人定要是善于沟通的人。

gossip (*disapproving*) a person who enjoys talking about other people's private lives 指喜欢传播流言蜚语的人、爱说长道短（或说三道四）的人：*Myra is a dear, but she's also a terrible gossip.* 迈拉是很可爱，但也是个讨厌的长舌妇。

talker a person who talks in a particular way or who talks a lot 指以某种方式说话的人、爱说话的人：*He's a very persuasive talker.* 他是一个说话很有说服力的人。◇ *She's a (great) talker* (= she talks a lot). 她很健谈。

SPEAKER OR TALKER? 用 speaker 还是 talker?

Talker is used when you are talking about how much sb talks or how well they talk. It is not used for the person who is or was talking. * talker 用以指说话多或少，或者话说得如何的人，不用以指正在或曾经在说话的人：~~*I looked round to see who the talker was.*~~ You can say that sb is *a good/persuasive speaker* but that means that they are good at making speeches. If you mean that they speak well in conversation, use **talker**. * good/persuasive speaker 指的是擅长演讲的人。如果指健谈或能言善辩的人就用 talker。

PATTERNS

- a **good/great** speaker/communicator/talker
- an **effective/excellent** speaker/communicator

speak·er·phone /ˈspiːkəfəʊn; *NAmE* -ərfoʊn/ *noun* a telephone that can be used without being held, because it contains a MICROPHONE and a LOUDSPEAKER 扬声电话（内置麦克风和扬声器，使用时无须拿起听筒）

spear /spɪə(r); *NAmE* spɪr/ *noun, verb*

■ ***noun*** **1** a weapon with a long wooden handle and a sharp metal point used for fighting, hunting and fishing in the past 矛；标枪 ➲ PICTURE AT SWORD **2** the long pointed STEM of some plants（某些植物的）嫩枝，幼芽 ➲ VISUAL VOCAB PAGE V33

■ ***verb*** **~ sth/sb** to throw or push a spear or other pointed object through sth/sb 用矛刺；用尖物刺穿：*They were standing in the river spearing fish.* 他们站在河里叉鱼。◇ *She speared an olive with her fork.* 她用叉子扎起一个橄榄。

spear·head /ˈspɪəhed; *NAmE* ˈspɪrhed/ *noun, verb*

■ ***noun*** [usually sing.] a person or group that begins an activity or leads an attack against sb/sth 先锋；前锋；先头部队

■ ***verb*** **~ sth** to begin an activity or lead an attack against sb/sth 做…的先锋；带头做；领先突击：*He is **spearheading a campaign** for a new stadium in the town.* 他正发起一项运动，呼吁在城里新建一座体育场。

spear·mint /ˈspɪəmɪnt; *NAmE* ˈspɪrm-/ *noun* [U] a type of MINT used especially in making sweets/candy and TOOTHPASTE 留兰香；绿薄荷：*spearmint chewing gum* 留兰香口香糖 ➲ COMPARE PEPPERMINT (1)

spec /spek/ *noun, verb*

■ ***noun*** (*also* **specs** *US*) a detailed description of sth, especially the design and materials needed to produce sth 规格：*We want the machine manufactured to our own spec.* 我们要求这台机器按我们自己的规格来制造。➲ SEE ALSO SPECIFICATION

IDM **on 'spec** (*informal*) when you do sth **on spec**, you are trying to achieve sth without organizing it in advance, but hoping you will be lucky 碰运气

■ ***verb*** **(-cc-)** **~ sth** to design and make sth to a particular standard 按特定标准设计并制造：*The camera is well specced at the price.* 就价钱来说，这台照相机的配置很不错。

speccy = SPECKY

spe·cial /ˈspeʃl/ *adj., noun*

■ ***adj.*** **1** [usually before noun] not ordinary or usual; different from what is normal 特殊的；特别的；不寻常的；不一般的 **SYN** **exceptional**: *The school will only allow this in special circumstances.* 学校只有在特殊情况下才会同意这种事。◇ *Some of the officials have special privileges.* 有些官员享受特权。◇ *There is **something special** about this place.* 这个地方有几分特别。**2** more important than others; deserving or getting more attention than usual 重要的；格外看重的；特别关照的：*What are your special interests?* 你有哪些主要的爱好？◇ *She's a very special friend.* 她是我特别要好的朋友。◇ *Our special guest on next week's show will be…* 我们下周节目的特邀嘉宾是… ◇ *Don't lose it—it's special.* 别丢了，这可不是一般东西。**3** organized or intended for a particular purpose 特设的；有专门目的的；起专门作用的：*a special event* 特设活动 ◇ *These teachers need special training.* 这些教师需要专门的培训。

S

4 ⚷ used by or intended for one particular person or group of people 专用的；专门针对…的；特有的：*She has a special way of smiling.* 她微笑的样子有些特别。◇ *He sent a special message to the men.* 他给那些人专门去了一封信。
5 ⚷ [only before noun] better or more than usual 更好的；格外的：*As an only child she got special attention.* 她是个独生女，所以备受关爱。◇ *Please take special care of it.* 请对它多加关照。➲ COMPARE ESPECIAL

■ *noun* **1** something that is not usually available but is provided for a particular purpose or on one occasion 特别活动（或节目等）；特制产品：*an election-night special on television* 选举之夜电视特别节目 ◇ *The menu changes regularly and there are daily specials to choose from.* 菜谱定期更换，而且每天都有特色菜供选择。**2** (*informal, especially NAmE*) a price for a particular product in a shop/store or restaurant that is lower than usual 特价：*There's a special on coffee this week.* 本周咖啡特价。

IDM **on 'special** (*especially NAmE*) on sale at a lower price for a short period of time（短期）特价：*The chocolates were on special at my local store.* 我家附近商店的巧克力在做特价。

ˈspecial agent *noun* a DETECTIVE who works for the FEDERAL government in the US, for example for the FBI 特工；特务

ˈSpecial Branch *noun* [U+sing./pl. v.] (*also* **the Special Branch** [sing.+sing./pl. v.]) the department of the British police force that deals with the defence of the country against political crimes and TERRORISM（英国警察部门的）政治保安处

ˌspecial ˈconstable *noun* (in Britain) a person who is not a professional police officer but who is trained to help the police force, especially during an emergency 临时警察，纠察（英国在非常时期协助警察维持治安）

ˌspecial deˈlivery *noun* [U] a service that delivers a letter, etc. faster than normal（信件等的）特快专递

ˌspecial deˈvelopment area (*also* **ˌspecial ˈarea**) *noun* an area of the UK for which special laws exist in order to help the economy to develop（英国）经济发展特区，经济开发区

ˌspecial eduˈcation *noun* [U] the education of children who have physical or learning problems 特殊教育（为有身体障碍或学习障碍的儿童而设）

ˌspecial efˈfects (*also* **SFX**) *noun* [pl.] unusual or exciting pieces of action in films/movies or television programmes, that are created by computers or clever photography to show things that do not normally exist or happen（电影或电视节目的）特技效果

ˌspecial ˈinterest group (*also* **ˌspecial ˈinterest**) *noun* (*especially NAmE*) a group of people who work together to achieve sth that they are particularly interested in, especially by putting pressure on the government, etc.（尤指对政府施压的）特别利益集团

spe·cial·ism /ˈspeʃəlɪzəm/ *noun* **1** [C] an area of study or work that sb SPECIALIZES in 专业；专长：*a business degree with a specialism in computing* 专修计算机技术的商业学位 ◇ *Dr Crane's specialism is tropical diseases.* 克莱恩博士的研究领域是热带病。**2** [U] the fact of SPECIALIZING in a particular subject 专业化

spe·cial·ist ⚷ /ˈspeʃəlɪst/ *noun* **1** ⚷ a person who is an expert in a particular area of work or study 专家：*a specialist in Japanese history* 日本史专家 **2** ⚷ a doctor who has SPECIALIZED in a particular area of medicine 专科医生：*a cancer specialist* 癌症专科医生 ➲ COMPARE GENERALIST ➲ WORDFINDER NOTE AT DOCTOR

> **WORDFINDER** 联想词： cardiologist, dermatologist, gynaecologist, neurologist, obstetrician, ophthalmologist, paediatrician, psychiatrist, radiologist

▶ **spe·cial·ist** *adj.* [only before noun]: *specialist magazines* 专业杂志 ◇ *You need some specialist advice.* 你需要咨询专业人士。

spe·ci·al·ity /ˌspeʃiˈæləti/ (*BrE*) (*also* **spe·cial·ty** *NAmE, BrE*) *noun* (*pl.* **-ies**) **1** a type of food or product that a restaurant or place is famous for because it is so good 特产；特色菜：*Seafood is a speciality on the island.* 海味是岛上的特产。◇ *local specialities* 土特产 ➲ WORDFINDER NOTE AT RESTAURANT **2** an area of work or study that sb gives most of their attention to and knows a lot about; sth that sb is good at 专业；专长：*My speciality is international tax law.* 我的专业是国际税法。

spe·cial·ize (*BrE also* **-ise**) /ˈspeʃəlaɪz/ *verb* [I] ~ (**in sth**) to become an expert in a particular area of work, study or business; to spend more time on one area of work, etc. than on others 专门研究（或从事）；专攻：*Many students prefer not to specialize too soon.* 很多学生不愿过早地确定专业。◇ *He specialized in criminal law.* 他专攻刑法。◇ *The shop specializes in hand-made chocolates.* 这家商店专营手工制作的巧克力。▶ **spe·cial·iza·tion, -isa·tion** /ˌspeʃəlaɪˈzeɪʃn; *NAmE* -ləˈz-/ *noun* [U, C]

spe·cial·ized (*BrE also* **-ised**) /ˈspeʃəlaɪzd/ *adj.* designed or developed for a particular purpose or area of knowledge 专用的；专业的；专门的：*specialized equipment* 专用设备 ◇ *specialized skills* 专门技能

ˌspecial ˈlicence *noun* (*BrE*) a licence allowing two people to get married at a time or place that is not usually allowed 结婚特别许可（批准在通常不允许的时间或地点结婚）

spe·cial·ly ⚷ /ˈspeʃəli/ *adv.* **1** ⚷ for a particular purpose, person, etc. 专门地；特意：*The ring was specially made for her.* 这枚戒指是为她定做的。◇ *a specially designed diet plan* 专门制订的饮食方案 ◇ *We came specially to see you.* 我们特意来看你。**2** (*informal*) more than usual or more than other things 格外；特别；尤其：*It will be hard to work today—specially when it's so warm and sunny outside.* 今天无心工作，尤其是外面这样风和日丽。◇ *I hate homework. Specially history.* 我讨厌家庭作业，特别是历史。➲ NOTE AT ESPECIALLY

ˌspecial ˈneeds *noun* [pl.] (*especially BrE*) needs that a person has because of mental or physical problems（智力或身体障碍者的）特殊需求：*She teaches children with special needs.* 她教的是有特殊需求的儿童。

ˌspecial ˈoffer *noun* [C, U] a product that is sold at less than its usual price, especially in order to persuade people to buy it; the act of offering goods in this way 特价商品；特价销售：*Shop around for special offers.* 去四处转转，看有没有特价商品。◇ *a special offer on perfume* 香水特价销售 ◇ *French wine is* **on special offer** *this week.* 法国葡萄酒本周特价销售。

ˌspecial ˈpleading *noun* [U] trying to persuade sb about sth by mentioning only the arguments that support your opinion and ignoring the arguments that do not support it（只谈有利于自己观点的论据的）诡辩

ˌspecial ˈschool *noun* a school for children who have physical or learning problems 特殊学校（为有身体障碍或学习障碍的儿童设立）

spe·cialty /ˈspeʃəlti/ *noun* (*pl.* **-ies**) (*especially NAmE* or *medical* 医) = SPECIALITY: *regional specialties* 地方特产 ◇ *specialty stores* 特产商店 ◇ *Her specialty is taxation law.* 她的专长是税法。◇ *Doctors training for General Practice must complete programmes in a number of specialties, including Paediatrics.* 接受全科培训的医生必须修完包括儿科学在内的多门专业课程。

spe·cies /ˈspiːʃiːz/ *noun* (*pl.* **spe·cies**) a group into which animals, plants, etc. that are able to breed with each other and produce healthy young are divided, smaller than a GENUS and identified by a Latin name 种，物种（分类上小于属）：*a rare species of beetle* 一种稀有甲虫 ◇ *There are many species of dog(s).* 狗有许多种。◇ *a conservation area for* **endangered species** 濒危物种保护区 ➲ WORDFINDER NOTE AT GREEN, BREED

the ˈspecies barrier *noun* [sing.] the natural system which is thought to prevent diseases spreading from one type of animal or plant to another 物种屏障（防止疾病在物种之间传播的自然机制）

spe·cies·ism /ˈspiːʃiːzɪzəm/ *noun* [U] (*disapproving*) the belief that humans are more important than animals, which causes people to treat animals badly 物种歧视（认为人类比动物重要，因此虐待动物）▶ **spe·cies·ist** *adj.*, *noun*

spe·cif·ic AW /spəˈsɪfɪk/ *adj.* **1** detailed and exact 明确的；具体的 SYN **precise**: *I gave you specific instructions.* 我给过你明确的指示。◇ *'I'd like your help tomorrow.' 'Can you **be more specific*** (= tell me exactly what you want)?' "我想让你明天来帮帮我。" "你能不能说得具体些？" **2** [usually before noun] connected with one particular thing only 特定的 SYN **particular**: *children's television programmes aimed at a specific age group* 针对特定年龄段的少儿电视节目 ◇ *The money was collected for a specific purpose.* 这笔钱是为一个特定用途而收的。◇ *children with specific learning difficulties* (= in one area only) 某一方面有学习困难的儿童 **3 ~ to sth** (*formal*) existing only in one place or limited to one thing 特有的；独特的 SYN **peculiar**: *a belief that is specific to this part of Africa* 非洲这一地区特有的一种观念

spe·cif·ic·al·ly AW /spəˈsɪfɪkli/ *adv.* **1** in a detailed and exact way 明确地；具体地：*I specifically told you not to go near the water!* 我明确告诉过你不要靠近水边！**2** connected with or intended for one particular thing only 特意；专门地：*liquid vitamins specifically designed for children* 专为儿童设计的维生素水剂 ◇ *a magazine aimed specifically at working women* 专门面向职业妇女的杂志 **3** used when you want to add more detailed and exact information 具体来说；确切地说：*The newspaper, or more specifically, the editor, was taken to court for publishing the photographs.* 那家报纸，更确切地说是那家报纸的编辑，因刊登那些照片而遭起诉。

speci·fi·ca·tion AW /ˌspesɪfɪˈkeɪʃn/ *noun* [C, U] a detailed description of how sth is, or should be, designed or made 规格；规范；明细单；说明书：*the technical specifications of the new model* (= of car) 新型号的技术规格 ◇ *The house has been built exactly **to our specifications**.* 房子完全是按照我们的工程设计书建造的。◇ *The office was furnished **to a high specification**.* 办公室是按高规格装潢的。

speˌcific ˈgravity *noun* [U] = RELATIVE DENSITY

speci·fi·city AW /ˌspesɪˈfɪsəti/ *noun* [U] (*formal*) the quality of being specific 明确性；具体性；独特性

spe·cif·ics AW /spəˈsɪfɪks/ *noun* [pl.] the details of a subject that you need to think about or discuss 详情；细节：*Okay, that's the broad plan—let's get down to the specifics.* 好，这是总的计划。下面来谈谈具体细节。

spe·cify AW /ˈspesɪfaɪ/ *verb* (**speci·fies, speci·fy·ing, speci·fied, speci·fied**) to state sth, especially by giving an exact measurement, time, exact instructions, etc. 具体说明；明确规定；详述；详列：**~ sth** *Remember to specify your size when ordering clothes.* 订购服装时记着要详细说明你要的号码。◇ **~ who, what, etc....** *The contract clearly specifies who can operate the machinery.* 合同明确规定谁可以操作机器。◇ **~ that...** *The regulations specify that calculators may not be used in the examination.* 考试规则明确规定考试时不得使用计算器。▶ **spe·ci·fi·able** AW /ˈspesɪfaɪəbl/ *adj.*

speci·men /ˈspesɪmən/ *noun* **1** a small amount of sth that shows what the rest of it is like 样品；样本；标本 SYN **sample**: *Astronauts have brought back specimens of rock from the moon.* 宇航员从月球带回了岩石标本。➲ COLLOCATIONS AT SCIENTIFIC **2** a single example of sth, especially an animal or a plant（尤指动植物的）单一实例：*The aquarium has some interesting specimens of unusual tropical fish.* 水族馆里有一些罕见的热带鱼，很有意思。◇ (*humorous*) *They were fine specimens of British youth!* 他们堪称英国青年的优秀代表！➲ SYNONYMS AT EXAMPLE **3** a small quantity of blood, URINE, etc. that is taken from sb and tested by a doctor（化验的）抽样，血样，尿样：*to **provide/take a specimen*** 提供血样；采血样

spe·cious /ˈspiːʃəs/ *adj.* (*formal*) seeming right or true but actually wrong or false 似是而非的；貌似有理的 SYN **misleading**: *a specious argument* 似是而非的论点

speck /spek/ *noun* a very small spot; a small piece of dirt, etc. 小点；污点：*The ship was now just a speck in the distance.* 此时，那艘船不过是远处的一个小点。◇ *specks of dust* 尘埃 ➲ SYNONYMS AT MARK

speckle /ˈspekl/ *noun* [usually pl.] a small coloured mark or spot on a background of a different colour 斑点；色斑 ➲ WORDFINDER NOTE AT PATTERN

speck·led /ˈspekld/ *adj.* covered with small marks or spots 布满斑点的；有色斑的 SYN **flecked**

specky (*also* **speccy**) /ˈspeki/ *adj.* (*BrE*, *offensive*) wearing glasses 戴眼镜的；四只眼的

specs /speks/ *noun* [pl.] **1** (*informal, especially BrE*) = GLASSES: *I need a new pair of specs.* 我需要一副新眼镜。**2** (*NAmE*) = SPEC

spec·tacle /ˈspektəkl/ *noun* **1 spectacles** [pl.] (*formal*) = GLASSES: *a pair of spectacles* 一副眼镜 ◇ *a spectacle case* (= to put your glasses in) 眼镜盒 **2** [C, U] a performance or an event that is very impressive and exciting to look at 精彩的表演；壮观的场面：*The carnival parade was a magnificent spectacle.* 狂欢节游行场面热烈，蔚为大观。**3** [C] a sight or view that is very impressive to look at 壮观的景象：*The sunset was a stunning spectacle.* 夕阳西斜，异常壮观。**4** [sing.] an unusual or surprising sight or situation that attracts a lot of attention 奇特的现象；出人意外的情况：*I remember the sad spectacle of her standing in her wedding dress, covered in mud.* 我记得她穿着婚纱、满身泥污站在那儿的凄惨样。

IDM **make a ˈspectacle of yourself** to draw attention to yourself by behaving or dressing in a ridiculous way in public 出洋相；出丑

spec·tacu·lar /spekˈtækjələ(r)/ *adj.*, *noun*

- ***adj.*** very impressive 壮观的；壮丽的；令人惊叹的 SYN **breathtaking**: *spectacular scenery* 壮丽的景色 ◇ *Messi scored a spectacular goal.* 梅西攻入了一个精彩进球。◇ *It was a spectacular achievement on their part.* 这是他们取得的一项了不起的成就。▶ **spec·tacu·lar·ly** *adv.*: *It has been a spectacularly successful year.* 这是成绩辉煌的一年。
- ***noun*** an impressive show or performance 壮观的场面；精彩的表演：*a Christmas TV spectacular* 精彩的圣诞节电视节目

spec·tate /spekˈteɪt/ *verb* [I] to watch sth, especially a sports event 观看（体育比赛等）

spec·ta·tor /spekˈteɪtə(r); *NAmE* ˈspekteɪtər/ *noun* a person who is watching an event, especially a sports event（尤指体育比赛的）观看者，观众 ➲ WORDFINDER NOTE AT SPORT

specˈtator sport *noun* a sport that many people watch; a sport that is interesting to watch 群众爱看的体育运动；观赏性体育运动

spec·tra PL. OF SPECTRUM

spec·tral /ˈspektrəl/ *adj.* **1** (*literary*) like a GHOST; connected with a ghost 鬼一般的；幽灵似的；鬼的；幽灵的 **2** (*specialist*) connected with a SPECTRUM 谱的；光谱的；频谱的：*spectral bands* 光谱带

spectre (*US* **spec·ter**) /ˈspektə(r)/ *noun* **1 ~ (of sth)** something unpleasant that people are afraid might happen in the future 恐惧；恐慌；忧虑：*The country is haunted by the spectre of civil war.* 内战仿佛一触即发，举国上下一片恐慌。◇ *These weeks of drought have once again **raised the spectre** of widespread famine.* 几星期来的干旱再次引起了群众对大饥荒的恐慌。**2** (*literary*) a GHOST 鬼；幽灵：*Was he a spectre returning to haunt her?* 是不是他的幽灵回来找她了？

spec·trom·eter /spek'trɒmɪtə(r); *NAmE* -'trɑːm-/ *noun* (*specialist*) a piece of equipment for measuring the WAVELENGTHS of SPECTRA 分光计；（光）谱仪

spec·tro·scope /'spektrəskəʊp; *NAmE* -skoʊp/ *noun* (*specialist*) a piece of equipment for forming and looking at SPECTRA 分光镜；看谱镜 ▸ **spec·tro·scop·ic** /ˌspektrə'skɒpɪk; *NAmE* -'skɑːp-/ *adj.*: *spectroscopic analysis* 光谱分析

spec·tros·copy /spek'trɒskəpi; *NAmE* -'trɑːs-/ *noun* [U] (*chemistry* 化, *physics* 物) the study of forming and looking at SPECTRA using spectrometers, spectroscopes, etc. 光谱学；光谱术

spec·trum /'spektrəm/ *noun* (*pl.* **spec·tra** /'spektrə/) **1** a band of coloured lights in order of their WAVELENGTHS, as seen in a RAINBOW and into which light may be separated 谱；光谱：*A spectrum is formed by a ray of light passing through a prism.* 一束光通过棱镜就会形成光谱。◇ *Red and violet are at opposite ends of the spectrum.* 红色和紫色位于光谱的两端。**2** a range of sound waves or several other types of wave 声谱；波谱；频谱：*the **electromagnetic/radio/sound spectrum*** 电磁波谱；射频频谱；声谱 **3** [usually sing.] a complete or wide range of related qualities, ideas, etc. 范围；各层次；系列；幅度：*a broad spectrum of interests* 广泛的兴趣范围 ◇ *We shall hear views from across the political spectrum.* 我们要听取各个政治派别的看法。

specu·late /'spekjuleɪt/ *verb* **1** [I, T] to form an opinion about sth without knowing all the details or facts 推测；猜测；推断：**~ (about/on/as to sth)** *We all speculated about the reasons for her resignation.* 我们大家都推测过她辞职的原因。◇ **~ why, how, etc....** *It is useless to speculate why he did it.* 对他为什么这么做妄加猜测毫无用处。◇ **~ that...** *We can speculate that the stone circles were used in some sort of pagan ceremony.* 我们可以推测，这些石头排成的圆圈是用于某种异教崇拜仪式的。➲ SYNONYMS AT PHOTOGRAPH

> ▼ **EXPRESS YOURSELF 情景表达**
>
> **Speculating 作出推测**
>
> In some exams, you have to talk about what you can see in a picture and speculate about the situation or a wider issue prompted by the picture. These are ways of saying what you think might be the case. 考试中有时需要谈论图画内容并据此就其情境或更广泛的问题作出推测，可使用以下表达方式：
>
> - ***I think it's likely that** these people know each other.* 我认为这些人可能彼此认识。
> - ***I imagine** she's his wife.* 我猜她是他的妻子。
> - *They **might/may/could** be related.* (*BrE* or *formal*, *NAmE*) 他们可能有亲属关系。
> - ***I would think/imagine/guess** they've been waiting for some time.* (*BrE*) 我猜他们已经等了一段时间。
> - ***I guess** that the car has broken down.* (*NAmE*) 我猜是车抛锚了。
> - *I think this has **probably** happened before.* 我觉得这事很可能以前发生过。
> - ***It looks to me as though** the woman is very angry.* 我看这女人好像很生气。
> - ***Perhaps/Probably/Possibly/It may be that/Maybe** there has been an accident.* (*BrE* or *formal*, *NAmE*) 可能出了事故。

2 [I] **~ (in/on sth)** to buy goods, property, shares, etc., hoping to make a profit when you sell them, but with the risk of losing money 投机；做投机买卖：*He likes to speculate on the stock market.* 他喜欢炒股。

specu·la·tion /ˌspekju'leɪʃn/ *noun* [U, C] **1** the act of forming opinions about what has happened or what might happen without knowing all the facts 推测；猜测；推断：**~ (that...)** *There was widespread speculation that she was going to resign.* 人们纷纷推测她将辞职。◇ *His private life is the subject of much speculation.* 他的私生活引起诸多猜测。◇ **~ (about/over sth)** *Today's announcement ends months of speculation about the company's future.* 今天的声明使得几个月来关于公司未来的种种猜测就此烟消云散。◇ *She dismissed the newspaper reports as **pure speculation**.* 她说报纸上的报道毫无根据，纯属臆断。◇ *Our speculations proved right.* 事实证明，我们的推断是对的。**2 ~ (in sth)** the activity of buying and selling goods or shares in a company in the hope of making a profit, but with the risk of losing money 投机买卖；炒股

specu·la·tive /'spekjələtɪv; *NAmE also* 'spekjəleɪtɪv/ *adj.* **1** based on guessing or on opinions that have been formed without knowing all the facts 推测的；猜测的；推断的 **2** showing that you are trying to guess sth 揣摩的；忖度的；试探的：*She cast a speculative look at Kate.* 她带着疑问的眼神看了凯特一眼。**3** (of business activity 商业活动) done in the hope of making a profit but involving the risk of losing money 投机性的；风险性的 ▸ **specu·la·tive·ly** *adv.*

specu·la·tor /'spekjuleɪtə(r)/ *noun* a person who buys and sells goods or shares in a company in the hope of making a profit 投机商；投机倒把者：*property speculators* 房地产投机商

specu·lum /'spekjələm/ *noun* (*medical* 医) a metal instrument that is used to make a hole or tube in the body wider so it can be examined 窥器；张开器

sped PAST TENSE, PAST PART. OF SPEED

speech 🔑 /spiːtʃ/ *noun* **1** 🔑 [C] **~ (on/about sth)** a formal talk that a person gives to an audience 演说；讲话；发言：*to **give/make/deliver a speech** on human rights* 就人权问题发表演讲 ◇ *He made the announcement **in a speech** on television.* 他在一次电视讲话中发表了这一声明。◇ *Several people made speeches at the wedding.* 有几个人在婚礼

> ▼ **SYNONYMS 同义词辨析**
>
> **speech**
>
> **lecture • address • talk • sermon**
>
> These are all words for a talk given to an audience. 以上各词均指讲话、发言。
>
> **speech** a formal talk given to an audience 指演说、讲话、发言：*Several people made speeches at the wedding.* 有几个人在婚礼上讲了话。
>
> **lecture** a talk given to a group of people to tell them about a particular subject, often as part of a university or college course 通常指大学里的讲座、讲课、演讲：*a lecture on the Roman army* 关于罗马军队的讲座 ◇ *a course/series of lectures* 讲座课程；系列讲座
>
> **address** a formal speech given to an audience 指演说、演讲：*a televised presidential address* 总统的电视演讲
>
> **SPEECH OR ADDRESS? 用 speech 还是 address?**
>
> A **speech** can be given on a public or private occasion; an **address** is always public. * speech 指公开或私下场合的讲话均可，而 address 总是指公开的演讲：~~*He gave an address at the wedding.*~~
>
> **talk** a fairly informal session in which sb tells a group of people about a subject 指相当不正式的报告、演讲：*She gave an interesting talk on her visit to China.* 她做了个关于她在中国访问的有趣报告。
>
> **sermon** a talk on a moral or religious subject, usually given by a religious leader during a service 指布道、讲道：*to preach a sermon* 布道
>
> **PATTERNS**
>
> - a **long/short** speech/lecture/address/talk/sermon
> - a **keynote** speech/lecture/address
> - to **write/prepare/give/deliver/hear** a(n) speech/lecture/address/talk/sermon
> - to **attend/go to** a lecture/talk

上讲了话。**2** [U] the ability to speak 说话的能力：*I seemed to have lost the* ***power of speech.*** 我好像话都说不出来了。◇ *a speech defect* 言语能力缺陷 ◇ ***freedom of speech*** (= the right to say openly what you think) 言论自由 **3** [U] the way in which a particular person speaks 说话方式：*Her speech was slurred—she was clearly drunk.* 她说话含混不清，显然是喝醉了。**4** [U] the language used when speaking 口语：*This expression is used mainly in speech, not in writing.* 这种表达主要用于口语，而不是书面语。◇ *speech sounds* 语音 **5** [C] a group of lines that an actor speaks in a play in the theatre（戏剧中的）台词：*She has the longest speech in the play.* 在这部剧中，她的台词最长。➲ WORDFINDER NOTE AT DRAMA, PLAY ➲ SEE ALSO FIGURE OF SPEECH

ˈspeech act *noun* (*linguistics* 语言) something that sb says, considered as an action, for example 'I forgive you' 言语行为（如 I forgive you）

ˈspeech bubble *noun* a circle around the words that sb says in a CARTOON 话泡泡（漫画中圈出人物所说的话的圆圈）

ˈspeech community *noun* all the people who speak a particular language or variety of a language（讲某语言或语言变体的）言语共同体，言语社区：*the Kodava speech community in India* 印度的果达古语社区 ◇ *speech communities such as high school students or hip hop fans* 中学生或嘻哈音乐迷之类的言语共同体

ˈspeech day *noun* an event held once a year in some British schools at which there are speeches and prizes（英国部分学校一年一度的）授奖演讲日

speechi·fy·ing /ˈspiːtʃɪfaɪɪŋ/ *noun* [U] (*informal, disapproving*) the act of making speeches in a very formal way, trying to sound important 煞有介事的讲话；装腔作势的演讲

speech·less /ˈspiːtʃləs/ *adj.* not able to speak, especially because you are extremely angry or surprised（尤指气得或惊讶得）说不出话的：*Laura was speechless with rage.* 劳拉气得说不出话来。▶ **speech·less·ly** *adv.* **speech·less·ness** *noun* [U]

ˈspeech marks *noun* [pl.] = QUOTATION MARKS

ˈspeech recognition (*also* **ˈvoice recognition**) *noun* [U] technology that allows a computer to understand spoken words（计算机）语音识别

ˈspeech synthesis *noun* [U] the production of speech from written language by a computer（计算机）语音合成，言语合成

ˌspeech ˈtherapy *noun* [U] special treatment to help people who have problems in speaking clearly, for example in pronouncing particular sounds 言语治疗；言语矫治 ▶ **ˌspeech ˈtherapist** *noun*

ˈspeech-writer *noun* a person whose job is to write speeches for a politician or public figure 演说稿撰写员

speed /spiːd/ *noun, verb*

■ *noun*

• **RATE OF MOVEMENT/ACTION** 运动／行动速率 **1** [C, U] the rate at which sb/sth moves or travels（运动的）速度，速率：*He reduced speed and turned sharp left.* 他减慢速度，向左急转。◇ *The train began to* ***pick up speed*** (= go faster). 火车开始加速。◇ *The car was* ***gathering speed.*** 汽车逐渐加速。◇ *a* ***speed*** *of 50 mph/80 kph* 每小时 50 英里／80 公里的速度 ◇ ***at high/low/full/top speed*** 以高速／低速／全速／最高速 ◇ ***at breakneck speed*** (= fast in a way that is dangerous) 以不要命的速度 ◇ *travelling at* ***the speed of light/sound*** 以光速／声速行进 ➲ SEE ALSO AIRSPEED, GROUND SPEED **2** [C, U] the rate at which sth happens or is done（发生或进行的）速度；进度：*the processing speed of the computer* 计算机的处理速度 ◇ *This course is designed so that students can progress at their own speed.* 这门课的设计思路是让学生自己掌握进度。◇ *We aim to increase the speed of delivery* (= how quickly goods are sent). 我们力争加快送货速度。**3** [U] the quality of being quick or rapid 快；迅速：*The accident was due to excessive speed.* 事故的原因在于速度过快。◇ *She was overtaken by the* ***speed of events*** (= things happened more quickly than she expected). 事态发展迅速为她始料所不及。◇ (*formal*) *A car flashed past them* ***at speed*** (= fast). 一辆汽车从他们身边疾驰而过。

• **IN PHOTOGRAPHY** 摄影 **4** [C] a measurement of how sensitive film for cameras, etc. is to light 感光度 **5** [C] the time taken by a camera SHUTTER to open and close 快门速度：*shutter speeds* 快门速度

• **ON BICYCLE/CAR** 自行车；汽车 **6** [C] (especially in compounds 尤用于构成复合词) a gear on a bicycle, in a car, etc. 排挡；速：*a four-speed gearbox* 四挡变速箱 ◇ *a ten-speed mountain bike* 十速山地自行车 ➲ WORDFINDER NOTE AT CYCLING

• **DRUG** 毒品 **7** [U] (*informal*) an illegal AMPHETAMINE drug that is taken to give feelings of excitement and energy 苯丙胺，安非他明（一种兴奋剂）

IDM **full speed/steam aˈhead** with as much speed or energy as possible 全速（或全力）向前 **up to ˈspeed (on sth)** **1** (of a person, company, etc. 人、公司等) performing at an expected rate or level （在某事上）达到应有的速度，达标：*the cost of* ***bringing*** *the chosen schools* ***up to speed*** 使选定的学校达标所需的费用 **2** (of a person 人) having the most recent and accurate information or knowledge 了解最新情况；跟上形势：*Are you up to speed yet on the latest developments?* 你了解最新的进展情况吗？ ➲ MORE AT HASTE, TURN *n.*

■ *verb* (**speed·ed**, **speed·ed**) **HELP** In senses 1 and 2 **sped** is also used for the past tense and past participle. 作第 1 及第 2 义时，过去式和过去分词也用 sped。

• **MOVE/HAPPEN QUICKLY** 快速运动／发生 **1** [I] + **adv./prep.** (*formal*) to move along quickly 快速前行：*He sped away on his bike.* 他飞快地骑着车走了。**2** [T] ~ **sb/sth + adv./prep.** (*formal*) to take sb/sth somewhere very quickly, especially in a vehicle 快速运送：*The cab speeded them into the centre of the city.* 出租汽车载着他们迅速驶往市中心。**3** [T] ~ **sth** (*formal*) to make sth happen more quickly 加速；促进：*The drugs will speed her recovery.* 这些药会加速她的康复。

• **DRIVE TOO FAST** 超速驾驶 **4** [I] (usually used in the progressive tenses 通常用于进行时) to drive faster than the speed that is legally allowed 超速驾驶；超速行驶：*The police caught him speeding.* 警察发现他超速行驶。

PHR V **ˌspeed ˈup** | **ˌspeed sth↔ˈup** to move or happen faster; to make sth move or happen faster（使）加速：*The train soon speeded up.* 火车很快加速了。◇ *Can you try and speed things up a bit?* 你能不能设法加快一点事情的进度？

speed·boat /ˈspiːdbəʊt; *NAmE* -boʊt/ *noun* a boat with a motor that can travel very fast 快艇 ➲ VISUAL VOCAB PAGE V59

ˈspeed breaker *noun* (*IndE*) a SPEED HUMP（设在路上的）减速垄，减速带

ˈspeed camera *noun* (*BrE*) a machine which takes pictures of vehicles that are being driven too fast. The pictures are then used as evidence so that the drivers can be punished.（拍摄超速车辆的）超速监控摄像机 ➲ COLLOCATIONS AT DRIVING

ˈspeed dating *noun* [U] meeting people at an event organized for single people who want to begin a romantic relationship, where you are allowed to spend only a few minutes talking to one person before you have to move on to meet the next person 快速相亲，闪电约会（为单身者安排的约会方式，每人只限与一人交谈几分钟即转往下一人）

ˈspeed hump (*especially BrE*) (*NAmE usually* **ˈspeed bump**) (*also BrE, informal* **ˌsleeping poˈliceman**) *noun* a raised area across a road that is put there to make traffic go slower（设在路上的）减速垄，减速带 ➲ WORDFINDER NOTE AT TRAFFIC

speed·ing /ˈspiːdɪŋ/ *noun* [U] the traffic offence of driving faster than the legal limit 超速驾驶；超速行驶 ➲ COLLOCATIONS AT DRIVING

S

ˈspeed limit *noun* the highest speed at which you can legally drive on a particular road（道路的）最高车速限制：*You should always keep to the speed limit.* 任何时候你都不得超过最高速度限制。◇ *to* ***break/exceed the speed limit*** 不遵守 / 超过限定速度◇ *The road has a 30 mph speed limit.* 这条公路限定最高时速 30 英里。➲ COLLOCATIONS AT DRIVING

speedo /ˈspiːdəʊ; *NAmE* -doʊ/ *noun* (*pl.* **-os**) **1** (*BrE, informal*) = SPEEDOMETER **2 Speedo™** [usually pl.] a SWIMMING COSTUME, especially a style of tight TRUNKS for men and boys（尤指）男式紧身游泳裤；游泳衣：*a pair of Speedos* 一条紧身游泳裤

speed·om·eter /spiːˈdɒmɪtə(r); *NAmE* -ˈdɑːm-/ (*also informal* **speedo**) *noun* an instrument in a vehicle which shows how fast the vehicle is going（车辆的）车速里程表 ➲ VISUAL VOCAB PAGE V56

ˈspeed-read *verb* [I, T] ~ (**sth**) to read sth very quickly, paying attention to the general meaning of sentences and phrases rather than to every word 快速阅读，速读（关注大意）▶ **ˈspeed-reading** *noun* [U]

ˈspeed skating *noun* [U] the sport of SKATING on ice as fast as possible 速度滑冰 ➲ COMPARE FIGURE-SKATING

speed·ster /ˈspiːdstə(r)/ *noun* (*informal*) **1** a person who drives a vehicle very fast 快速驾驶者；飙车者 **2** a machine or vehicle that works well at high speeds 高速运转的机器；快速行驶的车辆

ˈspeed trap (*BrE also* **ˈradar trap**) *noun* a place on a road where police use special equipment to catch drivers who are going too fast 汽车超速监视区

speed·way /ˈspiːdweɪ/ *noun* **1** [U] (*BrE*) the sport of racing motorcycles on a special track（摩托车）赛车运动 **2** [C] (*NAmE*) a special track for racing cars or motorcycles on（汽车或摩托车的）赛车跑道

speed·well /ˈspiːdwel/ *noun* [U, C] a small wild plant with bright blue or pinkish-white flowers 婆婆纳（开鲜艳蓝色或粉白色花的野生植物）

speedy /ˈspiːdi/ *adj.* (**speed·ier**, **speedi·est**) **1** happening or done quickly or without delay 迅速的；尽快的 SYN **rapid**：*We wish you* ***a speedy recovery*** (= from an illness or injury). 我们祝愿你早日康复。◇ *a speedy reply* 即时的答复 **2** moving or working very quickly 快速的；高速的：*speedy computers* 高速计算机 ➲ NOTE AT FAST ▶ **speed·ily** *adv.*：*All enquiries will be dealt with as speedily as possible.* 所有询问都将从速处理。

spele·olo·gist /ˌspiːliˈɒlədʒɪst; *NAmE* -ˈɑːlə-/ *noun* a scientist who studies CAVES or a person who goes into caves as a sport 洞穴学家；洞穴探险家 ➲ COMPARE CAVER, POTHOLER, SPELUNKER ▶ **spele·ology** /ˌspiːliˈɒlədʒi; *NAmE* -ˈɑːlə-/ *noun* [U]

spell 🔑 /spel/ *verb, noun*

■ *verb* (**spelt**, **spelt** /spelt/ or **spelled**, **spelled**) **1** 🔑 [T] ~ **sth** to say or write the letters of a word in the correct order 用字母拼；拼写：*How do you spell your surname?* 你的姓怎么拼？◇ *I thought her name was Catherine, but it's Kathryn spelt with a 'K'.* 我原以为她叫 Catherine，其实是 Kathryn，以 K 开头。**2** 🔑 [I, T] to form words correctly from individual letters 拼出，会拼（单词）：*I've never been able to spell.* 我一直不会拼写。◇ **~ sth + adj.** *You've spelt my name wrong.* 你把我的名字拼错了。➲ SEE ALSO MISSPELL **3** 🔑 [T] ~ **sth** (of letters of a word 构成单词的字母) to form words when they are put together in a particular order 拼作；拼成：*C—A—T spells 'cat'.* * C–A–T 拼作 cat。**4** [T] ~ **sth** (**for sb/sth**) to have sth, usually sth bad, as a result; to mean sth, usually sth bad 招致，意味着（通常指坏事）：*The crop failure spelt disaster for many farmers.* 对许多农民来说，庄稼歉收就意味着灾难。**5** [T] ~ **sb** (*NAmE, informal*) to replace for a short time sb who is doing a particular activity so that they can rest（短时间）替换，顶替：*Carter will be here in an hour to spell you.* 卡特一小时后过来替换你。

PHR V **ˌspell sth↔ˈout 1** to explain sth in a simple, clear way 解释明白；讲清楚：*You know what I mean—I'm sure I don't need to spell it out.* 你明白我的意思，肯定不需要我解释了。◇ **spell out why, what, etc.…** *Let me spell out why we need more money.* 我来说说清楚，我们为什么还需要钱。**2** to say or write the letters of a word in the right order 用字母拼；拼写：*Could you spell that name out again?* 你能不能把那个名字再拼一次？

■ *noun* **1** 🔑 [C] a short period of time during which sth lasts（持续的）一段时间：*a spell of warm weather* 一段天气温暖的日子◇ *a* ***cold/hot/wet/bright, etc. spell*** 一段寒冷、炎热、多雨、晴朗等的日子◇ *There will be rain at first, with* ***sunny spells*** *later.* 开始会有雨，雨后间晴。◇ *She went to the doctor complaining of* ***dizzy spells***. 她去找医生看病，说自己一阵一阵地头昏。**2** [C] a period of time doing sth or working somewhere（干某事或在某处工作的）一段时间：*She had a spell as a singer before becoming an actress.* 在当演员以前她唱过一阵子歌。◇ *I spent a* ***brief spell*** *on the 'Washington Post'.* 我曾在《华盛顿邮报》工作过一小段时间。**3** [C] words that are thought to have magic power or to make a piece of magic work; a piece of magic that happens when sb says these magic words 咒语；符咒；魔法：*a* ***magic spell*** 魔咒◇ *a book of spells* 咒语集◇ *The wizard recited a spell.* 巫师念了一道咒语。◇ ***to cast/put a spell on sb*** 对某人施魔法◇ ***to be under a spell*** (= affected by magic) 中了魔法 **4** [sing.] a quality that a person or thing has that makes them so attractive or interesting that they have a strong influence on you 魅力；魔力 SYN **charm**：*I completely* ***fell under her spell***. 我完全给她迷住了。IDM SEE WEAVE *v.*

spell·bind·ing /ˈspelbaɪndɪŋ/ *adj.* holding your attention completely 让人着魔的；迷人的 SYN **enthralling**：*a spellbinding performance* 使人入迷的演出

spell·bound /ˈspelbaʊnd/ *adj.* [not usually before noun] with your attention completely held by what you are listening to or watching 入迷；出神；着魔：*a storyteller who can hold audiences spellbound* 讲故事能让听众如痴如醉的人

spell·check /ˈspeltʃek/ *verb* ~ **sth** to use a computer program to check your writing to see if your spelling is correct（用计算机程序）检查拼写 ▶ **spell·check** *noun* = SPELLCHECKER

spell·checker /ˈspeltʃekə(r)/ *noun* a computer program that checks your writing to see if your spelling is correct（计算机中的）拼写检查程序

spell·er /ˈspelə(r)/ *noun* if sb is a **good/bad speller**, they find it easy/difficult to spell words correctly 拼写能力强（或差）的人

spell·ing 🔑 /ˈspelɪŋ/ *noun* **1** 🔑 [U] the act of forming words correctly from individual letters; the ability to do this 拼写；拼写能力：*a* ***spelling mistake*** 拼写错误◇ *the differences between British and American spelling* 英式英语和美式英语在拼写方面的区别◇ *My spelling is terrible.* 我的拼写很糟糕。**2** 🔑 [C] the way that a particular word is written 拼法：*a list of difficult spellings* 难拼单词表 ➲ WORDFINDER NOTE AT WORD

ˈspelling bee *noun* a competition in which people have to spell words 拼字比赛

spelt PAST TENSE, PAST PART. OF SPELL

spe·lunk·ing /spɪˈlʌŋkɪŋ/ (*NAmE*) (*especially BrE* **cav·ing**, *BrE* **pot·hol·ing**) *noun* [U] the sport or activity of going into CAVES under the ground 洞穴探察；洞穴探险 ➲ VISUAL VOCAB PAGE V44 ▶ **spe·lunk·er** /spɪˈlʌŋkə(r)/ *noun* (*NAmE*) (*especially BrE* **caver**, *BrE* **pot·holer**) ➲ COMPARE SPELEOLOGIST

spend 🔑 /spend/ *verb, noun*

■ *verb* (**spent**, **spent** /spent/) **1** 🔑 [T, I] to give money to pay for goods, services, etc. 用，花（钱）：**~ sth** *I've spent all my money already.* 我已经把我的钱全都花完了。◇ **~ sth on sth/on doing sth** *She spent £100 on a new dress.* 她花 100 英镑买了一条新连衣裙。◇ **~ (sth doing sth)** *The company has spent thousands of pounds updating their computer* *systems.* 公司花了几千英镑更新计算机系统。◇ *I just can't seem to stop spending.* 我似乎就是没法不花钱。**2** [T] to use time for a particular purpose; to pass time 花（时间）；度过：**~ sth + adv./prep.** *We spent the weekend in Paris.* 我们在巴黎度过了周末。◇ *How do you spend your spare time?* 你在业余时间干什么？◇ **~ sth on sth** *How long did you spend on your homework?* 你做家庭作业用了多长时间？◇ **~ sth doing sth** *I spend too much time watching television.* 我看电视花的时间太多。◇ **~ sth in doing sth** *Most of her life was spent in caring for others.* 她大半辈子的时间都用来照顾别人了。**3** [T, often passive] to use energy, effort, etc., especially until it has all been used 花费，消耗，用尽（精力等）：**~ sth on sth** *She spends too much effort on things that don't matter.* 她在一些无关紧要的事情上花费精力太多。◇ **~ itself** *The storm had finally spent itself.* 暴风雨终于停歇了。➲ SEE ALSO SPENT

IDM **spend the 'night with sb** **1** to stay with sb for a night 在某人家里住一夜：*My daughter's spending the night with a friend.* 我女儿要在一个朋友那里过夜。**2** (*also* **spend the 'night together**) to stay with sb for a night and have sex with them 和某人一起过夜并发生性关系 **spend a 'penny** (*old-fashioned, BrE*) people say 'spend a penny' to avoid saying 'use the toilet'（委婉说法，与 use the toilet 同义）解手，方便

■ ***noun*** [sing.] (*informal*) the amount of money spent for a particular purpose or over a particular length of time（为某目的或某段时间内的）花销，花费，开销

spend·er /ˈspendə(r)/ *noun* a person who spends money in the particular way mentioned 花钱…的人：*a big spender* (= who spends a lot of money) 花钱大手大脚的人

spend·ing /ˈspendɪŋ/ *noun* [U] the amount of money that is spent by a government or an organization（政府或其他机构的）开支，支出，花销：*to increase **public spending*** 增加公共开支 ➲ SYNONYMS AT COST

ˈspending money *noun* [U] money that you can spend on personal things for pleasure or entertainment 零花钱；零用钱

spend·thrift /ˈspendθrɪft/ *noun* (*disapproving*) a person who spends too much money or who wastes money 花钱无度的人；挥霍者 ▸ **spend·thrift** *adj.* [usually before noun]: *spendthrift governments* 花钱无度的政府机构

spendy /ˈspendi/ *adj.* (**spendier**, **spendiest**) (*informal*) **1** expensive 昂贵的；价格高的：*It's a really fun restaurant but a bit spendy.* 这是一家很有意思的餐馆，但就是有点贵。**2** spending a lot of money 花钱大方的；挥霍的：*He's spendy—he buys luxury cars new.* 他花钱毫不手软，买的都是全新的豪华轿车。

spent /spent/ *adj.* **1** [usually before noun] that has been used, so that it cannot be used again 用过已废的；失效的：*spent matches* 用过的火柴 **2** (*formal*) very tired 筋疲力尽的 SYN **exhausted**: *After the gruelling test, he felt totally spent.* 紧张的考试过后，他感觉筋疲力尽了。

IDM **a ˌspent ˈforce** a person or group that no longer has any power or influence 威势不再的人（或集团）；不再有影响力的人（或集团）➲ SEE ALSO SPEND

sperm /spɜːm; *NAmE* spɜːrm/ *noun* (*pl.* **sperm** or **sperms**) **1** [C] a cell that is produced by the sex organs of a male and that can combine with a female egg to produce young 精子：*He has a low **sperm count*** (= very few live male cells). 他的精液精子计数低。**2** [U] the liquid that is produced by the male sex organs that contains these cells 精液 SYN **semen** ➲ COLLOCATIONS AT LIFE

sperm·ato·zoon /ˌspɜːmətəˈzəʊən; *NAmE* ˌspɜːrmətəˈzoʊən/ *noun* (*pl.* **sperm·ato·zoa** /-ˈzəʊə; *NAmE* -ˈzoʊə/) (*biology* 生) a sperm 精子

ˈsperm bank *noun* a place where sperm is kept and then used to help women become pregnant artificially 精子库（保存精子以便帮助女子进行人工受孕）

spermi·cide /ˈspɜːmɪsaɪd; *NAmE* ˈspɜːrm-/ *noun* [U, C] a substance that kills sperm, used during sex to prevent the woman from becoming pregnant 杀精子剂 ▸ **spermi·cidal** /ˌspɜːmɪˈsaɪdl; *NAmE* ˌspɜːrm-/ *adj.* [only before noun]

ˈsperm whale *noun* a large WHALE that is hunted for its oil and fat 抹香鲸 ➲ VISUAL VOCAB PAGE V12

spew /spjuː/ *verb* **1** [I, T] to flow out quickly, or to make sth flow out quickly, in large amounts（使）喷出，涌出：**+ adv./prep.** *Flames spewed from the aircraft's engine.* 飞机发动机喷出火焰。◇ **~ sth + adv./prep.** *Massive chimneys were spewing out smoke.* 一座座高大的烟囱冒着烟。**2** [I, T] (*BrE, informal*) to VOMIT (= bring food from the stomach back out through the mouth) 呕吐：**~ (up)** *He spewed up on the pavement.* 他在人行道上吐了。◇ **~ sth (up)** *She spewed up the entire meal.* 她把吃的饭全吐出来了。

SPF /ˌes piː ˈef/ *abbr.* sun protection factor (a number that tells you how much protection a particular cream or liquid gives you from the harmful effects of the sun)（护肤霜等的）防晒指数，防晒系数

sphag·num /ˈsfæɡnəm/ (*also* **ˈSphagnum moss**) *noun* [U] a type of MOSS that grows in wet areas, used especially for planting plants in pots, making FERTILIZER, etc. 泥炭藓（尤用于盆种花草、积肥等）

sphere AW /sfɪə(r); *NAmE* sfɪr/ *noun* **1** (*geometry* 几何) a solid figure that is completely round, with every point on its surface at an equal distance from the centre 球；球体；球形 ➲ PICTURE AT SOLID **2** any object that is completely round, for example a ball 圆球；球状物 **3** an area of activity, influence or interest; a particular section of society 范围；领域；阶层；界 SYN **domain**: *the political sphere* 政界 ◇ *This area was formerly within the **sphere of influence** of the US.* 这一地区先前属于美国的势力范围。◇ *He and I moved in totally different social spheres.* 我和他进入了完全不同的社会圈子。**4 -sphere** (in nouns 构成名词) a region that surrounds a planet, especially the earth（包围地球等的大气的）层：*ionosphere* 电离层 ◇ *atmosphere* 大气层

spher·ic·al AW /ˈsferɪkl; *NAmE also* ˈsfɪr-/ *adj.* shaped like a sphere 球形的；球状的 SYN **round** ▸ **spher·ic·al·ly** AW /-kli/ *adv.*

spher·oid /ˈsfɪərɔɪd; *NAmE* ˈsfɪr-/ *noun* (*specialist*) a solid object that is approximately the same shape as a sphere 球（状）体；扁球体；椭球体

sphinc·ter /ˈsfɪŋktə(r)/ *noun* (*anatomy* 解) a ring of muscle that surrounds an opening in the body and can contract to close it 括约肌：*the anal sphincter* 肛门括约肌

sphinx /sfɪŋks/ *noun* (*often* **the Sphinx**) an ancient Egyptian stone statue of a creature with a human head and the body of a LION lying down. In ancient Greek stories the Sphinx spoke in RIDDLES. 斯芬克斯，狮身人面像（古埃及石像；在希腊神话中，斯芬克斯说话惯用谜语）

spic /spɪk/ *noun* (*taboo, slang, especially NAmE*) a very offensive word for a person from a country where Spanish is spoken, for example a Mexican or Puerto Rican 西班牙语区的人（如墨西哥人或波多黎各人，有强烈冒犯意）

IDM **ˌspic and ˈspan** = SPICK AND SPAN

spice /spaɪs/ *noun, verb*

■ ***noun*** **1** [C, U] one of the various types of powder or seed that come from plants and are used in cooking. Spices have a strong taste and smell.（调味）香料：*common spices such as ginger and cinnamon* 姜和肉桂等常见香料 ◇ *a spice jar* 香料瓶 ➲ VISUAL VOCAB PAGE V35 **2** [U] extra interest or excitement 额外的趣味（或刺激等）：*We need an exciting trip to add some spice to our lives.* 我们需要一次新奇的旅行来调剂一下生活。IDM SEE VARIETY

■ ***verb*** **1 ~ sth (up) (with sth)** to add spice to food in order to give it more flavour 在…中加香料 **2 ~ sth (up) (with sth)** to add interest or excitement to sth 给…增添趣味；使…变得刺激：*He exaggerated the details to spice up the story.* 他添油加醋，使故事更有趣味。

spick /spɪk/ *adj.*

IDM **ˌspick and ˈspan** (*also* **ˌspic and ˈspan**) [not usually before noun] neat and clean 整洁干净；清清爽爽：*Their house is always spick and span.* 他们家总是收拾得清清爽爽。➲ MORE LIKE THIS 13, page R26

spicy /ˈspaɪsi/ *adj.* (**spici·er**, **spici·est**) **1** (of food 食物) having a strong taste because spices have been used to flavour it 加有香料的；用香料调味的 **SYN** **hot** ➲ WORDFINDER NOTE AT TASTE **2** (*informal*) (of a story, piece of news, etc. 故事、新闻等) exciting and slightly shocking 刺激的；耸人听闻的 ▸ **spici·ness** *noun* [U]

spider /ˈspaɪdə(r)/ *noun* a small creature with eight thin legs. Many spiders spin webs (= nets of thin threads) to catch insects for food. 蜘蛛 ➲ VISUAL VOCAB PAGE V13

ˈ**spider monkey** *noun* a S American MONKEY with very long arms and legs and a long PREHENSILE tail 蜘蛛猴（栖于南美洲，四肢长，并有长卷尾）➲ VISUAL VOCAB PAGE V12

ˈ**spider's web** (*especially BrE*) (*also* **spiderweb** /ˈspaɪdəweb; *NAmE* -dər-/ *especially in NAmE*) (*also* **web**) *noun* a fine net of threads made by a spider to catch insects 蜘蛛网：(*figurative*) *to be caught in a spider's web of confusion* 陷入混乱不堪的局面 ➲ SEE ALSO COBWEB

spi·dery /ˈspaɪdəri/ *adj.* long and thin, like the legs of a spider（像蜘蛛腿一样）细长的：*spidery fingers* 修长的手指 ◇ *spidery writing* (= consisting of thin lines that are not very clear) 细长而不易辨认的笔画

spied PAST TENSE, PAST PART. OF SPY

spiel /ʃpiːl; spiːl/ *noun* (*informal, usually disapproving*) a long speech that sb has used many times, that is intended to persuade you to believe sth or buy sth 油嘴滑舌的游说；一长串招徕生意的套话

spies /spaɪz/ *noun* PL. OF SPY

spiff /spɪf/ *verb*

PHR V ˌ**spiff** ˈ**up** | ˌ**spiff sb/sth**↔ˈ**up** (*NAmE, informal*) to make yourself/sb/sth look neat and attractive 把…收拾得整齐漂亮；打扮；装扮

spif·fing /ˈspɪfɪŋ/ *adj.* (*BrE, old-fashioned, informal*) extremely good or pleasant 极好的；很棒的 **SYN** **excellent**

spiffy /ˈspɪfi/ *adj.* (*NAmE, informal*) attractive and fashionable 漂亮而时髦的

spigot /ˈspɪɡət/ *noun* **1** (*specialist*) a device in a tap/faucet that controls the flow of liquid from a container（龙头中的）塞，栓 **2** (*US*) any tap/faucet, especially one outdoors（尤指户外的）龙头

spike /spaɪk/ *noun, verb*

■ *noun* **1** [C] a thin object with a sharp point, especially a pointed piece of metal, wood, etc. 尖状物；尖头；尖刺：*a row of iron spikes on a wall* 墙头的一排尖铁 ◇ *Her hair stood up in spikes.* 她的头发一绺一绺地翘着。➲ SEE ALSO SPIKE HEEL **2** [C, usually pl.] a metal point attached to the SOLE of a sports shoe to prevent you from slipping while running（防滑）鞋钉 ➲ COMPARE CLEAT (3) **3** **spikes** [pl.] shoes fitted with these metal spikes, used for running（赛跑用的）钉鞋：*a pair of spikes* 一双钉鞋 **4** [C] a long pointed group of flowers that grow together on a single STEM 穗；穗状花序 **5** [C, usually sing.] (*informal, especially NAmE*) a sudden large increase in sth 猛增；急升：*a spike in oil prices* 油价的急剧上涨

■ *verb* **1** [T] **~ sb/sth (on sth)** to push a sharp piece of metal, wood, etc. into sb/sth; to injure sth on a sharp point 用尖物刺入（或扎破）**SYN** **stab** **2** [T] **~ sth (with sth)** to add alcohol, poison or a drug to sb's drink or food without them knowing 在…中偷偷掺入（烈酒、毒药或毒品）：*He gave her a drink spiked with tranquillizers.* 他给了她一杯偷偷放了镇静剂的饮料。◇ (*figurative*) *Her words were spiked with malice.* 她的话暗含恶意。**3** [T] **~ sth** to reject sth that a person has written or said; to prevent sth from happening or being made public 拒绝发表；阻止…传播；阻挠：*The article was spiked for fear of legal action against the newspaper.* 因担心被提起诉讼，报社未发表那篇文章。**4** [I] **~ (to sth)** (*especially NAmE*) to rise quickly and reach a high value 迅速升值；急剧增值：*The US dollar spiked to a three-month high.* 美元猛然升值到三个月来的最高价。

IDM **spike sb's** ˈ**guns** (*BrE*) to spoil the plans of an opponent 打乱对手的计划

spiked /spaɪkt/ *adj.* with one or more spikes 有尖刺的；带钉的：*spiked running shoes* 带钉的跑鞋 ◇ *short spiked hair* 刺猬头

ˌ**spike** ˈ**heel** *noun* a very thin high heel on a woman's shoe; a shoe with such a heel（女式鞋的）细高跟；细高跟鞋 **SYN** **stiletto**

spiky /ˈspaɪki/ *adj.* **1** having sharp points 有尖刺的：*spiky plants, such as cacti* 带刺的植物，如仙人掌 **2** (of hair 头发) sticking straight up from the head 刺猬式的 ➲ VISUAL VOCAB PAGE V65 **3** (*BrE*) (of people 人) easily annoyed or offended 动辄生气的；气量小的 ▸ **spiki·ness** *noun* [U]

spill /spɪl/ *verb, noun*

■ *verb* (**spilled**, **spilled** *or* **spilt**, **spilt** /spɪlt/) **1** [I, T] (especially of liquid 尤指液体) to flow over the edge of a container by accident; to make liquid do this（使）洒出，泼出，溢出：*Water had spilled out of the bucket onto the floor.* 桶里的水洒出来了，洒了一地。◇ **~ sth** *He startled her and made her spill her drink.* 她让他吓了一跳，把饮料弄洒了。◇ *Thousands of gallons of crude oil were spilled into the ocean.* 成千上万加仑的原油泄漏，流进了海洋。**2** [I] **+ adv./prep.** (of people 人) to come out of a place in large numbers and spread out 涌出；蜂拥而出：*The doors opened and people spilled into the street.* 门开了，人们涌上街道。◇ (*figurative*) *Light spilled from the windows.* 灯光从窗口照射出来。

IDM **spill the** ˈ**beans** (*informal*) to tell sb sth that should be kept secret or private 泄露秘密；说漏嘴 **spill (sb's)** ˈ**blood** (*formal or literary*) to kill or wound people 使流血；伤害；杀死 **spill your** ˈ**guts (to sb)** (*NAmE, informal*) to tell sb everything you know or feel about sth, because you are upset（向某人）倾诉心里话 ➲ MORE AT CRY *v.*

PHR V ˌ**spill sth**↔ˈ**out** | ˌ**spill** ˈ**out** to tell sb all about a problem etc. very quickly; to come out quickly 倾诉；涌出：*Has she been spilling out her troubles to you again?* 她是不是又向你诉苦了？◇ *When he started to speak, the words just spilled out.* 他一开口就滔滔不绝。ˌ**spill** ˈ**over (into sth)** **1** to fill a container and go over the edge 溢出；漫出：*She filled the glass so full that the water spilled over.* 她往杯子里倒水倒得太满，都溢出来了。◇ (*figurative*) *Her emotions suddenly spilled over.* 她突然就控制不住自己的感情了。**2** to start in one area and then affect other areas 波及：*Unrest has spilt over into areas outside the city.* 骚乱已经波及城市的周边地区。➲ RELATED NOUN OVERSPILL, SPILLOVER

■ *noun* **1** (*also formal* **spill·age**) [C, U] an act of letting a liquid come or fall out of a container; the amount of liquid that comes or falls out 洒出（量）；泼出（量）；溢出（量）；泄漏（量）：*Many seabirds died as a result of the oil spill.* 许多海鸟死于这次石油泄漏。◇ *I wiped up the coffee spills on the table.* 我把洒在桌上的咖啡擦掉。**2** [C] a long match, or a thin piece of twisted paper, used for lighting fires, oil lamps, etc.（点火用的）长梗火柴，纸捻 **3** [C, usually sing.] a fall, especially from a bicycle or a boat（尤指从自行车或船上）摔下，跌落：*to take a spill*（骑车）摔一跤 **IDM** SEE THRILL *n.*

spill·age /ˈspɪlɪdʒ/ *noun* [U, C] (*formal*) = SPILL: *Put the bottle in a plastic bag in case of spillage.* 把瓶子装在塑料袋里，以免洒得到处都是。

spilli·kins /ˈspɪlɪkɪnz/ (*BrE*) (*NAmE* **jack·straw**) *noun* [U] a game in which you remove a small stick from a pile, without moving any of the other sticks 挑棒游戏（挑出一堆小棒中的一根而不触动其他的小棒）

spill·over /ˈspɪləʊvə(r); *NAmE* -oʊ-/ *noun* [C, U] **1** something that is too large or too much for the place where it starts, and spreads to other places 容纳不下的部分；溢出部分：*A second room was needed for the spillover of staff and reporters.* 还需要一个房间给没有安置的员工和

记者。**2** the results or the effects of sth that have spread to other situations or places 影响

spill·way /ˈspɪlweɪ/ *noun* (*specialist*) a passage for the extra water from a DAM (= a wall across a river that holds water back) 溢洪道

spim /spɪm/ *noun* [U] (*informal*) advertising sent as messages on the Internet to people who have not asked for it（互联网）即时通信垃圾广告 ➲ COMPARE SPAM *n.* (2) **ORIGIN** From the letters for *SPam via Instant Messaging.* 源自 SPam via Instant Messaging 的缩写。

spin /spɪn/ *verb, noun*

■ *verb* (**spin·ning, spun, spun** /spʌn/)

• **TURN ROUND QUICKLY** 快速旋转 **1** [I, T] to turn round and round quickly; to make sth do this（使）快速旋转：(**+ adv./prep.**) *The plane was spinning out of control.* 飞机失去控制，进入尾旋状态。◇ *a spinning ice skater* 做旋转动作的溜冰者 ◇ *My head is spinning* (= I feel as if my head is going around and I can't balance). 我觉得天旋地转。◇ **~ (round/around)** *The dancers spun round and round.* 舞者不停地旋转。◇ **~ sth (round/around)** *to spin a ball/coin/wheel* 转动球 / 硬币 / 轮子 **2** [I, T] **~ (sb) round/around | + adv./prep.** to turn round quickly once; to make sb do this（使）急转身，猛转回头，急转弯：*He spun around to face her.* 他猛地回过身来，面对着她。

• **MAKE THREAD** 纺线 **3** [I, T] to make thread from wool, cotton, silk, etc. by twisting it 纺（线）；纺（纱）：*She sat by the window spinning.* 她坐在窗前纺线。◇ **~ sth** *to spin and knit wool* 纺毛线织毛活儿 ◇ **~ A into B** *spinning silk into thread* 把蚕丝纺成线 ◇ **~ B from A** *spinning thread from silk* 用蚕丝纺线

• **OF SPIDER/SILKWORM** 蜘蛛；蚕 **4** [T] **~ sth** to produce thread from its body to make a web or COCOON 吐（丝）；作（茧）；结（网）：*a spider spinning a web* 结网的蜘蛛

• **DRIVE/TRAVEL QUICKLY** 高速驾驶 / 行进 **5** [I] **+ adv./prep.** to drive or travel quickly 驾车飞驰；疾驰：*They went spinning along the roads on their bikes.* 他们骑自行车沿公路疾驰。

• **DRY CLOTHES** 甩干衣服 **6** [T] **~ sth** to remove the water from clothes that have just been washed, in a SPIN DRYER（用旋转式脱水机）甩干衣服

• **PRESENT INFORMATION** 陈述 **7** [T] **~ sth (as sth)** to present information or a situation in a particular way, especially one that makes you or your ideas seem good 有倾向性地陈述；（尤指）以有利于自己的口吻描述：*An aide was already spinning the senator's defeat as 'almost as good as an outright win'.* 一名助手已经开始将那位参议员的失败描述成"几乎是大获全胜"。

IDM **spin (sb) a ˈyarn, ˈtale, etc.** to try to make sb believe a long story that is not true 杜撰故事，编造故事（以让人信以为真）➲ MORE AT HEEL *n.*

PHR V **ˌspin ˈoff (from sth) | ˌspin sth↔ˈoff (from sth)** to happen or to produce sth as a new or unexpected result of sth that already exists 脱胎（于某事物）；（从某事物）派生，衍生；随之而产生：*products spinning off from favourite books* 从一些畅销书衍生出的产品 ➲ RELATED NOUN SPIN-OFF **ˌspin sth↔ˈoff** (*business* 商, *especially NAmE*) to form a new company from parts of an existing one 从…脱离出来（组建新公司）：*The transportation operation will be spun off into a separate company.* 运输部门将脱离出来组建为一家独立公司。**ˌspin sth↔ˈout** to make sth last as long as possible 拉长；拖长

■ *noun*

• **FAST TURNING MOVEMENT** 高速旋转 **1** [C, U] a very fast turning movement 高速旋转：*the earth's spin* 地球的自转 ◇ *the spin of a wheel* 轮子的转动 ◇ *Give the washing a short spin.* 把洗过的衣服稍稍甩一下。**2** [C, usually sing.] if an aircraft goes into a **spin**, it falls and turns round rapidly（飞机的）尾旋，螺旋式下坠

• **IN CAR** 乘汽车 **3** [C] (*informal, becoming old-fashioned*) a short ride in a car for pleasure 兜风：*Let's go for a spin.* 咱们兜风去吧。

• **IN TENNIS/CRICKET** 网球；板球 **4** [U] the way you make a ball turn very fast when you throw it or hit it 旋转：*She puts a lot of spin on the ball.* 她打出的球旋转得很厉害。◇ *a spin bowler* (= in CRICKET, a BOWLER who uses spin) 投旋转球的板球投球手 ➲ SEE ALSO TOPSPIN

• **ON INFORMATION** 陈述 **5** [sing., U] (*informal*) a way of presenting information or a situation in a particular way, especially one that makes you or your ideas seem good（尤指有利于自己的）导向性陈述：*Politicians put their own spin on the economic situation.* 政治家们对经济形势各执一词。

IDM **in a (flat) ˈspin** very confused, worried or excited 晕头转向；急得团团转；十分激动：*Her resignation put her colleagues in a spin.* 她的辞职令同事们摸不着头脑。

spina bif·ida /ˌspaɪnə ˈbɪfɪdə/ *noun* [U] a medical condition in which some bones in the SPINE have not developed normally at birth, often causing PARALYSIS (= loss of control or feeling) in the legs 脊柱裂（先天性椎管闭合不全）

spin·ach /ˈspɪnɪtʃ; -ɪdʒ/ *noun* [U] a vegetable with large dark green leaves that are cooked or eaten in salads 菠菜

spinal /ˈspaɪnl/ *adj.* [usually before noun] (*specialist*) connected with the SPINE (= the long bone in the back) 脊的；脊椎的；脊髓的：*spinal injuries* 脊椎损伤

ˌspinal ˈcolumn *noun* the SPINE 脊柱

ˌspinal ˈcord *noun* the mass of nerves inside the SPINE that connects all parts of the body to the brain 脊髓 ➲ VISUAL VOCAB PAGE V64

ˈspinal tap (*NAmE*) (*BrE* **ˌlumbar ˈpuncture**) *noun* the removal of liquid from the lower part of the SPINE with a hollow needle 腰椎穿刺（放液）

spin·dle /ˈspɪndl/ *noun* **1** a long straight part that turns in a machine, or that another part of the machine turns around 轴；心轴；指轴 **2** a thin pointed piece of wood used for spinning wool into thread by hand（手纺用的）绕线杆，纺锤

spindly /ˈspɪndli/ *adj.* (*informal, often disapproving*) very long and thin and not strong 长而纤弱的；细长而瘦弱的：*spindly legs* 细长的腿

ˈspin doctor *noun* (*informal*) a person whose job is to present information to the public about a politician, an organization, etc. in the way that seems most positive（政治人物、组织等的）舆论导向专家

ˌspin ˈdryer (*also* **ˌspin ˈdrier**) *noun* (*BrE*) a machine that partly dries clothes that you have washed by turning them round and round very fast to remove the water 旋转式脱水机；甩干机 ➲ COMPARE TUMBLE DRYER ▶ **ˌspin-ˈdry** *verb* **~ sth**

spine /spaɪn/ *noun* **1** the row of small bones that are connected together down the middle of the back 脊柱；脊椎 **SYN** **backbone** ➲ VISUAL VOCAB PAGE V64 **2** any of the sharp pointed parts like needles on some plants and animals（植物的）刺；（动物的）刺毛：*Porcupines use their spines to protect themselves.* 豪猪用身上的刺毛来自卫。➲ SEE ALSO SPINY **3** the narrow part of the cover of a book that the pages are joined to 书脊

ˈspine-chilling *adj.* (of a book, film/movie, etc. 书、电影等) frightening in an exciting way 令人毛骨悚然的 ➲ MORE LIKE THIS 10, page R26 ▶ **ˈspine-chiller** *noun*

spine·less /ˈspaɪnləs/ *adj.* **1** (*disapproving*) (of people 人) weak and easily frightened 没有骨气的；怯懦的 **2** (of animals 动物) having no SPINE (= the long bone in the back) 无脊椎的；无脊柱的 **3** (of animals or plants 动物或植物) having no SPINES (= sharp parts like needles) 无刺的

spi·net /spɪˈnet; *NAmE* ˈspɪnət/ *noun* **1** a kind of HARPSICHORD (= an early type of musical instrument), played like a piano 斯皮耐琴（小型拨弦键琴）**2** **~ piano/organ** (*US*) a small piano/electronic organ 小型钢琴 / 电子琴

ˈspine-tingling *adj.* (of an event, a piece of music, etc. 活动、乐曲等) enjoyable because it is very exciting or frightening 精彩刺激的；扣人心弦的

S

spin·naker /ˈspɪnəkə(r)/ *noun* a large extra sail on a racing YACHT that you use when the wind is coming from behind （赛艇的）大三角帆（顺风时用） ➲ VISUAL VOCAB PAGE V61

spin·ner /ˈspɪnə(r)/ *noun* **1** (in CRICKET 板球) a BOWLER who uses SPIN (4) when throwing the ball 投旋转球的投球手 **2** a person who spins thread 纺线者；纺纱工 **3** a device that spins around, used on a fishing line to attract fish（钓鱼用的）旋式诱饵

spin·ney /ˈspɪni/ *noun* (*BrE*) a small area of trees 小树林 SYN copse

spin·ning /ˈspɪnɪŋ/ *noun* [U] **1** the art or the process of twisting wool, etc. to make thread 纺线（手艺）；纺纱（手艺） **2 Spinning™** a type of exercise performed on an EXERCISE BIKE, usually in a class 动感单车

ˈ**spinning wheel** *noun* a simple machine that people used in their homes in the past for twisting wool, etc. It has a large wheel operated with the foot. 纺车（旧时的简易纺纱机，有一大轮，用脚操纵）

ˈ**spin-off** *noun* ~ (**from/of sth**) **1** an unexpected but useful result of an activity that is designed to produce sth else （意外但有用的）副产品，派生物：*commercial spin-offs from medical research* 医学研究引出的有商业价值的副产品 **2** a book, a film/movie, a television programme, or an object that is based on a book, film/movie or television series that has been very successful（根据成功的书、电影或电视剧制作的）派生作品，搭车产品：*The TV comedy series is a spin-off of the original movie.* 这部电视喜剧连续剧是电影原作的副产品。◇ *spin-off merchandise from the latest Disney movie* 根据最新的迪士尼影片开发的商品

spin·ster /ˈspɪnstə(r)/ *noun* (*old-fashioned, often disapproving*) a woman who is not married, especially an older woman who is not likely to marry 老处女；老姑娘 HELP This word should not now be used to mean simply a woman who is not married. 如今，不可用这个词泛指未婚女子。➲ COMPARE BACHELOR (1) ▶ **spin·ster·hood** /-hʊd/ *noun* [U]: *For most women, marriage used to bring a higher status than spinsterhood.* 从前，就多数妇女而言，结婚的比独身的更有地位。

spiny /ˈspaɪni/ *adj.* (of animals or plants 动物或植物) having sharp points like needles 有刺毛的；带刺的；多刺的 ➲ SEE ALSO SPINE (2)

S

ˌ**spiny ˈanteater** *noun* = ECHIDNA

spiral /ˈspaɪrəl/ *noun, adj., verb*

■ ***noun*** **1** a shape or design, consisting of a continuous curved line that winds around a central point, with each curve further away from the centre 螺旋形；螺旋式：*The birds circled in a slow spiral above the house.* 鸟儿在房子上空缓缓盘旋。**2** a continuous harmful increase or decrease in sth, that gradually gets faster and faster 逐渐加速上升（或下降）：*the destructive spiral of violence in the inner cities* 内城区日益严重的暴力行为 ◇ *measures to control the inflationary spiral* 控制日益恶化的通货膨胀的措施 ◇ *the **upward/downward spiral** of sales* 日渐上升 / 下降的销售额

■ ***adj.*** moving in a continuous curve that winds around a central point 螺旋形的；螺旋式的：*A snail's shell is spiral in form.* 蜗牛壳呈螺旋形。▶ **spir·al·ly** /ˈspaɪrəli/ *adv.*

■ ***verb*** (**-ll-**, *NAmE usually* **-l-**) **1** [I] (+ **adv./prep.**) to move in continuous circles, going upwards or downwards 螺旋式上升（或下降）；盘旋上升（或下降）：*The plane spiralled down to the ground.* 飞机盘旋降落。**2** [I] to increase rapidly 急剧增长：*the spiralling cost of health care* 急剧上涨的医疗费用 ◇ + **adv./prep.** *Prices are spiralling out of control.* 物价飞涨，失去控制。

PHR V ˌ**spiral ˈdown/ˈdownward** to decrease rapidly 急剧减少

ˌ**spiral-ˈbound** *adj.* (of a book 书) held together by wire which is wound through holes along one edge 螺旋装订的 ➲ VISUAL VOCAB PAGE V71

ˌ**spiral ˈstaircase** *noun* a set of stairs that curve upwards around a central post 螺旋式楼梯

spir·ant /ˈspaɪərənt/ (*NAmE*) (*also* **frica·tive** *BrE, NAmE*) *noun, adj.* (*phonetics* 语音) a speech sound made by forcing breath out through a narrow space in the mouth with the lips, teeth or tongue in a particular position, for example /f/ and /ʃ/ in *fee* and *she* 摩擦音；擦音 ▶ **spir·ant** (*also* **frica·tive**) *adj.* ➲ COMPARE PLOSIVE

spire /ˈspaɪə(r)/ *noun* a tall pointed structure on the top of a building, especially a church（教堂等顶部的）尖塔，尖顶

spirit 🔑 /ˈspɪrɪt/ *noun, verb*

■ ***noun***

• **MIND/FEELINGS/CHARACTER** 思想；感情；性格 **1** 🔑 [U, C] the part of a person that includes their mind, feelings and character rather than their body 精神；心灵：*the power of the human spirit to overcome difficulties* 人类克服困难的精神力量 **2** 🔑 **spirits** [pl.] a person's feelings or state of mind 情绪；心境：*to be in **high/low spirits*** 情绪高涨 / 低落 ◇ *You must try and **keep your spirits up*** (= stay cheerful). 你必须设法保持高昂的情绪。◇ *My **spirits sank** at the prospect of starting all over again.* 想到一切都得从头再来，我的情绪一下子低落了。**3** [C] (always with an adjective 总是与形容词连用) a person of the type mentioned （某种类型的）人：*a brave spirit* 勇敢的人 ◇ ***kindred spirits*** (= people who like the same things as you) 志趣相投的人 ➲ SEE ALSO FREE SPIRIT

• **COURAGE/DETERMINATION** 勇气；决心 **4** 🔑 [U] courage, determination or energy 勇气；志气；意志；活力：*Show a little **fighting spirit**.* 要表现出一点斗志。◇ *Although the team lost, they played with tremendous spirit.* 尽管输了，但队员表现得极为勇猛。◇ *They took away his freedom and broke his spirit.* 他们夺去了他的自由，摧垮了他的意志。

• **LOYAL FEELINGS** 忠心 **5** 🔑 [U, sing.] loyal feelings towards a group, team or society（对团体、队伍、社会的）忠心：*There's not much **community spirit** around here.* 这里集体精神比较薄弱。➲ SEE ALSO TEAM SPIRIT

• **ATTITUDE** 态度 **6** [sing.] a state of mind or mood; an attitude 心态；态度：*We approached the situation in the wrong spirit.* 我们以前对待局势的心态不对。◇ *'OK, I'll try.' '**That's the spirit**'* (= the right attitude). "好吧，我来试试。""这就对了。" ◇ *The party went well because everyone **entered into the spirit of things**.* 晚会很成功，因为每个人都很投入。➲ SEE ALSO PARTY SPIRIT

• **TYPICAL QUALITY** 根本属性 **7** [sing.] the typical or most important quality or mood of sth 本质；精髓；基本精神：*The exhibition captures the **spirit of the age/times**.* 这个展览会抓住了时代精神。

• **REAL MEANING** 真实意义 **8** [U] the real or intended meaning or purpose of sth 真实意义；实质：*Obey the spirit, not the letter* (= the narrow meaning of the words) *of the law.* 要依照法律的精神实质，而不是字面意思。

• **SOUL** 灵魂 **9** 🔑 [C] the soul thought of as separate from the body and believed to live on after death; a GHOST 灵魂；鬼魂；幽灵：*He is dead, but his spirit lives on.* 他死了，但他的灵魂将永存。◇ *It was believed that people could be possessed by evil spirits.* 从前，人们相信人有可能被恶魔缠身。➲ SEE ALSO HOLY SPIRIT

• **IMAGINARY CREATURE** 想象中的生灵 **10** [C] (*old-fashioned*) an imaginary creature with magic powers, for example, a FAIRY or an ELF 仙子；小精灵；小妖精

• **ALCOHOL** 酒精 **11** 🔑 [C, usually pl.] (*especially BrE*) a strong alcoholic drink 烈酒：*I don't drink whisky or brandy or any other spirits.* 我不喝威士忌和白兰地，也不喝其他烈性酒。**12** [U] a special type of alcohol used in industry or medicine 工业酒精；医用酒精 ➲ SEE ALSO METHYLATED SPIRIT, SURGICAL SPIRIT, WHITE SPIRIT

IDM **in ˈspirit** in your thoughts 在心里；在精神上：*I shall be with you in spirit* (= thinking about you though not with you physically). 我的心将和你在一起。**the ˌspirit is ˈwilling (but the ˌflesh is ˈweak)** (*humorous, saying*) you intend to do good things but you are too lazy, weak or busy to actually do them 心灵固然愿意，肉体却软弱；心有余而力不足；力不从心 **as/when/if the ˌspirit ˈmoves you** as/when/if you feel like it 要是愿意的话：*I'll go for a run this evening, if the spirit moves me.* 今晚要是有兴致的

话，我要去跑步。⊃ MORE AT FIGHT *v.*, RAISE *v.*

■ ***verb*** **~ sth + adv./prep.** to take sb/sth away in a quick, secret or mysterious way 偷偷带走；让人不可思议地弄走：*After the concert, the band was* ***spirited away*** *before their fans could get near them.* 音乐会结束后，乐队没等歌迷靠近就神秘地消失了。

spir·it·ed /ˈspɪrɪtɪd/ *adj.* [usually before noun] full of energy, determination or courage 精神饱满的；坚定的；勇猛的：*a spirited young woman* 充满朝气的年轻女子 ◇ *a spirited discussion* 热烈的讨论 ◇ *She put up a spirited defence in the final game.* 她在最后一场比赛中进行了顽强的防守。⊃ COMPARE DISPIRITED ⊃ SEE ALSO HIGH-SPIRITED, PUBLIC-SPIRITED ▸ **spir·it·ed·ly** *adv.*

spir·it·less /ˈspɪrɪtləs/ *adj.* (*formal*) without energy, enthusiasm or determination 没有生气的；无精打采的；淡漠的；沉闷的

ˈspirit level (*also* **level**) *noun* a glass tube partly filled with liquid, with a bubble of air inside. Spirit levels are used to test whether a surface is level, by the position of the bubble. 气泡式水准仪 ⊃ VISUAL VOCAB PAGE V21

spir·it·ual 🔑 /ˈspɪrɪtʃuəl/ *adj.*, *noun*

■ ***adj.*** [usually before noun] **1** 🔑 connected with the human spirit, rather than the body or physical things 精神的；心灵的：*a spiritual experience* 心灵体验 ◇ *spiritual development* 精神上的发展 ◇ *a lack of spiritual values in the modern world* 现代世界精神价值的缺失 ◇ *We're concerned about your* ***spiritual welfare****.* 我们担心你的心理健康。**OPP** **material** **2** 🔑 connected with religion 宗教的：*a spiritual leader* 宗教领袖 ⊃ COMPARE TEMPORAL ▸ **spir·itu·al·ly** /-tʃuəli/ *adv.*：*a spiritually uplifting book* 陶冶性灵的书

IDM **your ˌspiritual ˈhome** the place where you are happiest, especially a country where you feel you belong more than in your own country because you share the ideas and attitudes of the people who live there 在精神上认同的某个地方；精神家园

■ ***noun*** (*also* **ˌNegro ˈspiritual**) a religious song of the type originally sung by black SLAVES in America 灵歌（宗教歌曲，最初为美国黑人奴隶所唱）

spir·itu·al·ism /ˈspɪrɪtʃuəlɪzəm/ *noun* [U] the belief that people who have died can send messages to living people, usually through a MEDIUM (= a person who has special powers) 招魂说，招魂术（认为亡灵可通过巫师或以其他方式向活人传达信息）

spir·itu·al·ist /ˈspɪrɪtʃuəlɪst/ *noun* a person who believes that people who have died can send messages to living people 信奉招魂说的人

spir·itu·al·ity /ˌspɪrɪtʃuˈæləti/ *noun* [U] the quality of being concerned with religion or the human spirit 精神性；灵性

spir·it·ual·ized (*BrE also* **-ised**) /ˈspɪrɪtʃuəlaɪzd/ *adj.* (*formal*) raised to a spiritual level 达至精神层次的；精神化的：*She tends to have intense, spiritualized friendships.* 她和朋友往往关系紧密而且注重精神层面。

spit /spɪt/ *verb*, *noun*

■ ***verb*** (**spit·ting, spat, spat** /spæt/) **HELP** **spit** is also sometimes used for the past tense and past participle, especially in *NAmE* 过去式和过去分词有时也用 spit，尤其在美式英语中。

• **FROM MOUTH** 从嘴里 **1** [T] to force liquid, food, etc. out of your mouth 吐，唾（唾沫、食物等）：**~ sth (out)** *She took a mouthful of food and then suddenly spat it out.* 她吃了一口食物，突然又吐了出来。◇ **~ sth (from sth)** *He was spitting blood from a badly cut lip.* 他嘴唇伤得不轻，正不停地唾血。**2** [I] to force SALIVA (= the liquid that is produced in the mouth) out of your mouth, often as a sign of anger or lack of respect 啐唾沫（常表示愤怒或鄙视）：*He coughed and spat.* 他咳嗽一声，吐了口痰。◇ **~ at/on/in sb/sth** *The prisoners were spat on by their guards.* 监狱看守朝犯人身上吐唾沫。◇ *She spat in his face and went out.* 她朝他脸上啐了一口，然后走了出去。

• **SAY STH ANGRILY** 愤怒地说 **3** [T] to say sth in an angry or aggressive way 怒斥：**+ speech** *'You liar!' she spat.* "你撒谎！"她怒叱道。◇ **~ sth (at sb)** *He was dragged out of the court, spitting abuse at the judge and jury.* 他被拖出法庭，嘴里还不停地骂着法官和陪审团。

• **OF AN ANIMAL** 动物 **4** [I] to make a short angry sound（发怒时）发呼噜呼噜声：*Snakes spit and hiss when they are cornered.* 蛇陷入绝境时会发出嘶嘶呼呼的声音。

• **OF STH COOKING/BURNING** 烹煮／燃烧的东西 **5** [I] to make a noise and throw out fat, SPARKS, etc. 嗞嗞地冒油；噼啪作响；爆出火花：*sausages spitting in the frying pan* 在煎锅里嗞嗞冒油的香肠 ◇ *The logs on the fire crackled and spat.* 火中的木头噼啪作响，爆出火花。

• **RAIN** 雨 **6** [I] (*informal*) (only used in the progressive tenses 仅用于进行时) when **it is spitting**, it is raining lightly 下小雨

IDM **ˌspit it ˈout** (*informal*) usually used in orders to tell sb to say sth when they seem frightened or unwilling to speak 有话就讲；有什么尽管说出来：*If you've got something to say, spit it out!* 有什么话，你尽管说出来！ **spit ˈvenom/ˈblood** to show that you are very angry; to speak in an angry way 怒气冲天；咬牙切齿 **within ˈspitting distance (of sth)** (*BrE*) (*also* **within ˈshouting distance** *NAmE, BrE*) (*informal*) very close 很近

PHR V **ˌspit ˈup** (*NAmE, informal*) (especially of a baby 尤指婴儿) to VOMIT (= bring food from the stomach back out through the mouth) 呕吐

■ ***noun***

• **IN/FROM MOUTH**（从）嘴里 **1** [U] the liquid that is produced in your mouth 唾液；唾沫 **SYN** **saliva** **2** [C, usually sing.] the act of spitting liquid or food out of your mouth 啐唾沫；吐痰；吐食物

• **PIECE OF LAND** 一块陆地 **3** [C] a long thin piece of land that sticks out into the sea/ocean, a lake, etc. 岬；沙嘴 ⊃ VISUAL VOCAB PAGE V5

• **FOR COOKING MEAT** 烤肉 **4** [C] a long thin straight piece of metal that you put through meat to hold and turn it while you cook it over a fire 烤肉扦

IDM **ˌspit and ˈpolish** (*informal*) thorough cleaning and polishing of sth 彻底的擦洗

spite 🔑 /spaɪt/ *noun*, *verb*

■ ***noun*** [U] a feeling of wanting to hurt or upset sb 恶意；怨恨 **SYN** **malice**：*I'm sure he only said it* ***out of spite****.* 我相信他只是为了泄愤才那么说的。

IDM **in ˈspite of sth** 🔑 if you say that sb did sth **in spite of** a fact, you mean it is surprising that that fact did not prevent them from doing it 不管；尽管 **SYN** **despite**：*In spite of his age, he still leads an active life.* 尽管年事已高，他依旧过着一种忙碌的生活。◇ *They went swimming in spite of all the danger signs.* 他们无视那么多警告牌，还是去游泳了。◇ *English became the official language for business* ***in spite of the fact that*** *the population was largely Chinese.* 虽然当地居民主要是中国人，英语却成了商业上正式使用的语言。⊃ LANGUAGE BANK AT HOWEVER **in ˈspite of yourself** if you do sth **in spite of yourself**, you do it although you did not intend or expect to 不由自主地：*He fell asleep, in spite of himself.* 他还是不由自主地睡着了。

■ ***verb*** (only used in the infinitive with *to* 仅用于带 to 的不定式中) **~ sb** to deliberately annoy or upset sb 故意使烦恼；存心使苦恼：*They're playing the music so loud just to spite us.* 他们把音乐放得这么响就是存心要搅扰我们。**IDM** SEE NOSE *n.*

spite·ful /ˈspaɪtfl/ *adj.* behaving in an unkind way in order to hurt or upset sb 恶意的；居心不良的；故意使人苦恼的 **SYN** **malicious** ▸ **spite·ful·ly** /-fəli/ *adv.*：*'I don't need you,' she said spitefully.* "我不需要你。"她故意气他说。**spite·ful·ness** *noun* [U]

ˈspit-roast *verb* **~ sth** to cook meat on a SPIT (4) 用烤肉扦烤（肉）

ˌspitting ˈimage *noun*

IDM **be the spitting image of sb** to look exactly like sb else 和某人长得一模一样：*She's the spitting image of her mother.* 她长得酷似她的母亲。

spit·tle /ˈspɪtl/ *noun* [U] (*old-fashioned*) the liquid that forms in the mouth 唾沫；口水 **SYN** **saliva, spit**

S

spit·toon /spɪ'tuːn/ *noun* a container, used especially in the past, for people to SPIT into 痰盂

spiv /spɪv/ *noun* (*old-fashioned, BrE, slang, disapproving*) a man who makes his money by being dishonest in business, especially one who dresses in a way that makes people believe he is rich and successful 衣冠楚楚的奸商

splash /splæʃ/ *verb, noun*

■ ***verb*** **1** [I] + **adv./prep.** (of liquid 液体) to fall noisily onto a surface 泼洒；哗啦哗啦地溅；噼里啪啦地落：*Water splashed onto the floor.* 水哗的一声泼洒在地板上。◇ *Rain splashed against the windows.* 雨点啪啦啪啦地打在窗户上。**2** [T] to make sb/sth wet by making water, mud, etc. fall on them/it 把（水、泥等）泼在…上，溅在…上；朝…上泼（或溅）：**~ sth on/onto/over sb/sth** *He splashed cold water on his face.* 他把冷水往脸上泼。◇ **~ sb/sth with sth** *He splashed his face with cold water.* 他朝脸上泼冷水。◇ *My clothes were splashed with mud.* 我衣服上溅满了泥。◇ **~ sb/sth** *Stop splashing me!* 别溅我了！**3** [I] (+ **adv./prep.**) to move through water making drops fly everywhere （在水中）溅着水花行走，拍打着水游：*The kids were splashing through the puddles.* 孩子们哗啦哗啦地溅着水花从水坑里蹚过。◇ *People were having fun in the pool, swimming or just splashing around.* 人们在游泳池里或者游泳，或者只是拍打戏水，开心地玩着。**4** [T] **~ sth with sth** [usually passive] to decorate sth with areas of bright colour, not in a regular pattern 用（泼洒色斑）装饰：*The walls were splashed with patches of blue and purple.* 墙壁上随意泼了大块的蓝色和紫色。

PHR V **'splash sth across/over sth** to put a photograph, news story, etc. in a place where it will be easily noticed 把（照片、新闻报道等）安排在显著位置；在突出位置刊载 **,splash 'down** (of a SPACECRAFT 航天器) to land in the sea or ocean 溅落（在海洋里）➲ RELATED NOUN SPLASHDOWN **,splash 'out (on sth)** | **,splash sth↔'out (on/for sth)** (*BrE, informal*) to spend a lot of money on sth 花大笔的钱（买某物等）：*We're going to splash out and buy a new car.* 我们打算挥霍一下，买辆新车。◇ *He splashed out hundreds of pounds on designer clothes.* 他花了几百英镑买名牌服装。

■ ***noun*** **1** [C] the sound of sth hitting liquid or of liquid hitting sth 落水声；溅泼声：*We heard the splash when she fell into the pool.* 她掉进游泳池时我们听见扑通的一声。**2** [C] a small amount of liquid that falls onto sth; the mark that this makes 溅上的液体；溅洒后留下的污渍：*splashes of water on the floor* 洒在地板上的一摊摊水 ◇ *dark splashes of mud on her skirt* 溅在她裙子上的黑泥点 **3** [C] a small area of bright colour or light that contrasts with the colours around it 色块；光斑：*These flowers will give a splash of colour throughout the summer.* 这些花会给整个夏天增添一片亮丽的色彩。➲ WORDFINDER NOTE AT PATTERN **4** [sing.] (*informal*) a small amount of liquid that you add to a drink 掺入饮料的少量液体：*coffee with just a splash of milk* 只加了少量牛奶的咖啡 ➲ COMPARE DASH *n.* (3) **5** [sing.] an article in a newspaper, etc. that is intended to attract a lot of attention（报章等旨在招徕读者的）重点文章

IDM **make, cause, etc. a 'splash** (*informal*) to do sth in a way that attracts a lot of attention or causes a lot of excitement 引起广泛关注；引起轰动

splash·back /'splæʃbæk/ *noun* (*BrE*) a surface behind a sink or cooker/stove which protects the wall from liquids（洗涤槽或锅灶后壁的）防溅挡板 ➲ VISUAL VOCAB PAGE V26

splash·down /'splæʃdaʊn/ *noun* [C, U] a landing of a SPACECRAFT in the sea/ocean 溅落（指航天器坠入海洋）

splashy /'splæʃi/ *adj.* (**splash·ier, splashi·est**) (*especially NAmE*) bright and very easy to notice 鲜明醒目的；华丽而招摇的；大张声势的

splat /splæt/ *noun* [sing.] (*informal*) the sound made by sth wet hitting a surface with force（湿物落在平面上的）啪嗒声：*The tomato hit the wall with a splat.* 西红柿啪的一声打在墙上。▶ **splat** *adv.*: *The omelette fell splat onto the floor.* 煎蛋饼吧唧一下掉到了地上。➲ MORE LIKE THIS 3, page R25

splat·ter /'splætə(r)/ *verb* **1** [I] (+ **adv./prep.**) (of large drops of liquid 大滴的液体) to fall or hit sth noisily 啪嗒啪嗒地落下（或击打）：*Heavy rain splattered on the roof.* 大雨噼里啪啦地打在屋顶上。**2** [T, I] to drop or throw water, paint, mud, etc. on sb/sth; to make sb/sth wet or dirty by landing on them in large drops 把（水等）泼洒在…上；淋湿；溅污：**~ sb/sth (+ adv./prep.)** *The walls were splattered with blood.* 墙上血迹斑斑。◇ **+ adv./prep.** *Coffee had splattered across the front of his shirt.* 他的衬衣前襟上洒了一大片咖啡。

splay /spleɪ/ *verb* [T, I] **~ (sth) (out)** to make fingers, legs, etc. become further apart from each other or spread out; to be spread out wide apart 使（手指、腿等）叉开；使分开；张开；展开：*She lay on the bed, her arms and legs splayed out.* 她四肢摊开躺在床上。◇ *His long fingers splayed across her back.* 他把长长的手指叉开贴在她背上。

,splay-'foot *noun* a broad flat foot which turns away from the other foot 八字脚；外翻足 ▶ **,splay-'footed** *adj.*

spleen /spliːn/ *noun* **1** [C] a small organ near the stomach that controls the quality of the blood cells 脾：*a ruptured spleen* 破裂的脾 ➲ VISUAL VOCAB PAGE V64 **2** [U] (*literary*) anger 愤怒；怒气：*He* ***vented his spleen*** (= shouted in an angry way) *on the assembled crowd.* 他把怒气撒在了聚集的人群身上。➲ SEE ALSO SPLENETIC

splen·did /'splendɪd/ *adj., exclamation*

■ ***adj.*** (*especially BrE*) **1** very impressive; very beautiful 壮丽的；雄伟的；豪华的；华丽的：*splendid scenery* 壮丽的风景 ◇ *The hotel stands* ***in splendid isolation****, surrounded by moorland.* 那旅馆岿然独立，周围是一片高沼地。**2** (*old-fashioned*) excellent; very good 极佳的；非常好的 **SYN** **great**: *What a splendid idea!* 这主意妙极了！◇ *We've all had a splendid time.* 我们大家都玩得很开心。▶ **splen·did·ly** *adv.*: *You all played splendidly.* 你们都表现得很出色。

■ ***exclamation*** (*old-fashioned, especially BrE*) used to show that you approve of sth, or are pleased（表示赞许或满意）好极了，痛快：*You're both coming? Splendid!* 你们俩都要来？太好了！

splen·dif·er·ous /splen'dɪfərəs/ *adj.* (*informal, humorous*) extremely good or pleasant 极好的；美妙的

splen·dour (*especially US* **splen·dor**) /'splendə(r)/ *noun* **1** [U] grand and impressive beauty 壮丽；雄伟；豪华；华丽 **SYN** **grandeur**: *a view of Rheims Cathedral, in all its splendour* 尽显其宏伟气象的兰斯大教堂景色 ◇ *The palace has been restored to its former splendour.* 宫殿经过修葺，重现出昔日的富丽堂皇。**2** **splendours** [pl.] the beautiful and impressive features or qualities of sth, especially a place（尤指某地的）壮丽景色，恢弘气势：*the splendours of Rome* (= its fine buildings, etc.) 罗马的壮丽景色

splen·et·ic /splə'netɪk/ *adj.* (*formal*) often bad-tempered and angry 脾气坏的；常发怒的

splice /splaɪs/ *verb, noun*

■ ***verb*** **1 ~ sth (together)** to join the ends of two pieces of rope by twisting them together 绞接，捻接（两段绳子）**2 ~ sth (together)** to join the ends of two pieces of film, tape, etc. by sticking them together 胶接，黏结（胶片、磁带等）

IDM **get 'spliced** (*old-fashioned, BrE, informal*) to get married 结婚

■ ***noun*** the place where two pieces of film, tape, rope, etc. have been joined 胶接处；黏结处；绞接处

spli·cer /'splaɪsə(r)/ *noun* a person or machine that joins pieces of tape, cable, etc. together（磁带等的）胶接者；接片机；（电缆等的）绞接器

spliff /splɪf/ *noun* (*BrE, slang*) a cigarette containing CANNABIS 大麻烟卷

splint /splɪnt/ *noun* a long piece of wood or metal that is tied to a broken arm or leg to keep it still and in the right position（固定断肢的）夹板

splin·ter /ˈsplɪntə(r)/ *noun, verb*

■ ***noun*** a small, thin sharp piece of wood, metal, glass, etc. that has broken off a larger piece（木头、金属、玻璃等的）尖碎片，尖细条 **SYN** **shard**

■ ***verb*** **1** [I, T] (of wood, glass, stone, etc. 木头、玻璃、石头等) to break, or to make sth break, into small, thin sharp pieces（使）裂成碎片 **SYN** **shatter**: *The mirror cracked but did not splinter.* 镜子裂了，但没碎。◇ **~ sth** *The impact splintered the wood.* 木头被撞成了碎片。**2** [I] (of a group of people 团体) to divide into smaller groups that are no longer connected; to separate from a larger group 分裂；分离出来：*The party began to splinter.* 那个党开始分裂。◇ **~ (off) (from sth)** *Several firms have splintered off from the original company.* 从原公司分离出好几个企业。

ˈsplinter group *noun* a small group of people that has separated from a larger one, especially in politics（尤指政党的）小派别

split 🔑 /splɪt/ *verb, noun*

■ ***verb*** (**split·ting, split, split**)

• **DIVIDE** 分开 **1** 🔑 [T, I] **~ (sth)** to divide, or to make a group of people divide, into smaller groups that have very different opinions 分裂，使分裂（成不同的派别）：*a debate that has* ***split*** *the country* ***down the middle*** 使全国分成两大派的一场争论 ◇ *The committee split over government subsidies.* 在政府补贴的问题上，委员会出现了相互对立的意见。**2** 🔑 [T, I] to divide, or to make sth divide, into two or more parts 分开，使分开（成为几个部分）：**~ sth (into sth)** *She split the class into groups of four.* 她按四人一组把全班分成若干小组。◇ **~ (into sth)** *The results split neatly into two groups.* 结果恰巧分成两类。➲ SEE ALSO SPLIT SB UP **3** 🔑 [T] to divide sth into two or more parts and share it between different people, activities, etc. 分担；分摊；分享：**~ sth (with sb)** *She split the money she won with her brother.* 她把得到的钱与弟弟分了。◇ **~ sth between sb/sth** *His time is split between the London and Paris offices.* 他一半时间在伦敦的办事处，一半时间在巴黎的办事处。➲ SEE ALSO SPLIT STH↔UP

• **TEAR** 撕裂 **4** 🔑 [I, T] to tear, or to make sth tear, along a straight line（使）撕裂：*Her dress had split along the seam.* 她的连衣裙顺着接缝裂开了。◇ **~ (sth) open** *The cushion split open and sent feathers everywhere.* 垫子撕破了，羽毛掉得到处都是。◇ **~ sth** *Don't tell me you've split another pair of pants!* 你不会又把一条裤子撑破了吧！

• **CUT** 割伤 **5** [T] to cut sb's skin and make it BLEED 划破；割破；碰破：**~ sth open** *She split her head open on the cupboard door.* 她碰到碗橱门上把头碰破了。◇ **~ sth** *How did you split your lip?* 你怎么把嘴唇划破了？

• **END RELATIONSHIP** 断绝关系 **6** [I] (*informal*) to leave sb and stop having a relationship with them（和某人）断绝关系，分手；离开（某人）：**~ (with sb)** *The singer split with his wife last June.* 那歌手去年六月和妻子分手了。◇ **~ (from sb)** *She intends to split from the band at the end of the tour.* 她打算在巡回演出结束后离开乐队。➲ SEE ALSO SPLIT UP (WITH SB)

• **LEAVE** 离开 **7** [I] (*old-fashioned, informal*) to leave a place quickly（迅速）离开，走：*Let's split!* 咱们快走吧！

IDM **split the ˈdifference** (when discussing a price, etc.) to agree on an amount that is at an equal distance between the two amounts that have been suggested（讲价等）各让一步，折中 **split ˈhairs** to pay too much attention in an argument to differences that are very small and not important 在细节上过分纠缠 **split an inˈfinitive** to place an adverb between 'to' and the infinitive of a verb, for example to say 'to strongly deny a rumour'. Some people consider this to be bad English style. 使用分裂不定式（在 to 和动词不定式之间插入副词，如 to strongly deny a rumour，有人认为这种用法有语病） **split your ˈsides (laughing/with laughter)** to laugh a lot at sb/sth 笑破肚皮；笑弯腰 **split the ˈticket** (*US, politics* 政) to vote for candidates from more than one party 投两党或两党以上候选人的票 ➲ MORE AT MIDDLE *n.*

PHR V **ˌsplit aˈway/ˈoff (from sth)** | **ˌsplit sth↔aˈway/ˈoff (from sth)** to separate from, or to separate sth from, a larger object or group（使）脱离，分裂出去，分离：*A rebel faction has split away from the main group.* 一帮反叛者从核心组织中分裂了出去。◇ *The storm split a branch off from the main trunk.* 暴风雨把一根树枝从树干上刮了下来。**ˈsplit on sb (to sb)** (*BrE, informal*) to tell sb in authority about sth wrong, dishonest, etc. that sb else has done（向…）告发，揭发：*Don't worry—he won't split on us.* 别担心，他不会出卖我们的。**ˌsplit ˈup (with sb)** 🔑 to stop having a relationship with sb（和某人）断绝关系，分手：*My parents split up last year.* 我父母去年离婚了。◇ *She's split up with her boyfriend.* 她和男朋友分手了。**ˌsplit sb ˈup** to make two people stop having a relationship with each other 使断绝关系；拆散：*My friend is doing her best to split us up.* 我的朋友竭力想拆散我们。**ˌsplit sb ˈup** | **ˌsplit ˈup** 🔑 to divide a group of people into smaller parts; to become divided up in this way（把…）分成小组，化整为零：*We were split up into groups to discuss the question.* 我们分组讨论了那个问题。◇ *Let's split up now and meet again at lunchtime.* 我们现在先分开，午饭时再集合。**ˌsplit sth↔ˈup** 🔑 to divide sth into smaller parts 划分；分解：*The day was split up into 6 one-hour sessions.* 一天的活动分作 6 个时段，每个时段一小时。

■ ***noun***

• **DISAGREEMENT** 分歧 **1** 🔑 [C] (*informal*) a disagreement that divides a group of people or makes sb separate from sb else 分歧；分裂；分离：**~ (within sth)** *a damaging split within the party leadership* 党的领导层内部不利的分歧 ◇ **~ (with sb/sth)** *the years following his bitter split with his wife* 他和妻子痛苦分手后的那些年 ◇ **~ (between A and B)** *There have been reports of a split between the Prime Minister and the Cabinet.* 有报道说首相和内阁之间存在分歧。

• **DIVISION** 划分 **2** 🔑 [sing.] a division between two or more things; one of the parts that sth is divided into 划分；分别；份额：*He demanded a 50–50 split in the profits.* 他要求利润对半分成。

• **TEAR/HOLE** 裂缝；裂口 **3** 🔑 [C] a long crack or hole made when sth tears 裂缝；裂口：*There's a big split in the tent.* 帐篷上撕了一个大口子。

• **BANANA DISH** 香蕉甜食 **4** [C] a sweet dish made from fruit, especially a BANANA cut in two along its length, with cream, ice cream, etc. on top 香蕉船，水果船（将香蕉等纵切成条状作底，上覆奶油或冰淇淋等）：*a banana split* 香蕉船

• **BODY POSITION** 身体姿势 **5 the splits** [pl.] (*US also* **split** [sing.]) a position in which you stretch your legs flat across the floor in opposite directions with the rest of your body vertical 劈叉：*a gymnast* ***doing the splits*** 做劈叉的体操运动员

ˌsplit ˈend *noun* a hair on your head that has divided into parts at the end because it is dry or in poor condition 分叉的发梢

ˌsplit inˈfinitive *noun* (*grammar* 语法) the form of the verb with 'to', with an adverb placed between 'to' and the verb, as in *She seems to really like it*. Some people consider this to be bad English style. 分裂不定式（在 to 和动词不定式之间插入副词的不定式，如在句子 She seems to really like it，有人认为这种用法有语病）

ˌsplit-ˈlevel *adj.* (of a room, floor, etc. 房间、地板等) having parts at different levels 错层式的

ˌsplit ˈpea *noun* [usually pl.] a type of dried PEA, split into halves 干豌豆瓣

ˌsplit-persoˈnality disorder *noun* = MULTIPLE-PERSONALITY DISORDER

ˌsplit ˈscreen *noun* a way of displaying two or more pictures or pieces of information at the same time on a television, cinema or computer screen 分画面，分屏（在电视、电影或计算机屏幕上同时显示两个或两个以上的画面或文件）▶ **ˌsplit-ˈscreen** *adj.* [only before noun]: *a movie with several split-screen sequences* 一部有几个分画面镜头的电影

ˌsplit ˈsecond *noun* a very short moment of time 瞬间；刹那：*Their eyes met* ***for a split second.*** 在一刹那间，他们的目光交汇在了一起。

S

ˌ**split-ˈsecond** *adj.* [only before noun] done very quickly or very accurately 一瞬间作出的；做得非常精确的：*She had to make a split-second decision.* 她必须在瞬间作出决定。◇ *The success of the raid depended on* ***split-second timing.*** 袭击的成功取决于分秒不差的时间安排。

ˌ**split ˈshift** *noun* two separate periods of time that you spend working in a single day, with several hours between them 间隔班（工作时间分成间隔几小时的两段轮班）：*I work split shifts in a busy restaurant.* 我在一家繁忙的餐馆上间隔班。

splits·ville /ˈsplɪtsvɪl/ *noun* [sing.] (*NAmE, slang*) the end of a relationship 散伙；分手；离异：*Within three months of the honeymoon, it was splitsville for Ron and Mimi.* 罗恩和米米蜜月之后不到三个月就散伙了。

ˌ**split ˈticket** *noun* (in elections in the US) a vote in which sb votes for candidates from two different parties（在美国的各级选举中）投两党候选人的选票 ➲ COMPARE STRAIGHT TICKET ▶ ˌ**split-ˈticket** *adj.* [only before noun]：*a split-ticket vote* 投两党候选人的选票

split·ting /ˈsplɪtɪŋ/ *adj.* [only before noun] if you have a **splitting headache**, you have a very bad pain in your head（头痛）欲裂的

splodge /splɒdʒ; *NAmE* splɑːdʒ/ (*BrE*) (*also* **splotch** /splɒtʃ; *NAmE* splɑːtʃ/ *NAmE, BrE*) *noun* a large mark or spot of ink, paint, mud, etc.; a small area of colour or light 一块污渍；一片污迹；色块；光斑

splosh /splɒʃ; *NAmE* splɑːʃ/ *verb, noun* (*BrE, informal*)

■ *verb* [I] + **adv./prep.** to move through water, making soft sounds（在水里）啪嗒啪嗒地移动，溅泼着前行：*Children were sploshing about in the pool.* 孩子们在游泳池里哗哗地游来游去。

■ *noun* **1** the soft sound of sth moving through or falling into water 溅泼声；哗啦声 **2** a small amount of liquid that moves through the air 溅起的少量液体 ➲ MORE LIKE THIS 3, page R25

splurge /splɜːdʒ; *NAmE* splɜːrdʒ/ *noun, verb*

■ *noun* [usually sing.] (*informal*) an act of spending a lot of money on sth that you do not really need 乱花钱；糟蹋钱；挥霍

■ *verb* [T, I] ~ (**sth**) (**on sth**) (*informal*) to spend a lot of money on sth that you do not really need 乱花（钱）；糟蹋（钱）；挥霍

splut·ter /ˈsplʌtə(r)/ *verb, noun*

■ *verb* **1** [T, I] to speak quickly and with difficulty, making soft SPITTING sounds, because you are angry or embarrassed 气急败坏地说；慌张地说 SYN **sputter**：+ **speech** (**out**) *'But, but…you can't!' she spluttered.* "可是，可是…你不能啊！" 她急促而慌乱地说。◇ ~ (**with sth**) *Her father spluttered with indignation.* 她父亲气得说话都语无伦次了。**2** [I] to make a series of short EXPLOSIVE sounds 发噗噗声；发噼啪声 SYN **sputter**：*The firework spluttered and went out.* 花炮噼里啪啦地喷完后灭了。◇ *She fled from the blaze,* ***coughing and spluttering.*** 她从大火中逃出来，一边咳嗽，一边噗噗地吐气。

■ *noun* a short EXPLOSIVE sound 噗的一声；啪的一声：*The car started with a loud splutter.* 汽车突的一声发动了。

spoil /spɔɪl/ *verb, noun*

■ *verb* (**spoiled, spoiled** /spɔɪld/) (*BrE also* **spoilt, spoilt** /spɔɪlt/) **1** [T] ~ **sth** to change sth good into sth bad, unpleasant, useless, etc. 破坏；搞坏；糟蹋；毁掉 SYN **ruin**：*Our camping trip was spoilt by bad weather.* 天气不好，破坏了我们的露营旅行。◇ *Don't let him spoil your evening.* 别让他搞得你一晚上不开心。◇ *The tall buildings have spoiled the view.* 那些高楼大厦破坏了这一带的景致。◇ *Don't eat too many nuts—you'll* ***spoil your appetite*** (= will no longer be hungry at the proper time to eat). 别吃太多坚果，会影响你的食欲。◇ (*BrE*) *spoiled ballot papers* (= not valid because not correctly marked) 废选票 **2** [T] ~ **sb** to give a child everything that they ask for and not enough discipline in a way that has a bad effect on their character and behaviour 溺爱；娇惯；宠坏 SYN **over-indulge**：*She spoils those kids of hers.* 那几个孩子被她宠坏了。**3** [T] ~ **sb/yourself** to make sb/yourself happy by doing sth special 善待；格外关照：*Why not spoil yourself with a weekend in a top hotel?* 为什么不到顶级饭店度个周末，让自己享受享受呢？◇ *He really spoiled me on my birthday.* 我生日那天他真让我受宠若惊。**4** [I] (of food 食物) to become bad so that it can no longer be eaten 变坏；变质；腐败 SYN **go off**

IDM **be ˈspoiling for a fight** to want to fight with sb very much 按捺不住想打架 **spoil the ˌship for a haˈp'orth/haˈpennyworth of ˈtar** (*saying*) to spoil sth good because you did not spend enough money or time on a small but essential part of it 因小失大 ➲ MORE AT COOK *n.*

■ *noun* **1 the spoils** [pl.] (*formal* or *literary*) goods taken from a place by thieves or by an army that has won a battle or war 赃物；战利品；掠夺物 **2 spoils** [pl.] the profits or advantages that sb gets from being successful 成功所带来的好处；权力地位的连带利益：*the spoils of high office* 身居高位的连带利益 **3** [U] (*specialist*) waste material that is brought up when a hole is dug, etc.（开掘等时挖出的）弃土，废石方

spoil·age /ˈspɔɪlɪdʒ/ *noun* [U] (*specialist*) the decay of food which means that it can no longer be used（食物的）变质，腐败

spoil·er /ˈspɔɪlə(r)/ *noun* **1** a part of an aircraft's wing that can be raised in order to interrupt the flow of air over it and so slow the aircraft's speed（机翼的）扰流片 **2** a raised part on a fast car that prevents it from being lifted off the road when travelling very fast（汽车的）气流偏导器 **3** (*especially NAmE*) a candidate for a political office who is unlikely to win but who may get enough votes to prevent one of the main candidates from winning 选举中的搅局者（无望获胜但所得选票可能使某主要候选人无法当选）**4** a person or thing that intends or is intended to stop sb/sth being successful 阻碍…成功的人（或事物）；搞砸…的人（或事物）**5** information that you are given about what is going to happen in a film/movie, television series, etc. before it is shown to the public（在电影、电视剧等公映前的）剧情透露 **6** a newspaper story, book, etc. that is produced very quickly in order to take attention away from one produced by a COMPETITOR that appears at the same time（为竞争而迅速发表的）抵消影响的报道（或书籍等）

spoil·sport /ˈspɔɪlspɔːt; *NAmE* -spɔːrt/ *noun* (*informal*) a person who spoils other people's enjoyment, for example by not taking part in an activity or by trying to stop other people from doing it 扫兴的人：*Don't be such a spoilsport!* 别让人扫兴！

the ˈspoils system *noun* [sing.] the arrangement in US politics which allows the President to give government jobs to supporters after winning an election（美国当选总统把官职分给支持者的）政党分肥制，赐职制

spoilt /spɔɪlt/ (*BrE*) (*also* **spoiled** /spɔɪld/ *NAmE, BrE*) *adj.* (of a child 孩子) rude and badly behaved because they are given everything they ask for and not enough discipline 宠坏的；娇惯坏的：*a spoiled brat* 娇惯坏的淘气鬼 ◇ *He's* ***spoilt rotten*** (= a lot). 他给惯得一点样子都没有了。

IDM **be spoilt for ˈchoice** (*BrE*) to have such a lot of things to choose from that it is very difficult to make a decision（东西多得）挑花眼

spoke /spəʊk; *NAmE* spoʊk/ *noun* one of the thin bars or long straight pieces of metal that connect the centre of a wheel to its outer edge, for example on a bicycle 辐条；轮辐 ➲ VISUAL VOCAB PAGE V55

IDM **put a ˈspoke in sb's wheel** (*BrE*) to prevent sb from putting their plans into operation 破坏某人的计划；阻挠某人实行计划 ➲ SEE ALSO SPEAK

spoken /ˈspəʊkən; *NAmE* ˈspoʊ-/ *adj.* **1** involving speaking rather than writing; expressed in speech rather than in writing 口语的；口头的；以口头形式表达的：*spoken English* 英语口语 ◇ *spoken commands* 口头指令 **2** (following an adverb 用于副词后) speaking in the way mentioned 说话…的：*a quietly spoken man* 说话斯文的男人 ➲ SEE ALSO OUTSPOKEN

▼ **SYNONYMS 同义词辨析**

spoken

oral • vocal

These words all describe producing language using the voice, rather than writing. 以上各词均指口头的、口语的。

spoken (of language) produced using the voice; said rather than written 指口语的、口头的： *an exam in spoken English* 英语口语考试

oral [usually before noun] spoken rather than written 指口头的、口述的： *There will be a test of both oral and written French.* 将有一次法语口试和笔试。

SPOKEN OR ORAL? 用 spoken 还是 oral?

Both of these words can be used to refer to language skills and the communication of information. 上述两词均可用于语言技巧和信息交流： *spoken/oral French* 法语口语 ◇ *a spoken/oral presentation* 口头报告 In these cases **oral** is slightly more technical than **spoken**. **Oral** but not **spoken** can also be used with words such as *tradition*, *culture* and *legends* to talk about the way in which people pass stories down from one generation to the next, and in legal contexts followed by words such as *evidence* and *hearing*. 在上述例子中，oral 较 spoken 专业一些，oral 亦可与 tradition、culture 和 legends 等词连用，指故事代代相传的方式； spoken 则不能这样用。在法律语境中，oral 后可接 evidence 和 hearing 等词，spoken 则不能。

vocal [usually before noun] connected with the voice 指嗓音的、发音的： *vocal music* 声乐 ◇ *the vocal organs* (= the tongue, lips, etc.) 发声器官 NOTE **Vocal** is used to talk about the ability to produce sounds using the voice, and is often used in musical contexts when referring to singing. * vocal 关乎发音的能力，常用于音乐语境中，指歌唱。

PATTERNS

- spoken/oral **French/English/Japanese, etc.**
- spoken/oral **language skills**

ˈspoken for *adj.* [not before noun] already claimed or being kept for sb 已经有人要；留给某人： *I'm afraid you can't sit there—those seats are spoken for.* 恐怕您不能坐那儿，那些座位有人预订了。◇ (*old-fashioned*) *Liza is already spoken for* (= she is already married or has a partner). 莉莎已名花有主了。

the ˌspoken ˈword *noun* [sing.] language expressed in speech, rather than being written or sung 口头说的话

spokes·man /ˈspəʊksmən; *NAmE* ˈspoʊ-/, **spokes·woman** /ˈspəʊkswʊmən; *NAmE* ˈspoʊ-/ *noun* (*pl.* **-men** /-mən/, **-women** /-wɪmɪn/) a person who speaks on behalf of a group or an organization 发言人： *a police spokesman* 警方发言人 ◇ **~ for sb/sth** *A spokeswoman for the government denied the rumours.* 一位政府女发言人否认了那些传言。➲ NOTE AT GENDER ➲ MORE LIKE THIS 25, page R28

spokes·per·son /ˈspəʊkspɜːsn; *NAmE* ˈspoʊkspɜːrsn/ *noun* (*pl.* **-per·sons** or **-people**) **~ (for sb/sth)** a person who speaks on behalf of a group or an organization 发言人 ➲ MORE LIKE THIS 25, page R28

spon·dee /ˈspɒndiː; *NAmE* ˈspɑːn-/ *noun* (*specialist*) a unit of sound in poetry consisting of two strong or long syllables（诗歌的）扬扬格

sponge /spʌndʒ/ *noun, verb*

■ *noun* **1** [C] a piece of artificial or natural material that is soft and light and full of holes and can hold water easily, used for washing or cleaning（天然或人造、擦洗物品用的）海绵块： (*figurative*) *His mind was like a sponge, ready to absorb anything.* 他的脑子跟海绵似的，什么都能吸收。➲ VISUAL VOCAB PAGES V25, V65 **2** [U] artificial sponge used for filling furniture, CUSHIONS, etc.（用以填充家具、垫子等的）人造海绵 **3** [C] a simple sea creature with a light body full of holes, from which natural sponge is obtained 海绵动物 **4** [C, U] (*BrE*) = SPONGE CAKE: *a chocolate sponge* 巧克力海绵蛋糕

■ *verb* **1** [T] **~ sb/yourself/sth (down)** to wash sb/yourself/sth with a wet cloth or SPONGE 用湿布（或海绵）擦；揩拭 SYN **wipe**: *She sponged his hot face.* 她用湿毛巾擦了擦他那滚烫的脸。◇ *Take your jacket off and I'll sponge it down with water.* 把你的夹克脱下来，我要用海绵蘸上水把它擦一擦。 **2** [T] **~ sth + adv./prep.** to remove sth using a wet cloth or SPONGE 用湿布（或海绵）擦掉；揩去 SYN **wash**: *We tried to sponge the blood off my shirt.* 我们试着把我衬衫上的血迹擦掉。 **3** [I] **~ (off/on sb)** (*informal, disapproving*) to get money, food, etc. regularly from other people without doing anything for them or offering to pay 白要；白吃；揩油；蹭（饭等） SYN **scrounge**: *He spent his life sponging off his relatives.* 他靠在众亲属那儿蹭吃蹭喝过了一辈子。

ˈsponge bag (*also* **ˈtoilet bag**, **wash·bag**) (*all BrE*) (*NAmE* **ˈtoiletry bag**) *noun* a small bag for holding your soap, TOOTHBRUSH, etc. when you are travelling 盥洗用品袋 ➲ VISUAL VOCAB PAGE V25

ˈsponge bath *noun* (*NAmE*) an act of washing the whole of sb's body when they cannot get out of bed because they are sick, injured or old（为卧床不起者所做的）擦身浴，擦澡

ˈsponge cake (*also* **sponge**) *noun* [C, U] a light cake made from eggs, sugar and flour, with or without fat 海绵蛋糕；松蛋糕

ˌsponge ˈpudding *noun* [U, C] (*BrE*) a hot DESSERT (= a sweet dish) like a sponge cake that usually has jam or fruit on top 海绵布丁；松软布丁

spon·ger /ˈspʌndʒə(r)/ *noun* (*informal*) a person who gets money, food, etc. from other people without doing anything for them or offering to pay 吃白食的人；揩油者

spongi·form /ˈspʌndʒɪfɔːm; *NAmE* ˈspʌndʒɪfɔːrm/ *adj.* (*specialist*) having or relating to a structure with holes in it like a SPONGE 海绵状（组织）的 ➲ SEE ALSO BSE

spongy /ˈspʌndʒi/ *adj.* soft and able to absorb water easily like a SPONGE 海绵似的；柔软吸水的 SYN **springy**: *spongy moss* 海绵似的苔藓 ◇ *The ground was soft and spongy.* 土质松软，像海绵似的。◇ *The bread had a spongy texture.* 那种面包很松软。▶ **spon·gi·ness** *noun* [U]

spon·sor /ˈspɒnsə(r); *NAmE* ˈspɑːn-/ *noun, verb*

■ *noun* **1** a person or company that pays for a radio or television programme, or for a concert or sporting event, usually in return for advertising（广播电视节目、音乐会或体育赛事的）赞助者，赞助商： *The race organizers are trying to attract sponsors.* 比赛的组织者在想方设法吸引赞助者。 **2** a person who agrees to give sb money for a charity if that person succeeds in completing a particular activity 为慈善活动捐资的人；义赛（或义演等）捐款者： *I'm collecting sponsors for next week's charity run.* 我正在为下星期的募款赛跑征集捐款者。 **3** a person or company that supports sb by paying for their training or education（培训或教育的）资助者 **4** a person who introduces and supports a proposal for a new law, etc.（法案等的）倡议者，发起人，倡导者： *the sponsor of the new immigration bill* 新移民法案的倡议者 **5** a person who agrees to be officially responsible for another person 保人；保证人 **6** a person who presents a child for Christian BAPTISM or CONFIRMATION 代父（或母）；教父（或母）；（洗礼、坚信礼等的）引领人 SYN **godparent**

■ *verb* **1 ~ sth** (of a company, etc. 公司等) to pay the costs of a particular event, programme, etc. as a way of advertising 赞助（活动、节目等）： *sports events sponsored by the tobacco industry* 由烟草业赞助的体育赛事 **2 ~ sth** to arrange for sth official to take place 主办；举办；促成： *The US is sponsoring negotiations between the two sides.* 美国正在安排双方的谈判。 **3 ~ sb (for sth/to do sth)** to agree to give sb money for a charity if they complete a particular task 为慈善活动捐资；为义赛捐款： *Will you*

S

sponsor me for a charity walk I'm doing? 我正在参加竞走义赛，请您捐款好吗？◇ *a sponsored swim* 有赞助的慈善游泳活动 **4 ~ sb** (**through sth**) to support sb by paying for their training or education 资助（某人的培训或教育）：*She found a company to sponsor her through college.* 她找到一家愿资助她读完大学的公司。**5 ~ sth** to introduce a proposal for a new law, etc. 倡议，提交（法案等）：*The bill was sponsored by a Labour MP.* 这项议案是一位工党议员提交的。

spon·sor·ship /ˈspɒnsəʃɪp; *NAmE* ˈspɑːnsərʃɪp/ *noun* **1** [U, C] financial support from a sponsor 资助；赞助款：*a $50 million sponsorship deal* * 5 000 万美元的赞助协议 ◇ *The project needs to raise £8 million in sponsorship.* 这个项目需要筹集 800 万英镑的资助。◇ *We need to find sponsorships for the expedition.* 我们需要为这次探险找到赞助。**2** [U] the act of sponsoring sb/sth or being sponsored 资助；主办；倡议：*the senator's sponsorship of the job training legislation* 那位参议员对制定职业培训法规的倡议

spon·tan·eity /ˌspɒntəˈneɪəti; *NAmE* ˌspɑːn-/ *noun* [U] the quality of being spontaneous 自发性；自然

spon·tan·eous /spɒnˈteɪniəs; *NAmE* spɑːn-/ *adj.* **1** not planned but done because you suddenly want to do it 自发的；非筹划安排的：*a spontaneous offer of help* 主动提出帮助 ◇ *The audience burst into spontaneous applause.* 观众自发地鼓起掌来。**2** often doing things without planning to, because you suddenly want to do them 常心血来潮的 **3** (*specialist*) happening naturally, without being made to happen 自发的；自然的；自身造成的：*spontaneous remission of the disease* 疾病的自然缓解 **4** done naturally, without being forced or practised 自然的；非勉强的；无雕饰的：*a tape recording of spontaneous speech* 一段自然讲话的磁带录音 ◇ *a wonderfully spontaneous performance of the piece* 对那支乐曲极其淳朴自然的演奏 ▶ **spon·tan·eous·ly** *adv.*: *We spontaneously started to dance.* 我们情不自禁地跳起舞来。◇ *The bleeding often stops spontaneously.* 这种出血常常会自己停止。

sponˌtaneous comˈbustion *noun* [U] the burning of a mineral or vegetable substance caused by chemical changesinside it and not by fire or heat from outside 自燃

spoof /spuːf/ *noun, verb*

■ ***noun*** (*informal*) a humorous copy of a film/movie, television programme, etc. that exaggerates its main features（对电影、电视节目等的）滑稽模仿：*It's a spoof on horror movies.* 这是对恐怖片的滑稽模仿。

■ ***verb*** **1 ~ sth** to copy a film/movie, television programme, etc. in an amusing way by exaggerating its main features 滑稽地模仿（电影、电视节目等）：*It is a movie that spoofs other movies.* 这是一部夸张地模仿其他电影的影片。➲ WORDFINDER NOTE AT COMEDY **2 ~ sth** to send an email that appears to come from sb else's email address（冒用他人电邮地址）发送电邮；发送仿真电邮；电邮欺骗：*Someone has been spoofing my address.* 有人一直在冒用我的电邮地址发送电邮。▶ **spoof·ing** *noun* [U]

spook /spuːk/ *noun, verb*

■ ***noun*** (*informal*) **1** a GHOST 鬼：*a castle haunted by spooks* 闹鬼的城堡 **2** (*especially NAmE*) a SPY 间谍；特工：*a CIA spook* 中央情报局特工

■ ***verb*** [T, usually passive, I] ~ (**sb/sth**) (*informal, especially NAmE*) to frighten a person or an animal; to become frightened 吓；惊吓；受惊：*We were spooked by the strange noises and lights.* 那奇怪的声音和亮光把我们吓坏了。◇ *The horse spooked at the siren.* 警报器一响，马受惊了。

spooky /ˈspuːki/ *adj.* (**spook·ier**, **spooki·est**) HELP You can also use **more spooky** and **most spooky**. 亦可用 more spooky 和 most spooky。(*informal*) strange and frightening 怪异吓人的；阴森可怖的 SYN **creepy**: *a spooky old house* 阴森森的老房子 ◇ *I was just thinking about her when she phoned. Spooky!* 我正在想她，她就来电话了。你说怪不怪！

spool /spuːl/ *noun, verb*

■ ***noun*** (*especially NAmE*) = REEL (1): *a spool of thread* 一轴线 ➲ VISUAL VOCAB PAGE V45

■ ***verb*** **1** [T] **~ sth + adv./prep.** to wind sth onto or off a spool 把…绕到线轴上（或从线轴上绕下来）**2** [T, I] ~ (**sth**) (*computing* 计) to move data and store it for a short time, for example on a disk, especially before it is printed 假脱机（尤指打印前出现的操作情况）

spoon 🔑 /spuːn/ *noun, verb*

■ ***noun*** **1** 🔑 a tool that has a handle with a shallow bowl at the end, used for stirring, serving and eating food 勺；匙；调羹：*a soup spoon* 汤匙 ◇ *a wooden spoon* 木勺 ➲ VISUAL VOCAB PAGE V23 ➲ SEE ALSO DESSERTSPOON, GREASY SPOON, TABLESPOON, TEASPOON **2** = SPOONFUL IDM SEE BORN *v.*

■ ***verb*** **~ sth + adv./prep.** to lift and move food with a spoon 用勺舀：*She spooned the sauce over the chicken pieces.* 她用勺把沙司浇到鸡块上。

spoon·bill /ˈspuːnbɪl/ *noun* a large bird with long legs, a long neck and a beak that is wide and flat at the end 琵鹭

spoon·er·ism /ˈspuːnərɪzəm/ *noun* a mistake in which you change around the first sounds of two words by mistake when saying them, often with a humorous result, for example *well-boiled icicle* for *well-oiled bicycle* 首音误置（说话时误把两个单词的首音掉换，常造成滑稽效果）ORIGIN Named after **W.A. Spooner** (1844–1930), the head of New College, Oxford, who was said to have made many mistakes like this when he spoke. 名称源自斯普纳（W.A. Spooner, 1844–1930）。斯普纳曾任牛津大学新学院院长，据说他在讲话中出现过许多首音误置。

ˈspoon-feed *verb* **1** (*disapproving*) to teach people sth in a way that gives them too much help and does not make them think for themselves 填鸭式灌输；满堂灌：**~ sb** (**with sth**) *The students here do not expect to be spoon-fed.* 这儿的学生不希望教师满堂灌。◇ **~ sth to sb** *They had information spoon-fed to them.* 他们的知识是以满堂灌的方式传授给他们的。**2 ~ sb** to feed sb, especially a baby, with a spoon 用勺喂（婴儿）

spoon·ful /ˈspuːnfʊl/ (*also* **spoon**) *noun* the amount that a spoon can hold 一勺（的量）：*two spoonfuls of sugar* 两勺糖

spoor /spʊə(r); *NAmE* spʊr/ *noun* [sing.] a track or smell that a wild animal leaves as it travels（野兽走过留下的）足迹，嗅迹

spor·ad·ic /spəˈrædɪk/ *adj.* happening only occasionally or at intervals that are not regular 偶尔发生的；间或出现的；阵发性的；断断续续的 SYN **intermittent**: *sporadic fighting/gunfire/violence, etc.* 零星的战斗、一阵一阵的炮火、间或发生的暴力事件等 ◇ *sporadic outbreaks of the disease* 那种疾病的散发 ▶ **spor·ad·ic·al·ly** /-kli/ *adv.*: *She attended lectures only sporadically.* 她只是偶尔听听课。◇ *Fighting continued sporadically for two months.* 战斗断断续续地进行了两个月。

spore /spɔː(r)/ *noun* (*biology* 生) one of the very small cells that are produced by some plants and that develop into new plants 孢子：*Ferns, mosses and fungi spread by means of spores.* 蕨类植物、苔藓和真菌通过孢子传播蔓生。➲ COLLOCATIONS AT LIFE

spor·ran /ˈspɒrən; *NAmE* ˈspɑː-/ *noun* a flat bag, usually made of leather or fur, that is worn by men in front of the KILT as part of the Scottish national dress 毛皮袋（苏格兰男子民族服装的一部分，系在褶裥短裙前）

sport 🔑 /spɔːt; *NAmE* spɔːrt/ *noun, verb*

■ ***noun*** **1** 🔑 [U] (*BrE*) (*NAmE* **sports** [pl.]) activity that you do for pleasure and that needs physical effort or skill, usually done in a special area and according to fixed rules 体育运动：*There are excellent facilities for sport and recreation.* 有完善的体育娱乐设施。◇ *I'm not interested in sport.* 我对体育运动不感兴趣。◇ *the use of drugs in sport* 禁药在体育运动中的使用 ➲ WORDFINDER NOTE AT FIT

> **WORDFINDER** 联想词：athlete, champion, compete, fixture, match, record, spectator, stadium, tournament

2 🔑 [C] a particular form of sport（某项）体育运动：

What's your favourite sport? 你最喜欢哪一项体育运动？◇ ***team/water sports*** 集体项目；水上运动 ◇ *a sports club* 体育运动俱乐部 ➲ VISUAL VOCAB PAGES V47-52 ➲ SEE ALSO BLOOD SPORT, FIELD SPORTS, SPECTATOR SPORT, WINTER SPORTS **3** [C] (*AustralE, NZE, informal*) used as a friendly way of addressing sb, especially a man（用作友好称呼，尤指对男子）朋友，老兄，哥们儿：*Good on you, sport!* 老兄，你真行！**4** [U] (*formal*) enjoyment or fun 乐趣；消遣；玩笑；逗乐：*The comments were only made **in sport**.* 那些话只不过是开个玩笑。◇ ***to make sport of*** (= to joke about) ***sb/sth*** 开某人／某事的玩笑 **5** [C] (*biology* 生) a plant or an animal that is different in a noticeable way from its usual type 芽变；突变；变种

IDM **be a (good) 'sport** (*informal*) to be generous, cheerful and pleasant, especially in a difficult situation（尤指在困境中）开朗大度，讲交情：*She's a good sport.* 她很讲交情。◇ *Go on, be a sport* (= used when asking sb to help you). 来来来，别不够朋友。

■ ***verb*** **1** [T] **~ sth** to have or wear sth in a proud way 得意地穿戴；夸示；故意显示 SYN **wear**: *to sport a beard* 故意蓄着大胡子 ◇ *She was sporting a T-shirt with the company's logo on it.* 她穿了一件带有公司徽标的 T 恤衫，很是招摇。**2** [I] **+ adv./prep.** (*literary*) to play in a happy and lively way 开心活泼地玩；嬉戏

sport·ing /ˈspɔːtɪŋ; *NAmE* ˈspɔːrtɪŋ/ *adj.* **1** [only before noun] connected with sports 体育运动的：*a major sporting event* 一项重要的体育赛事 ◇ *a range of sporting activities* 一系列体育活动 ◇ *His main sporting interests are golf and tennis.* 他在体育方面主要爱好高尔夫球和网球。◇ (*NAmE*) *a store selling sporting goods* 经营体育用品的商店 **2** (*especially BrE*) fair and generous in your treatment of other people, especially in a game or sport 风格高的；有良好体育风尚的 OPP **unsporting** ▶ **sport·ing·ly** *adv.*: *He sportingly agreed to play the point again.* 他风格高，同意那一分重打。

IDM **a ˌsporting 'chance** a reasonable chance of success 比较有成功希望的机会

'sports car (*US also* **'sport car**) *noun* a low fast car, often with a roof that can be folded back 跑车（车身低，顶篷多可折叠）➲ VISUAL VOCAB PAGE V56

sports·cast /ˈspɔːtskɑːst; *NAmE* ˈspɔːrtskæst/ *noun* (*NAmE*) a television or radio broadcast of sports news or a sports event（电视台或广播电台的）体育节目

sports·cast·er /ˈspɔːtskɑːstə(r); *NAmE* ˈspɔːrtskæstər/ *noun* (*NAmE*) a person who introduces and presents a sportscast（电视台或广播电台的）体育节目播音员，体育比赛解说员

'sports centre (*especially US* **'sports center**) *noun* a building where the public can go to play many different kinds of sports, swim, etc. 体育中心（可进行多种体育活动）

'sports day (*BrE*) (*NAmE* **'field day**) *noun* a special day at school when there are no classes and children compete in sports events（学校的）运动会

'sports drink *noun* a type of cold drink that contains sugar and other ingredients that help restore energy during or after exercise 运动饮料

'sports jacket (*NAmE also* **'sport jacket**) *noun* a man's jacket for informal occasions, sometimes made of TWEED 男式便服外套；粗花呢夹克

sports·man /ˈspɔːtsmən; *NAmE* ˈspɔːrts-/, **sports·woman** /ˈspɔːtswʊmən; *NAmE* ˈspɔːrts-/ *noun* (*pl.* **-men** /-mən/, **-women** /-wɪmɪn/) (*especially BrE*) a person who plays a lot of sport, especially as a professional 运动员；体育运动爱好者；（尤指）职业运动员 SYN **athlete**: *a keen sportswoman* 热衷做体育运动的女子 ◇ *He is one of this country's top professional sportsmen.* 他是这个国家的顶级职业运动员。➲ NOTE AT GENDER ➲ MORE LIKE THIS 25, page R28

sports·man·like /ˈspɔːtsmənlaɪk; *NAmE* ˈspɔːrts-/ *adj.* behaving in a fair, generous and polite way, especially when playing a sport or game 有运动员风范的，有体育精神的（多指体育比赛中光明磊落、有气度）：*a sportsmanlike attitude* 光明磊落、互相敬重谦让的态度

sports·man·ship /ˈspɔːtsmənʃɪp; *NAmE* ˈspɔːrts-/ *noun* [U] fair, generous and polite behaviour, especially when playing a sport or game 运动员风范，体育精神（多指体育比赛中光明磊落、有气度）

sports·per·son /ˈspɔːtspɜːsn; *NAmE* ˈspɔːrtspɜːrsn/ *noun* (*pl.* **-persons** or **-people**) (*especially BrE*) a person who plays a lot of sport, especially as a professional 运动员；体育运动爱好者；（尤指）职业运动员 SYN **athlete** ➲ MORE LIKE THIS 25, page R28

'sports shirt (*NAmE also* **'sport shirt**) *noun* a man's shirt for informal occasions 男式运动衫

sports·wear /ˈspɔːtsweə(r); *NAmE* ˈspɔːrtswer/ *noun* [U] **1** (*especially BrE*) clothes that are worn for playing sports, or in informal situations 运动服装 **2** (*especially NAmE*) clothes that are worn in informal situations 便装

sports·woman *noun* (*pl.* **sports·women**) (*especially BrE*) ➲ SPORTSMAN

ˌsport u'tility vehicle *noun* (*abbr.* **SUV**) (*especially NAmE*) a type of large car, often with FOUR-WHEEL DRIVE and made originally for travelling over rough ground 运动型多功能车（四轮驱动、可在崎岖路段行驶）

sporty /ˈspɔːti; *NAmE* ˈspɔːrti/ *adj.* (**sport·ier**, **sporti·est**) (*informal*) **1** (*especially BrE*) liking or good at sport 爱好（或擅长）体育运动的：*I'm not very sporty.* 我不擅长体育运动。**2** (of clothes 衣服) bright, attractive and informal; looking suitable for wearing for sports 漂亮帅气的；适合运动时穿着的：*a sporty cotton top* 漂亮帅气的棉布上衣 **3** (of cars 汽车) fast and elegant 车型优美速度快的：*a sporty Mercedes* 一辆又快又靓的奔驰汽车

spot 🔑 /spɒt; *NAmE* spɑːt/ *noun, verb, adj.*

■ ***noun***

• SMALL MARK 斑点；点 **1** 🔑 a small round area that has a different colour or feels different from the surface it is on 斑点：*Which has spots, the leopard or the tiger?* 有斑点的是豹还是虎？◇ *The male bird has a red spot on its beak.* 雄鸟喙上有一个红点。◇ (*BrE*) *She was wearing a black skirt with white spots.* 她穿着一条黑底白点的裙子。➲ WORDFINDER NOTE AT PATTERN ➲ SEE ALSO BEAUTY SPOT (2), SUNSPOT ➲ SYNONYMS AT PATCH **2** 🔑 a small dirty mark on sth 污迹；污渍；脏点：*His jacket was covered with spots of mud.* 他的上衣满是泥点。◇ *rust spots* 锈斑 ➲ SYNONYMS AT MARK **3** 🔑 [usually pl.] a small mark or lump on a person's skin, sometimes with a yellow head to it（皮肤上的）丘疹，疱疹，粉刺；脓疱：*The baby's whole body was covered in small red spots.* 当时这孩子浑身布满小红疙瘩。◇ (*BrE*) *teenagers worried about their spots* 为长粉刺而烦恼的青少年 ➲ COMPARE PIMPLE, RASH *n.* (1), ZIT

• PLACE 地点 **4** 🔑 a particular area or place 地点；场所；处所：***a quiet/secluded/lonely, etc. spot*** 宁静、僻静、偏僻等的地方 ◇ *He showed me **the exact spot** where he had asked her to marry him.* 他把他当时向她求婚的确切地点指给我看。◇ *She stood **rooted to the spot** with fear* (= unable to move). 她吓得呆若木鸡地站在那里。◇ *a tourist spot* 旅游景点 ➲ SEE ALSO BLACK SPOT, BLIND SPOT, HOT SPOT, NIGHTSPOT, TROUBLE SPOT ➲ SYNONYMS AT PLACE

• SMALL AMOUNT 少量 **5** [usually sing.] **~ of sth** (*BrE, informal*) a small amount of sth 少量；一点 SYN **bit**: *He's in a spot of trouble.* 他遇到一点麻烦。**6** [usually pl.] **~ (of sth)** a small amount of a liquid 几滴，少许（液体）：*I felt a few spots of rain.* 我感觉掉雨点了。

• PART OF SHOW 一段节目 **7** a part of a television, radio, club or theatre show that is given to a particular entertainer or type of entertainment（电视、广播中或俱乐部、剧院演出中）某演员的固定节目，某类节目的固定栏目：*a **guest/solo spot*** 嘉宾节目；单人表演

• IN COMPETITION 竞赛 **8** a position in a competition or an event 排名位置：*two teams battling for top spot* 争夺冠军的两个队

• LIGHT 灯光 **9** (*informal*) = SPOTLIGHT (1)

IDM **in a (tight) 'spot** (*informal*) in a difficult situation 处于困境 **on the 'spot 1** immediately 当场；当下：*He*

S

answered the question on the spot. 他当场就回答了那个问题。◇ an on-the-spot parking fine 当场进行的违章停车罚款 **2** at the actual place where sth is happening 在现场：*An ambulance was on the spot within minutes.* 几分钟之内，一辆救护车便赶到现场。◇ *an on-the-spot report* 现场报道 **3** (*NAmE also* **in 'place**) in one exact place, without moving in any direction 在原地：*Running on the spot is good exercise.* 原地跑步是一种很好的锻炼。**put sb on the 'spot** to make sb feel awkward or embarrassed by asking them a difficult question（提出难题）使某人尴尬，使某人为难：*The interviewer's questions really put him on the spot.* 采访者的问题使他很下不来台。➲ MORE AT BRIGHT *adj.*, GLUE *v.*, HIT *v.*, KNOCK *v.*, LEOPARD, RIVET *v.*, SOFT, TIGHT *adj.*

■ ***verb*** (-tt-) **1** (not used in the progressive tenses 不用于进行时) to see or notice a person or thing, especially suddenly or when it is not easy to do so 看见；看出；注意到；发现：**~ sb/sth** *I finally spotted my friend in the crowd.* 我终于在人群中看见了我的朋友。◇ *I've just spotted a mistake on the front cover.* 我刚才在封面上发现了一处错误。◇ *Can you spot the difference between these two pictures?* 你能不能看出这两幅画有什么不同？◇ **~ sb/sth doing sth** *Neighbours spotted smoke coming out of the house.* 邻居们发现有烟从这所房子里冒出来。◇ **~ that…** *No one spotted that the gun was a fake.* 没有人留意到那是一支假枪。◇ **~ what, where, etc….** *I soon spotted what the mistake was.* 我很快就看出错误所在了。➲ SEE ALSO SPOTTER ➲ SYNONYMS AT SEE **2 ~ sb/sth sth** (*NAmE, sport* 体育) to give your opponent or the other team an advantage（对比赛对手）让分，让子，让步：*We spotted the opposing team two goals.* 我们让对手两个球。➲ MORE LIKE THIS 36, page R29

IDM **be spotted with sth** to be covered with small round marks of sth 满是…斑点：*His shirt was spotted with oil.* 他的衬衣上满是油点。

■ ***adj.*** [only before noun] (*business* 商) connected with a system of trading where goods are delivered and paid for immediately after sale 现货交易的；立即支付的：*spot prices* 现货价格

,spot 'check *noun* a check that is made suddenly and without warning on a few things or people chosen from a group to see that everything is as it should be 抽查；抽样检查：*to carry out random spot checks on vehicles* 对车辆进行随机抽检

'spot-fixing *noun* [U] (*BrE, sport* 体育) (especially in cricket) the act of deciding in a way that is not honest what the result of a particular part of a game will be before it is played（尤指板球运动）操纵比赛，比赛造假 ➲ COMPARE MATCH-FIXING

'spot kick *noun* (*BrE*) = PENALTY KICK

spot·less /'spɒtləs; *NAmE* 'spɑːt-/ *adj.* perfectly clean 极清洁的；非常洁净的 SYN **immaculate**：*a spotless white shirt* 洁白的衬衣 ◇ *She keeps the house spotless.* 她把家里收拾得一尘不染。◇ (*figurative*) *He has a spotless record so far.* 他的操行记录至今无任何污点。▸ **spot·less·ly** *adv.*：*spotlessly clean* 洁净得一尘不染

spot·light /'spɒtlaɪt; *NAmE* 'spɑːt-/ *noun, verb*

■ ***noun*** **1** (*also informal* **spot**) [C] a light with a single, very bright BEAM that can be directed at a particular place or person 聚光灯：*The room was lit by spotlights.* 房间被聚光灯照亮。➲ VISUAL VOCAB PAGE V22 **2 the spotlight** [U] the area of light that is made by a spotlight 聚光灯照亮的地方；聚光灯照明圈：*She stood alone on stage in the spotlight.* 她独自站在舞台的聚光灯下。**3 the spotlight** [U] attention from newspapers, television and the public 媒体和公众的注意：*Unemployment is once again **in the spotlight**.* 失业问题再次受到人们的关注。◇ *The issue will come **under the spotlight** when parliament reassembles.* 等议会重开的时候，这个问题将成为焦点。◇ *The report has **turned the spotlight on** the startling rise in street crime.* 这篇报道使人们将关注的目光投向街头犯罪激增的问题。

■ ***verb*** (**spot·lit**, **spot·lit** /-lɪt/) HELP Especially in sense 2, **spotlighted** is also used for the past tense and past participle. 第 2 义的过去式和过去分词也可用 spotlighted。**1 ~ sth** to shine a spotlight on sb/sth 用聚光灯照：*a spotlit stage* 聚光灯照亮的舞台 **2 ~ sth** to give special attention to a problem, situation, etc. so that people notice it 特别关注，突出报道（以使公众注意）SYN **highlight**：*The programme spotlights financial problems in the health service.* 节目突出报道了公共医疗机构的财政问题。

,spot 'on *adj.* [not before noun] (*BrE, informal*) exactly right 完全正确；对极了：*His assessment of the situation was spot on.* 他对形势的判断完全准确。

spot·ted /'spɒtɪd; *NAmE* 'spɑːt-/ (*also* **spotty**) *adj.* **1** (of cloth, etc. 织物等) having a regular pattern of round dots on it 有花点的：*a black and white spotted dress* 黑白点相间的连衣裙 **2** having marks on it, sometimes in a pattern 有斑点的：*a leopard's spotted coat* 豹的花斑皮毛

,spotted 'dick *noun* [U] (*BrE*) a hot DESSERT (= a sweet dish) like a SPONGE CAKE with dried fruit in it 葡萄干布丁

spot·ter /'spɒtə(r); *NAmE* 'spɑːt-/ *noun* **1** (especially in compounds 尤用于构成复合词) a person who looks for a particular type of thing or person, as a hobby or job 探子（爱好或专门搜寻物品或人才）：*a talent spotter* (= sb who visits clubs and theatres looking for new performers) 星探 ➲ SEE ALSO TRAINSPOTTER **2** (*also* **'spotter plane**) a plane used for finding out what an enemy is doing 侦察机

spotty /'spɒti; *NAmE* 'spɑːti/ *adj.* **1** (*BrE, usually disapproving*) (of a person 人) having a lot of spots on the skin 多丘疹的；多粉刺的 SYN **pimply**：*a spotty adolescent* 满脸粉刺的少年 ◇ *a spotty face* 布满丘疹的脸 **2** (*NAmE*) = PATCHY (2) **3** = SPOTTED：*a spotty dress* 带圆点的连衣裙

spouse /spaʊs; spaʊz/ *noun* (*formal* or *law* 律) a husband or wife 配偶 ▸ **spou·sal** /'spaʊzl; 'spaʊsl/ *adj.* [only before noun] (*formal*)：*spousal consent* 配偶的同意 ◇ *spousal abuse* 虐待配偶

spout /spaʊt/ *noun, verb*

■ ***noun*** **1** a pipe or tube on a container, that you can pour liquid out through（容器的）嘴：*the spout of a teapot* 茶壶嘴 ➲ VISUAL VOCAB PAGE V26 **2** a stream of liquid coming out of somewhere with great force（喷出的）水柱，液体柱 SYN **fountain**

IDM **be/go up the 'spout** (*BrE, slang*) to be/go wrong; to be spoilt or not working 弄错；搞糟；出问题；有毛病：*Well, that's my holiday plans gone up the spout!* 唉，我的休假计划全泡汤了！

■ ***verb*** **1** [T, I] to send out sth, especially a liquid, in a stream with great force; to come out of sth in this way 喷出；喷射 SYN **pour**：**~ sth (from sth)** *The wound was still spouting blood.* 伤口还在喷血。◇ **~ from/out of sth** *Clear water spouted from the fountains.* 清澈的水从喷泉中喷射出来。**2** [I] (of a WHALE 鲸) to send out a stream of water from a hole in its head 喷水 **3** [I, T] (*informal, disapproving*) to speak a lot about sth; to repeat sth in a boring or annoying way 滔滔不绝地说；喋喋不休地说：**~ (off/on) (about sth)** *He's always spouting off about being a vegetarian.* 他老把自己吃素挂在嘴边。◇ *What are you spouting on about now?* 你这会儿又在唠叨什么呢？◇ **~ sth** *He could spout poetry for hours.* 他聊起诗来一聊就是半天。◇ *She could do nothing but spout insults.* 她只会没完没了地骂人。

sprain /spreɪn/ *verb* **~ sth** to injure a joint in your body, especially your wrist or ankle, by suddenly twisting it 扭伤（关节）：*I stumbled and sprained my ankle.* 我摔了一跤，把脚脖子扭了。➲ COLLOCATIONS AT INJURY ➲ SYNONYMS AT INJURE ▸ **sprain** *noun*：*a bad ankle sprain* 踝关节严重扭伤

sprang PAST TENSE OF SPRING

sprat /spræt/ *noun* a very small European sea fish that is used for food 黍鲱（欧洲小海鱼，可食用）

sprawl /sprɔːl/ *verb, noun*

■ ***verb*** **1** [I] (+ adv./prep.) to sit or lie with your arms and legs spread out in a relaxed or awkward way 伸开四肢坐

（或躺）: *He was sprawling in an armchair in front of the TV.* 他伸开手脚坐在电视机前的一张扶手椅上。◇ *Something hit her and **sent her sprawling** to the ground.* 不知什么东西击中了她，把她打趴在地上。◇ *I tripped and **went sprawling**.* 我绊了一下，摔了个四脚朝天。 **2** [I] **+ adv./prep.** to spread in an untidy way; to cover a large area 蔓延；杂乱无序地拓展: *The town sprawled along the side of the lake.* 小镇顺着湖的边缘扩展。

■ ***noun*** **1** [C, usually sing., U] a large area covered with buildings that spreads from the city into the countryside in an ugly way（城市）杂乱无序拓展的地区: *attempts to control the fast-growing **urban sprawl*** 为控制城市过快过乱的拓展所作的努力 **2** [C, usually sing.] an act of spreading to cover a large area in an untidy way; sth that spreads like this 随意扩展；蔓延；蔓延物

sprawled /sprɔːld/ *adj.* sitting or lying with your arms and legs spread out in a lazy or awkward way 四肢摊开懒散地（或难看地）坐（或躺）着的: *He was lying sprawled in an armchair, watching TV.* 他四肢伸开正懒散地靠在扶手椅上看电视。

sprawl·ing /ˈsprɔːlɪŋ/ *adj.* [only before noun] spreading in an untidy way 蔓延的；杂乱无序拓展的: *a modern sprawling town* 一座杂乱无序拓展的现代城镇

spray 🔑 /spreɪ/ *noun, verb*

■ ***noun*** **1** 🔑 [U, C] very small drops of a liquid that are sent through the air, for example by the wind 浪花；水花；飞沫: *sea spray* 海上的浪花 ◇ *A cloud of fine spray came up from the waterfall.* 飞瀑溅起一片水雾。◇ (*figurative*) *a spray of machine-gun bullets* 一阵雨点般的机枪扫射 **2** 🔑 [U, C] (especially in compounds 尤用于构成复合词) a substance that is forced out of a container such as an AEROSOL, in very small drops 喷剂；喷雾的液体: *a can of insect spray* (= used to kill insects) 一罐喷雾杀虫剂 ◇ *body spray* 喷雾香水 ➲ **VISUAL VOCAB** PAGE V36 ➲ SEE ALSO HAIRSPRAY **3** 🔑 [C] a device or container, for example an AEROSOL, that you use to apply liquid in fine drops 喷雾器: *a throat spray* 喉头喷雾器 **4** [C] an act of applying liquid to sth in very small drops 喷雾；液体的喷洒: *I gave the plants a quick spray.* 我给这些花草略微喷了喷水。**5** [C] a small branch of a tree or plant, with its leaves and flowers or BERRIES, that you use for decoration（用作装饰的）小树枝，小花枝 SYN **sprig** **6** [C] an attractive arrangement of flowers or jewellery, that you wear（戴在身上的）一簇花，枝状饰物: *a spray of orchids* 一簇兰花

■ ***verb*** **1** 🔑 [T, I] to cover sb/sth with very small drops of a liquid that are forced out of a container or sent through the air 喷；喷洒；向…喷洒: **~ (sth) (on/onto/over sb/sth)** *Spray the conditioner onto your wet hair.* 往你的湿头发上喷些护发素。◇ *Champagne sprayed everywhere.* 香槟酒喷得到处都是。◇ **~ sb/sth (with sth)** *The crops are regularly sprayed with pesticide.* 庄稼定期喷洒杀虫剂。◇ **~ sth + adj.** *She's had the car sprayed blue.* 她让人把汽车喷成了蓝色。 **2** [T, I] to cover sb/sth with a lot of small things with a lot of force 向…扫射（或抛洒）；往…上撒: **~ sb/sth with sth** *The gunman sprayed the building with bullets.* 持枪歹徒向那座房子扫射。◇ **+ adv./prep.** *Pieces of glass sprayed all over the room.* 屋里到处落满了玻璃碎片。**3** [I] (especially of a male cat 尤指雄性猫科动物) to leave small amounts of URINE to mark its own area 撒尿（以示领地占有）

ˈspray can *noun* a small metal container that has paint in it under pressure and that you use to spray paint onto sth 喷雾罐；喷漆罐

spray·er /ˈspreɪə(r)/ *noun* a piece of equipment used for spraying liquid, especially paint or a substance used to kill insects that damage crops 喷漆器；喷雾器；喷枪: *a **paint/crop sprayer*** 喷漆器；农用喷雾器

ˈspray gun *noun* a device for spraying paint onto a surface, that works by air pressure 喷枪

ˈspray-on *adj.* [only before noun] (*especially BrE*) that you can spray onto sth/sb from a special container 喷雾式的；喷涂式的: *a spray-on water repellent for shoes* 鞋面防水喷雾

ˈspray paint *noun* [U] paint that is kept in a container under pressure and that you can spray onto sth 喷漆 ▶ **ˈspray-paint** *verb* **~ A (with B) | ~ B (on A)**

ˈspray tan *noun* an artificial SUNTAN, produced by spraying the skin with small drops of liquid containing special chemicals; the process of spraying the skin with this liquid 喷雾美黑；喷雾晒肤: *to get a spray tan* 将皮肤喷成古铜色 ▶ **ˈspray-tanned** *adj.* **ˈspray tanning** *noun* [U]

spread 🔑 /spred/ *verb, noun*

■ ***verb*** (**spread, spread**)

• **OPEN/ARRANGE** 展开；铺开 **1** 🔑 [T] **~ sth (out) (on/over sth)** to open sth that has been folded so that it covers a larger area than before 展开；打开: *to spread a cloth on a table* 在桌上铺桌布 ◇ *Sue spread the map out on the floor.* 休在地板上摊开地图。◇ *The bird spread its wings.* 鸟展开翅膀。**2** 🔑 [T] **~ sth (out) (on/over sth)** to arrange objects so that they cover a large area and can be seen easily 摊开；使散开: *Papers had been spread out on the desk.* 各种报纸摊在书桌上。**3** [T] to place the thumb and a finger of one hand on the screen of an electronic device such as a mobile/cell phone or small computer and move them apart to make the image on the screen larger, as though it is closer（在手机等电子装置的屏幕上）两指张开以放大图文: *Pinch and spread the text on screen to see a close-up.* 两指在屏幕上张开可以放大图文。 ➲ SEE ALSO PINCH *v.* (3)

• **ARMS/LEGS** 双臂；双腿 **4** 🔑 [T] **~ sth (out)** to move your arms, legs, fingers, etc. far apart from each other 张开；伸开: *She spread her arms and the child ran towards her.* 她张开双臂，孩子向她跑来。

• **AMONG PEOPLE** 在人们中间 **5** 🔑 [I, T] to affect or make sth affect, be known by, or be used by more and more people 传播；散布；（使）流传: (**+ adv./prep.**) *The disease spreads easily.* 这种疾病容易传播。◇ *Within weeks, his confidence had spread throughout the team.* 短短几个星期，他的信心感染了全体队员。◇ *Use of computers **spread rapidly** during that period.* 在那个时期，计算机的应用迅速普及开来。◇ **~ sth** *to **spread rumours/lies** about sb* 散布关于某人的谣言 / 谎言 ◇ *The disease is spread by mosquitoes.* 这种疾病通过蚊子传播。➲ **WORDFINDER NOTE** AT DISEASE

• **COVER LARGE AREA** 覆盖大面积 **6** 🔑 [I, T] to cover, or to make sth cover, a larger and larger area（使）蔓延，扩散，散开: (**+ adv./prep.**) *The fire rapidly spread to adjoining buildings.* 大火迅速蔓延到了邻近的建筑物。◇ *Water began to spread across the floor.* 水开始漫过地板。◇ *A smile spread slowly across her face.* 微笑慢慢在她脸上绽开。◇ **~ sth** *Using too much water could spread the stain.* 用水太多可能使污迹扩散。**7** 🔑 [T] **~ sb/sth** to cause sb/sth to be in a number of different places 使分散；使分布: *Seeds and pollen are spread by the wind.* 种子和花粉是随风传播的。◇ *We have 10 000 members spread all over the country.* 我们有 1 万名成员分布在全国各地。**8** [I] **~ (out) + adv./prep.** to cover a large area 延伸；伸展；扩张: *The valley spread out beneath us.* 山谷在我们下方延伸。

• **SOFT LAYER** 稀软的层面 **9** 🔑 [T, I] to put a layer of a substance onto the surface of sth; to be able to be put onto a surface 涂；敷: **~ (A on/over B)** *to spread butter on pieces of toast* 在烤面包片上抹黄油 ◇ **~ (B with A)** *pieces of toast spread with butter* 抹了黄油的烤面包片 ◇ *If the paint is too thick, it will not spread evenly.* 油漆如果太稠就涂不均匀。

• **DIVIDE/SHARE** 划分；分摊 **10** 🔑 [T] to separate sth into parts and divide them between different times or different people 分（若干次）进行；由（若干人）分摊: **~ sth** *Why not pay monthly and spread the cost of your car insurance?* 你为什么不把汽车保险费按月分期支付呢？◇ **~ sth (out) (over sth)** *A series of five interviews will be spread over two days.* 一共五次面谈，分两天进行。◇ **~ sth between sb/sth** *We attempted to spread the workload between the departments.* 我们试图把工作分摊给各部门。

IDM **spread like ˈwildfire** (of news, etc. 消息等) to become known by more and more people very quickly 像野火般蔓延；迅速传开 **spread your ˈnet** to consider a

S

wide range of possibilities or cover a large area, especially to try to find sb/sth 考虑到多种可能；大面积地排查；撒开网（寻找）：*They have spread their net far and wide in the search for a new team coach.* 他们撒开网四处物色新的球队教练。**spread your 'wings** to become more independent and confident and try new activities, etc. 展翅高飞（更自信地尝试新事物）**spread the 'word** to tell people about sth 散布消息 **spread yourself too 'thin** to try to do so many different things at the same time that you do not do any of them well 样样都抓，哪样都抓不好

PHR V **,spread 'out | ,spread yourself 'out 1** to stretch your body or arrange your things over a large area 伸展身体；摊开东西：*There's more room to spread out in first class.* 头等舱宽敞些，伸得开腿。◇ *Do you have to spread yourself out all over the sofa?* 你就非得躺下，把整个沙发全占了才行吗？ **2** to separate from other people in a group, to cover a larger area 散开：*The searchers spread out to cover the area faster.* 搜索人员分散开来，好更快地搜索这一地区。

■ ***noun***

• **INCREASE** 扩大 **1** [U] an increase in the amount or number of sth that there is, or in the area that is affected by sth 传播；散布；扩展；蔓延：*to prevent the spread of disease* 防止疾病的传播 ◇ *to encourage the spread of information* 促进信息的传播 ◇ *the spread of a city into the surrounding areas* 城市向周边地区的扩展 ➲ SEE ALSO MIDDLE-AGE SPREAD

• **RANGE/VARIETY** 广泛；多样 **2** [C, usually sing.] a range or variety of people or things 广泛；多样：*a **broad spread** of opinions* 各种各样的意见

• **ON BREAD** 面包 **3** [C, U] a soft food that you put on bread 抹在面包上的东西：*Use a low-fat spread instead of butter.* 不要抹黄油，抹点低脂肪的东西吧。◇ *cheese spread* 奶酪酱

• **AREA COVERED** 所占区域 **4** [C, usually sing.] ~ (**of sth**) the area that sth exists in or happens in 涉及区域；活动范围：*The company has a good geographical spread of hotels in this country.* 该公司在这个国家开设的饭店地理分布相当广。**5** [C, usually sing.] ~ (**of sth**) how wide sth is or the area that sth covers 宽度；面积；翼展：*The bird's wings have a spread of nearly a metre.* 这只鸟翼展近一米。

• **IN NEWSPAPER/MAGAZINE** 报刊 **6** [C] an article or advertisement in a newspaper or magazine, especially one that covers two opposite pages（尤指横贯两版的）文章，广告：*The story continued with **a double-page spread** on the inside pages.* 这篇报道在报纸的内页有横贯两版的后续部分。➲ SEE ALSO CENTRE SPREAD

• **MEAL** 餐食 **7** [C] (*informal*) a large meal, especially one that is prepared for a special occasion 丰盛的餐食：*They had laid on a huge spread for the party.* 他们为聚会安排了丰盛的食物。

• **OF LAND/WATER** 陆地；水域 **8** [C, usually sing.] ~ (**of sth**) (*NAmE*) an area of land or water 区域；一大片：*a vast spread of water* 浩瀚的水域 ◇ *They have a huge spread in California* (= a large farm or RANCH). 他们在加利福尼亚拥有大片的土地。

• **FINANCE** 金融 **9** [U] the difference between two rates or prices（两种价格或比率的）差额，差幅

• **ON BED** 床 **10** [C] (*NAmE*) = BEDSPREAD

,spread 'betting *noun* [U] a type of betting in which you bet money on whether you think the predicted outcome is too high or too low. The amount of money you win or lose depends on the extent to which you are right or wrong. 指数博彩，差额投注（判断预测的结果过高还是过低的博彩，输赢金额依判断的准确度而定）▸ **,spread 'bet** *noun*

spread·eagled /ˌspredˈiːɡld/ (*especially BrE*) (*NAmE usually* **spread·eagle**) *adj.* [not usually before noun] in a position with your arms and legs spread out 四肢摊开 ▸ **spread-eagle** *verb* ~ **sb**

spread·er /ˈspredə(r)/ *noun* a device or machine that spreads things 涂抹用具；涂抹器；散布机：*a muck spreader* 粪肥散布机

spread·sheet /ˈspredʃiːt/ *noun* a computer program that is used, for example, when doing financial or project planning. You enter data in rows and columns and the program calculates costs, etc. from it. The individual documents are also called spreadsheets.（计算机）电子表格程序，电子表格 ➲ WORDFINDER NOTE AT SOFTWARE

Sprech·ge·sang /ˈʃprexɡəzæŋ/ *noun* [U] (*music* 音, *from German*) a style of singing which is between speaking and singing 朗诵唱（介乎说话和歌唱之间的唱法）

spree /spriː/ *noun* **1** a short period of time that you spend doing one particular activity that you enjoy, but often too much of it（常指过分）玩乐，作乐；纵乐：*a **shopping/spending spree*** 疯狂购物；大肆花钱 ◇ *He's out on a spree.* 他到外面潇洒去了。**2** (used especially in newspapers 尤用于报章) a period of activity, especially criminal activity 一阵，一通（犯罪活动）：*to go on a killing spree* 一阵杀戮

sprig /sprɪɡ/ *noun* a small STEM with leaves on it from a plant or bush, used in cooking or as a decoration（烹饪或装饰用）带叶小枝：*a sprig of parsley/holly/heather* 一小枝欧芹 / 冬青 / 帚石楠

spright·ly /ˈspraɪtli/ (*also less frequent* **spry**) *adj.* (especially of older people 尤指年长者) full of life and energy 精力充沛的；精神矍铄的 SYN **lively**：*a sprightly 80-year-old* 精神矍铄的 80 岁老人 ➲ WORDFINDER NOTE AT OLD ▸ **spright·li·ness** *noun* [U]

spring 弹簧

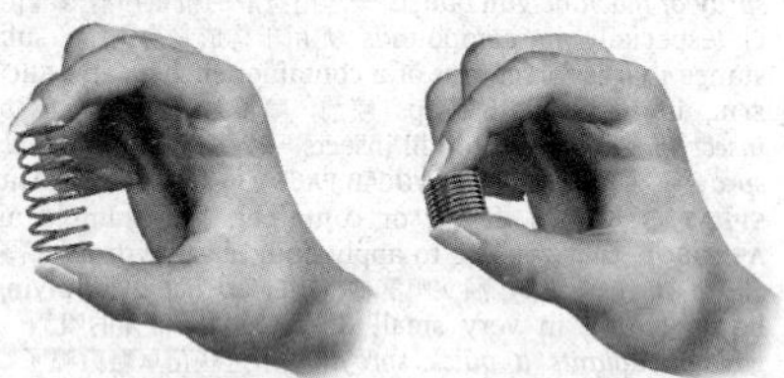

spring /sprɪŋ/ *noun, verb*

■ ***noun***

• **SEASON** 季节 **1** [U, C] the season between winter and summer when plants begin to grow 春天；春季：*flowers that bloom **in spring/in the spring*** 春天开的花 ◇ *He was born in the spring of 1944.* 他生于 1944 年春。◇ *There's a feeling of spring in the air today.* 今天可以感到一点春天的气息。◇ *spring flowers* 春天的花

• **TWISTED WIRE** 弹簧 **2** [C] a twisted piece of metal that can be pushed, pressed or pulled but which always returns to its original shape or position afterwards 弹簧；发条：*bed springs* 床垫弹簧 **3** [U] the ability of a spring to return to its original position 弹性；弹力：*The mattress has lost its spring.* 那个床垫失去弹性了。

• **WATER** 水 **4** [C] a place where water comes naturally to the surface from under the ground 泉：*a mountain spring* 山泉 ◇ *spring water* 泉水

• **CHEERFUL QUALITY** 活力 **5** [U, sing.] a cheerful, lively quality 活力；朝气：*She walked along **with a spring in her step.*** 她迈着轻快的步伐向前走去。

• **SUDDEN JUMP** 跳跃 **6** [C] a quick sudden jump upwards or forwards 跳；跃：*With a spring, the cat leapt on to the table.* 猫一跃跳上桌子。IDM SEE JOY

■ ***verb*** (**sprang** /spræŋ/, **sprung** /sprʌŋ/) (*NAmE also* **sprung, sprung**)

• **JUMP/MOVE SUDDENLY** 跳跃 **1** [I] (+ **adv./prep.**) (of a person or an animal 人或动物) to move suddenly and with one quick movement in a particular direction 跳；跃；蹦 SYN **leap**：*He turned off the alarm and sprang out of bed.* 他关上闹钟，从床上跳了下来。◇ *Everyone **sprang to their feet*** (= stood up suddenly) *when the principal walked in.* 校长进来时，所有的人都立刻站了起来。◇ *The cat crouched ready to spring.* 那猫弓起背准备跳。◇ (*figurative*) *to **spring to sb's defence/assistance*** (= to quickly defend or help sb) 连忙站出来保护 / 帮助某人 **2** [I] (of an object 物体) to move suddenly and violently 突然猛烈地移动：**+ adv./prep.** *The branch sprang back and hit him in the face.* 树枝弹回来打在他脸上。◇ **+ adj.** *She turned the key and the lid sprang open.* 她一拧钥匙，盖子啪地打开了。

- **SURPRISE** 使吃惊 **3** [T] to do sth, ask sth or say sth that sb is not expecting 突如其来地做；冷不防地问；突然说：**~ sth** *She sprang a surprise by winning the tournament.* 这次比赛她获得冠军，爆了个大冷门。◇ **~ sth on sb** *I'm sorry to **spring it on you**, but I've been offered another job.* 我很抱歉这样突然告诉您，我另有工作了。
- **APPEAR SUDDENLY** 突然出现 **4** [I] **+ adv./prep.** to appear or come somewhere suddenly 突然出现（或来到）：*Tears sprang to her eyes.* 她眼里一下子涌出了泪水。
- **FREE PRISONER** 救出被拘禁者 **5** [T] **~ sb** (*informal*) to help a prisoner to escape 帮助…逃跑（或越狱）；营救：*Plans to spring the hostages have failed.* 营救人质的计划失败了。

IDM **ˌspring into ˈaction | ˌspring into/to ˈlife** (of a person, machine, etc. 人、机器等) to suddenly start working or doing sth 突然工作（或行动）起来：*'Let's go!' he said, springing into action.* 他突然行动起来，说道："咱们走！"◇ *The town springs into life (= becomes busy) during the carnival.* 狂欢节期间，全城突然热闹起来。**spring a ˈleak** (of a boat or container 船舶或容器) to develop a hole through which water or another liquid can pass 出现裂缝；开裂漏水 **spring a ˈtrap 1** to make a trap for catching animals close suddenly 使捕兽器突然合上 **2** to try to trick sb into doing or saying sth; to succeed in this 设套诱使某人做（或说）➲ MORE AT HOPE *n.*, MIND *n.*

PHR V **ˈspring for sth** (*NAmE, informal*) to pay for sth for sb else（替别人）付…的账：*I'll spring for the drinks tonight.* 今晚的饮料我来付账。**ˈspring from sth** (*formal*) to be caused by sth; to start from sth 由某事物造成；起源于（或来自）某事物：*The idea for the novel sprang from a trip to India.* 写这部小说的想法源于一次去印度的旅行。**ˈspring from…** (*informal*) to appear suddenly and unexpectedly from a particular place 突如其来地从（某处）出现：*Where on earth did you spring from?* 你究竟是从哪儿冒出来的？**ˌspring ˈup** to appear or develop quickly and/or suddenly 迅速出现；突然兴起

spring·board /ˈsprɪŋbɔːd; *NAmE* -bɔːrd/ *noun* **1** a strong board that you jump on and use to help you jump high in DIVING and GYMNASTICS（跳水或体操中的）跳板 **2 ~ (for/to sth)** something that helps you start an activity, especially by giving you ideas（有助于开展某事的）基础，出发点：*The document provided a springboard for a lot of useful discussion.* 这份文件引发了许多有益的讨论。▶ **spring·board** *verb* [I, T]: **~ (sth) (into sth)** *The company expects that this strategic move would allow it to springboard into the US market.* 公司希望这次战略行动会成为公司进入美国市场的跳板。

spring·bok /ˈsprɪŋbɒk; *NAmE* -bɑːk/ *noun* **1** [C] a small ANTELOPE from southern Africa that can jump high into the air 跳羚（产于非洲南部，个头儿小，能跳得很高） **2 Springboks** [pl.] the name of the South African national RUGBY team 跳羚队（南非国家橄榄球队）

ˌspring ˈchicken *noun*

IDM **be no ˌspring ˈchicken** (*humorous*) to be no longer young 老大不小；不再年轻

ˌspring-ˈclean *verb* [T, I] **~ (sth)** to clean a house, room, etc. thoroughly, including the parts you do not usually clean 彻底打扫（房屋等）：*Fran decided to spring-clean the apartment.* 弗朗决定把房间彻底打扫一下。▶ **ˌspring ˈclean** *noun* [sing.] (*BrE*): *The place needed a good spring clean before we could move in.* 那地方得来个大扫除，然后我们才能搬进去。

ˌspring ˈgreens *noun* [pl.] leaves of young CABBAGE plants of certain types 嫩卷心菜叶

ˌspring-ˈloaded *adj.* containing a metal spring that presses one part against another 弹簧承载的；弹顶的

ˌspring ˈonion (*BrE*) (*NAmE* **ˌgreen ˈonion, scal·lion**) *noun* a type of small onion with a long green STEM and leaves. Spring onions are often eaten raw in salads. 小葱；香葱 ➲ VISUAL VOCAB PAGE V33

ˌspring ˈroll (*especially BrE*) *noun* a type of Chinese food consisting of a tube of thin PASTRY, filled with vegetables and/or meat and fried until it is crisp 春卷 ➲ SEE ALSO EGG ROLL

ˌspring ˈtide *noun* a TIDE in which there is a very great rise and fall of the sea, and which happens near the new moon and the full moon each month 大潮，朔望潮（在每个月的新月和满月期间发生）

spring·time /ˈsprɪŋtaɪm/ *noun* [U] the season of spring 春季；春天；春令：*a visit to Holland **in springtime/in the springtime*** 春季游览荷兰

springy /ˈsprɪŋi/ (**spring·ier, springi·est**) *adj.* **1** returning quickly to the original shape after being pushed, pulled, stretched, etc. 有弹性（或弹力）的：*We walked across the springy grass.* 我们走过松软的草地。**2** full of energy and confidence 矫健的；有活力的：*She's 73, but hasn't lost that youthful, springy step.* 她 73 岁了，但走起路来依旧矫健轻捷。

sprin·kle /ˈsprɪŋkl/ *verb, noun*

■ ***verb*** **1** [T] to shake small pieces of sth or drops of a liquid on sth 撒；洒；把…撒（或洒）在…上：**~ A on/onto/over B** *Sprinkle chocolate on top of the cake.* 给蛋糕洒上巧克力。◇ *She sprinkled sugar over the strawberries.* 她在草莓上撒了点糖。◇ **~ B with A** *She sprinkled the strawberries with sugar.* 她在草莓上撒了点糖。**2** [T, usually passive] **~ sth with sth** to include a few of sth in sth else 使某物包含少量的另一物；用…点缀 **SYN** **strew**：*His poems are sprinkled with quotations from ancient Greek.* 他的诗歌不时穿插有古希腊引文。**3** [I] (*NAmE*) if **it sprinkles**, it rains lightly 下小雨 **SYN** **drizzle**：*It's only sprinkling. We can still go out.* 雨不大，我们还可以出去。

■ ***noun*** [sing.] **1** = SPRINKLING：*Add a sprinkle of cheese and serve.* 再撒点奶酪，然后端上桌。**2** (*especially NAmE*) light rain 小雨：*We've only had a few sprinkles (of rain) recently.* 近来我们这里只下过几场小雨。

sprink·ler /ˈsprɪŋklə(r)/ *noun* **1** a device with holes in that is used to spray water in drops on plants, soil or grass 喷洒器；喷头 ➲ VISUAL VOCAB PAGE V20 **2** a device inside a building which automatically sprays out water if there is a rise in temperature because of a fire（建筑物内的）喷洒装置，消防喷淋，自动喷水灭火装置

sprin·kles /ˈsprɪŋklz/ *noun* (*NAmE*) (*BrE* **ˌhundreds and ˈthousands**) [pl.] extremely small pieces of coloured sugar, used to decorate cakes, etc.（装饰糕点等用的）着色珠子糖，糖屑

sprink·ling /ˈsprɪŋklɪŋ/ (*also* **sprin·kle**) *noun* a small amount of a substance that is dropped somewhere, or a number of things or people that are spread or included somewhere 少量（落、撒或包含的某种物质）；少数（分散在或包括在某处的人）：*Add a sprinkling of pepper.* 加一点胡椒粉。◇ *Most were men, but there was also a sprinkling of young women.* 多数是男人，不过也有为数不多的年轻妇女。

sprint /sprɪnt/ *verb, noun*

■ ***verb*** [I, T] to run or swim a short distance very fast 短距离快速奔跑（或游泳）；冲刺：**+ adv./prep.** *He sprinted for the line.* 他向终点线冲去。◇ *Three runners sprinted past.* 三名运动员飞跑了过去。◇ *She jumped out of the car and sprinted for the front door.* 她跳下车，朝前门跑去。◇ **~ sth** *I sprinted the last few metres.* 我全速跑完最后几米。

■ ***noun*** **1** a race in which the people taking part run, swim, etc. very fast over a short distance 短跑比赛；短距离速度竞赛：*a 100-metre sprint* * 100 米短跑 ◇ *the world sprint champion* 短跑世界冠军 ➲ VISUAL VOCAB PAGE V50 **2** [usually sing.] a short period of running, swimming, etc. very fast 短距离快速奔跑（或游泳等）；冲刺：*a sprint for the line* 向终点线的冲刺 ◇ *a sprint for the bus* 冲向公共汽车 ◇ *She won in a sprint finish.* 她在最后的冲刺中取得胜利。

▶ **sprint·er** *noun*

sprite /spraɪt/ *noun* (in stories) a small creature with magic powers, especially one that likes playing tricks（传说中的）小仙子，小精灵，小妖精

spritz /sprɪts/ *verb* **~ sth** to spray very small drops of liquid on sth quickly 喷：*Lightly spritz your hair with water.* 往你头发上稍微喷点水。▶ **spritz** *noun*

spritz·er /ˈsprɪtsə(r)/ *noun* a drink made with wine (usually white) mixed with either SODA WATER or SPARKLING mineral water (= with bubbles in it) 汽酒：*a white wine spritzer* 一杯白葡萄汽酒

sprocket wheel 链轮

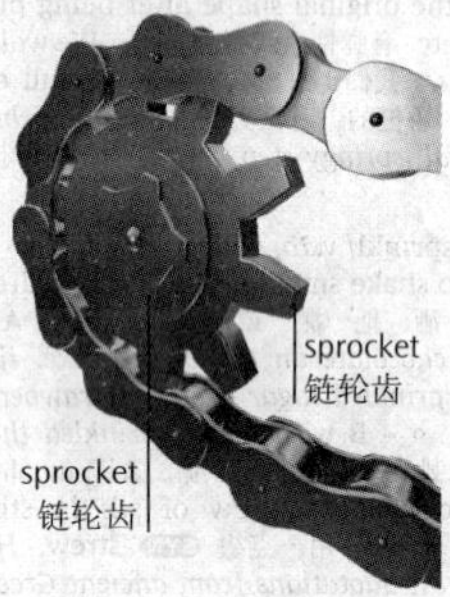

sprocket /ˈsprɒkɪt; *NAmE* ˈsprɑːkɪt/ *noun* **1** (*also* **ˈsprocket wheel**) a wheel with a row of teeth around the edge that connect with the holes of a bicycle chain or with holes in a film, etc. in order to turn it 链轮；输片齿轮 **2** one of the teeth on such a wheel 链轮齿；链齿

sprog /sprɒg; *NAmE* sprɑːg/ *noun* (*BrE, informal, humorous*) a child or baby 小孩；婴儿

sprout /spraʊt/ *verb, noun*

■ *verb* **1** [I] (of plants or seeds 植物或种子) to produce new leaves or BUDS; to start to grow 发芽；抽芽；抽条；生长：*new leaves sprouting from the trees* 树上长出的新叶 ◇ *The seeds will sprout in a few days.* 这些种子几天后就会发芽。**2** [I, T] to appear; to develop sth, especially in large numbers 出现；（使）涌现出：*Hundreds of mushrooms had sprouted up overnight.* 一夜之间长出来好几百朵蘑菇。◇ **~ sth** *The town has sprouted shopping malls, discos and nightclubs in recent years.* 最近几年，城里涌现出不少购物中心、迪斯科舞厅和夜总会。**3** [T, I] to start to grow sth; to start to grow on sb/sth 长出（某物）；（某物）长出：**~ sth** *Tim has sprouted a beard since we last saw him.* 我们上次见到蒂姆以后，蒂姆长出了胡子。◇ **~ from sth** *Hair sprouted from his chest.* 他胸前长出了毛。

■ *noun* **1** = BRUSSELS SPROUT **2** a new part growing on a plant 苗；新芽；嫩枝

spruce /spruːs/ *noun, verb, adj.*

■ *noun* **1** [C, U] an EVERGREEN forest tree with leaves like needles 云杉 **2** [U] the soft wood of the spruce, used, for example, in making paper 云杉木

■ *verb*

PHR V **ˌspruce ˈup** | **ˌspruce sb/sth/yourself↔ˈup** to make sb/sth/yourself clean and neat 打扮；把…收拾整洁：*She spruced up for the interview.* 她为参加面试打扮了一番。◇ *The city is sprucing up its museums and galleries.* 这座城市正在美化自己的博物馆和美术馆。

■ *adj.* (of people or places 人或处所) neat and clean in appearance 整洁的

spruit /spreɪt/ *noun* (*SAfrE*) a stream, sometimes one that only flows when there has been a lot of rain（只在雨季有水的）小河道，小溪

sprung /sprʌŋ/ *adj.* fitted with metal springs 装有弹簧的；弹簧支撑的：*a sprung mattress* 弹簧床垫 ➲ SEE ALSO SPRING *v.*

spry /spraɪ/ *adj.* = SPRIGHTLY

spud /spʌd/ *noun* (*especially BrE, informal*) a potato 土豆

spume /spjuːm/ *noun* [U] (*literary*) the mass of white bubbles that forms in waves when the sea is rough（海浪的）泡沫 SYN **foam**

spun PAST PART. OF SPIN

spunk /spʌŋk/ *noun* **1** [U] (*informal*) courage; determination 勇气；胆量；决心 **2** [U] (*BrE, taboo, slang*) = SEMEN **3** [C] (*informal, AustralE, informal*) a sexually attractive person 性感的人

spunky /ˈspʌŋki/ *adj.* (*informal*) **1** brave and determined; full of enthusiasm 勇敢坚定的；劲头十足的：*She is bright, tough and spunky.* 她聪明、顽强而且干劲十足。**2** (*AustralE, informal*) sexually attractive 性感的：*a top babe with a spunky boyfriend* 有个性感男友的绝色女子

spur /spɜː(r); *NAmE* spɜːr/ *noun, verb*

■ *noun* **1** a sharp pointed object that riders sometimes wear on the heels of their boots and use to encourage their horse to go faster 马刺；靴刺 **2** [usually sing.] **~ (to sth)** a fact or an event that makes you want to do sth better or more quickly 鞭策；激励；刺激；鼓舞 SYN **motivation**：*His speech was a powerful spur to action.* 他的讲话很有鼓动力。**3** an area of high ground that sticks out from a mountain or hill 山嘴；尖坡；支脉 **4** a road or a railway/railroad track that leads from the main road or line（公路或铁路的）支线，岔线

IDM **on the ˌspur of the ˈmoment** suddenly, without planning in advance 一时冲动之下；心血来潮：*I phoned him up on the spur of the moment.* 我一时冲动，给他打了电话。◇ *a spur-of-the-moment decision* 心血来潮的决定 **win/earn your ˈspurs** (*formal*) to achieve fame or success 获得名望；取得成功

■ *verb* (**-rr-**) **1** to encourage sb to do sth or to encourage them to try harder to achieve sth 鞭策；激励；刺激；鼓舞：**~ sb/sth (on) to sth/to do sth** *Her difficult childhood spurred her on to succeed.* 她艰辛的童年激励她取得成功。◇ **~ sb/sth into sth** *I was spurred into action by the letter.* 那封信激励我行动起来。◇ **~ sb/sth (on)** *The band has been spurred on by the success of their last single.* 最近一张单曲唱片的成功使乐队受到鼓舞。**2 ~ sth** to make sth happen faster or sooner 促进，加速，刺激（某事发生）：*The agreement is essential to spurring economic growth around the world.* 这项协议对于促进世界经济的增长是至关重要的。**3 ~ sth** to encourage a horse to go faster, especially by pushing the spurs on your boots into its side 策（马）前进；（尤指用马刺）策（马）加速

spuri·ous /ˈspjʊəriəs; *NAmE* ˈspjʊr-/ *adj.* **1** false, although seeming to be genuine 虚假的；伪造的：*He had managed to create the entirely spurious impression that the company was thriving.* 他设法制造出一种彻头彻尾的假象，让人误以为公司一派兴旺。**2** based on false ideas or ways of thinking 建立在错误的观念（或思想方法）之上的；谬误的：*a spurious argument* 谬误的论据 ▶ **spuri·ous·ly** *adv.*

spurn /spɜːn; *NAmE* spɜːrn/ *verb* **~ sb/sth** to reject or refuse sb/sth, especially in a proud way（尤指傲慢地）拒绝 SYN **shun**：*Eve spurned Mark's invitation.* 伊夫一口回绝了马克的邀请。◇ *a spurned lover* 遭到轻蔑拒绝的痴心爱慕者

spurt /spɜːt; *NAmE* spɜːrt/ *verb, noun*

■ *verb* **1** [I, T] (of liquid or flames 液体或火焰) to burst or pour out suddenly; to produce sudden, powerful streams of liquid or flames 喷出；冒出：**~ (from sth)** *Blood was spurting from her nose.* 血从她鼻子里汩汩流出来。◇ **~ out (of/from sth)** *Red and yellow flames spurted out of the fire.* 炉火吐出红色黄色的火焰。◇ **~ sth** *Her nose was spurting blood.* 她鼻子汩汩冒着血。◇ **~ sth + adv./prep.** *The volcano spurted clouds of steam and ash high into the air.* 火山把团团热气和灰尘喷向高空。**2** [I] **+ adv./prep.** to increase your speed for a short time to get somewhere faster（短暂地）加速前进；冲刺：*She spurted past me to get to the line first.* 她冲刺超过我，率先抵达终点线。

■ ***noun*** **1** an amount of liquid or flames that comes out of somewhere with great force 涌出的液体；喷出的火舌：*a great spurt of blood* 一大股急速喷出的血 **2** a sudden increase in speed, effort, activity or emotion for a short period of time（速度、干劲、活动或感情的）短时间激增，迸发：*You'd better* ***put on a spurt*** (= hurry up) *if you want to finish that work today.* 你要是想今天完成那项工作，最好狠加一把劲。◇ *Babies get very hungry during growth spurts.* 婴儿在猛长期会很饿。◇ *a sudden spurt of anger* 突然发作的怒火

IDM **in 'spurts** in short periods of great activity, powerful movement, etc., rather than in a steady, continuous way 一阵阵地；一股股地：*The water came out of the tap in spurts.* 水急速地从水龙头里喷出来。

sput·nik /'spʌtnɪk; 'spʊt-/ *noun* (*from Russian*) a SATELLITE of the type that was put into space by the Soviet Union（苏联）人造地球卫星，人造卫星

sput·ter /'spʌtə(r)/ *verb* **1** [I] if an engine, a lamp or a fire **sputters**, it makes a series of short EXPLOSIVE sounds（引擎、灯或火）发出噼啪声 SYN **splutter**：*sputtering fireworks* 噼啪作响的烟火 **2** [T] **+ speech** | **~ sth** to speak quickly and with difficulty, making soft SPITTING sounds, because you are angry or shocked 气急败坏地说；急促而语无伦次地说 SYN **splutter**：*'W-What?' sputtered Anna.* "什…什么？" 安娜气急败坏地说。

spu·tum /'spju:təm/ *noun* [U] (*medical* 医) liquid from the throat or lungs, especially when it is coughed up because of disease（尤指因疾病而咳出的）痰：*blood in the sputum* 痰中的血丝

spy /spaɪ/ *noun, verb*

■ ***noun*** (*pl.* **spies**) a person who tries to get secret information about another country, organization or person, especially sb who is employed by a government or the police 间谍；密探：*He was denounced as a foreign spy.* 有人告发他是外国间谍。◇ *a police spy* 警方密探 ◇ *a* ***spy plane/satellite*** (= used to watch the activities of the enemy) 间谍飞机 / 卫星 ◇ *Video spy cameras are being used in public places.* 隐蔽的摄像机在监视着公共场所。

■ ***verb*** (**spies**, **spy·ing**, **spied**, **spied**) **1** [I] to collect secret information about another country, organization or person 从事间谍活动；搜集情报：*He spied for his government for more than ten years.* 他做过十多年的政府间谍。**2** [T] **~ sb/sth** (*literary* or *formal*) to suddenly see or notice sb/sth 突然看见；发现：*In the distance we spied the Pacific for the first time.* 在远处，我们突然第一次看到了太平洋。

IDM **ˌspy out the 'land** to collect information before deciding what to do（事先）摸清情况，窥察虚实

PHR V **'spy on sb/sth** to watch sb/sth secretly 暗中监视，窥探（某人或事物）：*Have you been spying on me?* 你是不是一直在暗中监视我？ **ˌspy sth↔'out** to get information about sth 查明，了解清楚（某事）

spy·glass /'spaɪglɑ:s; *NAmE* -glæs/ *noun* a small TELESCOPE 小型望远镜

spy·hole /'spaɪhəʊl; *NAmE* -hoʊl/ *noun* a small hole in a door that you can look through to see who is on the other side before opening the door（门上的）观察孔，猫眼儿

spy·mas·ter /'spaɪmɑ:stə(r); *NAmE* -mæs-/ *noun* a person who controls a group of spies 间谍组织的首脑；间谍头子

spy·ware /'spaɪweə(r); *NAmE* -wer/ *noun* [U] software that enables sb to obtain secret information about sb else and their computer activities without their knowledge or permission 间谍软件（可窃取他人秘密及其计算机活动情况）：*Hackers can install spyware to get all your passwords.* 黑客可以安装间谍软件来获取你的所有密码。➲ SEE ALSO MALWARE

Sq. *abbr.* (used in written addresses) SQUARE（书写地址时用）广场：*6 Hanover Sq.* 汉诺威广场 6 号

sq (*also* **sq.** *especially in NAmE*) *abbr.* (in measurements) square 平方（用于度量）：*10 sq cm* * 10 平方厘米

SQC /ˌes kju: 'si:/ *abbr.* Scottish Qualifications Certificate (a record of all the courses and exams taken by students in Scotland in different subjects and at various levels, between the ages of approximately 15 and 19) 苏格兰资格证书（苏格兰约 15 到 19 岁的学生参加过的各个科目、各个等级考试的成绩记录）➲ SEE ALSO HIGHER, NQ

squab·ble /'skwɒbl; *NAmE* 'skwɑ:bl/ *verb* [I] **~ (with sb) (about/over sth)** to argue noisily about sth that is not very important（为小事）争吵，发生口角 SYN **bicker**：*My sisters were squabbling over what to watch on TV.* 我的姐妹正为看哪个电视节目争吵。▶ **squab·ble** *noun*：*family squabbles* 家庭内部的争吵 ◇ *There were endless squabbles over who should sit where.* 为谁该坐哪儿吵个没完没了。

squad /skwɒd; *NAmE* skwɑ:d/ *noun* [C+sing./pl. v.] **1** a section of a police force that deals with a particular type of crime（对付某类犯罪活动的）警察队伍：*the* ***drugs/fraud, etc. squad*** 缉毒队、反欺诈小组等 ➲ SEE ALSO FLYING SQUAD **2** (in sport 体育运动) a group of players, runners, etc. from which a team is chosen for a particular game or match 运动（代表）队：*the* ***Olympic/national squad*** 奥林匹克代表队；国家队 ◇ *They still have not named their squad for the World Cup qualifier.* 他们尚未确定参加世界杯预选赛的运动员名单。 **3** a small group of soldiers working or being trained together（军队的）班 ➲ SEE ALSO FIRING SQUAD **4** a group of people who have a particular task（特殊任务）小组，队 ➲ SEE ALSO DEATH SQUAD, HIT SQUAD

'squad car *noun* a police car 警车

squad·die /'skwɒdi; *NAmE* 'skwɑ:di/ *noun* (*BrE, slang*) a new soldier; a soldier of low rank 新兵蛋子；列兵

squad·ron /'skwɒdrən; *NAmE* 'skwɑ:d-/ *noun* [C+sing./pl. v.] a group of military aircraft or ships forming a section of a military force（空军或海军的）中队：*a* ***bomber/fighter squadron*** 轰炸机 / 战斗机中队

'squadron leader *noun* an officer of high rank in the British AIR FORCE（英国的）空军中队长，空军少校

squalid /'skwɒlɪd; *NAmE* 'skwɑ:lɪd/ *adj.* (*disapproving*) **1** (of places and living conditions 处所及生活环境) very dirty and unpleasant 肮脏的；邋遢的 SYN **filthy**：*squalid housing* 肮脏的房屋 ◇ *squalid, overcrowded refugee camps* 肮脏而拥挤的难民营 **2** (of situations or activities 情况或活动) involving low moral standards or dishonest behaviour 道德败坏的；丑恶的；卑鄙的 SYN **sordid**：*It was a squalid affair involving prostitutes and drugs.* 那是一桩涉及娼妓与毒品的丑事。

squall /skwɔ:l/ *noun, verb*

■ ***noun*** a sudden strong and violent wind, often with rain or snow during a storm 飑（常指暴风雨或暴风雪中突起的狂风）➲ WORDFINDER NOTE AT RAIN

■ ***verb*** [I] (usually used in the progressive tenses 通常用于进行时) (*disapproving*) to cry very loudly and noisily 大声啼哭；号哭：*squalling kids* 大声啼哭的孩子

squally /'skwɔ:li/ *adj.* (of weather 天气) involving sudden, violent and strong winds 有狂风的；刮飑的：*squally showers* 狂风阵雨

squalor /'skwɒlə(r); *NAmE* 'skwɑ:l-/ *noun* [U] dirty and unpleasant conditions 肮脏；邋遢：*the poverty and squalor of the slums* 贫民窟的贫穷和肮脏 ◇ *He had lost his job and was living* ***in squalor****.* 他丢了工作，过得很糟糕。

squan·der /'skwɒndə(r); *NAmE* 'skwɑ:n-/ *verb* **~ sth (on sb/sth)** to waste money, time, etc. in a stupid or careless way 浪费，挥霍（金钱、时间等）：*He squandered all his money on gambling.* 他把自己所有的钱都挥霍在赌博上了。

square 🔑 /skweə(r); *NAmE* skwer/ *adj., noun, verb, adv.*

■ ***adj.***

• SHAPE 形状 **1** 🔑 (*geometry* 几何) having four straight equal sides and four angles of 90° 正方形的；四方形的：*a square room* 正方形的房间 ➲ PICTURE AT PARALLELOGRAM **2** 🔑 forming an angle of 90° exactly or approximately

成直角的；方的：*The book had rounded, not square, corners.* 这本书是圆角的，而不是方角的。◇ *square shoulders* 宽而挺的肩膀 ◇ *He had a firm, square jaw.* 他的下巴方正显得很坚定。

- **MEASUREMENT** 量度 **3** used after a unit of measurement to say that sth measures the same amount on each of four sides（用于表示长度的单位后，表示某物四个边等长）…见方的：*a carpet four metres square* 四米见方的地毯 **4** (*abbr.* **sq**) used after a number to give a measurement of area（用于数字后表示面积）平方：*an area of 36 square metres* * 36 平方米的面积
- **BROAD/SOLID** 宽阔；结实 **5** used to describe sth that is broad or that looks solid in shape 宽阔的；结实的；厚实的：*a man of **square build*** 体格壮实的男子 ➲ SEE ALSO FOUR-SQUARE
- **LEVEL/PARALLEL** 相齐；平行 **6** [not before noun] ~ (**with sth**) level with or parallel to sth（和某物）相齐，平行：*tables arranged square with the wall* 顺着墙壁摆放的一些桌子
- **WITH MONEY** 钱 **7** (*informal*) if two people are **square**, neither of them owes money to the other 彼此无欠账的；两清的；结清账的：*Here's the £10 I owe you—now we're square.* 这是我欠你的 10 英镑，这下我们两清了。
- **IN SPORT** 体育运动 **8** ~ (**with sb**) if two teams are **square**, they have the same number of points 打平的；平局的：*The teams were **all square** at half-time.* 两队上半场打成平局。
- **FAIR/HONEST** 公平；诚实 **9** fair or honest, especially in business matters（尤指在生意上）公平的，公正的，诚实的：*a **square deal*** 公平交易 ◇ *Are you being square with me?* 你对我是以诚相待吗？
- **IN AGREEMENT** 一致 **10** ~ **with sth** in agreement with sth（和某事物）相一致的，相吻合的：*That isn't quite square with what you said yesterday.* 那跟你昨天所讲的不大吻合。
- **BORING** 乏味 **11** (*informal, disapproving*) (of a person 人) considered to be boring, for example because they are old-fashioned or work too hard at school 乏味的；古板的；太循规蹈矩的

IDM **a square 'meal** a good, satisfying meal 饱餐；丰盛的一餐：*He looks as though he hasn't had a square meal for weeks.* 看他那样子，就好像几个星期没吃过一顿像样的饭了。**a square 'peg (in a round 'hole)** (*informal*) a person who does not feel happy or comfortable in a particular situation, or who is not suitable for it 用非所长者；方枘圆凿

■ ***noun***

- **SHAPE** 形状 **1** [C] a shape with four straight sides of equal length and four angles of 90°; a piece of sth that has this shape 正方形；四方形；正方形物：*First break the chocolate into squares.* 先把巧克力掰成方块。◇ *The floor was tiled in squares of grey and white marble.* 地上铺的是灰白两色的大理石方砖。➲ SEE ALSO SET SQUARE, T-SQUARE
- **IN TOWN** 城镇 **2** [C] an open area in a town, usually with four sides, surrounded by buildings（通常为方形的）广场：*The hotel is just off the **main square**.* 旅馆就在大广场附近。◇ *the **market/town/village square*** 集市 / 镇 / 村广场 **3 Square** [sing.] (*abbr.* **Sq.**) (used in addresses 用于地址)：*They live at 95 Russell Square.* 他们住在拉塞尔广场 95 号。
- **MATHEMATICS** 数学 **4** [C] the number obtained when you multiply a number by itself 平方；二次幂：*The square of 7 is 49.* * 7 的平方是 49。
- **BORING PERSON** 乏味的人 **5** [C] (*informal, disapproving*) a person who is considered to be boring, for example because they are old-fashioned or because they work too hard at school 乏味的人；古板的人；老古董；书呆子

IDM **back to square 'one** a return to the situation you were in at the beginning of a project, task, etc., because you have made no real progress（因无进展）回到起点，从头再来：*If this suggestion isn't accepted, we'll be back to square one.* 如果这个建议得不到采纳，我们就得从头再来了。

■ ***verb***

- **SHAPE** 使成形 **1** to make sth have straight edges and corners 使成正方形；使成方形：~ **sth** *It was like trying to **square a circle**. That is, it was impossible.* 这就好比要把圆的变成方的。也就是说，是不可能的。◇ ~ **sth off** *The boat is rounded at the front but squared off at the back.* 这条船船头是圆的，船尾则是方的。
- **MATHEMATICS** 数学 **2** [usually passive] ~ **sth** to multiply a number by itself 使成平方；使成二次幂：*Three squared is written 3^2.* * 3 的平方写作 3^2。◇ *Four squared equals 16.* * 4 的平方等于 16。
- **SHOULDERS** 肩膀 **3** ~ **yourself/your shoulders** to make your back and shoulders straight to show you are ready or determined to do sth 挺直身子；挺起胸膛：*Bruno squared himself to face the waiting journalists.* 布鲁诺挺起胸膛面对等候的记者。
- **IN SPORT** 体育运动 **4** ~ **sth** (*especially BrE*) to make the number of points you have scored in a game or competition equal to those of your opponents（使）打成平局，打平：*His goal squared the game 1–1.* 他进了一球，使比赛打成 1:1 平。
- **PAY MONEY** 付钱 **5** ~ **sb** (*informal*) to pay money to sb in order to get their help 贿赂；收买；买通：*They must have squared the mayor before they got their plan underway.* 一定是买通了市长，他们的计划才得以实施。

PHR V **ˌsquare sth↔aˈway** [usually passive] (*NAmE*) to put sth in order; to finish sth completely 归整；办妥；了结 **ˌsquare ˈoff (against sb)** (*NAmE*) to fight or prepare to fight sb（和某人）打斗；摆好架势（和某人）打斗 **ˌsquare ˈup (to sb/sth) 1** to face a difficult situation and deal with it in a determined way 勇敢地面对；毅然面对 **2** to face sb as if you are going to fight them 气势汹汹地面对（某人）；摆好与（某人）打斗的架势 **ˌsquare ˈup (with sb)** to pay money that you owe（向某人）付清欠款；（与某人）结清账：*Can I leave you to square up with the waiter?* 我先走，你来和服务员结账好不好？**ˈsquare sth with sth | ˈsquare with sth** to make two ideas, facts or situations agree or combine well with each other; to agree or be CONSISTENT with another idea, fact or situation（使）与…一致，与…相符：*The interests of farmers need to be squared with those of consumers.* 农场主的利益需要同消费者的利益相符。◇ ***How can you square this with your conscience?*** 做这样的事你怎么能问心无愧呢？◇ *Your theory does not square with the facts.* 你的理论与事实不符。**ˈsquare sth with sb** to ask permission or check with sb that they approve of what you want to do 就…征得…同意（或认可）：*I think I'll be able to come, but I'll square it with my parents first.* 我想我能来，不过我要先征得我父母的同意。

■ ***adv.*** (only used *after* the verb 仅用于动词后) directly; not at an angle 正对着地；径直地 SYN **squarely**：*I looked her square in the face.* 我直视着她的脸。IDM SEE FAIR *adv.*

ˈsquare-bashing *noun* [U] (*BrE, informal*) training for soldiers, which involves marching and holding weapons in different positions（士兵的）队列训练

ˌsquare ˈbracket (*especially BrE*) (*NAmE usually* **bracket**) *noun* [usually pl.] either of a pair of marks, [ ], placed at the beginning and end of extra information in a text, especially comments made by an editor 方括号

squared /skweəd; *NAmE* skwerd/ *adj.* marked with squares; divided into squares 有正方形标记的；分成正方形形状的：*squared paper* 方格纸

ˈsquare dance *noun* **1** a traditional dance from the US in which groups of four couples dance together, starting the dance by facing each other in a square 方形舞，方块舞（美国传统舞蹈，每组四对男女面对面围成方形起舞）**2** a social event at which people dance square dances 方形舞会

square·head /ˈskweəhed; *NAmE* ˈskwer-/ *noun* (*informal, especially NAmE*) **1** a person who is stupid or not able to do sth 笨蛋；无能的人 **2** an offensive word for a person from Germany, Holland or Scandinavia; a person whose family originally came from there 北欧佬（含冒犯意，指德国、荷兰或斯堪的纳维亚人）；北欧裔人

ˈsquare knot *noun* (*NAmE*) = REEF KNOT

square·ly /ˈskweəli; *NAmE* ˈskwerli/ *adv.* (usually used *after* the verb 通常用于动词后) **1** directly; not at an angle or to one side 正对着地；径直地；不偏不倚地：*She looked at me squarely in the eye.* 她直直地看着我的眼睛。◇ *He stood squarely in front of them, blocking the entrance.* 他就对着他们站在那里，挡住入口。◇ (*figurative*) *We must meet the challenge squarely* (= not try to avoid it). 我们必须正面迎接这一挑战。**2** directly or exactly; without confusion 直截了当；明确无误；毫不含糊地：*The responsibility for the crisis rests squarely on the government.* 这一危机的责任全在政府。IDM SEE FAIRLY

the ˌSquare ˈMile *noun* [sing.] (*BrE, informal*) a name used for the City of London, where there are many banks and financial businesses 平方英里城（指伦敦金融城，为银行和金融业的聚集地）

ˌsquare ˈroot *noun* (*mathematics* 数) a number which when multiplied by itself produces a particular number 平方根：*The square root of 64 (√64) is 8 (8 × 8 = 64).* * 64 的平方根是 8。➲ COMPARE CUBE ROOT

squar·ish /ˈskweərɪʃ; *NAmE* ˈskwer-/ *adj.* almost square in shape 近似方形的；略呈方形的

squash /skwɒʃ; *NAmE* skwɑːʃ; skwɔːʃ/ *verb, noun*

■ ***verb*** **1** [T] to press sth so that it becomes soft, damaged or flat, or changes shape 压软（或挤软、压坏、压扁等）；把…压（或挤）变形：**~ sth/sb** *The tomatoes at the bottom of the bag had been squashed.* 袋底的西红柿给压烂了。◇ **~ sth against sth** *He squashed his nose against the window.* 他趴在窗户上，把鼻子都挤扁了。◇ **~ sth + adj.** *Squash your cans flat before recycling.* 把饮料罐压扁了再送去回收。➲ PICTURE AT SQUEEZE **2** [I, T] to push sb/sth or yourself into a space that is too small（使）挤进；塞入：**+ adv./prep.** *We all squashed into the back of the car.* 我们都挤到了汽车后部。◇ **~ sb/sth + adv./prep.** *How many people are they going to try and squash into this bus?* 他们打算把多少人塞进这辆公共汽车？◇ *She was squashed between the door and the table.* 她被挤在门和桌子中间。**3** [T] **~ sth** to stop sth from continuing; to destroy sth because it is a problem for you 打断；制止；去除；粉碎 SYN **quash**：*to squash a plan/an idea/a revolt* 使计划落空；否定想法；镇压反叛 ◇ *If parents don't answer children's questions, their natural curiosity will be squashed.* 如果父母不回答孩子的问题，就会挫伤他们好奇的天性。◇ *The statement was an attempt to squash the rumours.* 这份声明旨在辟谣。

PHR V **ˌsquash ˈup (against sb/sth)** | **ˌsquash sb/sth↔ˈup (against sb/sth)** to move so close to sb/sth else that it is uncomfortable（使）挤在一起：*We squashed up to make room for Sue.* 我们挤了挤，给休腾出个地方。◇ *I was squashed up against the wall.* 我被挤得紧贴墙壁。

■ ***noun*** **1** (*also formal* **ˈsquash rackets**) [U] a game for two players, played in a COURT surrounded by four walls, using RACKETS and a small rubber ball（软式）墙网球；壁球：*a squash court* 壁球场 ◇ *to play squash* 打壁球 ➲ VISUAL VOCAB PAGE V49 **2** [U, C] (*BrE*) a drink made with fruit juice, sugar and water 果汁饮料：*a glass of orange/lemon squash* 一杯橙汁 / 柠檬汁 ◇ *Two orange squashes, please.* 请来两杯橙汁。**3** [C, U] (*pl.* **squash** or **squashes**) a type of vegetable that grows on the ground. **Winter squash** have hard skin and orange flesh. **Summer squash** have soft yellow or green skin and white flesh. 南瓜小果（主要种类为笋瓜 winter squash 和西葫芦 summer squash）➲ VISUAL VOCAB PAGE V34 **4** [sing.] (*informal*) if sth is a **squash**, there is hardly enough room for everything or everyone to fit into a small space 拥挤的环境（或处所）：*It's a real squash with six of us in the car.* 我们六个人坐在这辆车上，可真够挤的。

squashy /ˈskwɒʃi; *NAmE* ˈskwɑːʃi; ˈskwɔːʃi/ *adj.* soft and easy to crush or squeeze 软而易压坏（或压扁）的

squat /skwɒt; *NAmE* skwɑːt/ *verb, noun, adj.*

■ ***verb*** (**-tt-**) **1** [I] **~ (down)** to sit on your heels with your knees bent up close to your body 蹲坐；蹲 **2** [I, T] **~ (sth)** to live in a building or on land which is not yours, without the owner's permission 偷住，擅自占用（房子或地方）：*They ended up squatting in the empty houses on Oxford Road.* 他们落得在牛津路偷住空房的境地。➲ WORDFINDER NOTE AT HOME

■ ***noun*** **1** (*especially BrE*) a building that people are living in without permission and without paying rent 偷住的房子：*to live in a squat* 擅自住在他人空着的房子里 **2** a squatting position of the body 蹲坐；蹲 **3** = SQUAT THRUST

■ ***adj.*** short and wide or fat, in a way that is not attractive 矮而宽的；矮胖的：*a squat tower* 矮而粗的塔 ◇ *a squat muscular man with a shaven head* 剃光头的矮壮男人

squat·ter /ˈskwɒtə(r); *NAmE* ˈskwɑːt-/ *noun* a person who is living in a building or on land without permission and without paying rent 擅自占用他人房子（或土地）的人

ˈsquat thrust (*also* **squat**) *noun* an exercise in which you start with your hands on the floor and your knees bent, and then quickly move both legs backwards and forwards together 俯撑下蹲促腿，俯撑腿屈伸（双手撑地下蹲后双腿同时前后跳动）

squaw /skwɔː/ *noun* (*old use*) a word for a Native American woman that is now often considered offensive 美洲印第安女人（常含冒犯意）

squawk /skwɔːk/ *verb* **1** [I] (of birds 鸟) to make a loud sharp sound 发出刺耳的尖叫声：*The parrot squawked and flew away.* 鹦鹉尖声叫了叫飞走了。**2** [T, I] (**+ speech**) to speak or make a noise in a loud, sharp voice because you are angry, surprised, etc. 尖声高叫；怒声叫嚷；吃惊地尖声说话：*'You did what?!' she squawked.* "你干了什么？！" 她惊叫道。▶ **squawk** *noun*：*The bird gave a startled squawk.* 鸟发出嘎嘎的惊叫声。◇ *a squawk of protest* 大声的抗议

squeak /skwiːk/ *verb, noun*

■ ***verb*** **1** [I] to make a short high sound that is not very loud 短促而尖厉地叫；吱吱叫；嘎吱作响：*My new shoes squeak.* 我的新鞋走路嘎吱嘎吱响。◇ *The mouse ran away, squeaking with fear.* 那只老鼠吓得尖叫着溜了。◇ *One wheel makes a horrible squeaking noise.* 一个车轮发出讨厌的吱吱声。**2** [T, I] (**+ speech**) to speak in a very high voice, especially when you are nervous or excited（尤指紧张或激动时）尖声说话：*'Let go of me!' he squeaked nervously.* "放开我！" 他紧张地尖叫道。**3** [I] **+ adv./prep.** to only just manage to win sth, pass a test, etc. 勉强通过；侥幸成功；险胜：*We squeaked into the final with a goal in the last minute.* 我们靠最后一分钟的进球得分侥幸进入决赛。

■ ***noun*** a short, high cry or sound, that is not usually very loud 短促而尖厉的叫声；吱吱声；尖叫声 ➲ SEE ALSO BUBBLE AND SQUEAK ➲ MORE LIKE THIS 3, page R25

squeak·er /ˈskwiːkə(r)/ *noun* (*informal, especially NAmE*) a competition or election won by only a small amount or likely to be won by only a small amount（很可能）以微弱优势赢得的比赛（或选举）；险胜的比赛（或选举）

squeaky /ˈskwiːki/ *adj.* making a short, high sound; squeaking 发短促尖叫声的；吱吱叫的；嘎吱作响的：*squeaky floorboards* 嘎吱作响的地板 ◇ *a high squeaky voice* 又高又尖的嗓子

ˌsqueaky ˈclean *adj.* (*informal*) **1** completely clean, and therefore attractive 非常干净的：*squeaky clean hair* 光洁的头发 **2** morally correct in every way; that cannot be criticized 品行完美的；一尘不染的；无可挑剔的

squeal /skwiːl/ *verb, noun*

■ ***verb*** **1** [I] to make a long, high sound 尖声长叫；发出长而尖的声音：*The pigs were squealing.* 猪尖叫着。◇ *The car squealed to a halt.* 汽车嘎的一声停了下来。◇ *Children were running around squealing with excitement.* 孩子们跑来跑去，兴奋地尖叫着。➲ MORE LIKE THIS 3, page R25 **2** [T, I] (**+ speech**) to speak in a very high voice, especially when you are excited or nervous（尤指激动或紧张时）尖声说，高声嚷着说：*'Don't!' she squealed.* "不要！" 她尖叫道。**3** [I] **~ (on sb)** (*informal, disapproving*) to give information, especially to the police, about sth illegal that sb has done 告密；告发

■ ***noun*** a long high cry or sound 拖长的尖叫声；长而尖的声音：*a squeal of pain* 疼痛的尖叫 ◇ *a squeal of delight* 快乐的尖叫 ◇ *He stopped with a squeal of brakes.* 他嘎的一声把车刹住了。

S

squeam·ish /ˈskwiːmɪʃ/ *adj.* **1** easily upset, or made to feel sick by unpleasant sights or situations, especially when the sight of blood is involved 易心烦意乱的；易恶心的；神经脆弱的 **2** not wanting to do sth that might be considered dishonest or immoral 诚实谨慎的；正派的 **3 the squeamish** *noun* [pl.] people who are squeamish 易心烦意乱的人；神经脆弱的人：*This movie is not for the squeamish.* 这部电影不是给神经脆弱的人看的。 ➲ MORE LIKE THIS 24, page R28 ▸ **squeam·ish·ness** *noun* [U]

squee·gee /ˈskwiːdʒiː/ *noun* **1** a tool with a rubber edge and a handle, used for removing water from smooth surfaces such as windows 橡皮刮水刷 ➲ VISUAL VOCAB PAGE V21 **2** (*also* **ˈsqueegee mop**) a tool for washing floors, that has a long handle with two thick pieces of soft material at the end, which may be squeezed together using a piece of machinery attached to the handle 胶棉拖把 ➲ VISUAL VOCAB PAGE V21

ˈsqueegee merchant *noun* (*BrE, informal*) a person who cleans the front windows of cars that have stopped in traffic and then asks the driver to pay them money, even if the driver did not want them to do it 要赖擦车仔（停车时不待车主允许便去擦挡风玻璃然后伸手要钱）

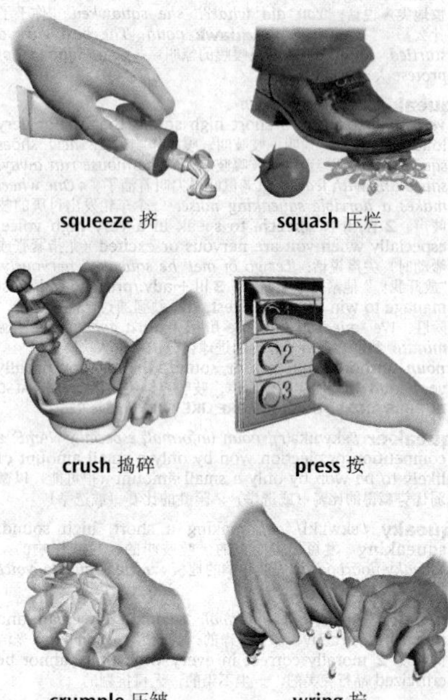

squeeze 挤　squash 压烂　crush 捣碎　press 按　crumple 压皱　wring 拧

squeeze 🔑 /skwiːz/ *verb, noun*

■ *verb*

• **PRESS WITH FINGERS** 用手指挤压 **1** 🔑 [T, I] ~ (**sth**) to press sth firmly, especially with your fingers 挤压；捏：*to squeeze a tube of toothpaste* 挤牙膏 ◇ *to squeeze the trigger of a gun* (= to fire it) 扣动枪的扳机 ◇ *He squeezed her hand and smiled at her.* 他捏了捏她的手，冲她笑笑。◇ *Just take hold of the tube and squeeze.* 拿住软管挤就行了。

• **GET LIQUID OUT** 挤出液体 **2** 🔑 [T] to get liquid out of sth by pressing or twisting it hard（从某物中）榨出，挤出，拧出：**~ sth out of/from sth** *to squeeze the juice from a lemon* 把柠檬的汁挤出来 ◇ (*figurative*) *She felt as if every drop of emotion had been squeezed from her.* 她觉得自己的激情似乎已经被榨尽了。◇ **~ sth (out)** *He took off his wet clothes and squeezed the water out.* 他脱下湿衣服，拧干了水。◇ *freshly squeezed orange juice* 现榨的橙汁 ◇ **~ sth + adj.** *Soak the cloth in warm water and then squeeze it dry.* 把衣服在温水里泡一下，然后把它拧干。

• **INTO/THROUGH SMALL SPACE** 进入 / 通过狭小的空间 **3** [T, I] to force sb/sth/yourself into or through a small space（使）挤入；挤过；塞入：**~ sb/sth into, through, etc. sth** *We managed to squeeze six people into the car.* 我们往那辆车上挤进了六个人。◇ (*figurative*) *We managed to squeeze a lot into a week* (= we did a lot of different things). 我们把很多事挤在一个星期里做完了。◇ **~ into, through, etc. sth** *to squeeze into a tight dress/a parking space* 勉强穿上一件紧身连衣裙；把车勉强挤进一个停车位 ◇ *to squeeze through a gap in the hedge* 从篱笆上的豁口挤过去 ◇ **~ through, in, past, etc.** *If you move forward a little, I can squeeze past.* 你朝前挪一挪，我就可以挤过去了。

• **THREATEN** 威胁 **4** [T] **~ sb (for sth)** (*informal*) to get sth by putting pressure on sb, threatening them, etc. 向…勒索（或榨取）；逼迫…给：*He's squeezing me for £500.* 他逼我拿出 500 英镑。

• **LIMIT MONEY** 限制金额 **5** [T] **~ sb/sth** to strictly limit or reduce the amount of money that sb/sth has or can use 严格限制，削减，紧缩（资金）：*High interest rates have squeezed the industry hard.* 高利率使这个行业举步维艰。

IDM **ˌsqueeze sb ˈdry** to get as much money, information, etc. out of sb as you can 榨取某人所拥有的一切；榨干某人的钱财；逼某人讲出所知道的一切

PHR V **ˌsqueeze sb/sth↔ˈin** to give time to sb/sth, although you are very busy 挤出时间见某人（或做某事）：*If you come this afternoon the doctor will try to squeeze you in.* 你要是今天下午来，大夫可以尽量挤时间给你看看。**ˌsqueeze sb/sth↔ˈout (of sth)** to prevent sb/sth from continuing to do sth or be in business 挤垮；把…挤出（某行业等）：*Supermarkets are squeezing out small shops.* 超市正挤垮小商店。**ˌsqueeze sth ˈout of/ˈfrom sb** to get sth by putting pressure on sb, threatening them, etc. 向…勒索（或榨取）；逼迫…给：*to squeeze a confession from a suspect* 逼迫嫌疑犯招供 **ˌsqueeze ˈup (against sb/sth)** | **ˌsqueeze sb↔ˈup (against sb/sth)** to move close to sb/sth so that you are pressed against them/it（使）挤紧：*There'll be enough room if we all squeeze up a little.* 大家稍稍挤一挤，地方就够了。◇ *I sat squeezed up against the wall.* 我被挤得紧贴着墙坐着。

■ *noun*

• **PRESSING WITH FINGERS** 用手指挤压 **1** 🔑 [C, usually sing.] an act of pressing sth, usually with your hands 挤压；捏：*He gave my hand a little squeeze.* 他轻轻捏了捏我的手。◇ *Give the tube another squeeze.* 把软管再挤一下。

• **OF LIQUID** 液体 **2** 🔑 [C] a small amount of liquid that is produced by pressing sth 榨出的液体；少量挤出的汁：*a squeeze of lemon juice* 挤出的一点儿柠檬汁

• **IN SMALL SPACE** 在狭小空间里 **3** [sing.] a situation where it is almost impossible for a number of people or things to fit into a small or restricted space 挤；塞：*It was* ***a tight squeeze*** *but we finally got everything into the case.* 箱子塞得很紧，不过我们最终还是把所有东西都装进去了。◇ *Seven people in the car was a bit of a squeeze.* 那辆车坐了七个人是有点挤。

• **REDUCTION IN MONEY** 钱的减少 **4** [C, usually sing.] a reduction in the amount of money, jobs, etc. available; a difficult situation caused by this（可获得的钱、工作岗位等的）减少，削减；拮据；经济困难：***a squeeze on*** *profits* 利润的减少 ◇ *We're really* ***feeling the squeeze*** *since I lost my job.* 自从我丢了工作后，我们的确感觉到手头拮据。◇ *a* ***credit squeeze*** 信贷紧缩

• **BOYFRIEND/GIRLFRIEND** 男 / 女朋友 **5** [sing.] (*informal, especially NAmE*) a boyfriend or girlfriend 男朋友；女朋友：*Who's his* ***main squeeze****?* 他最要好的女朋友是谁？

IDM **put the ˈsqueeze on sb (to do sth)** (*informal*) to put pressure on sb to act in a particular way; to make a situation difficult for sb 逼迫某人（做某事）；使某人处境困难

ˈsqueeze box *noun* (*informal*) an ACCORDION or a CONCERTINA（六角）手风琴

squelch /skweltʃ/ *verb* **1** [I] (+ **adv./prep.**) to make a wet sucking sound 发吧唧声，发扑哧声（如走在泥泞中似的）：*The mud squelched as I walked through it.* 我扑哧扑

哧地穿过泥泞。◇ *Her wet shoes squelched at every step.* 她的鞋湿了，走一步吧唧一声。◇ *We squelched across the muddy field.* 我们扑哧扑哧地穿过泥泞的田地。➲ MORE LIKE THIS 3, page R25 **2** [T] ~ **sth** (*NAmE*) to stop sth from growing, increasing or developing 制止；压制；遏制；限制 SYN **squash**: *to squelch a rumour/strike/fire* 制止谣言；镇压罢工；控制火势的蔓延 ▸ **squelch** *noun* [usually sing.]: *He pulled his foot out of the mud with a squelch.* 他扑哧一声从烂泥里拔出脚来。 **squelchy** *adj.*: *squelchy ground* 踩上去扑哧扑哧响的湿地

squib /skwɪb/ *noun* a small FIREWORK 小爆竹 IDM SEE DAMP *adj.*

squid /skwɪd/ *noun* [C, U] (*pl.* **squid** or **squids**) a sea creature that has a long soft body, eight arms and two TENTACLES (= long thin parts like arms) around its mouth, and that is sometimes used for food 枪乌贼；鱿鱼

squidgy /ˈskwɪdʒi/ *adj.* (*informal, especially BrE*) soft and wet, and easily SQUASHED 湿软易挤压的

squiffy /ˈskwɪfi/ *adj.* (*BrE, informal*) slightly drunk 微醉的

squig·gle /ˈskwɪgl/ *noun* a line, for example in sb's HANDWRITING, that is drawn or written in a careless way with twists and curls in it（写或画的）弯弯曲曲的线条；潦草的笔迹: *Are these dots and squiggles supposed to be your signature?* 这一堆点点画画就是你的签名吗？ ▸ **squig·gly** *adj.*

squil·lion /ˈskwɪljən/ *noun* (*informal, often humorous*) a very large number 无数；万千: *a squillion-dollar budget* 天文数字的预算

squint /skwɪnt/ *verb, noun*

■ ***verb*** **1** [I, T] to look at sth with your eyes partly shut in order to keep out bright light or to see better 眯着眼睛看: *to squint into the sun* 眯起眼睛看太阳 ◇ *She was squinting through the keyhole.* 她眯着眼从锁眼里看。◇ *He squinted at the letter in his hand.* 他眯着眼看手里的信。◇ ~ **sth** *When he squinted his eyes, he could just make out a house in the distance.* 他眯着眼睛，只能隐约看见远处有一所房子。 **2** [I] (*BrE*) (of an eye 眼睛) to look in a different direction from the other eye 斜视: *His left eye squints a little.* 他左眼有点斜视。 **3** [I] to have eyes that look in different directions （人）患斜视

■ ***noun*** **1** [C, usually sing.] a condition of the eye muscles which causes each eye to look in a different direction 斜视: *He was born with a squint.* 他生下来就斜视。 **2** [sing.] (*BrE, informal*) a short look 瞥；瞟: ***Have a squint at this.*** 你看看这个。

squire /ˈskwaɪə(r)/ *noun* **1** (*also* **Squire**) (in the past in England) a man of high social status who owned most of the land in a particular country area（英格兰旧时的）乡绅，大地主 **2 Squire** (*BrE, informal* or *humorous*) used by a man as a friendly way of addressing another man（男子对另一男子的友好称呼）先生: *What can I get you, Squire?* 您要点什么，先生？ **3** (in the past) a young man who was an assistant to a KNIGHT before becoming a knight himself（旧时骑士的）扈从

squire·archy /ˈskwaɪərɑːki; *NAmE* -ɑːrki/ *noun* [C+sing./pl. v.] (in the past in England) the people of high social status who owned large areas of land, considered as a social or political group（英格兰旧时的）地主阶层，乡绅阶层

squirm /skwɜːm; *NAmE* skwɜːrm/ *verb* **1** [I] to move around a lot making small twisting movements, because you are nervous, uncomfortable, etc.（因紧张、不舒服等）动来动去，来回扭动，坐卧不宁 SYN **wriggle**: (+ **adv./prep.**) *The children were squirming restlessly in their seats.* 孩子们在位子上心神不定地动来动去。◇ + **adj.** *Someone grabbed him but he managed to squirm free.* 有人抓住他，但他设法挣脱了。 **2** [I] to feel great embarrassment or shame 十分尴尬；羞愧难当；无地自容: *It made him squirm to think how badly he'd messed up the interview.* 一想到自己把面试搞得有多糟，他就觉得无地自容。

squir·rel /ˈskwɪrəl; *NAmE* ˈskwɜːrəl/ *noun, verb*

■ ***noun*** a small animal with a long thick tail and red, grey or black fur. Squirrels eat nuts and live in trees. 松鼠 ➲ VISUAL VOCAB PAGE V12 ➲ SEE ALSO GROUND SQUIRREL

■ ***verb*** (**-ll-**, *especially US* **-l-**)

PHR V **ˌsquirrel sth↔aˈway** to hide or store sth so that it can be used later 储藏；贮存: *She had money squirrelled away in various bank accounts.* 她把钱存在几个不同的银行账户上。

squir·rel·ly /ˈskwɪrəli; *NAmE* ˈskwɜːrəli/ *adj.* (*NAmE, informal*) **1** unable to keep still or be quiet 无法保持安静的；静不下来的: *squirrelly kids* 闹哄哄的孩子 **2** crazy 疯狂的；发疯的

squirt /skwɜːt; *NAmE* skwɜːrt/ *verb, noun*

■ ***verb*** **1** [T, I] to force liquid, gas, etc. in a thin fast stream through a narrow opening; to be forced out of a narrow opening in this way（使）喷射；喷 SYN **spurt**: ~ **sth** (+ **adv./prep.**) *The snake can squirt poison from a distance of a metre.* 这种蛇能把毒液喷一米远。◇ *I desperately squirted water on the flames.* 我拼命朝火上喷水。◇ (+ **adv./prep.**) *When I cut the lemon, juice squirted in my eye.* 我切柠檬时，柠檬汁溅到了我眼睛里。 **2** [T] to hit sb/sth with a stream of water, gas, etc.（用…）向…喷射 SYN **spray**: ~ **sb/sth** (**with sth**) *The children were squirting each other with water from the hose.* 孩子们用软水管相互喷水。◇ ~ **sth** (**at sb**) *He squirted a water pistol at me* (= made the water come out of it). 他用玩具水枪朝我喷水。

■ ***noun*** **1** a thin, fast stream of liquid that comes out of a small opening 喷射出的一股液体 SYN **spray**: *a squirt of perfume* 喷出的一股香水 **2** (*informal, disapproving*) a word used to refer to a short, young or unimportant person that you do not like or that you find annoying 小矮子；小屁孩；无名小辈

ˈsquirt gun *noun* (*NAmE*) = WATER PISTOL

squish /skwɪʃ/ *verb* (*informal*) **1** [I, T] ~ (**sth**) if sth soft **squishes** or **is squished**, it is crushed out of shape when it is pressed（被）压坏，挤坏 **2** [I] to make a soft wet sucking sound 发吧唧声；发吱嘎声

squishy /ˈskwɪʃi/ *adj.* (*informal*) soft and wet 湿软的；黏乎乎的

squit /skwɪt/ *noun* (*BrE*) **1** (*offensive*) a small or unimportant person 小人物；无名小卒；无足轻重的人 **2 the squits** (*also* **the squit·ters** /ˈskwɪtəz; *NAmE* -tərz/) [pl.] (*informal*) = DIARRHOEA

Sr (*also* **Snr**) (*both BrE*) (*also* **Sr.** *NAmE, BrE*) *abbr.* SENIOR 老；大 ➲ COMPARE JR

Sri, Srimati = SHRI, SHRIMATI

SS *abbr.* **1** SAINTS （基督教）圣人，圣徒: *SS Philip and James* 圣腓力和圣雅各 **2** /ˌes ˈes/ STEAMSHIP 汽船；轮船: *the SS Titanic* 泰坦尼克号邮轮

SSN /ˌes es ˈen/ *abbr.* SOCIAL SECURITY NUMBER（美国）社会保障号码

St *abbr.* **1** (*also* **st**) (*both BrE*) (*also* **St., st.** *NAmE, BrE*) (used in written addresses) Street（书写地址时用）街，路: *Fleet St* 弗利特街（或译舰队街） **2 St.** (*NAmE*) State 州 **3** (*also* **St.** *especially in NAmE*) SAINT（基督教）圣人，圣徒

st (*BrE*) (*also* **st.** *NAmE, BrE*) *abbr.* STONE (a British measurement of weight) 英石（英国重量单位）: *9st 2lb* * 9 英石 2 磅

stab /stæb/ *verb, noun*

■ ***verb*** (**-bb-**) **1** [T] ~ **sb** to push a sharp, pointed object, especially a knife, into sb, killing or injuring them（用刀等锐器）刺，戳，捅: *He was stabbed to death in a racist attack.* 他遭到种族主义者的袭击，被刺死了。◇ *She stabbed him in the arm with a screwdriver.* 她用螺丝刀在他胳膊上戳了一下。 **2** [T, I] to make a short, aggressive or violent movement with a finger or pointed object（用手指或尖物）戳，捅，刺 SYN **jab, prod**: ~ **sth** (**at/into/through sth**) *He stabbed his finger angrily at my chest.* 他气呼呼地用指头戳我的胸口。◇ ~ **sb/sth** (**with sth**) *She stabbed the air with her fork.* 她用叉子在空中比画。◇ ~ **at/into/through sth** (*figurative*) *The pain stabbed at his chest.* 他胸部疼得像

刀扎似的。

IDM **stab sb in the 'back** to do or say sth that harms sb who trusts you 在某人背后捅刀子；陷害（或中伤）信任你的人 **SYN** **betray**

■ ***noun*** **1** an act of stabbing or trying to stab sb/sth; a wound caused by stabbing 刺；戳；捅；刺（或戳、捅）的伤口：*He received several stabs in the chest.* 他胸部被刺了几刀。◇ *She died of a single* ***stab wound*** *to the heart.* 她因心脏被刺中一刀而身亡。 **2** a sudden sharp pain or unpleasant feeling 突然一阵剧痛（或难受的感觉）：*She felt a sudden* ***stab of pain*** *in the chest.* 她胸部突然感到一阵剧痛。◇ *a* ***stab of guilt/fear/pity/jealousy, etc.*** 一阵内疚、恐惧、怜悯、嫉妒等 **3** [usually sing.] (*informal*) an attempt to do sth 尝试；企图：**~ (at sth)** *He found the test difficult but nevertheless* ***made a good stab at*** *it.* 尽管他觉得试题很难，但还是尽力去做了。◇ **~ (at doing sth)** *Countless people* ***have had a stab at*** *solving the riddle.* 无数人试图解开这个谜。

IDM **a ˌstab in the 'back** (*informal*) an act that harms sb, done by a person they thought was a friend 背后捅刀子；对给予信任的人的陷害（或中伤）➲ MORE AT DARK *n.*

stab·bing /'stæbɪŋ/ *noun, adj.*

■ ***noun*** an occasion when a person is stabbed with a knife or other pointed object 持刀（或其他利器）伤人事件：*a fatal stabbing* 持刀伤人致死事件

■ ***adj.*** [usually before noun] (of pain 疼痛) very sharp, sudden and strong 突然而剧烈的；刀刺似的

sta·bil·ity **AW** /stə'bɪləti/ *noun* [U] the quality or state of being steady and not changing or being disturbed in any way (= the quality of being stable) 稳定（性）；稳固（性）：***political/economic/social stability*** 政治/经济/社会稳定 ◇ *the stability of the dollar on the world's money markets* 美元在世界货币市场上的稳定性 ◇ *Being back with their family should provide emotional stability for the children.* 回到家人身边会使儿童的情绪稳定下来。**OPP** **instability**

sta·bil·ize **AW** (*BrE also* **-ise**) /'steɪbəlaɪz/ *verb* [I, T] to become or to make sth become firm, steady and unlikely to change; to make sth stable（使）稳定，稳固：*The patient's condition stabilized.* 患者的病情稳定下来。◇ **~ sth** *government measures to stabilize prices* 政府稳定物价的措施 ◇ *Doctors stabilized the patient's condition.* 大夫们使患者的病情稳定下来。➲ COMPARE DESTABILIZE ▶ **sta·bil·iza·tion, -isa·tion** **AW** /ˌsteɪbəlaɪ'zeɪʃn; *NAmE* -lə'z-/ *noun* [U]：*economic stabilization* 经济稳定性

sta·bil·izer (*BrE also* **-iser**) /'steɪbəlaɪzə(r)/ *noun* **1** a device that keeps sth steady, especially one that stops an aircraft or a ship from rolling to one side 稳定装置；（航空器的）安定面；（船舶的）减摇装置 **2 stabilizers** [pl.] (*BrE*) (*NAmE* **'training wheels**) small wheels that are fitted at each side of the back wheel on a child's bicycle to stop it from falling over（儿童自行车后轮两侧的）稳定轮 ➲ VISUAL VOCAB PAGE V55 **3** (*specialist*) a chemical that is sometimes added to food or paint to stop the various substances in it from becoming separate 稳定剂

stable 🔑 **AW** /'steɪbl/ *adj., noun, verb*

> **WORD FAMILY**
> **stable** *adj.* (≠ unstable)
> **stability** *noun* (≠ instability)
> **stabilize** *verb*

■ ***adj.*** **1** 🔑 firmly fixed; not likely to move, change or fail 稳定的；稳固的；牢固的 **SYN** **steady**：*stable prices* 稳定的价格 ◇ *a stable relationship* 稳定的关系 ◇ *This ladder doesn't seem very stable.* 这架梯子好像不太稳。◇ *The patient's condition is stable* (= it is not getting worse). 患者病情稳定。**2** 🔑 (of a person 人) calm and reasonable; not easily upset 稳重的；沉稳的；持重的 **SYN** **balanced**：*Mentally, she is not very stable.* 她的心理状态不十分稳定。**3** (*specialist*) (of a substance 物质) staying in the same chemical or ATOMIC state（化学状态或原子状态）稳定的：*chemically stable* 化学状态稳定的 **OPP** **unstable** ▶ **sta·bly** /'steɪbli/ *adv.*

■ ***noun*** **1** 🔑 [C] a building in which horses are kept 马厩 ➲ WORDFINDER NOTE AT HORSE ➲ VISUAL VOCAB PAGE V3 **2** 🔑 (*BrE also* **stables**) [C+sing./pl. v.] an organization that keeps horses for a particular purpose（养马作特定用途的）养马场；马房：(*BrE*) *a* ***riding/racing stables*** 骑乘马/赛马养马场 ◇ *His stables are near Oxford.* 他的养马场在牛津附近。**3** [C] a group of RACEHORSES owned or trained by the same person 统称某人拥有（或训练）的赛马：*There have been just three winners from his stable this season.* 这个赛季他的马只有三匹获胜。**4** [sing.] a group of people who work or trained in the same place; a group of products made by the same company（在同一地方工作或训练的）一批人；（同一公司生产的）系列产品：*actors from the same stable* 同一剧团的演员 ◇ *the latest printer from the Epson stable* 爱普生系列最新款式打印机

■ ***verb*** **~ sth** to put or keep a horse in a stable 使（马）入厩；把（马）拴在马厩：*Where do you stable your pony?* 你的矮种马养在哪儿？

'stable boy, **'stable girl** (*BrE also* **'stable lad**) *noun* a person who works in a stable 饲养马的人；马倌；马夫

'stable companion *noun* = STABLEMATE (2)

ˌstable 'door (*BrE*) (*NAmE* **ˌDutch 'door**) *noun* a door which is divided into two parts so that the top part can be left open while the bottom part is kept shut 马厩式两截门（上下两部分可分别开关）

IDM **close, lock, etc. the stable door after the horse has 'bolted** (*BrE*) (*US* **close, etc. the barn door after the horse has e'scaped**) to try to prevent or avoid loss or damage when it is already too late to do so 马跑了才去关厩门；贼走关门，为时已晚

stable·man /'steɪblmæn/ *noun* (*pl.* **-men** /-men/) a person who works in a stable 饲养马的人；马倌；马夫

stable·mate /'steɪblmeɪt/ *noun* **1** a horse, especially a racing horse, from the same stable as another horse 同一马厩的马（尤指赛马）**2** (*also* **'stable companion**) a person or product from the same organization as another person or product 同机构的人（或产品）；同事；同伙：*the 'Daily Mirror' newspaper and its Scottish stablemate the 'Daily Record'*《每日镜报》及其苏格兰姊妹报《每日纪事报》

stab·ling /'steɪblɪŋ/ *noun* [U] buildings or space where horses can be kept 饲养马的场所

stac·cato /stə'kɑːtəʊ; *NAmE* -toʊ/ *adj., adv.* **1** (*music* 音, *from Italian*) with each note played separately in order to produce short, sharp sounds 断音的；断奏的；以断奏方式：*staccato sounds* 断奏音调 ◇ *The notes are played staccato.* 这些音要用断奏弹。**OPP** **legato** **2** with short, sharp sounds or movements 短促刺耳（的）；剧烈波动（的）：*a peculiar staccato voice* 特有的不连贯而且刺耳的嗓音 ◇ *staccato bursts of gunfire* 一阵阵噼里啪啦的枪炮声

stack /stæk/ *noun, verb*

■ ***noun*** **1** [C] a pile of sth, usually neatly arranged（通常指码放整齐的）一叠，一摞，一堆：*a stack of books* 一摞书 ◇ *a stack hi-fi system* (= where a radio, CD player, etc. are arranged on top of each other) 一套高保真组合音响 ➲ SEE ALSO HAYSTACK **2** [C] **~ (of sth)** (*informal, especially BrE*) a large number or amount of sth; a lot of sth 大量；许多；一大堆：*stacks of money* 许多钱 ◇ *There's a stack of unopened mail waiting for you at the house.* 家里有一大堆信等你拆呢。◇ *I've got stacks of work to do.* 我有一大堆活儿要做。**3** [C] a tall CHIMNEY, especially on a factory（尤指工厂的）大烟囱 ➲ SEE ALSO CHIMNEY STACK, SMOKESTACK **4 the stacks** [pl.] the part of a library, sometimes not open to the public, where books that are not often needed are stored（图书馆中贮藏使用频率较低的书的）书库 **5** [C] (*computing* 计) a way of storing information in a computer in which the most recently stored item is the first to be RETRIEVED (= found or got back) 栈；堆栈 **6** [C] (*geology* 地) a tall thin part of a CLIFF that has been separated from the land and stands on its own in the sea 海蚀柱 **IDM** SEE BLOW *v.*

■ ***verb*** **1** [T, I] **~ (sth) (up)** to arrange objects neatly in a pile; to be arranged in this way（使）放成整齐的一叠（或一摞、一堆）：*to stack boxes* 把箱子摞起来 ◇ *logs stacked up against a wall* 靠墙码放着的原木 ◇ *Do these chairs stack?*

这些椅子能摞起来吗？◇ *stacking chairs* 可摞在一起的椅子 **2** [T] **~ sth (with sth)** to fill sth with piles of things 使成叠（或成摞、成堆）地放在…；使码放在…：*They were busy stacking the shelves with goods.* 他们正忙着摆货物上架呢。 **3** [I, T] **~ (sth) (up)** if aircraft **stack (up)** or **are stacked (up)** over an airport, there are several flying around waiting for their turn to land（令飞机）分层盘旋等待着陆

IDM **'stack it** (*informal*) to fall over or off sth, especially in a way that makes you look silly and makes other people laugh（笨拙地）跌倒：*I tried a spin on the ice and stacked it.* 我试图在冰面上旋转，结果笨拙地跌倒了。

PHR V **,stack 'up 1** to keep increasing in quantity until there is a large pile, a long line, etc. 积聚成一大堆（或一长排等）：*Cars quickly stacked up behind the bus.* 公共汽车后面的汽车很快排成了长龙。 **2** (used especially in questions or in negatives 尤用于疑问句或否定句) to compare with sb/sth else; to be as good as sb/sth else（与其他人或事物）相比；比得上 **SYN** **measure up (to sth/sb)**: *Let's try him in the job and see how he stacks up.* 咱们让他干这活儿试试，看看他比别人干得怎么样。◇ **stack up against sb/sth** *A mobile home simply doesn't stack up against a traditional house.* 活动房屋怎么也比不上传统的房屋。 **3** (used especially in negatives 尤用于否定句) to seem reasonable; to make sense 看来合理；讲得通；合乎情理：*That can't be right. It just doesn't stack up.* 那不可能是对的，简直不合情理。

stacked /stækt/ *adj.* [not usually before noun] if a surface is **stacked with** objects, there are large numbers or piles of them on it 放有大量…；放有成叠（或成摞、成堆）…：*a table stacked with glasses* 摆满了玻璃杯的桌子

IDM **the cards/odds are stacked a'gainst you** you are unlikely to succeed because the conditions are not good for you 形势对你不利 **the cards/odds are stacked in your 'favour** you are likely to succeed because the conditions are good and you have an advantage 形势对你有利

sta·dium /ˈsteɪdiəm/ *noun* (*pl.* **sta·diums** or **sta·dia** /ˈsteɪdiə/) a large sports ground surrounded by rows of seats and usually other buildings 体育场；运动场：*a **football/sports stadium*** 足球场；运动场 ◇ *an **all-seater stadium*** 全座席体育场 ➲ WORDFINDER NOTE AT SPORT

staff /stɑːf; *NAmE* stæf/ *noun, verb*

■ ***noun* 1** [C, usually sing., U] all the workers employed in an organization considered as a group 全体职工（或雇员）：*medical staff* 全体医务人员 ◇ (*BrE*) *teaching staff* 全体教师 ◇ (*BrE*) *We have 20 part-time **members of staff**.* 我们有 20 名兼职员工。◇ (*NAmE*) ***staff members*** 职工 ◇ ***staff development/training*** 员工培训 ◇ *a **staff restaurant/meeting*** 职工食堂 / 大会 ◇ (*especially BrE*) *a lawyer **on the staff** of the Worldwide Fund for Nature* 任职于世界自然基金会的律师 ➲ COLLOCATIONS AT JOB ➲ SEE ALSO GROUND STAFF **2** [sing.] (*NAmE*) the people who work at a school, college or university, but who do not teach students（大、中、小学的）管理人员，行政人员：*students, faculty and staff* 学生和教职人员 **3** [C+sing./pl. v.] a group of senior army officers who help a commanding officer（军队的）全体参谋人员：*a staff officer* 参谋 ➲ SEE ALSO CHIEF OF STAFF, GENERAL STAFF **4** [C] (*old-fashioned* or *formal*) a long stick used as a support when walking or climbing, as a weapon, or as a symbol of authority 拐杖；棍棒；权杖 **5** (*especially NAmE*) (*pl.* **staves**) (*also* **stave**) [C] (*music* 音) a set of five lines on which music is written 五线谱 ➲ PICTURE AT MUSIC

IDM **the ,staff of 'life** (*literary*) a basic food, especially bread 主食；（尤指）面包

■ ***verb*** [T, usually passive] **~ sth** to work in an institution, a company, etc.; to provide people to work there 在…工作；任职于；为…配备职员：*The advice centre is staffed entirely by volunteers.* 在咨询中心工作的全部是志愿者。◇ *The charity provided money to staff and equip two hospitals.* 这个慈善机构提供资金装备了两家医院并配备了人员。◇ *a fully staffed department* 人员配备齐全的部门 ➲ SEE ALSO OVERSTAFFED, SHORT-STAFFED, UNDERSTAFFED ▸ **staf·fing** *noun* [U]: *staffing levels* 人员配备情况

> **▼ GRAMMAR POINT 语法说明**
>
> **staff**
>
> - In *BrE* **staff** (sense 1) can be singular 在英式英语中，staff（第 1 义）可作单数：*a staff of ten* (= a group of ten people) 职工十人 or plural 亦可作复数：*I have ten staff working for me.* 我手下有十名职员。If it is the subject of a verb, this verb is plural. 该词如果作动词的主语，动词用复数：*The staff in this shop are very helpful.* 这家店的员工非常乐意帮忙。
> - In *NAmE* **staff** (senses 1 and 2) can only be singular: *a staff of ten* (but not ~~*ten staff*~~). 在美式英语中，staff（第 1 及第 2 义）只能作单数，要说 a staff of ten（职工十人），而不能说 ten staff：*The staff in this store is very helpful.* 这家店的员工非常乐意帮忙。
> - The plural form **staffs** is less frequent but is used in both *BrE* and *NAmE* to refer to more than one group of people. 复数形式 staffs 较少用，但在英式英语和美式英语中均指两批或以上的职员：*the senator and his staff* (*singular*) 参议员及他的工作人员（单数）◇ *senators and their staffs* (*plural*) 参议员及他们各自的工作人员（复数）

staff·er /ˈstɑːfə(r); *NAmE* ˈstæf-/ *noun* (*NAmE*) a member of staff in a big organization（大机构）职员

'staff nurse *noun* (in Britain) a qualified hospital nurse（英国）医院护士

'staff officer *noun* a military officer who helps an officer of very high rank or who works at a military HEADQUARTERS or a government department 参谋

staff·room /ˈstɑːfruːm; -rʊm; *NAmE* ˈstæf-/ *noun* (*BrE*) a room in a school where teachers can go when they are not teaching 教师室；教员室

'staff sergeant *noun* a member of the army or the US AIR FORCE just above the rank of a SERGEANT 陆军上士；（美国）空军中士：*Staff Sergeant Bob Woods* 陆军上士鲍勃·伍兹

stag /stæg/ *noun* a male DEER 雄鹿 ➲ COMPARE BUCK *n.* (2), DOE, HART

IDM **go 'stag** (*NAmE, old-fashioned, informal*) (of a man 男子) to go to a party without a partner 不带女伴参加聚会

'stag beetle *noun* a large insect with a mouth that has parts like the horns of an animal 锹甲；鹿角甲虫

stage /steɪdʒ/ *noun, verb*

■ ***noun***

• **PERIOD/STATE** 时期；状态 **1** [C] a period or state that sth/sb passes through while developing or making progress（发展或进展的）时期，阶段，状态：*This technology is still in its **early stages**.* 这项技术还处于其早期开发状态。◇ *The children are at different stages of development.* 这些孩子处于不同的成长阶段。◇ *The product is at the design stage.* 产品处于设计阶段。◇ *People tend to work hard **at this stage** of life.* 人在这个人生阶段往往发奋努力。◇ ***At one stage** it looked as though they would win.* 有一段时间，他们好像大有获胜的希望。◇ *Don't worry about the baby not wanting to leave you—it's **a stage they go through**.* 宝宝不肯离开你别担心，他们总要经过这个阶段。

• **PART OF PROCESS** 程序 **2** [C] a separate part that a process, etc. is divided into 段；步；步骤 **SYN** **phase**: *We did the first stage of the trip by train.* 旅行的第一段我们乘的是火车。◇ *The police are building up a picture of the incident **stage by stage**.* 警方正逐步摸清那次事件的经过。◇ *The pay increase will be introduced **in stages*** (= not all at once). 加薪将分阶段进行。◇ *We can take the argument one stage further.* 我们可以把辩论更深入一步。➲ LANGUAGE BANK AT PROCESS[1]

• **THEATRE** 剧场 **3** [C] a raised area, usually in a theatre, etc. where actors, dancers, etc. perform（多指剧场中的）舞台：*The audience threw flowers onto the stage.* 观众把鲜花抛向舞台。◇ *There were more than 50 people **on stage** in one scene.* 有一场戏中舞台上的人有 50 多个。◇ *They marched **off stage** to the sound of trumpets.* 在号角声中，

他们阔步退下舞台。➲ SEE ALSO BACKSTAGE (1), OFFSTAGE (1), ONSTAGE ➲ WORDFINDER NOTE AT THEATRE

WORDFINDER 联想词： backdrop, costume, curtain, footlights, prop, proscenium, scenery, set, the wings

4 (*often* **the stage**) [sing.] the theatre and the world of acting as a form of entertainment 戏剧；戏剧表演；戏剧界：*His parents didn't want him to* ***go on the stage*** (= to be an actor). 他父母不想让他当演员。◇ *She was a popular star of* ***stage and screen*** (= theatre and cinema/movies). 她是观众喜爱的舞台银幕两栖明星。

• **IN POLITICS** 政界 **5** [sing.] an area of activity where important things happen, especially in politics（政治等活动的）领域；（政治）舞台：*She was forced to the centre of* ***the political stage.*** 她被推到了政治舞台的中心。◇ *Germany is playing a leading role on* ***the international stage.*** 德国在国际政治舞台上扮演着重要角色。➲ SEE ALSO CENTRE STAGE

• **CARRIAGE** 马车 **6** [C] (*old-fashioned, informal*) = STAGECOACH ➲ SEE ALSO LANDING STAGE

IDM **set the 'stage for sth** to make it possible for sth to happen; to make sth likely to happen 使某事成为可能；为某事铺平道路

■ *verb* **1 ~ sth** to organize and present a play or an event for people to see 上演；举办；举行：*to stage a ceremony/an event/an exhibition* 举行仪式 / 活动 / 展览 ◇ *The local theatre group is staging a production of 'Hamlet'.* 当地剧团在上演《哈姆雷特》。◇ *Birmingham has bid to stage the next national athletics championships.* 伯明翰申办下届全国田径锦标赛。**2 ~ sth** to organize and take part in action that needs careful planning, especially as a public protest 组织；筹划：*to* ***stage a strike/demonstration/march/protest*** 组织罢工 / 示威 / 游行 / 抗议活动 **3 ~ sth** to make sth happen 使发生；使出现：*The dollar* ***staged a recovery*** *earlier today.* 今天早些时候，美元出现回升。◇ *After five years in retirement, he* ***staged a comeback*** *to international tennis.* 退役五年之后，他重返国际网坛。

stage·coach /'steɪdʒkəʊtʃ; *NAmE* -koʊtʃ/ *noun* a large CARRIAGE pulled by horses, that was used in the past to carry passengers, and often mail, along a regular route（旧时的）驿站马车，公共马车

stage·craft /'steɪdʒkrɑːft; *NAmE* -kræft/ *noun* [U] skill in presenting plays in a theatre 舞台表演技巧；剧场表演艺术

S

'stage direction *noun* a note in the text of a play telling actors when to come on to or leave the stage, what actions to perform, etc. 舞台指示（剧本中关于演员上下场、表演动作等的说明）

,stage 'door *noun* the entrance at the back of a theatre used by actors, staff, etc. 剧场后门（供演职人员进出）

'stage fright *noun* [U] nervous feelings felt by performers before they appear in front of an audience 怯场（演员出场前的紧张不安）

stage·hand /'steɪdʒhænd/ *noun* a person whose job is to help move SCENERY, etc. in a theatre, to prepare the stage for the next play or the next part of a play 舞台工作人员（负责移动布景、准备道具等）

,stage 'left *adv.* on the left side of a stage in a theatre, as seen by an actor facing the audience（演员面对观众时的）舞台左侧

,stage-'manage *verb* **1 ~ sth** to act as stage manager for a performance in a theatre 担任舞台监督 **2 ~ sth** to arrange and carefully plan an event that the public will see, especially in order to give a particular impression 精心安排，周密策划（公共活动）

,stage 'manager *noun* the person who is responsible for the stage, lights, SCENERY, etc. during the performance of a play in a theatre 舞台监督 ➲ WORDFINDER NOTE AT PERFORMANCE

'stage name *noun* a name that an actor uses instead of his or her real name（演员的）艺名

,stage 'right *adv.* on the right side of a stage in a theatre, as seen by an actor facing the audience（演员面对观众时的）舞台右侧

'stage-struck *adj.* enjoying the theatre a lot and wishing very much to become an actor 醉心舞台渴望当演员的

,stage 'whisper *noun* **1** words that are spoken quietly by an actor to the audience and that the other people on stage are not supposed to hear 低声旁白（演员避开台上其他角色说给观众听的）**2** words that are spoken quietly by sb but that they in fact want everyone to hear 故意让所有人听见的悄悄话：*'I knew this would happen,' she said in a stage whisper.* "我早知道会出这样的事。" 她轻声说给所有人听。

stagey = STAGY

stag·fla·tion /stæg'fleɪʃn/ *noun* [U] an economic situation where there is high INFLATION (= prices rising continuously) but no increase in the jobs that are available or in business activity 滞胀（高通胀与低就业率或经济低迷并存）

stag·ger /'stægə(r)/ *verb* **1** [I, T] to walk with weak unsteady steps, as if you are about to fall 摇摇晃晃地走；蹒跚；踉跄 SYN **totter**: (+ **adv./prep.**) *The injured woman staggered to her feet.* 受伤的女人摇摇晃晃地站起身来。◇ *He staggered home, drunk.* 他喝醉酒，踉跄着回了家。◇ *We seem to stagger from one crisis to the next.* 我们仿佛在接连不断的危机中举步维艰。◇ (*figurative*) *The company is* ***staggering under the weight*** *of a £10m debt.* 公司在 1 000 万英镑债务的重压下步履艰难。◇ **~ sth** *I managed to stagger the last few steps.* 我好不容易跌跌撞撞走了这最后几步。**2** [T] to shock or surprise sb very much 使震惊；使大吃一惊 SYN **amaze**: **~ sb** *Her remarks staggered me.* 她的话让我震惊。◇ **it staggers sb that...** *It staggers me that the government is doing nothing about it.* 政府对此竟然不采取任何措施，我觉得不可思议。**3** [T] **~ sth** to arrange for events that would normally happen at the same time to start or happen at different times 使交错；使错开：*There were so many runners that they had to stagger the start.* 参加赛跑的选手很多，他们不得不把起跑点错开。
▸ **stag·ger** *noun*: *to walk with a stagger* 蹒跚着走

stag·gered /'stægəd; *NAmE* -gərd/ *adj.* **1** [not before noun] **~ (at/by sth)** | **~ (to hear, learn, see, etc.)** very surprised and shocked at sth you are told or at sth that happens 震惊；大吃一惊 SYN **amazed**: *I was staggered at the amount of money the ring cost.* 那戒指那么贵，我非常吃惊。**2** arranged in such a way that not everything happens at the same time 交错的；错开的：*staggered working hours* (= people start and finish at different times) 互相交错的工作时间

stag·ger·ing /'stægərɪŋ/ *adj.* (*rather informal*) so great, shocking or surprising that it is difficult to believe 令人难以相信的 SYN **astounding** ▸ **stag·ger·ing·ly** *adv.*: *staggeringly beautiful/expensive* 漂亮 / 昂贵得令人难以置信

sta·ging /'steɪdʒɪŋ/ *noun* **1** [C, U] the way in which a play is produced and presented on stage 演出形式；演出风格：*a modern staging of 'King Lear'* 以现代风格演出的《李尔王》**2** [U] a temporary platform used for standing or working on 临时工作台（或工作架）

'staging post *noun* a place where people, planes, ships, etc. regularly stop during a long journey 中途站（或机场、停靠码头）

stag·nant /'stægnənt/ *adj.* **1** **stagnant** water or air is not moving and therefore smells unpleasant（水或空气）不流动而污浊的 **2** not developing, growing or changing 停滞的；不发展的；无变化的 SYN **static**: *a stagnant economy* 停滞的经济

stag·nate /stæg'neɪt; *NAmE* 'stægneɪt/ *verb* **1** [I] to stop developing or making progress 停滞；不发展；不进步：*Profits have stagnated.* 利润原地踏步。◇ *I feel I'm stagnating in this job.* 我觉得，干这份工作我没有长进。**2** [I] to be or become stagnant 因不流动而变得污浊：*The water in the pond was stagnating.* 池塘里的水逐渐变成了死水。
▸ **stag·na·tion** /stæg'neɪʃn/ *noun* [U]: *a period of economic stagnation* 经济停滞时期

'**stag night** *noun* [usually sing.] **1** (*BrE*) the night before a man's wedding, often spent with his male friends 男子婚前夜（常与男性朋友一同度过）**2** (*BrE*) (*also* '**stag party** *BrE, NAmE*) (*NAmE* '**bachelor party**) a party that a man has with his male friends just before he gets married, often the night before 男子婚前聚会（只招待男性朋友）➲ COMPARE HEN PARTY ➲ WORDFINDER NOTE AT WEDDING

stagy (*also* **stagey**) /ˈsteɪdʒi/ *adj.* not natural, as if it is being acted by sb in a play 不自然的；做作的；演戏似的

staid /steɪd/ *adj.* (**staid·er**, **staid·est**) not amusing or interesting; boring and old-fashioned 没意思的；古板的；一本正经的

stain /steɪn/ *verb, noun*

■ ***verb*** **1** [T, I] to leave a mark that is difficult to remove on sth; to be marked in this way（被）玷污；留下污渍：**~ (sth) (with sth)** *I hope it doesn't stain the carpet.* 希望它别把地毯弄脏。◇ *This carpet stains easily.* 这块地毯不耐脏。◇ **~ sth + adj.** *The juice from the berries stained their fingers red.* 浆果汁把他们的手指染成了红色。**2** [T] to change the colour of sth using a coloured liquid 给…染色（或着色）：**~ sth** *to stain wood* 给木料上色 ◇ *Stain the specimen before looking at it under the microscope.* 先把标本染色，再放到显微镜下观察。◇ **~ sth + adj.** *They stained the floors dark brown.* 他们把地板涂成了深棕色。**3** [T] **~ sth** (*formal*) to damage the opinion that people have of sth 玷污，败坏（名声）：*The events had stained the city's reputation unfairly.* 这些事件使该市背上了不应有的恶名。

■ ***noun*** **1** [C] a dirty mark on sth, that is difficult to remove 污点；污渍：***a blood/a coffee/an ink, etc. stain*** 血迹、咖啡渍、墨痕等 ◇ ***stubborn stains*** (= that are very difficult to remove) 顽固的污渍 ◇ *How can I get this stain out?* 我怎么才能把这点污渍除去？◇ *The carpet has been treated so that it is **stain-resistant*** (= it does not stain easily). 这地毯已经过处理，不易挂污。➲ SYNONYMS AT MARK **2** [U, C] a liquid used for changing the colour of wood or cloth 染色剂；着色剂 **3** [sing.] **a ~ on sth** (*formal*) something that damages a person's reputation, so that people think badly of them（名声上的）污点

stained /steɪnd/ *adj.* (often in compounds 常构成复合词) covered with stains or marked with a stain 满是污痕的；沾有污渍的：*My dress was stained.* 我的连衣裙弄上了污渍。◇ *paint-stained jeans* 沾满油漆的牛仔裤 ➲ SYNONYMS AT DIRTY

ˌ**stained 'glass** *noun* [U] pieces of coloured glass that are put together to make windows, especially in churches 彩色玻璃

stain·less steel /ˌsteɪnləs ˈstiːl/ *noun* [U] a type of steel that does not RUST (= change colour) 不锈钢

stair 🔑 /steə(r); *NAmE* ster/ *noun* **1** 🔑 **stairs** [pl.] a set of steps built between two floors inside a building 楼梯：*We had to carry the piano up three **flights of stairs**.* 我们不得不抬着钢琴上了三段楼梯。◇ *The children ran **up/down the stairs**.* 孩子们跑上 / 跑下楼去。◇ ***at the bottom/top of the stairs*** 在楼梯下端 / 顶端 ◇ *He remembered passing her **on the stairs**.* 他记得在楼梯上与她擦肩而过。➲ SEE ALSO DOWNSTAIRS *n.*, UPSTAIRS *n.* **2** 🔑 [C] one of the steps in a set of stairs 梯级：*How many stairs are there up to the second floor?* 上到第三层一共有多少磴楼梯？➲ PICTURE AT STAIRCASE **3** [sing.] (*literary*) = STAIRCASE：*The house had a panelled hall and a fine oak stair.* 房子的门厅装有镶板墙裙，楼梯是用高级栎木建造的。▶ **stair** *adj.* [only before noun]: *the stair carpet* 楼梯地毯

IDM **below 'stairs** (*old-fashioned, BrE*) in the part of a house where the servants lived in the past（旧时）在仆人住的地方

stair·case /ˈsteəkeɪs; *NAmE* ˈsterk-/ *noun* a set of stairs inside a building including the posts and rails (= BANISTERS) that are fixed at the side（建筑物内的）楼梯：*a marble/stone/wooden staircase* 大理石 / 石头 / 木楼梯 ➲ SEE ALSO SPIRAL STAIRCASE

stair·lift /ˈsteəlɪft; *NAmE* ˈsterl-/ *noun* a piece of equipment in the form of a seat that sb can sit on to be moved up and down stairs, used by people who find it difficult to walk up and down stairs without help 座椅式升降器（供无法步行上下楼的人使用）

stair·way /ˈsteəweɪ; *NAmE* ˈsterweɪ/ *noun* a set of stairs inside or outside a building（建筑物内或外的）楼梯，阶梯

stair·well /ˈsteəwel; *NAmE* ˈsterwel/ *noun* [usually sing.] the space in a building in which the stairs are built 楼梯井（建筑物内楼梯占用的空间）

stake /steɪk/ *noun, verb*

■ ***noun*** **1** [C] a wooden or metal post that is pointed at one end and pushed into the ground in order to support sth, mark a particular place, etc. 桩；标桩；篱笆桩 ➲ VISUAL VOCAB PAGE V20 **2 the stake** [sing.] a wooden post that sb could be tied to in former times before being burnt to death (= killed by fire) as a punishment 火刑柱：*Joan of Arc was **burnt at the stake**.* 圣女贞德被处以火刑。**3** [C] money that sb invests in a company 股本；股份：*a 20% stake in the business* 那家公司 20% 的股份 **4** [sing.] **~ in sth** an important part or share in a business, plan, etc. that is important to you and that you want to be successful（在公司、计划等中的）重大利益，重大利害关系：*She has a personal stake in the success of the play.* 这出戏成功与否对她个人有重大利害关系。◇ *Many young people no longer feel they have a stake in society.* 很多年轻人不再觉得他们与社会休戚相关。**5** [C] something that you risk losing, especially money, when you try to predict the result of a race, game, etc., or when you are involved in an activity that can succeed or fail 赌注：*How much was the stake* (= how much did you bet)? 下了多少注？◇ *They were playing cards for **high stakes*** (= a lot of money). 他们当时正在打扑克，赌注很高。➲ WORDFINDER NOTE AT GAMBLING **6 stakes** [pl.] the money that is paid to the winners in horse racing 赛马奖金 **7 stakes** [U] used in the names of some horse races（用于某些赛马赛事的名称）…赛

IDM **at 'stake** that can be won or lost, depending on the

staircase 楼梯

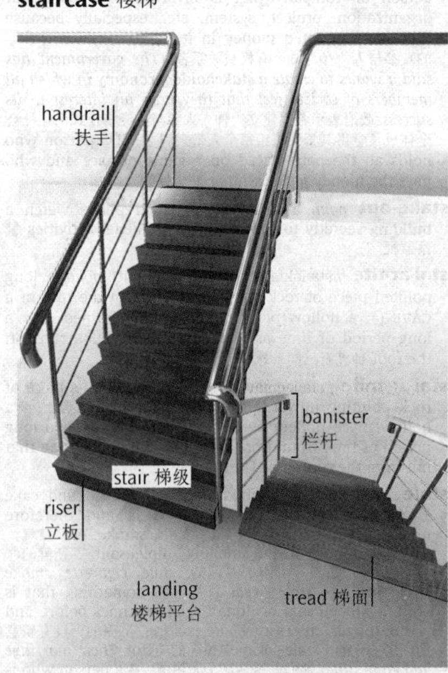

success of a particular action 成败难料；得失都可能；有风险：*We cannot afford to take risks when people's lives are at stake.* 在性命攸关的事情上，不容我们有闪失。◇ *The prize at stake is a place in the final.* 这次如果获胜，便能进入决赛。**go to the 'stake over/for sth** to be prepared to do anything in order to defend your opinions or beliefs 为坚持自己的观点（或信仰）甘冒一切危险；为维护自己的观点（或信仰）不惜赴汤蹈火 **in the... stakes** used to say how much of a particular quality a person has, as if they were in a competition in which some people are more successful than others（评论一个人的某种品质高或低）要是比…的话，论…：*John doesn't do too well in the personality stakes.* 论人格魅力，约翰很一般。➲ MORE AT UP *v.*

■ *verb* **1 ~ sth (on sth)** to risk money or sth important on the result of sth（就某事）以…打赌，拿…冒险 SYN **bet**: *He staked £25 on the favourite* (= for example, in horse racing). 他在那匹众人看好的马上押了 25 英镑。◇ *She staked her political career on tax reform, and lost.* 她把自己的政治前程押在税制改革上，结果赌输了。◇ *That's him over there—I'd **stake my life on it*** (= I am completely confident). 就是那边那个人，我敢拿脑袋打赌。**2 ~ sth (up)** to support sth with a stake (1) 用桩支撑：*to stake newly planted trees* 用木桩支撑新植的树

IDM **stake (out) a/your 'claim (to/for/on sth)** to say or show publicly that you think sth should be yours 公开宣布自己（对某物）的所有权；向公众表示某物应属于自己：*Adams staked his claim for a place in the Olympic team with his easy win yesterday.* 亚当斯昨天轻松获胜，这无异于告诉人们奥运代表队中应有他的位置。

PHR V **,stake sth↔'out 1** to clearly mark the limits of sth that you claim is yours 清楚地界定自认为属于自己的东西 **2** to state your opinion, position, etc. on sth very clearly 明确阐述自己的看法（或立场等）：*The President staked out his position on the issue.* 总统明确阐述了他在这个问题上的立场。**3** to watch a place secretly, especially for signs of illegal activity 监视：*Detectives had been staking out the house for several weeks.* 警探们已对这所房子监视了几个星期。➲ RELATED NOUN STAKE-OUT

stake·hold·er /'steɪkhəʊldə(r); *NAmE* -hoʊ-/ *noun* **1** a person or company that is involved in a particular organization, project, system, etc., especially because they have invested money in it（某组织、工程、体系等的）参与人，参与方；有权益关系者：*The government has said it wants to create a **stakeholder economy** in which all members of society feel that they have an interest in its success.* 政府表示希望建立一种人人参与的经济模式，让社会全体成员觉得其繁荣将给每个人带来利益。**2** a person who holds all the bets placed on a game or race and who pays the money to the winner 赌金保管人

'stake-out *noun* a situation in which police watch a building secretly to find evidence of illegal activities 警察监视

stal·ac·tite /'stæləktaɪt; *NAmE* stə'læktaɪt/ *noun* a long pointed piece of rock hanging down from the roof of a CAVE (= a hollow place underground), formed over a long period of time as water containing LIME runs off the roof 钟乳石（向下悬垂）

stal·ag·mite /'stæləgmaɪt; *NAmE* stə'læg-/ *noun* a piece of rock pointing upwards from the floor of a CAVE (= a hollow place underground), that is formed over a long period of time from drops of water containing LIME that fall from the roof 石笋（向上生长）

stale /steɪl/ *adj.* **1** (of food, especially bread and cake 食物，尤指面包和糕点) no longer fresh and therefore unpleasant to eat 不新鲜的 **2** (of air, smoke, etc. 空气、烟等) no longer fresh; smelling unpleasant 不新鲜的；（空气）污浊的；（烟味）难闻的：*stale cigarette smoke* 难闻的烟味儿 ◇ *stale sweat* 汗臭味 **3** something that is **stale** has been said or done too many times before and is no longer interesting or exciting 陈腐的；没有新意的；老掉牙的：*stale jokes* 老掉牙的笑话 ◇ *Their marriage had gone stale.* 他们的婚姻已了无热情。**4** a person who is **stale** has done the same thing for too long and so is unable to do it well or produce any new ideas（因持续做某事时间太长）厌倦的，腻烦的：*After ten years in the job, she felt stale and needed a change.* 在那个岗位干了十年之后，她觉得腻了，需要换换工作。▶ **stale·ness** *noun* [U]

stale·mate /'steɪlmeɪt/ *noun* **1** [U, C, usually sing.] a disagreement or a situation in a competition in which neither side is able to win or make any progress（辩论或竞赛中出现的）僵局，僵持局面 SYN **impasse**: *The talks ended in (a) stalemate.* 谈判陷入僵局，无果而终。**2** [U, sing.] (in CHESS 国际象棋) a situation in which a player cannot successfully move any of their pieces and the game ends without a winner 僵局；和棋 ➲ COMPARE CHECKMATE (1)

Sta·lin·ism /'stɑːlɪnɪzəm/ *noun* [U] the policies and beliefs of Stalin, especially that the Communist party should be the only party and that the central government should control the whole political and economic system 斯大林主义 ▶ **Sta·lin·ist** *adj., noun*

stalk /stɔːk/ *noun, verb*

■ *noun* **1** a thin STEM that supports a leaf, flower or fruit and joins it to another part of the plant or tree; the main STEM of a plant（叶）柄；（花）梗；（果实的）柄；（植物的）茎，秆：*flowers on long stalks* 长茎上的花 ◇ *celery stalks* 芹菜茎 ◇ *He ate the apple, stalk and all.* 他把那个苹果吃了个干净，连梗都没剩下。➲ VISUAL VOCAB PAGES V11, V32 **2** a long thin structure that supports sth, especially an organ in some animals, and joins it on to another part 柄；（动物的）肉柄，肉茎：*Crabs have eyes on stalks.* 螃蟹的眼睛长在肉柄上。

■ *verb* **1** [T, I] **~ (sth/sb)** to move slowly and quietly towards an animal or a person, in order to kill, catch or harm it or them 偷偷接近，潜近（猎物或人）：*The lion was stalking a zebra.* 狮子偷偷接近斑马。◇ *He stalked his victim as she walked home, before attacking and robbing her.* 她步行回家时，他偷偷地接近然后下手袭击，并且抢劫了她。**2** [T] **~ sb** to illegally follow and watch sb over a long period of time, in a way that is annoying or frightening（非法）跟踪，盯梢：*She claimed that he had been stalking her over a period of three years.* 她声称，三年来他一直在盯她的梢。**3** [I] **+ adv./prep.** to walk in an angry or proud way 怒冲冲地走；趾高气扬地走：*He stalked off without a word.* 他一言未发，怒冲冲地走了。**4** [T, I] **~ (sth)** to move through a place in an unpleasant or threatening way 令人厌恶地穿过；威胁地通过：*The gunmen stalked the building, looking for victims.* 这些持枪歹徒凶神恶煞般地打楼里走过，寻找袭击的目标。◇ (*figurative*) *Fear stalks the streets of the city at night.* 夜间，这座城市的大街小巷笼罩着恐怖气氛。

stalk·er /'stɔːkə(r)/ *noun* **1** a person who follows and watches another person over a long period of time in a way that is annoying or frightening 跟踪者；盯梢者 **2** a person who follows an animal quietly and slowly, especially in order to kill or capture it 悄悄接近猎物的猎人

stalk·ing /'stɔːkɪŋ/ *noun* [U] the crime of following and watching sb over a long period of time in a way that is annoying or frightening 跟踪罪

'stalking horse *noun* [sing.] **1** a person or thing that is used to hide the real purpose of a particular course of action 用以掩人耳目的人（或物）；用以掩蔽的事物 **2** a politician who competes against the leader of their party in order to see how much support the leader has; a stronger candidate can then compete against the leader more seriously（为试探对手支持率而推出的）掩护性候选人

stall /stɔːl/ *noun, verb*

■ *noun* **1** [C] a table or small shop with an open front that people sell things from, especially at a market 货摊，摊位，售货亭（尤指集市上的）SYN **stand**: *a market stall* 集市上的货摊 ➲ VISUAL VOCAB PAGE V3 ➲ SEE ALSO BOOKSTALL **2** [C] a section inside a farm building that is large enough for one animal to be kept in 牲畜棚；马厩；牛棚 **3** [C] (*especially NAmE*) a small area in a room, surrounded by glass, walls, etc., that contains a shower or toilet（房间内的）小隔间，淋浴室，洗手间 **4 the stalls** (*also* **the**

S

'**orchestra stalls**) (*both BrE*) [pl.] (*NAmE* **the orchestra** [sing.]) the seats that are nearest to the stage in a theatre（剧场的）正厅前排座位：*the front row of the stalls* 正厅第一排 ➲ WORDFINDER NOTE AT THEATRE **5** [C, usually pl.] the seats at the front of a church where the CHOIR (= singers) and priests sit（教堂内）唱诗班和牧师的座位 **6** [C, usually sing.] a situation in which a vehicle's engine suddenly stops because it is not getting enough power（车辆发动机的）熄火；（车辆的）抛锚 **7** [C, usually sing.] a situation in which an aircraft loses speed and goes steeply downwards（飞机的）失速

■ ***verb*** **1** [I, T] (of a vehicle or an engine 车辆或发动机) to stop suddenly because of a lack of power or speed; to make a vehicle or engine do this（使）熄火，抛锚：*The car stalled and refused to start again.* 汽车熄火打不着了。◇ **~ sth** *I stalled the car three times during my driving test.* 我考驾照时车子熄了三次火。**2** [I] **~ (on/over sth)** to try to avoid doing sth or answering a question so that you have more time 故意拖延（以赢得时间）：*They are still stalling on the deal.* 他们仍在拖时间，而不急于达成协议。◇ *'What do you mean?' she asked, **stalling for time**.* "你这是什么意思？" 她问，故意拖延着时间。**3** [T] **~ sb** to make sb wait so that you have more time to do sth 拖住（以赢得时间做某事）：*See if you can stall her while I finish searching her office.* 你看能不能拖住她，我好把她的办公室搜查完。**4** [T, I] **~ (sth)** to stop sth from happening until a later date; to stop making progress 暂缓；搁置；停顿：*attempts to revive the stalled peace plan* 旨在重新启动搁置了的和平计划的努力 ◇ *Discussions have once again stalled.* 讨论再次停顿下来。

stall·hold·er /'stɔːlhəʊldə(r); *NAmE* -hoʊ-/ *noun* (*BrE*) a person who sells things from a stall in a market, etc. 摊贩；货摊主

stal·lion /'stæliən/ *noun* a fully grown male horse, especially one that is used for breeding 牡马；（尤指）种马 ➲ COMPARE COLT (1), GELDING, MARE (1)

stal·wart /'stɔːlwət; *NAmE* -wərt/ *noun, adj.*

■ ***noun*** **~ (of sth)** a loyal supporter who does a lot of work for an organization, especially a political party（政党等组织的）忠诚拥护者，坚定分子

■ ***adj.*** [usually before noun] **1** loyal and able to be relied on, even in a difficult situation 忠诚的；忠实的 SYN **faithful**：*stalwart supporters* 忠实的拥护者 **2** (*formal*) physically strong 健壮的；强壮的

sta·men /'steɪmən/ *noun* (*specialist*) a small thin male part in the middle of a flower that produces POLLEN and is made up of a STALK supporting an ANTHER. The centre of each flower usually has several stamens. 雄蕊 ➲ VISUAL VOCAB PAGE V11

stam·ina /'stæmɪnə/ *noun* [U] the physical or mental strength that enables you to do sth difficult for long periods of time 耐力；耐性；持久力：*It takes a lot of stamina to run a marathon.* 跑马拉松需要很大的耐力。➲ WORDFINDER NOTE AT FIT ➲ COLLOCATIONS AT DIET

stam·mer /'stæmə(r)/ *verb, noun*

■ ***verb*** [I, T] to speak with difficulty, repeating sounds or words and often stopping, before saying things correctly 口吃；结结巴巴地说 SYN **stutter**：*Many children stammer but grow out of it.* 很多小孩口吃，但长大后就改过来了。◇ **+ speech** *'W-w-what?' he stammered.* "什…什…什么？" 他结巴着说。◇ **~ sth (out)** *She was barely able to stammer out a description of her attacker.* 她只能勉强结结巴巴地说一说袭击她的人是什么模样。▶ **stam·mer·er** *noun*

■ ***noun*** [sing.] a problem that sb has in speaking in which they repeat sounds or words or often pause before saying things correctly 口吃；结巴

stamp 🔑 /stæmp/ *noun, verb*

■ ***noun***

• **ON LETTER/PACKAGE** 信函；包裹 **1** 🔑 (*also formal* '**postage stamp**) [C] a small piece of paper with a design on it that you buy and stick on an envelope or a package before you post it 邮票：*a 62p stamp* 一枚 62 便士的邮票 ◇ *Could I have three first-class stamps, please?* 请给我拿三张第一类邮件的邮票。◇ *He has been collecting stamps since he was eight.* 他从八岁开始集邮。◇ *a **stamp album*** 集邮册 ➲ VISUAL VOCAB PAGE V45

• **PRINTING TOOL** 印章 **2** 🔑 [C] a tool for printing the date or a design or mark onto a surface 印；章；戳：*a date stamp* 日期戳 ➲ SEE ALSO RUBBER STAMP (1)

• **PRINTED DESIGN/WORDS** 印记 **3** 🔑 [C] a design or words made by stamping sth onto a surface 印记；戳记：*The passports, with the visa stamps, were waiting at the embassy.* 那些护照都加盖了签证章，在大使馆等待领取。◇ (*figurative*) *The project has the government's **stamp of approval**.* 工程已获得政府批准。

• **PROOF OF PAYMENT** 付款证明 **4** [C] a small piece of paper with a design on it, stuck on a document to show that a particular amount of money has been paid 印花：*a TV licence stamp* 电视收视许可证印花

• **CHARACTER/QUALITY** 特征；特性 **5** [sing.] **~ (of sth)** (*formal*) the mark or sign of a particular quality or person 特征；痕迹；烙印：*All his work **bears the stamp** of authority.* 他的一切工作都具有权威性。**6** [sing.] (*formal*) a kind or class, especially of people 类型，种类（尤指人）：*men of a different stamp* 另一类人

• **OF FOOT** 脚 **7** [sing.] an act or sound of stamping the foot 跺脚（声）；踩蹄（声）：*The stamp of hoofs alerted Isabel.* 马蹄声引起了伊莎贝尔的警觉。

■ ***verb***

• **FOOT** 脚 **1** 🔑 [T, I] **~ (sth)** to put your foot down heavily and noisily on the ground 跺（脚）；重踩；重踏：*I tried **stamping my feet** to keep warm.* 我跺了一阵脚想暖和暖和。◇ *Sam **stamped his foot** in anger.* 萨姆气得直跺脚。◇ *The audience were stamping and cheering.* 观众又是跺脚，又是欢呼。

• **WALK** 走 **2** [I] **+ adv./prep.** to walk with loud heavy steps 迈着重重的步伐走 SYN **stomp**：*She turned and stamped out of the room.* 她扭身嗵嗵地走出了房间。

• **PRINT DESIGN/WORDS** 盖印；盖章 **3** 🔑 [T, often passive] to print letters, words, a design, etc. onto sth using a special tool 在…上盖（字样或图案等）；把（字样或图案等）盖在…上：**~ A (with B)** *The box was stamped with the maker's name.* 盒子上盖有制作者的印章。◇ *Wait here to have your passport stamped.* 请在这里等候给护照盖章。◇ **~ B on A** *I'll stamp the company name on your cheque.* 我来给你的支票盖上公司的章。◇ *The maker's name was stamped in gold on the box.* 盒子上盖有制作者的金字印章。➲ SEE ALSO RUBBER-STAMP, STAMP STH ON STH

• **SHOW FEELING/QUALITY** 显露感情 / 性质 **4** [T, usually passive] to make a feeling show clearly on sb's face, in their actions, etc. 显示出（感情）：**~ A with B** *Their faces were stamped with hostility.* 他们的神情充满敌意。◇ **~ B over, across, etc. A** *The crime had revenge stamped all over it.* 从各方面看这次犯罪都是复仇行为。**5** [T] **~ sb as sth** to show that sb has a particular quality 表明（某人）是…：*Her success has stamped her as one of the country's top riders.* 她的成功表明她是全国最出色的骑手之一。

• **ON LETTER/PACKAGE** 信函；包裹 **6** [T, usually passive] **~ sth** to stick a stamp on a letter or package 在…上贴邮票

• **CUT OUT OBJECT** 冲压 **7** [T] **~ sth (out) (of/from sth)** to cut and shape an object from a piece of metal or plastic using a special machine or tool 冲压

PHR V '**stamp on sth** **1** to put your foot down with force on sth 用力踩：*The child stamped on the spider.* 小孩踩了那只蜘蛛一脚。**2** to stop sth from happening or stop sb from doing sth, especially by using force or authority 压制；镇压：*All attempts at modernization were stamped on by senior officials.* 旨在实现现代化的努力统统受到高级官员的压制。'**stamp sth on sth** to make sth have an important effect or influence on sth 在…上打上…印记；把…铭刻在…中：*She stamped her own interpretation on the role.* 她给那个角色注入了自己的诠释。,**stamp sth↔'out** **1** to get rid of sth that is bad, unpleasant or dangerous, especially by using force or a lot of effort（尤指通过武力或不懈努力）消除，消灭，镇压 SYN **eliminate**：*to stamp out racism* 消灭种族主义 **2** to put out a fire by bringing your foot down heavily on it 踩灭（火）

S

ˈ**stamp collecting** *noun* [U] the hobby of collecting stamps from different countries 集邮 ➲ VISUAL VOCAB PAGE V45 ▸ ˈ**stamp collector** *noun*

ˈ**stamp duty** *noun* [U] a tax in Britain on some legal documents 印花税

ˌ**stamped addressed ˈenvelope** *noun* (*abbr.* **SAE**) (*BrE*) an envelope on which you have written your name and address and put a stamp so that sb else can use it to send sth to you（写上姓名地址且贴有邮票的）回邮信封：*Please enclose a stamped addressed envelope to get your test results.* 请附姓名地址邮资俱全的信封，以便把化验结果寄给你。

stam·pede /stæmˈpiːd/ *noun, verb*

■ ***noun*** [C, usually sing.] **1** a situation in which a group of people or large animals such as horses suddenly start running in the same direction, especially because they are frightened or excited（人群的）奔逃，蜂拥；（兽群的）惊跑，狂奔：*A stampede broke out when the doors opened.* 门一开，人们蜂拥而出。**2** a situation in which a lot of people are trying to do or achieve the same thing at the same time 热潮；风尚；风气：*Falling interest rates has led to a stampede to buy property.* 不断下降的利率引发了一场购房热。

■ ***verb*** **1** [I, T] ~ **(sth)** (of large animals or people 兽群或人群) to run in a stampede; to make animals do this（使）狂奔，涌向：*a herd of stampeding elephants* 一群狂奔的大象 ◇ *A huge bunch of kids came stampeding down the corridor.* 一大群孩子顺着走廊涌了过来。**2** [T, usually passive] **~ sb (into sth/into doing sth)** to make sb rush into doing sth without giving them time to think about it 使仓促行事：*I refuse to be stampeded into making any hasty decisions.* 我不愿仓促行事，草率作决定。

ˈ**stamping ground** (*NAmE also* ˈ**stomping ground**) *noun* (*informal*) a place that sb likes and where they often go（某人）爱去的地方 SYN **haunt**

stance /stæns; *BrE also* stɑːns/ *noun* **1** ~ **(on sth)** the opinions that sb has about sth and expresses publicly（公开表明的）观点，态度，立场 SYN **position**：*What is the newspaper's stance on the war?* 那家报纸对这场战争持什么立场？**2** the way in which sb stands, especially when playing a sport（尤指体育运动中的）站立姿势

stanch /stɔːntʃ; stæntʃ/ *verb* (*especially NAmE*) = STAUNCH

stan·chion /ˈstæntʃən; ˈstɑːn-/ *noun* (*formal*) a vertical pole used to support sth（用以支撑的）杆，支柱

stand 🔑 /stænd/ *verb, noun*

■ ***verb*** (**stood, stood** /stʊd/)

• **ON FEET/BE VERTICAL** 站立；直立 **1** 🔑 [I] to be on your feet; to be in a vertical position 站立；立；直立：*She was too weak to stand.* 她虚弱得站都站不住。◇ *a bird standing on one leg* 单腿独立的鸟 ◇ ***Don't just stand there***—*do something!* 别光站着，干点什么！◇ *I was standing only a few feet away.* 当时我就站在几英尺远的地方。◇ *We all **stood around** in the corridor waiting.* 我们分散站在过道里等着。◇ *to **stand on your head/hands*** (= to be upside down, balancing on your head/hands) 用头 / 用手倒立 ◇ *After the earthquake, only a few houses were **left standing**.* 地震后只剩几座房子没倒。◇ **+ adj.** ***Stand still*** *while I take your photo.* 我给你照相，站着别动。**2** 🔑 [I] to get up onto your feet from another position 站起来；起立：*Everyone stood when the President came in.* 总统进来时大家都起立。◇ **~ up** *We stood up in order to get a better view.* 我们站起身来以便看得更清楚。

• **PUT UPRIGHT** 使直立 **3** [T] **~ sth/sb + adv./prep.** to put sth/sb in a vertical position somewhere 使直立；竖放；使站立：*Stand the ladder up against the wall.* 把梯子靠墙立好。◇ *I stood the little girl on a chair so that she could see.* 我让小女孩站到椅子上，好让她看得见。

• **BE IN PLACE/CONDITION** 位置；状态 **4** 🔑 [I] **+ adv./prep.** to be in a particular place 位于（某处）：*The castle stands on the site of an ancient battlefield.* 那座城堡坐落在一片古战场上。◇ *An old oak tree once stood here.* 以前这儿长着一棵老橡树。**5** [I] **(+ adj.)** to be in a particular condition or situation 处于（某种状态或情形）：*The house **stood** empty for a long time.* 那所房子空了好长一段时间。◇ *'You're wrong about the date—it was 1988.' '**I stand corrected**'* (= accept that I was wrong).' "你把日期搞错了，是 1988 年。""你说得对，是我搞错了。"◇ *You **never know where you stand with** her—one minute she's friendly, the next she'll hardly speak to you.* 你从来拿不准你和她的关系如何，她一会儿跟你亲热，一会儿连话也不大跟你说。◇ ***As things stand**, there is little chance of a quick settlement of the dispute.* 照目前的形势，尽快解决争端的可能微乎其微。

• **BE AT HEIGHT/LEVEL** 高度；水平 **6** [I] **+ noun** (not used in the progressive tenses 不用于进行时) to be a particular height 高度为；高达：*The tower stands 30 metres high.* 塔高 30 米。**7** [I] **~ at sth** to be at a particular level, amount, height, etc. 达特定水平（或数量、高度等）：*Interest rates stand at 3%.* 利率为 3%。◇ *The world record then stood at 6.59 metres.* 当时的世界纪录是 6.59 米。

• **OF CAR/TRAIN, ETC.** 汽车、火车等 **8** [I] **+ adv./prep.** to be in a particular place, especially while waiting to go somewhere 停；停靠：*The train standing at platform 3 is for London, Victoria.* 停在第 3 站台的火车开往伦敦维多利亚站。

• **OF LIQUID/MIXTURE** 液体；混合物 **9** [I] to remain still, without moving or being moved 停滞；不流动；搁置：*Mix the batter and let it stand for twenty minutes.* 搅好面糊以后，放上二十分钟。◇ *standing pools of rainwater* 雨水洼

• **OFFER/DECISION** 提议；决定 **10** [I] if an offer, a decision, etc. made earlier **stands**, it is still valid 保持有效；维持不变：*My offer still stands.* 我的出价仍然算数。◇ *The world record stood for 20 years.* 那项世界纪录 20 年未被打破。

• **BE LIKELY TO DO STH** 很可能 **11** [I] **~ to do sth** to be in a situation where you are likely to do sth 很可能做某事：*You stand to make a lot from this deal.* 你很可能会从这笔生意中大赚一笔。

• **HAVE OPINION** 观点 **12** [I] **~ (on sth)** to have a particular attitude or opinion about sth or towards sb（对某事）持某种态度，有某一观点，采取某种立场：***Where do you stand** on private education?* 你对私立教育持什么观点？

• **DISLIKE** 不喜欢 **13** 🔑 [T, no passive] (not used in the progressive tenses 不用于进行时) used especially in negative sentences and questions to emphasize that you do not like sb/sth（尤用于否定句和疑问句，强调不喜欢）容忍，忍受 SYN **bear**：**~ sb/sth** ***I can't stand*** *his brother.* 他弟弟让我受不了。◇ *I can't stand the sight of blood.* 一看见血我就难受。◇ ***I can't stand it*** *when you do that.* 你那么做，我受不了。◇ **~ doing sth** *She couldn't stand being kept waiting.* 叫她等着，她会受不了。◇ **~ sb/sth doing sth** *I can't stand people interrupting all the time.* 我不能容忍老有人打岔。◇ *How do you stand him being here all the time?* 他老在这儿，你怎么受得了呢？➲ SYNONYMS AT HATE

• **SURVIVE TREATMENT** 承受 **14** 🔑 [T] **~ sth** used especially with *can/could* to say that sb/sth can survive sth or can TOLERATE sth without being hurt or damaged（尤与 can 或 could 连用）经受，承受，经得起：*His heart won't stand the strain much longer.* 他的心脏对这种压力承受不了多久。◇ *Modern plastics can stand very high and very low temperatures.* 新型塑料能承受很高和很低的温度。

• **BUY DRINK/MEAL** 买饮料 / 餐点 **15** [T, no passive] to buy a drink or meal for sb 花钱请（某人喝饮料或吃饭）；买…请客：**~ sth** *He stood drinks all round.* 他请客，让大家喝了饮料。◇ **~ sb sth** *She was kind enough to stand us a meal.* 她真好，请我们吃了饭。

• **IN ELECTION** 选举 **16** 🔑 (*especially BrE*) (*NAmE usually* **run**) [I] **~ (for/as sth)** to be a candidate in an election 做候选人；参选：*He **stood for parliament*** (= tried to get elected as an MP). 他竞选过议会议员。◇ *She stood unsuccessfully as a candidate in the local elections.* 她参加过地方选举，但未能当选。

IDM HELP Idioms containing **stand** are at the entries for the nouns and adjectives in the idioms, for example **stand on ceremony** is at **ceremony**. 含 stand 的习语，都可在该等习语中的名词及形容词相关词条找到，如 stand on ceremony 在词条 ceremony 下。

PHR V ˌ**stand aˈside 1** to move to one side 站到一边；让开：*She stood aside to let us pass.* 她站到一边让我们过。**2** to not get involved in sth 不参与；不介入；置身事外：

S

Don't stand aside and let others do all the work. 不要袖手旁观，工作都让别人去做。**3** to stop doing a job so sb else can do it 退居一旁；让位于他人；靠边

ˌ**stand ˈback (from sth) 1** to move back from a place 往后站；退后：*The police ordered the crowd to stand back.* 警察命令人群往后退。**2** to be located away from sth 位于离…有一段距离的地方：*The house stands back from the road.* 房子离公路有一段距离。**3** to think about a situation as if you are not involved in it 置身事外（来考虑）：*It's time to stand back and look at your career so far.* 现在你该从旁观者的角度来审视一下自己迄今的职业生涯了。

ˌ**stand beˈtween sb/sth and sth** to prevent sb from getting or achieving sth 阻碍（某人获得某物）：*Only one game stood between him and victory.* 只要再赢一场比赛他就能胜出。

ˌ**stand ˈby 1** to be present while sth bad is happening but not do anything to stop it 袖手旁观；无动于衷：*How can you stand by and see him accused of something he didn't do?* 你怎么能眼睁睁看着他遭人诬陷呢？ RELATED NOUN BYSTANDER **2** to be ready for action 做好随时行动的准备；做好准备：*The troops are standing by.* 部队随时待命出动。 RELATED NOUN STANDBY ˈ**stand by sb** to help sb or be friends with them, even in difficult situations 支持；帮助；忠于：*her famous song, 'Stand by your man'* 她的著名歌曲《忠于你的男人》ˈ**stand by sth** to still believe or agree with sth you said, decided or agreed earlier 仍然遵守诺言（或协议等）：*She still stands by every word she said.* 她依旧恪守她说过的每一句话。

ˌ**stand ˈdown 1 stand down (as sth)** to leave a job or position 离职；退职；下台：*He stood down to make way for someone younger.* 他退下来好为年轻人让路。**2** (of a witness 证人) to leave the WITNESS BOX/STAND in court after giving evidence 退出证人席

ˈ**stand for sth** [no passive] **1** (not used in the progressive tenses 不用于进行时) to be an abbreviation or symbol of sth（指缩写或符号）是…意思，代表：*'The book's by T.C. Smith.' 'What does the 'T.C.' stand for?'* "这部书是 T.C. 史密斯写的。" "T.C. 是什么的缩写？" **2** to support sth 支持；主张：*I hated the organization and all it stood for* (= the ideas that it supported). 我厌恶那个组织，也厌恶它的一切主张。**3** **not stand for sth** to not let sb do sth or sth happen 容忍；忍受：*I'm not standing for it any longer.* 这种事我再也不能容忍了。

ˌ**stand ˈin (for sb)** to take sb's place 代替，顶替（某人） **SYN** **deputize**：*My assistant will stand in for me while I'm away.* 我不在期间，由我的助手代替我。 RELATED NOUN STAND-IN

ˌ**stand ˈout (as sth)** to be much better or more important than sb/sth 出色；杰出；更为重要：*Four points stand out as being more important than the rest.* 有四点比其余各点更为重要。 SEE ALSO OUTSTANDING (1) ˌ**stand ˈout (from/against sth)** to be easily seen; to be noticeable 显眼；突出：*The lettering stood out well against the dark background.* 那种字体在深色背景下十分醒目。◇ *She's the sort of person who **stands out in a crowd**.* 她是那种在人群中很显眼的人。

ˌ**stand ˈover sb** be near sb and watch them 监督；监视：*I don't like you standing over me while I'm cooking.* 我不喜欢做饭时你在一旁盯着我。

ˌ**stand ˈup** to be on your feet 站起；站立；起立：*There were no seats left so I had to stand up.* 没有座位了，所以我只好站着。◇ *You'll look taller if you **stand up straight**.* 站直身子，你会显得高些。ˌ**stand sb ˈup** (*informal*) to deliberately not meet sb you have arranged to meet, especially sb you are having a romantic relationship with（尤指恋人）故意失约使某人空等，放某人鸽子：*I've been stood up!* 人家让我空等一场！ˌ**stand ˈup for sb/sth** to support or defend sb/sth 支持；维护：*Always stand up for your friends.* 任何时候都要支持自己的朋友。◇ *You must stand up for your rights.* 你必须维护自己的权利。◇ *She had learnt to stand up for herself.* 她学会了自我保护。ˌ**stand ˈup (to sth)** to remain valid even when tested, examined closely, etc. 经得起（检验、审查等）：*His argument simply doesn't stand up to close scrutiny.* 他的论点完全经不起仔细推敲。◇ *I'm afraid this document will never stand up in a court of law.* 恐怕这份文件在法庭上是根本站不住的。ˌ**stand ˈup to sb** to resist sb; to not accept bad treatment from sb without complaining 抵抗；勇敢反对；不甘忍受某人的欺负（或不公平对待）：*It was brave of her to stand up to those bullies.* 她不向那几个坏蛋屈服，真是勇敢。ˌ**stand ˈup to sth** (of materials, products, etc. 材料、产品等) to remain in good condition despite rough treatment 能承受，经受得住，耐（…） **SYN** **withstand**：*The carpet is designed to stand up to a lot of wear and tear.* 这种地毯设计得十分耐用。

■ ***noun***

• **OPINION** 观点 **1** [usually sing.] **~ (on sth)** an attitude towards sth or an opinion that you make clear to people 态度；立场；观点：*to take a firm stand on sth* 在某事上采取坚定的立场 ◇ *He was criticized for his tough stand on immigration.* 他因在移民问题上立场强硬受到批评。

• **DEFENCE** 保卫 **2** [usually sing.] a strong effort to defend yourself or your opinion about sth 保卫；捍卫；维护；

▼ **SYNONYMS** 同义词辨析

stand

get up • stand up • rise • get to your feet • be on your feet

These words all mean to be in an upright position with your weight on your feet, or to put yourself in this position. 以上各词均含站立、直立、站起来之义。

stand to be in an upright position with your weight on your feet 指站立、直立：*She was too weak to stand.* 她虚弱得站都站不住。◇ ***Stand still** when I'm talking to you!* 我跟你说话，站着别动！ **NOTE** **Stand** is usually used with an adverb or prepositional phrase to show where or how sb stands, but sometimes another phrase or clause is used to show what sb does while they are standing. * stand 通常与副词或介词短语连用，表示站的地方或方式，但有时也与另一短语或从句连用，表明站着时在做某事：*We stood talking for a few minutes.* 我们站着谈了几分钟。◇ *He stood and looked out to sea.* 他站着向大海望去。

get up to get into a standing position from a sitting, kneeling or lying position 指从坐、跪或躺的姿势站起来：*Please don't get up!* 请不要站起来！

stand up to be in a standing position; to stand after sitting 指站立、起立：*Stand up straight!* 立正！◇ *Everyone would stand up when the teacher entered the classroom.* 老师走进教室时大家都会起立。

STAND, GET UP OR STAND UP? 用 stand、get up 还是 stand up?

Stand usually means 'to be in a standing position' but can also mean 'to get into a standing position'. **Stand up** can be used with either of these meanings, but its use is more restricted: it is used especially when sb tells sb or a group of people to stand. **Get up** is the most frequent way of saying 'get into a standing position', and this can be from a sitting, kneeling or lying position; if you **stand up**, this is nearly always after sitting, especially on a chair. If you want to tell sb politely that they do not need to move from their chair, use **get up**. * stand 通常含站立、直立之义，但亦含站起来、起来之义。stand up 用于上述两种意思均可，但其用法较受限制，主要用于指让某人或一群人站起来。get up 是表达从坐着、跪着或躺着的姿势站起来最常用的说法；stand up 则几乎总是指从坐着的姿势，尤指从椅子上站起来。如果想礼貌地告诉某人不必从椅子上起来，用 get up：~~*Please don't stand up!*~~

rise (*formal*) to get into a standing position from a sitting, kneeling or lying position 指从坐、跪或躺的姿势站起来：*Would you all rise, please, to welcome our visiting speaker.* 请大家起立，欢迎我们的演讲嘉宾。

get to your feet to stand up after sitting, kneeling or lying 指坐、跪或躺后站起来：*I helped her to get to her feet.* 我扶着她让她站起来。

be on your feet to be standing up 指站着：*I've been on my feet all day.* 我已经站了一整天。

S

抵抗：*We must* ***make a stand against*** *further job losses.* 我们必须采取措施，防止进一步裁员。◇ *the rebels' desperate last stand* 反叛者最后的疯狂抵抗

• **FOR SHOWING/HOLDING STH** 展示；摆放 **3** a table or a vertical structure that goods are sold from, especially in the street or at a market 货摊；售货亭 **SYN** **stall**：*a hamburger/newspaper stand* 汉堡包售卖亭；报摊 ➲ SEE ALSO NEWS STAND **4** (*especially BrE*) a table or a vertical structure where things are displayed or advertised, for example at an exhibition（展示或推介物品的）桌，台，摊位：***a display/an exhibition/a trade stand*** 展位；展销台 **5** (often in compounds 常构成复合词) a piece of equipment or furniture that you use for holding a particular type of thing 架；座：*a* ***bicycle/microphone/cake, etc. stand*** 自行车停靠架、麦克风架、蛋糕座等 ➲ VISUAL VOCAB PAGES V55, V72 ➲ SEE ALSO HATSTAND, MUSIC STAND, NIGHTSTAND, WASHSTAND

• **AT SPORTS GROUND** 体育场 **6** a large sloping structure at a STADIUM with rows where people sit or stand to watch the game 看台 ➲ SEE ALSO GRANDSTAND

• **IN COURT** 法庭 **7** [usually sing.] = WITNESS BOX：*He took* ***the stand*** *as the first witness.* 他第一个出庭作证。

• **IN CRICKET** 板球 **8** [usually sing.] the period of time in which two people who are BATTING (= hitting the ball) play together and score points 两个击球员同时在场上并跑动得分的阶段；双人配对：*Clinch and Harris shared an* ***opening stand*** *of 69.* 克林奇和哈里斯两位击球员，比赛一开始时搭档，共得 69 分。

• **FOR BAND/ORCHESTRA, ETC.** 乐队、交响乐队等 **9** a raised platform for a band, an ORCHESTRA, a speaker, etc.（用于演出或演讲等的）舞台，高台，台 ➲ SEE ALSO BANDSTAND

• **FOR TAXIS/BUSES, ETC.** 出租车、公共汽车等 **10** a place where taxis, buses, etc. park while they are waiting for passengers 停车处；站 ➲ COMPARE TAXI RANK

• **OF PLANTS/TREES** 植物；树 **11** ~ (**of sth**) (*specialist*) a group of plants or trees of one kind 林分：*a stand of pines* 松树丛

• **OF LAND** 土地 **12** (*SAfrE*) a piece of land that you can buy and use for building a house, etc. on（建房等用的）地皮，地块：*A developer bought the land and divided it into stands.* 开发商买下这块土地将其分为多块建筑用地。➲ SEE ALSO HANDSTAND, ONE-NIGHT STAND **IDM** SEE FIRM *adv.*

ˈstand-alone *adj.* [usually before noun] (especially of a computer 尤指计算机) able to be operated on its own without being connected to a larger system 独立的

stand·ard /ˈstændəd; *NAmE* -dərd/ *noun, adj.*

■ ***noun***

• **LEVEL OF QUALITY** 品质标准 **1** [C, U] ~ (**of sth**) a level of quality, especially one that people think is acceptable（品质的）标准，水平，规格，规范：*a fall in academic standards* 学术水准的下降 ◇ *We aim to maintain* ***high standards*** *of customer care.* 我们的宗旨是始终以高标准为顾客服务。◇ *The standard of this year's applications is very low.* 今年的申请标准很低。◇ *He failed to* ***reach the required standard****, and did not qualify for the race.* 他未能达到所要求的标准，因而不具备参赛资格。◇ *Her work is not* ***up to standard*** (= of a good enough standard). 她的工作不合格。◇ *Who* ***sets the standard*** *for water quality?* 水质标准由谁来制定？◇ *A number of Britain's beaches fail to* ***meet*** *European* ***standards*** *on cleanliness.* 英国有几处海滩不符合欧洲的清洁标准。◇ *In the shanty towns there are very poor* ***living standards.*** 棚户区的生活水平很低。➲ SEE ALSO STANDARD OF LIVING, SUBSTANDARD **2** [C, usually pl.] a level of quality that is normal or acceptable for a particular person or in a particular situation 正常的水平；应达到的标准：*You'd better* ***lower your standards*** *if you want to find somewhere cheap to live.* 要想找个便宜的地方住，你最好降低要求。◇ *It was a simple meal by Eddie's standards.* 在埃迪看来，那不过是一顿便饭。◇ *The equipment is slow and heavy* ***by modern standards.*** 按现代标准，那台设备又慢又笨重。

• **LEVEL OF BEHAVIOUR** 行为标准 **3** **standards** [pl.] a level of behaviour that sb considers to be morally acceptable 行为标准；道德水准：*a man of high moral standards* 道德水准高的人 ◇ *Standards aren't what they used to be.* 现在的行为标准和过去不一样了。➲ SEE ALSO DOUBLE STANDARD

• **UNIT OF MEASUREMENT** 度量衡标准 **4** [C] a unit of measurement that is officially used; an official rule used when producing sth 法定度量衡标准；法定含量；技术规范；产品规格：*a reduction in the weight standard of silver coins* 银币法定重量标准的降低 ◇ *industry standards* 工业标准 ➲ SEE ALSO GOLD STANDARD

• **FLAG** 旗帜 **5** [C] a flag that is used during official ceremonies, especially one connected with a particular military group 仪式上使用的旗帜；（尤指）军旗

• **SONG** 歌曲 **6** [C] a song that has been recorded by many different singers（很多歌手录制过的）经典曲目

■ ***adj.***

• **AVERAGE/NORMAL** 普通；正常 **1** average or normal rather than having special or unusual features 普通的；正常的；通常的；标准的：*A standard letter was sent to all candidates.* 给所有求职者均寄去了一封标准函。◇ *Televisions are a standard feature in most hotel rooms.* 电视机是多数旅馆房间里的标准设施。◇ *the standard rate of tax* (= paid by everyone) 标准税率 ◇ *It is* ***standard practice*** *to search visitors as they enter the building.* 对进入这栋建筑物的来访者进行搜查是例行做法。◇ *All vehicles come with a CD player* ***as standard.*** 所有汽车售出时通常都配有 CD 播放机。

• **SIZE/MEASUREMENT** 尺寸；量度 **2** [usually before noun] following a particular standard set, for example, by an industry（符合）标准的；按一定规格制作的：*standard sizes of clothes* 服装的标准尺寸

• **BOOK/WRITER** 著作；作者 **3** [only before noun] read by most people who are studying a particular subject 权威性的

• **LANGUAGE** 语言 **4** [usually before noun] (of spelling, pronunciation, grammar, etc. 拼写、读音、语法等) believed to be correct and used by most people 标准的；规范的：*Standard English* 规范的英语 ➲ COMPARE NON-STANDARD (1), SUBSTANDARD

ˈstandard-bearer *noun* a leader in a political group or campaign 旗手；领袖

ˌstandard deˈduction *noun* [usually sing.] (*US*) a fixed amount of money that you can earn free of tax 工资免税标准；工资免税额

ˌstandard deviˈation *noun* (*mathematics* 数) the amount by which measurements in a set vary from the average for the set 标准差；标准偏差

ˌstandard ˈerror *noun* (*statistics* 统计) a method of measuring how accurate an estimate is 标准误差（用于衡量估计的准确性）

ˈStandard Grade *noun* (in Scotland) an exam in a particular subject at a lower level than HIGHERS. Standard Grades are usually taken in a number of different subjects at the age of 16.（苏格兰）标准级别考试（学生通常在 16 岁时参加）➲ SEE ALSO NQ

stand·ard·ize (*BrE also* **-ise**) /ˈstændədaɪz; *NAmE* -dərd-/ *verb* ~ **sth** to make objects or activities of the same type have the same features or qualities; to make sth standard 使标准化；使符合标准（或规格）：*a standardized contract/design/test* 标准化合同 / 设计 / 考试 ▸ **stand·ard·iza·tion**，**-isation** /ˌstændədaɪˈzeɪʃn; *NAmE* -dərdəˈz-/ *noun* [U]：*the standardization of components* 部件的标准化

ˈstandard lamp (*BrE*) (*also* **ˈfloor lamp** *NAmE, BrE*) *noun* a tall lamp that stands on the floor 落地灯 ➲ VISUAL VOCAB PAGE V22

ˌstandard of ˈliving *noun* (*pl.* **standards of living**) the amount of money and level of comfort that a particular person or group has 生活水平

ˈstandard time *noun* [U] the official time of a country or an area 标准时

stand·by /ˈstændbaɪ/ *noun, adj.*

■ ***noun*** (*pl.* **stand·bys**) a person or thing that can always be used if needed, for example if sb/sth else is not available or if there is an emergency 后备人员；备用物品：*I always keep a pizza in the freezer as a standby.* 我总会在冰箱里放一个比萨饼以备不时之需。◇ *a standby electricity generator*

备用发电机

IDM **on 'standby 1** ready to do sth immediately if needed or asked 随时可以投入行动；处于待命状态；招之即来：*The emergency services were **put on standby** after a bomb warning.* 接到炸弹警报后，各应急服务机构进入待命状态。**2** ready to travel or go somewhere if a ticket or sth that is needed suddenly becomes available 候补座位（如临时有票或具备其他必要条件便可立即出发的）：*He was **put on standby** for the flight to New York.* 这班飞往纽约的班机，他候补待位。

▪ ***adj.*** [only before noun] a **standby** ticket for a flight, concert, etc. cannot be bought in advance and is only available a very short time before the plane leaves or the performance starts（机票、音乐会门票等）最后时刻出售的

'stand-down *noun* [U, C] a period when people, especially soldiers, relax after a period of duty or danger 停工休息期；（尤指士兵的）休整期

stand·ee /stæn'diː/ *noun* (*NAmE, ScotE*) a person who is standing, for example in a bus or at a concert 站立者；站立乘客；站票观众

'stand-in *noun* **1** a person who does sb's job for a short time when they are not available 代行职务者 **2** a person who replaces an actor in some scenes in a film/movie, especially dangerous ones（尤指影视中做危险动作的）替身演员

stand·ing /'stændɪŋ/ *adj., noun*

▪ ***adj.*** [only before noun] **1** existing or arranged permanently, not formed or made for a particular situation 长期存在的；永久性的；常设的：*a standing army* 常备军 ◇ (*BrE*) *a **standing charge*** (= an amount of money that you pay in order to use a service, such as gas or water) 长期支付的开销 ◇ *a **standing committee*** 常务委员会 ◇ *It's a **standing joke*** (= something that a group of people regularly laugh at). 那是一个活笑柄。◇ *We have a **standing invitation** to visit them anytime.* 他们邀请我们随时去他们家做客。**2** done from a position in which you are standing rather than sitting or running 站着进行的：*a **standing jump/start*** 立定跳远；站立式起跑 ◇ *The speaker got a **standing ovation*** (= people stood up to clap after the speech). 演讲者赢得了听众的起立鼓掌。➲ SEE ALSO FREE-STANDING

▪ ***noun*** **1** [U] the position or reputation of sb/sth within a group of people or in an organization 地位；级别；身份；名声 SYN **status**：*the **high/low standing** of politicians with the public* 在公众中声望高 / 低的政治人物 ◇ *The contract has no legal standing.* 那份合同在法律上没有约束力。**2** [U] the period of time that sth has existed 持续时间：*a friendship of many years' standing* 多年的友情 ➲ SEE ALSO LONG-STANDING **3 standings** [pl.] a list of people, teams, etc. showing their positions in a sports competition（运动员或运动队比赛成绩的）排名，名次

,standing 'order *noun* [C, U] an instruction that you give to your bank to pay sb a fixed amount of money from your account on the same day each week/month, etc.（客户给银行的）定期支付指示，经常性支付授权 ➲ COMPARE BANKER'S ORDER, DIRECT DEBIT

'standing room *noun* [U] space for people to stand in, especially in a theatre, sports ground, etc.（尤指剧场、体育场等）站立的空间：*standing room for 12 000 supporters* 可供 12 000 名支持者站立的地方 ◇ *It was **standing room only** at the concert* (= all the seats were sold). 音乐会只剩站票了。

'standing stone *noun* a tall vertical stone that was shaped and put up by PREHISTORIC people in western Europe（西欧）史前巨石柱

'stand-off *noun* ~ (**between A and B**) a situation in which no agreement can be reached（双方）僵持局面 SYN **deadlock**

,stand-off 'half (*also* **,fly 'half**) *noun* (in RUGBY 橄榄球) a player who plays behind the SCRUM HALF 传锋

stand-offish /,stænd 'ɒfɪʃ; *NAmE* 'ɔːf-; 'ɑːf-/ *adj.* (*informal*) not friendly towards other people 冷淡的；冷漠的；不友好的 SYN **aloof**

stand·out /'stændaʊt/ *noun* (*informal*) a person or thing that is very noticeable because they are or it is better, more impressive, etc. than others in a group 突出的人（或事物）▸ **stand·out** *adj.* [only before noun]: *the standout track on this album* 这张专辑里最突出的那首歌 ➲ MORE LIKE THIS 32, page R28

stand·pipe /'stændpaɪp/ *noun* a pipe that is connected to a public water supply and used to provide water outside a building 公用水管（用于在户外公共场所供水）

stand·point /'stændpɔɪnt/ *noun* [usually sing.] an opinion or a way of thinking about ideas or situations 立场；观点 SYN **perspective**：*a **political/theoretical, etc. standpoint*** 政治、理论等观点 ◇ *He is writing **from the standpoint of** someone who knows what life is like in prison.* 他从一个了解监狱生活的人的立场写作。

St Andrew's Day /,snt 'ændruːz deɪ; *NAmE* ,seɪnt/ *noun* 30 November, a Christian festival of the national SAINT of Scotland 圣安德烈节（11 月 30 日，纪念苏格兰主保圣人的基督教节日）

stand·still /'stændstɪl/ *noun* [sing.] a situation in which all activity or movement has stopped 停止；停顿；停滞 SYN **halt**：*The security alert **brought** the airport **to a standstill**.* 安全警戒使机场陷入停顿状态。◇ *Traffic in the northbound lane **is at a** complete **standstill**.* 北行车道的交通完全堵塞。

,stand-'to *noun* [U] the state of being ready to fight or attack 战备状态

'stand-up *adj., noun*

▪ ***adj.*** [only before noun] **1 stand-up** comedy consists of one person standing in front of an audience and telling jokes（喜剧节目）单人表演的，单口的 **2** (*especially BrE*) a **stand-up** argument, fight, etc. is one in which people shout loudly at each other or are violent towards each other（争论、打斗等）激烈的 **3** worn, used, etc. in a vertical position 直立的；挺立的：*a stand-up collar* 立领

▪ ***noun*** **1** [U] stand-up comedy 独角喜剧；单口相声：*When did you start doing stand-up?* 你什么时候开始表演独白喜剧的？**2** [C] a person who performs stand-up comedy 独白喜剧演员；单口相声演员：*She started out as a stand-up.* 她出道时是个独角喜剧演员。

stank PAST TENSE OF STINK

Stan·ley knife™ /'stænli naɪf/ *noun* (*BrE*) a very sharp knife with a blade in the shape of a triangle that can be replaced 斯坦利刀（刀刃锋利，呈三角形，可更换）

stanza /'stænzə/ *noun* (*specialist*) a group of lines in a repeated pattern that form a unit in some types of poem（诗的）节，段 SYN **verse** ➲ WORDFINDER NOTE AT POETRY

staphylo·coc·cus /,stæfɪlə'kɒkəs; *NAmE* -'kɑːk-/ *noun* (*medical* 医) a type of bacteria that can cause infections in some parts of the body such as the skin and eyes 葡萄球菌（可感染皮肤和眼睛等身体部位）

staple /'steɪpl/ *adj., noun, verb*

▪ ***adj.*** [only before noun] forming a basic, large or important part of sth 主要的；基本的；重要的：*The staple crop is rice.* 主要农作物为水稻。◇ *Jeans are a staple part of everyone's wardrobe.* 在每个人的衣橱里，牛仔裤是必不可少的。

▪ ***noun*** **1** a small piece of wire that is used in a device called a STAPLER and is pushed through pieces of paper and bent over at the ends in order to fasten the pieces of paper together 订书钉 ➲ VISUAL VOCAB PAGE V71 **2** a small piece of metal in the shape of a U that is hit into wooden surfaces using a HAMMER, used especially for holding electrical wires in place * U 形钉；U 形电线卡 **3** a basic type of food that is used a lot 基本食物；主食：*Aid workers helped distribute corn, milk and other staples.* 救助人员协助分发谷物、牛奶及其他基本食物。➲ WORDFINDER NOTE AT CROP **4** something that is produced by a country and is important for its economy（某国的）主要产品，支柱产品：*Rubber became the staple of the Malayan economy.* 橡胶成了马来亚经济的支柱产品。**5** ~ (**of sth**) a large or an

S

important part of sth 主要部分；重要内容：*Royal gossip is a staple of the tabloid press.* 围绕王室成员的飞短流长是小报的主要内容。

■ **verb** ~ **sth + adv./prep.** to attach one thing to another using a staple or staples 用订书钉装订：*Staple the invoice to the receipt.* 把发票订到收据上。◇ *Staple the invoice and the receipt together.* 把发票和收据订在一起。

ˌstaple ˈdiet *noun* [U, C] ~ **(of sth)** **1** the food that a person or an animal normally eats（某人或动物的）主要食物：*a staple diet of meat and potatoes* 以肉和土豆作为主要食物 ◇ *Bamboo is the panda's staple diet.* 大熊猫的基本食物是竹子。**2** something that is used a lot 家常便饭；主要内容；惯用手段：*Sex and violence seem to be the staple diet of television drama.* 性和暴力好像是电视剧离不开的内容。

ˈstaple gun *noun* a device for fixing paper to walls, etc. using STAPLES 钉枪，钉钉器（用以把纸钉到墙上等）

stapler /ˈsteɪplə(r)/ *noun* a small device used for putting staples into paper, etc. 订书机 ➲ VISUAL VOCAB PAGE V71

ˈstaple remover *noun* a small device used for removing staples from paper, etc.（订书钉）起钉器，拔钉器 ➲ VISUAL VOCAB PAGE V71

star 🔑 /stɑː(r)/ *noun, verb*

■ **noun**

• **IN SKY** 天空 **1** 🔑 [C] a large ball of burning gas in space that we see as a point of light in the sky at night 恒星；星：*There was a big moon and hundreds of stars were shining overhead.* 头顶是一轮明月和成百上千颗闪烁的星星。◇ *Sirius is the brightest star in the sky.* 天狼星是天空中最亮的一颗星。◇ *We camped out **under the stars**.* 我们露天宿营。➲ SEE ALSO FALLING STAR, LODESTAR (1), POLE STAR, SHOOTING STAR, STARRY

• **SHAPE** 形状 **2** 🔑 [C] an object, a decoration, a mark, etc., usually with five or six points, whose shape represents a star 星状物；星形饰物；星号：*a horse with a white star on its forehead* 前额有一块星形白斑的马 ◇ *a sheriff's star* 县治安官的星徽 ◇ *I've put a star by the names of the girls in the class.* 我在班里女生名字旁都画了一个星号。◇ *a four-star general* 四星上将

• **MARK OF QUALITY** 质量标志 **3** 🔑 [C, usually sing.] a mark that represents a star and tells you how good sth is, especially a hotel or restaurant（尤指旅馆或餐馆的）星级：***three-/four-/five-star** hotels* 三星级 / 四星级 / 五星级饭店 ◇ *What star rating does this restaurant have?* 这家餐馆是几星级的？

• **PERFORMER** 表演者 **4** 🔑 [C] a famous and excellent singer, performer, sports player, etc. 歌唱（或表演）明星；体坛高手；才华出众者：***pop/rock/Hollywood, etc. stars*** 流行音乐歌星、摇滚歌星、好莱坞影星等 ◇ *a **football/tennis, etc. star*** 足球、网球等明星 ◇ *He's so good—I'm sure he'll be a big star.* 他太棒了，我相信他会成为大明星的。◇ *She acts well but she hasn't got **star quality**.* 她演得不错，但缺少成为一个明星的素质。◇ *The best models receive **star treatment**.* 最优秀的模特儿会受到明星级的待遇。➲ SEE ALSO ALL-STAR, FILM STAR, MEGASTAR, MOVIE STAR, SUPERSTAR ➲ WORDFINDER NOTE AT ACTOR **5** 🔑 [C] a person who has the main part, or one of the main parts, in a film/movie, play, etc.（电影、戏剧等的）主角，主演：*She was the star of many popular television series.* 她在许多观众喜爱的电视连续剧中担任过主角。◇ *The **star of the show** was a young Italian singer.* 那台节目的主角是位年轻的意大利歌唱家。◇ *the **star role/part*** 主角 ➲ SEE ALSO STAR TURN

• **BEST OF GROUP** 最优秀者 **6** [C] (often used before another noun 常用于另一名词前) a person or thing that is the best of a group 最优秀（或出色、成功）者：*a star student* 最优秀的学生 ◇ *Paula is the star of the class.* 葆拉是班里的尖子。◇ *He was the **star performer** at the championships.* 他是那届锦标赛上的最佳运动员。◇ *The **star prize** is a weekend for two in Paris.* 特等奖是二人巴黎周末游。◇ *The monkey was **the star attraction*** (= the best or most popular act) *at the show.* 那只猴子是节目中最令人瞩目的明星。

• **HELPFUL PERSON** 提供帮助的人 **7** [C, usually sing.] (*informal*) used to show that you feel very grateful for sth that sb has done or that you think they are wonderful（表示万分感激或赞叹）：*Thanks! You're a star!* 多谢多谢！你真是个大好人！

• **INFLUENCE ON SB'S FUTURE** 对某人将来的影响 **8 stars** [pl.] a description of what sb thinks is going to happen to sb in the future, based on the position of the stars and planets when they were born 星象（根据人出生时天体的位置而描述的命运）SYN **horoscope**：*Do you read your stars in the paper?* 你读不读报上的星座运程，看自己的运气如何？

IDM **see ˈstars** (*informal*) to see flashes of light in front of your eyes, usually because you have been hit on the head（因头部被撞击等）两眼直冒金星 **ˈstars in your eyes** if sb has **stars in their eyes**, they have dreams of becoming famous, especially as an entertainer 成名的梦想；（尤指成为艺人的）明星梦 ➲ MORE AT REACH *v.*, THANK

■ **verb** (-rr-)

• **PERFORM IN MOVIE/PLAY** 在电影 / 戏剧中扮演角色 **1** 🔑 [I] ~ **(with/opposite sb)** **(in sth)** to have one of the main parts in a film/movie, play, etc. 主演；担任主角：*She starred opposite Cary Grant in 'Bringing up Baby'.* 她和加利 • 格兰特在《育婴奇谭》中联袂出演男女主角。◇ *No one has yet been chosen for the **starring role*** (= the main part). 主演还没选定。➲ COLLOCATIONS AT CINEMA **2** 🔑 [T, no passive] ~ **sb** if a film/movie, play, etc. **stars** sb, that person has one of the main parts 使主演；由…担任主角：*a movie starring Meryl Streep and Pierce Brosnan* 由梅丽尔 • 斯特里普和皮尔斯 • 布鲁斯南主演的电影 ◇ *The studio wants to star her in a sequel to last year's hit.* 制片厂为去年一部大获成功的影片筹拍续集，想聘她担任主角。➲ SEE ALSO CO-STAR *v.*

• **MARK WITH SYMBOL** 标记号 **3** [T, usually passive] ~ **sth** to put a symbol shaped like a star (= an ASTERISK) next to a word, etc. in order to make people notice it 给…标星号：*Treat all the sections that have been starred as priority.* 优先处理所有标星号的部分。➲ MORE LIKE THIS 36, page R29

ˌstar ˈanise *noun* [U, C] a small fruit in the shape of a star, used in cooking as a spice 八角茴香 ➲ VISUAL VOCAB PAGE V35

star·board /ˈstɑːbəd; *NAmE* ˈstɑːrbərd/ *noun* [U] the side of a ship or an aircraft that is on the right when you are facing forward（船舶或飞机的）右舷，右侧 ➲ COMPARE PORT *n.* (5)

star·burst /ˈstɑːbɜːst; *NAmE* ˈstɑːrbɜːrst/ *noun* a bright light in the shape of a star, or a shape that looks like a star exploding 星状亮光；星爆般的形状

starch /stɑːtʃ; *NAmE* stɑːrtʃ/ *noun, verb*

■ **noun** **1** [U, C] a white CARBOHYDRATE food substance found in potatoes, flour, rice, etc.; food containing this 淀粉；含淀粉的食物：*There's too much starch in your diet.* 你的日常饮食中淀粉含量太高。◇ *You need to cut down on starches.* 你得少吃些含淀粉的东西。**2** [U] starch prepared in powder form or as a spray and used for making clothes, sheets, etc. stiff（浆衣服、床单等用的）淀粉浆

■ **verb** [usually passive] ~ **sth** to make clothes, sheets, etc. stiff using starch 把（衣服、床单等）浆一浆：*a starched white shirt* 浆过的白衬衫

starchy /ˈstɑːtʃi; *NAmE* ˈstɑːrtʃi/ *adj.* **1** (of food 食物) containing a lot of starch 富含淀粉的 **2** (*informal, disapproving*) (of a person or their behaviour 人或行为) very formal; not friendly or relaxed 拘束的；古板的；拘泥的

ˈstar-crossed *adj.* (*literary*) not able to be happy because of bad luck or FATE 命运乖蹇的；不幸的：*Shakespeare's star-crossed lovers, Romeo and Juliet* 罗密欧和朱丽叶这一对莎士比亚笔下命途多舛的恋人

star·dom /ˈstɑːdəm; *NAmE* ˈstɑːrdəm/ *noun* [U] the state of being famous as an actor, a singer, etc. 明星的地位（或身份）：*The group is being **tipped for stardom*** (= people say they will be famous). 这支乐队被誉为明日之星。◇ *She **shot to stardom** in a Broadway musical.* 她在一部百老汇音乐剧中一炮而红。

star·dust /ˈstɑːdʌst; *NAmE* ˈstɑːrd-/ *noun* [U] **1** a magic quality that some famous people with a great natural

S

ability seem to have（天赋很高的名人似乎拥有的）魔力 **2** (*astronomy* 天) stars that are very far from the earth and appear like bright dust in the sky at night 星尘（远离地球的恒星，在夜空中看似明亮尘埃）

stare /steə(r); *NAmE* ster/ *verb, noun*

■ ***verb*** [I] ~ (**at sb/sth**) to look at sb/sth for a long time 盯着看；凝视；注视：*I screamed and everyone stared.* 我尖叫一声，众人都盯着我看。◇ *I stared blankly at the paper in front of me.* 我茫然地看着面前那张纸。◇ *He sat* ***staring into space*** (= looking at nothing). 他坐在那儿凝视着前方。◇ *She looked at them with dark staring eyes.* 她那双深色的眼睛专注地看着他们。

IDM **be staring sb in the 'face 1** to be obvious or easy to see 明摆着；显而易见：*The answer was staring us in the face.* 答案明摆在我们面前。**2** to be certain to happen 必定发生：*Defeat was staring them in the face.* 他们必遭失败。**be staring sth in the 'face** to be unable to avoid sth 不可避免：*They were staring defeat in the face.* 对他们来说，失败不可避免。

PHR V **,stare sb 'out** (*BrE*) (*also* **,stare sb 'down** *NAmE, BrE*) to look into sb's eyes for a long time until they feel embarrassed and are forced to look away 盯得某人转移目光（或慌了神）

▼ SYNONYMS 同义词辨析

stare

gaze • peer • glare

These words all mean to look at sb/sth for a long time. 以上各词均含盯着看、凝视、注视之义。

stare to look at sb/sth for a long time, especially with surprise or fear, or because you are thinking 尤指吃惊、害怕或深思地盯着看、凝视、注视：*I screamed and everyone stared.* 我尖叫一声，众人都盯着我看。

gaze (*rather formal*) to look steadily at sb/sth for a long time, especially with surprise or love, or because you are thinking 尤指吃惊、爱恋或深思地凝视、注视、盯着：*We all gazed at Marco in amazement.* 我们都惊异地注视着马可。

peer to look closely or carefully at sth, especially when you cannot see it clearly 尤指看不清楚时仔细看、端详

glare to look angrily at sb/sth for a long time 指怒目而视：*I looked at her and she glared stonily back.* 我看了她一眼，她便冷冷地回瞪我。

PATTERNS

- to stare/gaze/peer/glare **at** sb/sth
- to stare/gaze/peer/glare **suspiciously**
- to stare/gaze/peer **anxiously/intently**
- to stare/gaze/glare **wildly/fiercely**

■ ***noun*** an act of looking at sb/sth for a long time, especially in a way that is unfriendly or that shows surprise（尤指不友好或吃惊的）盯，凝视，注视：*She gave him a blank stare.* 她面无表情地直视着他。⊃ SYNONYMS AT LOOK

star·fish /'stɑːfɪʃ; *NAmE* 'stɑːrfɪʃ/ *noun* (*pl.* **star·fish**) a flat sea creature in the shape of a star with five arms 海星；星鱼

'star fruit *noun* (*pl.* **star fruit**) a green or yellow tropical fruit with a shape like a star 五敛子；杨桃

star·gazer /'stɑːɡeɪzə(r); *NAmE* 'stɑːrɡ-/ *noun* (*informal*) a person who studies ASTROLOGY or ASTRONOMY 占星术士；天文学家 ▶ **star·gaz·ing** *noun* [U]

stark /stɑːk; *NAmE* stɑːrk/ *adj., adv.*

■ ***adj.*** (**stark·er, stark·est**) **1** (*often disapproving*) looking severe and without any colour or decoration 毫无修饰的；荒凉的；粗陋的：*I think white would be too stark for the bedroom.* 我觉得卧室里用白色未免太素了。◇ *The hills stood stark against the winter sky.* 在冬日的天空下，小山了无生气。**2** unpleasant; real, and impossible to avoid 严酷的；赤裸裸的；真实而无法回避的 SYN **bleak**：*The author paints a stark picture of life in a prison camp.* 作者描绘出一幅冷酷而真实的战俘营生活画面。◇ *a stark choice* 残酷的抉择 ◇ *The remains of the building stand as a stark reminder of the fire.* 房子的断壁残垣是那场大火无情的见证。◇ *He now faces the* ***stark reality*** *of life in prison.* 他现在要面对狱中生活的严酷现实了。⊃ SYNONYMS AT PLAIN **3** very different to sth in a way that is easy to see（指区别）明显的，鲜明的 SYN **clear**：*stark differences* 鲜明的区别 ◇ *Social divisions in the city are stark.* 城市里各社会阶层有明确的分野。◇ *The good weather was* ***in stark contrast to*** *the storms of previous weeks.* 这时的好天气和前几个星期的暴风雨形成鲜明的对比。**4** [only before noun] complete and total 完全的；十足的 SYN **utter**：*The children watched in stark terror.* 孩子们极端恐惧地看着。▶ **stark·ly** *adv.*：*The interior is starkly simple.* 室内粗陋简朴。◇ *The lighthouse stood out starkly against the dark sky.* 在黑暗天空的映衬下，灯塔巍然兀立。◇ *We are starkly aware of the risks.* 我们完全清楚所面临的种种风险。**stark·ness** *noun* [U]

■ ***adv.*** ~ **naked** completely naked 一丝不挂；赤裸 IDM SEE RAVING *adv.*

stark·ers /'stɑːkəz; *NAmE* 'stɑːrkərz/ *adj.* [not before noun] (*BrE, informal*) not wearing any clothes 一丝不挂；赤裸 SYN **naked**

star·less /'stɑːləs; *NAmE* 'stɑːrləs/ *adj.* with no stars in the sky 没有星星的：*a starless night* 没有星星的夜晚

star·let /'stɑːlət; *NAmE* 'stɑːrlət/ *noun* a young woman actor who plays small parts and hopes to become famous 渴望成名的年轻女演员

star·light /'stɑːlaɪt; *NAmE* 'stɑːrl-/ *noun* [U] light from the stars 星光：*We walked home by starlight.* 我们借着星光走回家。

star·ling /'stɑːlɪŋ; *NAmE* 'stɑːrlɪŋ/ *noun* a common bird with dark shiny feathers and a noisy call 椋鸟

star·lit /'stɑːlɪt; *NAmE* 'stɑːrlɪt/ *adj.* with light from the stars 星光照耀的：*a starlit night* 星光照耀的夜晚

'star network *noun* (*computing* 计) a network in which computers are connected to a central unit, rather than to each other 星状网（通过中央主机连接）

,Star of 'David *noun* (*pl.* **Stars of David**) a star with six points that is used as a symbol of Judaism and the state of Israel 大卫之星，六角星（犹太教和以色列的标志）

starry /'stɑːri/ *adj.* [usually before noun] **1** (of the sky 天空) full of stars 布满星星的：*a beautiful starry night* 繁星满天的美丽夜晚 **2** looking like a star 像星星的：*starry flowers* 像星星似的花朵 **3** (of eyes 眼睛) shining like stars 闪闪发光的；明亮的

,starry-'eyed *adj.* (*informal*) full of emotion, hopes or dreams about sb/sth in a way that is not realistic 天真的；空想的

the ,Stars and 'Stripes *noun* [sing.] the national flag of the US 星条旗（美国国旗）

star·ship /'stɑːʃɪp; *NAmE* 'stɑːrʃ-/ *noun* (in SCIENCE FICTION 科幻小说) a large SPACECRAFT in which people or other creatures travel through space 星际飞船；星舰

'star sign (*also informal* **sign**) *noun* one of the twelve signs of the ZODIAC 星座（黄道十二宫之一）：*'What's your star sign?' 'Aquarius.'* "你是什么星座的？" "宝瓶座。"

the ,Star-,Spangled 'Banner *noun* [sing.] the national ANTHEM (= song) of the US《星条旗永不落》（美国国歌）

'star-struck *adj.* very impressed by famous people such as actors, football players, etc. 崇拜明星的；追星族的

'star-studded *adj.* including many famous performers 明星荟萃的：*a star-studded cast* 明星荟萃的演出阵容

start /stɑːt; *NAmE* stɑːrt/ *verb, noun*

■ ***verb***

• **DOING STH** 做事 **1** [T, I] to begin doing or using sth 开始，着手，动手（做或使用）：~ **sth** *I start work at nine.*

S

我每天九点开始工作。◇ *He's just started a new job.* 他刚刚着手一项新工作。◇ *I only started* (= began to read) *this book yesterday.* 我昨天才开始看这本书。◇ *We need to start* (= begin using) *a new jar of coffee.* 我们得新开一罐咖啡了。◇ *The kids start school next week.* 孩子们下星期开学。◇ **~ to do sth** *It started to rain.* 下起雨来了。◇ *Mistakes were starting to creep in.* 不知不觉间，开始出错了。◇ **~ doing sth** *She started laughing.* 她笑了起来。◇ **~ (on sth)** *It's a long story. Where shall I start?* 说来话长。我该从哪儿说起呢？◇ *It's time you started on your homework.* 你该做功课了。◇ *Can you start* (= a new job) *on Monday?* 你可以星期一就来上班吗？◇ **~ by doing sth** *Let's start by reviewing what we did last week.* 我们开始先来复习一下上星期学的内容。◇ **+ adj.** *The best professional musicians start young.* 卓有成就的音乐家很早就接触音乐。➲ NOTE AT BEGIN ➲ EXPRESS YOURSELF AT OPEN

• **HAPPENING** 发生 **2** 🔑 [I, T] to start happening; to make sth start happening （使）发生，开始进行：*When does the class start?* 什么时候上课？◇ *Have you any idea where the rumour started?* 你知不知道谣言是从哪儿传出来的？◇ **~ sth** *Who started the fire?* 谁放的火？◇ *Do you start the day with a good breakfast?* 你早晨起来会先好好吃一顿早饭吗？◇ *You're always trying to start an argument.* 你总是想挑起争论。◇ **~ sb/sth doing sth** *The news started me thinking.* 那条消息让我思考起来。

• **MACHINE/VEHICLE** 机器；车辆 **3** 🔑 [T, I] **~ (sth)** when you **start** a machine or a vehicle or it **starts**, it begins to operate 开动；发动；启动：*Start the engines!* 发动引擎！◇ *I can't get the car started.* 这辆车我发动不起来。◇ *The car won't start.* 这辆车发动不起来。

• **EXISTING** 存在 **4** 🔑 [I, T] to begin to exist; to make sth begin to exist （使）出现；发起；创办；开办：**~ (up)** *There are a lot of small businesses starting up in that area.* 小型企业在那一地区大量涌现。◇ **~ sth (up)** *They decided to start a catering business.* 他们决定开办一家酒席承办公司。

• **JOURNEY** 旅行 **5** 🔑 [I] **~ (out)** to begin a journey; to leave 出发；动身；起程 **SYN** **set off, set out**：*What time are we starting tomorrow?* 我们明天什么时候出发？

• **GOING/WALKING** 走 **6** [I] **+ adv./prep.** to begin to move in a particular direction 起身走向；向…而去：*I started after her* (= began to follow her) *to tell her the news.* 我起身朝她追去，好把消息告诉她。◇ *He started for the door, but I blocked his way.* 他向门口走去，但我挡住了他的去路。

• **IN PARTICULAR WAY/FROM PLACE/LEVEL** 方式；地方；层次 **7** 🔑 [I, T] to begin, or to begin sth such as a career, in a particular way that changed later 以…起步（或起家）；起初是：**~ as sth** *She started as a secretary but ended up running the department.* 她起初只是一个秘书，但最后掌管起了整个部门。◇ **~ out/off (as sth)** *The company started out with 30 employees.* 公司创立之初只有 30 名员工。◇ **~ sth (as sth)** *He started life as a teacher before turning to journalism.* 他开始当过教师，后来改行搞起了新闻。**8** 🔑 [I] **+ adv./prep.** to begin from a particular place, amount or situation （从…）开始；（由…）起：*The trail starts just outside the town.* 小径从刚出城的地方开始。◇ *Hotel prices start at €50 a night for a double room.* 旅馆的双人房间一宿 50 欧元起价。◇ *The evening started badly when the speaker failed to turn up.* 那天晚上的活动一开始挺糟糕，因为演讲者没有来。

• **MOVE SUDDENLY** 突然一动 **9** [I] to move suddenly and quickly because you are surprised or afraid 突然一惊 **SYN** **jump**：*The sudden noise made her start.* 突如其来的声音吓了她一跳。

IDM ˌ**don't (you) 'start** (*informal*) used to tell sb not to complain or be critical（制止某人抱怨或挑剔）别抱怨，别挑剔：*Don't start! I told you I'd be late.* 别抱怨啦！我跟你说过我要迟到的。**get 'started** to begin doing sth （使）开始；着手；动手：*It's nearly ten o'clock. Let's get started.* 快十点了，咱们开始吧。**you, he, she, etc. 'started it** (*informal*) you, he, she, etc. began a fight or an argument 是你（或他、她等）挑起来的：*'Stop fighting, you two!' 'He started it!'* "你们俩，别打了！""是他先动手的！" **'start something** (*informal*) to cause trouble 制造麻烦；惹是生非 **to 'start with 1** used when you are giving the first and most important reason for sth（给出首要理由）首先，第一：*To start with it's much too expensive...* 首先是太贵… **2** at the beginning 起初；开始时：*The club had only six members to start with.* 这家俱乐部起初仅有六名会员。◇ *I'll have melon to start with.* 我要先吃甜瓜。◇ *She wasn't keen on the idea to start with.* 她一开始并不喜欢这个主意。➲ MORE AT ALARM *n.*, BALL *n.*, FOOT *n.*

PHR V ˌ**start 'back** to begin to return somewhere 动身（或起程）返回 ˌ**start 'off 1** to begin to move 开始活动；动身：*The horse started off at a steady trot.* 马稳步小跑起来。**2** 🔑 to begin happening; to begin doing sth 进行（或开展）起来：*The discussion started off mildly enough.* 讨论颇为温和地开展起来。**3** 🔑 to begin by doing or being sth 首先进行；一开始是：*Let's start off with some gentle exercises.* 我们先来做点强度低的运动。◇ *We started off by introducing ourselves.* 我们一开始先自我介绍。◇ **+ adj.** *The leaves start off green but turn red later.* 树叶起先是绿色，到后来会变红。◇ **start off doing sth** *I started off working quite hard, but it didn't last.* 我一开始非常勤奋，

▼ SYNONYMS 同义词辨析

start

begin • start off • kick off • commence • open

These words are all used to talk about things happening from the beginning, or people doing the first part of sth. 以上各词均用以指事情开始发生或开始做某事。

start to begin to happen or exist; to begin in a particular way or from a particular point 指开始发生或存在、以…开始、以…为起点：*When does the class start?* 什么时候上课？

begin to start to happen or exist; to start in a particular way or from a particular point; to start speaking 指开始发生或存在、以…开始、以…为起点、开始讲话：*When does the concert begin?* 音乐会什么时候开始？

START OR BEGIN? 用 start 还是 begin?

There is not much difference in meaning between these words. **Start** is more frequent in spoken English and in business contexts; **begin** is more frequent in written English and is often used when you are describing a series of events. 上述两词在意义上无多大差别，start 较常用于口语和商业语境中，begin 较常用于书面语中，描述一系列事情：*The story begins on the island of Corfu.* 故事从科孚岛开始。**Start** is not used to mean 'begin speaking'. * start 不用以指开始讲话：~~'Ladies and gentlemen,' he started.~~

start off (*rather informal*) to start happening or doing sth; to start by doing or being sth 指进行或开展起来、首先进行、一开始是：*The discussion started off mildly enough.* 讨论颇为温和地开展起来。

kick off (*informal*) to start an event or activity, especially in a particular way; (of an event, activity, etc.) to start, especially in a particular way 尤指以…开始（活动）、（活动）以…开始：*Tom will kick off with a few comments.* 汤姆讲话时要先发表几点意见。◇ *The festival kicks off on Monday, September 13.* 节期从 9 月 13 日星期一开始。

commence (*formal*) to start happening 指开始发生：*The meeting is scheduled to commence at noon.* 会议定于午间召开。

open to start an event or activity in a particular way; (of an event, a film/movie or a book) to start, especially in a particular way 指以…开始（活动）、（活动、电影或书）以…开头 / 开篇：*The story opens with a murder.* 故事以一宗谋杀案作序幕。

PATTERNS

- to start/begin/start off/kick off/commence/open **with** sth
- to start/begin/start off/kick off/commence/open **by** doing sth
- to start/begin/start off/commence **as** sth
- a **campaign/season/meeting** starts/begins/starts off/kicks off/commences/opens
- a **film/movie/book** starts/begins/starts off/opens

但没有坚持下去。,**start sb 'off (on sth) 1** [no passive] to make sb begin doing sth 使开始（做某事）：*What started her off on that crazy idea?* 她怎么会有那样古怪的念头呢？◇ *Don't say anything to her—you'll start her off again* (= make her get angry). 什么也别跟她说，不然你又要惹她生气了。◇ **start sb off doing sth** *Kevin started us all off laughing.* 凯文把我们大家都逗笑了。**2** to help sb begin doing sth 帮助某人开始（做某事）：*My mother started me off on the piano when I was three.* 三岁时我母亲就让我开始练钢琴了。◇ **start sb off doing sth** *His father started him off farming.* 他父亲指点他做农活儿。**'start on sb** [no passive] to attack sb physically or with words（使用暴力或言语）向某人发起攻击 ,**start 'on at sb (about sth)** | ,**start 'on (at sb) about sth** (*informal*) to begin to complain about sth or criticize sb 开始责备（某人）；开始抱怨（某事）：*She started on at me again about getting some new clothes.* 她又就买新衣服的事情数落起我来。◇ *Don't start on about him not having a job.* 你不要埋怨他没工作。

,**start 'out 1** 🔑 to begin to do sth, especially in business or work 开始从事，着手（某工作）；从业：*to start out in business* 做起生意来 ◇ *She started out on her legal career in 2001.* 她于 2001 年开始从事法律工作。**2** to have a particular intention when you begin sth 最初想要；起先打算：**start out to do sth** *I started out to write a short story, but it soon developed into a novel.* 我起先打算写一篇短篇小说，但很快就写成了长篇小说。,**start 'over** (*especially NAmE*) to begin again 重新开始：*She wasn't happy with our work and made us start over.* 她对我们干的活儿不满意，要我们返工。,**start 'up** | ,**start sth↔'up** 🔑 to begin working, happening, etc.; to make sth do this（使）启动，发动，开始：*I heard his car start up.* 我听见他的汽车发动了。◇ *Start up the engines!* 发动引擎！➲ SEE ALSO START-UP

■ ***noun***

• **BEGINNING** 开始 **1** 🔑 [C, usually sing.] the point at which sth begins 开头；开端：*a perfect start to the day* 那一天的美好开端 ◇ *Things didn't look too hopeful at the start of the year.* 在年初，情况显得并不十分乐观。◇ *The meeting* ***got off to a good/bad start*** (= started well/badly). 会议有一个良好的 / 糟糕的开端。◇ *The trip was a disaster* ***from start to finish.*** 那次旅行从头到尾糟糕透顶。◇ *We've had problems* (***right***) ***from the start.*** 我们从（一）开始就遇到了困难。◇ (*informal*) *This could be the start of something big.* 这或许是要有大事的苗头。**2** 🔑 [sing.] the act or process of beginning sth 开始：*I'll paint the ceiling if you* ***make a start on*** *the walls.* 你要是动手刷墙，我就刷天花板吧。◇ *I want to make an early start in the morning.* 我想早上早点儿出发。◇ *She's moving abroad to make a* ***fresh start*** (= to begin a new life). 她要移居国外，开始新的生活。➲ SEE ALSO FALSE START, KICK-START *n.*

• **OPPORTUNITY** 机会 **3** 🔑 [C, usually sing.] the opportunity that you are given to begin sth in a successful way 起始优势；良好的基础条件：*They worked hard to give their children a good* ***start in life.*** 他们力争为孩子们的人生奠定一个良好的基础。◇ *The job gave him his start in journalism.* 那份工作是他加入新闻界的开始。

• **IN RACE** 比赛 **4 the start** [sing.] the place where a race begins 起点：*The runners lined up at the start.* 赛跑运动员在起跑线上一字排开。**5** [C, usually sing.] an amount of time or distance that sb has as an advantage over other people at the beginning of a race 起点优势（时间或距离）：*She went into the second round with a five-minute start on the rest of the cyclists.* 她进入第二轮，并取得比其他自行车选手提前五分钟出发的优势。◇ *I gave the younger children a start.* 我让年幼的孩子提前起跑。➲ SEE ALSO HEAD START **6** [C, usually pl.] (*sport* 体育) a race or competition that sb has taken part in（参加的）比赛：*She has been beaten only once in six starts.* 她参加了六次比赛，只败过一次。

• **SUDDEN MOVEMENT** 突然一动 **7** [C, usually sing.] an act of moving your body quickly and suddenly because you are surprised, afraid, etc. 突然一惊：*She woke from the dream* ***with a start.*** 她猛地一惊，从梦中醒来。◇ *You gave me quite a start!* 你吓了我一大跳！

IDM for a 'start (*informal*) used to emphasize the first of a list of reasons, opinions, etc.（强调一系列理由、意见等的第一条）首先：*I'm not working there—for a start, it's too far to travel.* 我不去那边干活儿。首先，路太远，去不了。➲ MORE AT FIT *n.*, FLYING START

start·er /ˈstɑːtə(r); *NAmE* ˈstɑːrt-/ *noun* **1** (*especially BrE*) (*NAmE usually* **ap·pe·tiz·er**) a small amount of food that is served before the main course of a meal（主菜之前的）开胃小吃，开胃品 ➲ COLLOCATIONS AT RESTAURANT ➲ COMPARE HORS D'OEUVRE **2** a person, horse, car, etc. that is in a race at the beginning 参赛人；参赛的马（或汽车等）：*Only 8 of the 28 starters completed the course.* *28 名参赛者中，只有 8 人完成了全程。➲ COMPARE NON-STARTER **3** a person who gives the signal for a race to start（赛跑等的）发令员 **4** a device used for starting the engine of a vehicle（发动机的）启动装置，启动器 **5** a person who begins doing a particular activity in the way mentioned 起步（或启动）…的人：*He was a* ***late starter*** *in the theatre* (= older than most people when they start). 他从事戏剧表演起步较晚。◇ *a* ***slow starter*** 做事起步慢的人 ➲ SEE ALSO SELF-STARTER **6** (often used as an adjective 常用作形容词) something that is intended to be used by sb who is starting to do sth 在起步阶段使用的；启动时用的：*a* ***starter home*** (= a small home for sb who is buying property for the first time) 供初次购房者购买的房屋 ◇ *a* ***starter kit/pack*** 入门工具包

IDM for 'starters (*informal*) used to emphasize the first of a list of reasons, opinions, etc., or to say what happens first（强调一系列理由、意见等的第一条或表示首先发生的事）首先，作为开头 **under ,starter's 'orders** (of a runner, rider, etc. 赛跑运动员、骑手等) waiting for a signal to start a race 等待发令员发令

'starting blocks (*also* **the blocks**) *noun* [pl.] the two blocks on the ground that runners push their feet against at the beginning of a race 起跑器 ➲ VISUAL VOCAB PAGE V50

'starting gate *noun* a barrier that is raised to let horses or dogs start running in a race（赛马或赛狗等比赛用的）起跑门

'starting pistol *noun* a gun used for signalling the start of a race（速度竞赛）发令枪

'starting point *noun* **1 ~ (for sth)** a thing, an idea or a set of facts that can be used to begin a discussion or process（讨论或过程的）起点，基础：*The article served as a useful starting point for our discussion.* 这篇文章成了我们展开讨论的良好起点。**2** the place where you begin a journey（旅行的）起点，出发点 ➲ MORE LIKE THIS 9, page R26

'starting price *noun* the final ODDS that are given for a horse or dog just before a race begins（赛马或赛狗的）临赛赔率

star·tle /ˈstɑːtl; *NAmE* ˈstɑːrtl/ *verb* to surprise sb suddenly in a way that slightly shocks or frightens them 使惊吓；使吓一跳；使大吃一惊：**~ sb/sth** *I didn't mean to startle you.* 我不是存心要吓唬你。◇ *The explosion startled the horse.* 爆炸声使马受了惊。◇ *I was startled by her question.* 她的问题让我大吃一惊。◇ **it startles sb to do sth** *It startled me to find her sitting in my office.* 发现她坐在我办公室里面，把我吓了一跳。➲ SYNONYMS AT SURPRISE ▶ **star·tled** /ˈstɑːtld; *NAmE* ˈstɑːrtld/ *adj.*: *She looked at him with startled eyes.* 她用吃惊的目光看着他。◇ *He looked startled.* 他显得很惊讶。◇ *She jumped back like a startled rabbit.* 她像受惊的兔子似的跳了回去。

start·ling /ˈstɑːtlɪŋ; *NAmE* ˈstɑːrt-/ *adj.* **1** extremely unusual and surprising 惊人的；让人震惊的：*a startling discovery* 惊人的发现 **2** (of a colour 颜色) extremely bright 极鲜亮的：*startling blue eyes* 蓝盈盈的眼睛 ▶ **start·ling·ly** *adv.*

'start-up *adj.*, *noun*

■ ***adj.*** [only before noun] connected with starting a new business or project（新企业或工程）开办阶段的，启动时期的：*start-up costs* 启动经费

■ ***noun*** a company that is just beginning to operate 新创公司；初创企业

S

ˌstar ˈturn *noun* [usually sing.] the main performer or entertainer in a show（节目的）主要演员，主要环节

star·va·tion /stɑːˈveɪʃn; *NAmE* stɑːrˈv-/ *noun* [U] the state of suffering and death caused by having no food 饥饿；挨饿；饿死：*to* ***die of/from starvation*** 饿死 ◇ *Millions will* ***face starvation*** *next year as a result of the drought.* 由于发生旱灾，明年将有数百万人面临饥饿的威胁。◇ *a* ***starvation diet*** (= one in which you do not have much to eat) 不足果腹的食物 ◇ *They were on* ***starvation wages*** (= extremely low wages). 他们挣的工资不够维持基本生活。

starve /stɑːv; *NAmE* stɑːrv/ *verb* **1** [I, T] to suffer or die because you do not have enough food to eat; to make sb suffer or die in this way （使）挨饿，饿死：*The animals were left to starve to death.* 那些动物只能等着饿死。◇ *pictures of starving children* 展示饥饿儿童的图片 ◇ *The new job doesn't pay as much but we won't starve!* 新工作的工资没有过去多，不过我们不至于挨饿！◇ **~ sb/yourself** *She's starving herself to try to lose weight.* 她试图通过节食来减肥。 **2 -starved** (in adjectives 构成形容词) not having sth that you need 缺乏…的；急需…的：*supply-starved rebels* 补给匮乏的反叛者 ➲ SEE ALSO CASH-STARVED

IDM **be ˈstarving (for sth)** (*also* **be ˈstarved** *especially in NAmE*) (*informal*) to feel very hungry 饿得很：*When's the food coming? I'm starving!* 食物什么时候上来？我快饿死了！

PHR V **ˌstarve sb into ˈsth/into ˈdoing sth** to force sb to do sth by not allowing them to get any food or money 断绝食物（或资金）来源以迫使某人做某事 **ˌstarve sb/sth of ˈsth** (*NAmE also* **ˌstarve sb/sth for ˈsth**) [usually passive] to not give sth that is needed 使某人（或事物）得不到所需要的：*I felt starved of intelligent conversation.* 让我感到痛苦的是无法与有识之士交谈。◇ *The department has been starved of resources.* 这个部门一直缺少资源。 **ˌstarve sb ↔ˈout (of sth)** to force sb to leave a particular building or area by not allowing them to get any food 以断绝食物来源迫使某人出来

stash /stæʃ/ *verb, noun*

■ ***verb*** **~ sth + adv./prep.** (*informal*) to store sth in a safe or secret place 存放；贮藏；隐藏：*She has a fortune* ***stashed away*** *in various bank accounts.* 她有一大笔钱存在几个不同的银行账户下。

■ ***noun*** [usually sing.] (*informal*) an amount of sth that is kept secretly 一批贮藏物：*a stash of money* 一笔存款

S

sta·sis /ˈsteɪsɪs/ *noun* [U, C] (*pl.* **sta·ses** /-siːz/) (*formal*) a situation in which there is no change or development 停滞；静止

stat /stæt/ *noun* (*informal*) = STATISTIC (3)

state 🔑 /steɪt/ *noun, adj., verb*

■ ***noun***

• **CONDITION OF SB/STH** 状态 **1** 🔑 [C] the mental, emotional or physical condition that a person or thing is in 状态；状况；情况：*a confused* ***state of mind*** 思绪纷乱 ◇ *He was in a state of permanent depression.* 他一直处于消沉状态。◇ *anxieties about the state of the country's economy* 对于国家经济状况的担忧 ◇ *The building is in a bad* ***state of repair*** (= needs to be repaired). 那座房子年久失修。◇ *She was in a* ***state of shock.*** 她震惊不已。◇ (*BrE, informal*) *Look at the state of you! You can't go out looking like that.* 看看你这副样子！你可不能就这么出去。◇ *You're* ***not in a fit state*** *to drive.* 你现在的状态不宜开车。 ➲ NOTE AT CONDITION

• **COUNTRY** 国家 **2** 🔑 (*also* **State**) [C] a country considered as an organized political community controlled by one government 国家：*the Baltic States* 波罗的海诸国 ◇ *European Union member states* 欧盟成员国 ➲ SEE ALSO CITY STATE, NATION STATE, POLICE STATE, WELFARE STATE ➲ NOTE AT COUNTRY

• **PART OF COUNTRY** 国家的一部分 **3** 🔑 (*also* **State**) [C] (*abbr.* **St.**) an organized political community forming part of a country 州；邦：*the states of Victoria and Western Australia* 维多利亚州和西澳大利亚州 ◇ *the southern states of the US* 美国南方各州

• **GOVERNMENT** 政府 **4** 🔑 (*also* **the State**) [U, sing.] the government of a country 政府：***matters/affairs of state*** 国家大事 ◇ *people who are financially dependent on the state* 依靠国家救济的人 ◇ *a state-owned company* 国营公司 ◇ *They wish to limit the power of the State.* 他们希望限制政府权力。

• **OFFICIAL CEREMONY** 正式礼仪 **5** [U] the formal ceremonies connected with high levels of government or with kings and queens（适用于国家元首或政府首脑的）正式礼仪，隆重仪式：*The president was driven* ***in state*** *through the streets.* 总统乘车隆重地从街上穿过。

• **THE US** 美国 **6 the States** [pl.] (*informal*) the United States of America 美国：*I've never been to the States.* 我从未去过美国。

IDM **be in/get into a ˈstate** (*informal, especially BrE*) **1** to be/become excited or anxious 兴奋；紧张；焦虑：*She was in a real state about her exams.* 她对考试感到很紧张。 **2** to be dirty or untidy 邋遢；凌乱；不整洁：*What a state this place is in!* 这地方真够乱的！ **in a state of ˈgrace** (in the Roman Catholic Church) having been forgiven by God for the wrong or evil things you have done（天主教指灵魂上没有大罪的状态）受天主眷爱，蒙受恩宠 **a state of afˈfairs** a situation 事态；情况；形势：*This state of affairs can no longer be ignored.* 再不能无视这种情况了。 ➲ SYNONYMS AT SITUATION **the state of ˈplay 1** the stage that has been reached in a process, etc. which has not yet been completed 进展情况；发展阶段：*What is the current state of play in the peace talks?* 和平谈判目前进展得怎么样？ **2** (*especially BrE*) the score in a sports match, especially in CRICKET（板球等比赛的）比分

■ ***adj.*** (*also* **State**) [only before noun]

• **GOVERNMENT** 政府 **1** 🔑 provided or controlled by the government of a country 国家提供（或控制）的：*state education* 公办教育 ◇ *families dependent on state benefits* (= in Britain, money given by the government to people who are poor) 靠政府救济金生活的家庭 ◇ *state secrets* (= information that could be harmful to a country if it were discovered by an enemy) 国家机密

• **OFFICIAL** 官方 **2** connected with the leader of a country attending an official ceremony 国事礼仪（或规格）的：*The Queen is on a state visit to Moscow.* 女王正对莫斯科进行国事访问。◇ *the state opening of Parliament* 隆重的议会开幕式 ◇ *the state apartments* (= used for official ceremonies) 国事活动厅

• **PART OF COUNTRY** 国家的一部分 **3** 🔑 connected with a particular state of a country, especially in the US 州的；邦的：*a* ***state prison/hospital/university, etc.*** 州监狱、州立医院、州立大学等 ◇ ***state police/troopers*** 州警察 ◇ *a state tax* 州税

■ ***verb*** **1** 🔑 to formally write or say sth, especially in a careful and clear way 陈述；说明；声明：**~ sth** *He has already stated his intention to run for election.* 他已声明打算参加竞选。◇ *The facts are clearly stated in the report.* 报道对事实真相作了清楚的说明。◇ *There is no need to* ***state the obvious*** (= to say sth that everyone already knows). 显而易见的事实就不必陈述了。◇ **~ how, what, etc....** *State clearly how many tickets you require.* 说清楚你需要多少张票。◇ **~ that...** *He stated categorically that he knew nothing about the deal.* 他明确表示对那笔交易一无所知。◇ **it is stated that...** *It was stated that standards at the hospital were dropping.* 据称，那家医院的医疗水准在不断下降。◇ **sth is stated to be/have sth** *The contract was stated to be invalid.* 那份合同宣布作废。 ➲ SYNONYMS AT DECLARE **2** [usually passive] **~ sth** to fix or announce the details of sth, especially on a written document 规定；公布：*This is not one of their stated aims.* 在他们宣布的目标里没有这一条。◇ *You must arrive at the time stated.* 你必须在规定时间到达。◇ *Do not exceed the stated dose* (= of medicine). 不要超过规定的剂量。

state·craft /ˈsteɪtkrɑːft; *NAmE* -kræft/ *noun* [U] skill in managing state and political affairs 治国才能；政务才能

the ˈState Department *noun* [sing.] the US government department of foreign affairs（美国）国务院

state·hood /ˈsteɪthʊd/ *noun* [U] **1** the fact of being an independent country and of having the rights and powers of a country 独立国家地位 **2** the condition of being one of the states within a country such as the

US or Australia 州（或邦）的地位：*West Virginia was granted statehood in 1863.* 西弗吉尼亚于 1863 年获准成为一个州。

ˈ**state house** *noun* [usually sing.] (in the US) a building in which a state LEGISLATURE (= parliament) meets（美国）州议会大厦

state·less /ˈsteɪtləs/ *adj.* not officially a citizen of any country 无国籍的 ▸ **state·less·ness** *noun* [U]

state·let /ˈsteɪtlət/ *noun* a small state, especially one that is formed when a larger state breaks up（尤指大国分裂后形成的）小国

ˌ**state ˈline** *noun* the line between two states in the US（美国）州界，州界线：*the Nevada-California state line* 内华达和加利福尼亚两州州界

state·ly /ˈsteɪtli/ *adj.* **1** impressive in size, appearance or manner 宏大的；壮观的；气宇不凡的；仪态高贵的 SYN **majestic**: *an avenue of stately chestnut trees* 两边有雄伟高大栗树的林荫道 ◇ *a tall, stately woman* 仪态高贵的高个子女人 **2** slow, formal and elegant 缓慢庄严的；优雅从容的：*a stately dance* 缓慢优雅的舞蹈 ◇ *The procession made its stately progress through the streets of the city.* 游行队伍缓慢而庄严地穿过城市的街道。▸ **state·li·ness** *noun* [U]

ˌ**stately ˈhome** *noun* (*BrE*) a large, impressive house of historical interest, especially one that the public may visit（具历史价值，尤指可供人参观的）豪华大宅 ➲ VISUAL VOCAB PAGE V15

state·ment /ˈsteɪtmənt/ *noun, verb*

■ *noun* **1** [C] something that you say or write that gives information or an opinion 说明；说法；表白；表态：*Are the following statements true or false?* 下面的说法对不对？◇ *Your statement is misleading.* 你的表述令人误解。◇ *Is that a statement or a question?* 这是在表态呢，还是提出问题呢？◇ *The play makes a strong political statement.* 这出戏表明一种鲜明的政治立场。➲ SEE ALSO FASHION STATEMENT **2** [C] ~ (**on/about sth**) a formal or official account of facts or opinions 声明；陈述；报告 SYN **declaration**: ***a formal/a public/a written/an official statement*** 正式 / 公开 / 书面 / 官方声明 ◇ *A government spokesperson **made a statement** to the press.* 政府发言人向新闻界发表了一份声明。◇ *The prime minister is expected to **issue a statement** on the policy change this afternoon.* 人们预计首相将在今天下午就政策的改变发表声明。◇ *The police asked me to **make a statement*** (= a written account of facts concerning a crime, used in court if legal action follows). 警方要求我写一份供述。**3** [C] a printed record of money paid, received, etc. 结算单；清单；报表：*The directors are responsible for preparing the company's financial statements.* 几位总监负责填写公司的财务报表。◇ *My bank sends me monthly statements.* 银行按月给我寄来结算单。➲ SEE ALSO BANK STATEMENT ➲ **WORDFINDER NOTE** AT BANK **4** [C] (in England and Wales) an official report on a child's special needs made by a local education authority（英格兰和威尔士地方教育部门针对儿童的特殊需求提供的）评估报告：*a statement of special educational needs* 特殊教育需求评估报告 **5** [U] (*formal*) the act of stating or expressing sth in words（文字）陈述，表述 SYN **expression**: *When writing instructions, clarity of statement is the most important thing.* 编写操作说明时，表述清晰明白至为重要。

IDM ˌ**make a ˈstatement** to express or reveal an opinion or a characteristic in a very clear way, although often without words 表明（意见或个性，但通常不是用语言）：*The cleaning staff extended their strike mainly to make a statement about how determined they were.* 清洁工人延长了罢工时间，主要目的是表明他们的决心。◇ *The way you dress makes a statement about you.* 你的衣着表明了你的性格。

■ *verb* [often passive] ~ **sb** (in England and Wales) to officially decide and report that a child has special needs for his or her education（英格兰和威尔士）对（儿童）做特殊教育需求评估：*statemented children* 评估认定须接受特殊教育的学童

ˌ**state of ˈsiege** *noun* a situation in which the government limits people's freedom to enter or leave a city, town or building 戒严（或封锁）状态

▼ **SYNONYMS** 同义词辨析

statement

comment • announcement • remark • declaration • observation

These are all words for sth that you say or write, especially sth that gives information or an opinion. 以上各词均指口头或书面的说明、宣布。

statement something that you say or write that gives information or an opinion, often in a formal way 通常指正式的说明、声明、陈述、报告：*A government spokesperson made a statement to the press.* 政府发言人向新闻界发表了一份声明。

comment something that you say or write that gives an opinion on sth or is a response to a question about a particular situation 指议论、评论、意见：*She made helpful comments on my work.* 她对我的工作提出了有益的意见。

announcement a spoken or written statement that informs people about sth 指公告、布告、通告：*the announcement of a peace agreement* 和平协议公告

remark something that you say or write that gives an opinion or thought about sb/sth 指谈论、言论、评述：*He made a number of rude remarks about the food.* 他对这食物作了许多无礼的评论。

declaration (*rather formal*) an official or formal statement, especially one that states an intention, a belief or a feeling, or that gives information 指官方或正式的公告、宣告、宣言、声明：*the declaration of war* 宣战

observation (*rather formal*) a comment, especially one based on sth you have seen, heard or read 尤指根据所见、所闻、所读而作的评论：*He began by making a few general observations about the report.* 开头他先对这个报告作了几点概括性的评论。

COMMENT, REMARK OR OBSERVATION? 用 comment、remark 还是 observation?

A **comment** can be official or private. A **remark** can be made in public or private but is always unofficial and the speaker may not have considered it carefully. An **observation** is unofficial but is usually more considered than a remark. * comment 既可是官方的也可是私下的；remark 既可是公开的也可是私下的，但总是非官方的，说话者可能未经深思熟虑；observation 是非官方的，但通常较 remark 多几分考虑。

PATTERNS

- a(n) statement/comment/announcement/remark/declaration/observation **about** sth
- a(n) statement/comment/observation **on** sth
- a(n) **public**/**official** statement/comment/announcement/declaration
- to **make** a(n) statement/comment/announcement/remark/declaration/observation
- to **issue** a(n) statement/announcement/declaration

ˌ**state of the ˈart** *adj.* using the most modern or advanced techniques or methods; as good as it can be at the present time 应用最先进技术（或方法）的；最先进的：*The system was state of the art.* 这一系统是当时最先进的。◇ *a state-of-the-art system* 目前最先进的系统

state·room /ˈsteɪtruːm; -rʊm/ *noun* **1** a private room on a large ship（轮船上的）特等客舱 **2** a room used by important government members, members of a royal family, etc. on formal occasions（政府要员或王室成员等使用的）会客厅，议事厅，国事活动厅

ˌ**state's atˈtorney** *noun* (*US*) a lawyer who represents a state in a court（美国）州检察官

ˈ**state school** *noun* **1** (*BrE*) (*NAmE* ˈ**public school**) a school that is paid for by the government and provides

S

free education 公立学校 ➲ COMPARE PRIVATE SCHOOL, PUBLIC SCHOOL (2) **2** (*NAmE*) = STATE UNIVERSITY

ˌstate's ˈevidence *noun* [U] (*US, law* 律) if a criminal **turns state's evidence**, he or she gives evidence against the people who committed a crime with him or her（刑事被告向法庭提供的）对同案犯不利的证据

state·side /ˈsteɪtsaɪd/ *adj., adv.* (*US, informal*) connected with the US; in or towards the US (used when the person speaking is not in the US)（用以在境外指美国）美国的（地），在美国的（地），去美国的（地）: *When are you next planning a trip stateside?* 你计划下一次什么时候去美国?

states·man /ˈsteɪtsmən/ *noun* (*pl.* **-men** /-mən/) a wise, experienced and respected political leader 政治家: *the party's **elder statesman*** 该党元老

states·man·like /ˈsteɪtsmənlaɪk/ *adj.* having or showing the qualities and abilities of a statesman 具有政治家风范的；像政治家的: *He was commended for his statesmanlike handling of the crisis.* 他处理那场危机时，因表现出政治家的才干而受到称赞。

states·man·ship /ˈsteɪtsmənʃɪp/ *noun* [U] skill in managing state affairs 政治才能；治国才干

states·per·son /ˈsteɪtspɜːsn; *NAmE* -pɜːrsn/ *noun* (*pl.* **-people**) a wise, experienced and respected political leader 政治家

ˌstates' ˈrights *noun* [pl.] (in the US) the rights of each state in relation to the national government, such as the right to make some laws and to have its own police force（美国的）州权（相对于国家政府的权力，如制定某些法律和拥有自己的警察）

ˌstate ˈtrooper (*also* **troop·er**) *noun* (*NAmE*) (in the US) a member of a State police force（美国）州警察

ˈstate university (*also* **ˈstate school**) *noun* (*both NAmE*) a university that is managed by a state of the US（美国）州立大学

state·wide /ˈsteɪtwaɪd/ *adj., adv.* happening or existing in all parts of a state of the US（美国）全州性的（地），在全州范围内的（地）: *a statewide election* 州选举 ◇ *She won 10% of the vote statewide.* 她赢得全州 10% 的选票。

S

static /ˈstætɪk/ *adj., noun*

■ ***adj.*** **1** not moving, changing or developing 静止的；静态的；停滞的: *Prices on the stock market, which have been static, are now rising again.* 股市价格一直停滞不动，现在又在上涨了。◇ *a static population level* 稳定的人口水平 **2** (*physics* 物) (of a force 力) acting as a weight but not producing movement 静力的: *static pressure* 静压 OPP **dynamic**

■ ***noun*** [U] **1** noise or other effects that disturb radio or television signals and are caused by particular conditions in the atmosphere 天电（干扰）**2** (*also* **ˌstatic elecˈtricity**) electricity that gathers on or in an object which is not a CONDUCTOR of electricity 静电: *My hair gets full of static when I brush it.* 我梳头时头发就有好多静电。**3 statics** the science that deals with the forces that balance each other to keep objects in a state of rest 静力学 ➲ COMPARE DYNAMIC (2) **4** (*NAmE, informal*) angry or critical comments or behaviour 抨击；指责；愤慨

sta·tin /ˈstætɪn/ *noun* a drug that people take to lower the level of CHOLESTEROL (= a substance in the body that can cause heart disease) in their blood. There are several types of statin. 胆固醇合成酶抑制剂；他汀

sta·tion 🔑 /ˈsteɪʃn/ *noun, verb*

■ ***noun***

• **FOR TRAINS/BUSES** 火车；公共汽车 **1** 🔑 a place where trains stop so that passengers can get on and off; the buildings connected with this 火车站: *I get off at the next station.* 我在下一站下车。◇ *the main station* 中心车站 ◇ *Penn Station* 宾州车站 ◇ *a **train station*** 火车站 ◇ (*BrE also*) *a **railway station*** 火车站 ◇ (*BrE*) ***a tube/an underground station*** 地铁站 ◇ (*NAmE*) ***a subway station*** 地铁站 ➲ WORDFINDER NOTE AT TRAIN **2** 🔑 (usually in compounds 通常构成复合词) a place where buses stop; the buildings connected with this 公共汽车站；长途汽车站: ***a bus/coach station*** 公共汽车 / 长途汽车站 HELP In Britain, the word **station** on its own usually refers to the train station. 在英国，station 单独使用时通常指火车站: *Can you tell me the way to the station?* 你能告诉我火车站怎么走吗? In the US it is usual to say which station you are talking about. 在美国，station 通常指明是什么车站: *the train station* 火车站 ◇ *the Greyhound Bus station* 灰狗巴士站

• **FOR WORK/SERVICE** 工作；服务 **3** 🔑 (usually in compounds 通常构成复合词) a place or building where a service is organized and provided or a special type of work is done 站；所；局: *a police station* 警察局 ◇ (*BrE*) *a **petrol station*** 加油站 ◇ (*NAmE*) *a **gas station*** 加油站 ◇ *an agricultural research station* 农业研究所 ◇ *a pollution monitoring station* 污染监测站 ➲ COMPARE SPACE STATION

• **RADIO/TV COMPANY** 广播 / 电视公司 **4** 🔑 (often in compounds 常构成复合词) a radio or television company and the programmes it broadcasts 电台；电视台: *a local **radio/TV station*** 地方广播电台 / 电视台 ◇ *He tuned to another station.* 他换了一个台。➲ WORDFINDER NOTE AT RADIO

• **SOCIAL POSITION** 社会地位 **5** (*old-fashioned* or *formal*) your social position 社会地位；身份: *She was definitely getting ideas **above her station**.* 她明显是抱有超出自己身份的想法。

• **POSITION** 位置 **6** a place where sb has to wait and watch or be ready to do work if needed 须坚守的位置；岗位: *You are not to leave your station without permission.* 未经允许，不得离开岗位。➲ SEE ALSO DOCKING STATION

• **LARGE FARM** 大农场 **7** (usually in compounds 通常构成复合词) a large sheep or CATTLE farm in Australia or New Zealand（澳大利亚或新西兰放养牛或羊的）大型牧场

• **FOR ARMY/NAVY** 陆军；海军 **8** a small base for the army or navy; the people living in it 军事基地；驻军: *a naval station* 海军基地 ➲ SEE ALSO ACTION STATIONS IDM SEE PANIC *n.*

■ ***verb***

• **ARMED FORCES** 武装部队 **1** [often passive] **~ sb + adv./prep.** to send sb, especially from one of the armed forces, to work in a place for a period of time 派驻；使驻扎: *troops stationed abroad* 驻扎在国外的部队

• **GO TO POSITION** 前往 **2 ~ sb/yourself + adv./prep.** (*formal*) to go somewhere and stand or sit there, especially to wait for sth; to send sb somewhere to do this 到某处站（或坐）；把…安置到（某处）: *She stationed herself at the window to await his return.* 她待在窗前等他回来。

ˈstation agent (*US*) (*BrE* **sta·tion·mas·ter**) *noun* a person in charge of a train station（火车站）站长

sta·tion·ary /ˈsteɪʃənri; *NAmE* -neri/ *adj.* **1** not moving; not intended to be moved 不动的；静止的；固定的；不可移动的: *I remained stationary.* 我待着没动。◇ *The car collided with a stationary vehicle.* 小汽车撞到一辆停着的车上。◇ *a stationary exercise bike* 固定式健身自行车 OPP **mobile 2** not changing in condition or quantity 不变的；稳定的 SYN **static**: *a stationary population* 稳定的人口

sta·tion·er /ˈsteɪʃənə(r)/ *noun* (*especially BrE*) **1** a person who owns or manages a shop selling stationery 文具商 **2 stationer's** (*pl.* **stationers**) a shop that sells stationery 文具店: *Is there a stationer's near here?* 这附近有没有文具店? ➲ MORE LIKE THIS 34, page R29

sta·tion·ery /ˈsteɪʃənri; *NAmE* -neri/ *noun* [U] **1** materials for writing and for using in an office, for example paper, pens and envelopes 文具 ➲ VISUAL VOCAB PAGE V71 **2** special paper for writing letters on 信纸；信笺 ➲ WORDFINDER NOTE AT STORE

ˈstation house *noun* (*NAmE*) = POLICE STATION

sta·tion·mas·ter /ˈsteɪʃnmɑːstə(r); *NAmE* -mæs-/ (*US also* **ˈstation agent**) *noun* a person in charge of a train station（火车站）站长

ˈstation wagon (*NAmE*) (*BrE* **eˈstate car, estate**) *noun* a car with a lot of space behind the back seats and a door at the back for loading large items 旅行轿车；客货两用车 ➲ VISUAL VOCAB PAGE V56

stat·ism /ˈsteɪtɪzəm/ *noun* [U] a political system in which the central government controls social and economic affairs 中央集权制 ▶ **stat·ist** *adj., noun*

stat·is·tic AW /stəˈtɪstɪk/ *noun* **1 statistics** (*also informal* **stats**) [pl.] a collection of information shown in numbers 统计数字；统计资料：*crime/unemployment, etc. statistics* 犯罪、失业等统计资料 ◇ *According to official statistics the disease killed over 500 people.* 根据官方的统计数字，500 多人死于这种疾病。◇ ***Statistics show** that far more people are able to ride a bicycle than can drive a car.* 统计资料表明，会骑自行车的人比会开汽车的人多得多。◇ *These statistics are misleading.* 这些统计资料会引起误解。➲ SEE ALSO VITAL STATISTICS (1) **2 statistics** (*also informal* **stats**) [U] the science of collecting and analysing statistics 统计学：*There is a compulsory course in statistics.* 有一门统计学的必修课。**3** (*also informal* **stat**) [C] a piece of information shown in numbers（一项）统计数据：*An important statistic is that 94 per cent of crime relates to property.* 一个重要数据是 94% 的犯罪同财产有关。◇ *I felt I was no longer being treated as a person but as a statistic.* 我感觉我不再被看作人，而被看作一个统计数字了。▶ **stat·is·tic·al** AW /stəˈtɪstɪkl/ *adj.*：*statistical analysis* 统计分析 **stat·is·tic·al·ly** AW /-kli/ *adv.*：*The difference between the two samples was not **statistically significant**.* 在统计学的意义上，这两个样品没有显著的差异。

stat·is·ti·cian AW /ˌstætɪˈstɪʃn/ *noun* a person who studies or works with statistics 统计学家；统计员

sta·tive /ˈsteɪtɪv/ *adj.* (*linguistics* 语言) (of verbs 动词) describing a state rather than an action. **Stative** verbs (for example *be, seem, understand, like, own*) are not usually used in the progressive tenses. 表示状态的 ➲ COMPARE DYNAMIC *adj.* (4)

stats /stæts/ *noun* (*informal*) = STATISTICS (1), (2)

ˈstat sheet *noun* (*NAmE*) a piece of paper or a document which gives details of sth in the form of numbers, especially of a team's or a player's performance 数据单，数据文件，统计表（以数字形式提供某事的细节，尤用于运动队或运动员的表现）

statu·ary /ˈstætʃuəri; *NAmE* -eri/ *noun* [U] (*formal*) statues 雕塑；雕像；塑像：*a collection of marble statuary* 一批大理石雕像

statue 🔑 /ˈstætʃuː/ *noun* a figure of a person or an animal in stone, metal, etc., usually the same size as in real life or larger 雕塑，雕像，塑像（大小通常等于或大于真人或实物）➲ COLLOCATIONS AT ART ➲ VISUAL VOCAB PAGE V3

statu·esque /ˌstætʃuˈesk/ *adj.* (*formal*) (usually of a woman 通常指女性) tall and beautiful in an impressive way; like a statue 又高又美的；雕塑般的 SYN **imposing**

statu·ette /ˌstætʃuˈet/ *noun* a small statue 小雕像；小塑像

stat·ure /ˈstætʃə(r)/ *noun* [U] (*formal*) **1** the importance and respect that a person has because of their ability and achievements 声望；名望：*an actress of considerable stature* 颇有名望的女演员 ◇ *The orchestra has **grown in stature**.* 这支管弦乐队的声望有所提高。**2** a person's height 身高；个子：*a woman of short stature* 身材矮小的女人 ◇ *He is small in stature.* 他个头小。

sta·tus 🔑 AW /ˈsteɪtəs; *NAmE also* ˈstætəs/ *noun* [usually sing.] **1** 🔑 [U, C] the legal position of a person, group or country 法律地位（或身份）：*They were granted refugee status.* 他们获得了难民身份。◇ *The party was denied legal status.* 那个党没有获得合法地位。**2** 🔑 [U, C, usually sing.] the social or professional position of sb/sth in relation to others 地位；身份；职位：*low status jobs* 地位低下的工作 ◇ *to have a high social status* 拥有很高的社会地位 ◇ *Women are only asking to be given equal status with men.* 妇女只是要求得到和男人平等的地位。◇ *She achieved celebrity status overnight.* 她一夜之间成为名流。**3** 🔑 [U] high rank or social position 高级职位；社会上层地位：*The job brings with it status and a high income.* 担任这一职务既有显贵的地位又有丰厚的收入。**4** 🔑 [U, C, usually sing.] the level of importance that is given to sth 重视（或崇尚）程度：*the high status accorded to science in our culture* 我们的文化对科学的高度崇尚 **5** [U] the situation at a particular time during a process（进展的）状况，情形：*What is the current status of our application for funds?* 我们申请资金目前进展如何？◇ *She updated her Facebook status to 'in a relationship'.* 她将她的脸书状态更新为"恋爱中"。

ˈstatus bar *noun* (*computing* 计) an area that you see along the bottom of your computer screen that gives you information about the program that you are using or the document that you are working on（电脑屏幕底部显示程序或文件信息的）状态条，状态列，状态栏

status quo /ˌsteɪtəs ˈkwəʊ; *NAmE* ˈkwoʊ/ *noun* [sing.] (*from Latin*) the situation as it is now, or as it was before a recent change 现状；原来的状况：*to **defend/restore the status quo*** 维持现状；恢复原来的状况 ◇ *conservatives who want to **maintain the status quo*** 想维持现状的保守派

ˈstatus symbol *noun* a possession that people think shows their high social status and wealth 社会地位与财富的象征：*Exotic pets are the latest status symbol.* 养珍禽异兽是表现社会地位的最时髦方式。

stat·ute /ˈstætʃuːt/ *noun* **1** a law that is passed by a parliament, council, etc. and formally written down 成文法；法令；法规：*Penalties are laid down **in the statute**.* 法规中有关于惩罚措施的规定。◇ *Corporal punishment was banned **by statute** in 1987.* * 1987 年通过的法令明文禁止体罚。**2** a formal rule of an organization or institution 章程；条例；规程：***Under the statutes** of the university they had no power to dismiss him.* 按大学的规章制度，校方无权开除他。

ˈstatute book *noun* a collection of all the laws made by a government 法典；法令全书；法规汇编：*It's not yet **on the statute book*** (= it has not yet become law). 这项内容还未成为正式法规。

ˈstatute law *noun* [U] all the written laws of a parliament, etc. as a group 制定法；成文法 ➲ COMPARE CASE LAW, COMMON LAW

ˌstatute of limiˈtations *noun* (*law* 律) the legal limit on the period of time within which action can be taken on a crime or other legal question 诉讼时效法；追诉时效法

statu·tory /ˈstætʃətri; *NAmE* -tɔːri/ *adj.* [usually before noun] fixed by law; that must be done by law 法定的；依法必须执行的：*The authority failed to carry out its statutory duties.* 主管部门未履行自己的法定职责。◇ *When you buy foods you have certain statutory rights.* 在购买食物时，你有一定的法定权利。▶ **statu·tor·ily** *adv.*

ˌstatutory ˈholiday *noun* (*CanE*) a public holiday that is fixed by law 法定假日

ˌstatutory ˈinstrument *noun* (*law* 律) a law or other rule which has legal status 行政立法性文件

ˌstatutory ofˈfence (*BrE*) (*NAmE* **ˌstatutory ofˈfense**) *noun* (*law* 律) a crime that is described by law and can be punished by a court 制定法上的犯罪

ˌstatutory ˈrape *noun* [U] (*NAmE, law* 律) the crime of having sex with sb who is not legally old enough 法定强奸罪；强奸幼女罪

staunch /stɔːntʃ/ *adj., verb*

■ ***adj.*** (**staunch·er**, **staunch·est**) strong and loyal in your opinions and attitude 忠实的；坚定的 SYN **faithful**：*a staunch supporter of the monarchy* 坚定地拥护君主制的人 ◇ *one of the president's staunchest allies* 总统最忠实的盟友之一 ◇ *a staunch Catholic* 笃信天主教的教徒 ▶ **staunch·ly** *adv.*：*She staunchly defended the new policy.* 她坚定地维护新政策。◇ *The family was staunchly Protestant.* 那一家人是忠实的新教徒。**staunch·ness** *noun* [U]

■ ***verb*** (*also* **stanch** *especially in NAmE*) **~ sth** (*formal*) to stop the flow of sth, especially blood 止住（血等的）流出

S

stave /steɪv/ *noun, verb*

■ *noun* **1** a strong stick or pole 棍；棒；木柱：*fence staves* 篱笆桩 **2** (*also* **staff**) (*music* 音) a set of five lines on which music is written 五线谱 ➲ PICTURE AT MUSIC

■ *verb* (**staved, staved** or **stove, stove** /stəʊv; *NAmE* stoʊv/)
PHR V **ˌstave sth↔ˈin** to break or damage sth by pushing it or hitting it from the outside 使向内塌陷；压凹；撞破：*The side of the boat was staved in when it hit the rocks.* 船触礁把船舷撞扁了。**ˌstave sth↔ˈoff** (**staved, staved**) to prevent sth bad from affecting you for a period of time; to delay sth 暂时挡住（坏事）；延缓，推迟（某事物）：*to stave off hunger* 暂时解饿

stay 🔑 /steɪ/ *verb, noun*

■ *verb* **1** 🔑 [I] to continue to be in a particular place for a period of time without moving away 停留；待：*to stay in bed* 待在床上 ◇ *'Do you want a drink?' 'No, thanks, I can't stay.'* "你要不要喝一杯？""不，谢谢，我不能久待。" ◇ *Stay there and don't move!* 待在那儿别动！◇ *We ended up staying for lunch.* 我们最终还是留了下来吃午饭。◇ *She* **stayed at home** (= did not go out to work) *while the children were young.* 孩子们小的时候，她没出去上班。◇ *I'm* **staying late** *at the office tonight.* 今晚我要在办公室待到很晚。◇ *My hat won't stay on!* 我的帽子怎么都戴不住！◇ *Can you* **stay behind** *after the others have gone and help me clear up?* 你能不能等别人走后留下来帮我收拾收拾？◇ *We stayed to see what would happen.* 我们留下来看会发生什么事。◇ ~ **doing sth** *They stayed talking until well into the night.* 他们待在那儿一直谈到深夜。HELP In spoken English **stay** can be used with **and** plus another verb, instead of with **to** and the infinitive, to show purpose or to tell somebody what to do. 口语中，stay 后面可接 and 加另一个动词，而不用 to 加不定式，以表示目的或要某人做某事：*I'll stay and help you.* 我留下来帮你。◇ *Can you stay and keep an eye on the baby?* 你可以留下来照看婴儿吗？**2** 🔑 [I] to continue to be in a particular state or situation 保持；继续是 SYN **remain**：**+ adj.** *He never stays angry for long.* 他生气时间从来不会长。◇ *I can't stay awake any longer.* 我困得再也熬不住了。◇ *The store stays open until late on Thursdays.* 这商店每星期四都会开到很晚。◇ **+ adv./prep.** *I don't know why they stay together* (= remain married or in a relationship). 我不知道他们为什么还在一起。◇ *Inflation stayed below 4% last month.* 上月的通货膨胀率保持在 4% 以下。◇ **+ noun** *We promised to stay friends for ever.* 我们约定永远做朋友。**3** 🔑 [I] to live in a place temporarily as a guest or visitor 暂住；逗留：*We found out we were staying in the same hotel.* 我们发现我们住在同一家旅馆里。◇ *My sister's coming to stay next week.* 下星期我妹妹要来住几天。◇ *He's staying with friends this weekend.* 这个周末他要和几个朋友一起过。◇ *I stayed three nights at my cousin's house.* 我在我表兄家住了三夜。HELP In Indian, Scottish and South African English **stay** can mean 'to live in a place permanently'. 在印度、苏格兰和南非英语中，stay 可以指定居：*Where do you stay* (= where do you live)? 你住在哪里？

IDM **be here to ˈstay | have come to ˈstay** to be accepted or used by most people and therefore a permanent part of our lives 为多数人所接受；得到普遍认可：*It looks like televised trials are here to stay.* 看来电视直播审判成了一种风气。**stay!** used to tell a dog not to move（叫狗）别动 **stay the ˈcourse** to continue doing sth until it has finished or been completed, even though it is difficult 坚持到底：*Very few of the trainees have stayed the course.* 极少受训者坚持到底。**stay your ˈhand** (*old-fashioned* or *literary*) to stop yourself from doing sth; to prevent you from doing sth 住手；不做（某事）**stay the ˈnight** (*especially BrE*) to sleep at sb's house for one night（在某人家）过夜：*You can always stay the night at our house.* 你什么时候都可以在我们家过夜。**stay ˈput** (*informal*) if sb/sth **stays put**, they continue to be in the place where they are or where they have been put 待在原地；留在原处 ➲ MORE AT CLEAR *adv.*, LOOSE *adj.*

PHR V **ˌstay aˈround** (*informal*) to not leave somewhere 待着不走；不离开：*I'll stay around in case you need me.* 我就待在这儿，也许你用得着我。**ˌstay aˈway (from sb/sth)** 🔑 to not go near a particular person or place 离开，不接近（某人）；不去（某处）：*I want you to stay away from my daughter.* 我要你离我女儿远远的。**ˌstay ˈin** to not go out or to remain indoors 不外出；待在室内：*I feel like staying in tonight.* 今晚我想待在家里。**ˌstay ˈon** to continue studying, working, etc. somewhere for longer than expected or after other people have left 留下来继续（学习、工作等）**ˌstay ˈout 1** to continue to be outdoors or away from your house at night 待在户外；不在家；（晚上）不回家 **2** (of workers 工人) to continue to be on strike 继续罢工 **ˌstay ˈout of sth 1** 🔑 to not become involved in sth that does not concern you 不介入；不干预 **2** 🔑 to avoid sth 避开；远离：*to stay out of trouble* 避免惹麻烦 **ˌstay ˈover** to sleep at sb's house for one night（在某人家）过夜 **ˌstay ˈup** to go to bed later than usual 深夜不睡；熬夜：*You've got school tomorrow. I don't want you staying up late.* 你明天要上学，我不想你熬夜。

■ *noun* **1** 🔑 a period of staying; a visit 停留；逗留（时间）；做客：*I enjoyed my stay in Prague.* 我在布拉格逗留期间过得很开心。◇ *an overnight stay* 留下过夜 **2** a rope or wire that supports a ship's MAST, a pole, etc.（船桅的）支索；（杆子等的）牵索，撑条 ➲ SEE ALSO MAINSTAY

IDM **a ˌstay of exeˈcution** (*law* 律) a delay in following the order of a court 缓期执行：*to grant a stay of execution* 准予缓期执行

ˈstay-at-home *noun, adj.*

■ *noun* (*informal, often disapproving*) a person who rarely goes out or does anything exciting 不爱出门的人；恋家的人；死气沉沉的人

■ *adj.* a **stay-at-home** mother or father is one who stays at home to take care of their children instead of going out to work 全职照顾家庭的

stay·cation /ˌsteɪˈkeɪʃn/ *noun* a holiday/vacation that you spend at or near your home 居家假；宅假；不出城度假 ➲ MORE LIKE THIS 1, page R25

stay·er /ˈsteɪə(r)/ *noun* (*BrE*) a person or an animal, especially a horse, with the ability to keep going in a tiring race or competition 有持久力的人；有耐力的动物（尤指赛马）

ˈstaying power *noun* [U] the ability to continue doing sth difficult or tiring until it is finished 持久力；耐力 SYN **stamina**

St Bernard /ˌsnt ˈbɜːnəd; *NAmE* ˌseɪnt bɜːrˈnɑːrd/ *noun* a large strong dog, originally from Switzerland, where it was trained to help find people who were lost in the snow 圣伯纳犬，瑞士救护犬（训练来搜寻雪地失踪者）

St Chris·to·pher /ˌsnt ˈkrɪstəfə; *NAmE* ˌseɪnt ˈkrɪstəfər/ *noun* a small MEDAL with a picture of St Christopher (the PATRON SAINT of travellers) on it, that some people wear or carry with them when they go on a journey because they believe it will protect them from danger 圣克里斯托弗像章（旅行者为求平安而佩戴或携带的旅行主保像章）

STD /ˌes tiː ˈdiː/ *noun* **1** the abbreviation for 'sexually transmitted disease' (a disease that is passed from one person to another during sexual activity) 性传播疾病（全写为 sexually transmitted disease）**2** (*BrE*) the abbreviation for 'subscriber trunk dialling' (a system of making direct telephone calls over long distances) 长途直拨电话（全写为 subscriber trunk dialling）

St David's Day /ˌsnt ˈdeɪvɪdz deɪ; *NAmE* ˌseɪnt/ *noun* 1 March, a Christian festival of the national SAINT of Wales, when many Welsh people wear a DAFFODIL 圣大卫节（3 月 1 日，纪念威尔士主保圣人的基督教节日，很多威尔士人佩戴黄水仙）

stead /sted/ *noun*

IDM **in sb's/sth's ˈstead** (*formal*) instead of sb/sth 代替某人（或某物）：*Foxton was dismissed and John Smith was appointed in his stead.* 福克斯顿被解职，受命接替他的是约翰·史密斯。**stand sb in good ˈstead** to be useful or helpful to sb when needed（需要时）对某人有用，对某人有利：*Your languages will stand you in good stead when it comes to finding a job.* 你懂得几种语言，找工作时就会显出优势。

stead·fast /ˈstedfɑːst; *NAmE* -fæst/ *adj.* (*literary, approving*) not changing in your attitudes or aims 坚定的；不动摇的 **SYN** **firm**: *steadfast loyalty* 忠贞不渝 ◇ **~ in sth** *He remained steadfast in his determination to bring the killers to justice.* 他要将杀人凶手绳之以法的决心一直没有动摇。 ▶ **stead·fast·ly** *adv.* **stead·fast·ness** *noun* [U]

steady 🔑 /ˈstedi/ *adj., verb, adv., exclamation*

■ ***adj.*** (**stead·ier, steadi·est**) **1** 🔑 developing, growing, etc. gradually and in an even and regular way（发展、增长等）稳步的，持续的，匀速的 **SYN** **constant**: *five years of steady economic growth* 经济持续五年的发展 ◇ *a steady decline in numbers* 数量逐渐下降 ◇ *We are making slow but steady progress.* 我们虽然缓慢但是在稳步前进。◇ *The castle receives a **steady stream** of visitors.* 前来参观城堡的游客流量保持稳定。 **2** 🔑 not changing and not interrupted 稳定的；恒定的 **SYN** **regular**: *His breathing was steady.* 他呼吸平稳。◇ *a **steady job/income*** 稳定的工作 / 收入 ◇ *She drove at a steady 50 mph.* 她以每小时 50 英里的稳定速度驾驶。◇ *They set off at a steady pace.* 他们以不紧不慢的速度出发了。◇ *a **steady boyfriend/girlfriend*** (= with whom you have a serious relationship or one that has lasted a long time) 关系稳定的男朋友 / 女朋友 ◇ *to have a steady relationship* 有稳定的关系 **3** 🔑 firmly fixed, supported or balanced; not shaking or likely to fall down 稳的；平稳的；稳固的: *He held the boat steady as she got in.* 他把船稳住，让她上了船。◇ *I met his steady gaze.* 我迎向他凝视的目光。◇ *Such fine work requires a good eye and a **steady hand**.* 做这样精细的工作，眼要尖，手要稳。 **OPP** **unsteady** **4** (of a person 人) sensible; who can be relied on 沉稳的；可靠的 ▶ **stead·ily** 🔑 *adv.*: *The company's exports have been increasing steadily.* 公司的出口量一直稳步增长。◇ *The situation got steadily worse.* 形势逐渐恶化。◇ *He looked at her steadily.* 他凝视着她。◇ *The rain fell steadily.* 雨不紧不慢地下着。 **steadi·ness** *noun* [U]

IDM **(as) steady as a ˈrock** extremely steady and calm; that you can rely on 十分可靠；稳如泰山；安如磐石 ➲ MORE LIKE THIS 14, page R26 ➲ MORE AT READY *adj.*

■ ***verb*** (**stead·ies, steady·ing, stead·ied, stead·ied**) **1** [T, I] **~ (yourself/sb/sth)** to stop yourself/sb/sth from moving, shaking or falling; to stop moving, shaking or falling 使稳；使平稳；稳住: *She steadied herself against the wall.* 她靠墙站稳。◇ *The lift rocked slightly, steadied, and the doors opened.* 电梯微微一晃又稳了下来，接着门开了。 **2** [I] to stop changing and become regular again 恢复平稳；稳定下来: *Her heartbeat steadied.* 她的心跳平稳下来。◇ **~ against sth** *The pound steadied against the dollar.* 英镑对美元的汇率稳定下来。 **3** [T] **~ sb/sth** to make sb/sth calm 使平静；使冷静；使镇定: *He took a few deep breaths to **steady his nerves**.* 他深深地吸了几口气，让自己平静下来。

■ ***adv.*** in a way that is steady and does not change or shake 稳定地；持续地；稳固地: *In trading today the dollar **held steady** against the yen.* 在今天的交易中，美元对日元的汇率保持稳定。

IDM **go ˈsteady (with sb)** (*old-fashioned, informal*) to have a romantic or sexual relationship with sb, in which you see the other person regularly（和情侣）关系稳定

■ ***exclamation*** (*informal*) **1 ~ on** (*becoming old-fashioned*) used to tell sb to be careful about what they are saying or doing, for example because it is extreme or not appropriate（要求对方注意言行）哎，注意点: *Steady on! You can't say things like that about somebody you've never met.* 注意点！你从没见过的人，不要那样议论人家。 **2** used to tell sb to be careful（提醒对方小心）注意，当心，小心: *Steady! Don't fall off.* 小心！别摔下来。

steak /steɪk/ *noun* **1** (*also less frequent* **beef·steak**) [U, C] a thick slice of good quality beef 牛排: ***fillet/rump/sirloin steak*** 里脊 / 臀肉 / 腰肉牛排 ◇ *How would you like your steak done?* 您要求您的牛排做到几成熟？◇ *a **steak knife*** (= one with a special blade for eating steak with) 牛排餐刀 ➲ VISUAL VOCAB PAGE V23 **2** [U, C] a thick slice of any type of meat 肉排；肉块: *pork steak* 猪排 ◇ *a gammon steak* 一厚片火腿 **3** [U] (often in compounds 常构成复合词) beef that is not of the best quality, often sold in small pieces and used in PIES, STEWS, etc. 碎牛肉（不是最佳部位，常剁碎出售，可以炖或做馅等）: ***braising/stewing steak*** 适合于炖的牛肉块 ◇ *a steak and kidney pie* 牛肉腰子馅饼 **4** [C] a large thick piece of fish 鱼排；鱼块: *a cod steak* 鳕鱼排

steak·house /ˈsteɪkhaʊs/ *noun* a restaurant that serves mainly steak 牛排餐馆

steak tar·tare /ˌsteɪk tɑːˈtɑː(r); *NAmE* tɑːrˈtɑːr; ˈtɑːrtər/ *noun* [U, C] (*from French*) a dish made with raw chopped beef and raw eggs 鞑靼牛排（用切碎的生牛肉加生鸡蛋等）

steal 🔑 /stiːl/ *verb, noun*

■ ***verb*** (**stole** /stəʊl; *NAmE* stoʊl/, **stolen** /ˈstəʊlən; *NAmE* ˈstoʊ-/) **1** 🔑 [I, T] to take sth from a person, shop/store, etc. without permission and without intending to return it or pay for it 偷；窃取: **~ (from sb/sth)** *We found out he'd been stealing from us for years.* 我们发现他从我们家偷东西已经好多年了。◇ **~ sth (from sb/sth)** *My wallet was stolen.* 我的钱包给人偷了。◇ ***I had** my wallet **stolen**.* 我的钱包给人偷了。◇ *Thieves stole jewellery worth over £10 000.* 窃贼偷走了价值 1 万多英镑的珠宝。◇ *It's a crime to handle stolen goods.* 经销赃物是犯法的。◇ (*figurative*) *to steal sb's ideas* 剽窃某人的观点 ➲ COLLOCATIONS AT CRIME **2** [I] + **adv./prep.** to move secretly and quietly so that other people do not notice you 偷偷地（或悄悄地）移动 **SYN** **creep**: *She stole out of the room so as not to wake the baby.* 她生怕惊醒婴儿，蹑手蹑脚地从房间里出来。◇ (*figurative*) *A chill stole over her body.* 她突然感到浑身发冷。 **3** [T] **~ sth** (in BASEBALL 棒球) to run to the next BASE before another player from your team hits the ball, so that you are closer to scoring 偷（垒）: *He tried to steal second base but was out.* 他试图盗二垒但被杀出局。

IDM **steal a ˈglance/ˈlook (at sb/sth)** to look at sb/sth quickly so that nobody sees you doing it 偷偷看…一眼 **steal sb's ˈheart** (*literary*) to make sb fall in love with you 博得某人的欢心 **steal a ˈkiss (from sb)** (*literary*) to kiss sb suddenly or secretly 突然吻一下；偷吻 **steal a ˈmarch (on sb)** [no passive] to gain an advantage over sb by doing sth before them 抢先（某人）一步；抢得先机 **steal the ˈshow** [no passive] to attract more attention and praise than other people in a particular situation 吸引更多的注意；抢风头: *As always, the children stole the show.* 和往常一样，最引人注意的是孩子们。 **steal sb's ˈthunder** to get the attention, success, etc. that sb else was expecting, usually by saying or doing what they had intended to say or do 抢了某人的风头（或功劳）；抢先讲（或做）

■ ***noun*** (*NAmE*) (in BASEBALL 棒球) the act of running to another BASE while the PITCHER is throwing the ball 盗垒

IDM **be a ˈsteal** (*informal, especially NAmE*) to be for sale at an unexpectedly low price 以极低价出售；很便宜: *This suit is a steal at $80.* 这套西服只卖 80 美元，跟白给差不多了。

stealth /stelθ/ *noun, adj.*

■ ***noun*** [U] the fact of doing sth in a quiet or secret way 偷偷摸摸；不声张的活动；秘密行动: *The government was accused of trying to introduce the tax **by stealth**.* 有人指责政府想不事声张地开征这种税。◇ *Lions rely on stealth when hunting.* 狮子捕食全凭偷袭。

■ ***adj.*** [only before noun] (of an aircraft 飞机) designed in a way that makes it difficult to be discovered by RADAR 隐形的: *a stealth bomber* 隐形轰炸机

ˈstealth tax *noun* (*BrE, disapproving*) a tax that is collected in a way that is not very obvious, so people are less aware that they are paying it 隐性税

stealthy /ˈstelθi/ *adj.* doing things quietly and secretly; done quietly and secretly 偷偷摸摸的；不声张的；秘密的: *a stealthy animal* 行动诡秘的动物 ◇ *a stealthy movement* 隐蔽的移动 ▶ **stealth·ily** /-ɪli/ *adv.*

steam 🔑 /stiːm/ *noun, verb*

■ ***noun*** [U] **1** 🔑 the hot gas that water changes into when it boils 水蒸气；蒸汽: *Steam rose from the boiling kettle.* 壶里的水开了，冒着蒸汽。 **2** 🔑 the power that is produced from steam under pressure, used to operate engines,

S

machines, etc. 蒸汽动力：*the introduction of steam in the 18th century* * 18 世纪蒸汽动力的采用 ◇ *steam power* 蒸汽动力 ◇ *the steam age* 蒸汽时代 ◇ *a **steam train/engine*** 蒸汽火车；蒸汽机 **3** very small drops of water that form in the air or on cold surfaces when warm air suddenly cools 水汽 SYN **condensation**: *She wiped the steam from her glasses.* 她擦去眼镜上的水汽。

IDM **full speed/steam a'head** with as much speed or energy as possible 全速前进；全力 **,get up/,pick up 'steam 1** (*informal*) to become gradually more powerful, active, etc. 声势逐渐强大；渐成气候；慢慢活跃起来：*His election campaign is beginning to get up steam.* 他的竞选活动逐渐形成声势。**2** (of a vehicle 车辆) to increase speed gradually 逐渐提速 **,let off 'steam** (*informal*) to get rid of your energy, anger or strong emotions by doing sth active or noisy 释放精力；发泄怒气；宣泄感情 **,run out of 'steam** (*informal*) to lose energy and enthusiasm and stop doing sth, or do it less well 筋疲力尽；丧失热情 **get, etc. somewhere under your own 'steam** (*informal*) to go somewhere without help from other people 靠自己的力量去某处

■ ***verb*** **1** [I] to send out steam 蒸发；散发蒸汽；冒水汽：*a mug of steaming hot coffee* 一大杯热气腾腾的咖啡 **2** [T, I] ~ (sth) to place food over boiling water so that it cooks in the steam; to be cooked in this way 蒸（食物）：*steamed fish* 蒸鱼 ➲ COLLOCATIONS AT COOKING ➲ VISUAL VOCAB PAGE V28 **3** [I] + **adv./prep.** (of a boat, ship, etc. 船舶等) to move using the power produced by steam 依靠蒸汽动力行驶：*The boat steamed across the lake.* 汽船从湖上驶过。**4** [I] + **adv./prep.** (especially of a person 尤指人) to go somewhere very quickly 快速行走；疾行：*He spotted her steaming down the corridor towards him.* 他看见她沿着走廊向他疾步走来。◇ (*figurative*) *The company is steaming ahead with its investment programme.* 公司正紧锣密鼓地实施自己的投资方案。

IDM **be/get (all) steamed 'up (about/over sth)** (*NAmE also* **be 'steamed (about sth)**) (*informal*) to be/become very angry or excited about sth（变得）非常气愤，非常激动

PHR V **,steam sth↔'off | ,steam sth 'off sth** to remove one piece of paper from another using steam to make the glue that is holding them together softer 用蒸汽使（纸张等）脱离（或分开）**,steam sth↔'open** to open an envelope using steam to make the glue softer 用蒸汽脱胶开启（信封）**,steam 'up | ,steam sth↔'up** to become, or to make sth become, covered with steam（使）蒙上水汽：*As he walked in, his glasses steamed up.* 他进去的时候，眼镜上起了一层雾。

steam·boat /ˈstiːmbəʊt; *NAmE* -boʊt/ *noun* a boat driven by steam, used especially in the past on rivers and along coasts 汽船；轮船

steam·er /ˈstiːmə(r)/ *noun* **1** a boat or ship driven by steam 汽船；轮船 ➲ SEE ALSO PADDLE STEAMER **2** a metal container with small holes in it, that is placed over a pan of boiling water in order to cook food in the steam 蒸锅；蒸笼 ➲ VISUAL VOCAB PAGE V28

steam·ing /ˈstiːmɪŋ/ *adj., noun*

■ ***adj.*** **1** (*informal*) very angry 非常愤怒的 **2** (*also* **,steaming 'hot**) very hot 非常热的

■ ***noun*** [U] (*informal*) a crime in which a group of thieves move quickly through a crowded public place, stealing things as they go 结伙沿路偷窃

steam·roll·er /ˈstiːmrəʊlə(r); *NAmE* -roʊ-/ *noun, verb*

■ ***noun*** a large slow vehicle with a ROLLER, used for making roads flat 蒸汽压路机

■ ***verb*** (*NAmE usually* **'steam roll**) [T, I] ~ **(sb/sth) (+ adv./prep.)** to defeat sb or force them to do sth, using your power or authority（凭借力量或权威）打败，压服，迫使：*The team steamrollered their way to victory.* 这支队以不可阻挡之势获得胜利。◇ *She knew that she'd let herself be steamrollered.* 她知道自己会屈服于对方的威势。

steam·ship /ˈstiːmʃɪp/ *noun* (*abbr.* **SS**) a ship driven by steam 汽船；轮船

'steam shovel *noun* (*especially NAmE*) a large machine for digging, that originally worked by steam（蒸汽）挖土机，挖掘机

steamy /ˈstiːmi/ *adj.* (**steam·ier**, **steami·est**) **1** full of steam; covered with steam 充满蒸汽的；蒙着水汽的：*a steamy bathroom* 水汽弥漫的浴室 ◇ *steamy windows* 蒙着一层水汽的窗户 ◇ *the steamy heat of Tokyo* 东京的潮湿闷热 **2** (*informal*) sexually exciting 色情的 SYN **erotic**

steed /stiːd/ *noun* (*literary* or *humorous*) a horse to ride on 坐骑

steel 🔑 /stiːl/ *noun, verb*

■ ***noun*** **1** 🔑 [U] a strong hard metal that is made of a mixture of iron and CARBON 钢：*the iron and steel industry* 钢铁工业 ◇ *The frame is made of steel.* 这个架子是钢制的。◇ *The bridge is reinforced with huge steel girders.* 这座桥用巨大的钢梁加固了。➲ SEE ALSO STAINLESS STEEL **2** 🔑 [U] the industry that produces steel 钢铁工业：*Steel used to be important in South Wales.* 以前钢铁工业在南威尔士很重要。◇ *steel workers* 炼钢工人 ◇ *a steel town* 一座钢城 **3** [C] a long thin straight piece of steel with a rough surface, used for rubbing knives on to make them sharp 钢制磨刀棒 ➲ VISUAL VOCAB PAGE V27 **4** [U] (*old use* or *literary*) weapons that are used for fighting 兵器：*the clash of steel* 刀剑交击的哐当声

IDM **of 'steel** having a quality like steel, especially a strong, cold or hard quality 钢铁般坚强（或冷漠、坚硬）的：*She felt a hand of steel* (= a strong, firm hand) *on her arm.* 她感觉一只有力的手抓住了她的胳膊。◇ *You need a cool head and **nerves of steel*** (= great courage). 你需要有冷静的头脑、非常的魄力。◇ *There was a hint of steel in his voice* (= he sounded cold and firm). 他的语调显得冷静而坚决。

■ ***verb*** to prepare yourself to deal with sth unpleasant 准备对付；下决心应付：**~ yourself (for/against sth)** *As she waited, she steeled herself for disappointment.* 她等着的时候，就冷了心不指望了。◇ **~ yourself to do sth** *He steeled himself to tell them the truth.* 他硬下心来把实情告诉了他们。

,steel 'band *noun* a group of musicians who play music on drums that are made from empty metal oil containers. Steel bands originally came from the West Indies. 钢鼓乐队（敲击用空油桶制成的鼓，源自西印度群岛）

,steel 'drum (*also* **,steel 'pan**) *noun* a musical instrument used in West Indian music, made from a metal oil container which is hit in different places with two sticks to produce different notes 钢鼓（用金属油桶制成的西印度乐器，用两根鼓棒敲击各处发出各种音调）➲ VISUAL VOCAB PAGE V37

,steel 'wool (*BrE also* **,wire 'wool**) *noun* [U] a mass of fine steel threads that you use for cleaning pots and pans, making surfaces smooth, etc. 钢丝球（用以擦洗或磨光）

steel·work·er /ˈstiːlwɜːkə(r); *NAmE* -wɜːrk-/ *noun* a person who works in a place where steel is made 炼钢工人

steel·works /ˈstiːlwɜːks; *NAmE* -wɜːrks/ *noun* (*pl.* **steel·works**) [C+sing./pl. v.] a factory where steel is made 炼钢厂

steely /ˈstiːli/ *adj.* **1** (of a person's character or behaviour 人的性格或行为) strong, hard and unfriendly 强硬的；冷冰冰的：*a cold, steely voice* 冷冰冰的腔调 ◇ *a look of steely determination* 一副下定决心、不可动摇的神态 **2** like steel in colour（色泽）似钢的：*steely blue eyes* 灰蓝色的眼睛 ▶ **steeli·ness** *noun* [U]

steep 🔑 /stiːp/ *adj., verb*

■ ***adj.*** (**steep·er**, **steep·est**) **1** 🔑 (of a slope, hill, etc. 斜坡、山等) rising or falling quickly, not gradually 陡的；陡峭的：*a **steep hill/slope/bank*** 陡峭的山；陡坡；陡岸 ◇ *a **steep climb/descent/drop*** 陡直的爬升 / 下降 / 下落 ◇ *a steep flight of stairs* 一段很陡的楼梯 ◇ *The path grew steeper as we climbed higher.* 我们越往上爬路就越陡。**2** 🔑 [usually before noun] (of a rise or fall in an amount 数量的上升或下降) sudden and very big 突然的；急剧的；大起大落的 SYN **sharp**: *a steep decline in the birth rate* 出生率的骤降 ◇ *a steep rise in unemployment* 失业率的暴升 **3** (*informal*) (of a price or demand 价格或要求) too much;

S

unreasonable 过高的；过分的；不合理的 SYN **expensive**: *£2 for a cup of coffee seems a little steep to me.* 一杯咖啡 2 英镑在我看来有点贵得离谱。▶ **steep·ly** adv.: *a steeply sloping roof* 大坡度房顶 ◇ *The path climbed steeply upwards.* 上去的路很陡。◇ *Prices rose steeply.* 物价猛涨。 **steep·ness** *noun* [U]

■ *verb*

IDM **be 'steeped in sth** (*formal*) to have a lot of a particular quality 深深浸淫；饱含（某品质）: *a city steeped in history* 历史古城

PHR V **'steep sth in sth** to put food in a liquid and leave it for some time so that it becomes soft and flavoured by the liquid 在（液体）中浸泡（食物） **'steep yourself in sth** (*formal*) to spend a lot of time thinking or learning about sth 沉浸于；潜心于: *They spent a month steeping themselves in Chinese culture.* 他们花了一个月时间潜心钻研中国文化。

steep·en /'stiːpən/ *verb* [I, T] ~ (**sth**) to become or to make sth become steeper （使）变陡: *After a mile, the slope steepened.* 过了一英里后，山坡变陡了。

steeple /'stiːpl/ *noun* a tall pointed tower on the roof of a church, often with a SPIRE on it （教堂的）尖塔

steeple·chase /'stiːpltʃeɪs/ (*also* **chase**) *noun* **1** a long race in which horses have to jump over fences, water, etc. 越野障碍赛马 ➲ COMPARE FLAT RACING **2** a long race in which people run and jump over gates and water, etc. around a track 障碍赛跑

steeple·chaser /'stiːpltʃeɪsə(r)/ *noun* a horse or a person that takes part in steeplechases 参加越野障碍赛马的马；障碍赛跑选手

steeple·jack /'stiːpldʒæk/ *noun* a person whose job is painting or repairing towers, tall CHIMNEYS, etc. 高空作业工人（粉刷或修理高塔、大烟囱等）

steer /stɪə(r); *NAmE* stɪr/ *verb, noun*

■ *verb* **1** [T, I] ~ (**sth/sb**) (+ **adv./prep.**) to control the direction in which a boat, car, etc. moves 驾驶（船、汽车等）；掌控方向盘: *He steered the boat into the harbour.* 他把船开进港。◇ (*figurative*) *He took her arm and steered her towards the door.* 他抓住她的胳膊，把她带往门口。◇ *You row and I'll steer.* 你划桨，我来掌舵。**2** [T, I] ~ (**sth**) (+ **adv./prep.**) (of a boat, car, etc. 船、汽车等) to move in a particular direction 行驶: *The ship steered a course between the islands.* 船在岛屿之间穿行。◇ *The ship steered into port.* 船驶进港口。**3** [T] ~ **sth** + **adv./prep.** to take control of a situation and influence the way in which it develops 操纵；控制；引导: *He managed to steer the conversation away from his divorce.* 他设法避开他离婚这话题。◇ *She steered the team to victory.* 她率领全队取得胜利。◇ *The skill is in steering a middle course between the two extremes.* 技巧就在于避开这两个极端，走中间路线。

IDM SEE CLEAR *adv.*

■ *noun* **1** [sing.] (*BrE*) a piece of advice or information that helps you do sth or avoid a problem 建议；劝告；忠告: *Can anyone give me a steer on this?* 有人能就这一点给我个建议吗？**2** [C] a BULL (= a male cow) that has been CASTRATED (= had part of its sex organs removed), kept for its meat 阉公牛；肉用公牛 ➲ COMPARE BULLOCK, OX (1)

steer·age /'stɪərɪdʒ; *NAmE* 'stɪr-/ *noun* [U] (in the past) the part of a ship where passengers with the cheapest tickets used to travel （旧时客轮的）统舱，大舱

steer·ing /'stɪərɪŋ; *NAmE* 'stɪr-/ *noun* [U] the machinery in a vehicle that you use to control the direction it goes in （车辆等的）转向装置 ➲ SEE ALSO POWER STEERING

'steering column *noun* the part of a car or other vehicle that the STEERING WHEEL is fitted on （汽车等的）转向柱

'steering committee (*also* **'steering group**) *noun* a group of people that a government or an organization chooses to direct an activity and to decide how it will be done 指导委员会；程序委员会

'steering wheel *noun* the wheel that the driver turns to control the direction that a vehicle goes in 方向盘；（操）舵轮 ➲ VISUAL VOCAB PAGE V56

stego·saur /'stegəsɔː(r)/ (*also* **stego·saurus** /ˌstegə'sɔːrəs/) *noun* a DINOSAUR with a small head, four legs and two rows of SPIKES along its back 剑龙（背部有三角形骨板的恐龙）

stein /staɪn/ *noun* (*from German*) a large decorated cup for drinking beer, usually made of EARTHENWARE and often with a lid 饰花大啤酒杯（多为陶质，常带盖）

stel·lar /'stelə(r)/ *adj.* [usually before noun] **1** (*specialist*) connected with the stars 星的；恒星的 ➲ COMPARE INTERSTELLAR **2** (*informal*) excellent 优秀的；精彩的；杰出的: *a stellar performance* 精彩的演出

stem /stem/ *noun, verb*

■ *noun* **1** the main long thin part of a plant above the ground from which the leaves or flowers grow; a smaller part that grows from this and supports flowers or leaves （花草的）茎；（花或叶的）梗，柄 ➲ VISUAL VOCAB PAGE V11 **2** the long thin part of a wine glass between the bowl and the base （高脚酒杯的）脚 ➲ VISUAL VOCAB PAGE V23 **3** the thin tube of a TOBACCO pipe 烟斗柄 **4** **-stemmed** (in adjectives 构成形容词) having one or more stems of the type mentioned 有…茎（或梗）的: *a long-stemmed rose* 一枝长茎玫瑰 **5** (*grammar* 语法) the main part of a word that stays the same when endings are added to it 词干: *'Writ' is the stem of the forms 'writes', 'writing' and 'written'.* * writ 是 writes、writing 和 written 三个词的词干。

IDM **from ˌstem to 'stern** all the way from the front of a ship to the back 从船头到船尾

■ *verb* (**-mm-**) ~ **sth** to stop sth that is flowing from spreading or increasing 阻止；封堵；遏止: *The cut was bandaged to stem the bleeding.* 伤口已包扎止血。◇ *They discussed ways of **stemming the flow** of smuggled drugs.* 他们讨论了遏制走私毒品流通的办法。◇ *The government had failed to **stem the tide** of factory closures.* 政府没有控制住工厂的倒闭潮。

PHR V **'stem from sth** (not used in the progressive tenses 不用于进行时) to be the result of sth 是…的结果；起源于；根源是 ➲ LANGUAGE BANK AT BECAUSE

'stem cell *noun* a basic type of cell which can divide and develop into cells with particular functions. All the different kinds of cells in the human body develop from stem cells. 干细胞

stem·ware /'stemweə(r); *NAmE* -wer/ *noun* [U] (*specialist*) glasses and glass bowls that have a STEM 有脚玻璃器皿

stench /stentʃ/ *noun* [sing.] a strong, very unpleasant smell 臭气；恶臭 SYN **reek**: *an overpowering stench of rotting fish* 腐烂的鱼臭气熏天 ◇ (*figurative*) *The stench of treachery hung in the air.* 到处都是可耻的叛变的气息。

sten·cil /'stensl/ *noun, verb*

■ *noun* a thin piece of metal, plastic or card with a design cut out of it, that you put onto a surface and paint over so that the design is left on the surface; the pattern or design that is produced in this way （印文字或图案用的）模板；（用模板印的）文字，图案

■ *verb* (**-ll-**, *NAmE also* **-l-**) [T, I] ~ (**sth**) to make letters or a design on sth using a stencil 用模板印（文字或图案）

steno /'stenəʊ; *NAmE* -noʊ/ *noun* (*pl.* **-os**) (*NAmE, informal*) **1** [C] = STENOGRAPHER **2** [U] = STENOGRAPHY

sten·og·raph·er /stə'nɒgrəfə(r); *NAmE* -'nɑːg-/ (*also informal* **steno**) *noun* (*especially NAmE*) a person whose job is to write down what sb else says, using a quick system of signs or abbreviations 速记员

sten·og·raphy /stə'nɒgrəfi; *NAmE* -'nɑːg-/ (*also informal* **steno**) *noun* [U] (*NAmE*) = SHORTHAND (1)

stent /stent/ *noun* (*medical* 医) a small support that is put inside a BLOOD VESSEL (= tube) in the body, for example in order to stop sth blocking it （防止栓塞等而植入的）血管支架

S

sten·tor·ian /sten'tɔːriən/ *adj.* (*formal*) (of a voice 嗓音) loud and powerful 洪亮的

step /step/ *noun, verb*

■ ***noun***

• **MOVEMENT/SOUND** 动作；声音 **1** [C] the act of lifting your foot and putting it down in order to walk or move somewhere; the sound this makes 迈步；脚步声：*a baby's first steps* 婴儿学步 ◇ *He **took a step** towards the door.* 他朝门口迈了一步。◇ *We heard steps outside.* 我们听见外面有脚步声。➲ SEE ALSO FOOTSTEP, GOOSE-STEP

• **WAY OF WALKING** 步履 **2** [C, usually sing.] the way that sb walks 步伐；步态：*He walked with a quick light step.* 他迈着轻快的步子走着。

• **DISTANCE** 距离 **3** [C] the distance that you cover when you take a step 一步（的距离）：*It's only a few steps further.* 再走几步就到了。◇ *He turned around and **retraced his steps*** (= went back the way he had come). 他转身原路往回走。◇ *She moved a step closer to me.* 她朝我靠近一步。◇ *The hotel is only a short step from the beach.* 旅馆离海滩只有几步路。

• **IN SERIES/PROCESS** 系列；过程 **4** [C] one of a series of things that you do in order to achieve sth 步骤；措施：*This was a first step towards a united Europe.* 这是朝着统一的欧洲迈出的第一步。◇ *It's a **big step** giving up your job and moving halfway across the world.* 你放弃工作搬到地球的另一端，可真不简单。◇ *We are **taking steps** to prevent pollution.* 我们正在采取措施防止污染。◇ *This won't solve the problem but it's **a step in the right direction**.* 这虽不能解决问题，却是朝正确方向迈出的一步。◇ *The new drug is a major **step forward** in the treatment of the disease.* 发现这种新药是治疗这一疾病的重大进展。➲ SYNONYMS AT ACTION **5** [C] one of a series of things that sb does or that happen, which forms part of a process 步；阶段 SYN **stage**: *Having completed the first stage, you can move on to step 2.* 第一阶段完成后，你就可以接着进行第二步了。◇ *I'd like to take this idea **a step further**.* 我想把这一思想深化一步。◇ *This was a big **step up*** (= to a better position) *in his career.* 这是他在事业上向前迈出的一大步。◇ *I'll explain it to you **step by step**.* 我来一步一步地给你解释。◇ *a **step-by-step** guide to building your own home* 自建房舍的分步骤指导手册

• **STAIR** 台阶 **6** [C] a surface that you put your foot on in order to walk to a higher or lower level, especially one of a series 台阶；梯级：*She was sitting on the bottom step of the staircase.* 她正坐在最下面一级楼梯上。◇ *We walked down some stone steps to the beach.* 我们走下几级石阶，来到海滩上。◇ *A short **flight of steps** led up to the door.* 上几磴台阶就到了门口。➲ VISUAL VOCAB PAGES V18, V21 ➲ SEE ALSO DOORSTEP *n.* (1)

• **IN DANCE** 舞蹈 **7** [C, usually pl.] a series of movements that you make with your feet and which form a dance 舞步 ➲ SEE ALSO QUICKSTEP ➲ WORDFINDER NOTE AT DANCE

• **EXERCISE** 健身运动 **8** [U] (often in compounds 常构成复合词) a type of exercise that you do by stepping on and off a raised piece of equipment 踏板操：*step aerobics* 有氧踏板操 ◇ *a step class* 踏板操训练班

• **LADDER** 梯子 **9 steps** [pl.] (*BrE*) a STEPLADDER 折梯；梯子：*a pair of steps* 一架折梯 ◇ *We need the steps to get into the attic.* 我们得踩着梯子才能爬到阁楼上去。

• **IN MUSIC** 音乐 **10** [C] (*NAmE*) the interval between two notes that are next to each other in a SCALE 音级；度 ➲ COMPARE TONE *n.* (7), SEMITONE

IDM **break 'step** to change the way you are walking so that you do not walk in the same rhythm as the people you are walking or marching with 走乱步伐 **fall into 'step (beside/with sb)** to change the way you are walking so that you start walking in the same rhythm as the person you are walking with（和某人）合上步伐，步调一致起来：*He caught her up and fell into step beside her.* 他赶上她，跟着她的步子往前走。**in/out of 'step (with sb/sth) 1** putting your feet on the ground in the right/wrong way, according to the rhythm of the music or the people you are moving with（和某人）步伐一致（或不一致）；（和音乐）合拍（或不合拍） **2** having ideas that are the same as or different from other people's（和某人）想法一致（或不一致）：*She was out of step with her colleagues.* 她和同事们想法不一样。 **mind/watch your 'step 1** to walk carefully 走路小心 **2** to behave in a careful and sensible way 言行小心谨慎 **one step ˌforward, two steps 'back** (*saying*) used to say that every time you make progress, sth bad happens that means that the situation is worse than before 进一步，退两步 **a/one step a'head (of sb/sth)** when you are **one step ahead** of sb/sth, you manage to avoid them or to achieve sth more quickly than they do 避开（某人或某事物）；领先（某人或某事物）一步 **a/one step at a 'time** when you do sth **one step at a time** you do it slowly and gradually 一步一步；逐步；按部就班

■ ***verb*** **(-pp-)** [I] **+ adv./prep.** to lift your foot and move it in a particular direction or put it on or in sth; to move a short distance 迈步；踩；踏；行走：*to step onto/off a bus* 上/下公共汽车 ◇ *I stepped forward when my name was called out.* 我听见叫我名字时向前迈了一步。◇ *She stepped aside to let them pass.* 她闪到一边让他们过去。◇ *We stepped carefully over the broken glass.* 我们小心翼翼地从碎玻璃上走了过去。◇ *I turned around quickly and stepped on his toes.* 我一个急转身，踩到了他的脚上。◇ (*figurative*) *Going into the hotel is like stepping back in time.* 走进这家旅馆就像是回到了过去。

IDM **step into the 'breach** to do sb's job or work when they are suddenly or unexpectedly unable to do it 临时顶替某人工作；临时顶缺 **step into sb's 'shoes** to continue a job or the work that sb else has started 接替某人的工作 **'step on it** (*informal*) used especially in orders to tell sb to drive faster（尤用以要求加速驾驶）开快点儿，赶快 **step on sb's 'toes** (*NAmE, informal*) = TREAD ON SB'S TOES **step out of 'line | be/get out of 'line** to behave badly or break the rules 表现不好；不守规矩；越轨；出格 **step up to the 'plate** (*especially NAmE*) to do what is necessary in order to benefit from an opportunity or deal with a crisis 开始行动，采取措施（以抓住机会或应对危机）：*It's important for world leaders to step up to the plate and honor their commitments on global warming.* 对世界领导人来说，重要的是开始行动，兑现他们在全球变暖问题上的承诺。

PHR V **ˌstep a'side/'down** to leave an important job or position and let sb else take your place 让位；退位 **ˌstep 'back (from sth)** to think about a situation calmly, as if you are not involved in it yourself 跳出（某事物的）圈子看问题：*We are learning to step back from ourselves and identify our strengths and weaknesses.* 我们正努力学会走出自我的樊篱，认清我们自身的优点和缺点。**ˌstep 'forward** to offer to help sb or give information 主动站出来（帮忙或提供信息）；自告奋勇 **ˌstep 'in** to help sb in a disagreement or difficult situation 居间调停；居中斡旋；施以援手：*A local businessman stepped in with a large donation for the school.* 当地一位商人出面捐了一大笔钱给学校。◇ *The team coach was forced to step in to stop the two athletes from coming to blows.* 运动队教练不得不介入，才使两个运动员没有动起手来。**ˌstep 'out** (*especially NAmE*) to go out 出去：*I'm just going to step out for a few minutes.* 我就出去一小会儿。**ˌstep 'up** to come forward 走上前去：*She stepped up to receive her prize.* 她走上前去领奖。◇ (*figurative*) *Employers have stepped up to help bridge the gap between education and work.* 雇主们已站出来帮助弥合教育与就业之间的鸿沟。**ˌstep sth↔'up** to increase the amount, speed, etc. of sth 增加，提高（数量、速度等）：*He has stepped up his training to prepare for the race.* 他为准备那场赛跑加强了训练。◇ *If he wants to win this election, he really needs to **step it up*** (= put in more effort). 如果他想赢得这次选举，必须加倍努力。

step- /step/ *combining form* (in nouns 构成名词) related as a result of one parent marrying again（因父母再婚而构成的亲缘关系）继…：*stepmother* 继母

step·brother /'stepbrʌðə(r)/ *noun* the son from an earlier marriage of your STEPMOTHER or STEPFATHER 继兄；继弟（继母与其前夫或继父与其前妻所生的儿子）➲ COMPARE HALF-BROTHER

'step change *noun* [usually sing.] (*BrE*) a big change or improvement in sth 巨大变化；显著进步（或改善）：*His speech called for a step change in attitudes to the*

S

environment in the 21st century. 他的演讲呼吁在21世纪彻底改变对待环境的态度。

step·child /ˈsteptʃaɪld/ *noun* (*pl.* **step·chil·dren** /-tʃɪldrən/) a child of your husband or wife by an earlier marriage 继子；继女

step·daugh·ter /ˈstepdɔːtə(r)/ *noun* a daughter that your husband or wife has from an earlier marriage to another person 继女

step·fam·ily /ˈstepfæməli/ *noun* (*pl.* **-ies**) the family that is formed when sb marries a person who already has children 有继子女的家庭；有继父（或继母）的家庭 ➲ WORDFINDER NOTE AT FAMILY

step·father /ˈstepfɑːðə(r)/ *noun* the man who is married to your mother but who is not your real father 继父

Step·ford wife /ˌstepfəd ˈwaɪf; *NAmE* -fərd/ *noun* a woman who does not behave or think in an independent way, always following the accepted rules of society and obeying her husband without thinking 斯特福德式妻子（缺乏独立性、只知遵守社会既定准则和顺从丈夫）：*She's gradually turning into a Stepford wife.* 她正逐渐变成一味顺从丈夫的妻子。 ➲ MORE LIKE THIS 17, page R27 **ORIGIN** From the title of the book and film/movie *The Stepford Wives*, in which a group of women who behave in this way are in fact robots. 源自小说和同名电影《斯特福德的妻子们》，影片中的女人实为机器人。

step·lad·der /ˈsteplædə(r)/ *noun* a short LADDER that is made of two parts, one with steps, that are joined together at the top, so that it can stand on its own or be folded flat for carrying or storing 折梯；梯子 ➲ VISUAL VOCAB PAGE V21

step·mother /ˈstepmʌðə(r)/ *noun* the woman who is married to your father but who is not your real mother 继母

step·ney /ˈstepni/ *noun* (*IndE*) a spare wheel for a car（汽车）备用轮胎

ˈstep-parent *noun* a stepmother or stepfather 继母；继父

steppe /step/ *noun* [C, usually pl., U] a large area of land with grass but few trees, especially in SE Europe and Siberia 草原；（尤指东南欧及西伯利亚树少的）干草原：*the vast Russian steppes* 辽阔的俄罗斯大草原

ˈstepping stone *noun* **1** one of a line of flat stones that you step on in order to cross a stream or river（小溪、小河中的）踏脚石 **2** something that allows you to make progress or begin to achieve sth 进身之阶；垫脚石；敲门砖：*a stepping stone to a more lucrative career* 涉足更赚钱的行业的敲门砖

step·sis·ter /ˈstepsɪstə(r)/ *noun* the daughter from an earlier marriage of your STEPMOTHER OR STEPFATHER 继姐，继妹（继母与其前夫或继父与其前妻所生的女儿）➲ COMPARE HALF-SISTER

step·son /ˈstepsʌn/ *noun* a son that your husband or wife has from an earlier marriage to another person 继子

step·wise /ˈstepwaɪz/ *adj.* **1** in a series of steps, rather than continuously 逐步的；逐渐的 **2** (*music* 音) (of a MELODY 旋律) moving in a way that uses only the notes that are next to each other in a SCALE（按音阶）级进的

-ster *suffix* (in nouns 构成名词) a person who is connected with or has the quality of 与…有关的人；有…品质的人：*gangster* 匪徒 ◇ *youngster* 年轻人

stereo /ˈsteriəʊ; *NAmE* -oʊ/ *noun* (*pl.* **-os**) **1** (*also* **ˈstereo system**) [C] a machine that plays CDs, etc., sometimes with a radio, that has two separate SPEAKERS so that you hear different sounds from each 立体声音响（系统）：*a **car/personal stereo*** 车用 / 个人立体声音响 ◇ *Let's put some music on the stereo.* 我们在立体声音响上放点音乐吧。 **2** [U] the system for playing recorded music, speech, etc. in which the sound is directed through two channels 立体声：*to broadcast **in stereo*** 用立体声广播 ➲ COMPARE MONO *n.* (1) ▶ **stereo** (*also formal* **stereo·phon·ic**) *adj.* [only before noun]: *stereo sound* 立体声 ➲ COMPARE QUADRAPHONIC

stereo·scop·ic /ˌsteriəˈskɒpɪk; *NAmE* -ˈskɑːpɪk/ *adj.* **1** (*specialist*) able to see objects with length, width and depth, as humans do 有立体视觉的：*stereoscopic vision* 立体视觉 **2** (of a picture, photograph, etc. 图画、照片等) that is made so that you see the objects in it with length, width, and depth when you use a special machine 有立体效果的 **SYN** three-D

stereo·type /ˈsteriətaɪp/ *noun, verb*

■ ***noun*** a fixed idea or image that many people have of a particular type of person or thing, but which is often not true in reality 模式化观念（或形象）；老一套；刻板印象：***cultural/gender/racial stereotypes*** 有关文化的 / 性别的 / 种族的旧框框 ◇ *He doesn't conform to the usual stereotype of the businessman with a dark suit and briefcase.* 他不同于人们一般印象中穿黑色西装、提公文包的商人形象。 ➲ COLLOCATIONS AT RACE ▶ **stereo·typ·ical** /ˌsteriəˈtɪpɪkl/ *adj.*: *the stereotypical image of feminine behaviour* 关于女性行为举止的模式化观念 **stereo·typ·ical·ly** *adv.*

■ ***verb*** [often passive] to form a fixed idea about a person or thing which may not really be true 对…形成模式化（或类型化）的看法：**~ sb** *Children from certain backgrounds tend to be stereotyped by their teachers.* 教师往往模式化地根据学生的某些背景把他们归类。◇ **~ sb as sth** *Why are professors stereotyped as absent-minded?* 为什么在人们心目中教授就一定健忘呢？ ▶ **stereo·typed** *adj.*: *a play full of stereotyped characters* 充斥着模式化人物的戏剧 **stereo·typ·ing** *noun* [U]: *sexual stereotyping* 性别的模式化

ster·ile /ˈsteraɪl; *NAmE* ˈsterəl/ *adj.* **1** (of humans or animals 人或动物) not able to produce children or young animals 不能生育的；不育的 **SYN** **infertile** ➲ COMPARE FERTILE **2** completely clean and free from bacteria 无菌的；消过毒的：*sterile bandages* 消毒绷带 ◇ *sterile water* 消过毒的水 **3** (of a discussion, an argument, etc. 讨论、争论等) not producing any useful result 无结果的；没有实际价值的 **SYN** **fruitless**: *a sterile debate* 没有结果的辩论 **4** lacking individual personality, imagination or new ideas 刻板的；无个性的；缺乏新意的：*The room felt cold and sterile.* 那房间让人觉得阴冷而没有生气。◇ *He felt creatively and emotionally sterile.* 他感觉自己既缺乏创意又没有充沛的感情。 **5** (of land 土地) not good enough to produce crops 贫瘠的 ▶ **ster·il·ity** /stəˈrɪləti/ *noun* [U]: *The disease can cause sterility in men and women.* 这种疾病可能导致男女不育。◇ *the meaningless sterility of statistics* 统计数字的枯燥无味 ◇ *She contemplated the sterility of her existence.* 她思量着自己空虚无聊的生活。

ster·il·ize (*BrE also* **-ise**) /ˈsterəlaɪz/ *verb* **1** [often passive] **~ sth** to kill the bacteria in or on sth 灭菌；消毒：*to sterilize surgical instruments* 给外科手术器械消毒 ◇ *sterilized milk/water* 消过毒的牛奶 / 水 **2** [usually passive] **~ sb/sth** to make a person or an animal unable to have babies, especially by removing or blocking their sex organs 使绝育 ▶ **ster·il·iza·tion, -isa·tion** /ˌsterəlaɪˈzeɪʃn; *NAmE* -ləˈz-/ *noun* [U, C]

ster·il·izer (*BrE also* **-iser**) /ˈsterəlaɪzə(r)/ *noun* a machine or piece of equipment that you use to make objects or substances completely clean and free from bacteria 灭菌器；杀菌设备；消毒器

ster·ling /ˈstɜːlɪŋ; *NAmE* ˈstɜːrlɪŋ/ *noun, adj.*

■ ***noun*** [U] the money system of Britain, based on the pound 英镑（英国货币）：*the value of sterling* 英镑的价值 ◇ *You can be paid in pounds sterling or American dollars.* 可以付你英镑，也可以付你美元。

■ ***adj.*** [usually before noun] (*formal*) of excellent quality 优秀的；杰出的：*He has done **sterling work** on the finance committee.* 他在财务委员会工作优异。

ˌsterling ˈsilver *noun* [U] silver of a particular standard of PURITY 标准纯银（达到规定的纯度）

stern /stɜːn; *NAmE* stɜːrn/ *adj., noun*

■ ***adj.*** (**stern·er, stern·est**) **1** serious and often disapproving; expecting sb to obey you 严厉的；苛刻的；要求别人服从的 **SYN** **strict**: *a stern face/expression/look* 严厉的面

S

容 / 表情 / 目光 ◇ *a stern warning* 严厉的警告 ◇ *Her voice was stern.* 她声调严厉。◇ *The police are planning sterner measures to combat crime.* 警方正制订更严厉的措施打击犯罪活动。**2** serious and difficult 严峻的；难对付的：*We face stern opposition.* 我们遇到激烈的反对。▶ **stern·ly** *adv.* **stern·ness** *noun* [U]

IDM **be made of sterner 'stuff** to have a stronger character and to be more determined in dealing with problems than other people 性格十分坚强；有很大的毅力

■ *noun* the back end of a ship or boat 船尾 ➲ VISUAL VOCAB PAGE V59 ➲ COMPARE BOW[1] *n.* (2), POOP *n.* (1) IDM SEE STEM *n.*

ster·num /ˈstɜːnəm; *NAmE* ˈstɜːrnəm/ *noun* (*pl.* **ster·nums** or **sterna** /-nə/) (*anatomy* 解) the BREASTBONE 胸骨 ➲ VISUAL VOCAB PAGE V64

ster·oid /ˈsterɔɪd; *BrE also* ˈstɪər-; *NAmE also* ˈstɪr-/ *noun* a chemical substance produced naturally in the body. There are several different steroids and they can be used to treat various diseases and are also sometimes used illegally by people playing sports to improve their performance. 类固醇；甾族化合物

stetho·scope /ˈsteθəskəʊp; *NAmE* -skoʊp/ *noun* an instrument that a doctor uses to listen to sb's heart and breathing 听诊器

stet·son (*BrE*) (*NAmE* **Stetson™**) /ˈstetsn/ *noun* a tall hat with a wide BRIM, worn especially by American COWBOYS 斯特森高顶宽边帽；牛仔帽

steve·dore /ˈstiːvədɔː(r)/ *noun* a person whose job is moving goods on and off ships 码头工人；码头装卸工 ➲ SEE ALSO DOCKER

stew /stjuː; *NAmE* stuː/ *noun, verb*

■ *noun* [U, C] a dish of meat and vegetables cooked slowly in liquid in a container that has a lid 炖的菜，煨的菜（有肉和蔬菜）：*beef stew and dumplings* 牛肉炖丸子 ◇ *I'm making a stew for lunch.* 我炖个菜中午吃。

IDM **get (yourself)/be in a 'stew (about/over sth)** (*informal*) to become/feel very anxious or upset about sth（为某事）坐立不安，心烦意乱

■ *verb* **1** [T, I] ~ (**sth**) to cook sth slowly, or allow sth to cook slowly, in liquid in a closed dish 炖；煨：*stewed apples* 炖苹果 ◇ *The meat needs to stew for two hours.* 这肉得炖两小时。➲ SEE ALSO STEWED **2** [I] (+ **adv./prep.**) to think or worry about sth 思考；担忧：*I've been stewing over the problem for a while.* 这个问题我已经考虑了一会儿。◇ *Leave him to stew.* 让他自个儿想想。

IDM **let sb stew in their own 'juice** (*informal*) to leave sb to worry and suffer the unpleasant effects of their own actions 让某人自作自受

stew·ard /ˈstjuːəd; *NAmE* ˈstuːərd/ *noun* **1** a man whose job is to take care of passengers on a ship, an aircraft or a train and who brings them meals, etc.（轮船、飞机或火车上的）乘务员，服务员 **2** a person who helps to organize a large public event, for example a race, public meeting, etc.（比赛、集会等大型公众活动的）统筹人 SYN **marshal** **3** a person whose job is to arrange for the supply of food to a college, club, etc.（大学、俱乐部等的）伙食管理员 ➲ SEE ALSO SHOP STEWARD **4** a person employed to manage another person's property, especially a large house or land（私人家中的）管家

stew·ard·ess /ˌstjuːəˈdes; ˈstjuːə-; *NAmE* ˈstuːərdəs/ *noun* **1** (*old-fashioned*) a female FLIGHT ATTENDANT（飞机上的）女乘务员；空中小姐 **2** a woman whose job is to take care of the passengers on a ship or train（轮船或火车上的）女乘务员，女服务员 ➲ NOTE AT GENDER

stew·ard·ship /ˈstjuːədʃɪp; *NAmE* ˈstuːərdʃɪp/ *noun* [U] (*formal*) the act of taking care of or managing sth, for example property, an organization, money or valuable objects 管理；看管；组织工作：*The organization certainly prospered under his stewardship.* 不可否认，这个组织在他的管理下兴旺了起来。

stewed /stjuːd; *NAmE* stuːd/ *adj.* (of tea 茶) tasting too strong and bitter because it has been left in the pot too long（因久泡）太酽的，泡苦了的

St George's Day /ˌsnt ˈdʒɔːdʒɪz deɪ; *NAmE* ˌseɪnt ˈdʒɔːrdʒɪz/ *noun* 23 April, the day of the national SAINT of England 圣乔治节（4 月 23 日，纪念英格兰主保圣人的节日）

STI /ˌes tiː ˈaɪ/ *noun* the abbreviation for 'sexually transmitted infection' (an infection that is passed from one person to another during sexual activity) 性传播感染，性行为造成的感染（全写为 sexually transmitted infection）

stick /stɪk/ *verb, noun*

■ *verb* (**stuck**, **stuck** /stʌk/)

• **PUSH STH IN** 推入 **1** [T, I] to push sth, usually a sharp object, into sth; to be pushed into sth 将…刺入（或插入）；刺；戳；插入：**~ sth + adv./prep.** *The nurse stuck the needle into my arm.* 护士把针扎进我的胳膊。◇ *Don't stick your fingers through the bars of the cage.* 不要把指头伸进笼子里。◇ **+ adv./prep.** *I found a nail sticking in the tyre.* 我发现轮胎上扎了一根钉子。

• **ATTACH** 粘贴 **2** [T, I] to fix sth to sth else, usually with a sticky substance; to become fixed to sth in this way 粘贴；粘住：**~ sth + adv./prep.** *He stuck a stamp on the envelope.* 他把一张邮票贴到信封上。◇ *We used glue to stick the broken pieces together.* 我们用胶把碎片粘到一起。◇ *I stuck the photos into an album.* 我把照片贴到相册上。◇ **+ adv./prep.** *Her wet clothes were sticking to her body.* 湿衣服贴在她身上。◇ *The glue's useless—the pieces just won't stick.* 这种胶不行，这几片东西根本粘不住。

• **PUT** 放置 **3** [T] **~ sth + adv./prep.** (*informal*) to put sth in a place, especially quickly or carelessly（尤指迅速或随手）放置：*Stick your bags down there.* 把你们的包搁到那儿吧。◇ *He stuck his hands in his pockets and strolled off.* 他把两手揣在口袋里溜达着走了。◇ *Can you stick this on the noticeboard?* 你能不能把这个贴到布告牌上？◇ *Peter stuck his head around the door and said, 'Coffee, anyone?'* 彼得从门后伸进头来问："咖啡，哪位要？"◇ (*informal*) *Stick 'em up!* (= Put your hands above your head—I have a gun!) 举起手来！**4** [T] **sb can stick sth** (*informal*) used to say in a rude and angry way that you are not interested in what sb has, offers, does, etc.（无礼或生气地表示）对…不感兴趣：*I got sick of my boss's moaning and told him he could stick the job.* 我烦透了老板的牢骚，便跟他说那活儿他自己干吧，我才不稀罕。

• **BECOME FIXED** 卡住 **5** [I] ~ (**in sth**) to become fixed in one position and impossible to move（在某物中）卡住，陷住，动不了 SYN **jam**：*The key has stuck in the lock.* 钥匙卡在锁里了。◇ *This drawer keeps sticking.* 这个抽屉老卡住。

• **DIFFICULT SITUATION** 困境 **6** [T] (*BrE, informal*) (usually used in negative sentences and questions 通常用于否定句和疑问句) to accept a difficult or unpleasant situation or person 容忍；忍受 SYN **stand**：**~ sth/sb** *I don't know how you stick that job.* 我不知道那活儿你怎么受得了。◇ *The problem is, my mother can't stick my boyfriend.* 问题是，我母亲不能接受我男朋友。◇ **~ doing sth** *John can't stick living with his parents.* 约翰受不了和父母住在一起。

• **BECOME ACCEPTED** 被接受 **7** [I] to become accepted 被接受；被证明成立：*The police couldn't **make the charges stick*** (= show them to be true). 警方无法证明那些指控成立。◇ *His friends called him Bart and **the name has stuck*** (= has become the name that everyone calls him). 朋友们称他巴特，这名字就叫开了。

• **IN CARD GAMES** 纸牌游戏 **8** [I] to not take any more cards 不再要牌 ➲ SEE ALSO STUCK

IDM **stick in your 'mind** (of a memory, an image, etc. 往事、形象等) to be remembered for a long time 经久不忘；铭记在心：*One of his paintings in particular sticks in my mind.* 他有一幅画我记得特别清楚。**stick in your 'throat/'craw** (*informal*) **1** (of words 话语) to be difficult or impossible to say 难以启齿；说不出口 **2** (of a situation 情况) to be difficult or impossible to accept; to make you angry 难以接受；无法接受；令人气愤 **stick your 'neck out** (*informal*) to do or say sth when there is a risk that you may be wrong 做不保险的事；说不保险的话；冒险 **stick to your 'guns** (*informal*) to refuse to change your mind about sth even when other people are trying to

S

persuade you that you are wrong 不听别人劝告；坚持己见；一意孤行 ➲ MORE AT BOOT *n.*, FINGER *n.*, KNIFE *n.*, MILE, MUD, NOSE *n.*, OAR, SORE *adj.*, TELL

PHR V **ˌstick aˈround** (*informal*) to stay in a place, waiting for sth to happen or for sb to arrive 不走开；待在原地：*Stick around; we'll need you to help us later.* 别走开，过一会儿我们还需要你帮忙呢。**ˈstick at sth** to continue to work in a serious and determined way to achieve sth 坚持不懈地做（某事）；持之以恒；锲而不舍：*If you want to play an instrument well, you've got to **stick at it**.* 要想练好一种乐器，你必须持之以恒。**ˈstick by sb** [no passive] to be loyal to a person and support them, especially in a difficult situation 坚持忠于；不离弃（某人）**ˈstick by sth** [no passive] to do what you promised or planned to do 信守，遵守，贯彻（承诺、计划等）：*They stuck by their decision.* 他们决心已下，矢志不渝。**ˌstick sth↔ˈdown** (*informal*) to write sth somewhere 写下；记下：*I think I'll stick my name down on the list.* 我想我还是把名字写到名单上吧。**ˌstick ˈout** to be noticeable or easily seen 醒目；显眼；引人注目 **SYN** **stand out (from/against sth)**: *They wrote the notice in big red letters so that it would stick out.* 他们用红色大字写出通知，这样会显眼一些。**ˌstick ˈout (of sth)** | **ˌstick sth↔ˈout (of sth)** 🔑 to be further out than sth else or come through a hole; to push sth further out than sth else or through a hole（使从某物中）伸出，探出，突出：*His ears stick out.* 他长着一对招风耳。◇ *She stuck her tongue out at me.* 她冲我吐了吐舌头。◇ *Don't stick your arm out of the car window.* 不要把胳膊伸出车窗。**ˌstick it/sth ˈout** (*informal*) to continue doing sth to the end, even when it is difficult or boring 坚持到底；忍受下去：*She didn't like the course but she **stuck it out** to get the certificate.* 她并不喜欢这门课，但为了拿证书还是耐着性子学完了。**ˌstick ˈout for sth** (*informal*) to refuse to give up until you get what you need or want 坚持要求；不得到…不罢休：*They are sticking out for a higher pay rise.* 他们坚持要求更大幅度地提高工资。**ˈstick to sth 1** 🔑 to continue doing sth despite difficulties 坚持（做某事，不怕困难）：*She finds it impossible to stick to a diet.* 饮食老受限制，她觉得受不了。**2** 🔑 to continue doing or using sth and not want to change it 坚持；维持；固守；坚持保留：*He promised to help us and he **stuck to his word*** (= he did as he had promised). 他答应过帮助我们，他没有失信。◇ *'Shall we meet on Friday this week?' 'No, let's stick to Saturday.'* "这个星期我们星期五见面怎么样？" "不，还是照旧在星期六吧。" ◇ *She stuck to her story.* 她坚持自己所说的。**ˌstick toˈgether** (*informal*) (of people 人) to stay together and support each other 团结在一起 **ˌstick ˈup** 🔑 to point upwards or be above a surface 竖立；向上突出：*The branch was sticking up out of the water.* 树枝从水下伸了出来。**ˌstick ˈup for sb/yourself/sth** [no passive] (*informal*) to support or defend sb/yourself/sth 支持，捍卫（某人、自己、某事物）：*Stick up for what you believe.* 你相信什么，就要捍卫它。◇ *She taught her children to stick up for themselves at school.* 她教育子女在学校要勇于自卫。◇ *Don't worry—I'll stick up for you.* 别担心，有我呢。**ˈstick with sb/sth** [no passive] (*informal*) **1** to stay close to sb so that they can help you 紧跟，不离开（某人，以便得到帮助）**2** to continue with sth or continue doing sth 持续；坚持：*They decided to stick with their original plan.* 他们决定继续执行原来的计划。

■ ***noun***

• **FROM TREE** 树木 **1** 🔑 [C] a thin piece of wood that has fallen or been broken from a tree 枝条；枯枝；柴火棍儿：*We collected dry sticks to start a fire.* 我们捡了些枯枝生起火来。◇ *The boys were throwing sticks and stones at the dog.* 男孩子们朝那条狗扔枝条扔石头。◇ *Her arms and legs were like sticks* (= very thin). 她胳膊和腿瘦得跟柴火棍儿似的。

• **FOR WALKING** 走路 **2** 🔑 [C] (*especially BrE*) = WALKING STICK: *The old lady leant on her stick as she talked.* 老太太说话时拄着拐棍。➲ SEE ALSO SHOOTING STICK, WHITE STICK

• **IN SPORT** 体育运动 **3** [C] a long thin object that is used in some sports to hit or control the ball 球棍：*a hockey stick* 曲棍球球棍 ➲ **VISUAL VOCAB** PAGE V48

• **LONG THIN PIECE** 条状物 **4** 🔑 [C] (often in compounds 常构成复合词) a long thin piece of sth 条状物；棍状物：*a stick of dynamite* 一根炸药棒 ◇ *carrot sticks* 胡萝卜条 ◇ (*NAmE*) *a stick of butter* 一条黄油 ➲ **VISUAL VOCAB** PAGE V36 ➲ SEE ALSO FRENCH STICK **5** [C] (often in compounds 常构成复合词) a thin piece of wood or plastic that you use for a particular purpose（木料或塑料制成的有特定用途的）棍，条，签：*pieces of pineapple on sticks* 一串串插在小棍上的菠萝块 ➲ SEE ALSO CHOPSTICK, COCKTAIL STICK, DRUMSTICK, MATCHSTICK, YARDSTICK (1)

• **OF GLUE, ETC.** 胶水等 **6** [C] a quantity of a substance, such as solid glue, that is sold in a small container with round ends and straight sides, and can be pushed further out of the container as it is used 一管，一支（胶棒等）➲ SEE ALSO LIPSTICK

• **IN PLANE/VEHICLE** 飞机；车辆 **7** [C] (*informal, especially NAmE*) the control stick of a plane（飞机的）操纵杆，驾驶杆 ➲ SEE ALSO JOYSTICK (2) **8** [C] (*informal, especially NAmE*) a handle used to change the gears of a vehicle（车辆的）变速杆，换挡杆 ➲ SEE ALSO GEAR LEVER, STICK SHIFT

• **FOR ORCHESTRA** 管弦乐队 **9** [C] a BATON, used by the person who CONDUCTS an ORCHESTRA 指挥棒

• **CRITICISM** 批评 **10** [U] (*BrE, informal*) criticism or severe words 批评；指责：*The referee **got a lot of stick** from the home fans.* 裁判饱受主队球迷的指责。

• **COUNTRY AREAS** 乡村地区 **11 the sticks** [pl.] (*informal, usually disapproving*) country areas, a long way from cities 边远乡村地区：*We live **out in the sticks**.* 我们住在偏远的乡村。

• **PERSON** 人 **12** [C] (*old-fashioned, BrE, informal*) a person 人；家伙：*He's not such a bad **old stick**.* 他老兄人不算坏。

HELP There are many other compounds ending in **stick**. You will find them at their place in the alphabet. 以 stick 结尾的复合词还有很多，可在各字母中的适当位置查到。 **IDM** SEE BEAT *v.*, BIG *adj.*, CARROT, CLEFT *adj.*, SHORT *adj.*, UP *v.*, WRONG *adj.*

sticks 棒状物

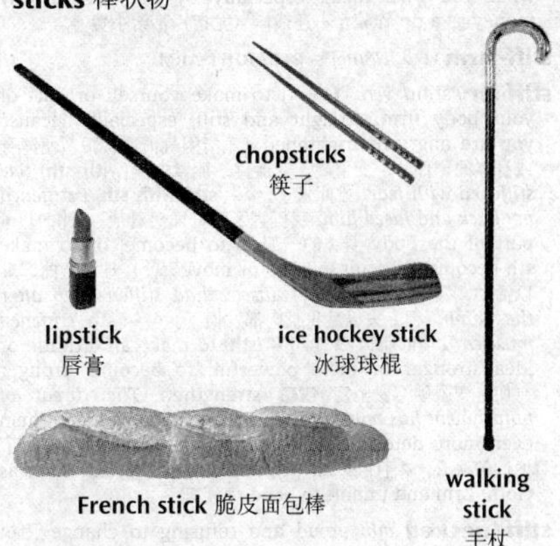

sticka·bil·ity /ˌstɪkəˈbɪləti/ *noun* [U] (*informal*) **1** (*NAmE also* **stick-to-itiveness**) the ability to keep doing sth, even if it is sometimes boring 持之以恒的能力；忍耐力 **SYN** **persistence, tenacity**: *The long list of jobs on her CV suggests a lack of stickability.* 她简历上的那一长串工作说明她没长性。**2** (of a website 网站) the ability to keep visitors interested for more than a short time（使访客长期感兴趣的）吸引力

stick·ball /ˈstɪkbɔːl/ *noun* [U] an informal game similar to BASEBALL, played with a stick and a rubber ball 棍球（用棍击橡胶球，类似于棒球的非正式运动）

stick·er /ˈstɪkə(r)/ *noun* a sticky label with a picture or message on it, that you stick onto sth 粘贴标签；贴纸：*bumper stickers* (= on cars) 汽车保险杠粘贴标签 ◇

S

a sticker album (= to collect stickers in) 粘贴标签收集册 ➲ SYNONYMS AT LABEL

'sticker price *noun* (*NAmE*) the price that is marked on sth, especially a car（尤指汽车的）标价

'sticker shock *noun* [U] (*NAmE*) the unpleasant feeling that people experience when they find that sth is much more expensive than they expected 价格震惊（发现价格比想象的要高得多）

'stick figure (*NAmE*) (*BrE* **'matchstick figure**) *noun* a picture of a person drawn only with thin lines for the arms and legs, a circle for the head, etc. 人物线条画；简笔人物画

'sticking plaster *noun* (*BrE*) = PLASTER (3)

'sticking point *noun* something that people do not agree on and that prevents progress in a discussion 分歧点；症结：*This was one of the major sticking points in the negotiations.* 这是谈判中主要的难点之一。

'stick insect *noun* a large insect with a long thin body that looks like a stick 竹节虫

'stick-in-the-mud *noun* (*informal, disapproving*) a person who refuses to try anything new or exciting 守旧的人；墨守成规的人

stickle·back /ˈstɪklbæk/ *noun* a small FRESHWATER fish with sharp points on its back 刺鱼

stick·ler /ˈstɪklə(r)/ *noun* ~ (**for sth**) a person who thinks that a particular quality or type of behaviour is very important and expects other people to think and behave in the same way 非常看重（某品质或行为）的人：*a stickler for punctuality* 非常注重守时的人

'stick-on *adj.* [only before noun] (of an object 物品) with glue on one side so that it sticks to sth 一面带黏胶的：*stick-on labels* 背胶标签

stick·pin /ˈstɪkpɪn/ *noun* (*NAmE*) a decorative pin that is worn on a tie to keep it in place, or as a piece of jewellery（领带的）装饰别针

'stick shift *noun* (*NAmE, informal*) **1** (*NAmE also* **gearshift**) (*BrE* **'gear lever**, **'gear·stick**) a handle used to change the gears of a vehicle 变速杆；换挡杆 **2** a vehicle that has a stick shift 手动变速车 ➲ COMPARE AUTOMATIC *n.* (2)

S

stick-to-itiveness /ˌstɪk ˈtuː ɪtəvnəs/ *noun* [U] (*NAmE, informal*) = STICKABILITY (1)

'stick-up *noun* (*informal, especially NAmE*) = HOLD-UP (2): *This is a stick-up!* 这是持枪抢劫！

sticky 🔑 /ˈstɪki/ *adj.*, *noun*

■ *adj.* (**stick·ier**, **sticki·est**) **1** 🔑 made of or covered in a substance that sticks to things that touch it 黏（性）的：*sticky fingers covered in jam* 粘满果酱的黏糊糊的手指 ◇ *Stir in the milk to make a soft but not sticky dough.* 把牛奶搅进去，和成软而不黏的面团。**2** 🔑 (of paper, labels, etc. 纸、标签等) with glue on one side so that you can stick it to a surface 一面带黏胶的 **3** (*informal*) (of the weather 天气) hot and damp 闷热的 **4** (*informal*) (of a person 人) feeling hot and uncomfortable 感到热得难受的 SYN **sweaty** **5** (*informal*) difficult or unpleasant 难办的；棘手的；让人为难的：*a sticky situation* 棘手的局面 **6** (*computing* 计) (of a website 网站) so interesting and well organized that the people who visit it stay there for a long time 用户黏着度高的；富有吸引力的 ▸ **stick·ily** /-ɪli/ *adv.* **sticki·ness** *noun* [U]

IDM **have sticky 'fingers** (*informal*) to be likely to steal sth 好偷东西的；有顺手牵羊的毛病 **a ˌsticky 'wicket** (*BrE, informal*) a difficult situation 困难的处境 ➲ MORE AT END *n.*

■ *noun* (*pl.* **-ies**) (*also* **'sticky note**) a small piece of sticky paper that you use for writing a note on, and that can be easily removed 告事贴 ➲ COMPARE POST-IT™

sticky·beak /ˈstɪkibiːk/ *noun* (*AustralE, NZE, informal*) a person who tries to find out information about other people's private lives in a way that is annoying or rude 爱打听的人；好探听隐私的人；包打听 ▸ **sticky·beak** *verb* [I]: *I don't mean to stickybeak, but when is he going to leave?* 我不是要多管闲事，但是他什么时候要离开呢？

'sticky tape *noun* [U] (*BrE*) = SELLOTAPE™

stiff 🔑 /stɪf/ *adj.*, *adv.*, *noun*, *verb*

■ *adj.* (**stiff·er**, **stiff·est**)

• **DIFFICULT TO BEND/MOVE** 不易弯曲 / 活动 **1** 🔑 firm and difficult to bend or move 不易弯曲（或活动）的；硬的；挺的：*stiff cardboard* 硬纸板 ◇ *a stiff brush* 硬刷子 ◇ *The windows were stiff and she couldn't get them open.* 窗户紧，她开不了。

• **MUSCLES** 肌肉 **2** 🔑 when a person is **stiff**, their muscles hurt when they move them 僵硬的；一动就疼的：*I'm really stiff after that bike ride yesterday.* 昨天骑了那趟自行车，我觉得浑身酸痛。◇ *I've got a **stiff neck**.* 我脖子发僵。

• **MIXTURE** 混合物 **3** 🔑 thick and almost solid; difficult to stir 稠的；难搅动的：*Whisk the egg whites until stiff.* 把蛋清打成稠的。

• **DIFFICULT/SEVERE** 困难；严厉 **4** more difficult or severe than usual 困难的；艰难的；严厉的；激烈的：*It was a **stiff climb** to the top of the hill.* 费了好大劲才爬到山顶。◇ *The company faces **stiff competition** from its rivals.* 公司遇到对手的激烈竞争。◇ *The new proposals have met with **stiff opposition**.* 新提案遭到强烈的反对。◇ *There are **stiff fines** for breaking the rules.* 违反规则要受重罚。◇ *a **stiff breeze/wind*** (= one that blows strongly) 强风

• **NOT FRIENDLY** 不友好 **5** (of a person or their behaviour 人或行为) not friendly or relaxed 不友好的；生硬的：*The speech he made to welcome them was stiff and formal.* 他那番欢迎他们的话讲得生硬刻板。

• **PRICE** 价格 **6** (*informal*) costing a lot or too much 高昂的；过高的：*There's a stiff $30 entrance fee to the exhibition.* 展览会的入场费高达 30 美元。

• **ALCOHOLIC DRINK** 酒 **7** [only before noun] strong; containing a lot of alcohol 烈性的；酒精度数高的：*a stiff whisky* 烈性威士忌

▸ **stiff·ly** 🔑 *adv.* **stiff·ness** *noun* [U]: *pain and stiffness in her legs* 她两腿又疼又僵的感觉

IDM (**keep**) **a stiff upper 'lip** to keep calm and hide your feelings when you are in pain or in a difficult situation（面对痛苦或困境）不动声色，沉着而不外露

■ *adv.* **1** (*informal*) very much; to an extreme degree 非常；极其：*be **bored/scared/worried stiff*** 非常厌烦 / 害怕 / 担心 **2 frozen ~** (of wet material 含水的东西) very cold and hard because the water has become ice（冻）僵；（冻）硬：*The clothes on the washing line were frozen stiff.* 挂在晾衣绳上的衣服冻硬了。◇ *I came home from the game frozen stiff* (= very cold). 我看完比赛回到家里，都快冻僵了。

■ *noun* (*slang*) the body of a dead person 死尸

■ *verb* **~ sb** (*NAmE, informal*) to cheat sb or not pay them what you owe them, especially by not leaving any money as a tip 诈骗；不还钱；（尤指）不给小费

ˌstiff-'arm *verb* (*NAmE*) = STRAIGHT-ARM

stiff·en /ˈstɪfn/ *verb* **1** [I, T] to make yourself or part of your body firm, straight and still, especially because you are angry or frightened（尤指因气愤或害怕，使浑身或身体的一部分）变僵硬，变僵直，绷紧：**~ (with sth)** *She stiffened with fear.* 她吓呆了。◇ **~ sth (with sth)** *I stiffened my back and faced him.* 我挺直了腰杆面对着他。**2** [I, T] (of part of the body 身体的一部分) to become, or to make sth become, difficult to bend or move（使）难以弯曲，难以活动，发僵：**~ (up)** *My muscles had stiffened up after the climb.* 爬上去以后我肌肉都发僵了。◇ **~ sth** *stiffened muscles* 发僵的肌肉 **3** [T, I] **~ (sth)** to make an attitude or idea stronger or more powerful; to become stronger（使）变强硬，变坚定 SYN **strengthen**: *The threat of punishment has only **stiffened their resolve*** (= made them even more determined to do sth). 惩罚的威胁益发坚定了他们的决心。**4** [T] **~ sth** (**with sth**) to make sth, such as cloth, firm and unable to bend 使硬挺

ˌstiff-'necked *adj.* proud and refusing to change 固执的；倔强的；犟的

stiffy /ˈstɪfi/ *noun* (*pl.* **-ies**) (*taboo, slang*) an ERECTION (1) of a man's PENIS（阴茎的）勃起

stifle /ˈstaɪfl/ *verb* **1** [T] **~ sth** to prevent sth from happening; to prevent a feeling from being expressed 压制；扼杀；阻止；抑制 SYN **suppress**: *She managed to stifle a yawn.* 她忍住了哈欠。◇ *They hope the new rules will not stifle creativity.* 他们希望新规则不会压制创新。◇ *The government failed to stifle the unrest.* 政府没有制止住动乱。**2** [I, T] to feel unable to breathe, or to make sb unable to breathe, because it is too hot and/or there is no fresh air（使）窒息，无法自如地呼吸，感觉窒闷 SYN **suffocate**: *I felt I was stifling in the airless room.* 在那间闷气的房间里我感觉都快憋死了。◇ **~ sb** *Most of the victims were stifled by the fumes.* 多数受害者是因烟雾窒息而死的。▶ **stif·ling** /ˈstaɪflɪŋ/ *adj.*: *a stifling room* 闷得让人透不过气来的房间 ◇ *'It's stifling in here—can we open a window?'* "这里闷得人难受，我们能不能开一扇窗户？" ◇ *At 25, she found family life stifling.* 她 25 岁时感到家庭生活令人窒息。 **stif·ling·ly** *adv.*: *The room was stiflingly hot.* 房间里热得人喘不上气来。

stigma /ˈstɪɡmə/ *noun* **1** [U, C, usually sing.] feelings of disapproval that people have about particular illnesses or ways of behaving 耻辱；羞耻: *the social stigma of alcoholism* 酗酒在社会上的恶名 ◇ *There is no longer any stigma attached to being divorced.* 离婚不再是什么丢脸的事。**2** [C] (*biology* 生) the part in the middle of a flower where POLLEN is received（花的）柱头 ➲ VISUAL VOCAB PAGE V11

stig·mata /ˈstɪɡmətə; stɪɡˈmɑːtə/ *noun* [pl.] marks that look like the wounds made by nails on the body of Jesus Christ, believed by some Christians to have appeared as holy marks on the bodies of some SAINTS 圣伤，圣痕（据信出现在某些圣徒身上，与耶稣身上钉子留下的伤痕相似）

stig·ma·tize (*BrE also* **-ise**) /ˈstɪɡmətaɪz/ *verb* [usually passive] **~ sb/sth** (*formal*) to treat sb in a way that makes them feel that they are very bad or unimportant 使感到羞耻；侮蔑 ▶ **stig·ma·tiza·tion, -isa·tion** /-ˈzeɪʃn; *NAmE* -təˈz-/ *noun* [U]

stile 梯磴

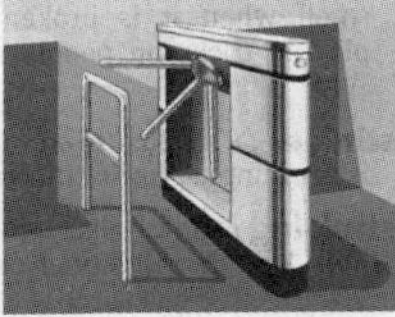
turnstile 旋转栅门

stile /staɪl/ *noun* a set of steps that help people climb over a fence or gate in a field, etc.（供人翻越田地等处所设的围栏、栅栏门等的）台阶，梯磴 ➲ VISUAL VOCAB PAGE V3

stil·etto /stɪˈletəʊ; *NAmE* -toʊ/ *noun* (*pl.* **-os** or **-oes**) **1** (*also* ˌ**stiletto** ˈ**heel**) (*especially BrE*) a woman's shoe with a very high narrow heel; the heel on such a shoe 细高跟女鞋；（女鞋的）细高跟 SYN **spike heel** ➲ VISUAL VOCAB PAGE V69 **2** a small knife with a narrow pointed blade 短剑；匕首

still 🔑 /stɪl/ *adv., adj., noun, verb*

■ ***adv.*** **1** 🔑 continuing until a particular point in time and not finishing 还；还是；仍然；依旧: *I wrote to them last month and I'm still waiting for a reply.* 我上个月给他们写了信，到现在还在等回音。◇ *Mum, I'm still hungry!* 妈，我还饿！◇ *Do you still live at the same address?* 你还住在原地址吗？◇ *There's still time to change your mind.* 你还有时间改变主意。◇ *It was, and still is, my favourite movie.* 那部影片以前是我最喜欢的，现在仍然是。**2** 🔑 despite what has just been said（虽然…）还是；但；不过: *We searched everywhere but we still couldn't find it.* 我们四处找，但还是没找到。◇ *The weather was cold and wet. Still, we had a great time.* 天气又冷又潮，不过我们仍旧玩得很开心。**3** used for making a comparison stronger（加强比较级）还要，更: *The next day was warmer still.* 第二天更暖和了。◇ *If you can manage to get two tickets that's better still.* 要是你能设法弄到两张票，那就更好了。**4 ~ more/another** even more 还有（更多）: *There was still more bad news to come.* 随后还传来了其他的坏消息。IDM SEE LESS *adv.*

■ ***adj.*** **1** 🔑 not moving; calm and quiet 静止的；平静的；安静的；寂静的: *still water* 平静的水面 ◇ ***Keep still*** *while I brush your hair.* 我给你梳头时你不要动。◇ *The kids found it hard to* ***stay still***. 孩子们觉得待着不动很难做到。◇ *Can't you* ***sit still***? 你就不能老老实实坐一会儿吗？◇ *We stayed in a village where* ***time has stood still*** (= life has not changed for many years). 我们待在一个时间似乎凝滞了的村子里。**2** with no wind 无风的: *a still summer's day* 无风的夏日 ◇ *the still night air* 夜间宁静的空气 **3** (*BrE*) (of a drink 饮料) not containing bubbles of gas; not FIZZY 不含碳酸气的；不起泡的: *still mineral water* 无汽矿泉水

IDM **the still of the ˈnight** (*literary*) the time during the night when it is quiet and calm 万籁俱寂的夜晚；夜阑人静 **a/the still small ˈvoice** (*literary*) the voice of God or your CONSCIENCE, that tells you to do what is morally right 上帝的教示；良心的呼唤 **still waters run ˈdeep** (*saying*) a person who seems to be quiet or shy may surprise you by knowing a lot or having deep feelings 静水流深；木讷寡言者也许胸藏丘壑

■ ***noun*** **1** a photograph of a scene from a film/movie or video（电影或录像的）定格画面；剧照: *a publicity still from his new movie* 他的新电影的宣传剧照 **2** a piece of equipment that is used for making strong alcoholic drinks（制酒的）蒸馏器: *a whisky still* 威士忌蒸馏器 ➲ SEE ALSO DISTIL (2)

■ ***verb*** [I, T] (*literary*) to become calm and quiet; to make sth calm and quiet（使）静止，平静，安静: *The wind stilled.* 风停了。◇ **~ sb/sth** *She spoke quietly to still the frightened child.* 她轻声安慰受到惊吓的孩子。◇ (*figurative*) *to still sb's doubts/fears* 消除某人的疑虑 / 恐惧

still·birth /ˈstɪlbɜːθ; *NAmE* -bɜːrθ/ *noun* [C, U] a birth in which the baby is born dead 死产

still·born /ˈstɪlbɔːn; *NAmE* -bɔːrn/ *adj.* **1** born dead 死产的: *a stillborn baby* 死产儿 **2** not successful; not developing 失败的；夭折的

ˌ**still ˈlife** *noun* [U, C] (*pl.* **still lifes**) the art of painting or drawing arrangements of objects such as flowers, fruit, etc.; a painting, etc. like this 静物画技法；静物画

still·ness /ˈstɪlnəs/ *noun* [U] the quality of being quiet and not moving 静止；安静；宁静: *The sound of footsteps on the path broke the stillness.* 小路上的脚步声打破了宁静。

stilt /stɪlt/ *noun* [usually pl.] **1** one of a set of posts that support a building so that it is high above the ground or water（支撑建筑物高出地面或水面的）桩子，支柱 **2** one of two long pieces of wood that have a step on the side that you can stand on, so that you can walk above the ground 高跷: *a circus performer* ***on stilts*** 马戏团里踩高跷的演员

stilt·ed /ˈstɪltɪd/ *adj.* (*disapproving*) (of a way of speaking or writing 言谈或写作) not natural or relaxed; too formal 生硬的；不自然的: *We made stilted conversation for a few moments.* 我们不自然地客套了一会儿。▶ **stilt·ed·ly** *adv.*

Stil·ton™ /ˈstɪltən/ *noun* [U, C] a type of English cheese with blue lines of MOULD running through it and a strong flavour 斯蒂尔顿干酪（一种英国奶酪，有蓝色霉纹，味浓）

stimu·lant /ˈstɪmjələnt/ *noun* (*formal*) **1** a drug or substance that makes you feel more awake and gives you more energy 兴奋剂: *Coffee and tea are mild stimulants.* 咖啡和茶是轻度兴奋剂。**2 ~ (to sth)** an event or activity that encourages more activity 有激励作用的事物

stimu·late /ˈstɪmjuleɪt/ *verb* **1 ~ sth** to make sth develop or become more active; to encourage sth 促进；激发；激励: *The exhibition has stimulated interest in her work.* 展览增进了人们对她作品的兴趣。◇ *The article can be used*

S

to stimulate discussion among students. 这篇文章可用来活跃学生的讨论。**2** to make sb interested and excited about sth 刺激；使兴奋：**~ sb** *Parents should give children books that stimulate them.* 父母应给孩子能启发他们的书。◇ *Both men and women are stimulated by erotic photos* (= sexually). 色情照片对男女都有刺激作用。◇ **~ sb to do sth** *The conference stimulated him to study the subject in more depth.* 这次会议促使他更深入地研究那个课题。**3 ~ sth** (*specialist*) to make a part of the body function 促进（身体某部分）的功能：*The women were given fertility drugs to stimulate the ovaries.* 那些妇女得到了促进卵巢功能的生育药。▶ **stimu·la·tion** /ˌstɪmjuˈleɪʃn/ *noun* [U]: *sensory/intellectual/ sexual/visual/physical stimulation* 感官 / 智力 / 性 / 视觉 / 身体刺激

stimu·lat·ing /ˈstɪmjuleɪtɪŋ/ *adj.* **1** full of interesting or exciting ideas; making people feel enthusiastic 趣味盎然的；激励人的；振奋人心的 **SYN** **inspiring**: *a stimulating discussion* 饶有趣味的讨论 ◇ *a stimulating teacher* 能够引发兴趣的老师 ➲ SYNONYMS AT INTERESTING **2** making you feel more active and healthy 增加活力的；增进健康的：*shower gel containing plant extracts that have a stimulating effect on the skin* 含有对皮肤有益的植物精华的沐浴凝胶

stimu·lus /ˈstɪmjələs/ *noun* (*pl.* **stim·uli** /-laɪ/) **~ (to/for sth)** | **~ (to do sth)** **1** [usually sing.] something that helps sb/sth to develop better or more quickly 促进因素；激励因素；刺激物：*Books provide children with ideas and a stimulus for play.* 书不仅给孩子们提供想法，而且使他们玩得更有意思。◇ *The new tax laws should act as a stimulus to exports.* 新税法应该能促进出口。**2** something that produces a reaction in a human, an animal or a plant（使生物产生反应的）刺激，刺激物：***sensory/verbal/visual** stimuli* 感官 / 言语 / 视觉刺激 ◇ *The animals were conditioned to respond to **auditory stimuli*** (= sounds). 经过训练，那些动物对声音形成了条件反射。

sting 🔑 /stɪŋ/ *verb, noun*

■ ***verb*** (**stung, stung** /stʌŋ/) **1** 🔑 [T, I] **~ (sb/sth)** (of an insect or a plant 昆虫或植物) to touch your skin or make a very small hole in it so that you feel a sharp pain 刺；蜇；叮：*I was stung on the arm by a wasp.* 我的胳膊给黄蜂蜇了一下。◇ *Be careful of the nettles—they sting!* 小心给荨麻扎着，荨麻有刺！**2** 🔑 [I, T] to feel, or to make sb feel, a sharp pain in a part of their body（使）感觉刺痛，感觉灼痛：*I put some antiseptic on the cut and it stung for a moment.* 我在割破的地方抹了点抗菌剂，一时间十分刺痛。◇ *My eyes were stinging from the smoke.* 烟熏得我眼睛疼。◇ **~ sth** *Tears stung her eyes.* 她流泪流得眼睛疼。➲ SYNONYMS AT HURT **3** [T] to make sb feel angry or upset 激怒；使不安：**~ sb** *He was stung by their criticism.* 他们的批评使他心烦意乱。◇ *They launched a stinging attack on the government.* 他们对政府进行了猛烈的抨击。◇ **~ sb to/into sth** *Their cruel remarks stung her into action.* 他们伤人的话激怒了她，使她采取了行动。◇ **~ sb into doing sth** *He was stung into answering in his defence.* 他被激怒了，不得不作出回应为自己辩护。**4** [T, often passive] **~ sb (for sth)** (*informal*) to charge sb more money than they expected; to charge sb who did not expect to pay 对（某人）敲竹杠；敲诈；欺诈：*I got stung for a £100 meal.* 我挨宰了，一顿饭吃了 100 英镑。

PHR V **ˈsting sb for sth** (*BrE, informal*) to borrow money from sb 向某人借钱

■ ***noun*** **1** 🔑 (*NAmE also* **sting·er**) [C] the sharp pointed part of an insect or a creature that can go into the skin leaving a small, painful and sometimes poisonous wound（昆虫的）螫针，刺；（植物的）刺，刺毛：*the sting of a bee* 蜜蜂的螫针 ◇ *The scorpion has a sting in its tail.* 蝎子尾巴上有螫针。➲ VISUAL VOCAB PAGE V13 **2** 🔑 [C] a wound that is made when an insect, a creature or a plant stings you 刺伤；蜇伤；叮伤：*A wasp or bee sting is painful but not necessarily serious.* 被黄蜂或蜜蜂蜇一下疼是疼，但未必碍事。**3** 🔑 [C, U] any sharp pain in your body or mind（身体或心灵的）剧痛，痛苦：*the sting of salt in a wound* 伤口上撒盐引起的剧痛 ◇ *He smiled at her, trying to **take the sting out of** his words* (= trying to make the situation less painful or difficult). 他冲她微微一笑，想使他的话不至于刺痛她。**4** [C] a clever secret plan by the police to catch criminals（警察为抓捕罪犯而设的）圈套：*a sting operation to catch heroin dealers in Detroit* 在底特律设圈套抓捕海洛因贩子的行动 **5** [C] (*especially NAmE*) a clever plan by criminals to cheat people out of a lot of money（罪犯诈骗钱财的）骗局，诡计

IDM **a ˌsting in the ˈtail** (*informal*) an unpleasant feature that comes at the end of a story, an event, etc. and spoils it 煞风景的结局

ˈstinging nettle *noun* = NETTLE

sting·ray /ˈstɪŋreɪ/ *noun* a large wide flat sea fish that has a long tail with a sharp sting in it that can cause serious wounds 魟（大型扁宽海鱼，尾长，有尖刺）

stingy /ˈstɪndʒi/ *adj.* (**stin·gier, stin·gi·est**) (*informal*) not given or giving willingly; not generous, especially with money 小气的；吝啬的 **SYN** **mean**: *You're stingy!* (= not willing to spend money) 你真小气！◇ *Don't be so stingy with the cream!* 别那么舍不得放奶油！▶ **stingi·ness** *noun* [U]

stink /stɪŋk/ *verb, noun*

■ ***verb*** (**stank** /stæŋk/, **stunk** /stʌŋk/ or **stunk, stunk**) (*informal*) **1** [I] **~ (of sth)** to have a strong, unpleasant smell 有臭味；有难闻的气味 **SYN** **reek**: *Her breath stank of garlic.* 她嘴里有股大蒜味。◇ ***It stinks** of smoke in here.* 这儿有股烟味。**2** [I] **~ (of sth)** to seem very bad, unpleasant or dishonest 让人觉得很糟糕；令人厌恶；似乎有不正当行为：*The whole business stank of corruption.* 这件事从头到尾都有腐败嫌疑。◇ *'What do you think of the idea?' 'I think **it stinks**.'* "你觉得这个主意怎么样？" "我觉得是个馊主意。"

PHR V **ˌstink sth↔ˈout** to fill a place with a strong, unpleasant smell 使充满臭味（或难闻气味）

■ ***noun*** (*informal*) **1** [C, usually sing.] a very unpleasant smell 恶臭；难闻气味 **SYN** **reek**: *the stink of sweat and urine* 难闻的汗味尿味 **2** [sing.] a lot of trouble and anger about sth 吵闹；争吵：*The whole business caused quite a stink.* 整件事引起了轩然大波。◇ ***We'll kick up a stink*** (= complain a lot and cause trouble) *if they try to close the school down.* 假如他们想关闭这所学校，我们就要大闹一场。

ˈstink bomb *noun* a container that produces a very bad smell when it is broken. Stink bombs are used for playing tricks on people. 臭弹（破碎时发出恶臭，用于恶作剧）

stink·er /ˈstɪŋkə(r)/ *noun* (*informal*) a person or thing that is very unpleasant or difficult 讨厌的人；棘手的事

stink·ing /ˈstɪŋkɪŋ/ *adj., adv.*

■ ***adj.*** **1** having a very strong, unpleasant smell 臭的；发恶臭的；十分难闻的：*I was pushed into a filthy, stinking room.* 我被推进一间又脏又臭的屋子里。**2** [only before noun] (*informal, especially BrE*) very bad or unpleasant 很糟糕的；令人讨厌的：*I've got a stinking cold.* 我得了这该死的感冒。**3** [only before noun] (*BrE, informal*) showing a lot of anger 愤怒不已的；气急败坏的：*I wrote them a stinking letter to complain.* 我给他们去信气愤地抱怨了一通。

■ ***adv.*** (*informal, usually disapproving*) extremely 极其；非常：*They must be **stinking rich**.* 他们一定富得流油。

stinky /ˈstɪŋki/ *adj.* (**stink·ier, stink·iest**) (*informal*) **1** having an extremely bad smell 发恶臭的；十分难闻的 **2** extremely unpleasant or bad 令人厌恶的；糟糕透顶的

stint /stɪnt/ *noun, verb*

■ ***noun*** **~ (as sth)** a period of time that you spend working somewhere or doing a particular activity 从事某项工作（或活动）的时间：*He **did a stint** abroad early in his career.* 他刚参加工作时在国外干过一段时间。◇ *a two-year stint in the Navy* 在海军服役两年

■ ***verb*** [I, T] (usually used in negative sentences 通常用于否定句) to provide or use only a small amount of sth 节省；吝惜：**~ (on sth)** *She never stints on the food at her parties.* 她举办聚会吃的东西从不小气。◇ **~ yourself** *We don't need to stint ourselves—have some more!* 我们没必要节省，多吃点！➲ SEE ALSO UNSTINTING

sti·pend /ˈstaɪpend/ *noun* (*formal*) an amount of money that is paid regularly to sb, especially a priest, as wages or money to live on（尤指神职人员的）生活津贴，薪俸；献仪：*a monthly stipend* 月俸 ◇ (*especially NAmE*) *a summer internship with a small stipend* 薪水微薄的暑期实习

sti·pen·diary /staɪˈpendiəri; *NAmE* -dieri/ *noun* (*pl.* **-ies**) (*also* **sti,pendiary 'magistrate**) (in Britain) a MAGISTRATE who is paid for his or her work（英国）受薪治安法官

stip·ple /ˈstɪpl/ *verb* [often passive] **~ sth** (*specialist*) to paint or draw sth using small dots or marks 点画；点彩画出 ▸ **stip·pling** /ˈstɪplɪŋ/ *noun* [U]

stipu·late /ˈstɪpjuleɪt/ *verb* (*formal*) to state clearly and firmly that sth must be done, or how it must be done 规定；明确要求 SYN **specify**: **~ sth** *A delivery date is stipulated in the contract.* 合同中规定了交货日期。◇ **~ that…** *The job advertisement stipulates that the applicant must have three years' experience.* 招聘广告明确要求应聘者必须有三年工作经验。◇ **~ what, how, etc.…** *The policy stipulates what form of consent is required.* 保险单规定了需要哪种知情同意书。▸ **stipu·la·tion** /ˌstɪpjuˈleɪʃn/ *noun* [C, U]: *The only stipulation is that the topic you choose must be related to your studies.* 唯一的要求是所选的题目必须与你的研究科目有关。

stir 🔑 /stɜː(r)/ *verb, noun*

■ ***verb*** (**-rr-**)

• **MIX** 使混合 **1** 🔑 [T] to move a liquid or substance around, using a spoon or sth similar, in order to mix it thoroughly 搅动；搅和；搅拌：**~ sth** *She stirred her tea.* 她搅了搅茶。◇ **~ sth into sth** *The vegetables are stirred into the rice while it is hot.* 趁米饭热时把蔬菜拌进去。◇ **~ sth in** *Stir in the milk until the sauce thickens.* 把牛奶搅进去，直到酱汁变稠为止。➲ SYNONYMS AT MIX ➲ COLLOCATIONS AT COOKING

• **MOVE** 移动 **2** [I, T] to move, or to make sth move, slightly（使）微动：*She heard the baby stir in the next room.* 她听见婴儿在隔壁动弹。◇ **~ sth/sb** *A slight breeze was stirring the branches.* 微风吹动着树枝。◇ *A noise stirred me from sleep.* 响声把我从睡梦中惊醒。**3** [I, T] to move, or to make sb move, in order to do sth（使）行动，活动：*You haven't stirred from that chair all evening!* 你坐在那把椅子上一晚上没动了！◇ **~ yourself/sb** *Come on, stir yourself. You're late!* 快，快走吧。你要迟到了！◇ *Their complaints have finally stirred him into action.* 他们的抱怨最终促使他采取了行动。

• **FEELINGS** 感觉 **4** [T] **~ sb** (**to sth**) to make sb excited or make them feel sth strongly 打动；激发：*a book that really stirs the imagination* 很能激发人的想象力的书 ◇ *She was stirred by his sad story.* 他那悲惨的故事打动了她。**5** [I] (of a feeling or a mood 感情或情绪) to begin to be felt 开始感到；逐渐产生；萌动；被唤起：*A feeling of guilt began to stir in her.* 她心里渐渐生出了内疚感。

• **CAUSE TROUBLE** 引起麻烦 **6** [T, I] **~ (it)** (*BrE, informal, disapproving*) to try to cause trouble 拨弄是非：*You're just stirring it!* 你这不是搬弄是非吗！➲ SEE ALSO STIRRER ➲ MORE LIKE THIS 36, page R29

IDM **stir the 'blood** to make sb excited 使人兴奋；激起热情 **stir your 'stumps** (*old-fashioned, BrE, informal*) to begin to move; to hurry 起身走；赶快

PHR V **ˌstir sb↔ˈup** to encourage sb to do sth; to make sb feel they must do sth 激励；鼓动 **ˌstir sth↔ˈup 1** to make people feel strong emotions 激起（感情）：*to stir up hatred* 激起仇恨 **2** to try to cause arguments or problems 挑起，煽动（争执或事端）：*to stir up a debate* 挑起争论 ◇ *Whenever he's around, he always manages to* ***stir up trouble.*** 只要有他在，他就总要挑起点事来。◇ *We've got enough problems without you trying to* ***stir things up.*** 我们麻烦事儿已经够多的了，你就别再挑拨是非了。**3** to make sth move around in water or air（水或空气中）搅起；吹起：*The wind stirred up a lot of dust.* 风吹起大量尘土。

■ ***noun* 1** [sing.] excitement, anger or shock that is felt by a number of people（一些人感到的）激动，愤怒，震动 SYN **commotion**: *Her resignation* ***caused quite a stir.*** 她的辞职引起很大震动。**2** [C, usually sing.] the action of stirring sth 搅动；搅和；搅拌：*Could you give the rice a stir?* 你把米饭搅一搅好吗？

'stir-crazy *adj.* (*informal, especially NAmE*) showing signs of mental illness because of being kept in prison（因遭囚禁而）精神失常的

'stir-fry *verb, noun* (*pl.* **-ies**)

■ ***verb*** **~ sth** to cook thin strips of vegetables or meat quickly by stirring them in very hot oil 翻炒；炒；煸：*stir-fried chicken* 油爆鸡 ➲ COLLOCATIONS AT COOKING ➲ VISUAL VOCAB PAGE V28

■ ***noun*** a hot dish made by stir-frying small pieces of meat, fish and/or vegetables 炒菜

stir·rer /ˈstɜːrə(r)/ *noun* (*BrE, informal, disapproving*) a person who likes causing trouble, especially between other people, by spreading secrets 喜欢制造事端的人；（尤指）好拨弄是非者

stir·ring /ˈstɜːrɪŋ/ *noun, adj.*

■ ***noun*** **~ (of sth)** the beginning of a feeling, an idea or a development（感情、想法或发展的）开始，出现，萌动，酝酿：*She felt a stirring of anger.* 她感觉自己忍不住要生气了。

■ ***adj.*** [usually before noun] causing strong feelings; exciting 令人激情澎湃的；激动人心的：*a stirring performance* 动人的表演 ◇ *stirring memories* 令人心潮澎湃的回忆

stir·rup /ˈstɪrəp/ *noun* one of the metal rings that hang down on each side of a horse's SADDLE, used to support the rider's foot 马镫 ➲ WORDFINDER NOTE AT HORSE

stitch /stɪtʃ/ *noun, verb*

■ ***noun* 1** [C] one of the small lines of thread that you can see on a piece of cloth after it has been sewn; the action that produces this（缝纫的）一针，针脚；缝：*Try to keep the stitches small and straight.* 针脚要尽量缝得小而直。➲ WORDFINDER NOTE AT SEW ➲ VISUAL VOCAB PAGE V45 **2** [C] one of the small circles of wool that you make around the needle when you are knitting（编织的）一针：*to* ***drop a stitch*** (= to lose one that you have made) 漏一针 **3** [C, U] (especially in compounds 尤用于构成复合词) a particular style of sewing or knitting that you use to make the pattern you want 缝法；针法；编织法：*chain stitch* 链式线步 **4** [C] a short piece of thread, etc. that doctors use to sew the edges of a wound together（缝合伤口的）缝线：*The cut needed eight stitches.* 这道伤口需要缝八针。➲ WORDFINDER NOTE AT OPERATION ➲ COLLOCATIONS AT INJURY **5** [C, usually sing.] a sudden pain in the side of your body, usually caused by running or laughing 肋部突然的疼痛（多由奔跑或笑引起）；岔气：*Can we slow down? I've got a stitch.* 我们慢一点好不好？我岔气了。

IDM **in 'stitches** (*informal*) laughing a lot 大笑不止；笑破肚皮：*The play* ***had us in stitches.*** 那出戏让我们笑得前仰后合。**not have a stitch 'on | not be wearing a 'stitch** (*informal*) to be naked 一丝不挂；赤裸 **a stitch in 'time (saves 'nine)** (*saying*) it is better to deal with sth immediately because if you wait it may become worse or more difficult and cause extra work 及时缝一针能省九针；小洞及时补，免遭大洞苦

■ ***verb* 1** **~ sth** (**+ adv./prep.**) to use a needle and thread to repair, join, or decorate pieces of cloth 缝；缝补 SYN **sew**: *Her wedding dress was stitched by hand.* 她的婚纱是手工缝制的。◇ (*figurative*) *An agreement was hastily stitched together* (= made very quickly). 仓促达成了一项协议。**2** **~ sth** (**up**) to sew the edges of a wound together 缝合（伤口）：*The cut will need to be stitched.* 这伤口需要缝合。

PHR V **ˌstitch sb↔ˈup** (*BrE, informal*) to cheat sb or put them in a position where they seem guilty of sth they have not done 算计某人；诬陷某人 **ˌstitch sth↔ˈup 1** to use a needle and thread to join things together 缝合 **2** (*informal*) to arrange or complete sth 办妥；做成：*to stitch up a deal* 做成一笔交易 ◇ *They think they have the US market stitched up.* 他们觉得美国市场已是万无一失。

stitch·ing /ˈstɪtʃɪŋ/ *noun* [U] a row of stitches（一行）针脚

'stitch-up *noun* (*BrE, informal*) a situation in which sb deliberately cheats you or causes you to be wrongly blamed for sth 故意欺骗；诬陷

St John's Wort /snt ˌdʒɒnz ˈwɜːt; *NAmE* seɪnt ˌdʒɑːnz ˈwɜːrt/ *noun* [U, C] a HERB with yellow flowers, used in medicines 金丝桃，圣约翰草（可入药）

stoat /stəʊt; *NAmE* stoʊt/ *noun* a small wild animal with a long body and brown fur that, in northern areas, turns white in winter. The white fur is called ERMINE. 白鼬

stock /stɒk; *NAmE* stɑːk/ *noun, verb, adj.*

■ ***noun***

• **SUPPLY** 供应 **1** [U, C] a supply of goods that is available for sale in a shop/store（商店的）现货，存货，库存：*We have a fast turnover of stock.* 我们的货物周转快。◇ *That particular model is not currently* ***in stock***. 那种型号目前没货。◇ *I'm afraid we're temporarily* ***out of stock***. 很遗憾，我们暂时脱销了。◇ *We don't carry a large stock of pine furniture.* 松木家具我们备货不多。➲ COLLOCATIONS AT SHOPPING **2** [C, U] ~ (**of sth**) a supply of sth that is available for use 储备物；备用物；供应物：*She's built up a good stock of teaching materials over the years.* 这些年来她积累了大量教学资料。◇ *Food stocks are running low.* 贮存的食物快吃完了。◇ *a country's* ***housing stock*** (= all the houses available for living in) 一个国家的住房保有量

• **FINANCE** 金融 **3** [U] the value of the shares in a company that have been sold 股本；资本 **4** [C, usually pl.] a share that sb has bought in a company or business 股份；股票：*stock prices* 股票价格 ◇ (*NAmE*) *to invest in* ***stocks and bonds*** 投资股票与债券 ➲ COMPARE SHARE *n.* (4) **5** [U, C] (*BrE*) money that is lent to a government at a fixed rate of interest; an official document that gives details of this 公债；公债券：*government stock* 政府债券 ◇ *to invest in* ***stocks and shares*** 投资债券与股票

• **FARM ANIMALS** 家畜 **6** [U] farm animals, such as cows and sheep, that are kept for their meat, wool, etc. 家畜；牲畜：*breeding stock* 种畜 ➲ SEE ALSO LIVESTOCK

• **FAMILY/ANCESTORS** 家族；祖先 **7** [U] **of farming, noble, French, etc.** ~ having the type of family or ANCESTORS mentioned 家族；世系；出身 SYN **descent**

• **FOOD** 食物 **8** [U, C] a liquid made by cooking bones, meat, etc. in water, used for making soups and sauces 高汤；原汤：*vegetable stock* 菜汤

• **FOR PUNISHMENT** 刑具 **9 stocks** [pl.] a wooden structure with holes for the feet, used in the past to lock criminals in as a form of punishment, especially in a public place 足枷 ➲ COMPARE PILLORY *n.*

• **RESPECT** 尊敬 **10** [U] (*formal*) the degree to which sb is respected or liked by other people 名声；声望；评价：*Their stock is high/low.* 他们的声望高 / 低。

• **OF GUN** 枪 **11** [C] the part of a gun that you hold against your shoulder when firing it 枪托

• **PLANT** 植物 **12** [U, C] a garden plant with brightly coloured flowers with a sweet smell 紫罗兰

• **THEATRE** 戏剧 **13** [C] (*NAmE*) = STOCK COMPANY (2) ➲ SEE ALSO LAUGHING STOCK, ROLLING STOCK

IDM **on the ˈstocks** in the process of being made, built or prepared 在制作（或建造、准备）中：*Our new model is already on the stocks and will be available in the spring.* 我们已着手生产新的款式，明年春天就可以上市。 **put ˈstock in sth** (*especially NAmE*) to have a particular amount of belief in sth（在某种程度上）相信，信任：*She no longer puts much stock in their claims.* 她再也不过于相信他们的断言了。 **take ˈstock (of sth)** to stop and think carefully about the way in which a particular situation is developing in order to decide what to do next（对某情况）加以总结，作出评估，进行反思 ➲ MORE AT LOCK *n.* ➲ SEE ALSO STOCKTAKING (2)

■ ***verb*** **1** ~ **sth** (of a shop/store 商店) to keep a supply of a particular type of goods to sell 存货：*Do you stock green tea?* 你们的库存有绿茶吗？ **2** [often passive] ~ **sth** (**with sth**) to fill sth with food, books, etc. 贮备，贮存（食物、书籍等）：*The pond was well stocked with fish.* 池塘里养了许多鱼。◇ *a well-stocked library* 藏书丰富的图书馆

PHR V **ˌstock sth↔ˈup** to fill sth with goods, food, etc. 在…中备足货品（或食物等）：*We need to stock up the freezer.* 我们需要在冰柜里存满东西。 **ˌstock ˈup (on/with sth)** to buy a lot of sth so that you can use it later 贮备，备足（某物）：*We ought to stock up on film before our trip.* 我们应该在旅行前备足胶卷。

■ ***adj.*** [only before noun] **1** (*disapproving*) a **stock** excuse, answer, etc. is one that is often used because it is easy and convenient, but that is not very original 老一套的；陈腐的：*'No comment,' was the actor's stock response.* "无可奉告。" 那位演员回答什么问题都是这一句老话。 **2** usually available for sale in a shop/store（商店里）常备的，通常有的 SYN **standard**：*stock sizes* 常备尺码

stock·ade /stɒˈkeɪd; *NAmE* stɑːˈk-/ *noun* a line or wall of strong wooden posts built to defend a place（防御用的）栅栏，围桩

stock·broker /ˈstɒkbrəʊkə(r); *NAmE* ˈstɑːkbroʊ-/ (*also* **broker**) *noun* a person or an organization that buys and sells shares for other people 证券（或股票）经纪人；证券（或股票）经纪商

ˈstockbroker belt *noun* [sing.] (*BrE*) an area outside a large city, where many rich people live（大城市外围的）富人住宅带

stock·brok·ing /ˈstɒkbrəʊkɪŋ; *NAmE* ˈstɑːkbroʊ-/ *noun* [U] the work of a stockbroker 证券（或股票）经纪业务

ˈstock car *noun* an ordinary car that has been made stronger for use in stock-car racing 改装赛车（经改装用以参加改装车赛的普通汽车）

ˈstock-car racing *noun* [U] (*BrE*) (*NAmE* **ˌdemolition ˈderby**) a type of race in which the competing cars are allowed to hit each other 改装车赛车（参赛车辆可以相互碰撞）

ˈstock company *noun* (*NAmE*) **1** a company owned by people who have shares in it 股份公司 **2** (*also* **stock**) a theatre company that does several different plays in a season; a REPERTORY company 保留剧目轮演剧团

ˈstock cube *noun* a solid CUBE made from the dried juices of meat or vegetables, sold in packs and used for making soups, sauces, etc. 固体汤料；汤块

ˈstock exchange *noun* [usually sing.] a place where shares in companies are bought and sold; all of the business activity involved in doing this 证券交易（所）；股票交易（所）：*the London Stock Exchange* 伦敦证券交易所 ◇ *to lose money on the stock exchange* 在股票交易中赔钱

stock·fish /ˈstɒkfɪʃ; *NAmE* ˈstɑːk-/ *noun* **1** [U] COD or similar fish that is dried without salt 淡鳕鱼干；淡鱼干 **2** [C] (*pl.* **stock·fish** or **stock·fishes**) (*SAfrE*) a large sea fish that is used for food 无须鳕（可食用）；好望角无须鳕

stock·hold·er /ˈstɒkhəʊldə(r); *NAmE* ˈstɑːkhoʊ-/ *noun* (*especially NAmE*) a person who owns STOCKS and shares in a business 股票持有人；股东

stock·inet (*also* **stock·in·ette**) /ˌstɒkɪˈnet; *NAmE* ˌstɑːk-/ *noun* [U] a type of soft cloth that stretches easily and is used for making bandages 弹性针织布料；松紧织物

stock·ing /ˈstɒkɪŋ; *NAmE* ˈstɑːk-/ *noun* **1** either of a pair of thin pieces of clothing that fit closely over a woman's legs and feet 长筒女袜：*a pair of silk stockings* 一双长筒丝袜 ➲ COMPARE TIGHTS (1) ➲ SEE ALSO BODY STOCKING **2** = CHRISTMAS STOCKING

IDM **in your ˌstocking(ed) ˈfeet** wearing socks or stockings but not shoes 只穿袜不穿鞋

ˈstocking filler (*BrE*) (*NAmE* **ˈstocking stuffer**) *noun* a small present that is put in a CHRISTMAS STOCKING 圣诞袜小礼物

ˌstock-in-ˈtrade *noun* [U] a person's **stock-in-trade** is sth that they do, say or use very often or too often 惯做的事（或说的话、用的东西）：*Famous people and their private lives are the stock-in-trade of the popular newspapers.* 名人和名人的私生活是通俗报纸惯有的内容。

stock·ist /ˈstɒkɪst; *NAmE* ˈstɑːk-/ *noun* (*BrE*) a shop/store or company that sells a particular product or type of goods（某种产品或某类货品的）专营商店 SYN **retailer**

S

stock·job·ber /ˈstɒkdʒɒbə(r); NAmE ˈstɑːkdʒɑːb-/ *noun* = JOBBER

stock·man /ˈstɒkmən; NAmE ˈstɑːk-/ *noun* (*pl.* **-men** /-mən/) **1** a man whose job is to take care of farm animals 畜牧工；饲养员 **2** (*NAmE*) a man who owns farm animals 牧场主 **3** (*NAmE*) a man who is in charge of the goods in a WAREHOUSE, etc. 仓库管理员

ˈstock market (*also* **market**) *noun* the business of buying and selling shares in companies and the place where this happens; a STOCK EXCHANGE 证券交易（所）；股票交易（所）；股市：*to make money on the stock market* 在股票市场上赚钱 ◇ *a stock market crash* (= when prices of shares fall suddenly and people lose money) 股票市场的暴跌 ➲ COLLOCATIONS AT ECONOMY

ˈstock option (*NAmE*) (*BrE* **ˈshare option**) *noun* a right given to employees to buy shares in their company at a fixed price 股票期权；认股选择权（员工按固定价格购买所属公司股票的权利）

stock·pile /ˈstɒkpaɪl; NAmE ˈstɑːk-/ *noun, verb*

■ ***noun*** a large supply of sth that is kept to be used in the future if necessary 囤聚的物资：*the world's stockpile of nuclear weapons* 全世界的核武器储备

■ ***verb*** **~ sth** to collect and keep a large supply of sth 大量储备

stock·pot /ˈstɒkpɒt; NAmE ˈstɑːkpɑːt/ *noun* a pot in which meat, fish, vegetables, or bones are cooked to make STOCK 汤锅

stock·room /ˈstɒkruːm; -rʊm; NAmE ˈstɑːk-/ *noun* a room for storing things in a shop/store, an office, etc. 仓库；贮藏室

ˌstock-ˈstill *adv.* without moving at all 静止地；一动不动地：*We stood stock-still watching the animals.* 我们一动不动地站着观看那些动物。

stock·tak·ing /ˈstɒkteɪkɪŋ; NAmE ˈstɑːk-/ *noun* [U] **1** (*especially BrE*) the process of making a list of all the goods in a shop/store or business 盘点；清点存货；盘货 ➲ COMPARE INVENTORY *n.* (2) **2** the process of thinking carefully about your own situation or position（自我）总结，评估，反思

stocky /ˈstɒki; NAmE ˈstɑːki/ *adj.* (**stock·ier**, **stocki·est**) (of a person 人) short, with a strong, solid body 矮壮的；敦实的 SYN **thickset** ▶ **stock·ily** *adv.*

stock·yard /ˈstɒkjɑːd; NAmE ˈstɑːkjɑːrd/ *noun* a place where farm animals are kept for a short time before they are sold at a market 牲畜栏，牲畜围场（用以安置牲畜，准备运往市场）

stodge /stɒdʒ; NAmE stɑːdʒ/ *noun* [U] (*BrE, informal, usually disapproving*) heavy food that makes you feel very full 吃下去感觉撑的食物；易饱的食物

stodgy /ˈstɒdʒi; NAmE ˈstɑːdʒi/ *adj.* (*informal, especially BrE*) **1** (of food 食物) heavy and making you feel very full 吃下去感觉撑的；易饱的 **2** serious and boring; not exciting 滞涩的；古板的；枯燥无味的

stoep /stuːp; stʊp/ *noun* (*SAfrE*) a raised area outside the door of a house, with a roof over it, where you can sit and relax, eat meals, etc. 屋前游廊；门廊

stogy (*also* **stogie**) /ˈstəʊgi; NAmE ˈstoʊgi/ *noun* (*pl.* **-ies**) (*NAmE*) a cheap cigar 廉价雪茄

stoic /ˈstəʊɪk; NAmE ˈstoʊɪk/ *noun* a person who is able to suffer pain or trouble without complaining or showing what they are feeling 斯多葛派人（对痛苦或困难能默默承受或泰然处之）▶ **stoic** (*also* **sto·ic·al**) *adj.*: *her stoic endurance* 她默默承受一切的坚忍性格 ◇ *his stoical acceptance of death* 他坦然面对死亡的态度 **sto·ic·al·ly** /-kli/ *adv.*

ORIGIN From the **Stoics**, a group of ancient Greek philosophers, who believed that wise people should not allow themselves to be affected by painful or pleasant experiences. 源自斯多葛学派 (Stoics)，古希腊哲学流派，认为智者不应为苦乐所动。

sto·icism /ˈstəʊɪsɪzəm; NAmE ˈstoʊ-/ *noun* [U] (*formal*) the fact of not complaining or showing what you are feeling when you are suffering 对痛苦的默默承受或泰然处之；坚忍：*She endured her long illness with stoicism.* 她默默忍受长期的病痛。

stoke /stəʊk; NAmE stoʊk/ *verb* **1** **~ sth (up) (with sth)** to add fuel to a fire, etc. 给…添加（燃料）：*to stoke up a fire with more coal* 往火里再添一些煤 ◇ *to stoke a furnace* 给炉子添煤 **2** **~ sth (up)** to make people feel sth more strongly 煽动；激起：*to stoke up envy* 激起妒忌 **3** **~ sth (up)** to make sth increase or develop more quickly 促使…的增加；刺激…的发展；加剧：*They were accused of stoking the crisis.* 他们被指控对这次危机起了推波助澜的作用。

PHR V **ˌstoke ˈup (on/with sth)** (*informal*) to eat or drink a lot of sth, especially so that you do not feel hungry later 吃饱；吃好；喝足：*Stoke up for the day on a good breakfast.* 早饭要吃得饱饱的，整整一天呢。

stoked /stəʊkt; NAmE stoʊkt/ *adj.* (*NAmE, informal*) excited and pleased about sth 兴奋的；满足的：*I'm really stoked that they chose me for the team.* 他们选我加入这个队，我兴奋极了。

stoker /ˈstəʊkə(r); NAmE ˈstoʊ-/ *noun* a person whose job is to add coal or other fuel to a fire, etc., especially on a ship or a steam train（尤指轮船或蒸汽机车上的）司炉

stok·vel /ˈstɒkfel; NAmE ˈstɑːk-/ *noun* (*SAfrE*) a group of people who agree to pay regular amounts of money and take turns to receive all or part of what is collected 集资互助组（成员定期缴纳款项并轮流领取全部或部分集资款）

stole /stəʊl; NAmE stoʊl/ *noun* a piece of clothing consisting of a wide band of cloth or fur, worn by a woman around the shoulders; a similar piece of clothing worn by a priest 女用披肩；（司祭佩戴的）圣带 ➲ SEE ALSO STEAL *v.*

stolid /ˈstɒlɪd; NAmE ˈstɑːl-/ *adj.* (*usually disapproving*) not showing much emotion or interest; remaining always the same and not reacting or changing 不动感情的；不关心的；淡漠的；无动于衷的 ▶ **stol·id·ly** *adv.* **stol·id·ity** /stəˈlɪdəti/ *noun* [U]

stoma /ˈstəʊmə; NAmE ˈstoʊ-/ *noun* (*pl.* **stomas** or **sto·mata** /ˈstəʊmətə; NAmE ˈstoʊ-/) **1** (*biology* 生) a tiny PORE (= hole) in the outer layer of a plant's leaf or STEM 气孔（植物叶或茎表皮的小孔）**2** (*biology* 生) a small opening like a mouth, in some animals（某些动物的）气门，呼吸孔 **3** (*medical* 医) an artificial opening made in an organ of the body, especially in the COLON or TRACHEA（尤指结肠或气管上的）造口

stom·ach 🔑 /ˈstʌmək/ *noun, verb*

■ ***noun*** 🔑 the organ inside the body where food goes when you swallow it; the front part of the body below the chest 胃；腹部：*stomach pains* 肚子疼 ◇ *an upset stomach* 胃部不适 ◇ (*BrE also*) *a stomach upset* 胃部不适 ◇ *It's not a good idea to drink* (= alcohol) ***on an empty stomach*** (= without having eaten anything). 空腹不宜喝酒。◇ *You shouldn't exercise* ***on a full stomach***. 你不应该吃饱了就运动。◇ *The attacker kicked him in the stomach.* 袭击者一脚踢在他肚子上。◇ *Lie on your stomach with your arms by your side.* 手臂放在两侧趴下。➲ COLLOCATIONS AT PHYSICAL ➲ VISUAL VOCAB PAGE V64 ➲ SEE ALSO TUMMY

IDM **have no ˈstomach for sth** **1** to not want to eat sth 不想吃…；对…没有胃口：*She had no stomach for the leftover stew.* 她不想吃剩下的炖菜。**2** to not have the desire or courage to do sth 没有做某事的欲望（或勇气）：*They had no stomach for a fight.* 他们不想打架。 **turn your ˈstomach** to make you feel upset, sick or disgusted 让某人反感（或恶心、厌恶）：*Pictures of the burnt corpses turned my stomach.* 那些烧焦的尸体的照片让我直恶心。➲ MORE AT BUTTERFLY, EYE *n.*, FEEL *v.*, PIT *n.*, PUMP *v.*, STRONG

■ ***verb*** (especially in negative sentences or questions 尤用于否定句或疑问句) **1** **~ sth** to approve of sth and be able to enjoy it; to enjoy being with a person 欣赏；欣然接受；喜欢和…相处：*I can't stomach violent films.* 我不喜欢暴力片。◇ *I find him very* ***hard to stomach***. 我觉得很难和

他相处。**2** **~ sth** to be able to eat sth without feeling ill/sick 能吃；吃得下：*She **couldn't stomach** any breakfast.* 她早上什么都吃不下。

'stomach ache *noun* [C, U] pain in or near your stomach 胃痛；腹痛

'stomach-churning (*also* **'stomach-turning**) *adj.* making you feel disgusted or that you want to VOMIT 令人反胃的；倒胃口的；令人恶心的：*The team daily faces stomach-churning crime scenes.* 这个小组每天都要面对让人反胃的犯罪现场。➲ MORE LIKE THIS 10, page R26

'stomach pump *noun* a machine with a tube that doctors use to remove poisonous substances from sb's stomach through their mouth 胃泵

stomp /stɒmp; *NAmE* stɑːmp; stɔːmp/ *verb* [I] **+ adv./prep.** (*informal*) to walk, dance, or move with heavy steps 迈着重重的步子走（或跳舞、移动）：*She stomped angrily out of the office.* 她怒气冲冲，重步走出办公室。

stompie /'stɒmpi; *NAmE* 'stɑːm-/ *noun* (*SAfrE, informal*) a cigarette that has been partly smoked; the end of a cigarette that is thrown away after it has been smoked （已经吸过的）半截烟；烟蒂

'stomping ground *noun* (*NAmE, informal*) = STAMPING GROUND

stone 🔑 /stəʊn; *NAmE* stoʊn/ *noun, verb*

■ ***noun***

• **HARD SUBSTANCE** 硬物质 **1** 🔑 [U] (often used before nouns or in compounds 常用于名词前或构成复合词) a hard solid mineral substance that is found in the ground, often used for building 石头；石料；岩石：*Most of the houses are built of stone.* 这些房子多数是用石头建造的。◇ *stone walls* 石墙 ◇ *a stone floor* 石地板 ◇ *a flight of stone steps* 一段石台阶 ➲ SEE ALSO DRYSTONE WALL, LIMESTONE, SANDSTONE, SOAPSTONE **2** 🔑 [C] (*especially BrE*) a small piece of rock of any shape 石块；石子：*a pile of stones* 一堆石块 ◇ *Some children were throwing stones into the lake.* 几个孩子正朝湖里扔石头。➲ SEE ALSO HAILSTONE, PHILOSOPHER'S STONE **3** 🔑 [C] (usually in compounds 通常构成复合词) a piece of stone shaped for a particular purpose（加工成某形状为某用途的）石块：*These words are carved on the stone beside his grave.* 在他的墓碑上刻着这样的话。➲ SEE ALSO CORNERSTONE, FOUNDATION STONE, GRAVESTONE, HEADSTONE, LODESTONE, MILLSTONE, PAVING STONE, STEPPING STONE (1), TOMBSTONE

• **JEWEL** 宝石 **4** [C] = PRECIOUS STONE

• **IN FRUIT** 水果 **5** [C] (*especially BrE*) (*NAmE usually* **pit**) a hard shell containing the nut or seed in the middle of some types of fruit 果核：***cherry/peach stones*** 樱桃核；桃核 ➲ VISUAL VOCAB PAGE V32

• **IN BODY** 体内 **6** [C] (often in compounds 常构成复合词) a small piece of hard material that can form in the BLADDER or KIDNEY and cause pain（膀胱或肾脏中的）结石：*kidney stones* 肾结石 ➲ SEE ALSO GALLSTONE

• **MEASUREMENT OF WEIGHT** 重量单位 **7** [C] (*pl.* **stone**) (*abbr.* **st**) (in Britain) a unit for measuring weight, equal to 6.35 kg or 14 pounds 英石（英国重量单位，相当于 6.35 千克或 14 磅）：*He weighs over 15 stone.* 他体重超过 15 英石。◇ *She's trying to lose a stone.* 她试图减去一英石的体重。

IDM **carved/set in 'stone** (of a decision, plan, etc. 决定、计划等) unable to be changed 不可改变；铁定；板上钉钉：*People should remember that our proposals aren't set in stone.* 人们应该记住我们的建议不是一成不变的。 **leave no stone un'turned** to try every possible course of action in order to find or achieve sth 千方百计；想尽办法 **a 'stone's throw** a very short distance away 很近的距离；不远处：*We live just a stone's throw from here.* 我们就住在附近。◇ *The hotel is within a stone's throw of the beach.* 旅馆离海滩很近。➲ MORE AT BLOOD *n.*, HEART, KILL *v.*, PEOPLE *n.*, ROLL *v.*

■ ***verb***

• **THROW STONES** 扔石块 **1** [usually passive] **~ sb/sth** to throw stones at sb/sth 向…扔石块；用石头砸：*Shops were looted and vehicles stoned.* 商店遭哄抢，车辆被砸坏。◇ ***to be stoned to death*** (= as a punishment) 用石头砸死（一种刑罚）

• **FRUIT** 水果 **2** (*BrE*) (*also* **pit** *NAmE, BrE*) **~ sth** to remove the stone from the inside of a fruit 去掉…的果核：*stoned black olives* 去核黑橄榄

IDM **,stone the 'crows** | **,stone 'me** (*old-fashioned, BrE*) used to express surprise, shock, anger, etc.（表示惊奇、震惊、气愤等）哎呀

the 'Stone Age *noun* [sing.] the very early period of human history when tools and weapons were made of stone 石器时代 (*figurative*): *My dad's taste in music is from the Stone Age* (= very old-fashioned). 我老爸的音乐品味都老得掉渣了。▸ **'stone-age** *adj.* [only before noun] (*figurative*): *stone-age* (= very out-of-date) *computers* 原始计算机

,stone 'circle *noun* a circle of large tall vertical stones from PREHISTORIC times, thought to have been used for religious or other ceremonies 史前环状巨石阵（据信用于宗教等的仪式）

,stone 'cold *adj.* completely cold, when it should be warm or hot 冰凉的；凉透的：*The soup was stone cold.* 汤全凉了。

IDM **,stone-cold 'sober** having drunk no alcohol at all 滴酒未沾；完全清醒

stoned /stəʊnd; *NAmE* stoʊnd/ *adj.* [not usually before noun] (*informal*) not behaving or thinking normally because of the effects of a drug such as MARIJUANA or alcohol（在毒品或酒精作用下）晕晕乎乎，飘飘然

,stone 'dead *adj.* completely dead or completely destroyed 完全死了的；完全毁坏的

,stone 'deaf *adj.* completely unable to hear 完全聋的；失聪的

stone·ground /'stəʊngraʊnd; *NAmE* 'stoʊn-/ *adj.* (of flour for bread, etc. 制作面包等的面粉) made by being crushed between heavy stones 石磨研磨的

stone·mason /'stəʊnmeɪsn; *NAmE* 'stoʊn-/ *noun* a person whose job is cutting and preparing stone for buildings 石工；石匠

stone·wall /,stəʊn'wɔːl; *NAmE* 'stoʊnwɔːl/ *verb* [T, I] **~ (sb/sth)** (especially in politics) to delay a discussion or decision by refusing to answer questions or by talking a lot 防守挡击（政治上指通过沉默或冗长发言等手段阻碍议事或拖延决议）

stone·ware /'stəʊnweə(r); *NAmE* 'stoʊnwer/ *noun* [U] pots, dishes, etc. made from CLAY that contains a small amount of the hard stone called FLINT 炻器；粗陶器；缸瓦器

stone·washed /'stəʊnwɒʃt; *NAmE* 'stoʊnwɔːʃt; -wɑːʃt/ *adj.* (of jeans, etc. 牛仔裤等) washed in a special way so that the cloth loses some colour and looks older 石磨水洗的

stone·work /'stəʊnwɜːk; *NAmE* 'stoʊnwɜːrk/ *noun* [U] the parts of a building that are made of stone（建筑物的）石造部分

stoni·ly /'stəʊnɪli; *NAmE* 'stoʊn-/ *adv.* in a way that shows a lack of feeling or sympathy 冷漠地；无情地；铁石心肠地：*She stared stonily at him for a minute.* 她冷冷地盯着他看了片刻。

stonk·er /'stɒŋkə(r); *NAmE* 'stɑːŋk-; 'stɔːŋk-/ *noun* (*BrE, informal*) an extremely large or impressive thing 特大型；令人印象深刻的事物

stonk·ing /'stɒŋkɪŋ; *NAmE* 'stɑːŋk-; 'stɔːŋk-/ *adj.* [usually before noun] (*BrE, informal*) extremely large or impressive 庞大的；绝妙的；出色的

stony /'stəʊni; *NAmE* 'stoʊni/ *adj.* (**stoni·er**, **stoni·est**) **1** having a lot of stones on it or in it 多石的；石头的：*stony soil* 多石的土壤 **2** showing a lack of feeling or sympathy 冷漠的；无情的；铁石心肠的 **SYN** **cold**: *They listened to him in stony silence.* 他们冷漠地静静听他讲。

IDM **fall on stony 'ground** to fail to produce the result or the effect that you hope for; to have little success

未产生预期的结果（或效果）；没有开花结果 **stony 'broke** = FLAT BROKE

ˌstony-'faced *adj.* not showing any friendly feelings 冷淡的；冷漠的

stood PAST TENSE, PAST PART. OF STAND

stooge /stuːdʒ/ *noun* **1** (*informal, usually disapproving*) a person who is used by sb to do things that are unpleasant or dishonest 受人驱使的人；奴才；走狗 **2** a performer in a show whose role is to appear silly so that the other performers can make jokes about him or her（供其他演员作弄打趣的）丑角

stool /stuːl/ *noun* **1** (often in compounds 常构成复合词) a seat with legs but with nothing to support your back or arms 凳子：*a bar stool* 酒吧高凳 ◇ *a piano stool* 钢琴凳 ➲ VISUAL VOCAB PAGES V24, V26, V40 **2** (*medical* 医) a piece of solid waste from your body 粪便；大便 IDM SEE TWO

'stool pigeon *noun* (*informal*) a person, especially a criminal, who helps the police to catch another criminal, for example by spending time with them and getting secret information（向警察提供情报的）线人，内线 SYN **informer**

stoop /stuːp/ *verb, noun*

■ ***verb*** **1** [I] ~ (**down**) to bend your body forwards and downwards 俯身；弯腰：*She stooped down to pick up the child.* 她俯身抱起孩子。◇ *The doorway was so low that he had to stoop.* 门廊很矮，他低下头才过去。**2** [I] to stand or walk with your head and shoulders bent forwards（站立或行走时）弓背：*He tends to stoop because he's so tall.* 他个子太高了，所以时常弓着背。

IDM **stoop so 'low** (**as to do sth**) (*formal*) to drop your moral standards far enough to do sth bad or unpleasant 卑鄙（或堕落）到…地步：*She was unwilling to believe anyone would stoop so low as to steal a ring from a dead woman's finger.* 她无法相信真有人会龌龊到这种地步，竟然从一个死去的女人手指上偷戒指。

PHR V **'stoop to sth** to drop your moral standards to do sth bad or unpleasant 卑鄙（或堕落）到做某事：*You surely don't think I'd stoop to that!* 你不会认为我会下作到那种地步吧！◇ **stoop to doing sth** *I didn't think he'd stoop to cheating.* 我觉得他总不至于作弊吧。

■ ***noun*** **1** [sing.] if sb has a **stoop**, their shoulders are always bent forward 曲背；驼背 **2** [C] (*NAmE*) a raised area outside the door of a house with steps leading up to it 门廊

stooped /stuːpt/ *adj.* **1** standing or walking with your head and shoulders bent forwards 弓背站立（或行走）的 **2** **stooped shoulders** are bent forwards 曲背的

stop /stɒp; *NAmE* stɑːp/ *verb, noun*

■ ***verb*** (**-pp-**)

• **NOT MOVE** 不动 **1** [I, T] to no longer move; to make sb/sth no longer move（使）停止，停下：*The car stopped at the traffic lights.* 汽车在交通信号灯前停了下来。◇ *We stopped for the night in Port Augusta.* 我们中途在奥古斯塔港停留过夜。◇ **~ sb/sth** *He was stopped by the police for speeding.* 他因超速行驶被警察截住了。

• **NOT CONTINUE** 不继续 **2** [I, T] to no longer continue to do sth; to make sb/sth no longer do sth（使）中断，停止：**~ (doing sth)** *That phone never stops ringing!* 那个电话没有不响的时候！◇ *Please stop crying and tell me what's wrong.* 快别哭了，告诉我出了什么事。◇ *She criticizes everyone and the trouble is, she* ***doesn't know when to stop***. 她谁都批评；而且，问题是她批评起来就没个完。◇ *Can't you just stop?* 你就不能停一停吗？◇ **~ sb/sth** *Stop me* (= make me stop talking) *if I'm boring you.* 你要是觉得我烦就打断我。◇ ***Stop it!*** *You're hurting me.* 住手！你把我弄疼了。◇ **~ what...** *Mike immediately stopped what he was doing.* 迈克立刻停下手头的事情。HELP Notice the difference between **stop doing sth** and **stop to do sth**: *'We stopped taking pictures'* means 'We were no longer taking pictures.'; *'We stopped to take pictures'* means 'We stopped what we were doing so that we could start taking pictures.' 注意 stop doing sth 和 stop to do sth 之间的区别：We stopped taking pictures 的意思是"我们不再照相了"；We stopped to take pictures 的意思是"我们停下正在做的事而去照相"。➲ EXPRESS YOURSELF AT INTERRUPT

• **END** 结束 **3** [I, T] to end or finish; to make sth end or finish（使）结束，终止：*When is this fighting going to stop?* 这场战斗要打到什么时候？◇ *The bus service stops at midnight.* 公共汽车午夜停止服务。◇ **~ doing sth** *Has it stopped raining yet?* 雨停了没有？◇ **~ sth** *Doctors couldn't stop the bleeding.* 医生止不住血。◇ *The referee was forced to stop the game because of heavy snow.* 由于下大雪，裁判被迫终止了比赛。

• **PREVENT** 阻止 **4** [T] to prevent sb from doing sth; to prevent sth from happening 阻止；阻碍；阻拦；防止：**~ sb/sth** *I want to go and you can't stop me.* 我要走，你拦不住我。◇ *We need more laws to stop pollution.* 我们需要制定更多法律来防止污染。◇ ***There's no stopping us now*** (= nothing can prevent us from achieving what we want to achieve). 现在什么都无法阻挡我们了。◇ **~ sb/sth from doing sth** ***There's nothing to stop you*** *from accepting the offer.* 你尽可以接受那个提议。◇ *You can't stop people from saying what they think.* 人们怎么想就会怎么说，你阻止不了。◇ **~ sb/sth doing sth** *You can't stop people saying what they think.* 人们怎么想就会怎么说，你阻止不了。

• **FOR SHORT TIME** 短时间 **5** [I] to end an activity for a short time in order to do sth 暂停，暂时中断（以便做某事）：**~ for sth** *I'm hungry. Let's stop for lunch.* 我饿了。我们停下来吃午饭吧。◇ **~ to do sth** *We stopped to admire the scenery.* 我们中途停下来欣赏一下风景。◇ *People just don't* ***stop to think*** *about the consequences.* 人们做事情就是不肯停下来想想后果。HELP In spoken English, **stop** can be used with **and** plus another verb, instead of with **to** and the infinitive, to show purpose. 口语中，stop 可以与 and 及另一动词连用，而不用带 to 的不定式表示目的：*He stopped and bought some flowers.* 他停下来买了些花。◇ *Let's stop and look at the map.* 咱们停一下看看地图。

• **NOT FUNCTION** 不工作 **6** [I, T] to no longer work or function; to make sth no longer work or function（使）停止工作，停止运转：*Why has the engine stopped?* 发动机怎么停了？◇ *I felt as if my heart had stopped.* 我觉得我的心好像都不跳了。◇ **~ sth** *I stopped the tape and pressed rewind.* 我停了磁带，按下倒回键。

• **STAY** 逗留 **7** [I] (*BrE, informal*) to stay somewhere for a short time, especially at sb's house 逗留，待，留下（做某事）：*I'm not stopping. I just came to give you this message.* 我不待了。我就是来告诉你这件事。◇ **~ for sth** *Can you stop for tea?* 你能留下来喝茶吗？

• **MONEY** 钱 **8** [T] to prevent money from being paid 止付；停付；扣除：**~ sth** ***to stop a cheque*** (= tell the bank not to pay it) 通知银行止付支票 ◇ **~ sth from sth** (*BrE*) *Dad threatened to stop £1 a week from our pocket money if we didn't clean our rooms.* 父亲威胁说，我们要是不把自己的房间收拾干净，他就每星期扣我们 1 英镑的零花钱。

• **CLOSE HOLE** 堵塞洞孔 **9** [T] **~ sth** (**up**) (**with sth**) to block, fill or close a hole, an opening, etc. 堵塞；塞住；阻塞：*Stop up the other end of the tube, will you?* 你把管子的另一头堵上好不好？◇ *I stopped my ears but still heard her cry out.* 我捂上耳朵，但还能听见她大声喊叫。

IDM **stop at 'nothing** to be willing to do anything to get what you want, even if it is dishonest or wrong 不择手段 **ˌstop the 'clock** to stop measuring time in a game or an activity that has a time limit（在计时比赛或活动中）停表 **ˌstop 'short** | **ˌstop sb 'short** to suddenly stop, or make sb suddenly stop, doing sth（使）突然停住：*He stopped short when he heard his name.* 听见有人喊他的名字，他突然停住了。**stop short of sth/of doing sth** to be unwilling to do sth because it may involve a risk, but to nearly do it 差一点儿没做某事；险些做出某事：*She stopped short of calling the president a liar.* 她差一点儿没说总统是骗子。➲ MORE AT TRACK *n.*

PHR V **ˌstop 'by** (**sth**) to make a short visit somewhere 过去坐坐；顺路造访：*I'll stop by this evening for a chat.* 今晚我想过去聊聊。◇ *Could you stop by the store on the way home for some bread?* 回家时你能不能顺路进那家店里买点面包？ **ˌstop 'in** (*BrE, informal*) to stay at home rather than go out 待在家里（不外出） **ˌstop 'off** (**at/in...**) to make a short visit somewhere during a trip in order to do sth 中途停留（在某处）：*We stopped off at a hotel for*

S

the night. 我们中途停下来在一家旅馆住了一宿。**ˌstop ˈout** (*BrE, informal*) to stay out late at night 夜里很晚不回家 **ˌstop ˈover (at/in…)** to stay somewhere for a short time during a long journey （长途旅行在某处）中途停留：*I wanted to stop over in India on the way to Australia.* 在去澳大利亚的途中我想在印度稍作停留。➲ RELATED NOUN STOPOVER **ˌstop ˈup** (*BrE, informal*) to stay up late 熬夜；迟睡

■ ***noun***

• **ACT OF STOPPING** 停止；阻止 **1** 🔑 an act of stopping or stopping sth; the state of being stopped 停止；终止；停留；阻止：*The trip included an overnight stop in Brussels.* 这次旅行需要在布鲁塞尔停留过夜。◇ *She* ***brought*** *the car* ***to a stop.*** 她停住汽车。◇ *Work has temporarily* ***come to a stop*** *while the funding is reviewed.* 资金审查期间工作暂停。◇ *It is time to* ***put a stop to*** *the violence.* 现在是终止暴行的时候了。◇ *Babies do not grow at a steady rate but* ***in stops and starts.*** 婴儿成长的速度并非一成不变，而是长长停停，停停长长。➲ SEE ALSO NON-STOP, WHISTLE-STOP

• **OF BUS/TRAIN** 公共汽车；火车 **2** 🔑 a place where a bus or train stops regularly for passengers to get on or off 车站：*I get off at the next stop.* 我在下一站下车。◇ *Is this your stop?* 你在这一站下车吗？➲ SEE ALSO BUS STOP, PIT STOP, REQUEST STOP

• **PUNCTUATION** 标点符号 **3** (*BrE*) = FULL STOP

• **MUSIC** 音乐 **4** a row of pipes on an organ that produce the different sounds（管风琴的）音管 **5** a handle on an organ that the player pushes in or pulls out to control the sound produced by the pipes（管风琴的）音栓

• **PHONETICS** 语音学 **6** a speech sound made by stopping the flow of air coming out of the mouth and then suddenly releasing it, for example /p/, /k/, /t/ 塞音 **SYN** **plosive** ➲ SEE ALSO GLOTTAL STOP **IDM** SEE FULL STOP *n.*, PULL *v.*

stop·cock /ˈstɒpkɒk; *NAmE* ˈstɑːpkɑːk/ (*also* **cock**) *noun* a tap that controls the flow of liquid or gas through a pipe （调节管道流量的）旋塞，活栓

stop·gap /ˈstɒpɡæp; *NAmE* ˈstɑːp-/ *noun* something that you use or do for a short time while you are looking for sth better 权宜之计；临时替代的东西：*The arrangement was only intended as a stopgap.* 这种安排不过是权宜之计而已。◇ *a stopgap measure* 临时措施

ˌstop-ˈgo (*especially BrE*) (*especially NAmE* **ˌstop-and-ˈgo**) *adj.* [usually before noun] (*disapproving*) **1** starting and then stopping 走走停停的：*stop-go driving in heavy traffic* 在交通繁忙的道路上走走停停的行驶 **2** used to describe the policy of first restricting and then encouraging economic activity and growth（形容经济政策）先紧缩后刺激的：*the damaging stop-go economic cycle* 经济上紧缩后刺激、刺激后紧缩的破坏性的循环

ˈstop light *noun* [C] **1** (*BrE*) a red TRAFFIC LIGHT 停车灯；红灯 **2** (*also* **stop·lights** [pl.]) (*NAmE*) = TRAFFIC LIGHT **3** (*NAmE*) = BRAKE LIGHT

stop·over /ˈstɒpəʊvə(r); *NAmE* ˈstɑːpoʊ-/ (*NAmE also* **lay·over**) *noun* a short stay somewhere between two parts of a journey 中途停留：*We had a two-day stopover in Fiji on the way to Australia.* 我们去澳大利亚时中途在斐济停留了两天。➲ COLLOCATIONS AT TRAVEL

stop·page /ˈstɒpɪdʒ; *NAmE* ˈstɑːp-/ *noun* **1** [C] a situation in which people stop working as part of a protest or strike 停工；罢工 **2** [C] (*sport* 体育) an interruption in the game for a particular reason 中断比赛：*Play resumed quickly after the stoppage.* 比赛中断后不久又继续进行。◇ ***stoppage time*** (= added on at the end of the game if there have been stoppages) 比赛补时时间 **3** [C] a situation in which sth does not move forward or is blocked 堵塞；阻塞：*a stoppage of blood to the heart* 通往心脏血液的阻塞 **4 stoppages** [pl.] (*old-fashioned, BrE, formal*) an amount of money that an employer takes from people's wages for tax and other payments（工资中用于纳税等的）扣除款

stop·per /ˈstɒpə(r); *NAmE* ˈstɑːp-/ (*NAmE also* **plug**) *noun* an object that fits into the top of a bottle to close it 瓶塞 ➲ VISUAL VOCAB PAGE V72 ▶ **stop·per** *verb* ~ **sth**

ˈstopping train *noun* (*BrE*) a train that stops at a lot of stations between main stations（铁路的）慢车

ˌstop ˈpress *noun* [U] late news that is added to a newspaper after printing has begun（报纸开印后临时插入的）最新消息

ˈstop street *noun* (*SAfrE*) a place where one road joins or crosses another at which there is a sign indicating that vehicles must stop before continuing 停车待行路口

stop·watch /ˈstɒpwɒtʃ; *NAmE* ˈstɑːpwɑːtʃ/ *noun* a watch that you can stop and start by pressing buttons, in order to time a race, etc. accurately（赛跑等计时用的）秒表，跑表，码表

stor·age /ˈstɔːrɪdʒ/ *noun* [U] **1** the process of keeping sth in a particular place until it is needed; the space where things can be kept 贮存，贮藏（空间）：*tables that fold flat for storage* 便于存放的折叠桌 ◇ *There's a lot of storage space in the loft.* 阁楼上有很大的存储空间。◇ *food storage facilities* 食物贮存设施 ◇ *We need more storage now.* 现在我们需要更多的贮存场所。➲ SEE ALSO COLD STORAGE **2** (*computing* 计) the process of keeping information, etc. on a computer; the way it is kept 存储（方式）：*the storage and retrieval of information* 信息的存储与检索 ◇ *data storage* 数据存储 **3** the process of paying to keep furniture, etc. in a special building until you want it 付费托管：*When we moved we had to put our furniture* ***in storage*** *for a while.* 搬家时我们不得不把家具送出去存放一阵子。

ˈstorage battery (*NAmE*) (*BrE* **ac·cu·mu·la·tor**) *noun* a large battery that you can fill with electrical power (= that you can RECHARGE) 蓄电池

ˈstorage heater *noun* (*BrE*) an electric HEATER that stores heat when electricity is cheaper, for example at night 蓄热电暖器

store 🔑 /stɔː(r)/ *noun, verb*

■ ***noun*** **1** 🔑 [C] a large shop that sells many different types of goods（大型）百货商店：*a big department store* 大型百货商店 ➲ SEE ALSO CHAIN STORE, VARIETY STORE ➲ WORDFINDER NOTE AT SHOP

> **WORDFINDER** 联想词：appliances, cookware, fashion, furnishings, hardware, linen, lingerie, menswear, stationery

2 🔑 [C] (*NAmE*) a shop, large or small 商店；店铺：*a health food store* 保健食品商店 ◇ *a liquor store* 出售酒类的商店 ➲ COLLOCATIONS AT SHOPPING ➲ VISUAL VOCAB PAGE V3 ➲ SEE ALSO CONSIGNMENT SHOP, CONVENIENCE STORE, GENERAL STORE, PACKAGE STORE **3** [C] a quantity or supply of sth that you have and use 贮存物；备用物：*her secret store of chocolate* 她私下存放的巧克力 ◇ *a vast store of knowledge* 丰富的知识 **4** [pl.] **stores** goods of a particular kind or for a particular purpose（某类或作某用途的）商品，物品：*medical stores* 医疗用品 **5** [C] (*often* **stores**) a place where goods of a particular kind are kept 仓库；贮藏所：*a grain store* 粮仓 ◇ *weapons stores* 武器库

IDM **in store (for sb)** waiting to happen to sb 即将发生（在某人身上）；等待着（某人）：*We don't know what life* ***holds in store*** *for us.* 我们不知道等待我们的将是什么样的生活。◇ *If she had known what* ***lay in store*** *for her, she would never have agreed to go.* 要是她事先知道会有什么遭遇的话，她是决不会同意去的。◇ *They think it'll be easy but they have a* ***surprise in store.*** 他们以为事情容易，到时候他们会吃惊的。**set/put (great, etc.) ˈstore by sth** to consider sth to be important（十分）看重，重视（某事物）：*She sets great store by her appearance.* 她十分看重自己的外貌。◇ *It is unwise to put too much store by these statistics.* 过分重视这些统计数字是不明智的。➲ MORE AT HIT *v.*, MIND *v.*

■ ***verb*** **1** 🔑 ~ **sth (away/up)** to put sth somewhere and keep it there to use later 贮存；贮藏；保存：*animals storing up food for the winter* 贮存过冬食物的动物 ◇ *He hoped the electronic equipment was safely stored away.* 他希望那些电子设备得到妥善保存。**2** 🔑 ~ **sth** to keep information or facts in a computer or in your brain（在计算机里）存

储；记忆：*Thousands of pieces of data are stored in a computer's memory.* 在计算机的存储器中存有成千上万条数据。

PHR V ˌ**store sth↔ˈup** to not express strong feelings or deal with problems when you have them, especially when this causes problems later（把强烈的感情或问题）郁积，憋在心里：*She had stored up all her anger and eventually snapped.* 她所有的愤怒郁积在一起，终于爆发了。◇ *By ignoring your feelings you are only* ***storing up trouble*** *for yourself.* 你回避自己的感受，将来会有麻烦的。

ˈ**store-bought** (*NAmE*) (*BrE* ˈ**shop-bought**) *adj.* [only before noun] bought from a shop/store and not made at home 从商店买的（而非家里做的）：*store-bought cookies* 在商店里买的饼干

ˈ**store-brand** (*US*) (*BrE* ˌ**own-ˈbrand**, ˌ**own-ˈlabel**) *adj.* used to describe goods that are marked with the name of the shop/store in which they are sold rather than with the name of the company that produced them 自有品牌的（指产品以商店自定的品牌出售）

ˈ**store card** *noun* a card that a particular shop/store provides for regular customers so that they can use it to buy goods that they will pay for later（商店发给老顾客的）赊账卡 ➲ COMPARE CREDIT CARD ➲ **WORDFINDER NOTE** AT BUY

ˈ**store detective** *noun* a person employed by a large shop/store to watch customers and make sure they do not steal goods 商店专抓行窃者的雇员

store·front /ˈstɔːfrʌnt; *NAmE* ˈstɔːrf-/ *noun* (*NAmE*) **1** (*BrE* **shop·front**) the outside of a shop/store that faces the street 商店门面；店面 **2** a room at the front of a shop/store 店面；铺面；铺面房：*They run their business from a small storefront.* 他们在一间狭小的铺面房中做生意。◇ *a storefront office* 设在店面房中的办公室 **3** a place on the Internet where you can buy goods and services 网上店铺；虚拟店面：*Welcome to our* ***online storefront.*** 欢迎到我们的网上店铺。

store·house /ˈstɔːhaʊs; *NAmE* ˈstɔːrh-/ *noun* **1** a building where things are stored 仓库；货栈 **SYN** **warehouse** **2 ~ of information, knowledge, etc.** a place or thing that has or contains a lot of information（信息或知识等的）宝库

store·keep·er /ˈstɔːkiːpə(r); *NAmE* ˈstɔːrk-/ *noun* (*especially NAmE*) = SHOPKEEPER

store·room /ˈstɔːruːm; -rʊm/ *noun* a room used for storing things 贮藏室

ˈ**store window** (*NAmE*) (*BrE* ˌ**shop ˈwindow**) (*also* **window**) *noun* the glass at the front of a shop/store and the area behind it where goods are shown to the public 商店橱窗

storey (*especially BrE*) (*especially US* **story**) /ˈstɔːri/ *noun* (*pl.* **stor·eys**, *NAmE* **stor·ies**) **1** a level of a building; a floor 楼层：*the* ***upper/lower storey*** *of the house* 房子的上面 / 下面一层 ◇ *a* ***single-storey/two-storey*** *building* 单层建筑物；两层楼房 ➲ SEE ALSO MULTI-STOREY at MULTI-STOREY CAR PARK **2 -storeyed** (*BrE*) (*NAmE* **-storied**) (in adjectives 构成形容词) (of a building 楼房) having the number of levels mentioned 有…层的：*a four-storeyed building* 四层楼房

▼ **WHICH WORD?** 词语辨析

storey / floor

- You use **storey** *BrE*/ **story** *NAmE* mainly when you are talking about the number of levels a building has. * storey（英式英语）/ story（美式英语）主要用以指建筑物的楼层数目：*a five-storey house* 一栋五层楼的房屋 ◇ *The office building is five storeys high.* 办公大楼有五层楼高。
- **Floor** is used mainly to talk about which particular level in the building someone lives on, goes to, etc. * floor 主要指居住或前往等的某楼层：*His office is on the fifth floor.* 他的办公室在五楼。

➲ NOTE AT FLOOR

stor·ied /ˈstɔːrid/ *adj.* (*NAmE*) **1** [only before noun] mentioned in stories; famous; well known 广为流传的；有名的；众所周知的：*the rock star's storied career* 那位摇滚歌星尽人皆知的演唱生涯 **2 -storied** = -STOREYED

stork /stɔːk; *NAmE* stɔːrk/ *noun* a large black and white bird with a long beak and neck and long legs, that lives near water but often builds its nest on the top of a high building. There is a tradition that says that it is storks that bring people their new babies. 鹳

storm /stɔːm; *NAmE* stɔːrm/ *noun, verb*

■ ***noun*** **1** very bad weather with strong winds and rain, and often THUNDER and LIGHTNING 暴风雨：***fierce/heavy/violent storms*** 狂风暴雨 ◇ *A few minutes later* ***the storm broke*** (= began). 不一会儿暴风雨降临了。◇ *I think we're* ***in for a storm*** (= going to have one). 我觉得暴风雨要来了。◇ *storm damage* 暴风雨造成的损害 ➲ NOTE AT RAIN ➲ **COLLOCATIONS** AT WEATHER **2** (in compounds 构成复合词) very bad weather of the type mentioned 和风暴有关的恶劣天气：*a* ***thunderstorm/snowstorm/sandstorm*** 雷暴；暴风雪；沙暴 ➲ SEE ALSO ELECTRICAL STORM, RAINSTORM **3 ~ (of sth)** a situation in which a lot of people suddenly express very strong feelings about sth（群情迸发的）浪潮：*a storm of protest* 抗议的浪潮 ◇ *A political* ***storm is brewing*** *over the Prime Minister's comments.* 首相的评论即将酝酿出一场政治风暴。**4 ~ of sth** a sudden loud noise that is caused by emotion or excitement（因激动或兴奋而爆发出的）暴风雨般的声音，轰鸣 **SYN** **roar**：*a storm of applause* 如雷掌声 ➲ SEE ALSO BRAINSTORM

IDM **a storm in a ˈteacup** (*BrE*) (*NAmE* **a tempest in a ˈteapot**) a lot of anger or worry about sth that is not important 大惊小怪，小题大做，茶杯里的风暴（小事引起的大风波） **take sth/sb by ˈstorm 1** to be extremely successful very quickly in a particular place or among particular people 在某处大获成功；迅速征服观众等：*The play took London by storm.* 这部剧很快就风靡伦敦。**2** to attack a place suddenly and capture it 突袭攻占某处 ➲ MORE AT CALM *n.*, PORT *n.*

■ ***verb*** **1** [T, I] to suddenly attack a place 突袭；攻占：**~ sth** *Police stormed the building and captured the gunman.* 警察突袭那栋楼房，抓获了持枪歹徒。◇ **~ into sth** *Soldiers stormed into the city at dawn.* 士兵在拂晓时分攻进城里。**2** [I] **+ adv./prep.** to go somewhere quickly and in an angry, noisy way 气呼呼地疾走；闯；冲：*She stormed into my office waving a newspaper.* 她挥舞着一张报纸怒气冲冲地闯进我的办公室。◇ *He burst into tears and stormed off.* 他突然大哭起来，气呼呼地跑了。**3** [T] **+ speech** to say sth in a loud angry way 怒吼；大发雷霆：*'Don't you know who I am?' she stormed.* "你不知道我是谁吗？" 她怒喝道。

ˈ**storm cloud** *noun* [usually pl.] a dark cloud that you see when bad weather is coming 暴风云：(*figurative*) *The storm clouds of revolution were gathering.* 乌云滚滚，山雨欲来，革命即将爆发。

ˈ**storm door** *noun* an extra door that is fitted to the outside door of a house, etc. to give protection from bad weather（用来防风、挡雨、御寒的）外重门

storm·ing /ˈstɔːmɪŋ; *NAmE* ˈstɔːrm-/ *adj.* [only before noun] (*BrE*) (of a performance 表现) very impressive; done with a lot of energy 出色的；精力充沛的；劲头十足的：*Arsenal scored three late goals in a storming finish.* 阿森纳队后来以三个进球轰轰烈烈地完成了比赛。

ˈ**storm-tossed** *adj.* [only before noun] (*literary*) affected or damaged by storms 在暴风雨中飘摇的；遭暴风雨损坏的

ˈ**storm trooper** *noun* a soldier who is specially trained for violent attacks, especially one in Nazi Germany in the 1930s and 1940s（尤指纳粹德国的）冲锋队员；突击队员

ˈ**storm water** *noun* [U] water covering the ground in large quantities because of heavy rain 暴雨积水；涝水

ˈ**storm window** *noun* an extra window that is fitted to a window of a house to give protection from bad weather 风雨防护窗，防风窗（防恶劣天气的外重窗）

S

stormy /ˈstɔːmi; *NAmE* ˈstɔːrmi/ *adj.* (**storm·ier**, **stormi·est**) **1** with strong winds and heavy rain or snow 有暴风雨（或暴风雪）的：*a dark and stormy night* 黑暗的暴风雨之夜 ◇ *stormy weather* 狂风暴雨的天气 ◇ *stormy seas* (= with big waves) 波涛汹涌的大海 **2** full of strong feelings and angry arguments 群情激愤的；激烈争吵的：*a stormy debate* 唇枪舌剑的辩论 ◇ *a stormy relationship* 冲突不断的关系

story /ˈstɔːri/ *noun* (*pl.* **-ies**) **1** ~ (**about/of sth/sb**) a description of events and people that the writer or speaker has invented in order to entertain people（虚构的）故事；小说：***adventure/detective/love, etc. stories*** 历险、侦探、爱情等小说 ◇ *a story about time travel* 一部关于穿越时间旅行的小说 ◇ *Shall I **tell you a story**?* 我给你讲个故事好吗？◇ *He **read** the children **a story**.* 他给孩子们读了一则故事。◇ *a **bedtime story*** 临睡前给小孩讲的故事 ➲ COLLOCATIONS AT LITERATURE ➲ SEE ALSO FAIRY STORY at FAIRY TALE, GHOST STORY, SHORT STORY

> **WORDFINDER 联想词**： comic, far-fetched, gripping, historical, mannered, moving, rambling, readable, tragic

2 ~ (**about/of sth/sb**) an account, often spoken, of what happened to sb or of how sth happened（真实情况的）叙述，描述：*It was many years before **the full story** was made public.* 许多年之后，事情的全貌才公之于众。◇ *The police didn't believe her story.* 警方不相信她对事情的描述。◇ *We must stick to our story about the accident.* 对事故的说法我们必须一口咬定，再不改口。◇ *I can't decide until I've heard **both sides of the story**.* 双方的说法都听了以后我才能作决定。◇ *It's a story of courage.* 这件事真体现了勇气。◇ *Many years later I returned to Africa but **that's another story*** (= I am not going to talk about it now). 多年以后我又重返非洲，不过这是后话了。➲ SEE ALSO COCK AND BULL STORY, HARD-LUCK STORY, LIFE STORY, SHAGGY-DOG STORY, SOB STORY, SUCCESS STORY, TALL STORY ➲ SYNONYMS AT REPORT **3** an account of past events or of how sth has developed 对往事的叙述：*He told us the story of his life.* 他对我们讲述了他的生活经历。◇ *the story of the Beatles* 披头士乐队的故事 ◇ *the story of the building of the bridge* 这座桥的建筑始末 **4** a report in a newspaper, magazine or news broadcast 新闻报道：*a front-page story* 头版报道 ◇ *Now for a summary of tonight's main news stories.* 现在是今晚主要新闻综述。➲ SEE ALSO COVER STORY, LEAD STORY **5** (*also* **story·line**) the series of events in a book, film/movie, play, etc.（书籍、电影、戏剧等的）情节 SYN **plot**：*Her novels always have the same basic story.* 她的小说基本情节都一样。**6** (*informal*) something that sb says which is not true 谎言；假话：*She knew the child had been **telling stories** again.* 她知道这孩子又在说谎了。**7** (*NAmE*) = STOREY

IDM **the story goes (that)...** | **so the story goes** used to describe sth that people are saying although it may not be correct 据说；传闻；谣传：*She never saw him again—or so the story goes.* 从此她再没有见过他，或者据说如此。**that's the ˌstory of my ˈlife** (*informal*) when you say **that's the story of my life** about an unfortunate experience you have had, you mean you have had many similar experiences 我就是这个命（表示一生中有很多类似的不幸经历）➲ MORE AT LIKELY *adj.*, LONG *adj.*, OLD, PITCH *v.*, TELL

story·board /ˈstɔːribɔːd; *NAmE* -bɔːrd/ *noun* a series of drawings or pictures that show the outline of the story of a film/movie, etc.（电影等的）剧情梗概系列图片 ▶ **story·board** *verb* ~ **sth** **storyboarding** *noun* [U]: *the storyboarding process* 分镜头脚本设计

story·book /ˈstɔːribʊk/ *noun* a book of stories for children 儿童故事书；童话书：*a picture in a storybook* 故事书中的插图 ◇ *storybook characters* 童话中的人物 ◇ *storybook adventures* (= like the ones in stories for children) 故事书里种种神奇的历险

story·line /ˈstɔːrilaɪn/ *noun* the basic story in a novel, play, film/movie, etc.（小说、戏剧、电影等的）故事情节，本事 SYN **plot** ➲ WORDFINDER NOTE AT PLOT

story·tell·er /ˈstɔːritelə(r)/ *noun* a person who tells or writes stories 讲故事的人；故事（或小说）作者 ▶ **story·tell·ing** *noun* [U]

stoup /stuːp/ *noun* (*specialist*) a stone container for holy water in a church（教堂的）圣水钵

stout /staʊt/ *adj.*, *noun*

■ ***adj.*** (**stout·er**, **stout·est**) **1** (of a person 人) rather fat 肥胖的；肥壮的 SYN **plump** **2** [usually before noun] strong and thick 粗壮结实的；厚实牢固的：*a stout pair of shoes* 一双厚实耐穿的鞋 **3** [usually before noun] brave and determined 顽强的；坚毅的；不屈不挠的：*He put up a stout defence in court.* 他在法庭上进行了顽强的辩护。▶ **stout·ly** *adv.*: *He was tall and stoutly built.* 他长得五大三粗的。◇ *'I disagree,' said Polly stoutly.* "我不同意。"波利拒不妥协地说。**stout·ness** *noun* [U]

■ ***noun*** [U, C] strong dark beer made with MALT or BARLEY 烈性黑啤酒

ˌstout-ˈhearted *adj.* (*old-fashioned, literary*) brave and determined 勇敢坚毅的

stove /stəʊv; *NAmE* stoʊv/ *noun* **1** a piece of equipment that can burn various fuels and is used for heating rooms（用于取暖的）炉子，火炉：*a **gas/wood-burning stove*** 烧煤气／木柴的火炉 **2** (*especially NAmE*) (*BrE also* **cook·er**) (*NAmE also* **range**) a large piece of equipment for cooking food, containing an oven and gas or electric rings on top（带烤箱、燃气炉或电炉的）厨房灶具，炉具：*She put a pan of water on the stove.* 她在灶上放了一锅水。◇ (*NAmE, BrE*) *Most people don't want to spend hours **slaving over a hot stove*** (= cooking). 人们大都不愿意老围着灶台转。➲ SEE ALSO STAVE *v.*

stove·top /ˈstəʊvtɒp; *NAmE* ˈstoʊvtɑːp/ *noun* (*NAmE*) (*BrE* **hob**) the top part of a cooker where food is cooked in pans; a similar surface that is built into a kitchen unit and is separate from the oven 炉盘；炉头：*stovetop cooking* 使用炉盘烹饪

stow /stəʊ; *NAmE* stoʊ/ *verb* ~ **sth** (**away**) (**in sth**) to put sth in a safe place 妥善放置；把…收好：*She found a seat, stowed her backpack and sat down.* 她找到一个座位，把背包放好，坐了下来。

PHR V **ˌstow aˈway** to hide in a ship, plane, etc. in order to travel secretly 无票偷乘（船、飞机等）➲ RELATED NOUN STOWAWAY

stow·age /ˈstəʊɪdʒ; *NAmE* ˈstoʊ-/ *noun* [U] space provided for stowing things away, in a boat or a plane（船或飞机上）存放物品处

stow·away /ˈstəʊəweɪ; *NAmE* ˈstoʊ-/ *noun* a person who hides in a ship or plane before it leaves, in order to travel without paying or being seen 偷乘船（或飞机）者

St Pat·rick's Day /ˌsnt ˈpætrɪks deɪ; *NAmE* ˌseɪnt/ *noun* 17 March, a Christian festival of the national SAINT of Ireland, when many Irish people wear a SHAMROCK 圣帕特里克节（3 月 17 日，纪念爱尔兰的主保圣人圣帕特里克的基督教节日，很多爱尔兰人佩戴三叶草）

strad·dle /ˈstrædl/ *verb* **1** ~ **sth/sb** to sit or stand with one of your legs on either side of sb/sth 骑；跨坐；分腿站立：*He swung his leg over the motorcycle, straddling it easily.* 他一骗腿轻而易举地骑上摩托车。**2** ~ **sth** to cross, or exist on both sides of, a river, a road or an area of land 跨过，横跨（河流、道路或一片土地）：*The mountains straddle the French-Swiss border.* 这座山脉横跨法国和瑞士边界。**3** ~ **sth** to exist within, or include, different periods of time, activities or groups of people 横跨，同属（不同时期、活动或群体）；两栖于（不同活动）：*a writer who straddles two cultures* 横贯两种文化的作家

strafe /strɑːf; *NAmE* streɪf/ *verb* ~ **sth** to attack a place with bullets or bombs from an aircraft flying low 低空扫射（或轰炸）

strag·gle /ˈstræɡl/ *verb* **1** [I] (**+ adv./prep.**) to grow, spread or move in an untidy way in different directions 蔓生；杂乱地蔓延；散布：*The town straggled to an end and the fields began.* 城边上横七竖八的建筑不再蔓延，田野展现出来。**2** [I] (**+ adv./prep.**) to move slowly behind a group of people that you are with so that you become separated from them 落伍；掉队；落在后面：*On the way the kids straggled behind us.* 在路上，那几个孩子落在了我们后面。

strag·gler /ˈstræɡlə(r)/ *noun* [usually pl.] a person or an animal that is among the last or the slowest in a group to do sth, for example, to finish a race or leave a place 落伍者；掉队者；落在最后的人（或动物）

strag·gly /ˈstræɡli/ *adj.* growing or hanging in a way that does not look tidy or attractive 蔓生的；杂乱地蔓延的：*a thin woman with grey, straggly hair* 灰发蓬乱的瘦女人

straight /streɪt/ *adv., adj., noun*

■ *adv.* (**straight·er, straight·est**)

• **NOT IN CURVE** 不弯曲 **1** not in a curve or at an angle; in a straight line 笔直地；平正地；成直线：*Keep **straight on** for two miles.* 一直向前走两英里。◇ *Can you stretch your arms out straighter?* 你能把胳膊伸得再直一些吗？◇ *He was too tired to walk straight.* 他累得走都走不直了。◇ *I can't shoot straight* (= accurately). 我射不准。◇ *She looked me straight in the eye.* 她直视着我。

• **IMMEDIATELY** 立刻 **2** by a direct route; immediately 直接；径直；立即：*Come straight home after school.* 放学后直接回家来。◇ *I was so tired I went straight to bed.* 我太累，径直上床睡了。◇ *She went straight from college to a top job.* 她大学一毕业就干上了一份优越的工作。◇ *I'm going to the library **straight after** the class.* 我一下课就马上去图书馆。◇ *I'll come **straight to the point**—your work isn't good enough.* 我开门见山地说吧，你的工作做得不够好。

• **IN LEVEL/CORRECT POSITION** 处于平正 / 合适的位置 **3** in or into a level or vertical position; in or into the correct position 正；直；平正地：*Sit up straight!* 坐直了！◇ *She pulled her hat straight.* 她把帽子拉正了。

• **HONESTLY** 如实 **4** honestly and directly 坦率地；直截了当地：*I told him straight that I didn't like him.* 我坦率地告诉他说我不喜欢他。◇ *Are you **playing straight** with me?* 你没跟我耍花招吧？

• **WITHOUT INTERRUPTION** 不间断 **5** continuously without interruption 连续不断地；一连：*They had been working for 16 hours straight.* 他们已经一连工作了 16 个小时。

IDM **go ˈstraight** (*informal*) to stop being a criminal and live an honest life 改邪归正；重新做人 **play it ˈstraight** to be honest and not try to trick sb 诚实无欺；公平正直 **ˌstraight aˈway** immediately; without delay 立即；马上 SYN **at once**: *I'll do it straight away.* 这件事我马上就做。 **ˌstraight from the ˈshoulder** if you say sth **straight from the shoulder**, you are being very honest and direct, even if what you are saying is critical 坦诚；直言不讳 **ˌstraight ˈoff/ˈout** (*informal*) without hesitating 毫不犹豫；直率：*She asked him straight off what he thought about it all.* 她率直地问他对这一切有什么想法。 **ˌstraight ˈup** (*BrE, informal*) used to ask if what sb has said is true or to emphasize that what you have said is true（询问或强调所说的话的真实性）真的，确实：*I saw it—straight up!* 我亲眼看见了，真的！ MORE AT HIT *v.*, HORSE *n.*, THINK *v.*

■ *adj.* (**straight·er, straight·est**)

• **WITHOUT CURVES** 不弯曲 **1** without a bend or curve; going in one direction only 直的：*a straight line* 直线 ◇ *a straight road* 笔直的公路 ◇ *long straight hair* (= without curls) 又长又直的头发 ◇ *a boat sailing **in a straight line*** 直线航行的船 ◇ *straight-backed chairs* 直背椅

• **CLOTHING** 服装 **2** not fitting close to the body and not curving away from the body 直筒型（非紧身）的：*a straight skirt* 直筒裙

• **AIM/BLOW** 瞄准；打击 **3** going directly to the correct place 准的；正中目标的：*a straight punch to the face* 不偏不倚打在脸上的一拳

• **IN LEVEL/CORRECT POSITION** 处于平正 / 合适的位置 **4** positioned in the correct way; level, vertical or parallel to sth 平正的；正的；直的；与…平行的：*Is my tie straight?* 我的领带正不正？

• **CLEAN/NEAT** 整洁 **5** [not usually before noun] clean and neat, with everything in the correct place 整洁；整齐；井井有条：*It took hours to get the house straight.* 用了好半天才把房子收拾出来。

• **HONEST** 坦诚 **6** honest and direct 坦诚的；直率的：*a straight answer to a straight question* 问得直率，答得坦诚 ◇ *I don't think you're being straight with me.* 我觉得你没有跟我坦诚相见。◇ *It's time for some **straight talking**.* 现在该开诚布公地谈谈了。 SYNONYMS AT HONEST

• **CHOICE** 选择 **7** [only before noun] simple; involving only two clear choices 简单明了的；非此即彼的：*It was a **straight choice** between taking the job and staying out of work.* 要么接受这份工作，要么继续失业，此外别无其他选择。◇ (*BrE*) *The election was a **straight fight** between the two main parties.* 那次选举是两大党直接交锋。

• **ACTOR/PLAY** 演员；戏剧 **8** [only before noun] (of an actor or a play 演员或戏剧) not connected with comedy or musical theatre, but with serious theatre 严肃的，正统的（与喜剧、音乐剧无关）

• **WITHOUT INTERRUPTION** 不间断 **9** [only before noun] one after another in a series, without interruption 连续的；不间断的 SYN **consecutive**: *The team has had five straight wins.* 这支队已连赢五场比赛了。

• **ALCOHOLIC DRINK** 酒精饮料 **10** (*NAmE*) (*BrE* **neat**) not mixed with water or anything else 纯的；不掺水（或其他东西）的

• **NORMAL/BORING** 规矩；无趣 **11** (*informal*) you can use **straight** to describe a person who is normal and ordinary, but who you consider dull and boring 规矩老实的；本分无趣的；正统的

• **SEX** 性 **12** (*informal*) HETEROSEXUAL 异性恋的 OPP **gay**

▶ **straight·ness** *noun* [U]

IDM **get sth ˈstraight** to make a situation clear; to make sure that you or sb else understands the situation 明确某事；把某事弄清楚：*Let's get this straight—you really had no idea where he was?* 我们把这个明确一下，你当时真的不知道他在哪儿？ **put/set sb ˈstraight (about/on sth)** to correct sb's mistake; to make sure that sb knows the correct facts when they have had the wrong idea or impression 纠正某人；指出某人的错误；使某人了解真相 **(earn/get) straight ˈA's** (*especially NAmE*) (to get) the best marks/grades in all your classes（成绩）全优：*a straight A student* 全优生 **the ˌstraight and ˈnarrow** (*informal*) the honest and morally acceptable way of living 诚实正当的生活；正路：*His wife is trying to keep him on the straight and narrow.* 他妻子想方设法让他要诚实正派。 **a straight ˈface** if you keep a **straight face**, you do not laugh or smile, although you find sth funny 绷着的脸；忍着不笑的脸 SEE ALSO STRAIGHT-FACED MORE AT RAMROD, RECORD *n.*

■ *noun*

• **SEX** 性 **1** (*informal*) a person who has sexual relationships with people of the opposite sex, rather than the same sex 异性恋者：*gays and straights* 同性恋者和异性恋者

• **OF ROAD/TRACK** 公路；跑道 **2** (*NAmE also* **straight·away**) a straight part of a RACETRACK or road 直道部分；直道 SEE ALSO HOME STRAIGHT

ˌstraight-ˈarm (*also* **ˌstiff-ˈarm**) (*both NAmE*) (*BrE* **ˌhand sb↔ˈoff**) *verb* ~ **sb** (in sport 体育运动) to push away a player who is trying to stop you, with your arm straight 伸直手臂挡开（对手）

ˌstraight ˈarrow *noun* (*NAmE, informal*) a person who is very honest or who never does anything exciting or different 老实巴交的人；循规蹈矩的人

straight·away /ˌstreɪtəˈweɪ/ *adv., noun*

■ *adv.* STRAIGHT

■ *noun* (*NAmE*) = STRAIGHT (2)

ˈstraight edge *noun* a strip of wood, metal or plastic with a straight edge used for drawing accurate straight lines, or checking them（用以画或测定直线的）直尺，标尺，规板

straight·en /ˈstreɪtn/ *verb* **1** [T, I] to become straight; to make sth straight（使）变直，变正：**~ sth (out)** *I straightened my tie and walked in.* 我把领带拉正，走了进去。◇ **~ (out)** *The road bends here then straightens out.* 公路在这儿拐弯，然后就直了。**2** [T, I] to make your body straight and vertical 挺直，端正（身体）：**~ sth** *He stood up and straightened his shoulders.* 他站起身，挺起肩膀。◇ **~ sth/**

S

yourself up *I straightened myself up to answer the question.* 我直起身来回答问题。◇ ~ (up) *Straighten up slowly, then repeat the exercise ten times.* 慢慢挺直身体，然后把这个动作重复十次。

PHR V ˌ**straighten sb↔ˈout** to help sb to deal with problems or understand a confused situation 帮人解决问题；为人解除困惑 ˌ**straighten sth↔ˈout** to deal with a confused situation by organizing things that are causing problems 清理；整顿：*I need time to straighten out my finances.* 我需要时间整理一下我的财务。ˌ**straighten sth↔ˈup** to make sth neat and tidy 整理；收拾整齐

straight·en·er /ˈstreɪtnə(r)/ *noun* **1 straight·en·ers** [pl.] = HAIR STRAIGHTENERS **2** any substance that you can use to make your hair straight 直发用品：*chemical straighteners* 化学直发剂

ˌ**straight-ˈfaced** *adj.* without laughing or smiling, even though you may be amused 绷着脸的；忍住不笑的

straight·for·ward AW /ˌstreɪtˈfɔːwəd; *NAmE* -ˈfɔːrwərd/ *adj.* **1** easy to do or to understand; not complicated 简单的；易懂的；不复杂的 SYN **easy**：*a straightforward process* 简单的过程 ◇ *It's quite straightforward to get here.* 来这儿相当容易。**2** (of a person or their behaviour 人或行为) honest and open; not trying to trick sb or hide sth 坦诚的；坦率的；率直的 ▶ **straight·for·ward·ly** *adv.*：*Let me put it more straightforwardly.* 我来把它说得更直截了当一些。**straight·for·ward·ness** *noun* [U]

straight·jacket *noun* = STRAITJACKET

ˌ**straight-ˈlaced** *adj.* = STRAIT-LACED

ˈ**straight man** *noun* a person in a show whose role is to provide the main entertainer with opportunities to make jokes（表演中）捧哏的配角

ˌ**straight ˈticket** *noun* (in elections in the US) a vote in which sb chooses all the candidates from the same party 清一色选票（美国选举中支持同一政党全部候选人的选票）➲ COMPARE SPLIT TICKET ▶ ˌ**straight-ˈticket** *adj.*：*straight-ticket voting* 选同一政党全部候选人的投票

strain 🔑 /streɪn/ *noun, verb*

■ *noun*

• **WORRY/ANXIETY** 担忧；焦虑 **1** 🔑 [U, C] pressure on sb/sth because they have too much to do or manage, or sth very difficult to deal with; the problems, worry or anxiety that this produces 压力；重负；重压之下出现的问题（或担忧等）：*Their marriage is **under great strain** at the moment.* 眼下他们的婚姻关系非常紧张。◇ *These repayments are **putting a strain on** our finances.* 偿还这些债务对我们的财务状况形成了压力。◇ *Relax, and let us **take the strain*** (= do things for you). 你歇一下，我们来顶一会儿。◇ *The transport service cannot cope with the strain of so many additional passengers.* 运输部门无法应对增加这么多乘客所带来的紧张局面。◇ *You will learn to cope with the **stresses and strains** of public life.* 你要学会应付公众人物生活的紧张和辛劳。◇ *I found it a strain having to concentrate for so long.* 我觉得这么长时间全神贯注挺累的。➲ SYNONYMS AT PRESSURE

• **PHYSICAL PRESSURE** 物理压力 **2** 🔑 [U, C] the pressure that is put on sth when a physical force stretches, pushes, or pulls it 压力；拉力；张力；应力：*The rope broke **under the strain**.* 绳子给拉断了。◇ *You should try not to place too much strain on muscles and joints.* 你要尽量不让肌肉和关节太吃力。◇ *The ground here cannot **take the strain** of a large building.* 这块地承受不住大型建筑的压力。◇ *The cable has a 140kg **breaking strain*** (= it will break when it is stretched or pulled by a force greater than this). 这种缆索的断裂应变力为 140 千克。

• **INJURY** 损伤 **3** [C, U] an injury to a part of your body, such as a muscle, that is caused by using it too much or by twisting it 劳损；拉伤；扭伤：*a calf/groin/leg strain* 腿肚子 / 腹股沟 / 腿部拉伤 ◇ *muscle strain* 肌肉劳损

• **TYPE OF PLANT/ANIMAL/DISEASE** 动植物 / 疾病种类 **4** [C] a particular type of plant or animal, or of a disease caused by bacteria, etc.（动、植物的）系，品系，品种；（疾病的）类型：*a new strain of mosquitoes resistant to the poison* 对这种毒药有抗药性的新品种蚊子 ◇ *This is only one of the many strains of the disease.* 这种病有许多类型，这只是其中之一。

• **IN SB'S CHARACTER** 性格 **5** [C, usually sing.] a particular tendency in the character of a person or group, or a quality in their manner 个性特点；性格倾向；禀性 SYN **streak**：*He had a definite strain of snobbery in him.* 他这个人明显有一股势利小人的气味。

• **OF MUSIC** 音乐 **6** [C, usually pl.] (*formal*) the sound of music being played or sung 乐曲；曲调；旋律：*She could hear the strains of Mozart through the window.* 她听见从窗户飘出的莫扎特的旋律。

■ *verb*

• **INJURE** 损伤 **1** [T] ~ **sth/yourself** to injure yourself or part of your body by making it work too hard 损伤；拉伤；扭伤：*to strain a muscle* 拉伤肌肉 ➲ SYNONYMS AT INJURE ➲ COLLOCATIONS AT INJURY

• **MAKE EFFORT** 尽力 **2** [T, I] to make an effort to do sth, using all your mental or physical strength 尽力；竭力；使劲：~ **sth to do sth** *I **strained my ears*** (= listened very hard) *to catch what they were saying.* 我竖起耳朵去听他们在说些什么。◇ ~ **sth** *Necks were strained for a glimpse of the stranger.* 大家伸长了脖子想看一看这个陌生人。◇ ~ **to do sth** *People were straining to see what was going on.* 人们翘首企足看发生了什么事。◇ ~ (**sth**) (**for sth**) *He burst to the surface, straining for air.* 他冲出水面，使劲吸气。◇ *Bend gently to the left without straining.* 轻轻向左弯，不要用力。

• **STRETCH TO LIMIT** 使达到极限 **3** [T] ~ **sth** to try to make sth do more than it is able to do 过度使用；使不堪承受：*The sudden influx of visitors is straining hotels in the town to the limit.* 游客突然涌入，城里的旅馆全都爆满。◇ *His constant complaints were straining our patience.* 他没完没了的抱怨让我们忍无可忍。◇ *The dispute has strained relations between the two countries* (= made them difficult). 这场争端使两国关系紧张起来。

• **PUSH/PULL HARD** 用力推 / 拉 **4** [I] + **adv./prep.** to push hard against sth; to pull hard on sth 用力推（或拉）；拉紧：*She strained against the ropes that held her.* 她使劲挣了挣拴着她的绳子。◇ *The dogs were **straining at the leash**, eager to get to the park.* 几条狗用力拽着皮带，急于要去公园。

• **SEPARATE SOLID FROM LIQUID** 过滤 **5** [T] to pour food, etc. through sth with very small holes in it, for example a SIEVE, in order to separate the solid part from the liquid part 滤；过滤：~ **sth** *Use a colander to strain the vegetables.* 把蔬菜放在漏筐里控控水。◇ ~ **sth off** *Strain off any excess liquid.* 滤掉多余的液体。

IDM **strain at the ˈleash** (*informal*) to want to do sth very much 急于；迫不及待：*Like all youngsters, he's straining at the leash to leave home.* 跟所有年轻人一样，他也急于离开家生活。**strain every ˈnerve/ˈsinew (to do sth)** (*formal*) to try as hard as you can to do sth 竭尽全力（做某事）➲ MORE AT CREAK *v.*

strained /streɪnd/ *adj.* **1** showing the effects of worry or pressure 神色不宁的；紧张的；憔悴的 SYN **tense**：*Her face looked strained and weary.* 她的脸色显得憔悴疲惫。◇ *He spoke in a low, strained voice.* 他焦虑地低声说话。**2** (of a situation 状况) not relaxed or friendly 紧张的；不友好的 SYN **tense**：*There was a strained atmosphere throughout the meeting.* 会议自始至终气氛紧张。◇ *Relations between the two families are strained.* 两家关系紧张。**3** not natural; produced by a deliberate effort 不自然的；做作的；勉强的 SYN **forced**：*She gave a strained laugh.* 她不自然地大笑了一声。

strain·er /ˈstreɪnə(r)/ *noun* a kitchen UTENSIL (= a tool) with a lot of small holes in it, used for separating solids from liquids 滤器；滤盆；滤网：*a tea-strainer* 滤茶器

strait /streɪt/ *noun* **1** (*also* **straits**) [pl.] (especially in the names of places 尤用于地名) a narrow passage of water that connects two seas or large areas of water 海峡；（连结两大水域的）水道：*the Strait(s) of Gibraltar* 直布罗陀海峡 **2 straits** [pl.] a very difficult situation especially because of lack of money（尤指经济拮据引起的）困境，境况窘迫：*The factory is **in dire straits**.* 工厂岌岌可危。◇

S

She found herself in desperate financial straits. 她发觉自己经济状况极为窘迫。

strait·ened /ˈstreɪtnd/ *adj.* [only before noun] (*formal*) without enough money or as much money as there was before 经济拮据的；穷困的；经济状况恶化的：*The family of eight was living* ***in straitened circumstances.*** 这个八口之家日子过得很拮据。

strait·jacket (*also* **straight·jacket**) /ˈstreɪtdʒækɪt/ *noun* **1** a piece of clothing like a jacket with long arms which are tied to prevent the person wearing it from behaving violently. Straitjackets are sometimes used to control people who are mentally ill. 约束衣，紧身衣（有时用以束缚精神病患者） **2** (*disapproving*) a thing that stops sth from growing or developing 束缚；桎梏；约束：*the straitjacket of taxation* 纳税的束缚

strait-laced (*also* **straight-laced**) /ˌstreɪt ˈleɪst/ *adj.* (*disapproving*) having strict or old-fashioned ideas about people's moral behaviour（在道德行为上）拘谨保守的，古板的

strand /strænd/ *noun, verb*

■ ***noun*** **1** a single thin piece of thread, wire, hair, etc.（线、绳、金属线、毛发等的）股，缕：*a strand of wool* 一股羊毛 ◇ *a few strands of dark hair* 几绺黑发 ◇ *She wore a single strand of pearls around her neck.* 她脖子上戴着单串珍珠。 **2** one of the different parts of an idea, a plan, a story, etc.（观点、计划、故事等的）部分，方面：*We heard every strand of political opinion.* 各派的政治观点我们都听到了。◇ *The author draws the different strands of the plot together in the final chapter.* 作者在最后一章把不同的情节线索归拢到了一起。 **3** (*literary* or *IrishE*) the land along the edge of the sea or ocean, or of a lake or river（海洋、湖或河的）岸，滨

■ ***verb*** [usually passive] **1 ~ sb** to leave sb in a place from which they have no way of leaving 使滞留：*The strike left hundreds of tourists stranded at the airport.* 这场罢工使成百上千的游客滞留在机场。 **2 ~ sth** to make a boat, fish, WHALE, etc. be left on land and unable to return to the water 使搁浅：*The ship was stranded on a sandbank.* 船在沙洲上搁浅了。

strange 🔑 /streɪndʒ/ *adj.* (**stran·ger, stran·gest**) **1** 🔑 unusual or surprising, especially in a way that is difficult to understand 奇怪的；奇特的；异常的：*A strange thing happened this morning.* 今天上午发生了一件怪事。◇ *She was looking at me in a very strange way.* 她用十分异样的目光看着我。◇ **~ (that)**… *It's strange (that) we haven't heard from him.* 奇怪，我们一直没有他的消息。◇ **~ (how…)** *It's strange how childhood impressions linger.* 童年的印象经久不忘，真是不可思议。◇ ***That's strange***—*the front door's open.* 怪事，正门开着。◇ *I'm looking forward to the exam,* ***strange as it may seem.*** 别人可能感到奇怪，我在盼望这场考试。◇ *There was* ***something strange*** *about her eyes.* 她的眼睛有些异常。◇ ***Strange to say,*** *I don't really enjoy television.* 说来奇怪，我不大喜欢看电视。 **2** 🔑 not familiar because you have not been there before or met the person before 陌生的；不熟悉的：*a strange city* 陌生的城市 ◇ *to wake up in a strange bed* 在陌生的床上醒来 ◇ *Never accept lifts from strange men.* 千万别搭陌生男人的车。◇ **~ to sb** *At first the place was strange to me.* 起先我对这个地方不熟悉。▶ **strange·ness** *noun* [U]

IDM **feel 'strange** 🔑 to not feel comfortable in a situation; to have an unpleasant physical feeling 感觉不自在；感觉不舒服：*She felt strange sitting at her father's desk.* 坐在父亲的书桌前，她感觉不自在。◇ *It was terribly hot and I started to feel strange.* 酷热难当，我逐渐感到不舒服。➲ MORE AT TRUTH

strange·ly 🔑 /ˈstreɪndʒli/ *adv.* in an unusual or surprising way 异常地；奇怪地；不可思议地：*She's been acting very strangely lately.* 近来她举止十分反常。◇ *The house was strangely quiet.* 房子里静得出奇。◇ *strangely shaped rocks* 奇形怪状的岩石 ◇ ***Strangely enough,*** *I don't feel at all nervous.* 真奇怪，我一点也不紧张。

stran·ger 🔑 /ˈstreɪndʒə(r)/ *noun* **1** 🔑 a person that you do not know 陌生人：*There was a* ***complete stranger*** *sitting at my desk.* 我书桌前坐着一个从未见过的陌生人。◇ *They got on well together although they were* ***total strangers.*** 尽管以前素未谋面，但他们相处融洽。◇ *We've told our daughter not to speak to strangers.* 我们告诉女儿不要和陌生人讲话。◇ **~ to sb** *She remained a stranger to me.* 我一直未能了解她。 **2** 🔑 a person who is in a place that they have not been in before 外地人；新来者：*Sorry, I don't know where the bank is. I'm a stranger here myself.* 对不起，我不知道银行在哪儿。我不是本地人。◇ **~ to…** *He must have been a stranger to the town.* 他当时一定是刚到这个镇子。

IDM **be no/a 'stranger to sth** (*formal*) to be familiar/not familiar with sth because you have/have not experienced it many times before 熟悉（或不熟悉）某事；习惯（或不习惯）某事：*He is no stranger to controversy.* 他对争论见得多了。

stran·gle /ˈstræŋɡl/ *verb* **1 ~ sb** to kill sb by squeezing or pressing on their throat and neck 扼死；勒死；掐死：*to strangle sb to death* 把某人掐死 ◇ *He strangled her with her own scarf.* 他用她自己的围巾把她勒死了。 **2 ~ sth** to prevent sth from growing or developing 抑制；压制；扼杀：*The current monetary policy is strangling the economy.* 现行货币政策抑制了经济的发展。

stran·gled /ˈstræŋɡld/ *adj.* (of a cry, sb's voice, etc. 哭声、说话声等) not clear because it stops before it has completely finished 哽塞的；哽咽的；顿住的：*There was a strangled cry from the other room.* 隔壁传来一声哽咽。

strangle·hold /ˈstræŋɡlhəʊld; *NAmE* -hoʊld/ *noun* [sing.] **1** a strong hold around sb's neck that makes it difficult for them to breathe 掐脖子；卡脖子 **2 ~ (on sth)** complete control over sth that makes it impossible for it to grow or develop well 压制；束缚：*The company now had a stranglehold on the market.* 这家公司现在垄断了市场。

stran·gler /ˈstræŋɡlə(r)/ *noun* a person who kills sb by squeezing their throat tightly 扼（或勒、掐）死人者

stran·gu·lated /ˈstræŋɡjuleɪtɪd/ *adj.* **1** (*medical* 医) (of a part of the body 身体一部分) squeezed so tightly that blood etc. cannot pass through it 绞窄性的 **2** (*formal*) (of a voice 声音) sounding as though the throat is tightly squeezed, usually because of fear or worry 嗓子被扼住似的，哽塞的（通常由于恐惧或担忧）：*He gave a strangulated squawk.* 他像嗓子被勒住似的嘎叫了一声。

stran·gu·la·tion /ˌstræŋɡjuˈleɪʃn/ *noun* [U] **1** the act of killing sb by squeezing their throat tightly; the state of being killed in this way 扼死；勒死；掐死：*to die of slow strangulation* 被缓慢勒死 **2** (*disapproving*) the act of preventing sth from growing or developing 抑制；压制；扼杀：*the strangulation of the human spirit* 对人的精神压制

strap /stræp/ *noun, verb*

■ ***noun*** a strip of leather, cloth or other material that is used to fasten sth, keep sth in place, carry sth or hold onto sth 带子：*the shoulder straps of her dress* 她连衣裙上的肩带 ◇ *a watch with a leather strap* 皮表带的手表 ➲ VISUAL VOCAB PAGES V55, V69

■ ***verb*** (**-pp-**) **1 ~ sth + adv./prep.** to fasten sb/sth in place using a strap or straps 用带子系（或捆、扎、扣）好：*He strapped the knife to his leg.* 他把刀绑到腿上。◇ *Everything had to be strapped down to stop it from sliding around.* 所有东西必须绑定，免得来回滑动。◇ *Are you strapped in (= wearing a seat belt in a car, plane, etc.)?* 您系好安全带了吗？ **2 ~ sth (up)** to wrap strips of material around a wound or an injured part of the body 包扎；给…打绷带 SYN **bandage**：*I have to keep my leg strapped up for six weeks.* 我的腿必须打六星期绷带。

strap·less /ˈstræpləs/ *adj.* (especially of a dress or BRA 尤指连衣裙或胸罩) without straps 无肩带的；无吊带的

strapped /stræpt/ *adj.* **~ (for cash, funds, etc.)** (*informal*) having little or not enough money 缺钱的；手头紧的

strap·ping /ˈstræpɪŋ/ *adj.* [only before noun] (*informal*) (of people 人) big, tall and strong 魁梧的；高大健壮的：*a strapping lad* 身材魁梧的小伙子

S

strappy /ˈstræpi/ *adj.* (**strap·pier**, **strap·pi·est**) (*informal*) (of shoes or clothes 鞋或衣服) having straps 有带子的：*white strappy sandals* 白色条带凉鞋

strata PL. OF STRATUM

strata·gem /ˈstrætədʒəm/ *noun* (*formal*) a trick or plan that you use to gain an advantage or to trick an opponent（为取胜或迷惑对手的）计策，计谋

stra·tegic AW /strəˈtiːdʒɪk/ (*also less frequent* **stra·tegic·al** /-dʒɪkl/) *adj.* [usually before noun] **1** done as part of a plan that is meant to achieve a particular purpose or to gain an advantage 根据全局而安排的；战略性的：*strategic planning* 全局性规划 ◇ *a strategic decision to sell off part of the business* 卖掉企业一部分的战略决策 ◇ *Cameras were set up at strategic points* (= in places where they would be most effective) *along the route.* 在沿途一些最佳位置架设了摄像机。**2** connected with getting an advantage in a war or other military situation 战略性的；战略上的：*Malta was of vital strategic importance during the war.* 在那次战争中，马耳他的战略意义至为关键。**3** (of weapons, especially nuclear weapons 武器，尤指核武器) intended to be fired at an enemy's country rather than used in a battle 战略性的 ➲ COMPARE TACTICAL (3) ▸ **stra·tegic·al·ly** AW /-kli/ *adv.*: *a strategically placed microphone* 安放在最佳位置的麦克风 ◇ *a strategically important target* 有重大战略意义的目标

strat·egist AW /ˈstrætədʒɪst/ *noun* a person who is skilled at planning things, especially military activities 战略家；善于筹划部署的人

strat·egy 🔑 AW /ˈstrætədʒi/ *noun* (*pl.* **-ies**) **1** 🔑 [C] a plan that is intended to achieve a particular purpose 策略；计策；行动计划：*the government's economic strategy* 政府的经济策略 ◇ **~ for doing sth** *to develop a strategy for dealing with unemployment* 制订解决失业问题的对策 ◇ **~ to do sth** *It's all part of an overall strategy to gain promotion.* 这都不过是一个向上爬的完整计划的一部分。**2** 🔑 [U] the process of planning sth or putting a plan into operation in a skilful way 策划；规划；部署；统筹安排：*marketing strategy* 营销策划 **3** 🔑 [U, C] the skill of planning the movements of armies in a battle or war; an example of doing this 战略；战略部署：*military strategy* 军事战略 ◇ *defence strategies* 防御部署 ➲ **COLLOCATIONS** AT WAR ➲ COMPARE TACTIC

S

strati·fi·ca·tion /ˌstrætɪfɪˈkeɪʃn/ *noun* [U] (*specialist*) the division of sth into different layers or groups 分层；成层：*social stratification* 社会阶层化

strat·ify /ˈstrætɪfaɪ/ *verb* (**strati·fies**, **strati·fy·ing**, **strati·fied**, **strati·fied**) [usually passive] **~ sth** (*formal* or *specialist*) to arrange sth in layers or STRATA（使）分层，成层：*a highly stratified society* 高度分化的社会 ◇ *stratified rock* 成层岩

strato·sphere /ˈstrætəsfɪə(r); *NAmE* -sfɪr/ *noun* **the stratosphere** [sing.] the layer of the earth's atmosphere between about 10 and 50 kilometres above the surface of the earth 平流层 ➲ COMPARE IONOSPHERE ▸ **strato·spher·ic** /ˌstrætəˈsferɪk; *NAmE also* -ˈsfɪr-/ *adj.*: *stratospheric clouds* 平流层云

IDM **in/into the ˈstratosphere** (*informal*) at or to an extremely high level 在（或到）极高水平：*The technology boom sent share prices into the stratosphere.* 科技热潮使得股价飙升到极高的水平。

stra·tum /ˈstrɑːtəm; *NAmE* ˈstreɪtəm/ *noun* (*pl.* **strata** /ˈstrɑːtə; *NAmE* ˈstreɪtə/) **1** (*geology* 地) a layer or set of layers of rock, earth, etc. 层；岩层；地层 **2** (*formal*) a class in a society 阶层：*people from all social strata* 来自不同社会阶层的人 ➲ **MORE LIKE THIS** 30, page R28

stra·tus /ˈstreɪtəs; ˈstrɑːtəs/ *noun* [U] (*specialist*) a type of cloud that forms a continuous grey sheet covering the sky 层云

stra·vaig (*also* **stra·vage**) /strəˈveɪɡ/ *verb* [I] (**+ adv./prep.**) (*IrishE, ScotE*) to walk around without an aim 游荡；徘徊；漫步

straw /strɔː/ *noun* **1** [U] STEMS of WHEAT or other grain plants that have been cut and dried. Straw is used for making MATS, hats, etc., for packing things to protect them, and as food for animals or for them to sleep on.（收割后干燥的）禾秆，麦秆，稻草：*a mattress filled with straw* 稻草填充的垫子 ◇ *a straw hat* 草帽 ➲ COMPARE HAY (1) **2** [C] a single STEM or piece of straw 一根禾秆（或麦秆、稻草）：*He was leaning over the gate chewing on a straw.* 他嘴里嚼着一根麦秆，靠到栅门上。**3** (*also* ˈ**drinking straw**) a thin tube of plastic or paper that you suck a drink through（喝饮料用的）吸管 ➲ VISUAL VOCAB PAGE V36

IDM **clutch/grasp at ˈstraws** to try all possible means to find a solution or some hope in a difficult or unpleasant situation, even though this seems very unlikely（在危难中）抓救命稻草，不放过任何微小的机会 **the last/final ˈstraw | the ˌstraw that breaks the camel's ˈback** the last in a series of bad events, etc. that makes it impossible for you to accept a situation any longer 压垮骆驼的最后一根稻草；终于使人不堪忍受的最后一件事（或因素等）**a straw in the ˈwind** (*BrE*) a small sign of what might happen in the future（预示发生某事的）迹象，苗头，征兆 ➲ MORE AT BRICK *n.*, DRAW *v.*

straw·berry /ˈstrɔːbəri; *NAmE* -beri/ *noun* (*pl.* **-ies**) a soft red fruit with very small yellow seeds on the surface, that grows on a low plant 草莓：*strawberries and cream* 草莓奶油 ◇ *strawberry plants* 草莓植株 ➲ VISUAL VOCAB PAGE V33

ˌ**strawberry ˈblonde** (*also* ˌ**strawberry ˈblond**) *adj.* (of hair 头发) a light reddish-yellow colour 草莓红色的；浅红黄色的

ˌ**straw ˈpoll** (*NAmE also* ˌ**straw ˈvote**) *noun* an occasion when a number of people are asked in an informal way to give their opinion about sth or to say how they are likely to vote in an election（选举前的）非正式民意测验

stray /streɪ/ *verb, adj., noun*

▪ *verb* **1** [I] (**+ adv./prep.**) to move away from the place where you should be, without intending to 迷路；偏离；走失：*He strayed into the path of an oncoming car.* 他偏到了一辆迎面驶来的汽车的行车路线上。◇ *Her eyes kept straying over to the clock on the wall.* 她的目光不时瞟向墙上的钟。**2** [I] (**+ adv./prep.**) to begin to think about or discuss a different subject from the one you should be thinking about or discussing 偏离正题；走神；离题：*My mind kept straying back to our last talk together.* 我老走神，一再回想起我们上次在一起交谈的情景。◇ *We seem to be straying from the main theme of the debate.* 我们似乎是偏离了辩论的主题。**3** [I] (of a person who is married or in a relationship 已婚或有固定关系者) to have a sexual relationship with sb who is not your usual partner 有外遇；拈花惹草

▪ *adj.* [only before noun] **1** (of animals normally kept as pets 常指宠物) away from home and lost; having no home 走失的；无主的：*stray dogs* 走失的狗 **2** separated from other things or people of the same kind 零星的；孤立的；离群的；走散的：*A civilian was killed by a stray bullet.* 一个平民被流弹打死。◇ *a few stray hairs* 几根散乱的头发

▪ *noun* **1** an animal that has got lost or separated from its owner or that has no owner 走失的宠物（或家畜）；无主的宠物（或家畜）➲ SEE ALSO WAIF **2** a person or thing that is not in the right place or is separated from others of the same kind 离群者；走散者；不在原位置的东西

streak /striːk/ *noun, verb*

▪ *noun* **1** a long thin mark or line that is a different colour from the surface it is on 条纹；条痕：*streaks of grey in her hair* 她头上的缕缕白发 ◇ *dirty streaks on the window* 窗户上的道道污痕 ➲ **SYNONYMS** AT MARK ➲ **WORDFINDER NOTE** AT PATTERN **2** a part of a person's character, especially an unpleasant part（尤指不好的）性格特征：*a ruthless/vicious/mean streak* 冷酷 / 邪恶 / 卑鄙的性格 ◇ *a streak of cruelty* 几分残忍 **3** a series of successes or failures, especially in a sport or in gambling（尤指体育比赛或赌博中）顺（或背）的时候，运气，手气：*a streak of good luck* 运气好 ◇ *to hit* (= have) *a* ***winning streak*** 碰上顺的时候 ◇ *to be on a* ***winning/losing streak*** 赶上顺的 / 背的时候 ◇ ***a lucky/an unlucky streak*** 运气好；运气不好 ➲ WORDFINDER NOTE AT GAMBLING

■ ***verb*** **1** [T] to mark or cover sth with streaks 在…上画条纹（或留下条痕）；使布满条纹（或条痕）：**~ sth** *Tears streaked her face.* 她脸上是道道泪痕。◇ *She's had her hair streaked* (= had special chemicals put on her hair so that it has attractive coloured lines in it). 她把头发做了挑染。◇ **~ sth with sth** *His face was streaked with mud.* 他脸上满是一条条的污泥。**2** [I] **+ adv./prep.** to move very fast in a particular direction 飞奔；疾驰 SYN **speed**: *A car pulled out and streaked off down the road.* 一辆汽车驶出后沿着公路疾驰而去。**3** [I] (**+ adv./prep.**) (*informal*) to run through a public place with no clothes on as a way of getting attention 裸奔

streak·er /ˈstriːkə(r)/ *noun* a person who runs through a public place with no clothes on as a way of getting attention 裸奔者

streaky /ˈstriːki/ *adj.* marked with lines of a different colour 有条纹（或条痕）的：*streaky blonde hair* 挑染的金发 ◇ *The wallpaper was streaky with grease.* 壁纸上道道油渍。◇ (*BrE*) *streaky bacon* (= with layers of fat in it) 五花咸肉

stream 🔑 /striːm/ *noun, verb*

■ ***noun*** **1** 🔑 a small narrow river 小河；溪：*mountain streams* 山涧 ➲ VISUAL VOCAB PAGE V3 ➲ SEE ALSO DOWNSTREAM, UPSTREAM, GULF STREAM **2** 🔑 **~ (of sth)** a continuous flow of liquid or gas 流；（液）流；（气）流：*A stream of blood flowed from the wound.* 一股鲜血从伤口流出来。➲ SEE ALSO BLOODSTREAM **3** 🔑 **~ (of sth/sb)** a continuous flow of people or vehicles（人）流；（车）流：*I've had a* ***steady stream*** *of visitors.* 我不断有客人。◇ *Cars filed past in an endless stream.* 汽车川流不息，鱼贯而过。**4** 🔑 **~ of sth** a large number of things that happen one after the other 一连串，接二连三，源源不断（的事情）：*a* ***constant stream of*** *enquiries* 接连不断的询问 ◇ *The agency provided me with a* ***steady stream*** *of work.* 这介绍所让我不断有活干。**5** (*especially BrE*) a group of students of the same age and level of ability in some schools（将同龄学生按能力编在一起的）班，组：*She was put into the fast stream.* 她被分在快班。

IDM **be/come on ˈstream** to be in operation or available 投产；投入使用：*The new computer system comes on stream next month.* 新的计算机系统下月投入使用。

■ ***verb*** **1** [I, T] (of liquid or gas 液体或气体) to move or pour out in a continuous flow; to produce a continuous flow of liquid or gas 流；流动；流出：(**+ adv./prep.**) *Tears streamed down his face.* 泪水顺着他的脸往下流。◇ *a streaming cold* (= with a lot of liquid coming from the nose) 流鼻涕的感冒 ◇ **~ with sth** *Her head was streaming with blood.* 她头上流着血。◇ **~ from sth** *Blood was streaming from her head.* 血从她头上流出来。◇ *Black smoke streamed from the exhaust.* 黑烟从排气管里冒出来。◇ **~ sth** *The exhaust streamed black smoke.* 排气管里冒出黑烟。**2** (of people or things 人或东西) [I] **+ adv./prep.** to move somewhere in large numbers, one after the other 鱼贯而行；一个接一个地移动：*People streamed across the bridge.* 桥上行人川流不息。**3** [I] to move freely, especially in the wind or water 飘动；飘扬：*Her scarf streamed behind her.* 她的围巾在身后飘动。**4** (*especially BrE*) (*NAmE usually* **track**) [T, usually passive] **~ sb** (in schools 学校) to put school students into groups according to their ability 按能力分班（或分组）：*Pupils are streamed for French and Maths.* 学生上法语课和数学课时按能力分成小组。**5** [T] **~ sth** (*computing* 计) to play video or sound on a computer by receiving it as a continuous stream, from the Internet for example, rather than needing to wait until the whole of the material has been DOWNLOADED 用流式传输，流播（无须待整个文件下载到计算机便可播放互联网上的视频或音频文件）

stream·er /ˈstriːmə(r)/ *noun* **1** a long narrow piece of coloured paper, used to decorate a place for a party or other celebration 装饰彩纸条 **2** a long narrow piece of cloth or other material 条幅；横幅

stream·ing /ˈstriːmɪŋ/ *noun* [U] **1** (*also* **band·ing**) (*both BrE*) the policy of dividing school students into groups of the same level of ability（把学生按能力）分班，分组：*Streaming within comprehensive schools is common practice.* 综合中学常把学生按能力分班。**2** a method of sending or receiving data, especially video, over a computer network（经计算机网络对视频等的）流式传输，串流播放

stream·line /ˈstriːmlaɪn/ *verb* [usually passive] **1 ~ sth** to give sth a smooth even shape so that it can move quickly and easily through air or water 使成流线型：*The cars all have a new streamlined design.* 这些汽车都是流线型新款。**2 ~ sth** to make a system, an organization, etc. work better, especially in a way that saves money 使（系统、机构等）效率更高；（尤指）使增产节约：*The production process is to be streamlined.* 生产流程还需改进。

ˌstream of ˈconsciousness *noun* [U] a continuous flow of ideas, thoughts, and feelings, as they are experienced by a person; a style of writing that expresses this without using the usual methods of description and conversation 意识流；意识流创作手法

street 🔑 /striːt/ *noun, adj.*

■ ***noun*** **1** 🔑 [C] (*abbr.* **St**, **st**) a public road in a city or town that has houses and buildings on one side or both sides 大街；街道：*The bank is just across the street.* 银行就在街对过。◇ *to walk* ***along/down/up the street*** 沿着街道走 ◇ *the town's narrow cobbled streets* 镇上狭窄的卵石街道 ◇ *92nd Street* 第 92 大街 ◇ *10 Downing Street* 唐宁街 10 号 ◇ *He is used to being recognized* ***in the street.*** 街上常有人认出他来，他习以为常了。◇ *a* ***street map/plan*** *of York* 约克街道地图 / 平面图 ◇ ***street theatre/musicians*** 街头戏剧 / 乐手 ◇ *My office is at* ***street level*** (= on the ground floor). 我的办公室在一楼。◇ *It's not safe to* ***walk the streets*** *at night.* 夜间在街上走不安全。➲ NOTE AT ROAD ➲ SEE ALSO BACKSTREET *n.*, HIGH STREET, SIDE STREET **2** [sing.] the ideas and opinions of ordinary people, especially people who live in cities, which are considered important（尤指城市里）街头民意：*The feeling I get from the street is that we have a good chance of winning this election.* 我从街头民意调查感觉到我们很有机会赢得这场选举。◇ *The* ***word on the street*** *is that it's not going to happen.* 民众普遍认为此事不会发生。

IDM (**out**) **on the ˈstreets/ˈstreet** (*informal*) without a home; outside, not in a house or other building 无家可归；流落街头；在外面大街上：*the problems of young people living on the streets* 年轻人流落街头的种种问题 ◇ *If it had been left to me I would have put him out on the street long ago.* 换了我，早就把他赶出家门了。**on/walking the ˈstreets** working as a PROSTITUTE 做妓女；靠卖淫为生 **ˈstreets ahead** (**of sb/sth**) (*BrE, informal*) much better or more advanced than sb/sth else（比某人或事物）好得多，先进得多：*a country that is streets ahead in the control of environmental pollution* 一个在整治环境污染方面远远走在前面的国家 **the streets are ˌpaved with ˈgold** (*saying*) used to say that it seems easy to make money in a place（表示在某地挣钱容易）遍地都是黄金 (**right**) **up your ˈstreet** (*especially BrE*) (*NAmE usually* (**right**) **up your ˈalley**) (*informal*) very suitable for you because it is sth that you know a lot about or are very interested in（正）适合你；（正）和你对口：*This job seems right up your street.* 这工作看来对你正合适。➲ MORE AT EASY *adj.*, HIT *v.*, MAN *n.*

■ ***adj.*** [only before noun] informal and based on the daily life of ordinary people in cities 街头的：*street sports such as skateboarding and skating* 街头运动，如滑板和溜冰 ◇ *street newspapers sold by the homeless* 无家可归者卖的街头报纸 ◇ *street culture/dance/law* 街头文化；街舞；法律普及

street·board /ˈstriːtbɔːd; *NAmE* -bɔːrd/ (*also* **Snake·board™**) *noun* two small boards joined with a short pole and with wheels on, which you stand on and ride as a sport 活

S

力板（用短横杆连接两块脚踏板构成，下有轮子）▸ **street·board·ing** (*also* **snake·board·ing**) *noun* [U]

street·car /ˈstriːtkɑː(r)/ (*also* **trol·ley**) (*both US*) (*BrE* **tram**, **tram·car**) *noun* a vehicle driven by electricity, that runs on rails along the streets of a town and carries passengers 有轨电车 ➲ VISUAL VOCAB PAGE V63

ˈstreet cred (*also* **cred**) (*informal*) (*also less frequent* **ˈstreet credibility**) *noun* [U] a way of behaving and dressing that is acceptable to young people, especially those who live in cities and have experienced the problems of real life 街头信誉，街头形象（青年人推崇的行为方式和着装风格，尤指城市青年）：*Those clothes do nothing for your street cred.* 穿那些衣服你可一点也不时髦。

ˌstreet ˈfurniture *noun* [U] (*specialist*) equipment such as road signs, street lights, etc. placed at the side of a road 街道设施（如路标、路灯等）

ˈstreet light (*also* **ˈstreet lamp**) *noun* a light at the top of a tall post in the street 路灯；街灯 ➲ COMPARE LAMP POST ➲ VISUAL VOCAB PAGE V3

ˈstreet people *noun* (*especially NAmE*) people who have no home and who live outside in a town（城市）无家可归者 **SYN** **homeless**

ˈstreet-smart *adj.* (*NAmE*) = STREETWISE ➲ COMPARE BOOK-SMART

ˈstreet smarts *noun* [pl.] (*NAmE, informal*) the knowledge and experience that is needed to deal with the difficulties and dangers of life in a big city 都市生活诀窍，都市人的精明，街头智慧（应对大都市生活的困难和危险所需的知识和经验）

ˌstreet ˈtheatre (*BrE*) (*NAmE* **ˌstreet ˈtheater**) *noun* [U] plays or other performances that are done in the street 街头戏剧；街头演出

ˈstreet value *noun* [usually sing.] a price for which sth that is illegal or has been obtained illegally can be sold（非法物品的）黑市价值：*drugs with a street value of over £1 million* 黑市价值超过 100 万英镑的毒品

street·walk·er /ˈstriːtwɔːkə(r)/ *noun* (*old-fashioned*) a PROSTITUTE who looks for customers on the streets 街头拉客的妓女

S

street·wise /ˈstriːtwaɪz/ (*NAmE also* **ˈstreet-smart**) *adj.* (*informal*) having the knowledge and experience that is needed to deal with the difficulties and dangers of life in a big city 适应都市生活的；有都市人的精明劲儿的

strength /streŋθ/ *noun*

- **BEING PHYSICALLY STRONG** 强壮；牢固 **1** [U, sing.] the quality of being physically strong 体力；力气；力量：*He pushed against the rock with all his strength.* 他用全力推那块石头。◇ *It may take a few weeks for you to build up your strength again.* 可能需要几个星期你才能恢复体力。◇ *He had a physical strength that matched his outward appearance.* 他的体力与外形相称。◇ **~ to do sth** *She didn't have the strength to walk any further.* 她再也走不动了。**2** [U] the ability that sth has to resist force or hold heavy weights without breaking or being damaged 强度：*the strength of a rope* 绳子的强度 ➲ SEE ALSO INDUSTRIAL-STRENGTH
- **BEING BRAVE** 勇敢 **3** [U, sing.] the quality of being brave and determined in a difficult situation 毅力；坚强决心；意志力量：*During this ordeal he was able to draw strength from his faith.* 在这次磨难中，他得以从自己的信仰中吸取力量。◇ *She has a remarkable **inner strength**.* 她有非凡的意志力。◇ *You have shown great **strength of character**.* 你表现得很有毅力。
- **POWER/INFLUENCE** 实力；势力 **4** [U] the power and influence that sb/sth has 实力：*Political power depends upon economic strength.* 政治权力取决于经济实力。◇ *Their superior military strength gives them a huge advantage.* 他们军事实力较强，占有巨大优势。◇ *to negotiate from a **position of strength*** 以实力地位谈判 ◇ *The rally was intended to be **a show of strength** by the socialists.* 社会主义者组织这次集会意在显示力量。
- **OF OPINION/FEELING** 意见；感情 **5** [U] how strong or deeply felt an opinion or a feeling is 强烈程度；深度：*the strength of public opinion* 公众舆论的强烈程度 ◇ *This view has recently gathered strength* (= become stronger or more widely held). 这种观点近来已为更多人接受了。◇ *I was surprised by the strength of her feelings.* 她感情之强烈让我吃惊。
- **ADVANTAGE** 优势 **6** [C] a quality or an ability that a person or thing has that gives them an advantage 优势；优点；长处：*The ability to keep calm is one of her many strengths.* 能够保持冷静是她的多项长处之一。◇ *the **strengths and weaknesses** of an argument* 一个论点的有力之处与薄弱之处
- **OF NATURAL FORCE** 自然力 **7** [U] how strong a natural force is 强度；力度：*the strength of the sun* 太阳的强度 ◇ *wind strength* 风力 ◇ *the strength and direction of the tide* 潮水的流速与方向
- **OF FLAVOUR** 味道 **8** [U, C] how strong a particular flavour or substance is 浓度；浓淡程度：*Add more curry powder depending on the strength required.* 按所要求的口味轻重再加点咖喱粉。◇ *a range of beers with different strengths* (= with different amounts of alcohol in them) 各种不同度数的啤酒
- **OF CURRENCY** 货币 **9** [U] how strong a country's CURRENCY (= unit of money) is in relation to other countries' CURRENCIES 强弱（程度）：*the strength of the dollar* 美元的强弱
- **NUMBER IN GROUP** 群体人数多寡 **10** [U] the number of people in a group, a team or an organization 人数多寡；人力：*The strength of the workforce is about to be doubled from 3 000 to 6 000.* 职工人数将翻一番，由 3 000 人增加到 6 000 人。◇ *The team will be back **at full strength*** (= with all the best players) *for the next match.* 这支队在下场比赛将恢复最佳的阵容。◇ *The protesters turned out **in strength*** (= in large numbers). 抗议者大量聚集。◇ *These cuts have left the local police force **under strength*** (= with fewer members than it needs). 这几次裁减造成地方警力不足。

IDM **go from ˌstrength to ˈstrength** to become more and more successful 越来越兴旺发达；不断取得成功：*Since her appointment the department has gone from strength to strength.* 自她上任以来，这个部门越来越兴旺了。**on the strength of sth** because sb has been influenced or persuaded by sth 凭借（或根据）某事物；在某事物的影响下：*I got the job on the strength of your recommendation.* 由于您的推荐，我得到了那份工作。➲ MORE AT TOWER *n.*

strength·en /ˈstreŋθn/ *verb* [I, T] to become stronger; to make sb/sth stronger 加强；增强；巩固：*Her position in the party has strengthened in recent weeks.* 最近几个星期以来，她在党内的地位有所增强。◇ *Yesterday the pound strengthened against the dollar.* 昨天，英镑对美元的汇率上升了。◇ *The wind had strengthened overnight.* 夜里，风更大了。◇ **~ sb/sth** *Repairs are necessary to strengthen the bridge.* 这座桥需要加固。◇ *The exercises are designed to strengthen your stomach muscles.* 这些活动目的在于增强你的腹部肌肉。◇ *The move is clearly intended to strengthen the President's position as head of state.* 这一举措显然意在巩固总统作为国家元首的地位。◇ *The new manager has strengthened the side by bringing in several younger players.* 新教练通过引进几名年轻队员加强了队伍的实力。◇ *Their attitude only strengthened his resolve to fight on.* 他们的态度反而使他坚定了继续战斗的决心。◇ *The new evidence will strengthen their case.* 新的证据将使他们的论据更为充分。**OPP** **weaken**

stren·u·ous /ˈstrenjuəs/ *adj.* **1** needing great effort and energy 费力的；繁重的；艰苦的 **SYN** **arduous**：*a strenuous climb* 艰难的攀登 ◇ *Avoid **strenuous exercise** immediately after a meal.* 刚吃完饭避免剧烈运动。◇ *How about a stroll in the park? **Nothing too strenuous**.* 在公园里散散步怎么样？不会太累的。**2** showing great energy and determination 劲头十足的；奋力的；顽强的：*The ship went down although **strenuous efforts** were made to save it.* 尽管人们为营救这条船作了很大的努力，它还是沉了。▸ **stren·u·ous·ly** *adv.*：*He still works out strenuously every morning.*

他仍然每天早晨努力锻炼。◇ *The government* ***strenuously*** *denies the allegations.* 政府坚称那些说法不是事实。

strep throat /ˌstrep ˈθrəʊt; *NAmE* ˈθroʊt/ *noun* (*NAmE, informal*) an infection of the throat 脓毒性咽喉炎

strepto·coc·cus /ˌstreptəˈkɒkəs; *NAmE* -ˈkɑːkəs/ *noun* (*pl.* **streptococci** /ˌstreptəˈkɒkaɪ; *NAmE* -ˈkɑːkaɪ/) (*medical* 医) a type of bacteria, some types of which can cause serious infections and illnesses 链球菌

stress 🔑 AW /stres/ *noun, verb*

■ ***noun***

• **MENTAL PRESSURE** 精神压力 **1** 🔑 [U, C] pressure or worry caused by the problems in sb's life 精神压力；心理负担；紧张：*Things can easily go wrong when people are* ***under stress.*** 人在压力之下，办事情就容易出差错。◇ *to suffer from stress* 有精神压力 ◇ *coping with stress* 应对压力 ◇ *She failed to withstand the* ***stresses and strains*** *of public life.* 她承受不了作为一个公众人物的生活压力和紧张。◇ ***stress-related*** *illnesses* 与精神压力有关的疾病 ◇ ***emotional/mental stress*** 情感 / 精神压力 ◇ *Stress is often a factor in the development of long-term sickness.* 心理压力常常是形成长期疾病的一个因素。◇ ***stress management*** (= dealing with stress) 对于压力的应对 ➲ SYNONYMS AT PRESSURE ➲ COLLOCATIONS AT DIET

• **PHYSICAL PRESSURE** 物理压力 **2** 🔑 [U, C] ~ (**on sth**) pressure put on sth that can damage it or make it lose its shape 压力；应力：*When you have an injury you start putting stress on other parts of your body.* 一旦受伤，你便会让身体其他部位受力。◇ *a* ***stress fracture*** *of the foot* (= one caused by such pressure) 足部应力性骨折

• **EMPHASIS** 强调 **3** [U] ~ (**on sth**) special importance given to sth 强调；重要性：*She* ***lays*** *great* ***stress on*** *punctuality.* 她十分注重守时。◇ *I think the company places too much stress on cost and not enough on quality.* 我认为公司对成本强调有余，而对质量重视不足。

• **ON WORD/SYLLABLE** 单词；音节 **4** 🔑 [U, C] (*phonetics* 语音) an extra force used when pronouncing a particular word or syllable 重音；重读：*We worked on pronunciation, stress and intonation.* 我们学习了语音、重读和语调。◇ ***primary/secondary stress*** 主重音；次重音 ◇ *In 'strategic' the stress falls on the second syllable.* * strategic 一词的重音在第二音节。➲ COMPARE INTONATION (1) ➲ WORDFINDER NOTE AT PRONUNCIATION

• **IN MUSIC** 音乐 **5** [U, C] extra force used when making a particular sound in music 加强（音）

• **ILLNESS** 疾病 **6** [U] illness caused by difficult physical conditions 环境恶劣引起的疾病：*Those most vulnerable to heat stress are the elderly.* 上了年纪的人最容易因受热而生病。

■ ***verb***

• **EMPHASIZE** 强调 **1** 🔑 [T] to emphasize a fact, an idea, etc. 强调；着重：~ **sth** *He stressed the importance of a good education.* 他强调了良好教育的重要性。◇ ~ **that...** *I must stress that everything I've told you is strictly confidential.* 我必须强调，我告诉你的一切都要严加保密。◇ + **speech** *'There is,' Johnson stressed, 'no real alternative.'* 约翰逊强调说："别无真正能够替代的办法。" ◇ **it is stressed that...** *It must be stressed that this disease is very rare.* 必须着重指出，这种病非常罕见。◇ ~ **how, what, etc....** *I cannot stress too much how important this is.* 这事的重要性我怎么强调都不过分。

• **WORD/SYLLABLE** 单词；音节 **2** 🔑 [T] ~ **sth** to give extra force to a word or syllable when saying it 重读；用重音读：*You stress the first syllable in 'happiness'.* * happiness 一词重读第一个音节。 **3** 🔑 [I, T] to become or make sb become too anxious or tired to be able to relax（使）焦虑不安，疲惫不堪：~ **out** *I try not to stress out when things go wrong.* 出问题时，我尽量不紧张。◇ ~ **sb** (**out**) *Driving in cities really stresses me (out).* 在城市里开车让我真的很紧张。

> ▼ SYNONYMS 同义词辨析
>
> **stress**
>
> **emphasize**
>
> These words both mean to give extra force to a syllable, word or phrase when you are saying it. 以上两词均含重读（音节、单词或短语）之义。
>
> **stress** to give extra force to a word or syllable when saying it 指重读、用重音读（单词或音节）：*You stress the first syllable in 'happiness'.* * happiness 一词重读第一个音节。
>
> **emphasize** to give extra force to a word or phrase when saying it, especially to show that it is important 指重读、强调（词或短语）、加强语气：*'Let nothing ... nothing,' he emphasized the word, 'tempt you.'* 他强调说："要抵制一切…一切的诱惑。"

stressed 🔑 AW /strest/ *adj.* **1** 🔑 (*also informal* ˌ**stressed** ˈ**out**) [not before noun] too anxious and tired to be able to relax 焦虑不安；心力交瘁 **2** (of a syllable 音节) pronounced with emphasis 重读的 OPP **unstressed** **3** [only before noun] (*specialist*) that has had a lot of physical pressure put on it 受压的；受应力的：*stressed metal* 受压金属

stress·ful AW /ˈstresfl/ *adj.* causing a lot of anxiety and worry 压力重的；紧张的：*a stressful job* 造成沉重压力的工作 ◇ *It was a stressful time for all of us.* 对我们所有人来说，那是一段艰难的时期。

ˈ**stress mark** *noun* a mark used to show where the stress is placed on a particular word or syllable 重音符号 ➲ SEE ALSO PRIMARY STRESS, SECONDARY STRESS

ˈ**stress-timed** *adj.* (*phonetics* 语音) (of a language 语言) having a regular rhythm of PRIMARY STRESSES. English is considered to be a stress-timed language. 重音节拍的（如英语）➲ COMPARE SYLLABLE-TIMED

stretch 🔑 /stretʃ/ *verb, noun*

■ ***verb***

• **MAKE BIGGER/LOOSER** 使变大 / 变松 **1** 🔑 [T, I] ~ (**sth**) to make sth longer, wider or looser, for example by pulling it; to become longer, etc. in this way 拉长；拽宽；撑大；抻松：*Is there any way of stretching shoes?* 有什么办法能把鞋撑大吗？◇ *This sweater has stretched.* 这件毛衣给撑得变形了。**2** 🔑 [I] (of cloth 织物) to become bigger or longer when you pull it and return to its original shape when you stop 有弹性（或弹力）：*The jeans stretch to provide a perfect fit.* 这条牛仔裤有弹性，可以完全贴身。

• **PULL TIGHT** 拉紧 **3** 🔑 [T] to pull sth so that it is smooth and tight 拉紧；拉直；绷紧：~ **sth** *Stretch the fabric tightly over the frame.* 把布在架子上绷紧。◇ ~ **sth + adj.** *Make sure that the rope is stretched tight.* 务必要把绳子拉紧。

• **YOUR BODY** 身体 **4** 🔑 [I, T] to put your arms or legs out straight and contract your muscles 伸展；舒展：*He stretched and yawned lazily.* 他伸了伸懒腰，打了个哈欠。◇ ~ **sth** *The exercises are designed to stretch and tone your leg muscles.* 这些活动目的在于伸展和增强你的腿部肌肉。

• **REACH WITH ARM** 伸手够着 **5** 🔑 [I, T] to put out an arm or a leg in order to reach sth 伸出，伸长（胳膊、腿）：+ **adv./prep.** *She stretched across the table for the butter.* 她伸手到桌子那头去拿黄油。◇ ~ **sth + adv./prep.** *I stretched out a hand and picked up the book.* 我伸出一只手，把书捡起来。

• **OVER AREA** 覆盖地域 **6** 🔑 [I] + **adv./prep.** to spread over an area of land 延伸；绵延 SYN **extend**：*Fields and hills stretched out as far as we could see.* 放眼望去，田野山丘绵延不绝。

• **OVER TIME** 时间 **7** [I] + **adv./prep.** to continue over a period of time 延续：*The town's history stretches back to before 1500.* 该镇的历史可以上溯到公元 1500 年以前。◇ *The talks look set to stretch into a second week.* 看来谈判十有八九要延续到下个星期了。

• **MONEY/SUPPLIES/TIME** 钱；物资；时间 **8** [I] ~ (**to sth**) (used in negative sentences and questions about an amount of money 用于否定句和疑问句，指一笔钱) to be enough to buy or pay for sth 足够买（或支付）：*I need a new car, but my savings won't stretch to it.* 我需要一辆新车，但我的积蓄不够。**9** [T] ~ **sb/sth** to make use of a lot of your

S

money, supplies, time, etc. （大量地）使用，消耗：*The influx of refugees has* ***stretched*** *the country's resources* ***to the limit.*** 难民的大量涌入把这个国家的资源消耗殆尽。◇ *We can't take on any more work—we're fully stretched as it is.* 我们不能再接受其他工作了，现在我们已经满负荷了。

• **SB'S SKILL/INTELLIGENCE** 技能；智力 **10** [T] **~ sb/sth** to make use of all sb's skill, intelligence, etc. 使竭尽所能；使全力以赴；使发挥出全部本领：*I need a job that will stretch me.* 我需要一份能让我充分发挥才智的工作。

• **TRUTH/BELIEF** 实情；信条 **11** [T] **~ sth** to use sth in a way that would not normally be considered fair, acceptable, etc. 滥用；随意歪曲：*He admitted that he had maybe* ***stretched the truth*** *a little* (= not been completely honest). 他承认可能有点言过其实了。◇ *The play's plot* ***stretches*** *credulity* ***to the limit.*** 这出戏的剧情简直就是胡编滥造。

IDM **stretch your 'legs** (*informal*) to go for a short walk after sitting for some time （久坐之后）散散步，活动活动腿脚：*It was good to get out of the car and stretch our legs.* 我们下了车活动活动腿脚，真不错。**stretch a 'point** to allow or do sth that is not usually acceptable, especially because of a particular situation 破例；通融 ➲ MORE AT RULE *n.*

PHR V **,stretch 'out | ,stretch yourself 'out** to lie down, usually in order to relax or sleep 躺下（通常为休息或睡觉）：*He stretched himself out on the sofa and fell asleep.* 他在沙发上躺下睡着了。

■ ***noun***

• **AREA OF LAND/WATER** 土地；水域 **1** [C] **~ (of sth)** an area of land or water, especially a long one 一片；一泓；一段：*an unspoilt stretch of coastline* 一段未破坏原貌的海岸线 ◇ *a particularly dangerous stretch of road* 特别危险的路段 ◇ *You rarely see boats on this stretch of the river.* 这一河段船只罕见。

• **PERIOD OF TIME** 一段时间 **2** [C] a continuous period of time （连续的）一段时间 **SYN** **spell**：*They worked in four-hour stretches.* 他们工作四小时一班。◇ *She used to read for hours* ***at a stretch*** (= without stopping). 她以前看书常常连看几小时。**3** [C, usually sing.] (*informal*) a period of time that sb spends in prison 服刑期：*He did a ten-year stretch for fraud.* 他因欺诈罪服刑十年。

• **OF BODY** 身体 **4** [C, U] an act of stretching out your arms or legs or your body and contracting the muscles; the state of being stretched 伸展；舒展：*We got out of the car and* ***had a good stretch.*** 我们下车好好舒展了一下身体。◇ *Only do these more difficult stretches when you are warmed up.* 要做了准备活动以后再做这些较难的伸展运动。◇ *Stay in this position and feel the stretch in your legs.* 保持这个姿势，体会腿部绷紧的感觉。

• **OF FABRIC** 织物 **5** [U] the ability to be made longer or wider without breaking or tearing 弹性；伸缩性：*You need a material with plenty of stretch in it.* 你需要一种弹性很大的布料。◇ *stretch jeans* 弹力牛仔裤

• **ON RACETRACK** 跑道 **6** [C, usually sing.] a straight part at the end of a racing track （终点）直道 **SYN** **straight**：*the* ***finishing/home stretch*** 终点直道 ◇ (*figurative*) *The campaign has entered its final stretch.* 竞选已进入最后冲刺阶段。

IDM **at full 'stretch** using as much energy as possible, or the greatest possible amount of supplies 竭尽全力；以最大财力物力：*Fire crews have been operating at full stretch.* 各消防队一直在全力以赴。**not by any stretch of the imagination | by no stretch of the imagination** used to say strongly that sth is not true, even if you try to imagine or believe it 任凭怎么想也不；再怎么说也不：*She could not, by any stretch of the imagination, be called beautiful.* 再怎么说，她也称不上漂亮。

stretch·er /ˈstretʃə(r)/ *noun, verb*

■ ***noun*** a long piece of strong cloth with a pole on each side, used for carrying sb who is sick or injured and who cannot walk 担架：*He was carried off on a stretcher.* 他被人用担架抬走了。◇ *stretcher cases* (= people too badly injured to be able to walk) 必须用担架抬的伤员 ➲ WORDFINDER NOTE AT ACCIDENT

■ ***verb*** **~ sb + adv./prep.** [usually passive] to carry sb somewhere on a stretcher 用担架抬：*He was stretchered off the pitch with a broken leg.* 他腿骨折了，从球场上抬了下去。

'stretcher-bearer *noun* a person who helps to carry a stretcher, especially in a war or when there is a very serious accident 抬担架者

,stretch 'limo *noun* (*also formal* **,stretch limou'sine**) a very large car that has been made longer so that it can have extra seats 超长豪华轿车

'stretch marks *noun* [pl.] the marks that are left on a person's skin after it has been stretched, particularly after a woman has been pregnant （尤指女性生育后的）妊娠纹

stretchy /ˈstretʃi/ *adj.* (**stretch·ier, stretchi·est**) that can easily be made longer or wider without tearing or breaking 有弹性的：*stretchy fabric* 有弹性的织物

strew /struː/ *verb* (**strewed, strewed** or **strewed, strewn** /struːn/) **1** [usually passive] to cover a surface with things 把…布满（或散布在）；在…上布满（或散播） **SYN** **scatter**：**~ A on, over, across, etc. B** *Clothes were strewn across the floor.* 衣服扔得满地都是。◇ **~ B with A** *The floor was strewn with clothes.* 满地都是衣服。◇ (*figurative*) *The way ahead is strewn with difficulties.* 前面的道路布满艰难险阻。**2** **~ sth** to be spread or lying over a surface 布满；撒满；散播在…上：*Leaves strewed the path.* 树叶落满小径。

strewth /struːθ/ *exclamation* (*old-fashioned, BrE, slang*) used to express surprise, anger, etc. （表示惊奇、愤怒等）哟，哎呀，天哪

stri·ation /straɪˈeɪʃn/ *noun* [usually pl.] (*specialist*) a striped pattern on sth, especially on a muscle （尤指肌肉上的）条纹

stricken /ˈstrɪkən/ *adj.* (*formal*) **1** seriously affected by an unpleasant feeling or disease or by a difficult situation 受煎熬的；患病的；遭受挫折的：*She raised her stricken face and begged for help.* 她仰起苦闷的脸，乞求帮助。◇ *We went to the aid of the stricken boat.* 我们前去救助那艘失事的船。◇ **~ with/by sth** *Whole villages were stricken with the disease.* 整村整村的人染上了这种病。◇ *He was stricken by a heart attack on his fiftieth birthday.* 他在五十岁生日那天心脏病发作。**2** (in compounds 构成复合词) seriously affected by the thing mentioned 遭受…的；受…之困的：*poverty-stricken families* 贫困家庭 ➲ SEE ALSO GRIEF-STRICKEN, HORROR-STRICKEN at HORROR-STRUCK, PANIC-STRICKEN

strict 🔑 /strɪkt/ *adj.* (**strict·er, strict·est**) **1** 🔑 that must be obeyed exactly 严格的（指必须恪守）：***strict rules/regulations/discipline*** 严格的规则 / 规章制度 / 纪律 ◇ *She left* ***strict instructions*** *that she was not to be disturbed.* 她严格指示不得打扰她。◇ *He told me* ***in the strictest confidence*** (= on the understanding that I would tell nobody else). 他相信我绝对口紧，便告诉了我。◇ *She's on a very strict diet.* 她正严格节食。**2** 🔑 demanding that rules, especially rules about behaviour, should be obeyed 要求严格的；严厉的：*a* ***strict teacher/parent/disciplinarian*** 严格的教师 / 父亲（或母亲） / 执行纪律者 ◇ *She's very strict about things like homework.* 她对作业之类的事要求非常严格。◇ *They were always very strict with their children.* 他们对子女一向十分严格。**3** 🔑 obeying the rules of a particular religion, belief, etc. exactly 恪守教规（或信条等）的：*a strict Muslim* 恪守教规的穆斯林 ◇ *a strict vegetarian* 纯粹的素食者 **4** [usually before noun] very exact and clearly defined 严密的；严谨的；精确的：*It wasn't illegal* ***in the strict sense*** (***of the word***). 严格说来，这不算违法。▶ **strictness** *noun* [U]

strict·ly 🔑 /ˈstrɪktli/ *adv.* **1** 🔑 with a lot of control and rules that must be obeyed 严格地：*She was brought up very strictly.* 她从小家教很严。◇ *The industry is strictly regulated.* 这个行业有严格的规章。**2** 🔑 used to emphasize that sth happens or must happen in all circumstances （强调在一切情况都是如此）绝对地，无论如何 **SYN** **absolutely**：*Smoking is strictly forbidden.* 严禁吸烟。◇ *My letter is, of course, strictly private and confidential.* 当然，

我的信纯属私人信件，务须保密。**3** in all details; exactly 完全地；确切地：*This is not strictly true.* 这不完全正确。**4** used to emphasize that sth only applies to one particular person, thing or situation（强调只适用于某人、物或情况）只，仅限于 SYN **purely**: *We'll look at the problem from a strictly legal point of view.* 我们将只从法律的角度来看待这个问题。◇ *I know we're friends, but this is strictly business.* 我知道我们是朋友，但这完全是公务。

IDM **'strictly speaking** if you are using words or rules in their exact or correct sense 严格说来：*Strictly speaking, the book is not a novel, but a short story.* 严格说来，这部小说不能算长篇，而是短篇。

stric·ture /ˈstrɪktʃə(r)/ *noun* (*formal*) **1** [usually pl.] ~ (**on sb/sth**) a severe criticism, especially of sb's behaviour 指摘；非难 **2** ~ (**against/on sth**) a rule or situation that restricts your behaviour 限制；约束；束缚 SYN **restriction**: *strictures against civil servants expressing political opinions* 对于公务员发表政治见解的禁令

stride /straɪd/ *verb, noun*

■ *verb* (*pt* **strode** /strəʊd; *NAmE* stroʊd/) [I] (not used in the perfect tenses 不用于完成时) **+ adv./prep.** to walk with long steps in a particular direction 大步走；阔步行走：*We strode across the snowy fields.* 我们大步流星地穿过雪封的旷野。◇ *She came striding along to meet me.* 她大步走上前来迎接我。

■ *noun* **1** one long step; the distance covered by a step 大步；一步（的距离） SYN **pace**[1]: *He crossed the room in two strides.* 他两大步跨到屋子另一头。◇ *I was gaining on the other runners **with every stride**.* 我正一步步赶上其他运动员。**2** your way of walking or running 步态；步伐：*his familiar purposeful stride* 他那熟悉而坚定的步伐 ◇ *She did not slow her stride until she was face to face with us.* 她没有放慢脚步，径直走到我们面前。**3** an improvement in the way sth is developing 进展；进步；发展：*We're **making great strides** in the search for a cure.* 在探索治疗办法方面，我们正不断取得重大进展。**4 strides** [pl.] (*AustralE, informal*) trousers/pants 裤子

IDM **get into your 'stride** (*BrE*) (*NAmE* **hit** (**your**) **'stride**) to begin to do sth with confidence and at a good speed after a slow, uncertain start 进入状态；开始顺利地做某事 **put sb off their 'stride** to make sb take their attention off what they are doing and stop doing it so well 使分心；拖某人后腿 (**match sb**) **ˌstride for 'stride** to keep doing sth as well as sb else, even though they keep making it harder for you 尽量不落后（于某人）**take sth in your 'stride** (*BrE*) (*NAmE* **take sth in 'stride**) to accept and deal with sth difficult without letting it worry you too much 从容处理；泰然处之 **without breaking 'stride** (*especially NAmE*) without stopping what you are doing 步调不变；阵脚不乱

stri·dent /ˈstraɪdnt/ *adj.* **1** having a loud, rough and unpleasant sound 刺耳的：*a strident voice* 刺耳的嗓音 ◇ *strident music* 刺耳的音乐 **2** aggressive and determined 强硬的；咄咄逼人的：*He is a strident advocate of nuclear power.* 他是发展核能的坚定拥护者。◇ *strident criticism* 猛烈的抨击 ▸ **stri·dency** /ˈstraɪdənsi/ *noun* [U] **stri·dent·ly** *adv.*

strife /straɪf/ *noun* **1** [U] (*formal* or *literary*) angry or violent disagreement between two people or groups of people 冲突；争斗；倾轧 SYN **conflict**: *civil strife* 内乱 ◇ *The country was torn apart by strife.* 这个国家被内部纷争搞得四分五裂。**2** (*AustralE, NZE*) trouble or difficulty of any kind 麻烦；纠纷；困难

strike /straɪk/ *verb, noun*

■ *verb* (**struck**, **struck** /strʌk/)

• **HIT SB/STH** 击打；碰撞 **1** [T] ~ **sb/sth** (*formal*) to hit sb/sth hard or with force 撞；碰；撞击；碰撞：*The ship struck a rock.* 船触礁了。◇ *The child ran into the road and was struck by a car.* 孩子跑到公路上给车撞了。◇ *The tree **was struck by lightning**.* 树遭到雷击。◇ *He fell, striking his head on the edge of the table.* 他摔倒了，头碰在桌子边上。◇ *The stone struck her on the forehead.* 那块石头击中她的额头。➲ SYNONYMS AT HIT **2** [T] ~ **sb/sth** (**sth**) (*formal*) to hit sb/sth with your hand or a weapon 打；击：*She struck him in the face.* 她掴了他一记耳光。◇ *He struck the table with his fist.* 他用拳头打桌子。◇ *Who struck the first blow* (= started the fight)? 是谁先动手的？

• **KICK/HIT BALL** 踢球；击球 **3** [T] ~ **sth** (*formal*) to hit or kick a ball, etc. 击打，踢（球等）：*He walked up to the penalty spot and struck the ball firmly into the back of the net.* 他走到罚球点，稳稳地把球踢入网内。

• **ATTACK** 攻击 **4** [I] to attack sb/sth, especially suddenly 突击；攻击：*The lion crouched ready to strike.* 狮子蹲身准备袭击。◇ *Police fear that the killer may strike again.* 警方担心杀人犯可能再次下手。

• **OF DISASTER/DISEASE** 灾难；疾病 **5** [I, T] to happen suddenly and have a harmful or damaging effect on sb/sth 侵袭；爆发：*Two days later tragedy struck.* 两天后悲剧发生了。◇ ~ **sb/sth** *The area was struck by an outbreak of cholera.* 那一地区爆发了霍乱。

• **THOUGHT/IDEA/IMPRESSION** 想法；念头；印象 **6** [T] (not used in the progressive tenses 不用于进行时) (of a thought or an idea 想法或念头) to come into sb's mind suddenly 突然想到；一下子想起；猛地意识到：~ **sb** *An awful thought has just struck me.* 刚才我脑子里突然闪过一个可怕的念头。◇ *I was struck by her resemblance to my aunt.* 我猛然发现她长得跟我姑姑很像。◇ **it strikes sb how, what, etc.…** *It suddenly struck me how we could improve the situation.* 我一下子明白我们如何能改善局面了。**7** [T] to give sb a particular impression 给（某人以…）印象；让（某人）觉得：~ **sb** (**as sth**) *His reaction struck me as odd.* 他的反应令我诧异。◇ *How does the idea strike you?* 你觉得这个主意怎么样？◇ *She strikes me as a very efficient person.* 在我眼里，她是个很干练的人。◇ **it strikes sb that…** *It strikes me that nobody is really in favour of the changes.* 我觉得没人真正赞成这些变动。

• **OF LIGHT** 光 **8** [T] ~ **sth** to fall on a surface 照在…上；照射：*The windows sparkled as the sun struck the glass.* 阳光照得玻璃窗熠熠闪光。

• **DUMB/DEAF/BLIND** 哑；聋；瞎 **9** [T] ~ **sb + adj.** [usually passive] to put sb suddenly into a particular state 顿时使处于某状态：***to be struck dumb/deaf/blind*** 一时什么也说不出 / 听不见 / 看不见

• **OF WORKERS** 工人 **10** [I] ~ (**for sth**) to refuse to work, because of a disagreement over pay or conditions 罢工：*The union has voted to strike for a pay increase of 6%.* 工会投票决定罢工，要求加薪6%。◇ *Striking workers picketed the factory.* 罢工的工人在工厂附近设置了纠察队。➲ WORDFINDER NOTE AT UNION

• **MATCH** 火柴 **11** [T, I] ~ (**sth**) to rub sth such as a match against a surface so that it produces a flame; to produce a flame when rubbed against a rough surface 擦，划（火柴）；击出（火星）：*to strike a match on a wall* 在墙上擦火柴 ◇ *The sword struck sparks off the stone floor.* 剑砍在石头地板上，火星飞溅。◇ *The matches were damp and he couldn't make them strike.* 火柴受潮了，他划不着。

• **OF CLOCK** 钟 **12** [I, T] to show the time by making a ringing noise, etc. 敲；鸣；报时 SYN **chime**: *Did you hear the clock strike?* 你听见钟响了吗？◇ ~ **sth** *The clock has just struck three.* 时钟刚刚敲过三点。

• **MAKE SOUND** 发出声音 **13** [T] ~ **sth** to produce a musical note, sound, etc. by pressing a key or hitting sth 弹奏；奏响；发出（声音）：*to strike a chord on the piano* 在钢琴上奏出和弦

• **GOLD/OIL, ETC.** 金、石油等 **14** [T] ~ **sth** to discover gold, oil, etc. by digging or DRILLING 开采出；钻探到：*They had struck oil!* 他们开采出了石油！

• **GO WITH PURPOSE** 有目的地走 **15** [I] ~ (**off/out**) to go somewhere with great energy or purpose 行进；加劲走：*We left the road and struck off across the fields.* 我们下了公路，穿过旷野往前走。

IDM **be 'struck by/on/with sb/sth** (*informal*) to be impressed or interested by sb/sth; to like sb/sth very much 被某人（或某物）打动；迷恋某人（或某物）：*I was struck by her youth and enthusiasm.* 她年轻热情，把我迷住了。◇ *We're not very struck on that new restaurant.* 我们不大看得上那家新餐馆。**strike a 'balance** (**between A and B**) to manage to find a way of being fair to two opposing things; to find an acceptable position which is between two things（在对立二者之间）找到折中办法；平衡（对立的双方）**strike a 'bargain/'deal** to make an

S

agreement with sb in which both sides have an advantage 达成（对双方都有利的）协议 **strike a blow for/against/at sth** to do sth in support of/against a belief, principle, etc. 维护（或损害）某种信念或原则等：*He felt that they had struck a blow for democracy.* 他感觉他们维护了民主制度。**strike fear, etc. into sb/sb's heart** (*formal*) to make sb be afraid, etc. 使某人感到恐惧等 **strike 'gold** to find or do sth that brings you a lot of success or money 打开成功（或财富）之门；踏上通往成功（或财富）之路：*He has struck gold with his latest novel.* 他凭借最新的一部小说叩开了成功之门。**strike it 'rich** (*informal*) to get a lot of money, especially suddenly or unexpectedly 暴富；（意外）发大财 **strike (it) 'lucky** (*informal*) to have good luck 交好运 **strike a 'pose/an 'attitude** to hold your body in a particular way to create a particular impression 摆出某种姿态 **strike while the iron is 'hot** (*saying*) to make use of an opportunity immediately 趁热打铁 ORIGIN This expression refers to a blacksmith making a shoe for a horse. He has to strike/hammer the iron while it is hot enough to bend into the shape of the shoe. 原意是指打马掌的铁匠必须趁热打铁才能将其弯成马蹄形。**within 'striking distance (of sth)** near enough to be reached or attacked easily; near enough to reach or attack sth easily 近在咫尺；在攻击距离之内：*The beach is within striking distance.* 海滩近在咫尺。◇ *The cat was now within striking distance of the duck.* 此时，猫就在可攻击鸭子的距离内。➲ MORE AT CHORD, HARD *adj.*, HOME *adv.*, LIGHTNING *n.*, NOTE *n.*, PAY DIRT

PHR V **'strike at sb/sth** **1** to try to hit sb/sth, especially with a weapon 朝…打去：*He struck at me repeatedly with a stick.* 他拿着棍子一再朝我打过来。**2** to cause damage or have a serious effect on sb/sth 损害；有损于；严重影响到：*to strike at the root of the problem* 从根源入手解决问题 ◇ *criticisms that* **strike at the heart of** *the party's policies* 直指该党政策之要害的批评意见 **,strike 'back (at/against sb)** to try to harm sb in return for an attack or injury you have received 反击；回击 **,strike sb 'down** [usually passive] **1** (of a disease, etc. 疾病等) to make sb unable to lead an active life; to make sb seriously ill; to kill sb 摧垮；使病倒；使丧命：*He was struck down by cancer at the age of thirty.* 他三十岁那年被癌症夺去了性命。**2** to hit sb very hard, so that they fall to the ground 击倒，撞倒（某人）**,strike sth ↔'down** (*especially NAmE*) to decide that a law is illegal and should not apply 取消，撤销（法规）：*The Supreme Court struck down a Texas state law.* 最高法院撤销了得克萨斯州的一条法律。**,strike sth↔'off** to remove sth with a sharp blow; to cut sth off 打掉；砍掉；砍下：*He struck off the rotten branches with an axe.* 他用斧子把枯树枝砍掉。**,strike sb/sth 'off (sth)** (*also* **,strike sb/sth 'from sth**) to remove sb/sth's name from sth, such as the list of members of a professional group 把某人（或某事物）除名：*Strike her name off the list.* 把她的名字从名单上删掉。◇ *The doctor was struck off* (= not allowed to continue to work as a doctor) *for incompetence.* 那名医生因不称职而被取消了执业资格。**,strike 'out** **1** to start being independent 独立出去；自立谋生：*I knew it was time I struck out on my own.* 我知道我该独立谋生了。**2** (*NAmE, informal*) to fail or be unsuccessful 失败；砸锅：*The movie struck out and didn't win a single Oscar.* 那部影片砸锅了，奥斯卡奖一项都没得着。**,strike 'out (at sb/sth)** **1** to aim a sudden violent blow at sb/sth 挥拳猛击；猛打：*He lost his temper and struck out wildly.* 他发了脾气，大打出手。**2** to criticize sb/sth, especially in a public speech or in a book or newspaper（尤指公开）抨击：*In a recent article she strikes out at her critics.* 她最近写了一篇文章，对批评她的人予以驳斥。**,strike 'out** | **,strike sb↔'out** (in BASEBALL 棒球) to fail to hit the ball three times and therefore not be allowed to continue hitting; to make sb do this（使）三击不中出局，三振出局 ➲ RELATED NOUN STRIKEOUT **,strike sth↔'out/'through** to remove sth by drawing a line through it 画掉；删去 SYN **cross sth↔out/through**：*The editor struck out the whole paragraph.* 编辑把整段全部删去了。**,strike 'out (for/towards sth)** to move in a determined way (towards sth)（奋力朝某处）去；赶往（某处）：*He struck out* (= started swimming) *towards the shore.* 他朝岸边游去。**,strike 'up (with sth)** | **,strike 'up sth** (of a band, an ORCHESTRA, etc. 乐队等) to begin to play a piece of music 开始演奏：*The orchestra struck up and the curtain rose.* 管弦乐队奏起音乐，幕启。◇ *The band struck up a waltz.* 乐队奏起一支华尔兹舞曲。**,strike 'up sth (with sb)** to begin a friendship, a relationship, a conversation, etc.（和某人）建立友谊，开始来往，交谈起来：*He would often strike up conversations with complete strangers.* 他爱和完全不相识的人攀谈。

■ ***noun***

• **OF WORKERS** 工人 **1** 🔑 a period of time when an organized group of employees of a company stops working because of a disagreement over pay or conditions 罢工；罢课；罢市：*the train drivers' strike* 火车司机罢工 ◇ *a strike by teachers* 教师举行的罢课 ◇ *an* ***unofficial/a one-day strike*** 未得到批准的 / 为期一天的罢工 ◇ *Air traffic controllers are threatening to* ***come out on/go on strike.*** 空中交通管制员威胁要举行罢工。◇ *Half the workforce are now* (***out***) ***on strike.*** 现在有半数职工罢工。◇ *The train drivers have voted to* ***take strike action.*** 火车司机投票表决采取罢工行动。◇ *The student union has called for a* ***rent strike*** (= a refusal to pay rent as a protest). 学生会呼吁拒缴房租。➲ SEE ALSO GENERAL STRIKE, HUNGER STRIKE

• **ATTACK** 攻击 **2** 🔑 a military attack, especially by aircraft dropping bombs 军事进攻；袭击；（尤指）空袭：*an* ***air strike*** 空袭 ◇ *They decided to launch a* ***pre-emptive strike.*** 他们决定发动先发制人的攻击。

• **HITTING/KICKING** 击；踢 **3** [usually sing.] an act of hitting or kicking sth/sb 击；打；踢：*His spectacular strike in the second half made the score 2–0.* 他在下半场令人叹为观止的一脚射门把比分改写为 2:0。➲ SEE ALSO BIRD STRIKE, LIGHTNING STRIKE

• **IN BASEBALL** 棒球 **4** an unsuccessful attempt to hit the ball 击球未中

• **IN BOWLING** 保龄球 **5** a situation in TENPIN BOWLING when a player knocks down all the pins with the first ball 全中（第一球撞倒全部十柱球）

• **DISCOVERY OF OIL** 石油的发现 **6** [usually sing.] a sudden discovery of sth valuable, especially oil（珍贵东西的）意外发现；（尤指石油的）发现

• **BAD THING/ACTION** 坏事；不利的行动 **7** (*NAmE*) ~ **(against sb/sth)** a bad thing or action that damages sb/sth's reputation（有损声誉的）不利因素，打击：*The amount of fuel that this car uses is a big strike against it.* 耗油量大是这辆车的一大缺点。

IDM **,three strikes and you're 'out** | **the ,three 'strikes rule** used to describe a law which says that people who commit three crimes will automatically go to prison 三振出局法（三次犯罪即入狱的法律）ORIGIN From baseball, in which a batter who misses the ball three times is out. 源自棒球，击球手三次击球不中即出局。

'strike-bound *adj.* unable to operate because employees have stopped working as a protest 因罢工而停顿的：*a strike-bound airport* 因罢工而陷于瘫痪的机场

'strike-breaker *noun* a person who continues to work while other employees are on strike; a person who is employed to replace people who are on strike 破坏罢工者；顶替罢工者工作的人 ➲ COMPARE BLACKLEG ► **'strike-breaking** *noun* [U]

'strike force *noun* [C+sing./pl. v.] a military or police force that is ready to act quickly when necessary 突击部队；警察快速行动部队

strike·out /'straɪkaʊt/ *noun* (in BASEBALL 棒球) a situation in which the player who is supposed to be hitting the ball has to stop because he or she has tried to hit the ball three times and failed（三击不中）出局；三振出局

striker /'straɪkə(r)/ *noun* **1** a worker who has stopped working because of a disagreement over pay or conditions 罢工者；罢课者；罢市者 **2** (in football (SOCCER) 足球) a player whose main job is to attack and try to score goals 前锋

'strike rate *noun* [usually sing.] (*sport* 体育) the number of times a player is successful in relation to the number of times they try to score or win 进球率；得分率

S

ˈ**strike zone** *noun* (in BASEBALL 棒球) the area between a BATTER's upper arms and their knees, to which the ball must be PITCHED 好球区，好球带（指击球手上臂和膝部之间的部位，投球必须投中此区）

strik·ing /ˈstraɪkɪŋ/ *adj.* **1** interesting and unusual enough to attract attention 引人注目的；异乎寻常的；显著的 SYN **marked**: *a striking feature* 显著的特征 ◊ *She bears **a striking resemblance** to her older sister.* 她酷似她姐姐。◊ ***In striking contrast to** their brothers, the girls were both intelligent and charming.* 姑娘们既聪明伶俐，又妩媚动人，跟她们的兄弟形成鲜明的对照。➲ LANGUAGE BANK AT SURPRISING **2** very attractive, often in an unusual way 妩媚动人的；标致的；俊秀的 SYN **stunning**: *striking good looks* 姣好的面容 ▸ **strik·ing·ly** *adv.*: *The two polls produced strikingly different results.* 两次投票产生的结果截然不同。◊ *She is strikingly beautiful.* 她美丽动人。

Strim·mer™ /ˈstrɪmə(r)/ *noun* (*BrE*) an electric garden tool held in the hands and used for cutting grass that is difficult to cut with a larger machine 草坪修剪器 ➲ VISUAL VOCAB PAGE V20

Strine /straɪn/ (*also* **strine**) *noun* (*informal*) **1** [U] Australian English, especially when spoken in an informal way and with a strong accent 斯确拉因（澳大利亚英语，尤指非正式且口音重的）**2** [C] an Australian 澳大利亚人 ▸ **Strine** *adj.*: *a Strine accent* 澳大利亚口音

string /strɪŋ/ *noun, verb, adj.*

■ ***noun***

• **FOR TYING/FASTENING** 捆 / 系用 **1** [U, C] material made of several threads twisted together, used for tying things together; a piece of string used to fasten or pull sth or keep sth in place 细绳；线；带子：*a **piece/length of string*** 一根 / 一段细绳 ◊ *He wrapped the package in brown paper and tied it with string.* 他用棕色包装纸把包裹包好，又用细绳捆上。◊ *The key is hanging on a string by the door.* 钥匙拴在门边的带子上。➲ PICTURE AT ROPE ➲ SEE ALSO DRAWSTRING, G-STRING, PURSE STRINGS

• **THINGS JOINED** 串接物 **2** [C] a set or series of things that are joined together, for example on a string 一串：*a string of pearls* 一串珍珠 ◊ *The molecules join together to form long strings.* 分子连接在一起形成长串。➲ VISUAL VOCAB PAGE V70

• **SERIES** 系列 **3** [C] a series of things or people that come closely one after another 一系列；一连串；一批：*a string of hits* 接二连三的成功 ◊ *He owns a string of racing stables.* 他有好多个赛马训练场。

• **COMPUTING** 计算机技术 **4** [C] a series of characters (= letters, numbers, etc.) 字符串

• **MUSICAL INSTRUMENTS** 乐器 **5** [C] a tightly stretched piece of wire, NYLON, or CATGUT on a musical instrument, that produces a musical note when the instrument is played 弦 ➲ VISUAL VOCAB PAGES V38, V40 **6 the strings** [pl.] the group of musical instruments in an ORCHESTRA that have strings, for example VIOLINS; the people who play them（管弦乐团的）弦乐器，弦乐器组：*The opening theme is taken up by the strings.* 开始的主旋律由弦乐继续发展。➲ VISUAL VOCAB PAGE V38 ➲ COMPARE BRASS (2), PERCUSSION, WOODWIND

• **ON TENNIS RACKET** 网球拍 **7** [C] any of the tightly stretched pieces of NYLON, etc. in a RACKET, used for hitting balls in TENNIS and some other games 弦

• **CONDITIONS** 条件 **8 strings** [pl.] special conditions or restrictions 特定条件（或限制）: *Major loans like these always come with strings.* 诸如此类的大宗贷款总有一些附带条件。◊ *It's a business proposition, pure and simple. **No strings attached.*** 这只是个业务建议，仅此而已。没有任何附带条件。

IDM **have another string/more strings to your bow** (*BrE*) to have more than one skill or plan that you can use if you need to 还另有一手；有两手准备 ➲ MORE AT APRON, LONG *adj.*, PULL *v.*

■ ***verb*** (**strung, strung** /strʌŋ/)

• **HANG DECORATION** 悬挂装饰物 **1** to hang or tie sth in place, especially as decoration 悬挂；系；扎：**~ sth + adv./prep.** *We strung paper lanterns up in the trees.* 我们把纸灯笼挂在树上。◊ **~ A on, along, in, etc. B** *Flags were strung out along the route.* 沿途悬挂着旗子。◊ **~ B with A** *The route was strung with flags.* 沿途悬挂着旗子。

• **JOIN THINGS** 串接东西 **2 ~ sth + adv./prep.** to put a series of small objects on string, etc.; to join things together with string, etc. 用线（或细绳等）串，把…连在一起 SYN **thread**: *She had strung the shells on a silver chain.* 她把贝壳串在一条银链子上。◊ (*figurative*) *carbon atoms strung together to form giant molecules* 连在一起构成巨分子的碳原子

• **RACKET/MUSICAL INSTRUMENT** 球拍；乐器 **3 ~ sth** to put a string or strings on a RACKET or musical instrument 给…装弦 ➲ SEE ALSO HIGHLY STRUNG

PHR V ˌ**string sb aˈlong** (*informal*) to allow sb to believe sth that is not true, for example that you love them, intend to help them, etc. 哄；愚弄：*She has no intention of giving you a divorce; she's just stringing you along.* 她无意跟你离婚，不过是骗着你玩的。ˌ**string aˈlong (with sb)** (*BrE, informal*) to go somewhere with sb, especially because you have nothing else to do 跟随；伴随 ˌ**string sth↔ˈout** to make sth last longer than expected or necessary 延长；拖长时间：*They seem determined to string the talks out for an indefinite period.* 他们好像一心要把谈判无限期地拖下去。➲ SEE ALSO STRUNG OUT (1) ˌ**string sth↔toˈgether** to combine words or phrases to form sentences 把（单词或短语）联成句子：*I can barely string two words together in Japanese.* 我那点日语把两个词连起来说都费劲。ˌ**string sb↔ˈup** (*informal*) to kill sb by hanging them, especially illegally（尤指非法地）吊死某人

■ ***adj.*** [only before noun]

• **MUSICAL INSTRUMENT** 乐器 **1** consisting of musical instruments that have strings; connected with these musical instruments 由弦乐器组成的；弦乐器的：*a string quartet* 弦乐四重奏 ◊ *a string player* 弦乐器演奏者

• **MADE OF STRING** 用线制成 **2** made of string or sth like string 线织的；线的：***a string bag/vest*** 网兜；网眼背心

ˌ**string ˈbass** *noun* a word for a DOUBLE BASS, used especially by JAZZ musicians 弦贝司；低音提琴（尤为爵士乐乐师用语）

ˌ**string ˈbean** *noun* **1** (*BrE*) = RUNNER BEAN **2** (*NAmE*) = GREEN BEAN

ˌ**stringed ˈinstrument** *noun* any musical instrument with strings that you play with your fingers or with a BOW² (3) 弦乐器 ➲ VISUAL VOCAB PAGE V38

strin·gent /ˈstrɪndʒənt/ *adj.* (*formal*) **1** (of a law, rule, regulation, etc. 法律、规则、规章等) very strict and that must be obeyed 严格的；严厉的：*stringent air quality regulations* 严格的空气质量管理条例 **2** (of financial conditions 财政状况) difficult and very strictly controlled because there is not much money 紧缩的；短缺的；银根紧的：*the government's stringent economic policies* 政府紧缩银根的经济政策 ▸ **strin·gency** /-nsi/ *noun* [U]: *a period of financial stringency* 财政紧缩时期 **strin·gent·ly** *adv.*: *The rules are stringently enforced.* 这些条例得到严格执行。

string·er /ˈstrɪŋə(r)/ *noun* a journalist who is not on the regular staff of a newspaper, but who often supplies stories for it特约记者 ➲ WORDFINDER NOTE AT JOURNALIST

ˌ**string ˈvest** *noun* (*especially BrE*) a man's VEST made from a type of cloth with a regular pattern of large holes（男式）网眼背心

stringy /ˈstrɪŋi/ *adj.* (*disapproving*) **1** (of hair 头发) long and thin and looking as if it has not been washed 细长而干枯的；细长而稀疏的 **2** (of food 食物) containing long thin pieces like string and difficult to chew 多筋的；纤维多而不嫩的；柴的：*tough, stringy meat* 又老筋又多的肉 **3** (of a person or part of their body 人或人体的一部分) thin so that you can see the muscles 瘦得露出筋的：*a stringy neck* 瘦得青筋毕露的脖子

S

strip /strɪp/ *verb, noun*

■ *verb* (-pp-)

• **TAKE OFF CLOTHES** 脱衣 **1** [I, T] to take off all or most of your clothes or another person's clothes 脱光衣服；脱掉大部分衣服；扒光…的衣服 SYN **undress**: *I stripped and washed myself all over.* 我脱掉衣服，把全身洗了洗。◇ **~ down to sth** *She stripped down to her underwear.* 她把衣服脱得只剩下了内衣。◇ **~ (sth) off** *We stripped off and ran down to the water.* 我们脱掉衣服，跑进水里。◇ **~ sb (to sth)** *He stood there* ***stripped to the waist*** (= he had no clothes on the upper part of his body). 他脱光了上衣站在那里。◇ **~ sb + adj.** *He was* ***stripped naked*** *and left in a cell.* 他被扒得一丝不挂，丢在一间牢房里。**2** [I] to take off your clothes as a form of entertainment; to perform a STRIPTEASE 进行脱衣表演；表演脱衣舞

• **REMOVE LAYER** 除去一层 **3** [T] to remove a layer from sth, especially so that it is completely exposed 除去，剥去（一层）；（尤指）剥光：**~ sth (off)** *Strip off all the existing paint.* 把现有的油漆全部刮掉。◇ *After the guests had gone, I stripped all the beds* (= removed all the sheets in order to wash them). 客人走后，我把被单床单全都撤了下来。◇ **~ A off/from B** *Deer had stripped all the bark off the tree.* 鹿把树皮全都啃光了。◇ **~ B of A** *Deer had stripped the tree of its bark.* 鹿啃掉了树皮。

• **REMOVE EVERYTHING** 拿走所有东西 **4** [T] to remove all the things from a place and leave it empty 从（某处）拿走所有东西；使（某处）空无一物：**~ sth (out)** *We had to strip out all the old wiring and start again.* 我们不得不将原有的线路全部拆除，从头再来。◇ **~ sth + adj.** *Thieves had stripped the house bare.* 窃贼把房子洗劫一空。

• **MACHINE** 机器 **5** [T] **~ sth (down)** to separate a machine, etc. into parts so that they can be cleaned or repaired 拆卸；拆开 SYN **dismantle**: *They taught us how to strip down a car engine and put it back together again.* 他们教我们拆卸、安装汽车引擎。

• **PUNISHMENT** 惩罚 **6** [T] **~ sb of sth** to take away property or honours from sb, as a punishment 剥夺；褫夺：*He was disgraced and stripped of his title.* 他名誉扫地，被取消了头衔。

PHR V **ˌstrip sth↔aˈway** **1** to remove a layer from sth 剥去；剥下；揭去：*First, you need to strip away all the old plaster.* 首先，你得把原来的灰泥全部刮掉。**2** to remove anything that is not true or necessary 揭去，揭穿，清除（虚假或不必要的东西）：*The movie aims to strip away the lies surrounding Kennedy's life.* 这部电影旨在揭穿有关肯尼迪生平的种种谎言。

■ *noun*

• **LONG, NARROW PIECE** 条状物 **1** a long narrow piece of paper, metal, cloth, etc.（纸、金属、织物等）条，带：*a strip of material* 一块布条 ◇ *Cut the meat into strips.* 把肉切成条。➲ SEE ALSO RUMBLE STRIP **2** a long narrow area of land, sea, etc.（陆地、海域等）狭长地带；带状水域：*the Gaza Strip* 加沙地带 ◇ *The islands are separated by a narrow strip of water.* 岛屿之间一衣带水。➲ SEE ALSO AIRSTRIP, LANDING STRIP

• **OF SPORTS TEAM** 运动队 **3** [usually sing.] (*BrE*) (*NAmE* **uniform**) the uniform that is worn by the members of a sports team when they are playing 队服：*Juventus in their famous black and white strip* 身穿他们闻名遐迩的黑白条队服的尤文图斯队 ◇ *the team's* ***away strip*** (= that they use when playing games away from home) 球队的客场队服 ➲ VISUAL VOCAB PAGE V48

• **TAKING CLOTHES OFF** 脱衣 **4** [usually sing.] an act of taking your clothes off, especially in a sexually exciting way and in front of an audience 脱衣舞：*to do a strip* 表演脱衣舞 ◇ *a strip show* 脱衣舞表演 ➲ SEE ALSO STRIPTEASE

• **STREET** 街道 **5** (*NAmE*) a street that has many shops, stores, restaurants, etc. along it 商业街：*Sunset Strip* 森塞特商业街

• **PICTURE STORY** 连环画 **6** (*NAmE*) = COMIC STRIP IDM SEE TEAR[1] *v.*

ˌstrip carˈtoon (*also* **cartoon**) *noun* (*BrE*) = COMIC STRIP

ˈstrip club (*also* **ˈstrip joint** *especially in NAmE*) *noun* a club where people go to watch performers take their clothes off in a sexually exciting way 脱衣舞夜总会

stripe /straɪp/ *noun* **1** a long narrow line of colour, that is a different colour from the areas next to it 条纹；线条：*a zebra's black and white stripes* 斑马的黑白条纹 ◇ *a white tablecloth with red stripes* 白地红条的桌布 ➲ SEE ALSO PINSTRIPE, STARS AND STRIPES ➲ WORDFINDER NOTE AT PATTERN **2** a narrow piece of cloth, often in the shape of a V, that is worn on the uniform of a soldier or police officer to show their rank（军装或警服上表示等级的）条，杠 **3** (*especially NAmE*) a type, category or opinion 种类；类型；观点：*politicians* ***of every stripe*** 形形色色的政界人士 ◇ *commentators* ***of all*** *political* ***stripes*** 持各种政治观点的评论员 ◇ *She's an educator* ***of a*** *very* ***different*** *stripe.* 她完全是另外一种类型的教育家。

striped /straɪpt/ (*BrE also, informal* **stripy**) *adj.* marked with a pattern of stripes 有条纹的：*a striped shirt* 条纹衬衫 ◇ *a blue and white striped jacket* 蓝白条上衣 ➲ VISUAL VOCAB PAGE V66

ˈstrip light *noun* a light consisting of a long glass tube that is used especially in offices, kitchens, etc. 长条状灯 ▸ **ˈstrip lighting** *noun* [U]

strip·ling /ˈstrɪplɪŋ/ *noun* (*old-fashioned* or *humorous*) a young man who is older than a boy but who does not seem to be a real man yet 年轻男子；小伙子

ˈstrip mall *noun* (*NAmE*) a line of shops/stores and restaurants beside a main road（公路旁边的）购物饮食街，商店街

ˈstrip mining *noun* [U] (*NAmE*) a type of mining in which coal is taken out of the ground near the surface 露天开采；露天剥采 ➲ SEE ALSO OPENCAST

ˌstripped-ˈdown *adj.* [usually before noun] **1** keeping only the most basic or essential features, with everything else removed 只保留最基本特征的；精简的；简约的：*a stripped-down version of the song* 这首歌的简约版 **2** (of a machine or vehicle 机器或车辆) taken to pieces, with all the parts removed 拆卸的；拆开的

strip·per /ˈstrɪpə(r)/ *noun* **1** [C] a performer who takes his or her clothes off in a sexually exciting way in front of an audience 脱衣舞演员：*a male stripper* 脱衣舞男演员 **2** [U, C] (especially in compounds 尤用于构成复合词) a substance or tool that is used for removing paint, etc. from sth 剥离剂；脱漆剂；剥离器：*paint stripper* 脱漆剂

ˈstrip search *noun* an act of searching a person for illegal drugs, weapons, etc., for example at an airport or in a prison, after they have been made to take off all their clothes（对怀疑非法携带毒品、武器等的人进行的）光身搜查 ▸ **ˈstrip-search** *verb* **~ sb**

strip·tease /ˈstrɪptiːz/ *noun* [C, U] a form of entertainment, for example in a bar or club, when a performer removes his or her clothes in a sexually exciting way, usually to music, in front of an audience 脱衣舞

stripy (*also* **stripey**) /ˈstraɪpi/ *adj.* (*BrE, informal*) = STRIPED: *a stripy jumper* 条纹套头毛衣

strive /straɪv/ *verb* (**strove** /strəʊv; *NAmE* stroʊv/, **striven** /ˈstrɪvn/ or *less frequent* **strived**, **strived**) [I] (*formal*) to try very hard to achieve sth 努力；奋斗；力争；力求：**~ (for sth)** *We encourage all members to strive for the highest standards.* 我们鼓励所有成员为达到最高标准而努力。◇ **~ (against sth)** *striving against corruption* 与腐败现象作斗争 ◇ **~ to do sth** *Newspaper editors all strive to be first with a story.* 报纸编辑都力争率先报道。▸ **striv·ing** *noun* [U, sing.]: *our striving for perfection* 我们争取完善的努力

strobe /strəʊb; *NAmE* stroʊb/ (*also* **ˈstrobe light**) *noun* a bright light that flashes rapidly on and off, used especially at DISCOS 频闪闪光灯（尤用于迪斯科舞厅）

strob·ing /ˈstrəʊbɪŋ; *NAmE* ˈstroʊb-/ *noun* [U] (*specialist*) the effect, sometimes seen in the lines and stripes in a television picture, of sudden movements or flashing 频闪，残影（有时出现于电视图像条纹中的突然抖动或闪光）

strode PAST TENSE OF STRIDE

stroke 🔑 /strəʊk; *NAmE* stroʊk/ *noun, verb*

■ ***noun***

• **HITTING MOVEMENT** 击打动作 **1** 🔑 an act of hitting a ball, for example with a BAT or RACKET 击球（动作）：*What a beautiful stroke!* 击球动作多漂亮呀！◇ *He won by two strokes* (= in GOLF, by taking two fewer strokes than his opponent). 他以少于对手两杆的成绩获胜。**2** a single movement of the arm when hitting sb/sth（打、击等的）一下，一击：*His punishment was six strokes of the cane.* 给他的惩罚是挨六教鞭。

• **IN SWIMMING/ROWING** 游泳；划船 **3** any of a series of repeated movements in swimming or ROWING 划水动作；划桨动作：*She took a few more strokes to reach the bank.* 她又划几下，游到了岸边。➲ WORDFINDER NOTE AT SWIM ➲ VISUAL VOCAB PAGE V48 **4** (often in compounds 常构成复合词) a style of swimming 游泳姿势：*Butterfly is the only stroke I can't do.* 只有蝶泳我不会。➲ SEE ALSO BACKSTROKE, BREASTSTROKE **5** the person who sets the speed at which everyone in a boat ROWS（指挥船上其他桨手的）尾桨手

• **GENTLE TOUCH** 抚摩 **6** [usually sing.] (*especially BrE*) an act of moving your hand gently over a surface, usually several times 轻抚；抚摩：*He gave the cat a stroke.* 他抚摩了一下猫。

• **OF PEN/BRUSH** 笔；刷子 **7** a mark made by moving a pen, brush, etc. once across a surface 一笔；一画；笔画：*to paint with fine brush strokes* 一小刷一小刷地刷漆 ◇ ***At the stroke of a pen*** (= by signing sth) *they removed thousands of people from the welfare system.* 他们大笔一挥，就把成千上万的人排除在福利制度之外。

• **ACTION** 行动 **8** ~ (**of sth**) a single successful action or event（成功的）举动；（高明的）举措；（巧妙的）办法；（成功的）事情：*Your idea was a* ***stroke of genius.*** 你的主意很高明。◇ *It was a* ***stroke of luck*** *that I found you here.* 我在这儿看见你纯属巧遇。◇ *It was a* ***bold stroke*** *to reveal the identity of the murderer on the first page.* 在头版上披露谋杀犯的身份，这是一个大胆的举措。◇ *She* ***never does a stroke*** (***of work***) (= never does any work). 她一向什么活儿都不干。➲ SEE ALSO MASTERSTROKE

• **OF CLOCK** 钟 **9** each of the sounds made by a clock or bell giving the hours 钟声；鸣；敲：*At the first stroke it will be 9 o'clock exactly.* 等到钟敲第一下时就是 9 点整。◇ ***on the stroke of*** *three* (= at 3 o'clock exactly) 三点整

• **ILLNESS** 疾病 **10** a sudden serious illness when a blood VESSEL (= tube) in the brain bursts or is blocked, which can cause death or the loss of the ability to move or to speak clearly 脑卒中；中风：*to* ***have/suffer a stroke*** 患中风 ◇ *The stroke left him partly paralysed.* 他因中风身体局部瘫痪了。

IDM **at a** (**single**) **'stroke | at one 'stroke** with a single immediate action 一下子；一举：*They threatened to cancel the whole project at a stroke.* 他们威胁要一下子砍掉整个项目。**put sb off their 'stroke** (*BrE*) to make sb make a mistake or hesitate in what they are doing 扰乱某人；使某人乱了方寸

■ ***verb***

• **TOUCH GENTLY** 轻抚 **1** 🔑 ~ **sth** (*especially BrE*) to move your hand gently and slowly over an animal's fur or hair 轻抚，抚摩（动物的毛皮）：*He's a beautiful dog. Can I stroke him?* 这只狗真漂亮，我可以摸一摸吗？➲ SEE ALSO PET *v.* (1) **2** 🔑 ~ **sth/sb** to move your hand gently over a surface, sb's hair, etc. 轻抚，抚摩（物体表面或头发等）：*He stroked her hair affectionately.* 他深情地抚摩着她的头发。

• **MOVE STH GENTLY** 轻挪 **3** ~ **sth + adv./prep.** to move sth somewhere with a gentle movement 轻挪；轻触；轻拭：*She stroked away his tears.* 她轻轻拭去他的眼泪。◇ *He stroked the ball between the posts.* 他轻轻一触，把球踢进门柱之间。

• **BE NICE TO SB** 待某人好 **4** ~ **sb** (*informal, especially NAmE*) to be very nice to sb, especially to get them to do what you want 待（某人）非常好；（尤指）顺着（某人）以便为自己办事

'stroke play (*also* **'medal play**) *noun* [U] a way of playing GOLF in which your score depends on the number of times you hit the ball in the whole game, rather than on the number of holes that you win（高尔夫球）比杆赛 ➲ COMPARE MATCH PLAY

stroll /strəʊl; *NAmE* stroʊl/ *verb, noun*

■ ***verb*** [I] (+ **adv./prep.**) to walk somewhere in a slow relaxed way 散步；溜达；闲逛：*People were strolling along the beach.* 人们在海滩漫步。

■ ***noun*** a slow relaxed walk 散步；溜达；闲逛：*We went for a stroll in the park.* 我们去公园散了散步。

stroll·er /'strəʊlə(r); *NAmE* 'stroʊ-/ *noun* **1** a person who is enjoying a slow relaxed walk 散步者；闲逛者 **2** (*NAmE*) (*BrE* **buggy, push·chair**) a small folding seat on wheels in which a small child sits and is pushed along 折叠式幼儿车；童车 ➲ PICTURE AT PUSHCHAIR

strong 🔑 /strɒŋ; *NAmE* strɔːŋ/ *adj.* (**strong·er** /'strɒŋɡə(r); *NAmE* 'strɔːŋɡər/, **strong·est** /-ɡɪst/)

> **WORD FAMILY**
> **strong** *adj.*
> **strongly** *adv.*
> **strength** *noun*
> **strengthen** *verb*

• **HAVING PHYSICAL POWER** 有体力 **1** 🔑 (of people, animals, etc. 人、动物等) having a lot of physical power so that you can lift heavy weights, do hard physical work, etc. 强壮的；强健的：*strong muscles* 强健的肌肉 ◇ *She wasn't a strong swimmer* (= she could not swim well). 她游泳不大行。◇ *He's strong enough to lift a car!* 他力气大得能抬起一辆汽车！**2** 🔑 (of a natural or physical force 自然力或物理力) having great power 强的；强劲的：*Stay indoors in the middle of the day, when the sun is strongest.* 中午阳光最强的时候待在室内。◇ *a* ***strong wind/current*** 强风；急流 ◇ *a strong magnet* 强磁铁 **3** 🔑 having a powerful effect on the body or mind（对身、心影响）强烈的，深刻的：*a strong drug* 强效药物

• **HAVING POWER OVER PEOPLE** 有影响力 **4** 🔑 having a lot of power or influence 有权势的；有影响的；有实力的：*a* ***strong leader/government*** 重权在握的领导人；强有力的政府 **5 the strong** [pl.] people who are rich or powerful 有钱人；有势者；强势群体

• **HARD TO RESIST/DEFEAT/ATTACK** 难以抵抗 / 击败 / 攻击 **6** 🔑 very powerful and difficult for people to fight against or defeat 强的；强大的；厉害的：*a strong team* 强队 ◇ (*figurative*) *The temptation to tell her everything was very strong.* 非常想把一切全都告诉她。**7** 🔑 (of an argument, evidence, etc. 论点、证据等) difficult to attack or criticize 难以辩驳的；确凿的：*There is strong evidence of a link between exercise and a healthy heart.* 有充分的证据证明锻炼有益于心脏健康。◇ *You have a strong case for getting your job back.* 你有充分的理由要求复职。

• **OPINION/BELIEF/FEELING** 观点；信念；感情 **8** [only before noun] (of a person 人) holding an opinion or a belief very firmly and seriously 坚决的；坚定的；不动摇的；始终不渝的 SYN **firm**：*a* ***strong supporter/opponent*** *of the government* 坚决拥护 / 反对政府的人 **9** 🔑 (of an opinion, a belief or a feeling 观点、信念或感情) very powerful 坚定的；强烈的；深厚的：*strong support for the government* 对政府的坚决拥护 ◇ *People have strong feelings about this issue.* 人们对这个问题反应强烈。

• **NOT EASILY BROKEN** 不易破碎 **10** 🔑 (of objects 物体) not easily broken or damaged; made well 坚固的；结实的：*a strong chair* 结实的椅子

• **NOT EASILY UPSET** 不脆弱 **11** 🔑 not easily upset or frightened; not easily influenced by other people 坚强的；不易受惊吓的；有主见的：*You need strong nerves to ride a bike in London.* 在伦敦骑自行车，你可得有胆量。◇ *It's difficult, I know. But be strong!* 我知道这不容易。不过要坚强！◇ *a strong personality* 坚强的个性 ➲ SEE ALSO HEADSTRONG, STRONG-MINDED, STRONG-WILLED

• **LIKELY TO SUCCEED** 有望成功 **12** 🔑 likely to succeed or happen 有望成功的；可能性大的：*a strong candidate for the job* 有望获得这份工作的人选 ◇ *You're* ***in a strong position*** *to negotiate a deal.* 你们很有希望通过谈判达成协议。◇ *There's* ***a strong possibility*** *that we'll lose the game.* 我们很有可能会输掉比赛。

• **GOOD AT STH** 擅长 **13** good at sth 擅长的；突出的：*The*

S

play has a very strong cast. 这部剧演员阵容强大。◇ *Mathematics was never my **strong point*** (= I was never very good at it). 数学从来不是我的强项。

- NUMBER 数目 **14** great in number 大量的；众多的：*There was a strong police presence at the demonstration.* 示威现场有大批警察。**15** used after numbers to show the size of a group（用于数字后，表示某集体的规模）多达…的，计有…的：*a 5 000-strong crowd* 多达 5 000 人的群众 ◇ *The crowd was 5 000 strong.* 聚集的人群有 5 000 人。
- HEALTHY 健康 **16** (of a person 人) not easily affected by disease; healthy 健康的；强壮的；身体好的：*Are you feeling stronger now after your rest?* 休息过后，你是不是感觉好些了？ ➲ SYNONYMS AT WELL
- FIRMLY ESTABLISHED 稳固 **17** firmly established; difficult to destroy 稳固的；牢固的：*a strong marriage* 巩固的婚姻 ◇ *The college has strong links with local industry.* 这所学院同当地产业界有牢固的联系。
- BUSINESS 商业 **18** (of prices, an economy, etc. 价格、经济等) having a value that is high or increasing 坚挺的；行情看涨的；呈强势的：*strong share prices* 行情看涨的股票价格 ◇ *The euro is getting stronger against the dollar.* 欧元对美元呈强势走向。**19** (of a business or an industry 企业或某行业) in a safe financial position 经营状况良好的；景气的：*Their catering business remained strong despite the recession.* 尽管出现经济衰退，他们的酒席承办生意仍然景气。
- EASY TO SEE/HEAR/FEEL/SMELL 易于看 / 听 / 感觉 / 嗅到 **20** easy to see, hear, feel or smell; very great or INTENSE 醒目的；响亮的；明显感觉得到的；浓烈的；强烈的：*a strong smell* 浓烈的气味 ◇ *a strong feeling of nausea* 强烈的恶心感觉 ◇ *a strong voice* (= loud) 洪亮的嗓音 ◇ *strong colours* 浓重的色彩 ◇ *a face with strong features* (= large and noticeable) 轮廓分明的面孔 ◇ *She spoke with a strong Australian accent.* 她说话带有浓重的澳大利亚口音。◇ *He was under strong pressure to resign.* 他承受着要辞职的巨大压力。
- FOOD 食物 **21** having a lot of flavour 味重的：*strong cheese* 味重的奶酪
- DRINKS 饮料 **22** containing a lot of a substance 浓的；酽的：*strong black coffee* 不加牛奶的浓咖啡
- WORDS 言辞 **23** (of words or language 言辞或言语) having a lot of force, often causing offence to people 强硬的；冒犯的：*The movie has been criticized for **strong language*** (= swearing). 这部电影因有脏话而受到批评。
- GRAMMAR 语法 **24** [usually before noun] (of a verb 动词) forming the past tense and past participle by changing a vowel, not by adding a regular ending, for example *sing, sang, sung* 强变化的（通过改变元音而不是加规则的词尾来构成动词过去式和过去分词，如 sing、sang、sung）
- PHONETICS 语音学 **25** [usually before noun] used to describe the way some words are pronounced when they have stress. For example, the strong form of *and* is /ænd/. 强读式的，重读的（某些词重读时的读音，如 and 的强式读音为 /ænd/） OPP **weak** ▸ **strong·ly** *adv.*：*a strongly built boat* 一艘造得结实的船 ◇ *a light shining strongly* 一盏发着强光的灯 ◇ *a strongly worded protest* 措辞强硬的抗议 ◇ *He was strongly opposed to the idea.* 他坚决反对那个主意。◇ *This is an issue I feel strongly about* (= I have firm opinions about). 这个问题我坚持自己的看法。◇ *The room smelt strongly of polish.* 那个房间里散发着浓浓的上光剂的气味。

IDM **be a bit 'strong** (*BrE, informal*) used to say that you think what sb has said is unfair or too critical（认为某人的话有失公允或过于苛刻时说）有点言重了 **be 'strong on sth 1** to be good at sth 擅长某事：*I'm not very strong on dates* (= I can't remember the dates of important events). 我不大记得住日期。**2** to have a lot of sth 某事物有很多；强于某一方面：*The report was strong on criticism, but short on practical suggestions.* 这份报告批评的话说得多，但可行的建议提得少。**be sb's 'strong suit** to be a subject that sb knows a lot about 为某人所长：*I'm afraid geography is not my strong suit.* 恐怕地理不是我的强项。**come on 'strong** (*informal*) to make your feelings clear in an aggressive way, especially your sexual feelings towards sb 言行过分；（尤指）露骨地调情 **going 'strong** (*informal*) to continue to be healthy, active or successful 保持健康；活跃依旧；兴盛不衰：*My grandmother is 90 and still going strong.* 我奶奶 90 岁了，还挺硬朗。**,have a ,strong 'stomach** to be able to see or do unpleasant things without feeling sick or upset 能忍受令人恶心的事 ➲ MORE AT CARD *n.*

'strong-arm *adj.* [only before noun] (*disapproving*) using threats or violence in order to make people do what you want 横施淫威的；以暴力强制的：*to use **strong-arm tactics** against your political opponents* 用强制手段对付政敌

strong·box /'strɒŋbɒks; *NAmE* 'strɔːŋbɑːks/ *noun* a strong, usually metal, box for keeping valuable things in 保险箱；保险柜

,strong 'force *noun* (*physics* 物) one of the four FUNDAMENTAL FORCES in the universe, which holds the parts of the NUCLEUS of an atom together 强力（宇宙四种基本力之一，将原子核各部分结合在一起） ➲ SEE ALSO ELECTROMAGNETISM, GRAVITY (1), WEAK FORCE

strong·hold /'strɒŋhəʊld; *NAmE* 'strɔːŋhoʊld/ *noun* **1** an area in which there is a lot of support for a particular belief or group of people, especially a political party 有广泛支持的地方；势力强大的地方：*a Republican stronghold/ a stronghold of Republicanism* 共和党势力强大的地区 **2** a castle or a place that is strongly built and difficult to attack 堡垒；要塞；据点 **3** an area where there are a large number of a particular type of animal（某种动物的）主要栖息地：*This valley is one of the last strongholds of the Siberian tiger.* 这条山谷是西伯利亚虎最后的几个主要栖息地之一。

strong·man /'strɒŋmæn; *NAmE* 'strɔːŋ-/ *noun* (*pl.* **-men** /-men/) **1** a leader who uses threats or violence to rule a country 铁腕人物；独裁者 **2** a physically very strong man, especially sb who performs in a CIRCUS（尤指马戏团里的）大力士

,strong-'minded *adj.* having strong opinions that are not easily influenced by what other people think or say 有主见的；坚持己见的 SYN **determined**

strong·room /'strɒŋruːm; -rʊm; *NAmE* 'strɔːŋ-/ *noun* a room, for example in a bank, with thick walls and a strong solid door, where valuable items are kept（银行等的）保险库

,strong 'safety *noun* (in AMERICAN FOOTBALL 美式足球) a defending player who plays opposite the attacking team's strongest side 强卫（针对攻方攻势最强的一边进行防守）

,strong-'willed *adj.* determined to do what you want to do, even if other people advise you not to 意志坚强的；坚持己见的

stron·tium /'strɒntiəm; 'strɒnʃ-; *NAmE* 'strɑːnt-; 'strɑːnʃ-/ *noun* [U] (*symb.* **Sr**) a chemical element. Strontium is a soft silver- white metal. 锶

strop /strɒp; *NAmE* strɑːp/ *noun* [sing.] (*BrE, informal*) a very bad mood when you are annoyed about sth 恼怒；懊恼：*Don't get in a strop —I'm only a few minutes late.* 别生气，我不过晚了几分钟。

strophe /'strəʊfi; *NAmE* 'stroʊfi/ *noun* (*specialist*) a group of lines forming a section of a poem 诗节 ➲ COMPARE STANZA ▸ **stroph·ic** /'strəʊfɪk; *NAmE* 'stroʊf-/ *adj.*

stroppy /'strɒpi; *NAmE* 'strɑːpi/ *adj.* (*BrE, informal*) (**strop·pier, strop·pi·est**) (of a person 人) easily annoyed and difficult to deal with 动辄生气的；性情暴躁的；易怒难处的：*Don't get stroppy with me—it isn't my fault!* 别冲我生气，这不是我的错！

strove PAST TENSE OF STRIVE

struck PAST TENSE, PAST PART. OF STRIKE

struc·tural AW /'strʌktʃərəl/ *adj.* [usually before noun] connected with the way in which sth is built or organized 结构（或构造）上的：*Storms have caused structural damage to hundreds of homes.* 几场暴风雨使几百间住房的结构受损。◇ *structural changes in society* 社会结构的变化 ▸ **struc·tur·al·ly** AW /-ərəli/ *adv.*：*The building is* *structurally sound.* 这座房子结构完好。◇ *The languages are structurally different.* 这些语言在结构上有差别。

ˌstructural engiˈneer *noun* a person whose job is to plan large buildings, bridges, etc. 结构工程师（设计大型建筑、桥梁等）

struc·tur·al·ism /ˈstrʌktʃərəlɪzəm/ *noun* [U] (in literature, language and social science 文学、语言及社会科学) a theory that considers any text as a structure whose various parts only have meaning when they are considered in relation to each other 结构主义（认为任何一篇文字为一结构体系，其各个部分只有在相互关系中才有意义）➲ COMPARE DECONSTRUCTION ▸ **struc·tur·al·ist** /-rəlɪst/ *noun, adj.*: *a structuralist approach* 结构主义方法

ˌstructural linˈguistics *noun*[U] the part of LINGUISTICS that deals with language as a system of related structures 结构主义语言学（把语言作为相关联的结构体系）

struc·ture 🔑 AW /ˈstrʌktʃə(r)/ *noun, verb*

■ ***noun* 1** 🔑 [U, C] the way in which the parts of sth are connected together, arranged or organized; a particular arrangement of parts 结构；构造：*the structure of the building* 这座建筑物的结构 ◇ *changes in the social and economic structure of society* 一个社会在社会结构和经济结构上的变化 ◇ *the grammatical structures of a language* 一种语言的语法结构 ◇ *a salary structure* 工资结构 **2** 🔑 [C] a thing that is made of several parts, especially a building 结构体；（尤指）建筑物：*a stone/brick/wooden structure* 石 / 砖 / 木结构建筑物 ➲ SYNONYMS AT BUILDING **3** 🔑 [U, C] the state of being well organized or planned with all the parts linked together; a careful plan 精心组织；周密安排；体系：*Your essay needs (a) structure.* 你这篇文章组织不好。

■ ***verb*** [usually passive] to arrange or organize sth into a system or pattern 使形成体系；系统安排；精心组织：**~ sth** *How well does the teacher structure the lessons?* 老师对课程组织安排得如何？◇ *Make use of the toys in structured group activities.* 在精心安排的分组活动中使用这些玩具。◇ **~ sth around sth** *The exhibition is structured around the themes of work and leisure.* 展览是围绕工作与休闲的主题来布置的。

▼ SYNONYMS 同义词辨析

structure

framework • form • composition • construction • fabric

These are all words for the way the different parts of sth combine together or the way that sth has been made. 以上各词均指事物各个不同部分的组合、构造。

structure the way in which the parts of sth are connected together or arranged; a particular arrangement of parts 指结构、构造：*the structure of the building/human body* 建筑物 / 人体结构 ◇ *the social structure of society* 社会的社会结构 ◇ *the grammatical structures of a language* 一种语言的语法结构 ◇ *a salary structure* 工资结构

framework a set of beliefs, ideas or rules that forms the basis of a system or society 指构成某个体系或社会基础的信仰、观点、准则：*The report provides a framework for further research.* 报告提供了进一步研究的原则。

form [U] the arrangement of parts in a whole, especially in a work of art or piece of writing（尤指艺术作品或文章的）结构、形式：*As a photographer, shape and form were more important to him than colour.* 作为摄影师，形状和结构对他来说比颜色更重要。

composition [U] (*rather formal*) the different parts or people that combine to form sth; the way in which they combine 指不同部分或人的构成、组合方式：*recent changes in the composition of the workforce* 劳动力组合最近的变化

construction [U] the way that sth has been built or made 指建造或构造：*ships of steel construction* 钢结构船

fabric (*rather formal*) the basic structure of a society or an organization that enables it to function successfully 指社会、机构等的基本结构：*This is a trend which threatens **the very fabric of society**.* 这趋势威胁社会的基本结构。

PATTERNS

- the **basic** structure/framework/form/composition/construction/fabric of sth
- a **simple**/**complex** structure/framework/form
- the **economic**/**political**/**social** structure/framework/composition/fabric of sth
- the **chemical**/**genetic** structure/composition of sth

stru·del /ˈstruːdl/ *noun* [U, C] (*from German*) a cake made from pieces of fruit, especially apple, rolled in thin PASTRY and baked 果馅卷（饼）

strug·gle 🔑 /ˈstrʌgl/ *verb, noun*

■ ***verb* 1** 🔑 [I] to try very hard to do sth when it is difficult or when there are a lot of problems 奋斗；努力；争取：**~ (for sth)** *a country struggling for independence* 为独立而奋斗的国家 ◇ *Shona **struggled for breath**.* 肖纳艰难地喘着气。◇ *life as a struggling artist* (= one who is very poor) 艺术家拮据的生活 ◇ **~ to do sth** *They struggled just to pay their bills.* 他们辛苦所得仅敷日用。**2** 🔑 [I] **+ adv./prep.** to move somewhere or do sth with difficulty 艰难地行进；吃力地进行：*I struggled up the hill with the heavy bags.* 我背着几个沉重的包吃力地爬上山去。◇ *Paul struggled out of his wheelchair.* 保罗挣扎着下了轮椅。**3** 🔑 [I] to fight against sb/sth in order to prevent a bad situation or result 斗争；抗争：**~ (against sb/sth)** *He struggled against cancer for two years.* 他同癌症抗争了两年。◇ **~ (with sb/sth)** *Lisa struggled with her conscience before talking to the police.* 莉萨经过一番良心上的斗争，终于对警方说了。**4** 🔑 [I] to fight sb or try to get away from them 搏斗；扭打；挣扎脱身：*I struggled and screamed for help.* 我挣扎着，高声呼救。◇ **~ together** *Ben and Jack struggled together on the grass.* 本和杰克在草地上扭打起来。◇ **~ with sb** *James was hit in the mouth as he struggled with the raiders.* 詹姆斯在同几个劫匪搏斗时嘴上挨了打。◇ **+ adj.** *How did she manage to **struggle free**?* 她是怎么逃脱的？ **5** [I] **~ (with sb) (for sth)** to compete or argue with sb, especially in order to get sth 争夺；辩论：*rival leaders struggling for power* 互相对立的领导人争夺权力

PHR V **ˌstruggle aˈlong/ˈon** to continue despite problems 在困难中坚持；勉力维持

■ ***noun* 1** 🔑 [C] a hard fight in which people try to obtain or achieve sth, especially sth that sb else does not want them to have 斗争；奋斗；努力：*a **power/leadership struggle*** 争夺权力；领导权的斗争 ◇ **~ (with sb) (for/against sth)** *a struggle for independence* 争取独立的斗争 ◇ **~ (with sb) (to do sth)** *He is engaged in a bitter struggle with his rival to get control of the company.* 为取得对公司的控制权，他正同对手进行一场激烈的斗争。◇ **~ (between A and B)** *the struggle between good and evil* 善恶之争 ◇ *She will not give up her children without a struggle.* 她不会轻易放弃自己的孩子。➲ SYNONYMS AT CAMPAIGN **2** 🔑 [C] a physical fight between two people or groups of people, especially when one of them is trying to escape, or to get sth from the other 搏斗；扭打；（尤指）抢夺，挣扎脱身：*There were no signs of a struggle at the murder scene.* 凶杀现场没有搏斗痕迹。➲ SYNONYMS AT FIGHT **3** 🔑 [sing.] **~ (to do sth)** something that is difficult for you to do or achieve 难事 SYN **effort**: *It was a real struggle to be ready on time.* 要按时做好准备确非易事。

strum /strʌm/ *verb* (**-mm-**) [I, T] **~ (on) sth** to play a GUITAR or similar instrument by moving your fingers up and down across the strings 弹奏（吉他等乐器）：*As she sang she strummed on a guitar.* 她边唱边弹吉他。

strum·pet /ˈstrʌmpɪt/ *noun* (*old use, disapproving*) a PROSTITUTE, or a woman who looks and behaves like one 妓女；婊子；淫妇

strung PAST TENSE, PAST PART. OF STRING

ˌstrung ˈout *adj.* [not before noun] **1** spread out in a line 一条线地伸展开来：*a group of riders strung out along the beach* 沿海滩散开的一队骑手 **2 ~ (on sth)** (*slang*) strongly affected by an illegal drug such as HEROIN（吸毒后）神志恍惚

ˌstrung ˈup *adj.* [not before noun] (*BrE, informal*) very nervous, worried or excited 十分紧张；非常焦虑；异常兴奋

strut /strʌt/ *verb, noun*

■ ***verb*** (**-tt-**) [I] to walk proudly with your head up and chest out to show that you think you are important 趾高气扬地走；高视阔步：*The players strutted and posed for the cameras.* 运动员昂首阔步，摆好姿势让拍照。

IDM **ˌstrut your ˈstuff** (*informal*) to proudly show your ability, especially at dancing or performing（尤指在跳舞或表演时）卖弄自己那一套，露一手

■ ***noun*** **1** a long thin piece of wood or metal used to support or make part of a vehicle or building stronger 支柱；撑杆；支杆；支撑 **2** [sing.] (*disapproving*) an act of walking in a proud and confident way 趾高气扬的步态；高视阔步的样子

strych·nine /ˈstrɪkniːn/ *noun* [U] a poisonous substance used in very small amounts as a medicine 士的宁；马钱子碱

St Swithin's Day /ˌsnt ˈswɪðɪnz deɪ; *NAmE* ˌseɪnt/ *noun* 15 July, a Christian festival. In Britain it is said that if it rains on this day it will rain for the next forty days. 圣斯威辛瞻礼日（7 月 15 日，基督教节日，在英国据说如该日下雨则将持续下雨四十天）

stub /stʌb/ *noun, verb*

■ ***noun*** **1** a short piece of a cigarette, pencil, etc. that is left when the rest of it has been used（烟、铅笔等的）残余部分，残端 **2** the small part of a ticket, cheque, etc. that you keep as a record when you have given the main part to sb 存根；票根 ➲ PICTURE AT MONEY

■ ***verb*** (**-bb-**) **~ your toe** (**against/on sth**) to hurt your toe by accident by hitting it against sth hard 脚趾不小心踢到…上

PHR V **ˌstub sth↔ˈout** to stop a cigarette, etc. from burning by pressing the end against sth hard 把（香烟等）弄灭

stub·ble /ˈstʌbl/ *noun* [U] **1** the lower short stiff part of the STEMS of crops such as WHEAT that are left in the ground after the top part has been cut and collected（作物收割后留在地里的）茬 **2** the short stiff hairs that grow on a man's face when he has not shaved recently 胡子茬 ➲ VISUAL VOCAB PAGE V65 ▸ **stub·bly** /ˈstʌbli/ *adj.*

stub·born /ˈstʌbən; *NAmE* -bərn/ *adj.* **1** (*often disapproving*) determined not to change your opinion or attitude 固执的；执拗的；顽固的；倔强的 SYN **obstinate**: *He was too stubborn to admit that he was wrong.* 他死不认错。◇ *She can be **as stubborn as a mule**.* 她可以倔得像头骡子。◇ *stubborn pride* 死要面子 ◇ *a stubborn resistance to change* 顽固抵制变革 ◇ *a stubborn refusal to listen* 硬是不听 **2** difficult to get rid of or deal with 难以去除（或对付）的 SYN **persistent**: *a **stubborn cough/stain*** 久治不愈的咳嗽；顽渍 ◇ *a stubborn problem* 难题 ▸ **stub·born·ly** *adv.*: *She stubbornly refused to pay.* 她怎么都不肯付钱。◇ *Unemployment remains stubbornly high.* 失业率居高不下。 **stub·born·ness** *noun* [U]

stubby /ˈstʌbi/ *adj., noun*

■ ***adj.*** [usually before noun] short and thick 短而粗的；矮壮的：*stubby fingers* 又短又粗的指头

■ ***noun*** (*pl.* **-ies**) (*AustralE, NZE*) **1** [C] (*informal*) a small fat bottle of beer usually holding 0.375 litres 矮胖啤酒瓶（容量通常为 0.375 升）**2 Stubbies™** [pl.] a pair of short trousers/pants for men 男式短裤

stucco /ˈstʌkəʊ; *NAmE* -koʊ/ *noun* [U] a type of PLASTER that is used for covering ceilings and the outside walls of buildings（涂墙壁或天花板用的）拉毛灰泥 ▸ **stuc·coed** *adj.*: *a stuccoed wall* 拉毛粉饰的墙

stuck /stʌk/ *adj.* [not before noun] ➲ SEE ALSO STICK *v.* **1** unable to move or to be moved 动不了；无法移动；卡住；陷住：*The wheels were stuck in the mud.* 车轮陷到了泥里。◇ *This drawer keeps **getting stuck**.* 这个抽屉动不动就卡住。◇ *She got the key stuck in the lock.* 她把钥匙卡在锁里了。◇ *I can't get out—I'm stuck.* 我出不去，我被卡住了。**2** in an unpleasant situation or place that you cannot escape from 陷（入）；困（于）：*We were stuck in traffic for over an hour.* 我们堵车堵了一个多小时。◇ *I hate being stuck at home all day.* 我讨厌整天困在家里出不去。**3 ~** (**on sth**) unable to answer or understand sth 被难住；答不上来；卡壳：*I got stuck on the first question.* 头一个问题我就答不上来。◇ *I'll help you if you're stuck.* 你要是难住了，我来帮你。**4 ~** (**for sth**) not knowing what to do in a particular situation 不知所措；（为某事）犯愁：*If you're stuck for something to do tonight, come out with us.* 你要是正愁今晚没事做，就跟我们一块儿出去吧。◇ *I've never known him to be stuck for words before.* 我从不知道他也会有词穷句蹇的时候。**5 ~ with sb/sth** (*informal*) unable to get rid of sb/sth that you do not want 摆脱不了；甩不掉：*I was stuck with him for the whole journey.* 一路上我一直没能摆脱他。

IDM **ˌget stuck ˈin | ˌget stuck ˈinto sth** (*BrE, informal*) to start doing sth in an enthusiastic way, especially to start eating 起劲地干起某事；（尤指）大吃起来 ➲ MORE AT GROOVE, ROCK *n.*, TIME WARP

ˌstuck-ˈup *adj.* (*informal, disapproving*) thinking that you are more important than other people and behaving in an unfriendly way towards them 自命不凡的；趾高气扬的 SYN **snobbish**

stud /stʌd/ *noun* **1** [C] a small piece of jewellery with a part that is pushed through a hole in your ear, nose, etc. 钉状首饰；耳钉；鼻钉：*diamond studs* 钻石耳钉 ➲ VISUAL VOCAB PAGE V70 **2** [C] a small round piece of metal that is attached to the surface of sth, especially for decoration（尤指装饰用的）饰钉，嵌钉：*a leather jacket with studs on the back* 后背有饰钉的皮夹克 **3** [C, usually pl.] (*BrE*) one of several small metal or plastic objects that are fixed to the bottom part of a FOOTBALL BOOT or running shoe（足球鞋或跑鞋上的）鞋钉 ➲ COMPARE CLEAT (3) **4** [C] a small metal object used in the past for fastening a COLLAR onto a shirt 领扣 ➲ SEE ALSO PRESS STUD **5** [C, U] an animal, especially a horse, that is kept for breeding; a place where animals, especially horses, are kept for breeding 种公畜；种马；种畜场；种马场：*a stud farm* 种马场 ◇ *The horse was retired from racing and **put out to stud*** (= kept for breeding). 那匹赛马被淘汰下来，留作种马。**6** [C] (*informal*) a man who has many sexual partners and who is thought to be sexually attractive 乱搞关系的男人；风流男子

stud·ded /ˈstʌdɪd/ *adj.* **1** decorated with small raised pieces of metal 用饰钉装饰的：*a studded leather belt* 饰钉装饰的皮带 **2 ~ with sth** having a lot of sth on or in it 布满（或有很多）…的：*The sky was clear and studded with stars.* 天空晴朗，繁星点点。◇ *an essay studded with quotations* 旁征博引的文章 ➲ SEE ALSO STAR-STUDDED ▸ **stud** *verb* (**-dd-**): *~ sth Stars studded the sky.* 繁星满天。

stu·dent /ˈstjuːdnt; *NAmE* ˈstuː-/ *noun* **1** a person who is studying at a university or college 大学生；研究生：*a **medical/science, etc. student*** 医科、理科等学生 ◇ *a **graduate/postgraduate/research student*** 研究生 ◇ *an **overseas student*** 留学生 ◇ *a **student teacher/nurse*** 实习教师 / 护士 ◇ *a **student grant/loan*** (= money that is given/lent to students to pay for their studies) 助学金；学生贷款 ◇ ***student fees*** (= to pay for the cost of teaching) 学费 ◇ *She's a student at Sussex University.* 她是萨塞克斯大学的学生。➲ SEE ALSO MATURE STUDENT **2** a person who is studying at a school, especially a SECONDARY SCHOOL 学生；（尤指）中学生：*a 15-year-old high school student* * 15 岁的中学生 ➲ COMPARE PUPIL (1) ➲ SEE ALSO A STUDENT **3 ~ of sth** (*formal*) a person who is very interested in a particular subject 研究者；学者：*a keen student of human nature* 热衷于探究人性的人

stu·dent·ship /ˈstjuːdəntʃɪp; *NAmE* ˈstuː-/ *noun* (*BrE*) one of a small number of places that a university gives to students who wish to continue studying or to do research after they have finished their degree; an amount of money that is given to a student who wins one of these places 学位后研修生资格（学生获得学位后在大学继续学习研究）；学位后研修生奖学金

ˌstudents' ˈunion (*also* **ˌstudent ˈunion**) *noun* **1** a building where students at a university or college can go to meet socially（大学或学院的）学生活动中心 **2** (*BrE*) an association of students at a particular university or college, concerned with students' rights, living conditions, etc.（大学或学院）学生会

ˌstudent ˈteaching (*US*) (*BrE* **ˈteaching practice**) *noun* [U] the part of a course for people who are training to become teachers which involves teaching classes of students 教学实习

▼SYNONYMS 同义词辨析

student

pupil • schoolboy/schoolchild/schoolgirl

These are all words for a child that attends school. 以上各词均指学生。

student a person who is studying in a school, especially an older child 指在校学习的学生，尤指较大的学生：*Students are required to be in school by 8.30.* 学生须在 8:30 以前到校。◇ *Any high school student could tell you the answer.* 随便一个高中生都可以告诉你答案。

pupil (*BrE*) a person who is being taught, especially a child in a school 指学生，尤指小学生：*The school has over 850 pupils.* 这所小学有 850 多名学生。 NOTE **Pupil** is used only in British English and is starting to become old-fashioned. **Student** is often preferred, especially by teachers and other people involved in education, and especially when talking about older children. * pupil 只用于英式英语，并已开始过时。现在尤其是教师和教育工作者，较常用 student，多指较大的学生。

schoolboy/schoolgirl/schoolchild a boy, girl or child who attends school 指学校的男生、女生、学童、小学生：*Since she was a schoolgirl she had dreamed of going on the stage.* 自从上学以来她就一直梦想着成为演员。 NOTE These words emphasize the age of the children or this period in their lives; they are less often used to talk about teaching and learning. * schoolboy/schoolgirl/schoolchild 强调童年或学龄时期，较少用于教与学：~~*an able schoolboy/schoolgirl/schoolchild*~~

PATTERNS

- a(n) **good/bright/able/brilliant/star/outstanding** student/pupil
- a **naughty** schoolboy/schoolgirl/schoolchild
- a **disruptive** student/pupil
- a(n) **ex-/former** student/pupil
- a **school** student/pupil
- to **teach** students/pupils/schoolboys/schoolgirls/schoolchildren

▼MORE ABOUT ... 补充说明

students

- A **student** is a person who is studying at a school, college, university, etc. * student 指在校学习的学生。
- An **undergraduate** is a student who is studying for their first degree at a university or college. * undergraduate 指大学里攻读学士学位的学生。
- In *BrE*, a **graduate** is a person who has completed a first degree at a university or college. In *NAmE* **graduate** is usually used with another noun and can also apply to a person who has finished high school. 在英式英语中，graduate 指大学本科毕业生。在美式英语中，graduate 通常与另一名词连用，亦可指中学毕业生：*a high school graduate* 中学毕业生 ◇ *a graduate student* 研究生
- A **postgraduate** is a person who has finished a first degree and is doing advanced study or research. This is the usual term in *BrE*, but it is formal in *NAmE* and **graduate student** is usually used instead. * postgraduate 指研究生，在英式英语中为常用词，在美式英语中则为正式用语，通常用 graduate student 取代。

stud·ied /ˈstʌdid/ *adj.* [only before noun] (*formal*) deliberate and carefully planned 刻意的；精心安排的：*She introduced herself with studied casualness.* 她故作轻松地做了自我介绍。

stu·dio 🔑 /ˈstjuːdiəʊ; *NAmE* ˈstuːdioʊ/ *noun* (*pl.* **-os**) **1** 🔑 a room where radio or television programmes are recorded and broadcast from, or where music is recorded（广播、电视的）录音室，录像室，演播室，制作室；（音乐）录音棚：*a* ***television studio*** 电视演播室 ◇ *a* ***studio audience*** (= one in a studio, that can be seen or heard as a programme is broadcast) 演播室现场的观众（或听众）◇ *a* ***recording studio*** 录音棚 **2** 🔑 a place where films/movies are made or produced 电影摄影棚 **3** 🔑 a company that makes films/movies 电影公司；电影制片厂：*She works for a major Hollywood studio.* 她在好莱坞一家大电影公司工作。◇ *a studio executive* 电影公司经理 **4** 🔑 a room where an artist works（艺术家的）工作室：*a sculptor's studio* 雕塑家的工作室 **5** a place where dancing is taught or where dancers practise（舞蹈）练功房：*a dance studio* 舞蹈练功房 **6** (*BrE also* **ˈstudio flat**) (*NAmE also* **ˈstudio apartment**) a small flat/apartment with one main room for living and sleeping in and usually a kitchen and bathroom 单间公寓（一个房间兼作起居室和卧室，通常带厨房和卫生间）

stu·di·ous /ˈstjuːdiəs; *NAmE* ˈstuː-/ *adj.* spending a lot of time studying or reading 勤奋的；好学的；用功的 SYN **scholarly**：*a studious young man* 勤奋的小伙子

stu·di·ous·ly /ˈstjuːdiəsli; *NAmE* ˈstuː-/ *adv.* in a way that is carefully planned and deliberate 刻意地；成心：*He studiously avoided answering the question.* 他刻意不去回答那个问题。

stud·muf·fin /ˈstʌdmʌfɪn/ *noun* (*informal, especially NAmE*) a man who is considered sexually attractive 性感的男人

study 🔑 /ˈstʌdi/ *noun, verb*

■ ***noun*** (*pl.* **-ies**)

• **ACTIVITY OF LEARNING** 学习 **1** 🔑 [U] the activity of learning or gaining knowledge, either from books or by examining things in the world 学习；研究：*a room set aside for* ***private study*** 单留出来的书房 ◇ ***academic/literary/scientific, etc. study*** 学术、文学、科学等研究 ◇ *It is important to develop good* ***study skills.*** 培养良好的学习方法很重要。◇ *Physiology is the study of how living things work.* 生理学是研究生物机能的学科。

WORDFINDER 联想词：course, distance learning, **education, exam**, further education, graduate, higher education, qualification, tertiary

2 🔑 **studies** [pl.] (*formal*) a particular person's learning activities, for example at a college or university 功课；课业；学业：*to continue your studies* 继续学业

• **ACADEMIC SUBJECT** 学科 **3** 🔑 **studies** [U+sing./pl. v.] used in the names of some academic subjects（用于某些学科名称）：*business/media/American studies* 商学；传媒学；美国研究

• **DETAILED EXAMINATION** 仔细检查 **4** 🔑 [U] the act of considering or examining sth in detail 细致考虑；仔细检查；审视：*These proposals deserve careful study.* 这些建议值得认真研究。**5** 🔑 [C] a piece of research that examines a subject or question in detail（专题）研究，调查：*to* ***make/carry out/conduct a study*** 开展一项研究 ◇ ***This study shows/confirms/suggests that...*** 这研究证明 / 证实 / 显示… ◇ *a detailed study of how animals adapt to their environment* 关于动物如何适应环境的细致研究 ➲ WORDFINDER NOTE AT SCIENCE ➲ **COLLOCATIONS** AT SCIENTIFIC ➲ SEE ALSO CASE STUDY

• **ROOM** 房间 **6** 🔑 [C] a room, especially in sb's home, used for reading and writing 书房

• **ART** 绘画 **7** [C] a drawing or painting of sth, especially one done for practice or before doing a larger picture 习作；试作；试画：*a study of Chartres Cathedral* 沙特尔大教

S

堂试画 ◇ *a nude study* 裸体画习作

- **MUSIC** 音乐 **8** (*also* **étude**) [C] a piece of music designed to give a player practice in technical skills 练习曲
- **PERFECT EXAMPLE** 典型 **9** [sing.] ~ (**in sth**) (*formal*) a perfect example of sth 典型；范例：*His face was a study in concentration.* 他脸上完全是一副全神贯注的表情。IDM SEE BROWN *adj.*

■ *verb* (**stud·ies**, **study·ing**, **stud·ied**, **stud·ied**)

- **LEARN** 学习 **1** [T, I] ~ (**for sth**) to spend time learning about a subject by reading, going to college, etc. 学习；攻读：~ (**sth**) *How long have you been studying English?* 你学英语多久了？◇ *Don't disturb Jane, she's studying for her exams.* 不要打扰简，她正在温习功课，准备考试呢。◇ ~ (**sth**) **at…** *My brother studied at the Royal College of Art.* 我哥哥曾就读于皇家美术学院。◇ ~ (**sth**) **under…** *a composer who studied under Nadia Boulanger* (= was taught by Nadia Boulanger) 曾师从纳迪亚·布朗热的作曲家 ◇ ~ **to do/be sth** *Nina is studying to be an architect.* 尼娜在学建筑。➲ COLLOCATIONS AT EDUCATION
- **EXAMINE CAREFULLY** 认真检查 **2** [T] ~ **sth** to watch or to look at sb/sth carefully in order to find out sth 审视；端详；细看：*Scientists are studying photographs of the planet for signs of life.* 科学家仔细察看行星照片，看有无生命迹象。◇ *He studied her face thoughtfully.* 他一边端详她的脸，一边沉思。◇ *Fran was studying the menu.* 弗兰在仔细地看菜单。**3** [T] to examine sth carefully in order to understand it 研究；调查：~ **sth** *We will study the report carefully before making a decision.* 我们将认真研究这份报告，然后再作决定。◇ ~ **how, what, etc.…** *The group will study how the region coped with the loss of thousands of jobs.* 该小组将考察这一地区是如何应对减少几千个工作岗位的局面的。➲ SYNONYMS AT EXAMINE

'study bedroom *noun* (*BrE*) a student's room containing a bed and a desk （学生宿舍的）书房兼寝室

'study hall *noun* [U] (*NAmE*) a period of time during the school day when students study quietly on their own, usually with a teacher present 自习课

stuff /stʌf/ *noun, verb*

■ *noun* [U] **1** (*informal, sometimes disapproving*) used to refer to a substance, material, group of objects, etc. when you do not know the name, when the name is not important or when it is obvious what you are talking about （事物名称不详、无关紧要或所指事物明显时用）东西，物品，玩意儿：*What's all that sticky stuff on the carpet?* 地毯上那黏乎乎的都是什么玩意儿？◇ *The chairs were covered in some sort of plastic stuff.* 椅子都包了一种塑料膜。◇ *This wine is good stuff.* 这酒不错。◇ (*disapproving*) *I don't know how you can eat that stuff!* 我不明白你怎么能吃那种东西！◇ *They sell stationery* ***and stuff*** (***like that***). 他们出售文具之类的东西。◇ *Where's all my stuff* (= my possessions)? 我那些东西都哪儿去了？◇ (*disapproving*) *Could you move all that stuff off the table?* 请你把桌上那些玩意儿全都拿走好不好？➲ SEE ALSO FOODSTUFF ➲ SYNONYMS AT THING **2** (*informal*) used to refer in a general way to things that people do, say, think, etc. （泛指）活儿，话，念头，东西：*I've got loads of stuff to do today.* 我今天有好多事儿要做。◇ *I like reading* ***and stuff***. 我喜欢看书什么的。◇ *The band did some* ***great stuff*** *on their first album.* 这支乐队首张专辑有几支很棒的曲子。◇ *This is all* ***good stuff***. *Well done!* 这一切都不错。干得漂亮！◇ *What's all this 'Mrs Smith' stuff? Call me Anna.* 哪来的什么"史密斯夫人"那一套？叫我安娜就好了。◇ *I don't believe in* ***all that stuff*** *about ghosts.* 我不信什么鬼呀魂呀的。**3** ~ (**of sth**) (*formal or literary*) the most important feature of sth; something that sth else is based on or is made from 基本特征；特质；根本；基础；原料：*The trip was magical; the stuff of which dreams are made.* 那次旅行很奇妙，宛如梦境。◇ *Parades and marches were* ***the very stuff of*** *politics in the region.* 游行示威是那一地区政治活动的基本内容。◇ *Let's see what stuff you're made of* (= what sort of person you are). 我们来看看你是怎样一个人。➲ SEE ALSO HOT STUFF

IDM **do your 'stuff** (*informal*) to do what you are good at or what you have been trained to do 施展自己的本事；露一手：*Some members of the team are just not doing their stuff* (= doing as well as they should). 队中几名成员压根儿没有使出自己的真本事。◇ (*figurative*) *The medicine has clearly done its stuff.* 这药显然起作用了。**not give a 'stuff** (*BrE, slang*) to not care at all about sth 一点不在乎 **,stuff and 'nonsense** ***exclamation*** (*old-fashioned, informal*) used to describe sth that is stupid or not true 废话；胡说八道 ➲ MORE AT KID *n.*, KNOW *v.*, STERN *adj.*, STRUT *v.*, SWEAT *v.*

■ *verb* **1** to fill a space or container tightly with sth 填满；装满；塞满；灌满：~ **A with B** *She had 500 envelopes to stuff with leaflets.* 她得在500个信封里装上传单。◇ ~ **B in, into, under, etc. A** *She had 500 leaflets to stuff into envelopes.* 她得把500份传单装进信封里。◇ ~ **sth** *The fridge is stuffed to bursting.* 冰箱满得都快撑破了。◇ ~ **sth + adj.** *All the drawers* ***were stuffed full of*** *letters and papers.* 所有抽屉里都放满了信函文件。**2** ~ **sth + adv./prep.** to push sth quickly and carelessly into a small space 把…塞进（或填进）SYN **shove**：*She stuffed the money under a cushion.* 她把钱塞到软垫底下。◇ *His hands were stuffed in his pockets.* 他两手插在口袋里。**3** ~ **sth** to fill a vegetable, chicken, etc. with another type of food 在（蔬菜、鸡等）里填入（另外一种食物）；给…装馅：*Are you going to stuff the turkey?* 你打算给火鸡加填料吗？◇ *stuffed peppers* 酿柿子椒 **4** (*informal*) to eat a lot of food or too much food; to give sb a lot or too much to eat （使）吃撑，吃足，吃得过饱：~ **sb/yourself** *He sat at the table stuffing himself.* 他坐在桌前大吃大嚼。◇ ~ **sb/yourself with sth** *Don't stuff the kids with chocolate before their dinner.* 正餐前不要给孩子一个劲地吃巧克力。◇ ~ **your face** *We stuffed our faces at the party.* 我们在聚会时都吃撑了。**5** [usually passive] ~ **sth** to fill the dead body of an animal with material and preserve it, so that it keeps its original shape and appearance 制作（动物）标本：*They had had their pet dog stuffed.* 他们请人把他们的宠物狗制成了标本。

IDM **get 'stuffed** (*BrE, informal*) used to tell sb in a rude and angry way to go away, or that you do not want sth 滚开；不稀罕 **'stuff it** (*informal*) used to show that you have changed your mind about sth or do not care about sth （表示改变了主意或不在乎）管它呢，去它的：*I didn't want a part in the play, then I thought—stuff it—why not?* 我本来没想在剧中扮演角色，然后又一想，管它呢，干吗不演？**you, etc. can stuff sth** (*informal*) used to tell sb in a rude and angry way that you do not want sth （粗暴或气愤地拒绝）还是收起你的宝贝吧：*I told them they could stuff their job.* 我告诉他们说我不稀罕他们的工作。

stuffed /stʌft/ *adj.* [not before noun] (*informal*) having eaten so much that you cannot eat anything else 饱 SYN **full**

,stuffed 'animal *noun* **1** (*especially NAmE*) (*BrE also* **,soft 'toy**) a toy in the shape of an animal, made of cloth and filled with a soft substance 填充玩具动物；（动物造型的）布绒玩具 ➲ VISUAL VOCAB PAGE V41 **2** a dead animal that has been STUFFED 动物标本：*stuffed animals in glass cases* 玻璃柜里的动物标本

,stuffed 'shirt *noun* (*informal, disapproving*) a person who is very serious, formal or old-fashioned 一本正经的人；古板的人；保守的人

,stuffed 'up *adj.* if you are **stuffed up**, your nose is blocked and you are not able to breathe easily 鼻子不通气；鼻塞

stuff·ing /'stʌfɪŋ/ *noun* [U] **1** (*NAmE also* **dress·ing**) a mixture of finely chopped food, such as bread, onions and HERBS, placed inside a chicken, etc. before it is cooked to give it flavour （烹饪前塞入鸡等膛内的）填料 **2** soft material used to fill CUSHIONS, toys, etc. （垫子、玩具等的）填充物 SYN **filling** IDM SEE KNOCK *v.*

stuffy /'stʌfi/ *adj.* (**stuff·ier**, **stuffi·est**) **1** (of a building, room, etc. 建筑物、房间等) warm in an unpleasant way and without enough fresh air 闷热的；闷人的；通风不畅的：*a stuffy room* 闷热的房间 ◇ *It gets very hot and stuffy in here in summer.* 这里夏天很热很闷。**2** (*informal, disapproving*) very serious, formal, boring or old-fashioned 一本正经的；古板的；无聊的；保守的：*a stuffy, formal family* 一本正经而又古板的一家人 ◇ *plain, stuffy clothes* 朴素刻板的衣服 **3** (*especially NAmE*) if you have a **stuffy**

nose, your nose is blocked because you have a cold（鼻子）不通的，堵住的；鼻塞的 ▶ **stuffi·ness** *noun* [U]

stul·ti·fy·ing /ˈstʌltɪfaɪɪŋ/ *adj.* (*formal*) making you feel very bored and unable to think of new ideas 乏味得使人呆滞的；使人思维迟钝的：*the stultifying effects of work that never varies* 一成不变的工作造成的使人呆滞的后果 ▶ **stul·tify** *verb* (**stul·ti·fies**, **stul·ti·fy·ing**, **stul·ti·fied**, **stul·ti·fied**) ~ **sb/sth** **stul·ti·fy·ing·ly** *adv.*

stum·ble /ˈstʌmbl/ *verb* **1** [I] to hit your foot against sth while you are walking or running and almost fall 绊脚 SYN **trip**: *The child stumbled and fell.* 孩子绊了一下，摔倒了。◇ ~ **over/on sth** *I stumbled over a rock.* 我在石头上绊了一下。**2** [I] + **adv./prep.** to walk or move in an unsteady way 跌跌撞撞地走；蹒跚而行：*We were stumbling around in the dark looking for a candle.* 黑暗中，我们东跌西撞地找蜡烛。**3** [I] ~ (**over/through sth**) to make a mistake or mistakes and stop while you are speaking, reading to sb or playing music（不顺畅地）说，读，演奏：*In her nervousness she stumbled over her words.* 她因紧张说话结结巴巴的。◇ *I stumbled through the piano piece with difficulty.* 我断断续续地好不容易弹完了那支钢琴曲。▶ **stum·ble** *noun*

PHR V **ˈstumble across/on/upon sth/sb** to discover sth/sb unexpectedly 意外发现；偶然遇见：*Police have stumbled across a huge drugs ring.* 警方无意中发现一个庞大的贩毒集团。 **ˈstumble into sth** to become involved in sth by chance 无意间涉足某事：*I stumbled into acting when I left college.* 我从大学出来后无意间进了演艺界。

ˈstumbling block *noun* ~ (**to sth**) | ~ (**to doing sth**) something that causes problems and prevents you from achieving your aim 障碍物；绊脚石 SYN **obstacle**

stump /stʌmp/ *noun, verb*

■ *noun* **1** [C] the bottom part of a tree left in the ground after the rest has fallen or been cut down 树墩；树桩 **2** [C] the end of sth or the part that is left after the main part has been cut, broken off or worn away 残余部分；残根；残段：*the stump of a pencil* 铅笔头 **3** [C] the short part of sb's leg or arm that is left after the rest has been cut off 残肢 **4** [C, usually pl.] (in CRICKET 板球) one of the set of three vertical wooden sticks (called **the stumps**) that form the WICKET（三柱门的）柱 **5 the stump** [sing.] (*informal, especially NAmE*) the fact of a politician going to different places before an election and trying to get people's support by making speeches（政治人物在选举前的）巡回演说：*The senator gave his standard stump speech.* 那位参议员进行了一次例行的竞选巡回演说。◇ *politicians* **on the stump** 作巡回演说的政治人物 IDM SEE STIR *v.*

■ *verb* **1** [T, usually passive] ~ **sb** (*informal*) to ask sb a question that is too difficult for them to answer or give them a problem that they cannot solve 把…难住；难倒 SYN **baffle**: *I'm stumped. I don't know how they got here before us.* 我搞不懂了。我不知道他们怎么比我们来得还早。◇ *Kate was* **stumped for words** (= unable to answer). 凯特张口结舌。**2** [I] + **adv./prep.** to walk in a noisy, heavy way, especially because you are angry or upset（尤指愤怒或烦恼时）脚步重重地走 SYN **stomp**: *He stumped off, muttering under his breath.* 他嘴里嘟哝着，脚步重重地走了。 **3** [I, T] + **adv./prep.** | ~ **sth** (*NAmE*) to travel around making political speeches, especially before an election（尤指在选举前）作巡回演说：*He stumped around the country trying to build up support.* 他在全国各地巡回演讲，争取更多的支持。**4** [T] ~ **sb** (in CRICKET 板球) (of a WICKETKEEPER) to put a BATSMAN out of the game by knocking off either of the BAILS (= the two pieces of wood that bridge the STUMPS) with the ball, when he or she is out of the area in which the ball can be hit, but not running（三柱门守门员用球打掉三柱门上的横木）使（击球手）出局

PHR V **ˌstump ˈup** (**for sth**) | **ˌstump ˈup sth** (**for sth**) (*BrE, informal*) to pay money for sth （为…）付钱，掏腰包 SYN **cough up**: *We were asked to stump up for the repairs.* 人家要我们出修理费。◇ *Who is going to stump up the extra money?* 额外的钱谁来出？

stumpy /ˈstʌmpi/ *adj.* (*disapproving*) short and thick 短而粗的 SYN **stubby**: *stumpy fingers* 又短又粗的手指 ◇ *a stumpy tail* 短而粗的尾巴

stun /stʌn/ *verb* (**-nn-**) **1** ~ **sb/sth** to make a person or an animal unconscious for a short time, especially by hitting them on the head 使昏迷；（尤指）打昏 SYN **knock sb↔out**: *The fall stunned me for a moment.* 那一下摔得我昏迷了片刻。◇ *The animals are stunned before slaughter.* 屠宰前要先把动物击昏。**2** ~ **sb** to surprise or shock sb so much that they cannot think clearly or speak 使震惊（或惊愕、目瞪口呆）SYN **astound** ➲ SYNONYMS AT SURPRISE **3** ~ **sb** to impress sb very much 给（某人）以深刻印象；使深深感动 SYN **amaze**: *They were stunned by the view from the summit.* 在峰顶看到的景色使他们惊叹不已。▶ **stunned** *adj.*: *She was too stunned to speak.* 她惊愕得说不出话来。◇ *There was a* **stunned silence** *when I told them the news.* 我把消息讲了后，他们惊愕得哑然一片。

stung PAST TENSE, PAST PART. OF STING

ˈstun grenade *noun* a small bomb that shocks people so that they cannot do anything, without seriously injuring them 眩晕弹，震撼手榴弹（使人无法动弹但不会造成重创）

ˈstun gun *noun* a weapon that makes a person or an animal unconscious or unable to move for a short time, usually by giving them a small electric shock 眩晕枪（一种使人或动物短时失去知觉或无法动弹的武器）

stunk PAST PART. OF STINK

stun·ner /ˈstʌnə(r)/ *noun* (*informal*) **1** a person (especially a woman) or a thing that is very attractive or exciting to look at 魅力十足的人（尤指女子）；绝妙的事物 **2** something, such as a piece of news, that is very surprising or shocking 令人震惊的事情（如新闻等）

stun·ning /ˈstʌnɪŋ/ *adj.* (*rather informal*) **1** extremely attractive or impressive 极有魅力的；绝妙的；给人以深刻印象的 SYN **beautiful**: *You look absolutely stunning!* 你看上去漂亮极了！◇ *a stunning view of the lake* 无比优美的湖光水色 **2** extremely surprising or shocking 令人惊奇万分的；令人震惊的：*He suffered a stunning defeat in the election.* 他在选举中惨败。▶ **stun·ning·ly** *adv.*: *stunningly beautiful* 极为美丽 ◇ *a stunningly simple idea* 一个简单得出奇的主意

stunt /stʌnt/ *noun, verb*

■ *noun* **1** a dangerous and difficult action that sb does to entertain people, especially as part of a film/movie（尤指电影中的）特技表演：*He did all his own stunts.* 所有特技都是他自己演的。◇ *a stunt pilot* 特技飞行员 ➲ COLLOCATIONS AT CINEMA **2** (*sometimes disapproving*) something that is done in order to attract people's attention 意在引人注意的花招；噱头：*a publicity stunt* 宣传噱头 **3** (*informal*) a stupid or dangerous act 愚蠢行为；危险举动：*I've had enough of her childish stunts.* 她那些幼稚的愚蠢行为我受够了。◇ *Don't you ever* **pull a stunt** *like that again!* 你再别那样逞能了！

■ *verb* ~ **sb/sth** to prevent sb/sth from growing or developing as much as they/it should 阻碍生长；妨碍发展；遏制：*The constant winds had stunted the growth of plants and bushes.* 老是刮风，花草、灌木长不大。◇ *His illness had not stunted his creativity.* 疾病没有扼杀他的创造力。

stunt·ed /ˈstʌntɪd/ *adj.* that has not been able to grow or develop as much as it should 发育不足的；生长不良的；未能充分发展的：*stunted trees* 没能长大的树 ◇ *the stunted lives of children deprived of education* 未受教育的孩子所过的局限生活

stunt·man /ˈstʌntmæn/, **stunt·woman** /ˈstʌntwʊmən/ *noun* (*pl.* **-men** /-men/, **-women** /-wɪmɪn/) a person whose job is to do dangerous things in place of an actor in a film/movie, etc.; a person who does dangerous things in order to entertain people（电影等中的）特技替身演员；特技表演者 ➲ WORDFINDER NOTE AT ACTOR ➲ MORE LIKE THIS 25, page R28

stu·pefy /ˈstjuːpɪfaɪ; *NAmE* ˈstuː-/ *verb* (**stu·pe·fies**, **stu·pe·fy·ing**, **stu·pe·fied**, **stu·pe·fied**) [often passive] ~ **sb** to surprise or shock sb; to make sb unable to think clearly 使

S

惊讶（或惊呆、思维不清、神志不清）：*He was stupefied by the amount they had spent.* 得知他们花了那么多钱，他都惊呆了。◇ *She was stupefied with cold.* 她给冻迷糊了。▶ **stu·pe·fac·tion** /ˌstjuːpɪˈfækʃn; *NAmE* ˌstuː-/ *noun* [U]

stu·pe·fy·ing /ˈstjuːpɪfaɪɪŋ; *NAmE* ˈstuː-/ *adj.* **1** making you unable to think clearly 使人思维不清的；令人神志不清的：*stupefying boredom* 腻烦得让人发傻 **2** very surprising or shocking 骇人的；令人震惊的 ▶ **stu·pe·fy·ing·ly** *adv.*: *The party was stupefyingly dull.* 这次聚会无聊透了。

stu·pen·dous /stjuːˈpendəs; *NAmE* stuː-/ *adj.* (*rather informal*) extremely large or impressive, especially greater or better than you expect 极大的；令人惊叹的；了不起的 **SYN** **staggering**: *stupendous achievements* 极大的成就 ◇ *stupendous costs* 惊人的花销 ▶ **stu·pen·dous·ly** *adv.*

stu·pid /ˈstjuːpɪd; *NAmE* ˈstuː-/ *adj., noun*

■ ***adj.*** (**stu·pider**, **stu·pidest**) **HELP** **more stupid** and **most stupid** are also common * more stupid 和 most stupid 也常用。**1** showing a lack of thought or good judgement 欠考虑的；糊涂的 **SYN** **foolish**, **silly**: *a stupid mistake* 愚蠢的错误 ◇ *It was a pretty stupid thing to do.* 做那样的事实在愚蠢。◇ *I was* ***stupid enough*** *to believe him.* 我可真够糊涂的，竟然相信他的话。◇ ***It was stupid of you*** *to get involved.* 你卷进去了，真是愚蠢。**2** (*disapproving*) (of a person 人) slow to learn or understand things; not clever or intelligent 笨的；傻的；脑子不好使的：*He'll manage—he isn't stupid.* 他可以的，他不笨。◇ *Forgetting my notes made me* ***look stupid****.* 我忘了带笔记，弄得自己像个傻瓜。**3** [only before noun] (*informal*) used to emphasize that you are annoyed with sb/sth（用以加强语气）讨厌的，恼人的：*I can't get the stupid thing open!* 这破玩意儿我怎么也打不开！◇ *Get your stupid feet off the chair!* 把你的臭脚从椅子上挪开！▶ **stu·pid·ly** *adv.*: *I stupidly agreed to lend him the money.* 我真傻，竟然同意借给他钱了。◇ *Todd stared stupidly at the screen.* 托德呆呆地盯着屏幕。

■ ***noun*** [sing.] (*informal*) if you call sb **stupid**, you are telling them, usually in a joking way, that you think they are not being very intelligent 傻子，笨蛋（常用于开玩笑）：*Yes, stupid, it's you I'm talking to!* 对，傻子，我在跟你说话呢！

stu·pid·ity /stjuːˈpɪdəti; *NAmE* stuː-/ *noun* (*pl.* **-ies**) **1** [U, C, usually pl.] behaviour that shows a lack of thought or good judgement 愚蠢行为；糊涂：*I couldn't believe my own stupidity.* 我干的蠢事我自己都不能相信。◇ *the errors and stupidities of youth* 年轻时犯的错误和做的蠢事 **2** [U] the state or quality of being slow to learn and not clever or intelligent 愚蠢；笨

stu·por /ˈstjuːpə(r); *NAmE* ˈstuː-/ *noun* [sing., U] a state in which you are unable to think, hear, etc. clearly, especially because you have drunk too much alcohol, taken drugs or had a shock（尤指由于醉酒、吸毒或惊吓而出现的）神志不清，恍惚，麻痹状态：*He drank himself into a stupor.* 他喝得烂醉。◇ *a drunken stupor* 酩酊大醉

sturdy /ˈstɜːdi; *NAmE* ˈstɜːrdi/ *adj.* (**stur·dier**, **stur·di·est**) **1** (of an object 物品) strong and not easily damaged 结实的；坚固的 **SYN** **robust**: *a sturdy pair of boots* 一双结实的靴子 ◇ *a sturdy table* 结实的桌子 **2** (of people and animals, or their bodies 人、动物或身体) physically strong and healthy 强壮的；健壮的：*a man of sturdy build* 体格健壮的男人 ◇ *sturdy legs* 强壮有力的腿 ◇ *a sturdy breed of cattle* 一种体格强壮的牛 **3** not easily influenced or changed by other people 坚决的；坚定的；顽强的 **SYN** **firm**, **determined**: *The village has always maintained a sturdy independence.* 这个村子始终顽强地保持着独立。▶ **stur·dily** /-ɪli/ *adv.*: *The boat was sturdily made.* 这艘船造得结实。◇ *a sturdily built young man* 体格健壮的年轻男子 ◇ *a sturdily independent community* 顽强地保持独立的社区 **stur·di·ness** *noun* [U]

stur·geon /ˈstɜːdʒən; *NAmE* ˈstɜːrdʒən/ *noun* [C, U] (*pl.* **stur·geon** or **stur·geons**) a large sea and FRESHWATER fish that lives in northern regions. Sturgeon are used for food and the eggs (called CAVIAR) are also eaten. 鲟

stut·ter /ˈstʌtə(r)/ *verb, noun*

■ ***verb*** **1** [T, I] to have difficulty speaking because you cannot stop yourself from repeating the first sound of some words several times 口吃；结结巴巴地说 **SYN** **stammer**: **+ speech** *'W-w-what?' he stuttered.* "什…什…什么？" 他结结巴巴地说。◇ **~ (sth)** *I managed to stutter a reply.* 我结结巴巴，好不容易应了一句。**2** [I] (of a vehicle or an engine 车辆或发动机) to move or start with difficulty, making short sharp noises or movements 突突地吃力行驶（或艰难启动、艰难运转）：*The car stuttered along in first gear.* 汽车挂了一挡，突突地缓缓前进。

■ ***noun*** [sing.] a speech problem in which a person finds it difficult to say the first sound of a word and repeats it several times 口吃；结巴：*He had a terrible stutter.* 他患严重口吃。

St ˈValentine's Day /ˌsnt ˈvæləntaɪnz deɪ; *NAmE* ˌseɪnt/ *noun* the day (14 February), when people send a card to the person that they love, often without signing their name on it 圣瓦伦丁节，情人节（2 月 14 日，人们常以匿名形式送情人卡）

sty /staɪ/ *noun* **1** (*pl.* **sties**) = PIGSTY **2** (*also* **stye**) (*pl.* **sties** or **styes**) an infection of the EYELID (= the skin above or below the eye) which makes it red and sore 麦粒肿；睑腺炎

Sty·gian /ˈstɪdʒiən/ *adj.* [usually before noun] (*literary*) very dark, and therefore frightening 黑黢黢的；阴森森的：*Stygian gloom* 阴森幽暗 ➲ MORE LIKE THIS 16, page R27 **ORIGIN** From the **Styx**, the river in the underworld which the souls of the dead had to cross in Greek myth. 源自 Styx 一词，即希腊神话中死人的灵魂必须渡过的冥河。

style **AW** /staɪl/ *noun, verb*

■ ***noun***

• **WAY STH IS DONE** 做事方式 **1** [C, U] **~ (of sth)** the particular way in which sth is done 方式；作风：*a style of management* 管理方式 ◇ *a management style* 管理方式 ◇ *furniture to suit your style of living* 适合你的生活方式的家具 ◇ *a study of different teaching styles* 对不同教学方式的研究 ◇ ***I like your style*** (= I like the way you do things). 我喜欢你做事的方式。◇ *Caution was* ***not her style*** (= not the way she usually behaved). 她不是那种谨小慎微的人。◇ *I'm surprised he rides a motorbike—I'd have thought big cars were* ***more his style*** (= what suited him). 没想到他骑的是摩托车。我还以为他开大轿车呢。➲ SEE ALSO LIFESTYLE

• **DESIGN OF CLOTHES/HAIR** 服式；发型 **2** [C] a particular design of sth, especially clothes 样式；款式：*We stock a wide variety of styles and sizes.* 我们有各种款式各种尺码的货品。◇ *Have you thought about having your hair in a shorter style?* 你有没有想过剪个短发型？➲ COLLOCATIONS AT FASHION ➲ SEE ALSO HAIRSTYLE **3** [U] the quality of being fashionable in the clothes that you wear（指服装）时新，时髦，流行式样：*style-conscious teenagers* 讲究时髦的青少年 ◇ *Short skirts are back* ***in style*** (= fashionable). 短裙子又流行起来了。

• **BEING ELEGANT** 格调优雅 **4** [U] the quality of being elegant and made to a high standard 优雅格调；精致性；品位；风度；气派：*The hotel has been redecorated but it's lost a lot of its style.* 旅馆已重新装修，但昔日的优雅格调所剩无几。◇ *She does everything with style and grace.* 她凡事都做得优雅得体。

• **OF BOOK/PAINTING/BUILDING** 书；画；建筑物 **5** [C, U] the features of a book, painting, building, etc. that make it typical of a particular author, artist, historical period, etc. 风格；体：*a style of architecture* 建筑风格 ◇ *a fine example of Gothic style* 哥特风格的佳例 ◇ *a parody written* ***in the style of*** *Molière* 一部模仿莫里哀风格的滑稽喜剧

• **USE OF LANGUAGE** 语言运用 **6** [U, C] the correct use of language 语言规范；好的文风：*It's not considered good style to start a sentence with 'but'.* 人们认为，一句话用 but 开头不是好的文风。◇ *Please follow* ***house style*** (= the rules of spelling, etc. used by a particular publishing company). 请遵循本社的行文格式。

• **-STYLE** …样式 **7** (in adjectives 构成形容词) having the type of style mentioned …式的；…风格的：*Italian-style gardens* 意大利风格的花园 ◇ *a buffet-style breakfast* 自助式早餐 ➲ SEE ALSO OLD-STYLE

• **IN A PLANT** 植物 **8** (*biology* 生) the long thin part of a flower that carries the STIGMA 花柱 ➲ VISUAL VOCAB PAGE V11

IDM in (great, grand, etc.) style in an impressive way 气派；隆重；气势非凡：*She always celebrates her birthday in style.* 她的生日总是过得很排场。◇ *He won the championship in great style.* 他赢得了冠军，尽显大将风度。➲ MORE AT CRAMP *v.*

■ *verb*

• CLOTHES/HAIR, ETC. 服装、头发等 **1** ~ sth to design, make or shape sth in a particular way 把…设计（或缝制、做）成某种式样：*an elegantly styled jacket* 式样高雅的上衣 ◇ *He'd had his hair styled at an expensive salon.* 他去一家豪华美发厅做了头发。

• GIVE NAME/TITLE 称呼 **2** ~ sb/sth/yourself + noun (*formal*) to give sb/sth/yourself a particular name or title 称呼；命名；称：*He styled himself Major Carter.* 他自称卡特少校。

PHR V **'style sth/yourself on sth/sb** to copy the style, manner or appearance of sb/sth 模仿…的风格（或举止、外观）SYN **model**：*a coffee bar styled on a Parisian cafe* 仿照巴黎一家咖啡馆而设计的咖啡馆 ◇ *He styled himself on Elvis Presley.* 他模仿埃尔维斯•普雷斯利唱歌。

'style sheet *noun* (*computing* 计) a file which is used for creating documents in a particular style 样式表，格式页（用以创建文档）

sty·li PL. OF STYLUS

styl·ing AW /ˈstaɪlɪŋ/ *noun* [U] **1** the act of cutting and/or shaping hair in a particular style（发型的）修剪，造型：*styling gel* 定型发胶 **2** the way in which sth is designed 式样；款式：*The car has been criticized for its outdated body styling.* 这种轿车因其过时的车身式样而受到批评。

styl·ish AW /ˈstaɪlɪʃ/ *adj.* (*approving*) fashionable; elegant and attractive 时髦的；新潮的；高雅的；雅致的 SYN **classy**：*his stylish wife* 他那时髦的妻子 ◇ *a stylish restaurant* 雅致的餐馆 ◇ *It was a stylish performance by both artists.* 这是两位艺术家演出的一场高雅节目。▸ **styl·ish·ly** *adv.* **styl·ish·ness** *noun* [U]

styl·ist /ˈstaɪlɪst/ *noun* **1** a person whose job is cutting and shaping people's hair 发型师 **2** a writer who takes great care to write or say sth in an elegant or unusual way 语言风格优美（或独特）的人；文体家 **3** a person whose job is to create or design a particular style or image for a product, a person, an advertisement, etc.（产品、人、广告等的）造型设计师，形象设计师 **4** a person who designs fashionable clothes 时装设计师 **5** (in sport or music 体育运动或音乐) a person who performs with style 表现得有格调的人

styl·is·tic /staɪˈlɪstɪk/ *adj.* [only before noun] connected with the style an artist uses in a particular piece of art, writing or music 风格上的；文体上的：*stylistic analysis* 风格分析 ◇ *stylistic features* 风格特点 ▸ **styl·is·tic·al·ly** /-kli/ *adv.*

styl·is·tics /staɪˈlɪstɪks/ *noun* [U] the study of style and the methods used in written language 文体学；风格学 ➲ MORE LIKE THIS 29, page R28

styl·ized AW (*BrE also* **-ised**) /ˈstaɪlaɪzd/ *adj.* drawn, written, etc. in a way that is not natural or realistic（绘画、写作等手法）非写实的：*a stylized drawing of a house* 用非写实手法画的一座房子 ◇ *the highly stylized form of acting in Japanese theatre* 日本戏剧中高度非写实的表演形式 ▸ **styl·iza·tion, -isa·tion** /ˌstaɪlaɪˈzeɪʃn; *NAmE* -ləˈz-/ *noun* [U]

Stylo·phone™ /ˈstaɪləfəʊn; *NAmE* -foʊn/ *noun* a small electronic musical instrument played by touching its keyboard with a STYLUS 斯笛洛风电子琴（用触笔弹奏）

sty·lus /ˈstaɪləs/ *noun* (*pl.* **sty·luses** or **sty·li** /ˈstaɪlaɪ/) **1** a device on a RECORD PLAYER that looks like a small needle and is placed on the record in order to play it（唱机的）唱针 **2** (*computing* 计) a special pen used to write text or draw an image on a special computer screen 触控笔（用以在电脑屏幕上书写、画画等）

sty·mie /ˈstaɪmi/ *verb* (**sty·mie·ing, sty·mying, sty·mied, sty·mied**) ~ sb/sth (*informal*) to prevent sb from doing sth that they have planned or want to do; to prevent sth from happening 阻挠；阻碍；阻止；妨碍 SYN **foil**

styp·tic /ˈstɪptɪk/ *adj.* (*medical* 医) able to stop the loss of blood from a wound 能止血的：*I use a styptic pencil on shaving cuts.* 我用止血笔处理刮胡子割破的伤口。

Styro·foam™ /ˈstaɪrəfəʊm; *NAmE* -foʊm/ *noun* [U] (*especially NAmE*) = POLYSTYRENE：*Styrofoam cups* 舒泰龙泡沫塑料杯

sua·sive /ˈsweɪsɪv/ *adj.* (*linguistics* 语言) (of verbs 动词) having a meaning that includes the idea of persuading 表劝说的；说服的 ▸ **sua·sion** /ˈsweɪʒn/ *noun* [U]

suave /swɑːv/ *adj.* (especially of a man 尤指男子) confident, elegant and polite, sometimes in a way that does not seem sincere 精明练达的；圆滑的 ▸ **suave·ly** *adv.*

sub /sʌb/ *noun, verb*

■ *noun* (*informal*) **1** = SUBMARINE **2** a substitute who replaces another player in a team 替补队员：*He came on as sub.* 他作为替补上场。**3** (*BrE*) a SUBSCRIPTION (= money that you pay regularly when you are a member of a club, etc.)（向俱乐部等定期交纳的）会员费 **4** (*BrE*) a SUBEDITOR 助理编辑；审校人 **5** (*NAmE, informal*) a SUBSTITUTE TEACHER 代课教师

■ *verb* **1** [T] ~ sb to replace a sports player with another player during a game（在比赛中）替换（队员）SYN **substitute**：*He was subbed after just five minutes because of a knee injury.* 他仅上场了五分钟便因膝部受伤被替换下场。**2** [I] ~ (for sb) to do sb else's job for them for a short time 暂代（某人）工作；替班 SYN **substitute 3** [T] ~ sth for sth to use sth instead of sth else, especially instead of the thing you would normally use 代用；替代（尤指通常使用的东西）SYN **substitute**：*For a lower-calorie version of the recipe, try subbing milk for cream.* 要降低这道菜的热量，可用牛奶代替奶油。**4** [T] ~ sb sth (*BrE, informal*) to lend sb money for a short time 短期借（款）给：*Could you sub me £50 till next week?* 借我 50 英镑，下星期还你，可以吗？

sub- /sʌb/ *prefix* **1** (in nouns and adjectives 构成名词和形容词) below; less than 在…以下；少于；低于；亚于；次于：*sub-zero temperatures* 零度以下气温 ◇ *a subtropical* (= almost tropical) *climate* 亚热带气候 ◇ *substandard* 低于标准的 **2** (in nouns and adjectives 构成名词和形容词) under 在…下面（或底下）：*subway* 地铁 ◇ *submarine* 潜艇 **3** (in verbs and nouns 构成动词和名词) a smaller part of sth 分支；分部；分：*subdivide* 再划分 ◇ *subset* 子集 ➲ MORE LIKE THIS 6, page R25

sub·al·tern /ˈsʌbltən; *NAmE* səˈbɔːltərn/ *noun* any officer in the British army who is lower in rank than a captain（英国）陆军中尉

ˌsub-ˈaqua *adj.* [only before noun] (*BrE*) connected with sports that are done underwater 水下运动的：*sub-aqua diving* 潜水 ◇ *sub-aqua equipment* 潜水设备

sub·atom·ic /ˌsʌbəˈtɒmɪk; *NAmE* -ˈtɑːm-/ *adj.* [usually before noun] (*physics* 物) smaller than, or found in, an atom 亚原子的；比原子小的；原子内的：*subatomic particles* 亚原子粒子

sub·clause /ˈsʌbklɔːz/ *noun* (*law* 律) one of the parts of a clause (= section) in a legal document（法律文件的）下设条款，次条款，子条款

sub·com·mit·tee /ˈsʌbkəmɪti/ *noun* [C+sing./pl. v.] a smaller committee formed from a main committee in order to study a particular subject in more detail（委员会内的）小组委员会

sub·com·pact /ˈsʌbkəmpækt/ *noun* (*NAmE*) a small car, smaller than a COMPACT 超小型汽车

sub·con·scious /ˌsʌbˈkɒnʃəs; *NAmE* -ˈkɑːn-/ *adj., noun*

■ *adj.* [usually before noun] connected with feelings that influence your behaviour even though you are not aware of them 下意识的；潜意识的：*subconscious desires* 下意识的欲望 ◇ *the subconscious mind* 潜意识 ➲ COMPARE CONSCIOUS, UNCONSCIOUS *adj.* (2) ▸ **sub·con·scious·ly**

S

adv.: *Subconsciously, she was looking for the father she had never known.* 她在下意识地寻找自己从未见过的父亲。

■ *noun* **the/your subconscious** [sing.] the part of your mind that contains feelings that you are not aware of 下意识；潜意识 ➲ COMPARE UNCONSCIOUS *n.*

sub·con·tin·ent /ˌsʌbˈkɒntɪnənt; *NAmE* -ˈkɑːn-/ *noun* [usually sing.] a large land mass that forms part of a continent, especially the part of Asia that includes India, Pakistan and Bangladesh 次大陆（尤指包括印度、巴基斯坦和孟加拉国在内的南亚次大陆）：*the Indian subcontinent* 印度次大陆

sub·con·tract *verb, noun*

■ *verb* /ˌsʌbkənˈtrækt; *NAmE* ˌsʌbˈkɑːntrækt/ to pay a person or company to do some of the work that you have been given a contract to do 分包；转包：**~ sth (to sb/sth)** *We subcontracted the work to a small engineering firm.* 我们把工作转包给了一家小型工程公司。◇ **~ sb/sth (to do sth)** *We subcontracted a small engineering firm to do the work.* 我们转包给了一家小型工程公司去干那项工作。▶ **sub·con·tract·ing** *noun* [U]

■ *noun* /ˌsʌbˈkɒntrækt; *NAmE* ˌsʌbˈkɑːntrækt/ a contract to do part of the work that has been given to another person or company 分包合同；转包合同

sub·con·tract·or /ˌsʌbkənˈtræktə(r); *NAmE* sʌbˈkɑːntræk-/ *noun* a person or company that does part of the work given to another person or company 分包商；分包人

sub·cul·ture /ˈsʌbkʌltʃə(r)/ *noun* (*sometimes disapproving*) the behaviour and beliefs of a particular group of people in society that are different from those of most people（某群体特有的）亚文化行为观念，次文化：*the **criminal/drug/youth, etc. subculture*** 犯罪、吸毒、青少年群体等的亚文化

sub·cuta·ne·ous /ˌsʌbkjuˈteɪniəs/ *adj.* [usually before noun] (*specialist*) under the skin 皮下的：*a subcutaneous injection* 皮下注射 ▶ **sub·cuta·ne·ous·ly** *adv.*

sub·dir·ec·tory /ˈsʌbdərektəri; -dɪ-; -daɪ-/ *noun* (*pl.* **-ies**) (*computing* 计) a DIRECTORY (= list of files or programs) which is inside another directory 子目录

sub·div·ide /ˈsʌbdɪvaɪd; ˌsʌbdɪˈvaɪd/ *verb* [T, often passive, I] **~ (sth) (into sth)** to divide sth into smaller parts; to be divided into smaller parts（被）再分割，再分

S

sub·div·ision *noun* **1** /ˌsʌbdɪˈvɪʒn/ [U] the act of dividing a part of sth into smaller parts 再分割；再分；细分 **2** /ˈsʌbdɪvɪʒn/ [C] one of the smaller parts into which a part of sth has been divided 进一步分成的部分；分支；分部：*a police subdivision* (= the area covered by one particular police force) 警察部门下属的管辖分区 ◇ *subdivisions within the Hindu caste system* 印度教种姓制度内的不同等级 **3** /ˈsʌbdɪvɪʒn/ [C] (*NAmE*) an area of land that has been divided up for building houses on（分割成小块的）建房土地

sub·due /səbˈdjuː; *NAmE* -ˈduː/ *verb* (*rather formal*) **1 ~ sb/sth** to bring sb/sth under control, especially by using force 制伏；征服；控制 SYN **defeat**: *Troops were called in to subdue the rebels.* 军队被调来镇压反叛者。**2 ~ sth** to calm or control your feelings 抑制，压制，克制（感情）SYN **suppress**: *Julia had to subdue an urge to stroke his hair.* 朱莉娅不得不克制住自己，不去抚摩他的头发。

sub·dued /səbˈdjuːd; *NAmE* -ˈduːd/ *adj.* **1** (of a person 人) unusually quiet, and possibly unhappy 闷闷不乐的；抑郁的；默不作声的：*He seemed a bit subdued to me.* 我觉得他当时有点闷闷不乐。◇ *She was in a subdued mood.* 她心情抑郁。◇ *The reception was a subdued affair.* 招待会开得冷冷清清的。**2** (of light or colours 光线或色彩) not very bright 柔和的：*subdued lighting* 柔和的灯光 **3** (of sounds 声音) not very loud 压低的；小声的：*a subdued conversation* 小声的谈话 **4** (of business activity 商业活动) not very busy; with not much activity 不活跃的；低迷的；萧条的：*a period of subdued trading* 贸易萧条时期

sub·edi·tor /ˌsʌbˈedɪtə(r)/ (*also informal* **sub**) *noun* (*BrE*) a person whose job is to check and make changes to the text of a newspaper or magazine before it is printed 助理编辑；审校人 ▶ **sub-edit** *verb* [I, T] **~ (sth)**

sub·group /ˈsʌbɡruːp/ *noun* a smaller group made up of members of a larger group 小组；（团体中的）部分

sub·head·ing /ˌsʌbˈhedɪŋ/ *noun* a title given to any of the sections into which a longer piece of writing has been divided 小标题；子标题

sub·human /ˌsʌbˈhjuːmən/ *adj.* (*disapproving*) not working or behaving like a normal human; not fit for humans 非人的；不齿于人类的；不适合人类的：*subhuman behaviour* 不齿于人类的行为 ◇ *They were living in subhuman conditions.* 他们生活在非人的条件下。➲ COMPARE INHUMAN, SUPERHUMAN

sub·ject 🔑 *noun, adj., verb*

■ *noun* /ˈsʌbdʒɪkt; -dʒekt/

• **OF CONVERSATION/BOOK** 谈话；书籍 **1** 🔑 a thing or person that is being discussed, described or dealt with 主题；题目；话题；题材；问题：*an unpleasant **subject of conversation*** 不愉快的话题 ◇ *books on many different subjects* 题材广泛的各种书籍 ◇ *a magazine article **on the subject of** space travel* 一篇谈航天旅行的杂志文章 ◇ *I have nothing more to say on the subject.* 关于这个问题，我再没有要说的了。◇ *I wish you'd **change the subject*** (= talk about sth else). 我希望你换个话题。◇ *How did we **get onto the subject of** marriage?* 我们怎么谈到婚姻问题上了？◇ *We seem to have **got off the subject** we're meant to be discussing.* 我们似乎偏离了应当讨论的题目。◇ *Nelson Mandela is the subject of a new biography.* 纳尔逊·曼德拉是一本新传记的传主。◇ *Climate change is still very much a **subject for debate**.* 气候变化很大程度上仍是一个争论的话题。

• **AT SCHOOL/COLLEGE** 学校 **2** 🔑 an area of knowledge studied in a school, college, etc. 学科；科目；课程：*Biology is my favourite subject.* 生物是我最喜欢的学科。

• **OF PICTURE/PHOTOGRAPH** 绘画；摄影 **3** a person or thing that is the main feature of a picture or photograph, or that a work of art is based on 表现对象；绘画（或拍摄）题材：*Focus the camera on the subject.* 把相机的焦距调到被拍对象上。◇ *Classical landscapes were a popular subject with many 18th century painters.* 古典风景画是 18 世纪许多画家所喜欢用的题材。

• **OF EXPERIMENT** 实验 **4** a person or thing being used to study sth, especially in an experiment 接受试验者；实验对象：*We need male subjects between the ages of 18 and 25 for the experiment.* 我们需要 18 至 25 岁之间的男性来接受试验。

• **GRAMMAR** 语法 **5** a noun, noun phrase or pronoun representing the person or thing that performs the action of the verb (*I* in *I sat down.*), about which sth is stated (*the house* in *the house is very old*) or, in a passive sentence, that is affected by the action of the verb (*the tree* in *the tree was blown down in the storm*) 主语 ➲ COMPARE OBJECT *n.* (4), PREDICATE *n.* ➲ **WORDFINDER NOTE** AT GRAMMAR

• **OF COUNTRY** 国家 **6** a person who has the right to belong to a particular country, especially one with a king or queen（尤指君主制国家的）国民，臣民：*a British subject* 英国国民

■ *adj.* /ˈsʌbdʒɪkt; -dʒekt/ (*formal*) **1 ~ to sth** likely to be affected by sth, especially sth bad 可能受…影响的；易遭受…的：*Flights are subject to delay because of the fog.* 由于有雾，航班可能延误。**2 ~ to sth** depending on sth in order to be completed or agreed 取决于；视…而定：*The article is ready to publish, subject to your approval.* 那篇文章准备好了，可以发表，就等你批准了。◇ *All the holidays on offer are subject to availability.* 所有拟订的度假行程，须能成行始可确定。**3 ~ to sth/sb** under the authority of sth/sb 受…支配；服从于：*All nuclear installations are subject to international safeguards.* 一切核设施均须执行国际防护措施。**4** [only before noun] controlled by the government of another country 受异族统治的；臣服的：*subject peoples* 被他国统治的民族

■ *verb* /səbˈdʒekt/ **~ sth (to sth)** (*formal*) to bring a country or group of people under your control, especially by using force 使臣服；使顺从；（尤指）压服：*The Roman Empire subjected most of Europe to its rule.* 罗马帝国把欧洲多数地区置于自己的统治之下。▶ **sub·jec·tion** /səbˈdʒekʃn/

noun [U]

PHR V **sub'ject sb/sth to sth** [often passive] to make sb/sth experience, suffer or be affected by sth, usually sth unpleasant 使经受；使遭受：*to be subjected to ridicule* 受到嘲笑 ◇ *The city was subjected to heavy bombing.* 那座城市遭受猛烈轰炸。◇ *The defence lawyers claimed that the prisoners had been subjected to cruel and degrading treatment.* 辩护律师声称囚犯遭到了残暴和侮辱性的对待。

➲ MORE LIKE THIS 21, page R27

sub·ject·ive /səb'dʒektɪv/ *adj.* **1** based on your own ideas or opinions rather than facts and therefore sometimes unfair 主观的（非客观的）：*a highly subjective point of view* 非常主观的看法 ◇ *Everyone's opinion is bound to be subjective.* 每个人的意见都必定是主观的。**2** (of ideas, feelings or experiences 思想、感情或经历) existing in sb's mind rather than in the outside world 主观的（非现实世界的）**3** [only before noun] (*grammar* 语法) the **subjective** case is the one which is used for the subject of a sentence 主语的；主格的 **OPP** **objective** ▸ **sub·ject·ive·ly** *adv.*: *People who are less subjectively involved are better judges.* 主观因素介入愈少，愈能作出恰当的判断。◇ *subjectively perceived changes* 主观感受到的变化 **sub·ject·iv·ity** /ˌsʌbdʒek'tɪvəti/ *noun* [U]: *There is an element of subjectivity in her criticism.* 她的批评有主观因素。

sub·ject·iv·ism /səb'dʒektɪvɪzəm/ *noun* [U] (*philosophy* 哲) the theory that all knowledge and moral values are subjective rather than based on truth that actually exists in the real world 主观主义；主观论

'subject matter *noun* [U] the ideas or information contained in a book, speech, painting, etc.（著作、讲话、绘画等的）主题，题材，主要内容：*The artist was revolutionary in both subject matter and technique.* 这位画家在内容和手法两方面都有重大创新。◇ *She's searching for subject matter for her new book.* 她要写一部新书，正寻找题材。

sub ju·dice /ˌsʌb 'dʒuːdəsi; -seɪ; -keɪ/ *adj.* [not usually before noun] (*from Latin*, *law* 律) if a legal case is **sub judice**, it is still being discussed in court and it is therefore illegal for anyone to talk about it in newspapers, etc. 在审理中，尚未裁决（任何人公诸报端等均属违法）

sub·ju·gate /'sʌbdʒuɡeɪt/ *verb* [usually passive] **~ sb/sth** (*formal*) to defeat sb/sth; to gain control over sb/sth 征服；制伏；使屈服；使服从：*a subjugated race* 被征服的民族 ◇ *Her personal ambitions had been subjugated to* (= considered less important than) *the needs of her family.* 她个人的雄心壮志让位给了家庭的需要。 ▸ **sub·ju·ga·tion** /ˌsʌbdʒu'ɡeɪʃn/ *noun* [U] (*formal*): *the subjugation of Ireland by England* 英格兰对爱尔兰的征服

sub·junct·ive /səb'dʒʌŋktɪv/ *noun* (*grammar* 语法) the form (or MOOD) of a verb that expresses wishes, possibility or UNCERTAINTY; a verb in this form 虚拟式；虚拟语气：*The verb is in the subjunctive.* 这个动词是虚拟语气。◇ *In 'I wish I were taller', 'were' is a subjunctive.* 在 I wish I were taller 中，were 是虚拟式。▸ **sub·junct·ive** *adj.*: *the subjunctive mood* 虚拟语气

sub·let /ˌsʌb'let/ *verb* (**sub·let·ting**, **sub·let**, **sub·let**) [T, I] **~ (sth) (to sb)** to rent to sb else all or part of a property that you rent from the owner 转租，分租（租来的物业）

➲ COLLOCATIONS AT HOUSE

ˌsub lieu'tenant *noun* an officer in the British navy just below the rank of LIEUTENANT（英国）海军中尉

sub·lim·ate /'sʌblɪmeɪt/ *verb* **~ sth** (*psychology* 心) to direct your energy, especially sexual energy, to socially acceptable activities such as work, exercise, art, etc. 升华，使高尚化（把性欲冲动等转移到工作、锻炼、艺术等社会可接受的活动中）**SYN** **channel** ▸ **sub·lim·ation** /ˌsʌblɪ'meɪʃn/ *noun* [U]

sub·lime /sə'blaɪm/ *adj.*, *noun*

■ *adj.* **1** of very high quality and causing great admiration 崇高的；壮丽的；宏伟的；令人赞叹的：*sublime beauty* 令人赞叹的美 ◇ *a sublime combination of flavours* 搭配巧妙的几种味道 **2** (*formal, often disapproving*) (of a person's behaviour or attitudes 人的行为或态度) extreme, especially in a way that shows they are not aware of what they are doing or are not concerned about what happens because of it 极端的；极端而盲目的；一味的：*the sublime confidence of youth* 年轻人目空一切的自信 ▸ **sub·lime·ly** *adv.*: *sublimely beautiful* 美得令人赞叹 ◇ *She was sublimely unaware of the trouble she had caused.* 她压根儿没察觉自己闹出了乱子。**sub·lim·ity** /sə'blɪməti/ *noun* [U]

■ *noun* **the sublime** [sing.] something that is sublime 崇高的事物；壮丽的景象；绝妙的东西：*He transforms the most ordinary subject into the sublime.* 经他一点化，极普通的题材也能变得令人叫绝。

IDM **from the sublime to the ri'diculous** used to describe a situation in which sth serious, important or of high quality is followed by sth silly, unimportant or of poor quality 从高超到荒谬；从高妙到低俗

sub·lim·inal /ˌsʌb'lɪmɪnl/ *adj.* affecting your mind even though you are not aware of it 下意识的；潜意识的：*subliminal advertising* 隐性广告 ▸ **sub·lim·in·al·ly** *adv.*

ˌsub-ma'chine gun *noun* a light MACHINE GUN that you can hold in your hands to fire 冲锋枪；轻型自动枪

sub·mar·ine /ˌsʌbmə'riːn; 'sʌbməriːn/ *noun*, *adj.*

■ *noun* (*also informal* **sub**) **1** a ship that can travel underwater 潜艇：*a nuclear submarine* 核潜艇 ◇ *a submarine base* 潜艇基地 ➲ WORDFINDER NOTE AT NAVY **2** (*also* **ˌsubmarine 'sandwich**, **hero**) (*all NAmE*) a long bread roll split open along its length and filled with various types of food 潜艇三明治，长卷三明治（用长卷面包纵向切开，内夹各种食物）

■ *adj.* [only before noun] (*specialist*) existing or located under the sea 水下的；海底的：*submarine plant life* 海底植物 ◇ *submarine cables* 海底电缆

sub·mar·iner /sʌb'mærɪnə(r); *NAmE also* ˌsʌbmə'riːnər/ *noun* a sailor who works on a submarine 潜艇水兵

sub·merge /səb'mɜːdʒ; *NAmE* -'mɜːrdʒ/ *verb* **1** [I, T] to go under the surface of water or liquid; to put sth or make sth go under the surface of water or liquid（使）潜入水中，没入水中，浸没，淹没：*The submarine had had time to submerge before the warship could approach.* 潜水艇没等军舰靠近就及时潜入水下了。◇ **~ sth** *The fields had been submerged by floodwater.* 农田被洪水淹没了。**2** [T] **~ sth** to hide ideas, feelings, opinions, etc. completely 湮没，湮灭，掩盖（思想、感情等）：*Doubts that had been submerged in her mind suddenly resurfaced.* 她心里早已湮灭的疑团突然又浮现出来。▸ **sub·merged** *adj.*: *Her submerged car was discovered in the river by police divers.* 她被河水淹没的汽车给警方的潜水员找到了。**sub·mer·sion** /səb'mɜːʃn; *NAmE* -'mɜːrʒn/ *noun* [U]

sub·mers·ible /səb'mɜːsəbl; *NAmE* -'mɜːrs-/ *adj.*, *noun*

■ *adj.* (*NAmE also* **sub·merg·ible** /səb'mɜːdʒəbl; *NAmE* səb'mɜːrdʒ-/) that can be used underwater 水下使用的：*a submersible camera* 水下摄影机

■ *noun* a SUBMARINE (= a ship that can travel underwater) that goes underwater for short periods 可潜船；潜水器

sub·mis·sion **AW** /səb'mɪʃn/ *noun* **1** [U] the act of accepting that sb has defeated you and that you must obey them 屈服；投降；归顺 **SYN** **surrender**: *a gesture of submission* 投降的手势 ◇ *to* ***beat/force/starve sb into submission*** 打得 / 强迫 / 饿得某人屈服 **2** [U, C] the act of giving a document, proposal, etc. to sb in authority so that they can study or consider it; the document, etc. that you give 提交；呈递；提交（或呈递）的文件、建议等：*When is the final date for the submission of proposals?* 呈交提案的最后日期是什么时候？◇ *They prepared a report for submission to the council.* 他们准备了一份报告要提交给理事会。◇ *All parties will have the opportunity to* ***make submissions*** *relating to this case.* 各方均有机会提交与此案有关的陈述。**3** [C] (*law* 律) a statement that is made to a judge in court（向法官提出的）看法，意见

sub·mis·sive /səb'mɪsɪv/ *adj.* too willing to accept sb else's authority and willing to obey them without questioning anything they want you to do 唯命是从的；顺从的；驯服的；听话的：*He expected his daughters to*

S

be meek and submissive. 他期望女儿都温顺听话。◇ *She followed him like a submissive child.* 她像个听话的孩子一样跟着他。**OPP** **assertive** ▶ **sub·mis·sive·ly** *adv.*: *'You're right and I was wrong,' he said submissively.* "你说得对，是我错了。" 他恭顺地说。 **sub·mis·sive·ness** *noun* [U]

sub·mit **AW** /səbˈmɪt/ *verb* (-tt-) **1** [T] ~ **sth** (**to sb/sth**) to give a document, proposal, etc. to sb in authority so that they can study or consider it 提交，呈递（文件、建议等）：*to* ***submit an application/a claim/a complaint*** 呈递申请书 / 书面要求；提交控诉书 ◇ *Completed projects must be submitted by 10 March.* 完成的方案必须在 3 月 10 日前提交。➲ WORDFINDER NOTE AT COMPETITION **2** [I, T] (*formal*) to accept the authority, control or greater strength of sb/sth; to agree to sth because of this 顺从；屈服；投降；不得已接受 **SYN** **give in** (**to sb/sth**), **yield**: ~ (**to sb/sth**) *She refused to submit to threats.* 面对威胁，她拒不低头。◇ ~ **yourself** (**to sb/sth**) *He submitted himself to a search by the guards.* 他接受卫兵搜查。**3** [T] ~ **that**... (*law* 律 or *formal*) to say or suggest sth 表示；认为；主张；建议：*Counsel for the defence submitted that the evidence was inadmissible.* 被告律师认为这一证据不可采纳。➲ MORE LIKE THIS 36, page R29

sub·nor·mal /ˌsʌbˈnɔːml; *NAmE* -ˈnɔːrml/ *adj.* **1** (*specialist*) lower than normal 低于正常的；正常值以下的；偏低的：*subnormal temperatures* 偏低的气温 **2** (*sometimes offensive*) having less than the normal level of intelligence 低能的；弱智的：*educationally subnormal children* 学习能力低下的儿童

sub·opti·mal /ˌsʌbˈɒptɪməl; *NAmE* -ˈɑːpt-/ *adj.* of less than the best standard or quality 次优的；未达最佳标准（或质量）的；非最理想的：*Some breeders keep their animals in suboptimal conditions.* 有些畜牧户在差强人意的环境下饲养牲畜。◇ *A score of 6 is optimal; 5 or less is suboptimal.* * 6 分最佳，5 分及以下为次优。➲ COMPARE OPTIMAL ▶ **sub·opti·mal·ly** *adv.*

sub·or·din·ate **AW** *adj., noun, verb*

■ ***adj.*** /səˈbɔːdɪnət; *NAmE* -ˈbɔːrd-/ **1** ~ (**to sb**) having less power or authority than sb else in a group or an organization 隶属的；从属的；下级的：*In many societies women are subordinate to men.* 在许多社会中，妇女都从属于男人。**2** ~ (**to sth**) less important than sth else 次要的 **SYN** **secondary**: *All other issues are subordinate to this one.* 所有其他问题都没有这一问题重要。

■ ***noun*** /səˈbɔːdɪnət; *NAmE* -ˈbɔːrd-/ a person who has a position with less authority and power than sb else in an organization 下级；部属 **SYN** **inferior**: *the relationship between subordinates and superiors* 上下级关系

■ ***verb*** /səˈbɔːdɪneɪt; *NAmE* -ˈbɔːrd-/ ~ **sb/sth** (**to sb/sth**) (*formal*) to treat sb/sth as less important than sb/sth else 把…置于次要地位；使从属于：*Safety considerations were subordinated to commercial interests.* 商业利益置于安全考虑之上。 ▶ **sub·or·din·ation** **AW** /səˌbɔːdɪˈneɪʃn; *NAmE* -ˌbɔːrd-/ *noun* [U]

suˌbordinate ˈclause (*also* **deˌpendent ˈclause**) *noun* (*grammar* 语法) a group of words that is not a sentence but adds information to the main part of a sentence, for example *when it rang* in *She answered the phone when it rang.* 从句；从属分句 ➲ COMPARE COORDINATE CLAUSE, MAIN CLAUSE

suˌbordinating conˈjunction *noun* (*grammar* 语法) a word that begins a subordinate clause, for example 'although' or 'because' 从属连词；主从连词；从属连接词 ➲ COMPARE COORDINATING CONJUNCTION

sub·orn /səˈbɔːn; *NAmE* səˈbɔːrn/ *verb* ~ **sb** (*law* 律) to pay or persuade sb to do sth illegal, especially to tell lies in court 收买，买通（使作伪证等）；唆使（他人犯法）：*to suborn a witness* 收买证人

sub·par /ˌsʌbˈpɑː(r)/ *adj.* (*especially NAmE*) below a level of quality that is usual or expected 不到一般（或预期）水平的；低于标准的：*a subpar performance* 低水平的演出

sub·plot /ˈsʌbplɒt; *NAmE* -plɑːt/ *noun* a series of events in a play, novel, etc. that is separate from but linked to the main story（戏剧、小说等的）次要情节，从属情节

sub·poena /səˈpiːnə/ *noun, verb*

■ ***noun*** (*law* 律) a written order to attend court as a witness to give evidence（传唤证人出庭的）传票

■ ***verb*** ~ **sb** (**to do sth**) (*law* 律) to order sb to attend court and give evidence as a witness 以传票传唤（证人出庭）：*The court subpoenaed her to appear as a witness.* 法庭传唤她出庭作证。➲ COLLOCATIONS AT JUSTICE

ˌsub-ˈpost office *noun* (*BrE*) a small local post office（本地的）小邮局；邮政所

ˌsub-ˈprime (*BrE*) (*NAmE* **ˌsubˈprime**) *adj.* (*finance* 财) connected with the practice of lending money to sb who is likely to have difficulty paying it back 次级的，次贷的（指贷款给信用差、可能无力还款的人）：*a subprime loan/mortgage* 次级贷款 / 按揭 ◇ *subprime lenders/borrowers* 次级放款人 / 借款人

sub·rou·tine /ˈsʌbruːtiːn/ (*also* **sub·pro·gram** /ˈsʌbprəʊɡræm; *NAmE* -proʊ-/) *noun* (*computing* 计) a set of instructions which perform a task within a program 子例程（程序中执行某任务的一系列指令）

sub-Saharan /ˌsʌb səˈhɑːrən/ *adj.* [only before noun] from or relating to areas in Africa that are south of the Sahara Desert 撒哈拉沙漠以南（非洲地区）的：*sub-Saharan Africa* 非洲撒哈拉沙漠以南的地区

sub·scribe /səbˈskraɪb/ *verb* **1** [I] ~ (**to sth**) to pay an amount of money regularly in order to receive or use sth 定期订购（或订阅等）：*Which journals does the library subscribe to?* 图书馆订有哪些报刊？◇ *We subscribe to several sports channels* (= on TV). 我们付费收看好几个体育频道。**2** [I] ~ (**to sth**) to arrange to have regular access to an electronic information service or other Internet service 订阅（电子信息服务或其他互联网服务）：*He subscribed to a newsgroup* (= on the Internet). 他成了一个网上新闻组的用户。◇ *To hear the full interview, subscribe to the free National Geographic News podcast.* 要听完整的采访，请订阅免费的《国家地理》新闻播客。**3** [I] ~ (**to sth**) to pay money regularly to be a member of an organization or to support a charity 定期交纳（会员费）；定期（向慈善机构）捐款；定期捐助：*He subscribes regularly to Amnesty International.* 他定期向大赦国际捐款。**4** [I] ~ (**for sth**) (*finance* 财) to apply to buy shares in a company 认购（股份）➲ SEE ALSO OVERSUBSCRIBED **5** [T, usually passive] ~ **sth** to apply to take part in an activity, use a service, etc. 申请；预订；报名：*The tour of Edinburgh is fully subscribed.* 去爱丁堡旅游的名额已经满了。

PHR V **subˈscribe to sth** (*formal*) to agree with or support an opinion, a theory, etc. 同意；赞成 **SYN** **believe in sth**: *The authorities no longer subscribe to the view that disabled people are unsuitable as teachers.* 当局不再支持残疾人不适宜做教师的观点。

sub·scriber /səbˈskraɪbə(r)/ *noun* **1** a person who pays money, usually once a year, to receive regular copies of a magazine or newspaper（报刊的）订阅人，订购者，订户 **2** a person who gives money regularly to help the work of an organization such as a charity（慈善机关等的）定期捐款者，定期捐助者 **3** a person who pays to receive a service 消费者；用户：*subscribers to cable television* 有线电视用户

sub·script /ˈsʌbskrɪpt/ *noun* **1** a letter, number or symbol that is written or printed below the normal line of writing or printing 下标（写或印在正常位置下方的字符）：*A subscript is used for secondary stress.* 次重音用下标表示。◇ *The subscript 'B' designates 'Brown'.* 下标的 B 表示 Brown。➲ COMPARE SUPERSCRIPT **2** (*computing* 计) a symbol, sometimes written as a subscript, used in a computer program to identify one part of an ARRAY (2)（阵列）标注，下标 ▶ **subscript** *adj.* [only before noun]

sub·scrip·tion /səbˈskrɪpʃn/ *noun* [C, U] **1** an amount of money you pay, usually once a year, to receive regular copies of a newspaper or magazine, etc.; the act of paying this money（报刊等的）订阅费，订购款；订阅，订购：*an annual subscription* 一年期订阅 ◇ ~ (**to/for sth**)

S

to take out a subscription to 'Newsweek' 订阅《新闻周刊》 ◇ *to **cancel/renew a subscription*** 退订；续订 ◇ *Copies are available by subscription.* 此刊物供订购。**2** a sum of money that you pay regularly to a charity, or to be a member of a club or to receive a service; the act of paying this money（向慈善机构的）定期捐款；（俱乐部的）会员费；（服务的）用户费；捐款（或会员费、服务费）的交纳 SYN **donation**: *a monthly subscription to Oxfam* 每月给乐施会的捐款 ➲ WORDFINDER NOTE AT CLUB **3** the act of people paying money for sth to be done 集体资助；集体捐助：*A statue in his memory was erected by **public subscription**.* 由公众捐资建起一座纪念他的雕像。➲ SYNONYMS AT PAYMENT

sub'scription concert *noun* (*BrE*) any of the concerts in a series for which the tickets are sold in advance 联票音乐会（预售系列音乐会中的一场）

sub·sec·tion /ˈsʌbsekʃn/ *noun* a part of a section, especially of a legal document 分部；分段；（尤指法律文件的）分款，分项 ➲ WORDFINDER NOTE AT DOCUMENT

sub·se·quent AW /ˈsʌbsɪkwənt/ *adj.* (*formal*) happening or coming after sth else 随后的；后来的；之后的；接后的：*subsequent generations* 后代 ◇ *Subsequent events confirmed our doubts.* 后来发生的事证实了我们的疑虑。◇ *Developments on this issue will be dealt with in a subsequent report.* 这个问题的发展将在以后的报道中予以说明。OPP **previous**

sub·se·quent·ly AW /ˈsʌbsɪkwəntli/ *adv.* (*formal*) afterwards; later; after sth else has happened 随后；后来；之后；接着：*The original interview notes were subsequently lost.* 采访记录原稿后来丢失了。◇ *Subsequently, new guidelines were issued to all employees.* 随后，新的准则发给了所有雇员。

'subsequent to *prep.* (*formal*) after; following 在…之后；继…之后：*There have been further developments subsequent to our meeting.* 在我们的会议之后又有新发展。

sub·ser·vi·ent /səbˈsɜːviənt; *NAmE* -ˈsɜːrv-/ *adj.* **1** ~ (**to sb/sth**) (*disapproving*) too willing to obey other people 恭顺的；驯服的；谄媚的；卑躬屈膝的：*The press was accused of being subservient to the government.* 有人指责新闻界一味迎合政府。**2** ~ (**to sth**) (*formal*) less important than sth else 次要；从属于：*The needs of individuals were subservient to those of the group as a whole.* 个人的需要服从于整个集体的需要。▶ **sub·ser·vi·ence** /-əns/ *noun* [U]

sub·set /ˈsʌbset/ *noun* (*specialist*) a smaller group of people or things formed from the members of a larger group 分组；小组；子集

sub·side /səbˈsaɪd/ *verb* **1** [I] to become calmer or quieter 趋于平静；平息；减弱；消退：*She waited nervously for his anger to subside.* 她提心吊胆地等他的怒气平息下来。◇ *I took an aspirin and the pain gradually subsided.* 我服了一片阿司匹林，疼痛逐渐缓解了。**2** [I] (of water 水) to go back to a normal level 回落；减退：*The flood waters gradually subsided.* 洪水缓缓回落。**3** [I] (of land or a building 地面或建筑物) to sink to a lower level; to sink lower into the ground 下沉；沉降；下陷：*Weak foundations caused the house to subside.* 由于地基不实，房子出现下陷。

sub·sid·ence /səbˈsaɪdns; ˈsʌbsɪdns/ *noun* [U] the process by which an area of land sinks to a lower level than normal, or by which a building sinks into the ground（地面或建筑物的）下沉，沉降，下陷

sub·sidi·ar·ity /səbˌsɪdiˈærəti; ˌsʌbsɪdi-; *NAmE* -ˈerəti/ *noun* [U] the principle that a central authority should not be very powerful, and should only control things which cannot be controlled by local organizations 辅助原则，辅从原则（中央权力机关应只控制地方上无法操控的事务）

sub·sid·iary AW /səbˈsɪdiəri; *NAmE* -dieri/ *adj., noun*
■ ***adj.*** **1** ~ (**to sth**) connected with sth but less important than it 辅助的；附带的；次要的 SYN **additional**: *subsidiary information* 辅助资料 ◇ *a subsidiary matter* 附带问题 ◇ (*BrE*) *I'm taking History as a **subsidiary subject*** (= one that is not studied in as great depth as a main subject). 我把历史课作为辅修科目。**2** (of a business company 公司) owned or controlled by another company 附属的；隶属的
■ ***noun*** (*pl.* **-ies**) a business company that is owned or controlled by another larger company 附属公司；子公司

sub·sid·ize AW (*BrE also* **-ise**) /ˈsʌbsɪdaɪz/ *verb* ~ **sb/sth** to give money to sb or an organization to help pay for sth; to give a subsidy 资助；补助；给…发津贴 SYN **fund**: *The housing projects are subsidized by the government.* 这些住房项目得到政府的补贴。◇ *She's not prepared to subsidize his gambling any longer.* 她再不愿意拿钱供他去赌博了。▶ **sub·sid·iza·tion**, **-isa·tion** /ˌsʌbsɪdaɪˈzeɪʃn; *NAmE* -dəˈz-/ *noun* [U]

sub·sidy AW /ˈsʌbsədi/ *noun* (*pl.* **-ies**) [C, U] money that is paid by a government or an organization to reduce the costs of services or of producing goods so that their prices can be kept low 补贴；补助金；津贴：*agricultural subsidies* 农业补贴 ◇ *to reduce the level of subsidy* 降低补贴标准 ➲ COLLOCATIONS AT FARMING

sub·sist /səbˈsɪst/ *verb* **1** [I] ~ (**on sth**) to manage to stay alive, especially with limited food or money（尤指靠有限的食物或钱）维持生活，度日：*Old people often subsist on very small incomes.* 老人往往靠十分微薄的收入艰难度日。**2** [I] (*formal*) to exist; to be valid 存在；有效：*The terms of the contract subsist.* 合同条款有效。

sub·sist·ence /səbˈsɪstəns/ *noun* [U] the state of having just enough money or food to stay alive 勉强维持生活：*Many families are living below the level of subsistence.* 许多家庭难以度日。◇ *to live below (the) **subsistence level*** 生活在基本生活水平线以下 ◇ *They had no visible means of subsistence.* 他们生计无着。◇ ***subsistence agriculture/farming*** (= growing enough only to live on, not to sell) 收成仅够自身口粮的自给农业 ◇ ***subsistence crops*** 生存作物 ◇ *He worked a 16-hour day for a **subsistence wage*** (= enough money to buy only basic items). 他一天工作 16 个小时，工资仅够勉强维持生计。

sub·soil /ˈsʌbsɔɪl/ *noun* [U] the layer of soil between the surface of the ground and the hard rock underneath it 底土；心土 ➲ COMPARE TOPSOIL

sub·son·ic /ˌsʌbˈsɒnɪk; *NAmE* -ˈsɑːn-/ *adj.* less than the speed of sound; flying at less than the speed of sound 亚声速的；亚声速飞行的 ➲ COMPARE SUPERSONIC

sub·stance 🔑 /ˈsʌbstəns/ *noun* **1** 🔑 [C] a type of solid, liquid or gas that has particular qualities 物质；物品；东西：*a **chemical/radioactive, etc. substance*** 化学、放射性等物质 ◇ ***banned/illegal substances*** (= drugs) 禁用 / 非法物品 ◇ *a sticky substance* 一种黏乎乎的东西 **2** [U] the quality of being based on facts or the truth 事实基础；根据：*It was malicious gossip, completely **without substance**.* 这是恶意造谣，完全没有事实根据。◇ *The commission's report **gives substance to** these allegations.* 委员会的报告为这些说法提供了事实根据。◇ *There is some substance in what he says.* 他的话是有一定根据的。**3** [U] the most important or main part of sth 主旨；要点；实质；基本内容：*Love and guilt form **the substance of** his new book.* 他的新书主要讲爱情与罪孽。◇ *I agreed with what she said **in substance**, though not with every detail.* 对于她所说的，虽然不是每个细节我都同意，但基本内容却是赞同的。**4** [U] (*formal*) importance 重要性 SYN **significance**: *matters of substance* 重大问题 ◇ *Nothing of any substance was achieved in the meeting.* 会议没有取得任何实质性成果。

IDM **a man/woman of 'substance** (*formal*) a rich and powerful man or woman 有钱有势的男人 / 女人

sub·standard /ˌsʌbˈstændəd; *NAmE* -ərd/ *adj.* not as good as normal; not acceptable 不达标的；不合格的 SYN **inferior**: *substandard goods* 次货

sub·stan·tial 🔑 /səbˈstænʃl/ *adj.* **1** 🔑 large in amount, value or importance 大量的；价值巨大的；重大的 SYN **considerable**: *substantial sums of money* 大笔大笔的钱 ◇ *a substantial change* 重大变化 ◇ *Substantial numbers of people support the reforms.* 相当多的人支持这些改革措施。◇ *He ate a substantial breakfast.* 他吃了一顿丰盛的

S

早餐。2 [usually before noun] (*formal*) large and solid; strongly built 大而坚固的；结实的；牢固的：*a substantial house* 结实的房子

sub·stan·tial·ly /səbˈstænʃəli/ *adj.* 1 very much; a lot 非常；大大地 SYN **considerably**: *The costs have increased substantially.* 成本大大提高了。◇ *The plane was substantially damaged in the crash.* 失事飞机损坏严重。2 (*formal*) mainly; in most details, even if not completely 基本上；大体上；总的来说：*What she says is substantially true.* 她的话大体符合事实。

sub·stan·ti·ate /səbˈstænʃieɪt/ *verb* ~ **sth** (*formal*) to provide information or evidence to prove that sth is true 证实；证明：*The results of the tests substantiated his claims.* 这些检验的结果证实了他的说法。▸ **sub·stan·ti·ation** /səbˌstænʃiˈeɪʃn/ *noun* [U]

sub·stan·tive /səbˈstæntɪv; ˈsʌbstəntɪv/ *adj., noun*

■ *adj.* (*formal*) dealing with real, important or serious matters 实质性的；本质上的；重大的；严肃认真的：*substantive issues* 实质性问题 ◇ *The report concluded that no substantive changes were necessary.* 报告的结论是，无须作任何重大变更。

■ *noun* (*old-fashioned, grammar* 语法) a noun 名词

sub·sta·tion /ˈsʌbsteɪʃn/ *noun* a place where the strength of electric power from a POWER STATION is reduced before it is passed on to homes and businesses 变电站；变电所

sub·sti·tute AW /ˈsʌbstɪtjuːt; *NAmE* -tuːt/ *noun, verb*

■ *noun* 1 a person or thing that you use or have instead of the one you normally use or have 代替者；代替物；代用品：*a meat substitute* 肉食替代品 ◇ *a substitute family* 收养家庭 ◇ ~ **for sb/sth** *Paul's father only saw him as a substitute for his dead brother.* 保罗的父亲只是把保罗当作他死去的哥哥来看待。◇ *The course teaches you the theory but **there's no substitute for** practical experience.* 这门课教的是理论，但没有任何东西能代替实践经验。◇ *The local bus service was a **poor substitute for** their car.* 他们坐当地的公交车，这比坐自己的汽车可差远了。2 (*also informal* **sub**) a player who replaces another player in a sports game 替补（运动员）：*He was brought on as (a) substitute after half-time.* 他作为替补队员在下半场上场。

■ *verb* [I, T] to take the place of sb/sth else; to use sb/sth instead of sb/sth else （以…）代替；取代：~ **for sb/sth** *Nothing can substitute for the advice your doctor is able to give you.* 大夫所能给你的忠告是无可替代的。◇ ~ **A for B** *Margarine can be substituted for butter in this recipe.* 做这道菜可以用人造黄油代替黄油。◇ ~ **B with/by A** *Butter can be substituted with margarine in this recipe.* 做这道菜可以用人造黄油代替黄油。◇ ~ **sb/sth** *Ronaldo was substituted in the second half after a knee injury* (= somebody else played instead of Ronaldo in the second half). 下半场罗纳尔多膝盖受伤被换下。 HELP When **for**, **with** or **by** are not used, as in the last example, it can be difficult to tell whether the person or thing mentioned is being used, or has been replaced by somebody or something else. The context will usually make this clear. 像最后一个例句这种情况，由于 for、with 或 by 均不出现，可能难以断定所说的人或事物是在使用的，还是被取代的，通常上下文能使意思明了。▸ **sub·sti·tu·tion** AW /ˌsʌbstɪˈtjuːʃn; *NAmE* -ˈtuː-/ *noun* [U, C]: *the substitution of low-fat spreads for butter* 用低脂的面包抹酱代替黄油 ◇ *Two substitutions were made during the game.* 比赛中换了两次人。

ˌsubstitute ˈteacher (*also informal* **sub**) (*both NAmE*) (*BrE* **supˈply teacher**) *noun* a teacher employed to do the work of another teacher who is away because of illness, etc. 代课教师

sub·strate /ˈsʌbstreɪt/ *noun* (*specialist*) a substance or layer which is under sth or on which sth happens, for example the surface on which a living thing grows and feeds 底物；底层；基底；基层

sub·stra·tum /ˈsʌbstrɑːtəm; *NAmE* ˈsʌbstreɪtəm/ *noun* (*pl.* **sub·strata** /ˈsʌbstrɑːtə; *NAmE* ˈsʌbstreɪtə/) (*specialist*) a layer of sth, especially rock or soil, that is below another layer（尤指岩石或土壤的）下卧层；底土层

sub·struc·ture /ˈsʌbstrʌktʃə(r)/ *noun* a base or structure that is below another structure and that supports it 基础；下部结构；下层建筑：*a substructure of timber piles* 木桩下部结构 ◇ (*figurative*) *the substructure of national culture* 民族文化的基础 ⊃COMPARE SUPERSTRUCTURE (1)

sub·sume /səbˈsjuːm; *NAmE* -ˈsuːm/ *verb* [usually passive] ~ **sth + adv./prep.** (*formal*) to include sth in a particular group and not consider it separately 将…归入（或纳入）：*All these different ideas can be subsumed under just two broad categories.* 所有这些不同的想法可归为两大类。

sub·tend /səbˈtend/ *verb* ~ **sth** (*geometry* 几何) (of a line or CHORD 直线或弦) to be opposite to an ARC or angle 对向（弧或角）

sub·ter·fuge /ˈsʌbtəfjuːdʒ; *NAmE* -tərf-/ *noun* [U, C] (*formal*) a secret, usually dishonest, way of behaving（通常指欺骗性）秘密手段；诡计

sub·ter·ra·nean /ˌsʌbtəˈreɪniən/ *adj.* [usually before noun] (*formal*) under the ground 地下的：*a subterranean cave* 地下洞穴

sub·text /ˈsʌbtekst/ *noun* a hidden meaning or reason for doing sth 字面背后的意思；潜台词；潜在原因

sub·title /ˈsʌbtaɪtl/ *noun, verb*

■ *noun* 1 [usually pl.] words that translate what is said in a film/movie into a different language and appear on the screen at the bottom. Subtitles are also used, especially on television, to help deaf people (= people who cannot hear well).（电影或电视上的）字幕：*a Polish film with English subtitles* 附有英语字幕的波兰影片 ◇ *Is the movie dubbed or are there subtitles?* 这部电影是配音的还是带字幕的？2 a second title of a book that appears after the main title and gives more information 副标题；小标题

■ *verb* [usually passive] to give a subtitle or subtitles to a book, film/movie, etc. 给…加副标题；给（电影等）加字幕：~ **sth** *a Spanish film subtitled in English* 一部加了英语字幕的西班牙影片 ◇ ~ **sth + noun** *The book is subtitled 'New language for new times'.* 这部书的副标题是“新时代的新语言”。⊃COMPARE DUB *v.* (2)

sub·tle /ˈsʌtl/ *adj.* (**sub·tler**, **sub·tlest**) HELP **more subtle** is also common * more subtle 也常用。1 (*often approving*) not very noticeable or obvious 不易察觉的；不明显的；微妙的：***subtle colours/flavours/smells, etc.*** 淡淡的色彩、味道、气味等 ◇ *There are **subtle differences** between the two versions.* 两个版本之间有一些细微的差异。◇ *She's been dropping subtle hints about what she'd like as a present.* 她不断隐隐暗示她喜欢什么样的礼物。2 (of a person or their behaviour 人或行为) behaving in a clever way, and using indirect methods, in order to achieve sth 机智的；机巧的；狡猾的：*I decided to try a more subtle approach.* 我决定智取。3 organized in a clever way 巧妙的：*a subtle plan* 巧妙的计划 ◇ *a subtle use of lighting in the play* 灯光在剧中的巧妙运用 4 good at noticing and understanding things 敏锐的；头脑灵活的：*The job required a subtle mind.* 那项工作需要一个头脑敏锐的人去做。▸ **subtly** /ˈsʌtli/ *adv.*: *Her version of events is subtly different from what actually happened.* 她对事件的描述跟实际发生的情况有些微妙的出入。◇ *Not very subtly, he raised the subject of money.* 他没有拐弯抹角，直接提出了钱的问题。

subtle·ty /ˈsʌtlti/ *noun* (*pl.* **-ies**) 1 [U] the quality of being subtle 细微；微妙；巧妙；敏锐：*It's a thrilling movie even though it lacks subtlety.* 这部电影虽说不算精巧，但还是扣人心弦的。2 [C, usually pl.] the small but important details or aspects of sth 细小但重要的地方；微妙之处：*the subtleties of language* 语言的微妙之处

sub·total /ˈsʌbtəʊtl; *NAmE* -toʊtl/ *noun* the total of a set of numbers which is then added to other totals to give a final number 部分和；小计

sub·tract /səbˈtrækt/ *verb* [T, I] ~ (**sth**) (**from sth**) to take a number or an amount away from another number or amount 减；减去 SYN **take**: *6 subtracted from 9 is 3.*

S

* 9 减 6 等于 3。OPP **add** ▶ **sub·trac·tion** /səb'trækʃn/ *noun* [U, C] ➲ COMPARE ADDITION (1)

sub·trop·ic·al /ˌsʌb'trɒpɪkl; *NAmE* -'trɑːp-/ (*also* **ˌsemi-'tropical**) *adj.* in or connected with regions that are near tropical parts of the world 亚热带的；副热带的

the sub·trop·ics /ˌsʌb'trɒpɪks; *NAmE* -'trɑːp-/ *noun* [pl.] the regions of the earth which are near the TROPICS 亚热带；副热带

sub·urb /'sʌbɜːb; *NAmE* -ɜːrb/ *noun* (*also NAmE, informal* **the burbs**) an area where people live that is outside the centre of a city 郊区；城外：*a suburb of London* 伦敦郊区 ◇ *a London suburb* 伦敦郊区 ◇ *They live **in the suburbs**.* 他们住在城外。➲ **WORDFINDER NOTE** AT CITY ➲ **COLLOCATIONS** AT TOWN

sub·ur·ban /sə'bɜːbən; *NAmE* -'bɜːrb-/ *adj.* **1** in or connected with a suburb 郊区的；城外的：*suburban areas* 郊区地带 ◇ *a suburban street* 郊区街道 ◇ *life in suburban London* 伦敦郊区的生活 ➲ **WORDFINDER NOTE** AT LOCATION **2** (*disapproving*) boring and ordinary 平淡乏味的；呆板的：*a suburban lifestyle* 平淡乏味的生活方式

sub·ur·ban·ite /sə'bɜːbənaɪt; *NAmE* -'bɜːrb-/ *noun* (*often disapproving*) a person who lives in the SUBURBS of a city 郊区居民

sub·ur·bia /sə'bɜːbiə; *NAmE* -'bɜːrb-/ *noun* [U] (*often disapproving*) the SUBURBS and the way of life, attitudes, etc. of the people who live there 郊区及其居民的生活方式（或态度等）

sub·ven·tion /səb'venʃn/ *noun* (*formal*) an amount of money that is given by a government, etc. to help an organization（政府等给予某机构的）资助金，补助金；拨款

sub·ver·sive /səb'vɜːsɪv; *NAmE* -'vɜːr-/ *adj.* trying or likely to destroy or damage a government or political system by attacking it secretly or indirectly 颠覆性的；暗中起破坏作用的 SYN **seditious** ▶ **sub·ver·sive** *noun*: *He was a known political subversive.* 他是一个有名的政治颠覆分子。**sub·ver·sive·ly** *adv.* **sub·ver·sive·ness** *noun* [U]

sub·vert /səb'vɜːt; *NAmE* -'vɜːrt/ *verb* (*formal*) **1** [T, I] ~ (**sth**) to try to destroy the authority of a political, religious, etc. system by attacking it secretly or indirectly 颠覆；暗中破坏 SYN **undermine** **2** [T] ~ **sth** to challenge sb's ideas or expectations and make them consider the opposite 策反；颠覆 SYN **undermine** ▶ **sub·ver·sion** /səb'vɜːʃn; *NAmE* -'vɜːrʒn/ *noun* [U]

sub·way /'sʌbweɪ/ *noun* **1** (*NAmE*) an underground railway/railroad system in a city 地铁；地铁交通：*the New York subway* 纽约地铁 ◇ *a **subway station/train*** 地铁站 / 列车 ◇ *a downtown subway stop* 闹市区的地铁站 ◇ *to **ride/take the subway*** 乘地铁 ➲ NOTE AT UNDERGROUND ➲ **VISUAL VOCAB** PAGE V63 **2** (*BrE*) a path that goes under a road, etc. which people can use to cross to the other side（穿越马路等的）地下人行道 SYN **underpass**

sub·woof·er /'sʌbwʊfə(r)/ *noun* (*specialist*) a part of a LOUDSPEAKER that produces very low sounds（扩音器的）低音炮，低音音箱

ˌsub-'zero *adj.* [usually before noun] (of temperatures 气温) below zero 零下的；零度以下的

suc·ceed 🔑 /sək'siːd/ *verb* **1** 🔑 [I] to achieve sth that you have been trying to do or get; to have the result or effect that was intended 达到目的；实现目标；办到；做成：*Our plan succeeded.* 我们的计划成功了。◇ ~ **in doing sth** *He succeeded in getting a place at art school.* 他被美术学校录取了。◇ *I tried to discuss it with her but **only succeeded** in making her angry* (= I failed and did the opposite of what I intended). 我本想跟她商量，结果却把她惹火了。➲ SEE ALSO SUCCESS **2** 🔑 [I] to be successful in your job, earning money, power, respect, etc. 成功；有成就；有作为：*You will have to work hard if you are to succeed.* 要想有所作为，你必须苦干。◇ ~ **in sth** *She doesn't have the ruthlessness required to succeed in business.* 要在生意场上干出一番名堂，她缺乏必要的冷酷心肠。◇ ~ **as sth** *He had hoped to succeed as a violinist.* 他曾希望做一名有成就的小提琴家。➲ SEE ALSO SUCCESS **3** [T] ~ **sb/sth** to come next after sb/sth and take their/its place or position 接替；继任；随后出现 SYN **follow**: *Who succeeded Kennedy as President?* 接替肯尼迪任总统的是谁？◇ *Their early success was succeeded by a period of miserable failure.* 他们起初获得成功，但随后有一段惨痛失败的时期。◇ *Strands of DNA are reproduced through **succeeding generations**.* * DNA（脱氧核糖核酸）链通过后代得到复制。➲ SEE ALSO SUCCESSION **4** [I] ~ (**to sth**) to gain the right to a title, property, etc. when sb dies 继承：*She succeeded to the throne* (= became queen) *in 1558.* 她于 1558 年继承王位。➲ SEE ALSO SUCCESSION

IDM **nothing succeeds like suc'cess** (*saying*) when you are successful in one area of your life, it often leads to success in other areas 一事成，百事顺

suc·cess 🔑 /sək'ses/ *noun* **1** 🔑 [U] the fact that you have achieved sth that you want and have been trying to do or get; the fact of becoming rich or famous or of getting a high social position 成功；胜利；发财；成名：*What's the secret of your success?* 你成功的秘诀是什么？◇ ~ (**in doing sth**) *I didn't **have much success in** finding a job.* 我找工作没什么结果。◇ ~ (**in sth**) *They didn't have much success in life.* 他们一生没取得多大成就。◇ *Confidence is **the key to success**.* 信心是成功的关键。◇ *economic success* 经济上的成功 ◇ *Their plan will probably **meet with little success**.* 他们的计划大概难有所成。◇ *She was surprised by the book's success* (= that it had sold a lot of copies). 那本书获得成功出乎她的意料。**2** 🔑 [C] a person or thing that has achieved a good result and been successful 成功的人（或事物）：*The party was a big success.* 这次聚会非常成功。◇ *He's proud of his daughter's successes.* 他为女儿的种种成就感到自豪。◇ *She wasn't a success as a teacher.* 她教书没教出什么名堂。◇ *He was determined to **make a success of** the business.* 他决心把这门生意做红火。OPP **failure** IDM SEE ROARING, SUCCEED, SWEET *adj.*

suc·cess·ful 🔑 /sək'sesfl/ *adj.* **1** 🔑 achieving your aims or what was intended 达到目的的；有成效的：~ (**in sth/in doing sth**) *They were successful in winning the contract.* 他们成功争取到了那份合同。◇ ~ (**at sth/at doing sth**) *I wasn't very successful at keeping the news secret.* 我没能把这条消息严格保密。◇ *We congratulated them on the successful completion of the project.* 我们祝贺他们项目顺利完成。**2** 🔑 having become popular and/or made a lot of money 获得成功的；有成就的：*The play was very successful on Broadway.* 那部剧在百老汇大获成功。◇ *a successful actor* 走红的演员 ◇ *The company has had another successful year.* 公司又度过了一个兴旺发达之年。OPP **unsuccessful** ▶ **suc·cess·ful·ly** 🔑 /-fəli/ *adv.* ➲ **SYNONYMS** ON NEXT PAGE

S

suc·ces·sion AW /sək'seʃn/ *noun* **1** [C, usually sing.] a number of people or things that follow each other in time or order 一连串；一系列；连续的人（或事物）SYN **series**: *a succession of visitors* 络绎不绝的来访者 ◇ *He's been hit by a succession of injuries since he joined the team.* 自入队以来他一再受伤。◇ *She has won the award for the third year **in succession**.* 这是她连续第三年获得此奖。◇ *They had three children **in quick succession**.* 短短几年间，他们接连生了三个孩子。◇ *The gunman fired three times **in rapid succession**.* 歹徒连开三枪。**2** [U] the regular pattern of one thing following another thing 交替；更迭：*the succession of the seasons* 四季的更迭 **3** [U] the act of taking over an official position or title; the right to take over an official position or title, especially to become the king or queen of a country 继承；继任；（尤指王位的）继承权：*He became chairman **in succession to** Bernard Allen.* 他接替伯纳德 • 艾伦任主席。◇ *She's third **in order of succession** to the throne.* 她在王位继承人顺位中排第三。➲ SEE ALSO SUCCEED ➲ **WORDFINDER NOTE** AT KING

suc'cession planning *noun* [U] (*business* 商) the process of training and preparing employees in a company or an organization so that there will always be sb to replace a senior manager who leaves（公司或机构的）继任规划，接班人培训规划

▼SYNONYMS 同义词辨析

successful

profitable • commercial • lucrative • economic

These words all describe sb/sth that is making or is likely to make money. 以上各词均指赚钱的、赢利的、有利可图的。

successful making a lot of money, especially by being popular 指赚钱的、成功的： *The play was very successful on Broadway.* 那出剧在百老汇大获成功。◇ *The company has had another successful year.* 公司又度过了一个兴旺发达之年。

profitable making a profit 指有利润的、赢利的： *a highly profitable business* 一家赢利很高的企业

commercial [only before noun] making or intended to make a profit 指赢利的、以获利为目的的： *The movie was not a commercial success* (= made no profit). 这部电影票房收入不佳。

lucrative (of business or work) producing or paying a large amount of money; making a large profit 指生意或工作赚大钱的、获利多的： *They do a lot of business in lucrative overseas markets.* 他们在利润丰厚的海外市场上生意很多。

economic (often used in negative sentences) (of a process, business or activity) producing enough profit to continue （常用于否定句中）指（工序、业务或活动）有利可图的、可赚钱的、合算的： *Small local shops stop being economic when a supermarket opens up nearby.* 附近有超市开业的话，当地的小商店就没有利润可赚了。

PATTERNS

- a successful/profitable/lucrative **business**
- a successful/profitable/lucrative **year**
- a(n) commercial/economic **success**

suc·ces·sive AW /sək'sesɪv/ *adj.* [only before noun] following immediately one after the other 连续的；接连的；相继的 SYN **consecutive**: *This was their fourth successive win.* 这是他们连续第四次获胜。◇ *Successive governments have tried to tackle the problem.* 历届政府都试图解决这个问题。▶ **suc·ces·sively** AW *adv.*: *This concept has been applied successively to painting, architecture and sculpture.* 这一概念相继应用于绘画、建筑和雕塑中。

S

suc·ces·sor AW /sək'sesə(r)/ *noun* ~ (**to sb/sth**) a person or thing that comes after sb/sth else and takes their/its place 接替者；继任者；接替的事物；后继的事物: *Who's the likely successor to him as party leader?* 谁较可能接替他担任党的领袖？◇ *Their latest release is a* ***worthy successor*** *to their popular debut album.* 继首张唱片大受欢迎之后，他们最新推出的专辑再获成功。➲ COMPARE PREDECESSOR

suc'cess story *noun* a person or thing that is very successful 获得巨大成功的人（或事物）

suc·cinct /sək'sɪŋkt/ *adj.* (*approving*) expressed clearly and in a few words 简明的；言简意赅的 SYN **concise**: *Keep your answers as succinct as possible.* 你们的答案要尽可能简洁明了。◇ *a succinct explanation* 简明的解释 ▶ **suc·cinct·ly** *adv.*: *You put that very succinctly.* 你说得十分简明扼要。 **suc·cinct·ness** *noun* [U]

suc·co·tash /'sʌkətæʃ/ *noun* [U] (*US*) a dish of CORN (MAIZE) and BEANS cooked together 煮玉米菜豆；沙可达玉米粥

Suc·coth /sʊ'kəʊt; 'sʌkəθ; *NAmE* 'su:koʊt; su:'koʊt/ (*also* ˌ**Feast of 'Tabernacles**) *noun* [U] a Jewish festival that takes place in the autumn/fall, during which shelters are made using natural materials 住棚节（秋季的犹太节日，期间会用天然材料搭棚）

suc·cour (*US* **suc·cor**) /'sʌkə(r)/ *noun, verb*

■ ***noun*** [U] (*literary*) help that you give to sb who is suffering or having problems 救助；救援；帮助

■ ***verb*** ~ **sb** (*literary*) to help sb who is suffering or having problems 救助；救援；帮助

suc·cu·bus /'sʌkjʊbəs/ *noun* (*pl.* **suc·cu·bi** /-baɪ/) (*literary*) a female evil spirit, supposed to have sex with a sleeping man（传说与睡眠中的男子交媾的）女淫妖 ➲ COMPARE INCUBUS (2)

suc·cu·lent /'sʌkjələnt/ *adj., noun*

■ ***adj.*** **1** (*approving*) (of fruit, vegetables and meat 水果、蔬菜和肉) containing a lot of juice and tasting good 汁多味美的 SYN **juicy**: *a succulent pear/steak* 汁多味美的梨；鲜美多汁的牛排 **2** (*specialist*) (of plants 植物) having leaves and STEMS that are thick and contain a lot of water 肉质的；多汁的 ▶ **suc·cu·lence** /-ləns/ *noun* [U]

■ ***noun*** (*specialist*) any plant with leaves and STEMS that are thick and contain a lot of water, for example a CACTUS 肉质植物

suc·cumb /sə'kʌm/ *verb* [I] to not be able to fight an attack, an illness, a TEMPTATION, etc. 屈服；屈从；抵挡不住（攻击、疾病、诱惑等）: *The town succumbed after a short siege.* 该城被围困不久即告失守。◇ **~ to sth** *His career was cut short when he succumbed to cancer.* 他的事业随着他死于癌症而中断。◇ *He finally succumbed to Lucy's charms and agreed to her request.* 他最终为露西的魅力所倾倒，答应了她的请求。

such /sʌtʃ/ *det., pron.* **1** of the type already mentioned（指上文）这样的，那样的，类似的: *They had been invited to a Hindu wedding and were not sure what happened on such occasions.* 有人邀请他们去参加一个印度教徒的婚礼，但他们不清楚这样的庆典会是怎样一种场面。◇ *He said he didn't have time or made* ***some such*** *excuse.* 他说他没时间或找了别的诸如此类的借口。◇ *She longed to find somebody who understood her problems, and in him she thought she had found such a person.* 她渴望找一个理解她困难的人，觉得他就是这样一个人。◇ *We were second-class citizens and they treated us* ***as such***. 我们是二等公民，他们也就这样对待我们。◇ *Accountants were boring. Such* (= that) *was her opinion before meeting Ian!* 做会计的个个乏味，在认识伊恩以前她一直是这样想的！**2** of the type that you are just going to mention（指后文）这样的，那样的，下述一类的: ***There is no such thing*** *as a free lunch.* 世上没有免费午餐之类的好事儿。◇ *Such advice as he was given* (= it was not very much) *has proved almost worthless.* 他所得到的那点建议结果证明几乎完全没用。◇ *The knot was fastened* ***in such a way*** *that it was impossible to undo.* 那个结系死了，没法解开。◇ *The damage was such that it would cost thousands to repair.* 损坏严重，要修好就得花几千块钱。**3** ~ **(is, was, etc.) sth that…** used to emphasize the great degree of sth（强调程度）这样，非常，如此程度: *This issue was of such importance that we could not afford to ignore it.* 这个问题十分重要，我们疏忽不得。◇ *Why are you in such a hurry?* 你干吗这么急匆匆的？◇ (*informal*) *It's such a beautiful day!* 天气多么好哇！◇ (*formal*) *Such is the elegance of this typeface that it is still a favourite of designers.* 这种字体很优美，至今仍深受设计人员喜欢。

IDM **... and such** and similar things or people 诸如此类的事物（或人）: *The centre offers activities like canoeing and sailing and such.* 这个中心开展划艇、帆船之类的活动。 **as 'such** as the word is usually understood; in the exact sense of the word 从字面意义看；严格说来: *The new job is not a promotion as such, but it has good prospects.* 担任这一新的职务算不上是真正的升职，不过有美好的前途。◇ *'Well, did they offer it to you?' 'No, not as such, but they said I had a good chance.'* "那么，他们把它给你了？""不，不完全是那样，可是他们说我很有希望。" **such as 1** for example 例如；…等: *Wild flowers such as primroses are becoming rare.* 报春花之类的野花越来越稀罕了。◇ *'There are loads of things to do.' 'Such as?'* (= give me an example) "该做的事有一大堆。""比如呢？" **2** of a kind that; like 像…这样；像…那种；诸如…之类: *Opportunities such as this did not come every day.* 这样的机会不是天天都有的。➲ LANGUAGE BANK AT E.G. ˌ**such as it 'is/they 'are** used to say that there is not much of sth or that it is of poor quality（数量不多或质量不好时说）虽说不多，尽管不好: *The food, such as it was, was served at nine o'clock.* 那饭虽说是粗茶淡饭，却到九点钟才端上来。

'such-and-such *pron., det.* (*informal*) used for referring to sth without saying exactly what it is（指没有明确说出的事物）某：*Always say at the start of an application that you're applying for such-and-such a job because...* 写求职信务须一开头就说明你申请某职务，因为…

such·like /ˈsʌtʃlaɪk/ *pron.* things of the type mentioned 诸如此类的事物：*You can buy brushes, paint, varnish and suchlike there.* 你在那儿能买到刷子、油漆、清漆之类的东西。▶ **such·like** *det.*：*food, drink, clothing and suchlike provisions* 食物、饮料、服装以及其他诸如此类的供应品

suck /sʌk/ *verb, noun*

■ *verb* **1** [T] ~ **sth** (+ **adv./prep.**) to take liquid, air, etc. into your mouth by using the muscles of your lips 吮吸；吸；咂；啜：*to suck the juice from an orange* 吸橙子的汁 ◇ *She was noisily sucking up milk through a straw.* 她正用吸管咕嘟咕嘟地喝牛奶。**2** [I, T] to keep sth in your mouth and pull on it with your lips and tongue 含在嘴里吸食：~ **at/on sth** *The baby sucked at its mother's breast.* 婴儿在吮吸母亲的奶。◇ *She sucked on a mint.* 她嘴里咂着一颗薄荷糖。◇ ~ **sth** *She sucked a mint.* 她嘴里咂着一颗薄荷糖。◇ *Stop sucking your thumb!* 别吮手指头！**3** [T] to take liquid, air, etc. out of sth 抽吸；抽取：~ **sth + adv./prep.** *The pump sucks air out through the valve.* 气泵通过阀门把空气抽出去。◇ ~ **sth + adj.** *Greenfly can literally suck a plant dry.* 蚜虫真能把一株植物吸干。**4** [T] ~ **sb/sth + adv./prep.** to pull sb/sth with great force in a particular direction（以巨大的力量）吸，吸引，使卷入：*The canoe was sucked down into the whirlpool.* 划艇被卷进了漩涡。**5 sth sucks** [I] (*slang*) used to say that sth is very bad（表示厌恶）臭，恶心：*Their new CD sucks.* 他们新出的唱片难听死了。➲ COMPARE ROCK *v.*

IDM **,suck it and 'see** (*BrE, informal*) used to say that the only way to know if sth is suitable is to try it 试试看 **,suck it 'up** (*NAmE, informal*) to accept sth bad and deal with it well, controlling your emotions 逆来顺受；忍气吞声 ➲ MORE AT DRY *adj.*, TEACH

PHR V **,suck sb 'in | ,suck sb 'into sth** [usually passive] to involve sb in an activity or a situation, especially one they do not want to be involved in 把某人卷入（某事）**,suck 'up (to sb)** (*informal, disapproving*) to try to please sb in authority by praising them too much, helping them, etc., in order to gain some advantage for yourself 奉承；巴结

■ *noun* [usually sing.] an act of sucking 吸；吮；啜；咂

suck·er /ˈsʌkə(r)/ *noun, verb*

■ *noun* **1** (*informal*) a person who is easily tricked or persuaded to do sth 容易上当受骗的人；没有主见的人 **2** ~ **for sb/sth** (*informal*) a person who cannot resist sb/sth or likes sb/sth very much 不由得对…入迷的人；酷爱…的人：*I've always been a sucker for men with green eyes.* 我一向对绿眼睛男人着迷。**3** a special organ on the body of some animals that enables them to stick to a surface（动物的）吸盘 ➲ VISUAL VOCAB PAGE V13 **4** a disc shaped like a cup, usually made of rubber or plastic, that sticks to a surface when you press it against it（橡胶或塑料等制成的）吸盘 **5** a part of a tree or bush that grows from the roots rather than from the main STEM or the branches and can form a new tree or bush 根出条 **6** (*NAmE, slang*) used to refer in a general way to a person or thing, especially for emphasis（泛指人或物，尤表示强调）家伙，东西，玩意儿：*The pilot said, 'I don't know how I got the sucker down safely.'* 飞行员说："我不知道是怎么把这玩意儿安全降落下来的。" **7** (*NAmE, informal*) = LOLLIPOP

■ *verb*

PHR V **,sucker sb 'into sth/into 'doing sth** (*NAmE, informal*) to persuade sb to do sth that they do not really want to do, especially by using their lack of knowledge or experience（尤指利用他人无知）欺骗，使上当：*I was suckered into helping.* 我受骗帮忙去了。

'sucker punch *noun* (*informal*) a blow that the person who receives it is not expecting 突如其来的一拳；毫无防备的一击 ▶ **'sucker punch** *verb* ~ **sb**

suckle /ˈsʌkl/ *verb* **1** [T] ~ **sb/sth** (of a woman or female animal 妇女或雌兽) to feed a baby or young animal with milk from the breast or UDDER 给…喂奶；给…哺乳：*a cow suckling her calves* 给小牛喂奶的母牛 ◇ (*old-fashioned*) *a mother suckling a baby* 给婴儿哺乳的母亲 **2** [I] (of a baby or young animal 婴儿或幼兽) to drink milk from its mother's breast or UDDER 吸奶；吃奶

suck·ling /ˈsʌklɪŋ/ *noun* (*old-fashioned*) a baby or young animal that is still drinking milk from its mother 乳儿；乳兽 IDM SEE MOUTH *n.*

'suckling pig *noun* [U, C] a young pig still taking milk from its mother, that is cooked and eaten（烤）乳猪

su·crose /ˈsuːkrəʊz; -krəʊs; *NAmE* -kroʊs; -kroʊz/ *noun* [U] (*chemistry* 化) the form of sugar that is obtained from SUGAR CANE and SUGAR BEET 蔗糖

suc·tion /ˈsʌkʃn/ *noun* [U] the process of removing air or liquid from a space or container so that sth else can be sucked into it or so that two surfaces can stick together 吸；抽吸；吸出：*Vacuum cleaners work by suction.* 真空吸尘器靠抽吸除尘。◇ *a suction pump/pad* 抽吸泵；吸力垫 ▶ **suc·tion** *verb* ~ **sth** (*specialist*)

sud·den /ˈsʌdn/ *adj.* happening or done quickly and unexpectedly 突然的；忽然的；骤然的：*a sudden change* 骤变 ◇ *Don't make any sudden movements.* 不要突然做动作。◇ *His death was very sudden.* 他死得很突然。◇ *It was only decided yesterday. It's all been very sudden.* 这是昨天才决定的，一切都非常突然。▶ **sud·den·ness** *noun* [U]

IDM **,all of a 'sudden** quickly and unexpectedly 突然；猛地：*All of a sudden someone grabbed me around the neck.* 猛不防有人抓住了我的脖子。

,sudden 'death *noun* [U] a way of deciding the winner of a game when the scores are equal at the end. The players or teams continue playing and the game ends as soon as one of them gains the lead. 突然死亡法（比赛出现平局时在加时赛中先得分者即为胜方）：*a sudden-death play-off in golf* 高尔夫球突然死亡法加赛

sud·den·ly /ˈsʌdənli/ *adv.* quickly and unexpectedly 突然；忽然；猛地；骤然：*'Listen!' said Doyle suddenly.* "你听！"多伊尔突然说。◇ *I suddenly realized what I had to do.* 我突然明白该怎么做了。◇ *It all happened so suddenly.* 一切都来得那么突然。

su·doku /ˌsuˈdəʊkuː; -ˈdɒk-; *NAmE* -ˈdoʊk-; -ˈdɑːk-/ *noun* [C, U] a number puzzle with nine squares, each containing nine smaller squares, in which you have to put the numbers one to nine so that a number appears only once in each of the nine squares and in each row of nine across and down the puzzle 数独游戏（九个大方格中各有九个小方格，要求在空格中填数字一到九，且纵、横排各不重复）：*He passes the time doing sudokus.* 他做数独游戏打发时间。➲ VISUAL VOCAB PAGE V43

suds /sʌdz/ (*also* **soap·suds**) *noun* **1** [pl.] a mass of very small bubbles that forms on top of water that has soap in it 肥皂泡沫 SYN **lather**：*She was up to her elbows in suds.* 她肘部以下都是肥皂沫子。**2** [U] (*old-fashioned, NAmE, informal*) beer 啤酒

sue /suː; *BrE also* sjuː/ *verb* **1** [T, I] ~ (**sb**) (**for sth**) to make a claim against sb in court about sth that they have said or done to harm you 控告；提起诉讼：*to sue sb for breach of contract* 控告某人违反合同 ◇ *to sue sb for $10 million* (= in order to get money from sb) 控告某人要求得到 1 000 万美元 ◇ *to sue sb for damages* 起诉某人要求赔偿损失 ◇ *They threatened to sue if the work was not completed.* 他们威胁说，如果不完成工作，就要提起诉讼。**2** [I] ~ **for sth** (*formal*) to formally ask for sth, especially in court（尤指在法庭上）提出请求：*to sue for divorce* 起诉要求离婚 ◇ *The rebels were forced to sue for peace.* 反叛者被迫求和。

suede /sweɪd/ *noun* [U] soft leather with a surface like VELVET on one side, used especially for making clothes and shoes 绒面革；仿麂皮：*a suede jacket* 绒面革夹克

suet /ˈsuːɪt; *BrE also* ˈsjuːɪt/ *noun* [U] hard fat from around the KIDNEYS of cows, sheep, etc., used in cooking（牛、

S

羊等肾周围的）板油：*suet pudding* (= one made using suet) 脂油布丁

suf·fer 🔑 /ˈsʌfə(r)/ *verb* **1** 🔑 [I] to be badly affected by a disease, pain, sadness, a lack of sth, etc.（因疾病、痛苦、悲伤等）受苦，受难，受折磨：*I hate to see animals suffering.* 我不忍心看动物受苦。◇ **~ from sth** *He suffers from asthma.* 他患有哮喘。◇ *road accident victims suffering from shock* 交通事故中受到惊吓的受害者 ◇ *Many companies are suffering from a shortage of skilled staff.* 许多公司苦于缺乏熟练员工。◇ **~ for sth** *He made a rash decision and now he is suffering for it.* 他当初草率决定，现在吃苦头了。**2** 🔑 [T] **~ sth** to experience sth unpleasant, such as injury, defeat or loss 遭受；蒙受：*He suffered a massive heart attack.* 他的心脏病发作很严重。◇ *The party suffered a humiliating defeat in the general election.* 该党在大选中惨败。◇ *The company suffered huge losses in the last financial year.* 公司在上一财政年度出现巨额亏损。**3** 🔑 [I] to become worse 变差；变糟：*His school work is suffering because of family problems.* 由于家庭问题，他的学业日渐退步。

IDM **not suffer fools ˈgladly** to have very little patience with people that you think are stupid 不愿迁就笨人；不能容忍愚蠢者

suf·fer·ance /ˈsʌfərəns/ *noun* [U]

IDM **on ˈsufferance** if you do sth **on sufferance**, sb allows you to do it although they do not really want you to 经勉强同意；由于（某人的）宽容：*He's only staying here on sufferance.* 他是经人勉强同意待在这儿的。

suf·fer·er /ˈsʌfərə(r)/ *noun* a person who suffers, especially sb who is suffering from a disease 患病者；受苦者；受难者：*cancer sufferers* 癌症患者 ◇ *She received many letters of support from fellow sufferers.* 许多和她有共同遭遇的人给她来信，表示支持。

suf·fer·ing 🔑 /ˈsʌfərɪŋ/ *noun* **1** 🔑 [U] physical or mental pain 疼痛；痛苦；折磨；苦难：*Death finally brought an end to her suffering.* 死亡终于结束了她的痛苦。◇ *This war has caused widespread human suffering.* 这场战争给许许多多的人带来了苦难。**2** **sufferings** [pl.] feelings of pain and unhappiness 痛苦；苦恼：*The hospice aims to ease the sufferings of the dying.* 临终关怀医院旨在减轻临终者的痛苦。

suf·fice /səˈfaɪs/ *verb* [I] (*formal*) (not used in the progressive tenses 不用于进行时) to be enough for sb/sth 足够；足以：*Generally a brief note or a phone call will suffice.* 通常写个便条或打个电话就足够了。◇ **~ to do sth** *One example will suffice to illustrate the point.* 举一个例子就足以说明这一点。

IDM **suffice (it) to say (that)...** used to suggest that although you could say more, what you do say will be enough to explain what you mean 无须多说；只需说…就够了

suf·fi·ciency **AW** /səˈfɪʃnsi/ *noun* [sing.] **~ (of sth)** (*formal*) an amount of sth that is enough for a particular purpose 足量；充足

suf·fi·cient 🔑 **AW** /səˈfɪʃnt/ *adj.* enough for a particular purpose; as much as you need 足够的；充足的：*Allow sufficient time to get there.* 留出充足的时间好赶过去。◇ **~ to do sth** *These reasons are not sufficient to justify the ban.* 这些理由不足以证明实施禁令有理。◇ **~ for sth/sb** *Is £100 sufficient for your expenses?* * 100 英镑够你花销吗？ **OPP** **insufficient** ➲ SEE ALSO SELF-SUFFICIENT ▶ **suf·fi·cient·ly** 🔑 **AW** *adv.*: *The following day she felt sufficiently well to go to work.* 第二天，她感觉好转，完全可以去上班了。

suf·fix /ˈsʌfɪks/ *noun* (*grammar* 语法) a letter or group of letters added to the end of a word to make another word, such as *-ly* in *quickly* or *-ness* in *sadness* 后缀，词尾（加在词尾，用以构成新词，如 quickly 中的 -ly 或 sadness 中的 -ness）➲ COMPARE AFFIX *n.*, PREFIX *n.* (1)

suf·fo·cate /ˈsʌfəkeɪt/ *verb* **1** [I, T] to die because there is no air to breathe; to kill sb by not letting them breathe air（使）窒息而死；（把…）闷死：*Many dogs have suffocated in hot cars.* 许多狗在热烘烘的汽车里给闷死了。◇ **~ sb/sth** *The couple were suffocated by fumes from a faulty gas fire.* 由于劣质煤气取暖器漏气，这对夫妇窒息而死。◇ *He put the pillow over her face and suffocated her.* 他用枕头捂住她的脸，把她憋死了。◇ (*figurative*) *She felt suffocated by all the rules and regulations.* 她受不了所有那些条条框框的束缚。**2** [I] **be suffocating** if it is **suffocating**, it is very hot and there is little fresh air 让人感觉闷热；憋气：*Can I open a window? It's suffocating in here!* 我可以打开窗户吗？这里面都快把人闷死了！▶ **suf·fo·ca·tion** /ˌsʌfəˈkeɪʃn/ *noun* [U]: *to die of suffocation* 窒息而死

suf·fo·cat·ing /ˈsʌfəkeɪtɪŋ/ *adj.* **1** making it difficult to breathe normally 令人呼吸困难的；闷的；使人窒息的 **SYN** **stifling**: *The afternoon heat was suffocating.* 下午热得让人透不过气来。**2** restricting what sb/sth can do 起扼制作用的；压制的；束缚性的：*Some marriages can sometimes feel suffocating.* 有些婚姻有时候让人觉得受到束缚。

suf·fra·gan /ˈsʌfrəgən/ (*also* **suffragan ˈbishop**) *noun* a BISHOP who is an assistant to a bishop of a particular DIOCESE 副主教

suf·frage /ˈsʌfrɪdʒ/ *noun* [U] the right to vote in political elections 选举权；投票权：*universal suffrage* (= the right of all adults to vote) 普选权 ◇ *women's suffrage* 妇女的选举权

suf·fra·gette /ˌsʌfrəˈdʒet/ *noun* a member of a group of women who, in Britain and the US in the early part of the 20th century, worked to get the right for women to vote in political elections（20 世纪初叶英国和美国的）妇女争取选举权团体的成员

suf·fuse /səˈfjuːz/ *verb* [often passive] **~ sb/sth (with sth)** (*literary*) (especially of a colour, light or feeling 尤指颜色、光线或感情) to spread all over or through sb/sth 布满；弥漫于；充满：*Her face was suffused with colour.* 她满脸通红。◇ *Colour suffused her face.* 她满脸通红。

Sufi /ˈsuːfi/ *noun* a member of a Muslim group who try to become united with God through prayer and MEDITATION and by living a very simple, strict life 苏非派信徒（伊斯兰教一教团成员，主张通过虔修默祷、生活简朴禁欲达到人主合一）▶ **Suf·ism** *noun* [U]

su·fur·ia /suːˈfuːriə/ *noun* (*EAfrE*) a metal pot used for cooking 金属锅；铁罐锅

sugar 🔑 /ˈʃʊgə(r)/ *noun, verb, exclamation*

■ ***noun*** **1** 🔑 [U] a sweet substance, often in the form of white or brown CRYSTALS, made from the juices of various plants, used in cooking or to make tea, coffee, etc. sweeter 食糖：*a **sugar plantation/refinery/bowl*** 甘蔗园；炼糖厂；糖罐 ◇ *This juice contains **no added sugar**.* 这种果汁没有加糖。◇ *Do you **take sugar*** (= have it in your tea, coffee, etc.)? 您放糖吗？➲ SEE ALSO BROWN SUGAR, CANE SUGAR, CASTER SUGAR, GRANULATED SUGAR, ICING SUGAR **2** 🔑 [C] the amount of sugar that a small spoon can hold or that is contained in a small CUBE, added to tea, coffee, etc. 一匙糖；一块方糖：*How many sugars do you take in coffee?* 您在咖啡里放几块方糖？**3** [C, usually pl.] (*specialist*) any of various sweet substances that are found naturally in plants, fruit, etc.（植物、水果等所含的）糖：*fruit sugars* 果糖 ◇ *a person's **blood sugar** level* (= the amount of GLUCOSE in their blood) 人的血糖含量 **4** [U] (*informal, especially NAmE*) a way of addressing sb that you like or love（爱称）宝贝儿，亲爱的：*See you later, sugar.* 回头见，亲爱的。

■ ***verb*** **~ sth** to add sugar to sth; to cover sth in sugar 在…中加糖；在…上撒糖；给…裹上糖衣 **IDM** SEE PILL *n.*

■ ***exclamation*** used to show that you are annoyed when you do sth stupid or when sth goes wrong (to avoid saying 'shit')（做了蠢事或出现差错时表示懊恼，用作shit的委婉语）哎呀，真是的：*Oh sugar! I've forgotten my book!* 哎呀！我忘记带书了！

ˈsugar beet *noun* [U] a plant with a large round root, from which sugar is made 糖用甜菜

S

ˈsugar cane *noun* [U] a tall tropical plant with thick STEMS from which sugar is made 甘蔗

ˈsugar-coat *verb* ~ **sth** to do sth that makes an unpleasant situation seem less unpleasant 美化，粉饰（不愉快的情况）

ˌsugar-ˈcoated *adj.* **1** covered with sugar 裹有糖的；包糖衣的 **2** (*disapproving*) made to seem attractive, in a way that tricks people 巧加粉饰的；使表面吸引人的：*a sugar-coated promise* 甜言蜜语的许诺

ˈsugar cube (*especially NAmE*) (*BrE also* **ˈsugar lump**) *noun* a small CUBE of sugar, used in cups of tea or coffee 方糖

ˈsugar daddy *noun* (*informal*) a rich older man who gives presents and money to a much younger woman, usually in return for sex 甜爹（对年轻女子慷慨大方的好色阔佬）

sug·ar·ing /ˈʃʊɡərɪŋ/ *noun* [U] **1** a way of removing hair from your skin using a mixture of sugar and water 糖水脱毛法 **2** the process of boiling juice from a MAPLE tree until it becomes sugar 槭糖熬制

ˈsugar lump (*also informal* **lump**) (*both BrE*) (*also* **ˈsugar cube** *NAmE, BrE*) *noun* a small CUBE of sugar, used in cups of tea or coffee 方糖

sugar·plum /ˈʃʊɡəplʌm; *NAmE* -ɡərp-/ *noun* (*especially NAmE*) a small round sweet/candy 小圆糖果；糖豆

ˈsugar snap (*also* **ˌsugar snap ˈpea**, **ˈsugar pea**) *noun* a type of PEA which is eaten while still in its POD（连荚食用）甜豌豆

sug·ary /ˈʃʊɡəri/ *adj.* **1** containing sugar; tasting of sugar 含糖的；甜的：*sugary snacks* 甜点心 **2** (*disapproving*) seeming too full of emotion in a way that is not sincere（态度等）甜腻腻的，媚人的；甜言蜜语的 SYN **sentimental**：*a sugary smile* 媚笑 ◇ *sugary pop songs* 甜腻腻的流行歌曲

sug·gest 🔑 /səˈdʒest; *NAmE also* səɡˈdʒ-/ *verb* **1** 🔑 to put forward an idea or a plan for other people to think about 建议；提议 SYN **propose**：~ **sth** (**to sb**) *May I suggest a white wine with this dish, Sir?* 先生，吃这道菜，我给您推荐一种白葡萄酒，好吗？ ◇ ~ **itself** (**to sb**) *A solution immediately suggested itself to me* (= I immediately thought of a solution). 我马上想到了一个解决办法。 ◇ ~ (**that**)… *I suggest* (*that*) *we go out to eat.* 我提议我们出去吃吧。 ◇ ~ **doing sth** *I suggested going in my car.* 我提议坐我的车去。 ◇ **it is suggested that…** *It has been suggested that bright children take their exams early.* 有人提议天资好的孩子提前考试。 ◇ (*BrE also*) *It has been suggested that bright children should take their exams early.* 有人提议天资好的孩子提前考试。 ➲ MORE LIKE THIS 27, page R28 ➲ LANGUAGE BANK AT ARGUE

▼ EXPRESS YOURSELF 情景表达

Making suggestions 提出建议

There are various ways of putting forward your suggestions. 提建议有多种方式：

- ***How about** going out for a walk on Saturday?* 星期六出去散散步怎么样？
- ***Shall we** ask Sarah to come along?* (*BrE* or *formal, NAmE*) 我们请萨拉一起去好吗？
- ***Should we** ask Sarah to come along?* (*especially NAmE*) 我们请萨拉一起去好吗？
- ***We could** go a bit earlier and have a drink first, **if you like**.* 如果你愿意，我们可以早点儿去，先喝一杯。
- ***What do you think of the idea** of sending this to the Research Department?* 把这送交研究部，你认为这个主意怎么样？
- ***Why don't you** try calling his landline?* 你为什么不试试打他的座机？
- ***Why not just** wait until they come back?* 为什么不干脆等到他们回来？
- ***Why not simply** explain your problem to them and see what they say?* (*BrE* or *formal, NAmE*) 为什么不把你的问题直接向他们解释？看看他们怎么说？

2 🔑 to tell sb about a suitable person, thing, method, etc. for a particular job or purpose 推荐；举荐 SYN **recommend**：~ **sb/sth for sth** *Who would you suggest for the job?* 要你说，谁适合做这个工作？ ◇ ~ **sb/sth as sth** *She suggested Paris as a good place for the conference.* 她推荐说，巴黎是举行这次会议的理想地点。 ◇ ~ **sb/sth** *Can you suggest a good dictionary?* 你能推荐一本好词典吗？ HELP You cannot 'suggest somebody something'. 不能说 suggest somebody something：~~*Can you suggest me a good dictionary?*~~ ◇ ~ **how, what, etc.…** *Can you suggest how I might contact him?* 我怎么才能联系上他，你能出个主意吗？ **3** 🔑 to put an idea into sb's mind; to make sb think that sth is true 使想到；使认为；表明 SYN **indicate**：~ (**that**)… *All the evidence suggests* (*that*) *he stole the money.* 所有证据都表明是他偷了钱。 ◇ ~ **sth** *The symptoms suggest a minor heart attack.* 症状显示这是轻微心脏病发作。 ◇ ~ **sth to sb** *What do these results suggest to you?* 照你看，这些结果说明什么呢？ **4** to state sth indirectly 暗示；言下之意是说 SYN **imply**：~ (**that**)… *Are you suggesting* (*that*) *I'm lazy?* 你言下之意是说我懒？ ◇ ~ **sth** *I would never suggest such a thing.* 我根本不会有这样的意思。

sug·gest·ible /səˈdʒestəbl; *NAmE also* səɡˈdʒ-/ *adj.* easily influenced by other people 易受他人影响的：*He was young and highly suggestible.* 当时他年轻，很容易受人影响。

sug·ges·tion 🔑 /səˈdʒestʃən; *NAmE also* səɡˈdʒ-/ *noun* **1** 🔑 [C] an idea or a plan that you mention for sb else to think about 建议；提议：*Can I make a suggestion?* 我提个建议好吗？ ◇ *Do you **have any suggestions**?* 你有什么建议吗？ ◇ ~ (**for/about/on sth**) *I'd like to hear your suggestions for ways of raising money.* 关于筹集资金的办法，我想听听你的意见。 ◇ *Are there any suggestions about how best to tackle the problem?* 这个问题最好怎样解决，大家有没有什么建议？ ◇ *We welcome any comments and suggestions on these proposals.* 对于这些方案的任何意见和建议，我们一概欢迎。 ◇ ~ (**that…**) *He agreed with my suggestion that we should change the date.* 他同意我提出的更改日期的建议。 ◇ *We are **open to suggestions*** (= willing to listen to ideas from other people). 我们愿意听取大家的建议。 ◇ *We need to get it there by four. **Any suggestions?*** 我们需要在四点以前把东西送过去。大家有什么办法吗？ **2** 🔑 [U, C, usually sing.] a reason to think that sth, especially sth bad, is true 使人作（尤其是不好的事情）推测的理由 SYN **hint**：~ **of sth** *A spokesman dismissed any suggestion of a boardroom rift.* 发言人的话打消了人们关于董事会不和的所有推测。 ◇ ~ **that…** *There was no suggestion that he was doing anything illegal.* 说他在从事非法活动无任何根据。 **3** [C, usually sing.] a slight amount or sign of sth 微量；些微；迹象 SYN **trace**：*She looked at me with just a suggestion of a smile.* 她看着我，脸上带着一丝笑意。 **4** [U] putting an idea into people's minds by connecting it with other ideas 暗示；联想：*Most advertisements work through suggestion.* 多数广告都是通过暗示发挥作用。 ◇ *the power of suggestion* 暗示力

IDM **at/on sb's sugˈgestion** because sb suggested it 根据某人的建议；在某人的提议下：*At his suggestion, I bought the more expensive printer.* 在他的建议下，我买了那台比较贵的打印机。

sug·gest·ive /səˈdʒestɪv; *NAmE also* səɡˈdʒ-/ *adj.* **1** ~ (**of sth**) reminding you of sth or making you think about sth 使人想起…的；引起联想的：*music that is suggestive of warm summer days* 使人想起温暖夏日的音乐 **2** making people think about sex 性暗示的；性挑逗的：*suggestive jokes* 黄色笑话 ▶ **sug·gest·ive·ly** *adv.*：*He leered suggestively.* 他色迷迷地斜瞟一眼。

sui·cidal /ˌsuːɪˈsaɪdl; *BrE also* ˌsjuːɪ-/ *adj.* **1** people who are **suicidal** feel that they want to kill themselves 想自杀的；有自杀倾向的：*On bad days I even felt suicidal.* 赶上不顺的日子，我都觉得不想活了。 ◇ *suicidal tendencies* 自杀倾向 **2** very dangerous and likely to lead to death; likely to cause very serious problems or disaster 自杀性的；有致命危险的；毁灭性的；灾难性的：*a suicidal leap into the swollen river* 不顾死活地跳进上涨的河水 ◇ ***It would***

S

be suicidal to risk going out in this weather. 在这种天气冒险出去，真是不要命了。◇ *The new economic policies could prove suicidal for the party.* 新经济政策可能给该党带来灾难性的后果。 ▸ **sui·cid·al·ly** /-dəli/ *adv.*: *suicidally depressed* 沮丧消沉得想自杀

sui·cide /ˈsuːɪsaɪd; *BrE also* ˈsjuːɪ-/ *noun* **1** [U, C] the act of killing yourself deliberately 自杀: *to **commit suicide*** 自杀 ◇ *an **attempted suicide*** (= one in which the person survives) 自杀未遂 ◇ *a **suicide letter/note*** (= written before sb tries to commit suicide) 绝命书 ◇ *a **suicide bomber*** (= who expects to die while trying to kill other people with a bomb) 自杀式爆炸者 ⊃ SEE ALSO ASSISTED SUICIDE **2** [U] a course of action that is likely to ruin your career, position in society, etc. 自杀性行为；自毁；自取灭亡的行为: *It would have been political suicide for him to challenge the allegations in court.* 假如当时他在法庭上质疑那些指控，那无异于自毁政治前程。**3** [C] (*formal*) a person who commits suicide 自杀者

ˈ**suicide pact** *noun* an agreement between two or more people to kill themselves at the same time（集体）自杀协议

sui generis /ˌsuːi ˈdʒenərɪs; ˈgenərɪs; ˌsuːaɪ/ *adj.* (*from Latin, formal*) different from all other people or things 独特的；特有的 SYN **unique**

suit 🔑 /suːt; *BrE also* sjuːt/ *noun, verb*

■ ***noun*** **1** 🔑 a set of clothes made of the same cloth, including a jacket and trousers/pants or a skirt 西服；西装；套装: *a business suit* 公务装 ◇ *a pinstripe suit* 一套细条纹西装 ◇ *a **two-/three-piece suit*** (= of two/three pieces of clothing) 一套两件 / 三件式西装 ⊃ VISUAL VOCAB PAGE V66 ⊃ SEE ALSO DINNER SUIT, JUMPSUIT, LEISURE SUIT, LOUNGE SUIT, SAILOR SUIT, SHELL SUIT, SWEATSUIT, TRACKSUIT, TROUSER SUIT **2** 🔑 a set of clothing worn for a particular activity（从事特定活动时穿的）成套服装: *a diving suit* 潜水服 ◇ *a suit of armour* 一套盔甲 ⊃ SEE ALSO BOILER SUIT, SPACESUIT, SWIMSUIT, WETSUIT **3** any of the four sets that form a PACK/DECK of cards（扑克牌中）所有同花色的牌: *The suits are called hearts, clubs, diamonds and spades.* 扑克牌的四种花色分别叫红桃、梅花、方块和黑桃。⊃ WORDFINDER NOTE AT CARD ⊃ VISUAL VOCAB PAGE V42 **4** = LAWSUIT: *to **file/bring a suit** against sb* 控告某人 ◇ *a divorce suit* 离婚诉讼 ⊃ SEE ALSO PATERNITY SUIT **5** [usually pl.] (*informal*) a person with an important job as a manager in a company or an organization, especially one thought of as being mainly concerned with financial matters or as having a lot of influence（具影响力的）高级管理人员（尤指财务方面的）IDM SEE BIRTHDAY, FOLLOW, STRONG

■ ***verb*** [no passive] (not used in the progressive tenses 不用于进行时) **1** 🔑 to be convenient or useful for sb 对（某人）方便；满足（某人）需要；合（某人）心意: **~ sb/sth** *Choose a computer to suit your particular needs.* 选一台适合你个人需要的电脑。◇ *If we met at 2, would that suit you?* 我们两点钟见面，你方便吗？◇ *If you want to go by bus, that **suits me fine**.* 要是你想坐公共汽车走，我也没问题。◇ *He can be very helpful, but only when it suits him.* 有时候他非常肯帮忙，不过那得合他心意。◇ **it suits sb to do sth** *It suits me to start work at a later time.* 对我来说，最好晚一点再开始工作。**2** 🔑 **~ sb** (especially of clothes, colours, etc. 尤指服装、颜色等) to make you look attractive 相配；合身: *Blue suits you. You should wear it more often.* 你适合穿蓝色，你该多穿蓝色衣服。◇ *I don't think this coat really suits me.* 我觉得这件大衣不大适合我穿。**3** **~ sb/sth** (*especially BrE*) (usually used in negative sentences 通常用于否定句) to be right or good for sb/sth 适合；适宜；有利于: *This hot weather doesn't suit me.* 天这么热，我真受不了。

IDM **suit your/sb's ˈbook** (*BrE, informal*) to be convenient or useful for you/sb 对某人方便（或有用） **suit sb ˌdown to the ˈground** (*BrE, informal*) to be very convenient or acceptable for sb 对某人非常方便；很合某人心意: *This job suits me down to the ground.* 这份工作我非常满意。 **ˌsuit yourˈself** (*informal*) **1** to do exactly what you would like 随自己的意愿: *I choose my assignments to suit myself.* 我根据自己的喜好选任务。**2** usually used in orders to tell sb to do what they want, even though it annoys you（表示听凭对方的意愿）自便，随便: *'I think I'll stay in this evening.' 'Suit yourself!'* "今晚我就不出去了。" "随你的便！"

PHR V ˈ**suit sth to sth/sb** to make sth appropriate for sth/sb 使适合（或适应）某事物（或人）: *He can suit his conversation to whoever he's with.* 无论跟谁说话，他都能说到一块儿。

suit·able 🔑 /ˈsuːtəbl; *BrE also* ˈsjuː-/ *adj.* right or appropriate for a particular purpose or occasion 合适的；适宜的；适当的；适用的: *a suitable candidate* 合适的人选 ◇ **~ for sth/sb** *This programme is not suitable for children.* 这个节目儿童不宜。◇ *a suitable place for a picnic* 适合野餐的地方 ◇ **~ to do sth** *I don't have anything suitable to wear for the party.* 我没有适合在聚会上穿的衣服。◇ *Would now be a suitable moment to discuss my report?* 现在讨论我的报告合适不合适？OPP **unsuitable** ▸ **suit·abil·ity** /ˌsuːtəˈbɪləti; *BrE also* ˌsjuː-/ *noun* [U]: *There is no doubt about her suitability for the job.* 毫无疑问，她适合做这个工作。

suit·ably /ˈsuːtəbli; *BrE also* ˈsjuː-/ *adv.* **1** in a way that is right or appropriate for a particular purpose or occasion 合适地；适宜地；适当地: *I am not really suitably dressed for a party.* 我穿这样的衣服参加聚会并不十分得体。◇ *suitably qualified candidates* 十分符合条件的人选 **2** showing the feelings, etc. that you would expect in a particular situation 如你所料地；自然: *He was suitably impressed when I told him I'd won.* 我告诉他我赢了，他当然觉得我真行。

suit·case 🔑 /ˈsuːtkeɪs; *BrE also* ˈsjuː-/ (*also* **case**) *noun* a case with flat sides and a handle, used for carrying clothes, etc. when you are travelling（旅行用的）手提箱: *to **pack/unpack a suitcase*** 把东西装进手提箱；取出手提箱里的东西 ⊃ VISUAL VOCAB PAGE V69

suite /swiːt/ *noun* **1** a set of rooms, especially in a hotel（尤指旅馆的）一套房间，套房: *a **hotel/private/honeymoon suite*** 旅馆 / 私人 / 蜜月套房 ◇ *a **suite of rooms/offices*** 一套房间；办公套房 ⊃ SEE ALSO EN SUITE ⊃ WORDFINDER NOTE AT HOTEL **2** a set of matching pieces of furniture 一套家具: *a **bathroom/bedroom suite*** 一套卫生间 / 卧室家具 ◇ (*BrE*) *a **three-piece suite** with two armchairs and a sofa* 由两张单人沙发和一张长沙发组成的三件套家具 **3** a piece of music made up of three or more related parts, for example pieces from an OPERA 组曲（由三个或更多相关部分组成）: *Stravinsky's Firebird Suite* 斯特拉文斯基的组曲《火鸟》**4** (*computing* 计) a set of related computer programs 套；套装软件: *a suite of software development tools* 一套软件开发工具

suit·ed 🔑 /ˈsuːtɪd; *BrE also* ˈsjuː-/ *adj.* [not before noun] **1** 🔑 right or appropriate for sb/sth 合适；适宜；适当: **~ (to sb/sth)** *She was **ideally suited** to the part of Eva Peron.* 她演爱娃 • 庇隆这个角色再合适不过了。◇ *This diet is suited to anyone who wants to lose weight fast.* 这食谱适合每一个希望迅速减肥的人。◇ **~ (for sb/sth)** *He is not really suited for a teaching career.* 他不大适合做教师。OPP **unsuited** **2** 🔑 if two people are **suited** or **well suited**, they are likely to make a good couple 般配的: *Jo and I are very well suited.* 我跟乔非常合得来。◇ *They were not suited to one another.* 他们俩彼此不配。OPP **unsuited** **3** wearing a suit, or a suit of the type mentioned 穿西装的；穿…套装的: *sober-suited city businessmen* 城市里那些穿着素净的西装的生意人

IDM ˌ**suited and ˈbooted** (*BrE, informal*) dressed in very smart clothes and shoes 西装革履；衣履光鲜

suit·ing /ˈsuːtɪŋ; *BrE also* ˈsjuːtɪŋ/ *noun* [U] cloth made especially of wool, used for making suits 西服毛料: *men's suiting* 男西装毛料

suitor /ˈsuːtə(r); *BrE also* ˈsjuː-; *NAmE* ˈsuːtər/ *noun* **1** (*old-fashioned*) a man who wants to marry a particular woman 求婚者 **2** (*business* 商) a company that wants to buy another company 有意收购另一公司的公司

su·kuma wiki /sʊˌkuːmə ˈwiːkiː/ *noun* [U] (*EAfrE*) a vegetable with dark green leaves that are cooked; KALE 羽衣

甘蓝（菜）：*a meal of ugali and sukuma wiki* 蒸玉米粉团加羽衣甘蓝菜的一餐

sul·fate, **sul·fide**, **sul·fur**, **sul·fur·ic acid** (*US*) = SULPHATE, SULPHIDE, SULPHUR, SULPHURIC ACID

sulk /sʌlk/ *verb, noun*
■ ***verb*** [I] (*disapproving*) to look angry and refuse to speak or smile because you want people to know that you are upset about sth 面有愠色；生闷气：*He went off to sulk in his room.* 他回到自己的房间，生起闷气来。
■ ***noun*** (*BrE also* **the sulks** [pl.]) a period of not speaking and being bad-tempered because you are angry about sth 愠怒；生闷气：*Jo was* ***in a sulk*** *upstairs.* 乔在楼上生闷气。◇ *to have the sulks* 满脸不高兴

sulky /ˈsʌlki/ *adj.* (*disapproving*) bad-tempered or not speaking because you are angry about sth 面有愠色的；生闷气的：*Sarah had looked sulky all morning.* 萨拉一上午都不高兴地板着脸。◇ *a sulky child* 闷闷不乐的孩子 ➲ WORDFINDER NOTE AT YOUNG ▶ **sulk·ily** /-ɪli/ *adv.* **sulki·ness** *noun* [U]

sul·len /ˈsʌlən/ *adj.* (*disapproving*) **1** bad-tempered and not speaking, either on a particular occasion or because it is part of your character 面有愠色的；闷闷不乐的；郁郁寡欢的：*Bob looked pale and sullen.* 鲍勃脸色苍白，闷闷不乐。◇ *She gave him a sullen glare.* 她满脸不高兴地瞪了他一眼。◇ *sullen teenagers* 面色阴郁的青少年 **2** (*literary*) (of the sky or weather 天空或天气) dark and unpleasant 阴沉的 ▶ **sul·len·ly** *adv.* **sul·len·ness** *noun* [U]

sully /ˈsʌli/ *verb* (**sul·lies**, **sully·ing**, **sul·lied**, **sul·lied**) (*formal* or *literary*) **1** ~ **sth** to spoil or reduce the value of sth 败坏；有损于 **2** ~ **sth** to make sth dirty 弄脏；玷污

sul·phate (*especially US* **sul·fate**) /ˈsʌlfeɪt/ *noun* [C, U] (*chemistry* 化) a COMPOUND of SULPHURIC ACID and a chemical element 硫酸盐：*copper sulphate* 硫酸铜 ➲ NOTE AT SULPHUR

sul·phide (*especially US* **sul·fide**) /ˈsʌlfaɪd/ *noun* [C, U] (*chemistry* 化) a COMPOUND of sulphur and another chemical element 硫化物 ➲ NOTE AT SULPHUR

sul·phur (*especially US* **sul·fur**) /ˈsʌlfə(r)/ *noun* [U] (*symb.* **S**) a chemical element. Sulphur is a pale yellow substance that produces a strong unpleasant smell when it burns and is used in medicine and industry. 硫；硫黄 HELP The spelling **sulfur** has been adopted by the International Union of Pure and Applied Chemistry and by the Royal Society of Chemistry in the UK. However, **sulphur** still remains the usual spelling in British, Irish, South African and Indian English. Both spellings are used in Canadian, Australian and New Zealand English.*sulfur这一拼写已为国际理论化学与应用化学联合会和英国皇家化学学会采用。不过，在英国、爱尔兰、南非和印度的英语中常见的拼写仍然是 sulphur。在加拿大、澳大利亚和新西兰的英语中，两种拼写均可使用。▶ **sul·phur·ous** (*especially US* **sul·fur·ous**) /ˈsʌlfərəs/ *adj.*：*sulphurous fumes* 燃烧硫黄产生的烟雾

ˌsulphur diˈoxide (*especially US* **ˌsulfur diˈoxide**) *noun* [U] (*symb.* SO_2) a poisonous gas with a strong smell, that is used in industry and causes air pollution 二氧化硫 ➲ NOTE AT SULPHUR

sul·phur·ic acid (*especially US* **sul·fur·ic acid**) /sʌlˌfjʊərɪk ˈæsɪd; *NAmE* -ˌfjʊr-/ *noun* [U] (*symb.* H_2SO_4) a strong clear acid 硫酸 ➲ NOTE AT SULPHUR

sul·tan /ˈsʌltən/ *noun* the title given to Muslim rulers in some countries 苏丹（某些国家穆斯林统治者的称号）：*the Sultan of Brunei* 文莱苏丹

sul·tana /sʌlˈtɑːnə; *NAmE* -ˈtænə/ *noun* **1** (*BrE*) (*NAmE* **ˌgolden ˈraisin**) a small dried GRAPE without seeds, used in cakes, etc. 无核小葡萄干（用于糕点等）**2** the wife, mother, sister or daughter of a sultan 苏丹女眷（指后妃、王太后、姊妹或女儿）

sul·tan·ate /ˈsʌltəneɪt/ *noun* **1** the rank or position of a SULTAN 苏丹的职位 **2** an area of land that is ruled over by a SULTAN 苏丹统治的领土：*the Sultanate of Oman* 阿曼苏丹国 **3** the period of time during which sb is a SULTAN 苏丹的统治时期

sul·try /ˈsʌltri/ *adj.* (**sul·trier**, **sul·tri·est**) **1** (of the weather or air 天气或空气) very hot and uncomfortable 闷热的 SYN **muggy**：*a sultry summer afternoon* 夏天一个闷热的下午 **2** (*formal*) (of a woman or her appearance 女子或其外表) sexually attractive; seeming to have strong sexual feelings 姿色迷人的；风情万种的；性感的 SYN **sexy**：*a sultry smile* 迷人的微笑 ◇ *a sultry singer* 嗓音撩人的歌手 ▶ **sul·tri·ness** *noun* [U]

sum AW /sʌm/ *noun, verb*
■ ***noun*** **1** [C] ~ (**of sth**) an amount of money 金额；款项：*You will be fined the sum of £200.* 你将被罚款 200 英镑。◇ *a large sum of money* 一大笔钱 ◇ *a six-figure sum* 一笔六位数的款项 ➲ SEE ALSO LUMP SUM **2** [C, usually sing.] ~ (**of sth**) the number you get when you add two or more numbers together 和；总和；总数：*The sum of 7 and 12 is 19.* *7 加 12 的和是 19。**3** (*also* **ˌsum ˈtotal**) [sing.] **the ~ of sth** all of sth, especially when you think that it is not very much 全部，一切（尤指数量不大）：*This is the sum of my achievements so far.* 这就是我目前的全部成就。**4** [C] a simple problem that involves calculating numbers 算术；（数字的）简单计算：*to* ***do a sum*** *in your head* 做心算 ◇ *I was good at sums at school.* 我上学时擅长算术。◇ *If I've got my sums right, I should be able to afford the rent.* 要是我算对了的话，我应该负担得起这笔租金。
IDM **be greater/more than the ˌsum of its ˈparts** to be better or more effective as a group than you would think just by looking at the individual members of the group 个体相加不如集体的力量大 **in ˈsum** (*formal*) used to introduce a short statement of the main points of a discussion, speech, etc. 总之；总而言之
■ ***verb*** (**-mm-**)
PHR V **ˌsum ˈup** | **ˌsum sth↔ˈup** **1** to state the main points of sth in a short and clear form 总结；概括 SYN **summarize**：***To sum up****, there are three main ways of tackling the problem…* 概括起来说，这一问题主要有三种解决办法…◇ **sum up what…** *Can I just sum up what we've agreed so far?* 我可否就我们目前已经达成的共识作个概括？➲ LANGUAGE BANK AT CONCLUSION **2** (of a judge 法官) to give a summary of the main facts and arguments in a legal case, near the end of a trial（审理结束前）作概述 ➲ RELATED NOUN SUMMING-UP **ˌsum sb/sth↔ˈup** **1** to describe or show the most typical characteristics of sb/sth, especially in a few words 简而言之：*Totally lazy—that just about sums him up.* 懒到家了，这大体上就是他的真实写照。**2** to form or express an opinion of sb/sth 估量；判断 SYN **size up**：*She quickly summed up the situation and took control.* 她很快就看出是怎么回事，并控制住局面。➲ RELATED NOUN SUMMING-UP

summa cum laude /ˌsʊmə ˌkʊm ˈlɔːdi; ˈlaʊdeɪ/ *adv., adj.* (*from Latin*) (in the US) at the highest level of achievement that students can reach when they finish their studies at college 以优异成绩（美国大学毕业的成绩等级，为三等优异成绩的第一等）：*He graduated summa cum laude from Harvard.* 他以最优异成绩从哈佛大学毕业。➲ COMPARE CUM LAUDE, MAGNA CUM LAUDE

sum·mar·ize AW (*BrE also* **-ise**) /ˈsʌməraɪz/ *verb* [T, I] ~ (**sth**) to give a summary of sth (= a statement of the main points) 总结；概括；概述：*The results of the research are summarized at the end of the chapter.* 在这一章末尾对研究结果作了总结。➲ LANGUAGE BANK AT CONCLUSION

sum·mary AW /ˈsʌməri/ *noun, adj.*
■ ***noun*** (*pl.* **-ies**) a short statement that gives only the main points of sth, not the details 总结；概括；概要：*The following is a summary of our conclusions.* 现将我们的几点结论综述如下。◇ *a news summary* 新闻综述 ◇ *a two-page summary of a government report* 一份两页的政府报告摘要 ◇ ***In summary****, this was a disappointing performance.* 总的来说，这场演出令人失望。
■ ***adj.*** [only before noun] **1** (*formal*) giving only the main points of sth, not the details 总结性的；概括的；概要的：*a summary financial statement* 财务汇总报表 ◇ *I made a summary report for the records.* 我对记录内容做了扼要报

S

告。**2** (*sometimes disapproving*) done immediately, without paying attention to the normal process that should be followed 从速从简的；即决的；草草的：***summary justice/execution*** 即决裁判；草草处决 ◇ *a summary judgement* 草草判决 ▸ **sum·mar·ily** /'sʌmərəli; *NAmE* sə'merəli/ *adv.*：*to be summarily dismissed/executed* 被草草开除 / 处决

sum·mat /'sʌmət; 'səmət/ *noun* (*NEngE, non-standard*) a way of writing a spoken form of 'something' (something 的一种书写形式)

sum·ma·tion AW /sʌ'meɪʃn/ *noun* **1** [usually sing.] (*formal*) a summary of what has been done or said 总结；概括：*What he said was a fair summation of the discussion.* 他这番话对讨论作了恰当的总结。**2** (*formal*) a collection of different parts that forms a complete account or impression of sb/sth 汇总物；综合体：*The exhibition presents a summation of the artist's career.* 展览全面体现了这位画家的艺术生涯。**3** (*NAmE, law* 律) a final speech that a lawyer makes near the end of a trial in court, after all the evidence has been given (判决前的) 证据总结

sum·mer 🔑 /'sʌmə(r)/ *noun* [U, C] the warmest season of the year, coming between spring and autumn/fall 夏天；夏季：*We're going away **in the summer**.* 夏天我们要外出。◇ *It's very hot here **in summer**.* 这里夏天很热。◇ *in the summer of 2009* 在 2009 年夏季 ◇ *late/early summer* 夏末；初夏 ◇ *this/next/last summer* 今年 / 下一个 / 上一个夏天 ◇ *a cool/hot/wet summer* 凉爽的 / 炎热的 / 多雨的夏天 ◇ *It is now **high summer*** (= the hottest part of summer). 正值盛夏。◇ *a summer's day* 夏日 ◇ *a summer dress* 夏天穿的连衣裙 ◇ *the **summer holidays/vacation*** 暑假 ◇ *two summers ago* 两年前 ➲ SEE ALSO INDIAN SUMMER (1) IDM SEE SWALLOW *n.*

'summer camp *noun* [C, U] (in the US) a place where children go during the summer and take part in sports and other activities 夏令营

'summer house *noun* **1** a small building in a garden/yard for sitting in in good weather (花园或院子里的) 凉亭 **2** (*also* **'summer home**) (*NAmE*) a house that sb lives in only during the summer 避暑别墅

ˌsummer 'pudding *noun* [C, U] (*BrE*) a cold DESSERT (= a sweet dish) made from BERRIES surrounded by slices of bread that have absorbed their juice 夏令布丁 (面包片围在浆果四周浸透果汁的冷盘甜食)

'summer school *noun* [C, U] courses that are held in the summer at a university or college or, in the US, at a school 暑期班 (一般在大学开设，美国中小学也有)

ˌsummer 'stock *noun* [U] (*NAmE*) the production of special plays and other entertainment in areas where people are on holiday/vacation (度假胜地的) 夏季特别娱乐表演，夏令剧目

'summer student *noun* (*CanE*) a student, especially a university student, who is working at a job for the summer 暑期工 (夏季打工的学生，尤指大学生)

'summer time (*BrE*) (*NAmE* **'daylight saving time**) *noun* [U] the period during which in some countries the clocks are put forward one hour, so that it is light for an extra hour in the evening 夏令时 (有些国家实行夏时制，将时钟拨快一小时，以节约照明能源)

sum·mer·time /'sʌmətaɪm; *NAmE* -mərt-/ *noun* [U] the season of summer 夏季；夏天；夏令：*It's beautiful here in (the) summertime.* 这里夏天很美。

sum·mery /'sʌməri/ *adj.* typical of or suitable for the summer 夏季的；夏季特有的；适合夏季的：*summery weather* 夏日的天气 ◇ *a light summery dress* 夏天穿的薄连衣裙 OPP **wintry**

ˌsumming-'up *noun* (*pl.* **summings-up**) **1** a speech that the judge makes near the end of a trial in court, in which he or she reminds the JURY about the evidence and the most important points in the case before the JURY makes its decision (审理结束前法官向陪审团作的) 证据总结 **2** an occasion when sb states the main points of an argument, etc. 总结；概括

sum·mit /'sʌmɪt/ *noun* **1** the highest point of sth, especially the top of a mountain 最高点；顶点；山顶：*We reached the summit at noon.* 中午时分我们抵达峰顶。◇ *This path leads to the summit.* 这条路通往山顶。◇ (*figurative*) *the summit of his career* 他事业的顶峰 ➲ WORDFINDER NOTE AT MOUNTAIN ➲ VISUAL VOCAB PAGE V5 **2** an official meeting or series of meetings between the leaders of two or more governments at which they discuss important matters (政府间的) 首脑会议；峰会：*a summit in Moscow* 在莫斯科举行的首脑会议 ◇ *a summit conference* 峰会 ➲ COLLOCATIONS AT INTERNATIONAL

sum·mon /'sʌmən/ *verb* **1** ~ **sb** (**to do sth**) (*formal*) to order sb to appear in court 传唤，传讯 (出庭) SYN **summons**: *He was summoned to appear before the magistrates.* 他被传唤在地方法院出庭。**2** ~ **sb** (**to sth**) | ~**sb to do sth** (*formal*) to order sb to come to you 召唤：*In May 1688 he was urgently summoned to London.* * 1688 年 5 月，他被紧急召往伦敦。◇ *She summoned the waiter.* 她召唤服务员过来。**3** ~ **sth** (*formal*) to arrange an official meeting 召集，召开 (会议) SYN **convene**: *to summon a meeting* 召集会议 **4** ~ **sth** (*formal*) to call for or try to obtain sth 吁求；请求；争取：*to **summon assistance/help/reinforcements*** 请求援助 / 帮助 / 增援 **5** ~ **sth** (**up**) to make an effort to produce a particular quality in yourself, especially when you find it difficult 鼓起；振作；使出 SYN **muster**: *She was trying to summon up the courage to leave him.* 当时她试图鼓起勇气离开他。◇ *I couldn't even summon the energy to get out of bed.* 我甚至连下床的力气都没有。

PHR V **ˌsummon sth↔'up** to make a feeling, an idea, a memory, etc. come into your mind 唤起；使想起 SYN **evoke**: *The book summoned up memories of my childhood.* 这本书唤起我童年的记忆。

sum·mons /'sʌmənz/ *noun, verb*

■ ***noun*** (*pl.* **sum·monses** /-zɪz/) **1** (*NAmE also* **cit·ation**) an order to appear in court (法院的) 传唤，传票：*to issue a summons against sb* 向某人发出传票 ◇ *The police have been unable to **serve a summons on** him.* 警方一直无法把传票送达他本人。◇ *She received a summons to appear in court the following week.* 她收到一张传票，让她下周出庭。**2** an order to come and see sb 召唤；召见令：*to obey a royal summons* 听从国王的召唤

■ ***verb*** to order sb to appear in court 传 (某人) 出庭；传唤 SYN **summon**: ~ **sb** (**for sth**) *She was summonsed for speeding.* 她因超速行车被传讯。◇ ~ **sb to do sth** *He was summonsed to appear in court.* 他被传唤出庭。

sumo /'suːməʊ; *NAmE* -moʊ/ (*also* **ˌsumo 'wrestling**) *noun* [U] a Japanese style of WRESTLING, in which the people taking part are extremely large 相扑：*a sumo wrestler* 相扑运动员

sump /sʌmp/ *noun* **1** a hole or hollow area in which liquid waste collects 集水坑；污水池 **2** (*NAmE also* **'oil pan**) the place under an engine that holds the engine oil (发动机下面的) 集油槽，油底壳

sump·tu·ous /'sʌmptʃuəs/ *adj.* (*formal*) very expensive and looking very impressive 华贵的；豪华的；奢华的：*a sumptuous meal* 盛宴 ◇ *We dined in sumptuous surroundings.* 我们在富丽堂皇的环境中用餐。▸ **sump·tu·ous·ly** *adv.* **sump·tu·ous·ness** *noun* [U]

ˌsum 'total *noun* [sing.] (*sometimes disapproving*) the whole of sth; everything 全部；一切；总共：*A photo, a book of poems and a gold ring—this was the sum total of his possessions.* 一张照片、一本诗集和一枚金戒指，这就是他的全部家当。

sun 🔑 /sʌn/ *noun, verb*

■ ***noun*** **1** **the sun**, **the Sun** [sing.] the star that shines in the sky during the day and gives the earth heat and light 太阳；日：*the sun's rays* 太阳的光线 ◇ *the **rising/setting sun*** 初升的 / 西下的太阳 ◇ ***The sun was shining** and birds were singing.* 阳光照耀，鸟儿啼啭。◇ *The sun was just* setting. 太阳刚往下落。➲COLLOCATIONS AT WEATHER

WORDFINDER 联想词: daylight, eclipse, equinox, ray, rise, solar, solstice, twilight, **the universe**

2 (*usually* **the sun**) [sing., U] the light and heat from the sun 太阳的光和热；阳光；日光 SYN **sunshine**: *the warmth of the afternoon sun* 下午温暖的阳光 ◇ *This room gets the sun in the mornings.* 这间屋子上午可以晒着太阳。 ◇ *We sat* ***in the sun.*** 我们坐在阳光下。◇ *The sun was blazing hot.* 阳光灼热逼人。◇ *Too much sun ages the skin.* 晒太阳过多会使皮肤衰老。◇ *We did our best to keep* ***out of the sun.*** 我们尽量避开阳光照射。◇ *They've booked a holiday* ***in the sun*** (= in a place where it is warm and the sun shines a lot). 他们已经预订好了去阳光充足的地方度假。◇ *Her face had obviously* ***caught the sun*** (= become red or brown) *on holiday.* 她的脸明显地在假期晒黑了。◇ *I was driving westwards and I* ***had the sun in my eyes*** (= the sun was shining in my eyes). 我驱车向西行驶，阳光直晃眼。➲SEE ALSO SUNNY (1) **3** [C] (*specialist*) any star around which planets move 恒星

IDM **under the 'sun** used to emphasize that you are talking about a very large number of things（强调事物数量很大）天下，世上，全世界：*We talked about everything under the sun.* 天南地北，我们无所不谈。 **with the 'sun** when the sun rises or sets 日出时；日落时：*I get up with the sun.* 我日出即起。➲MORE AT HAY, PLACE *n.*

■*verb* (-nn-) **~ yourself** to sit or lie in a place where the sun is shining on you 晒太阳：*We lay sunning ourselves on the deck.* 我们躺在甲板上晒太阳。

'sun-baked *adj.* **1** made hard and dry by the heat of the sun 晒得干硬的：*sun-baked earth* 被太阳烤干的土地 **2** receiving a lot of light and heat from the sun 太阳暴晒的；烈日下的：*sun-baked beaches* 太阳暴晒的海滩

sun·bathe /'sʌnbeɪð/ *verb* [I] to sit or lie in the sun, especially in order to go brown (get a SUNTAN) 沐日光浴；晒太阳 ➲NOTE AT BATH

sun·beam /'sʌnbiːm/ *noun* a stream of light from the sun（一束）阳光

sun·bed /'sʌnbed/ *noun* a bed for lying on under a SUNLAMP 太阳灯日光浴床 ➲COMPARE SUNLOUNGER

the Sun·belt /'sʌnbelt/ *noun* [sing.] the southern and south-western parts of the US that are warm for most of the year 阳光地带（美国南部和西南部地区，全年大部分时间气候温暖）

sun·block /'sʌnblɒk; *NAmE* -blɑːk/ *noun* [U, C] a cream that you put on your skin to protect it completely from the harmful effects of the sun 防晒霜；防晒油

sun·burn /'sʌnbɜːn; *NAmE* -bɜːrn/ *noun* [U] the condition of having painful red skin because you have spent too much time in the sun 晒斑；晒伤 ➲COMPARE SUNTAN

sun·burned /'sʌnbɜːnd; *NAmE* -bɜːrnd/ (*also* **sun·burnt** /'sʌnbɜːnt; *NAmE* -bɜːrnt/) *adj.* **1** suffering from sunburn 晒伤的：*Her shoulders were badly sunburned.* 她的肩膀严重晒伤了。**2** (*BrE*) (of a person or of skin 人或皮肤) having an attractive brown colour from being in the sun 晒得黝黑而好看的 SYN **tanned**: *She looked fit and sunburned.* 她看上去挺健康，晒得一身古铜色。

sun·burst /'sʌnbɜːst; *NAmE* -bɜːrst/ *noun* an occasion when the sun appears from behind the clouds and sends out bright streams of light 云开日出；阳光突现

sun·cream /'sʌnkriːm/ *noun* [U, C] (*especially BrE*) cream that you put on your skin to protect it from the harmful effects of the sun 防晒霜；防晒乳

sun·dae /'sʌndeɪ; -di/ *noun* a cold DESSERT (= a sweet dish) of ice cream covered with a sweet sauce, nuts, pieces of fruit, etc., usually served in a tall glass 圣代冰淇淋（加甜汁、果仁、水果粒等）

Sun·day /'sʌndeɪ; -di/ *noun* (*abbr.* **Sun.**) **1** [C, U] the day of the week after Saturday and before Monday, thought of as either the first or the last day of the week 星期日；星期天 HELP To see how **Sunday** is used, look at the examples at **Monday**. * Sunday 的用法见词条 Monday 下的示例。 ORIGIN From the Old English for 'day of the sun', translated from Latin *dies solis.* 源自古英语，原意为 day of the sun（太阳日），古英语则译自拉丁文 dies solis。**2** [C, usually pl.] (*BrE, informal*) a newspaper published on a Sunday 每逢星期日出版的报纸；星期日报

IDM **your ˌSunday 'best** (*informal, humorous*) your best clothes 自己最好的衣服 ➲MORE AT MONTH

'Sunday school *noun* [C, U] a class that is organized by a church or SYNAGOGUE where children can go for a short time on Sundays to learn about the Christian or Jewish religion 主日学校（基督教堂或犹太教堂在星期日为儿童提供宗教教育）

'sun deck *noun* the part of a ship where passengers can sit to enjoy the sun, or a similar area beside a restaurant or swimming pool（轮船的）日光甲板；（餐馆或游泳池旁边的）日光平台，晒台

sun·der /'sʌndə(r)/ *verb* **~ sth/sb (from sth/sb)** (*formal* or *literary*) to split or break sth/sb apart, especially by force（尤指强制地）分开，使分离，割裂 ➲SEE ALSO ASUNDER

sundial 日晷

sun·dial /'sʌndaɪəl/ *noun* a device used outdoors, especially in the past, for telling the time when the sun is shining. A pointed piece of metal throws a shadow on a flat surface that is marked with the hours like a clock, and the shadow moves around as the sun moves across the sky. 日晷

sun·down /'sʌndaʊn/ *noun* [U] (*especially NAmE*) the time when the sun goes down and night begins 日落时分 SYN sunset

sun·down·er /'sʌndaʊnə(r)/ *noun* (*BrE, informal*) an alcoholic drink, drunk around the time when the sun goes down 夕暮酒（夕阳西下时喝）

'sun-drenched *adj.* [only before noun] (*approving*) having a lot of hot sun 充满阳光的；阳光充足的：*sun-drenched Mediterranean beaches* 阳光充沛的地中海海滩

sun·dress /'sʌndres/ *noun* a dress that does not cover the arms, neck or shoulders, worn in hot weather 太阳裙，背心裙（领口低，无袖）

'sun-dried *adj.* [only before noun] (especially of food 尤指食物) dried naturally by the heat of the sun 晒干的：*sun-dried tomatoes* 晒干的西红柿

sun·dries /'sʌndriz/ *noun* [pl.] various items, especially small ones, that are not important enough to be named separately 杂物；杂项物品

sun·dry /'sʌndri/ *adj.* [only before noun] (*formal*) various; not important enough to be named separately 杂项的：*a watch, a diary and sundry other items* 一块手表、一本日记和其他一些零碎的东西

IDM **ˌall and 'sundry** (*informal*) everyone, not just a few special people 所有人；各色人等：*She was known to all and sundry as Bella.* 人人都叫她贝拉。◇ *The club is open to all and sundry.* 这个俱乐部什么人都可以加入。

sun·flower /'sʌnflaʊə(r)/ *noun* a very tall plant with large yellow flowers, grown in gardens or for its seeds and their oil that are used in cooking 向日葵；葵花：*sunflower oil* 葵花籽油 ➲VISUAL VOCAB PAGE V11

sung PAST PART. OF SING

S

sun·glasses /ˈsʌnglɑːsɪz; *NAmE* -glæs-/ (*also informal* **shades**) *noun* [pl.] a pair of glasses with dark glass in them that you wear to protect your eyes from bright light from the sun 太阳镜；墨镜：*a pair of sunglasses* 一副太阳镜 ➲ SEE ALSO DARK GLASSES

ˈ**sun hat** *noun* a hat worn to protect the head and neck from the sun 阔边遮阳帽 ➲ VISUAL VOCAB PAGE V70

sunk PAST PART. OF SINK

sunk·en /ˈsʌŋkən/ *adj.* **1** [only before noun] that has fallen to the bottom of the sea or the ocean, or of a lake or river 沉没的；沉入水底的 SYN **submerged**：*a sunken ship* 沉船 ◇ *sunken treasure* 沉在水底的财宝 **2** (of eyes or cheeks 眼睛或面颊) hollow and deep as a result of disease, getting old, or not having enough food 凹陷的，深陷的（尤因疾病、年老或饥饿）**3** [only before noun] at a lower level than the area around 低于周围平面的；低洼处的：*a sunken garden* 沉园

ˈ**sun-kissed** *adj.* [usually before noun] made warm or brown by the sun 晒暖的；晒黑的：*sun-kissed bodies on the beach* 沙滩上晒得黝黑的身体

sun·lamp /ˈsʌnlæmp/ *noun* a lamp that produces ULTRAVIOLET light that has the same effect as the sun and can turn the skin brown 太阳灯（能发出紫外线，与日照有相同效果）

sun·less /ˈsʌnləs/ *adj.* without any sun; receiving no light from the sun 无阳光的；阳光照不到的 SYN **gloomy**：*a sunless day* 无阳光的一天 OPP **sunny**

sun·light /ˈsʌnlaɪt/ *noun* [U] the light from the sun 阳光；日光：*a* ***ray/pool of sunlight*** 一束 / 一片阳光 ◇ ***shafts of bright sunlight*** 一道道明亮的阳光 ◇ *The morning sunlight flooded into the room.* 早晨的阳光泻入房间。

sun·lit /ˈsʌnlɪt/ *adj.* [usually before noun] receiving light from the sun 阳光照耀的：*sunlit streets* 阳光照耀的街道

ˈ**sun lounge** (*BrE*) (*also* **sun·room** *NAmE, BrE*) *noun* a room with large windows, and often a glass roof, that lets in a lot of light 日光室，阳光间（带大窗户，常有玻璃屋顶）

sun·loun·ger /ˈsʌnlaʊndʒə(r)/ *noun* (*BrE*) a chair with a long seat that supports your legs, used for sitting or lying on in the sun 日光浴椅；日光浴床 ➲ COMPARE LOUNGER, SUNBED ➲ VISUAL VOCAB PAGE V20

S

Sunni /ˈsʊni; ˈsʌni/ *noun* (*pl.* **Sunni** or **Sun·nis**) **1** [U] one of the two main branches of the Islamic religion 逊尼派（伊斯兰教两大派别之一）➲ COMPARE SHIA (1) **2** [C] a member of the Sunni branch of Islam 逊尼派穆斯林 ➲ COMPARE SHIITE ▶ **Sun·nite** /ˈsʊnaɪt; ˈsʌn-/ *adj.* [usually before noun]

sun·nies /ˈsʌniz/ [pl.] *noun* (*AustralE, NZE, informal*) SUNGLASSES 太阳镜；墨镜

sunny /ˈsʌni/ *adj.* (**sun·nier, sun·ni·est**) **1** with a lot of bright light from the sun 阳光充足的：*a sunny day* 阳光明媚的日子 ◇ *sunny weather* 艳阳高照的天气 ◇ *The outlook for the weekend is hot and sunny.* 预计本周末天气晴朗炎热。◇ *a sunny garden* 充满阳光的花园 ◇ *Italy was at its sunniest.* 当时意大利正值阳光最充沛的时节。**2** cheerful and happy 欢乐的；快乐的：*a sunny disposition* 开朗的性情

ˈ**sunny side** *noun* the side of sth that receives most light from the sun 晒着太阳的一边；向阳面：(*figurative*) *the sunny side of life* (= the more cheerful aspects of life) 人生的光明面
IDM ˌ**sunny side ˈup** (*NAmE*) (of an egg 蛋) fried on one side only 只煎一面的

sun·rise /ˈsʌnraɪz/ *noun* **1** [U] the time when the sun first appears in the sky in the morning 日出 SYN **dawn**：*We got up* ***at sunrise.*** 我们在日出时起床。**2** [C, usually sing.] the colours in the part of the sky where the sun first appears in the morning 朝霞：*the pinks and yellows of the sunrise* 一道道粉红和金黄的朝霞

ˈ**sunrise industry** *noun* a new industry, especially one connected with ELECTRONICS or computers, that is successful and growing 朝阳产业；（尤指与电子或计算机相关的）新兴产业 ➲ COMPARE SUNSET INDUSTRY

sun·roof /ˈsʌnruːf/ *noun* (*pl.* **-roofs**) a part of the roof of a car that you can open to let air and light in（汽车车顶可开启的）活动顶板，天窗

sun·room /ˈsʌnruːm; -rʊm/ (*especially NAmE*) (*BrE also* ˈ**sun lounge**) *noun* a room with large windows, and often a glass roof, that lets in a lot of light 日光室，阳光间（带大窗户，常有玻璃屋顶）

sun·screen /ˈsʌnskriːn/ *noun* [C, U] a cream or liquid that you put on your skin to protect it from the harmful effects of the sun 防晒霜；防晒油：*a high factor* (= strong) *sunscreen* 防晒系数高的防晒霜

sun·set /ˈsʌnset/ *noun, adj., verb*
■ ***noun*** **1** [U] the time when the sun goes down and night begins 日落；傍晚：*Every evening* ***at sunset*** *the flag was lowered.* 每天傍晚日落时都要降旗。**2** [C] the colours in the part of the sky where the sun slowly goes down in the evening 晚霞：*a spectacular sunset* 绚烂的晚霞 **3** [C] a fixed period of time after which a law or the effect of a law will end（法律的）自动废止期，效力消减期：*There is a five-year sunset on the new tax.* 新税种的有效施行期限为五年。
■ ***adj.*** [only before noun] **1** used to describe a colour that is like one of the colours in a sunset 霞红色的；浅橘红色的：*sunset yellow* 日落黄 **2** used to describe sth that is near its end, or that happens at the end of sth 衰落的；最后期的：*This is his sunset tour after fifty years as a singer.* 这是他五十年歌手生涯结束前最后一次巡回演出。**3** (of a law or the effect of a law 法律或法律效力) designed to end or to end sth after a fixed period of time 定期废止的：*a two-year sunset clause in the new law* 新法律中的一条实施期限为两年的"落日条款"
■ ***verb*** (**-tt-**) [I, T] ~ (**sth**) (of a law or the effect of a law 法律或法律效力) to end or to end sth after a fixed period of time（使）定期届满废止：*The tax relief will sunset after a year.* 税款减免将在一年后废止。

ˈ**sunset industry** *noun* an old industry that has started to become less successful 夕阳产业；夕阳工业 ➲ COMPARE SUNRISE INDUSTRY

ˈ**sunset provision** (*also* ˈ**sunset clause**) *noun* (*law* 律) part of a law, a rule or an agreement that states that it will no longer apply from a particular date 落日条款（法律、规定或协议中说明自某日期起即行废止的条款）

sun·shade /ˈsʌnʃeɪd/ *noun* **1** a light umbrella or other object such as an AWNING, that is used to protect people from hot sun 遮阳伞；遮阳篷：*a child's buggy fitted with a sunshade* 装有遮阳篷的婴儿车 ➲ VISUAL VOCAB PAGE V20 ➲ COMPARE PARASOL **2** **sunshades** [pl.] a pair of dark glasses that you wear to protect your eyes from bright light from the sun, especially ones that fix on to your ordinary glasses（尤指加在普通眼镜上的）太阳镜，墨镜

sun·shine /ˈsʌnʃaɪn/ *noun* [U] **1** the light and heat of the sun 阳光；日光：*the warm spring sunshine* 春天和煦的阳光 ➲ COLLOCATIONS AT WEATHER **2** (*informal*) happiness 欢乐；幸福：*She brought sunshine into our dull lives.* 她给我们乏味的生活带来了欢乐。**3** (*BrE, informal*) used for addressing sb in a friendly, or sometimes a rude way（友好地称呼某人，有时显得不礼貌）朋友，老兄：*Hello, sunshine!* 你好啊，老兄！◇ *Look, sunshine, who do you think you're talking to?* 喂，哥们儿，知道你在跟谁说话吗？ IDM SEE RAY

ˈ**sunshine law** *noun* (*US*) a law that forces government organizations to make certain types of information available to the public 阳光法，会议公开法（要求政府机构公开某些类型的信息）

sun·spot /ˈsʌnspɒt; *NAmE* -spɑːt/ *noun* a dark area that sometimes appears on the sun's surface（太阳）黑子

sun·stroke /ˈsʌnstrəʊk; *NAmE* -stroʊk/ *noun* [U] an illness with fever, weakness, headache, etc. caused by too much direct sun, especially on the head 日射病；中暑

sun·tan /ˈsʌntæn/ *noun* [usually sing.] = TAN (2): *Where have you been to get that suntan?* 你上哪儿去了，晒得黑黑的？ ➲ COMPARE SUNBURN ▶ **sun·tan** *adj.* [only before noun]: *suntan oil* 防晒油 **sun·tanned** *adj.* = TANNED: *a suntanned face* 晒得黝黑的脸庞

sun·trap /ˈsʌntræp/ *noun* a place that is sheltered from the wind and gets a lot of sun 避风向阳处

sun·up /ˈsʌnʌp/ *noun* [U] (*especially NAmE*) the time when the sun rises and day begins 日出

ˈsun-worship·per *noun* (*informal*) a person who enjoys lying in the sun very much 迷恋日光浴的人

sup /sʌp/ *verb* (**-pp-**) [I, T] ~ (**sth**) (*NEngE* or *old-fashioned*) to drink sth, especially in small amounts （小口地）喝；呷；啜 ▶ **sup** *noun*

super /ˈsuːpə(r); *BrE also* ˈsjuː-/ *adj., adv., noun*
- **adj.** (*informal, becoming old-fashioned*) extremely good 顶好的；超级的；顶呱呱的：*a super meal* 一顿美餐 ◇ *We had a super time in Italy.* 我们在意大利过得十分惬意。◇ *She was super* (= very kind) *when I was having problems.* 我遇到问题的时候，她待我好极了。
- **adv.** (*informal*) especially; particularly 特别；格外：*He's been super understanding.* 他特别体谅人。
- **noun 1** (*BrE, informal*) a SUPERINTENDENT in the police （英国的）警官；（美国的）警长 **2** (*NAmE*) a SUPERINTENDENT of a building （大楼的）管理人

super- /ˈsuːpə(r); *BrE also* ˈsjuː-/ *combining form* **1** (in adjectives, adverbs and nouns 构成形容词、副词和名词) extremely; more or better than normal 极；超；超级：*super-rich* 极富有的 ◇ *superhuman* 超出常人的 ◇ *superglue* 强力胶 **2** (in nouns and verbs 构成名词和动词) above; over 上；上方：*superstructure* 上层建筑 ◇ *superimpose* 使叠加

super·abun·dance /ˌsuːpərəˈbʌndəns; *BrE also* ˌsjuː-/ *noun* [sing., U] (*formal*) much more than enough of sth 过多；过剩 ▶ **super·abun·dant** *adj.*

super·annu·ated /ˌsuːpərˈænjueɪtɪd; *BrE also* ˌsjuː-/ *adj.* [usually before noun] (*formal* or *humorous*) (of people or things 人或东西) too old for work or to be used for their original purpose 年老不能工作的；陈旧不中用的；过时的：*superannuated rock stars* 过气摇滚歌星

super·annu·ation /ˌsuːpərˌænjuˈeɪʃn; *BrE also* ˌsjuː-/ *noun* [U] (*especially BrE*) a pension that you get, usually from your employer, when you stop working when you are old and that you pay for while you are working; the money that you pay for this （通常由原雇主发的）退休金，养老金

su·perb /suːˈpɜːb; sjuː-; *NAmE* suːˈpɜːrb/ *adj.* excellent; of very good quality 极佳的；卓越的；质量极高的：*a superb player* 一名杰出的运动员 ◇ *The car's in superb condition.* 这辆车车况极好。◇ *His performance was absolutely superb.* 他的表演精彩绝伦。◇ *You look superb.* 你看上去棒极了。➲ SYNONYMS AT EXCELLENT ▶ **su·perb·ly** *adv.*: *a superbly illustrated book* 一部配有精美插图的书 ◇ *She plays superbly.* 她演奏得好极了。

the ˈSuper Bowl™ *noun* an AMERICAN FOOTBALL game played every year to decide the winner of the National Football League 超级碗橄榄球赛（美国全国橄榄球联盟的年度冠军赛）

super·bug /ˈsuːpəbʌɡ; ˈsjuː-; *NAmE* ˈsuːpərb-/ *noun* a type of bacteria that cannot easily be killed by ANTIBIOTICS 超级细菌（抗生素不能轻易将其杀死）➲ SEE ALSO MRSA

super·cen·ter (*US*) (*BrE* **super·centre**) /ˈsuːpəsentə(r); ˈsjuː-; *NAmE* ˈsuːpər-/ *noun* (*especially US*) a very large shop/store, especially a grocery store that also sells lots of other goods 超大购物中心（尤指食品杂货超市）

super·charged /ˈsuːpətʃɑːdʒd; ˈsjuː-; *NAmE* ˈsuːpərtʃɑːrdʒd/ *adj.* **1** (of an engine 发动机) powerful because it is supplied with air or fuel at a pressure that is higher than normal （用增压器）增压的，提高功率的 **2** (*informal*) stronger, more powerful or more effective than usual 异常强烈的；格外强劲的；特别有效的：*supercharged words, like 'terrorism' or 'fascism'* 诸如 terrorism 或 fascism 等语义格外强烈的词 ▶ **super·charg·er** *noun*: *VW's supercharger for its 16-valve engine* 大众汽车 16 阀发动机专用增压器

super·cili·ous /ˌsuːpəˈsɪliəs; ˌsjuː-; *NAmE* ˌsuːpərˈs-/ *adj.* (*disapproving*) behaving towards other people as if you think you are better than they are 傲慢的；高傲的 **SYN** **superior** ▶ **super·cili·ous·ly** *adv.* **super·cili·ous·ness** *noun* [U]

super·com·puter /ˈsuːpəkəmpjuːtə(r); ˈsjuː-; *NAmE* ˈsuːpərk-/ *noun* a powerful computer with a large amount of memory and a very fast CENTRAL PROCESSING UNIT 巨型计算机；超级计算机

super·con·duct·iv·ity /ˌsuːpəˌkɒndʌkˈtɪvəti; ˌsjuː-; *NAmE* ˌsuːpərˌkɑːn-/ *noun* [U] (*physics* 物) the property (= characteristic) of some substances at very low temperatures to let electricity flow with no RESISTANCE 超导（电）性

super·con·duct·or /ˈsuːpəkəndʌktə(r); ˈsjuː-; *NAmE* ˈsuːpərk-/ *noun* (*physics* 物) a substance that has SUPERCONDUCTIVITY 超导体

super·con·tin·ent /ˈsuːpəkɒntɪnənt; ˈsjuː-; *NAmE* ˈsuːpərkɑːn-/ *noun* (*geology* 地) any of the very large areas of land, for example Gondwana or Laurasia, that existed millions of years ago 超大陆（存在于千百万年之前，如冈瓦纳古陆或劳亚古陆）

super-duper /ˌsuːpə ˈduːpə(r); ˌsjuː-; *NAmE* ˌsuːpər/ *adj.* (*old-fashioned, informal*) excellent 极好的；特好的

super·ego /ˌsuːpərˈiːɡəʊ; ˌsjuː-; *NAmE* ˌsuːpərˈiːɡoʊ/ *noun* [usually sing.] (*pl.* **-os**) (*psychology* 心) the part of the mind that makes you aware of right and wrong and makes you feel guilty if you do wrong 超我 ➲ COMPARE EGO (2), ID

super·fi·cial /ˌsuːpəˈfɪʃl; ˌsjuː-; *NAmE* ˌsuːpərˈf-/ *adj.* **1** (*often disapproving*) not studying or looking at sth thoroughly; seeing only what is obvious 粗略的；肤浅的；粗枝大叶的；浅薄的：*a superficial analysis* 粗略的分析 ◇ *The book shows only a superficial understanding of the historical context.* 这部书表现出对历史背景肤浅的理解。**2** appearing to be true, real or important until you look at it more carefully 表面的；外面的；外表的：*superficial differences/similarities* 表面的相异 / 相似之处 ◇ *When you first meet her, she gives a superficial impression of warmth and friendliness.* 初次见面时，她总给人以热情亲切的表面印象。**3** (of a wound or damage 伤口或损坏) only affecting the surface and therefore not serious 表层的；表皮的：*a superficial injury* 皮外伤 ◇ *superficial burns* 表面烧伤 **4** (*disapproving*) not concerned with anything serious or important and lacking any depth of understanding or feeling 浅薄的；肤浅的 **SYN** **shallow**: *a superficial friendship* 浅薄的交情 ◇ *The guests engaged in superficial chatter.* 客人闲聊起来。◇ *She's so superficial!* 她太肤浅了！**5** (*specialist*) of or on the surface of sth 表面的；浅表的：*superficial veins* 浅静脉 ◇ *a superficial deposit of acidic soils* 沉积在表层的酸性土壤 ▶ **super·fi·ci·al·ity** /ˌsuːpəˌfɪʃiˈæləti; ˌsjuː-; *NAmE* ˌsuːpərˌf-/ *noun* [U] **super·fi·cial·ly** /-ʃəli/ *adv.*

S

super·fine /ˈsuːpəfaɪn; ˈsjuː-; *NAmE* ˈsuːpərf-/ *adj.* (*specialist*) **1** extremely light or thin; made of extremely small pieces 极轻的；极细的：*superfine fibres* 微细的纤维 ◇ *superfine powder* 超细粉末 **2** of extremely good quality 质量极高的；特级的：*superfine cloth* 特级布料

su·per·flu·ous /suːˈpɜːfluəs; sjuː-; *NAmE* suːˈpɜːrf-/ *adj.* (*formal*) more than you need or want 过剩的；过多的；多余的 **SYN** **unnecessary**: *She gave him a look that made words superfluous.* 她看了他一眼，这已表明一切，无须多言了。▶ **su·per·flu·ity** /ˌsuːpəˈfluːəti; ˌsjuː-; *NAmE* ˌsuːpərˈf-/ *noun* [U, sing.] (*formal*) **su·per·flu·ous·ly** *adv.*

super·food /ˈsuːpəfuːd; ˈsjuː-; *NAmE* ˈsuːpər-/ *noun* a type of food that some people think is very good for you and helps to prevent disease 超级食品（一些人认为有益健康且可防病的食品）: *the health benefits of so-called superfoods* 所谓的超级食品对健康的益处

super·glue /ˈsuːpəgluː; ˈsjuː-; *NAmE* ˈsuːpərg-/ *noun* [U] a very strong glue that sticks very quickly and is used in small quantities for repairing things 强力胶

super·grass /ˈsuːpəgrɑːs; ˈsjuː-; *NAmE* ˈsuːpərgræs/ *noun* (*BrE, informal*) a criminal who informs the police about the activities of a large number of other criminals, usually in order to get a less severe punishment（为求得宽大处理）向警方告密的罪犯 ➲ COMPARE GRASS *n.* (5)

super·group /ˈsuːpəgruːp; ˈsjuː-; *NAmE* ˈsuːpərg-/ *noun* a very successful and very famous band that plays rock music, especially one whose members have already become famous in other bands（尤指成员已在其他乐队出名的）超级摇滚乐队

super·heated /ˌsuːpəˈhiːtɪd; ˌsjuː-; *NAmE* ˌsuːpərˈh-/ *adj.* (*physics* 物) **1** (of a liquid 液体) that has been heated under pressure above its boiling point without becoming a gas 过热的（加压加热至超过沸点而未变成气体）**2** (of a gas 气体) that has been heated above its temperature of SATURATION (= below which it becomes a liquid) 过热的（加热至超过饱和点）

super·heavy·weight /ˌsuːpəˈheviweɪt; ˌsjuː-; *NAmE* ˌsuːpərˈh-/ *noun* a BOXER of the heaviest class, weighing 91 kilograms or more 超重量级拳击手（体重为 91 公斤或以上）

super·hero /ˈsuːpəhɪərəʊ; ˈsjuː-; *NAmE* ˈsuːpərhɪroʊ; -hiːroʊ/ *noun* (*pl.* **-oes**) a character in a story, film/movie, etc. who has unusual strength or power and uses it to help people; a real person who has done sth unusually brave to help sb（小说、电影等中的）超级英雄；（现实中的）杰出英雄 **OPP** **supervillain**

super·high·way /ˌsuːpəˈhaɪweɪ; ˌsjuː-; *NAmE* ˌsuːpərˈh-/ *noun* (*NAmE, old-fashioned*) = INTERSTATE

super·human /ˌsuːpəˈhjuːmən; ˌsjuː-; *NAmE* ˌsuːpərˈh-/ *adj.* having much greater power, knowledge, etc. than is normal 超出常人的；非凡的 **SYN** **heroic**: *superhuman strength* 非凡的力量 ◊ *It took an almost **superhuman effort** to contain his anger.* 他以超常的克制力强压住怒火。➲ COMPARE SUBHUMAN

super·im·pose /ˌsuːpərɪmˈpəʊz; ˌsjuː-; *NAmE* ˌsuːpərɪmˈpoʊz/ *verb* **1** **~ sth (on/onto sth)** to put one image on top of another so that the two can be seen combined 使（图像甲）叠映在（图像乙）上: *A diagram of the new road layout was superimposed on a map of the city.* 新公路的规划示意图被叠映在该城市的地图上。**2** **~ sth (on/onto sth)** to add some of the qualities of one system or pattern to another one in order to produce sth that combines the qualities of both 使重叠；使叠加；使附加于: *She has tried to superimpose her own attitudes onto this ancient story.* 她尝试过把自己的看法加入这个古老的故事里。▸ **super·im·pos·it·ion** /ˌsuːpərˌɪmpəˈzɪʃn; *BrE also* ˌsjuː-/ *noun* [U]

super·in·junc·tion /ˈsuːpərɪndʒʌŋkʃn; *BrE also* ˈsjuːpər-/ *noun* (*BrE, informal*) an order made by a court that not only prevents information on a particular topic being made public but also states that nobody can say the order exists（法院的）超级禁制令（不仅禁止公开关于某事的任何消息，更禁止任何人透露有这一禁令的存在）: *The central issue concerns a footballer who had obtained a superinjunction preventing a girl from revealing secrets about an affair.* 重点消息是关于一名足球员取得了法院的超级禁止令，禁止一个女孩透露与他之间的风流韵事的秘密。

super·in·tend /ˌsuːpərɪnˈtend; *BrE also* ˌsjuː-/ *verb* **~ sth** (*formal*) to be in charge of sth and make sure that everything is working, being done, etc. as it should be 主管；监督；监管 **SYN** **supervise** ▸ **super·in·tend·ence** /-əns/ *noun* [U]

super·in·tend·ent /ˌsuːpərɪnˈtendənt; *BrE also* ˌsjuː-/ *noun* **1** a person who has a lot of authority and manages and controls an activity, a place, a group of workers, etc. 主管人；负责人；监管人；监督人: *a park superintendent* 公园负责人 ◊ *the superintendent of schools in Dallas* 达拉斯教育局长 **2** (*abbr.* **Supt**) (in Britain) a police officer just above the rank of CHIEF INSPECTOR（英国）警司（警阶为总督察的上一级）: *Superintendent Livesey* 利夫西警司 **3** (*abbr.* **Supt.**) (in the US) the head of a police department（美国）警察局长，总警监 **4** (*NAmE*) a person whose job is to be in charge of a building and make small repairs, etc. to it（大楼的）管理人

su·per·ior 🔑 /suːˈpɪəriə(r); sjuː-; *NAmE* suːˈpɪr-/ *adj., noun*
■ *adj.* **1** 🔑 **~ (to sb/sth)** better in quality than sb/sth else; greater than sb/sth else（在品质上）更好的；占优势的；更胜一筹的: ***vastly superior*** 强得多 ◊ *superior intelligence* 更强的智力 ◊ *This model is technically superior to its competitors.* 这一款式在技术上超过了与之竞争的产品。◊ *Liverpool were clearly the superior team.* 利物浦队明显更胜一筹。◊ *The enemy won because of their superior numbers* (= there were more of them). 敌人由于在人数上占优而取胜。**OPP** **inferior** **2** 🔑 **~ (to sb)** higher in rank, importance or position（在级别、重要性或职位上）更高的: *my superior officer* 我的上级军官 ◊ *superior status* 更高的地位 ◊ *a superior court of law* 上级法院 **OPP** **inferior** **3** (*disapproving*) showing by your behaviour that you think you are better than others 有优越感的；高傲的 **SYN** **arrogant**: *a superior manner* 神气活现的态度 ◊ *He always looks so superior.* 他总是显得那么有优越感。**4** (used especially in advertisements 尤用于广告) of very good quality; better than other similar things 质量卓越的；出类拔萃的；超群的: *superior apartments* 高级公寓套房
■ *noun* **1** a person of higher rank, status or position 级别（或地位、职位）更高的人；上级；上司: *your social superiors* 社会地位比自己高的人 ◊ *He's my **immediate superior*** (= the person directly above me). 他是我的顶头上司。◊ *I'm going to complain to your superiors.* 我要去找你的上级投诉。**OPP** **inferior** **2** used in titles for the head of a religious community（用作宗教团体领导的头衔）: *Mother Superior* 修女会院长

su·per·ior·ity /suːˌpɪəriˈɒrəti; sjuː-; *NAmE* suːˌpɪriˈɔːr-; -ˈɑːr-/ *noun* [U] **1** **~ (in sth)** | **~ (to/over sth/sb)** the state or quality of being better, more skilful, more powerful, greater, etc. than others 优越（性）；优势: *the superiority of this operating system* 这种操作系统的优越性 ◊ *to have **naval/air superiority*** (= more ships/planes than the enemy) 有海上/空中优势 **2** behaviour that shows that you think you are better than other people 优越感；神气活现的样子；盛气凌人的行为: *an air of superiority* 神气活现的样子 **OPP** **inferiority**

suˌperiˈority complex *noun* a feeling that you are better or more important than other people, often as a way of hiding your feelings of failure 自大情结，优越感（常为掩饰失败感）

su·per·la·tive /suˈpɜːlətɪv; sjuː-; *NAmE* suːˈpɜːrl-/ *adj., noun*
■ *adj.* **1** excellent 极佳的；卓越的；最优秀的 **SYN** **first-rate**: *a superlative performance* 精彩绝伦的演出 **2** (*grammar* 语法) relating to adjectives or adverbs that express the highest degree of sth, for example *best, worst, slowest* and *most difficult*（形容词或副词）最高级的 ➲ COMPARE COMPARATIVE *adj.* (3) ▸ **su·per·la·tive·ly** *adv.*
■ *noun* (*grammar* 语法) the form of an adjective or adverb that expresses the highest degree of sth（形容词或副词的）最高级: *It's hard to find enough superlatives to describe this book.* 用再多的盛赞之辞也难以描述这本书。➲ COMPARE COMPARATIVE *n.*

super·man /ˈsuːpəmæn; ˈsjuː-; *NAmE* ˈsuːpərm-/ *noun* (*pl.* **-men** /-men/) a man who is unusually strong or intelligent or who can do sth extremely well 有非凡才能的人；超人 ➲ COMPARE SUPERWOMAN

super·mar·ket 🔑 /ˈsuːpəmɑːkɪt; ˈsjuː-; *NAmE* ˈsuːpərmɑːrkət/ (*NAmE also* **ˈgrocery store**) *noun* a large shop/

store that sells food, drinks and goods used in the home. People choose what they want from the shelves and pay for it as they leave. 超级市场；超市

super·max /ˈsuːpəmæks; ˈsjuː-; *NAmE* ˈsuːpər-/ *noun* (*especially NAmE*) a maximum security prison, intended for very dangerous prisoners 顶级监狱（防备极为森严、为极危险的犯人设立的监狱）

super·model /ˈsuːpəmɒdl; ˈsjuː-; *NAmE* ˈsuːpərmɑːdl/ *noun* a very famous and highly paid fashion model 超级名模

super·nat·ural /ˌsuːpəˈnætʃrəl; ˌsjuː-; *NAmE* ˌsuːpərˈn-/ *adj.* **1** that cannot be explained by the laws of science and that seems to involve gods or magic 超自然的；神奇的；神灵魔怪的 SYN **paranormal**：*supernatural powers* 超自然力量 ◇ *supernatural strength* 神奇的力量 ➲ COMPARE NATURAL *adj.* (1) **2 the supernatural** *noun* [sing.] events, forces or powers that cannot be explained by the laws of science and that seem to involve gods or magic 超自然物；超自然力量；神奇怪异的事 SYN **the paranormal**：*a belief in the supernatural* 相信超自然力量 ▶ **super·nat·ur·al·ly** /-ˈnætʃrəli/ *adv.*

super·nova /ˌsuːpəˈnəʊvə; ˌsjuː-; *NAmE* ˌsuːpərˈnoʊvə/ *noun* (*pl.* **super·novae** /-viː/ or **super·novas**) (*astronomy* 天) a star that suddenly becomes much brighter because it is exploding 超新星 ➲ COMPARE NOVA

super·numer·ary /ˌsuːpəˈnjuːmərəri; ˌsjuː-; *NAmE* ˌsuːpərˈnuːməreri/ *adj.* (*formal*) more than you normally need; extra 多余的；过剩的；额外的

super·ordin·ate /ˌsuːpərˈɔːdɪnət; ˌsjuː-; *NAmE* -ˈɔːrd-/ (*also* **hyper·nym**) *noun* (*linguistics* 语言) a word with a general meaning that includes the meanings of other particular words, for example 'fruit' is the superordinate of 'apple', 'orange', etc. 上义词，上位词（如 fruit 是 apple、orange 等的上义词）➲ COMPARE HYPONYM ▶ **super·ordin·ate** *adj.* [only before noun] ➲ COMPARE SUBORDINATE *n.*

super·pose /ˌsuːpəˈpəʊz; ˌsjuː-; *NAmE* ˌsuːpərˈpoʊz/ *verb* (*formal* or *specialist*) ~ **sth** to put sth on or above sth else 把…放在上面；叠放：*They had superposed a picture of his head onto someone else's body.* 他们把他的头像贴在别人的身体上。▶ **super·pos·ition** /-pəˈzɪʃn/ *noun*

super·power /ˈsuːpəpaʊə(r); ˈsjuː-; *NAmE* ˈsuːpərp-/ *noun* one of the countries in the world that has very great military or economic power and a lot of influence, for example the US 超级大国

super·script /ˈsuːpəskrɪpt; ˈsjuː-; *NAmE* ˈsuːpərs-/ *noun* (*specialist*) a number, letter or symbol that is written or printed above the normal line of writing or printing 上标（写或印在正常位置上方的字符）➲ COMPARE SUBSCRIPT (1) ▶ **super·script** *adj.* [only before noun]

super·sede /ˌsuːpəˈsiːd; ˌsjuː-; *NAmE* ˌsuːpərˈs-/ *verb* ~ **sth/sb** [often passive] to take the place of sth/sb that is considered to be old-fashioned or no longer the best available 取代，替代（已过时或已非最佳选择的人或物）：*The theory has been superseded by more recent research.* 这一理论已为新近的研究所取代。

super·size /ˈsuːpəsaɪz; ˈsjuː-; *NAmE* ˈsuːpər-/ *adj.*, *verb*

■ ***adj.*** (*also* **super·sized**) bigger than normal 超大的：*supersize portions of fries* 超大份炸薯条 ◇ *supersized clothing* 超大码衣服

■ ***verb*** [T, I] ~ (**sb/sth**) to make sb/sth bigger; to become bigger （使）变大，更大；（使）膨胀：*We are being supersized into obesity* (= made very fat) *by the fast food industry.* 我们正被快餐业催肥。◇ *TV ads encourage kids to supersize.* 电视广告促使孩子变得越来越胖。

super·sonic /ˌsuːpəˈsɒnɪk; ˌsjuː-; *NAmE* ˌsuːpərˈsɑːnɪk/ *adj.* faster than the speed of sound 超声速的；超音速的：*a supersonic aircraft* 超声速飞机 ◇ *supersonic flight* 超声速飞行 ➲ COMPARE SUBSONIC

super·star /ˈsuːpəstɑː(r); ˈsjuː-; *NAmE* ˈsuːpərs-/ *noun* a very famous performer, for example an actor, a singer or a sports player 超级明星

super·state /ˈsuːpəsteɪt; ˈsjuː-; *NAmE* ˈsuːpərs-/ *noun* a very powerful state, especially one that is formed by several nations joining or working together 超级强国；（尤指由几个国家组成或进行合作的）超国家，政治共同体：*the European superstate* 欧洲超国家

super·sti·tion /ˌsuːpəˈstɪʃn; ˌsjuː-; *NAmE* ˌsuːpərˈs-/ *noun* [U, C] (*often disapproving*) the belief that particular events happen in a way that cannot be explained by reason or science; the belief that particular events bring good or bad luck 迷信；迷信观念（或思想）：*According to superstition, breaking a mirror brings bad luck.* 按照迷信的说法，摔碎镜子会带来噩运。➲ WORDFINDER NOTE AT LUCK

super·sti·tious /ˌsuːpəˈstɪʃəs; ˌsjuː-; *NAmE* ˌsuːpərˈs-/ *adj.* believing in superstitions迷信的；有迷信观念的：*superstitious beliefs* 迷信观念 ◇ *I'm superstitious about the number 13.* 我忌讳 13 这个数字。▶ **super·sti·tious·ly** *adv.*

super·store /ˈsuːpəstɔː(r); ˈsjuː-; *NAmE* ˈsuːpərs-/ *noun* a very large supermarket or a large shop/store that sells a wide variety of one type of goods 大型超市；大型商场：*a computer superstore* 计算机商城

super·struc·ture /ˈsuːpəstrʌktʃə(r); ˈsjuː-; *NAmE* ˈsuːpərs-/ *noun* **1** a structure that is built on top of sth, for example the upper parts of a ship or the part of a building above the ground （船舶的）上层建筑，船楼；（建筑物的）上部结构 ➲ COMPARE SUBSTRUCTURE **2** (*formal*) the systems and beliefs in a society that have developed from more simple ones （社会的）上层建筑

super·tank·er /ˈsuːpətæŋkə(r); ˈsjuː-; *NAmE* ˈsuːpərt-/ *noun* a very large ship for carrying oil, etc. 超级油轮

ˌSuper ˈTuesday *noun* [sing.] (*informal*) a day on which several US states hold PRIMARY elections 超级星期二（美国几个州的初选日）

super·vene /ˌsuːpəˈviːn; ˌsjuː-; *NAmE* ˌsuːpərˈv-/ *verb* [I] (*formal*) to happen, especially unexpectedly, and have a powerful effect on the existing situation （尤指意外）发生并带来重大影响

super·vil·lain /ˈsuːpəvɪlən; ˈsjuː-; *NAmE* ˈsuːpər-/ *noun* a very bad character in a story, especially one with magical powers （小说中的）超级恶棍，超级恶魔，超级反派 OPP **superhero**

super·vise /ˈsuːpəvaɪz; ˈsjuː-; *NAmE* ˈsuːpərv-/ *verb* [T, I] to be in charge of sb/sth and make sure that everything is done correctly, safely, etc. 监督；管理；指导；主管：~ (**sb/sth**) *to supervise building work* 监理建筑工程 ◇ ~ **sb doing sth** *She supervised the children playing near the pool.* 她照料着在水池附近玩的几个孩子。▶ **super·vi·sion** /ˌsuːpəˈvɪʒn; ˌsjuː-; *NAmE* ˌsuːpərˈv-/ *noun* [U, C]：*Very young children should not be left to play without supervision.* 不能让幼儿在没人照看的情况下独自玩耍。◇ *The drug should only be used* ***under medical supervision.*** 这种药须遵医嘱方可使用。◇ *I have weekly supervisions* (= meetings with a TUTOR or SUPERVISOR). 我每周同导师见一次面。

ˌsuperˈvision order *noun* (*law* 律) in the UK, an order made by a court which says that the local government or a PROBATION OFFICER must be responsible for a child, help them and check that they behave well 监督令（英国法院要求地方政府或缓刑监视官对少年进行监督）

super·visor /ˈsuːpəvaɪzə(r); ˈsjuː-; *NAmE* ˈsuːpərv-/ *noun* a person who supervises sb/sth 监督人；指导者；主管人：*I have a meeting with my supervisor about my research topic.* 我要就研究课题同导师见一次面。▶ **super·vis·ory** /ˌsuːpəˈvaɪzəri; ˌsjuː-; *NAmE* ˌsuːpərˈv-/ *adj.*：*She has a supervisory role on the project.* 她负责这个项目的监督工作。

super·woman /ˈsuːpəwʊmən; ˈsjuː-; *NAmE* ˈsuːpərw-/ *noun* (*pl.* **-women** /-wɪmɪn/) a woman who is unusually strong or intelligent or who can do sth extremely well, especially a woman who has a successful career and also takes care of her home and family 有非凡才能

S

的女子；超级女人（尤指事业和家庭都成功的）➲ COMPARE SUPERMAN

su·pine /ˈsuːpaɪn; *BrE also* ˈsjuː-/ *adj.* (*formal*) **1** lying flat on your back 仰卧的；平躺着的：*a supine position* 仰卧姿势 ➲ COMPARE PRONE (3) **2** (*disapproving*) not willing to act or disagree with sb because you are lazy or morally weak 得过且过的；苟安的；软弱的 ▸ **su·pine·ly** *adv.*

sup·per /ˈsʌpə(r)/ *noun* [U, C] the last meal of the day, either a main meal, usually smaller and less formal than dinner, or a SNACK eaten before you go to bed 晚饭；晚餐；夜宵：*I'll do my homework after supper.* 晚饭后我要做家庭作业。◇ *What's for supper?* 晚饭吃什么？◇ *We'll have an early supper tonight.* 今天我们要早点吃晚饭。➲ NOTE AT MEAL ➲ COMPARE TEA (6)

sup·plant /səˈplɑːnt; *NAmE* -ˈplænt/ *verb* ~ **sb/sth** (*formal*) to take the place of sb/sth (especially sb/sth older or less modern) 取代，替代（尤指年老者或落后于时代的事物）SYN **replace**

sup·ple /ˈsʌpl/ *adj.* **1** able to bend and move parts of your body easily into different positions（身体）柔软的，灵活的；柔韧性好的：*her slim, supple body* 她苗条灵活的身体 ◇ *These exercises will help to keep you supple.* 这些锻炼项目有助于保持身体的柔韧性。**2** soft and able to bend easily without cracking 易弯曲的；柔韧的：*Moisturizing cream helps to keep your skin soft and supple.* 保湿霜有助于保持皮肤柔软有弹性。▸ **supple·ness** *noun* [U]

sup·ple·ment AW *noun, verb*

■ ***noun*** /ˈsʌplɪmənt/ **1** a thing that is added to sth else to improve or complete it 增补（物）；补充（物）；添加物：***vitamin/dietary supplements*** (= VITAMINS and other foods eaten in addition to what you usually eat) 补充的维生素；补充膳食 ◇ ~ **to sth** *Industrial sponsorship is a supplement to government funding.* 工业界的赞助是对政府拨款的补充。**2** an extra separate section, often in the form of a magazine, that is sold with a newspaper（报纸的）增刊：*the Sunday **colour supplements*** 星期日彩色增刊 ➲ WORDFINDER NOTE AT NEWSPAPER **3** ~ (**to sth**) a book or a section at the end of a book that gives extra information or deals with a special subject（书籍的）补编，补遗，附录：*the supplement to the Oxford English Dictionary* 《牛津英语词典》补编 **4** (*BrE*) an amount of money that you pay for an extra service or item, especially in addition to the basic cost of a holiday/vacation 额外费用，附加费（尤指度假服务的）SYN **surcharge**：*There is a £10 supplement for a single room.* 住单间另付 10 英镑。◇ *Safety deposit boxes are available **at a supplement**.* 有贵重物品保管箱可供使用，费用另计。

■ ***verb*** /ˈsʌplɪment/ to add sth to sth in order to improve it or make it more complete 增补；补充：~ **sth with sth** *a diet supplemented with vitamin pills* 搭配有维生素片的饮食 ◇ ~ **sth** *He supplements his income by giving private lessons.* 他当家庭教师以补充收入。▸ **sup·ple·men·ta·tion** /ˌsʌplɪmenˈteɪʃn/ *noun* [U]

sup·ple·men·tary AW /ˌsʌplɪˈmentri/ (*especially BrE*) (*NAmE usually* **sup·ple·men·tal** /ˌsʌplɪˈmentl/) *adj.* provided in addition to sth else in order to improve or complete it 增补性的；补充性的；额外的；外加的 SYN **additional**：*supplementary information* 补充信息

supple,mentary ˈangle *noun* (*mathematics* 数) either of two angles which together make 180° 补角 ➲ COMPARE COMPLEMENTARY ANGLE

sup·ple·tion /səˈpliːʃn/ *noun* [U] (*linguistics* 语言) the use of a word as a particular form of a verb when the word is not related to the main form of the verb, for example 'went' as the past tense of 'go' 不规则词形屈折，异干互补（如 went 作为 go 的过去式）▸ **sup·ple·tive** /səˈpliːtɪv/ *adj.*

sup·pli·cant /ˈsʌplɪkənt/ (*also* **sup·pli·ant** /ˈsʌpliənt/) *noun* (*formal*) a person who asks for sth in a HUMBLE way, especially from God or a powerful person（尤指向神灵或有权势者）恳求者，哀求者，祈求者

sup·pli·ca·tion /ˌsʌplɪˈkeɪʃn/ *noun* [U, C] (*formal*) the act of asking for sth with a very HUMBLE request or prayer 恳求；哀求；祈求：*She knelt in supplication.* 她跪地祷求。

sup·plier /səˈplaɪə(r)/ *noun* a person or company that supplies goods 供应者；供货商；供货方：*a leading supplier of computers in the UK* 英国一家主要电脑供应商

sup·ply 🔑 /səˈplaɪ/ *noun, verb*

■ ***noun*** **1** 🔑 [C] an amount of sth that is provided or available to be used 供应量；供给量；储备：*The water supply is unsafe.* 供水不安全。◇ *Supplies of food are almost exhausted.* 贮存的食物快吃完了。◇ *We cannot guarantee adequate supplies of raw materials.* 我们不能保证提供充足的原料。◇ *Books were in **short supply*** (= there were not enough of them). 书籍供应短缺。**2** 🔑 **supplies** [pl.] the things such as food, medicines, fuel, etc. that are needed by a group of people, for example an army or EXPEDITION（军队或探险队等的）补给，补给品：*Our supplies were running out.* 我们的补给快用完了。◇ *a transport plane carrying food and **medical supplies** for refugees* 一架为难民运送食物和医疗用品的运输机 **3** 🔑 [U] the act of supplying sth 供应；供给；提供；补给：*The UN has agreed to allow the supply of emergency aid.* 联合国已同意允许提供紧急援助。◇ *A stroke can disrupt the supply of oxygen to the brain.* 中风可导致大脑供氧中断。◇ *The electricity supply* (= the system supplying electricity) *had been cut off.* 电力供应被切断了。

■ ***verb*** 🔑 (**sup·plies**, **sup·ply·ing**, **sup·plied**, **sup·plied**) to provide sb/sth with sth that they need or want, especially in large quantities（尤指大量）供应，供给，提供：~ **sth to sb/sth** *Foreign governments supplied arms to the rebels.* 一些外国政府向反叛者提供武器。◇ ~ **sb/sth with sth** *Foreign governments supplied the rebels with arms.* 一些外国政府向反叛者提供武器。◇ ~ **sb/sth** *Local schools supply many of the volunteers.* 许多志愿者来自当地学校。◇ *foods supplying our daily vitamin needs* 为我们提供日常所需维生素的食物

sup,ply and deˈmand *noun* [U] (*economics* 经) the relationship between the amount of goods or services that are available and the amount that people want to buy, especially when this controls prices 供求关系

supˈply chain *noun* [usually sing.] (*business* 商) the series of processes involved in the production and supply of goods, from when they are first made, grown, etc. until they are bought or used 供应链 ➲ WORDFINDER NOTE AT INDUSTRY

supˈply line *noun* a route along which food, equipment, etc. is transported to an army during a war（战争中军队的）补给线

supˈply-side *adj.* [only before noun] (*economics* 经) connected with the policy of reducing taxes in order to encourage economic growth 供应学派的（主张减税以刺激经济）

supˈply teacher (*BrE*) (*NAmE* **ˈsubstitute teacher**) *noun* a teacher employed to do the work of another teacher who is away because of illness, etc. 代课教师

sup·port 🔑 /səˈpɔːt; *NAmE* səˈpɔːrt/ *verb, noun*

■ ***verb***

• **ENCOURAGE/GIVE HELP** 鼓励；支持 **1** 🔑 to help or encourage sb/sth by saying or showing that you agree with them/it 支持；拥护；鼓励 SYN **back**：~ **sb/sth** *to support a proposal* 支持一项提议 ◇ *These measures are **strongly supported** by environmental groups.* 这些措施得到环境保护组织的大力支持。◇ *If you raise it at the meeting, I'll support you.* 如果你在会上提出这个问题，我将支持你。◇ ~ **sb/sth in sth** *The government supported the unions in their demand for a minimum wage.* 政府支持这些工会组织提出的确定最低工资的要求。**2** 🔑 ~ **sb** to give or be ready to give help to sb if they need it 帮助；援助：*an organization that supports people with AIDS* 一个向艾滋病患者提供援助的组织 ◇ *The company will support customers in Europe* (= solve their problems with a product). 这家公司将向欧洲客户提供技术支持。

• **PROVIDE MONEY, ETC.** 提供资金等 **3** 🔑 ~ **sth** to help or encourage sth to be successful by giving it money 资

S

助；赞助 SYN **sponsor**: *Several major companies are supporting the project.* 几家大公司正在对这一项目提供资助。 **4** ~ **sb/sth/yourself** to provide everything necessary, especially money, so that sb/sth can live or exist 养活；赡养；扶养；维持：*Mark has two children to support from his first marriage.* 马克得扶养他第一次婚姻生的两个孩子。◇ *He turned to crime to support his drug habit.* 他为维持吸毒的恶习而走上犯罪的道路。◇ *The atmosphere of Mars could not support life.* 生命无法在火星的大气环境下生存。

- **HOLD IN POSITION** 支撑 **5** ~ **sb/sth** to hold sb/sth in position; to prevent sb/sth from falling 支撑；支承；支护：*a platform supported by concrete pillars* 混凝土支柱支撑的平台 ◇ *Support the baby's head when you hold it.* 你抱婴儿时要把头扶好。
- **HELP PROVE STH** 证实 **6** ~ **sth** to help to show that sth is true 证实；提供依据 SYN **corroborate**: *The witness's story was not supported by the evidence.* 目击者的描述与证据不符。➲ LANGUAGE BANK AT EVIDENCE
- **SPORTS TEAM** 运动队 **7** ~ **sb/sth** (*BrE*) to like a particular sports team, watch their games, etc. 支持；喜爱：*Which team do you support?* 你喜欢哪个队？
- **POP/ROCK CONCERT** 流行 / 摇滚音乐会 **8** ~ **sb/sth** (of a band or singer 乐队或歌手) to perform in a pop or rock concert before the main performer（在流行或摇滚音乐会上）当助演，担任演出嘉宾：*They were supported by a local Liverpool band.* 利物浦当地的一支乐队为他们作助兴演出。➲ WORDFINDER NOTE AT CONCERT
- **COMPUTER** 计算机 **9** ~ **sth** (of a computer or computer system 计算机或计算机系统) to allow a particular program, language or device to be used with it 支持；支援：*This digital audio player supports multiple formats.* 这台数字音频播放器支持多种格式。

■ **noun**

- **ENCOURAGEMENT/MONEY** 鼓励；资金 **1** [U] ~ (**for sth**) encouragement and help that you give to sb/sth because you approve of them and want them to be successful 支持；拥护；鼓励；资助：*There is strong public support for the change.* 公众大力支持这一变革。◇ *Can I rely on your support* (= will you vote for me) *in the election?* 我能指望你投我的票吗？◇ *Only a few people spoke* ***in support of*** *the proposal.* 只有几个人表示支持这一提议。◇ *Local businesses have provided* ***financial support***. 当地企业提供了财政资助。◇ *She has no visible means of support* (= no work, income etc.). 她没有明确的生计来源。
- **HELP** 帮助 **2** [U] sympathy and help that you give to sb who is in a difficult or an unhappy situation 帮助；救助；援助：*Her family and friends have given her lots of support.* 家人和朋友给了她许多帮助。➲ SEE ALSO MORAL SUPPORT
- **HOLDING IN POSITION** 支撑 **3** [C] a thing that holds sth and prevents it from falling 支撑物；支承；支柱；支座：*The supports under the bridge were starting to bend.* 桥下的支柱开始弯曲。◇ (*figurative*) *When my father died, Jim was a real support.* 我父亲死后，吉姆成了真正的顶梁柱。 **4** [U] the act of holding sth firmly in position or preventing it from falling 支撑；支承；支护：*I wrapped a bandage around my ankle to give it some support.* 我在脚踝上缠上绷带，好把它固定住。◇ *She held on to his arm for support.* 她抓着他的胳膊，好站稳。 **5** [C] something you wear to hold an injured or weak part of your body firmly in position（身体部位的）支持器，托：*a* ***knee/back support*** 护膝；护背
- **PROOF** 证据 **6** [U] evidence that helps to show that sth is true or correct 证据；依据：*The statistics offer further support for our theory.* 这些统计数字为我们的理论提供了进一步的依据。
- **POP/ROCK CONCERT** 流行 / 摇滚音乐会 **7** [U] a band or singer who performs in a pop or rock concert before the main performer 助演嘉宾：*The support (act) has yet to be confirmed.* 助演尚未确定。
- **TECHNICAL HELP** 技术帮助 **8** [U] technical help that a company gives to customers using their computers or other products（公司向客户提供的）技术支持：*We offer free* ***technical support***. 我们免费提供技术支持。

sup·port·er /sə'pɔːtə(r); *NAmE* -'pɔːrt-/ *noun* **1** a person who supports a political party, an idea, etc. 支持者；拥护者：*a* ***strong/loyal/staunch supporter*** 积极的 / 忠实的 / 坚定的支持者 ◇ *Labour supporters* 工党的支持者 **2** (*BrE*) a person who supports a particular sports team（运动队的）支持者 SYN **fan**: *I'm an Arsenal supporter.* 我是阿森纳队的球迷。➲ SEE ALSO ATHLETIC SUPPORTER

sup'port group *noun* a group of people who meet to help each other with a particular problem 互助小组：*a support group for single parents* 单身父母互助小组

sup·port·ing /sə'pɔːtɪŋ; *NAmE* -'pɔːrt-/ *adj.* [only before noun] **1** a **supporting** actor in a play or film/movie has an important part but not the leading one（演员、角色）次要的；配角的：*The movie featured Robert Lindsay in* ***a supporting role***. 罗伯特・林赛在这部影片中担任配角。 **2** (*formal*) helping to show that sth is true 能确证的：*There was a wealth of supporting evidence.* 有大量证据。 **3** carrying the weight of sth 支承的；支撑的；承重的：*a supporting wall* 承重墙

sup·port·ive /sə'pɔːtɪv; *NAmE* -'pɔːrt-/ *adj.* giving help, encouragement or sympathy to sb 给予帮助的；支持的；鼓励的；同情的：*a supportive family* 支持自己的家人 ◇ *She was very supportive during my father's illness.* 在我父亲生病期间，她给了很多帮助。

sup·pose /sə'pəʊz; *NAmE* sə'poʊz/ *verb* **1** [I, T] to think or believe that sth is true or possible (based on the knowledge that you have)（根据所知）认为，推断，料想：*Getting a visa isn't as simple as you might suppose.* 办签证不像你想的那么容易。◇ *Prices will go up, I suppose.* 我觉得物价将会上涨。◇ ~ **sb/sth to be/have sth** (*formal*) *This combination of qualities is* ***generally supposed*** *to be extremely rare.* 一般认为，同时具有这样一些品质极为罕见。◇ ~ **sb/sth** (**to be/have**) **sth** | ~ **sb/sth + adj.** (*formal*) *She had supposed him* (*to be*) *very rich.* 她原以为他很有钱。◇ ~ **sb/sth + noun** (*formal*) *I had supposed his wife a younger woman.* 我原以为他妻子要更年轻。◇ ~ (**that**)... *I don't suppose for a minute that he'll agree* (= I'm sure that he won't). 我认为他决不会同意。◇ ***Why do you suppose*** *he resigned?* 你凭什么推断他辞职了呢？◇ ***There is no reason to suppose*** *she's lying.* 认为她在说谎完全没道理。◇ *I suppose you think it's funny, do you?* (= showing anger) 你好像觉得这很好笑，是不是？ HELP 'That' is nearly always left out, especially in speech. * that 一般都省去，在口语中尤其如此。 **2** [T] to pretend that sth is true; to imagine what would happen if sth were true 假定；假设；设想：~ (**that**)... *Suppose flights are fully booked on that day—which other day could we go?* 假定那天的航班都订满了，我们还可以在哪天走呢？◇ *Let us suppose, for example, that you are married with two children.* 比方说，我们假设你成家了，还有两个孩子。◇ ~ **sth** (*formal*) *The theory supposes the existence of life on other planets.* 这个理论假定其他行星存在生命。◇ ~ **sb/sth** (**to be/have**) **sth** | ~ **sb/sth + adj./noun** (*formal*) *Suppose him* (*to be*) *dead—what then?* 假设他死了，那怎么办？ **3** [I, T] used to make a statement, request or suggestion less direct or less strong（婉转表达）我看，要我说，要不：*I could take you in the car, I* ***suppose*** (= but I don't really want to). 要不你坐我的车。◇ *'Can I borrow the car?' '****I suppose so****.'* (= Yes, but I'm not happy about it.) "我能借这辆车吗？" "应该可以吧。" ◇ ~ (**that**)... ***I don't suppose*** (***that***) *I could have a look at your newspaper, could I?* 我能不能看看您的报纸？◇ *Suppose we take a later train?* 要不我们坐晚一点的火车？

IDM **be supposed to do/be sth 1** to be expected or required to do/be sth according to a rule, a custom, an arrangement, etc.（按规定、习惯、安排等）应当，应，该，须：*You're supposed to buy a ticket, but not many people do.* 按说应当买票，不过买的人不多。◇ *I thought we were supposed to be paid today.* 我以为我们今天会领到薪水呢。◇ *The engine doesn't sound like it's supposed to.* 发动机听起来不对劲。◇ *You were supposed to be here an hour ago!* 你本该在一小时以前就到这儿！◇ *How was I supposed to know you were waiting for me?* 我哪知道你在等我？◇ *'Yes and no.'* ***'What is that supposed to mean?'*** (= showing that you are annoyed) "是但又不是。" "这算什么意思呢？" ➲ EXPRESS YOURSELF AT HAVE TO **2** to be generally believed or expected to be/do sth 一般认为；人们普遍觉得会：*I haven't seen it myself, but it's supposed to* *be a great movie.* 这部电影我没看过，不过人们普遍认为很不错。**not be supposed to do sth** to not be allowed to do sth 不准；不应当；不得：*You're not supposed to walk on the grass.* 不准践踏草地。

sup·posed /sə'pəʊzd; *NAmE* sə'poʊzd/ *adj.* [only before noun] used to show that you think that a claim, statement or way of describing sb/sth is not true or correct, although it is generally believed to be 误以为的；误信的；所谓的 SYN **alleged**: *This is the opinion of the supposed experts.* 这是所谓专家的看法。◇ *When did this supposed accident happen?* 这场所谓的事故发生在什么时候？

sup·posed·ly /sə'pəʊzɪdli; *NAmE* -'poʊ-/ *adv.* according to what is generally thought or believed but not known for certain 据信；据传；据说 SYN **allegedly**: *The novel is supposedly based on a true story.* 据说这部小说取材于一个真实的故事。

sup·pos·ing /sə'pəʊzɪŋ; *NAmE* -'poʊ-/ *conj.* ~ (**that**) used to ask sb to pretend that sth is true or to imagine that sth will happen 假定；假设；设想：*Supposing (that) you are wrong, what will you do then?* 假设你错了，那你会怎么办？◇ *But supposing he sees us?* 可他要是看见我们呢？

sup·pos·ition /ˌsʌpə'zɪʃn/ *noun* (*formal*) **1** [C] ~ (**that...**) an idea that you think is true although you may not be able to prove it 推测的想法；推断的结论 SYN **assumption**: *The police are working on the supposition that he was murdered.* 警方正根据他被谋杀的假定展开调查。**2** [U] the act of believing or claiming that sth is true even though it cannot be proved 推测；推断：*The report is based entirely on supposition.* 这篇报道完全建立在推测的基础上。

sup·posi·tory /sə'pɒzətri; *NAmE* sə'pɑːzətɔːri/ *noun* (*pl.* **-ies**) a small piece of solid medicine that is placed in the RECTUM or VAGINA and left to dissolve gradually 栓剂

sup·press /sə'pres/ *verb* **1** ~ **sth** (*usually disapproving*) (of a government, ruler, etc. 政府、统治者等) to put an end, often by force, to a group or an activity that is believed to threaten authority 镇压；（武力）平定；压制 SYN **quash**: *The rebellion was brutally suppressed.* 叛乱遭到了残酷的镇压。**2** ~ **sth** (*usually disapproving*) to prevent sth from being published or made known 禁止（发表）；查禁；封锁：*The police were accused of suppressing vital evidence.* 警方被指隐瞒关键证据。**3** ~ **sth** to prevent yourself from having or expressing a feeling or an emotion 抑制；控制；忍住：*to suppress a smile* 忍住不笑 ◇ *She was unable to suppress her anger.* 她按捺不住怒火。**4** ~ **sth** to prevent sth from growing, developing or continuing 压制；阻止；抑制：*drugs that suppress the appetite* 抑制食欲的药

sup·pres·sant /sə'presnt/ *noun* a drug that is used to prevent one of the body's functions from working normally（对人体功能的）抑制药，抑制剂：*an appetite suppressant* 食欲抑制药

sup·pres·sion /sə'preʃn/ *noun* [U] the act of SUPPRESSING sth 镇压；压制；抑制：*the suppression of a rebellion* 对叛乱的镇压 ◇ *the suppression of emotion* 对感情的抑制

sup·pres·sor /sə'presə(r)/ *noun* a thing or person that SUPPRESSES sb/sth 镇压者；压制者；查禁者；抑制物：*the body's pain suppressors* 人体分泌的镇痛剂

sup·pur·ate /'sʌpjureɪt/ *verb* [I] (*formal*) (of a cut, wound, etc. 伤口等) to produce a thick yellow liquid (called PUS) because of infection 化脓 ▶ **sup·pur·ation** /ˌsʌpju'reɪʃn/ *noun* [U]

supra·nation·al /ˌsuːprə'næʃnəl; *BrE also* ˌsjuː-/ *adj.* (*formal*) involving more than one country 超国家的（指涉及不止一个国家）

supra·seg·men·tal /ˌsuːprəseg'mentl; *BrE also* ˌsjuː-/ *adj.* (*phonetics* 语音) relating to features of speech such as stress and INTONATION as opposed to individual speech sounds 超音段的（与单个语音相对的重音和音调等语音特征）

su·prema·cist /suː'preməsɪst; *BrE also* sjuː-/ *noun* a person who believes that their own race is better than others and should be in power 种族优越论者：*a white supremacist* 白人至上主义者

su·prem·acy /suː'preməsi; *BrE also* sjuː-/ *noun* [U] a position in which you have more power, authority or status than anyone else 至高无上；最大权力；最高权威；最高地位：*the battle for supremacy in the region* 争夺地区霸权的较量 ◇ *the dangerous notion of white supremacy* (= that white races are better than others and should control them) 危险的白人至上观念 ◇ ~ **over sb/sth** *The company has established total supremacy over its rivals.* 公司奠定了对竞争对手的绝对优势。

su·preme /suː'priːm; *BrE also* sjuː-/ *adj.* [usually before noun] **1** highest in rank or position（级别或地位）最高的，至高无上的：*the Supreme Commander of the armed forces* 武装部队的最高统帅 ◇ *the supreme champion* 绝对冠军 ◇ *It is an event in which she* ***reigns supreme.*** 这个比赛项目她所向无敌。**2** very great or the greatest in degree（程度）很大的，最大的：*to make the* ***supreme sacrifice*** (= die for what you believe in) 作出最大牺牲（为信仰牺牲生命）◇ *a supreme effort* 最大的努力 ◇ *She smiled with supreme confidence.* 她无比自信地微微一笑。

the Su,preme 'Being *noun* [sing.] (*formal*) God 上帝；无上的天主

the Su,preme 'Court (*also* **,High 'Court**) *noun* [sing.] the highest court in a country or state 最高法院；州最高法院

su·preme·ly /suː'priːmli; *BrE also* sjuː-/ *adv.* extremely 极其；极为：*supremely confident* 信心十足 ◇ *They managed it all supremely well.* 这件事他们干得极其出色。

su·premo /suː'priːməʊ; sjuː-; *NAmE* suː'priːmoʊ/ *noun* (*pl.* **-os**) (*BrE, informal*) a person who has the most power or authority in a particular business or activity（企业或活动的）最高领导人，总管，总指挥：*the Microsoft supremo, Bill Gates* 微软总裁比尔·盖茨

Supt (*also* **Supt.** *especially in NAmE*) *abbr.* (in the police force) SUPERINTENDENT（英国）警司；（美国）警长：*Chief Supt Pauline Clark* 波林·克拉克总警司

sura (*also* **surah**) /'sʊərə; *NAmE* 'sʊrə/ *noun* a chapter or section of the Koran（《古兰经》的）章

sur·charge /'sɜːtʃɑːdʒ; *NAmE* 'sɜːrtʃɑːrdʒ/ *noun, verb*

■ ***noun*** ~ (**on sth**) an extra amount of money that you must pay in addition to the usual price 额外费用；附加费；增收费 SYN **supplement**

■ ***verb*** ~ **sb** (**sth**) to make sb pay a surcharge 向（某人）收取额外费用：*We were surcharged £50 for travelling on a Friday.* 因为在星期五旅行，我们多付了 50 英镑。

sur·coat /'sɜːkəʊt; *NAmE* 'sɜːrkoʊt/ *noun* a piece of clothing without sleeves, worn in the past over a suit of ARMOUR 苏尔外套（旧时的无袖铠甲罩衣）

sure /ʃʊə(r); ʃɔː(r); *NAmE* ʃʊr/ *adj., adv.*

■ ***adj.*** (**surer, sur·est**) HELP You can also use **more sure** and **most sure**, especially in sense 1. 亦可用 more sure 和 most sure，尤用于第 1 义。**1** [not before noun] confident that you know sth or that you are right 确信；确知；肯定；有把握 SYN **certain**: *'Is that John over there?' 'I'm not sure.'* "那边那个人是约翰吗？" "我说不准。" ◇ *You don't sound very sure.* 听你这口气，你不大肯定。◇ ~ (**that**)... *I'm pretty sure (that) he'll agree.* 他会同意的，对此我有相当的把握。◇ *Are you sure you don't mind?* 你确实不在意？◇ ~ **of sth** *I hope you are sure of your facts.* 我希望你能肯定你说的都是事实。◇ ~ **about sth** *Are you sure about that?* 这事你肯定吗？◇ ~ **how, whether, etc....** *Ask me if you're not sure how to do it.* 你要是拿不准怎么干，就问我。◇ *I'm not sure whether I should tell you this.* 我拿不准该不该把这事告诉你。OPP **unsure** **2** [not before noun] certain that you will receive sth or that sth will happen 一定，必定，无疑（将会得到或发生）：~ **of sth** *You're always sure of a warm welcome there.* 到了那里你肯定会受到热烈欢迎。◇ ~ **of doing sth** *England must win this game to be sure of qualifying for the World Cup.* 英格兰队必须拿下这场比赛才能确保获得世界杯的参赛资格。**3** ~ **to do sth** certain to do sth or to happen 一定，必定，无疑（会做或会发生）：*The exhibition is sure to be popular.* 这一展览肯定受欢迎。◇ *It's sure to rain.* 一准会下雨。➲ SYNONYMS AT CERTAIN **4** [usually before noun] that can be trusted or relied on 不容置疑的；确切的；可靠的；保险的：*It's a* ***sure sign*** *of economic recovery.* 这是经济复苏的确切迹象。◇ *There's only one sure way to do it.* 做这件事只有一个保险的办法。◇ *He is a* ***sure bet*** *for the presidential nominations* (= certain to succeed). 他是总统候选人提名的铁定人选。➲ SYNONYMS AT CERTAIN **5** [usually before noun] steady and confident 沉着自信的；胸有成竹的：*We admired her sure touch at the keyboard.* 我们欣赏她沉着自信的弹奏风格。

IDM **be sure to do sth** used to tell sb to do sth 一定要，务必（去做某事）：*Be sure to give your family my regards.* 务必代我向你的家人问好。HELP In spoken English **and** plus another verb can be used instead of **to** and the infinitive. 口语中，可用 and 加动词代替带 to 的不定式：*Be sure and call me tomorrow.* 明天一定要打电话给我。**for 'sure** (*informal*) without doubt 无疑；肯定：*No one knows for sure what happened.* 没有人确切地知道发生了什么事。◇ *I think he'll be back on Monday, but I can't say for sure.* 我想他星期一会回来，不过我不敢肯定。◇ ***One thing is for sure***—*it's not going to be easy.* 有一点可以肯定，事情不会很容易。◇ (*NAmE*) *'Will you be there?' 'For sure.'* "你去吗？" "肯定去。" **make 'sure (of sth/that...)** **1** to do sth in order to be certain that sth else happens 确保；设法保证：*Make sure (that) no one finds out about this.* 绝对不要让任何人发现这件事。◇ *They scored another goal and made sure of victory.* 他们又进了一个球，这就赢定了。◇ *Our staff will do their best to make sure you enjoy your visit.* 我们的人员会竭尽全力使您访问愉快。**2** to check that sth is true or has been done 查明，核实，弄清（某事属实或已做）：*She looked around to make sure that she was alone.* 她往四下里看看，是不是只有她一个人。◇ *I think the door's locked, but I'll just go and make sure.* 我觉得门已经锁上了，不过我还是去看看好放心。**'sure of yourself** (*sometimes disapproving*) very confident 自信；自以为是：*She seems very sure of herself.* 她好像十分自信。**ˌsure 'thing** (*informal, especially NAmE*) used to say 'yes' to a suggestion or request（答应建议或要求）当然，一定：*'Are you coming?' 'Sure thing.'* "你来吗？" "当然。" **to be 'sure** (*formal*) used to admit that sth is true（承认属实）诚然，固然，无可否认：*He is intelligent, to be sure, but he's also very lazy.* 他固然聪明，但也很懒。

■ ***adv.*** (*informal, especially NAmE*) **1** used to say 'yes' to sb（表示同意）当然：*'Will you open the wine?' 'Sure, where is it?'* "你把葡萄酒打开好吗？" "没问题，酒在哪儿？" ◇ *Did it hurt? Sure it hurt.* 疼不疼？当然疼了。**2** used to emphasize sth that you are saying（加强语气）确实，的确：*Boy, it sure is hot.* 嗬，这天儿可真热。◇ *'Amazing view'. 'Sure is.'* "景色真美。" "没错。" ◇ *That song* ***sure as hell*** *sounds familiar.* 那首歌确实耳熟。◇ *He sure looked unhappy.* 他的确显得不高兴。**3** used to reply to sb who has just thanked you for sth（回答他人的感谢）不用客气，应该的：*'Thanks for the ride.' 'Sure—anytime.'* "谢谢你载我过来。" "不用客气，随时愿意效劳。"

IDM **(as) sure as eggs is 'eggs** (*old-fashioned, BrE, informal*) used to say that sth is definitely true 千真万确；的的确确 **ˌsure e'nough** used to say that sth happened as expected（表示不出所料）果真，果然：*I said he'd forget, and sure enough he did.* 我说他会忘记，他果然就忘了。

'sure-fire *adj.* [only before noun] (*informal*) certain to be successful or to happen as you expect 必定成功的；肯定会发生的：*a sure-fire success* 定能获得的成功

ˌsure-'footed (*also* **foot·sure**) *adj.* **1** not likely to fall when walking or climbing on rough ground 脚步稳的；不会摔倒的 **2** confident and unlikely to make mistakes, especially in difficult situations 沉着的；稳健的

sure·ly /ˈʃʊəli; ˈʃɔːli; *NAmE* ˈʃʊrli/ *adv.* **1** used to show that you are almost certain of what you are saying and want other people to agree with you（对自己的话很有把握，并希望他人同意）想必：*Surely we should do something about it?* 我们总得想个办法吧？◇ *It's surely only a matter of time before he is found, isn't it?* 找到他只是个时间问题，对不对？**2** used with a negative to show that sth surprises you and you do not want to believe it（用于否定句，表示难以置信）：*Surely you don't think I was responsible for this?* 你一定不会以为这是我的责任吧？◇ *'They're getting married.' '****Surely not!****'* "他们要结婚了。" "不会吧！" ◇ *They won't go, surely?* 他们不会真的要走吧？**3** (*formal*) without doubt; certainly 无疑；必定：*He knew that if help did not arrive soon they would surely die.* 他知道，如果救援不能很快到，他们必死无疑。**4** (*old-fashioned,*

▼ SYNONYMS 同义词辨析

sure

confident • convinced • certain • positive • clear

These words all describe sb who knows without doubt that sth is true or will happen. 以上各词均指确信、肯定、有把握。

sure [not before noun] without any doubt that you are right, that sth is true, that you will get sth or that sth will happen 指确信、肯定、有把握、必定：*'Is that John over there?' 'I'm not sure.'* "那边那个人是约翰吗？" "我说不准。" ◇ *Are you sure about that?* 这事你肯定吗？◇ *England must win this game to be sure of qualifying.* 英格兰队必须拿下这场比赛才能确保获得资格。NOTE **Sure** is often used in negative statements and questions, because there is some doubt or anxiety over the matter. If there is no doubt, people often say *quite sure*. * sure 常用于否定句和疑问句，表示有所怀疑或担忧。毫无疑问时常用 quite sure：*I'm quite sure (that) I left my bag here* (= I have no doubt about it). 我肯定是把包丢在这儿了。

confident completely sure that sth will happen in the way that you want or expect 指肯定、确信、有把握：*I'm quite confident that you'll get the job.* 我肯定你能得到那份工作。◇ *The team feels confident of winning.* 这个队觉得有把握取胜。NOTE **Confident** is a stronger and more definite word than **sure** and is more often used in positive statements, when you feel no anxiety. * confident 较 sure 语气强，而且更肯定，在无所担忧的情况下较常用于肯定句中。

convinced [not before noun] completely sure that sth is true or right, especially because the evidence seems to prove it or sb else has persuaded you to believe it 指坚信、深信、确信，尤指有证据证明或经说服：*I'm convinced that she's innocent.* 我坚信她是清白无辜的。

certain [not usually before noun] sure that you are right or that sth is true 指确信、肯定、无疑：*Are you absolutely certain about this?* 你对这事绝对确信无疑吗？

SURE OR CERTAIN? 用 sure 还是 certain？

Like **sure**, **certain** is often used in negative statements and questions. It is slightly more formal than **sure**; **sure** is more frequent, especially in spoken English. * certain 与 sure 一样，常用于否定句和疑问句中，但比 sure 稍正式些。sure 较常用，尤其是在口语中。

positive [not before noun] (*rather informal*) completely sure that sth is true 指有绝对把握、确信、肯定：*She was positive that he'd been there.* 她确信他曾到过那儿。◇ *'Are you sure?' 'Positive.'* "你肯定吗？" "绝对肯定。"

clear (often used in negative statements and questions) having no doubt or confusion about sth（常用于否定句与疑问句中）指无疑的、清楚的、明白的：*My memory isn't really clear on that point.* 那一点我记不太清楚了。

PATTERNS

- sure/confident/convinced/certain/positive/clear **about** sth
- sure/confident/convinced/certain **of** sth
- sure/confident/convinced/certain/positive/clear **that...**
- sure/certain/clear **who/what/how**, etc.
- **to feel** sure/confident/convinced/certain/positive
- **quite/absolutely/completely/fairly/pretty** sure/confident/convinced/certain/positive/clear
- **not altogether** sure/confident/convinced/certain/clear

S

NAmE, informal) used to say 'yes' to sb or to agree to sth（表示肯定或同意）当然 IDM SEE SLOWLY

▼ WHICH WORD? 词语辨析

surely / certainly

- You use **surely**, especially in *BrE*, to show that you are almost certain about what you are saying and you want other people to agree with you. * surely 表示对所说的话几乎肯定无疑，并希望别人同意自己的看法，尤用于英式英语： *Surely this can't be right?* 这不可能是对的吧？ **Surely** in negative sentences shows that something surprises you and you do not want to believe it. 在否定句中，surely 表示某事使人感到吃惊而不愿相信： *You're surely not thinking of going, are you?* 你不是想走吧？
- **Certainly** usually means 'without doubt' or 'definitely', and is used to show that you strongly believe something or to emphasize that something is really true. * certainly 常指无疑地、确定地，用以表示坚信某事或强调某事属实： *I'll certainly remember this trip!* 我绝不会忘记这次旅行！ In informal *NAmE* this would be 非正式的美式英语说法为： *I'll sure remember this trip!* 我绝不会忘记这次旅行！
- Compare 比较： *The meal was certainly too expensive* (= there is no doubt about it). 这顿饭的确太贵了（毫无疑问）。and 和： *The meal was surely too expensive?* (= that is my opinion. Don't you agree?) 这顿饭太贵了吧？（我这样认为，你不这样认为吗？）
- In formal language only, **surely** can be used to mean 'without doubt'. 只有在正式用语中，surely 才表示无疑： *This will surely end in disaster.* 这无疑将以灾难告终。

➲ NOTE AT COURSE, SURE

sure·ness /ˈʃʊənəs; ˈʃɔːn-; *NAmE* ˈʃʊrn-/ *noun* [U] the quality of being confident and steady; not hesitating or doubting 沉着自信；胸有成竹；有把握；确信不疑： *an artist's sureness of touch* 画家胸有成竹的笔触 ◇ *her sureness that she had done the right thing* 她确信自己做得对

surety /ˈʃʊərəti; ˈʃɔːr-; *NAmE* ˈʃʊr-/ *noun* [C, U] (*pl.* **-ies**) (*law* 律) **1** money given as a promise that you will pay a debt, appear in court, etc. 保证金： *She was granted bail with a surety of $500.* 她交了 500 美元保证金，获得保释。**2** a person who accepts responsibility if sb else does not pay a debt, appear in court, etc. 保证人；担保人： *to act as surety for sb* 为某人做担保人

surf /sɜːf; *NAmE* sɜːrf/ *noun, verb*

■ *noun* [U] large waves in the sea or ocean, and the white FOAM that they produce as they fall on the beach, on rocks, etc. 激浪；拍岸浪花： *the sound of surf breaking on the beach* 激浪拍岸的声音 ◇ *Sydney, surf capital of the world* (= where the sport of surfing is very popular) 世界冲浪之都悉尼 ➲ WORDFINDER NOTE AT SEA

■ *verb* **1** (*often* **go surfing**) [I, T] ~ (**sth**) to take part in the sport of riding on waves on a SURFBOARD 进行冲浪运动；冲浪 **2** [T] ~ **the Net/Internet** to use the Internet（互联网上）冲浪，漫游，浏览： *I was surfing the Net looking for information on Indian music.* 我正上网查找关于印度音乐的资料。

sur·face 🔑 /ˈsɜːfɪs; *NAmE* ˈsɜːrfɪs/ *noun, verb*

■ *noun* **1** 🔑 [C] the outside or top layer of sth 表面；表层；面： *an uneven road surface* 凹凸不平的路面 ◇ *We'll need a flat surface to play the game on.* 我们得有个平面才能玩这个游戏。◇ *Teeth have a hard surface layer called enamel.* 牙齿有一层叫做釉质的坚硬表层。◇ *a broad leaf with a large **surface area*** 表面积很大的阔叶 **2** 🔑 [C, usually sing.] the top layer of an area of water or land 水面；地面；液面： *the earth's surface* 地球表面 ◇ *These plants float on the surface of the water.* 这些植物漂浮在水面上。**3** 🔑 [C] the flat upper part of a piece of furniture, that is used for working on（家具的）顶面，操作台： *a work surface* 操作台 ◇ *She's cleaned all the kitchen surfaces.* 她把厨房的所有台面全都收拾干净了。**4** [sing.] the outer appearance of a person, thing or situation; the qualities that you see or notice, that are not hidden 表面；外表；外观： *Rage bubbled just below the surface of his mind.* 怒火在他心中燃烧，随时可能迸发。

IDM **on the ˈsurface** when not thought about deeply or thoroughly; when not looked at carefully 表面上；从外表看；乍一看： *It seems like a good idea on the surface but there are sure to be problems.* 这主意乍一看不错，但肯定存在问题。◇ *On the surface, he appeared unchanged.* 看外表他好像没变。➲ MORE AT SCRATCH *v.*

■ *verb* **1** [I] to come up to the surface of water 升到水面；浮出水面 SYN **emerge**: *The ducks dived and surfaced again several metres away.* 鸭子潜入水中，然后在几米外又钻出水面。**2** [I] to suddenly appear or become obvious after having been hidden for a while（隐藏或被掩盖一段时间后）露面，重新出现，显露，被披露 SYN **emerge**: *Doubts began to surface.* 质疑声开始出现。◇ *She surfaced again years later in London.* 多年后她又出现在伦敦。**3** [I] (*informal*) to wake up or get up after being asleep 醒来；起床： *He finally surfaced around noon.* 他终于在中午时分醒来。**4** [T] ~ **sth** to put a surface on a road, path, etc. 铺设（路面等）

ˈsurface mail *noun* [U] letters, etc. carried by road, rail or sea, not by air 水陆路邮件；平寄邮件

ˈsurface structure *noun* (*grammar* 语法) the structure of a well-formed sentence in a language, rather than its UNDERLYING form 表层结构 ➲ COMPARE DEEP STRUCTURE

ˌsurface ˈtension *noun* [U] (*specialist*) the property (= characteristic) of liquids by which they form a layer at their surface, and which makes sure that this surface covers as small an area as possible 表面张力

ˌsurface-to-ˈair *adj.* [only before noun] (especially of MISSILES 尤指导弹) fired from the ground or from ships and aimed at aircraft 地对空的；舰对空的

ˌsurface-to-ˈsurface *adj.* [only before noun] (especially of MISSILES 尤指导弹) fired from the ground or from ships and aimed at another point on the ground or a ship 地（或舰）对地（或舰）的

sur·fac·tant /sɜːˈfæktənt; *NAmE* sɜːrˈf-/ *noun* [C, U] **1** (*specialist*) a substance that reduces the SURFACE TENSION of a liquid, often forming bubbles in the liquid 表面活性剂（减少液体表面张力，常形成气泡）**2** (*medical* 医) a substance that keeps the lungs working well to prevent breathing problems 肺泡表面活性物质（维持肺部良好工作、防止呼吸困难）

ˌsurf and ˈturf *noun* [U] = SURF 'N' TURF

surf·board /ˈsɜːfbɔːd; *NAmE* ˈsɜːrfbɔːrd/ (*also* **board**) *noun* a long narrow board used for SURFING 冲浪板

sur·feit /ˈsɜːfɪt; *NAmE* ˈsɜːrfɪt/ *noun* [usually sing.] ~ (**of sth**) (*formal*) an amount that is too large 过量 SYN **excess**

surf·er /ˈsɜːfə(r); *NAmE* ˈsɜːrfər/ *noun* **1** a person who goes SURFING 进行冲浪运动的人 **2** (*also* **ˈNet surfer**) (*informal*) a person who spends a lot of time using the Internet（互联网上）网虫；冲浪者，漫游者 ➲ SEE ALSO SILVER SURFER

surfie /ˈsɜːfi; *NAmE* ˈsɜːrfi/ *noun* (*AustralE, NZE, informal*) a person who is enthusiastic about SURFING, especially a young man 冲浪迷（尤指男青年）

surf·ing /ˈsɜːfɪŋ; *NAmE* ˈsɜːrf-/ *noun* [U] **1** the sport of riding on waves while standing on a narrow board called a SURFBOARD 冲浪运动： *to go surfing* 去冲浪 ➲ VISUAL VOCAB PAGE V54 **2** the activity of looking at different things on the Internet in order to find sth interesting, or of changing between TV channels in order to find an interesting programme（互联网上）冲浪，漫游，浏览；换台（转换电视频道以寻找有趣节目）

ˈsurf lifesaver *noun* (*AustralE, NZE*) = LIFEGUARD

ˌsurf ’n’ ˈturf (*also* **ˌsurf and ˈturf**) *noun* [U] (*NAmE*) SEAFOOD and STEAK served together as a meal 海鲜牛排餐；海陆香鲜；海陆双拼

surge /sɜːdʒ; *NAmE* sɜːrdʒ/ *verb, noun*
■ ***verb* 1** [I] **+ adv./prep.** to move quickly and with force in a particular direction 涌；汹涌；涌动：*The gates opened and the crowd surged forward.* 大门打开了，人群向前涌去。◇ *Flood waters surged into their homes.* 洪水涌进了他们的房子。**2** [I] (**+ adv./prep.**) to fill sb with a strong feeling 使强烈地感到 **SYN sweep**：*Relief surged through her.* 她顿觉宽慰。**3** [I] (of prices, profits, etc. 物价、利润等) to suddenly increase in value 急剧上升；飞涨；激增：*Share prices surged.* 股价猛涨。➲ RELATED NOUN UPSURGE **4** [I] (of the flow of electrical power 电流) to increase suddenly 浪涌
■ ***noun* 1** ~ (**of sth**) a sudden increase of a strong feeling (强烈感情的) 突发 **SYN rush**：*She felt a sudden surge of anger.* 她突然感觉怒火中烧。◇ *a surge of excitement* 一阵兴奋 ➲ SEE ALSO UPSURGE **2** a sudden increase in the amount or number of sth; a large amount of sth (数量的) 急剧上升，激增；大量；一大批：~ (**in sth**) *a surge in consumer spending* 消费开支的激增 ◇ *We are having trouble keeping up with the recent surge in demand.* 对于近来出现的需求猛增，我们难以应对。◇ ~ (**of sth**) *After an initial surge of interest, there has been little call for our services.* 过了开始的一阵新鲜劲后，对我们服务的需求就变得很小。➲ SEE ALSO UPSURGE **3** ~ (**of sth**) a sudden, strong forward or upward movement 奔涌向前；突然的向上运动：*a tidal surge* 涨潮 **4** a sudden increase in the flow of electrical power through a system (电流) 浪涌：*An electrical surge damaged the computer's disk drive.* 电流浪涌损坏了计算机的磁盘驱动器。

sur·geon /ˈsɜːdʒən; *NAmE* ˈsɜːrdʒən/ *noun* a doctor who is trained to perform surgery (= medical operations that involve cutting open a person's body) 外科医生：***a brain/heart, etc. surgeon*** 脑外科、心脏外科等医生 ➲ COMPARE PHYSICIAN ➲ **WORDFINDER NOTE AT DOCTOR**

ˌSurgeon ˈGeneral *noun* (*pl.* **Surgeons General**) (in the US) the head of a public health service or of a medical service in the armed forces (美国) 卫生局局长，军医处长：*Surgeon General's warning: cigarette smoking causes cancer* 卫生局局长警告大家：吸烟致癌

sur·gery /ˈsɜːdʒəri; *NAmE* ˈsɜːrdʒ-/ *noun* (*pl.* **-ies**) **1** [U] medical treatment of injuries or diseases that involves cutting open a person's body and often removing or replacing some parts; the branch of medicine connected with this treatment 外科手术；外科学：***major/minor surgery*** 大手术；小手术 ◇ *to* ***undergo*** *heart* ***surgery*** 接受心脏手术 ◇ *He will require surgery on his left knee.* 他的左膝需要做手术。**HELP** In American English the countable form can be used. 美式英语可用复数形式：*She had three surgeries over ten days.* 她十天内做了三个手术。➲ **WORDFINDER NOTE** AT OPERATION ➲ **COLLOCATIONS** AT ILL ➲ SEE ALSO OPEN-HEART SURGERY, PLASTIC SURGERY **2** [U, C] (*BrE*) the time during which a doctor, dentist or VET is available to see patients 应诊时间：***morning/afternoon/evening surgery*** 上午 / 下午 / 晚间应诊时间 ◇ *surgery hours* 应诊时间 ◇ *Is there a surgery this evening?* 今晚有没有医生应诊？**3** [C] (*BrE*) (*NAmE* **office**) a place where a doctor, dentist or VET sees patients 诊室；门诊处：***a doctor's/dentist's surgery*** 医生的 / 牙医的诊室 **4** [C] (*BrE*) a time when people can meet their Member of Parliament to ask questions and get help (议员的) 接待时间：*a constituency surgery* 接待选区选民时间

sur·gi·cal /ˈsɜːdʒɪkl; *NAmE* ˈsɜːrdʒ-/ *adj.* [only before noun] used in or connected with surgery 外科的；外科手术的：*surgical procedures* 手术程序 ◇ *a surgical ward* (= for patients having operations) 外科手术病房 ▸ **sur·gi·cal·ly** /-kli/ *adv.*：*The lumps will need to be surgically removed.* 这些肿块需手术切除。

ˌsurgical ˈspirit (*BrE*) (*NAmE* **ˈrubbing alcohol**) *noun* [U] a clear liquid, consisting mainly of alcohol, used for cleaning wounds, etc. 医用酒精；消毒用酒精

surly /ˈsɜːli; *NAmE* ˈsɜːrli/ *adj.* (**sur·lier, sur·li·est**) bad-tempered and rude 脾气坏的；乖戾的；态度粗暴的：*a surly youth* 脾气暴躁的年轻人 ▸ **sur·li·ness** *noun* [U]

sur·mise *verb, noun*
■ ***verb*** /səˈmaɪz; *NAmE* sərˈm-/ [T, I] ~ (**sth**) | ~ (**that**)... | ~ **what, where, etc....** | **+ speech** (*formal*) to guess or suppose sth using the evidence you have, without definitely knowing 推测；猜测 **SYN conjecture**：*From the looks on their faces, I surmised that they had had an argument.* 看他们的脸色，我猜想他们之间发生了争执。
■ ***noun*** /ˈsɜːmaɪz; *NAmE* ˈsɜːrm-/ [U, C, usually sing.] (*formal*) a guess based on some facts that you know already 推测；猜测：*This is pure surmise on my part.* 这纯粹是我的猜测。

sur·mount /səˈmaʊnt; *NAmE* sərˈm-/ *verb* (*formal*) **1** ~ **sth** to deal successfully with a difficulty 克服；解决 **SYN overcome**：*She was well aware of the difficulties that had to be surmounted.* 她很清楚必须克服哪些困难。**2** [usually passive] ~ **sth** to be placed on top of sth 处于（某物）上面；置于（某物）顶端：*a high column surmounted by a statue* 顶端立着一尊雕像的高大的柱子

sur·name 🔑 /ˈsɜːneɪm; *NAmE* ˈsɜːrn-/ *noun* (*especially BrE*) a name shared by all the members of a family (written last in English names) 姓 ➲ COMPARE FAMILY NAME, LAST NAME

sur·pass /səˈpɑːs; *NAmE* sərˈpæs/ *verb* [T, I] ~ (**sb/sth/yourself**) (*formal*) to do or be better than sb/sth 超过；胜过；优于：*He hopes one day to surpass the world record.* 他希望有一天能刷新世界纪录。◇ *Its success has* ***surpassed all expectations***. 它所取得的成功远远超出了预期。◇ *Her cooking was always good, but this time she had* ***surpassed herself*** (= done better than her own high standards). 她的厨艺向来不错，但这一次她更是胜过以往。◇ *scenery of surpassing beauty* 无比优美的景色

sur·plice /ˈsɜːpləs; *NAmE* ˈsɜːrp-/ *noun* a loose white piece of clothing with wide sleeves worn by priests and singers in the CHOIR during church services (教士和唱诗班穿的) 白色罩衣

sur·plus /ˈsɜːpləs; *NAmE* ˈsɜːrp-/ *noun, adj.*
■ ***noun*** [C, U] **1** an amount that is extra or more than you need 过剩；剩余；过剩量；剩余额：*food surpluses* 过剩的食物 ◇ *Wheat was* ***in surplus*** *that year.* 那一年小麦过剩。**2** the amount by which the amount of money received is greater than the amount of money spent 盈余；顺差：*a trade surplus of £400 million* * 4 亿英镑的贸易顺差 ◇ *The balance of payments was* ***in surplus*** *last year* (= the value of exports was greater than the value of imports). 去年国际收支有盈余。➲ **COLLOCATIONS** AT INTERNATIONAL ➲ COMPARE DEFICIT (1)
■ ***adj.*** more than is needed or used 过剩的；剩余的；多余的：*surplus cash* 剩余的现金 ◇ *Surplus grain is being sold for export.* 过剩的谷物正销往国外。◇ ~ **to sth** *These items are* ***surplus to requirements*** (= not needed). 这几项不需要。

sur·prise 🔑 /səˈpraɪz; *NAmE* sərˈp-/ *noun, verb*
■ ***noun* 1** 🔑 [C] an event, a piece of news, etc. that is unexpected or that happens suddenly 意想不到（或突然）的事；令人惊奇的事（或消息等）：*What a nice surprise!* 真是让人惊喜！◇ *a surprise attack* 突然袭击 ◇ *There are few surprises in this year's budget.* 今年的预算案没有多少出人意料的地方。◇ *I have a surprise for you!* 我要告诉你一件你意想不到的事！◇ ***It comes as no surprise to*** *learn that they broke their promises.* 得知他们食言并不让人觉得意外。◇ *Her letter* ***came as a complete surprise***. 万万没想到会收到她的信。◇ *There are lots of* ***surprises in store for*** *visitors to the gallery.* 参观画展的人将会发现许多令他们惊奇的东西。◇ *Visitors to the gallery are* ***in for a few surprises***. 参观画展的人将会见到一些令他们惊奇的东西。**2** 🔑 [U, C] a feeling caused by sth happening suddenly or unexpectedly 惊奇；惊讶；意外：*a look of surprise* 惊讶的表情 ◇ *She looked up* ***in surprise***. 她惊讶地抬起头。◇ ~ (**at sth**) *He gasped* ***with surprise*** *at her strength.* 发现她有这么大的力气，他大吃一惊。◇ ~ (**at seeing, hearing, etc.**) *They couldn't conceal their surprise at seeing us together.* 看见我们在一起，他们表现出掩饰不住的诧异。◇ *I* ***got a surprise*** *when I saw the bill.* 一看账单我吃了一惊。◇ ***Much to my surprise***, *I passed.* 压根儿没想到，我及格了。◇ ***To***

S

everyone's surprise, the plan succeeded. 出乎所有人的意料，那个计划竟然取得了成功。◇ *Imagine our surprise when he walked into the room!* 你想象一下，他走进房间时，我们多么惊奇！ **3** [U] the use of methods that cause feelings of surprise 出人意表的做事方式；出奇制胜的策略：*A successful campaign should have* ***an element of surprise.*** 成功的宣传活动需有出奇制胜之处。

IDM **sur,prise, sur'prise** (*informal*) **1** (*ironic, often disapproving*) used to show that sth is not a surprise to you, as you could easily have predicted that it would happen or be true（认为不足为怪时说）：*One of the candidates was the manager's niece, and surprise, surprise, she got the job.* 求职者中有一个是经理的侄女，结果她被录用了。这有什么奇怪的呢。**2** used when giving sb a surprise（让某人感到意外时说）：*Surprise, surprise! Look who's here!* 想不到吧！看看这是谁！ **take sb/sth by sur'prise** to attack or capture sb/sth unexpectedly or without warning 突袭；出其不意地抓获：*The police took the burglars by surprise.* 警方出其不意地逮捕了入室窃贼。 **take sb by sur'prise** to happen unexpectedly so that sb is slightly shocked; to surprise sb 使某人惊诧；出乎某人意料：*His frankness took her by surprise.* 她没料到他竟如此坦率。

■ *verb* **1** to make sb feel surprised 使惊奇；使诧异；使感到意外：**~ sb** *It wouldn't surprise me if they got married soon.* 即使他们很快就结婚，我也不会感到意外。◇ **~ sb how, what, etc....** *It's always surprised me how popular he is.* 他怎么那么受欢迎，我百思不得其解。◇ **it surprises sb that...** *It surprises me that you've never sung professionally.* 想不到你从来没搞过专业演唱。◇ **it surprises sb to do sth** *Would it surprise you to know that I'm thinking of leaving?* 如果我告诉你我打算离开这里，你觉得意外吗？ **2** **~ sb** to attack, discover, etc., sb suddenly and unexpectedly 出其不意地攻击；使措手不及；无意中发现：*The army attacked at night to surprise the rebels.* 军队在夜间发起攻击，把叛乱者打了个措手不及。◇ *We arrived home early and surprised a burglar trying to break in.* 我们回家早，无意中发现一个窃贼正要入室行窃。

sur·prised /sə'praɪzd; *NAmE* sər'p-/ *adj.* feeling or showing surprise 惊奇的；惊讶的；觉得奇怪的；感觉意外的：*a surprised look* 惊讶的神色 ◇ *She looked surprised when I told her.* 我告诉她时她显得很惊讶。◇ **~ (at/by sb/sth)** *I was surprised at how quickly she agreed.* 我没想到她这么快就同意了。◇ *I'm surprised at you, behaving like that in front of the kids.* 我真想不到，当着孩子们的面你竟做出这种举动。◇ **~ (to see, hear, etc.)** *They were surprised to find that he'd already left.* 他们惊奇地发现他已经走了。◇ **~ (that...)** *You shouldn't be surprised (that) he didn't come.* 他没来，你不必感到意外。◇ ***Don't be surprised if*** *I pretend not to recognise you.* 要是我假装不认识你，你别觉得奇怪。◇ *'Will she cancel the party?'* ***'I wouldn't be surprised.'*** "她会取消这次聚会吗？" "即使取消我也不感到奇怪。" ➲ COMPARE UNSURPRISED

sur·pris·ing /sə'praɪzɪŋ; *NAmE* sər'p-/ *adj.* causing surprise 令人吃惊的；使人惊奇的；出人意料的；奇怪的：*It's not surprising (that) they lost.* 他们吃了败仗，不奇怪。◇ *We had a surprising amount in common.* 我们共同之处出奇地多。◇ *It's surprising what people will do for money.* 人为了钱什么干不出来，想想真令人愕然。▶ **sur·pris·ing·ly** *adv.* : *She looked surprisingly well.* 她看上去身体出奇地好。◇ *Surprisingly, he agreed straight away.* 真想不到，他马上同意了。◇ ***Not surprisingly*** *on such a hot day, the beach was crowded.* 在这样的大热天，海滩上人头攒动是不足为奇的。

▼ SYNONYMS 同义词辨析

surprise

startle • amaze • stun • astonish • take sb aback • astound

These words all mean to make sb feel surprised. 以上各词均含使惊奇、使诧异之义。

surprise to give sb the feeling that you get when sth happens that you do not expect or do not understand, or sth that you do expect does not happen; to make sb feel surprised 指使惊奇、使诧异、使感到意外：*The outcome didn't surprise me at all.* 这一结果完全在我的意料之中。

startle to surprise sb suddenly in a way that slightly shocks or frightens them 指惊吓、使吓一跳、使大吃一惊：*Sorry, I didn't mean to startle you.* 对不起，我不是存心要吓唬你。◇ *The explosion startled the horse.* 爆炸声使马受了惊。

amaze to surprise sb very much 指使惊奇、使惊愕、使惊诧：*Just the huge size of the place amazed her.* 仅仅地方之大就使她十分惊奇。

stun (*rather informal*) (often in newspapers) to surprise or shock sb so much that they cannot think clearly or speak（常用于报章）指使震惊、使惊愕、使目瞪口呆

astonish to surprise sb very much 指使十分惊讶、使大为惊奇：*The news astonished everyone.* 这消息使大家十分惊讶。

AMAZE OR ASTONISH? 用 amaze 还是 astonish?

These two words have the same meaning and in most cases you can use either. If you are talking about sth that both surprises you and makes you feel ashamed, use **astonish**. 上述两词意思相同，多数情况下可通用。如果指某事既使人惊愕又使人羞愧则用 astonish：*He was astonished by his own stupidity.* 他对自己的愚蠢感到十分震惊。

take sb aback [usually passive] (especially of sth negative) to surprise or shock sb （尤指不好的事）使大吃一惊、使震惊：*We were rather taken aback by her hostile reaction.* 她敌视的反应使我们大吃一惊。

astound to surprise or shock sb very much 指使震惊、使大惊：*His arrogance astounded her.* 他的傲慢使她震惊。

PATTERNS

- It surprises sb/startles sb/amazes sb/stuns sb/astonishes sb/takes sb aback/astounds sb
- to surprise/startle/amaze/stun/astonish/astound sb **that...**
- to surprise/amaze sb **what/how...**
- to surprise/startle/amaze/stun/astonish/astound sb **to know/find/learn/see/hear...**
- to be surprised/startled/stunned **into** (doing) sth

▼ LANGUAGE BANK 用语库

surprising

Highlighting interesting data 强调有趣的数据

- ***What is surprising*** *about these results* ***is that*** *boys are more likely to be left-handed than girls.* 这些结果令人吃惊的是男生比女生更可能是左撇子。
- ***Surprisingly****, boys are more likely to be left-handed than girls.* 令人吃惊的是男生比女生更可能是左撇子。
- ***Interestingly****, even when both parents are left-handed, there is still only a 26% chance of their children being left-handed.* 有趣的是即使父母都是左撇子，他们的孩子也只有 26% 的概率是左撇子。
- ***One of the most interesting*** *findings is that only 2% of the left-handers surveyed have two left-handed parents.* 研究结果中最有趣的一点是在受调查的左撇子中只有 2% 的人父母都是左撇子。
- ***It is interesting to note that*** *people are more likely to be left-handed if their mother is left-handed than if their father is.* 有趣的是，母亲是左撇子的人比父亲是左撇子的人更可能成为左撇子。
- ***The most striking*** *feature of these results* ***is that*** *left-handed mothers are more likely to have left-handed children.* 这些结果中最引人注目的一点是左撇子母亲更可能生左撇子孩子。

➲ LANGUAGE BANK AT CONTRAST, EMPHASIS, ILLUSTRATE, SIMILARLY

sur·real /səˈriːəl/ (*also less frequent* **sur·real·is·tic**) *adj.* very strange; more like a dream than reality, with ideas and images mixed together in a strange way 离奇的；怪诞的；梦幻般的；超现实的

sur·real·ism /səˈriːəlɪzəm/ *noun* [U] a 20th century style and movement in art and literature in which images and events that are not connected are put together in a strange or impossible way, like a dream, to try to express what is happening deep in the mind 超现实主义，超现实主义派（20 世纪文艺流派，以离奇怪诞的方式把无关联的形象和事情串连在一起）▸ **sur·real·ist** *adj.* [usually before noun]: *a surrealist painter/painting* 超现实主义画家 / 绘画 **sur·real·ist** *noun*: *the surrealist Salvador Dali* 超现实主义画家萨尔瓦多·达利

sur·real·is·tic /səˌriːəˈlɪstɪk/ *adj.* **1** = SURREAL **2** connected with surrealism 超现实主义的：*a surrealistic painting* 超现实主义绘画

sur·ren·der /səˈrendə(r)/ *verb, noun*
▪ *verb* **1** [I, T] to admit that you have been defeated and want to stop fighting; to allow yourself to be caught, taken prisoner, etc. 投降 SYN **give in (to sb/sth)**: **~ (to sb)** *The rebel soldiers were forced to surrender.* 叛军被迫投降。◇ **~ yourself (to sb)** *The hijackers eventually surrendered themselves to the police.* 劫机者最终向警方投降。➲ WORDFINDER NOTE AT PEACE **2** (*formal*) to give up sth/sb when you are forced to（被迫）放弃，交出 SYN **relinquish**: **~ sth/sb to sb** *He agreed to surrender all claims to the property.* 他同意放弃对那笔财产的一切权利要求。◇ *They surrendered their guns to the police.* 他们向警察交出了枪。◇ **~ sth/sb** *The defendant was released to await trial but had to surrender her passport.* 被告被释放候审，但须交出护照。
PHR V **surˈrender to sth | surˈrender yourself to sth** (*formal*) to stop trying to prevent yourself from having a feeling, habit, etc. and allow it to control what you do 听任（感情、习惯等）摆布（或发展）：*He finally surrendered to his craving for drugs.* 他最终克制不住，吸起毒来。
▪ *noun* [U, sing.] **1 ~ (to sb/sth)** an act of admitting that you have been defeated and want to stop fighting 投降：*They demanded (an)* ***unconditional surrender****.* 他们要求无条件投降。➲ COLLOCATIONS AT WAR **2** the fact of allowing yourself to be controlled by sth 屈服；屈从：*They accused the government of a surrender to business interests.* 他们指责政府唯商界利益是从。**3 ~ of sth (to sb)** an act of giving sth to sb else even though you do not want to, especially after a battle, etc.（尤指在战争等过后）放弃，交出：*They insisted on the immediate surrender of all weapons.* 他们坚持要求立即交出全部武器。

surˈrender value *noun* the amount of money that you get if you end a life insurance policy before its official end date（在到期之前终止人寿保险单所得的）解约退还金，退保价值

sur·rep·ti·tious /ˌsʌrəpˈtɪʃəs; *NAmE* ˌsɜːr-/ *adj.* done secretly or quickly, in the hope that other people will not notice 秘密的；趁人不注意赶紧进行的 SYN **furtive**: *She sneaked a surreptitious glance at her watch.* 她偷偷看了一眼手表。▸ **sur·rep·ti·tious·ly** *adv.*

sur·ro·gacy /ˈsʌrəgəsi; *NAmE* ˈsɜːr-/ *noun* [U] the practice of giving birth to a baby for another woman who is unable to have babies herself 代孕

sur·ro·gate /ˈsʌrəgət; *NAmE* ˈsɜːr-/ *adj.* (*formal*) used to describe a person or thing that takes the place of, or is used instead of, sb/sth else 替代的；代用的：*She saw him as a sort of surrogate father.* 在她心目中，他仿佛是能替代父亲角色的人。▸ **sur·ro·gate** *noun*

ˌsurrogate ˈmother *noun* a woman who gives birth to a baby for another woman who is unable to have babies herself 代孕母亲 ➲ WORDFINDER NOTE AT FAMILY

sur·round /səˈraʊnd/ *verb, noun*
▪ *verb* **1** to be all around sth/sb 围绕；环绕：**~ sth/sb** *Tall trees surround the lake.* 环湖都是大树。◇ *the membranes surrounding the brain* 脑膜 ◇ *As a child I was surrounded by love and kindness.* 幼年时我备受关爱。◇ **~ sth/sb with sth** *The lake is surrounded with/by trees.* 湖边树木环绕。**2** to move into position all around sb/sth, especially so as to prevent them from escaping; to move sb/sth into position in this way 包围；围住：**~ sb/sth** *Police surrounded the building.* 警方包围了那栋房子。◇ **~ sb/sth with sb/sth** *They've surrounded the building with police.* 他们派警察包围了那栋房子。**3 ~ sth/sb** to be closely connected with sth/sb 与…紧密相关；围绕：*publicity surrounding the divorce* 媒体围绕这桩离婚事件的报道 **4 ~ yourself with sb/sth** to choose to have particular people or things near you all the time 喜欢结交（某类人）；喜欢身边总有（某类东西）：*I like to surround myself with beautiful things.* 我喜欢身边老有漂亮的东西。
▪ *noun* a border or an area around the edge of sth, especially one that is decorated（物品的）框，饰边；周围 ➲ VISUAL VOCAB PAGE V22

sur·round·ing /səˈraʊndɪŋ/ *adj.* [only before noun] that is near or around sth 周围的；附近的：*Oxford and the surrounding area* 牛津及其周围地区

sur·round·ings /səˈraʊndɪŋz/ *noun* [pl.] everything that is around or near sb/sth 环境 SYN **environment**: *to work in pleasant surroundings* 在愉快的环境中工作 ◇ *The buildings have been designed to blend in with their surroundings.* 这些建筑物设计巧妙，与周围环境浑然一体。➲ SYNONYMS AT ENVIRONMENT

surˈround sound *noun* [U] a system for reproducing sound using several SPEAKERS (= the pieces of equipment that the sound comes out of) placed around the person listening in order to produce a more realistic sound 环绕音响系统；环绕立体声系统

sur·tax /ˈsɜːtæks; *NAmE* ˈsɜːrt-/ *noun* [U] a tax charged at a higher rate than the normal rate, on income above a particular level（对超过一定金额的收入征收的）附加税

sur·titles (*NAmE* **Sur·titles™**) /ˈsɜːtaɪtlz; *NAmE* ˈsɜːrt-/ *noun* [pl.] words that appear on a screen above or beside the stage to show or translate into a different language what is being sung in an OPERA, or spoken in a play in the theatre 台词译文字幕（打在歌剧院或戏院舞台上方或侧面）➲ WORDFINDER NOTE AT OPERA

sur·veil·lance /sɜːˈveɪləns; *NAmE* sɜːrˈv-/ *noun* [U] the act of carefully watching a person suspected of a crime or a place where a crime may be committed（对犯罪嫌疑人或可能发生犯罪的地方的）监视 SYN **observation**: *The police are keeping the suspects* ***under*** *constant* ***surveillance****.* 警方正对嫌疑人实施不间断监视。◇ ***surveillance cameras/equipment*** 监视摄像机 / 设备

sur·vey AW *noun, verb*
▪ *noun* /ˈsɜːveɪ; *NAmE* ˈsɜːrveɪ/ **1** an investigation of the opinions, behaviour, etc. of a particular group of people, which is usually done by asking them questions 民意调查；民意测验：*A recent survey showed 75% of those questioned were in favour of the plan.* 最近的民意调查显示，有 75% 的调查对象支持这项计划。◇ *The* ***survey revealed*** *that…* 民意测验显示… ◇ *to* ***conduct/carry out a survey*** 进行一项民意调查 **2** the act of examining and recording the measurements, features, etc. of an area of land in order to make a map or plan of it 测量；勘测；测绘：*an aerial survey* (= made by taking photographs from an aircraft) 航空测量 ◇ *a geological survey* 地质勘察 **3** (*BrE*) an examination of the condition of a house, etc., usually done for sb who is thinking of buying it（尤指为欲购房者所做的）房屋鉴定 **4** a general study, view or description of sth 总体研究；全面评述；概述：*a comprehensive survey of modern music* 现代音乐概述
▪ *verb* /səˈveɪ; *NAmE* sərˈveɪ/ **1 ~ sth** to look carefully at the whole of sth, especially in order to get a general impression of it 查看；审视；审察 SYN **inspect**: *The next morning we surveyed the damage caused by the fire.* 次日清早我们查看了火灾的破坏情况。◇ *He surveyed himself in the mirror before going out.* 出门前他对着镜子把自己审视了一番。**2 ~ sth** to study and give a general description of sth 总体研究；全面评述；概述：*This chapter briefly surveys the current state of European politics.* 本章对欧洲

S

政治的现状作了概述。**3 ~ sth** to measure and record the features of an area of land, for example in order to make a map or in preparation for building 测量；勘测；测绘 **4 ~ sth** (*BrE*) to examine a building to make sure it is in good condition（对建筑物的）鉴定，检查 **5** **~ sb/sth** to investigate the opinions or behaviour of a group of people by asking them a series of questions（对…）做民意调查，进行民意测验 SYN **interview**: *We surveyed 500 smokers and found that over three quarters would like to give up.* 我们对 500 名吸烟者进行了调查，发现有超过四分之三的人愿意戒烟。 ➲ MORE LIKE THIS 21, page R27

ˈsurvey course *noun* (*NAmE*) a college course that gives an introduction to a subject for people who are thinking about studying it further（大学的）概论课程，概况课程

sur·vey·or /səˈveɪə(r); *NAmE* sərˈv-/ *noun* **1** a person whose job is to examine and record the details of a piece of land（土地）测量员，勘测员 **2** (*BrE*) a person whose job is to examine a building to make sure it is in good condition, usually done for sb who is thinking of buying it（建筑物）鉴定人 **3** (*BrE*) an official whose job is to check that sth is accurate, of good quality, etc. 检验员；检验官：*the surveyor of public works* 市政工程检验官 ➲ SEE ALSO QUANTITY SURVEYOR

sur·viv·able /səˈvaɪvəbl; *NAmE* sərˈv-/ *adj.* (of an accident or experience 事故或经历) able to be survived 可幸免于难的；可幸存的：*a survivable air crash* 没有酿成死亡的飞机失事

sur·vival AW /səˈvaɪvl; *NAmE* sərˈv-/ *noun* **1** [U] the state of continuing to live or exist, often despite difficulty or danger 生存；存活；幸存：*the* ***struggle/battle/fight for survival*** 为生存而斗争 / 战斗 / 拼搏 ◇ *His only* ***chance of survival*** *was a heart transplant.* 只有进行心脏移植，他才有望活下去。◇ *Exporting is necessary for our economic survival.* 必须有出口，才能维持我们的经济。**2** [C] **~ (from sth)** something that has continued to exist from an earlier time 残存物；幸存事物 SYN **relic**: *The ceremony is a survival from pre-Christian times.* 这种仪式是从公元前遗留下来的。

IDM **the surˌvival of the ˈfittest** the principle that only the people or things that are best adapted to their surroundings will continue to exist 适者生存

sur·vival·ist /səˈvaɪvəlɪst; *NAmE* sərˈv-/ *noun* a person who prepares for a dangerous or an unpleasant situation such as a war by learning how to survive outdoors, practising how to use weapons, storing food, etc. 求生训练学员，户外生存受训者（为防备险恶状况而学习户外求生技能）▶ **sur·vival·ism** /səˈvaɪvəlɪzəm; *NAmE* sərˈv-/ *noun* [U]

surˈvival kit *noun* a set of emergency equipment, including food, medical supplies and tools 救生包（装有食物、医疗用品和工具）；救生器材

sur·vive AW /səˈvaɪv; *NAmE* sərˈv-/ *verb* **1** [I] to continue to live or exist 生存；存活；继续存在：*She was the last surviving member of the family.* 她是这家人中仅存的一员。◇ *Of the six people injured in the crash, only two survived.* 因这次撞车事故受伤的六人中，只有两人活了下来。◇ (*humorous*) *'How are you these days?' 'Oh, surviving.'* "你近来好吗？""嘻，凑合过吧。" ◇ *Don't worry, it's only a scratch—you'll survive.* 别担心，只不过是划伤，你没事的。◇ **~ from sth** *Some strange customs have survived from earlier times.* 有些奇怪的风俗是从早年留存下来的。◇ **~ on sth** *I can't survive on £40 a week* (= it is not enough for my basic needs). 一星期 40 英镑，我无法维持生活。◇ **~ as sth** *He survived as party leader until his second election defeat.* 直至第二次参选失败他才不再担任党的领导人。**2** [T] to continue to live or exist despite a dangerous event or time 幸存；幸免于难；艰难度过；**~ sth** *The company managed to survive the crisis.* 公司设法渡过了危机。◇ *Many birds didn't survive the severe winter.* 很多鸟死于这次严冬。◇ **~ sth + adj.** *Few buildings survived the war intact.* 战争之后没几座完好的建筑了。**3** [T] **~ sb/sth** to live or exist longer than sb/sth 比…活（或存在）的时间长 SYN **outlive**: *She survived her husband by ten years.* 丈夫死后她又活了十年。

sur·vivor AW /səˈvaɪvə(r); *NAmE* sərˈv-/ *noun* a person who continues to live, especially despite being nearly killed or experiencing great danger or difficulty 幸存者；生还者；挺过困难者：*the* ***sole/only survivor*** *of the massacre* 那场大屠杀的唯一幸存者 ◇ *The plane crashed in an area of dense jungle. There were no survivors.* 飞机坠落在一个丛林茂密的地区，无人生还。◇ *There are only a few survivors from the original team* (= members who remain in it while others have been replaced). 最初的队员只剩下几名了。◇ *She'll cope. She's one of life's great survivors* (= sb who deals very well with difficult situations). 她能挺过去。生活中什么样的困难她都能对付。

sus = SUSS

sus·cep·ti·bil·ity /səˌseptəˈbɪləti/ *noun* (*pl.* **-ies**) **1** [U, sing.] **~ (to sth)** the state of being very likely to be influenced, harmed or affected by sth 易受影响（或伤害等）的特性；敏感性；过敏性：*susceptibility to disease* 易患病的体质 **2** **susceptibilities** [pl.] a person's feelings which are likely to be easily hurt 感情脆弱处 SYN **sensibility**: *It was all carried out without any consideration for the susceptibilities of the bereaved family.* 这样做全然没有考虑到死者家人的感受。

sus·cep·tible /səˈseptəbl/ *adj.* **1** [not usually before noun] **~ (to sb/sth)** very likely to be influenced, harmed or affected by sb/sth 易受影响（或伤害等）；敏感；过敏：*He's highly susceptible to flattery.* 他爱听恭维话。◇ *Some of these plants are more susceptible to frost damage than others.* 这些植物中有一些较其他的易受霜冻危害。◇ *Salt intake may lead to raised blood pressure in susceptible adults.* 盐的摄入可能导致易病的成年人血压升高。**2** easily influenced by feelings and emotions 好动感情的；感情丰富的；善感的 SYN **impressionable**: *She was both charming and susceptible.* 她迷人而多情。**3 ~ (of sth)** (*formal*) allowing sth; capable of sth 容许…的；可能…的；可以…的：*Is this situation not susceptible of improvement by legislation?* 这种状况有没有可能通过立法加以改善？

sushi /ˈsuːʃi/ *noun* [U] a Japanese dish of small cakes of cold cooked rice, flavoured with VINEGAR and served with raw fish, etc. on top 寿司（日本食物，小糕饼状冷米饭配生鱼片等）：*a sushi bar* 寿司店

sus·pect *verb, noun, adj.*

> **WORD FAMILY**
> **suspect** *verb*
> **suspected** *adj.*
> **suspicion** *noun*
> **suspicious** *adj.*
> **suspiciously** *adv.*
> **suspect** *noun, adj.*

■ ***verb*** /səˈspekt/ (not used in the progressive tenses 不用于进行时) **1** [T, I] to have an idea that sth is probably true or likely to happen, especially sth bad, but without having definite proof 疑有，觉得（尤指坏事可能属实或发生）：**~ (sth)** *If you suspect a gas leak, do not strike a match or even turn on an electric light.* 假如你怀疑有煤气泄漏，不要划火柴，甚至连电灯都不要开。◇ *Suspecting nothing, he walked right into the trap.* 他毫无觉察，径直走入陷阱。◇ *As I had suspected all along, he was not a real policeman.* 他并不是真的警察，我一直就觉得不像。◇ **~ (that)...** *I began to suspect (that) they were trying to get rid of me.* 我开始觉察出，他们试图摆脱我。◇ **it is suspected that...** *It was suspected that the drugs had been brought into the country by boat.* 有人怀疑毒品是用船运入该国的。◇ **~ sb/sth to be/have sth** *She suspected him to be an impostor.* 她怀疑他是个冒名行骗者。**2** [T] to have an idea that sb is guilty of sth, without having definite proof 怀疑（某人有罪）：**~ sb/sth of sth** *He resigned after being suspected of theft.* 他被怀疑偷窃，随后就辞职了。◇ *The drug is suspected of causing over 200 deaths.* 人们怀疑这种药物造成 200 多人死亡。◇ **~ sb/sth** *Whom do the police suspect?* 警方怀疑谁？**3** [T] **~ sth** to be suspicious about sth; to not trust sth 怀疑；感觉有问题；不信任：*I suspected her motives in offering to help.* 她主动要帮忙，我怀疑她的动机。▶ **sus·pected** *adj.*: *a suspected broken arm* 怀疑骨折的胳膊 ◇ *suspected tax evasion* 逃税嫌疑 ◇ *suspected terrorists* 被怀疑从事恐怖主义活动的人

S

■***noun*** /ˈsʌspekt/ a person who is suspected of a crime or of having done sth wrong 嫌疑犯；嫌疑分子；可疑对象：*a murder suspect* 杀人嫌疑犯 ◇ *He is the **prime suspect** in the case.* 他是这个案子的首要嫌疑人。

■***adj.*** /ˈsʌspekt/ **1** that may be false and that cannot be relied on 不可信的；靠不住的 SYN **questionable**: *Some of the evidence they produced was highly suspect.* 他们出示的证据中有些相当成问题。**2** that you suspect to be dangerous or illegal 可疑的；可能有危险的；有违法嫌疑的 SYN **suspicious**: *a suspect package* (= one that may contain drugs, a bomb, etc.) 可疑包裹 ➲ MORE LIKE THIS 21, page R27

sus·pend AW /səˈspend/ *verb* **1 ~ sth/sb (from sth) (by/on sth)** (*formal*) to hang sth from sth else 悬；挂；吊：*A lamp was suspended from the ceiling.* 一盏吊灯悬在天花板上。◇ *Her body was found suspended by a rope.* 人们发现她的尸体吊在绳子上。**2 ~ sth** to officially stop sth for a time; to prevent sth from being active, used, etc. for a time 暂停；中止；使暂停发挥作用（或使用等）：*Production has been suspended while safety checks are carried out.* 在进行安全检查期间生产暂停。◇ *The constitution was suspended as the fighting grew worse.* 鉴于战斗趋于激烈，宪法暂停实施。◇ *In the theatre we willingly **suspend disbelief*** (= temporarily believe that the characters, etc. are real). 在剧院看戏时，我们自愿对一切暂不置疑。**3 ~ sth** to officially delay sth; to arrange for sth to happen later than planned 延缓；暂缓；推迟：*The introduction of the new system has been suspended until next year.* 新制度推迟到明年再行实施。◇ *to suspend judgement* (= delay forming or expressing an opinion) 暂不判断 **4** [usually passive] **~ sb (from sth)** to officially prevent sb from doing their job, going to school, etc. for a time 使暂时停职（或停学等）：*The police officer was suspended while the complaint was investigated.* 投诉调查期间，这名警员被暂停职务。**5 be suspended in sth** (*specialist*) to float in liquid or air without moving 悬浮 ➲ SEE ALSO SUSPENSION

susˌpended aniˈmation *noun* [U] **1** the state of being alive but not conscious or active 不省人事；假死 **2** a feeling that you cannot do anything because you are waiting for sth to happen 蛰伏状态

susˌpended ˈsentence *noun* a punishment given to a criminal in court which means that they will only go to prison if they commit another crime within a particular period of time 缓刑

sus·pend·er /səˈspendə(r)/ *noun* **1** [C, usually pl.] (*BrE*) (*NAmE* **gar·ter**) a short circle of ELASTIC for holding up a sock or STOCKING 吊袜带 **2 suspenders** (*NAmE*) (*BrE* **braces**) [pl.] long narrow pieces of cloth, leather, etc. for holding trousers/pants up. They are fastened to the top of the trousers/pants at the front and back and passed over the shoulders. 吊裤带；背带 ➲ VISUAL VOCAB PAGE V66

suˈspender belt *noun* (*BrE*) (*NAmE* **ˈgarter belt**) a piece of women's underwear like a belt, worn around the waist, used for holding STOCKINGS up（女用）吊袜腰带

sus·pense /səˈspens/ *noun* [U] a feeling of worry or excitement that you have when you feel that sth is going to happen, sb is going to tell you some news, etc.（对即将发生的事等的）担心；焦虑；兴奋；悬念：*a tale of mystery and suspense* 一个神秘莫测、充满悬念的故事 ◇ ***Don't keep us in suspense.** Tell us what happened!* 别让我们心老悬着了，告诉我们出了什么事！◇ *I couldn't bear the suspense a moment longer.* 这样提心吊胆，我一刻也受不了了。

sus·pen·sion AW /səˈspenʃn/ *noun* **1** [U, C] the act of officially removing sb from their job, school, team, etc. for a period of time, usually as a punishment 暂令停职（或停学、停赛等）：*suspension from school* 暂被停学 ◇ *The two players are appealing against their suspensions.* 这两名运动员请求取消对他们的停赛处罚。**2** [U, sing.] the act of delaying sth for a period of time, until a decision has been taken 暂缓；推迟；延期：*These events have led to the suspension of talks.* 这些事件导致谈判延期。**3** [U, C] the system by which a vehicle is supported on its wheels and which makes it more comfortable to ride in when the road surface is not even（车辆减震用的）悬挂系统 **4** [C, U] (*specialist*) a liquid with very small pieces of solid matter floating in it; the state of such a liquid 悬浮液；悬浮 ➲ SEE ALSO SUSPEND (5)

suˈspension bridge *noun* a bridge that hangs from steel cables that are supported by towers at each end 悬索桥；吊桥 ➲ VISUAL VOCAB PAGE V14

sus·pi·cion /səˈspɪʃn/ *noun* **1** [U, C] a feeling that sb has done sth wrong, illegal or dishonest, even though you have no proof 怀疑；嫌疑：*They drove away slowly to avoid arousing suspicion.* 他们缓缓驾车离去，以免引起怀疑。◇ *He was arrested **on suspicion of** murder.* 他因涉嫌谋杀而被捕。◇ **~ (that...)** *I have **a sneaking suspicion** that she's not telling the truth.* 我暗自怀疑她没讲实话。➲ SEE ALSO SUSPECT *n.* **2** [C] **~ (that...)** a feeling or belief that sth is true, even though you have no proof 感觉；看法：*I have a horrible suspicion that we've come to the wrong station.* 我感觉不妙，我们可能来错车站了。**3** [U, C] the feeling that you cannot trust sb/sth 猜疑；怀疑；不放心：*Their offer was greeted with some suspicion.* 他们的主动热情遭到一些猜疑。**4** [sing.] **~ of sth** (*formal*) a small amount of sth 少许；一点儿 SYN **hint**: *His mouth quivered in the suspicion of a smile.* 他嘴唇微微一颤，露出一丝笑意。

IDM **above/beyond suˈspicion** too good, honest, etc. to have done sth wrong, illegal or dishonest 无可置疑：*Nobody who was near the scene of the crime is above suspicion.* 犯罪现场附近的任何人都不能排除嫌疑。 **under suˈspicion (of sth)** suspected of doing sth wrong, illegal or dishonest 有嫌疑；涉嫌：*The whole family is currently under suspicion of her murder.* 目前这一家人都涉嫌谋杀她。◇ *A number of doctors **came under suspicion** of unethical behaviour.* 一些医生涉嫌有不道德行为。➲ MORE AT FINGER *n.*

sus·pi·cious /səˈspɪʃəs/ *adj.* **1 ~ (of/about sb/sth)** feeling that sb has done sth wrong, illegal or dishonest, without having any proof 感觉可疑的；怀疑的：*They became suspicious of his behaviour and contacted the police.* 他们开始觉得他行为可疑，便报了警。◇ *a suspicious look* 怀疑的神情 ◇ *You have a very **suspicious mind*** (= you always think that people are behaving in an illegal or dishonest way). 你疑心很重。**2** making you feel that sth is wrong, illegal or dishonest 令人怀疑的；可疑的：*Didn't you notice anything suspicious in his behaviour?* 你难道没有注意到他行为有可疑之处？◇ *She died in **suspicious circumstances**.* 她死得蹊跷。◇ *Police are not treating the fire as suspicious.* 警方认为这场火灾没有可疑之处。◇ *It was all very suspicious.* 这一切十分可疑。**3 ~ (of sb/sth)** not willing or able to trust sb/sth 不信任的；持怀疑态度的 SYN **sceptical**: *I was suspicious of his motives.* 我怀疑他的动机。◇ *Many were suspicious of reform.* 很多人对改革持怀疑态度。➲ SEE ALSO SUSPECT *adj.*

sus·pi·cious·ly /səˈspɪʃəsli/ *adv.* **1** in a way that shows you think sb has done sth wrong, illegal or dishonest 怀疑地；有疑心地：*The man looked at her suspiciously.* 那个男人以狐疑的目光看着她。**2** in a way that makes people think sth wrong, illegal or dishonest is happening 令人怀疑地；形迹（或神色等）可疑地：*Let me know if you see anyone acting suspiciously.* 如发现有人形迹可疑，你就告诉我。**3** in a way that shows you think there may be sth wrong with sth 以怀疑的态度；不信任地：*She eyed the fish on her plate suspiciously.* 她不放心地看着自己盘子里的鱼。

IDM **look/sound suspiciously like sth** (*often humorous*) to be very similar to sth 看／听上去与某事物相像得令人起疑：*Their latest single sounds suspiciously like the last one.* 他们的最新单曲唱片听着和前一张很像。

suss (*also* **sus**) /sʌs/ *verb* [T, I] **~ (sb/sth) (out) | ~ that... | ~ how, what, etc....** (*informal*) to realize sth; to understand the important things about sb/sth 意识到；认识到；发现：*I think I've **got him sussed*** (= now I understand him). 我想我已了解他了。◇ *If you want to succeed in business*

S

you have to suss out the competition. 要想在生意场上立足，你必须真正明白竞争是怎么回事。◇ *He cheated on her for years, but she never sussed.* 他有外遇多年了，但她从来没有察觉。

sussed /sʌst/ *adj.* (*BrE, informal*) knowing what you need to know about the situations and people around you, so that you are not easily tricked and are able to take care of yourself 有（处世）经验而不易上当的；门槛精的

sus·tain AW /səˈsteɪn/ *verb* **1 ~ sb/sth** to provide enough of what sb/sth needs in order to live or exist 维持（生命、生存）：*Which planets can sustain life?* 哪些行星可以维持生命的存在？ ◇ *The love and support of his family sustained him during his time in prison.* 家人的关爱和支持帮助他度过了狱中的岁月。**2 ~ sth** to make sth continue for some time without becoming less 使保持；使稳定持续 SYN **maintain**: *a period of sustained economic growth* 经济持续增长的时期 ◇ *a sustained attack* 持续的攻击 ◇ *She managed to sustain everyone's interest until the end of her speech.* 她使每个人兴趣盎然，一直听她把话讲完。**3 ~ sth** (*formal*) to experience sth bad 遭受；蒙受；经受 SYN **suffer**: *to **sustain damage/an injury/a defeat*** 遭受损失；受伤；遭到失败 ◇ *The company **sustained losses** of millions of dollars.* 公司遭受了数百万美元计的巨大损失。**4 ~ sth** to provide evidence to support an opinion, a theory, etc. 证明；证实 SYN **uphold**: *The evidence is not detailed enough to sustain his argument.* 这一证据过于笼统，不足以证明他的论点。**5 ~ sth** (*formal*) to support a weight without breaking or falling 支撑；承受住 SYN **bear**: *The ice will not sustain your weight.* 这冰承受不了你的体重。**6 ~ sth** (*law* 律) to decide that a claim, etc. is valid 认可；确认；准许；支持 SYN **uphold**: *The court sustained his claim that the contract was illegal.* 法庭支持他的主张，认定该合同不合法。◇ ***Objection sustained!*** (= said by a judge when a lawyer makes an OBJECTION in court) 反对有效！

sus·tain·able AW /səˈsteɪnəbl/ *adj.* **1** involving the use of natural products and energy in a way that does not harm the environment（对自然资源和能源的利用）不破坏生态平衡的，合理利用的：*sustainable forest management* 合理的森林管理 ◇ *an environmentally sustainable society* 保持生态环境平衡的社会 ➲ WORDFINDER NOTE AT GREEN **2** that can continue or be continued for a long time 可持续的：*sustainable economic growth* 经济的可持续增长 OPP **unsustainable** ▸ **sus·tain·abil·ity** AW /səˌsteɪnəˈbɪləti/ *noun* [U] **sus·tain·ably** *adv.*

sus·ten·ance AW /ˈsʌstənəns/ *noun* [U] (*formal*) **1** the food and drink that people, animals and plants need to live and stay healthy 食物；营养；养料：*There's not much sustenance in a bowl of soup.* 一碗汤没多少营养。◇ (*figurative*) *Arguing would only give further sustenance to his allegations.* 越是争论，他越会觉得自己那些说法有道理。**2 ~ (of sth)** the process of making sth continue to exist 维持；保持：*Elections are essential for the sustenance of parliamentary democracy.* 选举制度是维持议会民主所必不可少的。

sutra /ˈsuːtrə/ *noun* **1** a rule or statement in Sanskrit literature, or a set of rules （梵文的）箴言，格言，经 **2** a Buddhist or Jainist holy text（佛教或耆那教的）修多罗，经

sut·tee = SATI

su·ture /ˈsuːtʃə(r)/ *noun, verb*

■ ***noun*** (*medical* 医) a STITCH or stitches made when sewing up a wound, especially after an operation（尤指手术后伤口的）缝合，缝线

■ ***verb*** **~ sth** (*medical* 医) to sew up a wound 缝合（伤口）

SUV /ˌes juː ˈviː/ *noun* SPORT UTILITY VEHICLE

su·zer·ainty /ˈsuːzəremti; -rənti/ *noun* [U] (*formal*) the right of a country to rule over another country 宗主权

Sv *abbr.* SIEVERT

svelte /svelt; sfelt/ *adj.* (*approving*) (of a person, especially a woman 人，尤指女子) thin and attractive 苗条的；身材修长的

Sven·gali /svenˈɡɑːli/ *noun* a person who has the power to control another person's mind, make them do bad things, etc. 能控制他人思想的人；能使人干坏事（或唯命是从）的人 ➲ MORE LIKE THIS 17, page R27 ORIGIN From the name of a character in George du Maurier's novel *Trilby*. 源自乔治·杜·莫里哀的小说《软毡帽》中的人物斯文加利。

SW *abbr.* **1** (*especially BrE*) SHORT WAVE 短波：*SW and LW radio* 短波及长波无线电设备 **2** south-west; south-western 西南方（的）；西南部（的）：*SW Australia* 澳大利亚西南部

swab /swɒb; *NAmE* swɑːb/ *noun, verb*

■ ***noun*** **1** a piece of soft material used by a doctor, nurse, etc. for cleaning wounds or taking a sample from sb's body for testing（医用的）拭子，药签 **2** an act of taking a sample from sb's body, with a swab 用拭子对（人体）化验标本的采集：*to take a throat swab* 用棉签从咽部采集化验样品 ➲ WORDFINDER NOTE AT EXAMINE

■ ***verb*** (**-bb-**) **1 ~ sth** to clean or remove liquid from a wound, etc., using a swab 用拭子擦拭 **2 ~ sth (down)** to clean or wash a floor, surface, etc. using water and a cloth, etc. 擦洗，擦拭（地板等）

swad·dle /ˈswɒdl; *NAmE* ˈswɑːdl/ *verb* **~ sb/sth** (*old-fashioned*) to wrap sb/sth, especially a baby, tightly in clothes or a piece of cloth（用衣服或布）紧裹，包裹（尤指婴儿）

ˈswaddling clothes *noun* [pl.] strips of cloth used in the past for wrapping a baby tightly 包裹婴儿的布；襁褓

swa·deshi /swæˈdeʃi/ *adj.* (*IndE*) made in India from materials that have also been produced in India 印度国产的

swag /swæɡ/ *noun* **1** [U] (*old-fashioned, informal*) goods that have been stolen 被盗货品；赃物 SYN **loot** **2** [C, usually pl.] cloth that is hung in large curved folds as decoration, especially above a window（挂于窗户等上方的）装饰性布幔（或帷幕）**3** (*AustralE, NZE*) a pack of things tied or wrapped together and carried by a traveller（旅行者携带的）包裹；行囊 **4** [C, usually pl.] a bunch of flowers or fruit that is CARVED onto walls, etc. as decoration 垂花饰（雕刻装饰，形状为串起来的花、果等）

swag·ger /ˈswæɡə(r)/ *verb, noun*

■ ***verb*** [I] (+ **adv./prep.**) (*usually disapproving*) to walk in an extremely proud and confident way 神气十足地走；大摇大摆地走 SYN **strut**

■ ***noun*** [sing.] (*disapproving*) a way of walking or behaving that seems too confident 神气十足；大摇大摆

swag·man /ˈswæɡmæn/ *noun* (*pl.* **-men** /-men/) (*AustralE, NZE, old use*) a man who travels around looking for work, carrying his possessions wrapped in a cloth 背着行囊四处找工作的人

Swa·hili /swəˈhiːli; swɑːˈh-/ (*also* **Ki·swa·hili**) *noun* [U] a language widely used in E Africa, especially between people who speak different first languages 斯瓦希里语（通行于东非，尤作第二语言）

swain /sweɪn/ *noun* (*old use* or *humorous*) a young man who is in love 情郎

swal·low 🔑 /ˈswɒləʊ; *NAmE* ˈswɑːloʊ/ *verb, noun*

■ ***verb***

• **FOOD/DRINK** 食物；饮料 **1** 🔑 [T, I] to make food, drink, etc. go down your throat into your stomach 吞下；咽下：**~ (sth)** *Always chew food well before swallowing it.* 什么食物都要先嚼碎再吞咽。◇ *I had a sore throat and it hurt to swallow.* 当时我嗓子疼，咽东西就疼。◇ **~ sth + adj.** *The pills should be swallowed whole.* 这些药要吞服。

• **MOVE THROAT MUSCLES** 做吞咽动作 **2** 🔑 [I] to move the muscles of your throat as if you were swallowing sth, especially because you are nervous （由于紧张等）做吞咽动作：*She **swallowed hard** and told him the bad news.* 她使劲咽了口唾沫，把坏消息告诉了他。

• **COMPLETELY COVER** 完全覆盖 **3** [T, often passive] to take sb/sth in or completely cover it so that they cannot be seen or no longer exist separately 吞没；淹没；侵吞：~ **sb/sth** *I watched her walk down the road until she was swallowed by the darkness.* 我看着她沿公路越走越远，直至消失在黑暗中。◇ ~ **sb/sth up** *Large areas of countryside have been swallowed up by towns.* 大片大片的乡村地区被城镇吞噬。

• **USE UP MONEY** 用尽钱 **4** [T] ~ **sb/sth** (**up**) to use up sth completely, especially an amount of money 用尽，耗尽，花光（钱等）：*Most of my salary gets swallowed (up) by the rent and bills.* 我的工资大多支付房租和各种日常费用了。

• **BELIEVE** 相信 **5** [T] to accept that sth is true; to believe sth 相信；信以为真：~ **sth** *I found her excuse very* ***hard to swallow****.* 我觉得她的理由很难让人相信。◇ ~ **sth + adj.** *He told her a pack of lies, but she* ***swallowed it whole****.* 他对她讲了一堆假话，可她全都信以为真。

• **FEELINGS** 感情 **6** [T] ~ **sth** to hide your feelings 不流露；掩饰；抑制：*to swallow your doubts* 不流露怀疑 ◇ *You're going to have to* ***swallow your pride*** *and ask for your job back.* 你得放下架子，去求人家给你恢复原职。

• **ACCEPT INSULTS** 忍受侮辱 **7** [T] ~ **sth** to accept insults, criticisms, etc. without complaining or protesting 默默忍受（侮辱、批评等）：*I was surprised that he just sat there and swallowed all their remarks.* 让我吃惊的是他就坐在那儿默默地任凭他们评论。 IDM SEE BITTER *adj.*

■ *noun*

• **BIRD** 鸟 **1** a small bird with long pointed wings and a tail with two points, that spends the winter in Africa but flies to northern countries for the summer 燕

• **OF FOOD/DRINK** 食物；饮料 **2** an act of swallowing; an amount of food or drink that is swallowed at one time 咽；吞；一次吞咽的量；一口

IDM **one ˌswallow doesn't make a ˈsummer** (*saying*) you must not take too seriously a small sign that sth is happening or will happen in the future, because the situation could change 别略有好事就以为佳时已到；好事可能纯属偶然；一燕不成夏（不能单凭微小的迹象而下定论）

ˈswallow dive (*BrE*) (*NAmE* **ˈswan dive**) *noun* a DIVE performed with your arms stretched out sideways until you are close to the water 燕式跳水（接近水面前保持双臂向两侧张开）

ˈswallow hole *noun* = SINKHOLE

swam PAST TENSE OF SWIM

swami /ˈswɑːmi/ *noun* (also used as a title 亦用作称号) a Hindu religious teacher 印度教宗教教师：*Swami Vivekananda* 维韦卡南达导师（法号辨喜）

swamp /swɒmp; *NAmE* swɑːmp/ *noun, verb*

■ *noun* [C, U] an area of ground that is very wet or covered with water and in which plants, trees, etc. are growing 沼泽（地） SYN **marsh**: *tropical swamps* 热带沼泽 ▶ **swampy** *adj.*: *swampy ground* 沼泽地

■ *verb* [often passive] **1** to make sb have more of sth than they can deal with 使不堪承受；使疲于应对；使应接不暇 SYN **inundate**: ~ **sb/sth with sth** *The department was swamped with job applications.* 面对纷至沓来的求职申请，这个部门疲于应对。◇ ~ **sb/sth** *In summer visitors swamp the island.* 夏天，这个岛上游客熙熙攘攘，人满为患。**2** ~ **sth** to fill or cover sth with a lot of water 淹；淹没 SYN **engulf**: *The little boat was swamped by the waves.* 小船被大浪淹没了。

ˈswamp fever *noun* [U] **1** a serious disease that affects horses 沼泽热；马传染性贫血 **2** (*old-fashioned*) = MALARIA 疟疾

swamp·land /ˈswɒmplænd; *NAmE* ˈswɑːmp-/ *noun* [U, pl.] a large area of SWAMP 沼泽地

swan /swɒn; *NAmE* swɑːn/ *noun, verb*

■ *noun* a large bird that is usually white and has a long thin neck. Swans live on or near water. 天鹅

■ *verb* (**-nn-**) [I] **+ adv./prep.** (*informal, disapproving*) to go around enjoying yourself in a way that annoys other people or makes them jealous 悠游；悠然闲逛：*They've gone swanning off to Paris for the weekend.* 他们周末到巴黎潇洒去了。

ˈswan dive (*NAmE*) (*BrE* **ˈswallow dive**) *noun* a DIVE performed with your arms stretched out sideways until you are close to the water 燕式跳水（接近水面前保持双臂向两侧张开）

swank /swæŋk/ *verb* [I] (*old-fashioned, BrE, informal, disapproving*) to behave in way that is too proud or confident 炫耀；卖弄

swanky /ˈswæŋki/ (**swank·ier**, **swanki·est**) (*especially BrE*) (*also* **swank** *especially in NAmE*) *adj.* (*informal, approving*) fashionable and expensive in a way that is intended to impress people 摆阔的；时髦且豪华的：*a swanky new hotel* 时髦豪华的新旅馆

swan·song /ˈswɒnsɒŋ; *NAmE* ˈswɑːnsɔːŋ/ *noun* [sing.] the last piece of work produced by an artist, a musician, etc. or the last performance by an actor, ATHLETE, etc. （艺术家、音乐家等）最后的作品；（演员的）告别演出；（运动员的）告别比赛

swap (*also* **swop**) /swɒp; *NAmE* swɑːp/ *verb, noun*

■ *verb* (**-pp-**) **1** [I, T] to give sth to sb and receive sth in exchange 交换（东西）：~ (**sth**) (**with sb**) *I've finished this magazine. Can I swap with you?* 这本杂志我看完了，能跟你交换一下吗？◇ ~ **sth for sth** *I swapped my red scarf for her blue one.* 我用我的红围巾换了她的蓝围巾。◇ ~ **sth** *Can we swap places? I can't see the screen.* 咱俩交换一下座位好不好？我看不见银幕。◇ *We spent the evening in the pub* ***swapping stories*** (= telling each other stories) *about our travels.* 我们一晚上坐在酒吧里讲述各自的旅途经历。◇ ~ **sb sth for sth** *I swapped him my CD for his posters.* 我拿我的光盘换了他的海报。**2** [I] ~ (**over**) to start doing sb else's job, etc. while they do yours 交换（工作）：*I'll drive there and then we'll swap over on the way back.* 去的时候我开车，回来的时候咱俩再倒换过来。**3** [T] (*especially BrE*) to replace one person or thing with another 用…替换；把…换成；掉换：~ **sb/sth** (**for sb/sth**) *I think I'll swap this sweater for one in another colour.* 我想把这件毛衣换成其他颜色的。◇ ~ **sb/sth** (**over**) *I'm going to swap you over. Mike will go first and Jon will go second.* 我打算把你俩掉换一下。迈克先去，乔恩后去。
IDM SEE PLACE *n.*

■ *noun* **1** [usually sing.] an act of exchanging one thing or person for another 交换；掉换：*Let's* ***do a swap****. You work Friday night and I'll do Saturday.* 咱俩调个班吧。你星期五晚间上，我星期六上。**2** a thing or person that has been exchanged for another 交换物；被掉换者：*Most of my football stickers are swaps.* 我的足球贴纸多数都是跟别人换来的。

ˈswap meet *noun* (*especially NAmE*) an occasion at which people buy and sell or exchange items that interest them 物品交流会；收藏品交流会：*a swap meet for collectors of Star Trek memorabilia*《星际迷航》纪念品收藏者交流会

sward /swɔːd; *NAmE* swɔːrd/ *noun* [C, U] (*literary*) an area of grass 草地；草皮

swarm /swɔːm; *NAmE* swɔːrm/ *noun, verb*

■ *noun* ~ (**of sth**) **1** a large group of insects, especially BEES, moving together in the same direction 一大群（蜜蜂等昆虫）：*a swarm of bees/locusts/flies* 一大群蜜蜂 / 蝗虫 / 苍蝇 **2** a large group of people, especially when they are all moving quickly in the same direction 一大群，一大批（向同方向移动的人） SYN **horde**

■ *verb* **1** [I] **+ adv./prep.** (*often disapproving*) (of people, animals, etc. 人、动物等) to move around in a large group 成群地来回移动：*Tourists were swarming all over the island.* 岛上到处是旅游者熙来攘往。**2** (of BEES and other flying insects 蜜蜂或其他飞行昆虫) to move around together in a large group, looking for a place to live 成群地飞来飞去

PHR V **ˈswarm with sb/sth** to be full of people or things 到处是人（或物）；挤满：*The capital city is swarming with police.* 首都到处是警察。

S

swar·thy /ˈswɔːði; *NAmE* ˈswɔːrði/ *adj.* (especially of a person or their face 尤指人或人脸) having dark skin 肤色深的；皮肤黝黑的

swash /swɒʃ; *NAmE* swɔːʃ; swɑːʃ/ *noun* [sing.] (*specialist*) the flow of water up the beach after a wave has BROKEN（浪头拍岸后的）冲激，溅泼

swash·buck·ling /ˈswɒʃbʌklɪŋ; *NAmE* ˈswɔːʃ-; ˈswɑːʃ-/ *adj.* [only before noun] (especially of films/movies 尤指电影) set in the past and full of action, adventure, fighting with SWORDS, etc. 表现古代惊险打斗的；有传奇历险情节的：*a swashbuckling tale of adventure on the high seas* 公海上的传奇历险故事 ◊ *the swashbuckling hero of Hollywood epics* 好莱坞史诗片中的传奇英雄

swas·tika /ˈswɒstɪkə; *NAmE* ˈswɑːs-/ *noun* an ancient symbol in the form of a cross with its ends bent at an angle of 90°, used in the 20th century as the symbol of the German Nazi party 万字符

swat /swɒt; *NAmE* swɑːt/ *verb* (**-tt-**) **~ sth** to hit sth, especially an insect, using your hand or a flat object 拍，打（昆虫等） ▸ **swat** *noun*

swatch /swɒtʃ; *NAmE* swɑːtʃ/ *noun* a small piece of cloth used to show people what a larger piece would look or feel like（织物的小块）样品；布样

swathe /sweɪð/ *noun, verb*

■ ***noun*** (*also* **swath** /swɒθ; *NAmE* swɑːθ/) (*formal*) **1** a long strip of land, especially one on which the plants or crops have been cut（尤指割了庄稼的）一长条田地：*The combine had cut a swathe around the edge of the field.* 联合收割机把庄稼绕田边割了一长条。◊ *Development has affected vast swathes of our countryside.* 开发建设影响了乡村广大地区。**2** a large strip or area of sth 一长条；一长片：*The mountains rose above a swathe of thick cloud.* 群峰耸立在云海之上。

IDM **cut a ˈswathe through sth** (of a person, fire, etc. 人、火等) to pass through a particular area destroying a large part of it 把（某地的一大片）夷为平地；使…大部分遭受破坏

■ ***verb*** [usually passive] **~ sb/sth (in sth)** (*formal*) to wrap or cover sb/sth in sth 包；裹；覆盖：*He was lying on the hospital bed, swathed in bandages.* 他裹着绷带，躺在医院的病床上。

S

ˈSWAT team *noun* (*especially US*) a group of police officers who are especially trained to deal with violent situations. SWAT stands for 'Special Weapons and Tactics'. 特警队（SWAT 全写为 Special Weapons and Tactics）

sway /sweɪ/ *verb, noun*

■ ***verb*** **1** [I, T] to move slowly from side to side; to move sth in this way（使）摇摆，摇动：**(+ adv./prep.)** *The branches were swaying in the wind.* 树枝在风中摇曳。◊ *Vicky swayed and fell.* 维基摇晃着倒下了。◊ **~ sth (+ adv./prep.)** *They danced rhythmically, swaying their hips to the music.* 他们伴着音乐扭动屁股，有节奏地跳舞。**2** [T, often passive] **~ sb** to persuade sb to believe sth or do sth 说服；使相信；使动摇 SYN **influence**：*He's easily swayed.* 他很容易动摇。◊ *She wasn't swayed by his good looks or his clever talk.* 他相貌不凡，谈吐风趣，但她不为所动。

■ ***noun*** [U] **1** a movement from side to side 摇摆；摆动 **2** (*literary*) power or influence over sb 统治；势力；支配；控制；影响：*Rebel forces **hold sway** over much of the island.* 该岛很大一部分控制在叛军手里。◊ *He was quick to exploit those who fell **under his sway**.* 他毫不犹豫地利用受他控制的那些人。

swear 🔑 /sweə(r); *NAmE* swer/ *verb* (**swore** /swɔː(r)/, **sworn** /swɔːn; *NAmE* swɔːrn/) **1** 🔑 [I] to use rude or offensive language, usually because you are angry 咒骂；诅咒；说脏话：*She fell over and swore loudly.* 她摔倒了，大骂了一声。◊ **~ at sb/sth** *Why did you let him swear at you like that?* 你怎么听任他那样辱骂你呢？**2** 🔑 [T, no passive] to make a serious promise to do sth 郑重承诺；发誓要；表示决心要 SYN **vow**：**~ sth** *He swore revenge on the man who had killed his father.* 他发誓要向那个杀死他父亲的人报仇。◊ **~ (that)...** *I swear (that) I'll never leave you.* 我保证决不离开你。HELP 'That' is usually left out, especially in speech. * that 常省略，在口语中尤其如此。◊ **~ to do sth** *She made him swear not to tell anyone.* 她要他发誓不告诉任何人。**3** 🔑 [T] to promise that you are telling the truth 赌咒发誓地说；肯定地说：**~ (that)...** *She swore (that) she'd never seen him before.* 她明确表示自己以前从未见过他。◊ ***I could have sworn*** (= I am sure) *I heard the phone ring.* 我敢肯定我听见电话铃响了。◊ **~ to sb/on sth (that)...** *I swear to God I had nothing to do with it.* 我可以对天发誓，这跟我一点关系也没有。**4** 🔑 [I, T] to make a public or an official promise, especially in court（尤指在法庭上）发誓，郑重承诺：**~ (on sth)** *Witnesses were required to swear on the Bible.* 证人须手按《圣经》宣誓。◊ **~ that...** *Are you willing to stand up in court and swear that you don't recognize him?* 你愿出庭起誓说你不认识他吗？◊ **~ to do sth** *Remember, you have sworn to tell the truth.* 别忘记，你宣过誓要讲实话。◊ **~ sth** *Barons had to swear an oath of allegiance to the king.* 男爵须宣誓效忠国王。➲ MORE LIKE THIS 26, page R28 **5** [T] **~ sb to secrecy/silence** to make sb promise not to tell sth to anyone 使起誓（保密）：*Everyone was sworn to secrecy about what had happened.* 关于已发生的事，每个人都依照要求起誓不外传。➲ SEE ALSO SWORN (1)

IDM **swear ˈblind** (*informal*) to say that sth is definitely true 一口咬定 **swear like a ˈtrooper** (*old-fashioned, BrE*) to often use very rude or offensive language 满口脏话；动不动就破口大骂

PHR V **ˈswear by sb/sth** **1** to name sb/sth to show that you are making a serious promise 以…名义发誓；对…发誓：*I swear by almighty God that I will tell the truth.* 我向全能的上帝起誓，我以下所说句句属实。**2** (not used in the progressive tenses 不用于进行时) to be certain that sth is good or useful 极信赖；对…推崇备至：*She swears by meditation as a way of relieving stress.* 她深信冥想有助于缓解压力。**ˌswear sb↔ˈin | ˌswear sb ˈinto sth** [often passive] to make sb promise to do a job correctly, to be loyal to an organization, a country, etc. 使某人宣誓就职；使某人宣誓忠于某组织（或国家等）：*He was sworn in as president.* 他宣誓就任总统。◊ *The new prime minister was sworn into office.* 新首相宣誓就职。➲ RELATED NOUN SWEARING-IN **ˌswear ˈoff sth** (*informal*) to promise that you will not do or use sth again 保证不再做某事（或用某物）；发誓放弃…：*I decided to swear off burgers forever.* 我决心永远不再吃汉堡包。**ˈswear to sth** (*informal*) to say that sth is definitely true 一口咬定：*I think I put the keys back in the drawer, but I couldn't swear to it* (= I'm not completely sure). 我想我把钥匙放回抽屉里了，不过我不敢肯定。

swear·ing 🔑 /ˈsweərɪŋ; *NAmE* ˈswerɪŋ/ *noun* [U] rude or offensive language 诅咒语；骂人的话；脏话：*I was shocked at the swearing.* 我听到这脏话很震惊。

ˌswearing-ˈin *noun* [U, sing.] the act of publicly asking sb to promise to be loyal and perform their duties well when they start a new job, etc. 宣誓就职：*the swearing-in of the new President* 新总统的宣誓就职

ˈswear word *noun* a rude or offensive word, used, for example, to express anger（表示气愤等的）诅咒语，骂人的话，脏话 SYN **expletive**

sweat 🔑 /swet/ *noun, verb*

■ ***noun***

• **LIQUID ON SKIN** 汗水 **1** 🔑 [U] drops of liquid that appear on the surface of your skin when you are hot, ill/sick or afraid 汗 SYN **perspiration**：*beads of sweat* 汗珠 ◊ *She wiped the sweat from her face.* 她擦去脸上的汗水。◊ *By the end of the match, the sweat was pouring off him.* 到比赛结束时，他已经大汗淋漓了。➲ SEE ALSO SWEATY **2** 🔑 [usually sing.] the state of being covered with sweat 出汗；流汗；一身汗：*I woke up in a sweat.* 我醒来时浑身是汗。◊ *She completed the routine without even **working up a sweat**.* 她完成了一套常规动作，连一滴汗都没出。◊ *He **breaks out in a sweat** just at the thought of flying.* 他一想到飞行，就浑身冒汗。◊ *He started having night sweats.* 他开始夜间盗汗。➲ SEE ALSO COLD SWEAT

• **HARD WORK** 繁重的工作 **3** [U] hard work or effort 繁重的工作；艰苦的劳动；累活儿；艰苦努力：(*informal*) *Growing your own vegetables sounds like a lot of sweat.* 自己种菜吃，这恐怕很累吧。◇ (*literary*) *She achieved success by **the sweat of her brow*** (= by working very hard). 她靠吃苦流汗获得了成功。
• **CLOTHES** 衣服 **4 sweats** [pl.] (*informal, especially NAmE*) a SWEATSUIT or SWEATPANTS 运动服；运动裤：*I hung around the house all day in my sweats.* 我穿着运动服在家里晃荡了一整天。
IDM **be/get in a 'sweat (about sth)** to be/become anxious or frightened about sth（为某事）担心，焦虑，害怕 **break 'sweat** (*BrE*) (*NAmE* **break a 'sweat**) (*informal*) to use a lot of physical effort 花大力气；苦干：*He hardly needed to break sweat to reach the final.* 他几乎不费劲儿就取得了决赛权。**no 'sweat** (*informal*) used to tell sb that sth is not difficult or a problem when they thank you or ask you to do sth（回答致谢或请求）没什么，小事一桩：*'Thanks for everything.' 'Hey, no sweat!'* "谢谢你帮了这么多忙。" "哦，没什么！" ➲ MORE AT BLOOD *n.*
■ *verb*
• **PRODUCE LIQUID ON SKIN/SURFACE** 出汗；渗出液体 **1** 🔑 [I, T] when you **sweat**, drops of liquid appear on the surface of your skin, for example when you are hot, ill/sick or afraid 出汗；流汗 SYN **perspire**：*to sweat heavily* 汗流浃背 ◇ **~ sth** *He was **sweating buckets*** (= a lot). 他大汗淋漓。**2** [I] if sth **sweats**, the liquid that is contained in it appears on its surface（物体表面）渗出水分，结水珠：*The cheese was beginning to sweat.* 奶酪开始出水了。
• **WORK HARD** 努力工作 **3** [I] **~ (over sth)** to work hard at sth 艰苦努力；辛苦地干：*Are you still sweating over that report?* 你还在为那篇报道伤脑筋吗？
• **WORRY** 担心 **4** [I] (*informal*) to worry or feel anxious about sth 担心；焦虑；不安：*They really made me sweat during the interview.* 面试过程中，他们的确使我忐忑不安。
• **HEAT FOOD** 烹调 **5** [T, I] **~ (sth)** (*BrE*) if you **sweat** meat or vegetables or let them **sweat**, you heat them slowly with a little fat in a pan that is covered with a lid 焖
IDM **don't 'sweat it** (*NAmE, informal*) used to tell sb to stop worrying about sth 别担心；别发愁 **don't sweat the 'small stuff** (*NAmE, informal*) used to tell sb not to worry about small details or unimportant things 不要为鸡毛蒜皮的事伤脑筋 **sweat 'blood** (*informal*) to work very hard 苦干；卖命地工作 ➲ MORE AT GUT *n.*
PHR V **,sweat sth↔'off** to lose weight by doing a lot of hard exercise to make yourself sweat 通过排汗减轻体重 **,sweat it 'out** (*informal*) to be waiting for sth difficult or unpleasant to end, and be feeling anxious about it 熬过；焦急地等待到最后

sweat·band /'swetbænd/ *noun* a band of cloth worn around the head or wrist, for absorbing sweat（扎在头上或手腕上的）吸汗带

,sweated 'labour *noun* [U] (*BrE*) hard work that is done for low wages in poor conditions; the people who do this work 血汗活儿（劳动条件恶劣、工资低廉）；血汗劳工

sweat·er 🔑 /'swetə(r)/ *noun* a knitted piece of clothing made of wool or cotton for the upper part of the body, with long sleeves. In British English the word is used to describe a piece of clothing with no buttons. In American English a sweater can have buttons and be like a jacket. 毛衣，线衣（英式英语指套头无扣的；美式英语可指开襟有扣的）➲ VISUAL VOCAB PAGE V68

sweat·pants /'swetpænts/ (*also informal* **sweats**) *noun* [pl.] (*especially NAmE*) loose warm trousers/pants, usually made of thick cotton and worn for relaxing or playing sports in（厚长）运动裤

sweat·shirt /'swetʃɜːt; *NAmE* -ʃɜːrt/ *noun* a piece of clothing for the upper part of the body, with long sleeves, usually made of thick cotton and often worn for sports（长袖）运动衫

sweat·shop /'swetʃɒp; *NAmE* -ʃɑːp/ *noun* (*disapproving*) a place where people work for low wages in poor conditions 血汗工厂，血汗工场（工资低廉、劳动条件恶劣）➲ WORDFINDER NOTE AT POOR

sweat·suit /'swetsuːt; *BrE also* -sjuːt/ *noun* (*also informal* **sweats** [pl.]) (*both NAmE*) a sweatshirt and SWEATPANTS worn together, for relaxing or playing sports in（长袖）运动套装

sweaty /'sweti/ *adj.* (**sweat·ier, sweati·est**) **1** covered or damp with sweat 满是汗的；汗津津的；汗水湿透的：*sweaty feet* 汗湿的脚 ◇ *He felt all hot and sweaty.* 他感觉全身发热，满身是汗。**2** [only before noun] making you become hot and covered with sweat 热得让人出汗的：*It was sweaty work, under the hot sun.* 在火辣辣的太阳下干这活儿，让人汗流浃背。

swede /swiːd/ (*BrE*) (*NAmE* **ru·ta·baga**) (*ScotE* **tur·nip**) *noun* [C, U] a large round yellow root vegetable 芜菁甘蓝；大头菜 ➲ VISUAL VOCAB PAGE V34

sweep 🔑 /swiːp/ *verb, noun*
■ *verb* (**swept, swept** /swept/)
• **WITH BRUSH OR HAND** 用刷子或手 **1** 🔑 [T, I] to clean a room, surface, etc. using a BROOM (= a type of brush on a long handle) 扫；打扫；清扫：**~ (sth)** *to sweep the floor* 清扫地板 ◇ **~ sth + adj.** *The showroom had been emptied and swept clean.* 陈列室已经清理出来，打扫干净了。**2** 🔑 [T] **~ sth + adv./prep.** to remove sth from a surface using a brush, your hand, etc. 扫去；清除：*She swept the crumbs into the wastebasket.* 她把面包屑扫进废纸篓里。◇ *He swept the leaves up into a pile.* 他把树叶扫成一堆。
• **MOVE QUICKLY/WITH FORCE** 快速 / 猛烈移动 **3** [T] **~ sb/sth + adv./prep.** to move or push sb/sth suddenly and with a lot of force（迅猛地）推送，吹走，冲走，带走：*The little boat was swept out to sea.* 小船被吹到大海里去了。◇ *She let herself be swept along by the crowd.* 她任由自己被人流挟裹着前行。**4** [I, T] (of weather, fire, etc. 风、雨、雪、火等) to move suddenly and/or with force over an area or in a particular direction 猛烈吹过；掠过；席卷；横扫：**+ adv./prep.** *Rain swept in through the broken windows.* 雨水从破窗户灌进屋内。◇ **~ sth** *Strong winds regularly sweep the islands.* 这些岛上经常刮大风。
• **OF A PERSON** 人 **5** [I] **+ adv./prep.** to move quickly and/or smoothly, especially in a way that impresses or is intended to impress other people 步态轻盈地走；大模大样地走：*Without another word she swept out of the room.* 她再没说话，大模大样地走出房间。◇ (*figurative*) *He swept into the lead with an almost perfect performance.* 他以几近完美的表现跨入领先位置。**6** [T] **~ sth + adv./prep.** to move sth, especially your hand or arm, quickly and smoothly in a particular direction 挥动，舞动（手、臂等）：*He rushed to greet her, sweeping his arms wide.* 他张开双臂舞动着，冲过去迎接她。
• **OF FEELINGS** 感受 **7** [I] **+ adv./prep.** to suddenly affect sb strongly 突然袭来：*A wave of tiredness swept over her.* 她感到浑身疲惫。◇ *Memories came sweeping back.* 往事倏地又浮现在脑海中。
• **OF IDEAS/FASHIONS** 思想；时尚 **8** [I, T] to spread quickly 迅速传播：**+ adv./prep.** *Rumours of his resignation swept through the company.* 他辞职的传言在全公司传播开了。◇ **~ sth** *the latest craze sweeping America* 风靡美国的最新时尚
• **LOOK/MOVE OVER AREA** 扫视；掠过 **9** [I, T] to move over an area, especially in order to look for sth 扫视；掠过；搜索：**+ adv./prep.** *His eyes swept around the room.* 他把房间扫视了一遍。◇ **~ sth** *Searchlights swept the sky.* 探照灯在空中扫来扫去。
• **TOUCH SURFACE** 轻触表面 **10** [T] **~ sth** to move, or move sth, over a surface, touching it lightly（使）轻轻掠过，轻轻擦过：*Her dress swept the ground as she walked.* 她行走时衣裙拖在地上。
• **HAIR** 头发 **11** [T] **~ sth + adv./prep.** to brush, COMB, etc. your hair in a particular direction 梳；刷；掠：*Her hair was swept back from her face.* 她的头发是从前边往后梳的。
• **OF LANDSCAPE** 地貌 **12** [I] **+ adv./prep.** to form a long smooth curve 蜿蜒；呈缓坡延伸：*The hotel gardens sweep down to the beach.* 旅馆的花园呈缓坡一直延伸到海滩。

S

- **IN SPORT** 体育运动 **13** [T] **~ sth** (*NAmE*) to win all the games in a series of games against another team or all the parts of a contest（在系列比赛中）获得全部胜利，囊括各项冠军：*The Blue Jays have a chance to sweep the series.* 蓝鸟队有机会横扫系列赛。◇ *New Jersey swept Detroit last season.* 在上个赛季，新泽西队全胜底特律队。

IDM **sweep the 'board** to win all the prizes, etc. in a competition（在比赛中）囊括所有奖项 **,sweep sb off their 'feet** to make sb fall suddenly and deeply in love with you 使某人立刻迷上自己；使某人对自己一见倾心 **sweep (sb) to 'power** to win an election by a large number of votes; to make sb win an election with a large number of votes（使某人）以压倒性优势在选举中获胜 **sweep to 'victory** to win a contest easily 轻易赢得（竞赛）：*Obama swept to victory in 2008.* 奥巴马在 2008 年轻松取胜。**sweep sth under the 'carpet** (*US also* **sweep sth under the 'rug**) to try to stop people from finding out about sth wrong, illegal, embarrassing, etc. that has happened or that you have done 掩盖某事

PHR V **,sweep sb a'long/a'way** [usually passive] to make sb very interested or involved in sth, especially in a way that makes them forget everything else 使某人醉心；驱使某人专注：*They were swept along by the force of their emotions.* 他们受感情的力量所驱使。**,sweep sth↔a'side** to ignore sth completely 对…置之不理；不理会；全然无视：*All their advice was swept aside.* 他们所有的忠告全被当成了耳边风。**,sweep sth↔a'way** to get rid of sth completely 消灭；彻底消除；完全打消：*Any doubts had long since been swept away.* 一切怀疑早已完全消除。**,sweep sth↔'out** to remove all the dust, dirt, etc. from a room or building using a brush 打扫干净，清扫干净（房间等）**,sweep sb↔'up** to lift sb up with a sudden smooth movement 一把抱起某人：*He swept her up into his arms.* 他一把将她抱进怀里。

■ ***noun***

- **WITH BRUSH** 用刷子 **1** [C, usually sing.] an act of cleaning a room, surface, etc. using a BROOM 扫；打扫；清扫：*Give the room a good sweep.* 把房间好好打扫一下。
- **CURVING MOVEMENT** 挥动 **2** [C] a smooth curving movement 挥动；掠：*He indicated the door with a sweep of his arm.* 他一挥胳膊指向门。
- **LANDSCAPE** 地貌 **3** [C, usually sing.] a long, often curved, piece of road, river, coast, etc.（道路、河流、海岸等）一长段，绵延弯曲的地带，呈缓坡状的地带：*the broad sweep of white cliffs around the bay* 环绕海湾的一段白色悬崖
- **RANGE** 范围 **4** [U] the range of an idea, a piece of writing, etc. that considers many different things 广泛性；广博的范围；广度：*Her book covers the long sweep of the country's history.* 她的著作涵盖了该国漫长的历史。
- **MOVEMENT/SEARCH OVER AREA** 巡行；搜索 **5** [C] a movement over an area, for example in order to search for sth or attack sth 巡行；搜索；扫荡：*The rescue helicopter made another sweep over the bay.* 救援直升机在海湾上空又搜索了一遍。
- **CHIMNEY** 烟囱 **6** [C] = CHIMNEY SWEEP
- **GAMBLING** 赌博 **7** [C] (*NAmE also* **sweeps**) (*informal*) = SWEEPSTAKE
- **IN SPORT** 体育运动 **8** [C] (*NAmE*) a series of games that a team wins against another team; the fact of winning all the parts of a contest（两支球队对赛其中一方）全胜的一系列比赛；囊括冠军：*a World Series sweep* 在世界职业棒球系列赛中囊括冠军
- **TELEVISION** 电视 **9 the sweeps** [pl.] (*NAmE*) a time when television companies examine their programmes to find out which ones are the most popular, especially in order to calculate advertising rates 收视率调查（电视台为查明节目受欢迎度，尤为计算广告费）**IDM** SEE CLEAN *adj.*

sweep·er /'swiːpə(r)/ *noun* **1** a person whose job is to sweep sth 打扫者；清扫者；清洁工：*a road sweeper* 马路清洁工 **2** a thing that sweeps sth 清扫器；清洁器：*a carpet sweeper* 地毯清洁器 ➲ SEE ALSO MINESWEEPER **3** (in football (SOCCER) 足球) a player who plays behind the other defending players in order to try and stop anyone who passes them 自由中卫；清道夫

sweep·ing /'swiːpɪŋ/ *adj.* **1** [usually before noun] having an important effect on a large part of sth 影响广泛的；大范围的；根本性的：***sweeping reforms/changes*** 全面改革；彻底变化 ◇ *Security forces were given sweeping powers to search homes.* 安全部队获授入户搜查的绝对权力。**2** [usually before noun] (*disapproving*) too general and failing to think about or understand particular examples（过分）笼统的；一概而论的：***a sweeping generalization/statement*** 笼统的概括；一概而论的说法 **3 ~ victory** a victory by a large number of votes, etc.（在投票等中的）大胜，全胜 **4** [only before noun] forming a curved shape 弧线的；弯曲的：*a sweeping gesture* (= with your hand or arm) 挥动的动作 ◇ *a sweeping staircase* 弧形楼梯

sweep·stake /'swiːpsteɪk/ (*NAmE also* **sweep·stakes**) *noun* a type of betting in which the winner gets all the money bet by everyone else 赌金全赢制

sweet 🔑 /swiːt/ *adj., noun*

■ ***adj.*** (**sweet·er, sweet·est**)

- **FOOD/DRINK** 食物；饮料 **1** 🔑 containing, or tasting as if it contains, a lot of sugar 含糖的；甜的：*a cup of hot sweet tea* 一杯加糖热茶 ◇ *sweet food* 甜食 ◇ *I had a craving for something sweet.* 我馋甜的东西。◇ *This wine is too sweet for me.* 这种葡萄酒对我来说太甜了。➲ COMPARE BITTER *adj.*, SALTY (1) **OPP** **sour** ➲ **WORDFINDER NOTE AT TASTE**
- **SMELL** 气味 **2** 🔑 having a pleasant smell 香的；芳香的；芬芳的 **SYN** **fragrant**：*a sweet-smelling rose* 芬芳的玫瑰 ◇ *The air was sweet with incense.* 空气中弥漫着燃香的香气。
- **SOUND** 声音 **3** having a pleasant sound 悦耳的；好听的：*a sweet voice* 甜润的嗓音
- **PURE** 纯净 **4** pleasant and not containing any harmful substances 纯净的；清新的；新鲜的：*the sweet air of a mountain village* 山村的清新空气
- **SATISFYING** 令人满意 **5** making you feel happy and/or satisfied 令人愉快的；惬意的；舒畅的：*Goodnight.* ***Sweet dreams.*** 晚安。祝你做个甜蜜的梦。◇ *I can't tell you how sweet this victory is.* 取得这场胜利，别提多么痛快了。
- **ATTRACTIVE** 惹人喜爱 **6** (*especially BrE*) (especially of children or small things 尤指儿童或小物品) attractive 惹人喜爱的；可爱的 **SYN** **cute**：*His sister's a sweet young thing.* 他妹妹是个讨人喜欢的小家伙。◇ *You look sweet in this photograph.* 你这张照片照得很可爱。◇ *We stayed in a sweet little hotel on the seafront.* 我们住在海滨一家小巧玲珑的旅馆里。
- **KIND** 善良 **7** having or showing a kind character 善良的；好心的；和蔼的；温柔的：*She gave him her sweetest smile.* 她向他投以极温柔的一笑。◇ *It was* ***sweet of them*** *to offer to help.* 他们主动帮忙，真是好心人。
- **GOOD** 好 **8 Sweet!** (*especially NAmE, informal*) used to show that you approve of sth（表示赞许）好啊，太棒了：*Free tickets? Sweet!* 免费赠票？太棒了！

IDM **be 'sweet on sb** (*old-fashioned, informal*) to like sb very much in a romantic way 热恋某人 **have a sweet 'tooth** (*informal*) to like food that contains a lot of sugar 爱吃甜食 **in your ,own sweet 'time/'way** how and when you want to, even though this might annoy other people 任凭自己的意愿：*He always does the work, but in his own sweet time.* 工作他总是在做，但只在自己高兴的时候做。**keep sb 'sweet** (*informal*) to say or do pleasant things in order to keep sb in a good mood so that they will agree to do sth for you 讨好某人；哄着某人 **she's 'sweet** (*AustralE, NZE, informal*) everything is all right 一切都好 **sweet F'A | sweet Fanny 'Adams** (*BrE, informal*) nothing at all. People say 'sweet FA' to avoid saying 'fuck all'. 一点都没有，什么都没有（委婉说法，与 fuck all 同义）**sweet 'nothings** romantic words 情话：*to whisper sweet nothings in sb's ear* 向某人低诉喁喁情话 **the sweet smell of suc'cess** (*informal*) the pleasant feeling of being successful 成功的喜悦；成功的美妙滋味 ➲ MORE AT HOME *n.*, ROSE *n.*, SHORT *adj.*

■ ***noun***

- **FOOD** 食物 **1** 🔑 [C] (*BrE*) a small piece of sweet food, usually made with sugar and/or chocolate and eaten between meals 糖果 **SYN** **candy**：*a packet of boiled sweets* 一袋硬糖 ◇ *a sweet shop* 糖果店 **2** [C, U] (*BrE*) a sweet dish eaten at the end of a meal（餐后的）甜食，甜点 **SYN** **afters, dessert, pudding**：*I haven't made a sweet today.* 我今天没做甜点。◇ *Would you like some more sweet?* 你想

S

再吃点甜食吗？

• PERSON 人 **3** [U] (*old-fashioned*) a way of addressing sb that you like or love（称呼亲爱的人）亲爱的，宝贝儿：*Don't you worry, my sweet.* 你可别担心，宝贝儿。

ˌsweet-and-ˈsour *adj.* [only before noun] (of food 食物) cooked in a sauce that contains sugar and VINEGAR or lemon 甜酸的；糖醋的：*Chinese sweet-and-sour pork* 中式糖醋猪肉

sweet·bread /ˈswiːtbred/ *noun* [usually pl.] the THYMUS (= an organ in the neck) or the PANCREAS (= an organ near the stomach) of a young cow or sheep, eaten as food（食用的小牛或羊的）胸腺，胰脏

sweet·corn /ˈswiːtkɔːn; *NAmE* -kɔːrn/ (*NAmE also* **corn**) *noun* [U] the yellow seeds of a type of MAIZE (CORN) plant, also called sweetcorn, which grow on thick STEMS and are cooked and eaten as a vegetable（甜）玉米粒：(*BrE*) *tinned sweetcorn* 甜玉米粒罐头 ➲ VISUAL VOCAB PAGE V33 ➲ SEE ALSO CORN ON THE COB

sweet·en /ˈswiːtn/ *verb* **1** ~ **sth** to make food or drinks taste sweeter by adding sugar, etc. 使变甜；加糖于 **2** ~ **sb** (**up**) (*informal*) to try to make sb more willing to help you, agree to sth, etc. by giving them money, praising them, etc. 讨好；拉拢；哄；收买；恭维 **3** ~ **sth** to make sth more pleasant or acceptable 使令人愉快；使更合心意；改善；缓和 IDM SEE PILL *n.*

sweet·en·er /ˈswiːtnə(r)/ *noun* **1** [U, C] a substance used to make food or drink taste sweeter, used instead of sugar 甜味剂：*artificial sweetener(s)* 人造甜味剂 ➲ COLLOCATIONS AT DIET **2** [C] (*informal*) something that is given to sb in order to persuade them to do sth, especially when this is done in a secret or dishonest way 用以拉拢人的钱物；贿赂

sweet·heart /ˈswiːthɑːt; *NAmE* -hɑːrt/ *noun* **1** [sing.] (*informal*) used to address sb in a way that shows affection（用作称呼语）亲爱的，宝贝儿：*Do you want a drink, sweetheart?* 想喝一杯吗，亲爱的？ **2** [C] (*becoming old-fashioned*) a person with whom sb is having a romantic relationship 恋人；爱人；心上人：*They were childhood sweethearts.* 他们俩是青梅竹马。

sweetie /ˈswiːti/ *noun* (*informal*) **1** [C] (*BrE*) a child's word for a sweet/a piece of candy（儿童语）糖果 **2** [C] a person who is kind and easy to like 招人喜欢的人；可爱的人：*He's a real sweetie.* 他的确招人喜欢。**3** [sing.] used to address sb in a way that shows affection（用作称呼语）亲爱的

sweet·ish /ˈswiːtɪʃ/ *adj.* fairly sweet 有点甜的；带甜味的

sweet·ly /ˈswiːtli/ *adv.* **1** in a pleasant way 令人愉快地；可爱地：*She smiled sweetly at him.* 她朝他嫣然一笑。**2** in a way that smells sweet 气味芬芳地：*a sweetly scented flower* 气味芬芳的花 **3** in a way that is without difficulties or problems 顺利地；顺顺当当地：*Everything went sweetly and according to plan.* 一切按计划顺利进行。◇ *He headed the ball sweetly into the back of the net.* 他把球稳稳地顶入网窝。

sweet·meat /ˈswiːtmiːt/ *noun* (*old use*) a sweet/candy; any food preserved in sugar 糖果；甜食；蜜饯；果脯

sweet·ness /ˈswiːtnəs/ *noun* [U] **1** the quality of being pleasant 令人愉快；讨人喜欢：*a smile of great sweetness* 十分甜蜜的微笑 **2** the quality of tasting or smelling sweet 甜；芬芳：*The air was filled with the sweetness of mimosa.* 空气中弥漫着含羞草的芬芳。

IDM **be** (**all**) ˌ**sweetness and ˈlight** **1** (of a person 人) to be pleasant, friendly and polite 和蔼可亲；温文尔雅 **2** (of a situation 情况) to be enjoyable and easy to deal with 简单而有趣

ˌsweet ˈpea *noun* a climbing garden plant with pale flowers that have a sweet smell 香豌豆 ➲ VISUAL VOCAB PAGE V11

ˌsweet ˈpepper (*BrE also* **pep·per**) (*NAmE also* **ˈbell pepper**) *noun* a hollow fruit, usually red, green or yellow, eaten as a vegetable either raw or cooked 甜椒；柿子椒；灯笼椒 ➲ VISUAL VOCAB PAGE V34

ˌsweet poˈtato *noun* [C, U] a root vegetable that looks like a red potato, but that is yellow inside and tastes sweet 红薯；甘薯 ➲ VISUAL VOCAB PAGE V33

ˈsweet spot *noun* **1** the area on a BAT which hits the ball in the most effective way（球拍或球棒的）最佳击球点，甜区 **2** a location or combination of characteristics that produces the best results 最有效点；所有特点的完美组合：*This series aims to hit a sweet spot between romantic comedy and thriller.* 这连续剧想抓住浪漫喜剧和惊悚片的最佳结合点。

ˈsweet-talk *verb* ~ **sb** (**into sth/into doing sth**) (*disapproving*) to try to persuade sb to do sth by praising them and telling them things they like to hear 对…甜言蜜语；给…灌迷魂汤：*I can't believe you let him sweet-talk you into working for him!* 我无法相信，他几句好话就哄得你为他效力！
▸ **ˈsweet talk** *noun* [U]

sweet Wil·liam /ˌswiːt ˈwɪljəm/ *noun* a garden plant with groups of red, pink, or white flowers that smell sweet 美国石竹，须苞石竹（园林植物，开红色、粉红或白色芳香花簇）

swell /swel/ *verb, noun, adj.*

■ *verb* (**swelled** /sweld/, **swol·len** /ˈswəʊlən/; *NAmE* ˈswoʊlən/, **swelled**, **swelled**) **1** [I] ~ (**up**) to become bigger or rounder 膨胀；肿胀：*Her arm was beginning to swell up where the bee had stung her.* 她胳膊给蜜蜂蜇了，肿了起来。➲ WORDFINDER NOTE AT HURT **2** [I, T] to curve out or make sth curve out（使）凸出，鼓出：~ (**out**) *The sails swelled (out) in the wind.* 船帆鼓满了风。◇ ~ **sth** (**out**) *The wind swelled (out) the sails.* 风鼓起了帆。**3** [T, I] to increase or make sth increase in number or size（使）增加，增大，扩大：~ **sth** (**to sth**) *Last year's profits were swelled by a fall in production costs.* 去年因生产成本下降，利润有所增加。◇ *We are looking for more volunteers to swell the ranks* (= increase the number) *of those already helping.* 我们期盼有更多的志愿者加入，以壮大目前已在提供帮助的队伍。◇ ~ (**to sth**) *Membership has swelled to over 20 000.* 成员增加到 2 万余人。OPP **shrink** **4** [I] (of a sound 声音) to become louder 变得更响亮；增强：*The cheering swelled through the hall.* 欢呼声越来越大，响彻大厅。**5** [I] ~ (**with sth**) to be filled with a strong emotion 充满（激情）：*to swell with pride* 满腔自豪 ➲ SEE ALSO SWOLLEN

■ *noun* **1** [C, usually sing.] the movement of the sea when it rises and falls without the waves breaking 海浪的涌动；涌浪：*The boat was caught in a heavy* (= strong) *swell.* 船遇上了大涌浪。**2** [sing.] (*formal*) the curved shape of sth, especially a part of the body（尤指身体部位）凸起的形状，鼓出处，隆起处：*the firm swell of her breasts* 她挺拔的乳峰 **3** [sing.] a situation in which sth increases in size, number, strength, etc. 增加；增大；扩大；增强：*a growing swell of support* 越来越多的支持 ◇ *a swell of pride* 自豪感的增强 ➲ SEE ALSO GROUNDSWELL **4** [sing.] (of music or noise 乐音或噪声) a gradual increase in the volume of sth 逐渐增强 SYN **crescendo** **5** (*old-fashioned, informal*) an important or fashionable person 重要人士；时髦人物

■ *adj.* (*old-fashioned, NAmE, informal*) very good, enjoyable, etc. 很愉快的；极有趣的：*We had a swell time.* 我们过得开心极了。

swell·ing /ˈswelɪŋ/ *noun* **1** [U] the condition of being larger or rounder than normal (= of being SWOLLEN) 膨胀；肿胀：*Use ice to reduce the swelling.* 用冰敷消肿。**2** [C] a place on your body that has become larger or rounder than normal as the result of an illness or injury 肿胀处；浮肿处：*The fall left her with a painful swelling above her eye.* 她摔了一跤，眼睛上方起了一个包，挺疼的。

swel·ter /ˈsweltə(r)/ *verb* [I] to be very hot in a way that makes you feel uncomfortable 热得难受：*Passengers*

S

sweltered in temperatures of over 90°F. 在超过 90 华氏度的高温下，乘客热得要命。▶ **swel·ter·ing** *adj.* SYN **stifling**: *sweltering heat* 酷热难耐的高温 **swel·ter·ing·ly** *adv.*: *swelteringly hot* 酷热

swept PAST TENSE, PAST PART. OF SWEEP

ˌ**swept-ˈback** *adj.* [only before noun] **1** (of hair 头发) pulled back from your face 往后梳的；往后扎的 **2** (of an aircraft wing 机翼) pointing backwards 后掠的

ˈ**swept-up** *adj.* = UPSWEPT

swerve /swɜːv; *NAmE* swɜːrv/ *verb* [I] (especially of a vehicle 尤指车辆等) to change direction suddenly, especially in order to avoid hitting sb/sth 突然转向；急转弯：*She swerved sharply to avoid a cyclist.* 她猛地急转弯，以避开一个骑自行车的人。◇ *The bus suddenly swerved into his path.* 公共汽车突然拐到了他走的路上。◇ *The ball swerved into the net.* 球在空中划了一条弧线，进了球门。▶ **swerve** *noun*

swift /swɪft/ *adj., noun*

■ ***adj.*** (**swift·er, swift·est**) **1** happening or done quickly and immediately; doing sth quickly 迅即发生的；马上做出的；迅速的：*swift action* 迅速的行动 ◇ *a swift decision* 迅即作出的决定 ◇ **~ to do sth** *The White House was swift to deny the rumours.* 白宫立刻对这些传言予以否认。**2** moving very quickly; able to move very quickly 速度快的；敏捷的；矫健的：*a swift current* 湍急的水流 ◇ *a swift runner* 跑得飞快的人 ➲ NOTE AT FAST ▶ **swift·ly** *adv.*: *She moved swiftly to the rescue.* 她迅速赶来营救。**swift·ness** *noun* [U]

■ ***noun*** a small bird with long narrow wings, similar to a SWALLOW 雨燕

swig /swɪɡ/ *verb* (**-gg-**) **~ sth** (*informal*) to take a quick drink of sth, especially alcohol 大口喝（酒等）：*They sat around swigging beer from bottles.* 他们闲坐着，对着瓶子大口地喝啤酒。▶ **swig** *noun*: *She took a swig of wine.* 她喝了一大口葡萄酒。

swill /swɪl/ *verb, noun*

■ ***verb*** **1** [T] **~ sth (out/down)** (*especially BrE*) to clean sth by pouring large amounts of water in, on or through it 冲洗；灌洗；涮 SYN **rinse**: *She swilled the glasses with clean water.* 她用清水涮了杯子。**2** [T] **~ sth (down)** (*informal*) to drink sth quickly and/or in large quantities 大口喝；痛饮 **3** [T, I] to move, or to make a liquid move, in a particular direction or around a particular place（使）晃荡，摇动，流动：**~ sth + adv./prep.** *He swilled the juice around in his glass.* 他摇了摇杯子里的果汁。◇ **+ adv./prep.** *Water swilled around in the bottom of the boat.* 船底上的水来回晃荡。

■ ***noun*** **1** (*also* **pig·swill**) [U] a mixture of waste food and water that is given to pigs to eat（给猪吃的）泔脚，剩饭菜，馊水 **2** [U] (*informal*) drink or food that is unpleasant or of a poor quality 不好喝的饮料；难吃的食物；劣质饮料（或食物）**3** [C, usually sing.] (*informal*) a large amount of a drink that you take into your mouth 一大口饮料：*He had a quick swill of wine.* 他猛地灌下一大口葡萄酒。

swim /swɪm/ *verb, noun*

■ ***verb*** (**swim·ming, swam** /swæm/, **swum** /swʌm/) **1** [I, T] (of a person 人) to move through water in a horizontal position using the arms and legs 游水；游泳：*I can't swim.* 我不会游泳。◇ *The boys swam across the lake.* 男孩子们游到了湖对岸。◇ *They spent the day swimming and sunbathing.* 他们整整一天都在游泳和晒太阳。◇ **~ sth** *Can you swim backstroke yet?* 你会仰泳了吗？◇ *How long will it take her to swim the Channel?* 她游过英吉利海峡得用多长时间？➲ NOTE AT BATH

WORDFINDER 联想词： armband, dive, flipper, float, goggles, length, paddle, stroke, water wings

2 [I] **go swimming** to spend time swimming for pleasure 游泳（作为娱乐）：*I go swimming twice a week.* 我每星期游泳两次。**3** [I] (**+ adv./prep.**) (of a fish, etc. 鱼等) to move through or across water 游；游动：*A shoal of fish swam past.* 一群鱼游了过去。◇ *Ducks were swimming around on the river.* 鸭子在河面上游来游去。**4** [I] (*usually* **be swimming**) to be covered with a lot of liquid 浸；泡；洒满；充溢着：**~ (in sth)** *The main course was swimming in oil.* 主菜油汪汪的。◇ **~ (with sth)** *Her eyes were swimming with tears.* 她两眼噙满泪水。**5** [I] (of objects, etc. 物体等) to seem to be moving around, especially when you are ill/sick or drunk 仿佛在旋转，似在晃动（尤指生病或酒醉时的感觉）：*The pages swam before her eyes.* 书页仿佛在她眼前晃动。**6** [I] to feel confused and/or as if everything is spinning around 眩晕；感觉天旋地转：*His head swam and he swayed dizzily.* 他感觉天旋地转，摇晃起来。IDM SEE SINK *v.*

■ ***noun*** **1** [sing.] a period of time during which you swim 游泳：*Let's **go for a swim**.* 我们去游个泳吧。**2** (*especially NAmE*) (in compounds) related to or used for swimming（构成复合词）与游泳有关的，游泳时用的：*a swim meet* (= a swimming competition between teams) 游泳比赛 ◇ *swim trunks* 游泳裤

IDM **in the ˈswim (of things)** (*informal*) involved in things that are happening in society or in a particular situation 积极参与社会生活（或某活动）；合潮流

swim·mer /ˈswɪmə(r)/ *noun* a person who can swim; a person who is swimming 会游泳者；游泳者：*a **good/strong swimmer*** 水性好的人；擅长游泳的人 ◇ *They watched the swimmers splashing through the water.* 他们看着游泳的人扑通扑通溅着水花游过去。◇ *a shallow pool for **non-swimmers*** 供不会游泳的人用的浅水池

swim·ming /ˈswɪmɪŋ/ *noun* [U] the sport or activity of swimming 游泳；游泳运动：*Swimming is a good form of exercise.* 游泳是很好的锻炼方式。➲ VISUAL VOCAB PAGE V48

ˈ**swimming bath** *noun* [usually pl.] (*old-fashioned, BrE*) a public swimming pool inside a building 室内游泳池

ˈ**swimming cap** (*also* ˈ**swimming hat**) (*both BrE*) (*also* ˈ**bathing cap** *NAmE, BrE*) *noun* a soft rubber or plastic cap that fits closely over your head to keep your hair dry while you are swimming 游泳帽

ˈ**swimming costume** *noun* (*BrE*) = SWIMSUIT

swim·ming·ly /ˈswɪmɪŋli/ *adv.* (*informal*) without any problems or difficulties 顺利地；顺顺当当地：*We hope everything will **go swimmingly**.* 我们希望一切进展顺利。

ˈ**swimming pool** (*also* **pool**) *noun* **1** an area of water that has been created for people to swim in 游泳池：*an **indoor/outdoor swimming pool*** 室内 / 室外游泳池 ◇ *a **heated swimming pool*** 温水游泳池 ◇ *an **open-air swimming pool*** 露天游泳池 **2** the building that contains a public swimming pool 游泳场；游泳馆：*She trained five times a week at her local swimming pool.* 她每星期在当地的游泳池训练五次。

ˈ**swimming trunks** (*also* **trunks**) (*NAmE also* ˈ**swim trunks**) *noun* [pl.] a piece of clothing covering the lower part of the body and sometimes the top part of the legs, worn by men and boys for swimming（男式）游泳裤：*a pair of swimming trunks* 一条游泳裤 ➲ PICTURE AT TRUNK

swim·suit /ˈswɪmsuːt; *BrE also* -sjuːt/ *noun* (*BrE also* ˈ**swimming costume**) (*also* ˈ**bathing suit** *NAmE* or *old-fashioned*) a piece of clothing worn for swimming, especially the type worn by women and girls（尤指女式）游泳衣

swim·wear /ˈswɪmweə(r); *NAmE* -wer/ *noun* [U] clothing that you wear for swimming 游泳衣；泳装

swin·dle /ˈswɪndl/ *verb, noun*

■ ***verb*** to cheat sb in order to get sth, especially money, from them 诈骗；骗取：**~ sb (out of sth)** *They swindled him out of hundreds of dollars.* 他们诈骗了他好几百美元。◇ **~ sth (out of sb)** *They swindled hundreds of dollars out of him.* 他们诈骗了他好几百美元。▶ **swind·ler** /ˈswɪndlə(r)/ *noun* SYN **conman**

■ ***noun*** [usually sing.] a situation in which sb uses dishonest or illegal methods in order to get money from a company, another person, etc. 诈骗；骗取 SYN **con**: *an insurance swindle* 保险诈骗案

swine /swaɪn/ *noun* (*pl.* **swines** or **swine**) **1** [C] (*informal*) an unpleasant person 讨厌的人：*He's an arrogant little swine!* 他是个傲慢的小讨厌鬼！**2** [C] (*BrE, informal*) a difficult or an unpleasant thing or task 令人不愉快的事物；难处理的东西：*The car can be a swine to start.* 这辆车有时很难发动。**3 swine** [pl.] (*old use* or *specialist*) pigs 猪：*a herd of swine* 一群猪 ◇ *swine fever* (= a disease of pigs) 猪瘟 IDM SEE PEARL

'swine flu *noun* [U] **1** a serious illness that affects pigs 猪流感 **2** a serious illness spread between humans, that is GENETICALLY similar to swine flu in pigs, that in some cases causes death（人类感染的）猪流感（基因与猪流感相似，可引致死亡）

swine·herd /ˈswaɪnhɜːd; *NAmE* -hɜːrd/ *noun* (*old use*) a person whose job is to take care of pigs 养猪的人；猪倌

swing /swɪŋ/ *verb, noun*

■ *verb* (**swung, swung** /swʌŋ/)

- **HANG AND MOVE** 摆动 **1** [I, T] to move backwards or forwards or from side to side while hanging from a fixed point; to make sth do this（使）摆动，摇摆，摇荡：*His arms swung as he walked.* 他边走边摆着双臂。◇ *As he pushed her, she swung higher and higher* (= while sitting on a swing). 随着他推她，她在秋千上越荡越高。◇ **~ from sth** *A set of keys swung from her belt.* 她腰带上挂着的一串钥匙摆来摆去。◇ **~ sth** *He sat on the stool, swinging his legs.* 他坐在凳子上晃动着两条腿。**2** [I, T] to move from one place to another by holding sth that is fixed and pulling yourself along, up, etc. 纵身跃向；荡向；悬吊到：**+ adv./prep.** *The gunshot sent monkeys swinging away through the trees.* 枪声一响，猴子纷纷在树丛中飞跃荡走。◇ **~ yourself + adv./prep.** *He swung himself out of the car.* 他纵身跳下车。
- **MOVE IN CURVE** 弧线运动 **3** [I, T] to move or make sth move with a wide curved movement（使）弧线运动，转弯，转动：**+ adv./prep.** *A line of cars swung out of the palace gates.* 一队汽车拐出了宫门。◇ **~ sth + adv./prep.** *He swung his legs over the side of the bed.* 他把两腿移过来放下床。◇ **+ adj.** *The door swung open.* 门开了。◇ **~ sth + adj.** *She swung the door open.* 她把门推开。
- **TURN QUICKLY** 迅速转向 **4** [I, T] to turn or change direction suddenly; to make sth do this（使）突然转向，突然转身：**+ adv./prep.** *The bus swung sharply to the left.* 公共汽车猛地拐向左边。◇ **~ sth + adv./prep.** *He swung the camera around to face the opposite direction.* 他猛地将照相机转到相反的方向。
- **TRY TO HIT** 试图击中 **5** [I, T] to try to hit sb/sth（挥动某物）朝…打去：**~ at sb/sth** *She swung at me with the iron bar.* 她挥着铁棍朝我打来。◇ **~ sth (at sb/sth)** *He swung another punch in my direction.* 他朝着我这边又挥了一拳。
- **CHANGE OPINION/MOOD** 改变意见 / 情绪 **6** [I, T] to change or make sb/sth change from one opinion, mood, etc. to another（使）改变（意见、情绪等）：**~ (from A) (to B)** *The state has swung from Republican to Democrat.* 这个州原先支持共和党，现在倒向了民主党。◇ **~ (between A and B)** *His emotions swung between fear and curiosity.* 他时而害怕，时而好奇。◇ *The game could swing either way* (= either side could win it). 这场比赛胜负未卜。◇ **~ sb/sth (to sth)** *I managed to swing them round to my point of view.* 我设法使他们转而接受了我的观点。
- **DO/GET STH** 做；获得 **7** [T] (*informal*) to succeed in getting or achieving sth, sometimes in a slightly dishonest way（有时略微不正当地）获得，搞到，办成：**~ sth** *We're trying to* ***swing it*** *so that we can travel on the same flight.* 我们正在想法子，好坐上同一个航班。◇ **~ sb sth** *Is there any chance of you swinging us a couple of tickets?* 你有没有可能帮我们弄几张票？
- **OF MUSIC** 音乐 **8** [I] to have a strong rhythm 有强劲的节奏；节奏感强
- **OF PARTY** 聚会 **9** [I] (*informal*) if a party, etc. **is swinging**, there are a lot of people there having a good time 热闹；令人开心

IDM **swing the 'balance** = TIP THE BALANCE/SCALES **swing both 'ways** (*informal*) to be BISEXUAL (= sexually attracted to both men and women) 双性恋；既喜欢异性也喜欢同性 **ˌswing for the 'fences** (*NAmE*) to really try to achieve sth great, even when it is not reasonable to expect to be so successful 全力一搏；迎难而上：*entrepreneurs who think big and swing for the fences* 志向高远、迎难而上的企业家 **ˌswing into 'action** to start doing sth quickly and with a lot of energy 立即行动起来；马上大干起来 **ˌswing the 'lead** (*old-fashioned, BrE, informal*) (usually used in the progressive tenses 通常用于进行时) to pretend to be ill/sick when in fact you are not, especially to avoid work 装病偷懒：*I don't think there's anything wrong with her—she's just swinging the lead.* 我认为她没有什么病，只不过是在装病偷懒而已。ORIGIN The lead was a weight at the bottom of a line that sailors used to measure how deep water was when the ship was near land. 'Swinging the lead' was thought to be an easy task, and came to mean avoiding hard work. * lead 是船靠近陆地时水手测量水深用的水铊。swinging the lead 被认为是件轻松的工作，逐渐变成"逃避干重活"的意思。➲ MORE AT ROOM *n.*

PHR V **ˌswing 'by | 'swing by sth** (*NAmE, informal*) to visit a place or person for a short time 进某处一会儿；短暂拜访；看望某人一下 SYN **drop by/in/round**: *I'll swing by your house on the way home from work.* 下班回家路过时我会到你家一下。

■ *noun*

- **MOVEMENT** 运动 **1** [C] a swinging movement or rhythm 摆动；挥动；转动；强劲节奏：*He took a wild swing at the ball.* 他对准球猛地挥拍一击。◇ *the swing of her hips* 她臀部的扭动
- **OF OPINION/MOOD** 意见；情绪 **2** [C] a change from one opinion or situation to another; the amount by which sth changes 改变；改变的程度：*He is liable to abrupt* ***mood swings*** (= for example from being very happy to being very sad). 他的情绪容易大起大落。◇ *Voting showed a 10% swing to Labour.* 投票显示 10% 的人转而支持工党。
- **HANGING SEAT** 秋千 **3** [C] a seat for swinging on, hung from above on ropes or chains 秋千：*The kids were playing on the swings.* 孩子们在荡秋千。➲ VISUAL VOCAB PAGE V41
- **IN GOLF** 高尔夫球 **4** [sing.] the swinging movement you make with your arms and body when you hit the ball in the game of GOLF 挥杆动作：*I need to work on my swing.* 我需要改进挥杆动作。
- **MUSIC** 音乐 **5** [U] a type of JAZZ with a smooth rhythm, played especially by big dance bands in the 1930s 摇摆乐（流行于 20 世纪 30 年代）
- **JOURNEY** 行程 **6** [sing.] (*NAmE*) a quick journey, especially one made by a politician, in which sb visits several different places in a short time（尤指从政者在多处逗留的）短期快速行程：*a three-day campaign swing through California* 为期三天的加利福尼亚巡回竞选旅程

IDM **get in/into the 'swing (of sth)** (*informal*) to get used to an activity or a situation and become fully involved in it 熟悉（某种情况）；融入（某种活动或环境之中） **go with a 'swing** (*BrE*) **1** (of a party or an activity 聚会或活动) to be lively and enjoyable 热闹有趣；气氛热烈 **2** (of music 音乐) to have a strong rhythm 有强劲的节奏 **in full 'swing** having reached a very lively level 在热烈进行中；处于兴盛阶段：*When we arrived the party was already in full swing.* 我们赶到时，聚会已进入高潮。**ˌswings and 'roundabouts** (*BrE, informal*) used to say that there are advantages and disadvantages whatever decision you make（表示无论如何决定都有利有弊）有得必有失：*If you earn more, you pay more in tax, so it's all swings and roundabouts.* 赚的越多，缴的税也越多，所以有得必有失。

ˌswing 'bridge *noun* a bridge that can be moved to one side to allow tall ships to pass 平旋桥；平转桥

ˌswing 'door (*BrE*) (*NAmE* **ˌswinging 'door**) *noun* a door that you can open in either direction and that closes itself when you stop holding it open 双开式弹簧门

swinge·ing /ˈswɪndʒɪŋ/ *adj.* [usually before noun] (*BrE*) **1** large and likely to cause people problems, especially financial problems 巨额的；严重的；巨大的：*swingeing cuts in benefits* 补助金的大量削减 ◇ *swingeing tax increases* 征税大幅提高 **2** extremely critical of sb/sth 尖锐的；猛烈

S

的：*a swingeing attack on government policy* 猛烈抨击政府的政策

swing·er /ˈswɪŋə(r)/ *noun* (*old-fashioned, informal*) **1** a person who is fashionable and has an active social life 时髦活跃的人物 **2** a person who has sex with many different people 性开放者；滥交者

swing·ing /ˈswɪŋɪŋ/ *adj.* [usually before noun] (*old-fashioned, informal*) lively and fashionable 活跃而时髦的

ˌswinging ˈdoor (*NAmE*) (*BrE* **ˌswing ˈdoor**) *noun* a door that you can open in either direction and that closes itself when you stop holding it open 双开式弹簧门

ˈswing shift *noun* (*NAmE, informal*) the SHIFT (= period of time worked each day) from 3 or 4 o'clock in the afternoon until 11 or 12 at night; the workers who work this SHIFT 中班（从下午 3、4 点至夜里 11、12 点）；中班人员

ˌswing ˈstate *noun* (*politics* 政) (in an election for president in the US) a state where none of the candidates can be certain of getting the most support 摇摆州（指美国总统大选中无一候选人有把握获胜的州）➲ WORDFINDER NOTE AT CONGRESS

ˌswing ˈvote *noun* [C, sing.] (*NAmE*) the votes of people who do not always vote for the same political party and have not decided which party to vote for in an election 摇摆选票（指无一贯明确党派立场的选民举棋不定的选票）➲ WORDFINDER NOTE AT DEMOCRACY

ˌswing ˈvoter (*NAmE*) (*BrE* **ˌfloating ˈvoter**) *noun* a person who does not always vote for the same political party and who has not decided which party to vote for in an election 摇摆选民（不确定投哪一政党的票）

ˌswing-ˈwing *adj.* [only before noun] used to describe an aircraft wing that can be moved forward for landing, etc. and backward for rapid flight（飞机）可变后掠翼的

swipe /swaɪp/ *verb, noun*

■ *verb* **1** [I, T] ~ (**at**) **sb/sth** to hit or try to hit sb/sth with your hand or an object by swinging your arm 挥拳打；扬起巴掌打；挥起（物体）击打：*He swiped at the ball and missed.* 他挥棒击球但没击中。**2** [T] ~ **sth** (*informal*) to steal sth 偷窃 SYN **pinch** **3** [T] ~ **sth** to pass a plastic card, such as a credit card, through a special machine that is able to read the information that is stored on it 刷（磁卡）**4** [I, T] ~ (**sth**) (**on/across sth**) to move your finger quickly across the screen of an electronic device such as a mobile/cell phone or small computer in order to move text, pictures, etc. or give commands（用手指在手机等电子装置屏幕上）快速滑动，输入手势指令：*Switch on the phone and swipe your finger across the screen to unlock it.* 打开手机，在屏幕上滑动手指来解锁。

■ *noun* ~ (**at sb/sth**) (*informal*) **1** an act of hitting or trying to hit sb/sth by swinging your arm or sth that you are holding 抡打；挥击：*She **took a swipe at** him with her umbrella.* 她抡起雨伞朝他打去。**2** an act of criticizing sb/sth 批评；抨击：*He used the interview to **take a swipe at his critics**.* 他利用这次采访对批评他的人予以回击。

ˈswipe card *noun* a special plastic card with information recorded on it which can be read by an electronic device 磁卡；集成电路卡：*Access to the building is by swipe card only.* 刷磁卡才能进楼。➲ SEE ALSO KEY CARD

swirl /swɜːl; *NAmE* swɜːrl/ *verb, noun*

■ *verb* [I, T] to move around quickly in a circle; to make sth do this（使）打旋，旋动，起漩涡：(**+ adv./prep.**) *The water swirled down the drain.* 水打着漩流进了下水道。◇ *A long skirt swirled around her ankles.* 她的长裙在脚踝旁边摆动。◇ *swirling mists* 缭绕的薄雾 ◇ ~ **sth** (**+ adv./prep.**) *He took a mouthful of water and swirled it around his mouth.* 他含了一口水，漱了漱口。

■ *noun* **1** the movement of sth that twists and turns in different directions and at different speeds 打旋；旋动；漩涡 **2** a pattern or an object that twists in circles 螺旋形；漩涡状（物体）

swish /swɪʃ/ *verb, noun, adj.*

■ *verb* [I, T] to move quickly through the air in a way that makes a soft sound; to make sth do this 唰地（或嗖地、呼地等）挥动；（使）快速空中移动：(**+ adv./prep.**) *A large car swished past them and turned into the embassy gates.* 一辆大型轿车嗖地从他们身边驶过，拐进了大使馆的大门。◇ *The pony's tail swished.* 小马唰唰地甩着尾巴。◇ ~ **sth** (**+ adv./prep.**) *The pony swished its tail.* 小马唰唰地甩着尾巴。◇ *She swished her racket aggressively through the air.* 她咄咄逼人地把球拍挥舞得呼呼作响。

■ *noun* [sing.] the movement or soft sound made by sth moving quickly, especially through the air 快速的空中移动（或挥动、摆动等）；（快速空中挥动等的）唰唰声，嗖嗖声，呼呼声 ➲ MORE LIKE THIS 3, page R25

■ *adj.* (*BrE, informal*) looking expensive and fashionable 华贵入时的；豪华的 SYN **smart**：*a swish restaurant* 豪华餐馆

Swiss /swɪs/ *adj., noun* (*pl.* **Swiss**)

■ *adj.* from or connected with Switzerland 瑞士的

■ *noun* a person from Switzerland 瑞士人

ˌSwiss ˈArmy knife™ *noun* a small knife with several different blades and tools such as scissors, that fold into the handle 瑞士军刀（多功能小折叠刀）

ˈSwiss ball™ *noun* = EXERCISE BALL

ˌSwiss ˈchard *noun* [U] = CHARD

ˌSwiss ˈcheese *noun* [U, C] any hard cheese with holes in it 瑞士干酪（中间有孔）

ˌSwiss ˈroll (*BrE*) (*NAmE* **ˈjelly roll**) *noun* a thin flat cake that is spread with jam, etc. and rolled up 卷筒蛋糕（夹有果酱等）

switch 🔑 /swɪtʃ/ *noun, verb*

■ *noun* **1** 🔑 a small device that you press or move up and down in order to turn a light or piece of electrical equipment on and off（电路的）开关，闸，转换器：*a light switch* 电灯开关 ◇ *an on-off switch* 通断开关 ◇ *That was in the days before electricity was available **at the flick of a switch**.* 那是在过去，还没有到开关一响就有电的时代。◇ *Which switch do I press to turn it off?* 我按哪个开关就能把它关了？◇ *to throw a switch* (= to move a large switch) 扳动开关 ➲ WORDFINDER NOTE AT ELECTRICITY **2** a change from one thing to another, especially when this is sudden and complete（尤指突然彻底的）改变，转变：~ (**in/of sth**) *a switch of priorities* 轻重缓急的改变 ◇ ~ (**from A to B**) *She made the switch from full-time to part-time work when her first child was born.* 第一个孩子出生后她就从全职工作改为兼职工作。◇ *a policy switch* 政策的转变 **3** (*NAmE*) the POINTS on a railway/railroad line（铁路的）转辙器，道岔 **4** a thin stick that bends easily（细软）枝条；鞭子：*a riding switch* 马鞭

■ *verb* **1** 🔑 [I, T] to change or make sth change from one thing to another（使）改变，转变，突变：~ (**over**) (**from sth**) (**to sth**) *We're in the process of switching over to a new system of invoicing.* 我们正在转用新的发票制度。◇ ~ **between A and B** *Press these two keys to switch between documents on screen.* 按这两个键就可以在屏幕上的文件之间切换。◇ ~ **sth** (**over**) (**from sth**) (**to sth**) *When did you switch jobs?* 你什么时候调动工作的？**2** [T] to exchange one thing for another 交换；掉换；转换；对调 SYN **swap**：~ **sth** *The dates of the last two exams have been switched.* 最后两门考试的日期掉换了。◇ ~ **sth over/around/round** *I see you've switched the furniture around* (= changed its position). 我看出来你把家具重摆了。◇ ~ **sth with sth** *Do you think she'll notice if I switch my glass with hers?* 要是把我的杯子跟她的换了，你认为她看得出来吗？**3** [I, T] to do sb else's job for a short time or work during different hours so that they can do your job or work during your usual hours 调班；临时掉换工作时间 SYN **swap**：~ (**with sb**) *I can't work next weekend—will you switch with me?* 下个周末我不能上班，咱俩调个班好不好？◇ ~ **sth** (**with sb**) *Have you been able to switch your shift with anyone?* 你找着能跟你调班的人了吗？◇ ~ (**sth**) (**over/around/round**) *Can we switch our shifts around?* 我们可以换个班吗？

PHR V **ˌswitch ˈoff** (*informal*) to stop thinking about sth or paying attention to sth 不再想着；不再注意；失去兴趣：*When I hear the word 'football' I switch off* (= because

I am not interested in it). 我听见“足球”两个字就腻味。◇ *The only time he really switches off* (= stops thinking about work, etc.) *is when we're on vacation.* 只有在我们外出度假的时候，他才真正无牵无挂。 **ˌswitch ˈoff/ˈon | ˌswitch sth↔ˈoff/ˈon** to turn a light, machine, etc. off/on by pressing a button or switch 关 / 开（电灯、机器等）：*Please switch the lights off as you leave.* 离开的时候请关灯。◇ *How do you switch this thing on?* 这东西怎么开？ **ˌswitch ˈover | ˌswitch sth↔ˈover** (*BrE*) to change stations on a radio or television 换台；换频道

switch·back /ˈswɪtʃbæk/ *noun* **1** a road or railway/railroad track that has many sharp bends as it goes up a steep hill, or one that rises and falls steeply many times（公路或铁路坡道上的）之字形路线；（公路或铁路的）不断起伏的路线 **2** (*NAmE*) a 180 degree bend in a road that is going up a steep hill（陡坡路上的）急转弯，180 度的转弯 **3** (*old-fashioned, BrE*) = ROLLER COASTER

switch·blade /ˈswɪtʃbleɪd/ (*especially NAmE*) (*BrE also* **ˈflick knife**) *noun* a knife with a blade inside the handle that jumps out quickly when a button is pressed 弹簧刀

switch·board /ˈswɪtʃbɔːd; *NAmE* -bɔːrd/ *noun* the central part of a telephone system used by a company, etc., where telephone calls are answered and PUT THROUGH (= connected) to the appropriate person or department; the people who work this equipment（电话的）交换机，交换台，总机：*a switchboard operator* 交换台接线员 ◇ *Call the switchboard and ask for extension 410.* 你先打电话到总机，然后要求转分机 410。◇ *Hundreds of fans jammed the switchboard for over an hour.* 在一个多小时里，好几百个崇拜者打去电话，交换台应接不暇。

ˌswitched ˈon *adj.* **1** ~ (**to sth**) aware of new things that are happening 对新事物有认识的；懂时髦的：*We're trying to get people switched on to the benefits of healthy eating.* 我们正努力让大家意识到健康饮食的好处。◇ *an organization for switched-on young people* 一个新潮年轻人组织 **2** made to feel interested and excited 兴致勃发的；为之振奋的：*People get really switched on by this music.* 这首乐曲确实令人激情勃发。

ˈswitch-hitter *noun* (in BASEBALL 棒球) a player who can hit with the BAT on either side of their body 左右全能的击球手

switch·over /ˈswɪtʃəʊvə(r); *NAmE* -oʊ-/ *noun* a change from one system, method, policy, etc. to another（制度、方法、政策等的）转变，转换：*the switchover from analogue to digital TV* 从模拟到数字电视的转变

swivel /ˈswɪvl/ *noun, verb*

■ ***noun*** (often used as an adjective 常用作形容词) a device used to connect two parts of an object together, allowing one part to turn around without moving the other 转节；转环；旋轴；旋转接头：*a swivel chair* (= one on which the seat turns around without moving the base) 转椅 ➲ VISUAL VOCAB PAGE V71

■ ***verb*** (**-ll-**, *US* **-l-**) **1** [T, I] ~ (**sth**) (+ **adv./prep.**) to turn or make sth turn around a fixed central point（使）旋转，转动 SYN **spin**: *She swivelled the chair around to face them.* 她把椅子转过来朝着他们。**2** [I, T] ~ (**sth**) (+ **adv./prep.**) to turn or move your body, eyes or head around quickly to face another direction 转身；转动（身体、眼睛或头）SYN **swing**: *He swivelled around to look at her.* 他转过身来看着她。

swizz (*also* **swiz**) /swɪz/ *noun* [usually sing.] (*BrE, informal*) something unfair or disappointing 骗局；令人失望的事：*What a swizz!* 真令人失望！

swiz·zle stick /ˈswɪzl stɪk/ *noun* a stick used to remove the bubbles from SPARKLING drinks such as CHAMPAGNE（消除香槟酒等起泡饮料泡沫的）搅棒

swol·len /ˈswəʊlən; *NAmE* ˈswoʊlən/ *adj.* **1** (of a part of the body 身体的一部分) larger than normal, especially as a result of a disease or an injury 肿胀的；肿起来的：*swollen glands* 肿胀的腺体 ◇ *Her eyes were red and swollen from crying.* 她哭得两眼又红又肿。**2** (of a river 河流) containing more water than normal 涨水的；上涨的 ➲ SEE ALSO SWELL *adj.*

swoon /swuːn/ *verb* **1** [I] ~ (**over sb**) to feel very excited, emotional, etc. about sb that you think is sexually attractive, so that you almost become unconscious 痴迷；对（某人）神魂颠倒：*He's used to having women swooning over him.* 他对有女人痴迷于他司空见惯了。**2** [I] (*old-fashioned*) to become unconscious 昏厥；昏倒 SYN **faint** ▶ **swoon** *noun* [sing.] (*old-fashioned*): *to go into a swoon* 昏厥

swoop /swuːp/ *verb, noun*

■ ***verb*** **1** [I] (+ **adv./prep.**) (of a bird or plane 鸟或飞机) to fly quickly and suddenly downwards, especially in order to attack sb/sth（尤指为了袭击）向下猛冲，俯冲 SYN **dive**: *The aircraft swooped down over the buildings.* 飞机俯冲到那些建筑物上方。**2** [I] ~ (**on sb/sth**) (especially of police or soldiers 尤指警察或士兵) to visit or attack sb/sth suddenly and without warning 突然袭击；突击搜查；突然行动

■ ***noun*** **1** an act of moving suddenly and quickly through the air in a downward direction, as a bird does（鸟等的）向下猛冲，俯冲 SYN **dive** **2** ~ (**on sth/sb**) an act of arriving somewhere or attacking sth/sb in a way that is sudden and unexpected 突然袭击；突击搜查；突然行动 SYN **raid**: *Large quantities of drugs were found during a police swoop on the star's New York home.* 警方对这个明星在纽约的住所进行突击搜查，发现了大量毒品。IDM SEE FELL *adj.*

swoosh /swuːʃ/ *verb* [I] + **adv./prep.** to move quickly through the air in a way that makes a sound 嗖嗖地迅速移动：*Cars and trucks swooshed past.* 汽车和卡车嗖嗖地疾驶而过。▶ **swoosh** *noun* [sing.]

swop = SWAP

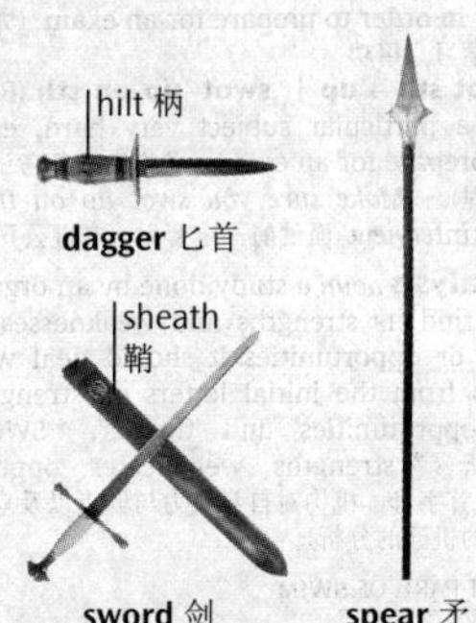

sword /sɔːd; *NAmE* sɔːrd/ *noun* a weapon with a long metal blade and a handle 剑；刀：*to* ***draw/sheathe a sword*** (= to take it out of/put it into its cover) 拔剑；把剑插入鞘 ➲ MORE LIKE THIS 20, page R27

IDM **put sb to the ˈsword** (*old-fashioned* or *literary*) to kill sb with a sword 用剑刺死某人 **a/the sword of ˈDamocles** (*literary*) a bad or an unpleasant thing that might happen to you at any time and that makes you feel worried or frightened 达摩克利斯之剑（喻指令人忧虑或畏惧的、随时可能降临的灾祸）ORIGIN From the legend in which **Damocles** had to sit at a meal at the court of Dionysius with a sword hanging by a single hair above his head. He had praised Dionysius' happiness, and Dionysius wanted him to understand how quickly happiness can be lost. 源自达摩克利斯（Damocles）在利剑下用餐的传说。达摩克利斯曾赞美狄俄尼索斯所享受的幸福，后者请他在宫中饮宴，命人将一把利剑用一根头发悬挂于他头顶，以此让他明白幸福易逝。 **turn swords into ˈploughshares** (*literary*) to stop fighting and return to peaceful activities 铸剑为犁；化干

戈为玉帛；偃武修文 ➲ MORE AT CROSS *v.*, DOUBLE-EDGED, PEN *n.*

ˈsword dance *noun* a Scottish dance in which people dance between and over SWORDS that are placed on the ground 剑舞（苏格兰舞蹈，在置于地上的刀剑间穿行）

sword·fish /ˈsɔːdfɪʃ; *NAmE* ˈsɔːrd-/ *noun* [C, U] (*pl.* **sword-fish**) a large sea fish with a very long thin pointed upper JAW 箭鱼；剑鱼

sword·play /ˈsɔːdpleɪ; *NAmE* ˈsɔːrd-/ *noun* [U] **1** the sport or skill of FENCING 击剑；剑术 **2** clever and amusing comments and replies that are made quickly 机智的巧辩 **SYN** **repartee**

swords·man /ˈsɔːdzmən; *NAmE* ˈsɔːrdz-/ *noun* (*pl.* **-men** /-mən/) (usually used with an adjective) a person who fights with a SWORD（通常与形容词连用）剑客，剑手：*a fine swordsman* 剑术高超的剑客

swords·man·ship /ˈsɔːdzmənʃɪp; *NAmE* ˈsɔːrdz-/ *noun* [U] skill in fighting with a SWORD 剑术

swore PAST TENSE OF SWEAR

sworn /swɔːn; *NAmE* swɔːrn/ *adj.* [only before noun] **1** made after you have promised to tell the truth, especially in court（尤指在法庭上）宣过誓的，宣誓证明的：*a sworn statement* 宣誓证词 **2** ~ **enemies** people, countries, etc. that have a strong hatred for each other 不共戴天的仇敌 ➲ SEE ALSO SWEAR

swot /swɒt; *NAmE* swɑːt/ *noun, verb*

■ ***noun*** (*BrE*) (*US* **grind**) (*informal, disapproving*) a person who spends too much time studying 只知一味用功学习的人；书呆子

■ ***verb*** (**-tt-**) [I] ~ (**for sth**) (*BrE, informal*) to study very hard, especially in order to prepare for an exam（尤指为准备考试）刻苦学习，用功

PHR V ˌ**swot sth↔ˈup** | ˌ**swot ˈup on sth** (*BrE, informal*) to study a particular subject very hard, especially in order to prepare for an exam（尤指为准备考试）刻苦学习（某门课程）：*Make sure you swot up on the company before the interview.* 面试前一定要用心掌握公司的情况。

ˈSWOT analysis *noun* a study done by an organization in order to find its strengths and weaknesses, and what problems or opportunities it should deal with. **SWOT** is formed from the initial letters of 'strengths', 'weaknesses', 'opportunities' and 'threats'. * SWOT 分析，强弱利弊分析（为 strengths、weaknesses、opportunities 和 threats 的首字母，机构对自身实力与弱点以及应处理的问题或应利用的机遇的分析）

swum PAST PART. OF SWIM

swung PAST TENSE, PAST PART. OF SWING

syb·ar·it·ic /ˌsɪbəˈrɪtɪk/ *adj.* [usually before noun] (*formal*) connected with a desire for pleasure 贪图享乐的；骄奢淫逸的：*his sybaritic lifestyle* 他骄奢淫逸的生活方式

syca·more /ˈsɪkəmɔː(r)/ *noun* **1** [C, U] (*especially BrE*) a European tree of the MAPLE family, with leaves that have five points and seeds shaped like a pair of wings 桐叶槭；欧亚槭 ➲ **VISUAL VOCAB PAGE V10** **2** [C] (*especially NAmE*) an American PLANE TREE 西卡莫；（美国）悬铃木 **3** [U] the valuable hard wood of the European sycamore 槭木

syco·phant /ˈsɪkəfænt/ *noun* (*formal, disapproving*) a person who praises important or powerful people too much and in a way that is not sincere, especially in order to get sth from them 阿谀奉承的人；谄媚者；拍马者 ► **syco·phancy** /ˈsɪkəfənsi/ *noun* [U] **syco·phan·tic** /ˌsɪkəˈfæntɪk/ *adj.*：*a sycophantic review* 献媚奉承的评论

syl·lab·ary /ˈsɪləbəri; *NAmE* -beri/ *noun* (*pl.* **-ies**) (*specialist*) a set of written characters representing syllables and used as an alphabet in some languages 音节文字；音节表

syl·lab·ic /sɪˈlæbɪk/ *adj.* (*phonetics* 语音) **1** based on syllables 音节的；分音节的：*syllabic stress* 音节重音 **2** (of a consonant 辅音) forming a whole syllable, for example /l/ in *settle* 成音节的

syl·lable /ˈsɪləbl/ *noun* any of the units into which a word is divided, containing a vowel sound and usually one or more consonants 音节：*a word with two syllables* 双音节单词 ◇ *a two-syllable word* 双音节单词 ◇ *'Potato' is stressed on the second syllable.* * potato 一词的重音在第二个音节上。**IDM** SEE WORD *n.*

ˈsyllable-timed *adj.* (*phonetics* 语音) (of a language 语言) having a regular rhythm of syllables 有规则音节节拍的；音节定速的 ➲ COMPARE STRESS-TIMED

syl·la·bub /ˈsɪləbʌb/ *noun* [C, U] (*BrE*) a cold DESSERT (= a sweet dish) made from cream that has been mixed very quickly with sugar, wine, fruit juice, etc. to make it thick 乳酒冻（用奶油加糖、葡萄酒、果汁等拌制）

syl·la·bus /ˈsɪləbəs/ *noun* (*pl.* **syl·la·buses** or *less frequent* **syl·labi** /ˈsɪləbaɪ/) a list of the topics, books, etc. that students should study in a particular subject at school or college 教学大纲 ➲ **COLLOCATIONS** AT EDUCATION ➲ COMPARE CURRICULUM

syl·lo·gism /ˈsɪlədʒɪzəm/ *noun* (*specialist*) a way of arguing in which two statements are used to prove that a third statement is true, for example: 'All humans must die; I am a human; therefore I must die.' 三段论（由两个前提得出结论的推理方法，如"凡人必有一死；我是人；所以我必有一死。"）► **syl·lo·gist·ic** /ˌsɪləˈdʒɪstɪk/ *adj.* [only before noun]

sylph /sɪlf/ *noun* **1** an imaginary spirit 气精；气仙 **2** a girl or woman who is thin and attractive 苗条女子

sylph·like /ˈsɪlflaɪk/ *adj.* (of a woman or girl 女人或少女) thin in an attractive way 体态轻盈柔美的；苗条的

syl·van /ˈsɪlvən/ *adj.* (*literary*) connected with forests and trees 森林的；树木的

sym·bi·osis /ˌsɪmbaɪˈəʊsɪs; *NAmE* -ˈoʊsɪs/ *noun* [U, C] (*pl.* **sym·bi·oses** /-ˈəʊsiːz; *NAmE* -ˈoʊsiːz/) **1** (*biology* 生) the relationship between two different living creatures that live close together and depend on each other in particular ways, each getting particular benefits from the other 共生（关系）**2** a relationship between people, companies, etc. that is to the advantage of both 合作关系；互惠互利的关系 ► **sym·bi·ot·ic** /-ˈɒtɪk; *NAmE* -ˈɑːtɪk/ *adj.*：*a symbiotic relationship* 一种互惠互利的关系 **sym·bi·ot·ic·al·ly** /ˌsɪmbaɪˈɒtɪkli; *NAmE* -ˈɑːtɪ-/ *adv.*

sym·bol **AW** /ˈsɪmbl/ *noun* **1** ~ (**of sth**) a person, an object, an event, etc. that represents a more general quality or situation 象征：*White has always been a symbol of purity in Western cultures.* 在西方文化中，白色一向象征纯洁。◇ *Mandela became a symbol of the anti-apartheid struggle.* 曼德拉成为反种族隔离斗争的象征。➲ **SYNONYMS** AT SIGN **2** ~ (**for sth**) a sign, number, letter, etc. that has a fixed meaning, especially in science, mathematics and music 符号；代号；记号：*What is the chemical symbol for copper?* 铜的化学符号是什么？◇ *A list of symbols used on the map is given in the index.* 这份地图所使用的符号全部列在索引中。➲ SEE ALSO SEX SYMBOL, STATUS SYMBOL

sym·bol·ic **AW** /sɪmˈbɒlɪk; *NAmE* -ˈbɑːlɪk/ *adj.* ~ (**of sth**) containing symbols, or being used as a symbol 使用象征的；作为象征的；象征性的：*The dove is symbolic of peace.* 鸽子是和平的象征。◇ *The Channel Tunnel has enormous symbolic significance for a united Europe.* 英吉利海峡隧道对于建立一个统一的欧洲具有重大的象征意义。◇ *The new regulations are largely symbolic* (= they will not have any real effect). 新的制度基本上是象征性的。► **sym·bol·ic·al·ly** **AW** /sɪmˈbɒlɪkli; *NAmE* -ˈbɑːlɪk-/ *adv.*：*a symbolically significant gesture* 有象征意义的姿态

sym·bol·ism **AW** /ˈsɪmbəlɪzəm/ *noun* [U] the use of symbols to represent ideas, especially in art and literature（尤指文艺中的）象征主义，象征手法 ➲ COLLOCATIONS

AT LITERATURE ▶ **sym·bol·ist** /ˈsɪmbəlɪst/ *adj., noun*: *the symbolist poet Rimbaud* 象征主义诗人兰波

sym·bol·ize AW (*BrE also* **-ise**) /ˈsɪmbəlaɪz/ *verb* **~ sth** to be a symbol of sth 象征；是…的象征；代表 SYN **represent**: *The use of light and dark symbolizes good and evil.* 用光明与黑暗来象征善与恶。◇ *He came to symbolize his country's struggle for independence.* 他逐渐成为祖国为争取独立而斗争的象征。

sym·met·rical /sɪˈmetrɪkl/ (*also* **sym·met·ric** /sɪˈmetrɪk/) *adj.* (of a body, a design, an object, etc. 身体、图案、物体等) having two halves, parts or sides that are the same in size and shape 对称的：*a symmetrical pattern* 对称的图案 OPP **asymmetric** ▶ **sym·met·ric·al·ly** /-kli/ *adv.*

sym·metry /ˈsɪmətri/ *noun* [U] **1** the exact match in size and shape between two halves, parts or sides of sth 对称：*the perfect symmetry of the garden design* 花园图案的完全对称 ➲ PICTURE AT AXIS **2** the quality of being very similar or equal 相似；相仿；相等：*the increasing symmetry between men's and women's jobs* 男女职业的日渐趋同

sym·pa·thet·ic 🔑 /ˌsɪmpəˈθetɪk/ *adj.* **1** 🔑 **~ (to/towards sb)** kind to sb who is hurt or sad; showing that you understand and care about their problems 同情的；有同情心的；表示同情的：*a sympathetic listener* 体恤别人的听者 ◇ *I did not feel at all sympathetic towards Kate.* 我对凯特一点也不同情。◇ *I'm here if you need a* ***sympathetic ear*** (= sb to talk to about your problems). 要是你想诉诉苦，那就跟我说吧。**2** 🔑 **~ (to/towards sb/sth)** showing that you approve of sb/sth or that you share their views and are willing to support them 赞同的；支持的：*to be sympathetic to the party's aims* 赞同该党的目标 ◇ *Russian newspapers are largely sympathetic to the president.* 俄罗斯报章大都支持总统。**3** (of a person 人) easy to like 让人喜欢的；招人喜爱的：*a* ***sympathetic character*** *in a novel* 小说中一个讨人喜欢的人物 ◇ *I don't find her a very sympathetic person.* 我觉得她并不十分招人喜欢。HELP This meaning is not very common and you should use **likeable** or **pleasant** instead. 这个词义不大常用，可用 likeable 或 pleasant 代替。OPP **unsympathetic** ▶ **sym·pa·thet·ic·al·ly** *adv.*: *to smile at sb sympathetically* 向某人微笑表示赞同 ◇ *We hope this application will be treated sympathetically* (= it will be approved). 我们希望这份申请能得到批准。

sym·pa·thize (*BrE also* **-ise**) /ˈsɪmpəθaɪz/ *verb* **1** [I, T] **~ (with sb/sth) | + speech** to feel sorry for sb; to show that you understand and feel sorry about sb's problems 同情：*I find it very hard to sympathize with him.* 我觉得很难去同情他。**2** [I] **~ with sb/sth** to support sb/sth 赞同；支持：*He has never really sympathized with the aims of Animal Rights activists.* 他从来没有真正赞同过动物权利保护者的目标。

sym·pa·thizer (*BrE also* **-iser**) /ˈsɪmpəθaɪzə(r)/ *noun* a person who supports or approves of sb/sth, especially a political cause or party 赞同者；支持者：*communist sympathizers* 共产主义的拥护者

sym·pathy 🔑 /ˈsɪmpəθi/ *noun* (*pl.* **-ies**) **1** 🔑 [U, C, usually pl.] the feeling of being sorry for sb; showing that you understand and care about sb's problems 同情：*to* ***express/feel sympathy*** *for sb* 向某人表示体恤；对某人感到同情 ◇ *I* ***have no sympathy for*** *Jan, it's all her own fault.* 我不同情简，那都是她自己的错。◇ *I wish he'd show me a little more sympathy.* 我多希望他能再体谅我一点。◇ ***Our*** *heartfelt* ***sympathy goes out*** *to the victims of the war.* 我们对战争的受害者表示由衷的同情。◇ (*formal*) *May* ***we offer*** *our deepest* ***sympathies*** *on the death of your wife.* 我们谨对尊夫人去世表示最深切的慰唁。➲ WORDFINDER NOTE AT SORRY **2** 🔑 [U, C, usually pl.] the act of showing support for or approval of an idea, a cause, an organization, etc. 赞同；支持：*The seamen went on strike* ***in sympathy with*** (= to show their support for) *the dockers.* 海员举行罢工，以表示对码头工人的支持。◇ *Her sympathies lie with the anti-abortion lobby.* 她支持反堕胎的团体。**3** [U] friendship and understanding between people who have similar opinions or interests 意气相投；志同道合：*There was no personal sympathy between them.* 他们个人之间全无相投之处。

IDM **in ˈsympathy with sth** happening because sth else has happened 因…而出现；相应发生：*Share prices slipped in sympathy with the German market.* 受德国市场影响，股票价格出现下跌。**out of ˈsympathy with sb/sth** not agreeing with or not wanting to support sb/sth 不赞成，不支持（某人或事物）

▼ **EXPRESS YOURSELF 情景表达**

Expressing sympathy 表达同情

If someone is ill, or something bad has happened to them, you can show them that you are sorry. 有人生病或遭遇不幸时，向他们表示同情可以这么说：

- ***I'm sorry you're not well. I hope you feel better soon.*** 你身体不适，我很难过。希望你尽快好起来。
- ***I am sorry to hear that.*** 听到这个消息我很难过。
- ***That's bad luck.*** 真是不幸。
- ***How awful for you.*** 这对你太糟糕了。
- ***I'm sorry for your loss*** (when sb has died). 你失去了亲人，我很难过。

sym·phony /ˈsɪmfəni/ *noun* (*pl.* **-ies**) a long complicated piece of music for a large ORCHESTRA, in three or four main parts (called MOVEMENTS) 交响乐；交响曲：*Beethoven's Fifth Symphony* 贝多芬的第五交响曲 ➲ COLLOCATIONS AT MUSIC ▶ **sym·phon·ic** /sɪmˈfɒnɪk; *NAmE* -ˈfɑːn-/ *adj.*: *Mozart's symphonic works* 莫扎特的交响乐作品

ˈsymphony orchestra *noun* a large ORCHESTRA that plays CLASSICAL music 交响乐团：*the Boston Symphony Orchestra* 波士顿交响乐团

sym·po·sium /sɪmˈpəʊziəm; *NAmE* -ˈpoʊ-/ *noun* (*pl.* **sym·po·sia** /-ziə/ or **sym·po·siums**) **~ (on sth)** a meeting at which experts have discussions about a particular subject; a small conference 专题讨论会；研讨会；小型讨论会

symp·tom /ˈsɪmptəm/ *noun* **1** a change in your body or mind that shows that you are not healthy 症状：*flu symptoms* 流感症状 ◇ *Look out for symptoms of depression.* 留心看有无抑郁症状。◇ *Symptoms include a headache and sore throat.* 症状包括头痛和咽喉疼痛。➲ WORDFINDER NOTE AT EXAMINE **2** a sign that sth exists, especially sth bad 征候；征兆 SYN **indication**: *The rise in inflation was just one symptom of the poor state of the economy.* 通胀上升不过是经济不景气的一个征候。➲ SYNONYMS AT SIGN

symp·tom·at·ic /ˌsɪmptəˈmætɪk/ *adj.* being a sign of an illness or a problem 作为症状的；（有）症状的；作为征候的：*a symptomatic infection* 有症状感染 ◇ **~ of sth** *These disagreements are symptomatic of the tensions within the party.* 出现意见分歧表明该党内部的关系紧张。

symp·tom·ize /ˈsɪmptəmaɪz/ *verb* **~ sth** (*US*) to be a sign or SYMPTOM of sth 是…的症状（或征候）

syn·aes·the·sia (*also* **syn·es·the·sia**) /ˌsɪnəsˈθiːziə; *NAmE* -ˈθiːʒə/ *noun* [U] (*biology* 生) the fact of experiencing some things in a different way from most other people, for example experiencing colours as sounds or shapes as tastes, or feeling sth in one part of the body when a different part is STIMULATED 联觉（对一种感官的刺激作用触发另一种感官知觉）

syna·gogue /ˈsɪnəɡɒɡ; *NAmE* -ɡɑːɡ/ *noun* a building where Jews meet for religious worship and teaching 犹太会堂；犹太教堂

syn·apse /ˈsaɪnæps; ˈsɪn-/ *noun* (*biology* 生) a connection between two nerve cells（神经元的）突触 ▶ **syn·ap·tic** /saɪˈnæptɪk; sɪˈn-/ *adj.*: *the synaptic membranes* 突触膜

sync (*also* **synch**) /sɪŋk/ *noun, verb* (*informal*)

■ *noun*

IDM **in ˈsync 1** moving or working at exactly the same time and speed as sb/sth else 同步：*The soundtrack is* ***not in sync*** *with the picture.* 音画不同步。**2** in agreement

S

with sb/sth; working well with sb/sth 一致；协调：*His opinions were in sync with those of his colleagues.* 他的看法和同事的一致。**out of 'sync** **1** not moving or working at exactly the same time and speed as sb/sth else 不同步 **2** not in agreement with sb/sth; not working well with sb/sth 不一致；不协调 ➲ SEE ALSO LIP-SYNC, SYNCHRONIZATION at SYNCHRONIZE

■ *verb* [T, I] = SYNCHRONIZE: **~ sth (up) (to/with sth)** *The live music isn't synced to the visuals.* 现场音乐跟画面不同步。◇ *How do I sync email across all my devices?* 我要如何在我所有的设备上设定电子邮件同步？◇ **~ (up) with/to sth** *Bluetooth technology will enable a cell phone to sync with a car's stereo speaker.* 蓝牙技术能使手机与汽车的立体声喇叭同步。

syn·chron·ic /sɪŋˈkrɒnɪk; *NAmE* -ˈkrɑːn-/ *adj.* (*linguistics* 语言) relating to a language as it is at a particular point in time（语言）共时的 ➲ COMPARE DIACHRONIC

syn·chron·icity /ˌsɪŋkrəˈnɪsəti/ *noun* [U] (*specialist*) the fact of two or more things happening at exactly the same time 同步性；同时发生

syn·chron·ize (*BrE also* **-ise**) (*also informal* **sync**, *informal* **synch**) /ˈsɪŋkrənaɪz/ *verb* **1** [I, T] to happen at the same time or to move at the same speed as sth; to make sth do this（使）同步，在时间上一致，同速进行：**~ (with sth)** *The soundtrack did not synchronize with the action.* 声迹与动作不同步。◇ **~ sth (with sth)** *Let's synchronize our watches* (= make them show exactly the same time). 咱们对一下表吧。**2** [T] to link data files between one computer or mobile device and another so that the information in the files on both machines is the same 使同步，使一致（使数据在不同的计算机或移动电子设备上同步更新）：**~ sth (between A and B)** *You can use the technology to synchronize data between computers.* 利用该技术可在计算机之间同步数据。◇ **~ sth (with sth)** *The phone lets you synchronize your calendar and contacts with your PC.* 这台手机可以将你的日程表和联系人信息与个人电脑同步。▶ **syn·chron·iza·tion, -isa·tion** /ˌsɪŋkrənaɪˈzeɪʃn; *NAmE* -nəˈz-/ (*also informal* **sync**) *noun* [U]

ˌsynchronized 'swimming (*BrE also* **-ised**) *noun* [U] a sport in which groups of SWIMMERS move in patterns in the water to music 花样游泳（组员伴着音乐同步进行）

syn·chron·ous /ˈsɪŋkrənəs/ *adj.* (*specialist*) happening or existing at the same time 同时发生（或存在）的；同步的；共时的

syn·cline /ˈsɪŋklaɪn/ *noun* (*geology* 地) an area of ground where layers of rock in the earth's surface have been folded into a curve that is lower in the middle than at the ends 向斜 ➲ COMPARE ANTICLINE

syn·co·pated /ˈsɪŋkəpeɪtɪd/ *adj.* (*music* 音) in **syncopated** rhythm the strong beats are made weak and the weak beats are made strong 切分的，切分音乐的（节拍强弱倒置）▶ **syn·co·pa·tion** /ˌsɪŋkəˈpeɪʃn/ *noun* [U]

syn·cope /ˈsɪŋkəpi/ *noun* [U] (*phonetics* 语音) the dropping of a sound or sounds in the middle of a word when it is spoken, for example the pronunciation of *library* as /ˈlaɪbri/ 词中语音省略（如将 library 发成 /ˈlaɪbri/）

syn·cre·tism /ˈsɪŋkrətɪzəm/ *noun* [U] **1** (*specialist*) the mixing of different religions, philosophies or ideas（不同宗教、哲学或思想的）融合 **2** (*linguistics* 语言) the mixing of different forms of the same word during the development of a language （语言发展过程中词的）屈折形式融合，铒合

syn·dic·al·ism /ˈsɪndɪkəlɪzəm/ *noun* [U] the belief that factories, businesses, etc. should be owned and managed by all the people who work in them 工团主义，工联主义（认为企业应由全体员工共同拥有及管理）

syn·dic·al·ist /ˈsɪndɪkəlɪst/ *noun* a person who believes in syndicalism 工团主义者；工联主义者 ▶ **syn·dic·al·ist** *adj.*

syn·di·cate *noun, verb*

■ ***noun*** /ˈsɪndɪkət/ a group of people or companies who work together and help each other in order to achieve a particular aim 辛迪加；企业联合组织；财团；私人联合会

■ ***verb*** /ˈsɪndɪkeɪt/ [usually passive] **~ sth** to sell an article, a photograph, a television programme, etc. to several different newspapers, etc. 把（文章、图片、电视节目等）出售给多个媒体：*His column is syndicated throughout the world.* 他的专栏文章在世界各地的报刊发表。▶ **syn·di·ca·tion** /ˌsɪndɪˈkeɪʃn/ *noun* [U]

syn·drome /ˈsɪndrəʊm; *NAmE* -droʊm/ *noun* **1** a set of physical conditions that show you have a particular disease or medical problem 综合征；综合症状：*PMS or premenstrual syndrome* 经前综合征 ◇ *This syndrome is associated with frequent coughing.* 这种综合症与经常咳嗽有关。➲ SEE ALSO AIDS, DOWN'S SYNDROME, ECONOMY CLASS SYNDROME, SICK BUILDING SYNDROME, TOURETTE'S SYNDROME **2** a set of opinions or a way of behaving that is typical of a particular type of person, attitude or social problem 典型意见；典型表现：*With teenagers, be prepared for the 'Me, me, me!' syndrome* (= they think of themselves first). 跟青少年在一起，对他们那种凡事只想到"我，我，我！"的典型心理不要大惊小怪。

syn·ec·doche /sɪˈnekdəki/ *noun* [U, C] (*specialist*) a word or phrase in which a part of sth is used to represent a whole, or a whole is used to represent a part of sth. For example, in 'Australia lost by two goals', *Australia* is used to represent the Australian team. 举偶法，提喻法（用局部代表整体或用整体代表局部的修辞手法）

syn·ergy /ˈsɪnədʒi; *NAmE* -ərdʒi/ *noun* [U, C] (*pl.* **-ies**) (*specialist*) the extra energy, power, success, etc. that is achieved by two or more people, companies or elements working together, instead of on their own 协同作用，协同增效作用（多方共同协作所产生的效果优于各自单独行动的效果）▶ **syn·er·gis·tic** /ˌsɪnəˈdʒɪstɪk; *NAmE* ˌsɪnər-/ *adj.* **syn·er·gis·tic·al·ly** /-kli/ *adv.*

synod /ˈsɪnəd; *BrE also* -nɒd/ *noun* an official meeting of Church members to discuss religious matters and make important decisions 教会会议

syno·nym /ˈsɪnənɪm/ *noun* a word or an expression that has the same or nearly the same meaning as another in the same language 同义词：*'Big' and 'large' are synonyms.* * big 和 large 是同义词。➲ COMPARE ANTONYM ➲ WORDFINDER NOTE AT WORD

syn·onym·ous /sɪˈnɒnɪməs; *NAmE* -ˈnɑːn-/ *adj.* **1** (of words or expressions 词语) having the same, or nearly the same, meaning 同义的 **2** **~ (with sth)** so closely connected with sth that the two things appear to be the same 等同于…的：*Wealth is not necessarily synonymous with happiness.* 财富未必等同于幸福。▶ **syn·onym·ous·ly** *adv.*

syn·onymy /sɪˈnɒnɪmi; *NAmE* -ˈnɑːn-/ *noun* [U] the fact of two or more words or expressions having the same meaning 同义；同义关系

syn·op·sis /sɪˈnɒpsɪs; *NAmE* -ˈnɑːp-/ *noun* (*pl.* **syn·op·ses** /-siːz/) a summary of a piece of writing, a play, etc.（著作、剧本等的）大纲，提要，概要，梗概 ▶ **syn·op·tic** /sɪˈnɒptɪk; *NAmE* -ˈnɑːp-/ *adj.* (*formal*)

syn·ovial /saɪˈnəʊviəl; sɪˈn-; *NAmE* sɪˈnoʊ-/ *adj.* (*biology* 生) (of a joint 关节) having a MEMBRANE (= a piece of very thin skin) containing liquid between the bones, which allows the joint to move freely（含）滑膜的

syn·tac·tic /sɪnˈtæktɪk/ *adj.* (*linguistics* 语言) connected with SYNTAX 句法的 ▶ **syn·tac·tic·al·ly** /-kli/ *adv.*: *to be syntactically correct* 在句法上正确

syn·tagm /ˈsɪntæm/ *noun* (*also* **syn·tagma** /sɪnˈtægmə/) (*linguistics* 语言) a unit of language consisting of sets of PHONEMES, words, or phrases that are arranged in order（语言）语段，结构段，结构体 ▶ **syn·tag·mat·ic** /ˌsɪntægˈmætɪk/ *adj.*

S

syn·tax /ˈsɪntæks/ *noun* [U] **1** (*linguistics* 语言) the way that words and phrases are put together to form sentences in a language; the rules of grammar for this 句法；句法规则 ➲ COMPARE MORPHOLOGY (2) **2** (*computing* 计) the rules that state how words and phrases must be used in a computer language 语法；句法；语构

synth /sɪnθ/ *noun* (*informal*) = SYNTHESIZER

syn·the·sis /ˈsɪnθəsɪs/ *noun* (*pl.* **syn·the·ses** /-siːz/) **1** [U, C] ~ (**of sth**) the act of combining separate ideas, beliefs, styles, etc.; a mixture or combination of ideas, beliefs, styles, etc. 综合；结合；综合体：*the synthesis of art with everyday life* 艺术与日常生活的结合 ◇ *a synthesis of traditional and modern values* 传统价值观和现代价值观的综合体 **2** [U] (*specialist*) the natural chemical production of a substance in animals and plants（物质在动植物体内的）合成：*protein synthesis* 蛋白质的合成 **3** [U] (*specialist*) the artificial production of a substance that is present naturally in animals and plants（人工的）合成：*the synthesis of penicillin* 青霉素的合成 **4** [U] (*specialist*) the production of sounds, music or speech by electronic means（用电子手段对声音、音乐或语音的）合成：*speech synthesis* 语音合成

syn·the·size (*BrE also* **-ise**) /ˈsɪnθəsaɪz/ *verb* **1** ~ **sth** (*specialist*) to produce a substance by means of chemical or BIOLOGICAL processes（通过化学手段或生物过程）合成 **2** ~ **sth** to produce sounds, music or speech using electronic equipment（音响）合成 **3** ~ **sth** to combine separate ideas, beliefs, styles, etc. 综合

syn·the·sizer (*BrE also* **-iser**) /ˈsɪnθəsaɪzə(r)/ (*also informal* **synth**) *noun* an electronic machine for producing different sounds. Synthesizers are used as musical instruments, especially for copying the sounds of other instruments, and for copying speech sounds. 音响合成器：*a speech synthesizer* 语音合成器 ➲ COMPARE KEYBOARD *n.* (3)

syn·thet·ic /sɪnˈθetɪk/ *adj., noun*

■ ***adj.*** **1** artificial; made by combining chemical substances rather than being produced naturally by plants or animals 人造的；（人工）合成的 **SYN** **man-made**: *synthetic drugs/fabrics* 合成药物/织物 ◇ *synthetic dyes* 合成染料 ➲ **SYNONYMS** AT **ARTIFICIAL** **2** (*also* **ag·glu·tin·ative**) (*linguistics* 语言) (of languages 语言) using changes to the ends of words rather than separate words to show the functions of words in a sentence 综合（型）的 ➲ COMPARE ANALYTIC (2) ▸ **syn·thet·ic·al·ly** /-kli/ *adv.*

■ ***noun*** an artificial substance or material 合成物；合成纤维（织物）；合成剂：*cotton fabrics and synthetics* 棉织物与合成织物

syph·ilis /ˈsɪfɪlɪs/ *noun* [U] a disease that gets worse over a period of time, spreading from the sexual organs to the skin, bones, muscles and brain. It is caught by having sex with an infected person. 梅毒 ▸ **syph·il·it·ic** /ˌsɪfɪˈlɪtɪk/ *adj.*

sy·phon = SIPHON

syr·inge /sɪˈrɪndʒ/ *noun, verb*

■ ***noun*** **1** (*also* **hypo·der·mic**, ˌ**hypodermic syˈringe**) a plastic or glass tube with a long hollow needle that is used for putting drugs, etc. into a person's body or for taking a small amount of blood from a person（皮下）注射器 **2** a plastic or glass tube with a rubber part at the end, used for sucking up liquid and then pushing it out 吸管；唧筒 ➲ **VISUAL VOCAB PAGE V72**

■ ***verb*** ~ **sth** to clean sb's ear by spraying liquid into it with a SYRINGE 用注射器清洗（耳朵）：*I had my ears syringed.* 我的耳朵已用注射器清洗干净。

syrup /ˈsɪrəp/ *noun* [U] **1** a sweet liquid made from sugar and water, often used in cans of fruit 糖水（罐头水果常用）：*pears in syrup* 糖水梨 **2** any thick sweet liquid made with sugar, used especially as a sauce 糖浆 ➲ SEE ALSO CORN SYRUP, GOLDEN SYRUP, MAPLE SYRUP

syr·upy /ˈsɪrəpi/ *adj.* **1** thick and sticky like syrup; containing syrup 糖浆般黏稠的；含糖浆的 **2** (*disapproving*) extremely emotional and romantic and therefore unpleasant; too SENTIMENTAL 缠绵的；过分多情的：*a syrupy romantic novel* 一部缠绵的言情小说

sys·tem 🔑 /ˈsɪstəm/ *noun* **1** 🔑 [C] an organized set of ideas or theories or a particular way of doing sth（思想或理论）体系；方法；制度；体制：*the British educational system* 英国的教育制度 ◇ ~ **for doing sth** *a new system for assessing personal tax bills* 新的个人税额估定办法 ◇ ~ **of sth** *a system of government* 政体 ➲ SEE ALSO BINARY (2), METRIC SYSTEM ➲ **WORDFINDER NOTE** AT GOVERNMENT

> **WORDFINDER** 联想词：capitalism, communism, **democracy**, dictatorship, fascism, imperialism, liberal, radical, socialism

2 🔑 [C] a group of things, pieces of equipment, etc. that are connected or work together 系统：*a transport system* 运输系统 ◇ *heating systems* 供热系统 ◇ *a stereo system* 立体声音响系统 ◇ *a security system* 保安系统 ➲ SEE ALSO ECOSYSTEM, EXPERT SYSTEM, OPERATING SYSTEM, PUBLIC ADDRESS SYSTEM, SOLAR SYSTEM **3** 🔑 [C] a human or an animal body, or a part of it, when it is being thought of as the organs and processes that make it function 身体；（器官）系统：*You have to wait until the drugs have passed out of your system.* 你必须等到药物排出体外。◇ *the male reproductive system* 男性生殖系统 ➲ SEE ALSO CENTRAL NERVOUS SYSTEM, DIGESTIVE SYSTEM, IMMUNE SYSTEM **4 the system** [sing.] (*informal, usually disapproving*) the rules or people that control a country or an organization, especially when they seem to be unfair because you cannot change them（尤指不公正的统治或管理）制度，体系，集团：*You can't* ***beat the system*** (= you must accept it). 你斗不过现行的体制。◇ *young people rebelling against the system* 反抗现行体制的年轻人

IDM **get sth out of your ˈsystem** (*informal*) to do sth so that you no longer feel a very strong emotion or have a strong desire 宣泄，排解，消解（强烈的感情或欲望）：*I was very angry with him, but now I feel I've got it out of my system.* 我当时很生他的气，不过现在我感觉气已经消了。

sys·tem·at·ic /ˌsɪstəˈmætɪk/ *adj.* done according to a system or plan, in a thorough, efficient or determined way 成体系的；系统的；有条理的；有计划有步骤的：*a* ***systematic approach to*** *solving the problem* 系统地解决问题的办法 ◇ *a systematic attempt to destroy the organization* 力图摧毁那个组织的有计划有步骤的行动 ◇ *The prisoner was subjected to systematic torture.* 犯人受到蓄意折磨。**OPP** **unsystematic** ▸ **sys·tem·at·ic·al·ly** /-kli/ *adv.*: *The search was carried out systematically.* 搜查已按照部署执行。

sys·tem·atize (*BrE also* **-ise**) /ˈsɪstəmətaɪz/ *verb* ~ **sth** (*formal*) to arrange sth according to a system 使系统化；使成体系；使条理化 **SYN** **organize** ▸ **sys·tem·atiza·tion**, **-isa·tion** /ˌsɪstəmətaɪˈzeɪʃn; *NAmE* -təˈz-/ *noun* [U]

sys·tem·ic /sɪˈstemɪk; sɪˈstiːmɪk/ *adj.* (*specialist*) **1** affecting or connected with the whole of sth, especially the human body 涉及全系统的；系统的；影响全身的；全身的 **2** **systemic** chemicals or drugs that are used to treat diseases in plants or animals enter the body of the plant or animal and spread to all parts of it（农药等）内吸的：*systemic weedkillers* 内吸除草剂 ▸ **sys·tem·ic·al·ly** *adv.*

ˈ**system operator** (*also* ˈ**systems operator**) *noun* (*computing* 计) a person who manages a computer system or an electronic communication service 计算机系统管理员；系统操作员；电子公告板管理员

ˈ**systems analyst** *noun* a person whose job is to analyse the needs of a business company or an organization and then design processes for working efficiently using computer programs 系统分析员 ▸ ˈ**systems analysis** *noun* [U]

ˈ**system unit** *noun* (*computing* 计) the main part of a computer, separate from the keyboard, mouse and monitor,

S

that contains the unit that controls all the other parts of the system 系统单元，系统部件（包含中央处理器，不含键盘、鼠标和显示器的电脑主体部分）➲ VISUAL VOCAB PAGE V73

sys·tole /ˈsɪstəli/ *noun* (*medical* 医) the stage of the heart's rhythm when the heart PUMPS blood 心缩期 ▶ **sys·tol·ic** /ˌsɪsˈtɒlɪk; *NAmE* -ˈtɑːl-/ *adj.*

Tt

T (*also* **t**) /tiː/ *noun* [C, U] (*pl.* **Ts, T's, t's** /tiːz/) the 20th letter of the English alphabet 英语字母表的第 20 个字母：*'Tin' begins with (a) T/'T'.* * tin 一词以字母 t 开头。➲ SEE ALSO T-BONE STEAK, T-JUNCTION, T-SHIRT, T-SQUARE
IDM **to a 'T/'tee** (*informal*) used to say that sth is exactly right for sb, succeeds in doing sth in exactly the right way, etc. （用以表示完全合适）恰好，丝毫不差：*Her new job suits her to a T.* 她的新工作对她再合适不过了。◇ *The novel captures the feeling of the pre-war period to a T.* 这部小说对战前时期的情怀把握得恰到好处。➲ MORE AT DOT *v.*

TA /ˌtiː ˈeɪ/ *noun* **1** (*BrE*) TERRITORIAL ARMY （英国）本土防卫义勇军；国防义勇军 **2** (*NAmE*) TEACHING ASSISTANT 助教

ta /tɑː/ *exclamation* (*BrE, slang*) thank you 谢谢

taa·rab /ˈtɑːrʌb/ *noun* [U] a type of music that is popular in E Africa, especially along the coast, and that is influenced by Arabian and Indian music 塔拉勃乐（受阿拉伯和印度音乐影响的东非流行乐，尤盛行于沿海地区）

tab /tæb/ *noun, verb*
■ ***noun*** **1** a small piece of paper, cloth, metal, etc. that sticks out from the edge of sth, and that is used to give information about it, or to hold it, fasten it, etc. 标签；签条；突耳；凸舌：*Insert tab A into slot 1* (= for example to make a model, box, etc.). 将凸舌 A 插入 1 号孔（如制作模型、盒子等）。**2** = TAB STOP **3** (*NAmE*) = PULL TAB **4** a bill for goods you receive but pay for later, especially for food or drinks in a restaurant or bar; the price or cost of sth （待付的）账单，账款；（尤指）餐饮账单；费用：*a bar tab* 酒吧账单 ◇ *Can I put it on my tab?* 我可以记账吗？◇ *The tab for the meeting could be $3 000.* 这次会议的费用可能达 3 000 美元。**5** (*informal*) a small solid piece of an illegal drug 药片，药丸（指毒品）：*a tab of Ecstasy* 一粒摇头丸 **6** = TABLATURE：*guitar tabs* 吉他奏法乐谱
IDM **keep (close) tabs on sb/sth** (*informal*) to watch sb/sth carefully in order to know what is happening so that you can control a particular situation 监视；密切注视：*It's not always possible to keep tabs on everyone's movements.* 监视每个人的行动并不总是能办得到的。➲ MORE AT PICK *v.*
■ ***verb*** (**-bb-**) **1** ~ **sb (as) sth** (*especially NAmE*) to say that sb is suitable for a particular job or role or describe them in a particular way 说（某人）适合于（某工作或角色）；把（某人）视为…：*He has been tabbed by many people as a future champion.* 许多人都说他是未来的冠军。**2** ~ **sth** to use the TAB KEY when you are using a keyboard 使用制表键

tab·ard /ˈtæbəd; -bɑːd; *NAmE* -bərd; -bɑːrd/ *noun* a simple piece of clothing consisting of back and front sections without sleeves, and a hole for the head 塔巴德式外衣，搭肩衫（由前后两片组成，无领无袖）

Tab·asco™ /təˈbæskəʊ; *NAmE* -koʊ/ *noun* [U] a red spicy sauce made from PEPPERS 塔巴斯科辣椒酱

tab·bou·leh /təˈbuːleɪ; *BrE also* ˈtæbuːleɪ/ *noun* [U] an Arab dish consisting of crushed WHEAT with chopped tomatoes, onions and HERBS 塔博勒色拉，麦粒番茄色拉（阿拉伯菜，用碎麦粒和切碎的番茄、洋葱和香草调制而成）

tabby /ˈtæbi/ *noun* (*pl.* **-ies**) (*also* **ˈtabby cat**) a cat with brown or grey fur marked with dark lines or spots 斑猫（毛皮灰色或褐色，带有深色斑条或斑点）

tab·er·nacle /ˈtæbənækl; *NAmE* -bərn-/ *noun* **1** [C] a place of worship for some groups of Christians （某些基督教派的）礼拜堂，会堂：*a Mormon tabernacle* 摩门教教堂 **2** **the tabernacle** [sing.] a small place of worship that could be moved, used by the Jews in ancient times when they were travelling in the desert 圣所，会幕（古代犹太人在沙漠旅途中拜神用）

ˈtab key (*also* **tab**, *formal* **tabu·la·tor**) *noun* a button on a keyboard that you use to move to a certain fixed position in a line of a document that you are typing （键盘上的）跳格键，制表键，Tab 键

tabla /ˈtæblə; ˈtʌb-/ *noun* a pair of small drums played with the hands and used in S Asian music, usually to accompany other instruments 塔布拉双鼓（用于南亚音乐中的成对小手鼓，通常作为伴奏乐器）

tab·lat·ure /ˈtæblətʃə(r)/ (*also* **tab**) *noun* [U, C] a way of representing musical notes on paper by showing the position of the fingers on a musical instrument rather than the actual notes; an example of this 符号记谱法，奏法记谱法（标明演奏者的手指位置）：*The book contains lyrics and guitar tablatures for over 100 songs.* 这本书有 100 多首带歌词的吉他六线谱记谱的歌曲。

table 🔑 /ˈteɪbl/ *noun, verb*
■ ***noun***
• **FURNITURE** 家具 **1** 🔑 a piece of furniture that consists of a flat top supported by legs 桌子；台子；几：*a kitchen table* 厨房用桌 ◇ *A table for two, please* (= in a restaurant). 请安排两人一桌的位子。◇ *I'd like to* ***book a table*** *for tonight* (= in a restaurant). 我想为今天晚上预订一个桌位。◇ *to* ***set the table*** (= to put the plates, knives, etc. on it for a meal) 摆餐具 ◇ (*BrE also*) *to* ***lay the table*** 摆餐具 ◇ *to* ***clear the table*** (= take away the dirty plates, etc. at the end of a meal) （餐后）清理餐桌 ◇ *He questioned her next morning over the breakfast table* (= during breakfast). 第二天早上，他一边吃着早餐一边查问她。◇ (*BrE, formal*) *Children must learn to behave* ***at table.*** 小孩必须学会吃饭时的规矩。◇ *a* ***billiard/snooker/pool table*** 台球 / 斯诺克 / 普尔球台 ➲ VISUAL VOCAB PAGE V44 **HELP** There are many compounds ending in **table**. You will find them at their place in the alphabet. 以 table 结尾的复合词很多，可在各字母中的适当位置查到。
• **PEOPLE** 人 **2** the people sitting at a table for a meal or to play cards, etc. （就餐或玩牌等的）一桌人：*He kept the whole table entertained with his jokes.* 他笑话不断，把全桌人逗得直乐。➲ SEE ALSO ROUND-TABLE
• **LIST OF FACTS/NUMBERS** 细目表；数字表 **3** 🔑 a list of facts or numbers arranged in a special order, usually in rows and columns 表；一览表：*a* ***table of contents*** (= a list of the main points or information in a book, usually at the front of the book) 目录 ◇ *Table 2 shows how prices and earnings have increased over the past 20 years.* 表 2 显示了过去 20 年来价格和收入的增长情况。➲ SEE ALSO PERIODIC TABLE
• **IN SPORT** 体育运动 **4** a list of sports teams, countries, schools, etc. that shows their position in a competition, etc. （竞赛等的）名次表，排名榜，积分表：*If Arsenal win this game they'll go to the top of the table.* 阿森纳队如果赢得这场比赛，就会登上积分榜榜首。◇ *school performance league tables* 学校排名表
• **MATHEMATICS** 数学 **5** = MULTIPLICATION TABLE：*Do you know your six times table?* 你会背六的乘法口诀吗？➲ SEE ALSO TURNTABLE, WATER TABLE
IDM **ˌbring sth to the ˈparty/ˈtable** to contribute sth useful to a discussion, project, etc. 为（讨论、项目等）作出贡献：*What Hislop brought to the table was real commitment and energy.* 希斯洛普作出的贡献是他全身心的投入和干劲。 **on the ˈtable** **1** (of a plan, suggestion, etc. 将计划、建议等) offered to people so that they can consider or discuss it 提供考虑；提交讨论：*Management have put several new proposals on the table.* 管理部门已将几项新的建议提交讨论。 **2** (*especially NAmE*) (of a plan, suggestion, etc. 计划、建议等) not going to be discussed or considered until a future date 搁置 **turn the ˈtables (on sb)** to change a situation so that you are now in a stronger position than the person who used to be in a stronger position than you 扭转形势；转变局面；转弱为强 ➲ MORE AT CARD *n.*, DRINK *v.*, WAIT *v.*
■ ***verb*** **1** ~ **sth** (*BrE*) to present sth formally for discussion （正式）提出，把…列入议事日程：*They have tabled a motion for debate at the next Party Conference.* 他们已经提出一项动议，在下次党的会议上进行辩论。 **2** ~ **sth**

T

(*NAmE*) to leave an idea, a proposal, etc. to be discussed at a later date（将主意、建议等）搁置：*They voted to table the proposal until the following meeting.* 他们投票决定把这项建议留到下次会议讨论。

tab·leau /ˈtæbləʊ; *NAmE* -loʊ/ *noun* (*pl.* **tab·leaux** /-ləʊ; -ləʊz; *NAmE* -loʊ; -loʊz/) **1** a scene showing, for example, events and people from history, that is presented by a group of actors who do not move or speak 舞台造型；静态画面：*The procession included a tableau of the Battle of Hastings.* 游行队伍中包括黑斯廷斯战役的人物造型。◇ (*figurative*) *She stood at the door observing the peaceful domestic tableau around the fire.* 她站在门口，看着炉火周围阖家祥和的景象。**2** a work of art, especially a set of statues, showing a group of people, animals, etc. 群像（尤指雕塑）

table·cloth /ˈteɪblklɒθ; *NAmE* -klɔːθ; -klɑːθ/ *noun* a cloth that you use for covering a table, especially when you have a meal（尤指餐桌的）桌布，台布 ➲ VISUAL VOCAB PAGE V23

ˈ**table dancing** *noun* [U] sexually exciting dancing which is performed close to a customer's table in a bar or club 桌边舞（酒吧或夜总会中的性感舞蹈）

table d'hôte /ˌtɑːbl ˈdəʊt; *NAmE* ˈdoʊt/ *adj.* (*from French*) a **table d'hôte** meal in a restaurant costs a fixed price and there are only a limited number of dishes to choose from 定餐的；套餐的：*the table d'hôte menu* 套餐菜单 ▸ **table d'hôte** *noun* [U]: *The restaurant offers both table d'hôte and à la carte.* 这家餐馆既供应套餐，也可单点。

ˈ**table football** (*BrE*) (*NAmE* **foosball**) *noun* [U] an indoor game for two people or teams, played by moving rows of small models of football (SOCCER) players in order to move a ball on a board that has marks like a football (SOCCER) field 桌上足球；足球机

ˈ**table lamp** *noun* a small lamp that you can put on a table, etc. 台灯 ➲ VISUAL VOCAB PAGE V22

table·land /ˈteɪbllænd/ *noun* a large area of high flat land 台地；高原 SYN **plateau**

ˈ**table linen** *noun* [U] the cloths that you use during a meal, for example TABLECLOTHS and NAPKINS 餐桌用布（如桌布、餐巾等）

ˈ**table manners** *noun* [pl.] the behaviour that is considered correct while you are having a meal at a table with other people 餐桌规矩；进餐礼节

ˈ**table mat** *noun* (*BrE*) a small piece of wood or cloth that you put under a hot dish or plate to protect the surface of the table 餐具垫；隔热桌垫

ˈ**table napkin** *noun* = NAPKIN (1)

table·spoon /ˈteɪblspuːn/ *noun* **1** a large spoon, used especially for serving food 餐匙，汤匙（尤用于分食物）➲ VISUAL VOCAB PAGE V23 **2** (*also* **table·spoon·ful** /-fʊl/) (*abbr.* **tbsp**) the amount a tablespoon can hold 一餐匙，一汤匙（的量）：*Add two tablespoons of water.* 加两汤匙的水。

tab·let 🔑 /ˈtæblət/ *noun* **1** 🔑 (*especially BrE*) a small round solid piece of medicine that you swallow 药片；片剂 SYN **pill**: *vitamin tablets* 维生素片 ◇ *Take two tablets with water before meals.* 每次两片，饭前用水冲服。**2** an amount of another substance in a small round solid piece 丸：*water purification tablets* 净水丸 **3** a flat piece of stone that has words written on it, especially one that has been fixed to a wall in memory of an important person or event（固定于墙上作纪念的）牌，碑，匾 SYN **plaque**: (*figurative*) *We can be very flexible—our entry requirements are not set in* ***tablets of stone*** (= they can be changed). 我们可以非常灵活，加入条件并非铁板钉钉。**4** (*also* **Tablet PC™**) a small computer that is easy to carry, with a large TOUCH SCREEN and sometimes without a physical keyboard 平板电脑 ➲ VISUAL VOCAB PAGE V73 **5** ~ **of soap** (*old-fashioned, formal*) a piece of soap 一块肥皂 **6** (*NAmE*) a number of pieces of paper for writing or drawing on, that are fastened together at one edge 便笺本；拍纸簿

ˈ**table tennis** (*BrE also, informal* ˈ**ping-pong**) (*NAmE also* ˈ**Ping-Pong™**) *noun* [U] a game played like TENNIS with BATS and a small plastic ball on a table with a net across it 乒乓球运动 ➲ VISUAL VOCAB PAGE V49

table·top /ˈteɪbltɒp; *NAmE* -tɑːp/ *noun* the top or the surface of a table 桌面；台面 ▸ **table·top** *adj.* [only before noun]: *a tabletop machine* (= that can be used on a table) 台式机器 ◇ (*BrE*) *a tabletop sale* (= where goods for sale are displayed on tables) 台面商品展销

ˌ**Tablet PˈC™** *noun* = TABLET (4)

table·ware /ˈteɪblweə(r); *NAmE* -wer/ *noun* [U] the word used in shops/stores, etc. for items that you use for meals, such as plates, glasses, knives and forks（商店用语）餐具

ˈ**table wine** *noun* [U, C] a fairly cheap wine, suitable for drinking with meals 佐餐葡萄酒

tab·loid /ˈtæblɔɪd/ *noun* **1** a newspaper with small pages (usually half the size of those in larger papers) 小报（版面通常比大报小一半）➲ COMPARE BERLINER, BROADSHEET **2** (*sometimes disapproving*) a newspaper of this size with short articles and a lot of pictures and stories about famous people, often thought of as less serious than other newspapers 通俗小报（文短图多，内容多为名人逸事，常被视为不太严肃）：*The story made the front page in all the tabloids.* 这件事成了所有小报的头版新闻。➲ COMPARE QUALITY NEWSPAPER ➲ SEE ALSO RED-TOP ▸ **tab·loid** *adj.* [only before noun]: *a serious paper in a new tabloid format* 一份以小报形式重新编排的严肃报纸 ◇ *tabloid journalists* 小报记者 ◇ *a tabloid newspaper* 通俗小报 ◇ *the tabloid press* 通俗小报界

taboo /təˈbuː/ *noun* (*pl.* **ta·boos**) ~ (**against/on sth**) **1** a cultural or religious custom that does not allow people to do, use or talk about a particular thing as people find it offensive or embarrassing（文化或宗教习俗方面的）禁忌，忌讳，戒律：*an incest taboo* 乱伦禁忌 ◇ *a taboo on working on a Sunday* 禁止星期日工作的习俗 ◇ *to* ***break/violate a taboo*** 触犯禁忌 ◇ *Death is one of the great taboos in our culture.* 在我们的文化中，"死亡"是一大忌。**2** a general agreement not to do sth or talk about sth 禁止；避讳：*The subject is still a taboo in our family.* 我们家仍然很避讳谈论这件事。▸ **taboo** *adj.*：*in the days when sex was a* ***taboo subject*** 在谈性色变的时代

taˈ**boo word** *noun* a word that many people consider offensive or shocking, for example because it refers to sex, the body or people's race 禁忌词

tabor /ˈteɪbə(r)/ *noun* a musical instrument like a small drum, used in the past 塔波鼓

ˈ**tab stop** (*also* **tab**) *noun* a fixed position in a line of a document that you are typing that shows where a piece of text or a column of figures, etc. will begin（打字）首行固定键位

tabu·lar /ˈtæbjələ(r)/ *adj.* [usually before noun] presented or arranged in a TABLE (= in rows and columns) 表格式的；列成表的；制成表的：*tabular data* 列成表的数据 ◇ *The results are presented* ***in tabular form.*** 结果以表格形式列出。

tab·ula rasa /ˌtæbjʊlə ˈrɑːzə/ *noun* (*pl.* **tab·ulae rasae** /ˌtæbjʊliː ˈrɑːziː/) (*from Latin, formal*) **1** a situation in which there are no fixed ideas about how sth should develop 虚静（指对未来发展没有既定的想法）**2** the human mind as it is at birth, with no ideas or thoughts in it 白板（指人出生时没有思想和观点的头脑）；白纸般的思想

tabu·late /ˈtæbjuleɪt/ *verb* ~ **sth** to arrange facts or figures in columns or lists so that they can be read easily 列成表格；列表显示 ▸ **tabu·la·tion** /ˌtæbjuˈleɪʃn/ *noun* [U, C]

tabu·la·tor /ˈtæbjuleɪtə(r)/ *noun* = TAB KEY

tacho·graph /ˈtækəɡrɑːf; *NAmE* -ɡræf/ *noun* a device that is used in vehicles such as large lorries/trucks and some types of buses to measure their speed, how far they have travelled and when the driver has stopped to rest（机动车的）行驶记录表

tach·om·eter /tæˈkɒmɪtə(r); *NAmE* -ˈkɑːm-/ *noun* a device that measures the rate that sth turns and is used to measure the speed of an engine in a vehicle 转速表（车辆发动机用）

tacit /ˈtæsɪt/ *adj.* [usually before noun] that is suggested indirectly or understood, rather than said in words 心照不宣的；不言而喻的；默示的：***tacit approval/support/knowledge*** 默许；暗中支持；了然于心的认识 ◇ *By* ***tacit agreement****, the subject was never mentioned again.* 根据达成的默契，这个话题从未再提起过。▶ **tacit·ly** *adv.*

taci·turn /ˈtæsɪtɜːn; *NAmE* -tɜːrn/ *adj.* (*formal*) tending not to say very much, in a way that seems unfriendly 不苟言笑的；沉默寡言的；缄默不语的 ▶ **taci·turn·ity** /ˌtæsɪˈtɜːnəti; *NAmE* -ˈtɜːrn-/ *noun* [U]

tack /tæk/ *noun, verb*

■ ***noun*** **1** [U, sing.] the way in which you deal with a particular situation; the direction of your words or thoughts 方针；方法；思路：*a complete* ***change of tack*** 方法的完全改变 ◇ *It was a brave decision to* ***change tack*** *in the middle of the project.* 在项目进行过程当中改变方针是个大胆的决定。◇ *When threats failed, she decided to* ***try/take a different tack****.* 威胁不成，她便决定变换策略。◇ *His thoughts wandered off* ***on another tack****.* 他走神想另一个问题了。**2** [C, U] (*specialist*) the direction that a boat with sails takes as it sails at an angle to the wind in order to fill its sails（帆船的）戗风调向，戗风行驶：*They were sailing on (a)* ***port/starboard tack*** (= with the wind coming from the left/right side). 他们正在左 / 右舷戗风行驶。**3** [C] a small nail with a sharp point and a flat head, used especially for fixing a carpet to the floor（尤指把地毯钉在地板上的）平头钉，大头钉：*a carpet tack* 地毯钉 ➲ COMPARE NAIL *n.* (2) **4** [C] (*NAmE*) = THUMBTACK ➲ **VISUAL VOCAB** PAGE V71 ➲ SEE ALSO BLU-TACK™ **5** [C] a long loose STITCH used for holding pieces of cloth together temporarily, before you sew them finally 粗线脚缝；假缝 ➲ **WORDFINDER NOTE** AT SEW **6** [U] (*specialist*) the equipment that you need for riding a horse, such as a SADDLE and BRIDLE 鞍辔；马具 ➲ **WORDFINDER NOTE** AT HORSE **IDM** SEE BRASS

■ ***verb*** **1** [T] **~ sth + adv./prep.** to fasten sth in place with a tack or tacks（用平头钉）钉住 **SYN** **nail**: *The carpet was tacked to the floor.* 地毯是用平头钉钉在地板上的。**2** [T] **~ sth (+ adv./prep.)** to fasten pieces of cloth together temporarily with long loose STITCHES before sewing them finally 绷；用粗线脚缝 **3** [I] (*specialist*) to change the direction of a sailing boat so that the wind blows onto the sails from the opposite side; to do this several times in order to travel in the direction that the wind is coming from 戗风行驶；换戗；作之字形航行

PHR V **ˌtack sth↔ˈon | ˌtack sth ˈonto sth** (*informal*) to add sth to sth that already exists, especially in a careless way（尤指漫不经心地）附加，增补，添加：*The poems were tacked on at the end of the book.* 这几首诗附在书的末尾。

tackie (*also* **tak·kie**) /ˈtæki/ *noun* (*SAfrE*) **1** a shoe with a rubber SOLE (= the part underneath), worn when dressing informally or for taking part in sports 胶底便鞋；运动鞋 ➲ COMPARE TRAINER **2** (*informal*) a tyre on a car, etc. 轮胎

tackle 🔑 /ˈtækl/ *verb, noun*

■ ***verb*** **1** 🔑 [T] **~ sth** to make a determined effort to deal with a difficult problem or situation 应付，处理，解决（难题或局面）：*The government is determined to tackle inflation.* 政府决心解决通货膨胀问题。**2** 🔑 [T] **~ sb (about sth)** to speak to sb about a problem or difficult situation 与某人交涉；向某人提起（问题或困难情况）**SYN** **confront**: *I tackled him about the money he owed me.* 我就他欠我钱的事与他进行了交涉。**3** [T, I] **~ (sb)** (in football (SOCCER), HOCKEY, etc. 足球、曲棍球等) to try and take the ball from an opponent 抢球；抢断；抢截；铲断：*He was tackled just outside the penalty area.* 他就在禁区外让对方把球抢断。**4** [I, T] **~ (sb)** (in RUGBY or AMERICAN FOOTBALL 橄榄球或美式足球) to make an opponent fall to the ground in order to stop them running 擒抱摔倒；阻截 **5** [T] **~ sb** to deal with sb who is violent or threatening you 抓获；擒获；给以颜色：*He tackled a masked intruder at his home.* 他在家里抓住了一个私自闯入的蒙面人。

■ ***noun*** **1** [C] an act of trying to take the ball from an opponent in football (SOCCER), etc.; an act of knocking an opponent to the ground in RUGBY or AMERICAN FOOTBALL（足球等）抢断球，阻截铲球；（橄榄球或美式足球）擒抱摔倒，阻截 ➲ **VISUAL VOCAB** PAGE V47 **2** [C] (*NAmE*) (in AMERICAN FOOTBALL 美式足球) a player whose job is to stop opponents by knocking them to the ground 阻截队员 **3** [U] the equipment used to do a particular sport or activity, especially fishing 用具；体育器材；（尤指）渔具 ➲ SEE ALSO BLOCK AND TACKLE **4** [U] (*BrE, slang*) a man's sexual organs 鸡巴；阳具

tack·ler /ˈtæklə(r)/ *noun* (*BrE*) a player who tries to TACKLE an opponent in some sports（某些体育运动的）阻截队员

tacky /ˈtæki/ *adj.* (**tack·ier, tacki·est**) **1** (*informal*) cheap, badly made and/or lacking in taste 低劣的；蹩脚的；俗气的；乏味的：*tacky souvenirs* 蹩脚的纪念品 ◇ *The movie had a really tacky ending.* 这部电影的结尾真差劲。**2** (of paint, glue, etc. 油漆、胶水等) not dry and therefore slightly sticky 未干透的；发黏的 ▶ **tacki·ness** *noun* [U]

taco /ˈtækəʊ; *NAmE* ˈtɑːkoʊ/ *noun* (*pl.* **-os**) (*from Spanish*) a type of Mexican food consisting of a crisp fried PANCAKE that is folded over and filled with meat, BEANS, etc. 墨西哥煎玉米粉卷（包着肉、豆等）

tact /tækt/ *noun* [U] the ability to deal with difficult or embarrassing situations carefully and without doing or saying anything that will annoy or upset other people（处事、言谈等的）圆通，老练，圆滑 **SYN** **sensitivity**: *Settling the dispute required great tact and diplomacy.* 解决这个争端需要十分老练和娴熟的外交手腕。◇ *She is not exactly known for her tact.* 她并不以策略见称。

tact·ful /ˈtæktfl/ *adj.* careful not to say or do anything that will annoy or upset other people 圆通的；得体的；不得罪人的 **SYN** **diplomatic**: *That wasn't a very tactful thing to say!* 说这种话可不太得体！◇ *I tried to find a tactful way of telling her the truth.* 我设法找一个妥善的办法，把实情告诉她。**OPP** **tactless** ▶ **tact·ful·ly** /-fəli/ *adv.*: *a tactfully worded reply* 措辞得体的答复 ◇ *I tactfully suggested he should see a doctor.* 我婉转地建议他去看医生。

tac·tic /ˈtæktɪk/ *noun* **1** [C, usually pl.] the particular method you use to achieve sth 策略；手段；招数：*They tried all kinds of tactics to get us to go.* 他们施尽所有的招数想让我们离开。◇ *This was just the latest in a series of* ***delaying tactics****.* 这只是一系列拖延战术中的一个新花招。◇ *The manager discussed tactics with his team.* 主教练和他的团队讨论了战术。◇ *Confrontation is not always the best tactic.* 对抗并非总是上策。◇ *It's time to try a change of tactic.* 现在是改弦易辙的时候了。**2 tactics** [pl.] the art of moving soldiers and military equipment around during a battle or war in order to use them in the most effective way 战术；兵法 ➲ COMPARE STRATEGY ➲ **WORDFINDER NOTE** AT ARMY

tac·tic·al /ˈtæktɪkl/ *adj.* **1** [usually before noun] connected with the particular method you use to achieve sth 战术上的；策略上的 **SYN** **strategic**: *tactical planning* 对策谋划 ◇ *to have a tactical advantage* 拥有战术上的优势 ◇ *Telling your boss you were looking for a new job was a* ***tactical error*** (= it was the wrong thing to do at that time). 你把正在另找工作的事告诉了老板，是个策略上的错误。**2** [usually before noun] carefully planned in order to achieve a particular aim 有谋略的；手段高明的；善于谋划的 **SYN** **strategic**: *a tactical decision* 高明的决策 ➲ SEE ALSO TACTICAL VOTING **3** [only before noun] (especially of weapons

T

尤指武器) used or having an effect over short distances or for a short time 战术的；短程的：*tactical weapons/missiles* 战术武器 / 导弹 ➲ COMPARE STRATEGIC (3) **4** [only before noun] connected with military tactics 作战的：*He was given tactical command of the operation.* 他被授以这次军事行动的作战指挥权。▶ **tac·tic·al·ly** /-kli/ *adv.*：*At the time, it was tactically the right thing to do.* 当时这样做在策略上是正确的。◇ *The enemy was tactically superior.* 敌人拥有战术上的优势。

ˌtactical ˈvoting *noun* [U] (*BrE*) the act of voting for a particular person or political party, not because you support them, but in order to prevent sb else from being elected（并非真心支持而是为防止他人当选的）战术投票，策略性投票

tac·ti·cian /tækˈtɪʃn/ *noun* a person who is very clever at planning the best way to achieve sth 有策略的人；手段高明的人

tact·ile /ˈtæktaɪl; *NAmE* -tl/ *adj.* [usually before noun] connected with the sense of touch; using your sense of touch 触觉的；有触觉的；能触知的：*tactile stimuli* 触觉刺激 ◇ *visual and tactile communication* 视觉和触觉交流 ◇ *tactile fabric* (= pleasant to touch) 手感好的织物 ◇ *tactile maps* (= that you can touch and feel) 触摸地图 ◇ *He's a very tactile man* (= he enjoys touching people). 他这个人很喜欢触碰别人身体。

tact·less /ˈtæktləs/ *adj.* saying or doing things that are likely to annoy or to upset other people 言行不得体的；得罪人的；不圆通的；没策略的 SYN **insensitive**：*a tactless remark* 不得体的话 ◇ *It was tactless of you to comment on his hair!* 你竟对他的头发说三道四，真是缺心眼！ OPP **tactful** ▶ **tact·less·ly** *adv.* **tact·less·ness** *noun* [U]

tad /tæd/ *noun* **a tad** [sing.] (*informal*) a very small amount 少量；一点儿：*Could you turn the sound down just a tad?* 你把音量调低一点儿好吗？ ▶ **a tad** *adv.*：*It's a tad too expensive for me.* 这对我来说稍微贵了一点儿。

tad·pole /ˈtædpəʊl; *NAmE* -poʊl/ (*NAmE also* **polli·wog**) *noun* a small creature with a large head and a small tail, that lives in water and is the young form of a FROG or TOAD 蝌蚪 ➲ VISUAL VOCAB PAGE V13

tae kwon do /ˌtaɪ ˌkwɒn ˈdəʊ; *NAmE* ˌkwɑːn ˈdoʊ/ *noun* [U] a Korean system of fighting without weapons, similar to KARATE 跆拳道

taf·feta /ˈtæfɪtə/ *noun* [U] a type of stiff shiny cloth made from silk or a similar material, used especially for making dresses 塔夫绸

Taffy /ˈtæfi/ *noun* (*pl.* **-ies**) (*also* **Taff** /tæf/) (*BrE, informal, often offensive*) a person from Wales 威尔士人

taffy /ˈtæfi/ *noun* (*pl.* **-ies**) [U, C] (*NAmE*) a type of soft sweet/candy made of brown sugar boiled until it is very thick and given different shapes and colours 太妃糖；乳脂糖

tag /tæg/ *noun, verb*

■ ***noun*** **1** [C] (often in compounds 常构成复合词) a small piece of paper, cloth, plastic, etc. attached to sth to identify it or give information about it 标签；标牌：*He put name tags on all his shirts.* 他给自己所有的衬衣都缝上了标有姓名的签条。◇ *a gift tag* (= tied to a present) 礼品签 ◇ *The police use electronic tags to monitor the whereabouts of young offenders on probation.* 警方利用电子跟踪器监视缓刑期间的青年罪犯。➲ SYNONYMS AT LABEL ➲ SEE ALSO PRICE TAG **2** [C, usually sing.] a name or phrase that is used to describe a person or thing in some way 称呼；诨名：*They are finally ready to drop the tag 'the new Beatles'.* 他们终于准备放弃"新披头士乐队"这一称谓。◇ *The 'lucky' tag stuck for years.* "幸运儿"这个诨名叫了好多年。**3** [C] (*linguistics* 语言) a word or phrase that is added to a sentence for emphasis, for example *I do* in *Yes, I do* 附加语（为加强语气，如 Yes, I do 一句中的 I do）➲ SEE ALSO QUESTION TAG **4** [C] (*computing* 计) a set of letters or symbols that are put before and after a piece of text or data in order to identify it or show that it is to be treated in a particular way 标志；标记；标签；标识符 **5** [C] a short QUOTATION or saying in a foreign language（外国语的）语录，引语，格言，谚语：*the Latin tag 'Si vis pacem, para bellum.'* (= if you want peace, prepare for war) 拉丁语格言："欲要和平，辄需备战。" **6** (*BrE also* **tig**) [U] a children's game in which one child chases the others and tries to touch one of them 捉人（儿童游戏）**7** [C] a symbol or name used by a GRAFFITI writer and painted in a public place（在公共场所涂鸦者用的）符号，名字

■ ***verb*** (**-gg-**) **1** ~ **sth/sb** to fasten a tag onto sth/sb 给…加上标签：*Each animal was tagged with a number for identification.* 每只动物都系上了标有号码的小牌，以便辨认。➲ SEE ALSO ELECTRONIC TAGGING **2** ~ **sb/sth as sth** to give sb/sth a name that describes what they are or do 把…称作；给…起诨名 SYN **label**：*The country no longer wanted to be tagged as a Third World nation.* 这个国家不愿意再被称为第三世界国家。**3** ~ **sth** (*computing* 计) to add a set of letters or symbols to a piece of text or data in order to identify it or to show that it is to be treated in a particular way（给…）加标识符，加标签 **4** ~ **sb/sth** to add a link to various users' PROFILES from a photo on a SOCIAL MEDIA website 给（社交网站上照片中的人）加标记（由此可添加链接至其个人资料）：*If you upload a photo, people can tag the people in it.* 如果你上传一张照片，人们可以标记照片上的人。◇ *The site lets you tag and share photographs.* 该网站支持标记和分享照片功能。**5** ~ **sth** to leave a name or mark on a piece of GRAFFITI to show who made it 在（涂鸦）上留名（或做标记）

PHR V **ˌtag aˈlong** (**behind/with sb**) to go somewhere with sb, especially when you have not been asked or invited 跟随，尾随（尤指未经同意或邀请） **ˌtag sth↔ˈon** | **ˌtag sth ˈonto sth** to add sth to the end of sth that already exists, especially in a careless way（尤指漫不经心地）给…加上，附加：*An apology was tagged onto the end of the letter.* 信的结尾顺便附了一句抱歉的话。

Taga·log /təˈgɑːlɒg; *NAmE* -lɔːg/ *noun* [U] the national language spoken in the Philippine islands 他加禄语（通行于菲律宾群岛）

ˈtag cloud *noun* a way of showing the most popular content on a website by using colour and size of type to show how important or frequent the TAGS added by users are 标签云（用不同颜色和字体大小来显示网站内容的关键词，以反映其重要性和热门程度）：*We have a tag cloud on the blogs homepage to help you with searching through our blogs by key word.* 我们的博客主页上有标签云，帮助您通过关键字查阅博客。

tag·ger /ˈtægə(r)/ *noun* **1** a person who writes or paints GRAFFITI in a public place, using a special symbol or name 留名涂鸦者：*It can take hours of time and thousands of dollars to fix the graffiti that one tagger can cause.* 清除一个留名者的涂鸦可能要花费几个小时和数千美元。**2** (*computing* 计) a piece of software that adds tags to a piece of text or data 标签软件；赋码软件

ta·gine (*also* **ta·jine**) /təˈʒiːn; təˈdʒiːn/ *noun* **1** [C, U] a hot dish made with meat and vegetables, cooked with liquid and spices in a closed container 塔吉锅炖菜（焖炖加调料的肉菜） **2** [C] a container made of CLAY, with a pointed lid, for cooking and serving tagine, originally used in North Africa 塔吉锅（陶质、尖盖、用于烹饪和上菜，源于北非）

taglia·telle /ˌtæljəˈteli; *NAmE* -ˈtɑːl-/ *noun* [U] (*from Italian*) PASTA in the shape of long flat strips 意大利扁面条

ˈtag line *noun* (*NAmE, informal*) **1** = PUNCHLINE **2** = SLOGAN

ˈtag question *noun* (*grammar* 语法) = QUESTION TAG

ˈtag team *noun* **1** a team of two WRESTLERS who take turns to fight in the same match（摔跤比赛中轮流出赛的）车轮战两人组 **2** (*informal, especially NAmE*) two people working or performing together 两人组；双人组合：*The show used a tag team of interviewers.* 节目采用了两人搭档提问访谈。

ta·hini /tɑːˈhiːni; təˈh-/ (*also* **ta·hina** /tɑːˈhiːnə; təˈh-/) *noun* [U] a thick mixture made with crushed SESAME seeds, eaten in the Middle East （中东）芝麻酱

t'ai chi ch'uan /ˌtaɪ tʃiː ˈtʃwɑːn/ (*also* **ˌt'ai 'chi**) *noun* [U] (*from Chinese*) a Chinese system of exercises consisting of sets of very slow controlled movements 太极拳

taiga /ˈtaɪgə/ *noun* [sing., U] forest that grows in wet ground in far northern regions of the earth 泰加林（北方湿地的针叶林）；北方针叶林：*the Siberian taiga* 西伯利亚针叶林

tail /teɪl/ *noun, verb*

■ ***noun***

• **OF BIRD/ANIMAL/FISH** 鸟兽；鱼 **1** [C] the part that sticks out and can be moved at the back of the body of a bird, an animal or a fish 尾；尾巴：*The dog ran up, wagging its tail.* 那条狗摇着尾巴跑上前去。◇ *The male has beautiful tail feathers.* 雄鸟有美丽的尾羽。➲ VISUAL VOCAB PAGE V12 ➲ SEE ALSO PONYTAIL

• **-TAILED** 有…尾巴 **2** (in adjectives 构成形容词) having the type of tail mentioned 有…尾巴的：*a white-tailed eagle* 白尾雕 ➲ MORE LIKE THIS 8, page R25

• **OF PLANE/SPACECRAFT** 飞机；宇宙飞船 **3** [C] the back part of a plane, SPACECRAFT, etc. 尾部；后部：*the tail wing* 尾翼 ➲ VISUAL VOCAB PAGE V57

• **BACK/END OF STH** 后部；末尾 **4** [C] ~ (**of sth**) a part of sth that sticks out at the back like a tail 尾状后部；尾状物：*the tail of a kite* 风筝的尾坠 **5** [C] ~ (**of sth**) the last part of sth that is moving away from you（离去事物的）末尾部分：*the tail of the procession* 游行队伍的末尾 ➲ SEE ALSO TAIL END

• **JACKET** 上衣 **6 tails** [pl.] (*also* **tail·coat** [C]) a long jacket divided at the back below the waist into two pieces that become narrower at the bottom, worn by men at very formal events 燕尾服；男式晚礼服：*The men all wore top hat and tails.* 男士都头戴高顶礼帽，身穿晚礼服。➲ SEE ALSO COAT-TAILS, SHIRT TAIL ➲ COMPARE DINNER JACKET, MORNING COAT

• **SIDE OF COIN** 硬币的面 **7 tails** [U] the side of a coin that does not have a picture of the head of a person on it, used as one choice when a coin is TOSSED to decide sth 硬币反面，硬币文面（没有头像的一面）➲ COMPARE HEAD *n.* (7)

• **PERSON WHO FOLLOWS SB** 跟踪者 **8** [C] (*informal*) a person who is sent to follow sb secretly and find out information about where that person goes, what they do, etc. 盯梢人；暗探：*The police have **put a tail on him**.* 警方已派人对他进行盯梢。

▶ **tail·less** *adj.*：*Manx cats are tailless.* 马恩岛猫没有尾巴。

IDM **on sb's 'tail** (*informal*) following behind sb very closely, especially in a car（尤指开车）盯梢，尾随 **the tail (is) wagging the 'dog** used to describe a situation in which the most important aspect is being influenced and controlled by sb/sth that is not as important（用以描述次要部分影响和支配主要部分）主次颠倒，喧宾夺主 **turn 'tail** to run away from a fight or dangerous situation （危急时刻）转身逃跑，逃逸，临阵脱逃 **with your tail between your 'legs** (*informal*) feeling ashamed or unhappy because you have been defeated or punished 无地自容；垂头丧气；灰溜溜 ➲ MORE AT CHASE *v.*, HEAD *n.*, NOSE *n.*, STING *n.*

■ ***verb*** ~ **sb** to follow sb closely, especially in order to watch where they go and what they do 跟踪；尾随；盯梢 SYN **shadow**：*A private detective had been tailing them for several weeks.* 私人侦探几个星期来一直在跟踪他们。IDM SEE TOP *v.*

PHR V **ˌtail a'way/'off** (*especially BrE*) to become smaller or weaker 变得越来越小（或弱）；逐渐消失：*The number of tourists tails off in October.* 十月份游客人数越来越少。◇ *'But why…?' Her voice tailed away.* "但是为什么…？"她的声音细了下去。**ˌtail 'back** (of traffic 车辆) to form a tailback 排成长队

tail·back /ˈteɪlbæk/ *noun* **1** [C] (*BrE*) a long line of traffic that is moving slowly or not moving at all, because sth is blocking the road （车辆因受阻而排成的）长队，长蛇阵 ➲ WORDFINDER NOTE AT TRAFFIC **2** [C, U] = HALF BACK (2), (3)

tail·board /ˈteɪlbɔːd; *NAmE* -bɔːrd/ *noun* = TAILGATE (1)

tail·bone /ˈteɪlbəʊn; *NAmE* -boʊn/ *noun* the small bone at the bottom of the SPINE 尾骨；尾椎 SYN **coccyx** ➲ VISUAL VOCAB PAGE V64

tail·coat /ˈteɪlkəʊt; *NAmE* -koʊt/ *noun* a long jacket divided at the back below the waist into two pieces that become narrower at the bottom, worn by men at formal events 燕尾服；男子晚礼服 SYN **tail**

ˌtail 'end *noun* [sing.] the very last part of sth 末尾；末端；尾端；结尾部分：*the tail end of the queue* 队尾

tail·gate /ˈteɪlgeɪt/ *noun, verb*

■ ***noun* 1** (*also* **tail·board**) a door at the back of a lorry/truck that opens downwards and that you can open or remove when you are loading or unloading the vehicle（卡车的）后拦板，后挡板 **2** the door that opens upwards at the back of a car that has three or five doors (called a HATCHBACK)（三门或五门轿车的）尾门，舱盖式后背门

■ ***verb* 1** [I, T] ~ (**sb/sth**) (*informal, especially NAmE*) to drive too closely behind another vehicle 紧跟（另一车辆）行驶 **2** [I] (*NAmE*) to eat food and drinks outdoors, served from the tailgate of a car 旅行野餐（打开轿车舱盖式后背门就餐）

'tail light *noun* a red light at the back of a car, bicycle or train（车辆的）尾灯，后灯 ➲ VISUAL VOCAB PAGE V56

tailor /ˈteɪlə(r)/ *noun, verb*

■ ***noun*** a person whose job is to make men's clothes, especially sb who makes suits, etc. for individual customers（尤指为顾客个别定制男装的）裁缝

■ ***verb*** to make or adapt sth for a particular purpose, a particular person, etc. 专门制作；定做：~ **sth to/for sb/sth** *Special programmes of study are tailored to the needs of specific groups.* 为满足特定群体的需要，特制了专门的课程。◇ ~ **sth to do sth** *Most travel agents are prepared to tailor travel arrangements to meet individual requirements.* 为了满足个别人士需要，大多数旅行社都愿意作出专门的旅游安排。

tailored /ˈteɪləd; *NAmE* -lərd/ *adj.* **1** (of clothes 衣服) made to fit well or closely 定做的；合身的：*a tailored jacket* 定做的夹克衫 **2** made for a particular person or purpose 特制的；专门的 SYN **tailor-made**

tailor·ing /ˈteɪlərɪŋ/ *noun* [U] **1** the style or the way in which a suit, jacket, etc. is made 裁剪式样；裁缝手艺：*Clever tailoring can flatter your figure.* 巧妙的裁剪可以使你的身材显得优美。**2** the job of making men's clothes（男装）裁缝业，成衣活

ˌtailor-'made *adj.* **1** ~ (**for sb/sth**) | ~ (**to sth/to do sth**) made for a particular person or purpose, and therefore very suitable 特制的；专门设置的；非常合适的：*a tailor-made course of study* 专门设置的课程 ◇ *a trip tailor-made just for you* 专门为你安排的旅行 ◇ *She seems tailor-made for the job* (= perfectly suited for it). 她似乎生来就是为了专门做这项工作的。**2** (of clothes 衣服) made by a TAILOR for a particular person 定做的 SYN **bespoke**：*a tailor-made suit* 定做的西服

tail·piece /ˈteɪlpiːs/ *noun* **1** ~ (**to sth**) a part that you add to the end of a piece of writing to make it longer or complete（文章结尾的）附加部分，续补部分 **2** (*music* 音) a piece of wood that the lower ends of the strings of some musical instruments are attached to（弦乐器的）系弦板

tail·pipe /ˈteɪlpaɪp/ *noun* (*especially NAmE*) = EXHAUST (2)

tail·plane /ˈteɪlpleɪn/ *noun* a small horizontal wing at the back of an aircraft（飞机的）横尾翼，水平尾翼 ➲ VISUAL VOCAB PAGE V57

T

tail·spin /ˈteɪlspɪn/ *noun* [sing.] **1** a situation in which a pilot loses control of an aircraft and it spins as it falls quickly towards the ground, with the back making larger circles than the front（飞机的）尾旋，尾螺旋 **2** a situation that suddenly becomes much worse and is not under control 恶化的局势；慌乱；混乱；失控：*Following the announcement, share prices went into a tailspin.* 公告宣布后，股市大跌。

tail·wind /ˈteɪlwɪnd/ *noun* a wind that blows from behind a moving vehicle, a runner, etc. 顺风 ⊃ COMPARE HEADWIND

taint /teɪnt/ *verb, noun*
■ ***verb*** [often passive] **~ sth** (**with sth**) (*formal*) to damage or spoil the quality of sth or the opinion that people have of sb/sth 使腐坏；污染；玷污，败坏（名声）：*The administration was tainted with scandal.* 丑闻使得政府声名狼藉。
▶ **taint·ed** *adj.*：*tainted drinking water* 受污染的饮用水
■ ***noun*** [usually sing.] the effect of sth bad or unpleasant that spoils the quality of sb/sth 腐坏；污染；玷污：*to be free from the taint of corruption* 不受腐败影响

tai·pan /ˈtaɪpæn/ *noun* (*from Chinese*) **1** a foreign person who is in charge of a business in China 大班（旧时对中国洋行老板的称呼） **2** an extremely poisonous Australian snake 太潘蛇（产于澳大利亚，剧毒）

ta·jine = TAGINE

take /teɪk/ *verb, noun*
■ ***verb*** (**took** /tʊk/, **taken** /ˈteɪkən/)
• **CARRY/LEAD** 携带；带领 **1** [T] to carry or move sth from one place to another 携带；拿走；取走；运走：**~ sth** (**with you**) *I forgot to take my bag with me when I got off the bus.* 我下公共汽车时忘了拿包。◇ **~ sth to sb/sth** *Take this to the bank for me, would you?* 请替我把这送到银行去好吗？◇ *Shall I take a gift to my host family?* 我要不要给主人家带件礼物呢？◇ **~ sb sth** *Shall I take my host family a gift?* 我要不要给主人家带件礼物呢？ **2** [T] to go with sb from one place to another, especially to guide or lead them 带去；引领：**~ sb** *It's too far to walk—I'll take you by car.* 步行路太远，我开车送你去。◇ **~ sb to sth** *A boy took us to our room.* 服务员带我们到房间。◇ **~ sb doing sth** *I'm taking the kids swimming later.* 我待会儿带孩子们去游泳。◇ **~ sb to do sth** *The boys were taken to see their grandparents most weekends.* 大多数周末都带着这些男孩去看望爷爷奶奶。 **3** [T] **~ sb/sth + adv./prep.** to make sb/sth go from one level, situation, etc. to another 使达到，把…推向，把…带到（另一个层次、层面等）：*Her energy and talent took her to the top of her profession.* 她凭着充沛的精力和天赋的才能达到了事业的顶峰。◇ *The new loan takes the total debt to $100 000.* 加上这笔新贷款，负债总额达到 10 万美元。◇ *I'd like to take my argument a stage further.* 我想把我的论点进行进一步的发挥。◇ *He believes he has the skills to take the club forward.* 他相信他有能力使俱乐部继续发展。◇ *We'll take the matter forward at our next meeting* (= discuss it further). 我们将在下一次会议上进一步讨论这个问题。
• **REACH AND HOLD** 伸手取 **4** [T] **~ sb/sth** to put your hands or arms around sb/sth and hold them/it; to reach for sb/sth and hold them/it 拿；抱；握；取；接：*I passed him the rope and he took it.* 我把绳子递给他，他接了过去。◇ *Free newspapers: please take one.* 报纸免费，请取一份。◇ *Can you take* (= hold) *the baby for a moment?* 你能先抱一下孩子吗？◇ *He took her hand/took her by the hand* (= held her hand, for example to lead her somewhere). 他拉着她的手。◇ *She took the child in her arms and kissed him.* 她把孩子搂在怀里亲吻他。
• **REMOVE** 移开 **5** [T] **~ sth/sb + adv./prep.** to remove sth/sb from a place or a person 拿开；取出；挪开：*Will you take your books off the table?* 把你的书从桌子上拿走好吗？◇ *The sign must be taken down.* 这个指示牌一定要摘下来。◇ *He took some keys out of his pocket.* 他从口袋里取出几把钥匙。◇ *My name had been taken off the list.* 我的名字从名单上画掉了。◇ *She was playing with a knife, so I took it away from her.* 她在玩一把刀子，于是我把刀子从她手里夺了过来。◇ (*informal*) *She was playing with a knife, so I took it off her.* 她在玩一把刀子，于是我把刀子从她手里夺了过来。◇ (*figurative*) *The new sports centre will* ***take the pressure off*** *the old one.* 新的体育中心将减轻老体育中心的压力。 **6** [T] **~ sth** to remove sth without permission or by mistake 擅自拿走；偷走；误拿：*Someone has taken my scarf.* 有人把我的围巾拿走了。◇ *Did the burglars take anything valuable?* 入室窃贼偷走了贵重的东西没有？◇ (*figurative*) *The storms* ***took the lives*** *of 50 people.* 这场暴风雨夺走了 50 人的生命。 **7** [T] to get sth from a particular source 从…中取出；取材于：**~ sth from sth** *The scientists are taking water samples from the river.* 科学家正从河中采水样。◇ *The machine takes its name from its inventor.* 这机器是用发明者的姓名命名的。◇ **~ sth out of sth** *Part of her article is taken straight* (= copied) *out of my book.* 她的文章有一部分是从我的书中抄来的。
• **CAPTURE** 捕获 **8** [T] to capture a place or person; to get control of sth 夺取；攻占；抓获；控制：**~ sth** (**from sb**) *The rebels succeeded in taking the town.* 反叛者攻占了那个城镇。◇ *The state has* ***taken control of*** *the company.* 政府已经接管了这家公司。◇ **~ sb + noun** *The rebels took him prisoner.* 反叛者把他俘虏了。◇ *He was* ***taken prisoner*** *by the rebels.* 他被反叛者俘虏了。
• **CHOOSE/BUY** 选择；购买 **9** [T] **~ sth** to choose, buy or rent sth 选中；买下；租用：*I'll take the grey jacket.* 我要那件灰色夹克衫。◇ *We took a room at the hotel for two nights.* 我们在旅馆开了个房间，住了两夜。 **10** [T] **~ sth** (*formal*) to buy a newspaper or magazine regularly 经常购买（某报纸或期刊）：*We take the 'Express'.* 我们订阅的是《快报》。
• **EAT/DRINK** 食用；饮用 **11** [T] **~ sth** to eat, drink, etc. sth 吃；喝；服（药）：*Do you take sugar in your coffee?* 你的咖啡里要放糖吗？◇ *The doctor has given me some medicine to take for my cough.* 医生已给我开了治咳嗽的药吃。◇ *He started taking drugs* (= illegal drugs) *at college.* 他上大学时开始吸毒。
• **MATHEMATICS** 数学 **12** [T] **~ A** (**away**) **from B | B ~ away A | ~ A away** (not used in the progressive tenses 不用于进行时) to reduce one number by the value of another 减去 **SYN** **subtract**：*Take 5 from 12 and you're left with 7.* * 12 减 5 得 7。◇ (*informal*) *80 take away 5 is 75.* * 80 减去 5 等于 75。
• **WRITE DOWN** 写下 **13** [T] **~ sth** to find out and record sth; to write sth down 记录；摘录；记下：*The police officer took my name and address.* 警察记下了我的姓名和地址。◇ *Did you* ***take notes*** *in the class?* 你在课堂上做了笔记吗？
• **PHOTOGRAPH** 拍照 **14** [T] **~ sth** to photograph sb/sth 拍照；照相；摄影：***to take a photograph/picture/snapshot*** *of sb/sth* 给（某人/某物）照相/拍照/拍快照 ◇ ***to have your picture/photo taken*** 让人给你拍照
• **MEASUREMENT** 计量 **15** [T] **~ sth** to test or measure sth 量取；测定：*to take sb's temperature* 给某人量体温 ◇ *I need to have my blood pressure taken.* 我需要量一下血压。
• **SEAT** 座位 **16** [T] **~ sth** to sit down in or use a chair, etc. 就（座）；占据（座位）：*Are these seats taken?* 这些座位有人吗？◇ *Come in;* ***take a seat.*** 进来，坐下。⊃ SYNONYMS AT SIT
• **GIVE EXAMPLE** 举例 **17** [T] **~ sb/sth** used to introduce sb/sth as an example 以…为例；将…作为例证：*Lots of couples have problems in the first year of marriage. Take Ann and Paul.* 在婚后头一年里，许多夫妇都出现一些问题。安和保罗就是个例子。
• **ACCEPT/RECEIVE** 接受；收到 **18** [T] (not usually used in the progressive tenses or in the passive 通常不用于进行时或被动语态) **~ sth** to accept or receive sth 接受；收到：*If they offer me the job, I'll take it.* 如果他们给我这份工作，我就接受。◇ *She was accused of taking bribes.* 她被控受贿。◇ *Does the hotel take credit cards?* 这家旅馆接受信用卡付款吗？◇ *I'll take the call in my office.* 我要在办公室里接这个电话。◇ *Why should I* ***take the blame*** *for somebody else's mistakes?* 我为什么要代人受过呢？◇ *If you* ***take my advice*** *you'll have nothing more to do with him.* 你要是听我的劝告，就不要再和他有什么瓜葛。◇ *Will you take $10 for the book* (= will you sell it for $10)? 这本书 10 美元你卖吗？◇ *The store took* (= sold goods worth) *$100 000 last week.* 这家商店上星期的营业额为 10 万美元。 **19** [T] (not usually used in the progressive tenses

通常不用于进行时) **~ sb** to accept sb as a customer, patient, etc. 接纳；接待（顾客、患者等）：*The school doesn't take boys* (= only has girls). 这所学校不收男生。◇ *The dentist can't take any new patients.* 这位牙科医生接待不了新患者了。 **20** [T] (not usually used in the progressive tenses 通常不用于进行时) **~ sth** to experience or be affected by sth 遭受；经受；承受：*The school took the full force of the explosion.* 这所学校在爆炸中毁坏最严重。◇ *Can the ropes **take the strain*** (= not break)? 这些绳子能承受住这一张力吗？◇ *The team took a terrible beating.* 这个队遭到惨败。 **21** 🔑 [T, no passive] **~ sth** (not usually used in the progressive tenses 通常不用于进行时) to be able to bear sth 忍受；容忍；承受：*She can't **take criticism**.* 她受不了批评。◇ *I don't think I can take much more of this heat.* 我觉得再也忍受不了这种高温了。◇ *I find his attitude a little **hard to take**.* 我觉得他的态度有点儿令人难以接受。 **22** 🔑 [T] **~ sth/sb + adv./prep.** to react to sth/sb in a particular way （以某种方式）对待，处理：*He took the criticism surprisingly well.* 他对待这一批评的态度竟意外地好。◇ *These threats are not to be taken lightly.* 这些威胁可不能等闲视之。◇ *I wish you'd take me seriously.* 我希望你认真对待我的话。◇ *She took it in the spirit in which it was intended.* 她根据其精神实质来认识此事。

• **CONSIDER** 考虑 **23** 🔑 [T] (not used in the progressive tenses 不用于进行时) to understand or consider sth in a particular way 领会；理解；考虑：**~ sth (as sth)** *She took what he said as a compliment.* 她把他说的看作是称誉。◇ *How am I supposed to take that remark?* 我应该怎么理解那话的意思？◇ *Taken overall, the project was a success.* 总的看来，这个项目是成功的。◇ **~ sth to do sth** *What did you take his comments to mean?* 你认为他的意见是什么意思？ **24** [T] (not used in the progressive tenses 不用于进行时) to consider sb/sth to be sb/sth, especially when you are wrong （尤指错误地）以为，把…看作；误认为：**~ sb/sth for sb/sth** *Even the experts took the painting for a genuine Van Gogh.* 连行家都误以为这幅画是凡高的真迹。◇ *Of course I didn't do it! **What do you take me for*** (= what sort of person do you think I am)? 那当然不是我干的！你把我当成什么人啦？◇ **~ sb/sth to be sb/sth** *I took the man with him to be his father.* 我误以为和他在一起的那个男人是他父亲。

• **HAVE FEELING/OPINION** 有感情 / 看法 **25** 🔑 [T] (not usually used in the progressive tenses 通常不用于进行时) **~ sth** to have a particular feeling, opinion or attitude 产生（感觉）；持有（看法）；采取（态度）：*My parents always **took an interest** in my hobbies.* 我父母总是关心重视我的爱好。◇ *Don't **take offence*** (= be offended) *at what I said.* 我讲的话你别见怪。◇ ***I took a dislike** to him.* 我对他产生了反感。◇ *He takes the view that children are responsible for their own actions.* 他的观点是孩子应对自己的行为负责。

• **ACTION** 行动 **26** 🔑 [T] **~ sth** to use a particular course of action in order to deal with or achieve sth 采取（措施）；采用（方法）：*The government is **taking action** to combat drug abuse.* 政府正在采取措施，打击滥用毒品。◇ *We need to take a different approach to the problem.* 我们应该采用另一种方法来解决这一问题。 **27** 🔑 [T] **~ sth** used with nouns to say that sb is doing sth, performing an action, etc. （与名词连用，表示举动、动作等）：*to take a step/walk/stroll* 迈步；散步；溜达 ◇ *to take a bath/shower/wash* 洗澡；淋浴；洗一洗 ◇ *to take a look/glance* 看一看；瞥一眼 ◇ *to take a bite/drink/sip* 咬 / 喝 / 呷一口 ◇ *to take a deep breath* 深吸一口气 ◇ *to take a break/rest* 暂歇一下；休息一下 ◇ (*BrE*) *No decision will be taken on the matter until next week.* 到下星期才会对这一问题作出决定。

• **FORM/POSITION** 形式；位置 **28** [T] **~ sth** to have a particular form, position or state 采用（形式）；就任（职位）；出现（状况）：*Our next class will take the form of a debate.* 我们下一堂课将采用辩论的形式。◇ *The new President takes office in January.* 新总统将于一月份就职。

• **TIME** 时间 **29** 🔑 [T, no passive, I] to need or require a particular amount of time 需要…时间；费时：**~ sth** *The journey to the airport takes about half an hour.* 到机场大约需要半小时。◇ **~ sth to do sth** *It takes about half an hour to get to the airport.* 到机场大概需要半小时。◇ *That cut is taking a long time to heal.* 那伤口需要很长时间才能愈合。◇ **~ sb sth (to do sth)** *It took her three hours to repair her bike.* 她花了三个小时修理自行车。◇ *It'll take her time to recover from the illness.* 她康复需要时间。◇ **~ sth for sb to do sth** *It'll **take time*** (= take a long time) *for her to recover from the illness.* 她的病需要很长时间才能痊愈。◇ **+ adv.** *I need a shower—I **won't take long**.* 我要冲个澡，用不了多长时间。 ➲NOTE AT LAST[1]

• **NEED** 需要 **30** [T, no passive] to need or require sth in order to happen or be done 需要；要求：**~ sb/sth to do sth** *It only takes one careless driver to cause an accident.* 只要有一个粗心大意的驾驶者便会发生车祸。◇ *It doesn't take much to make her angry.* 她动辄发脾气。◇ **~ sth** (*informal*) *He didn't take much persuading* (= he was easily persuaded). 不用费多少口舌就说服了他。 **31** [T, no passive] (not used in the progressive tenses 不用于进行时) **~ sth** (of machines, etc. 机器等) to use sth in order to work 使用；用：*All new cars take unleaded petrol.* 所有的新汽车都使用无铅汽油。

• **SIZE OF SHOES/CLOTHES** 鞋 / 衣服的尺码 **32** [T, no passive] (not used in the progressive tenses 不用于进行时) **~ sth** to wear a particular size in shoes or clothes 穿用（…尺码的鞋或衣服）：*What size shoes do you take?* 你穿多大号的鞋？

• **HOLD/CONTAIN** 装得下；包含 **33** [T, no passive] (not used in the progressive tenses 不用于进行时) **~ sth/sb** to have enough space for sth/sb; to be able to hold or contain a particular quantity 容纳；装；盛：*The bus can take 60 passengers.* 这辆公共汽车可载 60 名乘客。◇ *The tank takes 50 litres.* 这罐能容 50 升。

• **TEACH/LEAD** 讲授；带领 **34** [T] **~ sb (for sth)** | **~ sth** to be the teacher or leader in a class or a religious service 授（课）；主持（宗教仪式）：*The head teacher usually takes us for French.* 校长通常给我们上法语课。

• **STUDY** 学习 **35** [T] **~ sth** to study a subject at school, college, etc. 学习，读，修（课程）：*She is planning to take a computer course.* 她打算修一门计算机课。◇ *How many subjects are you taking this year?* 你今年修多少门课？

• **EXAM** 考试 **36** [T] **~ sth** to do an exam or a test 参加（考试或测验）：*When did you take your driving test?* 你什么时候参加的驾驶执照考试？

• **TRANSPORT/ROAD** 交通工具；道路 **37** [T] **~ sth** to use a form of transport, a road, a path, etc. to go to a place 乘坐，搭乘（交通工具）；取（道）；走（路线）：***to take the bus/plane/train*** 乘公共汽车 / 飞机 / 火车 ◇ *to take a cab* 乘出租汽车 ◇ *Take the second road on the right.* 第二个路口向右拐。◇ *It's more interesting to take the coast road.* 走海滨公路更有意思。

• **GO OVER/AROUND** 越过；绕路走 **38** [T] **~ sth (+ adv./prep.)** to go over or around sth 跨过；跳过；绕过：*The horse took the first fence well.* 那匹马轻快地跃过了第一道栅栏。◇ *He takes bends much too fast.* 他拐弯时车开得太快。

• **IN SPORTS** 体育运动 **39** [T] **~ sth** (of a player in a sports game 体育比赛中的运动员) to kick or throw the ball from a fixed or agreed position 踢；掷：*to **take a penalty/free kick/corner*** 主罚点球 / 任意球；开角球

• **VOTE/SURVEY** 投票；调查 **40** [T] **~ sth** to use a particular method to find out people's opinions 付诸（表决）；举行（投票）；进行（调查）：*to **take a vote/poll/survey*** 付诸表决；进行民意测验 / 调查

• **BE SUCCESSFUL** 成功 **41** [I] to be successful; to work 成功；起作用；行得通：*The skin graft failed to take.* 皮肤移植未能成功。

• **GRAMMAR** 语法 **42** [T] (not used in the progressive tenses 不用于进行时) **~ sth** (of verbs, nouns, etc. 动词、名词等) to have or require sth when used in a sentence or other structure （用于句子或其他结构中时）有，需要：*The verb 'rely' takes the preposition 'on'.* 动词 rely 需要和介词 on 连用。 ➲MORE LIKE THIS 33, page R28

IDM **HELP** Most idioms containing **take** are at the entries for the nouns and adjectives in the idioms, for example **take the biscuit** is at **biscuit**. 大多数含 take 的习语，都可在该等习语中的名词及形容词相关词条找到，如 take the biscuit 在词条 biscuit 下。 **I, you, etc. can't take sb 'anywhere** (*informal, often humorous*) used to say that you cannot trust sb to behave well in public （用以表示不相信某人会在公共场合行为得体）到哪儿都拿不出去 **have (got) what**

T

it ˈtakes (*informal*) to have the qualities, ability, etc. needed to be successful 具备（成功）所需要的一切条件（或素质、能力等） **take sth as it ˈcomes | take sb as they ˈcome** to accept sth/sb without wishing it/them to be different or without thinking about it/them very much in advance 安于现状；顺其自然：*She takes life as it comes.* 她对待生活的态度是顺其自然。 **ˈtake it (that...)** to suppose; to assume 假定；假设；设想；以为：*I take it you won't be coming to the party?* 我想你不会来参加聚会吧？ **take it from ˈme (that...)** (*informal*) used to emphasize that what you are going to say is the truth 我敢担保；我说的肯定没错：*Take it from me—he'll be a millionaire before he's 30.* 不信你等着瞧，他到不了 30 岁就会成为百万富翁。 **take it on/upon yourself to do sth** to decide to do sth without asking permission or advice 擅自作主；自作主张 **sb can take it or ˈleave it 1** used to say that you do not care if sb accepts or rejects your offer 要就要，不要就拉倒；取舍请便 **2** used to say that sb does not have a strong opinion about sth 可有可无；无所谓；无偏好：*Dancing? I can take it or leave it.* 跳舞？我跳不跳都行。 **take it/a lot ˈout of sb** (*informal*) to make sb physically or mentally tired 使精疲力竭；使心力交瘁：*Taking care of small children really takes it out of you.* 照看小孩确实会使你精疲力竭。 **take some/a lot of ˈdoing** (*informal*) to need a lot of effort or time; to be very difficult to do 费力；费时；难办；难做 **ˌtake ˈthat!** (*informal*) used as an exclamation when you are hitting sb or attacking them in some other way （打人时说）看打，接招

PHR V **ˌtake sb aˈback** [usually passive] to shock or surprise sb very much 使…震惊；使…大吃一惊

ˌtake ˈafter sb [no passive] **1** (not used in the progressive tenses 不用于进行时) to look or behave like an older member of your family, especially your mother or father （外貌或行为）像（父或母）：*Your daughter doesn't take after you at all.* 你女儿长得一点儿都不像你。 **2** (*NAmE, informal*) to follow sb quickly 追赶；跟踪：*I was afraid that if I started running the man would take after me.* 我害怕如果我跑起来，那人会追来。

ˌtake aˈgainst sb/sth [no passive] (*old-fashioned, BrE*) to start not liking sb/sth for no clear reason （说不清原因地）开始不喜欢

ˌtake sb/sth↔aˈpart (*informal*) **1** to defeat sb easily in a game or competition （运动或比赛）轻易打败，把…打得一败涂地 **2** to criticize sb/sth severely 严厉抨击 **ˌtake sth↔aˈpart** to separate a machine or piece of equipment into the different parts that it is made of 拆卸，拆散，拆开（机器等） **SYN** **dismantle**

ˌtake sth↔aˈway 1 to make a feeling, pain, etc. disappear 解除，消除（感情、痛苦等）：*I was given some pills to take away the pain.* 给我开了一些止痛药片。 **2** (*BrE*) (*NAmE* **ˌtake sth↔ˈout**) to buy cooked food at a restaurant and carry it away to eat, for example at home （从餐馆买饭菜等）带回食用；买外卖食物：*Two burgers to take away, please.* 请来两份汉堡包，带走。 ⇨ RELATED NOUN TAKEAWAY, TAKEOUT at TAKEAWAY **ˌtake aˈway from sth** [no passive] to make the effort or value of sth seem less 减少；减弱；贬低 **SYN** **detract**：*I don't want to take away from his achievements, but he couldn't have done it without my help.* 我不想贬低他的成就，但是如果没有我的帮助，他是做不成的。

ˌtake sb↔ˈback to allow sb, such as your husband, wife or partner, to come home after they have left because of a problem 允许（因不合而离去的配偶等）回家；与…重归于好 **ˌtake sb ˈback (to...)** to make sb remember sth 使回想起：*The smell of the sea took him back to his childhood.* 大海的气味使他回想起孩提时代。 **ˌtake sth↔ˈback 1** if you **take** sth **back** to a shop/store, or a shop/store **takes** sth **back**, you return sth that you have bought there, for example because it is the wrong size or does not work 退回；同意收回（退货） **2** to admit that sth you said was wrong or that you should not have said it 收回，撤回（说过的话）：*OK, I take it all back!* 好吧，我把我说过的话统统收回。

ˌtake sth↔ˈdown 1 to remove a structure, especially by separating it into pieces 拆掉；拆除；拆卸：*to take down a tent* 拆掉帐篷 **2** to pull down a piece of clothing worn below the waist without completely removing it 往下拽，拉低（下身衣服）：*to take down your trousers/pants* 把裤子 / 内裤往下拽一拽 **3** to write sth down 写下；记录：*Reporters took down every word of his speech.* 记者把他讲的每一句话都记录了下来。

ˌtake sb↔ˈin 1 to allow sb to stay in your home 留宿；收留：*to take in lodgers* 收房客 ◇ *He was homeless, so we took him in.* 他无家可归，我们便收留了他。 **2** [often passive] to make sb believe sth that is not true 欺骗；蒙骗 **SYN** **deceive**：*Don't be taken in by his charm—he's ruthless.* 不要被他那迷人的风度所蒙蔽，其实他冷酷无情。 ⇨ SYNONYMS AT CHEAT **ˌtake sth↔ˈin 1** to absorb sth into the body, for example by breathing or swallowing 吸入，吞入（体内）：*Fish take in oxygen through their gills.* 鱼用鳃吸取氧气。 ⇨ RELATED NOUN INTAKE **2** to make a piece of clothing narrower or tighter 改小，改瘦（衣服） **OPP** **let out** **3** [no passive] to include or cover sth 包括；包含：*The tour takes in six European capitals.* 这次旅游包括六个欧洲国家的首都。 **4** [no passive] to go to see or visit sth such as a film/movie 去看，观看（电影等）：*I generally take in a show when I'm in New York.* 我每次去纽约通常总会看一场演出。 **5** to take notice of sth with your eyes 注意到；看到：*He took in every detail of her appearance.* 他仔仔细细打量了她一番。 **6** to understand or remember sth that you hear or read 理解；领会；记住：*Halfway through the chapter I realized I hadn't taken anything in.* 这一章我读到一半才意识到我根本没有看懂。

ˌtake ˈoff 1 (of an aircraft, etc. 飞机等) to leave the ground and begin to fly 起飞：*The plane took off an hour late.* 飞机起飞晚了一个小时。 ⇨ RELATED NOUN TAKE-OFF **OPP** **land** **2** (*informal*) to leave a place, especially in a hurry 匆匆离去；急忙离开：*When he saw me coming he took off in the opposite direction.* 他见我走过来便赶快转身走了。 **3** (of an idea, a product, etc. 观念、产品等) to become successful or popular very quickly or suddenly 突然大受欢迎；迅速流行：*The new magazine has really taken off.* 这份新杂志真是大受欢迎。 **ˌtake sb↔ˈoff 1** to copy sb's voice, actions or manner in an amusing way （以诙谐的方式）模仿，学某人的样子 **SYN** **impersonate** **2** (in sports, entertainment, etc. 体育运动、娱乐等) to make sb stop playing, acting, etc. and leave the field or the stage 换下；中止；取消：*He was taken off after twenty minutes.* 二十分钟后，他被替换下场。 **ˌtake sth↔ˈoff 1** to remove sth, especially a piece of clothing from your/sb's body 脱下（衣服）；摘掉：*to take off your coat* 脱掉大衣 ◇ *He took off my wet boots and made me sit by the fire.* 他脱掉我湿漉漉的靴子，让我在火炉旁坐下。 **OPP** **put sth↔on** **2** to have a period of time as a break from work 休假；休息：*I've decided to take a few days off next week.* 我已决定下星期休息几天。 **3** [often passive] to stop a public service, television programme, performances of a show, etc. 取消；停演：*The show was taken off because of poor audience figures.* 该剧目因不卖座而停演了。 **4** to remove some of sb's hair, part of sb's body, etc. 剪掉（头发）；截去，切除（人体部位）：*The hairdresser asked me how much she should take off.* 理发师问我头发剪多少。 ◇ *The explosion nearly took his arm off.* 他的胳膊差点儿被炸掉。 **ˌtake yourself/sb ˈoff (to...)** (*informal*) to leave a place; to make sb leave a place （使）离去，走掉；带走 **ˌtake sb ˈoff sth** [often passive] to remove sb from sth such as a job, position, piece of equipment, etc. 调离，解除（工作、职务等）；撤掉，拆除（器械）：*The officer leading the investigation has been taken off the case.* 主持调查此案的警员已被撤下。 ◇ *After three days she was taken off the ventilator.* 三天之后给她摘掉了呼吸器。 **ˌtake sth ˈoff sth 1** to remove an amount of money or a number of marks, points, etc. in order to reduce the total 扣除，减去（款额、分数等）：*The manager took $10 off the bill.* 经理把账单上的金额减了 10 美元。 ◇ *That experience took ten years off my life* (= made me feel ten years older). 那段经历使我老了十岁。 **2** [often passive] to stop sth from being sold 停止销售：*The slimming pills were taken off the market.* 市场上已停止销售这种减肥药片。

ˌtake sb↔ˈon 1 (*especially BrE*) to employ sb 聘用；雇用：*to take on new staff* 雇用新员工 ◇ *She was taken on as*

a trainee. 她受聘当实习生。 **2** [no passive] to play against sb in a game or contest; to fight against sb（运动或比赛）同某人较量；反抗；与某人战斗： *to take somebody on at tennis* 与某人比赛打网球 ◇ *The rebels took on the entire Roman army.* 反叛者与整个罗马军队战斗。 **ˌtake sth↔ˈon** [no passive] to begin to have a particular quality, appearance, etc. 呈现，具有（特征、外观等）： *The chameleon can take on the colours of its background.* 变色龙可以变成周围环境的颜色。 ◇ *His voice took on a more serious tone.* 他说话的语气变得严肃起来。 **ˌtake sth/sb↔ˈon 1** to decide to do sth; to agree to be responsible for sth/sb 决定做；同意负责；承担（责任）： *I can't take on any extra work.* 我不能承担任何额外工作。 ◇ *We're not taking on any new clients at present.* 目前我们不接收新客户。 **2** (of a bus, plane or ship 公共汽车、飞机或船只) to allow sb/sth to enter 接纳（乘客）；装载： *The bus stopped to take on more passengers.* 公共汽车停下让其他乘客上车。 ◇ *The ship took on more fuel at Freetown.* 轮船在弗里敦停靠加燃料。

ˌtake sb↔ˈout to go to a restaurant, theatre, club, etc. with sb you have invited 带某人出去（到餐馆、剧院、俱乐部等） **ˌtake sb/sth↔ˈout** (*informal*) to kill sb or destroy sth 杀死；毁灭： *They took out two enemy bombers.* 他们摧毁了敌人的两架轰炸机。 **ˌtake sth↔ˈout 1** to remove sth from inside sb's body, especially a part of it 切除，摘除（人体内的一部分）： *How many teeth did the dentist take out?* 牙科医生拔了几颗牙？ **2** to obtain an official document or service 获得，领到（正式文件或服务）： *to **take out an insurance policy/a mortgage/a loan*** 买了一份保险；得到按揭贷款；获得贷款 ◇ *to take out an ad in a newspaper* 在报纸上刊登广告 **3** (*NAmE*) (*BrE* **ˌtake sth↔aˈway**) to buy cooked food at a restaurant and carry it away to eat, for example at home（从餐馆买饭菜等）带回食用；买外卖食物 ➲ RELATED NOUN TAKEAWAY, TAKEOUT at TAKEAWAY **ˌtake sth↔ˈout (against sb)** to start legal action against sb by means of an official document 发出（传票）： *The police have taken out a summons against the driver of the car.* 警方已向这辆汽车的驾驶人发出传票。 **ˌtake sth↔ˈout (of sth)** to obtain money by removing it from your bank account（从银行账户中）提取（款） **ˌtake sth ˈout of sth** to remove an amount of money from a larger amount, especially as a payment 扣除；减去；抽出： *The fine will be taken out of your wages.* 罚款将从你的工资中扣除。 **ˌtake it/sth ˈout on sb** to behave in an unpleasant way towards sb because you feel angry, disappointed, etc., although it is not their fault 向…发泄；拿…撒气： *OK, so you had a bad day. Don't take it out on me.* 好，这么说你今天遇上了很多倒霉事。可也别拿我当出气筒。 ◇ *She tended to take her frustrations out on her family.* 她心里不痛快总是在家里人身上发泄。 **ˌtake sb ˈout of himself/herself** to make sb forget their worries and become less concerned with their own thoughts and situation 使摆脱苦恼；为某人消愁

ˌtake ˈover (from sth) to become bigger or more important than sth else; to replace sth 占上风；取而代之： *Try not to let negative thoughts take over.* 尽量别受消极的想法左右。 ◇ *It has been suggested that mammals took over from dinosaurs 65 million years ago.* 有人提出哺乳动物是在 6 500 万年前取代恐龙的。 **ˌtake ˈover (from sb)** | **ˌtake sth↔ˈover (from sb) 1** 🔑 to begin to have control of or responsibility for sth, especially in place of sb else 接替；接任；接管；接手 **2** 🔑 to gain control of a political party, a country, etc. 控制，接管（政党、国家等）： *The army is threatening to take over if civil unrest continues.* 军方扬言如果内乱继续就实行军管。 **ˌtake sth↔ˈover** 🔑 to gain control of a business, a company, etc., especially by buying shares 接收，接管（企业、公司等，尤指通过购买股份）： *CBS Records was taken over by Sony.* 哥伦比亚广播公司的唱片公司已被索尼公司收购。 ➲ RELATED NOUN TAKEOVER

ˌtake sb ˈthrough sth to help sb learn or become familiar with sth, for example by talking about each part in turn 帮助某人深入了解；给某人解说： *The director took us through the play scene by scene.* 导演一幕一幕地给我们说戏。

ˈtake to sth [no passive] **1** to go away to a place, especially to escape from danger（尤指为逃避危险）逃往，躲到： *The rebels took to the hills.* 反叛者躲进山里。 **2** to begin to do sth as a habit 开始沉溺于；养成…习惯： **take to doing sth** *I've taken to waking up very early.* 我已形成习惯，醒得很早。 **3** to develop an ability for sth 培养…的能力： *She took to tennis as if she'd been playing all her life.* 她网球打得很好，好像一生都在从事这项运动似的。 **ˈtake to sb/sth** [no passive] to start liking sb/sth 开始喜欢；对…产生好感： *I took to my new boss immediately.* 我立刻对新老板产生了好感。 ◇ *He hasn't taken to his new school.* 他对新学校还没有产生兴趣。

ˌtake ˈup to continue, especially starting after sb/sth else has finished 继续；接下去： *The band's new album takes up where their last one left off.* 这个乐队的新唱片集是接上一集的乐曲录制的。 **ˌtake ˈup sth** 🔑 to fill or use an amount of space or time 占用（时间）；占据（空间）：

▼ **SYNONYMS 同义词辨析**

take

lead • escort • drive • show • walk • guide • usher • direct

These words all mean to go with sb from one place to another. 以上各词均含带去、引领之义。

take to go with sb from one place to another, for example in order to show them sth or to show them the way to a place 指带去、带路、引领： *It's too far to walk—I'll take you by car.* 步行路太远，我开车送你去。

lead to go with or go in front of sb in order to show them the way or to make them go in the right direction 指带路、领路、引领： *Firefighters led the survivors to safety.* 消防队员把幸存者带到了安全的地方。

escort to go with sb in order to protect or guard them or to show them the way 指护卫、护送： *The president arrived, escorted by twelve bodyguards.* 总统在十二名保镖的护送下到达。

drive to take sb somewhere in a car, taxi, etc. 指驾车送（人）： *My mother drove us to the airport.* 我母亲开车把我们送到了机场。

show to take sb to a particular place, in the right direction, or along the correct route 指引领、带领： *The attendant showed us to our seats.* 服务员把我们带到我们的座位。

walk to go somewhere with sb on foot, especially in order to make sure that they get there safely; to take an animal, especially a dog, for a walk or make an animal walk somewhere 指陪伴或护送（人）走、牵着或赶着（动物）走、遛（狗）： *He always walked her home.* 他经常护送她走回家。 ◇ *Have you walked the dog yet today?* 你今天遛狗了吗？

guide to show sb the way to a place, often by going with them; to show sb a place that you know well 指给某人领路（或导游）、指引： *She guided us through the busy streets.* 她带领我们穿过了繁忙的街道。 ◇ *We were guided around the museums.* 我们被领着参观了博物馆。

usher (*rather formal*) to politely take or show sb where they should go, especially within a building 指礼貌地引往、引导、引领，尤指在建筑物内： *She ushered her guests to their seats.* 她把客人引领到座位上。

direct (*rather formal*) to tell or show sb how to get somewhere or where to go 指给某人指路、为某人领路： *A young woman directed them to the station.* 一名年轻女子给他们指了去车站的路。

PATTERNS

- to take/lead/escort/drive/show/walk/guide/usher/direct sb **to/out of/into** sth
- to take/lead/escort/drive/show/walk/guide sb **around/round**
- to take/lead/escort/drive/walk sb **home**
- to take/lead/escort/guide sb **to safety**
- to lead/show **the way**

T

The table takes up too much room. 这张桌子太占地方。◇ *I won't take up any more of your time.* 我不再占用你的时间了。 **ˌtake sth↔ˈup 1** to make sth such as a piece of clothing shorter 将（衣服等）改短：*This skirt needs taking up.* 这条裙子需要改短。 **OPP let sth↔down 2** to learn or start to do sth, especially for pleasure（尤指为消遣）学着做，开始做：*They've taken up golf.* 他们学起打高尔夫球来了。◇ *She has taken up* (= started to learn to play) *the oboe.* 她学起吹双簧管来了。 **3** to start or begin sth such as a job 开始从事：*He takes up his duties next week.* 他下周就要开始履行职责。 **4** to join in singing or saying sth 一起唱；一齐说：*to take up the chorus* 加入合唱 ◇ *Their protests were later taken up by other groups.* 其他团体后来也加入了他们抗议的行列。 **5** to continue sth that sb else has not finished, or that has not been mentioned for some time 继续（他人未完成的事）；接着讲（以前提过的事）：*She took up the story where Tim had left off.* 她接着讲蒂姆未讲完的故事。◇ *I'd like to take up the point you raised earlier.* 我想继续谈一谈你早些时候提出的问题。 **6** to move into a particular position 进入，占据（位置）：*I took up my position by the door.* 我把住了门口。 **7** to accept sth that is offered or available 接受（建议或能得到的东西）：*to take up a challenge* 接受挑战 ◇ *She took up his offer of a drink.* 他请她喝一杯，她接受了。 **ˌtake ˈup with sb** (*informal*) to begin to be friendly with sb, especially sb with a bad reputation 开始结交（尤指名声不好的人） **ˌtake sb ˈup on sth 1** to question sb about sth, because you do not agree with them 质问；查问：*I must take you up on that point.* 那个问题我一定要找你问个明白。 **2** (*informal*) to accept an offer, a bet, etc. from sb 接受（提议、打赌等）：*Thanks for the invitation—we'll take you up on it some time.* 谢谢你的盛情邀请，改日我们一定奉陪。 **ˌtake sth ˈup with sb** to speak or write to sb about sth that they may be able to deal with or help you with 向…提出；与…交涉：*They decided to take the matter up with their MP.* 他们决定向本地区的下院议员反映这一问题。 **be ˌtaken ˈup with sth/sb** to be giving all your time and energy to sth/sb 致力于；专心于；对…一心一意

be ˈtaken with sb/sth to find sb/sth attractive or interesting 被…吸引；迷上；对…感兴趣：*We were all very taken with his girlfriend.* 我们都觉得他的女朋友非常讨人喜欢。◇ *I think he's quite taken with the idea.* 我认为他对这个想法十分感兴趣。

■ ***noun* 1** a scene or part of a film/movie that is filmed at one time without stopping the camera（不停机一次连续拍摄的）场景，镜头：*We managed to get it right in just two takes.* 我们仅拍摄了两个镜头就把这部分戏拍好了。 **2** [usually sing.] (*informal*) an amount of money that sb receives, especially the money that is earned by a business during a particular period of time 收入额；进项 **SYN takings**：*How much is my share of the take?* 我的那一份收入是多少？ **3 ~ on sth** (*informal*) the particular opinion or idea that sb has about sth 看法；意见：*What's his take on the plan?* 他对这项计划有什么意见？◇ *a new take on the Romeo and Juliet story* (= a way of presenting it) 对《罗密欧与朱丽叶》故事的重新演绎 ➲ SEE ALSO DOUBLE TAKE

IDM be on the ˈtake (*informal*) to accept money from sb for helping them in a dishonest or illegal way 受贿；贪赃枉法

take·away /ˈteɪkəweɪ/ (*BrE*) (*NAmE* **ˈtake-out**) (*also* **ˈcarry-out** *US, ScotE*) *noun* **1** a restaurant that cooks and sells food that you take away and eat somewhere else 外卖餐馆 **2** a meal that you buy at this type of restaurant 外卖的饭菜；外卖食物：*Let's have a takeaway tonight.* 咱们今晚吃一顿外卖的饭菜吧。

take·down /ˈteɪkdaʊn/ *noun* **1** a move in which a WRESTLER quickly gets his/her opponent down to the floor from a standing position（摔跤中将对手）摔倒，放倒 **2** (*informal*) an arrest or unexpected visit by the police（警方的）抓捕行动，临检，突检

ˈtake-home pay *noun* [U] the amount of money that you earn after you have paid tax, etc.（扣除税项等之后的）实得工资

ˈtake-off *noun* **1** [U, C] the moment at which an aircraft leaves the ground and starts to fly（飞机的）起飞：*The plane is ready for take-off.* 飞机准备随时起飞。◇ *take-off speed* 起飞速度 ◇ (*figurative*) *The local economy is poised for take-off.* 当地的经济蓄势待发。 **OPP landing** ➲ WORDFINDER NOTE AT PLANE **2** [C, U] the moment when your feet leave the ground when you jump 起跳 **3** [C] if you do a **take-off** of sb, you copy the way they speak or behave, in a humorous way to entertain people（对他人言行的）滑稽模仿 ➲ WORDFINDER NOTE AT COMEDY

take·over /ˈteɪkəʊvə(r); *NAmE* -oʊ-/ *noun* [C, U] **1** an act of taking control of a company by buying most of its shares 收购；接收；接管：*a **takeover bid** for the company* 收购这家公司的出价 ➲ WORDFINDER NOTE AT DEAL ➲ COLLOCATIONS AT BUSINESS **2** an act of taking control of a country, an area or a political organization by force（对国家、地区、政治组织等的）强行接管，控制

taker /ˈteɪkə(r)/ *noun* **1** [usually pl.] a person who is willing to accept sth that is being offered 接受者；收受人：*They won't find many takers for the house at that price.* 以这样的要价，他们不会为房子找到多少承让人的。 **2** (often in compounds 常构成复合词) a person who takes sth 接受者：*drug takers* 吸毒者 ◇ *It is better to be a giver than a taker.* 施比受有福。

ˈtake-up *noun* [U, sing.] the rate at which people accept sth that is offered or made available to them（福利等的）领受率：*a low take-up of government benefits* 政府救济金的低领取率

tak·ings /ˈteɪkɪŋz/ *noun* [pl.] (*BrE*) the amount of money that a shop/store, theatre, etc. receives from selling goods or tickets over a particular period of time（某一时期的）进账，票房收入：*The box office takings are up on last week.* 票房收入较上星期有所增长。

tak·kie = TACKIE

tala /ˈtɑːlə/ *noun* a traditional pattern of rhythm in CLASSICAL Indian music 塔拉（古印度音乐的传统节拍组合）

tal·cum pow·der /ˈtælkəm paʊdə(r)/ (*also informal* **talc** /tælk/) *noun* [U] a fine soft powder, usually with a pleasant smell, that you put on your skin to make it feel smooth and dry 滑石粉；爽身粉；扑粉

tale /teɪl/ *noun* **1** a story created using the imagination, especially one that is full of action and adventure（尤指充满惊险的）故事；历险记：*Dickens' 'A Tale of Two Cities'* 狄更斯的《双城记》◇ ***a fairy/moral/romantic, etc. tale*** 童话、寓言、爱情故事等 ➲ SEE ALSO FOLK TALE **2** an exciting spoken description of an event, which may not be completely true（精彩但不一定完全真实的）讲述，叙述：*I love listening to his tales of life at sea.* 我喜欢听他讲述他的海上生活。◇ *I've heard tales of people seeing ghosts in that house.* 我听说有人在那栋房子里见到过鬼。◇ *The team's **tale of woe** continued on Saturday* (= they lost another match). 上星期六这支队又遭败绩。◇ *Her experiences provide a **cautionary tale*** (= a warning) *for us all.* 她的经历成了我们大家的前车之鉴。 ➲ SEE ALSO TELLTALE *n.* **IDM** SEE OLD, TELL

tal·ent /ˈtælənt/ *noun* **1** [C, U] a natural ability to do sth well 天才；天资；天赋：*to **have** great artistic **talent*** 很有艺术天赋 ◇ *a man **of many talents*** 多才多艺的男子 ◇ **~ (for sth/for doing sth)** *She showed considerable talent for getting what she wanted.* 她很有天资，能够达成自己的目标。◇ *a **talent competition/contest*** (= in which people perform, to show how well they can sing, dance, etc.) 才艺选拔赛 **2** [U, C] people or a person with a natural ability to do sth well 有才能的人；人才；天才：*There is **a wealth of young talent** in British theatre.* 英国戏剧界年轻一代人才辈出。◇ *He is a great talent.* 他是个了不起的人才。 **3** [U] (*BrE, slang*) people who are sexually attractive（统称）性感的人：*He likes to spend his time chatting up the local talent.* 他喜欢把时间花在和当地的妞儿搭讪上。

tal·ent·ed /ˈtæləntɪd/ *adj.* having a natural ability to do sth well 有才能的；天才的；有才干的： *a talented player* 天才运动员

ˈtalent scout (*also* **scout**, **ˈtalent spotter**) *noun* a person whose job is to find people who are good at singing, acting, sport, etc. in order to give them work（歌唱、戏剧、体育运动等的）人才发掘者，新秀发现者，星探

ˈtalent show *noun* a performance, for example on television or in a school, in which people compete to show how well they can sing, dance, play a musical instrument, entertain by telling funny jokes or stories, etc. 才艺表演；达人秀；选秀节目

tal·is·man /ˈtælɪzmən/ *noun* an object that is thought to have magic powers and to bring good luck 护身符；驱邪物 ➲ WORDFINDER NOTE AT LUCK

talk /tɔːk/ *verb, noun*

■ *verb*

• SPEAK TO SB 与人说话 **1** [I, T] to say things; to speak in order to give information or to express feelings, ideas, etc. 说话；讲话；谈话： *Stop talking and listen!* 别说话，注意听！ ◇ *We talked on the phone for over an hour.* 我们在电话里谈了一个多小时。 ◇ ~ **(to/with sb)** **(about sb/sth)** *Who were you talking to just now?* 你刚才在跟谁说话？ ◇ *We looked around the school and talked with the principal.* 我们参观了那所学校，并跟校长进行了交谈。 ◇ *Ann and Joe* ***aren't talking*** *to each other right now* (= they refuse to speak to each other because they have argued). 安和乔两人现在互不理睬。 ◇ *When they get together, all they talk about is football.* 他们在一起时，谈论的都是足球。 ◇ ***What are you talking about?*** (= used when you are surprised, annoyed and/or worried by sth that sb has just said) 你在胡说什么？（对他人所言感到惊奇、不悦或担忧时用） ◇ ***I don't know what you're talking about*** (= used to say that you did not do sth that sb has accused you of). 我不知道你在说什么（表示自己没有做对方指责的事）。 ◇ ~ **of sth** *Mary is talking of looking for another job.* 玛丽说起要另找一份工作。 ◇ ~ **yourself + adj.** ***We talked ourselves hoarse,*** *catching up on all the news.* 我们互诉近况，把嗓子都说哑了。 ➲ WORDFINDER NOTE AT CONFERENCE

• DISCUSS 讨论 **2** [I, T] to discuss sth, usually sth serious or important 讨论，谈论，商谈，洽谈（通常指重大的事）： *This situation can't go on. We need to talk.* 这种情况不能再继续下去了。我们需要谈一谈。 ◇ *The two sides in the dispute say they are ready to talk.* 争执双方说他们愿意商谈。 ◇ ~ **(to/with sb)** **(about sth)** *Talk to your doctor if you're still worried.* 如果你仍然不放心，就找医生谈一谈。 ◇ ~ **sth** *to talk business* 谈正事

• SAY WORDS 说话 **3** [I, T] to say words in a language（用某种语言）讲，说： *The baby is just starting to talk.* 这婴儿刚开始咿呀学语。 ◇ ~ **in sth** *We couldn't understand them because they were talking in Chinese.* 我们听不懂他们在讲些什么，因为他们说的是中国话。 ◇ ~ **sth** *Are they talking Swedish or Danish?* 他们说的是瑞典语还是丹麦语？

• SENSE/NONSENSE 有理；无理 **4** [T] ~ **sth** to say things that are/are not sensible 说，讲（有理、无理的话）： *She talks a lot of sense.* 她讲得很在理。 ◇ (*BrE*) *You're talking rubbish!* 你胡说八道！ ◇ *See if you can* ***talk some sense into him*** (= persuade him to be sensible). 看你能否给他讲通道理。

• FOR EMPHASIS 加强语气 **5** [T] **be talking sth** (*informal*) used to emphasize an amount of money, how serious sth is, etc.（用以强调款额、情况严重程度等）讲的是，指的是： *We're talking £500 for three hours' work.* 咱们讲的可是工作三个小时酬金 500 英镑。

• ABOUT PRIVATE LIFE 私生活 **6** [I] to talk about a person's private life 说闲话；讲人坏话；嚼舌头 SYN **gossip**: *Don't phone me at work—****people will talk.*** 别在上班时给我打电话，人家会说闲话的。

• GIVE INFORMATION 提供信息 **7** [I] to give information to sb, especially unwillingly 供出消息；供认；招认： *The police questioned him but he refused to talk.* 警察审问他，但他拒不招供。

IDM **look who's ˈtalking | ˈyou can/can't talk | you're a ˈfine one to talk** (*informal*) used to tell sb that they should not criticize sb else for sth because they do the same things too（用以表示自己同样不对时不要批评别人）还有脸说别人： *'George is so careless with money.' 'Look who's talking!'* "乔治真是乱花钱。" "亏你还有脸说别人！" **now you're ˈtalking** (*informal*) used when you like what sb has suggested very much （表示赞同对方的话）你这算说对了，你所言正合我意 **ˈtalk about...** (*informal*) used to emphasize sth （用以强调）这才叫，真是…不得了： *Talk about mean! She didn't even buy me a card.* 这才叫吝啬呢！她连张贺卡都没给我买。 **talk ˈdirty** (*informal*) to talk to sb about sex in order to make them sexually excited

▼ SYNONYMS 同义词辨析

talk

discuss • speak • communicate • debate • consult

These words all mean to share news, information, ideas or feelings with another person or other people, especially by talking with them. 以上各词均含交流、交谈之义。

talk to speak in order to give information, express feelings or share ideas 指说话、讲话、谈话： *We talked on the phone for over an hour.* 我们在电话里谈了一个多小时。

discuss (*rather formal*) to talk and share ideas on a subject or problem with other people, especially in order to decide sth 指谈论、讨论、商量： *Have you discussed the problem with anyone?* 你与谁商量过这个问题吗？

NOTE You cannot say 'discuss about sth'. 不能说 discuss about sth： ~~*I'm not prepared to discuss about this on the phone.*~~

speak to talk to sb about sth; to have a conversation with sb 指谈话、交谈： *I've spoken to the manager about it.* 那件事我已经和经理谈过了。 ◇ *'Can I speak to Susan?' 'Speaking.'* (= at the beginning of a telephone conversation) "请问苏珊在吗？" "我就是。"

TALK OR SPEAK? 用 talk 还是 speak?

Speak can suggest a more formal level of communication than **talk**. You **speak** to sb about sth to try to achieve a particular goal or to tell them to do sth. You **talk** to sb in order to be friendly or to ask their advice. 与 talk 比较，speak 所指的交谈可能更正式。与某人交谈试图达到某一目的或让对方做某事用 speak，为表示友好或询问建议用 talk： *Have you talked to your parents about the problems you're having?* 你同你父母谈过你的问题吗？ ◇ *I've spoken to Ed about it and he's promised not to let it happen again.* 我已经同埃德谈过了，他答应不让这种事情再次发生。

communicate (*rather formal*) to exchange information or ideas with sb 指与某人交流信息或意见： *We only communicate by email.* 我们只通过电子邮件进行交流。 ◇ *Dolphins use sound to communicate with each other.* 海豚用声音相互沟通。 NOTE **Communicate** is often used when the speaker wants to draw attention to the means of communication used. 说话者要让人注意交流的方式时常用 communicate。

debate to discuss sth, especially formally, before making a decision or finding a solution （尤指正式）讨论、辩论： *Politicians will be debating the bill later this week.* 政界将在本周晚些时候讨论这项议案。

consult (*rather formal*) to discuss sth with sb in order to get their permission for sth, or to help you make a decision 指（与某人）商议、商量（以得到许可或帮助决策）： *You shouldn't have done it without consulting me.* 你不该不和我商量就做。

PATTERNS

- to talk/discuss sth/speak/communicate/debate/consult **with** sb
- to talk/speak **to** sb
- to talk/speak to sb/consult sb **about** sth
- to talk/speak **of** sth

T

说下流话 **talk a good 'game** (*NAmE*) to talk in a way that sounds convincing, but may not be sincere 说得好听；说得天花乱坠 **talk the hind leg off a 'donkey** (*informal*) to talk too much, especially about boring or unimportant things 唠叨个没完没了；喋喋不休 **talking of sb/sth** (*informal, especially BrE*) used when you are going to say more about a subject that has already been mentioned（继续谈论时用）提起，说起，谈及，至于：*Talking of Sue, I met her new boyfriend last week.* 谈到休，上星期我遇到了她的新男友。 **talk 'shop** (*usually disapproving*) to talk about your work with the people you work with, especially when you are also with other people who are not connected with or interested in it 说行话；三句话不离本行（尤指当着外行的面） **ˌtalk the 'talk** (*informal, sometimes disapproving*) to be able to talk in a confident way that makes people think you are good at what you do 说得头头是道：*You can talk the talk, but can you walk the walk?* (= can you act in a way that matches your words?) 你说得头头是道，可你能做到吗？ **talk through your 'hat** (*old-fashioned, informal*) to say silly things while you are talking about a subject you do not understand 胡说；信口开河；瞎扯 **talk 'tough (on sth)** (*informal, especially NAmE*) to tell people very strongly what you want 强硬地说；强烈地要求 **talk 'turkey** (*informal, especially NAmE*) to talk about sth seriously 郑重其事地谈；严肃认真地谈 **talk your way out of sth/of doing sth** to make excuses and give reasons for not doing sth; to manage to get yourself out of a difficult situation 靠能言善辩开脱；以话解围：*I managed to talk my way out of having to give a speech.* 我好说歹说总算逃脱了发言的差事。 **'you can/can't talk** (*informal*) = LOOK WHO'S TALKING **you're a 'fine one to talk** (*informal*) = LOOK WHO'S TALKING ➲ MORE AT DEVIL, KNOW *v.*, LANGUAGE, MONEY, SENSE *n.*, TURN *n.*

PHR V **ˌtalk a'round/'round sth** to talk about sth in a general way without dealing with the most important parts of it 拐弯抹角地说；不着边际地说 **'talk at sb** to speak to sb without listening to what they say in reply（不理会对方反应）对某人大发议论，滔滔不绝地对某人说 **ˌtalk 'back (to sb)** to answer sb rudely, especially sb in authority（尤指对掌权者）回嘴，顶嘴 ➲ RELATED NOUN BACK TALK **ˌtalk sb/sth↔'down** to help a pilot of a plane to land by giving instructions from the ground 引导（飞行员）着陆；引降 **ˌtalk sth↔'down** to make sth seem less important or successful than it really is 贬低；贬抑：*You shouldn't talk down your own achievements.* 你不该贬低自己的成绩。 **ˌtalk 'down to sb** to speak to sb as if they were less important or intelligent than you 以高人一等的口气说话 **ˌtalk sb 'into/'out of sth** to persuade sb to do/not to do sth 说服某人做/不做某事：*I didn't want to move abroad but Bill talked me into it.* 我本不想移居国外，但是比尔把我给说服了。◇ **talk sb into/out of doing sth** *She tried to talk him out of leaving.* 她极力劝他不要走。 **ˌtalk sth↔'out** to discuss sth thoroughly in order to make a decision, solve a problem, etc. 把…谈透；协商作出（决定）；协商解决（问题） **ˌtalk sth↔'over (with sb)** to discuss sth thoroughly, especially in order to reach an agreement or make a decision 详细讨论，详谈（以达成协议或作出决定）：*You'll find it helpful to talk things over with a friend.* 把情况和朋友详细聊一聊，你会觉得大有帮助。 **ˌtalk sb 'round (to sth)** (*BrE*) to persuade sb to accept sth or agree to sth 说服；劝说某人同意：*We finally managed to talk them round to our way of thinking.* 我们最后总算说服他们接受我们的想法。 **ˌtalk sb 'through sth** to explain to sb how sth works so that they can do it or understand it 给某人解说：*Can you talk me through the various investment options?* 你能给我详述可以选择的各种投资方法吗？ **ˌtalk sth↔'through** to discuss sth thoroughly until you are sure you understand it 把某事谈透 **ˌtalk sb/sth 'up** to describe sb/sth in a way that makes them sound better than they really are 过分夸奖；吹捧

■ ***noun***

• **CONVERSATION** 交谈 **1** [C] ~ (**with sb**) (**about sth**) a conversation or discussion 交谈；谈话；讨论；商讨：*I had a long talk with my boss about my career prospects.* 我和老板就我的事业前景进行了一次长谈。◇ *I had to have a heart-to-heart talk with her.* 我得推心置腹地和她谈一谈。 ➲ SYNONYMS AT DISCUSSION

• **FORMAL DISCUSSIONS** 正式讨论 **2** **talks** [pl.] formal discussions between governments or organizations（政府或组织之间正式的）洽谈，会谈，谈判：***arms/pay/peace, etc. talks*** 军备、工资、和平等谈判 ◇ *to **hold talks*** 举行会谈 ◇ ~ (**between A and B**) (**on/over sth**) *Talks between management and workers **broke down** over the issue of holiday pay.* 劳资双方就假日工资的谈判破裂了。◇ *A further **round of talks** will be needed if the dispute is to be resolved.* 要解决纠纷，还需再举行一轮谈判。

• **SPEECH** 讲话 **3** [C] ~ (**on sth**) a speech or lecture on a particular subject（专题）报告，演讲：*She gave a talk on her visit to China.* 她作了一次访华报告。 ➲ SYNONYMS AT SPEECH

• **WORDS WITHOUT ACTIONS** 空话 **4** [U] (*informal*) words that are spoken, but without the necessary facts or actions to support them 空话；空谈：*It's just talk. He'd never carry out his threats.* 这只不过是说说而已。他绝不会把他的恫吓付诸行动。◇ *Don't pay any attention to her—she's **all talk**.* 别听她的，她光说空话。

• **STORIES/RUMOURS** 传闻；谣言 **5** [U] ~ (**of sth/of doing sth**) | ~ (**that...**) stories that suggest a particular thing might happen in the future 传言；谣言；流言蜚语；揣测：*There was talk in Washington of sending in troops.* 华盛顿有派兵的传言。◇ *She dismissed the stories of her resignation as newspaper talk.* 她不理会有关她辞职的报道，认为那不过是报纸的谣言。

• **TOPIC/WAY OF SPEAKING** 话题；说话方式 **6** [U] (often in compounds 常构成复合词) a topic of conversation or a way of speaking 话题；说话方式：*business talk* 业务洽谈 ◇ *She said it was just **girl talk** that a man wouldn't understand.* 她说这是女生话题，男人是听不懂的。◇ *The book teaches you how to understand Spanish **street talk*** (= slang). 这本书教你如何理解西班牙俚语。◇ *It was tough talk, coming from a man who had begun the year in a hospital bed.* 这话出自年初住进医院的一位男子之口，语气很强硬。 ➲ SEE ALSO SMALL TALK, SWEET TALK at SWEET-TALK, TRASH TALK

IDM **the talk of sth** the person or thing that everyone is talking about in a particular place（某地人人谈论的）话题，谈论中心：*Overnight, she became **the talk of the town*** (= very famous). 一夜之间，她成了街头巷尾谈论的话题。 ➲ MORE AT FIGHT *v.*

talk·ative /ˈtɔːkətɪv/ *adj.* liking to talk a lot 爱多说话的；饶舌的；健谈的：*He's not very talkative, is he?* 他的话不多，是吧？◇ *She was in a talkative mood.* 她滔滔不绝，谈兴正浓。

talk·back /ˈtɔːkbæk/ *noun* [U] (*specialist*) a system that allows people working in a recording or broadcasting studio to talk to each other without their voices being recorded or heard on the radio（录音或播音室的）内部联络系统，内部对讲系统

talk·er /ˈtɔːkə(r)/ *noun* a person who talks in a particular way or who talks a lot 说话…的人；爱说话的人：*a brilliant talker* 能言善辩的人 ◇ *She's a (great) talker* (= she talks a lot). 她很健谈。◇ *He's more a talker than a doer* (= he talks instead of doing things). 他说得多做得少。 ➲ SYNONYMS AT SPEAKER **IDM** SEE FAST *adj.*

talkie /ˈtɔːki/ *noun* [usually pl.] (*old-fashioned, especially NAmE*) a film/movie that has sounds and not just pictures 有声电影 ➲ SEE ALSO WALKIE-TALKIE

ˌtalking 'drum *noun* a type of drum from W Africa whose sound can be changed in order to communicate different messages 话鼓（西非的一种可通过声音变化传递不同信息的鼓）

ˌtalking 'head *noun* (*informal*) a person on television who talks straight to the camera（电视上的）发言者头部特写：*The election broadcast consisted largely of talking heads.* 有关选举的电视广播主要播放发言者的特写镜头。

'talking point *noun* **1** (*BrE*) a subject that is talked about or discussed by many people 话题；论题：*The judge's decision became a legal talking point.* 法官的判决成了法律界谈论的中心。 **2** (*NAmE*) an item that sb will speak

T

about at a meeting, often one that supports a particular argument（常为支持某一论点的）论据

ˈ**talking shop** *noun* (*BrE, disapproving*) a place where there is a lot of discussion and argument but no action is taken（只讨论而无行动的）清谈俱乐部

ˈ**talking-to** *noun* [sing.] (*informal*) a serious talk with sb who has done sth wrong 训斥；申斥；责备；斥责：*to give sb a good talking-to* 狠狠训斥某人一顿

ˈ**talk radio** *noun* [U] radio programmes in which sb discusses a particular subject with people who telephone the radio station to give their opinions 电台听众热线节目

ˈ**talk show** *noun* **1** (*especially NAmE*) (*BrE also* ˈ**chat show**) a television or radio programme in which famous people are asked questions and talk in an informal way about their work and opinions on various topics（电视或电台的）访谈节目：*a talk-show host* 访谈节目主持人 **2** a television or radio programme in which a PRESENTER introduces a particular topic which is then discussed by the audience（电视或电台的）观众讨论节目，听众讨论节目

ˈ**talk time** *noun* [U] the amount of time that a mobile/cell phone can be used for calls without needing more power or more payments（手机的）通话时间，基本通话时间

talky /ˈtɔːki/ *adj.* (*informal*) **1** (of a film/movie, play or book 电影、戏剧或书) containing a lot of talk or conversation 讲话场景多的，有很多对话的：*The film is brilliantly animated, but it's overly talky and suffers from painfully slow pacing.* 这部电影的动画做得很棒，但对话太多，导致节奏慢得要命。 **2** (about a person 人) liking to talk a lot 爱多说话的；多嘴的；饶舌的；健谈的 SYN **talkative**

tall /tɔːl/ *adj.* (**tall·er, tall·est**) **1** (of a person, building, tree, etc. 人、建筑物、树木等) having a greater than average height 高的；高大的：*She's tall and thin.* 她身材高瘦。◇ *tall chimneys* 高高的烟囱 ◇ *the tallest building in the world* 世界上最高的建筑物 ◇ *a tall glass of iced tea* 一大杯冰茶 OPP **short** **2** used to describe or ask about the height of sb/sth （用以表示或询问高度）有…高，身高：*How tall are you?* 你身高多少？◇ *He's six feet tall and weighs 200 pounds.* 他身高六英尺，体重 200 磅。➲ NOTE AT HIGH ▶**tall·ness** *noun* [U]

IDM **stand ˈtall** (*especially NAmE*) to show that you are proud and able to deal with anything 趾高气扬；昂然挺立 **be a ˌtall ˈorder** (*informal*) to be very difficult to do 难以办到；要求苛刻 ➲ MORE AT OAK, WALK *v.*

tall·boy /ˈtɔːlbɔɪ/ (*BrE*) (*NAmE* **high·boy**) *noun* a tall piece of furniture with drawers, used for storing clothes in（带抽屉的）高衣柜

tal·low /ˈtæləʊ; *NAmE* -loʊ/ *noun* [U] animal fat used for making CANDLES, soap, etc.（用以制造蜡烛、肥皂等的）动物油脂

ˌ**tall ˈpoppy syndrome** *noun* [U] (*informal, especially AustralE*) the fact of criticizing people who are richer or more successful than others 高罂粟综合征（批评富有或成功的人）；仇富症；红眼病

ˌ**tall ˈstory** (*especially BrE*) (*NAmE usually* ˌ**tall ˈtale**) *noun* a story that is difficult to believe because what it describes seems exaggerated and not likely to be true 无稽之谈；荒诞不经的故事

tally /ˈtæli/ *noun, verb*

■ *noun* (*pl.* **-ies**) a record of the number or amount of sth, especially one that you can keep adding to 记录；积分表；账：*He hopes to improve on his tally of three goals in the past nine games.* 他希望提高在过去九场比赛中打进三球的纪录。◇ ***Keep a tally** of how much you spend while you're away.* 在外出期间，把你的花费都记录下来。

■ *verb* (**tal·lies, tally·ing, tal·lied, tal·lied**) **1** [I] ~ (**with sth**) to be the same as or to match another person's account of sth, another set of figures, etc.（说法、数字等）与…符合（或一致）；吻合 SYN **match up** (**with sth**): *Her report of what happened tallied exactly with the story of another witness.* 她对于事情的叙述和另一个证人的说法完全吻合。 **2** [T] ~ **sth** (**up**) to calculate the total number, cost, etc. of sth 计算（总的数目、成本等）；合计

ˌ**tally-ˈho** *exclamation* used in hunting for telling the dogs that a FOX has been seen 呔嗬（狩猎时的吆喝声，示意猎狗发现了狐狸）

the Tal·mud /ˈtælmʊd; *NAmE also* ˈtɑːl-/ *noun* [sing.] a collection of ancient writings on Jewish law and traditions《塔木德》（犹太古代法典） ▶ **Tal·mud·ic** /ˌtælˈmʊdɪk; -ˈmjuːd-; *NAmE also* ˌtɑːl-/ *adj.*

talon /ˈtælən/ *noun* a long sharp curved nail on the feet of some birds, especially BIRDS OF PREY (= birds that kill other creatures for food)（某些鸟类，尤指猛禽的）爪 ➲ VISUAL VOCAB PAGE V12

taluk /ˈtɑːlʊk/ (*also* **taluka** /ˈtɑːlʊkɑː/) *noun* (in some countries in S Asia) a smaller division of a district that governs itself（一些南亚国家的）自治小区

tam·ar·ind /ˈtæmərɪnd/ *noun* a tropical tree that produces fruit, also called tamarinds, that are often preserved and used in Asian cooking 罗望子树，酸豆（热带树木）；罗望子果，酸豆（常用于亚洲式烹调）

tam·bour /ˈtæmbʊə(r); *NAmE* -bʊr/ *noun* a type of drum 鼓

tam·bour·ine /ˌtæmbəˈriːn/ *noun* a musical instrument that has a round wooden frame, sometimes covered with plastic or skin, with metal discs around the edge. To play it you shake it or hit it with your hand. 铃鼓（蒙有塑料或皮面，鼓帮装有金属圆片，摇动或用手击打发声） ➲ VISUAL VOCAB PAGE V37

tame /teɪm/ *adj., verb*

■ *adj.* (**tamer, tam·est**) **1** (of animals, birds, etc. 兽、鸟等) not afraid of people, and used to living with them 养驯的；驯服的 OPP **wild** **2** (*informal*) not interesting or exciting 平淡无奇的；枯燥乏味的：*You'll find life here pretty tame after New York.* 这里的生活相当枯燥，与纽约形成对比。 **3** (*informal*) (of a person 人) willing to do what other people ask 听使唤的；温顺的：*I have a tame doctor who'll always give me a sick note when I want a day off.* 我的医生对我有求必应，我想要休一天假时，他总会给我开病假条。 ▶**tame·ly** *adv.* **tame·ness** *noun* [U]

■ *verb* ~ **sth** to make sth tame or easy to control 驯化；驯服；使易于控制：*Lions can never be completely tamed.* 狮子永远不能被完全驯化。◇ *She made strenuous efforts to tame her anger.* 她竭力压制心头怒火。

tamer /ˈteɪmə(r)/ *noun* (usually in compounds 通常构成复合词) a person who trains wild animals 驯兽师；驯养者：*a lion-tamer* 驯狮人

Tamil /ˈtæmɪl/ *noun* **1** [C] a member of a race of people living in Tamil Nadu in southern India and in Sri Lanka 泰米尔人（居住在印度南部泰米尔纳德邦和斯里兰卡） **2** [U] the language of the Tamils 泰米尔语 ▶**Tamil** *adj.*

Tam·many Hall /ˌtæməni ˈhɔːl/ *noun* a dishonest political organization that had a lot of influence in New York City in the 19th and early 20th centuries (sometimes used to refer to any dishonest political organization) 坦曼尼协会（19 世纪和 20 世纪初期操纵美国纽约市政界的腐败政治组织，有时泛指腐败政治组织）

tam-o'shanter /ˌtæməˈʃæntə(r)/ *noun* a round hat made of wool with a small ball made of wool in the centre, originally worn in Scotland 苏格兰宽顶羊毛圆帽（中央缀绒球）

tam·oxi·fen /təˈmɒksɪfen; *NAmE* -ˈmɑːks-/ *noun* [U] (*medical* 医) a drug that is used especially to treat breast cancer 三苯氧胺，他莫昔芬（尤用于治疗乳腺癌）

tamp /tæmp/ *verb* ~ **sth** (**down**) to press sth down firmly, especially into a closed space 捣实；压实；塞紧

Tam·pax™ /ˈtæmpæks/ *noun* [C, U] (*pl.* **Tam·pax**) a type of TAMPON 丹碧丝（卫生棉条）

tam·per /ˈtæmpə(r)/ *verb*

PHRV ˈ**tamper with sth** to make changes to sth without

T

permission, especially in order to damage it 篡改，擅自改动，胡乱摆弄（尤指有意破坏） SYN **interfere with**: *Someone had obviously tampered with the brakes of my car.* 显然有人鼓捣过我汽车的刹车。

'tamper-proof *adj.* something that is **tamper-proof** is specially designed so that it cannot be easily changed or damaged 防更改的；防损毁的： *a tamper-proof identity card* 防涂改身份卡

tamp·ing /'tæmpɪŋ/ *adj.* (*WelshE, informal*) very angry 非常愤怒的

tam·pon /'tæmpɒn; *NAmE* -pɑːn/ *noun* a specially shaped piece of cotton material that a woman puts inside her VAGINA to absorb blood during her PERIOD（妇女用的）月经棉条，卫生栓 ➲ COMPARE SANITARY TOWEL

tan /tæn/ *verb, noun, adj., abbr.*
■ *verb* (-nn-) **1** [I, T] ~ (sb/sth) if a person or their skin **tans** or **is tanned**, they become brown as a result of spending time in the sun（使）晒成褐色，晒黑 **2** [T] ~ sth to make animal skin into leather by treating it with chemicals 鞣（革）；硝（皮） IDM SEE HIDE *n.*
■ *noun* **1** [U] a yellowish-brown colour 棕黄色；黄褐色 **2** (*also* **sun·tan**) [C] the brown colour that sb with pale skin goes when they have been in the sun 晒成棕褐肤色；晒成的棕褐色： *to get a tan* 晒黑
■ *adj.* yellowish brown in colour 棕褐色的；棕黄色的
■ *abbr.* (*mathematics* 数) TANGENT 正切

tan·dem /'tændəm/ *noun* a bicycle for two riders, one behind the other 双座自行车；双人自行车 ➲ WORDFINDER NOTE AT CYCLING ➲ VISUAL VOCAB PAGE V55
IDM **in 'tandem (with sb/sth)** a thing that works or happens **in tandem** with sth else works together with it or happens at the same time as it 并行；并驾齐驱；同时实行

tan·doori /tæn'dʊəri; *NAmE* -'dʊri/ *noun* [U] (often used as an adjective 常用作形容词) a method of cooking meat on a long straight piece of metal (called a SPIT) in a CLAY oven called a **tandoor**, originally used in S Asia 唐杜里烹饪法（源自南亚，将肉插在金属棒上放入泥灶中烘烤）： *tandoori chicken* 唐杜里鸡 ◇ *a tandoori restaurant* 唐杜里餐馆

tang /tæŋ/ *noun* [usually sing.] a strong sharp taste or smell 强烈味道；刺鼻气味： *the tang of lemons* 清爽的柠檬味 ▸ **tangy** /'tæŋi/ *adj.* : *a refreshing tangy lemon flavour* 清新浓郁的柠檬香味

tan·gent /'tændʒənt/ *noun* **1** (*geometry* 几何) a straight line that touches the outside of a curve but does not cross it 切线 ➲ PICTURE AT CIRCLE **2** (*abbr.* **tan**) (*mathematics* 数) the RATIO of the length of the side opposite an angle in a RIGHT-ANGLED triangle to the length of the side next to it 正切 ➲ COMPARE COSINE, SINE
IDM **fly/go off at a 'tangent** (*BrE*) (*NAmE* **go off on a 'tangent**) (*informal*) to suddenly start saying or doing sth that does not seem to be connected to what has gone before 突然转换话题；突然改变行动

tan·gen·tial /tæn'dʒenʃl/ *adj.* **1** (*formal*) having only a slight or indirect connection with sth 稍微沾边的；离题的；不相干的： *a tangential argument* 牵强附会的论点 **2** (*geometry* 几何) of or along a tangent 正切的；切线的 ▸ **tan·gen·tial·ly** *adj.*

tan·ger·ine /ˌtændʒə'riːn; *NAmE* 'tændʒəriːn/ *noun* **1** [C] a type of small sweet orange with loose skin that comes off easily 橘 **2** [U] a deep orange-yellow colour 橘黄色；橘红色 ▸ **tan·ger·ine** *adj.* : *a tangerine evening gown* 橘红色的女晚礼服

tangi /'tæŋi/ *noun* (*NZE*) a Maori funeral, or meal that is held after the ceremony （毛利人的）葬礼，挽宴

tan·gible /'tændʒəbl/ *adj.* **1** [usually before noun] that can be clearly seen to exist 有形的；实际的；真实的： ***tangible benefits/improvements/results, etc.*** 实际的好处、改进、效果等 ◇ ***tangible assets*** (= a company's buildings, machinery, etc.) 有形资产 **2** that you can touch and feel 可触摸的；可触知的；可感知的： *The tension between them was **almost tangible**.* 他们之间的紧张关系几乎让人都感觉得出来。 OPP **intangible** ▸ **tan·gibly** /'tændʒəbli/ *adv.*

tan·gle /'tæŋgl/ *noun, verb*
■ *noun* **1** a twisted mass of threads, hair, etc. that cannot be easily separated （线、毛发等的）缠结的一团，乱团，乱糟糟的一堆： *a tangle of branches* 盘绕在一起的树枝 ◇ *Her hair was a mass of tangles.* 她的头发乱糟糟的。 **2** a state of confusion or lack of order 混乱；纷乱： *His financial affairs are in a tangle.* 他的财务一塌糊涂。 **3** (*informal*) a disagreement or fight 纠纷；不和；争执；打架
■ *verb* [T, I] ~ (sth) up to twist sth into an untidy mass; to become twisted in this way 使缠结；纠结；乱作一团： *She had tangled up the sheets on the bed as she lay tossing and turning.* 她在床上翻来覆去，把被单弄得乱成一团。
PHR V **'tangle with sb/sth** to become involved in an argument or a fight with sb/sth 争论；争吵；打架

tan·gled /'tæŋgld/ *adj.* **1** twisted together in an untidy way 缠结的；混乱的；紊乱的： *tangled hair/bed clothes* 凌乱的头发 / 床上用品 **2** complicated, and not easy to understand 复杂的；纠缠不清的： *tangled financial affairs* 错综复杂的财务

tango /'tæŋgəʊ; *NAmE* -goʊ/ *noun, verb*
■ *noun* (*pl.* **-os** /-gəʊz; *NAmE* -goʊz/) a fast S American dance with a strong beat, in which two people hold each other closely; a piece of music for this dance 探戈舞；探戈舞曲
■ *verb* (**tango·ing, tan·goed, tan·goed**) [I] to dance the tango 跳探戈舞
IDM **it takes 'two to tango** (*informal*) used to say that two people or groups, and not just one, are responsible for sth that has happened (usually sth bad)（常指坏事）一个巴掌拍不响，双方都有责任

tank /tæŋk/ *noun, verb*
■ *noun* **1** a large container for holding liquid or gas（贮放液体或气体的）箱，槽，罐： *a hot water tank* 热水箱 ◇ *a fuel tank* 燃料箱 ◇ *a fish tank* (= for keeping fish in) 鱼缸 ➲ VISUAL VOCAB PAGES V44, V55 ➲ SEE ALSO SEPTIC TANK, THINK TANK **2** (*also* **tank·ful** /-fʊl/) the contents of a tank or the amount it will hold 箱（或桶等）所装之物；一箱（或一桶等）的量： *We drove there and back on one tank of petrol.* 我们开车去那里来回用了一油箱汽油。 **3** a military vehicle covered with strong metal and armed with guns. It can travel over very rough ground using wheels that move inside metal belts. 坦克 **4** (*IndE*) an artificial pool, lake or RESERVOIR（人工）水池，湖，水库
■ *verb* **1** [I] (*NAmE*) (of a company or a product 公司或产品) to fail completely 彻底失败；破产；倒闭： *The company's shares tanked on Wall Street.* 这家公司的股票在华尔街彻底崩盘了。 **2** [T, I] ~ (sth) (*NAmE, sport* 体育) to lose a game, especially deliberately（尤指故意）输掉比赛： *She was accused of tanking the match.* 有人指责她故意输掉这场比赛。
PHR V **ˌtank (sth) 'up** (*NAmE*) to fill a car with petrol/gas 给（汽车）加油： *He tanked up and drove off.* 他给汽车加满油开走了。 ◇ *We stopped to tank the car up.* 我们停下来给汽车加油。

tank·ard /'tæŋkəd; *NAmE* -ərd/ *noun* a large, usually metal, cup with a handle, that is used for drinking beer from （通常为金属的）单柄大酒杯，啤酒杯

ˌtanked 'up (*BrE*) (*NAmE* **tanked**) *adj.* (*informal*) very drunk 喝得烂醉的

'tank engine *noun* a steam engine that carries its own fuel and water inside, rather than using another small truck（自带燃料的）水柜蒸汽机车

tank·er /'tæŋkə(r)/ *noun* a ship or lorry/truck that carries oil, gas or petrol/gas in large quantities 运送大量液体或气体的轮船（或卡车）；油轮；罐车；油槽车： *an oil tanker* 油轮 ➲ VISUAL VOCAB PAGE V62 ➲ SEE ALSO SUPERTANKER

tank·ini /ˌtæŋ'kiːni/ *noun* a SWIMSUIT in two pieces, consisting of a short top without sleeves and the bottom half of a BIKINI 坦基尼（两件套泳装，包括无袖短上衣和比基尼下裤）

ˈ**tank top** *noun* **1** (*BrE*) a sweater without sleeves 坎肩 **2** (*NAmE*) a piece of clothing like a T-SHIRT without sleeves 汗背心

tanned /tænd/ (*also* **sun·tanned**) *adj.* having a brown skin colour as a result of being in the sun 皮肤晒成褐色的；晒黑的

tan·ner /ˈtænə(r)/ *noun* a person whose job is to TAN animal skins to make leather 鞣皮工；硝皮匠；制革工人

tan·nery /ˈtænəri/ *noun* (*pl.* **-ies**) a place where animal skins are TANNED and made into leather 鞣皮厂；皮革厂

tan·nie /ˈtʌni/ *noun* (*SAfrE, informal*) **1** an aunt; a friendly form of address for a woman who is older than you 姑妈；姨妈；伯母；婶母；舅母；（用作称呼）大妈，大娘 **2** (*sometimes disapproving*) a woman, especially one with old-fashioned views or tastes 妇人；（尤指）古板的女人

tan·nin /ˈtænɪn/ (*also* ˌ**tannic** ˈ**acid**) *noun* [U] a yellowish or brownish substance found in the BARK of some trees and the fruit of many plants, used especially in making leather, ink and wine 单宁；单宁酸；鞣质 ▸ **tan·nic** /ˈtænɪk/ *adj.*

Tan·noy™ /ˈtænɔɪ/ *noun* (*BrE*) a system with LOUDSPEAKERS used for giving information in a public place 天朗扩音系统：*to make an announcement over the Tannoy* 通过天朗扩音系统发布通知

tan·tal·ize (*BrE also* **-ise**) /ˈtæntəlaɪz/ *verb* **~ sb/sth** to make you want sth that you cannot have or do （以可望而不可即之物）逗引，招惹 ▸ **tan·tal·iz·ing, -is·ing** *adj.*：*The tantalizing aroma of fresh coffee wafted towards them.* 新鲜咖啡那诱人的香味向他们飘来。◇ *a* ***tantalizing glimpse*** *of the future* 对未来令人向往的展望 **tan·tal·iz·ing·ly, -is·ing·ly** *adv.*：*The branch was tantalizingly out of reach.* 够不到那树枝，让人干着急。

tan·ta·lum /ˈtæntələm/ *noun* [U] (*symb.* **Ta**) a chemical element. Tantalum is a hard silver-grey metal used in the production of electronic parts and of metal plates and pins for connecting broken bones. 钽

tan·ta·mount /ˈtæntəmaʊnt/ *adj.* **~ to sth** (*formal*) having the same bad effect as sth else 无异于；等于；效果与…一样坏：*If he resigned it would be tantamount to admitting that he was guilty.* 他若辞职就等于承认自己有错。

tan·tra /ˈtæntrə/ *noun* **1** [C] an ancient Hindu or Buddhist text 坦陀罗；续；密续（古印度教或佛教的经文） **2** [U] behaviour based on these texts, including prayer and MEDITATION 坦陀罗神秘修炼；密教修行 ▸ **tan·tric** /ˈtæntrɪk/ *adj.* [usually before noun]

tan·trum /ˈtæntrəm/ *noun* a sudden short period of angry, unreasonable behaviour, especially in a child（尤指儿童）耍脾气，使性子：*to* ***have/throw a tantrum*** 发脾气 ◇ *Children often have* ***temper tantrums*** *at the age of two or thereabouts.* 儿童在两岁左右经常爱使性子。

Taoi·seach /ˈtiːʃəx/ *noun* the Prime Minister of the Irish Republic （爱尔兰共和国）总理

Tao·ism /ˈdaʊɪzəm; ˈtaʊ-/ *noun* [U] a Chinese philosophy based on the writings of Lao-tzu 道家 ▸ **Tao·ist** /ˈdaʊɪst; ˈtaʊ-/ *noun, adj.*

tap /tæp/ *verb, noun*

■ *verb* (**-pp-**) **1** [I, T] to hit sb/sth quickly and lightly 轻敲；轻拍；轻叩：**~ (away) (at sth)** *Someone tapped at the door.* 有人轻轻叩门。◇ *He was busy tapping away at his computer.* 他埋头敲着电脑键盘。◇ **~ sb/sth** *Ralph tapped me on the shoulder.* 拉尔夫轻轻地拍了拍我的肩膀。◇ *Tap the icon to open the app.* 点击图标打开应用程序。**2** [T, I] **~ (sth)** if you **tap** your fingers, feet, etc. or they **tap**, you hit them gently against a table, the floor, etc., for example to the rhythm of music （用…）轻轻叩击：*He kept tapping his fingers on the table.* 他不停地用手指轻轻敲着桌子。◇ *The music set everyone's feet tapping.* 乐曲使得每个人都用脚轻轻打起拍子来。**3** [T, I] to make use of a source of energy, knowledge, etc. that already exists 利用，开发，发掘（已有的资源、知识等）：**~ sth** *We need to tap the expertise of the people we already have.* 我们需要利用我们现有人员的专业知识。◇ **~ into sth** *The movie seems to tap into a general sentimentality about animals.* 这部电影似乎在激发人们对动物的普遍怜惜之情。**4** [T] **~ sth** (*especially BrE*) to fit a device to a telephone so that sb's calls can be listened to secretly （在电话上）安装窃听器，搭线窃听：*He was convinced his phone was being tapped.* 他确信自己的电话在被人窃听。➲ SEE ALSO WIRETAPPING **5** [T] **~ sth** to cut into a tree in order to get liquid from it 在（树）上切口（导出液体） **6** [T, usually passive] **~ sb** (*NAmE*) to choose sb to do a particular job 委任；指定（某人做某事）：*Richards has been tapped to replace the retiring chairperson.* 理查兹获得委任接替行将退任的主席。**7** [T] **~ sth** (*phonetics* 语音) to produce a TAP (6) 发轻拍音 SYN flap

PHR V ˈ**tap sb for sth** (*BrE, informal*) to persuade sb to give you sth, especially money 向…索要，向…乞讨（尤指钱） ˌ**tap sth↔ˈin/ˈout** to put information, numbers, letters, etc. into a machine by pressing buttons 输入，输出（信息、数字、字母等）：*Tap in your PIN number.* 输入你的个人身份识别号码。ˌ**tap sth↔ˈout 1** to hit a surface gently to the rhythm of music （跟着音乐节奏）轻轻打拍子：*She tapped out the beat on the table.* 她轻击桌面打着拍子。**2** to write sth using a computer or a mobile/cell phone （用计算机或移动电话）写，输入，键入：*I tapped out a text message to Mandy.* 我给曼迪发了一条短信。

■ *noun* **1** (*especially BrE*) (*NAmE usually* **fau·cet**) [C] a device for controlling the flow of water from a pipe into a bath/BATHTUB or SINK 水龙头；旋塞：*bath taps* 浴缸水龙头 ◇ *the* ***hot/cold tap*** (= the tap that hot/cold water comes out of) 热水 / 冷水龙头 ◇ ***Turn the tap on/off.*** 打开 / 关上龙头。◇ *Don't leave the tap running.* 别把水龙头开着白白流水。◇ *the sound of a* ***dripping tap*** 水龙头滴答的漏水声 ➲ PICTURE AT PLUG ➲ **VISUAL VOCAB** PAGES V25, V26 ➲ SEE ALSO TAP WATER **2** [C] a device for controlling the flow of liquid or gas from a pipe or container 龙头；旋塞：*a gas tap* 煤气阀门 ◇ *beer taps* 啤酒旋塞 **3** [C] a light hit with your hand or fingers 轻击；轻拍；轻敲；轻叩：*a* ***tap at/on*** *the door* 轻轻的叩门 ◇ *He felt a tap on his shoulder and turned round.* 他觉得有人轻轻拍他的肩膀便转过身来。**4** [C] an act of fitting a device to a telephone so that sb's telephone calls can be listened to secretly 电话窃听；搭线窃听：*a phone tap* 电话窃听 **5** [U] = TAP-DANCING **6** [C] (*phonetics* 语音) a speech sound which is produced by striking the tongue quickly and lightly against the part of the mouth behind the upper front teeth. The 't' in *later* in American English and the 'r' in *very* in some British accents are examples of taps. 轻拍音 SYN flap

IDM **on** ˈ**tap 1** available to be used at any time 可随时使用的：*We have this sort of information on tap.* 我们可随时向您提供这种资料。**2** beer that is **on tap** is in a BARREL with a tap on it （啤酒）装在有旋塞的桶里的，散装的 **3** (*NAmE*) something that is **on tap** is being discussed or prepared and will happen soon 协商中；准备中；即将发生

tapas /ˈtæpəs; -pæs/ *noun* [pl.] (*from Spanish*) small amounts of a variety of Spanish dishes, served with drinks in a bar 塔帕斯（酒吧中和饮料一起供应的各种西班牙风味小吃）

ˈ**tap dance** *noun* [U, C] a style of dancing in which you tap the rhythm of the music with your feet, wearing special shoes with pieces of metal on the heels and toes 踢踏舞 ▸ ˈ**tap dancer** *noun* ˈ**tap-dancing** (*also* **tap**) *noun* [U]

tape AW /teɪp/ *noun, verb*

■ *noun* **1** [U] a long narrow strip of MAGNETIC material that is used for recording sounds, pictures or information 磁带；录音带；录像带 ➲ SEE ALSO MAGNETIC TAPE, VIDEOTAPE *n.* **2** [C] a CASSETTE that contains sounds, or sounds and pictures, that have been recorded 录了音的盒式磁带；录了像的盒式磁带：*a* ***blank tape*** (= a tape that has nothing recorded on it) 空白盒式磁带 ◇ *I lent*

T

her my Bob Marley tapes. 我把我的鲍勃·马利音乐带借给了她。◇ *Police seized various books and tapes.* 警方扣留了各种图书和磁带。 **3** [U] a long narrow strip of material with a sticky substance on one side that is used for sticking things together 胶带；胶条： ***adhesive/sticky tape*** 黏胶带 ➲ SEE ALSO INSULATING TAPE, MASKING TAPE, SCOTCH TAPE™, SELLOTAPE™ **4** [C, U] a narrow strip of material that is used for tying things together or as a label（捆、系物品或作标记的）狭带，带子，线带，窄布条： *The papers were in a pile, tied together with a tape.* 报纸叠成一摞，用带子捆了起来。 ➲ SEE ALSO RED TAPE, TICKER TAPE **5** [C] a long narrow strip of material that is stretched across the place where a race will finish（赛跑场地的）终点线： *the finishing tape* 终点线 **6** [C] = TAPE MEASURE

■ ***verb*** **1 ~ sb/sth** to record sb/sth on MAGNETIC tape using a special machine 把…录在磁带上： *Private conversations between the two had been taped and sent to a newspaper.* 这两个人的私下谈话被录下音来送给了一家报纸。 **2 ~ sth** (**up**) to fasten sth by sticking or tying it with tape 用胶带粘住；用带子系紧： *Put it in a box and tape it up securely.* 把这个放进盒子里，再用带子系牢。 **3 ~ sth + adv./prep.** to stick sth onto sth else using sticky tape 用胶带粘贴： *Someone had taped a message on the door.* 有人用胶带把字条贴在了门上。 **4 ~ sth** (**up**) (*NAmE*) to tie a bandage firmly around an injury or a wound 用绷带包扎： *That's a nasty cut—come on, we'll get it all taped up.* 伤口很严重，快，咱们用绷带把它包扎起来。

IDM **have** (**got**) **sb/sth 'taped** (*BrE, informal*) to understand sb/sth completely and to have learned how to deal with them/it successfully 彻底了解；摸清楚…的底细： *He can't fool me—I've got him taped.* 他休想骗我，我把他的底细摸得一清二楚。

'tape measure (*also* **tape**, **'measuring tape**) *noun* a long narrow strip of plastic, cloth or FLEXIBLE metal that has measurements marked on it and is used for measuring the length of sth 卷尺；皮尺

taper /'teɪpə(r)/ *verb, noun*

■ ***verb*** [I, T] to become gradually narrower; to make sth become gradually narrower（使）逐渐变窄： *The tail tapered to a rounded tip.* 尾部越来越细，最后成了个圆尖。◇ **~ sth** *The pots are wide at the base and tapered at the top.* 这些壶底部粗，顶部细。

PHR V **,taper 'off** to become gradually less in number, amount, degree, etc.（数量、程度等）逐渐减少： *The number of applicants for teaching posts has tapered off.* 申请做教学工作的人数越来越少。 **,taper sth↔'off** to make sth become gradually less in number, amount, degree, etc. 使（数目等）逐渐减少；降低…程度： *They are gradually tapering off production of the older models.* 他们在逐步减少生产旧型号的产品。

■ ***noun*** **1** a long thin piece of wood, paper, etc. that is used for lighting fires or lamps（点火用的）木条，纸媒 **2** a long thin CANDLE 细长蜡烛 **3** [usually sing.] the way that sth gradually decreases in size, becoming thinner 渐减；逐渐缩小（或变细）

'tape-record *verb* **~ sth** to record sth on tape 用磁带录制： *a tape-recorded interview* 录音访谈

'tape recorder *noun* a machine that is used for recording and playing sounds on tape 录音机

'tape recording *noun* something that has been recorded on tape 磁带录音；磁带录像： *a tape recording of the interview* 访谈录音

tape·script /'teɪpskrɪpt/ *noun* the printed text of a recording of speech 录音文本

tap·es·try /'tæpəstri/ *noun* [C, U] (*pl.* **-ies**) a picture or pattern that is made by WEAVING coloured wool onto heavy cloth; the art of doing this 壁毯；挂毯；织锦；绣帷： *medieval tapestries* 中世纪的壁毯 ◇ *tapestry cushions* 织锦沙发靠垫 ◇ *crafts such as embroidery and tapestry* 诸如刺绣和织锦之类的手工艺 ▶ **tap·es·tried** *adj.* [only before noun]： *tapestried walls* 挂有绣帷的墙

tape·worm /'teɪpwɜːm; *NAmE* -wɜːrm/ *noun* a long flat WORM that lives in the INTESTINES of humans and animals 绦虫

'tap-in *noun* (in sport 体育运动) an easy light hit of the ball into the goal or hole from a close position 近距离轻松进球；轻拨入篮： *The pass left Tevez with a simple tap-in.* 这个传球使特维斯轻松破门。

tapi·oca /,tæpi'əʊkə; *NAmE* -'oʊkə/ *noun* [U] hard white grains obtained from the CASSAVA plant, often cooked with milk to make a DESSERT (= a sweet dish) 木薯淀粉

tapir /'teɪpə(r)/ *noun* an animal like a pig with a long nose, that lives in Central and S America and SE Asia 貘（生活在中南美洲和东南亚的长鼻猪状动物）

,tap-'penalty *noun* (in RUGBY 橄榄球) a situation where a player is allowed a free kick of the ball because the other team has broken a rule, and chooses to touch it lightly with the foot then immediately pick it up 轻踢罚球

tap·root /'tæpruːt/ *noun* the main root of a plant that grows straight downwards and produces smaller side roots（植物的）直根，主根

'tap water *noun* [U] water supplied through pipes to taps/faucets in a building 自来水： *Is the tap water safe to drink?* 这自来水喝了不会闹病吧？

tar /tɑː(r)/ *noun, verb*

■ ***noun*** [U] **1** a thick black sticky liquid that becomes hard when cold. Tar is obtained from coal and is used especially in making roads. 焦油；焦油沥青；柏油 **2** a substance similar to tar that is formed by burning TOBACCO（烟草点燃后产生的）焦油： *low-tar cigarettes* 焦油含量低的卷烟 IDM SEE SPOIL *v.*

■ ***verb*** (**-rr-**) **~ sth** to cover sth with tar 用沥青涂抹；用柏油铺： *a tarred road* 柏油路

IDM **tar and 'feather sb** to put tar on sb then cover them with feathers, as a punishment 把…浑身涂上沥青并粘上羽毛（作为惩罚）；严惩 **be tarred with the same 'brush** (**as sb**) to be thought to have the same faults, etc. as sb else 被认为是一路货色；被看成一丘之貉

tara·ma·sa·lata /,tærəməsə'lɑːtə/ *noun* [U] (*BrE*) a type of Greek food made from fish eggs 希腊红鱼子泥色拉；希腊鱼子酱

ta·ran·tula /tə'ræntʃələ/ *noun* a large spider covered with hair that lives in hot countries. Some types of tarantula have a poisonous bite. 捕鸟蛛

tardy /'tɑːdi; *NAmE* 'tɑːrdi/ *adj.* **~** (**in doing sth**) (*formal*) slow to act, move or happen; late in happening or arriving 行动缓慢的；拖拉的；迟缓的；迟到的： *The law is often tardy in reacting to changing attitudes.* 法律对变化中的观念常常反应迟缓。◇ *people who are tardy in paying their bills* 拖延付账的人 ◇ (*NAmE*) *to be tardy for school* 上学迟到 ▶ **tar·dily** /'tɑːdɪli; *NAmE* 'tɑːrd-/ *adv.* **tar·di·ness** *noun* [U]

tare /teə(r); *NAmE* ter/ *noun* (*literary* or *specialist*) a plant growing where you do not want it 莠草；杂草；稗子 SYN **weed**

tar·get AW /'tɑːɡɪt; *NAmE* 'tɑːrɡɪt/ *noun, verb*

■ ***noun*** **1** a result that you try to achieve 目标；指标： *business goals and targets* 经营目的和指标 ◇ *attainment targets* 成绩目标 ◇ ***Set yourself targets*** *that you can reasonably hope to achieve.* 给自己制订有望达到的指标。◇ *to* ***meet/achieve a target*** 完成目标 ◇ *a* ***target date*** *of April 2017* * 2017 年 4 月的预定日期 ◇ *The university will* ***reach its target*** *of 5 000 students next September.* 这所大学将于下个九月达到在校学生 5 000 人的目标。◇ *The new sports complex is* ***on target*** *to open in June.* 新建的体育中心将在六月份如期开放。◇ *a* ***target area/audience/group*** (= the particular area, audience, etc. that a product, programme, etc. is aimed at) 目标范围 / 观众 / 群体 ➲ COLLOCATIONS AT BUSINESS **2** an object, a person or a place that people aim at when attacking（攻击的）目标，对象：*They bombed military and civilian targets.* 他们轰炸了军事和民用目标。◇ **~ for sb/sth** *Doors and windows are an **easy target** for burglars.* 门窗被窃贼作为入室的目标容易得手。◇ *It's a **prime target*** (= an obvious target) *for terrorist attacks.* 这是恐怖分子攻击的首要目标。◇ **~ of sth** *(figurative) He's become the target of a lot of criticism recently.* 他最近成了众矢之的。 **3** an object that people practise shooting at, especially a round board with circles on it 靶；靶子：*to aim at a target* 瞄准靶子 ◇ *to **hit/miss the target*** 中靶；脱靶 ◇ ***target practice*** 射击练习 ➲ VISUAL VOCAB PAGE V44

▼ **SYNONYMS** 同义词辨析

target

objective • goal • object • end

These are all words for sth that you are trying to achieve. 以上各词均指目标、目的。

target a result that you try to achieve 指试图达到的目标、指标：*Set yourself targets that you can reasonably hope to achieve.* 给自己制订有望达到的指标。◇ *attainment targets in schools* 学校的成绩目标

objective *(rather formal)* something that you are trying to achieve 指正努力达到的目标、目的：*What is the main objective of this project?* 这个项目的主要目标是什么？

goal something that you hope to achieve 指希望达到的目标、目的：*He continued to pursue his goal of becoming an actor.* 他继续追求他成为演员的目标。

TARGET, OBJECTIVE OR GOAL? 用 target、objective 还是 goal?

A **target** is usually officially recorded in some way, for example by an employer or by a government committee. It is often specific, and in the form of figures, such as number of sales or exam passes, or a date. People often set their own **objectives**: these are things that they wish to achieve, often as part of a project or a talk they are giving. **Goals** are often long-term, and relate to people's life and career plans or the long-term plans of a company or organization. * target 通常为以某种方式正式记录的目标，如由雇主或政府委员会等制订，常为具体的数字，如销售量、考试及格率、日期等；objective 通常指为自己制订的、希望达到的目标，常为某一项目或发言的一部分；goal 通常指长远目标，与人生和职业规划或公司、机构的长远规划有关。

object the purpose of sth; sth that you plan to achieve 指目的、目标、宗旨：*The object is to educate people about road safety.* 目的就是教育大众注意交通安全。

end something that you plan to achieve 指计划达到的目的、目标：*He joined the society for political ends.* 他为了政治目的加入了这个协会。◇ *That's only OK if you believe that **the end justifies the means*** (= bad methods of doing sth are acceptable if the final result is good). 除非你认为只要目的正确可以不择手段，不然那是不可以接受的。 **NOTE** **End** is usually used in the plural or in particular fixed expressions. * end 常用复数或用于某些固定短语中。

PATTERNS

- to work **towards** a(n) target/objective/goal
- a(n) **ambitious/major/long-term/short-term/future** target/objective/goal
- **economic/financial/business** targets/objectives/goals
- to **set/agree on/identify/reach/meet/exceed** a(n) target/objective/goal
- to **achieve** a(n) target/objective/goal/end

■ ***verb*** (**tar·get·ing, tar·get·ed, tar·get·ed**) [usually passive] **1 ~ sb/sth** to aim an attack or a criticism at sb/sth 把…作为攻击目标；把…作为批评的对象：*The missiles were mainly targeted at the United States.* 导弹主要瞄准的是美国。◇ *The company has been targeted by animal rights groups for its use of dogs in drugs trials.* 这家公司因用狗做药物试验而成为动物保护团体批评的对象。 **2 ~ sb** to try to have an effect on a particular group of people 面向，把…对准（某群体）：*The campaign is clearly targeted at the young.* 这个宣传计划显然是针对青年人的。◇ *a new magazine that targets single men* 以单身男士为读者对象的新杂志 ▶ **tar·get·ed** *adj.*：*strategically targeted attacks* 战略上有针对性的攻击 ◇ *Emails are scanned for keywords in order to deliver targeted advertising.* 会对电子邮件进行关键字搜索，以便投放有针对性的广告。

'target language *noun* (*linguistics* 语言) **1** (*also* **'object language**) a language into which a text is being translated（翻译的）译文语言，译入语 **2** a foreign language that sb is learning（外语学习的）目标语言，对象语言，所学语

tar·iff /'tærɪf/ *noun* **1** a tax that is paid on goods coming into or going out of a country 关税 ➲ SYNONYMS AT TAX ➲ WORDFINDER NOTE AT TRADE ➲ COLLOCATIONS AT INTERNATIONAL **2** a list of fixed prices that are charged by a hotel or restaurant for rooms, meals, etc., or by a company for a particular service（旅馆、饭店或服务公司的）价目表，收费表：*mobile-phone tariffs* 手机话费单 **3** (*BrE, law* 律) a level of punishment for sb who has been found guilty of a crime 量刑标准

Tar·mac™ /'tɑːmæk; *NAmE* 'tɑːrmæk/ *noun* [U] **1** (*also less frequent* **tar·mac·adam** /ˌtɑːmə'kædəm; *NAmE* ˌtɑːrm-/) (*NAmE also* **black·top**) a black material used for making road surfaces, that consists of small stones mixed with TAR（用于铺路的）柏油碎石材料 **2 the tarmac** an area with a Tarmac surface, especially at an airport 柏油碎石路面；（尤指）柏油碎石停机坪：*Three planes were standing on the tarmac, waiting to take off.* 三架飞机停在跑道上，等候起飞。

tar·mac /'tɑːmæk; *NAmE* 'tɑːrmæk/ *verb* (**-ck-**) (*BrE*) **~ sth** to cover a surface with Tarmac™ 以柏油碎石铺筑（路面）：*tarmacked roads* 柏油碎石路面

tarn /tɑːn; *NAmE* tɑːrn/ *noun* a small lake in the mountains 冰川湖；山中小湖

tar·na·tion /tɑː'neɪʃn; *NAmE* tɑːr'n-/ *exclamation* (*old-fashioned, especially NAmE*) a word that people use to show that they are annoyed with sb/sth（表示恼怒）该死，讨厌

tar·nish /'tɑːnɪʃ; *NAmE* 'tɑːrnɪʃ/ *verb, noun*

■ ***verb*** **1** [I, T] if metal **tarnishes** or sth **tarnishes** it, it no longer looks bright and shiny（使）失去光泽，暗淡：*The mirrors had tarnished with age.* 这些镜子因年深日久而照影不清楚。◇ **~ sth** *The silver candlesticks were tarnished and dusty.* 银烛台都发乌了，满是灰尘。 **2** [T] **~ sth** to spoil the good opinion people have of sb/sth 玷污，败坏，损坏（名声等） **SYN** **taint**：*He hopes to improve the newspaper's somewhat tarnished public image.* 他希望改善报纸略有受损的公众形象。

■ ***noun*** [sing., U] a thin layer on the surface of a metal that makes it look dull and not bright（金属表面上的）暗锈

tarot /'tærəʊ; *NAmE* -roʊ/ *noun* [sing., U] a set of special cards with pictures on them, used for telling sb what will happen to them in the future 塔罗纸牌（用于占卜）

tar·paulin /tɑː'pɔːlɪn; *NAmE* tɑːr'p-/ (*also NAmE, informal* **tarp**) *noun* [C, U] a large sheet made of heavy WATERPROOF material, used to cover things with and to keep rain off 柏油帆布；（防水）油布

tar·ra·gon /'tærəgən/ *noun* [U] a plant with leaves that have a strong taste and are used in cooking as a HERB 龙蒿（用于烹调） ➲ VISUAL VOCAB PAGE V35

tarry /'tæri/ *verb* (**tar·ries, tarry·ing, tar·ried, tar·ried**) [I] (*old use* or *literary*) to stay in a place, especially when you ought to leave; to delay coming to or going from a place 逗留；耽搁 **SYN** **linger**

T

tar·sal /ˈtɑːsl; *NAmE* ˈtɑːrsl/ *noun* (*anatomy* 解) one of the small bones in the ankle and upper foot 跗骨（踝和脚上部的小骨）

tart /tɑːt; *NAmE* tɑːrt/ *noun, adj., verb*
■ ***noun*** **1** [C, U] an open PIE filled with sweet food such as fruit 甜果馅饼：*a strawberry tart* 草莓馅饼 ➲ COMPARE FLAN, QUICHE **2** [C] (*BrE, informal, disapproving*) a woman who you think behaves or dresses in a way that is immoral and is intended to make men sexually excited 放荡的女人；骚货 ➲ SEE ALSO TARTY **3** [C] (*slang*) a PROSTITUTE 妓女；野鸡
■ ***adj.*** **1** having a sour taste that may be pleasant or unpleasant 酸的；带酸味的：*tart apples* 酸苹果 ➲ WORDFINDER NOTE AT TASTE **2** [usually before noun] (of remarks, etc. 话语等) quick and unkind 尖酸的；刻薄的；辛辣的 SYN sharp：*a tart reply* 尖刻的答复 ▸ **tart·ly** *adv.*：*'Too late!' said my mother tartly.* "早干什么去了！"我母亲刻薄地说。 **tart·ness** *noun* [U]
■ ***verb***
PHR V ˌ**tart yourself ˈup** (*informal*) (especially of a woman 尤指女人) to make yourself more attractive by putting on nice clothes, jewellery, make-up, etc. 打扮得花枝招展；浓妆艳抹 ˌ**tart sth↔ˈup** (*informal*) to decorate or improve the appearance of sth, often in a way that other people do not think is attractive 把…装饰得俗气；把…弄得花里胡哨

tar·tan /ˈtɑːtn; *NAmE* ˈtɑːrtn/ *noun* **1** [U, C] a pattern of squares and lines of different colours and widths that cross each other at an angle of 90°, used especially on cloth, and originally from Scotland（尤指源自苏格兰织物的）花格图案，方格花纹：*a tartan rug* 花格小地毯 ➲ VISUAL VOCAB PAGE V66 **2** [C] a tartan pattern connected with a particular group of families (= a CLAN) in Scotland （与苏格兰某家族有关的）花格图案，方格花纹：*the MacLeod tartan* 麦克劳德花格图案 **3** [U] cloth, especially made of wool, that has a tartan pattern 花格布料；（尤指）苏格兰格呢 ➲ COMPARE PLAID

tar·tar /ˈtɑːtə(r); *NAmE* ˈtɑːrt-/ *noun* **1** [U] a hard substance that forms on teeth 牙石；牙垢 **2** [C] (*old-fashioned*) a person in a position of authority who is very bad-tempered 暴君；脾气暴躁的掌权者

tar·tare sauce (*NAmE* **tar·tar sauce**) /ˌtɑːtə ˈsɔːs; *NAmE* ˌtɑːrtər/ *noun* [U] a thick cold white sauce made from MAYONNAISE, chopped onions and CAPERS, usually eaten with fish 鞑靼酱，蛋黄沙司（用蛋黄酱、碎洋葱和刺山柑调制而成，通常为吃鱼的作料）

tar·tar·ic acid /tɑːˌtærɪk ˈæsɪd; *NAmE* tɑːrˌt-/ *noun* [U] (*chemistry* 化) a type of acid that is found in GRAPES that are not ready to eat 酒石酸（存在于葡萄中）

tarty /ˈtɑːti; *NAmE* ˈtɑːrti/ *adj.* (*disapproving*) (of a woman 女人) dressing or behaving in a way that is intended to attract sexual attention 风骚的；放荡的

Tar·zan /ˈtɑːzæn; *NAmE* ˈtɑːrz-/ *noun* a man with a very strong body 泰山（健壮的男子） ORIGIN From the novel *Tarzan of the Apes* by Edgar Rice Burroughs about a man who lived with wild animals. 源自埃德加・赖斯・巴勒斯的小说《人猿泰山》，其中的男主人公和野兽共同生活。

Taser™ /ˈteɪzə(r)/ *noun* a gun that fires DARTS that give a person a small electric shock and makes them unable to move for a short time 电击枪（发射电脉冲，使人暂时不能动弹） ▸ **taser** (*also* **tase** /teɪz/) *verb* **~ sb**

task 🔑 AW /tɑːsk; *NAmE* tæsk/ *noun, verb*
■ ***noun*** **1** 🔑 a piece of work that sb has to do, especially a hard or unpleasant one （尤指艰巨或令人厌烦的）任务，工作：*to **perform/carry out/complete/undertake a task*** 执行 / 完成 / 承担任务 ◇ ***a daunting/an impossible/a formidable/an unenviable, etc. task*** 令人望而生畏、不可能完成、艰巨、令人为难等的任务 ◇ ***a thankless task*** (= an unpleasant one that nobody wants to do and nobody thanks you for doing) 吃力不讨好的工作 ◇ *Our first task is to set up a communications system.* 我们的首项任务是架设通信系统。 ◇ *Detectives are now faced with **the task of** identifying the body.* 侦探现在面临辨认尸体这项任务。 ◇ *Getting hold of this information was **no easy task*** (= was difficult). 把这一情报搞到手绝不是件轻而易举的事。 **2** an activity which is designed to help achieve a particular learning goal, especially in language teaching（尤指语言教学中旨在帮助达到某一学习目的的）活动：*task-based learning* 任务型学习

IDM **take sb to ˈtask (for/over sth)** to criticize sb strongly for sth they have done 严厉地责备；申斥；训斥
■ ***verb*** [usually passive] **~ sb (with sth)** (*formal*) to give sb a task to do 交给某人（任务）；派给某人（工作）

> ▼ **SYNONYMS 同义词辨析**
>
> **task**
>
> **duties • mission • job • chore**
>
> These are all words for a piece of work that sb has to do. 以上各词均指任务、工作。
>
> **task** a piece of work that sb has to do, especially a difficult or unpleasant one 尤指艰巨或令人厌烦的任务、工作： *Our first task will be to set up a communications system.* 我们的首项任务是架设通信系统。
>
> **duties** tasks that are part of your job 指职责、任务： *Your duties will include setting up a new computer system.* 你的职责将包括建立一个新的计算机系统。
>
> **mission** an important official job that a person or group of people is given to do, especially when they are sent to another country 指官方使命、使团的使命： *They undertook a **fact-finding mission** in the region.* 他们承担了在该地区核查事实的工作。
>
> **job** a piece of work that sb has to do 指一项任务、一件工作： *I've got various jobs around the house to do.* 我在家里有各种各样的活儿要干。
>
> **TASK OR JOB? 用 task 还是 job?**
>
> A **task** may be more difficult than a **job** and require you to think carefully about how you are going to do it. A **job** may be sth small that is one of several jobs that you have to do, especially in the home; or a **job** can be sth that takes a long time and is boring and/or needs a lot of patience. * task 可能比 job 艰巨，需要仔细思考如何去做；job 可指许多要做的事情中的一件小事，尤指家务活；job 有时指费时、沉闷或需要极大耐心的工作。
>
> **chore** a task that you have to do regularly, especially one that you do in the home and find unpleasant or boring 指日常事务、例行工作，尤指令人厌烦或无聊的家务活： *household chores* 家务杂活
>
> **PATTERNS**
> - the task/mission/job/chore **of (doing)** sth
> - (a) **daily/day-to-day** task/duties/job/chore
> - (a) **routine** task/duties/mission/job/chore
> - (a/an) **easy/difficult** task/mission/job
> - (a) **household/domestic** task/duties/job/chore
> - to **do** a task/a job/the chores
> - to **finish** a task/a mission/a job/the chores
> - to **give sb** a task/their duties/a mission/a job/a chore

ˈ**task force** *noun* **1** a military force that is brought together and sent to a particular place 特遣部队 **2** a group of people who are brought together to deal with a particular problem （为解决某问题而成立的）特别工作组

task·mas·ter /ˈtɑːskmɑːstə(r); *NAmE* ˈtæskmæstər/ *noun* a person who gives other people work to do, often work that is difficult 工头；监工；督督人：*She was **a hard taskmaster**.* 她是个严厉的工头。

tas·sel /ˈtæsl/ *noun* a bunch of threads that are tied together at one end and hang from CUSHIONS, curtains, clothes, etc. as a decoration（靠垫、窗帘、衣服等的）流苏，穗，缨

tas·selled (*BrE*) (*US* **tas·seled**) /ˈtæsld/ *adj.* decorated with tassels 饰有流苏的；带穗的；有缨的

T

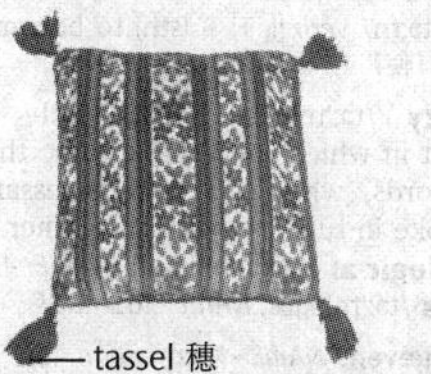

taste /teɪst/ *noun, verb*

■ ***noun***

• **FLAVOUR** 味 **1** [C, U] the particular quality that different foods and drinks have that allows you to recognize them when you put them in your mouth 味道；滋味： *a salty/bitter/sweet, etc. taste* 咸味、苦味、甜味等 ◇ *I don't like the taste of olives.* 我不喜欢橄榄的味道。◇ *This dish has an unusual combination of tastes and textures.* 这道菜的味道和口感搭配得很奇特。◇ *The soup has very little taste.* 这汤没什么味道。 ⊃ WORDFINDER NOTE AT EAT

WORDFINDER 联想词： bitter, bland, hot, pungent, savoury, sour, spicy, sweet, tart

• **SENSE** 感觉官能 **2** [U] the sense you have that allows you to recognize different foods and drinks when you put them in your mouth 味觉： *I've lost my sense of taste.* 我尝不出味道。

• **SMALL QUANTITY** 少量 **3** [C, usually sing.] a small quantity of food or drink that you try in order to see what it is like 少许尝的东西；一口；一点儿： *Just have a taste of this cheese.* 尝一点儿这种奶酪吧。

• **SHORT EXPERIENCE** 短暂经历 **4** [sing.] a short experience of sth 体验；尝试： *This was my **first taste** of live theatre.* 这是我初次在现场看戏。◇ *Although we didn't know it, this incident was **a taste of things to come**.* 尽管当时我们并不知道，但这件事是后来一系列事件的开端。

• **ABILITY TO CHOOSE WELL** 判断力 **5** [U] a person's ability to choose things that people recognize as being of good quality or appropriate 鉴赏力；欣赏力： *He has very **good taste** in music.* 他有很高的音乐欣赏力。◇ *They've got more money than taste.* 他们有钱，但品味不高。 ◇ *The room was furnished with taste.* 这个房间布置得很雅致。

• **WHAT YOU LIKE** 喜好 **6** [C, U] what a person likes or prefers 爱好；志趣： **~ (for sth)** *That trip gave me a taste for foreign travel.* 那次旅游使我产生了去国外旅行的兴趣。◇ **~ (in sth)** *She has very expensive tastes in clothes.* 她讲究穿高档的服装。 ◇ *The colour and style is **a matter of** personal **taste**.* 颜色和式样是个人爱好问题。 ◇ *Modern art is **not to everyone's taste**.* 现代艺术不见得适合每个人的口味。 ◇ *There are trips to suit all tastes.* 有适合各种喜好的旅游。

IDM **be in bad, poor, the worst possible, etc. 'taste** to be offensive and not at all appropriate 趣味低级；粗俗；不得体： *Most of his jokes were in very poor taste.* 他的笑话大多粗俗不堪。 **be in good, the best possible, etc. 'taste** to be appropriate and not at all offensive 适度；得体 **leave a bad/nasty 'taste in the mouth** (of events or experiences 事件或经历) to make you feel disgusted or ashamed afterwards 使后来感到厌恶（或羞耻）；留下坏印象 **to 'taste** in the quantity that is needed to make sth taste the way you prefer 按口味；适量： *Add salt and pepper to taste.* 适量放盐和胡椒粉。 ⊃ MORE AT ACCOUNT *v.*, ACQUIRE, MEDICINE

■ ***verb*** (not used in the progressive tenses 不用于进行时)

• **HAVE FLAVOUR** 有味道 **1** *linking verb* to have a particular flavour 有…味道： **+ adj.** *It tastes sweet.* 这有甜味儿。◇ **~ of sth** *The ice tasted of mint.* 这刨冰有薄荷味儿。 ◇ **~ like sth** *This drink tastes like sherry.* 这种酒味道像雪利酒。 **2 -tasting** (in adjectives 构成形容词) having a particular flavour 有…味道的： *foul-tasting medicine* 难吃的药

• **RECOGNIZE FLAVOUR** 辨味 **3** [T] **~ sth** (often used with *can* or *could* 常与 can 或 could 连用) to be able to recognize flavours in food and drink 尝出，品出（食品或饮料的味道）： *You can taste the garlic in this stew.* 在这炖肉里你可以尝出大蒜的味道。

• **TEST FLAVOUR** 尝味 **4** [T] **~ sth** to test the flavour of sth by eating or drinking a small amount of it 尝，品（味道） **SYN** **try**: *Taste it and see if you think there's enough salt in it.* 你尝尝看这够不够咸。

• **EAT/DRINK** 吃；喝 **5** [T] **~ sth** to eat or drink food or liquid 吃；喝： *I've never tasted anything like it.* 我从来没有吃过像这样的东西。

• **HAVE SHORT EXPERIENCE** 有短暂经历 **6** [T] **~ sth** to have a short experience of sth, especially sth that you want more of 浅尝；尝到甜头： *He had tasted freedom only to lose it again.* 他刚尝到了自由的甜头，却又失去了。

'taste bud *noun* [usually pl.] one of the small structures on the tongue that allow you to recognize the flavours of food and drink 味蕾

taste·ful /ˈteɪstfl/ *adj.* (especially of clothes, furniture, decorations, etc. 尤指衣服、家具、装饰等) attractive and of good quality and showing that the person who chose them can recognize good things 高雅的；雅致的；优美的 ▸ **taste·ful·ly** /-fəli/ *adv.* : *The bedroom was tastefully furnished.* 这卧室布置得很雅致。

taste·less /ˈteɪstləs/ *adj.* **1** having little or no flavour 无味的；不可口的： *tasteless soup* 淡而无味的汤 **2** offensive and not appropriate 不雅的；粗俗的；不得体的；煞风景的： *tasteless jokes* 粗俗的笑话 **3** showing a lack of the ability to choose things that people recognize as attractive and of good quality 俗气的；格调低的 ▸ **taste·less·ly** *adv.* **taste·less·ness** *noun* [U]

taster /ˈteɪstə(r)/ *noun* **1** a person whose job is to judge the quality of wine, tea, etc. by tasting it 试味员；品酒师；品茶员 **2** (*informal, especially BrE*) a small example of sth for you to try in order to see if you would like more of it（供尝试的）小样品

-tastic /ˈtæstɪk/ *suffix* (in adjectives 构成形容词) (*BrE, informal*) used to emphasize that sb/sth of a particular type is extremely good（某类人或物品中）极好的： *We have a toptastic line-up of stars for you tonight.* 今晚我们为您请来了最佳明星阵容。 ◇ *Try this new choctastic recipe!* 试试这种特别美味的巧克力新烹饪法吧！ ⊃ SEE ALSO POPTASTIC

tast·ing /ˈteɪstɪŋ/ *noun* an event at which people can try different kinds of food and drink, especially wine, in small quantities 品尝会： *a wine tasting* 品酒会

tasty /ˈteɪsti/ *adj.* (**tasti·er**, **tasti·est**) **1** (*approving*) having a strong and pleasant flavour 美味的；可口的；好吃的： *a tasty meal* 美餐 ◇ *something tasty to eat* 好吃的东西 **2** (*BrE, informal, sometimes offensive*) a word that some men use about women that they think are sexually attractive 风骚的，有味道的，性感的（男子用以形容性感女子） ▸ **tasti·ness** *noun* [U]

tat /tæt/ *noun* [U] (*BrE, informal*) goods that are cheap and of low quality 劣质货 ⊃ SEE ALSO TIT FOR TAT

ta-ta /ˌtæ ˈtɑː/ *exclamation* (*BrE, informal*) goodbye 再见： *Ta-ta for now!* 回头见！

tat·ami /təˈtɑːmi; ˈtætəmi/ *noun* (*from Japanese*) a traditional Japanese floor covering made from dried RUSHES 榻榻米（灯芯草日本地席）

tater /ˈteɪtə(r)/ *noun* [usually pl.] (*slang*) a potato 土豆；马铃薯；洋芋

tat·tered /ˈtætəd; *NAmE* -tərd/ *adj.* old and torn; in bad condition 破烂的；破旧的；褴褛的；破裂的： *tattered clothes* 破旧的衣服 ◇ (*figurative*) *tattered relationships* 破裂了的关系 ◇ (*figurative*) *the hotel's tattered reputation* 旅馆的败坏的名声

tat·ters /ˈtætəz; *NAmE* -tərz/ *noun* [pl.] clothes or pieces of cloth that are badly torn 破烂的衣服；破衣烂布

IDM **in tatters** **1** torn in many places 破烂不堪；破破烂烂： *His clothes were in tatters.* 他的衣服破旧不堪。 **2** ruined or badly damaged 被毁坏的；破败的；坍塌的 **SYN** **in shreds**: *Her reputation was in tatters.* 她已名誉扫地。

T

◇ *The government's education policy lies in tatters.* 政府的教育政策彻底破产了。

tat·tie /ˈtæti/ *noun* (*ScotE, informal*) a potato 马铃薯；土豆；洋芋

tat·tle /ˈtætl/ *verb* [I] ~ (**on sb**) (**to sb**) (*informal, disapproving, especially NAmE*) to tell sb, especially sb in authority, about sth bad that sb else has done 向当权者告发；（就某人不端行为）打小报告 **SYN** **tell on sb**

tat·tle·tale /ˈtætlteɪl/ (*NAmE*) (*BrE* **tell·tale**) *noun* (*informal, disapproving*) a child who tells an adult what another child has done wrong 向大人告另一个孩子状的小孩；小告密者

tat·too /təˈtuː; *NAmE* tæˈtuː/ *noun, verb*

■ ***noun*** (*pl.* **-oos**) **1** a picture or design that is marked permanently on a person's skin by making small holes in the skin with a needle and filling them with coloured ink 文身；（在皮肤上刺的）花纹：*His arms were covered in tattoos.* 他的胳膊上刺满了文身。 ➲ COLLOCATIONS AT FASHION **2** (*especially BrE*) an outdoor show by members of the armed forces that includes marching, music and military exercises 野外军事表演（包括齐步前进、军乐和军事演习） **3** [usually sing.] a rapid and continuous series of taps or hits, especially on a drum as a military signal 连续急促的敲击；（尤指军事上的）回营号，击鼓号

■ ***verb*** to mark sb's skin with a tattoo 将花纹刺在…上；给…文身：**~ A on B** *He had a heart tattooed on his shoulder.* 他让人给他在肩膀上刺了一颗心形图案。◇ **~ B** (**with A**) *His shoulder was tattooed with a heart.* 他的肩膀上刺了一颗心形图案。

tat·too·ist /təˈtuːɪst; *NAmE* tæˈt-/ *noun* a person who draws tattoos on people's skin, as a job 文身师；刺青师

tatty /ˈtæti/ *adj.* (*informal, especially BrE*) (**tat·tier, tat·ti·est**) in a bad condition because it has been used a lot or has not been cared for well 褴褛的；破烂的；破败的；邋遢的 **SYN** **shabby**: *a tatty carpet* 破旧的地毯

tau /tɔː; taʊ/ *noun* the 19th letter of the Greek alphabet (T, τ) 希腊字母表的第 19 个字母

taught PAST TENSE, PAST PART. OF TEACH

taunt /tɔːnt/ *verb, noun*

■ ***verb*** **~ sb** to try to make sb angry or upset by saying unkind things about them, laughing at their failures, etc. 辱骂；嘲笑；讽刺；奚落：*The other kids continually taunted him about his size.* 其他孩子不断地耻笑他的个头儿。

■ ***noun*** an insulting or unkind remark that is intended to make sb angry or upset 嘲笑（或讽刺、奚落等）的言辞：*Black players often had to endure racist taunts.* 黑人运动员经常得忍受种族歧视性的奚落。

taupe /təʊp; *NAmE* toʊp/ *noun* [U] a brownish-grey colour 褐灰色 ▸ **taupe** *adj.*

taur·ine /ˈtɔːriːn/ *noun* [U] an acid substance which is sometimes used in drinks that are designed to make you feel more active 牛磺酸，氨基乙磺酸（用于饮料，可提神）

Taurus /ˈtɔːrəs/ *noun* **1** [U] the second sign of the ZODIAC, the BULL 黄道第二宫；金牛宫；金牛（星）座 **2** [sing.] a person born when the sun is in this sign, that is between 21 April and 21 May 属金牛座的人（约出生于 4 月 21 日至 5 月 21 日） ▸ **Taur·ean** /ˈtɔːriən/ *noun, adj.*

taut /tɔːt/ *adj.* **1** stretched tightly 拉紧的；绷紧的：*Keep the rope taut.* 把绳子拉紧，别松开。 **2** showing that you are anxious or TENSE 显得紧张的（或焦虑的、不安的等）：*Her face was taut and pale.* 她神色紧张，脸色苍白。 **3** (of a person or their body 人或人体) with firm muscles; not fat 肌肉结实的；不虚胖的：*His body was solid and taut.* 他身体结实，肌肉发达。 **4** (of a piece of writing, etc. 文章等) tightly controlled, with no unnecessary parts in it 结构严谨的；紧凑的 ▸ **taut·ly** *adv.* **taut·ness** *noun* [U]

taut·en /ˈtɔːtn/ *verb* [I, T] ~ (**sth**) to become taut; to make sth taut （使）拉紧，绷紧

tau·tol·ogy /tɔːˈtɒlədʒi; *NAmE* -ˈtɑːl-/ *noun* [U, C] a statement in which you say the same thing twice in different words, when this is unnecessary, for example 'They spoke in turn, one after the other.' 同义反复；赘述 ▸ **tauto·logic·al** /ˌtɔːtəˈlɒdʒɪkl; *NAmE* -ˈlɑːdʒ-/ *adj.* **tau·tolo·gous** /tɔːˈtɒləgəs; *NAmE* -ˈtɑːl-/ *adj.*

tav·ern /ˈtævən; *NAmE* -vərn/ *noun* (*old use* or *literary*) a pub or an INN 酒馆；小旅店；客栈

taw·dry /ˈtɔːdri/ *adj.* (*disapproving*) **1** intended to be bright and attractive but cheap and of low quality 俗丽而不值钱的；俗气的；花里胡哨的：*tawdry jewellery* 俗丽便宜的首饰 **2** involving low moral standards; extremely unpleasant or offensive 粗俗的；下流的；卑鄙的；卑污的：*a tawdry affair* 卑鄙下流的勾当 ▸ **taw·dri·ness** *noun* [U]

tawny /ˈtɔːni/ *adj.* brownish-yellow in colour 黄褐色的；茶色的：*the lion's tawny mane* 狮子的黄褐色鬃毛

ˈtawny owl *noun* a reddish-brown or grey European BIRD OF PREY (= a bird that kills other creatures for food) of the OWL family 灰林鸮（产于欧洲的一种红褐色或灰色的鸮科猛禽）

tax /tæks/ *noun, verb*

■ ***noun*** [C, U] money that you have to pay to the government so that it can pay for public services. People pay tax according to their income and businesses pay tax according to their profits. Tax is also often paid on goods and services. 税；税款：*to* ***raise/cut taxes*** 增加 / 削减税收 ◇ ***tax increases/cuts*** 税款的增加 / 削减 ◇ *changes in* ***tax rates*** 税率的变化 ◇ *to pay over £1 000* ***in tax*** 缴纳 1 000 多英镑的税款 ◇ *profits* ***before/after tax*** 税前 / 税后利润 ◇ **~ on sth** *a tax on cigarettes* 香烟税 ➲ WORDFINDER NOTE AT PAY ➲ COLLOCATIONS AT ECONOMY ➲ SEE ALSO CORPORATION TAX, COUNCIL TAX, DIRECT TAX, INDIRECT TAX, INHERITANCE TAX, POLL TAX, ROAD TAX, SALES TAX,

▼ **SYNONYMS 同义词辨析**

tax

duty • customs • tariff • rates

These are all words for money that you have to pay to the government. 以上各词均指税款。

tax money that you have to pay to the government so that it can pay for public services 指税、税款：*income tax* 所得税 ◇ *tax cuts* 减税

duty a tax that you pay on things that you buy, especially those that you bring into a country 指购物税项，尤指进口货物缴纳的关税：*The company has to pay customs duties on all imports.* 该公司须为所有进口货物缴纳关税。

customs tax that is paid when goods are brought in from other countries 指关税、进口税

tariff a tax that is paid on goods coming into or going out of a country, often in order to protect industry from cheap imports 指（为使国内工业免遭廉价进口商品冲击而征收的）关税：*A general tariff was imposed on foreign imports.* 国外进口货物当时按普通税率征税。

rates (in Britain) a tax paid by businesses to a local authority for land and buildings that they use, and in the past also paid by anyone who owned a house 指（英国地方政府征收的）房地产税、房产税：*Business rates are very high in the city centre.* 市中心的商业房产税非常高。

PATTERNS

- (a) tax/duty/tariff/rates **on** sth
- to pay an amount of money **in** tax/duty/customs/rates
- to **pay** (a) tax/duty/customs/tariff/rates
- to **collect** taxes/duties/rates
- to **increase**/**raise**/**reduce** taxes/duty/tariffs/rates
- to **cut** taxes/duties/rates
- to **impose** a tax/duty/tariff
- to **put** a tax/duty **on** sth

T

STEALTH TAX, VALUE ADDED TAX, WITHHOLDING TAX

■ *verb* **1** ~ **sb/sth** to put a tax on sb/sth; to make sb pay tax 对…征税；课税；使纳税：*Any interest payments are taxed as part of your income.* 利息所得作为你收入的一部分要予以征税。◇ *His declared aim was to tax the rich.* 他宣布他的目的是向富人征税。 **2** ~ **sth** (*BrE*) to pay tax on a vehicle so that you may use it on the roads 缴纳车辆牌照税：*The car is taxed until July.* 这辆汽车的牌照税缴纳到了七月。 **3** ~ **sb/sth** to need a great amount of physical or mental effort 使负重担；使受压力；使大伤脑筋：*The questions did not tax me.* 那些问题没有让我费脑筋。◇ *The problem is currently **taxing the brains** of the nation's experts* (= making them think very hard). 目前这个问题使得全国的专家大伤脑筋。

PHR V **'tax sb with sth** (*formal*) to accuse sb of doing sth wrong （就某事）指责，责备，谴责…：*I taxed him with avoiding his responsibility as a parent.* 我指责他逃避做父亲的责任。

tax·able /'tæksəbl/ *adj.* (of money 钱) that you have to pay tax on 应纳税的；应课税的：*taxable income* 应课税的收入

tax·ation /tæk'seɪʃn/ *noun* [U] **1** money that has to be paid as taxes 税；税款；税金；税收：*to reduce taxation* 减税 **2** the system of collecting money by taxes 税制；征税；课税：*changes in the taxation structure* 税制结构的变化

'tax avoidance *noun* [U] ways of paying only the smallest amount of tax that you legally have to （合法）避税 ➲ COMPARE TAX EVASION

'tax bracket (*BrE also* **'tax band**) *noun* a range of different incomes on which the same rate of tax must be paid 税率等级，税级（同一税率的纳税收入等级段）：*There are now only two tax brackets—22% and 40%.* 现在纳税收入只有两个纳税档次：22% 和 40%。

'tax break *noun* a special advantage or reduction in taxes that the government gives to particular people or organizations 赋税优惠；减税

'tax collector *noun* a person whose job is collecting the tax that people must pay on the money they earn 收税员；税务员

'tax credit *noun* **1** money that is taken off your total tax bill 税收抵免 **2** money provided by the government to people who need financial help, especially if they have children or are on a low income （尤指政府向有子女或低收入者提供的）补助金，救济金

,tax-de'duct·ible *adj.* (of costs 费用) that can be taken off your income before the amount of tax that you have to pay is calculated 可减免课税的，应税收益额减免的（在计算所得税时可予以扣除）

,tax-de'ferred *adj.* (*NAmE*) that you only pay tax on later 延迟纳税的；延税的：*a tax-deferred savings plan* 延税储蓄计划

'tax disc *noun* = ROAD FUND LICENCE

'tax dodge *noun* (*informal*) a way of paying less tax, legally or illegally （合法或非法的）规避纳税 ▶ **'tax dodger** *noun*

'tax evasion *noun* [U] the crime of deliberately not paying all the taxes that you should pay （非法）逃税；偷税；漏税 ➲ COMPARE TAX AVOIDANCE

,tax-e'xempt *adj.* that is not taxed 免税的：*tax-exempt savings* 免收利息所得税的存款

'tax exile *noun* a rich person who has left their own country and gone to live in a place where the taxes are lower 跨境避税者，越国避税者（为少缴税而移居较低税地区的富人）

,tax-'free *adj.* (of money, goods, etc. 钱、货物等) that you do not have to pay tax on 免税的；不纳税的：*a tax-free allowance* 免税额 ▶ **,tax-'free** *adv.*

'tax haven *noun* a place where taxes are low and where people choose to live or officially register their companies because taxes are higher in their own countries 避税地，避税港（人们愿意居住或注册公司的低税率地方）

taxi /'tæksi/ *noun, verb*

■ *noun* **1** (*also* **cab**, **taxi·cab**) a car with a driver that you pay to take you somewhere. Taxis usually have METERS which show how much money you have to pay. 出租汽车；计程车；的士：*a **taxi driver/ride*** 出租汽车司机；乘出租车出行 ◇ *We'd better **take a taxi**.* 我们最好乘出租车。◇ *I came home **by taxi**.* 我是坐出租车回家的。◇ *to **order/hail/call a taxi*** 要 / 招呼 / 叫出租车 ➲ VISUAL VOCAB PAGE V63 **2** in some places in Africa, a small bus with a driver that you pay to take you somewhere. Taxis usually have fixed routes and stop wherever passengers need to get on or off. （非洲某些地方走固定路线、乘客可随时上下的）小公共汽车，小巴士 ➲ SEE ALSO DALA-DALA, MATATU

■ *verb* (**taxi·ing**, **tax·ied**, **tax·ied**) [I] (of a plane 飞机) to move slowly along the ground before taking off or after landing （起飞前或降落后在地面上）滑行

taxi·der·mist /'tæksɪdɜːmɪst; *NAmE* -dɜːrm-/ *noun* a person whose job is taxidermy 动物标本剥制师

taxi·dermy /'tæksɪdɜːmi; *NAmE* -dɜːrmi/ *noun* [U] the art of STUFFING dead animals, birds and fish with a special material so that they look like living ones and can be displayed 动物标本剥制术（将动物充填以支撑物，以表现出其生前外形）

tax·ing /'tæksɪŋ/ *adj.* needing a great amount of physical or mental effort 繁重的；费力的；伤脑筋的 SYN **demanding**：*a taxing job* 繁重的工作 ◇ *This shouldn't be too taxing for you.* 这对你来说不至于太费劲。➲ SYNONYMS AT DIFFICULT

'tax inspector *noun* (*BrE*) = INSPECTOR OF TAXES

'taxi rank (*BrE*) (*also* **'taxi stand** *NAmE, BrE*) *noun* a place where taxis park while they are waiting for passengers 出租汽车站；出租车停车处 ➲ VISUAL VOCAB PAGE V3

'taxi squad *noun* (in AMERICAN FOOTBALL 美式足球) **1** a group of players who practise with the first team but who do not play in games （不参加比赛的）陪练球队 **2** four extra players on a team who play when other players are injured （统称四名）替补队员

taxi·way /'tæksiweɪ/ *noun* the hard path that a plane uses as it moves to and from the RUNWAY (= the hard surface where planes take off and land) （飞机的）滑行道

tax·man /'tæksmæn/ *noun* (*pl.* **-men** /-men/) **1 the tax·man** [sing.] (*informal*) a way of referring to the government department that is responsible for collecting taxes 税务部门；税务机关：*He had been cheating the taxman for years.* 多年来他一直欺骗税务部门。 **2** [C] a person whose job is to collect taxes 收税员；税务员

tax·ono·mist /tæk'sɒnəmɪst; *NAmE* -'sɑːnə-/ *noun* a person who studies or is skilled in taxonomy 分类学家

tax·onomy /tæk'sɒnəmi; *NAmE* -'sɑːnə-/ *noun* (*pl.* **-ies**) **1** [U] the scientific process of CLASSIFYING things (= arranging them into groups) 分类学：*plant taxonomy* 植物分类学 **2** [C] a particular system of CLASSIFYING things 分类法；分类系统 ➲ WORDFINDER NOTE AT BREED ▶ **taxo·nom·ic** /,tæksə'nɒmɪk; *NAmE* -'nɑːmɪk/ *adj.*

tax·pay·er /'tækspeɪə(r)/ *noun* a person who pays tax to the government, especially on the money that they earn 纳税人

'tax relief (*also* **relief**) *noun* [U] a reduction in the amount of tax you have to pay 税款减免

'tax return *noun* an official document in which you give details of the amount of money that you have earned so that the government can calculate how much tax you have to pay 纳税申报单

'tax shelter *noun* a way of using or investing money so that you can legally avoid paying tax on it 避税方法（如用于消费、投资）

T

'tax year *noun* (*BrE*) = FINANCIAL YEAR

tay·berry /ˈteɪbəri; *NAmE* -beri/ *noun* (*pl.* **-ies**) a dark red soft fruit that is a combination of a BLACKBERRY and a RASPBERRY 泰莓（黑莓和悬钩子的杂交果实）

TB *abbr.* **1** /ˌtiː ˈbiː/ TUBERCULOSIS 结核病 **2** (in writing 书写形式) TERABYTE 太字节（计算机内存或数据单位）

Tb (*also* **Tbit**) *abbr.* (in writing 书写形式) TERABIT 太比特（计算机内存或数据单位）

TBA /ˌtiː biː ˈeɪ/ *abbr.* (used in notices about events 用于通告) to be announced 待宣布；待发表：*party with live band (TBA)* 乐队（待公布）现场伴奏的聚会

'T-bar *noun* **1** (*also* **'T-bar lift**) a machine which pulls two people up a mountain on SKIS together 丁字形吊椅（能同时送两人上山滑雪） **2** a T-shaped strip of leather, etc. on a shoe（鞋子上的）丁字形皮条（等）

TBC /ˌtiː biː ˈsiː/ *abbr.* (used in notices about events 用于通告) to be confirmed 待确认：*The four-day course will run from March 8–11 (TBC).* 这门四天的课程将从 3 月 8 日进行到 11 日（待确认）。

TBH (*also* **tbh**) *abbr.* (*informal*) (used in emails and TEXT MESSAGES to say that this is what you really think) to be honest 说实话（全写为 to be honest，用于电邮和短信）：*I don't know anything about it, TBH.* 说实话，我对此一无所知。

'T-bill *abbr.* (*NAmE, informal*) = TREASURY BILL

'T-bone steak *noun* a thick slice of beef containing a bone in the shape of a T 带骨牛排；T 字骨牛排

tbsp (*also* **tbs**) *abbr.* (*pl.* **tbsp** or **tbsps**) TABLESPOON (2) 一餐匙，一汤匙（的量）：*Add 3 tbsp sugar.* 加三汤匙的糖。

TCP/IP /ˌtiː siː ˌpiː aɪ ˈpiː/ *abbr.* (*computing* 计) transmission control protocol/Internet protocol (a system that controls the connection of computers to the Internet) * TCP / IP 协议，传输控制 / 网际协议（控制计算机接入互联网的系统）

TD /ˌtiː ˈdiː/ *noun* the abbreviation for 'Teachta Dála', 'Member of the Dáil' (a member of the LOWER HOUSE of the parliament of the Republic of Ireland)（爱尔兰共和国的）众议院议员，第一院议员（全写为 Teachta Dála，英语为 Member of the Dáil）

te (*BrE*) (*NAmE* **ti**) /tiː/ *noun* (*music* 音) the 7th note of a MAJOR SCALE 大调音阶的第 7 音

tea 🔑 /tiː/ *noun* **1** 🔑 [U, C] the dried leaves (called TEA LEAVES) of the tea bush 茶叶 ➲ SEE ALSO GREEN TEA **2** 🔑 [U, C] a hot drink made by pouring boiling water onto tea leaves. It may be drunk with milk or lemon and/or sugar added. 茶；茶水：*a* ***cup/mug/pot of tea*** 一杯 / 一茶缸子 / 一壶茶 ◇ ***lemon/iced tea*** 柠檬茶；冰茶 ◇ *Would you like tea or coffee?* 你喝茶还是喝咖啡？◇ *Do you take sugar in your tea?* 你的茶里放糖吗？ **3** 🔑 [C] a cup of tea 一杯茶：*Two teas, please.* 请来两杯茶。 **4** [U, C] a hot drink made by pouring boiling water onto the leaves of other plants（用其他植物的叶子沏的）热饮料：***camomile/mint/herb, etc. tea*** 春黄菊花茶、薄荷茶、药草茶等 ➲ SEE ALSO BEEF TEA **5** [U, C] the name used by some people in Britain for the cooked meal eaten in the evening, especially when it is eaten early in the evening 晚点，便餐（英国人傍晚时吃）：*You can have your tea as soon as you come home from school.* 你放学一回到家就可以吃晚点。 ➲ COMPARE DINNER, SUPPER **6** [U, C] (*BrE*) a light meal eaten in the afternoon or early evening, usually with SANDWICHES and/or biscuits and cakes and with tea to drink 茶点（在下午或傍晚，通常喝茶时还有三明治、饼干和蛋糕） ➲ NOTE AT MEAL ➲ SEE ALSO CREAM TEA, HIGH TEA

IDM **not for all the tea in 'China** (*old-fashioned*) not even for a great reward 无论报酬多高都不；无论有多大好处都不：*I wouldn't do your job. Not for all the tea in China!* 我才不做你的那份工作。有天大的好处也不干！ ➲ MORE AT CUP *n.*

teabag /ˈtiːbæg/ *noun* a small thin paper bag containing tea leaves, which you pour boiling water onto in order to make tea 袋泡茶；茶包

'tea break *noun* (*BrE*) a short period of time when people stop working and drink tea, coffee, etc. 喝茶休息时间；工间休息时间；茶歇

'tea caddy (*also* **caddy**) *noun* (*especially BrE*) a small box with a lid that you keep tea in 茶叶盒；茶叶罐

tea·cake /ˈtiːkeɪk/ *noun* (*BrE*) a small flat round cake made of a bread-like mixture, usually containing dried fruit 茶点饼（扁平状，常含有果干）：*toasted teacakes* 烘烤的茶点饼

tea·cart /ˈtiːkɑːt; *NAmE* -kɑːrt/ (*also* **'tea wagon**) (*both US*) (*BrE* **'tea trolley**) *noun* a small table on wheels that is used for serving drinks and food 茶具车；上菜车

'tea ceremony *noun* a Japanese ceremony in which tea is served and drunk according to complicated rules 茶道（日本沏茶和饮茶的礼仪）

teach 🔑 /tiːtʃ/ *verb* (**taught, taught** /tɔːt/) **1** 🔑 [I, T] to give lessons to students in a school, college, university, etc.; to help sb learn sth by giving information about it 教（课程）；讲授；教授：*She teaches at our local school.* 她在我们当地的学校任教。◇ *He taught for several years before becoming a writer.* 他教了几年书之后成为作家。◇ **~ sth** *I'll be teaching history and sociology next term.* 下学期我教历史和社会学。◇ (*NAmE*) *to* ***teach school*** (= teach in a school) 当学校教师 ◇ **~ sth to sb** *He teaches English to advanced students.* 他教高年级学生英语。◇ **~ sb sth** *He teaches them English.* 他教他们英语。 **2** 🔑 [T] to show sb how to do sth so that they will be able to do it themselves 教；训练：**~ (sb to do) sth** *Could you teach me to do that?* 你能教我干那活儿吗？◇ **~ sb how, what, etc.…** *My father taught me how to ride a bike.* 我父亲教会了我骑自行车。 **3** 🔑 [T] to make sb feel or think in a different way 教育；教导；使懂得（情理）：**~ sb to do sth** *She taught me to be less critical of other people.* 她教育我不要太苛求于人。◇ **~ (sb) that…** *My parents taught me that honesty was always the best policy.* 我父母教导我，诚实永

▼ VOCABULARY BUILDING 词汇扩充

Teach and teachers 教与教师

Verbs 动词

- **teach** 教：*John teaches French at the local school.* 约翰在当地学校教法语。◇ *She taught me how to change a tyre.* 她教会了我换轮胎。
- **educate** 教育：*Our priority is to educate people about the dangers of drugs.* 我们首先要做的是教育人们认识毒品的危害。
- **instruct** 讲授；指导：*Members of staff should be instructed in the use of fire equipment.* 应该指导全体职员学会使用消防设备。
- **train** 培养；训练：*She's a trained midwife.* 她是受过专门训练的助产士。◇ *He's training the British Olympic swimming team.* 他在训练英国的奥运游泳队。
- **coach** 辅导；训练：*He's the best football player I've ever coached.* 他是我训练过的最出色的足球运动员。◇ (*BrE*) *She coaches some of the local children in maths.* 她给当地一些孩子辅导数学。（英式英语）
- **tutor** 当…的教师；辅导：(*NAmE*) *She tutors some of the local children in math.* 她给当地一些孩子辅导数学。（美式英语）

Nouns 名词

- **teacher** 教师：*school/college teachers* 学校 / 大学教师
- **instructor** 教员；教练；指导员：*a swimming/science instructor* 游泳教练；自然科学教员
- **trainer** 训练员；教练；驯兽师：*a horse trainer* 驯马师 ◇ *Do you have a personal trainer?* 你有私人教练吗？
- **coach**（体育运动）教练；私人教练：*a football coach* 足球教练
- **tutor** 私人教师；家庭教师：*tutors working with migrant children* 教移民孩子的家庭教师

远是处世的最佳原则。◇ ~ sb sth *Our experience as refugees taught us many valuable lessons.* 我们流亡的经历给了我们许多宝贵的教训。 **4** [T, no passive] (*informal*) to persuade sb not to do sth again by making them suffer so much that they are afraid to do it 使引以为戒；惩戒： **~ sb to do sth** *Lost all your money? That'll teach you to gamble.* 你把钱都输光了？这是赌博给你的教训。◇ *I'll teach you to call* (= punish you for calling) *me a liar!* 你要说我撒谎，我就对你不客气！◇ **~ sb sth** *The accident* ***taught me a lesson*** *I'll never forget.* 这次事故给了我一个终生难忘的教训。 ➲ MORE LIKE THIS 33, page R28

IDM **teach your grandmother to suck 'eggs** (*BrE, informal*) to tell or show sb how to do sth that they can already do well, and probably better than you can 教奶奶嘬鸡蛋；在能人面前逞强；班门弄斧 **(you can't) teach an old dog new 'tricks** (*saying*) (you cannot) successfully make people change their ideas, methods of work, etc., when they have had them for a long time 老大（不）可教；（无法）改变人们长时间形成的思想（或做事方法等） **teach to the 'test** to teach students only what is necessary in order to pass a particular test, rather than help them develop a range of skills 应试教育；为考试而教学

teach·able /ˈtiːtʃəbl/ *adj.* **1** (of a subject 科目) that can be taught 适于教学的；可传授的 **2** (of a person 人) able to learn by being taught 可教的；能学的；善学的

teach·er /ˈtiːtʃə(r)/ *noun* a person whose job is teaching, especially in a school 教师；教员；老师；先生： *a* ***history/science, etc. teacher*** 历史、理科等教师 ◇ *primary school teachers* 小学教师 ◇ *There is a growing need for qualified teachers of Business English.* 对合格的商务英语教师的需求日益增长。 ➲ NOTE AT TEACH

ˌteacher ˈtraining *noun* [U] the process of teaching or learning the skills you need to be a teacher in a school 教师培训；师资培训 ▶ **ˌteacher ˈtrainer** *noun* : *experienced teachers and teacher trainers* 有经验的教师和培训师资的教师

ˈtea chest *noun* (*BrE*) a large light wooden box lined with metal in which tea is transported. Tea chests are sometimes used for transporting personal possessions, for example, when moving to another home. 茶叶箱（运输茶叶用的大木箱，搬家时可装个人物品）

ˈteach-in *noun* an informal lecture and discussion on a subject of public interest（以公众关注的事情等为题的）宣讲会，座谈会

teach·ing /ˈtiːtʃɪŋ/ *noun* **1** [U] the work of a teacher 教学；授课；指导： *She wants to go into teaching* (= make it a career). 她想从事教学工作。◇ *the teaching profession* 教学职业 **2** [C, usually pl., U] the ideas of a particular person or group, especially about politics, religion or society, that are taught to other people 教导；学说；教义；教诲： *the teachings of Lenin* 列宁的学说 ◇ *views that go against traditional Christian teaching* 与传统基督教教义相违的观点

ˈteaching assistant *noun* **1** a person who is not a qualified teacher who helps a teacher in a school 教学助理 **2** (*abbr.* **TA**) (*both NAmE*) (*also* **ˈteaching fellow** *US, BrE*) a GRADUATE student who teaches UNDERGRADUATE classes at a university or college, takes discussion or practical classes, marks written work, etc. 助教（担任本科生教学、组织讨论、上实践课、批改作业等工作的研究生）

ˈteaching practice (*BrE*) (*NAmE* **ˌstudent ˈteaching**) *noun* [U] the part of a course for people who are training to become teachers which involves teaching classes of students 教学实习

ˈtea cloth *noun* (*BrE*) = TEA TOWEL

ˈtea cosy (*BrE*) (*NAmE* **ˈtea cozy**) *noun* a cover placed over a TEAPOT in order to keep the tea warm 茶壶套；茶壶保温罩

tea·cup /ˈtiːkʌp/ *noun* a cup in which tea is served 茶杯 IDM SEE TEMPEST

ˈtea dance *noun* a social event held in the afternoon, especially in the past, at which people dance, drink tea, and eat a small meal（尤指旧时的）下午茶舞会

teak /tiːk/ *noun* [U] the strong hard wood of a tall Asian tree, used especially for making furniture 柚木（尤用以制造家具）

tea·ket·tle /ˈtiːketl/ *noun* a metal container with a lid, handle and a SPOUT, used for boiling water 烧水壶

teal /tiːl/ *noun* **1** [C] (*pl.* **teal**) a small wild DUCK 水鸭；短颈野鸭 **2** [U] (*especially NAmE*) a bluish-green colour 蓝绿色

ˈtea leaf *noun* a small piece of a dried leaf of the tea bush; used especially in the plural to describe what is left at the bottom of a cup or pot after the tea has been made 茶叶；茶叶渣

tea·light /ˈtiːlaɪt/ *noun* a small CANDLE that is used for decoration and which often gives off a pleasant smell 茶烛，工艺茶烛（蜡烛小，有些散发香味）

team AW /tiːm/ *noun, verb*

■ ***noun*** [C+sing./pl. v.] **1** a group of people who play a particular game or sport against another group of people（游戏或运动的）队： *a* ***football/baseball, etc. team*** 足球队、棒球队等 ◇ *a* ***team event*** (= one played by groups of people rather than individual players) 团体比赛项目 ◇ (*BrE*) *Whose team are you in?* 你是哪个队的？◇ (*NAmE*) *Whose team are you on?* 你是哪个队的？◇ *The team is/are not playing very well this season.* 这个队本赛季状态不佳。 **2** a group of people who work together at a particular job（一起工作的）组，班： *the sales team* 推销小组 ◇ *a* ***team leader/member*** 队长；队员 ◇ *A team of experts has/have been called in to investigate.* 一个专家小组已应召来进行调查。 **3** two or more animals that are used together to pull a CART, etc.（同拉一辆车等的）一组牲畜，联畜

IDM **ˌtake one for the ˈteam** (*informal*) to give up sth that is important to you or to do sth that is unpleasant in order to benefit your friends or colleagues 为集体牺牲自己的利益；为团队放弃个人利益： *Sometimes you have to take one for the team.* 有时为了团队必须得牺牲个人利益。

■ ***verb*** [usually passive] **~ sb/sth (with sb/sth)** to put two or more things or people together in order to do sth or to achieve a particular effect 使互相配合；使协作；使合作： *He was teamed with his brother in the doubles.* 他被安排和哥哥搭档参加双打。

PHR V **ˌteam ˈup (with sb)** to join with another person or group in order to do sth together 合作；（与某人）结成一队 **ˌteam sb/sth ˈup (with sb)** to put two or more people or things together in order to do sth or to achieve a particular effect 使互相配合；使协作；使合作

ˈteam handball *noun* [U] (*US*) = HANDBALL (1)

team·mate /ˈtiːmmeɪt/ *noun* a member of the same team or group as yourself 同队队员；队友

ˈteam player *noun* a person who is good at working as a member of a team, usually in their job 善于与团队合作的成员

ˌteam ˈspirit *noun* [U] (*approving*) the desire and willingness of people to work together and help each other as part of a team 合作精神；集体精神；团队精神

team·ster /ˈtiːmstə(r)/ *noun* (*NAmE*) a person whose job is driving a truck 卡车司机 SYN **trucker**

team·work /ˈtiːmwɜːk; *NAmE* -wɜːrk/ *noun* [U] the activity of working well together as a team 协同工作；配合： *She stressed the importance of good teamwork.* 她强调了团队合作的重要性。 ▶ **team·work·ing** *noun* [U] : *effective teamworking and problem-solving* 有效进行团队合作和解决问题 ◇ *teamworking skills* 团队合作的技巧

ˈtea party *noun* **1** a social event at which people eat cake, drink tea, etc. in the afternoon（午后的）茶会，茶话会 **2 the Tea Party** [sing.] a conservative political movement

T

in the US, begun in 2009 in protest against the government. In particular they want to reduce the amount of money that the national government spends and to cut taxes. 茶党（美国一个右翼政治运动，始于 2009 年抗议政府的行动，诉求缩减联邦政府开支和减税）

tea·pot /ˈtiːpɒt; *NAmE* -pɑːt/ *noun* a container with a SPOUT, a handle and a lid, used for making and serving tea 茶壶 ➲ VISUAL VOCAB PAGE V26 IDM ➤ SEE TEMPEST

tear[1] /teə(r); *NAmE* ter/ *verb, noun* ➲ SEE ALSO TEAR[2]

■ *verb* (**tore** /tɔː(r)/, **torn** /tɔːn; *NAmE* tɔːrn/)

• **DAMAGE** 损坏 **1** [T, I] to damage sth by pulling it apart or into pieces or by cutting it on sth sharp; to become damaged in this way 撕裂；撕碎；扯破；戳破 SYN **rip**: ~ (**sth**) (+ **adv./prep.**) *I tore my jeans on the fence.* 我的牛仔裤被篱笆划破了。◇ *I tore a hole in my jeans.* 我的牛仔裤刷了个窟窿。◇ *He tore the letter in two.* 他把信撕成两半。◇ *a torn handkerchief* 撕破的手帕 ◇ *Careful—the fabric tears very easily.* 小心，这种织物一撕就破。◇ ~ **sth** + **adj.** *I tore the package open.* 我把包裹撕开。 **2** [T] ~ **sth in sth** to make a hole in sth by force 撕开，划成，刺出，扯开（裂口或洞） SYN **rip**: *The blast tore a hole in the wall.* 墙被炸开了个洞。

• **REMOVE FROM STH/SB** 移开 **3** [T] ~ **sth** + **adv./prep.** to remove sth from sth else by pulling it roughly or violently 拉掉；撕掉；拔掉；扯掉 SYN **rip**: *The storm nearly tore the roof off.* 暴风雨差一点儿把屋顶掀掉。◇ *I tore another sheet from the pad.* 我从本子上又撕下一张纸。◇ *He tore his clothes off* (= took them off quickly and carelessly) *and dived into the lake.* 他把衣服从身上扯下，一头跳入湖中。 **4** [T] to pull yourself/sb away by force from sb/sth that is holding you or them 挣开；拽开；夺去；揪走：~ **yourself/sb from sb/sth** *She tore herself from his grasp.* 她挣脱了他紧紧抓着她的手。◇ ~ **yourself/sb** + **adj.** *He tore himself free.* 他挣脱了。

• **INJURE MUSCLE** 损伤肌肉 **5** [T] ~ **sth** to injure a muscle, etc. by stretching it too much 拉伤；拽伤：*a torn ligament* 拉伤的韧带

• **MOVE QUICKLY** 快速移动 **6** [I] + **adv./prep.** to move somewhere very quickly or in an excited way 飞跑；狂奔；疾驰：*He tore off down the street.* 他沿大街飞奔。◇ *A truck tore past the gates.* 卡车从大门前疾驰而过。

• **-TORN** 受…伤害 **7** (in adjectives 构成形容词) very badly affected or damaged by sth 深受…之苦的；饱经…摧残的：*to bring peace to a strife-torn country* 给一个饱经变乱创伤的国家带来和平 ◇ *a strike-torn industry* 深受罢工困扰的行业 ➲ SEE ALSO WAR-TORN

T

IDM ➤ **tear sb/sth aˈpart, to ˈshreds, to ˈbits, etc.** to destroy or defeat sb/sth completely or criticize them or it severely 彻底毁灭；彻底打败；严厉批评：*We tore the other team apart in the second half.* 我们在下半场把对方球队打得落花流水。◇ *The critics tore his last movie to shreds.* 影评家把他最近的一部影片说得一无是处。 ˌ**tear at your ˈheart** | ˌ**tear your ˈheart out** (*formal*) to strongly affect you in an emotional way 使伤心；使心如刀绞；使愁肠寸断 **tear your ˈhair (out)** (*informal*) to show that you are very angry or anxious about sth（因发怒、焦急而）撕扯自己的头发：*She's keeping very calm—anyone else would be tearing their hair out.* 她依旧泰然自若，换作别人早急坏了。(**be in**) **a tearing ˈhurry/ˈrush** (*especially BrE*) (to be) in a very great hurry 匆忙；急匆匆；风风火火 **be torn** (**between A and B**) to be unable to decide or choose between two people, things or feelings（在两者间）难以选择，左右为难：*I was torn between my parents and my friend.* 我在父母和朋友之间左右为难。 **tear sb ˈoff a strip** | **tear a ˈstrip off sb** (*BrE, informal*) to speak angrily to sb who has done sth wrong 怒斥；把…骂得狗血喷头 ˌ**that's ˈtorn it** (*BrE, informal*) used to say that sth has happened to spoil your plans（表示计划受挫）这可糟了 ➲ MORE AT HEART, LIMB, LOOSE *adj.*, PIECE *n.*, SHRED *n.*

PHR V ➤ ˌ**tear sb↔aˈpart/ˈup** to make sb feel very unhappy or worried 使不快；使担心 SYN **rip sb apart**: *It tears me apart to think I might have hurt her feelings.* 一想到我可能伤害了她的感情，我就感到痛心。 ˌ**tear sth↔aˈpart 1** to destroy sth violently, especially by pulling it to pieces 撕毁；撕碎：*The dogs tore the fox apart.* 几条狗把那只狐狸撕成了碎片。 **2** to make people in a country, an organization or other place fight or argue with each other 使四分五裂；使分崩离析：*Racial strife is tearing our country apart.* 种族冲突把我们国家搞得四分五裂。 **3** to search a place, making it look untidy and causing damage 把（某处）翻得凌乱不堪 SYN **rip sth apart**: *They tore the room apart, looking for money.* 他们为了找钱，把房间翻得乱七八糟。 ˈ**tear at sth** to pull or cut sth violently so that it tears 撕裂；扯开；撕破：*He tore at the meat with his bare hands.* 他徒手撕肉。 ˌ**tear yourself aˈway** (**from sth**) | ˌ**tear sth aˈway** (**from sth**) to leave somewhere even though you would prefer to stay there; to take sth away from somewhere 依依不舍地离开；忍痛离去；把…拿走：*Dinner's ready, if you can tear yourself away from the TV.* 开饭了，别舍不得离开电视了。◇ *She was unable to tear her eyes away from him* (= could not stop looking at him). 她恋恋不舍地望着他。 ˌ**tear sth↔ˈdown** to pull or knock down a building, wall, etc. 拆毁，拆除（建筑物、墙等） SYN **demolish** ˌ**tear ˈinto sb/sth 1** to attack sb/sth physically or with words 攻击；袭击；痛斥；抨击 **2** to start doing sth with a lot of energy 积极投入：*They tore into their food as if they were starving.* 他们狼吞虎咽地吃起饭来，好像饿坏了似的。 ˌ**tear sb↔ˈup** = TEAR SB/STH APART, TO SHREDS, TO BITS, ETC. ˌ**tear sth↔ˈup** to destroy a document, etc. by tearing it into pieces 撕毁，撕碎（文件等） SYN **rip sth up**: *She tore up all the letters he had sent her.* 她把他寄给她的信都撕了。◇ (*figurative*) *He accused the leader of tearing up the party's manifesto* (= of ignoring it). 他谴责领导人无视党的宣言。

■ *noun* a hole that has been made in sth by tearing 破洞；裂口；裂缝：*This sheet has a tear in it.* 这条床单上有个破洞。 IDM ➤ SEE WEAR *n.*

tear[2] /tɪə(r); *NAmE* tɪr/ *noun* [usually pl.] ➲ SEE ALSO TEAR[1] a drop of liquid that comes out of your eye when you cry 眼泪；泪珠；泪水：*A tear rolled down his face.* 一滴眼泪沿他的面颊流下来。◇ *She left the room* **in tears** (= crying). 她哭着离开了房间。◇ *He suddenly* **burst into tears** (= began to cry). 他突然放声大哭起来。◇ *As he listened to the music, his* **eyes filled with tears**. 他听着音乐，眼睛里噙着泪水。◇ *Their story will* **move you to tears** (= make you cry). 他们的故事会使你感动得落泪。◇ *They* **reduced her to tears** (= made her cry, especially by being cruel or unkind). 他们弄得她哭起来了。◇ *Ann* **wiped a tear** *from her eye.* 安擦去眼里的泪水。◇ *The memory* **brought a tear to her eye** (= made her cry). 她想起这事便热泪盈眶。◇ *Most of the audience was* **on the verge of tears**. 大多数观众都快流泪了。◇ *I was* **close to tears** *as I told them the news.* 我告诉他们这一消息时都快要哭了出来。◇ *Desperately she* **fought back the tears** (= tried not to cry). 她竭力忍住没让眼泪流出来。◇ *to* **shed tears** *of happiness* 喜极而泣 ◇ *tears of pain, joy, etc.* 痛苦、喜悦等的泪水 ◇ *The* **tears welled up** *in his eyes.* 他热泪盈眶。

▸ **teary** /ˈtɪəri; *NAmE* ˈtɪri/ *adj.*：*teary eyes* 泪眼 ◇ *a teary smile/goodbye* 含泪的微笑；挥泪告别 IDM ➤ SEE BLOOD *n.*, BORED, CROCODILE, END *v.*

tear·away /ˈteərəweɪ; *NAmE* ˈter-/ *noun* (*BrE, informal*) a young person who is difficult to control and often does stupid, dangerous and/or illegal things 小流氓；阿飞；不良青年 ➲ WORDFINDER NOTE AT YOUNG

tear·drop /ˈtɪədrɒp; *NAmE* ˈtɪrdrɑːp/ *noun* a single tear that comes from your eye 泪珠

tear duct /ˈtɪə dʌkt; *NAmE* ˈtɪr/ *noun* a tube through which tears pass from the tear GLANDS to the eye, or from the eye to the nose 鼻泪管 ➲ VISUAL VOCAB PAGE V64

tear·ful /ˈtɪəfl; *NAmE* ˈtɪrfl/ *adj.* **1** (of a person 人) crying, or about to cry 哭泣的；含泪的：*She suddenly became very tearful.* 她突然痛哭流涕。 **2** (of an event, etc. 事件等) at which people feel emotional and cry 令人伤心的；催人泪下的：*a tearful farewell* 挥泪送别 ▸ **tear·ful·ly** /-fəli/ *adv.* **tear·ful·ness** *noun* [U]

tear gas /ˈtɪə gæs; *NAmE* ˈtɪr/ *noun* [U] a gas that makes your eyes sting and fill with tears, used by the police or army to control crowds 催泪瓦斯；催泪性毒气

tear-jerker /ˈtɪə dʒɜːkə(r); *NAmE* ˈtɪr dʒɜːrkər/ *noun* (*informal*) a film/movie, story, etc. that is designed to make people feel sad 催人泪下的电影（或故事等）；"催泪弹" SYN weepy

tear-off /ˈteər ɒf; *NAmE* ˈter ɔːf; ɑːf/ *adj.* [only before noun] relating to sth that can be removed by being torn off, especially part of a sheet of paper（纸片等）可撕下的： *a tear-off slip* 可撕下的纸条

ˈtea room (*BrE also* **ˈtea shop**) *noun* a restaurant in which tea, coffee, cakes and SANDWICHES are served 茶室；茶馆

tear-stained /ˈtɪə steɪnd; *NAmE* ˈtɪr/ *adj.* (especially of sb's face or cheeks 尤指脸或面颊) wet with tears 布满泪痕的；泪水涟涟的

tease /tiːz/ *verb, noun*

■ ***verb*** **1** [I, T] **~ (sb) | ~ (sb) + speech** to laugh at sb and make jokes about them, either in a friendly way or in order to annoy or embarrass them 取笑；戏弄；揶揄；寻开心： *Don't get upset—I was only teasing.* 别不高兴，我只是在逗你玩。 ◇ *I used to get teased about my name.* 过去别人总拿我的名字开玩笑。 **2** [T] **~ sth** to annoy an animal, especially by touching it, pulling its tail, etc. 招惹，逗弄（动物） **3** [I, T] **~ (sb)** (*disapproving*) to make sb sexually excited, especially when you do not intend to have sex with them 挑逗，撩拨（异性） **4** [T] **~ sb (with sth)** to make sb want sth or become excited about sth by showing or offering them just a small part of it; to make sb want more of sth（用一小部分）逗惹，刺激；使想要更多： *Spring is here and we have already been teased with a glimpse of summer.* 春天来了，我们已经迫不及待地想要一睹夏日的风采。 ◇ *There are tempting menus to tease the taste buds.* 有挑逗味蕾的诱人的菜单。 **5** [T] **~ sth (+ adv./prep.)** to pull sth gently apart into separate pieces 梳理： *to tease wool into strands* 把羊毛梳成缕 **6** (*NAmE*) (*BrE* **back·comb**) [T] **~ sth** to COMB your hair in the opposite direction to the way it grows so that it looks thicker 倒梳（头发）使之蓬起

PHR V **ˌtease sth↔ˈout** **1** to remove knots from hair, wool, etc. by gently pulling or brushing it 梳理，梳通（毛发等） **2** to spend time trying to find out information or the meaning of sth, especially when this is complicated or difficult 探讨；深入研究；梳理清楚： *The teacher helped them tease out the meaning of the poem.* 老师帮助他们弄清楚那首诗的含义。

■ ***noun*** [usually sing.] **1** a person who likes to play tricks and jokes on other people, especially by telling them sth that is not true or by not telling them sth that they want to know 爱戏弄人的人；逗弄者；取笑者 **2** an act that is intended as a trick or joke 戏弄；捉弄；取笑 **3** (*disapproving*) a person who pretends to be attracted to sb, makes them sexually excited and then refuses to have sex with them 卖弄风骚的人；勾引人者

tea·sel (*also* **tea·zle**) /ˈtiːzl/ *noun* a plant which has large flowers with SPIKES, used in the past for brushing cloth to give it a smooth surface 川续断，起绒草（旧时用以使织物表面起绒）

teaser /ˈtiːzə(r)/ *noun* **1** (*informal*) a difficult problem or question 难题；棘手的问题 ➲ SEE ALSO BRAIN-TEASER **2** (*also* **ˈteaser ad**) an advertisement for a product that does not mention the name of the product or say much about it but is intended to make people interested and likely to pay attention to later advertisements 前导广告，悬念式广告（含蓄而引人好奇）

ˈtea set (*also* **ˈtea service**) *noun* a set consisting of a TEAPOT, sugar bowl, cups, plates, etc., used for serving tea （一套）茶具

ˈtea shop *noun* (*BrE*) = TEA ROOM

teas·ing·ly /ˈtiːzɪŋli/ *adv.* **1** in a way that is intended to make sb feel embarrassed, annoyed, etc. 戏弄地；取笑地 **2** in a way that suggests sth and makes sb want to know more 激起好奇心地 **3** in a way that is intended to make sb sexually excited 挑逗地；撩拨地

tea·spoon /ˈtiːspuːn/ *noun* **1** a small spoon for putting sugar into tea and other drinks 茶匙；小匙 ➲ VISUAL VOCAB PAGE V23 **2** (*also* **tea·spoon·ful** /-fʊl/) (*abbr.* **tsp**) the amount a teaspoon can hold 一茶匙（的量）： *Add two teaspoons of salt.* 加两小匙盐。

teat /tiːt/ *noun* **1** (*BrE*) (*NAmE* **nip·ple**) the rubber part at the end of a baby's bottle that the baby sucks in order to get milk, etc. from the bottle 奶嘴；橡胶乳头 **2** one of the parts of a female animal's body that the young animals suck in order to get milk （雌兽的）乳头，奶头

tea·time /ˈtiːtaɪm/ *noun* [U] (*BrE*) the time during the afternoon or early evening when people have the meal called tea （下午或傍晚的）茶点时间

ˈtea towel (*also* **ˈtea cloth**) (*both BrE*) (*NAmE* **dish·towel**) *noun* a small towel used for drying cups, plates, knives, etc. after they have been washed（擦拭已洗餐具的）茶巾，抹布 ➲ VISUAL VOCAB PAGE V26

ˈtea tree *noun* a small Australian and New Zealand tree. The oil from its leaves can be used to treat wounds and skin problems. 澳洲茶树（产于澳大利亚和新西兰，叶油可用于处理伤口和治疗皮肤病）

ˈtea trolley (*BrE*) (*US* **ˈtea·cart**, **ˈtea wagon**) *noun* a small table on wheels that is used for serving drinks and food 茶具车

tea·zle *noun* = TEASEL

tebi·bit /ˈtebibɪt/ *noun* (*abbr.* **Tib**, **Tibit**) (*computing* 计) = TERABIT (2)

tebi·byte /ˈtebibaɪt/ *noun* (*abbr.* **TiB**) (*computing* 计) = TERABYTE (2)

tech /tek/ *noun* **1** = TECHNOLOGY : *tech companies* 科技公司 **2** (*BrE, informal*) = TECHNICAL COLLEGE ➲ SEE ALSO HIGH-TECH, LOW-TECH

techie (*also* **techy**) /ˈteki/ *noun* (*pl.* **-ies**) (*informal*) a person who is expert in or enthusiastic about technology, especially computers 科技通；科技迷；（尤指）电脑通，电脑迷

tech·ne·tium /tekˈniːʃɪəm/ *noun* [U] (*symb.* **Tc**) a chemical element. Technetium is found naturally as a product of URANIUM or made artificially from MOLYBDENUM. 锝

tech·nical 🔑 AW /ˈteknɪkl/ *adj.* **1** 🔑 [usually before noun] connected with the practical use of machinery, methods, etc. in science and industry 技术的；技能的；工艺的： *We offer free technical support for those buying our software.* 我们向购买我们软件的顾客免费提供技术支持。 ◇ *a technical education* 技术教育 ◇ *technical drawing* (= especially taught as a school subject) 技术制图（尤指学校教学科目） **2** 🔑 [usually before noun] connected with the skills needed for a particular job, sport, art, etc. 专门技术的；技巧的；技艺的： *Skaters score extra points for technical complexity.* 滑冰运动员技巧难度大者获得额外加分。 **3** 🔑 connected with a particular subject and therefore difficult to understand if you do not know about that subject 专科的；专业的： *The article is full of technical terms.* 这篇文章满篇皆是专业术语。 ◇ *The guide is too technical for a non-specialist.* 这份手册对非专业人员来说太专业化了。 **4** 🔑 [only before noun] connected with the details of a law or set of rules 诉讼程序性的；技术性的： *Their lawyers spent days arguing over technical details.* 他们的律师花了好几天时间辩论诉讼程序细则。

ˈtechnical college (*also BrE, informal* **tech**) *noun* a college where students can study mainly practical subjects 工学院

ˌtechnical ˈfoul *noun* (in BASKETBALL 篮球) an act of breaking certain rules of the game, especially ones relating to fair play 技术犯规（尤指违反公平比赛）

ˌtechnical ˈhitch *noun* a temporary problem or difficulty, especially one caused by a piece of machinery or

T

equipment 暂时性问题（或困难）；（尤指）技术故障，机件故障

tech·ni·cal·ity /ˌteknɪˈkæləti/ *noun* (*pl.* **-ies**) **1 technicalities** [pl.] the small details of how to do sth or how sth works 技术性细节 **2** a small detail in a law or set of rules, especially one that does not seem fair 诉讼程序性细节，技术性细则（尤指似乎不合理的）：*She was released on a technicality* (= because of a small detail in the law). 根据诉讼程序上的一个细则，她获释了。

ˌtechnical ˈknockout *noun* (in BOXING 拳击运动) a victory when the opponent is still standing but is unable to continue fighting 技术性击倒（虽未被击倒但被认为已丧失继续比赛能力）

tech·nic·al·ly AW /ˈteknɪkli/ *adv.* **1** according to the exact meaning, facts etc. 根据确切意义地；严格按照事实地：*Technically (speaking), the two countries are still at war.* 严格说来，这两国仍在交战。◇ *It is still technically possible for them to win* (= but it seems unlikely). 从理论上讲，他们仍有获胜的可能性。 **2** in a way that is connected with the skills needed for a particular job, sport, art, etc. 在专业上；在技巧上；在技艺上：*As a musician, she is technically accomplished.* 作为乐师，她演奏技艺精湛。 **3** in a way that is connected with the practical use of machinery, methods, etc. in science and industry 在技术上；在技能上；在工艺上：*a technically advanced society* 科技先进的社会 ◇ *In those days recording sound was not technically possible.* 在那个时候，录音在技术上是不可能的。

ˌtechnical supˈport (*also informal* **ˌtech supˈport**) *noun* **1** [U] technical help that a company gives to customers using their computers or other products（公司为用户提供的）技术支持，技术支援：*All our software licences include technical support.* 我们的软件证书均包含技术支持。 **2** [U+sing./pl. v.] a department in a company that provides technical help to its workers or customers（公司的）技术支持部，技术支援部：*I called tech support and they fixed it.* 我给技术支持部打了电话，他们修好了。

tech·ni·cian /tekˈnɪʃn/ *noun* **1** a person whose job is keeping a particular type of equipment or machinery in good condition 技术员；技师：*laboratory technicians* 实验室技术员 **2** a person who is very skilled at the technical aspects of an art, a sport, etc.（艺术、体育等的）技巧精湛者，精于技巧者

Tech·ni·color™ /ˈteknɪkʌlə(r)/ *noun* [U] a process of producing colour film, as used in cinema films/movies 特艺彩色电影印片法；特艺彩色

tech·ni·col·our (*especially US* **tech·ni·color**) /ˈteknɪkʌlə(r)/ *noun* [U] (*informal*) the state of having many bright colours 鲜艳的色彩；五彩缤纷：*The rooms were painted in glorious technicolour.* 这些房间被粉刷得绚丽多彩。

tech·ni·kon /ˈteknɪkɒn; *NAmE* -kɑːn/ (*also informal* **tech**) *noun* (*SAfrE*) a type of college or university that teaches mainly practical subjects 工学院；职业技术大学

tech·nique AW /tekˈniːk/ *noun* **1** [C] a particular way of doing sth, especially one in which you have to learn special skills 技巧；技艺；工艺：*The artist combines different techniques in the same painting.* 这位艺术家在同一幅画中把不同的画法结合在一起。◇ *marketing techniques* 营销技巧 **2** [U, sing.] the skill with which sb is able to do sth practical 技术；技能：*Her technique has improved a lot over the past season.* 在过去的一个赛季里，她的技术大有长进。

techno /ˈteknəʊ; *NAmE* -noʊ/ *noun* [U] a type of fast, electronic dance music, typically with little or no singing 泰克诺音乐（一种节奏快、通常无歌声相伴的电子舞曲）

techno- /ˈteknəʊ; *NAmE* -noʊ/ *combining form* (in nouns, adjectives and adverbs 构成名词、形容词和副词) connected with technology 科技的；技术的；工艺的：*technophobe* (= a person who is afraid of technology) 科技恐惧者

techno·babble /ˈteknəʊbæbl; *NAmE* -noʊ-/ *noun* [U] (*informal, disapproving*) words or expressions connected with computers and technology that are difficult for ordinary people to understand 技术呓语（普通人难以理解的科技术语）

tech·noc·racy /tekˈnɒkrəsi; *NAmE* -ˈnɑːk-/ *noun* [U, C] (*pl.* **-ies**) a social or political system in which people with scientific knowledge have a lot of power 专家治国制度；专家政治

techno·crat /ˈteknəkræt/ *noun* an expert in science, engineering, etc. who has a lot of power in politics and/or industry 技术专家官员；技术官僚 ▸ **techno·crat·ic** /ˌteknəˈkrætɪk/ *adj.* [usually before noun]

tech·nolo·gist /tekˈnɒlədʒɪst; *NAmE* -ˈnɑːl-/ *noun* an expert in technology 技术专家；工艺师

tech·nol·ogy AW /tekˈnɒlədʒi; *NAmE* -ˈnɑːl-/ *noun* (*pl.* **-ies**) **1** [U, C] scientific knowledge used in practical ways in industry, for example in designing new machines 科技；工艺；工程技术；技术学；工艺学：*science and technology* 科学技术 ◇ *recent advances in medical technology* 医疗技术的新发展 ◇ *to make use of the most modern technologies* 利用最现代的技术 ➲ SEE ALSO HIGH TECHNOLOGY, INFORMATION TECHNOLOGY **2** [U] machinery or equipment designed using technology 技术性机器（或设备）：*The company has invested in the latest technology.* 这家公司已在尖端技术设备方面投资。 ▸ **techno·logic·al** AW /ˌteknəˈlɒdʒɪkl; *NAmE* -ˈlɑːdʒ-/ *adj.* : *technological advances* 科技进步 ◇ *technological change* 科技革新 ◇ *a major technological breakthrough* 重大科技突破 **techno·logic·al·ly** AW /-kli/ *adv.* : *technologically advanced* 技术上先进的

techno·phile /ˈteknəʊfaɪl; *NAmE* -noʊ-/ *noun* a person who is enthusiastic about new technology 新技术爱好者；新科技迷

techno·phobe /ˈteknəʊfəʊb; *NAmE* -noʊfoʊb/ *noun* a person who is afraid of, dislikes or avoids new technology 技术恐惧者（惧怕、厌恶或逃避新科技的人）

ˈtech support *noun* (*informal*) = TECHNICAL SUPPORT

techy = TECHIE

tec·ton·ic /tekˈtɒnɪk; *NAmE* -ˈtɑːnɪk/ *adj.* [only before noun] (*geology* 地) connected with the structure of the earth's surface 地壳构造的 ➲ SEE ALSO PLATE TECTONICS

teddy bear /ˈtedi beə(r); *NAmE* ber/ (*also* **teddy** *pl.* **-ies**) *noun* a soft toy BEAR 泰迪熊（一种柔软的毛绒玩具熊）➲ VISUAL VOCAB PAGE V41

ˈTeddy boy (*also informal* **ted** /ted/) *noun* (in Britain in the 1950s * 20 世纪 50 年代的英国) a member of a group of young men who liked ROCK AND ROLL music and who had their own style of dressing (usually wearing narrow trousers/pants, long jackets and pointed shoes) 阿飞（常穿紧身裤、长上衣、尖皮鞋，并热衷于摇滚乐的青年男子）

te·di·ous /ˈtiːdiəs/ *adj.* lasting or taking too long and not interesting 冗长的；啰嗦的；单调乏味的；令人厌烦的 SYN **boring**: *The journey soon became tedious.* 那次旅行不久就变得乏味起来。◇ *We had to listen to the tedious details of his operation.* 我们不得不听他唠叨他那次行动繁琐的细节。 ➲ SYNONYMS AT BORING ▸ **te·di·ous·ly** *adv.* **te·di·ous·ness** *noun* [U]

te·dium /ˈtiːdiəm/ *noun* [U] the quality of being boring 单调乏味；冗长；啰嗦 SYN **boredom**: *She longed for something to relieve the tedium of everyday life.* 她渴望有什么事情能排解她日常生活中的烦闷。

tee /tiː/ *noun, verb*

▪ *noun* **1** a flat area on a GOLF COURSE from which players hit the ball（高尔夫球场的）发球区，开球处：*to drive off from the first tee* 从第一发球区开球 ◇ *a tee shot* 开球处击球 **2** a small piece of plastic or wood that you stick in the ground to support a GOLF ball before you hit it（高尔夫球）球座 IDM SEE T

▪ *verb* (**teed, teed**)

PHR V **ˌtee ˈoff** to hit a GOLF ball from a tee, especially at the start of a match（尤指比赛开始时从高尔夫球座上）发球，开球 **ˌtee sb↔ˈoff** (*NAmE, informal*) to make sb angry or annoyed 使生气；使发火；使心烦 **ˌtee sth↔ˈup | ˌtee ˈup** to prepare to hit a GOLF ball by placing it on a tee（把高尔夫球置于球座上）准备击球

teed off /ˌtiːd ˈɒf; *NAmE* ˈɔːf; ˈɑːf/ *adj.* (*NAmE, informal*) annoyed or angry 给惹怒的；生气的

tee-hee /ˌtiː ˈhiː/ *exclamation* used to represent the sound of a quiet laugh（窃笑声）嘻嘻，嘿嘿 ➲ MORE LIKE THIS 3, page R25

teem /tiːm/ *verb* [I] (*usually* **be teeming**) (of rain 雨) to fall heavily 倾注；倾泻 SYN **pour**: *The rain was teeming down.* 大雨倾盆而下。◇ ***It was teeming with rain.*** 大雨如注。

PHR V **ˈteem with sth** (*usually* **be ˈteeming with sth**) to be full of people, animals, etc. moving around 充满，遍布，到处都是（移动着的人、动物等）: *The streets were teeming with tourists.* 大街上游人如织。◇ *a river teeming with fish* 盛产鱼的河流

teem·ing /ˈtiːmɪŋ/ *adj.* present in large numbers; full of people, animals, etc. that are moving around 大量的；充满（移动着的人、动物等）的；拥挤的： *teeming insects* 成群结队的昆虫 ◇ *the teeming streets of the city* 熙熙攘攘的城市街道

teen·age /ˈtiːneɪdʒ/ (*also informal* **teen** *especially in NAmE*) *adj.* [usually before noun] between 13 and 19 years old; connected with people of this age 十几岁的（指 13 至 19 岁）；青少年的： *teenage girls/boys* 十几岁的少女 / 少年 ◇ *teenage rebellion* 青少年的叛逆行为 ◇ *teen magazines* 青少年杂志 ➲ WORDFINDER NOTE AT AGE

teen·aged /ˈtiːneɪdʒd/ *adj.* between 13 and 19 years old 十几岁的（指 13 至 19 岁的）；青少年的： *They have two teenaged daughters.* 他们有两个十几岁的女儿。

teen·ager /ˈtiːneɪdʒə(r)/ (*also informal* **teen** *especially in NAmE*) *noun* a person who is between 13 and 19 years old（13 至 19 岁之间的）青少年，少男，少女： *a magazine aimed at teenagers* 以青少年为对象的杂志 ➲ WORDFINDER NOTE AT YOUNG

teens /tiːnz/ *noun* [pl.] the years of a person's life when they are between 13 and 19 years old 十几岁（13 至 19 岁之间）： *She began writing poetry **in her teens**.* 她从十几岁开始写诗。◇ *to be in your **early/late teens*** 现年十三四 / 十八九岁

teeny /ˈtiːni/ *adj.* (*informal*) (**teen·ier, teeni·est**) **1** (*also* **teeny-weeny** /ˌtiːni ˈwiːni/, **teensy** /ˈtiːnzi/, **teensy-weensy** /ˌtiːnzi ˈwiːnzi/) very small 很小的；极小的 SYN **tiny** ➲ MORE LIKE THIS 11, page R26 **2** connected with people between 13 and 19 years old 十几岁青少年的: *teeny magazines* 青少年杂志

teenybopper /ˈtiːnibɒpə(r); *NAmE* -bɑːp-/ *noun* (*old-fashioned, informal*) a young girl between the ages of about 10 and 13, who is very interested in pop music, fashionable clothes, etc. 时髦少女（喜好流行音乐和时髦服装，年龄在 10 至 13 岁之间）

tee·pee = TEPEE

ˈtee shirt = T-SHIRT

tee·ter /ˈtiːtə(r)/ *verb* [I] to stand or move in an unsteady way so that you look as if you are going to fall 摇晃；蹒跚行走；跟跄；摇摇欲坠： *She teetered after him in her high-heeled shoes.* 她穿着高跟鞋一步三晃地跟在他后面走。

IDM **teeter on the ˈbrink/ˈedge of sth** to be very close to a very unpleasant or dangerous situation 处在（灾难或危险）的边缘；濒临： *The country is teetering on the brink of civil war.* 这个国家正处在内战的边缘。

ˈteeter-totter *noun* (*NAmE*) = SEE-SAW (1)

teeth PL. OF TOOTH

teethe /tiːð/ *verb* [I] when a baby **is teething**, its first teeth are starting to grow（幼儿）出牙，长牙 ➲ WORDFINDER NOTE AT BABY

ˈteething troubles (*also* **ˈteething problems**) *noun* [pl.] small problems that a company, product, system, etc. has at the beginning（公司、产品、系统等的）初期遇到的小问题；创业阶段遇到的小麻烦

tee·total /ˌtiːˈtəʊtl; *NAmE* -ˈtoʊtl/ *adj.* never drinking alcohol 从不饮酒的；滴酒不沾的： *He's strictly teetotal.* 他绝对是滴酒不沾。 ▸ **tee·total·ism** *noun* [U]

tee·total·ler (*BrE*) (*US* **tee·total·er**) /ˌtiːˈtəʊtlə(r); *NAmE* -ˈtoʊ-/ *noun* a person who does not drink alcohol 不饮酒的人；滴酒不沾的人

TEFL /ˈtefl/ *abbr.* (*BrE*) teaching English as a foreign language 作为外语的英语教学

Tef·lon™ /ˈteflɒn; *NAmE* ˈteflɑːn/ *noun, adj.*

■ ***noun*** [U] a substance used especially to cover the inside of cooking pans, that stops food from sticking to them 特氟隆，聚四氟乙烯（不粘锅涂层材料）

■ ***adj.*** (especially of a politician 尤指从政者) still having a good reputation after making a mistake or doing sth that is not legal 扳不倒的（犯错误或违法后声誉不受损）： *The Teflon Prime Minister has survived another crisis.* 不倒翁首相又挺过了一次危机。

tel. (*also* **Tel.**) *abbr.* (in writing 书写形式) telephone number 电话号码

telco /ˈtelkəʊ; *NAmE* -koʊ/ *noun* (*pl.* **-os**) (used especially in newspapers 尤用于报章) a TELECOMMUNICATIONS company 电信公司： *Telcos were struggling to make money from broadband services.* 各家电信公司那时正努力通过宽带业务赢利。

tele- /ˈteli/ *combining form* (in nouns, verbs, adjectives and adverbs 构成名词、动词、形容词和副词) **1** over a long distance; far 远距离的；远的： *telepathy* 传心术 ◇ *telescopic* 望远的 **2** connected with television 电视的: *teletext* 图文电视 **3** done using a telephone 通过电话的: *telesales* 电话销售

tele·bank·ing /ˈtelibæŋkɪŋ/ *noun* [U] = TELEPHONE BANKING

tele·cam·era /ˈtelikæmərə/ *noun* a video camera used in VIDEOCONFERENCING（用于视频会议的）电视摄影机，远距离摄影机

tele·cast /ˈtelikɑːst; *NAmE* -kæst/ *noun* (*especially NAmE*) a broadcast on television 电视广播；电视节目 ▸ **tele·cast** *verb* (**tele·cast, tele·cast**) [usually passive]: **~ sth** *The event will be telecast simultaneously to nearly 150 cities.* 这一盛事将向近 150 个城市同时进行电视广播。**tele·cast·er** *noun*

tele·com·mu·ni·ca·tions /ˌtelikəˌmjuːnɪˈkeɪʃnz/ (*also informal* **tele·coms** /ˈtelikɒmz; *NAmE* -kɑːmz/) *noun* [pl.] the technology of sending signals, images and messages over long distances by radio, telephone, television, SATELLITE, etc. 电信；电讯： *technological developments in telecommunications* 电信技术的发展 ◇ *the telecommunications industry* 电信业 ▸ **tele·com·mu·ni·ca·tion** (*also informal* **tele·com** /ˈtelikɒm; *NAmE* -kɑːm/) *adj.* [only before noun]: *a telecommunication company* 电信公司

tele·com·mute /ˌtelikəˈmjuːt/ *verb* [I] to work from home, communicating with your office, customers and others by telephone, email, etc. 家庭办公，远距离工作（通过电话、电子邮件等与办公室、客户等进行联系） ▸ **tele·com·muter** *noun* SYN **teleworker** **tele·com·mut·ing** *noun* [U] SYN **teleworking**

tele·con·fer·ence /ˈtelikɒnfərəns; *NAmE* -kɑːn-/ *noun* a conference or discussion at which members are in different places and speak to each other using telephone and video connections 电话会议；电信会议；远程会议 ▸ **tele·con·fer·ence** *verb* [I] **tele·con·fer·enc·ing** /ˈtelikɒnfərənsɪŋ; *NAmE* -kɑːn-/ *noun* [U]

tele·film /ˈtelifɪlm/ *noun* a film/movie that is made specially to be shown on television 电视电影

T

tele·gen·ic /ˌtelɪˈdʒenɪk/ *adj.* a **telegenic** person looks good on television （人）适于拍摄电视的，适于上电视镜头的

tele·gram /ˈtelɪɡræm/ *noun* a message sent by TELEGRAPH and then printed and given to sb 电报（用电信号传递的信息）

tele·graph /ˈtelɪɡrɑːf; *NAmE* -ɡræf/ *noun, verb*
■ ***noun*** [U] a method of sending messages over long distances, using wires that carry electrical signals 电报（通信方式）
■ ***verb*** **1** [I, T] ~ **(sth)** to send a message by telegraph 发电报；用电报发送（电文）；电告 **2** [T] ~ **sth** to make it clear to people what you are going to do, often without intending to （无意中）流露（思想），泄露（动机）

tele·graph·ic /ˌtelɪˈɡræfɪk/ *adj.* connected with sending messages by telegraph 电报的；电报发送的： *You will need to arrange a telegraphic transfer from your bank to ours.* 你们得安排由你方银行将钱款电汇给我方银行。

ˈtelegraph pole (*BrE*) (*NAmE* **ˈtelephone post**) *noun* a tall wooden pole used for carrying telephone or telegraph wires high above the ground（电话或电报线路的）电线杆

tel·eg·raphy /təˈleɡrəfi/ *noun* [U] the process of sending messages by telegraph 电报通讯术

tele·kin·esis /ˌtelɪkɪˈniːsɪs; *BrE also* -kaɪˈn-/ *noun* [U] the ability to move objects without touching them, using mental powers 心灵致动；心灵遥感

tele·mark /ˈtelɪmɑːk; *NAmE* -mɑːrk/ *noun* [U] (in SKIING or SKI JUMPING 滑雪或跳台滑雪) a style of turning or landing with one SKI forward and bent knees 弓步式转弯；弓步单橇向前着地

tele·mar·ket·ing /ˈtelimɑːkɪtɪŋ; *NAmE* -mɑːrk-/ (*BrE also* **tele·sales**) *noun* [U] a method of selling things and taking orders for sales by telephone 电话销售；电话推销

tele·mat·ics /ˌtelɪˈmætɪks/ *noun* [U] the use or study of technology which allows information to be sent over long distances using computers 远程信息处理

tele·meter /ˈtelimiːtə(r)/ *noun* (*specialist*) a device for sending, receiving and measuring scientific data over a long distance 遥测装置；遥测仪 ▸ **tele·meter** *verb* : ~ **sth (to sth)** *Data from these instruments is telemetered to the laboratory.* 从这些仪器得到的数据用遥测仪传送到实验室。

tel·em·etry /təˈlemətri/ *noun* [U] (*specialist*) the process of using special equipment to send, receive and measure scientific data over long distances 遥测

tele·ology /ˌtiːliˈɒlədʒi; *NAmE* -ˈɑːlə-/ *noun* [U, sing.] (*philosophy* 哲) the theory that events and developments are meant to achieve a purpose and happen because of that 目的论（认为事物的发生和发展都是为了达到一定目的）▸ **teleo·logic·al** /ˌtiːliəˈlɒdʒɪkl; *NAmE* -ˈlɑːdʒ-/ *adj.*

tele·op·er·ate /ˌteliˈɒpəreɪt; *NAmE* -ˈɑːpə-/ *verb* ~ **sth (from sth)** to operate a machine which is not in the same place as you 远程操纵，遥控（机器）： *Equipment on the space station is teleoperated from earth.* 空间站上的设备是从地球遥控的。

tele·path·ic /ˌtelɪˈpæθɪk/ *adj.* **1** using telepathy 用传心术的；心灵感应的： *telepathic communication* 心灵感应交流 **2** (of a person 人) able to communicate by telepathy 会传心术的；有心灵感应的： *How do I know what he's thinking? I'm not telepathic!* 我怎么知道他在想什么？我又不会传心术！ ▸ **tele·path·ic·al·ly** /-kli/ *adv.*

tel·ep·athy /təˈlepəθi/ *noun* [U] the direct communication of thoughts or feelings from one person to another without using speech, writing, or any other normal method 传心术；通灵术；心灵感应

tele·phone /ˈtelɪfəʊn; *NAmE* -foʊn/ *noun, verb*
■ ***noun*** **1** [C, U] a system for talking to sb else over long distances, using wires or radio; a machine used for this 电话；电话机： *The* **telephone rang** *and Pat answered it.* 电话响起，帕特接了。◇ *You can reserve seats* **over the telephone**. 你可以打电话预订座位。◇ *I need to* **make a telephone call**. 我得打个电话。◇ ***telephone lines/networks/services*** 电话线路 / 网络 / 业务 ➲ COLLOCATIONS AT PHONE **2** [C] the part of the telephone that you hold in your hand and speak into （电话机的）受话器，听筒 SYN **handset, receiver** ➲ SEE ALSO PHONE *n.* (2)
IDM **be on the ˈtelephone 1** to be using the telephone 在打电话；在通电话： *He's on the telephone at the moment.* 他正在打电话。◇ *You're wanted* (= sb wants to speak to you) *on the telephone.* 有人打电话找你。 **2** (*BrE*) to have a telephone in your home or place of work（在家里或工作单位）装有电话机的： *We're not on the telephone at the cottage.* 我们的乡间别墅没有安装电话。
■ ***verb*** [I, T] (*formal, especially BrE*) to speak to sb by telephone 给某人打电话 SYN **call, phone**: *Please write or telephone for details.* 欲知详情，请来信或电话联系。◇ *He telephoned to say he'd be late.* 他来电话说要晚到一会儿。◇ ~ **sth** *You can telephone your order 24 hours a day.* 一天 24 小时你都可以打电话订购。◇ *I was about to telephone the police.* 我正要给警察打电话。➲ NOTE AT PHONE

ˌtelephone ˈbanking (*also* **ˈtele·bank·ing**) *noun* [U] activities relating to your bank account, which you do using the telephone 电话银行业务

ˈtelephone booth *noun* = PHONE BOOTH

ˈtelephone box *noun* (*BrE*) = PHONE BOX

ˈtelephone directory (*also* **ˈphone book**, **ˈtelephone book**) *noun* a book that lists the names, addresses and telephone numbers of people in a particular area 电话号码簿；电话簿： *to look up a number in the telephone directory* 在电话簿里查电话号码

ˈtelephone exchange (*also* **exchange**) *noun* a place where telephone calls are connected so that people can speak to each other 电话交换台；总机；电话局

ˈtelephone kiosk *noun* (*BrE*) = PHONE BOX

ˈtelephone number (*also* **ˈphone number**) *noun* the number of a particular telephone, that you use when you make a call to it 电话号码

ˈtelephone pole (*NAmE*) (*BrE* **ˈtelegraph pole**) *noun* a tall wooden pole used for carrying telephone or telegraph wires high above the ground（电话或电报线路的）电线杆

ˈtelephone tapping (*also* **ˈphone tapping**) *noun* [U] the practice of connecting a piece of equipment to a telephone in order to listen secretly to other people's telephone conversations 电话窃听

tel·eph·on·ist /təˈlefənɪst/ *noun* (*BrE*) = OPERATOR (2)

tel·eph·ony /təˈlefəni/ *noun* [U] the process of sending messages and signals by telephone 电话通讯

tele·photo lens /ˌtelifəʊtəʊ ˈlenz; *NAmE* -foʊtoʊ/ *noun* a camera LENS that produces a large image of an object that is far away and allows you to take photographs of it 摄远镜头；远距离照相镜头

tele·port /ˈtelipɔːt; *NAmE* -pɔːrt/ *verb* [I, T] ~ **(sb/sth)** (usually in SCIENCE FICTION) to move sb/sth immediately from one place to another a distance away, using special equipment; to be moved in this way（通常见于科幻作品）（被）远距离传送： *The search party was teleported down to the planet's surface.* 搜索队被传送到那个星球的表面。 ▸ **tele·por·ta·tion** /ˌtelipɔːˈteɪʃn; *NAmE* -pɔːrˈt-/ *noun* [U]

tele·print·er /ˈteliprɪntə(r)/ (*NAmE also* **tele·type·writer**) *noun* a machine that prints out TELEX messages that have been typed in another place and sent by telephone lines 电传打印机

tele·prompt·er /ˈteliprɒmptə(r); *NAmE* -prɑːm-/ (*especially NAmE*) (*BrE also* **Auto·cue™**) *noun* a device used by people who are speaking in public, especially on television, which displays the words that they have to say 电子提词器，自动提示器，讲词提示板（尤用于电视讲话时向说话人提示讲词）

tele·sales /ˈteliseɪlz/ (*BrE*) (*also* **tele·mar·ket·ing** *NAmE, BrE*) *noun* [U] a method of selling things and taking orders for sales by telephone 电话销售；电话推销

tele·scope /ˈtelɪskəʊp; *NAmE* -skoʊp/ *noun, verb*

▪ ***noun*** a piece of equipment shaped like a tube, containing LENSES, that you look through to make objects that are far away appear larger and nearer 望远镜：*to look at the stars through a telescope* 用望远镜观察星星 ➲ PICTURE AT BINOCULARS ➲ SEE ALSO RADIO TELESCOPE

▪ ***verb*** **1** [I, T] ~ (sth) to become shorter, or make sth shorter, by sliding sections inside one another （使）叠套缩短，叠缩 **2** [T] ~ **sth** (**into sth**) to reduce sth so that it happens in less time 缩短，精简，压缩（成…）：*Three episodes have been telescoped into a single programme.* 三集的内容被浓缩成了一个单独的节目。

tele·scop·ic /ˌtelɪˈskɒpɪk; *NAmE* -ˈskɑːpɪk/ *adj.* **1** connected with or using a telescope; making things look larger as a telescope does 望远镜的；望远的；放大的：*a rifle with a telescopic sight* 装有望远瞄准器的步枪 **2** made of sections that can slide into each other to make the object longer or shorter 可伸缩的；套叠的；套筒的：*a telescopic aerial* 可伸缩天线 ▸**tele·scop·ic·al·ly** /-kli/ *adv.*

tele·shop·ping /ˈteliʃɒpɪŋ; *NAmE* -ʃɑːp-/ *noun* [U] shopping that is done using the telephone or television 电话（或电视）购物

tele·text /ˈtelitekst/ *noun* [U] a service providing written news and information using television 图文电视；电视文字广播：*See if the results are* ***on teletext.*** 看看结果是否上了图文电视。

tele·thon /ˈteləθɒn; *NAmE* -θɑːn/ *noun* a very long television show, broadcast to raise money for charity（为募捐播放的）长时间的电视节目，马拉松式电视节目 ➲ WORDFINDER NOTE AT CHARITY ➲ MORE LIKE THIS 1, page R25

tele·type·writer /ˌteliˈtaɪpraɪtə(r)/ *noun* (*NAmE*) = TELEPRINTER

tele·van·gel·ist /ˌtelɪˈvændʒəlɪst/ *noun* (especially in the US) a person who appears regularly on television to try to persuade people to become Christians and to give money 电视福音布道者（在美国尤指定期在电视上劝人加入基督教及捐款者） ➲ MORE LIKE THIS 1, page R25 ▸**tele·van·gel·ism** *noun* [U]

tele·vise /ˈtelɪvaɪz/ *verb* [usually passive] ~ **sth** to broadcast sth on television 用电视播送：*a televised debate* 电视播送的辩论 ◇ *to televise a novel* 电视播送小说 ◇ *The speech will be televised live.* 这次演讲将由电视直播。

tele·vi·sion 🔑 /ˈtelɪvɪʒn/ *noun* (*abbr.* **TV**) **1** 🔑 (*also* **ˈtelevision set**) (*also BrE, informal* **telly**) [C] a piece of electrical equipment with a screen on which you can watch programmes with moving pictures and sounds 电视机：*a* ***colour television*** 彩色电视机 ◇ *a* ***widescreen television*** 宽屏幕电视机 ◇ *a* ***plasma screen television*** 等离子电视机 ◇ *to* ***turn the television on/off*** 打开 / 关闭电视机 **2** 🔑 (*also BrE, informal* **telly**) [U] the programmes broadcast on television 电视节目；电视：*We don't do much in the evenings except* ***watch television.*** 我们在晚上除了看电视不怎么干别的事。 ➲ WORDFINDER NOTE AT PROGRAMME **3** 🔑 [U] the system, process or business of broadcasting television programmes 电视系统；电视学；电视广播业：***satellite/terrestrial/cable/digital television*** 卫星 / 地面 / 有线 / 数字电视系统 ◇ *the television news* 电视新闻 ◇ *a television documentary* 电视纪录片 ◇ *a* ***television company/presenter*** 电视广播公司 / 节目主持人 ◇ *I'd like to work* ***in television*** (= for a television company). 我希望从事电视广播事业。 ➲ SEE ALSO CABLE TELEVISION, CLOSED-CIRCUIT TELEVISION

IDM **on** (**the**) **ˈtelevision** 🔑 (*also informal* **on TV**) (*also BrE, informal* **on the ˈtelly**) being broadcast by television; appearing in a television programme 电视播放的；上电视的；在电视上露面的：*What's on television tonight?* 今晚有什么电视节目？ ◇ *Is there anything good on the telly tonight?* 今晚电视有好节目吗？ ◇ *It was on TV yesterday.*

▼ **COLLOCATIONS 词语搭配**

Television 电视

Watching 观看

- **watch** television/TV/a show/(*BrE*) a programme/(*NAmE*) a program/a documentary/a pilot/a rerun/a repeat 看电视 / 电视节目 / 纪实电视节目 / 试播节目 / 重播的电视节目
- **see** (*especially BrE*) an ad/(*especially NAmE*) a commercial/the news/the weather 看广告 / 新闻 / 天气节目
- **catch/miss** a show/a programme/a program/an episode/the news 看 / 错过电视节目 / 电视连续剧的一集 / 新闻节目
- **pick up/reach for/grab** the remote (control) 拿起 / 伸手去拿 / 抓起遥控器
- **change/switch** channel 换频道
- **surf** (**through**)/(*especially NAmE*) **flip through**/(*especially BrE*) **flick through** the channels 快速浏览电视频道
- **sit in front of/switch on/switch off/turn on/turn off** the television/the TV/the TV set 坐在电视机前；开 / 关电视
- **have/install** satellite (TV)/cable (TV)/a satellite dish 有 / 安装卫星电视 / 有线电视 / 卫星电视碟形天线

Showing 播放

- **show** a programme/a documentary/an ad/a commercial 播放电视节目 / 纪实电视节目 / 广告
- **screen** a programme/a documentary 播放电视节目 / 纪实电视节目
- **run** an ad/a commercial 播放广告
- **broadcast**/(*especially NAmE*) **air/repeat** a show/a programme/a documentary/an episode/a series 播放 / 重播电视节目 / 纪实电视节目 / 电视连续剧的一集 / 系列节目
- **go out/air/be recorded** live 现场直播 / 录制
- **attract/draw** (**in**)/**pull** (**in**) viewers 吸引观众
- **be a hit with** viewers/audiences/critics 受到电视观众 / 观众 / 评论家的喜爱
- **get** (low/high) ratings 有（低 / 高）收视率

Appearing 演出

- **be on/appear on** television/TV/a TV show 在电视上 / 电视节目中露面
- **take part in** a phone-in/a game show/a quiz show/a reality TV show 参与热线直播节目 / 游戏节目 / 智力游戏节目 / 电视真人秀
- **host** a show/a programme/series/a game show/a quiz show/a talk show/(*BrE*) a chat show 主持电视节目 / 系列节目 / 游戏节目 / 智力游戏节目 / 访谈节目
- **be/become/work as** a(n) (*BrE*) TV presenter/talk-show host/sports commentator/anchorman/(*BrE*) newsreader 是 / 成为 / 当电视节目主持人 / 访谈节目主持人 / 体育运动实况解说员 / 新闻节目主持人 / 新闻播音员
- **read/present** the news 播报新闻
- **appear/perform** live (on TV) （在电视上）现场表演

Programme-making 节目制作

- **do/film/make** a show/a programme/a documentary/an episode/a pilot/a series/an ad/a commercial 拍摄电视节目 / 纪实电视节目 / 电视连续剧的一集 / 试播节目 / 系列节目 / 广告
- **work on** a soap (opera)/a pilot (episode)/a sitcom 制作肥皂剧 / 试播节目（的一集） / 情景喜剧
- **write/produce** a drama/sitcom/spin-off/comedy series 写 / 拍摄戏剧 / 情景喜剧 / 电视系列剧的派生作品 / 喜剧连续剧

T

昨天电视上播放了它。◇ *I recognize you. Aren't you on television?* 我认出你来了。你不是常上电视吗？

tele·vis·ual /ˌteliˈvɪʒuəl/ *adj.* relating to or suitable for television 电视的；适于电视的： *a major televisual event* 电视播放的大型活动

tele·work·ing /ˈteliwɜːkɪŋ; *NAmE* -wɜːrk-/ *noun* [U] (*BrE*) the practice of working from home, communicating with your office, customers and others by telephone, email, etc. 远程工作，远程操作（在家里工作，利用电话、电子邮件等与办公室、客户等联系） SYN **telecommuting** ▸ **teleworker** *noun* SYN **telecommuter**

telex /ˈteleks/ *noun, verb*

■ ***noun*** **1** [U] an international system of communication in which messages are typed on a special machine and sent by the telephone system 电传系统 **2** [C] a message sent or received by telex 电传；用户电报 **3** [C] (*informal*) a machine for sending and receiving messages by telex 电传机；电传收发机

■ ***verb*** [I, T] ~ (**sth**) to send a message by telex 发电传；以电传发出（电文）

tell /tel/ *verb* (**told, told** /təʊld; *NAmE* toʊld/)

• **GIVE INFORMATION** 提供信息 **1** [T] (of a person 人) to give information to sb by speaking or writing 告诉；告知： **~ sth to sb** *He told the news to everybody he saw.* 他逢人便讲这个消息。◇ **~ sb sth** *He told everybody he saw the news.* 他逢人便讲这个消息。◇ *Did she tell you her name?* 她告诉你她的姓名了吗？◇ ***What did I tell you?*** (= you should have listened to my advice) 我跟你说什么来着？◇ **~ sb** (**about sth**) *Why wasn't I told about the accident?* 为什么没人把这次事故告诉我？◇ **~ sb/yourself** (**that**)... *They've told us (that) they're not coming.* 他们已跟我们说过不来了。◇ *I **kept telling myself** (that) everything was OK.* 我不断告诉自己一切都没问题。◇ *Are you telling me you didn't have any help with this?* (= I don't believe what you have said) 你是说在这件事情上你没有得到过任何帮助吗？◇ **~ sb where, what, etc....** *Tell me where you live.* 告诉我你住哪儿。◇ **~ sb + speech** *'I'm ready to go now,' he told her.* "我现在可以走了。"他对她说。 ➲ NOTE AT SAY ➲ EXPRESS YOURSELF AT INFORMATION **2** [T] (of some writing, an instrument, a sign, etc. 文章、仪器、标记等) to give information about sth 提供（情况）；说明；显示： **~ sb sth** *The advertisement told us very little about the product.* 这则广告提供的产品情况很少。◇ **~ sb how, where, etc....** *This gauge tells you how much fuel you have left.* 这油表显示还剩有多少燃料。◇ **~ sb** (**that**)... *The sound of his breathing told her (that) he was asleep.* 她从他呼吸的声音中听出来他睡着了。

• **EXPRESS IN WORDS** 用言语表达 **3** [T] to express sth in words 讲述；说；表达： **~ sth** *to **tell stories/jokes/lies*** 讲故事；说笑话；撒谎 ◇ *Are you sure you're **telling the truth**?* 你说的真是实话吗？◇ **~ sb how, what, etc....** ***I can't tell you** how happy I am.* 我无法向你表达我多么高兴。

• **SECRET** 秘密 **4** [I] (*informal*) to let sb know a secret 泄露（秘密）；告发： *Promise you won't tell.* 你要保证不往外讲。◇ *'Who are you going out with tonight?' '**That would be telling!**'* (= it's a secret) "你今晚要和谁约会？" "那可不能讲！"（是个秘密）

• **ORDER** 命令 **5** [T] to order or advise sb to do sth 命令；指示；吩咐： **~ sb/yourself to do sth** *He was told to sit down and wait.* 有人吩咐他坐下等着。◇ *There was a sign telling motorists to slow down.* 有一个让汽车司机减速的指示牌。◇ *I kept telling myself to keep calm.* 我不断叮嘱自己要保持冷静。◇ **~ sb sth** *Do what I tell you.* 你要照我的吩咐做。◇ **~ sb** *Children must **do as they're told**.* 孩子们必须听话。◇ **~ sb what, when, etc....** *Don't tell me what to do!* 别跟我说该怎么办！◇ **~ sb** (**that**)... *The doctor told me (that) I should eat less fat.* 医生嘱咐我要少吃油腻。 ➲ SYNONYMS AT ORDER ➲ NOTE AT SAY

• **KNOW/JUDGE** 知道；判断 **6** [I, T] (not used in the progressive tenses 不用于进行时) to know, see or judge sth correctly 知道；看出；确切地判断： *I think he's happy. **It's hard to tell**.* 我想他是幸福的。这很难说。◇ ***As far as I can tell**, she's enjoying the course.* 据我判断，她喜欢这门课程。◇ **~** (**that**)... *I could tell (that) he was angry from his expression.* 从他的表情我看得出他生气了。◇ **~ how, if, etc....** *'That's not an original.' 'How can you tell?'* "那不是正本。" "你怎么知道的？" ◇ *The only way to tell if you like something is by trying it.* 要判定是否喜欢一件东西，唯一的办法是试一试。

• **DISTINGUISH** 辨别 **7** [T] (not used in the progressive tenses or in the passive 不用于进行时或被动语态) to distinguish one thing or person from another 识别；分辨；区分；辨认： **~ sth** *It was hard to **tell the difference between** the two versions.* 很难分辨出这两个版本有什么区别。◇ **~ A from B** *Can you tell Tom from his twin brother?* 你能分得出汤姆和他的孪生弟弟吗？ ◇ **~ A and B apart** *It's difficult to **tell them apart**.* 很难把他们区分开来。◇ **~ which, what, etc....** *The kittens look exactly alike—how can you **tell which is which**?* 这些小猫看上去一模一样，你怎么能分辨出哪只是哪只呢？

• **HAVE EFFECT** 有影响 **8** [I] **~** (**on sb**) to have an effect on sb/sth, especially a bad one 产生效果，发生影响（尤指负面影响）： *The strain was beginning to tell on the rescue team.* 过度的疲劳开始让救援队吃不消了。 ➲ MORE LIKE THIS 33, page R28

IDM **all ˈtold** with all people, etc. counted and included 合计；总共： *There are 52 people coming, all told.* 总共有52人要来。 **don't ˈtell me** (*informal*) used to say that you know or can guess what sb is going to say, especially because it is typical of them （用以表示知道或猜得出他人要说什么）不至于…吧，别又要说…了吧： *Don't tell me you were late again!* 你不至于又迟到了吧！ **I/I'll ˌtell you ˈwhat** (*informal*) used to introduce a suggestion 我的建议是；听我说： *I'll tell you what—let's stay in instead.* 听我说，咱们还是待在家里吧。 **I ˈtell you | I can ˈtell you | I'm ˈtelling you** (*informal*) used to emphasize what you are saying, especially when it is surprising or difficult to believe 我可以肯定地说；我敢说；确实： *It isn't cheap, I can tell you!* 我敢说，这并不便宜！◇ *I'm telling you, that's exactly what she said.* 我可以肯定地说，那正是她的原话。 **I ˈtold you** (**so**) (*informal*) used when sth bad has happened, to remind sb that you warned them about it and they did not listen to you 我提醒过你要出事；不听好人言，吃亏在眼前 **ˌlive, etc. to ˌtell the ˈtale** to survive a difficult or dangerous experience so that you can tell others what really happened 幸免于难之后向人讲述真实经历 **tell a ˈdifferent story/tale** to give some information that is different from what you expect or have been told 说的情况迥然不同；讲出来的是另一回事 **tell its own tale/story** to explain itself, without needing any further explanation or comment 不言而喻；不释自明；无须解释: *Her face told its own story.* 看她的面部表情，就什么都明白了。 **ˈtell me** (*informal*) used to introduce a question （用以引出问题）告诉我，跟我说实话： *Tell me, have you had lunch yet?* 跟我说实话，你吃过午餐没有？ **ˈtell me about it** (*informal*) used to say that you understand what sb is talking about and have had the same experience 你算说对了；的确： *'I get so annoyed with Steve!' 'Tell me about it. He drives me crazy.'* "史蒂夫把我烦透了！" "你算说对了。他快把我逼疯了。" **tell me aˈnother!** (*informal*) used to tell sb that you do not believe what they have said 不见得吧；我不相信；别瞎扯 **tell ˈtales** (**about sth/on sb**) to tell sb about sth that another person has done wrong 揭人短处；说长道短 ➲ RELATED NOUN TELLTALE **tell the ˈtime** (*BrE*) (*NAmE* **tell ˈtime**) to read the time from a clock, etc. （根据钟表等）说出时间；报时： *She's only five—she hasn't learnt to tell the time yet.* 她才五岁，还没有学会看钟表。 **tell sb where to get ˈoff/where they can get ˈoff** (*BrE, informal*) to make it clear to sb that you will no longer accept their bad behaviour 警告某人的行为不可容忍；不吃某人的这一套 **tell sb where to ˈput/ˈstick sth | tell sb what they can ˈdo with sth** (*informal*) to make it clear to sb that you are angry and are rejecting what they are offering you 别来这一套；让某人收起…的一套 **there's no ˈtelling** used to say that it is impossible to know what happened or will happen 无法知道；难以预料: *There's no telling how they'll react.* 说不准他们会有什么反应。 **to tell** (**you**) **the ˈtruth** (*informal*) used when admitting sth 说实话；老实说；说真的: *To tell the truth, I fell asleep in the middle of her talk.* 说实话，我在她讲话过程中睡着了。 **you can**

never 'tell | you never can 'tell (*saying*) you can never be sure, for example because things are not always what they appear to be 谁也拿不准；谁也说不清；很难说 **you're telling 'me!** (*informal*) I completely agree with you 我完全同意；的确如此 ➲ MORE AT HEAR, KISS *v.*, LITTLE *adj.*, THING, TIME *n.*, TRUTH

PHR V **ˌtell a'gainst sb** (*BrE, formal*) to be a disadvantage to sb 对…不利：*Her lack of experience told against her.* 她缺乏经验，这对她不利。 **'tell of sth** (*formal* or *literary*) to make sth known; to give an account of sth 公布；说明：*notices telling of the proposed job cuts* 公布拟裁员的通知 **ˌtell sb↔'off (for sth/for doing sth)** (*informal*) to speak angrily to sb for doing sth wrong 责备；斥责；责骂；数落 **SYN** **scold**：*I told the boys off for making so much noise.* 孩子们太吵，我把他们训斥了一顿。◇ *Did you get told off?* 你挨骂了没有？ ➲ RELATED NOUN TELLING-OFF **'tell on sb** (*informal*) to tell a person in authority about sth bad that sb has done 告发；打…的小报告；告…的状：*Promise not to tell on me!* 答应我，别告发我！

▼ **EXPRESS YOURSELF 情景表达**

Telling somebody to do something 让某人做某事

- *Could you wait here for a moment, **please**?* 请在这里等一会儿好吗？
- ***Would you** come through now?/**You can** come through now.* 你现在过来可以吗？/你现在可以过来了。
- ***Can you** send it up to my room, **please**?* 请把它送到我的房间里好吗？
- ***Just** sign here **for me, please**.* 请在这里给我签个名。
- ***I need you to** finish the report by Friday.* 我需要你在星期五之前把报告做好。
- ***Everyone has to** use the side entrance this week.* 本周所有人只能从侧门进出。
- ***You have to** sign these reports before submitting them.* 你提交这些报告之前必须在上面签字。

ˌtell-'all *adj.* [only before noun] (of a book, an interview in a newspaper or magazine, etc. 书或报刊上的访谈录等) in which sb, usually sb famous, admits sth that may shock people 坦白的，和盘托出的（通常指名人）：*a tell-all book/memoir/autobiography* 自我爆料的书/回忆录/自传

tell·er /'telə(r)/ *noun* **1** a person whose job is to receive and pay out money in a bank（银行的）出纳，出纳员 **2** a machine that pays out money automatically 出纳机；提款机：*automatic teller machines* 自动取款机 **3** a person whose job is to count votes, especially in a parliament（尤指议会投票时的）计票员 **4** (usually in compounds 通常构成复合词) a person who tells stories, etc. 说…的人；叙述者；讲故事的人；说书人：*a foul-mouthed teller of lies* 满嘴脏话的撒谎者 ➲ SEE ALSO FORTUNE TELLER, STORYTELLER

tell·ing /'telɪŋ/ *adj.* **1** having a strong or important effect; effective 强有力的；有明显效果的；显著的：*a telling argument* 有力的论据 **2** showing effectively what sb/sth is really like, but often without intending to 生动的；显露真实面目的，说明问题的（通常并非有意）：*The number of homeless people is a telling comment on the state of society.* 无家可归者的数量是社会状况的生动写照。▸ **tell·ing·ly** *adv.*

ˌtelling-'off *noun* [usually sing.] (*pl.* **tellings-off**) (*BrE, informal*) the act of speaking angrily to sb, especially a child, because they have done sth bad（尤指对儿童的）责备，责骂，数落，嗔怪

tell·tale /'telteɪl/ *adj.*, *noun*

■ *adj.* [only before noun] showing that sth exists or has happened 暴露实情的；能说明问题的：***telltale clues/marks/signs/sounds*** 能说明问题的种种线索/痕迹/迹象/声响 ◇ *The telltale smell of cigarettes told her that he had been in the room.* 那股明显的香烟味告诉她，他曾在这房间里待过。

■ *noun* (*BrE*) (*NAmE* **tat·tle·tale**) (*informal, disapproving*) a child who tells an adult what another child has done wrong 向大人告另一个孩子状的小孩儿；小告密者

tel·lur·ium /te'ljʊəriəm; *NAmE* te'lʊr-/ *noun* [U] (*symb.* **Te**) a chemical element. Tellurium is a shiny silver-white substance that breaks easily, found in SULPHIDE ORES. 碲

telly /'teli/ *noun* (*pl.* **-ies**) (*BrE, informal*) **1** [C] a television set 电视机 **SYN** **TV**：*He spends most evenings just sitting in front of the telly.* 他大部分晚上的时间都坐在电视机前。 **2** [U] the programmes broadcast on television 电视节目 **SYN** **TV**：*daytime telly* 日间电视节目 ◇ *Is there anything good on telly?* 电视上有好的节目吗？◇ *I don't want to **watch telly**.* 我不想看电视。

Tel·ugu /'teləgu:/ *noun* [U] a language spoken in Andhra Pradesh in SE India 泰卢固语（印度东南部安得拉邦的语言）

tem·blor /'temblə(r)/ *noun* (*NAmE*) an EARTHQUAKE (= a sudden, violent shaking of the earth's surface) 地震

tem·er·ity /tə'merəti/ *noun* [U] (*formal*) extremely confident behaviour that people are likely to consider rude 鲁莽；冒失；蛮勇：*He **had the temerity to** call me a liar!* 他竟敢说我撒谎！

temp /temp/ *noun, verb, abbr.*

■ *noun* a temporary employee in an office 临时雇员；临时工

■ *verb* [I] (*informal*) to do a temporary job or a series of temporary jobs 打临时工；做临时工作；打零工：*I've been temping for an employment agency.* 我一直在一家职业介绍所做临时工。 ➲ COLLOCATIONS AT JOB

■ *abbr.* (*also* **temp.** *especially in NAmE*) temperature 温度：*max temp 17°C* 最高温度 17 摄氏度

tem·per /'tempə(r)/ *noun, verb*

■ *noun* **1** [C, usually sing., U] if sb has a **temper**, they become angry very easily 脾气；易怒的性情：***a violent/short/quick, etc. temper*** 烈性子、急性子、火性子等 ◇ *He must learn to **control his temper**.* 他得学会捺住性子。◇ *She broke the plates in **a fit of temper**.* 她一气之下把盘子摔碎了。◇ *After an hour of waiting, **tempers began to fray*** (= people began to get angry). 等了一个小时后，大伙儿开始冒火了。 **2** [C, usually sing.] a short period of feeling very angry 怒气；火气；阵怒：*to **fly into a temper*** 勃然大怒 ◇ *She says awful things when she's **in a temper**.* 她一发脾气说话就难听。 **3** [C] the way that you are feeling at a particular time 心情；情绪；性情；心境 **SYN** **mood**：*Come back when you're in a better temper.* 心情好些时再回来。◇ *to be **in a bad/foul, etc. temper*** 心情不好、很坏等 **4 -tempered** (in adjectives 构成形容词) having a particular type of temper 有…脾气的；心情…的：***good-/bad-tempered*** 脾气好的/坏的 ◇ *a sweet-tempered child* 性情温和的小孩 **HELP** You will find other compounds ending in **-tempered** at their place in the alphabet. 其他以-tempered 结尾的复合词可在各字母中的适当位置查到。

IDM **lose/keep your 'temper (with sb)** to fail/manage to control your anger 发脾气；忍住怒火：*She lost her temper with a customer and shouted at him.* 她对一位顾客发了脾气，冲着他大喊大叫。◇ *I struggle to keep my temper with the kids when they misbehave.* 孩子们淘气时，我强捺住性子不发脾气。 ➲ MORE AT QUICK *adj.*

■ *verb* **1 ~ sth (with sth)** (*formal*) to make sth less severe by adding sth that has the opposite effect 使缓和；使温和：*Justice must be tempered with mercy.* 法外尚需施恩。 **2 ~ sth** (*specialist*) to make metal as hard as it needs to be by heating and then cooling it 使（金属）回火

tem·pera /'tempərə/ *noun* [U] a kind of paint in which the colour is mixed with egg and water; a method of painting that uses this kind of paint 蛋彩画颜料（用颜料与鸡蛋和水调和而成）；蛋彩画法

tem·pera·ment /'temprəmənt/ *noun* **1** [C, U] a person's or an animal's nature as shown in the way they behave or react to situations or people（人或动物的）气质，性

T

情，性格，禀性：*to have an artistic temperament* 有艺术家的气质 ◇ *a horse with an excellent temperament* 性情温顺的马 ◇ *She's a dreamer and a romantic* ***by temperament***. 她生性异想天开，浪漫多情。 **2** [U] the tendency to get emotional and excited very easily and behave in an unreasonable way 易冲动；（性情）暴躁；喜怒无常：*an actor given to displays of temperament* 性情喜怒无常的演员

tem·pera·men·tal /ˌtemprəˈmentl/ *adj.* **1** (*usually disapproving*) having a tendency to become angry, excited or upset easily, and to behave in an unreasonable way 喜怒无常的；容易激动的；反复无常的：*You never know what to expect with her. She's so temperamental.* 你永远说不清她要干什么。她一时一变。◇ (*figurative*) *The printer's being temperamental this morning.* 今天上午这台打印机时好时坏。 **2** connected with sb's nature and personality 气质的；性情的；性格的：*They are firm friends in spite of temperamental differences.* 他们尽管性格不同，但仍然友情甚笃。 ▸ **tem·pera·men·tal·ly** /-təli/ *adv.*：*I'm temperamentally unsuited to this job.* 我的性格不适合这种工作。

tem·per·ance /ˈtempərəns/ *noun* [U] **1** (*old-fashioned*) the practice of not drinking alcohol because of your moral or religious beliefs （由于道德或宗教信仰而实行的）戒酒，禁酒，滴酒不沾 **2** (*formal*) the practice of controlling your behaviour, the amount you eat, etc., so that it is always reasonable 自我克制；克己；节欲；节食 SYN **moderation**

tem·per·ate /ˈtempərət/ *adj.* **1** [usually before noun] (*specialist*) (of a climate or region 气候或地区) having a mild temperature without extremes of heat or cold 气候温和的；温带的 **2** (*formal*) behaving in a calm and controlled way 温和的；心平气和的；自我克制的 OPP **intemperate** ▸ **tem·per·ate·ly** *adv.*

ˈ**temperate zone** *noun* [C, usually sing.] (*specialist*) an area of the Earth that is not near the EQUATOR or the South or North Pole 温带

tem·pera·ture 🔑 /ˈtemprətʃə(r); *NAmE also* -tʃʊr/ *noun* [C, U] (*abbr.* **temp**) **1** 🔑 the measurement in degrees of how hot or cold a thing or place is 温度；气温：***high/low temperatures*** 高温；低温 ◇ ***a fall/drop in temperature*** 气温下降 ◇ ***a rise in temperature*** 气温升高 ◇ *The temperature has risen (by) five degrees.* 温度升高了五度。◇ *Heat the oven to a temperature of 200°C* (= degrees CENTIGRADE). 使烤箱的温度升至 200 摄氏度。◇ *Some places have had temperatures in the 40s* (= over 40° CENTIGRADE). 有些地方气温曾经超过 40 摄氏度。 ➲ SEE ALSO ABSOLUTE TEMPERATURE, ROOM TEMPERATURE **2** 🔑 the measurement of how hot sb's body is 体温：***to take sb's temperature*** (= measure the temperature of sb's body using a special instrument) 量体温 ◇ (*BrE*) *Does he* ***have a temperature*** (= is it higher than normal, because of illness)? 他发烧吗？◇ *She's* ***running a temperature*** (= it is higher than normal). 她在发烧。◇ *He's in bed with a temperature of 40°.* 他卧病在床，高烧 40 摄氏度。 HELP In *NAmE* you can *take sb's temperature* but in the other examples the word **fever** is used. 在美式英语中，可以用 take sb's temperature，但在其他几个示例中要用 fever 一词。 ➲ COMPARE FEVER (1)

IDM **raise/lower the ˈtemperature** to increase/decrease the amount of excitement, emotion, etc. in a situation 升 / 降温；增加 / 减少热烈程度等：*His angry refusal to agree raised the temperature of the meeting.* 他愤然拒不同意，使得会议的气氛紧张起来。

tem·pest /ˈtempɪst/ *noun* (*formal* or *literary*) a violent storm 大风暴；暴风雨；暴风雪

IDM **a tempest in a ˈteapot** (*NAmE*) (*BrE* **a storm in a ˈteacup**) a lot of anger or worry about sth that is not important 茶杯里的风暴；大惊小怪；小题大做

tem·pes·tu·ous /temˈpestʃuəs/ *adj.* **1** (*formal*) full of extreme emotions 激烈的；狂暴的；骚动的 SYN **stormy**：*a tempestuous relationship* 冲突不断的关系 **2** (*formal* or *literary*) caused by or affected by a violent storm 狂风暴雨的；大风暴的 SYN **stormy**：*tempestuous seas* 波涛汹涌的大海

tem·plate /ˈtempleɪt/ *noun* **1** a shape cut out of a hard material, used as a model for producing exactly the same shape many times in another material 样板；模板；型板 **2** a thing that is used as a model for producing other similar examples 样板；模框；标准：*If you need to write a lot of similar letters, set up a template on your computer.* 如果你需要写许多类似的信件，就在计算机上设一个模板。

tem·ple /ˈtempl/ *noun* **1** a building used for the worship of a god or gods, especially in religions other than Christianity （非基督教的）庙宇，寺院，神殿，圣堂：*the Temple of Diana at Ephesus* 以弗所的狄安娜神庙 ◇ *a* ***Buddhist/Hindu/Sikh temple*** 佛教 / 印度教 / 锡克教庙宇 ◇ (*NAmE*) *to go to temple* (= to a service in a SYNAGOGUE, where Jews worship) 去会堂礼拜 ➲ COLLOCATIONS AT RELIGION **2** each of the flat parts at the sides of the head, at the same level as the eyes and higher 太阳穴；鬓角；颞颥；颞部：*He had black hair, greying at the temples.* 他的头发是黑色的，但两鬓已见斑白。 ➲ VISUAL VOCAB PAGE V64

tempo /ˈtempəʊ; *NAmE* -poʊ/ *noun* [C, U] (*pl.* **-os**) **1** (*pl.* **tempi** /ˈtempiː/) the speed or rhythm of a piece of music （乐曲的）速度，拍子，节奏：***a slow/fast tempo*** 慢速；快速 ◇ *It's a difficult piece, with numerous changes of tempo.* 这支曲子节奏变化多，难度很大。 ➲ WORDFINDER NOTE AT SING **2** the speed of any movement or activity （运动或活动的）速度，节奏 SYN **pace**[1]：*the increasing tempo of life in Western society* 西方社会日益加速的生活节奏

tem·poral /ˈtempərəl/ *adj.* **1** (*formal*) connected with the real physical world, not spiritual matters 世间的；世俗的；现世的：*Although spiritual leader of millions of people, the Pope has no temporal power.* 教皇虽然是亿万人的精神领袖，但没有丝毫的世俗权力。 **2** (*formal*) connected with or limited by time 时间的：*a universe which has spatial and temporal dimensions* 有时空维度的宇宙 **3** (*anatomy* 解) near the TEMPLE(S) at the side of the head 太阳穴的；颞的：*the right temporal lobe of the brain* 大脑右颞叶

tem·por·ary 🔑 AW /ˈtemprəri; *NAmE* -pəreri/ *adj.* lasting or intended to last or be used only for a short time; not permanent 短暂的；暂时的；临时的：*temporary relief from pain* 短暂的解痛 ◇ *I'm looking for some* ***temporary work***. 我在找临时工作。◇ *They had to move into* ***temporary accommodation***. 他们不得不搬进临时住所。◇ ***a temporary measure/solution/arrangement*** 临时措施 / 解决办法 / 安排 ◇ *More than half the staff are temporary.* 半数以上的职员是临时雇员。 OPP **permanent** ➲ WORDFINDER NOTE AT WORK ▸ **tem·por·ar·ily** 🔑 AW /ˈtemprərəli; *NAmE* ˌtempəˈrerəli/ *adv.*：*We regret this service is temporarily unavailable.* 我们很抱歉暂时不能提供这一服务。 **tem·por·ari·ness** *noun* [U]

tem·por·ize (*BrE also* **-ise**) /ˈtempəraɪz/ *verb* [I] (*formal*) to delay making a decision or giving a definite answer, in order to gain time 拖延时间（不迅速作决定等）

tempt /tempt/ *verb* **1** to attract sb or make sb want to do or have sth, even if they know it is wrong 引诱；诱惑：**~ sb (into sth/into doing sth)** *I was tempted by the dessert menu.* 甜点菜单馋得我垂涎欲滴。◇ *Don't tempt thieves by leaving valuables clearly visible.* 别把贵重物品放在显眼处招贼。◇ **~ sb to do sth** *I was tempted to take the day off.* 我动了心，想那一天休假。 **2** to persuade or try to persuade sb to do sth that you want them to do, for example by offering them sth 劝诱；鼓动；怂恿；利诱：**~ sb (into sth/into doing sth)** *How can we tempt young people into engineering?* 我们怎么才能吸引年轻人学习工程学呢？◇ **~ sb to do sth** *Nothing would tempt me to live here.* 什么也吸引不了我到这里居住。

IDM **tempt ˈfate/ˈprovidence** to do sth too confidently in a way that might mean that your good luck will come to an end 玩命；冒险；鲁莽

temp·ta·tion /temp'teɪʃn/ *noun* **1** [C, U] the desire to do or have sth that you know is bad or wrong 引诱；诱惑：*the temptation of easy profits* 轻而易举获利的诱惑 ◇ *to* ***give way to/yield to temptation*** 经不住诱惑 ◇ *I couldn't* ***resist the temptation*** *to open the letter.* 我抑制不住好奇心把信打开了。◇ *Don't* ***put temptation in her way*** *by offering her a cigarette.* 别递烟来引诱她。 **2** [C] a thing that makes sb want to do or have sth that they know is bad or wrong 煽诱人的事物：*An expensive bicycle is a temptation to thieves.* 高档自行车对窃贼是个诱惑。

tempt·er /'temptə(r)/ *noun* a person who tries to persuade sb to do sth, especially sth bad or wrong 引诱者；诱惑者

tempt·ing /'temptɪŋ/ *adj.* something that is **tempting** is attractive, and makes people want to have it, do it, etc. 吸引人的；诱人的；有吸引力的：*It was a tempting offer.* 这是个诱人的提议。◇ *That cake looks very tempting.* 那蛋糕的样子让人嘴馋。◇ *It's tempting to speculate about what might have happened.* 大家不禁猜测，到底发生了什么事。 ▸ **tempt·ing·ly** *adv.*

temp·tress /'temptrəs/ *noun* (*old-fashioned* or *humorous*) a woman who TEMPTS sb, especially one who deliberately makes a man want to have sex with her 勾引人的女人；荡妇

tem·pura /'tempʊrə; tem'puːrə/ *noun* [U, C] a Japanese dish consisting of pieces of vegetables or fish that have been fried in BATTER (= a mixture of flour, egg and water) 天妇罗（日本食品，蔬菜或鱼裹面浆油炸而成）

ten 🔑 /ten/ *number* 10 十 HELP There are examples of how to use numbers at the entry for **five**. 数词用法示例见 five 条。

IDM **ˌten out of 'ten (for sth)** (*BrE, often ironic*) used to say that sb has guessed sth correctly or done sth very well 完全正确；得满分：*Not brilliant, Robyn, but I'll give you ten out of ten for effort.* 做得不算顶好，罗宾，但要论卖力气我给你打满分。 **ˌten to 'one** very probably 十之八九；非常可能：*Ten to one he'll be late.* 十之八九他会迟到。

ten·able /'tenəbl/ *adj.* **1** (of a theory, an opinion, etc. 理论、想法等) easy to defend against attack or criticism 说得过去的；站得住脚的：*a tenable position* 说得过去的观点 ◇ *The old idea that this work was not suitable for women was no longer tenable.* 认为这种工作不适合妇女的旧想法再也站不住脚了。 OPP **untenable** **2** [not before noun] (of a job, position, etc., especially in a university 尤指大学中的工作、职位等) that can be held for a particular period of time 可保有，可保持，可担任（一段时间）：*The lectureship is tenable for a period of three years.* 讲师这一职务任期三年。

ten·acious /tə'neɪʃəs/ *adj.* (*formal*) **1** that does not stop holding sth or give up sth easily; determined 紧握的；不松手的；坚持的：*a tenacious grip* 紧握 ◇ *She's a tenacious woman. She never gives up.* 她是个坚毅的人，从不放弃。◇ *The party has kept its tenacious hold on power for more than twenty years.* 这个政党已牢牢掌握大权二十多年。 **2** continuing to exist, have influence, etc. for longer than you might expect 顽强的；坚忍不拔的 SYN **persistent**：*a tenacious illness* 顽症 ▸ **ten·acious·ly** *adv.*：*Though seriously ill, he still clings tenaciously to life.* 他虽然病情严重，但仍顽强地活着。 **ten·acity** /tə'næsəti/ *noun* [U]: *They competed with skill and tenacity.* 他们竞争靠的是技术和顽强意志。

ten·ancy /'tenənsi/ *noun* (*pl.* **-ies**) **1** [C] a period of time that you rent a house, land, etc. for（房屋、土地等的）租用期限，租赁期限，租期：*a three-month tenancy* 三个月的租期 ◇ *a tenancy agreement* 租赁协议 ➲ COLLOCATIONS AT HOUSE **2** [C, U] the right to live or work in a building or on land that you rent（房屋或土地的）租用，租赁：*They had taken over the tenancy of the farm.* 他们承租了那个农场。

ten·ant /'tenənt/ *noun, verb*

▪ ***noun*** a person who pays rent for the use of a room, building, land, etc. to the person who owns it 房客；租户；佃户：*They had evicted their tenants for non-payment of rent.* 他们赶走了未交房租的房客。◇ *The decorating was done by a previous tenant.* 装修是一位前房客搞的。◇ *tenant farmers* (= ones who do not own their own farms) 佃农 ➲ WORDFINDER NOTE AT HOME ➲ COLLOCATIONS AT HOUSE

▪ ***verb*** [usually passive] **~ sth** to live or work in a place as a tenant（作为租赁者）居住，工作：*a tenanted farm* 租种的农场

tench /tentʃ/ *noun* (*pl.* **tench**) a European FRESHWATER fish 丁鲹（欧洲的一种淡水鱼）

tend 🔑 /tend/ *verb* **1** 🔑 [I] **~ to do sth** to be likely to do sth or to happen in a particular way because this is what often or usually happens 往往会；常常就：*Women tend to live longer than men.* 女人往往比男人长寿。◇ *When I'm tired, I tend to make mistakes.* 我累了就容易出错。◇ *It tends to get very cold here in the winter.* 这里冬天往往会很冷。◇ *People* ***tend to think*** *that the problem will never affect them.* 人们往往认为这个问题绝不会影响到他们。 ➲ LANGUAGE BANK AT GENERALLY **2** [I] **~ (to/towards sth)** to take a particular direction or often have a particular quality 趋向；走向；倾向；趋于：*His views tend towards the extreme.* 他的观点趋于偏激。◇ *Prices have tended downwards over recent years.* 近年来物价趋于下降。 **3** [T, I] to care for sb/sth 照料；照管；护理：**~ sb/sth** *a shepherd tending his sheep* 照看羊的牧人 ◇ *Doctors and nurses tended the injured.* 医生和护士护理受伤者。◇ *well-tended gardens* 精心照料的花园 ◇ **~ to sb/sth** *Ambulance crews were tending to the injured.* 救护车上的救护人员在照料受伤者。 **4** [T] **~ sth** (*NAmE*) to serve customers in a store, bar, etc. 招待，侍候，照顾，照料（商店、酒吧等的顾客）：*He had a job* ***tending bar*** *in San Francisco.* 他在旧金山做酒吧服务员。

ten·dency 🔑 /'tendənsi/ *noun* (*pl.* **-ies**) **1** 🔑 [C] if sb/sth has a particular **tendency**, they are likely to behave or act in a particular way 倾向；偏好；性情：*to* ***display*** *artistic, etc.* ***tendencies*** 显示出对艺术等的偏好 ◇ **~ (for sb/sth) (to do sth)** *I* ***have a tendency*** *to talk too much when I'm nervous.* 我紧张时总爱唠叨。◇ *There is a tendency for this disease to run in families.* 这种疾病易在家族里遗传。◇ **~ (to/towards sth)** *She has a strong natural tendency towards caution.* 她天生小心谨慎。 **2** 🔑 [C] **~ (for sb/sth) (to do sth)** | **~ (to/towards sth)** a new custom that is starting to develop 趋势；趋向 SYN **trend**：*There is a growing tendency among employers to hire casual staff.* 雇主雇用临时职员有增加的趋势。 **3** [C+sing./pl. v.] (*BrE*) a group within a larger political group, whose views are more extreme than those of the rest of the group（政党内的）极端派别

ten·den·tious /ten'denʃəs/ *adj.* (*formal, usually disapproving*) (of a speech, piece of writing, theory, etc. 演讲、文章、理论等) expressing a strong opinion that people are likely to disagree with 倾向性的；有偏见的；有争议的 SYN **controversial** ▸ **ten·den·tious·ly** *adv.* SYN **controversially** **ten·den·tious·ness** *noun* [U]

ten·der /'tendə(r)/ *adj., noun, verb*

▪ ***adj.*** (**ten·derer**, **ten·derest**) HELP **more tender** and **most tender** are also common * more tender 和 most tender 也常用。 **1** kind, gentle and loving 和善的；温柔的；亲切的；慈爱的：*tender words* 亲切的话语 ◇ *What he needs now is a lot of* ***tender loving care*** (= sympathetic treatment). 他现在需要的是充分的关心和爱护。 **2** (of food 食物) easy to bite through and cut 嫩的；柔软的：*This meat is extremely tender.* 这肉嫩得很。 OPP **tough** ➲ WORDFINDER NOTE AT CRISP **3** (of part of the body 身体部位) painful when you touch it 疼痛的；一触即痛的 SYN **sore** **4** easily hurt or damaged 易损坏的；纤弱的；脆弱的 SYN **delicate**：*tender young plants* 娇嫩的幼苗 ▸ **ten·der·ly** *adv.* **ten·der·ness** *noun* [U]

IDM **at a ˌtender 'age** | **at the tender age of...** used in connection with sb who is still young and does not have much experience 在少不更事的…岁时；在不谙世故的…岁上：*He left home at the tender age of 15.* 他 15 岁离家，

T

还少不更事。◇ *She shouldn't be having to deal with problems like this **at such a tender age**.* 她小小年纪涉世未深，实在不必应对这样的问题。

■ ***noun*** **1** a formal offer to supply goods or do work at a stated price 投标 SYN **bid**[1]: *Cleaning services have been **put out to tender*** (= companies have been asked to make offers to supply these services). 清洁工作已经对外招标。◇ *a competitive tender* 具有竞争力的投标 **2** a truck attached to a steam engine, carrying fuel and water（蒸汽机车的）煤水车 **3** a small boat, used for carrying people or goods between a larger boat and land（在大船和口岸之间载运人或货物的）供应船，补给船，交通船

■ ***verb*** **1** [I] ~ (**for sth**) to make a formal offer to supply goods or do work at a stated price 投标：*Local firms were invited to tender for the building contract.* 当地的公司被邀请投标承包建筑工程。**2** [T] ~ **sth** (**to sb**) (*formal*) to offer or give sth to sb 提议；提供；提出：*He has **tendered his resignation** to the Prime Minister.* 他已向首相递交辞呈。

ten·der·foot /'tendəfʊt; *NAmE* -dərf-/ *noun* (*pl.* **ten·der·feet** or **ten·der·foots**) (*NAmE, informal*) a person who is new to sth and not experienced 新手；初学者 SYN **greenhorn**

ˌtender-'hearted *adj.* having a kind and gentle nature 善良的；心肠软的；有恻隐之心的

ten·der·ize (*BrE also* **-ise**) /'tendəraɪz/ *verb* ~ **sth** to make meat softer and easier to cut and eat by preparing it in a particular way 使（肉）变嫩；使（肉）变软

ten·der·loin /'tendəlɔɪn; *NAmE* -dərl-/ *noun* [U] good quality meat from the back or side of a cow or pig（牛、猪的）里脊肉，嫩腰肉

ten·don /'tendən/ *noun* a strong band of TISSUE in the body that joins a muscle to a bone 腱 ➲ COLLOCATIONS AT INJURY

ten·dril /'tendrəl/ *noun* **1** a thin curling STEM that grows from a climbing plant. A plant uses tendrils to attach itself to a wall or other support.（攀缘植物的）卷须 ➲ VISUAL VOCAB PAGE V11 **2** (*literary*) a thin curling piece of sth such as hair 卷须状物（如鬈发）

tene·ment /'tenəmənt/ *noun* a large building divided into flats/apartments, especially in a poor area of a city（尤指城市贫困区的）经济公寓，廉租公寓：*a tenement block* 经济住宅街区

tenet /'tenɪt/ *noun* (*formal*) one of the principles or beliefs that a theory or larger set of beliefs is based on 原则；信条；教义：*one of the **basic/central tenets** of Christianity* 基督教的基本 / 主要信条之一

ten·fold /'tenfəʊld; *NAmE* -foʊld/ *adj., adv.* ➲ -FOLD

ˌten-gallon 'hat *noun* a large hat with a broad BRIM, traditionally worn by COWBOYS 高顶宽边帽（传统牛仔帽）

ten·ner /'tenə(r)/ *noun* (*BrE, informal*) £10 or a ten-pound note 十英镑；十英镑钞票：*You can have it for a tenner.* 你出十英镑，这就归你了。

ten·nis /'tenɪs/ (*also formal* **ˌlawn 'tennis**) *noun* [U] a game in which two or four players use RACKETS to hit a ball backwards and forwards across a net on a specially marked COURT 网球：*to **play tennis*** 打网球 ◇ ***a tennis player/tournament/club/court*** 网球运动员 / 锦标赛 / 俱乐部 / 场 ➲ VISUAL VOCAB PAGE V48

ˌtennis 'elbow *noun* [U] painful swelling of the elbow caused by too much repeated twisting of the arm 网球肘（胳膊经常扭动引起的肘部肿痛）

'tennis racket (*also* **'tennis rac·quet**) *noun* the RACKET that you use when you play tennis 网球拍

'tennis shoe (*NAmE also* **ath'letic shoe**) *noun* a sports shoe that is made of strong cotton cloth or leather 网球鞋

tenon /'tenən/ *noun* (*specialist*) an end of a piece of wood that has been cut to fit into a MORTISE so that the two are held together 雄榫；凸榫；榫头

tenor /'tenə(r)/ *noun, adj.*

■ ***noun*** **1** [C] a man's singing voice with a range just below the lowest woman's voice; a man with a tenor voice 男高音；男高音歌手 ➲ COMPARE ALTO *n.*, BARITONE (1), BASS[1] *n.* (2), COUNTERTENOR **2** [sing.] a musical part written for a tenor voice 男高音声部 **3** [sing.] **the ~ of sth** (*formal*) the general character or meaning of sth 大意；要旨；要领：*I was encouraged by the general tenor of his remarks.* 他话中的要点使我深受鼓舞。

■ ***adj.*** [only before noun] (of a musical instrument 乐器) with a range of notes similar to that of a tenor voice 次中音的：*a tenor saxophone* 次中音萨克斯管 ➲ COMPARE ALTO *adj.*, BASS[1] *adj.*, SOPRANO *adj.*

ˌten 'pence (*also* **ˌten pence 'piece, 10p** /ˌten 'piː/) *noun* a British coin worth ten pence 十便士硬币：*Have you got a ten pence piece?* 你有一枚十便士的硬币吗？

ten·pin /'tenpɪn/ *noun* **1** [C] any of the ten bottle-shaped objects that players try to knock over in the game of TENPIN BOWLING（十柱保龄球戏中的）瓶形滚柱，木瓶 **2** **ten·pins** [U] (*NAmE*) = TENPIN BOWLING

ˌtenpin 'bowling (*NAmE also* **ten·pins**) *noun* [U] a game in which players try to knock over tenpins by rolling a heavy ball at them, played indoors, especially in a BOWLING ALLEY 十柱保龄球戏 ➲ VISUAL VOCAB PAGE V44 ➲ COMPARE SKITTLE

tense AW /tens/ *adj., noun, verb*

■ ***adj.*** **1** (of a person 人) nervous or worried, and unable to relax 神经紧张的；担心的；不能松弛的：*He's a very tense person.* 他是个神经非常紧张的人。◇ *She sounded tense and angry.* 她的声音听起来又气又急。**2** (of a situation, an event, a period of time, etc. 形势、事件、时期等) in which people have strong feelings such as worry, anger, etc. that often cannot be expressed openly 令人紧张的（或焦虑的、满腹愤懑的等）：*I spent a tense few weeks waiting for the results of the tests.* 等候测试结果的这几个星期里我寝食不安。◇ *The atmosphere in the meeting was getting more and more tense.* 会议的气氛越来越紧张。**3** (of a muscle or other part of the body 肌肉或身体部位) tight rather than relaxed 绷紧的；不松弛的：*A massage will relax those tense muscles.* 按摩会使紧张的肌肉松弛。**4** (of wire, etc. 金属丝等) stretched tightly 拉紧的；绷紧的 SYN **taut** **5** (*phonetics* 语音) (of a speech sound 语音) produced with the muscles of the speech organs stretched tight 紧的；紧张音的 OPP **lax** ► **tense·ly** AW *adv.* **tense·ness** *noun* [U]

■ ***noun*** (*grammar* 语法) any of the forms of a verb that may be used to show the time of the action or state expressed by the verb（动词的）时，时态：***the past/present/future tense*** 过去 / 现在 / 将来时态 ➲ WORDFINDER NOTE AT GRAMMAR

■ ***verb*** [T, I] if you **tense** your muscles, or you or your muscles **tense**, they become tight and stiff, especially because you are not relaxed（使肌肉）拉紧，绷紧：~ **sth/yourself** (**up**) *She tensed her muscles in anticipation of the blow.* 眼看要挨打，她绷紧了肌肉。◇ *He tensed himself, listening to see if anyone had followed him.* 他竖起耳朵谛听是否有人跟踪。◇ ~ (**up**) *His muscles tensed as he got ready to run.* 他准备起跑时肌肉绷紧了。◇ *She tensed, hearing the strange noise again.* 再次听到那个奇怪的声音，她紧张起来。

IDM **be/get tensed 'up** to become or feel nervous or worried so that you cannot relax 变得神经紧张；变得焦虑不安

ten·sile /'tensaɪl; *NAmE* 'tensl/ *adj.* (*specialist*) **1** [only before noun] used to describe the extent to which sth can stretch without breaking 张力的；拉力的；抗张的：*the **tensile strength** of rope* 绳索的抗拉强度 **2** that can be drawn out or stretched 可拉长的；能伸长的；可延展的：*tensile cable* 可伸延的电缆

ten·sion 🔑 AW /'tenʃn/ *noun, verb*

■ ***noun*** **1** 🔑 [U, C, usually pl.] ~ (**between A and B**) a situation in which people do not trust each other, or feel unfriendly towards each other, and which may cause them to attack each other 紧张局势（或关系、状况）: *There is mounting tension along the border.* 边境局势日趋紧张。◇ ***international/racial/political tensions*** 国际紧张局势；种族间的紧张关系；政治上的紧张状况 **2** [C, U] ~ (**between A and B**) a situation in which the fact that there are different needs or interests causes difficulties 矛盾；对立: *There is often a tension between the aims of the company and the wishes of the employees.* 公司的目标和雇员的愿望之间经常存在矛盾。 **3** [U] a feeling of anxiety and stress that makes it impossible to relax（情绪上的）紧张，烦躁: ***nervous tension*** 神经紧张 ◇ *We laughed and that helped **ease the tension**.* 我们笑了，因而紧张的情绪得以缓和下来。 ➲ SYNONYMS AT PRESSURE **4** [U] the feeling of fear and excitement that is created by a writer or a film/movie director （作家或电影导演制造的）紧张气氛: *dramatic tension* 扣人心弦的紧张气氛 ◇ *As the movie progresses the tension builds.* 随着电影剧情的发展，气氛越来越紧张。 ➲ WORDFINDER NOTE AT PLOT **5** [U] the state of being stretched tight; the extent to which sth is stretched tight 拉伸；张力；拉紧状态；绷紧程度: *muscular tension* 肌肉绷紧 ◇ *Adjust the string tension of your tennis racket to suit your style of playing.* 调节网球拍的网张力，以配合你的打法。 ➲ SEE ALSO SURFACE TENSION

■ ***verb*** **~ sth** (*specialist*) to make a wire, sail, etc. tight and stretched（使金属线、帆等）拉紧，绷紧

ten·sor /ˈtensə(r); -sɔː(r)/ *noun* (*anatomy* 解) a muscle that TIGHTENS or stretches part of the body 张肌

tent /tent/ *noun* a shelter made of a large sheet of CANVAS, NYLON, etc. that is supported by poles and ropes fixed to the ground, and is used especially for camping 帐篷；帐棚: *to **put up/take down a tent*** 搭帐篷；拆帐篷 ◇ *to **pitch*** (= put up) ***a tent*** 搭帐篷 ◇ *Food will be served in the **hospitality tent*** (= for example at an outdoor show). 招待帐篷里会有食物供应。 ➲ SEE ALSO A-FRAME TENT, DOME TENT, FRAME TENT, OXYGEN TENT, PUP TENT, RIDGE TENT, WALL TENT

ten·tacle /ˈtentəkl/ *noun* **1** [C] a long thin part of the body of some creatures, such as SQUID, used for feeling or holding things, for moving or for getting food 触角；触手；触须: (*figurative*) *Tentacles of fear closed around her body.* 恐惧的阴影笼罩着她。 ➲ VISUAL VOCAB PAGE V13 **2 tentacles** [pl.] (*usually disapproving*) the influence that a large place, organization or system has and that is hard to avoid（大的地方、组织或系统难以避免的）影响，束缚，约束: *The tentacles of satellite television are spreading even wider.* 卫星电视的影响正日益扩大。

ten·ta·tive /ˈtentətɪv/ *adj.* **1** (of an arrangement, agreement, etc. 安排、协议等) not definite or certain because you may want to change it later 不确定的；不肯定的；暂定的: *We made a **tentative arrangement** to meet on Friday.* 我们暂定星期五见面。 ◇ *tentative conclusions* 初步结论 **2** not behaving or done with confidence 踌躇的；犹豫不定的；不果断的 SYN **hesitant**: *a tentative greeting* 怯声怯气的问候 ◇ *I'm taking the first **tentative steps** towards fitness.* 我试探性地开始实施健身计划。 ▶ **ten·ta·tive·ly** *adv.* **ten·ta·tive·ness** *noun* [U]

tent·ed /ˈtentɪd/ *adj.* consisting of tents; like a tent 由帐篷组成的；帐篷状的: *a tented village* 帐篷村

ten·ter·hooks /ˈtentəhʊks; *NAmE* -tərh-/ *noun* [pl.]
IDM (**be**) **on ˈtenterhooks** (*NAmE also* **be on ˌpins and ˈneedles**) (to be) very anxious or excited while you are waiting to find out sth or see what will happen 坐立不安；如坐针毡: *I've been on tenterhooks all week waiting for the results.* 整个星期我都在坐立不安，等待结果出来。
ORIGIN From **tenterhook**, a hook which in the past was used to keep material stretched on a drying frame during manufacture. 源自 tenterhook（拉幅钩），是过去把生产中的布料绷在干燥架上的一种钩子。

tenth /tenθ/ *ordinal number, noun*

■ ***ordinal number*** 10th 第十 HELP There are examples of how to use ordinal numbers at the entry for **fifth**. 序数词用法示例见 fifth 条。

■ ***noun*** each of ten equal parts of sth 十分之一 IDM SEE POSSESSION

ˈtent peg *noun* = PEG (2) ➲ PICTURE AT PEG

tenu·ous /ˈtenjuəs/ *adj.* **1** so weak or uncertain that it hardly exists 脆弱的；微弱的；缥缈的: *a tenuous hold on life* 命若游丝 ◇ *His links with the organization turned out to be, at best, tenuous.* 最后证实他与这个组织的关系充其量不过是不即不离罢了。 **2** extremely thin and easily broken 纤细的；薄的；易断的 ▶ **tenu·ous·ly** *adv.*

ten·ure /ˈtenjə(r)/ *noun* [U] **1** the period of time when sb holds an important job, especially a political one; the act of holding an important job（尤指重要政治职务的）任期，任职: *his four-year tenure as President* 他的四年总统任期 ◇ *She knew that tenure of high political office was beyond her.* 她知道自己与显赫的政治职位无缘。 **2** the right to stay permanently in your job, especially as a teacher at a university（尤指大学教师的）终身职位，长期聘用: *It's still extremely difficult to get tenure.* 要取得终身职位仍然极其困难。 **3** the legal right to live in a house or use a piece of land（房地产的）保有权，保有期

ten·ured /ˈtenjəd; *NAmE* -jərd/ *adj.* [usually before noun] **1** (of an official job 公职) that you can keep permanently 终身的；长期保有的: *a tenured post* 终身职位 **2** (of a person, especially a teacher at a university 尤指大学教师) having the right to keep their job permanently 获终身聘用的；享有终身职位的: *a tenured professor* 终身教授

tepee (*also* **tee·pee**) /ˈtiːpiː/ *noun* a type of tall tent shaped like a CONE, used by Native Americans in the past（美洲印第安人旧时使用的）圆锥形帐篷 ➲ SEE ALSO WIGWAM

tepid /ˈtepɪd/ *adj.* **1** slightly warm, sometimes in a way that is not pleasant 不冷不热的；微温的；温吞的 SYN **lukewarm**: *tepid tea* 温吞的茶 ◇ *a tepid bath* 温水浴 ➲ SYNONYMS AT COLD **2** not enthusiastic 不热情的；不热烈的 SYN **lukewarm**: *The play was greeted with tepid applause.* 这台戏只得到了零落的掌声。

te·quila /təˈkiːlə/ *noun* **1** [U, C] a strong alcoholic drink made in Mexico from a tropical plant 龙舌兰酒，特奎拉酒（墨西哥产的一种烈性酒） **2** [C] a glass of tequila 一杯龙舌兰酒

tera- /ˈterə/ *combining form* (in nouns; used in units of measurement 构成名词，用于计量单位) **1** 10^{12}, or 1 000 000 000 000 万亿，太（拉）（十进制，等于 1 000 000 000 000） **2** 2^{40}, or 1 099 511 627 776 太（拉）（二进制，等于 1 099 511 627 776）

tera·bit /ˈterəbɪt/ *noun* (*abbr.* **Tb, Tbit**) (*computing* 计) **1** a unit of computer memory or data, equal to one million million, or 10^{12} (= 1 000 000 000 000) BITS 万亿比特，太比特（十进制计算机内存或数据单位，等于 1 000 000 000 000 比特） **2** (*also* **tebi·bit**) a unit of computer memory or data, equal to 2^{40} (= 1 099 511 627 776) BITS 太比特（二进制计算机内存或数据单位，等于 1 099 511 627 776 比特）

tera·byte /ˈterəbaɪt/ *noun* (*abbr.* **TB**) (*computing* 计) **1** a unit of computer memory or data, equal to one million million, or 10^{12} (= 1 000 000 000 000) BYTES 万亿字节，太字节（十进制计算机内存或数据的单位，等于 1 000 000 000 000 字节） **2** (*also* **tebi·byte**) a unit of computer memory or data, equal to 2^{40} (= 1 099 511 627 776) BYTES 太字节（二进制计算机内存或数据的单位，等于 1 099 511 627 776 字节）

ter·bium /ˈtɜːbiəm; *NAmE* ˈtɜːrb-/ *noun* [U] (*symb.* **Tb**) a chemical element. Terbium is a silver-white metal used in LASERS, X-RAYS and television TUBES. 铽

ter·cen·ten·ary /ˌtɜːsenˈtiːnəri; *NAmE* ˌtɜːrsenˈtenəri/ *noun* (*pl.* **-ies**) the 300th anniversary of sth 三百周年纪念: *the tercentenary of the school's foundation* 建校三百周年纪念 ◇ *tercentenary celebrations* 三百周年庆典

ter·gi·ver·sate /ˈtɜːdʒɪvəseɪt; ˌtɜːdʒɪˈvɜːseɪt; *NAmE* tərˈdʒɪvərseɪt; ˈtɜːrdʒɪvərseɪt/ *verb* (*formal*) **1** [I] to make statements that deliberately hide the truth or that avoid

T

answering a question directly（说话）含糊其词，支吾，回避事实 **2** [I] to stop being loyal to one person, group, or religion and begin to support another 改变立场；背叛；变节 ▸ **ter·gi·ver·sa·tion** /ˌtɜːdʒɪvəˈseɪʃn; *NAmE* ˌtɜːrdʒɪvərˈseɪʃn/ *noun* [U, C]

teri·yaki /ˌterɪˈjɑːki; *BrE also* -ˈjæki/ *noun* [U, C] a Japanese dish consisting of meat or fish that has been left in a sweet sauce and then cooked 照烧（日本烹调方法，将肉或鱼加甜味酱汁烧烤）

term /tɜːm; *NAmE* tɜːrm/ *noun, verb*

■ ***noun*** ➲ SEE ALSO TERMS **1** [C] a word or phrase used as the name of sth, especially one connected with a particular type of language 词语；术语；措辞：*a **technical/legal/scientific, etc. term*** 技术、法律、科学等术语 ◇ *a term of abuse* 咒骂用语 ◇ *'Register' is the term commonly used to describe different levels of formality in language.* "语域"是一个术语，通常用以描述语言中用语的正式程度。 ➲ SYNONYMS AT WORD ➲ LANGUAGE BANK AT DEFINE **2** (*NAmE also* **tri·mes·ter**) [C, U] (especially in Britain) one of the three periods in the year during which classes are held in schools, universities, etc. 学期（尤用于英国，学校一年分三个学期）：*the **spring/summer/autumn/fall term*** 春季 / 夏季 / 秋季学期 ◇ *Many students now have paid employment **during term**.* 现在许多学生在上学期间就从事有薪工作。◇ (*BrE*) *It's nearly the **end of term**.* 学期快要结束了。◇ (*NAmE*) *the **end of the term*** 期终 ➲ SEE ALSO SEMESTER, TERMLY, TERM-TIME **3** [C] a period of time for which sth lasts; a fixed or limited time 期；期限；任期：*during the president's first **term of/in office*** 在总统的首届任期内 ◇ *He faces a maximum **prison/jail term** of 25 years.* 他面临 25 年的最高刑期。◇ *a long term of imprisonment* 长期监禁 **4** [sing.] (*formal*) the end of a particular period of time, especially one for which an agreement, etc. lasts 到期；期满：*the term of the loan* 贷款期限 ◇ *His life had reached its natural term.* 他已尽其天年。◇ (*medical* 医) *The pregnancy went to **full term*** (= lasted the normal length of time). 那次怀孕到了足月。 **5** [C] (*mathematics* 数) each of the various parts in a series, an EQUATION, etc.（数列、方程等的）项

IDM **in the ˈlong/ˈshort/ˈmedium term** used to describe what will happen a long, short, etc. time in the future 长 / 短 / 中期内：*Such a development seems unlikely, at least in the short term* (= it will not happen for quite a long time). 发生这样的情况看来可能性不大，起码短期之内应当如此。 ➲ MORE AT TERMS ➲ SEE ALSO LONG-TERM, MEDIUM-TERM, SHORT-TERM

■ ***verb*** [often passive] **~ sb/sth + noun/adj.** (*formal*) to use a particular name or word to describe sb/sth 把…称为；把…叫做：*At his age, he can hardly be termed a young man.* 到了这个年纪，他称不上是年轻人了。◇ *REM sleep is termed 'active' sleep.* 快速眼动睡眠称作"主动"睡眠。

ter·ma·gant /ˈtɜːməgənt; *NAmE* ˈtɜːrm-/ *noun* (*formal*) a woman who is very strict or who tries to tell people what to do, in an unpleasant way 苛刻的女人；专横的女人

ter·min·al AW /ˈtɜːmɪnl; *NAmE* ˈtɜːrm-/ *noun, adj.*

■ ***noun*** **1** a building or set of buildings at an airport where air passengers arrive and leave 航站楼；航空终点站：*A second terminal was opened in 2008.* 第二个航空站是 2008 年开始运营的。 ➲ WORDFINDER NOTE AT AIRPORT **2** a place, building or set of buildings where journeys by train, bus or boat begin or end（火车、公共汽车或船的）终点站：*a **railway/bus/ferry terminal*** 铁路 / 公共汽车终点站；渡船码头 **3** (*computing* 计) a piece of equipment, usually consisting of a keyboard and a screen that joins the user to a central computer system 终端；终端机 **4** (*specialist*) a point at which connections can be made in an electric CIRCUIT （电路的）端子，线接头：*a **positive/negative terminal*** 正极 / 负极端子

■ ***adj.*** **1** (of an illness or a disease 疾病) that cannot be cured and will lead to death, often slowly 晚期的；不治的；致命的：*He has terminal lung cancer.* 他患有晚期肺癌。◇ *The illness is usually terminal.* 这种病通常为不治之症。◇ (*figurative*) *She's suffering from terminal* (= very great) *boredom.* 她现在感到烦得要死。 ➲ WORDFINDER NOTE AT HEALTH **2** (of a person 人) suffering from an illness that cannot be cured and will lead to death 患绝症的；晚期的：*a terminal patient* 晚期病人 **3** certain to get worse and come to an end 不可救药的；无可挽回的：*The industry is **in terminal decline**.* 这个行业每况愈下，一蹶不振。 **4** [only before noun] (*formal* or *specialist*) at the end of sth 末端的；末梢的：*a terminal branch of a tree* 树顶枝条 ◇ *terminal examinations* (= at the end of a course, etc.) 期终考试 ▸ **ter·min·al·ly** /-nəli/ *adv.* : *a hospice for the terminally ill* 临终病人安养所 ◇ *a terminally dull film* 索然寡味的影片

ter·min·ate AW /ˈtɜːmɪneɪt; *NAmE* ˈtɜːrm-/ *verb* (*formal*) **1** [I, T] to end; to make sth end（使）停止，结束，终止：*Your contract of employment terminates in December.* 你的聘约十二月份到期。◇ **~ sth** *The agreement was terminated immediately.* 那项协议立即被终止了。 ◇ *to terminate a pregnancy* (= to perform or have an ABORTION) 终止妊娠（堕胎） **2** [I] (of a bus or train 公共汽车或火车) to end a journey/trip 到达终点站：*This train terminates at London Victoria.* 这趟列车的终点站是伦敦维多利亚火车站。

ter·min·ation AW /ˌtɜːmɪˈneɪʃn; *NAmE* ˌtɜːrm-/ *noun* **1** [U, C] (*formal*) the act of ending sth; the end of sth 结束；终止；末端；端：*Failure to comply with these conditions will result in termination of the contract.* 违反这些条款将导致合同终止。 **2** [C] (*medical* 医) a medical operation to end a PREGNANCY at an early stage 终止妊娠 SYN **abortion**

ter·min·ology /ˌtɜːmɪˈnɒlədʒi; *NAmE* ˌtɜːrməˈnɑːl-/ *noun* (*pl.* **-ies**) **1** [U, C] the set of technical words or expressions used in a particular subject （某学科的）术语：*medical terminology* 医学术语 ➲ SYNONYMS AT LANGUAGE **2** [U] words used with particular meanings 有特别含义的用语；专门用语：*The disagreement arose over a different use of terminology.* 分歧的缘起在于专门用语使用的不同。 ➲ SYNONYMS AT LANGUAGE ▸ **ter·mino·logic·al** /ˌtɜːmɪnəˈlɒdʒɪkl; *NAmE* ˌtɜːrmənəˈlɑːdʒ-/ *adj.*

ter·minus /ˈtɜːmɪnəs; *NAmE* ˈtɜːrm-/ *noun* (*pl.* **ter·mini** /ˈtɜːmɪnaɪ; *NAmE* ˈtɜːrm-/) the last station at the end of a railway/railroad line or the last stop on a bus route（铁路或公共汽车路线的）终点站

ter·mite /ˈtɜːmaɪt; *NAmE* ˈtɜːrm-/ *noun* an insect that lives in organized groups, mainly in hot countries. Termites do a lot of damage by eating the wood of trees and buildings. 白蚁：*a termite colony* 白蚁群

term·ly /ˈtɜːmli; *NAmE* ˈtɜːrm-/ *adj.* (*BrE*) happening in each of the periods that the school or college year is divided into 每学期的：*termly reports* 学期报告

ˈterm paper *noun* (in an American school or college) a long piece of written work that a student does on a subject that is part of a course of study（美国学校或大学的）学期论文

terms /tɜːmz; *NAmE* tɜːrmz/ *noun* [pl.] **1** the conditions that people offer, demand or accept when they make an agreement, an arrangement or a contract（协议、合同等的）条件，条款：*peace terms* 和平条件 ◇ ***Under the terms of the agreement**, their funding of the project will continue until 2015.* 根据协议条款，他们为这个项目提供资金，直到 2015 年为止。◇ *They failed to agree on the terms of a settlement.* 他们未能就和解的条件达成协议。◇ *These are the **terms and conditions** of your employment.* 这些是聘用你的条件。 **2** conditions that you agree to when you buy, sell, or pay for sth; a price or cost （交易的）条件；价钱；费用：*to buy sth **on easy terms*** (= paying for it over a long period) 按分期付款方式购买 ◇ *My terms are £20 a lesson.* 每教一堂课我收费 20 英镑。 **3** a way of expressing yourself or of saying sth 表达方式；措辞；说法：*We wish to protest in the **strongest possible terms*** (= to say we are very angry). 我们想要以最强硬的措辞抗议。◇ *I'll try to explain in simple terms.* 我会尽量讲得通俗易懂。◇ *The letter was brief, and **couched in** very polite **terms**.* 这封信内容简短，措辞特别客气。 ➲ SYNONYMS AT LANGUAGE

T

IDM be on good, friendly, bad, etc. 'terms (with sb) to have a good, friendly, etc. relationship with sb（与某人）关系好（或友好、不好等）: *I had no idea that you and he were on such intimate terms* (= were such close friends). 我还不知道你和他的关系这么密切。◇ *He is still on excellent terms with his ex-wife.* 他仍然和前妻保持着极好的关系。◇ *I'm on* ***first-name terms*** *with my boss now* (= we call each other by our first names). 现在我和老板交情很好，相互直呼其名。 **come to 'terms (with sb)** to reach an agreement with sb; to find a way of living or working together（与某人）达成协议，妥协 **come to 'terms with sth** to accept sth unpleasant by learning to deal with it 迁就顺从；接受（令人不快的事物）；适应（困难的处境）: *She is still coming to terms with her son's death.* 她还没有完全从儿子死亡的阴影中走出来。 **in terms of 'sth | in...terms** used to show what aspect of a subject you are talking about or how you are thinking about it 谈及；就…而言；在…方面: *The job is great in terms of salary, but it has its disadvantages.* 就薪金而言，这个工作倒是挺不错的，但也有一些不利之处。◇ *What does this mean in terms of cost?* 就费用而言，这意味着什么？ ◇ *In practical terms this law may be difficult to enforce.* 实际上，这条法规可能很难实施。◇ *The decision was disastrous in political terms.* 从政治上来看，这个决定是灾难性的。◇ *He's talking in terms of starting a completely new career.* 他正在谈论开创全新的事业。 **on your own 'terms | on sb's 'terms** according to the conditions that you or sb else decides 按照自己的条件；根据…的主张: *I'll only take the job on my own terms.* 我只会按照自己的条件接受这份工作。◇ *I'm not doing it on your terms.* 我不会按你的条件办的。 ➲ MORE AT CONTRADICTION, EQUAL *adj.*, SPEAK, UNCERTAIN

ˌterms of 'reference *noun* [pl.] the limits that are set on what an official committee or report has been asked to do（委员会或报告的）受委托权限，受权调查范围: *The matter, they decided, lay outside the commission's terms of reference.* 他们认定这个问题不在委员会受托权限之内。

'term-time *noun* [U] (*BrE*) the period of time when classes are held at a school, college, or university, as opposed to the holidays/vacations 学期（与假期相对而言） ▸ **'term-time** *adj.* [only before noun]: *Please give your term-time address.* 请提供你上学期间的住址。

tern /tɜːn; *NAmE* tɜːrn/ *noun* a bird with long pointed wings and a tail with two points that lives near the sea 燕鸥

ter·race /'terəs/ *noun* **1** [C] (*BrE*) (often in the names of streets 常用于街名) a continuous row of similar houses that are joined together in one block（相同的一排）排房，排屋: *12 Albert Terrace* 艾伯特排房 12 号 **2** [C] a flat, hard area, especially outside a house or restaurant, where you can sit, eat and enjoy the sun（尤指房屋或餐馆外的）露天平台，阳台: *a sun terrace* 阳台 ◇ *a roof terrace* 屋顶平台 ◇ *All rooms have a balcony or terrace.* 所有的房间都有阳台或露台。 ➲ SEE ALSO PATIO **3 terraces** [pl.] (*BrE*) the wide steps at a football (SOCCER) ground where people can stand to watch the game（足球场的）阶梯看台 **4** [C] one of a series of flat areas of ground that are cut into the side of a hill like steps so that crops can be grown there 梯田；阶地

ter·raced /'terəst/ *adj.* **1** (*BrE*) used to describe houses that form part of a terrace, or streets with houses in terraces 排房的；排屋的；排屋对着的街道的: *a terraced cottage* 排房式小屋 ◇ *terraced housing* 排屋式住房 ◇ *terraced streets* 排房对着的街道 **2** (of a slope or the side of a hill 斜坡或山坡) having a series of flat areas of ground like steps cut into it 梯田形的；阶地状的

ˌterraced 'house (*also less frequent* ˌ**terrace 'house**) (*both BrE*) (*NAmE* **'row house**, **town·house**) *noun* a house that is one of a row of houses that are joined together on each side 联排式住宅 ➲ VISUAL VOCAB PAGE V16

ter·ra·cing /'terəsɪŋ/ *noun* [U] **1** (*BrE*) an area with wide steps at a football (SOCCER) ground where people can stand to watch the game（足球场的）阶梯看台区 **2** a slope or the side of a hill that has had flat areas like steps cut into it 阶梯状坡地；阶梯形山坡

terra·cotta /ˌterə'kɒtə; *NAmE* -'kɑːtə/ *noun* [U] **1** reddish-brown CLAY that has been baked but not GLAZED, used for making pots, etc.（无釉的）赤陶土，赤陶 **2** a reddish-brown colour 赤褐色；土红色

terra firma /ˌterə 'fɜːmə; *NAmE* 'fɜːrmə/ *noun* [U] (*from Latin, usually humorous*) safe dry land, as contrasted with water or air 安全的陆地，坚实的大地（与水和空中相对而言） SYN **dry land**: *After two days at sea, it was good to be back on terra firma again.* 在海上度过两天之后，又回到使人觉得坚实的陆地，真是惬意。

terra·form /'terəfɔːm; *NAmE* -fɔːrm/ *verb* ~ **sth** to make a planet more like Earth, so that people can live on it 将（行星）地球化（以适合人类居住）

ter·rain /tə'reɪn/ *noun* [C, U] used to refer to an area of land when you are mentioning its natural features, for example, if it is rough, flat, etc. 地形；地势；地带: ***difficult/rough/mountainous, etc. terrain*** 难以通过的地带、崎岖不平的地形、山地等 ➲ SYNONYMS AT COUNTRY ➲ WORDFINDER NOTE AT EXPLORE

ter'rain park *noun* an outdoor area with special features designed for winter sports, especially SNOWBOARDING (= moving over snow on a special board) 地形公园（为单板滑雪等冬季户外运动特别设计的场地）

terra·pin /'terəpɪn/ *noun* a small TURTLE (= a REPTILE with a hard round shell), that lives in warm rivers and lakes in N America 水龟（生活在北美温带江河湖泊中） ➲ COMPARE TORTOISE

ter·rar·ium /te'reəriəm; *NAmE* -'rer-/ *noun* a glass container for growing plants in or for keeping small animals such as TURTLES or snakes in 生物育养箱；玻璃花园

ter·res·trial /tə'restriəl/ *adj.* **1** (*specialist*) (of animals and plants 动植物) living on the land or on the ground, rather than in water, in trees or in the air 陆地的；陆栖的；陆生的 **2** connected with the planet Earth 地球的；地球上的: *terrestrial life* 地球上的生物 ➲ COMPARE CELESTIAL, EXTRATERRESTRIAL *adj.* **3** (of television and broadcasting systems 电视和广播系统) operating on earth rather than from a SATELLITE 陆地上的，地面上的（与卫星相对而言）

ter·rible 🔑 /'terəbl/ *adj.* **1** 🔑 very unpleasant; making you feel very unhappy, upset or frightened 非常讨厌的；令人极不快的；可怕的: *a terrible experience* 令人极不愉快的经历 ◇ *What terrible news!* 多么骇人听闻的消息！ ◇ *I've just had a terrible thought.* 我刚刚产生了一个可怕的念头。 ➲ SYNONYMS ON NEXT PAGE **2** 🔑 causing great harm or injury; very serious 危害极大的；造成极大伤害的；非常严重的: *a terrible accident* 重大事故 ◇ *He had suffered terrible injuries.* 他受了重伤。 **3** 🔑 [not before noun] unhappy or ill/sick 不痛快；有病: *I feel terrible—I think I'll go to bed.* 我觉得难受，想去睡觉了。 **4** 🔑 (*informal*) of very bad quality; very bad 劣质的；劣等的；拙劣的: *a terrible meal* 劣质餐食 ◇ *Your driving is terrible!* 你的驾驶技术真是糟糕透了！ **5** 🔑 [only before noun] used to show the great extent or degree of sth bad 极度的；极其严重的: *a terrible mistake* 严重的错误 ◇ *to be in terrible pain* 处于极度痛苦之中 ◇ *The room was in a terrible mess.* 房间里脏乱不堪。◇ (*informal*) *I had a terrible job* (= it was very difficult) *to persuade her to come.* 为劝她来，我费尽了口舌。

ter·ribly 🔑 /'terəbli/ *adv.* **1** 🔑 (*especially BrE*) very 非常；很: *I'm terribly sorry—did I hurt you?* 非常抱歉，我伤着您了吗？ ◇ *It's terribly important for parents to be consistent.* 父母要做到始终如一，这是极为重要的。 **2** 🔑 very much; very badly 非常地；很厉害地: *I miss him terribly.* 我非常思念他。◇ *They suffered terribly when their son was killed.* 儿子遇难之后，他们悲痛欲绝。 ◇ *The experiment went terribly wrong.* 这次实验出了大问题。

ter·rier /'teriə(r)/ *noun* a small active dog. There are many types of terrier. 㹴（一种活泼的小狗） ➲ SEE ALSO BULL TERRIER, PIT BULL TERRIER, YORKSHIRE TERRIER

T

▼ SYNONYMS 同义词辨析

terrible

awful • horrible • dreadful • vile • horrendous

These words all describe sth that is very unpleasant. 以上各词均指事物令人不快的。

terrible very bad or unpleasant; making you feel unhappy, frightened, upset, ill, guilty or disapproving 指糟透了的、非常讨厌的、令人极不快的、可怕的、骇人的： *What terrible news!* 多么骇人听闻的消息！ ◇ *That's a terrible thing to say!* 说这话太难听了！

awful (*rather informal*) very bad or unpleasant; used to describe sth that you do not like or that makes you feel depressed, ill, guilty or disapproving 指很坏的、极讨厌的（用以形容令人沮丧、不舒服、内疚或不高兴的事物）： *That's an awful colour.* 那颜色难看得很。 ◇ *The weather last summer was awful.* 刚过去的夏季天气真糟糕。

horrible (*rather informal*) very unpleasant; used to describe sth that you do not like 指极坏的、十分讨厌的（用以形容令人不快的事物）： *The coffee tasted horrible.* 这咖啡难喝极了。

dreadful (*rather informal, especially BrE*) very bad or unpleasant; used to describe sth that you do not like or that you disapprove of 指糟糕透顶的、讨厌的（用以形容令人不快或反对的事物）： *What dreadful weather!* 多么讨厌的天气！

vile (*informal*) extremely bad or unpleasant 指糟糕透顶的、可恶的、极坏的： *There was a vile smell coming from the room.* 房间里传来令人恶心的气味。 ◇ *He was in a vile mood.* 他的心情坏极了。

horrendous (*rather informal*) extremely unpleasant and unacceptable 指讨厌得难以容忍的： *The traffic around the city was horrendous.* 城里的交通糟透了。

PATTERNS

- terrible/awful/horrible/dreadful **for** sb
- a(n) terrible/awful/horrible/dreadful/vile **thing**
- a(n) terrible/awful/horrible/vile **smell**
- terrible/awful/horrible/dreadful/vile/horrendous **conditions**
- terrible/awful/horrible/dreadful/vile **weather**
- terrible/awful/dreadful **news**

T

ter·rif·ic /tə'rɪfɪk/ *adj.* **1** (*informal*) excellent; wonderful 极好的；绝妙的；了不起的： *I feel absolutely terrific today!* 我今天的感觉真是好极了！ ◇ *She's doing a terrific job.* 她活儿干得真棒。 ➲ SYNONYMS AT GREAT **2** (*informal*) very large; very great 很大的；巨大的；异乎寻常的： *I've got a terrific amount of work to do.* 我有大量的工作要做。 ◇ *We drove along at a terrific speed.* 我们以极快的速度驱车行驶。

ter·rif·ic·al·ly /tə'rɪfɪkli/ *adv.* (*informal*) extremely (usually used about positive qualities) 极其，非常（通常用于正面性质）： *terrifically exciting* 极其令人兴奋

ter·ri·fied /'terɪfaɪd/ *adj.* very frightened 恐惧；很害怕： ~ (**of sb/sth**) *to be terrified of spiders* 惧怕蜘蛛 ◇ ~ (**of doing sth**) *I'm terrified of losing you.* 我真害怕失去你。 ◇ ~ (**that…**) *He was terrified (that) he would fall.* 他很害怕会跌倒。 ◇ ~ (**at sth**) *She was terrified at the thought of being alone.* 她一想到孤零零的独自一人就惊恐不安。 ➲ SYNONYMS AT AFRAID IDM SEE WIT

ter·rify /'terɪfaɪ/ *verb* (**ter·ri·fies**, **ter·ri·fy·ing**, **ter·ri·fied**, **ter·ri·fied**) ~ **sb** to make sb feel extremely frightened 使恐惧；使十分害怕；使惊吓： *Flying terrifies her.* 她害怕坐飞机。 ➲ SYNONYMS AT FRIGHTEN ▶ **ter·ri·fy·ing** *adj.* : *It was a terrifying experience.* 那是一次可怕的经历。 **ter·ri·fy·ing·ly** *adv.*

ter·rine /te'ri:n/ *noun* [U, C] a soft mixture of finely chopped meat, fish, etc. pressed into a container and served cold, especially in slices as the first course of a meal （罐装）肉糜，鱼酱

Ter·ri·tor·ial /ˌterə'tɔ:riəl/ *noun* (in Britain) a member of the Territorial Army （英国）本土防卫义勇军士兵

ter·ri·tor·ial /ˌterə'tɔ:riəl/ *adj.* **1** connected with the land or sea that is owned by a particular country 领土的： *territorial disputes* 领土争端 ◇ *Both countries feel they have territorial claims to* (= have a right to own) *the islands.* 两个国家都认为自己对这些岛屿拥有主权。 **2** (of animals, birds, etc. 兽、鸟等) guarding and defending an area of land that they believe to be their own 领域性的： *territorial instincts* 领域性本能 ◇ *Cats are very territorial.* 猫的领域性很强。 ▶ **ter·ri·tori·al·ity** /ˌterəˌtɔ:ri'æləti/ *noun* [U]: *the instinctive territoriality of some animals* 一些动物本能的领域性 **ter·ri·tori·al·ly** *adv.* : *The country was trying to expand territorially.* 这个国家在设法扩张领土。

the ˌTerritorial 'Army *noun* [sing.+sing./pl. v.] (*abbr.* **TA**) (in Britain) a military force of people who are not professional soldiers but who train as soldiers in their free time, now called the Army Reserve （英国）本土防卫义勇军，国防义勇军

ˌterritorial 'waters *noun* [pl.] the parts of a sea or an ocean which are near a country's coast and are legally under its control 领海

ter·ri·tory /'terətri; *NAmE* -tɔ:ri/ *noun* (*pl.* **-ies**) **1** [C, U] land that is under the control of a particular country or ruler 领土；版图；领地： ***enemy/disputed/foreign territory*** 敌方／有争议的／外国领土 ◇ *occupied territories* 被占领的土地 ◇ *They have refused to allow UN troops to be stationed in their territory.* 他们拒不允许联合国部队驻扎在他们的国土上。 ➲ WORDFINDER NOTE AT CONFLICT ➲ COLLOCATIONS AT WAR **2** [C, U] an area that one person, group, animal, etc. considers as their own and defends against others who try to enter it （个人、群体、动物等占据的）领域，管区，地盘： *Mating blackbirds will defend their territory against intruders.* 乌鸫交配时会保护自己的地盘，不允许外来者侵入。 ◇ (*figurative*) *This type of work is **uncharted territory** for us.* 我们从未涉足过这类工作。 ◇ (*figurative*) *Legal problems are Andy's territory* (= he deals with them). 法律问题由安迪负责处理。 **3** [C, U] an area of a town, country, etc. that sb has responsibility for in their work or another activity （某人负责的）地区： *Our representatives cover a very large territory.* 我们的代理人负责的地区很广。 **4** [U] a particular type of land （某类）地区；（某种）地方： *unexplored territory* 未勘察地区 ➲ WORDFINDER NOTE AT EXPLORE **5** (*also* **Territory**) [C] a country or an area that is part of the US, Australia or Canada but is not a state or PROVINCE （美国）准州；（澳大利亚）地区；（加拿大）地区： *Guam and American Samoa are US territories.* 关岛和美属萨摩亚是美国的准州。

IDM **ˌcome/ˌgo with the 'territory** to be a normal and accepted part of a particular job, situation, etc. 成为必然的部分（或结果）： *She has to work late most days, but in her kind of job that goes with the territory.* 她在大部分日子里都得加班，但根据她的工作性质，这是不可避免的。 ➲ MORE AT NEUTRAL *adj.*

ter·ror /'terə(r)/ *noun* **1** [U, sing.] a feeling of extreme fear 惊恐；恐惧；惊骇： *a feeling of **sheer/pure terror*** 胆战心惊 ◇ *Her eyes were wild with terror.* 她的眼睛里充满了恐惧。 ◇ *People fled from the explosion **in terror**.* 人们惊恐地逃离爆炸现场。 ◇ *She **lives in terror of*** (= is constantly afraid of) *losing her job.* 她一直胆战心惊地害怕丢了工作。 ◇ *Some women have a terror of losing control in the birth process.* 有些妇女惧怕在分娩过程中失去控制。 ◇ (*literary*) *The very name of the enemy **struck terror into** their hearts.* 他们一听到敌人的名字就心惊胆战。 ➲ SYNONYMS AT FEAR **2** [C] a person, situation or thing that makes you very afraid 可怕的人；恐怖的事；可怕的情况： *These street gangs have become the terror of the neighbourhood.* 这些街头少年团伙使得周围邻里谈之色变。 ◇ *Death **holds no terrors for*** (= does not frighten or worry) *me.* 死神是吓不倒我的。 ◇ *The terrors of the night were past.* 夜间那些恐怖的事情都已经成为过去。 **3** [U] violent action or the threat of violent action that is intended to cause fear, usually for political purposes（通常出于政治目的）恐怖行动，恐怖 SYN **terrorism**: *a campaign of terror* 恐怖运动 ◇ *terror tactics* 恐怖手段 ➲ SEE ALSO REIGN OF TERROR **4** [C] (*informal*) a person (usually a child) or an animal that causes you trouble or is difficult to control 讨厌鬼；小捣蛋：*Their kids are real little terrors.* 他们的小孩都是十足的讨厌鬼。

ter·ror·ism /ˈterərɪzəm/ *noun* [U] the use of violent action in order to achieve political aims or to force a government to act 恐怖主义：*an act of terrorism* 恐怖主义行动 ➲ WORDFINDER NOTE AT ATTACK ➲ COLLOCATIONS AT CRIME

ter·ror·ist /ˈterərɪst/ *noun* a person who takes part in terrorism 恐怖主义者；恐怖分子：*The terrorists are threatening to blow up the plane.* 恐怖分子扬言要炸毁飞机。◇ *a* ***terrorist attack/bomb/group*** 恐怖分子的袭击 / 炸弹 / 团体

ter·ror·ize (*BrE also* **-ise**) /ˈterəraɪz/ *verb* to frighten and threaten people so that they will not oppose sth or will do as they are told 恐吓；恫吓；威胁：**~ sb** *drug dealers terrorizing the neighbourhood* 使附近地区人心惶惶的毒品贩子 ◇ **~ sb into doing sth** *People were terrorized into leaving their homes.* 人们在恫吓之下离开家园。

ˈ**terror-stricken** *adj.* extremely frightened 胆战心惊的；惊恐万状的

terry /ˈteri/ *noun* [U] a type of soft cotton cloth that absorbs liquids and has a surface covered with raised LOOPS of thread, used especially for making towels 毛圈棉织物（多用以做毛巾）

terse /tɜːs; *NAmE* tɜːrs/ *adj.* using few words and often not seeming polite or friendly 简要的；简短生硬的：*a terse style* 生硬冷漠的风格 ◇ *The President issued a terse statement denying the charges.* 总统发表了一份简短的声明，否认那些指控。▶ **terse·ly** *adv.* **terse·ness** *noun* [U]

ter·tiary /ˈtɜːʃəri; *NAmE* ˈtɜːrʃieri; -ʃəri/ *adj.* third in order, rank or importance 第三的；第三位的；第三级的：*the tertiary sector* (= the area of industry that deals with services rather than materials or goods) 第三产业部门 ◇ (*BrE*) *tertiary education* (= at university or college level) 高等教育 ➲ COMPARE PRIMARY *adj.*, SECONDARY ➲ WORDFINDER NOTE AT STUDY

ˈ**tertiary college** *noun* (in Britain) a college that provides education for people aged 16 and older, but that is not a university 职业专科学校（英国为 16 岁以上的人提供教育的学院，但并非大学）

ˈ**tertiary industry** (*also* ˈ**service industry**) *noun* [U, C] (*economics* 经) the part of a country's economy that provides services 第三产业；服务业 ➲ COMPARE PRIMARY INDUSTRY, SECONDARY INDUSTRY

TESL /ˈtesl/ *abbr.* teaching English as a second language 作为第二语言的英语教学

TESOL /ˈtiːsɒl; ˈtesɒl; *NAmE* -sɑːl; -sɔːl/ *abbr.* **1** teaching English to speakers of other languages 对母语为非英语人士的英语教学 **2** (*NAmE*) teachers of English to speakers of other languages (an organization of teachers) 国际英语教师协会

tes·sel·lated /ˈtesəleɪtɪd/ *adj.* (*specialist*) made from small flat pieces arranged in a pattern 镶嵌铺面小块的；镶嵌花样的：*a tessellated pavement* 嵌花地面

test 🔑 /test/ *noun, verb*

■ *noun*

• **OF KNOWLEDGE/ABILITY** 知识；能力 **1** 🔑 an examination of sb's knowledge or ability, consisting of questions for them to answer or activities for them to perform 测验；考查：*an IQ/intelligence/aptitude test* 智商 / 智力 / 能力倾向测验 ◇ *to* ***take a test*** 参加测验 ◇ (*BrE*) *to* ***do a test*** 参加测验 ◇ **~ (on sth)** *a test on irregular verbs* 不规则动词测验 ◇ *to* ***pass/fail a test*** 通过 / 没有通过测验 ◇ (*BrE*) *a good mark* ***in the test*** 测验中取得的高分 ◇ (*NAmE*) *a good grade* ***on the test*** 优良的测验成绩 ➲ COLLOCATIONS AT EDUCATION ➲ NOTE AT EXAM ➲ SEE ALSO DRIVING TEST

• **OF HEALTH** 健康 **2** 🔑 a medical examination to discover what is wrong with you or to check the condition of your health（医疗上的）检查，化验，检验：*a test for AIDS* 艾滋病化验 ◇ *an eye test* 眼睛检查 ◇ *a pregnancy test* 妊娠检验 ◇ *When can I get my* ***test results****?* 我什么时候可以拿到化验结果？➲ SEE ALSO BLOOD TEST, BREATH TEST ➲ WORDFINDER NOTE AT EXAMINE

• **OF MACHINE/PRODUCT, ETC.** 机器、产品等 **3** 🔑 an experiment to discover whether or how well sth works, or to find out more information about it 试验；测试：*laboratory tests* 实验室测试 ◇ *a nuclear test* 核试验 ◇ *Tests have shown high levels of pollutants in the water.* 测试显示水中污染物质的含量很高。◇ *I'll run a diagnostic test to see why the server keeps crashing.* 我要做诊断测试，弄清为什么服务器总是不断地发生故障。➲ SEE ALSO ACID TEST, BLIND TEST, FIELD TEST at FIELD-TEST, MEANS TEST, ROAD TEST

• **OF STRENGTH, ETC.** 实力等 **4** a situation or an event that shows how good, strong, etc. sb/sth is 检验；考验：*The local elections will be a good test of the government's popularity.* 地方选举将是检验政府是否得人心的一个很好的试金石。

• **IN CRICKET, ETC.** 板球等 **5 Test** = TEST MATCH

IDM **put sb/sth to the** ˈ**test** to put sb/sth in a situation which will show what their or its true qualities are 使受考验；使受检验：*His theories have never really been put to the test.* 他的理论从未真正经受过检验。**stand the test of** ˈ**time** to prove to be good, popular, etc. over a long period of time 经得起时间的考验 ➲ MORE AT TEACH

■ *verb*

• **KNOWLEDGE/ABILITY** 知识；能力 **1** 🔑 [T, I] to find out how much sb knows, or what they can do by asking them questions or giving them activities to perform 测验；考查：**~ sb (on sth)** *Children are tested on core subjects at ages 7, 11 and 14.* 儿童在 7、11 和 14 岁时要接受核心课程的测验。◇ **~ (sth)** *We test your English before deciding which class to put you in.* 我们测验过你的英语后再决定把你分在哪一班。◇ *Schools use various methods of testing.* 学校采用各种各样的测试方法。 **2** [I] **~ well/badly** to perform well/badly in a test of knowledge or ability 在知识或能力测试中表现不错 / 糟糕：*students who tested well in reading* 阅读测试考得好的学生

• **HEALTH** 健康 **3** 🔑 [T, I] to examine the blood, a part of the body, etc. to find out what is wrong with a person, or to check the condition of their health 试验；检查；化验：**~ sb/sth** *to test sb's eyesight/hearing* 检查某人的视力 / 听力 ◇ **~ sb/sth for sth** *The doctor tested him for hepatitis.* 医生对他进行了肝炎病检查。◇ **+ adj. (for sth)** *to* ***test positive/negative*** 化验呈阳性 / 阴性 ◇ *Two athletes tested positive for steroids.* 两名运动员的类固醇试验呈阳性。

• **MACHINE/PRODUCT, ETC.** 机器、产品等 **4** 🔑 [T] to use or try a machine, substance, etc. to find out how well it works or to find out more information about it 试验；检验；测试：**~ sth** *Test your brakes regularly.* 要定期检验刹车。◇ **~ sth on sb/sth** *Our beauty products are not tested on animals.* 我们的美容产品不进行动物试验。◇ **~ sth for sth** *The water is regularly tested for purity.* 水的纯度定期受到检测。◇ **~ sth out** *They opened a single store in Europe to test out the market.* 他们在欧洲只开了一家商店，检验一下市场情况。➲ SEE ALSO FIELD-TEST **5** [I] **~ well/badly** (of a machine or product) to perform well/badly in a test of how well it works （机器或产品）测试结果良好 / 很差：*The ad had tested badly with consumers.* 测试结果表明消费者对这则广告的评价很差。

• **STRENGTH, ETC.** 实力等 **6** [T] **~ sb/sth** to be difficult and therefore need all your strength, ability, etc. 考验；检验：*The long climb tested our fitness and stamina.* 那次长距离爬山是对我们健康状况和耐力的考验。➲ SEE ALSO TESTING *n.*

IDM **test the** ˈ**waters** to find out what the situation is before doing sth or making a decision 摸清底细 ➲ MORE AT TRIED

PHR V ˈ**test for sth** | ˈ**test sth for sth** to examine sth to see if a particular substance, etc. is present 化验；检验；测试鉴定某物：*testing for oil* 化验确定是否含油 ◇ *The*

T

software has been tested for viruses. 这个软件已经过是否有病毒的测试。

test·able /ˈtestəbl/ *adj.* that can be tested 可检验的；可试验的；可验证的：*testable hypotheses* 可验证的假说

tes·ta·ment /ˈtestəmənt/ *noun* (*formal*) **1** [C, usually sing., U] ~ (**to sth**) a thing that shows that sth else exists or is true 证据；证明 SYN **testimony**: *The new model is a testament to the skill and dedication of the workforce.* 这种新型产品显示了全体员工的技术水平和敬业精神。 **2** [C] = WILL (3)：*This is the last will and testament of…* 这是…的临终遗嘱。 ➲ SEE ALSO NEW TESTAMENT, OLD TESTAMENT

ˈtest ban *noun* an agreement between countries to stop testing nuclear weapons 禁止核试验协定：*a test ban treaty* 禁止核试验条约

ˈtest bed *noun* a piece of equipment used for testing new machinery, especially aircraft engines 试验台；（尤指飞机发动机的）试验台架：(*figurative*) *The country is an ideal test bed for emerging technologies.* 这个国家是一个理想的新兴技术试验场。

ˈtest case *noun* a legal case or other situation whose result will be used as an example when decisions are being made on similar cases in the future（判决同类案件可援用的）判例

ˈtest drive *noun* an occasion when you drive a vehicle that you are thinking of buying so that you can see how well it works and if you like it（对想购买的车进行的）试验驾驶，试驾 ▶ **ˈtest-drive** *verb* ~ **sth**

test·er /ˈtestə(r)/ *noun* **1** a person or thing that tests sth 测试员；试验员；测试器；测试仪：*testers of new software* 新软件测试员 **2** a small container of a product, such as PERFUME, that you can try in a shop/store to see if you like it（商店里的）小包装试用品（如香水）

tes·tes PL. OF TESTIS

ˈtest flight *noun* a flight during which an aircraft or part of its equipment is tested （飞机的）试飞

tes·ticle /ˈtestɪkl/ *noun* either of the two organs that produce SPERM, located in a bag of skin below the PENIS 睾丸 ▶ **tes·ticu·lar** /tesˈtɪkjələ(r)/ *adj.* [only before noun]: *testicular cancer* 睾丸癌

test·ify /ˈtestɪfaɪ/ *verb* (**testi·fies, testi·fy·ing, testi·fied, testi·fied**) **1** [I, T] to make a statement that sth happened or that sth is true, especially as a witness in court （尤指出庭）作证：~ (**against/for sb**) *She refused to testify against her husband.* 她拒绝出庭作证指控丈夫。◇ *There are several witnesses who will testify for the defence.* 有几名证人愿意为被告作证。◇ ~ **about sth** *He was summoned to testify before a grand jury about his role in the affair.* 他被传唤出庭在大陪审团前就他在这一事件中的角色作证。◇ ~ **to sth/to doing sth** *Evans testified to receiving $200 000 in bribes.* 埃文斯出庭证实了收受 20 万美元贿赂的事情。◇ ~ (**that**)… *He testified (that) he was at the theatre at the time of the murder.* 他作证声称凶杀案发生时自己正在剧院。◇ **+ speech** *'I was approached by a man I did not recognize,' she testified.* "一个我不认识的男人和我接洽过。"她作证说。 **2** [T] ~ (**that**)… (*formal*) to say that you believe sth is true because you have evidence of it 证实；证明：*Too many young people are unable to write or spell well, as employers will testify.* 写作或拼写不好的年轻人太多了，这一点雇主都会证明。 **3** [I] (*especially NAmE*) to express your belief in God publicly 见证（上帝的存在）

PHR V **ˈtestify to sth** (*formal*) to show or be evidence that sth is true 作为某事的证明；表明；说明 SYN **evidence**: *The film testifies to the courage of ordinary people during the war.* 这部电影表明老百姓在战争期间是如何英勇。

tes·ti·mo·nial /ˌtestɪˈməʊniəl; *NAmE* -ˈmoʊ-/ *noun* **1** a formal written statement, often by a former employer, about sb's abilities, qualities and character; a formal written statement about the quality of sth 证明信；介绍信；推荐信：*a glowing testimonial* 充满赞誉的推荐信 ◇ *The catalogue is full of testimonials from satisfied customers.* 这份商品目录满篇皆是称心顾客的赞辞。 **2** a thing that is given or done to show admiration for sb or to thank sb 感谢信；纪念品；奖品；奖状：*a testimonial game* (= to raise money for a particular player) 纪念赛（为某位运动员筹款）

tes·ti·mony /ˈtestɪməni; *NAmE* -moʊni/ *noun* (*pl.* **-ies**) **1** [U, sing.] ~ (**to sth**) (*formal*) a thing that shows that sth else exists or is true 证明 SYN **testament**: *This increase in exports **bears testimony to** the successes of industry.* 出口增长证明了产业的成功。◇ *The pyramids are an eloquent testimony to the ancient Egyptians' engineering skills.* 金字塔是古埃及人非凡工程技术的明证。 **2** [C, U] a formal written or spoken statement saying what you know to be true, usually in court 证词；证言；口供：*a sworn testimony* 宣誓证词 ◇ *Can I refuse to give testimony?* 我能拒绝作证吗？

test·ing /ˈtestɪŋ/ *noun, adj.*

■ ***noun*** [U] the activity of testing sb/sth in order to find sth out, see if it works, etc. 试验；测试；检查：*nuclear testing* 核试验 ◇ *testing and assessment in education* 教育测试与评估

■ ***adj.*** (of a problem or situation 问题或情况) difficult to deal with and needing particular strength or abilities 棘手的；伤脑筋的；难应付的

ˈtesting ground *noun* **1** a place or situation used for testing new ideas and methods to see if they work （新思想、新方法的）试验场，试点 **2** a place used for testing machines, etc. to see if they work correctly （机器等的）试验场：*a piece of land in use as a tank testing ground* 用作坦克试验场的一块土地

tes·tis /ˈtestɪs/ *noun* (*pl.* **tes·tes** /ˈtestiːz/) (*anatomy* 解) a TESTICLE 睾丸

ˈTest match (*also* **Test**) *noun* a CRICKET or RUGBY match played between the teams of two different countries, usually as part of a series of matches on a tour（板球或橄榄球的）各国家队间的决赛阶段比赛

tes·tos·ter·one /teˈstɒstərəʊn; *NAmE* teˈstɑːstəroʊn/ *noun* a HORMONE (= chemical substance produced in the body) that causes men to develop the physical and sexual features that are characteristic of the male body 睾酮；睾丸素 ➲ COMPARE OESTROGEN, PROGESTERONE

ˈtest pilot *noun* a pilot whose job is to fly aircraft in order to test their performance （检验飞机性能的）试飞员

ˌtest ˈrun *noun* = TRIAL RUN

ˈtest tube *noun* a small glass tube, closed at one end, that is used in scientific experiments 试管 ➲ VISUAL VOCAB PAGE V72

ˈtest-tube baby *noun* a baby that grows from an egg that is FERTILIZED outside the mother's body and then put back inside to continue developing normally 试管婴儿 ➲ SEE ALSO IN VITRO

testy /ˈtesti/ *adj.* easily annoyed or irritated 易怒的；暴躁的 SYN **irritable** ▶ **test·ily** /-ɪli/ *adv.*：*'Leave me alone,' she said testily.* "别管我。"她不耐烦地说。

tet·anus /ˈtetənəs/ *noun* [U] a disease in which the muscles, especially the JAW muscles, become stiff, caused by bacteria entering the body through cuts or wounds 破伤风

tetchy /ˈtetʃi/ *adj.* bad-tempered; likely to get angry easily or without good reason 易怒的；暴躁的；动辄发怒的 SYN **irritable** ▶ **tetch·ily** /-ɪli/ *adv.*

tête-à-tête /ˌteɪt ɑː ˈteɪt/ *noun* (*from French*) a private conversation between two people 两人密谈；两人私语；促膝谈心

tether /ˈteðə(r)/ *verb, noun*

■ ***verb*** **1** ~ **sth** (**to sth**) to tie an animal to a post so that it cannot move very far 拴（牲畜） **2** to use a SMARTPHONE to connect a computer to the Internet 共享网络（利用智能手机的数据连线供电脑等接入互联网）

T

▸ **tethering** *noun* [U]
▪ ***noun*** a rope or chain used to tie an animal to sth, allowing it to move around in a small area（拴牲畜的）拴绳，拴链 IDM SEE END *n.*

tetra·he·dron /ˌtetrəˈhiːdrən; -ˈhed-/ *noun* (*geometry* 几何) a solid shape with four flat sides that are triangles 四面体 ➲ PICTURE AT SOLID

tet·ral·ogy /teˈtrælədʒi/ *noun* (*pl.* **-ies**) a group of four books, films/movies, etc. that have the same subject or characters 四部曲；四联剧

Tetra Pak™ /ˈtetrə pæk/ *noun* a type of cardboard container in which milk or other drinks are sold 利乐包装纸盒（用于包装牛奶等）

Teut·on·ic /tjuːˈtɒnɪk; *NAmE* tuːˈtɑːnɪk/ *adj.* [usually before noun] (*informal, often disapproving*) showing qualities considered typical of German people 德意志民族特点的；日耳曼人风格的；条顿的：*The preparations were made with Teutonic thoroughness.* 各项准备工作均以日耳曼人缜密的精神完成。

Tex-Mex /ˌteks ˈmeks/ *adj.* [only before noun] connected with the variety of Mexican cooking, music, etc. that is found in Texas and the SW part of the US 美国－墨西哥烹调的；美国－墨西哥音乐的；美国－墨西哥的

text 🔑 AW /tekst/ *noun, verb*
▪ ***noun*** **1** 🔑 [U] the main printed part of a book or magazine, not the notes, pictures, etc.（书籍或杂志的）正文，本文（并非附注、图片等）：*My job is to lay out the text and graphics on the page.* 我的工作是设计页面上的正文和图表。 **2** 🔑 [U] any form of written material 文本；文档：*a computer that can process text* 能处理文本的电脑 ◇ *printed text* 打印的文本 **3** [C] = TEXT MESSAGE **4** 🔑 [C] the written form of a speech, a play, an article, etc. 演讲稿；剧本；文稿：*The newspaper had printed the full text of the president's speech.* 报纸刊登了总统演讲的全文。 **5** 🔑 [C] a book, play, etc., especially one studied for an exam（尤指为了考试而学习的）课本，教科书，剧本：*a literary text* 文学课本 ◇ (*BrE*) *'Macbeth' is a* ***set text*** *this year.*《麦克白》是今年指定的必读剧目。 ➲ COLLOCATIONS AT LITERATURE **6** 🔑 [C] a piece of writing that you have to answer questions about in an exam or a lesson（考试或一课书中赖以回答问题的）文章 SYN **passage**: *Read the text carefully and then answer the questions.* 先仔细阅读文章，然后再回答问题。 **7** [C] (*NAmE*) = TEXTBOOK: *medical texts* 医学课本 **8** [C] a sentence or short passage from the Bible that is read out and discussed by sb, especially during a religious service（尤指宗教仪式上引用的）《圣经》经文
▪ ***verb*** [T, I] to send sb a written message using a mobile/cell phone（用手机给某人）发短信：**~ (sb)** *Text me when you're on your way.* 路上给我发短信吧。 ◇ *Kids seem to be texting non-stop these days.* 现在的孩子好像在不停地发短信。 ◇ **~ sb sth** *I'll text you the final score.* 我会发短信告诉你最终的比分。 ➲ SEE ALSO SMS *v.*, TEXT-MESSAGE at TEXT MESSAGE

text·book /ˈtekstbʊk/ *noun, adj.*
▪ ***noun*** (*NAmE also* **text**) a book that teaches a particular subject and that is used especially in schools and colleges 教科书；课本；教材：*a* ***school/medical/history, etc. textbook*** 学校、医学、历史等教科书 ➲ VISUAL VOCAB PAGE V72
▪ ***adj.*** [only before noun] used to describe sth that is done exactly as it should be done, in the best possible way 规范的；标准的：*a* ***textbook example*** *of how the game should be played* 这项比赛的标准示范

ˈ**text editor** *noun* (*computing* 计) a system or program that allows you to make changes to text 文本编辑系统（或程序）；文字编辑器

texter /ˈtekstə(r)/ *noun* a person who sends TEXT MESSAGES 发送（手机）短信息的人；短信发送者

tex·tile /ˈtekstaɪl/ *noun* **1** [C] any type of cloth made by WEAVING or knitting 纺织品：*a factory producing a range of textiles* 生产一系列纺织品的工厂 ◇ *the textile industry* 纺织工业 ◇ *a textile designer* 纺织品设计师 ➲ SYNONYMS AT FABRIC **2 textiles** [pl.] the industry that makes cloth 纺织业

ˈ**text message** (*also* **text**) *noun* a written message that you send using a mobile/cell phone（手机）短信息；短信：*Send a text message to this number to vote.* 请发短信到此号码参加投票。 ➲ COLLOCATIONS AT PHONE ▸ ˈ**text-message** (*also* **text**) *verb* [T, I]: **~ (sb) (sth)** *I text-messaged him to say we were waiting in the pub.* 我发短信告诉他我们在酒吧里等候。 ˈ**text-messaging** (*also* **text·ing**) *noun* [U]

text·speak /ˈtekstspiːk/ *noun* [U] (*informal*) the kind of language that is typically used in TEXT MESSAGES, for example short forms of words, initials, symbols, etc. 短信文，短信用语（尤用于手机短信的缩略词、首字母、符号等）

ˌ**text-to-ˈspeech** *noun* (*abbr.* **TTS**) [U] (*computing* 计) a computer program that converts text into spoken language 文本语音转换程序；语音朗读程序；文字至语音转换程序：*text-to-speech software* 文本语音转换软件 ◇ *a TTS package* 语音朗读软件包

text·ual AW /ˈtekstʃuəl/ *adj.* [usually before noun] connected with or contained in a text 文本的；篇章的：*textual analysis* 文本分析 ◇ *textual errors* 文本错误

tex·tural /ˈtekstʃərəl/ *adj.* (*specialist*) relating to texture 质地的；纹理的：*the textural characteristics of the rocks* 岩石的纹理特征

tex·ture /ˈtekstʃə(r)/ *noun* [C, U] **1** the way a surface, substance or piece of cloth feels when you touch it, for example how rough, smooth, hard or soft it is 质地；手感：*the soft texture of velvet* 天鹅绒柔软的质地 ◇ *She uses a variety of different colours and textures in her wall hangings.* 她悬挂的帷幔色彩和质地多姿多彩。 **2** the way food or drink tastes or feels in your mouth, for example whether it is rough, smooth, light, heavy, etc. 口感：*The two cheeses were very different in both taste and texture.* 这两种奶酪的味道和口感大不相同。 **3** the way that different parts of a piece of music or literature are combined to create a final impression（音乐或文学的）和谐统一感，神韵：*the rich texture of the symphony* 这首交响曲优美和谐的乐感

tex·tured /ˈtekstʃəd; *NAmE* -tʃərd/ *adj.* with a surface that is not smooth, but has a particular texture 起纹理的；质地不平的：*textured wallpaper* 起纹理的壁纸

ˌ**textured ˈvegetable protein** *noun* (*abbr.* **TVP**) a substance that looks like meat, but which is made from SOYA BEANS 结构性植物蛋白，植物组织蛋白，素肉（用大豆制成）

TFT /ˌtiː ef ˈtiː/ *noun* a piece of technology used to make flat screens for computers, mobile/cell phones, etc. (the abbreviation for thin film transistor) 薄膜晶体管（全写为 thin film transistor，电脑、手机等的平面屏幕制造技术）：*a 17 in TFT screen* * 17 英寸薄膜晶体管显示器

TG /ˌtiː ˈdʒiː/ *abbr.* TRANSFORMATIONAL GRAMMAR 转换语法

-th *suffix* **1** (in ordinal numbers 构成序数词): *sixth* 第六 ◇ *fifteenth* 第十五 ◇ *hundredth* 第一百 **2** (in nouns 构成名词) the action or process of（表示动作或过程）：*growth* 生长

thali /ˈtɑːli/ *noun* (*IndE*) **1** a metal plate on which food is served 金属餐盘 **2** a set meal at a restaurant（印度餐厅）套餐

thal·ido·mide /θəˈlɪdəmaɪd/ *noun* [U] a SEDATIVE drug which was used until the 1960s, when it was discovered that if given to pregnant women, it prevented some babies from developing normal arms and legs 酞胺哌啶酮，反应停（一种镇定药，20 世纪 60 年代发现孕妇服用后会导致胎儿四肢畸形而被禁用）

thal·lium /ˈθæliəm/ *noun* [U] (*symb.* **Tl**) a chemical element. Thallium is a soft silver-white metal whose COMPOUNDS are very poisonous. 铊

than 🔑 /ðən; *strong form* ðæn/ *prep.*, *conj.* **1** 🔑 used to introduce the second part of a comparison（用以引出比较的第二部分）比：*I'm older than her.* 我比她年龄大。◇ *There was more whisky in it than soda.* 那里面的威士忌比苏打水多。◇ *He loves me more than you do.* 他比你更爱我。◇ *It was much better than I'd expected.* 这比我预料的要好得多。◇ *You should know better than to behave like that.* 你应当明白事理，不该那么不懂规矩。◇ *I'd rather email than phone, if that's OK by you.* 如果你认为可以的话，我想发电邮而不打电话。 **2** 🔑 **more/less/fewer, etc. ~** used for comparing amounts, numbers, distances, etc.（比较数量、距离等）多于，小于，少于：*It never takes more than an hour.* 所用的时间从不会超过一个小时。◇ *It's less than a mile to the beach.* 离海滩不足一英里远。◇ *There were fewer than twenty people there.* 那里有不到二十个人。 **3** used in expressions showing that one thing happens straight after another（表示一事紧跟另一事发生）就：***No sooner*** *had I sat down* ***than*** *there was a loud knock on the door.* 我刚坐下就有人大声敲门。◇ ***Hardly*** *had we arrived* ***than*** *the problems started.* 我们刚到，问题就来了。 IDM SEE OTHER

thang /θæŋ/ *noun* (*NAmE, informal*) a way of saying or writing the word 'thing', that represents the pronunciation of the southern US 东西，事物（用于说话或书写，表示美国南方对 thing 一词的发音）

thank 🔑 /θæŋk/ *verb* to tell sb that you are grateful for sth 谢谢，感谢（某人）；（为某事）道谢：**~ sb for sth** *I must write and thank Mary for the present.* 我得写信感谢玛丽送给我这份礼物。◇ *In his speech, he thanked everyone for all their hard work.* 他在讲话中感谢大家各尽其力。◇ **~ sb for doing sth** *She said goodbye and thanked us for coming.* 她向我们道别，并感谢我们的光临。◇ **~ sb** *There's no need to thank me—I enjoyed doing it.* 不必谢我，我乐意效劳。

▼ **EXPRESS YOURSELF 情景表达**

Thanking somebody for something 表达谢意

When someone gives you something, or does something for you, you often want to say more than just a brief 'thank you'. 接受别人的馈赠或帮助后，想说的不仅仅是简单的"谢谢"，还有其他表达谢意的方式：

- ***Thank you very much.*** *It's very kind of you./You really shouldn't have.* 非常感谢。你真是太好了。/ 您真的不必那么客气。
- ***Thank you so much for coming.*** *It was really nice to see you.* 非常感谢你光临。见到你真高兴。
- ***I'm very grateful.*** 我非常感激。
- ***I do appreciate*** *your help.* 承蒙帮助，不胜感激。

Responses 回应：

- ***That's all right.*** 不用谢。
- ***Don't mention it.*** 不用客气。
- ***No problem.*** 别客气。
- ***My pleasure.*** 乐意效劳。
- ***I'm glad I could help.*** 很高兴能帮上忙。

IDM **have sb to thank (for sth)** used when you are saying who is responsible for sth 责怪；由…负责；多亏；归功于：*I have my parents to thank for my success.* 我的成功归功于我的父母。 **I'll thank you for sth/to do sth** (*formal*) used to tell sb that you are annoyed and do not want them to do sth （用以表示恼火，不让人做某事）请你…：*I'll thank you to mind your own business.* 请你少管闲事。 **thank 'God/'goodness/'heaven(s) (for sth)** 🔑 used to say that you are pleased about sth 谢天谢地：*Thank God you're safe!* 谢天谢地，你平安无事！◇ *'Thank goodness for that!' she said with a sigh of relief.* "这可要谢天谢地！"她宽慰地舒了一口气。 HELP Some people find the phrase **thank God** offensive. 有人认为 thank God 这一短语含冒犯意。 **thank your lucky 'stars** to feel very grateful and lucky about sth 真走运；吉星高照 **sb won't 'thank you for sth** used to say that sb will not be pleased or will be annoyed about sth 某人会因…而生气：*John won't thank you for interfering.* 你插手，约翰必定十分恼火。

thank·ful /'θæŋkfl/ *adj.* [not usually before noun] pleased about sth good that has happened, or sth bad that has not happened 感谢；感激；欣慰：**~ (to do sth)** *I was thankful to see they'd all arrived safely.* 看到他们都平安到达，我感到欣慰。◇ **~ (for sth)** *He wasn't badly hurt—that's something to be thankful for.* 他的伤不重，这倒是值得庆幸。◇ **~ (that...)** *I was thankful that he hadn't been hurt.* 他没有受伤，我感到很欣慰。 IDM SEE SMALL *adj.*

thank·ful·ly /'θæŋkfəli/ *adv.* **1** used to show that you are pleased that sth good has happened or that sth bad has been avoided （用以表示高兴）幸亏 SYN **fortunately**: *There was a fire in the building, but thankfully no one was hurt.* 大楼失火了，但幸好没有伤着人。 **2** in a pleased or grateful way 高兴地；感激地：*I accepted the invitation thankfully.* 我愉快地接受了邀请。

thank·less /'θæŋkləs/ *adj.* unpleasant or difficult to do and unlikely to bring you any rewards or thanks from anyone 让人不领情的；徒劳无益的；吃力不讨好的：*Sometimes being a mother and a housewife felt like* ***a thankless task.*** 做母亲和家庭主妇有时使人觉得好像是个受累不讨好的差使。

thanks 🔑 /θæŋks/ *exclamation, noun*

■ ***exclamation*** ➲ SEE ALSO THANK YOU *exclamation* **1** 🔑 used to show that you are grateful to sb for sth they have done（表示感激）感谢，谢谢：**~ (for doing sth)** *Thanks for lending me the money.* 多谢您借钱给我。◇ **~ (for sth)** ***Many thanks*** *for your support.* 多谢您的支持。◇ *'How are you?' 'Fine, thanks* (= thanks for asking).' "你好吗？" "挺好的，谢谢。" **2** 🔑 a polite way of accepting sth that sb has offered you（接受好意）好的，谢谢：*'Would you like a coffee?' 'Oh, thanks.'* "来杯咖啡好吗？" "好的，谢谢。" ◇ *'Here's the change.' '****Thanks very much****.'* "这是找你的零钱。" "非常感谢。" **3** 🔑 **no thanks** a polite way of refusing sth that sb has offered you（婉言谢绝）不用了，谢谢：*'Would you like some more?' 'No thanks.'* "再要一点儿吗？" "不要了，谢谢。"

■ ***noun*** 🔑 [pl.] **~ (to sb) (for sth)** words or actions that show that you are grateful to sb for sth 感谢；感激；谢意 SYN **gratitude**: *How can I ever express my thanks to you for all you've done?* 对你所做的一切，我怎么才能表达谢意？◇ *Thanks are due to all those who worked so hard for so many months.* 感谢这么多月来辛勤工作的每一个人。◇ *She murmured her thanks.* 她低声道谢。 ➲ SEE ALSO VOTE OF THANKS

IDM **no thanks to sb/sth** despite sb/sth; with no help from sb/sth 虽然；并非由于；不归功于：*We managed to get it finished in the end—no thanks to him* (= he didn't help). 我们终于把这件事完成了，但这没有他的什么功劳。 **thanks a lot** **1** 🔑 used to show that you are very grateful to sb for sth they have done（表示非常感激）多谢：*Thanks a lot for all you've done.* 多谢你所做的一切。 **2** (*ironic*) used to show that you are annoyed that sb has done sth because it causes trouble or difficulty for you（表示恼怒）多谢了：*'I'm afraid I've finished all the milk.' 'Well, thanks a lot!'* "对不起，我把牛奶都喝了。" "哦，多谢了！" **thanks to sb/sth** 🔑 (*sometimes ironic*) used to say that sth has happened because of sb/sth 幸亏；由于；因为：*It was all a great success—thanks to a lot of hard work.* 由于尽心竭力，这才大获成功。◇ *Everyone knows about it now, thanks to you!* 多亏了你，现在大家都知道了！

thanks·giv·ing /ˌθæŋks'ɡɪvɪŋ/ *noun* **1 Thanksgiving (Day)** [U, C] a public holiday in the US (on the fourth Thursday in November) and in Canada (on the second Monday in October), originally to give thanks to God for the HARVEST and for health 感恩节（美国定为十一月的第四个星期四，加拿大定为十月的第二个星期一，均为公休日）：*We always eat turkey on Thanksgiving.* 我们过感恩节时总是吃火鸡。◇ *Are you going home for Thanksgiving?* 你回家过感恩节吗？ ➲ COMPARE HARVEST FESTIVAL **2** [U] (*formal*) the expression of thanks to God 感恩（于上帝）

'thank you 🔑 *exclamation, noun*

■ ***exclamation*** ➲ SEE ALSO THANKS *exclamation* **1** 🔑 used to show that you are grateful to sb for sth they have done（表示感激）谢谢你：~ (**for sth**) *Thank you for your letter.* 谢谢你的来信。◇ ~ (**for doing sth**) *Thank you very much for sending the photos.* 非常感谢你寄给我这些照片。 **2** 🔑 a polite way of accepting sth that sb has offered you（接受好意）好，谢谢你：*'Would you like some help with that?' 'Oh, thank you.'* "这事你需要帮忙吗？" "需要，谢谢你。" **3** 🔑 **no thank you** a polite way of refusing sth that sb has offered you（婉言谢绝）不用了，谢谢你：*'Would you like some more cake?' 'No thank you.'* "你要再来点儿蛋糕吗？" "不要了，谢谢你。" **4** used at the end of a sentence to tell sb firmly that you do not need their help or advice（用于句末，坚决表示不需要帮助或劝告）谢谢：*'Shall I do that?' 'I can do it myself, thank you.'* "我来干好吗？" "我自己能干，谢谢。"

■ ***noun*** 🔑 [usually sing.] ~ (**to sb**) (**for sth**) an act, a gift, a comment, etc. intended to thank sb for sth they have done 感谢；谢意；酬谢；谢辞：*The actor sent a big thank you to all his fans for their letters of support.* 这位演员向所有来信表示支持的崇拜者表示万分感谢。◇ *She took the money without so much as a thank you.* 她接过钱，连一声谢谢都没说。◇ *a thank-you letter* 感谢信

that 🔑 *det., pron., conj., adv.*

■ ***det.*** /ðæt/ (*pl.* **those** /ðəʊz; *NAmE* ðoʊz/) **1** 🔑 used for referring to a person or thing that is not near the speaker or as near to the speaker as another（指较远的人或事物）那，那个：*Look at that man over there.* 瞧那边的那个男子。◇ *How much are those apples at the back?* 后边那些苹果什么价钱？ **2** 🔑 used for referring to sb/sth that has already been mentioned or is already known about （指已提到过或已知的人或事物）那，那个：*I was living with my parents at that time.* 那时候我和父母住在一起。◇ *That incident changed their lives.* 那次事件改变了他们的生活。◇ *Have you forgotten about that money I lent you last week?* 你忘记上星期我借给你的那笔钱了吧？◇ *That dress of hers is too short.* 她那件连衣裙太短了。

■ ***pron.*** /ðæt/ (*pl.* **those** /ðəʊz; *NAmE* ðoʊz/) **1** 🔑 used for referring to a person or thing that is not near the speaker, or not as near to the speaker as another（指较远的人或事物）那，那个：*Who's that?* 那是谁？◇ *That's Peter over there.* 那边那个人是彼得。◇ *Hello. Is that Jo?* 喂，是乔吗？◇ *That's a nice dress.* 那件连衣裙很漂亮。◇ *Those look riper than these.* 那些看上去比这些熟一些。 **2** 🔑 used for referring to sb/sth that has already been mentioned, or is already known about （指已提到过或已知的人或事物）那，那个：*What can I do about that?* 这事我可怎么办？◇ *Do you remember when we went to Norway? That was a good trip.* 你记得我们去挪威的情形吗？那次旅行真不错。◇ *That's exactly what I think.* 我正是那么想的。 **3** (*formal*) used for referring to people or things of a particular type （特指）那，那种，那些：*Those present were in favour of change.* 在座的人都赞成变革。◇ *There are those who say* (= some people say) *she should not have got the job.* 有些人说她本不该得到这份工作。◇ *Salaries are higher here than those in my country.* 这里的薪水比我国的高。 **4** 🔑 /ðət; ðæt/ (*pl.* **that**) used as a relative pronoun to introduce a part of a sentence which refers to the person, thing or time you have been talking about（用作关系代词，引导从句）：*Where's the letter that came yesterday?* 昨天来的信在哪儿？◇ *Who was it that won the US Open?* 在美国公开赛上获胜的是谁？◇ *The watch* (*that*) *you gave me keeps perfect time.* 您给我的那只表走得很准。◇ *The people* (*that*) *I spoke to were very helpful.* 我交谈过的人都很肯帮忙。◇ *It's the best novel* (*that*) *I've ever read.* 这是我读过的最佳小说。◇ *We moved here the year* (*that*) *my mother died.* 我们是我母亲去世那年搬来的。 HELP In spoken and informal written English **that** is nearly always left out when it is the object of the verb or is used with a preposition. 在口语和非正式的书面语中，作为动词宾语或与介词连用的 that 一般都省略。

IDM **and** (**all**) **'that** (*BrE, informal*) and everything else connected with an activity, a situation, etc. 等等；以及诸如此类的事物 SYN **and so forth**: *Did you bring the contract and* (*all*) *that?* 合同什么的你都带来了吗？ **that is** (**to say**) used to say what sth means or to give more information 也就是说；即；换句话说：*He's a local government administrator, that is to say a civil servant.* 他是地方政府的行政官员，也就是公务员。◇ *You'll find her very helpful—if she's not too busy, that is.* 你会觉得她很肯帮忙，那是说如果她不太忙的话。 ➲ LANGUAGE BANK AT I.E. **,that's 'it** (*informal*) **1** 🔑 used to say that sb is right, or is doing sth right（表示某人正确或做得对）就是这样，正是如此，对啦：*No, the other one… that's it.* 不，另一个…就是它。◇ *That's it, carry on!* 对啦！继续！ **2** 🔑 used to say that sth is finished, or that no more can be done（表示已完成或再也没有可做的了）好了，就这样吧：*That's it, the fire's out now.* 好了，现在火灭了。◇ *That's it for now, but if I get any news I'll let you know.* 现在就这些，如果再得到消息，我就通知你。◇ *A week to go, and that's it!* 还有一周，然后就完事了！ **3** used to say that you will not accept sth any longer（表示不再接受）行了，够了：*That's it, I've had enough!* 够了，我受够了！ **4** 🔑 used to talk about the reason for sth（表示理由）就是这个问题，就是这么回事：*So that's it—the fuse had gone.* 问题就出在这里，保险丝烧断了。◇ *You don't love me any more, is that it?* 你不再爱我啦，是不是这样？ **,that's 'that** (*informal*) used to say that your decision cannot be changed（表示决定不能更改）就是这样，就这样定了：*Well I'm not going, and that's that.* 好啦，我不去，就这么定了。

■ ***conj.*** /ðət; ðæt/ **1** 🔑 used after some verbs, adjectives and nouns to introduce a new part of the sentence（用于某些动词、形容词和名词后，引出从句）：*She said* (*that*) *the story was true.* 她说这件事是真的。◇ *It's possible* (*that*) *he has not received the letter.* 可能他还没有收到那封信。◇ *The fact* (*that*) *he's older than me is not relevant.* 他比我年纪大这一事实无关紧要。 HELP In spoken and informal written English **that** is usually left out after reporting verbs and adjectives. It is less often left out after nouns. 在口语和非正式的书面语中，在引出间接引语的动词和形容词之后的 that 通常省略，而在名词后的则一般不省略。 **2** 🔑 **so… that…** used to express a result（表示结果）如此…以致：*She was so tired* (*that*) *she couldn't think straight.* 她累得昏头昏脑。 HELP In informal English **that** is often left out. 在非正式英语中，that 常被省略。 **3** (*literary*) used for expressing a hope or a wish（表示希望或愿望）多么：*Oh that I could see him again!* 啊，我多么想能再看到他！

■ ***adv.*** /ðæt/ **1** used when saying how much or showing how long, big, etc. sth is with your hands（以手势表示长度、大小等时用）那样，那么：*I can't walk that far* (= as far as that). 我走不了那么远。◇ *It's about that long.* 大约有那么长。 **2 not** (**all**) ~ not very, or not as much as has been said 不很；不那么：*It isn't all that cold.* 天没那么冷。◇ *There aren't that many people here.* 这里并没有那么多人。 **3** (*BrE, informal*) used to emphasize how much（用以强调程度）那么：*I was that scared I didn't know what to do.* 我非常害怕，不知如何是好。

tha·ta·way /'ðætəweɪ/ *adv.* (*informal*) in that direction 朝那边；向那边：*They went thataway!* 他们往那边走了！

thatch /θætʃ/ *noun, verb*

■ ***noun*** **1** [U, C] dried STRAW, REEDS, etc. used for making a roof; a roof made of this material（作为屋顶材料的）茅草，稻草，芦苇；茅草屋顶；草屋顶：*a roof made of thatch* 茅草屋顶 ◇ *The thatch was badly damaged in the storm.* 茅草屋顶在暴风雨中遭到严重破坏。 **2** [sing.] ~ **of hair** (*informal*) thick hair on sb's head 浓密的头发

■ ***verb*** ~ **sth** to cover the roof of a building with thatch 用茅草盖屋顶 ▶ **thatched** /θætʃt/ *adj.*：*They live in a thatched cottage.* 他们住在茅舍里。 ➲ VISUAL VOCAB PAGE V16

thatch·er /'θætʃə(r)/ *noun* a person whose job is thatching roofs 盖茅草屋顶的人

Thatch·er·ite /'θætʃəraɪt/ *adj.* connected with or supporting the policies of the former British Prime Minister, Margaret Thatcher (= thought of as being right-wing)（支持）英国前首相玛格丽特・撒切尔政策的；（支持）右翼政策的 ▶ **Thatch·er·ite** *noun*

T

thaw /θɔː/ *verb, noun*

■ *verb* **1** [I] ~ (**out**) (of ice and snow 冰雪) to turn back into water after being frozen（结冰后）解冻，融化，融解 SYN **melt** OPP **freeze** ➲ WORDFINDER NOTE AT SNOW **2** [I] when **it thaws** or **is thawing**, the weather becomes warm enough to melt snow and ice 天气暖和得使冰雪融化（或解冻）: *It's starting to thaw.* 冰雪开始融化了。 **3** [I, T] ~ (**sth**) (**out**) to become, or to let frozen food become, soft or liquid ready for cooking（使冷冻食品）化冻: *Leave the meat to thaw completely before cooking.* 让冻肉完全化冻后再烹煮。 ➲ COMPARE DEFROST (1), DE-ICE, UNFREEZE (1) **4** [I, T] ~ (**sth**) (**out**) to become, or make sth become, a normal temperature after being very cold（使）回到正常温度，变暖: *I could feel my ears and toes start to thaw out.* 我觉得耳朵和脚趾暖和过来了。 **5** [I] ~ (**out**) to become more friendly and less formal 变得友好（或随和、不拘束）: *Relations between the two countries thawed a little after the talks.* 谈判后两国关系缓和了些。

■ *noun* **1** [C, usually sing.] a period of warmer weather following one of cold weather, causing snow and ice to melt 解冻时期；融化季节 **2** [sing.] ~ (**in sth**) a situation in which the relations between two enemy countries become more friendly（敌对国家之间）关系缓和

the /ðə; ði; *strong form* ðiː/ *definite article* **1** used to refer to sb/sth that has already been mentioned or is easily understood（指已提到或易领会到的人或事物）: *There were three questions. The first two were relatively easy but the third one was hard.* 有三个问题。头两个相对容易，第三个困难。◇ *There was an accident here yesterday. A car hit a tree and the driver was killed.* 昨天这里发生了一起事故。一辆小轿车撞到树上，驾车的人死了。◇ *The heat was getting to be too much for me.* 天气热得快让我受不了了。◇ *The nights are getting longer.* 夜越来越长。 **2** used to refer to sb/sth that is the only, normal or obvious one of their kind（指独一无二的、正常的或不言而喻的人或事物）: *the Mona Lisa*《蒙娜丽莎》◇ *the Nile* 尼罗河 ◇ *the Queen* 女王 ◇ *What's the matter?* 怎么回事？◇ *The phone rang.* 电话铃响了。◇ *I patted her on the back.* 我拍了拍她的背。◇ *How's the* (= your) *baby?* 宝宝好吗？ **3** used when explaining which person or thing you mean（解说时用）: *the house at the end of the street* 街尽头的房子 ◇ *The people I met there were very friendly.* 我在那里遇到的人很友善。◇ *It was the best day of my life.* 这是我一生中最美好的一天。◇ *You're the third person to ask me that.* 你是第三个问我那件事的人。◇ *Friday the thirteenth* 十三号，星期五 ◇ *Alexander the Great* 亚历山大大帝 **4** used to refer to a thing in general rather than a particular example（用以泛指）: *He taught himself to play the violin.* 他自学拉小提琴。◇ *The dolphin is an intelligent animal.* 海豚是聪明的动物。◇ *They placed the African elephant on their endangered list.* 他们把非洲大象列为濒危动物。◇ *I heard it on the radio.* 我从收音机里听到了这件事。◇ *I'm usually out during the day.* 白天我通常不在家。 **5** used with adjectives to refer to a thing or a group of people described by the adjective（与形容词连用，指事物或统称的人）: *With him, you should always expect the unexpected.* 在他身上你应随时料到有意想不到的事情发生。◇ *the unemployed* 失业者 ◇ *the French* 法国人 **6** used before the plural of sb's last name to refer to a whole family or a married couple（用于姓氏的复数形式前，指家庭或夫妇）: *Don't forget to invite the Jordans.* 别忘了邀请乔丹一家。 **7** enough of sth for a particular purpose（指特定用途的事物）足够，恰好: *I wanted it but I didn't have the money.* 我想买那东西，但钱不够。 **8** used with a unit of measurement to mean 'every'（与计量单位连用）每，一: *My car does forty miles to the gallon.* 我的车每加仑汽油跑四十英里。◇ *You get paid by the hour.* 你领的是时薪。 **9** used with a unit of time to mean 'the present'（与时间单位连用）当前的，本，此: *Why not have the dish of the day?* 何不试一下今天的特色菜？◇ *She's flavour of the month with him.* 她是他眼下的红人。 **10** /ðiː/ used, stressing *the*, to show that the person or thing referred to is famous or important（重读，表示所指的为知名或重要的人或事物）: *Sheryl Crow? Not 'the Sheryl Crow?* 雪瑞尔·克洛？莫不是大名鼎鼎的雪瑞尔·克洛？◇ *At that time London was 'the place to be.* 那时候伦敦是不可不去的地方。

IDM **the more, less, etc...., the more, less, etc....** used to show that two things change to the same degree（用以表示两个事物按照同一程度变化）越…越，愈…愈: *The more she thought about it, the more depressed she became.* 她越想这事越沮丧。◇ *The less said about the whole thing, the happier I'll be.* 对整个事情议论得越少，我越高兴。

the·atre (*especially US* **theater**) /ˈθɪətə(r); *NAmE* ˈθiːətər/ *noun* **1** [C] a building or an outdoor area where plays and similar types of entertainment are performed 戏院；剧场；露天剧场: *Broadway theatres* 百老汇的剧院 ◇ *an open-air theatre* 露天剧场 ◇ *How often do you* **go to the theatre**? 你多久看一次戏？ ➲ VISUAL VOCAB PAGE V3 ➲ SEE ALSO LECTURE THEATRE

> **WORDFINDER** 联想词: artistic director, auditorium, balcony, box office, circle, director, foyer, **stage**, the stalls

2 (*also* ˈ**movie theater**) (*both NAmE*) (*BrE* **cin·ema**) [C] a building in which films/movies are shown 电影院 **3** [U] plays considered as entertainment 戏剧: *an evening of live music and theatre* 现场演奏音乐戏剧晚会 ◇ (*BrE*) *I like music, theatre and cinema.* 我喜欢音乐、戏剧和电影。◇ *current ideas about what makes good theatre* (= what makes good entertainment when performed) 对何谓好戏剧的普遍看法 **4** [U] (*also* **the theatre** [sing.]) the work of writing, producing and acting in plays 戏剧工作；剧作；演出；上演: *I want to work in theatre.* 我想从事戏剧工作。◇ *He was essentially a man of the theatre.* 他本质上是个戏剧人。 **5** [C, U] (*BrE*) = OPERATING THEATRE: *a theatre sister* (= a nurse who helps during operations) 手术室护士长 ◇ *He's still* **in theatre**. 他仍在接受手术。 **6** [C, usually sing.] ~ (**of war, etc.**) (*formal*) the place in which a war or fighting takes place 战场；战区

theatre·goer (*especially US* **theater·goer**) /ˈθɪətəɡəʊə(r); *NAmE* ˈθiːətərɡoʊər/ (*also* **play·goer**) *noun* a person who goes regularly to the theatre 经常去戏院看戏的人；爱看戏的人 ▶ **theatre·going** (*especially US* **theater·going**) *adj.* [only before noun]: *the theatregoing public* 经常看戏的公众

ˌ**theatre-in-the-ˈround** (*especially US* ˌ**theater-in-the-ˈround**) *noun* [U] a way of performing plays on a stage which is surrounded by the audience 圆形剧场式演出

ˈ**theatre nurse** (*BrE*) (*NAmE* ˈ**scrub nurse**) *noun* a nurse with special training, who helps during operations 手术室护士

the·at·ri·cal /θiˈætrɪkl/ *adj.* **1** [only before noun] connected with the theatre 戏剧的；演剧的；剧场的: *a theatrical agent* 演员经纪人 **2** (*often disapproving*) (of behaviour 举止) exaggerated in order to attract attention or create a particular effect 演戏似的；夸张的；做作的: *a theatrical gesture* 夸张的姿势 ▶ **the·at·ri·cal·ly** /-kli/ *adv.*

the·at·ri·cal·ity /θiˌætrɪˈkæləti/ *noun* [U] the exaggerated quality of sth that is intended to attract attention or create a particular effect 戏剧性；夸张

the·at·ri·cals /θiˈætrɪklz/ *noun* [pl.] **1** performances of plays 戏剧演出: *amateur theatricals* 业余戏剧演出 **2** (*also* **the·at·rics** *especially in NAmE*) behaviour that is exaggerated and emotional in order to attract attention 戏剧化动作；矫揉造作

thee /ðiː/ *pron.* (*old use* or *dialect*) a word meaning 'you', used when talking to only one person who is the object of the verb（第二人称单数的宾格）你: *We beseech thee, O Lord.* 主啊，我们恳求您。 ➲ COMPARE THOU

theft /θeft/ *noun* [U, C] ~ (**of sth**) the crime of stealing sth from a person or place 偷；偷窃；盗窃罪: *car theft* 偷盗汽车 ◇ *Police are investigating the theft of computers from the company's offices.* 警方正在调查这家公司办公室里的计算机失窃案。 ➲ COMPARE BURGLARY, ROBBERY ➲ SEE ALSO IDENTITY THEFT, THIEF

T

their /ðeə(r); *NAmE* ðer/ *det.* (the possessive form of *they* * they 的所有格形式) **1** of or belonging to them 他们的；她们的；它们的：*Their parties are always fun.* 他们的聚会总是乐趣横生。◇ *Which is their house?* 哪座房子是他们的？ **2** used instead of *his* or *her* to refer to a person whose sex is not mentioned or not known（在提及性别不详的人时，用以代替 his 或 her）：*If anyone calls, ask for their number so I can call them back.* 如有人打电话来，问问他们的电话号码，这样我可以回电话。➲ NOTE AT GENDER

theirs /ðeəz; *NAmE* ðerz/ *pron.* (the possessive form of *they* * they 的所有格形式) of or belonging to them 他们的，她们的，它们的（所有物）：*Theirs are the children with very fair hair.* 他们的孩子是那些长着满头金发的。◇ *It's a favourite game of theirs.* 这是他们最喜爱的游戏。

the·ism /ˈθiːɪzəm/ *noun* [U] belief in the existence of God or gods 有神论 OPP **atheism**

them /ðəm; *strong form* ðem/ *pron.* (the object form of *they* * they 的宾格) **1** used when referring to people, animals or things as the object of a verb or preposition, or after the verb *be* 他们；她们；它们：*Tell them the news.* 把这消息告诉他们。◇ *What are you doing with those matches? Give them to me.* 你拿那些火柴做什么？把它们交给我。◇ *Did you eat all of them?* 你都吃光了吗？◇ *It's them.* 是他们。 **2** used instead of *him* or *her* to refer to a person whose sex is not mentioned or not known（指性别不详的人时，用以代替 him 或 her）：*If anyone comes in before I get back, ask them to wait.* 如果在我回来之前有人来，就请他等一等。

the·mat·ic AW /θɪˈmætɪk; θiː-/ *adj.* [usually before noun] connected with the theme or themes of sth 题目的；主题的：*the thematic structure of a text* 文本的主题结构 ▶ **the·mat·ic·al·ly** AW /-kli/ *adv.*：*The books have been grouped thematically.* 这些书籍已按主题进行了分类。

the͵matic ˈrole (*also* **ˈtheta role**) *noun* (*linguistics* 语言) the function that a noun phrase has in relation to a verb, for example AGENT or PATIENT 解元角色，主题角色（指与动词相关的名词短语的功能，如施动者或受动者）

theme AW /θiːm/ *noun, adj.*

■ ***noun*** **1** the subject or main idea in a talk, piece of writing or work of art（演讲、文章或艺术作品的）题目，主题，主题思想：*North American literature is the main theme of this year's festival.* 北美文学是今年艺术节的主题。◇ *The President stressed a favourite campaign theme—greater emphasis on education.* 总统强调了最受人欢迎的竞选主题——更加重视教育。◇ *The naked male figure was always the central theme of Greek art.* 男性裸体雕像总是希腊艺术的中心主题。◇ *The stories are all* ***variations on the theme*** *of unhappy marriage.* 这些故事讲来讲去无非是这样那样的不幸婚姻。➲ COLLOCATIONS AT LITERATURE **2** (*music* 音) a short tune that is repeated or developed in a piece of music（乐曲的）主题，主旋律 **3** = THEME MUSIC：*the theme from 'The Godfather'*《教父》的主题音乐 **4** (*old-fashioned, NAmE*) a short piece of writing on a particular subject, done for school（学生的）作文 **5** (*linguistics* 语言) the part of a sentence or clause that contains information that is not new to the reader or audience（句子的）主位；词干；主题 ➲ COMPARE RHEME

■ ***adj.*** (*BrE*) ~ **pub/bar/restaurant, etc.** a pub, bar, etc. that is designed to reflect a particular subject or period of history（反映某主题或历史时期的）主题酒馆（或酒吧、餐馆等）：*an Irish theme pub* 爱尔兰主题酒馆

themed /θiːmd/ *adj.* [usually before noun] (*BrE*) (of an event or a place of entertainment 事件或娱乐地点) designed to reflect a particular subject or period of history 特定主题的；特定历史时期的：*a themed restaurant* 以特定主题装饰的餐馆

ˈtheme music *noun* [U] (*also* **theme**, **ˈtheme song**, **ˈtheme tune** [C]) music that is played at the beginning and end and/or is often repeated in a film/movie, television programme, etc.（电影、电视节目的）主题音乐 ➲ COMPARE SIGNATURE TUNE

ˈtheme park *noun* a large park where people go to enjoy themselves, for example by riding on large machines such as ROLLER COASTERS, and where much of the entertainment is connected with one subject or idea 主题公园，主题乐园（娱乐项目大多围绕一个主题的大型公园）：*a western-style theme park* 西部风格主题乐园

them·self /ðəmˈself/ *pron.* (the reflexive form of *they*) used instead of *himself* or *herself* to refer to a person whose sex is not mentioned or not known（they 的反身形式，用以代替 himself 或 herself，指称性别不详的人）他自己，她自己：*Does anyone here consider themself a good cook?* 这里有人觉得自己烹饪很拿手吗？ HELP Although **themself** is fairly common, especially in spoken English, many people think it is not correct. * themself 很常见，特别是在口语中，但很多人认为不正确。

them·selves /ðəmˈselvz/ *pron.* **1** (the reflexive form of *they* * they 的反身形式) used when people or animals performing an action are also affected by it 他们自己；她们自己；它们自己：*They seemed to be enjoying themselves.* 他们好像玩得非常高兴。◇ *The children were arguing amongst themselves.* 孩子们在相互争论。◇ *They've bought themselves a new car.* 他们给自己买了一辆新车。 **2** used to emphasize *they* or a plural subject（用以强调 they 或复数主语）他们（或她们、它们）亲自，他们（或她们、它们）本身：*They themselves had had a similar experience.* 他们本身就曾有过类似的经历。◇ *Don and Julie paid for it themselves.* 唐和朱莉他们亲自付的款。 **3** used instead of *himself* or *herself* to refer to a person whose sex is not mentioned or not known（指性别不详的人时，用以代替 himself 或 herself）：*There wasn't anyone who hadn't enjoyed themselves.* 没有人不尽兴。 HELP Although this use of **themselves** is fairly common, especially in spoken English, many people think it is not correct. * themselves 的这一用法相当普遍，尤其在口语中，但许多人认为并不正确。

IDM **(all) by themˈselves** **1** alone; without anyone else（他们）独自，单独：*They wanted to spend the evening by themselves.* 他们想要单独度过这个夜晚。 **2** without help（他们）独立地：*They did the cooking by themselves.* 他们自己做了饭。 **(all) to themˈselves** for them alone; not shared with anyone 只供他们自己用

then /ðen/ *adv., adj.*

■ ***adv.*** **1** used to refer to a particular time in the past or future（指过去）当时，那时；（指将来）到那时，届时：*Life was harder then because neither of us had a job.* 那时生活比较艰苦，因为我俩都没有工作。◇ *Things were very different* ***back then.*** 以前那个时候情况大不相同。◇ *She grew up in Zimbabwe, or Rhodesia as it then was.* 她在津巴布韦长大，当时该地叫罗得西亚。◇ *I saw them at Christmas but haven't heard a thing* ***since then.*** 我在圣诞节见到过他们，但之后没听到过什么消息。◇ *I've been invited too, so I'll see you then.* 我也接到邀请，我们到那时见。◇ *There's a room free in Bob's house next week but you can stay with us* ***until then.*** 下星期鲍勃家会空出一个房间，不过在那之前你可以和我们住在一起。◇ *Call again next week. They should have reached a decision* ***by then.*** 下星期再来电话。到那时他们应该已作出决定了。◇ ***Just then*** (= at that moment) *there was a knock at the door.* 就在那时有人敲门了。◇ *She left in 1984 and* ***from then on*** *he lived alone.* 她于 1984 年离去，从那时起他便独自一人生活。◇ *I took one look at the car and offered to buy it* ***there and then/then and there*** (= immediately). 我只看了那辆汽车一眼，就当即表示要买下来。 **2** used to introduce the next item in a series of actions, events, instructions, etc. 然后；接着；其后；后来：*He drank a glass of whisky, then another and then another.* 他喝了杯威士忌，接着又喝了一杯，然后又喝了一杯。◇ *First cook the onions, then add the mushrooms.* 先炒洋葱，然后放进蘑菇。◇ *We lived in France and then Italy before coming back to England.* 我们在返回英格兰之前，先住在法国，后来住在意大利。 ➲ LANGUAGE BANK AT PROCESS[1] **3** used to show the logical result of a particular statement or situation 那么；因此；既然如此：*If you miss that train then you'll have to*

T

get a taxi. 如果你错过那趟火车，那就得坐出租汽车。◇ *'My wife's got a job in Glasgow.' 'I take it you'll be moving, then.'* "我妻子在格拉斯哥找了份工作。" "既然如此，我想你要搬家了。" ◇ *'You haven't done anything to upset me.' 'So what's wrong, then?'* "你没有做使我烦心的事。" "那你是怎么啦？" ◇ *Why don't you hire a car? Then you'll be able to visit more of the area.* 你怎么不租辆汽车？那样的话，你可以多参观些地方。 **4** used to introduce additional information 另外；还有；再者；而且：*She's been very busy at work **and then** there was all that trouble with her son.* 她工作一直很忙，另外还有儿子的一大堆麻烦事。 **5** (*formal*) used to introduce a summary of sth that has just been said 总之：*These, then, are the main areas of concern.* 总之，这些是人们主要关注的方面。 **6** used to show the beginning or end of a conversation, statement, etc.（表示交谈、陈述等的开始或结束）那么：*Right then, where do you want the table to go?* 那好吧，你要把桌子放在哪里呢？ ◇ *'I really have to go.' 'OK. Bye, then.'* "我真该走了。" "好，那就再见吧。" ◇ *OK then, I think we've just about covered everything on the agenda.* 就这样吧，我想我们几乎已把议程上所有的事项都讨论过了。

IDM **...and 'then some** (*informal*) used to emphasize the large amount or number of sth, and to say that you have not mentioned everything 而且还要多；而且远不止这些：*There are Indian, Chinese, Mexican, Thai restaurants… and then some!* 有印度、中国、墨西哥、泰国餐馆…，而且还有很多其他国家的餐馆！ **but 'then | then a'gain | but then a'gain** (*informal*) used to introduce additional information or information that contrasts with sth that has just been said（引出另外情况或相对照的情况）不过，可是话又说回来了：*She was early, but then again, she always is.* 她到得早，不过话又说回来了，她总是早到。 ◇ *'So you might accept their offer?' 'Yes, then again I might not.'* "这么说你也许会接受他们的提议了？" "是的，不过也可能不接受。" ➲ MORE AT NOW *adv.*

■ ***adj.*** [only before noun] used to describe sb who had a particular title, job, etc. at the time in the past that is being discussed 当时（任职等）的：*That decision was taken by the then president.* 那个决定是由当时的总统作出的。

thence /ðens/ *adv.* (*old use* or *formal*) from that place; following that 从那里；然后；随之：*They made their way from Spain to France and thence to England.* 他们从西班牙去了法国，再从那里去了英国。 ◇ *He was promoted to manager, thence to a partnership in the firm.* 他被提升为经理，然后又成了公司的合伙人。

thence·forth /ˌðensˈfɔːθ; *NAmE* -ˈfɔːrθ/ (*also* **thence·for·ward** /ˌðensˈfɔːwəd; *NAmE* -ˈfɔːrwərd/) *adv.* (*old use* or *formal*) starting from that time 从那时起；此后

theo- /ˈθiːəʊ; *NAmE* ˈθiːoʊ/ *combining form* (in nouns, adjectives and adverbs 构成名词、形容词和副词) connected with God or a god 上帝的；神的

the·oc·racy /θiˈɒkrəsi; *NAmE* θiˈɑːk-/ *noun* (*pl.* **-ies**) **1** [U] government of a country by religious leaders 神权政治；僧侣政体 **2** [C] a country that is governed by religious leaders 神权国；神权政治国家 ▸ **theo·crat·ic** /ˌθiːəˈkrætɪk/ *adj.*：*theocratic rule* 神权统治

the·odo·lite /θiˈɒdəlaɪt; *NAmE* θiˈɑːd-/ *noun* a piece of equipment used by SURVEYORS for measuring angles 经纬仪

theo·lo·gian /ˌθiːəˈləʊdʒən; *NAmE* -ˈloʊ-/ *noun* a person who studies theology 神学家；神学研究者

the·ology /θiˈɒlədʒi; *NAmE* -ˈɑːlə-/ *noun* (*pl.* **-ies**) **1** [U] the study of religion and beliefs 神学；宗教学；宗教信仰学：*a degree in Theology* 神学学位 ◇ *a theology student* 研究神学的人 **2** [C] a set of religious beliefs 宗教信仰：*the theologies of the East* 东方的种种宗教信仰 ▸ **theo·logic·al** /ˌθiːəˈlɒdʒɪkl; *NAmE* -ˈlɑːdʒ-/ *adj.*：(*BrE*) *a theological college* 神学院 ◇ (*NAmE*) *a theological seminary* 神学院 **theo·logic·al·ly** /-kli/ *adv.*

the·orem /ˈθɪərəm; *NAmE* ˈθiːə-; ˈθɪr-/ *noun* (*specialist*) a rule or principle, especially in mathematics, that can be proved to be true（尤指数学）定理 ➲ COLLOCATIONS AT SCIENTIFIC

the·or·etic·al AW /ˌθɪəˈretɪkl; *NAmE* ˌθiːə-/ *adj.* [usually before noun] **1** concerned with the ideas and principles on which a particular subject is based, rather than with practice and experiment 理论上的：*a theoretical approach* 理论研究方法 ◇ *theoretical physics* 理论物理 ◇ *The first year provides students with a sound theoretical basis for later study.* 第一年为学生以后的学习奠定坚实的理论基础。 OPP **experimental, practical** **2** that could possibly exist, happen or be true, although this is unlikely 理论上存在的；假设的：*It's a theoretical possibility.* 这是理论上存在的可能性。 ▸ **the·or·etic·al·ly** AW /-kli/ *adv.*：*theoretically sound conclusions* 理论上无懈可击的结论 ◇ *It is theoretically possible for him to overrule their decision, but highly unlikely.* 按理说他可以否定他们的决定，但是可能性很小。

the·or·ist AW /ˈθɪərɪst; *NAmE* ˈθiːə-; ˈθɪr-/ (*also* **the·or·et·ician** /ˌθɪərəˈtɪʃn; *NAmE* ˌθiːə-; ˌθɪr-/) *noun* a person who develops ideas and principles about a particular subject in order to explain why things happen or exist 理论家；理论工作者

the·or·ize (*BrE also* **-ise**) /ˈθɪəraɪz; *NAmE* ˈθiːə-/ *verb* [I, T] **~ (about/on sth) | ~ sth | ~ that…** to suggest facts and ideas to explain sth; to form a theory or theories about sth 从理论上说明；形成理论；理论化：*The study theorizes about the role of dreams in peoples' lives.* 这项研究从理论上说明了梦在人们生活中的作用。 ▸ **the·or·iz·ing, -is·ing** *noun* [U]

the·ory 🔑 AW /ˈθɪəri; *NAmE* ˈθɪri; ˈθiːəri/ *noun* (*pl.* **-ies**) **1** 🔑 [C, U] a formal set of ideas that is intended to explain why sth happens or exists 学说；论；说：*According to the theory of relativity, nothing can travel faster than light.* 根据相对论，任何东西都无法超越光速。 ➲ COLLOCATIONS AT SCIENTIFIC **2** 🔑 [U] the principles on which a particular subject is based 理论；原理；原则：*the theory and practice of language teaching* 语言教学理论与实践 **3** 🔑 [C] **~ (that…)** an opinion or idea that sb believes is true but that is not proved（未证明的）意见；看法；推测：*I have this theory that most people prefer being at work to being at home.* 依我看，多数人喜欢工作而不愿待在家里。

IDM **in 'theory** 🔑 used to say that a particular statement is supposed to be true but may in fact be wrong 理论上；按理说：*In theory, these machines should last for ten years or more.* 从理论上讲，这些机器应能用十年以上。 ◇ *That sounds fine in theory, but have you really thought it through?* 这话听起来很有道理，但是你真正全面考虑过没有？

the·oso·phy /θiˈɒsəfi; *NAmE* θiˈɑːs-/ *noun* **1** [U, C] a religious system of thought that tries to know God by means of MEDITATION, prayer, etc. 神智学（通过直接体验以认识上帝） **2 Theosophy** [U] the belief of a religious group, the Theosophical Society, started in New York in 1875 神智学会信仰（该会于 1875 年在纽约成立）

thera·peut·ic /ˌθerəˈpjuːtɪk/ *adj.* **1** [usually before noun] designed to help treat an illness 治疗的；医疗的；治病的：*the therapeutic properties of herbs* 草药的医疗效用 **2** helping you to relax 有助于放松精神的：*Painting can be very therapeutic.* 绘画可以使人完全放松。 ▸ **thera·peut·ic·al·ly** /-kli/ *adv.*

thera·peut·ics /ˌθerəˈpjuːtɪks/ *noun* [U] the branch of medicine concerned with the treatment of diseases 治疗学

ther·ap·ist /ˈθerəpɪst/ *noun* **1** (especially in compounds 尤用于构成复合词) a specialist who treats a particular type of illness or problem, or who uses a particular type of treatment（某治疗法的）治疗专家：*a speech therapist* 语言治疗师 ◇ *a beauty therapist* 美容师 ➲ SEE ALSO OCCUPATIONAL THERAPIST, PHYSIOTHERAPIST **2** = PSYCHOTHERAPIST

ther·apy /ˈθerəpi/ *noun* (*pl.* **-ies**) **1** [U, C] the treatment of a physical problem or an illness 治疗；疗法：*Most leukaemia patients undergo some sort of **drug therapy** (= treatment using drugs).* 大多数白血病患者都会接受某

种药物治疗。◇ ***alternative/complementary/natural therapies*** (= treatments that do not use traditional drugs) 替代 / 补充 / 自然疗法 ➲ COLLOCATIONS AT ILL **2** [U] = PSYCHOTHERAPY：*a therapy group* 心理治疗小组 ◇ *She's **in therapy**.* 她在接受心理治疗。➲ SEE ALSO CHEMOTHERAPY, GROUP THERAPY, HORMONE REPLACEMENT THERAPY, OCCUPATIONAL THERAPY, PHYSIOTHERAPY, RADIOTHERAPY, RETAIL THERAPY, SPEECH THERAPY

Thera·vada /ˌθerəˈvɑːdə/ (*also* **ˌTheraˌvada ˈBuddhism**) *noun* [U] one of the two major forms of Buddhism 上座部（佛教部派）➲ COMPARE MAHAYANA

there /ðeə(r); *NAmE* ðer/ *adv., exclamation*

■ ***adv.*** **1** **there is, are, was, were, etc.** used to show that sth exists or happens（表示存在或发生）：*There's a restaurant around the corner.* 拐角处有一家餐馆。◇ *There are two people waiting outside.* 有两个人正在外面等候。◇ *Has there been an accident?* 出过事故吗？◇ *I don't want there to be any misunderstanding.* 我不希望有任何误解。◇ *There seemed to be no doubt about it.* 此事似乎毫无疑问。◇ *There comes a point where you give up.* 现在你该放弃了。◇ *There remains the problem of finance.* 财政问题仍然存在。◇ *Suddenly there was a loud bang.* 突然发出砰的一声巨响。◇ (*informal*) *There's only four days left.* 只剩下四天了。◇ (*literary*) ***There once was** a poor farmer who had four sons.* 从前有一个贫苦的农夫，他有四个儿子。 **2** in, at or to that place or position 在那里；到那里；往那里：*We went on to Paris and stayed there eleven days.* 我们接着去了巴黎，在那里停留了十一天。◇ *I hope we get there in time.* 我希望我们及时到达那里。◇ *It's there, right in front of you!* 在那儿，就在你前面！◇ ***There it is**—just behind the chair.* 可找到它了，就在椅子后面。◇ *'Have you seen my pen?' 'Yes, it's **over there**.'* "你看见我的笔了吗？" "看见了，就在那儿。" ◇ *There are a lot of people **back there*** (= behind) *waiting to get in.* 后面有许多人等着进来。◇ *I'm not going **in there**—it's freezing!* 我不打算到那里面去，太冷了！◇ *We're **almost there*** (= we have almost arrived). 我们差不多快到了。◇ *Can I get **there and back** in a day?* 我去那里一天内能打来回吗？◇ *I left in 2008 and I haven't been **back there** since.* 我于 2008 年离开那里，从那以后再也没有回去过。◇ *Hello, is Bob there please?* (= used when calling sb on the phone) 喂，请问鲍勃在吗？◇ *I took one look at the car and offered to buy it **there and then/then and there*** (= immediately). 我只看了那辆汽车一眼，便当即表示要买下来。 **3** existing or available 存在的；现有的；可得到的：*I went to see if my old school was still there.* 我去看过母校是否依然存在。◇ *The money's there if you need it.* 你若需要用钱就来取好了。 **4** at that point (in a story, an argument, etc.)（故事、辩论等）在那一点上：*'I feel…' There she stopped.* "我觉得…" 她说到那儿停了下来。◇ *I don't agree with you there.* 在那一点上，我不敢与你苟同。 **5** used to attract sb's attention（用以引起注意）：*Hello, there!* 喂，你好！◇ *You there! Come back!* 说你呢！回来！◇ ***There you are!** I've been looking for you everywhere.* 原来你在这儿！我到处都把你找遍了。 **6** used to attract sb's attention to a particular person, thing or fact（用以引起对某人、事物或事实的注意）：*There's the statue I was telling you about.* 那就是我跟你们讲过的塑像。◇ *That woman there is the boss's wife.* 那边那个女人是老板的太太。◇ ***There goes** the last bus* (= we've just missed it). 最后一班公共汽车刚开走了。◇ ***There goes** the phone* (= it's ringing). 电话铃响了。◇ (*humorous*) ***There goes** my career!* (= my career is ruined) 我的前程就这么给毁了！◇ *So, **there you have it**: that's how it all started.* 就这样，你瞧：这就是整个事件的起因。 **7 ~ to do sth** used to show the role of a person or thing in a situation（表示人或事物在某一情况中的作用）：*The fact is, they're there to make money.* 真实的情况是，他们去那儿是为了赚钱。

IDM **ˌbeen ˈthere, ˌdone ˈthat** (*informal*) used to show that you think a place or an activity is not very interesting or impressive because you have already experienced it（表示已去过某地或做过某事而不再感兴趣）没意思，没劲，乏味：*Not Spain again! Been there, done that, got the T-shirt.* 别再提西班牙了！去过那儿了，没劲，就买了这件 T 恤。 **be ˈthere for sb** to be available if sb wants to talk to you or if they need help 随叫随到；不离…左右：*You know I'll always be there for you.* 你知道我将永远在你左右。 **by ˈthere** (*WelshE*) there; to there 在那里；到那里；往那里：*He's over by there.* 他在那儿。 **have been there beˈfore** (*informal*) to know all about a situation because you have experienced it 全都知道；亲身经历过 **not all ˈthere** (*informal*) not very intelligent, especially because of mental illness 傻乎乎；呆头呆脑 **ˌso ˈthere!** (*informal*) used to show that you are determined not to change your attitude or opinion 就是这样；我主意已定；没什么可商量的：*Well, you can't have it, so there!* 好啦，不给你了，就是这样！ **ˌthere it ˈis** (*informal*) that is the situation 情况就是这样：*It's crazy, I know, but there it is.* 我知道，那很疯狂，不过情况就是如此。 **ˈthere's a good boy, girl, dog, etc.** (*informal*) used to praise or encourage small children or animals（用以夸奖或勉励幼儿、动物）乖，乖孩子：*Finish your lunch, there's a good boy.* 把午饭吃完，乖孩子。 **there's lovely, nice, etc.** (*WelshE*) used to say that sth has a particular quality（表示有某种特性）真可爱，太好了 **ˌthere's ˈsth for you** (*informal*) used to say that sth is a very good example of sth 这才叫；这才称得上：*She visited him every day he was in the hospital. There's devotion for you.* 他住医院时，她每天都去探望他。这才叫做尽心尽力。◇ (*ironic*) *He didn't even say thank you. There's gratitude for you!* 他连个谢字都没说。瞧，这就是对你的感激！ **ˌthere or thereaˈbouts** (*BrE, informal*) used to say that sth is very good, even if it is not perfect（表示即使不完美也很好）差不多：*At the end of the tournament, he'll be there or thereabouts* (= he may not win, but he will be one of the best players). 锦标赛结束时，他不拔头筹也差不到哪里去。 **ˌthere, ˈthere!** (*informal*) used to persuade a small child to stop crying or being upset（劝说小孩不要唏哭或沮丧）好了，好了：*There, there! Never mind, you'll soon feel better.* 好了，好了！不要紧，你很快就会感到好一些了。 **ˌthere you ˈare** (*also* **ˌthere you ˈgo**) (*informal*) **1** used when giving sb a thing they want or have asked for 给你；这就是你要的；拿去吧：*There you are—that'll be £3.80, please.* 喏，给您，请付 3 英镑 80 便士。◇ *OK, there you go.* 好，给你。 **2** used when explaining or showing sth to sb（解释或示范时用）这就行了，就是这样：*You switch on, push in the DVD and there you are!* 你打开开关，把 DVD 推进去就行了！◇ *There you are! I told you it was easy!* 瞧，就是这样！我跟你说过这很容易！ **3** used when you are talking about sth that happens in a typical way or about a situation that cannot be changed（某事的发生方式）一贯如此；（某状况）无可更改：*There you go—that's what they're like.* 他们就是这个样子，一贯如此。◇ *I know it's not ideal but there you go…* 我知道这并不理想，但只好这样啦… **ˌthere you go aˈgain** (*informal*) used to criticize sb when they behave in a way that is typical of them（批评对方的一贯作风）你又来这一套了：*There you go again—jumping to conclusions.* 你又犯老毛病了，太快下结论了。➲ MORE AT HERE *adv.*

■ ***exclamation*** used to express satisfaction that you were right about sth or to show that sth annoys you（表示因说中某事而感到满意或表示烦恼）你瞧，好啦，得啦：*There now! What did I tell you?* (= you can see that I was right) 你瞧！我跟你说什么来着？◇ *There! That didn't hurt too much, did it?* 怎么样，那不太痛吧？◇ *There! You've gone and woken the baby!* 瞧！你一去就把孩子弄醒了！

there·abouts /ˌðeərəˈbaʊts; *NAmE* ˌðerə-/ *adv.* (usually used after *or* 通常用于 or 之后) **1** near the place mentioned 在那附近：*He comes from Leeds or thereabouts.* 他是利兹或其周边的人。 **2** used to say that a particular number, quantity, time, etc. is not exact（数量、时间等）大约，左右，上下：*They paid $100 000 or thereabouts for the house.* 他们买那房子花了大约 10 万美元。
IDM SEE THERE *adv.*

there·after /ˌðeərˈɑːftə(r); *NAmE* ˌðerˈæf-/ *adv.* (*formal*) after the time or event mentioned 之后；此后；以后：*She married at 17 and gave birth to her first child shortly thereafter.* 她 17 岁结婚，之后不久便生了第一个孩子。➲ COMPARE HEREAFTER *adv.* (2)

there·by AW /ˌðeəˈbaɪ; *NAmE* ˌðerˈbaɪ/ *adv.* (*formal*) used to introduce the result of the action or situation mentioned

T

因此；由此；从而：*Regular exercise strengthens the heart, thereby reducing the risk of heart attack.* 经常锻炼可以增强心脏机能，从而减少心脏病发作的危险。

there·fore 🔑 /ˈðeəfɔː(r); *NAmE* ˈðerf-/ *adv.* used to introduce the logical result of sth that has just been mentioned 因此；所以；因而：*He's only 17 and therefore not eligible to vote.* 他只有 17 岁，因此没有投票选举的资格。◇ *There is still much to discuss. We shall, therefore, return to this item at our next meeting.* 要讨论的问题还有很多。所以，我们将在下次会议上再讨论这项议题。

▼ LANGUAGE BANK 用语库

therefore

Ways of saying 'For this reason...'

"因此" 的种种表达方法

- *Today's children eat more junk food and get less exercise than previous generations of children. It is not surprising,* ***therefore****, that rates of childhood obesity are on the increase.* 当今的孩子比过去几代儿童吃的垃圾食品更多，锻炼更少。因此，肥胖儿童的比例逐渐升高并不奇怪。
- *Children who grow up on a diet of junk food find it difficult to change this habit later in life. It is essential,* ***therefore****, that parents encourage healthy eating from an early age.* 吃垃圾食品长大的孩子发现在日后的生活中很难改变这个习惯。因此，父母从孩子幼年开始就倡导健康饮食非常重要。
- *Children who grow up on a diet of junk food find it difficult to change this habit later in life.* ***For this reason****, /* ***This is why*** *it is essential that children eat healthily from an early age.* 吃垃圾食品长大的孩子在日后的生活中很难改变这个习惯。因此，孩子从幼年开始就健康饮食非常重要。
- *Eating habits formed in childhood tend to continue into adult life.* ***Thus****, the best way to prevent heart disease among adults is to encourage healthy eating from an early age.* 孩童时期形成的饮食习惯往往会延续到成年。因此，预防成年人心脏疾病的最好方法就是从小鼓励健康饮食。
- *Eating habits formed in childhood tend to continue into adult life,* ***hence*** *the importance of encouraging healthy eating from an early age.* 孩童时期形成的饮食习惯往往会延续到成年。因此，从小鼓励健康饮食尤为重要。

➲ LANGUAGE BANK AT CAUSE, CONSEQUENTLY, EMPHASIS, VITAL

there·from /ˌðeəˈfrɒm; *NAmE* ˌðerˈfrʌm/ *adv.* (*formal* or *law* 律) from the thing mentioned 由此；从那里：*The committee will examine the agreement and any problems arising therefrom.* 委员会将审查这项协议和由此引起的问题。

there·in /ˌðeərˈɪn; *NAmE* ˌðer-/ *adv.* (*law* 律 or *formal*) in the place, object, document, etc. mentioned 在那里，在其中（指提及的地点、物体、文件等）：*The insurance policy covers the building and any fixtures contained therein.* 保险单为这座大楼及其中所有的设施保了险。

IDM **therein lies...** used to emphasize the result or consequence of a particular situation 那一点就是；那方面便是；…就在那里：*He works extremely hard and therein lies the key to his success.* 他工作极其努力，这就是他成功的关键。

there·of /ˌðeərˈɒv; *NAmE* ˌðerˈʌv/ *adv.* (*law* 律 or *formal*) of the thing mentioned 在其中；由此：*Is the property or any part thereof used for commercial activity?* 这一财产或其中任何部分有用于商业活动吗？

there·on /ˌðeərˈɒn; *NAmE* ˌðerˈɑːn; -ˈɔːn/ *adv.* (*law* 律 or *formal*) on the thing mentioned 以…为根据；由…而产生：*a meeting to discuss the annual accounts and the auditors' report thereon* 讨论年度报表及其审计报告的会议

there's /ðeəz; *NAmE* ðerz/ *short form* **1** there is **2** there has

there·to /ˌðeəˈtuː; *NAmE* ˌðerˈtuː/ *adv.* (*law* 律 or *formal*) to the thing mentioned 附之；随之：*The lease entitles the holder to use the buildings and any land attached thereto.* 本租约持有人有权使用此建筑物以及所附属的土地。

there·under /ˌðeərˈʌndə(r); *NAmE* ˌðer-/ *adv.* (*law* 律 or *formal*) under the thing mentioned 在其下；据此：*This savings plan is only available under the Finance Act 1990 and any regulations made thereunder.* 这项储蓄计划只根据《1990 年金融法》及其下设规定提供。

there·upon /ˌðeərəˈpɒn; *NAmE* ˌðerəˈpɑːn/ *adv.* (*formal*) **1** immediately after the situation mentioned; as a direct result of the situation mentioned 立即；随即；因此；于是：*The audience thereupon rose cheering to their feet.* 观众随即起立欢呼。**2** on the thing mentioned 在其上：*a large notice with black letters printed thereupon* 印有黑体字的大幅告示

there·with /ˌðeəˈwɪð; -ˈwɪθ; *NAmE* ˌðerˈw-/ *adv.* (*old use* or *formal*) **1** with or in the thing mentioned 与此；与之 **2** soon or immediately after that 随即；立即

therm /θɜːm; *NAmE* θɜːrm/ *noun* a unit of heat, used in Britain for measuring a gas supply 撤姆（英国用以计量煤气的热量单位）

ther·mal /ˈθɜːml; *NAmE* ˈθɜːrml/ *adj., noun*

■ ***adj.*** [only before noun] **1** (*specialist*) connected with heat 热的；热量的：*thermal energy* 热能 **2** (of clothing 衣服) designed to keep you warm by preventing heat from escaping from the body 保暖的；防寒的：*thermal underwear* 保暖内衣裤 **3** (of streams, lakes, etc. 溪水、湖泊等) in which the water has been naturally heated by the earth 温暖的；热的：*thermal springs* 温泉 ▸ **ther·mal·ly** /-əli/ *adv.*

■ ***noun*** **1** [C] a rising current of warm air used, for example, by a GLIDER to gain height 上升的热气流 **2** **thermals** [pl.] (*especially BrE*) warm underwear that prevents heat from escaping from the body 保暖内衣裤

ˌthermal ˈimaging *noun* [U] (*specialist*) the process of producing an image of sth or finding out where sth is, using the heat that comes from it 热成像（利用物体所散发的热量形成图像或定位）：*Rescue teams are using thermal imaging to locate survivors of the earthquake.* 救援队伍正利用热成像确定地震幸存者的位置。

thermo- /ˈθɜːməʊ; *NAmE* -moʊ/ *combining form* (in nouns, adjectives and adverbs 构成名词、形容词和副词) connected with heat 热的：*thermonuclear* 热核的 ◇ *thermometer* 温度计

thermo·dynam·ics /ˌθɜːməʊdaɪˈnæmɪks; *NAmE* ˌθɜːrmoʊ-/ *noun* [U] the science that deals with the relations between heat and other forms of energy 热力学：*the laws of thermodynamics* 热力学定律 ➲ MORE LIKE THIS 29, page R28 ▸ **thermo·dynam·ic** *adj.*

therm·om·eter /θəˈmɒmɪtə(r); *NAmE* θərˈmɑːm-/ *noun* an instrument used for measuring the temperature of the air, a person's body, etc. 温度计；寒暑表；体温计：*a thermometer reading* 温度计读数

thermo·nuclear /ˌθɜːməʊˈnjuːkliə(r); *NAmE* ˌθɜːrmoʊˈnuːk-/ *adj.* connected with nuclear reactions that only happen at very high temperatures 热核的

thermo·plas·tic /ˌθɜːməʊˈplæstɪk; *NAmE* ˌθɜːrmoʊ-/ *noun* [U] (*specialist*) a plastic material that can be easily shaped and bent when it is heated, and that becomes hard when it is cooled 热塑（性）塑料

Ther·mos™ /ˈθɜːməs; *NAmE* ˈθɜːrməs/ (*BrE also* **ˈThermos flask**) (*NAmE also* **ˈThermos bottle**) *noun* a particular kind of VACUUM FLASK (= a container like a bottle with double walls with a VACUUM between them, used for keeping liquids hot or cold) 膳魔师保温（或保冷）瓶；保温瓶 ➲ COMPARE FLASK (2)

the thermo·sphere /ˈθɜːməsfɪə(r); *NAmE* ˈθɜːrməsfɪr/ *noun* [sing.] (*specialist*) the region of the atmosphere above the MESOSPHERE 热层

thermo·stat /ˈθɜːməstæt; *NAmE* ˈθɜːrm-/ *noun* a device that measures and controls the temperature of a machine or room, by switching the heating or cooling system on and off as necessary 温控器；恒温器 ▸ **thermo·stat·ic** /ˌθɜːməˈstætɪk; *NAmE* ˌθɜːrm-/ *adj.* [only before noun] **thermo·stat·ic·al·ly** /-kli/ *adv.*

the·saurus /θɪˈsɔːrəs/ *noun* (*pl.* **the·sauri** /θɪˈsɔːraɪ/ or **the·saur·uses** /-rəsɪz/) a book that lists words in groups that have similar meanings 类义词典；义类词典；同义词词典

these ➲ THIS *det., pron.*

thesis AW /ˈθiːsɪs/ *noun* (*pl.* **theses** /ˈθiːsiːz/) **1** ~ (**on sth**) a long piece of writing completed by a student as part of a university degree, based on their own research 论文；毕业论文；学位论文 **2** a statement or an opinion that is discussed in a logical way and presented with evidence in order to prove that it is true 命题；论题：*These latest findings support the thesis that sexuality is determined by nature rather than choice.* 这些最新发现证实了性取向取决于自然而非选择这一论点。 ➲ COLLOCATIONS AT SCIENTIFIC

thes·pian /ˈθespiən/ *noun* (*often humorous*) an actor 演员 ▸ **thes·pian** *adj.*

theta /ˈθiːtə/ *noun* the 8th letter of the Greek alphabet (Θ, θ) 希腊字母表的第 8 个字母

ˈtheta role *noun* = THEMATIC ROLE

they 🔑 /ðeɪ/ *pron.* (used as the subject of a verb 用作动词主语) **1** 🔑 people, animals or things that have already been mentioned or are easily identified 他们；她们；它们：*'Where are John and Liz?' 'They went for a walk.'* "约翰和利兹在哪儿？" "他们去散步了。" ◇ *They* (= the things you are carrying) *go on the bottom shelf.* 这些东西放在架子的底层。 **2** 🔑 used instead of *he* or *she* to refer to a person whose sex is not mentioned or not known (用以代替 he 或 she，指性别不详的人)：*If anyone arrives late they'll have to wait outside.* 谁要是迟到，他就得在外面等着。 ➲ NOTE AT GENDER **3** 🔑 people in general (泛指) 人们，人人，众人：*The rest, as they say, is history.* 其余的就尽人皆知，不须赘述了。 **4** 🔑 people in authority or experts 权威人士；上面 (指负责人)；专家：*They cut my water off.* 管事的把水给我掐了。 ◇ *They now say that red wine is good for you.* 现在专家说喝红葡萄酒对人有好处。

they'd /ðeɪd/ *short form* **1** they had **2** they would

they'll /ðeɪl/ *short form* they will

they're /ðeə(r); *NAmE* ðer; *weak form* ðər/ *short form* they are

they've /ðeɪv/ *short form* they have

thia·mine (*also* **thia·min**) /ˈθaɪəmɪn; -miːn/ *noun* [U] a VITAMIN of the B group, found in grains, BEANS and LIVER 维生素 B1，硫胺素（B 类维生素，存在于谷物、豆子和肝脏中）

thick 🔑 /θɪk/ *adj., noun, adv.*

▪ ***adj.*** (**thick·er**, **thick·est**)

• **DISTANCE BETWEEN SIDES** 厚度 **1** 🔑 having a larger distance between opposite sides or surfaces than other similar objects or than normal 厚的；粗的：*a thick slice of bread* 一片厚面包 ◇ *a thick book* (= one that has a lot of pages) 一本厚书 ◇ *a thick coat* (= one made of heavy cloth) 厚大衣 ◇ *thick fingers* 粗手指 ◇ *Everything was covered with a thick layer of dust.* 所有的东西都覆盖着厚厚的一层灰尘。 **2** 🔑 used to ask about or state the distance between opposite sides or surfaces（询问或说明厚度）有…厚：*How thick are the walls?* 这些墙有多厚？ ◇ *They're two feet thick.* 它们两英尺厚。

• **HAIR/FUR/TREES** 毛发；毛皮；树木 **3** 🔑 growing closely together in large numbers 浓密的；稠密的；茂密的：*thick dark hair* 浓密的黑发 ◇ *a thick forest* 茂密的森林

• **LIQUID** 液体 **4** 🔑 not flowing very easily 浓的；黏稠的：*thick soup* 浓汤 ◇ *The effect will be ruined if the paint is too thick.* 涂料太稠就会破坏效果。

• **FOG/SMOKE/AIR** 雾；烟；空气 **5** 🔑 difficult to see through; difficult to breathe in 能见度低的；浓的；阴霾的；浑浊的；不透气的：*The plane crashed in thick fog.* 飞机在大雾中坠毁。 ◇ *thick smoke* 浓烟 ◇ **~ with sth** *The air was thick with dust.* 空气由于灰尘弥漫而闷塞。 ◇ (*figurative*) *The atmosphere was thick with tension.* 气氛紧张得使人透不过气来。

• **WITH LARGE NUMBER/AMOUNT** 大量 **6** **~ with sb/sth** having a large number of people or a large amount of sth in one place 拥满；挤满；充满；弥漫：*The beach was thick with sunbathers.* 海滩上密密麻麻都是晒太阳的人。

• **STUPID** 愚蠢 **7** (*informal*) (of a person 人) slow to learn or understand things 迟钝的；愚笨的：*Are you thick, or what?* 你是傻还是怎么啦？

• **ACCENT** 口音 **8** (*sometimes disapproving*) easily recognized as being from a particular country or area 浓重的；明显的 SYN **strong**：*a thick Brooklyn accent* 浓重的布鲁克林口音

• **VOICE** 嗓音 **9** ~ (**with sth**) deep and not as clear as normal, especially because of illness or emotion 嘶哑的，不清的（尤指因疾病或激动所致）：*His voice was thick with emotion.* 他激动得连声音都嘶哑了。

• **FRIENDLY WITH SB** 友好 **10** ~ (**with sb**) (*informal*) very friendly with sb, especially in a way that makes other people suspicious 亲密的；十分友好的；过于亲近的：*You seem to be very thick with the boss!* 你好像和老板走得挺近的！ ➲ SEE ALSO THICKLY, THICKNESS

IDM **give sb/get a thick ˈear** (*BrE, informal*) to hit sb/be hit on the head as a punishment 打耳光；挨耳光 (**as**) **thick as ˈthieves** (*informal*) (of two or more people 两个或以上的人) very friendly, especially in a way that makes other people suspicious 非常友好；亲密无间；过从甚密 (**as**) **thick as two short ˈplanks** (*BrE, informal*) (of a person 人) very stupid 笨得像木头人；笨到极点 ➲ MORE LIKE THIS 14, page R26 **a thick ˈhead** (*informal*) a physical condition in which your head is painful or you cannot think clearly as a result of an illness or of drinking too much alcohol（由于疾病或饮酒过量）晕头涨脑，稀里糊涂 **your thick ˈhead** (*informal*) used to show that you are annoyed that sb does not understand sth（认为某人理解慢而恼火）笨脑瓜，木头脑瓜：*When will you get it into your thick head that I don't want to see you again!* 你那木头脑瓜什么时候才会明白我不想再见到你呢？ **a ˌthick ˈskin** the ability to accept criticism, insults, etc. without becoming upset 厚脸皮；不计较面子 OPP **a thin skin** ➲ SEE ALSO THICK-SKINNED ➲ MORE AT BLOOD *n.*, GROUND *n.*

▪ ***noun*** [U]

IDM **in the ˈthick of sth** involved in the busiest or most active part of sth 在…最繁忙的时候；处于…最活跃部分；在密集处 **through ˌthick and ˈthin** even when there are problems or difficulties 不顾艰难险阻；赴汤蹈火；同甘共苦：*He's supported the team for over ten years through thick and thin.* 十多年来，在任何情况下他都支持这个队。 ➲ MORE LIKE THIS 13, page R26

▪ ***adv.*** (**thick·er**, **thick·est**) in a way that produces a wide piece or deep layer of sth 厚厚地：*Make sure you cut the bread nice and thick.* 你一定要把面包片切得厚厚的，规规整整的。

IDM **lay it on ˈthick** (*informal*) to talk about sb/sth in a way that makes them or it seem much better or much worse than they really are; to exaggerate sth 夸大其词地褒贬；露骨地吹捧；过分贬低：*Praise them when necessary, but don't lay it on too thick.* 必要时要表扬他们，但不能言过其实。 **thick and ˈfast** quickly and in large quantities 又快又多；频频：*Questions were coming at them thick and fast.* 问题铺天盖地向他们而来。

thick·en /ˈθɪkən/ *verb* [I, T] to become thicker; to make sth thicker（使）变厚，变浓，变稠：*Stir until the sauce has thickened.* 不停地搅拌酱汁，直到搅稠为止。 ◇ *It was a dangerous journey through thickening fog.* 旅途中雾越来越大，险象环生。 ◇ **~ sth** *Thicken the stew with flour.* 给炖肉汁勾芡。 IDM SEE PLOT *n.*

T

thick·en·er /ˈθɪkənə(r)/ *noun* a substance used to make a liquid thicker 增稠剂：*paint thickeners* 油漆稠化剂

thicket /ˈθɪkɪt/ *noun* **1** a group of bushes or small trees growing closely together 灌木丛；树丛 **2** a large number of things that are not easy to understand or separate 错综复杂；盘根错节

thick·head /ˈθɪkhed/ (*also* **thicko**) *noun* (*BrE, informal*) a stupid person 傻瓜；笨蛋；呆子

thick·head·ed /ˌθɪkˈhedɪd/ *adj.* stupid 愚蠢的；笨的

thick·ly /ˈθɪkli/ *adv.* **1** in a way that produces a wide piece or deep layer of sth 厚厚地：*thickly sliced bread* 切成厚片的面包 ◇ *Apply the paint thickly in even strokes.* 涂颜料要厚，笔画要匀。 **2 ~ wooded, populated, etc.** having a lot of trees, people, etc. close together（树木、人口等）茂密，稠密 **3** in a deep voice that is not as clear as normal, especially because of illness or emotion 声音不清地，沙哑地（尤指因疾病或激动）

thick·ness /ˈθɪknəs/ *noun* **1** [U, C] the size of sth between opposite surfaces or sides 厚；厚度；粗 SYN **width**：*Use wood of at least 12 mm thickness.* 使用至少 12 毫米厚的木材。◇ *The board is available in four thicknesses.* 现有四种不同厚度的木板可供使用。 **2** [C] ~ **(of sth)** a layer of sth 层：*The jacket was lined with a double thickness* (= two layers) *of fabric.* 这件短上衣有两层衬里。

thicko /ˈθɪkəʊ; *NAmE* -oʊ/ *noun* (*pl.* **-os**) (*BrE, informal*) = THICKHEAD

thick·set /θɪkˈset/ *adj.* (especially of a man 尤指男子) having a strong heavy body 身体粗壮的；膀阔腰圆的；虎背熊腰的

ˌthick-ˈskinned *adj.* **1** (of a person 人) not easily upset by criticism or unkind comments 厚脸皮的；不计较脸面的；（对批评或侮辱）不易生气的 **2** (of fruit 水果) having a thick skin 皮厚的 OPP **thin-skinned**

thief /θiːf/ *noun* (*pl.* **thieves** /θiːvz/) a person who steals sth from another person or place 贼；小偷；窃贼：*a car/jewel, etc. thief* 偷汽车、珠宝等的窃贼 ➲ COLLOCATIONS AT CRIME ➲ SEE ALSO THEFT IDM SEE HONOUR *n.*, THICK *adj.*

thiev·ing /ˈθiːvɪŋ/ *noun* [U] (*informal*) the act of stealing things 偷窃 ▸ **thiev·ing** *adj.* (*informal*)：*You've no right to take that, you thieving swine!* 你没有权利把那拿走，你这个贪心的贼！

T

thigh /θaɪ/ *noun* **1** the top part of the leg between the knee and the hip 大腿；股 ➲ COLLOCATIONS AT PHYSICAL ➲ VISUAL VOCAB PAGE V64 **2** the top part of the leg of a chicken, etc., cooked and eaten（食用的鸡等的）大腿

ˈthigh bone *noun* the large thick bone in the top part of the leg between the hip and the knee 股骨 SYN **femur** ➲ VISUAL VOCAB PAGE V64

thim·ble /ˈθɪmbl/ *noun* a small metal or plastic object that you wear on the end of your finger to protect it when sewing 顶针；针箍

thimble·ful /ˈθɪmblfʊl/ *noun* a very small amount of a liquid, especially alcohol 少量液体（尤指酒）

thin /θɪn/ *adj., adv., verb*

■ *adj.* (**thin·ner, thin·nest**)

• NOT THICK 薄；细 **1** having a smaller distance between opposite sides or surfaces than other similar objects or than normal 薄的；细的：*Cut the vegetables into thin strips.* 把菜切成细条。◇ *A number of thin cracks appeared in the wall.* 墙上出现了许多细裂缝。 ◇ *The body was hidden beneath a thin layer of soil.* 尸体被埋在薄薄的一层土下面。◇ *a thin blouse* (= of light cloth) 薄薄的女衬衫 ➲ SEE ALSO PAPER-THIN ➲ NOTE AT NARROW

• NOT FAT 瘦 **2** (*sometimes disapproving*) (of a person or part of the body 人或身体部位) not covered with much flesh 瘦的：*He was tall and thin, with dark hair.* 他又高又瘦，满头黑发。◇ *She was looking pale and thin.* 她面黄肌瘦。◇ *He is as* **thin as a rake** (= very thin). 他骨瘦如柴。◇ *thin legs* 细腿

• HAIR 毛发 **3** not growing closely together or in large amounts 稀少的；稀疏的：*thin grey hair* 稀疏的花白头发

• LIQUID 液体 **4** containing more liquid than is normal or expected 稀薄的；淡的 SYN **runny**：*The sauce was thin and tasteless.* 这酱汁淡而无味。

• SMOKE 烟 **5** fairly easy to see through 能见度较高的；稀薄的：*They fought their way through where the smoke was thinner.* 他们挣扎着从烟雾稀薄的地方逃了出去。

• AIR 空气 **6** containing less OXYGEN than normal 稀薄的；含氧少的

• SOUND 声音 **7** (*disapproving*) high and weak 微弱的；尖细的；有气无力的：*Her thin voice trailed off into silence.* 她的声音越来越弱直至毫无声息。

• SMILE 微笑 **8** not sincere or enthusiastic 不真心实意的；冷淡的：*He gave a thin smile.* 他淡然一笑。

• LIGHT 光 **9** not very bright 微弱的；暗淡的：*the thin grey light of dawn* 浅灰色的晨曦

• POOR QUALITY 劣质 **10** of poor quality; lacking an important quality 质量差的；空乏的；拙劣的：*a thin excuse*

▼ **VOCABULARY BUILDING 词汇扩充**

Saying that somebody is thin 形容人瘦

Thin is the most usual word. * thin 为最常用词：*Steve is tall and thin and has brown hair.* 史蒂夫瘦高个儿，长着棕色的头发。 It is sometimes used with a negative meaning. 该词有时含贬义：*Mother looked thin and tired after her long illness.* 久病之后，母亲看上去很憔悴。

The following words all express praise or admiration. 下列词语均含褒义：

- **Slim** means pleasantly thin. It is often used to describe women who have controlled their weight by diet or exercise. * slim 指苗条、修长，常用以形容以节食或锻炼来控制体重的女子：*She has a beautifully slim figure.* 她的身材十分苗条。
- A **slender** girl or woman is thin and graceful. * slender 指女性身材苗条、纤细、修长。
- A **lean** man is thin and fit. * lean 指男子瘦而健康。
- **Willowy** describes a woman who is attractively tall and thin. * willowy 指女子身材高挑，婀娜多姿。

The following words are more negative in their meaning. 下列词语贬义较重：

- **Skinny** means very thin, often in a way that is not attractive. * skinny 指瘦得皮包骨、干瘦：*a skinny little kid* 瘦骨嶙峋的小孩
- **Bony** describes parts of the body when they are so thin that the bones can be seen. * bony 指人体某部位瘦得骨头突出：*the old man's bony hands* 这老人骨瘦如柴的双手
- **Scrawny** suggests that a person is thin, weak and not attractive. * scrawny 指人干瘪、骨瘦如柴：*a scrawny old woman* 骨瘦如柴的老妇
- **Gaunt** describes a person who is a little too thin and looks sad or ill. * gaunt 指人消瘦、憔悴。
- **Underweight** is used in medical contexts to describe people who are too thin because they are ill or have not had enough food. * underweight 在医学上指人因疾病或进食不足而没达到标准体重：*Women who smoke risk giving birth to underweight babies.* 抽烟的妇女生出的婴儿可能会体重不足。
- **Emaciated** describes a serious condition resulting from illness or lack of food. * emaciated 指因疾病或饥饿而枯瘦、消瘦。
- **Anorexic** is a medical term, but is now also used informally to describe a girl or woman who is so thin that you are worried about them. * anorexic（患厌食症的）为医学术语，不过现在作为非正式用语亦指女孩或女人瘦得可怜。

It is more acceptable to talk to somebody about how thin or slim they are than about how fat they are. 说人瘦或苗条比说人胖更容易让人接受。

➲ NOTE AT FAT

(= one that people are not likely to believe) 站不住脚的借口 ◇ *Their arguments all sound a little thin to me.* 他们的论据我听起来都觉得有点儿缺乏说服力。

▸ **thin·ness** /ˈθɪnnəs/ *noun* [U] ➲ SEE ALSO THINLY

IDM **be skating/walking on thin ˈice** to be taking a risk 履薄冰；冒风险 **disappear, vanish, etc. into thin ˈair** to disappear suddenly in a mysterious way 消失得无影无踪；不翼而飞；悄然而逝 **have a thin ˈtime (of it)** (*BrE, informal*) to have many problems or difficulties to deal with; to not be successful 遇到许多麻烦；过得不顺 **out of thin ˈair** from nowhere or nothing, as if by magic 凭空；无中生有地 **the thin end of the ˈwedge** (*especially BrE*) an event or action that is the beginning of sth more serious and/or unpleasant（不好的事物的）端倪，冰山一角 **thin on ˈtop** (*informal*) without much hair on the head 头发稀疏；谢顶：*He's starting to get a little thin on top* (= he's losing his hair). 他开始有点谢顶了。 **a ˌthin ˈskin** the lack of ability to accept criticism, insults, etc. without becoming upset 脸皮薄；顾及脸面 SYN **sensitive** OPP **a thick skin** ➲ SEE ALSO THIN-SKINNED ➲ MORE AT GROUND *n.*, LINE *n.*, SPREAD *v.*, THICK *n.*, WEAR *v.*

■ ***adv.*** (**thin·ner**, **thin·nest**) in a way that produces a thin piece or layer of sth 薄薄地：*Don't spread it too thin.* 不要涂得太薄。◇ *I like my bread sliced thin.* 我喜欢吃切成薄片的面包。

■ ***verb*** (-nn-)

• **LIQUID** 液体 **1** [T] ~ sth (**down**) (**with sth**) to make a liquid less thick or strong by adding water or another substance （掺水等）使稀薄，使变淡： *Thin the paint with water.* 用水把颜料调稀。

• **OF HAIR** 毛发 **2** [I] to become less thick 变稀疏；变稀少：*a middle-aged man with thinning hair* 头发逐渐稀少的中年男子

• **BECOME LESS THICK** 变稀少 **3** [I, T] to become less thick or fewer in number; to make sth less thick or fewer, for example by removing some things or people（使）变稀薄，变稀疏，变少： *The clouds thinned and the moon shone through.* 云层渐稀，透出了月光。◇ ~ **out** *The crowd had thinned out and only a few people were left.* 人群渐渐散去，只剩下几个人。◇ ~ **sth** (**out**) *Thin out the seedlings to about 10cm apart.* 把秧苗间成相隔 10 厘米。

thine /ðaɪn/ *pron., det.* (*old use*)

■ ***pron.*** a word meaning 'yours', used when talking to only one person （第二人称单数的物主代词）你的（所有物）

■ ***det.*** the form of *thy* that is used before a vowel or 'h', meaning 'your' （第二人称所有格单数 thy 的另一种形式，用于元音或 h 前）你的

thing 🔑 /θɪŋ/ *noun*

• **OBJECT** 物体 **1** 🔑 [C] an object whose name you do not use because you do not need to or want to, or because you do not know it 东西；物： *Can you pass me that thing over there?* 把那边那个东西递给我好吗？◇ *She's very fond of sweet things* (= sweet foods). 她非常喜欢吃甜食。◇ *He's just bought one of those exercise things.* 他刚买了一副健身器械。◇ *Turn that thing off while I'm talking to you!* 我在跟你说话，把那个玩意儿关掉！ **2** 🔑 [C] an object that is not alive in the way that people and plants are 物件；物品；事物： *Don't treat her like that—she's a person, not a thing!* 别那样对待她，她是人，不是物件！ ◇ *He's good at making things with his hands.* 他善于手工制作物品。◇ *She took no interest in the people and things around her.* 她对周围的人和事毫无兴趣。

• **POSSESSIONS/EQUIPMENT** 所有物；设备 **3** 🔑 **things** [pl.] (*rather informal*) objects, clothing or tools that belong to sb or are used for a particular purpose （个人的）用品，衣服；（某种）用具： *Shall I help you pack your things?* 我帮你打点行装好吗？ ◇ *Bring your swimming things with you.* 随身带上游泳用品。◇ *I'll just clear away the breakfast things.* 我这就收拾早餐餐具。◇ *Put your things* (= coat, etc.) *on and let's go.* 把你的衣服穿上，咱们就走。

• **ANYTHING** 任何东西 **4 a thing** [sing.] used with negatives to mean 'anything' in order to emphasize what you are saying 任何东西（用于否定句，加强语气）： *I haven't got a thing to wear!* 我没有一件可穿的衣服！ ◇ *There wasn't a thing we could do to help.* 没有什么我们能帮得上忙的。◇ *Ignore what he said—it **doesn't mean a thing**.* 别理睬他说的话，他那都是瞎说。

• **FACT/EVENT/SITUATION/ACTION** 事实；事件；情况；行为 **5** 🔑 [C] a fact, an event, a situation or an action; what sb says or thinks 事实；事件；情况；行为；话语；想法：*There are a lot of things she doesn't know about me.* 我有很多情况她都不了解。 ◇ *There's another thing I'd like to ask you.* 还有一件事我想问你。◇ *A terrible thing happened last night.* 昨天夜里发生了一件可怕的事情。◇ *He found **the whole thing*** (= the situation) *very boring.* 他觉得整件事情非常无聊。◇ *I've got loads of things to do today.* 今天我有许多事要做。◇ ***The main thing** to remember is to switch off the burglar alarm.* 最要紧的是记住关掉防盗报警器的开关。◇ *I like camping, climbing and **that sort of thing**.* 我喜欢露营、爬山之类的活动。◇ *She said **the first thing** that came into her head.* 她想到了什么就说什么。◇ *'Why did you tell her our secret?' 'I did **no such thing**!'* "你为什么把我们的秘密告诉她？" "我没干过这种事！" ◇ *Let's forget **the***

▼ **SYNONYMS** 同义词辨析

things

stuff • **property** • **possessions** • **junk** • **belongings** • **goods** • **valuables**

These are all words for objects or items, especially ones that you own or have with you at a particular time. 以上各词均指东西、物品，尤指个人拥有或随身携带的物件。

things (*rather informal*) objects, clothing or tools that you own or that are used for a particular purpose 指个人拥有或作特定用途的物品、衣服、用具： *Shall I help you pack your things?* 我帮你打点行装好吗？ ◇ *Bring your swimming things.* 随身带上游泳用品。

stuff [U] (*informal*) used to refer to a group of objects when you do not know their names, when the names are not important or when it is obvious what you are talking about 指名称不详、名称无关紧要或所指明确的东西、物品、玩意儿： *Where's all my stuff?* 我那些东西都哪儿去了？

property [U] (*rather formal*) a thing or things that are owned by sb 指所有物、财产、财物： *This building is government property.* 这座大楼是政府的财产。◇ *Be careful not to damage other people's property.* 小心别损坏别人的财物。

possessions things that you own, especially sth that can be moved 指个人财产、私人物品（尤指动产）： *Prisoners were allowed no personal possessions except letters and photographs.* 囚犯除信件和照片外不允许有任何私人物品。

junk [U] things that are considered useless or of little value 指无用的东西、无价值的东西： *I've cleared out all that old junk from the attic.* 我把阁楼里所有的废旧杂物都清除干净了。

belongings possessions that can be moved, especially ones that you have with you at a particular time 指动产，尤指随身物品： *Please make sure you have all your belongings with you when leaving the plane.* 请确保在下飞机前带好所有的随身物品。

goods (*technical* or *rather formal*) possessions that can be moved 指动产、（可搬运的）私人财产： *He was found guilty of **handling stolen goods**.* 他被判犯销赃罪。

valuables things that are worth a lot of money, especially small personal things such as jewellery or cameras 尤指私人的贵重物品（如首饰、相机等）： *Never leave cash or other valuables lying around.* 现金或其他贵重物品请勿乱放。

PATTERNS

- **personal** things/stuff/property/possessions/belongings
- to **collect**/**gather**/**pack** (up) your things/stuff/possessions/belongings
- to **search** sb's/your/the things/stuff/property/belongings
- to **go through** sb's/your/the things/stuff/belongings

T

whole thing (= everything). 咱们把所有事情都忘掉吧。 **6** 🔑 **things** [pl.] (*rather informal*) the general situation, as it affects sb 形势；局面；情况；事态：*Things haven't gone entirely to plan.* 事态没有完全按照计划发展。◇ (*informal*) *Hi, Jane! **How are things?*** 喂，简，近来怎么样？◇ ***Think things over** before you decide.* 先把情况考虑周全再作决定。◇ ***As things stand** at present, he seems certain to win.* 据目前情况看，他似乎胜券在握。◇ ***All things considered*** (= considering all the difficulties or problems), *she's done very well.* 通盘考虑起来，她干得很好。◇ *Why do you make things so difficult for yourself?* 你为什么这样跟自己过不去？ ➲ SYNONYMS AT SITUATION

• **WHAT IS NEEDED/RIGHT** 需要的 / 合适的事物 **7** 🔑 [C, usually sing.] what is needed or socially acceptable 需要的东西；适当的东西；合适的东西：*You need something to cheer you up—I know just the thing!* 你需要点什么使你高兴起来，我知道什么正合你的需要！◇ *to say **the right/wrong thing*** 说得体的 / 不得体的话 ◇ *The best thing to do is to apologize.* 道歉方是上策。

• **THINGS OF PARTICULAR TYPE** 某种类型的事物 **8 things** [pl.] (*formal*) (followed by an adjective 后接形容词) all that can be described in a particular way 所有…的事物；凡是…的东西：*She loves all things Japanese.* 凡是日本的东西她都喜欢。

• **CREATURE** 生物 **9** [C] (used with an adjective 与形容词连用) a living creature 生物；有生命的东西：*All living things are composed of cells.* 所有的生物都由细胞组成。

• **PERSON/ANIMAL** 人；动物 **10** [C] (with an adjective 与形容词连用) (*informal*) used to talk to or about a person or an animal, to show how you feel about them (指人或动物，带感情色彩) 人，家伙，东西：*You silly thing!* 你这个蠢货！◇ *You must be starving, you poor things.* 你们一定是饿坏了，你们这些可怜的家伙。◇ *The cat's very ill, poor old thing.* 这猫病得很厉害，真可怜。

IDM **A is 'one thing, B is a'nother | it's 'one thing to do A, it's a'nother thing to do B** B is very different from A, for example it is more difficult, serious or important …是一回事，…是另一回事；…和…截然不同：*Romance is one thing, marriage is quite another.* 爱情是一回事，婚姻却是另一回事。◇ *It's one thing to tease your sister, but it's another to hit her.* 逗你妹妹玩是一回事，但打她那就另当别论了。 **ˌall/ˌother things being 'equal** if the conditions stay the same; if other conditions are the same 如果所有条件保持不变；如果其他情况一样：*All things being equal, we should finish the job tomorrow.* 一切照常的话，我们明天应该完成这项工作。 **and 'things (like 'that)** (*informal*) used when you do not want to complete a list 等等；之类：*She likes nice clothes and things like that.* 她喜欢漂亮衣服之类的东西。◇ *I've been busy shopping and things.* 我一直忙于购物之类的事情。 **be all things to all 'men/'people 1** (of people 人) to please everyone by changing your attitudes or opinions to suit different people 使人人高兴；八面玲珑 **2** (of things 事物) to be understood or used in different ways by different people 仁者见仁，智者见智 **come to/be the same 'thing** to have the same result or meaning 结果相同；意义相同 **be a 'good thing (that)…** to be lucky that… 幸运的是；幸亏：*It's a good thing we got here early.* 幸亏我们早到了这儿。 **be no bad 'thing (that)…** used to say that although sth seems to be bad, it could have good results 并不是坏事；或许是好事：*We didn't want the press to get hold of the story, but it might be no bad thing.* 我们本不想让新闻界知道这事，但是知道了也许并非是坏事。 **be onto a good 'thing** to have found a job, situation or style of life that is pleasant or easy 找到称心的工作；过上舒心的日子；混得不错 **'do things to sb** (*informal*) to have a powerful emotional effect on sb 使某人十分激动；震撼某人：*That song just does things to me.* 一听到那首歌我就激动不已。 **do your own 'thing** (*informal*) to do what you want to do or what interests you, without thinking about other people; to be independent 做自己想做的事；照自己的意愿行事；独立自主；自行其是 **ˌfirst/ˌlast 'thing** early in the morning/late in the evening 一早 / 晚上最后（要做的事）：*I need the report on my desk first thing Monday morning.* 星期一一早这个报告就得放在我的办公桌上。 **ˌfirst things 'first** (*often humorous*) the most important matters must be dealt with first 最重要的事最早办；要事先办：*We have a lot to discuss, but, first things first, let's have a cup of coffee!* 我们有许多事要讨论，不过急事先办，咱们先喝杯咖啡吧！ **for 'one thing** used to introduce one of two or more reasons for doing sth （用以引出两个以上的理由之一）一来，一方面：*'Why don't you get a car?' 'Well, for one thing, I can't drive!'* "你为什么不买辆汽车呢？" "啊，首先，我不会开车！" **have a 'thing about sb/sth** (*informal*) to have a strong like or dislike of sb/sth in a way that seems strange or unreasonable （莫名其妙地）对…有好感，对…有偏见：*She has a thing about men with beards.* 她对留胡子的男人有强烈的感觉。 **it isn't my, his, etc. 'thing** it isn't sth that you really enjoy or are interested in 这不是我（或他等）真正喜欢的东西；并非…所好 **it's a… thing** (*informal*) it is sth that only a particular group

▼ **VOCABULARY BUILDING 词汇扩充**

Other words for thing 表示事物的其他词

Instead of using the word **thing**, try to use more precise and interesting words, especially in formal written English. 尽量使用更贴切和有意思的词代替 thing，尤其在正式的书面语中。

- **aspect** 方面：*That was the most puzzling aspect of the situation.* 那是整个局势中最令人费解的一面。(*…the most puzzling thing about…*)
- **attribute** 属性；特性；特质：*Curiosity is an essential attribute for a journalist.* 好奇心是新闻记者的基本素质。(*…an essential thing for a journalist to have.*)
- **characteristic** 特性；特征；特点：*This bird has several interesting characteristics.* 这种鸟有几个有趣的特征。(*There are several interesting things about this bird.*)
- **detail** 细节；详情：*I want to know every detail of what happened.* 我想了解所发生事情的全部详情。(*…everything about…*)
- **feature** 特征；特点；特色：*Noise is a familiar feature of city life.* 噪音是城市生活的常见特征。(*…a familiar thing in city life.*)
- **issue** 议题；课题：*She has campaigned on many controversial issues.* 她就许多具争议性的问题发起过运动。(*…many controversial things.*)
- **matter** 事情；情况；问题：*We have several important matters to deal with at this meeting.* 我们有几个重要问题要在这次会议上处理。(*…several important things…*)
- **point** 观点；论点；见解：*That's a very interesting point you made.* 你提出的这个观点很有意思。(*…a very interesting thing you said.*)
- **subject** 主题；题目；学科：*The book covers a number of subjects.* 本书涉及几个课题。(*…a number of things.*)
- **topic** 议题；话题；题目：*We discussed a wide range of topics.* 我们就广泛的话题进行了讨论。(*…a wide range of things.*)
- **trait** 个性；特征；特点：*Her generosity is one of her most attractive traits.* 慷慨大方是她最具魅力的个性之一。(*…one of the most attractive things about her.*)
- Don't use **thing** after an adjective when the adjective can be used on its own. 形容词可单独使用时，切勿在后面加 thing：*Having your own computer is very useful.* 自己有一台计算机用处很大。◇ ~~*Having your own computer is a very useful thing.*~~
- It is often more natural to use words like **something**, **anything**, etc. instead of **thing**. 以 something、anything 等词代替 thing 使用常常更自然：*I have something important to tell you.* 我有重要的事情要告诉你。◇ ~~*I have an important thing to tell you.*~~ ◇ *Do you want anything else?* 你还想要点儿别的什么吗？◇ ~~*Do you want any other thing?*~~
- It is more natural to say **a lot**, **a great deal**, **much**, etc. rather than **many things**. * a lot、a great deal、much 等词比 many things 说起来更自然：*I have so much to tell you.* 我要对你讲的事情太多了。◇ ~~*I have so many things to tell you.*~~ ◇ *She knows a lot about basketball.* 她对篮球很有研究。◇ ~~*She knows many things about basketball.*~~

understands 这是…的事（只有某群体才理解的）：*You wouldn't know what it means—it's a girl thing.* 你不会知道那是什么意思，那是女孩子家的事。 **know/tell sb a 'thing or two (about sb/sth)** (*informal*) to know/tell sb some useful, interesting or surprising information about sb/sth 了解 / 透露有用的（或有趣的、意外的）信息；有所了解 / 披露；见多识广：*She's been married five times, so she knows a thing or two about men!* 她结过五次婚，所以对男人有所了解。 **make a (big) 'thing of/about sth** (*informal*) to make sth seem more important than it really is 小题大做；大惊小怪；故弄玄虚 **not know, etc. the first thing a'bout sth/sb** to know nothing at all about sth/sb 对…一无所知；对…一窍不通 **not ˌquite the 'thing 1** not considered socially acceptable 不太合时宜；不太时兴；不得体：*It wouldn't be quite the thing to turn up in running gear.* 穿着跑步的运动服出现在这场合可不大成体统。**2** (*old-fashioned*) not healthy or normal 身体不舒服；感到不适 **(just) ˌone of those 'things** used to say that you do not want to discuss or think about sth bad or unpleasant that has happened, but just accept it 命中注定的事；难免的倒霉事；不可挽回的事：*It wasn't your fault. It was just one of those things.* 不是你的错。这是命中注定的事。 **ˌone (damned/damn) thing after a'nother** (*informal*) used to complain that a lot of unpleasant things keep happening to you（抱怨时用）倒霉事一桩接一桩 **ˌone thing leads to a'nother** used to suggest that the way one event or action leads to others is so obvious that it does not need to be stated （暗示事情的发展过程显而易见）一来二去，自然而然：*He offered me a ride home one night, and, well, one thing led to another and now we're married!* 一天晚上他让我搭车回家，唔，就这样自然发展，我们现在结婚了！ **be 'seeing/'hearing things** (*informal, humorous*) to imagine that you can see or hear sth that is in fact not there 产生幻觉 **there's only ˌone thing 'for it** there is only one possible course of action 这只有一个办法 **these ˌthings are sent to 'try us** (*saying*) used to say that you should accept an unpleasant situation or event because you cannot change it （表示无法改变，应该接受）这些都是对我们的考验（或磨炼） **the ˌthing 'is** 🔑 (*informal*) used to introduce an important fact, reason or explanation 事实是；主要原因是：*I'm sorry my assignment isn't finished. The thing is, I've had a lot of other work this week.* 对不起，我的任务没完成。主要原因是我这星期有许多其他工作要做。 **the ˌthing (about/with sth/sb) 'is** used to introduce a problem about sth/sb …的问题是：*The thing with Karl is, he's always late.* 卡尔的问题是，他总是迟到。 **the (whole)... thing** (*informal*) a situation or an activity of the type mentioned （纯粹的）…事；（完全是）…的活动：*She really didn't want to be involved in the whole family thing.* 她实在不想卷入家事之中。 **ˌthings that go ˌbump in the 'night** (*informal, humorous*) used to refer to GHOSTS and other SUPERNATURAL things that cannot be explained 夜里奇异可怕的响声；鬼魂；超自然现象 **too 'much of a good thing** used to say that, although sth is pleasant, you do not want to have too much of it 好事多了也觉得腻 **(what) with ˌone thing and a'nother** (*informal*) because you have been busy with various problems, events or things you had to do 因为事情一个接着一个；由于忙得不可开交：*I completely forgot her birthday, what with one thing and another.* 因为忙得不可开交，我把她的生日忘得一干二净。 ➲ MORE AT CHANCE *n.*, CLOSE² *adj.*, CLOSE² *adv.*, DAY, DECENT, DONE *adj.*, EASY *adv.*, NATURE, NEAR *adj.*, ONLY *adj.*, OVERDO, PUSH *v.*, REAL *adj.*, SCHEME *n.*, SHAPE *n.*, SURE *adj.*, TURN *v.*, WAY *n.*, WORK *v.*

thing·ummy /ˈθɪŋəmi/ *noun* (*pl.* **-ies**) (*also* **thing·ama·bob** /ˈθɪŋəməbɒb; *NAmE* -bɑːb/, **thing·uma·jig** /ˈθɪŋəmədʒɪɡ/, **thingy**) (*informal*) used to refer to a person or thing whose name you do not know or have forgotten, or which you do not want to mention（指不知、或忘记、或不想提及其名）某某，那个人，那东西：*It's one of those thingummies for keeping papers together.* 就是能收纳文件的那么一种东西。◇ *Is thingummy going to be there? You know, that woman from the Sales Department?* 某某人会去那儿吗？你知道，就是销售部的那个女的。

thingy /ˈθɪŋi/ *noun* (*pl.* **-ies**) = THINGUMMY

think 🔑 /θɪŋk/ *verb, noun*

■ *verb* (**thought, thought** /θɔːt/)

• **HAVE OPINION/BELIEF** 有看法 / 信念 **1** 🔑 [T, I] (not used in the progressive tenses 不用于进行时) to have a particular idea or opinion about sth/sb; to believe sth 认为；以为：**~ (that)...** *Do you think (that) they'll come?* 你认为他们会来吗？◇ *I thought I heard a scream.* 我好像听到了一声尖叫。◇ *I didn't think you liked sports.* 我原以为你不喜好运动。◇ ***Am I right in thinking** that you used to live here?* 我想你过去在这里住过，对吗？◇ *I think this is their house, but I'm not sure.* 我想这是他们的家，但不敢肯定。◇ *He ought to resign, I think.* 我看他应该辞职。◇ *We'll need about 20 chairs, **I should think**.* 我看我们需要大约 20 把椅子。◇ **it is thought that...** *It was once **thought that** the sun travelled around the earth.* 人们曾经认为太阳绕着地球转。◇ **~ sth (about sth)** *What did you think about the idea?* 你原先认为这个想法怎么样？◇ *Well, I like it. **What do you think?*** 嗯，我喜欢这个想法。你认为怎么样？◇ **~ so** *'Will we make it in time?' '**I think so**.'* "我们会及时完成吗？" "我想会的。" ◇ *'Is he any good?' '**I don't think so**.'* "他怎么样？" "我认为一般。" ◇ **~ sb/sth + adj.** *I think it highly unlikely that I'll get the job.* 我认为我得到这份工作的可能性极小。◇ *She thought him kind and generous.* 她认为他宽厚仁慈。◇ **sb/sth is thought to be sb/sth** *He's thought to be one of the richest men in Europe.* 他被认为是欧洲最富有的人之一。 ➲ LANGUAGE BANK AT ACCORDING TO, OPINION

• **USE MIND** 动脑筋 **2** 🔑 [I, T] to use your mind to consider sth, to form connected ideas, to try to solve problems, etc. 想；思考；思索；思想：*Are animals able to think?* 动物会思考吗？◇ *Let me think* (= give me time before I answer). 让我想一想。◇ **~ (about sth)** *I can't tell you now—I'll have to **think about it**.* 我现在无法告诉你，我得考虑一下。◇ *She **had thought** very **deeply** about this problem.* 她曾经对这个问题深深思考过。◇ *All he ever thinks about is money.* 他满脑子想的只是钱。◇ *I'm sorry, **I wasn't thinking*** (= said when you have upset or offended sb accidentally). 对不起，我太冒昧了。◇ **~ what, how, etc....** *He was trying to think what to do.* 他在努力想办法。 **3** 🔑 [T] (usually used in the progressive tenses 通常用于进行时) to have ideas, words or images in your mind 想；琢磨：**~ sth** *You're very quiet. What are you thinking?* 你一声不吭，在想什么？◇ **~ what, how, etc....** *I was just thinking what a long way it is.* 我刚才在琢磨路途太远了。◇ **+ speech** *'I must be crazy,' she thought.* "我准是疯了。" 她想。

• **IMAGINE** 想象 **4** 🔑 [T, no passive, I] to form an idea of sth; to imagine sth 猜想；想象；试想：**~ where, how, etc....** *We couldn't think where you'd gone.* 我们猜想不出来你到哪里去了。◇ *Just think how nice it would be to see them again.* 试想一下要是能再见到他们该有多好。◇ **~ (that)...** *I can't think (that) he would be so stupid.* 我不能想象他会这么蠢。◇ **~ (sth)** ***Just think**—we'll be lying on the beach this time tomorrow.* 想想看，明天这个时候我们就躺在海滩上了。◇ *If I'm late home, my mother always **thinks the worst**.* 如果我回家晚了，我母亲总是往最坏处想。◇ *Try to **think yourself** into the role.* 尽量发挥想象力，使自己进入角色。 ➲ SYNONYMS AT IMAGINE

• **EXPECT** 预料 **5** 🔑 [T] to expect sth 料想；预料；预期：**~ (that)...** *I never thought (that) I'd see her again.* 我从未料想到还会见到她。◇ *The job took longer than we thought.* 这项工作用的时间比我们预想的多。◇ *You'd think she'd have been grateful for my help* (= but she wasn't). 你还期望她会对我的帮助感恩戴德呢。◇ **~ to do sth** (*formal*) *Who would have thought to find you here?* 谁会料到你在这儿呢？

• **IN A PARTICULAR WAY** 以某种方式 **6** [I, T] (*informal*) [no passive] to think in a particular way or on a particular subject 只想；一心想；对…着迷：**+ adj.** *Let's think positive.* 咱们往好的方面想吧。◇ *You need to **think big*** (= aim to achieve a lot). 你要敢想。◇ **~ sth** *If you want to make money, you've got to think money.* 你要想赚钱，就得一门心思琢磨钱。

• **SHOWING ANGER/SURPRISE** 表示生气 / 吃惊 **7** [T] **~ (that)...**

T

used in questions to show that you are angry or surprised（用于问句，表示生气或吃惊）：*What do you think you're doing?* 你以为你在干什么？

- **BEING LESS DEFINITE/MORE POLITE** 不太肯定；较为婉转 **8** [T, I] used to make sth you say sound less definite or more polite（用于使话语不太肯定或较为婉转）：**~ (that)…** *I thought we could go out tonight.* 我本想我们今晚可以出去。◇ *Twenty guests are enough, I would have thought.* 我觉得二十位客人就够了。◇ ***Do you think*** *you could open the window?* 请打开窗子好吗？◇ **~ so** *'You've made a mistake.' 'I don't think so.'* "你出错了。""我想不会吧。"
- **INTEND** 打算 **9** [T, I] **~ (that…)** to intend sth; to have a plan about sth 打算；想要；计划：*I think I'll go for a swim.* 我想去游泳。◇ *I'm thinking in terms of about 70 guests at the wedding.* 我打算邀请 70 位嘉宾参加婚礼。
- **REMEMBER** 记忆 **10** [T] to remember sth; to have sth come into your mind 记得；想起：**~ to do sth** *I didn't think* (= it did not occur to me) *to tell her.* 我没有想到要告诉她。◇ **~ where, what, etc.…** *I can't think where I put the keys.* 我想不起把钥匙放在哪儿了。

IDM **come to 'think of it** used when you suddenly remember sth or realize that it might be important（用于突然想起某事或认识到其重要性）想起来了，的确：*Come to think of it, he did mention seeing you.* 想起来了，他确实提到看见过你。 **I ˌdon't 'think so** (*informal*) used to say very strongly that you do not agree with sth, or that sth is not possible 我想并非如此；我不这样认为；根本不可能：*Me? Fail? I don't think so.* 我？失败？我可不这样认为。 **if/when you 'think about it** used to draw attention to a fact that is not obvious or has not previously been mentioned（用以引起对不明显或未曾提到过的事情的注意）你想想看：*It was a difficult situation, when you think about it.* 仔细想来，当时处境是很困难的。 **I 'thought as much** that is what I expected or suspected 我早料到了；果然不出我所料：*'He said he'd forgotten.' 'I thought as much.'* "他说忘了。""果然不出我所料。" **ˌthink a'gain** to consider a situation again and perhaps change your idea or intention 重新考虑后另作打算（常指最终改变主意） **think a'loud/out 'loud** to say what your thoughts are as you have them 自言自语；边想边说；进行有声思考 **think 'better of it/of doing sth** to decide not to do sth after thinking further about it 深思熟虑后决定不做；一想又改变主意 **SYN** **reconsider**：*Rosie was about to protest but thought better of it.* 罗西刚要抗议，但又一想决定作罢。 **think (the) 'better of sb** to have a higher opinion of sb 对某人有较高的评价：*She has behaved appallingly—I must say I thought better of her.* 她的行为太恶劣了，看来我过去是高看了她。 **think nothing 'of it** (*formal*) used as a polite response when sb has said sorry to you or thanked you 别在意；没什么；别客气 **think 'nothing of sth/of doing sth** to consider an activity to be normal and not particularly unusual or difficult 不把…当一回事；对…等闲视之；觉得…无所谓：*She thinks nothing of walking thirty miles a day.* 她认为一天步行三十英里不足为奇。 **think on your 'feet** to be able to think and react to things very quickly and effectively without any preparation 思维敏捷；反应迅速 **ˌthink out of the 'box** to think about sth, or how to do sth, in a way that is new, different or shows imagination 跳出框框想问题；另辟蹊径 **'think straight** to think in a clear or logical way 思路清晰 **think 'twice about sth/about doing sth** to think carefully before deciding to do sth 三思而行；慎重考虑后

▼ **EXPRESS YOURSELF** 情景表达

Asking for somebody's opinion and involving others in a conversation
征求他人意见和邀请参与谈话

In a meeting or a discussion you may need to find out what other people think. In some exams, you have to show that you can control the conversation by asking for contributions from the examiner. 在会议或讨论中想知道别人的想法，或在某些考试中请主考人发表意见以显示你可以主导谈话，可用以下表达方式：

- *I would say it's OK in the city, but not in the country.* ***What do you think?*** 要我说，这在城市里还可以，但在乡村不行。你怎么看？
- *My feeling is that we could improve our performance.* ***Do you agree with that?*** 我觉得我们可以改善业绩。这么说你同意吗？
- ***What would you say*** *if we waited another month?* 如果我们再等一个月，你说怎么样？
- ***What about you?*** *Do you cycle?* 你呢？你会骑自行车吗？
- *Which place* ***do you think*** *is more dangerous?* 你认为哪个地方更危险？
- *The traffic's going faster there,* ***isn't it?/don't you think?*** 那里的交通畅通多了，是不是？/你不觉得吗？
- ***Would you say that*** *traffic's going faster there?* 你觉得那里的交通更加畅通了吗？
- *So this would be a better option,* ***right?*** (*NAmE, informal*) 那么，这会是更好的选择，对吧？

➲ EXPRESS YOURSELF AT SPECULATE

▼ **SYNONYMS** 同义词辨析

think

believe • feel • reckon • be under the impression

These words all mean to have an idea that sth is true or possible or to have a particular opinion about sb/sth. 以上各词均含以为、认为之义。

think to have an idea that sth is true or possible, although you are not completely certain; to have a particular opinion about sb/sth 指认为、以为某人/某事…但不肯定：*Do you think (that) they'll come?* 你认为他们会来吗？◇ *Well, I like it. What do you think?* 嗯，我喜欢这个。你认为怎么样？

believe to have an idea that sth is true or possible, although you are not completely certain; to have a particular opinion about sb/sth 指认为、以为：*Police believe (that) the man may be armed.* 警方认为那个人可能携有武器。

THINK OR BELIEVE? 用 think 还是 believe?

When you are expressing an idea that you have or that sb has of what is true or possible, **believe** is more formal than **think**. It is used especially for talking about ideas that other people have; **think** is used more often for talking about your own ideas. 表达自己或别人认为真实或有可能的想法时，believe 较 think 正式。believe 尤用于别人的想法；think 较常用于自己的想法：*Police believe…* 警方认为… ◇ *I think…* 我认为… When you are expressing an opinion, **believe** is stronger than **think** and is used especially for matters of principle; **think** is used more for practical matters or matters of personal taste. 表达意见时，believe 语气较 think 强烈，尤用于原则性事情；think 多用于实际事情或个人喜好。

feel to have a particular opinion about sth that has happened or about what you/sb ought to do 指认为（已发生的事情…）、相信（应该…）：*We all felt (that) we were unlucky to lose.* 我们都认为我们输了是运气不好。

reckon (*informal*) to think that sth is true or possible 指认为、以为：*I reckon (that) I'm going to get that job.* 我认为我会得到那份工作。

be under the impression that… to have an idea that sth is true 指以为某事…：*I was under the impression that the work had already been completed.* 我还以为已经完工了呢。

PATTERNS

- to think/believe/feel/reckon/be under the impression **that…**
- **It is** thought/believed/reckoned **that…**
- to **be** thought/believed/felt/reckoned **to be** sth
- to think/believe/feel sth **about** sb/sth
- to **sincerely/honestly/seriously/mistakenly** think/believe/feel

再决定：*You should think twice about employing someone you've never met.* 雇用素不相识的人应三思而行。 **think the world, highly, a lot, poorly, little, etc. of sb/sth** to have a very good, poor, etc. opinion of sb/sth 对…评价高（或不高）：*He thinks the world of his daughter.* 他非常器重女儿。◇ *I don't think much of her idea.* 我认为她的主意不怎么样。 **to think (that…)** used to show that you are surprised or shocked by sth（表示惊讶）想想看，想想…吧：*To think that my mother wrote all those books and I never knew!* 想想看，我母亲写了那么多部书，我竟然一无所知！ ➲ MORE AT FIT *adj.*, GREAT *adj.*, ILL *adv.*, LET *v.*, LIKE *v.*, OWN *v.*

PHR V **'think about/of sb/sth** 🔑 **1** 🔑 to consider sb/sth when you are doing or planning sth 考虑到；关心；替…着想：*Don't you ever think about other people?* 难道你就从来没有考虑过别人？ **2** 🔑 to consider doing sth 考虑，打算（做某事） **SYN** **contemplate**：**think about/of doing sth** *She's thinking of changing her job.* 她在考虑换工作。 **,think a'head (to sth)** to think about a future event or situation and plan for it 预先考虑；预想；预先计划 **,think 'back (to sth)** to think about sth that happened in the past 回想；追忆：*I keep thinking back to the day I arrived here.* 我不断回想起刚到这儿那一天的情景。 **,think for your'self** to form your own opinions and make decisions without depending on others 独立思考；自行决定 **'think of sth/sb 1** 🔑 to have an image or idea of sth/sb in your mind 想象到；对…有想法：*When I said that I wasn't thinking of anyone in particular.* 我说那话时，并没有想到任何具体的人。 **2** 🔑 to create an idea in your imagination 想出；构思出：*Can anybody think of a way to raise money?* 谁能想出个集资的办法？ ◇ *Have you thought of a name for the baby yet?* 你想好给孩子起什么名字没有？ **3** 🔑 [no passive] (used especially with *can* 尤与 can 连用) to remember sth/sb 记得；想起：*I can think of at least three occasions when he arrived late.* 我记得他至少迟到过三次。◇ *I can't think of her name at the moment.* 我一时想不起她的名字。 **'think of sb/sth as sb/sth** 🔑 to consider sb/sth in a particular way 把…看作；把…视为：*I think of this place as my home.* 我把这个地方当成了家。◇ *She is thought of as a possible director.* 人们认为她有可能成为董事。 ➲ SEE ALSO WELL THOUGHT OF **'think of sth** to imagine an actual or a possible situation 想一想；想象：*Just think of the expense!* 想想这笔开销吧！ ◇ **think of doing sth** *I couldn't think of letting you take the blame* (= I would not allow that to happen). 我没想到过让你承担责任。 **,think sth↔'out** to consider or plan sth carefully 认真考虑；仔细盘算：*It's a very well thought out plan.* 这个计划考虑得十分周密。 **,think sth↔'over** 🔑 to consider sth carefully, especially before reaching a decision （尤指在作决定前）仔细考虑，慎重思考：*He'd like more time to think things over.* 他希望有更多的时间把情况考虑周详。 **,think sth↔'through** to consider a problem or a possible course of action fully 充分考虑；全盘考虑；想透 **,think sth↔'up** 🔑 (*informal*) to create sth in your mind 想出；发明 **SYN** **devise, invent**：*Can't you think up a better excuse than that?* 难道你就想不出一个比这更好的借口？

■ ***noun*** [sing.]

IDM **have a 'think (about sth)** (*informal*) to think carefully about sth in order to make a decision about it 想一想，琢磨一下（以便作决定）：*I'll have a think and let you know tomorrow.* 我要好好想一想，明天告诉你。 **you've got another think 'coming** (*informal*) used to tell sb that they are wrong about sth and must change their plans or opinions 你还得想一想；你得改变计划（或主意）

think·able /'θɪŋkəbl/ *adj.* [not before noun] that you can imagine as a possibility 可以想象；想象得到：*Such an idea was scarcely thinkable ten years ago.* 十年前，这样的想法几乎是难以想象的。 **OPP** **unthinkable**

think·er /'θɪŋkə(r)/ *noun* **1** a person who thinks seriously, and often writes about important things, such as philosophy or science 思想家：*Einstein was one of the greatest thinkers of the 20th century.* 爱因斯坦是 20 世纪最伟大的思想家之一。 **2** a person who thinks in a particular way 思想…的人：*a clear thinker* 思路清晰的人

think·ing 🔑 /'θɪŋkɪŋ/ *noun, adj.*

■ ***noun*** [U] **1** 🔑 the process of thinking about sth 思想；思考；思维：*I had to do some quick thinking.* 我得迅速思考一番。 ➲ SEE ALSO LATERAL THINKING, WISHFUL THINKING **2** 🔑 ideas or opinions about sth 想法；见解：*What is the current thinking on this question?* 目前对这个问题的看法是什么？ ◇ *She explained the thinking behind the campaign.* 她解释了发动这场运动的想法。 **IDM** SEE WAY *n.*

■ ***adj.*** [only before noun] intelligent and able to think seriously about things 思想的；有理智的；有思考力的：*the thinking woman's magazine* 理性妇女的杂志

'thinking cap *noun*

IDM **put your 'thinking cap on** (*informal*) to try to solve a problem by thinking about it 动脑筋；通过思考努力解决问题

'think tank *noun* a group of experts who provide advice and ideas on political, social or economic issues（政治、社会、经济问题的）智囊团，智库，专家小组

thin·ly /'θɪnli/ *adv.* **1** in a way that produces a thin piece or layer of sth 细；瘦；薄：*Slice the potatoes thinly.* 把土豆切成薄片。 **2** with only a few things or people spread over a place so that there is a lot of space between them 稀疏；稀少：*a thinly populated area* 人烟稀少的地区 **3** in a way that is not sincere or enthusiastic 冷淡；冷漠：*She smiled thinly.* 她淡然一笑。 **4** in a way that does not hide the truth very well 容易识破的；显而易见的 **SYN** **barely**：*The novel is a thinly disguised autobiography.* 这部小说让人一眼就可以看出是部自传。

thin·ner /'θɪnə(r)/ *noun* [U, C] a substance that is added to paint, VARNISH, etc. to make it less thick（涂料、清漆等的）稀料，稀释剂

,thin-'skinned *adj.* **1** easily upset by criticism or insults 脸皮薄的；（对批评或侮辱）易生气的 **2** (of fruit 水果) having a thin skin 皮薄的 **OPP** **thick-skinned**

third 🔑 /θɜːd; *NAmE* θɜːrd/ *ordinal number, noun*

■ ***ordinal number*** 🔑 3rd 第三 **HELP** There are examples of how to use ordinal numbers at the entry for **fifth**. 序数词用法示例见 fifth 条。

IDM **third time 'lucky** (*US* **third time is the 'charm**) used when you have failed to do sth twice and hope that you will succeed the third time（但愿）第三次交好运；过一过二不过三

■ ***noun*** **1** 🔑 each of three equal parts of sth 三分之一 ➲ LANGUAGE BANK AT PROPORTION **2** ~ **(in sth)** a level of university degree at British universities, that is lower than average 三等学位（英国大学中低于平均水平的学位） ➲ COMPARE FIRST *n.* (6), SECOND[1] *n.* (7)

the ,third 'age *noun* [sing.] (*BrE*) the period of your life between MIDDLE AGE and OLD AGE, when you are still active 第三龄（中年和老年之间依然活跃的年龄段）

,third 'class *noun* **1** [U, sing.] (especially in the past) the cheapest and least comfortable part of a train, ship, etc.（尤指旧时火车、轮船等的）三等座，三等舱 **2** [U] (in the US) the class of mail used for sending advertisements, etc. 第三类邮件（在美国用以邮寄广告等） **3** [U, sing.] the lowest standard of degree given by a British university 第三等学位（英国大学颁发的最低标准学位）

'third-class *adj.* **1** (especially in the past) connected with the cheapest and least comfortable way of travelling on a train, ship, etc. 三等的（尤指旧时火车座位、轮船舱位等） **2** (in the US) connected with the class of mail used to send advertisements, etc. 第三类的（美国邮件等级） **3** [only before noun] used to describe the lowest standard of degree given by a British university 第三等的（英国大学学位） **4** (*disapproving*) (of people 人) less important than other people 第三等的；卑微的：*They are treated as third-class citizens.* 他们被当成三等公民对待。 ▶ **,third 'class** *adv.*：*to travel third class* 乘坐三等舱

,third de'gree *noun* [sing.]

IDM **give sb the ,third de'gree** (*informal*) to question sb for a long time and in a thorough way; to use threats or

T

violence to get information from sb 对某人逼供（或疲劳询问、刑讯）

ˌthird-deˈgree *adj.* **1 ~ burns** burns of the most serious kind, affecting TISSUE below the skin 三度（烧伤） **2** (*NAmE*) **~ murder, assault, robbery, etc.** murder, etc. of the least serious of three kinds 三级（谋杀、人身侵犯或抢劫等罪，程度最轻） ➲ COMPARE FIRST-DEGREE, SECOND-DEGREE

ˈthird-generation *adj.* (*abbr.* **3G**) **1** used to describe technology that has been developed to send data to mobile/cell phones, etc. at much higher speeds than were possible before 第三代移动通信技术的 **2** used to describe any technology that is being developed that is more advanced than the earlier two stages 第三代技术的

third·ly /ˈθɜːdli; *NAmE* ˈθɜːrd-/ *adv.* used to introduce the third of a list of points you want to make in a speech or piece of writing（用于讲话或文章中列举事项）第三，第三点：*Thirdly, I would like to say that…* 第三，我想说…

ˌthird ˈparty *noun* (*law* 律 or *formal*) a person who is involved in a situation in addition to the two main people involved 第三人；第三方；第三当事人；第三者

ˌthird-party inˈsurance *noun* [U] insurance that COVERS (= protects) you if you injure sb or damage sb's property 第三者保险，第三方责任险（保障受保人于被追讨赔偿时的损失）

the ˌthird ˈperson *noun* [sing.] **1** (*grammar* 语法) a set of pronouns and verb forms used by a speaker to refer to other people and things 第三人称：*'They are' is the third person plural of the verb 'to be'.* * they are 是动词 to be 的第三人称复数形式。 **2** a way of writing a novel, etc. as the experience of sb else, using third person forms 以第三人称叙述的文体：*a book written **in the third person*** 以第三人称写作的书 ➲ COMPARE FIRST PERSON, SECOND PERSON

ˌthird-ˈrate *adj.* of very poor quality 劣质的；三等的；三流的 **SYN** **inferior**：*a third-rate actor* 三流演员

the Third Reich /ˌθɜːd ˈraɪk; ˈraɪx; *NAmE* ˌθɜːrd/ *noun* [sing.] the Nazi rule of Germany between 1933 and 1945 第三帝国（1933 至 1945 年间的德国纳粹政权）

the ˌthird ˈsector *noun* [sing.] (*economics* 经) the part of an economy or a society that includes organizations that do not belong to the government and do not make a profit 第三部门（经济体或社会中不隶属政府也不以营利为目标的部分）：*The forum was aimed at key business leaders from across the private, public and third sectors in the region.* 此次论坛针对的是来自本地区私营、公共和第三部门的主要业界领袖。 ➲ SEE ALSO PRIVATE SECTOR, PUBLIC SECTOR

ˌthird ˈway *noun* [sing.] a course of action or political policy that is between two extreme positions 第三条道路（介乎两种极端立场之间的行动方案或政策）

the ˌThird ˈWorld *noun* [sing.] a way of referring to the poor or developing countries of Africa, Asia and Latin America, which is sometimes considered offensive 第三世界（指亚洲、非洲和拉丁美洲贫穷和落后的国家，该词有时被认为含有冒犯意）：*the causes of poverty and injustice in the Third World* 第三世界贫穷和不公正的原因 ◇ *Third-World debt* 第三世界债务 ➲ COMPARE FIRST WORLD

thirst /θɜːst; *NAmE* θɜːrst/ *noun, verb*

■ ***noun*** **1** [U, sing.] the feeling of needing or wanting a drink 口渴；干渴感：*He quenched his thirst with a long drink of cold water.* 他喝了好多冷水解渴。 ◇ *She woke up with a raging thirst and a headache.* 她醒来后，感到头痛，口渴难忍。 **2** [U] the state of not having enough water to drink 缺水；干渴：*Thousands are dying of thirst.* 成千上万的人都干渴得奄奄一息。 **3** [sing.] **~ (for sth)** a strong desire for sth 渴望；渴求 **SYN** **craving**：*a thirst for knowledge* 如饥似渴的求知欲

■ ***verb*** [I] (*old use*) to be thirsty 渴；想喝水

PHR V **ˈthirst for sth** (*literary*) to feel a strong desire for sth 渴望；渴求 **SYN** **crave**：*She thirsted for power.* 她渴望拥有权力。

thirsty 🔑 /ˈθɜːsti; *NAmE* ˈθɜːrsti/ *adj.* (**thirst·ier, thirsti·est**) **1** 🔑 needing or wanting to drink 渴的；口渴的：*We were hungry and thirsty.* 我们又饥又渴。 ◇ *Digging is thirsty work* (= makes you thirsty). 挖地是个使人口渴的活。 **2 ~ for sth** having a strong desire for sth 渴望；渴求；热望 **SYN** **hungry**：*He is thirsty for power.* 他拼命想掌权。 **3** (of plants, fields, etc. 植物、田地等) dry; in need of water 干旱的；缺水的 ▶ **thirst·ily** /-ɪli/ *adv.*：*Paul drank thirstily.* 保罗渴得拼命喝水。

thir·teen 🔑 /ˌθɜːˈtiːn; *NAmE* ˌθɜːrˈt-/ *number* 13 十三 ▶ **thir·teenth** 🔑 /ˌθɜːˈtiːnθ; *NAmE* ˌθɜːrˈt-/ *ordinal number, noun* **HELP** There are examples of how to use ordinal numbers at the entry for **fifth**. 序数词用法示例见 fifth 条。

thirty 🔑 /ˈθɜːti; *NAmE* ˈθɜːrti/ **1** 🔑 *number* 30 三十 **2** *noun* **the thirties** [pl.] numbers, years or temperatures from 30 to 39 三十几；三十年代 ▶ **thir·ti·eth** 🔑 /ˈθɜːtiəθ; *NAmE* ˈθɜːrt-/ *ordinal number, noun* **HELP** There are examples of how to use ordinal numbers at the entry for **fifth**. 序数词用法示例见 fifth 条。

IDM **in your ˈthirties** between the ages of 30 and 39 * 30 多岁

this 🔑 /ðɪs/ *det., pron., adv.*

■ ***det., pron.*** (*pl.* **these** /ðiːz/) **1** 🔑 used to refer to a particular person, thing or event that is close to you, especially compared with another（指较近的人或事物）这，这个：*How long have you been living in this country?* 你在这个国家居住多久啦？ ◇ *Well, make up your mind. Which do you want? This one or that one?* 哎，拿定主意。你要哪一个？这个还是那个？ ◇ *I think you'll find these more comfortable than those.* 我想你会觉得这些比那些更舒适。 ◇ *Is this your bag?* 这是你的包吗？ **2** 🔑 used to refer to sth/sb that has already been mentioned（指已提到过的人或事物）这，这个：*There was a court case resulting from this incident.* 这一事件引起一宗庭审案件。 ◇ *The boy was afraid and the dog had sensed this.* 男孩害怕了，狗已经察觉到这一点。 ◇ *What's this I hear about you getting married?* 我听说你结婚了，这是怎么回事？ **3** 🔑 used for introducing sb or showing sth to sb（介绍人或展示事物时用）这，这样：*Hello, this is Maria Diaz* (= on the telephone). 喂，我是玛丽亚・迪亚兹。 ◇ *Jo, this is Kate* (= when you are introducing them). 乔，这位是凯特。 ◇ *This is the captain speaking.* 我是船长。 ◇ *Listen to this.* 听听这个。 ◇ *Do it like this* (= in the way I am showing you). 照这样去做。 **4** 🔑 used with periods of time related to the present（与和现在有关的一段时间连用）今，本，这个，现在：*this week/month/year* 本周；本月；今年 ◇ *I saw her this morning* (= today in the morning). 今天早晨我见到过她。 ◇ *Do you want me to come this Tuesday* (= Tuesday of this week) *or next Tuesday?* 你要我本周二还是下周二来？ ◇ *Do it **this minute*** (= now). 现在就做。 ◇ *He never comes to see me **these days*** (= now, as compared with the past). 近来他一直不来看我。 **5 ~ sth of sb's** (*informal*) used to refer to sb/sth that is connected with a person, especially when you have a particular attitude towards it or them（尤指说话者抱有既定看法的人或事物）…的这个（或这些）：*These new friends of hers are supposed to be very rich.* 她的这些新朋友想必都很富有。 **6** (*informal*) used when you are telling a story or telling sb about sth（述说时用）有个：*There was this strange man sitting next to me on the plane.* 在飞机上有个奇怪的人坐在我身旁。 ◇ *I've been getting these pains in my chest.* 我胸部一直有一些疼痛感。

IDM **ˌthis and ˈthat | ˌthis, ˌthat and the ˈother** (*informal*) various things or activities 这样那样；各种事情；各种各样的活动：*'What did you talk about?' 'Oh, this and that.'* "你们谈什么来着？" "噢，无所不谈。" ➲ MORE LIKE THIS 13, page R26

■ ***adv.*** to this degree; so 这样；这么：*It's about this high* (= as high as I am showing you with my hands). 大约有这么高。 ◇ *I didn't think we'd get this far.* 我未曾想到我们会走得这么远。

this·tle /ˈθɪsl/ *noun* a wild plant with leaves with sharp points and purple, yellow or white flowers made up of a mass of narrow PETALS pointing upwards. The thistle is the national symbol of Scotland. 蓟（野生植物，叶有刺，花呈紫色、黄色或白色，为苏格兰民族象征） ➲ VISUAL VOCAB PAGE V11 ➲ MORE LIKE THIS 20, page R27

thistle·down /ˈθɪsldaʊn/ *noun* [U] a very light soft substance that contains THISTLE seeds and is blown from THISTLES by the wind 蓟种子冠毛

thither /ˈðɪðə(r)/ *adv.* (*old use*) to or towards that place 到那里；向那里 IDM SEE HITHER

tho' *adv.* an informal spelling of 'though' (though 的非正式拼法)

thong /θɒŋ; *NAmE* θɔːŋ; θɑːŋ/ *noun* **1** a narrow strip of leather that is used to fasten sth or as a WHIP（用以系物或做皮鞭的）皮条 **2** a pair of women's KNICKERS or men's UNDERPANTS that has only a very narrow strip of cloth, like a string, at the back（背后为绳子一样窄条的）内裤；丁字内裤 **3** (*NAmE, AustralE, NZE*) = FLIP-FLOP

thorax /ˈθɔːræks/ *noun* (*pl.* **thor·axes** or **thor·aces** /ˈθɔːrəsiːz/) **1** (*anatomy* 解) the part of the body that is surrounded by the RIBS, between the neck and the waist 胸；胸腔 **2** the middle section of an insect's body, to which the legs and wings are attached（昆虫的）胸，胸部 ➲ VISUAL VOCAB PAGE V13 ▶ **thor·acic** /θɔːˈræsɪk/ *adj.* [only before noun]

thor·ium /ˈθɔːriəm/ *noun* [U] (*symb.* **Th**) a chemical element. Thorium is a white RADIOACTIVE metal used as a source of nuclear energy. 钍（放射性化学元素）

thorn /θɔːn; *NAmE* θɔːrn/ *noun* **1** a small sharp pointed part on the STEM of some plants, such as ROSES（玫瑰之类植物的）刺，棘刺 ➲ VISUAL VOCAB PAGE V11 **2** a tree or bush that has thorns 带刺的树；荆棘 ➲ SEE ALSO BLACKTHORN, HAWTHORN **3** (*phonetics* 语音) the letter that was used in Old English and Icelandic to represent the sounds /θ/ and /ð/ and later written as *th* 刺形符，字母 ð（古英语和古冰岛语用的字母，表示 /θ/ 和 /ð/ 的发音，后书写为 th）

IDM **a thorn in sb's ˈflesh/ˈside** a person or thing that repeatedly annoys sb or stops them from doing sth 不断让人烦心的人（或事）；肉中刺；眼中钉

thorny /ˈθɔːni; *NAmE* ˈθɔːrni/ *adj.* (**thorn·ier**, **thorni·est**) **1** [usually before noun] causing difficulty or disagreement 棘手的；麻烦的；引起争议的 SYN **knotty**: *a thorny question/issue/problem* 棘手的问题 **2** having thorns 有刺的；多刺的：*a thorny bush* 有刺的灌木

thor·ough 🔑 /ˈθʌrə; *NAmE* ˈθɜːroʊ/ *adj.* **1** 🔑 done completely; with great attention to detail 彻底的；完全的；深入的；细致的：*a thorough knowledge of the subject* 对这一学科的透彻了解 ◇ *The police carried out a thorough investigation.* 警方展开了全面的调查。 **2** 🔑 [not usually before noun] (of a person 人) doing things very carefully and with great attention to detail 仔细周到；工作缜密：*She's very thorough and conscientious.* 她勤勤恳恳，一丝不苟。 **3** (*BrE, informal*) used to emphasize how bad or annoying sb/sth is 十足的；彻头彻尾的；完完全全的 SYN **complete**: *Everything was in a thorough mess.* 一切都是乱七八糟的。 ▶ **thor·ough·ness** *noun* [U]: *I was impressed by the thoroughness of the report.* 那份报告全面深入，给我留下了深刻的印象。 ◇ *I admire his thoroughness.* 我钦佩他办事认真仔细。

thor·ough·bred /ˈθʌrəbred; *NAmE* ˈθɜːroʊb-/ *noun* an animal, especially a horse, of high quality, that has parents that are both of the same breed 纯种动物，良种动物（尤指马） ➲ WORDFINDER NOTE AT HORSE ▶ **thor·ough·bred** *adj.*：*a thoroughbred mare* 纯种母马

thor·ough·fare /ˈθʌrəfeə(r); *NAmE* ˈθɜːroʊfer/ *noun* a public road or street used by traffic, especially a main road in a city or town 大街；大道；通衢

thor·ough·going /ˌθʌrəˈɡəʊɪŋ; *NAmE* ˌθɜːroʊˈɡoʊɪŋ/ *adj.* [only before noun] **1** very thorough; looking at every detail 彻底的；仔细的：*a thoroughgoing revision of the text* 对文本认真仔细的校订 **2** complete 完全的；全面的；彻底的：*a thoroughgoing commitment to change* 对变革的全面承诺

thor·ough·ly 🔑 /ˈθʌrəli; *NAmE* ˈθɜːr-/ *adv.* **1** 🔑 very much; completely 非常；极其；彻底；完全：*We thoroughly enjoyed ourselves.* 我们玩得痛快极了。 ◇ *I'm thoroughly confused.* 我完全给搞糊涂了。 ◇ *a thoroughly professional performance* 地道的专业表演 **2** 🔑 completely and with great attention to detail 彻底；仔细；缜密：*Wash the fruit thoroughly before use.* 把水果仔细清洗过后再用。 ◇ *The work had not been done very thoroughly.* 这工作做得不太认真。

those ➲ THAT *det., pron.*

thou /ðaʊ/ *pron.* (*old use* or *dialect*) a word meaning 'you', used when talking to only one person who is the subject of the verb（用作第二人称单数动词的主语）你，汝；尔 ➲ COMPARE THEE

though 🔑 /ðəʊ; *NAmE* ðoʊ/ *conj., adv.*

■ ***conj.*** **1** 🔑 despite the fact that 虽然；尽管；即使 SYN **although**: *Anne was fond of Tim, though he often annoyed her.* 安妮喜欢蒂姆，虽然他经常使她心烦。 ◇ *Though she gave no sign, I was sure she had seen me.* 尽管她没有示意，我还是确信她看见了我。 ◇ *His clothes, though old and worn, looked clean and of good quality.* 他的衣服虽然很旧，但看上去干干净净，质地很好。 ◇ *Strange though it may sound, I was pleased it was over.* 尽管听起来也许很奇怪，但我很高兴这都结束了。 **2** 🔑 used to add a fact or an opinion that makes the previous statement less strong or less important（用于主句后，引出补充说明，使语气变弱）不过，可是，然而：*They're very different, though they did seem to get on well when they met.* 他们大不相同，可是见面后好像还确实相处得不错。 ◇ *He'll probably say no, though it's worth asking.* 他很可能会拒绝，不过问一下有益无损。 ➲ NOTE AT ALTHOUGH IDM SEE AS *conj.*, EVEN *adv.*

■ ***adv.*** 🔑 used especially at the end of a sentence to add a fact or an opinion that makes the previous statement less strong or less important（尤用于句末补充说明，使语气减弱）不过，可是，然而：*Our team lost. It was a good game though.* 我们队输了，可是这也不失为一场好球。 ◇ *'Have you ever been to Australia?' 'No. I'd like to, though.'* "你去过澳大利亚吗？" "没有，不过我很想去。" ➲ NOTE AT ALTHOUGH

thought 🔑 /θɔːt/ *noun*

• **STH YOU THINK** 所想之事 **1** 🔑 [C] something that you think of or remember 想法；看法；主意；记忆：**~ of (sb/sth) doing sth** *I don't like the thought of you walking home alone.* 我不喜欢你一个人步行回家。 ◇ **~ of sth** *The very thought of it makes me feel sick.* 一想到这事就使我恶心。 ◇ **~ (that...)** *She was struck by the sudden thought that he might already have left.* 她突然想到他可能已经离去。 ◇ *I've just* **had a thought** (= an idea). 我刚想到一个主意。 ◇ *Would Mark be able to help? It's just a thought.* 马克能帮忙吗？仅仅是想到这一点而已。 ◇ *'Why don't you try the other key?' 'That's a thought!'* "你为什么不试试另一把钥匙？" "这倒是个主意！" ◇ *I'd like to hear your thoughts on the subject.* 我想听听你对这个问题的看法。

• **MIND/IDEAS** 心思；思想 **2** 🔑 **thoughts** [pl.] a person's mind and all the ideas that they have in it when they are thinking 心思；思想：*My thoughts turned to home.* 我想家了。

• **PROCESS/ACT OF THINKING** 思维过程；思考 **3** [U] the power or process of thinking 思考能力；思维过程；思考；思维：*A good teacher encourages independence of thought.* 好的教师鼓励独立思考。 ◇ *She was* **lost in thought** (= concentrating so much on her thoughts that she was not aware of her surroundings). 她陷入沉思。 **4** 🔑 [U] the act of thinking seriously and carefully about sth 考虑；深思 SYN **consideration**: *I've given the matter careful thought.* 我对这件事认真考虑过了。 ◇ *Not enough thought has gone into this essay.* 这篇文章很肤浅。

• **CARE/WORRY** 关心；忧虑 **5** [C] **~ (for sb/sth)** a feeling of

T

care or worry 关心；关怀；顾虑；忧虑： ***Spare a thought*** *for those without enough to eat this winter.* 请关心一下今冬食不果腹的人。 ◇ ***Don't give it another thought*** (= to tell sb not to worry after they have said they are sorry). 别多想了（让道了歉的人不再担心）。 ◇ ***It's the thought that counts*** (= used to say that sb has been very kind even if they have only done sth small or unimportant). 有这份心意就好。

• **INTENTION** 意向 **6** [U, C] an intention or a hope of doing sth 意图；打算；希望；念头： ~ (**of doing sth**) *She had given up all thought of changing her job.* 她打消了所有换工作的念头。 ◇ ~ (**of sth**) *He acted with no thoughts of personal gain.* 他这样做根本没有考虑个人得失。

• **IN POLITICS/SCIENCE, ETC.** 政治、科学等 **7** [U] ideas in politics, science, etc. connected with a particular person, group or period of history 思想；思潮： *feminist thought* 女权主义思想 ➲ SEE ALSO THINK *n.*

IDM **have ˌsecond ˈthoughts** to change your opinion after thinking about sth again （经考虑后）改变想法；（转念一想）改变主意 **on ˈsecond thoughts** (*BrE*) (*NAmE* **on ˈsecond thought**) used to say that you have changed your opinion （表示已改变想法）又一想，转念一想： *I'll wait here. No, on second thoughts, I'll come with you.* 我就在这儿等。不，再一想，我还是跟你一起走。 **without a second ˈthought** immediately; without stopping to think about sth further 立即；马上；不假思索： *He dived in after her without a second thought.* 他不假思索地随她跳入水中。 ➲ MORE AT COLLECT *v.*, FOOD, PAUSE *n.*, PENNY, PERISH, SCHOOL *n.*, TRAIN *n.*, WISH *n.*

thought·crime /ˈθɔːtkraɪm/ *noun* [U, C] an idea or opinion that is considered socially unacceptable or criminal 思想罪（被认为社会不接受或构成犯罪的想法或观点）
ORIGIN From George Orwell's novel *Nineteen Eighty-Four.* 源自乔治•奥威尔所著小说《一九八四》。

thought·ful /ˈθɔːtfl/ *adj.* **1** quiet, because you are thinking 沉思的；深思的；思考的： *He looked thoughtful.* 他一脸沉思的神情。 ◇ *They sat in thoughtful silence.* 他们坐着，沉思不语。 **2** (*approving*) showing that you think about and care for other people 体贴的；关心别人的；关切的 SYN **considerate, kind**： *It was very thoughtful of you to send the flowers.* 你送花来，想得真周到。 **3** showing signs of careful thought 缜密思考过的；深思熟虑的： *a player who has a thoughtful approach to the game* 对这场比赛缜密研究过对策的运动员 ▸ **thought·ful·ly** /-fəli/ *adv.*： *Martin looked at her thoughtfully.* 马丁若有所思地望着她。 ◇ *She used the towel thoughtfully provided by her host.* 她用了主人特意为她准备的毛巾。 **thought·ful·ness** *noun* [U]

thought·less /ˈθɔːtləs/ *adj.* (*disapproving*) not caring about the possible effects of your words or actions on other people 粗心大意的；欠考虑的；轻率的 SYN **inconsiderate**： *a thoughtless remark* 欠考虑的话 ▸ **thought·less·ly** *adv.* **thought·less·ness** *noun* [U]

ˈthought police *noun* [pl.] a group of people who are seen as trying to control people's ideas and stop them from having their own opinions 思想警察（被认为试图控制他人思想、禁止独立观点的集体）

ˈthought-provok·ing *adj.* making people think seriously about a particular subject or issue 发人深省的；引人深思的

thou·sand 🔑 /ˈθaʊznd/ *number* (*abbr.* **K**) **1** 🔑 1 000 一千 HELP You say **a, one, two, etc. thousand** without a final 's' on 'thousand'. **Thousands (of...)** can be used if there is no number or quantity before it. Always use a plural verb with **thousand** or **thousands**, except when an amount of money is mentioned. * thousand 与数词 a、one、two 等连用时，后面不加 s。若前面没有数目或数量，可用 thousands (of ...)。除指金额外，thousand 和 thousands 均用复数动词： *Four thousand (people) are expected to attend.* 预计有四千人出席。 ◇ *Two thousand (pounds) was withdrawn from the account.* 从账户中提取了两千（英镑）。 **2** 🔑 **a thousand** or **thousands (of...)** (*usually informal*) a large number 数以千计的；成千上万的；许许多多的： *There were thousands of people there.* 那里有成千上万的人。 **3 the thousands** the numbers from 1 000 to 9 999 * 1 000 到 9 999 间的数目；千位数： *The cost ran into the thousands.* 成本达到千位数。 HELP There are more examples of how to use numbers at the entry for **hundred**. 更多数词用法示例见 hundred 条。 IDM SEE BAT *v.*

thou·sandth 🔑 /ˈθaʊznθ/ *ordinal number, noun*
■ ***ordinal number*** 🔑 1 000th 第一千： *the city's thousandth anniversary* 这座城市的一千周年纪念
■ ***noun*** 🔑 each of one thousand parts of sth 千分之一： *a/one thousandth of a second* 千分之一秒

thrall /θrɔːl/ *noun*
IDM **in (sb's/sth's) ˈthrall | in ˈthrall to sb/sth** (*literary*) controlled or strongly influenced by sb/sth 受…控制；深受…影响

thrash /θræʃ/ *verb, noun*
■ ***verb*** **1** [T] ~ **sb/sth** to hit a person or an animal many times with a stick, etc. as a punishment （作为惩罚用棍子等）抽打，连续击打 SYN **beat 2** [I, T] to move or make sth move in a violent or uncontrolled way （使）激烈扭动，翻来覆去： ~ (**about/around**) *Someone was thrashing around in the water, obviously in trouble.* 有人在水里乱扑腾，显然遇到了危险。 ◇ ~ **sth** (**about/around**) *A whale was thrashing the water with its tail.* 一条鲸鱼不住地用尾巴击水。 ◇ *She thrashed her head from side to side.* 她把头摇得像拨浪鼓似的。 **3** [T] ~ **sb/sth** (*informal, especially BrE*) to defeat sb very easily in a game （赛事中）轻易击败，一举战胜： *Scotland thrashed England 5–1.* 苏格兰队以 5:1 大胜英格兰队。 ➲ COMPARE WHIP *v.* (5)
PHR V **ˌthrash sth↔ˈout** (*informal*) to discuss a situation or problem thoroughly in order to decide sth 彻底讨论，反复讨论（以便作出决定）
■ ***noun*** **1** [U] a type of loud rock music 快节奏重金属摇滚乐 **2** [C] (*old-fashioned, informal*) a party with music and dancing 载歌载舞的聚会

thrash·ing /ˈθræʃɪŋ/ *noun* **1** an act of hitting sb very hard, especially with a stick 棒打；殴打；痛打： *to give sb/get a thrashing* 痛打某人一顿；挨了一顿痛打 **2** (*informal*) a severe defeat in a game （比赛）大败，惨败

thread 🔑 /θred/ *noun, verb*
■ ***noun*** **1** 🔑 [U, C] a thin string of cotton, wool, silk, etc. used for sewing or making cloth （棉、毛、丝等的）线： *a needle and thread* 针线 ◇ *a robe embroidered with gold thread* 用金线绣的长袍 ◇ *the delicate threads of a spider's web* 蜘蛛网的纤丝 ➲ PICTURE AT ROPE ➲ **WORDFINDER NOTE** AT SEW ➲ **VISUAL VOCAB** PAGE V45 **2** [C] an idea or a feature that is part of sth greater; an idea that connects the different parts of sth 线索；脉络；思路；贯穿的主线： *A common thread runs through these discussions.* 这些讨论都贯穿着一条共同的主线。 ◇ *The author skilfully draws together the different threads of the plot.* 作者娴熟地把情节的各种线索串联在一起。 ◇ ***I lost the thread*** *of the argument* (= I could no longer follow it). 我再跟不上这论证的思路了。 **3** [C] ~ (**of sth**) a long thin line of sth 线状物；细细的一条： *A thread of light emerged from the keyhole.* 从锁眼里透出一丝光亮。 **4** [C] (*computing* 计) a series of connected messages on a MESSAGE BOARD on the Internet which have been sent by different people （互联网留言板上帖子的）系列相关信息，链式消息 **5** [C] the raised line that runs around the length of a screw and that allows it to be fixed in place by twisting 螺纹 ➲ **VISUAL VOCAB** PAGE V21 **6 threads** [pl.] (*old-fashioned, NAmE, slang*) clothes 衣服 IDM SEE HANG *v.*, PICK *v.*
■ ***verb*** **1** [T] ~ **sth** (+ **adv./prep.**) to pass sth long and thin, especially thread, through a narrow opening or hole 穿（针）；纫（针）；穿过： *to thread a needle (with cotton)* （用棉线）纫针 ◇ *to thread cotton through a needle* 用棉线纫针 ◇ *A tiny wire is threaded through a vein to the heart.* 一根细金属丝从静脉里穿到心脏。 **2** [I, T] to move or make sth move through a narrow space, avoiding things that are in the way （使）穿过；通过；穿行 SYN **pick your way** (**across, along, among, over, through sth**)： + **adv./prep.** *The waiters threaded between the crowded tables.* 服务员穿行在拥挤的餐桌之间。 ◇ ~ **your way** + **adv./prep.** *It took me a long time to thread my way through the crowd.* 我花了很长时间才从人群中挤过去。 **3** [T] ~ **sth** (**onto sth**) to

T

join two or more objects together by passing sth long and thin through them 穿成串；串在一起： *to thread beads (onto a string)*（在绳子上）把珠子串起来 **4** [T] **~ sth** to pass film, tape, string, etc. through parts of a piece of equipment so that it is ready to use 给…装入（胶片、磁带、丝弦等） **5** [T, usually passive] **~ sth (with sth)** to sew or twist a particular type of thread into sth 用…线缝；把…线绞入： *a robe threaded with gold and silver* 用金银线缝的长袍

thread·bare /ˈθredbeə(r); *NAmE* -ber/ *adj.* **1** (of cloth, clothing, etc. 织物、衣服等) old and thin because it has been used a lot 穿旧的；磨薄的；破旧的： *a threadbare carpet* 磨薄了的地毯 **2** (of an argument, excuse, etc. 论点、借口等) that does not have much effect, especially because it has been used too much 老一套的；陈腐的

thread·ed /ˈθredɪd/ *adj.* (*specialist*) (of a screw, etc. 螺钉等) having a THREAD (5) 有螺纹的

ˈthread vein *noun* a very thin VEIN, especially one that can be seen through the skin（尤指透过皮肤可见的）毛细血管

thread·worm /ˈθredwɜːm; *NAmE* -wɜːrm/ *noun* a small thin WORM that lives in the INTESTINES of humans and animals 线虫；蛲虫

threat /θret/ *noun* **1** [C, U] **~ (to do sth)** a statement in which you tell sb that you will punish or harm them, especially if they do not do what you want 威胁；恐吓： *to make threats against sb* 对某人进行威胁 ◇ *She is prepared to* ***carry out her threat*** *to resign.* 她以辞职作为要挟，已准备好付诸行动。 ◇ *He received* ***death threats*** *from right-wing groups.* 他收到了右翼团体的死亡恐吓。 ◇ *crimes involving violence or the threat of violence* 涉及暴力或暴力威胁的罪行 **2** [U, C, usually sing.] the possibility of trouble, danger or disaster 凶兆；不祥之兆： *These ancient woodlands are* ***under threat*** *from new road developments.* 新道路的修建可能对这些古老的林地造成破坏。 ◇ *There is a real threat of war.* 确有可能发生战争。 **3** [C, usually sing.] **~ (to sth)** a person or thing that is likely to cause trouble, danger, etc. 构成威胁的人；形成威胁的事物： *He is unlikely to be a threat to the Spanish player in the final.* 相信他不会在决赛中对这位西班牙运动员形成威胁。 ◇ *Drugs* ***pose a major threat to*** *our society.* 毒品对社会构成重大威胁。

threat·en /ˈθretn/ *verb* **1** [T] to say that you will cause trouble, hurt sb, etc. if you do not get what you want 扬言要；威胁；恐吓： **~ sb** *They broke my windows and threatened me.* 他们砸碎我的窗子并威胁我。 ◇ **~ sb with sth** *The attacker threatened them with a gun.* 袭击者用枪威胁他们。 ◇ *He was threatened with dismissal if he continued to turn up late for work.* 他受到警告，如果继续上班迟到，就被辞退。 ◇ **~ sth** *The threatened strike has been called off.* 扬言要进行的罢工被取消了。 ◇ **~ to do sth** *The hijackers threatened to kill one passenger every hour if their demands were not met.* 劫机者要挟说，如果他们的要求得不到满足，他们每过一小时就杀死一名乘客。 ◇ **~ that...** *They threatened that passengers would be killed.* 他们要挟说要杀死乘客。 **2** [I, T] to seem likely to happen or cause sth unpleasant 预示凶兆；有…危险： *A storm was threatening.* 暴风雨即将来临。 ◇ **~ to do sth** *This dispute threatens to split the party.* 这一分歧可能会造成党的分裂。 ◇ **~ sth** *The clouds threatened rain.* 乌云密布预示大雨将至。 **3** [T] **~ sth** to be a danger to sth 危及；对…构成威胁 SYN **endanger, at risk (from/of sth)**: *Pollution is threatening marine life.* 污染正危及海洋生物。

threat·en·ing /ˈθretnɪŋ/ *adj.* **1** expressing a threat of harm or violence 威胁的；恐吓的 SYN **menacing**: *threatening letters* 恐吓信 ◇ *threatening behaviour* 威胁行为 **2** (of the sky, clouds, etc. 天空、云等) showing that bad weather is likely 阴沉沉的；乌云密布的： *The sky was dark and threatening.* 天空乌云密布，阴沉沉的。 ▸ **threat·en·ing·ly** *adv.* : *He glared at her threateningly.* 他气势汹汹地瞪着她。

three /θriː/ *number* 3 三 HELP There are examples of how to use numbers at the entry for **five**. 数词用法示例见 five 条。

IDM **the three ˈRs** (*old-fashioned*) reading, writing and ARITHMETIC, thought to be the most important parts of a child's education 初等教育三要素（被视为儿童教育最重要部分的读、写、算） ➲ MORE AT TWO

ˌthree-card ˈtrick *noun* a game in which players bet money on which is the queen out of three cards lying face down 三牌猜王后（赌博戏，参加者猜三张正面朝下的纸牌中哪一张为王后）

ˌthree-ˈcornered *adj.* [usually before noun] **1** having three corners 三角形的；有三个角的；三隅的： *a three-cornered hat* 三角帽 **2** involving three people or groups 有三人参加的；有三个组的： *a three-cornered contest* 三方竞争

ˌthree-ˈD (*also* **3-D**) *noun* [U] the quality of having, or appearing to have, length, width and depth (= three DIMENSIONS) 三维；三度；立体： *These glasses allow you to see the film in three-D.* 这副眼镜让你能看立体电影。 ◇ *a three-D image* 立体视像

ˌthree-day eˈventing *noun* = EVENTING

ˌthree-diˈmension·al *adj.* having, or appearing to have, length, width and depth 三维的；立体的；三度空间的；有立体感的： *three-dimensional objects* 立体物体

three·fold /ˈθriːfəʊld; *NAmE* -foʊld/ *adj., adv.* ➲ -FOLD

ˌthree ˈfourths *noun* [pl.] (*US*) = THREE QUARTERS

three-legged race /ˌθriː ˈlegɪd reɪs/ *noun* a race in which people taking part run in pairs, the right leg of one runner being tied to the left leg of the other 二人三足赛跑，绑腿赛跑（参赛者两人一组，一人的右腿和另一人的左腿绑在一起）

ˌthree-line ˈwhip *noun* (in Britain) a written notice to Members of Parliament from their party leaders telling them that they must be present at a particular vote and must vote in a particular way 紧急通知（英国政党领袖要求其议员必须参加投票和如何投票的书面通知）

ˌthree-ˈpeat *noun* (*NAmE*) (used especially in newspapers 尤用于报章) an occasion when a person or team wins a competition for the third time, especially in sport（尤指在同一个体育比赛中的）第三次获胜，三连冠，三连霸 ▸ **ˌthree-ˈpeat** *verb* [I]

three·pence /ˌθriːˈpens; ˈθrepəns/ *noun* [U] (*BrE*) the sum of three old pence （旧时的）三便士

ˌthree-ˈpiece *adj.* [only before noun] consisting of three separate parts or pieces 三件一套的；由三部分组成的： *a* ***three-piece suit*** (= a set of clothes consisting of trousers/ pants, a jacket and a WAISTCOAT/VEST) 三件式套服（包括裤子、上衣和背心） ◇ (*BrE*) *a* ***three-piece suite*** (= a set of three pieces of furniture, usually a SOFA and two ARMCHAIRS) 三件一套的家具（通常为一张长沙发和两张单人沙发）

ˌthree-point ˈturn *noun* a method of turning a car in a small space so that it faces in the opposite direction, by driving forwards, then backwards, then forwards again, in a series of curves 三点转向（汽车在狭窄场所转弯掉头的方法，先向前，再后退，再向前进）

ˌthree-ˈquarter *adj.* [only before noun] used to describe sth which is three quarters of the usual size 四分之三的： *a three-quarter length coat* 七分长大衣

ˌthree ˈquarters (*US also* **ˌthree ˈfourths**) *noun* **~ (of sth)** three of the four equal parts into which sth may be divided 四分之三： *three quarters of an hour* 四十五分钟

ˌthree-ring ˈcircus *noun* [sing.] (*NAmE, informal*) a place or situation with a lot of confusing or amusing activity 有各种娱乐活动的场所；大型热闹的演出

three·some /ˈθriːsəm/ *noun* **1** [C+sing./pl. v.] a group of three people 三人一组；三人小组 **2** [C] an occasion when three people have sex together 三人性爱

T

ˈthree-star *adj.* [usually before noun] **1** having three stars in a system that measures quality. The highest standard is usually represented by four or five stars.（服务质量）三星级的：*a three-star hotel* 三星级宾馆 **2** (*NAmE*) having the third-highest military rank, and wearing uniform which has three stars on it（军阶）三星的：*a three-star general* 三星上将

ˌthree-ˈway *adj.* [only before noun] happening or working in three ways or directions, or between three people 三方面的；三向的；三人参加的：*a three-way switch* 三路开关 ◇ *a three-way discussion* 三人谈

thren·ody /ˈθrenədi/ *noun* (*pl.* **-ies**) (*specialist*) a song, poem or other expression of great sadness for sb who has died or for sth that has ended 挽歌；哀歌；悲诗；哀悼

thresh /θreʃ/ *verb* **1** [T] **~ sth** to separate grains of rice, WHEAT, etc. from the rest of the plant using a machine or, especially in the past, by hitting it with a special tool（用机器）使脱粒；（尤指旧时手持工具）打（稻、麦等） ➲ COLLOCATIONS AT FARMING **2** [I, T] **~ (sth)** to make, or cause sth to make, uncontrolled movements（使）剧烈扭动，翻滚 SYN **thrash** ▸**thresh·ing** *noun* [U]: *a threshing machine* 脱粒机

thresh·old /ˈθreʃhəʊld; *NAmE* -hoʊld/ *noun* **1** the floor or ground at the bottom of a DOORWAY, considered as the entrance to a building or room 门槛；门口：*She stood hesitating on the threshold.* 她站在门口，犹豫不决。◇ *He stepped across the threshold.* 他迈过门槛。 **2** the level at which sth starts to happen or have an effect 阈；界；起始点：*He has a low* ***boredom threshold*** (= he gets bored easily). 他极易感到乏味。◇ *I have a high* ***pain threshold*** (= I can suffer a lot of pain before I start to react). 我的痛阈很高。◇ *My earnings are just above the* ***tax threshold*** (= more than the amount at which you start paying tax). 我的收入刚刚超过税收起征点。 **3** [usually sing.] the point just before a new situation, period of life, etc. begins 开端；起点；入门：*She felt as though she was* ***on the threshold of*** *a new life.* 她觉得好像就要开始新生活了。

threw PAST TENSE OF THROW

thrice /θraɪs/ *adv.* (*old use* or *formal*) three times 三次；三倍

thrift /θrɪft/ *noun* [U] **1** (*approving*) the habit of saving money and spending it carefully so that none is wasted 节约；节俭 ➲ SEE ALSO SPENDTHRIFT **2** a wild plant with bright pink flowers that grows by the sea/ocean 海石竹（海边野生植物，花鲜艳，呈粉红色）

ˈthrift shop (*also* **ˈthrift store**) (*both NAmE*) (*BrE* **ˈcharity shop**) *noun* a shop/store that sells clothes and other goods given by people to raise money for a charity 慈善商店（通过出售捐赠的衣物等募集慈善资金）

thrifty /ˈθrɪfti/ *adj.* (*approving*) careful about spending money and not wasting things 节约的；节俭的 SYN **frugal**

thrill /θrɪl/ *noun, verb*

■ ***noun*** **1** a strong feeling of excitement or pleasure; an experience that gives you this feeling 震颤感；兴奋感；兴奋；激动；令人兴奋的经历：**~ (to do sth)** *It gave me a* ***big thrill*** *to meet my favourite author in person.* 能见到我最喜欢的作者本人使我感到兴奋不已。◇ **~ (of doing sth)** *the thrill of catching a really big fish* 捉到一条很大的鱼的兴奋 ◇ *She gets an obvious thrill out of performing.* 她显然从表演中得到一种兴奋感。 ➲ WORDFINDER NOTE AT ADVENTURE **2** a sudden strong feeling that produces a physical effect 一阵强烈的感觉：*A thrill of alarm ran through him.* 一阵惊恐的感觉传遍他的全身。

IDM **(the) thrills and ˈspills** (*informal*) the excitement that is involved in dangerous activities, especially sports（危险活动，尤指体育运动的）紧张和刺激 ➲ MORE LIKE THIS 12, page R26

■ ***verb*** **~ sb** to excite or please sb very much 使非常兴奋；使非常激动：*This band has thrilled audiences all over the world.* 这支乐队使全世界的观众狂热痴迷。◇ *I was thrilled by your news.* 你的消息使我兴奋极了。

PHR V **ˈthrill to sth** (*formal*) to feel very excited at sth 对…感到非常兴奋（或激动）

thrilled /θrɪld/ *adj.* very excited and pleased 非常兴奋；极为激动：**~ (about/at/with sth)** *He was thrilled at the prospect of seeing them again.* 他一想到有望再次见到他们便欣喜若狂。◇ **~ (to do sth)** *I was thrilled to be invited.* 我有幸受到邀请，感到非常兴奋。◇ **~ (that…)** (*BrE*) *She was* ***thrilled to bits*** (= extremely pleased) *that he'd been offered the job.* 她得知他得到了这份工作简直乐不可支。◇ *'Are you pleased?' 'I'm thrilled.'* "你高兴吗？" "我太兴奋了。" ➲ SYNONYMS AT GLAD

thrill·er /ˈθrɪlə(r)/ *noun* a book, play or film/movie with an exciting story, especially one about crime or SPYING（尤指关于罪案或间谍的）惊险小说（或戏剧、电影）

thrill·ing /ˈθrɪlɪŋ/ *adj.* exciting and enjoyable 惊险的；紧张的；扣人心弦的；令人兴奋不已的：*a thrilling experience/finish* 激动人心的经历 / 结局 ➲ SYNONYMS AT EXCITING ▸**thrill·ing·ly** *adv.*

ˈthrill ride *noun* a ride at an AMUSEMENT PARK that makes you feel very excited and frightened at the same time（游乐园的）惊险刺激乘骑，飞转

thrive /θraɪv/ *verb* [I] to become, and continue to be, successful, strong, healthy, etc. 兴旺发达；繁荣；蓬勃发展；旺盛；茁壮成长 SYN **flourish**：*New businesses thrive in this area.* 新企业在这一地区蓬勃兴起。◇ *These animals rarely thrive in captivity.* 这些动物栏养起来很少会肥壮。▸**thriv·ing** *adj.*：*a thriving industry* 兴盛的行业

PHR V **ˈthrive on sth** to enjoy sth or be successful at sth, especially sth that other people would not like 以某事为乐，因某事而有成（尤指别人不喜欢的事物）：*He thrives on hard work.* 他以苦干为乐事。

throat /θrəʊt; *NAmE* θroʊt/ *noun* **1** a passage in the neck through which food and air pass on their way into the body; the front part of the neck 咽喉；喉咙；颈前部：*a sore throat* 咽喉痛 ◇ *A sob caught in his throat.* 他泣不成声。◇ *He held the knife to her throat.* 他拿刀子顶着她的喉咙。◇ *Their throats had been cut.* 他们的咽喉被割断了。 **2 -throated** (in adjectives 构成形容词) having the type of throat mentioned 有…喉咙的；嗓子…的：*a deep-throated roar* 低沉的咆哮 ◇ *a blue-throated macaw* 一只蓝喉金刚鹦鹉 ➲ MORE LIKE THIS 8, page R25 ➲ SEE ALSO CUT-THROAT

IDM **be at each other's ˈthroats** (of two or more people, groups, etc. 两个以上的人或群体等) to be fighting or arguing with each other 打架斗殴；激烈争吵；吵架 **cut your own ˈthroat** to do sth that is likely to harm you, especially when you are angry and trying to harm sb else（尤指生气和要加害于人时）自食恶果，卡自己的脖子，自寻死路 **force/thrust/ram sth down sb's ˈthroat** (*informal*) to try to force sb to listen to and accept your opinions in a way that they find annoying 强加于人；强迫接受（观点） ➲ MORE AT CLEAR *v.*, FROG, JUMP *v.*, LUMP *n.*, STICK *v.*

throaty /ˈθrəʊti; *NAmE* ˈθroʊti/ *adj.* sounding low and rough 声音低沉的；嘶哑的：*a throaty laugh* 嘎嘎的笑声 ◇ *the throaty roar of the engines* 发动机的低沉轰鸣声 ▸**throat·ily** /-ɪli/ *adv.*

throb /θrɒb; *NAmE* θrɑːb/ *verb, noun*

■ ***verb*** **(-bb-) 1** [I] **~ (with sth)** (of a part of the body 身体部位) to feel a series of regular painful movements（有规律地）抽动，抽痛：*His head throbbed painfully.* 他的头一抽一跳地痛。◇ *My feet were throbbing after the long walk home.* 我走了很长的路回到家后，双脚阵阵作痛。 ➲ SYNONYMS AT HURT **2** [I] to beat or sound with a strong, regular rhythm （强烈有节奏地）跳动，搏动，震响 SYN **pulsate**：*The ship's engines throbbed quietly.* 船上的发动机有节奏地轻轻震动。◇ *a throbbing drumbeat* 咚咚的击鼓声 ◇ *The blood was throbbing in my veins.* 血液在我的血管里有节律地涌动着。◇ **~ with sth** (*figurative*) *His voice was throbbing with emotion.* 他的声音激动得颤抖。 ➲ MORE LIKE THIS 36, page R29

T

■ ***noun*** (*also* **throb·bing**) [sing.] a strong regular beat; a feeling of pain that you experience as a series of strong beats（强烈有规律的）跳动；阵阵的疼痛：*the throb of the machines* 机器有节奏的颤动 ◇ *My headache faded to a dull throbbing.* 我的头痛逐渐减轻，后来变得微微抽痛。 ➲ SEE ALSO HEART-THROB

throes /θrəʊz; *NAmE* θroʊz/ *noun* [pl.] violent pains, especially at the moment of death （尤指死亡时的）剧痛：*The creature went into its death throes.* 这个生命到了临终疼痛阶段。

IDM **in the throes of sth/of doing sth** in the middle of an activity, especially a difficult or complicated one 正在做，正忙于（尤指困难或复杂的活动）：*The country was in the throes of revolutionary change.* 国家正处于革命动荡中。

throm·bosis /θrɒmˈbəʊsɪs; *NAmE* θrɑːmˈboʊ-/ *noun* [C, U] (*pl.* **throm·boses** /-siːz/) (*medical* 医) a serious condition caused by a blood CLOT (= a thick mass of blood) forming in a blood VESSEL (= tube) or in the heart 血栓形成 ➲ SEE ALSO CORONARY THROMBOSIS, DEEP VEIN THROMBOSIS

throne /θrəʊn; *NAmE* θroʊn/ *noun* **1** [C] a special chair used by a king or queen to sit on at ceremonies（国王、女王的）御座，宝座 **2 the throne** [sing.] the position of being a king or queen 王位；王权；帝位：*Queen Elizabeth **came/succeeded to the throne** in 1952.* 伊丽莎白女王于 1952 年即位 / 登基。◇ *when Henry VIII was **on the throne*** (= was king) 亨利八世在位时 ➲ WORDFINDER NOTE AT KING IDM SEE POWER *n.*

throng /θrɒŋ; *NAmE* θrɔːŋ; θrɑːŋ/ *noun, verb*

■ ***noun*** (*literary*) a crowd of people 聚集的人群；一大群人：*We pushed our way through the throng.* 我们挤过人群。

■ ***verb*** [I, T] (*literary*) to go somewhere or be present somewhere in large numbers 群集；拥塞；拥向：**+ adv./prep.** *The children thronged into the hall.* 孩子们拥进了大厅。◇ **~ to do sth** *People are thronging to see his new play.* 人们成群结队地去看他的新戏。◇ **~ sth** *Crowds thronged the stores.* 各商店都挤满了人。

PHR V **ˈthrong with sb/sth | be ˈthronged with sb/sth** to be full of people, cars, etc. 挤满（人、汽车等）：*The cafes were thronging with students.* 小餐馆里都挤满了学生。◇ *The streets were thronged with people.* 条条大街都挤满了人。

throt·tle /ˈθrɒtl; *NAmE* ˈθrɑːtl/ *verb, noun*

■ ***verb*** **~ sb** to attack or kill sb by squeezing their throat in order to stop them from breathing 使窒息；掐死；勒死 SYN **strangle**：*He throttled the guard with his bare hands.* 他徒手掐死了卫兵。◇ (*humorous*) *I like her, although I could cheerfully throttle her at times* (= because she is annoying). 我喜欢她，虽然她有时烦得我想把她掐死。◇ (*figurative*) *The city is being throttled by traffic.* 这座城市的交通拥挤不堪。

PHR V **ˌthrottle (sth) ˈback/ˈdown/ˈup** to control the supply of fuel or power to an engine in order to reduce/increase the speed of a vehicle 调节油门；减速；加速：*I throttled back as we approached the runway.* 我们靠近跑道时，我减速了。

■ ***noun*** a device that controls the amount of fuel that goes into the engine of a vehicle, for example the ACCELERATOR in a car 节流阀；节流杆；风门；风门杆：*He drove along **at full throttle*** (= as fast as possible). 他全速驾车行驶。

through /θruː/ *prep., adv., adj.*

■ ***prep.*** HELP For the special uses of **through** in phrasal verbs, look at the entries for the verbs. For example **get through sth** is in the phrasal verb section at **get**. * through 在短语动词中的特殊用法见有关动词词条。如 get through sth 在词条 get 的短语动词部分。 **1** from one end or side of sth/sb to the other 从…一端至另一端；穿过；贯穿：*The burglar got in through the window.* 盗贼是从窗户进来的。◇ *The bullet went straight through him.* 子弹从他身上穿了过去。◇ *Her knees had gone through* (= made holes in) *her jeans.* 她的膝盖把牛仔裤磨破了。◇ *The sand ran through* (= between) *my fingers.* 沙子从我的手指缝间漏了下去。◇ *The path led through the trees to the river.* 这条小路穿过树林通向河边。◇ *The doctor pushed his way through the crowd.* 医生挤过人群。◇ *The Charles River flows through Boston.* 查尔斯河流经波士顿。 **2 see, hear, etc. ~ sth** to see, hear, etc. sth from the other side of an object or a substance 透过…看到；隔着…听到：*I couldn't hear their conversation through the wall.* 我隔墙听不到他们的交谈。◇ *He could just make out three people through the mist.* 透过薄雾他勉强能看出有三个人。 **3** from the beginning to the end of an activity, a situation or a period of time 自始至终；从头到尾：*The children are too young to sit through a concert.* 这些孩子年纪太小，音乐会没完就坐不住了。◇ *He will not live through the night.* 他活不过今天晚上了。◇ *I'm halfway through* (= reading) *her second novel.* 她的第二部小说我看了一半了。 **4** past a barrier, stage or test 通过（障碍、阶段或测试）；穿过：*Go through this gate, and you'll see the house on your left.* 你穿过这道大门，就看到左面的房子了。◇ *He drove through a red light* (= passed it when he should have stopped). 他开车闯了红灯。◇ *First I have to get through the exams.* 首先我必须通过这些考试。◇ *The bill had a difficult passage through Parliament.* 这项提案费了一番周折才在议会上通过。◇ *I'd never have got through it all* (= a difficult situation) *without you.* 假如没有您，我是绝对渡不过这个难关的。 **5** (*also informal* **thru**) (*both NAmE*) until, and including 直至，一直到（所指时间包括在内）：*We'll be in New York Tuesday through Friday.* 我们从星期二到星期五将一直待在纽约。 ➲ NOTE AT INCLUSIVE **6** by means of; because of 以；凭借；因为；由于：*You can only achieve success through hard work.* 你得孜孜不倦方能成功。◇ *It was through him* (= as a result of his help) *that I got the job.* 我全靠他的帮助才找到这份工作。◇ *The accident happened through no fault of mine.* 发生事故并不是我的过错。

■ ***adv.*** HELP For the special uses of **through** in phrasal verbs, look at the entries for the verbs. For example **carry sth through** is in the phrasal verb section at **carry**. * through 在短语动词中的特殊用法见有关动词词条。如 carry sth through 在词条 carry 的短语动词部分。 **1** from one end or side of sth to the other 从一端到另一端；通过：*Put the coffee in the filter and let the water run through.* 把咖啡放入过滤器里让水流过。◇ *The tyre's flat—the nail has gone right through.* 轮胎瘪了，让钉子扎穿了。◇ *The onlookers stood aside to let the paramedics through.* 围观的人闪开一条路，让医务辅助人员通过。◇ *The flood was too deep to drive through.* 洪水太深，汽车开不过去。 **2** from the beginning to the end of a thing or period of time 自始至终；从头至尾：*Don't tell me how it ends—I haven't read it all the way through yet.* 先别告诉我书的结尾，我还没有看完呢。◇ *I expect I'll struggle through until payday.* 我想我会挨到发薪日的。 **3** past a barrier, stage or test 通过（障碍、阶段或测试）：*The lights were red but he drove straight through.* 红灯亮着，但他开车闯了过去。◇ *Our team is through to* (= has reached) *the semi-finals.* 我们队打进了半决赛。 **4** travelling through a place without stopping or without people having to get off one train and onto another 直达；径直：*'Did you stop in Oxford on the way?' 'No, we drove straight through.'* "你路经牛津时停车了吗？" "没有，我一直开过来的。" ◇ *This train goes straight through to York.* 这列火车直达约克。 **5** connected by telephone（电话）接通着：*Ask to be **put through** to me personally.* 请接线员把电话直接接给我本人。◇ *I tried to call you but I couldn't **get through**.* 我给你打电话了，可是怎么也打不通。 **6** used after an adjective to mean 'completely'（用于形容词后）完全，彻底：*We got wet through.* 我们浑身上下都湿透了。

IDM **ˌthrough and ˈthrough** completely; in every way 完全；彻底；地地道道；彻头彻尾：*He's British through and through.* 他是地地道道的英国人。

■ ***adj.*** **1** [only before noun] **through** traffic travels from one side of a place to the other without stopping（交通旅行）直达的，直通的，全程的 **2** [only before noun] a **through** train takes you to the final place you want to get to and you do not have to get off and get on another train（火车）直达的，直通的 **3** [only before noun] a **through** road or route is open at both ends and allows

T

traffic to travel from one end to the other（道路或路线）直通的：*The village lies on a busy through road.* 那村庄坐落在一条繁忙的直达公路上。◇ ***No through road*** (= the road is closed at one end). 此路不通。 **4** [not before noun] ~ (**with sth/sb**) (*especially NAmE*) used to show that you have finished using sth or have ended a relationship with sb（使用）完成，结束；（关系）了结，断绝：*Are you through with that newspaper?* 你看完那份报纸了吗？◇ *Todd and I are through.* 托德和我吹了。

through·out /θruːˈaʊt/ *prep., adv.* **1** in or into every part of sth 各处；遍及：*They export their products to markets throughout the world.* 他们把产品出口到世界各地的市场。◇ *The house was painted white throughout.* 这所房子全都粉刷成了白色。 **2** during the whole period of time of sth 自始至终；贯穿整个时期：*The museum is open daily throughout the year.* 这个博物馆一年到头每天都开放。◇ *The ceremony lasted two hours and we had to stand throughout.* 仪式进行了两个小时，我们自始至终都得站着。

through·put /ˈθruːpʊt/ *noun* [U, C, usually sing.] (*specialist*) the amount of work that is done, or the number of people that are dealt with, in a particular period of time（某一时期内的）生产量，接待人数

through·way = THRUWAY

throw /θrəʊ; *NAmE* θroʊ/ *verb, noun*

■ ***verb*** (**threw** /θruː/, **thrown** /θrəʊn; *NAmE* θroʊn/)

• **WITH HAND** 用手 **1** [T, I] to send sth from your hand through the air by moving your hand or arm quickly 投；掷；抛；扔：~ (**sth**) *Stop throwing stones at the window!* 别朝窗户扔石头了！◇ *She threw the ball up and caught it again.* 她把球抛起来又接住。◇ *They had a competition to see who could throw the furthest.* 他们举行了一场比赛，看谁投得最远。◇ ~ **sth to sb** *Don't throw it to him, give it to him!* 别扔给他，递给他！◇ ~ **sb sth** *Can you throw me that towel?* 请把那条毛巾扔给我好吗？

• **PUT CARELESSLY** 漫不经心地放置 **2** [T] ~ **sth + adv./prep.** to put sth in a particular place quickly and carelessly 摔；丢；扔：*Just throw your bag down over there.* 把你的袋子就扔到那边吧。

• **MOVE WITH FORCE** 用力移动 **3** [T] to move sth suddenly and with force 猛推；使劲撞：~ **sth + adv./prep.** *The boat was thrown onto the rocks.* 那条船触礁了。◇ *The sea throws up all sorts of debris on the beach.* 大海把各种残骸碎片都冲上海滩。◇ ~ **sth + adj.** *I threw open the windows to let the smoke out.* 我猛力推开窗子，让烟散出去。

• **PART OF BODY** 身体部位 **4** [T] ~ **sth/yourself + adv./prep.** to move your body or part of it quickly or suddenly 猛动（头、臂、腿）；挺起（胸）；仰起（头）；挥动（拳头、手臂）：*He threw back his head and roared with laughter.* 他猛地仰起头哈哈大笑起来。◇ *I ran up and threw my arms around him.* 我跑上前去，张开双臂搂住他。◇ *Jenny threw herself onto the bed.* 珍妮一头倒在床上。

• **MAKE SB FALL** 使人摔倒 **5** [T] ~ **sb** to make sb fall quickly or violently to the ground 使迅猛地摔倒在地：*Two riders were thrown* (= off their horses) *in the second race.* 有两名骑手在第二场赛马中从马上摔了下来。

• **INTO PARTICULAR STATE** 处于某种状态 **6** [T, usually passive] ~ **sb/sth + adv./prep.** to make sb/sth be in a particular state 使处于，使陷入（某种状态）：*Hundreds were thrown out of work.* 数以百计的人遭到解雇。◇ *We were thrown into confusion by the news.* 我们被那消息弄得惊慌失措。◇ *The problem was suddenly thrown into sharp focus.* 这个问题突然引起人们的密切关注了。

• **DIRECT STH AT SB/STH** 指向某人/事物 **7** [T] ~ **sth on/at sb/sth** to direct sth at sb/sth 把…对准；向…作出；对…施加：*to throw doubt on the verdict* 对裁断产生怀疑 ◇ *to throw the blame on someone* 委过于人 ◇ *to throw accusations at someone* 对某人大加指责 ◇ *He threw the question back at me* (= expected me to answer it myself). 他反过来问我这个问题。

• **UPSET** 使烦恼 **8** [T] ~ **sb** (*informal*) to make sb feel upset, confused, or surprised 使心烦意乱；使困惑；使惊奇：*The news of her death really threw me.* 她的噩耗确实令我震惊。

• **DICE** 色子 **9** [T] ~ **sth** to roll a DICE or let it fall after shaking it; to obtain a particular number in this way 掷（色子）；掷出（色子的点数）：*Throw the dice!* 掷色子！◇ *He threw three sixes in a row.* 他一连掷出三个六点。

• **CLAY POT** 泥壶 **10** [T] ~ **sth** (*specialist*) to make a CLAY pot, dish, etc. on a POTTER'S WHEEL（在陶钧上）把…拉制成坯：*a hand-thrown vase* 手工拉制的陶瓶

• **LIGHT/SHADE** 光；影 **11** [T] ~ **sth** (+ **adv./prep.**) to send light or shade onto sth 照射（光线）；投射（阴影）：*The trees threw long shadows across the lawn.* 树木在草坪上投下长长的影子。

• **YOUR VOICE** 嗓音 **12** [T] ~ **your voice** to make your voice sound as if it is coming from another person or place 使变音；使嗓音听起来像来自他人（或别处） **SYN** **project**

• **A PUNCH** 一拳 **13** [T] ~ **a punch** to hit sb with your FIST 挥拳猛击；出拳

• **SWITCH/HANDLE** 开关；操作杆 **14** [T] ~ **sth** to move a switch, handle, etc. to operate sth 按动，扳动，推动（开关、操作杆等）

• **BAD-TEMPERED BEHAVIOUR** 发脾气 **15** [T] ~ **sth** to have a sudden period of bad-tempered behaviour, violent emotion, etc. 突然发作（脾气等）：*She'll throw a fit if she finds out.* 她要是发现了，一定会大发雷霆。◇ *Children often throw tantrums at this age.* 儿童在这个年龄经常犯脾气。

• **A PARTY** 聚会 **16** [T] ~ **a party** (*informal*) to give a party 举行聚会

• **IN SPORTS/COMPETITIONS** 体育运动；比赛 **17** [T] ~ **sth** (*informal*) to deliberately lose a game or contest that you should have won 故意输掉（本应获胜的比赛或竞赛）：*He was accused of having thrown the game.* 他被指责故意放

▼ **SYNONYMS** 同义词辨析

throw

toss • hurl • fling • chuck • lob • bowl • pitch

These words all mean to send sth from your hand through the air. 以上各词均含扔、投、掷、抛之义。

throw to send sth from your hand or hands through the air 指投、掷、抛、扔：*Some kids were throwing stones at the window.* 有些孩子在朝窗户扔石头。◇ *She threw the ball and he caught it.* 她把球抛出来，他接住了。

toss to throw sth lightly or carelessly 指轻轻或漫不经心地扔、抛、掷：*She tossed her jacket onto the bed.* 她把她的短上衣丢到床上。

hurl to throw sth violently in a particular direction 指猛扔、猛投、猛摔：*Rioters hurled a brick through the car's windscreen.* 暴徒把一块砖猛地扔向汽车，砸破了挡风玻璃。

fling to throw sb/sth somewhere with a lot of force, especially because you are angry or in a hurry 尤指生气地或急匆匆地用力扔、掷、抛、丢：*She flung the letter down onto the table.* 她把信摔在桌子上。

chuck (*especially BrE, informal*) to throw sth carelessly 指随便扔、抛：*I chucked him the keys.* 我把钥匙扔给了他。

lob (*informal*) to throw sth so that it goes high through the air 指往空中高扔、高抛、高掷：*They were lobbing stones over the wall.* 他们在朝墙那边扔石头。

bowl (in cricket) to throw the ball to the batsman（板球）指把球投给击球员

pitch (in baseball) to throw the ball to the batter（棒球）指把球投给击球员

PATTERNS

- to throw/toss/hurl/fling/chuck/lob/bowl/pitch sth **at/to** sb/sth
- to throw/toss/fling/chuck sth **aside/away**
- to throw/toss/hurl/fling/chuck/lob/bowl/pitch a **ball**
- to throw/toss/hurl/fling/chuck **stones/rocks/a brick**
- to throw/toss/hurl/fling sth **angrily**
- to throw/toss sth **casually/carelessly**

T

水，输掉了这场比赛。 ➲ MORE LIKE THIS 33, page R28

IDM HELP Idioms containing **throw** are at the entries for the nouns and adjectives in the idioms, for example **throw your hat into the ring** is at **hat**. 含 throw 的习语，都可在该等习语中的名词及形容词相关词条找到，如 throw your hat into the ring 在词条 hat 下。

PHR V **ˌthrow sth↔aˈside** to reject sth such as an attitude, a way of life, etc. 拒绝接受（某种看法、生活方式等） **ˈthrow yourself at sth/sb 1** to rush violently at sth/sb 冲向（人或物）；向…猛扑过去 **2** (*informal, disapproving*) (usually of a woman 通常指女人) to be too enthusiastic in trying to attract a sexual partner 撒娇；献媚；勾引 **ˌthrow sth↔aˈway 1** (*also* **ˌthrow sth↔ˈout**) to get rid of sth that you no longer want 扔掉；丢弃；抛弃：*I don't need that—you can throw it away.* 我不需要那东西，你可以把它扔了。◇ *That old chair should be thrown away.* 那把旧椅子应该扔掉了。 **2** to fail to make use of sth; to waste sth 失去；错过；浪费；白费：*to throw away an opportunity* 失去机会 ➲ SEE ALSO THROWAWAY **ˌthrow sth ˈback at sb** to remind sb of sth they have said or done in the past, especially to upset or annoy them（尤指为使人烦恼）使想起，提醒，重提 **ˌthrow sb ˈback on sth** [usually passive] to force sb to rely on sth because nothing else is available 迫使依靠（因别无他物）：*There was no TV so we were thrown back on our own resources* (= had to entertain ourselves). 没有电视机，所以我们只好自娱自乐了。 **ˌthrow sth↔ˈin 1** to include sth with what you are selling or offering, without increasing the price （免费）附送，额外赠送：*You can have the piano for $200, and I'll throw in the stool as well.* 你花 200 美元就可以买走这架钢琴，另外奉送这张琴凳。 **2** to add a remark to a conversation 加插评语（或感叹句等）：*Jack threw in the odd encouraging comment.* 杰克难得加了一句鼓励的话。 **ˌthrow yourself/sth ˈinto sth** to begin to do sth with energy and enthusiasm 投身于；热衷于；积极从事 **ˌthrow sth/sb↔ˈoff 1** to manage to get rid of sth/sb that is making you suffer, annoying you, etc. 摆脱；甩掉：*to throw off a cold/your worries/your pursuers* 治好伤风；消除忧虑；甩掉追踪者 **2** to take off a piece of clothing quickly and carelessly 匆匆脱掉，拽下，扯掉（衣服）：*She entered the room and threw off her wet coat.* 她一进屋就脱掉了湿漉漉的大衣。 **ˌthrow sth↔ˈon** to put on a piece of clothing quickly and carelessly 匆匆穿上（衣服）：*She just threw on the first skirt she found.* 她找到一条裙子就匆忙穿上。 **ˌthrow sth↔ˈopen (to sb) 1** to allow people to enter or visit a place where they could not go before（对…）开放；允许…进入 **2** to allow people to discuss sth, take part in a competition, etc. 允许…公开（讨论）；允许…参加（竞赛）：*The debate will be thrown open to the audience.* 这次辩论将允许观众参加。 **ˌthrow sb↔ˈout (of...)** to force sb to leave a place 撵走；轰走；逐出：*You'll be thrown out if you don't pay the rent.* 你不付房租就会被撵出去。 **ˌthrow sth↔ˈout 1** to say sth in a way that suggests you have not given it a lot of thought 脱口而出；随口说：*to throw out a suggestion* 随口提出建议 **2** to decide not to accept a proposal, an idea, etc. 拒不接受，否决（建议、想法等） **3** = THROW STH↔AWAY **4** to produce smoke, light, heat, etc. 冒（烟）；发（光）；散发出（热）：*a small fire that threw out a lot of heat* 散发出大量热量的小火炉 **5** to confuse sth or make it wrong 使混淆不清；打乱；使出错：*Our calculations of the cost of our trip were thrown out by changes in the exchange rate.* 我们旅行费用的计算因为汇率变动而完全打乱了。 **ˌthrow sb ˈover** (*old-fashioned*) to stop being friends with sb or having a romantic relationship with them 同某人绝交；抛弃某人 **ˌthrow sb↔toˈgether** [often passive] to bring people into contact with each other, often unexpectedly 使不期而遇；使意外聚在一起：*Fate had thrown them together.* 命运使他们聚在一起。 **ˌthrow sth↔toˈgether** to make or produce sth in a hurry 匆忙拼凑成；仓促制出：*I threw together a quick meal.* 我匆匆做了一顿便饭。 **ˌthrow ˈup** to VOMIT 呕吐 SYN **be sick**: *The smell made me want to throw up.* 这味道使得我想呕吐。 **ˌthrow sth↔ˈup 1** to VOMIT food 呕出（食物） SYN **sick sth↔up**: *The baby's thrown up her dinner.* 女婴把吃的东西吐了出来。 **2** to make people notice sth 使显眼；使引起注意：*Her research has thrown up some interesting facts.* 她的研究有些很有意思的发现。 **3** to build sth suddenly or in a hurry 突然建造；匆忙建造：*They're throwing up new housing estates all over the place.* 他们在这一带突然建起了新的居住区。 **4** to leave your job 辞职：*to throw up your career* 放弃事业

■ ***noun*** **1** the act of throwing sth, especially a ball or DICE 抛；扔；摔；投（球）；掷（色子）：*a well-aimed throw* 准确的投掷 ◇ *It's your throw* (= it's your turn to throw the dice). 轮到你掷（色子）了。◇ *He threw me to the ground with a judo throw.* 他用柔道摔法把我摔倒在地。 **2** the distance which sth is thrown 投掷的距离：*a javelin throw of 57 metres* * 57 米远的标枪投掷 **3** a loose cloth cover that can be thrown over a SOFA, etc.（沙发等的）套，罩 ➲ VISUAL VOCAB PAGE V22

IDM **$100, £50, etc. a ˈthrow** (*informal*) used to say how much items cost each 每件价格为；每件值：*The tickets for the dinner were £50 a throw.* 餐券每张 50 英镑。 ➲ MORE AT STONE *n.*

throw·away /ˈθrəʊəweɪ; *NAmE* ˈθroʊ-/ *adj.* [only before noun] **1 ~ line/remark/comment** something you say quickly without careful thought, sometimes in order to be funny 脱口而出的；顺嘴说出的；开玩笑的：*She was very upset at what to him was just a throwaway remark.* 对他来说这只是随口说说而已，而她听了却很不高兴。 **2** (of goods, etc. 货品等) produced cheaply and intended to be thrown away after use 用后丢弃的；一次性使用的 SYN **disposable**: *throwaway products* 一次性使用的产品 ◇ *We live in a throwaway society* (= a society in which things are not made to last a long time). 我们生活在一次性物品充斥的社会。

throw·back /ˈθrəʊbæk; *NAmE* ˈθroʊ-/ *noun* [usually sing.] **~ (to sth)** a person or thing that is similar to sb/sth that existed in the past 返祖者；返祖；返祖型的东西：*The car's design is a throwback to the 1960s.* 这种汽车的设计回到了 20 世纪 60 年代。

throw·er /ˈθrəʊə(r); *NAmE* ˈθroʊ-/ *noun* a person who throws sth 投掷者；投手：*a discus thrower* 铁饼运动员 ➲ SEE ALSO FLAMETHROWER

ˈthrow-in *noun* (in football (SOCCER) and RUGBY 足球和橄榄球) the act of throwing the ball back onto the playing field after it has gone outside the area 掷界外球；掷边线球

thrown PAST PART. OF THROW

ˈthrow pillow (*NAmE*) (*BrE* **ˈscatter cushion**) *noun* a small CUSHION that can be placed on furniture, on the floor, etc. for decoration（散放的）小装饰垫 ➲ VISUAL VOCAB PAGE V22

thru (*NAmE, informal*) = THROUGH *prep.* (5)

thrush /θrʌʃ/ *noun* **1** [C] a bird with a brown back and brown spots on its chest 鸫（一种背部为褐色、胸部有褐色斑点的鸟）：*a song thrush* 歌鸫 **2** [U] an infectious disease that affects the mouth and throat 鹅口疮；真菌性口炎 **3** [U] (*BrE*) (*NAmE* **ˈyeast infection**) an infectious disease that affects the VAGINA 念珠菌阴道炎

thrust /θrʌst/ *verb, noun*

■ ***verb*** (**thrust, thrust**) **1** [T, I] to push sth/sb suddenly or violently in a particular direction; to move quickly and suddenly in a particular direction 猛推；冲；搡；挤；塞：**~ sth/sb/yourself + adv./prep.** *He thrust the baby into my arms and ran off.* 他把婴儿往我怀里一塞就跑了。◇ *She thrust her hands deep into her pockets.* 她把双手深深插进口袋里。◇ (*figurative*) *He tends to thrust himself forward too much.* 他这个人太好强。◇ **+ adv./prep.** *She thrust past him angrily and left.* 她气呼呼地从他身旁挤过去走了。 **2** [I, T] **~ (at sb) (with sth) | ~ (sth at sb)** to make a sudden strong forward movement at sb with a weapon, etc. 刺；戳：*He thrust at me with a knife.* 他拿刀向我刺来。◇ *a thrusting movement* 冲刺动作 IDM SEE THROAT

PHR V **ˌthrust sth↔aˈside** to refuse to listen to sb's complaints, comments, etc. 置之一旁；置之不理：*All our objections were thrust aside.* 我们所有的异议都被置之不理。 **ˈthrust sth/sb on/upon sb** to force sb to accept

T

or deal with sth/sb that they do not want 把…强加于；强迫…接受；强人所难：*She was annoyed at having three extra guests suddenly thrust on her.* 突然又来了三位不速之客要她接待，她感到很恼火。

■ ***noun*** **1 the thrust** [sing.] the main point of an argument, a policy, etc.（论据、政策等的）要点，要旨，重点：*The thrust of his argument was that change was needed.* 他的论据要点是改革是必要的。 **2** [C] a sudden strong movement that pushes sth/sb forward 猛推；刺；戳；插：*He killed her with a thrust of the knife.* 他把她一刀刺死了。 **3** [U] (*specialist*) the force that is produced by an engine to push a plane, ROCKET, etc. forward（发动机推动飞机、火箭等的）推力，驱动力 IDM SEE CUT *n.*

thrust·er /ˈθrʌstə(r)/ *noun* a small engine used to provide extra force, especially on a SPACECRAFT 助力器；（尤指航天器的）推力器，推进器

thru·way (*also* **through·way**) /ˈθruːweɪ/ *noun* (*NAmE*) used in the names of some FREEWAYS (= important roads across or between states)（用于某些跨州或州际高速公路的名称中）过境道路，直达道路：*the New York State Thruway* 纽约州直达高速公路

thud /θʌd/ *noun, verb*

■ ***noun*** a sound like the one which is made when a heavy object hits sth else 砰的一声；扑通一声：*His head hit the floor with a dull thud.* 他的头砰的一声撞在了地板上。

■ ***verb*** **(-dd-)** **1** [I, T] **~ (sth) + adv./prep.** to fall or hit sth with a low dull sound 砰地落下；飕的一声击中：*His arrow thudded into the target.* 他的箭噗的一声射中靶子。 **2** [I] (*literary*) (especially of the heart 尤指心脏) to beat strongly 有力地跳动；怦怦地跳 ➲ MORE LIKE THIS 3, page R25, 36, page R29

thug /θʌɡ/ *noun* a violent person, especially a criminal 恶棍；暴徒；罪犯：*a gang of thugs* 一伙暴徒 ▸ **thug·gish** /ˈθʌɡɪʃ/ *adj.*：*thuggish brutality* 残忍的暴行

thug·gery /ˈθʌɡəri/ *noun* [U] (*formal*) violent, usually criminal, behaviour 暴行；罪恶行径

thu·lium /ˈθuːliəm; *BrE also* ˈθjuː-/ *noun* [U] (*symb.* **Tm**) a chemical element. Thulium is a soft silver-white metal. 铥

thumb 🔑 /θʌm/ *noun, verb*

■ ***noun*** **1** 🔑 the short thick finger at the side of the hand, slightly apart from the other four 拇指：*She still **sucks her thumb** when she's worried.* 她在忧虑时仍然会吸吮大拇指。 ➲ VISUAL VOCAB PAGE V64 ➲ SEE ALSO GREEN THUMB **2** 🔑 the part of a glove that covers the thumb（手套的）拇指部分：*There's a hole in the thumb.* 手套的拇指上有个窟窿。

IDM **be all (ˌfingers and) ˈthumbs** to be awkward with your hands so that you drop things or are unable to do sth 笨手笨脚；笨拙；手指不灵活 **hold ˈthumbs** (*SAfrE*) to hope that your plans will be successful or that sth will take place in the way that you want it to 希望（计划）成功；期望如愿以偿：*Let's hold thumbs that you get the job.* 我们期望你如愿得到这份工作啊。 **thumbs ˈup/ˈdown** (*informal*) used to show that sth has been accepted/rejected or that it is/is not a success 跷拇指（表示接受或成功）；拇指向下（表示拒绝或不成功）：*Their proposals **were given the thumbs down**.* 他们的建议遭到拒绝。 ◇ *It looks like it's thumbs up for their latest album.* 看样子他们的最新歌曲专辑成功了。 ORIGIN In contests in ancient Rome the public put their thumbs up if they wanted a gladiator to live, and down if they wanted him to be killed. 在古罗马的角斗中，公众若希望角斗士活就竖起拇指朝上，若希望他被杀死就伸出拇指朝下。 **under sb's ˈthumb** (of a person 人) completely controlled by sb 完全受人支配；受制于人 ➲ MORE AT RULE *n.*, SORE *adj.*, TWIDDLE *v.*

■ ***verb*** **1** [I, T] to make a signal with your thumb to passing drivers to ask them to stop and take you somewhere 跷起拇指请求搭乘（过路汽车）；示意请求搭便车：**+ adv./prep.** *He had thumbed all across Europe.* 他搭乘便车游遍了欧洲。 ◇ (*BrE*) **~ a lift** *We managed to thumb a lift with a lorry driver.* 我们竖起拇指招呼过路的卡车司机让我们搭上便车。 ◇ (*NAmE*) **~ a ride** *We managed to thumb a ride with a truck driver.* 我们竖起拇指招呼过路的卡车司机让我们搭上便车。 **2** [T] **~ sth (+ adv./prep.)** to touch or move sth with your thumb 用拇指摸；用拇指捋：*She thumbed off the safety catch of her pistol.* 她用拇指打开了手枪的保险栓。 ➲ SEE ALSO WELL THUMBED

IDM **thumb your ˈnose at sb/sth** to make a rude sign with your thumb on your nose; to show that you have no respect for sb/sth 嗤之以鼻；蔑视：*The company just thumbs its nose at the legislation on pollution.* 这家公司完全不把污染立法放在眼里。

PHR V **ˈthumb through sth** to turn the pages of a book quickly in order to get a general idea of what is in it 快速翻阅

ˈthumb drive *noun* (*NAmE*) = FLASH DRIVE

ˈthumb index *noun* a series of cuts in the edge of a book, with letters of the alphabet on them, to help you to find the section that you want more easily 拇指页标；书边标目；书边挖月索引

thumb·nail /ˈθʌmneɪl/ *noun* **1** the nail on the thumb 拇指甲 **2** (*also* **ˌthumbnail ˈimage**) (*computing* 计) a very small picture on a computer screen which shows you what a larger picture looks like, or what a page of a document will look like when you print it 索引图像；（打印预览）缩略图

ˌthumbnail ˈsketch *noun* a short description of sth, giving only the main details 简略描述

ˈthumb piano (*also* **sansa**) *noun* an African musical instrument consisting of a row of metal strips, that you play with your fingers and thumbs 拇指钢琴（非洲乐器，由一排金属簧片组成）

thumb·print /ˈθʌmprɪnt/ *noun* the mark made by the pattern of lines on the top of a person's thumb 拇指纹印

thumb·screw /ˈθʌmskruː/ *noun* an instrument that was used in the past for TORTURING people by crushing their thumbs 拇指夹（旧时的一种刑具）

thumb·suck /ˈθʌmsʌk/ *noun* [C, usually sing., U] (*SAfrE, informal, often disapproving*) a guess or estimate 猜测；估计：*Their sales projections are a total thumbsuck.* 他们的销售量预测纯属估计。

thumb·tack /ˈθʌmtæk/ (*also* **tack**) (*both NAmE*) (*BrE* **ˈdrawing pin**) *noun* a short pin with a large round flat head, used especially for fastening paper to a board or wall 图钉 ➲ VISUAL VOCAB PAGE V71

thump /θʌmp/ *verb, noun*

■ ***verb*** **1** [T, I] **~ (sb/sth) (+ adv./prep.)** to hit sb/sth hard, especially with your closed hand 重击；狠打；（尤指用拳）捶击：*He thumped the table angrily.* 他愤怒地用拳捶击桌子。 ◇ *She couldn't get her breath and had to be thumped on the back.* 她喘不上气来，不得不让人捶背。 ◇ (*informal*) *I'll thump you if you say that again.* 你若再说这话，我就把你揍扁。 ◇ (*figurative*) *He thumped out a tune* (= played it very loudly) *on the piano.* 他在钢琴上猛力弹奏了一支曲子。 **2** [I, T] to fall on or hit a surface hard, with a loud dull sound; to make sth do this（使）撞击，嘭地发出闷响：**+ adv./prep.** *A bird thumped against the window.* 一只鸟儿咚的一声撞在窗上。 ◇ **~ sth + adv./prep.** *He thumped the report down on my desk.* 他嘭的一声把报告摔在我的办公桌上。 **3** [I] to beat strongly 强有力地跳动；怦怦地跳：*My heart was thumping with excitement.* 我激动得心怦怦跳。 ➲ SEE ALSO TUB-THUMPING

■ ***noun*** **1** the sound of sth heavy hitting the ground or another object 重击声；碰撞声：*There was a thump as the truck hit the bank.* 卡车撞在马路边坡上，发出砰的一声巨响。 **2** (*informal*) an act of hitting sb/sth hard 重击；捶击：*She gave him a thump on the back.* 她在他背上重重打了一拳。

thump·ing /ˈθʌmpɪŋ/ *adj.* [only before noun] (*informal*) very big 很大的；巨大的 SYN **huge**: *a thumping majority* 压倒的多数 ▸ **thump·ing** *adv.* (*BrE*)：*He told us a thumping great lie.* 他对我们撒了一个弥天大谎。

T

thun·der /ˈθʌndə(r)/ *noun, verb*

■ ***noun*** [U] **1** the loud noise that you hear after a flash of LIGHTNING, during a storm 雷；雷声：*the rumble of distant thunder* 远处雷声隆隆 ◇ *a* ***clap/crash/roll of thunder*** 一声霹雳；一声巨雷；雷声隆隆 ◇ *Thunder crashed in the sky.* 霹雳在空中炸响。➲ COLLOCATIONS AT WEATHER **2** a loud noise like thunder 雷鸣般的响声；轰隆声：*the thunder of hooves* 隆隆的马蹄声 **IDM** SEE FACE *n.*, STEAL *v.*

■ ***verb*** **1** [I] when **it thunders**, there is a loud noise in the sky during a storm 打雷 **2** [I] to make a very loud deep noise 发出雷鸣般响声；轰隆隆地响 **SYN** **roar**：*A voice thundered in my ear.* 一个震耳欲聋的声音在我耳边响起。◇ *thundering traffic* 轰隆隆的来往车辆 **3** [I] **+ adv./prep.** to move very fast and with a loud deep noise 轰隆隆地快速移动 **SYN** **roar**：*Heavy trucks kept thundering past.* 重型卡车不断地隆隆驶过。**4** [T] **~ sth + adv./prep.** (*informal*) to make sth move somewhere very fast 使快速移动：*Essien thundered the ball past the goalie.* 埃辛砰的一脚将球踢过了守门员。**5** [I, T] (*literary*) to shout, complain, etc. very loudly and angrily 怒喝；大声斥责：**~ (sth)** *He thundered against the evils of television.* 他大声谴责电视的种种坏处。◇ **+ speech** *'Sit still!' she thundered.* "坐着别动！" 她怒喝道。

thun·der·bolt /ˈθʌndəbəʊlt; *NAmE* ˈθʌndərboʊlt/ *noun* a flash of LIGHTNING that comes at the same time as the noise of THUNDER and that hits sth 雷电；霹雳：*The news hit them like a thunderbolt* (= was very shocking). 这个消息犹如晴天霹雳使他们大为震惊。

thun·der·box /ˈθʌndəbɒks; *NAmE* ˈθʌndərbɑːks/ *noun* (*old-fashioned, BrE, informal*) a toilet, especially a simple one （简易）便桶，马桶

thun·der·clap /ˈθʌndəklæp; *NAmE* -dərk-/ *noun* a loud crash made by THUNDER 雷声；霹雳

thun·der·cloud /ˈθʌndəklaʊd; *NAmE* -dərk-/ *noun* a large dark cloud that produces THUNDER and LIGHTNING during a storm 雷雨云

thun·der·ous /ˈθʌndərəs/ *adj.* (*formal*) **1** very loud 雷鸣般的；声音很大的 **SYN** **deafening**：*thunderous applause* 雷鸣般的掌声 **2** looking very angry 怒容满面的；面色阴沉的；怒气冲冲的：*his thunderous expression* 他那气势汹汹的表情 ▸**thun·der·ous·ly** *adv.*

thun·der·storm /ˈθʌndəstɔːm; *NAmE* ˈθʌndərstɔːrm/ *noun* a storm with THUNDER and LIGHTNING and usually very heavy rain 雷雨；雷暴；雷雨交加

thun·der·struck /ˈθʌndəstrʌk; *NAmE* -dərs-/ *adj.* [not usually before noun] (*formal*) extremely surprised and shocked 大吃一惊 **SYN** **amazed**

thun·dery /ˈθʌndəri/ *adj.* (of weather 天气) with THUNDER; suggesting that THUNDER is likely 有雷的；可能要打雷的

Thurs·day 🔑 /ˈθɜːzdeɪ; -di; *NAmE* ˈθɜːrz-/ *noun* [C, U] (*abbr.* **Thur.**, **Thurs.**) the day of the week after Wednesday and before Friday 星期四 **HELP** To see how **Thursday** is used, look at the examples at **Monday**. * Thursday 的用法见词条 Monday 下的示例。**ORIGIN** From the Old English for 'day of thunder', translated from Latin *Jovis dies* 'Jupiter's day'. Jupiter was the god associated with thunder. 源自古英语，原意为 day of thunder（打雷日），古英语则译自拉丁文 Jovis dies (Jupiter's day)。Jupiter（朱庇特）为雷神。

thus 🔑 /ðʌs/ *adv.* (*formal*) **1** 🔑 in this way; like this 以此方式；如此；这样：*Many scholars have argued thus.* 许多学者都这样论证过。◇ *The universities have expanded, thus allowing many more people the chance of higher education.* 大学扩招了，这样就使更多人能有机会接受高等教育。**2** 🔑 as a result of sth just mentioned 因此；从而；所以 **SYN** **hence, therefore**：*He is the eldest son and thus heir to the title.* 他是长子，因此是这个封号的继承人。◇ *We do not own the building. Thus, it would be impossible for us to make any major changes to it.* 我们不是这栋楼房的业主，因此不能对它进行大改动。➲ LANGUAGE BANK AT THEREFORE **IDM** SEE FAR *adv.*

thwack /θwæk/ *verb* **~ sb/sth** to hit sb/sth hard, making a short loud sound 重击；拍打；使劲打 ▸**thwack** *noun*：*the thwack of bat on ball* 球拍击球 ➲ MORE LIKE THIS 3, page R25

thwart /θwɔːt; *NAmE* θwɔːrt/ *verb* [often passive] to prevent sb from doing what they want to do 阻止；阻挠；对…构成阻力 **SYN** **frustrate**：**~ sth** *to thwart sb's plans* 阻挠某人的计划 ◇ **~ sb (in sth)** *She* ***was thwarted in her attempt*** *to take control of the party.* 她控制这个政党的企图受阻了。

thx (*also* **tx**) *abbr.* (*informal*) thanks; thank you (used, for example, in text messages or TWEETS) 感谢，谢谢（thanks 或 thank you 的缩略形式，用于手机短信或推特信息）：*Thx for the info, everyone!* 信息收到，谢谢大家！

thy /ðaɪ/ *det.* (*old use*) a word meaning 'your', used when talking to only one person （用作第二人称单数所有格形式）你的：*Honour thy father and thy mother.* 要孝敬父母。**HELP** Before a vowel sound, the form is **thine** /ðaɪn/. 在元音前的形式是 thine。

thyme /taɪm/ *noun* [U] a plant with small leaves that have a sweet smell and are used in cooking as a HERB 百里香（一种植物，叶小，有香味，可作烹饪调味品）➲ VISUAL VOCAB PAGE V35

thy·mus /ˈθaɪməs/ (*also* **ˈthymus gland**) *noun* (*anatomy* 解) an organ in the neck that produces LYMPHOCYTES (= cells to fight infection) 胸腺

thy·roid /ˈθaɪrɔɪd/ (*also* **ˈthyroid gland**) *noun* (*anatomy* 解) a small organ at the front of the neck that produces HORMONES that control the way in which the body grows and functions 甲状腺

thy·self /ðaɪˈself/ *pron.* (*old use* or *dialect*) a word meaning 'yourself', used when talking to only one person （用作第二人称单数反身代词）你自己

ti (*NAmE*) (*BrE* **te**) /tiː/ *noun* (*music* 音) the 7th note of a MAJOR SCALE 大调音阶的第 7 音

tiara /tiˈɑːrə/ *noun* a piece of jewellery like a small crown decorated with PRECIOUS STONES, worn by a woman, for example a princess, on formal occasions 冠状头饰（女子用，如公主在正式场合戴的镶有宝石的王冠式头饰）

TiB *abbr.* (in writing 书写形式) TEBIBYTE 太字节（二进制计算机内存或数据单位）

Tib *abbr.* (*also* **Tibit**) (in writing 书写形式) TEBIBIT 太比特（二进制计算机内存或数据单位）

tibia /ˈtɪbiə/ *noun* (*pl.* **tib·iae** /-biiː/) (*anatomy* 解) the SHIN BONE 胫骨 ➲ VISUAL VOCAB PAGE V64 ➲ SEE ALSO FIBULA

tic /tɪk/ *noun* a sudden quick movement of a muscle, especially in your face or head, that you cannot control （尤指面部或头部肌肉的）抽搐

tick /tɪk/ *verb, noun*

■ ***verb*** **1** [I] (of a clock, etc. 钟表等) to make short, light, regular repeated sounds to mark time passing 发出滴答声；滴答地走时：*In the silence we could hear the clock ticking.* 寂静中，我们能听到钟表滴答作响。◇ *a ticking bomb* 滴答作响的定时炸弹 ◇ **~ away** *While we waited the taxi's meter kept ticking away.* 我们等候时，出租汽车的计程器一直在滴答滴答地走着。**2** [T] (*BrE*) (*NAmE* **check**) **~ sth** to put a mark (✓) next to an item on a list, an answer, etc. 标记号；打上钩；打对号：*Please tick the appropriate box.* 请在适合的方框内打钩。◇ *Tick 'yes' or 'no' to each question.* 在每个问题的"是"或"否"旁打钩。◇ *I've ticked the names of the people who have paid.* 我在已付款者的姓名旁画了钩。

IDM ˌ**tick all the/sb's ˈboxes** (*BrE, informal*) to do exactly the right things to please sb 投其所好；迎合众人 / 某人的喜好：*This is a movie that ticks all the boxes.* 这是一部适合众人口味的影片。**what makes sb ˈtick** what makes sb behave in the way that they do 使某人这样做的原因：*I've never really understood what makes her tick.* 我从未真正

弄懂她为什么这么做。

PHR V ˌ**tick aˈway/ˈby/ˈpast** (of time 时间) to pass 过去；流逝：*I had to get to the airport by two, and the minutes were ticking away.* 我必须在两点前赶到机场，时间正在一分一秒地过去。 ˌ**tick sth↔aˈway** (of a clock, etc. 钟表等) to mark the time as it passes 标示时间流逝：*The clock ticked away the minutes.* 钟表显示时间一分一秒地过去。 ˌ**tick sb↔ˈoff 1** (*BrE, informal*) to speak angrily to sb, especially a child, because they have done sth wrong 责备，斥责，责骂（尤指犯错的孩子） SYN **tell sb↔off (for sth/for doing sth)** ➲ RELATED NOUN TICKING OFF **2** (*NAmE, informal*) to make sb angry or annoyed 使生气；使烦恼 ˌ**tick sb/sth ˈoff** (*BrE*) (*NAmE* ˌ**check sb/sth ˈoff**) to put a mark (✓) beside a name or an item on a list to show that sth has been dealt with 给…画上钩；给…打核对号 ˌ**tick ˈover** (*BrE*) (usually used in the progressive tenses 通常用于进行时) **1** (of an engine 发动机) to run slowly while the vehicle is not moving 空转；怠速运转 SYN **idle 2** (of a business, a system, an activity, etc. 企业、系统、活动等) to keep working slowly without producing or achieving much （没有进展地）徐缓运作：*Just **keep things ticking over** while I'm away.* 在我外出期间，维持现状就行。

■ ***noun* 1** [C] (*BrE*) (*NAmE* ˈ**check mark**, **check**) a mark (✓) put beside a sum or an item on a list, usually to show that it has been checked or done or is correct 核对号；对号；钩号；记号：***Put a tick** in the appropriate box if you would like further information about any of our products.* 如想进一步了解我们任何产品的情况，请在适当的方框内打钩。 ➲ COMPARE CROSS *n.* (1), X *symbol* (4) **2** [C] a very small creature that bites humans and animals and sucks their blood. There are several types of tick, some of which can carry diseases. 蜱，壁虱，扁虱（吸血寄生虫，有些种类能传播疾病）：*a tick bite* 蜱叮咬之处 ➲ VISUAL VOCAB PAGE V13 **3** (*also* **tick·ing**) [U] a short, light, regularly repeated sound, especially that of a clock or watch （尤指钟表的）滴答声：*The only sound was the soft tick of the clock.* 唯一的响声是钟表轻轻的滴答声。 **4** [C] (*BrE, informal*) a moment 一会儿；一瞬间；一刹那；片刻：*Hang on a tick!* 等一会儿，别挂断电话！ ◇ *I'll be with you in two ticks.* 我马上就来。 **5** [U] (*old-fashioned, BrE, informal*) permission to delay paying for sth that you have bought 赊账；赊欠；赊购 SYN **credit**：*Can I have these **on tick**?* 我可以赊购这些东西吗？

tick·box /ˈtɪkbɒks; *NAmE* -bɑːks/ *noun* (*BrE*) = CHECKBOX

tick·er /ˈtɪkə(r)/ *noun* **1** = NEWS TICKER **2** (*old-fashioned, informal*) a person's heart （人的）心脏

ˈticker tape *noun* [U] (*especially NAmE*) (in the past) long narrow strips of paper with information, for example STOCK MARKET prices, printed on them by a special TELEGRAPH machine （旧时电传打字机用的）纸带：*a **ticker-tape parade** in the streets of New York* (= an occasion when people throw pieces of paper as part of a celebration, for example in honour of a famous person) 纽约街道上的抛纸带迎宾式

ticket 🔑 /ˈtɪkɪt/ *noun, verb*

■ ***noun* 1** 🔑 ~ (**for/to sth**) a printed piece of paper that gives you the right to travel on a particular bus, train, etc. or to go into a theatre, etc. 票；券；车票；戏票；入场券：*a **bus/theatre/plane, etc. ticket*** 公共汽车票、戏票、飞机票等 ◇ *free tickets to the show* 演出的免费入场券 ◇ *Tickets are available from the Arts Centre at £5.00.* 艺术中心有票，每张 5 英镑。 ◇ *a **ticket office/machine/collector*** 售票处；自动售票机；收票员 ◇ (*figurative*) *She hoped that getting this job would finally be her **ticket to success**.* 她希望得到这份工作将会使她踏上成功之途。 ➲ PICTURE AT LABEL ➲ SEE ALSO MEAL TICKET (2), RETURN TICKET, SEASON TICKET **2** 🔑 a printed piece of paper with a number or numbers on it, that you buy in order to have the chance of winning a prize if the number or numbers are later chosen 奖券；彩票：***a lottery/raffle ticket*** 彩票 ◇ *There are three winning tickets.* 有三张中奖的彩票。 **3** 🔑 a label that is attached to sth in a shop/store giving details of its price, size, etc. （商店中标明货物价格、尺码等的）标签 **4** an official notice that orders you to pay a FINE because you have done sth illegal while driving or parking your car （交通违章）通知单，罚款单 SYN **fine**：*a **parking/speeding ticket*** 违章停车／超速驾驶罚款单 **5** [usually sing.] (*especially NAmE*) a list of candidates that are supported by a particular political party in an election （政党在选举中所支持的）候选人名单：*She ran for office on the Democratic ticket.* 她作为民主党的候选人参加竞选。 ➲ SEE ALSO DREAM TICKET

IDM **be ˈtickets** (*SAfrE, informal*) be the end 结束；终结：*It's tickets for the team that loses.* 落败的球队就此止步。 **just the ˈticket** (*BrE also* **just the ˈjob**) (*informal, approving*) exactly what is needed in a particular situation 正需要的东西；求之不得的东西 **ˈthat's the ticket** (*old-fashioned, informal*) used to say that sth is just what is needed or that everything is just right 所需要的东西；一切正好 ➲ MORE AT SPLIT *v.*

■ ***verb* 1** ~ **sth/sb** (*specialist*) to produce and sell tickets for an event, a trip, etc.; to give sb a ticket 售票；给…门票；送票：*Passengers can now be ticketed electronically.* 旅客现在可以电子购票。 **2** [usually passive] ~ **sb** (*especially NAmE*) to give sb an official notice that orders them to pay a FINE because they have done sth illegal while driving or parking a car 发出交通违章通知单：*Park illegally, and you're likely to be ticketed.* 违章停车就可能收到罚款单。

ticket·ed /ˈtɪkɪtɪd/ *adj.* [usually before noun] a **ticketed** event is one for which you need a ticket to get in 须凭票入场的：*The museum holds both free and ticketed events.* 博物馆举办的活动既有免费入场的，也有凭票入场的。

IDM **be ˈticketed for sth** (*especially NAmE*) to be intended for a particular purpose 被指定为；被委派为

ticket·ing /ˈtɪkɪtɪŋ/ *noun* [U] the process of producing and selling tickets 售票：*ticketing systems* 售票系统

ˈticket tout *noun* (*BrE*) = TOUT

tickety-boo /ˌtɪkəti ˈbuː/ *adj.* [not before noun] (*old-fashioned, BrE, informal*) very good or successful, with no problems 非常好；妥当

tick·ing /ˈtɪkɪŋ/ *noun* [U] a type of strong cotton cloth that is often striped, used especially for making MATTRESS and PILLOW covers （尤指做床垫和枕芯套的）结实条纹棉布

ˌ**ticking ˈoff** *noun* [sing.] (*old-fashioned, BrE, informal*) the act of telling sb that they have done sth to make you angry 斥责；责骂；申斥 SYN **telling-off**

tickle /ˈtɪkl/ *verb, noun*

■ ***verb* 1** [T, I] ~ (**sb/sth**) to move your fingers on a sensitive part of sb's body in a way that makes them laugh 呵痒；胳肢：*The bigger girls used to chase me and tickle me.* 比我高大的女孩过去总是追赶着胳肢我。 ◇ *Stop tickling!* 别胳肢了！ **2** [T, I] ~ (**sth**) to produce a slightly uncomfortable feeling in a sensitive part of the body; to have a feeling like this （使）发痒：*His beard was tickling her cheek.* 他的胡须扎得她的面颊痒痒的。 ◇ *My throat tickles.* 我嗓子发痒。 ◇ *a tickling cough* 痒咳 **3** [T] to amuse and interest sb 逗乐；使高兴；使感兴趣；使满足：~ **sb/sth** *to tickle sb's imagination* 满足某人的想象力 ◇ ~ **sb to do sth** *I was tickled to discover that we'd both done the same thing.* 我高兴地发现我俩在做同样的事。

IDM **be tickled ˈpink** (*informal*) to be very pleased or amused 高兴极了；非常开心 **tickle sb's ˈfancy** (*informal*) to please or amuse sb 使觉得好玩；使开心：*See if any of these tickle your fancy.* 看看这里面是否有你喜欢的。

■ ***noun*** [usually sing.] **1** an act of tickling sb 呵痒；胳肢：*She gave the child a little tickle.* 她轻轻地胳肢孩子。 **2** a slightly uncomfortable feeling in a part of your body 痒；痒感：*to have a tickle in your throat* (= that makes you want to cough) 喉咙里发痒 IDM SEE SLAP *n.*

tick·lish /ˈtɪklɪʃ/ *adj.* **1** (of a person 人) sensitive to being tickled 怕痒的；易痒的：*Are you ticklish?* 你怕痒吗？ **2** (*informal*) (of a situation or problem 情况或问题) difficult to deal with, and possibly embarrassing 难对付的；难处理的；棘手的 SYN **awkward 3** (of a cough 咳嗽) that irritates your throat 使喉咙发痒的：*a dry ticklish cough* 喉咙发痒的干咳

tick-tock /ˌtɪk ˈtɒk; *NAmE* ˌtɪk ˈtɑːk/ *noun* [usually sing.] used to describe the sound of a large clock TICKING（大时钟的）滴答声 ➲ MORE LIKE THIS 3, page R25

ticky-tacky /ˌtɪki ˈtæki/ *noun* [U] (*NAmE, informal*) building material that is cheap and of low quality 廉价劣质建筑材料 ▶ **ticky-tacky** *adj.*

tic-tac-toe (*also* **tick-tack-toe**) /ˌtɪk tæk ˈtəʊ; *NAmE* ˈtoʊ/ (*NAmE*) (*BrE* ˌ**noughts and** ˈ**crosses**) *noun* [U] a simple game in which two players take turns to write Os or Xs in a set of nine squares. The first player to complete a row of three Os or three Xs is the winner. 井字游戏，圈叉游戏（二人轮流在井字形九格中画 O 或 X，先将三个 O 或 X 连成一线者为胜）➲ VISUAL VOCAB PAGE V42

tidal /ˈtaɪdl/ *adj.* connected with TIDES (= the regular rise and fall of the sea) 潮汐的；有潮的：*tidal forces* 潮汐力 ◇ *a tidal river* 感潮河

ˌ**tidal** ˈ**wave** *noun* **1** a very large ocean wave that is caused by a storm or an EARTHQUAKE, and that destroys things when it reaches the land 潮汐波；潮浪；海啸 **2 ~ (of sth)** a sudden increase in a particular feeling, activity or type of behaviour （情感或事物发展的）高涨阶段；高潮；浪潮；热潮：*a tidal wave of crime* 犯罪高峰

tid·bit /ˈtɪdbɪt/ (*NAmE*) (*BrE* **tit·bit**) *noun* a small special piece of food 小片食物 SYN **morsel**

tid·dler /ˈtɪdlə(r)/ *noun* (*BrE, informal*) a very small fish 小鱼

tid·dly /ˈtɪdli/ *adj.* (*BrE, informal*) **1** slightly drunk 微醉的；有醉意的 **2** very small 微小的 SYN **tiny**

tiddly·winks /ˈtɪdliwɪŋks/ *noun* [U] a game in which players try to make small plastic discs jump into a cup by pressing them on the edge with a larger disc 挑圆片游戏（用大圆片压小圆片的边缘使其弹入杯状容器）

tide /taɪd/ *noun, verb*

■ ***noun*** **1** [C, U] a regular rise and fall in the level of the sea, caused by the pull of the moon and sun; the flow of water that happens as the sea rises and falls 潮；潮汐；潮水：*the ebb and flow of the tide* 海潮的涨落 ◇ *The* **tide is in/out.** 涨潮／退潮了。◇ *Is the tide coming in or going out?* 是在涨潮还是在落潮？◇ *The body was washed up on the beach by the tide.* 尸体被潮水冲上了海滩。➲ SEE ALSO HIGH TIDE, LOW TIDE, NEAP TIDE, SPRING TIDE ➲ WORDFINDER NOTE AT COAST, SEA **2** [C, usually sing.] the direction in which the opinion of a large number of people seems to be moving 潮流；趋势；动向：*It takes courage to speak out against the tide of opinion.* 跟舆论趋向唱反调需要勇气。 **3** [C, usually sing.] a large amount of sth unpleasant that is increasing and is difficult to control （难以控制的）恶潮，怒潮：*There is anxiety about the* **rising tide** *of crime.* 犯罪率日益增长令人忧虑。 **4** [sing.] **~ of sth** a feeling that you suddenly have that gets stronger and stronger 高涨的情绪：*A tide of rage surged through her.* 一股怒火燃遍她的全身。 **5 -tide** [sing.] (*old use*) (in compounds 构成复合词) a time or season of the year 时节；季节：*Christmastide* 圣诞节节期

IDM **go, swim, etc. with/against the** ˈ**tide** to agree with/oppose the attitudes or opinions that most other people have 顺应／逆潮流；赶／反潮流 **the** ˈ**tide turned** | **turn the** ˈ**tide** used to say that there is a change in sb's luck or in how successful they are being 转变运气；改变形势

■ ***verb***

PHR V ˌ**tide sb** ˈ**over (sth)** [no passive] to help sb during a difficult period by providing what they need 帮助某人度过（困难时期）；协助某人克服（困难）：*Can you lend me some money to tide me over until I get paid?* 你能借些钱给我帮我凑合到发薪日吗？

tide·line /ˈtaɪdlaɪn/ *noun* a line left or reached by the sea when the tide is at its highest point （海滩上的）潮汐线

tide·mark /ˈtaɪdmɑːk; *NAmE* -mɑːrk/ *noun* **1** a line that is made by the sea on a beach at the highest point that the sea reaches （海滩上的）高潮痕 **2** (*BrE, informal*) a line that is left around the inside of a bath/BATHTUB by dirty water （污水在浴缸内侧留下的一圈）垢痕

ˈ**tide pool** (*NAmE*) (*BrE* ˈ**rock pool**) *noun* a small amount of water that collects between the rocks by the sea/ocean （海边）岩石区潮水潭 ➲ VISUAL VOCAB PAGE V5

tide·water /ˈtaɪdwɔːtə(r)/ *noun* **1** [C] (*NAmE*) an area of land at or near the coast 滨海地区；沿海低地 **2** [U, C] water that is brought by the TIDE 潮水

tid·ings /ˈtaɪdɪŋz/ *noun* [pl.] (*old-fashioned* or *humorous*) news 消息；音讯；音信：*I am the bearer of* **good tidings.** 我带来了好消息。◇ *He brought* **glad tidings.** 他带来了喜讯。

tidy 🔑 /ˈtaɪdi/ *adj., verb, noun*

■ ***adj.*** (**tidi·er, tidi·est**) **1** 🔑 (*especially BrE*) arranged neatly and with everything in order 整洁的；整齐的；井然有序的；井井有条的：*a tidy desk* 整洁的书桌 ◇ *She* **keeps** *her flat very* **tidy.** 她把她的单元房间保持得很整洁。◇ *I like everything to be* **neat and tidy.** 我喜欢一切都井井有条。OPP **untidy** **2** 🔑 (*especially BrE*) keeping things neat and in order 爱整洁的；爱整齐的：*I'm a tidy person.* 我这个人讲究整洁。◇ *tidy habits* 爱整齐的习惯 OPP **untidy** **3** [only before noun] (*informal*) a **tidy** amount of money is fairly large 高额的；可观的 SYN **considerable**：*It must have cost a tidy sum.* 这准花了相当大的一笔钱。◇ *a tidy profit* 可观的利润 ▶ **tidi·ly** *adv.*：*The room was very tidily arranged.* 这房间布置得整整齐齐。 **tidi·ness** *noun* [U]

■ ***verb*** 🔑 (**tidies, tidy·ing, tidied, tidied**) [I, T] (*especially BrE*) to make sth look neat by putting things in the place where they belong 使整洁；使整齐；使有条理；整理：*I spent all morning cleaning and tidying.* 我用了整个上午的时间清扫整理。◇ **~ up** *When you cook, could you please tidy up after yourself.* 请你在做饭时随手收拾干净。◇ **~ sth (up)** *to tidy (up) a room* 整理房间

PHR V ˌ**tidy sth↔a**ˈ**way** (*BrE*) to put things in the place where they belong, especially where they cannot be seen, so that a room appears tidy 收拾起来；拾掇起 ˌ**tidy sth↔**ˈ**up** to arrange or deal with sth so that it is well or correctly finished 收拾妥；整理好：*I tidied up the report before handing it in.* 我把报告整理好后才呈交。

■ ***noun*** (*pl.* **-ies**) (*BrE*) (especially in compounds 尤用于构成复合词) a container for putting small objects in, in order to keep a place tidy 盛零碎物品的容器：*a desk tidy* 案头文具盒

tie 🔑 /taɪ/ *verb, noun*

■ ***verb*** (**ties, tying, tied, tied**)

• **FASTEN WITH STRING/ROPE** 用线／绳扎牢 **1** 🔑 [T] **~ sth (+ adv./prep.)** to attach or hold two or more things together using string, rope, etc.; to fasten sb/sth with string, rope, etc. （用线、绳等）系，拴，绑，捆：*She tied the newspapers in a bundle.* 她把报纸扎成一捆。◇ *He had to tie her hands together.* 他不得不把她的双手绑在一起。◇ *They tied him to a chair with cable.* 他们用电缆把他绑在一把椅子上。◇ *Shall I tie the package or tape it?* 我把这个包裹捆起来还是贴胶带？◇ *I tie back my hair when I'm cooking.* 我做饭时把头发束在后面。 **2** 🔑 [T] **~ sth + adv./prep.** to fasten sth to or around sth else 将…系在…上；束紧；系牢；捆绑：*She tied a label on to the suitcase.* 她把签条系在衣箱上。 **3** 🔑 [T] **~ sth** to make a knot in a piece of string, rope, etc. （在线、绳上）打结，系扣：*to tie a ribbon* 系丝带 ◇ *Can you help me tie my tie?* 你能帮我打领带吗？◇ *Tie up your shoelaces!* 把你的鞋带系好！◇ *I tied a knot in the rope.* 我在绳子上打了个结。 **4** [I] **(+ adv./prep.)** to be closed or fastened with a knot, etc. 打结系牢；系上：*The skirt ties at the waist.* 裙子在腰部束紧。

• **CONNECT/LINK** 连接；联系 **5** [T, usually passive] **~ sb/sth (to sth/sb)** to connect or link sb/sth closely with sb/sth else 连接；联合；使紧密结合：*Pay increases are tied to inflation.* 提高工资和通货膨胀紧密相关。◇ *The house is tied to the job, so we'll have to move when I retire.* 这房子是为工作提供的，所以我退休后我们就得搬家。

• **RESTRICT** 限制 **6** [T, usually passive] to restrict sb and make them unable to do everything they want to 束缚；约束；限制：**~ sb** *to be tied by a contract* 受合同的约束 ◇ **~ sb to sth** *I want to work but I'm tied to the house with the baby.*

我想工作，但却被孩子拴在家里。◇ **~ sb to doing sth** *I don't want to be tied to coming home at a particular time.* 我不想受按钟点回家的束缚。

• **IN GAME/COMPETITION** 比赛；竞赛 **7** [I, T] (of two teams, etc. 两个队等) to have the same number of points 打成平局；得分相同 SYN **draw**: **~ (with sb)** *England tied 2–2 with Germany in the first round.* 在第一轮比赛中英格兰队与德国队以 2:2 打成平局。◇ **~ for sth** *They tied for second place.* 他们并列第二名。◇ **~ sth** *The scores are tied at 3–3.* 比分为 3:3 平。◇ *Last night's vote was tied.* 昨晚的表决得票相同。

• **MUSIC** 音乐 **8** [T] **~ sth** to join notes with a tie 用延音线连接（音符）➲ SEE ALSO TONGUE-TIED

IDM **tie sb/yourself (up) in 'knots** to become or make sb very confused （使）大惑不解，糊涂 **ˌtie one 'on** (*old-fashioned, NAmE, slang*) to get very drunk 喝醉；喝得烂醉 **ˌtie the 'knot** (*informal*) to get married 结婚；结成夫妻 ➲ MORE AT APRON, HAND *n.*

PHR V **ˌtie sb 'down (to sth/to doing sth)** to restrict sb's freedom, for example by making them accept particular conditions or by keeping them busy 限制；束缚；牵制：*Kids tie you down, don't they?* 孩子们把你给拖累住了吧？◇ *I don't want to tie myself down to coming back on a particular date.* 我不想限定自己在哪一天回来。 **ˌtie 'in (with sth)** to match or agree with sth 与…相配；与…相符：*This evidence ties in closely with what we already know.* 这一证据和我们已掌握的情况完全相符。 **ˌtie 'in (with sth) | ˌtie sth↔'in (with sth)** to link sth or be linked to sth; to happen, or arrange for sth to happen, at the same time as sth else （使）连接在一起，同时进行：*The concert will tie in with the festival of dance taking place the same weekend.* 音乐会将和周末举行的舞蹈会演同时进行。➲ RELATED NOUN TIE-IN **ˌtie sth↔'off** to put a knot in the end of sth; to close sth with string, thread, etc. 结扎；（用绳子、线等）封口：*to tie off a rope* 在绳子头上打结 ◇ *to tie off an artery* 结扎动脉血管 **ˌtie 'up | ˌtie sth↔'up 1** 🔑 to attach a boat to a fixed object with a rope （使船只）系泊，停靠：*We tied up alongside the quay.* 我们把船停靠在码头边上。◇ *We tied the boat up.* 我们把船停泊妥当。 **2** 🔑 to close sth with a knot; to be closed or fastened with a knot 系紧；捆牢；拴住；扎紧：*to tie up a garbage bag* 扎紧垃圾袋 **ˌtie sb↔'up 1** 🔑 to tie sb's arms and legs tightly so that they cannot move or escape 把某人捆绑起来：*The gang tied up a security guard.* 那群歹徒把一名保安人员捆绑起来。 **2** [usually passive] to keep sb busy so that they have no time for other things 把…缠住；使不能分身：*I'm tied up in a meeting until 3.* 我开会直到 3 点钟才能脱身。 **ˌtie sth↔'up 1** 🔑 to attach an animal to sth with a rope, chain, etc. （用绳索等把动物）拴住，拴到…上：*He left his dog tied up to a tree.* 他把狗拴在了树上。 **2** [usually passive] to connect or link sth to sth else 把…联系起来；使与…有关系：*Her behaviour is tied up with her feelings of guilt.* 她的行为与她的罪恶感有关。 ➲ RELATED NOUN TIE-UP (2) **3** [often passive] to invest money so that it is not easily available for use 占用，搁死（资金）：*Most of the capital is tied up in property.* 大部分资金都投在了房地产上无法动用。 **4** to deal with all the remaining details of sth 完成；处理完：*We are hoping to tie up the deal by tomorrow.* 我们希望能在明天前达成交易。◇ *I went into the office for an hour to* ***tie up any loose ends*** (= finish remaining small jobs). 我去了办公室一个小时，把未了结的零星事务处理完。

■ ***noun***

• **CLOTHES** 衣服 **1** 🔑 (*NAmE also* **neck·tie**) a long narrow piece of cloth worn around the neck, especially by men, with a knot in front 领带：***a collar and tie*** 衬衫加领带 ◇ *a striped silk tie* 带条纹的真丝领带 ➲ VISUAL VOCAB PAGE V66 ➲ SEE ALSO BLACK TIE, BOW TIE, OLD SCHOOL TIE, WHITE TIE

• **FOR FASTENING** 捆扎 **2** a piece of string or wire used for fastening or tying sth 绳子；金属丝；线：*ties for closing plastic bags* 封塑料袋用的捆扎绳

• **CONNECTION** 连接 **3** 🔑 [usually pl.] a strong connection between people or organizations 联系；关系；纽带：*family ties* 家族关系 ◇ *the ties of friendship* 友谊的纽带 ◇ *economic ties* 经济联系 ◇ *The firm has close ties with an American corporation.* 这家商行与一家美国公司关系密切。

• **RESTRICTION** 限制 **4** a thing that limits sb's freedom of action 束缚；约束；限制；牵累：*He was still a young man and he did not want any ties.* 他还年轻，不想有任何束缚。

• **IN GAME/COMPETITION** 比赛；竞赛 **5** a situation in a game or competition when two or more players have the same score 平局；得分相同；不分胜负：*The match ended in a tie.* 这场比赛以平局结束。 ➲ COMPARE DRAW *n.* (2) **6** (*BrE*) a sports match, especially a football (SOCCER) match, that is part of a larger competition （尤指足球）淘汰赛：*the first leg of the Cup tie between Leeds and Roma* 利兹队和罗马队在杯赛淘汰赛中的第一轮比赛

• **MUSIC** 音乐 **7** a curved line written over two notes of the same PITCH (= how high or low a note is) to show that they are to be played or sung as one note 延音线；延音连接线 ➲ PICTURE AT MUSIC

• **ON RAILWAY** 铁路 **8** (*NAmE*) (*BrE* **sleep·er**) one of the heavy pieces of wood or concrete on which the rails on a railway/railroad track are laid （铁路）轨枕，枕木 ➲ VISUAL VOCAB PAGE V63

tie·break /ˈtaɪbreɪk/ (*BrE*) (*NAmE* **tie·break·er**) *noun* (in TENNIS 网球) a period of extra play to decide who is the winner of a SET when both players have won six games 平分决胜局；抢七局

tie·breaker /ˈtaɪbreɪkə(r)/ *noun* **1** (*NAmE*) (*BrE* **tie·break**) (in TENNIS 网球) a period of extra play to decide who is the winner of a SET when both players have won six games 平分决胜局；抢七局 **2** an extra question in a competition to decide who is the winner when two or more of those taking part have equal scores 平分决胜比赛；（竞赛中比分相同时附加的）决胜负问题 ➲ WORDFINDER NOTE AT COMPETITION

tied /taɪd/ *adj.* [only before noun] (*BrE*) (of a house 房屋) rented to sb on the condition that they work for the owner 只租给雇工居住的：*a tied cottage on a farm* 农场里租给雇工的农舍

ˌtied 'house *noun* (*BrE*) a pub that is owned by a particular BREWERY (= a company that produces beer) and that mainly sells the beer which that brewery produces 酒厂酒吧（啤酒厂开设，主要卖自制啤酒）➲ COMPARE FREE HOUSE

'tie-dye *verb* **~ sth** to make patterns on cloth by tying knots in it or tying string around it before you put it in a DYE, so that some parts receive more colour than others 扎染（织物）

'tie-in *noun* a product such as a book or toy that is connected with a new film/movie, television programme, etc. （与新上演的电影或电视节目等）相关的产品（如书、玩具等）

tie·pin /ˈtaɪpɪn/ (*NAmE also* **'tie tack**) *noun* a small decorative pin that is worn on a tie to keep it in place 领带扣针；领带别针

tier /tɪə(r); *NAmE* tɪr/ *noun* **1** a row or layer of sth that has several rows or layers placed one above the other 级；阶；层：*a wedding cake with three tiers* 三层的结婚蛋糕 ◇ *The seating is arranged* ***in tiers.*** 座位是一级级排列的。 **2** one of several levels in an organization or a system 阶层；等级：*We have introduced an extra tier of administration.* 我们额外增加了一层管理。◇ *a two-tier system of management* 两级管理制

tiered /tɪəd; *NAmE* tɪrd/ *adj.* **1** arranged in tiers 阶梯式的；分层的：*tiered seating* 阶梯式座位 **2 -tiered** (in compounds 构成复合词) having the number of tiers mentioned …层的；…排的；…级的：*a two-tiered system* 两级系统

'tie-up *noun* **1 ~ (with sb/sth)** (*BrE*) an agreement between two companies to join together （两家公司的）联合，合作：*They're negotiating a tie-up with Ford.* 他们正在与福特公司洽谈合作事宜。 **2 ~ (between A and B)** (*BrE*) a connection between two or more things 联系；关系；关联：*a tie-up between politics and economics* 政治和经济之间的关系 **3** (*especially NAmE*) a situation in which sth stops

T

working or moving forward 停顿；停滞不前： *a traffic tie-up* 交通阻塞

TIFF /tɪf/ *noun* [U, C] (*computing* 计) the abbreviation for 'tagged image file format' (a form in which images can be stored and shown on a computer; an image created in this form) 标签式图像文件格式，TIFF 格式，TIFF 图像（全写为 tagged image file format）

tiff /tɪf/ *noun* (*informal*) a slight argument between close friends or lovers（朋友或情人之间的）争执，拌嘴，口角，吵嘴： *to have a tiff with sb* 与某人口角

tif·fin /ˈtɪfɪn/ *noun* [U] (*old-fashioned* or *IndE*) a small meal, especially lunch 简易饭菜（尤指午餐）

ˈtiffin carrier *noun* (*especially IndE*) a set of shallow metal food containers that fit on top of each other and that are attached together using a metal frame with a fastening device 层叠式金属餐盒（用金属框架连接在一起）

tig /tɪg/ *noun* [U] (*BrE*) = TAG (6)

tiger /ˈtaɪgə(r)/ *noun* a large wild animal of the cat family, that has yellowish fur with black lines (= STRIPES) and lives in parts of Asia 虎；老虎： *She **fought like a tiger** to be able to keep her children.* 她勇猛搏斗，以便能保住她的孩子。 ➲ COMPARE TIGRESS ➲ SEE ALSO PAPER TIGER

ˌtiger eˈconomy *noun* the economy of a country that is growing very quickly 小龙经济（指飞速发展的国家的经济）

tiger·ish /ˈtaɪgərɪʃ/ *adj.* like a tiger, especially in being aggressive or showing great energy 像虎的；凶猛有力的

tight /taɪt/ *adj., adv.*

■ ***adj.*** (**tight·er, tight·est**)

- **FIRM** 牢固 **1** held or fixed in position firmly; difficult to move or undo 牢固的；紧的；不松动的；难解开的： *He kept **a tight grip** on her arm.* 他紧紧握住她的胳膊。 ◇ *She twisted her hair into a tight knot.* 她把头发紧紧地挽了个发髻。 ◇ *The screw was so tight that it wouldn't move.* 螺丝钉太紧，拧不开。
- **CLOTHES** 衣服 **2** fitting closely to your body and sometimes uncomfortable 紧身的；紧贴的： *She was wearing a tight pair of jeans.* 她穿着一条紧身牛仔裤。 ◇ *These shoes are much too tight.* 这双鞋太紧了。 ◇ *The new sweater was **a tight fit**.* 这件新毛衣很贴身。 OPP **loose** ➲ SEE ALSO SKIN-TIGHT
- **CONTROL** 控制 **3** very strict and firm 严密的；严格的；严厉的： *to **keep tight control** over sth* 对某事严加控制 ◇ *We need tighter security at the airport.* 我们需要在机场实行更加严密的安全措施。
- **STRETCHED** 拉伸 **4** stretched or pulled so that it cannot stretch much further 拉紧的；绷紧的： *The rope was stretched tight.* 这绳子拉得很紧。
- **CLOSE TOGETHER** 紧密靠拢 **5** [usually before noun] with things or people packed closely together, leaving little space between them 装紧的；密集的；挤满的： *There was a tight group of people around the speaker.* 演讲人周围严严实实地挤了一群人。 ◇ *With six of us in the car it was **a tight squeeze**.* 小轿车里坐了我们六个人，挤得很。
- **MONEY/TIME** 金钱；时间 **6** difficult to manage with because there is not enough 紧的；拮据的；不宽裕的： *We have a very tight budget.* 我们的预算很紧。 ◇ *The president has a tight schedule today.* 总统今天的日程排满了。
- **EXPRESSION/VOICE** 表情；嗓音 **7** looking or sounding anxious, upset, angry, etc. 显得紧张的；忐忑不安的；生气的： *'I'm sorry,' she said, with a tight smile.* "对不起。" 她勉强一笑说。 ➲ SEE ALSO UPTIGHT (1)
- **PART OF BODY** 身体部位 **8** feeling painful or uncomfortable because of illness or emotion（由于疾病或情感）疼痛的，不适的，憋气的 SYN **constricted**: *He complained of having a tight chest.* 他主诉胸部憋闷。 ◇ *Her throat felt tight, just looking at her baby.* 她喉咙哽咽得说不出话来，只是看着她的婴儿。
- **RELATIONSHIP** 关系 **9** having a close relationship with sb else or with other people 亲密的；紧密的；密切的： *It was a tight community and newcomers were not welcome.* 这个社群内部很紧密，不太接纳新来的人。 ➲ SEE ALSO TIGHT-KNIT
- **BEND/CURVE** 弯曲；曲线 **10** curving suddenly rather than gradually 急转的；陡的： *The driver slowed down at a tight bend in the road.* 驾驶员在道路急转弯处慢了下来。 ◇ *The plane flew around in a tight circle.* 飞机绕着小圈盘旋。
- **CONTEST/RACE** 竞赛；赛跑 **11** with runners, teams, etc. that seem to be equally good 势均力敌的；不相上下的；旗鼓相当的 SYN **close²**: *a tight race* 势均力敌的赛跑
- **NOT GENEROUS** 不慷慨 **12** (*informal, disapproving*) not wanting to spend much money; not generous 小气的；吝啬的；不大方的 SYN **mean**: *He's very tight with his money.* 他花钱很抠门儿。
- **DRUNK** 喝醉 **13** [not usually before noun] (*old-fashioned, informal*) drunk 喝醉；醉醺醺 SYN **tipsy**
- **-TIGHT** 密封 **14** (in compounds 构成复合词) not allowing the substance mentioned to enter 不漏…的；不透…的；防…的： *measures to make your home weathertight* 使你家防风雨的措施 ➲ SEE ALSO AIRTIGHT, WATERTIGHT (1)

▸ **tight·ness** *noun* [U]

IDM **to keep a tight ˈrein on sb/sth** to control sb/sth carefully or strictly 对…严加控制（或约束）；牢牢驾驭 **run a tight ˈship** to organize sth in a very efficient way, controlling other people very closely 管理有方；严加控制 **a tight ˈspot/ˈcorner** a very difficult or dangerous situation 困境；险境

■ ***adv.*** (**tight·er, tight·est**) closely and firmly; tightly 紧紧地；牢固地： ***Hold tight!*** 抓紧了！ ◇ *My suitcase was packed tight.* 我的衣箱塞得满满的。 ◇ *His fists were clenched tight.* 他紧握双拳。 IDM SEE SIT, SLEEP *v.*

▼ **WHICH WORD?** 词语辨析

tight / tightly

- **Tight** and **tightly** are both adverbs that come from the adjective **tight**. They have the same meaning, but **tight** is often used instead of **tightly** after a verb, especially in informal language, and in compounds. * tight 和 tightly 均为源自形容词 tight 的副词，意思相同，但在动词后，尤其在非正式用语和复合词中，常用 tight 代替 tightly： *packed tight* 塞得紧紧的 ◇ *a tight-fitting lid* 严实的盖子 Before a past participle **tightly** is used. 过去分词前用 tightly： *clusters of tightly packed flowers* 一簇簇密密集的花

ˈtight-arse *noun* (*informal, disapproving*) **1** (*BrE*) a person who does not like spending money 吝啬鬼；铁公鸡 **2** (*BrE*) (*NAmE* **ˈtight-ass**) a person who controls their emotions and actions very carefully and does not like to break the rules 拘谨的人；拘泥的人 ▸ **ˈtight-arsed** (*BrE*) (*NAmE* **ˈtight-assed**) *adj.*

tight·en /ˈtaɪtn/ *verb* **1** [I, T] to become or make sth become tight or tighter（使）变紧，更加牢固： **~ (up)** *The rope holding the boat suddenly tightened and broke.* 系船的绳子突然绷断了。 ◇ *His mouth tightened into a thin line.* 他的嘴抿成了一道细缝。 ◇ **~ sth (up)** *to tighten a lid/screw/rope/knot* 拧紧盖子 / 螺钉；绷紧绳子；打紧结 ◇ *The nuts weren't properly tightened and the wheel came off.* 螺母没拧紧，轮子脱落了。 ◇ *She tightened her grip on his arm.* 她抓他的手臂抓得更紧了。 **2** [T] **~ sth** to make sth become stricter 使更加严格；加强： *to tighten security* 加强安全措施 OPP **loosen**

IDM **tighten your ˈbelt** to spend less money because there is less available 勒紧腰带（省吃俭用） ➲ SYNONYMS AT SAVE

PHR V **ˌtighten ˈup (on sth)** to become stricter or more careful 变得更加严格（或小心）： *Laws on gambling have tightened up recently.* 有关赌博的法律最近变得更加严厉。 ◇ *The police are tightening up on under-age drinking.* 警方正在采取更加严厉的措施对付未成年人饮酒的问题。

ˌtight ˈend *noun* (in AMERICAN FOOTBALL 美式足球) an attacking player who plays close to the TACKLE 边锋

T

ˌtight-ˈfisted *adj.* not willing to spend or give much money 吝啬的；小气的 SYN **mean, stingy**

ˌtight-ˈfitting *adj.* that fits very tightly or closely 紧身的；贴身的 SYN **close-fitting**: *a tight-fitting skirt* 紧身裙子

ˈtight head *noun* (in RUGBY 橄榄球) the player in the front row of a team in the SCRUM who is furthest from where the ball is put in 并列争球前边锋

ˌtight-ˈknit (*also* **ˌtightly-ˈknit**) *adj.* (of a family or community 家族或社群) with all the members having strong friendly relationships with one another 关系密切的；紧密团结的：*a tight-knit mining community* 紧密团结的矿工们

ˌtight-ˈlipped *adj.* **1** not willing to talk about sth 口紧的；缄口不语的；守口如瓶的 **2** keeping your lips pressed firmly together, especially because you are angry about sth 双唇紧闭的（尤指因生气）

tight·ly /ˈtaɪtli/ *adv.* closely and firmly; in a tight manner 紧紧地；牢固地；紧密地：*Her eyes were tightly closed.* 她的双眼紧闭着。◇ *He held on tightly to her arm.* 他紧紧抓住她的手臂。◇ *a tightly packed crowd of tourists* 挤得严严实实的旅游人群 ➲ NOTE AT TIGHT

tight·rope /ˈtaɪtrəʊp; *NAmE* -roʊp/ *noun* a rope or wire that is stretched tightly high above the ground and that performers walk along, especially in a CIRCUS（尤指马戏团表演用的）绷紧的绳索，绷紧的钢丝：*a tightrope walker* 走钢丝演员

IDM **tread/walk a ˈtightrope** to be in a difficult situation in which you do not have much freedom of action and need to be extremely careful about what you do 身处困境；如履薄冰

tights /taɪts/ *noun* [pl.] **1** (*BrE*) (*NAmE* **panty·hose**) a piece of clothing made of very thin cloth that fits closely over a woman's hips, legs and feet（女用）连裤袜，紧身裤：*a pair of tights* 一条连裤袜 ➲ COMPARE STOCKING (1) **2** a piece of clothing similar to tights but made of thicker cloth, worn especially by dancers（尤指舞蹈演员穿的）紧身衣裤

tight·wad /ˈtaɪtwɒd; *NAmE* -wɑːd/ *noun* (*NAmE, informal*) a person who hates to spend or give money 吝啬鬼；小气鬼；守财奴 SYN **miser**

tig·ress /ˈtaɪgrəs/ *noun* a female TIGER 雌老虎

tike *noun* = TYKE

tikka /ˈtɪkə; *BrE also* ˈtiːkə/ *noun* [U, C] a spicy S Asian dish consisting of pieces of meat or vegetables which have been left in a sauce and then cooked 帝卡烧焗肉片（或蔬菜）（南亚菜肴，将肉片或蔬菜用酱汁腌后烹煮而成）：*chicken tikka* 帝卡烧焗鸡肉片

til, ˈtil ➲ UNTIL

tilak /ˈtɪlæk/ *noun* a mark on the FOREHEAD of a Hindu, worn as a religious symbol or for decoration（印度教教徒标在前额代表教派或作装饰的）吉祥记

til·apia /tɪˈlæpiə; -ˈleɪp-; *NAmE* -ˈlɑːp-/ *noun* (*pl.* **til·apia** or **til·apias**) [C, U] a FRESHWATER fish found in hot countries that is used for food 罗非鱼

tilde /ˈtɪldə/ *noun* **1** the mark (˜) placed over letters in some languages and some vowels in the International Phonetic Alphabet to show how they should be pronounced, as in *España, São Paulo* and *penchant* /ˈpɒ̃ʃɒ̃/ 腭化符号（˜）（置于某些语言的字母和国际音标中某些元音符号之上，表示发音方法）**2** (*also* **ˌswung ˈdash**) the mark (~), used in this dictionary in some parts of an entry to represent the word in blue type at the top of the entry 波浪号，代字号（在本词典词条的某些地方用以代表首词）

tile /taɪl/ *noun, verb*

■ *noun* **1** a flat, usually square, piece of baked CLAY, carpet or other material that is used in rows for covering walls and floors（贴墙或铺地用的）瓷砖，地砖，小方地毯，片状材料：*ceramic floor tiles* 陶瓷地砖 ◇ *carpet tiles* 小方地毯 **2** a piece of baked CLAY that is used in rows for covering roofs（铺屋顶的）瓦，瓦片 ➲ VISUAL VOCAB PAGE V18 **3** any of the small flat pieces that are used in particular board games（棋盘游戏的）棋子 IDM SEE NIGHT

■ *verb* **1 ~ sth** to cover a surface with tiles 铺瓦；铺地砖；贴瓷砖：*a tiled bathroom* 铺瓷砖的浴室 **2 ~ sth** (*computing* 计) to arrange several windows on a computer screen so that they fill the screen but do not cover each other 平铺显示，并列显示，瓦片式显示（视窗）

tiler /ˈtaɪlə(r)/ *noun* a person whose job is to lay tiles 泥瓦匠；铺瓦工；贴砖工

til·ing /ˈtaɪlɪŋ/ *noun* [U] **1** an area covered with tiles 瓷砖面；地砖面；瓦屋顶 ➲ VISUAL VOCAB PAGE V25 **2** the work of covering a floor, wall, etc. with tiles 盖瓦；贴瓷砖；铺地砖

till /tɪl/ *conj., prep., noun, verb*

■ *conj., prep.* = UNTIL：*We're open till 6 o'clock.* 我们营业到 6 点钟。◇ *Can't you wait till we get home?* 难道你就不能等我们回到家吗？◇ *Just wait till you see it. It's great.* 你就等着直到看见它吧。好看极了。HELP **Till** is generally felt to be more informal than **until** and is used much less often in writing. At the beginning of a sentence, **until** is usually used. 一般认为 till 不如 until 正式，在书面语中不常用。句首通常用 until。

■ *noun* **1** (*BrE*) = CASH REGISTER **2** (*BrE, informal*) the place where you pay for goods in a large shop/store（大商店中的）交款处，收银台：*Please pay at the till.* 请在交款处付款。◇ *a long queue at the till* 收款处的长队 **3** (*especially NAmE*) the drawer where the money is put in a CASH REGISTER（现金出纳机的）放钱的抽屉 ➲ WORDFINDER NOTE AT SHOP IDM SEE FINGER *n.*

■ *verb* **~ sth** (*old use*) to prepare and use land for growing crops 耕作；犁地

till·age /ˈtɪlɪdʒ/ *noun* [U] (*old-fashioned*) **1** the process of preparing and using land for growing crops 耕地（包括整地和土壤中耕）**2** land that is used for growing crops 耕地

till·er /ˈtɪlə(r)/ *noun* a bar that is used to turn the RUDDER of a small boat in order to steer it（小船的）舵柄 ➲ COMPARE HELM

tilt /tɪlt/ *verb, noun*

■ *verb* **1** [I, T] to move, or make sth move, into a position with one side or end higher than the other（使）倾斜，倾侧 SYN **tip**: **(+ adv./prep.)** *Suddenly the boat tilted to one side.* 小船突然倾向一侧。◇ *The seat tilts forward, when you press this lever.* 按这个控制柄，座位就向前倾斜。◇ **~ sth (+ adv./prep.)** *His hat was tilted slightly at an angle.* 他的帽子有点歪。◇ *She tilted her head back and looked up at me with a smile.* 她仰起头含笑看着我。**2** [T, I] **~ (sth/sb) (in favour of/away from sth/sb)** to make sth/sb change slightly so that one particular opinion, person, etc. is preferred or more likely to succeed than another; to change in this way 使倾向于；使向…倾斜；偏向：*The conditions may **tilt the balance in favour of** the Kenyan runners.* 这些条件可能对肯尼亚赛跑运动员有利。◇ *Popular opinion has **tilted in favour** of the socialists.* 公众舆论已倒向社会党人一边。

IDM **tilt at ˈwindmills** to waste your energy attacking imaginary enemies 攻击假想敌；庸人自扰 ORIGIN From Cervantes' novel *Don Quixote*, in which the hero thought that the windmills he saw were giants and tried to fight them. 源自塞万提斯的长篇小说《堂吉诃德》，书中的主人公认为他看到的风车是巨人，于是与之展开搏斗。

PHR V **ˈtilt at sb/sth** (*BrE*) to attack sb/sth in speech or writing 抨击；攻击 **ˈtilt at sth** (*BrE*) to try to win sth 力争赢得某物：*He was tilting at the top prize.* 他在力争夺魁。

■ *noun* **1** [C, usually sing., U] a position in which one end or side of sth is higher than the other; an act of tilting sth to one side 倾斜；倾侧：*The table is at a slight tilt.* 这桌子有点儿倾斜。◇ *He answered with a tilt of his head.* 他歪着头回答。**2** [C] an attempt to win sth or defeat sb（意欲

赢得某物或战胜某人的）企图，尝试：*She aims to have a **tilt** at the world championship next year.* 她的目标是明年问鼎世界冠军。

IDM **(at) full 'tilt/'pelt** as fast as possible 全速；尽快

tim·ber /ˈtɪmbə(r)/ *noun* **1** [U] trees that are grown to be used in building or for making things （用于建筑或制作物品的）树木，林木；用材林：*the timber industry* 林木业 **2** [U] (*especially BrE*) (*NAmE usually* **lum·ber**) wood that is prepared for use in building, etc. （建筑等用的）木材，木料：*houses built of timber* 木屋 **3** [C, usually pl.] a long heavy piece of wood used in building a house or ship （建造房屋用的）大木料，栋木；（造船用的）肋材：*roof timbers* 房檩 **4 timber!** used to warn people that a tree that has been cut is about to fall （砍伐树木时喊）放树啦！

tim·bered /ˈtɪmbəd; *NAmE* -bərd/ *adj.* built of timbers; with a FRAMEWORK of timbers 木制的；木结构的 ➲ SEE ALSO HALF-TIMBERED

'tim·ber yard (*BrE*) (*NAmE* **lum·ber·yard**) *noun* a place where wood for building, etc. is stored and sold 木料场；贮木场

timbre /ˈtæmbə(r)/ *noun* (*formal*) the quality of sound that is produced by a particular voice or musical instrument 音质；音色；音品

Tim·buktu (*also* **Tim·buctoo**) /ˌtɪmbʌkˈtuː/ *noun* a place that is very far away 遥远的地方 ORIGIN From the name of a town in northern Mali. 源自马里北部城镇廷巴克图。

time /taɪm/ *noun, verb*

■ ***noun*** ➲ SEE ALSO TIMES

• **MINUTES/HOURS/YEARS, ETC.** 分钟、小时、年等 **1** [U] what is measured in minutes, hours, days, etc. （以分钟、小时、天等计量的）时间：*The changing seasons mark the **passing of time**.* 寒来暑往，斗转星移。◇ *A visit to the museum will take you **back in time** to the 1930s.* 参观这家博物馆就会使你回到 20 世纪 30 年代。◇ *time and space* 时间和空间 ◇ ***As time went by** we saw less and less of each other.* 随着时间的推移，我们见面越来越少。◇ *Perceptions change **over time*** (= as time passes). 观念随着时间的流逝而变化。➲ SEE ALSO FATHER TIME **2** [U] the time shown on a clock in minutes and hours （钟表所显示的）时间，钟点，时刻：***What time is it/What's the time?*** 几点了？◇ *Do you have the time?* 你知道现在几点了吗？◇ (*BrE*) ***What time do you make it?*** 你说现在几点了？◇ (*NAmE*) ***What time do you have?*** 你知道现在几点了吗？◇ *The time is now half past ten.* 现在是十点半。◇ (*BrE*) *Can she **tell the time** yet* (= say what time it is by looking at a clock)? 她会看钟表了吗？◇ (*NAmE*) *Can she **tell time** yet?* 她会看钟表了吗？◇ *My watch **keeps perfect time*** (= always shows the correct time). 我的表走得很准。◇ *Look at the time! We'll be late.* 看几点了！我们要迟到了。◇ ***This time tomorrow** I'll be in Canada.* 明天这个时候我就在加拿大了。**3** [U] the time measured in a particular part of the world （世界某一地区所计量的）时，时间：*Greenwich Mean Time* 格林尼治平时 ◇ *6 o'clock **local time*** 当地时间 6 点钟 ➲ SEE ALSO STANDARD TIME, SUMMER TIME **4** [U, C] the time when sth happens or when sth should happen （某事发生或应该发生的）时间，时候：*What time do you finish work?* 你什么时候下班？◇ *The baby loves bath time.* 这婴儿喜欢洗澡的时候。◇ ~ **(to do sth)** *I think it's time to go to bed.* 我想该睡觉了。◇ ~ **(for sth)** *It's time for lunch.* 午餐时间到了。◇ ~ **(that)**... *It's time the kids were in bed.* 孩子们该睡觉了。◇ ***By the time** you get there the meeting will be over.* 等你到了那里的时候，会议就该结束了。◇ *A computer screen shows arrival and departure times.* 电脑屏幕显示出到达和离开的时间。◇ *The train arrived right **on time*** (= at exactly the correct time). 火车准点到达。◇ *You'll feel differently about it **when the time comes*** (= when it happens). 到时候你就会有不同的感受了。➲ SEE ALSO ANY TIME, CLOSING TIME, DRIVE TIME, NIGHT-TIME, OPENING TIME

• **PERIOD** 时间段 **5** [U] ~ **(to do sth)** an amount of time; the amount of time available to work, rest, etc. 一段时间；（可用于工作、休息等的）一段时间：*Allow plenty of time to get to the airport.* 预留足够的时间到达机场。◇ *I can probably **make the time** to see them.* 我大概能腾出时间见他们。◇ *It **takes time** to make changes in the law.* 修改法律还有待时日。◇ *We have **no time to lose*** (= we must hurry). 我们不能耽误时间了！◇ *He spends most of his time working.* 他把大部分时间都花在工作上。◇ *She doesn't have much **free/spare time**.* 她没有多少空余时间。◇ *What a **waste of time**!* 太浪费时间了！◇ *I didn't finish the test—I **ran out of time**.* 我没答完试卷，我的时间不够了。◇ ***Time's up**—have you worked out the answer yet?* 时间到了，你得出答案了没有？◇ *He never takes any **time off*** (= time spent not working). 他从不休假。◇ *Jane's worked here **for some time*** (= for a fairly long period of time). 简在这儿工作已经有好些时候了。◇ *Do it now please—not in three hours' time* (= three hours from now). 请现在就干，而不是三个小时之后。◇ *The journey time is two hours.* 旅程时间为两个小时。➲ SEE ALSO RESPONSE TIME **6** **a time** [sing.] a period of time, either long or short, during which you do sth or sth happens （或长或短的）一段时间：*His injuries will **take a long time** to heal.* 他的伤需要很长一段时间才能好。◇ *I lived in Egypt **for a time**.* 我在埃及住过一阵子。◇ *The early morning is the best **time of day**.* 清晨是一天最好的时光。◇ *Her parents died **a long time ago**.* 她的父母很早以前就去世了。◇ ***At one time*** (= at a period of time in the past) *Emily was my best friend.* 埃米莉一度是我最好的朋友。◇ *Mr Curtis was the manager **in my time*** (= when I was working there). 我在那里工作时，柯蒂斯先生是经理。**7** [U, pl.] a period of history connected with particular events or experiences in people's lives 时期；时代；年代；世道：*The movie is set **at the time of** the Russian Revolution.* 这部电影以俄国革命时期为背景。◇ *in ancient times* 在古代 ◇ *the violent times we live in* (= the present period of history) 我们生逢的乱世 ◇ *Times are hard for the unemployed.* 对失业者来说，时世艰难。◇ ***Times have changed** since Grandma was young.* 世易时移，现在已不是祖母年轻时那会儿了。➲ SEE ALSO OLD-TIME

• **OCCASION/EVENT** 次；事件 **8** [C] an occasion when you do sth or when sth happens 次；回：***Every time** I hear that song I feel happy.* 我每次听到那首歌都感到很愉快。◇ ***Next time** you're here let's have lunch together.* 下次你到这里来，咱们一起吃午饭。◇ *He failed his driving test three times.* 他考了三次驾驶执照都没通过。◇ *He's determined to pass **this time**.* 这一回他决心要考及格。◇ *When was the **last time** you saw her?* 你上次是什么时候见到她的？◇ ***How many times*** (= how often) *do I have to tell you not to do that?* 我得要跟你说多少回不要做那种事？◇ (*especially NAmE*) *I remember **one time*** (= once) *we had to abandon our car in the snow.* 我记得有一次我们迫于无奈把汽车丢弃在雪地里。◇ (*formal*) ***At no time did** I give my consent to the plan.* 我从未同意过这项计划。HELP To talk about the first or the last time you do sth, use **the first/last time (that) I...**. 谈论第一次或最后一次做什么事情，可以说 the first/last time (that) I ...: *This is the first time (that) I've been to London.* 这是我第一次到伦敦。◇ ~~*This is the first time for me to go to London.*~~ ◇ *That was the last time (that) I saw her.* 那是我最后一次见她。**9** [C] an event or occasion that you experience in a particular way （以某种方式经历的）事件，时刻：*Did you **have a good time** in Spain?* 你在西班牙过得愉快吗？◇ *I had an awful time in the hospital.* 我住院的日子可真难熬。

• **FOR RACE** 赛跑 **10** [C, U] how long sb takes to run a race or complete an event （完成赛跑或竞赛项目的）所用时间：*The winner's time was 11.6 seconds.* 获胜者的时间是 11.6 秒。◇ *She completed the 500 metres **in record time*** (= faster than any previous runner). 她以破纪录的时间跑完了 500 米。◇ *one of the fastest times ever* 历来最快的成绩之一

• **IN MUSIC** 音乐 **11** [U] the number of beats in a BAR/MEASURE of music 拍子；节拍：*This piece is in four-four time.* 这首乐曲为四分之四拍。◇ *a slow waltz time* 缓慢的华尔兹节拍 ◇ *The conductor **beat time** with a baton.* 指挥用指挥棒打拍子。**12** [U] the correct speed and rhythm of a piece of music （乐曲正确的）速度，节奏：*Try and dance **in time to** the music* (= with the same speed and rhythm). 要跟上音乐的节奏跳舞。◇ *Clap your hands to **keep time*** (= sing or move with the correct speed and rhythm). 拍手以保持节奏。◇ *to play **in/out of time*** (= follow/not follow the correct speed and rhythm) 演奏得

T

合 / 不合节奏 ◇ *He always plays in perfect time.* 他演奏的节奏总是准确无误。 ➲ SEE ALSO BIG TIME *n.*, SMALL-TIME

IDM **(and) about 'time ('too) | (and) not before 'time** used to say that sth should have happened before now 早该发生；早该如此 **against 'time** if you do sth **against time**, you do it as fast as you can because you do not have much time 争分夺秒；抢时间：*They're working against time to try and get people out of the rubble alive.* 他们正在争分夺秒，设法把人们从瓦砾中活着救出来。 **ahead of/behind 'time** earlier/later than was expected 提前；拖后：*We finished 15 minutes ahead of time.* 我们提前 15 分钟完成。 **ahead of your 'time** having advanced or new ideas that other people use or copy later 超越时代的；有超前意识的；具有前瞻性的 **all the 'time | the whole 'time 1** ⚷ during the whole of a particular period of time（在某段时间内）一直，始终：*The letter was in my pocket all the time* (= while I was looking for it). 这信一直就在我的口袋里。 **2** ⚷ very often; repeatedly 经常；总是；老是：*She leaves the lights on all the time.* 她总是让灯亮着。 **at all 'times** ⚷ always 总是；随时；永远：*Our representatives are ready to help you at all times.* 我们的代表随时准备帮助你。 **at the 'best of times** even when the circumstances are very good 即使在最好的情况下：*He's never very happy at the best of times—he'll be much worse now!* 他即使在处境最好的时候也从未很高兴过，现在就更糟了！ **at the same 'time 1** ⚷ at one time; together 同时；一起：*She was laughing and crying at the same time.* 她又哭又笑。 **2** ⚷ used to introduce a contrasting fact, etc. that must be considered（用以引出必须予以考虑的相对情况）同时，也，然而，不过：*You have to be firm, but at the same time you should try and be sympathetic.* 你必须要严格，不过也应尽量怀有同情心。 **at a 'time** ⚷ separately or in groups of two, three, etc. on each occasion 每次；逐一；依次：*We had to go and see the principal one at a time.* 我们得逐一去见校长。 ◇ *She ran up the stairs two at a time.* 她一步两阶地跑上楼梯。 **at 'my, 'your, 'his, etc. time of life** at the age you are (especially when you are not young) 在…这样的年纪（尤指不年轻时）：*Eyesight doesn't get any better at my time of life.* 到我这把年纪，视力绝不会变好的。 **at 'times** ⚷ sometimes 有时；间或：*He can be really bad-tempered at times.* 他有的时候脾气可真坏。 **before my, your, his, etc. 'time 1** happening before you were born or can remember or before you lived, worked, etc. somewhere 在…出生（或记事、在世、工作等）之前：*'Were you taught by Professor Pascal?' 'No, he was before my time.'* "帕斯卡尔教授教过你吗？" "没有，他教书时我还没有入校呢。" **2** before the usual time in sb's life when sth happens 过早；提前 SYN **prematurely**: *She got old before her time.* 她过早地衰老了。 **behind the 'times** old-fashioned in your ideas, methods, etc.（思想、方法等）落伍，过时，陈旧 **do 'time** (*informal*) to spend time in prison 坐牢；蹲监狱 **every 'time** whenever there is a choice 无论何时；一有机会：*I don't really like cities—give me the countryside every time.* 我真不太喜欢城市，一有机会就让我去乡村吧。 **for the time 'being** for a short period of time but not permanently 暂时；眼下：*You can leave your suitcase here for the time being.* 你可以暂时把衣箱留在这儿。 **from ˌtime to 'time** ⚷ occasionally but not regularly 不时；有时；偶尔；间或：*She has to work at weekends from time to time.* 她偶尔周末还得工作。 **have a lot of time for sb/sth** (*informal, especially BrE*) to like and be interested in sb/sth 喜欢；对…感兴趣；愿意为…花时间 **have no time for sb/sth | not have much time for sb/sth** (*informal*) to dislike sb/sth 不喜欢；讨厌；不愿为…花时间：*I have no time for lazy people like Steve.* 我讨厌像史蒂夫这样的懒汉。 **have the ˌtime of your 'life** (*informal*) to enjoy yourself very much 过得很快乐；玩得痛快 **have time on your 'hands | have time to 'kill** (*informal*) to have nothing to do or not be busy 无所事事；没事可干；闲着 **in good 'time** early; with enough time so that you are not in a hurry 及早；有足够的时间 **(all) in good 'time** (*informal*) used to say that sth will be done or will happen at the appropriate time and not before 会按时做（或出现）；不消多久：*Be patient, Emily! All in good time.* 埃米莉，别急！快好了。 **in (less than/next to) 'no time** so soon or so quickly that it is surprising 短暂（或快）得令人吃惊；立刻；马上；一会儿：*The kids will be leaving home in no time.* 孩子们很快就要离开家了。 **in 'time** after a period of time when a situation has changed 经过一段时间之后；迟早；最后；终于 SYN **eventually**: *They learned to accept their stepmother in time.* 过了一段时间之后他们学着接受他们的继母。 **in time (for sth/to do sth)** ⚷ not late; with enough time to be able to do sth 来得及；及时：*Will we be in time for the six o'clock train?* 我们来得及赶上六点钟的那趟火车吗？ ◇ *The ambulance got there just in time* (= to save sb's life). 救护车及时赶到那里。 **in your own (good) 'time** (*informal*) when you are ready and not sooner 在准备停当时：*Don't hassle him! He'll do it in his own good time.* 别唠唠叨叨地烦他了！他准备好时就会做的。 **in your own time** in your free time and not when you usually work or study 在业余时间；在空闲时 **it's aˌbout/ˌhigh 'time** ⚷ (*informal*) used to say that you think sb should do sth soon 差不多 / 现在是…的时候了：*It's about time you cleaned your room!* 你该打扫自己的房间了！ **keep up/move with the 'times** to change and develop your ideas, way of working, etc. so that you do what is modern and what is expected 跟上时代；跟着潮流 **make good, etc. 'time** to complete a journey quickly 在路上花的时间很短：*We made excellent time and arrived in Spain in two days.* 我们一路很顺当，两天后就到了西班牙。 **'many a time | 'many's the time (that)...** (*old-fashioned*) many times; frequently 多次；常常；屡屡 **ˌnine times out of 'ten | ˌninety-ˌnine times out of a 'hundred** used to say that sth is usually true or almost always happens 十有八九；几乎总是：*Nine times out of ten she gives the right answer.* 她的答案十有八九是对的。 **(and) not before 'time** = (AND) ABOUT TIME (TOO) **not give sb the ˌtime of 'day** to refuse to speak to sb because you do not like or respect them 对某人厌弃不睬：*Since the success of her novel, people shake her hand who once wouldn't have given her the time of day.* 自从她的小说获得成功之后，曾经懒得答理她的人也跟她握起手来。 **(there is) no time like the 'present** (*saying*) now is the best time to do sth, not in the future 现在是做…的最佳时机；现在不做更待何时 **of all 'time** that has ever existed 自古以来；有史以来；从未有过：*Many rated him the best singer of all time.* 许多人认为他是有史以来最优秀的歌手。 ➲ SEE ALSO ALL-TIME **take your 'time (over sth) | take your 'time to do sth/doing sth 1** ⚷ to use as much time as you need without hurrying 从容不迫；慢慢来：*There's no rush—take your time.* 别着急，慢慢来。 **2** used to say you think sb is late or is too slow in doing sth 迟到；慢慢腾腾；磨磨蹭蹭：*You certainly took your time getting here!* 你真是姗姗来迟啊！ **take time 'out** to spend some time away from your usual work or activity in order to rest or do sth else instead 抽出时间（暂停工作或活动）；忙里偷闲：*She is taking time out from her music career for a year.* 她将抽出一年的时间，暂不从事音乐事业。 ➲ SYNONYMS AT REST **ˌtime after 'time | ˌtime and (ˌtime) a'gain** often; on many or all occasions 一次又一次；一再；屡屡；总是：*You will get a perfect result time after time if you follow these instructions.* 如果你遵循这些用法说明，每次都会得到最佳的效果。 **time and a 'half** one and a half times the usual rate of pay 通常工资的一倍半 ➲ SEE ALSO DOUBLE TIME **time 'flies** (*saying*) time seems to pass very quickly 时间过得真快；光阴似箭；时光飞逝：*How time flies! I've got to go now.* 时间过得真快！现在我得走了。 ◇ *Time has flown since the holiday began.* 假日一开始，时间就过得飞快。 ORIGIN This phrase is a translation of the Latin 'tempus fugit'. 此短语译自拉丁文 tempus fugit。 **time is 'money** (*saying*) time is valuable, and should not be wasted 时间就是金钱；一寸光阴一寸金 **time is on your 'side** used to say that sb can wait for sth to happen or can wait before doing sth 有的是时间（等待某事发生或做某事） **(the) next, first, second, etc. time 'round** on the next, first, etc. occasion that the same thing happens 同样的事情下次（或第一次等）发生时：*He repeated none of the errors he'd made first time round.* 他没有重复过首次所犯下的任何错误。 ◇ *This time round it was not so easy.* 这一次这事可就不那么容易了。 **time 'was (when)...** (*old-fashioned*) used to say that sth used to happen in the past 曾经有那么个时候…；那年

T

头… **time (alone) will 'tell | only time will 'tell** *(saying)* used to say that you will have to wait for some time to find out the result of a situation（只有）时间会证明：*Only time will tell if the treatment has been successful.* 只有时间才能证明这种疗法是否成功。 **the whole 'time** = ALL THE TIME ➲ MORE AT BEAT *v.*, BIDE, BORROW, BUY *v.*, CALL *v.*, COURSE *n.*, DAY, DEVIL, EASY *adj.*, FIRST *det.*, FORTH, FULLNESS, GAIN *v.*, GIVE *v.*, HARD *adj.*, HIGH *adj.*, KILL *v.*, LONG *adj.*, LOST, LUCK *n.*, MARK *v.*, MATTER *n.*, MOVE *v.*, NICK *n.*, NINETY, OLD, ONCE *adv.*, PASS *v.*, RACE *n.*, SIGN *n.*, STITCH *n.*, SWEET *adj.*, THIN *adj.*, THIRD *ordinal number*, WHALE

■ *verb*

• **ARRANGE TIME** 安排时间 **1** [often passive] to arrange to do sth or arrange for sth to happen at a particular time 为…安排时间；选择…的时机：**~ sth (for sth)** *She timed her arrival for shortly after 3.* 她定在 3 点钟刚过到达。◇ *Their request was **badly timed*** (= it was made at the wrong time). 他们的要求提出的时机不对。◇ *'I hope we're not too early.' 'You couldn't have timed it better!'* "我希望我们没有到得太早。" "你们来的时间再合适不过了。" ◇ **~ sth to do sth** *Publication of his biography was **timed to coincide with** his 70th birthday celebrations.* 他的传记特别安排在他的 70 寿诞庆典时出版。

• **MEASURE TIME** 计量时间 **2** to measure how long it takes for sth to happen or for sb to do sth 计时；测定…所需的时间：**~ sth (at sth)** *The winner was timed at 20.4 seconds.* 获胜者用的时间为 20.4 秒。◇ **~ how long...** *Time how long it takes you to answer the questions.* 记一下自己回答这些问题所需的时间。

• **IN SPORT** 体育运动 **3 ~ sth** to hit or kick a ball at a particular moment in a sports game 在某一时刻击球（或踢球）：*She timed the pass perfectly.* 她传球的时机掌握得恰到好处。◇ *a beautifully timed shot* 时机把握得绝妙的一击 ➲ SEE ALSO ILL-TIMED, MISTIME, TIMING, WELL TIMED

PHR V **ˌtime 'out | ˌtime sth 'out** (of a computer program or task) to turn off, or turn sth off, automatically after a particular length of time even if the user has not finished（计算机程序或任务）超时自动关闭：*My satellite connection timed out—it was so frustrating.* 我的卫星连接超时自动断开了，真令人沮丧。

ˌtime-and-'motion study *noun* a study to find out how efficient a company's working methods are 时间与动作研究（为评估生产或工作效率）

'time bomb *noun* **1** a bomb that can be set to explode at a particular time 定时炸弹 **2** a situation that is likely to cause serious problems in the future 潜在危险；隐患：*Rising unemployment is a political time bomb for the government.* 日益严重的失业问题对政府来说是一枚政治上的定时炸弹。

'time capsule *noun* a container that is filled with objects that people think are typical of the time they are living in. It is buried so that it can be discovered by people in the future. 时代文物贮藏器（收藏具有时代特征的物品）

'time card *noun* (*especially NAmE*) a piece of card on which the number of hours that sb has worked are recorded, usually by a machine 考勤卡；工作时间记录卡

'time clock *noun* a special clock that records the exact time that sb starts and finishes work 考勤钟；上下班计时钟

'time-consum·ing *adj.* taking or needing a lot of time 费时的；耗时间的：*a difficult and time-consuming process* 困难而又费时的过程

'time frame *noun* the length of time that is used or available for sth（用于某事的）一段时间

'time-honoured (*especially US* **-honored**) *adj.* respected because it has been used or done for a long time 古老而受到尊重的；历史悠久的；由来已久的：*They showed their approval in the time-honoured way* (= by clapping, for example). 他们以传统的方式表示同意。

time·keep·er /ˈtaɪmkiːpə(r)/ *noun* a person who records the time that is spent doing sth, for example at work or at a sports event（工作或运动比赛等的）时间记录员，计时员

IDM **be a good/bad 'timekeeper** to be regularly on time/late for work 经常按时 / 不按时上班

time·keep·ing /ˈtaɪmkiːpɪŋ/ *noun* [U] **1** a person's ability to arrive in time for things, especially work（尤指上班的）准时，守时 **2** the activity of recording the time sth takes 计时

'time lag (*also* **lag**, **'time lapse**) *noun* the period of time between two connected events（两件相关事件的）时间间隔，时滞：*There is a long time lag between when I do the work and when I get paid.* 我做工作和领薪水之间相隔很长一段时间。

'time-lapse *adj.* [only before noun] (of photography 摄影) using a method in which a series of individual pictures of a process are shown together so that sth that really happens very slowly is shown as happening very quickly 延时拍摄的：*a time-lapse sequence of a flower opening* 一组延时拍摄花蕾开放的镜头

time·less /ˈtaɪmləs/ *adj.* (*formal*) **1** not appearing to be affected by the passing of time or by changes in fashion 不受时间影响的；无时间性的；永不过时的：*her timeless beauty* 她的永恒的美丽 **2** existing or continuing forever 永存的；永远的；永恒的；永久的 SYN **unending**：*timeless eternity* 万古长存 ▸ **time·less·ly** *adv.* **time·less·ness** *noun* [U]

'time limit *noun* the length of time within which you must do or complete sth 时限；期限；限期：*We have to set a time limit for the work.* 我们得为这项工作规定个期限。◇ *The work must be completed within a certain time limit.* 这项工作必须在一定期限内完成。

time·line /ˈtaɪmlaɪn/ *noun* a horizontal line that is used to represent time, with the past towards the left and the future towards the right 时间线，时线（用以表示时间的水平线，左边表示过去，右边表示未来）

'time lock *noun* **1** a lock with a device which prevents it from being opened until a particular time 定时锁 **2** (*computing* 计) part of a program which stops the program operating after a particular time 定时锁程序块，锁时程序块，定时锁定程序（使程序停止运行）

time·ly /ˈtaɪmli/ *adj.* happening at exactly the right time 及时的；适时的 SYN **opportune**：*A nasty incident was prevented by the timely arrival of the police.* 警察的及时到来阻止了一次严重事件。◇ *This has been **a timely reminder** to us all.* 对我们大家来说这个提醒非常及时。OPP **untimely** ▸ **time·li·ness** *noun* [U]

'time machine *noun* (in SCIENCE FICTION stories 科幻小说) a machine that enables you to travel in time to the past or the future 时间机器（能使人往返于过去或未来）

time·out /ˈtaɪmaʊt/ *noun* **1** (*NAmE*) a short period of rest during a sports game（体育比赛中的）暂停 **2** (*computing* 计) an occasion when a process or program is automatically stopped after a certain amount of time because it has not worked successfully 超时；（自动）暂停

time·pass /ˈtaɪmpɑːs; *NAmE* ˈtaɪmpæs/ *noun* [U] (*IndE*) the action of spending time doing sth, especially sth that has no aim or is not very useful 消磨时光：*She wants to have a career rather than just a few years of timepass.* 她想有一份职业，而不是漫无目的地虚度几年时光。 ▸ **time·pass** *adj.* [only before noun]：*It's a good timepass film.* 这是一部很好的休闲娱乐片。

time·piece /ˈtaɪmpiːs/ *noun* (*formal*) a clock or watch 钟；表

ˌtime-'poor *adj.* having very little or no free time because you work all the time 缺乏空闲时间的：*products for customers who are time-poor but cash-rich* 面向没闲暇但有钱的顾客的产品

timer /ˈtaɪmə(r)/ *noun* (often in compounds 常构成复合词) a device that is used to measure the time that sth takes;

T

a device that starts or stops a machine working at a particular time 时计；计时器；跑表；定时器：*an oven timer* 烤箱定时器 ➲ VISUAL VOCAB PAGE V27 ➲ SEE ALSO EGG TIMER, OLD-TIMER

ˈtime-release *adj.* [usually before noun] releasing an active substance, for example a drug, a little at a time（药等）逐渐释放的，缓释的

times /taɪmz/ **1** *prep.* (*informal*) multiplied by 乘以：*Five times two is/equals ten* (= 5 × 2 = 10). 五乘以二等于十。 **2** *noun* [pl.] used in comparisons to show how much more, better, etc. sth is than sth else （用于比较）倍：*three times as long as sth* 某物的三倍长 ◇ *three times longer than sth* 比某物长两倍 ◇ *three times the length of sth* 三倍于某物的长度 ➲ LANGUAGE BANK AT PROPORTION

ˈtime-saving *adj.* [usually before noun] that reduces the amount of time it takes to do sth 节省时间的；省时的：*time-saving devices* 省时装置

time·scale /ˈtaɪmskeɪl/ *noun* the period of time that it takes for sth to happen or be completed（事情发生或完成所需要的）一段时间，期限：*What's the timescale for the project?* 这个项目的工期是多长？

ˈtime-server *noun* (*disapproving*) a person who does as little work as possible in their job because they are just waiting until they leave for another job or retire（跳槽或退休前）得过且过的人，混日子的人 ▶ **ˈtime-serving** *adj.*, *noun* [U]

time·share /ˈtaɪmʃeə(r); *NAmE* -ʃer/ *noun* **1** (*also* **ˈtime-sharing**) [U] an arrangement in which several people own a holiday/vacation home together and each uses it at a different time of the year 分时使用度假房的办法：*timeshare apartments* 分时度假用的套房 **2** [C] a holiday/vacation home that you own in this way 分时使用的度假房：*They have a timeshare in Florida.* 他们在佛罗里达有一套分时使用的度假房。

ˈtime sheet *noun* a piece of paper on which the number of hours that sb has worked are recorded 考勤表；工作时间记录单

ˈtime signal *noun* a sound or sounds that show the exact time of day, especially a series of short high sounds that are broadcast on the radio（尤指收音机播放的）报时信号

ˈtime signature *noun* (*music* 音) a sign at the start of a piece of music, usually in the form of numbers, showing the number of beats in each BAR/MEASURE（乐谱开头的）拍号 ➲ PICTURE AT MUSIC

ˈtime span *noun* a period of time 一段时间；时段：*These changes have occurred over a long time span.* 这些变化经过了很长一段时间才形成。

ˈtime switch *noun* a switch that can be set to start and stop a machine working automatically at a particular time （自动）计时开关，定时开关：*The heating is on a time switch.* 暖气靠定时开关自动供热。

time·table 🔑 /ˈtaɪmteɪbl/ *noun, verb*

■ *noun* **1** 🔑 (*especially BrE*) (*NAmE usually* **sched·ule**) a list showing the times at which particular events will happen 时间表；时刻表：*a bus/train timetable* (= when they arrive and leave) 公共汽车 / 火车时刻表 ◇ *We have a new timetable each term* (= showing the times of each class in school). 我们每个学期都有新的课程表。 ◇ *Sport is no longer so important in the school timetable* (= all the subjects that are taught at schools). 体育课在学校的课程表上已不再是重点课。 **2** 🔑 a plan of when you expect or hope particular events to happen 预定计划；时间安排 SYN **schedule**：*I have a busy timetable this week* (= I have planned to do many things). 这个星期我的时间安排得很紧。 ◇ *The government has set out its timetable for the peace talks.* 政府已制订出和平谈判的时间表。 ➲ NOTE AT AGENDA

■ *verb* [usually passive] ~ **sth** (**for sth**) (*especially BrE*) to arrange for sth to take place at a particular time 为…安排时间 SYN **schedule**：*A series of discussion groups have been timetabled for the afternoons.* 一系列小组讨论已安排在几个下午进行。 ▶ **time·tab·ling** *noun* [U]

ˈtime trial *noun* (in cycle racing and some other sports 自行车赛等体育运动) a race in which the people who are taking part race on their own in as fast a time as possible, instead of racing against each other at the same time 计时赛

ˈtime warp *noun* an imaginary situation, described for example in SCIENCE FICTION, in which it is possible for people or things from the past or the future to move to the present 时间错位（如科幻小说中所描写，过去或将来的人或事都可能移到现在）

IDM **be (stuck) in a ˈtime warp** not having changed at all from a time in the past although everything else has 停留在过去（毫无变化）

ˈtime-wasting *noun* [U] **1** the act of wasting time 浪费时间 **2** (*BrE*) (in sport 体育运动) the act of playing more slowly towards the end of a game to prevent the opposing team from scoring （比赛接近结束时为阻止对手得分的）拖延时间 ➲ COMPARE RUN DOWN/OUT THE CLOCK at CLOCK *n.* ▶ **ˈtime-waster** *noun*

ˈtime-worn *adj.* old and used a lot, and therefore damaged, or no longer useful or interesting 陈旧的；陈腐的；日久用坏的

ˈtime zone *noun* one of the 24 areas that the world is divided into, each with its own time that is one hour behind that of the time zone immediately to the east 时区

timid /ˈtɪmɪd/ *adj.* shy and nervous; not brave 羞怯的；胆怯的；缺乏勇气的：*He stopped in the doorway, too timid to go in.* 他在门口停住了脚步，不好意思进去。 ◇ *They've been rather timid in the changes they've made* (= they've been afraid to make any big changes). 他们对所进行的变革一直小心翼翼。 ◇ *a timid voice* 羞怯的声音 ▶ **tim·id·ity** /tɪˈmɪdəti/ *noun* [U] **tim·id·ly** *adv.*

tim·ing /ˈtaɪmɪŋ/ *noun* **1** [U, C] the act of choosing when sth happens; a particular point or period of time when sth happens or is planned 定时；时间的选择；（事情发生或计划安排的）特定时间：*The timing of the decision was a complete surprise.* 选择那个时间作决定，完全出人意料。 ◇ *Please check your flight timings carefully.* 请仔细核对航班时间。 **2** [U] the skill of doing sth at exactly the right time 时机的掌握；火候的把握：*an actor with a great sense of comic timing* 一位深谙把握时机引人发笑的演员 ◇ *Your timing is perfect. I was just about to call you.* 你来得正是时候。我正要给你打电话。 **3** [U] the repeated rhythm of sth; the skill of producing this 节奏；掌握节奏的技巧：*She played the piano confidently but her timing was not good.* 她钢琴弹得很自信，但是节奏掌握得不好。 **4** [U] (*specialist*) the rate at which an electric SPARK is produced in a vehicle's engine in order to make it work（汽车发动机的）点火时间控制

tim·or·ous /ˈtɪmərəs/ *adj.* (*literary* or *formal*) nervous and easily frightened 羞怯的；胆怯的；畏怯的 SYN **timid** ▶ **tim·or·ous·ly** *adv.*

tim·pani /ˈtɪmpəni/ (*also informal* **timps** /tɪmps/) *noun* [pl.] a set of large metal drums (also called KETTLEDRUMS) in an ORCHESTRA（管弦乐队的）定音鼓 ▶ **tim·pan·ist** *noun*

tin 🔑 /tɪn/ *noun* **1** 🔑 [U] (*symb.* **Sn**) a chemical element. Tin is a soft silver-white metal that is often mixed with other metals or used to cover them to prevent them from RUSTING. 锡：*a tin mine* 锡矿 ◇ *a tin box* 锡盒 **2** 🔑 [C] (*BrE*) (*also* ˌ**tin ˈcan**, **can** *NAmE*, *BrE*) ~ (**of sth**) a metal container in which food and drink is sold; the contents of one of these containers 罐；罐头盒；罐头：*a tin of beans* 一罐青豆 ◇ *Next, add two tins of tomatoes.* 然后，加两罐番茄。 ➲ VISUAL VOCAB PAGE V36 **3** 🔑 [C] (*BrE*) (*also* **can** *NAmE*, *BrE*) ~ (**of sth**) a metal container with a lid, in the shape of a CYLINDER, in which paint, glue, etc. is sold and stored; the contents of one of these containers（盛涂料、胶水等的）马口铁罐，白铁桶；罐装物：*a tin of varnish* 一罐清漆 ◇ *The bedroom needed three tins of*

T

paint (= in order to paint it). 卧室用了三桶涂料。 **4** [C] a metal container with a lid used for keeping food in 金属食品盒: *a biscuit/cake/cookie tin* 饼干 / 蛋糕 / 曲奇饼盒 ➲ VISUAL VOCAB PAGE V36 **5** [C] (*BrE*) (*NAmE* **pan**) a metal container used for cooking food in 烘焙用的金属器皿; 烤盘; 烤模: *a cake tin* 蛋糕烤盘 ➲ VISUAL VOCAB PAGE V28

IDM **(it) does (eˌxactly) what it says on the ˈtin** (*informal, saying*) used to say that sth is as good or effective as it claims to be, or that it really does what it claims to do. This expression is especially used when you are comparing publicity and advertisements with actual products. (尤用于比较广告宣传和实际产品) 和所说的一样好，名副其实: *I paid £150 for this camera and am more than happy with it. It does exactly what it says on the tin!* 我花 150 英镑买了这架照相机，真是十分令人满意。它和广告所说的别无二致!

ˌtin ˈcan *noun* = TIN (2)

tinc·ture /ˈtɪŋktʃə(r)/ *noun* [C, U] (*specialist*) a substance dissolved in alcohol for use as a medicine 酊剂

tin·der /ˈtɪndə(r)/ *noun* [U] dry material, especially wood or grass, that burns easily and can be used to light a fire 引火物; 火绒; 火种: *The fire started late Saturday in tinder-dry grass near the Snake River.* 大火是星期六晚些时候在斯内克河附近干枯的草地上燃起的。

tin·der·box /ˈtɪndəbɒks; *NAmE* ˈtɪndərbɑːks/ *noun* **1** a box containing dry material, used in the past for lighting a fire (旧时点火用的) 火绒盒，引火盒 **2** (*formal*) a situation that is likely to become dangerous 一触即发的形势

tine /taɪn/ *noun* (*specialist*) any of the points or sharp parts of, for example, a fork or the ANTLERS of a DEER (叉子等的) 尖头，尖齿; (鹿角的) 分叉 ➲ VISUAL VOCAB PAGE V23

tin·foil /ˈtɪnfɔɪl/ *noun* [U] metal made into very thin sheets, that is used for wrapping food, etc. (包裹食物等用的) 锡箔，锡纸

tinge /tɪndʒ/ *verb, noun*

■ ***verb*** [usually passive] **1 ~ sth (with sth)** to add a small amount of colour to sth (轻微地) 给…着色，给…染色: *white petals tinged with blue* 略带蓝色的白花瓣 **2 ~ sth (with sth)** to add a small amount of a particular emotion or quality to sth 使略带…感情 (或性质): *a look of surprise tinged with disapproval* 带有几分不满的惊奇神情

■ ***noun*** [usually sing.] a small amount of a colour, feeling or quality 微量，少许，一丝，几分 (颜色、感情或性质): *to feel a tinge of envy* 感到几分妒忌 ◇ *There was a faint pink tinge to the sky.* 天空略带一点淡淡的粉红色。 ➲ SYNONYMS AT COLOUR

tin·gle /ˈtɪŋɡl/ *verb, noun*

■ ***verb*** **1** [I] (of a part of your body 身体部位) to feel as if a lot of small sharp points are pushing into it 感到刺痛: *The cold air made her face tingle.* 冷空气冻得她的脸发痛。 ◇ *a tingling sensation* 刺痛感 ➲ SYNONYMS AT HURT **2** [I] **~ with sth** to feel an emotion strongly 强烈地感到: *She was still tingling with excitement.* 她仍然兴奋不已。

■ ***noun*** [usually sing.] (*also* **ting·ling** [sing., U]) **1** a slight stinging or uncomfortable feeling in a part of your body 刺痛感 **2** an exciting or uncomfortable feeling of emotion 激动感; 兴奋感; 震颤: *to feel a tingle of excitement* 感到一阵激动

tin·gly /ˈtɪŋɡli/ *adj.* causing or experiencing a slight feeling of tingling 引起 (或感到) 轻微刺痛的: *a tingly sensation* 刺痛感

tin·ker /ˈtɪŋkə(r)/ *noun, verb*

■ ***noun*** (in the past) a person who travelled from place to place, selling or repairing things (旧时走街串巷的) 小炉匠，补锅匠，白铁匠

■ ***verb*** [I] **~ (with sth)** to make small changes to sth in order to repair or improve it, especially in a way that may not be helpful (尤指不起作用地) 小修补，小修理

tin·kle /ˈtɪŋkl/ *noun, verb*

■ ***noun*** [usually sing.] **1** (*also* **tink·ling** [sing., U]) a light high ringing sound 丁零声; 当啷响: *the tinkle of glass breaking* 玻璃破碎发出的当啷声 **2** (*old-fashioned, BrE, informal*) a telephone call 电话通话 **3** (*informal*) an act of URINATING 撒尿; 小便: *to have a tinkle* 撒尿

■ ***verb*** [I, T] **~ (sth)** to make a series of light high ringing sounds; to make sth produce this sound (使) 发出叮当声，丁零响: *A bell tinkled as the door opened.* 房门一开，铃声丁零响了。 ◇ *tinkling laughter* 银铃般的笑声

tinned /tɪnd/ (*BrE*) (*also* **canned** *NAmE, BrE*) *adj.* (of food 食物) preserved in a can 罐装的: *tinned fruit* 罐头水果

tin·nitus /ˈtɪnɪtəs/ *noun* [U] (*medical* 医) an unpleasant condition in which sb hears ringing in their ears 耳鸣

tinny /ˈtɪni/ *adj., noun*

■ ***adj.*** (*especially BrE, disapproving*) **1** having a high thin sound like small pieces of metal hitting each other (声音) 尖细的，尖声尖气的，如金属片碰撞声般的 **2** having a taste like metal 有金属味的: *The beer tasted tinny.* 这啤酒喝起来有金属味。

■ ***noun*** (*also* **tin·nie**) (*pl.* **-ies**) (*AustralE, NZE, informal*) a can of beer 一罐啤酒

ˈtin opener (*BrE*) (*also* **ˈcan opener** *NAmE, BrE*) *noun* a kitchen UTENSIL (= a tool) for opening tins of food 开罐器; 罐头刀; 罐头起子 ➲ VISUAL VOCAB PAGE V27

ˌTin Pan ˈAlley *noun* [U] (*old-fashioned, informal*) people who write and publish popular songs 流行歌曲作者和发行人 ORIGIN From the name of the part of New York where many such people worked in the past. 源自旧时纽约的流行歌曲作者和发行人聚集区名称。

tin·plate /ˈtɪnpleɪt/ *noun* [U] a metal material made from iron and steel and covered with a layer of tin 镀锡铁皮; 马口铁

tin·pot /ˈtɪnpɒt; *NAmE* -pɑːt/ *adj.* [only before noun] (*disapproving*) (especially of a leader or government 尤指领导人或政府) not important and of little worth or use 无足轻重的; 不起作用的: *a tinpot dictator* 领导无方的独裁者

tin·sel /ˈtɪnsl/ *noun* [U] strips of shiny material like metal, used as decorations, especially at Christmas (尤指圣诞节时装饰用的) 光片，金属箔，金属丝

Tin·sel·town /ˈtɪnsltaʊn/ *noun* [U] (*informal*) a way of referring to Hollywood in California, the centre of the US movie industry 星光熠熠之城 (指位于加利福尼亚的美国电影业中心好莱坞)

tint /tɪnt/ *noun, verb*

■ ***noun*** **1** a shade or small amount of a particular colour; a faint colour covering a surface 色调; 淡色彩; (一层) 淡色，浅色: *leaves with red and gold autumn tints* 金秋时节略呈红黄色的树叶 ◇ *the brownish tint of an old photo* 旧照片的淡褐色 ➲ SYNONYMS AT COLOUR **2** an artificial colour used to change the colour of your hair; the act of colouring the hair with a tint 染发剂; 染发: *a blond tint* 金黄色染发剂 ◇ *to have a tint* 染发

■ ***verb*** **1** [usually passive] **~ sth (with sth)** to add a small amount of colour to sth 为…轻微染色; 给…略微着色 **2 ~ sth** to change the colour of sb's hair with a tint 染 (发)
▸ **tint·ed** *adj.*: *tinted glasses* 有色眼镜

ˌT-interˈsec·tion (*NAmE*) (*BrE* **ˈT-junction**) *noun* a place where one road joins another but does not cross it, so that the roads form the shape of the letter T 丁字路口

tin·tin·nabu·la·tion /ˌtɪntɪnæbjuˈleɪʃn/ *noun* [U, C] (*formal*) a ringing sound 叮当声; 丁零声

ˌtin ˈwhistle (*also* **ˌpenny ˈwhistle**) *noun* a simple musical instrument like a short pipe with six holes, that you play by blowing 六孔小笛; 六孔哨

tiny 🔑 /ˈtaɪni/ *adj.* (**tini·er**, **tini·est**) very small in size or amount 极小的; 微小的; 微量的: *a tiny baby* 纤弱的婴儿 ◇ *Only a tiny minority hold such extreme views.* 只有极少数人持这样极端的观点。 IDM SEE PATTER *n.*

-tion ➲ -ION

T

tip /tɪp/ *noun, verb*

■ ***noun***

• **END OF STH** 末端 **1** the thin pointed end of sth 尖端；尖儿；端：*the tips of your fingers* 手指尖 ◇ *the tip of your nose* 你的鼻尖 ◇ *the northern tip of the island* 岛的北端 ➲ SEE ALSO FINGERTIP **2** a small part that fits on or over the end of sth（装在顶端的）小部件：*a walking stick with a rubber tip* 带橡皮头的手杖 ➲ SEE ALSO FELT-TIP PEN, FILTER TIP

• **ADVICE** 建议 **3** a small piece of advice about sth practical 指点；实用的提示 SYN **hint**： **~ (on/for doing sth)** *handy tips for buying a computer* 购买电脑几点有用的提示 ◇ **~ (on/for sth)** *useful tips on how to save money* 几个省钱的窍门儿 **4** (*informal*) a secret or expert piece of advice about what the result of a competition, etc. is likely to be, especially about which horse is likely to win a race（尤指有关赛马的）内幕消息，指点： *a **hot tip** for the big race* 赛马大赛的最新内幕消息 **5** (*NAmE*) (*also* **'tip-off** *especially in BrE*) (*informal*) secret information that sb gives, for example to the police, to warn them about an illegal activity that is going to happen 举报；密报；线报： *The man was arrested after an anonymous tip.* 有人匿名举报后，那个人被抓了起来。

• **EXTRA MONEY** 额外的钱 **6** a small amount of extra money that you give to sb, for example sb who serves you in a restaurant 小费；小账：*to **leave a tip*** 留小费 ◇ *He **gave** the waiter **a** generous **tip**.* 他给了服务员很多小费。

• **FOR RUBBISH** 垃圾 **7** (*BrE*) a place where you can take rubbish/garbage and leave it 垃圾场；垃圾堆

• **UNTIDY PLACE** 脏乱处 **8** (*BrE, informal, disapproving*) an untidy place 脏乱的地方 SYN **dump**： *Their flat is a tip!* 他们的寓所简直是个猪窝！

IDM **on the tip of your 'tongue** if a word or name is **on the tip of your tongue**, you are sure that you know it but you cannot remember it 话在嘴边上（却一时想不起来） **the tip of the 'iceberg** only a small part of a much larger problem（问题的）冰山一角

■ ***verb*** (**-pp-**)

• **LEAN/POUR/PUSH AT AN ANGLE** 倾斜地倚 / 倒 / 推 **1** [I, T] to move so that one end or side is higher than the other; to move sth into this position （使）倾斜，倾倒，翻覆 SYN **tilt**： **(+ adv./prep.)** *The boat tipped to one side.* 船向一边倾斜。◇ *The seat tips forward to allow passengers into the back.* 座位向前放倒，好让乘客进入车的后部。◇ **~ sth (+ adv./prep.)** *She tipped her head back and laughed loudly.* 她把头一仰，哈哈大笑起来。 **2** [T] **~ sth/sb + adv./prep.** to make sth/sb come out of a container or its/their position by holding or lifting it/them at an angle 倒出；倾倒；倾覆： *She tipped the dirty water down the drain.* 她把脏水倒入了下水道。◇ *The bus stopped abruptly, nearly tipping me out of my seat.* 公共汽车突然刹车，差点儿把我从座位上甩出去。 **3** [T] **~ sth + adv./prep.** to touch sth lightly so that it moves in a particular direction 轻触；轻碰： *The goalkeeper just managed to tip the ball over the crossbar.* 守门员刚好把球捅出球门的横梁。

• **LEAVE RUBBISH** 丢垃圾 **4** [I, T] **~ (sth)** (*BrE*) to leave rubbish/garbage somewhere outdoors in order to get rid of it （在户外）倒垃圾： *'No tipping.'* (= for example, on a notice) "此处禁止倒垃圾。"

• **GIVE EXTRA MONEY** 额外付款 **5** [I, T] to give sb an extra amount of money to thank them for sth they have done for you as part of their job 给小费；付小账： *Americans were always welcome because they tended to tip heavily.* 美国人总是受欢迎，因为他们往往给很多小费。◇ **~ sb** *Did you remember to tip the waiter?* 你记得给服务员小费了吗？◇ **~ sb sth** *She tipped the porter a dollar.* 她给了行李工一美元的小费。

• **PREDICT SUCCESS** 预测成功 **6** [T] (*especially BrE*) to say in advance that sb/sth will be successful 预言…获胜；事先说…会成功： **~ sb/sth (for sth)** *The band is being tipped for the top.* 人们说这支乐队将位居榜首。◇ **~ sb/sth as sth** *The senator has been tipped by many as a future president.* 许多人猜测这位参议员将会继任总统。◇ **~ sb/sth to do sth** *The actor is tipped to win an Oscar for his performance.* 这位演员因表演出色而被认为有望获得奥斯卡奖。

• **COVER END** 覆盖端头 **7** [T, usually passive] **~ sth (with sth)** to cover the end or edge of sth with a colour, a substance, etc. （用颜色、物质等）覆盖…的末端，遮盖…的边： *The wings are tipped with yellow.* 翅膀的尖端呈黄色。

IDM **it is/was 'tipping (it) down** (*BrE, informal*) it is/was raining heavily 大雨倾盆；大雨如注 **tip the 'balance/'scales** (*also* **swing the 'balance**) to affect the result of sth in one way rather than another 使天平倾斜；使结果倾向某方；起决定性作用： *In an interview, smart presentation can tip the scales in your favour.* 在面试中，机敏的表现是一种有利的条件。 **tip your 'hand** (*NAmE*) (*BrE* **show your 'hand/'cards**) to make your plans or intentions known 摊牌；让对方摸着底细；公开自己的意图 **tip the scales at sth** to weigh a particular amount 重量为： *He tipped the scales at just over 80 kilos.* 他称得体重刚过 80 公斤。 **tip sb the 'wink | tip the 'wink to sb** (*BrE, informal*) to give sb secret information that they can use to gain an advantage for themselves 给某人密送情报 ➲ MORE AT HAT

PHR V **,tip sb↔'off (about sth)** (*informal*) to warn sb about sth that is going to happen, especially sth illegal 暗中警告，私下告诫，密报（尤指非法的事情）： *Three men were arrested after police were tipped off about the raid.* 警方获得有关袭击的密报后，逮捕了三个人。◇ **tip sb off that...** *They were tipped off that he might be living in Wales.* 他们探得风声，他现在可能住在威尔士。 ➲ RELATED NOUN TIP-OFF **,tip 'up/'over | ,tip sth↔'up/'over** to fall or turn over; to make sth do this （使）跌倒，倾覆： *The mug tipped over, spilling hot coffee everywhere.* 杯子倒了，热咖啡溅得到处都是。◇ *We'll have to tip the sofa up to get it through the door.* 我们必须把沙发翻转过来才能搬过房门。

'tip-off *noun* (*especially BrE*) (*NAmE usually* **tip**) (*informal*) secret information that sb gives, for example to the police, to warn them about an illegal activity that is going to happen 举报；密告；线报： *The man was arrested after an anonymous tip-off.* 有人匿名举报后，那个人被抓了起来。

tip·per /'tɪpə(r)/ *noun* **1** (used with an adjective 与形容词连用) a person who gives sb a TIP (= a small amount of extra money to thank them for doing sth as part of their job) of the size mentioned 给…小费者；给赏钱者： *She says that Americans are usually big tippers.* 她说美国人通常给小费很大方。 **2** (*also* **'tipper lorry/truck**) a lorry/truck with a container part that can be moved into a sloping position so that its load can slide off at the back 翻斗卡车；自卸货卡车

tip·pet /'tɪpɪt/ *noun* a long piece of fur worn in the past by a woman around the neck and shoulders, with the ends hanging down in front; a similar piece of clothing worn by judges, priests, etc. 蒂皮特披巾（旧时的女式毛皮披巾）；（法官、教士等所披的）黑色圣带

Tipp-Ex™ /'tɪpeks/ *noun* [U] (*BrE*) a liquid, usually white, that you use to cover mistakes that you make when you are writing or typing, and that you can write on top of; a type of CORRECTION FLUID 迪美斯修正液；修正液 ▸ **tip·pex** *verb* : **~ sth (out)** *I tippexed out the mistakes.* 我用修正液涂改了错误。

'tipping point *noun* the point at which the number of small changes over a period of time reaches a level where a further small change has a sudden and very great effect on a system or leads to an idea suddenly spreading quickly among a large number of people（个案积累终成大趋势的）引爆点，爆发点

tip·ple /'tɪpl/ *noun, verb*

■ ***noun*** [usually sing.] (*informal, especially BrE*) an alcoholic drink 含酒精饮料： *His favourite tipple was rum and lemon.* 他最爱喝的饮料是朗姆酒加柠檬汁。

■ ***verb*** [I, T] **~ (sth)** (*informal, especially BrE*) to drink alcohol 饮酒 ▸ **tip·pler** /'tɪplə(r)/ *noun*

tip·ster /'tɪpstə(r)/ *noun* **1** a person who tells you, often in exchange for money, which horse is likely to win a race, so that you can bet on it and win money 提供赛马情报的人（常指贩卖情报者） **2** (*especially NAmE*) a person who gives information to the police about a crime or criminal（犯罪行为等的）举报者，告密者

tipsy /ˈtɪpsi/ *adj.* (*informal*) slightly drunk 微醉的；略有醉意的 **SYN** **tight**

tip·toe /ˈtɪptəʊ; *NAmE* -toʊ/ *noun, verb*

■ ***noun***

IDM **on ˈtiptoe/ˈtiptoes** standing or walking on the front part of your foot, with your heels off the ground, in order to make yourself taller or to move very quietly 踮着脚；蹑手蹑脚：*She had to stand on tiptoe to reach the top shelf.* 她得踮着脚才能够到顶层搁架。◇ *We crept around on tiptoes so as not to disturb him.* 我们蹑手蹑脚地在周围走动，以免惊动他。

■ ***verb*** [I] (**+ adv./prep.**) to walk using the front parts of your feet only, so that other people cannot hear you 踮着脚走；蹑手蹑脚地走：*I tiptoed over to the window.* 我踮着脚走到窗前。

ˌtip-ˈtop *adj.* [usually before noun] (*informal*) excellent 极好的；头等的；一流的：*The house is **in tip-top condition**.* 这座房子的状况没得挑。

ˈtip-up *adj.* (of a seat 座位) moving up into a vertical position when nobody is sitting in it（无人坐时）自动上翻的，自动收起的

tir·ade /taɪˈreɪd; *NAmE* ˈtaɪreɪd/ *noun* ~ (**against sb/sth**) a long angry speech criticizing sb/sth or accusing sb of sth（批评或指责性的）长篇激烈讲话：*She launched into a tirade of abuse against politicians.* 她发表了长篇演说，愤怒地谴责政客。

tire 🔑 /ˈtaɪə(r)/ *verb, noun*

■ ***verb*** [I, T] ~ (**sb**) to become tired and feel as if you want to sleep or rest; to make sb feel this way（使）疲劳，疲倦，困倦：*Her legs were beginning to tire.* 她的双腿开始感到累了。◇ *He has made a good recovery but still tires easily.* 他已康复得不错，但仍然容易感到疲劳。

IDM **never tire of doing sth** to do sth a lot, especially in a way that annoys people 不厌其烦地做：*He went to Harvard—as he never tires of reminding us.* 他上过哈佛，他总是不厌其烦地一再提醒我们这一点。

PHR V **ˈtire of sth/sb** to become bored with sth/sb or begin to enjoy it/them less 对…感到厌倦；对…腻烦：*They soon tired of the beach and went for a walk.* 他们很快对海滩腻烦了，便去散步。 **ˌtire sb/yourself ˈout** 🔑 to make sb/yourself feel very tired 使感到筋疲力尽；使感到疲惫不堪 ➲ SEE ALSO TIRED

■ ***noun*** 🔑 (*NAmE*) (*BrE* **tyre**) a thick rubber ring that fits around the edge of a wheel of a car, bicycle, etc. 轮胎：*a **front tire*** 前胎 ◇ *a **back/rear tire*** 后胎 ◇ *to **pump up** a tire* 给轮胎打气 ◇ *a **flat/burst/punctured tire*** 瘪了的/爆了的/扎了的轮胎 ◇ ***bald/worn tires*** 磨平的/磨损的轮胎 ◇ *to check your tire pressure* 检查胎压 ➲ VISUAL VOCAB PAGES V55, V56 ➲ SEE ALSO SPARE TYRE (1)

tired 🔑 /ˈtaɪəd; *NAmE* ˈtaɪərd/ *adj.* **1** 🔑 feeling that you would like to sleep or rest; needing rest 疲倦的；疲劳的；困倦的 **SYN** **weary**：*to **be/look/feel tired*** 感到/显得/觉得疲惫 ◇ *I'm too tired even to think.* 我累得连想也不愿意想。◇ *They were cold, hungry and **tired out*** (= very tired). 他们又冷又饿，疲惫不堪。◇ *tired feet* 疲劳的双脚 ➲ WORDFINDER NOTE AT SLEEP **2** 🔑 feeling that you have had enough of sb/sth because you no longer find them/it interesting or because they make you angry or unhappy 厌倦；厌烦：~ **of sb/sth** *I'm **sick and tired** of all the arguments.* 我对所有这些争论烦透了。◇ ~ **of doing sth** *She was tired of hearing about their trip to India.* 她听腻了他们的印度之行。 **3** boring because it is too familiar or has been used too much 陈旧的；陈腐的；陈词滥调的：*He always comes out with the same tired old jokes.* 他总是讲些千篇一律老掉牙的笑话。 ▶ **tired·ly** *adv.*：*He shook his head tiredly.* 他厌倦地摇了摇头。 **tired·ness** *noun* [U] ➲ SEE ALSO DOG-TIRED

ˈtire iron *noun* (*NAmE*) a metal tool for taking tyres off wheels 拆轮胎棒

tire·less /ˈtaɪələs; *NAmE* ˈtaɪərləs/ *adj.* (*approving*) putting a lot of hard work and energy into sth over a long period of time 不知疲倦的；不觉疲劳的；精力充沛的 **SYN** **indefatigable**：*a tireless campaigner for human rights* 不屈不挠的人权运动参与者 ▶ **tire·less·ly** *adv.*

tire·some /ˈtaɪəsəm; *NAmE* ˈtaɪərsəm/ *adj.* making you feel annoyed 讨厌的；令人厌烦的；烦人的 **SYN** **annoying**：*Buying a house can be a very tiresome business.* 买房子有时是件很麻烦的事。◇ *The children were being very tiresome.* 这些孩子非常讨人嫌。 ▶ **tire·some·ly** *adv.*

tir·ing 🔑 /ˈtaɪərɪŋ/ *adj.* making you feel the need to sleep or rest 令人困倦的；使人疲劳的；累人的 **SYN** **exhausting**：*It had been a long tiring day.* 这一天让人感到又累又长。

'tis /tɪz/ *short form* (*old use*) it is

tis·sue /ˈtɪʃuː; *BrE also* ˈtɪsjuː/ *noun* **1** [U] (*also* **tissues** [pl.]) a collection of cells that form the different parts of humans, animals and plants（人、动植物细胞的）组织：***muscle/brain/nerve, etc. tissue*** 肌肉、大脑、神经等组织 ◇ *scar tissue* 瘢痕组织 **2** [C] a piece of soft paper that absorbs liquids, used especially as a HANDKERCHIEF（尤指用作手帕的）纸巾，手巾纸：*a box of tissues* 一盒纸巾 **3** (*also* **ˈtissue paper**) [U] very thin paper used for wrapping and packing things that break easily（用于包装易碎物品的）薄纸，绵纸

IDM **a ˌtissue of ˈlies** (*literary*) a story, an excuse, etc. that is full of lies 一派谎言

tit /tɪt/ *noun* **1** [usually pl.] (*also* **titty**) (*taboo, slang*) a woman's breast or NIPPLE（女人的）奶子，奶头，乳头 **2** (*BrE, slang*) a stupid person 蠢货；笨蛋；窝囊废 **3** a small European bird. There are several types of tit. 山雀：*a great tit* 大山雀 ➲ SEE ALSO BLUE TIT

Titan /ˈtaɪtn/ (*also* **titan**) *noun* (*formal*) a person who is very large, strong, intelligent or important 巨人；高人；伟人 ➲ MORE LIKE THIS 16, page R27 **ORIGIN** From the **Titans**, who in Greek mythology were the older gods who were defeated in a battle with Zeus. 源自提坦诸神（Titans），在希腊神话中被宙斯打败的众巨神。

ti·tan·ic /taɪˈtænɪk/ *adj.* (*formal*) very large, important, strong or difficult 巨大的；极重要的；强大的；极艰巨的：*a titanic struggle between good and evil* 善与恶之间的一场大搏斗

ti·tan·ium /tɪˈteɪniəm/ *noun* [U] (*symb.* **Ti**) a chemical element. Titanium is a silver-white metal used in making various strong light materials. 钛

tit·bit /ˈtɪtbɪt/ (*BrE*) (*NAmE* **tid·bit**) *noun* **1** a small special piece of food 小片食物 **SYN** **morsel** **2** a small but interesting piece of news 花絮；趣闻；逸事 **SYN** **snippet**：*titbits of gossip* 蜚短流长

titch /tɪtʃ/ *noun* (*BrE, informal, often humorous*) used as a way of talking about or addressing a very small person（用于谈论或称呼）小不点儿，娃儿

titchy /ˈtɪtʃi/ *adj.* (*BrE, informal*) very small 很小的

ˌtit for ˈtat *noun* [U] a situation in which you do sth bad to sb because they have done the same to you 以牙还牙；针锋相对；一报还一报：*the routine tit for tat when countries expel each other's envoys* 国家相互驱逐对方使节这种惯常的报复行动 ◇ *tit-for-tat assassinations by rival gangs* 敌对团伙冤冤相报的暗杀

tithe /taɪð/ *noun* **1** (in the past) a tenth of the goods that sb produced or the money that they earned, that was paid as a tax to support the Church（旧时按固定比例给教会的）什一税 **2** (in some Christian Churches today) a tenth of a person's income, that they give to the Church（现在某些教友按收入的十分之一给基督教教会的）什一捐献

tit·il·late /ˈtɪtɪleɪt/ *verb* [I, T] (*often disapproving*) to interest or excite sb, especially in a sexual way 使兴奋；煽情；煽动情欲：*titillating pictures* 煽动情欲的图画 ◇ ~ **sth** *a story intended to titillate the imagination of the public* 意欲煽动公众想象力的故事 ▶ **tit·il·la·tion** /ˌtɪtɪˈleɪʃn/ *noun* [U]

titi·vate /ˈtɪtɪveɪt/ *verb* **~ sth** to improve the appearance of sb/sth by making small changes 打扮；装扮；装点

title /ˈtaɪtl/ *noun, verb*

■ ***noun*** **1** [C] the name of a book, poem, painting, piece of music, etc.（书、诗歌、图画、乐曲等的）名称，标题，题目：*His poems were published under the title of 'Love and Reason'.* 他的诗是以《爱情与理智》为题发表的。◇ *the* ***title track*** *from their latest CD* (= the song with the same title as the disc) 他们最新 CD 的同名主打歌 ◇ *She has sung the title role in 'Carmen'* (= the role of Carmen in that OPERA). 她在《卡门》中演唱卡门的角色。 ➲ WORDFINDER NOTE AT BOOK **2** [C] a particular book or magazine（书刊的）一种，一本：*The company publishes twenty new titles a year.* 这家公司一年出版二十种新书。 **3** [C] a word in front of a person's name to show their rank or profession, whether or not they are married, etc.（人名前表示地位、职业、婚否等的）称号，头衔，职称，称谓：*The present duke inherited the title from his father.* 现在的公爵承袭的是他父亲的爵位。◇ *Give your name and title* (= Mr, Miss, Ms, Dr, etc.). 报出你的姓名和称谓。 ➲ NOTE AT NAME **4** [C] a name that describes a job 职位名称；职称：*The official title of the job is 'Administrative Assistant'.* 这个职位的正式名称为"行政助理"。 **5** [C] the position of being the winner of a competition, especially a sports competition（竞赛、体育比赛的）冠军：*the world heavyweight title* 重量级世界拳击冠军 ◇ *She has three world titles.* 她已获得三项世界冠军。 **6** [U, C] **~ (to sth/to do sth)** (*law* 律) the legal right to own sth, especially land or property; the document that shows you have this right（尤指土地或财产的）所有权，所有权凭证，房地契

■ ***verb*** [usually passive] **~ sth + noun** to give a book, piece of music, etc. a particular name（给书、乐曲等）加标题，定题目：*Their first album was titled 'Made in Valmez'.* 他们的第一张专辑定名为 Made in Valmez。

ˈtitle bar *noun* (*computing* 计) a bar at the top of a computer screen, which shows the name of the program and file that is on the screen（计算机屏幕顶端的）标题栏

titled /ˈtaɪtld/ *adj.* having a title such as Lord, LADY, etc. 有头衔的；有爵位的

ˈtitle deed *noun* [usually pl.] a legal document proving that sb is the owner of a particular house, etc. 房契；产权契约；所有权凭证

ˈtitle-holder *noun* **1** a person or team that has defeated all the other people or teams taking part in an important competition 冠军；冠军得主：*the current Olympic title-holder* 本届奥林匹克运动会冠军 **2** (*specialist, NAmE*) the legal owner of sth 法定所有人；合法所有人

ˈtitle page *noun* a page at the front of a book that has the title and the author's name on it（书的）标题页，书名页，扉页

ti·trate /taɪˈtreɪt; tɪ-/ *verb* **~ sth** (*chemistry* 化) to find out how much of a particular substance is in a liquid by measuring how much of another substance is needed to react with it 滴定测量（液体中的物质） ▶ **ti·tra·tion** /-ˈtreɪʃn/ *noun* [U]

tit·ter /ˈtɪtə(r)/ *verb* [I] to laugh quietly, especially in a nervous or embarrassed way（尤指紧张或尴尬地）傻笑，嗤嗤地笑；窃笑 SYN **giggle** ▶ **tit·ter** *noun*

tittle-tattle /ˈtɪtl tætl/ *noun* [U] (*informal, disapproving*) unimportant talk, usually not true, about other people and their lives 闲聊；蜚短流长；张家长李家短 SYN **gossip** ➲ MORE LIKE THIS 11, page R26

titty /ˈtɪti/ *noun* (*pl.* **-ies**) (*slang*) = TIT (1)

titu·lar /ˈtɪtjulə(r); *NAmE* -tʃə-/ *adj.* [only before noun] **1** (*formal*) having a particular title or status but no real power or authority 名义上的；有名无实的；徒有虚名的 SYN **nominal**：*the titular head of state* 名义上的国家元首 **2** the **titular** character of a book, play, film/movie, etc. is the one mentioned in the title 标题的；被用作标题的 SYN **eponymous**

tizzy /ˈtɪzi/ (*also* **tizz** /tɪz/) *noun* [sing.] (*informal*) a state of nervous excitement or confusion 紧张；慌张；慌乱：*She was in a real tizzy before the meeting.* 她在会前感到心慌意乱。

ˈT-junction (*BrE*) (*NAmE* **ˌT-interˈsection**) *noun* a place where one road joins another but does not cross it, so that the roads form the shape of the letter T 丁字路口

TLC /ˌtiː el ˈsiː/ *noun* [U] (*informal*) the abbreviation for 'tender loving care' (care that you give sb to make them feel better) 亲切的照料（全写为 tender loving care）：*What he needs now is just rest and a lot of TLC.* 他现在需要的只是休息和充分的亲切关怀。

Tlin·git /ˈtlɪŋɡɪt/ *noun* (*pl.* **Tlin·git** or **Tlin·gits**) a member of a Native American people, many of whom live in the US state of Alaska 特林吉特人（美洲土著，很多居于美国阿拉斯加州）

TM /ˌtiː ˈem/ *abbr.* **1** TRADEMARK 商标 **2** (*US* **T.M.**) TRANSCENDENTAL MEDITATION 超觉静坐（静思默念真言）

tme·sis /ˈtmiːsɪs/ *noun* [U, C] (*pl.* **tme·ses** /-siːz/) (*linguistics* 语言) the use of a word or words in the middle of another word, for example 'abso-bloody-lutely' 分割插入法（在词的中间插入其他词，如 abso-bloody-lutely）；插词

TMI (*also* **tmi**) *abbr.* (*informal*) (used in emails or TEXT MESSAGES to say that sb has given some personal information that is embarrassing) too much information 信息过多，说得太多（电邮或手机短信用语，表示对方透露了令人难堪的个人隐私，全写为 too much information）：*I needed to go to the bathroom very badly—sorry, TMI!* 我急着要上厕所。噢，我说太多了！

TNT /ˌtiː en ˈtiː/ *noun* [U] a powerful EXPLOSIVE 三硝基甲苯；梯恩梯；黄色炸药

to /tə; *before vowels* tu; *strong form* tuː/ *prep., infinitive marker, adv.*

■ ***prep.*** HELP For the special uses of **to** in phrasal verbs, look at the entries for the verbs. For example **see to sth** is in the phrasal verb section at **see**. * to 在短语动词中的特殊用法见有关动词词条。如 see to sth 在词条 see 的短语动词部分。 **1** in the direction of sth; towards sth 向，朝，往，对着（某方向或某处）：*I walked to the office.* 我朝办公室走去。◇ *It fell to the ground.* 它掉到了地上。◇ *It was on the way to the station.* 那是在去火车站的路上。◇ *He's going to Paris.* 他就要去巴黎了。◇ *my first visit to Africa* 我对非洲的第一次访问 ◇ *He pointed to something on the opposite bank.* 他指向对岸的某样东西。 ◇ *Her childhood was spent travelling from place to place.* 她的童年是在不断迁移中度过的。 **2** **~ the sth (of sth)** located in the direction mentioned from sth 位于…方向：*Place the cursor to the left of the first word.* 把光标置于第一个单词的左边。◇ *There are mountains to the north.* 北面有山。 **3** as far as sth 到，达（某处）：*The meadows lead down to the river.* 牧场一直延伸到河边。◇ *Her hair fell to her waist.* 她的长发一直垂到腰部。 **4** reaching a particular state 到，达（某种状态）：*The vegetables were cooked to perfection.* 这些蔬菜烧的火候恰到好处。◇ *He tore the letter to pieces.* 他把信撕碎了。◇ *She sang the baby to sleep.* 她唱着歌把孩子哄睡了。◇ *The letter reduced her to tears* (= made her cry). 那封信让她落泪了。 ◇ *His expression changed from amazement to joy.* 他的表情由惊变喜。 **5** used to show the end or limit of a range or period of time（表示范围或一段时间的结尾或界限）到，至：*a drop in profits from $105 million to around $75 million* 利润从 1.05 亿美元降到 7 500 万美元左右 ◇ *I'd say he was 25 to 30 years old* (= approximately 25 or 30 years old). 我猜他在 25 至 30 岁之间。◇ *I like all kinds of music from opera to reggae.* 我喜欢各种音乐，从歌剧到雷盖都喜欢。 ◇ *We only work from Monday to Friday.* 我们仅从星期一工作到星期五。◇ *I watched the programme from beginning to end.* 这个节目我从头看到了尾。 **6** before the start of sth 在…开始之前；离；差：*How long is it to lunch?* 离吃午饭还有多久？ ◇ (*especially BrE*) *It's five to ten* (= five minutes before ten o'clock). 现在是十点差五分。 **7** used to show the person or thing that receives sth（引出接受者）给，予，向：*He gave it to his sister.* 他把那给了他的妹妹。◇ *I'll explain to you where everything goes.* 我会向你解释所有东西的摆放位置。◇ *I am deeply grateful to my parents.* 我打心里感谢我的父母。◇ *Who did she address the letter to?* 那封信她是写给谁的？◇ (*formal*) *To whom did she address the letter?* 那封信她是写给谁的？ **8** used to show the person or thing that is affected by an action（引出受事者或受体）对于，关于：*She is devoted to her family.* 她深深爱着自己的家庭。◇ *What have you done to your hair?* 你怎么把头发弄成这个样子？ **9** used to show that two things are attached or connected（表示两件事物相接或相连）：*Attach this rope to the front of the car.* 把这绳子系在小轿车的前面。 **10** used to show a relationship between one person or thing and another（表示两人或事物之间的关系）属于，归于，关于，对于：*She's married to an Italian.* 她嫁给了一个意大利人。◇ *the Japanese ambassador to France* 日本驻法大使 ◇ *the key to the door* 这个门的钥匙 ◇ *the solution to this problem* 解决这个问题的办法 **11** directed towards; concerning 指向；关于：*It was a threat to world peace.* 这是对世界和平的威胁。◇ *She made a reference to her recent book.* 她提到了自己最近的那本书。 **12** used to introduce the second part of a comparison or RATIO（引出比较或比率的第二部分）比：*I prefer walking to climbing.* 我喜欢散步多于喜欢爬山。◇ *The industry today is nothing to what it once was.* 这一行业的现状与昔日的盛况相比微不足道。◇ *We won by six goals to three.* 我们以六比三获胜。 **13** used to show a quantity or rate（表示数量或比率）等于，每，一：*There are 2.54 centimetres to an inch.* 一英寸等于 2.54 厘米。◇ *This car does 30 miles to the gallon.* 这辆汽车每加仑汽油可行驶 30 英里。➲ COMPARE PER **14** in honour of sb/sth 向…表示敬意：*a monument to the soldiers who died in the war* 阵亡将士纪念碑 ◇ *Let's drink to Julia and her new job.* 让咱们为朱莉娅和她的新工作干杯。 **15** while sth else is happening or being done 伴随；随同：*He left the stage to prolonged applause.* 他在经久不息的掌声中退下了舞台。 **16** used after verbs of movement to mean 'with the intention of giving sth'（用于表示动作的动词之后）为了给，以提供：*People rushed to her rescue and picked her up.* 人们冲上前来把她救起。 **17** used to show sb's attitude or reaction to sth（表示态度或反应）适合，符合，致使：*His music isn't really to my taste.* 他的音乐不太合我的口味。◇ *To her astonishment, he smiled.* 使她惊讶的是，他笑了。 **18** used to show what sb's opinion or feeling about sth is（表示看法或感觉）按…的看法，据…认为：*It sounded like crying to me.* 在我听来这像哭。

■ ***infinitive marker*** HELP **To** is often used before the base form of a verb to show that the verb is in the infinitive. The infinitive is used after many verbs and also after many nouns and adjectives. * to 常用于原形动词之前，表示该动词为不定式。不定式用于许多动词之后，也用于许多名词和形容词之后。 **1** used to show purpose or intention（表示目的或意图）：*I set out to buy food.* 我动身去买吃的。◇ *I am going to tell you a story.* 我要给你们讲一个故事。◇ *She was determined to do well.* 她决心要做好。◇ *His aim was to become president.* 他的目的是当总统。◇ *To be honest with you, I don't remember what he said.* 跟你说实话，我不记得他说过什么了。 **2** used to show the result of sth（表示结果）：*She managed to escape.* 她设法逃走了。◇ *It was too hot to go out.* 天太热，不能出去。◇ *He couldn't get close enough to see.* 他无法靠近看个清楚。 **3** used to show the cause of sth（表示原因）：*I'm sorry to hear that.* 我听到这消息很难过。 **4** used to show an action that you want or are advised to do（表示想做或让做的事情）：*I'd love to go to France this summer.* 今年夏天我想去法国。◇ *The leaflet explains how to apply for a place.* 这本小册子介绍如何申请职位。◇ *I don't know what to say.* 我不知道说什么好。 HELP **To** can also be used without a following verb when the missing verb is easy to understand. * to 后面的动词如省略后仍容易理解时也可省略：*He asked her to come but she said she didn't want to.* 他让她来，但她说不想来。 **5** used to show sth that is known or reported about a particular person or thing（表示已知或转述的事情）：*The house was said to be haunted.* 据说这座房子里闹鬼。 **6** used to show that one action immediately follows another（表示一个动作紧跟另一动作）：*I reached the station only to find that my train had already left.* 我到了车站，却发现我要搭乘的火车已经开走了。 **7 am, is, are, was, were ~** used to show that you must or should do sth 必须；一定；应该：*You are not to talk during the exam.* 考试期间不许说话。◇ *She was to be here at 8.30 but she didn't arrive.* 她应该在 8:30 到这里，但是没有到。

■ ***adv.*** (usually of a door 通常指门) in or into a closed position 关着；关闭；关上：*Push the door to.* 推门关上。➲ SEE ALSO TOING

IDM **,to and 'fro** backwards and forwards 往返地；来回地：*She rocked the baby to and fro.* 她来回摇动着婴儿。 HELP For the special uses of **to** in phrasal verbs, look at the entries for the verbs. For example **set to** is in the phrasal verb section at **set**. * to 在短语动词中的特殊用法见有关动词词条。如 set to 在词条 set 的短语动词部分。

toad /təʊd; *NAmE* toʊd/ *noun* **1** a small animal like a FROG but with a drier and less smooth skin, that lives on land but breeds in water (= is an AMPHIBIAN) 蟾蜍；癞蛤蟆 ➲ VISUAL VOCAB PAGE V13 **2** (*informal, disapproving*) an unpleasant person 讨厌的人；使人恶心的人

,toad-in-the-'hole *noun* [U] a British dish of SAUSAGES cooked in BATTER 裹面糊烤香肠（一种英国菜）

toad·stool /'təʊdstu:l; *NAmE* 'toʊd-/ *noun* a FUNGUS with a round flat or curved head and a short STEM. Many types of toadstool are poisonous. 伞菌（其中许多是有毒的）➲ COMPARE MUSHROOM *n.*

toady /'təʊdi; *NAmE* 'toʊdi/ *noun, verb*

■ ***noun*** (*pl.* **-ies**) (*informal, disapproving*) a person who treats sb more important with special kindness or respect in order to gain their favour or help 谄媚者；马屁精 SYN **sycophant**

■ ***verb*** (**toad·ies, toady·ing, toad·ied, toad·ied**) [I] **~ (to sb)** (*disapproving*) to treat sb more important with special kindness or respect in order to gain their favour or help 拍马；奉承；谄媚

toast /təʊst; *NAmE* toʊst/ *noun, verb*

■ ***noun*** **1** [U] slices of bread that have been made brown and crisp by heating them on both sides in a toaster or under a GRILL 烤面包片；吐司：*cheese on toast* 烤面包片加奶酪 ◇ *a piece of toast* 一块烤面包片 ◇ *two* ***slices/rounds of toast*** 两片烤面包片 ➲ SEE ALSO FRENCH TOAST **2** [C] **~ (to sb/sth)** the act of a group of people wishing sb happiness, success, etc. by drinking a glass of sth, especially alcohol, at the same time 干杯；祝酒；敬酒：*I'd like to* ***propose a toast*** *to the bride and groom.* 我提议为新娘新郎干杯。◇ *The committee* ***drank a toast*** *to the new project.* 委员会为这项新计划干杯。 **3** [sing.] **the ~ of...** a person who is praised by a lot of people in a particular place because of sth that they have done well（在某领域）广受赞誉的人，有口皆碑的人：*The performance made her the toast of the festival.* 她的演出使她在会演中备受推崇。

IDM **be 'toast** (*informal*) to be likely to die or be destroyed 会死；要完蛋：*One mistake and you're toast.* 要是出一次错，你就完了。

■ ***verb*** **1** [T] **~ sb/sth** to lift a glass of wine, etc. in the air and drink it at the same time as other people in order to wish sb/sth success, happiness, etc. 为…举杯敬酒；为…干杯：*The happy couple were toasted in champagne.* 人们举起香槟酒为这对幸福的伉俪干杯。◇ *We toasted the success of the new company.* 我们为新公司的成功干杯。 **2** [T, I] **~ (sth)** to make sth, especially bread, turn brown by heating it in a toaster or close to heat; to turn brown in this way 烤（尤指面包）；把…烤得焦黄：*a toasted sandwich* 烤过的三明治 ◇ *Place under a hot grill until the nuts have toasted.* 把这些坚果放在高温烤架下面烤熟。➲ COLLOCATIONS AT COOKING **3** [T] **~ sth** to warm a part of your body by placing it near a fire 烤火；取暖；使暖和

toast·er /'təʊstə(r); *NAmE* 'toʊ-/ *noun* an electrical machine that you put slices of bread in to make toast（电的）烤面包片器；吐司炉 ➲ VISUAL VOCAB PAGE V26

T

toastie /ˈtəʊsti; *NAmE* ˈtoʊsti/ *noun* (*BrE*) a SANDWICH that has been TOASTED 烤三明治；吐司三明治

ˈ**toasting fork** *noun* a fork with a long handle used for TOASTING bread in front of a fire 烤面包长叉

toast·mas·ter /ˈtəʊstmɑːstə(r); *NAmE* ˈtoʊstmæstər/ *noun* a person who introduces the speakers at a formal dinner and calls for people to drink sth together in honour of particular people (= proposes TOASTS) 宴会主持人；致祝酒词的人

toasty /ˈtəʊsti; *NAmE* ˈtoʊ-/ *adj.* (*especially NAmE*) warm and comfortable 暖烘烘的；温暖舒适的

to·bacco /təˈbækəʊ; *NAmE* -koʊ/ *noun* [U, C] (*pl.* **-os**) the dried leaves of the tobacco plant that are used for making cigarettes, smoking in a pipe or chewing 烟叶；烟草：*The government imposed a ban on tobacco advertising* (= the advertising of cigarettes and all other forms of tobacco). 政府下令禁止做烟草广告。

to·bac·con·ist /təˈbækənɪst/ *noun* **1** a person who owns, manages or works in a shop/store selling cigarettes, tobacco for pipes, etc. 烟草店老板；烟草商 **2 to·bac·con·ist's** (*pl.* **to·bac·con·ists**) a shop/store that sells cigarettes, tobacco, etc. 烟草店：*There's a tobacconist's on the corner.* 街角处有一家烟草店。 ➲ MORE LIKE THIS 34, page R29

to·bog·gan /təˈbɒɡən; *NAmE* -ˈbɑːɡ-/ *noun, verb*

■ ***noun*** a long light narrow SLEDGE (= a vehicle that slides over snow) sometimes curved up in front, used for sliding down slopes 长雪橇；平底长雪橇

■ ***verb*** [I] to travel down a slope on snow or ice using a toboggan 坐长雪橇滑行 ▶ **to·bog·gan·ing** *noun* [U]

toc·cata /təˈkɑːtə/ *noun* a piece of music for a keyboard instrument which includes difficult passages designed to show the player's skill 托卡塔（用键盘乐器演奏的乐曲，其中有的乐段难度很大，以显示演奏者的技艺）

toc·sin /ˈtɒksɪn; *NAmE* ˈtɑːk-/ *noun* (*old use*) a warning bell or signal 警钟；警戒信号

tod /tɒd; *NAmE* tɑːd/ *noun*

IDM **on your ˈtod** (*old-fashioned, BrE, informal*) on your own; alone 独自；单独

today 🔑 /təˈdeɪ/ *adv., noun*

■ ***adv.*** **1** 🔑 on this day 在今天；在今日：*I've got a piano lesson later today.* 今天晚些时候我有一堂钢琴课。◇ *The exams start* ***a week today/today week*** (= one week from now). 考试于下周的今天开始。**2** 🔑 at the present period 现在；当今；当代 SYN **nowadays**：*Young people today face a very difficult future at work.* 如今的年轻人面临着充满困难的工作前景。

■ ***noun*** [U] **1** 🔑 this day 今天；今日：*Today is her tenth birthday.* 今天是她的十岁生日。◇ *The review is in today's paper.* 这篇评论刊登在今天的报纸上。◇ *I'm leaving a week from today.* 我下周的今天动身。**2** 🔑 the present period of time 现在；当今；当代：*today's young people* 当代青年

tod·dle /ˈtɒdl; *NAmE* ˈtɑːdl/ *verb* **1** [I] when a young child who has just learnt to walk **toddles**, he/she walks with short, unsteady steps （幼儿学步时）摇摇摆摆地走，蹒跚行走 **2** [I] + **adv./prep.** (*informal*) to walk or go somewhere 步行；去：*She toddles down to the park most afternoons.* 多数下午她都溜达着去公园。◇ *I locked the door and then toddled off to bed.* 我锁上房门，然后就上床睡觉去了。

tod·dler /ˈtɒdlə(r); *NAmE* ˈtɑːd-/ *noun* a child who has only recently learnt to walk 学步的幼儿；刚学会走路的孩子

toddy /ˈtɒdi; *NAmE* ˈtɑːdi/ *noun* [C, U] (*pl.* **-ies**) a drink made with strong alcohol, sugar, hot water and sometimes spices 托迪酒（用烈酒加糖、热水或香料等调配而成）

tod·ger /ˈtɒdʒə(r); *NAmE* ˈtɑːdʒər/ *noun* (*BrE, informal*) a man's PENIS 阴茎

to-do /tə ˈduː/ *noun* [sing.] (*informal, becoming old-fashioned*) unnecessary excitement or anger about sth 忙乱；喧嚷；大惊小怪；吵吵嚷嚷 SYN **fuss**：*What a to-do!* 真是太大惊小怪了！

to-ˈdo list *noun* a list of tasks that you have to do 待办事项清单：*A marathon has been on my to-do list for 20 years.* 跑一次马拉松是我 20 年来一直计划要做的事情。

toe 🔑 /təʊ; *NAmE* toʊ/ *noun, verb*

■ ***noun*** **1** 🔑 one of the five small parts that stick out from the foot 脚趾：*the* ***big/little toe*** (= the largest/smallest toe) 大脚趾；小脚趾 ◇ *I stubbed my toe on the step.* 我的脚趾踢在了台阶上。◇ *Can you* ***touch your toes***? (= by bending over while keeping your legs straight) 你直腿弯腰够得着你的脚趾吗？ ➲ VISUAL VOCAB PAGE V64 **2** 🔑 the part of a sock, shoe, etc. that covers the toes（袜、鞋等的）足尖部；鞋头 ➲ VISUAL VOCAB PAGE V69 **3 -toed** (in adjectives 构成形容词) having the type or number of toes mentioned 有…脚趾的：*open-toed sandals* 露脚趾的凉鞋 ◇ *a three-toed sloth* 三趾树懒 ➲ SEE ALSO PIGEON-TOED

IDM **keep sb on their ˈtoes** to make sure that sb is ready to deal with anything that might happen by doing things that they are not expecting（通过出其不意的行动）使保持警觉：*Surprise visits help to keep the staff on their toes.* 突击巡察有助于使员工不致懈怠偷懒。 **make sb's ˈtoes curl** to make sb feel embarrassed or uncomfortable 使人尴尬；使人难为情 ➲ SEE ALSO TOE-CURLING ➲ MORE AT DIG *v.*, DIP *v.*, HEAD *n.*, STEP *v.*, TOP *n.*, TREAD *v.*

■ ***verb***

IDM **toe the ˈline** (*NAmE also* **toe the ˈmark**) to say or do what sb in authority tells you to say or do, even if you do not share the same opinions, etc. 顺从当局（或集体）；遵循…路线：*to toe the party line* 遵循党的路线

toe·cap /ˈtəʊkæp; *NAmE* ˈtoʊ-/ *noun* a piece of metal or leather that covers the front part of a shoe or boot to make it stronger （鞋或靴尖的）外包头

ˈ**toe-curling** *adj.* (*informal*) extremely embarrassing because of being very bad or silly 令人无地自容的；丢人现眼的 ➲ MORE LIKE THIS 10, page R26 ▶ ˈ**toe-curlingly** *adv.*：*a toe-curlingly awful movie* 非常令人反感的电影

TOEFL™ /ˈtəʊfl; *NAmE* ˈtoʊfl/ *noun* the abbreviation for 'Test of English as a Foreign Language' (a test of a person's level of English that is taken in order to go to a university in the US) 托福考试（外国学生入读美国大学须参加的英语水平考试，全写为 Test of English as a Foreign Language）

toe·hold /ˈtəʊhəʊld; *NAmE* ˈtoʊhoʊld/ *noun* **1** a position in a place or an activity which you hope will lead to more power or success 初步的地位；立足点：*The firm is anxious to gain a toehold in Europe.* 这家公司急于在欧洲找个立脚点。 **2** a very small hole or space on a CLIFF, just big enough to put your foot in when you are climbing （攀登时可放进脚去的）小立足点，小支撑点

TOEIC™ /ˈtəʊɪk; *NAmE* ˈtoʊɪk/ *noun* [U] the abbreviation for 'Test of English for International Communication' (a test that measures your ability to read and understand English if it is not your first language) 托业考试（作为外语的英语阅读和理解能力的考试，全写为 Test of English for International Communication）

toe·nail /ˈtəʊneɪl; *NAmE* ˈtoʊ-/ *noun* the nail on a toe 趾甲 ➲ VISUAL VOCAB PAGE V64

toe·rag /ˈtəʊræɡ; *NAmE* ˈtoʊ-/ *noun* (*BrE, slang*) used as a rude and offensive way of addressing sb you do not like or that you are angry with 浑蛋；废物

ˈ**toe-tapping** *adj.* (*informal*) (of music 音乐) lively and making you want to move your feet 欢快的；轻松明快的

toey /ˈtəʊi; *NAmE* ˈtoʊi/ *adj.* (*AustralE, NZE, informal*) (of a person or an animal) nervous or not able to keep still （人或动物）神经紧张的，焦急不安的，躁动的

toff /tɒf; *NAmE* tɑːf/ *noun* (*BrE, informal*) a disapproving way of referring to sb from a high social class 纨绔子弟；花花公子

tof·fee /ˈtɒfi; *NAmE* ˈtɔːfi; ˈtɑːfi/ *noun* [U, C] a hard sticky sweet/candy made by heating sugar, butter and water together and allowing it to cool 太妃糖；乳脂糖

IDM **can't do sth for ˈtoffee** (*old-fashioned, BrE, informal*) if sb **can't do sth for toffee**, they are very bad at doing it 做某事很糟糕；不能胜任某事：*He can't dance for toffee!* 他根本不会跳舞！

ˈtoffee apple (*BrE*) (*NAmE* **ˈcandy apple**) *noun* an apple covered with a thin layer of hard toffee and fixed on a stick 太妃苹果（外涂奶油乳脂，用签子插起）

ˈtoffee-nosed *adj.* (*old-fashioned, BrE, informal*) behaving as if you are better than other people, especially those of a lower social class 势利眼的；妄自尊大的；目空一切的 **SYN** **snobbish**

tofu /ˈtəʊfuː; *NAmE* ˈtoʊfuː/ (*also* **ˈbean curd**) *noun* [U] a soft white substance that is made from SOYA and used in cooking, often instead of meat 豆腐

tog /tɒg; *NAmE* tɑːg/ *noun, verb*

■ ***noun*** **1** **togs** [pl.] (*informal, becoming old-fashioned*) clothes, especially ones that you wear for a particular purpose （尤指专用的）衣服，服装：*running togs* 跑步装 **2** (*BrE*) a unit for measuring the warmth of DUVETS, etc. 托格（显示羽绒被褥等保暖性的热阻计量单位）

■ ***verb*** (**-gg-**)

IDM **be ˌtogged ˈout/ˈup (in sth)** (*informal*) to be wearing clothes for a particular activity or occasion 穿着（适合某种活动或场合）的服装：*They were all togged up in their skiing gear.* 他们全都身着滑雪服。

toga /ˈtəʊgə; *NAmE* ˈtoʊgə/ *noun* a loose outer piece of clothing worn by the citizens of ancient Rome 托加袍（古罗马市民穿的宽松大袍）

to·gether 🔑 /təˈgeðə(r)/ *adv., adj.*

■ ***adv.*** **HELP** For the special uses of **together** in phrasal verbs, look at the entries for the verbs. For example **pull yourself together** is in the phrasal verb section at **pull**. * together 在短语动词中的特殊用法见有关动词词条。如 pull yourself together 在词条 pull 的短语动词部分。**1** 🔑 with or near to sb/sth else; with each other 在一起；共同：*We grew up together.* 我们是在一块儿长大的。◇ *Together they climbed the dark stairs.* 他们一起登上黑洞洞的楼梯。◇ *Get all the ingredients together before you start cooking.* 把所有的材料放在一起再开始烹饪。◇ *Stay **close together**—I don't want anyone to get lost.* 紧紧靠在一起，我不想把谁给丢了。**2** 🔑 so that two or more things touch or are joined to or combined with each other 以使接触（或相结合）；到一起：*He rubbed his hands together in satisfaction.* 他满意地擦搓着双手。◇ *She nailed the two boards together.* 她把两块木板钉在了一起。◇ *Mix the sand and cement together.* 把沙子和水泥混合在一起。◇ ***Taken together**, these factors are highly significant.* 这些因素综合起来看就很重要了。◇ *He has **more money than the rest of us put together**.* 他的钱比我们所有人的加在一起还多。**3** 🔑 (of two people 两个人) in a close relationship, for example a marriage 关系密切；有婚姻关系：*They split up after ten years together.* 他们在一起生活了十年之后分手了。**4** 🔑 in or into agreement 一致；协调：*After the meeting the two sides in the dispute were no closer together.* 会面之后，争论的双方立场差距依然如故。**5** 🔑 at the same time 同时；一起；一齐：*They both spoke together.* 他们两人同时发言。◇ (*informal*) ***All together now**: 'Happy birthday to you…'* 现在大家一齐唱："祝你生日快乐…" **6** **for hours, days, etc. ~** (*formal*) for hours, days, etc. without stopping 接连…地；连续…地；…不间断地：*She sat for hours together just staring into space.* 她连续几个小时坐在那里怔怔地望着前面。

IDM **together with 1** 🔑 including 包括…在内：*Together with the Johnsons, there were 12 of us in the villa.* 包括约翰逊一家在内，别墅里总共有我们 12 个人。**2** 🔑 in addition to; as well as 加之；和；连同；同…一起：*I sent my order, together with a cheque for £40.* 我把订单连同一张 40 英镑的支票一起寄出去。

■ ***adj.*** (*informal, approving*) (of a person 人) well organized and confident 自信而妥实的：*He's incredibly together for someone so young.* 他这个人年纪轻轻，办事如此稳当，真是了不起。

to·gether·ness /təˈgeðənəs; *NAmE* -ðərn-/ *noun* [U] the happy feeling you have when you are with people you like, especially family and friends（尤指家庭或朋友的）和睦相处，亲密无间，团结友爱

tog·gle /ˈtɒgl; *NAmE* ˈtɑːgl/ *noun, verb*

■ ***noun*** **1** a short piece of wood, plastic, etc. that is put through a LOOP of thread to fasten sth, such as a coat or bag, instead of a button（大衣或口袋等上木质或塑料的）栓扣钉，棒形纽扣，套索扣 ➲ VISUAL VOCAB PAGE V68 **2** (*also* **ˈtoggle switch**) (*computing* 计) a key on a computer that you press to change from one style or operation to another, and back again 转换键；切换键

■ ***verb*** [I, T] (*computing* 计) to press a key or set of keys on a computer keyboard in order to turn a feature on or off, or to move from one program, etc. to another（两种状态之间）切换，转换：**~ (between A and B)** *He toggled between the two windows.* 他在两个窗口之间来回切换。◇ **~ sth** *This key toggles various views of the data.* 按此键可切换数据的各种视图。➲ WORDFINDER NOTE AT COMMAND

ˈtoggle switch *noun* **1** an electrical switch which you move up and down or backwards and forwards 拨动开关；钮子开关 **2** (*computing* 计) = TOGGLE (2)

toil /tɔɪl/ *verb, noun*

■ ***verb*** (*formal*) **1** [I] to work very hard and/or for a long time, usually doing hard physical work（长时间）苦干，辛勤劳作 **SYN** **slave** **2** [I] **+ adv./prep.** to move slowly and with difficulty 艰难缓慢地移动；跋涉 **SYN** **slog**: *They toiled up the hill in the blazing sun.* 他们冒着炎炎烈日艰难地一步一步爬上山冈。▶ **toil·er** *noun*

■ ***noun*** [U] (*formal* or *literary*) hard unpleasant work that makes you very tired 苦工；劳累的工作：*a life of hardship and toil* 艰难劳苦的一生 ➲ SEE ALSO TOILS

toi·let 🔑 /ˈtɔɪlət/ *noun* **1** 🔑 [C] a large bowl attached to a pipe that you sit on or stand over when you get rid of waste matter from your body 坐便器；抽水马桶：*Have you flushed the toilet?* 你冲厕所了吗？◇ (*BrE*) *I need to go **to the toilet*** (= use the toilet). 我得去趟洗手间。◇ *a toilet seat* 马桶座圈 ◇ *toilet facilities* 卫生设施 ◇ *Do you **need the toilet**?* 你需要用洗手间吗？ ➲ VISUAL VOCAB PAGE V25 **2** 🔑 (*BrE*) (*NAmE* **bath·room**) [C] a room containing a toilet 厕所；卫生间；盥洗室：*Every flat has its own bathroom and toilet.* 每套公寓都带有洗澡间和盥洗室。◇ *Who's in the toilet?* 谁在用厕所？ **3** 🔑 (*BrE*) [C] (*also* **toi·lets** [pl.]) a room

▼ **BRITISH/AMERICAN 英式 / 美式英语**

toilet / bathroom

- In *BrE*, but not in *NAmE*, the room that has a toilet in it is usually referred to as a **toilet**. This room in people's houses can also be called the **lavatory**, or informally, the **loo**. An extra downstairs toilet in a house can be called the **cloakroom**. In public places, especially on signs, the words **toilets**, **Gents** (for men's toilets) or **Ladies** (for women's toilets) are used for a room or small building containing several toilets. You might also see **WC** or **Public Conveniences** on some signs. 在英式英语而非美式英语中，厕所一般称为 toilet，住宅中的厕所亦可称为 lavatory 或（非正式用法）loo。住宅楼下附加的厕所可叫做 cloakroom。在公共场所，尤其在指示牌上，toilets、Gents（男厕所）或 Ladies（女厕所）指有几个小间的厕所。有的指示牌亦可能用 WC 或 Public Conveniences。
- In *NAmE* the room that contains a toilet is usually called the **bathroom**, never the **toilet**. A room with a toilet in a public place can also be called a **restroom**, **ladies' room**, **women's room** or **men's room**. **Washroom** is also used, especially in Canada. 在美式英语中，厕所一般称为 bathroom，从不叫 toilet。公共厕所亦可称为 restroom、ladies' room、women's room 或 men's room，还可用 washroom，尤其是在加拿大。

T

or small building containing several toilets, each in a separate smaller room（有几个分隔坐便器的）厕所间，厕所：*public toilets* 公共厕所 ◇ *Could you tell me where the ladies' toilet is, please?* 请问哪里有女厕所？ **4** [U] (*old-fashioned*) the process of washing and dressing yourself, arranging your hair, etc. 梳洗；打扮

'toilet bag *noun* (*BrE*) = SPONGE BAG

'toilet paper (*also* **'toilet tissue**) *noun* [U] thin soft paper used for cleaning yourself after you have used the toilet 卫生纸；手纸：*a roll of toilet paper* 一卷卫生纸 ➲ VISUAL VOCAB PAGE V25

toi·let·ries /'tɔɪlətriz/ *noun* [pl.] things such as soap or TOOTHPASTE that you use for washing, cleaning your teeth, etc.（香皂、牙膏等）洗漱用品 ➲ VISUAL VOCAB PAGE V25

'toilet roll *noun* (*BrE*) a roll of toilet paper 卫生纸卷；手纸卷 ➲ PICTURE AT ROLL

'toiletry bag (*NAmE*) (*BrE* **'sponge bag, 'toilet bag, wash·bag**) *noun* a small bag for holding your soap, TOOTHBRUSH, etc. when you are travelling 盥洗用品袋 ➲ VISUAL VOCAB PAGE V25

'toilet soap *noun* [U, C] soap that you use for washing yourself 香皂

'toilet-train *verb* [usually passive] **~ sb** to teach a small child to use the toilet 训练（幼儿）上厕所 ▸ **'toilet-trained** *adj.* **'toilet-training** *noun* [U]

'toilet water *noun* [U, C] a kind of PERFUME (= a pleasant smelling liquid for the skin) that has water added to it and is not very expensive 花露水

toils /tɔɪlz/ *noun* [pl.] (*formal* or *literary*) if you are caught in **the toils** of an unpleasant feeling or situation, you cannot escape from it 牢笼；罗网 SYN **snare**

toing /'tuːɪŋ/ *noun*

IDM **,toing and 'froing 1** movement or travel backwards and forwards between two or more places 来回运动；往返旅行；来来往往：*All this toing and froing between London and New York takes it out of him.* 这样没完没了地在伦敦和纽约之间来回奔波使得他疲惫不堪。 **2** a lot of unnecessary or repeated activity or discussion 翻来覆去地做（或讨论）；忙乱；折腾：*After a great deal of toing and froing, I decided not to change jobs after all.* 好一番折腾之后，我最终决定还是不换工作。

T

toke /təʊk; *NAmE* toʊk/ *noun* (*informal*) an act of breathing in smoke from a cigarette containing MARIJUANA 吸一口（大麻烟） ▸ **toke** *verb* [I]

token /'təʊkən; *NAmE* 'toʊ-/ *noun, adj.*

■ *noun* **1** a round piece of metal or plastic used instead of money to operate some machines or as a form of payment（用以启动某些机器或用作支付方式的）代币，专用辅币：*a parking token* 停车专用辅币 **2** (*BrE*) a piece of paper that you pay for and that sb can exchange for sth in a shop/store 代金券：*a £20 book/record/gift token* 价值20 英镑的书券 / 唱片券 / 礼物券 **3** a piece of paper that you can collect when you buy a particular product and then exchange for sth 赠券；礼券：*Collect six tokens for a free T-shirt.* 收集到六张礼券可以换一件 T 恤衫。**4** something that is a symbol of a feeling, a fact, an event, etc.（感觉、事实、事件等的）象征，标志，表示，信物 SYN **expression, mark**：*Please accept this small gift as a token of our gratitude.* 区区薄礼，以表谢忱，请笑纳。

IDM **by the same 'token** for the same reasons 由于同样的原因；同样地：*The penalty for failure will be high. But, by the same token, the rewards for success will be great.* 失败就要付出沉重的代价，同样，成功就会获得很大的回报。

■ *adj.* [only before noun] **1** involving very little effort or feeling and intended only as a way of showing other people that you think sb/sth is important, when really you are not sincere 装样子的；装点门面的；敷衍的：*The government has only made a token gesture towards helping the unemployed.* 政府只不过是做做样子表示了一下对失业者的帮助。◇ *There was one token woman on the committee* (= a woman who is included in the group to make it look as if women are always included, although that is not true). 委员会中有一位装点门面的女性委员。 **2** done as a symbol to show that you are serious about sth and will keep a promise or an agreement or do more later 象征性的；作为标志的：*The government agreed to send a small token force to the area.* 政府同意派遣一小支象征性的部队到那一地区。◇ *a one-day token strike* 一天的象征性罢工 **3** (of a small amount of money 小额款项) that you pay or charge sb only as a symbol, because a payment is expected 象征性支付（或收取）的 SYN **nominal**：*We charge only a token fee for use of the facilities.* 我们对使用这些设施只收取象征性的费用。

token·ism /'təʊkənɪzəm; *NAmE* 'toʊ-/ *noun* [U] (*disapproving*) the fact of doing sth only in order to do what the law requires or to satisfy a particular group of people, but not in a way that is really sincere 装点门面；表面文章；敷衍了事；应付差事：*Appointing one woman to the otherwise all-male staff could look like tokenism.* 给原本清一色的男职员队伍增派一位女性会显得是装点门面。

to·kol·oshe /'tɒkɒlɒʃ; *NAmE* 'tɑːkəlɑːʃ/ *noun* (*SAfrE*) an evil imaginary creature that some people believe can harm you while you are sleeping 托克洛希（传说中能趁人睡眠时进行伤害的邪恶精灵）

Tok Pisin /,tɒk 'pɪzən; -sən; *NAmE* ,tɑːk/ (*also* **Pidgin**) *noun* [U] a CREOLE language based on English, used in Papua New Guinea 新美拉尼西亚语（巴布亚新几内亚使用的一种以英语为基础的克里奥尔语）

told PAST TENSE, PAST PART. OF TELL

tol·er·able /'tɒlərəbl; *NAmE* 'tɑːl-/ *adj.* (*formal*) **1** fairly good, but not of the best quality 尚好的；过得去的；还可以的 SYN **reasonable**：*a tolerable degree of success* 说得过去的成功 **2** that you can accept or bear, although unpleasant or painful 可接受的；可忍受的；可容忍的 SYN **bearable**：*At times, the heat was barely tolerable.* 有时天气炎热得几乎令人难以忍受。 OPP **intolerable** ▸ **tol·er·ably** /'tɒlərəbli; *NAmE* 'tɑːl-/ *adv.*：*He plays the piano tolerably (well).* 他钢琴弹得还算不错。

tol·er·ance /'tɒlərəns; *NAmE* 'tɑːl-/ *noun* **1** [U] **~ (of/for sb/sth)** the willingness to accept or TOLERATE sb/sth, especially opinions or behaviour that you may not agree with, or people who are not like you 忍受；容忍；宽容；宽恕：*She had no tolerance for jokes of any kind.* 她容不得开任何玩笑。◇ *religious tolerance* 宗教上的包容 ◇ *a reputation for tolerance towards refugees* 对难民宽容的美誉 ➲ SEE ALSO ZERO TOLERANCE OPP **intolerance 2** [C, U] **~ (to sth)** the ability to suffer sth, especially pain, difficult conditions, etc. without being harmed 忍耐力；忍受性；耐力；耐量：*tolerance to cold* 耐寒力 ◇ *Tolerance to alcohol decreases with age.* 酒量随年龄的增大而减少。 **3** [C, U] (*specialist*) the amount by which the measurement of a value can vary without causing problems 公差；容限：*They were working to a tolerance of 0.0001 of a centimetre.* 他们在按 0.0001 厘米的公差加工。

tol·er·ant /'tɒlərənt; *NAmE* 'tɑːl-/ *adj.* **1 ~ (of/towards sb/sth)** able to accept what other people say or do even if you do not agree with it 忍受的；容忍的；宽容的：*He has a very tolerant attitude towards other religions.* 他对其他宗教持非常包容的态度。 **2 ~ (of sth)** (of plants, animals or machines 植物、动物或机器) able to survive or operate in difficult conditions 能在困难条件下生存（或操作）的；能耐…的：*The plants are tolerant of frost.* 这些植物耐霜。 OPP **intolerant** ▸ **tol·er·ant·ly** *adv.*

tol·er·ate /'tɒləreɪt; *NAmE* 'tɑːl-/ *verb* **1** to allow sb to do sth that you do not agree with or like 容许，允许（不同意或不喜欢的事物） SYN **put up with sb/sth**：**~ sth** *Their relationship was tolerated but not encouraged.* 他们的关系得到了允许，但不宜鼓励。◇ *This sort of behaviour will not be tolerated.* 这种行为是不能容许的。 ◇ **~ (sb/sth) doing/being/having sth** *She refused to tolerate being called a liar.* 她拒不接受被称为撒谎者。 **2 ~ sb/sth** to accept sb/sth that is annoying, unpleasant, etc. without complaining 忍受；容忍；包容 **SYN** **put up with sb/sth**: *There is a limit to what one person can tolerate.* 一个人的容忍是有限度的。◇ *I don't know how you tolerate that noise!* 我不知道你怎么能忍受那样的噪音！ **3 ~ sth** to be able to be affected by a drug, difficult conditions, etc. without being harmed（对药物）有耐受性；能经受（困难条件）：*She tolerated the chemotherapy well.* 她对化疗的耐受力很强。◇ *Few plants will tolerate sudden changes in temperature.* 很少植物经受得住气温的突然变化。

tol·er·ation /ˌtɒləˈreɪʃn; *NAmE* ˌtɑːl-/ *noun* [U] a willingness to allow sth that you do not like or agree with to happen or continue 忍受；容忍；宽容；容许 **SYN** **tolerance**: *religious toleration* 宗教上的宽容

toll /təʊl; *NAmE* toʊl/ *noun, verb*

■ ***noun*** **1** [C] money that you pay to use a particular road or bridge（道路、桥梁的）通行费：*motorway tolls* 高速公路通行费 ◇ *a* **toll road/bridge** 收费道路 / 桥梁 ➲ SYNONYMS AT RATE ➲ WORDFINDER NOTE AT TRAFFIC **2** [C, usually sing.] the amount of damage or the number of deaths and injuries that are caused in a particular war, disaster, etc.（战争、灾难等造成的）毁坏；伤亡人数：*The official* **death toll** *has now reached 7 000.* 官方公布的死亡人数现已达 7 000 人。◇ *the war's growing casualty toll* 不断增长的战争伤亡人数 **3** [sing.] the sound of a bell ringing with slow regular strokes（缓慢而有规律的）钟声 **4** [C] (*NAmE*) a charge for a telephone call that is calculated at a higher rate than a local call 长途电话费

IDM **take a heavy ˈtoll (on sb/sth)** | **take its ˈtoll (on sb/sth)** to have a bad effect on sb/sth; to cause a lot of damage, deaths, suffering, etc. 产生恶果；造成重大损失（或伤亡、灾难等）：*Illness had taken a heavy toll on her.* 疾病对她的身体造成极大的损害。◇ *The recession is taking its toll on the housing markets.* 经济衰退使住房市场遭受着重大损失。

■ ***verb*** [I, T] when a bell **tolls** or sb **tolls** it, it is rung slowly many times, especially as a sign that sb has died（缓慢而有规律地）敲（钟）；（尤指）鸣（丧钟）：**~ (for sb)** *The Abbey bell tolled for those killed in the war.* 大教堂为战争中的死难者鸣钟。◇ **~ sth** *The bell tolled the hour.* 鸣钟报时。◇ (*figurative*) *The revolution* **tolled the death knell** (= signalled the end) *for the Russian monarchy.* 那场革命敲响了俄国君主制的丧钟。

toll·booth /ˈtəʊlbuːð; *NAmE* ˈtoʊlbuːθ/ *noun* a small building by the side of a road where you pay to drive on a road, go over a bridge, etc.（道路、桥梁的）收费亭，收费站

ˌtoll-ˈfree *adj.* (*NAmE*) (of a telephone call to an organization or a service 打给机构或服务部门的电话) that you do not have to pay for 免费的：*a toll-free number* 免费电话号码 ➲ SEE ALSO FREEPHONE

toll·house cookie /ˌtəʊlhaʊs ˈkʊki; *NAmE* ˌtoʊl-/ *noun* (*US*) a crisp sweet biscuit/cookie that contains small pieces of chocolate 碎粒巧克力曲奇

ˈtoll plaza *noun* (*US*) a row of TOLLBOOTHS across a road（道路上的）收费站，收费区，收费广场

Tom /tɒm; *NAmE* tɑːm/ *noun*

IDM **any/every ˌTom, ˌDick or ˈHarry** (*usually disapproving*) any ordinary person rather than the people you know or people who have special skills or qualities（不熟悉或无特长的）任何人；闲人；生人：*We don't want any Tom, Dick or Harry using the club bar.* 我们不想随便让什么人都来使用会所的酒吧。

tom /tɒm; *NAmE* tɑːm/ *noun* = TOMCAT

toma·hawk /ˈtɒməhɔːk; *NAmE* ˈtɑːm-/ *noun* a light AXE used by Native Americans 印第安战斧（美洲土著的一种武器）

to·mato 🔑 /təˈmɑːtəʊ; *NAmE* təˈmeɪtoʊ/ *noun* [C, U] (*pl.* **-oes**) a soft fruit with a lot of juice and shiny red skin that is eaten as a vegetable either raw or cooked 番茄；西红柿：*a bacon, lettuce and tomato sandwich* 熏肉生菜番茄三明治 ◇ *sliced tomatoes* 番茄片 ◇ *tomato plants* 番茄植株 ➲ VISUAL VOCAB PAGE V34

tomb /tuːm/ *noun* a large grave, especially one built of stone above or below the ground 坟墓；冢

tom·bola /tɒmˈbəʊlə; *NAmE* tɑːmˈboʊlə/ *noun* [U, C] (*BrE*) a game in which you buy tickets with numbers on them. If the number on your ticket is the same as the number on one of the prizes, you win the prize. "翻筋斗" 赌戏（一种抽彩摇奖法）

tom·boy /ˈtɒmbɔɪ; *NAmE* ˈtɑːm-/ *noun* a young girl who enjoys activities and games that are traditionally considered to be for boys 假小子，野丫头（喜欢男孩玩意儿的女孩子）

tomb·stone /ˈtuːmstəʊn; *NAmE* -stoʊn/ *noun* a large, flat stone that lies over a grave or stands at one end, that shows the name, age, etc. of the person buried there 墓碑 ➲ COMPARE GRAVESTONE, HEADSTONE

tom·cat /ˈtɒmkæt; *NAmE* ˈtɑːm-/ (*also* **tom**) *noun* a male cat 公猫；雄猫

tome /təʊm; *NAmE* toʊm/ *noun* (*formal*) a large heavy book, especially one dealing with a serious topic（尤指严肃的）大部头书，巨著

tom·fool /ˌtɒmˈfuːl; *NAmE* ˌtɑːm-/ *noun* (*old-fashioned*) a silly person 傻瓜；笨蛋

tom·fool·ery /tɒmˈfuːləri; *NAmE* tɑːm-/ *noun* [U] (*old-fashioned*) silly behaviour 愚蠢的行为 **SYN** **foolishness**

Tommy /ˈtɒmi; *NAmE* ˈtɑːmi/ *noun* (*old use, informal*) a British soldier 英国兵

ˈtommy gun *noun* a type of SUB-MACHINE GUN 汤普森冲锋枪

tommy·rot /ˈtɒmirɒt; *NAmE* ˈtɑːmirɑːt/ *noun* [U] (*old-fashioned*) nonsense 废话；胡说

tom·og·raphy /təˈmɒɡrəfi; *NAmE* -ˈmɑːɡ-/ *noun* [U] a way of producing an image of the inside of the human body or a solid object using X-RAYS or ULTRASOUND 层析成像，层析术（利用 X 射线或超声波清楚显示体内结构）

to·mor·row 🔑 /təˈmɒrəʊ; *NAmE* təˈmɔːroʊ; -ˈmɑːr-/ *adv., noun*

■ ***adv.*** on or during the day after today 在明天；在明日：*I'm off now. See you tomorrow.* 我走了。明天见。◇ *She's leaving tomorrow.* 她明天就走了。◇ (*especially BrE*) *They arrive* **a week tomorrow/tomorrow week** (= after a week, starting from tomorrow). 他们将于从明天算起一星期后到达。**IDM** SEE JAM *n.*

■ ***noun*** [U] **1** 🔑 the day after today 明天；明日：*Today is Tuesday, so tomorrow is Wednesday.* 今天是星期二，那么明天就是星期三。◇ **tomorrow afternoon/morning/night/evening** 明天下午 / 上午 / 夜里 / 晚上 ◇ *I'll see you* **the day after tomorrow**. 我们后天见。◇ *The announcement will appear in tomorrow's newspapers.* 这份通告将于明日见报。◇ *I want it done by tomorrow.* 我希望这件事最迟明天做好。 **2** 🔑 the future 未来；将来；来日：*Who knows what changes tomorrow may bring?* 谁知道将来会有什么变化？◇ *Tomorrow's workers will have to be more adaptable.* 未来的工人必须具有更强的适应性。

IDM **do sth as if/like there's no toˈmorrow** to do sth a lot or as though you do not care what effects it will have 不顾后果地一个劲…：*I ate as if there was no tomorrow.* 我狼吞虎咽地吃着。◇ *She spends money like there's no tomorrow.* 她拼命花钱，就像过了今天没有明天似的。

ˈtom-tom *noun, verb*

■ ***noun*** **1** a medium-sized drum, which may be part of a DRUM KIT 桶子鼓（有时是成套鼓乐器的组成部分）➲ VISUAL VOCAB PAGE V37 **2** a drum, often played with the hands, especially in Asian or Native American cultures（尤指亚洲或美洲土著文化中的）咚咚鼓，手鼓

■ ***verb*** (*IndE*) **~ (about) sth** to make sth known or to talk with too much pride about it 大肆宣扬；得意洋洋地谈论

ton 🔑 /tʌn/ *noun* **1** 🔑 [C] (*pl.* **tons** or **ton**) a unit for measuring weight, in Britain 2 240 pounds (**long ton**) and in

T

the US 2 000 pounds (**short ton**) 吨（英国为 2 240 磅，即长吨；美国为 2 000 磅，即短吨）：(*informal*) *What have you got in this bag? It weighs a ton!* 你这口袋里装的是什么？重死了！ ➲ COMPARE TONNE **2** [C] a unit for measuring the size of a ship. 1 ton is equal to 100 CUBIC feet. 注册吨，吨位（船舶大小的计量单位，1 吨等于 100 立方英尺） **3 tons** [pl.] (*informal*) a lot 大量；许多：*They've got tons of money.* 他们腰缠万贯。◇ *I've still got tons to do.* 我还有许多事要做。 **4 a/the ton** (*BrE, informal*) 100, especially when connected with a speed of 100 miles per hour * 100；（尤指）每小时 100 英里的速度：*He was caught doing a ton.* 他被发现以每小时 100 英里的速度行车。

IDM **like a ton of 'bricks** (*informal*) very heavily; very severely 非常沉重；极为严厉：*Disappointment hit her like a ton of bricks.* 她大失所望。◇ *They **came down on him like a ton of bricks*** (= criticized him very severely). 他们狠狠批评了他一顿。

tonal /'təʊnl; *NAmE* 'toʊnl/ *adj.* **1** (*specialist*) relating to tones of sound or colour 音调的；声调的；色调的 **2** (*music* 音) having a particular KEY 调性的 OPP **atonal** ▸ **tonal·ly** *adv.*

ton·al·ity /təʊ'næləti; *NAmE* toʊ-/ *noun* [U, C] (*pl.* **-ies**) (*music* 音) the quality of a piece of music that depends on the KEY in which it is written 调性

tone /təʊn; *NAmE* toʊn/ *noun, verb*

■ ***noun***

• **OF VOICE** 腔调 **1** [C] the quality of sb's voice, especially expressing a particular emotion 语气；口气；腔调；口吻：*speaking in **hushed/low/clipped/measured, etc. tones*** 以压低、低沉、短促、缓慢谨慎等的语调讲话 ◇ *a conversational tone* 交谈的语气 ◇ *a tone of surprise* 惊奇的口气 ◇ *Don't speak to me in that **tone of voice*** (= in that unpleasant way). 别用那种口吻跟我讲话。◇ *There's no need to **take that tone** with me—it's not my fault we're late.* 不必那样跟我拿腔拿调的。我们来晚了，可不是我的错。

• **CHARACTER/ATMOSPHERE** 特征；气氛 **2** [sing.] the general character and attitude of sth such as a piece of writing, or the atmosphere of an event 风格；特色；气氛；情调：*The overall tone of the book is gently nostalgic.* 这本书整体格调是温情的怀旧。◇ *She **set the tone for** the meeting with a firm statement of company policy.* 她坚定地说明了公司的方针，为会议定下了调子。◇ *Trust you to **lower the tone of the conversation*** (= for example by telling a rude joke). 管保你会降低谈话的格调（如讲粗俗的笑话）。◇ *The article was moderate **in tone** and presented both sides of the case.* 这篇文章基调温和，不偏不倚。

• **OF SOUND** 声音 **3** [C] the quality of a sound, especially the sound of a musical instrument or one produced by electronic equipment（尤指乐器或电子音响设备的）音质，音色：*the full rich tone of the trumpet* 小号饱满嘹亮的音色 ◇ *the volume and tone controls on a car stereo* 汽车立体声系统音量和音质的控制装置

• **COLOUR** 颜色 **4** [C] a shade of a colour 色调；明暗；影调：*a carpet in warm tones of brown and orange* 棕色和橘黄色的暖色调地毯

• **OF MUSCLES/SKIN** 肌肉；皮肤 **5** [U] how strong and firm your muscles or skin are（肌肉）结实度，健壮度；（皮肤）紧致性：*how to improve your **muscle/skin tone*** 如何使肌肉结实 / 皮肤紧致

• **ON TELEPHONE** 电话 **6** [C] a sound heard on a telephone line（打电话时听到的）声音信号：(*BrE*) *the **dialling tone*** 拨号音 ◇ (*NAmE*) *the **dial tone*** 拨号音 ◇ *Please speak after the tone* (= for example as an instruction on an answering machine). 听到信号后请讲话。

• **IN MUSIC** 音乐 **7** (*BrE*) (*US* **'whole step**) [C] one of the five longer INTERVALS in a musical SCALE, for example the INTERVAL between C and D or between E and F# 全音 ➲ COMPARE SEMITONE, STEP *n.* (10) ➲ WORDFINDER NOTE AT SING

• **PHONETICS** 语音学 **8** [C] the PITCH (= how high or low a sound is) of a syllable in speaking（说话的）声调，音调：*a **rising/falling tone*** 升调；降调 **9** a particular PITCH pattern on a syllable in languages such as Chinese, that can be used to distinguish different meanings（字的）声调；字调 ➲ WORDFINDER NOTE AT PRONUNCIATION

• **-TONED** 有…音调 **10** (in adjectives 构成形容词) having the type of tone mentioned 有…音调的（或音质的、色调的）：*a bright-toned soprano* 声音嘹亮的女高音 ◇ *olive-toned skin* 黄褐色的皮肤

■ ***verb***

• **MUSCLES/SKIN** 肌肉；皮肤 **1** [T] ~ **sth** (**up**) to make your muscles, skin, etc. firmer and stronger 使更健壮；使更结实；使更有力：*Massage will help to tone up loose skin under the chin.* 按摩有助于使颏下松弛的皮肤紧起来。◇ *a beautifully toned body* 优美矫健的身体

• **COLOUR** 颜色 **2** [I] ~ (**in**) (**with sth**) (*BrE*) to match the colour of sth 与…协调；与…相配：*The beige of his jacket toned (in) with the cream shirt.* 他那夹克的米黄色与乳白色的衬衫非常协调。

PHR V **,tone sth↔'down 1** to make a speech, an opinion, etc. less extreme or offensive 使（讲话、意见等）缓和；使温和：*The language of the article will have to be toned down for the mass market.* 这篇文章的措辞必须缓和一下以适合大众市场。 **2** to make a colour less bright 使（颜色）柔和

,tone-'deaf *adj.* unable to hear the difference between musical notes 不能辨别音高的

'tone language *noun* a language in which differences in TONE (9) can change the meaning of words 声调语言（声调变化构成不同的语义）

tone·less /'təʊnləs; *NAmE* 'toʊn-/ *adj.* (of a voice, etc. 声音等) dull or flat; not expressing any emotion or interest 单调的；呆板的；沉闷的 ▸ **tone·less·ly** *adv.*

'tone poem *noun* a piece of music that is intended to describe a place or express an idea 音诗（文学性的管弦乐曲）

toner /'təʊnə(r); *NAmE* 'toʊ-/ *noun* [U, C] **1** a type of ink used in machines that print or photocopy（打印机或复印机使用的）墨粉 **2** a liquid or cream used for making the skin on your face firm and smooth 护肤霜；爽肤水

'tone unit (*also* **'tone group**) *noun* (*phonetics* 语音) the basic unit of INTONATION in a language which consists of one or more syllables with a complete PITCH movement 语调单位（即有完整音高变化的一个或多个音节）

tongs /tɒŋz; *NAmE* tɔːŋz; tɑːŋz/ *noun* [pl.] **1** a tool with two long parts that are joined at one end, used for picking up and holding things 夹剪；夹具；钳子；烧瓶钳：*a pair of tongs* 一把夹剪 ➲ VISUAL VOCAB PAGES V27, V28, V72 **2** (*also* **'curling tongs**) (*both BrE*) (*NAmE* **curling iron**) a tool that is heated and used for curling hair 烫发钳；卷发钳

IDM SEE HAMMER *n.*

tongue /tʌŋ/ *noun, verb*

■ ***noun*** **1** [C] the soft part in the mouth that moves around, used for tasting, swallowing, speaking, etc. 舌；舌头：*He clicked his tongue to attract their attention.* 他咂嘴发出啧啧声以吸引他们的注意。◇ *She ran her tongue over her lips.* 她用舌头舔着嘴唇。◇ *It's very rude to **stick your tongue out** at people.* 向别人吐舌头是非常不礼貌的。 **2** [U, C] the tongue of some animals, cooked and eaten 口条：*a slice of ox tongue* 一片牛口条 **3** [C] (*formal* or *literary*) a language 语言：*None of the tribes speak the same tongue.* 这些部落所说的语言都不相同。◇ *I tried speaking to her in her native tongue.* 我试着用她的本族语和她说话。➲ SEE ALSO MOTHER TONGUE **4** [sing.] a particular way of speaking 说话方式：*He has a sharp tongue.* 他说话尖酸刻薄。◇ (*formal*) *I'll thank you to **keep a civil tongue in your head*** (= speak politely). 请你说话讲究礼貌。➲ SEE ALSO SILVER TONGUE **5 -tongued** (in adjectives 构成形容词) speaking in the way mentioned 有…说话方式的；说话…的：*sharp-tongued* 说话尖刻的 **6** [C] a long narrow piece of leather under the LACES on a shoe 鞋舌 ➲ VISUAL VOCAB PAGE V69 **7** [C] ~ (**of sth**) (*literary*) something that is long and narrow and shaped like a tongue 舌状物：*a tongue of flame* 火舌

IDM **get your 'tongue around/round sth** to pronounce a difficult word correctly 正确发出（难读单词）的音 **,hold** your 'tongue/'peace (*old-fashioned*) to say nothing although you would like to give your opinion 忍住不说；保持缄默 **roll/slip/trip off the 'tongue** to be easy to say or pronounce 容易说（或发音）；顺口：*It's not a name that exactly trips off the tongue, is it?* 这个名字叫起来拗口，是不是？ **set 'tongues wagging** (*informal*) to cause people to start talking about sb's private affairs 惹得满城风雨；使议论纷纷；招闲话 **with your tongue in your 'cheek | with tongue in 'cheek** if you say sth **with your tongue in your cheek**, you are not being serious and mean it as a joke 说说而已；半开玩笑地 ➲ MORE AT BITE *v.*, FIND *v.*, LOOSE *adj.*, LOOSEN, SLIP *n.*, TIP *n.*, WATCH *v.*

■ *verb* **1 ~ sth** to stop the flow of air into a wind instrument with your tongue in order to make a note 吹奏（管乐器） **2 ~ sth** to LICK sth with your tongue 舔

ˌtongue and 'groove *noun* [U] wooden boards that have a long cut along one edge and a long RIDGE along the other, which are used to connect them together 企口接合板；榫槽接合板

'tongue depressor (*NAmE*) (*BrE* **spat·ula**) *noun* a thin flat instrument that doctors use for pressing the tongue down when they are examining sb's throat 压舌板，压舌器（医生诊症用）

ˌtongue-in-'cheek *adj.* not intended seriously; done or said as a joke 言不由衷的；随便说说的；开玩笑的：*a tongue-in-cheek remark* 一句戏言 ► **ˌtongue-in-'cheek** *adv.*：*The offer was made almost tongue-in-cheek.* 这种提议差不多只是说说而已。

'tongue-tied *adj.* not able to speak because you are shy or nervous（因害羞或紧张）张口结舌的，说不出话来的

'tongue-twister *noun* a word or phrase that is difficult to say quickly or correctly, such as 'She sells sea shells on the seashore.' 绕口令

tonic /'tɒnɪk; *NAmE* 'tɑːn-/ *noun* **1** (*also* **'tonic water**) [U, C] a clear FIZZY drink (= with bubbles in it) with a slightly bitter taste, that is often mixed with a strong alcoholic drink, especially GIN or VODKA 奎宁水，汤力水（一种味微苦、常加于烈性酒中的有气饮料）：*a gin and tonic* 一杯杜松子酒奎宁水 **2** [C] a medicine that makes you feel stronger and healthier, taken especially when you feel tired 补药；滋补品：*herbal tonics* 滋补草药 **3** [C, U] a liquid that you put on your hair or skin in order to make it healthier 护发液；护肤液：*skin tonic* 护肤液 **4** [C, usually sing.] (*old-fashioned*) anything that makes people feel healthier or happier 使精神振奋的东西：*The weekend break was just the tonic I needed.* 周末休息正是我所需要的养精蓄锐的机会。 **5** [C] (*music* 音) the first note of a SCALE of eight notes 主音（自然音阶中的第一音） **6** (*also* **ˌtonic 'syllable**) [C] (*phonetics* 语音) the syllable in a TONE UNIT on which a change in PITCH takes place 语调音节，语调核心（区别音高变化的音节）

ˌtonic ˌsol-'fa *noun* = SOL-FA

ton·ify /'təʊnɪfaɪ; *NAmE* 'toʊn-/ *verb* (**toni·fies, toni·fy·ing, toni·fied, toni·fied**) **~ sth** to make a part of the body firmer, smoother and stronger, by exercise or by applying special creams, etc.（通过锻炼或涂特殊的护肤霜等）改善（身体部位）状况

to·night 🔑 /tə'naɪt/ *adv., noun*

■ *adv.* 🔑 on or during the evening or night of today 在今夜；在今晚：*Will you have dinner with me tonight?* 今天晚上和我一起吃饭好吗？ ◇ *It's cold tonight.* 今天晚上很冷。

■ *noun* 🔑 [U] the evening or night of today 今夜；今晚：*Here are tonight's football results.* 现在报告今晚足球比赛的结果。◇ *Tonight will be cloudy.* 今天夜间多云。

ton·nage /'tʌnɪdʒ/ *noun* [U, C] **1** the size of a ship or the amount it can carry, expressed in tons（表示船舶大小或载重量的）吨位 **2** the total amount that sth weighs（某物的）总重量

tonne 🔑 /tʌn/ (*pl.* **tonnes** or **tonne**) (*also* **ˌmetric 'ton**) *noun* a unit for measuring weight, equal to 1 000 kilograms 吨（等于 1 000 公斤）：*a record grain harvest of 236m tonnes* 创纪录的 2.36 亿公吨谷物收获量 ◇ *a 17-tonne truck* * 17 吨卡车 ➲ COMPARE TON (1)

ton·sil /'tɒnsl; *NAmE* 'tɑːnsl/ *noun* either of the two small organs at the sides of the throat, near the base of the tongue 扁桃体：*I've had my tonsils out* (= removed). 我的扁桃体已被切除了。➲ VISUAL VOCAB PAGE V64

ton·sil·lec·tomy /ˌtɒnsə'lektəmi; *NAmE* ˌtɑːn-/ *noun* (*pl.* **-ies**) (*medical* 医) a medical operation to remove the TONSILS 扁桃体切除术

ton·sil·litis /ˌtɒnsə'laɪtɪs; *NAmE* ˌtɑːn-/ *noun* [U] an infection of the tonsils in which they become swollen and sore 扁桃体炎

ton·sure /'tɒnʃə(r); *NAmE* 'tɑːn-/ *noun* the part of a MONK's or priest's head that has been shaved（僧侣或教士的）头顶剃光部位

Tony /'təʊni; *NAmE* 'toʊni/ *noun* (*pl.* **Tonys**) an award given in the US for achievement in the theatre 托尼奖（美国的舞台剧成就奖）

tony /'təʊni; *NAmE* 'toʊni/ *adj.* (*NAmE, informal, becoming old-fashioned*) fashionable and expensive 豪华的；时兴而昂贵的

too 🔑 /tuː/ *adv.* **1** 🔑 used before adjectives and adverbs to say that sth is more than is good, necessary, possible, etc.（用于形容词和副词前）太，过于，过度：*He's far too young to go on his own.* 他年纪太小，不能独自一人去。◇ *This is too large a helping for me/This helping is too large for me.* 这一份太多，我吃不了。◇ *Is it too much to ask for a little quiet?* 请略微安静一点儿，这个要求过分吗？◇ *The dress was too tight for me.* 这件连衣裙我穿太瘦了。◇ *It's too late to do anything about it now.* 现在进行任何补救都为时太晚。◇ *Accidents like this happen* ***all too*** (= much too) *often.* 这类事故发生得太频繁了。 **2** 🔑 (usually placed at the end of a clause 通常置于句末) also; as well 也；又；还：*Can I come too?* 我也可以来吗？◇ *When I've finished painting the bathroom, I'm going to do the kitchen too.* 我油漆完浴室后，还要油漆厨房。 ➲ NOTE AT ALSO ➲ SEE ALSO ME-TOO **3** used to comment on sth that makes a situation worse（评说某事物使情况更糟）而且，还：*She broke her leg last week—and on her birthday too!* 她上星期把腿摔断了，而且还是在她生日那一天！ **4** 🔑 very 很；非常：*I'm not too sure if this is right.* 这是否正确，我没有太大把握。◇ *I'm just going out—I won't be too long.* 我正要出去，用不了多长时间。◇ *She's* ***none too*** (= not very) *clever.* 她不很聪明。 **5** used to emphasize sth, especially your anger, surprise or agreement with sth（用以强调生气、惊奇或同意等）：*'He did apologize eventually.' 'I should think so too!'* "他终于道歉了。" "我想他应该如此！" ◇ *'She gave me the money.' 'About time too!'* "她把那钱给我了。" "早该这样！"

IDM **be too 'much (for sb)** 🔑 to need more skill or strength than you have; to be more difficult, annoying, etc. than you can bear 非…力所能及；非…所能忍受 ➲ MORE AT RIGHT *adj.*

took PAST TENSE OF TAKE

tool 🔑 /tuːl/ *noun, verb*

■ *noun* **1** 🔑 an instrument such as a hammer, SCREWDRIVER, SAW, etc. that you hold in your hand and use for making things, repairing things, etc. 工具：*garden tools* 园艺工具 ◇ *a cutting tool* 切削工具 ◇ *power tools* (= using electricity) 电动工具 ◇ *Always select the right tool for the job.* 一定要选对干活的工具。 ➲ VISUAL VOCAB PAGE V21 **2** 🔑 a thing that helps you to do your job or to achieve sth（有助于做工或完成某事的）用具，器具，手段，方法：*research tools like questionnaires* 问卷之类的研究手段 ◇ *The computer is now an invaluable tool for the family doctor.* 计算机现在是家庭医生非常有用的工具。 ◇ *Some of them carried the guns which were* ***the tools of their trade*** (= the things they needed to do their job). 他们有些人携带着喷枪，那是干他们那一行的器具。 **3** a person who is used or controlled by another person or group 受人利用

T

的人；工具：*The prime minister was an unwitting tool of the president.* 首相不知不觉被总统利用了。**4** (*taboo, slang*) a PENIS 鸡巴；屌 IDM SEE DOWN *v.*

■ *verb* [I] + **adv./prep.** (*NAmE, informal*) to drive around in a vehicle 驱车兜风；驾车到处跑

PHR V ˌ**tool ˈup** | ˌ**tool sb/sth↔ˈup** (*specialist*) to get or provide sb/sth with the equipment, etc. that is necessary to do or produce sth 获得（或提供）必要的设备；给…配置装备：*The factory is not tooled up to produce this type of engine.* 这家工厂还没有装置生产这类发动机的设备。

tool·bar /ˈtuːlbɑː(r)/ *noun* (*computing* 计) a row of symbols (= ICONS) on a computer screen, SMARTPHONE, etc. that show the different things that you can do with a particular program（计算机、手机等屏幕上的）工具栏

tool·box /ˈtuːlbɒks; *NAmE* -bɑːks/ *noun* a box with a lid for keeping tools in 工具箱 ➲ VISUAL VOCAB PAGE V21

tooled /tuːld/ *adj.* (of leather 皮革) decorated with patterns made with a special heated tool 热烫花的；压花的

tool·kit /ˈtuːlkɪt/ *noun* **1** a set of tools in a box or bag（装在箱子或包里的）一套工具；工具箱；工具包 **2** (*computing* 计) a set of software tools 配套软件；软件包；工具箱 **3** the things that you need in order to achieve sth 配备用品；装备

tool·maker /ˈtuːlmeɪkə(r)/ *noun* a person or company that makes tools, especially ones used in industry（尤指工业用）工具制造者，工具制造厂 ▸ **tool·mak·ing** /ˈtuːlmeɪkɪŋ/ *noun* [U]

tool·tip /ˈtuːltɪp/ *noun* (*computing* 计) a message that appears when you move a CURSOR over an image, a symbol, a link, etc. on a computer screen 工具提示，提示框，提示条（把光标移到电脑屏幕上的图像、符号、链接等处时出现的信息）：*Moving your mouse over an icon displays a tooltip explaining its function.* 将鼠标移到图标上，会显示提示条解释其功能。

toonie /ˈtuːni/ *noun* (*CanE*) the Canadian two-dollar coin 两加元硬币

toot /tuːt/ *noun, verb*

■ *noun* a short high sound made by a car horn or a whistle（喇叭、哨子等发出的）嘟嘟声：*She gave a sharp toot on her horn.* 她高声按响了喇叭。

■ *verb* [I, T] (*especially BrE*) when a car horn **toots** or you **toot** it, it makes a short high sound（使汽车喇叭）发出短促尖锐的声音，发出嘟嘟声：*the sound of horns tooting* 鸣喇叭的声音 ◇ ~ **sth** *Toot your horn to let them know we're here.* 按按喇叭，告诉他们我们到了。IDM SEE HORN *n.* ➲ MORE LIKE THIS 3, page R25

tooth 🔑 /tuːθ/ *noun* (*pl.* **teeth** /tiːθ/) **1** 🔑 any of the hard white structures in the mouth used for biting and chewing food 牙；齿：*I've just* ***had a tooth out*** *at the dentist's.* 我刚在牙科诊所拔了一颗牙。◇ *to* ***brush/clean your teeth*** 刷牙 ◇ ***tooth decay*** 龋齿 ◇ *She answered* ***through clenched teeth*** (= opening her mouth only a little because of anger). 她咬牙切齿地回答。◇ *The cat* ***sank its teeth into*** *his finger.* 那只猫狠狠咬住了他的手指。➲ COLLOCATIONS AT PHYSICAL ➲ VISUAL VOCAB PAGE V64 ➲ SEE ALSO BUCK TEETH, FALSE TEETH, MILK TOOTH, WISDOM TOOTH **2** a narrow pointed part that sticks out of an object 齿状部分；齿：*the teeth on a saw* 锯齿 ➲ VISUAL VOCAB PAGE V68 ➲ SEE ALSO FINE-TOOTH COMB

IDM **cut your teeth on sth** to do sth that gives you your first experience of a particular type of work 从…中获得初步经验；初次涉足 **cut a ˈtooth** (of a baby 婴儿) to grow a new tooth 出牙；长出新牙 **get your ˈteeth into sth** (*informal*) to put a lot of effort and enthusiasm into sth that is difficult enough to keep you interested 专注于，全力投入（有一定难度的事）：*Choose an essay topic that you can really get your teeth into.* 选择一个你可以真正悉心钻研的论文题目。**have ˈteeth** (*informal*) (of an organization, a law, etc. 组织、法律等) to be powerful and effective 具有强大威力；有杀伤力 **in the teeth of sth 1** despite problems, opposition, etc. 不管，不顾，尽管遇到（困难、反对等）：*The new policy was adopted in the teeth of fierce criticism.* 新政策尽管受到强烈的批评，但还是被采用了。**2** in the direction that a strong wind is coming from 顶着，迎着（强风）：*They crossed the bay in the teeth of a howling gale.* 他们顶着呼啸的狂风渡过了海湾。**set sb's ˈteeth on edge** (of a sound or taste 声音或味道) to make sb feel physically uncomfortable 使感到身体不舒服：*Just the sound of her voice sets my teeth on edge.* 我一听到她的声音就浑身不舒服。➲ MORE AT ARMED, BARE *v.*, BIT, EYE *n.*, EYE TEETH, FIGHT *v.*, GNASH, GRIT *v.*, HELL, KICK *v.*, KICK *n.*, LIE² *v.*, LONG *adj.*, RED *adj.*, SKIN *n.*, SWEET *adj.*

tooth·ache /ˈtuːθeɪk/ *noun* [U, C, usually sing.] a pain in your teeth or in one tooth 牙痛：(*BrE*) *I've got toothache.* 我牙疼。◇ (*NAmE, BrE*) *I've got a toothache.* 我牙疼。

tooth·brush /ˈtuːθbrʌʃ/ *noun* a small brush for cleaning your teeth 牙刷 ➲ VISUAL VOCAB PAGE V25

ˌ**toothbrush mousˈtache** *noun* a short MOUSTACHE cut with square corners（修剪成方形的）牙刷形胡子

toothed /tuːθt; tuːðd/ *adj.* [only before noun] **1** (*specialist*) having teeth 有齿的：*a toothed whale* 齿鲸 **2 -toothed** (in compounds 构成复合词) having the type of teeth mentioned 有…齿的：*a gap-toothed smile* 露出稀疏牙齿的微笑 ➲ MORE LIKE THIS 8, page R25

the ˈtooth fairy *noun* [sing.] an imaginary creature that is said to take away a tooth that a small child leaves near his or her bed at night and to leave a coin there in its place 牙仙子（传说会取去幼儿脱落并放于床边的乳齿，在原处留下一枚钱币）

tooth·less /ˈtuːθləs/ *adj.* **1** having no teeth 无牙的；无齿的：*a toothless old man* 没牙的老头 ◇ *She gave us a toothless grin.* 她张开没牙的嘴巴对我们笑了笑。**2** having no power or authority 人微言轻的；没有权威的；不起作用的

tooth·paste /ˈtuːθpeɪst/ *noun* [U] a substance that you put on a brush and use to clean your teeth 牙膏 ➲ VISUAL VOCAB PAGE V25

tooth·pick /ˈtuːθpɪk/ *noun* a short pointed piece of wood or plastic used for removing bits of food from between the teeth 牙签

tooth·some /ˈtuːθsəm/ *adj.* (*humorous*) (of food 食物) tasting good 美味的；可口的 SYN **tasty**

toothy /ˈtuːθi/ *adj.* a **toothy** smile shows a lot of teeth（笑时）露齿的，多齿的

too·tle /ˈtuːtl/ *verb* (*informal*) **1** [I] + **adv./prep.** to walk, drive, etc. somewhere without hurrying 信步；闲逛；溜达；不慌不忙地开车 **2** [I, T] ~ (**sth**) to produce a series of notes by blowing into a musical instrument 连续吹（乐器）；发出一连串的嘟嘟声

toot·sies /ˈtʊtsɪz/ *noun* [pl.] (*informal*) (used by or when speaking to young children 儿语) toes or feet 脚趾；脚丫

top 🔑 /tɒp; *NAmE* tɑːp/ *noun, adj., verb*

■ *noun*

• **HIGHEST POINT** 最高点 **1** 🔑 [C] the highest part or point of sth 顶；顶部；顶端：*She was standing* ***at the top*** *of the stairs.* 她站在楼梯的顶端。◇ *Write your name at the top.* 把你的姓名写在上端。◇ *The title is* ***right at the top*** *of the page.* 标题就在页面的顶端。◇ *He filled my glass* ***to the top.*** 他把我的杯子斟得满满的。◇ *We climbed to the* ***very top*** *of the hill.* 我们爬到了山的最高点。◇ *Snow was falling on the mountain tops.* 山顶上正在下雪。◇ (*BrE*) *the top of the milk* (= the cream that rises to the top of a bottle of milk) 牛奶表面的奶皮 ◇ *The wind was blowing in the tops of the trees.* 风儿吹拂着树梢。➲ SEE ALSO ROOFTOP, TREETOP

• **UPPER SURFACE** 上层表面 **2** 🔑 [C] the upper flat surface of sth 表面；上面：*Can you polish the top of the table?* 请把桌面擦亮好吗？◇ *a desk top* 桌面 ➲ SEE ALSO HARDTOP, ROLL-TOP DESK, TABLETOP

• **HIGHEST RANK** 最高等级 **3** 🔑 [sing.] **the ~ (of sth)** the highest or most important rank or position 最高的级别；最重要的职位：*He's at the top of his profession.* 他正处于

事业的巅峰。◇ *She is determined to make it to the top* (= achieve fame or success). 她决心要出人头地。◇ *They finished the season at the top of the league.* 他们打完这个赛季之后积分高居联赛的榜首。◇ *We have a lot of things to do, but packing is at the* ***top of the list****.* 我们有许多事情要做，但首先是打点行装。◇ *This decision came from the top.* 这个决定是由最高领导作出的。

• **FARTHEST POINT** 最远点 **4** [sing.] **the ~ of sth** the end of a street, table, etc. that is farthest away from you or from where you usually come to it 尽头；远端：*I'll meet you at the top of Thorpe Street.* 我会和你在索普大街的尽头碰面。

• **OF PEN/BOTTLE** 笔；瓶子 **5** [C] a thing that you put on the end of sth to close it 帽；盖；塞：*Where's the top of this pen?* 这支笔的笔帽在哪儿？◇ *a bottle with a screw top* 带螺旋盖儿的瓶子 ➲ SYNONYMS AT LID ➲ VISUAL VOCAB PAGE V36

• **CLOTHING** 衣服 **6** [C] a piece of clothing worn on the upper part of the body 上衣：*I need a top to go with this skirt.* 我需要一件上衣来配这条裙子。◇ *a* ***tracksuit/pyjama/bikini top*** 运动服上衣；睡衣 / 比基尼泳装的上部 ➲ SEE ALSO CROP TOP

• **LEAVES OF PLANT** 植物的叶子 **7** [C, usually pl.] the leaves of a plant that is grown mainly for its root（根菜作物的）茎叶：*Remove the green tops from the carrots.* 去掉胡萝卜的绿叶。

• **AMOUNT OF MONEY** 款额 **8 tops** [pl.] used after an amount of money to show that it is the highest possible（用于款额后）最高额：*It couldn't have cost more than £50, tops.* 这东西的价格最高不会超过 50 英镑。

• **BEST** 最好 **9 tops** [pl.] (*old-fashioned, informal*) a person or thing of the best quality 最优秀的人；最好的东西；精华：*Among sports superstars she's (the) tops.* 她在超级体育明星中独占鳌头。◇ *In the survey the Brits come out tops for humour.* 这项调查显示，英国人的幽默是首屈一指的。

• **TOY** 玩具 **10** [C] a child's toy that spins on a point when it is turned round very quickly by hand or by a string 陀螺：*She was so confused—her mind was* ***spinning like a top****.* 她如坠五里雾中，被搞得晕头转向。➲ SEE ALSO BIG TOP

IDM **at the top of the 'tree** in the highest position or rank in a profession or career（在行业、事业中）高居首位，处于顶峰 **at the top of your 'voice** as loudly as possible 高声地；放声地；扯着喉咙地：*She was screaming at the top of her voice.* 她在声嘶力竭地尖叫。 **come out on 'top** to win a contest or an argument（在比赛或辩论中）名列前茅，先拔头筹：*In most boardroom disputes he tends to come out on top.* 在大多数董事会议的辩论中，他往往占据上风。 **from ˌtop to 'bottom** going to every part of a place in a very thorough way 从上到下；彻底地：*We cleaned the house from top to bottom.* 我们把房子彻底打扫了一遍。 **from ˌtop to 'toe** completely; all over 从头到脚；浑身上下；全部：*She was dressed in green from top to toe.* 她从头到脚穿了一身绿。 **get on 'top of sb** to be too much for sb to manage or deal with 使吃不消；使应接不暇：*All this extra work is getting on top of him.* 这么多的额外工作快使他吃不消了。 **get on 'top of sth** to manage to control or deal with sth 设法驾驭；处理：*How will I ever get on top of all this work?* 我究竟怎样才处理得了这么多的工作？ **off the ˌtop of your 'head** (*informal*) just guessing or using your memory, without taking time to think carefully or check the facts 单凭猜测（或记忆）；信口地；不假思索地：*I can't remember the name off the top of my head, but I can look it up for you.* 我一时想不起这个名字，不过我可以给你查一查。 **on 'top 1** on the highest point or surface 在上面；在顶部：*a cake with cream on top* 上面浇有奶油的蛋糕 ◇ *Stand on top and look down.* 站在顶上俯视。◇ *He's going bald on top* (= on the top of his head). 他谢顶了。 **2** in a leading position or in control 处于领先地位；控制局面：*She remained on top for the rest of the match.* 在比赛的余下部分她一直领先。 **3** in addition 另外；加之：*Look, here's 30 dollars, and I'll buy you lunch on top.* 你看，这是给你的 30 美元，另外我还会给你买午餐。 **on top of sth/sb 1** on, over or covering sth/sb 在…上面；在…上方；覆盖着：*Books were piled on top of one another.* 书一本一本地摞在一起。◇ *Many people were crushed when the building collapsed on top of them.* 那座楼房倒塌时砸伤了下面许多人。 **2** in addition to sth 除…之外：*He gets commission on top of his salary.* 他除了薪金之外还拿佣金。◇ *On top of everything else, my car's been stolen.* 我所有的东西都被盗，连汽车也给偷走了。 **3** very close to sth/sb 紧挨着；与…紧靠着：*We were all living on top of each other in that tiny apartment.* 我们都挤着住在那套小小的公寓里。 **4** in control of a situation 控制着；掌握着：*Do you think he's really on top of his job?* 你认为他真的能做好他的工作吗？ **on ˌtop of the 'world** very happy or proud 欢天喜地；心满意足；非常自豪 **ˌover the 'top** (*abbr.* **OTT**) (*informal, especially BrE*) done to an exaggerated degree and with too much effort 过分；过火；过头：*His performance is completely over the top.* 他的表演完全过火了。◇ *an over-the-top reaction* 过头的反应 **ˌtake sth from the 'top** (*informal*) to go back to the beginning of a song, piece of music, etc. and repeat it 从头再唱（或再奏等）：*OK, everybody, let's take it from the top.* 好，咱们大家从头再唱一遍。 **up 'top** (*BrE, informal*) used to talk about a person's intelligence（指人的智力）头脑，脑子：*He hasn't got much up top* (= he isn't very intelligent). 他没有多少脑子。 ➲ MORE AT BLOW *v.*, HEAP *n.*, PILE *n.*, THIN *adj.*

■ ***adj.*** [usually before noun] **1** highest in position, rank or degree（位置、级别或程度）最高的：*He lives on the top floor.* 他住在顶层。◇ *She kept her passport in the top drawer.* 她把护照存放在最上层抽屉里。◇ *He's one of the top players in the country.* 他是国内最优秀的运动员之一。◇ *She got the top job.* 她得到了那个最高职位。◇ *He finished top in the exam.* 他考试得了第一名。◇ *She got top marks for her essay.* 她的论文得了最高分。◇ *They're top of the league.* 他们是联赛的领头羊。◇ *The athletes are all on top form* (= performing their best). 运动员都处于最佳竞技状态。◇ *Welfare reform is a top priority for the government.* 福利改革是政府的当务之急。◇ *The car was travelling at top speed.* 那辆汽车全速行驶。 **2** (*BrE, informal*) very good 很好的；极棒的；顶呱呱的：*He's a top bloke.* 他是个大好人。

■ ***verb*** (-pp-)

• **BE MORE** 多出 **1 ~ sth** to be higher than a particular amount 高于，超过（某一数量）：*Worldwide sales look set to top $1 billion.* 全球销售额看来很可能要超过 10 亿美元。

• **BE THE BEST** 是最好 **2 ~ sth** to be in the highest position on a list because you are the most successful, important, etc. 居…之首；为…之冠：*The band topped the charts for five weeks with their first single.* 这支乐队的第一张单曲唱片有五个星期高居最畅销流行音乐唱片榜榜首。

• **PUT ON TOP** 置于顶端 **3** [usually passive] **~ sth (with sth)** to put sth on the top of sth else 把（某物）放在…的上面：*fruit salad topped with cream* 上面浇了奶油的水果色拉

• **SAY/DO STH BETTER** 说 / 做得更好 **4 ~ sth** to say or do sth that is better, funnier, more impressive, etc. than sth that sb else has said or done in the past 胜过，优于，压倒（前人所做）：*I'm afraid the other company has topped your offer* (= offered more money). 很抱歉，另一家公司出价比你们高。

• **KILL YOURSELF** 自杀 **5 ~ yourself** (*BrE, informal*) to kill yourself deliberately 自杀

• **CLIMB HILL** 爬山 **6 ~ sth** (*literary*) to reach the highest point of a hill, etc. 到达山顶；达到顶端

IDM **to top/cap it 'all** (*informal*) used to introduce the final piece of information that is worse than the other bad things that you have just mentioned 更有甚者；最糟糕的是 **ˌtop and 'tail sth** (*BrE*) to cut the top and bottom parts off fruit and vegetables to prepare them to be cooked or eaten 去掉（水果、蔬菜）的两端；砍掉…的两头 ➲ MORE LIKE THIS 13, page R26

PHR V **ˌtop sth↔'off (with sth)** to complete sth successfully by doing or adding one final thing 以…圆满结束；用…完成 **ˌtop 'out (at sth)** if sth **tops out** at a particular price, speed, etc. it does not rise any higher（价格、速度等）达到顶点，到最高点：*Inflation topped out at 12%.* 通货膨胀最高达到了 12%。 **ˌtop sth↔'up** (*especially BrE*) **1** to fill a container that already has some liquid in it with more liquid 装满，注满（未满的容器）：*Top the car up with oil before you set off.* 出发前给车加满油。◇ *Top the*

T

oil up before you set off. 出发前加满油。 **2** to increase the amount of sth to the level you want or need 补足；将…增加到所需的量： *She relies on tips to top up her wages.* 她靠小费弥补工资的不足。◇ (*BrE*) *I need to top up my mobile phone* (= pay more money so you can make more calls). 我需要给手机充够值。 ➲ RELATED NOUN TOP-UP **ˌtop sb ˈup** (*especially BrE*) to fill sb's glass or cup with sth more to drink 给…的杯子斟满（饮料）： *Can I top you up?* 把你的杯子加满好吗？ ➲ RELATED NOUN TOP-UP (2)

topaz /ˈtəʊpæz; *NAmE* ˈtoʊ-/ *noun* [C, U] a clear yellow SEMI-PRECIOUS stone 黄玉： *a topaz ring* 黄宝石戒指

ˌtop ˈbrass *noun* [sing.+sing./pl. v.] (*informal*) = BRASS (5)

ˌtop-ˈclass *adj.* of the highest quality or standard 头等的；第一流的；顶级的： *a top-class performance* 顶级的表演

top·coat /ˈtɒpkəʊt; *NAmE* ˈtɑːpkoʊt/ *noun* **1** the last layer of paint put on a surface（油漆等的）外涂层 ➲ COMPARE UNDERCOAT **2** (*old-fashioned*) an OVERCOAT 大衣

ˌtop ˈdog *noun* [usually sing.] (*informal*) a person, group or country that is better than all the others, especially in a situation that involves competition（尤指竞争中的）夺魁者，优胜者

ˌtop ˈdollar *noun*

IDM **pay, earn, charge, etc. top ˈdollar** (*informal*) pay, earn, charge, etc. a lot of money 支付（或赚得、收取等）一大笔钱： *If you want the best, you have to pay top dollar.* 你想要最好的，就得花大钱。◇ *We can help you get top dollar when you sell your house.* 您卖房子我们能帮您卖个好价钱。

ˌtop-ˈdown *adj.* **1** (of a plan, project, etc. 计划、项目等) starting with a general idea to which details are added later 从总体到具体的；自上而下的；先总后分的 ➲ COMPARE BOTTOM-UP **2** starting from or involving the people who have higher positions in an organization（组织或机构中）自上而下的，与高层有关的： *a top-down management style* 自上而下的管理方式

ˌtop ˈdrawer *noun* [sing.] if sb/sth is out of **the top drawer**, they are of the highest social class or of the highest quality（社会地位的）最上层，最高层；精华 ▸ **ˌtop-ˈdrawer** *adj.*

topee = TOPI

ˌtop-ˈend *adj.* [only before noun] among the best, most expensive, etc. examples of sth 最高档的；最昂贵的；最高级的： *Many people are upgrading their mobiles to top-end models.* 很多人不断将手机升级到最高档的款式。

ˌtop-ˈflight *adj.* of the highest quality; the best or most successful 第一流的；最高档的；最佳的；最成功的

ˌtop ˈgear *noun* [U] the highest gear in a vehicle（车辆变速器的）最高挡： *They cruised along **in top gear**.* 他们驾车高速行驶。◇ (*figurative*) *Her career is moving into top gear.* 她的事业正如日中天。

ˌtop-ˈgrossing *adj.* [only before noun] earning more money than other similar things or people 赚钱最多的；收入最高的： *the top-grossing movie of 2013* * 2013 年票房收入最高的影片

ˌtop ˈhat (*also informal* **top·per**) *noun* a man's tall black or grey hat, worn with formal clothes on very formal occasions 高顶礼帽 ➲ VISUAL VOCAB PAGE V70

ˌtop-ˈheavy *adj.* **1** too heavy at the top and therefore likely to fall 上部过重的；头重脚轻的 **2** (of an organization 组织) having too many senior staff compared to the number of workers 高级职员过多的；将多兵少的

ˌtop-ˈhole *adj.* (*old-fashioned, BrE, informal*) excellent 极好的；很棒的

topi (*also* **topee**) /ˈtəʊpi; *NAmE* ˈtoʊpi; toʊˈpiː/ *noun* a light hard hat worn to give protection from the sun in very hot countries 遮阳帽；通草帽

topi·ary /ˈtəʊpiəri; *NAmE* ˈtoʊpieri/ *noun* [U] the art of cutting bushes into shapes such as birds or animals 树木造型；绿雕塑

topic 🔑 **AW** /ˈtɒpɪk; *NAmE* ˈtɑːp-/ *noun* a subject that you talk, write or learn about 话题；题目；标题： *The main **topic of conversation** was Tom's new girlfriend.* 交谈的主要话题是汤姆的新女友。◇ *The article covered a wide range of topics.* 这篇文章讨论了一系列广泛的论题。

IDM **on ˈtopic** appropriate or relevant to the situation 切题： *Keep the text short and on topic.* 文章要简短切题。◇ *Let's get back on topic.* 我们回到正题上来吧。 **off ˈtopic** not appropriate or relevant to the situation 离题；跑题： *That comment is completely off topic.* 这个评论完全脱离主题。◇ *He keeps veering off topic.* 他总是偏离主题。

top·ic·al **AW** /ˈtɒpɪkl; *NAmE* ˈtɑːp-/ *adj.* **1** connected with sth that is happening or of interest at the present time 有关时事的；当前关注的；热门话题的： *a topical joke/reference* 时事笑话；提及热门话题 ◇ *topical events* 当前人们所关注的事件 **2** (*medical* 医) connected with, or put directly on, a part of the body （身体）局部的，表面的 ▸ **top·ic·al·ity** /ˌtɒpɪˈkæləti; *NAmE* ˌtɑːp-/ *noun* [U, sing.]

top·knot /ˈtɒpnɒt; *NAmE* ˈtɑːpnɑːt/ *noun* a way of arranging your hair in which it is tied up on the top of your head 顶髻

top·less /ˈtɒpləs; *NAmE* ˈtɑːp-/ *adj.* (of a woman 女人) not wearing any clothes on the upper part of the body so that her breasts are not covered 上身裸露的；不穿上装的： *a topless model* 上身裸露的模特儿 ◇ *a topless bar* (= where the female staff are topless) 女招待不穿上装的酒吧 ▸ **top·less** *adv.* : *to sunbathe topless* 裸露着上身沐日光浴

ˌtop-ˈlevel *adj.* [only before noun] involving the most important or best people in a company, an organization or a sport 顶级的；最高级别的： *a top-level meeting* 最高级会谈 ◇ *top-level tennis* 顶级网球比赛

top·most /ˈtɒpməʊst; *NAmE* ˈtɑːpmoʊst/ *adj.* [only before noun] (*formal*) highest 最高的；最上面的： *the topmost branches of the tree* 树顶的枝丫

ˌtop-ˈnotch *adj.* (*informal*) excellent; of the highest quality 最好的；卓越的；第一流的

ˌtop of the ˈrange (*BrE*) (*NAmE* **ˌtop of the ˈline**) *adj.* [usually before noun] used to describe the most expensive of a group of similar products （同类产品中）最昂贵的，最高价的： *Our equipment is top of the range.* 我们的设备是最昂贵的。◇ *our top-of-the-range model* 我们最昂贵的产品型号

top·og·raphy /təˈpɒɡrəfi; *NAmE* təˈpɑːɡ-/ *noun* [U] (*specialist*) the physical features of an area of land, especially the position of its rivers, mountains, etc.; the study of these features 地形；地貌；地势；地形学： *a map showing the topography of the island* 这个岛的地形图 ▸ **topo·graph·ic·al** /ˌtɒpəˈɡræfɪkl; *NAmE* ˌtɑːpə-/ (*also* **topo·graph·ic** /ˌtɒpəˈɡræfɪk; *NAmE* ˌtɑːpə-/) *adj.* : *a topographical map/feature* 地形图；地貌 **topo·graph·ic·al·ly** /-kli/ *adv.*

top·ology /təˈpɒlədʒi; *NAmE* -ˈpɑːl-/ *noun* [U, C] (*specialist*) the way the parts of sth are arranged and related 拓扑结构；构相： *The Canadian banking topology is relatively flat, with a few large banks controlling the entire market.* 加拿大银行业结构相对简单，由几家大银行控制着整个市场。

topo·nym /ˈtɒpənɪm; *NAmE* ˈtɑːp-/ *noun* (*specialist*) a place name 地名

topos /ˈtɒpɒs; *NAmE* ˈtoʊpɑːs; ˈtɑːp-/ *noun* (*pl.* **topoi** /ˈtɒpɔɪ; *NAmE* ˈtoʊ-; ˈtɑː-/) (*specialist*) a traditional subject or idea in literature（文学的）传统主题，传统观念

top·per /ˈtɒpə(r); *NAmE* ˈtɑːp-/ *noun* (*informal*) **1** = TOP HAT **2** (*IndE*) a student who gets the highest results in the class 尖子生；成绩最好的学生

top·ping /ˈtɒpɪŋ; *NAmE* ˈtɑːp-/ *noun* [C, U] a layer of food that you put on top of a dish, cake, etc. to add flavour or to make it look nice（菜肴、蛋糕等上的）浇汁，浇料，配料，佐料

top·ple /ˈtɒpl; *NAmE* ˈtɑːpl/ *verb* **1** [I, T] to become unsteady and fall down; to make sth do this（使）失去平衡而坠落，倒塌，倒下：**+ adv./prep.** *The pile of books toppled over.* 那一摞书倒了。◇ **~ sb/sth + adv./prep.** *He brushed past, toppling her from her stool.* 他经过时蹭了她一下，使她从凳子上摔了下来。**2** [T] **~ sb/sth** to make sb lose their position of power or authority 打倒；推翻；颠覆 **SYN overthrow**: *a plot to topple the President* 推翻总统的阴谋

ˌtop-ˈranking *adj.* [only before noun] of the highest rank, status or importance in an organization, a sport, etc.（组织、运动等中）最高级的，最重要的

ˌtop-ˈrated *adj.* [only before noun] most popular with the public 最受欢迎的；一流的：*a top-rated TV show* 最受欢迎的电视节目

top·sail /ˈtɒpseɪl; ˈtɒpsl; *NAmE* ˈtɑːpseɪl; ˈtɑːpsl/ *noun* [usually sing.] the sail attached to the upper part of the MAST of a ship 上桅帆

ˌtop ˈsecret *adj.* that must be kept completely secret, especially from other governments（尤指对他国政府）最高机密的，绝密的：*This information has been classified top secret.* 这一情报被归为绝密类别。◇ *top-secret documents* 绝密文件

ˌtop-ˈshelf *adj.* [only before noun] **1** (*BrE*) including pictures of naked people and/or sexual acts 含色情内容的：*top-shelf magazines/DVDs* 色情杂志 / 影碟 **2** (*especially NAmE*) of the highest class 一流的：*It is a top-shelf law firm.* 那是一家顶级律师事务所。

top·side /ˈtɒpsaɪd; *NAmE* ˈtɑːp-/ *noun* [U] (*BrE*) a piece of beef that is cut from the upper part of the leg 牛上股肉

top·soil /ˈtɒpsɔɪl; *NAmE* ˈtɑːp-/ *noun* [U] the layer of soil nearest the surface of the ground 表土；表土层 ➲ COMPARE SUBSOIL

top·spin /ˈtɒpspɪn; *NAmE* ˈtɑːp-/ *noun* [U] (*sport* 体育) the fast forward spinning movement that a player can give to a ball by hitting or throwing it in a special way（球的）上旋

topsy-turvy /ˌtɒpsi ˈtɜːvi; *NAmE* ˌtɑːpsi ˈtɜːrvi/ *adj.* (*informal*) in a state of great confusion 乱七八糟的；杂乱无章的；颠三倒四的：*Everything's topsy-turvy in my life at the moment.* 现在我的生活全都被打乱了。

ˌtop ˈtable (*BrE*) (*NAmE* **ˌhead ˈtable**) *noun* the table at which the most important guests sit at a formal dinner（正式宴会上的）主桌

the ˌtop ˈten *noun* [pl.] the ten pop records that have sold the most copies in a particular week（一周）流行音乐十大畅销唱片

ˈtop-up *noun* (*BrE*) **1** a payment that you make to increase the amount of money, etc. to the level that is needed 附加付款：*a phone top-up* (= to buy more time for calls) 电话充值费 ◇ *Students will have to pay top-up fees* (= fees that are above the basic level). 学生必须交附加费用。**2** (*informal*) an amount of a drink that you add to a cup or glass in order to fill it again（重新斟满杯子的）补充饮料：*Can I give anyone a top-up?* 我来给哪位添酒好吗？

ˈtop-up card *noun* a card that you buy for a mobile/cell phone so that you can make more calls to the value of the card 手机充值卡

toque /təʊk; *NAmE* toʊk/ *noun* **1** a woman's small hat 托克小女帽；无边（或小帽边）女帽 **2** (*CanE*) a close-fitting hat made of wool, sometimes with a ball of wool on the top 绒线保暖帽，绒线无边帽（有时顶部饰绒球）

tor /tɔː(r)/ *noun* a small hill with rocks at the top, especially in parts of SW England（尤指英格兰西南部的）突岩

Torah /ˈtɔːrɑː; tɔːˈrɑː/ *noun* [usually sing., U] (*usually* **the Torah**) (in Judaism 犹太教) the law of God as given to Moses and recorded in the first five books of the Bible 托拉，律法书，摩西五经（《圣经》中的首五卷）

torch /tɔːtʃ; *NAmE* tɔːrtʃ/ *noun, verb*

■ *noun* **1** (*BrE*) (*also* **flash·light** *NAmE, BrE*) a small electric lamp that uses batteries and that you can hold in your hand 手电筒：*Shine the torch on the lock while I try to get the key in.* 我插钥匙时，请用手电筒照着锁头。**2** (*NAmE*) = BLOWTORCH **3** a long piece of wood that has material at one end that is set on fire and that people carry to give light 火炬；火把：*a flaming torch* 燃烧着的火炬 ◇ *the Olympic torch* 奥林匹克火炬 ◇ (*figurative*) *They struggled to keep the torch of idealism and hope alive.* 他们为使理想主义和希望的火炬不熄灭而奋斗。

IDM **put sth to the ˈtorch** (*literary*) to set fire to sth deliberately 将…付之一炬 ➲ MORE AT CARRY

■ *verb* **~ sth** to set fire to a building or vehicle deliberately in order to destroy it 放火烧，纵火烧（建筑物或汽车）

torch·light /ˈtɔːtʃlaɪt; *NAmE* ˈtɔːrtʃ-/ *noun* [U] the light that is produced by an electric torch or by burning torches 手电筒光；火炬的光亮

ˈtorch song *noun* a type of sad romantic song about feelings of love for a person who does not share those feelings 单恋情歌；情殇曲；失恋情歌 ▸ **ˈtorch singer** *noun*

tore PAST TENSE OF TEAR[1]

torea·dor /ˈtɒriədɔː(r); *NAmE* ˈtɔːr-/ *noun* a man, especially one riding a horse, who fights BULLS to entertain people, for example in Spain（西班牙等地、尤指骑马的）斗牛士

tor·ment *noun, verb*

■ *noun* /ˈtɔːment; *NAmE* ˈtɔːrm-/ [U, C] (*formal*) extreme suffering, especially mental suffering; a person or thing that causes this（尤指精神上的）折磨，痛苦；苦难之源 **SYN anguish**: *the cries of a man **in torment*** 一个备受折磨的人的喊叫声 ◇ *She suffered years of mental torment after her son's death.* 儿子去世后，她多年悲痛欲绝。◇ *The flies were a terrible torment.* 苍蝇一度肆虐。

■ *verb* /tɔːˈment; *NAmE* tɔːrˈm-/ **1 ~ sb** (*formal*) to make sb suffer very much 使备受折磨；使痛苦；烦扰 **SYN plague**: *He was tormented by feelings of insecurity.* 他苦于没有安全感。**2 ~ sb/sth** to annoy a person or an animal in a cruel way because you think it is amusing 戏弄；捉弄；纠缠 **SYN torture** ➲ MORE LIKE THIS 21, page R27

tor·ment·or /tɔːˈmentə(r); *NAmE* tɔːrˈm-/ *noun* (*formal*) a person who causes sb to suffer 折磨人的人；折磨者

torn PAST PART. OF TEAR[1]

tor·nado /tɔːˈneɪdəʊ; *NAmE* tɔːrˈneɪdoʊ/ *noun* (*pl.* **-oes** or **-os**) a violent storm with very strong winds which move in a circle. There is often also a long cloud which is narrower at the bottom than the top. 龙卷风；旋风 ➲ WORDFINDER NOTE AT DISASTER, WIND[1] ➲ COLLOCATIONS AT WEATHER

tor·pedo /tɔːˈpiːdəʊ; *NAmE* tɔːrˈpiːdoʊ/ *noun, verb*

■ *noun* (*pl.* **-oes**) a long narrow bomb that is fired under the water from a ship or SUBMARINE and that explodes when it hits a ship, etc. 鱼雷 ➲ WORDFINDER NOTE AT NAVY

■ *verb* (**tor·pe·does**, **tor·pe·do·ing**, **tor·pe·doed**, **tor·pe·doed**) **1 ~ sth** to attack a ship or make it sink using a torpedo 用鱼雷袭击（或击沉） **2 ~ sth** to completely destroy the possibility that sth could succeed 彻底破坏，完全摧毁（某事成功的可能性）：*Her comments had torpedoed the deal.* 她的一番话使得那笔交易彻底告吹。

tor·pid /ˈtɔːpɪd; *NAmE* ˈtɔːrpɪd/ *adj.* (*formal*) not active; with no energy or enthusiasm 不活泼的；迟钝的；有气无力的；懒散的 **SYN lethargic**

tor·por /ˈtɔːpə(r); *NAmE* ˈtɔːrp-/ *noun* [U, sing.] (*formal*) the state of not being active and having no energy or enthusiasm 迟钝；死气沉沉；懒散 **SYN lethargy**: *In the heat they sank into a state of torpor.* 炎热的天气使得他们委靡不振。

torque /tɔːk; *NAmE* tɔːrk/ *noun* [U] (*specialist*) a twisting force that causes machinery, etc. to ROTATE (= turn around)（使机器等旋转的）转矩

T

tor·rent /'tɒrənt; NAmE 'tɔːr-; 'tɑːr-/ *noun* **1** a large amount of water moving very quickly 急流；激流；湍流；洪流：*After the winter rains, the stream becomes a **raging torrent**.* 冬雨过后，溪流湍急。◇ *The rain was coming down **in torrents**.* 大雨如注。 **2** a large amount of sth that comes suddenly and violently 迸发；连发；狂潮 **SYN** **deluge**: *a **torrent of abuse/criticism*** 连珠炮似的谩骂 / 批评 ◇ *a torrent of words* 滔滔不绝的话语

tor·ren·tial /tə'renʃl/ *adj.* (of rain 雨) falling in large amounts 倾泻的；如注的

tor·rid /'tɒrɪd; NAmE 'tɔːr-; 'tɑːr-/ *adj.* [usually before noun] **1** full of strong emotions, especially connected with sex and love （尤指情爱）热烈的，狂热的，热情洋溢的 **SYN** **passionate**: *a torrid love affair* 狂热的恋情 **2** (*formal*) (of a climate or country 气候或国家) very hot or dry 炎热而干燥的；酷热的；灼热的：*a torrid summer* 酷热的夏季 **3** (*BrE*) very difficult 艰难的：*They face a torrid time in tonight's game.* 他们在今晚的比赛中面临一场恶战。

'torrid zone *noun* [sing.] (*specialist*) an area of the earth near the EQUATOR 热带 **SYN** **the tropics**

tor·sion /'tɔːʃn; NAmE 'tɔːrʃn/ *noun* [U] (*specialist*) twisting, especially of one end of sth while the other end is held fixed （物体等一端固定的）扭转

torso /'tɔːsəʊ; NAmE 'tɔːrsoʊ/ *noun* (*pl.* **-os**) **1** the main part of the body, not including the head, arms or legs（身体的）躯干 **SYN** **trunk** **2** a statue of a torso 躯干雕像

tort /tɔːt; NAmE tɔːrt/ *noun* [C, U] (*law* 律) something wrong that sb does to sb else that is not criminal, but that can lead to action in a CIVIL court 侵权行为（不构成刑事犯罪但可引起民事诉讼）

torte /'tɔːtə; tɔːt; NAmE 'tɔːrtə; tɔːrt/ *noun* [C, U] a large cake filled with a mixture of cream, chocolate, fruit, etc. 奶油巧克力水果大蛋糕

tor·tilla /tɔː'tiːə; NAmE tɔːr't-/ *noun* (*from Spanish*) **1** a thin Mexican PANCAKE made with CORN (MAIZE) flour or WHEAT flour, usually eaten hot and filled with meat, cheese, etc. 墨西哥薄馅饼（用玉米面或白面制成，通常加肉、奶酪等为馅，热食） **2** a Spanish dish made with eggs and potatoes fried together 西班牙土豆炒鸡蛋

tor'tilla chip *noun* a small flat hard piece of food, often shaped like a triangle, made from CORN (MAIZE) 脆玉米片（通常为三角形）

T

tor·toise /'tɔːtəs; NAmE 'tɔːrtəs/ *noun* a REPTILE with a hard round shell, that lives on land and moves very slowly. It can pull its head and legs into its shell. 陆龟；龟 ➲ VISUAL VOCAB PAGE V13 ➲ COMPARE TERRAPIN, TURTLE (2)

tor·toise·shell /'tɔːtəsʃel; 'tɔːtəʃel; NAmE 'tɔːrt-/ *noun* **1** [U] the hard shell of a TURTLE, especially the type with orange and brown marks, used for making COMBS and small decorative objects 龟甲；龟板；玳瑁壳 **2** (*NAmE also* **'calico cat**) [C] a cat with black, brown, orange and white fur（毛色为黄褐黑白相间的）家猫 **3** [C] a BUTTERFLY with orange and brown marks on its wings（翅膀带黄褐色斑点的）蛱蝶

tor·tu·ous /'tɔːtʃuəs; NAmE 'tɔːrtʃ-/ *adj.* [usually before noun] (*formal*) **1** (*usually disapproving*) not simple and direct; long, complicated and difficult to understand 拐弯抹角的；含混不清的；冗长费解的 **SYN** **convoluted**: *tortuous language* 含混不清的语言 ◇ *the long, tortuous process of negotiating peace* 漫长而曲折的和平谈判过程 **2** (of a road, path, etc. 道路、小径等) full of bends 弯弯曲曲的；逶迤的；蜿蜒的 **SYN** **winding** ▸ **tor·tu·ous·ly** *adv.*

tor·ture /'tɔːtʃə(r); NAmE 'tɔːrtʃ-/ *noun, verb*

■ ***noun*** [U, C] **1** the act of causing sb severe pain in order to punish them or make them say or do sth 拷打；拷问；酷刑：*Many of the refugees have suffered torture.* 许多难民都遭受过拷打。◇ *the use of torture* 施酷刑 ◇ *terrible instruments of torture* 可怕的刑讯工具 ◇ *His confessions were made **under torture**.* 他被屈打成招。◇ *I heard stories of gruesome tortures in prisons.* 我听说过监狱里令人毛骨悚然的刑讯。 **2** (*informal*) mental or physical suffering; sth that causes this （精神上或肉体上的）折磨，痛苦；折磨人的事物：*The interview was sheer torture from start to finish.* 这次面试从头至尾使人备受煎熬。

■ ***verb*** [often passive] **1** to hurt sb physically or mentally in order to punish them or make them tell you sth 拷打；拷问；严刑逼供：**~ sb** *Many of the rebels were captured and tortured by secret police.* 反叛者中许多人被捕并遭受到秘密警察的酷刑。◇ **~ sb into doing sth** *He was tortured into giving them the information.* 他受不住酷刑被迫向他们供出了情报。 **2 ~ sb** to make sb feel extremely unhappy or anxious 使痛苦；使苦恼；使焦急；使受煎熬 **SYN** **torment**: *He spent his life tortured by the memories of his childhood.* 童年的记忆使他痛苦了一辈子。 ▸ **tor·turer** /'tɔːtʃərə(r); NAmE 'tɔːrtʃ-/ *noun*

tor·tured /'tɔːtʃəd; NAmE 'tɔːrtʃərd/ *adj.* [only before noun] suffering severely; involving a lot of suffering and difficulty 遭受重创的；饱受煎熬的：*a tortured mind* 饱受煎熬的心灵

Tory /'tɔːri/ *noun* (*pl.* **-ies**) (*informal*) a member or supporter of the British Conservative party 英国保守党党员（或支持者）：*The Tories* (= the Tory party) *lost the election.* 英国保守党在选举中失败。 ▸ **Tory** *adj.* [usually before noun]: *the Tory party* 英国保守党 ◇ *Tory policies* 英国保守党的政策 **Tory·ism** *noun* [U]

tosa /'təʊsə; NAmE 'toʊ-/ *noun* a large strong dog originally kept for fighting 土佐犬

tosh /tɒʃ; NAmE tɑːʃ/ *noun* [U] (*old-fashioned, BrE, slang*) nonsense 胡说；废话 **SYN** **rubbish**

toss /tɒs; NAmE tɔːs; tɑːs/ *verb, noun*

■ ***verb***

• **THROW** 扔 **1** [T] to throw sth lightly or carelessly （轻轻或漫不经心地）扔，抛，掷：**~ sth + adv./prep.** *I tossed the book aside and got up.* 我把书丢在一边，站了起来。◇ **~ sth to sb** *He tossed the ball to Anna.* 他把球抛给了安娜。◇ **~ sb sth** *He tossed Anna the ball.* 他把球抛给了安娜。 ➲ SYNONYMS AT THROW

• **YOUR HEAD** 头 **2** [T] **~ sth** to move your head suddenly upwards, especially to show that you are annoyed or impatient 甩（头，以表示恼怒或不耐烦）：*She just tossed her head and walked off.* 她头一甩，走开了。

• **SIDE TO SIDE/UP AND DOWN** 左右；上下 **3** [I, T] to move or make sb/sth move from side to side or up and down （使）摇摆，挥动，颠簸：*Branches were tossing in the wind.* 树枝随风摇曳。◇ *I couldn't sleep but kept **tossing and turning** in bed all night.* 我彻夜在床上辗转反侧不能成眠。◇ **~ sb/sth** *Our boat was being tossed by the huge waves.* 我们的船随着巨浪颠簸。

• **IN COOKING** 烹调 **4** [T] **~ sth** to shake or turn food in order to cover it with oil, butter, etc. 摇匀；翻动（以沾油、奶酪等）：*Drain the pasta and toss it in melted butter.* 把面条的汤控干，在融化了的黄油里搅拌。 **5** [T] **~ a pancake** (*BrE*) to throw a PANCAKE upwards so that it turns over in the air and you can fry the other side 把（煎饼）颠起翻面

• **COIN** 硬币 **6** [T, I] to throw a coin in the air in order to decide sth, especially by guessing which side is facing upwards when it lands （为…）掷硬币决定；掷币猜边儿 **SYN** **flip**: **~ sth** *Let's toss a coin.* 咱们掷硬币猜边儿决定吧。◇ (*especially BrE*) **~ (sb) for sth** *There's only one ticket left—I'll toss you for it.* 只剩一张票，我来与你掷币决定给谁。◇ (*BrE*) **~ up (for sth)** *We tossed up to see who went first.* 我们掷硬币决定谁先去。◇ (*BrE*) **~ up between A and B** (*figurative*) *He had to toss up between* (= decide between) *paying the rent or buying food.* 他不得不在付房租和买食品之间作出决定。 ➲ RELATED NOUN TOSS-UP

PHR V **,toss 'off | ,toss sb/yourself 'off** (*BrE, taboo, slang*) to give yourself sexual pleasure by rubbing your sex organs; to give sb sexual pleasure by rubbing their sex organs 手淫；对某人行手淫 **SYN** **masturbate** **,toss sth↔'off** (*BrE*) to produce sth quickly and without much thought or effort 未经思索（或费力）很快做完

■ ***noun*** [usually sing.]

• **OF COIN** 硬币 **1** an act of throwing a coin in the air in order to decide sth 掷硬币决定：*The final result was decided on/by the toss of a coin.* 最后的结果是掷硬币决定的。◇ ***to win/lose the toss*** (= to guess correctly/wrongly which side of a coin will face upwards when it lands on the ground after it has been thrown in the air) 猜中 / 猜错所掷硬币朝上的一面

• **OF HEAD** 头 **2 ~ of your head** an act of moving your head suddenly upwards, especially to show that you are annoyed or impatient 向上甩头，猛仰头（尤指表示恼怒或不耐烦）：*She dismissed the question with a toss of her head.* 她一扬头，对这一问题不予理睬。

• **THROW** 扔 **3** an act of throwing sth, especially in a competition or game（尤指比赛或游戏中）投掷：*a toss of 10 metres* * 10 米远的投掷

IDM **not give a 'toss (about sb/sth)** (*BrE, slang*) to not care at all about sb/sth 毫不介意；满不在乎 ➲ MORE AT ARGUE

toss·er /ˈtɒsə(r); *NAmE* ˈtɔːs-; ˈtɑːs-/ *noun* (*BrE, slang*) a stupid or unpleasant person 蠢货；傻蛋；讨厌鬼

toss·pot /ˈtɒspɒt; *NAmE* ˈtɔːspɑːt; ˈtɑːspɑːt/ *noun* (*BrE, slang*) an offensive word for an unpleasant or stupid person（含冒犯意）讨厌鬼，蠢货

ˈtoss-up *noun* [sing.] (*informal*) a situation in which either of two choices, results, etc. is equally possible（两种选择、结果等的）同样可能，均等机会：*'Have you decided on the colour yet?' 'It's a toss-up between the blue and the green.'* "你决定了要什么颜色没有？""在蓝色和绿色之间实在难以取舍。"

tot /tɒt; *NAmE* tɑːt/ *noun, verb*

■ ***noun* 1** (*informal*) a very young child 幼儿 **2** (*especially BrE*) a small amount of a strong alcoholic drink in a glass 小杯烈酒

■ ***verb*** (**-tt-**)

PHR V **ˌtot sth↔ˈup** (*informal, especially BrE*) to add together several numbers or amounts in order to calculate the total 把…加起来；计算…的总和 **SYN** **add up**

total 🔑 /ˈtəʊtl; *NAmE* ˈtoʊtl/ *adj., noun, verb*

■ ***adj.*** [usually before noun] **1** 🔑 being the amount or number after everyone or everything is counted or added together 总的；总计的；全体的；全部的：*the total profit* 利润总额 ◇ *This brought the total number of accidents so far this year to 113.* 这使得今年迄今为止发生事故的总数达到 113 起。◇ *The club has a total membership of 300.* 这家俱乐部的成员总数为 300 人。 **2** 🔑 including everything 彻底的；完全的 **SYN** **complete**：*The room was in total darkness.* 房间里一片漆黑。◇ *They wanted a total ban on handguns.* 他们要求彻底禁止拥有手枪。◇ *The evening was a total disaster.* 晚会彻底搞砸了。◇ *I can't believe you'd tell a total stranger about it!* 我不能相信你会把这事告诉一个素昧平生的人！

■ ***noun*** the amount you get when you add several numbers or amounts together; the final number of people or things when they have all been counted 总数；总额；合计；总计：*You got 47 points on the written examination and 18 on the oral, making a total of 65.* 你笔试得了 47 分，口试得了 18 分，总分 65 分。◇ *His businesses are worth a combined total of $3 billion.* 他的企业加在一起总值 30 亿美元。◇ *Out of a total of 15 games, they only won 2.* 在总共 15 场比赛中，他们只胜了 2 场。◇ *The repairs came to over £500* ***in total*** (= including everything). 修理费总共 500 多英镑。➲ SEE ALSO GRAND TOTAL, RUNNING TOTAL, SUM TOTAL

■ ***verb*** (**-ll-**, *US* **-l-**) **1 ~ sth** to reach a particular total 总数达；共计：*Imports totalled $1.5 billion last year.* 去年的进口总额达 15 亿美元。 **2 ~ sth/sb (up)** to add up the numbers of sth/sb and get a total 把…加起来；计算…的总和：*Each student's points were totalled and entered in a list.* 每个学生的总分都已计算出来并列入表中。 **3 ~ sth** (*informal, especially NAmE*) to damage a car very badly, so that it is not worth repairing it 彻底毁坏（汽车）➲ SEE ALSO WRITE STH↔OFF (2) at WRITE

to·tali·tar·ian /təʊˌtæləˈteəriən; *NAmE* toʊˌtæləˈter-/ *adj.* (*disapproving*) (of a country or system of government 国家或政府体制) in which there is only one political party that has complete power and control over the people 极权主义的 ▸ **to·tali·tar·ian·ism** /-ɪzəm/ *noun* [U]

to·tal·ity /təʊˈtæləti; *NAmE* toʊ-/ *noun* [C, U] (*formal*) the state of being complete or whole; the whole number or amount 全体；全部；整个；总数；总额：*The seriousness of the situation is difficult to appreciate* ***in its totality***. 很难从全局上理解局势的严重性。

to·tal·iza·tor (*BrE also* **-isa·tor**) /ˈtəʊtəlaɪzeɪtə(r); *NAmE* ˈtoʊt-/ (*also* **to·tal·izer, -iser** /ˈtəʊtəlaɪzə(r); *NAmE* ˈtoʊt-/) *noun* a device for showing the number and amount of bets put on a race 赌金数额显示器（用于赛马等）

to·tal·ly 🔑 /ˈtəʊtəli; *NAmE* ˈtoʊ-/ *adv.* completely 完全；全部地；整个地：*They come from totally different cultures.* 他们来自完全不同的文化。◇ *I'm still not totally convinced that he knows what he's doing.* 我仍然不完全相信他明白自己在干什么。◇ *This behaviour is totally unacceptable.* 这种行为是完全不能接受的。◇ (*informal, especially NAmE*) *'She's so cute!' 'Totally!'* (= I agree) "她真是精明过人！""一点不错！" ◇ (*informal*) *It's a totally awesome experience.* 这是个棒极了的经历。

ˌtotal ˌquality ˈmanagement *noun* [U] (*abbr.* **TQM**) a system of management that considers that every employee in an organization is responsible for keeping the highest standards in every aspect of the company's work 全面质量管理，全面品质管理（认为机构中每个雇员都有责任在各方面按最高标准工作的管理体系）

tote /təʊt; *NAmE* toʊt/ *noun, verb*

■ ***noun* 1** (*also* **the Tote**) [sing.] a system of betting on horses in which the total amount of money that is bet on each race is divided among the people who bet on the winners（赛马的）赌金计算系统 **2** (*also* **'tote bag**) [C] (*NAmE*) a large bag for carrying things with you 大手提袋；大提包

■ ***verb* 1 ~ sth** (*informal, especially NAmE*) to carry sth, especially sth heavy 携带，搬运（尤指重物）：*We arrived, toting our bags and suitcases.* 我们拎着包拖着行李箱到了那里。 **2 -toting** (in adjectives 构成形容词) carrying the thing mentioned 携带…的：*gun-toting soldiers* 持枪的士兵

totem /ˈtəʊtəm; *NAmE* ˈtoʊ-/ *noun* an animal or other natural object that is chosen and respected as a special symbol of a community or family, especially among Native Americans; an image of this animal, etc.（尤指美洲土著的）图腾；图腾形象 ▸ **to·tem·ic** /təʊˈtemɪk; *NAmE* toʊ-/ *adj.*：*totemic animals* 图腾动物

ˈtotem pole *noun* **1** a tall wooden pole that has symbols and pictures (called TOTEMS) CARVED or painted on it, traditionally made by Native Americans 图腾柱 **2** (*NAmE, informal*) a range of different levels in an organization, etc.（机构等内的）等级，级别：*I didn't want to be* ***low man on the totem pole*** *for ever.* 我不想永远当小人物。

t'other /ˈtʌðə(r)/ *adj., pron.* (*BrE, dialect*) the other（两者中的）另一个；其余的：*I saw it t'other day.* 几天前我见过它。◇ *They were talking of this, that and t'other.* 他们谈这，谈那，无所不谈。

toto ➲ IN TOTO

tot·ter /ˈtɒtə(r); *NAmE* ˈtɑːt-/ *verb* **1** [I] (+ **adv./prep.**) to walk or move with weak unsteady steps, especially because you are drunk or ill/sick 蹒跚；踉跄；跌跌撞撞 **SYN** **stagger** **2** [I] to be weak and seem likely to fall 摇摇欲坠；摇摇晃晃：*the tottering walls of the castle* 城堡摇摇欲坠的墙壁 ◇ (*figurative*) *a tottering dictatorship* 濒临瓦解的独裁统治

totty /ˈtɒti; *NAmE* ˈtɑːti/ *noun* [U] (*BrE, slang*) sexually attractive women (an expression used by men, and usually offensive to women) 骚货；浪货

tou·can /ˈtuːkæn/ *noun* a tropical American bird that is black with some areas of very bright feathers, and that has a very large beak 鹞鹉，巨嘴鸟（分布于美洲热带地区，羽毛鲜艳，喙很大）

touch /tʌtʃ/ *verb, noun*

■ *verb*

• **WITH HAND/PART OF BODY** 用手或身体部位 **1** [T] **~ sb/sth** to put your hand or another part of your body onto sb/sth 触摸；碰：*Don't touch that plate—it's hot!* 别碰那个盘子，烫手！◇ *Can you touch your toes?* (= bend and reach them with your hands) 你直腿弯腰够得着你的脚趾吗？◇ *I touched him lightly on the arm.* 我轻轻碰了碰他的手臂。◇ *He has hardly touched the ball all game.* 他整场比赛几乎没碰到过球。◇ (*figurative*) *I must do some more work on that article—I haven't touched it all week.* 我还得在那篇文章上再下点儿功夫，我整整一个星期没有碰它了。

• **NO SPACE BETWEEN** 无间隙 **2** [I, T] (of two or more things, surfaces, etc. 两个或以上的东西、表面等) to be or come so close together that there is no space between 接触；触及：*Make sure the wires don't touch.* 一定不要让金属线搭在一起。◇ **~ sth** *Don't let your coat touch the wet paint.* 你的外衣别蹭着还没有干的油漆。◇ *His coat was so long it was almost touching the floor.* 他的大衣太长，差不多拖到地板上了。

• **MOVE STH/HIT SB** 移动东西；打人 **3** [T] (often in negative sentences 常用于否定句) **~ sth/sb** to move sth, especially in such a way that you damage it; to hit or harm sb 移动；碰到；打（人）；使受伤：*I told you not to touch my things.* 我告诉过你不要动我的东西。◇ *He said I kicked him, but I never touched him!* 他说我踢他了，可是我从来就没碰过他！

• **AFFECT SB/STH** 影响某人/某事物 **4** [T] **~ sb/sth (to do sth)** to make sb feel upset or sympathetic 感动；触动；使同情：*Her story touched us all deeply.* 她的故事使我们大家深受感动。**5** [T] **~ sb/sth** (*old-fashioned* or *formal*) to affect or concern sb/sth 影响；与…有关：*These are issues that touch us all.* 这些问题与我们大家都有关系。

• **EAT/DRINK/USE** 吃；喝；用 **6** [T] (usually in negative sentences 通常用于否定句) **~ sth** to eat, drink or use sth 吃；喝；使用：*You've hardly touched your food.* 你没怎么吃东西啊。◇ *He hasn't touched the money his aunt left him.* 他还没动过他姑妈留给他的钱。

• **EQUAL SB** 与…等同 **7** [T] (usually in negative sentences 通常用于否定句) **~ sb** to be as good as sb in skill, quality, etc. 与…媲美；比得上；抵得过：*No one can touch him when it comes to interior design.* 在室内设计方面，没有人能比得上他。

• **REACH LEVEL** 达到水平 **8** [T] **~ sth** to reach a particular level, etc. 达到（某一水平等）：*The speedometer was touching 90.* 速度表显示时速达 90 英里。

• **BE INVOLVED WITH** 被牵涉 **9** [T] **~ sth/sb** to become connected with or work with a situation or person 与…有关；从事；与…共事：*Everything she touches turns to disaster.* 什么事她一插手就会糟糕。◇ *His last two movies have been complete flops and now no studio will touch him.* 他的前两部电影彻底失败了，现在没有制片厂愿意用他。

• **OF SMILE** 微笑 **10** [T] **~ sth** to be seen on sb's face for a short time（在脸上）闪现，掠过：*A smile touched the corners of his mouth.* 他的嘴角闪现出一丝笑意。

IDM **be touched with sth** to have a small amount of a particular quality 略微带点儿；轻微呈现：*His hair was touched with grey.* 他的头发有些斑白。**not touch sb/sth with a 'bargepole** (*BrE*) (*NAmE* **not touch sb/sth with a ten-foot 'pole**) (*informal*) to refuse to get involved with sb/sth or in a particular situation 决不与…有任何牵扯；拒不牵扯到…中去 **touch 'base (with sb)** (*informal*) to make contact with sb again 再次联系 **touch 'bottom 1** to reach the ground at the bottom of an area of water 触到水底 **2** to reach the worst possible state or condition 到最坏境况；到最低点；跌到谷底 **ˌtouch 'wood** (*BrE*) (*NAmE* **ˌknock on 'wood**) (*saying*) used when you have just mentioned some way in which you have been lucky in the past, to avoid bringing bad luck（表示希望继续走好运）：*I've been driving for over 20 years and never had an accident—touch wood!* 我开车 20 多年从来没出过车祸，但愿好运常在！➲ MORE AT CHORD, FORELOCK, HAIR, NERVE *n.*, RAW *n.*

PHR V **ˌtouch 'down 1** (of a plane, SPACECRAFT, etc. 飞机、航天器等) to make contact with the ground as it lands 着陆；降落：(*figurative*) *Tornadoes touched down in Alabama and Louisiana.* 龙卷风在亚拉巴马州和路易斯安那州登陆了。➲ RELATED NOUN TOUCHDOWN (1) **2** (in RUGBY 橄榄球) to score a TRY by putting the ball on the ground behind the other team's goal line（在对方球门线后）持球触地得分；达阵 ➲ RELATED NOUN TOUCHDOWN (2) **'touch sb for sth** (*informal*) to persuade sb to give or lend you sth, especially money 向…要，劝说…借给（尤指钱）**ˌtouch sth↔'off** to make sth begin, especially a difficult or violent situation 触发，引发，引起（困难或暴力的局面）**'touch on/upon sth** to mention or deal with a subject in only a few words, without going into detail 谈及；提及：*In his speech he was only able to touch on a few aspects of the problem.* 他在演讲中只能涉及这个问题的几个方面。**ˌtouch sb↔'up** (*BrE*, *informal*) to touch sb sexually, usually in a way that is not expected or welcome（常指强行猥亵地）触摸 **SYN** **grope** **ˌtouch sth↔'up** to improve sth by changing or adding to it slightly（稍加）修饰，润色，修改：*She was busy touching up her make-up in the mirror.* 她正忙着对着镜子补妆。

■ *noun*

• **SENSE** 感觉 **1** [U] the sense that enables you to be aware of things and what they are like when you put your hands and fingers on them 触觉；触感：*the sense of touch* 触觉

• **WITH HAND/PART OF BODY** 用手或身体部位 **2** [C, usually sing.] an act of putting your hand or another part of your body onto sb/sth 触摸；触；碰：*The gentle touch of his hand on her shoulder made her jump.* 他的手轻轻地触了一下她肩膀便使她跳了起来。◇ *All this information is readily available* **at the touch of a button** (= by simply pressing a button). 这么多的资料，按下按钮便可毫不费力地查到。◇ *This type of engraving requires a delicate touch.* 这种雕刻要求手法轻巧。

• **WAY STH FEELS** 给人的感觉 **3** [sing.] the way that sth feels when you put your hand or fingers on it or when it comes into contact with your body 触摸时的感觉：*The body was cold* **to the touch**. 这具尸体摸上去是冰冷的。◇ *material with a smooth silky touch* 摸起来光滑得像丝绸一样的料子 ◇ *He could not bear the touch of clothing on his sunburnt skin.* 他忍受不住衣服磨蹭他那被太阳灼伤的皮肤。

• **SMALL DETAIL** 细节 **4** [C] a small detail that is added to sth in order to improve it or make it complete 修饰；润色；装点：*I spent the morning* **putting the finishing touches** *to the report.* 我花了一个上午为这个报告做最后的润色。◇ *Meeting them at the airport was a nice touch.* 到机场迎接他们是一个妙招。

• **WAY OF DOING STH** 办事方法 **5** [sing.] a way or style of doing sth 作风；风格；手法：*She prefers to answer any fan mail herself for a more personal touch.* 她喜欢针对每一位崇拜者的来信，亲自予以回复。◇ *Computer graphics will give your presentation the professional touch.* 计算机绘图将会使你的演示具有专业特色。◇ *He couldn't find his magic touch with the ball today* (= he didn't play well). 他今天施展不出神奇的球技。◇ *This meal is awful. I think I'm* **losing my touch** (= my ability to do sth). 这顿饭太难吃了。我想我的烹调技艺在走下坡路。

• **SMALL AMOUNT** 微量 **6** [C, usually sing.] **~ of sth** a very small amount 一点儿；少许 **SYN** **trace**：*There was a touch of sarcasm in her voice.* 她的话音中有点儿讥讽的意味。

• **SLIGHTLY** 轻微 **7** **a touch** [sing.] slightly; a little 轻微；稍许：*The music was a touch too loud for my liking.* 这音乐有点太吵，不合我的口味。

• **IN FOOTBALL/RUGBY** 足球；橄榄球 **8** [U] the area outside the lines that mark the sides of the playing field 边线以外的区域：*He kicked the ball into touch.* 他把球踢出了边线。

IDM **be, get, keep, etc. in 'touch (with sb)** to communicate with sb, especially by writing to them or telephoning them（与…）有（或进行、保持等）联系：*Are you still in touch with your friends from college?* 你和大学的同学还有联系吗？◇ *Thanks for showing us your products—we'll be in touch.* 谢谢给我们介绍你们的产品，我们将会保持联系。◇ *I'm trying to get in touch with Jane. Do you have* *her number?* 我正在设法和简取得联系。你有她的电话号码吗？ ◇ *Let's keep in touch.* 咱们保持联系。 ◇ *I'll put you in touch with someone in your area.* 我将安排你和你那个地区的一个人进行联系。 **be, keep, etc. in 'touch (with sth)** to know what is happening in a particular subject or area 了解（某课题或领域的情况）: *It is important to keep in touch with the latest research.* 及时了解最新研究情况很重要。 **be out of 'touch (with sb)** to no longer communicate with sb, so that you no longer know what is happening to them 失去联系；不再了解（某人的）情况 **be, become, etc. out of 'touch (with sth)** to not know or understand what is happening in a particular subject or area 不再了解，不懂得（某课题或领域）的情况: *Unfortunately, the people making the decisions are out of touch with the real world.* 令人遗憾的是，制定决策的人不了解实情。 **an easy/a soft 'touch** (*informal*) a person that you can easily persuade to do sth, especially to give you money （尤指在钱财方面）有求必应的人，耳根子软的人: *Unfortunately, my father is no soft touch.* 可惜，我父亲并非有求必应。 **lose 'touch (with sb/sth)** **1** to no longer have any contact with sb/sth 失去联系: *I've lost touch with all my old friends.* 我与所有的老朋友都失去了联系。 **2** to no longer understand sth, especially how ordinary people feel 不再了解（尤指一般人的想法） ➲ MORE AT COMMON *adj.*, KICK *v.*, LIGHT *adj.*

ˌtouch-and-'go *adj.* [not usually before noun] (*informal*) used to say that the result of a situation is uncertain and that there is a possibility that sth bad or unpleasant will happen 不确定；无把握；很难说；吉凶未卜: *She's fine now, but it was touch-and-go for a while* (= there was a possibility that she might die). 她现在好了，可是她曾一度病危。

touch·down /'tʌtʃdaʊn/ *noun* **1** [C, U] the moment when a plane or SPACECRAFT lands （飞机或航天器的）着陆，降落，接地 **SYN** **landing** **2** [C] (in RUGBY 橄榄球) an act of scoring points by putting the ball down on the area of ground behind the other team's GOAL LINE （在对方球门线后）持球触地；达阵 **3** [C] (in AMERICAN FOOTBALL 美式足球) an act of scoring points by crossing the other team's GOAL LINE while carrying the ball, or receiving the ball when you are over the other team's GOAL LINE 达阵（持球越过对方球门线或在对方球门线后接球）

tou·ché /'tu:ʃeɪ; *NAmE* tu:'ʃeɪ/ *exclamation* (*from French*) used during an argument or a discussion to show that you accept that sb has answered your comment in a clever way and has gained an advantage by making a good point （承认对方言之有理，答话切中要害）一针见血，一语破的

touched /tʌtʃt/ *adj.* [not before noun] **1** feeling happy and grateful because of sth kind that sb has done; feeling emotional about sth 感激；受感动；激动: ~ **(by sth)** *She was touched by their warm welcome.* 她对他们的热烈欢迎十分感动。 ◇ *She was touched by the plight of the refugees.* 难民的困境使她受到触动。 ◇ ~ **(that...)** *I was touched that he still remembered me.* 他仍然记得我，使我十分感动。 **2** (*old-fashioned, informal*) slightly crazy 神经兮兮；疯疯癫癫

ˌtouch 'football *noun* [U] (*NAmE*) a type of AMERICAN FOOTBALL in which touching is used instead of TACKLING 触身式橄榄球（利用身体接触而不是擒抱的美式足球） ➲ COMPARE FLAG FOOTBALL

touch·ing /'tʌtʃɪŋ/ *adj.* causing feelings of pity or sympathy; making you feel emotional 令人同情的；感人的；动人的 **SYN** **moving**: *It was a touching story that moved many of us to tears.* 那是一个让我们许多人落泪的动人故事。 ▸ **touch·ing·ly** *adv.*

'touch judge *noun* (in RUGBY 橄榄球) a LINESMAN 边线裁判员；巡边员

touch·less /'tʌtʃləs/ *adj.* used to describe technology that allows you to give instructions by making movements rather than by touching any part 非接触式的；自动感应的: *Hand dryers are available with push button or touchless automatic operation.* 干手器有使用按钮操作的，也有非接触式自动运转的。

touch·line /'tʌtʃlaɪn/ *noun* a line that marks the side of the playing field in football (SOCCER), RUGBY, etc. （足球、橄榄球等场地的）边线

touchpad /'tʌtʃpæd/ (*also* **trackpad**) *noun* (*computing* 计) a device which you touch in different places in order to operate a program （操作程序的）触摸板，触控板

touch·paper /'tʌtʃpeɪpə(r)/ *noun* a piece of paper that burns slowly, that you light in order to start a FIREWORK burning （焰火的）火硝纸，导火纸

'touch screen *noun* (*computing* 计) a screen on a computer, TABLET (4), etc. which allows you to give instructions to the computer by touching areas on it （计算机、平板电脑等的）触摸屏

touch·stone /'tʌtʃstəʊn; *NAmE* -stoʊn/ *noun* [usually sing.] ~ **(of/for sth)** (*formal*) something that provides a standard against which other things are compared and/or judged 试金石；检验标准: *the touchstone for quality* 检验质量的标准

'Touch-Tone™ *adj.* (of a telephone or telephone system 电话或电话系统) producing different sounds when different numbers are pushed 按钮式拨号的

'touch-type *verb* [I] to type without having to look at the keys of a TYPEWRITER or keyboard （不看键盘）按指法打字；盲打

'touch-up *noun* a quick improvement made to the appearance or condition of sth 润色；修饰；装点: *My lipstick needed a touch-up.* 我的口红需要补一下。

touchy /'tʌtʃi/ *adj.* (**touch·ier, touchi·est**) **1** [not usually before noun] ~ **(about sth)** (of a person 人) easily upset or offended 易烦恼；易生气；易怒 **SYN** **sensitive**: *He's a little touchy about his weight.* 他有点忌讳别人说他胖。 **2** [usually before noun] (of a subject 课题) that may upset or offend people and should therefore be dealt with carefully 敏感性的；需要小心处理的；棘手的 **SYN** **delicate, sensitive** ▸ **touchi·ness** *noun* [U]

ˌtouchy-'feely *adj.* (*informal, usually disapproving*) expressing emotions too openly 露骨地表示情感的 ➲ MORE LIKE THIS 11, page R26

tough 🔑 /tʌf/ *adj., noun, verb*

■ ***adj.*** (**tough·er, tough·est**)

• **DIFFICULT** 困难 **1** 🔑 having or causing problems or difficulties 艰苦的；艰难的；棘手的: *a tough childhood* 苦难的童年 ◇ *It was a tough decision to make.* 那是个很难作的决定。 ◇ *She's been having **a tough time of it*** (= a lot of problems) *lately.* 她最近的日子一直很难熬。 ◇ *He faces the toughest test of his leadership so far.* 他面临迄今为止对自己的领导工作最严峻的考验。 ◇ *It can be tough trying to juggle a career and a family.* 要事业家庭两不误，有时会很艰难。

• **STRICT/FIRM** 严格；坚定 **2** 🔑 demanding that particular rules be obeyed and showing a lack of sympathy for any problems or suffering that this may cause 严厉的；强硬的；无情的: ~ **(on sb/sth)** *Don't be too tough on him—he was only trying to help.* 别对他要求过高，他只是想帮忙。 ◇ ~ **(with sb/sth)** *It's about time teachers started to **get tough with** bullies.* 现在教师要对横行霸道的学生开始采取严厉措施了。 ◇ *The school **takes a tough line on*** (= punishes severely) *cheating.* 学校对作弊行为的惩罚很严厉。 **OPP** **soft**

• **STRONG** 强壮 **3** 🔑 strong enough to deal successfully with difficult conditions or situations 坚强的；健壮的；能吃苦耐劳的；坚韧不拔的: *a tough breed of cattle* 耐劣等饲养条件的牛种 ◇ *He's not tough enough for a career in sales.* 他干推销这一行缺少足够的韧劲。 ◇ *She's a **tough cookie/customer*** (= sb who knows what they want and is not easily influenced by other people). 她是个有主见的人。 **4** 🔑 (of a person 人) physically strong and likely to be violent 彪悍的；粗暴的；粗野的: *You think you're so tough, don't you?* 你以为自己够厉害的，是不是？ ◇ *He plays the **tough guy** in the movie.* 他在电影中扮演硬汉。

• **MEAT** 肉 **5** 🔑 difficult to cut or chew 难切开的；嚼不烂

T

的；老的 OPP **tender** ➲ WORDFINDER NOTE AT CRISP
• NOT EASILY DAMAGED 不易损坏 **6** not easily cut, broken, torn, etc. 坚固的；不易切开（或打破、撕破等）的： *a tough pair of shoes* 一双结实的鞋子 ◇ *The reptile's skin is tough and scaly.* 这种爬行动物的皮肤坚韧并带有鳞片。
• UNFORTUNATE 不幸 **7** ~ (**on sb**) (*informal*) unfortunate for sb in a way that seems unfair 不幸的；倒霉的： *It was tough on her being dropped from the team like that.* 她就这样被队里刷了下来，真是倒霉。◇ (*ironic*) *'I can't get it finished in time.' 'Tough!* (= I don't feel sorry about it.) *'* "我无法按时完成。""活该倒霉！"
▸ **tough·ly** *adv.* **tough·ness** *noun* [U]

IDM (**as**) **tough as old 'boots** | (**as**) **tough as 'nails** (*informal*) **1** very strong and able to deal successfully with difficult conditions or situations 很强壮；坚韧不拔；雷打不动 **2** not feeling or showing any emotion 铁石心肠；不为所动 ➲ MORE LIKE THIS 14, page R26 **tough 'luck** (*informal*) **1** used to show sympathy for sth unfortunate that has happened to sb （表示同情）真不幸，真不走运： *'I failed by one point.' 'That's tough luck.'* "我差一分没及格。""运气真不好。" **2** (*ironic*) used to show that you do not feel sorry for sb who has a problem （表示并不同情）该你倒霉： *'If you take the car, I won't be able to go out.' 'Tough luck!'* "如果你把车开走，我就出不去了。""该你倒霉！" ➲ MORE AT ACT *n.*, GOING *n.*, HANG *v.*, NUT *n.*, TALK *v.*

■ ***noun*** (*old-fashioned, informal*) a person who regularly uses violence against other people 粗暴的人；暴徒；恶棍

■ ***verb***

PHR V **,tough sth↔'out** to stay firm and determined in a difficult situation 坚持；挨过： *You're just going to have to tough it out.* 你只好硬着头皮撑到底了。

tough·en /'tʌfn/ *verb* **1** [T, I] ~ (**sth**) (**up**) to become or make sth stronger, so that it is not easily cut, broken, etc. （使）坚硬，坚固： *toughened glass* 钢化玻璃 **2** [T] ~ **sth** (**up**) to make sth such as laws or rules stricter 加强，强化（法律、规定等）： *The government is considering toughening up the law on censorship.* 政府正在考虑强化书报电影审查方面的法律。 **3** [T] ~ **sb** (**up**) to make sb stronger and more able to deal with difficult situations 使更坚强；使坚韧

toughie /'tʌfi/ *noun* (*informal*) **1** a person who is determined and not easily frightened 坚定勇敢的人；无畏的人 **2** a very difficult choice or question 艰难的选择；难题

,tough 'love *noun* [U] the fact of helping sb who has problems by dealing with them in a strict way because you believe it is good for them 严厉的爱（为帮助而严厉对待有问题的人）

,tough-'minded *adj.* dealing with problems and situations in a determined way without being influenced by emotions 坚定理智的；坚强面对现实的 SYN **hard-headed**

tou·pee /'tu:peɪ; *NAmE* tu:'peɪ/ (*also informal* **rug** *especially in NAmE*) *noun* a small section of artificial hair, worn by a man to cover an area of his head where hair no longer grows （男用）小型遮秃假发

tour /tʊə(r); tɔ:(r); *NAmE* tʊr/ *noun, verb*

■ ***noun*** **1** ~ (**of/round/around sth**) a journey made for pleasure during which several different towns, countries, etc. are visited 旅行；旅游： *a walking/sightseeing, etc. tour* 徒步、观光等旅行 ◇ *a **coach tour** of northern France* 乘长途汽车在法国北部旅游 ◇ *a **tour operator*** (= a person or company that organizes tours) 旅游经营商 ➲ SYNONYMS AT TRIP ➲ COLLOCATIONS AT TRAVEL ➲ SEE ALSO PACKAGE TOUR, WHISTLE-STOP **2** an act of walking around a town, building, etc. in order to visit it 游览；参观；观光： *We were given a **guided tour*** (= by sb who knows about the place) *of the palace.* 我们由导游带领参观游览了那座宫殿。◇ *a **tour guide*** 导游 ◇ *a **tour of inspection*** (= an official visit of a factory, classroom, etc. made by sb whose job is to check that everything is working as expected) 视察 **3** an official series of visits made to different places by a sports team, an ORCHESTRA, an important person, etc. 巡回比赛（或演出等）；巡视： *The band is currently on a nine-day tour of France.* 这支乐队目前正在法国进行九天的巡回演出。◇ *The band is **on tour** in France.* 这支乐队正在法国巡回演出。◇ *a concert tour* 巡回音乐会 ◇ *The Prince will visit Boston on the last leg* (= part) *of his American tour.* 亲王美国之行的最后一站是波士顿。◇ *The soldiers all used to do a six-month **tour of duty** in Northern Ireland.* 士兵过去都要在北爱尔兰服役六个月。

■ ***verb*** [T, I] to travel around a place, for example on holiday/vacation, or to perform, to advertise sth, etc. 在…旅游；在…巡回演出（或做宣传广告等）： ~ **sth** *He toured America with his one-man show.* 他在美国进行了个人巡回演出。◇ *She toured the country promoting her book.* 她在全国巡回推销自己的书。 ◇ ~ **around sth** *We spent four weeks touring around Europe.* 我们花了四个星期周游欧洲。

tour de force /,tʊə də 'fɔ:s; *NAmE* ,tʊr də 'fɔ:rs/ *noun* (*pl.* **tours de force** /,tʊə də 'fɔ:s; *NAmE* ,tʊr də 'fɔ:rs/) (*from French*) an extremely skilful performance or achievement 绝技；特技；杰作： *a cinematic tour de force* 电影杰作

Tour·ette's syn·drome /tʊ'rets sɪndrəʊm; *NAmE* -droʊm/ *noun* [U] (*medical* 医) a DISORDER of the nerves in which a person makes a lot of small movements and sounds that they cannot control, including using swear words 图雷特综合征，多发性抽动秽语综合征（特征为不自主且反复出现的肌肉痉挛和发声）

tour·ism /'tʊərɪzəm; 'tɔ:r-; *NAmE* 'tʊr-/ *noun* [U] the business activity connected with providing accommodation, services and entertainment for people who are visiting a place for pleasure 旅游业；观光业： *The area is heavily dependent on tourism.* 这个地区非常依赖旅游业。 ◇ *the tourism industry* 旅游业 ➲ COLLOCATIONS AT TRAVEL ➲ SEE ALSO AGRITOURISM

tour·ist /'tʊərɪst; 'tɔ:r-; *NAmE* 'tʊr-/ *noun* **1** a person who is travelling or visiting a place for pleasure 旅游者；观光者；游客： *busloads of foreign tourists* 一车一车的外国观光客 ◇ *a popular **tourist attraction/destination/resort*** 为游客所喜爱的旅游景点 / 目的地 / 胜地 ◇ *the **tourist industry/sector*** 旅游业 / 部门 ◇ *Further information is available from the local **tourist office**.* 进一步详情可向当地的旅游办事处查询。 ➲ WORDFINDER NOTE AT HOLIDAY ➲ COLLOCATIONS AT TRAVEL

WORDFINDER 联想词： abroad, backpack, border, guide, passport, resort, sightseeing, **travel**, visa

2 (*BrE*) a member of a sports team that is playing a series of official games in a foreign country （在国外参加）巡回比赛的运动队队员

'tourist class *noun* [U] the cheapest type of ticket or accommodation that is available on a plane or ship or in a hotel （飞机、轮船的）二等舱（或票），经济舱（或票）；（旅馆的）旅游客房，最便宜的客房

'tourist trap *noun* (*informal, disapproving*) a place that attracts a lot of tourists and where food, drink, entertainment, etc. is more expensive than normal 敲游客竹杠的地方

tour·isty /'tʊərɪsti; 'tɔ:r-; *NAmE* 'tʊr-/ *adj.* (*informal, disapproving*) attracting or designed to attract a lot of tourists 吸引很多游客的；为吸引游客设计的： *Jersey is the most touristy of the islands.* 这些岛屿中就数泽西岛最能吸引游客。◇ *a shop full of touristy souvenirs* 摆满旅游纪念品的商店

tour·na·ment /'tʊənəmənt; 'tɔ:n-; 'tɜ:n-; *NAmE* 'tʊrn-; 'tɜ:rn-/ *noun* **1** (*NAmE, less frequent* **tour·ney**) a sports competition involving a number of teams or players who take part in different games and must leave the competition if they lose. The competition continues until there is only the winner left. 锦标赛；联赛： *a golf/squash/tennis, etc. tournament* 高尔夫球、壁球、网球等锦标赛 ➲ WORDFINDER NOTE AT SPORT **2** a competition in the Middle Ages between soldiers on HORSEBACK fighting to show courage and skill （中世纪的）骑马比武

tour·ney /'tʊəni; 'tɜ:ni; *NAmE* 'tʊrni; 'tɜ:rni/ *noun* (*NAmE*) = TOURNAMENT (1)

tour·ni·quet /ˈtʊənɪkeɪ; *NAmE* ˈtɜːrnəkət/ *noun* a piece of cloth, etc. that is tied tightly around an arm or a leg to stop the loss of blood from a wound （扎在手臂或腿上的）止血带

tou·sle /ˈtaʊzl/ *verb* [usually passive] **~ sth** to make sb's hair untidy 弄乱（头发）；使蓬乱 ▶ **tou·sled** *adj.*: *a boy with blue eyes and tousled hair* 头发蓬乱的蓝眼睛男孩

tout /taʊt/ *verb, noun*
■ *verb* **1** [T] **~ sb/sth (as sth)** to try to persuade people that sb/sth is important or valuable by praising them/it 标榜；吹捧；吹嘘：*She's being touted as the next leader of the party.* 她被吹捧为该党的下一任领导人。**2** [I, T] (*especially BrE*) to try to persuade people to buy your goods or services, especially by going to them and asking them directly 兜售；推销：**~ (for sth)** *the problem of unlicensed taxi drivers touting for business at airports* 没有执照的出租汽车司机在机场揽生意的问题 ◇ **~ sth** *He's busy touting his client's latest book around London publishers.* 他正忙于向伦敦多家出版商兜售他的委托人的一部新书。**3** [I, T] (*BrE*) (*NAmE* **scalp**) **~ (sth)** to sell tickets for a popular event illegally, at a price that is higher than the official price, especially outside a theatre, STADIUM, etc.（尤指在剧院、体育场等外以高价）倒卖门票，卖黑市票
■ *noun* (*also* ˈ**ticket tout**) (*both BrE*) (*NAmE* **scalp·er**) a person who buys tickets for concerts, sports events, etc. and then sells them to other people at a higher price（音乐会、体育比赛等的）倒卖门票的人，票贩子

tout court /ˌtuː ˈkʊə(r); ˈkɔː(r); *NAmE* ˈkuːr/ *adv.* (*from French*) simply, with nothing to add 简单地；仅仅：*It was a lie, tout court.* 那只不过是谎言。

tow /təʊ; *NAmE* toʊ/ *verb, noun*
■ *verb* **~ sth (away)** to pull a car or boat behind another vehicle, using a rope or chain（用绳索或链条）拖，拉，牵引，拽：*Our car was towed away by the police.* 我们的汽车被警察拖走了。 ➲ SYNONYMS AT PULL ➲ SEE ALSO TOW BAR, TOW ROPE
■ *noun* [sing.] an act of one vehicle pulling another vehicle using a rope or chain（车、船等的）牵引，拽引：*The car broke down and we had to get somebody to give us a tow.* 汽车抛锚了，我们只得让人拖走。◇ *a tow truck* 牵引车
IDM **in tow 1** (*informal*) if you have sb **in tow**, they are with you and following closely behind 紧随着；陪伴着：*She turned up with her mother in tow.* 她露面了，后面紧跟着她的母亲。 **2** if a ship is taken **in tow**, it is pulled by another ship（船）被拖着走

to·wards /təˈwɔːdz; *NAmE* tɔːrdz/ (*also* **to·ward** /təˈwɔːd; *NAmE* tɔːrd/ *especially in NAmE*) *prep.* **1** in the direction of sb/sth 向；朝；对着：*They were heading towards the German border.* 他们正前往德国边界。◇ *She had her back towards me.* 她背对着我。**2** getting closer to achieving sth 趋向，接近，将近（完成某事）：*This is a first step towards political union.* 这是走向政治上联合的第一步。 **3** close or closer to a point in time 接近，将近（某一时间）：*towards the end of April* 将近四月底 **4** in relation to sb/sth 对；对于；关于：*He was warm and tender towards her.* 他对她既热情又温柔。◇ *our attitude towards death* 我们对死亡的态度 **5** with the aim of obtaining sth, or helping sb to obtain sth 以…为目标（或目的）；用于：*The money will go towards a new school building* (= will help pay for it). 这笔资金将用于修建新校舍。

ˈ**tow bar** *noun* a bar fixed to the back of a vehicle for TOWING (= pulling) another vehicle （用以牵引拖车的）牵引杆，拖杆

towel /ˈtaʊəl/ *noun, verb*
■ *noun* a piece of cloth or paper used for drying things, especially your body 毛巾；手巾；抹布；纸巾：*Help yourself to a clean towel.* 请随便拿一条干净毛巾用。◇ *a* **hand/bath towel** (= a small/large towel) 手巾；浴巾 ◇ *a* **beach towel** (= a large towel used for lying on in the sun) 沙滩太阳浴巾 ◇ *a* **kitchen towel** (= a piece of paper from a roll that you use to clean up liquid, etc. in the kitchen) 厨房用清洁纸巾 ➲ VISUAL VOCAB PAGE V25 ➲ SEE ALSO PAPER TOWEL, SANITARY TOWEL, TEA TOWEL
IDM **throw in the** ˈ**towel** (*informal*) to admit that you have been defeated and stop trying 认输；承认失败；放弃努力
■ *verb* (**-ll-**, *NAmE also* **-l-**) **~ yourself/sb/sth (down)** to dry yourself/sb/sth with a towel 用毛巾擦干

tow·el·ling (*BrE*) (*US* **tow·el·ing**) /ˈtaʊəlɪŋ/ *noun* [U] a type of soft cotton cloth that absorbs liquids, used especially for making towels 毛巾布；毛巾料：*a towelling bathrobe* 毛巾布浴衣

ˈ**towel rail** (*BrE*) (*NAmE* ˈ**towel rack**) *noun* a bar or frame for hanging towels on in a bathroom 毛巾架 ➲ VISUAL VOCAB PAGE V25

tower /ˈtaʊə(r)/ *noun, verb*
■ *noun* **1** a tall narrow building or part of a building, especially of a church or castle 塔；建筑物的塔形部分；（尤指教堂或城堡的）塔楼：*a* **clock/bell tower** 钟楼 ◇ *the Tower of London* 伦敦塔 ◇ *the Eiffel Tower* 埃菲尔铁塔 **2** (often in compounds 常构成复合词) a tall structure used for sending television or radio signals （电视或无线电信号的）发射塔：*a television tower* 电视塔 **3** (usually in compounds 通常构成复合词) a tall piece of furniture used for storing things 高柜；高架子：*a CD tower* 光盘柜 ➲ SEE ALSO CONTROL TOWER, COOLING TOWER, IVORY TOWER, WATCHTOWER, WATER TOWER
IDM **a** ˌ**tower of** ˈ**strength** a person that you can rely on to help, protect and comfort you when you are in trouble（危难时的）可依靠的人，主心骨
■ *verb*
PHR V ˌ**tower** ˈ**over/a**ˈ**bove sb/sth 1** to be much higher or taller than the people or things that are near 高于，超过（附近的人或物）：*The cliffs towered above them.* 悬崖峭壁高耸于他们上方。◇ *He towered over his classmates.* 他的个儿比班里其他同学高出一大截。 **2** to be much better than others in ability, quality, etc. （在能力、品质等方面）胜过，远远超过（其他）：*She towers over other dancers of her generation.* 她远远超过同时代的舞蹈演员。

ˈ**tower block** *noun* (*BrE*) a very tall block of flats/apartments or offices 高层建筑；公寓大楼；办公大楼

tower·ing /ˈtaʊərɪŋ/ *adj.* [only before noun] **1** extremely tall or high and therefore impressive 高大的；高耸的；屹立的：*towering cliffs* 高耸的悬崖 **2** of extremely high quality 卓越的；杰出的；出色的：*a towering performance* 出色的表演 **3** (of emotions 情感) extremely strong 强烈的；激烈的：*a towering rage* 勃然大怒

tow·line /ˈtəʊlaɪn; *NAmE* ˈtoʊ-/ *noun* = TOW ROPE

town /taʊn/ *noun* **1** [C, U] a place with many houses, shops/stores, etc. where people live and work. It is larger than a village but smaller than a city. 镇；市镇；集镇：*a university town* 大学城 ◇ *They live in a rough part of town.* 他们居住在一个社会秩序混乱的城区。◇ *The nearest town is ten miles away.* 最近的集镇离这里有十英里远。◇ *We spent a month in the French town of Le Puy.* 我们在一个叫勒皮的法国小镇里待了一个月。 ➲ SEE ALSO SMALL-TOWN HELP You will find other compounds ending in **town** at their place in the alphabet. 其他以 town 结尾的复合词可在各字母中的适当位置查到。 **2** **the town** [sing.] the people who live in a particular town （某一市镇的）居民，市民：*The whole town is talking about it.* 全镇的人都在议论这件事。 **3** [U] the area of a town where most of the shops/stores and businesses are （城镇的）商业区：*Can you give me a lift into town?* 我可以搭你的车到商业区去吗？ ➲ SEE ALSO DOWNTOWN, MIDTOWN, OUT-OF-TOWN (1), UPTOWN **4** [U] (*especially NAmE*) a particular town where sb lives and works or one that has just been referred to （生活、工作或刚提到的）城镇：*I'll be in town next week if you want to meet.* 如果你想见面的话，我下个星期在城里。◇ *He married a girl from out of town.* 他娶了一个外地姑娘。 ➲ SEE ALSO OUT-OF-TOWN (1) **5** [sing., U] life in towns or cities as opposed to life in the country 城市生活（与乡村生活相对）：*Pollution is just one of the disadvantages of living in the town.* 污染只是生

T

活在城里的不利条件之一。➲ WORDFINDER NOTE AT CITY

IDM **go to 'town (on sth)** (*informal*) to do sth with a lot of energy, enthusiasm, etc., especially by spending a lot of money（尤指花大钱）大干一番 **(out) on the 'town** (*informal*) visiting restaurants, clubs, theatres, etc. for entertainment, especially at night （尤指夜里）去娱乐场所玩：*a night on the town* 去娱乐场所作乐的夜晚 ◇ *How about going out on the town tonight?* 今晚出去痛痛快快地玩一玩怎么样？ ➲ MORE AT GAME *n.*, MAN *n.*, PAINT *v.*

ˌtown and 'gown *noun* [U] the relationship between the people who live permanently in a town where there is a university and the members of the university 大学城居民与师生的关系

ˌtown 'centre *noun* (*BrE*) the main part of a town, where the shops/stores are 市中心；（城镇的）商业中心 ➲ COMPARE DOWNTOWN

ˌtown 'clerk *noun* **1** (*NAmE*) a public officer in charge of the records of a town 镇书记员（主管档案） **2** (*BrE*) in the past, the person who was the secretary of, and gave legal advice to, the local government of a town（旧时的）镇政府秘书兼法律顾问

ˌtown 'crier (*also* **crier**) *noun* (in the past) a person whose job was to walk through a town shouting news, official ANNOUNCEMENTS, etc. （旧时沿街高声传报消息等的）街头公告员

townee = TOWNIE (1)

ˌtown 'hall *noun* a building containing local government offices and, in Britain, usually a hall for public meetings, concerts, etc. 镇公所；市政厅；（英国）市镇集会所

'town house *noun* **1** a house in a town owned by sb who also has a house in the country（另有乡村住房者的）城市住宅 **2** a tall narrow house in a town that is part of a row of similar houses 联排式住宅：*an elegant Georgian town house* 一套具有乔治王朝时期风格的典雅排房 ➲ VISUAL VOCAB PAGE V16 **3** (*usually* **'townhouse**) (*NAmE*) = ROW HOUSE

townie /'taʊni/ *noun* (*disapproving*) **1** (*also* **townee**) a person who lives in or comes from a town or city, especially sb who does not know much about life in the countryside（尤指不了解乡村生活的）城里人 **2** (*NAmE*) a person who lives in a town with a college or university but does not attend or work at it（大学城中不上大学或不在大学工作的）居民，老百姓 **3** (*BrE, informal*) a member of a group of young people who live in a town, all wear similar clothes, such as TRACKSUITS and caps, and often behave badly 阿飞，城市小流氓（穿着类似，行为不端）

ˌtown 'meeting *noun* a meeting when people in a town come together to discuss problems that affect the town and to give their opinions on various issues 镇民大会

ˌtown 'planner *noun* = PLANNER (1)

ˌtown 'planning (*also* **plan·ning**) *noun* [U] the control of the development of towns and their buildings, roads, etc. so that they can be pleasant and convenient places for people to live in; the subject that studies this 城市规划；城市规划学

town·scape /'taʊnskeɪp/ *noun* **1** what you see when you look at a town, for example from a distance 城市风景；城镇景观：*an industrial townscape* 工业城市景象 **2** (*specialist*) a picture of a town 城镇风景画 ➲ COMPARE LANDSCAPE *n.*, SEASCAPE

town·ship /'taʊnʃɪp/ *noun* **1** (in South Africa in the past) a town or part of a town that black people had to live in, and where only black people lived（旧时南非的）黑人城镇，黑人居住区 **2** (in the US or Canada) a division of a county that is a unit of local government 镇区（美国和加拿大县以下一级的地方政府）

towns·people /'taʊnzpiːpl/ (*also* **towns·folk** /'taʊnsfəʊk; *NAmE* -foʊk/) *noun* [pl.] people who live in towns, not in the countryside; the people who live in a particular town 镇民；市民；城里人；（某一城镇的）居民

▼ **COLLOCATIONS 词语搭配**

Town and country 城镇与乡村

Town 城镇

- **live in** a city/a town/an urban environment/(*informal*) a concrete jungle/the suburbs/shanty towns/slums 住在城里 / 镇上 / 城区 / 混凝土丛林 / 郊区 / 棚户区 / 贫民窟
- **live** (*especially NAmE*) downtown/in the downtown area/(*BrE*) in the city centre 住在市中心
- **enjoy/like** the hectic pace of life/the hustle and bustle of city life 喜欢忙碌的生活节奏 / 城市生活的热闹
- **cope with** the stress/pressure of urban life 应对城市生活的压力
- **get caught up in** the rat race 卷入大城市里为财富、权力等的疯狂追逐中
- **prefer/seek** the anonymity of life in a big city 更喜欢 / 追求大城市里人与人互不相识的生活
- **be drawn by/resist** the lure of the big city 被大城市的诱惑所吸引；抵御大城市的诱惑
- **head for** the bright lights (of the big city/New York) 奔向（大城市 / 纽约）五光十色的生活
- **enjoy/love** the vibrant/lively nightlife 享受 / 喜爱充满生机的夜生活
- **have/be close to** all the amenities 拥有 / 紧靠各种便利设施
- **be surrounded by** towering skyscrapers/a soulless urban sprawl 被高耸入云的摩天大楼 / 毫无生气的城市拓展区所包围
- **use/travel by/rely on** (*BrE*) public transport/(*NAmE*) public transportation 使用 / 出行乘坐 / 依赖公共交通
- **put up with/get stuck in/sit in** massive/huge/heavy/endless/constant traffic jams 忍受 / 陷入大面积 / 严重的 / 没完没了的 / 持续的交通堵塞
- **tackle/ease/reduce/relieve/alleviate** the heavy/severe traffic congestion 处理 / 缓解严重的交通堵塞
- **be affected/choked/damaged by** pollution 受到污染的影响；被污染呛得透不过气；受到污染的伤害

Country 乡村

- **live** in a village/the countryside/an isolated area/a rural backwater/(*informal*) the sticks 住在村里 / 乡村 / 偏僻的地区 / 落后的乡村 / 偏远的乡村地区
- **enjoy/like** the relaxed/slower pace of life 享受 / 喜欢悠闲 / 缓慢的生活节奏
- **enjoy/love/explore** the great outdoors 享受 / 喜欢 / 探索蓝天碧野
- **look for/find/get/enjoy** a little peace and quiet 寻找 / 找到 / 得到 / 享受一点宁静与安宁
- **need/want** to get back/closer to nature 需要 / 想要回去 / 接近大自然
- **be surrounded by** open/unspoilt/picturesque countryside 四周被空旷的 / 未被污染的 / 风景如画的乡村环绕
- **escape/quit/get out of/leave** the rat race 逃离 / 退出城市中你死我活的竞争
- **seek/achieve** a better/healthy work-life balance 寻求 / 达到工作与生活更好的 / 健康的平衡
- **downshift** to a less stressful life 选择压力较小的生活
- **seek/start** a new life in the country 在乡村寻求 / 开始一种新的生活
- (*BrE, informal*) **up sticks**/(*NAmE, informal*) **pull up stakes** and move to/head for... 突然迁居到…
- **create/build/foster** a strong sense of community 树立 / 培养强烈的社群意识
- **depend on/be employed in/work in** agriculture 依赖 / 从事农业
- **live off/farm/work** the land 靠土地为生；耕种土地
- **tackle/address** the problem of rural unemployment 解决农村失业问题

T

tow·path /ˈtəʊpɑːθ; *NAmE* ˈtoʊpæθ/ *noun* a path along the bank of a river or CANAL, that was used in the past by horses pulling boats (called BARGES) 纤道，纤路（旧时河流沿岸马拉驳船所走的路）

ˈtow rope (*also* **tow·line**) *noun* a rope that is used for pulling sth along, especially a vehicle 纤绳；拖缆；拖索

ˈtow truck (*especially NAmE*) (*BrE usually* **ˈbreakdown truck**) *noun* a truck that is used for taking cars away to be repaired when they have had a breakdown（把故障车辆拖去修理的）牵引车，救险车 ➲ VISUAL VOCAB PAGE V62

tox·ae·mia (*BrE*) (*NAmE* **tox·emia**) /tɒkˈsiːmiə; *NAmE* tɑːk-/ *noun* [U] (*medical* 医) infection of the blood by harmful bacteria 毒血症 **SYN** **blood poisoning**

toxic /ˈtɒksɪk; *NAmE* ˈtɑːk-/ *adj.* **1** containing poison; poisonous 有毒的；引起中毒的：*toxic chemicals/fumes/gases/substances* 有毒的化学品 / 烟雾 / 气体 / 物质 ◇ *to dispose of toxic waste* 处理有毒废料 ◇ *Many pesticides are highly toxic.* 许多杀虫剂毒性很大。 ➲ WORDFINDER NOTE AT GREEN **2** ~ **debt/loan/asset/investment** a level of debt or high-risk investment that causes very serious problems for a bank or other financial institution 有毒的（指能引致银行或其他金融机构出现严重问题的高水平债务或高风险投资） **3** [usually before noun] (*informal*) (of a person 人) having a very unpleasant personality, especially in the way they like to control and influence other people in a dishonest way 卑鄙无耻的；（尤指）爱摆布人的

tox·icity /tɒkˈsɪsəti; *NAmE* tɑːk-/ *noun* (*pl.* **-ies**) (*specialist*) **1** [U] the quality of being poisonous; the extent to which sth is poisonous 毒性；毒力：*substances with high levels of toxicity* 毒性大的物质 **2** [C] the effect that a poisonous substance has 毒性作用；毒性反应：*Minor toxicities of this drug include nausea and vomiting.* 这种药的轻微毒性反应包括恶心和呕吐。

toxi·col·ogy /ˌtɒksɪˈkɒlədʒi; *NAmE* ˌtɑːksɪˈkɑːl-/ *noun* [U] the scientific study of poisons 毒理学；毒物学 ▸ **toxi·colo·gical** /ˌtɒksɪkəˈlɒdʒɪkl; *NAmE* ˌtɑːksɪkəˈlɑːdʒɪkl/ *adj.* **toxi·colo·gist** /-dʒɪst/ *noun*

ˌtoxic ˈshock syndrome *noun* [U] a serious illness in women caused by harmful bacteria in the VAGINA, connected with the use of TAMPONS 中毒性休克综合征

toxin /ˈtɒksɪn; *NAmE* ˈtɑːk-/ *noun* a poisonous substance, especially one that is produced by bacteria in plants and animals 毒素（尤指生物体内细菌产生的毒物）

toxo·plas·mo·sis /ˌtɒksəʊplæzˈməʊsɪs; *NAmE* ˌtɑːksoʊplæzˈmoʊsɪs/ *noun* [U] (*medical* 医) a disease that can be dangerous to a baby while it is still in its mother's body, caught from infected meat, soil, or animal FAECES 弓形体病，弓形虫病（对胎儿有害，由感染病菌的肉、土壤或动物粪便传染）

toy /tɔɪ/ *noun, adj., verb*

■ ***noun*** **1** an object for children to play with 玩具：*cuddly/soft toys* 毛绒玩具 ◇ *The children were playing happily with their toys.* 孩子们正高兴地玩着玩具。 ➲ VISUAL VOCAB PAGE V41 **2** an object that you have for enjoyment or pleasure rather than for a serious purpose 玩物；玩意儿 **SYN** **plaything**：*executive toys* 行政人员的玩意儿 ◇ *His latest toy is the electric drill he bought last week.* 他的新玩意儿是他上星期买的电钻。

■ ***adj.*** [only before noun] **1** made as a copy of a particular thing and used for playing with 玩具的；作玩具的：*a toy car* 玩具汽车 ◇ *toy soldiers* 玩具士兵 **2** (of a dog 狗) of a very small breed 个头很小的；小体型品种的：*a toy poodle* 小鬈毛狗

■ ***verb***

PHR V **ˈtoy with sth** **1** to consider an idea or a plan, but not very seriously and not for a long time 不太认真地考虑；把…当儿戏 **SYN** **flirt with**：*I did briefly* **toy with the idea of** *living in France.* 我确实闪过定居法国的念头。 **2** to play with sth and move it around carelessly or without thinking 玩耍；戏弄；摆弄：*He kept toying nervously with his pen.* 他一直精神紧张地摆弄着钢笔。 ◇ *She hardly ate a thing, just toyed with a piece of cheese on her plate.* 她几乎没吃一点东西，只是拨弄着碟子里的一块奶酪。

ˈtoy boy *noun* (*BrE*) (*NAmE* **ˈboy toy**) (*informal, humorous*) a woman's male lover who is much younger than she is（比情妇年轻得多的）小情夫，小男友

toyi-toyi /ˈtɔɪ tɔɪ/ *noun* [U] (*SAfrE*) a type of dance or march, used as a form of protest, in which you repeatedly move one leg up and down followed by the other 托弋托弋舞（或游行）（作为抗议示威，左右交替踢腿）

TQM /ˌtiː kjuː ˈem/ *abbr.* TOTAL QUALITY MANAGEMENT 全面质量管理；全面品质管理

trace **AW** /treɪs/ *verb, noun*

■ ***verb*** **1** ~ **sb/sth (to sth)** to find or discover sb/sth by looking carefully for them/it 查出；找到；发现；追踪 **SYN** **track sb/sth↔down**：*We finally traced him to an address in Chicago.* 我们终于追查到他在芝加哥的一个地址。 **2** ~ **sth (back) (to sth)** to find the origin or cause of sth 追溯；追究：*She could trace her family tree back to the 16th century.* 她能把本族家谱追溯到 16 世纪。 ◇ *The leak was eventually traced to a broken seal.* 最后查出泄漏是由于密封处破裂所致。 ◇ *The police traced the call* (= used special electronic equipment to find out who made the telephone call) *to her ex-husband's number.* 警方用追踪装置查出是她前夫的电话号码打出的电话。 ➲ WORDFINDER NOTE AT RELATION **3** ~ **sth (from sth) (to sth)** to describe a process or the development of sth 描绘（事物的过程或发展）；追述；记述：*Her book traces the town's history from Saxon times to the present day.* 她的书描述的是这个市镇从撒克逊时代到现在的历史。 **4** ~ **sth (out)** to draw a line or lines on a surface 画（线）：*She traced a line in the sand.* 她在沙地上画了一条线。 **5** ~ **sth** to follow the shape or outline of sth 绘出，勾画出（轮廓）：*He traced the route on the map.* 他在地图上勾画出了路线。 ◇ *A tear traced a path down her cheek.* 一滴眼泪沿着她的面颊流了下来。 **6** ~ **sth** to copy a map, drawing, etc. by drawing on transparent paper (= TRACING PAPER) placed over it （用透明纸覆盖在地图、绘画等上）复制，描摹

■ ***noun*** **1** [C, U] a mark, an object or a sign that shows that sb/sth existed or was present 痕迹；遗迹；踪迹：*It's exciting to discover traces of earlier civilizations.* 发现早期文明的遗迹，真令人兴奋。 ◇ *Police searched the area but found* **no trace of** *the escaped prisoners.* 警方搜索了那一地区，但未发现越狱逃犯的任何踪迹。 ◇ *Years of living in England had eliminated* **all trace of** *her American accent.* 她多年居住在英国，美国口音已荡然无存。 ◇ *The ship had vanished* **without (a) trace**. 那艘船消失得无影无踪。 **2** [C] ~ **of sth** a very small amount of sth 微量；少许：*The post-mortem revealed traces of poison in his stomach.* 验尸发现他胃中有微量毒物。 ◇ *She spoke without a trace of bitterness.* 她说话时一点儿也不伤感。 **3** [C] (*specialist*) a line or pattern on paper or a screen that shows information that is found by a machine 描记图；轨迹；迹线；扫描线：*The trace showed a normal heart rhythm.* 描记图显示心率正常。 **4** [C] ~ **on sb/sth** a search to find out information about the identity of sb/sth, especially what number a telephone call was made from （对信息的）跟踪，追踪：*The police ran a trace on the call.* 警察对那次通话进行了追踪。 **5** [C, usually pl.] one of the two long pieces of leather that fasten a CARRIAGE or CART to the horse that pulls it 挽绳；套绳 **IDM** SEE KICK *v.*

trace·able **AW** /ˈtreɪsəbl/ *adj.* ~ **(to sb/sth)** if sth is **traceable**, you can find out where it came from, where it has gone, when it began or what its cause was 可追溯的；可追踪的；可追本溯源的：*Most telephone calls are traceable.* 大多数电话都可查出是从哪里打来的。

ˈtrace element *noun* **1** a chemical substance that is found in very small amounts 痕量元素 **2** a chemical substance that living things, especially plants, need only in very small amounts to be able to grow well 微量元素（生物，尤指植物，生长所需要的微量的化学物质）

tracer /ˈtreɪsə(r)/ *noun* **1** a bullet or SHELL (= a kind of bomb) that leaves a line of smoke or flame behind it 曳光弹 **2** (*specialist*) a RADIOACTIVE substance that can be seen in the human body and is used to find out what is happening inside the body 示踪剂

tra·cery /ˈtreɪsəri/ *noun* (*pl.* **-ies**) **1** [U] (*specialist*) a pattern of lines and curves in stone on the top part of some church windows 花色窗棂，窗花格（某些教堂窗户顶部的石制花饰） **2** [U, C, usually sing.] (*literary*) an attractive pattern of lines and curves 精美花饰图案

tra·ceur /ˈtreɪsə(r); ˌtræˈsɜː(r)/ *noun* a person who takes part in the sport of PARKOUR 跑酷者

trachea /trəˈkiːə; *NAmE* ˈtreɪkiə/ *noun* (*pl.* **trach·eas** or **trach·eae** /-kiːiː/) (*anatomy* 解) the tube in the throat that carries air to the lungs 气管 SYN **windpipe** ➲ VISUAL VOCAB PAGE V64

trache·ot·omy /ˌtrækiˈɒtəmi; *NAmE* ˌtreɪkiˈɑːt-/ *noun* (*pl.* **-ies**) (*medical* 医) a medical operation to cut a hole in sb's trachea so that they can breathe 气管切开术

tra·cing /ˈtreɪsɪŋ/ *noun* a copy of a map, drawing, etc. that you make by drawing on a piece of transparent paper placed on top of it 描摹；摹图；描图

ˈtracing paper *noun* [U] strong transparent paper that is placed on top of a drawing, etc. so that you can follow the lines with a pen or pencil in order to make a copy of it 描图纸；摹图纸

track /træk/ *noun, verb*

■ ***noun***

• **ROUGH PATH** 崎岖不平的小路 **1** [C] a rough path or road, usually one that has not been built but that has been made by people walking there （人踩出的）小道，小径：*a muddy track through the forest* 穿过森林的泥泞小径 ➲ VISUAL VOCAB PAGE V5 ➲ SEE ALSO CART TRACK

• **MARKS ON GROUND** 地面上的痕迹 **2** [C, usually pl.] marks left by a person, an animal or a moving vehicle（人、动物或车辆留下的）足迹，踪迹；车辙：*We followed the bear's tracks in the snow.* 我们跟着熊在雪地上留下的足迹走。◇ *tyre tracks* 轮胎印迹

• **FOR TRAIN** 火车 **3** [C, U] rails that a train moves along 轨道：*railway/railroad tracks* 铁路轨道 ◇ *India has thousands of miles of track.* 印度有数千英里的铁道。➲ WORDFINDER NOTE AT TRAIN **4** [C] (*NAmE*) a track with a number at a train station that a train arrives at or leaves from （火车站有编号的）轨道，站台：*The train for Chicago is on track 9.* 开往芝加哥的列车停靠在 9 号站台。➲ NOTE AT PLATFORM

• **FOR RACES** 赛跑 **5** [C] a piece of ground with a special surface for people, cars, etc. to have races on （赛跑、赛车等的）跑道：*a running track* 赛跑跑道 ◇ *a Formula One Grand Prix track* (= for motor racing) 一级方程式大奖赛赛道 ➲ SEE ALSO DIRT TRACK (2), TRACK AND FIELD

• **DIRECTION/COURSE** 方向；路线 **6** [C] the path or direction that sb/sth is moving in （移动的）路径，路线，方向：*Police are **on the track of*** (= searching for) *the thieves.* 警察正在追踪窃贼。◇ *She is on the **fast track** to promotion* (= will get it quickly). 她现在升迁在望。➲ SEE ALSO ONE-TRACK MIND

• **ON TAPE/CD** 录音磁带；光盘 **7** [C] a piece of music or song on a record, tape or CD（唱片、录音磁带或光盘的）一首乐曲，一首歌曲：*a track from their latest album* 他们最新唱片专辑里的一首歌曲 **8** [C] part of a tape, CD or computer disk that music or information can be recorded on （录音磁带、光盘或计算机磁盘的）音轨，声道：*a sixteen track recording studio* 十六声道录音室 ◇ *She sang on the backing track.* 她是唱和声的。➲ SEE ALSO SOUNDTRACK

• **FOR CURTAIN** 幕帘 **9** [C] a pole or rail that a curtain moves along （幕帘的）滑轨，滑道

• **ON LARGE VEHICLE** 大型车辆 **10** [C] a continuous belt of metal plates around the wheels of a large vehicle such as a BULLDOZER that allows it to move over the ground （推土机等的）履带

IDM **ˌback on ˈtrack** going in the right direction again after a mistake, failure, etc. 重新步入正确轨道；恢复正常：*I tried to get my life back on track after my divorce.* 离婚之后我力图使生活恢复正常。 **be ˌon ˈtrack** to be doing the right thing in order to achieve a particular result 步入正轨；做法对头：*Curtis is on track for the gold medal.* 柯蒂斯正踏上夺取金牌之途。 **keep/lose track of sb/sth** to have/not have information about what is happening or where sb/sth is 了解 / 不了解…的动态；与…保持 / 失去联系：*Bank statements help you keep track of where your money is going.* 银行账单有助于你了解你的资金使用情况。◇ *I lost all track of time* (= forgot what time it was). 我完全忘了时间。 **make ˈtracks** (*informal*) to leave a place, especially to go home 离去（尤指回家） **on the right/wrong ˈtrack** thinking or behaving in the right/wrong way 思路对头 / 不对头；做法对路 / 不对路 **stop/halt sb in their ˈtracks | stop/halt/freeze in your ˈtracks** to suddenly make sb stop by frightening or surprising them; to suddenly stop because sth has frightened or surprised you （使由于恐惧或吃惊）突然止步；（使）怔住：*The question stopped Alice in her tracks.* 这个问题问得艾丽斯张口结舌无以答对。➲ MORE AT BEAT *v.*, COVER *v.*, HOT *adj.*, WRONG *adj.*

■ ***verb***

• **FOLLOW** 跟随 **1** [T, I] ~ (**sb/sth**) to find sb/sth by following the marks, signs, information, etc., that they have left behind them 跟踪；追踪：*hunters tracking and shooting bears* 追踪射猎熊的猎人 **2** [T] ~ **sb/sth** | ~ **where, how, etc....** to follow the movements of sb/sth, especially by using special electronic equipment （尤指用特殊电子设备）跟踪，追踪：*We continued tracking the plane on our radar.* 我们继续用雷达追踪那架飞机。 **3** [T] ~ **sb/sth** | ~ **where, how, etc....** to follow the progress or development of sb/sth 跟踪（进展情况）：*The research project involves tracking the careers of 400 graduates.* 这个研究项目对 400 名毕业生的事业发展情况进行跟踪调查。➲ SEE ALSO FAST-TRACK

• **OF CAMERA** 摄影机 **4** [I] + **adv./prep.** to move in relation to the thing that is being filmed 跟踪摄影；移动摄影：*The camera eventually tracked away.* 摄影机最终将镜头推远。

• **SCHOOL STUDENTS** 学校学生 **5** [T] (*NAmE*) = STREAM (4)

• **LEAVE MARKS** 留下痕迹 **6** [T] ~ **sth** (+ **adv./prep.**) (*especially NAmE*) to leave dirty marks behind you as you walk 留下（脏）足迹：*Don't track mud on my clean floor.* 别在我干净的地板上踩上泥脚印。

PHR V **ˌtrack sb/sth↔ˈdown** to find sb/sth after searching in several different places 搜寻到；跟踪找到；追查到 SYN **trace**: *The police have so far failed to track down the attacker.* 警方至今未能追捕到攻击者。

ˌtrack and ˈfield (*NAmE*) (*BrE* **ath·let·ics**) *noun* sports that people compete in, such as running and jumping 田径运动 ➲ VISUAL VOCAB PAGE V50

track·ball /ˈtrækbɔːl/ (*also* **ˈtracker ball**, **roller·ball**) *noun* (*computing* 计) a device containing a ball that is used instead of a mouse to move the CURSOR around the screen 跟踪球；光标运动球；轨迹球

track·er /ˈtrækə(r)/ *noun* a person who can find people or wild animals by following the marks that they leave on the ground 追踪者；跟踪者；追踪人（或野兽）的人

ˈtracker ball *noun* (*computing* 计) = TRACKBALL

ˈtracker dog *noun* a dog that has been trained to help the police find people or EXPLOSIVES （受过训练协助搜寻人或炸药的）警犬，搜救犬

ˈtrack event *noun* [usually pl.] a sports event that is a race run on a track, rather than jumping or throwing sth 径赛项目 ➲ VISUAL VOCAB PAGE V50 ➲ COMPARE FIELD EVENT

ˈtracking station *noun* a place where people follow the movements of aircraft, etc. in the sky by RADAR or radio （用雷达或无线电追踪飞机等动向的）跟踪站

ˈtrack·less trol·ley (*US*) (*BrE* **trol·ley·bus**) *noun* a bus driven by electricity from a cable above the street 无轨电车

track·pad /'trækpæd/ *noun* = TOUCHPAD

'track record *noun* all the past achievements, successes or failures of a person or an organization（个人或组织的）业绩记录：*He has a proven track record in marketing.* 他有可靠的营销业绩记录。

track·suit /'træksuːt/ (*also* **'jogging suit**) *noun* a warm loose pair of trousers/pants and matching jacket worn for sports practice or as informal clothes（运动练习时或作便衣穿的）宽松暖和的衣裤；运动服 ➲ COMPARE SHELL SUIT

tract /trækt/ *noun* **1** (*biology* 生) a system of connected organs or TISSUES along which materials or messages pass（连通身体组织或器官的）道，束：*the digestive tract* 消化道 ◇ *a nerve tract* 神经束 **2** an area of land, especially a large one 大片土地；地带 SYN **stretch**：*vast tracts of forest* 大片大片的森林 **3** (*sometimes disapproving*) a short piece of writing, especially on a religious, moral or political subject, that is intended to influence people's ideas（尤指宣扬宗教、伦理或政治的）短文，传单，小册子

tract·able /'træktəbl/ *adj.* (*formal*) easy to deal with or control 易处理的；易驾驭的 SYN **manageable** OPP **intractable** ▸ **tract·abil·ity** /ˌtræktə'bɪləti/ *noun* [U]

'tract house (*also* **'tract home**) *noun* (*NAmE*) a modern house built on an area of land where a lot of other similar houses have also been built（设计类似的）住宅区房屋

trac·tion /'trækʃn/ *noun* [U] **1** the action of pulling sth along a surface; the power that is used for doing this 牵引；拖拉；牵引力；拉力 **2** a way of treating a broken bone in your body that involves using special equipment to pull the bone gradually back into its correct place 牵引（使体内断骨复位的疗法）：*He spent six weeks in traction after he broke his leg.* 他腿部骨折后做了六个星期的牵引治疗。 **3** the force that stops sth, for example the wheels of a vehicle, from sliding on the ground（车轮等对地面的）附着摩擦力

'traction engine *noun* a vehicle, driven by steam or DIESEL oil, used in the past for pulling heavy loads（旧时用以拖重物的）牵引机车，牵引车

trac·tor /'træktə(r)/ *noun* **1** a powerful vehicle with two large and two smaller wheels, used especially for pulling farm machinery 拖拉机；牵引机 ➲ WORDFINDER NOTE AT FARM ➲ VISUAL VOCAB PAGES V3, V63 **2** (*NAmE*) the front part of a tractor-trailer, where the driver sits（牵引式挂车的）牵引车，拖车头

'tractor-trailer (*also* **'trailer truck**) *noun* (*NAmE*) a large lorry/truck with two sections, one in front where the driver sits and one behind for carrying goods. The sections are connected by a FLEXIBLE joint so that the tractor-trailer can turn corners more easily. 牵引式挂车；铰接式卡车；载重拖车 ➲ VISUAL VOCAB PAGE V62 ➲ SEE ALSO ARTICULATED

trad /træd/ (*also less frequent* **'trad jazz**) (*both BrE*) *noun* [U] traditional JAZZ in the style of the 1920s, with free playing (= IMPROVISATION) against a background of fixed rhythms and combinations of notes 传统爵士乐（有 20 世纪 20 年代的风格、固定的节奏及和声，可即兴发挥）➲ SEE ALSO DIXIELAND

trad·able (*also* **trade·able**) /'treɪdəbl/ *adj.* (*specialist*) that you can easily buy and sell or exchange for money or goods 可买卖的；可交易的 SYN **marketable**

trade /treɪd/ *noun, verb*

■ ***noun*** **1** [U] the activity of buying and selling or of exchanging goods or services between people or countries 贸易；买卖；商业；交易：***international/foreign trade*** 国际 / 对外贸易 ◇ *Trade between the two countries has increased.* 两国之间的贸易增长了。◇ *the international trade in oil* 国际石油贸易 ◇ *the arms/drugs, etc. trade* 军火、毒品等交易 ➲ COLLOCATIONS AT BUSINESS, INTERNATIONAL ➲ SEE ALSO BALANCE OF TRADE, FAIR-TRADE, FREE TRADE

WORDFINDER 联想词： boom, **business**, commerce, embargo, import, market, monopoly, sanction, tariff

2 [C] a particular type of business 行业；职业；生意：*the* ***building/food/tourist, etc. trade*** 建筑业、食品业、旅游业等 ◇ *He works in the* ***retail trade*** (= selling goods in shops/stores). 他做零售工作。 ➲ SEE ALSO RAG TRADE **3** **the trade** [sing.+sing./pl. v.] a particular area of business and the people or companies that are connected with it 同业；同行；同人：*They offer discounts to the trade* (= to people who are working in the same business). 他们对同行业的人给予折扣。◇ *a* ***trade magazine/journal*** 行业杂志 / 期刊 ➲ SEE ALSO STOCK-IN-TRADE **4** [U, C] the amount of goods or services that you sell 营业额；交易量 SYN **business**：*Trade was very good last month.* 上月的交易量很大。 **5** [U, C] a job, especially one that involves working with your hands and that requires special training and skills（尤指手工）职业；手艺；行当：*He was a carpenter* ***by trade***. 他以木工为业。◇ *When she leaves school, she wants to learn a trade.* 她毕业后想学一门手艺。◇ *She was surrounded by* ***the tools of her trade*** (= everything she needs to do her job). 她周围都是她干活用的工具。 ➲ SYNONYMS AT WORK IDM SEE JACK *n.*, PLY *v.*, ROARING, TRICK *n.*

■ ***verb*** **1** [I, T] to buy and sell things 做买卖；做生意；从事贸易： **~ (in sth) (with sb)** *The firm openly traded in arms.* 这家公司公开买卖军火。◇ *Early explorers traded directly with the Indians.* 早期的探险者与印第安人直接进行交易。◇ *trading partners* (= countries that you trade with) 贸易伙伴 ◇ **~ sth (with sb)** *Our products are now traded worldwide.* 我们的产品现在销往世界各地。 **2** [I] to exist and operate as a business or company 营业；营运：*The firm has now ceased trading.* 这家商行现已停业。◇ **~ as sb/sth** *They traded as 'Walker and Son'.* 他们以"沃克父子公司"之名营业。 **3** [I, T] **~ (sth)** to be bought and sold, or to buy and sell sth, on a STOCK EXCHANGE（在证券交易所）交易，买卖：*Shares were trading at under half their usual value.* 那些股票以低于通常价值的一半买卖。 **4** [T] to exchange sth that you have for sth that sb else has 互相交换；以物易物： **~ (sb) sth** *to* ***trade secrets/insults/jokes*** 互换秘密；对骂；互说笑话 ◇ **~ sth for sth** *She traded her posters for his CD.* 她以海报换取他的光盘。◇ **~ sth with sb** *I wouldn't mind* ***trading places*** *with her for a day.* 我不介意和她掉换一天位置。

PHR V **'trade at sth** (*US*) to buy goods or shop at a particular store 在（某商店）购物 **ˌtrade 'down** to spend less money on things than you used to 降低消费：*Shoppers are trading down and looking for bargains.* 到商店买东西的人都降低消费，寻找减价货。 **ˌtrade sth↔'in** to give sth used as part of the payment for sth new 以旧物折价换新物；折价贴换：*He traded in his old car for a new Mercedes.* 他把旧汽车折价添钱买了辆新奔驰。 ➲ RELATED NOUN TRADE-IN **ˌtrade sth↔'off (against/for sth)** to balance two things or situations that are opposed to each other 权衡；平衡；使协调：*They were attempting to trade off inflation against unemployment.* 他们正力求在通货膨胀和失业之间进行协调。 ➲ RELATED NOUN TRADE-OFF **'trade on sth** (*disapproving*) to use sth to your own advantage, especially in an unfair way（为私利不公正地）利用 SYN **exploit**：*They trade on people's insecurity to sell them insurance.* 他们利用人们的不安全感向他们推销保险。 **ˌtrade 'up 1** to sell sth in order to buy sth more expensive 卖次买好；（卖掉原有的以便）买更贵的东西：*We're going to trade up to a larger house.* 我们打算卖掉房子，再买一座大点的。 **2** to give sth you have used as part of the payment for sth more expensive 以旧物折价添钱买较贵的东西；折价贴换

'trade balance *noun* = BALANCE OF TRADE

'trade deficit (*also* **'trade gap**) *noun* [usually sing.] a situation in which the value of a country's imports is greater than the value of its exports 外贸逆差；贸易赤字

the ˌTrade De'scriptions Act *noun* [sing.] (in Britain) a law that states that goods must be described honestly

T

when they are advertised or sold《商品说明法》（英国规定商品出售或做广告必须如实说明）: *You could get them under the Trade Descriptions Act for that!* 你可以就那一点指控他们违反了《商品说明法》!

ˈtrade fair (*also* **ˈtrade show**) *noun* an event at which many different companies show and sell their products 商品展销会；商品交易会

ˈtrade-in *noun* a method of buying sth by giving a used item as part of the payment for a new one; the used item itself 折旧贴换交易；以旧折价换新；折价旧物: *the trade-in value of a car* 一辆汽车的以旧换新抵价 ◇ *Do you have a trade-in?* 你有折价的旧物品吗? ➲ SEE ALSO PART EXCHANGE

trade·mark /ˈtreɪdmɑːk; *NAmE* -mɑːrk/ *noun, verb*

■ ***noun*** **1** (*abbr.* **TM**) a name, symbol or design that a company uses for its products and that cannot be used by anyone else 商标: *'Big Mac' is McDonald's best-known trademark.* "巨无霸"是麦当劳最著名的商标。 **2** a special way of behaving or dressing that is typical of sb and that makes them easily recognized（人的行为或衣着的）特征，标记

■ ***verb*** to register sth as a trademark 把…注册为商标: *They have trademarked the name in the US and the UK.* 他们已在美国和英国将这个名称注册为商标。

ˈtrade name *noun* **1** = BRAND NAME **2** a name that is taken and used by a company for business purposes（公司的）商号，牌号，字号

ˈtrade-off *noun* ~ (**between sth and sth**) the act of balancing two things that are opposed to each other（在相互对立的两者间的）权衡，协调: *a trade-off between increased production and a reduction in quality* 对产量增加和质量下降的权衡

trader /ˈtreɪdə(r)/ *noun* a person who buys and sells things as a job 商人；经商者；买卖人: ***small/independent/local traders*** 小的/独立的/当地的商人 ◇ ***bond/currency traders*** 债券/货币交易人

ˈtrade route *noun* (in the past) the route that people buying and selling goods used to take across land or sea（旧时的）商队路线，商船航线

ˈtrade school *noun* (*NAmE*) a school where students go to learn a trade 中等职业学校

ˌtrade ˈsecret *noun* a secret piece of information that is known only by the people at a particular company 商业秘密: *The recipe for their drink is a closely guarded trade secret.* 他们饮料的配方是严格保守的商业秘密。

ˈtrade show *noun* = TRADE FAIR

trades·man /ˈtreɪdzmən/ *noun* (*pl.* **-men** /-mən/) **1** a person whose job involves going to houses to sell or deliver goods 上门推销商；送货员 **2** (*especially BrE*) a person who sells goods, especially in a shop/store（尤指在商店里售货的）商人；店主 SYN **shopkeeper** **3** (*especially NAmE*) a skilled person, especially one who makes things by hand 工匠；手艺人

trades·people /ˈtreɪdzpiːpl/ *noun* [pl.] **1** people whose job involves selling goods or services, especially people who own a shop/store（统称）商人，商店主人 **2** people whose job involves training and special skills, for example CARPENTERS 手艺人；工匠

the ˌTrades ˌUnion ˈCongress *noun* [sing.] = TUC

ˌtrade ˈsurplus *noun* a situation in which the value of a country's exports is greater than the value of its imports 外贸盈余；贸易顺差

ˌtrade ˈunion (*BrE also* **ˌtrades ˈunion**) *noun* = UNION (1) ▸ **ˌtrade ˈunionism** *noun* [U]: *the history of trade unionism* 工会主义的历史

ˌtrade ˈunionist (*also* **ˌtrades ˈunionist, union·ist**) *noun* a member of a trade/labor union 工会会员

ˈtrade-up *noun* a sale of an object in order to buy sth similar but better and more expensive 卖次买好；以次换好的买卖

ˈtrade winds *noun* [pl.] strong winds that blow all the time towards the EQUATOR and then to the west 信风，贸易风（稳定吹向赤道再向西）

trad·ing 🔑 /ˈtreɪdɪŋ/ *noun* [U] the activity of buying and selling things 贸易；经商；营业；交易: *new laws on Sunday trading* (= shops being open on Sundays) 关于星期日营业的新法律 ◇ *Supermarkets everywhere reported excellent trading in the run-up to Christmas.* 各地超市报告说圣诞节前生意火爆。 ◇ *Shares worth $8 million changed hands during a day of hectic trading.* 当日交投活跃，股票交易达 800 万美元。

ˈtrading card *noun* (*especially NAmE*) one of a set of cards, often showing sports players or other famous people on them, that children collect and exchange with one another 集换式卡牌（儿童收集并相互交换的运动员或明星等卡牌）

ˈtrading estate *noun* (*BrE*) an area of land, often on the edge of a city or town, where there are a number of businesses and small factories（城镇边缘的）工商业区 ➲ COMPARE INDUSTRIAL ESTATE

ˈtrading floor *noun* an area in a STOCK EXCHANGE or bank where shares and other SECURITIES are bought and sold（证券交易所或银行的）交易大厅

ˈtrading post *noun* a small place in an area that is a long way from any town, used as a centre for buying and selling goods (especially in N America in the past)（尤指北美旧时偏远地区的）贸易站

trad·ition 🔑 AW /trəˈdɪʃn/ *noun* [C, U] a belief, custom or way of doing sth that has existed for a long time among a particular group of people; a set of these beliefs or customs 传统；传统的信仰（或风俗）: ***religious/cultural, etc. traditions*** 宗教、文化等传统 ◇ *This region is **steeped in tradition**.* 这个地区有着深厚的传统。 ◇ *The company has a **long tradition** of fine design.* 这家公司的优秀设计历史悠久。 ◇ *The British are said to love tradition* (= to want to do things in the way they have always been done). 据说英国人热爱传统。 ◇ *They **broke with tradition*** (= did things differently) *and got married quietly.* 他们打破传统，毫不声张地结了婚。 ◇ ***By tradition**, children play tricks on 1 April.* 按照传统风俗，儿童在 4 月 1 日捣乱戏弄别人。 ◇ *There's a tradition in our family that we have a party on New Year's Eve.* 我们家有个传统，新年除夕要办家庭聚会。 ◇ *He's a politician **in the tradition of*** (= similar in style to) *Kennedy.* 他是位具有肯尼迪风格的从政者。

trad·ition·al 🔑 AW /trəˈdɪʃənl/ *adj.* **1** 🔑 being part of the beliefs, customs or way of life of a particular group of people, that have not changed for a long time 传统的；习俗的；惯例的: *traditional dress* 传统服装 ◇ ***It's traditional** in America to eat turkey on Thanksgiving Day.* 感恩节时吃火鸡是美国的传统。 **2** 🔑 (*sometimes disapproving*) following older methods and ideas rather than modern or different ones 传统的；因袭的；守旧的 SYN **conventional**: *traditional methods of teaching* 传统的教学方法 ◇ *Their marriage is very traditional.* 他们的婚姻十分守旧。 ▸ **trad·ition·al·ly** 🔑 AW /-ʃənəli/ *adv.*: *The festival is traditionally held in May.* 这个节日按照传统是在五月份过的。 ◇ *Housework has traditionally been regarded as women's work.* 家务劳动历来被认为是妇女的事。

trad·ition·al·ism /trəˈdɪʃənəlɪzəm/ *noun* [U] the belief that customs and traditions are more important for a society than modern ideas 传统主义（认为传统习俗比现代思想对社会更重要）

trad·ition·al·ist AW /trəˈdɪʃənəlɪst/ *noun* a person who prefers tradition to modern ideas or ways of doing things 传统主义者 ▸ **trad·ition·al·ist** *adj.*

ˈtrad jazz *noun* [U] = TRAD

T

tra·duce /trəˈdjuːs; *NAmE* -ˈduːs/ *verb* **~ sb** (*formal*) to say things about sb that are unpleasant or not true 诽谤；中伤；诋毁 SYN **slander**

traf·fic /ˈtræfɪk/ *noun, verb*

■ ***noun*** [U] **1** the vehicles that are on a road at a particular time 路上行驶的车辆；交通：***heavy/rush-hour traffic*** 繁忙的 / 高峰时刻的交通 ◇ ***local/through traffic*** 当地 / 过境车辆 ◇ *There's always a lot of traffic at this time of day.* 每天这个时候总是有很多来往车辆。◇ *They were **stuck in traffic** and missed their flight.* 他们遇到了塞车，没赶上班机。◇ *a plan to reduce **traffic congestion*** 减少交通拥堵的计划 ◇ ***traffic police*** (= who control traffic on a road or stop drivers who are breaking the law) 交通警察 ◇ *The delay is due simply to the **volume of traffic**.* 延误完全是因为交通拥挤。➲ WORDFINDER NOTE AT CAR ➲ COLLOCATIONS AT DRIVING

WORDFINDER 联想词：clamp, cone, contraflow, pedestrian, roadworks, speed hump, tailback, toll, zebra crossing

2 the movement of ships, trains, aircraft, etc. along a particular route （沿固定路线的）航行，行驶，飞行：*transatlantic traffic* 横渡大西洋的航行 ◇ *air traffic control* 空中交通管制 **3** the movement of people or goods from one place to another 运输；人流；货流：***commuter/freight/passenger traffic*** 市郊间上下班运输；货运；客运 ◇ *the traffic of goods between one country and another* 一国与另一国间的货物运输 **4** the movement of messages and signals through an electronic communication system 信息流量；通信（量）：*the computer servers that manage global Internet traffic* 管理全球互联网通信的计算机服务器 **5 ~ (in sth)** illegal trade in sth （非法的）交易，买卖：*the traffic in firearms* 非法军火交易

■ ***verb*** **(-ck-) 1** [T, I, usually passive] **~ (in) sb** to move people illegally, especially in order to make them work in bad conditions without proper payment 非法贩卖人口（尤指迫使他们充当廉价劳工）：*The women had been trafficked and forced into prostitution.* 这些妇女被贩卖，被逼迫卖淫。◇ *The cartel is now trafficking in illegal immigrants.* 这一集团正从事贩卖非法移民的勾当。**2** [T, I] **~ (in) sth** to buy and sell sth illegally （非法）进行…交易，做…买卖：*Smugglers were trafficking arms across the border to the rebels.* 走私分子越境将武器贩卖给叛乱者。◇ *to traffic in drugs* 买卖毒品 ▶ **traf·fick·er** *noun*：*a drugs trafficker* 毒品贩子 **traf·fick·ing** *noun* [U]：*drug trafficking* 贩毒 ◇ *human trafficking* (= moving people illegally in order to make them work in bad conditions and without proper payment) 非法贩卖人口

ˈtraffic calming *noun* [U] (*BrE*) ways of making roads safer, especially for people who are walking or riding bicycles, by building raised areas, etc. to make cars go more slowly 道路安全措施，减缓机动车车速措施（如在马路设置凸面使车辆减速，保障行人及骑自行车者的安全）

ˈtraffic circle (*also* **ro·tary**) (*both NAmE*) (*BrE* **round·about**) *noun* a place where two or more roads meet, forming a circle that all traffic must go around in the same direction （交通）环岛

ˈtraffic cone *noun* = CONE (3)

ˈtraffic island (*BrE also* **island**, **ref·uge**) *noun* an area in the middle of a road where you can stand and wait for cars to go past until it is safe for you to cross 安全岛（供行人避让车辆）

ˈtraffic jam *noun* a long line of vehicles on a road that cannot move or that can only move very slowly 堵车；交通阻塞：*We were **stuck in a traffic jam**.* 我们遇上了交通阻塞。➲ COLLOCATIONS AT DRIVING

ˈtraffic light *noun* [C] (*also* **ˈtraffic lights** [pl.]) (*NAmE also* **stop·lights** [pl.]) a signal that controls the traffic on a road, by means of red, orange and green lights that show when you must stop and when you can go 交通信号灯：*Turn left at the traffic lights.* 在交通信号灯处向左拐。➲ VISUAL VOCAB PAGE V3

ˈtraffic warden *noun* (*BrE*) a person whose job is to check that people do not park their cars in the wrong place or for longer than is allowed, and to report on those who do or tell them that they have to pay a FINE （处理违章停车的）交通管理员

tra·gedian /trəˈdʒiːdiən/ *noun* (*formal*) **1** a person who writes tragedies for the theatre 悲剧作家 **2** an actor in tragedies 悲剧演员

tra·gedy /ˈtrædʒədi/ *noun* [C, U] (*pl.* **-ies**) **1** a very sad event or situation, especially one that involves death 悲惨的事；不幸；灾难；惨案：***It's a tragedy** that she died so young.* 她英年早逝是一大悲哀。◇ ***Tragedy struck** the family when their son was hit by a car and killed.* 这个家庭惨遭不幸，他们的儿子被汽车撞死了。◇ *The whole affair **ended in tragedy**.* 整个事件以悲剧而告终。**2** a serious play with a sad ending, especially one in which the main character dies; plays of this type 悲剧；悲剧作品：*Shakespeare's tragedies* 莎士比亚的悲剧 ◇ *Greek tragedy* 希腊悲剧 ➲ COMPARE COMEDY (1)

tra·gic /ˈtrædʒɪk/ *adj.* **1** making you feel very sad, usually because sb has died or suffered a lot 悲惨的；悲痛的；可悲的：*He was killed in a tragic accident at the age of 24.* 他 24 岁时在一次悲惨的事故中丧命。◇ *Cuts in the health service could have tragic consequences for patients.* 减少公共医疗卫生服务可能对病人造成悲惨的后果。◇ *It would be tragic if her talent remained unrecognized.* 若她一直怀才不遇，那就可悲了。**2** [only before noun] connected with tragedy (= the style of literature) 悲剧的：***a tragic actor/hero*** 悲剧演员 / 男主角 ➲ WORDFINDER NOTE AT STORY ▶ **tra·gic·al·ly** /-kli/ *adv.*：*Tragically, his wife was killed in a car accident.* 他的妻子在车祸中不幸身亡。◇ *He died tragically young.* 他英年早逝。

ˌtragic ˈirony *noun* [U] (*specialist*) a technique in literature in which a character's actions or thoughts are known to the reader or audience but not to the other characters in the story 悲剧性讽示（故事中某个人物的行为或想法为读者或观众所知却不为故事中其他人物所知的表现手法）

tragi·com·edy /ˌtrædʒiˈkɒmədi; *NAmE* -ˈkɑːm-/ *noun* [C, U] (*pl.* **-ies**) **1** a play that is both funny and sad; plays of this type 悲喜剧；悲喜剧作品 **2** an event or a situation that is both funny and sad 悲喜交加的事情（或局面）▶ **tragi·com·ic** /-ˈkɒmɪk; *NAmE* -ˈkɑːm-/ *adj.*

trail /treɪl/ *noun, verb*

■ ***noun*** **1** a long line or series of marks that is left by sb/sth （长串的）痕迹，踪迹，足迹：*a trail of blood* 一连串血迹 ◇ *tourists who **leave a trail** of litter everywhere they go* 一路乱丢垃圾的游客 ◇ *The hurricane left a trail of destruction behind it.* 飓风过后满目疮痍。**2** a track, sign or smell that is left behind and that can be followed, especially in hunting （尤指打猎时跟踪的）踪迹，足迹，臭迹：*The hounds were following the fox's trail.* 猎犬追踪着狐狸的气味。◇ *The police are still **on the trail of** the escaped prisoner.* 警方仍在追捕逃犯。◇ *Fortunately the **trail was still warm*** (= clear and easy to follow). 庆幸的是痕迹仍然清晰可循。◇ *The **trail had gone cold**.* 臭迹已经消失了。➲ WORDFINDER NOTE AT HUNT **3** a path through the countryside （乡间的）小路，小径：*a trail through the forest* 穿过森林的小路 ➲ SEE ALSO NATURE TRAIL **4** a route that is followed for a particular purpose （特定）路线，路径：*a **tourist trail*** (= of famous buildings) 游览路线 ◇ *politicians on the **campaign trail*** (= travelling around to attract support) 进行巡回宣传的政治人物 IDM SEE BLAZE *v.*, HIT *v.*, HOT *adj.*

■ ***verb*** **1** [T, I] to pull sth behind sb/sth, usually along the ground; to be pulled along in this way （被）拖，拉：**~ sth** *A jeep trailing a cloud of dust was speeding in my direction.* 一辆吉普车拖着一股扬尘，朝我疾驰而来。◇ *I trailed my hand in the water as the boat moved along.* 我把手放在水里，让小船拖着往前划行。◇ **(+ adv./prep.)** *The bride's dress trailed behind her.* 新娘的结婚礼服拖在身后。**2** [I] **+ adv./prep.** to walk slowly because you are tired or bored, especially behind sb else （尤指跟在他人后面）疲惫地走，没精打采地慢走，磨蹭：*The kids trailed around after us while we shopped for clothes.* 我们在商店买衣服时，孩子们无精打采地跟在后面。**3** [I, T] (used especially in the progressive tenses 尤用于进行时) to be losing a game or other contest （在比赛或其他竞赛中）落后，失利，失败： *United were trailing 2–0 at half-time.* 联队在上半场结束时以 0:2 落后。◇ **~ by sth** *We were trailing by five points.* 我们落后五分。◇ **~ in sth** *This country is still trailing badly in scientific research.* 这个国家在科研方面仍然大大滞后。◇ **~ sb/sth** *The Conservatives are trailing Labour in the opinion polls.* 在民意测验中保守党的支持率落后于工党。 **4** [T] **~ sb/sth** to follow sb/sth by looking for signs that show you where they have been 跟踪；追踪： *The police trailed Dale for days.* 警方跟踪了戴尔多日。 **5** [I] to grow or hang downwards over sth or along the ground; to move downwards over sth 蔓生；蔓延；向下移动： *trailing plants* 蔓生植物 ◇ *He had tears trailing down his cheeks.* 他的眼泪顺着双颊流了下来。

PHR V **,trail a'way/'off** (of sb's speech 话语) to become gradually quieter and then stop 声音逐渐减弱到停止；逐渐消失： *His voice trailed away to nothing.* 他的声音越来越小，最后消失了。◇ **+ speech** *'I only hope…', she trailed off.* "我只希望…" 她的声音越来越小，最后听不到了。

'trail bike *noun* a light motorcycle that can be used on rough ground 越野摩托车

trail·blazer /'treɪlbleɪzə(r)/ *noun* a person who is the first to do or discover sth and so makes it possible for others to follow 创始人；先驱；拓荒者；开路先锋 ➲ COMPARE BLAZE A TRAIL at BLAZE *v.* ▶ **trail·blaz·ing** *adj.* [usually before noun]: *trailblazing scientific research* 创新的科学研究

trail·er /'treɪlə(r)/ *noun* **1** a truck, or a container with wheels, that is pulled by another vehicle 拖车；挂车： *a car towing a trailer with a boat on it* 拖着一辆载有小船的拖车的小汽车 ➲ **VISUAL VOCAB** PAGE V63 ➲ SEE ALSO TRACTOR-TRAILER **2** (*NAmE*) (*BrE* **mobile home**) a vehicle without an engine, that can be pulled by a car or truck or used as a home or an office when it is parked （拖车式）活动房屋，活动工作室： *a **trailer park*** (= an area where trailers are parked and used as homes) 拖车式活动房屋停车场 **3** (*NAmE*) = MOBILE HOME (1) ➲ **VISUAL VOCAB** PAGE V16 **4** (*especially BrE*) (*NAmE usually* **preview**) a series of short scenes from a film/movie or television programme, shown in advance to advertise it （电影或电视节目的）预告片 ➲ **SYNONYMS** AT ADVERTISEMENT

'trailer trash *noun* [U] (*NAmE, informal, offensive*) a way of referring to poor white people from a low social class 住活动房屋的废物（指地位低下的贫困白人）

'trailer truck *noun* (*NAmE*) = TRACTOR-TRAILER

,trailing 'edge *noun* (*specialist*) the rear edge of sth moving, especially an aircraft wing （移动物体，尤指机翼的）后缘 ➲ **VISUAL VOCAB** PAGE V57

train 🔑 /treɪn/ *noun, verb*

■ *noun* **1** 🔑 a railway/railroad engine pulling a number of coaches/cars or trucks, taking people and goods from one place to another 火车；列车： *to **get on/off a train*** 上 / 下火车 ◇ *I like travelling **by train**.* 我喜欢乘火车旅行。◇ *a **passenger/commuter/goods/freight train*** 客运 / 市郊通勤 / 货运列车 ◇ *to **catch/take/get the train** to London* 赶上 / 乘坐 / 搭乘开往伦敦的火车 ◇ *a **train journey/driver*** 火车旅程 / 司机 ◇ *You have to **change trains** at Reading.* 你得在雷丁换乘火车。 ➲ **VISUAL VOCAB** PAGE V63 ➲ SEE ALSO GRAVY TRAIN, ROAD TRAIN, WAGON TRAIN

WORDFINDER 联想词： aisle, buffet, carriage, connection, locomotive, luggage rack, platform, station, track

2 a number of people or animals moving in a line 列队行进的人（或动物）；队列；行列： *a camel train* 骆驼队 **3** [usually sing.] a series of events or actions that are connected 一系列相关的事情（或行动）： *His death set in motion a **train of events** that led to the outbreak of war.* 他的死引发了一系列的事件，从而导致了战争的爆发。 **4** the part of a long formal dress that spreads out on the floor behind the person wearing it 拖裾，裙裾（长礼服的曳地部分）

IDM **bring sth in its 'train** (*formal*) to have sth as a result 带来…后果： *Unemployment brings great difficulties in its train.* 失业带来了重重困难。 **in sb's 'train** (*formal*) following behind sb 跟随…之后： *In the train of the rich and famous came the journalists.* 记者蜂拥在豪绅名流之后。 **set sth in 'train** (*formal*) to prepare or start sth 安排；准备；开始： *That telephone call set in train a whole series of events.* 那个电话把一整套事项安排好了。 **a train of 'thought** the connected series of thoughts that are in your head at a particular time 思路；思绪： *The phone ringing interrupted my train of thought.* 电话铃声打断了我的思路。

■ *verb* **1** 🔑 [T, I] to teach a person or an animal the skills for a particular job or activity; to be taught in this way 训练；培训；接受训练： **~ sb/sth** *badly trained staff* 缺乏训练的员工 ◇ **~ sb/sth to do sth** *They train dogs to sniff out drugs.* 他们训练狗嗅出毒品。 ◇ **~ (sb) (as/in/for sth)** *He trained as a teacher before becoming an actor.* 他在成为演员之前受过师资培训。 ◇ *All members of the team have trained in first aid.* 全队队员都接受过急救培训。 ◇ **~ to do/be sth** *Sue is training to be a doctor.* 休正在接受医生培训。 **2** 🔑 [I, T] to prepare yourself/sb for a particular activity, especially a sport, by doing a lot of exercise; to prepare a person or an animal in this way 进行…训练；（尤指）进行体育锻炼；训练（人或动物）： **~ (for/in sth)** *athletes training for the Olympics* 为迎战奥林匹克运动会而进行训练的运动员 ◇ **~ sb/sth (for/in sth)** *She trains horses.* 她是驯马的。 ◇ *He trains the Olympic team.* 他训练奥林匹克队。 **3** [T] to develop a natural ability or quality so that it improves 教育；培养…的能力（或素质）： **~ sth** *An expert with a trained eye will spot the difference immediately.* 训练有素、眼光敏锐的专家会马上发现差别所在。 ◇ **~ sth to do sth** *You can train your mind to think positively.* 你可以培养自己有乐观思想的能力。 **4** [T] **~ sth (around/along/up, etc.)** to make a plant grow in a particular direction 使（植物）朝某方向生长；修整： *Roses had been trained around the door.* 玫瑰被修整得围绕着门口生长。

PHR V **'train sth at/on sb/sth** to aim a gun, camera, light, etc. at sb/sth 把（枪口、照相机、灯光等）瞄准，对准

train·ee /,treɪ'niː/ *noun* a person who is being taught how to do a particular job 接受培训者；实习生；见习生： *a management trainee* 管理培训生 ◇ *a trainee teacher* 实习教师 ➲ **COLLOCATIONS** AT JOB

train·er /'treɪnə(r)/ *noun* **1** (*also* **'training shoe**) (*both BrE*) (*NAmE* **sneak·er**) [usually pl.] a shoe that you wear for sports or as informal clothing 运动鞋；便鞋： *a pair of trainers* 一双运动鞋 ➲ **VISUAL VOCAB** PAGE V69 ➲ SEE ALSO CROSS-TRAINER (2) **2** a person who teaches people or animals to perform a particular job or skill well, or to do a particular sport 教员；驯兽师；教练员： *teacher trainers* 培训师资的教员 ◇ *a racehorse trainer* 赛马驯马师 ◇ *Her trainer had decided she shouldn't run in the race.* 她的教练决定她不应参加赛跑。 ➲ SEE ALSO PERSONAL TRAINER

train·ing 🔑 /'treɪnɪŋ/ *noun* [U] **1** 🔑 **~ (in sth/in doing sth)** the process of learning the skills that you need to do a job 训练；培训： *staff training* 职工培训 ◇ *Few candidates had received any training in management.* 没有几个应聘者接受过管理培训。 ◇ *a training course* 培训课程 ➲ **COLLOCATIONS** AT EDUCATION, JOB

WORDFINDER 联想词： apprentice, certificate, coaching, college, course, intern, probation, qualify, work experience

2 🔑 the process of preparing to take part in a sports competition by doing physical exercises （为参加体育比赛而进行的）训练，锻炼： *to be **in training** for a race* 在进行赛前训练

'training college *noun* (*BrE*) a college that trains people for a job or profession 专科学院；职业（培训）学院： *a police training college* 警察学院

'training shoe *noun* (*BrE*) = TRAINER (1)

'training wheels (*NAmE*) (*BrE* **sta·bil·izers**) *noun* [pl.] small wheels that are fitted at each side of the back

T

wheel on a child's bicycle to stop it from falling over（儿童自行车后轮两侧的）稳定轮 ➲ VISUAL VOCAB PAGE V55

train·man /ˈtreɪnmən/ *noun* (*pl.* **-men** /-mən/) (*NAmE*) a member of the team of people operating a train 列车员；乘务员

ˈtrain set *noun* a toy train, together with the track that it runs on, a toy station, etc. 玩具火车（包括铁轨、车站等的成套玩具）

train·spot·ter /ˈtreɪnspɒtə(r); *NAmE* -spɑːt-/ *noun* (*BrE*) **1** a person who collects the numbers of railway engines as a hobby（作为业余爱好）收集机车号码的人 **2** (*disapproving*) a person who is interested in the details of a subject that other people think are boring 过分注重细节的人 ▸ **ˈtrain·spot·ting** *noun* [U]

ˈtrain wreck *noun* **1** an accident in which a train crashes into sth else or comes off the track 列车撞车事故；列车脱轨事故 **2** (*informal, figurative*) a situation, a person's life, etc. that people find extremely interesting because it lacks order, is very bad or is unsuccessful 混乱失序的局面，灾难式的人生（因太过混乱、糟糕或倒霉而使人们觉得有趣）：*She gives a train wreck of a performance in the movie.* 她在电影中的演出烂透了。◇ *This guy is a train wreck.* 这个男人的人生简直就是一场灾难。➲ COMPARE CAR CRASH (2)

traipse /treɪps/ *verb* [I] + **adv./prep.** (*informal*) to walk somewhere slowly when you are tired and unwilling 疲惫地走；拖沓地行走；磨蹭

trait /treɪt/ *noun* a particular quality in your personality（人的个性的）特征，特性，特点：*personality traits* 个性特点 ➲ WORDFINDER NOTE AT CHARACTER

trai·tor /ˈtreɪtə(r)/ *noun* ~ (**to sb/sth**) a person who gives away secrets about their friends, their country, etc. 背叛者；叛徒；卖国贼：*He was seen as a traitor to the socialist cause.* 他被视为社会主义事业的叛徒。◇ *She denied that she had **turned traitor*** (= become a traitor). 她否认自己叛变了。

trai·tor·ous /ˈtreɪtərəs/ *adj.* (*formal*) giving away secrets about your friends, your country, etc. 背叛的；叛国的；卖国的 ▸ **trai·tor·ous·ly** *adv.*

tra·jec·tory /trəˈdʒektəri/ (*pl.* **-ies**) *noun* (*specialist*) the curved path of sth that has been fired, hit or thrown into the air（射体在空中的）轨道，弹道，轨迹：*a missile's trajectory* 导弹的弹道 ◇ (*figurative*) *My career seemed to be on a downward trajectory.* 我的事业似乎在走下坡路。

tram /træm/ (*also* **tram·car**) (*both BrE*) (*US* **street·car**, **trol·ley**) *noun* a vehicle driven by electricity, that runs on rails along the streets of a town and carries passengers 有轨电车：*a tram route* 有轨电车路线 ➲ VISUAL VOCAB PAGE V63

tram·lines /ˈtræmlaɪnz/ *noun* [pl.] **1** the rails in the street that trams run on 电车轨道 **2** (*BrE*) (*NAmE* **alley**) (*informal*) the pair of parallel lines on a TENNIS or BADMINTON COURT that mark the extra area that is used when four people are playing（网球或羽毛球球场两侧的）双打边线

tram·mel /ˈtræml/ *verb* (**-ll-**, *especially US* **-l-**) [often passive] ~ **sb/sth** (*formal*) to limit sb's freedom of movement or activity 限制，束缚，阻碍（某人的活动自由）SYN **restrict** ➲ COMPARE UNTRAMMELLED

tramp /træmp/ *noun, verb*

■ *noun* **1** (*also* **hobo**) [C] a person with no home or job who travels from place to place, usually asking people in the street for food or money 流浪汉；流浪乞丐 **2** [sing.] **the ~ of sb/sth** the sound of sb's heavy steps 沉重的脚步声：*the tramp of marching feet* 行进中沉重的脚步声 **3** [C, usually sing.] a long walk 长途步行；徒步旅行 SYN **trek**: *We had a long tramp home.* 我们是经过长途跋涉回家的。**4** (*old-fashioned, NAmE, disapproving*) a woman who has many sexual partners 淫妇；荡妇

■ *verb* (*also NAmE, informal* **tromp**) [I, T] to walk with heavy or noisy steps, especially for a long time（尤指长时间地）重步行走，踏，踩：(**+ adv./prep.**) *We tramped across the wet grass to look at the statue.* 我们踏过湿漉漉的草地去看那座雕像。◇ *the sound of tramping feet* 沉重的脚步声 ◇ **~ sth** *She's been tramping the streets looking for a job.* 她一直在大街上四处奔走寻找工作。

tramp·ing /ˈtræmpɪŋ/ *noun* [U] (*NZE*) the activity of going for long walks over rough country, carrying all the food and equipment that you need 长途徒步旅行（带足食物和装备穿越崎岖地区）▸ **tramper** *noun*

tram·ple /ˈtræmpl/ *verb* **1** [T, I] to step heavily on sb/sth so that you crush or harm them/it with your feet 踩碎；踩伤；践踏：**~ sb/sth** *People were **trampled underfoot** in the rush for the exit.* 有人在拼命涌向出口时被踩在脚下。◇ *He was **trampled to death** by a runaway horse.* 他被一匹脱缰的马踩死了。◇ **~ sb/sth down** *The campers had trampled the corn down.* 野营的人践踏了庄稼。◇ **~ on/over sth** *Don't trample on the flowers!* 勿踏花草！**2** [I] **~ (on/over) sb/sth** to ignore sb's feelings or rights and treat them as if they are not important 践踏，摧残（人权、心灵等）：*The government is trampling on the views of ordinary people.* 政府在践踏民意。

tram·po·line /ˈtræmpəliːn/ *noun, verb*

■ *noun* a piece of equipment that is used in GYMNASTICS for doing jumps in the air. It consists of a sheet of strong material that is attached by springs to a frame. 蹦床，跳床，弹床（体操器械）➲ VISUAL VOCAB PAGE V41

■ *verb* [I] to jump on a trampoline 在蹦床上弹跳 ▸ **tram·po·lin·ing** *noun* [U]

tram·way /ˈtræmweɪ/ *noun* the rails that form the route for a TRAM 有轨电车轨道

trance /trɑːns; *NAmE* træns/ *noun* **1** [C] a state in which sb seems to be asleep but is aware of what is said to them, for example if they are HYPNOTIZED 昏睡状态；催眠状态：*to **go/fall into a trance*** 进入 / 陷入昏睡状态 **2** [C] a state in which you are thinking so much about sth that you do not notice what is happening around you 出神；发呆 SYN **daze** **3** (*also* **ˈtrance music**) [U] a type of electronic dance music with HYPNOTIC rhythms and sounds 迷幻音乐

tranche /trɑːnʃ/ *noun* (*finance* 财, *BrE*) one of the parts into which an amount of money or a number of shares in a company is divided（款额或股份的）一份，一部分

tranny (*also* **tran·nie**) /ˈtræni/ *noun* (*pl.* **-ies**) (*informal*) **1** a TRANSSEXUAL or TRANSVESTITE 变性者；易性癖者；易装癖者 **2** (*especially BrE*) a TRANSISTOR radio 晶体管收音机 **3** a TRANSPARENCY (1) 幻灯片；透明正片

tran·quil /ˈtræŋkwɪl/ *adj.* (*formal*) quiet and peaceful 安静的；平静的；安宁的 SYN **serene**: *a tranquil scene* 静谧的景象 ◇ *the tranquil waters of the lake* 平静无波的湖水 ◇ *She led a tranquil life in the country.* 她过着恬静的乡村生活。▸ **tran·quil·lity** (*especially BrE*) (*NAmE usually* **tran·quil·ity**) /træŋˈkwɪləti/ *noun* [U] **tran·quil·ly** *adv.*

tran·quil·lize (*also* **-ise**) (*both BrE*) (*NAmE* **tran·quil·ize**) /ˈtræŋkwəlaɪz/ *verb* **~ sb/sth** to make a person or an animal calm or unconscious, especially by giving them a drug (= a TRANQUILLIZER)（尤指用镇定剂）使平静，使安定

tran·quil·lizer (*also* **-iser**) (*both BrE*) (*NAmE* **tran·quil·izer**) /ˈtræŋkwəlaɪzə(r)/ *noun* a drug used to reduce anxiety 安定药；镇静剂：*She's on* (= is taking) *tranquillizers.* 她在服用镇静剂。

trans- /trænz; træns/ *prefix* **1** (in adjectives 构成形容词) across; beyond 横穿；通过；超越：*transatlantic* 横渡大西洋的 ◇ *transcontinental* 横贯大陆的 **2** (in verbs 构成动词) into another place or state 进入（另一地方）；成为（另一状态）：*transplant* 移植 ◇ *transform* 转变 ➲ MORE LIKE THIS 6, page R25

trans·act /trænˈzækt/ *verb* [T, I] **~ (sth) (with sb)** (*formal*) to do business with a person or an organization（与人或组织）做业务，做交易：*buyers and sellers transacting business* 进行交易的买方和卖方

T

trans·ac·tion /træn'zækʃn/ *noun* **1** [C] ~ (**between A and B**) a piece of business that is done between people, especially an act of buying or selling （一笔）交易，业务，买卖 **SYN deal**: *financial transactions between companies* 公司之间的财务往来 ◇ *commercial transactions* 商业交易 **2** [U] ~ **of sth** (*formal*) the process of doing sth 办理；处理：*the transaction of government business* 处理政府事务

trans·at·lan·tic /ˌtrænzət'læntɪk/ *adj.* [only before noun] **1** crossing the Atlantic Ocean 横渡大西洋的；横越大西洋的：*a transatlantic flight* 横越大西洋的飞行 **2** connected with countries on both sides of the Atlantic Ocean 大西洋两岸国家的：*a transatlantic alliance* 大西洋两岸国家联盟 **3** on or from the other side of the Atlantic Ocean 在大西洋彼岸的；来自大西洋彼岸的：*to speak with a transatlantic accent* 说话带大西洋对岸的口音

trans·ceiver /træn'siːvə(r)/ *noun* a radio that can both send and receive messages 无线电收发两用机

tran·scend /træn'send/ *verb* ~ **sth** (*formal*) to be or go beyond the usual limits of sth 超出，超越（通常的界限）**SYN exceed**

tran·scend·ent /træn'sendənt/ *adj.* (*formal*) going beyond the usual limits; extremely great 卓越的；杰出的；极其伟大的 ▶ **tran·scend·ence** /-dəns/ *noun* [U]: *the transcendence of God* 上帝的至高无上

tran·scen·den·tal /ˌtrænsen'dentl/ *adj.* [usually before noun] going beyond the limits of human knowledge, experience or reason, especially in a religious or spiritual way （尤指宗教或精神方面）超验的，玄奥的：*a transcendental experience* 超验的感受

ˌtranscenˌdental mediˈtation (*BrE*) (*NAmE* **Transcendental Meditation™**) *noun* [U] (*abbr.* **TM**) a method of making yourself calm by thinking deeply in silence and repeating a special phrase to yourself many times 超觉静坐（静思默念真言）

trans·con·tin·en·tal /ˌtrænzˌkɒntɪ'nentl; ˌtræns-; *NAmE* -ˌkɑːn-/ *adj.* crossing a continent 横贯大陆的；穿越大陆的：*a transcontinental railway/railroad* 横贯大陆的铁路

tran·scribe /træn'skraɪb/ *verb* **1** to record thoughts, speech or data in a written form, or in a different written form from the original 记录；抄录；把…转成（另一种书写形式）：~ **sth** *Clerks transcribe everything that is said in court.* 书记员把法庭上所说的话全都记录在案。◇ *The interview was recorded and then transcribed.* 采访谈话先录了音，然后再抄录出来。◇ ~ **sth into sth** *How many official documents have been transcribed into Braille for blind people?* 有多少官方文件已经转成盲文供盲人阅读？ **2** ~ **sth** (*specialist*) to show the sounds of speech using a special PHONETIC alphabet 用音标标音 **3** ~ **sth** (**for sth**) to write a piece of music in a different form so that it can be played by another musical instrument or sung by another voice 改编（乐曲，以适合其他乐器或声部）：*a piano piece transcribed for the guitar* 为吉他改编的钢琴曲

tran·script /'trænskrɪpt/ *noun* **1** (*also* **tran·scrip·tion**) a written or printed copy of words that have been spoken 抄本；誊本；打印本：*a transcript of the interview* 采访内容的文字稿 **2** (*especially NAmE*) an official record of a student's work that shows the courses they have taken and the marks/grades they have achieved 学生成绩报告单

tran·scrip·tion /træn'skrɪpʃn/ *noun* **1** [U] the act or process of representing sth in a written or printed form 抄写；誊写；打印：*errors made in transcription* 抄写错误 ◇ *phonetic transcription* 标音 **2** [C] = TRANSCRIPT (1)：*The full transcription of the interview is attached.* 现附上采访记录文本的全文。 **3** [C] something that is represented in writing 书面标注的事物：*This dictionary gives phonetic transcriptions of all headwords.* 本词典所有词目都注出了音标。 **4** [C] a change in the written form of a piece of music so that it can be played on a different instrument or sung by a different voice （乐曲的）改编

trans·ducer /trænz'djuːsə(r); træns-; *NAmE* -'duːsər/ *noun* (*specialist*) a device for producing an electrical signal from another form of energy such as pressure 换能器；变换器

tran·sept /'trænsept/ *noun* (*architecture* 建) either of the two wide parts of a church shaped like a cross, that are built at RIGHT ANGLES to the main central part（十字形教堂的）耳堂 ⊃ COMPARE NAVE

tran·sex·ual = TRANSSEXUAL

ˌtrans-fatty ˈacid (*also* **ˌtrans-ˈfat**) *noun* [C, U] a type of fat produced when oils are changed by a chemical process into solids, for example to make MARGARINE. Trans-fatty acids are believed to encourage the harmful development of CHOLESTEROL. 反式脂肪酸：*foods that are low in trans-fatty acids* 低反式脂肪酸食物 ⊃ SEE ALSO MONOUNSATURATED FAT, POLYUNSATURATED FAT, SATURATED FAT, UNSATURATED FAT

trans·fer 🔑 **AW** *verb, noun*

■ ***verb*** /træns'fɜː(r)/ (**-rr-**)

• **TO NEW PLACE** 到新地方 **1** 🔑 [I, T] to move from one place to another; to move sth/sb from one place to another（使）转移，搬迁：~ (**from…**) (**to…**) *The film studio is transferring to Hollywood.* 这家电影制片厂正迁往好莱坞。◇ (*especially NAmE*) *If I spend a semester in Madrid, will my credits transfer?* 如果我在马德里上一学期的课，我的学分能转过来吗？◇ ~ **sth/sb** (**from…**) (**to…**) *How can I transfer money from my bank account to his?* 怎么才能把我账户上的钱转到他的账户上呢？◇ *The patient was transferred to another hospital.* 患者转送到了另一家医院。◇ (*especially NAmE*) *I couldn't transfer all my credits from junior college.* 我无法把我在专科学校的所有学分都转过来。

• **TO NEW JOB/SCHOOL/SITUATION** 到新的工作 / 学校 / 环境 **2** 🔑 [I, T] to move from one job, school, situation, etc. to another; to arrange for sb to move（使）调动；转职；转学；改变（环境）：~ (**from…**) (**to…**) *Children usually transfer to secondary school at 11 or 12.* 儿童通常在 11 或 12 岁时升读中学。◇ *He transferred to UCLA after his freshman year.* 他读完大学一年级后，转学到加利福尼亚大学洛杉矶分校。◇ ~ **sb** (**from…**) (**to…**) *Ten employees are being transferred from the sales department.* 十名雇员已调离销售部。

• **FEELING/DISEASE/POWER** 感觉；疾病；权力 **3** [T, I] ~ (**sth**) (**from…**) (**to…**) if you **transfer** a feeling, a disease, or power, etc., or if it **transfers** from one person to another, the second person has it, often instead of the first 转移（感情）；传染（疾病）；让与，转让（权力等）：*Joe had already transferred his affections from Lisa to Cleo.* 乔已移情别恋，把爱意从莉萨转移到了克利奥身上。◇ *This disease is rarely transferred from mother to baby* (= so that the baby has it as well as the mother). 这种疾病很少由母亲传给婴儿。

• **PROPERTY** 财产 **4** [T] ~ **sth** (**to sb**) to officially arrange for sth to belong to sb else or for sb else to control sth 转让；让与 **SYN sign sth↔over** (**to sb**): *He transferred the property to his son.* 他把财产转让给了儿子。

• **IN SPORT** 体育运动 **5** [I, T] (*especially BrE*) to move, or to move sb, to a different sports team, especially a professional football (SOCCER) team 转会，使转会（尤指职业足球队）：~ (**from…**) (**to…**) *He transferred to Everton for £6 million.* 他以 600 万英镑的转会费转到埃弗顿队。◇ ~ **sb** (**from…**) (**to…**) *He was transferred from Spurs to Arsenal for a huge fee.* 他以巨额转会费从热刺队转到阿森纳队。

• **TO NEW VEHICLE** 换乘交通工具 **6** [I, T] to change to a different vehicle during a journey; to arrange for sb to change to a different vehicle during a journey（使在旅途中）转乘，换乘，倒车：~ (**from…**) (**to…**) *I transferred at Bahrain for a flight to Singapore.* 我在巴林转乘飞往新加坡的班机。◇ ~ **sb** (**from…**) (**to…**) *Passengers are transferred from the airport to the hotel by taxi.* 旅客自机场改乘出租汽车到旅馆。

• **INFORMATION/MUSIC, ETC.** 信息、音乐等 **7** 🔑 [T, I] to copy information, music, an idea, etc. from one method of recording or presenting it to another; to be recorded or presented in a different way 转存，转录（资料、音乐等）；改编：~ **sth** (**from sth**) (**to sth**) *You can transfer data to a memory stick in a few seconds.* 你可以在几秒钟

内将数据转存到 U 盘。◇ ~ (**from sth**) (**to sth**) *The novel does not transfer well to the movies.* 这部小说不太适宜改编成电影。➲ MORE LIKE THIS 36, page R29

■ ***noun*** /ˈtrænsfɜː(r)/

• **CHANGE OF PLACE/JOB/SITUATION** 地点 / 工作 / 环境的改变 **1** 🔑 [U, C] the act of moving sb/sth from one place, group or job to another; an occasion when this happens 搬迁; 转移; 调动; 变换: *electronic **data transfer*** 电子数据传输 ◇ *the transfer of currency from one country to another* 货币从一国到另一国的汇划 ◇ *He has asked for a transfer to the company's Paris branch.* 他要求调到公司的巴黎分部。◇ *After the election there was a swift **transfer of power**.* 大选之后权力迅速交接。

• **IN SPORT** 体育运动 **2** [U, C] the act of moving a sports player from one club or team to another （运动员）转会: *It was the first goal he had scored since his transfer from Chelsea.* 这是他从切尔西队转会过来之后的第一记入球。◇ *a transfer fee* 转会费 ◇ *to be **on the transfer list*** (= available to join another club) 在转会名单上

• **CHANGE OF VEHICLE** 转车 **3** [U, C] an act of changing to a different place, vehicle or route when you are travelling （旅途中的）中转，换乘，改变路线: *The transfer from the airport to the hotel is included in the price.* 票价包括从机场转车到旅馆的费用。

• **TRAIN/BUS TICKET** 火车 / 公共汽车票 **4** [C] (*NAmE*) a ticket that allows a passenger to continue their journey on another bus or train 转车票; 换乘票

• **PICTURE** 图画 **5** [C] (*especially BrE*) (*NAmE usually* **decal**) a picture or design that can be removed from a piece of paper and stuck onto a surface, for example by being pressed or heated 转印图画，转印图案（利用挤压或加热，可从纸上转印到物体的表面）

• **PSYCHOLOGY** 心理学 **6** [U] (*psychology* 心) the process of using behaviour which has already been learned in one situation in a new situation 迁移（将已习得的行为在新的情况下应用）➲ SEE ALSO LANGUAGE TRANSFER

trans·fer·able AW /trænsˈfɜːrəbl/ *adj.* that can be moved from one place, person or use to another 可转移的; 可调动的; 可转让的; 可转录的; 可中转的: *This ticket is not transferable* (= it may only be used by the person who has bought it). 此票不得转让。◇ *We aim to provide our students with **transferable skills*** (= that can be used in different jobs). 我们的目的是让学生掌握可用于不同工作的技术。▶ **trans·fer·abil·ity** /ˌtræns,fɜːrəˈbɪləti/ *noun* [U]

trans·fer·ence AW /ˈtrænsfərəns; *NAmE* trænsˈfɜːrəns/ *noun* [U] (*specialist* or *formal*) the process of moving sth from one place, person or use to another 转移; 转递; 调动; 转让: *the transference of heat from the liquid to the container* 热量从液体到容器的传导

trans·fer·ral /trænsˈfɜːrəl/ *noun* [U] the action of transferring sth or sb 转移; 调动; 转换

ˈtransfer student *noun* (*NAmE*) a student at a college or university who has completed classes at another college or university after leaving high school （大学）转学生

trans·fig·ure /trænsˈfɪɡə(r); *NAmE* -ɡjər/ *verb* [often passive] ~ **sb/sth** (*literary*) to change the appearance of a person or thing so that they look more beautiful 使改观; 美化…的外表 ▶ **trans·fig·ur·ation** /ˌtræns,fɪɡəˈreɪʃn; *NAmE* -ɡjəˈr-/ *noun* [U, sing.]

trans·fix /trænsˈfɪks/ *verb* [usually passive] ~ **sb** to make sb unable to move because they are afraid, surprised, etc. 使（因恐惧、惊愕等而）动弹不得; 使惊呆 SYN **paralyse**: *Luisa stood transfixed with shock.* 路易莎大吃一惊，站在那里呆若木鸡。

trans·form 🔑 AW /trænsˈfɔːm; *NAmE* -ˈfɔːrm/ *verb* **1** 🔑 ~ **sth/sb** (**from sth**) (**into sth**) to change the form of sth 使改变形态 SYN **convert**: *The photochemical reactions transform the light into electrical impulses.* 光化学反应使光变为电脉冲。**2** 🔑 ~ **sth/sb** (**from sth**) (**into sth**) to completely change the appearance or character of sth, especially so that it is better 使改变外观（或性质）; 使改观: *A new colour scheme will transform your bedroom.* 新的色彩调配将使你的卧室焕然一新。◇ *It was an event that would transform my life.* 那是能够彻底改变我一生的一件事。

trans·form·ation AW /ˌtrænsfəˈmeɪʃn; *NAmE* -fərˈm-/ *noun* **1** [C, U] a complete change in sb/sth （彻底的）变化，改观，转变，改革: *The way in which we work has **undergone a** complete **transformation** in the past decade.* 在过去的十年里，我们的工作方式经历了彻底的变革。◇ *What a transformation! You look great.* 真是判若两人！你看上去真神气。◇ ~ (**from sth**) (**to/into sth**) *the country's transformation from dictatorship to democracy* 这个国家由独裁到民主的转变 **2** [U] used in South Africa to describe the process of making institutions and organizations more DEMOCRATIC（用于南非）民主改革: *a lack of transformation in the private sector* 在私营部门缺乏民主改革 ▶ **trans·form·ation·al** /-ʃənl/ *adj.*

ˌtransforˌmational ˈgrammar *noun* [U] (*abbr.* **TG**) (*linguistics* 语言) a type of grammar that describes a language as a system that has a deep structure which changes in particular ways when real sentences are produced 转换语法（将语言描述为有深层结构的系统，在产出真实句子时按特定方式转换）

trans·form·er /trænsˈfɔːmə(r); *NAmE* -ˈfɔːrm-/ *noun* a device for reducing or increasing the VOLTAGE of an electric power supply, usually to allow a particular piece of electrical equipment to be used 变压器

trans·fu·sion /trænsˈfjuːʒn/ *noun* [C, U] **1** = BLOOD TRANSFUSION **2** ~ **of sth** the act of investing extra money in a place or an activity that needs it 追加投资; （资金的）注入: *The project badly needs a transfusion of cash.* 这个项目急需追加现金投资。▶ **trans·fuse** *verb*: ~ **sth** (**into sb/sth**) *to transfuse blood into a patient* 给病人输血

trans·gen·der /trænzˈdʒendə(r); træns-/ *adj.* relating to TRANSSEXUALS and TRANSVESTITES 变性（者）的; 易性癖（者）的; 易装癖（者）的: *transgender issues* 关于变性的有争议的问题 ▶ **trans·gen·dered** *adj.*

trans·gen·ic /ˌtrænzˈdʒenɪk; ˌtræns-/ *adj.*, *noun* (*biology* 生)

■ ***adj.*** (of a plant or an animal 植物或动物) having GENETIC material introduced from another type of plant or animal 转基因的 SYN **genetically modified**: *transgenic crops* 转基因作物 ▶ **trans·gen·ic·ally** /-kli/ *adv.*

■ ***noun*** **1** **trans·gen·ics** [pl.] the study or practice of creating transgenic plants or animals 转基因学; 转基因（做法） **2** [C] a transgenic plant or animal 转基因植物（或动物）

trans·gress /trænzˈɡres; træns-/ *verb* ~ **sth** (*formal*) to go beyond the limit of what is morally or legally acceptable 越轨; 违背（道德）; 违犯（法律）▶ **trans·gres·sion** /trænzˈɡreʃn; træns-/ *noun* [C, U] **trans·gres·sor** *noun*

trans·hu·mance /trænsˈhjuːməns; *NAmE* trænz-/ *noun* [U] (*specialist*) the practice of moving animals to different fields in different seasons, for example to higher fields in summer and lower fields in winter 迁移性放牧

tran·si·ent /ˈtrænziənt; *NAmE* ˈtrænʃnt/ *adj.*, *noun*

■ ***adj.*** (*formal*) **1** continuing for only a short time 短暂的; 转瞬即逝的; 倏忽的 SYN **fleeting**, **temporary**: *the transient nature of speech* 言语的即逝性 **2** staying or working in a place for only a short time, before moving on 暂住的; 过往的; 临时的: *a city with a large transient population* (= of students, temporary workers, etc.) 有大量流动人口的城市 ▶ **tran·si·ence** /-əns/ *noun* [U]: *the transience of human life* 人生的短暂

■ ***noun*** (*especially NAmE*) a person who stays or works in a place for only a short time, before moving on 暂住某地的人; 过往旅客; 临时工

tran·sis·tor /trænˈzɪstə(r); -ˈsɪst-/ *noun* **1** a small electronic device used in computers, radios, televisions, etc. for controlling an electric current as it passes along a CIRCUIT 晶体管 **2** (*also* **tranˌsistor ˈradio**) (*also informal* **tranny** *especially in BrE*) a small radio with transistors 晶体管收音机

T

tran·sit AW /ˈtrænzɪt; -sɪt/ *noun, verb*
■ *noun* **1** [U] the process of being moved or carried from one place to another 运输；运送；搬运；载运：*The cost includes transit.* 成本中包括运费。◇ *goods damaged **in transit*** 在运输中损坏的货物 ◇ *transit times* 运送时间 **2** [U, C, usually sing.] the act of going through a place on the way to somewhere else 通过；经过；通行；过境；中转：*the transit lounge at Vienna airport* 维也纳机场中转候机室 ◇ *a **transit visa*** (= one that allows a person to pass through a country but not to stay there) 过境签证 **3** [U] (*NAmE*) the system of buses, trains, etc. which people use to travel from one place to another 交通运输系统：*the city's **mass/public transit** system* 城市的公共交通运输系统
■ *verb* [T, I] ~ (**sth**) to pass across or through an area 穿过；经过；越过：*The ship is currently transiting the Gulf of Mexico.* 这艘船现在正穿越墨西哥湾。

ˈ**transit camp** *noun* a camp that provides temporary accommodation for REFUGEES 临时难民营

tran·si·tion AW /trænˈzɪʃn; -ˈsɪʃn/ *noun, verb*
■ *noun* [U, C] the process or a period of changing from one state or condition to another 过渡；转变；变革；变迁：~ (**from sth**) (**to sth**) *the transition from school to full-time work* 从学校到全职工作的过渡阶段 ◇ *He will remain head of state during the **period of transition** to democracy.* 在向民主政体过渡时期，他仍将是国家首脑。◇ ~ (**between A and B**) *We need to ensure a smooth transition between the old system and the new one.* 我们需要确保新旧制度的平稳过渡。◇ *This course is useful for students who are **in transition*** (= in the process of changing) *from one training programme to another.* 对转换培训项目的学生来说，这一课程很有用。
■ *verb* [I, T] to change or to make sth change from one state or condition to another （使）过渡，转变，变迁：*They transitioned from print journalism to the digital world.* 他们由纸媒过渡到了数字世界。◇ ~ **sb/sth** *They decided to transition the farm to organic.* 他们决定将农场转型为有机农场。▶ **tran·si·tion·al** AW /-ʃənl/ *adj.*：*a transitional period* 过渡时期 ◇ *a transitional government* 过渡政府

tranˈsition metal (*also* **tranˈsition element**) *noun* (*chemistry* 化) one of the group of metals in the centre of the PERIODIC TABLE (= a list of all the chemical elements) which form coloured COMPOUNDS and often act as CATALYSTS (= substances that make chemical reactions happen faster) 过渡金属（位于元素周期表中心的一组金属元素，可形成有色化合物，常作为催化剂）

tran·si·tive /ˈtrænsətɪv/ *adj.* (*grammar* 语法) (of verbs 动词) used with a DIRECT OBJECT 及物的：*In 'She wrote a letter', the verb 'wrote' is transitive and the word 'letter' is the direct object.* 在 She wrote a letter 一句中，动词 wrote 是及物动词，letter 一词是直接宾语。OPP **intransitive** ▶ **tran·si·tive·ly** *adv.*：*The verb is being used transitively.* 这个动词在此用作及物动词。

tran·si·tiv·ity /ˌtrænsəˈtɪvəti; ˌtrænz-/ *noun* [U] (*grammar* 语法) the fact of whether a particular verb is TRANSITIVE or INTRANSITIVE （动词的）及物性

tran·si·tory AW /ˈtrænsətri; *NAmE* -tɔːri/ *adj.* (*formal*) continuing for only a short time 暂时的；片刻的；转瞬即逝的 SYN **fleeting, temporary**：*the transitory nature of his happiness* 他昙花一现的幸福

ˈ**Transit van™** *noun* (*BrE*) a type of large van that is used for delivering goods, carrying equipment, etc. 货运车；全顺车

trans·late 🔑 /trænsˈleɪt; trænz-/ *verb* **1** 🔑 [T, I] to express the meaning of speech or writing in a different language 翻译；译：~ **sth** (**from sth**) (**into sth**) *He translated the letter into English.* 他把这封信译成了英文。◇ *Her books have been translated into 24 languages.* 她的书被译成了 24 种语言。◇ *Can you help me translate this legal jargon into plain English?* 你能帮助我用浅显易懂的英语来说明这一法律术语吗？◇ ~ **sth** (**as sth**) *'Suisse' had been wrongly translated as 'Sweden'.* * Suisse 被错译成 Sweden（瑞典）。◇ ~ (**from sth**) (**into sth**) *I don't speak Greek so Dina offered to translate for me.* 我不懂希腊语，于是迪娜主动给我翻译。◇ *My work involves translating from German.* 我的工作包括德语翻译。➲ WORDFINDER NOTE AT LANGUAGE **2** 🔑 [I] to be changed from one language to another 被翻译；被译成：*Most poetry does not translate well.* 诗歌大多翻译不好。◇ ~ **as sth** *The Welsh name translates as 'Land's End'.* 这个威尔士语的地名可译成"地之角"。**3** [T, I] to change sth, or to be changed, into a different form （使）转变，变为：~ **sth** (**into sth**) *It's time to translate words into action.* 是把言语化为行动的时候了。◇ ~ **into sth** *I hope all the hard work will translate into profits.* 我希望所有的辛勤劳动都会有回报。**4** [T, I] ~ (**sth**) (**as sth**) to understand sth in a particular way or give sth a particular meaning （以某种方式）理解；给予（某种含义）SYN **interpret**：*the various words and gestures that we translate as love* 我们理解为爱的各种言语和姿势

trans·la·tion 🔑 /trænsˈleɪʃn; trænz-/ *noun* **1** 🔑 [U] ~ (**from sth**) (**into sth**) | ~ (**of sth**) (**into sth**) the process of changing sth that is written or spoken into another language 翻译；译：*an error in translation* 误译 ◇ *He specializes in translation from Danish into English.* 他专门从事把丹麦文译成英文的工作。◇ *The book loses something **in translation**.* 此书在翻译过程中丢失了一些原意。◇ *The irony is **lost in translation**.* 原文的反语用法在翻译中丢失了。**2** 🔑 [C, U] a text or work that has been changed from one language into another 译文；译本；译作：*The usual translation of 'glasnost' is 'openness'.* * glasnost 一词通常译为 openness（公开性）。◇ *a **rough translation*** (= not translating everything exactly) 粗略的翻译 ◇ *a **literal translation*** (= following the original words exactly) 直译 ◇ *a **free translation*** (= not following the original words exactly) 意译 ◇ *a **word-for-word translation*** 字字对应的翻译 ◇ *I have only read Tolstoy **in translation**.* 我只读过托尔斯泰作品的译本。◇ *a copy of Dryden's translation of the Aeneid* 一本德莱顿翻译的史诗《埃涅阿斯纪》 **3** [U] ~ (**of sth**) **into sth** the process of changing sth into a different form 转变；转化：*the translation of theory into practice* 从理论到实践的转化

trans·la·tor /trænsˈleɪtə(r); trænz-/ *noun* a person who translates writing or speech into a different language, especially as a job （尤指专职）翻译，译员，译者，翻译家：*She works as a translator of technical texts.* 她的工作是科技翻译。➲ COMPARE INTERPRETER (1)

trans·lit·er·ate /trænsˈlɪtəreɪt; trænz-/ *verb* ~ **sth** (**into/as sth**) (*formal*) to write words or letters using letters of a different alphabet or language 移译；音译 ▶ **trans·lit·er·ation** /ˌtrænsˌlɪtəˈreɪʃn; ˌtrænz-/ *noun* [C, U]

trans·lu·cent /trænsˈluːsnt; trænz-/ *adj.* (*formal*) allowing light to pass through but not transparent 半透明的 ▶ **trans·lu·cence** /-sns/ (*also* **trans·lu·cency** /-snsi/) *noun* [U]

trans·mi·gra·tion /ˌtrænzmaɪˈɡreɪʃn; ˌtræns-/ *noun* [U] the passing of a person's soul after their death into another body （死后灵魂的）转生，转世

trans·mis·sion AW /trænsˈmɪʃn; trænz-/ *noun* (*formal*) **1** [U] the act or process of passing sth from one person, place or thing to another 传送；传递；传达；传播；传染 SYN **transfer**：*the transmission of the disease* 这种疾病的传播 ◇ *the risk of transmission* 传染的危险 **2** [U] the act or process of sending out an electronic signal or message or of broadcasting a radio or television programme（电子信号或信息的）发射，发送；（电台或电视节目的）播送：*the transmission of computer data along telephone lines* 计算机数据沿电话线的传输 ◇ *a break in transmission* (= of a radio or television broadcast) *due to a technical fault* 技术故障造成的播送中断 **3** [C] a radio or television message or broadcast （电台或电视）信息，广播：*a live transmission from Sydney* 来自悉尼的现场直播 **4** [U, C] the system in a vehicle by which power is passed from the engine to the wheels （车辆的）传动装置，变速器

trans·mit AW /trænsˈmɪt; trænz-/ *verb* (**-tt-**) **1** [T, I] ~ (**sth**) (**from…**) (**to…**) to send an electronic signal, radio or television broadcast, etc. 传送；输送；发射；播送：*signals* *transmitted from a satellite* 从卫星传送来的信号 ◇ *The ceremony was transmitted live by satellite to over fifty countries.* 典礼通过卫星向五十多个国家进行了实况转播。 ◇ *a short-wave radio that can transmit as well as receive* 收发两用的短波无线电装置 **2** [T] (*formal*) to pass sth from one person to another 传播；传染 SYN **transfer**：~ **sth** *sexually transmitted diseases* 性传播疾病 ◇ ~ **sth to sb** *Parents can unwittingly transmit their own fears to their children.* 父母自己的恐惧有可能在无意中感染孩子。 **3** [T] ~ **sth** (*specialist*) to allow heat, light, sound, etc. to pass through 传（热、声等）；透（光等）；使通过 SYN **conduct**

trans·mit·ter /trænsˈmɪtə(r); trænz-/ *noun* **1** a piece of equipment used for sending electronic signals, especially radio or television signals （尤指电台或电视信号的）发射机，发射台，发报台 ➲ COMPARE RECEIVER (2) **2** ~ **of sth** (*formal*) a person or thing that transmits sth from one person or thing to another 传送者；传输者；传播者；传染媒介：*Emphasis was placed on the school as a transmitter of moral values.* 人们强调学校为道德价值观的传输者。

trans·mog·rify /ˌtrænzˈmɒgrɪfaɪ; ˌtræns-; *NAmE* -ˈmɑːg-/ *verb* (**trans·mog·ri·fies, trans·mog·ri·fy·ing, trans·mog·ri·fied, trans·mog·ri·fied**) ~ **sb/sth** (*often humorous*) to change sb/sth completely, especially in a surprising way （尤指出乎意料地）使完全改变 SYN **transform** ▶ **trans·mog·ri·fi·ca·tion** /ˌtrænzˌmɒgrɪfɪˈkeɪʃn; ˌtræns-; *NAmE* -ˌmɑːg-/ *noun* [U]

trans·mute /trænzˈmjuːt; træns-/ *verb* [T, I] ~ (**sth**) (**into sth**) (*formal*) to change, or make sth change, into sth different （使）变化，变质，变形 SYN **transform**：*It was once thought that lead could be transmuted into gold.* 有人曾经认为铅可以变成黄金。 ▶ **trans·mu·ta·tion** /ˌtrænzmjuːˈteɪʃn; ˌtræns-/ *noun* [C, U]

trans·nation·al /ˌtrænzˈnæʃnəl; ˌtræns-/ *adj.* (*business* 商) existing in or involving many different countries 跨国的；多国的：*transnational corporations* 跨国公司

tran·som /ˈtrænsəm/ *noun* **1** a bar of wood or stone across the top of a door or window （门窗上端的）横档，横楣 **2** (*NAmE*) = FANLIGHT

trans·par·ency /trænsˈpærənsi/ *noun* (*pl.* **-ies**) **1** (*also informal* **tranny**) [C] a picture printed on a piece of film, usually in a frame, that can be shown on a screen by shining light through the film 幻灯片；透明正片 SYN **slide**：*an overhead transparency* (= used with an OVERHEAD PROJECTOR) 高射投影透明正片 **2** [U] the quality of sth, such as glass, that allows you to see through it 透明；透明性 **3** [U] the quality of sth, such as an excuse or a lie, that allows sb to see the truth easily 显而易见；一目了然：*They were shocked by the transparency of his lies.* 他们感到震惊的是他竟睁着眼睛说瞎话。 **4** [U] the quality of sth, such as a situation or an argument, that makes it easy to understand 易懂；清楚；透明度：*a need for greater transparency in legal documents* 对法律文件更简明易懂的需求 ◇ *The police reforms will ensure greater transparency and accountability.* 警察机构的改革将确保更大程度的透明度和问责性。

trans·par·ent 🔑 /trænsˈpærənt/ *adj.* **1** 🔑 (of glass, plastic, etc. 玻璃、塑料等) allowing you to see through it 透明的；清澈的：*The insect's wings are almost transparent.* 这昆虫的翅膀几乎是透明的。 OPP **opaque** **2** (of an excuse, a lie, etc. 借口、谎言等) allowing you to see the truth easily 易识破的；易看穿的；显而易见的 SYN **obvious**：*a man of transparent honesty* 一看就很诚实的人 ◇ *a transparent attempt to buy votes* 明显收买选票的企图 ◇ *Am I that transparent?* (= are my intentions that obvious?) 我的意图就那么明显吗？ **3** (of language, information, etc. 语言、信息等) easy to understand 易懂的：*a campaign to make official documents more transparent* 简化公文语言的运动 OPP **opaque** ▶ **trans·par·ent·ly** *adv.*：*transparently obvious* 显而易见

tran·spir·ation /ˌtrænspɪˈreɪʃn/ *noun* [U] (*biology* 生) the process of water passing out from the surface of a plant or leaf 蒸腾（水分通过植物体表或叶子的散失过程） ➲ COMPARE PERSPIRATION

tran·spire /trænˈspaɪə(r)/ *verb* (*formal*) **1** [T] (not usually used in the progressive tenses 通常不用于进行时) ~ **that…** if **it transpires that** sth has happened or is true, it is known or has been shown to be true 公开；透露；为人所知：*It transpired that the gang had had a contact inside the bank.* 据报这伙歹徒在银行里有内应。 ◇ *This story, it later transpired, was untrue.* 后来得知，此事纯属凭空假造。 **2** [I] to happen 发生：*You're meeting him tomorrow? Let me know what transpires.* 你明天和他见面吗？把见面的情况告诉我。 **3** [I, T] ~ (**sth**) (*biology* 生) when plants or leaves **transpire**, water passes out from their surface （植物）水分蒸发，蒸腾

trans·plant *verb, noun*

■ *verb* /trænsˈplɑːnt; trænz-; *NAmE* -ˈplænt/ **1** ~ **sth** (**from sb/sth**) (**into sb/sth**) to take an organ, skin, etc. from one person, animal, part of the body, etc. and put it into or onto another 移植（器官、皮肤等）：*Surgeons have successfully transplanted a liver into a four-year-old boy.* 外科医生成功地给一个四岁的男孩移植了肝脏。 ◇ *Patients often reject transplanted organs.* 患者通常排斥移植的器官。 ➲ COMPARE IMPLANT *v.* (2) **2** ~ **sth** to move a growing plant and plant it somewhere else 移栽，移种，移植（植物） **3** ~ **sb/sth** (**from…**) (**to…**) (*formal*) to move sb/sth to a different place or environment 使迁移；使移居：*Japanese production methods have been transplanted into some British factories.* 日本的生产方法已被引进到一些英国的工厂。 ▶ **trans·plan·ta·tion** /ˌtrænsplɑːnˈteɪʃn; ˌtrænz-; *NAmE* -plæn-/ *noun* [U]：*liver transplantation* 肝脏移植 ◇ *the transplantation of entire communities overseas* 整个整个的社群向海外的迁移

■ *noun* /ˈtrænsplɑːnt; ˈtrænz-; *NAmE* -plænt/ **1** [C, U] a medical operation in which a damaged organ, etc. is replaced with one from another person （器官等的）移植：*to have a heart transplant* 接受心脏移植 ◇ *a transplant operation* 移植手术 ◇ *a shortage of suitable kidneys for transplant* 适合移植的肾脏的短缺 ➲ WORDFINDER NOTE AT OPERATION ➲ COLLOCATIONS AT ILL **2** [C] an organ, etc. that is used in a transplant operation 移植器官：*There is always a chance that the body will reject the transplant.* 身体总是有排斥移植器官的可能。 ➲ COMPARE IMPLANT *n.*

tran·spon·der /trænsˈpɒndə(r); *NAmE* -ˈpɑːn-/ *noun* (*specialist*) a piece of equipment that receives radio signals and automatically sends out another signal in reply 应答器；转发器；应答机

trans·port 🔑 AW *noun, verb*

■ *noun* /ˈtrænspɔːt; *NAmE* -spɔːrt/ **1** 🔑 (*especially BrE*) (*NAmE usually* **trans·por·ta·tion**) [U] a system for carrying people or goods from one place to another using vehicles, roads, etc. 交通运输系统：*air/freight/road transport* 空运；货运；公路运输 ◇ *the government's transport policy* 政府的交通运输政策 ➲ SEE ALSO PUBLIC TRANSPORT **2** 🔑 (*BrE*) (*NAmE* **trans·por·ta·tion**) [U] a vehicle or method of travel 交通车辆；运输工具；旅行方式：*Applicants must have their own transport.* 申请人必须有自己的交通工具。 ◇ *Transport to and from the airport is included in the price.* 价格中包括往返机场的交通费。 ◇ *His bike is his only* **means of transport**. 自行车是他唯一的代步工具。 **3** 🔑 [U] (*especially BrE*) (*also* **trans·por·ta·tion** *NAmE, BrE*) the activity or business of carrying goods from one place to another using lorries/trucks, trains, etc. 运输；运送；输送；搬运：*The goods were damaged during transport.* 货物在运输期间受损。 ◇ *controls on the transport of nuclear waste* 运输核废料的管制措施 **4** [C] a ship, plane or lorry/truck used for carrying soldiers, supplies, etc. from one place to another （运送部队、给养等的）运输船，运输机，运输卡车 **5 transports** [pl.] ~ **of sth** (*literary*) strong feelings and emotions 强烈的情感；激情；激动：*to be in transports of delight* 兴高采烈

■ *verb* /trænˈspɔːt; *NAmE* -ˈspɔːrt/ **1** 🔑 ~ **sth/sb** (+ **adv./prep.**) to take sth/sb from one place to another in a vehicle （用交通工具）运输，运送，输送：*to transport goods/passengers* 运送货物 / 旅客 **2** 🔑 ~ **sth** (+ **adv./prep.**) to move sth somewhere by means of a natural process （以

T

自然方式）运输，输送，传播 SYN carry: *The seeds are transported by the wind.* 这些种子是由风传播的。◇ *Blood transports oxygen around the body.* 血把氧气输送到全身。**3 ~ sb (+ adv./prep.)** to make sb feel that they are in a different place, time or situation 使产生身临其境的感觉: *The book transports you to another world.* 这本书会把你带到另一个世界。 **4 ~ sb (+ adv./prep.)** (in the past) to send sb to a far away place as a punishment （旧时）流放: *British convicts were transported to Australia for life.* 英国的囚犯被终生流放到澳大利亚。

trans·port·able /træn'spɔːtəbl; *NAmE* -'spɔːrt-/ *adj.* [not usually before noun] that can be carried or moved from one place to another, especially by a vehicle 可运输；可运送；可输送

trans·por·ta·tion AW /ˌtrænspɔː'teɪʃn; *NAmE* -pɔːr't-/ *noun* [U] **1** (*especially NAmE*) = TRANSPORT (1): *the transportation industry* 运输业 ◇ *public transportation* (= the system of buses, trains, etc. provided for people to travel from one place to another) 公共交通运输系统 ◇ *The city is providing free transportation to the stadium from downtown.* 本市现在提供从市中心到体育场的免费交通。◇ *the transportation of heavy loads* 重载运输 ◇ *transportation costs* 运费 **2** (in the past) the act of sending criminals to a place that is far away as a form of punishment （旧时的）流放

'transport cafe *noun* (*BrE*) a CAFE at the side of a main road that serves cheap food and is used mainly by lorry/truck drivers（供长途卡车司机用餐的）路边小餐馆 ⊃ COMPARE TRUCK STOP

trans·port·er AW /træn'spɔːtə(r); *NAmE* -'spɔːrt-/ *noun* a large vehicle used for carrying heavy objects, for example other vehicles 大型载重运输车: *a car transporter* 装运汽车的运输车 ⊃ VISUAL VOCAB PAGE V62

trans·pose /træn'spəʊz; *NAmE* -'spoʊz/ *verb* [often passive] **1 ~ sth** (*formal*) to change the order of two or more things 使掉换顺序 SYN **reverse** **2 ~ sth (from sth) (to sth)** (*formal*) to move or change sth to a different place or environment or into a different form 使转移；使换位；使变形 SYN **transfer**: *The director transposes Shakespeare's play from 16th century Venice to present-day England.* 导演把莎士比亚的戏剧从 16 世纪的威尼斯改成当代的英国。**3 ~ sth** (*music* 音) to write or play a piece of music or a series of notes in a different key 使（乐曲）变调，移调 ▸ **trans·pos·ition** /ˌtrænspə'zɪʃn/ *noun* [C, U]

trans·sex·ual (*also* **tran·sex·ual**) /trænz'sekʃuəl; træns-/ (*also informal* **tranny**) *noun* a person who feels emotionally that they want to live, dress, etc. as a member of the opposite sex, especially one who has a medical operation to change their sexual organs 易性癖者；（经外科手术后的）变性人

tran·sub·stan·ti·ation /ˌtrænsəbˌstænʃi'eɪʃn/ *noun* [U] the belief that the bread and wine of the COMMUNION service become the actual body and blood of Jesus Christ after they have been BLESSED, even though they still look like bread and wine 变体论（指面饼和葡萄酒经祝圣后变成基督的体血，只留下饼酒的外形）

trans·verse /'trænzvɜːs; 'træns-; *NAmE* -vɜːrs/ *adj.* [usually before noun] (*specialist*) placed across sth 横（向）的；横断的；横切的 SYN **diagonal**: *A transverse bar joins the two posts.* 一根横杆连接着两根立柱。

ˌtransverse 'wave *noun* (*specialist*) a wave that VIBRATES at 90° to the direction in which it is moving 横波 ⊃ COMPARE LONGITUDINAL WAVE

trans·vest·ite /trænz'vestaɪt; træns-/ (*also informal* **tranny**) *noun* a person, especially a man, who enjoys dressing as a member of the opposite sex 有异性装扮癖的人，易装癖者（尤指男性） ▸ **trans·vest·ism** /trænz'vestɪzəm; træns-/ *noun* [U]

trap /træp/ *noun, verb*

■ ***noun***

• **FOR ANIMALS** 动物 **1** a piece of equipment for catching animals （捕捉动物的）陷阱，罗网，夹，捕捉器: *a fox with its leg in a trap* 被夹子夹住腿的狐狸 ◇ *A trap was laid, with fresh bait.* 陷阱设置好，还投放了新诱饵。⊃ SEE ALSO MOUSETRAP

• **TRICK** 计谋 **2** a clever plan designed to trick sb, either by capturing them or by making them do or say sth that they did not mean to do or say 圈套；诡计: *She had set a trap for him and he had walked straight into it.* 她给他设下圈套，他就径直钻了进去。⊃ SEE ALSO BOOBY TRAP, RADAR TRAP, SAND TRAP, TOURIST TRAP

• **BAD SITUATION** 恶劣处境 **3** [usually sing.] an unpleasant situation from which it is hard to escape （难以逃脱的）困境，牢笼: *the unemployment trap* 失业的困境 ◇ *Some women see marriage as a trap.* 有些妇女把婚姻视作围城。⊃ SEE ALSO DEATHTRAP, POVERTY TRAP

• **CARRIAGE** 马车 **4** a light CARRIAGE with two wheels, pulled by a horse 双轮轻便马车: *a pony and trap* 一匹矮马拉的双轮轻便马车

• **MOUTH** 嘴 **5** (*slang*) mouth 嘴；口 SYN **gob**: *Shut your trap!* (= a rude way of telling sb to be quiet) 闭上你的臭嘴！◇ *to keep your trap shut* (= to not tell a secret) 嘴上有把门儿的

• **FOR RACING DOG** 赛狗 **6** a CAGE from which a GREYHOUND (= a type of dog) is let out at the start of a race 隔栏（赛狗开始时把狗从中放出）

• **IN GOLF** 高尔夫球 **7** (*especially NAmE*) = BUNKER (3)

IDM **to fall into/avoid the trap of doing sth** to do/avoid doing sth that is a mistake but which seems at first to be a good idea 掉进/避免掉进陷阱: *Parents often fall into the trap of trying to do everything for their children.* 家长经常陷入极力为子女操办一切的误区。⊃ MORE AT SPRING *v.*

■ ***verb*** (**-pp-**)

• **IN DANGEROUS/BAD SITUATION** 处境危险/恶劣 **1** [often passive] **~ sb (+ adv./prep.)** to keep sb in a dangerous place or bad situation that they want to get out of but cannot 使落入险境；使陷入困境: *Help! I'm trapped!* 救命啊！我给困住了！◇ *They were trapped in the burning building.* 他们被困在燃烧着的楼房里。◇ *We became trapped by the rising floodwater.* 我们被上涨的洪水困住了。◇ *He was trapped in an unhappy marriage.* 他陷入不幸的婚姻之中。◇ *I feel trapped in my job.* 我觉得被工作缠住了。

• **PART OF BODY/CLOTHING** 身体/衣服部位 **2 ~ sth (+ adv./prep.)** to have part of your body, your clothing, etc. held in a place so tightly that you cannot remove it and it may be injured or damaged 卡住；夹住；绊住；缠住: *I trapped my coat in the car door.* 我的外衣被汽车门夹住了。◇ *The pain was caused by a trapped nerve.* 这疼痛是由于神经受压迫引起的。

• **CATCH** 捕捉 **3 ~ sth** to catch or keep sth in a place and prevent it from escaping, especially so that you can use it 收集；吸收: *Solar panels trap energy from the sun.* 太阳能电池板吸收太阳能。 **4 ~ sb/sth (+ adv./prep.)** to force sb/sth into a place or situation that they cannot escape from, especially in order to catch them 把…逼进，迫使…进入（不能逃脱的地方）: *The escaped prisoners were eventually trapped in an underground garage and recaptured.* 越狱逃犯终于给追逼到地下汽车库，再次被捕。**5 ~ sth** to catch an animal in a trap 设陷阱捕捉，用捕捉器捕捉（动物）: *Raccoons used to be trapped for their fur.* 人们过去经常猎取浣熊，以获得其毛皮。

• **TRICK** 计谋 **6 ~ sb (into sth/into doing sth)** to trick sb into sth 使陷入圈套；使中计；使上当: *He felt he had been trapped into accepting the terms of the contract.* 他觉得自己是中了圈套才接受这合同条款的。

trap·door /'træpdɔː(r)/ *noun* a small door in a floor or ceiling 地板门；（天花板上的）活板门，通风门，活动天窗

trap·eze /trə'piːz; *NAmE* træ-/ *noun* a wooden or metal bar hanging from two pieces of rope high above the ground, used especially by CIRCUS performers（尤指马戏团演员使用的）高空秋千，吊架: *a trapeze artist* 高空秋千表演者

tra·pez·ium /trəˈpiːziəm/ *noun* (*pl.* **tra·pez·iums** or **tra·pezia** /trəˈpiːziə/) (*geometry* 几何) **1** (*BrE*) (*NAmE* **trap·ez·oid**) a flat shape with four straight sides, one pair of opposite sides being parallel and the other pair not parallel 梯形 **2** (*NAmE*) (*BrE* **trap·ez·oid**) a flat shape with four straight sides, none of which are parallel 不规则四边形

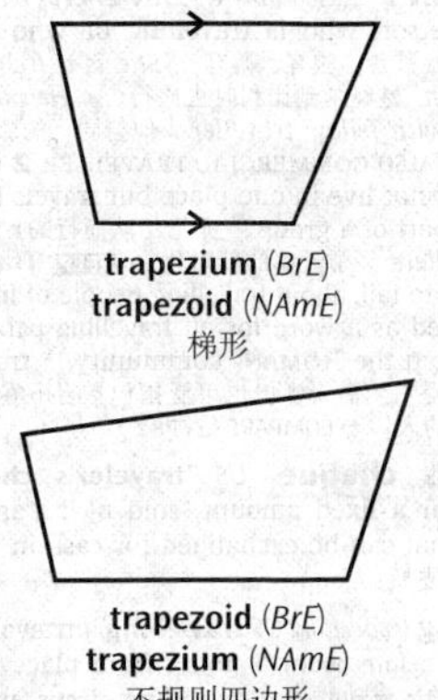

trapezium (*BrE*)
trapezoid (*NAmE*)
梯形

trapezoid (*BrE*)
trapezium (*NAmE*)
不规则四边形

trap·ez·oid /ˈtræpəzɔɪd/ *noun* (*geometry* 几何) **1** (*BrE*) (*NAmE* **tra·pez·ium**) a flat shape with four straight sides, none of which are parallel 不规则四边形 ➲ PICTURE AT TRAPEZIUM **2** (*NAmE*) (*BrE* **tra·pez·ium**) a flat shape with four straight sides, one pair of opposite sides being parallel and the other pair not parallel 梯形

trap·per /ˈtræpə(r)/ *noun* a person who traps and kills animals, especially for their fur 捕杀动物者（尤指为获取毛皮）

trap·pings /ˈtræpɪŋz/ *noun* [pl.] ~ (**of sth**) (*formal, especially disapproving*) the possessions, clothes, etc. that are connected with a particular situation, job or social position （与某一处境、职业或社会地位有关的）身外之物，标志，服装：*They enjoyed all the trappings of wealth.* 他们享有所有象征财富的东西。

Trap·pist /ˈtræpɪst/ *adj.* belonging to a group of MONKS who have very strict rules, including a rule that they must not speak 特拉普派的（有严格教规，包括缄口苦修的修道士组织） ▶ **Trap·pist** *noun*

trash /træʃ/ *noun, verb*

■ ***noun*** [U] **1** (*NAmE*) things that you throw away because you no longer want or need them 废物；垃圾 ➲ NOTE AT RUBBISH **2** (*informal, disapproving*) objects, writing, ideas, etc. that you think are of poor quality 劣质品；拙劣的作品；糟粕；谬论：*What's this trash you're watching?* 你看的这个乌七八糟的节目是什么？◇ (*especially BrE*) *He's talking trash* (= nonsense). 他在胡说八道。 **3** (*NAmE, informal*) an offensive word used to describe people that you do not respect 窝囊废；废物；没出息的人：***white trash*** (= poor white people, especially those living in the southern US) 贫贱的白人 ➲ SEE ALSO TRAILER TRASH

■ ***verb*** (*informal*) **1** ~ **sth** to damage or destroy sth 损坏；毁坏：*The band was famous for trashing hotel rooms.* 这帮人以破坏旅馆房间出名。 **2** ~ **sth/sb** to criticize sth/sb very strongly 抨击；谴责 **3** ~ **sth** (*NAmE*) to throw away sth that you do not want 丢弃；把…抛弃：*I'm leaving my old toys here—if you don't want them, just trash them.* 我把我的旧玩具留在这里，你不要就扔掉好了。

'trash can *noun* (*NAmE*) **1** (*BrE* **'litter bin**) a container for people to put rubbish/garbage in, in the street or in a public building （街道上或公共建筑物里的）垃圾箱，废物箱 **2** = GARBAGE CAN

'trash talk (*also* **'trash talking**) *noun* [U] (*NAmE, informal*) a way of talking which is intended to make sb, especially an opponent, feel less confident 口水战（为令对手等丧失自信心）；打击对手士气的言论 ➲ COMPARE SLEDGING (2)

trashy /ˈtræʃi/ *adj.* (*informal*) (**trash·ier, trashi·est**) of poor quality; with no value 蹩脚的；无价值的 SYN **rubbishy**: *trashy TV shows* 无聊的电视节目

trat·toria /ˌtrætəˈriːə/ *noun* (*from Italian*) an Italian restaurant serving simple food 意大利餐馆（或便餐店）

trauma /ˈtrɔːmə; *NAmE* ˈtraʊmə/ *noun* **1** [U] (*psychology* 心) a mental condition caused by severe shock, especially when the harmful effects last for a long time 精神创伤 **2** [C, U] an unpleasant experience that makes you feel upset and/or anxious 痛苦经历；挫折：*She felt exhausted after the traumas of recent weeks.* 她经受了最近几个星期的痛苦之后感到精疲力竭。 **3** [U, C] (*medical* 医) an injury 损伤；外伤：*The patient suffered severe brain trauma.* 患者的大脑受到严重损伤。

trau·mat·ic /trɔːˈmætɪk; *NAmE* traʊˈm-/ *adj.* **1** extremely unpleasant and causing you to feel upset and/or anxious 痛苦的；极不愉快的：*a traumatic experience* 不幸的经历 ◇ *Divorce can be traumatic for everyone involved.* 离婚对所有相关的人都会造成痛苦。 **2** [only before noun] (*psychology* 心 or *medical* 医) connected with or caused by trauma 创伤的；外伤的；损伤的：*traumatic amnesia* 创伤性遗忘 ➲ SEE ALSO POST-TRAUMATIC STRESS DISORDER ▶ **trau·mat·ic·al·ly** /-kli/ *adv.*

trau·ma·tize (*BrE also* **-ise**) /ˈtrɔːmətaɪz; *NAmE* ˈtraʊm-/ *verb* [usually passive] ~ **sb** to shock and upset sb very much, often making them unable to think or work normally 使受精神创伤

trav·ail /ˈtræveɪl; trəˈveɪl/ *noun* [U, pl.] (*old use* or *literary*) an unpleasant experience or situation that involves a lot of hard work, difficulties and/or suffering 艰苦劳动；煎熬；艰辛；痛苦

travel 🔑 /ˈtrævl/ *verb, noun*

■ ***verb*** (**-ll-**, *especially US* **-l-**) **1** 🔑 [I, T] to go from one place to another, especially over a long distance 长途行走；旅行；游历：*to travel around the world* 周游世界 ◇ *I go to bed early if I'm travelling the next day.* 如果第二天要去旅行我就早睡。◇ *I love travelling by train.* 我喜欢乘火车旅行。◇ *We always travel first class.* 我们总坐头等舱旅行。◇ *We travelled to California for the wedding.* 我们到加利福尼亚去参加婚礼。◇ *When I finished college I* ***went travelling*** *for six months* (= spent time visiting different places). 我大学毕业后在外旅行了六个月。◇ ~ **sth** *He travelled the length of the Nile in a canoe.* 他乘独木舟游完尼罗河的全程。◇ *I travel 40 miles to work every day.* 我每天奔波 40 英里去上班。 **2** 🔑 [I] (+ **adv./prep.**) to go or move at a particular speed, in a particular direction, or a particular distance （以某速度、朝某方向或在某距离内）行进，转送，传播：*to travel at 50 miles an hour* 以每小时 50 英里的速度行进 ◇ *Messages travel along the spine from the nerve endings to the brain.* 信息从神经末梢沿脊柱传送到大脑。◇ *News travels fast these days.* 如今消息传播得很快。 **3** [I] (of food, wine, an object, etc. 食物、葡萄酒、物体等) to be still in good condition after a long journey 经长途运输仍不变质；经得住长途运输：*Some wines do not travel well.* 有些葡萄酒经不住长途运输。 **4** [I] (+ **adv./prep.**) (of a book, an idea, etc. 书籍、思想等) to be equally successful in another place and not just where it began 盛行各地；广为流传：*Some writing travels badly in translation.* 有些作品经翻译后流传不广。 **5** [I] to go fast 走得快；快速行进：*Their car can really travel!* 他们的车开得可真快！ **6** [I] (in BASKETBALL 篮球) to move while you are holding the ball, in a way that is not allowed 持球走；（带球）走步 ➲ MORE LIKE THIS 36, page R29

IDM **travel 'light** to take very little with you when you go on a trip 轻装上路

■ ***noun*** **1** 🔑 [U] the act or activity of travelling 旅行；旅游；游历：***air/rail/space, etc. travel*** 乘飞机、乘火车、乘

T

航天器等 ◇ *travel expenses* 旅费 ◇ *The job involves a considerable amount of **foreign travel**.* 这个工作要经常出差去国外。◇ *the travel industry* 旅游业 ◇ *travel sickness* 晕车 ◇ *a **travel bag/clock*** (= for use when travelling) 旅行包；旅行钟 ◇ *The pass allows **unlimited travel** on all public transport in the city.* 持有乘车证可乘坐市内所有的公共交通工具，次数不限。 **2** 🔑 **travels** [pl.] time spent travelling, especially in foreign countries and for pleasure（出国）旅游，旅行：*The novel is based on his travels in India.* 这部长篇小说是根据他的印度之行写成的。◇ *When are you off **on your travels*** (= going travelling)? 你们什么时候动身外出旅行？ ➲ WORDFINDER NOTE AT HOLIDAY, JOURNEY, PLANE, TOURIST

'travel agency *noun* a company that arranges travel and/or accommodation for people going on a holiday/vacation or journey 旅行社

'travel agent *noun* **1** a person or business whose job is to make arrangements for people wanting to travel, for example buying tickets or arranging hotel rooms 旅行代办人；旅行代理商 ➲ COLLOCATIONS AT TRAVEL **2 travel agent's** (*pl.* **travel agents**) a shop/store where you can go to arrange a holiday/vacation, etc. 旅行社：*He works in a travel agent's.* 他在一家旅行社工作。 ➲ MORE LIKE THIS 34, page R29 ➲ SEE ALSO TRAVEL AGENCY

trav·ela·tor (*also* **trav·ola·tor**) /ˈtrævəleɪtə(r)/ *noun* a moving path, especially at an airport （尤指机场的）自动人行道

trav·elled (*especially US* **trav·eled**) /ˈtrævld/ *adj.* (usually in compounds 通常构成复合词) **1** (of a person 人) having travelled the amount mentioned 有过…次旅行的；到过…地方的：*a much-travelled man* 见多识广的人 **2** (of a road, etc. 路等) used the amount mentioned（常有人或不常有人）走的：*The path was steeper and less travelled than the previous one.* 这条小路比刚才那条陡，走的人少。

trav·el·ler 🔑 (*especially US* **trav·el·er**) /ˈtrævələ(r)/ *noun* **1** 🔑 a person who is travelling or who often travels 旅行者；旅游者；旅客；游客：*She is a frequent traveller to Belgium.* 她经常到比利时去旅行。◇ *He passed the time chatting with fellow travellers.* 他与同行的旅客闲聊消磨时间。 ➲ SEE ALSO COMMERCIAL TRAVELLER **2** (*BrE*) a person who does not live in one place but travels around, especially as part of a group （尤指结队而行的）漂泊者：*New Age travellers* 经常迁移的新时代人 HELP **Traveller** is used especially to talk about travelling people of Irish origin, but is also used as a word for all travelling people, including people from the ROMANI community. * traveller 尤指经常迁移的爱尔兰裔人，但也可泛指包括吉卜赛人在内的所有经常迁移的人。 ➲ COMPARE GYPSY

'traveller's cheque (*US* **'traveler's check**) *noun* a cheque for a fixed amount, sold by a bank or TRAVEL AGENT, that can be exchanged for cash in foreign countries 旅行支票

trav·el·ling (*especially US* **trav·el·ing**) /ˈtrævəlɪŋ/ *adj., noun*
■ *adj.* [only before noun] **1** going from place to place 旅行的；巡回的；流动的：*a **travelling circus/exhibition/performer, etc.*** 巡回马戏团、展览、表演者等 ◇ *the travelling public* 旅游爱好者们 ◇ (*BrE*) ***travelling people*** (= people

▼ **COLLOCATIONS 词语搭配**

Travel and tourism 旅游和旅游业

Holidays/vacations 假期

- **have/take** (*BrE*) a holiday/(*NAmE*) a vacation/a break/a day off/(*BrE*) a gap year 休假；短期休假；休一天假；休空缺年假
- **go on/be on** holiday/vacation/leave/honeymoon/safari/a trip/a tour/a cruise/a pilgrimage 去 / 在度假 / 休假 / 度蜜月 / 游猎 / 旅游 / 观光 / 乘船游览 / 朝圣
- **go** backpacking/camping/hitchhiking/sightseeing 去背包旅行 / 露营 / 搭顺风车旅行 / 观光游览
- **plan** a trip/a holiday/a vacation/your itinerary 计划旅行 / 假期 / 行程
- **book** accommodation/a hotel room/a flight/tickets 预订住宿 / 酒店房间 / 航班 / 票
- **have/make/cancel** a reservation/(*especially BrE*) booking 预订；取消预订
- **rent** a villa/(*both BrE*) a holiday home/a holiday cottage 租一座度假别墅 / 一个度假住所 / 一座度假小别墅
- (*especially BrE*) **hire**/(*especially NAmE*) **rent** a car/bicycle/moped 租借一辆汽车 / 自行车 / 摩托自行车
- **stay in** a hotel/a bed and breakfast/a youth hostel/a villa/(*both BrE*) a holiday home/a caravan 住在酒店 / 提供住宿和早餐的旅馆 / 青年旅舍 / 度假别墅 / 度假住所 / 旅行拖车里
- **cost/charge $100 a/per night for** a single/double/twin/standard/(*BrE*) en suite room 单人房 / 双人房 / 标间 / 套房一晚花费 / 要价 100 美元
- **check into/out of** a hotel/a motel/your room 入住 / 结账离开酒店 / 汽车旅馆 / 房间
- **pack/unpack** your suitcase/bags 把东西装进手提箱 / 旅行包；取出手提箱 / 旅行包里的东西
- **call/order** room service 打电话叫 / 叫客房服务
- **cancel/cut short** a trip/holiday/vacation 取消 / 缩短旅程 / 假期

Foreign travel 出国旅行

- **apply for/get/renew** a/your passport 申请 / 拿到 / 续签护照
- **take out/buy/get** travel insurance 获得 / 购买 / 取得旅游保险
- **catch/miss** your plane/train/ferry/connecting flight 赶上 / 错过飞机 / 火车 / 渡船 / 转乘航班
- **fly (in)/travel in** business/economy class 乘坐商务 / 经济舱飞行 / 旅行
- **make/have** a brief/two-day/twelve-hour stopover/(*NAmE also*) layover in Hong Kong 在香港作短暂的 / 两天的 / 十二小时的中途停留
- **experience/cause/lead to** delays 遇上 / 引起 / 导致延误
- **check (in)/collect/get/lose** (your) (*especially BrE*) luggage/(*especially NAmE*) baggage 托运 / 取 / 弄丢行李
- **be charged for/pay** excess baggage 被收取 / 支付超重行李费
- **board/get on/leave/get off** the aircraft/plane/ship/ferry 上 / 下飞机 / 船 / 渡船
- **taxi down/leave/approach/hit/overshoot** the runway 在跑道上滑行；离开 / 接近 / 降落在 / 冲出跑道
- **experience/hit/encounter** severe turbulence 遇到强烈的气流
- **suffer from/recover from/get over your** jet lag/travel sickness 遭受时差反应 / 晕车；从时差反应 / 晕车恢复过来；克服时差反应 / 晕车

The tourist industry 旅游业

- **attract/draw/bring** tourists/visitors 吸引游客
- **encourage/promote/hurt** tourism 鼓励 / 促进 / 损害旅游业
- **promote/develop** ecotourism 促进 / 发展生态旅游
- **build/develop/visit** a tourist/holiday/(*especially BrE*) seaside/beach/ski resort 建立 / 开发 / 参观旅游 / 假日 / 海滨 / 海滩 / 滑雪胜地
- **work for/be operated by** a major hotel chain 就职于一家大型连锁酒店；由一家大型连锁酒店经营
- **be served by/compete with** low-cost/(*especially NAmE*) low-fare/budget airlines 由廉价航空公司提供服务；与廉价航空公司竞争
- **book sth through/make a booking through/use** a travel agent 通过旅行社预订；经旅行社代办
- **contact/check with** your travel agent/tour operator 联系旅行社；向旅行社咨询
- **book/be on/go on** a package deal/holiday/tour 预订 / 进行 / 去包价旅游
- **buy/bring back** (tacky/overpriced) souvenirs 购买 / 带回（低劣的 / 定价过高的）纪念品

T

who have no fixed home, especially those living in a community that moves from place to place, also known as 'travellers') 不断迁移的人 **2** used when you travel 旅行用的: *a travelling clock* 旅行钟

■ ***noun*** [U] the act of travelling 旅行: *The job requires a lot of travelling.* 这个工作要求经常出差。◇ ***a travelling companion*** 旅伴

ˌtravelling ˈsalesman (*especially US* **ˌtraveling ˈsalesman**) *noun* (*old-fashioned*) = SALES REPRESENTATIVE

trav·el·ogue (*NAmE also* **trav·elog**) /ˈtrævəlɒɡ; *NAmE* -lɔːɡ; -lɑːɡ/ *noun* a film/movie, broadcast or piece of writing about travel 旅行纪录片；旅游广播节目；游记

ˈtravel-sick *adj.* (*BrE*) feeling sick because you are travelling in a vehicle 晕车的；晕船的；晕机的 ▶ **ˈtravel-sickness** (*BrE*) (*also* **ˈmotion sickness** *NAmE, BrE*) *noun* [U]

tra·verse *verb, noun*

■ ***verb*** /trəˈvɜːs; *NAmE* -ˈvɜːrs/ **~ sth** (*formal* or *specialist*) to cross an area of land or water 横过；横越；穿过；横渡

■ ***noun*** /ˈtrævɜːs; *NAmE* -vɜːrs/ (in mountain climbing 爬山) an act of moving sideways or walking across a steep slope, not climbing up or down it; a place where this is possible or necessary（在陡坡上的）侧向移动，横过，横越；可横越的地方

trav·esty /ˈtrævəsti/ *noun* (*pl.* **-ies**) **~ (of sth)** something that does not have the qualities or values that it should have, and as a result is often shocking or offensive 嘲弄；歪曲 **SYN** **parody**: *The trial was a travesty of justice.* 这一审判是对正义的嘲弄。

trav·ola·tor = TRAVELATOR

trawl /trɔːl/ *verb, noun*

■ ***verb*** **1** [T, I] to search through a large amount of information or a large number of people, places, etc. looking for a particular thing or person 查阅（资料）；搜集，搜罗，网罗（人或物）：**~ sth** (**for sth/sb**) *She trawled the shops for bargains.* 她到各商店搜罗便宜货。◇ **~ (through sth) (for sth/sb)** *The police are trawling through their files for similar cases.* 警方正在档案中查阅类似案件。 **2** [I] **~ (for sth)** to fish for sth by pulling a large net with a wide opening through the water 用拖网捕鱼 ➲ WORDFINDER NOTE AT FISHING

■ ***noun*** **1** a search through a large amount of information, documents, etc.（对资料、文件等的）查阅: *A quick trawl through the newspapers yielded five suitable job adverts.* 快速翻阅一下报纸便找到五则适合的招聘广告。 **2** (*also* **ˈtrawl net**) a large net with a wide opening, that is dragged along the bottom of the sea by a boat in order to catch fish （海上捕鱼用的）拖网

trawl·er /ˈtrɔːlə(r)/ *noun* a fishing boat that uses large nets that it drags through the sea behind it 拖网渔船

tray /treɪ/ *noun* **1** a flat piece of wood, metal or plastic with raised edges, used for carrying or holding things, especially food 盘；托盘；碟: *He brought her breakfast in bed on a tray.* 他把早餐用托盘给她送到床上。◇ *She came in with a tray of drinks.* 她端着一托盘饮料走进来。◇ *a tea tray* 茶盘 **2** (often in compounds 常构成复合词) a shallow plastic box, used for various purposes（各种用途的）浅塑料盒: *a seed tray* (= for planting seeds in) 育苗盘 ◇ *a cat's litter tray* 猫的便盆 ➲ VISUAL VOCAB PAGES V36, V71 ➲ SEE ALSO BAKING TRAY at BAKING SHEET, IN TRAY, OUT TRAY

TRC /ˌtiː ɑː ˈsiː; *NAmE* ɑːr/ *abbr.* Truth and Reconciliation Commission (an organization that was established in South Africa to investigate how people had been treated unfairly in the past) 真相与调解委员会（南非组织，调查以往的不公平待遇事件）

treach·er·ous /ˈtretʃərəs/ *adj.* **1** that cannot be trusted; intending to harm you 不可信任的；背叛的；奸诈的 **SYN** **deceitful**: *He was weak, cowardly and treacherous.* 他软弱、胆怯、奸诈。◇ *lying, treacherous words* 阴险的谎话 **2** dangerous, especially when seeming safe 有潜在危险的: *The ice on the roads made driving conditions treacherous.* 路上的冰对驾车构成了隐患。 ▶ **treach·er·ous·ly** *adv.*

treach·ery /ˈtretʃəri/ *noun* [U, C] (*pl.* **-ies**) behaviour that involves not being loyal to sb who trusts you; an example of this 背叛；变节；背信弃义: *an act of treachery* 背叛行为

trea·cle /ˈtriːkl/ *noun* [U] (*BrE*) **1** (*NAmE* **mo·las·ses**) a thick black sweet sticky liquid produced when sugar is REFINED (= made pure), used in cooking（制糖时产生的）糖浆，糖蜜 **2** = GOLDEN SYRUP

trea·cly /ˈtriːkli/ *adj.* **1** (*BrE*) like treacle 像糖浆的；糖蜜似的: *a treacly brown liquid* 糖浆状的棕色液体 **2** expressing feelings of love in a way that seems false or exaggerated 虚情假意的；过分多情的: *treacly music* 甜腻腻的音乐

tread /tred/ *verb, noun*

■ ***verb*** (**trod** /trɒd; *NAmE* trɑːd/, **trod·den** /ˈtrɒdn; *NAmE* ˈtrɑːdn/ or **trod**) **1** [I] **~ (on/in/over sth/sb)** (*especially BrE*) to put your foot down while you are stepping or walking 踩；踏；践踏: *Ouch! You trod on my toe!* 唉哟！你踩着我的脚指头了！◇ *Careful you don't tread in that puddle.* 小心，别踩着那水坑。 **2** [T] **~ sth (+ adv./prep.)** to crush or press sth with your feet 踩碎；践踏 **SYN** **trample**: *Don't tread ash into the carpet!* 别把烟灰踩进地毯里！◇ *The wine is still made by treading grapes in the traditional way.* 这种葡萄酒仍然是以传统的方法踩碎葡萄酿制的。 **3** [T, I] **~ (sth)** (*formal* or *literary*) to walk somewhere 行走；步行；走: *Few people had trod this path before.* 以前没有多少人走过这条小路。◇ *He was treading quietly and cautiously.* 他蹑手蹑脚地走着。

IDM **tread ˈcarefully, ˈwarily, etc.** to be very careful about what you do or say 小心谨慎地说；小心翼翼地做: *The government will have to tread very carefully in handling this issue.* 政府在处理这个问题时须慎之又慎。 **ˌtread a difficult, dangerous, solitary, etc. ˈpath** to choose and follow a particular way of life, way of doing sth, etc. 走一条困难、危险、孤独等的人生道路（指选择特定的生活方式或处事方法）: *A restaurant has to tread the tricky path between maintaining quality and keeping prices down.* 餐馆必须在保证质量和价格低廉之间走出一条困难的折中之路。 **ˌtread on sb's ˈheels** to follow sb closely 紧随某人之后；步人后尘 **ˌtread on sb's ˈtoes** (*especially BrE*) (*NAmE usually* **ˌstep on sb's ˈtoes**) (*informal*) to offend or annoy sb, especially by getting involved in sth that is their responsibility 激怒，得罪，冒犯（尤指因插手他人职责） **ˌtread ˈwater** **1** to keep yourself vertical in deep water by moving your arms and legs 踩水（摆动四肢使身体在深水中保持直立） **2** to make no progress while you are waiting for sth to happen 裹足不前；徘徊观望 ➲ MORE AT FOOL *n.*, LINE *n.*, TIGHTROPE

■ ***noun*** **1** [sing.] the way that sb walks; the sound that sb makes when they walk 步法；步态；脚步声: *I heard his heavy tread on the stairs.* 我听到他在楼梯上的沉重脚步声。 **2** [C, U] the raised pattern on the surface of a tyre on a vehicle （轮胎的）胎面；外胎花纹: *The tyres were worn below the legal limit of 1.6 mm of tread.* 这些轮胎磨损得已低于胎面 1.6 毫米的法定厚度。 **3** [C] the upper surface of a step or stair（台阶或楼梯的）踏步板，梯面，踏面 ➲ PICTURE AT STAIRCASE ➲ COMPARE RISER (2)

treadle /ˈtredl/ *noun* (especially in the past) a device worked by the foot to operate a machine （尤指旧时驱动机器的）踏板

tread·mill /ˈtredmɪl/ *noun* **1** [sing.] work or a way of life that is boring or tiring because it involves always doing the same things 枯燥无味的工作（或生活方式）: *I'd like to escape the office treadmill.* 我想摆脱办公室的枯燥工作。 **2** [C] (especially in the past) a large wheel turned by the weight of people or animals walking on steps around its inside edge, and used to operate machinery（尤指旧时由人或牲畜踩动踏板使之转动的）踏车 **3** [C] an exercise machine that has a moving surface that you can walk or run on while remaining in the same place（锻炼身体的）跑步机，健走机 ➲ VISUAL VOCAB PAGE V46

trea·son /ˈtriːzn/ (*also* **ˌhigh ˈtreason**) *noun* [U] the crime of doing sth that could cause danger to your country,

T

such as helping its enemies during a war 危害国家罪，叛国罪（如战时通敌）▸ **treas·on·able** /'triːzənəbl/ *adj.*：*a treasonable act* 叛国行为

treas·ure /'treʒə(r)/ *noun, verb*

■ *noun* **1** [U] a collection of valuable things such as gold, silver and jewellery 金银财宝；珠宝；财富：*buried treasure* 埋藏的财宝 ◇ *a pirate's treasure chest* 海盗的财宝箱 **2** [C, usually pl.] a highly valued object 极贵重的物品；珍宝；宝物；珍品：*the priceless art treasures of the Uffizi Gallery* 乌菲齐美术馆收藏的无价艺术瑰宝 **3** [sing.] a person who is much loved or valued 备受宠爱（或器重）的人；心肝宝贝儿

■ *verb* ~ **sth** to have or keep sth that you love and that is extremely valuable to you 珍视；珍爱；珍重；珍藏 SYN **cherish**：*I treasure his friendship.* 我珍重他的友谊。◇ *This ring is my most treasured possession.* 这枚戒指是我最珍爱的财产。

'**treasure house** *noun* a place that contains many valuable or interesting things 宝库；宝地：*The area is a treasure house of archaeological relics.* 这个地区是古文物遗迹的宝库。

'**treasure hunt** *noun* a game in which players try to find a hidden prize by answering a series of questions that have been left in different places 寻宝游戏（回答问题以获得匿藏的奖品）

treas·urer /'treʒərə(r)/ *noun* a person who is responsible for the money and accounts of a club or an organization （俱乐部或组织的）司库，会计，出纳，财务主管 ➲ WORDFINDER NOTE AT CLUB

'**treasure trove** *noun* **1** [U, C, usually sing.] valuable things that are found hidden and whose owner is unknown 无主财宝 **2** [C, usually sing.] a place, book, etc. containing many useful or beautiful things 宝藏，宝库（贮藏珍宝、知识等）

treas·ury /'treʒəri/ *noun* (*pl.* **-ies**) **1 the Treasury** [sing.+ sing./pl. v.] (in Britain, the US and some other countries) the government department that controls public money （英国、美国和其他一些国家的）财政部 **2** [C] a place in a castle, etc. where valuable things are stored（城堡等中的）金银财宝库，宝库

'**treasury bill** (*also informal* '**T-bill**) *noun* a type of investment sold by the US government in which a fixed amount of money is paid back on a certain date（美国）短期国库券

treat /triːt/ *verb, noun*

■ *verb*

• **BEHAVE TOWARDS SB/STH** 对待 **1** to behave in a particular way towards sb/sth 以…态度对待；以…方式对待：~ **sb/sth (with sth)** *to treat people with respect/consideration/suspicion, etc.* 对人尊敬、体谅、怀疑等 ◇ *Treat your keyboard with care and it should last for years.* 爱惜你的键盘，这样就可以使用很多年。◇ ~ **sb/sth like sth** *My parents still treat me like a child.* 我父母仍然把我当成孩子。◇ ~ **sb/sth as sth** *He was treated as a hero on his release from prison.* 他获释出狱时被当成英雄看待。

• **CONSIDER** 考虑 **2** ~ **sth as sth** to consider sth in a particular way 把…看作；把…视为：*I decided to treat his remark as a joke.* 我决定把他的话当作戏言。 **3** ~ **sth + adv./prep.** to deal with or discuss sth in a particular way 处理；讨论：*The question is treated in more detail in the next chapter.* 下一章中对这一问题有更详尽的阐述。

• **ILLNESS/INJURY** 疾病；损伤 **4** ~ **sb (for sth) (with sth)** to give medical care or attention to a person, an illness, an injury, etc. 医疗；医治；治疗：*She was treated for sunstroke.* 她因中暑而接受治疗。◇ *The condition is usually treated with drugs and a strict diet.* 这种病通常用药物和严格控制饮食进行治疗。➲ COLLOCATIONS AT INJURY

• **USE CHEMICAL** 用化学品 **5** ~ **sth (with sth)** to use a chemical substance or process to clean, protect, preserve, etc. sth （利用化学物质或反应）处理，保护，保存：*to treat crops with insecticide* 给庄稼喷洒杀虫剂 ◇ *wood treated with preservative* 经过防腐处理的木材

• **PAY FOR STH ENJOYABLE** 花钱享受 **6** ~ **sb/yourself (to sth)** to pay for sth that sb/you will enjoy and that you do not usually have or do 招待；款待；请（客）；买（可享受的东西）：*She treated him to lunch.* 她请他吃午饭。◇ *Don't worry about the cost—I'll treat you.* 别担心费用，我来替你付。◇ *I'm going to treat myself to a new pair of shoes.* 我打算给自己买双新鞋。

▸ **treat·able** *adj.*：*a treatable infection* 能治疗的传染病

IDM **treat sb like 'dirt** (*informal*) to treat sb with no respect at all 视某人如粪土；把…视为草芥；蔑视

PHR V **'treat sb to sth** to entertain sb with sth special 用…招待；以…款待：*The crowd were treated to a superb display of tennis.* 观众看了一场非常精彩的网球赛，大饱眼福。

■ *noun* something very pleasant and enjoyable, especially sth that you give sb or do for them 乐事；乐趣；款待：*We took the kids to the zoo* ***as a special treat.*** 我们特地带孩子们到动物园去，让他们开心一下。◇ *You've never been to this area before? Then you're in for a real treat.* 你以前从来没有到过这一地区？那么你一定会喜之不尽。◇ *When I was young chocolate was a treat.* 我年轻的时候，吃巧克力是一种难得的享受。◇ *Let's go out for lunch—**my treat*** (= I will pay). 咱们到外面去吃午餐，我请客。➲ SYNONYMS AT PLEASURE

IDM **a 'treat** (*BrE, informal*) extremely well or good 极为有效；棒极了：*His idea worked a treat* (= was successful). 他的主意棒极了。➲ MORE AT TRICK *n.*

trea·tise /'triːtɪs; -tɪz/ *noun* ~ **(on sth)** (*formal*) a long and serious piece of writing on a particular subject（专题）论文

treat·ment /'triːtmənt/ *noun* **1** [U, C] ~ **(for sth)** something that is done to cure an illness or injury, or to make sb look and feel good 治疗；疗法；诊治：*He is receiving treatment for shock.* 他正在接受休克治疗。◇ *She is **responding well to treatment.*** 她经过治疗大有起色。◇ *to require **hospital/medical treatment*** 需要住院 / 药物治疗 ◇ *There are various treatments available for this condition.* 对这种病情有各种疗法。◇ *Guests at the health spa receive a range of beauty treatments.* 客人在休闲健身中心可接受各种美容服务。➲ WORDFINDER NOTE AT HEALTH ➲ COLLOCATIONS AT ILL

> **WORDFINDER** 联想词：acupuncture, chiropractor, complementary medicine, herbalism, holistic, homeopathy, hypnotist, massage, reflexology

2 [U] a way of behaving towards or dealing with a person or thing 对待；待遇：*the brutal treatment of political prisoners* 对政治犯的残酷虐待 ◇ *Certain city areas have been singled out for special treatment.* 某些城区已划出要进行特别治理。 **3** [U, C] a way of dealing with or discussing a subject, work of art, etc. 处理；讨论；论述：*Shakespeare's treatment of madness in 'King Lear'* 莎士比亚在《李尔王》中对疯癫的处理手法 **4** [U, C] a process by which sth is cleaned, or protected against sth （净化或防治）处理，加工：*a sewage **treatment plant*** 污水处理厂 ◇ ~ **for sth** *an effective treatment for dry rot* 防治干腐病的有效方法

treaty /'triːti/ *noun* (*pl.* **-ies**) a formal agreement between two or more countries （国家之间的）条约，协定：*the Treaty of Rome* 《罗马条约》◇ *a peace treaty* 和平协定 ◇ *to **draw up/sign/ratify a treaty*** 起草 / 签署 / 正式批准条约 ◇ *Under **the terms of the treaty,** La Rochelle was ceded to the English.* 根据这个条约的条款，拉罗谢尔割让给了英国人。➲ WORDFINDER NOTE AT ALLY, PEACE ➲ COLLOCATIONS AT WAR

treble /'trebl/ *noun, verb, det., adj.*

■ *noun* **1** [U] the high tones or part in music or a sound system（音乐或音响系统的）高音，高音部：*to turn up the treble on the stereo* 把立体声唱机的高音音量调大 ➲ COMPARE BASS[1] *n.* (1) **2** [C] a child's high voice; a boy who sings with a treble voice 童声高音；唱高音的男童歌手 ➲ COMPARE SOPRANO *n.* **3** [sing.] a musical part written for a treble voice 高音声部 **4** [sing.] (*BrE*) three successes in a row 三连胜：*The victory completed a treble for the horse's owner.* 这次胜利使得马主获得三连胜。

■ ***verb*** [I, T] to become, or to make sth, three times as much or as many（使）成三倍，增加两倍 **SYN triple**: *Cases of food poisoning have trebled in the last two years.* 在过去的两年里，食物中毒事件增加了两倍。◇ **~ sth** *He trebled his earnings in two years.* 他在两年间收入增加了两倍。

■ ***det.*** [usually before noun] three times as much or as many 三倍的；三重的：*Capital expenditure was treble the 2013 level.* 资本支出是 2013 年的三倍。

■ ***adj.*** [only before noun] high in tone 高音的；高声的：*a treble voice* 高嗓音 ◇ *the **treble clef*** (= the symbol in music showing that the notes following it are high) 高音谱号 ➲ PICTURE AT MUSIC ➲ COMPARE BASS[1] *adj.*

tree /triː/ *noun* a tall plant that can live a long time. Trees have a thick central wooden TRUNK from which branches grow, usually with leaves on them. 树；树木；乔木：*an oak tree* 橡树 ◇ *to **plant a tree*** 植树 ◇ *to **chop/cut down a tree*** 砍倒一棵树 ◇ *They followed a path through the trees.* 他们沿着林间小路走着。➲ COLLOCATIONS AT LIFE ➲ VISUAL VOCAB PAGE V10 ➲ COMPARE BUSH (1), SHRUB ➲ SEE ALSO BAY TREE, CHRISTMAS TREE, FAMILY TREE, GUM TREE, PLANE TREE

IDM **be out of your 'tree** (*informal*) to be behaving in a crazy or stupid way, perhaps because of drugs or alcohol（因药物或酒精等）发疯，发傻 ➲ MORE AT APPLE, BARK *v.*, FOREST, GROW, TOP *n.*, WOOD

'tree diagram *noun* a diagram with lines that divide more and more as you move to lower levels to show the relationships between processes, people etc.（表示层级关系的）树形图

'tree house *noun* a structure built in the branches of a tree, usually for children to play on 树上小屋（搭建在树枝间，通常供儿童游戏用）

'tree-hugger *noun* (*informal, usually disapproving*) a person who cares very much about the environment and tries to protect it 抱树人，环保狂（指过度热衷环保的人）

tree·less /ˈtriːləs/ *adj.* without trees 无树木的：*a treeless plain* 没有树木的平原

tree·line /ˈtriːlaɪn/ *noun* [sing.] a level of land, for example on a mountain, above which trees will not grow 林线（山上等树木生长的上限）

'tree structure *noun* (*computing* 计) a diagram that uses lines that divide into more and more lines to show the various levels of a computer program, and how each part relates to a part in the level above（计算机程序的）树形结构图

'tree surgeon (*also formal* **ar·bor·ist**) *noun* a person whose job is treating trees that are damaged or have a disease, especially by cutting off branches, to try to preserve them 树木修补者；树木修整专家 ▶ **'tree surgery** *noun* [U]

tree·top /ˈtriːtɒp; *NAmE* -tɑːp/ *noun* [usually pl.] the branches at the top of a tree 树梢：*birds nesting in the treetops* 在树梢上筑巢的鸟

tre·foil /ˈtrefɔɪl; ˈtriːfɔɪl/ *noun* **1** (*specialist*) a plant whose leaves are divided into three similar parts, for example CLOVER 车轴草；百脉根；三叶植物 **2** a decoration or a design shaped like a trefoil leaf 三叶形装饰（或图案）

trek /trek/ *noun, verb*

■ ***noun*** **1** a long, hard walk lasting several days or weeks, especially in the mountains 长途跋涉，艰难的旅程（尤指在山区）**2** (*informal*) a long walk 远距离行走 **SYN tramp**: *It's a long trek into town.* 到商业区去要走很长的路。

■ ***verb*** (**-kk-**) **1** [I] (**+ adv./prep.**) (*informal*) to make a long or difficult journey, especially on foot（尤指徒步）长途跋涉：*I hate having to trek up that hill with all the groceries.* 我很不愿意得带着这么多吃用杂物爬上那个山头。**2** (*also* **go trekking**) [I] (**+ adv./prep.**) to spend time walking, especially in mountains and for enjoyment and interest（尤指在山中）远足，徒步旅行：*We went trekking in Nepal.* 我们去尼泊尔徒步旅行。◇ *During the expedition, they trekked ten to thirteen hours a day.* 在探险期间，他们每天都要走十到十三个小时。➲ SEE ALSO PONY-TREKKING

trel·lis /ˈtrelɪs/ *noun* [C, U] a light frame made of long narrow pieces of wood that cross each other, used to support climbing plants（支撑攀缘植物的）棚，架；攀缘架 ➲ VISUAL VOCAB PAGE V20

trem·ble /ˈtrembl/ *verb, noun*

■ ***verb*** **1** [I] **~ (with sth)** to shake in a way that you cannot control, especially because you are very nervous, excited, frightened, etc.（因紧张、激动、惊慌等）颤抖，哆嗦，抖动，战栗：*My legs were trembling with fear.* 我吓得双腿直发抖。◇ *Her voice trembled with excitement.* 她激动得声音颤抖。◇ *He opened the letter with trembling hands.* 他双手哆嗦着把信打开。 **2** [I] to shake slightly 颤动；轻轻摇晃 **SYN quiver**: *leaves trembling in the breeze* 在微风中摇曳的树叶 **3** [I] to be very worried or frightened 极担心；焦虑；恐惧：*I trembled at the thought of having to make a speech.* 我一想到得发表演讲心里就发怵。

■ ***noun*** [C, usually sing.] (*also* **trem·bling** [C, U]) a feeling, movement or sound of trembling 颤抖；战栗；哆嗦：*a tremble of fear* 恐惧引起的颤抖 ◇ *She tried to control the trembling in her legs.* 她竭力控制住颤抖的双腿。

trem·bly /ˈtrembli/ *adj.* (*informal*) shaking from fear, cold, excitement, etc. 发抖的；战栗的；哆嗦的

tre·men·dous /trəˈmendəs/ *adj.* **1** very great 巨大的；极大的 **SYN huge**: *a tremendous explosion* 巨大的爆炸声 ◇ *A tremendous amount of work has gone into the project.* 大量的工作已投入到这项工程。 **2** extremely good 极好的；精彩的；了不起的 **SYN remarkable**: *It was a tremendous experience.* 这是个了不起的经历。 ▶ **tre·men·dous·ly** *adv.*：*tremendously exciting* 极其令人兴奋

trem·olo /ˈtreməlәʊ; *NAmE* -loʊ/ *noun* (*pl.* **-os**) (*music* 音, *from Italian*) a special effect in singing or playing a musical instrument made by repeating the same note or two notes very quickly（演唱或乐器演奏的）震音

tremor /ˈtremə(r)/ *noun* **1** a small EARTHQUAKE in which the ground shakes slightly 轻微地震；小震；微震：*an earth tremor* 地动 **2** a slight shaking movement in a part of your body caused, for example, by cold or fear（由于寒冷或恐惧引起的）颤抖，战栗，哆嗦 **SYN quiver**: *There was a slight tremor in his voice.* 他的声音略微有点儿颤抖。

tremu·lous /ˈtremjələs/ *adj.* (*literary*) shaking slightly because you are nervous; causing you to shake slightly（因紧张）颤抖的，战栗的；使打战的；使颤动的 **SYN trembling**: *a tremulous voice* 颤抖的声音 ◇ *He was in a state of tremulous excitement.* 他激动得直发抖。 ▶ **tremu·lous·ly** *adv.*

trench /trentʃ/ *noun* **1** a long deep hole dug in the ground, for example for carrying away water 沟；渠 **2** a long deep hole dug in the ground in which soldiers can be protected from enemy attacks (for example in northern France and Belgium in the First World War) 战壕，堑壕（如第一次世界大战期间在法国北部和比利时开挖的）：*life in the **trenches*** 战壕生活 ◇ *trench warfare* 堑壕战 **3** (*also* **ˌocean 'trench**) a long deep narrow hole in the ocean floor 海沟；大洋沟

tren·chant /ˈtrentʃənt/ *adj.* (*formal*) (of criticism, remarks, etc. 批评、言语等) expressed strongly and effectively, in a clear way 尖锐的；有效的；鲜明的 **SYN incisive** ▶ **tren·chant·ly** *adv.*

'trench coat *noun* a long loose coat, worn especially to keep off rain, with a belt and pockets in the style of a military coat（有口袋和系带的军装式）雨衣，大衣

trench·er /ˈtrentʃə(r)/ *noun* a wooden plate used in the past for serving food（旧时端饭菜用的）大木盘

ˌtrench 'foot *noun* [U] a painful condition of the feet, in which the flesh begins to decay and die, caused by being in mud or water for too long 壕沟足（因在泥水中时间过长而造成足部皮肉坏死）

trend 🔑 AW /trend/ *noun* a general direction in which a situation is changing or developing 趋势；趋向；倾向；动态；动向：***economic/social/political trends*** 经济/社会/政治趋势 ◇ ~ (**towards sth**) *There is a **growing trend** towards earlier retirement.* 提早退休者有增加的趋势。◇ ~ (**in sth**) ***current trends** in language teaching* 当前语言教学的趋势 ◇ ***a downward/an upward trend** in sales* 销售额下滑/上升的趋势 ◇ *You seem to have **set*** (= started) *a new **trend**.* 看来你们是开了一个新风气。◇ *This trend is being reversed* (= is going in the opposite direction). 这种倾向正在向相反的方向转变。◇ *One region is attempting to **buck*** (= oppose or resist) *the **trend** of economic decline.* 有一个地区试图在经济衰退的趋势中逆流而上。◇ *The **underlying trend** of inflation is still upwards.* 通货膨胀的潜在趋势仍然是上升的。➲ LANGUAGE BANK AT FALL

WORDFINDER 联想词： boom, decline, dip, fluctuate, level off/out, peak, plateau, plummet, slump

trend·set·ter /'trendsetə(r)/ *noun* (*often approving*) a person who starts a new fashion or makes it popular 新潮倡导者；创新风的人 ▶ **trend·set·ting** *adj.* [only before noun]

trendy /'trendi/ *adj., noun*

■ ***adj.*** (**trend·ier**, **trendi·est**) (*informal*) very fashionable 时髦的；赶时髦的：*trendy clothes* 时髦的衣服 ▶ **trend·ily** *adv.* **trendi·ness** *noun* [U]

■ ***noun*** (*pl.* **-ies**) (*BrE, informal, usually disapproving*) a trendy person 爱时髦的人；赶时髦的人：*young trendies from art college* 艺术院校时髦的年轻人

trepi·da·tion /ˌtrepɪ'deɪʃn/ *noun* [U] (*formal*) great worry or fear about sth unpleasant that may happen 惊恐；恐惧；惊惶；不安

tres·pass /'trespəs/ *verb, noun*

■ ***verb*** **1** [I] ~ (**on sth**) to enter land or a building that you do not have permission or the right to enter 擅自进入，非法侵入（他人的土地或建筑物）：*He told me I was trespassing on private land.* 他说我在擅闯私人土地。 **2** [I] (*old use*) to do sth wrong 做错事

PHR V **'trespass on sth** (*formal*) to make unfair use of sb's time, help, etc. 滥用，不公正地利用（别人的时间、帮助等） SYN **encroach**：*I mustn't trespass on your time any longer.* 我不能再占用你的时间了。

■ ***noun*** **1** [U, C] an act of trespassing on land 非法侵入（他人土地） **2** [C] (*old use*) something that you do that is morally wrong 罪过 SYN **sin**

tres·pass·er /'trespəsə(r)/ *noun* a person who goes onto sb's land without their permission 非法进入者：*The notice read: 'Trespassers will be prosecuted.'* 告示上写着"非请莫入，违者必究"。

tresses /'tresɪz/ *noun* [pl.] (*literary*) a woman's long hair（女性的）长发 SYN **lock**

tres·tle /'tresl/ *noun* a wooden or metal structure with two pairs of sloping legs. Trestles are used in pairs to support a flat surface, for example the top of a table.（放置桌面等成对的）支架，条凳

'trestle table *noun* a table that consists of a wooden top supported by trestles 支架台；搁板桌

trews /truːz/ *noun* [pl.] trousers/pants, especially when they are made of TARTAN （尤指格子呢的）裤子，短裤

trey /treɪ/ *noun* (in BASKETBALL 篮球) a shot that scores three points 三分球

tri- /traɪ/ *combining form* (in nouns and adjectives 构成名词和形容词) three; having three 三；有三的：*tricycle* 三轮脚踏车 ◇ *triangular* 三角的

triad /'traɪæd/ *noun* (*formal*) a group of three related people or things 三人组合；三位一体；三件一套

tri·age /'triːɑːʒ; *NAmE* triː'ɑːʒ/ *noun* [U] (in a hospital 医院) the process of deciding how seriously ill/sick or injured a person is, so that the most serious cases can be treated first 患者鉴别分类；伤员鉴别分类；治疗类选法

trial 🔑 /'traɪəl/ *noun, verb*

■ ***noun***

• LAW 法律 **1** 🔑 [U, C] a formal examination of evidence in court by a judge and often a JURY, to decide if sb accused of a crime is guilty or not （法院的）审讯，审理，审判：*a murder trial* 谋杀案的审理 ◇ *He's **on trial** for murder.* 他因涉嫌谋杀而受审。◇ *She will **stand trial/go on trial** for fraud.* 她因涉嫌诈骗将受到审判。◇ *The men were arrested but not **brought to trial**.* 这些人已被逮捕但并未送交法院审判。◇ *The case never **came to trial**.* 这个案件从未开庭审理。◇ *She is awaiting trial on corruption charges.* 她因被控贪污正等候审判。◇ *He did not receive a fair trial.* 他没有受到公正的审判。◇ *She was detained without trial.* 她未经审讯便被羁押。➲ WORDFINDER NOTE AT LAW ➲ COLLOCATIONS AT JUSTICE

WORDFINDER 联想词： accuse, appeal, counsel, defendant, evidence, **justice**, offence, plea, prosecution

• TEST 试验 **2** 🔑 [C, U] the process of testing the ability, quality or performance of sb/sth, especially before you make a final decision about them （对能力、质量、性能等的）试验，试用：*The new drug is undergoing clinical trials.* 这种新药正在进行临床试验。◇ *She agreed to employ me for **a trial period**.* 她同意试用我一段时间。◇ *The system was introduced **on a trial basis** for one month.* 这个制度已引进试行一个月。◇ *a **trial separation*** (= of a couple whose marriage is in difficulties) 试验性分居 ◇ *We had the machine **on trial** for a week.* 这台机器我们已经试用了一个星期。◇ *a **trial of strength*** (= a contest to see who is stronger) 实力的较量 ➲ COLLOCATIONS AT SCIENTIFIC

• IN SPORT 体育运动 **3** [C, usually pl.] (*NAmE also* **try·out**) a competition or series of tests to find the best players for a sports team or an important event 预赛；选拔赛：*Olympic trials* 奥林匹克运动会选拔赛

• FOR ANIMALS 动物 **4** [C, usually pl.] an event at which animals compete or perform 比赛；表演：*horse trials* 马匹比赛

• DIFFICULT EXPERIENCE 艰难经历 **5** [C] an experience or a person that causes difficulties for sb 令人伤脑筋的事；惹麻烦的人；考验：*the **trials and tribulations** of married life* 婚姻生活的考验与磨炼 ◇ ~ **to sb** *She was a sore trial to her family at times.* 她有时让家人伤透了脑筋。

IDM **ˌtrial and 'error** the process of solving a problem by trying various methods until you find a method that is successful 反复试验；不断摸索：*Children learn to use computer programs **by trial and error**.* 儿童通过反复摸索才学会运用计算机程序。

■ ***verb*** (**-ll-**, *NAmE* **-l-**) [T, I] ~ (**sth**) (*BrE*) to test the ability, quality or performance of sth to see if it will be effective or successful 测试（能力、质量、性能等）；试验；试用

'trial balloon *noun* (*especially NAmE*) something that you say or do to find out what people think about a course of action before you take it 试探性言论（或行动）

ˌtrial 'run (*also* **ˌtest 'run**) *noun* a test of how well sth new works, so that you can see if any changes are necessary（对新事物的）初步试验，试行

'trials riding *noun* **'trials biking**, **obˌserved 'trials** [U+sing./pl. v.] the sport of riding a specially designed motorcycle or bicycle through a course that has objects on the ground, which is designed to test a rider's ability 极限骑行运动（使用特制摩托车或自行车，考验骑行者通过障碍物的能力）

tri·angle 🔑 /'traɪæŋɡl/ *noun* **1** 🔑 a flat shape with three straight sides and three angles; a thing in the shape of a triangle 三角形；三角形物体：(*BrE*) *a right-angled triangle* 直角三角形 ◇ (*NAmE*) *a right triangle* 直角三角形 ◇ *Cut the sandwiches into triangles.* 把三明治切成三角形。 **2** a simple musical instrument that consists of a long piece of metal bent into the shape of a triangle, that you hit with another piece of metal 三角铁（打击乐器） ➲ VISUAL VOCAB PAGE V37 **3** a situation involving three people in a complicated relationship 三角关系：*a love triangle* 三角恋爱 ➲ SEE ALSO ETERNAL TRIANGLE **4** (*NAmE*) (*BrE* **'set square**) an instrument for drawing

T

straight lines and angles, made from a flat piece of plastic or metal in the shape of a triangle with one angle of 90° 三角板；三角尺

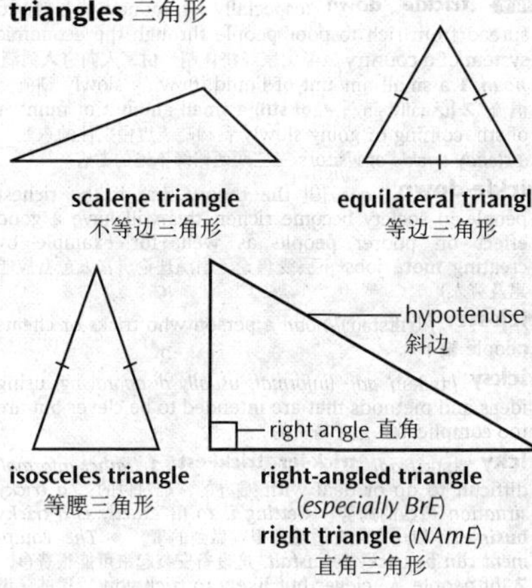

tri·angu·lar /traɪˈæŋɡjələ(r)/ *adj.* **1** shaped like a triangle 三角的；三角形的 **2** involving three people or groups 涉及三人的；三组的；三方面的：*a triangular contest in an election* 竞选中三位候选人的角逐

tri·angu·la·tion /traɪˌæŋɡjuˈleɪʃn/ *noun* [U] (*specialist*) a method of finding out distance and position, usually on a map, by measuring the distance between two fixed points and then measuring the angle from each of these to the third point （通常在地图上做的）三角测量，三角定位

triˌanguˈlation point *noun* = TRIG POINT

tri·ath·lon /traɪˈæθlən/ *noun* a sporting event in which people compete in three different sports, usually swimming, cycling and running 铁人三项；三项全能运动 ➲ COMPARE BIATHLON, DECATHLON, HEPTATHLON, PENTATHLON

tri·bal /ˈtraɪbl/ *adj., noun*

■ *adj.* [usually before noun] connected with a tribe or tribes 部落的；部族的：*tribal art* 部落艺术 ◇ *tribal leaders* 部落首领

■ *noun* a member of a tribe, especially in S Asia （尤指南亚的）部落成员

tri·bal·ism /ˈtraɪbəlɪzəm/ *noun* [U] **1** behaviour, attitudes, etc. that are based on being loyal to a tribe or other social group 部落习性；种族意识；部落主义 **2** the state of being organized in a tribe or tribes 部落制度

ˈtri-band *adj.* (of a mobile/cell phone) able to use three different ranges of radio waves so that it can be used in different regions of the world （手机）三频的

tribe /traɪb/ *noun* **1** (*sometimes offensive*) (in developing countries) a group of people of the same race, and with the same customs, language, religion, etc., living in a particular area and often led by a chief 部落：*tribes living in remote areas of the Amazonian rainforest* 居住在亚马孙河雨林偏远地区的部落 **2** (*usually disapproving*) a group or class of people, especially of one profession （尤指同一职业的）一伙（人），一帮（人），一类（人）：*He had a sudden outburst against the whole tribe of actors.* 他突然对所有的演员非常反感。 **3** (*biology* 生) a group of related animals or plants （动物或植物的）群，族：*a tribe of cats* 猫族 **4** (*informal* or *humorous*) a large number of people 大群，大帮，大批（人）：*One or two of the grandchildren will be there, but not the whole tribe.* 一两个孙子孙女会去那里，但并不是所有的人。

tribes·man /ˈtraɪbzmən/, **tribes·woman** /-wʊmən/ *noun* (*pl.* **-men** /-mən/, **-women** /-wɪmɪn/) a member of a tribe 部落成员

tribes·people /ˈtraɪbzpiːpl/ *noun* [pl.] the people who belong to a particular tribe 部落成员

tribu·la·tion /ˌtrɪbjuˈleɪʃn/ *noun* [C, U] (*literary* or *humorous*) great trouble or suffering 忧患；苦难；磨难；痛苦：*the tribulations of modern life* 现代生活的苦恼

tri·bu·nal /traɪˈbjuːnl/ *noun* [C+sing./pl. v.] a type of court with the authority to deal with a particular problem or disagreement 特别法庭；裁判所：*an international war crimes tribunal* 国际战争罪法庭 ◇ *a military tribunal* 军事法庭 ➲ SEE ALSO INDUSTRIAL TRIBUNAL

trib·une /ˈtrɪbjuːn/ *noun* **1** an official elected by the people in ancient Rome to defend their rights; a popular leader（古罗马由平民选出的）保民官；受拥戴的领袖 **2** a raised area that sb stands on to make a speech in public （公开演讲的）讲坛

tribu·tary /ˈtrɪbjətri; *NAmE* -teri/ *noun* (*pl.* **-ies**) a river or stream that flows into a larger river or a lake （流入大河或湖泊的）支流 ➲ WORDFINDER NOTE AT RIVER ➲ VISUAL VOCAB PAGE V5 ▶ **tribu·tary** *adj.* [only before noun]: *a tributary stream* 支流

trib·ute /ˈtrɪbjuːt/ *noun* **1** [U, C] ~ (**to sb**) an act, a statement or a gift that is intended to show your respect or admiration, especially for a dead person （尤指对死者的）致敬，颂词；悼念；致哀；吊唁礼物：*At her funeral her oldest friend* ***paid tribute to*** *her life and work.* 在葬礼上，与她相识最久的老朋友对她的一生和工作给予了高度的赞扬。◇ *This book is a fitting tribute to the bravery of the pioneers.* 本书是对先驱们大无畏精神恰如其分的献礼。◇ *floral tributes* (= gifts of flowers at a funeral) 葬礼献花 **2** [sing.] ~ **to sth/sb** showing the good effects or influence of sth/sb （良好效果或影响的）体现，显示：*His recovery is a tribute to the doctors' skill.* 他的康复充分显示了各位医生高超的医术。 **3** [U, C] (especially in the past) money given by one country or ruler to another, especially in return for protection or for not being attacked （尤指旧时一国向他国交纳的）贡品，贡金

ˈtribute band *noun* a group of musicians who play the music of a famous band and copy the way they look and sound 翻唱乐队；致敬乐队

trice /traɪs/ *noun*

IDM **in a ˈtrice** very quickly or suddenly 转眼之间；弹指一挥间；瞬息间 SYN **instant**: *He was gone in a trice.* 转眼之间他就没影儿了。

tri·ceps /ˈtraɪseps/ *noun* (*pl.* **tri·ceps**) the large muscle at the back of the top part of the arm 三头肌 ➲ COMPARE BICEPS

tri·cera·tops /traɪˈserətɒps; *NAmE* -tɑːps/ *noun* (*pl.* **tri·cera·tops** or **tri·cera·topses**) a large DINOSAUR with two large horns and one small horn on its very large head 三角龙

trich·ology /trɪˈkɒlədʒi; *NAmE* -ˈkɑːl-/ *noun* [U] the study of the hair and SCALP 毛发学 ▶ **trich·olo·gist** /trɪˈkɒlədʒɪst; *NAmE* -ˈkɑːl-/ *noun*

trick 🔑 /trɪk/ *noun, verb, adj.*

■ *noun*

• **STH TO CHEAT SB** 用以骗人 **1** 🔑 something that you do to make sb believe sth which is not true, or to annoy sb as a joke 诡计；花招；骗局；把戏：*They had to think of a trick to get past the guards.* 他们只好想出个计谋骗过岗哨。◇ *The kids are always* ***playing tricks on*** *their teacher.* 孩子们经常耍些花招戏弄老师。 ➲ SEE ALSO CONFIDENCE TRICK, DIRTY TRICK (2)

• **STH CONFUSING** 令人困惑的事 **2** 🔑 something that confuses you so that you see, understand, remember, etc. things in the wrong way 引起错觉（或记忆紊乱）的事物：*One of the problems of old age is that your memory* *can start to* ***play tricks*** *on you.* 老年人的问题之一是记忆可能紊乱起来。◇ *Was there somebody standing there or was it* ***a trick of the light****?* 是真的有人站在那儿还是光线引起的错觉？

• **ENTERTAINMENT** 娱乐 **3** a clever action that sb/sth performs as a way of entertaining people 戏法；把戏：*He amused the kids with conjuring tricks.* 他变戏法逗得孩子们直乐。◇ *a card trick* 纸牌戏法 ➲ SEE ALSO HAT-TRICK

• **GOOD METHOD** 好方法 **4** [usually sing.] a way of doing sth that works well; a good method 技巧；诀窍；窍门：***The trick is*** *to pick the animal up by the back of its neck.* 窍门在于抓住动物的后脖颈把它提起来。◇ *He used the old trick of attacking in order to defend himself.* 他采用了以攻为守的老招数。

• **IN CARD GAMES** 纸牌游戏 **5** the cards that you play or win in a single part of a card game 一圈；一墩；一圈所打（或赢）的牌：*I won six tricks in a row.* 我接连赢了六墩牌。

IDM **a bag/box of ˈtricks** (*informal*) a set of methods or equipment that sb can use 一套措施；全部法宝 **be up to your (old) ˈtricks** (*informal, disapproving*) to be behaving in the same bad way as before 故伎重演；耍老花招 **do the ˈtrick** (*informal*) to succeed in solving a problem or achieving a particular result 奏效；起作用；达到目的：*I don't know what it was that did the trick, but I am definitely feeling much better.* 我不知道是什么起的作用，但是我确实觉得好多了。 **every trick in the ˈbook** every available method, whether it is honest or not 无所不用其极；浑身解数：*He'll try every trick in the book to stop you from winning.* 他将使尽浑身解数阻止你取胜。 **have a ˈtrick, some more ˈtricks, etc. up your sleeve** to have an idea, some plans, etc. that you keep ready to use if it becomes necessary 袖藏玄机；胸有成竹；自有锦囊妙计 **ˌtrick or ˈtreat** said by children who visit people's houses at Halloween and threaten to play tricks on people who do not give them sweets/candy 是请吃糖，还是想遭殃（万圣节时儿童挨家索要糖果用语，扬言若不给糖就捣乱戏弄别人） **the ˌtricks of the ˈtrade** the clever ways of doing things, known and used by people who do a particular job or activity（某一行业或活动的）绝招，绝活，门道，生意经 **ˌturn a ˈtrick** (*NAmE, slang*) to have sex with sb for money 接客卖淫 ➲ MORE AT MISS *v.*, TEACH

■ ***verb*** to make sb believe sth which is not true, especially in order to cheat them 欺骗；欺诈：**~ sb** *I'd been tricked and I felt stupid.* 我被人骗了，觉得自己真傻。◇ **~ your way + adv./prep.** *He managed to trick his way past the security guards.* 他想方设法骗过保安员走了过去。➲ SYNONYMS AT CHEAT

PHR V **ˌtrick sb ˈinto sth/into doing sth** to make sb do sth by means of a trick 骗某人做某事：*He tricked me into lending him £100.* 他骗我借给了他 100 英镑。 **ˌtrick sb ˈout of sth** to get sth from sb by means of a trick 从某人处骗走某物：*She was tricked out of her life savings.* 她被骗走了一生的积蓄。 **ˌtrick sb/sth↔ˈout (in/with sth)** (*literary*) to dress or decorate sb/sth in a way that attracts attention 打扮（或装饰）得引人注目

■ ***adj.*** [only before noun] **1** intended to trick sb 意在欺骗的；容易使人上当的：*It was a* ***trick question*** (= one to which the answer seems easy but actually is not). 那是个容易使人上当的问题。◇ *It's all done using* ***trick photography*** (= photography that uses clever techniques to show things that do not actually exist or are impossible). 这都是利用特技摄影产生的假象。 **2** (*NAmE*) (of part of the body 身体部位) weak and not working well 虚弱有毛病的：*a trick knee* 膝软

trick·ery /ˈtrɪkəri/ *noun* [U] the use of dishonest methods to trick people in order to achieve what you want 欺骗；欺诈；耍花招；招摇撞骗 SYN **deception**

trickle /ˈtrɪkl/ *verb, noun*

■ ***verb*** **1** [I, T] to flow, or to make sth flow, slowly in a thin stream （使）滴，淌，小股流淌：**(+ adv./prep.)** *Tears were trickling down her cheeks.* 眼泪顺着她的面颊流了下来。◇ **~ sth (+ adv./prep.)** *Trickle some oil over the salad.* 往色拉上滴些油。 **2** [I, T] **~ (sth) + adv./prep.** to go, or to make sth go, somewhere slowly or gradually 慢慢走；（使）缓慢移动：*People began trickling into the hall.* 人们开始缓步进入大厅。◇ *News is starting to trickle out.* 消息渐渐传了出来。

PHR V **ˌtrickle ˈdown** (especially of money 尤指钱) to spread from rich to poor people through the economic system of a country （经国家经济体制）由富人向穷人涓滴

■ ***noun*** **1** a small amount of liquid, flowing slowly 细流；涓流 **2** [usually sing.] **~ (of sth)** a small amount or number of sth, coming or going slowly 稀稀疏疏缓慢来往的东西：*a steady trickle of visitors* 三三两两络绎不绝的游客

ˈtrickle-down *noun* [U] the theory that if the richest people in society become richer, this will have a good effect on poorer people as well, for example by creating more jobs 下层受惠论，涓滴理论（富人愈富应能惠及穷人）

trick·ster /ˈtrɪkstə(r)/ *noun* a person who tricks or cheats people 骗子

tricksy /ˈtrɪksi/ *adj.* (*informal, usually disapproving*) using ideas and methods that are intended to be clever but are too complicated 过于精密的

tricky /ˈtrɪki/ *adj.* (**trick·ier**, **tricki·est**) **1** (*rather informal*) difficult to do or deal with 难办的；难对付的：*a tricky situation* 微妙的局势 ◇ *Getting it to fit exactly is a* ***tricky business****.* 使这完全合适是件很难做到的事。◇ *The equipment can be tricky to install.* 这设备安装起来可能很费事。 **2** (of people 人) clever but likely to trick you 狡猾的；诡计多端的 SYN **crafty**

tri·col·our (*US* **tri·color**) /ˈtrɪkələ(r); *NAmE* ˈtraɪkʌlər/ *noun* [C] a flag which has three bands of different colours, especially the French and Irish national flags 三色旗（尤指法国和爱尔兰的国旗）

tri·cycle /ˈtraɪsɪkl/ (*also informal* **trike**) *noun* a vehicle similar to a bicycle, but with one wheel at the front and two at the back 三轮脚踏车 ➲ VISUAL VOCAB PAGE V55

tri·dent /ˈtraɪdnt/ *noun* a weapon used in the past that looks like a long fork with three points 三叉戟（旧时武器）

tried /traɪd/ *adj.* ➲ SEE ALSO TRY *v.*

IDM **ˌtried and ˈtested/ˈtrusted** (*BrE*) (*NAmE* **ˌtried and ˈtrue**) that you have used or relied on in the past successfully 经过考验的；可靠的；可信赖的：*a tried and tested method for solving the problem* 解决这个问题的可靠办法 ➲ MORE LIKE THIS 13, page R26

tri·en·nial /traɪˈeniəl/ *adj.* happening every three years 每三年一次的；每三年的

trier /ˈtraɪə(r)/ *noun* a person who tries very hard at what they are doing and does their best 工作尽心尽力的人；勤勤恳恳的人

trifle /ˈtraɪfl/ *noun, verb*

■ ***noun*** **1 a trifle** [sing.] (used as an adverb 用作副词) (*formal* or *humorous*) slightly 稍微；一点儿：*She seemed a trifle anxious.* 她似乎有点儿焦急。 **2** [C] something that is not valuable or important 小事；琐事；不值钱的东西：*$1 000 is a mere trifle to her.* * 1 000 美元对她来说不过是区区小数。 **3** [C, U] (*BrE*) a cold DESSERT (= a sweet dish) made from cake and fruit with wine and/or jelly poured over it, covered with CUSTARD and cream 葡萄酒蛋糕，屈莱弗（在蛋糕和水果上浇葡萄酒或果冻，上覆蛋奶冻等）

■ ***verb***

PHR V **ˈtrifle with sb/sth** (*formal*) (used especially in negative sentences 尤用于否定句) to treat sb/sth without genuine respect 怠慢；小看：*He is not a person to be trifled with.* 他这个人怠慢不得。

trif·ling /ˈtraɪflɪŋ/ *adj.* (*formal*) small and not important 琐碎的；微不足道的；无足轻重的；不重要的 SYN **trivial**：*trifling details* 琐碎细节

trig·ger AW /ˈtrɪɡə(r)/ *noun, verb*

■ ***noun*** **1** the part of a gun that you press in order to fire it （枪的）扳机：*to* ***pull/squeeze the trigger*** 扣扳机 ◇ *He kept his finger on the trigger.* 他的手指一直勾着扳机。 **2** **~ (for sth)** | **~ (to sth/to do sth)** something that is the cause of a particular reaction or development, especially a bad one （尤指引发不良反应或发展的）起因，诱因： *The trigger for the strike was the closure of yet another factory.* 触发这次罢工的是又一家工厂被关闭了。 **3** the part of a bomb that causes it to explode 触发器；引爆器： *nuclear triggers* 核引爆器

■ ***verb*** **1 ~ sth** (**off**) to make sth happen suddenly 发动；引起；触发 **SYN** **set off**: *Nuts can trigger off a violent allergic reaction.* 坚果可以引起严重的过敏反应。 **2 ~ sth** to cause a device to start functioning 开动；起动 **SYN** **set off**: *to trigger an alarm* 触发警报器

'trigger-happy *adj.* (*informal, disapproving*) too willing and quick to use violence, especially with guns 以开枪为乐的；好斗的；爱动武的；动辄开枪的

trig·onom·etry /ˌtrɪɡəˈnɒmətri; *NAmE* -ˈnɑːm-/ *noun* [U] the type of mathematics that deals with the relationship between the sides and angles of triangles 三角学 ➲ WORDFINDER NOTE AT MATHS ▸ **trig·ono·met·ric** /ˌtrɪɡənəˈmetrɪk/ (*also* **trig·ono·met·ric·al** /-kl/) *adj.*

trig point /ˈtrɪɡ pɔɪnt/ (*also* **triˌangu'lation point**) *noun* (*specialist*) a position on a high place used as a REFERENCE POINT, especially by people who make and use maps. It is usually marked on the ground by a short stone PILLAR. （地图制作和使用者设的）三角点

tri·graph /ˈtraɪɡrɑːf; *NAmE* -ɡræf/ *noun* (*linguistics* 语言) a combination of three letters representing one sound, for example 'sch' in German 三合字母；三字母一音

trike /traɪk/ *noun* (*informal*) = TRICYCLE

tri·lat·eral /ˌtraɪˈlætərəl/ *adj.* involving three groups of people or three countries 三边的；三方的： *trilateral talks* 三方会谈 ➲ COMPARE BILATERAL (1), MULTILATERAL, UNILATERAL

trilby /ˈtrɪlbi/ *noun* (*pl.* **-ies**) (*especially BrE*) a man's soft hat with a narrow BRIM and the top part pushed in from front to back （男式）软毡帽 ➲ VISUAL VOCAB PAGE V70

tri·lin·gual /ˌtraɪˈlɪŋɡwəl/ *adj.* **1** able to speak three languages equally well 会说三种语言的： *He is trilingual in English, Spanish and Danish.* 他能讲英语、西班牙语和丹麦语三种语言。 **2** using three languages; written in three languages 使用三种语言的；用三种语言写的： *trilingual education* 三语教育 ◇ *a trilingual menu* 三语菜单

trill /trɪl/ *noun, verb*

■ ***noun*** **1** a repeated short high sound made, for example, by sb's voice or by a bird （人的）颤声，短促尖声；（鸟的）啼啭，唧唧啾啾 **2** (*music* 音) the sound made when two notes next to each other in the musical SCALE are played or sung quickly several times one after the other 颤音 **3** (*also* **roll**) (*phonetics* 语音) a sound, usually a /r/, produced by making the tongue VIBRATE against a part of the mouth 颤音

■ ***verb*** **1** [I] to make repeated short high sounds （连续）发颤音，发短促的响声 **SYN** **warble**: *A phone trilled on the desk.* 办公桌上的电话丁零零地响了。◇ *The canary was trilling away happily.* 那只金丝雀唧唧啾啾地欢唱个不停。 **2** [T] **+ speech** to say sth in a high cheerful voice 欢快地高声说 **SYN** **warble**: *'How wonderful!' she trilled.* "太妙了！"她高兴地喊道。 **3** [T] **~ sth** (*phonetics* 语音) to pronounce a /r/ sound by making a trill (3) 发 r 颤音 ➲ COMPARE ROLL *v.* (10)

tril·lion /ˈtrɪljən/ *number* **1** 1 000 000 000 000; one million million 万亿；兆 **HELP** You say **a, one, two, several, etc. trillion** without a final 's' on 'trillion'. **Trillions (of...)** can be used if there is no number or quantity before it. Always use a plural verb with **trillion** or **trillions**. 说 a, one, two, several, etc. trillion 时，trillion 后面不加 s。若前面没有数目或数量，可用 trillions (of ...)。trillion 和 trillions 均用复数动词。 **2 a trillion** or **trillions** (**of...**) (*informal*) a very large amount 大量；无数 **HELP** There are more examples of how to use numbers at the entry for **hundred**. 更多数词用法示例见 hundred 条。 **3** (*old-fashioned, BrE*) one million million million; 1 000 000 000 000 000 000 百万兆

tri·lo·bite /ˈtraɪləʊbaɪt; *NAmE* ˈtraɪlə-/ *noun* a small sea creature that lived millions of years ago and is now a FOSSIL 三叶虫（生活于几百万年前的小型海洋生物，已成化石）

tril·ogy /ˈtrɪlədʒi/ *noun* (*pl.* **-ies**) a group of three books, films/movies, etc. that have the same subject or characters（书籍、电影等的）三部曲；三部剧

trim /trɪm/ *verb, noun, adj.*

■ ***verb*** (**-mm-**) **1 ~ sth** to make sth neater, smaller, better, etc., by cutting parts from it 修剪；修整： *to trim your hair* 理发 ◇ *to trim a hedge* (*back*) 修剪树篱 ◇ (*figurative*) *The training budget had been trimmed by £10 000.* 培训预算削减了 1 万英镑。 **2 ~ sth** (**off sth**) | **~ sth** (**off/away**) to cut away unnecessary parts from sth 切去，割掉，剪下，除去（不必要的部分）： *Trim any excess fat off the meat.* 把多余的肥膘从肉上切掉。◇ *I trimmed two centimetres off the hem of the skirt.* 我把裙子的下摆剪短了两厘米。 **3** [usually passive] **~ sth** (**with sth**) to decorate sth, especially around its edges 装饰，修饰，点缀（尤指某物的边缘）： *gloves trimmed with fur* 毛皮镶边的手套

IDM **ˌtrim your ˈsails 1** to arrange the sails of a boat to suit the wind so that the boat moves faster 随风扬帆；见风转舵 **2** to reduce your costs 减少开支；削减费用

PHR V **ˌtrim ˈdown** | **ˌtrim sth↔ˈdown** to become smaller in size; to make sth smaller （使）变小；缩减： *Using the diet he's trimmed down from 90 kilos to 70.* 通过控制饮食，他的体重从 90 公斤减到了 70 公斤。

■ ***noun*** **1** [C, usually sing.] an act of cutting a small amount off sth, especially hair （尤指毛发的）修剪： *a wash and trim* 洗头理发 ◇ *The hedge needs a trim.* 这树篱得修剪了。 **2** [U, sing.] material that is used to decorate clothes, furniture, cars, etc., especially along the edges, by being a different colour, etc. （衣服、家具、汽车等的）饰物，边饰，装饰配件： *The car is available with black or red trim* (= the colour of the seats). 这款汽车的座椅有黑红两种颜色。◇ *a blue jacket with a white trim* 镶有白边的蓝色上衣

IDM **in** (**good, etc.**) **ˈtrim** (*informal*) in good condition or order 状态良好；健康极佳；井然有序： *He* ***keeps in trim*** *by running every day.* 他每天跑步保持身体健康。◇ *The team need to* ***get in trim*** *for the coming season.* 这个球队需要为下个赛季做好准备。

■ ***adj.*** **1** (of a person 人) looking thin, healthy and attractive 苗条的；修长的；健康优雅的： *She has kept very trim.* 她的身材保持得很苗条。◇ *a trim figure* 修长的身材 **2** neat and well cared for 整齐的；精心照管的；井然有序的 **SYN** **well kept**: *a trim garden* 精心管理的花园

tri·maran /ˈtraɪməræn/ *noun* a fast sailing boat like a CATAMARAN, but with three HULLS instead of two 三体帆船

tri·mes·ter /traɪˈmestə(r)/ *noun* **1** (*medical* 医) a period of three months during the time when a woman is pregnant 妊娠期（以三个月为单位）： *the first trimester of pregnancy* 妊娠的头三个月 **2** (*NAmE*) = TERM (2)： *The school year is divided into three trimesters.* 一学年分三个学期。 ➲ COMPARE SEMESTER

trim·mer /ˈtrɪmə(r)/ *noun* a machine for cutting the edges of bushes, grass and HEDGES（树丛、花草、树篱的）修剪机： *a hedge trimmer* 树篱修剪机

trim·ming /ˈtrɪmɪŋ/ *noun* **1 trimmings** (*NAmE also* **fixings**) [pl.] the extra things that it is traditional to have for a special meal or occasion （菜肴的）配料；额外的事物： *a splendid feast of turkey with* ***all the trimmings*** 备有各种配料的丰盛火鸡大餐 **2 trimmings** [pl.] the small pieces of sth that are left when you have cut sth 修剪下来的东西；剪屑： *hedge trimmings* 树篱修剪下来的碎枝叶 **3** [U, C, usually pl.] material that is used to decorate sth, for example along its edges 装饰材料；镶边饰物： *a white blouse with blue trimming* 有蓝色饰边的白衬衫

trin·ity /ˈtrɪnəti/ *noun* [sing.] **1 the Trinity** (in Christianity 基督教) the union of Father, Son and HOLY SPIRIT as one God 三位一体（圣父、圣子及圣灵合为上帝） **2** (*formal*) a group of three people or things 三人小组；三件一套；三合一

trin·ket /ˈtrɪŋkɪt/ *noun* a piece of jewellery or small decorative object that is not worth much money（价值不高的）小首饰，小装饰物

trio /ˈtriːəʊ; *NAmE* ˈtriːoʊ/ *noun* (*pl.* **-os**) **1** [C+sing./pl. v.] a group of three people or things 三人小组；三件一套；三合一 ➲ COMPARE DUO (1) **2** [C+sing./pl. v.] a group of three musicians or singers who play or sing together 三重奏乐团；三重唱组合 **3** [C] a piece of music for three musicians or singers 三重奏（曲）；三重唱（曲）：*a trio for piano, oboe and bassoon* 钢琴、双簧管及大管三重奏 ➲ COMPARE DUET

trip /trɪp/ *noun, verb*

■ ***noun* 1** a journey to a place and back again, especially a short one for pleasure or a particular purpose（尤指短程往返的）旅行，旅游，出行：*Did you have a good trip?* 你旅行顺利吗？◇ *We* ***went on a trip*** *to the mountains.* 我们到山里去旅游了。◇ *a* ***day trip*** (= lasting a day) 一日游 ◇ *a* ***boat/coach trip*** 乘船/长途汽车旅行 ◇ *a* ***business/school/shopping trip*** 出差；学校旅行；去商场购物 ◇ *They* ***took a trip*** *down the river.* 他们沿河往下游旅行。◇ *We had to* ***make several trips*** *to bring all the equipment over.* 我们往返了几次才把全部设备运过来。➲ COLLOCATIONS AT TRAVEL ➲ SEE ALSO EGO TRIP, FIELD TRIP, ROUND TRIP **2** (*slang*) the experience that sb has if they take a powerful drug that affects the mind and makes them imagine things（服用毒品后所产生的）幻觉，迷幻感受：*an acid (= LSD) trip* 迷幻药产生的幻觉 **3** an act of falling or nearly falling down, because you hit your foot against sth 绊；绊倒 IDM SEE GUILT *n.*

■ ***verb*** (**-pp-**) **1** [I] to catch your foot on sth and fall or almost fall 绊；绊倒：*She tripped and fell.* 她绊了一下摔倒了。◇ **~ over/on sth** *Someone will trip over that cable.* 有人会让那条电缆绊倒的。◇ **~ over/up** *Be careful you don't trip up on the step.* 你小心别在台阶上绊倒了。**2** [T] **~ sb** (*also* **trip sb up**) to catch sb's foot and make them fall or almost fall 将…绊倒；使跌倒：*As I passed, he stuck out a leg and tried to trip me up.* 我经过时，他伸出腿来想把我绊倒。**3** [I] **+ adv./prep.** (*literary*) to walk, run or dance with quick light steps 脚步轻快地走（或跑、跳舞）：*She said goodbye and tripped off along the road.* 她说了声再见就连蹦带跳地沿路走了。**4** [T] **~ sth** to release a switch, etc. or to operate sth by doing so 触发（开关）；（松开开关）开动：*to trip a switch* 打开开关 ◇ *Any intruders will trip the alarm.* 任何非法入室者都会触响报警器。**5** [I] (*informal*) to be under the influence of a drug that makes you HALLUCINATE（服用毒品后）产生幻觉 IDM SEE MEMORY LANE, TONGUE *n.*

PHRV ˌ**trip ˈup** | ˌ**trip sb**↔ˈ**up** to make a mistake; to deliberately make sb do this（故意使）犯错误：*Read the questions carefully, because the examiners sometimes try to trip you up.* 要仔细把问题看清楚，因为出卷人有时故意让你出错。

tri·par·tite /traɪˈpɑːtaɪt; *NAmE* -ˈpɑːrt-/ *adj.* [usually before noun] (*formal*) having three parts or involving three people, groups, etc. 有三部分的；涉及三人的；三方参加的

tripe /traɪp/ *noun* [U] **1** the LINING of a cow's or pig's stomach, eaten as food 食用牛肚（或猪肚）；百叶 **2** (*informal*) something that sb says or writes that you think is nonsense or not of good quality 废话；胡说；拙劣的文章 SYN **garbage, rubbish**

ˈ**trip hop** *noun* [U] a type of dance music which is a mixture of HIP HOP and REGGAE, has a slow beat, and is intended to create a relaxed atmosphere 迷幻舞曲（结合嘻哈和雷盖音乐元素、节奏缓慢）

triple /ˈtrɪpl/ *adj., verb*

■ ***adj.*** [only before noun] **1** having three parts or involving three people or groups 三部分的；三人的；三组的：*a triple heart bypass operation* 心脏三处分流手术 ◇ *a triple alliance* 三方同盟 ◇ *They're showing a* ***triple bill*** *of horror movies* (= three horror movies one after the other). 他们正在连演三部恐怖片。**2** three times as much or as many as sth 三倍的；三重的：*The amount of alcohol in his blood was triple the legal maximum.* 他血液中的酒精含量为法定最高限量的三倍。◇ *Its population is about triple that of Venice.* 它的人口大约是威尼斯的三倍。▶ **triply** /ˈtrɪpli/ *adv.*

■ ***verb*** [I, T] **~ (sth)** to become, or to make sth, three times as much or as many 成为三倍；使增至三倍 SYN **treble**: *Output should triple by next year.* 到明年产量应增至三倍。

the ˈtriple jump *noun* [sing.] a sporting event in which people try to jump as far forward as possible with three jumps. The first jump lands on one foot, the second on the other and the third on both feet. 三级跳远

trip·let /ˈtrɪplət/ *noun* **1** one of three children born at the same time to the same mother 三胞胎中的一个 **2** (*music*

▼ SYNONYMS 同义词辨析

trip

journey • tour • expedition • excursion • outing • day out

These are all words for an act of travelling to a place. 以上各词均指旅行、旅游。

trip an act of travelling from one place to another, and usually back again 通常指往返的旅行：*a business trip* 出差 ◇ *a five-minute trip by taxi* 五分钟的出租车车程

journey an act of travelling from one place to another, especially when they are a long way apart 尤指长途旅行：*a long and difficult journey across the mountains* 漫长而艰难的翻山旅行

TRIP OR JOURNEY? 用 trip 还是 journey?

A **trip** usually involves you going to a place and back again; a **journey** is usually one-way. A **trip** is often shorter than a **journey**, although it does not have to be. * trip 通常为往返旅行，journey 通常为单程旅行。trip 的行程常较 journey 短，但并非一定如此：*a trip to New York* 去纽约的旅行 ◇ *a round-the-world trip* 环球旅行 It is often short in time, even if it is long in distance. **Journey** is more often used when the travelling takes a long time and is difficult. In North American English **journey** is not used for short trips. 即使距离远，trip 所花时间常常不长。如果旅程长且艰难较常用 journey。在美式英语中，journey 不用以指短途旅行：(*BrE*) *What is your journey to work like?* 你上班的路程如何？

tour a journey made for pleasure during which several different places are visited 指游览多地的旅行、旅游：*a tour of Bavaria* 巴伐利亚之旅

expedition an organized journey with a particular purpose, especially to find out about a place that is not well known 指远征、探险、考察：*the first expedition to the South Pole* 首次去南极的探险

excursion a short trip made for pleasure, especially one that has been organized for a group of people 尤指集体远足、短途旅行：*We went on an all-day excursion to the island.* 我们到岛上去游览了一整天。

outing a short trip made for pleasure or education, usually with a group of people and lasting no more than a day 指集体出外游玩或学习，通常不超过一天：*The children were on a day's outing from school.* 孩子们离校游览了一天。

day out a trip to somewhere for a day, especially for pleasure 指一日游：*We had a day out at the beach.* 我们在海滩玩了一天。

PATTERNS

- a(n) **foreign/overseas** trip/journey/tour/expedition
- a **bus/coach/train/rail** trip/journey/tour
- to **go on** a(n) trip/journey/tour/expedition/excursion/outing/day out
- to **set out/off on** a(n) trip/journey/tour/expedition/excursion
- to **make** a(n) trip/journey/tour/expedition/excursion

T

音）a group of three equal notes to be played or sung in the time usually taken to play or sing two of the same kind 三连音

trip·li·cate /'trɪplɪkət/ *noun*

IDM **in 'triplicate** **1** done three times 做过三次：*Each sample was tested in triplicate.* 每种样品都做过三次检验。**2** (of a document 文件) copied twice, so that there are three copies in total 一式三份 ➲ COMPARE DUPLICATE *n.*

tri·pod /'traɪpɒd; *NAmE* -pɑːd/ *noun* a support with three legs for a camera, TELESCOPE, etc.（照相机、望远镜等的）三脚架 ➲ VISUAL VOCAB PAGE V72

trip·per /'trɪpə(r)/ *noun* (*BrE*) a person who is visiting a place for a short time for pleasure（短程）旅游者：*a day tripper* 一日游者

trip·tych /'trɪptɪk/ *noun* (*specialist*) a picture that is painted or CARVED on three pieces of wood placed side by side, especially one over an ALTAR in a church 三联画；三联雕刻；（尤指）三折圣像画

trip·wire /'trɪpwaɪə(r)/ *noun* a wire that is stretched close to the ground as part of a device for catching sb/sth if they touch it 绊索；绊网

tri·reme /'traɪriːm/ *noun* a long flat ship with three rows of OARS on each side, used in war by the ancient Greeks and Romans（古希腊和古罗马人的）三层划桨战船

tri·shaw /'traɪʃɔː/ *noun* a light vehicle with three wheels and PEDALS, used in SE Asia to carry passengers（东南亚载客用的）三轮脚踏车

trite /traɪt/ *adj.* (of a remark, an opinion, etc. 言语、想法等) dull and boring because it has been expressed so many times before; not original 老生常谈的；陈腐的；老一套的 SYN **banal** ▸ **trite·ly** *adv.* **trite·ness** *noun* [U]

tri·tium /'trɪtiəm/ *noun* [U] (*symb.* **T**) an ISOTOPE (= a different form) of hydrogen with a mass that is three times that of the usual isotope 氚（氢的同位素）

tri·umph /'traɪʌmf/ *noun, verb*

▪ *noun* **1** [C, U] a great success, achievement or victory 巨大成功；重大成就；伟大胜利：*one of the greatest triumphs of modern science* 现代科学最重大的成就之一 ◇ **~ over sb/sth** *It was a personal triumph over her old rival.* 这是她对老对头的个人胜利。**2** [U] the feeling of great satisfaction or joy that you get from a great success or victory（巨大成功或胜利的）心满意足，喜悦，狂喜：*a shout of triumph* 喜悦的欢呼声 ◇ *The winning team returned home* ***in triumph.*** 球队奏凯而归。**3** [sing.] **a ~ (of sth)** an excellent example of how successful sth can be（成功的）典范，楷模：*Her arrest was a triumph of international cooperation.* 她的被捕是国际合作的成果。

▪ *verb* [I] **~ (over sb/sth)** to defeat sb/sth; to be successful 打败；战胜；成功：*As is usual in this kind of movie, good triumphs over evil in the end.* 像这类电影的一贯结局一样，善良战胜了邪恶。◇ *France triumphed 3–0 in the final.* 法国队在决赛中以 3:0 获胜。

tri·umph·al /traɪ'ʌmfl/ *adj.* [usually before noun] done or made in order to celebrate a great success or victory 庆祝成功（或胜利）的；凯旋的

tri·umph·al·ism /traɪ'ʌmfəlɪzəm/ *noun* [U] (*disapproving*) behaviour that celebrates a victory or success in a way that is too proud and intended to upset the people you have defeated 耀武扬威；扬扬得意 ▸ **tri·umph·al·ist** *adj.*

tri·umph·ant /traɪ'ʌmfənt/ *adj.* **1** very successful in a way that causes great satisfaction 高奏凯歌的；大获全胜的；巨大成功的：*They emerged triumphant in the September election.* 他们在九月份的选举中大获全胜。**2** showing great satisfaction or joy about a victory or success 欢欣鼓舞的；扬扬得意的；耀武扬威的：*a triumphant smile* 得意扬扬的笑容 ▸ **tri·umph·ant·ly** *adv.*

tri·um·vir·ate /traɪ'ʌmvərət/ *noun* (*formal*) a group of three powerful people or groups who control sth together 三人领导小组；三人统治集团；三方执政集团

trivet /'trɪvɪt/ *noun* a metal stand that you can put a hot dish, etc. on（垫热菜盘等用的）金属架

trivia /'trɪviə/ *noun* [U] **1** unimportant matters, details or information 琐事；细枝末节：*We spent the whole evening discussing domestic trivia.* 我们整个晚上谈论家庭琐事。**2** (usually in compounds 通常构成复合词) facts about many subjects that are used in a game to test people's knowledge（智力测验比赛用的）各种科目的知识：*a trivia quiz* 知识面宽的问答比赛

triv·ial /'trɪviəl/ *adj.* not important or serious; not worth considering 不重要的；琐碎的；微不足道的：*a trivial detail* 细枝末节 ◇ *I know it* ***sounds trivial****, but I'm worried about it.* 我知道这事听起来微不足道，但我还是放心不下。◇ *I'll try to fix it—but it's not trivial* (= it may be difficult to fix). 我会设法修好，不过这并非易事。▸ **trivi·al·ly** /-iəli/ *adv.*

trivi·al·ity /ˌtrɪvi'æləti/ *noun* (*pl.* **-ies**) (*disapproving*) **1** [C] a matter that is not important 琐事；小事：*I don't want to waste time on trivialities.* 我不想把时间浪费在一些琐碎小事上。**2** [U] the state of being unimportant or dealing with unimportant things 微不足道；琐碎；无足轻重：*His speech was one of great triviality.* 他的讲话根本无足轻重。

trivi·al·ize (*BrE also* **-ise**) /'trɪviəlaɪz/ *verb* **~ sth** (*usually disapproving*) to make sth seem less important, serious, difficult, etc. than it really is 使显得琐碎（或不重要、不难等）；轻视 ▸ **trivi·al·iza·tion, -isa·tion** /ˌtrɪviəlaɪ'zeɪʃn; *NAmE* -lə'z-/ *noun* [U]

tro·chee /'trəʊkiː; *NAmE* 'troʊkiː/ *noun* (*specialist*) a unit of sound in poetry consisting of one strong or long syllable followed by one weak or short syllable（诗的）扬抑格，长短格 ▸ **tro·cha·ic** /trəʊ'keɪɪk; *NAmE* troʊ-/ *adj.*

trod PAST TENSE OF TREAD

trod·den PAST PART. OF TREAD

trog /trɒg; *NAmE* trɑːg/ *noun* (*BrE, informal*) a person with bad social skills and low intelligence 不受欢迎的笨人；呆子

trog·lo·dyte /'trɒglədaɪt; *NAmE* 'trɑːg-/ *noun* a person living in a CAVE, especially in PREHISTORIC times（尤指史前时期的）穴居人 SYN **cave dweller**

troika /'trɔɪkə/ *noun* (*formal*) a group of three politicians, organizations or countries working together 三人领导小组；三头政治；三巨头；三国集团

troil·ism /'trɔɪlɪzəm/ *noun* [U] sexual activity involving three people 三方性爱

Tro·jan /'trəʊdʒən; *NAmE* 'troʊ-/ *noun, adj.* a person from the ancient city of Troy in Asia Minor（小亚细亚古城）特洛伊人

IDM **work like a 'Trojan** (*old-fashioned*) to work very hard 埋头苦干；卖力干活

Trojan 'horse *noun* **1** a person or thing that is used to trick an enemy in order to achieve a secret purpose 特洛伊木马；（来自外部的）颠覆分子（或活动）**2** (*computing* 计) a computer program that seems to be helpful but that is, in fact, designed to destroy data, etc.（特洛伊）木马程序（一种欺骗程序，看起来有用，实际却旨在毁坏数据等）ORIGIN From the story in which the ancient Greeks hid inside a hollow wooden statue of a horse in order to enter the city of their enemies, Troy. 源自传说，古希腊人为了潜入敌城特洛伊而藏在空心的木马中。

troll /trɒl; trəʊl; *NAmE* troʊl/ *noun, verb*

▪ *noun* **1** (in Scandinavian stories) a creature that looks like an ugly person. Some trolls are very large and evil, others are small and friendly but like to trick people.（斯堪的纳维亚传说中的）山精，巨怪，友善顽皮的侏儒 **2** (*informal*) a message to a discussion group on the Internet that sb deliberately sends to make other people angry; a person who sends a message like this "投饵"，恶意挑衅的帖子（在互联网讨论组张贴）；"投饵"人；发挑衅帖子的人

▪ *verb* **1** [I] **~ (for sth)** (*especially NAmE*) to catch fish by pulling a line with BAIT on it through the water behind a

T

boat 曳绳钓（鱼）；拖钓 **2** [T, I] (*informal*) to search for or try to get sth 搜查；搜索；设法得到：**~ sth for sth** *He trolled the Internet for advice on the disease.* 他搜索互联网寻求治疗这种病的建议。◇ **~ for sth** *Both candidates have been trolling for votes.* 两个候选人一直都在拉票。**3** [I, T] **~ (sb/sth)** to write false or insulting messages in Internet CHAT ROOMS, BLOGS, etc. in order to make other people angry （在网络聊天室、博客等上）发表虚假或侮辱性的言论（以激怒别人），发恶意挑衅的帖子

trol·ley /ˈtrɒli; *NAmE* ˈtrɑːli/ *noun* **1** (*BrE*) (*NAmE* **cart**) a small vehicle with wheels that can be pushed or pulled along and is used for carrying things 手推车；手拉车：*a* ***shopping/supermarket/luggage trolley*** 购物 / 超市 / 行李手推车 ➲ VISUAL VOCAB PAGE V36 **2** (*BrE*) (*US* **cart, wagon**) a small table on very small wheels, used for carrying or serving food or drink （运或送食品、饮料的）小推车，台车：*a drinks trolley* 饮料车 ◇ *a tea trolley* 茶具车 **3** (*US*) = STREETCAR

IDM **off your ˈtrolley** (*BrE, informal*) crazy; stupid 失去理智；疯疯癫癫；愚蠢

trol·ley·bus /ˈtrɒlibʌs; *NAmE* ˈtrɑːl-/ (*BrE*) (*US* **ˈtrackless trolley**) *noun* a bus driven by electricity from a cable above the street 无轨电车

ˈtrolley car *noun* (*old-fashioned, US*) = STREETCAR

trol·leyed (*also* **trollied**) /ˈtrɒlid; *NAmE* ˈtrɑː-/ *adj.* [not usually before noun] (*BrE, informal*) extremely drunk 酩酊大醉；烂醉：*I can't remember what happened as I got* ***trollied.*** 我喝得酩酊大醉，不记得发生了什么。

trol·lop /ˈtrɒləp; *NAmE* ˈtrɑːləp/ *noun* (*old-fashioned, offensive*) **1** a woman who has many sexual partners 荡妇；娼妇 **2** a woman who is very untidy 邋遢的女人；懒婆娘

trom·bone /trɒmˈbəʊn; *NAmE* trɑːmˈboʊn/ *noun* a large BRASS musical instrument that you blow into, with a sliding tube used to change the note 长号 ➲ VISUAL VOCAB PAGE V37

trom·bon·ist /trɒmˈbəʊnɪst; *NAmE* trɑːmˈboʊ-/ *noun* a person who plays the trombone 长号手

tromp /trɒmp; *NAmE* trɑːmp/ *verb* (*NAmE, informal*) = TRAMP

trompe l'œil /ˌtrɒmp ˈlɔɪ; *NAmE* ˌtrɔːmp/ *noun* (*pl.* **trompe l'œils** /ˌtrɒmp ˈlɔɪ; *NAmE* ˌtrɔːmp/) (*from French*) a painting or design intended to make the person looking at it think that it is a real object 视幻觉画，视幻觉图（逼真和写实达到乱真程度）

troop /truːp/ *noun, verb*

■ ***noun*** **1 troops** [pl.] soldiers, especially in large groups 军队；部队；士兵：*They announced the withdrawal of 12 000 troops from the area.* 他们宣布从这个地区撤军 12 000 人。◇ *The president decided to* ***send in the troops.*** 总统决定派驻军队。◇ *Russian troops* 俄国军队 ➲ COLLOCATIONS AT WAR **2** [C] one group of soldiers, especially in tanks or on horses 连队；坦克连；骑兵连：(*figurative*) *A troop of guests was moving towards the house.* 一群客人朝那房子走去。**3** [C] a local group of SCOUTS 童子军中队 ▶ **troop** *adj.* [only before noun]：*troop movements* (= of soldiers) 部队的调动

■ ***verb*** [I] **+ adv./prep.** (used with a plural subject 与复数主语连用) to walk somewhere together as a group 成群结队而行；列队行进：*After lunch we all trooped down to the beach.* 午餐后我们都成群结队走向海滩。

troop·er /ˈtruːpə(r)/ *noun* **1** a soldier of low rank in the part of an army that uses tanks or horses 坦克兵；骑兵 **2** (*NAmE*) = STATE TROOPER IDM SEE SWEAR

troop·ship /ˈtruːpʃɪp/ *noun* a ship used for transporting soldiers 部队运输船；运兵船

trop ➲ DE TROP

trope /trəʊp; *NAmE* troʊp/ *noun* (*specialist*) **1** a word or phrase that is used in a way that is different from its usual meaning in order to create a particular mental image or effect. METAPHORS and SIMILES are tropes. 转义词语；比喻词语 **2** a theme that is important or repeated in literature, films/movies, etc. （文学、电影等中的）重要主题，一再重复的主题：*the trope of the mad scientist in horror movies* 恐怖电影中一再重复的疯狂科学家的主题

troph·ic /ˈtrəʊfɪk; ˈtrɒf-; *NAmE* ˈtroʊfɪk/ *adj.* (*biology* 生) **1** relating to feeding, and to the food necessary for growth 营养的；营养有关的 **2** (of a HORMONE or its effect 激素或其作用) causing the release of another HORMONE or other substance into the blood 引起其他激素（或物质）分泌的；有分泌作用的

ˌtrophic ˈlevel *noun* (*specialist*) each of several levels in an ECOSYSTEM (= all the plants and animals in a particular area and their relationship with their surroundings). Each level consists of living creatures that share the same function in the FOOD CHAIN and get their food from the same source. （生态系统的）营养级

trophy /ˈtrəʊfi; *NAmE* ˈtroʊfi/ *noun, adj.*

■ ***noun*** (*pl.* **-ies**) **1** an object such as a silver cup that is given as a prize for winning a competition （颁发给竞赛获胜者的）奖品，奖杯，奖座 ➲ PICTURE AT MEDAL **2 Trophy** used in the names of some competitions and races in which a trophy is given to the winner （用于竞赛或赛跑名称）奖，奖杯 **3** an object that you keep to show that you were successful in sth, especially hunting or war （尤指狩猎或战争中获得的）纪念品，战利品

■ ***adj.*** [only before noun] **~ building/art/girlfriend, etc.** (*informal, disapproving*) an impressive or beautiful thing or person that you have in order to make other people admire you 炫耀的；摆阔的；招摇的：*We don't need a trophy building for our business.* 我们的企业不需要豪华奢侈的建筑。

ˈtrophy wife *noun* (*informal, disapproving*) a young attractive woman who is married to an older man and thought of as a trophy (= sth that shows that you are successful and impresses other people) （年长男人用以炫耀的）花瓶妻子

trop·ic /ˈtrɒpɪk; *NAmE* ˈtrɑːpɪk/ *noun* **1** [C, usually sing.] one of the two imaginary lines drawn around the world 23° 26′ north (**the Tropic of Cancer**) or south (**the Tropic of Capricorn**) of the EQUATOR 回归线（北回归线称 the Tropic of Cancer，南回归线称 the Tropic of Capricorn） **2 the tropics** [pl.] the area between the two tropics, which is the hottest part of the world 热带；热带地区 SYN **torrid zone** ➲ WORDFINDER NOTE AT EARTH

trop·ic·al /ˈtrɒpɪkl; *NAmE* ˈtrɑːp-/ *adj.* coming from, found in or typical of the tropics 热带的；来自热带的；产于热带的：*tropical fish* 热带鱼 ◇ *tropical Africa* 热带非洲 ◇ *a tropical island* 位于热带地区的岛 ➲ WORDFINDER NOTE AT CLIMATE

tro·pism /ˈtrəʊpɪzəm; ˈtrɒp-; *NAmE* ˈtroʊpɪzəm/ *noun* [U] (*biology* 生) the action of a living thing turning all or part of itself in a particular direction, towards or away from sth such as a source of light （生物的）向性

the tropo·sphere /ˈtrɒpəsfɪə(r); *NAmE* ˈtroʊpəsfɪr; ˈtrɑːp-/ *noun* [sing.] (*specialist*) the lowest layer of the earth's atmosphere, between the surface of the earth and about 6–10 kilometres above the surface 对流层（大气的最低层，在地球表面和 6 至 10 公里上空之间）

trot /trɒt; *NAmE* trɑːt/ *verb, noun*

■ ***verb*** (**-tt-**) **1** [I] (of a horse or its rider 马或骑马者) to move forward at a speed that is faster than a walk and slower than a CANTER 快步；疾走；小跑 **2** [T] **~ sth (+ adv./prep.)** to ride a horse in this way 骑马小跑：*She trotted her pony around the field.* 她骑着小马绕场慢跑。**3** [I] **+ adv./prep.** (of a person or an animal 人或动物) to run or walk fast, taking short quick steps 小步快跑；碎步急行：*The children trotted into the room.* 孩子们小跑着进了房间。**4** [I] **+ adv./prep.** (*informal*) to walk or go somewhere 步行；走；到…去：*The guide led the way and we trotted along behind him.* 向导在前面带路，我们跟在他的后面走。IDM SEE HOT *adj.*

PHR V ˌ**trot sth↔ˈout** (*informal, disapproving*) to give the same excuses, facts, explanations, etc. for sth that have often been used before 重复，翻出（老一套的借口、事实、解释等）：*They trotted out the same old excuses for the lack of jobs in the area.* 他们又用那老一套的借口解释这个地区缺少就业机会的问题。

■ ***noun*** **1** [sing.] a trotting speed, taking short quick steps （指速度）慢跑，小跑，小步快跑，疾走：*The horse slowed to a trot.* 那马放慢速度在小跑。◇ *The girl* ***broke into a trot*** *and disappeared around the corner.* 那姑娘突然小步跑了起来，拐过街角不见了。 **2** [C] a period of trotting （指活动）小跑；一阵小跑

IDM **on the ˈtrot** (*BrE, informal*) **1** one after the other 接连地；接二连三；一个接着一个 **SYN** **succession**: *They've now won three games on the trot.* 他们现在已经连胜三场比赛。 **2** busy all the time 忙个不停：*I've been on the trot all day.* 我一整天忙得不可开交。

troth /trəʊθ; *NAmE* trɑːθ/ *noun* **IDM** SEE PLIGHT *v.*

Trot·sky·ist /ˈtrɒtskiɪst; *NAmE* ˈtrɑːt-/ (*also* **Trot·sky·ite** /ˈtrɒtskiaɪt; *NAmE* ˈtrɑːt-/) *noun* a supporter of the political ideas of Leon Trotsky, especially that SOCIALISM should be introduced all over the world by means of revolution 托洛茨基分子 ▸ **Trot·sky·ist** (*also* **Trot·sky·ite**) *adj.*

trot·ter /ˈtrɒtə(r); *NAmE* ˈtrɑːt-/ *noun* **1** a pig's foot, especially when cooked and eaten as food （尤指煮熟供食用的）猪蹄，猪脚 **2** a horse that has been trained to TROT fast in races （受过快步马赛训练的）快步马

trou·ba·dour /ˈtruːbədɔː(r)/ *noun* (*literary*) a writer and performer of songs or poetry (after the French travelling performers of the 11th-13th centuries) 游吟诗人（因 11-13 世纪法国的巡回表演者而得名）

trouble 🔑 /ˈtrʌbl/ *noun, verb*

■ ***noun***

• **PROBLEM/WORRY** 问题；忧虑 **1** 🔑 [U, C] a problem, worry, difficulty, etc. or a situation causing this 问题；忧虑；困难；苦恼：*We* ***have trouble*** *getting staff.* 我们在招聘雇员方面有困难。◇ *He could* ***make trouble for me*** *if he wanted to.* 他要是想找麻烦就能给我找麻烦。◇ **~ (with sb/sth)** ***The trouble with you is*** *you don't really want to work.* 你的问题在于你并不是很想工作。◇ *We've never* ***had*** *much* ***trouble with*** *vandals around here.* 我们这一带从来没有多少破坏公物的问题。◇ ***Her trouble is*** *she's incapable of making a decision.* 她的问题是自己没有能力作决定。◇ ***The trouble is*** (= what is difficult is) *there aren't any trains at that time.* 麻烦的是当时没有火车。◇ ***The only trouble is*** *we won't be here then.* 唯一的麻烦是到那时我们就不在这儿了。◇ *No, I don't know his number—I have quite enough trouble remembering my own.* 不，我不知道他的号码，我光记自己的号码就够困难的了。◇ *financial troubles* 财政困难 ◇ *She was on the phone for an hour telling me her troubles.* 她在电话上用了一个小时向我倾诉她的种种烦恼。◇ *Our troubles aren't over yet.* 我们的麻烦还没有完呢。 ➲ SEE ALSO TEETHING TROUBLES

• **ILLNESS/PAIN** 疾病；疼痛 **2** 🔑 [U] illness or pain 疾病；疼痛：*back trouble* 背痛 ◇ *I've been having trouble with my knee.* 我一直膝盖痛。 ➲ SYNONYMS AT ILLNESS

• **WITH MACHINE** 机器 **3** 🔑 [U] something that is wrong with a machine, vehicle, etc. （机器、车辆等的）故障：*mechanical trouble* 机械故障

• **DIFFICULT/VIOLENT SITUATION** 困难 / 暴力局面 **4** 🔑 [U] a situation that is difficult or dangerous; a situation in which you can be criticized or punished 困境；险境；可能受到批评（或处罚）的情形：*The company* ***ran into trouble*** *early on, when a major order was cancelled.* 这家公司早些时候有一个大订单被撤销，因此陷入了困境。◇ *A yachtsman* ***got into trouble*** *off the coast and had to be rescued.* 一个驾驶帆船的人在海上遇险须要救援。◇ *If I don't get this finished in time, I'll be* ***in trouble****.* 我如不按时把这完成就要倒霉了。◇ *He's* ***in trouble with*** *the police.* 他犯事落入了警察的手里。◇ *My brother was always* ***getting me into trouble*** *with my parents.* 以前我弟弟经常连累我遭父母的责难。 **5** 🔑 [U] an angry or violent situation 纷争；动乱；骚乱：*The police were expecting trouble after the match.* 警方预料比赛后会有骚乱。◇ *If you're not in by midnight, there'll be trouble* (= I'll be very angry). 你要是半夜前不回家，我就让你有好戏看。◇ *He had to throw out a few drunks who were causing trouble in the bar.* 他不得不轰走几个在酒吧里闹事的醉鬼。

• **EXTRA EFFORT** 额外努力 **6** 🔑 [U] **~ (to sb)** extra effort or work 额外努力（或工作）；烦扰；打扰；麻烦 **SYN** **bother**: *I don't want to* ***put you to a lot of trouble****.* 我不想给你添很多的麻烦。◇ *I'll get it if you like, that will* ***save you the trouble of*** *going out.* 如果你愿意的话我去取，省得你还得出去。◇ *Making your own yogurt* ***is more trouble than it's worth****.* 自己做酸奶很麻烦，不值得。◇ *She* ***went to a lot of trouble*** *to find the book for me.* 她不辞劳苦把书给我找到了。◇ *He thanked me for my trouble and left.* 他感谢我尽了力便走了。◇ *Nothing is ever* ***too much trouble*** *for her* (= she's always ready to help). 她从不把麻烦当回事。◇ *I can call back later—it's* ***no trouble*** (= I don't mind). 我可以过一会儿回电话，没关系。◇ *I hope the children weren't too much trouble.* 我希望这些孩子没有太烦人。

• **IN NORTHERN IRELAND** 北爱尔兰 **7** **the Troubles** [pl.] the time of political and social problems in Northern Ireland, especially after 1968, when there was violence between Catholics and Protestants about whether Northern Ireland should remain part of the UK 动乱时期（尤指 1968 年后，天主教徒和新教徒之间就北爱尔兰是否应继续附属于英国而引发的暴力冲突）

IDM **get sb into ˈtrouble** (*old-fashioned*) to make a woman who is not married pregnant 使…未婚先孕 **give (sb) (some, no, any, etc.) ˈtrouble** to cause problems or difficulties 给（或没有给）…造成麻烦（或烦恼、困难）：*My back's been giving me a lot of trouble lately.* 我的后背最近一直疼痛。◇ *The children didn't give me any trouble at all when we were out.* 我们外出时孩子们一点儿也没给我添麻烦。 **look for ˈtrouble** to behave in a way that is likely to cause an argument, violence, etc. 自找麻烦；自寻烦恼；惹是生非：*Drunken youths hang around outside looking for trouble.* 喝醉的年轻人在街头游荡滋事。 **take trouble over/with sth | take trouble doing/to do sth** to try hard to do sth well 尽心尽力地做；费力地做：*They take a lot of trouble to find the right person for the right job.* 他们竭力寻找合适的人选。 **take the trouble to do sth** to do sth even though it involves effort or difficulty 不辞辛劳地做；不厌其烦地做 **SYN** **effort**: *She didn't even take the trouble to find out how to spell my name.* 她嫌麻烦，甚至连我的姓名如何拼写都不想搞清楚。 **a trouble ˌshared is a trouble ˈhalved** (*saying*) if you talk to sb about your problems and worries, instead of keeping them to yourself, they seem less serious 诉说烦恼，一半自消（向人倾诉，愁苦就会减少） ➲ MORE AT ASK *v.*

■ ***verb***

• **MAKE SB WORRIED** 使忧虑 **1** [T] **~ sb** to make sb worried or upset 使忧虑；使烦恼；使苦恼：*What is it that's troubling you?* 是什么事使得你愁眉苦脸？

• **DISTURB** 打扰 **2** [T] (often used in polite requests 常用于客气的请求) to disturb sb because you want to ask them sth 劳驾；费神；麻烦 **SYN** **bother**: **~ sb** *Sorry to trouble you, but could you tell me the time?* 对不起打扰您一下，请问几点了？◇ **~ sb with sth** *I don't want to trouble the doctor with such a small problem.* 我不想为了这个小毛病麻烦医生。◇ (*formal*) **~ sb to do sth** *Could I trouble you to open the window, please?* 劳驾，请您把窗户打开好吗？

• **MAKE EFFORT** 努力 **3** [I] **~ to do sth** (*formal*) (usually used in negative sentences 通常用于否定句) to make an effort to do sth 费神；费事；费力 **SYN** **bother**: *He rushed into the room without troubling to knock.* 他连门也懒得敲就闯进屋去。

• **CAUSE PAIN** 造成痛苦 **4** [T] **~ sb** (of a medical problem 健康问题) to cause pain 使疼痛；折磨：*My back's been troubling me again.* 我的背又在一直疼了。 **IDM** SEE POUR

troubled /ˈtrʌbld/ *adj.* **1** (of a person 人) worried and anxious 忧虑的；烦恼的；不安的：*She looked into his troubled face.* 她仔细打量着他那张布满愁容的脸。 **2** (of a place, situation or time 地方、局势或时间) having a lot of problems 麻烦多的；混乱的；扰乱的：*a troubled*

T

marriage 坎坷的婚姻 ◇ *We live in **troubled times**.* 我们生逢乱世。

trouble·maker /ˈtrʌblmeɪkə(r)/ *noun* a person who often causes trouble, especially by involving others in arguments or encouraging them to complain about people in authority 麻烦制造者；搬弄是非者；捣乱者；闹事者

trouble·shoot /ˈtrʌblʃuːt/ *verb* **1** [I, T] ~ (**sth**) to analyse and solve serious problems for a company or other organization （为公司、机构等）分析解决（难题） **2** [I, T] ~ (**sth**) (*computing* 计) to identify and correct faults in a computer system 检修，排除（系统错误） ▶ **trouble·shoot·ing** *noun* [U]

trouble·shoot·er /ˈtrʌblʃuːtə(r)/ *noun* a person who helps to solve problems in a company or an organization （公司或机构中）解决困难者

trouble·some /ˈtrʌblsəm/ *adj.* causing trouble, pain, etc. over a long period of time 令人烦恼的；讨厌的；令人痛苦的 SYN **annoying, irritating**: *a troublesome cough/child/problem* 烦人的咳嗽；让人心烦的孩子；棘手的问题

ˈ**trouble spot** *noun* a place or country where trouble often happens, especially violence or war 不安定的地区；动乱的国家；（尤指）经常发生暴力（或战争）的地方

trough /trɒf; *NAmE* trɔːf/ *noun* **1** [C] a long narrow open container for animals to eat or drink from 槽；饲料槽；饮水槽 **2 the trough** [sing.] (*informal*) if you say that people have their noses **in the trough**, you mean that they are trying to get a lot of money for themselves 钱槽；钱眼 **3** [C] (*specialist*) a long narrow region of low air pressure between two regions of higher pressure 低压槽 ➲ COMPARE RIDGE *n.* (3) **4** [C] a period of time when the level of sth is low, especially a time when a business or the economy is not growing 低谷；（企业或经济的）低潮，萧条阶段: *There have been **peaks and troughs** in the long-term trend of unemployment.* 长期以来失业率一直时起时伏。 **5** [C] a low area between two waves in the sea, or two hills（海浪间的）波谷；（小山间的）槽谷，盆状洼地

trounce /traʊns/ *verb* ~ **sb** (*formal*) to defeat sb completely 彻底打败；击溃: *Brazil trounced Italy 5–1 in the final.* 在决赛中巴西队以 5:1 狂胜意大利队。

troupe /truːp/ *noun* [C+sing./pl. v.] a group of actors, singers, etc. who work together （演员、歌手等的）班子，表演团

trouper /ˈtruːpə(r)/ *noun* (*informal*) an actor or other person who has a lot of experience and who you can depend on 角儿；台柱子演员；可靠的人；主心骨

trou·ser /ˈtraʊzə(r)/ *verb* ~ **sth** (*BrE, informal*) to take or earn an amount of money 收受；赚得 SYN **pocket**

trou·sers 🔑 /ˈtraʊzəz; *NAmE* -zərz/ (*especially BrE*) (*NAmE usually* **pants**) *noun* [pl.] a piece of clothing that covers the body from the waist down and is divided into two parts to cover each leg separately 裤子: *a pair of grey trousers* 一条灰裤子 ◇ *I was still **in short trousers*** (= still only a boy) *at the time.* 我那时还在穿着短裤呢（还只是个小男孩）。 ◇ *He dropped his trousers.* 他脱了裤子。 ➲ VISUAL VOCAB PAGE V66 ▶ **trou·ser** *adj.* [only before noun]: *trouser pockets* 裤兜 IDM SEE CATCH *v.*, WEAR *v.*

ˈ**trouser suit** (*BrE*) (*NAmE* **pant·suit**) *noun* a woman's suit of jacket and trousers/pants （女子的）衣裤套装

trous·seau /ˈtruːsəʊ; *NAmE* -soʊ/ *noun* (*pl.* **trous·seaus** or **trous·seaux** /-səʊz; *NAmE* -soʊz/) (*old-fashioned*) the clothes and other possessions collected by a woman who is soon going to get married, to begin her married life with 嫁妆；妆奁

trout /traʊt/ *noun* **1** [C, U] (*pl.* **trout**) a common FRESHWATER fish that is used for food. There are several types of trout. 鲑；鲑鳟鱼；鳟鱼: *rainbow trout* 虹鳟 ◇ *trout fishing* 捕鳟鱼 ◇ *Shall we have trout for dinner?* 我们正餐吃鳟鱼好吗？ ➲ VISUAL VOCAB PAGE V12 **2** [C, usually sing.] (*usually* **old trout**) (*informal, disapproving*) a bad-tempered or annoying old woman 恶婆子；讨厌的老太婆

trove /trəʊv; *NAmE* troʊv/ *noun* ➲ TREASURE TROVE

trowel /ˈtraʊəl/ *noun* **1** a small garden tool with a curved blade for lifting plants and digging holes 小铲子（园艺工具） ➲ VISUAL VOCAB PAGE V20 **2** a small tool with a flat blade, used in building for spreading CEMENT or PLASTER （抹泥灰或砂浆用的）瓦刀，镘刀，抹子

IDM **lay it on with a ˈtrowel** (*informal*) to talk about sb/sth in a way that makes them or it seem much better or much worse than they really are; to exaggerate sth 过分地吹捧；言过其实；过分贬低: *He was laying the flattery on with a trowel.* 他吹捧得天花乱坠。

troy /trɔɪ/ *noun* [U] a system for measuring PRECIOUS METALS and PRECIOUS STONES 金衡制（用于称量贵重金属和宝石）

tru·ancy /ˈtruːənsi/ *noun* [U] the practice of staying away from school without permission 旷课；逃学

tru·ant /ˈtruːənt/ *noun* a child who stays away from school without permission 旷课的小学生 ▶ **tru·ant** *verb* [I]: *A number of pupils have been truanting regularly.* 不少小学生经常旷课。

IDM **play ˈtruant** (*BrE*) (*NAmE, old-fashioned, informal* **play ˈhooky**) to stay away from school without permission 旷课；逃学 ➲ COLLOCATIONS AT EDUCATION ➲ SEE ALSO BUNK OFF at BUNK *v.*, SKIVE

truce /truːs/ *noun* an agreement between enemies or opponents to stop fighting for an agreed period of time; the period of time that this lasts 停战协定；休战；停战期: *to **call/break a truce*** 宣布休战；破坏停战协定 ➲ WORDFINDER NOTE AT PEACE ➲ COLLOCATIONS AT WAR

truck 🔑 /trʌk/ *noun, verb*

■ *noun* **1** 🔑 (*especially NAmE*) (*BrE also* **lorry**) a large vehicle for carrying heavy loads by road 卡车；货运汽车: *a truck driver* 卡车司机 ➲ COLLOCATIONS AT DRIVING ➲ VISUAL VOCAB PAGE V62 **2** 🔑 (*BrE*) (*NAmE* **car**) an open railway vehicle for carrying goods or animals （铁路上运送货物或动物的）敞篷车，无盖车皮: *a cattle truck* 敞篷运牛车厢 **3** 🔑 a vehicle that is open at the back, used for carrying goods, soldiers, animals, etc.（运送货物、士兵、动物等后面敞开的）载重汽车: *a delivery/garbage/farm truck* 送货车；垃圾车；农用卡车 **4** 🔑 a vehicle for carrying things, that is pulled or pushed by hand（运送东西的）手推车，手拉车 ➲ SEE ALSO FORKLIFT TRUCK, PICKUP TRUCK at PICKUP *n.* (1), SALT TRUCK

IDM **have/want no truck with sb/sth** to refuse to deal with sb; to refuse to accept or consider sth 拒不与…打交道；拒不接受；拒不考虑: *We in this party will have no truck with illegal organizations.* 我们党的成员绝不与非法组织有来往。

■ *verb* ~ **sth** (+ **adv./prep.**) (*especially NAmE*) to take sth somewhere by truck 用卡车装运 ▶ **truck·ing** *noun* [U]: *trucking companies* 货车运输公司

truck·er /ˈtrʌkə(r)/ *noun* (*especially NAmE*) a person whose job is driving a truck 卡车司机

ˈ**truck farm** (*US*) (*BrE* ˌ**market ˈgarden**) *noun* a type of farm where vegetables are grown for sale 蔬菜农场 ▶ ˈ**truck farmer** *noun* ˈ**truck farming** *noun* [U]

truck·load /ˈtrʌkləʊd; *NAmE* -loʊd/ *noun* ~ (**of sb/sth**) the amount of sb/sth that fills a truck (often used to express the fact that an amount is large) 货车荷载；一卡车（的量）；大量

ˈ**truck stop** *noun* (*NAmE*) a place at the side of a main road where lorry/truck drivers can stop for a time and can rest, get sth to eat, etc. 长途卡车服务站；公路小餐馆 ➲ COMPARE TRANSPORT CAFE

trucu·lent /ˈtrʌkjələnt/ *adj.* (*formal, disapproving*) tending to argue or be bad-tempered; slightly aggressive 爱争吵的；粗暴的；好斗的；寻衅的 ▶ **trucu·lence** /-ləns/ *noun* [U] **trucu·lent·ly** *adv.*

trudge /trʌdʒ/ *verb, noun*

■ ***verb*** [I] to walk slowly or with heavy steps, because you are tired or carrying sth heavy（因疲劳或负重而）步履沉重地走，缓慢地走，费力地走： **+ noun** *He trudged the last two miles to the town.* 他步履艰难地走完最后两英里到了城里。◇ **+ adv./prep.** *The men trudged up the hill, laden with supplies.* 这些人背着补给品疲惫地往山上爬。

■ ***noun*** [sing.] a long tiring walk 徒步跋涉；疲惫的长途步行

true /truː/ *adj., adv., noun*

> **WORD FAMILY**
> **true** *adj.* (≠ untrue)
> **truth** *noun*
> **truthful** *adj.* (≠ untruthful)
> **truthfully** *adv.*
> **truly** *adv.*

■ ***adj.*** (**truer, tru·est**)

• **CORRECT** 正确 **1** connected with facts rather than things that have been invented or guessed 符合事实的；确实的；如实的： *Indicate whether the following statements are* ***true or false.*** 标出下列说法是对还是错。◇ *Is it true she's leaving?* 她要走是真的吗？◇ *All the rumours turned out to be true.* 所有的传闻结果都确有其事。◇ *That's not strictly* (= completely) *true.* 那不完全正确。◇ *The novel is based on* ***a true story.*** 这部小说是根据真人真事写成的。◇ *His excuse just doesn't* ***ring*** (= sound) ***true.*** 他的借口听起来就不真实。◇ *Unfortunately, these findings do not* ***hold true*** (= are not valid) *for women and children.* 遗憾的是，这些调查结果不适用于妇女和儿童。◇ *The music is dull and uninspiring, and* ***the same is true of*** *the acting.* 音乐沉闷枯燥毫不动人，表演也是。◇ *You never spoke a truer word* (= used to emphasize that you agree with what sb has just said). 你说的一点不假。 **OPP untrue**

• **REAL** 真正 **2** real or exact, especially when this is different from how sth seems 实质的，真正的（而非表面上的）： *the true face of war* (= what it is really like rather than what people think it is like) 战争的真实面目 ◇ *The true cost of these experiments to the environment will not be known for years to come.* 这些实验对环境造成的确切代价在未来数年内是看不见的。◇ *He reveals his true character to very few people.* 他没有向什么人显露过他的真实性格。 **3** [usually before noun] having the qualities or characteristics of the thing mentioned 名副其实的；真正的： *It was true love between them.* 他们是真心相爱。◇ *He's a true gentleman.* 他是个正人君子。◇ *The painting is a masterpiece in the truest sense of the word.* 这幅画是名副其实的杰作。◇ *He is credited with inventing the first true helicopter.* 他被认为是发明第一架真正的直升机的人。

• **ADMITTING FACT** 承认事实 **4** used to admit that a particular fact or statement is correct, although you think that sth else is more important （承认事实或说法正确，但有更重要的考虑）确实，的确： *It's true that he could do the job, but would he fit in with the rest of the team?* 他确实能做这项工作，但他是否能和团队其他人配合得好呢？ ◇ *'We could get it cheaper.' 'True, but would it be as good?'* "我们可以买得再便宜一点儿。" "话是这么说，但是质量是不是一样好呢？" ➲ LANGUAGE BANK AT NEVERTHELESS

• **LOYAL** 忠实 **5** showing respect and support for a particular person or belief in a way that does not change, even in different situations 忠诚的；忠心耿耿的；忠实的： *a true friend* 忠实的朋友 ◇ **~ to sb/sth** *She has always been true to herself* (= done what she thought was good, right, etc.). 她一贯坚持按自己的信念办事。◇ *He was* ***true to his word*** (= did what he promised to do). 他信守诺言。

• **ACCURATE** 精确 **6 ~ (to sth)** being an accurate version or copy of sth 精确的；与正本无异的；逼真的： *The movie is not true to the book.* 这部电影并非忠于原著。 **7** [not usually before noun] (*old-fashioned* or *literary*) straight and accurate 正而准： *His aim was true* (= he hit the target). 他瞄得很准。

IDM **come 'true** (of a hope, wish, etc. 希望、愿望等) to become reality 实现；成为现实： *Winning the medal was like* ***a dream come true.*** 获得这枚奖牌好比梦想成真。 **too ˌgood to be 'true** used to say that you cannot believe that sth is as good as it seems 好得难以令人相信： *'I'm afraid you were quoted the wrong price.' 'I thought it was too good to be true.'* "很抱歉，给你报错价了。" "我也觉得价格低得令人难以置信。" **your true 'colours** (*often disapproving*) your real character, rather than the one that you usually allow other people to see 本性；本来面目 **true to 'form** used to say that sb is behaving in the way that you expect them to behave, especially when this is annoying 跟往常一样；一如既往；合乎本性 **true to 'life** (of a book, film/movie, etc. 书、电影等) seeming real rather than invented 真实的；逼真的；惟妙惟肖；活灵活现 ➲ MORE AT RING[2] *v.*, TRIED

> ▼ **SYNONYMS 同义词辨析**
>
> **true**
>
> **right • correct**
>
> These words all describe sth that cannot be doubted as fact and includes no mistakes. 以上各词均指某事确实、真实、确切。
>
> **true** connected with facts rather than things that have been invented or guessed 指合乎事实的、确实的、如实的： *Are the following statements* ***true or false?*** 下列说法是对还是错？◇ *Is it* ***true*** *(****that****) she's leaving?* 她要走是真的吗？
>
> **right** that is true and cannot be doubted as a fact 指正确的、真实的： *I got about half the answers right.* 我的回答约有一半是正确的。◇ *What's the right time?* 现在的准确时间是几点？
>
> **correct** right according to the facts and without any mistakes 指准确无误的、正确的： *Only one of the answers is correct.* 这些答案中只有一个是正确的。◇ *Check that all the details are correct.* 检查所有这些细节是否准确无误。
>
> **RIGHT OR CORRECT?** 用 right 还是 correct?
>
> **Correct** is more formal than **right** and is more likely to be used in official or formal instructions or documents.
> * correct 较 right 正式，更多用于官方或正式的说明或文件中。
>
> **PATTERNS**
> • right/correct **about** sb/sth
> • the true/right/correct **answer**
> • the right/correct **time**

■ ***adv.*** (*old-fashioned* or *literary*)

• **STRAIGHT** 径直 **1** in a direct line 笔直地；不偏不斜地： *The arrow flew straight and true to the target.* 箭不偏不斜地朝靶子飞去。

• **CORRECTLY** 正确地 **2 speak ~** to tell the truth 直言相告；实话实说： *He had spoken truer than he knew.* 他说得比他知道的还确切。

■ ***noun***

IDM **ˌout of 'true** if an object is **out of true**, it is not straight or in the correct position 歪七扭八；位置不正；偏斜

ˌtrue-'blue *adj.* **1** (*BrE*) strongly supporting the British Conservative Party （英国）坚决支持保守党的，忠于保守党的： *true-blue Tory voters* 忠于保守党的投票人 **2** (*especially NAmE*) being a loyal supporter of a particular person, group, principle, etc.; being a typical example of sth （对人、团体、原则等）忠贞不渝的，坚定不移的；典型的；有代表性的： *a true-blue Californian* 典型的加利福尼亚人

ˌtrue-'life *adj.* [only before noun] a **true-life** story is one that actually happened rather than one that has been invented 真人真事的；确有其事的；写实的

ˌtrue 'north *noun* [U] north according to the earth's AXIS (= the imaginary line through the earth's centre from north to south) 真北（以地轴北极为正北） ➲ COMPARE MAGNETIC NORTH

truf·fle /ˈtrʌfl/ *noun* **1** an expensive type of FUNGUS that grows underground, used in cooking 块菌（生长于地下，可食用，价格昂贵） **2** a soft round sweet/candy made of chocolate 圆形巧克力软糖

trug /trʌɡ/ *noun* a shallow BASKET used for carrying garden tools, plants, etc.（装园艺用具、植物等的）浅筐

tru·ism /ˈtruːɪzəm/ *noun* a statement that is clearly true and does not therefore add anything interesting or important to a discussion 不言而喻的道理；自明之理；老生常谈

truly /ˈtruːli/ *adv.* **1** used to emphasize that a particular statement, feeling, etc. is sincere or genuine（用于说法、感觉等）真诚地，诚恳地，衷心地：*I'm truly sorry that things had to end like this.* 事情落到这样的结局，我从内心里感到歉疚。 **2** used to emphasize a particular quality（指性质）真正，确实：*a truly memorable occasion* 的确值得纪念的盛事 **3** used to emphasize that a particular description is accurate or correct（指描述）确切，准确，精确，确实：*a truly democratic system of government* 真正的民主政体 ◇ (*informal*) *Well, **really and truly**, things were better than expected.* 啊，情况的的确确比预计的要好。

IDM **yours truly 1 Yours Truly** (*NAmE, formal*) used at the end of a formal letter before you sign your name（用于正式信函末尾署名前） **2** (*informal, often humorous*) I/me 鄙人：*Steve came first, Robin second, and yours truly came last.* 史蒂夫最先，罗宾第二，鄙人最后。 ➲ MORE AT WELL *adv.*

trump /trʌmp/ *noun, verb*

■ *noun* **1** (*also* **ˈtrump card**) [C] (in some card games) a card that belongs to the SUIT (= one of the four sets in a PACK/DECK of cards) that has been chosen for a particular game to have a higher value than the other three suits（某些纸牌游戏的一张）王牌，主牌，将牌：*I played a trump and won the trick.* 我打出一张主牌，赢了那一墩。 **2 trumps** [U+sing./pl. v.] (in some card games) the SUIT that has been chosen for a particular game to have a higher value than the other three suits（某些纸牌游戏的）王牌花色，主牌花色：*What's trumps?* 王牌是什么？◇ *Clubs are trumps.* 梅花是主牌。 ➲ WORDFINDER NOTE AT CARD

IDM **ˌcome up/ˌturn up ˈtrumps** to do what is necessary to make a particular situation successful, especially when this is sudden or unexpected 打出王牌；做有助于获得（意外）成功的事：*I didn't honestly think he'd pass the exam but he came up trumps on the day.* 说实话我以为他考试及不了格，但是那天他发挥出色，考得不错。

■ *verb* **1 ~ sth (with sth)** (in some card games 某些纸牌游戏) to play a trump card that beats sb else's card 出王牌赢（牌）；出王牌压掉（他人的牌） **2 ~ sth/sb** to beat sth that sb says or does by saying or doing sth even better 赢；胜过；打败

PHR V **ˌtrump sth↔ˈup** to make up a false story about sb/sth, especially accusing them of doing sth wrong 诬陷；捏造；编造：*She was arrested on a trumped-up charge.* 她以莫须有的罪名被捕。

ˈtrump card *noun* **1** = TRUMP (1) **2** something that gives you an advantage over other people, especially when they do not know what it is and you are able to use it to surprise them 王牌；绝招；杀手锏

trump·ery /ˈtrʌmpəri/ *noun* [U] (*old-fashioned*) objects of little value 实际价值低的东西 ▶ **trump·ery** *adj.*

trum·pet /ˈtrʌmpɪt/ *noun, verb*

■ *noun* **1** a BRASS musical instrument made of a curved metal tube that you blow into, with three VALVES for changing the note 小号；喇叭 ➲ VISUAL VOCAB PAGE V37 **2** a thing shaped like a trumpet, especially the open flower of a DAFFODIL 喇叭形物；（尤指）绽开的水仙花 ➲ VISUAL VOCAB PAGE V11 IDM SEE BLOW *v.*

■ *verb* **1** [T] **~ sth (as sth)** | **+ speech** to talk about sth publicly in a proud or enthusiastic way 宣扬；鼓吹；吹嘘：*to trumpet somebody's achievements* 吹嘘某人的成就 ◇ *Their marriage was trumpeted as the wedding of the year.* 他们的联姻被宣扬成年度婚礼。 **2** [I] (especially of an ELEPHANT 尤指大象) to make a loud noise 吼叫

trum·pet·er /ˈtrʌmpɪtə(r)/ *noun* a person who plays the trumpet 号手；号兵；小号吹奏者

trun·cate /trʌŋˈkeɪt; *NAmE* ˈtrʌŋkeɪt/ *verb* [usually passive] **~ sth** (*formal*) to make sth shorter, especially by cutting off the top or end 截短，缩短，删节（尤指掐头或去尾）：*My article was published in truncated form.* 我的文章以节录的形式发表了。 ▶ **trun·ca·tion** *noun* [U, C]

trun·cheon /ˈtrʌntʃən/ *noun* (*especially BrE*) = BATON (1)

trun·dle /ˈtrʌndl/ *verb* **1** [I, T] **~ (sth) + adv./prep.** to move or roll somewhere slowly and noisily; to move sth slowly and noisily, especially sth heavy, with wheels（使缓慢、轰鸣地）移动，滚动：*A train trundled across the bridge.* 一列火车隆隆驶过大桥。 **2** [I] **+ adv./prep.** (of a person 人) to walk slowly with heavy steps 沉重缓慢地走

PHR V **ˌtrundle sth↔ˈout** (*disapproving, especially BrE*) to mention or do sth that you have often mentioned or done before 重提某事；故伎重演：*A long list of reasons was trundled out to justify their demands.* 他们重复一大串理由，说明他们的要求正当。

trunks 树干；象鼻；大箱子；男式游泳裤

trunk /trʌŋk/ *noun* **1** [C] the thick main STEM of a tree, that the branches grow from 树干 ➲ VISUAL VOCAB PAGE V10 **2** (*NAmE*) (*BrE* **boot**) [C] the space at the back of a car that you put bags, cases, etc. in（汽车后部的）行李厢 ➲ VISUAL VOCAB PAGE V56 **3** [C] the long nose of an ELEPHANT 象鼻 ➲ VISUAL VOCAB PAGE V12 **4 trunks** [pl.] = SWIMMING TRUNKS **5** [C] a large strong box with a lid used for storing or transporting clothes, books, etc. 大箱子；大衣箱 ➲ VISUAL VOCAB PAGE V69 **6** [C, usually sing.] the main part of the human body apart from the head, arms and legs（人的）躯干 ➲ SEE ALSO TORSO (1)

ˈtrunk call *noun* (*old-fashioned, BrE*) a telephone call to a place that is a long distance away but in the same country（国内）长途电话

ˈtrunk road *noun* (*BrE*) an important main road 公路干线；干道

truss /trʌs/ *noun, verb*

■ *noun* **1** a special belt with a thick piece of material, worn by sb suffering from a HERNIA in order to support the muscles 疝带（疝病患者所用） **2** a frame made of pieces of wood or metal used to support a roof, bridge, etc.（支撑屋顶、桥梁等的）桁架，构架

■ *verb* **1 ~ sb/sth (up)** to tie up sb's arms and legs so that they cannot move 把（人的双臂和双腿）捆紧，缚牢 **2 ~ sth** to tie the legs and wings of a chicken, etc. before it is cooked（在烹煮鸡等前）把腿和翅膀束紧

trust /trʌst/ *noun, verb*

■ ***noun*** **1** [U] ~ (**in sb/sth**) the belief that sb/sth is good, sincere, honest, etc. and will not try to harm or trick you 相信；信任；信赖：*Her trust in him was unfounded.* 她对他的信任毫无道理。◇ *a partnership **based on trust*** 建立在互相信任基础上的合伙关系 ◇ *It has taken years to **earn their trust**.* 花了好多年才赢得他们的信任。◇ *If you **put your trust in** me, I will not let you down.* 你要是信赖我，我就不会让你失望。◇ *She will not **betray your trust*** (= do sth that you have asked her not to do). 她不会辜负你对她的信任。◇ *He was appointed to a **position of trust*** (= a job involving a lot of responsibility, because people trust him). 他被委以重任。 **2** [C, U] (*law* 律) an arrangement by which an organization or a group of people has legal control of money or property that has been given to sb, usually until that person reaches a particular age; an amount of money or property that is controlled in this way 委托；信托；信托财产：*He **set up a trust** for his children.* 他为子女安排好了信托财产。◇ *The money will be **held in trust** until she is 18.* 这笔钱将由人代管到她 18 岁为止。◇ *Our fees depend on the value of the trust.* 我们的费用视信托金额而定。 ➲ SEE ALSO UNIT TRUST **3** [C] (*law* 律) an organization or a group of people that invests money that is given or lent to it and uses the profits to help a charity 受托基金机构；受托团体：*a charitable trust* 慈善基金机构 **4** [C] (*business* 商, *especially NAmE*) a group of companies that work together illegally to reduce competition, control prices, etc. 托拉斯（为减少竞争、操纵价格等而非法联合的企业组织）：*anti-trust laws* 反托拉斯法

IDM **in sb's 'trust | in the trust of sb** being taken care of by sb 由某人保管（或照管）：*The family pet was left in the trust of a neighbour.* 这家的宠物委托邻居代管。 **take sth on 'trust** to believe what sb says even though you do not have any proof or evidence to show that it is true 听信；轻信；贸然相信

■ ***verb*** **1** to have confidence in sb; to believe that sb is good, sincere, honest, etc. 信任；信赖；相信（某人的善良、真诚等）：**~ sb** *She trusts Alan implicitly.* 她绝对信任艾伦。◇ **~ sb to do sth** *You can trust me not to tell anyone.* 你可以相信我不会跟任何人讲。 **2 ~ sth** to believe that sth is true or correct or that you can rely on it 相信；认为可靠：*He trusted her judgement.* 他相信她的判断力。◇ *Don't trust what the newspapers say!* 别相信报纸上的话！ **3 ~ (that)...** (*formal*) to hope and expect that sth is true 想；希望；期望：*I trust (that) you have no objections to our proposals?* 我想你不反对我们的建议吧？

IDM **not trust sb an 'inch** to not trust sb at all 对…根本不相信 **trust 'you, 'him, 'her, etc. (to do sth)** (*informal*) used when sb does or says sth that you think is typical of them （认为某人言行一贯如此时说）管保，保证：*Trust John to forget Sue's birthday!* 管保约翰会把休的生日忘了！ ➲ MORE AT TRIED

PHR V **'trust in sb/sth** (*formal*) to have confidence in sb/sth; to believe that sb/sth is good and can be relied on 相信；信任；信赖：*She needs to trust more in her own abilities.* 她需要更加相信自己的能力。 **'trust to sth** [no passive] to put your confidence in sth such as luck, chance, etc. because there is nothing else to help you 依靠，依赖（运气、机会等）：*I stumbled along in the dark, trusting to luck to find the right door.* 我摸黑跌跌撞撞地往前走，希望凭运气能找对门。 **'trust sb with sth/sb** to give sth/sb to a person to take care of because you believe they would be very careful with it/them 托付；托交；把…委托给某人照管：*I'd trust her with my life.* 她是我可以性命相托的人。

trust·ee /trʌ'stiː/ *noun* **1** a person or an organization that has control of money or property that has been put into a TRUST for sb （财产的）受托人，信托机构 **2** a member of a group of people that controls the financial affairs of a charity or other organization （慈善事业或其他机构的）受托人

trustee·ship /trʌ'stiːʃɪp/ *noun* [U, C] **1** the job of being a trustee 受托人职责 **2** the responsibility for governing a particular region, given to a country by the United Nations Organization; a region that is governed by another country in this way 托管（联合国委托某一国家管理某一地区）；托管地区

▼ **SYNONYMS 同义词辨析**

trust

depend on sb/sth • rely on sb/sth • count on sb/sth • believe in sb

These words all mean to believe that sb/sth will do what you hope or expect of them or that what they tell you is correct or true. 以上各词均含相信、信任、信赖之义。

trust to believe that sb is good, honest, sincere, etc. and that they will do what you expect of them or do the right thing; to believe that sth is true or correct 指相信、信任、信赖：*You can trust me not to tell anyone.* 你可以相信我不会跟任何人讲。◇ *Don't trust what you read in the newspapers!* 别相信你在报纸上读到的！

depend on/upon sb/sth (often used with *can/cannot/could/could not*) to trust sb/sth to do what you expect or want, to do the right thing, or to be true or correct （常与 can/cannot/could/could not 连用）指相信、信赖、指望：*He was the sort of person you could depend on.* 他是你可以信赖的人。◇ *Can you depend on her version of what happened?* 你相信她对所发生事情的描述吗？

rely on/upon sb/sth (used especially with *can/cannot/could/could not* and *should/should not*) to trust sb/sth to do what you expect or want, or to be honest, correct or good enough （尤与 can/cannot/could/could not 和 should/should not 连用）指信任、信赖：*Can I rely on you to keep this secret?* 我能相信你会保守这个秘密吗？◇ *You can't rely on any figures you get from them.* 你不能相信从他们那儿得到的任何数据。

TRUST, DEPEND OR RELY ON/UPON SB/STH? 用 trust、depend 还是 rely on/upon sb/sth?

You can **trust** a person but not a thing or system. You can **trust** sb's *judgement* or *advice*, but not their support. You can **depend on** sb's *support*, but not their judgement or advice. **Rely on/upon sb/sth** is used especially with *you can/could* or *you should* to give advice or a promise.
* trust 的宾语可以是人，但不能是物或制度；trust 后还可接 sb's judgement 或 advice，但不能接 sb's support；depend on 后可跟 sb's support，但不能跟 sb's judgement 或 advice；rely on/upon sb/sth 尤与 you can/could 或 you should 连用，以给予建议或承诺：~~*I don't really rely on his judgement.*~~ ◇ *You can't really rely on his judgement.* 你不能真的相信他的判断。

count on sb/sth (often used with *can/cannot/could/could not*) to be sure that sb will do what you need them to do, or that sth will happen as you want it to happen （常与 can/cannot/could/could not 连用）指可信赖、依靠、指望（某人做某事）、确信（某事会发生）：*I'm counting on you to help me.* 我就靠你帮我啦。◇ *We can't count on the good weather lasting.* 我们不能指望这样好的天气会持久。

believe in sb to feel that you can trust sb and/or that they will be successful 指信赖、信任、相信某人会成功：*They need a leader they can believe in.* 他们需要一个可以信赖的领导。

PATTERNS

- to trust/depend on/rely on/count on sb/sth **to do sth**
- to trust/believe **in** sb/sth
- to trust/rely on **sb's advice/judgement**
- to depend on/rely on/count on **sb's support**
- to **completely** trust/depend on/rely on/believe in sb/sth

'trust fund *noun* money that is controlled for sb by an organization or a group of people 信托基金

trust·ing /'trʌstɪŋ/ *adj.* tending to believe that other people are good, honest, etc. 轻信的；轻易信赖别人的：*If you're too trusting, other people will take advantage of you.* 如果你过于轻信，其他人就会打你的主意。 ▶ **trust·ing·ly** *adv.*

T

'trust territory *noun* a region governed by the United Nations Organization or by another country that has been chosen by the United Nations Organization （联合国或其委托国家的）托管领地

trust·worthy /'trʌstwɜːði; *NAmE* -wɜːrði/ *adj.* that you can rely on to be good, honest, sincere, etc. 值得信任的；可信赖的；可靠的 **SYN** **reliable** ▸ **trust·worthi·ness** *noun* [U]

trusty /'trʌsti/ *adj., noun*

■ ***adj.*** [only before noun] (*old use* or *humorous*) that you have had a long time and have always been able to rely on （长期以来）可信任的，可信赖的；忠实的 **SYN** **reliable**: *a trusty friend* 忠实的朋友 ◇ *She spent years touring Europe with her trusty old camera.* 她带着她那架忠心耿耿的照相机在欧洲周游多年。

■ ***noun*** (*pl.* **-ies**) (*informal*) a prisoner who is given special advantages because of good behaviour 模范囚犯（由于表现好而受到优待）

truth /truːθ/ *noun* (*pl.* **truths** /truːðz/) **1** **the truth** [sing.] the true facts about sth, rather than the things that have been invented or guessed 真相；实情；事实；真实情况： *Do you think she's **telling the truth**?* 你认为她在讲实话吗？ ◇ *We are determined to get at* (= discover) *the truth.* 我们决心查出真相。◇ ***The truth** (**of the matter**) **is** we can't afford to keep all the staff on.* 实际情况是我们无力继续聘用所有的职员。 ◇ *I don't think you are telling me **the whole truth** about what happened.* 我认为你没有把事情的全部真相都告诉我。 **2** [U] the quality or state of being based on fact 真实；真实性： *There is no truth in the rumours.* 这些谣言毫无根据。 ◇ *There is not **a grain of truth** in what she says.* 她说的没有一句真话。 **OPP** **falsity** **3** [C] a fact that is believed by most people to be true 真理： *universal truths* 普遍真理 ◇ *She was forced to face up to a few unwelcome truths about her family.* 她不得不正视有关她家的几桩尴尬事。 ➲ COMPARE UNTRUTH (1) ➲ SEE ALSO HALF-TRUTH, HOME TRUTH

IDM **if** (**the**) **ˌtruth be 'known/'told** used to tell sb the true facts about a situation, especially when these are not known by other people （用于说出真相）说实话，说真的，老实说 **in 'truth** (*formal*) used to emphasize the true facts about a situation （强调真实情况）的确，事实上： *She laughed and chatted but was, in truth, not having much fun.* 她虽然又是笑又是侃，但实际上玩得并不开心。 **ˌnothing could be ˌfurther from the 'truth** used to say that a fact or comment is completely false 大错特错；假到极点；荒谬绝伦 **to tell** (**you**) **the 'truth** (*informal*) used when admitting sth （承认某事）说实话，老实说： *To tell you the truth, I'll be glad to get home.* 说实话，能回家我会很高兴。 **ˌtruth is stranger than 'fiction** (*saying*) used to say that things that actually happen are often more surprising than stories that are invented 现实比虚构更不可思议 (**the**) **ˌtruth will 'out** (*saying*) used to say that people will find out the true facts about a situation even if you try to keep them secret 真相终将大白于天下；纸包不住火；终会水落石出 ➲ MORE AT BEND *v.*, ECONOMICAL, MOMENT

'truth drug *noun* a drug that is believed to be able to put sb into a state where they will answer questions with the truth 吐真药；坦白药

truth·ful /'truːθfl/ *adj.* **1** ~ (**about sth**) (of a person 人) saying only what is true 诚实；讲真话；坦率 **SYN** **honest**: *They were less than truthful about their part in the crime.* 关于自己在这次犯罪中所起的作用，他们讲的绝非实情。 ◇ *Are you being completely truthful with me?* 你跟我讲的全是真话吗？ **2** (of a statement 陈述) giving the true facts about sth 真实的；如实的： *a truthful answer* 坦诚的回答 **OPP** **untruthful** ▸ **truth·ful·ly** /-fəli/ *adv.* : *She answered all their questions truthfully.* 她如实回答了他们的所有问题。 **truth·ful·ness** *noun* [U]

try /traɪ/ *verb, noun*

■ ***verb*** (**tries, try·ing, tried, tried**) **1** [I, T] to make an attempt or effort to do or get sth 试图；想要；设法；努力： *I don't know if I can come but I'll try.* 我不知道是否能来，但我尽可能来。 ◇ **~ to do sth** *What are you trying to do?* 你想要做什么？ ◇ *I tried hard not to laugh.* 我强忍住不笑出来。 ◇ **~ your best/hardest** (**to do sth**) *She tried her best to solve the problem.* 她尽了最大的努力解决这个问题。 ◇ *Just try your hardest.* 请尽力而为吧。 **HELP** In spoken English **try** can be used with **and** plus another verb, instead of with **to** and the infinitive. 口语中，try 可以和 and 加另一动词连用，而不和 to 及动词不定式连用： *I'll try and get you a new one tomorrow.* 我明天会设法给你个新的。 ◇ *Try and finish quickly.* 尽快完成。 In this structure, only the form **try** can be used, not **tries**, **trying** or **tried**. 在这一结构中，只能用 try 的形式，而不能用 tries、trying 或 tried。 ➲ MORE LIKE THIS 26, page R28 **2** [T] to use, do or test sth in order to see if it is good, suitable, etc. 试；试用；试做；试验： **~ sth** *Have you tried this new coffee? It's very good.* 你尝过这种新咖啡吗？好极啦。 ◇ *'Would you like to try some raw fish?' 'Why not? **I'll try anything once!**'* "你想尝点儿生鱼片吗？" "好哇，我什么都想尝一点儿！" ◇ *Have you ever tried windsurfing?* 你玩过帆板运动吗？ ◇ ***Try** these shoes **for size**—they should fit you.* 试试这双鞋的大小，你穿应该合脚。 ◇ *She tried the door, but it was locked.* 她推了推那扇门，但门锁着。 ◇ **~ doing sth** *John isn't here. Try phoning his home number.* 约翰不在这儿。给他家里打电话试试看。 **HELP** Notice the difference between **try to do sth** and **try doing sth**: *'You should try to eat more fruit'* means 'You should make an effort to eat more fruit.'; *'You should try eating more fruit'* means 'You should see if eating more fruit will help you' (to feel better, for example). 注意 try to do sth 和 try doing sth 之间的区别：You should try to eat more fruit 的意思是"你应该尽量多吃些水果"；You should try eating more fruit 的意思是"你应该试试多吃些水果（看看身体是不是会好些）"。 **3** [T] to examine evidence in court and decide whether sb is innocent or guilty 审理；审讯；审判： **~ sb** (**for sth**) *He was tried for murder.* 他因谋杀罪而受审。◇ **~ sth** *The case was tried before a jury.* 此案是由陪审团参加审理的。

IDM **ˌnot for want/lack of 'trying** used to say that although sb has not succeeded in sth, they have tried very hard 并非努力不够；已经尽力了： *They haven't won a game yet, but it isn't for want of trying.* 他们还没赢过一场比赛，但并不是由于拼劲不足。 **try your 'hand** (**at sth**) to do sth such as an activity or a sport for the first time 初试身手 **ˌtry it 'on** (**with sb**) (*BrE, informal, disapproving*) **1** to behave badly towards sb or try to get sth from them, even though you know this will make them angry 对…粗野无礼；要弄；向…行骗： *Children often try it on with new teachers.* 儿童经常设法戏弄新来的老师。 **2** to try to start a sexual relationship with sb 试图与（某人）发生性关系 **try your 'luck** (**at sth**) to do sth that involves risk or luck, hoping to succeed 碰运气： *My grandparents emigrated to Canada to try their luck there.* 我的祖父母移民到加拿大去碰碰运气。 **try sb's 'patience** to make sb feel impatient 使忍无可忍；使不耐烦 ➲ MORE AT DAMNEDEST, LEVEL *adj.*, THING

PHR V **'try for sth** to make an attempt to get or win sth 试图获得；力争赢得 **ˌtry sth↔'on** to put on a piece of clothing to see if it fits and how it looks 试穿（衣物）： *Try the shoes on before you buy them.* 鞋子要先穿上试一试再买。 **ˌtry 'out for sth** (*especially NAmE*) to compete for a position or place in sth, or to be a member of a team 参加…选拔（或试演）： *She's trying out for the school play.* 她正在参加学校戏剧演员甄选。 ➲ RELATED NOUN TRY-OUT (2) **ˌtry sb/sth↔'out** (**on sb**) to test or use sb/sth in order to see how good or effective they are 试用（某人）；测试；试验： *They're trying out a new presenter for the show.* 他们正在为这个节目试用一名新的主持人。 ➲ RELATED NOUN TRYOUT (1)

■ ***noun*** (*pl.* **tries**) **1** [usually sing.] an act of trying to do sth 尝试；试图；努力 **SYN** **attempt**: *I doubt they'll be able to help but it's **worth a try*** (= worth asking them). 我不敢肯定他们能够帮得上忙，但不妨试一试。 ◇ **~** (**at sth/at doing sth**) *Why don't you **have a try** at convincing him?* 为什么你不试试说服他？ ◇ (*NAmE*) *The US negotiators decided to **make another try at** reaching a settlement.* 美国的谈判者决定再作一番努力，力争达成和解。 ◇ *I don't think I'll be any good at tennis, but I'll **give it a try**.* 我不认为我有

打网球的特长，但是我会试一试。◇ (*informal*) *'What's that behind you?' '**Nice try** (= at making me turn round), but you'll have to do better than that!'* "看你身后是什么？""好个鬼花招，不过你要的手法还不够高明！" **2** (in RUGBY 橄榄球) an act of scoring points by touching the ground behind your opponents' GOAL LINE with the ball 在对方球门线后带球触地；持球触地得分：*to score a try* 带球触地得分

ˌ**try-and-ˈbuy** *adj.* [only before noun] (especially of computer programs and equipment 尤指计算机程序和设备) that can be used free for a limited period of time, during which you can decide whether you want to buy it or not 先试后买的

try·ing /ˈtraɪɪŋ/ *adj.* annoying or difficult to deal with 令人厌烦的；难对付的：*These are trying times for all of us.* 对我们所有人来说，这是最难熬的时期。

try·out /ˈtraɪaʊt/ *noun* **1** an act of testing how good or effective sb/sth is before deciding whether to use them in the future 检查衡量潜力；考核潜力 **2** (*NAmE*) (*BrE* **trial**) a competition or series of tests to find the best players for a sports team or an important event 预赛；选拔赛

tryst /trɪst/ *noun* (*literary* or *humorous*) a secret meeting between lovers（情人的）约会，幽会

tsar (*also* **tzar**, **czar**) /zɑː(r)/ *noun* **1** the title of the EMPEROR of Russia in the past 沙皇（旧时俄国皇帝的称号）：*Tsar Nicholas II* 沙皇尼古拉二世 **2** (in compounds 构成复合词) (*informal*) an official whose job is to advise the government on policy in a particular area（在某领域向政府提供有关政策的建议的）政府顾问，政府高级官员：(*BrE*) *a drugs tsar* 毒品问题顾问 ◇ (*NAmE*) *a drug tsar* 毒品问题顾问

tsar·ina (*also* **tzar·ina**, **czar·ina**) /zɑːˈriːnə/ *noun* the title of the EMPRESS of Russia in the past （旧时俄国的）女沙皇，沙皇皇后

tsar·ism (*also* **tzar·ism**, **czar·ism**) /ˈzɑːrɪzəm/ *noun* [U] the Russian system of government by a tsar, which existed before 1917 （1917 年之前的）俄国沙皇政体 ▸ **tsar·ist** (*also* **tzar·ist**, **czar·ist**) *noun, adj.*

tsetse fly /ˈtsetsi flaɪ/ *noun* an African fly that bites humans and animals and sucks their blood and can spread a disease called SLEEPING SICKNESS 舌蝇，采采蝇（非洲苍蝇，叮咬人和动物，吸血传染昏睡病）

ˈ**T-shirt** (*also* ˈ**tee shirt**) *noun* an informal shirt with short sleeves and no COLLAR or buttons, or just a few buttons at the top * T 恤衫；短袖汗衫 ➲ VISUAL VOCAB PAGE V68

tsk tsk /ˌtəsk ˈtəsk/ *exclamation* used in writing to represent the sound you make with your tongue when you disapprove of something（用于书写，表示不赞成）啧啧：*So you were out drinking again last night were you? Tsk tsk!* 这么说你昨晚又外出喝酒了，对吗？啧啧！ ➲ MORE LIKE THIS 2, page R25

tsotsi /ˈtsɒtsi; *NAmE* ˈtsɑːt-/ *noun* (*SAfrE*) a young black criminal 黑人少年犯

Tsotsi·taal /ˈtsɒtsitɑːl; *NAmE* ˈtsɑːt-/ *noun* [U] (*SAfrE*) a simple form of language that includes words from Afrikaans and African languages, used especially between young black people in cities or TOWNSHIPS 南非塔尔语（包含南非荷兰语和非洲语言中一些词汇的简单语言，尤用于非洲城镇年轻黑人之间）

tsp *abbr.* (*pl.* **tsp** or **tsps**) TEASPOON (2) 一茶匙（的量）：*1 tsp chilli powder* 一茶匙辣椒粉

ˈ**T-square** *noun* a plastic or metal instrument in the shape of a T for drawing or measuring RIGHT ANGLES (= of 90°) 丁字尺；曲尺

tsu·nami /tsuːˈnɑːmi/ *noun* (*from Japanese*) an extremely large wave in the sea caused, for example, by an EARTHQUAKE 海啸 SYN **tidal wave** ➲ WORDFINDER NOTE AT DISASTER

TTYL (*also* **ttyl**) *abbr.* (*informal*) (used especially at the end of a text message or email) talk to you later 以后再聊（全写为 talk to you later）：*OK, I've gotta fly. Bye. TTYL.* 好了，我得赶紧走了。再见。回头再聊。

tub /tʌb/ *noun* **1** a large round container without a lid, used for washing clothes in, growing plants in, etc. 盆；桶：*There were tubs of flowers on the balcony.* 阳台上有一盆盆的花。 **2** a small wide, usually round, plastic or paper container with a lid, used for food, etc.（塑料或纸的）饭盒，食品盒：*a tub of margarine* 一盒人造黄油 ➲ VISUAL VOCAB PAGE V36 **3** (*informal, especially NAmE*) = BATHTUB：*They found her lying in the tub.* 他们发现她躺在浴缸里。 ➲ SEE ALSO HOT TUB

tuba /ˈtjuːbə; *NAmE* ˈtuːbə/ *noun* a large BRASS musical instrument that you play by blowing, and that produces low notes 大号（低音铜管乐器） ➲ VISUAL VOCAB PAGE V37

tubal /ˈtjuːbl; *NAmE* ˈtuːbl/ *adj.* (*medical* 医) connected with the FALLOPIAN TUBES 输卵管的：*a tubal pregnancy* 输卵管妊娠

tubby /ˈtʌbi/ *adj.* (*informal*) (of a person 人) short and slightly fat 矮胖的 SYN **stout**

tube 🔑 /tjuːb; *NAmE* tuːb/ *noun*

• **PIPE** 管 **1** 🔑 [C] a long hollow pipe made of metal, plastic, rubber, etc., through which liquids or gases move from one place to another （金属、塑料、橡皮等制成的）管，管子 ➲ SEE ALSO CATHODE RAY TUBE, INNER TUBE, TEST TUBE **2** 🔑 [C] a hollow object in the shape of a pipe or tube 管状物：*a bike's inner tube* 自行车内胎 ◇ *the cardboard tube from the centre of a toilet roll* 手纸卷中央的硬纸管

• **CONTAINER** 容器 **3** 🔑 [C] ~ (**of sth**) a long narrow container made of soft metal or plastic, with a lid, used for holding thick liquids that can be squeezed out of it（由软金属或塑料制成的带盖的、盛膏状物的）软管：*a tube of toothpaste* 一管牙膏 ➲ VISUAL VOCAB PAGE V36 **4** (*AustralE, informal*) a can of beer 一罐啤酒：*a tube of lager* 一罐拉格啤酒

• **PART OF BODY** 身体部位 **5** [C] a part inside the body that is shaped like a tube and through which air, liquid, etc. passes 管状器官；管；道：*bronchial tubes* 支气管 ➲ VISUAL VOCAB PAGE V64 ➲ SEE ALSO FALLOPIAN TUBE

• **UNDERGROUND RAILWAY** 地下铁道 **6** (*also* **The Tube™**) [sing.] (*BrE*) the underground railway system in London 伦敦地下铁道：*a **tube station/train*** 地铁车站 / 列车 ◇ *We came **by tube**.* 我们乘地铁来的。 ➲ NOTE AT UNDERGROUND

• **TELEVISION** 电视 **7 the tube** [sing.] (*NAmE, informal*) the television 电视；电视机

• **IN EAR** 耳朵 **8** (*NAmE*) (*BrE* **grom·met**) [C] a small tube placed in a child's ear in order to DRAIN liquid from it 鼓室通气管；中耳引流管

IDM **go down the ˈtube/ˈtubes** (*informal*) (of a plan, company, situation, etc. 计划、公司、情况等) to fail 失败；落空；完蛋；吹了：*The education system is going down the tubes.* 这种教育体系就要垮台了。

tuber /ˈtjuːbə(r); *NAmE* ˈtuː-/ *noun* the short thick round part of an underground STEM or root of some plants, such as potatoes, which stores food and from which new plants grow 块茎（某些植物的肉质地下茎）；块根 ▸ **tu·ber·ous** /ˈtjuːbərəs; *NAmE* ˈtuː-/ *adj.*

tu·ber·cle /ˈtjuːbəkl; *NAmE* ˈtuːb-/ *noun* **1** (*anatomy* 解, *biology* 生) a small round lump, especially on a bone or on the surface of an animal or plant 结节；疣粒；小块茎 **2** (*medical* 医) a small swollen area in the lung caused by TUBERCULOSIS （肺）结核结节

tu·ber·cu·losis /tjuːˌbɜːkjuˈləʊsɪs; *NAmE* tuːˌbɜːrkjəˈloʊsɪs/ *noun* [U] (*abbr.* **TB**) a serious infectious disease in which swellings appear on the lungs and other parts of the body 结核病 ▸ **tu·ber·cu·lar** /tjuːˈbɜːkjələ(r); *NAmE* tuːˈbɜːrk-/ *adj.*：*a tubercular infection* 结核病感染

ˈ**tube top** (*NAmE*) (*BrE* ˈ**boob tube**) *noun* a piece of women's clothing that is made of cloth that stretches and covers the chest（女人的）紧身平口胸衣

'tube well *noun* a pipe with holes in the sides near the end, that is put into the ground and used with a PUMP operated by hand to bring water up from under the ground 管井

tub·ing /'tju:bɪŋ; *NAmE* 'tu:bɪŋ/ *noun* [U] metal, plastic, etc. in the shape of a tube 管；管状物；金属管；塑料管：*a length of copper tubing* 一截铜管 ➲ VISUAL VOCAB PAGE V72

'tub-thumping *noun* [U] (*BrE, disapproving*) the act of giving your opinions about sth in a loud and aggressive way 咄咄逼人的演讲；大吹大擂的宣扬 ▶ **'tub-thumping** *adj.* [only before noun]

tu·bu·lar /'tju:bjələ(r); *NAmE* 'tu:-/ *adj.* **1** made of tubes or of parts that are shaped like tubes 管子构成的；有管状部分的：*a tubular metal chair* 用金属管做的椅子 **2** shaped like a tube 管状的

ˌtubular 'bells *noun* [pl.] a musical instrument which sounds like a set of bells, consisting of a row of hanging metal tubes that are hit with a stick 管钟（打击乐器，由一排悬挂的金属管组成）

TUC /ˌti: ju: 'si:/ *abbr.* Trades Union Congress (an organization to which many British trade/labor unions belong) 英国职工大会（统辖英国多个工会）

tuck /tʌk/ *verb, noun*

■ *verb* **1 ~ sth + adv./prep.** to push, fold or turn the ends or edges of clothes, paper, etc. so that they are held in place or look neat 把（衣服、纸张等的边缘）塞进，折叠，卷起：*She tucked up her skirt and waded into the river.* 她撩起裙子蹚水走进河里。◇ *The sheets should be tucked in neatly* (= around the bed). 床单的四边应整整齐齐地掖在褥垫下面。◇ *Tuck the flap of the envelope in.* 把信封的口盖塞进信封里。 **2 ~ sth + adv./prep.** to put sth into a small space, especially to hide it or keep it safe or comfortable 把…塞进狭窄的空间；把…藏入；收藏：*She tucked her hair (up) under her cap.* 她把头发拢起来塞进帽子里。◇ *He sat with his legs tucked up under him.* 他盘着腿坐着。◇ *The letter had been tucked under a pile of papers.* 那封信压在了一摞文件下面。 **3 ~ sth + adv./prep.** to cover sb with sth so that they are warm and comfortable 用…盖住；用…围紧；用…裹严：*She tucked a blanket around his legs.* 她拿一条毯子把他的双腿裹好。

PHR V **ˌtuck sth↔a'way 1 be tucked away** to be located in a quiet place, where not many people go 坐落在，位于（僻静的地方）：*The shop is tucked away down a backstreet.* 这家店铺位于一条僻静的小巷。 **2** to hide sth somewhere or keep it in a safe place 收藏起；使隐藏：*She kept his letters tucked away in a drawer.* 她把他的来信收藏在抽屉里。◇ *They have thousands of pounds tucked away in a savings account.* 他们把几千英镑存在一个储蓄账户上。 **3** (*BrE, informal*) to eat a lot of food 大吃；拼命吃；暴食 **ˌtuck sb 'in/'up** to make sb feel comfortable in bed by pulling the covers up around them 把…的被子掖好：*I tucked the children in and said goodnight.* 我给孩子们盖好被子说晚安。 **ˌtuck 'in | ˌtuck 'into sth** (*BrE, informal*) to eat a lot of food, especially when it is done quickly and with enthusiasm 痛快地吃；狼吞虎咽地吃：*Come on, tuck in everyone!* 来呀，大家痛痛快快地吃吧！◇ *He was tucking into a huge plateful of pasta.* 他在狼吞虎咽地吃一大盘意大利面。

■ *noun* **1** [C] a fold that is sewn into a piece of clothing or cloth, either for decoration or to change the shape of it （衣服或织物的）褶，打褶 **2** [C] (*informal*) a medical operation in which skin and/or fat is removed to make sb look younger or thinner 去赘皮手术；减肥手术 **3** [U] (*old-fashioned, BrE, informal*) food, especially sweets, etc. eaten by children at school 食物，零食（尤指儿童在学校吃的糖果等）

tuck·er /'tʌkə(r)/ *noun* [U] (*AustralE, NZE, informal*) food 食物 **IDM** SEE BIB

Tudor /'tju:də(r); *NAmE* 'tu:-/ *adj.* connected with the time when kings and queens from the Tudor family ruled England (1485–1603) （英格兰）都铎王朝时代的：*Tudor architecture* 都铎式建筑

Tues·day 🔑 /'tju:zdeɪ; -di; *NAmE* 'tu:-/ *noun* [C, U] (*abbr.* **Tue.**, **Tues.**) the day of the week after Monday and before Wednesday 星期二 **HELP** To see how **Tuesday** is used, look at the examples at **Monday**. * Tuesday 的用法见词条 Monday 下的示例。 **ORIGIN** Originally translated from the Latin for 'day of Mars' *dies Marti* and named after the Germanic god *Tiw*. 译自拉丁文 dies Marti，原意为 day of Mars（战神日），以日耳曼神 Tiw（蒂乌）命名。

tuft /tʌft/ *noun* **~ (of sth)** a number of pieces of hair, grass, etc. growing or held closely together at the base （在底部丛生或聚集的）一绺毛发，一丛草

tuft·ed /'tʌftɪd/ *adj.* [usually before noun] having a tuft or tufts; growing in tufts 成束的；成簇的；丛生的；簇生的：*a tufted carpet* 簇绒地毯 ◇ *a tufted duck* 冠凫

tug /tʌg/ *verb, noun*

■ *verb* **(-gg-) 1** [I, T] to pull sth hard, often several times （常为几次用力）拉，拖，拽：**~ (at/on sth)** *She tugged at his sleeve to get his attention.* 她拽了拽他的袖子引起他的注意。◇ (*figurative*) *a sad story that **tugs at your heart-strings*** (= makes you feel sad) 令人心酸的故事 ◇ **~ sth** *The baby was tugging her hair.* 婴儿直扯她的头发。◇ **~ sth + adj.** *He tugged the door open.* 他用力拉开了门。 **2** [T] **~ sth + adv./prep.** to pull sth hard in a particular direction （朝某一方向用力）拉，拖，拽：*He tugged the hat down over his head.* 他把帽子往下拉了拉遮住脸。 ➲ SYNONYMS AT PULL **IDM** SEE FORELOCK

■ *noun* **1** (*also* **tug·boat** /'tʌgbəʊt; *NAmE* -boʊt/) a small powerful boat for pulling ships, especially into a HARBOUR or up a river 拖船 ➲ VISUAL VOCAB PAGE V59 **2** a sudden hard pull （突然的）猛拉，猛拽：*I felt a tug at my sleeve.* 我觉得有人用力拽了一下我的袖子。◇ *She gave her sister's hair a sharp tug.* 她猛地使劲扯了一下她姐姐的头发。 **3** [usually sing.] a sudden strong emotional feeling 一股强烈的感情：*a tug of attraction* 一阵强烈的吸引

ˌtug of 'love *noun* [sing.] (*BrE, informal*) a situation in which a child's parents are divorced or no longer living together and are fighting over who the child should live with （离异或分居父母对孩子的）监护权争夺

ˌtug of 'war *noun* [sing., U] **1** a sporting event in which two teams pull at opposite ends of a rope until one team drags the other over a line on the ground 拔河 **2** a situation in which two people or groups try very hard to get or keep the same thing （两人或两组的）激烈争夺

tu·ition /tju'ɪʃn; *NAmE* tu-/ *noun* [U] **1 ~ (in sth)** (*formal*) the act of teaching sth, especially to one person or to people in small groups （尤指对个人或小组的）教学，讲授，指导：*She received private tuition in French.* 她由私人教授法语。 ➲ COLLOCATIONS AT EDUCATION **2** (*also* **tu'ition fees** [pl.]) the money that you pay to be taught, especially in a college or university （尤指大专院校的）学费

tuk-tuk (*also* **tuk tuk**) /'tʊk tʊk/ *noun* (in some countries) a vehicle with three wheels and an engine, typically with open sides, that is used as a taxi （某些国家的）嘟嘟车，三轮出租摩托车

tulip /'tju:lɪp; *NAmE* 'tu:-/ *noun* a large, brightly coloured spring flower, shaped like a cup, on a tall STEM 郁金香 ➲ VISUAL VOCAB PAGE V11

tulle /tju:l; *NAmE* tu:l/ *noun* [U] a type of soft fine cloth made of silk, NYLON, etc. and full of very small holes, used especially for making VEILS and dresses 绢网，丝网眼纱，网眼织物（尤用以制作面纱或连衣裙）

tum /tʌm/ *noun* (*BrE, informal*) a person's stomach or the area around the stomach 胃；肚子

tum·ble /'tʌmbl/ *verb, noun*

■ *verb* **1** [I, T] **~ (sb/sth) + adv./prep.** to fall downwards, often hitting the ground several times, but usually without serious injury; to make sb/sth fall in this way （使）跌倒，摔倒，滚落，翻滚下来：*He slipped and tumbled down the stairs.* 他脚一滑滚下了楼梯。 **2** [I] **~ (down)** to fall suddenly and in a dramatic way 倒塌；坍塌：*The scaffolding came tumbling down.* 脚手架突然倒塌。◇ (*figurative*) *World records tumbled at the last Olympics.* 在上届奥林匹克运动会上世界纪录被大幅刷新。➲ SEE ALSO TUMBLEDOWN **3** [I] to fall rapidly in value or amount（价格或数量）暴跌，骤降：*The price of oil is still tumbling.* 油价仍在急遽下跌。 **4** [I] **+ adv./prep.** to move or fall somewhere in a relaxed, uncontrolled, or noisy way 翻滚；打滚；翻腾；轻松地倒下：*A group of noisy children tumbled out of the bus.* 一群吵吵嚷嚷的孩子一窝蜂地下了公共汽车。◇ *Thick golden curls tumbled down over her shoulders.* 厚厚的金色鬈发垂在她的肩上。 **5** [I] to perform ACROBATICS on the floor, especially SOMERSAULTS (= a jump in which you turn over completely in the air) 表演杂技；翻跟头；（尤指）做空翻动作

PHR V **ˈtumble to sth/sb** (*BrE, informal*) to suddenly understand sth or be aware of sth 顿悟；突然意识到

■ ***noun*** **1** [C, usually sing.] a sudden fall 跌倒；滚落；暴跌：*The jockey **took a nasty tumble** at the third fence.* 骑师在第三道栅栏处给重重摔下马来。◇ *Share prices **took a sharp tumble** following news of the merger.* 合并消息传出，股价随即暴跌。➲ SEE ALSO ROUGH AND TUMBLE **2** [sing.] **~ (of sth)** an untidy group of things 混乱的一堆；杂乱不堪的一团：*a tumble of blond curls* 蓬乱的金色鬈发

tumble·down /ˈtʌmbldaʊn/ *adj.* [usually before noun] (of a building 建筑物) old and in a poor condition so that it looks as if it is falling down 破败不堪的；摇摇欲坠的 **SYN** **dilapidated**

ˌtumble ˈdryer (*also* **ˌtumble-ˈdrier**) (*both BrE*) *noun* a machine that uses hot air to dry clothes after they have been washed 滚筒式（衣服）烘干机 ➲ COMPARE SPIN DRYER

tum·bler /ˈtʌmblə(r)/ *noun* **1** a glass for drinking out of, with a flat bottom, straight sides and no handle or STEM（无柄无脚、平底直壁的）玻璃杯 ➲ VISUAL VOCAB PAGE V23 **2** (*also* **tum·bler·ful** /-fʊl/) the amount held by a tumbler 一平底玻璃杯（的量） **3** (*old-fashioned*) an ACROBAT who performs SOMERSAULTS (= a jump in which you turn over completely in the air) 翻筋斗杂技演员

tumble·weed /ˈtʌmblwiːd/ *noun* [U] a plant that grows like a bush in the desert areas of N America and Australia. In the autumn/fall, it breaks off just above the ground and is blown around like a ball by the wind. 风滚草（生长于北美和澳洲沙漠地区，秋季在地面处折落，随风像球一样到处滚动）

tum·bril /ˈtʌmbrəl/ *noun* an open vehicle used for taking people to their deaths at the GUILLOTINE during the French Revolution（法国大革命期间押送囚犯去断头台的）死囚车

tu·mes·cent /tjuːˈmesnt; *NAmE* tuː-/ *adj.* (*formal*) (especially of parts of the body 尤指身体部位) larger than normal, especially as a result of sexual excitement（尤指由于性冲动而）胀大的 **SYN** **swollen** ▶ **tu·mes·cence** /-sns/ *noun* [U]

tummy /ˈtʌmi/ *noun* (*pl.* **-ies**) (*informal*) (used especially by children or when speaking to children 尤为儿语或对儿童说话时用) the stomach or the area around the stomach 胃；肚子：*Mum, my tummy hurts.* 妈妈，我肚子痛。◇ *to have (a) tummy ache* 肚子痛 ◇ *a **tummy bug/upset*** (= an illness when you feel sick or VOMIT) 反胃

ˈtummy button *noun* (*BrE, informal*) = NAVEL

tu·mour (*especially US* **tu·mor**) /ˈtjuːmə(r); *NAmE* ˈtuː-/ *noun* a mass of cells growing in or on a part of the body where they should not, usually causing medical problems 瘤；肿瘤；肿块：*a brain tumour* 脑瘤 ◇ *a **benign/malignant*** (= harmless/harmful) *tumour* 良性 / 恶性肿瘤

tu·mult /ˈtjuːmʌlt; *NAmE* ˈtuː-/ *noun* [U, C, usually sing.] (*formal*) **1** a confused situation in which there is usually a lot of noise and excitement, often involving large numbers of people 骚乱；骚动；混乱；喧哗 **2** a state in which your thoughts or feelings are confused 心烦意乱；思绪不宁

tu·mul·tu·ous /tjuːˈmʌltʃuəs; *NAmE* tuː-/ *adj.* [usually before noun] **1** very loud; involving strong feelings, especially feelings of approval 嘈杂的；喧嚣的；热烈的；欢腾的：*tumultuous applause* 热烈的欢呼声 ◇ *a **tumultuous reception/welcome*** 热情的接待；热烈的欢迎 **2** involving a lot of change and confusion and/or violence 动荡的；动乱的；狂暴的 **SYN** **tempestuous**：*the tumultuous years of the English Civil War* 英国内战的动乱年代

tu·mu·lus /ˈtjuːmjələs; *NAmE* ˈtuː-/ *noun* (*pl.* **tu·muli** /-laɪ/) (*specialist*) a large pile of earth built over the grave of an important person in ancient times 冢；（古墓的）坟头

tun /tʌn/ *noun* (*old-fashioned*) a large round wooden container for beer, wine, etc. 大酒桶；大啤酒桶 **SYN** **barrel**

tuna /ˈtjuːnə; *NAmE* ˈtuːnə/ *noun* [C, U] (*pl.* **tuna** or **tunas**) (*also* **ˈtuna fish**) (*BrE also, less frequent* **tunny**) a large sea fish that is used for food 金枪鱼：*fishing for tuna* 捕金枪鱼 ◇ *tuna steaks* 金枪鱼排 ◇ *a tin/can of tuna in vegetable oil* 一罐植物油浸金枪鱼罐头

tun·dra /ˈtʌndrə/ *noun* [U] the large flat Arctic regions of northern Europe, Asia and N America where no trees grow and where the soil below the surface of the ground is always frozen 冻原，苔原（树木不生，底土常年冰冻的北极地区）

tune 🔑 /tjuːn; *NAmE* tuːn/ *noun, verb*

■ ***noun*** 🔑 [C] a series of musical notes that are sung or played in a particular order to form a piece of music 曲调；曲子：*He was humming a familiar tune.* 他低声哼着一支熟悉的小曲。◇ *I don't know the title but I recognize the tune.* 我不知道曲名，但听得出这曲调。◇ *It was a catchy tune* (= song). 这是一首悦耳易记的曲子。◇ *a football song sung **to the tune of*** (= using the tune of) *'When the saints go marching in'* 用《圣者的行进》的曲调唱的足球歌 ➲ COLLOCATIONS AT MUSIC ➲ SEE ALSO SIGNATURE TUNE, THEME TUNE at THEME MUSIC

IDM **be ˌin/ˌout of ˈtune (with sb/sth)** to be/not be in agreement with sb/sth; to have/not have the same opinions, feelings, interests, etc. as sb/sth（与…）协调 / 不协调，一致 / 不一致，融洽 / 不融洽：*These proposals are perfectly in tune with our own thoughts on the subject.* 这些建议与我们在这个问题上的想法完全一致。◇ *The President is out of tune with public opinion.* 总统与公众舆论大唱反调。 **be ˌin/ˌout of ˈtune** to be/not be singing or playing the correct musical notes to sound pleasant 音调正确 / 不正确；演奏合调 / 走调：*None of them could sing in tune.* 他们中没有一个人能唱得合调。◇ *The piano is out of tune.* 钢琴音走调了。 **to the tune of sth** (*informal*) used to emphasize how much money sth has cost（用于强调）总额达，总数为：*The hotel has been refurbished to the tune of a million dollars.* 这家旅馆重新装修花费达一百万美元。➲ MORE AT CALL *v.*, CHANGE *v.*, DANCE *v.*, PAY *v.*, SING

■ ***verb*** **1 ~ sth** to adjust a musical instrument so that it plays at the correct PITCH（为乐器）调音，校音：*to tune a guitar* 给吉他调弦 **2 ~ sth** to adjust an engine so that it runs smoothly and as well as possible 调整，调节（发动机） **3** [usually passive] **~ sth (in) (to sth)** to adjust the controls on a radio or television so that you can receive a particular programme or channel（给收音机、电视等）调谐，调频道：*The radio was tuned (in) to the BBC World Service.* 收音机调到了英国广播公司国际广播电台。◇ (*informal*) ***Stay tuned*** *for the news coming up next.* 别换台，下面的新闻马上就来。 **4 ~ sth (to sth)** to prepare or adjust sth so that it is suitable for a particular situation 调整；使协调；使适合：*His speech was tuned to what the audience wanted to hear.* 他在演讲中专讲听众爱听的话。

PHR V **ˌtune ˈin (to sth)** to listen to a radio programme or watch a television programme 收听（收音机广播节目）；收看（电视节目） **ˌtune ˈin to sb/sth** to become aware of other people's thoughts and feelings, etc. 理解，体谅（他人的思想感情等） **ˌtune ˈout | ˌtune sb/sth↔ˈout** to stop listening to sth 不理睬；思想开小差：*When she started talking about her job, he just tuned out.* 在她开始

谈她工作的时候，他走神了。 **,tune 'up | ,tune sth↔'up** to adjust musical instruments so that they can play together（乐队等为乐器）调音，定弦：*The orchestra was tuning up as we entered the hall.* 我们进入音乐厅时，管弦乐队正在调音。

,tuned 'in *adj.* [not before noun] ~ **(to sth)** aware of what is happening in a particular situation （对情况）了解，掌握：*The resort is tuned in to the tastes of young and old alike.* 这个度假胜地适合各种口味，老少皆宜。

tune·ful /'tju:nfl; *NAmE* 'tu:nfl/ *adj.* having a pleasant tune or sound 音调优美的；声音悦耳的 **OPP tuneless** ▶ **tune·ful·ly** /-fəli/ *adv.* **tune·ful·ness** *noun* [U]

tune·less /'tju:nləs; *NAmE* 'tu:n-/ *adj.* not having a pleasant tune or sound 不好听的；不成曲调的；没腔没调的 **OPP tuneful** ▶ **tune·less·ly** *adv.*

tuner /'tju:nə(r); *NAmE* 'tu:-/ *noun* **1** (especially in compounds 尤用于构成复合词) a person who tunes musical instruments, especially pianos （乐器的）调音者，调弦者；（尤指）钢琴调音师 **2** the part of a radio, television, etc. that you move in order to change the signal and receive the radio or television station that you want （收音机、电视机等的）调谐钮，调谐键 **3** an electronic device that receives a radio signal and sends it to an AMPLIFIER so that it can be heard （接收无线电信号传输到放大器的）调谐器

tune·smith /'tju:nsmɪθ; *NAmE* 'tu:n-/ *noun* (*informal*) a person who writes popular music 流行音乐作曲家

tung·sten /'tʌŋstən/ *noun* [U] (*symb.* **W**) a chemical element. Tungsten is a very hard silver-grey metal, used especially in making steel and in FILAMENTS for LIGHT BULBS. 钨

tunic /'tju:nɪk; *NAmE* 'tu:-/ *noun* **1** a loose piece of clothing covering the body down to the knees, usually without sleeves, as worn in ancient Greece and Rome （古希腊、古罗马时期长及膝的）短袍 **2** a piece of women's clothing like a tunic, that reaches to the hips and is worn over trousers/pants or a skirt （长及臀部，罩于裤或裙外的）女式宽上衣 **3** (*BrE*) a tightly fitting jacket worn as part of a uniform by police officers, soldiers, etc. （警察、士兵等的）紧身制服上衣

'tuning fork *noun* a small metal instrument with two long parts joined together at one end, that produces a particular musical note when you hit it and is used in TUNING musical instruments 音叉（一种校音器） ➲ **MORE LIKE THIS** 9, page R26

'tuning peg *noun* = PEG (4) ➲ PICTURE AT PEG

tun·nel 🔑 /'tʌnl/ *noun, verb*

■ *noun* **1** 🔑 a passage built underground, for example to allow a road or railway/railroad to go through a hill, under a river, etc. 地下通道；地道；隧道：*a **railway/railroad tunnel*** 铁路隧道 ◇ *the Channel Tunnel* 英吉利海峡隧道 ➲ SEE ALSO WIND TUNNEL **2** an underground passage made by an animal（动物的）洞穴通道 **IDM** SEE LIGHT *n.*

■ *verb* (-**ll**-, *NAmE also* -**l**-) [I, T] to dig a tunnel under or through the ground 开凿隧道；挖地道： **+ adv./prep.** *The engineers had to tunnel through solid rock.* 工程师须要在坚实的岩石中开凿隧道。◇ **~ your way + adv./prep.** *The rescuers tunnelled their way in to the trapped miners.* 救援人员挖地道通向那些被困的矿工。

,tunnel 'vision *noun* [U] **1** (*medical* 医) a condition in which sb cannot see things that are not straight ahead of them 视野收缩，视野狭窄（只能看正前方的人或物） **2** (*disapproving*) an inability to see or understand all the aspects of a situation, an argument, etc. instead of just one part of it 一孔之见；井蛙之见

tunny /'tʌni/ *noun* (*pl.* **tunny**) (*BrE*) = TUNA

tup·pence (*also* **two·pence**) /'tʌpəns/ *noun* [U] (*BrE, informal*) the sum of two pence 两便士

IDM not care/give 'tuppence for sb/sth to think that sb/sth is not important or that they have no value 认为…无关紧要；认为…没有价值

tup·penny /'tʌpəni/ *adj.* [only before noun] (*BrE, informal*) = TWOPENNY

Tup·per·ware™ /'tʌpəweə(r); *NAmE* 'tʌpərwer/ *noun* [U] plastic containers used mainly for storing food 特百惠塑料容器（主要用于贮存食物）

tur·ban /'tɜ:bən; *NAmE* 'tɜ:rbən/ *noun* **1** a long piece of cloth wound tightly around the head, worn, for example, by Muslim or Sikh men （穆斯林或锡克教男教徒等用的）包头巾 **2** a woman's hat that looks like a turban （女用）头巾帽 ▶ **tur·baned** /'tɜ:bənd; *NAmE* 'tɜ:rb-/ *adj.*：*turbaned Sikhs* 包着头巾的锡克教徒

tur·bid /'tɜ:bɪd; *NAmE* 'tɜ:rbɪd/ *adj.* (*formal*) (of liquid 液体) full of mud, dirt, etc. so that you cannot see through it 浑浊的；污浊不清的 **SYN muddy** ▶ **tur·bid·ity** /tɜ:'bɪdəti; *NAmE* tɜ:r'b-/ *noun* [U]

tur·bine /'tɜ:baɪn; *NAmE* 'tɜ:rb-/ *noun* a machine or an engine that receives its power from a wheel that is turned by the pressure of water, air or gas 涡轮机；汽轮机 ➲ SEE ALSO WIND TURBINE

turbo·char·ger /'tɜ:bəʊtʃɑ:dʒə(r); *NAmE* 'tɜ:rboʊtʃɑ:rdʒər/ (*also* **turbo** *pl.* **-os**) *noun* a system driven by a turbine that gets its power from an engine's EXHAUST gases. It sends the mixture of petrol/gas and air into the engine at high pressure, making it more powerful. 涡轮增压器 ▶ **turbo·charge** *verb*： **~ sth** *turbocharged engines* 涡轮增压发动机

turbo·jet /'tɜ:bəʊdʒet; *NAmE* 'tɜ:rboʊ-/ *noun* **1** a TURBINE engine that produces forward movement by forcing out a stream of hot air and gas behind it 涡轮喷气发动机 **2** a plane that gets its power from this type of engine 涡轮喷气飞机

turbo·prop /'tɜ:bəʊprɒp; *NAmE* 'tɜ:rboʊprɑ:p/ *noun* **1** a TURBINE engine that produces forward movement by turning a PROPELLER (= a set of spinning blades) 涡轮螺旋桨发动机 **2** a plane that gets its power from this type of engine 涡轮螺旋桨飞机

tur·bot /'tɜ:bət; *NAmE* 'tɜ:rbət/ *noun* [C, U] (*pl.* **tur·bot** or **tur·bots**) a large flat European sea fish that is used for food 大菱鲆（产于欧洲的一种可食用比目鱼）

tur·bu·lence /'tɜ:bjələns; *NAmE* 'tɜ:rb-/ *noun* [U] **1** a situation in which there is a lot of sudden change, confusion, disagreement and sometimes violence 骚乱；动乱；动荡；混乱 **SYN upheaval** **2** a series of sudden and violent changes in the direction that air or water is moving in （空气和水的）湍流，涡流，紊流：*We experienced severe turbulence during the flight.* 我们在飞行中遇到了强烈的气流。 ➲ COLLOCATIONS AT TRAVEL

tur·bu·lent /'tɜ:bjələnt; *NAmE* 'tɜ:rb-/ *adj.* [usually before noun] **1** in which there is a lot of sudden change, confusion, disagreement and sometimes violence 动荡的；动乱的；骚动的；混乱的：*a short and turbulent career in politics* 短暂动荡的政治生涯 ◇ *a turbulent part of the world* 世界上动荡不安的地区 **2** (of air or water 空气或水) changing direction suddenly and violently 汹涌的；猛烈的；湍动的：*The aircraft is designed to withstand turbulent conditions.* 这架飞机是为经受猛烈的气流而设计的。◇ *a turbulent sea/storm* (= caused by turbulent water/air) 波涛汹涌的大海；狂风暴雨 **3** (of people 人) noisy and/or difficult to control 骚动的；混乱而难以控制的 **SYN unruly**：*a turbulent crowd* 骚动的人群

turd /tɜ:d; *NAmE* tɜ:rd/ *noun* (*taboo, slang*) **1** a lump of solid waste from the BOWELS 粪块；粪球；粪团：*dog turds* 狗屎堆 **2** an offensive word for an unpleasant person 臭狗屎（对不喜欢的人的冒犯语）

tur·een /tju'ri:n; tə'ri:n/ *noun* a large deep dish with a lid, used for serving vegetables or soup （盛菜或汤的）有盖海碗；汤碗

turf /tɜ:f; *NAmE* tɜ:rf/ *noun, verb*

■ *noun* (*pl.* **turfs** or **turves** /tɜ:vz; *NAmE* tɜ:rvz/) **1** [U, C] short grass and the surface layer of soil that is held together by its roots; a piece of this that has been cut from the ground and is used especially for making LAWNS (= the area of grass in a garden/yard) 草皮；（铺草坪用的）草皮块：*newly laid turf* 新铺的草皮 ◇ *(especially BrE) the hallowed turf of Wimbledon, etc.* (= the grass used for playing a sport on) 温布尔登等被视为神圣的运动场草皮 **2** [U, C] PEAT that is cut to be used as fuel; a piece of this 泥煤；泥炭；泥煤块；泥炭块 **3 the turf** [sing.] the sport of horse racing 赛马 **4** [U] *(informal)* the place where sb lives and/or works, especially when they think of it as their own（自己的）地盘，势力范围：*He feels more confident on* ***home turf***. 他在主场感到更有信心。

■ ***verb*** ~ sth to cover an area of ground with turf 用草皮覆盖

PHR V **ˌturf sb ˈout (of sth)** | **ˌturf sb ˈoff (sth)** *(BrE, informal)* to make sb leave a place, an organization, etc. 赶出，驱逐出（地方、组织等） **SYN** **throw sb↔out (of…)**: *He was turfed out of the party.* 他已被驱逐出党。◇ *The boys were turfed off the bus.* 男孩们被赶下了公共汽车。

ˈturf accountant *noun (BrE, formal)* = BOOKMAKER

ˈturf war *noun* a violent disagreement between two groups of people about who should control a particular area, activity or business（地盘、势力范围等的）争夺战；地盘之争：*a vicious turf war between rival gangs of drug dealers* 对立贩毒团伙之间的猛烈火拼

tur·gid /ˈtɜːdʒɪd; *NAmE* ˈtɜːrdʒɪd/ *adj. (formal)* **1** (of language, writing, etc. 语言、文章等) boring, complicated and difficult to understand 枯燥无味的；晦涩难懂的 **2** swollen; containing more water than usual 肿胀的；膨胀的；肿大的：*the turgid waters of the Thames* 上涨的泰晤士河水

tur·ista /tuˈrɪstə/ *noun* [U] *(NAmE, informal)* DIARRHOEA that is suffered by sb who is visiting a foreign country 旅行者腹泻；水土不服造成的腹泻

tur·key /ˈtɜːki; *NAmE* ˈtɜːrki/ *noun (pl.* **-eys***)* **1** [C] a large bird that is often kept for its meat, eaten especially at Christmas in Britain and at Thanksgiving in the US 吐绶鸡；火鸡 ➲ VISUAL VOCAB PAGE V12 **2** [U] meat from a turkey 火鸡肉：*roast turkey* 烤火鸡肉 **3** [C] *(NAmE, informal)* a failure 失败：*His latest movie is a real turkey.* 他最近的那部电影是一大败笔。 **4** [C] *(NAmE, informal)* a stupid or useless person 笨蛋；草包 ➲ SEE ALSO COLD TURKEY

IDM SEE TALK *v.*

ˈturkey shoot *noun (informal, especially NAmE)* a battle or contest in which one side is much stronger than the other and able to win very easily 一边倒的战争（或比赛）

Turk·ish /ˈtɜːkɪʃ; *NAmE* ˈtɜːrkɪʃ/ *adj., noun*

■ ***adj.*** from or connected with Turkey 土耳其的

■ ***noun*** [U] the language of Turkey 土耳其语

ˌTurkish ˈbath *noun* a type of bath in which you sit in a room full of hot steam, have a MASSAGE and then a cold shower or bath; a building where this treatment takes place 土耳其浴；蒸汽浴；蒸汽浴室

ˌTurkish ˈcoffee *noun* [U, C] very strong, usually very sweet, black coffee 土耳其咖啡（通常很甜，不加牛奶）

ˌTurkish deˈlight *noun* [U, C] a sweet/candy made from a substance like jelly that is flavoured with fruit and covered with fine white sugar 土耳其软糖，拌砂软糖（一种外粘白糖面的胶质糖果）

tur·meric /ˈtɜːmərɪk; *NAmE* ˈtɜːrm-/ *noun* [U] a yellow powder made from the root of an Asian plant, used in cooking as a spice, especially in CURRY 姜黄根粉（用作烹饪调料，尤用于做咖喱） ➲ VISUAL VOCAB PAGE V35

tur·moil /ˈtɜːmɔɪl; *NAmE* ˈtɜːrm-/ *noun* [U, sing.] a state of great anxiety and confusion 动乱；骚动；混乱；焦虑 **SYN** **confusion**：*emotional/mental/political turmoil* 纷乱的情绪；精神上的混乱；政治动乱 ◇ *His statement* ***threw*** *the court* ***into turmoil***. 他的陈述使得法庭陷入一片混乱。◇ *Her mind was* ***in*** *(a)* ***turmoil***. 她心乱如麻。

turn 🔑 /tɜːn; *NAmE* tɜːrn/ *verb, noun*

■ ***verb***

• **MOVE ROUND** 转动 **1** 🔑 [I, T] to move or make sth move around a central point（使）转动，旋转：*The wheels of the car began to turn.* 汽车的轮子开始转动起来。◇ *I can't get the screw to turn.* 我拧不动这个螺丝钉。◇ **~ sth (+ adv./prep.)** *He turned the key in the lock.* 他转动钥匙开锁。◇ *She turned the wheel sharply to the left.* 她猛地向左打方向盘。

• **CHANGE POSITION/DIRECTION** 改变位置 / 方向 **2** 🔑 [I, T] to move your body or part of your body so as to face or start moving in a different direction 转身；扭转（身体部位）：*We turned and headed for home.* 我们转身朝家走去。◇ *She turned to look at me.* 她转过头来看着我。◇ **+ adv./prep.** *He turned back to his work.* 他回去继续工作。◇ *I turned away and looked out of the window.* 我扭过脸去望着窗外。◇ **~ sth (+ adv./prep.)** *He turned his back to the wall.* 他转身背对着墙。◇ *She turned her head away.* 她把头扭向别处。➲ SEE ALSO TURN OVER **3** 🔑 [T] **~ sth + adv./prep.** to move sth so that it is in a different position or facing a different direction 翻转；翻动；把…翻过来：*She turned the chair on its side to repair it.* 她把椅子翻转过来修理。◇ *Turn the sweater inside out before you wash it.* 你把针织套衫里面翻过来再洗。➲ SEE ALSO TURN STH↔OVER **4** 🔑 [I, T] to change the direction you are moving or travelling in; to make sth change the direction it is moving in （使）改变方向；转弯：**~ (into sth)** *He turned into a narrow street.* 他拐进了一条狭窄的街道。◇ **~ sth** *The man* ***turned the corner*** *and disappeared.* 那男人转过街角就没影了。◇ **~ sth into sth** *I turned the car into the car park.* 我转弯把汽车开进了停车场。 **5** 🔑 [I] **(+ adv./prep.)** (of a road or river 道路或河流) to curve in a particular direction 转向；转弯：*The road turns to the left after the church.* 这条路过了教堂之后向左转弯。

• **AIM/POINT** 瞄准；指向 **6** [T, I] to aim or point sth in a particular direction 朝着；向…方向；对准：**~ sth (on/to sb/sth/yourself)** *Police turned water cannon on the rioters.* 警察把高压水枪对准了闹事者。◇ *He turned the gun on himself.* 他把枪口对准了自己。◇ *She looked at him then turned her attention back to me.* 她看了看他，然后又把注意力转回到我的身上。◇ **~ to sb/sth/yourself** *His thoughts turned to his dead wife.* 他想起了自己已故的妻子。

• **OF TIDE IN SEA** 海潮 **7** [I] to start to come in or go out 开始涨（或落）：*The tide is turning—we'd better get back.* 涨潮了，我们最好回去吧。

• **LET SB/STH GO** 松开 **8** [T] to make or let sb/sth go into a particular place or state （使）松开，释放：**~ sth + adv./prep.** *They turned the horse into the field.* 他们把马松开放到牧场里。◇ **~ sth + adj.** *to turn the dogs loose* 把狗放开

• **FOLD** 折叠 **9** [T] **~ sth + adv./prep.** to fold sth in a particular way 折起；翻转：*She turned down the blankets and climbed into bed.* 她掀开毯子爬上床去。◇ *He turned up the collar of his coat and hurried out into the rain.* 他竖起大衣领子，冒雨匆匆走了。

• **CARTWHEEL/SOMERSAULT** 侧手翻；筋斗 **10** [T, no passive] **~ sth** to perform a movement by moving your body in a circle 表演（身体旋转动作）：*to turn cartwheels/somersaults* 做侧手翻；翻筋斗

• **PAGE** 书页 **11** 🔑 [T, I] if you **turn** a page of a book or magazine, you move it so that you can read the next page 翻，翻动（书页）：**~ sth** *He sat turning the pages idly.* 他坐在那里无所事事地翻着书。◇ **~ to sth** *Turn to p.23.* 翻到第 23 页。

• **GAME** 比赛 **12** [I, T] **~ (sth) (around)** if a game **turns** or sb **turns** it, it changes the way it is developing so that a different person or team starts to win （使）逆转

• **BECOME** 变成 **13** 🔑 *linking verb* to change into a particular state or condition; to make sth do this （使）变成，成为：**+ adj.** *The leaves were turning brown.* 叶子变黄。◇ *The weather has turned cold.* 天气变得寒冷了。◇ *He turned nasty when we refused to give him the money.* 我们不给他钱，他变得穷凶极恶。◇ *He decided to* ***turn professional***. 他决定转为职业人员。◇ **~ sth + adj.** *The heat turned the milk sour.* 炎热的天气使得牛奶变酸了。◇ **+ noun** *She turned a deathly shade of white when she heard the news.* 她听到这个消息时面如死灰。◇ *He's a lawyer turned politician* (= he used to be a lawyer but is now a politician). 他以前是个律师，现在成为政治家了。➲ NOTE AT BECOME

T

• **AGE/TIME** 年龄；时间 **14** *linking verb* (not used in the progressive tenses 不用于进行时) **+ noun** to reach or pass a particular age or time 到达，超过（某一年龄或时间）：*She turns 21 in June.* 她到六月份就满 21 岁了。◇ *It's turned midnight.* 已过了午夜。

• **STOMACH** 胃 **15** [I, T] **~ (your stomach)** when your stomach **turns** or sth **turns** your stomach, you feel as though you will VOMIT 作呕；恶心；使（胃）不适

• **WOOD** 木材 **16** [T] **~ sth** to shape sth on a LATHE（在车床上）车削：*to turn a chair leg* 在车床上车椅子腿 ◇ *turned boxes and bowls* 车削成的盒和碗

IDM **HELP** Most idioms containing **turn** are at the entries for the nouns and adjectives in the idioms, for example **not turn a hair** is at **hair**. 大多数含 turn 的习语，都可在该等习语中的名词及形容词相关词条找到，如 not turn a hair 在词条 hair 下。 **as it/things turned 'out** as was shown or proved by later events 正如后来表明的；果然如此；果不其然：*I didn't need my umbrella, as it turned out* (= because it didn't rain). 我果然没用上我的伞。 **be well, badly, etc. turned 'out** to be well, badly, etc. dressed 穿着打扮得好（或不好等） **turn round/around and do sth** (*informal*) used to report what sb says or does, when this is surprising or annoying（用以报告令人吃惊或不快的言行）竟会：*How could she turn round and say that, after all I've done for her?* 我为她做了这么多，她怎么竟会说出那种话来？

PHR V **ˌturn aˈgainst sb | ˌturn sb aˈgainst sb** to stop or make sb stop being friendly towards sb （使）与…反目成仇，变得敌对：*She turned against her old friend.* 她与老朋友翻脸了。◇ *After the divorce he tried to turn the children against their mother.* 他离婚后企图教唆子女反对他们的母亲。

ˌturn aˈround/ˈround | ˌturn sb/sth aˈround/ˈround 🔑 to change position or direction so as to face the other way; to make sb/sth do this （使）翻身，转身，翻转：*Turn around and let me look at your back.* 转过身去让我看看你的后背。◇ *I turned my chair round to face the fire.* 我把椅子转过来面向火炉。**ˌturn aˈround/ˈround | ˌturn sth↔aˈround/ˈround** if a business, economy, etc. **turns around** or sb **turns it around**, it starts being successful after it has been unsuccessful for a time （使企业、经济等）好转，扭转，有起色 ⊃ RELATED NOUN TURNAROUND

ˌturn sb↔aˈway (from sth) to refuse to allow sb to enter a place 把某人拒之门外；不准某人进入：*Hundreds of people were turned away from the stadium* (= because it was full). 体育场满座，数百人被拒之门外。◇ *They had nowhere to stay so I couldn't turn them away.* 他们无处安身，所以我不能把他们打发走。

ˌturn ˈback | ˌturn sb/sth↔ˈback 🔑 to return the way you have come; to make sb/sth do this（使）原路返回，往回走：*The weather became so bad that they had to turn back.* 天气变得非常恶劣，他们不得不循原路折回。◇ (*figurative*) *We said we would do it—there can be no turning back.* 我们说过要干这事，不能反悔。◇ *Our car was turned back at the border.* 我们的汽车在边境被挡了回来。 ⊃ SYNONYMS AT RETURN

ˌturn sb/sth↔ˈdown 🔑 to reject or refuse to consider an offer, a proposal, etc. or the person who makes it 拒绝，顶回（提议、建议或提议人）：*Why did she turn down your invitation?* 她为什么谢绝你的邀请？◇ *He has been turned down for ten jobs so far.* 他迄今申请了十份工作都遭到拒绝。◇ *He asked her to marry him but she turned him down.* 他请求她嫁给他，但是她回绝了。 **ˌturn sth↔ˈdown** 🔑 to reduce the noise, heat, etc. produced by a piece of equipment by moving its controls 把…调低；关小：*Please turn the volume down.* 请把音量调低些。◇ **+ adj.** *He turned the lights down low.* 他把灯光调得暗了一些。

ˌturn ˈin 1 to face or curve towards the centre 朝内；向内拐：*Her feet turn in.* 她的两脚呈内八字。 **2** (*old-fashioned*) to go to bed 上床睡觉 **ˌturn sb↔ˈin** (*informal*) to take sb to the police or sb in authority because they have committed a crime 把…扭送（到警察局）；使自首：*She threatened to turn him in to the police.* 她扬言要把他交给警方。◇ *He decided to turn himself in.* 他决定到警察局去自首。 **ˌturn sth↔ˈin 1** to give back sth that you no longer need 交还，退还（不再需要的东西）：*You must turn in your pass when you leave the building.* 你离开大楼时必须交还通行证。 **2** (*especially NAmE*) to give sth to sb in authority 上交；呈交；提交：*They turned in a petition with 80 000 signatures.* 他们递交了一份有 8 万人签名的请愿书。◇ *I haven't even turned in Monday's work yet.* 我连星期一的作业还没交呢。 **3** to achieve a score, performance, profit, etc. 取得（分数）；完成（表演）；获得（利润）：*The champion turned in a superb performance to retain her title.* 上届冠军表现十分出色，卫冕成功。 **ˌturn ˈin on yourself** to become too concerned with your own problems and stop communicating with others 忙于自己的事情而不与人交往；闭门谢客

ˌturn (from sth) ˈinto sth 🔑 to become sth 变成某事物：*Our dream holiday turned into a nightmare.* 我们梦想的假日变成了一场噩梦。◇ *In one year she turned from a problem child into a model student.* 一年内，她从问题儿童变成了模范学生。 **ˌturn sb/sth (from sth) ˈinto sth** 🔑 to make sb/sth become sth 使（从…）变成：*Ten years of prison had turned him into an old man.* 十年大狱使他变成了一个老头。◇ *The prince was turned into a frog by the witch.* 王子被女巫变成了一只青蛙。

ˌturn ˈoff | ˌturn ˈoff sth [no passive] to leave a road in order to travel on another 拐弯；转入另一条路：*Is this where we turn off?* 这儿是我们换道的地方吗？◇ *The jet began to turn off the main runway.* 那架喷气式飞机开始拐出主跑道。 **ˌturn ˈoff** (*informal*) to stop listening to or thinking about sb/sth 不再听；不再想：*I couldn't understand the lecture so I just turned off.* 我听不懂讲课，所以也就不听了。 **ˌturn sb↔ˈoff 1** to make sb feel bored or not interested 使厌烦；使失去兴趣：*People had been turned off by both candidates in the election.* 大选中的两位候选人都让人觉得扫兴。 **2** to stop sb feeling sexually attracted; to make sb have a feeling of disgust 使（异性）失去兴趣；使厌恶 ⊃ RELATED NOUN TURN-OFF **ˌturn sth↔ˈoff** 🔑 to stop the flow of electricity, gas, water, etc. by moving a switch, button, etc. 关掉，截断（电流、煤气、水等）：*to turn off the light* 关上灯 ◇ *Please turn the television off before you go to bed.* 睡觉前请关上电视。

ˈturn on sb to attack sb suddenly and unexpectedly 突然攻击：*The dogs suddenly turned on each other.* 那两条狗突然互相撕咬了起来。◇ *Why are you all turning on me* (= criticizing or blaming me)? 你们怎么突然都冲我来了？

ˈturn on sth [no passive] **1** to depend on sth 依靠；依…而定；取决于：*Much turns on the outcome of the current peace talks.* 事情主要取决于当前和谈的结果。 **2** [no passive] to have sth as its main topic 以…为主题：*The discussion turned on the need to raise standards.* 这次讨论的主要议题是提高标准的必要性。 **ˌturn sb↔ˈon** (*informal*) to make sb excited or interested, especially sexually 使性兴奋；使感兴趣：*Jazz has never really turned me on.* 我对爵士乐从未真正产生过兴趣。◇ *She gets turned on by men in uniform.* 她看到穿制服的男人就欲火攻心。 ⊃ RELATED NOUN TURN-ON **ˌturn sb ˈon (to sth)** (*informal*) to make sb become interested in sth or to use sth for the first time 使对…感兴趣；使首次使用：*He turned her on to jazz.* 他使她对爵士乐产生了兴趣。 **ˌturn sth↔ˈon** 🔑 to start the flow of electricity, gas, water, etc. by moving a switch, button, etc. 接通（电流、煤气、水等）；打开：*to turn on the heating* 打开供热系统 ◇ *I'll turn the television on.* 我来打开电视机。◇ (*figurative*) *He really knows how to* ***turn on the charm*** (= suddenly become pleasant and attractive). 他确实懂得如何一展魅力。

ˌturn ˈout 1 to be present at an event 出席（某项活动）；在场：*A vast crowd turned out to watch the procession.* 有一大群人出来观看游行队伍。 ⊃ RELATED NOUN TURNOUT **2** (used with an adverb or adjective, or in questions with *how* 与副词或形容词连用，或用于以 how 引导的疑问句) to happen in a particular way; to develop or end in a particular way …地发展（或发生）；结果…：*Despite our worries everything turned out well.* 尽管我们都很担心，结果一切都顺利。◇ *You never know how your children will turn out.* 很难说子女将来的发展怎样。◇ **+ adj.** *If the day turns out wet, we may have to change our plans.* 如果那天下雨的话，我们可能得改变计划。 **3** to point away from the centre 向外；朝外：*Her toes turn out.* 她的脚趾向外撇。 **4** 🔑 to be discovered to be; to prove to be 原来是；证明是；结果是： **turn out that**… *It turned out that she was a friend of my sister.* 她原来是我姐姐的朋友。◇ **turn out to be/have sth** *The job turned out to be harder than we thought.* 这工作结果比我们想象的要难。◇ *The house they had offered us turned out to be a tiny apartment.* 他们向我们提供的房子原来是很小的公寓套间。 **ˌturn sb/sth↔ˈout** to produce sb/sth 制造；生产；培养出：*The factory turns out 900 cars a week.* 这家工厂每周生产 900 辆汽车。 **ˌturn sb ˈout (of/from sth)** to force sb to leave a place 赶走；逐出；撵走 **ˌturn sth↔ˈout 1** to switch a light or a source of heat off 关掉（灯或热源）；熄灭：*Remember to turn out the lights when you go to bed.* 临睡前别忘了关灯。 **2** (*BrE*) to clean sth thoroughly by removing the contents and organizing them again 腾空；彻底清理：*to turn out the attic* 把阁楼腾空清扫 **3** to empty sth, especially your pockets 弄空，掏净（尤指口袋） **4** to make sth point away from the centre 使向外；使朝外：*She turned her toes out.* 她把脚趾向外撇。

ˌturn ˈover 1 ⚿ to change position so that the other side is facing towards the outside or the top 翻身；翻转：*If you turn over you might find it easier to get to sleep.* 你若翻个身，也许入睡容易些。◇ *The car skidded and turned over.* 汽车打滑向一侧翻倒了。◇ (*figurative*) *The smell made my stomach turn over* (= made me feel sick). 这气味让我反胃。 **2** (of an engine 发动机) to start or to continue to run 发动；转动；继续运转 **3** to change to another channel when you are watching television 变换（电视频道） **ˌturn ˈover sth** to do business worth a particular amount of money in a particular period of time 营业额为…；做金额为…的生意：*The company turns over £3.5 million a year.* 这家公司一年的营业额为 350 万英镑。 ➲ RELATED NOUN TURNOVER (1) **ˌturn sth↔ˈover 1** ⚿ to make sth change position so that the other side is facing towards the outside or the top 使翻个儿；使翻转：*Brown the meat on one side, then turn it over and brown the other side.* 把肉的一面烤黄，然后翻转过来，再烤另一面。 **2** to think about sth carefully 认真思考；深思熟虑：*She kept turning over the events of the day in her mind.* 她脑子里不断琢磨当天发生的事。 **3** (of a shop/store 商店) to sell goods and replace them 周转；销货和进货：*A supermarket will turn over its stock very rapidly.* 超市的货物周转得很快。 ➲ RELATED NOUN TURNOVER (3) **4** (*informal*) to steal from a place 从…偷窃：*Burglars had turned the house over.* 盗贼把这所房子盗窃一空。 **5** to make an engine start running 发动（引擎） **ˌturn sb↔ˈover to sb** to deliver sb to the control or care of sb else, especially sb in authority 移交，送交（他人看管，尤指当局）：*Customs officials turned the man over to the police.* 海关官员把那个男子移交给警方看管。 **ˌturn sth↔ˈover to sb** to give the control of sth to sb 把…移交给（他人管理）：*He turned the business over to his daughter.* 他把这个企业交给了女儿管理。 **ˌturn sth↔ˈover to sth** to change the use or function of sth 改变，转变（用途或功能）：*The factory was turned over to the manufacture of aircraft parts.* 这家工厂转产飞机部件。

ˈturn to sb/sth ⚿ to go to sb/sth for help, advice, etc. 向…求助（或寻求指教等）：*She has nobody she can turn to.* 她求助无门。

ˌturn ˈup 1 ⚿ to be found, especially by chance, after being lost （尤指失去后偶然）被发现，被找到：*Don't worry about the letter—I'm sure it'll turn up.* 别为那封信担心，我相信会找到的。 **2** ⚿ (of a person 人) to arrive 到达；来到；露面：*We arranged to meet at 7.30, but she never turned up.* 我们约好 7:30 碰头，但她根本没露面。 **3** (of an opportunity 机会) to happen, especially by chance 偶然出现；到来：*He's still hoping something* (= for example, a job or a piece of luck) *will turn up.* 他仍然在希望会有机会出现。 ➲ RELATED NOUN TURN-UP (2) **ˌturn sth↔ˈup 1** ⚿ to increase the sound, heat, etc. of a piece of equipment 开大，调高（音量、热量等）：*Could you turn the TV up?* 你能把电视机的音量开大些吗？◇ **+ adj.** *The music was turned up loud.* 音乐的音量开大了。 **2** (*BrE*) to make a piece of clothing shorter by folding and sewing it up at the bottom 将（衣服的底边）折起缝好；改短 OPP **let sth↔down** ➲ RELATED NOUN TURN-UP (1) **3** to find sth 找到；发现：*Our efforts to trace him turned up nothing.* 我们辛辛苦苦跟踪他，却无功而返。

■ ***noun*** [C]

• **MOVEMENT** 活动 **1** ⚿ an act of turning sb/sth around 转动；旋动：*Give the handle a few turns.* 转动几下把手。

• **OF ROAD/VEHICLE** 道路；车辆 **2** ⚿ a change in direction in a vehicle （车辆的）转弯，转向：***Make a left/right turn*** *into West Street.* 向左 / 右拐入西大街。 ➲ SEE ALSO THREE-POINT TURN, U-TURN **3** (*especially NAmE*) (*BrE also* **turning**) a place where a road leads away from the one you are travelling on 岔路口；拐弯处；转弯处 **4** a bend or corner in a road （道路的）弯道，转弯处：*a lane full of* ***twists and turns*** 弯弯曲曲的小巷

• **TIME** 时间 **5** ⚿ the time when sb in a group of people should or is allowed to do sth （依次轮到的）机会：*When it's your turn, take another card.* 轮到你时，再抓一张牌。 ◇ *Please* ***wait your turn.*** 请等着轮到你。◇ ***Whose turn is it*** *to cook?* 轮到谁做饭了？◇ *Steve* ***took a turn*** *driving while I slept.* 我睡觉时，史蒂夫接着开车。

• **CHANGE** 变化 **6** an unusual or unexpected change in what is happening （异乎寻常或意外的）变化，转变：*a surprising* ***turn of events*** 意想不到的事态变化 ◇ *His health has* ***taken a turn for the worse*** (= suddenly got worse). 他的健康状况突然恶化。◇ *Events took a dramatic turn in the weeks that followed.* 在以后的几周里，事态急转直下。 ◇ *The book is,* ***by turns,*** *funny and very sad.* 这部书时而妙趣横生，时而悲悲戚戚。 ➲ SEE ALSO ABOUT-TURN

• **PERFORMANCE** 表演 **7** a short performance or piece of entertainment such as a song, etc. 短小节目：*Everyone got up on stage to do a turn.* 每个人都登台表演了一个小节目。 ➲ SEE ALSO STAR TURN

• **WALK** 步行 **8** (*old-fashioned*) a short walk 散步；转一圈：*We took a turn around the park.* 我们在公园里转了一圈。

• **ILLNESS** 疾病 **9** (*old-fashioned*) a feeling of illness （疾病的）一阵发作；不适感：*a funny turn* (= a feeling that you may faint) 感到一阵晕眩

IDM **at every ˈturn** everywhere or every time you try and do sth 处处；事事；每次：*At every turn I met with disappointment.* 我事事都不顺心。 **(do sb) a good ˈturn** (to do) sth that helps sb （为某人做）好事，善事；（做）有助于某人的事：*Well, that's my good turn for the day.* 好啦，这就是我今天做的好事。 **done to a ˈturn** cooked for exactly the right amount of time 烹调得恰到火候 **give sb a ˈturn** (*old-fashioned*) to frighten or shock sb 使大吃一惊；吓某人一跳 **in ˈturn 1** ⚿ one after the other in a particular order 依次；轮流；逐个：*The children called out their names in turn.* 孩子们逐一自报姓名。 **2** as a result of sth in a series of events 相应地；转而：*Increased production will, in turn, lead to increased profits.* 增加生产会继而增加利润。 **ˌone good ˌturn deserves aˈnother** (*saying*) you should help sb who has helped you 善须善报；要以德报德；好人应得好报 **on the ˈturn** (*especially BrE*) going to change soon 即将变化：*His luck is on the turn.* 他就要时来运转了。 **speak/talk ˌout of ˈturn** to say sth that you should not because it is the wrong situation or because it offends sb 说话出格（或冒失、鲁莽、不合时宜） **take ˈturns (in sth/to do sth)** ⚿ (*BrE also* **take it in ˈturns**) if people **take turns** or **take it in turns** to do sth, they do it one after the other to make sure it is done fairly 依次；轮流：*The male and female birds take turns in sitting on the eggs.* 雄鸟和雌鸟轮流伏窝。◇ *We take it in turns to do the housework.* 我们轮流做家务。 **the ˌturn of the ˈcentury/ˈyear** the time when a new century/year starts 世纪之交；新年伊始；辞旧迎新之际：*It was built at the turn of the century.* 这是在世纪之交修建的。 **a ˌturn of ˈmind** a particular way of thinking about things 思维方式；思想方法 **a ˌturn of ˈphrase** a particular way of describing sth 措辞；表达方式；描述方式 **a ˌturn of the ˈscrew** an extra amount of pressure, CRUELTY, etc. added to a situation that is already difficult to bear or understand 雪上加霜 **a ˌturn of ˈspeed** a sudden increase in your speed or rate of progress; the ability to suddenly increase your speed 突然加速；加快进度；突然加快的能力：*He put on an impressive turn of speed in the last lap.* 他在最后一圈猛然加速。 ➲ MORE AT HAND *n.*, SERVE *v.*

turn·about /ˈtɜːnəbaʊt; NAmE ˈtɜːrn-/ *noun* [sing.] ~ (**in sth**) a sudden and complete change in sb/sth 突变；一百八十度的大转弯；变卦 **SYN reversal**

turn·around /ˈtɜːnəraʊnd; NAmE ˈtɜːrn-/ (*BrE also* **turn·round**) *noun* [usually sing.] **1** the amount of time it takes to unload a ship or plane at the end of one journey and load it again for the next one（轮船、飞机的）终点装卸时间 **2** the amount of time it takes to do a piece of work that you have been given and return it（接活到交活之间的）周转期，时限 **3** a situation in which sth changes from bad to good 好转；起色；转机：*a turnaround in the economy* 经济好转 **4** a complete change in sb's opinion, behaviour, etc.（观点、行为等的）彻底转变

turn·coat /ˈtɜːnkəʊt; NAmE ˈtɜːrnkoʊt/ *noun* (*disapproving*) a person who leaves one political party, religious group, etc. to join one that has very different views 叛徒；变节者；叛逆

turn·ing /ˈtɜːnɪŋ; NAmE ˈtɜːrnɪŋ/ (*BrE*) (*also* **turn** *NAmE, BrE*) *noun* a place where a road leads away from the one you are travelling on 岔路口；拐弯处；转弯处：*Take the first turning on the right.* 在第一个路口向右拐。◇ *I think we must have taken a wrong turning somewhere.* 我觉得我们一定是在什么地方拐错了路。

ˈ**turning circle** *noun* the smallest circle that a vehicle can turn around in（车辆掉头用的）最小转向圆，最小回转圆

ˈ**turning point** *noun* ~ (**in sth**) the time when an important change takes place, usually with the result that a situation improves 转折点；转机；转捩点：*The promotion marked a turning point in her career.* 这次提升标志着她事业上的转折点。

tur·nip /ˈtɜːnɪp; NAmE ˈtɜːrnɪp/ *noun* [C, U] **1** a round white, or white and purple, root vegetable 蔓菁；芜菁 ➲ VISUAL VOCAB PAGE V34 **2** (*ScotE*) = SWEDE ➲ VISUAL VOCAB PAGE V34

turn·key /ˈtɜːnkiː; NAmE ˈtɜːrn-/ *adj.* (especially of computer systems 尤指计算机系统) complete and ready to use immediately 交钥匙的；完整并可立即使用的

ˈ**turn-off** *noun* **1** a place where a road leads away from another larger or more important road 岔道；支路：*We missed the turn-off for the airport.* 我们错过了通往机场的岔道。**2** [usually sing.] (*informal*) a person or thing that people do not find interesting, attractive or sexually exciting 扫兴的人（或事）；厌烦的人（或事）；引不起性欲的人（或物）：*The city's crime rate is a serious turn-off to potential investors.* 这个城市的犯罪率使得潜在的投资者望而却步。◇ *I find beards a real turn-off.* 我觉得胡子确实令人厌恶。

ˈ**turn-on** *noun* [usually sing.] (*informal*) a person or thing that people find sexually exciting 引起性欲的人（或物）

turn·out /ˈtɜːnaʊt; NAmE ˈtɜːrn-/ *noun* [C, usually sing., U] **1** the number of people who attend a particular event 出席人数；到场人数：*This year's festival attracted a record turnout.* 今年的节日吸引的参加者之多创了纪录。**2** the number of people who vote in a particular election 投票人数：*a high/low/poor turnout* 参加投票的人数很多 / 很少 / 寥寥无几 ◇ *a 60% turnout of voters* * 60% 的投票率

turn·over /ˈtɜːnəʊvə(r); NAmE ˈtɜːrnoʊ-/ *noun* **1** [C, usually sing., U] ~ (**of sth**) the total amount of goods or services sold by a company during a particular period of time（一定时期内的）营业额，成交量：*an annual turnover of $75 million* * 7 500 万美元的年营业额 ◇ *a fall in turnover* 营业额的下降 ➲ COLLOCATIONS AT BUSINESS **2** [sing.] ~ (**of sb**) the rate at which employees leave a company and are replaced by other people 人事变更率；人员调整率：*a high turnover of staff* 很高的人员变更率 **3** [sing.] ~ (**of sth**) the rate at which goods are sold in a shop/store and replaced by others（商店的）货物周转率，销售比率：*a fast turnover of stock* 快速的存货周转 **4** [C] a small PIE in the shape of a triangle or half a circle, filled with fruit or jam 三角馅饼，半圆馅饼（以水果或果酱作馅）

turn·pike /ˈtɜːnpaɪk; NAmE ˈtɜːrn-/ (*also* **pike**) (*both NAmE*) *noun* a wide road, where traffic can travel fast for long distances and that drivers must pay a TOLL to use 收费公路

turn·round /ˈtɜːnraʊnd; NAmE ˈtɜːrn-/ *noun* (*BrE*) = TURNAROUND

ˈ**turn signal** (*NAmE*) (*BrE* **in·di·ca·tor**) (*also informal* **blink·er** *NAmE, BrE*) *noun* a light on a vehicle that flashes to show that the vehicle is going to turn left or right 转向灯；方向灯 ➲ VISUAL VOCAB PAGE V56

turn·stile /ˈtɜːnstaɪl; NAmE ˈtɜːrn-/ *noun* a gate at the entrance to a public building, STADIUM, etc. that turns in a circle when pushed, allowing one person to go through at a time 旋转栅门（常设于公共建筑、体育场等入口处）➲ PICTURE AT STILE

turn·table /ˈtɜːnteɪbl; NAmE ˈtɜːrn-/ *noun* **1** the round surface on a RECORD PLAYER that you place the record on to be played（唱机上的）唱盘 **2** a large round surface that is able to move in a circle and onto which a railway/railroad engine is driven in order to turn it to go in the opposite direction（铁路机车的）转台，旋车盘

ˈ**turn-up** *noun* (*BrE*) **1** (*NAmE* **cuff**) [C] the bottom of the leg of a pair of trousers/pants that has been folded over on the outside（裤脚的）外翻边，外卷边 **2** [sing.] (*informal*) something surprising or unexpected that happens 奇异的事；意想不到的事：*He actually offered to help? That's a turn-up for the books!* 他居然提出要帮忙？这真是太阳从西边出来了！

tur·pen·tine /ˈtɜːpəntaɪn; NAmE ˈtɜːrp-/ (*also informal* **turps** /tɜːps; NAmE tɜːrps/) *noun* [U] a clear liquid with a strong smell, used especially for making paint thinner and for cleaning paint from brushes and clothes 松节油

tur·pi·tude /ˈtɜːpɪtjuːd; NAmE ˈtɜːrpətuːd/ *noun* [U] (*formal*) very immoral behaviour 堕落；卑鄙；邪恶 **SYN wickedness**

tur·quoise /ˈtɜːkwɔɪz; NAmE ˈtɜːrk-/ *noun* **1** [C, U] a blue or greenish-blue SEMI-PRECIOUS stone 绿松石：*a turquoise brooch* 绿松石胸针 **2** [U] a greenish-blue colour 绿松石色；青绿色 ▸ **tur·quoise** *adj.*：*a turquoise dress* 一条青绿色的连衣裙

tur·ret /ˈtʌrət; NAmE ˈtɜːrət/ *noun* **1** a small tower on top of a wall or building, especially a castle（尤指城堡的）塔楼，角楼 ➲ VISUAL VOCAB PAGE V15 **2** a small metal tower on a ship, plane or TANK that can usually turn around and from which guns are fired（战舰、飞机或坦克的）炮塔，回转炮塔，活动射击装置

tur·ret·ed /ˈtʌrətɪd; NAmE ˈtɜːr-/ *adj.* [usually before noun] having one or more turrets 有塔楼的；有角楼的

tur·tle /ˈtɜːtl; NAmE ˈtɜːrtl/ *noun* **1** (*NAmE also* ˈ**sea turtle**) a large REPTILE with a hard round shell, that lives in the sea 海龟 ➲ VISUAL VOCAB PAGE V13 **2** (*NAmE, informal*) any REPTILE with a large shell, for example a TORTOISE or TERRAPIN（任何种类的）龟；陆龟；水龟；鳖

IDM turn ˈ**turtle** (of a boat 船) to turn over completely while sailing（在航行中）倾覆，翻

ˈ**turtle dove** *noun* a wild DOVE[1] (1) (= a type of bird) with a pleasant soft call, thought to be a very loving bird 斑鸠

turtle·neck /ˈtɜːtlnek; NAmE ˈtɜːrtl-/ *noun* **1** (*also* ˌ**turtle-neck** ˈ**sweater**) a sweater with a high part fitting closely around the neck 高领套头衫 **2** (*NAmE*) (*BrE* ˈ**polo neck**) a high round COLLAR made when the neck of a piece of clothing is folded over; a piece of clothing with a polo neck 高圆翻领；高圆翻领衣服 ➲ VISUAL VOCAB PAGE V68

turves PL. OF TURF

tusk /tʌsk/ *noun* either of the long curved teeth that stick out of the mouth of ELEPHANTS and some other animals（象和某些其他动物的）长牙 ➲ VISUAL VOCAB PAGE V12 ➲ SEE ALSO IVORY (1)

T

tus·sle /ˈtʌsl/ *noun, verb*

■ ***noun*** ~ **(for/over sth)** a short struggle, fight or argument especially in order to get sth 扭打，争斗，争执（尤指为了争得物品）： *He was injured during a tussle for the ball.* 他在争球时受了伤。

■ ***verb*** [I] ~ **(with sb/sth)** to fight or compete with sb/sth, especially in order to get sth 扭打，争斗（尤指为了争夺物品）： *The children were tussling with one another for the ball.* 孩子们在你抢我夺地争球。

tus·sock /ˈtʌsək/ *noun* a small area of grass that is longer and thicker than the grass around it（比周围的草密而高的）草丛 ▸**tus·socky** *adj.*： *tussocky grass* 丛生草

tut /tʌt/ (*also* ˌ**tut-ˈtut**) *exclamation, noun* used as the written or spoken way of showing the sound that people make when they disapprove of sth （作书面语或口语，表示不赞成的咂嘴声）啧啧： *Tut-tut, I expected better of you.* 啧啧，我没想到你会这样。 ◇ *tuts of disapproval* 不同意的啧啧声 ➲ **MORE LIKE THIS** 2, page R25 ▸ **tut** (*also* ˌ**tut-ˈtut**) *verb* (**-tt-**) [I]： *He tut-tutted under his breath.* 他轻声咂咂嘴。

tutee /tjuːˈtiː; *NAmE* tuː-/ *noun* a person who is taught or given advice by a TUTOR 受辅导者；受指导者

tu·tel·age /ˈtjuːtəlɪdʒ; *NAmE* ˈtuː-/ *noun* [U] (*formal*) **1** the teaching and instruction that one person gives to another 教导；指导；辅导 **SYN** **tuition** **2** the state of being protected or controlled by another person, organization or country （人、组织、国家等给予的）保护，监护，托管： *parental tutelage* 家长的监护

tutor /ˈtjuːtə(r); *NAmE* ˈtuː-/ *noun, verb*

■ ***noun*** **1** a private teacher, especially one who teaches an individual student or a very small group 家庭教师；私人教师 **2** (*especially BrE*) a teacher whose job is to pay special attention to the studies or health, etc. of a student or a group of students 导师；指导教师： *his history tutor* 他的历史导师 ◇ *He was my* ***personal tutor*** *at university.* 他是我大学时的个人指导教师。 ◇ *She's in my* ***tutor group*** *at school.* 她在学校里是指导我的那个小组的成员。 **3** (*BrE*) a teacher, especially one who teaches adults or who has a special role in a school or college（负责成人教育或在学校里有特别任务的）教师： *a part-time adult education tutor* 兼职的成人教育教师 **4** (*NAmE*) an assistant LECTURER in a college（大专院校的）助教 **5** a book of instruction in a particular subject, especially music 课本；（尤指）音乐课本： *a violin tutor* 小提琴课本

■ ***verb*** **1** [T] ~ **sb (in sth)** to be a tutor to an individual student or a small group; to teach sb, especially privately 进行单独（或小组）辅导；任…的私人教师；指导： *He tutors students in mathematics.* 他教学生数学。 **2** [I] to work as a tutor 当家庭教师；任大学导师： *Her work was divided between tutoring and research.* 她的工作分为导师工作和研究工作。

tu·tor·ial /tjuːˈtɔːriəl; *NAmE* tuː-/ *noun, adj.*

■ ***noun*** **1** a period of teaching in a university that involves discussion between an individual student or a small group of students and a tutor （大学导师的）个别辅导时间，辅导课 ➲ **WORDFINDER NOTE** AT **UNIVERSITY** **2** a short book or computer program that gives information on a particular subject or explains how sth is done 教程；辅导材料；使用说明书： *An online tutorial is provided.* 在线辅导可供查阅。

■ ***adj.*** connected with the work of a tutor 导师的；私人教师的；辅导的： *tutorial staff* 辅导人员 ◇ (*BrE*) *a tutorial college* (= a private school that prepares students for exams) 私立考试辅导学校

tutti-frutti /ˌtuːti ˈfruːti/ *noun* [U] a type of ice cream that contains pieces of fruit of various kinds 什锦水果冰淇淋

tutu /ˈtuːtuː/ *noun* a BALLET dancer's skirt made of many layers of material. Tutus may be either short and stiff, sticking out from the waist, or long and bell-shaped. 芭蕾舞裙

tu-whit, tu-whoo /təˌwɪt təˈwuː/ *noun* used to represent the sound that an OWL makes（猫头鹰的叫声）嘟噫－嘟呼 ➲ **MORE LIKE THIS** 4, page R25

tux·edo /tʌkˈsiːdəʊ; *NAmE* -doʊ/ *noun* (*pl.* **-os**) (*also informal* **tux** /tʌks/) (*especially NAmE*) **1** (*BrE also* ˈ**dinner suit**) a black or white jacket and trousers/pants, worn with a BOW TIE at formal occasions in the evening （配蝶形领结的）成套无尾晚礼服 **2** (*also* ˈ**dinner jacket**) a black or white jacket worn with a BOW TIE at formal occasions in the evening （配蝶形领结的）晚礼服上衣，无尾礼服上衣 **ORIGIN** From Tuxedo Park in New York, where it was first worn. 源自纽约的塔克西多公园，此处最早有人穿这种服装。

TV 🔑 /ˌtiː ˈviː/ *noun* [C, U] television 电视；电视机： *What's on TV tonight?* 今晚电视有什么节目？ ◇ *We're buying a new TV with the money.* 我们要用这笔钱买一台新电视机。 ◇ *Almost all homes have at least one* ***TV set.*** 差不多每家都至少有一台电视机。 ◇ *All rooms have a bathroom and colour TV.* 所有的房间都有洗澡间和彩色电视机。 ◇ ***a TV series/show/programme*** 电视系列片 / 节目 ◇ ***satellite/cable/digital TV*** 卫星 / 有线 / 数字电视 ◇ *She's a highly paid TV presenter.* 她是高薪电视节目主持人。 ➲ **COLLOCATIONS AT TELEVISION** ➲ **VISUAL VOCAB** PAGE V22 ➲ **SEE ALSO** PAY TV

ˌ**TV ˈdinner** *noun* a meal that you can buy already cooked and prepared, that you only have to heat up before you can eat it （加热即可食用的）方便快餐，熟食快餐

TVP™ /ˌtiː ˌviː ˈpiː/ *abbr.* TEXTURED VEGETABLE PROTEIN 结构性植物蛋白；植物组织蛋白；素肉

twad·dle /ˈtwɒdl; *NAmE* ˈtwɑːdl/ *noun* [U] (*old-fashioned, informal*) something that has been said or written that you think is stupid and not true 胡说八道；蠢话；废话；拙劣的文字 **SYN** **nonsense**

twain /tweɪn/ *number* (*old use*) two 二

IDM **never the ˌtwain shall ˈmeet** (*saying*) used to say that two things are so different that they cannot exist together 二者永远合不到一起；泾渭分明；大相径庭

twang /twæŋ/ *noun, verb*

■ ***noun*** [usually sing.] **1** used to describe a way of speaking, usually one that is typical of a particular area and especially one in which the sounds are produced through the nose as well as the mouth 鼻音（通常指方言） **2** a sound that is made when a tight string, especially on a musical instrument, is pulled and released （乐器等的）拨弦声

■ ***verb*** [I, T] to make a sound like a tight wire or string being pulled and released; to make sth do this 弹拨；（使）发出弹拨声，发出嘣的一声： *The bed springs twanged.* 这床的弹簧嘣嘣响。 ◇ ~ **sth** *Someone was twanging a guitar in the next room.* 隔壁有人在弹吉他。

'twas /twɒz; *NAmE* twʌz/ *abbr.* (*literary*) it was

twat /twæt; twɒt; *NAmE* twɑːt/ *noun* (*taboo, slang, especially BrE*) **1** an offensive word for an unpleasant or stupid person 讨厌鬼；蠢材 **2** an offensive word for the outer female sex organs 屄

tweak /twiːk/ *verb, noun*

■ ***verb*** **1** ~ **sth** to pull or twist sth suddenly 扭；拧；扯： *She tweaked his ear playfully.* 她拧他的耳朵逗着玩儿。 **2** ~ **sth** to make slight changes to a machine, system, etc. to improve it 稍稍调整（机器、系统等）： *I think you'll have to tweak these figures a little before you show them to the boss.* 我想你得略微改动一下这些数字再让老板过目。

■ ***noun*** **1** a sharp pull or twist 扭；拧；扯： *She gave his ear a tweak.* 她拧了一下他的耳朵。 **2** a slight change that you make to a machine, system, etc. to improve it （对机器、系统等的）轻微调整

twee /twiː/ *adj.* (*BrE, informal, disapproving*) very pretty, in a way that you find unpleasant and silly; appearing SENTIMENTAL 矫揉造作的；花里胡哨的；故作多情的： *The room was decorated with twee little pictures of animals.* 这个房间里挂满了花哨的动物小图片。

tweed /twiːd/ *noun* **1** [U] a type of thick rough cloth made of wool that has small spots of different coloured thread in it （杂色）粗花呢：*a tweed jacket* 粗花呢短上衣 **2 tweeds** [pl.] clothes made of tweed 粗花呢服装

Tweedle·dum and Tweedle·dee /ˌtwiːdlˌdʌm ən twiːdlˈdiː/ *noun* [pl.] two people or things that are not different from each other 无差别的两个人（或事物）；半斤八两 ➲ MORE LIKE THIS 17, page R27 **ORIGIN** From two characters in *Through the Looking Glass* by Lewis Carroll who look the same and say the same things. 源自刘易斯・卡罗尔所著小说《镜中世界》中的两个角色。

tweedy /ˈtwiːdi/ *adj.* **1** made of or looking like tweed 粗花呢制的；像粗花呢的：*a tweedy jacket* 粗花呢夹克 **2** (*BrE, informal, often disapproving*) used to describe the sort of person who often wears tweeds and therefore shows that they belong to the social class of rich people who live in the country（经常身穿呢子衣服）乡绅的，乡绅派头的

tween /twiːn/ (*also* **tween·er** *especially BrE*, **tween·ager** /ˈtwiːneɪdʒə(r)/) *noun* a child between the ages of about 10 and 12 * 10 至 12 岁之间的少年 **SYN** **pre-teen**

tween·er /ˈtwiːnə(r)/ *noun* **1** = TWEEN **2** a person or thing that is between two categories, classes or age groups 介乎两者之间的人（或事物）：*The film is a tweener, neither indie nor mainstream.* 这部影片既非独立制作，也不属于主流，而是介于两者之间。

tweet /twiːt/ *noun, verb*

■ *noun* **1** the short high sound made by a small bird（小鸟的）唧啾，吱喳 ➲ MORE LIKE THIS 4, page R25 **2** (*also* **twitter**) a message sent using the Twitter SOCIAL NETWORKING service 运用推特社交网络发送的信息

■ *verb* = TWITTER (1), (3)

tweet·able /ˈtwiːtəbl/ *adj.* suitable to send out as a message on the Twitter SOCIAL NETWORKING service 可通过推特发送的；可在推特上分享的：*I'll give you the tweetable summary of the plan.* 我会发给你这份计划书的概要，它能通过推特发送。

tweet·er /ˈtwiːtə(r)/ *noun* a LOUDSPEAKER for reproducing the high notes in a SOUND SYSTEM （音响系统的）高频扬声器 ➲ COMPARE WOOFER

tweez·ers /ˈtwiːzəz; *NAmE* -ərz/ *noun* [pl.] a small tool with two long thin parts joined together at one end, used for picking up very small things or for pulling out hairs 镊子；小夹钳：*a pair of tweezers* 一把镊子 ➲ VISUAL VOCAB PAGE V25

ˌTwelfth ˈNight *noun* [U] **1** January 6th, the day of the Christian festival of EPIPHANY 主显节，显现节（1 月 6 日，基督教节日） **2** the evening of January 5th, the day before EPIPHANY, which traditionally marks the end of Christmas celebrations 主显节前夕，显现节前夕（1 月 5 日夜，传统上标志着圣诞节期的结束）

twelve 🔑 /twelv/ *number* 12 十二 ▸ **twelfth** 🔑 /twelfθ/ *ordinal number, noun* **HELP** There are examples of how to use ordinal numbers at the entry for **fifth**. 序数词用法示例见 fifth 条。

twelve·month /ˈtwelvmʌnθ/ *noun* [sing.] (*old use*) a year 十二个月；一年

ˈtwelve-note (*also* **do·deca·phon·ic**, **ˈtwelve-tone**) *adj.* [only before noun] (*music* 音) used to describe a system of music which uses the twelve notes in the scale equally rather than using a particular KEY 十二音的，十二音体系的

twenty 🔑 /ˈtwenti/ **1** 🔑 *number* 20 二十 **2** *noun* **the twenties** [pl.] numbers, years or temperatures from 20 to 29 二十几；二十年代 ▸ **twen·ti·eth** 🔑 /ˈtwentiəθ/ *ordinal number, noun* **HELP** There are examples of how to use ordinal numbers at the entry for **fifth**. 序数词用法示例见 fifth 条。

IDM **in your ˈtwenties** between the ages of 20 and 29 * 20 多岁

ˌtwenty-ˈfirst *noun* [sing.] (*informal, especially BrE*) a person's 21st birthday and the celebrations for this occasion * 21 岁生日；21 岁生日庆典

ˌtwenty-ˌfour ˈseven (*also* **24/7**) *adv.* (*informal*) twenty-four hours a day, seven days a week (used to mean 'all the time') 一天二十四小时，一星期七天（用以表示"全天候"）：*He's on duty twenty-four seven.* 他不分昼夜地天天上班。

ˌtwenty ˈpence (*also* **ˌtwenty pence ˈpiece, 20p** /ˌtwenti ˈpiː/) *noun* a British coin worth 20 pence * 20 便士硬币：*You need two 20ps for the machine.* 你得往这机器里放两枚 20 便士的硬币。

ˌtwenty-ˌtwenty ˈvision (*also* **20/20 vision**) *noun* [U] the ability to see perfectly 绝好的视力

'twere /twɜː(r)/ *abbr.* (*old use*) it were

twerk /twɜːk/ *verb* [I] (*informal*) to dance to popular music with the body bent low and the hips moving forwards and backwards 跳甩臀舞 ▸ **twerk·ing** *noun* [U]

twerp /twɜːp; *NAmE* twɜːrp/ *noun* (*old-fashioned, informal*) a stupid or annoying person 笨蛋；讨厌鬼

twice 🔑 /twaɪs/ *adv.* **1** 🔑 two times; on two occasions 两次；两遍：*I don't know him well; I've only met him twice.* 我跟他不熟悉，只见过两次面。◇ *They go there **twice a week/month/year**.* 他们每星期 / 每月 / 每年去那里两次。◇ *a **twice-monthly/yearly** newsletter* 半月 / 半年刊的简讯 **2** 🔑 double in quantity, rate, etc. 两倍：*an area twice the size of Wales* 两倍于威尔士大小的地区 ◇ *Cats sleep twice as much as people.* 猫睡觉的时间比人长一倍。◇ *At 56 he's twice her age.* 他 56 岁，年龄比她大一倍。

IDM **twice ˈover** not just once but twice 不止一次，而是两次：*There was enough of the drug in her stomach to kill her twice over.* 她胃中的药物足够毒死她两次的。➲ MORE AT LIGHTNING *n.*, ONCE *adv.*, THINK *v.*

twid·dle /ˈtwɪdl/ *verb, noun*

■ *verb* [I, T] to twist or turn sth with your fingers often because you are nervous or bored（常因紧张或无聊）旋弄，摆弄，捻弄（物件）：**~ with sth** *He twiddled with the radio knob until he found the right programme.* 他转动了一会儿收音机旋钮才找到了合意的节目。◇ **~ sth** *She was twiddling the ring on her finger.* 她摆弄着手指上的戒指。

IDM **twiddle your thumbs** **1** to move your thumbs around each other with your fingers joined together 抱手旋弄大拇指 **2** to do nothing while you are waiting for sth to happen（等待之际）无所事事

■ *noun* **1** a twist or turn 拧；转动：*a twiddle of the knob* 转动一下旋钮 **2** a decorative twist in a pattern, piece of music, etc.（图案等的）修饰性曲线，螺旋形线条；（乐曲的）装饰音：*twiddles on the clarinet* 单簧管的装饰音

twid·dly /ˈtwɪdli/ *adj.* (*BrE, informal*) detailed or complicated 琐碎的；繁杂的 **SYN** **fiddly**

twig /twɪɡ/ *noun, verb*

■ *noun* a small very thin branch that grows out of a larger branch on a bush or tree 细枝；小枝；嫩枝 ➲ VISUAL VOCAB PAGE V10

■ *verb* (-gg-) [I, T] **~ (sth) | ~ what... | ~ (that)...** (*BrE, informal*) to suddenly understand or realize sth（突然地）懂得，理解，明白，意识到：*Haven't you twigged yet?* 难道你还不明白？◇ *I finally twigged what he meant.* 我终于弄明白了他的意思。

twi·light /ˈtwaɪlaɪt/ *noun, adj.*

■ *noun* [U] **1** the faint light or the period of time at the end of the day after the sun has gone down 暮色；薄暮；黄昏：*It was hard to see him clearly **in the twilight**.* 在朦胧的暮色中很难看清他。◇ *We went for a walk along the beach **at twilight**.* 黄昏时分我们沿着海滩散步。➲ WORDFINDER NOTE AT SUN **2 the ~ (of sth)** the final stage of sth when it becomes weaker or less important than it was 没落时期；衰退期；晚期：*the twilight years* (= the last years of your life) 暮年

■ *adj.* [only before noun] **1** (*formal*) used to describe a state in which things are strange and mysterious, or where things are kept secret and do not seem to be part of the real world 奇妙神秘的；虚幻的：*the **twilight world** of the occult* 魔法的虚幻世界 ◇ *They lived in the **twilight zone** on the fringes of society.* 他们生活在社会边缘光怪陆离之处。 **2** used to describe a situation or area of thought that is not clearly defined （局面或思想领域）朦胧的，模糊的，界限不清的

twi·lit /'twaɪlɪt/ *adj.* (*literary*) lit by twilight 暮色苍茫的；昏暗朦胧的

twill /twɪl/ *noun* [U] a type of strong cloth that is made in a particular way to produce a surface of raised DIAGONAL lines 斜纹布：*a cotton twill skirt* 斜纹布裙子

'twill /twɪl/ *abbr.* (*old use*) it will

twin /twɪn/ *noun, verb, adj.*

■ ***noun*** **1** one of two children born at the same time to the same mother 孪生儿之一；双胞胎之一：*She's expecting twins.* 她怀着双胞胎。 ➲ COLLOCATIONS AT CHILD ➲ SEE ALSO CONJOINED TWIN, FRATERNAL TWIN, IDENTICAL TWIN, SIAMESE TWIN **2** one of two similar things that make a pair 一对相像的事物之一

■ ***verb*** (**-nn-**) **1** [usually passive] **~ sth** (**with sth**) to make a close relationship between two towns or areas 使结成姊妹城市；使结成友好地区：*Oxford is twinned with Bonn in Germany.* 牛津和德国的波恩结成了友好城市。 **2 ~ sth** (**with sth**) to join two people or things closely together 使（两人或两事物）紧密结合；使耦合；使相连：*The opera twins the themes of love and death.* 这出歌剧把爱与死的主题紧密结合在一起。

■ ***adj.*** [only before noun] **1** used to describe one of a pair of children who are twins 孪生之一的；双胞胎之一的：***twin boys/girls*** 孪生男孩／女孩 ◇ ***a twin brother/sister*** 孪生兄弟／姐妹中的一个 **2** used to describe two things that are used as a pair 成对的；成双的：*a ship with twin propellers* 有双螺旋桨的船 **3** used to describe two things that are connected, or present or happening at the same time 双重的；双联的；两个同时发生的：*The prison service has the twin goals of punishment and rehabilitation.* 监狱有惩罚和改造双重目的。

ˌtwin 'bed *noun* **1** [usually pl.] one of a pair of single beds in a room （成对的）一张单人床：*Would you prefer twin beds or a double?* 你们喜欢一对单人床还是一张双人床？ **2** (*NAmE*) (*BrE* **ˌsingle 'bed**) a bed big enough for one person 单人床：*sheets to fit a twin bed* 单人床的床单 ➲ VISUAL VOCAB PAGE V24

ˌtwin-'bedded *adj.* (of a room 房间) having two single beds in it 有两张单人床的

ˌtwin 'bedroom *noun* a room in a hotel, etc. that has two single beds （旅馆等的）有两张单人床的房间

twine /twaɪn/ *noun, verb*

■ ***noun*** [U] strong string that has two or more STRANDS (= single thin pieces of thread or string) twisted together （两股或多股的）线，绳；合股线；麻绳

■ ***verb*** [I, T] **~** (**sth**) **around/round/through/in sth** to wind or twist around sth; to make sth do this （使）盘绕，缠绕，围绕：*ivy twining around a tree trunk* 缠绕在树干上的藤蔓 ◇ *She twined her arms around my neck.* 她用双臂搂着我的脖子。

ˌtwin-'engined *adj.* (of an aircraft 飞机) having two engines 双发动机的；双引擎的

twinge /twɪndʒ/ *noun* **1** a sudden short feeling of pain （一阵）剧痛，刺痛：*He **felt a twinge** in his knee.* 他感到膝盖一阵剧痛。 **2 ~** (**of sth**) a sudden short feeling of an unpleasant emotion （一阵）不快，难过，痛苦：*a twinge of disappointment* 一阵失望

twin·kle /'twɪŋkl/ *verb, noun*

■ ***verb*** **1** [I] to shine with a light that keeps changing from bright to faint to bright again 闪耀；闪烁：*Stars twinkled in the sky.* 星星在天空中闪烁。 ◇ *twinkling lights in the distance* 远处闪耀的点点灯光 ➲ SYNONYMS AT SHINE **2** [I] **~** (**with sth**) | **~** (**at sb**) if your eyes **twinkle**, you have a bright expression because you are happy or excited （眼睛因高兴或兴奋）闪光，发亮：*twinkling blue eyes* 闪闪发亮的蓝眼睛 ◇ *Her eyes twinkled with merriment.* 她高兴得双眸闪闪发亮。

■ ***noun*** [sing.] **1** an expression in your eyes that shows you are happy or amused about sth （眼睛的）闪亮；欣喜的神情：*He looked at me with a **twinkle in his eye**.* 他目光熠熠地望着我。 **2** a small light that keeps changing from bright to faint to bright again 闪烁；闪耀；闪光：*the twinkle of stars* 星星的闪烁 ◇ *the twinkle of the harbour lights in the distance* 远处港口灯光的闪烁

twink·ling /'twɪŋklɪŋ/ *noun* [sing.] (*old-fashioned, informal*) a very short time 瞬间；转眼；一眨眼；一刹那

IDM **in the ˌtwinkling of an 'eye** very quickly 瞬息之间；转眼之间 SYN **instant**

twin·set /'twɪnset/ *noun* a woman's matching sweater and CARDIGAN that are designed to be worn together 女式套装毛衣（配套穿的套头和开襟毛衣）

ˌtwin 'town *noun* one of two towns in different countries that have a special relationship with each other （不同国家间）结成姊妹城的两个城市之一：*a visit to Lyon, Birmingham's twin town in France* 对伯明翰在法国的友好城市里昂的访问

twirl /twɜːl; *NAmE* twɜːrl/ *verb, noun*

■ ***verb*** **1** [I, T] **~** (**sb**) (**around/round**) to move or dance round and round; to make sb do this （使）旋转，转动：*She twirled around in front of the mirror.* 她对着镜子转动身子。 ◇ *He held her hand and twirled her around.* 他牵着她的手，让她旋转。 **2** [T] **~ sth** (**around/about**) to make sth turn quickly and lightly round and round 使轻快地转动；使旋转 SYN **spin**：*He twirled his hat in his hand.* 他快速旋转着手里的帽子。 ◇ *She sat twirling the stem of the glass in her fingers.* 她坐在那里用手指捻动着高脚酒杯的柄脚。 **3** [T] **~ sth** to twist or curl sth with your fingers （用手指）缠绕，盘绕，卷曲：*He kept twirling his moustache.* 他不停地用手指卷胡须。

■ ***noun*** the action of a person spinning around once （人）旋转一周：*Kate **did a twirl** in her new dress.* 凯特穿着新连衣裙转了一圈。

twist /twɪst/ *verb, noun*

■ ***verb***

• **BEND INTO SHAPE** 弯曲成形 **1** [T] **~ sth** (**into sth**) to bend or turn sth into a particular shape 使弯曲，使扭曲（成一定形状）：*Twist the wire to form a circle.* 把铁丝弯成一个环。 **2** [T, I] to bend or turn sth into a shape or position that is not normal or natural; to be bent or turned in this way （使）弯曲变形，扭曲变形：**~ sth** (**+ adv./prep.**) *He grabbed me and twisted my arm behind my back.* 他抓住我，把我的胳膊扭到背后。 ◇ (**+ adv./prep.**) *Her face twisted in anger.* 她气得脸都变形了。

• **TURN BODY** 转动身体 **3** [T, I] to turn part of your body around while the rest stays still 扭转，转动（身体部位）：**~ sth** (**+ adv./prep.**) *He twisted his head around to look at her.* 他扭过头去看她。 ◇ (**+ adv./prep.**) *She twisted in her chair when I called her name.* 我唤她的名字时，她坐在座椅上转过身来。 **4** [I, T] to turn your body with quick sharp movements and change direction often （猛地将身体）转动，旋转，扭动：*I **twisted and turned** to avoid being caught.* 我左躲右闪免得被捉住。 ◇ **+ adv./prep.** *She tried unsuccessfully to twist free.* 她试图挣脱身子，但无济于事。 ◇ **~ sth/yourself + adv./prep.** *He managed to twist himself round in the restricted space.* 他设法在有限的空间内转过身来。

• **TURN WITH HAND** 用手转动 **5** [T] **~ sth** (**+ adv./prep.**) to turn sth around in a circle with your hand （用手）转动，旋转：*Twist the knob to the left to open the door.* 向左转动手柄把门打开。 ◇ *Nervously I twisted the ring on my finger.* 我紧张地转动着手指上的戒指。

• **OF ROADS/RIVERS** 道路；河流 **6** [I] to bend and change direction often 曲折；蜿蜒；盘旋：*The road **twists and turns** along the coast.* 道路沿着海滨蜿蜒曲折。 ◇ *narrow twisting streets* 狭窄弯曲的街道 ◇ *a twisting staircase* 盘旋而上的楼梯

• **ANKLE/WRIST/KNEE** 踝；腕；膝 **7** [T] **~ sth** to injure part

T

of your body, especially your ankle, wrist or knee, bending it in an awkward way 扭伤；崴伤：*She fell and twisted her ankle.* 她摔了一下，把脚崴了。

• **WIND AROUND** 缠绕 **8** [T] ~ sth (+ adv./prep.) to wind sth around or through an object 使缠绕；缭绕；盘绕：*She twisted a scarf around her head.* 她用一条围巾裹住了头。◇ *The telephone cable has* ***got twisted*** (= wound around itself). 电话线缠绕在一起了。 **9** [I] ~ (round/around sth) to move or grow by winding around sth 蠕动；盘绕；缠绕生长：*A snake was twisting around his arm.* 一条蛇缠绕在他的手臂上。

• **FACTS** 事实 **10** [T] ~ sth to deliberately change the meaning of what sb has said, or to present facts in a particular way, in order to benefit yourself or harm sb else（故意）歪曲，曲解 SYN **misrepresent**：*You always twist everything I say.* 你总是歪曲我说的每一句话。◇ *The newspaper was accused of twisting the facts.* 这家报纸被指责歪曲事实。

• **THREADS** 线 **11** [T] ~ sth (into sth) to turn or wind threads, etc. together to make sth longer or thicker 捻，搓，绞（线等）：*They had twisted the sheets into a rope and escaped by climbing down it.* 他们把床单绞成绳子，缘绳而下逃走了。

IDM **twist sb's 'arm** (*informal*) to persuade or force sb to do sth 劝说；强迫；生拉硬拽；施加压力 ➲ MORE AT KNIFE *n.*, LITTLE FINGER

PHR V **,twist sth↔'off** to turn and pull sth with your hand to remove it from sth 拧开；扭脱：*I twisted off the lid and looked inside.* 我拧开盖子往里面看。◇ *a twist-off top* 一拧即开的盖儿

■ ***noun***

• **ACTION OF TURNING** 旋转 **1** [C] the action of turning sth with your hand, or of turning a part of your body 转动；旋转；搓；捻；拧；扭动：*She gave the lid another twist and it came off.* 她又拧了一下，盖儿开了。◇ *He gave a shy smile and a little twist of his head.* 他羞怯地笑了笑，略微扭了一下头。

• **UNEXPECTED CHANGE** 意外变化 **2** [C] an unexpected change or development in a story or situation（故事或情况的）转折，转变，突然变化：*the twists and turns of his political career* 他政治生涯的一波三折 ◇ *The story has taken another twist.* 故事情节再一次变化。◇ *The disappearance of a vital witness added a* ***new twist*** *to the case.* 一名重要证人失踪，令诉讼出现了新的变数。◇ *By a curious* ***twist of fate*** *we met again only a week or so later.* 由于命运巧妙的安排，大约只过了一周我们又相逢了。
➲ WORDFINDER NOTE AT PLOT

• **IN ROAD/RIVER** 道路；河流 **3** [C] a sharp bend in a road or river 急转弯处；曲折处：*The car followed the* ***twists and turns*** *of the mountain road.* 汽车沿着弯弯曲曲的山路行驶。

• **SHAPE** 形状 **4** [C] a thing that has been twisted into a particular shape 螺旋状的东西；卷曲物；捻合成的东西：*mineral water with a twist of lemon* 加了一卷柠檬皮的矿泉水

• **DANCE** 舞蹈 **5** **the twist** [sing.] a fast dance that was popular in the 1960s, in which you twist from side to side 扭摆舞（盛行于 20 世纪 60 年代）

IDM **round the bend/twist** (*informal, especially BrE*) crazy 发疯；疯狂：*She's gone completely round the twist.* 她完全疯了。➲ MORE AT KNICKERS

twist·ed /'twɪstɪd/ *adj.* **1** bent or turned so that the original shape is lost 扭曲的；弯曲的；变形的：*After the crash the car was a mass of twisted metal.* 那辆车撞成了一堆扭曲的废铁。◇ *a twisted ankle* (= injured by being turned suddenly) 扭伤的踝关节 ◇ *She gave a small twisted smile.* 她不自然地微微一笑。➲ PICTURE AT CURVED **2** (of a person's mind or behaviour 人的思想或行为) not normal; strange in an unpleasant way 怪僻的；偏执的：*Her experiences had left her* ***bitter and twisted.*** 她的经历使她变得愤愤不平，性情乖僻。

twist·er /'twɪstə(r)/ *noun* (*NAmE, informal*) a violent storm that is caused by a powerful spinning column of air 旋风；龙卷风 SYN **tornado**

twisty /'twɪsti/ *adj.* (especially of a road 尤指道路) having many bends or turns 弯弯曲曲的；蜿蜒曲折的 SYN **winding, zigzag**

twit /twɪt/ *noun* (*informal, especially BrE*) a silly or annoying person 笨蛋；傻瓜；讨厌鬼

twitch /twɪtʃ/ *verb, noun*

■ ***verb*** **1** [I, T] ~ (sth) if a part of your body **twitches**, or if you **twitch** it, it makes a sudden quick movement, sometimes one that you cannot control 痉挛；抽搐；抽动：*Her lips twitched with amusement.* 她忍俊不禁地颤动着嘴唇。◇ *The cats watched each other, their tails twitching.* 两只猫晃动着尾巴彼此对视着。 **2** [T, I] ~ (sth) to give sth a short sharp pull; to be pulled in this way 急拉；猛拽；猛地被扯动：*He twitched the package out of my hands.* 他猛地从我手中拽走了包裹。◇ *The curtains twitched as she rang the bell.* 她按铃时窗帘被猛地拉动了一下。

■ ***noun*** **1** a sudden quick movement that you cannot control in one of your muscles 颤搐；痉挛；抽动：*She has a twitch in her left eye.* 她左眼跳了一下。◇ *a nervous twitch* 神经性颤搐 **2** a sudden quick movement or feeling 闪动；晃动；急拉；（一阵）感觉：*He greeted us with a mere twitch of his head.* 他只晃了一下头算是和我们打过招呼。◇ *At that moment she felt the first twitch of anxiety.* 那一刻她第一次感到一阵焦虑。

twitch·er /'twɪtʃə(r)/ *noun* (*BrE, informal*) a person who is very keen on finding and watching rare birds 观鸟痴，赏鸟迷（热衷发现和观赏珍稀鸟类）

twitchy /'twɪtʃi/ *adj.* (*informal*) **1** nervous or anxious about sth 神经紧张的；焦急的；焦虑不安的 SYN **jittery** **2** making sudden quick movements 抽搐的；抽动的；痉挛的

Twit·ter™ /'twɪtə(r)/ *noun* [U] a SOCIAL NETWORKING service that allows you to send out short regular messages about what you are doing, that people can access on the Internet or on their mobile/cell phones 推特（通过互联网或手机访问并发送即时短信息的社交网络服务）➲ COMPARE MICROBLOGGING, TWEET *n.* (2)

twit·ter /'twɪtə(r)/ *verb, noun*

■ ***verb*** **1** (*also* **tweet**) [I] when birds **twitter**, they make a series of short high sounds（鸟）唧啾，叽喳，啁啾 **2** [I, T] ~ (on) (about sth) | + speech (*especially BrE*) to talk quickly in a high excited voice, especially about sth that is not very important 唧唧喳喳地说话 **3** (*also* **tweet**) [I, T] ~ (sth) to send a message using the TWITTER™ SOCIAL NETWORKING service 用推特发信息

■ ***noun*** [sing.] **1** (*also* **twit·tering**) a series of short high sounds that birds make（鸟的）唧啾声，叽叽叫声 **2** (*informal*) a state of nervous excitement 兴奋；紧张；激动 **3** = TWEET (2)

Twit·ter·verse /'twɪtəvɜːs; *NAmE* 'twɪtərvɜːrs/ (*usually* **the Twit·ter·verse**) (*also* **the Twit·ter·sphere** /ðə 'twɪtəsfɪə(r); *NAmE* ðə 'twɪtərsfɪr/) *noun* [sing.] (*informal*) all the messages that are sent using the Twitter SOCIAL NETWORKING service, viewed as a network of people communicating with each other 推特圈；推特世界

'twixt /twɪkst/ *prep.* (*old use*) between 在…中间；在…之间
IDM SEE SLIP *n.*

two /tuː/ *number* 2 二 HELP There are examples of how to use numbers at the entry for **five**. 数词用法示例见 five 条。➲ MORE LIKE THIS 20, page R27

IDM **a 'day, 'moment, 'pound, etc. or two** one or a few days, moments, pounds, etc. 一两天（或一会儿、一两镑等）：*May I borrow it for a day or two?* 这个我可以借用一两天吗？ **fall between two 'stools** (*BrE*) to fail to be or to get either of two choices, both of which would have been acceptable 两头落空；鸡飞蛋打 **in 'two** in or into two pieces or halves 一分为二；成两半：*He broke the bar of chocolate in two and gave me half.* 他把巧克力掰成两半，给了我一块。 **in ,twos and 'threes** two or three at a time; in small numbers 三三两两；稀稀拉拉：*People arrived in twos and threes.* 人们三三两两地到了。 **it takes two to do sth** (*saying*) one person cannot be completely responsible for sth 双方都有责任；一个巴掌拍不响：*You* *can't put all the blame on him. It takes two to make a marriage.* 你不能全责怪他，结婚是两个人的事。**not have two beans, brain cells, etc. to rub to'gether** (*informal*) to have no money; to be very stupid, etc. 不名一文（或没有脑子等） **put ˌtwo and ˌtwo to'gether** to guess the truth from what you see, hear, etc. 根据所见所闻推断：*He's inclined to* ***put two and two together and make five*** (= reaches the wrong conclusion from what he sees, hears, etc.). 他爱捕风捉影，听风就是雨。**that makes 'two of us** (*informal*) I am in the same position or I agree with you 我也一样；我也有同感：*'I'm tired!' 'That makes two of us!'* "我累了！""我也是一样！" **two ˌsides of the same 'coin** used to talk about two ways of looking at the same situation 同一事物的两个方面 ➲ MORE AT MIND *n.*, SHAKE *n.*

'two-bit *adj.* [only before noun] (*informal, especially NAmE*) not good or important 不好的；微不足道的；不重要的：*She wanted to be more than just a two-bit secretary.* 她并不想只做一个人微言轻的小秘书。

ˌtwo 'bits *noun* [pl.] (*old-fashioned, NAmE, informal*) 25 cents（货币）25 分

ˌtwo-di'mension·al *adj.* flat; having no depth; appearing to have only two DIMENSIONS 平面的；无深度的；二度空间的；二维的：*a two-dimensional drawing* 平面图 ◇ (*figurative*) *The novel was criticized for its two-dimensional characters* (= that did not seem like real people). 这部小说因人物缺乏深度而受到批评。

ˌtwo-'edged *adj.* **1** (of a blade, knife, etc. 刃、刀等) having two sharp edges for cutting 双刃的；双锋的 **2** having two possible meanings or results, one good and one bad 有好坏两种含义（或结果）的；双关的；有利有弊的：*a two-edged remark* 双关语 ◇ *Fame can be* ***a two-edged sword.*** 名声是把双刃剑。

ˌtwo-'faced *adj.* (*informal, disapproving*) not sincere; not acting in a way that supports what you say that you believe; saying different things to different people about a particular subject 两面派的；言行不一的；阴一套阳一套的 **SYN** **hypocritical**

ˌtwo 'fingers *noun* [pl.] (*BrE, informal*) a sign that you make by holding up your hand with the inside part facing towards you and making a V-shape with your first and second fingers (used as a way of being rude to other people)（手心向里，表示侮蔑的）V 字形手势：*I gave him the two fingers.* 我对他做了一个侮辱性的手势。➲ COMPARE V-SIGN

two·fold /'tuːfəʊld; *NAmE* -foʊld/ *adj.* (*formal*) **1** consisting of two parts 由两部分组成的；有两部分的：*The problem was twofold.* 这个问题分两个部分。**2** twice as much or as many 两倍的：*a twofold increase in demand* 需求增加了一倍 ▶ **two·fold** *adv.*：*Her original investment has increased twofold.* 她原先的投资已经增加到两倍。

ˌtwo-'handed *adj.* using or needing both hands 用双手的；需要双手的：*a two-handed backhand* (= in TENNIS) 双手握拍反手击球 ◇ *a two-handed catch* 用双手接的球

ˌtwo-'hander *noun* (*especially BrE*) a play that is written for only two actors 双人物戏剧

twonk /twɒŋk; *NAmE* twɑːŋk/ *noun* (*BrE, slang*) a stupid person 傻瓜；笨蛋

ˌtwo 'pence (*also* **ˌtwo pence 'piece, 2p** /ˌtuː 'piː/) *noun* a British coin worth two pence（英国的）两便士硬币

two·pence /'tʌpəns/ *noun* (*BrE*) = TUPPENCE

two·penny (*also informal* **tup·penny**) /'tʌpəni; *NAmE also* 'tuːpeni/ *adj.* (*BrE*) costing or worth two old pence 值两旧便士的：*a twopenny stamp* 一枚两便士的邮票

ˌtwo-'piece *noun* a set of clothes consisting of two matching pieces of clothing, for example a skirt and jacket or trousers/pants and a jacket 两件一套的衣服；两件式 ▶ **ˌtwo-'piece** *adj.* [only before noun]：*a two-piece suit* 两件式西装

'two-ply *adj.* (of wool, wood or other material 毛线、木材或其他材料) with two threads or thicknesses 双股的；双层的

ˌtwo-'seater *noun* a vehicle, an aircraft or a piece of furniture with seats for two people 双座车辆（或飞机、家具） ➲ VISUAL VOCAB PAGE V22

two·some /'tuːsəm/ *noun* a group of two people who do sth together（共事的）两人组 **SYN** **pair**

'two-star *adj.* [usually before noun] **1** having two stars in a system that measures quality. The highest standard is usually represented by four or five stars.（服务质量）两星级的：*a two-star hotel* 两星级宾馆 **2** (*NAmE*) having the fourth-highest military rank, and wearing uniform which has two stars on it（军阶）两星的

'two-step *noun* a dance with long, sliding steps; the music for this dance 两步舞；两步舞曲

'two-stroke *adj.* (of an engine or vehicle 发动机或车辆) with a PISTON that makes two movements, one up and one down, in each power CYCLE 二冲程的 ➲ COMPARE FOUR-STROKE

'two-time *verb* **~ sb** (*informal*) to not be faithful to a person you have a relationship with, especially a sexual one, by having a secret relationship with sb else at the same time 对（情人或爱人）不忠：*Are you sure he's not two-timing you?* 你肯定他没有背着你另有所爱？ ▶ **'two-timer** *noun*

'two-tone *adj.* [only before noun] having two different colours or sounds 两色的；双音的

'twould /twʊd/ *abbr.* (*old use*) it would

ˌtwo-ˌup ˌtwo-'down *noun* (*BrE, informal*) a house with two rooms on the bottom floor and two bedrooms upstairs 两上两下的房屋（楼下两室，楼上两卧室）

ˌtwo-'way *adj.* [usually before noun] **1** moving in two different directions; allowing sth to move in two different directions 双行的；双向的：*two-way traffic* 双向交通 ◇ *two-way trade* 双向贸易 ◇ *a two-way switch* (= that allows electric current to be turned on or off from either of two points) 双路开关 **2** (of communication between people 人际交流) needing equal effort from both people or groups involved 相互的；彼此的；有来有往的：*Friendship is a two-way process.* 友谊是一种相互的关系。 **3** (of radio equipment, etc. 无线电设备等) used both for sending and receiving signals 收发两用的

ˌtwo-way 'mirror *noun* a piece of glass that is a mirror on one side, but that you can see through from the other 单向透明玻璃镜（一面是镜子，但从镜后可看到镜前面）

ty·coon /taɪ'kuːn/ *noun* a person who is successful in business or industry and has become rich and powerful（企业界的）大亨，巨头，巨子：***a business/property/media tycoon*** 产业大亨；房地产巨头；传媒巨子

tyke (*also* **tike**) /taɪk/ *noun* (*informal*) **1** a small child, especially one who behaves badly 小孩子；小淘气；小调皮鬼 **2** (*BrE*) a person from Yorkshire 约克郡人

tym·pa·num /'tɪmpənəm/ *noun* (*pl.* **tym·pa·nums** or **tym·pana** /'tɪmpənə/) (*anatomy* 解) the EARDRUM 鼓膜；耳膜

type /taɪp/ *noun, verb*

■ *noun* **1** [C] **~ (of sth)** a class or group of people or things that share particular qualities or features and are part of a larger group; a kind or sort 类型；种类：*different racial types* 不同的人种 ◇ *a rare blood type* 罕见的血型 ◇ *There are three main types of contract(s).* 有三种主要的合同。◇ *Bungalows are a type of house.* 平房是一种房屋。◇ *She mixes with all types of people.* 她和各种类型的人打交道。◇ *She mixes with people of all types.* 她和各种类型的人打交道。◇ *I love this type of book.* 我喜欢这类书籍。◇ *I love these types of books.* 我喜欢这些种类的书籍。◇ (*informal*) *I*

T

love these type of books. 我爱读这些种类的书籍。◇ *What do you charge for this type of work?* 这种活你收多少钱？◇ *What do you charge for work of this type?* 这种活你收多少钱？◇ *It is the first car of its type to have this design feature.* 这是同类型汽车中首部具备这种设计特点的。 **2** [sing.] (*informal*) a person of a particular character, with particular features, etc. 具有某种特征的人；典型： *She's the artistic type.* 她是艺术家一类的人。◇ *He's not the type to be unfaithful.* 他不是背信弃义的那种人。◇ *She's **not my type*** (= not the kind of person I am usually attracted to). 她不是我喜欢的那种人。 **3 -type** (in adjectives 构成形容词) having the qualities or features of the group, person or thing mentioned 属于…类型的；具有…特征的： *a police-type badge* 一枚警徽 ◇ *a continental-type cafe* 有欧洲大陆特色的小餐馆 **4** [U] letters that are printed or typed （印刷或打印的）文字，字符，字体： *The type was too small for me to read.* 这种印刷文字太小，我看不清。◇ *The important words are in bold type.* 重点词是用黑体字印刷的。

■ ***verb*** **1** [I, T] to write sth using a computer or TYPEWRITER （用计算机或打字机）打字： *How fast can you type?* 你打字有多快？◇ *typing errors* 打字错误 ◇ **~ sth (out/in/up)** *This letter will need to be typed (out) again.* 这封信需要再打一遍。◇ *Type (in) the filename, then press 'Return'.* 键入文件名称，再按"回车"键。◇ *Has that report been **typed up** yet?* 那份报告打出来没有？ **2** [T] **~ sb/sth** (*specialist*) to find out the group or class that a person or thing belongs to 测定…的类型；分型；定型： *Blood samples were taken from patients for typing.* 已采集患者的血样供测定血型用。

type·cast /ˈtaɪpkɑːst; *NAmE* -kæst/ *verb* (**type·cast, type·cast**) [usually passive] **~ sb (as sth)** if an actor is **typecast**, he or she is always given the same kind of character to play 让（演员）总演同一类型的角色： *She didn't want to be typecast as a dumb blonde.* 她不想总是演傻乎乎的金发女郎一类的角色。

type·face /ˈtaɪpfeɪs/ *noun* a set of letters, numbers, etc. of a particular design, used in printing （印刷用的）字体： *I'd like the heading to be in a different typeface from the text.* 我希望标题和正文使用不同的字体。

type·script /ˈtaɪpskrɪpt/ *noun* [C, U] a copy of a text or document that has been typed （打印出的）文稿，文件；打字稿

type·set·ter /ˈtaɪpsetə(r)/ *noun* a person, machine or company that prepares a book, etc. for printing 排字工人；排字机；排字公司 ▶ **type·set** *verb* (**type·set·ting, type·set, type·set**)： **~ sth** *Pages can now be typeset on-screen.* 现在可以屏幕排版。 **type·set·ting** *noun* [U]: *computerized typesetting* 计算机排版

type·writer /ˈtaɪpraɪtə(r)/ *noun* a machine that produces writing similar to print. It has keys that you press to make metal letters or signs hit a piece of paper through a strip of cloth covered with ink. 打字机 ➲ SEE ALSO TYPIST

type·writ·ing /ˈtaɪpraɪtɪŋ/ *noun* = TYPING

type·writ·ten /ˈtaɪprɪtn/ *adj.* written using a typewriter or computer （用打字机或计算机）打字的，打印的

ty·phoid /ˈtaɪfɔɪd/ (*also less frequent* ˌ**typhoid ˈfever**) *noun* [U] a serious infectious disease that causes fever, red spots on the chest and severe pain in the BOWELS, and sometimes causes death 伤寒： *a typhoid epidemic* 伤寒的流行

ty·phoon /taɪˈfuːn/ *noun* a violent tropical storm with very strong winds 台风 ➲ COMPARE CYCLONE, HURRICANE

ty·phus /ˈtaɪfəs/ *noun* [U] a serious infectious disease that causes fever, headaches, purple marks on the body and often death 斑疹伤寒

typ·ical /ˈtɪpɪkl/ *adj.* **1** having the usual qualities or features of a particular type of person, thing or group 典型的；有代表性的 SYN **representative**: *a typical Italian cafe* 典型的意大利式小餐馆 ◇ *This is a typical example of Roman pottery.* 这是一件典型的罗马陶器。◇ **~ of sb/sth** *This meal is typical of local cookery.* 这是有当地风味的饭菜。◇ **~ for sb/sth** *The weather at the moment is not typical for July.* 现在的天气并不是七月份常有的。 OPP **atypical** **2** happening in the usual way; showing what sth is usually like 一贯的；平常的 SYN **normal**: *A typical working day for me begins at 7.30.* 我的工作日一般在 7:30 开始。 OPP **untypical** **3** **~ (of sb/sth)** (*often disapproving*) behaving in the way that you expect 不出所料；特有的： *It was typical of her to forget.* 她这个人就是爱忘事。◇ *He spoke with typical enthusiasm.* 他以其特有的热情讲话。◇ (*informal*) *She's late again—typical!* 她又迟到了，一贯如此！

typ·ic·al·ly /ˈtɪpɪkli/ *adv.* **1** used to say that sth usually happens in the way that you are stating 通常；一般： *The factory typically produces 500 chairs a week.* 这家工厂通常每周生产 500 把椅子。◇ *A typically priced meal will be around $10.* 一餐通常的价格为 10 美元左右。 **2** in a way that shows the usual qualities or features of a particular type of person, thing or group 典型地；具有代表性地： *typically American hospitality* 美国人特有的殷勤好客 ◇ *Mothers typically worry about their children.* 母亲总爱挂念自己的子女。 **3** in the way that you expect sb/sth to behave 不出所料；果然： *Typically, she couldn't find her keys.* 她果然又找不着自己的钥匙了。◇ *He was typically modest about his achievements.* 他一如既往，对自己的成就很谦虚。

typ·ify /ˈtɪpɪfaɪ/ *verb* (**typi·fies, typi·fy·ing, typi·fied, typi·fied**) (not usually used in the progressive tenses 通常不用于进行时) **1 ~ sth** to be a typical example of sth 作为…的典型；是…的典范： *clothes that typify the 1960s* * 20 世纪 60 年代典型的服装 ◇ *the new style of politician, typified by the Prime Minister* 以首相为代表的新型政治家风格 **2 ~ sth** to be a typical feature of sth 成为…的特征： *the haunting guitar melodies that typify the band's music* 反映这个乐队音乐特色的萦绕心头的吉他乐曲

typ·ing /ˈtaɪpɪŋ/ (*also less frequent* **type·writ·ing**) *noun* [U] **1** the activity or job of using a TYPEWRITER or computer to write sth （用打字机或计算机）打字： *to do the typing* 打字 ◇ *typing errors* 打字错误 ◇ *a **typing pool*** (= a group of people who share a company's typing work) 打字小组 **2** writing that has been done on a TYPEWRITER or computer （用打字机或计算机打的）打字稿，文稿

typ·ist /ˈtaɪpɪst/ *noun* **1** a person who works in an office typing letters, etc. 打字员 **2** a person who uses a TYPEWRITER or computer keyboard （用打字机或计算机键盘的）打字者： *I'm quite a fast typist.* 我打字相当快。

typo /ˈtaɪpəʊ; *NAmE* -poʊ/ *noun* (*pl.* **-os**) (*informal*) a small mistake in a typed or printed text 打字（或排印）文稿的小错误

typ·og·raph·er /taɪˈpɒɡrəfə(r); *NAmE* -ˈpɑːɡ-/ *noun* a person who is skilled in typography 印刷工人；排字工

typ·og·raphy /taɪˈpɒɡrəfi; *NAmE* -ˈpɑːɡ-/ *noun* [U] the art or work of preparing books, etc. for printing, especially of designing how text will appear when it is printed 印刷术；排印；版面设计 ▶ **typo·graph·ic·al** /ˌtaɪpəˈɡræfɪkl/ (*also* **typo·graph·ic** /ˌtaɪpəˈɡræfɪk/) *adj.*： *a typographical error* 排印错误 ◇ *typographic design* 印刷版面设计 **typo·graph·ic·al·ly** /-kli/ *adv.*

typ·ology /taɪˈpɒlədʒi; *NAmE* -ˈpɑːl-/ *noun* (*pl.* **-ies**) (*specialist*) a system of dividing things into different types 类型学

tyr·an·nical /tɪˈrænɪkl/ (*also formal* **tyr·an·nous** /ˈtɪrənəs/) *adj.* using power or authority over people in an unfair and cruel way 暴君的；专横的；残暴的 SYN **autocratic, dictatorial**

tyr·an·nize (*BrE also* **-ise**) /ˈtɪrənaɪz/ *verb* [T, I] to use your power to treat sb in a cruel or unfair way 对…施行暴政；专横地对待： **~ sb/sth** *a father tyrannizing his children* 专横地对待子女的父亲 ◇ **~ over sb/sth** *a political leader who tyrannizes over his people* 对人民施行暴政的政治头领 ➲ SEE ALSO TYRANT

T

tyr·an·no·saur /tɪˈrænəsɔː(r); taɪ-/ (*also* **tyr·an·no·saurus** /tɪˌrænəˈsɔːrəs/) *noun* a very large DINOSAUR that stood on two legs, had large powerful JAWS and two short front legs 霸王龙

tyr·anny /ˈtɪrəni/ *noun* [U, C] (*pl.* **-ies**) **1** unfair or cruel use of power or authority 暴虐；专横；苛政；专政：*a victim of oppression and tyranny* 压迫和暴政的受害者 ◇ *The children had no protection against the tyranny of their father.* 孩子们无法抵御其父的虐待。◇ *the tyrannies of Nazi rule* 纳粹统治的暴行 ◇ (*figurative*) *These days it seems we must all submit to the tyranny of the motor car.* 如今，似乎所有人都离不开汽车了。 **2** the rule of a tyrant; a country under this rule 暴君统治；暴君统治的国家 SYN **dictatorship**：*Any political system refusing to allow dissent becomes a tyranny.* 任何不允许不同政见的政治体制都会变成专制。

tyr·ant /ˈtaɪrənt/ *noun* a person who has complete power in a country and uses it in a cruel and unfair way 暴君；专制君主；暴虐的统治者 SYN **dictator**：*The country was ruled by a succession of tyrants.* 这个国家接连遭受暴君的统治。◇ (*figurative*) *His boss is a complete tyrant.* 他的老板是个不折不扣的暴君。

tyre (*BrE*) (*NAmE* **tire**) /ˈtaɪə(r)/ *noun* a thick rubber ring that fits around the edge of a wheel of a car, bicycle, etc. 轮胎：*a* ***front tyre*** 前胎 ◇ *a* ***back/rear tyre*** 后胎 ◇ *to pump up a tyre* 给轮胎打气 ◇ *a* ***flat/burst/punctured tyre*** 瘪了的／爆了的／扎了的轮胎 ◇ ***bald/worn tyres*** 磨平的／磨损的轮胎 ➲ COLLOCATIONS AT DRIVING ➲ VISUAL VOCAB PAGES V55, V56 ➲ SEE ALSO SPARE TYRE (1) IDM SEE KICK *v.*

tyro /ˈtaɪrəʊ; *NAmE* -roʊ/ *noun* (*pl.* **-os**) a person who has little or no experience of sth or is beginning to learn sth 初学者；新手；生手 SYN **novice**

tzar, **tzar·ina**, **tzar·ism**, **tzar·ist** = TSAR, TSARINA, TSARISM, TSARIST

T

Uu

U /juː/ *noun, abbr.*

■ ***noun*** (*also* **u**) [C, U] (*pl.* **Us, U's, u's** /juːz/) the 21st letter of the English alphabet 英语字母表的第 21 个字母： *'Under' begins with (a) U/'U'.* * under 一词以字母 u 开头。 ➲ SEE ALSO U-BOAT, U-TURN

■ ***abbr.*** (*BrE*) universal (the label of a film/movie that is suitable for anyone including children) * U 类影片（适合所有观众）： *Aladdin, certificate U* * U 类电影《阿拉丁》

'U-bend *noun* a section of pipe shaped like a U, especially one that carries away used water（尤指污水管的）U 形弯头，马蹄弯头，U 形管

uber- (*also* **über-**) /ˈuːbə(r)/ *combining form* (*from German, informal*) (in nouns and adjectives 构成名词和形容词) of the greatest or best kind; to a very large degree 最好的；超级的： *His girlfriend was a real uber-babe, with long blonde hair and a big smile.* 他的女友是个超级靓妞，一头长长的金发，脸上带着灿烂的笑容。◇ *This stylish new restaurant is futuristic and uber-cool.* 这家时尚的新餐馆设计极其超前，真是超酷。

ubi·qui·tous /juːˈbɪkwɪtəs/ *adj.* [usually before noun] (*formal* or *humorous*) seeming to be everywhere or in several places at the same time; very common 似乎无所不在的；十分普遍的： *the ubiquitous bicycles of university towns* 大学城里处处可见的自行车 ◇ *the ubiquitous movie star, Tom Hanks* 尽人皆知的影星汤姆·汉克斯 ▸ **ubi·qui·tous·ly** *adv.* **ubi·quity** /juːˈbɪkwəti/ *noun* [U]: *the ubiquity of the mass media* 大众传媒的无所不在

'U-boat *noun* a German SUBMARINE (= a ship that can travel underwater)（德国）U 潜艇

ubuntu /ʊˈbʊntʊ/ *noun* [U] (*SAfrE*) the idea that people are not only individuals but live in a community and must share things and care for each other 班图精神，社团关爱精神（生活在集体中，大家必须分享物品并互相关心）： *The* ***concept of ubuntu*** *involves deep concern for others and having sound morals.* 班图精神包含对他人的深切关爱和具备良好的道德。◇ *The rekindling of* ***the spirit of Ubuntu*** *will restore tolerance and dialogue.* 班图精神的复苏将重建宽容与对话。

u.c. *abbr.* (in writing 书写形式) UPPER CASE 大写字体

UCAS /ˈjuːkæs/ *abbr.* (in Britain) Universities and Colleges Admissions Service (an official organization that deals with applications to study at universities and colleges)（英国）高校招生服务处

UDA /ˌjuː diː ˈeɪ/ *abbr.* Ulster Defence Association (an illegal military organization in Northern Ireland that wants Northern Ireland to remain part of the UK) 北爱尔兰防务协会

udder /ˈʌdə(r)/ *noun* an organ shaped like a bag that produces milk and hangs underneath the body of a cow, GOAT, etc.（母牛、母羊等的）乳房

UDR /ˌjuː diː ˈɑː(r)/ *abbr.* Ulster Defence Regiment (a branch of the British army in Northern Ireland, now forming part of the Royal Irish Regiment) 北爱尔兰防卫军（英军的一部分）

UEFA /juˈeɪfə/ *abbr.* Union of European Football Associations 欧足联；欧洲足球协会联合会

U-ey /ˈjuːi/ *noun* (*informal, especially AustralE*) a turn of 180° that a vehicle makes so that it can move forwards in the opposite direction（汽车等的）U 形转弯，180 度转弯 SYN **U-turn**

UFO (*also* **ufo**) /ˌjuː ef ˈəʊ; ˈjuːfəʊ; *NAmE* ˌjuː ef ˈoʊ; ˈjuːfoʊ/ *noun* (*pl.* **UFOs** or **ufos**) the abbreviation for 'Unidentified Flying Object' (a strange object that some people claim to have seen in the sky and believe is a SPACECRAFT from another planet) 不明飞行物，幽浮（全写为 Unidentified Flying Object） ➲ COMPARE FLYING SAUCER

ufol·ogy /juːˈfɒlədʒi; *NAmE* -ˈfɑːl-/ *noun* [U] the study of UFOs 不明飞行物学；幽浮学

ugali /uːˈɡɑːli/ *noun* [U] (*EAfrE*) a type of food made with flour from MAIZE (CORN) or MILLET, usually eaten with meat or vegetable STEW 玉米（或粟米）粉团，米粉糕（通常和炖肉或蔬菜一起吃）

UGC /ˌjuː dʒiː ˈsiː/ *abbr.* user-generated content (any data or media created by individual users of a website and available for others to use) 用户生成内容，用户原创内容（全写为 user-generated content）： *Consumers between 25 and 54 years old were the biggest content drivers, contributing 70% of all UGC.* * 25 至 54 岁的用户是最大的内容增长动力，贡献用户生成内容的 70%。

ugh (*also* **urgh**) *exclamation* the way of writing the sound /ɜː/ or /ʊx/ that people make when they think that sth is disgusting or unpleasant（表示厌恶或不快）咳，呸： *Ugh! How can you eat that stuff?* 咳！你怎么能吃那玩意儿呢？ ➲ MORE LIKE THIS 2, page R25

Ugli™ /ˈʌɡli/ (*also* **'Ugli fruit**) *noun* a large CITRUS fruit with a rough, yellowish-orange skin and sweet flesh with a lot of juice 丑橘（大柑橘类水果，果皮粗糙，呈淡橙色，果肉甜而多汁）

ugly /ˈʌɡli/ *adj.* (**ug·lier, ugli·est**) **1** unpleasant to look at 丑陋的；难看的 SYN **unattractive**: *an ugly face* 丑陋的面孔 ◇ *an ugly building* 难看的建筑 **2** (of an event, a situation, etc. 事件、局势等) unpleasant or dangerous; involving threats or violence 令人不快的；危险的；险恶的；凶险的： *an ugly incident* 危险事件 ◇ *There were ugly scenes in the streets last night as rioting continued.* 昨晚暴乱持续之际，街上险象环生。 ▸ **ugli·ness** *noun* [U] IDM SEE REAR *v.*, SIN *n.*

ˌugly 'duckling *noun* a person or thing that at first does not seem attractive or likely to succeed but that later becomes successful or much admired 丑小鸭（初似平庸后来出众的人或事物） ORIGIN From the title of a story by Hans Christian Andersen, in which a young swan thinks it is an ugly young duck until it grows up into a beautiful adult swan. 源自安徒生童话，讲述一只小天鹅一直认为自己是只丑小鸭，长大后却变成了美丽的天鹅。

uh *exclamation* the way of writing the sound /ʌ/ or /ɜː/ that people make when they are not sure about sth, when they do not hear or understand sth you have said, or when they want you to agree with what they have said（表示不肯定、不清楚或征求同意）嗯，唔： *Uh, yeah, I guess so.* 嗯，对，我想是这样。◇ *'Are you ready yet?' 'Uh? Oh. Yes.'* "你准备好了吗？" "嗯？噢，好了。" ◇ *We can discuss this another time, uh?* 这事咱们以后再说，嗯？ ➲ MORE LIKE THIS 2, page R25

UHF /ˌjuː eɪtʃ ˈef/ *abbr.* ultra-high frequency (a range of radio waves used for high-quality radio and television broadcasting) 超高频

'uh-huh *exclamation* the way of writing the sound /ˈʌ hʌ/ that people make when they understand or agree with what you have said, when they want you to continue or when they are answering 'Yes'（表示理解、赞同、希望对方继续或作肯定答复）嗯，哦，喔，啊： *'Did you read my note?' 'Uh-huh.'* "你看了我的条子没有？" "嗯。" ➲ MORE LIKE THIS 2, page R25

'uh-oh (*also* **'oh-oh**) *exclamation* the way of writing the sound /ˈʌ əʊ/ that people make when they want to say that they have done sth wrong or that they think there will be trouble（表示做错了事或感到有麻烦）哎哟，哦唷： *Uh-oh. I forgot to write that letter.* 哦唷，我忘了写那封信了。◇ *Uh-oh! Turn the TV off. Here comes Dad!* 哎哟！把电视关掉！爸爸来了！ ➲ MORE LIKE THIS 2, page R25

UHT /ˌjuː eɪtʃ ˈtiː/ *abbr.* (*BrE*) ultra heat treated. UHT milk has been heated to a very high temperature in order to make it last for a long time. 经高温处理的

ˈuh-uh *exclamation* the way of writing the sound /ˈʌ ʌ/ that people make when they are answering 'No' to a question （表示否定回答） ➲ MORE LIKE THIS 2, page R25

uja·maa /ˌʊdʒæˈmɑː/ *noun* [U] (in Tanzania) SOCIALISM （坦桑尼亚）乌贾马，社会主义

UK (*also* **U.K.** *especially in US*) /juː ˈkeɪ/ *abbr.* UNITED KINGDOM 英国；联合王国

uku·lele /juːkəˈleɪli/ *noun* a musical instrument with four strings, like a small GUITAR 尤克里里（四弦小吉他）

ulcer /ˈʌlsə(r)/ *noun* a sore area on the outside of the body or on the surface of an organ inside the body which is painful and may BLEED or produce a poisonous substance 溃疡：*a stomach ulcer* 胃溃疡 ➲ SEE ALSO MOUTH ULCER

ul·cer·ate /ˈʌlsəreɪt/ *verb* [I, T, usually passive] ~ (**sth**) (*medical* 医) to become, or make sth become, covered with ulcers （使）形成溃疡，溃烂 ▸ **ul·cer·ation** /ˌʌlsəˈreɪʃn/ *noun* [U, C]

ulna /ˈʌlnə/ *noun* (*pl.* **ulnae** /-niː/) (*anatomy* 解) the longer bone of the two bones in the lower part of the arm between the elbow and the wrist, on the side opposite the thumb 尺骨 ➲ SEE ALSO RADIUS (3) ➲ VISUAL VOCAB PAGE V64

ul·ter·ior /ʌlˈtɪəriə(r); *NAmE* -ˈtɪr-/ *adj.* [only before noun] (of a reason for doing sth 行事的理由) that sb keeps hidden and does not admit 隐秘的；不可告人的；秘密的；矢口否认的：*She must have some **ulterior motive** for being nice to me—what does she really want?* 她对我这么好，一定别有用心。她到底想干什么呢？ ➲ MORE LIKE THIS 32, page R28

ul·tim·ate 🔑 AW /ˈʌltɪmət/ *adj., noun*
■ ***adj.*** [only before noun] **1** 🔑 happening at the end of a long process 最后的；最终的；终极的 SYN **final**：*our ultimate **goal/aim/objective/target*** 我们最终的目的 / 目标 ◇ *We will accept ultimate responsibility for whatever happens.* 无论出什么事情，我们愿承担全部责任。◇ *The ultimate decision lies with the parents.* 最后的决定权握在父母手中。 **2** 🔑 most extreme; best, worst, greatest, most important, etc. 极端的；最好（或坏、伟大、重要等）的：*This race will be the ultimate test of your skill.* 这次竞赛将是对你的技能的最大考验。◇ *Silk sheets are the ultimate luxury.* 丝绸床单是顶级奢侈品。 **3** from which sth originally comes 根本的；基本的；基础性的 SYN **basic, fundamental**：*the ultimate truths of philosophy and science* 哲学与科学的终极原理
■ ***noun*** [sing.] **the ~ in sth** (*informal*) the best, most advanced, greatest, etc. of its kind 最好（或先进、伟大等）的事物；极品；精华：*the ultimate in modern design* 现代设计的最高代表

ˈUltimate Fighting™ (*also* **ˈExtreme Fighting**) *noun* [U] a sport that combines different styles of fighting such as BOXING, WRESTLING and MARTIAL ARTS and in which there are not many rules 终极搏击，终极格斗（结合拳击、摔跤和武术等，规则不多）

ul·tim·ate·ly 🔑 AW /ˈʌltɪmətli/ *adv.* **1** 🔑 in the end; finally 最终；最后；终归：*Ultimately, you'll have to make the decision yourself.* 最终你还是得自己拿主意。◇ *A poor diet will ultimately lead to illness.* 不合理的饮食终将导致疾病。 **2** at the most basic and important level 最基本地；根本上：*All life depends ultimately on oxygen.* 一切生命归根到底都要依赖氧气。

ul·ti·matum /ˌʌltɪˈmeɪtəm/ *noun* (*pl.* **ul·ti·matums** or **ul·ti·ma·ta**) a final warning to a person or country that if they do not do what you ask, you will use force or take action against them 最后通牒：*to issue an ultimatum* 发出最后通牒

ultra /ˈʌltrə/ *noun* a person who holds extreme views, especially in politics （尤指政治上的）过激分子，极端主义者

ultra- /ˈʌltrə/ *prefix* (in adjectives and nouns 构成形容词和名词) extremely; beyond a particular limit 极；超过某限度：*ultra-modern* 超现代的 ◇ *ultraviolet* 紫外线的 ➲ COMPARE INFRA- ➲ MORE LIKE THIS 6, page R25

ˌultra-high ˈfrequency *noun* [U] = UHF

ultra·light /ˈʌltrəlaɪt/ (*NAmE*) (*BrE* **micro·light**) *noun* a very small light aircraft for one or two people 微型飞机 ➲ VISUAL VOCAB PAGE V58

ultra·mar·ine /ˌʌltrəməˈriːn/ *noun* [U] a bright blue colour 群青色；佛青色

ultra·short /ˌʌltrəˈʃɔːt; *NAmE* -ˈʃɔːrt/ *adj.* (of radio waves 无线电波) having a very short WAVELENGTH (shorter than 10 metres), with a FREQUENCY greater than 30 MEGAHERTZ 超短的 ➲ COMPARE LONG WAVE, MEDIUM WAVE, SHORT WAVE

ultra·son·ic /ˌʌltrəˈsɒnɪk; *NAmE* -ˈsɑːn-/ *adj.* [usually before noun] (of sounds 声音) higher than humans can hear 超声的：*ultrasonic waves* 超声波

ultra·sound /ˈʌltrəsaʊnd/ *noun* **1** [U] sound that is higher than humans can hear 超声 **2** [U, C] a medical process that produces an image of what is inside your body 超声波扫描检查：*Ultrasound showed she was expecting twins.* 超声波扫描显示她怀了双胞胎。 ➲ WORDFINDER NOTE AT EXAMINE

ultra·vio·let /ˌʌltrəˈvaɪələt/ (*abbr.* **UV**) *adj.* [usually before noun] (*physics* 物) of or using ELECTROMAGNETIC waves that are just shorter than those of VIOLET light in the SPECTRUM and that cannot be seen 紫外线的；利用紫外线的：*ultraviolet rays* (= that cause the skin to go darker) 紫外线 ◇ *an ultraviolet lamp* 紫外线灯 ➲ COMPARE INFRARED

ulu·late /ˈjuːljʊleɪt; ˈʌljʊleɪt; *NAmE* ˈʌljʊl-/ *verb* [I] (*literary*) to give a long cry 嚎叫；大叫；长啸 SYN **wail** ▸ **ulu·la·tion** /-leɪʃn/ *noun* [U, C]

um *exclamation* the way of writing the sound /ʌm/ or /əm/ that people make when they hesitate, or do not know what to say next （表示犹豫或说话中间停顿）嗯，唔：*Um, I'm not sure how to ask you this…* 嗯，我不知道该怎么问你这个… ➲ MORE LIKE THIS 2, page R25

umami /uːˈmɑːmi/ *noun* [U] a taste found in some foods that is neither sweet, sour, bitter nor salty 鲜味：*Tomatoes have lots of umami.* 西红柿味道特鲜。

umber /ˈʌmbə(r)/ *noun* [U] a dark brown or yellowish-brown colour used in paints （油漆中用的）棕土色，赭土色

um·bil·ical cord /ʌmˌbɪlɪkl ˈkɔːd; *NAmE* ˈkɔːrd/ *noun* a long piece of TISSUE that connects a baby to its mother before it is born and is cut at the moment of birth 脐带 ➲ WORDFINDER NOTE AT BIRTH

um·bil·icus /ʌmˈbɪlɪkəs; ˌʌmbɪˈlaɪkəs/ *noun* (*pl.* **um·bil·ici** /ʌmˈbɪlɪsaɪ; ˌʌmbɪˈlaɪsaɪ; -kaɪ/ or **um·bil·icuses**) (*specialist*) the NAVEL 脐

umbra /ˈʌmbrə/ *noun* (*pl.* **um·bras** or **um·brae** /ˈʌmbriː/) (*specialist*) **1** the darkest part of a shadow 本影（影子中光源完全照射不到的部分） **2** the area on the earth or the moon which is the darkest during an ECLIPSE （日食或月食期间地球或月球的）本影 ➲ COMPARE PENUMBRA

um·brage /ˈʌmbrɪdʒ/ *noun*
IDM **take ˈumbrage (at sth)** (*formal* or *humorous*) to feel offended, insulted or upset by sth, often without a good reason 认为受到冒犯（或羞辱）；（无故）感到不快 SYN **offence**

um·brella 🔑 /ʌmˈbrelə/ *noun* **1** 🔑 (*also BrE, informal* **brolly**) an object with a round folding frame of long straight pieces of metal covered with material, that you use to protect yourself from the rain or from hot sun 伞；雨伞；阳伞：*I put up my umbrella.* 我撑开伞。◇ *colourful beach umbrellas* 五彩缤纷的海滩遮阳伞 ➲ COMPARE PARASOL (2), SUNSHADE (1) **2** a thing that contains or includes many different parts or elements 综合体；总体；整体：*Many previously separate groups are now*

U

operating under the umbrella of a single authority. 许多原本分散的团体现归一个单一的机构领导。◇ *an* ***umbrella organization/group/fund*** 综合机构 / 团体 / 基金◇ *'Contact sports' is an* ***umbrella term*** *for a variety of different sports.* "身体接触式运动"是多种不同体育运动的总称。**3** a country or system that protects people 保护国（或体系）；保护伞；庇护

um·faan /ʊmˈfɑːn/ *noun* (*pl.* **um·faans** or **ba·fana** /bɑːˈfɑːnə/) (*SAfrE*) **1** a young black man who is not married 未婚黑人男青年 **2** a young black boy 黑人男孩

um·laut /ˈʊmlaʊt/ *noun* the mark placed over a vowel in some languages to show how it should be pronounced, as over the *u* in the German word *für*（元音的）变音符 ➲ COMPARE ACUTE ACCENT, CIRCUMFLEX, GRAVE², TILDE

UMPC /ˌjuː em piː ˈsiː/ *noun* (*computing* 计) the abbreviation for 'ultra-mobile personal computer' (a very small computer that is easy to carry, often with a touch screen and sometimes without a physical keyboard) 超便携个人电脑，超级移动电脑（全写为 ultra-mobile personal computer）

um·pire /ˈʌmpaɪə(r)/ *noun, verb*

■ ***noun*** (*also NAmE, informal* **ump**) (in sports such as TENNIS and BASEBALL 网球、棒球等体育运动) a person whose job is to watch a game and make sure that rules are not broken 裁判员 ➲ COMPARE REFEREE *n.* (1)

■ ***verb*** [I, T] to act as an umpire（为…）做裁判员，当裁判：*We need someone to umpire.* 我们得找个人当裁判。◇ **~ sth** *to umpire a game of baseball* 做棒球赛裁判

ump·teen /ˌʌmpˈtiːn/ *det.* (*informal*) very many 大量；很多：*I've told this story umpteen times.* 这个故事我已讲了无数次了。▶ **ump·teen** *pron.*：*Umpteen of them all arrived at once.* 他们大伙都一块儿来了。 **ump·teenth** /ˌʌmpˈtiːnθ/ *det.*：*'This is crazy,' she told herself* ***for the umpteenth time*** (= she had done it many times before). "这简直疯了！"她已无数次这般地自言自语着。

UN (*also* **U.N.** *especially in US*) /ˌjuː ˈen/ *abbr.* United Nations (an association of many countries that aims to help economic and social conditions improve and to solve political problems in the world in a peaceful way) 联合国：*the UN Security Council* 联合国安理会◇ *a UN peacekeeping plan* 联合国维和计划

un- /ʌn/ *prefix* **1** (in adjectives, adverbs and nouns 构成形容词、副词和名词) not; the opposite of 不；未；非；反：*unable* 不能◇ *unconsciously* 无意识地◇ *untruth* 虚假 **2** (in verbs that describe the opposite of a process 构成表示相反过程的动词)：*unlock* 开锁◇ *undo* 解开 ➲ MORE LIKE THIS 6, page R25

'un /ən/ *pron.* (*BrE, informal*) a way of saying or writing 'one'（等于 one）：*That was a good 'un.* 那个东西不错。◇ *The little 'uns* (= the small children) *couldn't keep up.* 那些小不点儿跟不上了。

un·abashed /ˌʌnəˈbæʃt/ *adj.* not ashamed, embarrassed or affected by people's disapproval, when other people would be 不在乎的；不害羞的；不难为情的 OPP **abashed** ▶ **un·abashed·ly** /-ʃɪdli/ *adv.*

un·abated /ˌʌnəˈbeɪtɪd/ *adj.* [not usually before noun] (*formal*) without becoming any less strong 不减；未变弱：*The rain* ***continued unabated.*** 雨势一直没减弱。

un·able ⚷ /ʌnˈeɪbl/ *adj.* [not before noun] **~ to do sth** (*rather formal*) not having the skill, strength, time, knowledge, etc. to do sth 没有所需技能（或力量、时间、知识等）；未能；无法：*He lay there, unable to move.* 他躺在那里动弹不得。◇ *I tried to contact him but was unable to.* 我试着跟他联系，却没联系上。OPP **able**

un·abridged /ˌʌnəˈbrɪdʒd/ *adj.* (of a novel, play, speech, etc. 小说、戏剧、讲演等) complete, without being made shorter in any way（版本）完整的；未删节的 OPP **abridged**

un·ac·cent·ed /ʌnˈæksentɪd/ *adj.* **1** (of sb's speech 讲话) having no regional or foreign accent 不带地方（或外国）口音的；无口音的 **2** (*phonetics* 语音) (of a syllable 音节) having no stress 非重读的

un·accept·able ⚷ /ˌʌnəkˈseptəbl/ *adj.* that you cannot accept, allow or approve of 不能接受（或允许、同意）的：*Such behaviour is totally unacceptable in a civilized society.* 这种行为在文明社会是完全不能接受的。◇ *Noise from the factory has reached an unacceptable level.* 工厂的噪声达到了难以容忍的地步。OPP **acceptable** ▶ **un·accept·ably** /-bli/ *adv.*：*unacceptably high levels of unemployment* 奇高的失业率

un·accom·pan·ied AW /ˌʌnəˈkʌmpənid/ *adj.* **1** (*formal*) without a person going together with sb/sth 无人陪伴（或同行）的：*No unaccompanied children allowed.* 儿童无大人陪伴不许进入。◇ ***unaccompanied luggage/baggage*** (= travelling separately from its owner) 托运的行李 **2** (*music* 音) performed without anyone else playing or singing at the same time 无伴奏的；无伴唱的：*a sonata for unaccompanied violin* 无伴奏小提琴奏鸣曲 **3** (*formal*) **~ by sth** not together with a particular thing 没有；不伴有：*Mere words, unaccompanied by any violence, cannot amount to an assault.* 只有言语而未伴随暴力不能算攻击。

un·account·able /ˌʌnəˈkaʊntəbl/ *adj.* (*formal*) **1** impossible to understand or explain 无法理解的；难以解释的 SYN **inexplicable**：*For some unaccountable reason, the letter never arrived.* 不知何故，那封信始终未寄到。**2 ~ (to sb/sth)** not having to explain or give reasons for your actions to anyone 无须解释（或说明）的；不负责的：*Too many government departments are unaccountable to the general public.* 有太多的政府部门不对社会大众负责。OPP **accountable**

un·account·ably /ˌʌnəˈkaʊntəbli/ *adv.* (*formal*) in a way that is very difficult to explain; without any obvious reason 难以解释地；莫名其妙地；无明显原因地 SYN **inexplicably**：*He has been unaccountably delayed.* 他被莫名其妙地耽误了。

un·account·ed for /ˌʌnəˈkaʊntɪd fɔː(r)/ *adj.* [not before noun] **1** a person or thing that is **unaccounted for** cannot be found and people do not know what has happened to them or it 下落不明；失踪：*At least 300 civilians are unaccounted for after the bombing raids.* 遭轰炸袭击之后，至少有 300 名平民下落不明。**2** not explained 未解释；未说明：*In the story he gave the police, half an hour was left unaccounted for.* 他对警察的陈述中有半个小时的事情未交代清楚。

un·accus·tomed /ˌʌnəˈkʌstəmd/ *adj.* (*formal*) **1 ~ to sth/to doing sth** not in the habit of doing sth; not used to sth 不习惯；不适应：*He was unaccustomed to hard work.* 他不习惯艰苦工作。◇ *I am unaccustomed to being told what to do.* 我没有听人使唤的习惯。**2** [usually before noun] not usual, normal or familiar 反常的；不一般的；不熟悉的：*The unaccustomed heat made him weary.* 反常的炎热令他虚弱无力。OPP **accustomed**

un·achiev·able /ˌʌnəˈtʃiːvəbl/ *adj.* that you cannot manage to reach or obtain 难以达到的；无法获得的：*unachievable goals* 难以实现的目标 OPP **achievable**

un·acknow·ledged /ˌʌnəkˈnɒlɪdʒd; *NAmE* -ˈnɑːl-/ *adj.* **1** not receiving the thanks or praise that is deserved 未得到应有的感激（或赞赏）的：*Her contribution to the research went largely unacknowledged.* 她对这项研究的贡献大都被忽略了。**2** that people do not admit as existing or true; that people are not aware of 不被承认存在（或真实）的；未被意识到的：*unacknowledged feelings* 下意识的感情 **3** not publicly or officially recognized 未得到公开（或正式）承认的；非正式的：*the unacknowledged leader of the group* 这个团体非正式任命的首领

un·ac·quaint·ed /ˌʌnəˈkweɪntɪd/ *adj.* **~ (with sth/sb)** (*formal*) not familiar with sth/sb; having no experience of sth 不熟悉；无经验：*visitors unacquainted with local customs* 不谙当地风俗的游客 OPP **acquainted**

un·adjust·ed /ˌʌnəˈdʒʌstɪd/ *adj.* (*statistics* 统计) (of figures 数字) not adjusted according to particular facts or circumstances 未调整的；调整前的：*Unadjusted figures which do not take tourism into account showed that unemployment fell in July.* 不含旅游业的调整前数字表明七月份失业率下降。

un·adorned /ˌʌnəˈdɔːnd; *NAmE* -ˈdɔːrnd/ *adj.* (*formal*) without any decoration 不加装饰的；简朴的 **SYN simple**: *The walls were plain and unadorned.* 墙壁朴素无华。

un·adul·ter·ated /ˌʌnəˈdʌltəreɪtɪd/ *adj.* **1** [usually before noun] you use **unadulterated** to emphasize that sth is complete or total 完全的；十足的；不折不扣的 **SYN undiluted**: *For me, the holiday was sheer unadulterated pleasure.* 对我来说，这个假期是百分之百的赏心乐事。**2** not mixed with other substances; not ADULTERATED 纯的；不掺杂质的 **SYN pure**: *unadulterated foods* 未掺杂其他物质的食物

un·ad·ven·tur·ous /ˌʌnədˈventʃərəs/ *adj.* not willing to take risks or try new and exciting things 不愿冒险（或尝试新奇事物）的 **SYN cautious OPP adventurous**

un·affect·ed **AW** /ˌʌnəˈfektɪd/ *adj.* **1 ~ (by sth)** not changed or influenced by sth; not affected by sth 未被改变的；未受影响的；无动于衷的：*People's rights are unaffected by the new law.* 新法规没有影响人民的权利。◇ *Some members of the family may remain unaffected by the disease.* 这家族有些人可能不会受到这种疾病的影响。**2** (*approving*) (of a person or their behaviour 人或行为) natural and sincere 真诚自然的；真挚的；不做作的 **OPP affected**

un·affili·ated /ˌʌnəˈfɪlieɪtɪd/ *adj.* **~ (with sth)** not belonging to or connected with a political party or a large organization 独立的；无党派（或组织）的 **SYN independent OPP affiliated**

un·afford·able /ˌʌnəˈfɔːdəbl; *NAmE* -əˈfɔːrd-/ *adj.* costing so much that people do not have enough money to pay for it 买不起的；负担不起的：*Health insurance is now unaffordable for many people.* 如今很多人买不起健康保险。**OPP affordable**

un·afraid /ˌʌnəˈfreɪd/ *adj.* [not before noun] (*formal*) not afraid or nervous; not worried about what might happen 不害怕；不畏惧；不紧张；无顾忌：**~ (of sth)** *She was unafraid of conflict.* 她不怕发生冲突。◇ **~ (to do sth)** *He's unafraid to speak his mind.* 他勇于说出心里的话。

un·aid·ed **AW** /ʌnˈeɪdɪd/ *adj., adv.* (*formal*) without help from anyone or anything 无外援的；独力的：*He can now walk unaided.* 他现在能独自行走了。

un·ali·en·able /ʌnˈeɪliənəbl/ *adj.* = INALIENABLE

un·alloyed /ˌʌnəˈlɔɪd/ *adj.* (*formal*) not mixed with anything else, such as negative feelings 纯真的；纯粹的 **SYN pure**: *unalloyed joy* 纯粹的快乐

un·alter·able **AW** /ʌnˈɔːltərəbl/ *adj.* (*formal*) that cannot be changed 不可更改的；无法改变的 **SYN immutable**: *the unalterable laws of the universe* 不可改变的宇宙法则

un·altered **AW** /ʌnˈɔːltəd; *NAmE* -tərd/ *adj.* that has not changed or been changed 未改变的；未被改变的：*This practice has **remained unaltered** for centuries.* 这种习俗已数百年未变。

un·am·bigu·ous **AW** /ˌʌnæmˈbɪɡjuəs/ *adj.* clear in meaning; that can only be understood in one way 意思清楚的；明确的；毫不含糊的；无歧义的：*an unambiguous statement* 明确的陈述 ◇ *The message was clear and unambiguous—'Get out!'* 这其中的含义明确无疑——“滚开！” **OPP ambiguous** ▸ **un·am·bigu·ous·ly** **AW** *adv.*

un·am·bi·tious /ˌʌnæmˈbɪʃəs/ *adj.* **1** (of a person 人) not interested in becoming successful, rich, powerful, etc. 无抱负的；无名利心的 **2** not involving a lot of effort, time, money, etc. or anything new 不费功夫（或时间、金钱等）的；不铺张的：*an unambitious plan* 平实的计划 **OPP ambitious**

ˌun-Aˈmerican *adj.* against American values or interests 与美国人价值（或兴趣）相反的；非美国的

unan·im·ity /ˌjuːnəˈnɪməti/ *noun* [U] complete agreement about sth among a group of people 一致同意；全体赞同

unani·mous /juˈnænɪməs/ *adj.* **1** if a decision or an opinion is **unanimous**, it is agreed or shared by everyone in a group（决定或意见）一致的，一致同意的：*a unanimous vote* 全体一致的表决 ◇ *unanimous support* 一致的拥护 ◇ *The decision was not unanimous.* 这项决定没有得到一致通过。**2 ~ (in sth)** if a group of people are **unanimous**, they all agree about sth（团体）意见一致的，一致同意某事的：*Local people are unanimous in their opposition to the proposed new road.* 当地居民一致反对拟建的新公路。▸ **unani·mous·ly** *adv.*: *The motion was passed unanimously.* 动议获一致通过。

un·announced /ˌʌnəˈnaʊnst/ *adj.* happening without anyone being told or warned in advance 未通知的；未预告的；未打招呼的：*She just turned up unannounced on my doorstep.* 她未打招呼就来到我家门口了。◇ *an unannounced increase in bus fares* 公共汽车票价未经公告的上涨

un·answer·able /ʌnˈɑːnsərəbl; *NAmE* ʌnˈæn-/ *adj.* **1** an **unanswerable** argument, etc. is one that nobody can question or disagree with 无可争辩的；不容反对的 **SYN irrefutable**: *They presented an unanswerable case for more investment.* 他们提出了一个无可争辩的理由，要求增加投资。**2** an **unanswerable** question is one that has no answer or that you cannot answer 无答案的；无法回答的

un·answered /ʌnˈɑːnsəd; *NAmE* -sərd/ *adj.* **1** (of a question, problem, etc. 提问、问题等) that has not been answered 未回答的；未解答的；悬而未决的：*Many questions about the crime **remain unanswered**.* 这桩罪行涉及的许多问题仍然没有答案。**2** (of a letter, telephone call, etc. 信函、电话等) that has not been replied to 未回复（或答复）的：*unanswered letters* 未答复的信件

un·antici·pated **AW** /ˌʌnænˈtɪsɪpeɪtɪd/ *adj.* (*formal*) that you have not expected or predicted; that you have not anticipated 没想到的；未预料到的：*unanticipated costs* 预料之外的费用

un·apolo·get·ic /ˌʌnəˌpɒləˈdʒetɪk; *NAmE* -ˌpɑːl-/ *adj.* not saying that you are sorry about sth, even in situations in which other people might expect you to 不致歉的；不道歉的 **OPP apologetic** ▸ **un·apolo·get·ic·al·ly** /-kli/ *adv.*

un·appeal·ing /ˌʌnəˈpiːlɪŋ/ *adj.* not attractive or pleasant 不诱人的；无魅力的；令人不快的：*The room was painted in an unappealing shade of brown.* 这屋子漆成了难看的棕色。◇ *The prospect of studying for another five years was distinctly unappealing.* 未来还需要再学五年，真是让人厌烦。**OPP appealing**

un·appe·tiz·ing (*BrE also* **-is·ing**) /ʌnˈæpɪtaɪzɪŋ/ *adj.* (of food 食物) unpleasant to eat; looking as if it will be unpleasant to eat 难吃的；倒胃口的；看似难吃的 **OPP appetizing**

un·appre·ci·ated **AW** /ˌʌnəˈpriːʃieɪtɪd/ *adj.* [not usually before noun] not having your work or your qualities recognized and enjoyed by other people; not appreciated 无人赏识；不被欣赏；无人感激：*He was in a job where he felt unappreciated and undervalued.* 他以前的工作未让他感到受赏识和重视。

un·approach·able **AW** /ˌʌnəˈprəʊtʃəbl; *NAmE* -ˈproʊ-/ *adj.* (of a person 人) unfriendly and not easy to talk to 不友好的；难接近的；不好说话的 **OPP approachable**

un·argu·able /ʌnˈɑːɡjuəbl; *NAmE* -ˈɑːrɡ-/ *adj.* (*formal*) that nobody can disagree with 无可争辩的；不容置疑的：*unarguable proof* 不容置疑的证据 ➲ COMPARE ARGUABLE ▸ **un·argu·ably** *adv.*: *She is unarguably one of the country's finest athletes.* 她无疑是全国最优秀的运动员之一。

un·armed /ˌʌnˈɑːmd; *NAmE* ˌʌnˈɑːrmd/ *adj.* **1** not carrying a weapon 不带武器的；非武装的：*unarmed civilians* 没有武装的平民 **2** not involving the use of weapons 不使用武器的；徒手的：*The soldiers were trained in unarmed combat.* 士兵接受徒手格斗训练。**OPP armed**

U

un·ashamed /ˌʌnəˈʃeɪmd/ *adj.* feeling no shame or embarrassment about sth, especially when people might expect you to 不害臊的；不感觉难为情的；恬不知耻的 ➲ COMPARE ASHAMED ▶ **un·ashamed·ly** /ˌʌnəˈʃeɪmɪdli/ *adv.*: *She wept unashamedly.* 她不顾羞耻地哭了起来。◇ *an unashamedly sentimental song* 一首夸张的伤感歌曲

un·asked /ˌʌnˈɑːskt; NAmE ˌʌnˈæskt/ *adj.* **1** an **unasked** question is one that you have not asked even though you would like to know the answer 没发问的；未出口的 **2** without being invited or asked 未获邀请的；未经要求的：*He came to the party unasked.* 他未经邀请就来参加聚会了。◇ *She brought him, unasked, the relevant file.* 她主动把有关案卷带给了他。

unˈasked-for *adj.* that has not been asked for or requested 未经要求的；非请求的：*unasked-for advice* 主动提出的建议

un·assail·able /ˌʌnəˈseɪləbl/ *adj.* (*formal*) that cannot be destroyed, defeated or questioned 无法摧毁的；不可战胜的；不容置疑的：*The party now has an unassailable lead.* 这个党的领先地位现在坚不可摧。◇ *Their ten-point lead puts the team in an almost unassailable position.* 他们以十分领先的优势使整个球队处于难以撼动的地位。

un·assigned AW /ˌʌnəˈsaɪnd/ *adj.* not given to or reserved for any particular person or purpose 未分配的；未保留的

un·assist·ed AW /ˌʌnəˈsɪstɪd/ *adj.* not helped by anyone or anything 无人帮助的；不靠外援的；独力的 SYN **unaided**: *She could not move unassisted.* 她不能够独力活动。

un·assum·ing /ˌʌnəˈsjuːmɪŋ; NAmE ˌʌnəˈsuː-/ *adj.* (*approving*) not wanting to draw attention to yourself or to your abilities or status 不爱出风头的；不爱炫耀的；谦逊的 SYN **modest**

un·attached AW /ˌʌnəˈtætʃt/ *adj.* **1** not married or involved in a romantic relationship 未婚的；单身的；未恋爱的 SYN **single**: *He was still unattached at the age of 34.* 他 34 岁时还是单身。**2** not connected with or belonging to a particular group or organization 不属于团体或组织的；无所属的；无党派的；独立的 ➲ COMPARE ATTACHED (1)

un·attain·able AW /ˌʌnəˈteɪnəbl/ *adj.* impossible to achieve or reach 无法得到的；难以达到的：*an unattainable goal* 难以达到的目标 OPP **attainable**

un·attend·ed /ˌʌnəˈtendɪd/ *adj.* (*formal*) without the owner present; not being watched or cared for 主人不在场的；无人看管（或照料）的：*unattended vehicles* 无人看管的车辆 ◇ *Never leave young children unattended.* 小孩绝不能无人看管。

un·attract·ive /ˌʌnəˈtræktɪv/ *adj.* **1** not attractive or pleasant to look at 不悦目的；不漂亮的；难看的：*an unattractive brown colour* 难看的棕色 **2** not good, interesting or pleasant 不好的；无趣的；令人反感的：*one of the unattractive aspects of the free market economy* 自由市场经济糟糕的一个方面 OPP **attractive** ▶ **un·attract·ive·ly** *adv.*

un·author·ized (*BrE also* **-ised**) /ʌnˈɔːθəraɪzd/ *adj.* without official permission 未经许可（或批准）的：*No access for unauthorized personnel.* 未经允许不得入内。OPP **authorize**

un·avail·able AW /ˌʌnəˈveɪləbl/ *adj.* [not usually before noun] ~ (**to sb/sth**) **1** that cannot be obtained 无法得到；难以获得：*Such luxuries are unavailable to ordinary people.* 此等奢侈品普通百姓是难以获得的。**2** not able or not willing to see, meet or talk to sb 不能（或不愿）见面；不能（或不愿）交谈：*The minister was* **unavailable for comment.** 部长无法接受访问作出评论。OPP **available** ▶ **un·avail·abil·ity** *noun* [U]

un·avail·ing /ˌʌnəˈveɪlɪŋ/ *adj.* (*formal*) without success 徒劳的；无成果的 SYN **unsuccessful**: *Their efforts were unavailing.* 他们的努力都付诸东流。

un·avoid·able /ˌʌnəˈvɔɪdəbl/ *adj.* impossible to avoid or prevent 无法避免的；难以预防的：*unavoidable delays* 不可避免的延误 OPP **avoidable** ▶ **un·avoid·ably** /-əbli/ *adv.*: *I was unavoidably delayed.* 我无奈被耽搁了。

un·aware AW /ˌʌnəˈweə(r); NAmE -ˈwer/ *adj.* [not before noun] not knowing or realizing that sth is happening or that sth exists 不知道；没意识到；未察觉：**~ of sth** *He was completely unaware of the whole affair.* 他对整件事情一无所知。◇ **~ that…** *She was unaware that I could see her.* 她没想到我能看见她。OPP **aware** ▶ **un·aware·ness** *noun* [U]

un·awares /ˌʌnəˈweəz; NAmE -ˈwerz/ *adv.* **1** when not expected 猝然；出其不意地；冷不防：*The camera had* **caught her unawares.** 她毫无防备地被拍摄下来。◇ *The announcement* **took me unawares.** 这项声明令我感到意外。◇ *She came upon him unawares when he was searching her room.* 他在翻她屋子时，冷不防被她撞见了。**2** (*formal*) without noticing or realizing 不留神地；未注意到；不知不觉地：*He slipped unawares into sleep.* 他不知不觉地睡着了。

un·bal·ance /ˌʌnˈbæləns/ *verb* **1** **~ sth** to make sth no longer balanced, for example by giving too much importance to one part of it 使不平衡；使失去均衡 **2** **~ sb/sth** to make sb/sth unsteady so that they are likely to fall down 使失去重心（或平衡）；使倾覆 **3** **~ sb** to make sb slightly crazy or mentally ill 使心理不平衡；使精神失常

un·bal·anced /ˌʌnˈbælənst/ *adj.* **1** [not usually before noun] (of a person 人) slightly crazy; mentally ill 心理不平衡；精神失常 **2** [usually before noun] giving too much or too little importance to one part or aspect of sth 不持平的；偏颇的；失衡的：*an unbalanced article* 持论偏颇的文章 ◇ *an unbalanced diet* 不均衡的饮食

unban /ˌʌnˈbæn/ *verb* (**-nn-**) **~ sth** to allow sth that was banned before 开放；解禁 OPP **ban**

un·bear·able /ʌnˈbeərəbl; NAmE -ˈber-/ *adj.* too painful, annoying or unpleasant to deal with or accept 难耐的；无法接受的；难以处理的 SYN **intolerable**: *The heat was becoming unbearable.* 炎热开始变得难以忍受。◇ *unbearable pain* 无法忍受的疼痛 ◇ *He's been unbearable since he won that prize.* 他得奖以后变得很难相与。OPP **bearable** ▶ **un·bear·ably** /-əbli/ *adv.*: *unbearably hot* 酷热难当

un·beat·able /ʌnˈbiːtəbl/ *adj.* **1** (of a team, player, etc. 团队、运动员等) impossible to defeat 难以击败的；打不垮的 SYN **invincible** **2** (of prices, value, etc. 价格、价值等) impossible to improve 已达极限的；难以竞争的：*unbeatable offers* 最优惠的报价

un·beat·en /ʌnˈbiːtn/ *adj.* (*sport* 体育) not having been defeated 未尝败绩的；未败过的：*The team are unbeaten in their last four games.* 这个队在最近的四场比赛中从未输过。◇ *They will be putting their* **unbeaten record** *to the test next Saturday.* 下周六他们的不败纪录将要受到考验。

un·be·com·ing /ˌʌnbɪˈkʌmɪŋ/ *adj.* (*formal*) **1** not suiting a particular person 不合适的；不相称的 SYN **unflattering**: *She was wearing an unbecoming shade of purple.* 她穿着一身不相配的紫色衣服。**2** ~ (**to/of sb**) not appropriate or acceptable 不恰当；不得体；不可接受 SYN **inappropriate**: *He was accused of conduct unbecoming to an officer.* 他被谴责行为有失官员身份。OPP **becoming**

un·be·fit·ting /ˌʌnbɪˈfɪtɪŋ/ *adj.* ~ (**of/for/to sb/sth**) (*formal*) not suitable or good enough for sb/sth 不合适的；不适宜的；不得体的：*His behaviour is unbefitting of a university professor.* 他的行为与大学教授的身份不相符。◇ *The amount of litter in the streets is unbefitting for a historic city.* 街道上垃圾之多与历史名城不协调。

un·be·known /ˌʌnbɪˈnəʊn; NAmE -ˈnoʊn/ (*also less frequent* **un·be·knownst** /ˌʌnbɪˈnəʊnst; NAmE -ˈnoʊnst/) *adj.* **~ to sb** (*formal*) without the person mentioned knowing 瞒着；背着：*Unbeknown to her they had organized a surprise party.* 他们瞒着她筹备了一个给她意外惊喜的聚会。

un·belief /ˌʌnbɪˈliːf/ *noun* [U] (*formal*) lack of belief, or the state of not believing, especially in God, a religion, etc.

（对上帝的）不相信；无（宗教）信仰 ➲ COMPARE BELIEF (3), DISBELIEF

un·believ·able /ˌʌnbɪˈliːvəbl/ *adj.* **1** (*informal*) used to emphasize how good, bad or extreme sth is 非常好（或坏、极端）的；难以置信的；惊人的 SYN **incredible**: *We had an unbelievable* (= very good) *time in Paris.* 我们在巴黎的日子快活极了。◇ *Conditions in the prison camp were unbelievable* (= very bad). 集中营的生活条件糟糕透了。◇ *The cold was unbelievable* (= it was extremely cold). 天气冷极了。◇ ***It's unbelievable that*** (= very shocking) *they have permitted this trial to go ahead.* 令人震惊的是他们竟允许进行这项审讯。**2** very difficult to believe and unlikely to be true 难以相信的；不真实的 SYN **incredible**: *I found the whole story bizarre, not to say unbelievable.* 我觉得整个事件经过荒诞不经，更不用说不可信了。▶ **un·believ·ably** *adv.*: *unbelievably bad/good* 坏得 / 好得令人难以置信 ◇ *Unbelievably it actually works.* 难以相信的是，它确实有效。

un·believer /ˌʌnbɪˈliːvə(r)/ *noun* (*formal*) a person who does not believe, especially in God, a religion, etc. 无（宗教）信仰的人；（尤指）不信上帝的人 OPP **believer**

un·believ·ing /ˌʌnbɪˈliːvɪŋ/ *adj.* (*formal*) feeling or showing that you do not believe sb/sth 不相信的；怀疑的：*She stared at us with unbelieving eyes.* 她用疑惑的眼睛看着我们。◇ *He gazed at the letter, unbelieving.* 他两眼盯着信，满腹狐疑。

un·bend /ˌʌnˈbend/ *verb* (**un·bent**, **un·bent** /ˌʌnˈbent/) **1** [I] to relax and become less strict or formal in your behaviour or attitude （在行为或态度上）放松；变得无拘束；随和 **2** [T, I] ~ (**sth**) to make sth that was bent become straight; to become straight 拉直；抻直；变直

un·bend·ing /ˌʌnˈbendɪŋ/ *adj.* (*often disapproving*) unwilling to change your opinions, decisions, etc. 顽固的；固执的；倔强的 SYN **inflexible**

un·biased AW /ʌnˈbaɪəst/ *adj.* fair and not influenced by your own or sb else's opinions, desires, etc. 公正的；不偏不倚的；无偏见的 SYN **impartial**: *unbiased advice* 客观的忠告 ◇ *an unbiased judge* 公正的法官 OPP **biased**

un·bid·den /ʌnˈbɪdn/ *adj.* (*literary*) (usually used after the verb 通常置于动词后) without being asked, invited or expected 未经要求；未被邀请；擅自 SYN **unasked**: *He walked into the room unbidden.* 他径自走进了屋子。

un·bleached /ʌnˈbliːtʃt/ *adj.* not made whiter by the use of chemicals; not bleached 未漂白的：*unbleached flour* 未经漂白的面粉

un·blem·ished /ʌnˈblemɪʃt/ *adj.* (*formal*) not spoiled, damaged or marked in any way 完好的；无损的；无污点的：*He had an unblemished reputation.* 他的名声白璧无瑕。◇ *her pale unblemished skin* 她那白皙光洁的皮肤

un·blink·ing /ʌnˈblɪŋkɪŋ/ *adj.* (*formal*) if sb has an **unblinking stare** or looks with **unblinking eyes**, they look very steadily at sth and do not BLINK 不眨眼的；目不转睛的 ▶ **un·blink·ing·ly** *adv.*

un·block /ˌʌnˈblɒk; *NAmE* -ˈblɑːk/ *verb* ~ **sth** to clean sth, for example a pipe, by removing sth that is blocking it 疏通（管道等）；清除…障碍

un·born /ˌʌnˈbɔːn; *NAmE* -ˈbɔːrn/ *adj.* [usually before noun] not yet born 未出世的；未出生的：*her unborn baby* 她未出世的宝宝

un·bound·ed /ʌnˈbaʊndɪd/ *adj.* (*formal*) having, or seeming to have, no limits （似）无限的；无尽的；无穷的 SYN **boundless, infinite**: *her unbounded energy* 她的无限精力

un·bowed /ˌʌnˈbaʊd/ *adj.* (*literary*) not defeated or not ready to accept defeat 不败的；不屈的；不服输的：*The losing team left the field* ***bloody but unbowed.*** 那支队一番苦战下离开球场，虽败犹荣。

un·break·able /ʌnˈbreɪkəbl/ *adj.* impossible to break 无法打破的；牢不可破的 SYN **indestructible**: *This new material is virtually unbreakable.* 这种新材料实际上是不碎的。OPP **breakable**

un·bridge·able /ʌnˈbrɪdʒəbl/ *adj.* an **unbridgeable** gap or difference between two people or groups or their opinions is one that cannot be closed or made less wide （分歧、意见等）无法弥合的；无法沟通的

un·bridled /ʌnˈbraɪdld/ *adj.* [usually before noun] (*formal*) not controlled and therefore extreme 无节制的；奔放的；极端的：*unbridled passion* 奔放的激情

un·broken /ʌnˈbrəʊkən; *NAmE* -ˈbroʊ-/ *adj.* **1** not interrupted or disturbed in any way 连续的；不间断的：*a single unbroken line* 一条连续的线 ◇ *30 years of virtually unbroken peace* * 30 年几乎未间断的和平 ◇ *my first night of unbroken sleep since the baby was born* 自孩子出世以来我睡的头一个囫囵觉 **2** (of a record in a sport, etc. 体育运动等的纪录) that has not been improved on 未改写的；未被打破的；未被超过的

un·buckle /ˌʌnˈbʌkl/ *verb* ~ **sth** to undo the BUCKLE of a belt, shoe, etc. 解开，松开（皮带、鞋子等）的扣

un·bur·den /ˌʌnˈbɜːdn; *NAmE* -ˈbɜːrdn/ *verb* **1** ~ **yourself/sth** (**of sth**) (**to sb**) (*formal*) to talk to sb about your problems or sth you have been worrying about, so that you feel less anxious 倾诉；诉说；诉苦：*She needed to unburden herself to somebody.* 她需要找个人诉诉心里的苦衷。**2** ~ **sb/sth** (**of sth**) to take sth that causes a lot of work or worry away from sb/sth 给…解除（负担）；分忧 OPP **burden**

un·but·ton /ˌʌnˈbʌtn/ *verb* ~ **sth** to undo the buttons on a piece of clothing 解开纽扣：*He unbuttoned his shirt.* 他解开衬衣扣子。OPP **button**

un·but·toned /ˌʌnˈbʌtnd/ *adj.* informal and relaxed 非正式的；轻松的；无拘束的：*Staff respond well to her unbuttoned style of management.* 职工对她洒脱的管理风格反应很好。

unˈcalled for *adj.* (of behaviour or remarks 行为或言论) not fair or appropriate 不公允的；不适当的；不恰当的 SYN **unnecessary**: *His comments were uncalled for.* 他的评论有失公允。◇ *uncalled-for comments* 不恰当的言论

un·canny /ʌnˈkæni/ *adj.* strange and difficult to explain 异常的；难以解释的 SYN **weird**: *I had an uncanny feeling I was being watched.* 我有种被人监视的奇怪感觉。◇ *It was uncanny really, almost as if she knew what I was thinking.* 真是不可思议，她好像知道我在想什么似的。▶ **un·can·nily** /-ɪli/ *adv.*: *He looked uncannily like someone I knew.* 他酷似我认识的一个人。

unˈcared for *adj.* not taken care of 无人照看的 SYN **neglected**: *The garden looked uncared for.* 这花园似乎无人管理。◇ *an uncared-for garden* 一个无人照料的花园

un·car·ing /ʌnˈkeərɪŋ; *NAmE* -ˈker-/ *adj.* (*disapproving*) not sympathetic about the problems or suffering of other people 冷漠的；无同情心的 SYN **callous** OPP **caring**

un·ceas·ing /ʌnˈsiːsɪŋ/ *adj.* (*formal*) continuing all the time 持续不断的；连绵不绝的 SYN **incessant**: *unceasing efforts* 不懈的努力 ◇ *Planes passed overhead with unceasing regularity.* 每隔一段时间总有飞机从头顶飞过。▶ **un·ceas·ing·ly** *adv.*: *Snow fell unceasingly.* 飞雪连绵。

un·cen·sored /ʌnˈsensəd; *NAmE* -sərd/ *adj.* (of a report, film/movie, etc. 报告、电影等) not CENSORED (= having had parts removed that are not considered suitable for the public) 未作删剪的；未经审查的：*an uncensored newspaper article* 一篇未经删剪的报纸文章

un·cere·mo·ni·ous /ˌʌnˌserəˈməʊniəs; *NAmE* -ˈmoʊ-/ *adj.* (*formal*) done roughly and rudely 粗暴无礼的；粗野的：*He was bundled out of the room with unceremonious haste.* 他被粗暴地轰出屋外。➲ COMPARE CEREMONIOUS

un·cere·mo·ni·ous·ly /ˌʌnˌserəˈməʊniəsli; *NAmE* -ˈmoʊ-/ *adv.* (*formal*) in a rough or rude way, without caring about a person's feelings 粗野地；粗暴无礼地：*They dumped his belongings unceremoniously on the floor.* 他们粗暴地把他的物品摔到地板上。

U

un·cer·tain 🔑 /ʌn'sɜːtn; *NAmE* ʌn'sɜːrtn/ *adj.* **1** 🔑 [not before noun] ~ (**about/of sth**) feeling doubt about sth; not sure 无把握；犹豫；拿不准：*They're both uncertain about what to do.* 他们两人都拿不定主意该怎么办。◇ *I'm still uncertain of my feelings for him.* 我仍不能肯定我对他的感情。**OPP certain** ➲ EXPRESS YOURSELF AT CERTAIN **2** 🔑 likely to change, especially in a negative or unpleasant way 多变的；难预料的：*Our future looks uncertain.* 我们似乎前途渺茫。◇ *a man of uncertain temper* 脾气令人捉摸不透的男人 **3** 🔑 not definite or decided 不确定的；未决定的 **SYN unclear**：*It is uncertain what his role in the company will be.* 他在公司担当什么职务尚未决定。**4** not confident 信心不足的；迟疑的 **SYN hesitant**：*The baby took its first uncertain steps.* 宝宝迈出了最初的蹒跚脚步。
IDM in ˌno unˌcertain 'terms clearly and strongly 明确有力地；毫不含糊地：*I told him what I thought of him in no uncertain terms.* 我直言不讳地说出了我对他的看法。

un·cer·tain·ly /ʌn'sɜːtnli; *NAmE* -'sɜːrtn-/ *adv.* without confidence 犹豫地；迟疑地 **SYN hesitantly**：*They smiled uncertainly at one another.* 他们犹豫地相视而笑。

un·cer·tainty /ʌn'sɜːtnti; *NAmE* -'sɜːrtn-/ *noun* (*pl.* **-ies**) **1** [U] the state of being uncertain 犹豫；迟疑；无把握：*There is considerable uncertainty about the company's future.* 这家公司的前景相当渺茫。◇ *He had an air of uncertainty about him.* 他显出将信将疑的神情。**2** [C] something that you cannot be sure about; a situation that causes you to be or feel uncertain 拿不定的事；令人无把握的局面：*life's uncertainties* 人生的不可知因素 ◇ *the uncertainties of war* 战争带来的不确定性

un·chal·lenge·able /ʌn'tʃælɪndʒəbl/ *adj.* that cannot be questioned or argued with; that cannot be challenged 不可争辩的；不容置辩的；不可挑战的：*unchallengeable evidence* 无可置辩的证据

un·chal·lenged /ʌn'tʃælɪndʒd/ *adj.* **1** not doubted; accepted without question; not challenged 不被怀疑的；完全接受的；没有异议的：*She could not allow such a claim to go **unchallenged**.* 她不能对这样的要求听之任之。**2** (of a ruler or leader, or their position 统治者、领袖或其地位) not opposed by anyone 无人反对的；稳固的：*He is in a position of unchallenged authority.* 他拥有绝对的权威。**3** without being stopped and asked to explain who you are, what you are doing, etc. 无阻挡的；未受盘查的：*I walked into the building unchallenged.* 我畅行无阻地走进大楼。

un·change·able /ʌn'tʃeɪndʒəbl/ *adj.* that cannot be changed 不可改变的：*unchangeable laws* 不变的定律 ➲ COMPARE CHANGEABLE

un·changed /ʌn'tʃeɪndʒd/ *adj.* [not usually before noun] that has stayed the same and not changed 不变；没有变化：*My opinion remains unchanged.* 我的看法一如既往。

un·chan·ging /ʌn'tʃeɪndʒɪŋ/ *adj.* that always stays the same and does not change 永恒的；不变的：*unchanging truths* 永恒的真理

un·char·ac·ter·is·tic /ʌnˌkærəktə'rɪstɪk/ *adj.* ~ (**of sb**) not typical of sb; not the way sb usually behaves （指人的行为）非典型的；非通常的；表现奇怪的：*The remark was quite uncharacteristic of her.* 这话很不像是她说的。**OPP characteristic** ▸ **un·char·ac·ter·is·tic·al·ly** /-kli/ *adv.*：*The children had been uncharacteristically quiet.* 孩子们显得异样的安静。

un·char·it·able /ʌn'tʃærɪtəbl/ *adj.* unkind and unfair in the way that you judge people 刻薄的；苛刻的；冷酷的：*uncharitable thoughts* 刻薄的想法 **OPP charitable** ▸ **un·char·it·ably** /-əbli/ *adv.*

un·chart·ed **AW** /ˌʌn'tʃɑːtɪd; *NAmE* -'tʃɑːrt-/ *adj.* [usually before noun] **1** that has not been visited or investigated before; not familiar 人迹罕至的；无人涉足的；陌生的：*They set off into the country's uncharted interior.* 他们出发前往这个国家人迹罕至的内陆。◇ (*figurative*) *The party is sailing in **uncharted waters*** (= a situation it has not been in before). 这个党面临一种崭新的局势。◇ (*figurative*) *I was moving into **uncharted territory*** (= a completely new experience) *with this relationship.* 这个关系让我开始有全新的体验。**2** not marked on a map 地图上未绘出（或未标明）的：*The ship hit an uncharted rock.* 船撞在海图上未标示的岩石上。

un·check /ˌʌn'tʃek/ *verb* [T] to remove a mark (✓) from a box on an electronic form to show that you do not want sth （在电子表格上）取消勾选

un·checked /ˌʌn'tʃekt/ *adj.* if sth harmful is **unchecked**, it is not controlled or stopped from getting worse 不加约束的；不受限制的；放任的：*The fire was allowed to burn unchecked.* 大火肆虐，不受控制。◇ *The rise in violent crime must not **go unchecked**.* 暴力犯罪的增长必须加以制止。◇ *The plant will soon choke ponds and waterways **if left unchecked**.* 如不控制这种植物的生长，池塘和水道很快就要被阻塞。

un·chris·tian /ˌʌn'krɪstʃən/ *adj.* not showing the qualities you expect of a Christian; not kind or thinking about other people's feelings 无基督教徒品质的；不慈善的；不为他人着想的 **OPP Christian**

un·civil /ˌʌn'sɪvl/ *adj.* (*formal*) not polite 失礼的；粗鲁的 **OPP civil** ➲ SEE ALSO INCIVILITY

un·civ·il·ized (*BrE also* **-ised**) /ʌn'sɪvəlaɪzd/ *adj.* (*disapproving*) **1** (of people or their behaviour 人或行为) not behaving in a way that is acceptable according to social or moral standards 不合社会（或道德）规范的；无教养的 **2** (of people or places 人或地方) not having developed a modern culture and way of life 未开化的；远离文明的：*I have worked in the wildest and most uncivilized parts of the world.* 我曾在世界上最荒凉、最原始的地区工作过。**OPP civilized**

un·claimed /ˌʌn'kleɪmd/ *adj.* that nobody has claimed as belonging to them or being owed to them 无人认领的；无人索取的

un·clas·si·fied /ʌn'klæsɪfaɪd/ *adj.* **1** (of documents, information, etc. 文件、信息等) not officially secret; available to everyone 非机密的；公开的 **OPP classified** **2** (*specialist*) that has not been CLASSIFIED as being the member of a particular group 未分类的；无类别的：(*BrE*) *A high proportion of candidates get low or unclassified grades* (= their work is not good enough to receive a grade). 有很大部分的考生成绩很差或没有成绩。**3** (*BrE*) (of a road 道路) not large or important enough to be given a number （因并非大路而）未编号的

uncle 🔑 /'ʌŋkl/ *noun* **1** 🔑 the brother of your mother or father; the husband of your aunt 舅父；叔父；伯父；姑父；姨父：*Uncle Ian* 伊恩叔叔 ◇ *I'm going to visit my uncle.* 我要去看我舅舅。◇ *I've just become an uncle* (= because your brother/sister has had a baby). 我刚当上叔叔（或舅舅）。**2** used by children, with a first name, to address a man who is a close friend of their parents （儿童用语，称呼父母的同辈男性朋友）叔叔，伯伯 **IDM** ➤ SEE BOB

un·clean /ˌʌn'kliːn/ *adj.* **1** (*formal*) dirty and therefore likely to cause disease 肮脏的，不洁净的（因而容易致病）：*unclean water* 不清洁的水 **OPP clean** **2** considered to be bad, immoral or not pure in a religious way, and therefore not to be touched, eaten, etc. 邪恶的；不洁的；（宗教上所指）不洁净的 **SYN impure**：*unclean thoughts* 邪念 ◇ *unclean food* 不洁的食物

un·clear /ˌʌn'klɪə(r); *NAmE* -'klɪr/ *adj.* **1** not clear or definite; difficult to understand or be sure about 不清楚的；不确定的；难以掌握的：*His motives are unclear.* 他的用意不明。◇ *It is unclear whether there is any damage.* 有无损坏尚不清楚。◇ *Your diagrams are unclear.* 你的图表不清楚。**2** ~ (**about sth**) | ~ (**as to sth**) not fully understanding sth 不完全明白；不理解 **SYN uncertain**：*I'm unclear about what you want me to do.* 我不太明白你要我做什么。

ˌUncle 'Sam *noun* (*informal*) a way of referring to the United States of America or the US government (sometimes shown as a tall man with a white beard and a tall hat) 山姆大叔（指美国或美国政府，有时被塑造成有白

胡子、戴大礼帽的高个子男人）：*He owed $20 000 in tax to Uncle Sam.* 他欠美国政府 2 万美元税款。➲ MORE LIKE THIS 18, page R27

Uncle 'Tom *noun* (*taboo, offensive*) sometimes used in the past to refer to a black man who wants to please or serve white people 汤姆大叔（旧时有时用以指想讨好或侍奉白人的黑人男子）**ORIGIN** From a character in the novel *Uncle Tom's Cabin* by Harriet Beecher Stowe. 源自哈丽雅特·比彻·斯托所著长篇小说《汤姆叔叔的小屋》中的人物。

un·clothed /ˌʌnˈkləʊðd; *NAmE* -ˈkloʊðd/ *adj.* (*formal*) not wearing any clothes 赤裸的；裸体的；一丝不挂的 **SYN** **naked** **OPP** **clothed**

un·clut·tered /ˌʌnˈklʌtəd; *NAmE* -tərd/ *adj.* (*approving*) not containing too many objects, details or unnecessary items 简洁的；整洁的；利落的 **SYN** **tidy** **OPP** **cluttered**

un·coil /ˌʌnˈkɔɪl/ *verb* [I, T] to become or make sth straight after it has been wound or twisted round in a circle （使盘卷的东西）展开，打开；拉直：*The snake slowly uncoiled.* 蛇慢慢地展开了盘着的身体。◇ **~ sth/itself** *to uncoil a rope* 打开盘卷的绳索

un·col·oured (*especially US* **un·col·ored**) /ˌʌnˈkʌləd; *NAmE* -ərd/ *adj.* with no colour; with no colour added 无色的；不加色的

un·combed /ˌʌnˈkəʊmd; *NAmE* -ˈkoʊmd/ *adj.* (of hair 头发) that has not been brushed or COMBED; very untidy 未梳理的；蓬乱的

un·com·fort·able 🔑 /ʌnˈkʌmftəbl; *BrE also* -fət-; *NAmE also* -fərt-/ *adj.* **1** 🔑 (of clothes, furniture, etc. 衣服、家具等) not letting you feel physically comfortable; unpleasant to wear, sit on, etc. 使人不舒服的；令人不舒适的：*uncomfortable shoes* 不舒适的鞋子 ◇ *I couldn't sleep because the bed was so uncomfortable.* 这床太不舒服了，我睡不着觉。**OPP** **comfortable** **2** 🔑 not feeling physically relaxed, warm, etc. 感到难受的；感觉不舒服（或不暖和等）的：*I was sitting in an extremely uncomfortable position.* 我坐着的姿势难受极了。◇ *She still finds it uncomfortable to stand without support.* 她仍觉得没有支撑站着不太舒服。**OPP** **comfortable** **3** 🔑 anxious, embarrassed or afraid and unable to relax; making you feel like this （使）焦虑的；尴尬的；害怕的；不自在的：*He looked distinctly uncomfortable when the subject was mentioned.* 提到这个话题，他明显表现出不安。◇ *There was an uncomfortable silence.* 有一种令人不安的寂静。**OPP** **comfortable** **4** unpleasant or difficult to deal with 棘手的；麻烦的；难处理的：*an uncomfortable fact* 令人头痛的事实 ◇ *I had the uncomfortable feeling that it was my fault.* 我内心惴惴不安，觉得那是我的过错。

un·com·fort·ably /ʌnˈkʌmftəbli; *BrE also* -fət-; *NAmE also* -fərt-/ *adv.* **1** in a way that makes you feel anxious or embarrassed; in a way that shows you are anxious or embarrassed 令人不安（或尴尬）地；显得不安（或尴尬）地：*I became uncomfortably aware that no one else was laughing.* 我难堪地意识到别人都没有笑。◇ *Her comment was uncomfortably close to the truth.* 她的评论逼近真相，令人局促不安。◇ *He shifted uncomfortably in his seat when I mentioned money.* 我提到钱时，他便坐不住了。**2** in a way that is not physically comfortable 不舒服地；难受地：*I was feeling uncomfortably hot.* 我觉得酷热难当。◇ *She perched uncomfortably on the edge of the table.* 她将就坐在桌边上，非常难受。

un·com·mit·ted /ˌʌnkəˈmɪtɪd/ *adj.* **~ (to sb/sth)** not having given or promised support to a particular person, group, belief, action, etc. 未作承诺的；未表态的：*The party needs to canvass the uncommitted voters.* 这个党需要向未表明态度的选民游说拉票。➲ COMPARE COMMITTED

un·com·mon /ʌnˈkɒmən; *NAmE* -ˈkɑːm-/ *adj.* **1** not existing in large numbers or in many places 不常有的；罕见的；稀罕的 **SYN** **unusual, rare**：*an uncommon occurrence* 不寻常的事情 ◇ *Side effects from the drug are uncommon.* 这药很少有副作用。◇ *It is* **not uncommon** *for college students to live at home.* 大学生住在家里并不少见。◇ *Red squirrels are uncommon in England.* 红松鼠在英格兰很少见。**OPP** **common** **2** (*formal* or *literary*) unusually large in degree or amount; great 程度深的；特别大的 **SYN** **remarkable**：*She showed uncommon pleasure at his arrival.* 他的到来令她异常欢喜。

un·com·mon·ly /ʌnˈkɒmənli; *NAmE* -ˈkɑːm-/ *adv.* (*formal*) **1** to an unusual degree; extremely 极其；极端地；非凡地：*an uncommonly gifted child* 一个天赋异禀的儿童 **2** not often; not usually 不经常；罕见；不平常：*Not uncommonly, there is a great deal of rain in August.* 八月份降雨量大并非异常。

un·com·mu·ni·ca·tive **AW** /ˌʌnkəˈmjuːnɪkətɪv/ *adj.* (*disapproving*) (of a person 人) not willing to talk to other people or give opinions 不爱说话的；寡言少语的；缄默的 **SYN** **taciturn** **OPP** **communicative**

un·com·peti·tive /ˌʌnkəmˈpetətɪv/ *adj.* (*business* 商) not cheaper or better than others and therefore not able to compete equally 无竞争力的；竞争力弱的：*an uncompetitive industry* 无竞争力的行业 ◇ *uncompetitive prices* 缺乏竞争力的价格 **OPP** **competitive**

un·com·plain·ing /ˌʌnkəmˈpleɪnɪŋ/ *adj.* (*approving*) not saying that you are unhappy about a difficult or unpleasant situation; not saying that you are in pain 任劳任怨的；不抱怨的 ▸ **un·com·plain·ing·ly** *adv.*

un·com·pleted /ˌʌnkəmˈpliːtɪd/ *adj.* that has not been finished 未完成的；未竟的；未竣工的：*an uncompleted project* 未完成的项目

un·com·pli·cated /ʌnˈkɒmplɪkeɪtɪd; *NAmE* -ˈkɑːm-/ *adj.* simple; without any difficulty or confusion 简单的；率真的；容易的；不混乱的 **SYN** **straightforward**：*an easy-going, uncomplicated young man* 一个随和、率直的男青年 ◇ *Why can't I have an uncomplicated life?* 我为什么不能过一种简朴的生活？**OPP** **complicated**

un·com·pli·men·tary /ʌnˌkɒmplɪˈmentri; *NAmE* -ˌkɑːm-/ *adj.* rude or insulting 无礼的；贬抑的；污辱性的：*uncomplimentary remarks* 不客气的话 ➲ COMPARE COMPLIMENTARY (2)

un·com·pre·hend·ing /ʌnˌkɒmprɪˈhendɪŋ; *NAmE* -ˌkɑːm-/ *adj.* (*formal*) (of a person 人) not understanding a situation or what is happening 不理解的；茫然的；不领会的 ▸ **un·com·pre·hend·ing·ly** *adv.*：*She looked at him uncomprehendingly.* 她一脸茫然地注视着他。

un·com·prom·is·ing /ʌnˈkɒmprəmaɪzɪŋ; *NAmE* -ˈkɑːm-/ *adj.* unwilling to change your opinions or behaviour 不让步的；不妥协的；强硬的：*an uncompromising attitude* 强硬的态度 ◇ *He has a reputation for being tough and uncompromising.* 他的严厉和强硬态度是出了名的。▸ **un·com·prom·is·ing·ly** *adv.*

un·con·cealed /ˌʌnkənˈsiːld/ *adj.* [usually before noun] (of an emotion, etc. 感情等) that you do not try to hide 不掩饰的；不隐藏的；明显的 **SYN** **obvious**：*unconcealed curiosity* 表露无遗的好奇心

un·con·cern /ˌʌnkənˈsɜːn; *NAmE* -ˈsɜːrn/ *noun* [U] (*formal*) a lack of care, interest or worry about sth that other people would care about 冷漠；不关心；无兴趣 **SYN** **indifference**：*She received the news with apparent unconcern.* 她接到这消息时显然无动于衷。➲ COMPARE CONCERN *n.* (1)

un·con·cerned /ˌʌnkənˈsɜːnd; *NAmE* -ˈsɜːrnd/ *adj.* **1 ~ (about/by sth)** not worried or anxious about sth because you feel it does not affect you or is not important 冷淡的；漠视的；漫不经心的：*He drove on, apparently unconcerned about the noise the engine was making.* 他继续驾车前进，对发动机发出的噪声显然毫不在意。**2 ~ (with sb/sth)** not interested in sth 不关心的；无兴趣的：*Young people are often unconcerned with political issues.* 青年人对政治问题往往漠不关心。**OPP** **concerned** ▸ **un·con·cern·ed·ly** /ˌʌnkənˈsɜːnɪdli/ *adv.*

un·con·di·tion·al /ˌʌnkənˈdɪʃənl/ *adj.* without any conditions or limits 无条件的；无限制的；绝对的：*the unconditional surrender of military forces* 军队的无条件投降 ◇

U

*She gave her children **unconditional love**.* 她将爱毫无保留地给了她的孩子。 OPP **conditional** ▶ **un·con·di·tion·al·ly** /-ʃənəli/ *adv.*

un·con·di·tioned /ˌʌnkənˈdɪʃnd/ *adj.* (*psychology* 心) (of behaviour 行为) not trained or influenced by experience; natural 非条件的： *an unconditioned response* 无条件反应

un·con·fined AW /ˌʌnkənˈfaɪnd/ *adj.* (*formal*) not limited in space, range or amount 不受限制的；无限的： *The animals have unconfined access to pasture.* 这些动物是散养的。◇ *When the news came through joy was unconfined.* 听到消息时无比喜悦。

un·con·firmed /ˌʌnkənˈfɜːmd; *NAmE* -ˈfɜːrmd/ *adj.* that has not yet been proved to be true or confirmed 未经证实的；未被认可的；未确认的： *unconfirmed rumours* 未证实的传言 ◇ *Unconfirmed reports said that at least six people had been killed.* 未经证实的报道称至少有六人丧生。

un·con·gen·ial /ˌʌnkənˈdʒiːniəl/ *adj.* (*formal*) **1** (of a person 人) not pleasant or friendly; not like yourself 不友善的；性情不相投的： *uncongenial company* 脾气不相投的同伴 **2 ~ (to sb)** (of a place, job, etc. 地方、工作等) not pleasant; not making you feel relaxed; not suitable for your personality 不愉快的；令人紧张的；不适宜的： *an uncongenial atmosphere* 不和谐的气氛 **3 ~ (to sth)** not suitable for sth; not encouraging sth 不适合的；不利的： *The religious climate at the time was uncongenial to new ideas.* 当时的宗教气候容不得新思想。 OPP **congenial**

un·con·nect·ed /ˌʌnkəˈnektɪd/ *adj.* not related or connected in any way 不相关的；无联系的： *The two crimes are apparently unconnected.* 这两起犯罪显然没有关联。◇ **~ with/to sth** *My resignation was totally unconnected with recent events.* 我的辞职与最近的事件毫不相干。

un·con·quer·able /ʌnˈkɒŋkərəbl; *NAmE* -ˈkɑːŋ-/ *adj.* too strong to be defeated or changed 不可战胜的；坚不可摧的；难以改变的 SYN **invincible**

un·con·scion·able /ʌnˈkɒnʃənəbl; *NAmE* -ˈkɑːn-/ *adj.* [usually before noun] (*formal*) **1** (of an action, etc. 行动等) so bad, immoral, etc. that it should make you feel ashamed 违背良心的 **2** (*often humorous*) too great, large, long, etc. 过分的；过于大（或多、长等）的 SYN **excessive**

un·con·scious 🔑 /ʌnˈkɒnʃəs; *NAmE* -ˈkɑːn-/ *adj., noun*

■ *adj.* **1** 🔑 in a state like sleep because of an injury or illness, and not able to use your senses 无知觉的；昏迷的；不省人事的： *She was **knocked unconscious**.* 她被打昏了。◇ *They found him lying unconscious on the floor.* 他们发现他晕倒在地板上。 **2** 🔑 (of feelings, thoughts, etc. 感情、思想等) existing or happening without you realizing or being aware; not deliberate or controlled 无意识的；自然流露的： *unconscious desires* 自然流露的欲望 ◇ *The brochure is full of unconscious humour.* 这本小册子妙趣横生。 ➲ COMPARE SUBCONSCIOUS *adj.* **3** 🔑 **~ of sb/sth** not aware of sb/sth; not noticing sth; not conscious 未察觉；未意识到；未注意 SYN **oblivious**： *She is unconscious of the effect she has on people.* 她没有察觉自己对大众的影响。◇ *He was quite unconscious of the danger.* 他丝毫没有意识到危险。 OPP **conscious**

■ *noun* **the unconscious** [sing.] (*psychology* 心) the part of a person's mind with thoughts, feelings, etc. that they are not aware of and cannot control but which can sometimes be understood by studying their behaviour or dreams 无意识（不察觉的心理活动） ➲ COMPARE SUBCONSCIOUS *n.*

un·con·scious·ly /ʌnˈkɒnʃəsli; *NAmE* -ˈkɑːn-/ *adv.* without being aware 无意地；不知不觉地： *Perhaps, unconsciously, I've done something to offend her.* 我也许无意中做了什么得罪她的事。 OPP **consciously**

un·con·scious·ness /ʌnˈkɒnʃəsnəs; *NAmE* -ˈkɑːn-/ *noun* [U] a state like sleep caused by injury or illness, when you are unable to use your senses 昏迷；无知觉状态： *He had lapsed into unconsciousness.* 他陷入了昏迷状态。

un·con·sid·ered /ˌʌnkənˈsɪdəd; *NAmE* -ərd/ *adj.* (*formal*) not thought about, or not thought about with enough care 未经（或欠）考虑的；未经深思熟虑的： *I came to regret my unconsidered remarks.* 我对我那些考虑不周的言辞开始感到后悔。

un·con·sol·able /ˌʌnkənˈsəʊləbl; *NAmE* -ˈsoʊl-/ *adj.* = INCONSOLABLE ▶ **un·con·sol·ably** /-əbli/ *adv.* = INCONSOLABLY

un·con·sti·tu·tion·al AW /ˌʌnˌkɒnstɪˈtjuːʃənl; *NAmE* -kɑːnstəˈtuː-/ *adj.* not allowed by the CONSTITUTION of a country, a political system or an organization 违背宪法的；违反宪章（或章程）的 OPP **constitutional** ▶ **un·con·sti·tu·tion·al·ly** /-ʃənəli/ *adv.*

un·con·strained AW /ˌʌnkənˈstreɪnd/ *adj.* not restricted or limited 不受约束的；自由的： *unconstrained growth* 自然生长 ➲ SEE ALSO CONSTRAIN (2)

un·con·tam·in·ated /ˌʌnkənˈtæmɪneɪtɪd/ *adj.* not harmed or spoilt by sth (for example, dangerous substances) 未被损害的；未受污染的： *uncontaminated water* 未被污染的水 OPP **contaminate**

un·con·ten·tious /ˌʌnkənˈtenʃəs/ *adj.* (*formal*) not likely to cause disagreement between people 没有（或不容易）引起争议的： *The proposal is relatively uncontentious.* 这个建议并没有什么重大的争议。 OPP **contentious**

un·con·test·ed /ˌʌnkənˈtestɪd/ *adj.* without any opposition or argument 无争议的；无人反对的： *an uncontested election/divorce* 无争议的选举/离婚 ◇ *These claims have **not gone uncontested**.* 这些说法并非无人提出异议。

un·con·trol·lable /ˌʌnkənˈtrəʊləbl; *NAmE* -ˈtroʊ-/ *adj.* that you cannot control or prevent 无法控制的；难以防止的；禁不住的： *an uncontrollable temper* 控制不住的脾气 ◇ *uncontrollable bleeding* 止不住的流血 ◇ *I had an uncontrollable urge to laugh.* 我忍不住想笑。◇ *The ball was uncontrollable.* 球控制不住了。◇ *He's an uncontrollable child* (= he behaves very badly and cannot be controlled). 他是个难以管教的孩子。 ▶ **un·con·trol·lably** /-əbli/ *adv.*： *She began shaking uncontrollably.* 她不由自主地哆嗦起来。

un·con·trolled 🔑 /ˌʌnkənˈtrəʊld; *NAmE* -ˈtroʊld/ *adj.* **1** 🔑 (of emotions, behaviour, etc. 感情、行为等) that sb cannot control or stop 抑制不住的；无法制止的： *uncontrolled anger* 克制不住的愤怒 ◇ *The thoughts rushed into my mind uncontrolled.* 各种想法如潮水般涌上我的心头。 **2** 🔑 that is not limited or managed by law or rules 不受法律（或规则）制约的；无序的： *the uncontrolled growth of cities* 城市的无规划发展 ◇ *uncontrolled dumping of toxic wastes* 有毒废弃物的胡乱弃置 ➲ COMPARE CONTROLLED (2)

un·con·tro·ver·sial AW /ˌʌnˌkɒntrəˈvɜːʃl; *NAmE* ˌʌnkɑːntrəˈvɜːrʃl/ *adj.* not causing, or not likely to cause, any disagreement 无争议的；不会引起不和的： *an uncontroversial opinion* 无争议的意见 ◇ *He chose an uncontroversial topic for his speech.* 他为自己的演讲选择了一个不会引起争议的话题。 OPP **controversial** ➲ COMPARE NON-CONTROVERSIAL

un·con·ven·tion·al AW /ˌʌnkənˈvenʃənl/ *adj.* (*often approving*) not following what is done or considered normal or acceptable by most people; different and interesting 不因循守旧的；不因袭的；新奇的 SYN **unorthodox**： *an unconventional approach to the problem* 解决这个问题的非常规方法 ◇ *unconventional views* 新奇的观点 OPP **conventional** ▶ **un·con·ven·tion·al·ity** /ˌʌnkənvenʃəˈnæləti/ *noun* [U] **un·con·ven·tion·al·ly** /-ʃənəli/ *adv.*

un·con·vinced AW /ˌʌnkənˈvɪnst/ *adj.* not believing or not certain about sth despite what you have been told 不信服的；未被说服的： **~ (of sth)** *I remain unconvinced of the need for change.* 我仍怀疑改革的必要性。◇ **~ (by sth)** *She seemed unconvinced by their promises.* 她似乎不相信他们的许诺。◇ **~ (that…)** *The jury were unconvinced that he was innocent.* 陪审团不相信他是无辜的。 OPP **convinced**

un·con·vin·cing /ˌʌnkənˈvɪnsɪŋ/ *adj.* not seeming true or real; not making you believe that sth is true 似乎不真实

U

的；不令人信服的；难以相信的：*I find the characters in the book very unconvincing.* 我觉得书中的人物很不真实。◇ *She managed a weak, unconvincing smile.* 她勉强挤出一丝笑意。OPP **convincing** ▶ **un·con·vin·cing·ly** *adv.*

un·cooked /ˌʌnˈkʊkt/ *adj.* not cooked 未烹煮的；生的 SYN **raw**: *Eat plenty of uncooked fruit and vegetables.* 要多吃生的水果和蔬菜。

un·cool /ˌʌnˈkuːl/ *adj.* (*informal*) not considered acceptable by fashionable young people 不时髦的；不帅的；不潇洒的；不"酷"的 OPP **cool**

un·co·opera·tive /ˌʌnkəʊˈɒpərətɪv; *NAmE* -koʊˈɑːp-/ *adj.* not willing to be helpful to other people or do what they ask 不愿合作的；不愿配合的 SYN **unhelpful** OPP **cooperative**

un·co·or·din·ated /ˌʌnkəʊˈɔːdɪneɪtɪd; *NAmE* -koʊˈɔːrd-/ *adj.* **1** if a person is **uncoordinated**, they are not able to control their movements well, and are therefore not very skilful at some sports and physical activities 动作不协调的；不灵便的；手脚笨拙的 **2** (of movements or parts of the body 动作或身体部位) not controlled; not moving smoothly or together 不协调的；不灵活的 **3** (of plans, projects, etc. 计划、项目等) not well organized; with no thought for how the different parts work together 不缜密的；无通盘安排的；缺乏全面考虑的

un·cork /ˌʌnˈkɔːk; *NAmE* -ˈkɔːrk/ *verb* **~ sth** to open a bottle by removing the CORK from the top 打开…的瓶塞 OPP **cork**

un·cor·rob·or·ated /ˌʌnkəˈrɒbəreɪtɪd; *NAmE* -ˈrɑːb-/ *adj.* (of a statement or claim 声明或要求) not supported by any other evidence; not having been CORROBORATED 无确证的；未经证实的 SYN **unconfirmed**

un·count·able /ʌnˈkaʊntəbl/ (*also* ˌ**non-ˈcount**) *adj.* (*grammar* 语法) a noun that is **uncountable** cannot be made plural or used with *a* or *an*, for example *water*, *bread* and *information* （名词）不可数的 OPP **countable** ➲ COMPARE COUNTLESS

ˈ**uncount noun** *noun* (*grammar* 语法) an uncountable noun 不可数名词 OPP **count noun**

un·couple /ˌʌnˈkʌpl/ *verb* **~ sth (from sth)** to remove the connection between two vehicles, two parts of a train, etc. 使（车辆、车厢等）分离；分开（连在一起的两个）

un·couth /ʌnˈkuːθ/ *adj.* (of a person or their behaviour 人或行为) rude or socially unacceptable 粗鲁的；无礼的；无教养的 SYN **coarse**: *uncouth laughter* 粗野的笑声 ◇ *an uncouth young man* 一个无教养的年轻人

un·cover /ʌnˈkʌvə(r)/ *verb* **1 ~ sth** to remove sth that is covering sth 揭开盖子：*Uncover the pan and let the soup simmer.* 揭开锅盖，让汤再慢火煨一下。**2 ~ sth** to discover sth that was previously hidden or secret 发现；揭露；揭发：*Police have uncovered a plot to kidnap the President's son.* 警方发现了一个绑架总统之子的阴谋。

un·covered /ʌnˈkʌvəd; *NAmE* -ərd/ *adj.* not covered by anything 裸露的；暴露的；无覆盖的：*His head was uncovered.* 他光着头。

un·crit·ic·al /ˌʌnˈkrɪtɪkl/ *adj.* (*usually disapproving*) not willing to criticize sb/sth or to judge whether sb/sth is right or wrong 不愿批评的；不置可否的；不得罪人的：*Her uncritical acceptance of everything I said began to irritate me.* 我说什么她都不论对错一概接受，这倒惹我不耐烦起来。OPP **critical** ▶ **un·crit·ic·al·ly** /-ɪkli/ *adv.*

un·crowd·ed /ʌnˈkraʊdɪd/ *adj.* not full of people 不拥挤的；人少的：*The beach was pleasantly uncrowded.* 海滩上人不多，很是惬意。OPP **crowded**

un·crowned /ˌʌnˈkraʊnd/ *adj.* (of a king or queen 国君) not yet CROWNED 尚未加冕的

IDM **the ˌuncrowned ˈking/ˈqueen (of sth)** the person considered to be the best, most famous or successful in a particular place or area of activity 无冕之王（某地区或领域中最杰出的人）

unc·tion /ˈʌŋkʃn/ *noun* [U] **1** the act of pouring oil on sb's head or another part of their body as part of an important religious ceremony （宗教上的）傅油礼 ➲ SEE ALSO EXTREME UNCTION **2** (*formal, disapproving*) behaviour or speech that is not sincere and that expresses too much praise or admiration of sb 虚情假意的行为（或讲话）；奉承；甜言蜜语

unc·tu·ous /ˈʌŋktjuəs; *NAmE* -tʃuəs/ *adj.* (*formal, disapproving*) friendly or giving praise in a way that is not sincere and which is therefore unpleasant 谄媚的；油滑的；拍马奉迎的 ▶ **unc·tu·ous·ly** *adv.*

un·culti·vated /ʌnˈkʌltɪveɪtɪd/ *adj.* (of land 土地) not used for growing crops 未经耕作的；未开垦的 OPP **cultivated**

un·cul·tured AW /ˌʌnˈkʌltʃəd; *NAmE* -tʃərd/ *adj.* (of people 人) not well educated; not able to understand or enjoy art, literature, etc. 缺乏教养的；不文雅的；粗俗的 OPP **cultured**

un·curl /ˌʌnˈkɜːl; *NAmE* -ˈkɜːrl/ *verb* [I, T] to become straight, or to make sth become straight, after being in a curled position （使由盘卷姿势）伸直；抻直：*The snake slowly uncurled.* 那条蛇慢慢地伸开了蜷缩的身子。◇ **~ sth/itself** *The cat uncurled itself and jumped off the wall.* 那猫伸直了腰跳下墙头。OPP **curl up**

uncut /ˌʌnˈkʌt/ *adj.* **1** left to grow; not cut short 未割的；未剪的：*The uncut grass came up to her waist.* 未割的草齐了她的腰。**2** (of a book, film/movie, etc. 书籍、电影等) left in its complete form; without any parts removed; not CENSORED 未删节的；未删剪的；未审查的：*the original uncut version* 未删节的原版 **3** (of a PRECIOUS STONE 宝石) not shaped by cutting 未雕琢的；未加工的：*uncut diamonds* 未雕琢的钻石

un·dam·aged /ʌnˈdæmɪdʒd/ *adj.* not damaged or spoilt 未损坏的；未毁坏的：*There was a slight collision but my car was undamaged.* 虽有轻微碰撞，但我的汽车没有损坏。◇ *He emerged from the court case with his reputation undamaged.* 他挺过了官司，名声没有受损。

un·dated /ˌʌnˈdeɪtɪd/ *adj.* **1** without a date written or printed on it 未注日期的：*an undated letter* 一封没写日期的信 **2** of which the date is not known 日期不明的；时间不详的：*undated archaeological remains* 时间未确定的考古遗迹 ➲ COMPARE DATED

un·daunt·ed /ˌʌnˈdɔːntɪd/ *adj.* [not usually before noun] (*formal*) still enthusiastic and determined, despite difficulties or disappointment 顽强；百折不挠；坚强不屈 SYN **undeterred**: *He seemed undaunted by all the opposition to his idea.* 尽管他的思想屡遭非难，他似乎仍然百折不挠。

un·decided /ˌʌndɪˈsaɪdɪd/ *adj.* [not usually before noun] **1** not having made a decision about sb/sth 未拿定主意；犹豫不决：**~ (about sb/sth)** *I'm still undecided (about) who to vote for.* 我还拿不定主意投谁的票。◇ **~ (as to sth)** *He was undecided as to what to do next.* 他对下一步要做什么犹豫不决。**2** not having been decided 尚未被确定；悬而未决：*The venue for the World Cup remains undecided.* 世界杯的举办地点尚未确定。➲ COMPARE DECIDED (2)

un·declared /ˌʌndɪˈkleəd; *NAmE* -ˈklerd/ *adj.* not admitted to; not stated in an open way; not having been declared 未承认的；未声明的；未申报的：*No income should remain undeclared.* 一切收入均应申报。◇ *Undeclared goods* (= that the customs are not told about) *may be confiscated.* 未报关的物品可能被没收。

un·defeat·ed /ˌʌndɪˈfiːtɪd/ *adj.* (especially in sport 尤用于体育运动) not having lost or been defeated 不败的；未尝败绩的：*They are undefeated in 13 games.* 他们 13 场比赛未被打败过。◇ *the undefeated world champion* 全胜的世界冠军

un·defend·ed /ˌʌndɪˈfendɪd/ *adj.* **1** not protected or guarded 不设防的；不加防御的 SYN **unprotected**: *undefended borders* 不设防边界 **2** if a case in court is **undefended**, no defence is made against it 无抗辩的；不作辩护的

U

un·defined AW /ˌʌndɪˈfaɪnd/ *adj.* not made clear or definite 未阐明的；未限定的：*The money was lent for an undefined period of time.* 这笔钱无限期借出。

un·de·lete /ˌʌndɪˈliːt/ *verb* [T, I] ~ (**sth**) (*computing* 计) to cancel an action of DELETING a document, a file, text, etc. on a computer, so that it appears again 取消删除；恢复（已删除的文件等）

un·demand·ing /ˌʌndɪˈmɑːndɪŋ/ *adj.* **1** not needing a lot of effort or thought 不费力的；不费神的；轻松容易的：*an undemanding job* 轻松的工作 **2** (of a person 人) not asking for a lot of attention or action from other people 不强求的；不要求照顾的；随和的 OPP **demanding**

un·demo·crat·ic /ˌʌndeməˈkrætɪk/ *adj.* against or not acting according to the principles of DEMOCRACY 不民主的；专横的；霸道的：*undemocratic decisions* 专制的决定 ◇ *an undemocratic regime* 专制政权 OPP **democratic** ▸ **un·demo·crat·ic·al·ly** /-kli/ *adv.*：*an undemocratically elected government* 非民选政府 ◇ *He was accused of acting undemocratically.* 他被指责作风专制。

un·demon·stra·tive /ˌʌndɪˈmɒnstrətɪv; *NAmE* -ˈmɑːn-/ *adj.* not showing feelings openly, especially feelings of affection 喜怒不形于色的；不流露感情的 OPP **demonstrative**

un·deni·able AW /ˌʌndɪˈnaɪəbl/ *adj.* true or certain; that cannot be denied 不可否认的；确凿的 SYN **indisputable**：*He had undeniable charm.* 他具有不可否认的魅力。◇ *It is an undeniable fact that crime is increasing.* 犯罪在增长是无可争辩的事实。OPP **deniable** ▸ **un·deni·ably** /-əbli/ *adv.*：*undeniably impressive* 确实令人赞叹

under /ˈʌndə(r)/ *prep., adv., adj.*

■ ***prep.*** **1** in, to or through a position that is below sth 在（或到、通过）…下面：*Have you looked under the bed?* 你看了床底下没有？◇ *She placed the ladder under* (= just lower than) *the window.* 她把梯子立在窗户下面。◇ *The dog squeezed under the gate and ran into the road.* 狗从门底下钻出去，跑到大路上去了。 **2** below the surface of sth; covered by sth 在…表面下；由…覆盖着：*The boat lay under several feet of water.* 那条船沉在水下好几英尺处。 **3** less than; younger than 少于；小于；不足；比…年轻：*an annual income of under £10 000* 不到 1 万英镑的年收入 ◇ *It took us under an hour.* 这事花了我们不到一小时。◇ *Nobody under 18 is allowed to buy alcohol.* 未满 18 岁者不得买酒。 **4** used to say who or what controls, governs or manages sb/sth 由…控制（或管理、经营）：*The country is now under martial law.* 这个国家目前在戒严中。◇ *The coinage was reformed under Elizabeth I* (= when she was queen). 英国币制在伊丽莎白一世时代作了改革。◇ *She has a staff of 19 working under her.* 她手下有 19 个职员工作。◇ *Under its new conductor, the orchestra has established an international reputation.* 在新指挥的领导下，这个乐团建立了国际声誉。 **5** according to an agreement, a law or a system 根据，按照（协议、法律或制度）：*A man was detained under the Mental Health Act.* 根据《精神卫生法》，一名男子被拘留。◇ *Under the terms of the lease you had no right to sublet the property.* 按租约条款的规定，你无权转租这房产。◇ *Is the television still under guarantee?* 这台电视机还在保修期内吗？ **6** experiencing a particular process在…过程中：*The hotel is still under construction.* 旅馆还在兴建中。◇ *The matter is under investigation.* 此事正在调查中。 **7** affected by sth 由…造成；受…影响：*The wall collapsed under the strain.* 墙壁因承受不了重压而坍塌了。◇ *I've been feeling under stress lately.* 我最近感到压力很大。◇ *I'm under no illusions about what hard work this will be.* 对于这项工作的辛苦，我从不存错误的幻想。◇ *You'll be under anaesthetic, so you won't feel a thing.* 你将被麻醉，所以什么也感觉不到。 **8** using a particular name 用，以（某一名字）：*She also writes under the pseudonym of Barbara Vine.* 她也用芭芭拉·瓦因的化名从事写作。 **9** found in a particular part of a book, list, etc. 在…项下；在（书等中的）某部分：*If it's not under 'sports', try looking under 'games'.* 如果在"体育运动"项下查不到，就试试"游戏"项吧。

■ ***adv.*** **1** below sth 在下面：*He pulled up the covers and crawled under.* 他揭开被子钻到里面。 **2** below the surface of water 在水下：*She took a deep breath and stayed under for more than a minute.* 她深吸了一口气，然后潜水一分多钟。◇ *The boat was going under fast.* 小船正迅速下沉。 **3** less; younger 少于；小于；较年轻：*prices of ten dollars and under* 不高于十美元的价格 ◇ *children aged 12 and under* * 12 岁及以下的儿童 **4** in or into an unconscious state 在昏迷中；陷入昏迷状态：*He felt himself going under.* 他觉得自己将要昏厥。

■ ***adj.*** [only before noun] lower; underneath 较低的；下面的：*the under layer* 下面的一层 ◇ *the under surface of a leaf* 叶子的背面

under- /ˈʌndə(r)/ *prefix* **1** (in nouns and adjectives 构成名词和形容词) below; beneath 在下面；在…之下：*undergrowth* 下层灌木丛 ◇ *undercover* 暗中的 **2** (in nouns 构成名词) lower in age or rank（年龄）较小；（级别）较低：*the under-fives* 五岁以下的儿童 ◇ *an undergraduate* 大学生 **3** (in adjectives and verbs 构成形容词和动词) not enough 不足；未：*underripe* 未成熟的 ◇ *undercooked* 未煮熟的 ➲ MORE LIKE THIS 6, page R25

under·achieve /ˌʌndərəˈtʃiːv/ *verb* [I] to do less well than you could do, especially in school work（尤指学习上）未发挥水平，未展现实力 ▸ **under·achieve·ment** *noun* [U] **under·achiever** *noun*

under·age /ˈʌndəreɪdʒ/ *adj.* [only before noun] done by people who are too young by law 未达到法定年龄的人所做的；未成年人的：*underage drinking* 未成年饮酒 ➲ SEE ALSO AGE *n.*

under·arm /ˈʌndərɑːm; *NAmE* -ɑːrm/ *adj., adv.*

■ ***adj.*** **1** [only before noun] connected with a person's ARMPIT 腋窝的；腋下的：***underarm hair/deodorant/sweating*** 腋毛；腋下除臭剂；腋下出汗 **2** an **underarm** throw of a ball is done with the hand kept below the level of the shoulder 下手（或低手）投球的 ➲ COMPARE OVERARM

■ ***adv.*** if you throw, etc. **underarm**, you throw keeping your hand below the level of your shoulder 下手地，低手地（投球等）➲ COMPARE OVERARM

under·belly /ˈʌndəbeli; *NAmE* -dərb-/ *noun* [sing.] **1** the weakest part of sth that is most easily attacked 脆弱点；薄弱环节：*The trade deficit remains the **soft underbelly** of the US economy.* 贸易赤字仍是美国经济的软肋。 **2** the underneath part of an animal（动物的）下腹部，腩：(*figurative*) *He became familiar with the dark underbelly of life in the city* (= the parts that are usually hidden). 他逐渐熟悉都市生活的阴暗面。

under·bid /ˌʌndəˈbɪd; *NAmE* -dərˈb-/ *verb* (**under·bid·ding**, **under·bid**, **under·bid**) ~ **sb/sth** to make a lower bid than sb else, for example when trying to win a contract 投标出价低于（竞争对手）

under·brush /ˈʌndəbrʌʃ; *NAmE* -dərb-/ (*NAmE*) (*also* **under·growth** *BrE, NAmE*) *noun* [U] a mass of bushes and plants that grow close together under trees in woods and forests（林木下的）下层灌木丛

under·car·riage /ˈʌndəkærɪdʒ; *NAmE* -dərk-/ (*also* **ˈland·ing gear**) *noun* the part of an aircraft, including the wheels, that supports it when it is landing and taking off（飞行器的）起落装置 ➲ VISUAL VOCAB PAGE V57

under·charge /ˌʌndəˈtʃɑːdʒ; *NAmE* ˌʌndərˈtʃɑːrdʒ/ *verb* [I, T] ~ (**sb**) (**for sth**) to charge too little for sth, usually by mistake（因疏忽）少收（…的）款项 OPP **overcharge**

under·class /ˈʌndəklɑːs; *NAmE* ˈʌndərklæs/ *noun* [sing.] a social class that is very poor and has no status 社会底层；贫困阶层：*The long-term unemployed are becoming a new underclass.* 长期失业的人正形成新的贫困阶层。

under·class·man /ˌʌndəˈklɑːsmən; *NAmE* -dərˈklæs-/, **under·class·woman** /ˌʌndəˈklɑːswʊmən; *NAmE* -dərˈklæs-/ *noun* (*pl.* **-men** /-mən/, **-women** /-wɪmɪn/) (in the US) a student in the first or second year of HIGH SCHOOL or college 低年级学生（美国中学或大学一、二年级的学生）➲ COMPARE UPPERCLASSMAN

U

under·clothes /ˈʌndəkləʊðz; *NAmE* ˈʌndərkloʊðz/ *noun* [pl.] (*also* **under·cloth·ing** /-kləʊðɪŋ; *NAmE* -kloʊ-/ [U]) (*formal*) = UNDERWEAR

under·coat /ˈʌndəkəʊt; *NAmE* ˈʌndərkoʊt/ *noun* [C, U] a layer of paint under the final layer; the paint used for making this 底涂层；内涂层；底层涂料 ➲ COMPARE TOPCOAT (1)

under·cook /ˌʌndəˈkʊk; *NAmE* -dərˈk-/ *verb* [usually passive] **~ sth** to not cook sth for long enough, with the result that it is not ready to eat 未煮透

under·cover /ˌʌndəˈkʌvə(r); *NAmE* -dərˈk-/ *adj.* [usually before noun] working or done secretly in order to find out information for the police, a government, etc. 秘密工作的；暗中做的；私下进行的：*an **undercover agent*** 密探 ◇ *an **undercover operation/investigation*** 秘密行动 / 调查 ➲ WORDFINDER NOTE AT POLICE ▶ **under·cover** *adv.*：*The illegal payments were discovered by a journalist **working undercover**.* 这些非法付款是一位暗中查访的新闻记者发现的。

under·cur·rent /ˈʌndəkʌrənt; *NAmE* -dərkɜːr-/ *noun* **~ (of sth)** a feeling, especially a negative one, that is hidden but whose effects are felt 潜在的情绪（尤指负面的） **SYN** **undertone**：*I detect an undercurrent of resentment towards the new proposals.* 我察觉到对新提案有一股潜在的不满情绪。

under·cut *verb, noun*

■ *verb* /ˌʌndəˈkʌt; *NAmE* ˌʌndərˈkʌt/ (**under·cut·ting**, **under·cut**, **under·cut**) **1 ~ sb/sth** to sell goods or services at a lower price than your COMPETITORS 削价竞争；以低于（竞争对手）的价格出售：*to undercut sb's prices* 以低于对手的价格求售 ◇ *We were able to undercut our European rivals by 5%.* 我们能以低于我们的欧洲对手 5% 的价格出售。**2 ~ sb/sth** to make sb/sth weaker or less likely to be effective 削弱；使降低效力 **SYN** **undermine**：*Some members of the board were trying to undercut the chairman's authority.* 委员会的某些成员试图削弱主席的权力。

■ *noun* /ˈʌndəkʌt; *NAmE* ˈʌndərkʌt/ a way of cutting sb's hair in which the hair is left quite long on top but the hair on the lower part of the head is cut much shorter 大盖儿头发型；帽盔式发型；华盖式发型

under·devel·oped /ˌʌndədɪˈveləpt; *NAmE* -dərdɪ-/ *adj.* (of a country, society, etc. 国家、社会等) having few industries and a low standard of living 工业不发达的；生活水平低的；低度开发的 ➲ COMPARE DEVELOPED (1), DEVELOPING, UNDEVELOPED (2) **HELP** 'A **developing** country' is now the usual expression. 现在常用 developing country（发展中国家）。▶ **under·devel·op·ment** *noun* [U]

under·dog /ˈʌndədɒg; *NAmE* ˈʌndərdɔːg; -dɑːg/ *noun* a person, team, country, etc. that is thought to be in a weaker position than others and therefore not likely to be successful, win a competition, etc. 处于劣势的人（或团队、国家等）；弱者；比赛前不被看好者：*Before the game we were definitely the underdogs.* 我们在赛前绝对不被看好。◇ *In politics, he was a champion of the underdog* (= always fought for the rights of weaker people). 在政治上，他总是为弱势群体争取权益。**OPP** **overdog**

under·done /ˌʌndəˈdʌn; *NAmE* -dərˈd-/ *adj.* not completely cooked 未煮熟的；欠火的 ➲ COMPARE WELL DONE, OVERDO (3)

under·employed /ˌʌndərɪmˈplɔɪd/ *adj.* not having enough work to do; not having work that makes full use of your skills and abilities 未充分就业的（指就业不足、没有足够的工作可做，或所做的工作未能充分发挥技能）

under·esti·mate **AW** *verb, noun*

■ *verb* /ˌʌndərˈestɪmeɪt/ **1 ~ sth | ~ what, how, etc....** to think or guess that the amount, cost or size of sth is smaller than it really is 低估；对…估计不足：*to underestimate the cost of the project* 低估项目的成本 ◇ *We underestimated the time it would take to get there.* 我们低估了抵达那里所需的时间。**2 ~ sb/sth** to not realize how good, strong, determined, etc. sb really is 对…认识不足（或重视不够）；低估；轻视：*Never underestimate your opponent.* 决不可低估你的对手。**OPP** **overestimate** ➲ COMPARE UNDERRATE

■ *noun* /ˌʌndərˈestɪmət/ (*also* **under·esti·ma·tion** /ˌʌndərˌestɪˈmeɪʃn/ [C, U]) an estimate about the size, cost, etc. of sth that is too low 低估；轻视：*My guess of 400 proved to be a serious underestimate.* 我猜 400，结果证明是严重的低估。**OPP** **overestimate**

under·expose /ˌʌndərɪkˈspəʊz; *NAmE* -ˈspoʊz/ *verb* [usually passive] **~ sth** to allow too little light to reach the film when you take a photograph 使曝光不足 **OPP** **overexpose**

under·fed /ˌʌndəˈfed; *NAmE* -dərˈf-/ *adj.* having had too little food to eat 食物不足的；没吃饱的 **SYN** **malnourished** **OPP** **overfed**

under·floor /ˌʌndəˈflɔː(r); *NAmE* -dərˈf-/ *adj.* [only before noun] placed underneath the floor 在地板下面的：*underfloor heating* 设在地板下面的供暖系统

under·foot /ˌʌndəˈfʊt; *NAmE* -dərˈf-/ *adv.* under your feet; on the ground where you are walking 在脚下；在（脚下的）地面上：*The ground was dry and firm underfoot.* 脚下踩的土地又干又硬。◇ *I was nearly **trampled underfoot** by the crowd of people rushing for the door.* 冲向大门的人群险些把我踩在脚下。

under·fund·ed /ˌʌndəˈfʌndɪd; *NAmE* -dərˈf-/ *adj.* (of an organization, a project, etc. 机构、项目等) not having enough money to spend, with the result that it cannot function well 资金不足的；缺乏资金的：***seriously/chronically underfunded*** 严重 / 长期缺乏资金

under·gar·ment /ˈʌndəgɑːmənt; *NAmE* -dərgɑːrm-/ *noun* (*old-fashioned* or *formal*) a piece of underwear 内衣

under·go **AW** /ˌʌndəˈgəʊ; *NAmE* ˌʌndərˈgoʊ/ *verb* (**under·goes** /-ˈgəʊz; *NAmE* -ˈgoʊz/, **under·went** /-ˈwent/, **under·gone** /-ˈgɒn; *NAmE* -ˈgɔːn; -ˈgɑːn/) **~ sth** to experience sth, especially a change or sth unpleasant 经历，经受（变化、不快的事等）：*to **undergo tests/trials/repairs*** 经受考验；接受检修 ◇ *My mother **underwent** major **surgery** last year.* 我母亲去年动过大手术。◇ *Some children **undergo a** complete **transformation** when they become teenagers.* 一些儿童进入青少年期会完全变成另一个人。

under·gradu·ate /ˌʌndəˈgrædʒuət; *NAmE* -dərˈg-/ *noun* a university or college student who is studying for their first degree 本科生：*a first-year undergraduate* 大学一年级学生 ◇ *an **undergraduate course/student/degree*** 大学本科课程 / 学生 / 学位 ➲ NOTE AT STUDENT

under·ground 🔑 *adj., adv., noun*

■ *adj.* /ˌʌndəˈgraʊnd; *NAmE* -dərˈg-/ [only before noun] **1** 🔑 under the surface of the ground 地下的；地面以下的：*underground passages/caves/streams* 地下通道 / 洞穴 / 溪流 ◇ *underground cables* 地下电缆 ➲ COMPARE OVERGROUND **2** operating secretly and often illegally, especially against a government 秘密的，非法的，暗中的，地下的（尤指反政府的）：*an underground resistance movement* 地下抵抗运动

■ *adv.* /ˌʌndəˈgraʊnd; *NAmE* -dərˈg-/ **1** 🔑 under the surface of the ground 在地下；在地面下：*Rescuers found victims trapped several feet underground.* 营救人员发现有受难者被困在地下几英尺处。◇ *toxic waste buried deep underground* 深埋在地下的有毒废弃物 **2** in or into a secret place in order to hide from the police, the government, etc. 隐蔽地；隐匿地：*He **went underground** to avoid arrest.* 他隐藏起来以防被捕。

■ *noun* /ˈʌndəgraʊnd; *NAmE* -dərg-/ **1** (*often* **the Underground**) (*BrE*) (*NAmE* **sub·way**) [sing.] an underground railway/railroad system in a city（城市的）地下铁路系统，地铁：*underground stations* 地铁车站 ◇ *the London Underground* 伦敦地铁 ◇ *I always travel by underground.* 我总是乘地铁。➲ VISUAL VOCAB PAGE V63 ➲ COMPARE METRO *n.* (1), TUBE (6) **2 the underground** [sing.+sing./pl. v.] a secret political organization, usually working against the government of a country 秘密政治组织；（反

U

政府）地下组织 **3** (*IndE*) a person who works against the government as a member of a secret political organization 反政府地下组织成员

▼ **BRITISH/AMERICAN** 英式 / 美式英语

underground / subway / metro / tube

- A city's underground railway/railroad system is usually called the **underground** (often **the Underground**) in *BrE* and the **subway** in *NAmE*. Speakers of *BrE* also use **subway** for systems in American cities and **metro** for systems in other European countries. **The Metro** is the name for the systems in Paris and Washington, D.C. London's system is often called **the Tube**. 城市的地铁系统在英式英语中通常称为 underground（常作 the Underground），在美式英语中为 subway。说英式英语的人指美国城市的地铁亦用 subway，而指其他欧洲国家的地铁则用 metro。the Metro 为巴黎和华盛顿市的地铁名称；伦敦的地铁通常称作 the Tube。

the ˌunderground eˈconomy (*NAmE*) (*BrE* **the ˌblack eˈconomy**) *noun* [sing.] business activity or work that is done without the knowledge of the government or other officials so that people avoid paying tax on the money they earn 地下经济活动；黑市经济

under·growth /ˈʌndəgrəʊθ; *NAmE* ˈʌndərgroʊθ/ (*BrE*) (*NAmE also* **under·brush**) *noun* [U] a mass of bushes and plants that grow close together under trees in woods and forests 下木层：*They used their knives to clear a path through the dense undergrowth.* 他们用刀在浓密的灌木丛中劈开一条小路。◇ *The murder weapon was found concealed in undergrowth.* 杀人凶器被发现藏在灌木丛中。

under·hand /ˌʌndəˈhænd; *NAmE* -dərˈh-/ (*also less frequent* **under·hand·ed** /-ˈhændɪd/) *adj.* (*disapproving*) secret and dishonest 秘密的；阴险的；狡诈的；卑鄙的：*I would never have expected her to behave in such an underhand way.* 我从未想到她的行为竟如此阴险。

under·in·sured /ˌʌndərɪnˈʃʊəd; -ˈʃɔːd; *NAmE* -ˈʃʊrd/ *adj.* not having enough insurance protection 保险（额）不足的

under·lay /ˈʌndəleɪ; *NAmE* ˈʌndərleɪ/ *noun* [U, C] a layer of thick material placed under a carpet to protect it 地毯衬垫

U

under·lie AW /ˌʌndəˈlaɪ; *NAmE* ˌʌndərˈlaɪ/ *verb* (**under·lying**, **under·lay** /-ˈleɪ/, **under·lain** /-ˈleɪn/) [no passive] **~ sth** (*formal*) to be the basis or cause of sth 构成…的基础；作为…的原因：*These ideas underlie much of his work.* 他的作品大部分都是以这些主题思想为基础。◇ *It is a principle that underlies all the party's policies.* 这是贯穿该党各项政策的一条准则。➲ SEE ALSO UNDERLYING

under·line /ˌʌndəˈlaɪn; *NAmE* -dərˈl-/ (*also* **under·score** *especially in NAmE*) *verb* **1 ~ sth** to draw a line under a word, sentence, etc. 在（词语等下）画线；画底线标出 **2** to emphasize or show that sth is important or true 强调；突出：**~ sth** *The report underlines the importance of pre-school education.* 这份报告强调学前教育的重要性。◇ **~ how, what, etc....** *Her question underlined how little she understood him.* 她的问题表明她多么不了解他。◇ **~ that...** *The report underlined that the project enjoyed considerable support in both countries.* 这份报告强调该项目得到两国的极大支持。◇ **it is underlined that...** *It should be underlined that these are only preliminary findings.* 需要强调的是，这些只是初步的研究结果。

under·ling /ˈʌndəlɪŋ; *NAmE* ˈʌndərlɪŋ/ *noun* (*disapproving*) a person with a lower rank or status 走卒；喽啰；手下；下属 SYN **minion**

under·lying AW /ˌʌndəˈlaɪɪŋ; *NAmE* -dərˈl-/ *adj.* [only before noun] **1** important in a situation but not always easily noticed or stated clearly 根本的；潜在的；隐含的：*The underlying assumption is that the amount of money available is limited.* 隐含的假定是可用的资金有限。◇ *Unemployment may be an underlying cause of the rising crime rate.* 失业可能是犯罪率攀升的潜在原因。**2** existing under the surface of sth else 表面下的；下层的：*the underlying rock formation* 地表下的岩石结构 ➲ SEE ALSO UNDERLIE

under·manned /ˌʌndəˈmænd; *NAmE* -dərˈm-/ *adj.* (of a hospital, factory, etc. 医院、工厂等) not having enough people working in order to be able to function well 人手不足的；编制不足的；缺编的 SYN **understaffed** OPP **overmanned**

under·men·tioned /ˌʌndəˈmenʃnd; *NAmE* -dərˈm-/ *adj.* (*BrE, formal*) used in a book or document to refer to sth that is mentioned later （用于书或文件）下述的

under·mine /ˌʌndəˈmaɪn; *NAmE* -dərˈm-/ *verb* **1 ~ sth** to make sth, especially sb's confidence or authority, gradually weaker or less effective 逐渐削弱（信心、权威等）；使逐步减少效力：*Our confidence in the team has been seriously undermined by their recent defeats.* 他们最近的几次失利已严重动摇了我们对该队的信心。◇ *This crisis has undermined his position.* 这场危机已损害了他的地位。**2 ~ sth** to make sth weaker at the base, for example by digging under it 从根基处破坏；挖…的墙脚

under·neath 🔑 /ˌʌndəˈniːθ; *NAmE* -dərˈn-/ *prep., adv., noun*

■ ***prep., adv.*** **1** 🔑 under or below sth else, especially when it is hidden or covered by the thing on top 在…底下；隐藏（或掩盖）在下面：*The coin rolled underneath the piano.* 硬币滚到了钢琴底下。◇ *This jacket's too big, even with a sweater underneath.* 即使里面穿一件毛衣，这件外套也太大了。**2** 🔑 used to talk about sb's real feelings or character, as opposed to the way they seem to be （指真实的感情或性格）在…表象之下：*Underneath her cool exterior she was really very frightened.* 她外表冷静，其实内心十分害怕。◇ *He seems bad-tempered, but he's very soft-hearted underneath.* 他表面脾气暴躁，实则菩萨心肠。

■ ***noun*** **the underneath** [sing.] the lower surface or part of sth （物体的）下表面，底面，底部，下部：*She pulled the drawer out and examined the underneath carefully.* 她拉开抽屉仔细查看底部。

under·nour·ished /ˌʌndəˈnʌrɪʃt; *NAmE* -dərˈnɜːr-/ *adj.* in bad health because of a lack of food or a lack of the right type of food 营养不良的；缺乏营养的 SYN **mal·nourished**：*severely undernourished children* 严重营养不良的儿童 ▶ **under·nour·ish·ment** /-ˈnʌrɪʃmənt; *NAmE* -ˈnɜːr-/ *noun* [U]

under·paid /ˌʌndəˈpeɪd; *NAmE* -dərˈp-/ *adj.* not paid enough for the work you do 报酬过低的；酬不抵劳的：*Nurses complain of being* ***overworked and underpaid***. 护士抱怨工作劳累过度而报酬过低。

under·pants /ˈʌndəpænts; *NAmE* -dərp-/ *noun* [pl.] **1** (*also informal* **pants**) (*BrE*) a piece of men's underwear worn under their trousers/pants （男用）内裤，衬裤 **2** (*NAmE*) a piece of underwear worn by men or women under trousers/pants, a skirt, etc. （男、女）内裤，衬裤

under·pass /ˈʌndəpɑːs; *NAmE* ˈʌndərpæs/ *noun* a road or path that goes under another road or railway/railroad track 下穿式立交桥；地下通道 ➲ COMPARE OVERPASS

under·pay /ˌʌndəˈpeɪ; *NAmE* -dərˈp-/ *verb* (**under·paid**, **under·paid** /ˌʌndəˈpeɪd; *NAmE* -dərˈp-/) [usually passive] **~ sb** to pay sb too little money, especially for their work 给…报酬过低；少付…工资 OPP **overpay** ▶ **under·pay·ment** *noun* [U, C]

under·per·form /ˌʌndəpəˈfɔːm; *NAmE* ˌʌndərpərˈfɔːrm/ *verb* [I] to not be as successful as was expected 发挥不好；表现不理想

under·pin /ˌʌndəˈpɪn; *NAmE* -dərˈp-/ *verb* (**-nn-**) **1 ~ sth** (*formal*) to support or form the basis of an argument, a claim, etc. 加强，巩固，构成（…的基础等）：*The report* *is underpinned by extensive research.* 这份报告以广泛的研究为基础。 **2** ~ **sth** (*specialist*) to support a wall by putting metal, concrete, etc. under it 加固（墙）基 ▶ **under·pin·ning** *noun* [C, U]

under·play /ˌʌndəˈpleɪ; *NAmE* -dərˈp-/ *verb* ~ **sth** (*especially BrE*) to make sth seem less important than it really is 低调处理；降低…的重要性 SYN **play down, downplay** OPP **overplay**

under·pre·pared /ˌʌndəprɪˈpeəd; *NAmE* ˌʌndərprɪˈperd/ *adj.* not having done enough preparation for sth you have to do 准备不充分的；准备不足的

under·priced /ˌʌndəˈpraɪst; *NAmE* -dərˈp-/ *adj.* something that is **underpriced** is sold at a price that is too low and less than its real value 定价过低的；售价过低的

under·priv·il·eged /ˌʌndəˈprɪvəlɪdʒd; *NAmE* -dərˈp-/ *adj.* **1** [usually before noun] having less money and fewer opportunities than most people in society 在社会中处于弱势的；贫苦的；机遇少的；底层的 SYN **disadvantaged**: *underprivileged sections of the community* 社区的弱势阶层 ◇ *educationally/socially underprivileged groups* 教育上 / 社会上处于弱势地位的群体 ➲ COMPARE PRIVILEGED **2 the underprivileged** *noun* [pl.] people who are underprivileged 弱势群体；贫困阶层

under·rate /ˌʌndəˈreɪt/ *verb* ~ **sb/sth** to not recognize how good, important, etc. sb/sth really is 过低评价；低估：*He's seriously underrated as a writer.* 他是被严重低估的一位作家。 ◇ *an underrated movie* 一部未得到应有评价的电影 ➲ COMPARE OVERRATE, UNDERESTIMATE *v.*

ˌunder-reˈhearsed *adj.* (of a play or other performance 戏剧或其他表演) that has not been prepared and practised enough 排演不够的；练习过少的；准备不充分的

ˌunder-ˌrepreˈsent·ed *adj.* not having as many representatives as would be expected or needed 代表人数不够的；代表名额不足的：*Women are under-represented at senior levels in business.* 商界高层的女性代表不足。

ˌunder-ˌreˈsourced AW *adj.* not provided with as much money or as many staff, materials, etc. as are needed 缺乏资源的；资金（或人手、材料等）不足的：*Nurses are overstretched and the hospital is seriously under-resourced.* 护士超负荷工作，医院人手严重不足。

under·score *verb, noun*

■ *verb* /ˌʌndəˈskɔː(r); *NAmE* -dərˈs-/ (*especially NAmE*) = UNDERLINE

■ *noun* /ˈʌndəskɔː(r); *NAmE* -dərs-/ (*computing* 计) the symbol (_) that is used to draw a line under a letter or word and used in computer commands and in Internet addresses 下划线，底线（用于字母下划线或计算机命令和互联网地址中）

under·sea /ˈʌndəsiː; *NAmE* ˈʌndərsiː/ *adj.* [only before noun] found, used or happening below the surface of the sea 海面下的；海底的：*undersea cables/earthquakes* 海底电缆 / 地震

under·sec·re·tary /ˌʌndəˈsekrətri; *NAmE* ˌʌndərˈsekrəteri/ *noun* (*pl.* **-ies**) **1** (in Britain) a senior CIVIL SERVANT in charge of one part of a government department（英国）政务次官 ➲ COMPARE PERMANENT UNDERSECRETARY **2** (in Britain) a junior minister who reports to the minister in charge of a government department（英国）副大臣，次长 **3** (in the US) an official of high rank in a government department, directly below a member of a cabinet（美国）副部长，副国务卿

under·sell /ˌʌndəˈsel; *NAmE* ˌʌndərˈsel/ *verb* (**un·der·sold, un·der·sold** /ˌʌndəˈsəʊld; *NAmE* ˌʌndərˈsoʊld/) **1** ~ **sth** to sell goods or services at a lower price than your COMPETITORS 以低于（竞争者）的价格出售；竞价销售 **2** ~ **sth** to sell sth at a price lower than its real value 赔本出售；压价销售 **3** ~ **sb/sth/yourself** to make people think that sb/sth is not as good or as interesting as they really are 降低人们对…的印象；贬损：*Don't undersell yourself at the interview.* 面试时不可过分自谦。

under·shirt /ˈʌndəʃɜːt; *NAmE* ˈʌndərʃɜːrt/ (*NAmE*) (*BrE* **vest**) *noun* a piece of underwear worn under a shirt, etc. next to the skin（衬衣等里面贴身穿的）背心，汗衫 ➲ COMPARE SINGLET

under·shoot /ˌʌndəˈʃuːt; *NAmE* -dərˈʃ-/ *verb* (**under·shot, under·shot** /-ˈʃɒt; *NAmE* -ˈʃɑːt/) **1** [I, T] ~ (**sth**) to fail to reach the intended level, target, etc. 未达预期水平；未达标 **2** [I, T] ~ (**sth**) (of an aircraft 飞机) to land before reaching the RUNWAY 未达跑道着陆 ▶ **under·shoot** *noun*

under·shorts /ˈʌndəʃɔːts; *NAmE* ˈʌndərʃɔːrts/ *noun* [pl.] (*NAmE*) UNDERPANTS that are worn by men（男用）内裤，衬裤

under·side /ˈʌndəsaɪd; *NAmE* -dərs-/ *noun* the side or surface of sth that is underneath 下侧；底面；底部；下表面 SYN **bottom**

the under·signed /ˌʌndəˈsaɪnd; *NAmE* -dərˈs-/ *noun* (*pl.* **the under·signed**) (*formal*) the person who has signed that particular document（文件的）签字人，具名人，签署人：*We, the undersigned, agree to…* 我们，本文件的具名人，同意…

under·sized /ˌʌndəˈsaɪzd; *NAmE* -dərˈs-/ *adj.* not as big as normal 小于正常（或一般）的

under·skirt /ˈʌndəskɜːt; *NAmE* ˈʌndərskɜːrt/ *noun* a skirt that is worn under another skirt as underwear 衬裙

under·sold PAST TENSE, PAST PART. OF UNDERSELL

under·spend /ˌʌndəˈspend; *NAmE* -dərˈs-/ *verb* (**under·spent, under·spent** /-ˈspent/) [I, T] to not spend enough money on sth, especially when money has been made available for sth but still not spent（尤指在资金已具备的情况下对…）投资不够，花费不足：~ (**on sth**) *The inquiry found that the company had seriously underspent on safety equipment.* 调查发现，公司对安全设备的投资严重不足。 ◇ ~ **sth** *We've underspent our budget this year.* 我们今年的花费少于预算。 ▶ **under·spend** *noun* [sing.] (*BrE*)：*a £1 million underspend* 少花的 100 万英镑

under·staffed /ˌʌndəˈstɑːft; *NAmE* ˌʌndərˈstæft/ *adj.* [not usually before noun] not having enough people working and therefore not able to function well 人员不足；人手太少 SYN **undermanned** OPP **overstaffed**

under·stand 🔑 /ˌʌndəˈstænd; *NAmE* -dərˈs-/ *verb* (**under·stood, under·stood** /-ˈstʊd/) (not used in the progressive tenses 不用于进行时)

> **WORD FAMILY**
> **understand** *verb* (≠ misunderstand)
> **understandable** *adj.*
> **misunderstood** *adj.*
> **understanding** *adj., noun* (≠ misunderstanding)

• **MEANING** 意思 **1** 🔑 [T, I] to know or realize the meaning of words, a language, what sb says, etc. 懂；理解；领会：~ (**sth**) *Can you understand French?* 你懂法语吗？ ◇ *Do you understand the instructions?* 你懂得这些指令的意思吗？ ◇ *She didn't understand the form she was signing.* 她弄不懂她正在签署的表格。 ◇ *I'm not sure that I understand. Go over it again.* 我不敢说我搞懂了。请再来一遍吧。 ◇ *I don't want you doing that again. Do you understand?* 我不许你再这样做。你听明白了吗？ ◇ ~ **what…** *I don't understand what he's saying.* 我不明白他在说些什么。 ➲ EXPRESS YOURSELF AT EXPLAIN

• **HOW STH WORKS/HAPPENS** 运作；发生 **2** 🔑 [T, I] to know or realize how or why sth happens, how it works or why it is important 了解；认识到；明了：~ (**sth**) *Doctors still don't understand much about the disease.* 医生对这种疾病仍了解不多。 ◇ *No one is answering the phone—I can't understand it.* 没人接电话，我不知道是怎么回事。 ◇ ~ **why, what, etc.…** *I could never understand why she was fired.* 我怎么也不明白她为何被解雇。 ◇ ~ **sb/sth doing sth** *I just can't understand him taking the money.* 我真想不通他为什么会偷钱。 ◇ (*formal*) *I just can't understand his taking the money.* 我真想不通他为什么会偷钱。 ◇ ~ **that…** *He was the first to understand that we live in a knowledge economy.* 他最早认识到我们正处于知识经济的时代。

• **KNOW SB** 了解某人 **3** 🔑 [T, I] to know sb's character, how they feel and why they behave in the way they do 了解；谅解；体谅：**~ sb** *Nobody understands me.* 没有人了解我。◇ *He doesn't understand women at all.* 他根本就不了解女性。◇ **~ what, how, etc....** *They understand what I have been through.* 他们对我的遭遇很同情。◇ **~ (that...)** *I quite understand that you need some time alone.* 我很理解你需要独自静一会。◇ *If you want to leave early, I'm sure he'll understand.* 如果你想早些离开，我相信他会体谅的。◇ **~ sb doing sth** *I quite understand you needing some time alone.* 我很理解你需要独自静一会。

▼ **SYNONYMS** 同义词辨析

understand

see • get • follow • grasp • comprehend

These words all mean to know or realize sth, for example why sth happens, how sth works or what sth means. 以上各词均含懂得、理解、认识到之义。

understand to know or realize the meaning of words, a language, what sb says, etc; to know or realize how or why sth happens, how it works or why it is important 指懂、理解、领会（词义、语言、话语等），了解、认识到、明白（事情如何或为何发生、如何起作用或为何重要等）：*I don't understand the instructions.* 我不懂这些指令的意思。◇ *Doctors still don't understand much about the disease.* 医生对这种疾病还了解不多。

see to understand what is happening, what sb is saying, how sth works or how important sth is 指理解、明白、领会（正在发生的事、某人的话、某事如何起作用或重要性如何）：*'It opens like this.' 'Oh, I see.'* "这样就打开了。" "哦，我明白了。" ◇ *Oh yes, **I see what you mean**.* 噢，我明白你的意思了。

get (*informal*) to understand a joke, what sb is trying to tell you, or a situation that they are trying to describe 指理解、明白（笑话、某人试图告知的事或描述的情况）：*She didn't get the joke.* 她听不懂那个笑话。◇ *I don't get you.* 我搞不懂你的意思。

follow to understand an explanation, a story or the meaning of sth 指理解、明白（说明、故事、意思）：*Sorry—I don't quite follow.* 对不起，我不太懂你的话。◇ *The plot is almost impossible to follow.* 故事情节几乎叫人不明所以。

grasp to come to understand a fact, an idea or how to do sth 指理解、领会、领悟、明白（事实、想法或如何做某事）：*They failed to grasp the importance of his words.* 他们没有理解他的话的重要性。

UNDERSTAND OR GRASP? 用 understand 还是 grasp?

You can use **understand** or **grasp** for the action of realizing the meaning or importance of sth for the first time. 第一次意识到某事的意义或重要性可用 understand 或 grasp：*It's a difficult concept for children to understand/grasp.* 对孩子来说，这是一个很难理解的概念。Only **understand** can be used to talk about languages, words or writing. 只有 understand 可用于理解语言、词汇或文章等：~~*I don't grasp French/the instructions.*~~

comprehend (often used in negative statements) (*formal*) to understand a fact, idea or reason （常用于否定句中）指理解、领悟、明白（事实、想法或原因）：*The concept of infinity is almost impossible for the human mind to comprehend.* 无穷的概念几乎是人类的大脑无法理解的。

PATTERNS

- to understand/see/get/follow/grasp/comprehend **what/why/how...**
- to understand/see/grasp/comprehend **that...**
- to understand/see/get/grasp **the point/idea** (of sth)
- to be **easy/difficult/hard** to understand/see/follow/grasp/comprehend
- to **fully** understand/see/grasp/comprehend sth

• **THINK/BELIEVE** 认为；相信 **4** [T] (*formal*) to think or believe that sth is true because you have been told that it is 得知；据信；认为：**~ (that)...** *I understand (that) you wish to see the manager.* 我听说您想见经理。◇ *Am I to understand that you refuse?* 你是告诉我你拒绝了？◇ **~ sb/sth to be/have sth** *The Prime Minister is understood to have been extremely angry about the report.* 据说首相对这份报告大为恼火。◇ **it is understood that...** *It is understood that the band are working on their next album.* 据说这个乐队正在录制他们的下一张专辑。

• **BE AGREED** 得到赞同 **5** [T] **it is understood that...** to agree sth with sb without it needing to be said 默认；默许；不言而喻：*I thought it was understood that my expenses would be paid.* 我原以为对方已同意支付我的费用。

• **MISSING WORD** 省略的字 **6** [T, usually passive] **~ sth** to realize that a word in a phrase or sentence is not expressed and to supply it in your mind 领会；清楚；推断出：*In the sentence 'I can't drive', the object 'a car' is understood.* 在 I can't drive 一句中，宾语 a car 是不言自明的。

IDM **ˌmake yourself underˈstood** to make your meaning clear, especially in another language （尤指用另一种语言）把自己的意思说清楚：*He doesn't speak much Japanese but he can make himself understood.* 他不大会讲日语，不过尚能勉强表达意思。➲ MORE AT GIVE *v.*

under·stand·able /ˌʌndəˈstændəbl; *NAmE* -dərˈs-/ *adj.* **1** (of behaviour, feelings, reactions, etc. 行为、感情、反应等) seeming normal and reasonable in a particular situation 合情理的；正常的；可以理解的 SYN **natural**: *Their attitude is **perfectly understandable**.* 他们的态度是完全可以理解的。◇ *It was an understandable mistake to make.* 那是一个情有可原的失误。**2** (of language, documents, etc. 语言、文件等) easy to understand 易懂的 SYN **comprehensible**: *Warning notices must be readily understandable.* 警示性公告必须明白易懂。

under·stand·ably /ˌʌndəˈstændəbli; *NAmE* -dərˈs-/ *adv.* in a way that seems normal and reasonable in a particular situation 可以理解地；正常地；合乎情理地 SYN **naturally**: *They were understandably disappointed with the result.* 他们对结果感到失望是可以理解的。

under·stand·ing 🔑 /ˌʌndəˈstændɪŋ; *NAmE* -dərˈs-/ *noun, adj.*

■ ***noun*** **1** 🔑 [U, sing.] **~ (of sth)** the knowledge that sb has about a particular subject or situation 理解；领悟；了解：*The committee has little or no understanding of the problem.* 委员会对这个问题了解不多或根本不了解。◇ *The existence of God is beyond human understanding* (= humans cannot know whether God exists or not). 上帝的存在与否超出人类所能理解的范畴。**2** 🔑 [C, usually sing.] an informal agreement （非正式的）协议：*We finally **came to an understanding** about what hours we would work.* 我们最终就工作时间问题取得了一致意见。◇ *We have this understanding that nobody talks about work over lunch.* 我们有个默契：吃午饭时谁也不许谈工作。**3** 🔑 [U, sing.] the ability to understand why people behave in a particular way and the willingness to forgive them when they do sth wrong 理解；谅解；体谅：*We must tackle the problem with sympathy and understanding.* 我们必须以同情和谅解的态度来处理这个问题。◇ *We are looking for a better understanding between the two nations.* 我们正在寻求两国间的进一步了解。**4** 🔑 [U, C] **~ (of sth)** the particular way in which sb understands sth 理解；看法；解释；意见 SYN **interpretation**: *My understanding of the situation is...* 我对形势的看法是… ◇ *The statement is open to various understandings.* 这个声明可以有各种不同的诠释。

IDM **on the understanding that...** (*formal*) used to introduce a condition that must be agreed before sth else can happen 条件是…：*They agreed to the changes on the understanding that they would be introduced gradually.* 他们同意这些改革，条件是须要逐步进行。

■ ***adj.*** showing sympathy for other people's problems and being willing to forgive them when they do sth wrong 善解人意的；富有同情心的；体谅人的 SYN **sympathetic**: *She has very understanding parents.* 她的父母对她非常宽容。▸ **under·stand·ing·ly** *adv.*

U

under·state /ˌʌndəˈsteɪt; *NAmE* -dərˈs-/ *verb* **~ sth** to state that sth is smaller, less important or less serious than it really is 轻描淡写；避重就轻地说：*It would be a mistake to understate the seriousness of the problem.* 淡化问题的严重性是错误的。**OPP** **overstate**

under·stated /ˌʌndəˈsteɪtɪd; *NAmE* -dərˈs-/ *adj.* (*approving*) if a style, colour, etc. is **understated**, it is pleasing and elegant in a way that is not too obvious 淡雅的；素雅的；柔和的；不过分的 **SYN** **subtle**

under·state·ment /ˈʌndəsteɪtmənt; *NAmE* -dərs-/ *noun* **1** [C] a statement that makes sth seem less important, impressive, serious, etc. than it really is 保守的说法；不充分的叙述：*To say we were pleased is an understatement* (= we were extremely pleased). 说我们高兴，那是轻描淡写。◇ *'These figures are a bit disappointing.' 'That's got to be* ***the understatement of the year.***' "这些数字有点令人失望。" "那一定是本年度最保守的说法了。" **2** [U] the practice of making things seem less impressive, important, serious, etc. than they really are 淡化；低调说法：*typical English understatement* 典型的英国式低调说法 ◇ *He always goes for subtlety and understatement in his movies.* 他总是在自己的电影中运用细腻刻画和淡化手法。**OPP** **overstatement**

under·stood PAST TENSE, PAST PART. OF UNDERSTAND

under·storey (*NAmE* **under·story** *pl.* **-stories**) /ˈʌndəstɔːri; *NAmE* ˈʌndər-/ *noun* a layer of plants, bushes, etc. that is found underneath the main CANOPY of a forest (= the top leaves and branches of the trees that form a thick layer) 下木层（上层林冠下的林木）

under·study /ˈʌndəstʌdi; *NAmE* -dərs-/ *noun, verb*
▪ *noun* (*pl.* **-ies**) **~ (to sb)** an actor who learns the part of another actor in a play so that they can play that part if necessary 候补演员；替角 ⊃WORDFINDER NOTE AT ACTOR
▪ *verb* (**under·stud·ies**, **under·study·ing**, **under·stud·ied**, **under·stud·ied**) **~ sb/sth** to learn a part in a play as an understudy; to act as an understudy to sb 排练当候补演员；做替角

under·take **AW** /ˌʌndəˈteɪk; *NAmE* -dərˈt-/ *verb* (**under·took** /-ˈtʊk/, **under·taken** /-ˈteɪkən/) (*formal*) **1** **~ sth** to make yourself responsible for sth and start doing it 承担；从事；负责：*to* ***undertake a task/project*** 承担一个任务 / 项目 ◇ *University professors both teach and* ***undertake research.*** 大学教授既要教学又要从事研究工作。◇ *The company has announced that it will undertake a full investigation into the accident.* 公司已经宣布将对这次事故进行全面调查。**2** **~ to do sth** | **~ that...** to agree or promise that you will do sth 承诺；允诺；答应：*He undertook to finish the job by Friday.* 他答应星期五之前完成这一工作。

under·taker /ˈʌndəteɪkə(r); *NAmE* -dərt-/ (*also formal* **ˈfuneral director**) (*NAmE also* **mor·ti·cian**) *noun* a person whose job is to prepare the bodies of dead people to be buried or CREMATED, and to arrange funerals 殡葬承办人；殡仪服务员

under·tak·ing **AW** /ˌʌndəˈteɪkɪŋ; *NAmE* -dərˈt-/ *noun* **1** [C] a task or project, especially one that is important and/or difficult（重大或艰巨的）任务，项目，事业；企业 **SYN** **venture**：*He is interested in buying the club as a commercial undertaking.* 他有意购买那个俱乐部作为投资。◇ *In those days, the trip across country was a dangerous undertaking.* 那个时期，越野旅行是一件危险的事情。**2** [C] (*formal*) an agreement or a promise to do sth 承诺；保证；许诺；答应：**~ (to do sth)** *a government undertaking to spend more on education* 政府增加教育经费的承诺 ◇ **~ (that...)** *The landlord gave a written undertaking that the repairs would be carried out.* 房东书面保证将进行维修。**3** /ˈʌndəteɪkɪŋ; *NAmE* -dərt-/ [U] the business of an undertaker 殡仪业；丧葬业

ˌunder-the-ˈcounter *adj.* (*informal*) illegal 台面下的；非法的；私下的；暗中的

under·tone /ˈʌndətəʊn; *NAmE* ˈʌndərtoʊn/ *noun* **~ (of sth)** a feeling, quality or meaning that is not expressed directly but is still noticeable from what sb says or does 蕴涵的感情（或特质、意思）；寓意；弦外之音 **SYN** **undercurrent**：*His soft words contained an undertone of warning.* 他温和的话中蕴涵着警告之意。◇ *The play does not have the political undertones of the novel.* 这部戏没有小说的那种政治寓意。⊃COMPARE OVERTONE
IDM **in an ˈundertone** | **in ˈundertones** in a quiet voice 低声地；小声地

under·took **AW** PAST TENSE OF UNDERTAKE

under·tow /ˈʌndətəʊ; *NAmE* ˈʌndərtoʊ/ *noun* [usually sing.] **1** a current in the sea or ocean that moves in the opposite direction to the water near the surface 潜流：*The children were carried out to sea by the strong undertow.* 强大的潜流把孩子们卷到海里去了。**2** **~ (of sth)** a feeling or quality that influences people in a particular situation even though they may not really be aware of it 潜在的倾向（或特质）；感染力

under·trial /ˈʌndətraɪəl; *NAmE* ˈʌndər-/ *noun* (*IndE*) a person who has been charged with a crime 候审者：*The undertrials will appear in court next week.* 候审者将于下周出庭。

under·used /ˌʌndəˈjuːzd; *NAmE* -dərˈj-/ (*also formal* **under·util·ized**) *adj.* not used as much as it could or should be 未充分利用的；浪费的 ▶ **under·use** /ˌʌndəˈjuːs; *NAmE* -dərˈj-/ (*also formal* **under·util·iza·tion**) *noun* [U]

under·util·ized (*BrE also* **-ised**) /ˌʌndəˈjuːtəlaɪzd; *NAmE* -dərˈj-/ *adj.* (*formal*) = UNDERUSED ▶ **under·util·iza·tion, -isa·tion** /ˌʌndəˌjuːtəlaɪˈzeɪʃn; *NAmE* -dərˌjuːtələˈz-/ *noun* [U] = UNDERUSE

under·value /ˌʌndəˈvæljuː; *NAmE* -dərˈv-/ *verb* [usually passive] **~ sb/sth** to not recognize how good, valuable or important sb/sth really is 低估；对…认识不足；轻视：*Education is currently undervalued in this country.* 现在这个国家对教育重视不够。◇ *He believes his house has been undervalued.* 他认为自己的房子估值太低。**OPP** **overvalue**

under·water 🔑 /ˌʌndəˈwɔːtə(r); *NAmE* -dərˈw-/ *adj.* [only before noun] found, used or happening below the surface of water 水下的；用于水下的；水下发生的：*underwater creatures* 水生动物 ◇ *an underwater camera* 水下摄影机 ▶ **under·water** 🔑 *adv.*：*Take a deep breath and see how long you can stay underwater.* 深吸一口气，看你能在水里待多久。

under·way /ˌʌndəˈweɪ; *NAmE* -dərˈw-/ *adj.* [not before noun]
IDM **underway** = UNDER WAY at WAY

under·wear 🔑 /ˈʌndəweə(r); *NAmE* ˈʌndərwer/ *noun* [U] (*also formal* **under·clothes**, **under·cloth·ing**) clothes that you wear under other clothes and next to the skin 内衣；衬衣：*She packed one change of underwear.* 她打行李时带了一套换洗的内衣。

under·weight /ˌʌndəˈweɪt; *NAmE* -dərˈw-/ *adj.* (especially of a person 尤指人) weighing less than the normal or expected weight 体重不足的；未达到正常体重的：*She is a few pounds underweight for* (= in relation to) *her height.* 就其身高而言，她的体重还差几磅。**OPP** **overweight** ⊃COLLOCATIONS AT DIET

under·went PAST TENSE OF UNDERGO

under·whelmed /ˌʌndəˈwelmd; *NAmE* -dərˈw-/ *adj.* (*informal, humorous*) not impressed with or excited about sth at all 无动于衷的；毫不激动的：*We were distinctly underwhelmed by the director's speech.* 主任的讲话显然令我们感觉索然无味。⊃COMPARE OVERWHELM

under·whelm·ing /ˌʌndəˈwelmɪŋ; *NAmE* -dərˈw-/ *adj.* (*informal, humorous*) not impressing or exciting you at all 平庸的；索然无味的：*the contrast between his overwhelming guitar-playing and his underwhelming singing* 他那激昂的吉他演奏与其味同嚼蜡的歌唱之间的反差

under·wired /ˌʌndəˈwaɪəd; *NAmE* ˌʌndərˈwaɪərd/ (*BrE*) (*NAmE* **under·wire** /ˌʌndəˈwaɪə(r); *NAmE* ˌʌndərˈwaɪər/)

U

adj. (of a BRA 胸罩) having a thin metal strip sewn into the bottom half of each CUP to improve the shape 钢托式的（罩杯下半部缝金属撑条）；用金属条定型的

under·world /ˈʌndəwɜːld; *NAmE* ˈʌndərwɜːrld/ *noun* [sing.] **1** the people and activities involved in crime in a particular place 黑社会；黑道；犯罪集团：*the criminal underworld* 罪恶的黑社会 ◇ *the Glasgow underworld* 格拉斯哥的黑社会 **2 the underworld** (in MYTHS and LEGENDS, for example those of ancient Greece 神话、传说中的) the place under the earth where people are believed to go when they die 阴间；冥府；阴曹地府

under·write /ˌʌndəˈraɪt; *NAmE* -dərˈr-/ *verb* (**under·wrote** /-ˈrəʊt; *NAmE* -ˈroʊt/, **under·writ·ten** /-ˈrɪtn/) (*specialist*) **1** ~ **sth** to accept financial responsibility for an activity so that you will pay for special costs or for losses it may make 承担经济责任（包括支付特别费用或损失） **2** ~ **sth** to accept responsibility for an insurance policy so that you will pay money in case loss or damage happens 承担保险责任；承保 ➲ WORDFINDER NOTE AT INSURANCE **3** ~ **sth** to agree to buy shares that are not bought by the public when new shares are offered for sale 包销，承销（未获认购的新发行股份）

under·writer /ˈʌndəraɪtə(r)/ *noun* **1** a person or organization that underwrites insurance policies, especially for ships（尤指船只的）承保人，保险商 **2** a person whose job is to estimate the risks involved in a particular activity and decide how much sb must pay for insurance 核保人（对投保项目进行风险评估并决定保险费率）

un·des·cend·ed /ˌʌndɪˈsendɪd/ *adj.* (*medical* 医) (of a TESTICLE 睾丸) staying inside the body instead of moving down normally into the SCROTUM 未下降（入阴囊）的；内隐的

un·deserved /ˌʌndɪˈzɜːvd; *NAmE* -ˈzɜːrvd/ *adj.* that sb does not deserve and therefore unfair 不应得的；冤枉的；不公正的：*The criticism was totally undeserved.* 这批评纯属冤枉人。◇ *an undeserved victory* 不该得到的胜利 ▸ **un·deserved·ly** /ˌʌndɪˈzɜːvɪdli; *NAmE* -ˈzɜːrv-/ *adv.*

un·deserv·ing /ˌʌndɪˈzɜːvɪŋ; *NAmE* -ˈzɜːrv-/ *adj.* ~ (**of sth**) (*formal*) not deserving to have or receive sth 不够格的；不相当的；不配的：*He was undeserving of her affections.* 他不配得到她的爱。**OPP** **deserving**

un·desir·able /ˌʌndɪˈzaɪərəbl/ *adj., noun*

■ *adj.* not wanted or approved of; likely to cause trouble or problems 不想要的；不得人心的；易惹麻烦的：***undesirable consequences/effects*** 不良后果 / 影响 ◇ *It would be highly undesirable to increase class sizes further.* 再增加班级人数，是大家都极不愿意的。◇ *prostitution and other undesirable practices* 卖淫和其他不良勾当 **OPP** **desirable** ▸ **un·desir·ably** /-əbli/ *adv.*

■ *noun* [usually pl.] a person who is not wanted in a particular place, especially because they are considered dangerous or criminal 不受欢迎的人；不良分子：*He's been mixing with drug addicts and other undesirables.* 他一直跟瘾君子和其他不良分子混在一起。

un·detect·able /ˌʌndɪˈtektəbl/ *adj.* impossible to see or find 看不见的；察觉不出的；发现不了的：*The sound is virtually undetectable to the human ear.* 这声音实际上是人耳难以听得到的。**OPP** **detectable**

un·detect·ed /ˌʌndɪˈtektɪd/ *adj.* not noticed by anyone 未被注意的：*How could anyone break into the palace undetected?* 怎么会有人神不知、鬼不觉地潜入皇宫呢？◇ *The disease often* ***goes/remains undetected*** *for many years.* 这种疾病经常潜伏多年而不被察觉。

un·deterred /ˌʌndɪˈtɜːd; *NAmE* -ˈtɜːrd/ *adj.* if sb is **undeterred** by sth, they do not allow it to stop them from doing sth 顽强的；坚毅的；不屈不挠的

un·devel·oped /ˌʌndɪˈveləpt/ *adj.* **1** (of land 土地) not used for farming, industry, building, etc. 未开垦的；未利用的；未开发的 **2** (of a country 国家) not having modern industries, and with a low standard of living 不发达的；落后的 **3** not grown to full size 发育不良的；未充分发育的：*undeveloped limbs* 发育不全的四肢 ➲ COMPARE UNDERDEVELOPED

un·did PAST TENSE OF UNDO

un·dies /ˈʌndiz/ *noun* [pl.] (*informal*) underwear 内衣；衬衣

un·dif·fer·en·ti·ated /ˌʌndɪfəˈrenʃieɪtɪd/ *adj.* having parts that you cannot distinguish between; not split into different parts or sections 无法区分的；分不开的；一体的：*a view of society as an undifferentiated whole* 认为社会是一个统一整体的观点 ◇ *an undifferentiated target audience* 不分类的目标观众

un·dig·ni·fied /ʌnˈdɪɡnɪfaɪd/ *adj.* causing you to look silly and to lose the respect of other people 不像样的；不成体统的；不体面的；不庄重的：*There was an undignified scramble for the best seats.* 大家争抢最好的位子，真是有失体统。**OPP** **dignified**

un·diluted /ˌʌndaɪˈluːtɪd; *BrE also* -ˈljuːtɪd/ *adj.* **1** (of a liquid 液体) not made weaker by having water added to it; not having been DILUTED 未掺水的；未稀释的 **2** (of a feeling or quality 感情或品质) not mixed or combined with anything and therefore very strong 真挚的；纯洁的；浓烈的；醇厚的 **SYN** **unadulterated**

un·dimin·ished **AW** /ˌʌndɪˈmɪnɪʃt/ *adj.* that has not become smaller or weaker 未减少的；未衰的；未减弱的：*They continued with undiminished enthusiasm.* 他们热情依旧地继续着。

un·dis·charged /ˌʌndɪsˈtʃɑːdʒd; *NAmE* -ˈtʃɑːrdʒd/ *adj.* (*law* 律) an **undischarged** BANKRUPT is a person who has been officially stated to be bankrupt by a court but who still has to pay his or her debts（破产者）未清偿债务的

un·dis·cip·lined /ʌnˈdɪsəplɪnd/ *adj.* lacking control and organization; behaving badly 无组织纪律的；没规矩的；缺乏管教的 **OPP** **disciplined**

un·dis·closed /ˌʌndɪsˈkləʊzd; *NAmE* -ˈkloʊzd/ *adj.* not made known or told to anyone; not having been DISCLOSED 未披露的；未公开的；保密的：*He was paid an undisclosed sum.* 他得到了一笔数目不详的钱。

un·dis·cov·ered /ˌʌndɪsˈkʌvəd; *NAmE* -ərd/ *adj.* that has not been found or noticed; that has not been discovered 未找到（或注意到）的；未被发现的：*a previously undiscovered talent* 以前没被发掘的天才

un·dis·guised /ˌʌndɪsˈɡaɪzd/ *adj.* (especially of a feeling 尤指感情) that you do not try to hide from other people; not DISGUISED 坦诚的；率直的；不加掩饰的：*a look of undisguised admiration* 不加掩饰的仰慕神情

un·dis·mayed /ˌʌndɪsˈmeɪd/ *adj.* [not before noun] (*formal*) not worried or frightened by sth unpleasant or unexpected 处变不惊的；不惊恐的；镇定 **SYN** **undaunted**

un·dis·puted /ˌʌndɪˈspjuːtɪd/ *adj.* **1** that cannot be questioned or proved to be false; that cannot be DISPUTED 不容置疑的；毫无疑问的；不可争辩的 **SYN** **irrefutable**：*undisputed facts* 不容置疑的事实 **2** that everyone accepts or recognizes 广为接受的；公认的：*the undisputed champion of the world* 公认的世界冠军

un·dis·tin·guished /ˌʌndɪˈstɪŋɡwɪʃt/ *adj.* not very interesting, successful or attractive 乏味的；平凡的；无特色的；不吸引人的：*an undistinguished career* 平凡的职业生涯 **OPP** **distinguished**

un·dis·turbed /ˌʌndɪˈstɜːbd; *NAmE* -ˈstɜːrbd/ *adj.* **1** [not usually before noun] not moved or touched by anyone or anything 未被移动（或触及） **SYN** **untouched**：*The treasure had lain undisturbed for centuries.* 那份珍宝安然无恙地存放了几个世纪。**2** not interrupted by anyone 未受惊扰的；未被打搅的 **SYN** **uninterrupted**：*She succeeded in working undisturbed for a few hours.* 她终于得以安安静静地工作了几个小时。**3** [not usually before noun] ~ (**by sth**) not affected or upset by sth 平静；镇定；泰然自若 **SYN** **unconcerned**：*He seemed undisturbed by the news of her death.* 他对她的死讯似乎无动于衷。➲ COMPARE DISTURBED

un·div·ided /ˌʌndɪˈvaɪdɪd/ *adj.* **1** not split into smaller parts; not divided 未划分的；未分开的；完整的：*an undivided Church* 未分立支派的教会 **2** [usually before noun] total; complete; not divided 完全的；全部的；专注的：*undivided loyalty* 赤胆忠心 ◇ *You must be prepared to give the job your* ***undivided attention***. 你必须准备好全心全意地投入工作。

undo 🔑 /ʌnˈduː/ *verb* (**un·does** /ʌnˈdʌz/, **un·did** /ʌnˈdɪd/, **un·done** /ʌnˈdʌn/) **1** 🔑 **~ sth** to open sth that is fastened, tied or wrapped 打开；解开；拆开：*to* ***undo a button/knot/zip, etc.*** 解开纽扣、解开绳结、拉开拉锁等 ◇ *to* ***undo a jacket/shirt, etc.*** 解开上衣、衬衫等 ◇ *I undid the package and took out the books.* 我打开包裹取出书来。 **OPP** **do sth↔up** **2 ~ sth** to cancel the effect of sth 消除，取消，废止（某事的影响）：*He undid most of the good work of the previous manager.* 他把前任经理的大部分功绩都毁掉了。◇ *It's not too late to try and* ***undo*** *some of* ***the damage***. 想办法补救部分损失还为时不晚。◇ *UNDO* (= a command on a computer that cancels the previous action) 撤销（计算机的还原指令） **3** [usually passive] **~ sb/sth** (*formal*) to make sb/sth fail 打败；挫败：*The team was undone by the speed and strength of their opponents.* 这个队伍被对手的速度和力量打败了。

un·dock /ʌnˈdɒk; *NAmE* -ˈdɑːk/ *verb* **~ sth** (*computing* 计) to remove a computer from a DOCKING STATION 使出坞 **OPP** **dock**

un·docu·ment·ed /ˌʌnˈdɒkjumentɪd; *NAmE* -ˈdɑːk-/ *adj.* **1** not supported by written evidence 无书面证据的：*undocumented accusations* 无书面证据的指控 **2** not having the necessary documents, especially permission to live and work in a foreign country 无必要证件的；（尤指在外国）无居住证的，无执照的：*undocumented immigrants* 无证移民

un·do·ing /ʌnˈduːɪŋ/ *noun* [sing.] the reason why sb fails at sth or is unsuccessful in life 失败的原因 **SYN** **downfall**：*That one mistake was his undoing.* 他一失足即成千古恨。

un·done /ʌnˈdʌn/ *adj.* [not usually before noun] **1** (especially of clothing 尤指衣服) not fastened or tied 未扣；未系；松开：*Her blouse had* ***come undone***. 她的衬衫扣松开了。 **2** (especially of work 尤指工作) not finished 未完成；未竟：*Most of the work had been left undone.* 大部分工作还没有做完。 **3** (*old use*) (of a person 人) defeated and without any hope for the future 完蛋；一蹶不振；无出头之日

un·doubt·ed /ʌnˈdaʊtɪd/ *adj.* [usually before noun] used to emphasize that sth exists or is definitely true 无疑的；确实的；千真万确的 **SYN** **indubitable**：*She has an undoubted talent as an organizer.* 她的确有组织才能。 ▸ **un·doubt·ed·ly** *adv.*：*There is undoubtedly a great deal of truth in what he says.* 他所说的的确大部分都是实情。

undreamed-of /ʌnˈdriːmd ɒv; *NAmE* ʌv/ (*also* **undreamt-of** /ʌnˈdremt ɒv; *NAmE* ʌv/ *especially in BrE*) *adj.* much more or much better than you thought was possible 意想不到的；做梦都没想到的：*undreamed-of success* 意想不到的成功

un·dress /ʌnˈdres/ *verb, noun*

■ *verb* [I, T] to take off your clothes; to remove sb else's clothes （给…）脱衣服：*She undressed and got into bed.* 她解衣上床了。◇ **~ sb** *to undress a child* 给小孩脱衣服 ◇ *He* ***got undressed*** *in a small cubicle next to the pool.* 他在游泳池旁的小更衣室里脱掉了衣服。 **OPP** **dress**

■ *noun* [U] (*formal*) the fact of sb wearing no, or few, clothes 裸体；赤身：*He appeared at the window in a* ***state of undress***. 他光着身子出现在窗前。

un·dressed /ʌnˈdrest/ *adj.* [not usually before noun] not wearing any clothes 赤裸；一丝不挂：*She began to* ***get undressed*** (= remove her clothes). 她开始脱去衣服。 **OPP** **dressed**

un·drink·able /ʌnˈdrɪŋkəbl/ *adj.* not good or pure enough to drink 不适合饮用的；不能喝的 **OPP** **drinkable**

undue /ˌʌnˈdjuː; *NAmE* ˌʌnˈduː/ *adj.* [only before noun] (*formal*) more than you think is reasonable or necessary 不适当的；过分的；过度的 **SYN** **excessive**：*They are taking undue advantage of the situation.* 他们过分利用了这种情势。◇ *The work should be carried out without undue delay.* 进行这项工作不得有不当的延误。◇ *We did not want to put any undue pressure on them.* 我们并不想给他们施加过多的压力。 ➲ COMPARE DUE *adj.* (6)

un·du·late /ˈʌndjuleɪt; *NAmE* -dʒə-/ *verb* [I] (*formal*) to go or move gently up and down like waves 起伏；波动；荡漾：*The countryside undulates pleasantly.* 原野起伏，景色宜人。 ➲ WORDFINDER NOTE AT LANDSCAPE

un·du·lat·ing /ˈʌndjuleɪtɪŋ; *NAmE* ˈʌndʒəleɪtɪŋ/ *adj.* shaped like a wave or moving up and down like a wave 波浪形的；波动的；起伏的：*undulating countryside/fields/terrain/ground* 起伏不平的乡野 / 田野 / 地势 / 地面 ◇ *undulating flight/movement/motion* 颠簸的飞行；波浪形的移动 / 运动

un·du·la·tion /ˌʌndjuˈleɪʃn; *NAmE* -dʒə-/ *noun* [C, U] a smooth curving shape or movement like a series of waves 波浪形；起伏；波动；荡漾

un·duly /ˌʌnˈdjuːli; *NAmE* ˌʌnˈduːli/ *adv.* (*formal*) more than you think is reasonable or necessary 过分；过度；不适当地 **SYN** **excessively**：*He did not sound unduly worried at the prospect.* 他的口气听上去对前景并不十分担忧。◇ *The levels of pollution in this area are unduly high.* 本地区的污染程度过高。◇ *The thought did not disturb her unduly.* 这个想法并没有让她过分烦恼。 ➲ COMPARE DULY

un·dying /ʌnˈdaɪɪŋ/ *adj.* [only before noun] lasting for ever 永恒的；永久的；不朽的 **SYN** **eternal**：*undying love* 永恒的爱

un·earned /ˌʌnˈɜːnd; *NAmE* ˌʌnˈɜːrnd/ *adj.* [usually before noun] used to describe money that you receive but do not earn by working 非劳动所得的：*Declare all* ***unearned income***. 一切非劳动所得的收入都要申报。

un·earth /ʌnˈɜːθ; *NAmE* ʌnˈɜːrθ/ *verb* **1 ~ sth** to find sth in the ground by digging 挖掘；发掘；使出土 **SYN** **dig sth↔up**：*to unearth buried treasures* 挖掘地下埋藏的珍宝 **2 ~ sth** to find or discover sth by chance or after searching for it （偶然或经搜寻）发现，找到 **SYN** **dig sth↔up**：*I unearthed my old diaries when we moved house.* 我们搬家时，我偶然发现了自己以前的日记。◇ *The newspaper has unearthed some disturbing facts.* 报纸揭发了一些令人不安的真相。

un·earth·ly /ʌnˈɜːθli; *NAmE* -ˈɜːrθ-/ *adj.* [usually before noun] very strange; not natural and therefore frightening 怪异的；异常的；非自然的；恐怖的：*an unearthly cry* 令人毛骨悚然的喊声 ◇ *an unearthly light* 奇异的光

IDM **at an unearthly ˈhour** (*informal*) very early, especially when this is annoying 很早；过分的早：*The job involved getting up at some unearthly hour to catch the first train.* 这工作需要起大早赶头班火车。

un·ease /ʌnˈiːz/ (*also* **un·easi·ness** /ʌnˈiːzinəs/) *noun* [U, sing.] the feeling of being worried or unhappy about sth 不安；忧虑 **SYN** **anxiety**：*a* ***deep feeling/sense of unease*** 深刻的忧虑感 / 忧患意识 ◇ *There was a growing unease about their involvement in the war.* 他们卷入战争令人们感到日益不安。◇ *He was unable to hide his unease at the way the situation was developing.* 他无法掩饰对局势演变的忧虑。

un·easy /ʌnˈiːzi/ *adj.* **1** feeling worried or unhappy about a particular situation, especially because you think that sth bad or unpleasant may happen or because you are not sure that what you are doing is right 担心的；忧虑的；不安的 **SYN** **anxious**：*an uneasy laugh* 不自然的大笑 ◇ **~ about sth** *He was beginning to feel distinctly uneasy about their visit.* 他对他们的造访明显地感到不安起来。◇ **~ about doing sth** *She felt uneasy about leaving the children with them.* 把孩子托付给他们，她心里七上八下的。 ➲ SYNONYMS AT WORRIED **2** not certain to last; not safe or

U

settled 不稳定的；靠不住的；不确定的：*an uneasy peace* 不会持久的和平 ◇ *The two sides eventually reached an uneasy compromise.* 双方最终达成了暂时的妥协。**3** that does not enable you to relax or feel comfortable 令人不安的；令人不舒服的；不安稳的：*She woke from an* ***uneasy sleep*** *to find the house empty.* 她睡得不安稳，醒来时发现屋子里空无一人。**4** used to describe a mixture of two things, feelings, etc. that do not go well together 不和谐的；不协调的；矛盾的：*an* ***uneasy mix*** *of humour and violence* 幽默与暴力的矛盾组合 ◇ *Old farmhouses and new villas stood together in uneasy proximity.* 破旧的农舍与崭新的别墅比肩而立，很不协调。▶ **un·eas·ily** /ʌn'iːzɪli/ *adv.*：*I wondered uneasily what he was thinking.* 我惴惴不安，不知他到底在想什么。◇ *She shifted uneasily in her chair.* 她忐忑不安地在椅子上移动。◇ *His socialist views* ***sit uneasily*** *with his huge fortune.* 他拥有大量财富，这与他的社会主义观点格格不入。

un·eat·able /ʌn'iːtəbl/ *adj.* (of food 食物) not good enough to be eaten 不能吃的；不宜食用的 ➲ SEE ALSO INEDIBLE

un·eat·en /ʌn'iːtn/ *adj.* not eaten 未吃的：*Bill put the uneaten food away.* 比尔把没吃的食物收了起来。

un·eco·nom·ic /ˌʌnˌiːkə'nɒmɪk; ˌʌnˌek-; *NAmE* -'nɑːm-/ *adj.* **1** (of a business, factory, etc. 企业、工厂等) not making a profit 不赢利的；不赚钱的 SYN **unprofitable**：*uneconomic industries* 不赚钱的行业 OPP **economic** **2** = UNECONOMICAL

un·eco·nom·ic·al AW /ˌʌnˌiːkə'nɒmɪkl; ˌʌnˌek-; *NAmE* -'nɑːm-/ (*also* **un·eco·nom·ic**) *adj.* ~ (**to do sth**) using too much time or money, or too many materials, and therefore not likely to make a profit 浪费的；不节俭的；不经济的：*It soon proved uneconomical to stay open 24 hours a day.* 每天 24 小时营业很快就证明是不经济的。OPP **economical**

un·edify·ing /ʌn'edɪfaɪɪŋ/ *adj.* (*formal, especially BrE*) unpleasant in a way that makes you feel disapproval 讨厌的；令人厌恶的；有伤风化的：*the unedifying sight of the two party leaders screeching at each other* 两党党魁狺狺对吠的讨厌情景 ➲COMPARE EDIFYING

un·edu·cated /ʌn'edʒukeɪtɪd/ *adj.* having had little or no formal education at a school; showing a lack of education 未受教育的；未教化的；缺乏教养的：*an uneducated workforce* 缺乏教育的劳动力 ◇ *an uneducated point of view* 无知的观点 ➲COMPARE EDUCATED

U

un·elect·ed /ˌʌnɪ'lektɪd/ *adj.* not having been chosen by people in an election 未当选的；落选的：*unelected bureaucrats* 未当选的官僚

un·emo·tion·al /ˌʌnɪ'məʊʃənl; *NAmE* -'moʊ-/ *adj.* not showing your feelings 不露感情的；不动声色的；平静的：*an unemotional speech* 心平气和的讲话 ◇ *She seemed very cool and unemotional.* 她显得十分冷静。OPP **emotional** ▶ **un·emo·tion·al·ly** *adv.*

un·employ·able /ˌʌnɪm'plɔɪəbl/ *adj.* lacking the skills or qualities that you need to get a job 不宜雇用的（因缺乏所需技能或资质不足） OPP **employable**

un·employed 🔑 /ˌʌnɪm'plɔɪd/ *adj.* without a job although able to work 失业的；待业的；下岗的 SYN **jobless**：*How long have you been unemployed?* 你失业多久了？◇ *an unemployed builder* 失业的建筑工人 ➲ COLLOCATIONS AT UNEMPLOYMENT ▶ **the un·employed** 🔑 *noun* [pl.]：*a programme to get the* ***long-term unemployed*** *back to work* 协助长期失业者恢复工作的计划 ◇ *I've joined the ranks of the unemployed* (= I've lost my job). 我加入了失业者的行列。

un·employ·ment 🔑 /ˌʌnɪm'plɔɪmənt/ *noun* [U] **1** 🔑 the fact of a number of people not having a job; the number of people without a job 失业；失业人数：*an area of* ***high/low unemployment*** 失业率高 / 低的地区 ◇ ***rising/falling unemployment*** 上升的 / 下降的失业率 ◇ *It was a time of* ***mass unemployment***. 当时有大批人失业。◇ *measures to help* ***reduce/tackle unemployment*** 旨在减少失业 / 缓解失业情况的措施 ◇ *the* ***level/rate*** *of* ***unemployment*** 失业人数；失业率 ◇ ***unemployment benefit/statistics*** 失业补贴 / 统计资料 ➲ COLLOCATIONS AT ECONOMY **2** 🔑 the state of not having a job 无业；没有工作：*Thousands of young people are facing* ***long-term unemployment***. 成千上万的青年正面临长期待业状况。➲ COMPARE EMPLOYMENT **3** (*US*) = UNEMPLOYMENT BENEFIT：*Since losing his job, Mike has been collecting unemployment.* 自从丢了工作之后，迈克一直在领取失业救济金。➲ WORDFINDER NOTE AT POOR

▼**COLLOCATIONS 词语搭配**

Unemployment 失业

Losing your job 失业

- **lose** your job 失业
- (*BrE*) **become/be made** redundant 被裁减
- **be offered/take** voluntary redundancy/early retirement 被要求 / 选择自愿裁退 / 提前退休
- **face/be threatened with** dismissal/(*BrE*) the sack/(*BrE*) compulsory redundancy 面临被解职 / 被裁 / 强制裁员；受到解职 / 被裁 / 强制裁员的威胁
- **dismiss/fire/**(*especially BrE*) **sack** an employee/a worker/a manager 解雇雇员 / 工人 / 经理
- **lay off** staff/workers/employees 解雇员工 / 工人 / 雇员
- (*AustralE, NZE, SAfrE*) **retrench** workers 缩减人员
- **cut/reduce/downsize/slash** the workforce 裁减员工
- (*BrE*) **make** staff/workers/employees redundant 裁员

Being unemployed 失业；待业；下岗

- **be** unemployed/out of work/out of a job 失业
- **seek/look for** work/employment 找工作
- **be on/collect/draw/get/receive** (*both BrE*) unemployment benefit/Jobseeker's Allowance 领取失业补助金
- **be/go/live/sign** (*BrE, informal*) on the dole 领取失业救济金
- **claim/draw/get** (*BrE, informal*) the dole 领取失业救济金
- **be on/qualify for** (*NAmE*) unemployment (compensation) 领取 / 有资格领取失业补偿金
- **be/go/live/depend** (*NAmE*) on welfare 靠社会保障金过活
- **collect/receive** (*NAmE*) welfare 领取社会保障金
- **combat/tackle/cut/reduce** unemployment 防止 / 解决 / 减少失业

unem'ployment benefit (*BrE*) (*US* **unemˌployment compen'sation, unemployment**) *noun* [U] (*also* **un·em'ployment benefits** [pl.]) money paid by the government to sb who is unemployed 失业补贴（或津贴）；失业救济金：*people on* (= receiving) *unemployment benefit* 领取失业救济金的人 ◇ *Applications for unemployment benefits dropped last month.* 上个月申请失业津贴的人数下降了。➲SEE ALSO JOBSEEKER'S ALLOWANCE

un·en·cum·bered /ˌʌnɪn'kʌmbəd; *NAmE* -bərd/ *adj.* **1** not having or carrying anything heavy or anything that makes you go more slowly 无负担的；没有阻碍的；不受妨碍的 **2** (of property 地产) not having any debts left to be paid 没有作为抵押的

un·end·ing /ʌn'endɪŋ/ *adj.* seeming to last for ever 无尽的；源源不断的；不竭的：*a seemingly unending supply of money* 似乎源源不断的资金供应

un·en·dur·able /ˌʌnɪn'djʊərəbl; *NAmE* -'dʊr-/ *adj.* (*formal*) too bad, unpleasant, etc. to bear 无法容忍的；难以忍受的 SYN **unbearable**：*unendurable pain* 难以忍受的痛苦

un·envi·able /ʌn'enviəbl/ *adj.* [usually before noun] difficult or unpleasant; that you would not want to have 艰难的；讨厌的；不值得羡慕的：*She was given the* ***unenviable task*** *of informing the losers.* 让她去通知失败的人，真不是什么好差事。OPP **enviable**

un·equal /ʌnˈiːkwəl/ *adj.* **1** [usually before noun] in which people are treated in different ways or have different advantages in a way that seems unfair 不平等的；不均衡的；不公平的 SYN **unfair**: *an unequal distribution of wealth* 财富的分配不均 ◇ *an unequal contest* 不公平竞争 **2** ~ (**in sth**) different in size, amount, etc.（面积、数量等）不相等的，不同的：*The sleeves are unequal in length.* 这两只衣袖不一样长。◇ *The rooms upstairs are of unequal size.* 楼上的房间大小不同。 **3** ~ **to sth** (*formal*) not capable of doing sth 力所不及；不胜任：*She felt unequal to the task she had set herself.* 她觉得难以完成给自己定下的任务。 OPP **equal** ▸ **un·equal·ly** /-kwəli/ *adv.*

un·equalled (*US* **un·equaled**) /ʌnˈiːkwəld/ *adj.* better than all others 无比的；无双的；出类拔萃的 SYN **unparalleled**: *an unequalled record of success* 空前的成功纪录

un·equivo·cal /ˌʌnɪˈkwɪvəkl/ *adj.* (*formal*) expressing your opinion or intention very clearly and firmly 表达明确的；毫不含糊的；斩钉截铁的 SYN **unambiguous**: *an unequivocal rejection* 明确的拒绝 ◇ *The answer was an unequivocal 'no'.* 回答是个干脆利落的"不"字。 OPP **equivocal** ➲ SYNONYMS AT PLAIN ▸ **un·equivo·cal·ly** /-kəli/ *adv.*

un·err·ing /ʌnˈɜːrɪŋ/ *adj.* always right or accurate 万无一失的；一贯正确（或精确）的 SYN **unfailing**: *She had an unerring instinct for a good business deal.* 她有天生擅长做生意的本事。 ▸ **un·err·ing·ly** *adv.*

UNESCO /juːˈneskəʊ; *NAmE* -koʊ/ (*also* **Unesco**) *abbr.* United Nations Educational, Scientific and Cultural Organization 联合国教科文组织；联合国教育、科学及文化组织

un·eth·ic·al AW /ʌnˈeθɪkl/ *adj.* not morally acceptable 不道德的：*unethical behaviour* 不道德行为 OPP **ethical** ▸ **un·eth·ic·al·ly** /-kli/ *adv.*

un·even /ʌnˈiːvn/ *adj.* **1** not level, smooth or flat 凹凸不平的；不平坦的：*The floor felt uneven under his feet.* 他觉得脚下的地板高低不平。 OPP **even** **2** not following a regular pattern; not having a regular size and shape 无定型的；不规则的；无规律的 SYN **irregular**: *Her breathing was quick and uneven.* 她的呼吸急促不匀。◇ *uneven teeth* 不整齐的牙齿 OPP **even** **3** not having the same quality in all parts 质量不稳定的：*an uneven performance* (= with some good parts and some bad parts) 时好时坏的表现 **4** (of a contest or match 竞争或比赛) in which one group, team or player is much better than the other 实力悬殊的；一边倒的；不在同一水平的 SYN **unequal** OPP **even** **5** organized in a way that is not regular and/or fair 不均衡的；不公平的；不规则的 SYN **unequal**: *an uneven distribution of resources* 资源的不均衡分配 OPP **even** ▸ **un·even·ly** *adv.* **un·even·ness** *noun* [U]

unˌeven ˈbars (*NAmE*) (*BrE* **asymˌmetric ˈbars**) *noun* [pl.] two bars on posts of different heights that are used by women for doing GYMNASTIC exercises on 高低杠（女子体操器械）

un·event·ful /ˌʌnɪˈventfl/ *adj.* in which nothing interesting, unusual or exciting happens 平淡无奇的；平凡的；缺乏刺激的：*an uneventful life* 平淡的一生 OPP **eventful** ▸ **un·event·ful·ly** /-fəli/ *adv.*: *The day passed uneventfully.* 这一天平平淡淡地过去了。

un·ex·cep·tion·able /ˌʌnɪkˈsepʃənəbl/ *adj.* **1** (*formal*) not giving any reason for criticism 无可指责的；无从挑剔的；无懈可击的：*a man of unexceptionable character* 一个品格完美的男子 **2** (*informal*) not very new or exciting 不新奇的；不刺激的；不令人振奋的

un·ex·cep·tion·al /ˌʌnɪkˈsepʃənl/ *adj.* not interesting or unusual 乏味的；平常的；不突出的；普通的 SYN **unremarkable** ➲ COMPARE EXCEPTIONAL

un·ex·cit·ing /ˌʌnɪkˈsaɪtɪŋ/ *adj.* not interesting; boring 枯燥的；乏味的；无聊的 OPP **exciting**

un·ex·pect·ed 🔑 /ˌʌnɪkˈspektɪd/ *adj.* if sth is **unexpected**, it surprises you because you were not expecting it 出乎意料的；始料不及的：*an unexpected result* 意想不到的结果 ◇ *an unexpected visitor* 不速之客 ◇ *The announcement was not entirely unexpected.* 这个通告并非完全出乎意料。 ▸ **the unexpected** 🔑 *noun* [sing.]: *Police officers must be prepared for the unexpected.* 警察必须随时准备应付意外事件。 **un·ex·pec·ted·ly** 🔑 *adv.*: *They had arrived unexpectedly.* 他们意外地到达了。◇ *an unexpectedly large bill* 出乎意料的高额账单 ◇ *The plane was unexpectedly delayed.* 飞机意外地延误了。◇ *Not unexpectedly, most local business depends on tourism.* 并非出人意料的是，当地的大部分生意依靠旅游业。 **un·ex·pect·ed·ness** *noun* [U] ➲ COMPARE EXPECT, EXPECTED

un·ex·pired /ˌʌnɪkˈspaɪəd; *NAmE* -ˈspaɪərd/ *adj.* [usually before noun] (of an agreement or a period of time 协议或限期) still valid; not yet having come to an end or EXPIRED 有效的；未过期的

un·ex·plained /ˌʌnɪkˈspleɪnd/ *adj.* for which the reason or cause is not known; that has not been explained 原因不详的；未解释的；未说明的：*an unexplained mystery* 解释不清的奥妙 ◇ *He died in unexplained circumstances.* 他死因不明。

un·ex·ploded /ˌʌnɪkˈspləʊdɪd; *NAmE* -ˈsploʊ-/ *adj.* [only before noun] (of a bomb, etc. 炸弹等) that has not yet exploded 未爆炸的

un·ex·plored /ˌʌnɪkˈsplɔːd; *NAmE* -ˈsplɔːrd/ *adj.* **1** (of a country or an area of land 国家或地域) that nobody has investigated or put on a map; that has not been explored 无人涉足的；未画进地图的；未经勘察的 **2** (of an idea, a theory, etc. 想法、理论等) that has not yet been examined or discussed thoroughly 未经彻底研究（或探讨）的

un·ex·pressed /ˌʌnɪkˈsprest/ *adj.* (of a thought, a feeling or an idea 思想、感情或意见) not shown or made known in words, looks or actions; not expressed 未表现出的；未表达的；未表示的

un·ex·pur·gated /ʌnˈekspəgeɪtɪd; *NAmE* -pərg-/ *adj.* (of a text) complete and containing all the original material, even if it is offensive（文稿）未经删节的：*This is the full unexpurgated version of the diaries.* 这是日记的足本。

un·fail·ing /ʌnˈfeɪlɪŋ/ *adj.* that you can rely on to always be there and always be the same 可靠的；一贯的；永久的：*unfailing support* 一贯的支持 ◇ *She fought the disease with* ***unfailing good humour.*** 她始终抱乐观态度同疾病斗争。 ▸ **un·fail·ing·ly** *adv.*: *unfailingly loyal/polite* 一贯地忠心耿耿 / 彬彬有礼

un·fair 🔑 /ˌʌnˈfeə(r); *NAmE* -ˈfer/ *adj.* not right or fair according to a set of rules or principles; not treating people equally 不公正的；不公平的；待人不平等的 SYN **unjust**: *unfair criticism* 不公正的批评 ◇ ~ (**on/to sb**) *It seems unfair on him to make him pay for everything.* 让他承担一切费用似乎对他不公平。◇ *It would* ***be unfair*** *not to let you have a choice.* 不让你有所选择是不公平的。◇ *They had been given an* ***unfair advantage.*** 他们得到了不公正的好处。◇ ***unfair dismissal*** (= a situation in which sb is illegally dismissed from their job) 不公平解雇 ◇ *measures to prevent unfair competition between member countries* 防止成员国之间不公平竞争的措施 ◇ *Life seems so unfair sometimes.* 人生有时似乎非常不公平。◇ *It's so unfair!* 这太不公平了！ OPP **fair** ▸ **un·fair·ly** 🔑 *adv.*: *She claims to have been unfairly dismissed.* 她声言遭到无理解雇。◇ *The tests discriminate unfairly against older people.* 这些测验对年纪较大的人不公平。 **un·fair·ness** *noun* [U]

un·faith·ful /ʌnˈfeɪθfl/ *adj.* ~ (**to sb**) having sex with sb who is not your husband, wife or usual partner 不忠的；通奸的：*Have you ever been unfaithful to him?* 你对他是否有过不忠行为？ OPP **faithful** ▸ **un·faith·ful·ness** *noun* [U]

un·famil·iar /ˌʌnfəˈmɪliə(r)/ *adj.* **1** that you do not know or recognize 陌生的；不熟悉的；不认识的：*She felt uneasy in the unfamiliar surroundings.* 她在陌生的环境中感到局促不安。◇ ~ **to sb** *Please highlight any terms that are unfamiliar to you.* 请把你们不熟悉的用语都标示出来。

U

2 ~ **with sth** not having any knowledge or experience of sth 无…的知识（或经验）：*an introductory course for students who are unfamiliar with computers* 为不了解计算机的学生开设的入门课程 OPP **familiar** ▸ **un·famili·ar·ity** /ˌʌnfəˌmɪliˈærəti/ *noun* [U]

un·fash·ion·able /ʌnˈfæʃnəbl/ *adj.* not popular or fashionable at a particular time 不时兴的；不时髦的；过时的：*an unfashionable part of London* 伦敦一个老旧的角落 ◇ *unfashionable ideas* 守旧的思想 OPP **fashionable** ▸ **un·fash·ion·ably** *adv.*：*a man with unfashionably long hair* 留着过时长发的男人

un·fas·ten /ʌnˈfɑːsn; *NAmE* ʌnˈfæsn/ *verb* ~ **sth** to undo sth that is fastened 解开；松开；打开：*to unfasten a belt/button, etc.* 解开皮带、纽扣等 OPP **fasten**

un·fath·om·able /ʌnˈfæðəməbl/ *adj.* (*formal*) **1** too strange or difficult to be understood 难以理解的；莫测高深的：*an unfathomable mystery* 难以解释的奥秘 **2** if sb has an **unfathomable** expression, it is impossible to know what they are thinking（表情）难以琢磨的，微妙的

un·favour·able (*especially US* **un·favor·able**) /ʌnˈfeɪvərəbl/ *adj.* (*formal*) **1** ~ (**for/to sth**) (of conditions, situations, etc. 条件、形势等) not good and likely to cause problems or make sth more difficult 不利的；有害的：*The conditions were unfavourable for agriculture.* 这些条件不利于农业。◇ *an unfavourable exchange rate* 不利的汇率 **2** showing that you do not approve of or like sb/sth 不赞成的；否定的；不喜欢的：*an unfavourable comment* 负面的评论 ◇ *The documentary presents him in a very* ***unfavourable light.*** 这部纪录片从十分负面的角度来描绘他。◇ *an* ***unfavourable comparison*** (= one that makes one thing seem much worse than another) 使相形见绌的比较 OPP **favourable** ▸ **un·favour·ably** (*BrE*) (*NAmE* **un·favor·ably**) *adv.*：*In this respect, Britain* ***compares unfavourably*** *with other European countries.* 在这方面，英国比欧洲其他各国要逊色。

un·fazed /ʌnˈfeɪzd/ *adj.* (*informal*) not worried or surprised by sth unexpected that happens 未受干扰；不担忧的；泰然自若的 OPP **faze**

un·feas·ible /ʌnˈfiːzəbl/ *adj.* not possible to do or achieve 不可行的；难以实现的 OPP **feasible**

un·feel·ing /ʌnˈfiːlɪŋ/ *adj.* not showing care or sympathy for other people 漠不关心的；无情的；无怜悯心的

un·feigned /ʌnˈfeɪnd/ *adj.* (*formal*) real and sincere 真诚的；真挚的；不虚伪的 SYN **genuine**：*unfeigned admiration* 由衷的钦佩 ➲ MORE LIKE THIS 20, page R27

un·fenced /ʌnˈfenst/ *adj.* (of a road or piece of land 道路或土地) without fences beside or around it 无护栏的；无围栏的

un·fet·tered /ʌnˈfetəd; *NAmE* -tərd/ *adj.* (*formal*) not controlled or restricted 无限制的；不受约束的；自由的：*an unfettered free market* 不受约束的自由市场

un·filled /ʌnˈfɪld/ *adj.* **1** if a job or position is **unfilled**, nobody has been chosen for it（职位）空缺的 **2** if a pause in a conversation is **unfilled**, nobody speaks（谈话中）停顿的 **3** an **unfilled** cake has nothing inside it（糕饼）无馅的 **4** (*especially NAmE*) if an order for goods is **unfilled**, the goods have not been supplied（订单）未交货的

un·fin·ished /ʌnˈfɪnɪʃt/ *adj.* not complete; not finished 未做完的；未完成的：*We have some* ***unfinished business*** *to settle.* 我们还有些没做完的事要处理。

unfit /ʌnˈfɪt/ *adj.* **1** not of an acceptable standard; not suitable 不合格的；不适合的；不适宜的：~ (**for sth**) *The housing was* ***unfit for human habitation.*** 这种住房不适合居住。◇ *The food on offer was* ***unfit for human consumption.*** 那些特价食品不适宜让人食用。◇ ~ (**to eat, drink, live in, etc.**) *This water is unfit to drink.* 这水不宜饮用。◇ *Most of the buildings are unfit to live in.* 这些楼房多数不适合居住。◇ ~ (**to do sth**) *They described him as unfit to govern.* 他们认为他这个人不适合做管理工作。◇ (*specialist*) *Many of the houses were condemned as unfit.* 这些房屋有许多被批评为不适宜居住。◇ (*specialist*) *The court claims she is an unfit mother.* 法庭声称她是个不称职的母亲。 **2** not capable of doing sth, for example because of illness（因病等）不能做某事，不宜做事：~ **for sth** *He's still unfit for work.* 他还不宜工作。◇ ~ **to do sth** *The company's doctor found that she was unfit to carry out her normal work.* 公司的医生认为，她不宜从事原来的工作。 **3** (*especially BrE*) (of a person 人) not in good physical condition; not fit, because you have not taken exercise 健康状况欠佳；身体状态差：*The captain is still unfit and will miss tonight's game.* 队长身体状态仍不好，将不会出战今晚的比赛。OPP **fit** ▸ **un·fit·ness** *noun* [U]

un·fit·ted /ʌnˈfɪtɪd/ *adj.* ~ **for sth** | ~ **to do sth** (*formal*) not suitable for sth 不适于；不适合：*She felt herself unfitted for marriage.* 她觉得自己不适宜结婚。

un·flag·ging /ˌʌnˈflæɡɪŋ/ *adj.* [usually before noun] remaining strong; not becoming weak or tired 蓬勃的；不松懈的；不减弱的；不倦的 SYN **tireless**：*unflagging energy* 无穷的精力

un·flap·pable /ˌʌnˈflæpəbl/ *adj.* (*informal*) able to stay calm in a difficult situation 处变不惊的；镇定的；冷静的 SYN **imperturbable**

un·flat·ter·ing /ʌnˈflætərɪŋ/ *adj.* making sb/sth seem worse or less attractive than they really are 贬损的；有损形象的；不恭维的：*an unflattering dress* 难看的连衣裙 ◇ *unflattering comments* 贬抑的评论 OPP **flattering**

un·flinch·ing /ʌnˈflɪntʃɪŋ/ *adj.* remaining strong and determined, even in a difficult or dangerous situation 不屈不挠的；果敢的；坚定的；不畏缩的 SYN **steadfast**：*unflinching loyalty* 坚贞不渝的忠诚 ◇ *an unflinching stare* 毫不畏惧的注视 ▸ **un·flinch·ing·ly** *adv.* ➲ SEE ALSO FLINCH

un·focused (*also* **un·focussed**) /ʌnˈfəʊkəst; *NAmE* -ˈfoʊ-/ *adj.* **1** (especially of eyes 尤指眼睛) not looking at a particular thing or person; not having been focused 目光分散的；漫不经心的：*an unfocused look* 茫然的眼神 **2** (of plans, work, etc. 计划、工作等) not having a clear aim or purpose; not well organized or clear 目的不明确的；组织不严密的；松散的：*The research is too unfocused to have any significant impact.* 这一次的研究太零散，难以发挥重大的作用。◇ *unfocused questions* 漫无边际的问题

un·fold /ʌnˈfəʊld; *NAmE* ʌnˈfoʊld/ *verb* **1** [T, I] ~ (**sth**) to spread open or flat sth that has previously been folded; to become open and flat（使）展开；打开：*to unfold a map* 展开地图 ◇ *She unfolded her arms.* 她张开双臂。OPP **fold 2** [I, T] to be gradually made known; to gradually make sth known to other people（使）逐渐展现；展示；透露：*The audience watched as* ***the story unfolded*** *before their eyes.* 观众看着剧情逐渐地展开。◇ ~ **sth** (**to sb**) *She unfolded her tale to us.* 她向我们倾吐了她的故事。

un·follow /ˌʌnˈfɒləʊ; *NAmE* ˌʌnˈfɑːloʊ/ *verb* [T, I] to decide to stop receiving messages from a particular person, group, etc. on the Twitter SOCIAL NETWORKING service by removing them from the list of people you receive messages from（在推特等社交网站上）取消关注

un·forced /ʌnˈfɔːst; *NAmE* ʌnˈfɔːrst/ *adj.* **1** (especially in sports 尤用于体育运动) an **unforced** error is one that you make by playing badly, not because your opponent has caused you to make a mistake by their skilful play（失误）自己造成的，非受迫性的 **2** natural; done without effort 自然的；轻易的；不费力的：*unforced humour* 自然的幽默

un·fore·see·able /ˌʌnfɔːˈsiːəbl; *NAmE* -fɔːrˈs-/ *adj.* that you cannot predict or FORESEE 无法预见的；难以预测的：*Building a dam here could have* ***unforeseeable consequences*** *for the environment.* 在这里修建水坝可能会对环境造成无法预料的后果。OPP **foreseeable**

un·fore·seen /ˌʌnfɔːˈsiːn; *NAmE* -fɔːrˈs-/ *adj.* that you did not expect to happen 未想到的；始料不及的 SYN **unexpected**：***unforeseen delays/problems*** 意外的延误 /

问题 ◇ *The project was running late owing to* ***unforeseen circumstances.*** 这个项目因意外情况而拖延了。➲ COMPARE FORESEE

un·for·get·table /ˌʌnfəˈgetəbl; *NAmE* -fərˈg-/ *adj.* if sth is **unforgettable**, you cannot forget it, usually because it is so beautiful, interesting, enjoyable, etc. 难以忘怀的；令人难忘的 **SYN** **memorable** ➲ COMPARE FORGETTABLE

un·for·giv·able /ˌʌnfəˈgɪvəbl; *NAmE* -fərˈg-/ *adj.* if sb's behaviour is **unforgivable**, it is so bad or unacceptable that you cannot forgive the person 不可原谅的；难以饶恕的 **SYN** **inexcusable** **OPP** **forgivable** ▸ **un·for·giv·ably** *adv.*

un·for·giv·ing /ˌʌnfəˈgɪvɪŋ; *NAmE* -fərˈg-/ *adj.* (*formal*) **1** (of a person 人) unwilling to forgive other people when they have done sth wrong 不饶人的；不宽容的；不肯原谅的 **OPP** **forgiving** **2** (of a place, situation, etc. 地方、局面等) unpleasant and causing difficulties for people 让人为难的；难应付的；棘手的

un·formed /ˌʌnˈfɔːmd; *NAmE* ˌʌnˈfɔːrmd/ *adj.* (*formal*) not fully developed 发展不充分的；未成形的；不成熟的：*unformed ideas* 不成熟的意见

un·forth·com·ing /ˌʌnfɔːθˈkʌmɪŋ; *NAmE* -fɔːrθ-/ *adj.* not wanting to help or give information about sth 不愿帮忙的；口紧的；不露口风的 **SYN** **reticent**：*He was very unforthcoming about what had happened.* 他对发生的事守口如瓶。**OPP** **forthcoming**

un·for·tu·nate 🔑 /ʌnˈfɔːtʃənət; *NAmE* -ˈfɔːrtʃ-/ *adj.*, *noun*

■ *adj.* **1** 🔑 having bad luck; caused by bad luck 不幸的；倒霉的 **SYN** **unlucky**：*He was unfortunate to lose in the final round.* 他不幸在最后一轮输了。◇ *It was an unfortunate accident.* 那是一次不幸的事故。**OPP** **fortunate** **2** 🔑 (*formal*) if you say that a situation is **unfortunate**, you wish that it had not happened or that it had been different 令人遗憾的；可惜的 **SYN** **regrettable**：*She described the decision as 'unfortunate'.* 她把这项决定说成是"令人遗憾"。◇ *It was unfortunate that he couldn't speak English.* 可惜他不会讲英语。◇ *You're putting me in a* ***most unfortunate*** *position.* 你正在把我推入十分可悲的处境。➲ LANGUAGE BANK AT IMPERSONAL **3** embarrassing and/or offensive 令人尴尬的；不适当的；得罪人的：*It was an unfortunate choice of words.* 那是一种不恰当的措辞。

■ *noun* (*literary*) a person who does not have much luck, money, etc. 不幸的人：*one of life's unfortunates* 人生中的不幸者之一

un·for·tu·nate·ly 🔑 /ʌnˈfɔːtʃənətli; *NAmE* -ˈfɔːrtʃ-/ *adv.* used to say that a particular situation or fact makes you sad or disappointed, or gets you into a difficult position 不幸地；遗憾地；可惜地；可悲地 **SYN** **regrettably**：*Unfortunately, I won't be able to attend the meeting.* 真可惜我不能参加这次会议。◇ *I can't make it, unfortunately.* 很遗憾，我来不及。◇ *Unfortunately for him, the police had been informed and were waiting outside.* 算他倒霉，警察已得到消息，就在外边等着。◇ *It won't be finished for a few weeks. Unfortunately!* 这工作得过几周才能完成。很遗憾！**OPP** **fortunately**

un·found·ed **AW** /ʌnˈfaʊndɪd/ *adj.* not based on reason or fact 莫须有的；无端的；没理由的；不依据事实的：***unfounded allegations/rumours, etc.*** 缺乏依据的指控、无中生有的谣言等 ◇ *Speculation about a divorce* ***proved totally unfounded.*** 有关离婚的猜测证实纯属无稽之谈。

un·freeze /ˌʌnˈfriːz/ *verb* (**un·froze** /-ˈfrəʊz; *NAmE* -ˈfroʊz/, **un·frozen** /-ˈfrəʊzn; *NAmE* -ˈfroʊzn/) **1** [T, I] ~ (**sth**) if you **unfreeze** sth that has been frozen or very cold, or it **unfreezes**, it melts or warms until it reaches a normal temperature （使）解冻，化冻，融化 ➲ COMPARE DEFROST (1), DE-ICE, THAW *v.* (3) **2** [T] ~ **sth** to remove official controls on money or an economy 解冻；解除（对资金的冻结或经济方面的限制）：*The party plans to unfreeze some of the cash held by local government.* 这个党计划将地方政府冻结的一部分现款解冻。**OPP** **freeze**

un·friend /ˌʌnˈfrend/ (*also* **de·friend**) *verb* [T] (*informal*) to remove sb from a list of friends or contacts on a SOCIAL NETWORKING website （在社交网站上）删除好友：*If a Facebook friend suddenly becomes your boss, do you unfriend them?* 如果你脸书上的朋友突然成为你的老板，你会将他从好友名单中删除吗？◇ *Young adults are more likely to unfriend.* 年轻人更容易删除好友。

un·friend·ly 🔑 /ʌnˈfrendli/ *adj.* not kind or pleasant to sb 不友好的；冷漠的；有敌意的：*an unfriendly atmosphere* 不友好的气氛 ◇ ~ (**to/towards sb**) *There's no need to be so unfriendly towards them.* 没必要对他们这么不客气。◇ *the use of* ***environmentally unfriendly*** *products* (= that harm the environment) 危害环境的产品的使用 **OPP** **friendly** ▸ **un·friend·li·ness** *noun* [U]

un·ful·filled /ˌʌnfʊlˈfɪld/ *adj.* **1** (of a need, wish, etc. 需要、愿望等) that has not been satisfied or achieved 未满足的；未实现的；未兑现的：***unfulfilled ambitions/hopes/promises, etc.*** 未实现的抱负、希望、诺言等 **2** if a person feels **unfulfilled**, they feel that they could achieve more in their life or work 壮志未酬的；宏图未展的 **OPP** **fulfilled**

un·ful·fil·ling /ˌʌnfʊlˈfɪlɪŋ/ *adj.* not causing sb to feel satisfied and useful 不能使人感到满足的；不令人称心的：*an unfulfilling job* 不能令人感到满足的工作

un·funny /ʌnˈfʌni/ *adj.* not funny or amusing, especially when sth is supposed to be funny 索然无味的；没意思的；无趣的：*The show was deeply unfunny.* 这场演出毫无趣味。

un·furl /ˌʌnˈfɜːl; *NAmE* ˌʌnˈfɜːrl/ *verb* [I, T] when sth that is curled or rolled tightly **unfurls**, or you **unfurl** it, it opens （使卷紧的东西）打开，展开：*The leaves slowly unfurled.* 叶子慢慢地展开了。◇ ~ **sth** *to unfurl a flag* 展开旗子

un·fur·nished /ʌnˈfɜːnɪʃt; *NAmE* -ˈfɜːrn-/ *adj.* without furniture 无家具的：*We rented an unfurnished apartment.* 我们租了一套不带家具的公寓。**OPP** **furnished**

unga /ˈʊŋə/ *noun* [U] (*EAfrE*) flour made from MAIZE (CORN), used to make UGALI 玉米粉（用来做玉米粉糕）

un·gain·ly /ʌnˈgeɪnli/ *adj.* moving in a way that is not smooth or elegant 笨手笨脚的；（举止）不雅观的，难看的 **SYN** **awkward**：*He was a tall, ungainly boy of 18.* 他是个个子高而笨拙的 18 岁小伙子。

un·gentle·man·ly /ʌnˈdʒentlmənli/ *adj.* (of a man's behaviour 男子的行为) not polite or pleasant; not acceptable 不礼貌的；无教养（或风度）的 **OPP** **gentlemanly**

un·glam·or·ous /ʌnˈglæmərəs/ *adj.* not attractive or exciting; dull 无魅力的；不刺激的；枯燥的：*an unglamorous job* 乏味的工作 **OPP** **glamorous**

un·glued /ʌnˈgluːd/ *adj.*

IDM **come unˈglued** (*NAmE*, *informal*) **1** to become very upset 十分烦恼；心情烦乱 **2** if a plan, etc. **comes unglued**, it does not work successfully （计划等）不顺利，效果不佳

un·god·ly /ʌnˈgɒdli; *NAmE* -ˈgɑːd-/ *adj.* (*old-fashioned*) not showing respect for God; evil 亵渎神灵的；不敬神的；邪恶的 **OPP** **godly**

IDM **at an ungodly ˈhour** very early or very late and therefore annoying 一大早（或很晚）；在十分不便的时间

un·gov·ern·able /ʌnˈgʌvənəbl; *NAmE* -ˈgʌvərn-/ *adj.* **1** (of a country, region, etc. 国家、地区等) impossible to govern or control 无法管治的；难以控制的 **2** (*formal*) (of a person's feelings 感情) impossible to control 抑制不住的；无法控制的 **SYN** **uncontrollable**：*ungovernable rage* 难以抑制的暴怒

un·gra·cious /ʌnˈgreɪʃəs/ *adj.* (*formal*) not polite or friendly, especially towards sb who is being kind to you （尤指对别人的善意）不客气的，失礼的 **OPP** **gracious** ▸ **un·gra·cious·ly** *adv.*

un·gram·mat·ical /ˌʌngrəˈmætɪkl/ *adj.* not following the rules of grammar 违反语法规则的；不合语法的 **OPP** **grammatical**

U

un·grate·ful /ʌnˈgreɪtfl/ *adj.* not showing or expressing thanks for sth that sb has done for you or given to you 不领情的；忘恩负义的 OPP grateful ▸ **un·grate·ful·ly** /-fəli/ *adv.*

un·guard·ed /ʌnˈgɑːdɪd; *NAmE* -ˈgɑːrd-/ *adj.* **1** not protected or watched 无防备的；无警戒的；无保护的：*The museum was unguarded at night.* 这个博物馆夜里无人看守。◇ *an unguarded fire* (= that has nothing to stop people from burning themselves on it) 无防护设施的火堆 **2** (of a remark, look, etc. 话语、神情等) said or done carelessly, at a time when you are not thinking about the effects of your words or are not paying attention 不小心的；不谨慎的；不留神的：*an unguarded remark* 轻率的言论 ◇ *It was something I'd let out* ***in an unguarded moment.*** 那是我一不留神说漏了嘴的话。➲ COMPARE GUARDED

un·guent /ˈʌŋgwənt/ *noun* [C, U] (*formal*) a soft substance that is used for rubbing onto the skin to heal it 药膏；软膏

un·gu·late /ˈʌŋgjʊlət; -leɪt/ *noun* (*specialist*) any animal which has HOOFS, such as a cow or horse 有蹄类动物

un·hand /ˌʌnˈhænd/ *verb* **~ sb** (*old-fashioned* or *humorous*) to release a person that you are holding 放开…的手

un·hap·pily /ʌnˈhæpɪli/ *adv.* **1** in an unhappy way 难过地；怏怏不乐地：*He sighed unhappily.* 他难过地叹息了一声。**2** used to say that a particular situation or fact makes you sad or disappointed 遗憾地；不幸地；可惜地 SYN **unfortunately**：*Unhappily, such good luck is rare.* 遗憾的是，这样的好运太少了。◇ *His wife, unhappily, died five years ago.* 他的妻子不幸于五年前去世了。OPP **happily**

un·happy 🔑 /ʌnˈhæpi/ *adj.* (**un·hap·pier**, **un·happi·est**) HELP **more unhappy** and **most unhappy** are also common * more unhappy 和 most unhappy 也常用。**1** 🔑 not happy; sad 不快乐的；不幸福的；难过的；悲伤的：*to* ***be/look/seem/sound unhappy*** 感到 / 看来 / 似乎 / 听起来不愉快 ◇ *an unhappy childhood* 不快乐的童年 ◇ *I didn't realize but he was* ***deeply unhappy*** *at that time.* 我没有察觉到他那时非常不开心。**2** 🔑 **~ (about/at/with sth)** not pleased or satisfied with sth 不悦的；不高兴的；不满的：*They were unhappy with their accommodation.* 他们对住处不满意。◇ *He was unhappy at being left out of the team.* 他对未能入选该队感到不高兴。**3** (*formal*) unfortunate or not suitable 不幸的；不适当的：*an unhappy coincidence* 不幸的巧合 ◇ *It was an unhappy choice of words.* 那样用词是不适当的。▸ **un·hap·pi·ness** *noun* [U]

U

un·harmed /ʌnˈhɑːmd; *NAmE* ʌnˈhɑːrmd/ *adj.* not injured or damaged; not harmed 未受伤的；未受损害的

UNHCR /juː en ˌeɪtʃ siː ˈɑː(r)/ *abbr.* United Nations High Commission for Refugees (an organization whose function is to help and protect REFUGEES) 联合国难民事务高级专员办事处

un·healthy /ʌnˈhelθi/ *adj.* **1** not having good health; showing a lack of good health 不健康的；虚弱的：*They looked poor and unhealthy.* 他们看起来贫病交加。◇ *unhealthy skin* 不健康的皮肤 ◇ *His eyeballs were an unhealthy yellow.* 他的眼球是不健康的蜡黄色。**2** harmful to your health; likely to make you ill/sick 损害健康的；对身体有害的；会致病的：*unhealthy living conditions* 有碍健康的生活条件 ◇ *an* ***unhealthy diet/lifestyle*** 不良的饮食 / 生活方式 **3** not normal and likely to be harmful 反常的；不良的；有害的 SYN **unwholesome**：*He had an unhealthy interest in disease and death.* 他对疾病与死亡有一种病态的兴趣。OPP **healthy** ▸ **un·health·ily** /-ɪli/ *adv.* **un·healthi·ness** *noun* [U]：*the unhealthiness of suppressing emotions* 抑制情绪对健康的坏处

un·heard /ʌnˈhɜːd; *NAmE* ʌnˈhɜːrd/ *adj.* **1** that nobody pays attention to 无人理会的；未被注意的：*Their protests* ***went unheard.*** 他们的抗议无人理会。**2** not listened to or heard 未被听的；未听到的：*a previously unheard tape of their conversations* 以前未听过的他们谈话的录音带

unheard-of /ʌnˈhɜːd ɒv; *NAmE* ʌnˈhɜːrd ʌv/ *adj.* that has never been known or done; very unusual 前所未闻的；空前的；很反常的：*He'd dyed his hair, which was almost unheard-of in the 1960s.* 他染了头发，这在 20 世纪 60 年代是罕见的事。◇ *It is almost unheard-of for a new band to be offered such a deal.* 一支新乐队得到这样的一份合同，几乎是空前的。

un·heat·ed /ʌnˈhiːtɪd/ *adj.* having no form of heating 无供暖设施的；无暖气的：*an unheated bathroom* 无暖气的浴室 OPP **heated**

un·heed·ed /ʌnˈhiːdɪd/ *adj.* (*formal*) that is heard, seen or noticed but then ignored 遭视而不见的；遭听而不闻的；被忽视的：*Her warning* ***went unheeded.*** 她的警告没有引起重视。➲ COMPARE HEED *v.*

un·help·ful /ʌnˈhelpfl/ *adj.* not helpful or useful; not willing to help sb 无益的；无用的；不愿帮助的：*an unhelpful response* 于事无补的反应 ◇ *The taxi driver was being very unhelpful.* 那个出租车司机不肯帮忙。OPP **helpful** ▸ **un·help·ful·ly** /-fəli/ *adv.*

un·her·ald·ed /ʌnˈherəldɪd/ *adj.* (*formal*) not previously mentioned; happening without any warning 未曾提及的；突如其来的；突然发生的

un·hesi·tat·ing /ʌnˈhezɪteɪtɪŋ/ *adj.* done or given immediately and confidently 果断的；坚决的；毫不迟疑的：*He gave an unhesitating 'yes' when asked if he would go through the experience again.* 问到是否愿意再有一次这样的经历时，他毫不迟疑地表示愿意。▸ **un·hesi·tat·ing·ly** *adv.*

un·hin·dered /ʌnˈhɪndəd; *NAmE* -dərd/ *adj.* without anything stopping or preventing the progress of sb/sth 不受阻挡的；没有障碍的；畅通无阻的：*She had unhindered access to the files.* 她可任意直接存取档案。◇ *He was able to* ***pass unhindered*** *through several military checkpoints.* 他畅行无阻地通过了好几处军事检查站。➲ SEE ALSO HINDER

un·hinge /ʌnˈhɪndʒ/ *verb* [usually passive] **~ sb** to make sb mentally ill 使精神失常（或错乱）

un·hitch /ʌnˈhɪtʃ/ *verb* **~ sth** to undo sth that is tied to sth else 解开；分开；卸掉：*to unhitch a trailer* 卸掉拖车 ➲ SEE ALSO HITCH *v.*

un·holy /ʌnˈhəʊli; *NAmE* -ˈhoʊ-/ *adj.* **1** dangerous; likely to be harmful 危险的；有害的：*an* ***unholy alliance*** *between the medical profession and the pharmaceutical industry* 医疗界与医药业的不当联盟 **2** not respecting the laws of a religion 不守教规的；亵渎神明的；罪恶的 OPP **holy 3** [only before noun] (*informal*) used to emphasize how bad sth is 过分的；极端的；无法容忍的：*She wondered how she had got into this unholy mess.* 她不知道自己如何弄得如此狼狈不堪。

un·hook /ʌnˈhʊk/ *verb* **~ sth (from sth)** to remove sth from a hook; to undo the hooks on clothes, etc. 从钩子上取下；解开（衣物等）的钩子：*He unhooked his coat from the door.* 他从门上取下外衣。◇ *She unhooked her bra.* 她解开了胸罩。

un·hur·ried /ʌnˈhʌrid; *NAmE* -ˈhɜːr-/ *adj.* (*formal*) relaxed and calm; not done too quickly 从容的；不慌不忙的 OPP **hurried** ▸ **un·hur·ried·ly** *adv.*：*Lynn walked unhurriedly into the kitchen.* 林恩不慌不忙地走进了厨房。

un·hurt /ʌnˈhɜːt; *NAmE* ʌnˈhɜːrt/ *adj.* [not before noun] not injured or harmed 未受伤；未受伤害；平安；安然无恙 SYN **unharmed**：*He escaped from the crash unhurt.* 他平安逃过了这场车祸。OPP **hurt**

un·hygien·ic /ˌʌnhaɪˈdʒiːnɪk; *NAmE usually* -ˈdʒen-/ *adj.* not clean and therefore likely to cause disease or infection 不清洁的；不卫生的；易致病（或感染）的 OPP **hygienic**

uni /ˈjuːni/ *noun* (*BrE, informal*) university 大学：*friends from uni* 大学校友 ◇ *Where were you* ***at uni?*** 你在哪儿上的大学？

uni- /ˈjuːni/ *combining form* (in nouns, adjectives and adverbs 构成名词、形容词和副词) one; having one 单；独；一：*uniform* 制服 ◇ *unilaterally* 单方面地

uni·cam·eral /ˌjuːnɪˈkæmərəl/ *adj.* (*specialist*) (of a parliament 议会) that has only one main governing body 单院的；一院（制）的

UNICEF /ˈjuːnɪsef/ *abbr.* United Nations Children's Fund (an organization within the United Nations that helps to take care of the health and education of children all over the world) 联合国儿童基金会

uni·cel·lu·lar /ˌjuːnɪˈseljələ(r)/ *adj.* (*biology* 生) (of a living thing 生物) consisting of only one cell 单细胞的：*unicellular organisms* 单细胞生物

uni·corn /ˈjuːnɪkɔːn; *NAmE* -kɔːrn/ *noun* (in stories) an animal like a white horse with a long straight horn on its head （传说中的）独角兽

uni·cycle /ˈjuːnɪsaɪkl/ (*also* **mono·cycle**) *noun* a vehicle that is similar to a bicycle but that has only one wheel 独轮脚踏车 ➲ VISUAL VOCAB PAGE V55

un·iden·ti·fi·able AW /ˌʌnaɪˈdentɪfaɪəbl/ *adj.* impossible to identify 无法辨认的；难以确认的；无法识别的：*He had an unidentifiable accent.* 他的口音难以识别。◇ *Many of the bodies were unidentifiable except by dental records.* 许多尸体若不是靠牙科病历就无法辨认。OPP **identifiable**

un·iden·ti·fied /ˌʌnaɪˈdentɪfaɪd/ *adj.* not recognized or known; not identified 未知的；不明的；未确认的：*an unidentified virus* 尚未确定的病毒 ◇ *The painting was sold to an unidentified American dealer* (= his or her name was not given). 这幅画卖给了一名未披露姓名的美国商人。

ˌUnifiˈcation Church *noun* a religious and political organization begun in Korea in 1954 by Sun Myung Moon 统一教团（1954 年由文鲜明成立于韩国）

uni·form 🔑 AW /ˈjuːnɪfɔːm; *NAmE* -fɔːrm/ *noun, adj.*

■ ***noun*** **1** 🔑 [C, U] the special set of clothes worn by all members of an organization or a group at work, or by children at school 制服；校服：*a **military/police/nurse's uniform*** 军装；警服；护士制服 ◇ *soldiers **in uniform*** 穿军装的军人 ◇ *The hat is part of the **school uniform**.* 这帽子是校服的一部分。◇ *Do you have to **wear uniform**?* 你非得穿制服不可吗？ **2** [C, usually sing., U] (*NAmE*) (*BrE* **strip**) the clothes worn by the members of a sports team when they are playing （运动队）队服：*a striped baseball uniform* 条纹棒球服 ◇ *the team's **away uniform*** (= that they use when playing games away from home) 该队的客场队服 **3** [sing., U] the type of clothes that a person or group usually wears 清一色服装；统一服装：*my standard teenage uniform of sweatshirt and jeans* 我少年时代标准的衣着：运动衫和牛仔裤

■ ***adj.*** 🔑 not varying; the same in all parts and at all times 一致的；统一的；一律的：*uniform rates of pay* 统一的薪资标准 ◇ *The walls were a uniform grey.* 墙壁一律都是灰色。◇ *Growth has not been uniform across the country.* 全国各地的发展程度不一。◇ *uniform lines of terraced houses* (= they all looked the same) 整齐的一列列排房 ▶ **uni·form·ity** AW /ˌjuːnɪˈfɔːməti/ *noun* [U, sing.]: *They tried to ensure uniformity across the different departments.* 他们努力保证各部门之间的统一。◇ *the drab uniformity of the houses* 这些房屋的千篇一律 **uni·form·ly** AW *adv.*：*The principles were applied uniformly across all the departments.* 这些原则统一适用于所有部门。◇ *The quality is uniformly high.* 质量一律很高。◇ *Pressure must be uniformly distributed over the whole surface.* 压力必须均匀分布于整个表面。

uni·formed /ˈjuːnɪfɔːmd; *NAmE* -fɔːrmd/ *adj.* wearing a uniform 穿制服的：*a uniformed chauffeur* 穿制服的司机

unify AW /ˈjuːnɪfaɪ/ *verb* (**uni·fies**, **uni·fy·ing**, **uni·fied**, **uni·fied**) ~ **sth** to join people, things, parts of a country, etc. together so that they form a single unit 统一；使成一体；使一元化：*The new leader hopes to unify the country.* 新领袖希望把国家统一起来。◇ *the task of unifying Europe* 统一欧洲的大业 ◇ *a unified transport system* 统一的运输体系 ▶ **uni·fi·ca·tion** AW /ˌjuːnɪfɪˈkeɪʃn/ *noun* [U]: *the unification of Germany* 德国的统一

uni·lat·eral /ˌjuːnɪˈlætrəl/ *adj.* done by one member of a group or an organization without the agreement of the other members 单方的：*a unilateral decision* 单方面的决定 ◇ *a unilateral declaration of independence* 单方面宣布独立 ◇ *They were forced to take unilateral action.* 他们被迫采取单方面行动。◇ *They had campaigned vigorously for **unilateral nuclear disarmament*** (= when one country gets rid of its nuclear weapons without waiting for other countries to do the same). 他们曾致力于单方面裁减核武器运动。➲ COMPARE BILATERAL, MULTILATERAL, TRILATERAL ▶ **uni·lat·eral·ly** /-rəli/ *adv.*

uni·lat·eral·ism /ˌjuːnɪˈlætrəlɪzəm/ *noun* [U] belief in or support of unilateral action, especially the policy of getting rid of nuclear weapons without waiting for other countries to do the same 单边主义（信仰和支持单方面行动，尤指单方面销毁核武器的政策） ▶ **uni·lat·eral·ist** *noun*：*the defeat of the unilateralists on nuclear disarmament* 核武器裁军单边主义者的失败 **uni·lat·eral·ist** *adj.*：*unilateralist defence policy* 单边主义防御政策

un·imagin·able /ˌʌnɪˈmædʒɪnəbl/ *adj.* (*formal*) impossible to think of or to believe exists; impossible to imagine 难以置信的；不可想象的：*unimaginable wealth* 难以想象的财富 ◇ *This level of success would have been unimaginable just last year.* 如此成就在去年都是不敢想象的。OPP **imaginable** ▶ **un·imagin·ably** *adv.*

un·imagina·tive /ˌʌnɪˈmædʒɪnətɪv/ *adj.* lacking in original or new ideas 无创意的；缺乏想象力的 SYN **dull**：*an unimaginative solution to a problem* 毫无创意的解决方法 ◇ *a boring unimaginative man* 一个乏味、没有想象力的男人 OPP **imaginative**

un·im·paired /ˌʌnɪmˈpeəd; *NAmE* -ˈperd/ *adj.* (*formal*) not damaged or spoiled 未被损坏的；未毁坏的：*Although he's ninety, his mental faculties remain unimpaired.* 他虽年届九旬，但头脑仍然清晰。OPP **impaired**

un·im·peach·able /ˌʌnɪmˈpiːtʃəbl/ *adj.* (*formal, approving*) that you cannot doubt or question 不容置疑的；无可指摘的；无可怀疑的：*evidence from an unimpeachable source* 来源可靠的证据

un·im·peded /ˌʌnɪmˈpiːdɪd/ *adj.* (*formal*) with nothing blocking or stopping sb/sth 无障碍的；无阻挡的：*an unimpeded view of the bay* 一览无余的海湾风光 ◇ *free and unimpeded trade* 自由顺畅的贸易

un·im·port·ant 🔑 /ˌʌnɪmˈpɔːtnt; *NAmE* -ˈpɔːrtnt/ *adj.* not important 不重要的；次要的；无足轻重的：*unimportant details* 细枝末节 ◇ ***relatively/comparatively unimportant*** 相对 / 比较次要的 ◇ *They dismissed the problem as unimportant.* 他们认为这个问题无关紧要而不予理会。◇ *This consideration was not unimportant.* 这项考虑并非无关紧要。◇ *I was just a young girl from a small town and I felt very unimportant.* 当时我只是个从小镇出来的小女孩，自觉十分渺小。▶ **un·im·port·ance** *noun* [U]

un·im·pressed /ˌʌnɪmˈprest/ *adj.* ~ (**by/with sb/sth**) not thinking that sb/sth is particularly good, interesting, etc.; not impressed by sb/sth 印象平平的；无深刻印象的

un·im·pres·sive /ˌʌnɪmˈpresɪv/ *adj.* ordinary; not special in any way 普通的；平庸的；毫无特色的：*His academic record was unimpressive.* 他的学业成绩平平。OPP **impressive**

un·inflect·ed /ˌʌnɪnˈflektɪd/ *adj.* (*linguistics* 语言) (of a word or language 词或语言) not changing its form to show different functions in grammar 无屈折变化的；无屈折的

un·in·forma·tive /ˌʌnɪnˈfɔːmətɪv; *NAmE* -ˈfɔːrm-/ *adj.* not giving enough information 不详细的；信息不足的：*The reports of the explosion were brief and uninformative.* 有关爆炸事件的报道很简略，未及详情。OPP **informative**

un·in·formed /ˌʌnɪnˈfɔːmd; *NAmE* -ˈfɔːrmd/ *adj.* having or showing a lack of knowledge or information about sth 知识（或信息）贫乏的；蒙昧的；无知的：*an **uninformed comment/criticism*** 无知的话语 / 批评 ◇ *The public is generally uninformed about these diseases.* 大众对这些疾病普遍知之甚少。OPP **informed**

U

un·in·hab·it·able /ˌʌnɪnˈhæbɪtəbl/ *adj.* not fit to live in; impossible to live in 不宜居住的；无法居住的：*The building was totally uninhabitable.* 这栋大楼根本没法住人。**OPP** **habitable**

un·in·hab·it·ed /ˌʌnɪnˈhæbɪtɪd/ *adj.* with no people living there; not INHABITED 无人居住的；无人烟的；荒凉的：*an uninhabited island* 荒岛

un·in·hib·it·ed /ˌʌnɪnˈhɪbɪtɪd/ *adj.* behaving or expressing yourself freely without worrying about what other people think 纵情的；无拘无束的；随心所欲的 **SYN** **unrestrained**：*uninhibited dancing* 纵情的舞蹈 **OPP** **inhibited**

the un·initi·ated /ˌʌnɪˈnɪʃieɪtɪd/ *noun* [pl.] people who have no special knowledge or experience of sth 无专门知识（或经验）的人；门外汉；外行：*To the uninitiated the system seems too complicated.* 对外行而言，这个系统似乎过于复杂。▶ **un·initi·ated** *adj.*

un·in·jured **AW** /ʌnˈɪndʒəd; *NAmE* -dʒərd/ *adj.* [not usually before noun] not hurt or injured in any way 安然无恙；毫无损伤 **SYN** **unhurt**：*They escaped from the crash uninjured.* 他们安然逃过了撞车事故。

un·in·spired /ˌʌnɪnˈspaɪəd; *NAmE* -ˈspaɪərd/ *adj.* not original or exciting 无创意的；不激励人心的；乏味的 **SYN** **dull** **OPP** **inspired**

un·in·spir·ing /ˌʌnɪnˈspaɪərɪŋ/ *adj.* not making people interested or excited不吸引人的；不令人鼓舞的：*The view from the window was uninspiring.* 窗外的景色平凡无奇。**OPP** **inspiring**

un·in·stall /ˌʌnɪnˈstɔːl/ *verb* ~ **sth** (*computing* 计) to remove a program from a computer 卸载（程序）：*Uninstall any programs that you no longer need.* 将不再需要的程序全部卸载。

un·in·sur·able /ˌʌnɪnˈʃʊərəbl; -ˈʃɔːrə-; *NAmE* -ˈʃʊrə-/ *adj.* something that is **uninsurable** cannot be given insurance because it involves too much risk（因风险太大而）不可予以保险的

un·in·sured /ˌʌnɪnˈʃʊəd; -ˈʃɔːd; *NAmE* -ˈʃʊrd/ *adj.* not having insurance; not covered by insurance 未保险的；无保险的：*an uninsured driver* 没有保险的驾驶员 ◇ *an uninsured claim* 未保过险的索赔

un·in·tel·li·gent **AW** /ˌʌnɪnˈtelɪdʒənt/ *adj.* not intelligent 愚笨的；迟钝的；不聪明的：*He was not unintelligent, but he was lazy.* 他并非不聪明，不过就是懒。

un·in·tel·li·gible /ˌʌnɪnˈtelɪdʒəbl/ *adj.* impossible to understand 难以理解的；难懂的 **SYN** **incomprehensible**：*She turned away and muttered something unintelligible.* 她转向一旁，嘴里不知咕哝些什么。◇ ~ **to sb** *A lot of the jargon they use is unintelligible to outsiders.* 他们所用的大量行话是外人听不懂的。**OPP** **intelligible** ▶ **un·in·tel·li·gib·ly** /-əbli/ *adv.*

un·in·tend·ed /ˌʌnɪnˈtendɪd/ *adj.* an **unintended** effect, result or meaning is one that you did not plan or intend to happen 非计划的；无意的；无心的

un·in·ten·tion·al /ˌʌnɪnˈtenʃənl/ *adj.* not done deliberately, but happening by accident 无意的；非故意的；偶然的：*Perhaps I misled you, but it was quite unintentional* (= I did not mean to). 也许我误导了你，但那绝不是有意的。**OPP** **intentional** ▶ **un·in·ten·tion·al·ly** /-ʃənəli/ *adv.*：*They had unintentionally provided wrong information.* 他们无意中提供了错误的信息。

un·inter·est·ed /ʌnˈɪntrəstɪd; -trest-/ *adj.* ~ (**in sb/sth**) not interested; not wanting to know about sb/sth 不感兴趣的；冷淡的；漠不关心的：*He was totally uninterested in sport.* 他对体育运动毫无兴趣。◇ *She seemed cold and uninterested.* 她似乎很冷漠且不感兴趣。➲ NOTE AT INTERESTED

un·inter·est·ing /ʌnˈɪntrəstɪŋ; -trest-/ *adj.* not attracting your attention or interest; not interesting 不吸引人的；无趣的；无聊的 ➲ NOTE AT INTERESTED

un·inter·rupt·ed /ˌʌnˌɪntəˈrʌptɪd/ *adj.* not stopped or blocked by anything; continuous and not interrupted 不受阻挡的；不间断的；持续不断的：*We had an uninterrupted view of the stage.* 我们能清楚地看见舞台。◇ *eight hours of uninterrupted sleep* 八个小时未受干扰的睡眠 ◇ *We managed to eat our meal uninterrupted by phone calls.* 我们总算吃了一顿没有电话打搅的安生饭。

un·in·vited /ˌʌnɪnˈvaɪtɪd/ *adj.* doing sth or going somewhere when you have not been asked or invited to, especially when sb does not want you to 未经要求的；未获邀请的；不速而至的：*uninvited guests at a party* 聚会上的不速之客 ◇ *He turned up uninvited.* 他不请自到了。

un·in·vit·ing /ˌʌnɪnˈvaɪtɪŋ/ *adj.* not attractive or pleasant 无吸引力的；不诱人的：*The water looked cold and uninviting.* 这水看上去凉冰冰的，让人不想下去。**OPP** **inviting**

un·in·volved **AW** /ˌʌnɪnˈvɒlvd; *NAmE* -ˈvɑːlvd/ *adj.* ~ (**in/with sth**) not taking part in sth; not connected with sb/sth, especially on an emotional level（尤指感情方面）不投入的，不相关的：*My mum was distant and cold and very uninvolved in my life.* 我妈妈疏远冷漠，对我的生活全不过问。**OPP** **involved**

union /ˈjuːniən/ *noun* **1** (*also* ˌ**trade** ˈ**union**) (*BrE also* ˌ**trades** ˈ**union**) (*NAmE also* ˈ**labor union**) [C] an organization of workers, usually in a particular industry, that exists to protect their interests, improve conditions of work, etc. 工会：***I've joined the union.*** 我已经加入工会。◇ *a* ***union member*** 工会会员

> **WORDFINDER** 联想词：ballot, closed shop, collective bargaining, industrial action, labour, picket, **protest**, representative, strike

2 [C] an association or a club for people or organizations with the same interest 协会；联合会；会社；俱乐部：*the Scottish Rugby Union* 苏格兰橄榄球协会 ➲ SEE ALSO STUDENTS' UNION (2) **3** [C] a group of states or countries that have the same central government or that agree to work together 同盟；联盟；联邦：*the former Soviet Union* 前苏维埃联邦 ◇ *the European Union* 欧洲联盟 **4 Union** [sing.] the US (used especially at the time of the Civil War)（尤指内战时期的）美利坚合众国，美国：*the Union and the Confederacy* 合众国与南部邦联 ◇ *the State of the Union address by the President* 美国总统向国会发表的国情咨文 **5** [U, sing.] the act of joining two or more things together; the state of being joined together; the act of two people joining together 联合；结合；合并：*a summit to discuss economic and monetary union* 商讨经济和货币联盟的高峰会议 ◇ *Northern Ireland's union with Britain* 北爱尔兰同英国的联合 ◇ *sexual union* 性结合 **6** [C] (*old-fashioned*) a marriage 结为夫妻；婚姻：*Their union was blessed with six children.* 他们婚后幸得六个儿女。

union·ist /ˈjuːniənɪst/ *noun* **1** = TRADE UNIONIST **2 Union·ist** a person who believes that Northern Ireland should stay part of the United Kingdom 统一主义者，统一派（主张北爱尔兰继续为英国的一部分）**3 Union·ist** a supporter of the Union during the Civil War in the US（美国内战时期的）合众国拥护者，合众派成员 ▶ **union·ism** /ˈjuːniənɪzəm/ *noun* [U]

union·ize (*BrE also* **-ise**) /ˈjuːniənaɪz/ *verb* [T, I] ~ (**sth**) to organize people to become members of a trade/labor union; to become a member of a trade/labor union 组织（或成立）工会；加入工会：*a unionized workforce* 有工会组织的劳动力 ◇ *They were forbidden to unionize.* 他们被禁止成立工会。▶ **union·iza·tion**, **-isa·tion** /ˌjuːniənaɪˈzeɪʃn; *NAmE* -nəˈz-/ *noun* [U]

the ˌ**Union** ˈ**Jack** *noun* [sing.] the name for the national flag of the United Kingdom 联合王国国旗；英国国旗

unique **AW** /juˈniːk/ *adj.* **1** being the only one of its kind 唯一的；独一无二的：*Everyone's fingerprints are unique.* 每个人的指纹都是独一无二的。**HELP** You can use **absolutely**, **totally** or **almost** with **unique** in this meaning. 作此义时可用 absolutely、totally 或 almost 修饰 unique。**2** very special or unusual 独特的；罕见的：*a unique talent* 奇才 ◇ *The preview offers a unique opportunity to see the show without the crowds.* 预展提供了看展览但不

挨挤的难得机会。◇ *The deal will put the company in a unique position to export goods to Eastern Europe.* 这项协议给予这家公司向东欧输出商品的特殊地位。**HELP** You can use **more**, **very**, etc. with **unique** in this meaning. 作此义时可用 more、very 等修饰 unique。**3** ~ **(to sb/sth)** belonging to or connected with one particular person, place or thing（某人、地或事物）独具的，特有的：*an atmosphere that is unique to New York* 纽约所独具的气氛 ◇ *The koala is unique to Australia.* 树袋熊是澳大利亚独有的。▶ **unique·ly** AW *adv.*：*Her past experience made her uniquely suited to lead the campaign.* 她以往的经历使她格外适合领导这场运动。◇ *The UK, uniquely, has not had to face the problem of mass unemployment.* 唯有英国无须面对大量失业的问题。◇ *He was a uniquely gifted teacher.* 他是个天赋异禀的天才教师。**unique·ness** AW *noun* [U]：*The author stresses the uniqueness of the individual.* 这位作者强调个人的独特性。

uni·sex /ˈjuːnɪseks/ *adj.* intended for or used by both men and women 男女皆宜的；不分性别的：*a unisex hair salon* 男女美发店 ◇ *unisex jeans* 男女都能穿的牛仔裤

uni·son /ˈjuːnɪsn/ *noun*

IDM **in ˈunison (with sb/sth)** **1** if people do or say sth **in unison**, they all do it at the same time（做事、说话）一起，一齐 **2** if people or organizations are working **in unison**, they are working together, because they agree with each other 一致行动；协调地 **3** (*music* 音) if singers or musicians sing or play **in unison**, they sing or play notes at the same PITCH or at one or more OCTAVES apart（歌唱或演奏）齐声，同音，同度

unit /ˈjuːnɪt/ *noun*
- **SINGLE THING** 单个事物 **1** a single thing, person or group that is complete by itself but can also form part of sth larger 单独的事物（或人、群体）；单位；单元：*The cell is the unit of which all living organisms are composed.* 细胞是构成一切生物的单位。◇ *The* ***basic unit*** *of society is the family.* 社会的基本单位是家庭。**2** (*business* 商) a single item of the type of product that a company sells 一件（商品）；单位：*The game's selling price was $15 per unit.* 这游戏的售价为每套 15 美元。◇ *What's the* ***unit cost****?* 单位成本是多少钱？
- **GROUP OF PEOPLE** 群体 **3** a group of people who work or live together, especially for a particular purpose 班组；小队：***army/military/police units*** 陆军 / 军事 / 警察分队 ◇ *Medical units were operating in the disaster area.* 医疗小组正在灾区工作。
- **IN HOSPITAL** 医院 **4** a department, especially in a hospital, that provides a particular type of care or treatment 科；病区：*the intensive care unit* 重症监护室 ◇ *a maternity unit* 妇产科
- **FURNITURE** 家具 **5** a piece of furniture, especially a cupboard, that fits with and matches others of the same type 配套家具组件；（尤指）成套家具中的柜子：*a fitted kitchen with white units* 用白色组件的厨房 ◇ ***floor/wall units*** 地板 / 墙壁组合件 ◇ ***bedroom/kitchen/storage units*** 卧室 / 厨房 / 贮藏室组合设备 ➲ VISUAL VOCAB PAGE V26
- **MEASUREMENT** 计量 **6** ~ **(of sth)** a fixed quantity, etc. that is used as a standard measurement 单位；单元：*a* ***unit of time/length/weight*** 时间 / 长度 / 重量单位 ◇ *a* ***unit of currency****, such as the euro or the dollar* 货币单位，如欧元或美元 ◇ *Women are advised not to drink more than fourteen units of alcohol per week.* 建议妇女每周饮酒不超过十四个酒精单位。
- **SMALL MACHINE** 小机器 **7** a small machine that has a particular purpose or is part of a larger machine 装置；机件；部件；元件：*a waste disposal unit* 废物销毁器 ◇ *the central processing unit of a computer* 电脑的中央处理器
- **IN TEXTBOOK** 课本 **8** one of the parts into which a TEXTBOOK or a series of lessons is divided 单元；课：*The present perfect is covered in Unit 8.* 现在完成时在第 8 单元讲解。
- **FLAT/APARTMENT/HOUSE** 公寓；住宅 **9** (*also* **ˈhome unit**) (*AustralE, NZE*) a single flat/apartment or house in a building or group of buildings containing a number of them（一）套；单元
- **NUMBER** 数字 **10** any whole number from 0 to 9 个位数：*a column for the tens and a column for the units* 十位数栏和个位数栏

Uni·tar·ian /ˌjuːnɪˈteəriən; *NAmE* -ˈter-/ *noun* a member of a Christian Church that does not believe in the TRINITY and has no formal teachings 上帝一位论派，一位论派（属于不信仰三位一体的基督教派别）▶ **Uni·tar·ian** *adj.* **Uni·tar·ian·ism** /-ɪzəm/ *noun* [U]

uni·tary /ˈjuːnətri; *NAmE* -teri/ *adj.* **1** (*specialist*) (of a country or an organization 国家或机构) consisting of a number of areas or groups that are joined together and are controlled by one government or group 集中的；统一的；中央集权制的：*a single unitary state* 单一中央集权制国家 ◇ (*BrE*) ***a unitary authority*** (= a type of local council, introduced in some areas from 1995 to replace existing local governments which consisted of county and district councils) 单一自治体，自治体监察委员会（1995 年起在某些地区实行的地方理事会，代替原有的郡、区政府）**2** (*formal*) single; forming one unit 单一的；形成单一个体的

unite /juˈnaɪt/ *verb* **1** [I] to join together with other people in order to do sth as a group（为某事）联合，联手，团结：**~ in sth** *Local resident groups have* ***united in opposition*** *to the plan.* 当地居民团体已联合起来反对这项计划。◇ **~ in doing sth** *We will unite in fighting crime.* 我们将联手打击犯罪。◇ **~ (behind/against sb/sth)** *Will they unite behind the new leader?* 他们会联手支持新领导人吗？◇ *Nationalist parties united to oppose the government's plans.* 民族主义党派联合反对政府的计划。**2** [T, I] to make people or things join together to form a unit; to join together（与某人或集体）联结，联合；统一：**~ (sb/sth)** *A special bond unites our two countries.* 一种特殊的纽带把我们两国联结起来。◇ *His aim was to unite Italy.* 他的目标是统一意大利。◇ *The two countries united in 1887.* 两国于 1887 年合并。◇ **~ (sb/sth) (with sb/sth)** *She unites keen business skills with a charming personality.* 她兼具敏锐的商业技能和个人魅力。

united /juˈnaɪtɪd/ *adj.* **1** (of countries 国家) joined together as a political unit or by shared aims 联合的；统一的：*the United States of America* 美利坚合众国 ◇ *efforts to build a united Europe* 建立统一欧洲的努力 **2** (of people or groups 人或群体) in agreement and working together 和谐的；一致的；团结的：*We need to become a more united team.* 我们要成为一支更加团结的队伍。◇ *They are united in their opposition to the plan.* 他们一致反对这个计划。◇ *We should present* ***a united front*** (= an appearance of being in agreement with each other). 我们要表现得团结一致。**3** used in the names of some teams and companies（用于团队和公司名称）：*Manchester United* 曼彻斯特联队 ◇ *United Biscuits* 联合饼干公司

the Uˌnited ˈFree Church *noun* [sing.] a church formed in Scotland in 1900 from the union of the Free Church of Scotland and the United Presbyterian Church（苏格兰）联合自由长老会（1900 年由苏格兰自由长老会和联合长老会联合于苏格兰成立）

the Uˌnited ˈKingdom *noun* [sing.] (*abbr.* **(the) UK**) England, Scotland, Wales and Northern Ireland (considered as a political unit) 英国；联合王国

the Uˌnited ˈNations *noun* [sing.+sing./pl. v.] (*abbr.* **(the) UN**) an association of many countries which aims to improve economic and social conditions and to solve political problems in the world in a peaceful way 联合国

the ˌUnited Nations Seˈcurity Council *noun* = SECURITY COUNCIL

the Uˌnited ˈStates (of Aˈmerica) *noun* (*abbr.* **(the) US, (the) USA**) a large country in N America consisting of 50 states and the District of Columbia 美国；美利坚合众国 **HELP** Although **United States** is sometimes found with a plural verb after it, this is quite rare and it is much more common to use a singular verb. * United States 后有时用复数动词，但很罕见，用单数动词要常见得多。➲ NOTE AT AMERICAN

U

ˌunit ˈtrust (*BrE*) (*NAmE* **ˈmutual fund**) *noun* a company that offers a service to people by investing their money in various different businesses 单位信托投资公司，共同基金（代客户进行不同组合的投资）

unity /ˈjuːnəti/ *noun* (*pl.* **-ies**) **1** [U, sing.] the state of being in agreement and working together; the state of being joined together to form one unit 团结一致；联合；统一：*European unity* 欧洲的统一 ◇ *a plea for unity within the party* 要求党内团结的呼吁 ◇ *unity of purpose* 目标一致 OPP **disunity** **2** [U] (in art, etc. 艺术等) the state of looking or being complete in a natural and pleasing way 完整；完美；和谐；协调：*The design lacks unity.* 这项设计整体不够协调。 **3** [C] (in literature and theatre 文学、戏剧) any of the principles of CLASSICAL or NEOCLASSICAL theatre that restrict the action of a play to a single story, day and place（情节、时间和地点的）统一性，一致性；三一律：*the unities of action, time and place* 要求情节、时间和地点一致的三一律 **4** [sing.] (*formal*) a single thing that may consist of a number of different parts 统一体；联合体；整体：*If society is to exist as a unity, its members must have shared values.* 社会若要成为一个统一的群体，它的成员就必须有共同的价值观。 **5** [U] (*mathematics* 数) the number one（数目或数字）一

Univ. *abbr.* (in writing 书写形式) University 大学

uni·ver·sal /ˌjuːnɪˈvɜːsl; *NAmE* -ˈvɜːrsl/ *adj.* **1** done by or involving all the people in the world or in a particular group 普遍的；全体的；全世界的；共同的：*Such problems are a universal feature of old age.* 这类问题是老年人的通病。 ◇ *Agreement on this issue is almost universal.* 这个问题几乎取得全体一致的意见。 ◇ ***universal suffrage*** (= the right of all the people in a country to vote) 普选权 **2** true or right at all times and in all places 普遍存在的；广泛适用的：*universal facts about human nature* 人性的普遍现象 ▸ **uni·ver·sal·ity** /ˌjuːnɪvɜːˈsæləti; *NAmE* -vɜːrˈs-/ *noun*：*the universality of religious experience* 宗教行为的普遍性

ˌUniˌversal Coˌordinated ˈTime *noun* = UTC

ˌuniˌversal ˈgrammar *noun* [U, C] (*linguistics* 语言) the set of rules that is thought to be able to describe all languages 普遍语法（据信能够描述所有语言的一系列规则）

ˌuniˌversal ˈindicator *noun* (*chemistry* 化) a substance that changes colour when another substance touches it, indicating whether it is an acid or an ALKALI 通用指示剂（通过颜色变化显示物质的酸碱性）

U

uni·ver·sal·ly /ˌjuːnɪˈvɜːsəli; *NAmE* -ˈvɜːrs-/ *adv.* **1** by everyone 全体地；一致地；共同地：*to be universally accepted* 得到普遍接受 **2** everywhere or in every situation 到处；随时随地；在各种情况下：*This treatment is not universally available.* 这种疗法不是到处都有的。 ◇ *The theory does not apply universally.* 这个理论并非放之四海而皆准。

ˌUniˌversal ˌTime Coˈordinated *noun* = UTC

uni·verse 🔑 /ˈjuːnɪvɜːs; *NAmE* -vɜːrs/ *noun* **1** 🔑 **the universe** [sing.] the whole of space and everything in it, including the earth, the planets and the stars 宇宙；天地万物；万象：*theories of how the universe began* 关于宇宙形成的各种理论 ➲ WORDFINDER NOTE AT SUN

> **WORDFINDER** 联想词： asteroid, astronomy, comet, constellation, cosmic, galaxy, meteorite, orbit, **space**

2 [C] a system of stars, planets, etc. in space outside our own（已知宇宙以外的）宇宙：*The idea of a parallel universe is hard to grasp.* 平行宇宙的概念是很难理解的。 ◇ (*figurative*) *He lives in a little universe of his own.* 他生活在自己的小天地里。 **3** [sing.] a particular area of experience or activity（某种）经验（或活动）领域；体系：*the moral universe* 道德体系

uni·ver·sity 🔑 /ˌjuːnɪˈvɜːsəti; *NAmE* -ˈvɜːrs-/ *noun* [C, U] (*pl.* **-ies**) (*abbr.* **Univ.**) an institution at the highest level of education where you can study for a degree or do research（综合性）大学；高等学府：*Is there a university in this town?* 这座城市有没有大学？ ◇ *Ohio State University* 俄亥俄州立大学 ◇ *the University of York* 约克大学 ◇ *York University* 约克大学 ◇ (*BrE*) *Both their children are* ***at university.*** 他们的两个孩子都在上大学。 ◇ (*BrE*) *He's hoping* ***to go to university*** *next year.* 他希望明年能上大学。 ◇ *a* ***university course/degree/lecturer*** 大学课程 / 学位 / 讲师 ➲ COLLOCATIONS AT EDUCATION ➲ NOTE AT COLLEGE ➲ SEE ALSO STATE UNIVERSITY

> **WORDFINDER** 联想词： degree, dissertation, **education**, graduate, hall of residence, lecture, major, seminar, tutorial

IDM **the university of ˈlife** (*informal*) the experience of life thought of as giving sb an education, instead of the person gaining formal qualifications 人生大学（生活体验，相对于正式学历）：*a degree from the university of life* 人生大学学位

Unix™ /ˈjuːnɪks/ *noun* [U] (*computing* 计) an OPERATING SYSTEM which can be used by many people at the same time * Unix 操作系统（可供多人同时使用）

un·just /ˌʌnˈdʒʌst/ *adj.* not deserved or fair 不公平的；不公正的；非正义的：*an unjust law* 不公正的法律 OPP **just** ▸ **un·just·ly** *adv.*：*She felt that she had been unjustly treated.* 她觉得自己受到了不公平的待遇。

un·jus·ti·fi·able /ʌnˈdʒʌstɪfaɪəbl/ *adj.* (of an action 行动) impossible to excuse or accept because there is no good reason for it 不可原谅的；无法接受的；无正当理由的 SYN **indefensible**：*an unjustifiable delay* 无理的拖延 OPP **justifiable** ▸ **un·jus·ti·fi·ably** /-əbli/ *adv.*

un·jus·ti·fied AW /ʌnˈdʒʌstɪfaɪd/ *adj.* not fair or necessary 不公正的；不正当的；不必要的 SYN **unwarranted**：*The criticism was wholly unjustified.* 这样的批评完全是不公平的。 OPP **justified**

un·kempt /ˌʌnˈkempt/ *adj.* (*formal*) (especially of sb's hair or general appearance 尤指头发或外貌) not well cared for; not neat or tidy 不整洁的；凌乱的；不修边幅的 SYN **dishevelled**：*greasy, unkempt hair* 油乎乎乱蓬蓬的头发

un·kind 🔑 /ˌʌnˈkaɪnd/ *adj.* ~ **(to sb/sth)** **(to do sth)** unpleasant or unfriendly; slightly cruel 不友善的；不亲切的；不客气的；刻薄的：*an unkind remark* 不友善的话 ◇ *He was never actually unkind to them.* 其实他从没有对他们不好。 ◇ *It would be unkind to go without him.* 甩掉他那就太不够朋友了。 OPP **kind** ▸ **un·kind·ly** *adv.*：*'That's your problem,' she remarked unkindly.* "那是你的问题。" 她刻薄地说。 **un·kind·ness** *noun* [U]

un·know·able /ʌnˈnəʊəbl; *NAmE* -ˈnoʊ-/ *adj.* (*formal*) that cannot be known 无法知道的；不可知的：*a distant, unknowable divine power* 遥远不可知的神力

un·know·ing /ʌnˈnəʊɪŋ; *NAmE* -ˈnoʊ-/ *adj.* [usually before noun] (*formal*) not aware of what you are doing or what is happening 没意识到的；未察觉的；无知的：*He was the unknowing cause of all the misunderstanding.* 他无意中引起了这一切误会。 ➲ COMPARE KNOWING ▸ **un·know·ing·ly** *adv.*：*She had unknowingly broken the rules.* 她无意中犯了规。

un·known 🔑 /ˌʌnˈnəʊn; *NAmE* -ˈnoʊn/ *adj.*, *noun*

■ ***adj.*** **1** 🔑 ~ (to sb) not known or identified 未知的；不详的；未被确认的：*a species of insect previously unknown to science* 科学上以前尚未了解的一种昆虫 ◇ *He was trying,* ***for some unknown reason,*** *to count the stars.* 不知何故，他试图数星星。 ◇ *The man's identity remains unknown.* 这名男子的身份还是个谜。 **2** 🔑 (of people 人) not famous or well known 不出名的；无名的：*an unknown actor* 没有名气的演员 ◇ *The author is virtually unknown outside Poland.* 在波兰以外，这位作者实际上鲜为人知。 **3** 🔑 never happening or existing 从未发生的；从不存在的：*The disease is as yet unknown in Europe* (= there have been no cases there). 这种疾病至今尚未在欧洲出现过。 ◇ ***It was not unknown for*** *people to have to wait several hours* (= it happened sometimes). 人们得等几个小时的事时有发生。

IDM **an ˌunknown ˈquantity** a person or thing whose qualities or abilities are not yet known 未知数（指尚不清楚，有待证实的人或事物） **unknown to sb** without the person mentioned being aware of it …尚不知道；把…

蒙在鼓里：*Unknown to me, he had already signed the agreement.* 他背着我已签了协议。

■ ***noun*** **1 the unknown** [sing.] places or things that are not known about 未知的地方（或事物）：*a journey into the unknown* 探险之旅 ◇ *a fear of the unknown* 对未知事物的恐惧 **2** [C] a person who is not well known 无名者；不出名的人：*A young unknown played the leading role.* 演主角的是一个名不见经传的年轻人。**3** [C] a fact or an influence that is not known 不明的情况；未知的因素：*There are so many unknowns in the proposal.* 这项提案中的未知数太多了。**4** [C] (*mathematics* 数) a quantity that does not have a known value 未知数；未知量：*X and Y in the equation are both unknowns.* 等式中的 X 和 Y 都是未知数。

the ˌUnknown ˈSoldier *noun* [sing.] a soldier who has been killed in a war, whose body has not been identified, and who is buried in special ceremony. The **Unknown Soldier** is a symbol for all the soldiers killed in a particular war or in wars generally. 无名战士（在特别葬礼上埋葬的阵亡无名军人，象征某场或所有战争中的阵亡将士）：*the tomb of the Unknown Soldier* 无名战士墓

un·lace /ʌnˈleɪs/ *verb* **~ sth** to undo the LACES of shoes, clothes, etc. 解开（鞋子、衣服等）的带子 **OPP lace**

un·laden /ˌʌnˈleɪdn/ *adj.* (*specialist*) (of a vehicle 车辆等) not loaded 未负载的；空车的：*a vehicle with an unladen weight of 3 000 kg* 净重 3 吨的汽车 ➲ COMPARE LADEN

un·law·ful /ʌnˈlɔːfl/ *adj.* (*formal*) not allowed by the law 不合法的；非法的；违法的 **SYN illegal OPP lawful** ▸ **un·law·ful·ly** /-fəli/ *adv.*

unˌlawful ˈkilling *noun* (*law* 律) a murder or other killing which is considered a crime, for example when a person dies because sb is careless 非法杀人（包括因疏忽导致他人死亡）：*The two police officers were accused of unlawful killing.* 这两名警员被控非法杀人。

un·lead·ed /ˌʌnˈledɪd/ *adj.* (of petrol/gas 汽油) not containing LEAD² (1) and therefore less harmful to the environment 无铅的；不含铅的 **OPP leaded** ▸ **un·lead·ed** *noun* [U]：*Unleaded is cheaper than diesel.* 无铅汽油比柴油便宜。

un·learn /ˌʌnˈlɜːn; *NAmE* ˌʌnˈlɜːrn/ *verb* **~ sth** to deliberately forget sth that you have learned, especially sth bad or wrong 故意忘却（尤指错事或坏事）；抛弃：*You'll have to unlearn all the bad habits you learned with your last piano teacher.* 你必须丢掉你的前任钢琴老师所教的一切坏习惯。

un·leash /ʌnˈliːʃ/ *verb* **~ sth (on/upon sb/sth)** to suddenly let a strong force, emotion, etc. be felt or have an effect 发泄；突然释放；使爆发：*The government's proposals unleashed a storm of protest in the press.* 政府的提案引发了新闻界的抗议浪潮。

un·leav·ened /ˌʌnˈlevnd/ *adj.* (of bread 面包) made without any YEAST and therefore flat 未发酵的；不加酵母的；死面的 ➲ SEE ALSO LEAVEN *v.*

un·less /ənˈles/ *conj.* **1** used to say that sth can only happen or be true in a particular situation 除非；除非在…情况下：*You won't get paid for time off unless you have a doctor's note.* 除非你有医生证明，否则你不上班便拿不到工资。◇ *I won't tell them—not unless you say I can.* 我绝不告诉他们，除非你允许。◇ *Unless I'm mistaken, she was back at work yesterday.* 除非是我记错了，她是昨天回来上班的。◇ *He hasn't got any hobbies—unless you call watching TV a hobby.* 他没有什么爱好，除非你把看电视也称作爱好。**2** used to give the only situation in which sth will not happen or be true 若非；如果不：*I sleep with the window open unless it's really cold.* 天气若不很冷，我总开着窗户睡觉。◇ *Unless something unexpected happens, I'll see you tomorrow.* 如果不出意外，我明天去看你。◇ *Have a cup of tea—unless you'd prefer a cold drink?* 喝杯茶吧，还是你喜欢冷饮？ **HELP Unless** is used to talk about a situation that could happen, or something that could be true, in the future. If you know that something has not happened or that sth is not true, use **if … not**. 指将来可能发生或可能真实的情况用 unless。如果知道没有发生或不真实则用 if … not：*If you weren't always in such a hurry* (= but you are), *your work would be much better.* 你若不是总是那么匆忙完成的话，你的工作质量会好很多。◇ ~~*Your work would be much better unless you were always in such a hurry.*~~

un·let·tered /ˌʌnˈletəd; *NAmE* -tərd/ *adj.* (*formal*) unable to read 不识字的；文盲的

un·licensed AW /ʌnˈlaɪsnst/ *adj.* without a licence 无执照的；无许可证的：*an unlicensed vehicle* 无牌照车辆 **OPP licensed**

un·like /ˌʌnˈlaɪk/ *prep., adj., verb*

■ ***prep.*** **1** different from a particular person or thing 不像；与…不同：*Music is quite unlike any other art form.* 音乐与其他艺术形式迥然不同。◇ *The sound was **not unlike** that of birds singing.* 这声音有点像鸟鸣。**2** used to contrast sb/sth with another person or thing（用于对比）与…不同：*Unlike most systems, this one is very easy to install.* 本系统与多数系统不同，极易安装。➲ LANGUAGE BANK AT CONTRAST **3** not typical of sb/sth 非…的特征：*It's very unlike him to be so late.* 迟到这么久可实在不像他平时的作风。**OPP like**

■ ***adj.*** [not before noun] (of two people or things 两个人或事物) different from each other 不同；不像；相异：*They are both teachers. Otherwise they are quite unlike.* 他们两位都是教师；除此之外他们迥然不同。➲ COMPARE ALIKE *adj.*, LIKE *adj.*

■ ***verb*** [T] (*informal*) **~ sth** to show that you no longer like or agree with sth on a SOCIAL NETWORKING service, news website, BLOG, etc. by pressing a special button（在社交网络、新闻网站、博客等上）对…取消点赞 ➲ COMPARE UNFRIEND

un·like·ly /ʌnˈlaɪkli/ *adj.* (**un·like·lier**, **un·likeli·est**) **HELP more unlikely** and **most unlikely** are the usual forms 常用 more unlikely 和 most unlikely。**1** not likely to happen; not probable 不大可能发生的：**~ (to do sth)** *The project seemed unlikely to succeed.* 这个项目似乎难以成功。◇ **~ (that…)** *It's most* (= very) *unlikely that she'll arrive before seven.* 她几乎不可能在七点前到达。◇ ***In the unlikely event of** a problem arising, please contact the hotel manager.* 万一出现问题，请找旅馆经理。➲ EXPRESS YOURSELF AT LIKELY **2** [only before noun] not the person, thing or place that you would normally think of or expect 非心目中的；意料之外的：*He seems a most unlikely candidate for the job.* 他似乎是最不适合担任这项工作的人选。◇ *They have built hotels in the most unlikely places.* 他们把旅馆建在最冷门的地方。**3** [only before noun] difficult to believe 难以相信的；不能信服的 **SYN implausible**：*She gave me an unlikely explanation for her behaviour.* 她对自己行为的解释很难令我信服。**OPP likely** ▸ **un·like·li·hood** /ʌnˈlaɪklihʊd/ *noun* [U] **un·like·li·ness** /-nəs/ *noun* [U]

un·lim·it·ed /ʌnˈlɪmɪtɪd/ *adj.* as much or as many as is possible; not limited in any way 尽量多的；任意多的；无限制的：*The ticket gives you unlimited travel for seven days.* 凭本车票在七日内可自由乘车不受限制。◇ *The court has the power to impose an unlimited fine for this offence.* 法庭有权对这一违法行为罚款，额度不受限制。◇ *You will be allowed unlimited access to the files.* 你可以无限制使用这些档案。

un·lined /ˌʌnˈlaɪnd/ *adj.* **1** not marked with lines 无线条的；无皱纹的：*unlined paper/skin* 无横格的纸；无皱纹的皮肤 **2** (of a piece of clothing, etc. 衣服等) made without an extra layer of cloth on the inside 无衬里的 **OPP lined**

un·list·ed /ˌʌnˈlɪstɪd/ *adj.* **1** not on a published list, especially of STOCK EXCHANGE prices 未列表公布的；（尤指证券）未挂牌的，未上市的：*an unlisted company* 非上市公司 **2** (of a telephone number 电话号码) not listed in the public telephone book, at the request of the owner of the telephone. The telephone company will not give unlisted numbers to people who ask for them. 未登入电话簿的 ➲ SEE ALSO EX-DIRECTORY

U

unlit /ˌʌnˈlɪt/ *adj.* **1** dark because there are no lights or the lights are not switched on 黑暗的；无灯光的：*an unlit passage* 无灯光的通道 **2** not yet burning 未点燃的：*an unlit cigarette* 未点燃的香烟 **OPP lighted**

un·load /ˌʌnˈləʊd; *NAmE* ˌʌnˈloʊd/ *verb* **1** [T, I] to remove things from a vehicle or ship after it has taken them somewhere（从车、船上）卸，取下：**~ sth from sth** *Everyone helped to unload the luggage from the car.* 大家都帮着从汽车上卸行李。◇ **~ (sth)** *This isn't a suitable place to unload the van.* 这个地方不适宜卸车。◇ *The truck driver was waiting to unload.* 卡车司机在等着卸货。**OPP load** **2** [T] **~ sth** to remove the contents of sth after you have finished using it, especially the bullets from a gun or the film from a camera 拆掉，退出，取出（子弹或胶卷等）**OPP load** **3** [T] **~ sth/sb (on/onto sb)** (*informal*) to pass the responsibility for sb/sth to sb else 推卸（责任）；甩掉（包袱）：*It's his problem, not something he should unload onto you.* 那是他的事，他不该把问题甩给你。**4** [T] **~ sth (on/onto sb/sth)** (*informal*) to get rid of or sell sth, especially sth illegal or of bad quality 脱手，卖掉（尤指非法物品或次品）：*They want to unload their shares at the right price.* 他们想在价格合适的时候卖掉股票。

un·lock /ˌʌnˈlɒk; *NAmE* ˌʌnˈlɑːk/ *verb* **1 ~ sth** to undo the lock of a door, window, etc., using a key（用钥匙）开…的锁：*to unlock the door* 打开门锁 **OPP lock** **2 ~ sth** to discover sth and let it be known 发现；揭示；揭开：*The divers hoped to unlock some of the secrets of the seabed.* 潜水员希望揭开海底的一些秘密。 **3 ~ sth** to enable a mobile/cell phone to use any network rather than only one particular one 解除（手机）的网络锁定：*Have an old phone lying around? Unlock it and keep it as a spare.* 有闲置的旧手机？把它解除网络锁定留作备用吧。

un·locked /ˌʌnˈlɒkt; *NAmE* ˌʌnˈlɑːkt/ *adj.* not locked 未锁的：*Don't leave your desk unlocked.* 请不要忘记锁好办公桌。

unlooked-for /ʌnˈlʊkt fɔː(r)/ *adj.* (*formal*) not expected 没想到的；不期的；意外的：*unlooked-for developments* 意料之外的发展

un·loose /ˌʌnˈluːs/ (*also* **un·loosen** /ʌnˈluːsn/) *verb* **~ sth** (*old-fashioned* or *formal*) to make sth loose 松开；解开：*He unloosed his tie.* 他松开了领带。

un·loved /ˌʌnˈlʌvd/ *adj.* (*formal*) not loved by anyone 无人喜欢（或疼爱）的：*unloved children* 无人疼爱的孩子

un·love·ly /ˌʌnˈlʌvli/ *adj.* (*formal*) not attractive 不好看的；不动人的；不美观的：*an unlovely building* 不美观的建筑物

U

un·luck·ily /ʌnˈlʌkɪli/ *adv.* unfortunately; as a result of bad luck 不幸地；遗憾地；倒霉地：*He was injured in the first game and unluckily missed the final.* 他第一场比赛就受了伤，遗憾地未能参加决赛。**OPP luckily**

un·lucky /ʌnˈlʌki/ *adj.* (**un·luck·ier**, **un·lucki·est**) **HELP** You can also use **more unlucky** and **most unlucky**. 亦可用 more unlucky 和 most unlucky。**1 ~ (to do sth)** having bad luck or happening because of bad luck; not lucky 不幸的；倒霉的；不顺利的 **SYN unfortunate**：*He was very unlucky not to win.* 他不幸输了。◇ *By some unlucky chance, her name was left off the list.* 倒霉的是，名单上没有她的名字。**2 ~ (to do sth)** causing bad luck 不吉利的；晦气的：*Some people think it's unlucky to walk under a ladder.* 有些人认为从梯子下面走过不吉利。◇ *Thirteen is often considered an unlucky number.* 十三常被认为是不吉利的数字。**OPP lucky**

un·made /ˌʌnˈmeɪd/ *adj.* **1** an **unmade** bed is not ready for sleeping in because the sheets, etc. have not been arranged neatly（床）未铺好的 **2** (*BrE*) an **unmade** road does not have a hard smooth surface（道路）未铺路面的

un·man·age·able /ʌnˈmænɪdʒəbl/ *adj.* difficult or impossible to control or deal with 难以控制（或处理）的；无法对付的 **OPP manageable**

un·man·ly /ʌnˈmænli/ *adj.* (*formal*) not having the qualities that are admired or expected in a man 非男子汉的；无男子气概的 **OPP manly**

un·manned /ˌʌnˈmænd/ *adj.* if a machine, a vehicle, a place or an activity is **unmanned**, it does not have or need a person to control or operate it 无（需）人操作的；无（需）人控制的；自控的：*an unmanned spacecraft* 无人驾驶宇宙飞船 ◇ *an unmanned Mars mission* 无人火星探测 **OPP manned**

un·man·ner·ly /ʌnˈmænəli; *NAmE* -nərli/ *adj.* (*formal*) not having or showing good manners; not polite 没有礼貌的；没教养的

un·marked /ʌnˈmɑːkt; *NAmE* ʌnˈmɑːrkt/ *adj.* **1** without a sign or words to show what or where sth is 无标志的；无标记的；无记号的：*an unmarked police car* 无标识的警车 ◇ *He was buried in an unmarked grave.* 他埋在一处无名冢下。➲ COMPARE MARKED (1) **2** (*especially BrE*) (of a player in a team game, especially football (SOCCER) 比赛队员，尤指足球运动员) with no player from the other team staying close to prevent them from getting the ball 无人盯防的：*He headed the ball to the unmarked Gray.* 他把球顶给了无人盯防的格雷。**3** (*linguistics* 语言) (of a word or form of a word 词或词形) not showing any particular feature or style, such as being formal or informal 无标记的 **OPP marked**

un·mar·ried /ˌʌnˈmærid/ *adj.* not married 未婚的；独身的 **SYN single**：*an unmarried mother* 未婚母亲

un·mask /ˌʌnˈmɑːsk; *NAmE* ˌʌnˈmæsk/ *verb* **~ sb/sth** to show the true character of sb, or a hidden truth about sth 使露出真相；揭露；暴露 **SYN expose**：*to unmask a spy* 揭发间谍

un·matched /ˌʌnˈmætʃt/ *adj.* **~ (by sb/sth)** (*formal*) better than all others 无双的；无比的：*He had a talent unmatched by any other politician of this century.* 他的才华是本世纪其他政坛人物望尘莫及的。

un·mem·or·able /ʌnˈmemərəbl/ *adj.* that cannot be remembered because it was not special 容易遗忘（或忘怀）的 **OPP memorable**

un·men·tion·able /ʌnˈmenʃənəbl/ *adj.* [usually before noun] too shocking or embarrassing to be mentioned or spoken about 不可提及的；不宜述说的；难以启齿的：*an unmentionable disease* 羞于启齿的疾病

unmet /ˌʌnˈmet/ *adj.* (*formal*) (of needs, etc. 需要等) not satisfied 未满足的：*a report on the unmet needs of elderly people* 有关老年人生活所需不足的报告

un·mind·ful /ʌnˈmaɪndfl/ *adj.* **~ of sb/sth** (*formal*) not giving thought or attention to sb/sth 不注意的；不留心的；漫不经心的 **OPP mindful**

un·miss·able /ʌnˈmɪsəbl/ *adj.* that you must not miss because it is so good 不能错过的；不可失掉的：*an unmissable opportunity* 不能错过的良机

un·mis·tak·able (*also less frequent* **un·mis·take·able**) /ˌʌnmɪˈsteɪkəbl/ *adj.* that cannot be mistaken for sb/sth else 不会弄错的；确定无疑的；清楚明白的：*Her accent was unmistakable.* 她的口音是很明显的。◇ *the unmistakable sound of gunfire* 清清楚楚的枪炮声 ▶ **un·mis·tak·ably** (*also less frequent* **un·mis·take·ably**) /-əbli/ *adv.*：*His accent was unmistakably British.* 他明显地操英国口音。

un·miti·gated /ʌnˈmɪtɪɡeɪtɪd/ *adj.* [only before noun] used to mean 'complete', usually when describing sth bad 完全的，十足的，彻底的（通常指坏事）**SYN absolute**：*The evening was an unmitigated disaster.* 这一晚完全是一场灾难。➲ SEE ALSO MITIGATE

un·modi·fied **AW** /ˌʌnˈmɒdɪfaɪd; *NAmE* -ˈmɑːd-/ *adj.* not MODIFIED 未更改的；未修改的

un·mol·est·ed /ˌʌnməˈlestɪd/ *adj.* [not usually before noun] (*formal*) not disturbed or attacked by sb; not prevented from doing sth 不受打搅（或攻击）；未受阻挠；不被干涉

un·moti·vated **AW** /ˌʌnˈməʊtɪveɪtɪd; *NAmE* -ˈmoʊ-/ *adj.* **1** not having interest in or enthusiasm for sth, especially work or study（尤指对工作或学习）缺乏动机的，不感兴趣

的，无热情的：*unmotivated students* 缺乏动力的学生 **2** without a reason or MOTIVE 无缘由的；无动机的：*an unmotivated attack* 无缘无故的攻击 OPP **motivated**

un·moved /ˌʌnˈmuːvd/ *adj.* ~ (**by sth**) not feeling pity or sympathy, especially in a situation where it would be normal to do so 冷漠的；无同情心的；无动于衷的：*Alice seemed totally unmoved by the whole experience.* 艾丽斯似乎对整个经过十分冷漠。◇ *She pleaded with him but he remained unmoved.* 她苦苦哀求，可是他仍无动于衷。

un·mov·ing /ˌʌnˈmuːvɪŋ/ *adj.* (*formal*) not moving 不动的；静止的：*He stood, unmoving, in the shadows.* 他一动不动地站在阴暗处。

un·music·al /ˌʌnˈmjuːzɪkl/ *adj.* **1** (of a sound 声音) unpleasant to listen to 难听的；刺耳的；不悦耳的：*His voice was harsh and unmusical.* 他的声音刺耳难听。**2** (of a person 人) unable to play or enjoy music 不擅长音乐的；对音乐无兴趣的 OPP **musical**

un·named /ˌʌnˈneɪmd/ *adj.* whose name is not given or not known 未披露姓名的；不知姓名的：*information from an unnamed source* 不愿透露姓名的人提供的消息 ◇ *Two casualties, as yet unnamed, are still in the local hospital.* 两个尚不知姓名的伤者仍在当地医院。

un·nat·ural /ʌnˈnætʃrəl/ *adj.* **1** different from what is normal or expected, or from what is generally accepted as being right 不自然的；勉强的；反常的：*It seems unnatural for a child to spend so much time alone.* 一个孩子独自一人待那么长时间似乎有点反常。◇ *There was an unnatural silence and then a scream.* 一阵反常的寂静，接着便是一声尖叫。◇ *unnatural sexual practices* 反常的性行为 ◇ *He gave an unnatural smile* (= that did not seem genuine). 他勉强笑了笑。**2** different from anything in nature 不正常的；怪异的：*Her leg was bent at an unnatural angle.* 她的腿弯曲的角度反常。◇ *an unnatural death* (= one not from natural causes) 非正常死亡 OPP **natural** ▶ **un·nat·ur·al·ly** /-rəli/ *adv.*：*She was, **not unnaturally**, very surprised at the news.* 这消息自然让她大吃一惊。◇ *His eyes were unnaturally bright.* 他的眼睛异常明亮。

un·neces·sary 🔑 /ʌnˈnesəsəri; *NAmE* -seri/ *adj.* **1** 🔑 not needed; more than is needed 不需要的；不必要的；多余的 SYN **unjustified**：*unnecessary expense* 不必要的花费 ◇ *They were found guilty of causing unnecessary suffering to animals.* 他们因虐待动物而被判有罪。◇ *All this fuss is **totally unnecessary**.* 这场纷扰是完全可以避免的。OPP **necessary** **2** 🔑 (of remarks, etc. 言语等) not needed in the situation and likely to be offensive 不必要（且容易开罪于人）的 SYN **uncalled for**：*That last comment was a little unnecessary, wasn't it?* 那最后一点评论有点多余，是吧？ ▶ **un·neces·sar·ily** /ʌnˈnesəsərəli; *NAmE* ˌʌnˌnesəˈserəli/ *adv.*：*There's no point worrying him unnecessarily.* 没有必要让他过于担心。◇ *unnecessarily complicated instructions* 过分复杂的指令

un·nerve /ˌʌnˈnɜːv; *NAmE* ˌʌnˈnɜːrv/ *verb* ~ **sb** to make sb feel nervous or frightened or lose confidence 使紧张；使恐惧；使丧失信心：*His silence unnerved us.* 他的沉默令我们心里发慌。◇ *She appeared strained and a little unnerved.* 她看起来神色不安，有点心慌。▶ **un·nerv·ing** *adj.* **un·nerv·ing·ly** *adv.*

un·noticed /ˌʌnˈnəʊtɪst; *NAmE* -ˈnoʊ-/ *adj.* [not before noun] not seen or noticed 未被看见；未受到注意；被忽视：*His kindness did not **go unnoticed** by his staff.* 他的厚道员工了然于心。

un·num·bered /ˌʌnˈnʌmbəd; *NAmE* -bərd/ *adj.* not marked with a number; not NUMBERED 未编号的；未标号的：*unnumbered seats* 未编号的座位

UNO /juː en ˈəʊ; ˈjuːnəʊ; *NAmE* ˈoʊ; -noʊ/ *abbr.* United Nations Organization 联合国组织 ➲ SEE ALSO UNITED NATIONS

un·ob·jec·tion·able /ˌʌnəbˈdʒekʃənəbl/ *adj.* (*formal*) (of an idea, etc. 看法等) that you can accept 可以接受的；无异议的 SYN **acceptable**

un·ob·served /ˌʌnəbˈzɜːvd; *NAmE* -ˈzɜːrvd/ *adj.* without being seen 不被看见（或发现）的：*It's not easy for somebody to get into the building unobserved.* 进入这栋大楼而不被发现很不容易。

un·ob·tain·able AW /ˌʌnəbˈteməbl/ *adj.* [not usually before noun] that cannot be obtained 得不到；无法得到 OPP **obtainable**

un·ob·tru·sive /ˌʌnəbˈtruːsɪv/ *adj.* (*formal, often approving*) not attracting unnecessary attention 不张扬的；不招摇的：*The service at the hotel is efficient and unobtrusive.* 那旅馆的服务既有效率，又沉稳低调。OPP **obtrusive** ▶ **un·ob·tru·sive·ly** *adv.*：*Dora slipped unobtrusively in through the back door.* 多拉悄悄地从后门溜了进去。

un·occu·pied /ˌʌnˈɒkjupaɪd; *NAmE* -ˈɑːk-/ *adj.* **1** empty, with nobody living there or using it 空着的；闲置的；无人占用的：*an unoccupied house* 闲置的房屋 ◇ *I sat down at the nearest unoccupied table.* 我在最近的一张空桌旁坐了下来。**2** (of a region or country 地区或国家) not controlled by foreign soldiers 未沦陷的；未被敌人占领的：*unoccupied territory* 未沦陷的领土 OPP **occupied**

un·offi·cial /ˌʌnəˈfɪʃl/ *adj.* **1** that does not have permission or approval from sb in authority 未经正式批准的；非官方的；非正式的：*an unofficial agreement/strike* 未经批准的协议 / 罢工 ◇ *Unofficial estimates put the figure at over two million.* 非官方的估计数字为 200 万以上。**2** that is not part of sb's official business 非公事的；私事的；私人的：*The former president paid an unofficial visit to China.* 前总统到中国进行了私人访问。OPP **official** ▶ **un·offi·cial·ly** /-ʃəli/ *adv.*

un·opened /ʌnˈəʊpənd; *NAmE* -ˈoʊ-/ *adj.* not opened yet 未开启的；未打开的：*The letter was returned unopened.* 信被原封不动地退回了。

un·opposed /ˌʌnəˈpəʊzd; *NAmE* -ˈpoʊzd/ *adj.* [not usually before noun] not opposed or stopped by anyone 无人反对；无阻挠：*The party leader was re-elected unopposed.* 这个党派的领袖再次顺利当选。

un·organ·ized (*BrE also* **-ised**) /ʌnˈɔːɡənaɪzd; *NAmE* -ˈɔːrɡ-/ *adj.* **1** (of workers 工人) without a trade/labor union or other organization to represent or support them 没有工会的；没有成立组织的 **2** = DISORGANIZED **3** not having been organized 无组织的；无系统的；杂乱无章的：*unorganized data* 杂乱的数据 ➲ COMPARE ORGANIZED (1)

un·ortho·dox /ʌnˈɔːθədɒks; *NAmE* ʌnˈɔːrθədɑːks/ *adj.* different from what is usual or accepted 非正统的；非传统的；不正规的：*unorthodox methods* 非正统的方法 OPP **orthodox** ➲ COMPARE HETERODOX

un·pack /ˌʌnˈpæk/ *verb* **1** [T, I] ~ (**sth**) to take things out of a suitcase, bag, etc. 打开（箱、包等）取；从（箱、包等中）取出：*I unpacked my bags as soon as I arrived.* 我一到达就打开行李袋，把东西取出来。◇ *She unpacked all the clothes she needed and left the rest in the case.* 她取出所有要穿的衣服，其余的都留在箱子里。◇ *She went to her room to unpack.* 她回到自己的房间打开行李取出衣物。OPP **pack** **2** [T] ~ **sth** to separate sth into parts so that it is easier to understand 分析；剖析：*to unpack a theory* 剖析一个理论

un·paid /ˌʌnˈpeɪd/ *adj.* **1** not yet paid 未付的；未偿付的：*unpaid bills* 未付的账单 **2** done or taken without payment 无偿的；不付报酬的：*unpaid work* 无偿劳动 ◇ *unpaid leave* 不带薪的休假 OPP **paid** **3** (of people 人) not receiving payment for work that they do 不领报酬的；义务的：*unpaid volunteers* 不领报酬的志愿者 OPP **paid**

un·pal·at·able /ʌnˈpælətəbl/ *adj.* ~ (**to sb**) **1** (of facts, ideas, etc. 事实、意见等) unpleasant and not easy to accept 令人不快的；难以接受的 SYN **distasteful**：*Only then did I learn the unpalatable truth.* 直到那时我才得知令人难以接受的真相。**2** not pleasant to taste 难吃的；不可口的：*unpalatable food* 难吃的食物 OPP **palatable**

un·par·al·leled AW /ʌnˈpærəleld/ *adj.* (*formal*) used to emphasize that sth is bigger, better or worse than

U

anything else like it 无比的；无双的；空前的；绝无仅有的 SYN **unequalled**: *It was an unparalleled opportunity to develop her career.* 这是她发展自己的事业的绝好机会。◇ *The book has enjoyed a success unparalleled in recent publishing history.* 这本书在近期出版史上是空前的成功。➲ COMPARE PARALLEL *adj.*

un·par·don·able /ʌn'pɑːdnəbl; *NAmE* -'pɑːrd-/ *adj.* that cannot be forgiven or excused 不可饶恕的；不可原谅的 SYN **unforgivable, inexcusable** OPP **pardonable**

un·par·lia·men·tary /ˌʌnˌpɑːlə'mentri; *NAmE* -ˌpɑːrl-/ *adj.* against the accepted rules of behaviour in a parliament 违反议会行为准则的；违反议会惯例的：*unparliamentary language* 不适于在议会使用的言语

un·pat·ri·ot·ic /ˌʌnˌpætri'ɒtɪk; *NAmE* -ˌpeɪtri'ɑːt-/ *adj.* not supporting your own country 无爱国心的；不爱国的 OPP **patriotic**

un·per·turbed /ˌʌnpə'tɜːbd; *NAmE* ˌʌnpər'tɜːrbd/ *adj.* not worried or anxious 不担忧的；平静的；镇静的；镇定的：*She seemed unperturbed by the news.* 她听到这消息似乎并不惊慌。OPP **perturbed**

un·pick /ˌʌn'pɪk/ *verb* ~ **sth** to take out STITCHES from a piece of sewing or knitting 拆去…的缝线；拆（编织物）的针脚

un·placed /ˌʌn'pleɪst/ *adj.* (*BrE*) not one of the first three to finish in a race or competition（速度比赛或竞争）未进入前三名的，未获名次的

un·planned /ˌʌn'plænd/ *adj.* not planned in advance 未计划（或筹划）的；意外的：*an unplanned pregnancy* 意外怀孕

un·play·able /ˌʌn'pleɪəbl/ *adj.* (*especially BrE*) **1** not able to be played; impossible to play on or with（乐曲）无法演奏的；（球）接不住的；（运动场）不能用于比赛的：*The ball was unplayable* (= it was hit so well that it was impossible to hit it back). 那个球没法接。➲ COMPARE PLAYABLE **2** (of a sportsperson or team) playing so well that it is impossible to beat them（运动员或运动队）发挥出色而难以击败的：*When they're good, they're unplayable.* 他们打得好时是战无不胜的。

un·pleas·ant /ʌn'pleznt/ *adj.* **1** not pleasant or comfortable 令人不快的；不舒服的 SYN **disagreeable**: *an unpleasant experience* 不愉快的经历 ◇ *The minerals in the water made it unpleasant to drink.* 水里的矿物质使得这水挺难喝的。**2** ~ (**to sb**) not kind, friendly or polite 不和蔼的；不客气的；不礼貌的：*He was very unpleasant to me.* 他对我很凶。◇ *She said some very unpleasant things about you.* 她说了你一些坏话。OPP **pleasant** ▸ **un·pleas·ant·ly** *adv.*: *The drink is very sweet, but not unpleasantly so.* 这饮料非常甜，但并不腻。◇ *He laughed unpleasantly.* 他笑得令人讨厌。

U

un·pleas·ant·ness /ʌn'plezntnəs/ *noun* [U] bad feeling or arguments between people 不和；反目；争执

un·plug /ˌʌn'plʌg/ *verb* (-gg-) ~ **sth** to remove the plug of a piece of electrical equipment from the electricity supply 拔掉…的电源插头 OPP **plug in**

Un·plugged™ /ˌʌn'plʌgd/ *adj.* (sometimes after noun 有时用于名词后) (of pop or ROCK music or musicians 流行乐、摇滚乐或音乐人) performed or performing with ACOUSTIC rather than electric instruments 不插电的（用原音乐器）：*an Unplugged concert* 不插电音乐会 ◇ *Bob Dylan Unplugged* 鲍勃•迪伦不插电演出

un·pol·luted /ˌʌnpə'luːtɪd/ *adj.* that has not been POLLUTED (= made dirty by harmful substances) 未被污染的；干净的

un·popu·lar /ʌn'pɒpjələ(r); *NAmE* -'pɑːp-/ *adj.* not liked or enjoyed by a person, a group or people in general 没人缘儿的；不受欢迎的；不得人心的：*an unpopular choice* 不普遍的选择 ◇ *an unpopular government* 不得人心的政府 ◇ ~ **with/among sb** *The proposed increase in income tax proved deeply unpopular with the electorate.* 增加所得税的建议令选民十分不满。OPP **popular** ▸ **un·popu·lar·ity** /ˌʌnˌpɒpju'lærəti; *NAmE* -ˌpɑːp-/ *noun* [U]: *the growing unpopularity of the military regime* 军政府日益不得人心

un·pre·ced·ent·ed AW /ʌn'presɪdentɪd/ *adj.* that has never happened, been done or been known before 前所未有的；空前的；没有先例的：*The situation is unprecedented in modern times.* 这种情况在现代还没有出现过。▸ **un·pre·ced·ent·ed·ly** *adv.*: *a period of unprecedentedly high food prices* 食物空前昂贵的时期

un·pre·dict·able AW /ˌʌnprɪ'dɪktəbl/ *adj.* **1** that cannot be predicted because it changes a lot or depends on too many different things 无法预言的；不可预测的；难以预料的：*unpredictable weather* 变幻莫测的天气 ◇ *The result is entirely unpredictable.* 结果是完全无法预料的。**2** if a person is **unpredictable**, you cannot predict how they will behave in a particular situation（人）善变的，难以捉摸的 OPP **predictable** ▸ **un·pre·dict·abil·ity** AW /ˌʌnprɪˌdɪktə'bɪləti/ *noun* [U]: *the unpredictability of the English weather* 英国天气的变幻莫测 **un·pre·dict·ably** *adv.*

un·pre·ju·diced /ʌn'predʒədɪst/ *adj.* not influenced by an unreasonable fear or dislike of sth/sb; willing to consider different ideas and opinions 公正的；无成见的；无偏见的；一视同仁的 OPP **prejudiced**

un·pre·medi·tated /ˌʌnpriː'medɪteɪtɪd/ *adj.* (*formal*) (of a crime or bad action 罪行或恶行) not planned in advance 非预谋的；非事先策划的 OPP **premeditated**

un·pre·pared /ˌʌnprɪ'peəd; *NAmE* -'perd/ *adj.* **1** ~ (**for sth**) not ready or not expecting sth 无准备的；没有预料的；无防备的：*She was totally unprepared for his response.* 她对他的反应毫无准备。**2** ~ (**to do sth**) (*formal*) not willing to do sth 不乐意的；不情愿的；不甘心的：*She was unprepared to accept that her marriage was over.* 她不愿相信她的婚姻已经结束。OPP **prepared**

un·pre·pos·sess·ing /ˌʌnˌpriːpə'zesɪŋ/ *adj.* (*formal*) not attractive; not making a good or strong impression 不讨人喜欢的；不吸引人的；让人无良好（或深刻）印象的 SYN **unattractive** ➲ COMPARE PREPOSSESSING

un·pre·ten·tious /ˌʌnprɪ'tenʃəs/ *adj.* (*approving*) not trying to appear more special, intelligent, important, etc. than you really are 谦虚谨慎的；不事张扬的；不爱炫耀的 OPP **pretentious**

un·prin·cipled AW /ʌn'prɪnsəpld/ *adj.* (*formal*) without moral principles 不道德的 SYN **dishonest** OPP **principled**

un·print·able /ʌn'prɪntəbl/ *adj.* (of words or comments 语言或评论) too offensive or shocking to be printed and read by people（因冒犯或令人震惊）不宜刊印的，不宜发表的 OPP **printable**

un·prob·lem·at·ic /ˌʌnˌprɒblə'mætɪk; *NAmE* -ˌprɑːb-/ (*also less frequent* **un·prob·lem·at·ic·al** /-ɪkl/) *adj.* not having or causing problems 没有问题的；不惹麻烦的 OPP **problematic** ▸ **un·prob·lem·at·ic·al·ly** /-kli/ *adv.*

un·pro·duct·ive /ˌʌnprə'dʌktɪv/ *adj.* not producing very much; not producing good results 产量少的；效果不佳的；无益的：*unproductive land* 贫瘠的土地 ◇ *an unproductive meeting* 事倍功半的会议 ◇ *I've had a very unproductive day.* 我这一天什么事都没干成。OPP **productive** ▸ **un·pro·duct·ive·ly** *adv.*

un·pro·fes·sion·al /ˌʌnprə'feʃənl/ *adj.* not reaching the standard expected in a particular profession 未达专业水平的；违反职业道德的：*She was found guilty of unprofessional conduct.* 她因违反职业道德而被判罪。OPP **professional** ➲ COMPARE NON-PROFESSIONAL ▸ **un·pro·fes·sion·al·ly** /-ʃənəli/ *adv.*

un·prof·it·able /ʌn'prɒfɪtəbl; *NAmE* -'prɑːf-/ *adj.* **1** not making enough financial profit 不赢利的；无利可图的：*unprofitable companies* 不赚钱的公司 **2** (*formal*) not bringing any advantage 无益的；没好处的 OPP **profitable** ▸ **un·prof·it·ably** /-əbli/ *adv.*

un·prom·is·ing /ʌn'prɒmɪsɪŋ; *NAmE* -'prɑːm-/ *adj.* not likely to be successful or show good results 不乐观的；难有好结果的 OPP **promising**

un·prompt·ed /ʌn'prɒmptɪd; *NAmE* -'prɑːm-/ *adj.* said or done without sb asking you to say or do it 主动的；自发的：*Quite unprompted, Sam started telling us exactly what had happened that night.* 萨姆完全出于主动，开始把那天夜里发生的事一一向我们说了出来。 ➲SEE ALSO PROMPT *v.*

un·pro·nounce·able /ˌʌnprə'naʊnsəbl/ *adj.* (of a word, especially a name 词语，尤指名字) too difficult to pronounce 难发音的；拗口的 **OPP** **pronounceable**

un·pro·tect·ed /ˌʌnprə'tektɪd/ *adj.* **1** not protected against being hurt or damaged 未受保护的；未设防的 **2** not covered to prevent it from causing damage or injury 无防护罩的；无掩护的：*Machinery was often unprotected and accidents were frequent.* 机器常裸露着，因此事故频仍。 **3** (of sex 性交) done without using a CONDOM 未用避孕套的；无防护的

un·proven /ʌn'pruːvn/ *adj.* not proved or tested 未验证的；未经检验的：*unproven theories* 未证实的理论 ➲COMPARE PROVEN

un·pro·voked /ˌʌnprə'vəʊkt; *NAmE* -'voʊkt/ *adj.* (especially of an attack 尤指攻击) not caused by anything the person being attacked has said or done 未受挑衅的；无端的：*an act of unprovoked aggression* 无端的侵犯行为 ◇ *Her angry outburst was totally unprovoked.* 她暴跳如雷完全是无理取闹。 ➲SEE ALSO PROVOKE

un·pub·lished **AW** /ʌn'pʌblɪʃt/ *adj.* not published 未出版的；未发表的；未公开的：*an unpublished novel* 未出版的小说

un·pun·ished /ʌn'pʌnɪʃt/ *adj.* not punished 未受惩罚的：*He promised that the murder would not **go unpunished**.* 他保证不会让凶手逍遥法外。

un·put·down·able /ˌʌnpʊt'daʊnəbl/ *adj.* (*informal*) (of a book 书) so exciting or interesting that you cannot stop reading it 使人着迷的；令人爱不释手的

un·quali·fied /ˌʌn'kwɒlɪfaɪd; *NAmE* -'kwɑːl-/ *adj.* **1** not having the right knowledge, experience or qualifications to do sth 不合格的；没资格的：*an unqualified instructor* 不合格的教员 ◇ **~ to do sth** *I feel unqualified to comment on the subject.* 我觉得没有资格对此事发表意见。 ◇ **~ for sth** *He was totally unqualified for his job as a senior manager.* 他担任高级经理职务完全不够格。 **2** /ʌn'kwɒlɪfaɪd; *NAmE* -'kwɑːl-/ [usually before noun] complete; not limited by any negative qualities 完全的；绝对的；无保留的；无限制条件的：*The event was not an unqualified success.* 这件事并非百分之百的成功。 ◇ *I gave her my unqualified support.* 我全力支持她。 **OPP** **qualified**

un·quench·able /ʌn'kwentʃəbl/ *adj.* (*formal*) that cannot be satisfied 满足不了的；止不住的：*He had an **unquenchable thirst** for life.* 他有着极其强烈的求生欲。 ➲SEE ALSO QUENCH

un·ques·tion·able /ʌn'kwestʃənəbl/ *adj.* (*formal*) that cannot be doubted 无疑的；无可非议的；确实的：*a man of unquestionable honesty* 绝对诚实的人 **OPP** **questionable** ▸ **un·ques·tion·ably** /-əbli/ *adv.*：*It was unquestionably a step in the right direction.* 这无疑是朝正确方向迈出的一步。

un·ques·tioned /ʌn'kwestʃənd/ *adj.* (*formal*) **1** so obvious that it cannot be doubted 显而易见的；无可争议的；毋庸置疑的；公认的：*His courage remains unquestioned.* 他的勇敢仍然不容置疑。 **2** accepted as right or true without really being considered 不假思索而认可的；盲目接受的：*an unquestioned assumption* 盲目接受的假设

un·ques·tion·ing /ʌn'kwestʃənɪŋ/ *adj.* (*formal*) done or given without asking questions, expressing doubt, etc. 不加质询的；不表示怀疑（等）的：*unquestioning obedience* 绝对的服从 ▸ **un·ques·tion·ing·ly** *adv.*

un·quiet /ˌʌn'kwaɪət/ *adj.* [usually before noun] (*literary*) not calm; anxious and RESTLESS 不平静的；焦躁不安的；心神不宁的

un·quote /ˌʌn'kwəʊt; *NAmE* ˌʌn'kwoʊt/ *verb* **IDM** SEE QUOTE *v.*

un·ravel /ʌn'rævl/ *verb* (**-ll-**, *US* **-l-**) **1** [T, I] **~ (sth)** if you **unravel** threads that are twisted, WOVEN or knitted, or if they **unravel**, they become separated（把缠或织在一起的线）解开，拆散，松开：*I unravelled the string and wound it into a ball.* 我把绳子解开并绕成一个球。 **2** [I] (of a system, plan, relationship, etc. 系统、计划、关系等) to start to fail or no longer stay together as a whole 解体；崩溃；瓦解 **3** [T, I] **~ (sth)** to explain sth that is difficult to understand or is mysterious; to become clearer or easier to understand 阐释；说明；澄清；变得清楚易懂：*The discovery will help scientists unravel the mystery of the Ice Age.* 这一发现将有助于科学家揭开冰期的奥秘。

un·read /ˌʌn'red/ *adj.* (of a book, etc. 书籍等) that has not been read 未读的；未阅的：*a pile of unread newspapers* 一摞未看的报纸

un·read·able /ʌn'riːdəbl/ *adj.* **1** (of a book, etc. 书籍等) too dull or difficult to be worth reading（因枯燥晦涩而）不值一读的，难以卒读的 **2** = ILLEGIBLE **3** if sb's face or expression is **unreadable**, you cannot tell what they are thinking or feeling（面部表情）揣摩不透的，难以捉摸的 **4** (*computing* 计) (of a computer file, disk, etc. 计算机文件、磁盘等) containing information that a computer is not able to read 无法读取的；打不开的

un·real /ˌʌn'rɪəl; *NAmE* ˌʌn'riːəl/ *adj.* **1** so strange that it is more like a dream than reality 奇异的；虚幻的；梦幻般的：*The party began to take on an unreal, almost nightmarish quality.* 聚会开始呈现出虚幻、近乎梦魇般的气氛。 **2** not related to reality 不真实的；脱离现实的 **SYN** **unrealistic**：*Many people have unreal expectations of what marriage will be like.* 许多人对婚姻生活抱有不切实际的憧憬。 **3** (*informal*) used to say that you like sth very much or that sth surprises you（表示十分喜爱或惊讶）：*'That's unreal!' she laughed.* "这怎么可能！"她笑了起来。 ▸ **un·real·ity** /ˌʌnri'æləti/ *noun* [U]

un·real·is·tic /ˌʌnrɪə'lɪstɪk; *NAmE* -riːə-/ *adj.* not showing or accepting things as they are 不切实际的；不实事求是的：*unrealistic expectations* 不切实际的期望 ◇ ***It is unrealistic to** expect them to be able to solve the problem immediately.* 指望他们能够立即解决问题是不现实的。 **OPP** **realistic** ▸ **un·real·is·tic·al·ly** /-kli/ *adv.*：*These prices are unrealistically high.* 这些价格高得离谱。

un·real·ized (*BrE also* **-ised**) /ˌʌn'riːəlaɪzd; *BrE also* -'rɪəl-/ *adj.* **1** not achieved or created 未实现的；未完成的；未成为现实的：*an unrealized ambition* 没有实现的抱负 ◇ *Their potential is unrealized.* 他们没有发挥出潜力。 **2** (*finance* 财) not sold or changed into the form of money 未变现的：*unrealized assets* 未变现资产

un·rea·son·able 🔑 /ʌn'riːznəbl/ *adj.* not fair; expecting too much 不合理的；不公正的；期望过高的：*The job was beginning to make unreasonable demands on his free time.* 他的闲暇时间开始被工作过分地侵占了。 ◇ *The fees they charge are not unreasonable.* 他们的收费还算合理。 ◇ ***It would be unreasonable to** expect somebody to come at such short notice.* 要求人家随传随到，太不近人情了吧。 ◇ *He was being totally unreasonable about it.* 他在这件事上蛮不讲理。 **OPP** **reasonable** ▸ **un·rea·son·able·ness** *noun* [U] **un·rea·son·ably** /-əbli/ *adv.*

un·rea·son·ing /ʌn'riːzənɪŋ/ *adj.* [usually before noun] (*formal*) not based on facts or reason 没根据的；缺乏理性的；无缘无故的 **SYN** **irrational**：*unreasoning fear* 无端的恐惧

un·rec·og·niz·able (*BrE also* **-is·able**) /ˌʌnrekəg'naɪzəbl/ *adj.* (of a person or thing 人或事物) so changed or damaged that you do not recognize them or it 变得（或损坏得）难以辨认的；无法识别的：*He was unrecognizable without his beard.* 他刮掉胡子，无人认得出他了。 **OPP** **recognizable**

un·rec·og·nized (*BrE also* **-ised**) /ʌn'rekəgnaɪzd/ *adj.* **1** that people are not aware of or do not realize is important 未被意识到的；被忽略的；不受重视的：*The problem*

U

of ageism in the workplace often ***goes unrecognized.*** 工作场所的年龄歧视问题常被忽视。 **2** (of a person 人) not having received the admiration they deserve for sth that they have done or achieved 被埋没的；未得到赏识的

un·re·con·struct·ed /ˌʌnriːkənˈstrʌktɪd/ *adj.* [only before noun] (*disapproving*) (of people and their beliefs 人及信仰) not having changed, although the situation they are in has changed 僵化的；顽固守旧的；不顺应形势的

un·re·cord·ed /ˌʌnrɪˈkɔːdɪd; *NAmE* -ˈkɔːrd-/ *adj.* not written down or recorded 未写下的；未记录的；未录音的：*Many crimes* ***go unrecorded.*** 许多罪行都未记录在案。

un·re·fined /ˌʌnrɪˈfaɪnd/ *adj.* **1** (of a substance 物质) not separated from the other substances that it is combined with in its natural form 未精制的；未提炼的：*unrefined sugar* 原糖 **2** (of a person or their behaviour 人或行为) not polite or educated 粗俗的；不文雅的；缺乏教养的 **OPP refined**

un·re·gen·er·ate /ˌʌnrɪˈdʒenərət/ *adj.* (*formal*) not trying to change your bad habits or bad behaviour 恶习不改的；不思悔改的

un·regu·lated AW /ˌʌnˈreɡjuleɪtɪd/ *adj.* not controlled by laws or regulations 不受法规约束的；不受管制的

un·re·lated /ˌʌnrɪˈleɪtɪd/ *adj.* **1** not connected; not related to sth else 无关联的；不相关的 **SYN unconnected**：*The two events were totally unrelated.* 这两件事毫不相干。 **2** (of people, animals, etc. 人、动物等) not belonging to the same family 不属于同一家族（或同一科等）的；无亲缘关系的 **OPP related**

un·re·lent·ing /ˌʌnrɪˈlentɪŋ/ *adj.* (*formal*) **1** (of an unpleasant situation 令人不快的局面) not stopping or becoming less severe 持续的；不缓和的；势头不减的 **SYN relentless**：*unrelenting pressure* 持续不断的压力 ◇ *The heat was unrelenting.* 炎热没有减弱的迹象。 **2** if a person is **unrelenting**, they continue with sth without considering the feelings of other people 不留情的 **SYN relentless**：*He was unrelenting in his search for the truth about his father.* 他不顾一切地搜集有关他父亲的事实真相。 ▶ **un·re·lent·ing·ly** *adv.*

un·re·li·able AW /ˌʌnrɪˈlaɪəbl/ *adj.* that cannot be trusted or depended on 不可靠的；不能信赖的：*The trains are notoriously unreliable.* 火车不准点是出了名的。 ◇ *He's totally unreliable as a source of information.* 他提供的消息完全不可信。 **OPP reliable** ▶ **un·re·li·abil·ity** /ˌʌnrɪˌlaɪəˈbɪləti/ *noun* [U]：*the unreliability of some statistics* 某些统计资料的不可靠性

un·re·lieved /ˌʌnrɪˈliːvd/ *adj.* (*formal*) (of an unpleasant situation 令人不快的情况) continuing without changing 持续不变的；未缓和的

un·re·mark·able /ˌʌnrɪˈmɑːkəbl; *NAmE* -ˈmɑːrk-/ *adj.* ordinary; not special or remarkable in any way 一般的；平常的；平凡的；平庸的：*an unremarkable life* 平淡的生活

un·re·marked /ˌʌnrɪˈmɑːkt; *NAmE* -ˈmɑːrkt/ *adj.* (*formal*) not noticed 未被注意：*His absence* ***went unremarked.*** 没有人注意到他不在场。

un·re·mit·ting /ˌʌnrɪˈmɪtɪŋ/ *adj.* (*formal*) never stopping 不停的；不懈的；持续不断的：*unremitting hostility* 从未化解的敌视 ▶ **un·re·mit·ting·ly** *adv.*：*unremittingly gloomy weather* 持续的阴沉天气

un·re·peat·able /ˌʌnrɪˈpiːtəbl/ *adj.* **1** too offensive or shocking to be repeated （因冒犯或令人震惊）不宜重提的，不堪重复的：*He called me several unrepeatable names.* 他骂了我几句不堪入耳的话。 **2** that cannot be repeated or done again 不可重复的；不能重演的：*an unrepeatable experience* 不可重复的经历 **OPP repeatable**

un·re·pent·ant /ˌʌnrɪˈpentənt/ *adj.* showing no shame about your actions or beliefs 不思悔改的；不悔悟的；顽固不化的 **OPP repentant** ▶ **un·re·pent·ant·ly** *adv.*

un·re·port·ed /ˌʌnrɪˈpɔːtɪd; *NAmE* -ˈpɔːrt-/ *adj.* not reported to the police or sb in authority or to the public 未举报的；未报告的；未报道的：*Many cases of bullying* ***go unreported.*** 很多欺凌案件都没有人告发。

un·rep·re·sen·ta·tive /ʌnˌreprɪˈzentətɪv/ *adj.* ~ **(of sb/sth)** not typical of a group of people or things and therefore not useful as a source of information about that group 不典型的；无代表性的 **SYN untypical**：*an unrepresentative sample* 缺乏代表性的样品 **OPP representative**

un·re·quit·ed /ˌʌnrɪˈkwaɪtɪd/ *adj.* (*formal*) (of love 爱情) not returned by the person that you love 没有回报的；单方面的；单相思的 ➲ COMPARE REQUITE

un·re·served /ˌʌnrɪˈzɜːvd; *NAmE* -ˈzɜːrvd/ *adj.* **1** (of seats in a theatre, etc. 剧院的座位等) not paid for in advance; not kept for the use of a particular person 未被预订的；非保留的 **2** (*formal*) complete and without any doubts 完全的；彻底的；无保留的：*He offered us his unreserved apologies.* 他诚恳地向我们道了歉。

un·re·served·ly /ˌʌnrɪˈzɜːvɪdli; *NAmE* -ˈzɜːrv-/ *adv.* completely; without hesitating or having any doubts 完全地；坦诚地；无条件地；无保留地：*We apologize unreservedly for any offence we have caused.* 若有得罪，我们深表歉意。

un·re·solved AW /ˌʌnrɪˈzɒlvd; *NAmE* -ˈzɑːlvd; -ˈzɔːlvd/ *adj.* (*formal*) (of a problem or question 问题或提问) not yet solved or answered; not having been resolved 未克服的；未解答的；未解决的

un·re·spon·sive AW /ˌʌnrɪˈspɒnsɪv; *NAmE* -ˈspɑːn-/ *adj.* ~ **(to sth)** (*formal*) not reacting to sb/sth; not giving the response that you would expect or hope for 无反应的；未答复的；反应迟钝的：*a politician who is unresponsive to the mood of the country* 对国民情绪毫无反应的政客 **OPP responsive**

un·rest /ʌnˈrest/ *noun* [U] a political situation in which people are angry and likely to protest or fight 动荡；动乱；骚动：***industrial/civil/social/political/popular unrest*** 工业/平民/社会/政治/民众动乱 ◇ *There is growing unrest in the south of the country.* 这个国家的南方日益动荡不安。 ➲ COLLOCATIONS AT WAR

un·re·strained AW /ˌʌnrɪˈstreɪnd/ *adj.* (*formal*) not controlled; not having been RESTRAINED 无节制的；放纵的；不加制约的：*unrestrained aggression* 肆无忌惮的侵犯

un·re·strict·ed AW /ˌʌnrɪˈstrɪktɪd/ *adj.* not controlled or limited in any way 没有限制的 **SYN unlimited**：*We have unrestricted access to all the facilities.* 我们可随意使用一切设施。 **OPP restricted**

un·re·ward·ed /ˌʌnrɪˈwɔːdɪd; *NAmE* -ˈwɔːrd-/ *adj.* not receiving the success that you are trying to achieve 无回报的；未果的；未获成功的：*Real talent often* ***goes unrewarded.*** 真正的人才常被埋没。

un·re·ward·ing /ˌʌnrɪˈwɔːdɪŋ; *NAmE* -ˈwɔːrd-/ *adj.* (of an activity, etc. 活动等) not bringing feelings of satisfaction or achievement 不令人满足的；未能给人成就感的 **OPP rewarding**

un·ripe /ˌʌnˈraɪp/ *adj.* not yet ready to eat （食物）未成熟的：*unripe fruit* 未熟的水果 **OPP ripe**

un·rivalled (*especially BrE*) (*NAmE usually* **un·rivaled**) /ʌnˈraɪvld/ *adj.* (*formal*) better or greater than any other 无与伦比的；无双的 **SYN unsurpassed**

un·roll /ʌnˈrəʊl; *NAmE* ʌnˈroʊl/ *verb* **1** [T, I] ~ **(sth)** if you **unroll** paper, cloth, etc. that was in a roll or if it **unrolls**, it opens and becomes flat （使纸张、织物等）展开，摊开，铺开：*We unrolled our sleeping bags.* 我们打开了睡袋。 ➲ COMPARE ROLL *v.* (5) **2** [I] (of events 事情) to happen one after another in a series 相继出现；连续发生：*We watched the events unroll before the cameras.* 我们眼看着事态的发展一一呈现在镜头前。

un·round·ed /ˌʌnˈraʊndɪd/ *adj.* (*phonetics* 语音) (of a speech sound 语音) pronounced with the lips not forming a narrow round shape 非圆唇的 **OPP rounded**

U

un·ruf·fled /ʌn'rʌfld/ *adj.* (of a person 人) calm 平静的；镇定的；沉着的 SYN **unperturbed**: *He remained unruffled by their accusations.* 对于他们的指控他处之泰然。

un·ruled /ˌʌn'ru:ld/ *adj.* (of paper 纸) not having printed lines on it 未印横格的；无平行线的

un·ruly /ʌn'ru:li/ *adj.* difficult to control or manage 难以控制（或管理）的；难以驾驭的 SYN **disorderly**: *an unruly class* 难管教的班级 ◇ *unruly behaviour* 无法无天的行为 ◇ *unruly hair* (= difficult to keep looking neat) 难梳理的头发 ▶ **un·ru·li·ness** *noun* [U]

un·sad·dle /ʌn'sædl/ *verb* **1** [T, I] ~ **(sth)** to take the saddle off a horse 给（马）解鞍；卸马鞍 **2** [T] ~ **sb** to throw a rider off 把…掀下马；使落马 SYN **unseat**

un·safe /ʌn'seɪf/ *adj.* **1** (of a thing, a place or an activity 东西、地方或活动) not safe; dangerous 不安全的；危险的：*The roof was declared unsafe.* 已宣布屋顶有安全隐患。◇ *It was considered unsafe to release the prisoners.* 释放这些囚犯被认为是危险的。◇ *unsafe sex* (= for example, sex without a CONDOM) 不安全的性行为 **2** (of people 人) in danger of being harmed 身处险境的：*He felt unsafe and alone.* 他感到既危险又孤单。 **3** (*BrE, law* 律) (of a decision in a court of law 法庭判决) based on evidence that may be false or is not good enough 证据不可靠（或不足）的：*Their convictions were declared unsafe.* 先前给他们的定罪已经宣布证据不足。 OPP **safe**

un·said /ʌn'sed/ *adj.* [not before noun] thought but not spoken （想到却）未说出：*Some things are better left unsaid.* 有些事情还是不说出来好。

un·sale·able (*also* **un·sal·able**) /ʌn'seɪləbl/ *adj.* that cannot be sold, because it is not good enough or because nobody wants to buy it 无销路的；难以售出的 OPP **saleable**

un·salt·ed /ʌn'sɔ:ltɪd; *BrE also* -'sɒlt-; *NAmE* -'sɑ:lt-/ *adj.* (especially of food 尤指食物) without added salt 未放盐的；不加盐的：*unsalted butter* 无盐黄油

un·sani·tary /ʌn'sænətri; *NAmE* -teri/ *adj.* (*especially NAmE*) = INSANITARY

un·sat·is·fac·tory /ˌʌnˌsætɪs'fæktəri/ *adj.* not good enough 不够好的；不能令人满意的 SYN **inadequate, unacceptable** OPP **satisfactory** ▶ **un·sat·is·fac·tor·ily** /-tərəli/ *adv.*

un·sat·is·fied /ʌn'sætɪsfaɪd/ *adj.* **1** (of a need, demand, etc. 需要、要求等) not dealt with 未处理的；未解决的；未满足的 **2** (of a person 人) not having got what you hoped; not having had enough of sth 不如意的；失望的；未得到满足的 ➲ COMPARE DISSATISFIED, SATISFIED (1)

un·sat·is·fy·ing /ˌʌn'sætɪsfaɪɪŋ/ *adj.* not giving you any satisfaction 不令人满意（或感到满足）的 OPP **satisfying**: *a shallow, unsatisfying relationship* 淡薄而不令人满意的关系

un·sat·ur·ated fat /ʌnˌsætʃəreɪtɪd 'fæt/ *noun* [U, C] a type of fat found in nuts, seeds and vegetable oils that does not encourage the harmful development of CHOLESTEROL 不饱和脂肪：*Avocados are high in unsaturated fat.* 油梨富含不饱和脂肪。➲ SEE ALSO MONOUNSATURATED FAT, POLYUNSATURATED FAT, SATURATED FAT, TRANS-FATTY ACID

un·savoury (*especially US* **un·savory**) /ʌn'seɪvəri/ *adj.* unpleasant or offensive; not considered morally acceptable 讨厌的；无礼的；声名狼藉的；不道德的：*an unsavoury incident* 令人厌恶的事件 ◇ *Her friends are all pretty unsavoury characters.* 她的朋友尽是些不三不四的人。➲ MORE LIKE THIS 23, page R27

un·scathed /ʌn'skeɪðd/ *adj.* [not before noun] not hurt 未受伤害；未受伤 SYN **unharmed**: *The hostages emerged from their ordeal unscathed.* 人质历尽磨难后安然生还。

un·sched·uled AW /ʌn'ʃedju:ld; *NAmE* ʌn'skedʒu:ld/ *adj.* that was not planned in advance 未事先计划的；非计划中的 SYN **unplanned**: *an unscheduled stop* 计划外的停顿

un·sci·en·tif·ic /ˌʌnˌsaɪən'tɪfɪk/ *adj.* (*often disapproving*) not scientific; not done in a careful, logical way 不科学的；非科学的；违背科学方法的：*an unscientific approach to a problem* 非科学的解决问题方式 ➲ COMPARE NON-SCIENTIFIC

un·scram·ble /ˌʌn'skræmbl/ *verb* **1** ~ **sth** to change a word, message, television signal, etc. that has been sent in a code so that it can be read or understood 使（信息、信号等）还原；译出（密码）；解码 OPP **scramble 2** ~ **sth** to arrange sth that is confused or in the wrong order in a clear correct way 整理；清理；使条理化

un·screw /ˌʌn'skru:/ *verb* **1** [T, I] ~ **(sth)** to undo sth by twisting or turning it; to become undone in this way （被）旋松，拧开：*I can't unscrew the lid of this jar.* 这个瓶盖儿我拧不开。 **2** [T] ~ **sth** to take the screws out of sth 拧下…的螺丝：*You'll have to unscrew the handles to paint the door.* 要漆这扇门，你得把螺丝拧开，卸下门把手。

un·script·ed /ʌn'skrɪptɪd/ *adj.* (of a speech, broadcast, etc. 讲演、广播等) not written or prepared in detail in advance 无底稿的；未详细准备的 OPP **scripted**

un·scru·pu·lous /ʌn'skru:pjələs/ *adj.* without moral principles; not honest or fair 不道德的；无道德原则的；不诚实的；不公正的 SYN **unprincipled**: *unscrupulous methods* 不公正的方法 OPP **scrupulous** ▶ **un·scru·pu·lous·ly** *adv.* **un·scru·pu·lous·ness** *noun* [U]

un·sea·son·able /ʌn'si:znəbl/ *adj.* unusual for the time of year 不合季节的；违反时令的：*unseasonable weather* 反常的天气 OPP **seasonable** ▶ **un·sea·son·ably** /-əbli/ *adv.*：*unseasonably warm* 反常地温暖

un·sea·son·al /ʌn'si:zənl/ *adj.* not typical of or not suitable for the time of year 无季节特征的；不合节令的：*unseasonal weather* 不合节令的天气 OPP **seasonal**

un·seat /ˌʌn'si:t/ *verb* **1** ~ **sb** to remove sb from a position of power 罢免；解除职务；赶下台 **2** ~ **sb** to make sb fall off a horse or bicycle 使摔下马（或自行车）：*The horse unseated its rider at the first fence.* 马在过第一道篱障时把骑手掀了下来。

un·seed·ed /ʌn'si:dɪd/ *adj.* not chosen as a SEED in a sports competition, especially in TENNIS 未被列为种子选手的；（尤指网球运动员）非种子的：*unseeded players* 非种子选手 OPP **seeded**

un·see·ing /ˌʌn'si:ɪŋ/ *adj.* (*literary*) not noticing or really looking at anything although your eyes are open 心不在焉地看着的 ▶ **un·see·ing·ly** *adv.*：*They stared unseeingly at the wreckage.* 他们看着残骸发愣。

un·seem·ly /ʌn'si:mli/ *adj.* (*old-fashioned* or *formal*) (of behaviour, etc. 行为等) not polite or suitable for a particular situation 不礼貌的；不得体的；不相宜的 SYN **improper** OPP **seemly**

un·seen /ˌʌn'si:n/ *adj.* **1** that cannot be seen 看不见的；无形的：*unseen forces* 无形的力量 ◇ *He was killed by a single shot from an unseen soldier.* 一个埋伏的士兵一枪就把他打死了。◇ *I managed to slip out of the room unseen.* 我总算偷偷地溜出了屋子。 **2** not previously seen 前所未见的；未被发现的：*unseen dangers* 未预见的危险 ◇ *The exam consists of an essay and an* ***unseen translation****.* 考试包括一篇作文和一篇即席翻译。 IDM SEE SIGHT *n.*

un·self·con·scious /ˌʌnself'kɒnʃəs; *NAmE* -'kɑ:n-/ *adj.* not worried about or aware of what other people think of you 不管（或不注意）别人看法的；不怯场的；大方自然的 OPP **self-conscious** ▶ **un·self·con·scious·ly** *adv.*

un·self·ish /ʌn'selfɪʃ/ *adj.* giving more time or importance to other people's needs, wishes, etc. than to your own 无私的；忘我的；不谋私利的 SYN **selfless**: *unselfish motives* 无私的动机 OPP **selfish** ▶ **un·self·ish·ly** *adv.* **un·self·ish·ness** *noun* [U]

un·sen·ti·men·tal /ˌʌnˌsentɪ'mentl/ *adj.* not having or expressing emotions such as love or pity; not allowing such emotions to influence what you do 没有（或不流露）感情的；不感情用事的 OPP **sentimental**

U

un·ser·vice·able /ʌnˈsɜːvɪsəbl; *NAmE* -ˈsɜːrv-/ *adj.* not suitable to be used 不适用的；不正常运转的 OPP **serviceable**

un·set·tle /ˌʌnˈsetl/ *verb* **~ sb** to make sb feel upset or worried, especially because a situation has changed 使心神不宁；扰乱；使担忧：*Changing schools might unsettle the kids.* 转学可能会让孩子感到不安。

un·set·tled /ʌnˈsetld/ *adj.* **1** (of a situation 形势) that may change; making people uncertain about what might happen 多变的；不安定的；不平稳的；动荡不安的：*These were difficult and unsettled times.* 那是个艰难而动荡的时期。◇ *The weather has been very unsettled* (= it has changed a lot). 天气一直变幻莫测。**2** not calm or relaxed 不镇静的；心绪不宁的；不安的：*They all felt restless and unsettled.* 他们都感到焦躁不安。**3** (of an argument, etc. 争论等) that continues without any agreement being reached 无休止的；未解决的 SYN **unresolved** **4** (of a bill, etc. 账单等) not yet paid 未支付的；未付清的

un·set·tling /ʌnˈsetlɪŋ/ *adj.* making you feel upset, nervous or worried 令人不安（或紧张、担忧）的

un·shaded /ˌʌnˈʃeɪdɪd/ *adj.* (of a source of light 光源) without a SHADE or other covering 无（灯）罩的；无遮蔽的：*an unshaded light bulb* 没有灯罩的电灯泡

un·shak·able (*also* **un·shake·able**) /ʌnˈʃeɪkəbl/ *adj.* (of a feeling or an attitude 感情或态度) that cannot be changed or destroyed 不能改变的；不可动摇的；坚定不移的；坚不可摧的 SYN **firm**

un·shaken /ʌnˈʃeɪkən/ *adj.* **~ (in sth)** not having changed a particular feeling or attitude 坚定的；未动摇的：*They remain unshaken in their loyalty.* 他们仍然忠贞不渝。

un·shaven /ˌʌnˈʃeɪvn/ *adj.* not having shaved or been shaved recently 未刮脸的；未剃须的：*He looked pale and unshaven.* 他面色苍白，胡子也没刮。◇ *his unshaven face* 他那张没刮的脸 ➲COMPARE SHAVEN

un·sight·ly /ʌnˈsaɪtli/ *adj.* not pleasant to look at 难看的；不雅观的；不悦目的 SYN **ugly**

un·skilled /ˌʌnˈskɪld/ *adj.* not having or needing special skills or training 无特长的；无（需）特别技能的；无（需）专门训练的：*unskilled manual workers* 非熟练体力劳动者 ◇ *unskilled work* 无需特别技能的工作 OPP **skilled**

un·smil·ing /ʌnˈsmaɪlɪŋ/ *adj.* (*formal*) not smiling; looking unfriendly 不苟言笑的；表情冷漠的：*His eyes were hard and unsmiling.* 他目光严厉冷峻。▶ **un·smil·ing·ly** *adv.*

U

un·soci·able /ʌnˈsəʊʃəbl; *NAmE* -ˈsoʊ-/ *adj.* **1** not enjoying the company of other people; not friendly 不爱交际的；不合群的 OPP **sociable** **2** = UNSOCIAL

un·social /ˌʌnˈsəʊʃl; *NAmE* ˌʌnˈsoʊʃl/ (*also less frequent* **un·soci·able**) (*BrE*) *adj.* outside the normal times of working 非正常工作时间的；正常工作时间以外的：*I work long and unsocial hours.* 我工作时间长，且在非正常时间上班。

un·sold /ˌʌnˈsəʊld; *NAmE* ˌʌnˈsoʊld/ *adj.* not bought by anyone未售出的；无人购买的：*Many of the houses remain unsold.* 这些房屋有许多尚未售出。

un·soli·cit·ed /ˌʌnsəˈlɪsɪtɪd/ *adj.* not asked for and sometimes not wanted 未经要求的；自发的；自我推荐的：*unsolicited advice* 主动提出的忠告

un·solved /ˌʌnˈsɒlvd; *NAmE* ˌʌnˈsɑːlvd/ *adj.* not having been solved 未解决的；未破解的：*an unsolved murder/mystery/problem* 未侦破的谋杀案；未解开的谜团；未解决的问题

un·sophis·ti·cated /ˌʌnsəˈfɪstɪkeɪtɪd/ *adj.* **1** not having or showing much experience of the world and social situations 单纯的；阅历浅的；涉世不深的；不谙世故的：*unsophisticated tastes* 单纯的爱好 **2** simple and basic; not complicated 基本的；简单的；不复杂的 SYN **crude**：*unsophisticated equipment* 简单的基本设备 OPP **sophisticated**

un·sorted /ˌʌnˈsɔːtɪd; *NAmE* -ˈsɔːrt-/ *adj.* not sorted, or not arranged in any particular order 未分类的；未排序的：*a pile of unsorted papers* 一沓未整理的文件

un·sound /ˌʌnˈsaʊnd/ *adj.* **1** not acceptable; not holding acceptable views 不稳妥的；观点不正确的：*ideologically unsound* 意识上不妥 ◇ *The use of disposable products is considered ecologically unsound.* 使用一次性产品被认为是没有顾及对生态的影响。**2** containing mistakes; that you cannot rely on 有错误的；靠不住的 SYN **unreliable**：*The methods used were unsound.* 所使用的方法不可靠。**3** (of a building, etc. 建筑物等) in poor condition; weak and likely to fall down 破旧的；摇摇欲坠的：*The roof is structurally unsound.* 这屋顶结构不牢固。 OPP **sound** ▶ **un·sound·ness** *noun* [U]

IDM **of ˌunsound ˈmind** (*law* 律) not responsible for your actions because of a mental illness 精神失常，神志不清（无须对自己的行为负责）

un·spar·ing /ʌnˈspeərɪŋ; *NAmE* -ˈsper-/ *adj.* **~ (in sth)** (*formal*) **1** not caring about people's feelings 无情的；严厉的：*She is unsparing in her criticism.* 她批评人毫不留情。◇ *an unsparing portrait of life in the slums* 对贫民窟生活无情的摹写 **2** giving or given generously 慷慨的；大方的；不吝啬的：*He won his mother's unsparing approval.* 他赢得了母亲毫无保留的赞同。 ➲COMPARE SPARING ▶ **un·spar·ing·ly** *adv.*

un·speak·able /ʌnˈspiːkəbl/ *adj.* (*literary, usually disapproving*) that cannot be described in words, usually because it is so bad 难以说出口的；不堪入耳的 SYN **indescribable** ▶ **un·speak·ably** /-əbli/ *adv.*

un·speci·fied AW /ˌʌnˈspesɪfaɪd/ *adj.* not stated clearly or definitely; not having been SPECIFIED 未说明的；不明确的：*The story takes place at an unspecified date.* 故事发生的日期不明。

un·spec·tacu·lar /ˌʌnspekˈtækjələ(r)/ *adj.* not exciting or special 平凡的；平淡的；普通的：*He had a steady but unspectacular career.* 他的事业稳定但平淡无奇。

un·spoiled /ˌʌnˈspɔɪld/ (*BrE also* **un·spoilt** /ˌʌnˈspɔɪlt/) *adj.* (*approving*) **1** (of a place 地方) beautiful because it has not been changed or built on 有自然美的；未遭破坏的 **2** (of a person 人) not made unpleasant, bad-tempered, etc. by being praised too much 未被宠坏的；未被捧杀的 OPP **spoilt**

un·spoken /ˌʌnˈspəʊkən; *NAmE* -ˈspoʊ-/ *adj.* (*formal*) not stated; not said in words but understood or agreed between people 未说出的；未表达的；默契的；心照不宣的 SYN **unstated**：*an unspoken assumption* 隐含的假定 ◇ *Something unspoken hung in the air between them.* 他们之间有些心照不宣的事还没有解决。

un·sport·ing /ˌʌnˈspɔːtɪŋ; *NAmE* -ˈspɔːrt-/ *adj.* (*disapproving*) not fair or generous in your behaviour or treatment of others, especially of an opponent in a game 不公平的；不光明正大的；（尤指）缺乏体育道德的 OPP **sporting**

un·sports·man·like /ˌʌnˈspɔːtsmənlaɪk; *NAmE* -ˈspɔːrts-/ *adj.* (*disapproving*) not behaving in a fair, generous and polite way, especially when playing a sport or game 没有运动员风范的，无体育精神的（尤指体育比赛中不光明磊落、无气度）：*unsportsmanlike conduct* 有失运动员风度的行为

un·stable AW /ʌnˈsteɪbl/ *adj.* **1** likely to change suddenly 不稳定的；易变的；变化莫测的 SYN **volatile**：*The political situation remains highly unstable.* 政局仍然十分动荡。**2** if people are **unstable**, their behaviour and emotions change often and suddenly because their minds are upset （行为、情绪）反复无常的，不稳定的 ➲ SYNONYMS AT MENTALLY **3** likely to move or fall 易动（或倒下）的；不稳固的 **4** (*specialist*) (of a substance 物质) not staying in the same chemical or ATOMIC state 不稳定的：*chemically unstable* 化学上不稳定的 OPP **stable** ➲SEE ALSO INSTABILITY

un·stated /ʌnˈsteɪtɪd/ *adj.* (*formal*) not stated; not said in words but understood or agreed between people 未说出的；未用语言表达的；心照不宣的 SYN **unspoken**：*Their* *reasoning was based on a set of unstated assumptions.* 他们的推理是以一系列未说明的假定为基础的。

un·steady /ʌnˈstedi/ *adj.* **1** not completely in control of your movements so that you might fall 站不稳的；摇晃的：*She is still a little* ***unsteady on her feet*** *after the operation.* 手术以后她还有点站不稳。**2** shaking or moving in a way that is not controlled 颤抖的；抖动的：*an unsteady hand* 颤抖的手 OPP **steady** ▶ **un·stead·ily** /-ɪli/ *adv.* **un·steadi·ness** *noun* [U]

un·stint·ing /ʌnˈstɪntɪŋ/ *adj.* given or giving generously 慷慨的；大方的；无限的：*unstinting support* 全力的支持 ◇ **~ in sth** *They were unstinting in their praise.* 他们赞不绝口。▶ **un·stint·ing·ly** *adv.*

un·stop·pable /ʌnˈstɒpəbl; *NAmE* -ˈstɑːp-/ *adj.* that cannot be stopped or prevented 无法遏止的；不能防止的：*an unstoppable rise in prices* 无法遏止的价格上涨 ◇ *On form, the team was simply unstoppable.* 若状态良好，这个队简直势不可当。

un·stressed AW /ʌnˈstrest/ *adj.* (*phonetics* 语音) (of a syllable 音节) pronounced without emphasis 非重读的；轻读的 OPP **stressed**

un·struc·tured AW /ʌnˈstrʌktʃəd; *NAmE* -tʃərd/ *adj.* without structure or organization 结构凌乱的；无条理的；紊乱的

un·stuck /ˌʌnˈstʌk/ *adj.*
IDM **ˌcome unˈstuck 1** to become separated from sth it was stuck or fastened to 未粘住；脱离；松开：*The flap of the envelope had come unstuck.* 信封的封口没粘牢，张开了。**2** (*BrE, informal*) (of a person, plan, etc. 人、计划等) to fail completely, with bad results 彻底失败；一败涂地

un·sub·scribe /ˌʌnsəbˈskraɪb/ *verb* [I, T] **~ (from sth)** | **~ sb/sth** (*computing* 计) to remove your email address from an Internet MAILING LIST 取消订阅电邮的登记；取消订阅 ➲ WORDFINDER NOTE AT WEB

un·sub·stan·ti·ated /ˌʌnsəbˈstænʃieɪtɪd/ *adj.* (*formal*) not proved to be true by evidence 未经证实的；未被证明的 SYN **unsupported**: *an* ***unsubstantiated claim/rumour, etc.*** 未经证实的说法、传言等

un·suc·cess·ful /ˌʌnsəkˈsesfl/ *adj.* not successful; not achieving what you wanted to 不成功的；失败的；落空的：*His efforts to get a job proved unsuccessful.* 他求职的努力都落空了。◇ *They were unsuccessful in meeting their objectives for the year.* 他们未能达到年度目标。◇ *She made several unsuccessful attempts to see him.* 她几次想见他都未如愿。OPP **successful** ▶ **un·suc·cess·ful·ly** *adv.*

un·suit·able /ʌnˈsuːtəbl; *BrE also* -ˈsjuː-/ *adj.* **~ (for sb/sth)** not right or appropriate for a particular person, purpose or occasion 不适当的；不适宜的；不合适的：*He was wearing shoes that were totally unsuitable for climbing.* 他穿了一双完全不适合登山的鞋子。OPP **suitable** ▶ **un·suit·abil·ity** *noun* [U] **un·suit·ably** *adv.*: *They were unsuitably dressed for the occasion.* 他们的穿着在那种场合很不得体。

un·suit·ed /ʌnˈsuːtɪd; *BrE also* -ˈsjuː-/ *adj.* **1 ~ (to/for sth)** | **~ (to do sth)** not having the right or necessary qualities for sth 不合格的；不胜任的；不适宜的：*He is unsuited to academic work.* 他不适合做学术工作。◇ *She was totally unsuited for the job.* 她根本不能胜任这项工作。**2** if two people are **unsuited** to each other they do not have the same interests, etc. and are therefore not likely to make a good couple（人）志趣不相投的，不相配的，不般配的 OPP **suited**

un·sul·lied /ʌnˈsʌlid/ *adj.* (*literary*) not spoiled by anything; still pure or in the original state 未被玷污的；保持洁净的；纯洁的 SYN **unspoiled**

un·sung /ˌʌnˈsʌŋ/ *adj.* [usually before noun] (*formal*) not praised or famous but deserving to be 被埋没的；未被颂扬的：*the unsung heroes of the war* 战争中的无名英雄

un·sup·port·ed /ˌʌnsəˈpɔːtɪd; *NAmE* -ˈpɔːrt-/ *adj.* **1** (of a statement, etc. 声明等) not proved to be true by evidence 未经证实的 SYN **unsubstantiated**: *Their claims are unsupported by research findings.* 他们的说法未能得到研究结果的证实。**2** not helped or paid for by sb/sth else 无资助的；自力更生的：*She has brought up three children unsupported.* 她独力将三个孩子抚养成人。**3** not physically supported 无支撑物的：*Sections of the structure have been left unsupported.* 这个结构有几部分没有支撑。

un·sure /ˌʌnˈʃʊə(r); ˌʌnˈʃɔː(r); *NAmE* -ˈʃʊr/ *adj.* [not before noun] **1** not certain of sth; having doubts 无把握；不确知；犹豫：**~ about/of sth** *There were a lot of things I was unsure about.* 有许多事情我没把握。◇ **~ how, what, etc....** *I was unsure how to reply to this question.* 我拿不准该如何回答这个问题。◇ **~ of/as to how, what, etc....** *He was unsure of what to do next.* 他对下一步该做什么犹豫不定。◇ *They were unsure as to what the next move should be.* 下一步该做什么他们心里没底。**2 ~ (of yourself)** lacking confidence in yourself 缺乏自信：*Like many women, deep down she was unsure of herself.* 和许多女性一样，她内心深处缺乏自信。OPP **sure**

un·sur·passed /ˌʌnsəˈpɑːst; *NAmE* ˌʌnsərˈpæst/ *adj.* (*formal*) better or greater than any other 无比的；卓绝的；出类拔萃的 SYN **unrivalled**

un·sur·prised /ˌʌnsəˈpraɪzd; *NAmE* -sərˈp-/ *adj.* [not usually before noun] not surprised 不觉得惊奇：*She appeared totally unsurprised at the news.* 她对这消息一点都不显得惊奇。

un·sur·pris·ing /ˌʌnsəˈpraɪzɪŋ; *NAmE* -sərˈp-/ *adj.* not causing surprise 不令人惊讶的；不足为奇的 OPP **surprising** ▶ **un·sur·pris·ing·ly** *adv.*: *Unsurprisingly, the plan failed.* 果然不出所料，计划失败了。

un·sus·pect·ed /ˌʌnsəˈspektɪd/ *adj.* not predicted or known; that you were not previously aware of 未预料到的；未知的；未觉察到的

un·sus·pect·ing /ˌʌnsəˈspektɪŋ/ *adj.* [usually before noun] feeling no suspicion; not aware of danger or of sth bad 毫不怀疑的；无危险意识的；无戒备心的：*He had crept up on his unsuspecting victim from behind.* 他从背后悄悄逼近了那毫无戒备的受害者。

un·sus·tain·able AW /ˌʌnsəˈsteɪnəbl/ *adj.* that cannot be continued at the same level, rate, etc. 不能持续的；无法维持的：*unsustainable growth* 难以持续的增长 OPP **sustainable**

un·sweet·ened /ˌʌnˈswiːtnd/ *adj.* (of food or drinks 食物或饮料) without sugar or a similar substance having been added 未加糖的；未加甜味素的

un·swerv·ing /ʌnˈswɜːvɪŋ; *NAmE* -ˈswɜːrv-/ *adj.* (*formal*) strong and not changing or becoming weaker 坚定的；不懈的；始终如一的：***unswerving loyalty/support, etc.*** 始终如一的忠诚、支持等

un·sym·pa·thet·ic /ˌʌnˌsɪmpəˈθetɪk/ *adj.* **1 ~ (to/towards sb)** not feeling or showing any sympathy 无同情心的；不表示同情的；冷漠的：*I told him about the problem but he was totally unsympathetic.* 我把麻烦事告诉了他，但他完全无动于衷。**2 ~ (to/towards sth)** not in agreement with sth; not supporting an idea, aim, etc.（与…）不一致的；有分歧的；（与某意见、目的等）相违的：*The government was unsympathetic to public opinion.* 政府违背了民意。**3** (of a person 人) not easy to like; unpleasant 不招人喜欢的 OPP **sympathetic** ▶ **un·sym·pa·thet·ic·al·ly** /-kli/ *adv.*: *'You've only got yourself to blame,' she said unsympathetically.* "你只能怪你自己。"她冷漠地说。

un·sys·tem·at·ic /ˌʌnˌsɪstəˈmætɪk/ *adj.* not organized into a clear system 无系统的；紊乱的；杂乱无章的 OPP **systematic** ▶ **un·sys·tem·at·ic·al·ly** /-kli/ *adv.*

un·taint·ed /ʌnˈteɪntɪd/ *adj.* **~ (by sth)** (*formal*) not damaged or spoiled by sth unpleasant; not TAINTED 未受损害的；未被污染的；未被玷污的

un·tal·ent·ed /ʌnˈtæləntɪd/ *adj.* without a natural ability to do sth well 无天赋的；没有特别天分的 OPP **talented**

un·tamed /ˌʌnˈteɪmd/ *adj.* allowed to remain in a wild state; not changed, controlled or influenced by anyone; not TAMED 野性的；未驯服的；未受抑制的；未调教的

un·tan·gle /ˌʌnˈtæŋɡl/ *verb* **1 ~ sth (from sth)** to undo string, hair, wire, etc. that has become twisted or has knots in it 解开，松开（结子等） **2 ~ sth** to make sth that is complicated or confusing easier to deal with or understand 整理；理清

un·tapped /ˌʌnˈtæpt/ *adj.* available but not yet used 未利用的；未开发的；蕴藏的：*untapped reserves of oil* 未开采的石油储量

un·ten·able /ʌnˈtenəbl/ *adj.* (*formal*) (of a theory, position, etc. 理论、地位等) that cannot be defended against attack or criticism 难以捍卫的；站不住脚的；不堪一击的：*His position had become untenable and he was forced to resign.* 他的地位已难以维持，因此他被迫辞职。**OPP tenable**

un·test·ed /ˌʌnˈtestɪd/ *adj.* not tested; of unknown quality or value 未经试验（或考验）的

un·think·able /ʌnˈθɪŋkəbl/ *adj.* **~ (for sb) (to do sth) | ~ (that...)** impossible to imagine or accept 难以想象的；不可思议的；难以置信的 **SYN inconceivable**：*It was unthinkable that she could be dead.* 她竟然去世了，真是很难相信。**OPP thinkable** ▸ **the un·think·able** *noun* [sing.]：*Suddenly the unthinkable happened and he drew out a gun.* 突然，难以相信的事情发生了，他拔出了手枪。◇ *The time has come to* ***think the unthinkable*** (= consider possibilities that used to be unacceptable). 现在该开始考虑以前不予考虑的事情了。

un·think·ing /ʌnˈθɪŋkɪŋ/ *adj.* (*formal*) not thinking about the effects of what you do or say; not thinking much about serious things 不计后果的；考虑不周的；不动脑筋的 **SYN thoughtless** ▸ **un·think·ing·ly** *adv.*

un·tidy 🔑 /ʌnˈtaɪdi/ *adj.* (**un·tidi·er, un·tidi·est**) **1** 🔑 not neat or well arranged; in a state of confusion 不整洁的；不整齐的；凌乱的：*an untidy desk* 凌乱的办公桌 ◇ *untidy hair* 蓬乱的头发 **2** 🔑 (of a person 人) not keeping things neat or well organized 无条理的；不修边幅的：*Why do you have to be so untidy?* 你为什么非得这么邋遢？**OPP tidy** ▸ **un·tidi·ly** /-ɪli/ *adv.* **un·tidi·ness** *noun* [U]

untie /ʌnˈtaɪ/ *verb* **~ sth** to undo a knot in sth; to undo sth that is tied 解开…的结；打开：*to untie a knot* 解开绳结 ◇ *I quickly untied the package and peeped inside.* 我迅速拆开包裹，往里瞥了一眼。◇ *He untied the rope and pushed the boat into the water.* 他解开缆绳，把小船推入水中。

until 🔑 /ənˈtɪl/ *conj., prep.* (*also informal* **till, til, 'til**) up to the point in time or the event mentioned 到…时；直到…为止：*Let's wait until the rain stops.* 咱们等雨停了吧。◇ *Until she spoke I hadn't realized she wasn't English.* 直到她开口说话我才知道她不是英格兰人。◇ *You're not going out until you've finished this.* 你没把这事做完就不准出去。◇ *Until now I have always lived alone.* 直到现在，我一直独自生活。◇ *They moved here in 2009. Until then they'd always been in the London area.* 他们 2009 年搬到这里，之前一直住在伦敦地区。◇ *He continued working up until his death.* 他一直工作到去世。◇ *The street is full of traffic* ***from morning till night.*** 街上从早到晚车水马龙。◇ *You can stay on the bus until London* (= until you reach London). 你可以不用下车，直到公车到达伦敦。

un·time·ly /ʌnˈtaɪmli/ *adj.* (*formal*) **1** happening too soon or sooner than is normal or expected 过早的；不到时间的；突然的 **SYN premature**：*She met a tragic and* ***untimely death*** *at 25.* 她于 25 岁时不幸猝然辞世。**2** happening at a time or in a situation that is not suitable 不合时宜的；不适时的 **SYN ill-timed**：*His interruption was untimely.* 他的插话不是时候。**OPP timely**

un·tir·ing /ʌnˈtaɪərɪŋ/ *adj.* (*approving*) continuing to do sth for a long period of time with a lot of effort and/or enthusiasm 不知疲劳的；孜孜不倦的；坚持不懈的 **SYN tireless**

un·titled /ˌʌnˈtaɪtld/ *adj.* (of a work of art 艺术品) without a title 无题的（表示不标明题目或没有名称）

unto /ˈʌntə; *before vowels* ˈʌntu/ *prep.* (*old use*) **1** to or towards sb/sth 朝；向；到；对：*The angel appeared unto him in a dream.* 在梦中天使出现在他面前。**2** until a particular time or event 直到；到…为止：*The knights swore loyalty unto death.* 骑士们宣誓至死效忠。

un·told /ˌʌnˈtəʊld; *NAmE* ˌʌnˈtoʊld/ *adj.* **1** [only before noun] used to emphasize how large, great, unpleasant, etc. sth is 难以形容的（大、恶劣等） **SYN immeasurable**：*untold misery/wealth* 极度的痛苦；巨额财富 ◇ *These gases cause* ***untold damage*** *to the environment.* 这些气体对环境造成难以估计的破坏。**2** (of a story 故事) not told to anyone 未讲过的；未叙述的

un·touch·able /ʌnˈtʌtʃəbl/ *adj., noun*

■ *adj.* **1** a person who is **untouchable** is in a position where they are unlikely to be punished or criticized 不可处罚（或批评）的；管不了的：*Given his political connections, he thought he was untouchable.* 他有一些政界关系，所以自以为谁也管不了他。**2** that cannot be touched or changed by other people 不可触及（或改变）的：*The department's budget is untouchable.* 这个部门的预算是不容变动的。**3** (in India in the past) belonging to or connected with the Hindu social class (or CASTE) that was considered by other classes to be the lowest （旧时印度）贱民的，不可接触者的

■ *noun* (*often* **Untouchable**) (in India in the past) a member of a Hindu social class (or CASTE) that was considered by other classes to be the lowest （旧时印度）贱民，不可接触者

un·touched /ʌnˈtʌtʃt/ *adj.* [not usually before noun] **1 ~ (by sth)** not affected by sth, especially sth bad or unpleasant; not damaged 未受影响；未被损害；原封未动：*The area has remained relatively untouched by commercial development.* 相对而言，这个地区至今没怎么受到商业开发的影响。**2** (of food or drink 食物或饮料) not eaten or drunk 未食用（或饮用）；未动：*She left her meal untouched.* 她的饭连动都没动。**3** not changed in any way 未改变；未修改：*The final clause in the contract will be left untouched.* 合同的最后一项条款将不作改动。

un·to·ward /ˌʌntəˈwɔːd; *NAmE* ʌnˈtɔːrd/ *adj.* unusual and unexpected, and usually unpleasant 异常的；意外的；不幸的；棘手的：*That's the plan—unless* ***anything untoward*** *happens.* 计划就这么定了，除非出现异常情况。◇ *He had noticed* ***nothing untoward.*** 他没有注意到有何特殊情况。

un·trained /ˌʌnˈtreɪnd/ *adj.* **~ (in sth)** not trained to perform a particular job or skill; without formal training in sth 没有训练的；未经正规培训的：*untrained in keyboard skills* 未经键盘操作技能训练的 ◇ *untrained teachers* 未经正规培训的教师 ◇ ***To the untrained eye,*** *the products look remarkably similar.* 这些产品在没有受过专门训练的人看来几乎一模一样。

un·tram·melled (*especially US* **un·tram·meled**) /ʌnˈtræmld/ *adj.* **~ (by sth)** (*formal*) not restricted or limited by sth 不受限制的；无拘束的；自由自在的 ➲ COMPARE TRAMMEL

un·treat·ed /ˌʌnˈtriːtɪd/ *adj.* **1** not receiving medical treatment 没有接受治疗的：*If untreated, the illness can become severe.* 若不加以治疗，病情就可能会变得很严重。**2** (of substances 物质) not made safe by chemical or other treatment 未处理的：*untreated sewage* 未处理的污水 **3** (of wood 木材) not treated with substances to preserve it 未经防护处理的

un·tried /ˌʌnˈtraɪd/ *adj.* **1** without experience of doing a particular job 没有经验的：*She chose two untried actors for the leading roles.* 她选了两个没有经验的演员饰演主角。**2** not yet tried or tested to discover if it works or is successful 未检验的；未经考验（或试验）的 **SYN untested**：*This is a new and relatively untried procedure.* 这是个未经多少试验的新程序。

U

un·true /ʌn'tru:/ *adj.* **1** not true; not based on facts 不真实的；假的；无事实根据的：*These accusations are totally untrue.* 这些指控纯属捏造。◇ *an untrue claim* 不真实的说法 ◇ *It **is untrue to say** that something like this could never happen again.* 说这类事情再也不会发生是毫无事实根据的。**2** ~ (**to sb/sth**) (*formal*) not loyal to sb/sth 不忠实的；不忠诚的 SYN **unfaithful**：*If he agreed to their demands, he would have to be untrue to his principles.* 假使答应他们的要求，他就得背叛自己的原则。OPP **true**

un·trust·worthy /ʌn'trʌstwɜ:ði; *NAmE* -wɜ:rði/ *adj.* that cannot be trusted 不可靠的；不能信赖（或信任）的 OPP **trustworthy**

un·truth /ˌʌn'tru:θ/ *noun* (*pl.* **un·truths** /ˌʌn'tru:ðz; -'tru:θs/) **1** [C] (*formal*) a lie. People often say 'untruth' to avoid saying 'lie'. (lie 的委婉说法) 妄语，诳语，假话 ➲ COMPARE TRUTH (1) **2** [U] the state of being false 虚伪；虚假；不真实

un·truth·ful /ʌn'tru:θfl/ *adj.* saying things that you know are not true 说谎的；不说实话的 OPP **truthful** ▶ **un·truth·ful·ly** /-fəli/ *adv.*

un·turned /ˌʌn'tɜ:nd; *NAmE* ˌʌn'tɜ:rnd/ *adj.* IDM SEE STONE *n.*

un·tutored /ˌʌn'tju:təd; *NAmE* ˌʌn'tu:tərd/ *adj.* (*formal*) not having been formally taught about sth 未接受正规教育的；未受过正式训练的

un·typ·ical /ʌn'tɪpɪkl/ *adj.* ~ (**of sb/sth**) not typical 不典型的；无代表性的；无特征的：*an untypical example* 非典型的例子 ◇ *Schools in this area are quite untypical of schools in the rest of the country.* 这个地区的学校根本不能代表全国其他地区的学校。◇ *All in all, it had been a **not untypical** day* (= it had been very like other days). 总而言之，那一天平平常常，并没有什么特别。OPP **typical** ➲ COMPARE ATYPICAL ▶ **un·typ·ic·al·ly** /-kli/ *adv.*

un·usable /ʌn'ju:zəbl/ *adj.* in such a bad condition or of such low quality that it cannot be used（破得或差得）不能使用的；破烂不堪的 OPP **usable**

un·used[1] /ˌʌn'ju:zd/ *adj.* not being used at the moment; never having been used 没用着的；闲着的；未用过的 ➲ COMPARE DISUSED

un·used[2] /ʌn'ju:st/ *adj.* not having much experience of sth and therefore not knowing how to deal with it; not used to sth 经验少；不习惯；不熟悉；不惯于：**~ to sth** *This is an easy routine, designed for anyone who is unused to exercise.* 这是一套简单的固定动作，是为不常锻炼的人设计的。◇ **~ to doing sth** *She was unused to talking about herself.* 她不习惯谈论自己。OPP **used**[1]

un·usual 🔑 /ʌn'ju:ʒuəl; -ʒəl/ *adj.* **1** 🔑 different from what is usual or normal 特别的；不寻常的；罕见的 SYN **uncommon**：***It's unusual** for the trees to flower so early.* 这种树这么早开花很少见。◇ *She has a very unusual name.* 她的名字很特别。◇ *It's **not unusual** for young doctors to work a 70-hour week* (= it happens often). 年轻的医生每周工作 70 小时并不罕见。**2** 🔑 different from other similar things and therefore interesting and attractive 独特的；与众不同的；别致的：*an unusual colour* 特别的颜色

un·usual·ly 🔑 /ʌn'ju:ʒuəli; -ʒəli/ *adv.* **1** 🔑 used before adjectives to emphasize that a particular quality is greater than normal（置于形容词前，用以强调）特别地，极，非常：*unusually high levels of radiation* 超高的辐射强度 ◇ *an unusually cold winter* 异常寒冷的冬天 **2** 🔑 used to say that a particular situation is not normal or expected 不寻常地；意想不到地：*Unusually for him, he wore a tie.* 他破例打了一条领带。

un·utter·able /ʌn'ʌtərəbl/ *adj.* [only before noun] (*formal*) used to emphasize how great a particular emotion or quality is 难以言表的；说不出的：*unutterable sadness* 无法形容的悲伤 ▶ **un·utter·ably** /-əbli/ *adv.*

un·var·nished /ʌn'vɑ:nɪʃt; *NAmE* -'vɑ:rn-/ *adj.* **1** [only before noun] (*formal*) with nothing added 不加掩饰的；质朴的；坦率的：*It was the plain unvarnished truth.* 这是简单确凿的事实。**2** (of wood, etc. 木材等) not covered with VARNISH 未加涂层的；未涂清漆的

un·vary·ing /ʌn'veərɪŋ; *NAmE* -'veri-; -'væri-/ *adj.* (*formal*) never changing 从无变化的；固定的；恒久的：*an unvarying routine* 不变的常规

un·veil /ˌʌn'veɪl/ *verb* **1** ~ **sth** to remove a cover or curtain from a painting, statue, etc. so that it can be seen in public for the first time 为…揭幕；揭开…上的覆盖物；拉开…的帷幔：*The Queen unveiled a plaque to mark the official opening of the hospital.* 女王主持揭幕式，标志着医院正式启用。**2** ~ **sth** to show or introduce a new plan, product, etc. to the public for the first time（首次）展示，介绍，推出；将…公之于众 SYN **reveal**：*They will be unveiling their new models at the Motor Show.* 他们将在汽车展上首次推出自己的新型汽车。

un·voiced /ˌʌn'vɔɪst/ *adj.* **1** thought about but not expressed in words（想法）未用语言表达的，未说出的 **2** (*phonetics* 语音) (of consonants 辅音) produced without moving your VOCAL CORDS; not VOICED 清音的；不带声的 SYN **voiceless**：*unvoiced consonants such as 'p' and 't'* 清辅音如 /p/ 和 /t/

un·waged /ˌʌn'weɪdʒd/ *adj.* (*BrE*) **1** (of a person 人) not earning money by working 无工资收入的；不挣钱的 OPP **waged** **2** (of work 工作) for which you are not paid 无偿的；无报酬的 SYN **unpaid** **3 the unwaged** *noun* [pl.] people who are unwaged 无工作报酬者

un·want·ed /ˌʌn'wɒntɪd; *NAmE* -'wɑ:nt-; -'wɔ:nt-/ *adj.* that you do not want 不需要的；多余的；不受欢迎的：*unwanted advice* 多余的劝告 ◇ *unwanted pregnancies* 非意愿妊娠 ◇ *It is very sad when children **feel unwanted*** (= feel that other people do not care about them). 小孩觉得没有人爱是很悲惨的。

un·war·rant·ed /ʌn'wɒrəntɪd; *NAmE* -'wɔ:r-; -'wɑ:r-/ *adj.* (*formal*) not reasonable or necessary; not appropriate 不合理的；不必要的；无正当理由的；不适当的 SYN **unjustified**：*Much of the criticism was totally unwarranted.* 这种批评基本上是毫无道理的。

un·wary /ʌn'weəri; *NAmE* -'weri/ *adj.* **1** [only before noun] not aware of the possible dangers or problems of a situation and therefore likely to be harmed in some way 不警觉的；不提防的 ➲ COMPARE WARY **2 the unwary** *noun* [pl.] people who are unwary 粗心的人；不警觉的人：*The stock market is full of traps for the unwary.* 对无风险意识的人而言，股票市场充满了陷阱。

un·washed /ˌʌn'wɒʃt; *NAmE* -'wɔ:ʃt; -'wɑ:ʃt/ *adj.* not washed; dirty 未洗涤的；肮脏的：*a pile of unwashed dishes* 一堆未洗的碟子 ◇ *Their clothes were dirty and their hair unwashed.* 他们衣服肮脏，头发未洗。

un·waver·ing /ʌn'weɪvərɪŋ/ *adj.* (*formal*) not changing or becoming weaker in any way 不动摇的；坚定的；始终如一的：*unwavering support* 坚定不移的支持 ▶ **un·waver·ing·ly** *adv.*

un·wel·come /ʌn'welkəm/ *adj.* not wanted 不需要的；不受欢迎的；多余的：*an unwelcome visitor* 不受欢迎的访客 ◇ *To avoid attracting unwelcome attention he kept his voice down.* 为避免引起不必要的注意，他把声音压低了。OPP **welcome**

un·wel·com·ing /ʌn'welkəmɪŋ/ *adj.* **1** (of a person 人) not friendly towards sb who is visiting or arriving（对造访者）不亲切的，不热情的，冷淡的 **2** (of a place 地方) not attractive; looking uncomfortable to be in 不惬意的；无亲切感的；不温馨的 OPP **welcoming**

un·well /ʌn'wel/ *adj.* [not before noun] (*rather formal*) ill/sick 有恙；染病；不适；不舒服：*She said she was feeling unwell and went home.* 她说她感觉不舒服回家了。OPP **well**

un·whole·some /ˌʌn'həʊlsəm; *NAmE* -'hoʊl-/ *adj.* **1** harmful to health; not looking healthy 有损健康的；不健康的；不卫生的 **2** that you consider unpleasant or not natural 令人不快的；讨厌的；不自然的 SYN **unhealthy** OPP **wholesome**

U

un·wieldy /ʌnˈwiːldi/ *adj.* **1** (of an object 东西) difficult to move or control because of its size, shape or weight 笨重的；笨拙的；不灵巧的 SYN **cumbersome** **2** (of a system or group of people 体制或团体) difficult to control or organize because it is very large or complicated 难控制（或操纵、管理）的；运转不灵的；尾大不掉的

un·will·ing /ʌnˈwɪlɪŋ/ *adj.* **1** [not usually before noun] ~ (**to do sth**) not wanting to do sth and refusing to do it 不情愿；不愿意：*They are unwilling to invest any more money in the project.* 他们不想在这个项目上再增加投资。◇ *She was unable, or unwilling, to give me any further details.* 她不能，或不愿意，向我提供进一步的细节。**2** [only before noun] not wanting to do or be sth, but forced to by other people 勉强的；无奈的；迫不得已的 SYN **reluctant**：*an unwilling hero* 自己不愿却被抬举的英雄 ◇ *He became the unwilling object of her attention.* 他受到她的青睐实非所愿。OPP **willing** ▸ **un·will·ing·ly** *adv.* **un·will·ing·ness** *noun* [U]

un·wind /ˌʌnˈwaɪnd/ *verb* (**un·wound**, **un·wound** /ˌʌnˈwaʊnd/) **1** [T, I] ~ (**sth**) (**from sth**) to undo sth that has been wrapped into a ball or around sth 解开，打开，松开（卷绕之物）：*to unwind a ball of string* 解开一团绳 ◇ *He unwound his scarf from his neck.* 他从脖子上解下围巾。◇ *The bandage gradually unwound and fell off.* 绷带逐渐松开脱落了。**2** [I] to stop worrying or thinking about problems and start to relax 放松；轻松 SYN **relax, wind down**：*Music helps me unwind after a busy day.* 音乐使我在忙碌一天后得以放松。

un·wise /ˌʌnˈwaɪz/ *adj.* ~ (**to do sth**) showing a lack of good judgement 愚蠢的；不明智的；轻率的 SYN **foolish**：*It would be unwise to comment on the situation without knowing all the facts.* 不全面了解情况就对局势妄加评论是不明智的。◇ *an unwise investment* 不明智的投资 OPP **wise** ▸ **un·wise·ly** *adv.*：*Perhaps unwisely, I agreed to help.* 我答应帮忙，这也许太轻率了。

un·wit·ting /ʌnˈwɪtɪŋ/ *adj.* [only before noun] not aware of what you are doing or of the situation you are involved in 不知情的；糊里糊涂的；无意的：*He became an unwitting accomplice in the crime.* 他糊里糊涂地成了犯罪的帮凶。◇ *She was the unwitting cause of the argument.* 她无意中引起了这场争执。

un·wit·ting·ly /ʌnˈwɪtɪŋli/ *adv.* without being aware of what you are doing or the situation that you are involved in 糊里糊涂地；茫然；无意地：*She had broken the law unwittingly, but still she had broken it.* 她并非故意犯法，但毕竟是犯了法。OPP **wittingly**

U

un·wont·ed /ʌnˈwəʊntɪd; *NAmE* -ˈwoʊn-/ *adj.* (*formal*) not usual or expected 不平常的；异常的；罕见的；没想到的：*He spoke with unwonted enthusiasm.* 他讲话显得出人意料的热心。

un·work·able /ʌnˈwɜːkəbl; *NAmE* -ˈwɜːrk-/ *adj.* not practical or possible to do successfully 不切实际的；难以实行的；行不通的：*an unworkable plan* 不切实际的计划 ◇ *The law as it stands is unworkable.* 照现在的情形，这条法律是难以执行的。OPP **workable**

un·world·ly /ʌnˈwɜːldli; *NAmE* -ˈwɜːrld-/ *adj.* **1** not interested in money or the things that it buys 不慕金钱的；对钱财无兴趣的 **2** lacking experience of life 不谙世故的；天真的 SYN **naive** OPP **worldly** **3** having qualities that do not seem to belong to this world 非现世的；非尘世的；超凡的：*The landscape had a stark, unworldly beauty.* 那景色有一种简朴、超凡的美。

un·wor·ried /ʌnˈwʌrid; *NAmE* -ˈwɜːr-/ *adj.* [not usually before noun] (*formal*) not worried; calm; relaxed 坦然；平静；轻松：*She appeared unworried by criticism.* 她看上去并不在乎挨批评。

un·worthy /ʌnˈwɜːði; *NAmE* ʌnˈwɜːrði/ *adj.* (*formal*) **1** ~ (**of sth**) not having the necessary qualities to deserve sth, especially respect 不值得（尊重）的；不配的：*He considered himself unworthy of the honour they had bestowed on him.* 他认为自己不配得到大家赋予他的荣誉。OPP **worthy** **2** ~ (**of sb**) not acceptable from sb, especially sb who has an important job or high social position 格格不入的；不能接受的；（与…的身份）不相称的 SYN **unbefitting**：*Such opinions are unworthy of educated people.* 知识分子发表这样的言论有失身份。▸ **un·worthi·ness** *noun* [U]：*feelings of unworthiness* 自卑感

un·wound PAST TENSE, PAST PART. OF UNWIND

un·wrap /ʌnˈræp/ *verb* (**-pp-**) ~ **sth** to take off the paper, etc. that covers or protects sth 打开（或解开、拆开）…的包装：*Don't unwrap your present until your birthday.* 生日礼物要等到你生日那天再打开。OPP **wrap up**

un·writ·ten /ˌʌnˈrɪtn/ *adj.* **1** ~ **law, rule, agreement, etc.** a law, etc. that everyone knows about and accepts even though it has not been made official 非书面的，不成文的，惯常的（法律、规定、协议等）：*an unwritten understanding that nobody leaves before five o'clock* 五点钟之前谁都不离开的默契 **2** (of a book, etc. 书等) not yet written 未写的；未写完的：*The photographs were to be included in his as yet unwritten autobiography.* 这些照片准备要收入他那尚未写的自传之中。

un·yield·ing /ʌnˈjiːldɪŋ/ *adj.* (*formal*) **1** if a person is **unyielding**, they are not easily influenced and they are unlikely to change their mind 坚定的；顽强不屈的；固执的 SYN **inflexible** **2** an **unyielding** substance or object does not bend or break when pressure is put on it 不弯曲的；坚固的

unzip /ˌʌnˈzɪp/ *verb* (**-pp-**) **1** [T, I] ~ (**sth**) if you **unzip** a piece of clothing, a bag, etc., or if it **unzips**, you open it by undoing the ZIP that fastens it 拉开…的拉锁；…的拉锁被拉开 OPP **zip up** **2** [T] ~ **sth** (*computing* 计) to return a file to its original size after it has been COMPRESSED (= made smaller) （文件）解压缩 SYN **decompress** OPP **zip**

up /ʌp/ *adv., prep., adj., verb, noun*

■ ***adv.*** HELP For the special uses of **up** in phrasal verbs, look at the entries for the verbs. For example **break up** is in the phrasal verb section at **break**. * up 在短语动词中的特殊用法见有关动词词条。如 break up 在词条 break 的短语动词部分。**1** towards or in a higher position 向（或在）较高位置；向上；在上面：*He jumped up from his chair.* 他从椅子上跳起来。◇ *The sun was already up* (= had risen) *when they set off.* 他们出发时太阳已经升起来了。◇ *They live up in the mountains.* 他们住在山区。◇ *It didn't take long to put the tent up.* 没用多长时间就搭完帐篷了。◇ *I pinned the notice up on the wall.* 我把通知钉在墙上了。◇ *Lay the cards face up* (= facing upwards) *on the table.* 把纸牌正面朝上摆在桌子上。◇ *You look nice with your hair up* (= arranged on top of or at the back of your head). 你把头发向上梳很好看。◇ ***Up you come!*** (= said when lifting a child) 举高高喽！**2** to or at a higher level 向（或在）较高水平；加大；增高：*She turned the volume up.* 她把音量调大了。◇ *Prices are still going up* (= rising). 物价还在上涨。◇ *United were 3–1 up at half-time.* 半场结束时，联队以 3:1 领先。◇ *The wind is getting up* (= blowing more strongly). 风渐渐大起来了。◇ *Sales are* ***well up*** *on last year.* 销量比去年大幅增加。➲ LANGUAGE BANK AT INCREASE **3** to the place where sb/sth is 朝（某人或某物）的方向；向…的地方：*A car drove up and he got in.* 一辆汽车开过来，他就上了车。◇ *She went straight up to the door and knocked loudly.* 她径直走到门前大声敲门。**4** to or at an important place, especially a large city 到，朝，在（重要地方，尤指大城市）：*We're going up to New York for the day.* 我们要上纽约一天。◇ (*BrE, formal*) *His son's up at Oxford* (= Oxford University). 他儿子在上牛津大学。**5** to a place in the north of a country 向（国家北部的地方）；向（北方）：*They've moved* ***up north.*** 他们已搬到北部去了。◇ *We drove up to Inverness to see my father.* 我们开车北上因弗内斯去看我父亲。**6** into pieces or parts 成碎片；分开：*She tore the paper up.* 她把纸撕得粉碎。◇ *They've had the road up* (= with the surface broken or removed) *to lay some pipes.* 他们挖开了路面以便敷设管线。◇ *How shall we divide up the work?* 我们怎么分工呢？**7** completely 完全；彻底地：*We ate all the food up.* 我们把食物吃光了。◇ *The stream has dried up.* 小溪已经干涸了。**8** so as to be formed or brought together （以便）形成，聚拢： *The government agreed to set up a committee of inquiry.* 政府同意成立一个调查委员会。◇ *She gathered up her belongings.* 她收拾起她的私人物品。 **9** so as to be finished or closed （以便）完结，关闭： *I have some paperwork to finish up.* 我有些文案工作要做完。◇ *Do your coat up; it's cold.* 把上衣扣上，天凉了。 **10** (of a period of time 一段时间) finished; over 已结束；已过去： *Time's up. Stop writing and hand in your papers.* 时间到了。不要再写了，把试卷交上来。 **11** out of bed 未上床；起床： *I stayed up late* (= did not go to bed until late) *last night.* 我昨晚熬夜了。◇ (*BrE*) *He's* ***up and about*** *again after his illness.* 他病愈后又能起来活动了。 **12** (*informal*) used to say that sth is happening, especially sth unusual or unpleasant （尤指异常或不愉快的事情）发生，出现： *I could tell* ***something was up*** *by the looks on their faces.* 从他们的脸色我就知道出事了。◇ ***What's up?*** (= What is the matter?) 怎么回事？◇ ***What's up with*** *him? He looks furious.* 他怎么了？他看上去怒气冲冲的。◇ *Is anything up? You can tell me.* 出什么事了吗？跟我说吧。 **HELP** In *NAmE* **What's up?** can just mean 'What's new?' or 'What's happening?' There may not be anything wrong. 在美式英语中，what's up 可以是 what's new 或 what's happening 的意思，可能没有什么不对头的事。

IDM **be up to sb** to be sb's duty or responsibility; to be for sb to decide 是…的职责（或责任）；由…决定： *It's not up to you to tell me how to do my job.* 还轮不到你来告诉我怎么做我的事。◇ *Shall we eat out or stay in? It's up to you.* 咱们是到外面吃饭还是待在家里？你决定吧。 **not be 'up to much** (*BrE*) to be of poor quality; to not be very good 质量差；不很好： *His work isn't up to much.* 他的活儿做得不怎么样。 **up against sth** (*informal*) facing problems or opposition 遇到问题；遭到反对： *Teachers are up against some major problems these days.* 老师们最近面临着一些重大问题。◇ *She's really* ***up against it*** (= in a difficult situation). 她确实陷入了困境。 **ˌup and 'down** **1** moving upwards and downwards 起伏；上下波动： *The boat bobbed up and down on the water.* 小船在水面颠簸。 **2** in one direction and then in the opposite direction 来回；往复： *She was pacing up and down in front of her desk.* 她在办公桌前踱来踱去。 **3** sometimes good and sometimes bad 时好时坏： *My relationship with him was up and down.* 我跟他的关系忽冷忽热。 **4** (*NAmE, informal*) if you swear **up and down** that sth is true, you say that it is definitely true 绝对地；肯定地；完全地 **ˌup and 'running** (of a system, for example a computer system 系统，如计算机系统) working; being used 在运转；在使用中： *By that time the new system should be up and running.* 到那时这个新系统应该会运转起来了。 **up before sb/sth** appearing in front of sb in authority for a judgement to be made about sth that you have done 到…面前接受裁决；出庭受审： *He came up before the local magistrate for speeding.* 他因超速驾驶到当地法庭受审。 **up for sth** **1** on offer for sth 提供作…： *The house is up for sale.* 这所房子正待出售。 **2** being considered for sth, especially as a candidate 正被考虑，被提名（作候选人等）： *Two candidates are up for election.* 有两位候选人被提名参选。 **3** (*informal*) willing to take part in a particular activity 愿意参与（某活动）： *We're going clubbing tonight. Are you* ***up for it?*** 我们今晚去夜总会，你愿意来吗？ **'up there** (*informal*) among or almost the best, worst, most important, etc. （是或差不多是最好、最差、最重要等）之列，之一： *It may not have been the worst week of my life but it's up there.* 这可能不是我一生中最糟糕的一周，但也差不远了。◇ *OK, it's not my absolute dream, but it's up there.* 是的，那不是我的终极梦想，不过也差不远了。 **up to sth** **1** as far as a particular number, level, etc. 达到（某数量、程度等）；至多有： *I can take up to four people* (= but no more than four) *in my car.* 我的汽车最多能载四个人。◇ *The temperature went up to 35°C.* 气温上升到了 35 摄氏度。 **2** (*also* **up until sth**) not further or later than sth; until sth 直到；不多于；不迟于： *Read up to page 100.* 读到第 100 页。◇ *Up to now he's been very quiet.* 到目前为止，他一直很安静。 **3** as high or as good as sth 与…一样高（或好）： *Her latest book isn't up to her usual standard.* 她的新作没有达到她平常的水准。 **4** (*also* **up to doing sth**) physically or mentally capable of sth （体力或智力上）能胜任： *He's not up to the job.* 他无法胜任这项工作。◇ *I don't feel up to going to work today.* 我觉得不舒服，今天不能去上班。 **5** (*informal*) doing sth, especially sth bad 正在干，从事着（尤指坏事）；在捣鬼： *What's she up to?* 她在捣什么鬼？◇ *What've you been up to?* 你一直在搞什么名堂？◇ *I'm sure he's* ***up to no good*** (= doing sth bad). 我敢说他在打什么坏主意。

■ ***prep.*** **1** to or in a higher position somewhere 向，在（较高位置）： *She climbed up the flight of steps.* 她爬上了那段楼梯。◇ *The village is further up the valley.* 村庄在山谷的更深处。 **2** along or further along a road or street 沿着；顺着： *We live just up the road, past the post office.* 我们就住在路的前面，刚过邮局的地方。 **3** towards the place where a river starts 向…上游；溯流而上： *a cruise up the Rhine* 乘船沿莱茵河溯流而上

IDM **up and down sth** in one direction and then in the opposite direction along sth 沿…来来回回： *I looked up and down the corridor.* 我来回扫视着走廊。 **ˌup 'yours!** (*taboo, slang*) an offensive way of being rude to sb, for example because they have said sth that makes you angry （愤怒地回应）去你的

■ ***adj.*** **1** [only before noun] directed or moving upwards 向上的；往上移动的： *an up stroke* 上提笔画 ◇ *the up escalator* 上行自动扶梯 **2** [not before noun] (*informal*) cheerful; happy or excited 高兴；快乐；激动： *The mood here is resolutely up.* 这里的气氛十分热闹。 **3** [not before noun] (of a computer system 计算机系统) working 在运行： *Our system should be up by this afternoon.* 到今天下午，我们的电脑系统应该运行起来了。

■ ***verb*** (-pp-) **1** [I] **up and…** (*informal* or *humorous*) to suddenly move or do sth unexpected 突然移动；突然做（意想不到的事）： *He* ***upped and left*** *without telling anyone.* 他突然起身不辞而别。 **2** [T] **~ sth** to increase the price or amount of sth 提高…的价格（或数量） **SYN** **raise**: *The buyers upped their offer by £1 000.* 买方把出价增加了 1 000 英镑。

IDM **ˌup 'sticks** (*BrE*) (*NAmE* **ˌpull up 'stakes**) (*informal*) to suddenly move from your house and go to live somewhere else 突然迁居 ➲ MORE AT ANTE

■ ***noun***

IDM **on the 'up** increasing or improving 在增长；在改善中： *Business confidence is on the up.* 商业信心正在增强。 **on the ˌup and 'up** (*informal*) **1** (*BrE*) becoming more and more successful 蒸蒸日上；日益兴旺；越来越好： *The club has been on the up and up since the beginning of the season.* 从本季开始，这个俱乐部便日益欣欣向荣。 **2** (*NAmE*) = ON THE LEVEL： *The offer seems to be on the up and up.* 这一提议似乎是坦诚可信的。 **ˌups and 'downs** the mixture of good and bad things in life or in a particular situation or relationship 浮沉；兴衰；荣辱

up- /ʌp/ *prefix* (in adjectives, verbs and related nouns 构成形容词、动词和相关的名词) higher; upwards; towards the top of sth 更高；向上；朝顶部： *upland* 高地 ◇ *upturned* 向上翘的 ◇ *upgrade* 升级 ◇ *uphill* 上坡 ➲ MORE LIKE THIS 6, page R25

ˌup-'anchor *verb* [I] (of a ship or its CREW 轮船或船员) to raise the ANCHOR from the water in order to be ready to sail 起锚（准备开航）

ˌup-and-'coming *adj.* likely to be successful and popular in the future 有前途的；前程似锦的： *up-and-coming young actors* 前程似锦的年轻演员

up·beat /ˈʌpbiːt/ *adj.* (*informal*) positive and enthusiastic; making you feel that the future will be good 乐观的；快乐的；积极向上的 **SYN** **optimistic**: *The tone of the speech was upbeat.* 这次讲话的语气颇为乐观。◇ *The meeting ended on an upbeat note.* 会议在乐观的气氛中结束。 **OPP** **downbeat**

up·braid /ʌpˈbreɪd/ *verb* **~ sb (for sth/for doing sth)** (*formal*) to criticize sb or speak angrily to them because you do not approve of sth that they have said or done 申斥；训斥；责骂 **SYN** **reproach**

up·bring·ing /ˈʌpbrɪŋɪŋ/ *noun* [sing., U] the way in which a child is cared for and taught how to behave while it is growing up 抚育；养育；教养；培养： *to have had a*

U

sheltered upbringing 受到呵护的养育 ◇ *He was a Catholic by upbringing.* 他因受家庭熏陶，从小就是个天主教徒。

UPC /juː piː ˈsiː/ *abbr.* (*NAmE, specialist*) Universal Product Code 通用产品代码；通用商品条码：*The Universal Product Code symbol, also known as the 'barcode', is printed on products for sale and contains information that a computer can read.* 通用产品代码符号，亦称"条码"，印在出售的商品上，其中含有计算机能识别的信息。

up·chuck /ˈʌptʃʌk/ *verb* [I, T] ~ (sth) (*NAmE, informal*) to VOMIT 呕吐

up·com·ing /ˈʌpkʌmɪŋ/ *adj.* [only before noun] going to happen soon 即将发生（或来临）的：*the upcoming presidential election* 即将举行的总统选举 ◇ *a single from the band's upcoming album* 选自该乐队即将发行的专辑的一首单曲

ˌup-ˈcountry *adj.* [only before noun] connected with an area of a country that is not near large towns 内地的；偏远的；偏僻的 ▶ **ˌup-ˈcountry** *adv.*

up·cycle /ˈʌpsaɪkl/ *verb* ~ **sth** to treat an item that has already been used in such a way that you make sth of greater quality or value than the original item 升级改造；再生利用：*Plastic straws have been upcycled into jewellery.* 塑料吸管升级改造成首饰。➲ SEE ALSO RECYCLE (1) ▶ **upcycled** *adj.*：*This wallet is made from 98% upcycled bicycle inner tubes.* 这个钱包 98% 是由再生利用的自行车内胎制成的。

up·date *verb, noun*

▪ *verb* /ˌʌpˈdeɪt/ **1** ~ **sth** to make sth more modern by adding new parts, etc. 使现代化；更新：*It's about time we updated our software.* 我们的软件应该更新了。**2** to give sb the most recent information about sth; to add the most recent information to sth 向…提供最新信息；给…增加最新信息 **SYN** **bring up to date**：~ **sb** (**on sth**) *I called the office to update them on the day's developments.* 我给办公室打电话告诉他们当天最新的发展。◇ ~ **sth** *Our records are regularly updated.* 我们的记录定期更新。

▪ *noun* /ˈʌpdeɪt/ **1** ~ (**on sth**) a report or broadcast that gives the most recent information about sth; a new version of sth containing the most recent information 最新报道；最新消息；最新进展：*a news update* 最新新闻报道 **2** (*computing* 计) the most recent improvements to a computer program that are sent to users of the program （计算机程序的）更新，最新校正数据

updo /ˈʌpduː/ *noun* (*informal*) (*pl.* **updos**) long hair that is pulled away from the face and fastened on top or at the back of the head 高髻；盘发；盘头

upend /ʌpˈend/ *verb* ~ **sb/sth** to turn sb/sth upside down 翻倒；倒放；使颠倒：*The bicycle lay upended in a ditch.* 自行车翻倒在一条小水沟里。

up·field /ˌʌpˈfiːld/ *adv.* (*sport* 体育) towards your opponent's end of the playing field 向前场；朝前场

up·front /ˌʌpˈfrʌnt/ *adj.* **1** ~ (**about sth**) not trying to hide what you think or do 坦率的；诚实的；直爽的 **SYN** **honest, frank**：*He's been upfront about his intentions since the beginning.* 他从一开始就坦白说出了他的意图。**2** [only before noun] paid in advance, before other payments are made 预付的；预交的：*There will be an upfront fee of 4%.* 将收取 4% 的预付费。➲ SEE ALSO UP FRONT at FRONT *n.*

up·grad·ation /ˌʌpgreɪˈdeɪʃn; ˌʌpgrəˈd-/ *noun* [U] (*IndE*) the fact of UPGRADING sth 升级；改善；提高：*the upgradation of civic facilities in large cities* 大城市市政设施的改进

up·grade /ˌʌpˈgreɪd; *NAmE also* ˈʌpgreɪd/ *verb* [often passive] **1** ~ **sth** to make a piece of machinery, computer system, etc. more powerful and efficient 使（机器、计算机系统等）升级；提高；改进 **2** ~ **sb** (**to sth**) to give sb a more important job 提升；提拔 **SYN** **promote 3** ~ **sb** (**to sth**) to give sb a better seat on a plane, room in a hotel, etc. than the one that they have paid for 提高（飞机乘客、旅馆住客等的）待遇；优待 **4** ~ **sth** to improve the condition of a building, etc. in order to provide a better service 提高（设施、服务等的）档次；改善；使升格：*to upgrade the town's leisure facilities* 改善镇里的休闲设施 ➲ COMPARE DOWNGRADE ▶ **up·grade** /ˈʌpgreɪd/ *noun* ➲ MORE LIKE THIS 21, page R27

up·heav·al /ʌpˈhiːvl/ *noun* [C, U] a big change that causes a lot of confusion, worry and problems 剧变；激变；动乱；动荡 **SYN** **disruption**：*the latest upheavals in the education system* 最近教育制度上的种种变更 ◇ *I can't face the upheaval of moving house again.* 我无法忍受再次搬家的折腾。◇ *a period of emotional upheaval* 情绪波动很大的时期

up·hill /ˌʌpˈhɪl/ *adj., adv.*

▪ *adj.* **1** sloping upwards 上坡的：*an uphill climb/slope* 向上的攀爬；上坡 ◇ *The last part of the race is all uphill.* 赛跑的最后一段全是上坡路。**OPP** **downhill 2** ~ **battle, struggle, task, etc.** an argument or a struggle that is difficult to win and takes a lot of effort over a long period of time 漫长而艰难的，费力的（战斗、斗争、任务等）

▪ *adv.* towards the top of a hill or slope 向山上；朝上坡方向：*We cycled uphill for over an hour.* 我们骑自行车爬了一个多小时的坡。◇ *The path slopes steeply uphill.* 小径直上陡峭的山坡。**OPP** **downhill**

up·hold /ʌpˈhəʊld; *NAmE* -ˈhoʊld/ *verb* (**up·held, up·held** /-ˈheld/) **1** ~ **sth** to support sth that you think is right and make sure that it continues to exist 支持，维护（正义等）：*We have a duty to uphold the law.* 维护法律是我们的责任。**2** ~ **sth** (especially of a court of law 尤指法庭) to agree that a previous decision was correct or that a request is reasonable 维持（原判）；受理（申诉）：*to uphold a conviction/an appeal/a complaint* 维持原判；受理上诉 / 申诉 ▶ **up·hold·er** *noun*：*an upholder of traditional values* 支持传统价值观的人

up·hol·ster /ʌpˈhəʊlstə(r); *NAmE* -ˈhoʊl-/ *verb* [usually passive] ~ **sth** (**in sth**) to cover a chair, etc. with soft material (= PADDING) and cloth 为（椅子等）装软垫（或套子等）

up·hol·ster·er /ʌpˈhəʊlstərə(r); *NAmE* -ˈhoʊl-/ *noun* a person whose job is to upholster furniture 家具装饰商

up·hol·stery /ʌpˈhəʊlstəri; *NAmE* -ˈhoʊl-/ *noun* [U] **1** soft covering on furniture such as ARMCHAIRS and SOFAS 家具装饰品（或衬垫等） **2** the process or trade of UPHOLSTERING 家具装饰；家具装饰业

up·keep /ˈʌpkiːp/ *noun* [U] **1** ~ (**of sth**) the cost or process of keeping sth in good condition 保养（费）；维修（费） **SYN** **maintenance**：*Tenants are responsible for the upkeep of rented property.* 承租人应负责维修租用的房产。**2** ~ (**of sb/sth**) the cost or process of giving a child or an animal the things that they need 抚养（费）；喂养（成本）：*He makes payments to his ex-wife for the upkeep of their children.* 他向前妻支付子女的抚养费。

up·land /ˈʌplənd/ *noun* [usually pl.] an area of high land that is not near the coast （内陆）高地；山地 ▶ **up·land** *adj.* [only before noun]：*upland agriculture* 山区农业

up·lift *noun, verb*

▪ *noun* /ˈʌplɪft/ [U, sing.] **1** the fact of sth being raised or of sth increasing 提高；抬高；增长；增加：*an uplift in sales* 销售的增长 ◇ *an uplift bra* (= that raises the breasts) 挺高式乳罩 **2** a feeling of hope and happiness 振奋；鼓舞：*The news gave them a much needed uplift.* 这消息给他们带来了及时的鼓舞。**3** (*also* **up·thrust**) (*geology* 地) the process or result of land being moved to a higher level by movements inside the earth （地壳的）隆起，上升；抬升

▪ *verb* /ˌʌpˈlɪft/ ~ **sb** (*formal*) to make sb feel happier or give sb more hope 鼓励；激励；使振奋

up·lift·ed /ˌʌpˈlɪftɪd/ *adj.* **1** [not before noun] feeling happy and full of hope 兴冲冲；意气昂扬 **2** (*literary*) lifted upwards 抬起的；昂起的；举起的：*a sea of uplifted faces* 一张张扬起的脸

up·lift·ing /ˌʌpˈlɪftɪŋ/ *adj.* making you feel happier or giving you more hope 令人振奋的；鼓舞人心的；催人奋进的：*an uplifting experience/speech* 令人振奋的经历 / 演说

U

up·light·er /ˈʌplaɪtə(r)/ (*also* **up·light** /ˈʌplaɪt/) *noun* a lamp in a room that is designed to send light upwards 上射灯 ➲ COMPARE DOWNLIGHTER

up·link /ˈʌplɪŋk/ *noun* (*specialist*) a communications link to a SATELLITE （卫星通信的）上行链路

up·load *verb, noun*
■ *verb* /ˌʌpˈləʊd; *NAmE* -ˈloʊd/ ~ **sth** (*computing* 计) to send data onto another computer 上传 **OPP** **download** ➲ COLLOCATIONS AT EMAIL
■ *noun* /ˈʌpləʊd; *NAmE* -loʊd/ (*computing* 计) data that has been moved to a larger computer system from a smaller one 上载（或上传）的数据 **OPP** **download**

up·mar·ket /ˌʌpˈmɑːkɪt; *NAmE* -ˈmɑːrk-/ (*especially BrE*) (*NAmE also* **up·scale**) *adj.* [usually before noun] designed for or used by people who belong to a high social class or have a lot of money 高档的；高级的：*an upmarket restaurant* 高级餐厅 **OPP** **downmarket** ▶ **up·mar·ket** (*BrE*) (*NAmE* **up·scale**) *adv.*：*The company has been forced to move more upmarket.* 这家公司被迫进一步转向高端市场。

upon /əˈpɒn; *NAmE* əˈpɑːn; əˈpɔːn/ *prep.* **1** (*formal, especially BrE*) = ON：*The decision was based upon two considerations.* 这一决定基于两种考虑。**HELP** Although the word **upon** has the same meaning as **on**, it is usually used in more formal contexts or in phrases such as：*once upon a time* and：*row upon row of seats*. * upon 与 on 同义，但通常用于较正式的场合或 once upon a time 和 row upon row of seats 等短语中。**2** ... **upon**... used to emphasize that there is a large number or amount of sth （强调数目或数量大）：*mile upon mile of dusty road* 绵延数英里尘土飞扬的道路 ◇ *thousands upon thousands of letters* 成千上万封信件

IDM **(almost) uˈpon you** if sth in the future is **almost upon you**, it is going to arrive or happen very soon 近在咫尺；即将来临：*The summer season was almost upon them again.* 转眼间他们又要过夏天了。➲ MORE AT ONCE *adv.*

upper /ˈʌpə(r)/ *adj., noun*
■ *adj.* [only before noun] **1** located above sth else, especially sth of the same type or the other of a pair 上边的，上面的，上层的（尤指同类或一对中的一个）：*the upper lip* 上嘴唇 ◇ *the upper deck* 上层甲板 **2** at or near the top of sth 上部的；靠上部的：*the upper arm* 上臂 ◇ *the upper slopes of the mountain* 靠近山顶的斜坡 ◇ *a member of the upper middle class* 中上层社会的人 ◇ *salaries at the upper end of the pay scale* 工资级别最高的薪金 ◇ *There is an upper limit of £20 000 spent on any one project.* 任何项目都有一个 2 万英镑的经费上限。**3** (of a place 地方) located away from the coast, on high ground or towards the north of an area 内陆的；高地的；向北部的：*the upper reaches of the river* 河流的上游 **OPP** **lower**[1]

IDM **gain, get, have, etc. the ˌupper ˈhand** to get an advantage over sb so that you are in control of a particular situation 占上风；处于有利地位；有优势；有控制权 ➲ MORE AT STIFF *adj.*
■ *noun* [usually pl.] **1** the top part of a shoe that is attached to the SOLE 鞋帮；靴面：*shoes with leather uppers* 皮鞋 ➲ VISUAL VOCAB PAGE V69 **2** (*informal*) a drug that makes you feel excited and full of energy 兴奋剂 ➲ COMPARE DOWNER (1)

IDM **on your ˈuppers** (*BrE, informal*) having very little money 手头拮据；困窘

ˌupper ˈcase *noun* [U] (*specialist*) capital letters (= the large form of letters, for example A, B, C rather than a, b, c) 大写字母：*Headings should be in upper case.* 标题应该大写。◇ *upper-case letters* 大写字母 ➲ COMPARE LOWER CASE

ˌupper ˈchamber *noun* = UPPER HOUSE

the ˌupper ˈclass *noun* [sing.] (*also* **the ˌupper ˈclasses** [pl.]) the groups of people that are considered to have the highest social status and that have more money and/or power than other people in society 上流社会；上等阶层：*a member of the upper class/upper classes* 上流社会人士 ▶ **ˌupper ˈclass** *adj.*：*Her family is very upper class.* 她家世显赫。◇ *an upper-class accent* 上流社会的腔调 ➲ COMPARE LOWER CLASS at LOWER CLASSES, MIDDLE CLASS, WORKING CLASS

upper·class·man /ˌʌpəˈklɑːsmən; *NAmE* ˌʌpərˈklæs-/, **upper·class·woman** /ˌʌpəˈklɑːswʊmən; *NAmE* ˌʌpərˈklæs-/ *noun* (*pl.* **-men** /-mən/, **-women** /-wɪmɪn/) (in the US) a student in the last two years of HIGH SCHOOL or college 高年级学生（美国中学或大学的最高两个年级的学生）➲ COMPARE UNDERCLASSMAN

the ˌupper ˈcrust *noun* [sing.+sing./pl. v.] (*informal*) the people who belong to the highest social class 上流社会的人；上层人士；达官显贵 **SYN** **aristocracy** ▶ **ˌupper-ˈcrust** *adj.*

upper·cut /ˈʌpəkʌt; *NAmE* ˈʌpərkʌt/ *noun* (in boxing 拳击运动) a way of hitting sb on the chin, in which you bend your arm and move your hand upwards 上钩拳

ˌupper ˈhouse (*also* **ˌupper ˈchamber**) (*also* **ˌsecond ˈchamber** *especially in BrE*) *noun* [sing.] one of the parts of a parliament in countries which have a parliament that is divided into two parts. In Britain it is the House of Lords and in the US it is the Senate. 上议院；（英国）贵族院；（美国）参议院 ➲ COMPARE LOWER HOUSE

upper·most /ˈʌpəməʊst; *NAmE* ˈʌpərmoʊst/ *adj., adv.*
■ *adj.* **1** [usually before noun] (*formal*) higher or nearer the top than other things 最高的；最上端的；最上面的：*the uppermost branches of the tree* 树顶端的枝桠 **2** [not usually before noun] more important than other things in a particular situation 最重要；最关键：*These thoughts were **uppermost in my mind**.* 我心里想的最多的就是这些事。
■ *adv.* (*formal*) in the highest position; facing upwards 处于最高位置；面向上地：*Place the material on a flat surface, shiny side uppermost.* 把材料放在平面上，有光的一面朝上。

ˈupper school *noun* (*BrE*) a school, or the classes in a school, for older students, usually between the ages of 14 and 18 高中，高中班（通常为 14 至 18 岁的学生而设）➲ COMPARE LOWER SCHOOL, MIDDLE SCHOOL

up·pity /ˈʌpəti/ *adj.* (*old-fashioned, informal*) behaving as if you are more important than you really are, especially when this means that you refuse to obey orders 傲慢的；自视甚高（而不服从）的

up·raised /ˌʌpˈreɪzd/ *adj.* lifted upwards 举起的；扬起的：*She strode towards them, her fist upraised.* 她举着拳头，大步迈向他们。

up·right /ˈʌpraɪt/ *adj., adv., noun*
■ *adj.* **1** (of a person 人) not lying down, and with the back straight rather than bent 直立的；挺直的：*an upright posture* 直立的姿势 ◇ *Gradually raise your body into an upright position.* 慢慢起身，成直立状态。**2** placed in a vertical position 竖直的；直立的；垂直的：*Keep the bottle upright.* 保持瓶子直立。◇ *an upright freezer* (= one that is taller than it is wide) 立式冰柜 ◇ *an upright piano* (= one with vertical strings) 一台立式钢琴 **3** (of a person 人) behaving in a moral and honest way 正直的；诚实的；规矩的 **SYN** **upstanding**：*an upright citizen* 正直的公民 **IDM** SEE BOLT *adv.*
■ *adv.* in or into a vertical position 竖立着；垂直着：*She sat upright in bed.* 她挺直地坐在床上。◇ *He managed to pull himself upright.* 他设法挺直了身子。
■ *noun* **1** a long piece of wood, metal or plastic that is placed in a vertical position, especially in order to support sth （支撑用的）直柱，立柱，立放构件 **2** = UPRIGHT PIANO

up·right·ness /ˈʌpraɪtnəs/ *noun* [U] behaviour or attitudes that are very moral and honest 正直的行为（或态度）；诚实；公正

ˌupright piˈano (*also* **up·right**) *noun* a piano in which the strings are vertical 立式钢琴 ➲ VISUAL VOCAB PAGE V40 ➲ COMPARE GRAND PIANO, SPINET

U

up·ris·ing /ˈʌpraɪzɪŋ/ *noun* ~ (**against sth**) a situation in which a group of people join together in order to fight against the people who are in power 起义；暴动；造反 SYN **rebellion, revolt**: *an armed uprising against the government* 反政府的武装起义 ◇ *a* ***popular uprising*** (= by the ordinary people of the country) 平民暴动 ◇ *to crush/suppress an uprising* 粉碎 / 镇压暴动 ➲ WORDFINDER NOTE AT PROTEST

up·river /ˌʌpˈrɪvə(r)/ *adv.* = UPSTREAM

up·roar /ˈʌprɔː(r)/ *noun* [U, sing.] **1** a situation in which people shout and make a lot of noise because they are angry or upset about sth 吵闹；喧嚣；叫喊：*The room was in (an) uproar.* 屋子里一片嘈杂。◇ *Her comments provoked (an) uproar from the audience.* 她的评论激起了听众的鼓噪。**2** a situation in which there is a lot of public criticism and angry argument about sth that sb has said or done 骚动；怨愤 SYN **outcry**: *The article caused (an) uproar.* 这篇文章引起了轩然大波。

up·roari·ous /ʌpˈrɔːriəs/ *adj.* [usually before noun] **1** in which there is a lot of noise and people laugh or shout a lot 喧闹的；热烈的；吵吵嚷嚷的：*an uproarious party* 热闹的聚会 **2** extremely funny 滑稽的；极可笑的；令人捧腹的：*an uproarious story* 令人捧腹的故事 ▸ **up·roari·ous·ly** *adv.*: *The audience laughed uproariously.* 观众哄然大笑。◇ *uproariously funny* 滑稽得令人捧腹

up·root /ˌʌpˈruːt/ *verb* **1** [T] ~ **sth** to pull a tree, plant, etc. out of the ground 将…连根拔起 **2** [I, T] to leave a place where you have lived for a long time; to make sb do this （使）离开家园（或熟悉的地方等）：*We decided to uproot and head for Scotland.* 我们决定迁往苏格兰。◇ ~ **yourself/sb** *If I accept the job, it will mean uprooting my family and moving to Italy.* 如果我接受了这份工作，那将意味着我得举家搬迁到意大利去。

up·rush /ˈʌprʌʃ/ *noun* [sing.] ~ **of sth** (*formal*) a sudden feeling of sth such as joy or fear （快乐或惧怕等感觉的）突发，突涌：*an uprush of joy* 涌上心头的一阵喜悦

ups-a-daisy /ˈʊpsə deɪzi; ˈʌpsə/ *exclamation* = UPSY-DAISY

up·scale /ˌʌpˈskeɪl/ *adj., verb*

■ *adj.* [usually before noun] (*NAmE*) (*also especially BrE* **up·mar·ket**) designed for or used by people who belong to a high social class or have a lot of money 高档的；高级的 OPP **downscale** ▸ **up·scale** (*NAmE*) (*BrE* **up·mar·ket**) *adv.*

■ *verb* **1** ~ **sth** to make sth better, bigger or more powerful 改进；扩大；升级：*The pilot project will begin in three areas and then be upscaled to the entire state.* 该试点项目将先在三个地区推行，然后扩展至整个州。**2** ~ **sth** to change a product so that it will be used or bought by people who have more money or belong to a higher social class 使（产品）更高档

up·sell /ˈʌpsel/ *verb* (**upsold, upsold** /ˈʌpsəʊld; *NAmE* -soʊld/) [I] (*business* 商) to persuade a customer to buy more products or a more expensive product than they originally intended 向上端推销（指劝说顾客购买更多或更贵的产品）：*You can usually upsell to about half the customers.* 通常可以说服大约一半的顾客掏更多的钱买东西。▸ **up·sell·ing** /ˈʌpselɪŋ/ *noun* [U] (*business* 商)：*You can make great profits from upselling.* 可以通过向上端推销赚取很高的收益。

upset 🔑 *verb, adj., noun*

■ *verb* /ʌpˈset/ (**up·set·ting, upset, upset**) **1** 🔑 to make sb/yourself feel unhappy, anxious or annoyed 使烦恼；使心烦意乱；使生气 SYN **distress**: ~ **sb/yourself** *This decision is likely to upset a lot of people.* 这项决定很可能会使许多人不快。◇ *Don't upset yourself about it—let's just forget it ever happened.* 你别为这事烦恼了，咱们就只当它没发生过。◇ **it upsets sb that…** *It upset him that nobody had bothered to tell him about it.* 让他不高兴的是，谁也没把这件事告诉他。◇ **it upsets sb to do sth** *It upsets me to think of her all alone in that big house.* 想到她孤身一人守着那所大房子，我就感到不舒服。**2** ~ **sth** to make a plan, situation, etc. go wrong 打乱；搅乱：*He arrived an hour late and upset all our arrangements.* 他迟到了一个小时，把我们的一切安排都打乱了。**3** ~ **sb's stomach** to make sb feel sick after they have eaten or drunk sth 使（肠胃）不适 **4** ~ **sth** to make sth fall over by hitting it by accident 打翻；碰倒；使倾覆：*She stood up suddenly, upsetting a glass of wine.* 她蓦然起身，碰倒了一杯酒。

IDM **upset the ˈapple cart** to cause problems for sb or spoil their plans, arrangements, etc. 制造麻烦；打乱计划（或安排等）

■ *adj.* /ˌʌpˈset/ **1** 🔑 [not before noun] ~ (**about sth**) | ~ (**that…**) unhappy or disappointed because of sth unpleasant that has happened 难过；不高兴；失望；沮丧：*There's no point getting upset about it.* 犯不着为此事难过。**2** 🔑 **an ˌupset ˈstomach** an illness in the stomach that makes you feel sick or have DIARRHOEA 肠胃不适；腹泻

■ *noun* /ˈʌpset/ **1** [U] a situation in which there are problems or difficulties, especially when these are unexpected （意外的）混乱，困扰，麻烦：*The company has survived the recent upset in share prices.* 这家公司撑过了最近股价的动荡。◇ *His health has not been improved by all the upset at home.* 家中的纷乱使他的健康毫无起色。**2** [C] (in a competition 竞赛) a situation in which a person or team beats the person or team that was expected to win 意外的结果；爆冷门 **3** [C] an illness in the stomach that makes you feel sick or have DIARRHOEA 肠胃病；腹泻：*a stomach upset* 拉肚子 **4** [U, C] feelings of unhappiness and disappointment caused by sth unpleasant that has happened 不痛快；烦闷；失望；苦恼：*It had been the cause of much emotional upset.* 那便是使人情绪一落千丈的原因。

up·set·ting 🔑 /ʌpˈsetɪŋ/ *adj.* making you feel unhappy, anxious or annoyed 令人不快（或忧虑、苦恼）的：*an upsetting experience* 令人苦恼的经历

up·shift /ˈʌpʃɪft/ *verb* [I] (*NAmE*) to change into a higher gear in a vehicle 换高挡（开车等加速）

the up·shot /ˈʌpʃɒt; *NAmE* -ʃɑːt/ *noun* [sing.] the final result of a series of events （一系列事件的）结局，结果 SYN **outcome**: *The upshot of it all was that he left college and got a job.* 这一切的最终结果是他离开大学并找了份工作。

up·side /ˈʌpsaɪd/ *noun* [sing.] the more positive aspect of a situation that is generally bad （糟糕局面的）好的一面，光明的一面，正面 OPP **downside**

ˌupside ˈdown 🔑 *adv.* in or into a position in which the top of sth is where the bottom is normally found and the bottom is where the top is normally found 颠倒；倒转；翻转：*The canoe floated upside down on the lake.* 独木舟底朝天漂浮在湖面上。OPP **right side up** ▸ **ˌupside ˈdown** 🔑 *adj.* [not usually before noun]: *The painting looks like it's upside down to me.* 在我看来这幅画好像是上下颠倒了。

IDM **turn sth ˌupside ˈdown 1** to make a place untidy when looking for sth 把…翻得乱七八糟；使凌乱不堪：*The police turned the whole house upside down looking for clues.* 警察为查找线索把整所房子翻得乱七八糟。**2** to cause large changes and confusion in a person's life 给（某人生活）造成大的变化（或混乱）：*His sudden death turned her world upside down.* 他的遽然离世使她的生活完全乱套了。

up·si·lon /ʌpˈsaɪlən; ˈʊpsɪlɒn; *NAmE* ˈʊpsɪlɑːn/ *noun* the 20th letter of the Greek alphabet (Υ, υ) 希腊字母表的第 20 个字母

up·skill /ˈʌpskɪl/ *verb* [T, I] ~ (**sb**) (*business* 商) to teach sb new skills; to learn new skills （使）提高技能；（使）学习新技能：*The company has invested heavily in upskilling its workforce.* 公司在提高员工的技能方面投资很大。▸ **up·skill·ing** /ˈʌpskɪlɪŋ/ *noun* [U]

up·stage /ˌʌpˈsteɪdʒ/ *adv., adj., verb*

■ *adv., adj.* at or towards the back of the stage in a theatre 在（或向）舞台后部（的）OPP **downstage**

■ *verb* ~ **sb** to say or do sth that makes people notice you more than the person that they should be interested in 抢…的镜头；把对…的注意吸引过来：*She was furious*

U

at being upstaged by her younger sister. 她被妹妹抢去风头，感到气愤不已。

up·stairs /ˌʌpˈsteəz; NAmE -ˈsterz/ *adv., noun*

■ *adv.* up the stairs; on or to a floor of a house or other building higher than the one that you are on 在（或向）楼上；在（或向）上一层：*The cat belongs to the people who live upstairs.* 这猫是楼上人家的。◇ *I carried her bags upstairs.* 我把她的包拿到楼上。◇ *She went upstairs to get dressed.* 她上楼换衣服去了。**OPP** **downstairs** ▶ **up·stairs** *adj.* [only before noun]: *an upstairs room* 楼上的房间 **IDM** SEE KICK *v.*

■ *noun* [sing.] the floor or floors in a building that are above the ground floor 二楼；二楼以上各层；楼上：*We've converted the upstairs into an office.* 我们把楼上改成了办公室。**OPP** **downstairs**

up·stand·ing /ˌʌpˈstændɪŋ/ *adj.* [usually before noun] (*formal*) behaving in a moral and honest way 正直的；正派的；诚实的 **SYN** **upright**：*an upstanding member of the community* 群体中正直的一分子

IDM **be upˈstanding** (*BrE, formal*) used in a formal situation to tell people to stand up（用于正式场合）请起立：*Ladies and gentlemen, please be upstanding and join me in a toast to the bride and groom.* 各位来宾，请大家起立，我们一起为新娘新郎干一杯。

up·start /ˈʌpstɑːt; NAmE -stɑːrt/ *noun* (*disapproving*) a person who has just started in a new position or job but who behaves as if they are more important than other people, in a way that is annoying 自命不凡的新上任者；狂妄自大的新手

up·state /ˌʌpˈsteɪt/ *adv.* (*US*) in or to a part of a state that is far from its main cities, especially a northern part 在（或向）州的乡野地区（尤指北部）：*They retired and went to live upstate.* 他们退休后移居到州的乡野地区去了。▶ **up·state** *adj.* [only before noun]: *upstate New York* 纽约的北部

up·stream /ˌʌpˈstriːm/ (*also less frequent* **up·river**) *adv.* ~ (**of/from sth**) along a river, in the opposite direction to the way in which the water flows 向（或在）上游；逆流：*The nearest town is about ten miles upstream.* 最近的城镇大约在沿河向上十英里处。◇ *upstream of/from the bridge* 在桥的上游 **OPP** **downstream**

up·surge /ˈʌpsɜːdʒ; NAmE -sɜːrdʒ/ *noun* [usually sing.] (*formal*) a sudden large increase in sth 急剧上升；飙升；猛增：~ (**in sth**) *an upsurge in violent crime* 暴力犯罪的猛增 ◇ ~ (**of sth**) *a recent upsurge of interest in his movies* 最近他的电影掀起的一阵热潮

up·swell /ˈʌpswel/ (*also* **up·swell·ing** /ˈʌpswelɪŋ/) *noun* [sing.] ~ **of sth** (*formal*) an increase in sth, especially a feeling（尤指感觉的）增加，上涨，上涌：*a huge upswell of emotion* 膨胀的激情

up·swept /ˈʌpswept/ (*also* **ˈswept-up**) *adj.* curved or sloping upwards 向上弯曲的；向上倾斜的：*an upswept moustache* 翘胡子

up·swing /ˈʌpswɪŋ/ *noun* [usually sing.] ~ (**in sth**) a situation in which sth improves or increases over a period of time 改进；改善；上升；进步 **SYN** **upturn**：*an upswing in economic activity* 经济活动的增加 ◇ *an upswing in the team's fortunes* 这支队伍鸿运高照

upsy-daisy /ˈʊpsi deɪzi; ˈʌpsi/ (*also* **ups-a-daisy**, **oops-a-daisy**) *exclamation* said when you have made a mistake, dropped sth, fallen down, etc. or when sb else has（自己或他人出错、掉东西、摔倒等时说）天哪，哎呀

up·take /ˈʌpteɪk/ *noun* [U, sing.] **1** ~ (**of sth**) the use that is made of sth that has become available（对现有东西的）使用，利用，应用：*There has been a high uptake of the free training.* 免费培训有很多人参加。**2** ~ (**of sth**) (*specialist*) the process by which sth is taken into a body or system; the rate at which this happens 吸收；吸收速度：*the uptake of oxygen by muscles* 肌肉对氧气的吸收

IDM **be ˌquick/ˌslow on the ˈuptake** (*informal*) to be quick/slow to understand sth 领悟得快 / 慢：*Is he always this slow on the uptake?* 他总是理解得这么慢吗？

up·tempo /ˈʌptempəʊ; NAmE -poʊ/ *adj.* (especially of music 尤指音乐) fast 快节奏的；节奏渐快的：*uptempo dance tunes* 快节奏舞曲

up·thrust /ˈʌpθrʌst/ *noun* [U] **1** (*physics* 物) the force with which a liquid or gas pushes up against an object that is floating in it（液体或气体对漂浮物的）上推力 **2** (*geology* 地) = UPLIFT

up·tick /ˈʌptɪk/ *noun* (*economics* 经, *NAmE*) a small increase in the level or value of sth（程度或价值的）小幅上升：*The futures market is showing an uptick.* 期货市场正小幅上扬。**OPP** **downtick**

up·tight /ˌʌpˈtaɪt/ *adj.* ~ (**about sth**) (*informal*) **1** anxious and/or angry about sth 紧张不安的；愤怒的：*Relax! You're getting too uptight about it.* 放松点儿！你对这事太紧张了。**2** (*especially NAmE*) nervous about showing your feelings 局促的；拘谨的；紧张的：*an uptight teenager* 腼腆的少年

up·time /ˈʌptaɪm/ *noun* [U] the time during which a machine, especially a computer, is working（计算机等的）运行时间 **OPP** **downtime**

ˌup to ˈdate *adj.* **1** modern; fashionable 现代的；最新的；时髦的；新式的：*This technology is bang up to date* (= completely modern). 这项技术是最新的。◇ *up-to-date clothes* 时髦服装 ◇ *up-to-date equipment* 最新的设备 **2** having or including the most recent information 拥有（或包含）最新信息的：*We are keeping up to date with the latest developments.* 我们时刻留意最新的发展情况。◇ *up-to-date records* 最新的记录 ◇ *She* ***brought him up to date*** *with what had happened.* 她让他知道最新的情况。➲ SEE ALSO OUT OF DATE

ˌup-to-the-ˈminute *adj.* [usually before noun] **1** having or including the most recent information 最新的；时新的；即时的：*up-to-the-minute news* 最新消息 **2** modern; fashionable 现代化的；时髦的；流行的：*up-to-the-minute designs* 最时髦的设计 ➲ SEE ALSO UP TO THE MINUTE at MINUTE[1] *n.*

up·town /ˌʌpˈtaʊn/ *adv., adj.* (*NAmE*)

■ *adv.* in or to the parts of a town or city that are away from the centre, where people live 离开市中心；在（或向）市郊：*They live in an apartment uptown.* 他们住在市郊的一套公寓。◇ *We walked uptown a couple of blocks until we found a cab.* 我们向市郊走了好几条街才找到一辆出租车。➲ COMPARE DOWNTOWN, MIDTOWN

■ *adj.* **1** [only before noun] in, to or typical of the parts of a town or city that are away from the centre, where people live 在（或向）市郊住宅区的；市郊住宅区的：*an uptown train* 开往市郊住宅区的火车 **2** typical of an area of a town or city where people have a lot of money 富人区的：*uptown prices* 富人区的价格 ◇ *an uptown girl* 富人区的姑娘

up·trend /ˈʌptrend/ *noun* [sing.] (*NAmE*) a situation in which business activity or performance increases or improves over a period of time（商业活动的）上升趋势，改善，增强，活跃 **OPP** **downtrend**

up·turn /ˈʌptɜːn; NAmE -tɜːrn/ *noun* [usually sing.] ~ (**in sth**) a situation in which sth improves or increases over a period of time 回升；好转；改善；提高 **SYN** **upswing**：*an upturn in the economy* 经济的好转 ◇ *The restaurant trade is on the upturn.* 餐厅业正在复苏。**OPP** **downturn**

up·turned /ˌʌpˈtɜːnd; NAmE ˌʌpˈtɜːrnd/ *adj.* [usually before noun] **1** pointing or facing upwards 向上翘的；面朝上的：*an upturned nose* (= that curves upwards at the end) 翘鼻子 ◇ *She looked down at the sea of upturned faces.* 她俯视着一大片仰起的脸孔。**2** turned upside down 颠倒的；翻转的；倒着的：*She sat on an upturned box.* 她坐在一个倒放的箱子上。

uPVC /ˌjuː ˌpiː ˌviː ˈsiː/ *noun* [U] the abbreviation for 'unplasticized polyvinyl chloride' (a strong plastic used to make window frames and pipes) 硬质聚氯乙烯（全

U

写为 unplasticized polyvinyl chloride，用以制作窗框和管子的坚固塑料）

up·ward /ˈʌpwəd; *NAmE* -wərd/ *adj.* [only before noun] **1** pointing towards or facing a higher place 向上的；朝上的；向高处的：*an upward gaze* 举目凝望 **2** increasing in amount or price （数量、价格）上升的，上涨的，增长的：*an upward movement in property prices* 房地产价格的上升 OPP **downward**

ˌupwardly ˈmobile *adj.* moving towards a higher social position, usually in which you become richer 走向上层社会的；走向富裕的；步步高升的：*upwardly mobile immigrant groups* 步步高升的移民群体 ◇ *an upwardly mobile lifestyle* 日益阔绰的生活方式 ▶ **ˌupward moˈbility** *noun* [U]

up·wards /ˈʌpwədz; *NAmE* -wərdz/ (*especially BrE*) (*also* **up·ward** *especially in NAmE*) *adv.* **1** towards a higher place or position 向上；向高处：*A flight of steps led upwards to the front door.* 一段台阶往上通向正门。◇ *Place your hands on the table with the palms facing upwards.* 把手放在桌子上，手心朝上。OPP **downwards** **2** towards a higher amount or price （数量、价格）上升，上涨，提高：*Bad weather forced the price of fruit upwards.* 恶劣的天气迫使水果价格上涨。◇ *The budget has been revised upwards.* 预算已经上调。OPP **downwards** **3 ~ of sth** more than the amount or number mentioned 在…以上；大于；超过：*You should expect to pay upwards of £50 for a hotel room.* 酒店每个房间预计至少要 50 英镑。

up·wind /ˌʌpˈwɪnd/ *adv., adj.* in the opposite direction to the way in which the wind is blowing 逆风；顶风：*to sail upwind* 逆风行船 ◇ *The house was upwind of the factory and its smells* (= the wind did not blow the smells towards the house). 这房子坐落在工厂的上风处，闻不到工厂的气味。OPP **downwind**

ur- /ʊə(r); *NAmE* ʊr/ *prefix* (*formal*) earliest or original 最早的；原始的

ur·an·ium /juˈreɪniəm/ *noun* [U] (*symb.* **U**) a chemical element. Uranium is a heavy, silver-white, RADIOACTIVE metal, used mainly in producing nuclear energy. 铀（放射性化学元素）

Ura·nus /ˈjʊərənəs; jʊˈreɪnəs; *NAmE* ˈjʊr-; jʊˈr-/ *noun* the planet in the SOLAR SYSTEM that is 7th in order of distance from the sun 天王星

urban /ˈɜːbən; *NAmE* ˈɜːrbən/ *adj.* [usually before noun] **1** connected with a town or city 城市的；都市的；城镇的：*damage to both urban and rural environments* 对城乡环境的破坏 ◇ *urban areas* 城镇地区 ◇ *urban life* 城市生活 ◇ *urban development* (= the process of building towns and cities or making them larger) 城市发展 ◇ ***urban renewal/regeneration*** (= the process of improving the buildings, etc. in the poor parts of a town or city) 城市更新 ◇ *efforts to control **urban sprawl*** (= the spread of city buildings into the countryside) 控制城市蔓延的努力 ⊃ COMPARE RURAL ⊃ **WORDFINDER NOTE** AT CITY, LOCATION **2** connected with types of music such as RHYTHM AND BLUES and REGGAE that are played by black musicians 都市音乐的，城市音乐的（如节奏布鲁斯音乐、雷盖音乐）：*today's urban music scene* 当今的城市音乐圈 ◇ *urban radio shows* 城市音乐广播节目

ur·bane /ɜːˈbeɪn; *NAmE* ɜːrˈb-/ *adj.* (especially of a man 尤指男子) good at knowing what to say and how to behave in social situations; appearing relaxed and confident 温文儒雅的；练达的；从容不迫的 ▶ **ur·bane·ly** *adv.* **ur·ban·ity** /ɜːˈbænəti; *NAmE* ɜːrˈb-/ *noun* [U]

ur·ban·ite /ˈɜːbənaɪt; *NAmE* ˈɜːrb-/ *noun* a person who lives in a town or city 城市居民

ur·ban·ized (*BrE also* **-ised**) /ˈɜːbənaɪzd; *NAmE* ˈɜːrb-/ *adj.* **1** (of an area, a country, etc. 地区、国家等) having a lot of towns, streets, factories, etc. rather than countryside 城市化的 **2** (of people 人) living and working in towns and cities rather than in the country 生活于城市的；在都市工作的：*an increasingly urbanized society* 城镇居民日益增加的社会 ▶ **ur·ban·iza·tion, -isa·tion** /ˌɜːbənaɪˈzeɪʃn; *NAmE* ˌɜːrbənəˈz-/ *noun* [U]

ˌurban ˈmyth (*also* **ˌurban ˈlegend**) *noun* a story about an amusing or strange event that is supposed to have happened, which is often repeated and which many people believe is true 都市传奇（街谈巷议的传闻或趣事）

ur·chin /ˈɜːtʃɪn; *NAmE* ˈɜːrtʃɪn/ *noun* **1** (*old-fashioned*) a young child who is poor and dirty, often one who has no home 贫穷肮脏的儿童；流浪儿：*a dirty little street urchin* 肮脏的街头小乞丐 **2** = SEA URCHIN

Urdu /ˈʊəduː; ˈɜːduː; *NAmE* ˈʊrduː; ˈɜːrduː/ *noun* [U] the official language of Pakistan, also widely used in India 乌尔都语（巴基斯坦的官方语言，印度也通用）

-ure *suffix* (in nouns 构成名词) the action, process or result of …的行动（或过程、结果等）：*closure* 关闭 ◇ *failure* 失败

urea /juˈriːə/ *noun* [U] (*specialist*) a clear substance containing NITROGEN that is found especially in URINE 尿素；脲

ur·ethra /juˈriːθrə/ *noun* (*anatomy* 解) the tube that carries liquid waste out of the body. In men and male animals SPERM also flows along this tube. 尿道 ▶ **ur·eth·ral** *adj.* [only before noun]

ur·eth·ritis /ˌjʊərəˈθraɪtɪs; *NAmE* ˌjʊr-/ *noun* [U] (*medical* 医) infection of the urethra 尿道炎

urge /ɜːdʒ; *NAmE* ɜːrdʒ/ *verb, noun*

■*verb* **1** to advise or try hard to persuade sb to do sth 敦促；催促；力劝：**~ sb to do sth** *She urged him to stay.* 她力劝他留下。◇ **~ that…** *The report urged that all children be taught to swim.* 这份报告呼吁教所有的儿童游泳。◇ **~ (sb) + speech** *'Why not give it a try?' she urged (him).* "为什么不试一试呢？"她敦促（他）道。⊃ **SYNONYMS** AT RECOMMEND **2** **~ sth (on/upon sb)** to recommend sth strongly 大力推荐；竭力主张：*The situation is dangerous and the UN is urging caution.* 局势岌岌可危，联合国力主谨慎行事。**3** **~ sb/sth + adv./prep.** (*formal*) to make a person or an animal move more quickly and/or in a particular direction, especially by pushing or forcing them 驱赶；鞭策：*He urged his horse forward.* 他策马前行。

PHR V **ˌurge sb↔ˈon** to encourage sb to do sth or support them so that they do it better 鼓励；激励；为…加油：*She could hear him urging her on as she ran past.* 她跑过他面前时，听到他在为她加油。

■*noun* a strong desire to do sth 强烈的欲望；冲动：*sexual urges* 性冲动 ◇ **~ to do sth** *I had a sudden urge to hit him.* 我突然很想揍他一顿。

ur·gent /ˈɜːdʒənt; *NAmE* ˈɜːrdʒ-/ *adj.* **1** that needs to be dealt with or happen immediately 紧急的；紧迫的；迫切的 SYN **pressing**: *an urgent appeal for information* 紧急呼吁提供信息 ◇ *a problem that requires urgent attention* 需要紧急处理的问题 ◇ *'Can I see you for a moment?' 'Is it urgent?'* "我能见你一下吗？""有急事吗？" ◇ *Mark the message 'urgent', please.* 请在通知上注明"急件"。◇ *The law is **in urgent need of** reform.* 这项法律亟待修订。**2** showing that you think that sth needs to be dealt with immediately 催促的；急切的：*an urgent whisper* 急切的耳语 ▶ **ur·gen·cy** /-dʒənsi/ *noun* [U, sing.]: *This is a matter of some urgency.* 这件事相当紧迫。◇ *The attack added a new urgency to the peace talks.* 这次攻击事件使和平谈判愈加紧迫。**ur·gent·ly** *adv.*: *New equipment is urgently needed.* 急需新设备。◇ *I need to speak to her urgently.* 我得马上跟她谈谈。◇ *'We must find him,' she said urgently.* "我们必须找到他。"她急切地说。

urgh /əx; *NAmE* ərx/ *exclamation* = UGH: *Urgh! There's a dead fly in my coffee!* 呸！我的咖啡里有只死苍蝇！

ur·inal /jʊəˈraɪnl; ˈjʊərɪnl; *NAmE* ˈjʊrənl/ *noun* a type of toilet for men that is attached to the wall; a room or building containing urinals （男用）小便池，小便器；男厕所

urin·ary /ˈjʊərɪnəri; NAmE ˈjʊrəneri/ *adj.* [usually before noun] (*medical* 医) connected with URINE or the parts of the body through which it passes 尿的；泌尿的；尿路的

urin·ate /ˈjʊərɪneɪt; NAmE ˈjʊrən-/ *verb* [I] (*formal* or *specialist*) to get rid of URINE from the body 排尿；小便 ▶ **urin·ation** /ˌjʊərɪˈneɪʃn; NAmE ˌjʊrəˈn-/ *noun* [U]

urine /ˈjʊərɪn; -raɪn; NAmE ˈjʊrən/ (*also informal* **wee** *especially in BrE*) *noun* [U] the waste liquid that collects in the BLADDER and that you pass from your body 尿；小便

URL /ˌjuː ɑːr ˈel/ *abbr.* (*computing* 计) uniform/universal resource locator (typically, the address of a WORLD WIDE WEB page) 统一资源定位地址，URL 地址（全写为 uniform/universal resource locator） ➲ WORDFINDER NOTE AT WEBSITE

URN /ˌjuː ɑːr ˈen/ *abbr.* (*computing* 计) uniform/universal resource name (a standard way of identifying a book, film, journal, computer file, etc.) 统一资源名称（全写为 uniform/universal resource name，一种资源定位方式） ➲ COMPARE URL

urn /ɜːn; NAmE ɜːrn/ *noun* **1** a tall decorated container, especially one used for holding the ASHES of a dead person 瓮；（尤指）骨灰缸 **2** a large metal container with a tap, used for making and/or serving tea or coffee （带龙头的）茶水桶，咖啡桶：*a tea urn* 茶水桶

ur·ology /jʊəˈrɒlədʒi; NAmE jʊˈrɑːl-/ *noun* [U] (*medical* 医) the scientific study of the URINARY system 泌尿外科学 ▶ **uro·logic·al** /ˌjʊərəˈlɒdʒɪkl; NAmE ˌjʊrəˈlɑːdʒ-/ *adj.* **ur·olo·gist** /-dʒɪst/ *noun*

Ursa Major /ˌɜːsə ˈmeɪdʒə(r); NAmE ˌɜːrsə/ (*also* **the ˌGreat ˈBear**) *noun* [sing.] (*astronomy* 天) a large group of stars that can be clearly seen from the northern HEMISPHERE 大熊（星）座

Ursa Minor /ˌɜːsə ˈmaɪnə(r); NAmE ˌɜːrsə/ (*also* **the ˌLittle ˈBear**) *noun* [sing.] a group of stars that can be clearly seen from the northern HEMISPHERE and that includes the POLE STAR 小熊（星）座

ur·sine /ˈɜːsaɪn; NAmE ˈɜːrs-/ *adj.* [usually before noun] (*specialist* or *literary*) connected with BEARS; like a bear 与熊有关的；像熊的

ur·ti·caria /ˌɜːtɪˈkeəriə; NAmE ˌɜːrtɪˈkeriə/ (*also* **nettle·rash**, **hives**) *noun* [U] (*medical* 医) red spots on the skin that ITCH (= make you want to scratch), caused by an ALLERGIC reaction, for example to certain foods 荨麻疹

US (*also* **U.S.** *especially in US*) /ˌjuː ˈes/ *abbr.* UNITED STATES (OF AMERICA) 美国；美利坚合众国：*She became a US citizen.* 她成了美国公民。◇ *the US dollar* 美元

us 🔑 /əs; *strong form* ʌs/ *pron.* (the object form of *we* * we 的宾格) **1** 🔑 used when the speaker or writer and another or others are the object of a verb or preposition, or after the verb *be* 我们：*She gave us a picture as a wedding present.* 她赠给我们一幅画作结婚礼物。◇ *We'll take the dog with us.* 我们要把狗带上。◇ *Hello, it's us back again.* 嘿！我们又回来了。**2** (*BrE, informal*) me 我：*Give us the newspaper, will you?* 把报纸给我好吗？

USA (*also* **U.S.A.** *especially in US*) /ˌjuː es ˈeɪ/ *abbr.* UNITED STATES OF AMERICA 美国；美利坚合众国：*Do you need a visa for the USA?* 你需要美国签证吗？

us·able /ˈjuːzəbl/ *adj.* that can be used; in good enough condition to be used 能用的；可用的；适用的：*The bike is rusty but usable.* 自行车生锈了，但还能骑。◇ *How can we display this data in a usable form?* 我们如何把这些数据以实用形式展示出来呢？ OPP **unusable** ▶ **usability** *noun* [U]: *They are improving the accessibility and usability of government websites.* 他们正在改进政府网站的可访问性和实用性。

USAF /ˌjuː es eɪ ˈef/ *abbr.* United States Air Force 美国空军

usage /ˈjuːsɪdʒ; ˈjuːz-/ *noun* **1** [U, C] the way in which words are used in a language （词语的）用法，惯用法：*current English usage* 当代英语惯用法 ◇ *It's not a word in common usage.* 这不是一个常用词。**2** [U] the fact of sth being used; how much sth is used 使用；利用；利用率：*land usage* 土地的利用 ◇ *Car usage is predicted to increase.* 汽车的使用率预计会增长。

USB /ˌjuː es ˈbiː/ *abbr.* (*computing* 计) universal serial bus (the system for connecting other pieces of equipment to a computer) 通用串行总线（连接计算机外接设备的系统）：*All new PCs now have USB sockets.* 新的个人计算机现在都有通用串行总线插孔。◇ *a USB port* 通用串行总线端口

USˈB drive (*also informal* **USˈB stick**) *noun* = FLASH DRIVE ➲ VISUAL VOCAB PAGE V73

USCIS /ˌjuː es siː aɪ ˈes/ *abbr.* United States Citizenship and Immigration Services (the US government department that deals with people from other countries who want to visit or live in the US or to become a US citizen, part of the Department of Homeland Security) 美国公民及移民事务署（隶属美国国土安全部）

use 🔑 *verb, noun*

■ *verb* /juːz/ (**used**, **used** /juːzd/) **1** 🔑 [T] to do sth with a machine, a method, an object, etc. for a particular purpose 使用；利用；运用：**~ sth** *Can I use your phone?* 我可以用一下你的电话吗？◇ *Have you ever used this software before?* 你以前用过这种软件吗？◇ *How often do you use* (= travel by) *the bus?* 你多长时间坐一次公共汽车？◇ *They were able to achieve a settlement without using military force.* 他们没有诉诸武力就解决了问题。◇ *I have some information you may be able to use* (= to get an advantage from). 我有些可能对你有用的信息。◇ **~ sth for sth/for doing sth** *The blue files are used for storing old invoices.* 蓝色卷宗是用来存放旧发票的。◇ **~ sth to do sth** *Police used tear gas to disperse the crowds.* 警察用了催泪瓦斯驱散人群。◇ **~ sth as sth** *The building is currently being used as a warehouse.* 这所房子目前用作仓库。◇ *You can't keep using your bad back as an excuse.* 你不能老拿腰疼当托辞呀。**2** 🔑 [T] **~ sth** to take a particular amount of a liquid, substance, etc. in order to achieve or make sth 消耗：*This type of heater uses a lot of electricity.* 这种加热器耗电量很大。◇ *I hope you haven't used all the milk.* 希望你没有把牛奶都用掉了。**3** 🔑 [T] **~ sth** to say or write particular words or a particular type of language 说，写，使用（词语或语言）：*The poem uses simple language.* 这首诗用语简单。◇ *That's a word I never use.* 那是我从来不用的字眼。◇ *You have to use the past tense.* 要使用过去时。**4** [T] **~ sb** (*disapproving*) to be kind, friendly, etc. to sb with the intention of getting an advantage for yourself from them （施展手段）利用（别人） SYN **exploit**: *Can't you see he's just **using you for his own ends**?* 你难道看不出他在利用你谋求私利吗？◇ *I felt used.* 我觉得被人利用了。**5** [T, I] **~ (sth)** to take illegal drugs 吸（毒）；服用（毒品）：*Most of the inmates have used drugs at some point in their lives.* 大多数囚犯都在人生的某个阶段服用过毒品。◇ (*slang*) *She's been using since she was 13.* 她从 13 岁起就吸毒。

IDM **I, you, etc. could use sth** (*informal*) used to say that you would like to have sth very much 恨不得；巴不得；非常想：*I think we could all use a drink after that!* 我想我们在事情办完之后都得痛快地喝一杯！ **use your ˈhead** (*BrE also* **use your ˈloaf**) (*informal*) used to tell sb to think about sth, especially when they have asked for your opinion or said sth stupid 你动动脑子；你仔细想想：*'Why don't you want to see him again?' 'Oh, use your head!'* "你为什么不愿再见到他？""唔，你好好想想吧！" ORIGIN From rhyming slang, in which **loaf of bread** stands for 'head'. 源自同韵俚语 loaf of bread，代表 head 的意思。

PHR V **ˌuse sth↔ˈup** 🔑 to use all of sth so that there is none left 用尽；吃光：*Making soup is a good way of using up leftover vegetables.* 把剩下的蔬菜全部用来做汤是个好主意。

■ *noun* /juːs/ **1** 🔑 [U, sing.] the act of using sth; the state of being used 用；使用；得到利用：*A ban was imposed on the use of chemical weapons.* 化学武器已被禁止使用。◇ *The software is designed for use in schools.* 这个软件是为学校应用设计的。◇ *I'm not sure that this is the most valuable use of my time.* 我不能肯定我的时间这样安排最有

U

价值。◇ *The chapel was built in the 12th century and is still* **in use** *today.* 这座小教堂建于 12 世纪，今天仍在使用。◇ *The bar is* **for the use of** *members only.* 酒吧仅供会员使用。**2** [C, U] a purpose for which sth is used; a way in which sth is or can be used 用途；功能；用法：*I'm sure you'll think of a use for it.* 我相信你会给这东西找到用途的。◇ *This chemical has a wide range of industrial uses.* 这种化学品在工业上用途广泛。➲SEE ALSO SINGLE-USE **3** [U] ~ (**of sth**) the right or opportunity to use sth, for example sth that belongs to sb else 使用权；使用的机会：*I have the use of the car this week.* 这辆汽车本周归我使用。**4** [U] the ability to use your mind or body 运用头脑（或身体）的能力；功能：*He lost the use of his legs* (= became unable to walk) *in an accident.* 他在一次事故中失去了双腿的功能。

IDM **be no 'use (to sb)** (*also formal* **be of no 'use**) to be useless 无用：*You can throw those away—they're no use to anyone.* 那些东西你可以扔了，它们对谁都没用。**be of 'use (to sb)** (*formal*) to be useful 有用；有帮助：*Can I be of any use* (= can I help)? 有什么要我帮忙的吗？**come into/go out of, etc. 'use** to start/stop being used 开始 / 停止使用：*When did this word come into common use?* 这个词是什么时候普遍使用起来的？**have its/their/your 'uses** (*informal, often humorous*) to be useful sometimes 有时用得着的；偶尔可派上用场：*I know you don't like him, but he has his uses.* 我知道你不喜欢他，但他有时还用得着。**have no 'use for sb** to dislike sb 讨厌（或憎恶）…的人：*I've no use for people who don't make an effort.* 我厌恶那些不努力的人。**have no 'use for sth** to not need sth 不需要；用不着 **it's no 'use (doing sth) | what's the 'use (of doing sth)?** used to say that there is no point in doing sth because it will not be successful or have a good result 没有意义；没有用处：*What's the use of worrying about it?* 为此事操心有什么用呢？◇ *It's no use—I can't persuade her.* 没用，我劝不了她。**make 'use of sth/sb** to use sth/sb, especially in order to get an advantage 使用；利用（以谋私利等）：*We could make better use of our resources.* 我们可以更有效地利用我们的资源。**put sth to good 'use** to be able to use sth for a purpose, and get an advantage from doing so 有效使用（或利用）：*She'll be able to put her languages to good use in her new job.* 她在新工作中应该可以好好运用她会的各种语言。

used[1] /juːst/ *adj.* familiar with sth because you do it or experience it often 习惯于；适应：~ **to doing sth** *I'm not used to eating so much at lunchtime.* 我不习惯午饭吃那么多。◇ ~ **to sth** *I found the job tiring at first but I soon* **got used to** *it.* 起初我觉得这份工作很累人，但很快就习惯了。➲NOTE AT USED TO

U

used[2] /juːzd/ *adj.* [usually before noun] that has belonged to or been used by sb else before 用过的；旧的；二手的 SYN **second-hand**：*used cars* 二手汽车

used to /'juːst tə; *before vowels and finally* 'juːst tu/ *modal verb* (*negative* **didn't use to** /dɪdnt 'juːs tə; dɪdnt 'juːs tu/, *BrE also, old-fashioned or formal* **used not to**, *short form* **usedn't to** /'juːsnt tə; *before vowels and finally* 'juːsnt tu/) used to say that sth happened continuously or frequently during a period in the past（用于过去持续或经常发生的事）曾经：*I used to live in London.* 我曾经在伦敦居住过。◇ *We used to go sailing on the lake in summer.* 从前的夏天，我们经常泛舟湖上。◇ *I didn't use to like him much when we were at school.* 以前我们是同学时，我并不太喜欢他。◇ *You used to see a lot of her, didn't you?* 你过去常见她，是吧？➲NOTE AT MODAL

use·ful /'juːsfl/ *adj.* **1** that can help you to do or achieve what you want 有用的；有益的；实用的；有帮助的：*a useful gadget* 有用的小器具 ◇ ~ (**to do sth**) *It can be useful to write a short summary of your argument first.* 先把你的论点纲要写下来可能会有帮助。◇ ~ (**to sb**) *He might be useful to us.* 我们也许用得上他。◇ ~ (**for sth/for doing sth**) *These plants are particularly useful for brightening up shady areas.* 这些植物特别有助于让背阴的地方明亮起来。◇ *Don't just sit watching television—* **make yourself useful!** 别光坐着看电视，帮一下忙吧！◇ *This information could* **prove useful.** 这条信息往后也许有用。◇ *Your knowledge of German may* **come in useful** (= be useful in a particular situation). 你的德文知识可能会派上用场。◇ *Some products can be recycled at the end of their useful life.* 有些产品过了有效使用年限后是可以回收再利用的。**2** (*BrE, informal*) good; of the right standard 好的；合格的 SYN **competent**：*He's a very useful player.* 他是个很棒的运动员。▶ **use·ful·ly** /-fəli/ *adv.*：*The money could be more usefully spent on new equipment.* 这笔钱用来购置新设备可能会更有价值。

use·ful·ness /'juːsfəlnəs/ *noun* [U] the fact of being useful or possible to use 有用；实用；可用性：*There are doubts about the usefulness of these tests.* 这些试验是否有用，人们有所保留。◇ *The building has outlived its usefulness.* 这座楼房已超过使用年限了。

use·less /'juːsləs/ *adj.* **1** not useful; not doing or achieving what is needed or wanted 无用的；无效的；无价值的：*This pen is useless.* 这支笔没用了。◇ ~ (**to do sth**) *He knew it was useless to protest.* 他知道抗议是徒劳的。◇ ~ (**doing sth**) *It's useless worrying about it.* 为这事担心无济于事。◇ *She tried to work, but it was useless* (= she wasn't able to). 她很想做事，但力不从心。**2** ~ (**at sth/at doing sth**) (*informal*) not very good at sth; not able to do things well 差劲的；不行的；不擅长的：*I'm useless at French.* 我的法语不太行。◇ *Don't ask her to help. She's useless.* 别求她帮忙。她没那个能耐。▶ **use·less·ly** *adv.* **use·less·ness** *noun* [U]

▼WHICH WORD? 词语辨析

used to / be used to

- Do not confuse **used to do sth** with **be used to sth.** 不要混淆 used to do sth 与 be used to sth。
- You use **used to do sth** to talk about something that happened regularly or was the case in the past, but is not now * used to do sth 指过去惯常做某事，而现在则不了：*I used to smoke, but I gave up a couple of years ago.* 我以前抽烟，但几年前就戒掉了。
- You use **be used to sth/to doing sth** to talk about something that you are familiar with so that it no longer seems new or strange to you * be used to sth / to doing sth 指习惯于、适应于：*We're used to the noise from the traffic now.* 现在我们已经适应车辆往来的噪音了。◇ *I'm used to getting up early.* 我习惯早起。You can also use **get used to sth** 亦可用 get used to sth：*Don't worry—you'll soon get used to his sense of humour.* 别担心，你不久就会适应他的幽默感。◇ *I didn't think I could ever get used to living in a big city after living in the country.* 我觉得我在农村住了之后就无法适应大城市的生活了。

▼GRAMMAR POINT 语法说明

used to

- Except in negatives and questions, the correct form is **used to**. 除在否定句和疑问句中之外，正确的形式为 used to：*I used to go there every Saturday.* 我以前每星期六都去那儿。◇ ~~*I use to go there every Saturday.*~~
- To form questions, use *did.* 构成疑问句用 did：*Did she use to have long hair?* 她过去留长发吗？Note that the correct spelling is **use to**, not 'used to'. 注意：正确的拼写为 use to，而非 used to。
- The negative form is usually **didn't use to**, but in *BrE* this is quite informal and is not usually used in writing. 否定式通常为 didn't use to，但在英式英语中，此形式相当口语化，通常不用于书面语中。
- The negative form **used not to** (*rather formal*) and the question form **used you to…?** (*old-fashioned and very formal*) are only used in *BrE*, usually in writing. 否定式 used not to（相当正式）和疑问式 used you to ...?（过时且非常正式）只用于英式英语，而且通常作书面语。

Use·net /ˈjuːznet/ *noun* [U] (*computing* 计) a service on the Internet used by groups of users who email each other because they share a particular interest * Usenet 网，友思网，新闻组（世界性的新闻组网络系统）

user /ˈjuːzə(r)/ *noun* **1** a person or thing that uses sth 使用者；用户：*road users* 道路的使用者 ◇ *computer software users* 计算机软件用户 ◇ *a user manual* 使用说明书 ➲ SEE ALSO END USER **2** (*slang*) a person who uses illegal drugs 瘾君子；吸毒者

ˈuser fee *noun* (*NAmE*) a tax on a service that is provided for the public 使用费（某些税捐）

ˌuser-ˈfriend·ly *adj.* easy for people who are not experts to use or understand 方便非专业用户的；便于使用的；易于掌握的 ▸ **ˌuser-ˈfriendli·ness** *noun* [U]

ˌuser-ˈgenerated *noun* connected with material on a website that has been contributed by the people who use the website 用户生成的；用户原创的：*user-generated content* 用户原创内容

ˈuser group *noun* a group of people who use a particular thing and who share information about it, especially people who share information about computers on the Internet 用户组，用户群（使用同一产品或服务并交流信息）

user·name /ˈjuːzəneɪm; *NAmE* -zərn-/ *noun* (*computing* 计) the name you use in order to be able to use a computer program or system（使用计算机程序或系统时用以识别身份的）用户名：*Please enter your username.* 请键入你的用户名。

usher /ˈʌʃə(r)/ *noun, verb*

■ ***noun*** **1** a person who shows people where to sit in a church, public hall, etc. 引座员 **2** an official who has special responsibilities in court, for example allowing people in and out of the court（法院的）传达员，门卫，门房 **3** a friend of the BRIDEGROOM at a wedding, who has special duties 男傧相

■ ***verb*** **~ sb + adv./prep.** to take or show sb where they should go 把…引往；引导；引领：*The secretary ushered me into his office.* 秘书把我领进他的办公室。 ➲ SYNONYMS AT TAKE

PHR V **ˌusher sth↔ˈin** (*formal*) to be the beginning of sth new or to make sth new begin 开创；开始；开启：*The change of management ushered in fresh ideas and policies.* 更换领导班子带来了新思想和新政策。

ush·er·ette /ˌʌʃəˈret/ *noun* (*especially BrE, old-fashioned*) a woman whose job is to lead people to their seats in a theatre or cinema/movie theater 女引座员

USN /ˌjuː es ˈen/ *abbr.* United States Navy 美国海军

USP /ˌjuː es ˈpiː/ *noun* (*business* 商) the abbreviation for 'unique selling proposition' or 'unique selling point' (a feature of a product or service that makes it different from all the others that are available and is a reason for people to choose it) 独特卖点（全写为 unique selling proposition 或 unique selling point，指产品或服务吸引顾客的特色）：*You need to come up with a USP.* 你得想出个独特的卖点来。

USS /ˌjuː es ˈes/ *abbr.* United States Ship (used before the name of a ship in the US navy) 美国船（用于美国海军舰船的名称前）：*USS Oklahoma* 美国军舰俄克拉何马号

USSR /ˌjuː es es ˈɑː(r)/ *abbr.* (the former) Union of Soviet Socialist Republics（前）苏联，苏维埃社会主义共和国联盟

ustad /ʊsˈtɑːd/ *noun* (*IndE*) an expert or a highly skilled person, especially a musician 专家，大师（尤指音乐家）：*She learned classical music from an ustad.* 她曾向一名大师学习古典音乐。

usual /ˈjuːʒuəl; -ʒəl/ *adj.* **1** that happens or is done most of the time or in most cases 通常的；寻常的；惯常的 SYN **normal**：*She made all the usual excuses.* 她找了些非常司空见惯的借口。◇ *He came home later than usual.* 他回家比平时晚了些。◇ *She sat in her usual seat at the back.* 她坐在后排平时惯坐的位子上。◇ *He didn't sound like his usual happy self.* 他听起来不像平常那个乐天派了。◇ **~ (for sb/sth) (to do sth)** ***It is usual to*** *start a speech by thanking everybody for coming.* 讲话前先感谢大家光临，这是惯例。 ➲ COMPARE UNUSUAL **2 the usual** *noun* [sing.] (*informal*) what usually happens; what you usually have, especially the drink that you usually have 惯常的事物；（尤指）常喝的饮料

IDM **as usual** in the same way as what happens most of the time or in most cases 照例；照旧；像往常一样：*Steve, as usual, was the last to arrive.* 史蒂夫照例来得最晚。◇ *As usual at that hour, the place was deserted.* 跟平常那个时刻一样，那地方空荡荡的。◇ *Despite her problems, she carried on working as usual.* 尽管她有困难，她照样继续工作。 ➲ MORE AT BUSINESS, PER

usu·al·ly /ˈjuːʒuəli; -ʒəli/ *adv.* in the way that is usual or normal; most often 通常地；正常地；一般地；经常地：*I'm usually home by 6 o'clock.* 我一般 6 点钟回到家。◇ *We usually go by car.* 我们通常开汽车去。◇ *How long does the journey usually take?* 这段旅程通常需要多长时间？

us·urer /ˈjuːʒərə(r)/ *noun* (*old-fashioned, disapproving*) a person who lends money to people at unfairly high rates of interest 放高利贷者

us·uri·ous /juːˈʒʊəriəs; *NAmE* juːˈʒʊr-/ *adj.* (*formal*) lending money at very high rates of interest 放高利贷的；收取高利的

usurp /juːˈzɜːp; *NAmE* -ˈzɜːrp/ *verb* **~ sb/sth** (*formal*) to take sb's position and/or power without having the right to do this 篡夺；侵权 ▸ **usurp·ation** /ˌjuːzɜːˈpeɪʃn; *NAmE* -zɜːrˈp-/ *noun* [U, C] **usurp·er** *noun*

usury /ˈjuːʒəri/ *noun* [U] (*old-fashioned, disapproving*) the practice of lending money to people at unfairly high rates of interest 放高利贷；高利盘剥

UTC /ˌjuː tiː ˈsiː/ (*also* **Coˌordinated Uniˌversal ˈTime, ˌUniˌversal Coˌordinated ˈTime**) *abbr.* the abbreviation for 'Universal Time Coordinated' (the time based on ATOMIC CLOCKS, used as the basis for legal time in most countries) 协调世界时（全写为 Universal Time Coordinated，基于原子钟的时间，在大多数国家用作法定基准时间） ➲ COMPARE GMT

Utd *abbr.* UNITED 联合的；统一的；一致的；团结的

Ute /juːt/ *noun* (*pl.* **Ute** or **Utes**) a member of a Native American people many of whom live in the US states of Colorado and Utah 犹他人（美洲土著，很多居于美国科罗拉多州和犹他州）

ute /juːt/ *noun* (*AustralE, NZE, informal*) a vehicle with low sides and no roof at the back used, for example, by farmers（农用）小卡车，轻型货车 SYN **pickup**

uten·sil /juːˈtensl/ *noun* (*formal*) a tool that is used in the house（家庭）用具，器皿；家什：***cooking/kitchen utensils*** 炊具；厨房用具 ➲ VISUAL VOCAB PAGE V27

uterus /ˈjuːtərəs/ *noun* (*anatomy* 解) the organ in women and female animals in which babies develop before they are born 子宫 SYN **womb** ▸ **uter·ine** /ˈjuːtəraɪn/ *adj.* [only before noun] ➲ SEE ALSO INTRAUTERINE DEVICE

utili·tar·ian /ˌjuːtɪlɪˈteəriən; *NAmE* -ˈter-/ *adj.* **1** (*formal*) designed to be useful and practical rather than attractive 实用的；功利的；实惠的 **2** (*philosophy* 哲) based on or supporting the ideas of utilitarianism 功利主义的

utili·tar·ian·ism /ˌjuːtɪlɪˈteəriənɪzəm; *NAmE* -ˈter-/ *noun* [U] (*philosophy* 哲) the belief that the right course of action is the one that will produce the greatest happiness of the greatest number of people 功利主义

util·ity AW /juːˈtɪləti/ *noun, adj.*

■ ***noun*** (*pl.* **-ies**) **1** [C] a service provided for the public, for example an electricity, water or gas supply 公用事业：*the administration of* ***public utilities*** 公共事业的管理 ➲ COLLOCATIONS AT HOUSE **2** [U] (*formal*) the quality of being useful 实用；效用；有用 SYN **usefulness** **3** [C] (*computing* 计) a piece of computer software that performs a particular task 实用程序；公用程序；工具

■ ***adj.*** [only before noun] that can be used for several different purposes 多用途的；多效用的；多功能的：*an all-round utility player* (= one who can play equally well in several different positions in a sport) 全面型选手

u'tility room *noun* a room, especially in a private house, that contains large pieces of equipment such as a WASHING MACHINE, FREEZER, etc. 杂物室，杂用间（放置洗衣机、电冰箱等大体积家用器具）

u'tility vehicle (*also* **u'tility truck**) *noun* a small truck with low sides designed for carrying light loads 轻载小卡车；轻型货车

util·ize AW (*BrE also* **-ise**) /'juːtəlaɪz/ *verb* **~ sth (as sth)** (*formal*) to use sth, especially for a practical purpose 使用；利用；运用；应用 SYN **make use of**: *The Romans were the first to utilize concrete as a building material.* 罗马人首先使用混凝土作建筑材料。◇ *The resources at our disposal could have been better utilized.* 我们所掌握的资源本来可以利用得更好。 ▶ **util·iza·tion**, **-isa·tion** AW /ˌjuːtəlaɪ'zeɪʃn; *NAmE* -lə'z-/ *noun* [U]

ut·most /'ʌtməʊst; *NAmE* -moʊst/ *adj., noun*

■ ***adj.*** (*also less frequent* **ut·ter·most**) [only before noun] greatest; most extreme 最大的；极度的：*This is a matter of the utmost importance.* 这是个极其重要的问题。◇ *You should study this document with the utmost care.* 你对这份文件的研究应该慎之又慎。

■ ***noun*** [sing.] the greatest amount possible 最大量；最大限度；极限；最大可能：*Our resources are strained to the utmost.* 我们的资源极端紧缺。◇ ***He did his utmost*** (= tried as hard as possible) *to persuade me not to go.* 他使尽浑身解数劝我别去。

uto·pia /juː'təʊpiə; *NAmE* -'toʊ-/ (*also* **Uto·pia**) *noun* [C, U] an imaginary place or state in which everything is perfect 乌托邦；空想的完美境界 ➲ MORE LIKE THIS 17, page R27 ORIGIN From the title of a book by Sir Thomas More, which describes a place like this. 源自托马斯·莫尔爵士所著的书名，书中描绘了这样一个地方。

uto·pian /juː'təʊpiən; *NAmE* -'toʊ-/ (*also* **Uto·pian**) *adj.* having a strong belief that everything can be perfect, often in a way that does not seem to be realistic or practical 乌托邦的；空想完美主义的：*utopian ideals* 不切实际的理想 ◇ *a utopian society* 乌托邦式社会 ▶ **uto·pian·ism** (*also* **Uto·pian·ism**) *noun* [U]

utter /'ʌtə(r)/ *adj., verb*

■ ***adj.*** [only before noun] used to emphasize how complete sth is 完全的；十足的；彻底的：*That's complete and utter nonsense!* 那纯属一派胡言！◇ *To my utter amazement she agreed.* 令我大感意外的是，她同意了。◇ *He felt an utter fool.* 他觉得自己蠢到家了。 ➲ MORE LIKE THIS 32, page R28

▶ **ut·ter·ly** *adv.*: *We're so utterly different from each other.* 我们之间有着天壤之别。◇ *She utterly failed to convince them.* 她根本没有说服他们。

■ ***verb*** **~ sth** (*formal*) to make a sound with your voice; to say sth 出声；说；讲：*to utter a cry* 发出喊叫声 ◇ *She did not **utter a word** during lunch* (= said nothing). 进午餐时，她一言未发。

ut·ter·ance /'ʌtərəns/ *noun* (*formal*) **1** [U] the act of expressing sth in words 用言语的表达；说话：*to give utterance to your thoughts* 把你的想法说出来 **2** [C] something that you say 话语；言论：*one of her few recorded public utterances* 她仅有的几次公开讲话录音之一

ut·ter·most /'ʌtəməʊst; *NAmE* 'ʌtərmoʊst/ *adj., noun* [sing.] = UTMOST

'U-turn *noun* **1** a turn of 180° that a vehicle makes so that it can move forwards in the opposite direction（汽车等的）U 形转弯，180 度转弯：*to do/make a U-turn* 掉头 **2** (*informal*) a complete change in policy or behaviour, usually one that is embarrassing（政策、行为上令人尴尬的）彻底转变，180 度大转变

UUP /ˌjuː juː 'piː/ *abbr.* Ulster Unionist Party (a political party in Northern Ireland that wants it to remain part of the United Kingdom) 北爱尔兰统一党（主张北爱尔兰为英国的一部分）

UV /ˌjuː 'viː/ *abbr.* ULTRAVIOLET 紫外线的；利用紫外线的：*UV radiation* 紫外辐射

UVA /ˌjuː viː 'eɪ/ *noun* [U] ULTRAVIOLET RAYS that are relatively long 长波紫外线；紫外线 A 波段：*UVA rays* 长波紫外线

UVB /ˌjuː viː 'biː/ *noun* [U] ULTRAVIOLET RAYS that are relatively short 中波紫外线；紫外线 B 波段：*UVB rays* 中波紫外线

UVC /ˌjuː viː 'siː/ *noun* [U] ULTRAVIOLET RAYS that are very short and do not get through the OZONE LAYER 短波紫外线，紫外线 C 波段（不能穿过臭氧层）：*UVC radiation* 短波紫外辐射

uvula /'juːvjələ/ *noun* (*pl.* **uvu·lae** /-liː/) (*anatomy* 解) a small piece of flesh that hangs from the top of the inside of the mouth just above the throat 腭垂；小舌；悬雍垂 ➲ VISUAL VOCAB PAGE V64

uvu·lar /'juːvjələ(r)/ *adj.* (*phonetics* 语音) (of a consonant 辅音) produced by placing the back of the tongue against or near the uvula 小舌（部位发出）的

UX /ˌjuː 'eks/ *abbr.* (*computing* 计) user experience (what it is like for sb to use a particular product such as a website, for example how easy or pleasant it is to use) 用户体验（全写为 user experience）

ux·or·ial /ʌk'sɔːriəl/ *adj.* (*formal*) connected with a wife 与妻子有关的

Uzi™ /'uːzi/ *noun* a type of SUB-MACHINE GUN designed in Israel 乌齐冲锋枪（以色列设计）

U

V /viː/ *noun, abbr., symbol*

■***noun*** (*also* **v**) (*pl.* **Vs**, **V's**, **v's** /viːz/) **1** [C, U] the 22nd letter of the English alphabet 英语字母表的第 22 个字母：*'Violin' begins with (a) V/'V'.* * violin 一词以字母 v 开头。**2** a thing shaped like a V * V 形物：*Ahead was the deep V of a gorge with water pouring down it.* 前面是陡深的 V 字形峡谷，水流倾泻而下。➲ SEE ALSO V-CHIP, V-NECK, V-SIGN

■***abbr.*** (in writing 书写形式) VOLT 伏，伏特（电压单位）：*a 1.5 V battery* * 1.5 伏电池

■***symbol*** (*also* **v**) the number 5 in ROMAN NUMERALS（罗马数字）5

v /viː/ *abbr.* **1** (*also* **vs** *especially in NAmE*) (in sport or in a legal case 体育运动或法律案件) VERSUS (= against) 对；对抗：*England v West Indies* 英格兰队对西印度群岛队 ◇ *the State vs Kramer* (= a case in a court of law) 州政府诉克雷默案 **2** (in writing 书写形式) (*BrE, informal*) very 很；非常；十分：*I was v pleased to get your letter.* 来信收到，很高兴。**3** VIDE（指示语，用于书等中）参见，参阅，另见

vac /væk/ *noun* (*BrE, informal*) a university vacation（大学的）假期

va·cancy /ˈveɪkənsi/ *noun* (*pl.* **-ies**) **1** [C] a job that is available for sb to do（职位的）空缺；空职；空额：***job vacancies*** 职位空缺 ◇ *a temporary vacancy* 临时空缺 ◇ ~ (**for sb/sth**) *vacancies for bar staff* 酒吧职员的空缺 ◇ ***to fill a vacancy*** 填补空额 ➲ SYNONYMS AT JOB **2** [C] a room that is available in a hotel, etc.（旅馆等的）空房，空间：*I'm sorry, we have no vacancies.* 对不起，我们这里客满。➲ WORDFINDER NOTE AT HOTEL **3** [U] lack of interest or ideas 无兴趣；无主意；空虚 SYN **emptiness**：*the vacancy of her expression* 她那茫然若失的表情

va·cant /ˈveɪkənt/ *adj.* **1** (of a seat, hotel room, house, etc. 座位、旅馆房间、房屋等) empty; not being used 空着的；未被占用的 SYN **unoccupied**：*vacant properties* 未被占用的房地产 ◇ *The seat next to him was vacant.* 他旁边的座位空着。◇ (*especially NAmE*) *a* ***vacant lot*** (= a piece of land in a city that is not being used) 一块闲置的地皮 ➲ COMPARE ENGAGED (4), OCCUPIED (1) **2** (*formal*) if a job in a company is **vacant**, nobody is doing it and it is available for sb to take（职位）空缺的：*When the post finally fell* (= became) *vacant, they offered it to Fiona.* 这个职位最终空出来之后，他们把它给了菲奥纳。◇ (*BrE*) ***Situations Vacant*** (= a section in a newspaper where jobs are advertised) 招聘广告栏目 **3** (of a look, an expression, etc. 目光、表情等) showing no sign that the person is thinking of anything 无神的；呆滞的；茫然的；若有所失的：*a vacant look* 呆滞的目光 ▶ **va·cant·ly** *adv.*：*to stare vacantly* 茫然瞪视

ˌ**vacant posˈsession** *noun* [U] (*BrE, specialist*) the fact of owning a house that is empty because the people who lived there have moved out 无（实际）占有

vac·ate /vəˈkeɪt; veɪˈk-; *NAmE also* ˈveɪkeɪt/ *verb* (*formal*) **1** ~ **sth** to leave a building, seat, etc., especially so that sb else can use it 搬出，腾出，空出（建筑物、座位等）：*Guests are requested to vacate their rooms by noon on the day of departure.* 房客务请在离开之日的中午以前腾出房间。**2** ~ **sth** to leave a job, position of authority, etc. so that it is available for sb else 辞（职）；让（位）

va·cation 🔑 /vəˈkeɪʃn; veɪˈk-/ *noun, verb*

■***noun*** **1** 🔑 [C] (in Britain) one of the periods of time when universities or courts of law are closed; (in the US) one of the periods of time when schools, colleges, universities or courts of law are closed（英国大学的）假期；（美国学校的）假期；（法庭的）休庭期：*the* ***Christmas/Easter/summer vacation*** 圣诞节 / 复活节假期；暑假 ◇ (*BrE*) *the* ***long vacation*** (= the summer vacation) 暑假 ➲ SEE ALSO VAC **2** 🔑 (*NAmE*) (*BrE* **holi·day**) [U, C] a period of time spent travelling or resting away from home 度假：*They're* ***on vacation*** *in Hawaii right now.* 他们此时正在夏威夷度假。◇ *You look tired—you should* ***take a vacation***. 你看上去很累，应该休假了。◇ *The job includes two weeks' paid vacation.* 这份工作包括两周的带薪假期。◇ ***a vacation home*** 度假之家 ➲ COLLOCATIONS AT TRAVEL ➲ NOTE AT HOLIDAY

■***verb*** [I] (*NAmE*) (*BrE* **holi·day**) to spend a holiday somewhere 度假；休假：*They are currently vacationing in Florida.* 他们目前正在佛罗里达度假。

va·cation·er /vəˈkeɪʃənə(r); veɪˈk-/ (*NAmE*) (*BrE* **holiday-maker**) *noun* a person who is visiting a place on holiday/vacation 度假者

vac·cin·ate /ˈvæksɪneɪt/ *verb* [often passive] ~ **sb** (**against sth**) to give a person or an animal a vaccine, especially by INJECTING it, in order to protect them against a disease 给…接种疫苗：*I was vaccinated against tetanus.* 我接种了破伤风疫苗。➲ WORDFINDER NOTE AT DISEASE ➲ COLLOCATIONS AT ILL ➲ COMPARE IMMUNIZE, INOCULATE ▶ **vac·cin·ation** /ˌvæksɪˈneɪʃn/ *noun* [C, U]：*Make sure your vaccinations are up to date.* 一定要接种最新的疫苗。◇ *vaccination against typhoid* 伤寒疫苗的接种

vac·cine /ˈvæksiːn; *NAmE* vækˈsiːn/ *noun* [C, U] a substance that is put into the blood and that protects the body from a disease 疫苗：*a measles vaccine* 麻疹疫苗 ◇ *There is no vaccine against HIV infection.* 现在还没有防止感染艾滋病病毒的疫苗。

vacil·late /ˈvæsəleɪt/ *verb* [I] (*formal*) to keep changing your opinion or thoughts about sth, especially in a way that annoys other people 观点（或立场等）摇摆；动摇 SYN **waver** ▶ **va·cil·la·tion** /ˌvæsəˈleɪʃn/ *noun* [U, C]

vacu·ity /vəˈkjuːəti/ *noun* [U] (*formal*) lack of serious thought or purpose 空虚；茫然；缺乏思考

vacu·ole /ˈvækjuəʊl; *NAmE* -oʊl/ *noun* **1** (*biology* 生) a small space within a cell, usually filled with liquid（细胞内的）液泡，泡 **2** (*medical* 医) a small hole in the TISSUE of the body, usually caused by disease（身体组织中由疾病等造成的）空泡

vacu·ous /ˈvækjuəs/ *adj.* (*formal*) showing no sign of intelligence or sensitive feelings 空洞的；空洞无物的：*a vacuous expression* 茫然的表情 ▶ **vacu·ous·ly** *adv.* **vacu·ous·ness** *noun* [U]

vac·uum /ˈvækjuəm/ *noun, verb*

■***noun*** **1** a space that is completely empty of all substances, including all air or other gas 真空：*a vacuum pump* (= one that creates a vacuum) 真空泵 ◇ ***vacuum-packed foods*** (= in a package from which most of the air has been removed) 真空包装的食品 **2** [usually sing.] a situation in which sb/sth is missing or lacking 真空状态；空白；空虚：*His resignation has created a vacuum which cannot easily be filled.* 他的引退造成了难以填补的空白。**3** [usually sing.] the act of cleaning sth with a vacuum cleaner（用真空吸尘器所做的）清洁，清扫：*to give a room a quick vacuum* 用吸尘器把房间迅速清扫一下

IDM **in a ˈvacuum** existing separately from other people, events, etc. when there should be a connection 与世隔绝；脱离实际：*This kind of decision cannot ever be made in a vacuum.* 这种决定绝不能脱离实际。

■***verb*** [T, I] ~ (**sth**) to clean sth using a vacuum cleaner 用真空吸尘器清扫 SYN **hoover**：*Have you vacuumed the stairs?* 你用吸尘器清扫楼梯了吗？

ˈ**vacuum cleaner** (*BrE also* **Hoover™**) *noun* an electrical machine that cleans floors, carpets, etc. by sucking up dirt and dust 真空吸尘器 ➲ VISUAL VOCAB PAGE V21

ˈ**vacuum flask** (*also* **flask**) (*both BrE*) (*US* ˈ**vacuum bottle**) *noun* a container like a bottle with double walls with a vacuum between them, used for keeping liquids hot or cold 真空瓶；保温瓶；热水瓶；冰瓶 ➲ COMPARE THERMOS™

V

vade mecum /ˌvɑːdi ˈmeɪkəm/ *noun* (*from Latin, formal*) a book or written guide which you keep with you all the time, because you find it helpful（常备的）手册，便览

vaga·bond /ˈvæɡəbɒnd; *NAmE* -bɑːnd/ *noun* (*old-fashioned, disapproving*) a person who has no home or job and who travels from place to place 流浪汉；无业游民；漂泊者

va·gar·ies /ˈveɪɡəriz/ *noun* [pl.] (*formal*) changes in sb/sth that are difficult to predict or control 奇思遐想；游移不定；变幻莫测

va·gina /vəˈdʒaɪnə/ *noun* the passage in the body of a woman or female animal between the outer sex organs and the WOMB 阴道 ▸ **va·ginal** /vəˈdʒaɪnl/ *adj.* **va·gi·nal·ly** *adv.*

va·grancy /ˈveɪɡrənsi/ *noun* [U] (*law* 律) the crime of living on the streets and BEGGING (= asking for money) from people 流浪罪；流浪行乞

va·grant /ˈveɪɡrənt/ *noun* (*formal* or *law* 律) a person who has no home or job, especially one who BEGS (= asks for money) from people 无业游民；流浪者；（尤指）乞丐 ▸ **va·grant** *adj.* [only before noun]

vague /veɪɡ/ *adj.* (**vaguer, vaguest**) **1** not clear in a person's mind（思想上）不清楚的，含糊的，不明确的，模糊的：*to have a* ***vague impression/memory/recollection*** *of sth* 对某事印象 / 记忆模糊 ◇ *They had only a* ***vague idea*** *where the place was.* 他们只是大概知道那个地方的位置。 **2** ~ (**about sth**) not having or giving enough information or details about sth 不具体的；不详细的；粗略的：*She's a little vague about her plans for next year.* 她对她明年的计划还不太确定。 ◇ *The politicians made vague promises about tax cuts.* 政界人物的减税承诺言辞含混。 ◇ *He was accused of being deliberately vague.* 他被指责为故意含糊其词。 ◇ *We had only a vague description of the attacker.* 我们只有那个袭击者的粗略描述。 **3** (of a person's behaviour 人的行为) suggesting a lack of clear thought or attention 茫然的；糊涂的；心不在焉的 SYN **absent-minded**：*His vague manner concealed a brilliant mind.* 他大智若愚。 **4** not having a clear shape 不清楚的；模糊的；朦胧的 SYN **indistinct**：*In the darkness they could see the vague outline of a church.* 他们在黑暗中能看到一座教堂的朦胧轮廓。 ➲ MORE LIKE THIS 20, page R27 ▸ **vague·ness** *noun* [U]

vague·ly /ˈveɪɡli/ *adv.* **1** in a way that is not detailed or exact 不详细地；含糊地；不确切地：*a vaguely worded statement* 措辞含糊的声明 ◇ *I can vaguely remember my first day at school.* 我还依稀记得我第一天上学的情景。 **2** slightly 略微；稍微：*There was something vaguely familiar about her face.* 她有点儿面熟。 ◇ *He was vaguely aware of footsteps behind him.* 他仿佛意识到背后有脚步声。 **3** in a way that shows that you are not paying attention or thinking clearly 心不在焉地：*He smiled vaguely, ignoring her questions.* 他漫不经心地笑了笑，没有理会她的问题。

vain /veɪn/ *adj.* **1** that does not produce the result you want 徒劳的；枉然的；无结果的 SYN **useless**：*She closed her eyes tightly* ***in a vain attempt*** *to hold back the tears.* 她紧闭双眼，却无法忍住眼泪。 ◇ *I knocked loudly* ***in the vain hope*** *that someone might answer.* 我敲门敲得很响，希望有人应声，却是徒然。 **2** (*disapproving*) too proud of your own appearance, abilities or achievements 自负的；自视过高的 SYN **conceited**：*She's too vain to wear glasses.* 她太爱虚荣，不肯戴眼镜。 ➲ SEE ALSO VANITY (1)

IDM **in ˈvain** without success 枉费心机；徒劳无益；白费力气：*They tried in vain to persuade her to go.* 他们极力劝说她去，但枉费了一番口舌。 ◇ *All our efforts were in vain.* 我们的所有努力都付诸东流了。 ➲ MORE AT NAME *n.*

vain·glori·ous /ˌveɪnˈɡlɔːriəs/ *adj.* (*literary, disapproving*) too proud of your own abilities or achievements 自负的；自命不凡的；自吹自擂的 ▸ **vain·glory** /ˌveɪnˈɡlɔːri/ *noun* [U]

vain·ly /ˈveɪnli/ *adv.* without success 徒劳地；不成功地；白费力地：*He shouted after them, vainly trying to attract their attention.* 他在他们的后面高喊，想引起他们的注意，却是徒劳。

val·ance /ˈvæləns/ *noun* **1** a narrow piece of cloth like a short curtain that hangs around the frame of a bed, under a shelf, etc.（床架等四周的）短帷幔，布帘 ➲ VISUAL VOCAB PAGE V24 **2** (*especially NAmE*) = PELMET

vale /veɪl/ *noun* (*old use* or *literary*) (also used in modern place names 也用于现代地名) a valley 谷；山谷：*a wooded vale* 树木茂密的山谷 ◇ *the Vale of the White Horse* 白马谷

val·edic·tion /ˌvælɪˈdɪkʃn/ *noun* [C, U] (*formal*) the act of saying goodbye, especially in a formal speech（尤指正式演讲中的）告别，告别辞

val·edic·tor·ian /ˌvælɪdɪkˈtɔːriən/ *noun* (*NAmE*) the student who has the highest marks/grades in a particular group of students and who gives the valedictory speech at a GRADUATION ceremony（毕业典礼上）致告别辞的最优生

val·edic·tory /ˌvælɪˈdɪktəri/ *adj.* [usually before noun] (*formal*) connected with saying goodbye, especially at a formal occasion（尤在正式场合）告别的，告辞的：*a valedictory speech* 告别演说

va·lency /ˈveɪlənsi/ *noun* [C, U] (*pl.* **-ies**) (*also* **va·lence** /ˈveɪləns/ *especially in NAmE*) **1** (*chemistry* 化) a measurement of the power of an atom to combine with others, by the number of HYDROGEN atoms it can combine with or DISPLACE 价；化合价；原子价：*Carbon has a valency of 4.* 碳的化合价是 4 价。 ➲ WORDFINDER NOTE AT ATOM, CHEMISTRY **2** (*linguistics* 语言) the number of GRAMMATICAL elements that a word, especially a verb, combines with in a sentence 组配数限，配价（一个词，尤指动词，在句子中结合的语法成分的数目）

val·en·tine /ˈvæləntaɪn/ *noun* **1** (*also* **ˈvalentine card**) a card that you send to sb that you love on St Valentine's Day (14 February), often without putting your name on it（在 2 月 14 日常以匿名寄送的）圣瓦伦丁节情人卡 **2** a person that you send a valentine to（收到情人节卡片的）情人

ˈValentine's Day ➲ ST VALENTINE'S DAY

val·er·ian /vəˈlɪəriən; *NAmE* -ˈlɪr-/ *noun* [U] a drug obtained from the root of a plant with the same name, used to make people feel calmer 缬草根（从缬草根提取的镇定药）

valet *noun, verb*

■ ***noun*** /ˈvæleɪ; ˈvælɪt; *NAmE also* væˈleɪ/ **1** a man's personal servant who takes care of his clothes, serves his meals, etc.（照管男子衣食等的）贴身仆人，仆从 **2** a hotel employee whose job is to clean the clothes of hotel guests（旅馆中）为顾客洗衣服的服务员 **3** (*NAmE*) a person who parks your car for you at a hotel or restaurant（旅馆或餐厅）为顾客停车的服务员

■ ***verb*** /ˈvælɪt/ **1** [T] ~ **sth** (*BrE*) to clean a person's car thoroughly, especially on the inside 彻底清洗（尤指车内）：*a car valeting service* 清洗汽车服务 **2** [I] to perform the duties of a valet 侍候；服侍

Val·halla /vælˈhælə/ *noun* [U] (in ancient Scandinavian stories 古斯堪的纳维亚神话) a palace in which some chosen men who had died in battle went to live with the god Odin for ever 瓦尔哈拉殿堂（阵亡将士与奥丁神永久生活的宫殿）

vali·ant /ˈvæliənt/ *adj.* (*especially literary*) very brave or determined 英勇的；勇敢的；果敢的；坚定的 SYN **courageous**：*valiant warriors* 勇敢的武士 ◇ *She made a* ***valiant attempt*** *not to laugh.* 她试图强忍住不笑出来。 ▸ **vali·ant·ly** *adv.*

valid 🔑 AW /ˈvælɪd/ *adj.* **1** 🔑 that is legally or officially acceptable（法律上）有效的；（正式）认可的：*a valid passport* 有效的护照 ◇ *a bus pass valid for 1 month* 公共汽车月票 ◇ *They have a valid claim to compensation.* 他们有要求赔偿的合法权利。 **2** based on what is logical or true 符合逻辑的；合理的；有根据的；确凿的：*She had valid reasons for not supporting the proposals.* 她有充分的理由不支持这些建议。 ◇ *The point you make is perfectly* valid. 你提出的论点完全站得住脚。 **3** (*computing* 计) that is accepted by the system 有效的；系统认可的： *a valid password* 有效密码 OPP **invalid** ▶ **val·id·ly** AW *adv.*： *The contract had been validly drawn up.* 这份合同已依据法律草拟妥当。

val·id·ate AW /ˈvælɪdeɪt/ *verb* (*formal*) **1** ~ **sth** to prove that sth is true 证实；确认；确证： *to validate a theory* 证实理论 OPP **invalidate** **2** ~ **sth** to make sth legally valid 使生效；使有法律效力： *to validate a contract* 使合同生效 OPP **invalidate** **3** ~ **sth** to state officially that sth is useful and of an acceptable standard 批准；确认…有效；认可： *Check that their courses have been validated by a reputable organization.* 要确保他们的课程获得有声望机构的承认。 **4** to recognize the value of a person or their feelings or opinions; to make sb feel valued 承认（某人）的价值；认同（某人的感受或观点）；使感到受重视： ~ **sb/sth** *Be sure to validate your child's feelings—don't minimize them.* 一定要重视孩子的感受，千万不要不当回事。 ◇ ~ **sb/sth as sth** *She seemed to need his admiration to validate her as a person.* 她似乎需要他的赞赏来肯定自己的存在价值。 ▶ **val·id·ation** AW /ˌvælɪˈdeɪʃn/ *noun* [U, C]

val·id·ity AW /vəˈlɪdəti/ *noun* [U] **1** the state of being legally or officially acceptable （法律上的）有效，合法性；（正式的）认可： *The period of validity of the agreement has expired.* 本协议的有效期已过。 **2** the state of being logical and true 符合逻辑；正当；正确： *We had doubts about the validity of their argument.* 我们对他们的论点的正确性有过怀疑。

val·ise /vəˈliːz; *NAmE* vəˈliːs/ *noun* (*old-fashioned*) a small bag for carrying clothes, used when you are travelling （装衣服的）小旅行包

Val·ium™ /ˈvæliəm/ *noun* [U] a drug used to reduce anxiety 安定；地西泮

Val·kyrie /ˈvælkɪri; vælˈkɪəri; *NAmE* vælˈkɪri; -ˈkaɪri/ *noun* (in ancient Scandinavian stories 古斯堪的纳维亚神话) one of the twelve female servants of the god Odin, who selected men who had been killed in battle and took them to VALHALLA 瓦尔基里（奥丁神十二侍女之一，负责挑选阵亡者并将他们带到瓦尔哈拉殿堂）

val·ley 🔑 /ˈvæli/ *noun* an area of low land between hills or mountains, often with a river flowing through it; the land that a river flows through 谷；山谷；溪谷；流域： *a small town set in a valley* 坐落在溪谷中的小镇 ◇ *a wooded valley* 树木茂盛的山谷 ◇ *the valley floor* 谷底 ◇ *the Shenandoah Valley* 谢南多厄谷 ➲ **WORDFINDER NOTE** AT MOUNTAIN ➲ VISUAL VOCAB PAGE V5

ˈ**Valley Girl** *noun* (*NAmE, informal*) a girl from a rich family who is only interested in things like shopping, thought to be typical of one of those living in the San Fernando Valley of California 谷地富家女（只热衷于购物等，被认为是加利福尼亚州圣费尔南多谷地富家女的典型）

val·our (*especially US* **valor**) /ˈvælə(r)/ *noun* [U] (*literary*) great courage, especially in war （尤指战争中的）英勇，勇气 SYN **bravery** ▶ **val·or·ous** /ˈvælərəs/ *adj.* IDM SEE DISCRETION

valu·able 🔑 /ˈvæljuəbl/ *adj.* **1** 🔑 ~ (**to sb/sth**) very useful or important 很有用的；很重要的；宝贵的： *a valuable experience* 宝贵的经验 ◇ *The book provides valuable information on recent trends.* 此书就近来的发展趋势提供了宝贵的信息。 ◇ *This advice was to* **prove valuable**. 这忠告证明是有益的。 **2** 🔑 worth a lot of money 很值钱的；贵重的： *valuable antiques* 贵重的古玩 ◇ *Luckily, nothing valuable was stolen.* 幸运的是，没有贵重物品失窃。 OPP **valueless, worthless** ➲ COMPARE INVALUABLE, PRICELESS (1) ➲ MORE LIKE THIS 23, page R27

valu·ables /ˈvæljuəblz/ *noun* [pl.] things that are worth a lot of money, especially small personal things such as jewellery, cameras, etc. （尤指私人的）贵重物品 ➲ SYNONYMS AT THING

valu·ation /ˌvæljuˈeɪʃn/ *noun* [C, U] **1** a professional judgement about how much money sth is worth; its estimated value （专业）估价；估定的价值；估值： *Surveyors carried out a valuation of the property.* 鉴定人员对这处房产作了估价。 ◇ *Experts set a high valuation on the painting.* 专家对这幅画估价很高。 ◇ *land valuation* 土地的估价 **2** (*formal*) a judgement about how useful or important sth is; its estimated importance 评价；评估： *She puts a high valuation on trust between colleagues.* 她很看重同事间的信任。

value 🔑 /ˈvæljuː/ *noun, verb*

> **WORD FAMILY**
> **value** *noun, verb*
> **valuable** *adj.*
> **invaluable** *adj.* (≠ valueless)
> **valuables** *noun*

■ ***noun***

• **HOW MUCH STH IS WORTH** 价值 **1** 🔑 [U, C] how much sth is worth in money or other goods for which it can be exchanged （商品）价值： *to* **go up/rise/increase in value** 升值 ◇ *to* **go down/fall/drop in value** 贬值 ◇ *rising property values* 上涨中的房地产价值 ◇ *The winner will receive a prize* **to the value of** *£1 000.* 获胜者将得到价值为 1 000 英镑的奖项。 ◇ *Sports cars tend to* **hold their value** *well.* 跑车往往很能保值。 ➲ SYNONYMS AT PRICE ➲ SEE ALSO MARKET VALUE, STREET VALUE **2** 🔑 [U] (*especially BrE*) how much sth is worth compared with its price （与价格相比的）值，划算程度： *to be* **good/excellent value** (= worth the money it costs) 很 / 极为合算 ◇ *to be* **bad/poor value** (= not worth the money it costs) 不上算；不值 ◇ *Larger sizes give the best* **value for money**. 较大尺寸的最划算。

• **BEING USEFUL/IMPORTANT** 有用；重要 **3** 🔑 [U] the quality of being useful or important 用途；积极作用 SYN **benefit**: *The value of regular exercise should not be underestimated.* 经常锻炼的好处不应低估。 ◇ *The arrival of canals was* **of great value** *to many industries.* 运河的出现对许多行业具有重大的意义。 ◇ *to* **be of little/no value** *to sb* 对某人没什么 / 毫无帮助 ◇ *This ring has great* **sentimental value** *for me.* 这枚戒指对我来说很有纪念意义。 ◇ *I suppose it has a certain* **novelty value** (= it's interesting because it's new). 我觉得这有一定的新意。 ◇ *food with a high nutritional value* 营养价值高的食物 ◇ *The story has very little news value.* 这件事没有什么新闻价值。

• **BELIEFS** 信念 **4** 🔑 **values** [pl.] beliefs about what is right and wrong and what is important in life 是非标准；生活准则；价值观： *moral values* 道德信条 ◇ *a return to traditional values in education, such as firm discipline* 恢复传统的教育准则，如严格的纪律 ◇ *The young have a completely different* **set of values** *and expectations.* 年轻人有一整套截然不同的价值观和期望。

> ▼ **SYNONYMS** 同义词辨析
>
> **valuable**
>
> **precious • priceless • irreplaceable**
>
> These words all describe sth that is worth a lot of money or very important to sb. 以上各词均用以形容物品值钱、宝贵。
>
> **valuable** worth a lot of money 指值钱的、贵重的： *The thieves took three pieces of valuable jewellery.* 窃贼盗走了三件贵重的首饰。
>
> **precious** rare and worth a lot of money; loved or valued very much 指珍稀的、珍贵的、宝贵的： *a precious Chinese vase, valued at half a million pounds* 价值 50 万英镑的稀世中国花瓶 ◇ *precious memories of our time together* 我们共度时光的珍贵回忆
>
> **priceless** extremely valuable; loved or valued very much 指无价的、极珍贵的、极宝贵的： *a priceless collection of antiques* 价值连城的古文物收藏
>
> **irreplaceable** too valuable or special to be replaced 指因贵重或独特而不能替代的
>
> **PATTERNS**
> • valuable/precious/priceless/irreplaceable **possessions**
> • valuable/precious/priceless **antiques/jewels/jewellery**

V

• MATHEMATICS 数学 **5** [C] the amount represented by a letter or symbol 值；数值：*Let y have the value 33.* 假设 y 的值为 33。

■ *verb*

• CONSIDER IMPORTANT 认为重要 **1** (not used in the progressive tenses 不用于进行时) to think that sb/sth is important 重视；珍视：**~ sb/sth (as sth)** *I really value him as a friend.* 我真的把他视为好朋友。◇ **~ sb/sth (for sth)** *The area is valued for its vineyards.* 这个地区因它的葡萄园而受到重视。◇ *a valued member of staff* 职工中受重视的一员

• DECIDE WORTH 决定价值 **2** [usually passive] **~ sth (at sth)** to decide that sth is worth a particular amount of money 给…估价；给…定价：*The property has been valued at over $2 million.* 这处房地产估价为 200 多万美元。

ˌvalue ˈadded tax *noun* [U] = VAT

ˌvalue-ˈfree *adj.* not influenced by personal opinions 不受主观价值影响的；客观的

ˈvalue judgement (*also* **ˈvalue judgment** *especially in NAmE*) *noun* [C, U] (*sometimes disapproving*) a judgement about how good or important sth is, based on personal opinions rather than facts （根据主观意见的）价值判断

ˌvalue-ˈladen *adj.* influenced by personal opinions 受主观价值影响的；主观的：*'Freedom fighter' is a value-laden word.* "自由战士"是个带有主观判断的词。

value·less /ˈvæljuːləs/ *adj.* (*formal*) without value or worth 没有价值的；不值钱的 SYN **worthless** OPP **valuable**

valuer /ˈvæljuːə(r)/ *noun* a person whose job is to estimate how much property, land, etc. is worth （房地产等的）估价人

valve /vælv/ *noun* **1** a device for controlling the flow of a liquid or gas, letting it move in one direction only 阀；阀门；活门；气门 ➲ VISUAL VOCAB PAGE V55 **2** a structure in the heart or in a VEIN that lets blood flow in one direction only （心脏或血管的）瓣（膜） **3** a device in some BRASS musical instruments for changing the note （铜管乐器的）阀键，活塞 ➲ VISUAL VOCAB PAGE V37

vam·oose /vəˈmuːs/ *verb* [I] (*old-fashioned, informal*) to leave quickly 匆匆离去；迅速走开；开溜

vamp /væmp/ *noun* (*old-fashioned, disapproving*) a sexually attractive woman who tries to control men 妖妇（利用色相控制男性）

vam·pire /ˈvæmpaɪə(r)/ *noun* (in stories 传说) a dead person who leaves his or her grave at night to suck the blood of living people 吸血鬼（夜间走出坟墓吸吮活人血的游魂）

ˈvampire bat *noun* a S American BAT (= an animal like a mouse with wings) that sucks the blood of other animals 吸血蝠（产于美洲热带，吸吮其他动物的血）

vam·pir·ism /ˈvæmpaɪərɪzəm/ *noun* [U] the behaviour or practices of VAMPIRES 吸血鬼行为；吸血

van /væn/ *noun* **1** a covered vehicle with no side windows in its back half, usually smaller than a lorry/truck, used for carrying goods or people 客货车；厢式送货车：*a furniture van* 运家具的货车 ◇ *a police van* (= for carrying police officers or prisoners) 警车 ◇ *a delivery van* 送货车 ◇ *a van driver* 客货车司机 ➲ VISUAL VOCAB PAGE V62 **2** (*NAmE*) a covered vehicle with side windows, usually smaller than a lorry/truck, that can carry about twelve passengers 面包车（通常为 12 座左右） **3** (*BrE*) a closed coach/car on a train for carrying bags, cases, etc. or mail （铁路上运送包裹、邮件等的）车厢：*a luggage van* 装运行李的车厢

IDM **in the ˈvan** (*BrE, formal*) at the front or in the leading position 处于前沿；处于领先地位

van·adium /vəˈneɪdiəm/ *noun* [U] (*symb.* **V**) a chemical element. Vanadium is a soft poisonous silver-grey metal that is added to some types of steel to make it stronger. 钒

ˈvan conversion *noun* (*US*) = CONVERSION VAN

van·dal /ˈvændl/ *noun* a person who deliberately destroys or damages public property 故意破坏公物者

van·dal·ism /ˈvændəlɪzəm/ *noun* [U] the crime of destroying or damaging sth, especially public property, deliberately and for no good reason 故意破坏公共财物罪；恣意毁坏他人财产罪：*an act of vandalism* 恣意破坏公共财物的行为 ➲ COLLOCATIONS AT CRIME

van·dal·ize (*BrE also* **-ise**) /ˈvændəlaɪz/ *verb* [usually passive] **~ sth** to damage sth, especially public property, deliberately and for no good reason 故意破坏，肆意破坏（尤指公共财物）

vane /veɪn/ *noun* a flat blade that is moved by wind or water and is part of the machinery in a WINDMILL, etc. （风车等的）叶片，翼，轮叶 ➲ SEE ALSO WEATHERVANE

van·guard /ˈvæŋɡɑːd; *NAmE* -ɡɑːrd/ *noun* (*usually* **the vanguard**) [sing.] **1** the leaders of a movement in society, for example in politics, art, industry, etc. （政治、艺术、工业等社会活动的）领导者，先锋，先驱者：*The company is proud to be* ***in the vanguard of*** *scientific progress.* 这家公司以处于科学发展的领先地位而自豪。**2** the part of an army, etc. that is at the front when moving forward to attack the enemy 先头部队；前卫；尖兵 OPP **rearguard**

van·illa /vəˈnɪlə/ *noun, adj.*

■ ***noun*** [U] a substance obtained from the BEANS of a tropical plant, also called vanilla, used to give flavour to sweet foods, for example ice cream 香草醛，香草香精（从热带植物香子兰豆中提取，用于冰淇淋等甜食）：(*BrE*) *vanilla essence* 香子兰精 ◇ (*NAmE*) *vanilla extract* 香子兰精 ◇ (*BrE*) *a vanilla pod* 香子兰蒴果 ◇ (*NAmE*) *a vanilla bean* 香子兰豆

■ ***adj.*** **1** flavoured with vanilla 有香子兰香味的；香草味的：*vanilla ice cream* 香草冰淇淋 **2** (*informal*) ordinary; not special in any way 普通的；寻常的；毫无特色的：*The city is pretty much plain vanilla.* 这座城市相当一般化。

van·il·lin /vəˈnɪlɪn/ *noun* [U] a strong-smelling chemical which gives VANILLA its smell 香草醛；香兰素

van·ish /ˈvænɪʃ/ *verb* **1** [I] to disappear suddenly and/or in a way that you cannot explain （莫名其妙地）突然消失：*The magician vanished in a puff of smoke.* 魔术师在一股烟雾中突然不见了。◇ *My glasses seem to have vanished.* 我的眼镜似乎不翼而飞了。◇ *He* ***vanished without trace***. 他消失得无影无踪。 **2** [I] to stop existing 不复存在；消亡；绝迹：*the vanishing woodlands of Europe* 不断消失的欧洲林地 ◇ *All hopes of a peaceful settlement had now vanished.* 和平解决的全部希望现已化为泡影。IDM SEE ACT *n.*, FACE *n.*

ˈvanishing point *noun* [usually sing.] (*specialist*) the point in the distance at which parallel lines appear to meet 灭点

van·ity /ˈvænəti/ *noun* (*pl.* **-ies**) **1** [U] (*disapproving*) too much pride in your own appearance, abilities or achievements 自负；自大；虚荣；虚荣心：*She had no personal vanity* (= about her appearance). 她对自己的相貌毫不自负。➲ SEE ALSO VAIN (2) **2** [U] (*literary*) the quality of being unimportant, especially compared with other things that are important （尤指与其他重大事物相比）渺小，无所谓，不重要：*the vanity of human ambition in the face of death* 个人抱负在死亡面前的微不足道 **3 vanities** [pl.] behaviour or attitudes that show people's vanity 自负的行为；虚荣的态度；过分的骄傲：*Politics is too often concerned only with the personal vanities of politicians.* 政治常常仅与政界人士的个人虚荣有关。**4** (*also* **ˈvanity table**) [C] = DRESSING TABLE

ˈvanity case *noun* a small bag or case with a mirror in it, used for carrying make-up 小化妆包；小梳妆盒

ˈvanity unit *noun* (*BrE*) a WASHBASIN fixed into a flat surface with cupboards underneath （下方设有橱柜的）组合式盥洗盆，嵌入式盥洗盆 ➲ VISUAL VOCAB PAGE V25

van·quish /ˈvæŋkwɪʃ/ *verb* ~ **sb/sth** (*literary*) to defeat sb completely in a competition, war, etc. 完全征服；彻底击败；战胜 SYN **conquer**

the van·quished /ˈvæŋkwɪʃt/ *noun* [pl.] (*literary*) people who have been completely defeated in a competition, war, etc. 战败者；被完全征服的人；败阵者

vant·age point /ˈvɑːntɪdʒ pɔɪnt; *NAmE* ˈvæn-/ (*also formal* **vant·age**) *noun* a position from which you watch sth; a point in time or a situation from which you consider sth, especially the past （观察事物的）有利地点；（尤指回顾过去的）有利时刻，有利形势：*The cafe was a good vantage point for watching the world go by.* 从这家小餐馆能清楚地看到人生百态。◇ *From the vantage point of the present, the war seems to have achieved nothing.* 依目前的情况来看，这场战争似乎一无所获。

vapid /ˈvæpɪd/ *adj.* (*formal*) lacking interest or intelligence 乏味的；枯燥的；愚蠢的 SYN **dull** ▶ **vap·id·ity** /vəˈpɪdəti/ *noun* [U]

vapor (*NAmE*) = VAPOUR

va·por·ize (*BrE also* **-ise**) /ˈveɪpəraɪz/ *verb* [I, T] ~ (**sth**) (*specialist*) to turn into gas; to make sth turn into gas （使）汽化，蒸发 ▶ **va·por·iza·tion, -isa·tion** /ˌveɪpəraɪˈzeɪʃn; *NAmE* -rəˈz-/ *noun* [U]

va·por·ous /ˈveɪpərəs/ *adj.* (*formal*) full of vapour; like vapour 充满蒸气的；似蒸气的：*clouds of vaporous air* 团团雾气

va·pour (*especially US* **vapor**) /ˈveɪpə(r)/ *noun* [C, U] a mass of very small drops of liquid in the air, for example steam 蒸气；潮气；雾气：*water vapour* 水蒸气

ˈvapour trail (*especially US* **ˈva·por trail**) *noun* the white line that is left in the sky by a plane （飞机在高空留下的）水汽尾迹，凝结尾迹，拉烟

va·pour·ware (*especially US* **va·por·ware**) /ˈveɪpəweə(r); *NAmE* -pərwer/ *noun* [U] (*computing* 计) a piece of software or other computer product that has been advertised but is not available to buy yet, either because it is only an idea or because it is still being written or designed 雾件（已做广告但尚未上市的计算机程序或产品）

vari·abil·ity AW /ˌveəriəˈbɪləti; *NAmE* ˌver-; ˌvær-/ *noun* [U] the fact of sth being likely to vary 可变性；易变性；反复不定：*climatic variability* 气候的多变性 ◇ *a degree of variability in the exchange rate* 汇率的变化幅度

vari·able AW /ˈveəriəbl; *NAmE* ˈver-; ˈvær-/ *adj., noun*

▪ *adj.* **1** often changing; likely to change 多变的；易变的；变化无常的 SYN **fluctuating**: *variable temperatures* 变化不定的气温 ◇ *The acting is of variable quality* (= some of it is good and some of it is bad). 表演时好时坏。➲ COMPARE INVARIABLE **2** able to be changed 可更改的；可变的：*The drill has variable speed control.* 这钻机有变速控制。◇ *variable lighting* 亮度可调的照明设备 ▶ **vari·ably** AW /-iəbli/ *adv.*

▪ *noun* a situation, number or quantity that can vary or be varied 可变情况；变量；可变因素：*With so many variables, it is difficult to calculate the cost.* 有这么多的可变因素，很难计算出成本。◇ *The temperature remained constant while pressure was a variable in the experiment.* 做这实验时温度保持不变，但压力可变。OPP **constant**

vari·ance AW /ˈveəriəns; *NAmE* ˈver-; ˈvær-/ *noun* [U, C] (*formal*) the amount by which sth changes or is different from sth else 变化幅度；差额：*variance in temperature* 温差 ◇ *a note with subtle variances of pitch* 音高有细微变化的音符

IDM **at ˈvariance (with sb/sth)** (*formal*) disagreeing with or opposing sb/sth 看法不一；矛盾；冲突：*These conclusions are totally at variance with the evidence.* 这些结论与证据完全相悖。

vari·ant AW /ˈveəriənt; *NAmE* ˈver-; ˈvær-/ *noun* ~ (**of/on sth**) a thing that is a slightly different form or type of sth else 变种；变体；变形：*This game is a variant of baseball.* 这种运动是由棒球演变而来的。▶ **vari·ant** *adj.* [only before noun]：*variant forms of spelling* 不同的拼写形式

vari·ation 🔑 AW /ˌveəriˈeɪʃn; *NAmE* ˌver-/ *noun* **1** 🔑 [C, U] ~ (**in/of sth**) a change, especially in the amount or level of sth （数量、水平等的）变化，变更，变异：*The dial records very slight variations in pressure.* 该刻度盘能显示很微小的压力变化。◇ *Currency exchange rates are always subject to variation.* 货币的兑换率总在波动。◇ ***regional/seasonal variation*** (= depending on the region or time of year) 地区性 / 季节性变化 **2** 🔑 [C] ~ (**on sth**) a thing that is different from other things in the same general group 变异的东西；变种；变体：*This soup is a spicy variation on a traditional favourite.* 这种汤是在一种受欢迎的传统汤羹中加了香料。**3** [C] ~ (**on sth**) (*music* 音) any of a set of short pieces of music based on a simple tune repeated in a different and more complicated form 变奏；变奏曲：*a set of variations on a theme by Mozart* 以莫扎特某一乐曲为主题的一组变奏曲 ◇ (*figurative*) *His numerous complaints are all **variations on a theme*** (= all about the same thing). 他的满腹牢骚说来道去都是为了一件事。

vari·cose vein /ˌværɪkəʊs ˈveɪn; *NAmE* -koʊs/ *noun* a VEIN, especially one in the leg, which has become swollen and painful （尤指腿部的）静脉曲张

var·ied 🔑 AW /ˈveərid; *NAmE* ˈverid; ˈvær-/ *adj.* (*usually approving*) **1** 🔑 of many different types 各种各样的；形形色色的；不相同的：*varied opinions* 各种不同的意见 ◇ *a wide and varied selection of cheeses* 种类繁多的可供选购的奶酪 **2** 🔑 not staying the same, but changing often 变化的；多变的；不同的：*He led a full and varied life.* 他过着丰富多彩的生活。

varie·gated /ˈveəriəgeɪtɪd; ˈveərɪg-; *NAmE* ˈver-/ *adj.* **1** (*specialist*) having spots or marks of a different colour 斑驳的；有斑点的：*a plant with variegated leaves* 斑叶植物 ➲ VISUAL VOCAB PAGE V11 **2** (*formal*) consisting of many different types of thing or person 五花八门的；形形色色的

var·iety 🔑 /vəˈraɪəti/ *noun* (*pl.* **-ies**) **1** 🔑 [sing.] ~ (**of sth**) several different sorts of the same thing （同一事物的）不同种类，多种式样：*There is **a wide variety of** patterns to choose from.* 有种类繁多的图案可供选择。◇ *He resigned for a variety of reasons.* 他由于种种原因辞职了。◇ *This tool can be used in a variety of ways.* 这一工具有多种用途。◇ *I was impressed by the variety of dishes on offer.* 所供应的菜肴之丰盛让我叹服。HELP A plural verb is needed after **a/an (large, wide, etc.) variety of**…. 在 a / an (large, wide, etc.) variety of ... 之后谓语动词要用复数：*A variety of reasons were given.* 给出了多个理由。**2** 🔑 [U] the quality of not being the same or not doing the same thing all the time 变化；多样化；多变性 SYN **diversity**: *We all need variety in our diet.* 我们都需要饮食多样化。◇ *We want more variety in our work.* 我们希望我们的工作多变点儿花样。**3** 🔑 [C] ~ (**of sth**) a type of a thing, for example a plant or language, that is different from the others in the same general group （植物、语言等的）变种，变体；异体；品种：*Apples come in a great many varieties.* 苹果的品种繁多。◇ *a rare variety of orchid* 兰花的稀有品种 ◇ *different varieties of English* 各类英语 ◇ *My cooking is of the 'quick and simple' variety.* 我做饭属于既快捷又简单的那一类。**4** (*NAmE also* **vaude·ville**) [U] a form of theatre or television entertainment that consists of a series of short performances, such as singing, dancing and funny acts 综艺节目：***a variety show/theatre*** 综艺节目 / 剧场

IDM **variety is the spice of ˈlife** (*saying*) new and exciting experiences make life more interesting 经历丰富多彩才令生活充满乐趣

vaˈriety meats *noun* [pl.] (*NAmE*) = OFFAL

vaˈriety store *noun* (*old-fashioned, NAmE*) a shop/store that sells a wide range of goods at low prices （廉价）杂货店，杂货铺

vari·fo·cals /ˈveərɪfəʊklz; *NAmE* ˈverɪfoʊklz/ *noun* [pl.] a pair of glasses in which each LENS varies in thickness from the upper part to the lower part. The upper part

V

is for looking at things at a distance, and the lower part is for looking at things that are close to you. 渐进多焦镜（镜片由上至下用于看远、近距离的东西）➲ COMPARE BIFOCALS ▶ **vari·focal** *adj.* ➲ COMPARE BIFOCAL at BIFOCALS

vari·ous /ˈveəriəs; *NAmE* ˈver-; ˈvær-/ *adj.* **1** several different 各种不同的；各种各样的 SYN **diverse**: *Tents come in various shapes and sizes.* 帐篷有各种各样的形状和大小。◇ *She took the job for various reasons.* 她由于种种原因接受了这份工作。◇ *There are various ways of doing this.* 做这一工作的方法有很多。 **2** (*formal*) having many different features 具有多种特征的；多姿多彩的 SYN **diverse**: *a large and various country* 一个多姿多彩的大国

vari·ous·ly /ˈveəriəsli; *NAmE* ˈver-; ˈvær-/ *adv.* (*formal*) in several different ways, usually by several different people 以各种方式；不同地： *He has been **variously described** as a hero, a genius and a bully.* 他被描述为英雄、天才、恶霸，不一而足。◇ *The cost has been variously estimated at between £10 million and £20 million.* 对成本的估计众说纷纭，从 1 000 万英镑到 2 000 万英镑不等。

var·mint /ˈvɑːmɪnt; *NAmE* ˈvɑːrm-/ *noun* (*old-fashioned, informal*) **1** a person, especially a child, who causes trouble 惹是生非的人；（尤指）顽童，小淘气 **2** a wild animal, especially a FOX, that causes problems 害兽（尤指狐狸）

var·nish /ˈvɑːnɪʃ; *NAmE* ˈvɑːrnɪʃ/ *noun, verb*

■ ***noun*** [U, C] a liquid that is painted onto wood, metal, etc. and that forms a hard shiny transparent surface when it is dry 清漆 ➲ SEE ALSO NAIL VARNISH at NAIL POLISH ➲ VISUAL VOCAB PAGE V65

■ ***verb*** to put varnish on the surface of sth 给…涂清漆；上清漆；涂指甲油： **~ sth** *The doors are then stained and varnished.* 这些门还要染色涂清漆。◇ (*BrE*) *Josie was sitting at her desk, varnishing her nails.* 乔西坐在书桌旁，涂着指甲油。◇ **~ sth + noun** *Her nails were varnished a brilliant shade of red.* 她的指甲上涂了一层鲜亮的红指甲油。

var·sity /ˈvɑːsəti; *NAmE* ˈvɑːrs-/ *noun, adj.*

■ ***noun*** [C, U] (*pl.* **-ies**) **1** (*NAmE*) the main team that represents a college or HIGH SCHOOL, especially in sports competitions（尤指体育比赛中大中学校的）代表队，校队 **2** (*BrE, old use* or *IndE* or *SAfrE*) university 大学： *She's still at varsity.* 她还在上大学。

■ ***adj.*** [only before noun] (*BrE, informal*) used when describing activities connected with the universities of Oxford and Cambridge, especially sports competitions（常用于牛津和剑桥两大学的体育比赛）大学的： *the varsity match* 大学体育比赛

vary AW /ˈveəri; *NAmE* ˈveri; ˈværi/ *verb* (**vary·ing, var·ied, var·ied**) **1** [I] **~ (in sth)** (of a group of similar things 一组类似的事物) to be different from each other in size, shape, etc.（大小、形状等）相异，不同，有别： *The students' work varies considerably in quality.* 学生作业的质量甚是参差不齐。◇ *The quality of the students' work varies considerably.* 学生作业的质量甚是参差不齐。◇ *New techniques were introduced with **varying degrees of** success.* 引进新技术的成功程度不尽相同。 **2** [I] to change or be different according to the situation（根据情况）变化，变更，改变： **~ with sth** *The menu varies with the season.* 菜单随季节而变动。◇ **~ according to sth** *Prices vary according to the type of room you require.* 价格随要求的房间类型而有所变化。◇ **~ from sth to sth** ◇ **~ (between A and B)** *Class numbers vary between 25 and 30.* 班级人数从 25 到 30 不等。◇ *'What time do you start work?' **'It varies.'*** "你几点钟开始工作？""没准儿。" **3** [T] **~ sth** to make changes to sth to make it slightly different（略为）变更，改变： *The job enables me to vary the hours I work.* 这份工作使我能够调整工作时间。

> **WORD FAMILY**
> **vary** *verb*
> **varied** *adj.*
> **variable** *adj.*
> **variation** *noun*
> **various** *adj.*
> **variety** *noun*

vas·cu·lar /ˈvæskjələ(r)/ *adj.* [usually before noun] (*specialist*) of or containing VEINS (= the tubes that carry liquids around the bodies of animals and plants) 血管的；脉管的；维管的

vas def·er·ens /ˌvæs ˈdefərenz/ *noun* (*pl.* **vasa def·er·entia** /ˌveɪsə defəˈrenʃiə/) (*anatomy* 解) the tube through which SPERM pass from the TESTIS on their way out of the body 输精管

vase /vɑːz; *NAmE* veɪs; veɪz/ *noun* a container made of glass, etc., used for holding cut flowers or as a decorative object 花瓶；装饰瓶： *a vase of flowers* 一瓶花 ➲ VISUAL VOCAB PAGE V22

vas·ec·tomy /vəˈsektəmi/ *noun* (*pl.* **-ies**) (*medical* 医) a medical operation to remove part of each of the tubes in a man's body that carry SPERM, after which he is not able to make a woman pregnant 输精管切除术

Vas·el·ine™ /ˈvæsəliːn/ *noun* [U] a thick soft clear substance that is used on skin to heal or protect it, or as a LUBRICANT to stop surfaces from sticking together 凡士林

vaso·con·stric·tion /ˌveɪzəʊkənˈstrɪkʃn; *NAmE* -zoʊ-/ *noun* [U] (*biology* 生 or *medical* 医) a process in which BLOOD VESSELS become narrower, which tends to increase BLOOD PRESSURE 血管收缩（可导致血压增高）

vaso·di·lation /ˌveɪzəʊdaɪˈleɪʃn; *NAmE* -zoʊ-/ *noun* [U] (*biology* 生 or *medical* 医) a process in which BLOOD VESSELS become wider, which tends to reduce BLOOD PRESSURE 血管舒张（可导致血压降低）

vas·sal /ˈvæsl/ *noun* **1** a man in the Middle Ages who promised to fight for and be loyal to a king or other powerful owner of land, in return for being given land to live on 封臣，家臣（中世纪为国王或其他权贵效忠的受封者） **2** a country that depends on and is controlled by another country 附庸国；属国

vast /vɑːst; *NAmE* væst/ *adj.* extremely large in area, size, amount, etc. 辽阔的；巨大的；庞大的；大量的 SYN **huge**: *a vast area of forest* 莽莽苍苍的森林 ◇ *a vast crowd* 一大群人 ◇ *a vast amount of information* 大量信息 ◇ *At dusk bats appear **in vast numbers**.* 蝙蝠于傍晚时分大批出现。◇ *His business empire was vast.* 他的企业规模庞大。◇ *In **the vast majority** of cases, this should not be a problem.* 在绝大多数情况下，这应该不成问题。 ▶ **vast·ness** *noun* [U, C]: *the vastness of space* 太空的浩瀚无垠

vast·ly /ˈvɑːstli; *NAmE* ˈvæstli/ *adv.* very much 非常；很： *I'm a vastly different person now.* 我现在已判若两人了。◇ *The quality of the training has vastly improved.* 训练的质量已经大幅度提高。

VAT /ˌviː eɪ ˈtiː; væt/ *noun* [U] (*BrE*) the abbreviation for 'value added tax' (a tax that is added to the price of goods and services) 增值税（全写为 value added tax）: *Prices include VAT.* 价格中含增值税。◇ *£27.50 + VAT* 27.50 英镑加增值税

vat /væt/ *noun* a large container for holding liquids, especially in industrial processes（尤指工业用）大桶，大盆，瓮，缸，罐： *distilling vats* 蒸馏罐 ◇ *a vat of whisky* 一大桶威士忌

Vati·can /ˈvætɪkən/ *noun* **the Vatican** **1** [sing.] the group of buildings in Rome where the POPE lives and works 梵蒂冈（罗马教宗居住和办公的地方） **2** [sing.+sing./pl. v.] the centre of government of the Roman Catholic Church 梵蒂冈（天主教教廷） ➲ MORE LIKE THIS 19, page R27

vaude·ville /ˈvɔːdəvɪl/ *noun* [U] **1** (*NAmE*) = VARIETY (4) **2** (*BrE also* **ˈmusic hall**) a type of entertainment popular in the late 19th and early 20th centuries, including singing, dancing and comedy（盛行于 19 世纪末 20 世纪初的）歌舞杂耍表演

ˈvaudeville theater (*NAmE*) (*BrE* **ˈmusic hall**) *noun* a theatre used for popular entertainment in the late 19th and early 20th centuries 歌舞杂耍戏院

V

vault /vɔːlt/ *noun, verb*
■ ***noun*** **1** a room with thick walls and a strong door, especially in a bank, used for keeping valuable things safe（尤指银行的）金库，保险库 **2** a room under a church or in a CEMETERY, used for burying people（教堂的）地下墓室；（坟地的）墓穴 **3** a roof or ceiling in the form of an ARCH or a series of ARCHES 穹顶；拱顶；穹隆 **4** a jump made by vaulting 撑物跳高；撑竿跳 ➲ SEE ALSO POLE VAULT
■ ***verb*** [I, T] to jump over an object in a single movement, using your hands or a pole to push you（用手支撑或撑竿）跳跃，腾跃：**~ over sth** *She vaulted over the gate and ran up the path.* 她用手一撑跃过栅栏门沿着小路跑去。◇ **~ sth** *to vault a fence* 跃过篱笆墙 ➲ SEE ALSO POLE VAULT

vault·ed /ˈvɔːltɪd/ *adj.* (*architecture* 建) made in the shape of an ARCH or a series of ARCHES; having a ceiling or roof of this shape 拱形的；有拱顶的：*a vaulted ceiling/cellar* 拱形天花板 / 地窖 ➲ VISUAL VOCAB PAGE V14

vault·ing /ˈvɔːltɪŋ/ *noun* [U] (*architecture* 建) a pattern of ARCHES in a ceiling or roof（天花板或屋顶的）拱形结构

ˈvaulting horse (*also* **horse**) *noun* a large object with legs, and sometimes handles, that GYMNASTS use to vault over（体操器械）跳马

vaunt·ed /ˈvɔːntɪd/ *adj.* [usually before noun] (*formal*) proudly talked about or praised as being very good, especially when this is not deserved 被吹嘘的；被夸耀的：*Their **much vaunted** reforms did not materialize.* 他们大肆吹嘘的改革并没有实现。

va-va-voom /ˌvɑː vɑː ˈvuːm; ˌvæ væ/ *noun* [U] (*informal*) the quality of being exciting or sexually attractive 令人兴奋的特性；性感 ORIGIN First used in the 1950s in the US to represent the sound of a car engine running. * 20 世纪 50 年代在美国首次使用，表示汽车发动机运转的声音。

VC /ˌviː ˈsiː/ *noun* [sing.] the abbreviation for 'Victoria Cross' (a MEDAL for special courage that is given to members of the British and Commonwealth armed forces) 维多利亚十字勋章（全写为 Victoria Cross，授予英国和英联邦军队中特别英勇的官兵）：*He was awarded the VC.* 他荣获维多利亚十字勋章。◇ *Captain Edward Bell VC* 维多利亚十字勋章获得者爱德华 • 贝尔上尉

ˈV-chip *noun* a computer chip in a television RECEIVER that can be programmed to block material that contains sex and violence 童锁；V 芯片（装入电视接收器阻断含有色情和暴力内容的节目）

VCR /ˌviː siː ˈɑː(r)/ *noun* (*especially NAmE*) the abbreviation for 'video cassette recorder' (a machine which is used to play videos or to record programmes from a television) 录像机（全写为 video cassette recorder）

VD /ˌviː ˈdiː/ *abbr.* (*old-fashioned*) VENEREAL DISEASE 性病

veal /viːl/ *noun* [U] meat from a CALF (= a young cow) 小牛肉；牛犊肉

vec·tor /ˈvektə(r)/ *noun* **1** (*mathematics* 数) a quantity that has both size and direction 向量；矢量：*Acceleration and velocity are both vectors.* 加速度和速度都是矢量。➲ COMPARE SCALAR **2** (*biology* 生) an insect, etc. that carries a particular disease from one living thing to another（传染疾病的）介体，载体 **3** (*specialist*) a course taken by an aircraft（航空器的）航线

Veda /ˈveɪdə; ˈviːdə/ *noun* an ancient holy text of Hinduism《吠陀》（印度教古经文）

Vedic /ˈveɪdɪk; ˈviːd-/ *adj., noun*
■ ***adj.*** relating to the Vedas《吠陀》有关的
■ ***noun*** [U] the language of the Vedas《吠陀》梵语

vee·jay /ˈviː dʒeɪ/ *noun* = VIDEO JOCKEY

veep /viːp/ *noun* (*NAmE, informal*) VICE-PRESIDENT 副总统

veer /vɪə(r); *NAmE* vɪr/ *verb* **1** [I] + **adv./prep.** (especially of a vehicle 尤指车辆) to change direction suddenly 突然变向；猛然转向 SYN **swerve**：*The bus veered onto the wrong side of the road.* 公共汽车突然驶入了逆行道。**2** [I] + **adv./prep.** (of a conversation or way of behaving or thinking 说话、行为或思想) to change in the way it develops 偏离；改变；转变：*The debate veered away from the main topic of discussion.* 争论脱离了讨论的主题。◇ *His emotions veered between fear and anger.* 他的情绪变化不定，一会儿恐惧一会儿生气。**3** [I] + **adv./prep.** (*specialist*) (of the wind 风) to change direction 改变方向：*The wind veered to the west.* 风向转西。

veg /vedʒ/ *noun, verb*
■ ***noun*** [U, C] (*pl.* **veg**) (*BrE, informal*) a vegetable or vegetables 蔬菜：*a fruit and veg stall* 水果蔬菜摊位 ◇ *He likes the traditional **meat and two veg** for his main meal.* 他主餐喜欢传统的一荤两素。
■ ***verb*** (-gg-)
PHR V **ˌveg ˈout** (*informal*) to relax by doing sth that needs very little effort, for example watching television 消遣；休闲

vegan /ˈviːɡən/ *noun* a person who does not eat any animal products such as meat, milk or eggs. Some vegans do not use animal products such as silk or leather. 严格素食主义者（不吃肉、奶、蛋等，有的不用动物产品）

Vege·bur·ger™ /ˈvedʒibɜːɡə(r); *NAmE* -bɜːrɡ-/ *noun* = VEGGIE BURGER

Vege·mite™ /ˈvedʒɪmaɪt/ *noun* [U] (*AustralE, NZE*) a dark substance made from YEAST, spread on bread, etc. 维吉麦酱（由酵母制成，呈黑色，抹在面包等食物上食用）

vege·table /ˈvedʒtəbl/ *noun* **1** (*also informal, especially in NAmE* **veg·gie**) a plant or part of a plant that is eaten as food. Potatoes, BEANS and onions are all vegetables. 蔬菜：***green vegetables*** (= for example CABBAGE) 绿色蔬菜 ◇ ***root vegetables*** (= for example CARROTS) 块根蔬菜 ◇ *a salad of raw vegetables* 生菜色拉 ◇ ***a vegetable garden/patch/plot*** 菜园；菜畦；菜地 ◇ *vegetable matter* (= plants in general) 植物质 ➲ VISUAL VOCAB PAGES V33-34 ➲ COMPARE ANIMAL *n.* (3), FRUIT *n.* (1), MINERAL (1) **2** (*BrE also* **cab·bage**) a person who is physically alive but not capable of much mental or physical activity, for example because of an accident or illness 植物人：*Severe brain damage turned him into a vegetable.* 严重的脑损伤使他变成了植物人。**3** a person who has a boring life 生活单调乏味的人：*Since losing my job I've been a vegetable.* 失业以来我感到百无聊赖。

vege·tal /ˈvedʒətl/ *adj.* (*formal*) connected with plants 植物的

vege·tar·ian /ˌvedʒəˈteəriən; *NAmE* -ˈter-/ (*also informal* **veg·gie**) *noun* a person who does not eat meat or fish 素食者；吃素的人：*Is she a vegetarian?* 她是素食者吗？➲ COMPARE FRUITARIAN, HERBIVORE ▸ **vege·tar·ian** *adj.*：*Are you vegetarian?* 你只吃素食吗？◇ *a vegetarian diet* (= with no meat or fish in it) 素食食谱 ◇ *a vegetarian restaurant* (= that serves no meat or fish) 素食餐馆 **vege·tar·ian·ism** /-ɪzəm/ *noun* [U]

vege·tate /ˈvedʒəteɪt/ *verb* [I] (of a person 人) to spend time doing very little and feeling bored 过无聊生活；无所用心

vege·tated /ˈvedʒəteɪtɪd/ *adj.* having the amount of plant life mentioned 有…植物的；植物…的：*a **densely/sparsely vegetated** area* 植物茂密的 / 稀疏的地区

vege·ta·tion /ˌvedʒəˈteɪʃn/ *noun* [U] plants in general, especially the plants that are found in a particular area or environment（统称）植物；（尤指某地或环境的）植被，植物群落，草木：*The hills are covered in lush green vegetation.* 这片丘陵草木茂盛，郁郁葱葱。

vege·ta·tive /ˈvedʒɪtətɪv; *NAmE* -teɪtɪv/ *adj.* **1** relating to plant life 植物的；植物性的 **2** (*medical* 医) (of a person 人) alive but showing no sign of brain activity 植物人状态的 ➲ SEE ALSO PERSISTENT VEGETATIVE STATE

veg·gie /ˈvedʒi/ *noun* (*informal*) **1** = VEGETARIAN：*He's turned veggie* (= become a vegetarian). 他改吃素了。**2** (*especially NAmE*) = VEGETABLE ▸ **veg·gie** *adj.*

'veggie burger (*also* **Vege·bur·ger™**) *noun* a BURGER made with vegetables, especially BEANS, instead of meat 素汉堡包

vehe·ment /'viːəmənt/ *adj.* showing very strong feelings, especially anger（感情）强烈的，激烈的；（尤指）愤怒的 SYN **forceful**: ***a vehement denial/attack/protest, etc.*** 强烈的否认、攻击、抗议等 ◇ *He had been vehement in his opposition to the idea.* 他一直强烈反对这一主张。▶ **vehe·mence** /-məns/ *noun* [U] **vehe·ment·ly** *adv.*: *The charge was vehemently denied.* 这一指责遭到了断然否认。

ve·hicle AW /'viːəkl; *NAmE also* 'viːhɪkl/ *noun* **1** (*rather formal*) a thing that is used for transporting people or goods from one place to another, such as a car or lorry/truck 交通工具；车辆：*motor vehicles* (= cars, buses, lorries/trucks, etc.) 机动车辆 ◇ *Are you the driver of this vehicle?* 你是这辆汽车的驾驶员吗？◇ *rows of parked vehicles* 一排排停放的车辆 ➲ VISUAL VOCAB PAGES V62, V63 **2** ~ (**for sth**) something that can be used to express your ideas or feelings or as a way of achieving sth（赖以表达思想、感情或达到目的的）手段，工具：*Art may be used as a vehicle for propaganda.* 艺术可以用作宣传的工具。◇ *The play is an ideal vehicle for her talents.* 这部戏是她施展才华的理想机会。

ve·hicu·lar /və'hɪkjələ(r); *NAmE* viː'h-/ *adj.* (*formal*) intended for vehicles or consisting of vehicles 供车辆等使用的；车辆的；运输工具的：*vehicular access* 车辆入口 ◇ *The road is closed to vehicular traffic.* 此路禁止车辆通行。

veil /veɪl/ *noun, verb*

■ ***noun*** **1** a covering of very thin transparent material worn, especially by women, to protect or hide the face, or as part of a hat, etc.（尤指女用的）面纱，面罩：*a bridal veil* 新娘的面纱 **2** a piece of cloth worn by NUNS over the head and shoulders（修女的）头巾 **3** [sing.] (*formal*) something that stops you from learning the truth about a situation 掩饰；掩盖；借口；托辞：*Their work is carried out behind a veil of secrecy.* 他们的工作是在秘密掩护下进行的。◇ *It would be better to* ***draw a veil*** *over what happened next* (= not talk about it). 最好把之后发生的事情掩盖起来。 **4** [sing.] (*formal*) a thin layer that stops you from seeing sth 薄薄的遮盖层：*The mountain tops were hidden beneath a veil of mist.* 山顶笼罩在薄雾中。

IDM **take the 'veil** (*old-fashioned*) to become a NUN 当修女

■ ***verb*** **1** ~ **sth/yourself** to cover your face with a veil 戴面纱；戴面罩 **2** ~ **sth** (*literary*) to cover sth with sth that hides it partly or completely 遮掩；掩饰 SYN **shroud**: *A fine drizzle began to veil the hills.* 蒙蒙的细雨渐渐笼罩了群山。

veiled /veɪld/ *adj.* **1** not expressed directly or clearly because you do not want your meaning to be obvious 含蓄的；掩饰的：*a* ***thinly veiled*** *threat* 几乎不加掩饰的威胁 ◇ *She made a* ***veiled reference to*** *his past mistakes.* 她含蓄地提到了他过去所犯的错误。 **2** wearing a veil 戴面纱的；蒙面的：*a mysterious veiled woman* 戴面纱的神秘女人

vein /veɪn/ *noun* **1** [C] any of the tubes that carry blood from all parts of the body towards the heart 静脉：*the jugular vein* 颈静脉 ➲ COMPARE ARTERY (1) ➲ SEE ALSO DEEP VEIN THROMBOSIS, VARICOSE VEIN **2** [C] any of the very thin tubes that form the frame of a leaf or an insect's wing 叶脉；翅脉 **3** [C] a narrow strip of a different colour in some types of stone, wood and cheese 纹理；纹路；条纹 **4** [C] a thin layer of minerals or metal contained in rock 矿脉；矿脉床；矿层；岩脉 SYN **seam**: *a vein of gold* 金矿脉 **5** [sing.] ~ (**of sth**) an amount of a particular quality or feature in sth（某种素质或特征的）量：*They had tapped a rich vein of information in his secretary.* 他们从他的秘书那里摸到了大量信息。 **6** [sing., U] a particular style or manner 风格；方式：*A number of other people commented* ***in a similar vein***. 其他一些人也以类似的腔调评论。◇ *'And that's not all,' he continued in angry vein.* "那还不算全部呢。"他生气地继续说道。

veined /veɪnd/ *adj.* having or marked with veins or thin lines 有静脉的；有叶脉的；有翅脉的；有纹理的：*thin blue-veined hands* 青筋暴突的瘦弱的双手 ◇ *veined marble* 有纹理的大理石

vein·ing /'veɪnɪŋ/ *noun* [U] a pattern of veins or thin lines 静脉纹；纹理：*the blue veining in Gorgonzola cheese* 戈尔贡佐拉干酪的蓝纹

vein·ous /'veɪnəs/ *adj.* (*specialist*) having VEINS that are very noticeable 静脉明显的

velar /'viːlə(r)/ *noun* (*phonetics* 语音) a speech sound made by placing the back of the tongue against or near the back part of the mouth, for example /k/ or /g/ in the English words *key* and *go* 软腭音，舌根音（如 /k/ 或 /g/）▶ **velar** *adj.*

Vel·cro™ /'velkrəʊ; *NAmE* -kroʊ/ *noun* [U] a material for fastening clothes, etc. with two different surfaces, one rough and one smooth, that stick to each other when they are pressed together 维克罗搭扣；魔术贴 ➲ VISUAL VOCAB PAGE V68

veld /velt/ *noun* [U] (in South Africa) flat open land with grass and no trees（南非的）无树草原 ➲ COMPARE PAMPAS, PRAIRIE, SAVANNAH, STEPPE

vel·lum /'veləm/ *noun* [U] **1** material made from the skin of a sheep, GOAT or CALF, used for making book covers and, in the past, for writing on（书封或旧时书写用的）羊皮纸，犊皮纸 **2** smooth cream-coloured paper used for writing on 仿羊皮纸；仿犊皮纸

vel·oci·rap·tor /və,lɒsɪ'ræptə(r); *NAmE* -,lɑːs-/ *noun* a small DINOSAUR that moved fairly quickly 伶盗龙；迅猛龙；疾走龙

vel·ocity /və'lɒsəti; *NAmE* -'lɑːs-/ *noun* [U, C] (*pl.* **-ies**) **1** (*specialist*) the speed of sth in a particular direction（沿某一方向的）速度：*the velocity of light* 光速 ◇ ***to gain/lose velocity*** 加速；减速 ◇ *a* ***high-velocity*** *rifle* 高速步枪 **2** (*formal*) high speed 高速；快速：*Jaguars can move with an astonishing velocity.* 美洲豹跑起来速度惊人。

velo·drome /'velədrəʊm; *NAmE* -droʊm/ *noun* a track or building used for cycle racing（自行车或摩托车的）赛车场 ➲ WORDFINDER NOTE AT CYCLING

vel·our /və'lʊə(r); *NAmE* və'lʊr/ *noun* [U] a type of silk or cotton cloth with a thick soft surface like VELVET 丝绒；拉绒织物；维罗绒

velum /'viːləm/ *noun* (*pl.* **vela** /'viːlə/) (*anatomy* 解) a layer of TISSUE that covers sth, especially the soft PALATE inside the mouth 罩膜；缘膜

vel·vet /'velvɪt/ *noun* [U] a type of cloth made from silk, cotton or NYLON, with a thick soft surface 丝绒；立绒；经绒；天鹅绒：*a velvet dress* 天鹅绒连衣裙 ◇ *velvet curtains/drapes* 天鹅绒窗帘 / 帷幕 IDM SEE IRON *adj.*

vel·vet·een /,velvə'tiːn/ *noun* [U] a type of cotton cloth that looks like VELVET but is less expensive 棉绒；平绒；纬绒

vel·vety /'velvəti/ *adj.* pleasantly smooth and soft 光滑柔软的；柔和的：*velvety skin* 柔软的皮肤 ◇ *a velvety red wine* 醇厚的红葡萄酒

vena cava /,viːnə 'keɪvə/ *noun* (*pl.* **venae cavae** /,viːniː 'keɪviː/) (*anatomy* 解) either of the two VEINS that take blood without OXYGEN in it towards the heart 腔静脉

venal /'viːnl/ *adj.* (*formal*) prepared to do dishonest or immoral things in return for money 贪赃枉法的；见利忘义的 SYN **corrupt**: *venal journalists* 唯利是图的记者 ▶ **ve·nal·ity** /viː'næləti/ *noun* [U]

vend /vend/ *verb* ~ **sth** (*formal*) to sell sth 售卖

ven·detta /ven'detə/ *noun* **1** a long and violent disagreement between two families or groups, in which people are murdered in return for previous murders 家族世仇；团伙仇杀 SYN **feud** **2** ~ (**against sb**) a long argument or disagreement in which one person or group does or says things to harm another 积怨；宿怨；长期不和：*He has accused the media of pursuing a vendetta against him.*

他指责媒体长期跟他过不去。◇ *She conducted a **personal vendetta** against me.* 她对我有宿仇。

vending machine /ˈvendɪŋ məʃiːn/ *noun* a machine from which you can buy cigarettes, drinks, etc. by putting coins into it（出售香烟、饮料等的）投币式自动售货机

vend·or /ˈvendə(r)/ *noun* **1** a person who sells things, for example food or newspapers, usually outside on the street 小贩；摊贩：*street vendors* 街头小贩 **2** (*formal*) a company that sells a particular product（某种产品的）销售公司：*software vendors* 软件销售商 **3** (*law* 律) a person who is selling a house, etc.（房屋等的）卖主 ➲ COMPARE SELLER (1)

ven·eer /vəˈnɪə(r); *NAmE* vəˈnɪr/ *noun, verb*

■ *noun* **1** [C, U] a thin layer of wood or plastic that is glued to the surface of cheaper wood, especially on a piece of furniture 饰面薄板，薄片镶饰（尤用于家具上）**2** [sing.] ~ (**of sth**) (*formal*) an outer appearance of a particular quality that hides the true nature of sb/sth 虚假的外表；虚饰：*Her veneer of politeness began to crack.* 她那彬彬有礼的伪装开始露馅儿了。

■ *verb* ~ **sth** (**with/in sth**) to cover the surface of sth with a veneer of wood, etc.（用薄片镶饰等）饰面，覆盖

ven·er·able /ˈvenərəbl/ *adj.* **1** (*formal*) **venerable** people or things deserve respect because they are old, important, wise, etc.（因年高、显要、智慧等）令人尊重的，值得敬重的，受敬佩的：*a venerable old man* 德高望重的老人 ◇ *a venerable institution* 令人仰慕的机构 **2 the Venerable...** [only before noun] (in the Anglican Church) a title of respect used when talking about an ARCHDEACON（对圣公会会吏长的尊称）尊者：*the Venerable Martin Roberts* 尊者马丁·罗伯茨 **3 the Venerable...** [only before noun] (in the Roman Catholic Church) a title given to a dead person who is very holy but who has not yet been made a SAINT 真福（天主教会对列入圣品前的已故圣洁者的尊称）

ven·er·ate /ˈvenəreɪt/ *verb* ~ **sb/sth** (**as sth**) (*formal*) to have and show a lot of respect for sb/sth, especially sb/sth that is considered to be holy or very important 敬重；崇敬；敬仰 SYN **revere** ▸ **ven·er·ation** /ˌvenəˈreɪʃn/ *noun* [U]: *The relics were objects of veneration.* 这些圣人遗物是备受敬奉之物。

ven·ereal /vəˈnɪəriəl; *NAmE* -ˈnɪr-/ *adj.* [only before noun] relating to diseases spread by sexual contact 性病的；性交传染的：*a venereal infection* 性传染病

veˌnereal diˈsease *noun* [C, U] (*abbr.* **VD**) (*old-fashioned*) a disease that is caught by having sex with an infected person 性病

ven·etian blind /vəˌniːʃn ˈblaɪnd/ *noun* a covering for a window that has flat horizontal plastic or metal strips going across it that you can turn to let in as much light as you want 百叶窗帘 ➲ VISUAL VOCAB PAGE V22

ven·geance /ˈvendʒəns/ *noun* [U] (*formal*) the act of punishing or harming sb in return for what they have done to you, your family or friends 报复；报仇；复仇 SYN **revenge**: *a desire for vengeance* 复仇心 ◇ ~ **on/upon sb** *to take vengeance on sb* 对某人进行报复 ◇ *He swore vengeance on his child's killer.* 他发誓要找杀害他孩子的凶手报仇。

IDM **with a ˈvengeance** (*informal*) to a greater degree than is expected or usual 程度更深地；出乎意料地：*She set to work with a vengeance.* 她加倍努力地工作起来。

venge·ful /ˈvendʒfl/ *adj.* (*formal*) showing a desire to punish sb who has harmed you 心存报复的；图谋复仇的 ▸ **venge·ful·ly** /-fəli/ *adv.*

ve·nial /ˈviːniəl/ *adj.* [usually before noun] (*formal*) (of a SIN or mistake 罪过或错误) not very serious and therefore able to be forgiven 轻微而可原谅的

ven·ison /ˈvenɪsn; -zn/ *noun* [U] meat from a DEER 鹿肉

Venn dia·gram /ˈven daɪəgræm/ *noun* (*mathematics* 数) a picture showing SETS (= groups of things that have a shared quality) as circles that cross over each other, to show which qualities the different sets have in common 维恩图，文氏图（用圆表示集合之间的关系）

Venn diagram 文氏图

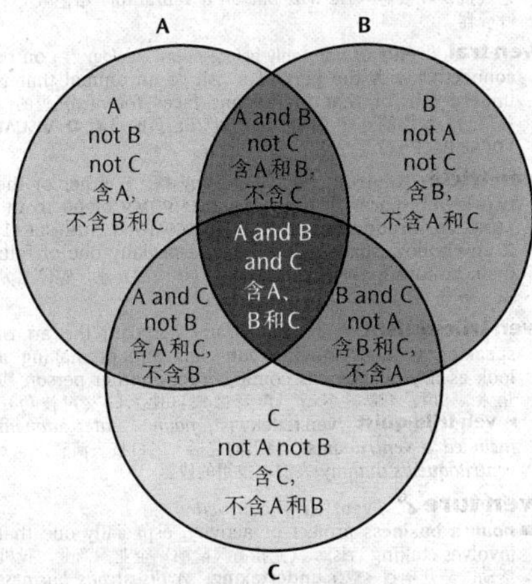

venom /ˈvenəm/ *noun* [U] **1** the poisonous liquid that some snakes, spiders, etc. produce when they bite or sting you（毒蛇、蜘蛛等分泌的）毒液 **2** (*formal*) strong bitter feeling; hatred and a desire to hurt sb 恶毒；怨恨；恶意；歹心：*a look of pure venom* 恶狠狠的样子 IDM SEE SPIT *v.*

ven·om·ous /ˈvenəməs/ *adj.* **1** (of a snake, etc. 蛇等) producing venom 分泌毒液的；有毒的 **2** (*formal*) full of bitter feeling or hatred 恶毒的；恶意的；充满仇恨的：*a venomous look* 恶狠狠的样子 ▸ **ven·om·ous·ly** *adv.*

ven·ous /ˈviːnəs/ *adj.* (*specialist*) of or contained in VEINS (= the tubes that carry liquids around the bodies of animals and plants) 静脉的；静脉中的；叶脉的：*venous blood* 静脉血

vent /vent/ *noun, verb*

■ *noun* **1** an opening that allows air, gas or liquid to pass out of or into a room, building, container, etc.（空气、气体、液体的）出口，进口，漏孔：***air/heating vents*** 通气孔；热风孔 ➲ VISUAL VOCAB PAGE V56 ➲ COMPARE REGISTER *n.* (4) **2** (*specialist*) the opening in the body of a bird, fish, REPTILE or other small animal, through which waste matter is passed out（鸟、鱼等小动物的）肛门 **3** a long thin opening at the bottom of the back or side of a coat or jacket（大衣等的）衩口，开衩，背衩

IDM **give** (**full**) **vent to sth** (*formal*) to express a feeling, especially anger, strongly（充分）表达；（淋漓尽致地）发泄：*She gave full vent to her feelings in a violent outburst.* 她大发脾气以宣泄情绪。

■ *verb* ~ **sth** (**on sb**) (*formal*) to express feelings, especially anger, strongly 表达，发泄（感情，尤指愤怒）：*He vented his anger on the referee.* 他把气撒在裁判身上。

ven·ti·late /ˈventɪleɪt/ *verb* **1** ~ **sth** to allow fresh air to enter and move around a room, building, etc. 使（房间、建筑物等）通风；使通气：*a well-ventilated room* 通风良好的房间 ◇ *The bathroom is ventilated by means of an extractor fan.* 这个浴室使用抽风扇通风。**2** ~ **sth** (*formal*) to express your feelings or opinions publicly 公开表达（感情或意见）SYN **air** ▸ **ven·ti·la·tion** /ˌventɪˈleɪʃn/ *noun* [U]: *a ventilation shaft* 通风井 ◇ *Make sure that there is adequate ventilation in the room before using the paint.* 在使用油漆前确保室内通风充足。

V

ven·ti·la·tor /ˈventɪleɪtə(r)/ *noun* **1** a device or an opening for letting fresh air come into a room, etc. 通风设备；通风口 **2** a piece of equipment with a PUMP that helps sb to breathe by sending air in and out of their lungs 通气机；呼吸器：*He was put on a ventilator.* 给他戴上了呼吸器。

ven·tral /ˈventrəl/ *adj.* [only before noun] (*biology* 生) on or connected with the part of a fish or an animal that is underneath (or that in humans faces forward) 腹的；腹部的；腹侧的：*a fish's ventral fin* 鱼的腹鳍 ➲ VISUAL VOCAB PAGE V12

ven·tricle /ˈventrɪkl/ *noun* (*anatomy* 解) **1** either of the two lower spaces in the heart that PUMP blood to the LUNGS or around the body 心室 ➲ COMPARE AURICLE (1) **2** any hollow space in the body, especially one of four main hollow spaces in the brain （体内的）室，腔；（尤指）脑室

ven·trilo·quism /venˈtrɪləkwɪzəm/ *noun* [U] the art of speaking without moving your lips and of making it look as if your voice is coming from another person 腹语术，口技（嘴唇不动、声音像来自他人的发声技巧） ▸ **ven·trilo·quist** /venˈtrɪləkwɪst/ *noun*：*Entertainment included a ventriloquist.* 演出的包括一名口技表演者。◇ *a ventriloquist's dummy* 表演口技用的傀儡

ven·ture 🔑 /ˈventʃə(r)/ *noun, verb*

■ ***noun*** a business project or activity, especially one that involves taking risks （尤指有风险的）企业，商业，投机活动，经营项目 SYN **undertaking**：*A disastrous business venture lost him thousands of dollars.* 一个彻底失败的经营项目使他损失成千上万美元。➲ SEE ALSO JOINT VENTURE

■ ***verb*** **1** 🔑 [I] **+ adv./prep.** to go somewhere even though you know that it might be dangerous or unpleasant 敢于去（危险或令人不快的地方）：*They ventured nervously into the water.* 他们紧张地硬着头皮下水。◇ *He's never ventured abroad in his life.* 他一生中从来不敢出国。**2** [T] (*formal*) to say or do sth in a careful way, especially because it might upset or offend sb 小心地说，谨慎地做（尤指会使人烦恼或不快的事）：**~ sth** *She hardly dared to venture an opinion.* 她几乎不敢亮明观点。◇ **~ to do sth** *I ventured to suggest that she might have made a mistake.* 我小心地提醒说她可能出了差错。◇ **+ speech** *'And if I say no?' she ventured.* "那么我要是说不呢？"她试探说。◇ **~ that...** *He ventured that the data might be flawed.* 他大胆地推测说数据可能有误差。**3** [T] **~ sth (on sth)** to risk losing sth valuable or important if you are not successful at sth 冒着（失去贵重或重要的东西）的危险 SYN **gamble**：*It was wrong to venture his financial security on such a risky deal.* 他牺牲自己的财务安全去做风险这么大的交易是错误的。

IDM **nothing ˈventured, nothing ˈgained** (*saying*) used to say that you have to take risks if you want to achieve things and be successful 不敢冒险就一事无成；不入虎穴，焉得虎子

PHR V **ˈventure into/on sth** to do sth, even though it involves risks 冒险做：*This is the first time the company has ventured into movie production.* 这是这家公司首次涉足电影制作。

ˈventure ˈcapital *noun* [U] (*business* 商) money that is invested in a new company to help it develop, which may involve a lot of risk 风险资本（投入新公司的资金，风险很大）➲ COMPARE WORKING CAPITAL

ˈVenture Scout *noun* (in some countries) a member of the senior branch of the SCOUT ASSOCIATION for young people between the ages of about 15 and 20 （某些国家）深资童军，奋进童子军（年龄约为 15 至 20 岁）➲ COMPARE EXPLORER SCOUT

ven·ture·some /ˈventʃəsəm; *NAmE* -tʃərs-/ *adj.* (*formal* or *literary*) willing to take risks 大胆的；好冒险的 SYN **daring**

venue /ˈvenjuː/ *noun* a place where people meet for an organized event, for example a concert, sporting event or conference 活动场地（如音乐厅、体育比赛场馆、会场）：*The band will be playing at 20 different venues on their UK tour.* 这个乐队在英国巡回演出期间将在 20 个不同的地点演出。◇ *Please note the change of venue for this event.* 请注意：这次活动的地点有变。➲ SYNONYMS AT PLACE ➲ WORDFINDER NOTE AT CONCERT, CONFERENCE

Venus /ˈviːnəs/ *noun* the planet in the SOLAR SYSTEM that is second in order of distance from the sun, between Mercury and the earth 金星；太白星

Venus fly·trap /ˌviːnəs ˈflaɪtræp/ *noun* a small CARNIVOROUS (= flesh-eating) plant with leaves that trap insects by closing quickly around them 捕蝇草（用叶子捕捉后消化昆虫）

ver·acity /vəˈræsəti/ *noun* [U] (*formal*) the quality of being true; the habit of telling the truth 真实；真实性；诚实 SYN **truth, truthfulness**：*They questioned the veracity of her story.* 他们质疑她所述事情的真实性。

ver·anda (*also* **ver·an·dah**) /vəˈrændə/ *noun* **1** (*especially BrE*) (*NAmE usually* **porch**) a platform with an open front and a roof, built onto the side of a house on the ground floor （房屋底层有顶半敞的）走廊，游廊：*After dinner, we sat talking on the veranda.* 饭后我们坐在游廊上交谈。**2** (*AustralE, NZE*) a roof over the part of the street where people walk in front of a shop/store （店铺面街上方的）遮檐 SYN **awning**

verb /vɜːb; *NAmE* vɜːrb/ *noun* (*grammar* 语法) a word or group of words that expresses an action (such as *eat*), an event (such as *happen*) or a state (such as *exist*) 动词：***regular/irregular verbs*** 规则 / 不规则动词 ◇ ***transitive/intransitive verbs*** 及物 / 不及物动词 ➲ SEE ALSO PHRASAL VERB

ver·bal /ˈvɜːbl; *NAmE* ˈvɜːrbl/ *adj.* **1** relating to words 文字的；言语的；词语的：*The job applicant must have good verbal skills.* 应聘这份工作的人必须具有良好的语言表达技能。◇ *non-verbal communication* (= expressions of the face, GESTURES, etc.) 非语言交际 **2** spoken, not written 口头（而非书面）的：*a* ***verbal agreement/warning*** 口头协议 / 警告 ◇ *verbal instructions* 口头指示 ➲ COMPARE ORAL *adj.* (1) **3** (*grammar* 语法) relating to verbs 动词的：*a verbal noun* 动名词

ver·bal·ize (*BrE also* **-ise**) /ˈvɜːbəlaɪz; *NAmE* ˈvɜːrb-/ *verb* [T, I] **~ (sth)** (*formal*) to express your feelings or ideas in words 用言语（或文字）表达 SYN **put**：*He's a real genius but he has difficulty verbalizing his ideas.* 他确实是个天才，但不太会表达自己的想法。

ver·bal·ly /ˈvɜːbəli; *NAmE* ˈvɜːrb-/ *adv.* in spoken words and not in writing or actions 口头上（而非书面或行动上）：*The company had received complaints both verbally and in writing.* 这家公司收到了口头和书面的投诉。

ver·ba·tim /vɜːˈbeɪtɪm; *NAmE* vɜːrˈb-/ *adj., adv.* exactly as spoken or written 一字不差的（地）；逐字的（地）SYN **word for word**：*a verbatim report* 一字不差的报告 ◇ *He reported the speech verbatim.* 他逐字报道了那篇讲话。

ver·bena /vɜːˈbiːnə; *NAmE* vɜːrˈb-/ *noun* [U, C] a garden plant with bright flowers 马鞭草（庭院花卉，花鲜艳）

ver·bi·age /ˈvɜːbiɪdʒ; *NAmE* ˈvɜːrb-/ *noun* [U] (*formal, disapproving*) the use of too many words, or of more difficult words than are needed, to express an idea 冗词；赘语；晦涩

ver·bose /vɜːˈbəʊs; *NAmE* vɜːrˈboʊs/ *adj.* (*formal, disapproving*) using or containing more words than are needed 冗长的；啰嗦的；唠叨的 SYN **long-winded**：*a verbose speaker/style* 啰里啰嗦的演讲者；长篇大论 ▸ **ver·bos·ity** /vɜːˈbɒsəti; *NAmE* vɜːrˈbɑːs-/ *noun* [U]

ver·dant /ˈvɜːdnt; *NAmE* ˈvɜːrdnt/ *adj.* (*literary*) (of grass, plants, fields, etc. 草、植物、田地等) fresh and green 嫩绿的；碧绿的；青翠的

ver·dict /ˈvɜːdɪkt; *NAmE* ˈvɜːrd-/ *noun* **1** a decision that is made by a JURY in court, stating if sb is considered guilty of a crime or not （陪审团的）裁定，裁决，裁断：*Has the jury* ***reached a verdict****?* 陪审团作出裁定了吗？◇ *The jury* ***returned a verdict*** (= gave a verdict) *of guilty.* 陪审团作出了有罪的裁决。➲ COLLOCATIONS AT JUSTICE ➲

V

SEE ALSO MAJORITY VERDICT, OPEN VERDICT **2 ~ (on sth/sb)** a decision that you make or an opinion that you give about sth, after you have tested it or considered it carefully（经过检验或认真考虑后的）决定，结论，意见：*The coroner* ***recorded a verdict*** *of accidental death.* 验尸官得出了意外死亡的结论。◇ *The panel will* ***give their verdict*** *on the latest video releases.* 专家组将就最近发行的录像提出他们的意见。◇ *Well, what's your verdict?* 那么，你有何意见呢？

ver·di·gris /ˈvɜːdɪgriː; -griːs; *NAmE* ˈvɜːrd-/ *noun* [U] the greenish substance which forms, for example on roofs, when COPPER reacts with the air 铜绿，碱式碳酸铜（铜遇空气发生反应形成）

ver·dure /ˈvɜːdjə(r); *NAmE* ˈvɜːrd-/ *noun* [U] (*literary*) thick green plants growing in a particular place 青葱的草木；郁郁葱葱的植物

verge /vɜːdʒ; *NAmE* vɜːrdʒ/ *noun, verb*

■ ***noun*** (*BrE*) a piece of grass at the edge of a path, road, etc.（路边的）小草地，绿地：*a grass verge* 长了草的路边 ➲ COMPARE SOFT SHOULDER

IDM **on/to the verge of sth/of doing sth** very near to the moment when sb does sth or sth happens 濒于；接近于；行将：*He was on the verge of tears.* 他差点儿哭了出来。◇ *They are on the verge of signing a new contract.* 他们即将签订一份新的合同。

■ ***verb***

PHR V **ˈverge on sth** to be very close to an extreme state or condition 极接近；濒于 SYN **border on sth**：*Some of his suggestions verged on the outrageous.* 他的一些建议都快到了荒唐的地步。

ver·ger /ˈvɜːdʒə(r); *NAmE* ˈvɜːrdʒ-/ *noun* (*especially BrE*) an official whose job is to take care of the inside of a church and to perform some simple duties during church services 教堂司事

ver·ify /ˈverɪfaɪ/ *verb* (**veri·fies**, **veri·fy·ing**, **veri·fied**, **veri·fied**) (*formal*) **1** to check that sth is true or accurate 核实；查对；核准：**~ sth** *We have no way of verifying his story.* 我们无法核实他的说法。◇ **~ that...** *Please verify that there is sufficient memory available before loading the program.* 请在核实有足够的内存后再载入程序。◇ **~ whether, what, etc....** *I'll leave you to verify whether these claims are true.* 我让你来查核这些说法是否属实。**2 ~ sth | ~ that...** to show or say that sth is true or accurate 证明；证实 SYN **confirm**：*Her version of events was verified by neighbours.* 她对这些事件的说法已得到邻居的证实。▶ **veri·fi·able** /ˈverɪfaɪəbl/ *adj.*：*a verifiable fact* 可核实的事实 **veri·fi·ca·tion** /ˌverɪfɪˈkeɪʃn/ *noun* [U]：*the verification of hypotheses* 对假说的证实

ver·ily /ˈverɪli/ *adv.* (*old use*) really; truly 真正地；真实地

veri·sim·ili·tude /ˌverɪsɪˈmɪlɪtjuːd; *NAmE* -tuːd/ *noun* [U] (*formal*) the quality of seeming to be true or real 貌似真实；逼真 SYN **authenticity**：*To add verisimilitude, the stage is covered with sand for the desert scenes.* 为了更加逼真，舞台上铺满了沙子作为沙漠的场景。

ver·it·able /ˈverɪtəbl/ *adj.* [only before noun] (*formal* or *humorous*) a word used to emphasize that sb/sth can be compared to sb/sth else that is more exciting, more impressive, etc. 十足的；名副其实的；不折不扣的 SYN **positive**：*The meal that followed was a veritable banquet.* 随后摆上的饭菜俨然是一桌宴席。

ver·ity /ˈverəti/ *noun* (*pl.* **-ies**) **1** [usually pl.] (*formal*) a belief or principle about life that is accepted as true（关于生命的）信念，准则，真理：*the* ***eternal verities*** *of life* 生命永恒的真理 **2** [U] (*old use*) truth 真理；客观事实

vermi·celli /ˌvɜːmɪˈtʃeli; *NAmE* ˌvɜːrm-/ *noun* [U] **1** PASTA in the shape of very thin sticks, often broken into small pieces and added to soups 意大利细面条（常折碎做汤等）**2** (*BrE*) small pieces of chocolate in the shape of very thin sticks broken into pieces, used to decorate cakes 碎条巧克力（用以装饰糕点）

ver·mil·ion /vəˈmɪliən; *NAmE* vərˈm-/ *adj.* bright red in colour 鲜红的；朱红的 ▶ **ver·mil·ion** *noun* [U]

ver·min /ˈvɜːmɪn; *NAmE* ˈvɜːrmɪn/ *noun* [pl.] **1** wild animals or birds that destroy plants or food, or attack farm animals and birds 害兽；害鸟：*On farms the fox is considered vermin and treated as such.* 在农场里狐狸被当成有害动物来对待。**2** insects that live on the bodies of animals and sometimes humans 体外寄生虫；害虫：*The room was crawling with vermin.* 这房间里虱蚤横行。**3** (*disapproving*) people who are very unpleasant or dangerous to society 蟊贼；歹徒；害人虫

ver·min·ous /ˈvɜːmɪnəs; *NAmE* ˈvɜːrm-/ *adj.* (*formal*) covered with vermin 有害虫的；布满寄生虫的

ver·mouth /ˈvɜːməθ; *NAmE* vərˈmuːθ/ *noun* [U] a strong wine, flavoured with HERBS and spices, often mixed with other drinks as a COCKTAIL 味美思酒，苦艾酒（以多种香草制成，常用以调配鸡尾酒）

ver·nacu·lar /vəˈnækjələ(r); *NAmE* vərˈn-/ *noun* **1** (*usually* **the vernacular**) [sing.] the language spoken in a particular area or by a particular group, especially one that is not the official or written language 方言；土语 **2** [U] (*specialist*) a style of ARCHITECTURE concerned with ordinary houses rather than large public buildings（建筑的）民间风格 ▶ **ver·nacu·lar** *adj.*

ver·nal /ˈvɜːnl; *NAmE* ˈvɜːrnl/ *adj.* [only before noun] (*formal* or *literary*) connected with the season of spring 春季的：*the vernal equinox* 春分

ver·nis·sage /ˌvɜːnɪˈsɑːʒ; *NAmE* ˌvɜːrn-/ *noun* (*pl.* **ver·nis·sages** /ˌvɜːnɪˈsɑːʒ; *NAmE* ˌvɜːrn-/) an occasion when a few invited people can look at paintings before they go on show to the public（画展开幕前的）特邀来宾观摩

ver·ruca /vəˈruːkə/ (*BrE*) (*NAmE* **ˈplantar wart**) *noun* a small hard lump like a WART on the bottom of the foot, which can be easily spread from person to person（长在脚底上，容易传染的）疣

ver·sa·tile /ˈvɜːsətaɪl; *NAmE* ˈvɜːrsətl/ *adj.* (*approving*) **1** (of a person 人) able to do many different things 多才多艺的；有多种技能的；多面手的：*He's a versatile actor who has played a wide variety of parts.* 他是个多才多艺的演员，扮演过各种各样的角色。**2** (of food, a building, etc. 食物、建筑物等) having many different uses 多用途的；多功能的：*Eggs are easy to cook and are an extremely versatile food.* 鸡蛋容易烹煮，怎么做着吃都行。▶ **ver·sa·til·ity** /ˌvɜːsəˈtɪləti; *NAmE* ˌvɜːrs-/ *noun* [U]：*She is a designer of extraordinary versatility.* 她是位特别多才多艺的设计师。

verse /vɜːs; *NAmE* vɜːrs/ *noun* **1** [U] writing that is arranged in lines, often with a regular rhythm or pattern of RHYME 诗；韵文 SYN **poetry**：*Most of the play is written in verse, but some of it is in prose.* 这剧本大部分是用韵文写的，不过有一些是用散文。➲ SEE ALSO BLANK VERSE, FREE VERSE ➲ WORDFINDER NOTE AT POETRY **2** [C] a group of lines that form a unit in a poem or song 诗节；歌曲的段落：*a hymn with six verses* 一首六节的赞美诗 **3 verses** [pl.] (*old-fashioned*) poetry 诗：*a book of comic verses* 打油诗集 **4** [C] any one of the short NUMBERED divisions of a chapter in the Bible（《圣经》的）节 IDM SEE CHAPTER

versed /vɜːst; *NAmE* vɜːrst/ *adj.* **~ in sth** having a lot of knowledge about sth, or skill at sth 精通的；熟练的 SYN **expert, practised**：*He was* ***well versed*** *in employment law.* 他精通雇佣法。

ver·si·fi·ca·tion /ˌvɜːsɪfɪˈkeɪʃn; *NAmE* ˌvɜːrs-/ *noun* [U] (*formal*) the art of writing poetry in a particular pattern; the pattern in which poetry is written 诗格；诗律；诗体；韵律

vers·ify /ˈvɜːsɪfaɪ; *NAmE* ˈvɜːrs-/ *verb* (**ver·si·fies**, **ver·si·fy·ing**, **ver·si·fied**, **ver·si·fied**) [I, T] **~ (sth)** (*formal, sometimes disapproving*) to write sth in verse 以诗体写 ▶ **ver·si·fier** *noun*

V

ver·sion AW /ˈvɜːʃn; -ʒn; NAmE ˈvɜːrʒn/ *noun* **1** a form of sth that is slightly different from an earlier form or from other forms of the same thing 变体；变种；型式：*There are two versions of the game, a long one and a short one.* 这游戏有两个版本，一长一短。◇ *the **latest version** of the software package* 软件包的最新版本 ◇ *the **de luxe/luxury version*** 豪华型 ⇨ SEE ALSO BETA VERSION **2** a description of an event from the position of a particular person or group of people （从不同角度的）说法，描述：*She gave us her version of what had happened that day.* 她从她的角度向我们描述了那天发生的事情。◇ *Their versions of how the accident happened conflict.* 他们对事故发生情况的说法相互矛盾。⇨ SYNONYMS AT REPORT **3** a film/movie, play, piece of music, etc. that is based on a particular piece of work but is in a different form, style or language （电影、剧本、乐曲等的）版本，改编形式，改写本：*the film version of 'War and Peace'* 根据《战争与和平》改编的电影 ◇ *The English version of the novel is due for publication next year.* 这部小说的英文译本预定明年出版。⇨ SEE ALSO AUTHORIZED VERSION, COVER VERSION

verso /ˈvɜːsəʊ; NAmE ˈvɜːrsoʊ/ *noun* (*pl.* **-os**) (*specialist*) the page on the left side of an open book （书的）左页，偶数页；（书页的）背面 OPP **recto**

ver·sus /ˈvɜːsəs; NAmE ˈvɜːrsəs/ *prep.* (*abbr.* **v**, **vs**) **1** (*sport* 体育 or *law* 律) used to show that two teams or sides are against each other （表示两队或双方对阵）对，诉，对抗：*It is France versus Brazil in the final.* 决赛是法国队对巴西队。◇ *in the case of the State versus Ford* 在州政府诉福特公司的案件中 **2** used to compare two different ideas, choices, etc. （比较两种不同想法、选择等）与…相对，与…相比：*It was the promise of better job opportunities versus the inconvenience of moving away and leaving her friends.* 可能会有较好的就业前景，但麻烦的是要搬走并远离她的朋友。

ver·tebra /ˈvɜːtɪbrə; NAmE ˈvɜːrt-/ *noun* (*pl.* **ver·te·brae** /-reɪ; -riː/) any of the small bones that are connected together to form the SPINE 椎骨；脊椎 ⇨ VISUAL VOCAB PAGE V64 ▶ **ver·te·bral** *adj.* [only before noun]

ver·te·brate /ˈvɜːtɪbrət; NAmE ˈvɜːrt-/ *noun* (*specialist*) any animal with a BACKBONE, including all MAMMALS, birds, fish, REPTILES and AMPHIBIANS 脊椎动物（包括所有哺乳动物、鸟类、鱼类、爬行动物和两栖动物）⇨ COMPARE INVERTEBRATE ▶ **ver·te·brate** *adj.*

ver·tex /ˈvɜːteks; NAmE ˈvɜːrt-/ *noun* (*pl.* **ver·ti·ces** /-tɪsiːz/ or **ver·texes**) **1** (*geometry* 几何) a point where two lines meet to form an angle, especially the point of a triangle or CONE opposite the base （三角形或锥形的）顶点；角顶 ⇨ PICTURE AT SOLID **2** (*specialist*) the highest point or top of sth 至高点；顶点

ver·ti·cal /ˈvɜːtɪkl; NAmE ˈvɜːrt-/ *adj., noun*

■ *adj.* **1** (of a line, pole, etc. 线、杆等) going straight up or down from a level surface or from top to bottom in a picture, etc. 竖的；垂直的；直立的：*the vertical axis of the graph* 图的纵轴 ◇ *The cliff was almost vertical.* 那悬崖几乎是垂直的。◇ *There was a vertical drop to the ocean.* 至海洋有一段垂直落差。⇨ COMPARE HORIZONTAL *adj.* **2** having a structure in which there are top, middle and bottom levels 纵向的：*a vertical flow of communication* 上下级纵向交流 ▶ **ver·ti·cal·ly** /-kli/ *adv.*

■ *noun* (*usually* **the vertical**) a vertical line or position 垂直线；垂直位置 SYN **perpendicular**：*The wall is several degrees off the vertical.* 这堵墙倾斜了有好几度。

ver·tigin·ous /vɜːˈtɪdʒɪnəs; NAmE vɜːrˈt-/ *adj.* (*formal*) causing a feeling of vertigo 引起眩晕的 SYN **dizzying**：*From the path there was a vertiginous drop to the valley below.* 从小路向谷底望去令人眩晕。

ver·tigo /ˈvɜːtɪɡəʊ; NAmE ˈvɜːrtɪɡoʊ/ *noun* [U] the feeling of DIZZINESS and fear, and of losing your balance, that is caused in some people when they look down from a very high place （从高处俯视时感到的）眩晕，头晕目眩

V

verve /vɜːv; NAmE vɜːrv/ *noun* [U, sing.] energy, excitement or enthusiasm 精力；激情；热情；热忱 SYN **gusto**：*It was a performance of verve and vitality.* 这是一场充满激情与活力的演出。

very /ˈveri/ *adv., adj.*

■ *adv.* (*abbr.* **v**) **1** used before adjectives, adverbs and determiners to mean 'in a high degree' or 'extremely' （置于形容词、副词和限定词前）很，非常，十分，极：*very small* 很小 ◇ *very quickly* 极快 ◇ *Very few people know that.* 很少有人知道那件事。◇ *Thanks very much.* 非常感谢。◇ *'Do you like it?' 'Yeah, I do. **Very much**.'* "你喜欢吗？""是的，我喜欢，非常喜欢。" ◇ *'Is it what you expected?' 'Oh yes, **very much so**.'* "这是你所期望的吗？""啊，是的，非常期望如此。" ◇ *'Are you busy?' 'Not very.'* "你忙吗？""不太忙。" ◇ *The new building has been very much admired.* 这座新建筑物是人见人夸。◇ *I'm **not very*** (= not at all) *impressed.* 我觉得并不怎么样。◇ *I'm very very grateful.* 我万分感激。**2** used to emphasize a superlative adjective or before *own* （强调形容词最高级或置于 own 前）完全，十足：*They wanted the **very best** quality.* 他们要最好的质量。◇ *Be there by six **at the very latest**.* 至迟不要超过六点到达那里。◇ *At last he had his **very own** car* (= belonging to him and to nobody else). 他终于有了完全属于他自己的汽车。**3 the ~ same** exactly the same 完全同样；完全同一：*Mario said the very same thing.* 马里奥说的完全是同一件事。

■ *adj.* [only before noun] **1** used to emphasize that you are talking about a particular thing or person and not about another （特指人或事物）正是的，恰好的，同一的 SYN **actual**：*Those were her very words.* 这些都是她的原话。◇ *He might be phoning her **at this very moment**.* 他也许这会儿正在给她打电话呢。◇ *That's **the very thing** I need.* 那正是我需要的东西。**2** used to emphasize an extreme place or time （强调极限的地点或时间）最…的，极端的，十足的：*It happens at the very beginning of the book.* 这事发生在书的一开头。**3** used to emphasize a noun （加强名词的语气）仅仅的，唯独的，甚至于 SYN **mere**：*The*

▼ **GRAMMAR POINT 语法说明**

very / very much

- **Very** is used with adjectives, past participles used as adjectives, and adverbs. * very 与形容词、作形容词的过去分词或副词连用：*I am very hungry.* 我很饿。◇ *I was very pleased to get your letter.* 收到你的信我非常高兴。◇ *You played very well.* 你演得很好。But notice this use. 但注意：*I'm **very much afraid** that your son may be involved in the crime.* 我非常担忧，你儿子可能与这桩罪案有牵连。
- **Very** is not used with past participles that have a passive meaning. **Much**, **very much** or **greatly** (*formal*) are usually used instead. 含被动意义的过去分词不与 very 连用，而通常用 much、very much 或 greatly（正式用语）：*Your help was very much appreciated.* 非常感谢您的帮助。◇ *He was much loved by everyone.* 他深受大家的爱戴。◇ *She was greatly admired.* 她很受赞赏。
- **Very** is used to emphasize superlative adjectives. * very 用以强调形容词最高级：*my very best work* 我最好的工作 ◇ *the very youngest children* 这些最小的孩子 However, with comparative adjectives **much**, **very much**, **a lot**, etc. are used. 形容词比较级则用 much、very much、a lot 等：*Your work is very much better.* 你的工作要好得多。◇ *much younger children* 小得多的孩子
- **Very** is not used with adjectives and adverbs that already have an extreme meaning. You are more likely to use an adverb such as *absolutely*, *completely*, etc. 含极端意义的形容词和副词不用 very，而常用 absolutely、completely 等副词：*She was absolutely furious.* 她愤怒极了。◇ *I'm completely exhausted.* 我完全筋疲力尽了。◇ *You played really brilliantly.* 你的表现真是棒极了。
- **Very** is not used with verbs. Use **very much** instead. 动词不用 very，而用 very much：*We enjoyed staying with you very much.* 我们非常喜欢待在你这里。

very thought of drink made him feel sick. 他一想到酒就觉得恶心。◇ *'I can't do that!' she gasped, appalled at the very idea.* "那事我可不能干！"她一听到这个想法便惊得倒抽一口冷气。IDM SEE EYE *n.*

ˌvery high ˈfrequency *noun* [U] = VHF

Very light /ˈveri laɪt/ *noun* a bright coloured light that is fired from a gun as a signal from a ship that it needs help（船上发出的）求援信号弹

ves·icle /ˈvesɪkl/ *noun* **1** (*biology* 生) a small bag or hollow structure in the body of a plant or an animal（动植物体内的）泡囊 **2** (*medical* 医) a small swelling filled with liquid under the skin 小疱 SYN **blister**

ves·pers /ˈvespəz; *NAmE* -pərz/ *noun* [U] the service of evening prayer in some Christian Churches（基督教某些教派的）晚课，晚祷 ➲ COMPARE EVENSONG, MATINS

ves·sel /ˈvesl/ *noun* **1** (*formal*) a large ship or boat 大船；轮船：*ocean-going vessels* 远洋轮船 **2** (*old use* or *specialist*) a container used for holding liquids, such as a bowl, cup, etc.（盛液体的）容器，器皿：*a Bronze Age drinking vessel* 青铜器时代的饮具 **3** a tube that carries blood through the body of a person or an animal, or liquid through the parts of a plant（人或动物的）血管，脉管；（植物的）导管 ➲ SEE ALSO BLOOD VESSEL

vest /vest/ *noun, verb*

■ ***noun*** **1** (*BrE*) (*NAmE* **under·shirt**) a piece of underwear worn under a shirt, etc. next to the skin（衬衣等里面贴身穿的）背心，汗衫：*a cotton vest* 棉汗衫 ➲ COMPARE SINGLET **2** a special piece of clothing that covers the upper part of the body 坎肩；（外面穿的）背心：*a bullet-proof vest* 防弹背心 ◇ *a running vest* 赛跑背心 **3** (*NAmE*) (*BrE* **waist·coat**) a short piece of clothing with buttons down the front but no sleeves, usually worn over a shirt and under a jacket, often forming part of a man's suit（西服的）背心 ➲ VISUAL VOCAB PAGE V66

■ ***verb***

PHR V **ˈvest in sb/sth** (*law* 律) (of power, property, etc. 权力、财产等) to belong to sb/sth legally（合法地）属于，归属 **ˈvest sth in sb | ˈvest sb with sth** [often passive] (*formal*) **1** to give sb the legal right or power to do sth 授予，赋予，给予（合法权利或权力）：*Overall authority is vested in the Supreme Council.* 一切权力属于最高议会。◇ *The Supreme Council is vested with overall authority.* 最高议会拥有一切权力。**2** to make sb the legal owner of land or property 使合法拥有（土地或财产）

ˌvested ˈinterest *noun* ~ (**in sth**) a personal reason for wanting sth to happen, especially because you get some advantage from it 既得利益：*They have a vested interest in keeping the club as exclusive as possible.* 他们希望俱乐部尽可能地限制会员加入以从中受益。◇ *Vested interests* (= people with a vested interest) *are opposing the plan.* 既得利益集团在反对这项计划。

ves·ti·bule /ˈvestɪbjuːl/ *noun* **1** (*formal*) an entrance hall of a large building, for example where hats and coats can be left 前厅，门厅（如可放衣帽处）**2** (*specialist*) a space at the end of a coach/car on a train that connects it with the next coach/car 通过台（列车两个车厢间的连接处）

ves·tige /ˈvestɪdʒ/ *noun* (*formal*) **1** a small part of sth that still exists after the rest of it has stopped existing 残留部分；遗迹 SYN **trace**：*the last vestiges of the old colonial regime* 旧殖民制度最后的残余 **2** usually used in negative sentences, to say that not even a small amount of sth exists（通常用于否定句）丝毫，一点儿：*There's not a vestige of truth in the rumour.* 这个谣传毫无真实可言。

ves·tigial /veˈstɪdʒiəl/ *adj.* [usually before noun] (*formal* or *specialist*) remaining as the last small part of sth that used to exist 残留的；残余的；退化的：*vestigial traces of an earlier culture* 早期文化的遗迹 ◇ *It is often possible to see the vestigial remains of rear limbs on some snakes.* 在某些蛇身上常可看到退化后肢的痕迹。

vest·ment /ˈvestmənt/ *noun* [usually pl.] a piece of clothing worn by a priest during church services（司祭在礼拜仪式上穿的）祭衣，祭服

ves·try /ˈvestri/ *noun* (*pl.* **-ies**) a room in a church where a priest prepares for a service by putting on special clothes and where various objects used in worship are kept（教堂的）祭衣室 SYN **sacristy**

vet /vet/ *noun, verb*

■ ***noun*** **1** (*especially BrE*) (*NAmE usually* **vet·er·in·ar·ian**) (*also BrE, formal* **ˈveterinary surgeon**) a person who has been trained in the science of animal medicine, whose job is to treat animals who are sick or injured 兽医 **2 vet's** (*pl.* **vets**) the place where a vet works 兽医诊所：*I've got to take the dog to the vet's tomorrow.* 明天我得把狗带到兽医诊所去诊治。**3** (*NAmE, informal*) = VETERAN (2)：*a Vietnam vet* 参加过越战的老兵

■ ***verb*** (**-tt-**) **1** ~ **sb** to find out about a person's past life and career in order to decide if they are suitable for a particular job 审查（某人过去的生活和职业）SYN **screen**：*All candidates are carefully vetted for security reasons.* 出于安全考虑，所有的求职申请人都要经过严格的审查。➲ SEE ALSO POSITIVE VETTING **2** ~ **sth** to check the contents, quality, etc. of sth carefully 仔细检查，审查（内容、质量等）SYN **screen**：*All reports are vetted before publication.* 所有报道都要经过仔细检查后才能发表。

vetch /vetʃ/ *noun* [U, C] a plant of the PEA family. There are several types of vetch, one of which is used as food for farm animals. 巢菜，野豌豆（有一种可作饲料）

vet·eran /ˈvetərən/ *noun* **1** a person who has a lot of experience in a particular area or activity 经验丰富的人；老手：*the veteran American actor, Clint Eastwood* 美国资深演员克林特•伊斯特伍德 **2** (*also NAmE, informal* **vet**) a person who has been a soldier, sailor, etc. in a war 退伍军人；老兵；老战士；老水兵：*war veterans* 经历过战争的老战士 ◇ *a Vietnam vet* 参加过越战的老兵

ˌveteran ˈcar *noun* (*BrE*) a car made before 1919 老爷车（1919 年以前生产的汽车）➲ COMPARE VINTAGE *adj.* (2)

ˈVeterans Day *noun* a holiday in the US on 11 November, in honour of members of the armed forces and others who have died in war 退伍军人节（美国纪念阵亡将士的日子，定于 11 月 11 日）➲ SEE ALSO MEMORIAL DAY, REMEMBRANCE SUNDAY

vet·er·in·ar·ian /ˌvetərɪˈneəriən; *NAmE* -ˈner-/ *noun* (*NAmE*) = VET (1)

vet·er·in·ary /ˈvetnri; ˈvetrənəri; *NAmE* ˈvetərəneri/ *adj.* [only before noun] connected with caring for the health of animals 兽医的：***veterinary medicine/science*** 兽医学

ˈveterinary surgeon *noun* (*BrE, formal*) = VET (1)

veto /ˈviːtəʊ; *NAmE* -toʊ/ *noun, verb*

■ ***noun*** (*pl.* **-oes**) **1** [C, U] the right to refuse to allow sth to be done, especially the right to stop a law from being passed or a decision from being taken 否决权：*The British government used its veto to block the proposal.* 英国政府行使其否决权阻止了这项提案。◇ *to have the* ***power/right of veto*** 有否决权 ◇ *the use of the presidential veto* 总统否决权的行使 **2** [C] ~ (**on sth/on doing sth**) an occasion when sb refuses to allow sth to be done 拒绝认可；禁止 SYN **ban**：*For months there was a veto on employing new staff.* 有好几个月禁止雇用新职员。

■ ***verb*** (**ve·toes**, **veto·ing**, **ve·toed**, **ve·toed**) **1** ~ **sth** to stop sth from happening or being done by using your official authority (= by using your veto) 行使否决权；拒绝认可；禁止：*Plans for the dam have been vetoed by the Environmental Protection Agency.* 修建大坝的计划已被环境保护局否决。➲ COLLOCATIONS AT POLITICS **2** ~ **sth** to refuse to accept or do what sb has suggested 拒不接受；反对；否定 SYN **rule sb/sth↔out**：*I wanted to go camping but the others quickly vetoed that idea.* 我想去野营，但这个想法很快遭到了其他人的反对。

vex /veks/ *verb* ~ **sb** (*old-fashioned* or *formal*) to annoy or worry sb 使恼火；使烦恼；使忧虑 ▶ **vex·ing** *adj.*：*a vexing problem* 令人烦恼的问题

V

vex·ation /vek'seɪʃn/ *noun* (*old-fashioned* or *formal*) **1** [U] the state of feeling upset or annoyed 烦恼；恼火；伤脑筋；心烦意乱 **2** [C] a thing that upsets or annoys you 令人心烦（或恼火）的事

vex·atious /vek'seɪʃəs/ *adj.* (*old-fashioned* or *formal*) making you feel upset or annoyed 使人烦恼的；令人恼火的

vexed /vekst/ *adj.* **1** ~ **question/issue** a problem that is difficult to deal with （问题等）棘手的，伤脑筋的 SYN **thorny**: *The conference spent days discussing the vexed question of border controls.* 会议花了几天的时间讨论边境管制这个难题。 **2** ~ (**at/with sb/sth**) (*old-fashioned*) upset or annoyed （人）恼火，烦恼，伤脑筋

VHF /ˌviː eɪtʃ 'ef/ *abbr.* very high frequency (a range of radio waves used for high-quality broadcasting) 甚高频，特高频 （用于高质量广播的无线电波段）

via 🔑 AW /'vaɪə; 'viːə/ *prep.* **1** 🔑 through a place 经由，经过（某一地方）: *We flew home via Dubai.* 我们乘飞机经迪拜回国。 **2** by means of a particular person, system, etc. 通过，凭借（某人、系统等）: *I heard about the sale via Jane.* 我从简那里听说了这次大减价。 ◇ *The news programme came to us via satellite.* 新闻节目是通过卫星传送到我们这里来的。

vi·able /'vaɪəbl/ *adj.* **1** that can be done; that will be successful 可实施的；切实可行的 SYN **feasible**: *a* ***viable option/proposition*** 切实可行的选择 / 提议 ◇ *There is no* ***viable alternative.*** 没有其他可行的措施。 ◇ *to be* ***commercially/politically/financially/economically viable*** 在商业上 / 政治上 / 财政上 / 经济上可行 **2** (*biology* 生) capable of developing and surviving independently 可生存的；能独立发展的；能独立生存的；可生长发育的: *viable organisms* 可存活的生物 ▶ **via·bil·ity** /ˌvaɪə'bɪləti/ *noun* [U]: *commercial viability* 商业上的可行性

via·duct /'vaɪədʌkt/ *noun* a long high bridge, usually with ARCHES, that carries a road or railway/railroad across a river or valley 高架桥（通常有拱，横跨河道或山谷连通公路或铁路） ➲ VISUAL VOCAB PAGE V14

Viagra™ /vaɪ'æɡrə/ *noun* [U] a drug used to treat IMPOTENCE in men 万艾可，威而刚，"伟哥"（一种治疗阳痿的药物）

vial /'vaɪəl/ *noun* (*especially NAmE*) = PHIAL

vibes /vaɪbz/ *noun* [pl.] **1** (*also formal* **vi·bra·tions**) (*also* **vibe** [sing.]) (*informal*) a mood or an atmosphere produced by a particular person, thing or place 情绪；气氛；氛围: ***good/bad vibes*** 好 / 坏情绪 ◇ *The vibes weren't right.* 这气氛不对头。 **2** = VIBRAPHONE : *a jazzy vibes backing* 爵士乐的颤音琴伴奏

V

vi·brant /'vaɪbrənt/ *adj.* **1** full of life and energy 充满生机的；生气勃勃的；精力充沛的 SYN **exciting**: *a vibrant city* 充满生机的城市 ◇ *Thailand is at its most vibrant during the New Year celebrations.* 在欢度新年期间，泰国举国欢腾。 **2** (of colours 颜色) very bright and strong 鲜艳的；醒目的 SYN **brilliant**: *The room was decorated in vibrant reds and yellows.* 那房间是由鲜艳的红黄两色装饰的。 ➲ SYNONYMS AT BRIGHT **3** (of music, sounds, etc. 音乐、声音等) loud and powerful 响亮的；洪亮的；强劲的: *vibrant rhythms* 强有力的节奏 ▶ **vi·brancy** /-brənsi/ *noun* [U] **vi·brant·ly** *adv.*

vi·bra·phone /'vaɪbrəfəʊn; *NAmE* -foʊn/ *noun* [C] (*also informal* **vibes** [pl.]) a musical instrument used especially in JAZZ, that has two rows of metal bars that you hit, and a motor that makes them vibrate 颤音琴（常用于爵士乐）

vi·brate /vaɪ'breɪt; *NAmE usually* 'vaɪbreɪt/ *verb* [I, T] to move or make sth move from side to side very quickly and with small movements （使）振动，颤动，摆动: ~ (**sth**) *Every time a train went past the walls vibrated.* 每当火车驶过，这些墙都会震动。 ◇ ~ **with sth** *The atmosphere seemed to vibrate with tension.* 气氛似乎紧张得发颤。

vi·bra·tion /vaɪ'breɪʃn/ *noun* **1** [C, U] a continuous shaking movement or feeling 震动；颤动；抖动；（感情的）共鸣: *We could feel the vibrations from the trucks passing outside.* 我们可以感到外面卡车经过时的颤动。 ◇ *a reduction in the level of vibration in the engine* 发动机震动程度的下降 **2 vibrations** [pl.] (*formal*) = VIBES (1)

vi·brato /vɪ'brɑːtəʊ; *NAmE* -toʊ/ *noun* [U, C] (*pl.* **-os**) (*music* 音, *from Italian*) a shaking effect in singing or playing a musical instrument, made by rapid slight changes in PITCH (= how high or low a sound is) （演唱或演奏的）颤音效果，颤音

vi·bra·tor /vaɪ'breɪtə(r)/ *noun* an electrical device that produces a continuous shaking movement, used in MASSAGE or for sexual pleasure （用于按摩或产生性快感的）颤动按摩器，震动器

vicar /'vɪkə(r)/ *noun* **1** (*especially BrE*) an Anglican priest who is in charge of a church and the area around it (called a PARISH) （圣公会的）代牧，教区牧师 **2** (*NAmE*) a priest in the US Episcopal Church （美国圣公会的）牧师 ➲ COMPARE CURATE[1], MINISTER *n.* (2), PRIEST (1), RECTOR (1)

vic·ar·age /'vɪkərɪdʒ/ *noun* a vicar's house 代牧住宅

vic·ari·ous /vɪ'keəriəs; *NAmE* vaɪ'ker-/ *adj.* [only before noun] felt or experienced by watching or reading about sb else doing sth, rather than by doing it yourself 间接感受到的: *He got a vicarious thrill out of watching his son score the winning goal.* 他看着儿子射入获胜的一球，也同样感到欣喜若狂。 ▶ **vic·ari·ous·ly** *adv.*

vice /vaɪs/ *noun* **1** [U] criminal activities that involve sex or drugs （与性或毒品有关的）罪行: *plain-clothes detectives from the vice squad* 取缔性或毒品犯罪行动队的便衣侦探 **2** [U, C] evil or immoral behaviour; an evil or immoral quality in sb's character 恶行；不道德行为；堕落；邪恶: *The film ended most satisfactorily: vice punished and virtue rewarded.* 这部电影有个令人满意的结局：邪恶受到惩治，美德得到报偿。 ◇ *Greed is a terrible vice.* 贪婪是一种恶习。 ◇ (*humorous*) *Cigarettes are my only vice.* 我唯一的罪过就是爱抽烟。 **3** (*especially BrE*) (*NAmE usually* **vise**) [C] a tool with two metal blocks that can be moved together by turning a screw. The vice is used to hold an object firmly while work is done on it. 台钳；虎钳: *He held my arm in a* ***vice-like*** (= very firm) ***grip.*** 他的手像虎钳一样紧紧抓住了我的手臂。 ➲ VISUAL VOCAB PAGE V21

vice- /vaɪs/ *combining form* (in nouns and related adjectives 构成名词和相关的形容词) next in rank to sb and able to represent them or act for them 副；代理: *vice-captain* 副舰长

ˌvice 'admiral *noun* an officer of very high rank in the navy 海军中将

ˌvice 'chancellor *noun* the head of a university in Britain, who is in charge of the work of running the university. (Compare the CHANCELLOR, who is the official head of a university but only has duties at various ceremonies.) （英国大学）校长

ˌvice-'president *noun* (*abbr.* **VP**) **1** the person below the president of a country in rank, who takes control of the country if the president is not able to 副总统；国家副主席 **2** (*NAmE*) a person in charge of a particular part of a business company （商业公司的）副总裁，副总经理: *the vice-president of sales* 负责销售的副总裁 ▶ **ˌvice-presi'dential** *adj.* [usually before noun]

vice·roy /'vaɪsrɔɪ/ *noun* (often used as a title 常用作头衔) (in the past) a person who was sent by a king or queen to govern a COLONY （旧时受君主委派管治殖民地的）总督

vice versa /ˌvaɪs 'vɜːsə; ˌvaɪsi; *NAmE* 'vɜːrsə/ *adv.* used to say that the opposite of what you have just said is also true 反过来也一样；反之亦然: *You can cruise from Cairo to Aswan or vice versa* (= also from Aswan to Cairo). 你可以乘船从开罗游览到阿斯旺，也可以从阿斯旺游览到开罗。

vi·cin·ity /və'sɪnəti/ **the vicinity** *noun* [sing.] the area around a particular place 周围地区；邻近地区；附近：*Crowds gathered* ***in the vicinity of*** *Trafalgar Square.* 成群结队的人聚集在特拉法尔加广场周围。◇ *There is no hospital* ***in the immediate vicinity.*** 附近没有医院。

vi·cious /'vɪʃəs/ *adj.* **1** violent and cruel 狂暴的；残酷的 SYN **brutal**：*a vicious attack* 猛烈的攻击 ◇ *a vicious criminal* 凶残的罪犯 ◇ *She has a vicious temper.* 她性情暴虐。**2** (of animals 动物) aggressive and dangerous 凶猛危险的：*a vicious dog* 恶犬 **3** (of an attack, criticism, etc. 攻击、批评等) full of hatred and anger 充满仇恨的；严厉的：*She wrote me a vicious letter.* 她给我写了一封严厉的信。**4** (*informal*) very bad or severe 恶劣的；严重的：*a vicious headache* 剧烈的头痛 ◇ *a vicious spiral of rising prices* 物价的恶性持续上涨 ▶ **vi·cious·ly** *adv.* **vi·cious·ness** *noun* [U]：*Police were shocked by the viciousness of the assault.* 警方对这一攻击的残忍感到震惊。

ˌvicious 'circle *noun* [sing.] a situation in which one problem causes another problem which then makes the first problem worse 恶性循环 ⊃ COMPARE VIRTUOUS CIRCLE

vi·cis·si·tude /vɪ'sɪsɪtjuːd; *NAmE* -tuːd/ *noun* [usually pl.] (*formal*) one of the many changes and problems in a situation or in your life, that you have to deal with 变迁；人生的沉浮；兴衰枯荣

vic·tim 🔑 /'vɪktɪm/ *noun* **1** 🔑 a person who has been attacked, injured or killed as the result of a crime, a disease, an accident, etc. 受害者；罹难者；罹病者；牺牲品：***murder/rape, etc. victims*** 谋杀案、强奸案等受害者 ◇ ***accident/earthquake/famine, etc. victims*** 事故、地震、饥荒等的罹难者 ◇ ***AIDS/cancer/stroke, etc. victims*** 艾滋病、癌症、中风等患者 ◇ *victims of crime* 犯罪的受害者 ◇ *She was the* ***innocent victim*** *of an arson attack.* 她是一起纵火案的无辜受害者。◇ *Schools are the latest victims of cuts in public spending.* 学校是削减公共开支的最新的牺牲品。⊃ WORDFINDER NOTE AT ACCIDENT **2** 🔑 a person who has been tricked 受骗者；上当的人 SYN **target**：*They were the victims of a cruel hoax.* 他们成了一大骗局的上当受骗者。⊃ SEE ALSO FASHION VICTIM **3** an animal or a person that is killed and offered as a SACRIFICE 为祭祀杀死的动物（或人）；祭品；牺牲：*a sacrificial victim* 祭品

IDM **fall 'victim (to sth)** (*formal*) to be injured, damaged or killed by sth 受伤；受损；被害

vic·tim·ize (*BrE also* **-ise**) /'vɪktɪmaɪz/ *verb* [often passive] **~ sb** to make sb suffer unfairly because you do not like them, their opinions, or sth that they have done （不正当地）使受害，使受苦：*For years the family had been victimized by racist neighbours.* 多年来这家人因邻居怀有种族偏见而饱受欺凌。◇ *The union claimed that some of its members had been victimized for taking part in the strike.* 工会声称有些会员因参加罢工而受到迫害。▶ **vic·tim·iza·tion, -isa·tion** /ˌvɪktɪmaɪ'zeɪʃn; *NAmE* -mə'z-/ *noun* [U]

vic·tim·less /'vɪktɪmləs/ *adj.* a **victimless** crime is one in which nobody seems to suffer or be harmed （犯罪行为）无受害人的，不侵害他人的

ˌvictim sup'port *noun* [U] a service provided by the police that helps people who are victims of crime 受害人援助（警方提供）

vic·tor /'vɪktə(r)/ *noun* (*literary*) the winner of a battle, competition, game, etc. 胜利者；获胜者

Vic·toria Cross /vɪkˌtɔːriə 'krɒs; *NAmE* 'krɔːs/ *noun* (*abbr.* **VC**) a MEDAL for special courage that is given to members of the British and Commonwealth armed forces 维多利亚十字勋章（授予英勇的英国及英联邦军人）

Vic·tor·ian /vɪk'tɔːriən/ *adj.*, *noun*

■ ***adj.*** **1** connected with the period from 1837 to 1901 when Queen Victoria ruled Britain （英国）维多利亚女王时代（1837–1901 年）的：*Victorian architecture* 维多利亚女王时代的建筑 ◇ *the Victorian age* 维多利亚时代 **2** having the attitudes that were typical of society during Queen Victoria's REIGN 持维多利亚时代观点的：*Victorian attitudes to sex* (= being easily shocked by sexual matters) 维多利亚时代的性爱观 ◇ *She advocated a return to Victorian values* (= hard work, pride in your country, etc.). 她提倡恢复维多利亚时代的价值观念。

■ ***noun*** a British person who was alive during the period from 1837 to 1901, when Queen Victoria ruled 维多利亚时代的英国人

Vicˌtoria 'sponge *noun* [C, U] a type of SPONGE CAKE that is made with fat in the mixture 维多利亚海绵蛋糕

vic·tori·ous /vɪk'tɔːriəs/ *adj.* having won a victory; that ends in victory 胜利的；获胜的；战胜的 SYN **successful, triumphant**：*the victorious army/team* 胜利之师；获胜的队 ◇ **~ in sth** *He* ***emerged victorious*** *in the elections.* 他在竞选中脱颖而出获得胜利。▶ **vic·tori·ous·ly** *adv.*

vic·tory 🔑 /'vɪktəri/ *noun* (*pl.* **-ies**) [C, U] **~ (over/against sb/sth)** success in a game, an election, a war, etc. 胜利；成功：*the team's 3–2 victory against Poland* 该队以 3:2 战胜波兰队 ◇ *to* ***win a victory*** 获得胜利 ◇ *a* ***decisive/narrow victory*** 决定性的胜利；险胜 ◇ *an election victory* 选举胜利 ◇ *She is confident of victory in Saturday's final.* 她对在星期六决赛中取得胜利充满信心。◇ ***victory celebrations/parades*** 胜利的庆祝活动 / 游行 ⊃ SEE ALSO MORAL VICTORY

IDM **roar, romp, sweep, etc. to victory** to win sth easily 轻易取胜；大获全胜：*He swept to victory in the final of the championship.* 他在锦标赛的决赛中轻而易举地获胜。

vict·ual·ler /'vɪtlə(r)/ (*also* **ˌlicensed 'victualler**) *noun* (*BrE*, *law* 律) a person who is legally allowed to sell alcoholic drinks 持证售酒者

vict·uals /'vɪtlz/ *noun* [pl.] (*old-fashioned*) food and drink 饮食；食物及饮料

vi·cuña /vɪ'kuːnjə/ *noun* a wild animal with a long neck and very soft wool, which lives in S America. Vicuñas are related to LLAMAS. 骆马（产于南美的骆驼科动物）

vide /'viːdeɪ/ *verb* (*abbr.* **v**) **~ sth** used (meaning 'see') as an instruction in books to tell the reader to look at a particular book, passage, etc. for more information （指示语，用于书等中）参见，参阅，另见

video 🔑 /'vɪdiəʊ; *NAmE* -oʊ/ *noun*, *verb*

■ ***noun*** (*pl.* **-os**) **1** 🔑 [U] a system of recording moving pictures and sound, either using VIDEOTAPE or a digital method of storing data 录像系统：*A wedding is the perfect subject for video.* 婚礼是极好的录像主题。◇ *the use of video in schools* 学校对电影电视录像的使用 **2** (*also* **'video clip**) [C] a short film or recording of an event, made using digital technology and viewed on a computer, especially over the Internet 视频；视频剪辑：*The school made a short* ***promotional video.*** 学校录制了一条宣传短片。◇ *Upload your videos and share them with friends and family online.* 上传你的视频，与朋友和家人在线分享。**3** [C] (*also* **'music video**) a short film made by a pop or rock band to be shown with a song when it is played on television or online 音乐短片 **4** 🔑 (*also* **video·tape**) [U, C] a type of MAGNETIC tape used for recording moving pictures and sound; a box containing this tape, also called a **video cassette** 录像带；盒式录像带 **5** 🔑 [C] a copy of a film/movie, programme, etc. that is recorded on VIDEOTAPE （指制品）录像，录影：*a* ***home video*** (= not a professional one) 家庭录像 ⊃ COLLOCATIONS AT CINEMA **6** [C] (*BrE*) = VIDEO CASSETTE RECORDER

■ ***verb*** (*also formal* **video·tape**) **~ sth/sb** (*especially BrE*) to record a television programme using a VIDEO CASSETTE RECORDER; to film sb/sth using a video camera 录电视节目；给…录像：*Videoing students can be a useful teaching exercise.* 给学生录像可以成为有用的教学活动。

'video camera *noun* a special camera for making video films 摄像机 ⊃ SEE ALSO CAMCORDER

'video card (*also* **'graphics adapter**) *noun* (*computing* 计) a device that allows images to be shown on a computer screen 视频卡

V

ˌ**video caˈssette recorder** *noun* (*abbr.* **VCR**) (*also* **video**, ˌ**video caˈssette player**, ˈ**video recorder**) a piece of equipment used to record and play films/movies and TV programmes on video 盒式录像机

video·con·fer·en·cing /ˈvɪdiəʊkɒnfərənsɪŋ; *NAmE* ˈvɪdioʊkɑːn-/ *noun* [U] a system that enables people in different parts of the world to have a meeting by watching and listening to each other using video screens 电视会议；视频会议；视像会议

ˈ**video diary** *noun* a series of video recordings made by sb over a period of time, in which they record their experiences, thoughts and feelings 录影日记；影音日记

video·disc /ˈvɪdiəʊdɪsk; *NAmE* -oʊ-/ *noun* [U, C] a plastic disc that you can record films/movies and programmes on, for showing on a television screen 视盘；影碟 ➲ SEE ALSO DVD

ˈ**video game** *noun* a game in which you press buttons to control and move images on a screen 电子游戏

ˈ**video jockey** (*also* **VJ**, **vee·jay**) *noun* a person who introduces music videos on television 电视音乐节目主持人

video·phone /ˈvɪdiəʊfəʊn; *NAmE* -oʊfoʊn/ *noun* a type of telephone with a screen that enables you to see the person you are talking to 可视电话；电视电话

video·tape /ˈvɪdiəʊteɪp; *NAmE* -oʊ-/ *noun, verb*

■ ***noun*** [U, C] = VIDEO (4)

■ ***verb*** **~ sth** (*formal*) = VIDEO：*a videotaped interview* 录像访谈

video·tex /ˈvɪdiəʊteks; *NAmE* -oʊ-/ *noun* [U] (*US*) = VIEWDATA

vi·deshi /vɪˈdeʃi/ *adj., noun* (*IndE*)

■ ***adj.*** not Indian or not made in India 非印度的；非印度制造的：*Videshi fruit is much more expensive than locally produced fruit.* 非印度原产水果比印度本地产的贵得多。➲ COMPARE DESI *adj.* (1)

■ ***noun*** a person who does not come from India 非印度人

vie /vaɪ/ *verb* (**vying** /ˈvaɪɪŋ/, **vied**, **vied**) [I] (*formal*) to compete strongly with sb in order to obtain or achieve sth 激烈竞争；争夺 **SYN** **compete**：**~ (with sb) (for sth)** *She was surrounded by men all vying for her attention.* 她周围尽是争相博取她青睐的男子。◇ *a row of restaurants vying with each other for business* 彼此争抢生意的一排饭馆 ◇ **~ (to do sth)** *Screaming fans vied to get closer to their idol.* 尖声喊叫的崇拜者争先恐后地涌向他们的偶像。

V

view 🔑 /vjuː/ *noun, verb*

■ ***noun***

• **OPINION** 想法 **1** 🔑 [C] a personal opinion about sth; an attitude towards sth （个人的）看法，意见，见解；态度：*to have **different/conflicting/opposing views*** 有不同的 / 矛盾的 / 相反的观点 ◇ *to have **strong political views*** 持强硬的政治观点 ◇ **~ (about/on sth)** *His views on the subject were well known.* 他对这个问题的看法众所周知。◇ *This evidence **supports the view** that there is too much violence on television.* 这一证据证实了人们认为电视节目中有太多暴力的看法。◇ *We **take the view** that it would be wrong to interfere.* 我们所持的态度是：干涉是错误的。◇ ***In my view** it was a waste of time.* 依我看，这是浪费时间。◇ *What is needed is a frank **exchange of views**.* 需要的是坦诚地交换意见。➲ SEE ALSO POINT OF VIEW ➲ LANGUAGE BANK AT ACCORDING TO, OPINION

• **WAY OF UNDERSTANDING** 理解方式 **2** 🔑 [sing.] **~ (of sth)** a way of understanding or thinking about sth （理解或思维的）方法，方式：*He has an optimistic view of life.* 他乐观地看待人生。◇ *the Christian view of the world* 基督教的世界观 ◇ *The traditional view was that marriage was meant to last.* 传统的观念是结成夫妻就要白头到老。➲ SEE ALSO WORLD VIEW

• **WHAT YOU CAN SEE** 可看到的东西 **3** 🔑 [U, sing.] used when you are talking about whether you can see sth or whether sth can be seen in a particular situation 观看；看；视野；视域；视线：*The lake soon **came into view**.* 那湖很快映入眼帘。◇ *The sun disappeared **from view**.* 太阳看不见了。◇ *There was nobody **in view**.* 一个人也看不见。◇ *Sit down—you're blocking my view.* 坐下，你挡住我的视线了。◇ *I didn't have a good view of the stage.* 我看不清舞台。➲ SYNONYMS AT SIGHT **4** 🔑 [C] what you can see from a particular place or position, especially beautiful countryside （从某处看到的）景色，风景；（尤指）乡间美景：*There were magnificent views of the surrounding countryside.* 四周乡间的景色壮观秀丽。◇ *The view from the top of the tower was spectacular.* 从塔顶远眺景色蔚为壮观。◇ *a **sea/mountain view*** 海景；山景 ◇ *I'd like a room with a view.* 我想要一个可以观看风景的房间。

• **PHOTOGRAPH/PICTURE** 照片；图画 **5** [C] a photograph or picture that shows an interesting place or scene 风景照；风景画：*a book with views of Paris* 一本巴黎风光画册

• **CHANCE TO SEE STH** 观看的机会 **6** (*also* **view·ing**) [C] a special chance to see or admire sth （一次）观看；一睹；一览：*a **private view*** (= for example, of an art exhibition) 画展预展

IDM **have, etc. sth in ˈview** (*formal*) to have a particular aim, plan, etc. in your mind 心中有…目的（或打算等） **SYN** **have sb/sth in mind** **in full ˈview (of sb/sth)** completely visible, directly in front of sb/sth 完全看得见；在眼皮底下：*He was shot in full view of a large crowd.* 他在众目睽睽之下被人枪杀了。 **in view of sth** (*formal*) considering sth 鉴于；考虑到；由于：*In view of the weather, the event will now be held indoors.* 由于天气的缘故，这项赛事将在室内进行。 **on ˈview** being shown in a public place so that people can look at it 在展出；陈列着；展览着 **with a view to sth/to doing sth** (*formal*) with the intention or hope of doing sth 为了；指望：*He's painting the house with a view to selling it.* 他在粉刷房子，想把它卖掉。➲ MORE AT BIRD *n.*, DIM *adj.*, HEAVE *v.*, LONG *adj.*

■ ***verb***

• **THINK ABOUT STH** 思考 **1** 🔑 to think about sb/sth in a particular way 把…视为；以…看待：**~ (sb/sth as sth)** *When the car was first built, the design was viewed as highly original.* 这种车刚造出时，其设计被认为是独具匠心。◇ *How do you view your position within the company?* 你如何看待自己在公司中的位置？◇ **~ sb/sth with sth** *She viewed him with suspicion.* 她对他心存怀疑。➲ SYNONYMS AT REGARD

▼ **SYNONYMS** 同义词辨析

view

sight • **scene** • **panorama**

These are all words for a thing that you can see, especially from a particular place. 以上各词均指景色，尤指从某处看到的风景。

view what you can see from a particular place or position, especially beautiful natural scenery 指从某处看到的景色、风景，尤指自然美景：*The cottage had a delightful sea view.* 这小屋可以看到宜人的海景。

sight a thing that you see or can see, especially sth that is impressive or unusual 指看见或看得见的事物、景象，尤指壮观、奇特的景象：*It's a spectacular sight as the flamingos lift into the air.* 一群红鹳飞向空中，景象十分壮观。

scene a view that you see, especially one with people and/or animals moving about and doing things 指景象、景色，尤指有人和 / 或动物活动的风光：*It was a delightful rural scene.* 那是赏心悦目的乡村风光。

panorama a view of a wide area of land 指全景：*The tower offers a breathtaking panorama of Prague.* 从塔上可看到壮丽的布拉格全景。

PATTERNS

- a view/panorama **of** sth
- a **beautiful**/**breathtaking** view/sight/scene/panorama
- a **magnificent**/**spectacular** view/sight/panorama
- to **take in** the view/sight/scene
- to **admire** the view/sight

- **LOOK AT STH** 看 **2** 🔑 **~ sth** (*formal*) to look at sth, especially when you look carefully 看；观看；（尤指）仔细察看：*People came from all over the world to view her work.* 人们从世界各地涌来欣赏她的作品。◇ *A viewing platform gave stunning views over the valley.* 从观景台向山谷望去，景色之壮观令人叹为观止。➲ SYNONYMS AT LOOK **3** **~ sth** (*formal*) to visit a house, etc. with the intention of buying or renting it 查看，察看（房子等，以便购买或租用）：*The property can only be viewed by appointment.* 察看这处房产须预约。
- **WATCH TV, FILM/MOVIE** 看电视 / 电影 **4** **~ sth** (*formal*) to watch television, a film/movie, etc. 看，观看（电视、电影等）：*The show has a viewing audience of six million* (= six million people watch it). 这个节目有六百万观众观看。◇ *an opportunity to view the movie before it goes on general release* 在公开放映之前观看这部影片的机会 ➲ SYNONYMS AT LOOK

view·data /ˈvjuːdeɪtə; *NAmE also* -dætə/ (*US also* **video·tex**) *noun* [U] an information system in which computer data is sent along telephone lines and shown on a television screen 视传，视传系统，视频数据传送系统（通过电话线路传输计算机数据并在电视屏上显示）

view·er /ˈvjuːə(r)/ *noun* **1** a person watching television 电视观众：*The programme attracted millions of viewers.* 这个节目吸引了数百万电视观众。➲ COLLOCATIONS AT TELEVISION **2** a person who looks at or considers sth 观看者；观察者：*Some of her art is intended to shock the viewer.* 她的某些艺术作品旨在震撼观赏者。◇ *viewers of the current political scene* 当前政治局面的观察家 **3** a device for looking at SLIDES (= photographs on special film), for example a small box with a light in it （幻灯片）观看器；幻灯机

viewer·ship /ˈvjuːəʃɪp; *NAmE* ˈvjuːər-/ *noun* [usually sing.] the number or type of people who watch a particular television programme or television channel （电视节目或频道的）观众人数，观众类型

view·find·er /ˈvjuːfaɪndə(r)/ *noun* the part of a camera that you look through to see the area that you are photographing （照相机的）取景器

view·point /ˈvjuːpɔɪnt/ *noun* **1** **~ (on sth)** a way of thinking about a subject 观点；看法 **SYN** **point of view**: *Try looking at things from a different viewpoint.* 试试从不同的角度观察事物。◇ *She will have her own viewpoint on the matter.* 她对这个问题会有她自己的看法。◇ *From a practical viewpoint, I'd advise you not to go.* 从实际角度考虑，我劝你不要去。**2** a direction or place from which you look at sth 角度 **SYN** **angle**: *The artist has painted the scene from various viewpoints.* 那位画家从各种角度把这一景色画了下来。➲ SEE ALSO POINT OF VIEW

view·port /ˈvjuːpɔːt; *NAmE* -pɔːrt/ *noun* **1** (*computing* 计) an area inside a frame on a screen, for viewing information （电脑屏幕的）视点，视埠，视口 **2** a window in a SPACECRAFT （宇宙飞船的）观察窗，观察孔

vigil /ˈvɪdʒɪl/ *noun* [C, U] a period of time when people stay awake, especially at night, in order to watch a sick person, say prayers, protest, etc. （看护病人、祷告、抗议等的）不眠时间；（尤指）值夜，守夜祈祷：*His parents **kept a** round-the-clock **vigil** at his bedside.* 他父母日夜守护在他的床边。

vigi·lant /ˈvɪdʒɪlənt/ *adj.* (*formal*) very careful to notice any signs of danger or trouble 警觉的；警惕的；警戒的；谨慎 **SYN** **alert, watchful**: *A pilot must remain vigilant at all times.* 飞行员必须随时保持警惕。▸ **vigi·lance** /-əns/ *noun* [U] **SYN** **watchfulness**: *She stressed the need for constant vigilance.* 她强调必须时常保持警惕。 **vigi·lant·ly** *adv.*

vigi·lante /ˌvɪdʒɪˈlænti/ *noun* (*sometimes disapproving*) a member of a group of people who try to prevent crime or punish criminals in their community, especially because they think the police are not doing this （尤指认为警方不力而自发组织的）治安会会员 ▸ **vigi·lant·ism** /ˌvɪdʒɪˈlæntɪzəm/ *noun* [U]

vi·gnette /vɪnˈjet/ *noun* (*formal*) **1** a short piece of writing or acting that clearly shows what a particular person, situation, etc. is like （清晰展示人物特征、局势等的）短文，简介，花絮；（表演）片段，小品 **2** a small picture or drawing, especially on the first page of a book （尤指书名页上的）小花饰，小插图

vig·or·ous /ˈvɪɡərəs/ *adj.* **1** very active, determined or full of energy 充满活力的；果断的；精力充沛的 **SYN** **energetic**: *a vigorous campaign against tax fraud* 坚决打击骗税的运动 ◇ *a vigorous opponent of the government* 坚决反对政府的人 ◇ *Take **vigorous exercise** for several hours a week.* 每周做几个小时剧烈运动。**2** strong and healthy 强壮的；强健的：*a vigorous young man* 身强力壮的年轻人 ◇ *This plant is a vigorous grower.* 这种植物生长起来茂盛苗壮。▸ **vig·or·ous·ly** *adv.*

vig·our (*especially US* **vigor**) /ˈvɪɡə(r)/ *noun* [U] energy, force or enthusiasm 精力；力量；活力；热情 **SYN** **vitality**: *He worked with renewed vigour and determination.* 他将重燃起来的活力和热情投入到工作中。

Vi·king /ˈvaɪkɪŋ/ *noun* a member of a race of Scandinavian people who attacked and sometimes settled in parts of NW Europe, including Britain, in the 8th to the 11th centuries 维京人，北欧海盗（斯堪的纳维亚部落成员，8–11 世纪时劫掠英国等西北欧部分地区，有时在当地定居）

vile /vaɪl/ *adj.* (**viler, vil·est**) **1** (*informal*) extremely unpleasant or bad 糟糕透顶的；可恶的；极坏的 **SYN** **disgusting**: *a vile smell* 令人恶心的气味 ◇ *The weather was really vile most of the time.* 天气大部分时间都糟糕得很。◇ *He was in a vile mood.* 他的心情坏极了。➲ SYNONYMS AT TERRIBLE **2** (*formal*) morally bad; completely unacceptable 邪恶的；令人完全不能接受的 **SYN** **wicked**: *the vile practice of taking hostages* 扣押人质的卑劣行径 ▸ **vile·ly** /ˈvaɪlli/ *adv.* **vile·ness** *noun* [U]

vil·ify /ˈvɪlɪfaɪ/ *verb* (**vili·fies, vili·fy·ing, vili·fied, vili·fied**) **~ sb/sth (as sth)** | **~ sb/sth (for sth/for doing sth)** (*formal*) to say or write unpleasant things about sb/sth so that other people will have a low opinion of them 污蔑；诽谤；诋毁；中伤 **SYN** **malign, revile** ▸ **vili·fi·ca·tion** /ˌvɪlɪfɪˈkeɪʃn/ *noun* [U]: *the vilification of single parents by right-wing politicians* 右翼政客对单亲父母的诋毁

villa /ˈvɪlə/ *noun* **1** (*BrE*) a house where people stay on holiday/vacation 度假别墅：*We rented a holiday villa in Spain.* 我们在西班牙租了一座假日别墅。**2** a house in the country with a large garden, especially in southern Europe （尤指南欧的）乡间庄园 **3** (*BrE*) a large house in a town （城内的）豪宅：*a Victorian villa in North London* 伦敦北部的维多利亚式豪宅 **4** (in Roman times 古罗马时代) a country house or farm with land attached to it （附有土地的）乡间宅第，别墅，庄园

vil·lage 🔑 /ˈvɪlɪdʒ/ *noun* **1** 🔑 [C] a very small town located in a country area 村庄；村镇：*We visited towns and villages all over Spain.* 我们走遍了西班牙的城镇和村庄。◇ *a **fishing/mountain/seaside village*** 渔村；山村；滨海村 ◇ (*especially BrE*) *the village shop* 乡村商店 ◇ *Her books are about village life.* 她的书是关于乡村生活的。➲ VISUAL VOCAB PAGE V3 **HELP** Do not use **village** to talk about small towns in the US. In *NAmE* **village** is used for a small place in another country that seems more old-fashioned than a town in the US. 在美国说小村镇不用 village。在美式英语中，village 用于指其他国家看似比美国小村镇古老的小地方。**2** 🔑 **the village** [sing.] (*especially BrE*) the people who live in a village 乡村居民；村民：*The whole village was invited to the party.* 全村的人都获邀参加聚会。

ˌvillage ˈidiot *noun* a person in a village who is thought to be stupid; a stupid person 愚笨的村人；蠢人

vil·la·ger /ˈvɪlɪdʒə(r)/ *noun* a person who lives in a village 村民；乡村居民；乡下人

vil·lain /ˈvɪlən/ *noun* **1** the main bad character in a story, play, etc. （小说、戏剧等中的）主要反面人物，反派主角，坏人：*He often plays the part of the villain.* 他经常扮演反面人物。➲ WORDFINDER NOTE AT CHARACTER **2** a person

V

who is morally bad or responsible for causing trouble or harm 恶棍；坏蛋： *the heroes and villains of the 20th century* * 20 世纪的英雄豪杰与罪魁祸首 ◇ *Industrialized nations are the real environmental villains.* 工业化国家是破坏环境的真正元凶。 **3** (*informal*) a criminal 罪犯

IDM **the 'villain of the piece** (*especially humorous*) the person or thing that is responsible for all the trouble in a situation 元凶；祸首；症结

vil·lain·ous /ˈvɪlənəs/ *adj.* [usually before noun] (*formal*) very evil; very unpleasant 邪恶的；可憎的

vil·lainy /ˈvɪləni/ *noun* [U] (*formal* or *humorous*) immoral or cruel behaviour 邪恶行为；罪恶

vil·lein /ˈvɪleɪn/ *noun* (in the Middle Ages) a poor man who had to work for a richer man in return for a small piece of land to grow food on （中世纪的）农奴，隶农

vil·lus /ˈvɪləs/ *noun* (*pl.* **villi** /ˈvɪlaɪ; -liː/) (*biology* 生) any one of the many small thin parts shaped like fingers that stick out from some surfaces on the inside of the body (for example in the INTESTINE). Villi increase the area of these surfaces so that substances can be absorbed by the body more easily. 绒毛（在小肠内壁等）

vim /vɪm/ *noun* [U] (*old-fashioned, informal*) energy 精力；活力；力量

vin·ai·grette /ˌvɪnɪˈɡret/ *noun* [U] a mixture of oil, VINEGAR and various HERBS, etc., used to add flavour to a salad 色拉调味汁（用油、醋和各种香草等混合而成） **SYN** **French dressing**

vin·da·loo /ˌvɪndəˈluː/ *noun* [U, C] (*pl.* **-oos**) a very spicy Indian dish, usually containing meat or fish 辛辣咖喱肉，辛辣咖喱鱼（印度菜肴）： *lamb vindaloo* 辛辣咖喱羊肉

vin·di·cate /ˈvɪndɪkeɪt/ *verb* (*formal*) **1** **~ sth** to prove that sth is true or that you were right to do sth, especially when other people had a different opinion 证实；证明有理 **SYN** **justify**: *I have every confidence that this decision will be fully vindicated.* 我完全相信这一决定的正确性将得到充分证明。 **2** **~ sb** to prove that sb is not guilty when they have been accused of doing sth wrong or illegal 澄清（责难或嫌疑）；证明（某人）无罪（责）： *New evidence emerged, vindicating him completely.* 新证据出现了，证明他完全是无辜的。 ▶ **vin·di·ca·tion** /ˌvɪndɪˈkeɪʃn/ *noun* [U, sing.]: *Anti-nuclear protesters regarded the Chernobyl accident as a clear vindication of their campaign.* 反核示威者认为，切尔诺贝利核电站核泄漏事故清楚地表明他们的反核运动是正确的。

vin·dic·tive /vɪnˈdɪktɪv/ *adj.* trying to harm or upset sb, or showing that you want to, because you think that they have harmed you 想复仇的；报复性的；怀恨的 **SYN** **spiteful**: *He accused her of being vindictive.* 他指责她存心报复。 ◇ *a vindictive comment* 报复性的言论 ▶ **vin·dic·tive·ly** *adv.* **vin·dic·tive·ness** *noun* [U]

V

vine /vaɪn/ *noun* **1** a climbing plant that produces GRAPES 葡萄藤： *grapes on the vine* 藤上的葡萄 ◇ *vine leaves* 葡萄叶 ➲ SEE ALSO GRAPEVINE **2** any climbing plant with long thin STEMS; one of these STEMS 藤本植物；攀缘植物；藤；藤蔓

vin·egar /ˈvɪnɪɡə(r)/ *noun* [U] a liquid with a bitter taste made from MALT (= a type of grain) or wine, used to add flavour to food or to preserve it 醋： *malt/wine vinegar* 麦芽醋；葡萄酒醋 ◇ *onions pickled in vinegar* 用醋泡制的洋葱 ➲ SEE ALSO BALSAMIC VINEGAR

vin·egary /ˈvɪnɪɡəri/ *adj.* having a taste or smell that is typical of vinegar 醋的；酸的；有醋味的： *a vinegary wine* 酸葡萄酒

vine·yard /ˈvɪnjəd; *NAmE* -jərd/ *noun* a piece of land where GRAPES are grown in order to produce wine; a business that produces wine from the GRAPES it grows in a vineyard （为酿酒而种植的）葡萄园；（以自产葡萄进行生产的）葡萄酒厂 ➲ VISUAL VOCAB PAGE V3 ➲ COMPARE WINERY

vino /ˈviːnəʊ; *NAmE* -noʊ/ *noun* [U] (*informal, humorous*) wine 葡萄酒；果酒

vin·tage /ˈvɪntɪdʒ/ *noun, adj.*

■ *noun* **1** the wine that was produced in a particular year or place; the year in which it was produced 特定年份（或地方）酿制的酒；酿造年份： *the 1999 vintage* * 1999 年酿制的葡萄酒 ◇ *2005 was a particularly fine vintage.* * 2005 年是特别好的酿酒年份。 **2** [usually sing.] the period or season of gathering GRAPES for making wine 采摘葡萄酿酒的期间（或季节）；葡萄收获期（或季节）： *The vintage was later than usual.* 这次葡萄的收获季节比往常晚。

■ *adj.* [only before noun] **1** **vintage** wine is of very good quality and has been stored for several years （葡萄酒）优质的，上等的，佳酿的 **2** (*BrE*) (of a vehicle 车辆) made between 1919 and 1930 and admired for its style and interest 古色古香的（指 1919–1930 年间制造，车型和品味受人青睐的） ➲ COMPARE VETERAN CAR **3** typical of a period in the past and of high quality; the best work of the particular person （过去某个时期）典型的，优质的；（某人的）最佳作品的： *a collection of vintage designs* 优秀设计选编 ◇ *vintage TV drama* 最佳电视剧 ◇ *The opera is vintage Rossini.* 这部歌剧是罗西尼的最佳代表作。 **4** **~ year** a particularly good and successful year 成绩卓著的一年；成功的一年： *2008 was not a vintage year for the movies.* * 2008 年对电影业来说不是个好年景。

vint·ner /ˈvɪntnə(r)/ *noun* (*old-fashioned, formal*) a person whose business is buying and selling wines or a person who grows GRAPES and makes wine 葡萄酒商；葡萄酒酿制者

vinyl /ˈvaɪnl/ *noun* [U] **1** a strong plastic that can bend easily, used for making wall, floor and furniture coverings, book covers, and, especially in the past, records 乙烯基；乙烯基塑料；（尤指旧时）压制唱片的塑料 **2** records made of vinyl, in contrast to CDs 乙烯基唱片；黑胶唱片： *My dad had to buy CDs of all the albums he already owned on vinyl.* 我爸爸就是要买他已有的所有黑胶唱片的 CD 版。

viol /ˈvaɪəl/ *noun* an early type of musical instrument with strings, shaped like a VIOLIN 维奥尔琴（一种早期的拉弦乐器）

viola /viˈəʊlə; *NAmE* -ˈoʊ-/ *noun* a musical instrument with strings, that you hold under your chin and play with a BOW² (3). A viola is larger than a VIOLIN and plays lower notes. 中提琴： *a viola player* 中提琴手 ➲ VISUAL VOCAB PAGE V38

vio·late **AW** /ˈvaɪəleɪt/ *verb* **1** **~ sth** (*formal*) to go against or refuse to obey a law, an agreement, etc. 违反，违犯，违背（法律、协议等） **SYN** **flout**: *to violate international law* 违反国际法 **2** **~ sth** (*formal*) to disturb or not respect sb's peace, PRIVACY, etc. 侵犯（隐私等）；使人不得安宁；搅扰： *She accused the press photographers of violating her privacy.* 她指责新闻摄影记者侵犯了她的隐私。 **3** **~ sth** to damage or destroy a holy or special place 亵渎，污损（神圣之地） **SYN** **desecrate**: *to violate a grave* 亵渎坟墓 **4** **~ sb** (*literary* or *old-fashioned*) to force sb to have sex 强奸；奸污 **SYN** **rape** ▶ **vio·la·tion** **AW** /ˌvaɪəˈleɪʃn/ *noun* [U, C]: *They were in open violation of the treaty.* 他们公然违反条约。 ◇ *gross violations of human rights* 对人权的粗暴践踏 **vio·la·tor** *noun*

vio·lence /ˈvaɪələns/ *noun* [U] **1** violent behaviour that is intended to hurt or kill sb 暴力；暴行： ***crimes/acts/threats of violence*** 暴力犯罪 / 行为 / 威胁 ◇ **~ (against sb)** *He condemned the protesters' **use of violence** against the police.* 他谴责抗议者对警察使用暴力。 ◇ ***domestic violence*** (= between family members) 家庭暴力 ◇ *Why do they always have to **resort to violence**?* 为什么他们总是非要诉诸暴力不可呢？ ◇ ***Violence broke out/erupted** inside the prison last night.* 昨晚监狱里发生了暴力事件。 ◇ *Is there too much sex and violence on TV?* 电视上有太多的色情和暴力吗？ **2** physical or emotional force and energy 狂热；激情；激烈的力量： *The violence of her feelings surprised him.* 她感情之强烈使他吃惊。

vio·lent /ˈvaɪələnt/ *adj.* **1** involving or caused by physical force that is intended to hurt or kill sb 暴力的；强暴的： ***violent crime*** 暴力犯罪 ◇ *Students were involved in violent clashes with the police.* 学生和警察发生了暴力冲突。◇ *He met with a **violent death*** (= he was murdered, killed in a fight, etc.). 他遭暴力致死。◇ *Her husband was a violent man.* 她丈夫是个粗暴的人。◇ *The crowd suddenly **turned violent**.* 人群中突然有人开始大打出手。◇ *Children should not be allowed to watch violent movies* (= that show a lot of violence). 不应允许儿童看暴力电影。 **2** showing or caused by very strong emotion 感情强烈的；激情的；由激情引起的： *There was a violent reaction from the public.* 公众的反应强烈。 **3** very strong and sudden 猛烈的；剧烈的；强烈的 SYN **intense, severe**: *I took a violent dislike to him.* 我很讨厌他。◇ *a violent explosion* 剧烈的爆炸 ◇ *a violent change* 急剧的变化 ◇ *a violent headache* 剧烈的头痛 **4** (of a colour 颜色) extremely bright 强烈的；鲜艳夺目的： *Her dress was a violent pink.* 她的连衣裙是非常鲜艳的粉红色。

vio·lent·ly /ˈvaɪələntli/ *adv.* **1** with great energy or strong movement, especially caused by a strong emotion such as fear or hatred 强烈地；激烈地： *She shook her head violently.* 她拼命摇头。◇ *to shiver violently* 剧烈地颤抖 **2** very strongly or severely 猛烈地；厉害地： *He was violently sick.* 他病得很厉害。◇ *They are violently opposed to the idea.* 他们强烈反对这个想法。 **3** in a way that involves physical violence 凶猛地；凶狠地；强烈地： *The crowd reacted violently.* 人群反应强烈。

vio·let /ˈvaɪələt/ *noun* **1** [C] a small wild or garden plant with purple or white flowers with a sweet smell that appear in spring 紫罗兰 **2** [U] a bluish-purple colour 蓝紫色；紫罗兰色： *dressed in violet* 身着蓝紫色衣服的 ▸ **vio·let** *adj.* : *violet eyes* 蓝紫色的眼睛 IDM SEE SHRINK *v.*

vio·lin /ˌvaɪəˈlɪn/ *noun* a musical instrument with strings, that you hold under your chin and play with a BOW² (3) 小提琴： *Brahms' violin concerto* 勃拉姆斯的小提琴协奏曲 ➲ VISUAL VOCAB PAGE V38 ➲ COMPARE VIOLA ➲ SEE ALSO FIDDLE *n.* (1)

vio·lin·ist /ˌvaɪəˈlɪnɪst/ *noun* a person who plays the violin 小提琴手；小提琴演奏者

vio·list *noun* **1** /viˈəʊlɪst; *NAmE* -ˈoʊl-/ a person who plays a VIOLA 中提琴手；中提琴演奏者 **2** /ˈvaɪəlɪst/ a person who plays a VIOL 维奥尔琴手；维奥尔琴演奏者

vio·lon·cello /ˌvaɪələnˈtʃeləʊ; *NAmE* -loʊ/ *noun* (*pl.* **-os**) (*formal*) = CELLO

VIP /ˌviː aɪ ˈpiː/ *noun* the abbreviation for 'Very Important Person' (a famous or important person who is treated in a special way) 要人，贵宾（全写为 Very Important Person） SYN **celebrity, dignitary**: *the VIP lounge* 贵宾厅 ◇ *to get **the VIP treatment*** 得到贵宾待遇

viper /ˈvaɪpə(r)/ *noun* **1** a small poisonous snake 蝰蛇（一种小毒蛇） **2** (*formal*) a person who harms other people 毒如蛇蝎的人；险恶的人

vir·ago /vɪˈrɑːɡəʊ; *NAmE* -ɡoʊ/ *noun* (*pl.* **-os**) (*literary, disapproving*) a woman who is aggressive and tries to tell people what to do 爱支使人的女性；泼妇；悍妇

viral /ˈvaɪrəl/ *adj.* **1** like or caused by a virus 病毒的；病毒性的；病毒引起的： ***a viral infection*** 病毒性感染 **2** used to describe a piece of information, a video, an image, etc. that is sent rapidly over the Internet from one person to another （信息、视频、图像等）在网上快速传播的： *a viral email* 快速传播的电子邮件 ◇ *Within 24 hours, the video **went viral** on YouTube and Facebook.* 在 24 小时内，该视频在影片分享网站和脸书上疯传。

ˈviral marketing *noun* [U] a way of advertising in which information about a company's products or services is sent by email to people who then send it on by email to other people they know 病毒式营销（通过互联网用户之间的电邮进行广告宣传）

vir·gin /ˈvɜːdʒɪn; *NAmE* ˈvɜːrdʒ-/ *noun, adj.*

■ *noun* **1** [C] a person who has never had sex 处女；童男 **2 the (Blessed) Virgin** [sing.] the Virgin Mary, mother of Jesus Christ 童贞马利亚（耶稣之母） **3** [C] a person who has no experience of a particular activity 无…经验的人；新手： *a political virgin* 无政治经验的人 ◇ *an Internet virgin* 网络新手

■ *adj.* **1** [usually before noun] in its original pure or natural condition and not changed, touched or spoiled 未开发的；原始状态的；天然的；未遭破坏的： ***virgin forest/land/territory*** 原始森林；处女地；未开发地区 ◇ ***virgin snow*** (= fresh and not marked) 新雪 **2** [only before noun] with no sexual experience 处女的；贞洁的；童贞的： *a virgin bride* 贞洁的新娘 ◇ *the **virgin birth*** (= the belief that Mary was a virgin before and after giving birth to Jesus) 圣母马利亚童贞生子

vir·gin·al /ˈvɜːdʒɪnl; *NAmE* ˈvɜːrdʒ-/ *adj.* of or like a virgin; pure and innocent 处女（般）的；童贞的；贞洁的；纯真的： *She was dressed in virginal white.* 她穿了一身洁白无瑕的衣服。

Vir·ginia creep·er /vəˌdʒɪniə ˈkriːpə(r); *NAmE* vərˌdʒ-/ *noun* [U, C] a climbing plant, often grown on walls, with large leaves that turn red in the autumn/fall 五叶地锦，弗吉尼亚爬山虎（常蔓生于墙上，叶大，秋季变成红色）

vir·gin·ity /vəˈdʒɪnəti; *NAmE* vərˈdʒ-/ *noun* [U] the state of being a virgin 处女状态；童贞；原始状态： *He **lost his virginity*** (= had sex for the first time) *when he was 18.* 他在 18 岁时失去童贞。

Virgo /ˈvɜːɡəʊ; *NAmE* ˈvɜːrɡoʊ/ *noun* **1** [U] the 6th sign of the ZODIAC, the VIRGIN 黄道第六宫；室女宫；室女（星）座 **2** [C] (*pl.* **-os**) a person born when the sun is in this sign, that is between 23 August and 23 September, approximately 属室女座的人（约出生于 8 月 23 日至 9 月 23 日）

vir·id·ian /vɪˈrɪdiən/ *noun* [U] (*specialist*) a bluish-green PIGMENT used in art; the colour of this pigment 铬绿（颜料）；铬绿色；青绿色

vir·ile /ˈvɪraɪl; *NAmE* ˈvɪrəl/ *adj.* (*usually approving*) **1** (of men 男子) strong and full of energy, especially sexual energy 强壮的；精力充沛的；（尤指）性机能强的 **2** having or showing the strength and energy that is considered typical of men 有阳刚之气的；有男子气概的；雄浑的： *a virile performance* 雄壮的演奏 ◇ *virile athleticism* 雄健的体魄

vir·il·ity /vəˈrɪləti/ *noun* [U] **1** sexual power in men （男性的）性功能，生殖力： *displays of male virility* 男子生殖力的表现 ◇ *a need to prove his virility* 需要证明他有生殖能力 **2** strength or energy 力量；活力： *economic virility* 经济活力

vir·ology /vaɪˈrɒlədʒi; *NAmE* -ˈrɑːl-/ *noun* [U] the scientific study of viruses and the diseases caused by them 病毒学 ▸ **vir·olo·gist** /vaɪˈrɒlədʒɪst; *NAmE* -ˈrɑːl-/ *noun*

vir·tual AW /ˈvɜːtʃuəl; *NAmE* ˈvɜːrtʃ-/ *adj.* [only before noun] **1** almost or very nearly the thing described, so that any slight difference is not important 很接近的；几乎…的；事实上的；实际上的；实质上的： *The country was sliding into a state of virtual civil war.* 这个国家实际上正逐渐进入内战状态。◇ *The company has a virtual monopoly in this area of trade.* 这家公司实质上已经垄断了这种贸易。◇ *He married a virtual stranger.* 他娶了一个几乎素不相识的女子。 **2** made to appear to exist by the use of computer software, for example on the Internet （通过计算机软件，如在互联网上）模拟的，虚拟的： *New technology has enabled development of an online 'virtual library'.* 新技术已经使在线"虚拟图书馆"的发展成为可能。

vir·tu·al·ly AW /ˈvɜːtʃuəli; *NAmE* ˈvɜːrtʃ-/ *adv.* **1** almost or very nearly, so that any slight difference is not important 几乎；差不多；事实上；实际上： *to be virtually impossible* 几乎不可能 ◇ ***Virtually all** students will be exempt from the tax.* 差不多所有的学生都可免此税项。◇ *He virtually admitted he was guilty.* 他实际上已承认自己有罪。◇ *This year's results are virtually the same as last*

V

year's. 今年的结果几乎和去年的一样。 **2** (*computing* 计) by the use of computer software that makes sth appear to exist; using VIRTUAL REALITY technology 模拟；虚拟；以模拟现实技术

ˌvirtual ˈmemory (*also* **ˌvirtual ˈstorage**) *noun* [U] (*computing* 计) part of a computer's HARD DISK that can be used when the main memory is full 虚拟存储（器），虚拟内存（计算机硬盘的一部分，可在主内存已满时使用）

ˌvirtual reˈality *noun* [U] images and sounds created by a computer that seem almost real to the user, who can affect them by using SENSORS （计算机创造的）虚拟现实，拟境（用户可使用传感器与之互动）

ˌvirtual ˈworld *noun* images, sounds and text used by a computer to create a world where people can communicate with each other, play games and pretend to live another life （计算机）虚拟世界

vir·tue /ˈvɜːtʃuː; *NAmE* ˈvɜːrtʃuː/ *noun* **1** [U] (*formal*) behaviour or attitudes that show high moral standards 高尚的道德；正直的品性；德行：*He led a life of virtue.* 他过着高尚的生活。◇ *She was certainly no* ***paragon of virtue!*** 她绝不是道德高尚的典范！ **2** [C] a particular good quality or habit 美德；优秀品质；良好习惯：*Patience is not one of her virtues, I'm afraid.* 恐怕她没有耐心。 **3** [C, U] an attractive or useful quality 优点；长处；用处 **SYN** **advantage**：*The plan* ***has the virtue of*** *simplicity.* 这项计划的优点是简单。◇ *He was extolling the virtues of the Internet.* 他赞扬了互联网的长处。◇ *They could see* ***no virtue*** *in discussing it further.* 他们看不到再讨论下去有什么用处。

IDM **by/in virtue of sth** (*formal*) by means of or because of sth 凭借；依靠；由于；因为：*She got the job by virtue of her greater experience.* 她由于经验较为丰富而得到了那份工作。 **make a ˌvirtue of neˈcessity** to manage to gain an advantage from sth that you have to do and cannot avoid 不得已而力争有所得 **ˌvirtue is its own reˈward** (*saying*) the reward for acting in a moral or correct way is the knowledge that you have done so, and you should not expect more than this, for example praise from other people or payment 施恩无他图，有德便是报；美德本身就是报偿 ➲ MORE AT EASY *adj.*

vir·tu·os·ity /ˌvɜːtʃuˈɒsəti; *NAmE* ˌvɜːrtʃuˈɑːs-/ *noun* [U] (*formal*) a very high degree of skill in performing or playing （表演或演奏方面的）高超技艺，精湛演技：*technical virtuosity* 技术的娴熟 ◇ *a performance of breathtaking virtuosity* 技艺令人叫绝的演出

vir·tu·oso /ˌvɜːtʃuˈəʊsəʊ; -ˈəʊzəʊ; *NAmE* ˌvɜːrtʃuˈoʊsoʊ; -ˈoʊzoʊ/ *noun, adj.*

▪ ***noun*** (*pl.* **vir·tu·osos** or **vir·tu·osi** /-siː; -ziː/) a person who is extremely skilful at doing sth, especially playing a musical instrument 技艺超群的人；（尤指）演奏家：*a piano virtuoso* 钢琴演奏家

▪ ***adj.*** [only before noun] showing extremely great skill 技艺精湛的；技巧超群的：*a virtuoso performance* 技艺精湛的表演 ◇ *a virtuoso pianist* 钢琴大师

vir·tu·ous /ˈvɜːtʃuəs; *NAmE* ˈvɜːrtʃ-/ *adj.* **1** (*formal*) behaving in a very good and moral way 品行端正的；品德高的；有道德的 **SYN** **irreproachable**：*a wise and virtuous man* 博学多识的君子 ◇ *She lived an entirely virtuous life.* 她一生品行端正。 **2** (*disapproving* or *humorous*) claiming to behave better or have higher moral standards than other people 自命不凡的；自命清高的：*He was feeling virtuous because he had finished and they hadn't.* 因为他完成了而他们没有，他自以为了不起。▶ **vir·tu·ous·ly** *adv.*

ˌvirtuous ˈcircle *noun* (*formal*) a series of events in which each one seems to increase the good effects of the previous one 良性循环 ➲ COMPARE VICIOUS CIRCLE

viru·lent /ˈvɪrələnt; -rjəl-/ *adj.* **1** (of a disease or poison 疾病或毒物) extremely dangerous or harmful and quick to have an effect 致命的；恶性的；剧毒的 **2** (*formal*) showing strong negative and bitter feelings 狠毒的；恶毒的；不共戴天的：*virulent criticism* 恶意的批评 ◇ *virulent nationalism* 不共戴天的民族主义 ▶ **viru·lence** /-ləns/ *noun* [U] **viru·lent·ly** *adv.*

virus 🔑 /ˈvaɪrəs/ *noun* **1** 🔑 a living thing, too small to be seen without a MICROSCOPE, that causes infectious disease in people, animals and plants 病毒；滤过性病毒：*the flu virus* 流感病毒 ◇ *a virus infection* 病毒感染 ➲ WORDFINDER NOTE AT DISEASE ➲ COLLOCATIONS AT ILL, LIFE **2** 🔑 (*informal*) a disease caused by a virus 病毒性疾病；病毒病：*There's a virus going around the office.* 办公室里流行着一种病毒性疾病。 **3** 🔑 instructions that are hidden within a computer program and are designed to cause faults or destroy data （计算机程序中的）病毒 ➲ COLLOCATIONS AT EMAIL ➲ SEE ALSO VIRAL (1)

visa /ˈviːzə/ *noun* a stamp or mark put in your passport by officials of a foreign country that gives you permission to enter, pass through or leave their country （护照的）签证：*to* ***apply for a visa*** 申请签证 ◇ ***an entry/a tourist/a transit/an exit visa*** 入境 / 旅游 / 过境 / 出境签证 ➲ WORDFINDER NOTE AT HOLIDAY, TOURIST

vis·age /ˈvɪzɪdʒ/ *noun* (*literary*) a person's face （人的）脸，面容

vis-à-vis /ˌviːz ɑː ˈviː/ *prep.* (*from French*) **1** in relation to 关于；对于：*Britain's role vis-à-vis the United States* 英国对美国的作用 **2** in comparison with 和…相比；与…相较：*It was felt that the company had an unfair advantage vis-à-vis smaller companies elsewhere.* 人们感到这家公司与其他地方的小公司相比占有不公平的优势。

vis·cera /ˈvɪsərə/ *noun* [pl.] (*anatomy* 解) the large organs inside the body, such as the heart, lungs and stomach 内脏；脏腑

vis·ceral /ˈvɪsərəl/ *adj.* **1** (*literary*) resulting from strong feelings rather than careful thought （未经过认真思考而）出自内心的，发自肺腑的：*She had a visceral dislike of all things foreign.* 凡是外国的东西，她都打心眼儿里讨厌。 **2** (*specialist*) relating to the viscera 内脏的；脏腑的

vis·cid /ˈvɪsɪd/ *adj.* (*formal* or *specialist*) sticky and SLIMY 黏稠的；黏质的：*the viscid lining of the intestine* 肠黏膜

vis·cose /ˈvɪskəʊz; -kəʊs; *NAmE* -koʊz; -koʊs/ *noun* [U] (*especially BrE*) a chemical made from CELLULOSE, used to make FIBRES which can be used to make clothes, etc. 黏胶

vis·count /ˈvaɪkaʊnt/ *noun* (in Britain) a NOBLEMAN of a rank below an EARL and above a BARON 子爵（英国贵族，低于伯爵而高于男爵）

vis·count·cy /ˈvaɪkaʊntsi/ *noun* the rank or position of a viscount 子爵爵位（或地位）

vis·count·ess /ˈvaɪkaʊntəs/ *noun* **1** a woman who has the rank of a VISCOUNT 女子爵 **2** the wife of a VISCOUNT 子爵夫人

vis·cous /ˈvɪskəs/ *adj.* (*specialist*) (of a liquid 液体) thick and sticky; not flowing freely 黏稠的；黏滞的 ▶ **vis·cos·ity** /vɪˈskɒsəti; *NAmE* -ˈskɑːs-/ *noun* [U]

vise (*NAmE*) (*especially BrE* **vice**) /vaɪs/ *noun* [C] a tool with two metal blocks that can be moved together by turning a screw. The vise is used to hold an object firmly while work is done on it. 台钳；虎钳：*He held my arm in a vise-like* (= very firm) ***grip***. 他的手像虎钳一样紧紧抓住了我的手臂。 ➲ VISUAL VOCAB PAGE V21

visi·bil·ity **AW** /ˌvɪzəˈbɪləti/ *noun* [U] **1** how far or well you can see, especially as affected by the light or the weather 可见度；能见度；能见距离：***good/poor/bad/zero visibility*** 能见度高 / 低 / 差 / 为零 ◇ *Visibility was down to about 100 metres in the fog.* 雾中的能见距离降到了大约 100 米。◇ *The car has excellent* ***all-round visibility*** (= you can see what is around you very easily from it). 这辆车四周的视野极好。 **2** the fact or state of being easy to see 可见性；明显性：***high visibility*** *equipment for cyclists* 骑自行车人配备的高可见性的设备 ◇ *The advertisements were intended to increase the company's visibility in the marketplace* (= to make people more aware of their products and services). 那些广告旨在使这家公司在市场中更加引人注目。

vis·ible AW /ˈvɪzəbl/ *adj.* **1** that can be seen 看得见的；可见的：*The house is **clearly visible** from the beach.* 从海滩可以清楚地看到那所房子。◇ *Most stars are not **visible to the naked eye**.* 大多数星星肉眼看不见。**2** that is obvious enough to be noticed 明显的；能注意到的 SYN **obvious**：*visible benefits* 显而易见的实惠 ◇ *a visible police presence* 明显有警察在场 ◇ *He showed no visible sign of emotion.* 他丝毫不露声色。◇ *She made a visible effort to control her anger.* 看得出她竭力控制自己不发火。➲ COMPARE INVISIBLE

ˌvisible miˈnority *noun* (*CanE*) a group whose members are clearly different in race from those of the majority race in a society 显性少数民族（与占社会主体的民族明显不同）

vis·ibly AW /ˈvɪzəbli/ *adv.* in a way that is easily noticeable 易察觉地；明显地：*He was visibly shocked.* 看得出他大为震惊。◇ *She paled visibly at the news.* 她听到这消息时脸色明显地变得苍白。

vi·sion AW /ˈvɪʒn/ *noun* **1** [U] the ability to see; the area that you can see from a particular position 视力；视野：*to have **good/perfect/poor/blurred/normal vision*** 视力好／极好／差／模糊／正常 ◇ ***20–20 vision*** (= the ability to see perfectly) * 20–20 的视力 ◇ *Cats have good **night vision**.* 猫的夜视能力强。◇ *The couple moved outside her **field of vision**.* 这对夫妇离开了她的视野。◇ *He glimpsed something on the edge of his vision.* 他斜眼瞥见了点什么。➲ SYNONYMS AT SIGHT ➲ SEE ALSO TUNNEL VISION **2** [C] an idea or a picture in your imagination 想象；幻象：*He had a vision of a world in which there would be no wars.* 他幻想有一个没有战争的世界。◇ *I **had visions** of us getting hopelessly lost.* 我想象我们完全迷失了方向。**3** [C] a dream or similar experience, especially of a religious kind 梦幻；幻象；神示；异象：*The idea came to her in a vision.* 她在神示中想到了这个主意。**4** [U] the ability to think about or plan the future with great imagination and intelligence 想象力；眼力；远见卓识 SYN **foresight**：*a leader of vision* 有远见的领袖 **5** [C] **a ~ (of sth)** (*literary*) a person of great beauty or who shows the quality mentioned 俊男；天仙；有…气质的人：*She was a vision in white lace.* 她穿着白色蕾丝的衣服美极了。◇ *a vision of loveliness* 可爱的人 **6** [U] the picture on a television or cinema/movie theater screen（电视或影院屏幕的）影像，画面：*We apologize for the loss of vision.* 很抱歉没法显示画面。

vi·sion·ary /ˈvɪʒənri; *NAmE* -ʒəneri/ *adj., noun*

■***adj.*** **1** (*approving*) original and showing the ability to think about or plan the future with great imagination and intelligence 有眼力的；有创见的；有远见卓识的：*a visionary leader* 有远见卓识的领袖 **2** relating to dreams or strange experiences, especially of a religious kind 梦幻的；耽于幻想的；（尤指）宗教异象的；神示的：*visionary experiences* 异象体验

■***noun*** (*pl.* **-ies**) (*usually approving*) a person who has the ability to think about or plan the future in a way that is intelligent or shows imagination 有眼力的人；有远见卓识的人

visit /ˈvɪzɪt/ *verb, noun*

■***verb*** **1** [T] **~ sb/sth** to go to see a person or a place for a period of time 访问；拜访；看望；参观：*She went to visit relatives in Wales.* 她去威尔士看望亲戚了。◇ *The Prime Minister is visiting Japan at the moment.* 首相目前正在访问日本。◇ *You should visit your dentist at least twice a year.* 你应该每年至少去看两次牙科医生。**2** [T] **~ sth** (*computing* 计) to go to a website on the Internet 访问（互联网上的网站）：*For more information, visit our website.* 欲知详情，请访问我们的网站。➲ WORDFINDER NOTE AT WEB **3** [I, T] to stay somewhere for a short time（短暂地）作客，逗留：*We don't live here. We're just visiting.* 我们不住在这里，只作短期停留。◇ **~ sth** *The lake is also visited by seals in the summer.* 夏天也有海豹游到这湖里来。**4** [T] **~ sth** to make an official visit to sb, for example to perform checks or give advice 视察；巡视：*government inspectors visiting schools* 视察学校的政府督学

PHR V **ˈvisit sth on/upon sb/sth** (*old use*) to punish sb/sth 对…进行惩罚：*The sins of the fathers are visited upon the children* (= children are blamed or suffer for what their parents have done). 父辈造的孽报应到子女头上。**ˈvisit with sb** (*NAmE*) to spend time with sb, especially talking socially 与某人聊天；与某人闲谈：*Come and visit with me some time.* 找个时间来跟我聊聊吧。

■***noun*** **1** **~ (to sb/sth)** **(from sb)** an occasion or a period of time when sb goes to see a place or person and spends time there 访问；参观；游览；逗留；看望：*It's my first visit to New York.* 这是我第一次去纽约。◇ *They're on an **exchange visit** to France.* 他们到法国进行互访。◇ *If you have time, **pay a visit to** the local museum.* 你若有空，参观一下当地的博物馆。◇ *We had a visit from the police last night.* 昨晚警察来我们家了。◇ *Is this a **social visit**, or is it business?* 这是社交性的拜访，还是业务性的？◇ *a visit to the doctor* 看医生 ◇ (*BrE*) *a **home visit*** (= when your doctor visits you) 上门出诊 ➲ SEE ALSO FLYING VISIT **2** (*computing* 计) an occasion when sb looks at a website on the Internet（到网站的）访问：*Visits to our website have doubled in a year.* 我们网站的访问人次一年内翻了一番。**3** **~ (with sb)** (*NAmE, informal*) an occasion when two or more people meet to talk in an informal way 碰头；会面

vis·it·ation /ˌvɪzɪˈteɪʃn/ *noun* **1** [U] (*NAmE*) the right of a parent who is divorced or separated from his or her partner to visit a child who is living with the partner（离婚父母对子女的）探视权：*She is seeking more liberal visitation with her daughter.* 她正在争取对女儿有更自由的探视权。◇ *visitation rights* 探视子女的权利 ➲ COMPARE ACCESS *n.* (2) **2** [C, U] **~ (of/from sb/sth)** (*formal*) an official visit, especially to check that rules are being obeyed and everything is as it should be 视察；巡视 **3** [C] **~ (of/from sb/sth)** (*formal*) an unexpected appearance of sth, for example a GHOST（神灵等的）显现，显示，出现 **4** [C] **~ (of sth)** (*formal*) a disaster that is believed to be a punishment from God（视为上帝惩罚的）天灾，灾难，灾祸：*a visitation of plague* 天降瘟疫

vis·it·ing /ˈvɪzɪtɪŋ/ *adj.* [only before noun] a **visiting** professor or lecturer is one who is teaching for a fixed period at a particular university or college, but who normally teaches at another one（指教授或讲师）客座的

ˈvisiting card (*BrE*) (*NAmE* **ˈcalling card**) (*also* **card** *BrE, NAmE*) *noun* (especially in the past) a small card with your name on it which you leave with sb after, or instead of, a formal visit（尤指旧时访客留下或其他人用以表示到访的）名片，拜帖 ➲ COMPARE BUSINESS CARD

vis·it·or /ˈvɪzɪtə(r)/ *noun* **~ (to…)** a person who visits a person or place 来访者；访问者；参观者；游客：*We've got visitors coming this weekend.* 本周末我们有客人来访。◇ *Do you get many visitors?* 来探望你的人多吗？◇ *She's a frequent visitor to the US.* 她经常去美国。◇ *The theme park attracts 2.5 million visitors a year.* 这个主题乐园每年吸引 250 万游客。◇ *How can we attract more visitors to our website?* 我们如何才能吸引更多人访问我们的网站呢？➲ SEE ALSO HEALTH VISITOR

ˈvisitors' book *noun* a book in which visitors write their names, addresses and sometimes comments, for example, at a hotel or place of public interest 来客登记簿；来宾留言簿；游客意见簿

visor /ˈvaɪzə(r)/ *noun* **1** a part of a helmet that can be pulled down to protect the eyes and face（头盔上的）面甲，面罩，护面 ➲ VISUAL VOCAB PAGE V70 **2** a curved piece of plastic, etc. worn on the head above the eyes to protect them from the sun 遮阳帽舌 **3** a small piece of plastic, etc. inside the front window of a car that can be pulled down to protect the driver's eyes from the sun（汽车内挡风玻璃上方的）遮阳板 ➲ VISUAL VOCAB PAGE V56 **4** (*NAmE*) = BILL (9)

vista /ˈvɪstə/ *noun* **1** (*literary*) a beautiful view, for example, of the countryside, a city, etc.（农村、城市等的）景色，景观 SYN **panorama** **2** (*formal*) a range of things that

V

might happen in the future （未来可能发生的）一系列情景，一连串事情 SYN **prospect**: *This new job could open up whole new vistas for her.* 这项新工作可能给她开辟全新的前景。

vis·ual AW /ˈvɪʒuəl/ *adj., noun*
■ ***adj.*** of or connected with seeing or sight 视力的；视觉的： *I have a very good visual memory.* 我过目不忘。◇ *the visual arts* 视觉艺术 ◇ *The building makes a tremendous visual impact.* 这栋建筑物给人以极其深刻的视觉印象。 ▶ **visu·al·ly** AW /ˈvɪʒuəli/ *adv.*： ***visually handicapped/impaired*** 有视力障碍的；视力受损的 ◇ *visually exciting* 视觉上令人兴奋
■ ***noun*** a picture, map, piece of film, etc. used to make an article or a talk easier to understand or more interesting 视觉资料（指说明性的图片、影片等）： *He used striking visuals to get his point across.* 他用醒目的视觉资料解释他的观点。

ˌvisual ˈaid *noun* [usually pl.] a picture, video, etc. used in teaching to help people to learn or understand sth 直观教具

ˌvisual ˈfield *noun* (*specialist*) = FIELD OF VISION

visu·al·ize AW (*BrE also* **-ise**) /ˈvɪʒuəlaɪz/ *verb* **1** to form a picture of sb/sth in your mind 使形象化；想象；构思；设想 SYN **imagine**： **~ sb/sth/yourself (as sth)** *Try to visualize him as an old man.* 尽量设想他是一位老人。◇ **~ what, how, etc.…** *I can't visualize what this room looked like before it was decorated.* 我想象不出这个房间在装修之前是什么样子。◇ **~ sb/sth/yourself doing sth** *It can help to visualize yourself making your speech clearly and confidently.* 设想自己口齿清晰和充满信心地演讲是很有助益的。◇ **~ doing sth** *She couldn't visualize climbing the mountain.* 她想象不出如何攀登这座大山。 **2 ~ sth** to make sth visible to the eye 使可视化；使看得见： *Ultrasound is a technique that uses sound waves to visualize internal structures.* 超声波扫描检查是利用声波透视人体内部结构的技术。 ▶ **visu·al·iza·tion**, **-isa·tion** AW /ˌvɪʒuəlaɪˈzeɪʃn; *NAmE* -ləˈz-/ *noun* [U, C]

vita /ˈviːtə/ *noun* (*US*) = CURRICULUM VITAE

vital /ˈvaɪtl/ *adj.* **1** necessary or essential in order for sth to succeed or exist 必不可少的；对…极重要的： **~ (for sth)** *the vitamins that are vital for health* 保持健康必不可少的维生素 ◇ **~ (to sth)** *Good financial accounts are vital to the success of any enterprise.* 妥善的财务账目对任何公司的成功都是极其重要的。 ◇ *Reading is **of vital importance** in language learning.* 阅读在语言学习中至关重要。 ◇ *The police play **a vital role** in our society.* 警察在我们的社会中起着极其重要的作用。 ◇ **~ that…** *It is vital that you keep accurate records when you are self-employed.* 干个体的要准确记录账目，这十分重要。 ◇ **~ to do sth** *It was vital to show that he was not afraid.* 最重要的是要表现出他毫无畏惧。 ➲ SYNONYMS AT ESSENTIAL ➲ LANGUAGE BANK AT EMPHASIS, IMPERSONAL **2** [only before noun] connected with or necessary for staying alive 生命的；维持生命所必需的： *the **vital organs*** (= the brain, heart, lungs, etc.) 重要脏器 **3** (of a person 人) full of energy and enthusiasm 生气勃勃的；充满生机的；热情洋溢的 SYN **dynamic**

> **▼ LANGUAGE BANK 用语库**
>
> **vital**
>
> Saying that something is necessary 表达某事是必要的
>
> - ***It is vital that** journalists can verify the accuracy of their reports.* 新闻记者能够核实其报道的准确性，这一点至关重要。
> - *Journalists play a **vital/crucial** role in educating the public.* 新闻记者对教育公众起着极其重要的作用。
> - *Public trust is a **crucial** issue for all news organizations.* 对所有新闻机构来说，公众的信任是至关重要的问题。
> - *The ability to write well is **essential** for any journalist.* 好的笔头功夫对任何一个新闻记者都是非常重要的。
> - *The Internet has become an **indispensable** tool for reporters.* 互联网已经成为记者不可或缺的工具。
> - *In journalism, accuracy is **paramount**/…**is of paramount importance**.* 在新闻工作中，准确至关重要。
> - ***It is imperative that** journalists maintain the highest possible standards of reporting.* 新闻记者的当务之急是尽可能保持最高水平的报道。
>
> ➲ SYNONYMS AT ESSENTIAL
> ➲ LANGUAGE BANK AT EMPHASIS, IMPERSONAL

vi·tal·ity /vaɪˈtæləti/ *noun* [U] energy and enthusiasm 生命力；活力；热情 SYN **vigour**: *She is bursting with vitality and new ideas.* 她朝气蓬勃，满脑子新主意。

vi·tal·ly /ˈvaɪtəli/ *adv.* extremely; in an essential way 极其；绝对： *Education is **vitally important** for the country's future.* 教育对国家的未来是至关重要的。

the vi·tals /ˈvaɪtlz/ *noun* [pl.] (*old-fashioned* or *humorous*) the organs of the body that are essential for staying alive, for example the brain, heart, lungs, etc. （维持生命的）重要器官

ˌvital ˈsign *noun* [usually pl.] (*medical* 医) a measurement that shows that sb is alive, such as the rate of their breathing, their body temperature or their HEARTBEAT 生命体征（如呼吸、体温、心搏等）

ˌvital staˈtistics *noun* [pl.] **1** figures that show the number of births and deaths in a country 生命统计，人口动态统计（显示一国出生和死亡的人口数字） **2** (*BrE, informal*) the measurements of a woman's chest, waist and hips 女子三围尺寸

vita·min /ˈvɪtəmɪn; *NAmE* ˈvaɪt-/ *noun* a natural substance found in food that is an essential part of what humans and animals eat to help them grow and stay healthy. There are many different vitamins. 维生素；维他命： *breakfast cereals enriched with vitamins* 增加了维生素的谷物早餐食品 ◇ *vitamin deficiency* 维生素缺乏 ◇ *vitamin pills* 维生素丸 ➲ COLLOCATIONS AT DIET

ˌvitamin ˈC (*also* **asˌcorbic ˈacid**) *noun* [U] a vitamin found in fruits such as oranges and lemons, and in green vegetables 维生素 C，维他命 C，抗坏血酸（存在于柑橘、柠檬等水果和绿色蔬菜）： *Oranges are rich in vitamin C.* 柑橘里含有丰富的维生素 C。

viti·ate /ˈvɪʃieɪt/ *verb* [usually passive] **~ sth** (*formal*) to spoil or reduce the effect of sth 使失效；削弱效用

viti·cul·ture /ˈvɪtɪkʌltʃə(r); ˈvaɪt-/ *noun* [U] (*specialist*) the science or practice of growing GRAPES 葡萄栽培学；葡萄栽培术；葡萄栽培

vit·re·ous /ˈvɪtriəs/ *adj.* (*specialist*) hard, shiny and transparent like glass 玻璃质的；玻璃状的；透明的： *vitreous enamel* 玻璃釉

ˌvitreous ˈhumour (*especially US* **ˌvitreous ˈhumor**) *noun* [U] (*anatomy* 解) the transparent jelly-like substance inside the eye （眼睛的）玻璃体液 ➲ COMPARE AQUEOUS HUMOUR

vit·rify /ˈvɪtrɪfaɪ/ *verb* (**vit·ri·fies**, **vit·ri·fy·ing**, **vit·ri·fied**, **vit·ri·fied**) [I, T] **~ (sth)** (*specialist*) to change or make sth change into glass, or a substance like glass 使成玻璃（状物质）；使玻璃化 ▶ **vit·ri·fi·ca·tion** /ˌvɪtrɪfɪˈkeɪʃn/ *noun* [U]

vit·riol /ˈvɪtriəl/ *noun* [U] (*formal*) very cruel and bitter comments or criticism 尖刻无情的话（或批评） SYN **abuse**

vit·ri·ol·ic /ˌvɪtriˈɒlɪk; *NAmE* -ˈɑːlɪk/ *adj.* (*formal*) (of language or comments 言语或评论) full of anger and hatred 愤怒的；恶意的；尖酸刻薄的 SYN **bitter**: *The newspaper launched a vitriolic attack on the president.* 这家报纸对总统发起了一场恶意的攻击。

vitro ➲ IN VITRO

vi·tu·per·ation /vɪˌtjuːpəˈreɪʃn; *NAmE* vaɪˌtuː-/ *noun* [U] (*formal*) cruel and angry criticism 辱骂；斥责；责骂 SYN abuse ▸ **vi·tu·pera·tive** /vɪˈtjuːpərətɪv; *NAmE* vaɪˈtuːpəreɪtɪv/ *adj.* : *a vituperative attack* 谩骂式的攻击

viva¹ /ˈviːvə/ *exclamation* used for expressing support for sb or sth （表示拥护）万岁

viva² /ˈvaɪvə/ *noun* (*BrE*) = VIVA VOCE

viv·ace /vɪˈvɑːtʃeɪ/ *noun* (*music* 音, *from Italian*) a piece of music to be played in a quick lively way 活板 ▸ **viv·ace** *adv., adj.*

viv·acious /vɪˈveɪʃəs; *NAmE also* vaɪˈv-/ *adj.* (*approving*) (especially of a woman 尤指女子) having a lively, attractive personality 可爱的；活泼的；动人的： *He had three pretty, vivacious daughters.* 他有三个活泼漂亮的女儿。 ▸ **viv·acious·ly** *adv.* **viv·acity** /vɪˈvæsəti; *NAmE also* vaɪˈv-/ *noun* [U]: *He was charmed by her beauty and vivacity.* 他被她的美丽与活泼迷住了。

viv·ar·ium /vaɪˈveəriəm; vɪˈv-; *NAmE* -ˈver-/ *noun* (*pl.* **viv·ar·ia** /vaɪˈveəriə; vɪˈv-; *NAmE* -ˈver-/) a container for keeping live animals in, especially for scientific study 生态缸（用于饲养动物作科研用途等）

viva voce /ˌvaɪvə ˈvəʊtʃi; *NAmE* ˈvoʊtʃi/ (*BrE also* **viva**) *noun* (*from Latin*) a spoken exam, especially in a British university （尤指英国大学的）口试

vive la dif·fer·ence /ˌviːv lɑː ˌdɪfəˈrɒns; *NAmE* -ˈrɑːns/ *exclamation* (*from French, humorous*) used to show that you think it is good that there is a difference between two people or things, especially a difference between men and women （尤用以赞同男女有别）差别万岁

vivid /ˈvɪvɪd/ *adj.* **1** (of memories, a description, etc. 记忆、描述等) producing very clear pictures in your mind 清晰的；生动的；逼真的 SYN **graphic**: *vivid memories* 清晰的记忆 ◇ *He gave a vivid account of his life as a fighter pilot.* 他生动地描述了他那战斗机飞行员的生活。 **2** (of light, colours, etc. 光、颜色等) very bright 鲜明的；耀眼的；鲜艳的；强烈的： *vivid blue eyes* 碧蓝的眼睛 ➲ SYNONYMS AT BRIGHT **3** (of sb's imagination 人的想象) able to form pictures of ideas, situations, etc. easily in the mind 丰富的 ▸ **viv·id·ly** *adv.* : *I vividly remember the day we first met.* 我对我们第一次相见的那天记忆犹新。 **viv·id·ness** *noun* [U]: *the vividness of my dream* 我的梦境的清晰逼真

viv·ip·ar·ous /vɪˈvɪpərəs/ *adj.* (*biology* 生) (of an animal 动物) producing live babies from its body rather than eggs 胎生的 ➲ COMPARE OVIPAROUS, OVOVIVIPAROUS

vivi·sec·tion /ˌvɪvɪˈsekʃn/ *noun* [U] the practice of doing experiments on live animals for medical or scientific research 活体解剖

vivo ➲ IN VIVO

vixen /ˈvɪksn/ *noun* **1** a female FOX (= a wild animal of the dog family) 雌狐 **2** (*old-fashioned*) an unpleasant and bad-tempered woman 泼妇；悍妇；母夜叉

viz. /vɪz/ *adv.* (*formal, especially BrE*) used to introduce a list of things that explain sth more clearly or are given as examples 即；就是 SYN **namely**: *four major colleges of surgery, viz. London, Glasgow, Edinburgh and Dublin* 四所主要的外科学院，即伦敦、格拉斯哥、爱丁堡和都柏林

viz·ier /vɪˈzɪə(r); *NAmE* vɪˈzɪr/ (*also* **wazir**) *noun* an important official in some Muslim countries in the past 维齐尔（旧时某些伊斯兰国家的高官）

VJ /ˈviː dʒeɪ/ *noun* = VIDEO JOCKEY

VLE /ˌviː el ˈiː/ *noun* (*BrE*) the abbreviation for 'virtual learning environment' (a software system for teaching and learning using the Internet) 虚拟学习环境（全写为 virtual learning environment，利用互联网教学的软件系统）

vlei /fleɪ/ *noun* (*SAfrE*) [C, U] an area of low land that is always soft and wet; a shallow natural pool of water 沼泽地；积水洼地；浅湖

ˈV-mail *noun* [U] *NAmE* **ˈV-mail™** = VOICEMAIL : *He insistently calls, texts and leaves V-mail messages.* 他没完没了地打电话，发短信，还在语音信箱里留言。

ˈV-neck *noun* an opening for the neck in a piece of clothing shaped like the letter V; a piece of clothing with a V-neck * V 形领；V 字领；鸡心领；V 形领服装： *a V-neck sweater* 鸡心领套衫 ◇ *a navy V-neck* 一件海军蓝的V形领衣服 ➲ VISUAL VOCAB PAGE V68 ➲ PICTURE AT NECK ▸ **ˈV-necked** *adj.* : *a V-necked sweater* 鸡心领套衫

VOA /ˌviː əʊ ˈeɪ; *NAmE* oʊ/ *abbr.* VOICE OF AMERICA 美国之音（广播电台）

vo·cabu·lary 🔑 /vəˈkæbjələri; *NAmE* -leri/ *noun* [C, U] (*pl.* **-ies**) **1** 🔑 all the words that a person knows or uses （某人掌握或使用的）词汇，词汇量： *to have a* ***wide/limited vocabulary*** 词汇量大 / 有限 ◇ *your* ***active vocabulary*** (= the words that you use) 你的主动词汇 ◇ *your* ***passive vocabulary*** (= the words that you understand but don't use) 你的被动词汇 ◇ *Reading will increase your vocabulary.* 阅读会增加你的词汇量。 ◇ *The word 'failure' is not in his vocabulary* (= for him, failure does not exist). 在他的词典中没有"失败"这个词。 ➲ SYNONYMS AT LANGUAGE ➲ SEE ALSO DEFINING VOCABULARY **2** 🔑 all the words in a particular language （某一语言的）词汇，词汇量： *When did the word 'bungalow' first enter the vocabulary?* * bungalow 一词何时进入（英语）词汇中的？ ➲ SYNONYMS AT LANGUAGE **3** the words that people use when they are talking about a particular subject （某学科中所使用的）词汇： *The word has become part of advertising vocabulary.* 这个单词已经成了广告用语。 ➲ SYNONYMS AT LANGUAGE **4** (*also informal* **vocab** /ˈvəʊkæb; *NAmE* ˈvoʊkæb/) a list of words with their meanings, especially in a book for learning a foreign language （尤指外语教科书中附有释义的）词汇表 ➲ WORDFINDER NOTE AT WORD

vocal /ˈvəʊkl; *NAmE* ˈvoʊkl/ *adj., noun*

■ ***adj.*** **1** [only before noun] connected with the voice 嗓音的；发声的： *vocal music* 声乐 ◇ *the vocal organs* (= the tongue, lips, etc.) 发声器官 ➲ SYNONYMS AT SPOKEN ➲ WORDFINDER NOTE AT SING **2** telling people your opinions or protesting about sth loudly and with confidence 大声表达的；直言不讳的： *He has been very vocal in his criticism of the government's policy.* 他对政府政策的批评一直是直言不讳。 ◇ *The protesters are a small but vocal minority.* 抗议者人数不多但敢于直言。

■ ***noun*** [usually pl.] the part of a piece of music that is sung, rather than played on a musical instrument （乐曲中的）歌唱部分，声乐部分： *backing vocals* 伴唱 ◇ *In this recording Armstrong himself is* ***on vocals.*** 在这个录音中阿姆斯特朗亲自领唱。

ˌvocal ˈcords *noun* [pl.] the thin strips of TISSUE in the throat that are moved by the flow of air to produce the voice 声带

vo·cal·ic /vəʊˈkælɪk; *NAmE* voʊ-/ *adj.* (*phonetics* 语音) relating to or consisting of a vowel or vowels 元音的；元音性的 ➲ COMPARE CONSONANTAL

vo·cal·ist /ˈvəʊkəlɪst; *NAmE* ˈvoʊ-/ *noun* a singer, especially in a pop, rock or JAZZ band （尤指流行音乐、摇滚乐或爵士乐乐队的）歌手，歌唱者： *a* ***lead/guest/backing vocalist*** 领唱 / 特邀 / 伴唱歌手 ➲ COMPARE INSTRUMENTALIST

vo·cal·iza·tion (*BrE also* **-isa·tion**) /ˌvəʊkəlaɪˈzeɪʃn; *NAmE* ˌvoʊkələˈzeɪʃn/ *noun* (*formal*) **1** [C] a word or sound that is produced by the voice 说出的话；嗓音；歌声： *the vocalizations of animals* 动物发出的声音 **2** [U] the process of producing a word or sound with the voice 说话；发声；唱歌；发嗓音

vo·cal·ize (*BrE also* **-ise**) /ˈvəʊkəlaɪz; *NAmE* ˈvoʊ-/ *verb* (*formal*) **1** [T] **~ sth** to use words to express sth 用言语表达 SYN **articulate, express**: *Showing children pictures sometimes helps them to vocalize their ideas.* 让儿童看图画有时有助于他们用言语表达思想。 **2** [I, T] **~ (sth)** to say or sing sounds or words 说（话）；唱（歌）；哼；发声： *Your baby will begin to vocalize long before she can talk.* 你的宝宝在她会说话前很早就要开始咿呀发声了。

V

vo·cal·ly /ˈvəʊkəli; *NAmE* ˈvoʊ-/ *adv.* **1** in a way that uses the voice 用嗓音；口头上：*to communicate vocally* 口头交流 **2** by speaking in a loud and confident way 大声地；直言不讳地：*They protested vocally.* 他们直言不讳地提出了抗议。

vo·ca·tion /vəʊˈkeɪʃn; *NAmE* voʊ-/ *noun* **1** [C] a type of work or way of life that you believe is especially suitable for you（认为特别适合自己的）工作，职业，生活方式 SYN **calling**: *Nursing is not just a job—it's a vocation.* 护理不仅仅是一项工作，而且还是一种职业。◇ *She believes that she has found her true vocation in life.* 她相信自己找到了真正适合自己的生活方式。◇ *You missed your vocation—you should have been an actor.* 你干错行了，你本该当演员。➲ COLLOCATIONS AT JOB **2** [C, U] ~ (**for sth**) a belief that a particular type of work or way of life is especially suitable for you（认为某种工作或生活方式特别适合自己的）信心，使命感：*He has a vocation for teaching.* 他是教书的材料。◇ *She is a doctor with a strong sense of vocation.* 她是一位具有强烈使命感的医生。**3** [C, U] a belief that you have been chosen by God to be a priest or NUN 圣召；神召：*a vocation to the priesthood* 司铎圣召

vo·ca·tion·al /vəʊˈkeɪʃənl; *NAmE* voʊ-/ *adj.* connected with the skills, knowledge, etc. that you need to have in order to do a particular job 职业的；职业技术的；业务知识的：***vocational education/qualifications/training*** 职业教育 / 资格 / 培训

voˈcational school *noun* [C, U] (in the US) a school that teaches skills that are necessary for particular jobs（美国）职业学校，技术学校

voca·tive /ˈvɒkətɪv; *NAmE* ˈvɑːk-/ *noun* (*grammar* 语法) (in some languages 用于某些语言) the form of a noun, a pronoun or an adjective used when talking to a person or thing 呼格；呼格词；呼语 ➲ COMPARE ABLATIVE, ACCUSATIVE, DATIVE, GENITIVE, NOMINATIVE ▶ **voca·tive** *adj.*：*the vocative case* 呼格

vo·cif·er·ous /vəˈsɪfərəs; *NAmE* voʊˈs-/ *adj.* (*formal*) expressing your opinions or feelings in a loud and confident way 大声疾呼的；喧嚣的；大叫大嚷的 SYN **strident**: *vociferous protests* 高声的抗议 ◇ *a vociferous critic of the president's stance* 猛烈批评总统所持态度的人 ▶ **vo·cif·er·ous·ly** *adv.*：*to complain vociferously* 大声地抱怨

vod·cast /ˈvɒdkɑːst; *NAmE* ˈvɑːdkæst/ *noun* a videocast (a PODCAST with video content) 视频播客：*She plans to create a vodcast tour of her studio for the Art at Work month.* 她计划为"工作中的艺术"月活动制作一个介绍她的工作室的视频播客。▶ **vod·cast·ing** *noun* [U]: *Many newspapers are choosing to use podcasting and vodcasting to reach a wider audience.* 多家报纸开始选择利用有声和视频播客以扩大读者群。

V

vodka /ˈvɒdkə; *NAmE* ˈvɑːdkə/ *noun* **1** [U, C] a strong clear alcoholic drink, made from grain, originally from Russia 伏特加（原产于俄国的烈性酒）**2** [C] a glass of vodka 一杯伏特加酒：*I'll have a vodka and lime.* 我要喝一杯来檬伏特加。

voet·stoots /ˈfʊtstʊəts; *NAmE* ˈfʊtstʊts/ *adj., adv.* (*SAfrE*) (*law* 律) (of a sale or purchase) without guarantee; at the buyer's risk （销售或购买）没有担保（的）；由买方承担风险（的）：*They bid 3m rand voetstoots or 5m rand if the property was renovated.* 若房产按现状出售，他们出价 300 万兰特；若对房产进行翻修，他们出价 500 万兰特。

vogue /vəʊg; *NAmE* voʊg/ *noun* [C, usually sing., U] ~ (**for sth**) a fashion for sth 流行；时髦；风行；风尚：*the vogue for child-centred education* 以孩子为中心的教育潮流 ◇ *Black is* ***in vogue*** *again.* 黑色又成了流行色。➲ COLLOCATIONS AT FASHION

voice /vɔɪs/ *noun, verb*

■ *noun*

• **SOUND FROM MOUTH** 口中发出的声音 **1** [C, U] the sound or sounds produced through the mouth by a person speaking or singing 嗓音；说话声；歌唱声：*I could hear voices in the next room.* 我能听到隔壁说话的声音。◇ *to speak* ***in a deep/soft/loud/quiet, etc. voice*** 低沉地说、轻柔地说、大声地说、轻声地说等 ◇ *'I promise,' she said in a* ***small voice*** (= a quiet, shy voice). "我保证。"她小声说。◇ *to* ***raise/lower your voice*** (= to speak louder/more quietly) 提高 / 压低嗓门 ◇ ***Keep your voice down*** (= speak quietly). 说话轻一些。◇ *Don't take that* ***tone of voice*** *with me!* 别用那种腔调和我说话。◇ *Her voice shook with emotion.* 她激动得声音颤抖。◇ *'There you are,' said a voice behind me.* "你来啦。"我身后一个声音说道。◇ *When did his* ***voice break*** (= become deep like a man's)? 他的嗓音什么时候变粗的？◇ *He was suffering from flu and had* ***lost his voice*** (= could not speak). 他患了流感，嗓子哑了。◇ *She has a good singing voice.* 她有一副很好的歌喉。◇ *She was* ***in good voice*** (= singing well) *at the concert tonight.* 她在今晚的音乐会上唱得不错。

• **-VOICED** 嗓音… **2** (in adjectives 构成形容词) having a voice of the type mentioned 有…嗓音的；嗓音…的：*low-voiced* 嗓门低的 ◇ *squeaky-voiced* 嗓音尖细的

• **OPINION** 看法 **3** [sing.] ~ (**in sth**) the right to express your opinion and influence decisions 发言权；发表意见的权利；影响：*Employees should* ***have a voice*** *in the decision-making process.* 雇员在决策的过程中应该有发言权。**4** [C] a particular attitude, opinion or feeling that is expressed; a feeling or an opinion that you become aware of inside yourself 呼声；意见；态度；心声：*He pledged that his party would listen to the voice of the people.* 他保证他的政党愿意倾听人民的呼声。◇ *Very few* ***dissenting voices*** *were heard on the right of the party.* 在党的右翼听不到什么不同的政见。◇ *the* ***voice of reason/sanity/conscience*** 理性的 / 理智的 / 良心的声音 ◇ *'Coward!' a tiny* ***inner voice*** *insisted.* "胆小鬼！"内心一个小声音坚持说。

• **GRAMMAR** 语法 **5** [sing.] **the active/passive ~** the form of a verb that shows whether the subject of a sentence performs the action (*the active voice*) or is affected by it (*the passive voice*) 主动 / 被动语态

• **PHONETICS** 语音学 **6** [U] sound produced by movement of the VOCAL CORDS used in the pronunciation of vowels and some consonants 浊音（声带振动发出的元音和某些辅音）➲ SEE ALSO VOICED, VOICELESS

IDM **give voice to sth** to express your feelings, worries, etc. 表露心声；表白心迹 **make your ˈvoice heard** to express your feelings, opinions, etc. in a way that makes people notice and consider them（为引起他人注意）发表意见，表达感情 **with ˌone ˈvoice** as a group; with everyone agreeing 异口同声；众口一词：*The various opposition parties speak with one voice on this issue.* 在这个问题上各反对党派众口一词。➲ MORE AT FIND *v.*, SOUND *n.*, STILL *adj.*, TOP *n.*

■ *verb*

• **GIVE OPINION** 发表意见 **1** ~ **sth** to tell people your feelings or opinions about sth 表示，表达，吐露（感情或意见）：*to* ***voice complaints/criticisms/doubts/objections, etc.*** 表示不满、批评、怀疑、异议等 ◇ *A number of parents have* ***voiced concern*** *about their children's safety.* 一些家长对他们子女的安全表示了担心。

• **PHONETICS** 语音学 **2** ~ **sth** to produce a sound with a movement of your VOCAL CORDS as well as your breath 发浊音；发嗓音 ➲ COMPARE UNVOICED (2), VOICELESS

ˈvoice box *noun* the area at the top of the throat that contains the VOCAL CORDS 喉 SYN **larynx**

voiced /vɔɪst/ *adj.* (*phonetics* 语音) (of consonants 辅音) produced by moving your VOCAL CORDS. For example, the consonants /b/, /d/ and /g/ are voiced. 浊音性的；带声的 OPP **unvoiced** ➲ WORDFINDER NOTE AT PRONUNCIATION

voice·less /ˈvɔɪsləs/ *adj.* (*phonetics* 语音) (of consonants 辅音) produced without moving your VOCAL CORDS. For example, the consonants /p/, /t/ and /k/ are voiceless. 清音的 SYN **unvoiced** OPP **voiced**

voice·mail /ˈvɔɪsmeɪl/ (*also* **ˈV-mail™**) *noun* [U] an electronic system which can store telephone messages, so that sb can listen to them later 语音信箱；电话留言 ➲ WORDFINDER NOTE AT CALL

the ˌVoice of Aˈmerica *noun* [sing.] (*abbr.* **VOA**) an official US government service that broadcasts news and other programmes in English and many other languages around the world 美国之音（广播电台）

ˈvoice-over *noun* information or comments in a film/movie, television programme, etc. that are given by a person who is not seen on the screen （电影或电视节目的）解说，画外音：*She earns a lot of money doing voice-overs for TV commercials.* 她为电视广告配音收入很高。

voice·print /ˈvɔɪsprɪnt/ *noun* (*specialist*) a printed record of a person's speech, showing the different FREQUENCIES and lengths of sounds as a series of waves 声纹（显示个人说话声音频率和长度的打印记录）

ˈvoice recognition *noun* [U] **1** technology that allows a computer to identify a voice （计算机）声音识别 **2** = SPEECH RECOGNITION

void /vɔɪd/ *noun, adj., verb*

■ ***noun*** [usually sing.] (*formal* or *literary*) a large empty space 空间；空白；真空；空虚：*Below him was nothing but a black void.* 他下面只是一片漆黑。◇ (*figurative*) *The void left by his mother's death was never filled.* 他母亲死后留下的空虚感永远没能填补上。

■ ***adj.*** **1** ~ **of sth** (*formal*) completely lacking sth 缺乏；没有 SYN **devoid**：*The sky was void of stars.* 天空没有一颗星星。 **2** (*law* 律) (of a contract, an agreement etc. 合同、协议等) not valid or legal 无效的：*The agreement was declared void.* 该协议已宣布无效。 **3** (*formal*) empty 空的；空空如也的：*void spaces* 空位 IDM ➤ SEE NULL

■ ***verb*** **1** ~ **sth** (*law* 律) to state officially that sth is no longer valid 使无效；宣布…作废；取消 SYN **invalidate, nullify** **2** ~ **sth** (*formal*) to empty waste matter from the BLADDER or BOWELS 排泄，排放（大小便）

ˈvoid deck *noun* (*SEAsianE*) the ground floor of a block of flats/apartments, which is left empty and is usually for the use of all the people who live in the building 公寓楼大堂（在底层，常为公用）

voile /vɔɪl/ *noun* [U] a type of cloth made of cotton, wool or silk that is almost transparent, used for making clothes 巴里纱（用以制衣的一种棉、毛或丝的近乎透明的织物）

VoIP /vɔɪp/ (*also* **ˌIP teˈlephony**) *noun* [U] the abbreviation for 'voice over Internet protocol' (a telephone system that allows users to make and receive calls using the Internet) * IP 电话，网络电话（全写为 voice over Internet protocol，通过互联网来传送语音的电话系统）

vol. AW *abbr.* VOLUME 卷；册：*the Complete Works of Byron Vol. 2* 《拜伦全集》第 2 卷

vola·tile /ˈvɒlətaɪl; *NAmE* ˈvɑːlətl/ *adj.* **1** (*often disapproving*) (of a person or their moods 人或其情绪) changing easily from one mood to another 易变的；无定性的；无常性的：*a highly volatile personality* 反复无常的个性 **2** (of a situation 情况) likely to change suddenly; easily becoming dangerous 可能急剧波动的；不稳定的；易恶化的 SYN **unstable**：*a highly volatile situation from which riots might develop* 可能会出现动乱的极不稳定的局势 ◇ *a volatile exchange rate* 剧烈波动的汇率 **3** (*specialist*) (of a substance 物质) that changes easily into a gas 易挥发的；易发散的：*Petrol is a volatile substance.* 汽油是挥发性物质。▶ **vola·til·ity** /ˌvɒləˈtɪləti; *NAmE* ˌvɑːl-/ *noun* [U]

vol-au-vent /ˈvɒl ə vɒ̃; *NAmE* ˌvɔːl oʊ ˈvɑ̃ː/ *noun* (*BrE, from French*) a small round case of light PASTRY filled with meat, fish, etc. in a cream sauce, often eaten with your fingers at parties 酥皮馅饼（以肉、鱼等加奶油作馅的小圆千层酥）

vol·can·ic /vɒlˈkænɪk; *NAmE* vɑːl-; vɔːl-/ *adj.* caused or produced by a volcano 火山的；火山引起的；火山产生的：*volcanic rocks* 火山岩 ◇ *volcanic eruptions* 火山喷发 ➲ WORDFINDER NOTE AT LANDSCAPE

vol·cano /vɒlˈkeɪnəʊ; *NAmE* vɑːlˈkeɪnoʊ; vɔːlˈkeɪnoʊ/ *noun* (*pl.* **-oes** or **-os**) a mountain with a large opening at the top through which gases and LAVA (= hot liquid rock) are forced out into the air, or have been in the past 火山：*An active volcano may erupt at any time.* 活火山会随时喷发。◇ *a dormant volcano* (= one that is not active at present) 休眠火山 ◇ *an extinct volcano* (= one that is no longer active) 死火山 ➲ WORDFINDER NOTE AT MOUNTAIN

vol·can·ology /ˌvɒlkəˈnɒlədʒi; *NAmE* ˌvɑːlkəˈnɑːl-; ˌvɔːlkəˈnɑːl-/ (*also* **vul·can·ology**) *noun* [U] the scientific study of volcanoes 火山学

vole /vəʊl; *NAmE* voʊl/ *noun* a small animal like a mouse or RAT that lives in fields or near rivers 田鼠 ➲ SEE ALSO WATER VOLE

vol·ition /vəˈlɪʃn; *NAmE also* voʊˈl-/ *noun* [U] (*formal*) the power to choose sth freely or to make your own decisions 意志力；自愿选择；自行决断 SYN **free will**：*They left entirely **of their own volition*** (= because they wanted to). 他们完全是自愿离开的。

vol·ley /ˈvɒli; *NAmE* ˈvɑːli/ *noun, verb*

■ ***noun*** **1** (in some sports, for example TENNIS or football (SOCCER) 某些体育运动，如网球或足球) a hit or kick of the ball before it touches the ground 截击空中球；凌空击球（或踢球）：*She hit a forehand volley into the net.* 她正手截击球未过网。 **2** a lot of bullets, stones, etc. that are fired or thrown at the same time （子弹的）群射，齐发；（石块的）齐投：*A volley of shots rang out.* 一排子弹呼啸而出。◇ *Police fired a volley over the heads of the crowd.* 警察朝人群头顶上方射出一排子弹。 **3** a lot of questions, comments, insults, etc. that are directed at sb quickly one after the other （质问、评论、辱骂等的）接连发出 SYN **torrent**：*She faced a volley of angry questions from her mother.* 她受到母亲一连串愤怒的质问。

■ ***verb*** [T, I] ~ **(sth)** (in some sports, for example TENNIS or football (SOCCER) 某些体育运动，如网球或足球) to hit or kick the ball before it touches the ground 拦截（空中球）；截击；凌空抽射：*He volleyed the ball into the back of the net.* 他凌空一脚把球踢入网窝。

vol·ley·ball /ˈvɒlibɔːl; *NAmE* ˈvɑːl-; ˈvɔːl-/ *noun* [U] a game in which two teams of six players use their hands to hit a large ball backwards and forwards over a high net while trying not to let the ball touch the ground on their own side 排球运动 ➲ SEE ALSO BEACH VOLLEYBALL

volt /vəʊlt; vɒlt; *NAmE* voʊlt/ *noun* (*abbr.* **V**) a unit for measuring the force of an electric current 伏，伏特（电压单位）：*a high security fence with 5 000 volts passing through it* 通有 5 000 伏电流的森严铁丝网

volt·age /ˈvəʊltɪdʒ; *NAmE* ˈvoʊlt-/ *noun* [U, C] electrical force measured in volts 电压；伏特数：***high/low voltage*** 高压；低压

volte-face /ˌvɒlt ˈfɑːs; *NAmE* ˌvɔːlt/ *noun* [sing.] (*formal*) a complete change of opinion or plan （意见或计划的）大转变，完全转变 SYN **about-turn**：*This represents a volte-face in government thinking.* 这代表着政府观点的彻底转变。

volt·meter /ˈvəʊltmiːtə(r); *NAmE* ˈvoʊlt-/ *noun* an instrument for measuring VOLTAGE 电压表；伏特计

vol·uble /ˈvɒljʊbl; *NAmE* ˈvɑːljə-/ *adj.* (*formal*) **1** talking a lot, and with enthusiasm, about a subject 健谈的；滔滔不绝的：*Evelyn was very voluble on the subject of women's rights.* 伊夫林谈起女权这个话题口若悬河。 **2** expressed in many words and spoken quickly 流利的；明快的：*voluble protests* 振振有词的抗议 ▶ **vol·ubly** /ˈvɒljʊbli; *NAmE* ˈvɑːljə-/ *adv.*

vol·ume 🔑 AW /ˈvɒljuːm; *NAmE* ˈvɑːl-; -jəm/ *noun* **1** 🔑 [U, C] the amount of space that an object or a substance fills; the amount of space that a container has 体积；容积；容量：*How do you measure the volume of a gas?* 你如何计量气体的体积？◇ *jars of different volumes* 不同容量的罐子 **2** 🔑 [U, C] the amount of sth 量；额：*the sheer **volume*** (= large amount) *of business* 大量业务 ◇ *This work has grown in volume recently.* 这项工作的量最近增加了。◇ *New roads are being built to cope with the increased volume of traffic.* 正在修建新的道路以应付增加

V

了的交通量。◇ *Sales volumes fell 0.2% in June.* 六月份的销售额下降了 0.2%。 **3** [U] the amount of sound that is produced by a television, radio, etc. 音量；响度： *to turn the volume up/down* 把音量调大 / 调小 **4** [C] (*abbr.* **vol.**) a book, that is part of a series of books （成套书籍中的）一卷，一册： *an encyclopedia in 20 volumes* 一套 20 卷的百科全书 **5** [C] (*formal*) a book 书： *a library of over 50 000 volumes* 藏书 5 万多册的图书馆 ◇ *a slim volume of poetry* 薄薄的一本诗集 **6** [C] (*abbr.* **vol.**) a series of different issues of the same magazine, especially all the issues for one year 卷，合订本（同一杂志的一系列期刊，尤指一年的）： *'New Scientist' volume 142, number 3* 《新科学家》第 142 卷第 3 期 IDM SEE SPEAK

vo·lu·min·ous /və'lu:mɪnəs/ *adj.* (*formal*) **1** (of clothing 衣服) very large; having a lot of cloth 肥大的；宽松的；用布料多的 SYN **ample**： *a voluminous skirt* 肥大的裙子 **2** (of a piece of writing, a book, etc. 文章、书等) very long and detailed 浩繁的；大部头的；长篇的；冗长的 **3** (of a container, piece of furniture, etc. 容器、家具等) very large 很大的： *I sank down into a voluminous armchair.* 我一下子坐在了宽大的扶手椅里。▶ **vo·lu·min·ous·ly** *adv.*

volu·mize (*BrE also* **-ise**) /'vɒljʊmaɪz; *NAmE* 'vɑ:l-/ *verb* ~ **sth** to make hair look thicker 使（头发）显得浓密；使（头发）丰盈 ▶ **volu·mizer** /'vɒljʊmaɪzə(r); *NAmE* 'vɑ:l-/ *noun*

vol·un·tar·ily AW /'vɒləntrəli; *NAmE* ˌvɑ:lən'terəli/ *adv.* **1** willingly; without being forced 自愿地；自动地；主动地： *He was not asked to leave—he went voluntarily.* 没人让他走，是他主动走的。 **2** without payment; free 无偿地；义务地： *The fund is voluntarily administered.* 这个基金是无偿管理的。

vol·un·tary AW /'vɒləntri; *NAmE* 'vɑ:ləntəri/ *adj., noun*

■ *adj.* **1** done willingly, not because you are forced 自愿的；志愿的；主动的；自告奋勇的： *a voluntary agreement* 自愿协议 ◇ *Attendance on the course is purely voluntary.* 听这门课纯粹是自愿的。◇ *to pay* ***voluntary contributions*** *into a pension fund* 自愿向退休基金交款 ◇ (*BrE*) *He took* ***voluntary redundancy.*** 他选择了自愿裁汰。 OPP **compulsory** **2** [usually before noun] (of work 工作) done by people who choose to do it without being paid 自愿性的；无偿的；义务性的： *I do some* ***voluntary work*** *at the local hospital.* 我在当地医院从事一些义务性工作。◇ *She works there* ***on a voluntary basis.*** 她自愿在那里无偿工作。◇ ***voluntary services/bodies/agencies/organizations*** (= organized, controlled or supported by people who choose to do this and are usually not paid) 义务性服务 / 团体 / 机构 / 组织 ◇ ***the voluntary sector*** (= organizations which are set up to help people and which do not make a profit, for example charities) 非营利机构 ➲ WORDFINDER NOTE AT WORK **3** [only before noun] (of a person 人) doing a job without wanting to be paid for it 自愿的；志愿的；义务的；自发的： *a voluntary worker* 志愿工作者 **4** (*specialist*) (of movements of the body 人体活动) that you can control 随意的；可以控制的 OPP **involuntary**

■ *noun* (*pl.* **-ies**) a piece of music played before, during or after a church service, usually on an organ 仪式终始曲，即兴曲（通常用风琴在教堂礼拜仪式前后或期间演奏）

V

ˌVoluntary ˌService Over'seas *noun* [U] (*abbr.* **VSO**) a British charity that sends skilled people such as doctors and teachers to work in other countries as volunteers 海外志愿者服务社（英国外派医生、教师等技术人士的慈善机构）

vol·un·teer AW /ˌvɒlən'tɪə(r); *NAmE* ˌvɑ:lən'tɪr/ *noun, verb*

■ *noun* **1** a person who does a job without being paid for it 义务工作者；志愿者： *volunteer helpers* 无偿援助者 ◇ *Schools need volunteers to help children to read.* 学校需要义务工作者帮助儿童阅读。 ➲ WORDFINDER NOTE AT CHARITY **2** a person who offers to do sth without being forced to do it 自告奋勇者；主动做某事的人： *Are there any volunteers to help clear up?* 有自愿帮助清扫的人吗？ **3** a person who chooses to join the armed forces without being forced to join 志愿兵；义勇兵 ➲ COMPARE CONSCRIPT *n.*

■ *verb* **1** [I, T] to offer to do sth without being forced to do it or without getting paid for it 自愿做；义务做；无偿做： **~ to do sth** *Jill volunteered to organize a petition.* 吉尔自告奋勇组织请愿。◇ **~ (for/as sth)** *Several staff members volunteered for early retirement.* 几位职员自愿提前退休。◇ **~ sth (for/as sth)** *He volunteered his services as a driver.* 他自愿服务充当司机。 **2** [T] **~ sth | + speech** to suggest sth or tell sb sth without being asked 主动建议（或告诉）： *to volunteer advice* 主动提出忠告 **3** [I] **~ (for sth) | ~ to do sth** to join the army, etc. without being forced to 自愿参军；当志愿兵： *to volunteer for military service* 自愿服兵役 **4** [T] **~ sb (for/as sth) | ~ sb to do sth** to suggest sb for a job or an activity, even though they may not want to do it （未经当事人同意）举荐： *They volunteered me for the job of interpreter.* 他们擅自指定由我担任口头翻译。

the ˌVolunteer Re'serve Forces *noun* [pl.] the parts of the British armed forces for people who are volunteers and train in their free time so they can be used in a national emergency （英国）志愿兵员预备役部队

vol·un·tour·ism /ˌvɒlən'tʊərɪzəm; -'tɔ:r-; *NAmE* ˌvɑ:lən'tʊrɪzəm/ *noun* [U] a form of TOURISM in which travellers work without pay, usually for a charity, in countries they are visiting 公益旅游，义工旅游（旅游者在到访的国家做慈善义务工作） ▶ **vol·un·tour·ist** *noun*

vo·lup·tu·ary /və'lʌptʃuəri; *NAmE* -ueri/ *noun* (*pl.* **-ies**) (*formal, usually disapproving*) a person who enjoys physical, especially sexual, pleasures very much 骄奢淫逸者；纵欲者

vo·lup·tu·ous /və'lʌptʃuəs/ *adj.* **1** (*formal*) (of a woman 女人) attractive in a sexual way with large breasts and hips 体态丰满的；性感的；肉感的 SYN **buxom**： *a voluptuous woman* 体态丰满的女人 ◇ *a voluptuous body* 丰满性感的身体 **2** (*literary*) giving you physical pleasure 令人舒服的；舒适的 SYN **sensual**： *voluptuous perfume* 芬芳馥郁的香水 ▶ **vo·lup·tu·ous·ly** *adv.* **vo·lup·tu·ous·ness** *noun* [U]

vomit /'vɒmɪt; *NAmE* 'vɑ:m-/ *verb, noun*

■ *verb* (*also informal* ˌ**throw** '**up**) [I, T] to bring food from the stomach back out through the mouth 呕；吐；呕吐 SYN **be sick**： *The smell made her want to vomit.* 那气味使得她想要吐。◇ **~ sth up** *He had vomited up his supper.* 他把晚饭吃的东西都吐了出来。 ◇ **~ sth** *The injured man was vomiting blood.* 那受伤的人在吐血。➲ SEE ALSO SICK *v.*

■ *noun* [U] food from the stomach brought back out through the mouth 呕吐物

voo·doo /'vu:du:/ *noun* [U] a religion that is practised especially in Haiti and involves magic and WITCHCRAFT 伏都教，巫毒教（尤指在海地奉行的一种宗教，涉及魔法和巫术）

vor·acious /və'reɪʃəs/ *adj.* (*formal*) **1** eating or wanting large amounts of food 饭量大的；贪吃的；狼吞虎咽的 SYN **greedy**： *a voracious eater* 贪吃的人 ◇ *to have a* ***voracious appetite*** 胃口极大 **2** wanting a lot of new information and knowledge （对信息、知识）渴求的；求知欲强的 SYN **avid**： *a voracious reader* 求知欲极强的读者 ◇ *a boy with a voracious and undiscriminating appetite for facts* 一个如饥似渴地寻求事实的男孩 ▶ **vor·acious·ly** *adv.* **vor·acity** /və'ræsəti/ *noun* [U]

vor·tex /'vɔ:teks; *NAmE* 'vɔ:rt-/ *noun* (*pl.* **vor·texes** or **vor·ti·ces** /-tɪsi:z/) **1** (*specialist*) a mass of air, water, etc. that spins around very fast and pulls things into its centre 低涡；涡旋；旋涡 SYN **whirlpool, whirlwind** **2** (*literary*) a very powerful feeling or situation that you cannot avoid or escape from 感情（或局势）的旋涡： *They were caught up in a whirling vortex of emotion.* 他们陷入了感情旋涡。

vo·tary /'vəʊtəri; *NAmE* 'voʊt-/ *noun* (*pl.* **-ies**) **~ of sb/sth** (*formal*) a person who worships or loves sb/sth 仰慕者；爱好者；信仰者： *a votary of John Keats* 约翰·济慈的崇拜者

vote /vəʊt; *NAmE* voʊt/ *noun, verb*

■ ***noun*** **1** [C] ~ (**for/against sb/sth**) a formal choice that you make in an election or at a meeting in order to choose sb or decide sth 选票；票：*There were 21 votes for and 17 against the motion, with 2 abstentions.* 这项动议有 21 票赞成，17 票反对，2 票弃权。◇ *The motion was passed by 6 votes to 3.* 这项动议以 6 票对 3 票获得通过。◇ *The chairperson has the* ***casting/deciding vote.*** 主席可投决定票。◇ *The Green candidate won over 3 000 of the* ***14 000 votes cast.*** 绿党候选人在 14 000 张投票总数中获得了 3 000 多张选票。➲ WORDFINDER NOTE AT DEBATE **2** [C] ~ (**on sth**) an occasion when a group of people vote on sth 投票；选举；表决：*to* ***have/take a vote*** *on an issue* 就一问题进行表决 ◇ *The issue was* ***put to the vote.*** 这一问题被付诸表决。◇ *The vote was unanimous.* 表决一致通过。➲ SYNONYMS AT ELECTION **3** **the vote** [sing.] the total number of votes in an election 投票总数；选票总数：*She obtained 40% of the vote.* 她获得 40% 的选票。◇ *The party increased their share of the vote.* 这个政党得票份额有所增长。**4** **the vote** [sing.] the vote given by a particular group of people, or for a particular party, etc.（某一群体的）投票总数；（某一政党等的）得票总数：*the student vote* 学生的投票总数 ◇ *the Labour vote* 工党得票总数 **5** **the vote** [sing.] the right to vote, especially in political elections（尤指政治选举中的）投票权，选举权，表决权：*In Britain and the US, people get the vote at 18.* 在英国和美国，国民 18 岁开始有选举权。➲ SEE ALSO BLOCK VOTE ➲ WORDFINDER NOTE AT PARLIAMENT

■ ***verb*** **1** [I, T] to show formally by marking a paper or raising your hand which person you want to win an election, or which plan or idea you support 投票（赞成 / 反对）；表决（支持 / 不支持）；选举：~ (**for/against sb/sth**) *Did you vote for or against her?* 你投了她的赞成票还是反对票？◇ *How did you vote at the last election?* 在上次选举中你是怎么投的票？◇ ~ **in favour of sth** *Over 60% of members voted in favour of* (= for) *the motion.* * 60% 以上的成员对这一动议投了赞成票。◇ ~ (**on sth**) *We'll listen to the arguments on both sides and then vote on it.* 我们将先听取双方的论点，然后再表决。◇ *Only about half of the electorate bothered to vote.* 只有约半数的选民参加了投票。◇ ~ **sth** *We voted Democrat in the last election.* 我们在上次选举中投了民主党的票。◇ ~ **to do sth** *Parliament voted to set up an independent inquiry into the matter.* 议会表决对这个问题进行独立调查。➲ COLLOCATIONS AT POLITICS **2** [T, usually passive] ~ **sb/sth + noun** to choose sb/sth for a position or an award by voting 选出，推举（某人担任某职）；表决（授奖给某人）：*He was voted most promising new director.* 他当选为最有前途的新导演。**3** [T, usually passive] ~ **sth + noun** to say that sth is good or bad 表明，认为，公认（某事好或坏）：*The event was voted a great success.* 大家认为这项活动很成功。**4** [T] ~ **sb/yourself sth** to agree to give sb/yourself sth by voting 投票同意：*The directors have just voted themselves a huge pay increase.* 董事们刚刚投票同意给他们自己大幅度提高工资。**5** [T] ~ (**that**)... to suggest sth or support a suggestion that sb has made 提议；建议；支持（建议）：*I vote (that) we go out to eat.* 我提议我们到外面去吃饭。

IDM **ˌvote with your ˈfeet** to show what you think about sth by going or not going somewhere 用脚投票（用去或不去某处表示想法）：*Shoppers voted with their feet and avoided the store.* 购物者对那家商店避而远之。

PHR V **ˌvote sb/sth↔ˈdown** to reject or defeat sb/sth by voting for sb/sth else 投票否决；投票击败 **ˌvote sb ˈin** | **ˌvote sb ˈinto/ˈonto sth** to choose sb for a position by voting 投票选出…任职：*He was voted in as treasurer.* 他当选为司库。◇ *She was voted onto the board of governors.* 她获选入董事会。**ˌvote sb ˈout** | **ˌvote sb ˈout of/ˈoff sth** to dismiss sb from a position by voting 投票免去…的职务：*He was voted out of office.* 经投票他被免去了职务。**ˌvote sth↔ˈthrough** to bring a plan, etc. into effect by voting for it 投票通过（计划等）：*A proposal to merge the two companies was voted through yesterday.* 两家公司合并的建议已于昨日投票通过。

ˌvote of ˈconfidence *noun* [usually sing.] a formal vote to show that people support a leader, a political party, an idea, etc.（表示支持领导人、政党、看法等的）信任票

▼ COLLOCATIONS 词语搭配

Voting in elections 在选举中投票

Running for election 参加选举

- **conduct/hold** an election/a referendum 举行选举 / 全民公决
- (*especially NAmE*) **run for** office/election/governor/mayor/president/the White House 竞选公职；参加竞选；竞选州长 / 市长 / 总统 / 美国总统
- (*especially BrE*) **stand for** election/office/Parliament/the Labour Party/a second term 参加竞选；竞选公职 / 议会议员；当工党候选人；竞选连任
- **hold/call/contest** a general/national election 举行 / 要求 / 角逐大选 / 全国选举
- **launch/run** a presidential election campaign 开始总统竞选活动
- **support/back** a candidate 支持候选人
- **sway/convince/persuade** voters/the electorate 说服选民 / 全体选民
- **appeal to/attract/woo/target** (*NAmE*) swing voters/(*BrE*) floating voters 吸引游离选民；寻求游离选民的支持；瞄准游离选民
- **fix/rig/steal** an election/the vote 操纵选举；暗中舞弊获取选票

Voting 投票

- **go to/be turned away from** (*especially BrE*) a polling station/(*NAmE*) a polling place 去 / 被拒绝进入投票站投票
- **cast** a/your vote/ballot (for sb) 投（某人）一票
- **vote for** the Conservative candidate/the Democratic party 投票给保守党候选人 / 民主党
- **mark/spoil** your ballot paper 在选票上做标记；投废票
- **count** (*BrE*) the postal votes/(*especially NAmE*) the absentee ballots 清点邮寄选票数
- **go to/be defeated at** the ballot box 去投票箱投票；竞选失败
- **get/win/receive/lose** votes 赢得 / 失去选票
- **get/win** (60% of) the popular/black/Hispanic/Latino/Muslim vote 赢得大众 / 黑人 / 拉美裔 / 穆斯林 (60%) 的选票
- **win** the election/(*in the US*) the primaries/a seat in Parliament/a majority/power 赢得大选 /（美国的）初选 / 议会中的一个席位 / 多数票 / 权力
- **lose** an election/the vote/your majority/your seat 在选举中失败；失去多数人的支持 / 席位
- **win/come to power in** a landslide (victory) (= with many more votes than any other party) 以压倒多数的选票获胜 / 掌权
- **elect/re-elect sb** (**as**) mayor/president/an MP/senator/congressman/congresswoman 选举 / 再度选举某人为市长 / 总统 / 议员 / 参议员 / 国会议员 / 国会女议员

Taking power 掌权

- **be sworn** into office/in as president 宣誓就职 / 就任总统
- **take/administer** (*in the US*) the oath of office （美国）宣誓就职；听取就职宣誓
- **swear/take** (*in the UK*) an/the oath of allegiance （英国）宣誓效忠
- **give/deliver** (*in the US*) the president's inaugural address 发表（美国）总统就职演说
- **take/enter/hold/leave** office 就职；任职；离职
- **appoint sb** (**as**) ambassador/governor/judge/minister 任命某人为大使 / 州长 / 法官 / 部长
- **form** a government/a cabinet 组建政府 / 内阁
- **serve** two terms as prime minister/in office 任两届总理；两届任职

➲ COLLOCATIONS AT ECONOMY, POLITICS

V

ˌvote of ˌno ˈconfidence *noun* [usually sing.] a formal vote to show that people do not support a leader, a political party, an idea, etc. （表示不支持领导人、政党、看法等的）不信任票

ˌvote of ˈthanks *noun* [usually sing.] a short formal speech in which you thank sb for sth and ask other people to join you in thanking them 谢辞

voter /ˈvəʊtə(r); *NAmE* ˈvoʊ-/ *noun* a person who votes or has the right to vote, especially in a political election （尤指政治性选举的）投票人，选举人，有选举权的人： *A clear majority of voters were in favour of the motion.* 绝大多数选民赞成这一动议。◇ *Only 60% of eligible voters actually used their vote.* 只有 60% 的符合资格的选民行使了选举权。 ➲COLLOCATIONS AT VOTE ➲SEE ALSO FLOATING VOTER, SWING VOTER

vot·ing /ˈvəʊtɪŋ; *NAmE* ˈvoʊ-/ *noun* [U] the action of choosing sb/sth in an election or at a meeting 投票；选举；表决： *He was eliminated in the first round of voting.* 他在第一轮投票中被淘汰。 ◇ *Voting will take place on May 1.* 投票将于 5 月 1 日进行。◇ *tactical voting* 有策略的投票 ◇ *to be of voting age* 到了选举年龄

ˈvoting booth *noun* (*especially NAmE*) = POLLING BOOTH

ˈvoting machine *noun* a machine in which votes can be recorded automatically, used, for example, in the US 选票计算器；投票记录机；计票机

vo·tive /ˈvəʊtɪv; *NAmE* ˈvoʊ-/ *adj.* [usually before noun] (*specialist*) presented to a god as a sign of thanks （向上帝）还愿的，表示谢恩的： *votive offerings* 还愿奉献物

vouch /vaʊtʃ/ *verb*

PHR V **ˈvouch for sb/sth** (*formal*) to say that you believe that sb will behave well and that you will be responsible for their actions 替…担保（或保证）： *Are you willing to vouch for him?* 你愿意为他担保吗？ ◇ *I can vouch for her ability to work hard.* 我保证她能够努力工作。 **ˈvouch for sth** (*formal*) to say that you believe that sth is true or good because you have evidence for it （因有证据而）为…作证 SYN **confirm**： *I was in bed with the flu. My wife can vouch for that.* 我患流感卧床休息了。我的妻子可为此作证。

vouch·er /ˈvaʊtʃə(r)/ *noun* a printed piece of paper that can be used instead of money to pay for sth, or that allows you to pay less than the usual price of sth 代币券；票券： *a voucher for a free meal* 免费用餐券 ◇ *a travel voucher* 旅游券 ◇ *This discount voucher entitles you to 10% off your next purchase.* 凭这张优惠券你下次购物可打九折。 ➲ SEE ALSO LUNCHEON VOUCHER ➲WORDFINDER NOTE AT BUY

V

vouch·safe /ˌvaʊtʃˈseɪf/ *verb* **~ sth (to sb) | ~ sb sth | ~ that… | + speech** (*old-fashioned* or *formal*) to give, offer or tell sth to sb, especially in order to give them a special advantage 赐予，给予，告知（尤指为给特别的好处）： *He vouchsafed to me certain family secrets.* 他让我知道了某些家庭秘密。

vow /vaʊ/ *noun, verb*

■*noun* a formal and serious promise, especially a religious one, to do sth （尤指宗教的）誓，誓言，誓约： *to **make/take a vow*** 立誓；发誓 ◇ *to **break/keep a vow*** 违反／履行誓约 ◇ *to break your **marriage vows*** 背弃婚姻誓约 ◇ *Nuns take **a vow of** chastity.* 修女矢发贞洁愿。 ➲COLLOCATIONS AT MARRIAGE

■*verb* to make a formal and serious promise to do sth or a formal statement that is true 起誓；立誓；发誓： **~ to do sth** *She vowed never to speak to him again.* 她发誓再也不和他说话了。◇ **~ (that)…** *He vowed (that) he had not hurt her.* 他起誓他没有伤害过她。 ◇ **~ sth** *They vowed eternal friendship.* 他们立誓要友谊长存。◇ **+ speech** *'I'll be back,' she vowed.* "我会回来的。"她发誓道。

vowel /ˈvaʊəl/ *noun* (*phonetics* 语音) **1** a speech sound in which the mouth is open and the tongue is not touching the top of the mouth, the teeth, etc., for example /ɑː, e, ɔː/ 元音： *vowel sounds* 元音 ◇ *Each language has a different vowel system.* 每种语言都有不同的元音系统。 **2** a letter that represents a vowel sound. In English the vowels are a, e, i, o and u. 元音字母 ➲COMPARE CONSONANT *n.* (1) ➲SEE ALSO DIPHTHONG

vox pop /ˌvɒks ˈpɒp; *NAmE* ˌvɑːks ˈpɑːp/ *noun* [C, U] (*BrE, informal*) the opinion of members of the public, especially when it is broadcast or published （尤指广播或发表的）公众舆论

voy·age /ˈvɔɪɪdʒ/ *noun, verb*

■*noun* a long journey, especially by sea or in space 航行；（尤指）航海，航天： *an around-the-world voyage* 环球航行 ◇ *a voyage in space* 航天 ◇ *The Titanic sank on its **maiden voyage*** (= first journey). 泰坦尼克号首航便沉没了。◇ (*figurative*) *Going to college can be a voyage of self-discovery.* 上大学可以算作自我发现之行。 ➲WORDFINDER NOTE AT EXPLORE

■*verb* [I] **+ adv./prep.** (*literary*) to travel, especially in a ship and over a long distance 航行；远行；（尤指）远航

voy·ager /ˈvɔɪɪdʒə(r)/ *noun* (*old-fashioned* or *literary*) a person who goes on a long journey, especially by ship to unknown parts of the world 航行者；远行者；（尤指）远航探险者

voy·eur /vwaɪˈɜː(r); vɔɪˈɜː(r)/ *noun* (*disapproving*) **1** a person who gets pleasure from secretly watching people who are naked or having sex 窥阴癖者（喜欢偷窥他人裸体或性交） **2** a person who enjoys watching the problems and private lives of others 刺探隐秘者（喜欢刺探他人的问题或私生活） ▶ **voy·eur·ism** /vwaɪˈɜːrɪzəm; vɔɪˈɜː-/ *noun* [U] **voy·eur·is·tic** /ˌvwaɪəˈrɪstɪk; ˌvɔɪəˈr-/ *adj.*： *a voyeuristic interest in other people's lives* 对他人生活怀有窥秘癖的兴趣

VP /ˌviː ˈpiː/ *abbr.* VICE-PRESIDENT 副总统；副总裁

vroom /vruːm/ *noun* [U] used to represent the loud sound made by a vehicle moving very fast （车辆高速行驶时发出的）呜的一声： *Vroom! A sports car roared past.* 呜的一声，一辆跑车疾驶而过。 ➲MORE LIKE THIS 3, page R25

vs *abbr.* (*especially NAmE*) (in writing 书写形式) VERSUS （体育运动）对，对阵；（法律案件）诉；与…相比

ˈV-sign *noun* a sign that you make by holding up your hand and making a V-shape with your first and second fingers. When the PALM (= inside part) of your hand is facing away from you, the sign means 'victory'; when the palm is facing towards you the sign is used as a way of being rude to other people. * V 字形手势（手心向外表示胜利，手心向内表示侮辱） ➲COMPARE TWO FINGERS

VSO /ˌviː es ˈəʊ; *NAmE* ˈoʊ/ *abbr.* VOLUNTARY SERVICE OVERSEAS 海外志愿者服务社（英国外派专业人员的慈善机构）

VTOL /ˌviː tiː əʊ ˈel; *NAmE* oʊ/ *abbr.* vertical take-off and landing (used to refer to an aircraft that can take off and land by going straight up or straight down) （飞机）垂直起落

vul·can·ized (*BrE also* **-ised**) /ˈvʌlkənaɪzd/ *adj.* (*specialist*) (of rubber 橡胶) treated with SULPHUR at great heat to make it stronger 硫化的

vul·can·ology /ˌvʌlkəˈnɒlədʒi; *NAmE* -ˈnɑːl-/ *noun* [U] = VOLCANOLOGY

vul·gar /ˈvʌlgə(r)/ *adj.* **1** not having or showing good taste; not polite, elegant or well behaved 庸俗的；粗俗的；粗野的；不雅的 SYN **coarse, in bad taste**： *a vulgar man* 粗俗的男人 ◇ *vulgar decorations* 俗里俗气的装饰 ◇ *She found their laughter and noisy games coarse and rather vulgar.* 她觉得他们的笑声和吵吵闹闹的游戏趣味低下，俗不可耐。 **2** rude and likely to offend 粗野的；粗鲁的；下流的 SYN **crude**： *vulgar jokes* 低俗的笑话 ▶ **vul·gar·ly** *adv.*： *He eyed her vulgarly.* 他色迷迷地瞅着她。

ˌvulgar ˈfraction *noun* (*BrE*) a FRACTION (= a number less than one) that is shown as numbers above and below a line 普通分数： *¾ and ⅝ are vulgar fractions.* * ¾ 和 ⅝ 均为普通分数。 ➲COMPARE DECIMAL FRACTION at DECIMAL *n.*

vul·gar·ian /vʌl'geəriən; *NAmE* -'ger-/ *noun* (*formal*) a person who does not have polite manners or good taste 粗俗的人；庸俗的人

vul·gar·ism /'vʌlgərɪzəm/ *noun* (*formal*) a rude word or expression, especially one relating to sex（尤指与性有关的）粗鄙词语

vul·gar·ity /vʌl'gærəti/ *noun* [U, C] the fact of being rude or not having good taste; a rude object, picture, etc. 庸俗；粗野；下流；庸俗的物品（或图画等）：*She was offended by the vulgarity of their jokes.* 他们那些粗俗的笑话使她大为不快。◇ *a pornographic magazine full of vulgarities* 充满下流图片的色情杂志

vul·gar·ize (*BrE also* **-ise**) /'vʌlgəraɪz/ *verb* ~ **sth** (*formal, disapproving*) to spoil sth by changing it so that it is more ordinary than before and not of such a high standard 使庸俗化；使通俗化 ▶ **vul·gar·iza·tion**, **-isa·tion** /ˌvʌlgəraɪ'zeɪʃn; *NAmE* -rə'z-/ *noun* [U]

ˌvulgar 'Latin *noun* [U] the spoken form of Latin which was used in the western part of the Roman Empire 民间拉丁语（罗马帝国西部使用的拉丁口语）

the Vul·gate /'vʌlgeɪt; -gət/ *noun* [sing.] the main Latin version of the Bible prepared in the late 4th century《圣经》通俗拉丁文本（完成于 4 世纪后期）

vul·ner·able /'vʌlnərəbl/ *adj.* ~ (**to sb/sth**) weak and easily hurt physically or emotionally（身体上或感情上）脆弱的，易受…伤害的：*to be vulnerable to attack* 易受攻击 ◇ *She looked very vulnerable standing there on her own.* 她独自站在那里，看上去弱不禁风。◇ *In cases of food poisoning, young children are especially vulnerable.* 遇到食物中毒，幼儿尤其容易受危害。◇ *The sudden resignation of the financial director put the company in a very vulnerable position.* 财务部主任的突然辞职使得这家公司岌岌可危。▶ **vul·ner·abil·ity** /ˌvʌlnərə'bɪləti/ *noun* [U]: ~ (**of sb/sth**) (**to sth**) *financial vulnerability* 在财政上易受打击 ◇ *the vulnerability of newborn babies to disease* 新生婴儿容易患病 **vul·ner·ably** /-əbli/ *adv.*

vul·pine /'vʌlpaɪn/ *adj.* (*formal*) of or like a FOX 狐狸的；狐狸似的；狡猾的

vul·ture /'vʌltʃə(r)/ *noun* **1** a large bird, usually without feathers on its head or neck, that eats the flesh of animals that are already dead 兀鹫；秃鹫：*vultures circling/wheeling overhead* 在头顶上空盘旋的兀鹫 ➲ VISUAL VOCAB PAGE V12 **2** a person who hopes to gain from the troubles or sufferings of other people 乘人之危的人；趁火打劫的人

vulva /'vʌlvə/ *noun* (*anatomy* 解) the outer opening of the female sex organs 外阴；女阴

vuvu·zela™ /ˌvuːvuː'zeɪlə/ *noun* (*SAfrE*) a long plastic instrument in the shape of a TRUMPET, that makes a very loud noise when you blow it and is popular with football fans in South Africa 呜呜祖拉，巫巫兹拉（南非足球迷使用的塑料长喇叭）

vying PRES. PART. OF VIE

Ww

W /ˈdʌbljuː/ *noun, abbr.*

■ ***noun*** (*also* **w**) [C, U] (*pl.* **Ws, W's, w's** /ˈdʌbljuːz/) the 23rd letter of the English alphabet 英语字母表的第 23 个字母：*'Water' begins with (a) W/'W'.* * water 一词以字母 w 开头。

■ ***abbr.*** **1** west; western 西方（的）；西部（的）**2** WATT 瓦；瓦特：*a 100W light bulb* * 100 瓦的电灯泡

W-2 form /ˌdʌbljuː ˈtuː fɔːm; *NAmE* fɔːrm/ *noun* (in the US) an official document that an employer gives to an employee that shows the amount of pay and tax for the year（美国雇主发给雇员的）全年薪资和纳税表

wack /wæk/ *adj.* (*informal, especially US*) **1** very bad; not of good quality 很差的；劣质的：*That movie was really wack.* 那部电影糟透了。**2** very strange 很奇怪的；怪异的

wacko /ˈwækəʊ; *NAmE* -koʊ/ *adj., noun* (*informal*)

■ ***adj.*** crazy; not sensible 古怪的；发疯的；不理智的：*wacko opinions* 古怪的看法

■ ***noun*** (*pl.* **-os** or **-oes**) (*especially NAmE*) a crazy person 疯子

wacky (*also* **whacky**) /ˈwæki/ *adj.* (**wack·ier, wacki·est**) (*informal*) funny or amusing in a slightly crazy way 古怪的；滑稽可笑的；疯疯癫癫的 **SYN** **zany**：*wacky ideas* 滑稽可笑的想法 ◇ *Some of his friends are pretty **wild and wacky** characters.* 他的一些朋友是那种放荡不羁又怪里怪气的人。

wad /wɒd; *NAmE* wɑːd/ *noun, verb*

■ ***noun*** **1** a thick pile of pieces of paper, paper money, etc. folded or rolled together（纸张、钞票等的）卷，沓，捆：*He pulled a thick wad of £10 notes out of his pocket.* 他从衣袋里掏出厚厚的一沓面额 10 英镑的钞票。◇ (*BrE, slang*) *They had a wad/wads of money* (= a large amount). 他们有大把大把的钱。**2** a mass of soft material, used for blocking sth or keeping sth in place 用以填塞（或填衬等）的软材料；填料；填絮；衬料：*The nurse used a wad of cotton wool to stop the bleeding.* 护士用了一团脱脂棉止血。

■ ***verb*** (**-dd-**) **1 ~ sth (up)** (*especially NAmE*) to fold or press sth into a tight wad 将…揉成团；使成沓；使成卷 **2 ~ sth** to fill sth with soft material for warmth or protection（用柔软的材料）填塞，填充，衬垫

wad·ding /ˈwɒdɪŋ; *NAmE* ˈwɑːdɪŋ/ *noun* [U] soft material that you wrap around things to protect them（柔软的）填料，填絮，衬垫

wad·dle /ˈwɒdl; *NAmE* ˈwɑːdl/ *verb* [I] (**+ adv./prep.**) to walk with short steps, swinging from side to side, like a DUCK（鸭子似的）蹒跚行走，摇摆地行走 ▸ **wad·dle** *noun* [sing.]：*She walked with a waddle.* 她走起路来步履蹒跚。

W

wade /weɪd/ *verb* **1** [I, T] to walk with an effort through sth, especially water or mud 跋涉，涉，蹚（水或淤泥等）：(**+ adv./prep.**) *He waded into the water to push the boat out.* 他蹚进水里把船推出来。◇ *Sometimes they had to wade waist-deep through mud.* 有时他们得通过齐腰深的泥浆。◇ **~ sth** *They waded the river at a shallow point.* 他们在水浅处蹚过河。**2** (*NAmE*) (*BrE* **pad·dle**) [I] to walk or stand with no shoes or socks in shallow water in the sea, a lake, etc. 蹚水；赤足涉水

PHR V **ˌwade ˈin | ˌwade ˈinto sth** (*informal*) to enter a fight, a discussion or an argument in an aggressive or not very sensitive way 强行加入，介入，插手（打架、讨论、争论等）：*The police waded into the crowd with batons.* 警察挥舞着警棍冲入人群。◇ *You shouldn't have waded in with all those unpleasant accusations.* 你本不该插一杠子，横加指责，让人难受。**ˌwade ˈinto sb** (*informal*) to attack sb with words in an angry aggressive way 抨击 **ˌwade ˈthrough sth** [no passive] to deal with or read sth that is boring and takes a lot of time 艰难地处理；费力地阅读：*I spent the whole day wading through the paperwork on my desk.* 我一整天都在伏案处理文件。

wader /ˈweɪdə(r)/ *noun* **1** (*also* **ˈwading bird**) [C] any of several different types of bird with long legs that feed in shallow water 涉禽；涉水鸟 **2 waders** [pl.] long rubber boots that reach up to your THIGH, that you wear for standing in water, especially when fishing（涉水捕鱼等穿的）高筒防水胶靴：*a pair of waders* 一双高筒防水胶靴

wadi /ˈwɒdi; *NAmE* ˈwɑːdi/ *noun* (in the Middle East and N Africa) a valley or channel that is dry except when it rains（中东和北非仅在雨后才有水的）干谷，干河谷

ˈwading pool (*NAmE*) (*BrE* **ˈpaddling pool**) *noun* a shallow swimming pool for children to play in, especially a small plastic one that you fill with water（尤指小型的塑料）浅水池，嬉水池

wafer /ˈweɪfə(r)/ *noun* **1** a thin crisp light biscuit/cookie, often eaten with ice cream 威化饼，薄脆饼（常与冰淇淋同吃）**2** a very thin round piece of special bread given by the priest during COMMUNION 圣饼；圣体；面饼 **3 ~ (of sth)** a very thin piece of sth 薄片

ˌwafer-ˈthin *adj.* very thin 很薄的 ➲ COMPARE PAPER-THIN

waf·fle /ˈwɒfl; *NAmE* ˈwɑːfl; ˈwɔːfl/ *noun, verb*

■ ***noun*** **1** [C] a crisp flat cake with a pattern of squares on both sides, often eaten with sweet sauce, cream, etc. on top 华夫饼，蛋奶烘饼（两面有方块图案，常涂以糖浆、奶油等）：*a waffle iron* (= for making waffles with) 蛋奶烘饼烤模 **2** [U] (*BrE, informal*) language that uses a lot of words but does not say anything important or interesting 胡扯；废话连篇：*The report is just full of waffle.* 这份报告只是一大堆废话。

■ ***verb*** **1** [I] **~ (on) (about sth)** (*BrE, informal, disapproving*) to talk or write using a lot of words but without saying anything interesting or important 胡扯；耍贫嘴；絮叨；胡写：*The principal waffled on about exam results but no one was listening.* 校长絮絮叨叨地谈着考试结果，但是谁也没有听进去。**2** [I] **~ (on/over sth)** (*NAmE, informal*) to be unable to decide what to do about sth or what you think about sth 拿不定主意；三心二意：*The senator was accused of waffling on major issues.* 人们指责参议员在主要问题上立场模糊。

waft /wɒft; *NAmE* wɑːft; wæft/ *verb, noun*

■ ***verb*** [I, T] to move, or make sth move, gently through the air（随风）飘荡；使飘荡；吹拂 **SYN** **drift**：**+ adv./prep.** *The sound of their voices wafted across the lake.* 他们的声音飘过湖面传到了另一边。◇ *Delicious smells wafted up from the kitchen.* 香喷喷的味道从厨房飘了出来。◇ **~ sth + adv./prep.** *The scent of the flowers was wafted along by the breeze.* 微风传花香。

■ ***noun*** (*formal*) a smell or a line of smoke carried through the air 一阵，一股（在空气中飘荡的味或烟）：*wafts of perfume/smoke* 阵阵香气；缕缕青烟

Wag /wæg/ *noun* (*BrE, informal*) one of a group of 'wives and girlfriends' of famous men, especially members of a sports team（名人的，尤指运动队明星的）妻子女友团成员：*Wags at the World Cup* 世界杯足球赛中的太太女友团

wag /wæg/ *verb, noun*

■ ***verb*** (**-gg-**) **1** [T, I] **~ (sth)** if a dog **wags** its tail, or its tail **wags**, its tail moves from side to side several times （狗）摇，摆动（尾巴）；（狗尾巴）摇，摆动 **2** [T] **~ sth** to shake your finger or your head from side to side or up and down, often as a sign of disapproval 摆动，摇（头或手指，常表示不赞成）**3** [T] **~ sth** (*AustralE, NZE*) to stay away from school without permission 逃学：*to wag school* 逃学 **IDM** SEE TAIL *n.*, TONGUE *n.*

■ ***noun*** **1** (*old-fashioned, especially BrE*) a person who enjoys making jokes 老开玩笑的人；爱闹着玩的人 **SYN** **joker** **2** a wagging movement 摇摆；摆动

wage 🔑 /weɪdʒ/ *noun, verb*

■ ***noun*** 🔑 [sing.] (*also* **wages** [pl.]) a regular amount of money that you earn, usually every week, for work or services（通常指按周领的）工资，工钱：*wages of £200 a week* 一星期 200 英镑的工资 ◇ *a **weekly wage** of £200* 周薪 200英镑 ◇ ***wage cuts*** 减薪 ◇ *a **wage increase** of 3%* * 3% 的加薪 ◇ (*BrE*) *a **wage rise** of 3%* * 3% 的加薪 ◇ ***wage demands/claims/settlements*** 工资要求；工资和解协议 ◇ *Wages are paid on Fridays.* 每星期五发工资。◇ *There are* extra benefits for people on **low wages**. 低薪者有额外补助。◇ *The staff have agreed to a voluntary* **wage freeze** (= a situation in which wages are not increased for a time). 全体员工已经同意自愿冻结工资。➲ SYNONYMS AT INCOME ➲ WORDFINDER NOTE AT PAY ➲ COLLOCATIONS AT FINANCE ➲ COMPARE SALARY ➲ SEE ALSO LIVING WAGE, MINIMUM WAGE

■ *verb* to begin and continue a war, a battle, etc. 开始，发动，进行，继续（战争、战斗等）：**~ sth** *The rebels have waged a guerrilla war since 2007.* 叛乱分子自 2007 年以来一直在进行游击战。◇ **~ sth against/on sb/sth** *He alleged that a press campaign was being waged against him.* 他声称有人正在对他发起新闻攻势。

waged /weɪdʒd/ *adj.* **1** (of a person 人) having regular paid work 领工资的；有定期付酬工作的：*waged workers* 有固定工作者 **2** (of work 工作) for which you are paid 支取工资的；带薪的：*waged employment* 有酬雇用 **3 the waged** *noun* [pl.] people who have regular paid work 工薪族；（统称）拿工资的人 OPP **unwaged**

'wage earner *noun* a person who earns money, especially a person who works for wages 挣钱的人；挣工资的人：*We have two wage earners in the family.* 我们家有两个人挣钱。

'wage packet *noun* (*BrE*) = PAY PACKET

wager /ˈweɪdʒə(r)/ *noun, verb*

■ *noun* (*old-fashioned* or *formal*) an arrangement to risk money on the result of a particular event 打赌 SYN **bet**

■ *verb* (*old-fashioned* or *formal*) **1** [I, T] to bet money 打赌；押（赌注）SYN **bet**：**~ on sth** *She always wagered on an outsider.* 她总是把赌注押在不大可能获胜的马上。◇ **~ sth (on sth)** *to wager £50 on a horse* 在一匹马上押 50 英镑的赌注 ◇ **~ sth/sb that…** *I had wagered a great deal of money that I would beat him.* 我下了大赌注打赌，这次比赛我会赢他的。**2** [T] **~ (that)…** used to say that you are so confident that sth is true or will happen that you would be willing to bet money on it 打赌；打包票 SYN **bet**：*I'll wager that she knows more about it than she's saying.* 我敢打赌，她知道的比她说的要多。

wag·gish /ˈwæɡɪʃ/ *adj.* (*old-fashioned*) funny, clever and not serious 诙谐的；打趣的：*waggish remarks* 俏皮话

wag·gle /ˈwæɡl/ *verb* [T, I] **~ (sth)** (*informal*) to make sth move with short movements from side to side or up and down; to move in this way（使）上下移动，来回摆动：*Can you waggle your ears?* 你能让耳朵来回动吗？
▸ **wag·gle** *noun*

Wag·ner·ian /vɑːɡˈnɪəriən; *NAmE* -ˈnɪr-/ *adj.* **1** related to the music of the German COMPOSER Richard Wagner; typical of this music 瓦格纳乐曲的，瓦格纳作品风格的（指德国作曲家理查德·瓦格纳）**2** (*humorous*) very big or great, or in a style that is too serious or exaggerated 巨大的；极大的；过于严肃（或夸张）的：*a hangover of Wagnerian proportions* 强烈的宿醉反应

wagon /ˈwæɡən/ *noun* **1** (*BrE*) (*NAmE* **'freight car**) a railway/railroad truck for carrying goods（铁路）货车车厢，车皮 **2** (*BrE also* **wag·gon**) a vehicle with four wheels, pulled by horses or OXEN and used for carrying heavy loads 四轮载重马车（或牛车）**3** (*also* **cart**) (*both NAmE*) (*BrE* **trol·ley**) a small table on very small wheels, used for carrying or serving food or drink（运或送食品、饮料的）小推车，台车 ➲ SEE ALSO BANDWAGON, STATION WAGON

IDM **be/go on the 'wagon** (*informal*) to not drink alcohol, either for a short time or permanently（短期或永久地）不喝酒，戒酒，滴酒不沾

wag·on·load /ˈwæɡənləʊd; *NAmE* -loʊd/ *noun* an amount of goods carried on a wagon 货车车厢载荷；马车载荷

'wagon train *noun* a long line of WAGONS and horses, used by people travelling west in N America in the 19th century（19 世纪美国人向西部迁移的）马拉篷车队

wag·tail /ˈwæɡteɪl/ *noun* a small bird with a long tail that moves up and down when the bird is walking 鹡鸰（走动时长尾上下摆动）

wah-wah /ˈwɑː wɑː/ *noun* [U] (*music* 音) a special effect made on electric musical instruments, especially the GUITAR, which varies the quality of the sound（尤指吉他等电子乐器发出的）哇音；"哇哇"音响效果

waif /weɪf/ *noun* a small thin person, usually a child, who looks as if they do not have enough to eat 瘦小的人；（通常指）面黄肌瘦的小孩：*the* ***waifs and strays*** *of our society* (= people with no home) 我们社会的弃儿
▸ **'waif-like** *adj.*：*waif-like young girls* 面黄肌瘦的女孩子

wail /weɪl/ *verb, noun*

■ *verb* **1** [I] to make a long loud high cry because you are sad or in pain（因悲伤或疼痛）哭号，恸哭：*The little girl was wailing miserably.* 那小女孩难过得号啕大哭。◇ *women wailing and weeping* 痛哭流涕的妇女 **2** [T, I] to cry or complain about sth in a loud high voice 大声呼叫；哀号；高声抱怨 SYN **moan**：**+ speech** *'It's broken,' she wailed.* "打碎了。"她大声叫道。◇ **~ (about sth)** *There's no point wailing about something that happened so long ago.* 事情早已发生，痛哭流涕也于事无补。**3** [I] (of things 物体) to make a long loud high sound 发出尖厉的声音；呼啸：*Ambulances raced by with sirens wailing.* 救护车高声鸣笛疾驰而过。▸ **wail·ing** /ˈweɪlɪŋ/ *noun* [sing., U]：*a high-pitched wailing* 高声哭号

■ *noun* a long loud high cry expressing pain or sadness; a sound similar to this（疼痛或悲伤时发出的）号啕，哀号 SYN **moan**：*a wail of despair* 绝望的哀号 ◇ *the distant wail of sirens* 远处警报器的鸣响

wains·cot /ˈweɪnskət/ *noun* (*old use*) = SKIRTING BOARD

waist 🔑 /weɪst/ *noun* **1** 🔑 the area around the middle of the body between the RIBS and the hips, often narrower than the areas above and below 腰；腰部：*He put his arm around her waist.* 他搂住了她的腰。◇ *She was paralysed* ***from the waist down*** (= in the area below her waist). 她从腰部以下都瘫痪了。◇ *The workmen were* ***stripped to the waist*** (= wearing no clothes on the top half of their bodies). 工人光着上身。➲ COLLOCATIONS AT PHYSICAL ➲ VISUAL VOCAB PAGE V64 **2** 🔑 the part of a piece of clothing that covers the waist（衣服的）腰部，腰：*a skirt with an elasticated waist* 腰部有松紧带的裙子 **3 -waisted** (in adjectives 构成形容词) having the type of waist mentioned 有…腰身的；腰身…的：*a high-waisted dress* 高腰连衣裙

waist·band /ˈweɪstbænd/ *noun* the strip of cloth that forms the waist of a piece of clothing, especially at the top of a skirt or trousers/pants 衣服腰；腰头；（尤指）裙腰，裤腰：*an elasticated waistband* 松紧腰身

waist·coat /ˈweɪskəʊt; *NAmE usually* ˈweskət; *also* ˈweɪskoʊt/ (*BrE*) (*NAmE* **vest**) *noun* a short piece of clothing with buttons down the front but no sleeves, usually worn over a shirt and under a jacket, often forming part of a man's suit（西服的）背心 ➲ VISUAL VOCAB PAGE V66

,waist-'deep *adj., adv.* up to the waist 齐腰深（的）；上至腰部（的）：*The water was waist-deep.* 水齐腰深。◇ *We waded waist-deep into the muddy water.* 我们蹚进齐腰深的泥水里。

,waist-'high *adj., adv.* high enough to reach the waist 齐腰高（的）；高至腰部（的）：*waist-high grass* 齐腰高的草 ◇ *The grass had grown waist-high.* 草长得齐腰高了。

waist·line /ˈweɪstlaɪn/ *noun* **1** the amount that a person measures around the waist, used to talk about how fat or thin they are 腰围：*an expanding waistline* 逐渐增大的腰围 **2** the place on a piece of clothing where your waist is（衣服的）腰部，腰 SYN **waist**

wait 🔑 /weɪt/ *verb, noun*

■ *verb* **1** 🔑 [I, T] to stay where you are or delay doing sth until sb/sth comes or sth happens 等；等待；等候：*She rang the bell and waited.* 她按铃后等候着。◇ **+ adv./prep.** *Have you been waiting long?* 你等了很久了吗？◇ *I've been waiting (for) twenty minutes.* 我等了二十分钟。◇ *I'll wait outside until the meeting's over.* 我会在外面等到会议结束。

◇ ~ **for sb/sth** *Wait for me!* 等等我！◇ ~ **for sb/sth to do sth** *We're waiting for the rain to stop before we go out.* 我们要等到雨停了再出去。◇ ~ **to do sth** *Hurry up! We're waiting to go.* 快点儿，我们等着走呢。◇ ~ **your turn** *You'll just have to wait your turn* (= wait until your turn comes). 你得等着轮到你才行。**2** [I, T] to hope or watch for sth to happen, especially for a long time（尤指长期地）希望，盼望，期待：~ (**for sth**) *Leeds United had waited for success for eighteen years.* 利兹联队企盼夺冠已经十八年了。◇ *This is just the opportunity I've been waiting for.* 这正是我一直在期待的机会。◇ ~ **for sb/sth to do sth** *He's waiting for me to make a mistake.* 他正盼着我出错呢。◇ ~ **your chance** *I waited my chance and slipped out when no one was looking.* 我等待时机，趁没人注意时溜了出去。**3** **be waiting** [I] (of things 事物) to be ready for sb to have or use 准备妥；在手边；可得到；可使用：~ (**for sb**) *There's a letter waiting for you at home.* 家里有你一封信。◇ ~ **to do sth** *The hotel had a taxi waiting to collect us.* 旅馆召了辆出租车等着接我们。**4** [I] to be left to be dealt with at a later time because it is not urgent 推迟；搁置；延缓：*I've got some calls to make but they* ***can wait*** *until tomorrow.* 我有几个电话要打，不过可以等到明天再说。

IDM **an ˌaccident/a diˌsaster waiting to ˈhappen** a thing or person that is very likely to cause danger or a problem in the future because of the condition it is in or the way they behave 隐患 **I, they, etc. can't ˈwait/can hardly ˈwait** used when you are emphasizing that sb is very excited about sth or keen to do it（我、他们等）迫不及待：*The children* ***can't wait for*** *Christmas to come.* 孩子们等圣诞节都等不及了。◇ *I can hardly wait to see him again.* 我迫不及待地想再次见到他。**keep sb ˈwaiting** to make sb have to wait or be delayed, especially because you arrive late（尤指因迟到）让人等候，使人耽搁：*I'm sorry to have kept you waiting.* 对不起，让你久等了。**ˌwait and ˈsee** used to tell sb that they must be patient and wait to find out about sth later 耐心等待；等着瞧：*We'll just have to wait and see—there's nothing we can do at the moment.* 我们只得等等看，眼下没有法子。◇ *a wait-and-see policy* 等待观望的政策 ◇ *'Where are we going?' 'Wait and see!'* "我们到哪里去？" "等着瞧吧！" **wait at ˈtable** (*formal*) to serve food to people, for example at a formal meal 伺候进餐；（往饭桌上）端饭上菜 **ˈwait for it** (*informal, especially BrE*) **1** used to say that you are about to tell sb sth that is surprising or amusing（要说出令人吃惊或高兴的事情）听着，听好了：*They're off on a trip, to—wait for it—the Maldives!* 他们出去旅行了，去的地方是，听好了，马尔代夫！**2** used to tell sb not to start doing sth yet, but to wait until you tell them（让人在得到通知前别做某事）等候通知 **wait a minute/moment/second 1** to wait for a short time 等一会儿；稍等一下：*Can you wait a second while I make a call?* 你能等一会儿让我打个电话吗？**2** used when you have just noticed or remembered sth, or had a sudden idea（刚注意到、想起某事或突然想出了主意）且慢，等一等：*Wait a minute—this isn't the right key.* 等一等，不是这把钥匙。**wait on sb hand and ˈfoot** (*disapproving*) to take care of sb's needs so well that they do not have to do anything for themselves 过分照顾；让…饭来张口，衣来伸手 **wait ˈtables** (*NAmE*) to work serving food to people in a restaurant（在餐馆）端盘子，招待顾客 **ˈwait till/until...** (*informal*) used to show that you are very excited about telling or showing sth to sb（兴奋地表示或展示某事物）等到…吧：*Wait till you see what I've found!* 你等着看我发现了什么吧！**what are we ˈwaiting for?** (*informal*) used to suggest that you should all start doing what you have been discussing（建议都应开始去做商议中的事）我们还在等什么呢 **what are you ˈwaiting for?** (*informal*) used to tell sb to do sth now rather than later（让人马上就干而不要往后拖）你还等什么呢：*If the car needs cleaning, what are you waiting for?* 如果这辆汽车需要清洗，你还在等什么呢？(**just**) **you ˈwait** used to emphasize a threat, warning or promise（用以加强威胁、警告或允诺的语气）你就等着吧，你就等着瞧：*I'll be famous one day, just you wait!* 我有朝一日会出名的，你就等着瞧吧！➲ MORE AT DUST *n.*, WING *n.*

PHR V **ˌwait aˈbout/aˈround** to stay in a place, with nothing particular to do, for example because you are expecting sth to happen or sb to arrive 白白等着；空等 **ˌwait beˈhind** (*especially BrE*) to stay after other people have gone, especially to speak to sb privately 等到他人走后留下来（尤指为与人私下谈话）**ˌwait ˈin** (*BrE*) to stay at home because you are expecting sb to come, telephone, etc. 在家等候（人、电话等）**ˈwait on sb** to act as a servant to sb, especially by serving food to them 伺候，服侍，招待（尤指进餐）**ˈwait on sth/sb** (*informal, especially NAmE*) to wait for sth to happen before you do or decide sth 等待…（才采取行动或作出决定）：*She is waiting on the result of a blood test.* 她在等验血结果。**ˌwait sth↔ˈout** to wait until an unpleasant event has finished 等待（令人不快的事情）结束：*We sheltered in a doorway to wait out the storm.* 我们躲避在一个门洞里等候暴风雨过去。**ˌwait ˈup** (*NAmE*) used to ask sb to stop or go more slowly so that you can join them 等一等，慢点走（以便自己赶上）**ˌwait ˈup** (**for sb**) to wait for sb to come home at night before you go to bed 熬夜，不睡觉（等人回家）

■ ***noun*** [usually sing.] ~ (**for sb/sth**) an act of waiting; an amount of time waited 等候；等待；等待的时间：*We had* ***a long wait*** *for the bus.* 我们等公共汽车等了很长时间。◇ *He now faces an agonizing two-month wait for the test results.* 他现在要苦苦等待两个月才能拿到测验结果。IDM SEE LIE[1] *v.*

wait·er /ˈweɪtə(r)/ (*feminine* **wait·ress**) *noun* a person whose job is to serve customers at their tables in a restaurant, etc.（餐馆等的）服务员，侍者：*I'll ask the waitress for the bill.* 我要让女服务员拿账单来。◇ *Waiter, could you bring me some water?* 服务员，给我送点儿水来好吗？➲ NOTE AT GENDER ➲ **WORDFINDER NOTE** AT RESTAURANT ➲ SEE ALSO DUMB WAITER, SERVER (4) ➲ **MORE LIKE THIS** 25, page R28

wait·ing /ˈweɪtɪŋ/ *noun* [U] **1** the fact of staying where you are or delaying doing sth until sb/sth comes or sth happens 等候；等待：***No waiting*** (= on a sign at the side of the road, telling vehicles that they must not stop there). 禁止停车（路牌指示）**2** the fact of working as a waiter or waitress 当侍者；当服务员 ➲ SEE ALSO WAITRESSING

ˈwaiting game *noun* [sing.] a policy of waiting to see how a situation develops before you decide how to act 伺机而动的策略

ˈwaiting list *noun* a list of people who are waiting for sth such as a service or medical treatment that is not yet available（服务或医疗的）等候者名单：*There are no places available right now but I'll* ***put you on a waiting list.*** 现时没有空位，但我会把你列入等候者名单的。◇ *There's a waiting list to join the golf club.* 等着加入高尔夫球俱乐部的有一长队人呢。◇ (*BrE*) *The government has promised to cut hospital waiting lists.* 政府已许诺减少排队看病的人数。

ˈwaiting room *noun* a room where people can sit while they are waiting, for example for a bus or train, or to see a doctor or dentist 等候室；候车室；候诊室 ➲ **MORE LIKE THIS** 9, page R26

ˈwait list *noun* (*NAmE*) = WAITING LIST: *She was on a wait list for a liver transplant.* 她的名字当时在肝移植等候者名单上。

ˈwait-list *verb* ~ **sb** (*NAmE*) to put sb's name on a WAITING LIST 列入等候者名单：*He's been wait-listed for a football scholarship to Stanford.* 他已被列入斯坦福大学的美式足球奖学金等候者名单。

wait·person /ˈweɪtpɜːsn; *NAmE* ˈweɪtpɜːrsn/ *noun* (*pl.* **-persons**) (*NAmE*) a person whose job is to serve customers at their tables in a restaurant, etc.（餐馆等的）服务员；侍应生 ➲ **MORE LIKE THIS** 25, page R28

wait·ress /ˈweɪtrəs/ *noun* ➲ WAITER ➲ **MORE LIKE THIS** 25, page R28

wait·ress·ing /ˈweɪtrəsɪŋ/ *noun* [U] the job of being a waitress 女服务员工作：*I did some waitressing when I was a student.* 我当学生时做过侍应生。

W

wait·staff /ˈweɪtstɑːf; *NAmE* ˈweɪtstæf/ *noun* [U] (*NAmE*) the people whose job is to serve customers at their tables in a restaurant, etc.（统称，餐馆等的）服务人员；全体侍应生

waive /weɪv/ *verb* **~ sth** to choose not to demand sth in a particular case, even though you have a legal or official right to do so 放弃（权利、要求等）SYN **forgo**

waiver /ˈweɪvə(r)/ *noun* (*law* 律) a situation in which sb gives up a legal right or claim; an official document stating this（对合法权利或要求的）弃权；弃权声明

wake /weɪk/ *verb, noun*

■ ***verb*** (**woke** /wəʊk; *NAmE* woʊk/, **woken** /ˈwəʊkən; *NAmE* ˈwoʊkən/) **1** [I, T] to stop sleeping; to make sb stop sleeping 醒；醒来；唤醒；弄醒：**~ (up)** *What time do you usually wake up in the morning?* 通常你早晨几点钟醒？◇ *I always wake early in the summer.* 我夏天总是醒得早。◇ *Wake up! It's eight o'clock.* 醒醒吧！已经八点钟了。◇ **~ to sth** (*formal*) *They woke to a clear blue sky.* 他们醒来时天空碧蓝。◇ **~ from sth** (*formal*) *She had just woken from a deep sleep.* 她刚从熟睡中醒来。◇ **~ to do sth** *He woke up to find himself alone in the house.* 他醒来时发现屋里只有他一个人。◇ **~ sb (up)** *Try not to wake the baby up.* 尽量别把孩子弄醒。◇ *I was woken by the sound of someone moving around.* 有人来回走动的响声把我吵醒了。➲ NOTE AT AWAKE **2** [T] **~ sth** (*literary* or *formal*) to make sb remember sth or feel sth again 唤起（记忆）；使再次感觉到：*The incident woke memories of his past sufferings.* 这件事唤起了他对往昔苦难的回忆。

IDM **wake ˌup and smell the ˈcoffee** (*informal*) (usually in orders 通常用于命令) used to tell sb to become aware of what is really happening in a situation, especially when this is sth unpleasant 要清醒面对现实

PHR V **ˌwake ˈup** to become more lively and interested 活跃起来；更感兴趣：*Wake up and listen!* 打起精神注意听！➲ SEE ALSO WAKE *v.* **ˌwake sb↔ˈup** to make sb feel more lively 使活跃；使清醒：*A cold shower will soon wake you up.* 你冲个凉水澡，很快就清醒了。◇ *The class needs waking up.* 应该让这个班活跃起来。➲ SEE ALSO WAKE *v.* (1) **ˌwake ˈup to sth** to become aware of sth; to realize sth 意识到；认识到：*He hasn't yet woken up to the seriousness of the situation.* 他还没有意识到形势的严重性。

■ ***noun*** **1** an occasion before or after a funeral when people gather to remember the dead person, traditionally held the night before the funeral to watch over the body before it is buried（葬礼前的）守夜；守灵 **2** the track that a boat or ship leaves behind on the surface of the water（船只航行时的）尾流，伴流，航迹 ➲ VISUAL VOCAB PAGE V5

IDM **in the wake of sb/sth** coming after or following sb/sth 随…之后而来；跟随在…后：*There have been demonstrations on the streets in the wake of the recent bomb attack.* 在近来的轰炸之后，大街上随即出现了示威游行。◇ *A group of reporters followed in her wake.* 一群记者跟随在她的身后。◇ *The storm left a trail of destruction in its wake.* 暴风雨过处满目疮痍。

wake·board·ing /ˈweɪkbɔːdɪŋ; *NAmE* -bɔːrd-/ *noun* [U] the sport of riding on a short wide board called a **wakeboard** while being pulled along through the water by a fast boat 尾流滑水运动（由快艇牵引，用尾波板进行）▶ **wake·board** *verb* [I] ➲ VISUAL VOCAB PAGE V54

wake·ful /ˈweɪkfl/ *adj.* (*formal*) **1** not sleeping; unable to sleep 失眠的；不能入睡的 SYN **sleepless**: *He lay wakeful all night.* 他躺在床上彻夜未眠。**2** (of a period at night 夜间一段时间) spent with little or no sleep 没怎么睡的；不眠的 SYN **sleepless**: *She had spent many wakeful nights worrying about him.* 她度过了许多不眠之夜，为他担心。
▶ **wake·ful·ness** *noun* [U]

waken /ˈweɪkən/ *verb* (*formal*) **1** [I, T] to wake, or make sb wake, from sleep 醒来；睡醒；唤醒；弄醒：**~ (up)** *The child had just wakened.* 这孩子刚醒。◇ **~ sb (up)** *I was wakened by a knock at the door.* 敲门声把我吵醒了。➲ NOTE AT AWAKE **2** [T] **~ sth** to make sb remember sth or feel sth again 唤起（记忆）；使感觉到：*The dream wakened a forgotten memory.* 那梦唤起了一段忘却的记忆。

ˈwake-up call *noun* **1** a telephone call that you arrange to be made to you at a particular time, for example in a hotel, in order to wake you up 催醒电话；叫早电话：*I asked for a wake-up call at 6.30 a.m.* 我请他们在早晨 6:30 打电话叫醒我。**2** an event that makes people realize that there is a problem that they need to do sth about 让人警醒的事：*These riots should be a wake-up call for the government.* 这些暴乱该为政府敲响警钟了。

wakey-wakey /ˌweɪki ˈweɪki/ *exclamation* (*BrE, informal, humorous*) used to tell sb to wake up（用以叫醒别人）醒醒

wak·ing /ˈweɪkɪŋ/ *adj.* [only before noun] used to describe time when you are awake 醒着的；不眠的：*She spends all her waking hours caring for her mother.* 她不睡觉的时候都在照看母亲。▶ **wak·ing** *noun* [U]: *the dreamlike state between waking and sleeping* 似睡非睡的梦境状态

Wal·dorf salad /ˌwɔːldɔːf ˈsæləd; *NAmE* -dɔːrf/ *noun* [U, C] a salad made from apples, nuts, CELERY and MAYONNAISE (= sauce made with egg and oil) 沃尔多夫色拉（用苹果、果仁、芹菜、蛋黄酱制作而成）

walk /wɔːk/ *verb, noun*

■ ***verb*** **1** [I, T] to move or go somewhere by putting one foot in front of the other on the ground, but without running 走；行走；步行：*The baby is just learning to walk.* 这孩子刚学走路。◇ *'How did you get here?' 'I walked.'* "你怎么到这儿来的？""我走路来的。"◇ **+ adv./prep.** *He walked slowly away from her.* 他慢慢地从她身旁走开。◇ *The door opened and Jo walked in.* 门开了，乔走了进来。◇ *She missed the bus and had to walk home.* 她没赶上公共汽车，只好步行回家。◇ *The school is* ***within easy walking distance of*** *the train station.* 学校离火车站不远，不费劲就走到了。◇ **~ sth** *Children here walk several miles to school.* 这里的孩子去上学要步行好几英里。**2** (*also* **go walking**) (*both especially BrE*) [I, T] to spend time walking for pleasure 徒步旅行；散步：**(+ adv./prep.)** *We're going walking in the mountains this summer.* 今年夏天我们打算到山里去徒步旅行。◇ *I walked across Scotland with a friend.* 我和一个朋友徒步穿越了苏格兰。◇ **~ sth** *They love walking the moors.* 他们喜欢到沼泽地散步。**3** [T] **~ sb + adv./prep.** to go somewhere with sb on foot, especially in order to make sure they get there safely 陪伴…走；护送…走：*He always walked her home.* 他经常护送她走回家。**4** [T] **~ sth (+ adv./prep.)** to take an animal for a walk; to make an animal walk somewhere 牵着（动物）走；遛；赶着…走：*They walk their dogs every day.* 他们每天遛狗。➲ SYNONYMS AT TAKE **5** [I] (*informal*) to disappear; to be taken away 不翼而飞；被盗走：*Lock up any valuables. Things tend to walk here* (= be stolen). 把贵重物品锁起来。这里的东西常会不翼而飞。**6** [I] (*literary*) (of a GHOST 鬼魂) to appear 出现；出没；显灵

IDM **run before you can ˈwalk** to do things that are difficult, without learning the basic skills first 不会走就跑；没掌握基本功就做难事 **walk the ˈbeat** (of police officers 警察) to walk around the area that they are responsible for 在辖区值勤巡逻 **walk ˈfree** to be allowed to leave court, etc., without receiving any punishment 获无罪释放 **ˈwalk it** (*informal*) **1** to go somewhere on foot instead of in a vehicle 徒步前往 **2** (*BrE*) to easily achieve sth that you want 轻易获得；轻易取胜：*It's not a difficult exam. You'll walk it!* 这次考试不难。你会轻松通过的！**walk sb off their ˈfeet** (*informal*) to make sb walk so far or so fast that they are very tired 使走得筋疲力尽 **walk off the ˈjob** (*NAmE*) to stop working in order to go on strike（离开岗位）罢工 **walk the ˈplank** (in the past) to walk along a board placed over the side of a ship and fall into the sea, as a punishment 走跳板（旧时强迫受害人在置于船舷外的跳板上行走而致落水）**walk the ˈstreets** to walk around the streets of a town or city（在城镇里）穿街走巷；在大街上闲逛：*Is it safe to walk the streets alone at night?* 夜间独自一人在大街上行走安全吗？**walk ˈtall** to feel proud and confident 昂首阔步；趾高气扬 **ˌwalk the ˈwalk** (*informal, approving*) to act in a way that shows people you are really good at what you do, and not just good at

W

talking about it 言行一致：*You can talk the talk but can you walk the walk?* 你说得头头是道，可是你做得到吗？ ➲ MORE AT AIR *n.*, AISLE, LINE *n.*, MEMORY LANE, THIN *adj.*, TIGHTROPE

PHR V **ˌwalk aˈway (from sb/sth)** to leave a difficult situation or relationship, etc. instead of staying and trying to deal with it（从困难的处境或关系中）脱身，一走了之 **ˌwalk aˈway with sth** (*informal*) to win or obtain sth easily 轻易取胜；轻易获得：*She walked away with the gold medal.* 她轻松地摘走了金牌。**ˌwalk ˈin on sb/sth** to enter a room when sb in there is doing sth private and does not expect you 冷不丁进屋撞见 **ˌwalk ˈinto sth** (*informal*) **1** to become involved in an unpleasant situation, especially because you were not sensible enough to avoid it 不意落入，不明智地陷入（不愉快的境地）：*I realized I'd walked into a trap.* 我意识到自己稀里糊涂落入了陷阱。**2** to succeed in getting a job very easily 轻易获得（工作）**ˌwalk ˈinto sth/sb** to crash into sth/sb while you are walking, for example because you do not see them 走路时撞着（人或东西）**ˌwalk ˈoff** to leave a person or place suddenly because you are angry or upset 愤然离去；拂袖而去 **ˌwalk sth↔ˈoff** to go for a walk after a meal so that you feel less full 散步消食：*We walked off a heavy Sunday lunch.* 我们星期日午餐吃得特别多，散散步帮助消化。**ˌwalk ˈoff with sth** (*informal*) **1** to win sth easily 轻易取胜 **2** to take sth that is not yours; to steal sth 顺手牵羊；顺便偷走 **ˌwalk ˈout** (*informal*) (of workers 工人) to stop working in order to go on strike（离开岗位）罢工 ➲ RELATED NOUN WALKOUT (1) **ˌwalk ˈout (of sth)** 🔑 to leave a meeting, performance, etc. suddenly, especially in order to show your disapproval 突然离去，退场，退席（尤为表示异议）**ˌwalk ˈout (on sb)** (*informal*) to suddenly leave sb that you are having a relationship with and that you have a responsibility for 遗弃，抛弃，舍弃，离开（某人） **SYN** **desert**：*How could she walk out on her kids?* 她怎么能遗弃自己的孩子呢？**ˌwalk ˈout (on sth)** (*informal*) to stop doing sth that you have agreed to do before it is completed 半途而废；半截撂挑子：*I never walk out on a job half done.* 我做工作从不半途而废。**ˌwalk (all) ˈover sb** (*informal*) **1** to treat sb badly, without considering them or their needs 苛刻对待：*She'll always let him walk all over her.* 她对他总是逆来顺受。**2** to defeat sb easily 轻而易举地打败；轻取 ➲ RELATED NOUN WALKOVER (1) **ˌwalk sb ˈthrough sth** to help sb learn or become familiar with sth, by showing them each stage of the process in turn（循序渐进地）教；逐步引导：*She walked me through a demonstration of the software.* 她一步步地给我演示软件。 ➲ RELATED NOUN WALK-THROUGH (2) **ˌwalk ˈup (to sb/sth)** 🔑 to walk towards sb/sth, especially in a confident way（尤指自信地）向…走去，走近

■ ***noun*** **1** 🔑 [C] a journey on foot, usually for pleasure or exercise 行走；步行；徒步旅行；散步：*Let's go for a walk.* 咱们去散散步吧。◇ *I like to have a walk in the evenings.* 我喜欢晚上散步。◇ *She's taken the dog for a walk.* 她带着狗去散步了。◇ *He set out on the long walk home.* 他动身走很长的路回家了。◇ *The office is ten minutes' walk from here.* 从这里去办公室要步行十分钟。◇ *a ten-minute walk* 步行十分钟的路程 ◇ *It's only a short walk to the beach.* 步行到海滩没多远。**2** 🔑 [C] a path or route for walking, usually for pleasure; an organized event when people walk for pleasure 散步的小路；步行的路径；（为游玩而组织的）徒步旅行：*a circular walk* 环形步行路径 ◇ *There are some interesting walks in the area.* 这一带有几条有趣的小径。◇ *a guided walk around the farm* 由向导引路绕农场走一圈 **3** [sing.] a way or style of walking; the act or speed of walking rather than running 步态；步行速度：*I recognized him by his walk.* 我根据他走路的样子认出了他。◇ *The horse slowed to a walk.* 那匹马慢下来缓步而行。**4** [C] (*NAmE*) a SIDEWALK or path 人行道；小路

IDM **a ˌwalk in the ˈpark** (*informal*) a thing that is very easy to do or deal with 易事；轻而易举的事：*The role isn't exactly a walk in the park.* 这个角色绝非闲庭散步。**a walk of ˈlife** a person's job or position in society 行业；职业；地位；阶层 **SYN** **background**：*She has friends from all walks of life.* 她在社会各界中都有朋友。

▼**VOCABULARY BUILDING 词汇扩充**

Ways of walking 走路的方式

- **creep** 蹑手蹑脚地走；缓慢（或悄悄）地走：*He could hear someone creeping around downstairs.* 他听得见有人在楼下蹑手蹑脚走来走去的声音。
- **limp** 一瘸一拐地走；跛行：*One player limped off the field with a twisted ankle.* 一个球员拖着扭伤的脚踝一瘸一拐地走下场。
- **pace** 徘徊：*I found him in the corridor nervously pacing up and down.* 我看到他在走廊里焦虑不安地走来走去。
- **pad** 放轻脚步走：*She spent the morning padding about the house in her slippers.* 她一个早上都穿着拖鞋在房子里轻轻地走来走去。
- **plod** 沉重缓慢地走；步履艰难地走：*They wearily plodded home through the rain.* 他们冒着雨疲惫而吃力地走回家。
- **shuffle** 拖着脚走：*The queue gradually shuffled forward.* 排队等候的人慢慢向前挪动。
- **stagger** 摇摇晃晃地行走；蹒跚：*They staggered out of the pub, completely drunk.* 他们烂醉如泥，踉踉跄跄地走出了酒馆。
- **stomp** 噔噔地走或跳舞：*She stomped out of the room, slamming the door behind her.* 她噔噔地走出了屋子，随手砰的一声把门关上。
- **stroll** 漫步；闲逛；溜达：*Families were strolling around the park.* 游人一家一家地在公园四处漫步。
- **tiptoe** 踮着脚走路：*They tiptoed upstairs so they wouldn't wake the baby.* 他们踮着脚上楼，以免吵醒婴儿。
- **trudge** 缓慢而吃力地走；步履艰难地走：*We trudged up the hill.* 我们步履艰难地一步一步往山上爬。

walk·about /ˈwɔːkəbaʊt/ *noun* **1** (*BrE*) an occasion when an important person walks among ordinary people to meet and talk to them（要人的）出巡 **2** (*AustralE*) a journey (originally on foot) that is made by an Australian Aboriginal in order to live in the traditional manner（澳大利亚土著为回归传统生活而进行的）短期丛林漫游

IDM **go ˈwalkabout 1** (*informal*) to be lost or not where you should be 迷路；丢失：*My rucksack seems to have gone walkabout.* 我的旅行包好像是丢了。**2** (of an Australian Aboriginal) to go into the country away from white society in order to live in the traditional manner（澳大利亚土著远离白人社会到乡间）进行丛林漫游

walk·er /ˈwɔːkə(r)/ *noun* **1** (*especially BrE*) a person who walks, usually for pleasure or exercise 步行者；散步的人；徒步旅行者：*The coastal path is a popular route for walkers.* 这条海滨小路是散步者很喜欢走的路径。**2 a fast, slow, etc. ~** a person who walks fast, slow, etc. 走路快（或慢等）的人 **3** (*NAmE*) (*BrE* **Zim·mer frame™**, *informal* **Zim·mer**) a metal frame that people use to help them to walk, for example people who are old or who have sth wrong with their legs 助行器：*He now needs a walker to get around.* 他现在走动需要助行架。➲ PICTURE AT FRAME **4** (*NAmE*) (*BrE* **ˈbaby walker**) a frame with wheels and a HARNESS for a baby who can walk around a room, supported by the frame（幼儿）学步车

walk·ies /ˈwɔːkiz/ *noun* [pl.] (*BrE, informal*) a walk with a dog 遛狗：*to go for walkies* 去遛狗

walkie-talkie /ˌwɔːki ˈtɔːki/ *noun* (*informal*) a small radio that you can carry with you and use to send or receive messages 步话机；无线电通话机

ˈwalk-in *adj.* [only before noun] **1** large enough to walk into 大得能走进去的：*a walk-in closet* 小贮藏室 **2** not arranged in advance; where you do not need to arrange a time in advance 未经预约的；无须事先约定的：*a walk-in interview* 未经预约的访谈 ◇ *a walk-in clinic* 无须预约的诊所

walk·ing /ˈwɔːkɪŋ/ *noun, adj.*
■ ***noun*** [U] **1** (*especially BrE*) the activity of going for walks in the countryside for exercise or pleasure 行走；步行；散步；徒步旅行：*to* **go walking** 去散步 ◇ *walking boots* 便靴 ◇ *a walking holiday in Scotland* 苏格兰的徒步旅行假日 ➲ SEE ALSO POWER WALKING **2** the sport of walking a long distance as fast as possible without running 竞走
■ ***adj.*** [only before noun] (*informal*) used to describe a human or living example of the thing mentioned 似人的；活的：*She's a walking dictionary* (= she knows a lot of words). 她是部活字典。

ˈwalking bus *noun* (in Britain) a way for a group of children to walk safely in a group with an adult to and from school, along a route that passes by the children's homes 步行巴士（英国小学生由成人带领，结队步行安全上学和回家）

ˈwalking papers *noun* [pl.] (*NAmE, informal*) the letter or notice dismissing sb from a job 解雇函；解雇通知书

ˈwalking stick (*also* **stick** *especially in BrE*) *noun* a stick that you carry and use as a support when you are walking 手杖；拐棍 ➲ PICTURE AT STICK

the ˌwalking ˈwounded *noun* [pl.] people who have been injured in a battle or an accident but who are still able to walk（战争或事故中）尚能走路的伤员

Walk·man™ /ˈwɔːkmən/ *noun* (*pl.* **-mans** /-mənz/) a type of PERSONAL STEREO 随身听（小型立体声音响）

ˈwalk-on *adj.* ~ **part/role** used to describe a very small part in a play or film/movie, without any words to say（指戏剧或电影中无台词的）小角色，龙套角色

walk·out /ˈwɔːkaʊt/ *noun* **1** a sudden strike by workers（突然的）罢工 **2** the act of suddenly leaving a meeting as a protest against sth（为表示抗议而突然的）退场，退席

walk·over /ˈwɔːkəʊvə(r); *NAmE* -oʊ-/ *noun* **1** an easy victory in a game or competition（比赛或竞赛中的）轻易取得的胜利 **2** a victory given to a player or team because their opponent did not take part（因对手无法参赛的）不战而胜

ˈwalk-through *noun* **1** an occasion when you practise a performance, etc. without an audience being present 排演；排练；彩排 **2** a careful explanation of the details of a process 逐步解释

ˈwalk-up *noun* (*NAmE*) a tall building with stairs but no lift/elevator; an office or a flat/apartment in such a building 无电梯的大楼；无电梯大楼中的办公室（或公寓套房）

walk·way /ˈwɔːkweɪ/ *noun* a passage or path for walking along, often outside and raised above the ground（常为户外高出地面的）人行通道，走道

wall /wɔːl/ *noun, verb*
■ ***noun*** **1** a long vertical solid structure, made of stone, brick or concrete, that surrounds, divides or protects an area of land 城墙；围墙；隔墙：*The fields were divided by stone walls.* 这些田地由石墙分隔。◇ *He sat on the wall and watched the others playing.* 他坐在墙头上看别人玩耍。➲ VISUAL VOCAB PAGE V18 ➲ SEE ALSO SEA WALL **2** any of the vertical sides of a building or room 墙；壁；墙壁：*I'm going to paint the walls white and the ceiling pink.* 我打算把墙壁刷成白色，把天花板刷成粉红色。◇ *Hang the picture* **on the wall** *opposite the window.* 把这张画挂在对着窗的墙上。◇ *She leaned against the wall.* 她倚靠着墙。➲ COLLOCATIONS AT DECORATE **3** something that forms a barrier or stops you from making progress 屏障；隔阂；壁垒：*The boat struck a solid wall of water.* 船撞上一道水幕。◇ *The investigators were confronted by* **a wall of silence.** 调查人员碰了壁，问谁谁都默不作声。**4** the outer layer of sth hollow such as an organ of the body or a cell of an animal or a plant（身体器官或动植物细胞等的）外壁：*the abdominal wall* 腹壁 ◇ *the wall of an artery* 动脉血管壁
IDM **go to the ˈwall** (*informal*) (of a company or an organization 公司或机构) to fail because of lack of money（因缺少资金）走投无路，失败，破产，陷于绝境 **off the ˈwall** (*informal*) unusual and amusing; slightly crazy 奇妙的；有点儿出格的：*Some of his ideas are really off the wall.* 他有些想法真是十分新奇。◇ *off-the-wall ideas* 奇妙的想法 **up the ˈwall** (*informal*) crazy or angry 发狂；愤怒：*That noise is driving me up the wall.* 那噪音让我都快疯了。◇ *I mustn't be late or Dad will go up the wall.* 我不能晚了，否则爸爸会发脾气的。**ˌwalls have ˈears** (*saying*) used to warn people to be careful what they say because other people may be listening 隔墙有耳 ➲ MORE AT BACK *n.*, BOUNCE *v.*, BRICK *n.*, FLY *n.*, FOUR, HANDWRITING, HEAD *n.*, HIT *v.*, WRITING
■ ***verb*** [usually passive] ~ **sth** to surround an area, a town, etc. with a wall or walls 用墙把…围住：*a walled city* 有城墙的城市
PHR V **ˌwall sth↔ˈin** [usually passive] to surround sth/sb with a wall or barrier 把（人或东西）围到屏障等里面 **ˌwall sth↔ˈoff** [usually passive] to separate one place or area from another with a wall 用墙把…隔开 **ˌwall sb↔ˈup** [usually passive] to keep sb as a prisoner behind walls 把…关在大墙后；监禁 **ˌwall sth↔ˈup** [usually passive] to fill an opening with a wall, bricks, etc. so that you can no longer use it（用墙、砖等把通路）堵住，封死

wal·laby /ˈwɒləbi; *NAmE* ˈwɑːl-/ *noun* (*pl.* **-ies**) an Australian animal like a small KANGAROO, that moves by jumping on its strong back legs and keeps its young in a POUCH (= a pocket of skin) on the front of the mother's body 沙袋鼠（袋鼠科动物，产于澳大利亚）

wal·lah /ˈwɒlə; *NAmE* ˈwɑːlə/ *noun* **1** (*informal* or *IndE*) a person connected with a particular job 与…工作有关的人；从事…工作的人：*office wallahs* 办公室人员 **2** (*IndE*) a person who was born in or lives in the country or area mentioned 出生于某国（或某地）的人；某国（或某地）居民：*a Delhi wallah* 德里人

ˈwall anchor (*NAmE*) (*BrE* **Rawl·plug™**, **ˈwall plug**) *noun* a small plastic tube, closed at one end, that you put into a wall to hold a screw（塑料制）墙锚；墙栓

wall·chart /ˈwɔːltʃɑːt; *NAmE* -tʃɑːrt/ *noun* a large piece of paper on which there is information, fixed to a wall for people to look at 挂图

wall·cov·er·ing /ˈwɔːlkʌvərɪŋ/ *noun* [U, C] WALLPAPER or cloth used to decorate the walls in a room 覆盖墙壁的装饰；壁纸；墙布

wal·let /ˈwɒlɪt; *NAmE* ˈwɑːl-; ˈwɔːl-/ *noun* **1** (*NAmE also* **bill·fold**) a small flat folding case made of leather or plastic used for keeping paper money and credit cards in（放钞票、信用卡的）钱包，皮夹子 ➲ VISUAL VOCAB PAGE V69 **2** (*BrE*) a flat leather, plastic or cardboard case for carrying documents in（携带文件用的）皮夹，塑料夹，硬纸夹：*a document wallet* 文件夹

wall·flower /ˈwɔːlflaʊə(r)/ *noun* **1** a garden plant with yellow, orange or red flowers with a sweet smell that appear in late spring 桂竹香（一种园艺植物，暮春开花，呈黄、橙或红色）**2** (*informal*) a person who does not dance at a party because they do not have sb to dance with or because they are too shy（舞会或聚会上因无舞伴或腼腆）待在一旁的人，壁花

wall·ing /ˈwɔːlɪŋ/ *noun* [U] **1** material from which a wall is built 砌墙的材料：*stone walling* 砌墙石料 **2** the act or skill of building a wall or walls 砌墙；垒墙；垒墙技术：*a firm that does paving and walling* 从事铺路砌墙的公司

ˌwall-ˈmounted *adj.* fixed onto a wall 固定在墙上的：*wall-mounted lights* 壁灯

wal·lop /ˈwɒləp; *NAmE* ˈwɑːl-/ *noun, verb*
■ ***noun*** [sing.] (*informal*) a heavy powerful hit 痛打；猛击
■ ***verb*** (*informal*) **1** ~ **sb/sth** to hit sb/sth very hard 痛打；猛击 SYN **thump** **2** ~ **sb/sth** to defeat sb completely in a contest, match, etc.（在竞赛、比赛等中）彻底击败，大胜 SYN **thrash**：*We walloped them 6–0.* 我们以 6:0 把他们打得落花流水。

W

wal·lop·ing /ˈwɒləpɪŋ; NAmE ˈwɑːl-/ *noun, adj.* (*informal*)

▪ ***noun*** [usually sing.] **1** a heavy defeat 大败；惨败：*Our team got a real walloping last week.* 我们队上星期一败涂地。**2** an act of hitting sb very hard several times, often as a punishment（连续）痛打，狠揍

▪ ***adj.*** [only before noun] very big 很大的；巨大的：*They had to pay a walloping great fine.* 他们不得不缴一大笔罚款。

wal·low /ˈwɒləʊ; NAmE ˈwɑːloʊ/ *verb, noun*

▪ ***verb*** **1** [I] ~ (**in sth**) (of large animals or people 大动物或人) to lie and roll about in water or mud, to keep cool or for pleasure（为保持凉爽或嬉戏在烂泥、水里）打滚，翻滚：*hippos wallowing in the river* 在河里打滚的河马 ◇ *He loves to wallow in a hot bath after a game.* 他在比赛后喜欢泡个热水澡。**2** [I] ~ **in sth** (*often disapproving*) to enjoy sth that causes you pleasure 沉湎；放纵：*She wallowed in the luxury of the hotel.* 她沉湎于旅馆豪华奢侈的享乐之中。◇ *to wallow in **despair/self-pity*** (= to think about your unhappy feelings all the time and seem to be enjoying them) 陷入绝望；顾影自怜

▪ ***noun*** [sing.] an act of wallowing（在烂泥或水里的）打滚嬉戏，翻滚：*pigs having a wallow in the mud* 在烂泥中打滚的猪

ˈwall painting *noun* a picture painted straight onto the surface of a wall 壁画

wall·paper /ˈwɔːlpeɪpə(r)/ *noun, verb*

▪ ***noun*** [U] **1** thick paper, often with a pattern on it, used for covering the walls and ceiling of a room 壁纸；墙纸：*wallpaper paste* 贴壁纸用的糨糊 ◇ *a roll of wallpaper* 一卷壁纸 ◇ *to hang wallpaper* 贴壁纸 ➲ **COLLOCATIONS** AT DECORATE **2** (*computing* 计) the background pattern or picture that you choose to have on the screen of your computer, mobile/cell phone, etc.（计算机、手机等屏幕上的）壁纸，桌面背景

▪ ***verb*** (*also* **paper**) [T, I] ~ (**sth**) to put wallpaper onto the walls of a room 往（屋里墙上）贴壁纸

ˈwall plug *noun* = RAWLPLUG™

ˈWall Street *noun* [U] the US financial centre and STOCK EXCHANGE in New York City (used to refer to the business that is done there) 华尔街（美国纽约金融中心和证券交易所所在地）：*Share prices fell on Wall Street today.* 今日纽约证券交易所的股价下跌。◇ *Wall Street responded quickly to the news.* 华尔街对这一消息反应迅速。

ˈwall tent (*NAmE*) (*BrE* **ˈframe tent**) *noun* a large tent with a roof and walls that do not slope much 框架式大帐篷（篷顶和篷壁形成的坡度很小）➲ COMPARE DOME TENT, RIDGE TENT

ˌwall-to-ˈwall *adj.* [only before noun] **1** covering the floor of a room completely 覆盖整个地板的：***wall-to-wall carpets/carpeting*** 满铺地毯 ➲ **VISUAL VOCAB** PAGE V24 **2** (*informal*) continuous; happening or existing all the time or everywhere 连续的；无时不在的；到处存在的：*wall-to-wall TV sports coverage* 连续的电视体育报道

W

wally /ˈwɒli; NAmE ˈwɔːli; ˈwɑːli/ *noun* (*pl.* **-ies**) (*BrE, informal*) a stupid person 傻瓜；笨蛋；白痴

wal·nut /ˈwɔːlnʌt/ *noun* **1** [C] the light brown nut of the walnut tree that has a rough surface and a hard round shell in two halves 核桃；胡桃 ➲ **VISUAL VOCAB** PAGE V35 **2** (*also* **ˈwalnut tree**) [C] the tree on which walnuts grow 核桃树；胡桃树 **3** [U] the brown wood of the walnut tree, used in making furniture 核桃木；胡桃木

wal·rus /ˈwɔːlrəs/ *noun* an animal like a large SEAL (= a sea animal with thick fur, that eats fish and lives around coasts), that has two long outer teeth called TUSKS and lives in Arctic regions 海象（形似海豹，獠牙较长，栖息在北极海域）

ˌwalrus mouˈstache *noun* (*informal*) a long thick MOUSTACHE that hangs down on each side of the mouth 海象胡子（浓密且两端下垂的唇上长胡须）

Walter Mitty /ˌwɔːltə ˈmɪti; NAmE ˌwɔːltər/ *noun* a person who imagines that their life is full of excitement and adventures when it is in fact just ordinary 幻想多彩生活的人 ➲ **MORE LIKE THIS** 17, page R27 **ORIGIN** From the name of the main character in James Thurber's story *The Secret Life of Walter Mitty.* 源自詹姆斯•瑟伯所著小说《沃尔特•米蒂的秘密生活》中主人公的名字。

waltz /wɔːls; wɔːlts/ *noun, verb*

▪ ***noun*** a dance in which two people dance together to a regular rhythm; a piece of music for this dance 华尔兹舞；华尔兹舞曲；圆舞曲：*to dance a/the waltz* 跳华尔兹舞 ◇ *a Strauss waltz* 施特劳斯圆舞曲

▪ ***verb*** **1** [I, T] to dance a waltz 跳华尔兹舞：(**+ adv./prep.**) *I watched them waltzing across the floor.* 我望着他们跳着华尔兹在舞池中旋转。◇ **~ sb + adv./prep.** *He waltzed her around the room.* 他带着她满屋跳华尔兹舞。**2** [I] **+ adv./prep.** (*informal*) to walk or go somewhere in a very confident way 大摇大摆地走：*I don't like him waltzing into the house as if he owned it.* 我不喜欢他像房主似的大摇大摆走进屋来。**3** [I] ~ (**through sth**) to complete or achieve sth without any difficulty 轻易完成；轻而易举地取得：*The recruits have waltzed through their training.* 新招收的成员轻松顺利地完成了训练。

PHR V **ˌwaltz ˈoff** (**with sth/sb**) (*informal*) to leave a place or person in a way that is very annoying, often taking sth that is not yours 令人讨厌地离开（常带走不属于自己的东西）：*He just waltzed off with my car!* 他顺手牵羊开走了我的汽车！

WAN /wæn/ *noun* (*pl.* **WANs**) (*computing* 计) the abbreviation for 'wide area network' (a system in which computers in different places are connected, usually over a large area) 广域网（全写为 wide area network，将大范围内不同地方的电脑联网的系统）➲ COMPARE LAN

wan /wɒn; NAmE wɑːn/ *adj.* looking pale and weak 苍白无力的；无血色的；憔悴的：*his grey, wan face* 他那苍白憔悴的面孔 ◇ *She gave me a wan smile* (= showing no energy or enthusiasm). 她勉强向我微微一笑。▸ **wanly** *adv.*: *He smiled wanly.* 他惨然一笑。

wa·nan·chi /wəˈnæntʃi/ *noun* [pl.] (*EAfrE*) ordinary people; the public 普通百姓；民众 ➲ SEE ALSO MWANANCHI

wand /wɒnd; NAmE wɑːnd/ *noun* **1** (*also* **ˌmagic ˈwand**) a straight thin stick that is held by sb when performing magic or magic tricks 魔杖：*The fairy waved her wand and the table disappeared.* 那仙女魔杖一挥，桌子不翼而飞。◇ *You can't expect me to just **wave a** (**magic**) **wand** and make everything all right again.* 你不能指望我挥动一下魔杖，便一切又平安无事了。**2** any object in the shape of a straight thin stick 棍；棒；杆；杖：*a mascara wand* 睫毛刷 ➲ **VISUAL VOCAB** PAGE V65

wan·der /ˈwɒndə(r); NAmE ˈwɑːn-/ *verb, noun*

▪ ***verb*** **1** [I, T] to walk slowly around or to a place, often without any particular sense of purpose or direction 闲逛；漫游；游荡：**+ adv./prep.** *She wandered aimlessly around the streets.* 她在大街上漫无目的地到处游荡。◇ *We wandered back towards the car.* 我们溜达着回到汽车那里。◇ **~ sth** *The child was found wandering the streets alone.* 那孩子被发现独自在大街上瞎转。**2** [I] to move away from the place where you ought to be or the people you are with 偏离（正道）；走失；离散 **SYN** **stray**: **~ away/off** *The child wandered off and got lost.* 那孩子走散后迷路了。◇ **~ from/off sth** *They had wandered from the path into the woods.* 他们离开小路消失在树林里。**3** [I] (of a person's mind or thoughts 人的思想或想法) to stop being directed on sth and to move without much control to other ideas, subjects, etc. 走神；神志恍惚；（思想）开小差 **SYN** **drift**: *It's easy to be distracted and **let your attention wander**.* 很容易走神分散了注意力。◇ *Try not to **let your mind wander**.* 尽量别让你的思想开小差。◇ **~ away, back, to, etc. sth** *Her thoughts wandered back to her youth.* 她浮想联翩，思绪回到了青春岁月。**4** [I] (of a person's eyes 人的眼睛) to move slowly from looking at one thing to looking at another thing or in other directions 慢慢地移开：*She **let her gaze wander**.* 她东瞅瞅西望望。◇ **+ adv./prep.** *His eyes wandered towards the photographs on the wall.* 他的目光慢慢地移向墙上的照片。**5** [I] (**+ adv./prep.**) (of a road or river 道路或河流) to curve instead of following a straight course 蜿蜒；迂回曲折：*The road wanders along through the hills.* 这条路蜿蜒曲折地穿过山丘。

■**noun** [sing.] a short walk in or around a place, usually with no special purpose 游荡；溜达；闲逛；徘徊：*I went to the park and had a wander around.* 我去公园转了一圈。

wan·der·er /ˈwɒndərə(r); *NAmE* ˈwɑːn-/ *noun* a person who keeps travelling from place to place with no permanent home 漂泊者；漫游者；流浪者

wan·der·ings /ˈwɒndərɪŋz; *NAmE* ˈwɑːn-/ *noun* [pl.] (*literary*) journeys from place to place, usually with no special purpose 漫游；流浪；漂泊

wan·der·lust /ˈwɒndəlʌst; *NAmE* ˈwɑːndərl-/ *noun* [U] (*from German*) a strong desire to travel 漫游癖；旅行癖

wane /weɪn/ *verb, noun*

■**verb 1** [I] to become gradually weaker or less important 衰落；衰败；败落；减弱 SYN **decrease, fade**: *Her enthusiasm for the whole idea was waning rapidly.* 她对整个想法的热情迅速冷淡了下来。**2** [I] (of the moon 月亮) to appear slightly smaller each day after being round and full 缺；亏 OPP **wax** IDM SEE WAX *v.*

■**noun** [sing.]

IDM **on the ˈwane** becoming smaller, less important or less common 变小；衰落；减弱；败落 SYN **decline**: *Her popularity has been on the wane for some time.* 她的人气一段时间以来江河日下。

wan·gle /ˈwæŋɡl/ *verb* (*informal*) to get sth that you or another person wants by persuading sb or by a clever plan 把…弄到手；设法获得；搞：**~ sth** *She had wangled an invitation to the opening night.* 她弄到了一张首映之夜的请柬。◇ *We should be able to* **wangle it** *so that you can start tomorrow.* 我们应该能设法安排你明天启程。◇ *He managed to* **wangle his way** *onto the course.* 他终于设法修读了这一科目。◇ **~ sth from/out of sb** *I'll try to wangle some money out of my parents.* 我要设法从父母那里哄出些钱来。◇ **~ sb sth** *He had wangled her a seat on the plane.* 他为她弄到了一个飞机上的座位。

wank /wæŋk/ *verb, noun*

■**verb** [I] (*BrE, taboo, slang*) to MASTURBATE 手淫

■**noun** [usually sing.] (*BrE, taboo, slang*) an act of MASTURBATION 手淫

wank·er /ˈwæŋkə(r)/ *noun* (*BrE, taboo, slang*) an offensive word used to insult sb, especially a man, and to show anger or dislike 无能者，下流坯子（尤用以侮辱男性）：*a bunch of wankers* 一群下流坯子

wanna /ˈwɒnə; *NAmE* ˈwɔːnə; ˈwɑːnə/ (*informal, nonstandard*) the written form of the word some people use to mean 'want to' or 'want a', which is not considered to be correct 要，想要个（书写形式，有人用以表示 want to 或 want a。此用法被视为不正确）：*I wanna go.* 我想走。◇ *Wanna drink?* (= Do you want…) 要杯饮料吗？HELP You should not write this form unless you are copying somebody's speech. 除非转述他人话语，否则不应写成这种形式。➲ MORE LIKE THIS 5, page R25

wan·nabe /ˈwɒnəbi; *NAmE* ˈwɑːn-; ˈwɔːn-/ *noun* (*informal, disapproving*) a person who behaves, dresses, etc. like sb famous because they want to be like them（名人的）崇拜模仿者

want /wɒnt; *NAmE* wɑːnt; wɔːnt/ *verb, noun*

■**verb** [T] (not usually used in the progressive tenses 通常不用于进行时)

• **WISH** 希望 **1** to have a desire or a wish for sth 要；想要；希望：**~ sth** *Do you want some more tea?* 你再要点儿茶吗？◇ *She's always wanted a large family.* 她一直希望生一大群孩子。◇ ***All I want is*** *the truth.* 我只想知道实情。◇ *Thanks for the present—it's* ***just what I wanted.*** 感谢赠我这份礼物，这正是我想要的。◇ *I can do whatever I want.* 我想干什么就可以干什么。◇ ***The last thing I wanted was*** *to upset you.* 我最不希望做的事就是惹你不高兴。◇ *The party wants her as leader.* 这个政党希望由她做领袖。◇ **~ (to do sth)** *What do you want to do tomorrow?* 明天你想做什么？◇ *'It's time you did your homework.' 'I don't want to!'* "你该做作业了。""我就是不想做！"◇ *There are two points which I wanted to make.* 我想要指出的有两点。◇ ***I just wanted*** *to know if everything was all right.* 我只是想知道是否一切都好。◇ (*informal*) *You can come too,* ***if you want.*** 如果你想来也可以来。◇ **~ sb/sth to do sth** *Do you want me to help?* 你要我帮忙吗？◇ *We didn't want this to happen.* 我们并不希望发生这样的事情。◇ *I want it (to be) done as quickly as possible.* 我希望这件事尽快完成。HELP Notice that you cannot say 'want that…'. 注意不能说 want that ...: ~~*I want that you do it quickly.*~~ When the infinitive is used after **want**, it must have **to**. * want 后用不定式时，必须带 to: ~~*I want study in America.*~~ ◇ **~ sb/sth doing sth** *I don't want you coming home so late.* 我不希望你这么晚回家。◇ **~ sb/sth + adj.** *Do you want your coffee black or white?* 你的咖啡里加不加奶？➲ MORE LIKE THIS 26, page R28

• **NEED** 需要 **2** (*informal*) to need sth 需要：**~ sth** *We'll want more furniture for the new office.* 我们的新办公室需要添些家具。◇ *What this house wants is a good clean.* 这房子需要好好打扫一下。◇ **~ doing sth** *The plants want watering daily.* 这些植物需要天天浇水。◇ **~ to be/have sth** *The plants want to be watered daily.* 这些植物需要天天浇水。**3** [usually passive] **~ sb (+ adv./prep.)** to need sb to be present in the place or for the purpose mentioned 需要…在场：*She's wanted immediately in the director's office.* 她得马上到主任办公室去。◇ *Excuse me, you're wanted on the phone.* 对不起，有你的电话。➲ SEE ALSO WANTED

• **SHOULD/OUGHT TO** 应该 **4 ~ to do sth** (*informal*) used to give advice to sb, meaning 'should' or 'ought to'（用于提出建议）应该：*If possible, you want to avoid alcohol.* 你应尽可能避免饮酒。◇ *He wants to be more careful.* 他应多加小心。◇ *You don't want to do it like that.* 你不应那样做。

• **FEEL SEXUAL DESIRE** 有性欲 **5 ~ sb** to feel sexual desire for sb 对…有性欲

• **LACK** 缺少 **6 ~ sth** (*formal*) to lack sth 缺少；缺乏 SYN **short**: *He doesn't want courage.* 他有的是勇气。

IDM **not want to ˈknow (about sth)** (*informal*) to take no interest in sth because you do not care about it or it is too much trouble 不想知道；不愿理会：*I've tried to ask her advice, but she doesn't want to know* (= about my problems). 我尝试向她请教，但她却不愿理会。◇ *'How much was it?'* ***'You don't want to know.'*** (= it is better if you don't know) "这要多少钱？""你还是不知道的好。" **want ˈrid of sb/sth** (*BrE, informal*) to want to be free of sb/sth that has been annoying you or that you do not want 想摆脱；想甩掉：*Are you trying to say you want rid of me?* 你是在说要甩掉我吗？ **what do you ˈwant?** used to ask sb in a rude or angry way why they are there or what they want you to do（语带指责）你在这里干什么；你要我干什么 ➲ MORE AT NONE *pron.*, PART *n.*, TRUCK *n.*, WASTE *v.*, WAY *n.*

PHR V **ˈwant for sth** (especially in negative sentences 尤用于否定句) (*formal*) to lack sth that you really need 缺少，短缺（真正需要的东西）：*He's ensured that his children will want for nothing* (= will have everything they need).

▼**MORE ABOUT ...** 补充说明

offers and invitations 提议和邀请

- **Would you like…?** is the most usual polite question form for offers and invitations, especially in *BrE*. * Would you like ...? 是最常见的礼貌提议和邀请疑问式，尤用于英式英语：*Would you like a cup of coffee?* 喝杯咖啡好吗？
- **Do you want…?** is less formal and more direct. It is more common in *NAmE* than in *BrE*. * Do you want ...? 较非正式且更直接，在美式英语中比在英式英语中常见：*We're going to a club tonight. Do you want to come with us?* 今晚我们要去俱乐部，你想和我们一起去吗？
- **Would you care…?** is very formal and now sounds old-fashioned. * Would you care ...? 很正式，听起来显得过时。

W

他得到保证他的子女将什么也不会缺少。**want sth from/out of sth/sb** to hope to get sth from a particular experience or person 希望从…中得到：*I had to discover what I really wanted out of life.* 我得弄清楚我到底要从生活中得到什么。◇ *What do you want from me?* 你要从我这里得到什么？**,want 'in/'out** (*informal, especially NAmE*) to want to come in or out of a place 想进来（或出去）：*The dog wants in.* 那条狗想进来。**,want 'in | ,want 'in/'into sth** (*informal*) to want to be involved in sth 想要参与；希望涉足：*He wants in on the deal.* 他希望参与这宗交易。**,want 'out | ,want 'out of sth** (*informal*) to want to stop being involved in sth 想要退出：*Jenny was fed up. She wanted out.* 珍妮厌倦了，她想要退出。

■ ***noun*** (*formal*)

• **STH YOU NEED** 需要的东西 **1** [C, usually pl.] something that you need or want 需要的东西；想望的东西：*She spent her life pandering to the wants of her children.* 她一生都在设法满足子女的需要。

• **LACK** 缺少 **2** [U, sing.] **~ of sth** (*formal*) a situation in which there is not enough of sth; a lack of sth 缺少；缺乏；不足：*a want of adequate medical facilities* 缺少足够的医疗设施

• **BEING POOR** 贫穷 **3** [U] (*formal*) the state of being poor, not having food, etc. 贫穷；贫困；匮乏：*Visitors to the slums were clearly shocked to see so many families living* ***in want.*** 到过贫民窟的人看到有这么多的家庭生活在贫苦之中显然震惊不已。

IDM **for (the) want of sth** because of a lack of sth; because sth is not available 因为缺乏…：*The project failed for want of financial backing.* 这个项目由于缺少财政支援而告吹。◇ *We call our music 'postmodern' for the want of a better word.* 由于没有更合适的词来表达，我们把我们的音乐称作"后现代风格"。**in want of sth** (*formal*) needing sth 需要（某事物）：*The present system is in want of a total review.* 目前的系统需要全面的复查。**not for (the) want of doing sth** used to say that if sth is not successful, it is not because of a lack of effort 并非办事不力：*If he doesn't manage to convince them, it won't be for* ***want of trying*** (= he has tried hard). 如果他没能使他们信服，这倒不是由于努力不够。

'want ads *noun* [pl.] (*NAmE*) = CLASSIFIED ADVERTISEMENTS

want·ed /'wɒntɪd; *NAmE* 'wɑːn-/ *adj.* being searched for by the police, in connection with a crime 受通缉的：*He is wanted by the police in connection with the deaths of two people.* 他因与两条人命有关而受到警方通缉。◇ *Italy's most wanted man* 意大利头号通缉犯

want·ing /'wɒntɪŋ; *NAmE* 'wɑːn-; 'wɔːn-/ *adj.* [not before noun] (*formal*) **1 ~ (in sth)** not having enough of sth 缺少；缺乏；不足 **SYN** **lacking**：*The students were certainly not wanting in enthusiasm.* 学生们当然不乏热情。**2 ~ (in sth)** not good enough 欠缺；不够好；不令人满意：*This explanation is wanting in many respects.* 这一解释在很多方面不能令人满意。◇ *The new system was tried and* ***found wanting.*** 这一新系统经测试发现不够好。

wan·ton /'wɒntən; *NAmE* 'wɑːn-/ *adj.* (*formal*) **1** [usually before noun] causing harm or damage deliberately and for no acceptable reason 恶意的；不怀好意的；恣意的：*wanton destruction* 肆意破坏 ◇ *a wanton disregard for human life* 全然不顾人的死活 **2** (*old-fashioned, disapproving*) (usually of a woman 通常指女人) behaving in a very immoral way; having many sexual partners 淫荡的；淫乱的；水性杨花的 ▸ **wan·ton·ly** *adv.* **wan·ton·ness** *noun* [U]

WAP /wæp/ *abbr.* wireless application protocol (a technology that links devices such as mobile/cell phones to the Internet) 无线应用协议（全写为 wireless application protocol，使手机等连接互联网的技术）：*a WAP-enabled phone* 可无线上网的电话

wap·iti /'wɒpɪti; *NAmE* 'wɑːp-/ *noun* (*pl.* **wap·iti**) (*NAmE also* **elk**) a very large N American DEER 马鹿 ➲ PICTURE AT ELK

war 🔑 /wɔː(r)/ *noun* **1** 🔑 [U, C] a situation in which two or more countries or groups of people fight against each other over a period of time 战争；战争状态：*the Second World War* 第二次世界大战 ◇ *the threat of (a) nuclear war* 核战争威胁 ◇ *to* ***win/lose a/the war*** 战胜；战败 ◇ *the* ***war between*** *England and Scotland* 英格兰和苏格兰之间的战争 ◇ *England's* ***war with/against*** *Scotland* 英格兰和/对苏格兰的战争 ◇ *It was the year Britain* ***declared war on*** *Germany.* 那是英国对德国宣战的那一年。◇ *Social and political problems led to* ***the outbreak*** (= the beginning) ***of war.*** 社会和政治问题导致了战争的爆发。◇ *Where were you living when* ***war broke out?*** 战争爆发时你住在哪儿？◇ *The government does not want to* ***go to war*** (= start a war) *unless all other alternatives have failed.* 除非所有其他方法都行不通，否则政府不希望开战。◇ *How long have they been* ***at war?*** 他们交战有多长时间了？◇ *a* ***war hero*** 战斗英雄 ◇ (*formal*) *In the Middle Ages England* ***waged war*** *on France.* 在中世纪，英格兰向法国发动了战争。◇ *More troops are being despatched to the* ***war zone.*** 更多的部队被派往作战地区。◇ (*formal*) *the* ***theatre of war*** (= the area in which fighting takes place) 战区 ➲ WORDFINDER NOTE AT CONFLICT ➲ SEE ALSO CIVIL WAR, COLD WAR, COUNCIL OF WAR, PHONEY WAR, POST-WAR, PRISONER OF WAR, WARRING, WORLD WAR **2** 🔑 [C, U] a situation in which there is aggressive competition between groups, companies, countries, etc.（群体、公司、国家之间的）竞争，斗争，对抗，冲突：*the class war* 阶级斗争 ◇ *a trade war* 贸易战 ➲ SEE ALSO PRICE WAR **3** 🔑 [U, sing.] **~ (against/on sb/sth)** a fight or an effort over a long period of time to get rid of or stop sth unpleasant（为消灭有害事物的）长期斗争；顽强抵御：*The government* ***has declared war on*** *drug dealers.* 政府已向贩毒分子宣战。◇ *We seem to be winning the war against crime.* 我们在打击犯罪方面似乎已做出成绩。➲ SYNONYMS AT CAMPAIGN

IDM **have been in the 'wars** (*informal*) to have been injured in a fight or an accident 打架受伤；在事故中受伤：*You look like you've been in the wars—who gave you that black eye?* 看样子你打架受伤了，是谁把你打得鼻青眼肿？**a ,war of 'nerves** an attempt to defeat your opponents by putting pressure on them so that they lose courage or confidence 神经战（利用心理压力摧毁对方的斗志）**a ,war of 'words** a bitter argument or disagreement over a period of time between two or more people or groups 舌战；论战：*the political war of words over tax* 有关税收问题的政治论战 ➲ MORE AT FAIR *adj.*

war·ble /'wɔːbl; *NAmE* 'wɔːrbl/ *verb* **1** [T, I] **~ (sth) | + speech** (*humorous*) to sing, especially in a high voice that is not very steady（尤指用颤音高声）唱：*He warbled his way through the song.* 整个歌曲他是用高颤音唱的。**2** [I, T] **~ (sth)** (of a bird 鸟) to sing with rapidly changing notes 啭鸣 ▸ **war·ble** *noun*

warb·ler /'wɔːblə(r); *NAmE* 'wɔːrbl-/ *noun* a small bird. There are many types of warbler, some of which have a musical call. 莺（有些能发出悦耳的啭鸣）

war·chalk·ing /'wɔːtʃɔːkɪŋ; *NAmE* 'wɔːr-/ *noun* [U] (*informal*) the action of drawing a symbol on the wall of a building to show that you can get a free Internet connection near that place 免费上网标记（在墙上标示附近可免费上网）

'war chest *noun* an amount of money that a government or an organization has available to spend on a particular plan, project, etc. 专用款项；专款

'war crime *noun* a cruel act that is committed during a war and is against the international rules of war 战争罪行（违反国际战争公约的战时行为）

'war criminal *noun* a person who has committed war crimes 战犯

'war cry *noun* a word or phrase that is shouted by people fighting in a battle in order to give themselves courage and to frighten the enemy（作战时鼓舞士气的）喊杀声，呐喊声

ward /wɔːd; *NAmE* wɔːrd/ *noun, verb*

■ ***noun*** **1** a separate room or area in a hospital for people with the same type of medical condition 病房；病室：

W

a maternity/surgical/psychiatric/children's, etc. ward 产科、外科、精神科、儿科等病房 ◇ *He worked as a nurse on the children's ward.* 他在儿科病房当护士。➲ WORDFINDER NOTE AT HOSPITAL **2** (in Britain) one of the areas into which a city is divided and which elects and is represented by a member of the local council（英国城市中可选出一位地方议员的）区，选区 **3** (*law* 律) a person, especially a child, who is under the legal protection of a court or another person (called a GUARDIAN) 受监护人（受法院或监护人保护的人，尤指儿童）: *The child was made a **ward of court**.* 这个孩子由法院监护。

■ *verb*

PHR V ˌ**ward sb/sth**↔ˈ**off** to protect or defend yourself against danger, illness, attack, etc. 防止，避免，抵御（危险、疾病、攻击等）: *to ward off criticism* 受到批评后为自己开脱 ◇ *She put up her hands to ward him off.* 她举起双手把他挡开。

-ward (*also less frequent* **-wards**) *suffix* (in adjectives 构成形容词) in the direction of 向…的: *backward* 向后的 ◇ *eastward* 向东的 ◇ *homeward* 回家去的 ▶ **-wards** (*also* **-ward** *especially in NAmE*) (in adverbs 构成副词): *onwards* 向前 ◇ *forwards* 向前

ˈ**war dance** *noun* a dance that is performed by members of some peoples, for example before battle or to celebrate a victory 战舞（某些民族在战前动员或祝捷时跳）

war·den /ˈwɔːdn; *NAmE* ˈwɔːrdn/ *noun* **1** a person who is responsible for taking care of a particular place and making sure that the rules are obeyed 管理人；看守人；监护人: *a forest warden* 护林员 ◇ (*BrE*) *the warden of a youth hostel* 青年旅舍的管理员 ➲ SEE ALSO CHURCHWARDEN, DOG WARDEN, GAME WARDEN, TRAFFIC WARDEN **2** (*especially NAmE*) the person in charge of a prison 监狱长 **3** (in Britain), a title given to the head of some colleges and institutions（英国）学院院长，协会会长，机构主管:

▼ **COLLOCATIONS** 词语搭配

War and peace 战争与和平

Starting a war 开战

- **declare/make/wage** war (on sb/sth)（向…）宣战 / 挑起战争 / 发动战争
- **go to** war (against/with sb)（向…）开战
- **cause/spark/provoke/foment/quell** unrest 引起 / 平息骚乱
- **incite/lead/crush/suppress** a revolt/rebellion 煽动 / 领导 / 镇压起义 / 叛乱
- **launch/mount/carry out** a surprise/terrorist attack 发起 / 实施突然 / 恐怖袭击
- **prevent/halt/represent** an escalation of the conflict 防止 / 阻止 / 表明冲突升级
- **be torn apart by/be on the brink of** civil war 被内战搞得四分五裂；濒于内战
- **enter/invade/occupy** sb's territory 进入 / 侵略 / 占领某人的领土
- **lead/launch/resist/repel** an invasion 领导 / 发起 / 抵制 / 击退武装入侵

Military operations 军事行动

- **adopt/develop/implement/pursue** a military strategy 采用 / 发展 / 实施 / 执行军事战略
- **carry out/execute/perform** military operations/manoeuvres/(*especially US*) maneuvers 执行军事行动 / 军事演习
- **send/deploy/station/pull back/withdraw** troops 派遣 / 部署 / 派驻 / 撤回部队
- **go on/fly/carry out** a reconnaissance/rescue mission 进行 / 驾机执行 / 执行侦察 / 营救任务
- **train/equip/deploy** army/military/combat units 训练 / 装备 / 部署陆军 / 军事 / 作战分队
- **lead/launch/conduct** a raid/a surprise attack/an (air/airborne/amphibious) assault (on sb) 领导 / 发起 / 实施（对某人的）突然袭击 /（空中 / 空投部队 / 登陆）攻击
- **employ/use** guerrilla tactics 采用游击战术
- **conduct/wage** biological/guerrilla warfare 进行 / 发动生物战 / 游击战
- **fight/crush/defeat** the rebels/the insurgency 设法战胜 / 镇压 / 挫败叛乱者 / 叛乱
- **suffer/inflict** a crushing defeat 遭受惨败；大获全胜
- **achieve/win** a decisive victory 赢得决定性的胜利
- **halt/stop** the British/German/Russian advance 阻止英国 / 德国 / 俄罗斯的前进
- **order/force** a retreat 命令 / 强迫撤退

Fighting 作战

- **join/serve in** the army/navy/air force 加入陆军 / 海军 / 空军；在陆军 / 海军 / 空军部队服役
- **be/go/remain/serve** on active duty 在服现役
- **serve/complete/return from** a tour of duty 在服役；服役完毕；服役归来
- **be sent** to the front (line) 被派往前线
- **attack/strike/engage/defeat/kill/destroy** the enemy 袭击 / 攻击敌人；与敌人交战；击败 / 杀死 / 消灭敌人
- **see/report/be engaged in** heavy fighting 目睹 / 报道 / 参与激战
- **call for/be met with** armed resistance 要求 / 遭遇武装抵抗
- **come under** heavy/machine-gun/mortar fire 冒着激烈的 / 机关枪的 / 迫击炮的射击
- **fire** a machine-gun/mortar shells/rockets (at sb/sth)（对…）发射机关枪 / 迫击炮弹 / 火箭弹
- **shoot** a rifle/a pistol/bullets/missiles 步枪 / 手枪射击；发射子弹 / 导弹
- **launch/fire** a cruise/ballistic/anti-tank missile 发射巡航 / 弹道 / 反坦克导弹
- **use** biological/chemical/nuclear weapons 使用生物 / 化学 / 核武器
- **inflict/suffer/sustain** heavy losses/casualties 遭受惨重损失 / 伤亡
- **be hit/killed by** enemy/friendly/artillery fire 被敌军 / 友军 / 炮火击中 / 射死
- **become/be held as** a prisoner of war 成为战俘；作为战俘被监禁

Civilians in war 战争中的平民

- **harm/kill/target/protect** innocent/unarmed civilians 伤害 / 杀死 / 瞄准 / 保护无辜的 / 手无寸铁的平民
- **cause/avoid/limit/minimize** civilian casualties/collateral damage 导致 / 避免 / 限制 / 最大限度减少平民伤亡 / 附带性破坏
- **impose/enforce/lift** a curfew 强制实行 / 解除宵禁
- **engage in/be a victim of** ethnic cleansing 参与种族清洗；成为种族清洗的受害者
- **be sent to** an internment/a concentration camp 被送到俘虏拘留营 / 集中营
- **accept/house/resettle** refugees fleeing from war 接受 / 收容 / 安置战争难民
- **fear/threaten** military/violent reprisals 害怕 / 扬言要军事 / 暴力报复
- **commit/be accused of** war crimes/crimes against humanity/genocide 犯 / 被指控犯战争罪 / 反人类罪 / 种族灭绝罪

Making peace 和解

- **make/bring/win/achieve/maintain/promote** peace 促使 / 带来 / 赢得 / 实现 / 保持 / 促进和平
- **call for/negotiate/broker/declare** a ceasefire/a temporary truce 要求 / 商谈 / 协商 / 宣布停战 / 暂时休战
- **sign** a ceasefire agreement 签署停战协议
- **call for/bring/put an end to** hostilities 要求发动 / 引发 / 结束战争
- **demand/negotiate/accept** the surrender of sb/sth 强烈要求 / 商讨 / 接受…投降
- **establish/send (in)** a peacekeeping force 建立 / 派遣维和部队
- **negotiate/conclude/ratify/sign/accept/reject/break/violate** a peace treaty 商讨 / 达成 / 正式批准 / 签署 / 接受 / 拒绝 / 破坏 / 违反和平协定

W

the Warden of Wadham College, Oxford 牛津大学沃德姆学院院长

war·der /ˈwɔːdə(r); *NAmE* ˈwɔːrd-/ (*feminine* **ward·ress** /ˈwɔːdrəs; *NAmE* ˈwɔːrd-/) *noun* (*BrE*) a person who guards prisoners in a prison（监狱的）看守；狱吏 ➲ COMPARE GUARD *n.* (1) ➲ **WORDFINDER NOTE** AT PRISON

ward·robe /ˈwɔːdrəʊb; *NAmE* ˈwɔːrdroʊb/ *noun* **1** a large cupboard for hanging clothes in which is either a piece of furniture or (in British English) built into the wall 衣柜；衣橱；（英国）放置衣物的壁橱：*a fitted wardrobe* 入墙衣柜 ➲ **VISUAL VOCAB** PAGE V24 ➲ COMPARE CLOSET *n.* **2** [usually sing.] the clothes that a person has（一个人的）全部衣物：*everything you need for your summer wardrobe* 需要的所有夏装 ➲ **COLLOCATIONS** AT FASHION **3** [usually sing.] the department in a theatre or television company that takes care of the clothes that actors wear（剧院或电视公司的）服装部，戏装保管室

ˈwardrobe mistress, **ˈwardrobe master** *noun* a person whose job is to take care of the clothes that the actors in a theatre company, etc. wear on stage（剧团等的）服装保管员

ward·room /ˈwɔːdruːm; -rʊm; *NAmE* ˈwɔːrd-/ *noun* a room in a ship, especially a WARSHIP, where the officers live and eat（尤指军舰上的）军官起居室，军官餐厅

-wards ➲ -WARD

ward·ship /ˈwɔːdʃɪp; *NAmE* ˈwɔːrd-/ *noun* [U] (*law* 律) the fact of a child being cared for by a GUARDIAN (= a person who is not his or her parent) or of being protected by a court（监护人或法院对儿童的）监护，保护 ➲ SEE ALSO WARD *n.* (3)

ware /weə(r); *NAmE* wer/ *noun* **1** [U] (in compounds 构成复合词) objects made of the material or in the way or place mentioned 用某材料（或以某方式、在某地）制造的物品：*ceramic ware* 陶瓷制品 ◇ *a collection of local ware* 一批当地器皿 ◇ *basketware* 篮筐制品 ➲ SEE ALSO EARTHENWARE, FLATWARE, GLASSWARE, SILVERWARE (2) **2** [U] (in compounds 构成复合词) objects used for the purpose or in the room mentioned 作…用的器皿；…室的物品：*bathroom ware* 浴室用品 ◇ *ornamental ware* 装饰品 ◇ *homeware* 家居用品 ➲ SEE ALSO KITCHENWARE, TABLEWARE **3 wares** [pl.] (*old-fashioned*) things that sb is selling, especially in the street or at a market（尤指小商贩在大街上或市场里出售的）物品：*He travelled from town to town selling his wares.* 他走乡串镇出售自己的货品。

ware·house /ˈweəhaʊs; *NAmE* ˈwerh-/ *noun* a building where large quantities of goods are stored, especially before they are sent to shops/stores to be sold 仓库；货栈；货仓 ➲ **WORDFINDER NOTE** AT INDUSTRY ➲ **VISUAL VOCAB** PAGE V15

ware·hous·ing /ˈweəhaʊzɪŋ; *NAmE* ˈwerh-/ *noun* [U] the practice or business of storing things in a warehouse 仓储；仓储业

war·fare /ˈwɔːfeə(r); *NAmE* ˈwɔːrfer/ *noun* [U] **1** the activity of fighting a war, especially using particular weapons or methods 战；作战；战争：***air/naval/guerrilla, etc. warfare*** 空战、海战、游击战等 ◇ *countries engaged in warfare* 参战国 ➲ **COLLOCATIONS** AT WAR ➲ SEE ALSO BIOLOGICAL WARFARE, CHEMICAL WARFARE, GERM WARFARE **2** the activity of competing in an aggressive way with another group, company, etc.（群体、公司等之间的）斗争，竞争，冲突：***class/gang warfare*** 阶级 / 帮派斗争 ◇ *The debate soon degenerated into open warfare.* 争论很快恶化，演变成了公开的论战。➲ SEE ALSO PSYCHOLOGICAL WARFARE

war·farin /ˈwɔːfərɪn; *NAmE* ˈwɔːrf-/ *noun* [U] a substance that is used as a poison to kill RATS and also for people as a medicine to make the blood thinner, for example in the treatment of THROMBOSIS 华法林，苄丙酮香豆素钠（用作灭鼠剂或抗凝血剂）

ˈwar game *noun* **1** a practice battle that is used to test military plans and equipment 作战演习；军事演习 **2** a game or activity in which imaginary battles are fought, for example by moving models of soldiers, ships, etc. around on a table, or on a computer 战争游戏（用模型士兵、战舰等在桌面或计算机上进行）

ˈwar gaming *noun* [U] the activity of playing war games (2) 战争游戏

war·head /ˈwɔːhed; *NAmE* ˈwɔːrhed/ *noun* the EXPLOSIVE part of a MISSILE（导弹的）弹头：*nuclear warheads* 核弹头

war·horse /ˈwɔːhɔːs; *NAmE* ˈwɔːrhɔːrs/ *noun* **1** (in the past) a large horse used in battle（旧时）军马，战马 **2** (*informal*) an old soldier or politician who has a lot of experience 久经沙场的老兵；老练的政治家

wari·ly, **wari·ness** ➲ WARY

war·like /ˈwɔːlaɪk; *NAmE* ˈwɔːrl-/ *adj.* (*formal*) **1** aggressive and wanting to fight 好战的；好斗的；尚武的 **SYN** **belligerent**：*a warlike nation* 好战的民族 **2** connected with fighting wars 战争的；与战争有关的；军事的 **SYN** **military**：*warlike preparations* 战备

war·lock /ˈwɔːlɒk; *NAmE* ˈwɔːrlɑːk/ *noun* a man who is believed to have magic powers, especially evil ones（尤指邪恶的）男巫，术士

war·lord /ˈwɔːlɔːd; *NAmE* ˈwɔːrlɔːrd/ *noun* (*disapproving*) the leader of a military group that is not official and that fights against other groups within a country or an area 军阀

warm 🔑 /wɔːm; *NAmE* wɔːrm/ *adj., verb, noun, adv.*

■ ***adj.*** (**warm·er**, **warm·est**)

• **AT PLEASANT TEMPERATURE** 温度宜人 **1** 🔑 at a fairly high temperature in a way that is pleasant, rather than being hot or cold 温暖的；暖和的：*a warm breeze* 和煦的微风 ◇ *Wash the blouse in warm soapy water.* 这件女衬衫要用温的肥皂水洗。◇ *It's **nice and warm** in here.* 这里暖烘烘的。◇ *Are you warm enough?* 你够暖和吗？◇ *The children jumped up and down to **keep warm**.* 孩子们上下跳动保持身体暖和。◇ *You'll be **as warm as toast** in here.* 你在这里会感到暖烘烘的。

• **CLOTHES/BUILDINGS** 衣服；建筑物 **2** 🔑 keeping you warm or staying warm in cold weather 保暖的；保温的：*a warm pair of socks* 一双暖和的袜子 ◇ *This sleeping bag is very warm.* 这条睡袋很暖和。◇ *a warm house* 温暖的房屋

• **FRIENDLY** 友善 **3** 🔑 showing enthusiasm and/or affection; friendly 温情的；热心的；友好的：*His smile was warm and friendly.* 他的微笑热情而友好。◇ *The speaker was given **a warm welcome/reception**.* 演讲者受到热烈的欢迎。◇ *Please send her my warmest congratulations.* 请代我向她致以最热烈的祝贺。

• **COLOURS** 颜色 **4** (of colours 颜色) containing red, orange or yellow, which creates a pleasant, comfortable and relaxed feeling or atmosphere 暖色调的：*The room was decorated in warm shades of red and orange.* 这房间是用红和橙的这些暖色调装饰的。

• **IN GAME** 游戏 **5** [not before noun] used to say that sb has almost guessed the answer to sth or that they have almost found sb/sth that has been hidden 即将猜中；接近答案；即将找到：*Keep guessing—you're getting warmer.* 接着猜，你离答案越来越近了。

▶ **warm·ly** /ˈwɔːmli; *NAmE* ˈwɔːrmli/ *adv.*: *They were warmly dressed in coats and scarves.* 他们身着大衣，围着围巾，穿得暖暖和和。◇ *The play was warmly received by the critics.* 评论家对这出戏反应热烈。➲ SEE ALSO WARMTH

■ ***verb***

• **MAKE/BECOME WARM** （使）变暖 **1** 🔑 [T, I] to make sth/sb warm or warmer; to become warm or warmer（使）温暖，变暖和：**~ sth/sb/yourself** (**up**) *I'll warm up some milk.* 我来热些牛奶。◇ *Come in and warm yourself by the fire.* 进来烤火暖和暖和吧。◇ *The alcohol warmed and relaxed him.* 这酒使他浑身发暖轻松起来。◇ **~** (**up**) *As the climate warms (up) the ice caps will melt.* 随着气候变暖，冰盖将融化。

• **BECOME FRIENDLY** 变得友好 **2** [I, T] **~** (**sb**) to become more friendly, loving, etc.; to make sb feel or become more friendly, loving, etc.（使）变得更友好，变得更温情 ➲ SEE ALSO GLOBAL WARMING, HOUSE-WARMING

IDM **warm the 'cockles (of sb's 'heart)** (*BrE*) to make sb feel happy or sympathetic 使人内心感到高兴（或同情）➲ MORE AT DEATH

PHR V **ˌwarm 'down** to do gentle exercises to help your body relax after doing a particular sport or activity（在体育运动或活动后）做放松运动 ➲ RELATED NOUN WARM-DOWN **'warm to/towards sb** to begin to like sb 开始喜欢上（某人）：*I warmed to her immediately.* 我立即喜欢上了她。**'warm to/towards sth** to become more interested in or enthusiastic about sth 对…更加感兴趣（或热衷）：*The speaker was now warming to her theme.* 演讲者就她的主题越讲越起劲。**ˌwarm 'up 1** to prepare for physical exercise or a performance by doing gentle exercises or practice（为体育活动或表演）做适应性练习，做准备活动；热身 ➲ RELATED NOUN WARM-UP **2** (of a machine, an engine, etc. 机器、发动机等) to run for a short time in order to reach the temperature at which it will operate well 暖机；预热 **ˌwarm 'up | ˌwarm sb/sth ↔'up** to become more lively or enthusiastic; to make sb/sth more lively or enthusiastic（使）活跃起来，热情起来：*The party soon warmed up.* 聚会很快活跃起来。**ˌwarm sth↔'up** to heat previously cooked food again for eating 把（冷饭菜）热一热

■ *noun*

• PLACE 地方 **1 the warm** [sing.] a place where the temperature is warm 暖和的地方：*Come inside into the warm.* 进来暖和暖和。

■ *adv.* (**warm·er, warm·est**) (*informal*) in a way that makes you feel warm 使人暖和地；温暖地 **SYN** **warmly**: *Wrap up warm before you go outside!* 穿得暖和些再出去！

ˌwarm-'blooded *adj.* (of animals 动物) having a warm blood temperature that does not change if the temperature around them changes 温血的；恒温的 ➲ COMPARE COLD-BLOODED (2), HOT-BLOODED

'warm-down *noun* [usually sing.] a series of gentle exercises that you do to help your body relax after doing a particular sport or activity（锻炼后的）缓和运动，放松运动，收操

warm·er /ˈwɔːmə(r); *NAmE* ˈwɔːrmər/ *noun* (especially in compounds 尤用于构成复合词) a piece of clothing, a device, etc. that warms sb/sth 保温衣；保温器；加热器：*a plate warmer* 暖盘器 ➲ SEE ALSO LEG WARMER

ˌwarm-'hearted *adj.* (of a person 人) kind, friendly and sympathetic 热心肠的；友好的；富有同情心的 ➲ COMPARE COLD-HEARTED

warm·ing /ˈwɔːmɪŋ; *NAmE* ˈwɔːrmɪŋ/ *noun* [U] the process of making sth, or of becoming, warm or warmer 加温；温暖；暖和；变暖：*atmospheric warming* 大气层变暖 ➲ SEE ALSO GLOBAL WARMING ▶ **warm·ing** *adj.*: *the warming rays of the sun* 暖融融的太阳光线 ◇ *a warming drink* 热饮

'warming pan *noun* a metal container with a long handle that, in the past, was filled with hot coals and used to warm beds（旧时的）长柄炭炉，长柄暖床器

war·mon·ger /ˈwɔːmʌŋɡə(r); *NAmE* ˈwɔːrmʌŋɡər/ *noun* (*formal, disapproving*) a person, especially a politician or leader, who wants to start a war or encourages people to start a war 战争贩子 ▶ **war·mon·ger·ing** *noun* [U] **war·mon·ger·ing** *adj.* [only before noun]

warmth /wɔːmθ; *NAmE* wɔːrmθ/ *noun* [U] **1** the state or quality of being warm, rather than hot or cold 温暖；暖和：*She felt the warmth of his arms around her.* 她感到了他双臂搂着她的温暖。◇ *The animals huddled together for warmth.* 那些动物依偎在一起取暖。◇ *He led the child into the warmth and safety of the house.* 他把这孩子领到家里享受温暖和安全。**2** the state or quality of being enthusiastic and/or friendly 热情；友情：*They were touched by the warmth of the welcome.* 他们受到了热情欢迎，很感动。

'warm-up *noun* [usually sing.] **1** a short practice or a series of gentle exercises that you do to prepare yourself for doing a particular sport or activity（体育运动等前的）适应性活动，准备活动；热身练习：*warm-up exercises* 热身练习 **2** a short performance of music, comedy, etc. that is intended to prepare the audience for the main show 暖场表演（正式表演开始前上演的短小音乐、喜剧等节目）：*a warm-up act* 暖场表演

warn /wɔːn; *NAmE* wɔːrn/ *verb* **1** [T, I] to tell sb about sth, especially sth dangerous or unpleasant that is likely to happen, so that they can avoid it 提醒注意（可能发生的事）；使警惕：**~ sb** *I tried to warn him, but he wouldn't listen.* 我设法提醒过他，可他就是不听。◇ *If you're thinking of getting a dog,* ***be warned****—they take a lot of time and money.* 如果你想养条狗，有话说在前头，那可既费时间又费钱。◇ **~ (sb) about/against sb/sth** *He warned us against pickpockets.* 他提醒我们要提防小偷。◇ **~ (sb) of sth** *Police have warned of possible delays.* 警方已经通知交通可能受阻。◇ **~ (sb) that…** *She was warned that if she did it again she would lose her job.* 她被警告说如果她再这样做就会丢掉工作。◇ **~ sb what, how, etc.…** *I had been warned what to expect.* 有人事先告诉过我要出什么事。◇ **~ (sb) + speech** *'Beware of pickpockets,' she warned (him).* "当心扒手。" 她提醒（他）道。**2** [I, T] to strongly advise sb to do or not to do sth in order to avoid danger or punishment 劝告（使有所防备）；警告；告诫 **SYN** **advise**: **~ (sb) against/about sth** *The guidebook warns against walking alone at night.* 这本指南告诫夜间不要单独行走。◇ **~ sb (to do sth)** *He warned Billy to keep away from his daughter.* 他警告比利离他女儿远点。**3** [T] **~ sb (for sth)** (in sport, etc. 体育运动等) to give sb an official warning after they have broken a rule 警告：*The referee warned him for dangerous play.* 裁判警告他有危险动作。

PHR V **ˌwarn sb 'off (sth) 1** to tell sb to leave or stay away from a place or person, especially in a threatening way（尤指以威胁的方式）叫…离开，告诫…不要靠近：*The farmer warned us off his land when we tried to camp there.* 我们想在那里露营，可是农场主警告我们不得靠近他的土地。**2** to advise sb not to do sth or to stop doing sth 劝…不要做；建议…停止做：**warn sb off doing sth** *We were warned off buying the house.* 有人劝我们不要购买这所房子。

▼ **EXPRESS YOURSELF 情景表达**

Warning people of danger 警示危险

You may need to tell someone that they are in danger or advise them not to do something dangerous. 告诉他人有危险或劝其远离危险：

- ***Look out!*** *There's a car coming.* 当心！有辆车开过来。
- ***Be careful.*** *It can be quite dangerous on that path.* 小心，那条小路有时挺危险的。
- ***Watch out.*** *That's not a very safe place at night.* 当心点儿，那个地方晚上不是很安全。
- ***Make sure you keep hold of your bag.*** 一定要拿好自己的包。
- ***I wouldn't do that if I were you.*** 如果我是你，我不会那么做。

warn·ing /ˈwɔːnɪŋ; *NAmE* ˈwɔːrn-/ *noun* **1** [C, U] a statement, an event, etc. telling sb that sth bad or unpleasant may happen in the future so that they can try to avoid it（就可能发生的意外等提出的）警告，警示；先兆：*Doctors* ***issued a warning against*** *eating any fish caught in the river.* 医生发出警告不要吃在那条河里捕的鱼。◇ *to give sb* ***fair/advance/adequate warning*** *of sth* 就某事向某人发出充分的 / 预先的 / 足够的警告 ◇ *The bridge collapsed* ***without (any) warning.*** 那座桥在没有任何先兆的情况下坍塌了。◇ *Let me give you* ***a word of warning.*** 我来提醒你一句。◇ *a government* ***health warning*** 政府关于健康的忠告 ➲ SEE ALSO EARLY WARNING **2** [C] a statement telling sb that they will be punished if they continue to behave in a particular way（就将要遭受的处罚等提出的）警告，警戒 **SYN** **caution**: *to give sb a* ***verbal/written/***

final warning 向某人发出口头 / 书面 / 最后警告 ▸ **warn·ing** *adj.* [only before noun]: *She had ignored the* **warning signs** *of trouble ahead.* 她没有理会警示前方危险的标志。◇ *Police fired a number of* **warning shots**. 警方多次鸣枪警告。◇ ***Warning bells began to ring*** (= it was a sign that sth was wrong) *when her letters were returned unopened.* 当她的信原封不动被退回时，不祥之感就来了。

ˌwarning ˈtriangle *noun* (*BrE*) a red triangle that a driver puts on the road next to his or her car as a warning to other drivers when the car has stopped because of a fault, an accident, etc.（发生故障或车祸等使用的）三角警示架，三角警示牌

warp /wɔːp; *NAmE* wɔːrp/ *verb, noun*

■ *verb* **1** [I, T] ~ (**sth**) to become, or make sth become, twisted or bent out of its natural shape, for example because it has become too hot, too damp, etc.（使）扭曲，弯曲，变形：*The window frames had begun to warp.* 窗框已经开始变形。**2** [T] ~ **sth** to influence sb so that they begin to behave in an unacceptable or shocking way 使（行为等）不合情理；使乖戾：*His judgement was warped by prejudice.* 他因偏见而判断有误。

■ *noun* **the warp** [sing.] (*specialist*) the threads on a LOOM (= a machine used for making cloth) that other threads are passed over and under in order to make cloth（织布机上的）经线，经纱 ➲ COMPARE WEFT ➲ SEE ALSO TIME WARP

war·paint /ˈwɔːpeɪnt; *NAmE* ˈwɔːrp-/ *noun* [U] **1** paint that some peoples, for example Native American peoples, put on their bodies and faces before fighting a battle（美国土著等）出征前涂在身上和脸上的颜料 **2** (*informal, humorous*) make-up, especially when it is thick or bright（尤指浓重的）化妆

war·path /ˈwɔːpɑːθ; *NAmE* ˈwɔːrpæθ/ *noun*

IDM **(be/go) on the ˈwarpath** (*informal*) (to be) angry and wanting to fight or punish sb（怒不可遏）准备开火

warped /wɔːpt; *NAmE* wɔːrpt/ *adj.* **1** (*disapproving*) (of a person 人) having ideas that most people think are strange or unpleasant 思想反常的；乖戾的：*a warped mind* 扭曲的心灵 ◇ *a warped sense of humour* 畸形的幽默感 **2** bent or twisted and not in the normal shape 弯曲的；扭曲的；变形的

war·plane /ˈwɔːpleɪn; *NAmE* ˈwɔːrp-/ *noun* a military plane that is designed for fighting in the air or dropping bombs 军用飞机（战斗机、轰炸机等）➲ WORDFINDER NOTE AT AIRCRAFT

ˈwarp speed *noun* [sing.] (*informal, humorous*) a very fast speed 极高速 **ORIGIN** From the US television series *Star Trek*, in which a 'warp drive' allowed space travel at speeds faster than the speed of light. 源自美国电视剧《星际迷航》，其中的"曲相推进"能使空间旅行速度超过光速。

war·rant /ˈwɒrənt; *NAmE* ˈwɔːr-; ˈwɑːr-/ *noun, verb*

■ *noun* **1** [C] a legal document that is signed by a judge and gives the police authority to do sth 执行令；授权令：*an arrest warrant* 逮捕证 ◇ ~ **for sth** *They* **issued a warrant** *for her arrest.* 当局发出了逮捕她的令状。◇ ~ **to do sth** *They had a warrant to search the house.* 他们有搜查这座房子的搜查令。➲ SEE ALSO DEATH WARRANT, SEARCH WARRANT **2** [C] ~ (**for sth**) a document that gives you the right to receive money, services, etc.（接受款项、服务等的）凭单，许可证 **3** [U] ~ (**for sth/for doing sth**) (*formal*) (usually in negative sentences 通常用于否定句) an acceptable reason for doing sth（做某事的）正当理由，依据：*There is no warrant for such criticism.* 这种批评毫无根据。

■ *verb* (*formal*) to make sth necessary or appropriate in a particular situation 使有必要；使正当；使恰当 **SYN** **justify**: ~ **sth** *Further investigation is clearly warranted.* 进一步调查显然是必要的。◇ ~ (**sb/sth**) **doing sth** *The situation scarcely warrants their/them being dismissed.* 这种情况很难证明解雇他们是正当的。➲ SEE ALSO UNWARRANTED

IDM **I/I'll warrant (you)** (*old-fashioned*) used to tell sb that you are sure of sth and that they can be sure of it too 我给你打保票；我向你保证

ˈwarrant officer *noun* a member of one of the middle ranks in the army, the British AIR FORCE and the US navy 准尉（陆军、英国空军和美国海军的中级军衔）：*Warrant Officer Gary Owen* 加里•欧文准尉

war·ranty /ˈwɒrənti; *NAmE* ˈwɔːr-; ˈwɑːr-/ *noun* (*pl.* **-ies**) [C, U] a written agreement in which a company selling sth promises to repair or replace it if there is a problem within a particular period of time（商品）保用单 **SYN** **guarantee**: *The television comes with a full two-year warranty.* 这台电视机有整两年的保修期。◇ *Is the car still* **under warranty**? 这辆汽车仍在保修期内吗？

war·ren /ˈwɒrən; *NAmE* ˈwɔːr-; ˈwɑːr-/ *noun* = RABBIT WARREN: (*figurative*) *The offices were a warren of small rooms and passages.* 这些办公室房间小，通道窄。

war·ring /ˈwɔːrɪŋ/ *adj.* [only before noun] involved in a war 战争的；交战的；敌对的：*A ceasefire has been agreed by the country's three warring factions.* 这个国家的交战三方已达成停火协议。

war·rior /ˈwɒriə(r); *NAmE* ˈwɔːr-/ *noun* (*formal*) (especially in the past) a person who fights in a battle or war（尤指旧时的）武士，勇士，斗士：*a warrior nation* (= whose people are skilled in fighting) 善战的民族 ◇ *a Zulu warrior* 祖鲁人的勇士

war·ship /ˈwɔːʃɪp; *NAmE* ˈwɔːrʃɪp/ *noun* a ship used in war 军舰；舰艇 ➲ WORDFINDER NOTE AT NAVY

wart /wɔːt; *NAmE* wɔːrt/ *noun* **1** a small hard lump that grows on your skin and that is caused by a virus 疣；瘊子；肉赘 **2** (*NAmE*) = VERRUCA

IDM **ˌwarts and ˈall** (*informal*) including all the bad or unpleasant features of sb/sth 包括所有的缺点；不隐瞒缺点；不遮丑：*She still loves him, warts and all.* 她仍然爱他，不管他有什么缺点。

wart·hog /ˈwɔːthɒg; *NAmE* ˈwɔːrthɑːg/ *noun* an African wild pig with two large outer teeth called TUSKS and lumps like warts on its face 疣猪（非洲野猪，有一对獠牙，脸部有疣）

war·time /ˈwɔːtaɪm; *NAmE* ˈwɔːrt-/ *noun* [U] the period during which a country is fighting a war 战时：*Different rules applied in wartime.* 战时实施不同的规定。▸ **war·time** *adj.* [only before noun]: *Fruit was a luxury in wartime Britain.* 在战时的英国，水果是一种奢侈品。➲ COMPARE PEACETIME

ˈwar-torn *adj.* [only before noun] a **war-torn** country or area is severely affected by the fighting that is taking place there 受战争严重破坏的；饱受战争蹂躏的

warty /ˈwɔːti; *NAmE* ˈwɔːrti/ *adj.* covered with WARTS 有疣的；长着瘊子的

ˈwar widow *noun* a woman whose husband was killed in a war 战争遗孀

wary /ˈweəri; *NAmE* ˈweri/ *adj.* (**wari·er**, **wari·est**) careful when dealing with sb/sth because you think that there may be a danger or problem（对待人或事物时）小心的，谨慎的，留神的，小心翼翼的 **SYN** **cautious**: ~ (**of sb/sth**) *Be wary of strangers who offer you a ride.* 提防那些主动让你搭车的陌生人。◇ ~ (**of doing sth**) *She was wary of getting involved with him.* 她唯恐和他有牵连。◇ *He gave her a wary look.* 他留意地看了她一眼。◇ *The police will need to* **keep a wary eye on** *this area of town* (= watch it carefully, in case there is trouble). 警方必须密切注意这一带城区。➲ COMPARE UNWARY ▸ **wari·ly** /ˈweərəli; *NAmE* ˈwerəli/ *adv.*: *The cat eyed him warily.* 那只猫警惕地注视着他。**wari·ness** *noun* [U, sing.]: *feelings of wariness* 小心谨慎 ◇ *There was a wariness in her tone.* 她的语气中透出一丝谨慎。

was /wəz; *strong form* wɒz; *NAmE strong form* wʌz/ ➲ BE

was·abi /wəˈsɑːbi/ *noun* [U] (*from Japanese*) a root vegetable with a strong taste like HORSERADISH, used in Japanese cooking, especially with raw fish 山嵛菜，山葵（辣味块根蔬菜，尤用于生鱼等日本食物）

wash 🔑 /wɒʃ; *NAmE* wɑːʃ; wɔːʃ/ *verb, noun*

▪ *verb* **1** 🔑 [T] to make sth/sb clean using water and usually soap 洗；洗涤：**~ sth/sb** *These jeans need washing.* 这条牛仔裤该洗了。◇ *to wash the car* 洗车 ◇ *to wash your hands* 洗手 ◇ *Wash the fruit thoroughly before eating.* 把水果彻底洗干净后再吃。◇ **~ sth from sth** *She washed the blood from his face.* 她把他脸上的血洗掉。◇ **~ sth/sb + adj.** *The beach had been washed clean by the tide.* 海滩让潮水冲刷得干干净净。➲ SYNONYMS AT CLEAN **2** 🔑 [I, T] (*especially BrE*) to make yourself clean using water and usually soap 洗澡；洗脸；洗手：*I washed and changed before going out.* 我洗了个澡，换好衣服，然后才出去。◇ **~ yourself** *She was no longer able to wash herself.* 她再也不能给自己洗澡了。**3** [I] (**+ adv./prep.**) (of clothes, cloth, etc. 衣服、织物等) to be able to be washed without losing colour or being damaged 耐洗；洗后不退色（或破损）：*This sweater washes well.* 这件套衫很耐洗。**4** [I, T] (of water 水) to flow or carry sth/sb in a particular direction （向着某一方向）流动；冲向：**+ adv./prep.** *Water washed over the deck.* 水从甲板上流过。◇ **~ sth/sb + adv./prep.** *Pieces of the wreckage were* ***washed ashore.*** 沉船残骸的碎片被冲到了岸上。◇ *He was* ***washed overboard*** *by a huge wave.* 一个巨浪把他从船上掀进海里。

IDM **wash your dirty linen in 'public** (*BrE, disapproving*) to discuss your personal affairs in public, especially sth embarrassing 公开谈论个人的事；（尤指）家丑外扬 **wash your 'hands of sb/sth** to refuse to be responsible for or involved with sb/sth 拒绝对…负责；脱离关系；洗手不干：*When her son was arrested again she washed her hands of him.* 她的儿子再次被捕，她就与他脱离了关系。**sth won't/doesn't 'wash (with sb)** used to say that sb's explanation, excuse, etc. is not valid or that you/sb else will not accept it（解释、借口等）对某人来说站不住脚，令某人不能接受：*That excuse simply won't wash with me.* 那种托辞根本不能令我信服。

PHR V **,wash sb/sth↔a'way** 🔑 (of water 水) to remove or carry sb/sth away to another place 冲掉；冲走：*Part of the path had been washed away by the sea.* 部分小路已被海浪冲坏。**,wash sth↔'down (with sth)** **1** to clean sth large or a surface with a lot of water 冲洗，冲刷（大件物品或表面）：*Wash down the walls before painting them.* 先把墙冲洗后再粉刷。**2** to drink sth after, or at the same time as, eating sth 配着食物喝（饮料）：*For lunch we had bread and cheese, washed down with beer.* 我们午餐吃的是面包和奶酪，喝的是啤酒。**,wash 'off** 🔑 to be removed from the surface of sth or from clothes by washing 被冲洗掉；被洗掉：*Those grease stains won't wash off.* 那些油渍洗不掉。**,wash sth↔'off (sth)** 🔑 to remove sth from the surface of sth or from clothes by washing（从某物表面或衣服上）冲洗掉，洗掉：*Wash that mud off your boots before you come in.* 先把你靴子上的泥冲洗掉再进来。**,wash 'out** 🔑 (of a dirty mark 污迹) to be removed from clothes by washing （从衣服上）被洗掉：*These ink stains won't wash out.* 这些墨渍洗不掉。**,wash sth↔'out** **1** 🔑 to wash the inside of sth to remove dirt, etc. 洗净，清洗（某物的内部）：*to wash out empty bottles* 把空瓶子里面洗干净 **2** to remove a substance from sth by washing 把…洗掉：*Wash the dye out with shampoo.* 用洗发剂把染发剂洗掉。**3** (of rain 雨) to make a game, an event, etc. end early or prevent it from starting 使（比赛等）提前结束；阻止…的举行：*The game was completely washed out.* 这场比赛因下雨根本无法进行。➲ RELATED NOUN WASHOUT **,wash 'over sb** **1** (*also* **,wash 'through sb**) (*literary*) (of a feeling 感觉) to suddenly affect sb strongly, so that they are not aware of anything else 冲动；升腾：*Waves of nausea washed over him.* 他突然感到阵阵恶心。**2** to happen to or around sb without affecting them（周围发生的事情）对…无多大影响：*She manages to let criticism just wash over her.* 她没有让别人的批评影响到自己。**,wash 'up** **1** 🔑 (*BrE*) (*also* **do the dishes** *NAmE, BrE*) to wash plates, glasses, etc. after a meal 洗刷饭后的杯盘等 ➲ RELATED NOUN WASHING-UP **2** 🔑 (*NAmE*) to wash your face and hands 洗脸和手：*Go and get washed up.* 去洗洗脸和手。**,wash sth↔'up** **1** (*BrE*) to wash dishes after a meal 洗刷（吃饭用过的盘子等）：*I didn't wash up the pans.* 我没有刷锅。**2** (of water 水) to carry sth onto land 把…冲到陆地上：*The body was found washed up on a beach.* 有人发现尸体被冲上了海滩。

▪ *noun* **1** [C, usually sing.] (*especially BrE*) an act of cleaning sb/sth using water and usually soap 洗；洗涤；清洗；洗刷：*These towels are ready for a wash.* 这些毛巾需要洗了。◇ *I'll just* ***have a quick wash*** *before dinner.* 我只是很快地洗一洗就吃饭。◇ *I'm doing a dark wash* (= washing all the dark clothes together). 我在集中洗深色的衣服。◇ *Your shirt's* ***in the wash*** (= being washed or waiting to be washed). 你的衬衣正在洗。◇ *My sweater shrank in the wash.* 我的套衫洗后缩水了。◇ *That blouse shouldn't look like that after only two washes.* 那件女衬衫只洗过两水，不应该变成这个样子。➲ SEE ALSO CAR WASH **2 the wash** [sing.] an area of water that has waves and is moving a lot, especially after a boat has moved through it; the sound made by this（尤指船过后划出的）水流，波浪；波浪拍打声：*The dinghy was rocked by the wash of a passing ferry.* 驶过的渡船掀起的波浪把小艇冲得摇摇晃晃。◇ *They listened to the wash of waves on the beach.* 他们听着波浪拍击海滩的声音。**3** [C] a thin layer of a liquid, especially paint, that is put on a surface 薄涂层（尤指涂料）：*The walls were covered with a pale yellow wash.* 墙壁刷了一层薄的浅黄色涂料。➲ SEE ALSO WHITEWASH *n.* (1) **4** [C, U] a liquid containing soap, used for cleaning your skin 肥皂液：*an antiseptic skin wash* 抗菌净肤液 ➲ SEE ALSO MOUTHWASH

IDM **it will (all) come out in the 'wash** (*informal*) **1** used to say that the truth about a situation will be made known at some time in the future 终将水落石出；将会真相大白 **2** used to make sb less anxious by telling them that any problems or difficulties will be solved in the future（用以劝人不要太着急）问题终会解决的，困难将会被克服的

wash·able /ˈwɒʃəbl; *NAmE* ˈwɑːʃ-; ˈwɔːʃ-/ *adj.* that can be washed without being damaged 可洗的；耐洗的：*machine washable* (= that can be washed in a washing machine) 可机洗的

wash·bag /ˈwɒʃbæg; *NAmE* ˈwɔːʃ-; ˈwɑːʃ-/ *noun* (*BrE*) = SPONGE BAG

wash·basin /ˈwɒʃbeɪsn; *NAmE* ˈwɑːʃ-; ˈwɔːʃ-/ (*also* **basin**) (*both especially BrE*) (*also* **sink** *NAmE, BrE*) (*also especially NAmE* **wash·bowl**) *noun* a large bowl that has taps/faucets and is fixed to the wall in a bathroom, used for washing your hands and face in（浴室内固定在墙上有水龙头的）洗脸盆 ➲ VISUAL VOCAB PAGE V25

wash·board /ˈwɒʃbɔːd; *NAmE* ˈwɑːʃbɔːrd; ˈwɔːʃ-/ *noun* a board with a surface with RIDGES on it, used in the past for rubbing clothes on when washing them; a similar board played as a musical instrument（洗衣用）搓板；（打击乐器）刮板

wash·cloth /ˈwɒʃklɒθ; *NAmE* ˈwɑːʃklɔːθ; ˈwɔːʃ-/ (*NAmE*) (*BrE* **flan·nel, face·cloth**) *noun* a small piece of cloth used for washing yourself（洗擦身体用的）小毛巾

wash·day /ˈwɒʃdeɪ; *NAmE* ˈwɑːʃ-; ˈwɔːʃ-/ (*also* **'washing day**) *noun* the day in sb's house when the clothes, etc. are washed, especially when this happens on the same day each week（尤指每周固定的）洗衣日

,washed 'out *adj.* **1** (of cloth, clothes or colours 织物、衣服或颜色) no longer brightly coloured, often as a result of frequent washing（洗后）退色的：*She didn't like jeans that looked too washed out.* 她不喜欢看起来退色厉害的牛仔裤。◇ *a pair of washed-out old jeans* 一条洗得退了色的旧牛仔裤 ◇ *The walls were a washed-out blue colour.* 墙壁是一种退了色的蓝色。**2** (of a person 人) pale and tired 苍白无力的；疲惫的 **SYN** **exhausted**：*He always looks washed out at the end of the week.* 他在周末总是满脸倦色。

,washed 'up *adj.* (*informal*) no longer successful and unlikely to succeed again in the future（事业等）告吹的，完蛋：*Her singing career was all washed up by the time she was 27.* 她到 27 岁时歌唱生涯就告终了。

wash·er /ˈwɒʃə(r); *NAmE* ˈwɑːʃ-; ˈwɔːʃ-/ *noun* **1** a small flat ring made of rubber, metal or plastic placed between

W

two surfaces, for example under a NUT (2) to make a connection tight（螺母等的）垫圈 ➲ VISUAL VOCAB PAGE V21 **2** (*informal*) a WASHING MACHINE 洗衣机 ➲ SEE ALSO DISHWASHER

ˌwasher-ˈdryer *noun* an electric machine that washes and dries clothes, etc. 洗衣烘干机

ˌwasher-ˈup *noun* (*BrE, informal*) a person who washes dishes 洗碟子的人

wash·er·wom·an /ˈwɒʃəwʊmən; *NAmE* ˈwɑːʃər-; ˈwɔːʃər-/ *noun* (*pl.* **-women** /-wɪmɪn/) a woman in the past whose job was to wash clothes, etc. for other people（旧时的）洗衣女工

wash·ing 🔑 /ˈwɒʃɪŋ; *NAmE* ˈwɑːʃ-; ˈwɔːʃ-/ *noun* [U] **1** 🔑 the act of cleaning sth using water and usually soap 洗；洗涤；洗刷；冲洗：*a gentle shampoo for frequent washing* 供经常洗发用的柔性洗发剂 ◇ *I* ***do the washing*** (= wash the clothes) *in our house.* 我在家里洗衣服。➲ SEE ALSO BRAINWASHING at BRAINWASH **2** 🔑 (*BrE*) clothes, sheets, etc. that are waiting to be washed, being washed or have just been washed 待洗的（或正在洗的、刚洗过的）衣物：*a pile of dirty washing* 一堆待洗的脏衣物 ◇ *Would you* ***hang the washing out*** (= hang it outside to dry)? 你把刚洗过的衣服晾在外面好吗？

ˈwashing day *noun* = WASHDAY

ˈwashing line *noun* (*BrE*) = CLOTHES LINE

ˈwashing machine *noun* an electric machine for washing clothes 洗衣机

ˈwashing powder *noun* [U] (*BrE*) soap or DETERGENT in the form of powder for washing clothes 洗衣粉

ˈwashing soda *noun* [U] = SODIUM CARBONATE

ˌwashing-ˈup (*BrE*) *noun* [U] **1** the act of washing plates, glasses, pans, etc. after a meal（饭后）刷洗餐具：*If you cook, I'll* ***do the washing-up***. 如果你做饭，我就洗碗。◇ *a washing-up bowl* 洗碟盆 **2** the dirty plates, glasses, pans, etc. that have to be washed after a meal（饭后的）待洗餐具：*The sink was still full of last night's washing-up.* 洗涤槽里仍然摆满了昨天晚上没洗刷的餐具。

washing-ˈup liquid *noun* [U] (*BrE*) liquid soap for washing dishes, pans, etc.（刷洗餐具的）洗涤液

wash·out /ˈwɒʃaʊt; *NAmE* ˈwɑːʃ-; ˈwɔːʃ-/ *noun* (*informal*) an event, etc. that is a complete failure, especially because of rain 因雨取消的事；彻底失败的事情

wash·room /ˈwɒʃruːm; -rʊm; *NAmE* ˈwɑːʃ-; ˈwɔːʃ-/ *noun* (*CanE* or *old-fashioned, NAmE*) a toilet/bathroom, especially one that is in a public building（尤指公共建筑物内的）洗手间，厕所

wash·stand /ˈwɒʃstænd; *NAmE* ˈwɑːʃ-; ˈwɔːʃ-/ *noun* (especially in the past) a special table in a bedroom that holds a BASIN for washing yourself in（尤指旧时卧室内的）盥洗台

wash·tub /ˈwɒʃtʌb; *NAmE* ˈwɑːʃ-; ˈwɔːʃ-/ *noun* (in the past) a large metal container for washing clothes, etc. in（旧时的）洗衣盆

wasn't /ˈwɒznt; *NAmE also* ˈwʌznt/ *short form* was not

Wasp /wɒsp; *NAmE* wɑːsp/ (*also* **WASP**) *noun* (*especially NAmE, usually disapproving*) the abbreviation for 'White Anglo-Saxon Protestant' (a white American whose family originally came from northern Europe and is therefore thought to be from the most powerful section of society) 白种盎格鲁－撒克逊新教徒（全写为 White Anglo-Saxon Protestant，祖先来自北欧，被认为是美国社会中势力最强大的白人）：*a privileged Wasp background* 享有特权的盎格鲁－撒克逊裔白人新教徒出身

wasp /wɒsp; *NAmE* wɑːsp/ *noun* a black and yellow flying insect that can sting 黄蜂；胡蜂：*a wasp sting* 黄蜂蜇伤 ◇ *a wasps' nest* 黄蜂窝 ➲ VISUAL VOCAB PAGE V13

wasp·ish /ˈwɒspɪʃ; *NAmE* ˈwɑːs-/ *adj.* (*formal*) expressing criticism or showing that sb is annoyed 尖刻的；恼怒的 ▸ **wasp·ish·ly** *adv.*

was·sail /ˈwɒseɪl; *NAmE* ˈwɑːs-/ *verb* (*old use*) **1** [I] to enjoy yourself by drinking alcohol with others 饮酒狂欢；纵酒欢闹 **2** [I] to go from house to house at Christmas time singing CAROLS（挨户唱歌）报圣诞佳音 ▸ **was·sail·er** *noun*

wast·age /ˈweɪstɪdʒ/ *noun* **1** [U, sing.] ~ (**of sth**) the fact of losing or destroying sth, especially because it has been used or dealt with carelessly 耗费；损耗；浪费：*It was a new production technique aimed at minimizing wastage.* 这是一项旨在使损耗减至最低的新生产技术。**2** [U] the amount of sth that is wasted 损耗量；耗费量；浪费量：*There is little wastage from a lean cut of meat.* 瘦肉基本上没有损耗。**3** [U] (*BrE*) the loss of employees because they stop working or move to other jobs; the number of students who do not finish a particular course of study（雇员的）减员；（学生的）流失人数：*Half of the posts will be lost through* ***natural wastage***. 有一半的职位通过自然减员将会丧失。◇ *student wastage rates* 学生流失率

waste 🔑 /weɪst/ *verb, noun, adj.*

■ *verb*

• **NOT USE WELL** 使用不当 **1** 🔑 to use more of sth than is necessary or useful 浪费；滥用：**~ sth** *to waste time/food/energy* 浪费时间 / 食物 / 能源 ◇ **~ sth on sth** *Why waste money on clothes you don't need?* 为什么浪费钱买你不需要的衣服呢？◇ **~ sth (in) doing sth** *She* ***wasted no time*** *in rejecting the offer* (= she rejected it immediately). 她当即拒绝了提议。◇ *You're* ***wasting your time*** *trying to explain it to him* (= because he will not understand). 你跟他解释是在浪费时间。**2 ~ sth (on sb/sth)** to give, say, use, etc. sth good where it is not valued or used in the way that it should be 白费；糟蹋：*Don't waste your sympathy on him—he got what he deserved.* 别把你的同情心白白浪费在他的身上，他是咎由自取。◇ *Her comments were not wasted on Chris* (= he understood what she meant). 她对克里斯的一席话没有白费。 **3** 🔑 [usually passive] to not make good or full use of sb/sth 未充分利用；使…屈才：**~ sb/sth** *It was a wasted opportunity.* 这白白浪费了一次机会。◇ **~ sb/sth as sth** *You're wasted as a sales manager—you should have been an actor.* 你当销售经理屈才了，你本应该做演员。

• **KILL SB** 杀人 **4 ~ sb** (*informal, especially NAmE*) to get rid of sb, usually by killing them 干掉；把…废了；杀死

• **DEFEAT SB** 打败 **5 ~ sb** (*NAmE, informal*) to defeat sb very badly in a game or competition（游戏或比赛中）大胜，把…打得落花流水

IDM **waste your ˈbreath** to say sth that nobody takes any notice of 白费唇舌 **ˌwaste not, ˈwant not** (*saying*) if you never waste anything, especially food or money, you will always have it when you need it 勤俭节约，吃穿不缺

PHR V **ˌwaste aˈway** (of a person 人) to become thin and weak, especially because of illness（尤指因病）变得瘦弱 ➲ SEE ALSO EMACIATED

■ *noun*

• **NOT GOOD USE** 非充分利用 **1** 🔑 [U, sing.] ~ (**of sth**) the act of using sth in a careless or unnecessary way, causing it to be lost or destroyed 浪费；滥用：*I hate unnecessary waste.* 我憎恨不必要的浪费。◇ *It seems such a waste to throw good food away.* 把好好的食物扔掉似乎太浪费了。◇ *I hate to see good food* ***go to waste*** (= be thrown away). 我不愿看到好好的食物被扔掉。◇ *The report is critical of the department's waste of resources.* 报告批评了这个部门对资源的浪费。◇ *What a waste of paper!* 多么浪费纸啊！**2** 🔑 [sing.] a situation in which it is not worth spending time, money, etc. on sth 白费；糟蹋：*These meetings are a complete* ***waste of time***. 这些会议完全是白费时间。◇ *They believe the statue is a waste of taxpayers' money.* 他们认为这座雕像糟蹋了纳税人的钱。

• **MATERIALS** 材料 **3** 🔑 [U] (*also* **wastes** [pl.]) materials that are no longer needed and are thrown away 废料；废物；弃物；垃圾：***household/industrial waste*** 生活垃圾；工业废料 ◇ *toxic wastes* 有毒废物 ◇ ***waste disposal*** (= the process of getting rid of waste) 废物处理

WORDFINDER 联想词： drain, dump, effluent, exhaust, fly-tip, incinerator, landfill, rubbish, sewage

4 (*also* ˌ**waste ˈmatter**) [U] material that the body gets rid of as solid or liquid material 粪便：*The farmers use both animal and human waste as fertilizer.* 农民把牲畜和人类的粪便都用作肥料。

• **LAND** 土地 **5 wastes** [pl.] (*formal*) a large area of land where there are very few people, animals or plants 人烟稀少的地区；荒芜地区；荒原：*the frozen wastes of Siberia* 西伯利亚的冻土荒原

IDM **a waste of ˈspace** (*informal*) a person who is useless or no good at anything 无用的人；干什么都不行的人；废物；饭桶

■ ***adj.*** [usually before noun]

• **LAND** 土地 **1** not suitable for building or growing things on and therefore not used 荒芜的；废弃的 **SYN** **derelict**: *The car was found on a piece of waste ground.* 那辆车是在一块荒地里发现的。

• **MATERIALS** 材料 **2** no longer needed for a particular process and therefore thrown away 废弃的；丢弃的；无用的：*waste plastic* 废塑料

IDM **lay sth ˈwaste | lay ˈwaste (to) sth** (*formal*) to destroy a place completely 彻底毁坏（某地）；把…夷为平地

waste·bas·ket /ˈweɪstbɑːskɪt; *NAmE* -bæs-/ (*NAmE*) (*BrE* ˌ**waste-ˈpaper basket**) *noun* a BASKET or other container for waste paper, etc. 废纸篓；废纸箱 ➲ PICTURE AT BASKET ➲ VISUAL VOCAB PAGES V22, V71

ˈ**waste bin** *noun* (*BrE*) a container that you put rubbish/garbage in 垃圾箱；垃圾桶

wasted /ˈweɪstɪd/ *adj.* **1** [only before noun] (of an action 行动) unsuccessful because it does not produce the result you wanted 徒劳无功的；白费的：*We had a wasted trip—they weren't in.* 我们白跑了一趟，他们不在。**2** too thin, especially because of illness（尤指因病）瘦骨嶙峋的，瘦弱的：*thin wasted legs* 枯瘦的双腿 **3** (*slang*) strongly affected by alcohol or drugs 极度迷醉的

ˈ**waste-disposal unit** (*also* ˈ**waste disposer**) *noun* (*NAmE usually* ˈ**garbage dis·posal**, **dis·posal**) a machine connected to the waste pipe of a kitchen SINK, for cutting food waste into small pieces 食物垃圾处理器（安装于厨房水槽下方，可粉碎厨余垃圾）

waste·ful /ˈweɪstfl/ *adj.* using more of sth than is necessary; not saving or keeping sth that could be used 浪费的；挥霍的：*The whole process is wasteful and inefficient.* 整个程序既浪费又低效。◇ ~ **of sth** *an engine that is wasteful of fuel* 费燃料的发动机 ▸ **waste·ful·ly** /-fəli/ *adv.* **waste·ful·ness** *noun* [U]

waste·land /ˈweɪstlænd/ *noun* [C, U] an area of land that cannot be used or that is no longer used for building or growing things on 荒地；荒原；不毛之地：*industrial wasteland* 工业废地 ◇ *the desert wastelands of Arizona* 亚利桑那州的荒漠 ◇ (*figurative*) *The mid 1970s are seen as a cultural wasteland for rock music.* * 20 世纪 70 年代中期被视为摇滚乐的文化荒漠。

ˌ**waste ˈpaper** *noun* [U] paper that is not wanted and is thrown away 废纸

ˌ**waste-ˈpaper basket** (*BrE*) (*NAmE* **waste·basket**) *noun* a BASKET or other container for waste paper, etc. 废纸篓；废纸箱 ➲ PICTURE AT BASKET ➲ VISUAL VOCAB PAGES V22, V71

ˈ**waste product** *noun* a useless material or substance produced while making sth else 工业垃圾；（生产中的）无用副产品

waster /ˈweɪstə(r)/ *noun* **1** (often in compounds 常构成复合词) a person or thing that uses too much of sth in an unnecessary way 浪费…的人；耗费…的东西：*He's a time-waster.* 他总是浪费时间。**2** (*informal, disapproving*) a person who is useless or no good at anything 废物；无用的人；饭桶；酒囊饭袋

waste·water /ˈweɪstwɔːtə(r); *NAmE also* -wɑːt-/ *noun* [U] (*especially NAmE*) used water that contains waste substances from homes, factories and farms 废水：*municipal water and wastewater systems* 市政用水和废水系统 ◇ *a wastewater treatment plant* 废水处理厂 ➲ COMPARE SEWAGE

wast·ing /ˈweɪstɪŋ/ *adj.* a **wasting** disease or illness is one that causes sb to gradually become weaker and thinner（指疾病）消耗性的，使消瘦的，使虚弱的

wast·rel /ˈweɪstrəl/ *noun* (*literary*) a lazy person who spends their time and/or money in a careless and stupid way 花花公子；浪荡子；二流子

watch /wɒtʃ; *NAmE* wɑːtʃ/ *verb, noun*

■ ***verb*** **1** [T, I] to look at sb/sth for a time, paying attention to what happens 看；注视；观看；观察：~ **sb/sth** *to watch television/a football game* 看电视 / 足球比赛 ◇ ~ **sth for sth** *He watched the house for signs of activity.* 他注视着那所房子里的动静。◇ ~ (**for sth**) *He watched for signs of activity in the house.* 他注视着那所房子里的动静。◇ *'Would you like to play?' 'No thanks—I'll just watch.'* "你想玩吗？" "不啦，谢谢。我就看看好了。" ◇ *We watched to see what would happen next.* 我们注视着下一步要发生的事情。◇ ~ **what, how, etc....** *Watch what I do, then you try.* 你注意看我的动作，然后试着做。◇ ~ **sb/sth doing sth** *She watched the kids playing in the yard.* 她看着孩子们在院子里玩。◇ ~ **sb/sth do sth** *They watched the bus disappear into the distance.* 他们注视着公共汽车消失在远方。➲ SYNONYMS AT LOOK **2** [T] ~ **sb/sth** (**for sb**) to take care of sb/sth for a short time（短时间）照看，看护，照管：*Could you watch my bags for me while I buy a paper?* 我去买份报纸，你能替我照看一下我的包吗？**3** (*BrE also* **mind**) [T] (*informal*) to be careful about sth 小心；当心；留意：~ **sth/yourself** *Watch yourself!* (= be careful, because you're in a dangerous situation) 当心！◇ *Watch your bag—there are thieves around.* 小心你的提包，这里有小偷。◇ *I have to watch every penny* (= be careful what I spend). 我必须掂量着花每一分钱。◇ *Watch your head on the low ceiling.* 天花板很低，当心别碰着头。◇ ~ **where, what, etc....** *Hey, watch where you're going!* 嘿，瞧着点路！

IDM **watch the ˈclock** (*disapproving*) to be careful not to work longer than the required time; to think more about when your work will finish than about the work itself 盯着钟表（算计着不超过规定的工作时间，或只盼望下班而无心工作）➲ SEE ALSO CLOCK-WATCHER **a watched ˌpot never ˈboils** (*saying*) used to say that when you are impatient for sth to happen, time seems to pass very slowly 心急水不开（越心急，时间过得越慢）ˈ**watch it** (*informal*) used as a warning to sb to be careful 当心；留神；注意 **watch your ˈmouth/ˈtongue** to be careful what you say in order not to offend sb or make them angry 说话当心；嘴上留个把门的 **watch this ˈspace** (*informal*) used in orders, to tell sb to wait for more news about sth to be announced（用于命令）等待下面发表的消息：*I can't tell you any more right now, but watch this space.* 目前我不能跟你多说，等着听下面发表的消息吧。**watch the ˈtime** to be sure that you know what the time is, so that you finish sth at the correct time, or are not late for sth 注意时间（以便按时完成或到达）：*I'll have to watch the time. I need to leave early today.* 我得看着点时间。今天我要早走。**watch the ˈworld go by** to relax and watch people in a public place 闲看人来人往；静观众生百态：*We sat outside a cafe, watching the world go by.* 我们坐在一家小餐馆外面，望着眼前来来往往的人们。➲ MORE AT LANGUAGE, STEP *n.*

PHR V ˈ**watch for sb/sth** to look and wait for sb/sth to appear or for sth to happen 观察等待（某人出现或发生某事）：*The cat was on the wall, watching for birds.* 那只猫在墙上伺机捕捉鸟儿。ˌ**watch ˈout** (*informal*) used to warn sb about sth dangerous 小心；留神；注意：*Watch out! There's a car coming!* 小心！汽车来了！ˌ**watch ˈout for sb/sth** **1** to make an effort to be aware of what is happening, so that you will notice if anything bad or unusual happens 密切注意；留意：*The cashiers were asked to watch out for forged banknotes.* 要求出纳员注意伪钞。**2** to be careful of sth 小心；当心：*Watch out for the stairs—they're steep.* 小心楼梯，这些台阶很陡。

W

ˌwatch ˈover sb/sth (*formal*) to take care of sb/sth; to guard and protect sb/sth 照管；监督；保护

■ *noun* **1** [C] a type of small clock that you wear on your wrist, or (in the past) carried in your pocket 表；手表；（旧时的）怀表：*She kept looking anxiously at her watch.* 她焦急不安地一个劲儿看表。◇ *My watch is fast/slow.* 我的表快 / 慢了。➲ PICTURE AT CLOCK ➲ SEE ALSO STOPWATCH, WRISTWATCH **2** [sing., U] the act of watching sb/sth carefully in case of possible danger or problems 注意；注视；监视；观察：*The police have* ***mounted a watch*** *outside the hotel.* 警方已在旅馆外面布置人监视。◇ *I'll* ***keep watch*** *while you go through his papers* (= watch and warn you if somebody is coming). 你查阅他的文件，我来放哨。◇ *The government is* ***keeping a close watch*** *on how the situation develops.* 政府正在密切注视着形势的发展。➲ SEE ALSO NEIGHBOURHOOD WATCH **3** [C, U] a fixed period of time, usually while other people are asleep, during which sb watches for any danger so that they can warn others, for example on a ship; the person or people who do this 值班（人）；警戒（人）；守夜（人）：*I'm* ***on first watch.*** 我值第一班。◇ *I go* ***on watch*** *in an hour.* 我一个小时后值班。➲ SEE ALSO NIGHTWATCHMAN

IDM **be on the ˈwatch (for sb/sth)** to be looking carefully for sb/sth that you expect to see, especially in order to avoid possible danger 小心提防；警戒：*Be on the watch for thieves.* 要提防小偷。➲ MORE AT CLOSE² *adj.*

watch·able /ˈwɒtʃəbl; *NAmE* ˈwɑːtʃ-/ *adj.* (*informal*) entertaining or pleasant to watch 值得一看的

watch·band /ˈwɒtʃbænd; *NAmE* ˈwɑːtʃ-/ (*NAmE*) (*also* **ˈwatch strap** *BrE, NAmE*) *noun* a thin strip of leather, etc. for fastening your watch around your wrist 表带

watch·dog /ˈwɒtʃdɒg; *NAmE* ˈwɑːtʃdɔːg/ *noun* a person or group of people whose job is to check that companies are not doing anything illegal or ignoring people's rights （监督公司活动及监护人们权利的）监察人，监察团体：*a consumer watchdog* 消费者监察人 ➲ COMPARE GUARD DOG

watch·er /ˈwɒtʃə(r); *NAmE* ˈwɑːtʃ-/ *noun* (often in compounds 常构成复合词) a person who watches and studies sb/sth regularly …观察家；…观察员：*an industry/a market watcher* 行业 / 市场观察员 ➲ SEE ALSO BIRDWATCHER, CLOCK-WATCHER

watch·ful /ˈwɒtʃfl; *NAmE* ˈwɑːtʃ-/ *adj.* paying attention to what is happening in case of danger, accidents, etc. 注意的；警惕的；提防的：*Her expression was watchful and alert.* 她露出一副察言观色、处处提防的表情。◇ *His mother* ***kept a watchful eye on*** *him.* 他的母亲特别留心他。◇ *The children played* ***under the watchful eye of*** *their teacher.* 孩子们在老师的看护下玩耍。 ▸ **watch·ful·ly** /-fəli/ *adv.* **watch·ful·ness** *noun* [U]

ˌwatching ˈbrief *noun* [sing.] the task of watching a group, especially a political organization, to make sure that it is doing everything it should and nothing wrong or illegal （尤指对政治组织的）监视，监督

watch·maker /ˈwɒtʃmeɪkə(r); *NAmE* ˈwɑːtʃ-/ *noun* a person who makes and repairs watches and clocks as a job 钟表匠；钟表制造人；修表匠

watch·man /ˈwɒtʃmən; *NAmE* ˈwɑːtʃ-/ *noun* (*pl.* **-men** /-mən/) (*old-fashioned*) a man whose job is to guard a building, for example a bank, an office building or a factory, especially at night （夜间）保安员，看守人，警卫员 ➲ SEE ALSO NIGHTWATCHMAN

ˈwatch strap (*NAmE also* **ˈwatch·band**) *noun* a thin strip of leather, etc. for fastening your watch around your wrist 表带

watch·tower /ˈwɒtʃtaʊə(r); *NAmE* ˈwɑːtʃ-/ *noun* a tall tower from which soldiers, etc. watch when they are guarding a place 瞭望塔；岗楼

watch·word /ˈwɒtʃwɜːd; *NAmE* ˈwɑːtʃwɜːrd/ *noun* a word or phrase that expresses sb's beliefs or attitudes, or that explains what sb should do in a particular situation 口号；标语；格言：*Quality is our watchword.* 品质至上是我们的口号。

water /ˈwɔːtə(r); *NAmE also* ˈwɑːt-/ *noun, verb*

■ *noun* **1** [U] a liquid without colour, smell or taste that falls as rain, is in lakes, rivers and seas, and is used for drinking, washing, etc. 水：*a glass of water* 一杯水 ◇ ***drinking water*** 饮用水 ◇ *water pollution* 水污染 ◇ ***clean/dirty water*** 净水；脏水 ◇ *water shortages* 缺水 ◇ *There is hot and cold* ***running water*** *in all the bedrooms.* 所有的卧室里都有冷热自来水。➲ SEE ALSO BATHWATER **2** [U] an area of water, especially a lake, river, sea or ocean 大片的水；水域；（尤指）江，河，湖，海：*We walked down to the water's edge.* 我们步行到水边去。◇ *She fell into the water.* 她失足落水。◇ ***shallow/deep water*** 浅 / 深水域 ◇ *In the lagoon the water was calm.* 环礁湖里风平浪静。➲ SEE ALSO BACKWATER, BREAKWATER **3** **waters** [pl.] the water in a particular lake, river, sea or ocean （某一江、河、湖、海的）水域：*the grey waters of the River Clyde* 克莱德河灰蒙蒙的河水 ◇ *This species is found in* ***coastal waters*** *around the Indian Ocean.* 在环印度洋沿岸的海域有这一物种。**4** [U] the surface of a mass of water （一片）水面：*She dived under the water.* 她潜入水下。◇ *The leaves floated on the water.* 叶片漂浮在水面上。➲ SEE ALSO UNDERWATER **5** **waters** [pl.] an area of sea or ocean belonging to a particular country （某个国家的）领海，海域：*We were still in British waters.* 我们仍在英国的领海上。◇ *fishing in international waters* 在国际海域捕鱼 ➲ SEE ALSO TERRITORIAL WATERS **6** **waters** [pl.] **murky, uncharted, stormy, dangerous, etc. ~** used to describe a situation, usually one that is difficult, dangerous or not familiar 不明朗（或未知的、困难、危险等）局面：*The conversation got into the murky waters of jealousy and relationships.* 交谈进入到爱妒交织的复杂话题。◇ *The government has warned of stormy waters ahead.* 政府已告诫说，以后的局势将很严峻。HELP There are many other compounds ending in **water**. You will find them at their place in the alphabet. 以 water 结尾的复合词还有很多，可在各字母中的适当位置查到。

IDM **by water** (*formal*) using a boat or ship 乘船；由水路 **it's (all) water under the ˈbridge** used to say that sth happened in the past and is now forgotten or no longer important 已成往事；往事云烟 **like ˈwater** (*informal*) in large quantities 大量地：*He spends money like water.* 他挥霍无度。**not hold ˈwater** (*informal*) if an argument, an excuse, a theory, etc. does not **hold water**, you cannot believe it （论点、借口、理论等）站不住脚，不合情理 **sb's ˈwaters break** when a pregnant woman's **waters break**, the liquid in her WOMB passes out of her body just before the baby is born 羊水破（即将分娩）**(like) water off a ˌduck's ˈback** (*informal*) used to say that sth, especially criticism, has no effect on sb/sth （像）耳边风；水过鸭背：*I can't tell my son what to do; it's water off a duck's back with him.* 我无法告诉我儿子该做什么，他根本听不进去。➲ MORE AT BLOOD *n.*, BLOW *v.*, COLD *adj.*, DEAD *adj.*, DEEP *adj.*, DIP *v.*, DUCK *n.*, FISH *n.*, HEAD *n.*, HELL, HORSE *n.*, HOT *adj.*, PASS *v.*, POUR, STILL *adj.*, TEST *v.*, TREAD *v.*

■ *verb* **1** [T] **~ sth** to pour water on plants, etc. 给…浇水；灌溉：*to* ***water the plants/garden*** 给花草 / 花园浇水 **2** [I] (of the eyes 眼睛) to become full of tears 充满眼泪：*The smoke made my eyes water.* 烟熏得我直流眼泪。**3** [I] (of the mouth 嘴) to produce SALIVA 流口水：*The smells from the kitchen made our mouths water.* 厨房里的香味馋得我们直流口水。**4** [T] **~ sth** to give water to an animal to drink 给…水喝；饮（动物）：*to water the horses* 饮马 ◇ (*humorous*) *After a tour of the grounds, the guests were* ***fed and watered.*** 客人们游览场地之后，给招待得酒足饭饱。**5** [T, usually passive] **~ sth** (*specialist*) (of a river, etc. 河流等) to provide an area of land with water 流经；给（某地）供水：*The valley is watered by a stream.* 这山谷有一条小溪流过。**6** [T] **~ sth** to add water to an alcoholic drink 往（酒里）掺水；给…加水：*watered wine* 掺了水的葡萄酒

PHR V **ˌwater sth↔ˈdown** **1** to make a liquid weaker by adding water 加水冲淡（液体）；掺水稀释 SYN **dilute** **2** [usually passive] to change a speech, a piece of writing, etc. in order to make it less strong or offensive 缓和（说话、文章等的）语气；使变得轻描淡写 SYN **dilute**

the 'Water Bearer *noun* [sing.] = AQUARIUS (1)

water·bed /ˈwɔːtəbed; *NAmE* ˈwɔːtərbed; ˈwɑːtərbed/ *noun* a bed with a rubber or plastic MATTRESS that is filled with water 水床（铺橡胶或塑料充水床垫的床）

water·bird /ˈwɔːtəbɜːd; *NAmE* ˈwɔːtərbɜːrd; ˈwɑːt-/ *noun* a bird that lives near and walks or swims in water, especially rivers or lakes（尤指江河湖泊中的）水鸟，水禽

'water biscuit *noun* (*BrE*) a thin crisp plain biscuit, usually eaten with butter and/or cheese 薄脆饼干（通常加黄油、奶酪食用）

water·board·ing /ˈwɔːtəbɔːdɪŋ; *NAmE* ˈwɔːtərbɔːrd-; ˈwɑːt-/ *noun* [U] a way of trying to force sb to give you information by pouring water onto their face while making them lie on their back, so that they feel as if they are DROWNING 水刑（逼供）

water·borne /ˈwɔːtəbɔːn; *NAmE* ˈwɔːtərbɔːrn; ˈwɑːt-/ *adj.* spread or carried by water 水传播的；水源传染的；经水路的；水运的：*cholera and other waterborne diseases* 霍乱等经水传染疾病 ◇ *waterborne goods* 水运货物 ➲ COMPARE AIRBORNE (2)

'water buffalo *noun* (*pl.* **water buf·falo** or **water buf·faloes**) a large Asian animal of the cow family, used for pulling vehicles and farm equipment in tropical countries 印度水牛（亚洲挽畜）

'water butt (*BrE*) (*NAmE* **'rain barrel**) *noun* a large BARREL for collecting rain as it flows off a roof（接房檐雨水的）雨水桶 ➲ VISUAL VOCAB PAGE V20

'water cannon *noun* a machine that produces a powerful flow of water, used by the police to control crowds of people 水炮（警方用以驱散人群）

the 'Water Carrier *noun* [sing.] = AQUARIUS (1)

'water chestnut *noun* the thick round white root of a tropical plant that grows in water, often used in Chinese cooking 荸荠

'water clock *noun* (in the past) a clock that used the flow of water to measure time 水钟，漏壶（旧时利用水流计时）

'water closet *noun* (*abbr.* **WC**) (*old-fashioned*) a toilet 盥洗室；厕所

water·col·our (*especially US* **water·color**) /ˈwɔːtəkʌlə(r); *NAmE* ˈwɔːtərk-; ˈwɑːt-/ *noun* **1** **watercolours** [pl.] paints that you mix with water, not oil, and use for painting pictures 水彩（颜料）➲ COLLOCATIONS AT ART **2** [C] a picture painted with these paints 水彩画 ➲ WORDFINDER NOTE AT PAINTING

water·col·our·ist (*especially US* **water·col·or·ist**) /ˈwɔːtəkʌlərɪst; *NAmE* ˈwɔːtər-/ *noun* a person who paints with watercolours 水彩画作者；水彩画家

'water-cooled *adj.* (of machines, etc. 机器等) cooled using water 水冷的

'water cooler *noun* **1** a machine, for example in an office, that cools water and supplies it for drinking 饮水冷却器 **2** used when referring to a place where office workers talk in an informal way, for example near the water cooler 职员聊天处（饮水冷却器附近等的办公室人员闲谈处）：*It was a story they'd shared around the water cooler.* 这件事成为他们工作之余闲聊的谈资。

water·course /ˈwɔːtəkɔːs; *NAmE* ˈwɔːtərkɔːrs; ˈwɑːt-/ *noun* (*specialist*) a stream or an artificial channel for water 河道；水道；沟渠；渠道

water·cress /ˈwɔːtəkres; *NAmE* ˈwɔːtərk-; ˈwɑːt-/ *noun* [U] a water plant with small round green leaves and thin STEMS. It has a strong taste and is often eaten raw in salads. 水田芥，豆瓣菜，西洋菜（水生植物，有辛香味）

ˌwatered 'silk *noun* [U] a type of shiny silk cloth with a pattern on it that looks like water in waves 波纹绸

water·fall /ˈwɔːtəfɔːl; *NAmE* ˈwɔːtərf-; ˈwɑːt-/ *noun* a place where a stream or river falls from a high place, for example over a CLIFF or rock 瀑布 ➲ WORDFINDER NOTE AT RIVER ➲ VISUAL VOCAB PAGE V5

'water feature *noun* an artificial area of water, or structure with water flowing through it, which is intended to make a garden more attractive and interesting（花园中的）人工水景 ➲ VISUAL VOCAB PAGE V20

'water fountain *noun* (*NAmE*) = DRINKING FOUNTAIN

water·fowl /ˈwɔːtəfaʊl; *NAmE* ˈwɔːtərf-; ˈwɑːt-/ *noun* [usually pl.] (*pl.* **water·fowl**) a bird that can swim and lives near water, especially a DUCK or GOOSE 水鸟；水禽（尤指鸭或鹅）

water·front /ˈwɔːtəfrʌnt; *NAmE* ˈwɔːtərf-; ˈwɑːt-/ *noun* [usually sing.] a part of a town or an area that is next to water, for example in a HARBOUR 滨水路；滨水区；码头区：*a waterfront apartment* 一套滨水公寓

'water gun *noun* (*NAmE*) = WATER PISTOL

water·hole /ˈwɔːtəhəʊl; *NAmE* ˈwɔːtərhoʊl; ˈwɑːt-/ (*also* **'watering hole**) *noun* a place in a hot country, where animals go to drink（热带国家动物饮水的）水坑，水池

'water ice *noun* [U, C] (*BrE*) = SORBET

'watering can *noun* a metal or plastic container with a handle and a long SPOUT, used for pouring water on plants（浇花草用的）洒水壶，喷壶 ➲ VISUAL VOCAB PAGE V20

'watering hole *noun* **1** = WATERHOLE **2** (*informal, humorous*) a bar or place where people go to drink 酒吧；酒馆

'watering place *noun* (*old-fashioned*) a town with a natural supply of MINERAL WATER where people go for their health 矿泉疗养地 **SYN** **spa**

'water jump *noun* an area of water that horses or runners have to jump over in a race or competition（障碍赛马或赛跑等中需越过的）水沟障碍

water·less /ˈwɔːtələs; *NAmE* ˈwɔːtərləs; ˈwɑːt-/ *adj.* with no water 无水的；干的：*a waterless barren region* 干旱的荒芜地区

'water level *noun* [U, C] the height that the surface of a mass of water rises or falls to, or the height it is at 水位

'water lily *noun* a plant that floats on the surface of water, with large round flat leaves and white, yellow or pink flowers 睡莲

water·line /ˈwɔːtəlaɪn; *NAmE* ˈwɔːtərl-; ˈwɑːt-/ *noun* **the waterline** [sing.] the level that the water reaches along the side of a ship（船的）水线，吃水线

water·logged /ˈwɔːtəlɒgd; *NAmE* ˈwɔːtərlɔːgd; ˈwɑːt-/ *adj.* **1** (of soil, a field, etc. 土壤、田地等) so full of water that it cannot hold any more and becomes flooded 水浸的；水涝的；水淹的：*They couldn't play because the pitch was waterlogged.* 因球场泡水他们未能进行比赛。**2** (of a boat, etc. 船等) so full of water that it can no longer float 进水满舱的；浸满水下沉的

Water·loo /ˌwɔːtəˈluː; *NAmE* ˌwɔːtərˈluː; ˌwɑːt-/ *noun* [sing.] **sb's ~** a final defeat for sb 最终的失败；毁灭性打击：*This was the point at which he was to* ***meet his Waterloo****.* 这就是他最终失败之处。**ORIGIN** From the battle of **Waterloo** in 1815, in which the British (under the Duke of Wellington) and the Prussians finally defeated Napoleon. 源自 1815 年的滑铁卢战役。在那场战役中，英国人（在威灵顿公爵的率领下）和普鲁士人最终打败了拿破仑。

'water main *noun* a large underground pipe that supplies water to buildings, etc. 给水干管；总水管

water·mark /ˈwɔːtəmɑːk; *NAmE* ˈwɔːtərmɑːrk; ˈwɑːt-/ *noun* a symbol or design in some types of paper, which can be seen when the paper is held against the light（纸张上的）水印 ➲ SEE ALSO HIGH-WATER MARK, LOW-WATER MARK

W

ˈwater meadow *noun* [usually pl.] a field near a river that is often flooded（河边经常让水淹的）浸水草地，草甸

water·melon /ˈwɔːtəmelən; *NAmE* ˈwɔːtərm-; ˈwɑːt-/ *noun* [C, U] a type of large MELON with hard, dark green skin, red flesh and black seeds 西瓜 ➲ VISUAL VOCAB PAGE V32

water·mill /ˈwɔːtəmɪl; *NAmE* ˈwɔːtərm-; ˈwɑːt-/ *noun* a MILL next to a river in which the machinery for GRINDING grain into flour is driven by the power of the water turning a wheel 水磨；水力磨粉机

ˈwater moccasin *noun* = COTTONMOUTH

ˈwater pistol (*NAmE also* **ˈwater gun**, **ˈsquirt gun**) *noun* a toy gun that shoots water 玩具喷水手枪

ˈwater polo *noun* [U] a game played by two teams of people swimming in a swimming pool. Players try to throw a ball into the other team's goal. 水球运动

ˈwater power *noun* [U] power produced by the movement of water, used to drive machinery or produce electricity 水力；水能

water·proof /ˈwɔːtəpruːf; *NAmE* ˈwɔːtərpruːf; ˈwɑːt-/ *adj.*, *noun*, *verb*
- *adj.* that does not let water through or that cannot be damaged by water 不透水的；防水的；耐水的：*waterproof clothing* 防水衣 ◇ *a waterproof camera* 防水照相机
- *noun* [usually pl.] a piece of clothing made from material that does not let water through 防水衣物；雨衣：*You'll need waterproofs* (= a waterproof jacket and trousers/pants). 你会用得着雨衣裤的。
- *verb* ~ sth to make sth waterproof 使不透水；使防水

ˈwater rat *noun* = WATER VOLE

ˈwater-repellent *adj.* a material, etc. that is **water-repellent** is specially treated so that water runs off it rather than going into it（材料等经处理后）拒水的，防水的：*a water-repellent coating* 防水涂层

ˈwater-resist·ant *adj.* that does not let water through easily 有抗水作用的；防水的：*a water-resistant jacket* 防水上衣

water·shed /ˈwɔːtəʃed; *NAmE* ˈwɔːtərʃed; ˈwɑːt-/ *noun* **1** [C] ~ (**in sth**) an event or a period of time that marks an important change 转折点，分界线，分水岭（标志着重大变化的事件或时期）：*The middle decades of the 19th century marked a watershed in Russia's history.* * 19 世纪中叶标志着俄国历史的转折点。**2** [C] a line of high land where streams on one side flow into one river, and streams on the other side flow into a different river 分水线；分水岭；分水界 **3 the watershed** [sing.] (in Britain) the time before which programmes that are not considered suitable for children may not be shown on television（英国）儿童不宜节目可在电视上播放的起始时间：*the 9 o'clock watershed* 可开播儿童不宜电视节目的晚上 9 点钟时限

water·side /ˈwɔːtəsaɪd; *NAmE* ˈwɔːters-; ˈwɑːt-/ *noun* [sing.] the area at the edge of a river, lake, etc. 水边；河边；湖滨；海滨：*They strolled down to the waterside.* 他们漫步向水边走去。◇ *a waterside cafe* 一家水滨小餐馆

water·ski /ˈwɔːtəskiː; *NAmE* ˈwɔːtərs-; ˈwɑːt-/ *verb*, *noun*
- *verb* [I] to SKI on water while being pulled by a fast boat 水橇滑水；进行滑水运动 ▸ **water·ski·ing** *noun* [U]: *We snorkelled and did some waterskiing.* 我们玩了浮潜，还玩了一会儿水橇。➲ VISUAL VOCAB PAGE V54
- *noun* either of the pair of long flat boards on which a person stands in order to waterski 滑水橇

ˈwater softener *noun* [U, C] a device or substance that removes particular minerals, especially CHALK, from water 硬水软化器；软水剂

ˈwater sports *noun* [pl.] sports that are done on or in water, for example sailing and WATERSKIING 水上运动

water·spout /ˈwɔːtəspaʊt; *NAmE* ˈwɔːtərs-; ˈwɑːt-/ *noun* a column of water that is pulled up from the sea during a storm by a rapidly spinning column of air 水龙卷；海龙卷

ˈwater strider (*NAmE*) (*BrE* **ˈpond skater**) *noun* an insect which moves quickly across the surface of water 黾蝽；水黾

ˈwater supply *noun* [C, U] the water provided for a town, an area or a building; the act of or system for supplying water to a town, etc. 给水；供水；给水系统；供水系统：*a* ***clean/contaminated water supply*** 洁净的 / 受污染的水源 ◇ *to improve the water supply to rural villages* 改善乡村供水系统

ˈwater table *noun* [usually sing.] (*specialist*) the level at and below which water is found in the ground 地下水位

water·tight /ˈwɔːtətaɪt; *NAmE* ˈwɔːtərt-; ˈwɑːt-/ *adj.* **1** that does not allow water to get in or out 不透水的；防水的；水密的：*a watertight container* 不漏水的容器 **2** (of an excuse, a plan, an argument, etc. 借口、计划、论点等) carefully prepared so that it contains no mistakes, faults or weaknesses 严密的；无懈可击的；天衣无缝的：*a watertight alibi* 无法驳倒的不在犯罪现场证据 ◇ *The case has to be made watertight.* 理据必须做到无懈可击。

ˈwater tower *noun* a tall structure with a tank of water at the top from which water is supplied to buildings in the area around it（自来）水塔

ˈwater vole (*BrE*) (*also* **ˈwater rat**) *noun* an animal like a RAT that swims and lives in a hole beside a river or lake 水䶄，水田鼠，水鼠（穴居于溪流、湖泊旁）

water·way /ˈwɔːtəweɪ; *NAmE* ˈwɔːtərw-; ˈwɑːt-/ *noun* a river, CANAL, etc. along which boats can travel 水路；航道：*inland waterways* 内河航道 ◇ *a navigable waterway* 可通航的水路

water·wheel /ˈwɔːtəwiːl; *NAmE* ˈwɔːtərw-; ˈwɑːt-/ *noun* a wheel turned by the movement of water, used, especially in the past, to drive machinery（尤指旧时的）水轮，水车

ˈwater wings *noun* [pl.] (*old-fashioned*) a pair of plastic bags filled with air that children wear on their arms when they learn to swim（儿童学游泳时套在胳膊上的）双翼式浮水袋 ➲ WORDFINDER NOTE AT SWIM

water·works /ˈwɔːtəwɜːks; *NAmE* ˈwɔːtərwɜːrks; ˈwɑːt-/ *noun* (*pl.* **water·works**) **1** [C+sing./pl. v.] a building with machinery for supplying water to an area 自来水厂 **2** [pl.] (*informal* or *humorous*) the organs of the body through which URINE (= waste water) is passed（人体的）排水系统；泌尿系统

IDM **turn on the ˈwaterworks** (*informal, disapproving*) to start crying, especially in order to get sympathy or attention 开始哭鼻子（尤指为博得同情或引人关注）

watery /ˈwɔːtəri; *NAmE* ˈwɑːt-/ *adj.* **1** of or like water; containing a lot of water 水的；似水的；含水的；水分很多的：*a watery fluid* 稀薄的流体 ◇ *His eyes were red and watery.* 他两眼发红，泪水汪汪。◇ (*literary*) *She was rescued from a* ***watery grave*** (= saved from DROWNING). 她从龙王爷那里被救了回来。**2** weak and/or pale 虚弱的；苍白无力的：*a watery sun* 惨淡的太阳 ◇ *His eyes were a watery blue.* 他的眼睛是淡蓝色的。◇ *a watery smile* (= weak and without much feeling) 淡然一笑 **3** (of food, drink, etc. 食物、饮料等) containing too much water; thin and having no taste 水分过多的；稀薄无味的：*watery soup* 稀薄无味的汤

Wat·ford /ˈwɒtfəd; *NAmE* ˈwɑːtfərd/ *noun* (*BrE*) a town in Hertfordshire, north of London, that is considered to mark the northern limit of the area of London and SE England. The expression **north of Watford** means the parts of Britain outside this area. 沃特福德（赫特福德郡城镇，被视为伦敦地区和英格兰东南部北界限的标志）：*civil servants who seem to think the world ends north of Watford* 似乎把沃特福德以北当作天涯海角的公务员

watt /wɒt; *NAmE* wɑːt/ *noun* (*abbr.* **W**) a unit for measuring electrical power 瓦，瓦特（电功率单位）：*a 60-watt light bulb* * 60 瓦的电灯泡

W

watt·age /ˈwɒtɪdʒ; *NAmE* ˈwɑːt-/ *noun* [U] (*specialist*) an amount of electrical power expressed in watts 瓦数；瓦特数

wat·tle /ˈwɒtl; *NAmE* ˈwɑːtl/ *noun* **1** [U] sticks twisted together as a material for making fences, walls, etc. 编条结构（用于编筑篱笆、围墙等）：*walls made of* ***wattle and daub*** 泥笆墙 **2** [C] a piece of red skin that hangs down from the throat of a bird such as a TURKEY（火鸡等禽类喉部的）红色肉垂 **3** [C, U] (*especially AustralE*) a name for various types of ACACIA tree 金合欢树

wave 🔑 /weɪv/ *noun, verb*

■ ***noun***

• **OF WATER** 水 **1** 🔑 [C] a raised line of water that moves across the surface of the sea, ocean, etc. 海浪；波浪；波涛：*Huge* ***waves were breaking*** *on the shore.* 巨浪拍打着海岸。◇ *Surfers flocked to the beach to* ***ride the waves.*** 冲浪者集聚到海滩去冲浪。◇ *the gentle sound of* ***waves lapping*** 波浪轻轻拍打的声音 ◇ *Children were playing* ***in the waves.*** 孩子们在海浪中嬉戏。◇ *Seagulls bobbed* ***on the waves.*** 海鸥随海浪一起一伏。◇ *The wind made little waves on the pond.* 风吹得池水起了涟漪。➲ WORDFINDER NOTE AT SEA ➲ VISUAL VOCAB PAGE V5 ➲ SEE ALSO TIDAL WAVE (1)

• **OF ACTIVITY/FEELING** 活动；感觉 **2** 🔑 [C] a sudden increase in a particular activity or feeling 汹涌的行动（或思想）态势；心潮；风潮：*a* ***wave of opposition/protest/violence, etc.*** 反对、抗议、暴力等的浪潮 ◇ ***a crime wave*** 犯罪潮 ◇ *A wave of fear swept over him.* 一阵恐惧传遍他的全身。◇ *Guilt and horror flooded her* ***in waves.*** 歉疚和恐惧一阵阵涌上她的心头。◇ *A wave of panic spread through the crowd.* 一阵恐慌传遍人群。➲ SEE ALSO BRAINWAVE, HEATWAVE

• **LARGE NUMBER** 大量 **3** 🔑 [C] a large number of people or things suddenly moving or appearing somewhere 涌现的人（或事物）；涌动的人（或物）：*Wave after wave of aircraft passed overhead.* 一批又一批飞机从上空掠过。➲ SEE ALSO NEW WAVE

• **MOVEMENT OF ARM/HAND/BODY** 臂 / 手 / 身体的动作 **4** 🔑 [C] a movement of your arm and hand from side to side 挥臂；挥手；招手；摆手：*She declined the offer with a wave of her hand.* 她摆了摆手谢绝了这一提议。◇ ***He gave us a wave*** *as the bus drove off.* 公共汽车开走时他向我们挥了挥手。**5 the wave** (*NAmE*) (*BrE* ˌ**Mexican ˈwave**) [sing.] a continuous movement that looks like a wave on the sea, made by a large group of people, especially people watching a sports game, when one person after another stands up, raises their arms, and then sits down again 人浪（尤指体育比赛中看台上的观众依次站起坐下而形成的波浪状场面）

• **OF HEAT/SOUND/LIGHT** 热；声；光 **6** 🔑 [C] the form that some types of energy such as heat, sound, light, etc. take as they move 波；波状运动：***radio/sound/ultrasonic waves*** 无线电波；声波；超声波 ➲ SEE ALSO AIRWAVES, LONG WAVE, MEDIUM WAVE, MICROWAVE *n.* (2), SHOCK WAVE, SHORT WAVE, SOUND WAVE

• **IN HAIR** 头发 **7** [C] if a person's hair has **a wave** or **waves**, it is not straight but curls slightly 拳曲；波浪 ➲ SEE ALSO PERMANENT WAVE

• **SEA** 海洋 **8 the waves** [pl.] (*literary*) the sea 大海 ➲ SEE ALSO WAVY

IDM **make ˈwaves** (*informal*) to be very active in a way that makes people notice you, and that may sometimes cause problems 咋咋呼呼；大肆张扬 ➲ MORE AT CREST *n.*, RIDE *v.*

■ ***verb***

• **MOVE HAND/ARM** 挥动手 / 臂 **1** 🔑 [I, T] to move your hand or arm from side to side in the air in order to attract attention, say hello, etc. 挥手；招手；摆手；挥臂：*The people on the bus waved and we waved back.* 公共汽车上的人挥手致意，我们也向他们挥手。◇ **~ at/to sb** *Why did you wave at him?* 你为什么向他招手？◇ **~ sth (about/around)** *A man in the water was shouting and waving his arms around frantically.* 水里有个人大喊大叫，拼命摆动着双臂。◇ **~ sth at sb** *She waved her hand dismissively at the housekeeper.* 她轻蔑地朝客房服务员挥了挥手。◇ **~ sb sth** *My mother was crying as I* ***waved her goodbye.*** 我向母亲挥手告别时她哭了。◇ **~ sth to sb** *My mother was crying as I* ***waved goodbye*** *to her.* 我向母亲挥手告别时她哭了。**2** 🔑 [I, T] to show where sth is, show sb where to go, etc. by moving your hand in a particular direction 挥手指引，挥手示意（方向）：**+ adv./prep.** *She waved vaguely in the direction of the house.* 她含糊地朝房子的方向挥了挥手。◇ **~ sth/sb + adv./prep.** ***'He's over there,' said Ali, waving a hand*** *towards some trees.* "他在那儿。" 阿里说着朝几棵树挥了挥手。◇ *I showed my pass to the security guard and he waved me through.* 我向保安员出示了通行证，他挥手让我通过。**3** 🔑 [T] to hold sth in your hand and move it from side to side 挥舞，挥动（手中之物）：**~ sth** *Crowds lined the route, waving flags and cheering.* 人群沿路线排成行，挥舞着旗子欢呼。◇ **~ sth + adv./prep.** *'I'm rich!' she exclaimed, waving the money under his nose.* "我发财了！" 她在他的鼻子下面舞动着钞票喊道。

• **MOVE FREELY** 自由移动 **4** 🔑 [I] to move freely and gently, for example in the wind, while one end or side is held in position（一端固定地）飘扬，飘动，摇晃，起伏：*The flag waved in the breeze.* 旗子在微风中飘扬。

• **HAIR** 头发 **5** [I] to curl slightly 略呈波形；拳曲：*His hair waves naturally.* 他天生一头鬈发。**6** [T] **~ sth** to make sb's hair curl slightly 使…略呈波形；烫（发）：*She's had her hair waved.* 她烫发了。

IDM **like waving a red flag in front of a ˈbull** (*US*) (*BrE* **a red rag to a ˈbull**) something that is likely to make sb very angry 斗牛的红布；激起人怒火的事物 ➲ MORE AT FLAG *n.*

PHR V ˌ**wave sth↔aˈside/aˈway** to not accept sth because you do not think it is necessary or important 对…置之不理；不理会 **SYN** **dismiss**: *My objections to the plan were waved aside.* 我对这项计划的反对意见未被理会。 ˌ**wave sth/sb↔ˈdown** to signal to a vehicle or its driver to stop by waving your hand 对（汽车或司机）挥手示意停下；挥手叫停 ˌ**wave sb↔ˈoff** to wave goodbye to sb as they are leaving 挥手送别

wave·band /ˈweɪvbænd/ *noun* = BAND (6): *a radio set with medium and short wavebands* 中短波段收音机

ˌ**wave-cut ˈplatform** *noun* (*specialist*) an area of land between the CLIFFS and the sea which is covered by water when the sea is at its highest level 海蚀台地（悬崖和海之间的地面，涨潮时被水覆盖）

wave·form /ˈweɪvfɔːm; *NAmE* -fɔːrm/ *noun* (*physics* 物) a curve showing the shape of a wave at a particular time 波形

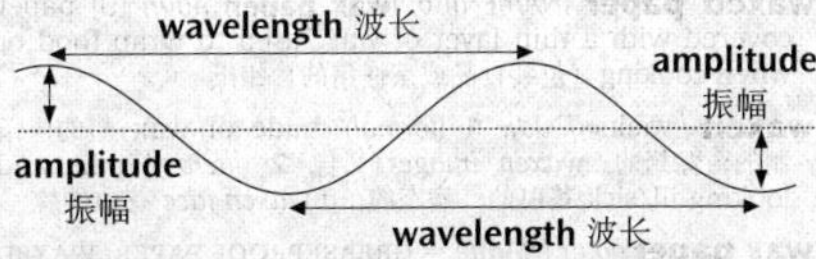

wave·length /ˈweɪvleŋθ/ *noun* **1** the distance between two similar points on a wave of energy, such as light or sound 波长 **2** the size of a radio wave that is used by a particular radio station, etc. for sending signals or broadcasting programmes（广播电台等使用的）频道，波道

IDM **be on the same ˈwavelength | be on sb's ˈwavelength** (*informal*) to have the same way of thinking or the same ideas or feelings as sb else 具有（与他人）相同的思路；合拍；与…所见略同

wave·let /ˈweɪvlət/ *noun* (*literary*) a small wave on the surface of a lake, the sea or the ocean（湖面或海面的）鳞波，涟漪

ˈ**wave machine** *noun* a machine that makes waves in the water in a swimming pool（游泳池内的）造波机

waver /ˈweɪvə(r)/ *verb* **1** [I] to be or become weak or unsteady 减弱；动摇；颤抖：*His voice wavered with emotion.* 他激动得嗓音发抖。◇ *Her determination never*

W

wavered. 她的决心从未动摇过。◇ *She never wavered in her determination to succeed.* 她要取得成功的决心从未动摇过。**2** [I] ~ (**between A and B**) | ~ (**on/over sth**) to hesitate and be unable to make a decision or choice 踌躇；犹豫不决；举棋不定 SYN **hesitate**: *She's wavering between buying a house in the city or moving away.* 她举棋不定，不知是在这个城市里买所房子，还是迁居他处。**3** [I] (especially of light 尤指光) to move in an unsteady way 摇曳；闪烁；忽明忽暗 ▸ **waver·er** /ˈweɪvərə(r)/ *noun*: *The strength of his argument convinced the waverers.* 他以有力的论据说服了那些摇摆不定的人。

wavy /ˈweɪvi/ *adj.* (**wavi·er, wavi·est**) having curves; not straight 起伏不平的；波浪形的；拳曲的: *brown wavy hair* 棕色鬈发 ◇ *a pattern of wavy lines* 波浪形线条图案 ➲ PICTURE AT CURVED

wax /wæks/ *noun, verb*

■ ***noun*** [U] **1** a solid substance that is made from BEESWAX or from various fats and oils and used for making CANDLES, polish, models, etc. It becomes soft when it is heated. 蜡；蜂蜡；动物蜡；植物蜡；石蜡: *styling wax for the hair* 定型发蜡 ◇ *floor wax* 地板蜡 ◇ *wax crayons* 蜡笔 ◇ *wax polish* 上光蜡 ➲ SEE ALSO PARAFFIN WAX, SEALING WAX **2** a soft sticky yellowish substance that is found in your ears 耳垢；耳屎 IDM SEE BALL *n.*

■ ***verb*** **1** [T] ~ **sth** to polish sth with wax 给…打蜡 **2** [T, usually passive] ~ **sth** to cover sth with wax 给…上蜡；给…涂蜡: *waxed paper* 蜡纸 ◇ *a waxed jacket* 上过蜡的夹克 **3** [T, often passive] ~ **sth** to remove hair from a part of the body using wax 用蜡除去…上的毛: *to wax your legs/to have your legs waxed* 用蜡除去你腿上的毛 **4** [I] (of the moon 月亮) to seem to get gradually bigger until its full form is visible 渐圆；渐满 OPP **wane** **5** [I] + **lyrical, eloquent, sentimental, etc.** (*formal*) to become LYRICAL, etc. when speaking or writing 说话变得（热情、雄辩、伤感等）起来: *He waxed lyrical on the food at the new restaurant.* 他对这家新餐馆的菜肴越说越来劲。

IDM ˌ**wax and ˈwane** (*literary*) to increase then decrease in strength, importance, etc. over a period of time（力量、重要性等）兴衰枯荣，盛衰；阴晴圆缺 ➲ MORE LIKE THIS 13, page R26

ˈ**wax bean** *noun* (*NAmE*) a type of BEAN that is a long thin yellow POD, cooked and eaten whole as a vegetable 黄荚种菜豆；黄刀豆；蜡豆

ˈ**waxed paper** (*NAmE also* ˈ**wax paper**) *noun* [U] paper covered with a thin layer of wax, used to wrap food or when cooking（包装食品或烹饪用的）蜡纸

waxen /ˈwæksn/ *adj.* **1** (*formal*) made of wax 蜡的；蜡制的；涂蜡的: *waxen images* 蜡像 **2** (*literary*) pale and looking ill/sick 苍白的；病态的: *a waxen face* 苍白的脸

ˈ**wax paper** *noun* (*NAmE*) = GREASEPROOF PAPER, WAXED PAPER

W

wax·work /ˈwækswɜːk; *NAmE* -wɜːrk/ *noun* **1** a model of a person that is made of wax 蜡像；蜡人 **2** **wax·works** (*pl.* **wax·works**) (*especially BrE*) (*NAmE usually* ˈ**wax museum**) a museum where you can see wax models of famous people 蜡像馆

waxy /ˈwæksi/ *adj.* made of wax; looking or feeling like wax 蜡制的；似蜡的；质地光滑的

way /weɪ/ *noun, adv.*

■ ***noun***

• **METHOD/STYLE** 方法；方式 **1** [C] a method, style or manner of doing sth 方法；手段；途径；方式: ~ **to do sth** *That's not the right way to hold a pair of scissors.* 那样拿剪刀不对。◇ (*informal, disapproving*) ***That's no way*** *to speak to your mother!* 不能那样跟你妈妈说话！◇ ~ **of doing sth** *I'm not happy with this way of working.* 我不喜欢这种工作方法。◇ ~ (**that…**) *It's not what you say, it's the way that you say it.* 问题不在于你说什么，而在于你怎么说。◇ *I **hate the way** she always criticizes me.* 我讨厌她一贯批评我的方式。◇ *I told you we should have done it my way!* 我跟你说过我们原本应该用我的方法来做这事。◇ *Infectious diseases can be acquired in several ways.* 传染病的感染途径有几种。◇ *I generally get what I want **one way or another*** (= by some means). 我一般总能想方设法得到我想要的东西。➲ SEE ALSO THIRD WAY

• **BEHAVIOUR** 行为 **2** [C] a particular manner or style of behaviour 作风；风度；样子: *They grinned at her **in a friendly way**.* 他们友好地对她咧嘴笑了笑。◇ ***It was not his way** to admit that he had made a mistake.* 承认自己犯了错误可不是他一贯的作风。◇ *Don't worry, if she seems quiet—**it's just her way**.* 如果她看上去不爱说话，别担心，她就是这么个人。◇ *He was showing off, **as is the way** with adolescent boys.* 他在炫耀，青春期的男孩都是这个样子。**3 ways** [pl.] the typical way of behaving and living of a particular group of people（群体的）行为方式，生活方式，习俗: *After ten years I'm used to the strange British ways.* 十年之后，我习惯了英国人的奇异习俗。

• **ROUTE/ROAD** 路线；道路 **4** [C, usually sing.] ~ (**from…**) (**to…**) a route or road that you take in order to reach a place 路线；路；道路: *the **best/quickest/shortest way** from A to B* 从甲地到乙地最好的 / 最快的 / 最近的路线 ◇ *Can you **tell me the way** to Leicester Square?* 你能告诉我去莱斯特广场的路吗？◇ *to **ask sb the way*** 向某人问路 ◇ *We went **the long way round**.* 我们绕了一个大圈子。**5** [C, usually sing.] the route along which sb/sth is moving; the route that sb/sth would take if there was nothing stopping them/it 行进路线；通路: ***Get out of my way!** I'm in a hurry.* 让开！我有急事。◇ *Riot police with shields were blocking the demonstrators' way.* 手持盾牌的防暴警察堵住了示威者的路。◇ *We fought our way through the dense vegetation.* 我们在茂密的植被中开出一条通路。◇ *Unfortunately they ran into a snowstorm along the way.* 他们不幸在途中遇上了暴风雪。➲ SEE ALSO RIGHT OF WAY **6** [C] a road, path or street for travelling along 路；小径；街道: *There's a way across the fields.* 有一条路穿过田地。➲ SEE ALSO FREEWAY, HIGHWAY, MOTORWAY, RAILWAY, WATERWAY **7** **Way** used in the names of streets（用于街道名称）路，道: *106 Headley Way* 黑德利路 106 号

• **DIRECTION** 方向 **8** [C, usually sing.] **which, this, that, etc.** ~ a particular direction; in a particular direction 某方向；往某方向: *Which way did they go?* 他们往哪边去了？◇ *We just missed a car coming **the other way**.* 我们差点被一辆对面开过来的汽车撞上。◇ *Look **both ways*** (= look left and right) *before crossing the road.* 横过马路前要朝左右两边看一看。◇ *Make sure that sign's **the right way up**.* 一定不要把这招牌挂颠倒了。◇ *Kids were running **this way and that*** (= in all directions). 孩子们四处奔跑。◇ *They decided to split the money four ways* (= between four different people). 他们决定把钱分成四份。◇ (*figurative*) *Which way* (= for which party) *are you going to vote?* 你打算投哪边的票？➲ SEE ALSO EACH WAY, ONE-WAY, THREE-WAY, TWO-WAY

• **FOR ENTERING/LEAVING** 进入；离去 **9** [C, usually sing.] a means of going into or leaving a place, such as a door or gate 出入通道；门口: *the **way in/out*** 入口；出口 ◇ *They escaped out the back way.* 他们从后门逃走了。➲ SEE ALSO COMPANIONWAY

• **DISTANCE/TIME** 距离；时间 **10** [sing.] (*also NAmE, informal* **ways**) a distance or period of time between two points（两点之间的）距离，时间段: *A little way up on the left is the Museum of Modern Art.* 前面不远左手边就是现代艺术博物馆。◇ *September was **a long way off**.* 那时离九月份还有很长一段时间。◇ (*figurative*) *The area's wine industry still has **a way to go** to full maturity.* 这个地区的酿酒业还远远没有完全成熟。◇ *You came **all this way** to see us?* 你大老远地跑来看我们？◇ (*NAmE, informal*) *We still have **a ways to go**.* 我们还有很大的差距。

• **AREA** 地区 **11** [sing.] (*informal*) an area, a part of a country, etc. 地区；地带: *I think he lives somewhere **over** Greenwich **way**.* 我想他住在格林尼治那一带。◇ *I'll stop by and see you next time I'm **down your way**.* 下次我去你那一带时会顺道去看你的。

• **ASPECT** 方面 **12** [C] a particular aspect of sth 方面 SYN **respect**: *I have changed in every way.* 我已经完完全全变了。◇ *It's been quite a day, **one way and another*** (= for several reasons). 从几方面看，这是不寻常的一天。

• **CONDITION/STATE** 情况；状态 **13** [sing.] a particular condition or state 情况；状态: *The economy's **in a bad way**.* 经

济状况很糟。◇ *I don't know how we're going to manage, the way things are.* 按目前这样的情况，我不知道我们要如何应付。

IDM **across the 'way** (*BrE also* **over the 'way**) on the other side of the street, etc. 在街对面；在…对面：*Music blared from the open window of the house across the way.* 从街对面那栋房子开着的窗户里传出嘈杂的音乐声。 **ˌall the 'way 1** 🔑 (*also* **the ˌwhole 'way**) during the whole journey/period of time 一路上；自始至终：*She didn't speak a word to me all the way back home.* 回家的一路上，她没对我说过一句话。**2** completely; as much as it takes to achieve what you want 完全地；无保留地：*I'm fighting him all the way.* 我在全力和他对抗。◇ *You can feel that the audience is with her all the way.* 你可以感觉到听众完全支持她。 **(that's/it's) always the 'way** (*informal*) used to say that things often happen in a particular way, especially when it is not convenient（表示经常如此，尤用于贬义）总是这样，老是 **any way you 'slice it** (*NAmE, informal*) however you choose to look at a situation 无论你如何看待 **'be/be 'born/be 'made that way** (of a person 人) to behave or do things in a particular manner because it is part of your character 天性如此；生下就这样：*It's not his fault he's so pompous—he was born that way.* 他如此自命不凡并不是他的错，他天生就是这种性格。 **be ˌset in your 'ways** to have habits or opinions that you have had for a long time and that you do not want to change 积习难改；禀性难移；执拗 **by the 'way** 🔑 (*also* **by the 'by/'bye**) (*informal*) used to introduce a comment or question that is not directly related to what you have been talking about 顺便提一下；捎带说一声；附带问一句：*By the way, I found that book you were looking for.* 顺便提一下，我找到了你在寻找的那本书。◇ *What's the time, by the way?* 顺便问一句，几点钟了？◇ *Oh by the way, if you see Jackie, tell her I'll call her this evening.* 啊，对了，你要是看到杰基，告诉她我今晚给她打电话。 **by way of sth** by a route that includes the place mentioned 路经；经过；经由 SYN **via**：*The artist recently arrived in Paris from Bulgaria by way of Vienna.* 这位艺术家最近从保加利亚途经维也纳到了巴黎。◇ *She came to TV by way of drama school.* 她是念过戏剧学校后到电视台的。 **by way of/in the way of sth** as a form of sth; for sth; as a means of sth 作为…的形式；为了；作为…的手段：*He received £600 by way of compensation from the company.* 他得到那家公司 600 英镑的赔偿。◇ *She rolled her eyes by way of an answer and left.* 她转动了一下眼睛作为回答就走了。 **come your 'way** to happen to you by chance, or when you were not expecting it 意外落在…头上；偶尔发生在…身上：*He took whatever came his way.* 无论什么事落到他的头上，他都认了。 **cut both/two 'ways** (of an action, argument, etc. 行动、论点等) to have two opposite effects or results 两面都行得通（或说得通）；有利也有弊 **either way | one way or the other** used to say that it does not matter which one of two possibilities happens, is chosen or is true 两者都一样：*Was it his fault or not? Either way, an explanation is due.* 是他的错或不是？无论是不是，都得有个解释。◇ *We could meet today or tomorrow—I don't mind one way or the other.* 我们可以在今天或明天见面，哪一天对我都行。 **every 'which way** (*informal*) in all directions 四面八方；向各处：*Her hair tumbled every which way.* 她的头发乱得像鸡窝。 **get into/out of the way of (doing) sth** to become used to doing sth/to lose the habit of doing sth 养成（或丢掉）…的习惯：*The women had got into the way of going up on the deck every evening.* 这些女人养成了每天晚上到平台去的习惯。 **get in the way of** to prevent sb from doing sth; to prevent sth from happening 挡…的路；妨碍：*He wouldn't allow emotions to get in the way of him doing his job.* 他不会让感情妨碍自己的工作。 **get/have your own 'way** to get or do what you want, especially when sb has tried to stop you 一意孤行；为所欲为：*She always gets her own way in the end.* 到最后总是她说了算。 **give 'way** to break or fall down 断裂；倒塌；塌陷：*The pillars gave way and a section of the roof collapsed.* 这些立柱坍塌了，一部分屋顶坠落下来。◇ *Her numb leg gave way beneath her and she stumbled clumsily.* 她那麻木了的腿一软，她便重重地摔了一跤。 **give 'way (to sb/sth) 1** to stop resisting sb/sth; to agree to do sth that you do not want to do 屈服；退让；让步：*He refused to give way on any of the points.* 他拒绝在任何一点上让步。**2** (*BrE*) to allow sb/sth to be or go first 让…在先；让…先行：*Give way to traffic already on the roundabout.* 让已上环状交叉路的车辆先行。 **give way to sth 1** to allow yourself to be very strongly affected by sth, especially an emotion 让自己陷于（某种情绪等）：*Flinging herself on the bed, she gave way to helpless misery.* 她一头扑倒在床上，痛苦不堪。**2** to be replaced by sth 被…代替：*The storm gave way to bright sunshine.* 暴风雨过后阳光灿烂。 **go all the 'way (with sb)** (*informal*) to have full SEXUAL INTERCOURSE with sb （与某人）尽情地性交 **go a long/some way towards doing sth** to help very much/a little in achieving sth（对做某事）帮助很大 / 不大，作用很大 / 不大：*The new law goes a long way towards solving the problem.* 新的法律十分有助于解决这一问题。 **go out of your 'way (to do sth)** to make a special effort to do sth 特地；格外努力：*He would always go out of his way to be friendly towards her.* 他总是特意向她表示友好。 **go your own 'way** to do as you choose, especially when sb has advised you against it 一意孤行；我行我素：*It's best to let her go her own way if you don't want a fight.* 你要不想吵架的话，最好是随她去好了。 **go sb's way 1** to travel in the same direction as sb 与…同路：*I'm going your way—I'll walk with you.* 咱们同路，我和你一起走。**2** (of events 事情) to go well for you; to be in your favour 进行顺利；对…有利：*By the third round he knew the fight was going his way.* 拳击打到第三回合，他知道形势对自己很有利。 **go the way of all 'flesh** (*saying*) to die 长逝；走向人生终点 **have it your 'own way!** (*informal*) used to say in an angry way that although you are not happy about sth that sb has said, you are not going to argue 随你的便好了：*Oh OK, then. Have it your own way.* 啊，好啦。随你的便吧。 **have it/things/everything your 'own way** to have what you want, especially by opposing other people 为所欲为；一意孤行 **have a way of doing sth** used to say that sth often happens in a particular way, especially when it is out of your control …是常有的事（尤指无法控制的事）：*First love affairs have a way of not working out.* 第一次恋爱常常不成功。 **have a way with sb/sth** to be good at dealing with sb/sth 善于应付；善于处理；有办法对付：*He has a way with small children.* 他很会逗小孩。◇ *She has a way with words* (= is very good at expressing herself). 她善于辞令。 **have/want it 'both ways** to have or want to have the advantages of two different situations or ways of behaving that are impossible to combine （想）两全其美：*You can't have it both ways. If you can afford to go out all the time, you can afford to pay off some of your debts.* 你不可能做到两全其美。如果你有钱整天外出玩乐，就能还掉一部分债。 **have your (wicked) way with sb** (*old-fashioned, humorous*) to persuade sb to have sex with you 把…勾到手 **in a big/small way** on a large/small scale 大 / 小规模地：*The new delivery service has taken off in a big way.* 新的递送服务迅速走红。◇ *Many people are investing in a small way in the stock market.* 许多人都在小量地向证券市场投资。 **in ˌmore ways than 'one** used to show that a statement has more than one meaning（所说的话）不止一个意思；在很多方面：*With the first goal he used his head in more ways than one.* 他进第一个球时从多方面动了脑筋。 **in her, his, its, etc. (own) 'way** in a manner that is appropriate to or typical of a person or thing but that may seem unusual to other people 以…的特有方式：*I expect she does love you in her own way.* 我想她的确是以她特有的方式爱你。 **in a 'way | in 'one way | in 'some ways** to some extent; not completely 在某种程度上；不完全地：*In a way it was one of our biggest mistakes.* 从某种意义上来说，这是我们所犯的最大错误之一。 **in the/sb's 'way** 🔑 stopping sb from moving or doing sth 妨碍；挡着…的路：*You'll have to move—you're in my way.* 你得挪一挪，你挡了我的路。◇ *I left them alone, as I felt I was in the way.* 我留下他们单独在一起，因为我觉得我碍他们的事。 **in the way of sth** used in questions and negative sentences to talk about the types of sth that are available（用于问句或否定句）关于，就…而言：*There isn't much in the way of entertainment in this place.* 这个地方没有多少娱乐活动。 **keep/stay**

W

out of sb's 'way 🔑 to avoid sb 规避；避开；躲开 **look the other 'way** to deliberately avoid seeing sb/sth 故意避而不看：*Prison officers know what's going on, but look the other way.* 狱警知道出了什么事，但扭过头去装作没看见。**lose your 'way 1** 🔑 to become lost 迷失方向；迷路：*We lost our way in the dark.* 我们在黑暗中迷了路。**2** to forget or move away from the purpose or reason for sth 忘记宗旨；背离…的意图：*I feel that the project has lost its way.* 我觉得这个项目已经背离了原来的意图。**make your 'way (to/towards sth)** to move or get somewhere; to make progress 去；前往；到…地方去；前进：*Will you be able to* **make your own way** *to the airport* (= get there without help, a ride, etc.)? 你能自己去机场吗？◇ *Is this your plan for* **making your way in the world**? 这就是你要出人头地的计划吗？**make 'way (for sb/sth)** to allow sb/sth to pass; to allow sb/sth to take the place of sb/sth 让…通过；给…让路；让出位置：*Make way for the Lord Mayor!* 给市长大人让路！◇ *Tropical forest is felled to make way for grassland.* 热带森林被砍伐，腾出地方做草地。**,my way or the 'highway** (*NAmE, informal*) used to say that sb else has either to agree with your opinion or to leave 要么听我的，要么走人 **(there are) no two ways a'bout it** (*saying*) used to show that you are certain about sth 肯定无疑；别无他途：*It was the wrong decision—there are no two ways about it.* 这是错误的决定，毫无疑问。**(there is) ,no 'way** 🔑 (*informal*) used to say that there is no possibility that you will do sth or that sth will happen 不可能；决不；不行；没门儿：*'Do you want to help?' 'No way!'* "你想帮忙吗？""没门！"◇ *No way am I going to drive them there.* 我无论如何都不会开车把他们送到那里去。◇ *There's no way we could afford that sort of money.* 我们无论如何都花不起那种钱。**on your/the/its 'way 1** 🔑 going or coming 即将去（或来）；就要去（或来）：*I'd better be on my way* (= I must leave) *soon.* 我最好还是快点儿走。◇ *The letter should be on its way to you.* 那封信该快到你那里了。**2** 🔑 during the journey 在路上；在行进中：*He stopped for breakfast on the way.* 他中途停下吃早点。◇ *She grabbed her camera and bag on her way out.* 她出门时一把抓起照相机和提包。**3** (of a baby 婴儿) not yet born 尚未出生的：*They've got three kids and one on the way.* 他们有三个孩子，还有一个尚未出生。**the ,other way 'round 1** 🔑 in the opposite position, direction or order 颠倒过来；相反；反过来：*I think it should go on the other way round.* 我想这应该以相反的方式继续下去。**2** 🔑 the opposite situation 相反的情况：*I didn't leave you. It was the other way round* (= you left me). 我没有离开你。是你离开了我。**,out of the 'way 1** 🔑 no longer stopping sb from moving or doing sth 不再挡路；不再碍事：*I moved my legs out of the way so that she could get past.* 我挪开腿让她过去。◇ *I didn't say anything until Dad was out of the way.* 我直到爸爸不再打扰之后才说话。**2** finished; dealt with 结束；处理完：*Our region is poised for growth once the election is out of the way.* 大选一结束，我们地区就准备大展拳脚。**3** used in negative sentences to mean 'unusual'（用于否定句）奇特的，不寻常的，罕见的：*She had obviously noticed nothing out of the way.* 她显然没发现异常情况。➲ SEE ALSO OUT-OF-THE-WAY **,out of your 'way** not on the route that you planned to take 不在计划走的路线上：*I'd love a ride home—if it's not out of your way.* 我很想搭你的车回家，如果这不叫你绕路的话。**see your 'way ('clear) to doing sth/to do sth** to find that it is possible or convenient to do sth 觉得有可能做某事；认为便于做某事：*Small builders cannot see their way clear to take on many trainees.* 小建筑商认为不可能招收很多见习生。**see which way the 'wind is blowing** to get an idea of what is likely to happen before doing sth 看看风向；观察势头；摸清可能发生的情况 **(not) stand in sb's 'way** to (not) prevent sb from doing sth（不）妨碍别人：*If you believe you can make her happy, I won't stand in your way.* 如果你相信你能使她幸福，我不会妨碍你的。**that's the way the cookie 'crumbles** (*informal*) that is the situation and we cannot change it, so we must accept it 情况就是这样；没有别的办法 **there's more than ,one way to skin a 'cat** (*saying, humorous*) there are many different ways to achieve sth（要做成某事）方法不止一个，有的是办法 **to 'my way of thinking** in my opinion 我认为；依我看；依我之见 **under 'way** (*also* **under·way**) having started 已经开始；在进行中：*Preparations are well under way for a week of special events in May.* 五月份特别活动周的准备工作已经顺利开展。**a/the/sb's way of 'life** 🔑 the typical pattern of behaviour of a person or group（个人或群体的）特有的行为模式，典型生活方式：*the American way of life* 美国人的生活方式 **the ,way of the 'world** the way that most people behave; the way that things happen, which you cannot change 大多数人的行为模式；世道；事情发生的规律：*The rich and powerful make the decisions—that's the way of the world.* 有钱有势者说了算，这就是世道。**,ways and 'means** the methods and materials available for doing sth（做某事现有的）方法和资源，手段和财力：*ways and means of raising money* 筹资办法 **a way 'into sth** (*also* **a way 'in to sth**) something that allows you to join a group of people, an industry, etc. that it is difficult to join, or to understand sth that it is difficult to understand（加入难以进入的群体、行业等的）敲门砖；（弄懂难以理解的事物的）窍门，诀窍 **the way to sb's 'heart** the way to make sb like or love you 赢得某人喜爱的办法；攻心策：*The way to a man's heart is through his stomach* (= by giving him good food). 取得男人欢心的方法就是让他吃好。**way to 'go!** (*NAmE, informal*) used to tell sb that you are pleased about sth they have done 干得好：*Good work, guys! Way to go!* 伙计们，活儿不错！干得好！**,work your 'way through college, round the world, etc.** to have a job or series of jobs while studying, travelling, etc. in order to pay for your education, etc. 勤工俭学；半工半读；边挣钱边周游世界 **,work your way 'through sth** to do sth from beginning to end, especially when it takes a lot of time or effort 自始至终做（尤指耗费时间或力量的事）：*She worked her way through the pile of documents.* 她从头至尾处理了那一堆文件。**,work your way 'up** to move regularly to a more senior position in a company 逐步升职；按部就班晋升：*He worked his way up from messenger boy to account executive.* 他从送信员一步一步晋升为客户经理。➲ MORE AT CHANGE *v.*, CLAW *v.*, CLEAR *v.*, DOWNHILL *adj.*, EASY *adj.*, ERROR, FAMILY *n.*, FEEL *v.*, FIND *v.*, HARD *adj.*, HARM *n.*, HEAD *n.*, KNOW *v.*, LAUGH *v.*, LIE² *v.*, LONG *adj.*, MEND *v.*, MIDDLE *adj.*, OPEN *v.*, ORDINARY, PARTING *n.*, PAVE, PAY *v.*, PICK *v.*, RUB *v.*, SEPARATE *adj.*, SHAPE *n.*, SHOW *v.*, SMOOTH *v.*, SWEET *adj.*, SWING *v.*, TALK *v.*, WELL *adv.*, WILL *n.*, WRONG *adj.*

■ ***adv.* 1** 🔑 (used with a preposition or an adverb 与介词或副词连用) very far; by a large amount 很远；大量：*She finished the race* **way ahead** *of the other runners.* 她遥遥领先于其他选手跑到终点。◇ *I must be going home; it's* **way past** *my bedtime.* 我得回家了，早过了我的就寝时间了。◇ *The price is* **way above** *what we can afford.* 这价格大大超过了我们的支付能力。◇ *They live* **way out** *in the suburbs.* 他们住在很偏远的郊区。◇ *This skirt is way* (= a lot) *too short.* 这条裙子太短了。◇ *I guessed that there would be a hundred people there, but I was* **way out** (= wrong by a large amount). 我估计那里会有一百人，但是我大错特错了。**2** (used with an adjective 与形容词连用) (*informal, especially NAmE*) very 非常；极其：*Things just got way difficult.* 事情变得太困难了。◇ *I'm way glad to hear that.* 听到这个消息，我太高兴了。

IDM **'way back (in…)** a long time ago 很久以前：*I first met him way back in the 80s.* 我和他初次见面早在80年代。

way·farer /ˈweɪfeərə(r); *NAmE* -fer-/ *noun* (*old-fashioned* or *literary*) a person who travels from one place to another, usually on foot（徒步）旅行者

way·lay /weɪˈleɪ/ *verb* (**way·laid**, **way·laid** /-ˈleɪd/) **~ sb** to stop sb who is going somewhere, especially in order to talk to them or attack them 拦截（尤其是为了谈话或袭击）；拦路：*I got waylaid on my way here.* 我在来这里的路上遭到了拦路抢劫。

way·mark /ˈweɪmɑːk; *NAmE* -mɑːrk/ *noun* (*BrE*) a mark or sign on a route in the countryside to show the way to people who are walking, etc.（乡间步道等的）路标：*Turn right where you see a waymark arrow.* 看到箭头路标就向右转。▸ **way·marked** /-mɑːkt; *NAmE* -mɑːrkt/ *adj.*: *waymarked routes* 有路标的路线

W

ˌway ˈout *noun* **1** (*BrE*) a door used for leaving a building（建筑物的）出口 **SYN** **exit** **2** a way of escaping from a difficult situation（困境的）出路：*She was in a mess and could see no way out.* 她陷入困境，找不到出路。

IDM **on the way ˈout** **1** as you are leaving 在离开的途中 **2** going out of fashion 开始过时

ˌway-ˈout *adj.* (*old-fashioned, informal*) unusual or strange 稀奇的；非传统的；前卫的 **SYN** **weird**：*way-out ideas* 离奇的想法

way·point /ˈweɪpɔɪnt/ *noun* **1** a place where you stop during a journey（旅途中的）停留处 **2** (*specialist*) the COORDINATES, checked by a computer, of each stage of a flight or journey by sea 航路点（飞行或航海每一阶段的坐标点）

-ways *suffix* (in adjectives and adverbs 构成形容词和副词) in the direction of 在…方向（的）；朝…方向（的）：*lengthways* 纵向的 ◇ *sideways* 向一侧的

the ˌWays and ˈMeans Committee *noun* [sing.+sing./pl. v.] a group of members of the US House of Representatives which makes suggestions about laws concerning tax and trade in order to provide money for the US government 美国众议院筹款委员会（就税收和贸易法规提出建议以便为政府提供资金）

way·side /ˈweɪsaɪd/ *noun* [sing.] the area at the side of a road or path 路边；路旁：*a wayside inn* 路边的客店 ◇ *wild flowers growing by the wayside* 路旁长的野花

IDM **fall by the ˈwayside** to fail or be unable to make progress 半途而废；中辍

ˈway station *noun* (*especially NAmE*) a place where people stop to eat or rest during a long journey（长途旅行中的）小站，小饭馆

way·ward /ˈweɪwəd; *NAmE* -wərd/ *adj.* (*formal*) difficult to control 难以控制的；任性的；倔强的 **SYN** **headstrong**：*a wayward child* 任性的孩子 ◇ *wayward emotions* 反复无常的情绪 ► **way·ward·ness** *noun* [U]

wazir /wəˈzɪə(r); *NAmE* -ˈzɪr/ *noun* = VIZIER

wazoo /wæˈzuː/ *noun* (*US, slang*) a person's bottom (the part they sit on) or ANUS 屁股；屁眼

IDM **ˌout/ˌup the waˈzoo** in large numbers or amounts 数目很大；大量

wazungu /wəˈzʊŋgʊ/ PL. OF MZUNGU

Wb *abbr.* WEBER 韦伯（磁通量单位）

WC /ˌdʌbljuː ˈsiː/ *noun* (*BrE* or *NAmE, old-fashioned*) (on signs and doors in public places) toilet (the abbreviation for 'water closet') 盥洗室，厕所（全写为 water closet，见于公共场所的指示牌和厕所门上）

w/c *abbr.* (in writing 书写形式) (*BrE*) week commencing (the week that begins on the date mentioned) 从（提到之）日开始的一周：*the schedule for w/c 19 November* 从 11 月 19 日开始一周的日程

we 🔑 /wi; *strong form* wiː/ *pron.* (used as the subject of a verb 用作动词的主语) **1** 🔑 I and another person or other people; I and you 我们；咱们：*We've moved to Atlanta.* 我们已经搬到亚特兰大了。◇ *We'd* (= the company would) *like to offer you the job.* 我们公司想聘你做这一工作。◇ *Why don't we go and see it together?* 咱们为什么不一起去看看呢？ **2** 🔑 people in general 人们：*We should take more care of our historic buildings.* 我们应该更加爱护有历史意义的建筑。 ➲ SEE ALSO ROYAL 'WE'

weak 🔑 /wiːk/ *adj.* (**weaker**, **weakest**)

• **NOT PHYSICALLY STRONG** 身体虚弱 **1** 🔑 not physically strong 虚弱的；无力的：*She is still weak after her illness.* 她病后仍然虚弱。◇ *His legs felt weak.* 他觉得两腿发软。◇ *She suffered from a weak heart.* 她心脏不好。

• **LIKELY TO BREAK** 易破 **2** 🔑 that cannot support a lot of weight; likely to break 不牢固的；易损坏的；易破的：*That bridge is too weak for heavy traffic.* 那座桥不太牢固，承受不住过多的车辆。

• **WITHOUT POWER** 没有能力 **3** 🔑 easy to influence; not having much power 易受影响的；懦弱的；软弱无力的：*a weak and cowardly man* 一个懦弱胆怯的男子 ◇ *In a weak moment* (= when I was easily persuaded) *I said she could borrow the car.* 我一时心软，同意她借用汽车。◇ *a weak leader* 软弱的领导人 ◇ *The unions have always been weak in this industry.* 在这个行业，工会一直没有权威。

• **POOR/SICK PEOPLE** 穷人；病人 **4** **the weak** *noun* [pl.] people who are poor, sick or without power 穷人；病人；弱者

• **CURRENCY/ECONOMY** 货币；经济 **5** 🔑 not FINANCIALLY strong or successful 疲软的；萧条的：*a weak currency* 疲软的货币 ◇ *The economy is very weak.* 经济十分萧条。

• **NOT GOOD AT STH** 不善于 **6** 🔑 not good at sth 不善于；不擅长；（能力）弱的：*a weak team* 弱队 ◇ **~ in sth** *I was always weak in the science subjects.* 我总是学不好理科。

• **NOT CONVINCING** 欠缺说服力 **7** 🔑 that people are not likely to believe or be persuaded by 不能令人信服的；不能说服人的 **SYN** **unconvincing**：*weak arguments* 无说服力的论据 ◇ *I enjoyed the movie but I thought the ending was very weak.* 我喜欢这部电影，但是觉得结尾很牵强。

• **HARD TO SEE/HEAR** 难以看见 / 听到 **8** 🔑 not easily seen or heard 微弱的；隐约的：*a weak light/signal/sound* 微弱的光线 / 信号 / 声音

• **WITHOUT ENTHUSIASM** 缺乏热情 **9** done without enthusiasm or energy 淡漠的；无活力的；无生气的：*a weak smile* 淡淡的微笑 ◇ *He made a weak attempt to look cheerful.* 他有气无力地摆出高兴的样子。

• **LIQUID** 液体 **10** 🔑 a weak liquid contains a lot of water 稀的；稀薄的；稀释的：*weak tea* 淡茶

• **POINT/SPOT** 点；处 **11** 🔑 **~ point/spot** the part of a person's character, an argument, etc. that is easy to attack or criticize 弱点；缺点；不足之处：*The team's weak points are in defence.* 这个队的弱点在防守。◇ *He knew her weak spot where Steve was concerned.* 他知道史蒂夫是她的软肋。

• **GRAMMAR** 语法 **12** a **weak** verb forms the past tense and past participle by adding a regular ending and not by changing a vowel. In English this is done by adding *-d*, *-ed* or *-t* (for example *walk, walked*).（动词）规则的，弱（变化）的

• **PHONETICS** 语音学 **13** (of the pronunciation of some words 某些单词的发音) used when there is no stress on the word. For example, the weak form of *and* is /ən/ or /n/, as in *bread and butter* /ˌbred n ˈbʌtə(r)/. 轻读的；非重读的 **OPP** **strong**

IDM **ˌweak at the ˈknees** (*informal*) hardly able to stand because of emotion, fear, illness, etc.（因激动、恐惧、疾病等）两腿发软：*His sudden smile made her go weak at the knees.* 他突然笑了笑，使得她两膝发软。 **the weak link (in the ˈchain)** the point at which a system or an organization is most likely to fail 薄弱环节 ➲ MORE AT SPIRIT *n.*

weak·en /ˈwiːkən/ *verb* **1** [T, I] **~ (sb/sth)** to make sb/sth less strong or powerful; to become less strong or powerful（使）虚弱，衰弱；减弱；削弱：*The team has been weakened by injury.* 这个队因伤实力减弱。 ◇ *The new evidence weakens the case against her.* 新的证据削弱了诉她的案由。◇ *His authority is steadily weakening.* 他的权威日趋减弱。 **OPP** **strengthen** **2** [T, I] **~ (sth)** to make sth less physically strong; to become less physically strong 使强度减弱；削弱：*The explosion had weakened the building's foundations.* 爆炸松动了这座楼房的地基。◇ *She felt her legs weaken.* 她觉得两腿无力。 **3** [I, T] to become or make sb become less determined or certain about sth 使（肯定程度）减弱；动摇；犹豫：*You must not agree to do it. Don't weaken.* 你们一定不能同意做这件事。别心软。◇ **~ sth** *Nothing could weaken his resolve to continue.* 什么也不能削弱他继续下去的决心。

ˈweak force *noun* (*specialist*) one of the four FUNDAMENTAL FORCES in the universe, which is produced between PARTICLES in an atom 弱力（宇宙四种基本力之一，产生于原子中的粒子之间） ➲ SEE ALSO ELECTROMAGNETISM, GRAVITY (1), STRONG FORCE

ˌweak-ˈkneed *adj.* (*informal*) lacking courage or strength 缺乏勇气的；意志薄弱的；不坚决的

W

weak·ling /ˈwiːklɪŋ/ *noun* (*disapproving*) a person who is not physically strong 瘦弱的人；弱不禁风的人

weak·ly /ˈwiːkli/ *adv.* in a weak way 虚弱地；软弱无力地；懦弱地；冷淡地：*She **smiled weakly** at them.* 她勉强朝他们笑笑。◇ *'I'm not sure about it,' he said weakly.* "这我说不准。" 他支吾说。

weak·ness /ˈwiːknəs/ *noun* **1** [U] lack of strength, power or determination 软弱；虚弱；疲软；衰弱；懦弱：*The sudden weakness in her legs made her stumble.* 她突然两腿发软踉跄了一下。◇ *the weakness of the dollar against the pound* 美元对英镑的疲软 ◇ *He thought that crying was **a sign of weakness**.* 他认为哭是懦弱的表现。OPP **strength** **2** [C] a weak point in a system, sb's character, etc.（系统、性格等的）弱点，缺点，不足：*It's important to know your own **strengths and weaknesses**.* 了解自己的优缺点很重要。◇ *Can you spot the weakness in her argument?* 你能指出她论点中的不足之处吗？OPP **strength** **3** [C, usually sing.] ~ (**for sth/sb**) difficulty in resisting sth/sb that you like very much（对人或事物的）迷恋，无法抗拒：*He has a weakness for chocolate.* 他爱吃巧克力。

weal /wiːl/ *noun* a sore red mark on sb's skin where they have been hit（挨打造成的）红肿伤痕

wealth /welθ/ *noun* **1** [U] a large amount of money, property, etc. that a person or country owns 钱财；财产；财物；财富：*a person of wealth and influence* 有钱有势的人 ◇ *His personal wealth is estimated at around $100 million.* 他个人的财产估计为 1 亿美元左右。◇ *the **distribution of wealth** in Britain* 英国财富的分配 ➲ COLLOCATIONS AT FINANCE **2** [U] the state of being rich 富有；富裕；富足：*The purpose of industry is to create wealth.* 勤劳的目的是致富。◇ *Good education often depends on wealth.* 良好的教育经常依靠良好的经济条件。**3** [sing.] ~ **of sth** a large amount of sth 大量；丰富；众多；充裕：*a wealth of information* 大量的信息 ◇ *The new manager brings **a great wealth of experience** to the job.* 新任经理为这项工作带来了丰富的经验。➲ COMPARE RICHNESS

wealthy /ˈwelθi/ *adj.* (**wealth·ier**, **wealthi·est**) **1** having a lot of money, possessions, etc. 富有的；富裕的；富饶的 SYN **rich**：*a wealthy nation* 富国 ◇ *The couple are said to be fabulously wealthy.* 据说这对夫妇家财万贯。◇ *They live in a wealthy suburb of Chicago.* 他们住在芝加哥郊区的一处富人区。➲ SYNONYMS AT RICH **2 the wealthy** *noun* [pl.] people who are rich 富人；有钱人；阔人 ➲ MORE LIKE THIS 24, page R28

wean /wiːn/ *verb* ~ **sb/sth** (**off/from sth**) to gradually stop feeding a baby or young animal with its mother's milk and start feeding it with solid food 使（婴儿或动物幼崽）断奶

PHR V **ˈwean sb off/from sth** to make sb gradually stop doing or using sth 使逐渐戒除恶习（或避免依赖…）：*The doctor tried to wean her off sleeping pills.* 医生设法使她逐渐停止服用安眠药片。**ˈwean sb on sth** [usually passive] to make sb experience sth regularly, especially from an early age 使…经常经历（尤指从早年）：*He was weaned on a diet of rigid discipline and duty.* 他自幼受到严格纪律和职责的约束。

weapon /ˈwepən/ *noun* **1** an object such as a knife, gun, bomb, etc. that is used for fighting or attacking sb 武器；兵器；凶器：*nuclear weapons* 核武器 ◇ *a **lethal/deadly weapon*** 致命武器 ◇ *The police still haven't found the **murder weapon**.* 警方仍未找到谋杀的凶器。◇ *He was charged with carrying an **offensive weapon**.* 他被指控携带攻击性武器。➲ WORDFINDER NOTE AT ARMY ➲ COLLOCATIONS AT WAR ➲ SEE ALSO BIOLOGICAL WEAPON, CHEMICAL WEAPON **2** something such as knowledge, words, actions, etc. that can be used to attack or fight against sb/sth 武器，手段，工具（指用作攻击或斗争的知识、言语、行动等）：*Education is the only weapon to fight the spread of the disease.* 教育是战胜这一疾病蔓延的唯一手段。◇ *Guilt is the **secret weapon** for the control of children.* 愧疚是控制儿童的秘密武器。IDM SEE DOUBLE-EDGED

weap·on·ize (*BrE also* **-ise**) /ˈwepənaɪz/ *verb* ~ **sth** to make sth suitable for use as a weapon 使适合用作武器；使武器化：*They may have weaponized quantities of anthrax.* 他们可能已将大量炭疽制成了武器。▸ **weap·on·iza·tion**, **-isa·tion** /ˌwepənaɪˈzeɪʃn; *NAmE* -nəˈz-/ *noun* [U]

ˌweapon of ˌmass deˈstruction *noun* (*abbr.* **WMD**) a weapon such as a nuclear weapon, a CHEMICAL WEAPON or a BIOLOGICAL WEAPON that can cause a lot of destruction and kill many people 大规模杀伤性武器（如核武器、化学武器和生物武器）

weap·on·ry /ˈwepənri/ *noun* [U] all the weapons of a particular type or belonging to a particular country or group（总称某一类型或某国、某组织的）武器，兵器：*high-tech weaponry* 高科技武器 ◇ *US weaponry* 美国的军械

wear /weə(r); *NAmE* wer/ *verb, noun*

■ *verb* (**wore** /wɔː(r)/, **worn** /wɔːn; *NAmE* wɔːrn/)

• **CLOTHING/DECORATION** 衣服；饰物 **1** [T] ~ **sth** to have sth on your body as a piece of clothing, a decoration, etc. 穿；戴；佩戴：*She was wearing a new coat.* 她穿了一件新外衣。◇ *Do I have to wear a tie?* 我得系领带吗？◇ *Was she wearing a seat belt?* 她系着安全带吗？◇ *He wore glasses.* 他戴着眼镜。◇ *All delegates must wear a badge.* 所有代表都要佩戴徽章。◇ *She always wears black* (= black clothes). 她总是穿黑色衣服。➲ COLLOCATIONS AT FASHION

• **HAIR** 须发 **2** [T] to have your hair in a particular style; to have a beard or MOUSTACHE 蓄，留（发、须等）：~ **sth + adj.** *She wears her hair long.* 她梳着长发。◇ ~ **sth** *to wear a beard* 留胡须

• **EXPRESSION ON FACE** 面部表情 **3** [T] ~ **sth** to have a particular expression on your face 流露，面带，呈现（某种神态）：*He wore a puzzled look on his face.* 他脸上流露出迷惑不解的神情。◇ *His face wore a puzzled look.* 他脸上流露出迷惑不解的神情。

• **DAMAGE WITH USE** 用坏 **4** [I, T] to become, or make sth become thinner, smoother or weaker through continuous use or rubbing 磨损；消耗；用旧：*The carpets are starting to wear.* 地毯渐渐磨坏了。◇ **+ adj.** *The sheets have worn thin.* 床单已经磨薄了。◇ ~ **sth + adj.** *The stones have been worn smooth by the constant flow of water.* 不停的流水把这些石头冲刷得很光滑。**5** [T] ~ **sth + adv./prep.** to make a hole, path, etc. in sth by continuous use or rubbing 穿破；磨出（洞）；踩出（路）；冲出（沟）：*I've **worn holes** in all my socks.* 我把我所有的袜子都穿破了。

• **STAY IN GOOD CONDITION** 保持良好状况 **6** [I] ~ **well** to stay in good condition after being used for a long time 耐用；耐穿；耐磨；耐久：*That carpet is wearing well, isn't it?* 这地毯很耐用，是不是？◇ (*figurative, humorous*) *You're wearing well—only a few grey hairs!* 你一点儿都不显老，只有几根灰白头发！

• **ACCEPT/ALLOW** 接受；允许 **7** [T] (usually used in questions and negative sentences 通常用于问句和否定句) ~ **sth** (*BrE, informal*) to accept or allow sth, especially sth that you do not approve of 接受，容许（尤指不赞成的事物）

IDM **wear your ˌheart on your ˈsleeve** to allow your feelings to be seen by other people 让感情外露；把心事挂在脸上 **wear ˈthin** to begin to become weaker or less acceptable 开始变弱；变得不受欢迎；变得兴趣索然：*These excuses are wearing a little thin* (= because we've heard them so many times before). 这些托辞让人听得有点儿腻烦。**wear the ˈtrousers** (*BrE*) (*NAmE* **wear the ˈpants**) (*often disapproving*) (especially of a woman 尤指女人) to be the person in a marriage or other relationship who makes most of the decisions（在婚姻等关系中）处于支配的位置，起指挥的作用 ➲ MORE AT SHOE *n.*

PHR V **ˌwear aˈway** | **ˌwear sth↔aˈway** to become, or make sth become, gradually thinner or smoother by continuously using or rubbing it（因重复使用而）变薄，变光滑；磨薄；磨光：*The inscription on the coin had worn away.* 铸在这枚硬币上的文字已磨平了。◇ *The steps had been worn away by the feet of thousands of pilgrims.* 成千上万的朝圣者把台阶踏得磨损了。**ˌwear ˈdown** | **ˌwear sth↔ˈdown** to become, or make sth become, gradually smaller or smoother by continuously using or rubbing it（因重复使用或磨擦而）变小，变光滑；磨短：*Notice how*

W

the tread on this tyre has worn down. 注意这个轮胎的花纹磨损的程度。ˌ**wear sb/sth↔ˈdown** to make sb/sth weaker or less determined, especially by continuously attacking or putting pressure on them or it over a period of time（尤指通过不断攻击或施加压力）使衰弱，使意志薄弱：*Her persistence paid off and she eventually wore me down.* 她不屈不挠，最终把我拖垮了。ˌ**wear ˈoff** 🔑 to gradually disappear or stop 逐渐消失；消逝；逐渐停止：*The effects of the drug will soon wear off.* 这麻醉药品的作用将很快消失。ˌ**wear ˈon** (of time 时间) to pass, especially in a way that seems slow 慢慢地过去；（光阴）荏苒：*As the evening wore on, she became more and more nervous.* 随着夜色渐深，她越来越紧张。ˌ**wear ˈout** | ˌ**wear sth↔ˈout** 🔑 to become, or make sth become, thin or no longer able to be used, usually because it has been used too much 磨薄；穿破；磨损；用坏：*He wore out two pairs of shoes last year.* 去年他穿坏了两双鞋。ˌ**wear yourself/sb ˈout** 🔑 to make yourself/sb feel very tired 使疲乏；使筋疲力尽；使厌烦：*The kids have totally worn me out.* 孩子们简直把我烦透了。◇ *You'll wear yourself out if you carry on working so hard.* 你要是继续这样拼命工作，身体会吃不消的。

■ ***noun*** [U]

• **CLOTHING** 衣服 **1** (usually in compounds 通常构成复合词) used especially in shops/stores to describe clothes for a particular purpose or occasion（尤用于商店）…时穿的衣服，…装：***casual/evening, etc. wear*** 便装、晚礼服等 ◇ ***children's/ladies' wear*** 童装；女装 ➲ SEE ALSO FOOTWEAR, MENSWEAR, SPORTSWEAR, UNDERWEAR **2** the fact of wearing sth 衣着；穿着；穿戴；佩戴：*casual clothes for everyday wear* 平时穿的休闲服 ◇ *These woollen suits are not designed for wear in hot climates.* 这些毛料西服不是为炎热气候下穿着设计的。➲ **SYNONYMS** AT CLOTHES

• **USE** 使用 **3** the amount or type of use that sth has over a period of time 使用量（或形式）；耐用性；经久性：*You should get years of wear out of that carpet.* 那条地毯你可使用很多年。

• **DAMAGE** 损坏 **4** the damage or loss of quality that is caused when sth has been used a lot 磨损；用坏；耗损：*His shoes were beginning to show signs of wear.* 他那双鞋看样子快穿坏了。

IDM ˌ**wear and ˈtear** the damage to objects, furniture, property, etc. that is the result of normal use（正常使用造成的）磨损，损耗，损坏：*The insurance policy does not cover damage caused by normal wear and tear.* 保险单不保正常使用所造成的坏损。➲ **MORE LIKE THIS** 12, page R26 ➲ MORE AT WORSE *n.*

wear·able /ˈweərəbl; *NAmE* ˈwer-/ *adj.* (of clothes, etc. 衣服等) pleasant and comfortable to wear; suitable to be worn 穿戴舒适的；可穿戴的；适于穿戴的

wear·er /ˈweərə(r); *NAmE* ˈwer-/ *noun* the person who is wearing sth; a person who usually wears the thing mentioned 穿戴者；佩戴人；常穿戴…的人：*The straps can be adjusted to suit the wearer.* 这些背带可进行调整以适合使用者。◇ *contact lens wearers* 戴隐形眼镜的人

wear·ing /ˈweərɪŋ; *NAmE* ˈwer-/ *adj.* that makes you feel very tired mentally or physically 令人精疲力竭的；使人疲倦的；令人厌烦的 **SYN** **exhausting**

weari·some /ˈwɪərisəm; *NAmE* ˈwɪr-/ *adj.* (*formal*) that makes you feel very bored and tired 乏味的；令人疲劳的；使人厌倦的 **SYN** **tedious**

weary /ˈwɪəri; *NAmE* ˈwɪri/ *adj., verb*

■ ***adj.*** (**weari·er**, **weari·est**) **1** very tired, especially after you have been working hard or doing sth for a long time（尤指长时间努力工作后）疲劳的，疲倦的，疲惫的：*a weary traveller* 疲惫不堪的旅行者 ◇ *She suddenly felt old and weary.* 她突然感到了衰老和疲倦。◇ *a weary sigh* 疲倦的叹息 **2** (*literary*) making you feel tired or bored 使人疲劳的；使人厌烦的：*a weary journey* 使人疲乏的旅程 **3** ~ **of sth/of doing sth** (*formal*) no longer interested in or enthusiastic about sth（对…）不再感兴趣，不再热心，感到不耐烦：*Students soon grow weary of listening to a parade of historical facts.* 学生们很快便对听连串史实厌烦起来。▶ **wear·ily** /ˈwɪərəli; *NAmE* ˈwɪr-/ *adv.*: *He closed his eyes wearily.* 他疲惫地闭上了眼睛。**weari·ness** *noun* [U]

■ ***verb*** (**wear·ies**, **weary·ing**, **wear·ied**, **wear·ied**) **1** [T] ~ **sb** (*formal*) to make sb feel tired 使疲劳；使疲倦 **SYN** **tire** **2** [I] ~ **of sth/of doing sth** to lose your interest in or enthusiasm for sth（对…）失去兴趣，失去热情 **SYN** **tire**: *She soon wearied of his stories.* 她很快就厌烦了他的故事。

weasel /ˈwiːzl/ *noun, verb*

■ ***noun*** a small wild animal with reddish-brown fur, a long thin body and short legs. Weasels eat smaller animals. 鼬；黄鼠狼

■ ***verb*** (-**ll**-, *NAmE* -**l**-)

PHR V ˌ**weasel ˈout** (**of sth**) (*informal, disapproving, especially NAmE*) to avoid doing sth that you ought to do or have promised to do 逃避，推诿（责任或已作出的承诺）：*He's now trying to weasel out of our agreement.* 他现在正设法逃避在我们协议中应承担的义务。

ˈ**weasel word** *noun* [usually pl.] (*informal, disapproving*) a word that has little meaning, or more than one meaning, that you use when you want to avoid saying sth in a clear or direct way 滑头话；含糊其词的话；推诿词

wea·ther 🔑 /ˈweðə(r)/ *noun, verb*

■ ***noun*** [U] **1** 🔑 the condition of the atmosphere at a particular place and time, such as the temperature, and if there is wind, rain, sun, etc. 天气；气象：***hot/cold/wet/fine/summer/windy, etc. weather*** 炎热、寒冷、下雨、晴朗、夏天、刮风等的天气 ◇ *Did you have* ***good weather*** *on your trip?* 你旅途中天气好吗？◇ *I'm not going out in this weather!* 这种天气我不会出门的！◇ *There's going to be* ***a change in the weather.*** 天气将有变化。◇ ***if the weather holds/breaks*** (= if the good weather continues/changes) 如果天气还是这么好 / 变坏 ◇ *The weather is very changeable at the moment.* 现时天气变化无常。◇ *'Are you going to the beach tomorrow?' 'It depends on the weather.'* "你明天打算去海滩吗？" "那要看天气而定。" ◇ *We'll have the party outside,* ***weather permitting*** (= if it doesn't rain). 天气允许的话，我们就在室外举行这次聚会。 ◇ ***a weather map/chart*** 气象图 ◇ *a weather report* 气象报告 **2** 🔑 **the weather** (*informal*) a report of what the weather will be like, that is on the radio or television, or in the newspapers 气象预报：*to listen to the weather* 收听气象预报

IDM **in ˈall weathers** in all kinds of weather, good and bad 不论天气好坏；风雨无阻：*She goes out jogging in all weathers.* 无论天气好坏，她都出去慢跑锻炼。**keep a ˈweather eye on sb/sth** to watch sb/sth carefully in case you need to take action 对…随时留意；对…小心提防 **under the ˈweather** (*informal*) if you are or feel **under the weather**, you feel slightly ill/sick and not as well as usual 略有不适；不得劲 ➲ MORE AT BRASS, HEAVY *adj.* ➲ **COLLOCATIONS** ON NEXT PAGE

■ ***verb*** **1** [I, T] to change, or make sth change, colour or shape because of the effect of the sun, rain or wind（因受风吹、日晒、雨淋等，使）退色，变色，变形：*This brick weathers to a warm pinkish-brown colour.* 这块砖经日晒雨淋退成了带粉红的暖褐色。◇ ~ **sth** *Her face was weathered by the sun.* 她的脸晒黑了。**2** [T] ~ **sth** to come safely through a difficult period or experience 经受住；平安地度过（困难时期）：*The company just managed to weather the recession.* 这家公司勉强度过了衰退期。◇ *She refuses to resign, intending to* ***weather the storm*** (= wait until the situation improves again). 她拒绝辞职，想要经受住这次风暴的考验。

ˈ**weather balloon** *noun* a BALLOON that carries instruments into the atmosphere to measure weather conditions 气象气球

ˈ**weather-beaten** *adj.* [usually before noun] (especially of a person or their skin 尤指人或人的皮肤) rough and damaged because the person spends a lot of time outside（因风吹日晒）粗糙的，晒黑的，受损的

wea·ther·board /ˈweðəbɔːd; *NAmE* ˈweðərbɔːrd/ (*also* **clap·board** *especially in NAmE*) *noun* one of a series of long, narrow, horizontal pieces of wood, each with one edge thicker than the other. They are fixed to the outside walls of a house with the bottom of one over the top of the one below, to cover the wall and protect

W

it from rain and wind. 封檐板；风雨板：*a weatherboard house* 安装了封檐板的房屋 ▸ **'wea·ther·boarded** /-ðəbɔːdɪd; *NAmE* -ðərbɔːrdɪd/ *adj.* **'wea·ther·board·ing** /-ðəbɔːdɪŋ; *NAmE* -ðərbɔːrdɪŋ/ *noun* [U]

'weather centre (*BrE*) (*US* **'weather bureau**) *noun* a place where information about the weather is collected and reports are prepared 气象局；气象站；气象中心

weathercock 风信鸡

wea·ther·cock /ˈweðəkɒk; *NAmE* ˈweðərkɑːk/ *noun* a WEATHERVANE in the shape of a male chicken (called a COCK or ROOSTER)（公鸡形）风向标；风信鸡

'weather forecast (*also* **fore·cast**) *noun* a description, for example on the radio or television, of what the weather will be like tomorrow or for the next few days 天气预报

wea·ther·ing /ˈweðərɪŋ/ *noun* [U] the action of sun, rain or wind on rocks, making them change shape or colour（岩石的）风化

wea·ther·ize (*BrE also* **-ise**) /ˈweðəraɪz/ *verb* **~ sth** (*NAmE*) to protect a building against the effects of cold weather, for example by providing INSULATION 使（建筑物）提供御寒性能

wea·ther·man /ˈweðəmæn; *NAmE* -ðərm-/ (*pl.* **-men** /-men/), **wea·ther·girl** /ˈweðəgɜːl; *NAmE* -ðərgɜːrl/ *noun* (*informal*) a person on radio or television whose job is describing the weather and telling people what it is going to be like 气象播音员 ➲ **MORE LIKE THIS** 25, page R28

wea·ther·proof /ˈweðəpruːf; *NAmE* -ðərp-/ *adj.* that is not affected by weather; that protects sb/sth from wind and rain 不受气候影响的；全天候的；防风雨的：*The finished roof should be weatherproof for years.* 修过的屋顶应该能维持好几年都不会漏雨。◇ *a weatherproof jacket* 风雨短上衣

'weather station *noun* a place where weather conditions are studied and recorded 气象站

'weather strip (*NAmE*) (*BrE* **'draught excluder**) *noun* a piece of material that helps to prevent cold air coming through a door, window, etc.（门窗等的）密封条

wea·ther·vane /ˈweðəveɪn; *NAmE* -ðərv-/ *noun* a metal object on the roof of a building that turns easily in the wind and shows which direction the wind is blowing from 风向标；风标 ➲ SEE ALSO WEATHERCOCK

weave /wiːv/ *verb, noun*

■ ***verb*** (**wove** /wəʊv; *NAmE* woʊv/, **woven** /ˈwəʊvn; *NAmE* ˈwoʊvn/) **HELP** In sense 4 **weaved** is used for the past tense and past participle. 作第 4 义时过去式和过去分词用 weaved。**1** [T, I] to make cloth, a carpet, a BASKET, etc. by crossing threads or strips across, over and under each other by hand or on a machine called a LOOM（用手或机器）编，织：**~ A from B** *The baskets are woven from strips of willow.* 这些篮子是用柳条编的。◇ **~ B into A** *The strips*

▼ **COLLOCATIONS** 词语搭配

The weather 天气

Good weather 好天气

- **be bathed in/bask in/be blessed with/enjoy** bright/brilliant/glorious sunshine 沐浴着 / 享受着明媚的 / 灿烂的阳光
- the sun **shines/warms sth/beats down (on sth)** 太阳照耀着 / 温暖着 / 照射在…
- the sunshine **breaks/streams through sth** 阳光穿过…
- fluffy/wispy clouds **drift across the sky** 绒毛般的 / 一缕缕云彩在空中飘过
- a gentle/light/stiff/cool/warm/sea breeze **blows in/comes in off the sea** 微风 / 轻风 / 强风 / 凉爽的风 / 暖风 / 海风从海上吹来
- the snow **crunches beneath/under sb's feet/boots** 积雪在…脚下 / 靴子下嘎吱作响

Bad weather 坏天气

- thick/dark/storm clouds **form/gather/roll in/cover the sky/block out the sun** 厚厚的云层 / 乌云 / 暴风云形成 / 聚集 / 大量聚集 / 遮住天空 / 挡住太阳
- the sky **darkens/turns black** 天空变暗 / 变黑
- a fine mist **hangs in the air** 一丝薄雾弥漫在空气中
- a dense/heavy/thick fog **rolls in** 浓雾滚滚而来
- the rain **falls/comes down (in buckets/sheets)/pours down** 下雨了；大雨倾盆而下；大雨滂沱
- snow **falls/comes down/covers sth** 雪花飘落 / 覆盖着…
- the wind **blows/whistles/howls/picks up/whips through sth/sweeps across sth** 风刮 / 嗖嗖地刮 / 呼啸而过 / 愈刮愈大 / 刮过… / 掠过…
- strong/gale-force winds **blow/gust (up to 80 mph)** 狂风大作（高达每小时 80 英里的速度）
- a storm **is approaching/is moving inland/hits/strikes/rages** 暴风雨即将降临 / 向内陆移动 / 来临 / 袭来 / 肆虐
- thunder **rolls/rumbles/sounds** 雷声隆隆
- (forked/sheet) lightning **strikes/hits/flashes**（叉状的 / 片状的）闪电袭来 / 闪过
- a (blinding/snow) blizzard **hits/strikes/blows/rages**（令人目眩的）暴风雪袭来 / 大作 / 肆虐
- a tornado **touches down/hits/strikes/destroys sth/rips through sth** 龙卷风袭击 / 摧毁… / 撕裂…
- **forecast/expect/predict** rain/snow/a category-four hurricane 预报有雨 / 雪 / 四级飓风
- (*NAmE*) **pour (down)**/ (*BrE*) **pour (down) with** rain 下瓢泼大雨
- **get caught in/seek shelter from/escape** the rain 遇上下雨；寻找避雨处；躲雨
- **be covered/shrouded in** mist/a blanket of fog 笼罩在雾霭之中 / 厚厚的一层雾中
- **be in for/brave/shelter from** a/the storm 即将遇到 / 勇敢面对 / 躲避暴风雨
- **hear** rolling/distant thunder 听到隆隆的 / 远处的雷声
- **be battered/buffeted by** strong winds 遭受强风肆虐；被强风吹得左右摇摆
- (*BrE*) **be blowing** a gale 在刮大风
- **battle against/brave** the elements 与恶劣天气搏斗；冒着风雨

The weather improves 天气好转

- the sun **breaks through the clouds** 太阳破云而出
- the sky **clears/brightens (up)/lightens (up)** 天放晴了
- the clouds **part/clear** 乌云散去
- the rain **stops/lets up/holds off** 雨停了 / 小了 / 延迟了
- the wind **dies down** 风逐渐平息
- the storm **passes** 暴风雨过去了
- the mist/fog **lifts/clears** 薄雾 / 雾消散了

W

of willow are woven into baskets. 用柳条编成篮子。◇ **~ sth together** *threads woven together* 织在一起的线 ◇ **~ (sth)** *Most spiders weave webs that are almost invisible.* 大多数蜘蛛可结成几乎看不见的网。◇ *She is skilled at spinning and weaving.* 她是纺织能手。**2** [T] **~ A (out of/from B) | ~ B (into A)** to make sth by twisting flowers, pieces of wood, etc. together（用…）编成：*She deftly wove the flowers into a garland.* 她灵巧地把花编成了一个花环。**3** [T] to put facts, events, details, etc. together to make a story or a closely connected whole（把…）编成，编纂成，编造（故事等）：**~ (sth into) sth** *to weave a narrative* 编故事 ◇ **~ sth together** *The biography weaves together the various strands of Einstein's life.* 这部传记把爱因斯坦一生的各个方面编纂成书。**4** (**weaved, weaved**) [I, T] to move along by running and changing direction continuously to avoid things that are in your way 迂回行进，穿行（以避开障碍）：**+ adv./prep.** *She was weaving in and out of the traffic.* 她在来往的车辆中穿来穿去。◇ *The road weaves through a range of hills.* 这条路在群山中绕来绕去。◇ **~ your way + adv./prep.** *He had to weave his way through the milling crowds.* 他不得不在来回乱转的人群中穿梭而行。

IDM **weave your 'magic | weave a 'spell (over sb)** (*especially BrE*) to perform or behave in a way that is attractive or interesting, or that makes sb behave in a particular way（对某人）施展魔力；发挥（对某人的）影响力：*Will Ronaldo be able to weave his magic against Italy on Wednesday?* 罗纳尔多星期三能施展其魔力击败意大利队吗？

■ ***noun*** the way in which threads are arranged in a piece of cloth that has been woven; the pattern that the threads make 编法；织法；编织式样

weaver /ˈwiːvə(r)/ *noun* a person whose job is weaving cloth 织布工；编织工

'weaver bird *noun* a tropical bird that builds large nests by weaving sticks and pieces of grass together in a complicated way 织布鸟，织巢鸟（栖息于热带，能用枝条和草编筑结构复杂的大鸟巢）

weav·ing /ˈwiːvɪŋ/ *noun* **1** [U] the activity of making cloth by WEAVING 织布；编织 **2** [C] an article that is made by WEAVING especially one that is used for decoration（尤指用作装饰的）编织物，编织品

web 🔑 /web/ *noun* **1** 🔑 [C] = SPIDER'S WEB: *A spider had spun a perfect web outside the window.* 蜘蛛在窗外结了一张完整的网。➲ VISUAL VOCAB PAGE V13 **2** 🔑 [C] a complicated pattern of things that are closely connected to each other 网状物；网络；错综复杂的事物：*a web of streets* 纵横交错的街道 ◇ *We were caught in a* ***tangled web*** *of relationships.* 我们陷入了错综复杂的人际关系网络。**3** 🔑 **the Web** (*also* **the web**) [sing.] = WORLD WIDE WEB: *I found the information* ***on the Web.*** 我在万维网上找到了这条消息。➲ COLLOCATIONS AT EMAIL

> **WORDFINDER 联想词：** access, blog, browse, chat, google, navigate, search engine, unsubscribe, visit

4 [C] a piece of skin that joins the toes of some birds and animals that swim, for example DUCKS and FROGS 蹼

Web 2.0 /ˌweb tuː pɔɪnt ˈəʊ; *NAmE* ˈoʊ/ *noun* [U] the developments in the way that people use the Internet that allow users free access and give them more control over the information 互联网 2.0（指互联网应用方式的新发展，允许用户免费上网并对信息有更多的支配权）

web·bed /webd/ *adj.* [only before noun] a bird or an animal (such as a DUCK or FROG) that has **webbed feet** has pieces of skin between the toes 有蹼的 ➲ VISUAL VOCAB PAGE V12

web·bing /ˈwebɪŋ/ *noun* [U] strong strips of cloth that are used to make belts, etc., and to support the seats of chairs, etc.（用以制作带子等的）带状结实织物

web·cam /ˈwebkæm/ *noun* a video camera that is connected to a computer so that what it records can be seen on a website or on another computer as it happens 网络摄像机；网络摄影机；网路摄影头 ➲ VISUAL VOCAB PAGE V73

web·cast /ˈwebkɑːst; *NAmE* ˈwebkæst/ *noun* a live broadcast that is sent out on the Internet 网络直播；网播

'Web-enabled *adj.* able to be connected to and used with the Internet 能上网的：*a Web-enabled interface* 网络接口界面

weber /ˈveɪbə(r)/ *noun* (*abbr.* **Wb**) (*physics* 物) a unit for measuring the amount of magnetic force that passes through a point in a magnetic field 韦伯（磁通量单位）

web·head /ˈwebhed/ *noun* (*informal*) a person who uses the Internet a lot 网虫；网民

'web hosting *noun* [U] the activity or business of providing space to store websites, access to them and other services related to them 虚拟主机服务；网站托管；网页寄存：*If you are starting your own business you can buy affordable web hosting or host your own website.* 如果自己创业，你可以购买负担得起的虚拟主机或自行存储网站。◇ *a web hosting business/company/provider/service* 网站托管业务 / 公司 / 供应商 / 服务

webi·nar /ˈwebmɑː(r)/ *noun* a presentation or SEMINAR (= a meeting for discussion or training) that is conducted over the Internet 网上研讨会；在线讲座：*Our company uses webinars to train representatives in other countries.* 我们公司用网上研讨会的方式对派驻其他国家的销售代表进行培训。

webli·og·raphy /ˌwebliˈɒɡrəfi; *NAmE* -ˈɑːɡ-/ *noun* (*pl.* **-ies**) a list of websites or electronic works about a particular subject that have been used by a person writing an article, etc. 网络参考书目；网路书目：*a Poe webliography* 爱伦·坡网络书目 ◇ *a selected webliography on new Irish poetry* 爱尔兰新诗网络参考目录

web·log /ˈweblɒɡ; *NAmE* ˈweblɔːɡ; ˈweblɑːɡ/ *noun* = BLOG

web·master /ˈwebmɑːstə(r); *NAmE* -mæs-/ *noun* (*computing* 计) a person who is responsible for particular pages of information on the World Wide Web（万维网）站点管理员，网络管理员

'web page *noun* a document that is connected to the World Wide Web and that anyone with an Internet connection can see, usually forming part of a website 网页：*We learned how to create and register a new web page.* 我们学会了如何制作和注册一个新网页。

web·site 🔑 /ˈwebsaɪt/ *noun* a place connected to the Internet, where a company or an organization, or an individual person, puts information 网站：*I found this information* ***on their website.*** 我在他们的网站上发现了这一信息。◇ *For current prices please* ***visit our website.*** 有关目前的价格，请访问我们的网站。➲ COLLOCATIONS AT EMAIL ➲ VISUAL VOCAB PAGE V74

> **WORDFINDER 联想词：** bookmark, cookie, domain, home page, hyperlink, landing page, online, social media, URL

web·zine /ˈwebziːn/ *noun* a magazine published on the Internet, not on paper 网络杂志

wed /wed/ *verb* (**wed·ded, wed·ded** or **wed, wed**) [I, T] (not used in the progressive tenses 不用于进行时) (*old-fashioned* or used in newspapers 过时用法或用于报章) to marry 结婚；娶；嫁：*The couple plan to wed next summer.* 这俩人计划在夏天结婚。◇ **~ sb** *Rock star to wed top model* (= in a newspaper HEADLINE). 摇滚歌星与顶级名模结成伉俪。

we'd /wiːd; wid/ *short form* **1** we had **2** we would

wed·ded /ˈwedɪd/ *adj.* **1 ~ to sth** (*formal*) if you are **wedded** to sth, you like or support it so much that you are not willing to give it up 执着；献身；全力以赴：*She's wedded to her job.* 她专心致志地工作。**2** [usually before noun] (*old-fashioned* or *formal*) legally married 已婚的；已完婚的：*your* ***lawfully wedded*** *husband* 你的合法丈夫 ◇ *to live together in* ***wedded bliss*** 一起过着幸福美满的婚姻生活 **3** [not before noun] **~ (to sth)** (*formal* or *literary*) combined or united with sth 结合在一起；融为一体

wed·ding /ˈwedɪŋ/ *noun* a marriage ceremony, and the meal or party that usually follows it 婚礼；结婚庆典：*a **wedding present*** 结婚礼物 ◇ *a **wedding ceremony/reception*** 结婚典礼；婚宴 ◇ *Have you been invited to their wedding?* 他们有没有邀请你参加婚礼？◇ *She looked beautiful on her **wedding day**.* 她在自己的婚礼那天看起来很漂亮。◇ *All her friends could hear **wedding bells*** (= they thought she would soon get married). 所有的朋友仿佛已听到了她婚礼的钟声。➲ COLLOCATIONS AT MARRIAGE ➲ SEE ALSO DIAMOND WEDDING, GOLDEN WEDDING, SHOTGUN WEDDING, SILVER WEDDING, WHITE WEDDING

WORDFINDER 联想词： best man, bride, ceremony, engaged, honeymoon, **marriage**, propose, reception, stag night

ˈwedding anniversary *noun* the celebration every year of the date when two people were married 结婚纪念日：*Today's our wedding anniversary.* 今天是我们的结婚纪念日。

ˈwedding band *noun* a wedding ring in the form of a plain band, usually of gold 结婚戒指（通常为金质净面）➲ VISUAL VOCAB PAGE V70

ˈwedding breakfast *noun* (*BrE, formal*) a special meal after a marriage ceremony 婚宴

ˈwedding cake *noun* [C, U] a cake covered with ICING, and usually with several layers, eaten at a wedding party 结婚蛋糕

ˈwedding dress *noun* a dress that a woman wears at her wedding, especially a long white one 婚纱

ˈwedding ring *noun* a ring that is given during a marriage ceremony and worn afterwards to show that you are married 结婚戒指 ➲ VISUAL VOCAB PAGE V70

ˈwedding tackle *noun* [U] (*BrE, slang*) a man's sexual organs 鸡巴；阳具

wedge /wedʒ/ *noun, verb*

■ ***noun*** **1** a piece of wood, rubber, metal, etc. with one thick end and one thin pointed end that you use to keep a door open, to keep two things apart, or to split wood or rock 楔子；三角木：*He hammered the wedge into the crack in the stone.* 他用锤子把楔子砸入石缝里。◇ (*figurative*) *I don't want to **drive a wedge** between the two of you* (= to make you start disliking each other). 我不想在你们俩中间挑起不和。**2** something that is shaped like a wedge or that is used like a wedge 楔形物；用作楔子的东西：*a wedge of cake* 一角蛋糕 ◇ *shoes with wedge heels* 坡跟鞋 ➲ VISUAL VOCAB PAGE V69 **3** a shoe with a wedge heel (= one that forms a solid block with the bottom part of the shoe) 坡跟鞋：*a pair of wedges* 一双坡跟鞋 **4** a GOLF CLUB that has its face (= the part that you hit the ball with) at an angle（高尔夫球）楔形铁头球杆，挖起杆 IDM SEE THIN *adj.*

■ ***verb*** **1 ~ sth + adv./prep.** to put or squeeze sth tightly into a narrow space, so that it cannot move easily 将…挤入（或塞进、插入）SYN **jam**：*The boat was now wedged between the rocks.* 船卡在了岩石之间。◇ *She wedged herself into the passenger seat.* 她挤进了旅客座椅中。**2 ~ sth (+ adj.)** to make sth stay in a particular position, especially open or shut, by placing sth against it 把…楔牢（或楔住）：*to wedge the door open* 用楔子卡住门让它开着

ˈwedge issue *noun* (*NAmE*) an important and difficult political issue, used by a political party to draw supporters away from an opposing party 楔子问题，楔子议题（政党借以离间对手支持者的重大政治难题）

wedgie /ˈwedʒi/ *noun* (*informal*) an act of lifting sb up by his/her underwear, usually done as a joke 抓着内裤提起某人（作为玩笑）

wed·lock /ˈwedlɒk; *NAmE* -lɑːk/ *noun* [U] (*old-fashioned* or *law* 律) the state of being married 婚姻；已婚状态：*children born **in/out of wedlock*** (= whose parents are/are not married) 婚生 / 非婚生子女

Wed·nes·day /ˈwenzdeɪ; -di/ *noun* [C, U] (*abbr.* **Wed.**, **Weds.**) the day of the week after Tuesday and before Thursday 星期三 HELP To see how **Wednesday** is used, look at the examples at **Monday**. * Wednesday 的用法见词条 Monday 下的示例。ORIGIN Originally translated from the Latin for 'day of Mercury' *Mercurii dies* and named after the Germanic god *Odin*. 译自拉丁文 Mercurii dies，原意为 day of Mercury（水星日），以日耳曼神 Odin（奥丁）命名。

wee /wiː/ *adj., noun, verb*

■ ***adj.*** (*informal*) **1** (*especially ScotE*) very small in size 很小的；极小的：*a wee girl* 娇小的女孩 **2** small in amount; little 微量的；很少的；一丁点儿的：*Just a wee drop of milk for me.* 给我一丁点儿奶就行。◇ *I felt **a wee bit** guilty about it.* 我对此觉得有点儿愧疚。

IDM **the wee small ˈhours** (*ScotE*) (*NAmE* **the wee ˈhours**) = THE SMALL/EARLY HOURS

■ ***noun*** (*also* **ˈwee-wee**) (*informal, especially BrE*) (often used by young children or when you are talking to them 常用作儿语) **1** [sing.] an act of passing liquid waste (called URINE) from your body 尿尿；撒尿：***to do/have a wee*** 尿尿 **2** [U] = URINE：*a puddle of wee* 一摊尿

■ ***verb*** (*also* **ˈwee-wee**) [I] (*informal, especially BrE*) (often used by young children or when you are talking to them 常用作儿语) to pass liquid waste (called URINE) from the body 尿尿；撒尿：*Do you need to wee?* 你要撒尿吗？

weed /wiːd/ *noun, verb*

■ ***noun*** **1** [C] a wild plant growing where it is not wanted, especially among crops or garden plants 杂草，野草（尤指庄稼或花园中的）：*The yard was overgrown with weeds.* 这座庭院杂草丛生。**2** [U] any wild plant without flowers that grows in water and forms a green floating mass 水草 **3 the weed** [sing.] (*humorous*) TOBACCO or cigarettes 烟草；烟叶；香烟；烟卷：*I wish I could give up the weed* (= stop smoking). 但愿我能把烟戒掉。**4** [U] (*informal*) the drug CANNABIS 大麻烟 **5** [C] (*BrE, informal, disapproving*) a person with a weak character or body 懦弱的人；体弱的人

■ ***verb*** [T, I] **~ (sth)** to take out weeds from the ground 除（地面的）杂草：*I've been weeding the flower beds.* 我一直在除花坛里的杂草。

PHR V **ˌweed sth/sb↔ˈout** to remove or get rid of people or things from a group because they are not wanted or are less good than the rest 清除，剔除，淘汰（不需要的或较差的人或物）

weed·kill·er /ˈwiːdkɪlə(r)/ *noun* [U, C] a substance that is used to destroy weeds 除草剂；除莠剂

weedy /ˈwiːdi/ *adj.* (**weed·ier**, **weedi·est**) **1** (*informal, disapproving*) having a thin weak body 瘦弱的；弱不禁风的：*a weedy little man* 瘦弱矮小的男子 **2** full of or covered with weeds 杂草丛生的；长满杂草的

ˌWee ˈFree *noun* a member of the part of the Free Church of Scotland that did not join with the United Presbyterian Church in 1900 to form the United Free Church（1900 年未与苏格兰联合长老会共同成立联合自由长老会的）苏格兰自由长老会少数派成员

week /wiːk/ *noun* **1** a period of seven days, either from Monday to Sunday or from Sunday to Saturday 周；星期；礼拜：***last/this/next week*** 上 / 本 / 下星期 ◇ *It rained all week.* 整个星期都在下雨。◇ *What **day of the week** is it?* 今天星期几？◇ *He comes to see us **once a week**.* 他每周来看望我们一次。**2** any period of seven days 一周；七天的时间：*a **two-week** vacation* 两周假期 ◇ *The course lasts five weeks.* 这门课程为期五周。◇ ***a week ago today*** (= seven days ago) 一周前的今天 ◇ *She'll be back **in a week**.* 她一周后回来。**3** the five days other than Saturday and Sunday（除星期六和星期日以外的）五天：*They live in town **during the week** and go to the country for the weekend.* 他们从星期一到星期五住在城里，周末到乡下去。◇ (*BrE*) *I never have the time to go out **in the week**.* 我从星期一到星期五从来没有时间外出参加社交活动。**4** the part of the week when you go to work 工作周（一个星期中的工作时间）：*a 35-hour week* * 35 小时的工作周 ◇

W

The firm is introducing a shorter ***working week****.* 这家公司要采用较短的周工作时间。

IDM **today, tomorrow, Monday, etc. 'week** (*BrE*) (*also* **a ˌweek (from) to'day, etc.** *NAmE, BrE*) seven days after the day that you mention 一周后的今天（或明天、星期一等）: *I'll see you Thursday week.* 我们下星期四见。 **ˌweek after 'week** (*informal*) continuously for many weeks 一个星期又一个星期；一周接一周；一连数周: *Week after week the drought continued.* 干旱持续了好多个星期。 **ˌweek by 'week** as the weeks pass 一个星期一个星期地；每过一周: *Week by week he grew a little stronger.* 每过一星期他都更健壮一点儿。 **week ˌin, week 'out** happening every week 一周又一周；每个星期都；每周均无例外: *Every Sunday, week in, week out, she goes to her parents for lunch.* 她每个星期天都毫无例外地到她父母那里吃午饭。 **a ˌweek next/on/this 'Monday, etc. | a ˌweek to'morrow, etc.** (*BrE*) (*also* **a ˌweek from 'Monday, etc.** *NAmE, BrE*) seven days after the day that you mention 一周后的今天（或明天、星期一等）: *It's my birthday a week on Tuesday.* 一周后的星期二是我的生日。 **a ˌweek 'yesterday, last 'Monday, etc.** (*especially BrE*) seven days before the day that you mention 一个星期前的昨天（或星期一等）: *She started work a week yesterday.* 她在一个星期前的昨天就开始工作了。 ➲ MORE AT OTHER

week·day /ˈwiːkdeɪ/ *noun* any day except Saturday and Sunday 周工作日（星期一至星期五的任何一天）: *The centre is open from 9 a.m. to 6 p.m. on weekdays.* 本中心星期一至星期五上午 9 点至下午 6 点开放。 ▶ **week·days** *adv.*: *open weekdays from 9 a.m. to 6 p.m.* 星期一至星期五上午 9 点至下午 6 点开放

week·end /ˌwiːkˈend; *NAmE* ˈwiːkend/ *noun, verb*

■ ***noun*** **1** Saturday and Sunday 星期六和星期日；周末: *Are you doing anything* ***over the weekend****?* 你在周末有什么安排吗？ ◇ *Have a good weekend!* 周末愉快！ ◇ *It happened* ***on the weekend of*** *24 and 25 April.* 事情发生在 4 月 24 日和 25 日那个周末。 ◇ (*BrE*) *The office is closed* ***at the weekend****.* 本办事处星期六和星期日不办公。 ◇ (*especially NAmE*) *The office is closed* ***on the weekend****.* 本办事处星期六和星期日不办公。 ◇ (*BrE, informal*) *I like to go out* ***on a weekend****.* 我喜欢周末外出参加社交活动。 ◇ *We go skiing most weekends in winter.* 我们在冬天的周末大多去滑雪。 ➲ SEE ALSO DIRTY WEEKEND, LONG WEEKEND **2** Saturday and Sunday, or a slightly longer period, as a holiday/vacation 星期六和星期日（或略长一点的）休息时间: *He won a weekend for two in Rome.* 他赢得双人去罗马度周末的奖项。 ◇ *a weekend break* 周末假日

■ ***verb*** [I] **+ adv./prep.** to spend the weekend somewhere （在某处）过周末，度周末: *They're weekending in Paris.* 他们正在巴黎度周末。

week·end·er /ˌwiːkˈendə(r)/ *noun* **1** a person who visits or lives in a place only on Saturdays and Sundays 周末游人（或来客等） **2** (*AustralE, informal*) a house in the country that people go to for weekends and holidays/vacations 周末度假屋（供度周末或假日用的乡间房屋）

ˌweekend 'warrior *noun* (*NAmE*) a person who works all week, especially in an office or other indoor job, and uses the weekends to go out and do more active and/or dangerous physical activities 周末战士（仅在周末外出参加剧烈惊险体育活动的人，尤指室内工作者）

'week-long *adj.* lasting for a week 持续一星期的；为期一周的: *a week-long visit to Rome* 到罗马进行为期一周的访问 ◇ *week-long courses* 为期一周的课程

week·ly /ˈwiːkli/ *adj., noun*

■ ***adj.*** happening, done or published once a week or every week 每周的: *weekly meetings* 周会 ◇ *a weekly magazine* 周刊 ▶ **week·ly** *adv.*: *Employees are paid weekly.* 雇员按周领工资。 ◇ *The newspaper is published twice weekly.* 这份报纸每周出版两次。

■ ***noun*** (*pl.* **-ies**) a newspaper or magazine that is published every week 周报；周刊

week·night /ˈwiːknaɪt/ *noun* any night of the week except Saturday, Sunday and sometimes Friday night 工作日夜晚（除星期六和星期日以外的任何夜晚，有时亦不含星期五晚上）: *I have to stay in on weeknights.* 除了星期六和星期日外我每天夜里都得待在家里。

weenie /ˈwiːni/ *noun* (*NAmE, informal*) **1** (*disapproving*) a person who is not strong, brave or confident 懦弱的人；窝囊废 **SYN** **wimp**: *Don't be such a weenie!* 别这么窝囊！ **2** = FRANKFURTER **3** (*slang*) a word for a PENIS, used especially by children 小鸡鸡（指阴茎，尤用于儿语）

weeny /ˈwiːni/ *adj.* (**ween·ier, weeni·est**) (*informal*) extremely small 极小的 **SYN** **tiny**: *Weren't you just a weeny bit scared?* 难道你就一点儿都不害怕吗？ ➲ SEE ALSO TEENY (1)

weep /wiːp/ *verb, noun*

■ ***verb*** (**wept, wept** /wept/) **1** [I, T] (*formal* or *literary*) to cry, usually because you are sad（通常因悲伤）哭泣，流泪: *She started to weep uncontrollably.* 她不由自主地哭了起来。 ◇ ***I could have wept*** *thinking about what I'd missed.* 想到所失去的东西，我真想痛哭一场。 ◇ **~ for/with sth** *He wept for joy.* 他高兴得流泪了。 ◇ **~ at/over sth** *I do not weep over his death.* 他死了我也不哭。 ◇ **~ sth** *She wept bitter tears of disappointment.* 她失望得痛哭流涕。 ◇ **~ to do sth** *I wept to see him looking so sick.* 看到他病成那个样子我怆然泪下。 ◇ **+ speech** *'I'm so unhappy!' she wept.* "我好难过啊！" 她哭着说道。 **2** [I] (usually used in the progressive tenses 通常用于进行时) (of a wound 伤口) to produce liquid 流出，渗出（液体）: *His legs were covered with weeping sores* (= sores which had not healed). 他的双腿有多处红肿流脓的伤口。

■ ***noun*** [sing.] an act of crying 哭泣；落泪: *Sometimes you feel better for a good weep.* 有时候你痛痛快快哭上一场就会觉得好受些。

weep·ing /ˈwiːpɪŋ/ *adj.* [only before noun] (of some trees 某些树木) with branches that hang downwards 有下垂枝条的: *a* ***weeping willow/fig/birch*** 垂柳；枝条下垂的无花果树 / 桦树

weepy /ˈwiːpi/ *adj., noun*

■ ***adj.*** (*informal*) sad and tending to cry easily 悲伤欲哭的；眼泪汪汪的；动不动就哭的: *She was feeling tired and weepy.* 她感到累得想哭。

■ ***noun*** (*also* **weepie**) (*pl.* **-ies**) (*informal*) a sad film/movie or play that makes you want to cry 催人泪下的电影（或戏剧）；令人伤感的电影（或戏剧） **SYN** **tear-jerker**

wee·vil /ˈwiːvl/ *noun* a small insect with a hard shell, that eats grain, nuts and other seeds and destroys crops 象鼻虫，象甲，豆象（吃谷物、坚果和种子，危害作物的小甲虫）

'wee-wee *noun, verb* = WEE

the weft /weft/ (*also less frequent* **the woof**) *noun* [sing.] the threads that are twisted under and over the threads that are held on a LOOM (= a frame or machine for making cloth)（织布机上的）纬线，纬纱 ➲ COMPARE WARP *n.*

weigh /weɪ/ *verb* **1** *linking verb* (**+ noun**) to have a particular weight 有…重；重: *How much do you weigh* (= how heavy are you)? 你体重多少？ ◇ *She weighs 60 kilos.* 她体重为 60 公斤。 ◇ *These cases* ***weigh a ton*** (= are very heavy). 这些箱子重得很。 **2** [T] **~ sb/sth/yourself** to measure how heavy sb/sth is, usually by using SCALES 称重量，量体重（通常用磅秤）: *He weighed himself on the bathroom scales.* 他用浴室磅秤量体重。 ◇ *She weighed the stone in her hand* (= estimated how heavy it was by holding it). 她用手掂了掂那块石头的重量。 **3** [T] to consider sth carefully before making a decision 认真考虑；权衡；斟酌: **~ sth (up)** *You must weigh up the pros and cons* (= consider the advantages and disadvantages of sth). 你必须权衡利弊。 ◇ *She weighed up all the evidence.* 她慎重地考虑了所有的证据。 ◇ **~ (up) sth against sth** *I weighed the benefits of the plan against the risks involved.* 我认真考虑了这个计划的优点和有关的风险。 **4** [I] **~ (with sb) (against sb/sth)** to have an influence on sb's opinion or the result of sth（对看法或结果）有影响；有分量: *His past record* ***weighs heavily against*** *him.* 他过去的记录对他很不利。 **5** [T] **~ anchor** to lift an ANCHOR out of the water and into a boat before sailing away 起（锚）

W

IDM **weigh your 'words** to choose your words carefully so that you say exactly what you mean 推敲；斟酌字句
PHR V **,weigh sb↔'down** to make sb feel worried or anxious 使烦恼；使焦虑；使忧心忡忡 SYN **burden**: *The responsibilities of the job are weighing her down.* 这项工作的责任压得她喘不过气来。◇ *He is weighed down with guilt.* 他由于内疚而心神不定。 **,weigh sb/sth↔'down** to make sb/sth heavier so that they are not able to move easily 压得…难以移动；压弯：*I was weighed down with baggage.* 我被行李压得走不动路。 **,weigh 'in (at sth)** to have your weight measured, especially before a contest, race, etc.（尤指赛前）量体重：*Both boxers weighed in at several pounds below the limit.* 两个拳击手赛前量的体重都比规定限度少几磅。 ➲ RELATED NOUN WEIGH-IN **,weigh 'in (with sth)** (*informal*) to join in a discussion, an argument, an activity, etc. by saying sth important, persuading sb, or doing sth to help（在讨论、辩论等中）发表有分量的意见，发挥作用：*We all weighed in with our suggestions.* 我们都提出了有分量的建议。◇ *Finally the government weighed in with financial aid.* 最后政府提供了财政支援。 **'weigh on sb/sth** to make sb anxious or worried 加重…的思想负担；使焦虑不安；使担忧：*The responsibilities* **weigh heavily** *on him.* 他肩负重任，寝食不安。◇ *Something was weighing on her mind.* 她心事重重。 **,weigh sth↔'out** to measure an amount of sth by weight 称出（一定重量的东西）：*She weighed out a kilo of flour.* 她称出一千克面粉。 **,weigh sb↔'up** to form an opinion of sb by watching or talking to them（通过观察或谈话）形成对…的看法，品评

weigh·bridge /'weɪbrɪdʒ/ *noun* a machine for weighing vehicles and their loads, usually with a platform onto which the vehicle is driven 桥秤，地秤，地磅，称量台（用以称车等及其装载量）

'weigh-in *noun* the occasion when the weight of a BOXER, JOCKEY, etc. is checked officially（对拳击手、骑师等正式的）称体重

'weighing machine *noun* a machine for weighing large objects or for weighing people in a public place 称量机；衡器

weight 🔑 /weɪt/ *noun*, *verb*

■ *noun*

• **BEING HEAVY** 重 **1** 🔑 [U, C] how heavy sb/sth is, which can be measured in, for example, kilograms or pounds 重量；分量：*It is about 76 kilos* **in weight**. 这东西重约 76 千克。◇ *Bananas are sold by weight.* 香蕉按重量出售。◇ *In the wild, this fish can reach a weight of 5lbs.* 这种鱼在自然生存环境中可以长到 5 磅重。◇ *She is trying to* **lose weight** (= become less heavy and less fat). 她正在设法减肥。◇ *He's* **put on/gained weight** (= become heavier and fatter) *since he gave up smoking.* 他戒烟后体重增加了。◇ *Sam has a weight problem* (= is too fat). 萨姆太胖了。◇ *No more for me. I have to* **watch my weight**. 我不再吃了。我得控制体重。 ➲ COLLOCATIONS AT DIET ➲ SEE ALSO OVERWEIGHT, UNDERWEIGHT **2** 🔑 [U] the fact of being heavy 重：*He staggered a little* **under the weight of** *his backpack.* 他身上的背包压得他有点步履蹒跚。◇ *I just hoped the branch would* **take my weight**. 我真希望树枝经得住我的体重。◇ *The pillars have to support the weight of the roof.* 这些立柱必须支撑起屋顶的重量。◇ *Don't put any weight on that ankle for at least a week.* 至少要一个星期别让那个脚踝承重。 ➲ SEE ALSO DEAD WEIGHT

• **HEAVY OBJECT** 重物 **3** 🔑 [C] an object that is heavy 重物：*The doctor said he should not lift heavy weights.* 医生建议他别拿重物。 **4** [C] an object used to keep sth in position or as part of a machine（用于固定某物或用作机器部件的）重体，重物：*weights on a fishing line* 钓线上的坠 ➲ SEE ALSO PAPERWEIGHT

• **RESPONSIBILITY/WORRY** 责任；忧心 **5** [sing.] ~ (**of sth**) a great responsibility or worry 重任；重担；重压；压力 SYN **burden**: *The full weight of responsibility falls on her.* 全部的重任都落在了她的肩上。◇ *The news was certainly a* **weight off my mind** (= I did not have to worry about it any more). 这个消息真是去掉了我心头的重担。◇ *Finally telling the truth was* **a great weight off my shoulders**. 最后讲了实话使我如释重负。

• **INFLUENCE/STRENGTH** 影响；实力 **6** [U] importance, influence or strength 重要性；影响力；实力：*The many letters of support* **added weight** *to the campaign.* 许多声援信增加了这场运动的影响力。◇ *The President has now offered to* **lend his weight to** *the project.* 总统现已主动表示支持这个项目。◇ *Your opinion* **carries weight** *with the boss.* 你的意见对老板有影响。◇ *How can you ignore* **the sheer weight of** *medical opinion?* 你怎么能忽视医生意见的绝对重要性呢？◇ *The weight of evidence against her is overwhelming.* 对她不利的证据确凿，无法抵赖。

• **FOR MEASURING/LIFTING** 测量；举重 **7** [C, U] a unit or system of units by which weight is measured 重量单位；衡制：*tables of weights and measures* 度量衡表 ◇ ***imperial/metric weight*** 英制 / 公制重量 **8** [C] a piece of metal that is known to weigh a particular amount and is used to measure the weight of sth, or lifted by people to improve their strength and as a sport 砝码；秤砣；秤锤；杠铃片；哑铃：*a set of weights* 一组砝码 ◇ *She lifts weights as part of her training.* 举杠铃是她锻炼的一部分。◇ *He does a lot of* **weight training**. 他进行大量的举重训练。 ➲ MORE LIKE THIS 20, page R27

IDM **take the weight off your feet** (*informal*) to sit down and rest, especially when you are tired（尤指疲乏时）坐下歇歇脚，坐下喘口气：*Come and sit down and take the weight off your feet for a while.* 来坐下歇一会儿吧。 **throw your 'weight about/around** (*informal*) to use your position of authority or power in an aggressive way in order to achieve what you want 仗势欺人；盛气凌人 **throw/put your weight behind sth** to use all your influence and power to support sth 鼎力支持；全力相助 **weight of 'numbers** the combined power, strength or influence of a group 人多势众；团队力量（或影响）：*They won the argument by sheer weight of numbers.* 他们纯粹靠人多势众在争论中获胜。 ➲ MORE AT GROAN *v.*, PULL *v.*, PUNCH *v.*, WORTH *adj.*

■ *verb*

• **ATTACH HEAVY OBJECT** 附上重物 **1** ~ **sth** (**down**) (**with sth**) to attach a weight to sth in order to keep it in the right position or make it heavier 在…上加重量；使负重；（用重物）固定：*The fishing nets are weighted with lead.* 这些渔网是靠铅坠下沉的。

• **GIVE IMPORTANCE** 重视 **2** [usually passive] ~ **sth** to give different values to things to show how important you think each of them is compared with the others 使加权：*The results of the survey were weighted to allow for variations in the sample.* 这次调查的结果进行了加权处理，以包容样本中的偏差。◇ *a* ***weighted vote*** (= one that is worth more than a single vote) 加权选票 ◇ (*NAmE*) *a* ***weighted grade*** (= given at school for a course that is more advanced or harder and so has a higher value) 加权分数

weight·ed /'weɪtɪd/ *adj.* [not before noun] arranged in such a way that a particular person or thing has an advantage or a disadvantage 有利（或不利）于 SYN **biased**: ~ **towards sb/sth** *The proposal is weighted towards smaller businesses.* 这项提议对小型企业有利。◇ ~ **against sb/sth** *Everything seemed weighted against them.* 一切似乎都与他们过不去。◇ ~ **in favour of sb/sth** *The course is heavily weighted in favour of engineering.* 这门课程非常侧重于工程学。

weight·ing /'weɪtɪŋ/ *noun* **1** [U] (*BrE*) extra money that you get paid for working in a particular area because it is expensive to live there（发放给在生活费用高的地区工作的人的）额外津贴，生活补贴 **2** [C, U] a value that you give to each of a number of things to show how important it is compared with the others 加权值：*Each of the factors is given a weighting on a scale of 1 to 10.* 每种因素按 1 至 10 之间的数值加权。◇ *Each question in the exam has equal weighting.* 考试中每道题的分值相等。

weight·less /'weɪtləs/ *adj.* having no weight or appearing to have no weight, for example because there is no GRAVITY 无重量的；似无重量的；失重的：*Astronauts work in weightless conditions.* 宇航员在失重的条件下工作。 ➲ WORDFINDER NOTE AT SPACE ▶ **weight·less·ness** *noun* [U]

weight·lift·ing /ˈweɪtlɪftɪŋ/ *noun* [U] the sport or activity of lifting heavy weights 举重 ▸ **weight·lift·er** *noun*

weighty /ˈweɪti/ *adj.* (**weight·ier**, **weighti·est**) (*formal*) **1** important and serious 严重的；重要的；重大的：*weighty matters* 重大事情 **2** heavy 重的；沉重的：*a* ***weighty volume/tome*** 大部头书 ▸ **weight·ily** /-ɪli/ *adv.* **weighti·ness** *noun* [U]

weir /wɪə(r); *NAmE* wɪr/ *noun* a low wall or barrier built across a river in order to control the flow of water or change its direction 堰；拦河坝；导流坝

weird /wɪəd; *NAmE* wɪrd/ *adj., verb*

■ ***adj.*** (**weird·er**, **weird·est**) **1** very strange or unusual and difficult to explain 奇异的；不寻常的；怪诞的 SYN **strange**：*a weird dream* 离奇的梦 ◇ *She's a really weird girl.* 她真是个古怪的女孩。◇ *He's got some weird ideas.* 他有些怪念头。◇ *It's really weird seeing yourself on television.* 看到自己上了电视感觉怪怪的。◇ *the* ***weird and wonderful*** *creatures that live beneath the sea* 奇异美丽的海底生物 **2** strange in a mysterious and frightening way 离奇的；诡异的 SYN **eerie**：*She began to make weird inhuman sounds.* 她开始发出可怕的非人的声音。 ▸ **weird·ly** *adv.*：*The town was weirdly familiar.* 这个城镇怪面熟的。**weird·ness** *noun* [U]

■ ***verb***

PHR V ˌ**weird sb ˈout** (*informal*) to seem strange or worrying to sb and make them feel uncomfortable 使感到奇怪；使感到烦恼；使感到不舒服：*The whole concept really weirds me out.* 这整个想法让我觉得十分怪异。

weirdo /ˈwɪədəʊ; *NAmE* ˈwɪrdoʊ/ *noun* (*pl.* **-os** /-əʊz; *NAmE* -oʊz/) (*informal, disapproving*) a person who looks strange and/or behaves in a strange way（长相或行为）古怪的人；怪人

welch /weltʃ; welʃ/ *verb* = WELSH

wel·come /ˈwelkəm/ *verb, adj., noun, exclamation*

■ ***verb*** **1** [T, I] to say hello to sb in a friendly way when they arrive somewhere（打招呼）欢迎（某人的到来）：~ (**sb**) *They were at the door to welcome us.* 他们在门口迎接我们。◇ *a welcoming smile* 欢迎的微笑 ◇ **~ sb to sth** *It is a pleasure to welcome you to our home.* 很高兴欢迎您光临舍下。**2** [T] **~ sb** to be pleased that sb has come or has joined an organization, activity, etc. 欢迎（新来的人）；迎新：*They* ***welcomed*** *the new volunteers* ***with open arms*** (= with enthusiasm). 他们热烈欢迎这些新的志愿者。**3** [T] **~ sth** to be pleased to receive or accept sth 乐意接纳；欣然接受：*I'd welcome any suggestions.* 任何建议我都会愉快地听取。◇ *I* ***warmly welcome*** *this decision.* 我热烈欢迎这一决定。◇ *In general, the changes they had made were to be welcomed.* 总的来说，他们所作的这些变动都会被欣然接受。

■ ***adj.*** **1** that you are pleased to have, receive, etc. 令人愉快的；受欢迎的：*a welcome sight* 赏心悦目的景象 ◇ *Your letter was very welcome.* 很高兴收到你的信。◇ *The fine weather* ***made a welcome change.*** 天气转晴，令人心旷神怡。**2** (of people 人) accepted or wanted somewhere 受欢迎的；受款待的：*Children are always welcome at the hotel.* 儿童在旅馆里总是受到款待。◇ *Our neighbours* ***made us welcome*** *as soon as we arrived.* 我们一到就受到了邻居们的欢迎。◇ *I had the feeling we were not welcome at the meeting.* 我有种感觉，人家并不欢迎我们参加这个会议。 **3** **~ to do sth** (*informal*) used to say that you are happy for sb to do sth if they want to（表示乐于让某人做某事）可随意：*They're welcome to stay here as long as they like.* 他们在这里愿意住多久就住多久。**4** **~ to sth** (*informal*) used to say that you are very happy for sb to have sth because you definitely do not want it（表示十分乐于让他人取去自己不想要的事物）尽管…好了：*It's an awful job. If you want it, you're* ***welcome to it!*** 这事真难办。你要是想做就交给你做好了！

IDM **you're ˈwelcome** used as a polite reply when sb thanks you for sth 别客气；不用谢；哪里话：*'Thanks for your help.' 'You're welcome.'* "多谢你的帮助。" "别客气。"

■ ***noun*** **1** [C, U] something that you do or say to sb when they arrive, especially sth that makes them feel you are happy to see them 迎接；接待；欢迎：*Thank you for your warm welcome.* 感谢你们的热情接待。◇ *The winners were* ***given an*** *enthusiastic* ***welcome*** *when they arrived home.* 获胜者奏凯而归时受到了热烈欢迎。◇ *a* ***speech/smile of welcome*** 欢迎词；欢迎的微笑 ◇ *to receive a* ***hero's welcome*** 受到英雄般的欢迎 **2** [C] the way that people react to sth, which shows their opinion of it（表明看法的）反应方式，对待，接受：*This new comedy deserves a* ***warm welcome.*** 这出新喜剧值得受到热烈欢迎。◇ *The proposals were* ***given a*** *cautious* ***welcome*** *by the trade unions.* 这些建议得到了工会审慎的接受。

IDM **outstay/overstay your ˈwelcome** to stay somewhere as a guest longer than you are wanted 做客太久而不再受欢迎

■ ***exclamation*** used as a GREETING to tell sb that you are pleased that they are there 欢迎：*Welcome home!* 欢迎归来！◇ *Welcome to Oxford!* 欢迎您来到牛津！◇ *Good evening everybody. Welcome to the show!* 诸位，晚上好。欢迎观看本次演出！

ˈwelcome mat *noun*

IDM **lay, put, roll, etc. out the ˈwelcome mat (for sb)** (*especially NAmE*) to make sb feel welcome; to try to attract visitors, etc. 使感到受欢迎；设法吸引（客人等）

ˌwelcome to ˈcountry (*also* **Welcome to Country**) *noun* (*AustralE*) a formal welcome to the traditional land of an Aboriginal people by one or more members of the local Aboriginal community（澳大利亚由当地土著主持的）土著家园欢迎仪式

wel·com·ing /ˈwelkəmɪŋ/ *adj.* **1** (of a person 人) friendly towards sb who is visiting or arriving（对来访或到达的人）欢迎的，热情的，友好的 **2** (of a place 地方) attractive and looking comfortable to be in 令人感到惬意的；舒适的 OPP **unwelcoming**

weld /weld/ *verb, noun*

■ ***verb*** **1** [T, I] to join pieces of metal together by heating their edges and pressing them together 焊接；熔接；锻接：**~ (sth)** *to weld a broken axle* 焊接一条断裂的轴 ◇ **~ A (on) (to B)** *The car has had a new wing welded on.* 这辆汽车焊上了一块新挡泥板。◇ **~ A and B (together)** *All the parts of the sculpture have to be welded together.* 这件雕塑所有的部件都必须焊接在一起。**2** [T] to unite people or things into a strong and effective group 使紧密结合；使连成整体：**~ sb/sth into sth** *They had welded a bunch of untrained recruits into an efficient fighting force.* 他们把一群未经训练的新兵打造成了一支有战斗力的部队。◇ **~ sth together** *The crisis helped to weld the party together.* 这场危机促使整个党紧密地团结在一起。

■ ***noun*** a joint made by welding 焊接点；焊接处

weld·er /ˈweldə(r)/ *noun* a person whose job is welding metal 焊工

wel·fare AW /ˈwelfeə(r); *NAmE* -fer/ *noun* [U] **1** the general health, happiness and safety of a person, an animal or a group（个体或群体的）幸福，福祉，安康 SYN **well-being**：*We are concerned about the child's welfare.* 我们关注那个孩子的福祉。**2** practical or financial help that is provided, often by the government, for people or animals that need it（政府给予的）福利：*The state is still the main provider of welfare.* 政府仍然是福利的主要提供者。◇ *child welfare* 儿童福利 ◇ *a social welfare programme* 社会福利计划 ◇ ***welfare provision/services/work*** 福利供给 / 机构 / 工作 ➲ WORDFINDER NOTE AT CHARITY **3** (*especially NAmE*) (*BrE also* ˌ**social seˈcurity**) money that the government pays regularly to people who are poor, unemployed, sick, etc. 社会保障金（政府定期向贫穷、失业、患病等人员发放）：*They would rather work than live* ***on welfare.*** 他们更愿工作而不愿靠社会保障金过活。➲ COLLOCATIONS AT UNEMPLOYMENT

ˌwelfare ˈstate *noun* **1** (*often* **the Welfare State**) [usually sing.] a system by which the government provides a range of free services to people who need them, for example medical care, money for people without work, care for old people, etc. 福利制度（由政府向有需要的人提供各种免费服务，如医疗、失业救济金、对老人的照顾等） **2** [C] a country that has such a system 福利国家

W

wel·kin /ˈwelkɪn/ *noun* [U] (*literary* or *old use*) the sky or heaven 天空；苍穹

IDM **let/make the welkin ˈring** to make a very loud noise 响彻云霄

well /wel/ *adv., adj., exclamation, noun, verb*

■ *adv.* (**bet·ter** /ˈbetə(r)/, **best** /best/) **1** in a good, right or acceptable way 好；对；令人满意地：*The kids all behaved well.* 孩子们都很有礼貌。◇ *The conference was very well organized.* 这次会议组织得很好。◇ ***Well done!*** (= expressing admiration for what sb has done) 干得好！◇ *His campaign was not **going well**.* 他的竞选活动进展得不顺利。◇ *These animals make very good pets if treated well* (= with kindness). 这些动物若得到善待会成为很好的宠物。◇ *People **spoke well of*** (= spoke with approval of) *him.* 人们对他的评价很高。◇ *She **took it very well*** (= did not react too badly), *all things considered.* 总的说来，她的反应还挺不错。◇ *They lived well* (= in comfort and spending a lot of money) *and were generous with their money.* 他们生活优裕，花钱大方。◇ *She was determined to marry well* (= marry sb rich and/or with a high social position). 她决意嫁给有钱有势的人。**2** thoroughly and completely 完全地；彻底地；全部地：*Add the lemon juice and mix well.* 加进柠檬汁并搅拌均匀。◇ *The surface must be well prepared before you start to paint.* 一定要把表面打磨好再开始油漆。◇ *How well do you know Carla?* 你对卡拉有多了解？◇ *He's well able to take care of himself.* 他完全能够自理。◇ (*BrE, informal*) *I was well annoyed, I can tell you.* 我跟你说吧，我那时气坏了。**3** to a great extent or degree 很；相当；大大地；远远地：*He was driving at well over the speed limit.* 他当时开车的速度远远超过了限制。◇ *a well-loved tale* 深受喜爱的故事 ◇ *The castle is **well worth** a visit.* 这座城堡很值得参观。◇ *He liked her **well enough*** (= to a reasonable degree) *but he wasn't going to make a close friend of her.* 他够喜欢她的，但并不打算和她结为密友。**4 can/could well** easily 容易地；轻松地：*She could well afford to pay for it herself.* 她自己完全买得起。**5 can/could/may/might well** probably 很可能：*You may well be right.* 你很可能是对的。◇ ***It may well be that** the train is delayed.* 火车很可能晚点了。**6 can/could/may/might well** with good reason 有充分理由；合理地：*I can't very well leave now.* 我现在离开不太合适。◇ *I couldn't very well refuse to help them, could I?* 我没有理由拒绝帮助他们，是不是？◇ *'What are we doing here?' '**You may well ask*** (= I don't really know either).' "我们在这儿干什么呢？""你算问对了（我也不知道）。"

IDM **as well (as sb/sth)** in addition to sb/sth; too 除…之外；也；还：*Are they coming as well?* 他们也来吗？◇ *They sell books as well as newspapers.* 他们既卖报也卖书。◇ *She is a talented musician as well as being a photographer.* 她不但是个摄影师而且还是个天才的音乐家。➲ NOTE AT ALSO **be doing ˈwell** to be getting healthier after an illness; to be in good health after a birth（病后）康复，恢复良好；（产后）平安，健康：*Mother and baby are doing well.* 母子平安。**(you, etc.) may/might as well be hanged/hung for a ˌsheep as (for) a ˈlamb** (*saying*) if you are going to be punished for doing sth wrong, whether it is a big or small thing, you may as well do the big thing 与其偷羊羔被绞死，不如偷只羊；一不做，二不休 **be well on the way to sth/doing sth** to have nearly achieved sth and be going to achieve it soon 即将达到；将要成就：*She is well on the way to recovery.* 她就要康复了。◇ *He is well on the way to establishing himself among the top ten players in the world.* 他很快就会成为排名世界前十位的选手。**be ˌwell ˈout of sth** (*BrE, informal*) to be lucky that you are not involved in sth 幸运地与…无关；幸亏没有卷入 **be ˌwell ˈup in sth** to know a lot about sth 精通；熟悉：*He's well up in all the latest developments.* 他对所有的最新发展情况都了如指掌。**do ˈwell** to be successful 成功：*Jack is doing very well at school.* 杰克在学校里学习成绩斐然。**do ˈwell by sb** to treat sb generously 善待；慷慨对待 **do ˈwell for yourself** to become successful or rich 成功；发家致富 **do ˈwell out of sb/sth** to make a profit or get money from sb/sth 获利于；从…中获取钱财 **do ˈwell to do sth** to be sensible or wise to do sth 做…明智（或聪明）：*He **would do well to** concentrate more on his work.* 他最好还是更加集中精力在工作上。◇ *You did well to sell when the price was high.* 你在价钱高的时候出售，真明智。**leave/let well aˈlone** (*BrE*) (*NAmE* **let well enough aˈlone**) to not get involved in sth that does not concern you 不管闲事；事不关己高高挂起：*When it comes to other people's arguments, it's better to leave well alone.* 遇到别人争论时，最好别插嘴。**may/might (just) as well do sth** to do sth because it seems best in the situation that you are in, although you may not really want to do it 做…倒也无妨；只好做（某事）：*If no one else wants it, we might as well give it to him.* 如果没人要这个，我们不妨

▼ **SYNONYMS 同义词辨析**

well

all right • OK • fine • healthy • strong • fit

These words all describe sb who is not ill and is in good health. 以上各词均形容人健康、身体好。

well [not usually before noun] (*rather informal*) in good health 指健康、身体好：*I'm not feeling very well.* 我感觉身体不太好。◇ *Is he well enough to travel?* 他身体怎么样，能够旅行吗？NOTE **Well** is used especially to talk about your own health, to ask sb about their health or to make a comment on it. * well 尤用以谈自己的健康、询问别人的健康或谈论身体情况。

all right [not before noun] (*rather informal*) not feeling ill; not injured 指感觉身体还好、没有生病、没有受伤：*Are you feeling all right?* 你感觉还好吗？

OK [not before noun] (*informal*) not feeling ill; not injured 指感觉身体还好、没有生病、没有受伤：*She says she's OK now, and will be back at work tomorrow.* 她说她现在身体还可以，明天就回来上班。

ALL RIGHT OR OK? 用 all right 还是 OK?

These words are slightly less positive than the other words in this group. They are both used in spoken English to talk about not actually being ill or injured, rather than being positively in good health. Both are rather informal but **OK** is slightly more informal than **all right**. 上述两词比同组其他词的肯定含意稍弱一些，两词均用于口语中，指没有生病、安然无恙，而非确定身体健康；两词均相当非正式，不过 OK 较 all right 还要非正式些。

fine [not before noun] (not used in negative statements) (*rather informal*) completely well （不用于否定句）指身体很好、健康：*'How are you?' 'Fine, thanks.'* "你好吗？""很好，谢谢。" NOTE **Fine** is used especially to talk about your health, especially when sb asks you how you are. It is also used to talk about sb's health when you are talking to sb else. Unlike **well** it is not often used to ask sb about their health or make a comment on it. * fine 尤用于回应别人的询问，表示自己身体很健康；与人谈话时，亦可用以指另一人身体健康。与 well 不一样，fine 通常不用于询问别人的身体状况或者谈论对方身体情况：~~*Are you keeping fine?*~~

healthy in good health and not likely to become ill 指健康、健壮：*Keep healthy by exercising regularly.* 经常锻炼以保持健康。

strong in good health and not suffering from an illness 指健康、身体好：*After a few weeks she was feeling stronger.* 几周之后她感觉身体好些了。NOTE **Strong** is often used to talk about becoming healthy again after an illness. * strong 常用以指病后恢复健康。

fit (*especially BrE*) in good physical health, especially because you take regular physical exercise 指健壮，尤指因经常锻炼而身体健康：*I go swimming every day in order to keep fit.* 我每天游泳以保持健康。

PATTERNS

- all right/OK/fit **for** sth
- all right/OK/fit **to do sth**
- to **feel**/**look** well/all right/OK/fine/healthy/strong/fit
- to **keep** (sb) well/healthy/fit
- **perfectly** well/all right/OK/fine/healthy/fit
- **physically** well/healthy/strong/fit

W

给他吧。,**well and 'truly** (*informal*) completely 完全；彻底：*By that time we were well and truly lost.* 那时候我们已经完全迷路了。**'well away** (*BrE, informal*) **1** having made good progress 有很大进步；大有进展：*If we got Terry to do that, we'd be well away.* 假若我们让特里干这事，我们就会有很大成绩。**2** drunk or fast asleep 酒醉；沉睡 ,**well 'in (with sb)** (*informal*) to be good friends with sb, especially sb important 是某人（尤指要人）的好友：*She seems to be well in with all the right people.* 她似乎和所有大人物都关系很好。➲ MORE AT BLOODY[1], FUCKING, JOLLY *adv.*, KNOW *v.*, MEAN *v.*, PRETTY *adv.*

■ ***adj.*** (**bet·ter, best**) **1** [not usually before noun] in good health 健康；身体好：*I don't feel very well.* 我觉得身体不太好。◇ *Is she well enough to travel?* 她身体怎么样，能够旅行吗？◇ ***Get well soon!*** (= for example, on a card) 愿早日康复！◇ *I'm better now, thank you.* 我现在好些了，谢谢您。◇ (*informal*) *He's not a well man.* 他身体不太好。**2** [not before noun] in a good state or position 状态良好；情况良好：*It seems that **all is not well** at home.* 看来家中并非事事如意。◇ ***All's well that ends well*** (= used when sth has ended happily, even though you thought it might not). 结果好就算一切都好。**3** [not before noun] (**as**) ~ (**to do sth**) sensible; a good idea 明智；可取；好主意：*It would be **just as well** to call and say we might be late.* 还是打个电话说一声我们可能到得晚些比较好。◇ (*formal*) *It would be well to start early.* 最好还是早点动身。

IDM ,**all very 'well (for sb) (to do sth)** (*informal*) used to criticize or reject a remark that sb has made, especially when they were trying to make you feel happier about sth（用于批评或反驳）某人尽可做某事：*It's all very well for you to say it doesn't matter, but I've put a lot of work into this and I want it to be a success.* 你说这无所谓当然容易，可是我却已经花费很大力气而且想要取得成功。,**all well and 'good** (*informal*) quite good but not exactly what is wanted 好倒是好（但并不完全合乎心意）：*That's all well and good, but why didn't he call her to say so?* 那好倒是好，可是他为什么不给她打电话这样说呢？

▼ **GRAMMAR POINT 语法说明**

well

- Compound adjectives beginning with **well** are generally written with no hyphen when they are used alone after a verb, but with a hyphen when they come before a noun. 以 well 开头的复合形容词单独用于动词后一般不用连字符，但用于名词前要用连字符：*She is well dressed.* 她衣着入时。◇ *a well-dressed woman* 穿着考究的女人 The forms without hyphens are given in the entries in the dictionary, but forms with hyphens can be seen in some examples. 本词典的词条给出了无连字符的形式，有连字符的形式则可在某些例句中见到。
- The comparative and superlative forms of these are usually formed with **better** and **best**. 这些复合形容词的比较级和最高级通常由 better 和 best 构成：*better-known poets* 较著名的诗人 ◇ *the best-dressed person in the room* 这屋里穿着最考究的人

■ ***exclamation*** **1** used to express surprise, anger or relief（表示惊奇、愤怒或宽慰）哎呀，哟，啊，好啦：***Well, well***—*I would never have guessed it!* 哟，哟，我怎么也不会猜到那儿去！◇ ***Well, really!*** *What a thing to say!* 啊，真是的！这么说太不像话了！◇ *Well, thank goodness that's over!* 好啦，谢天谢地，这件事总算过去了！**2** used to show that you accept that sth cannot be changed（承认某事不可改变）唉，好吧：*Well, it can't be helped.* 唉，这没有办法。◇ *'We lost.' '**Oh, well**. Better luck next time.'* "我们输了。" "啊，算了。愿下次交好运。" **3** used to agree to sth, rather unwillingly（勉强同意）嗯，好吧：*Well, I suppose I could fit you in at 3.45.* 好吧，我想可以在 3:45 见你。◇ *Oh, **very well**, then, if you insist.* 啊，那好吧，如果你坚持的话。**4** used when continuing a conversation after a pause（停顿后继续交谈）唔，这个，噢：*Well, as I was saying…* 噢，我刚才是说… **5** used to say that sth is uncertain（表示不肯定）哦：*'Do you want to come?' 'Well, I'm not sure.'* "你想来吗？" "哦，我还说不准。" **6** used to show that you are waiting for sb to say sth（等待别人说话）嘿，嗨：*Well? Are you going to tell us or not?* 嗯？你想不想告诉我们？**7** used to mark the end of a conversation（结束交谈）就这样，好啦：*Well, I'd better be going now.* 就这样，我现在该走了。**8** used when you are pausing to consider your next words（说话时稍微停顿）对了，噢：*I think it happened, well, towards the end of last summer.* 我想事情发生在，对了，快到上个夏末的时候。**9** used when you want to correct or change sth that you have just said（纠正或改变刚说过的话时用）：*There were thousands of people there—well, hundreds, anyway.* 那里有数以千计的人，噢，至少几百人。

IDM **well I 'never ('did)!** (*old-fashioned*) used to express surprise（表示惊奇）哟，我可从未做过（或听说过）这样的事 ➲ MORE AT SAY *v.*

■ ***noun*** **1** a deep hole in the ground from which people obtain water. The sides of wells are usually covered with brick or stone and there is usually some covering or a small wall at the top of the well. 井；水井 **2** = OIL WELL **3** a narrow space in a building that drops down from a high to a low level and usually contains stairs or a lift/elevator 楼梯井；电梯井道 ➲ SEE ALSO STAIRWELL **4** (*BrE*) the space in front of the judge in a court, where the lawyers sit（法庭中的）律师席

■ ***verb*** **1** [I] ~ (**up**) (of a liquid 液体) to rise to the surface of sth and start to flow 涌出；冒出；流出；溢出：*Tears were welling up in her eyes.* 她热泪盈眶。**2** [I] ~ (**up**) (*literary*) (of an emotion 情感) to become stronger 涌起；迸发：*Hate welled up inside him as he thought of the two of them together.* 他一想到他们俩在一起就恨得咬牙切齿。

we'll /wiːl; wil/ *short form* **1** we will **2** we shall

,**well ad'justed** *adj.* (of a person 人) able to deal with people, problems and life in general in a normal, sensible way 能适应环境的；能自如地待人接物的；稳重的 ➲ COMPARE MALADJUSTED

,**well ad'vised** *adj.* [not before noun] ~ (**to do sth**) acting in the most sensible way 审慎；稳妥：*You **would be well advised to** tackle this problem urgently.* 你还是抓紧处理这个问题为好。➲ COMPARE ILL-ADVISED

,**well ap'pointed** *adj.* (*formal*) having all the necessary equipment; having comfortable and attractive furniture, etc. 设备齐全的；陈设讲究的

,**well at'tended** *adj.* attended by a lot of people 有许多人出席的；座无虚席的：*a well-attended conference* 与会者甚多的会议

,**well 'balanced** *adj.* **1** containing a sensible variety of the sort of things or people that are needed 很均衡的；很均匀的：*a well-balanced diet* 均衡的饮食 ◇ *The team was not well balanced.* 这个队的队员配备得不是很均衡。**2** (of a person or their behaviour 人或行为) sensible and emotionally in control 通情达理的；头脑清醒的；情绪稳定的：*His response was well balanced.* 他的反应很沉着。

,**well be'haved** *adj.* behaving in a way that other people think is polite or correct 彬彬有礼的；行为端正的：*a well-behaved child* 规规矩矩的孩子 ◇ *The audience was surprisingly well behaved.* 观众令人出奇地守秩序。

'**well-being** *noun* [U] general health and happiness 健康；安乐；康乐：***emotional/physical/psychological well-being*** 情绪 / 身体 / 心理健康 ◇ *to have **a sense of well-being*** 有一种安适愉快的感觉

,**well 'born** *adj.* (*formal*) from a rich family or a family of high social class 出身高贵的；出身名门的

,**well 'bred** *adj.* (*old-fashioned, formal*) having or showing good manners; typical of a high social class 有教养的；有涵养的；知书达理的；高贵的：*a well-bred young lady* 一位有教养的少女 ◇ *She was too well bred to show her disappointment.* 她很有涵养，没有表露出她的失望。OPP **ill-bred**

,**well 'built** *adj.* **1** (of a person 人) with a solid, strong body 身强力壮的；体格健美的 **2** (of a building or machine 建筑或机器) strongly made 结实的；坚固的

W

ˌwell conˈnected *adj.* (*formal*) (of a person 人) having important or rich friends or relatives 与达官豪富有亲友关系的；社会关系强固的

ˌwell ˈcut *adj.* (of clothes 衣服) made well and therefore probably expensive 做工精细的；考究的

ˌwell deˈfined *adj.* easy to see or understand 易于辨认理解的；明确的；规定得清楚的；界限分明的：*well-defined rules* 明确的规则 ◇ *These categories are not well defined.* 这些类别划分得不太明确。**OPP ill-defined**

ˌwell deˈveloped *adj.* fully developed; fully grown 发育良好的；完善的；健全的：*He had a well-developed sense of his own superiority.* 他的个人优越感十足。

ˌwell disˈposed *adj.* ~ (**towards/to sb/sth**) having friendly feelings towards sb or a positive attitude towards sth 和善亲切的；怀有好感的 **OPP ill-disposed**

ˌwell ˈdocumented *adj.* having a lot of written evidence to prove, support or explain it 证据充分的；有大量文件证明的：*The problem is well documented.* 这个问题有很多依据。◇ *well-documented facts* 证据充分的事实

ˌwell ˈdone *adj.* (of food, especially meat 食物，尤指肉) cooked thoroughly or for a long time 熟透的；煮透了的：*He prefers his steak well done.* 他喜欢吃全熟的牛排。➲ COMPARE RARE (3), UNDERDONE

ˌwell ˈdressed *adj.* wearing fashionable or expensive clothes 衣着入时的；穿着讲究的：*This is what today's well-dressed man is wearing.* 这是当今时髦男子的穿着。

ˌwell ˈearned *adj.* much deserved 完全应得的；理当有的；当之无愧的：*a well-earned rest* 应有的休息

ˌwell enˈdowed *adj.* **1** (*informal, humorous*) (of a woman 女人) having large breasts 乳房大的 **2** (*informal, humorous*) (of a man 男人) having large GENITALS 阴茎大的；生殖器大的 **3** (of an organization 组织) having a lot of money 资金充足的：*well-endowed colleges* 资金充足的学院

ˌwell eˈstablished *adj.* having a respected position, because of being successful, etc. over a long period 地位稳固的；树立起声誉的；得到确认的：*a well-established firm* 久享盛誉的商行 ◇ *He is now well established in his career.* 他现在已经在事业上稳住了根基。

ˌwell ˈfed *adj.* having plenty of good food to eat regularly 吃得好的；营养足的：*well-fed family pets* 喂得肥肥胖胖的家庭宠物 ◇ *The animals all looked well fed and cared for.* 这些动物看上去都得到了精心的饲养和照料。

ˌwell ˈformed *adj.* (of sentences 句子) written or spoken correctly according to the rules of grammar 符合语法规则的；结构完整的

ˌwell ˈfounded (*also less frequent* **ˌwell ˈgrounded**) *adj.* having good reasons or evidence to cause or support it 理由充足的；有根据的；有事实依据的：*well-founded suspicions* 有根据的怀疑 ◇ *His fear turned out to be well founded.* 他的恐惧证明是有道理的。**OPP ill-founded**

ˌwell ˈgroomed *adj.* (of a person 人) looking clean, neat and carefully dressed 整洁且衣着得体的

ˌwell ˈgrounded *adj.* **1** ~ **in sth** having a good training in a subject or skill 功底深的；基础扎实的 **2** = WELL FOUNDED

ˌwell ˈheeled *adj.* (*informal*) having a lot of money 有钱的；富有的 **SYN rich, wealthy**

ˌwell ˈhung *adj.* **1** (of meat 肉) having been left for several days before being cooked in order to improve the flavour 适度风干的 **2** (of a man 男子) (*informal*) having a large PENIS 大阴茎的；生殖器硕大下垂的

ˌwell inˈformed *adj.* having or showing knowledge or information about many subjects or about one particular subject 见多识广的；消息灵通的；知识渊博的：*a well-informed decision* 有见识的决定 **OPP ill-informed**

wel·ling·ton /ˈwelɪŋtən/ (*also* **ˌwellington ˈboot**, *informal* **welly**) (*all BrE*) (*NAmE* **ˌrubber ˈboot**) *noun* one of a pair of long rubber boots, usually reaching almost up to the knee, that you wear to stop your feet getting wet 威灵顿长筒靴；及膝胶靴：*a pair of wellingtons* 一双高筒胶靴 ➲ VISUAL VOCAB PAGE V69

ˌwell inˈtentioned *adj.* intending to be helpful or useful but not always succeeding very well 出于好心的，好心好意的，善意的（但往往事与愿违）**SYN well meaning**

ˌwell ˈkept *adj.* **1** kept neat and in good condition 保持整齐的；妥善保管的；悉心照料的：*well-kept gardens* 照料得井井有条的花园 **2** (of a secret 秘密) known only to a few people 保守得好的；严守的

ˌwell ˈknown *adj.* **1** known about by a lot of people 众所周知的；著名的；出名的 **SYN famous**：*a well-known actor* 著名演员 ◇ *His books are not well known.* 他写的书不太有名。**2** (of a fact 事实) generally known and accepted 为人所熟知的（或熟悉的、认可的）：*It is a well-known fact that caffeine is a stimulant.* 咖啡因是兴奋剂，这是人所共知的事实。

ˌwell ˈmannered *adj.* (*formal*) having good manners 行为端正的；举止得当的；有礼貌的 **SYN polite OPP ill-mannered**

ˌwell ˈmatched *adj.* able to live together, play or fight each other, etc. because they are similar in character, ability, etc. 匹配的；相匹敌的；不相上下的：*a well-matched couple* 天生的一对 ◇ *The two teams were well matched.* 这两个队势均力敌。

ˌwell ˈmeaning *adj.* intending to do what is right and helpful but often not succeeding 出于好心的，好心好意的，善意的（但常事与愿违）**SYN well intentioned**：*a well-meaning attempt to be helpful* 尝试帮忙的善意举动 ◇ *He's very well meaning.* 他用心良苦。

ˌwell ˈmeant *adj.* done, said, etc. in order to be helpful but often not succeeding 本意良好的，出于好心的，善意的（但常事与愿违）：*well-meant comments* 善意的批评 ◇ *His offer was well meant.* 他的提议是出于好心。

well·ness /ˈwelnəs/ *noun* [U] (*especially NAmE*) the state of being healthy 健康

well-ˈnigh *adv.* (*formal*) almost 几乎；差不多；可谓：*Defence was well-nigh impossible against such opponents.* 遇到这样的对手几乎防不胜防。

ˌwell ˈoff *adj.* **1** (**better off**) having a lot of money 富有的；富裕的 **SYN rich**：*a well-off family* 富裕家庭 ◇ *They are much better off than us.* 他们比我们富得多。➲ SYNONYMS AT RICH **2** (**better off, best off**) in a good situation 境况良好：*I've got my own room so I'm well off.* 我有自己的房间，所以还不错。◇ *Some people don't know when they're well off.* 有些人身在福中不知福。**OPP badly off**

IDM be well ˈoff for sth (*BrE*) to have enough of sth（某事物）充裕：*We're well off for jobs around here* (= there are many available). 我们这里工作机会很多。

ˌwell ˈoiled *adj.* operating smoothly and well 运转顺畅的；一帆风顺的：*The system ran like a well-oiled machine.* 这个系统运行得就像一台上了油的机器。

ˌwell ˈpaid *adj.* earning or providing a lot of money 报酬（或薪金）丰厚的：*well-paid managers* 高薪经理 ◇ *The job is very well paid.* 这个职位工资很高。

ˌwell preˈserved *adj.* not showing many signs of age; kept in good condition 不显老的；保养得好的

ˌwell ˈread *adj.* having read many books and therefore having gained a lot of knowledge 博览群书的；博学的

ˌwell ˈrounded *adj.* **1** having a variety of experiences and abilities and a fully developed personality 全才的；通才的；全面发展的：*well-rounded individuals* 全面发展的人 **2** providing or showing a variety of experience, ability, etc. 全面的；面面俱到的：*a well-rounded education* 通才教育 **3** (of a person's body 人体) pleasantly round in shape 丰满的

W

ˌwell ˈrun *adj.* managed smoothly and well 运转良好的；经营得好的：*a well-run hotel* 经营良好的旅馆

ˌwell ˈspoken *adj.* having a way of speaking that is considered correct or elegant 言语得体的；谈吐文雅的

well·spring /ˈwelsprɪŋ/ *noun* (*literary*) a supply or source of a particular quality, especially one that never ends （永不枯竭的）源泉，来源

ˌwell ˈthought of *adj.* respected, admired and liked 受敬重的；令人钦佩的；受喜爱的：*Their family has always been well thought of around here.* 他们家在这一带一直颇受敬重。

ˌwell thought ˈout *adj.* carefully planned 经过深思熟虑的；计划周密的

ˌwell ˈthumbed *adj.* a **well-thumbed** book has been read many times （书）被翻旧了的，翻阅过很多遍的

ˌwell ˈtimed *adj.* done or happening at the right time or at an appropriate time 适时的；不早不晚的 **SYN** **timely**：*a well-timed intervention* 及时的介入 ◇ *Your remarks were certainly well timed.* 你的话说得确实正是时候。**OPP** **ill-timed**

ˌwell-to-ˈdo *adj.* having a lot of money 有钱的；富有的；富裕的 **SYN** **rich, wealthy**：*a well-to-do family* 富裕家庭 ◇ *They're very well-to-do.* 他们很阔绰。

ˌwell ˈtravelled (*BrE*) (*NAmE* **ˌwell ˈtraveled**) *adj.* **1** (of a person 人) having travelled to many different places 旅行经历丰富的；去过很多地方的 **2** (of a route 路线) used by a lot of people 交通频繁的；人流量大的

ˌwell ˈtried *adj.* used many times before and known to be successful 屡试不爽的；屡屡证明行之有效的：*a well-tried method* 屡试不爽的方法

ˌwell ˈtrodden *adj.* (*formal*) (of a road or path 道路或小径) much used 常有人走的

ˌwell ˈturned *adj.* (*formal*) expressed in an elegant way 措辞优雅的：*a well-turned phrase* 文雅的言辞

ˌwell ˈused *adj.* used a lot 使用得多的；频繁使用的：*a well-used path* 行人很多的小路

ˈwell-wisher *noun* a person who wants to show that they support sb and want them to be happy, successful, etc. （以行动）表示祝愿者

ˌwell ˈworn *adj.* **1** worn or used a lot or for a long time 破旧的；破烂不堪的；使用很久的：*a well-worn jacket* 穿得破旧了的夹克 ◇ *Most British visitors beat a well-worn path to the same tourist areas of the US.* 大多数英国游客总沿着一条老路线参观相同的美国旅游景点。**2** (of a phrase, story, etc. 短语、故事等) heard so often that it does not sound interesting any more 听腻了的；使用过多的；陈腐的 **SYN** **hackneyed**

welly /ˈweli/ *noun, verb*

■ *noun* (*pl.* **-ies**) (*BrE, informal*) = WELLINGTON：*a pair of green wellies* 一双绿色的长筒靴

IDM **give it some ˈwelly** (*BrE, informal*) to use a lot of physical effort 用很大的力气

■ *verb* (**wel·lies**, **welly·ing**, **wel·lied**, **wel·lied**) **~ sth** (+ **adv./prep.**) (*BrE, informal*) to hit or kick sth very hard 重击；猛踢：*He wellied the ball over the bar.* 他一脚猛射，球从横梁上飞出。

Welsh /welʃ/ *noun, adj.*

■ *noun* **1** [U] the Celtic language of Wales 威尔士语：*Do you speak Welsh?* 你说威尔士语吗？**2 the Welsh** [pl.] the people of Wales 威尔士人

■ *adj.* of or connected with Wales, its people or its language 威尔士的；威尔士人的；威尔士语的：*Welsh poetry* 威尔士诗歌

welsh /welʃ/ (*also* **welch**) *verb* [I] **~ (on sb/sth)** (*disapproving, informal*) to not do sth that you have promised to do, for example to not pay money that you owe 说话不算数；赖账；耍赖皮：*'I'm not in the habit of welshing on deals,' said Don.* 唐说："我做生意没有说话不算数的习惯。"

the ˌWelsh Asˈsembly (*also* **the ˌNational Asˌsembly for ˈWales**) *noun* [sing.] the group of people who are elected as a government for Wales with limited independence from the British Parliament that includes the power to make certain laws 威尔士议会

ˌWelsh ˈdresser *noun* (*BrE*) = DRESSER (1)

ˌWelsh ˈrarebit (*also* **rare·bit**) *noun* [U] a hot dish of cheese melted on TOAST 威尔士干酪吐司（烤面包片上浇有熔化奶酪）

welt /welt/ *noun* a raised mark on the skin where sth has hit or rubbed you （撞击或擦伤所致的）红肿 **SYN** **weal**

wel·ter /ˈweltə(r)/ *noun* [sing.] **~ of sth** (*formal*) a large and confusing amount of sth 杂乱的一堆：*a welter of information* 一大堆杂乱的信息

wel·ter·weight /ˈweltəweɪt; *NAmE* -tərw-/ *noun* a BOXER weighing between 61 and 67 kilograms, heavier than a LIGHTWEIGHT 次中量级拳击手（体重在 61 至 67 公斤之间）：*a welterweight champion* 次中量级拳击冠军

wench /wentʃ/ *noun* (*old use* or *humorous*) a young woman 少妇；少女

wend /wend/ *verb* [T, I] **~ (your way)** (+ **adv./prep.**) (*old use* or *literary*) to move or travel slowly somewhere （缓慢地）走，去，行，往：*Leo wended his way home through the wet streets.* 利奥沿着潮湿的街道缓缓地朝家走去。

Wendy house /ˈwendi haʊs/ *noun* (*BrE*) = PLAYHOUSE (2)

went PAST TENSE OF GO

wept PAST TENSE, PAST PART. OF WEEP

were /wə(r); *strong form* wɜː(r)/ ➲ BE

we're /wɪə(r); *NAmE* wɪr/ *short form* we are

weren't /wɜːnt/ *short form* were not

were·wolf /ˈweəwʊlf; *NAmE* ˈwerw-/ *noun* (*pl.* **-wolves** /-wʊlvz/) (in stories) a person who sometimes changes into a WOLF, especially at the time of the full moon （传说中，尤指在月圆时）变成狼的人，狼人

Wer·nicke's area /ˈwɜːnɪkəz eəriə; ˈveənɪkəz; *NAmE* ˈwɜːrnɪkəz eriə; ˈvern-/ *noun* (*anatomy* 解) an area in the brain concerned with understanding language 韦尼克区（大脑中的语言理解区）

west 🔑 /west/ *noun, adj., adv.*

■ *noun* [U, sing.] (*abbr.* **W**) **1** 🔑 (*usually* **the west**) the direction that you look towards to see the sun go down; one of the four main points of the COMPASS 西；西方：*Which way is west?* 哪边是西？◇ *Rain is spreading from the west.* 雨正从西边袭来。◇ *He lives* **to the west of** (= further west than) *the town.* 他住在这个城镇以西的地方。➲ PICTURE AT COMPASS ➲ COMPARE EAST *n.*, NORTH *n.*, SOUTH *n.* **2** 🔑 **the West** Europe, N America and Canada, contrasted with Eastern countries 西方（与东方国家相对照的欧洲和北美）：*I was born in Japan, but I've lived in the West for some years now.* 我出生在日本，但已在西方居住了一些年了。**3 the West** (*NAmE*) the western side of the US 美国西部：*the history of the American West* 美国西部的历史 ➲ SEE ALSO MIDWEST, WILD WEST **4 the West** (in the past) Western Europe and N America, when contrasted with the Communist countries of Eastern Europe （旧时与共产党执政的东欧国家相对应的）西方国家，西欧及北美：*East-West relations* 东西方关系

■ *adj.* [only before noun] (*abbr.* **W**) **1** 🔑 in or towards the west 西方的；向西的；西部的：*West Africa* 西非 ◇ *the west coast of Scotland* 苏格兰西海岸 **2** 🔑 a **west wind** blows from the west 西风的；西方吹来的 ➲ COMPARE WESTERLY *adj.*

■ *adv.* 🔑 towards the west 向西；朝西：*This room faces west.* 这个房间朝西。

west·bound /ˈwestbaʊnd/ *adj.* travelling or leading towards the west 西行的；向西的：*westbound traffic* 西行车辆 ◇ *the westbound carriageway of the motorway* 高速公路的西向车道

W

the ˌWest ˈCoast *noun* [sing.] the states on the west coast of the US, especially California 美国西海岸（尤指加利福尼亚州）

the ˌWest ˈEnd *noun* [sing.] the western area of central London where there are many theatres, shops/stores and hotels 西伦敦，伦敦西区（即伦敦市中心西部的戏院、商店和旅馆聚集区）

west·er·ly /ˈwestəli; *NAmE* -ərli/ *adj., noun*
■ *adj.* **1** [only before noun] in or towards the west 西方的；向西的；西部的：*travelling in a westerly direction* 向西行进 **2** [usually before noun] (of winds 风) blowing from the west 从西方吹来的：*westerly gales* 从西面刮来的大风 ➲ COMPARE WEST *adj.*
■ *noun* (*pl.* **-ies**) a wind that blows from the west 西风：*light westerlies* 微微的西风

west·ern /ˈwestən; *NAmE* -ərn/ *adj., noun*
■ *adj.* **1** [only before noun] (*abbr.* **W**) (*also* **Western**) located in the west or facing west 西方的；向西的；西部的：*western Spain* 西班牙西部 ◇ *Western Europe* 西欧 ◇ *the western slopes of the mountain* 山的西坡 **2** (*usually* **Western**) connected with the west part of the world, especially Europe and N America 西方的；西方国家的；（尤指）欧美的：*Western art* 西方艺术 ➲ SEE ALSO COUNTRY AND WESTERN
■ *noun* a film/movie or book about life in the western US in the 19th century, usually involving COWBOYS（描写 19 世纪美国西部，尤指有关牛仔生活的）西部电影，西部小说

west·ern·er /ˈwestənə(r); *NAmE* -ərn-/ *noun* **1** a person who comes from or lives in the western part of the world, especially western Europe or N America 西方人；（尤指）欧美人 **2 Westerner** a person who was born in or who lives in western Canada or the US（加拿大或美国）西部人

west·ern·iza·tion (*BrE also* **-isa·tion**) /ˌwestənaɪˈzeɪʃn; *NAmE* -ərnəˈz-/ *noun* [U] the process of becoming WESTERNIZED 西方化；西化；欧美化

west·ern·ize (*BrE also* **-ise**) /ˈwestənaɪz; *NAmE* -ərn-/ *verb* [usually passive] **~ sth** to bring ideas or ways of life that are typical of western Europe and N America to other countries 使西方化；使欧美化：*The islands have been westernized by the growth of tourism.* 旅游业的增长已经使这些岛西方化了。▸ **west·ern·ized, -ised** /ˈwestənaɪzd; *NAmE* ˈwestərnaɪzd/ *adj.*：*a westernized society* 西方化了的社会

west·ern·most /ˈwestənməʊst; *NAmE* -ərnmoʊst/ *adj.* located furthest west 最西的；最西端的；最西部的：*the westernmost tip of the island* 岛的最西端

W

the West Indies /ˌwest ˈɪndɪz; ˌwest -diːz/ *noun* [pl.] several groups of islands between the Caribbean and the Atlantic, that include the Antilles and the Bahamas 西印度群岛（位于加勒比海和大西洋之间，包括安的列斯群岛和巴哈马群岛）▸ **ˌWest ˈIndian** *adj.* **ˌWest ˈIndian** *noun*

West·min·ster /ˈwestmɪnstə(r)/ *noun* [U] the British parliament and government 威斯敏斯特（英国议会及政府）：*The rumours were still circulating at Westminster.* 当时谣言依然在英国议会和政府流传。 ORIGIN From the name of the part of London with the Houses of Parliament, Downing Street and many government offices. 源自伦敦威斯敏斯特区，为英国议会大厦、唐宁街及许多政府机关所在地。

ˌwest-north-ˈwest *noun* [sing.] (*abbr.* **WNW**) the direction at an equal distance between west and north-west 西西北；西北西 ▸ **ˌwest-north-ˈwest** *adv.*

the ˈWest Side *noun* [sing.] the western part of Manhattan in New York City which includes Broadway and Central Park 曼哈顿西区（在美国纽约市，包括百老汇和中央公园）

ˌwest-south-ˈwest *noun* [sing.] (*abbr.* **WSW**) the direction at an equal distance between west and south-west 西西南；西南西 ▸ **ˌwest-south-ˈwest** *adv.*

west·wards /ˈwestwədz; *NAmE* -wərdz/ (*also* **west·ward**) *adv.* towards the west 向西；朝西：*to turn westwards* 向西转 ▸ **west·ward** *adj.*：*in a westward direction* 方向朝西

wet /wet/ *adj., verb, noun*
■ *adj.* (**wet·ter, wet·test**) **1** covered with or containing liquid, especially water 潮的；湿的；潮湿的：*wet clothes* 湿衣服 ◇ *wet grass* 湿草 ◇ *You'll* **get wet** (= in the rain) *if you go out now.* 你要是现在出去会被淋湿的。◇ *Try not to get your shoes wet.* 尽量别弄湿了鞋子。◇ *His face was wet with tears.* 他泪流满面。◇ *We were all* **soaking wet** (= extremely wet). 我们都成了落汤鸡。◇ *Her hair was still* **dripping wet**. 她的头发仍然湿淋淋的。◇ *My shirt was* **wet through** (= completely wet). 我的衬衣湿透了。**2** (of weather, etc. 天气等) with rain 有雨的；下雨的：*a wet day* 下雨天 ◇ *a wet climate* 多雨的气候 ◇ ***It's wet*** *outside.* 外边下雨了。◇ *It's going to be wet tomorrow.* 明天有雨。◇ *It was the wettest October for many years.* 这是多年来下雨最多的一个十月份。**3** (of paint, ink, etc. 油漆、墨水等) not yet dry 尚未干的：*Keep off! Wet paint.* 油漆未干，请勿靠近！**4** if a child or its NAPPY/DIAPER is **wet**, its nappy/diaper is full of URINE（儿童）尿湿了尿布的；（尿布）尿湿的 **5** (*BrE*) (of a person 人) (*informal, disapproving*) lacking a strong character 窝囊的；没有骨气的 SYN **feeble, wimpish**：*'Don't be so wet,' she laughed.* "别这么窝囊。" 她笑道。➲ MORE LIKE THIS 35, page R29 ▸ **wetly** *adv.* **wet·ness** *noun* [U]
IDM **all ˈwet** (*NAmE, informal*) completely wrong 完全错

▼ **SYNONYMS 同义词辨析**

wet

moist • damp • soaked • drenched • saturated

These words all describe things covered with or full of liquid, especially water. 以上各词均形容物体等潮的、湿的。

wet covered with or full of liquid, especially water 指潮的、湿的、潮湿的：*The car had skidded on the wet road.* 汽车在湿路上打滑了。◇ *You'll get wet (= in the rain) if you go out now.* 你现在出去就会被淋湿。

moist slightly wet, often in a way that is pleasant or useful 指微湿的、湿润的、润泽的，常指是舒适或有益的：*a lovely rich moist cake* 可爱的松软味浓的蛋糕

damp slightly wet, often in a way that is unpleasant 指微湿的、潮湿的、湿度大的，常指令人不舒服的：*The cottage was cold and damp.* 这小屋又冷又湿。

soaked (*rather informal*) very wet 指湿透了：*You're soaked through!* (= completely wet) 你都湿透了！

drenched very wet 指湿透了：*We were caught in the storm and came home drenched to the skin.* 我们遇上了暴雨，回到家时浑身湿透了。

SOAKED OR DRENCHED? 用 soaked 还是 drenched?

Both of these words can be used with *with* or *in*. 上述两词均可与 with 或 in 连用：*soaked/drenched with/in sweat/blood* 大汗淋漓；浸透了鲜血 **Soaked** but not usually **drenched** can also be used before a noun.
* soaked 亦可用于名词前，drenched 通常不这样用：*their soaked clothes* 他们湿透了的衣服 ◇ ~~*their drenched clothes*~~

saturated very wet 指湿透、浸透：*The ground is completely saturated: it would be pointless to plant anything.* 地已经浸透，种什么东西都是白搭。

PATTERNS
- wet/moist/damp/soaked/drenched/saturated **with** sth
- soaked/drenched **in** sth
- sb's **coat**/**shirt**/**shoes**/**clothes**/**hair** is/are wet/damp/soaked/drenched
- wet/moist/damp/saturated **ground**/**earth**
- to **get** wet/moist/damp/soaked/drenched/saturated

的；大错特错 (**still**) ˌ**wet behind the ˈears** (*informal, disapproving*) young and without much experience 乳臭未干；少不更事；没见过世面 **SYN** **naive** ➲ MORE AT FOOT *n.*

■ *verb* (**wet·ting, wet, wet** or **wet·ting, wet·ted, wet·ted**) **~ sth** to make sth wet 使潮湿；把…弄湿：*Wet the brush slightly before putting it in the paint.* 把刷子弄湿点再去沾油漆。

IDM **wet the/your ˈbed** [no passive] to URINATE in your bed by accident 尿床：*It is quite common for small children to wet their beds.* 小孩尿床是常有的事。**ˈwet yourself | wet your ˈpants/ˈknickers** [no passive] to URINATE in your underwear by accident 尿裤子

■ *noun* **1 the wet** [sing.] wet weather; rain 雨天；雨：*Come in out of the wet.* 快进来，别淋着。**2** [U] liquid, especially water 液体；（尤指）水：*The dog shook the wet from its coat.* 狗抖掉了毛上的水。**3** [C] (*BrE, disapproving*) a conservative politician who supports MODERATE policies rather than extreme ones 保守党温和派成员：*Tory wets* 保守党的温和派 **4** [C] (*BrE, informal, disapproving*) a person who lacks a strong character 窝囊废；软骨头 **SYN** **wimp**

wet·back /ˈwetbæk/ *noun* (*US, taboo, slang*) an offensive word for a Mexican person, especially one who enters the US illegally 湿背人（从墨西哥到美国的移民，尤指非法入境者）

ˌ**wet ˈblanket** *noun* (*informal, disapproving*) a person who is not enthusiastic about anything and who stops other people from enjoying themselves 泼冷水的人；扫兴的人

ˈ**wet dock** *noun* a place for ships to stay in order to be repaired, have goods put onto them, etc., in which there is enough water for the ship to float 湿船坞 ➲ COMPARE DRY DOCK

ˌ**wet ˈdream** *noun* a sexually exciting dream that a man has that results in an ORGASM 梦遗；（梦中）遗精

ˈ**wet fish** *noun* [U] (*BrE*) fresh raw fish for sale in a shop, etc.（供出售的）鲜鱼

wet·land /ˈwetlənd/ *noun* [C, U] (*also* **wetlands** [pl.]) an area of wet land 湿地；沼泽地：*The wetlands are home to a large variety of wildlife.* 湿地是多种野生动物的栖息地。▸ **wet·land** *adj.* [only before noun]: *wetland birds* 湿地鸟类

ˈ**wet look** *noun* [sing.] the appearance of hair being shiny and wet, obtained by using hair GEL or by treating it with chemicals（头发的）湿润亮泽，湿亮感 ▸ ˈ**wet-look** *adj.*: *wet-look hair gel* 保湿亮发胶

ˈ**wet nurse** *noun* (usually in the past) a woman employed to feed another woman's baby with her own breast milk（通常指旧时的）奶妈，乳母

ˈ**wet room** *noun* (*BrE*) a bathroom in which the shower is not separated from the rest of the room 非干湿分离卫生间；淋浴洗手间

wet·suit /ˈwetsuːt; *BrE also* -sjuːt/ *noun* a piece of clothing made of rubber that fits the whole body closely, worn, for example, by people swimming underwater or sailing 潜水衣 ➲ VISUAL VOCAB PAGE V44

wet·ware /ˈwetweə(r); *NAmE* -wer/ *noun* [U] (*computing* 计) the human brain, considered as a computer program or system 湿件（被视为计算机程序或系统的人脑）

we've /wiːv; wiv/ *short form* we have

whack /wæk/ *verb, noun*

■ *verb* **1 ~ sb/sth** (*informal*) to hit sb/sth very hard 猛打；重击；狠揍：*She whacked him with her handbag.* 她用手提包狠狠地打他。◇ *James whacked the ball over the net.* 詹姆斯猛力把球击过网去。**2 ~ sth + adv./prep.** (*informal*) to put sth somewhere without much care 草草放下：*Just whack your bags in the corner.* 就把你的包丢在角落里吧。**3 ~ sb** (*NAmE, slang*) to murder sb 谋杀

■ *noun* [usually sing.] (*informal*) **1** the act of hitting sb/sth hard; the sound made by this 重击；重击声：*He gave the ball a good whack.* 他猛击了一下球。◇ *I heard the whack of the bullet hitting the wood.* 我听到子弹砰的一声击中了木头。**2** (*BrE*) a share of sth; an amount of sth 份儿；一份；量：*Don't leave all the work to her. Everyone should do their fair whack.* 别把所有的工作都让她做。大家应合理分担一下。◇ *You have to pay the full whack. There are no reductions.* 你得付全额。没有折扣。◇ *He charges **top whack*** (= the highest amount possible). 他索要最高价。

IDM **out of ˈwhack** (*informal, especially NAmE*) **1** no longer correct or working properly 不对头；有毛病；运行不正常：*The system is clearly out of whack.* 这个系统明显是运行不正常。◇ *All the traveling had thrown my body out of whack.* 这一路旅行已经使我的身体出了毛病。**2** not agreeing with or the same as sth else 不一致；不一样：*Expectations and reality got out of whack.* 期望和现实之间出现了差距。

whacked /wækt/ (*also* ˌ**whacked ˈout**) *adj.* [not usually before noun] (*BrE, informal*) very tired 筋疲力尽；累垮了：*I'm whacked!* 我累死了！

whack·ing /ˈwækɪŋ/ (*also* ˈ**whacking great**) *adj.* (*BrE, informal*) used to emphasize how big or how much sth is（强调体积或数额）巨大的，极大的 **SYN** **whopping**: *a whacking great hole in the roof* 房顶上一个巨大的窟窿 ◇ *They were fined a whacking £100 000.* 他们被罚了 10 万英镑的巨款。

whacko (*also* **wacko**) /ˈwækəʊ; *NAmE* -koʊ/ *adj.* (*informal*) crazy 疯狂的；发狂的

whacky /ˈwæki/ = WACKY

whale /weɪl/ *noun* a very large animal that lives in the sea and looks like a very large fish. There are several types of whale, some of which are hunted. 鲸：*whale meat* 鲸肉 ➲ SEE ALSO BLUE WHALE, KILLER WHALE, PILOT WHALE, SPERM WHALE

IDM **have a ˈwhale of a time** (*informal*) to enjoy yourself very much; to have a very good time 玩得很痛快；过得非常快活

whale·bone /ˈweɪlbəʊn; *NAmE* -boʊn/ *noun* [U] a thin hard substance found in the upper JAW of some types of whale, used in the past to make some clothes stiffer 鲸须，鲸骨（几种鲸上腭的角质薄片，旧时用以支撑衣服）

whaler /ˈweɪlə(r)/ *noun* **1** a ship used for hunting whales 捕鲸船 **2** a person who hunts whales 捕鲸人

whal·ing /ˈweɪlɪŋ/ *noun* [U] the activity or business of hunting and killing WHALES 捕鲸（业）

wham /wæm/ *exclamation* (*informal*) **1** used to represent the sound of a sudden, loud hit（突然的重击声）砰，嘭：*The bombs went down—wham!—right on target.* 炸弹落了下来，砰！正好击中目标。**2** used to show that sth that is unexpected has suddenly happened（表示意外的事情突然发生）：*I saw him yesterday and—wham!—I realized I was still in love with him.* 我昨天看到他了。我猛地一下子意识到我仍然爱着他。➲ MORE LIKE THIS 3, page R25

whammy /ˈwæmi/ *noun* (*pl.* **-ies**) (*informal*) an unpleasant situation or event that causes problems for sb/sth 晦气；倒霉事：*With this government we've had a double whammy of tax increases and benefit cuts.* 自从这任政府上台以来，我们又是增加税收又是减少补贴，倒了双倍的霉。

ORIGIN From the 1950s American cartoon *Li'l Abner*, in which one of the characters could **shoot a whammy** (put a curse on sb) by pointing a finger with one eye open, or a **double whammy** with both eyes open. 源自 20 世纪 50 年代美国的漫画《利尔·阿布纳》。其中一个人物睁一只眼时用手指指着可施一个诅咒，睁两只眼睛可施两个诅咒。

wha·nau /ˈfɑːnaʊ/ *noun* (*pl.* **wha·nau**) (*NZE*) a family or community of related families who live together in the same area（生活在同一地区的）大家庭，家族

wharf /wɔːf; *NAmE* wɔːrf/ *noun* (*pl.* **wharves** /wɔːvz; *NAmE* wɔːrvz/ or **wharfs**) a flat structure built beside the sea or a river where boats can be tied up and goods unloaded 码头

what 🔑 /wɒt; *NAmE* wɑːt; wʌt/ *pron., det.* **1** 🔑 used in questions to ask for particular information about

W

sb/sth 什么：*What is your name?* 你叫什么名字？◇ *What* (= what job) *does he do?* 他是做什么工作的？◇ *What time is it?* 现在什么时候了？◇ *What kind of music do you like?* 你喜欢什么音乐？➲ COMPARE WHICH (1) **2** the thing or things that; whatever …的事物；无论什么；凡是…的事物：*What you need is a good meal.* 你需要的是一顿美餐。◇ *Nobody knows what will happen next.* 没有人知道接下来将会发生什么事。◇ *I spent what little time I had with my family.* 我仅有的一点儿时间都和家人在一起度过了。**3** used to say that you think that sth is especially good, bad, etc. 多么；真；太：*What awful weather!* 天气太糟糕了！◇ *What a beautiful house!* 多么漂亮的房子啊！

IDM **and 'what not | and what 'have you** (*informal*) and other things of the same type 以及其他同样的东西；诸如此类：*It's full of old toys, books and what not.* 这里全都是旧玩具、书籍，以及这类的东西。**get/give sb what 'for** (*informal*) to be punished/punish sb severely（受到）严惩；（被）痛打一顿，申斥一顿：*I'll give her what for if she does that again.* 她若再这样做，看我怎么收拾她。**or 'what** (*informal*) **1** used to emphasize your opinion（强调看法）：*Is he stupid or what?* 他真是傻透了。**2** used when you are not sure about sth（表示不肯定）还是别的什么：*I don't know if he's a teacher or what.* 我不知道他是个教师还是别的什么。◇ *Are we going now or what?* 我们现在走还是不走？**what?** (*informal*) **1** used when you have not heard or have not understood sth（没听见或没听懂时说）什么：*What? I can't hear you.* 什么？我听不见你说话。**2** used to show that you have heard sb and to ask what they want（听到对方的话并问他们要什么）什么事，要什么：*'Mummy!' 'What?' 'I'm thirsty.'* "妈咪！" "什么事？" "我渴。" **3** used to express surprise or anger（惊讶或愤怒时说）什么，竟有这种事，真的：*'It will cost $500.' 'What?'* "这东西要花 500 美元。" "真的？" ◇ *'I asked her to marry me.' 'You what?'* "我向她求婚了。" "你说什么？" **'what about…?** (*informal*) **1** used to make a suggestion（提出建议）…怎么样：*What about a trip to France?* 到法国去旅游一趟如何？**2** used to introduce sb/sth into the conversation（用以引出话题）…怎么样：*What about you, Joe? Do you like football?* 你呢，乔？你喜欢足球吗？ **'what-d'you-call-him/-her/-it/-them | 'what's-his/-her/-its/-their-name** used instead of a name that you cannot remember（记不得名字时说）你叫他（或她、它、他们）什么来着：*She's just gone out with old what-d'you-call-him.* 她刚和老…，你叫他什么来着，一块儿出去的。**what for?** for what purpose or reason? 为何目的；为何理由：*What is this tool for?* 这个工具是干什么用的？◇ *What did you do that for* (= why did you do that)? 你为何做那事？◇ *'I need to see a doctor.' 'What for?'* "我得去看医生。" "看什么病？" **what if…?** what would happen if? 要是…会怎么样呢：*What if the train is late?* 火车要是晚点会怎么样呢？◇ *What if she forgets to bring it?* 要是她忘记带来，会怎么样呢？**what 'of it?** (*informal*) used when admitting that sth is true, to ask why it should be considered important（承认某事属实，想知道为何重要）那又怎么样呢，那有什么关系呢：*Yes, I wrote the article. What of it?* 是的，文章是我写的。那又怎么样呢？**what's ˌup with 'that?** (*especially NAmE*) used to suggest that sth you have heard is a stupid idea or does not make sense 怎么回事（表示听到的话愚蠢或无聊）：*They dropped their best player. What's up with that?* 他们弃用了最佳队员。怎么回事？**what's 'what** (*informal*) what things are useful, important, etc. 什么事物有用（或重要等）：*She certainly knows what's what.* 她当然知道轻重缓急。**what's with sb?** (*NAmE, informal*) used to ask why sb is behaving in a strange way（询问某人为何行为古怪）…怎么啦：*What's with you? You haven't said a word all morning.* 你怎么啦？整个上午你一句话都没说。**what's with sth?** (*NAmE, informal*) used to ask the reason for sth（询问原因）为什么，怎么：*What's with all this walking? Can't we take a cab?* 怎么就这么一直走？难道我们就不能打辆出租车吗？**what with sth** used to list the various reasons for sth（列举各种理由）由于，因为：*What with the cold weather and my bad leg, I haven't been out for weeks.* 由于天气很冷，我的腿又不好，我已经好几个星期没有出门了。

whatch·am·acall·it /ˈwɒtʃəməkɔːlɪt; *NAmE* ˈwɑːt-; ˈwʌt-/ *noun* (*informal*) used when you cannot think of the name of sth（想不起名称时说）叫什么来着：*Have you got a whatchamacallit? You know… a screwdriver?* 你有一把…叫什么来着的？嗯…螺丝刀吗？

what·ever /wɒtˈevə(r); *NAmE* wət-; wɑːt-/ *det., pron., adv.*

■ ***det., pron.*** **1** any or every; anything or everything 任何；每一；任何事物；一切事物：*Take whatever action is needed.* 采取任何必要的行动。◇ *Do whatever you like.* 你喜欢做什么就做什么。**2** used when you are saying that it does not matter what sb does or what happens, because the result will be the same（表示做什么或发生什么都没关系，因结果都一样）无论什么，不管什么：*Whatever decision he made I would support it.* 无论他作出什么决定我都会支持的。◇ *You have our support, whatever you decide.* 不管你作何决定，都会得到我们的支持。**3** (*especially BrE*) used in questions to express surprise or confusion（用于问句，表示惊讶或困惑）到底是什么，究竟是什么：*Whatever do you mean?* 你究竟是什么意思？◇ *Chocolate-flavoured carrots! Whatever next?* 巧克力味的胡萝卜！接下来到底还想吃什么？**4** (*informal, ironic*) used as a reply to tell sb that you do not care what happens or that you are not interested in what they are talking about（用于回应，表示不在乎或不感兴趣）或许吧，无所谓：*'You should try a herbal remedy.' 'Yeah, whatever.'* "你应该试一试草药疗法。" "是啊，或许吧。" **5** (*informal*) used to say that you do not mind what you do, have, etc. and that anything is acceptable（表示不在乎，什么都可接受）什么都可以：*'What would you like to do today?' 'Whatever.'* "今天你想做什么呢？" "做什么都可以。"

IDM **or what'ever** (*informal*) or sth of a similar type 诸如此类；等等：*It's the same in any situation: in a prison, hospital or whatever.* 这在什么场合都一样：在监狱、医院或诸如此类的地方。**what'ever you do** used to warn sb not to do sth under any circumstances（警告某人绝不要做某事）无论如何：*Don't tell Paul, whatever you do!* 无论如何都不要告诉保罗！

■ ***adv.*** **1** (*also* **what·so·ever** /ˌwɒtsəʊˈevə(r); *NAmE* ˌwʌtsoʊˈevər; ˌwɑːtsoʊˈevər/) **no, nothing, none, etc.** ~ not at all; not of any kind 一点儿都（不）；丝毫（不）；什么都（没有）：*They received no help whatever.* 他们没有得到一点儿帮助。◇ *'Is there any doubt about it?' 'None whatsoever.'* "对此有怀疑吗？" "丝毫没有。" **2** (*informal*) used to say that it does not matter what sb does, or what happens, because the result will be the same 不管发生什么：*We told him we'd back him whatever.* 我们告诉他，在任何情况下我们都会支持他。

what·not /ˈwɒtnɒt; *NAmE* ˈwɑːtnɑːt/ *noun* [U] **and ~** (*informal*) used when you are referring to sth, but are not being exact and do not mention its name（由于拿不准而不指名）某种东西，不可名状的东西：*It's a new firm. They make toys and whatnot.* 这是家新的公司。他们制作玩具和别的小玩意儿。

whats·it /ˈwɒtsɪt; *NAmE* ˈwɑːt-; ˈwʌt-/ *noun* (*informal, especially BrE*) used when you cannot think of the word or name you want, or do not want to use a particular word（想不起名称或不想指明时说）什么来着，某某玩意儿：*I've got to make a whatsit for the party. That's it—a flan.* 我得给聚会制作一个什么东西来着。想起来了，一个果馅饼。

wheat /wiːt/ *noun* [U] a plant grown for its grain that is used to produce the flour for bread, cakes, PASTA, etc.; the grain of this plant 小麦；小麦粒：*wheat flour* 小麦制的面粉 ➲ COLLOCATIONS AT FARMING ➲ VISUAL VOCAB PAGE V35

IDM **sort out/separate the ˌwheat from the 'chaff** to distinguish useful or valuable people or things from ones that are not useful or have no value 识别优劣；分清好坏；去芜存菁

the 'Wheat Belt *noun* [sing.] the western central region of the US including the Great Plains where wheat is an important crop 小麦带（包括大平原在内的美国中西部小麦产区）

W

wheat·germ /ˈwiːtdʒɜːm; *NAmE* -dʒɜːrm/ *noun* [U] the centre of the wheat grain, which is especially good for your health 麦芽；小麦胚芽

wheat·ish /ˈwiːtɪʃ/ *adj.* (*IndE*) (of a person's skin or face) light brown or pale gold, like WHEAT that is fully grown and ready to be picked（人的皮肤或脸）浅棕色的，淡金色的，小麦色的：*He has a wheatish complexion.* 他面色是小麦色。

wheat·meal /ˈwiːtmiːl/ *noun* [U] a type of flour made from wheat, that uses more of the grain than WHITE FLOUR 小麦粉；全麦面粉

whee /wiː/ *exclamation* used to express excitement（激动时发出的声音）哟，啊

whee·dle /ˈwiːdl/ *verb* (*disapproving*) to persuade sb to give you sth or do sth by saying nice things that you do not mean（用言语）哄 SYN **coax**: **~ sth (out of sb)** *The kids can always wheedle money out of their father.* 孩子们总是能从父亲那里哄出钱来。◇ **~ sb into doing sth** *She wheedled me into lending her my new coat.* 她用花言巧语哄我把新大衣借给了她。◇ **+ speech** *'Come on, Em,' he wheedled.* "快点，爱玛。" 他哄道。

wheel 🔑 /wiːl/ *noun, verb*

▪ *noun*

• **ON/IN VEHICLES** 车辆 **1** 🔑 [C] one of the round objects under a car, bicycle, bus, etc. that turns when it moves 轮；车轮；轮子：*He braked suddenly, causing the front wheels to skid.* 他猛然刹车，使得前车轮打滑了。◇ *One of the boys was pushing the other along in a little box* ***on wheels.*** 一个男孩用下面装着轮子的小箱子推着另一个男孩。**2** 🔑 [C, usually sing.] the round object used to steer a car, etc. or ship（汽车等的）方向盘；（轮船的）舵轮：*This is the first time I've sat* ***behind the wheel*** *since the accident.* 这是出车祸以来我头一次坐在方向盘前。◇ *A car swept past with Laura* ***at the wheel.*** 劳拉驱车疾驰而过。◇ *Do you want to* ***take the wheel*** *(= drive) now?* 你现在想开车吗？➲ SEE ALSO HELM, STEERING WHEEL **3 wheels** [pl.] (*informal*) a car 汽车：*At last he had his own wheels.* 他终于有了自己的汽车。

• **IN MACHINE** 机器 **4** 🔑 [C] a flat round part in a machine 机轮：*gear wheels* 齿轮 ➲ SEE ALSO CARTWHEEL (2), CATHERINE WHEEL, FERRIS WHEEL, MILL WHEEL, SPINNING WHEEL, WATERWHEEL

• **ORGANIZATION/SYSTEM** 组织；系统 **5 wheels** [pl.] **~ (of sth)** an organization or a system that seems to work like a complicated machine that is difficult to understand 错综复杂的机构（或系统）：*the* ***wheels of bureaucracy/commerce/government, etc.*** 复杂的官僚、商务、政府等机构 ◇ *It was Rob's idea. I merely* ***set the wheels in motion*** (= started the process). 这是罗布的主意。我只不过是让它运作起来而已。

• **-WHEELED** 有…轮 **6** (in adjectives 构成形容词) having the number or type of wheels mentioned 有…轮的：*a sixteen-wheeled lorry* 十六轮大卡车

• **-WHEELER** 有…轮子的车 **7** (in nouns 构成名词) a car, bicycle, etc. with the number of wheels mentioned 有…轮子的汽车（或自行车等）：*a three-wheeler* 三轮机动车

IDM ˌ**wheels within** ˈ**wheels** a situation which is difficult to understand because it involves complicated or secret processes and decisions 错综复杂；盘根错节：*There are wheels within wheels in this organization—you never really know what is going on.* 这个机构里错综复杂，你永远搞不清到底是怎么回事。➲ MORE AT COG, GREASE *v.*, OIL *v.*, REINVENT, SHOULDER *n.*, SPOKE

▪ *verb*

• **MOVE STH WITH WHEELS** 用轮子移动 **1** [T] **~ sth (+ adv./prep.)** to push or pull sth that has wheels 推（或拉）有轮之物：*She wheeled her bicycle across the road.* 她推着自行车穿过了马路。**2** [T] **~ sb/sth (+ adv./prep.)** to move sb/sth that is in or on sth that has wheels 用有轮之物推动（或拉动、移动）…：*The nurse wheeled him along the corridor.* 护士推着他沿楼道走。

• **MOVE IN CIRCLE** 旋转 **3** [I] **(+ adv./prep.)** to move or fly in a circle 转动；旋转；打转；盘旋：*Birds wheeled above us in the sky.* 鸟儿在我们上空盘旋。

• **TURN QUICKLY** 快速转向 **4** [I, T] to turn quickly or suddenly and face the opposite direction; to make sb/sth do this（使）迅速转身，猛然转身：**(+ adv./prep.)** *She wheeled around and started running.* 她突然转身就跑。◇ **~ sb/sth (+ adv./prep.)** *He wheeled his horse back to the gate.* 他突然掉转马头返回到大门。

IDM ˌ**wheel and** ˈ**deal** (usually used in the progressive tenses 通常用于进行时) to do a lot of complicated deals in business or politics, often in a dishonest way（在商界或政界）工于心计；（以不正当的方式）进行纷繁复杂的交易，周旋 ➲ MORE LIKE THIS 12, page R26

PHR V ˌ**wheel sth**↔ˈ**out** to show or use sth to help you do sth, even when it has often been seen or heard before 故伎重演：*They wheeled out the same old arguments we'd heard so many times before.* 他们又弹起了我们听过多次的老调。

ˈ**wheel arch** *noun* a space in the body of a vehicle over a wheel, shaped like an ARCH 车轮拱罩；轮拱

wheel·bar·row /ˈwiːlbærəʊ; *NAmE* ˈwiːlbæroʊ/ (*also* **bar·row**) *noun* a large open container with a wheel and two handles that you use outside to carry things 独轮手推车 ➲ VISUAL VOCAB PAGE V20

wheel·base /ˈwiːlbeɪs/ *noun* [sing.] (*specialist*) the distance between the front and back wheels of a car or other vehicle（汽车或其他机动车辆的）轴距；（机车的）轮组定距

wheel·chair /ˈwiːltʃeə(r); *NAmE* -tʃer/ *noun* a special chair with wheels, used by people who cannot walk because of illness, an accident, etc. 轮椅：*Does the hotel have* ***wheelchair access?*** 这家旅馆有轮椅通道吗？◇ *He's* ***been confined to a wheelchair*** *since the accident.* 他从那次出事以后就离不开轮椅了。◇ *wheelchair users* 坐轮椅的人

ˈ**wheel clamp** *noun* (*BrE*) = CLAMP (2), DENVER BOOT

wheeler-dealer /ˌwiːlə ˈdiːlə(r)/ *noun* (*informal*) a person who does a lot of complicated deals in business or politics, often in a dishonest way（商界或政界的）工于心计的人，进行复杂交易的人

wheel·house /ˈwiːlhaʊs/ *noun* a small CABIN with walls and a roof on a ship where the person steering stands at the wheel（船上的）操舵室，驾驶室

wheelie /ˈwiːli/ *noun* (*informal*) a trick that you can do on a bicycle or motorcycle by balancing on the back wheel, with the front wheel off the ground（骑自行车或摩托车将前轮抬起的）后轮支撑车技：*to do a wheelie* 做后轮支撑的特技

ˈ**wheelie bin** *noun* (*BrE, informal*) a large container with a lid and wheels, that you keep outside your house and use for putting rubbish in（带盖的）有轮大垃圾筒

wheel·wright /ˈwiːlraɪt/ *noun* a person whose job is making and repairing wheels, especially wooden ones 车轮修造工（尤指木轮的）

wheeze /wiːz/ *verb, noun*

▪ *verb* [I, T] to breathe noisily and with difficulty 喘；喘息；喘鸣：*He was coughing and wheezing all night.* 他整夜又咳嗽又喘。◇ **+ speech** *'I have a chest infection,' she wheezed.* "我胸部受到了感染。" 她呼哧呼哧地说。

▪ *noun* [usually sing.] **1** the high whistling sound that your chest makes when you cannot breathe easily 喘息声；喘鸣声；呼吸发出的哨音；呼哧呼哧声 **2** (*old-fashioned, BrE, informal*) a clever trick or plan 花招；计谋

wheezy /ˈwiːzi/ *adj.* making the high whistling sound that your chest makes when you cannot breathe easily 喘息的；喘鸣的；气喘吁吁的；呼哧呼哧响的：*I'm wheezy today.* 我今天感到喘不上气来。◇ *a wheezy cough* 喘鸣性咳 ▸ **wheez·ily** /-ɪli/ *adv.* **wheezi·ness** *noun* [U]

whelk /welk/ *noun* a small SHELLFISH that can be eaten 蛾螺（有些可食用）

whelp /welp/ *noun, verb*

▪ *noun* (*specialist*) a young animal of the dog family; a PUPPY or CUB 小狗；幼犬；（犬科动物的）幼兽

W

■*verb* [I, T] ~ (sth) (*formal*) (of a female dog 母狗) to give birth to a PUPPY or PUPPIES 下（崽）；产（仔）

when 🔑 /wen/ *adv., pron., conj.*
■*adv.* **1** 🔑 (used in questions 用于问句) at what time; on what occasion 什么时候；何时；什么情况下；什么场合下：*When did you last see him?* 你上次什么时候见到他的？ ◇ *When can I see you?* 我什么时候可以见你？ ◇ *When* (= in what circumstances) *would such a solution be possible?* 什么情况下可以这么解决？ **2** 🔑 used after an expression of time to mean 'at which' or 'on which'（用于时间的表达方式之后）在那时，其时：*Sunday is the only day when I can relax.* 星期日是我唯一可以休息的日子。◇ *There are times when I wonder why I do this job.* 有时候我也不明白自己为什么要干这个工作。**3** 🔑 at which time; on which occasion 其时；当时；当场：*The last time I went to Scotland was in May, when the weather was beautiful.* 我上次去苏格兰是在五月份，那时的天气好极了。
■*pron.* 🔑 what/which time 什么时候；何时：*Until when can you stay?* 你可以待到什么时候？ ◇ *'I've got a new job.' 'Since when?'* "我有了份新工作。""什么时候开始的？"
■*conj.* **1** 🔑 at or during the time that 在…时候；当…时；在…期间：*I loved history when I was at school.* 我上学时喜欢历史。**2** 🔑 after 在…之后：*Call me when you've finished.* 你完成后就打电话给我。**3** 🔑 at any time that; whenever 在任何…时候：*Can you spare five minutes when it's convenient?* 方便时能占用你五分钟时间吗？ **4** 🔑 just after which 一…就；刚…就：*He had just drifted off to sleep when the phone rang.* 他刚睡着电话铃就响了。**5** 🔑 considering that 考虑到；既然：*How can they expect to learn anything when they never listen?* 既然他们从不听讲，他们怎么能指望学到东西呢？ **6** although 虽然；然而；可是：*She claimed to be 18, when I know she's only 16.* 她自称是 18 岁，可是我知道她才 16 岁。 IDM SEE AS *conj.*

whence /wens/ *adv.* (*old use*) from where 从何处；从哪里：*They returned whence they had come.* 他们从哪里来又回到哪里去了。

when·ever 🔑 /wen'evə(r)/ *conj., adv.*
■*conj.* **1** 🔑 at any time that; on any occasion that 在任何…的时候；无论何时；在任何…的情况下：*You can ask for help whenever you need it.* 你如果需要帮助随时可以提出来。**2** 🔑 every time that 每当；每次：*Whenever she comes, she brings a friend.* 她每次来都带着个朋友。◇ *The roof leaks whenever it rains.* 屋顶每逢下雨就漏。◇ *We try to help* ***whenever possible.*** 只要有可能我们都尽量帮忙。**3** used when the time when sth happens is not important 别的什么时候（也可以）；任何时间（都行）：*'When do you need it by?' 'Saturday or Sunday. Whenever.'* "你什么时候需要这个东西？""星期六或星期日。哪一天都行。" ◇ *It's not urgent—we can do it next week or whenever.* 这不着急，我们可以在下星期或别的什么时候做。
■*adv.* used in questions to mean 'when', expressing surprise（用于问句，表示惊奇）究竟什么时候：*Whenever did you find time to do all that cooking?* 你怎么有时间做了这么多菜？

W

where 🔑 /weə(r); *NAmE* wer/ *adv., conj.*
■*adv.* **1** 🔑 in or to what place or situation 在哪里；到哪里；处于哪种情形：*Where do you live?* 你住在哪儿？ ◇ *I wonder where they will take us to.* 我不知道他们要把我们带到哪里去。◇ *Where* (= at what point) *did I go wrong in my calculations?* 我计算中什么地方出了差错？ ◇ *Where* (= in what book, newspaper, etc.) *did you read that?* 你在哪儿读到这个的？ ◇ *Just where* (= to what situation or final argument) *is all this leading us?* 这一切到底是要将我们引向何处？ **2** 🔑 used after words or phrases that refer to a place or situation to mean 'at, in or to which'（用于表示地点或情况的词语后）在那（地方），到那（地方）：*It's one of the few countries where people drive on the left.* 这是为数不多的几个靠左行驶的国家之一。**3** 🔑 the place or situation in which 在那里；在该处；在该情况下：*We then moved to Paris, where we lived for six years.* 我们随后移居巴黎，在那里住了六年。
■*conj.* (in) the place or situation in which（在）…的地方；（在）…情况下：*This is where I live.* 这是我住的地方。◇ *Sit where I can see you.* 坐在我能看到你的地方。◇ *Where people were concerned, his threshold of boredom was low.* 涉及人的事情，他便极易感到厌烦。◇ *That's where* (= the point in the argument at which) *you're wrong.* 这就是你的错误所在。

where·abouts *noun, adv.*
■*noun* /'weərəbaʊts; *NAmE* 'wer-/ [U+sing./pl. v.] the place where sb/sth is（人或物）所在的地方；下落；行踪：*His whereabouts are/is still unknown.* 他仍下落不明。
■*adv.* /ˌweərə'baʊts; *NAmE* ˌwer-/ used to ask the general area where sb/sth is（用以询问大概的地方）在什么地方，在哪里：*Whereabouts did you find it?* 你在哪儿找到它的？

where·as 🔑 AW /ˌweər'æz; *NAmE* ˌwer-/ *conj.* **1** 🔑 used to compare or contrast two facts（用以比较或对比两个事实）然而，但是，尽管：*Some of the studies show positive results, whereas others do not.* 有一些研究结果令人满意，然而其他的则不然。 ➲ LANGUAGE BANK AT CONTRAST **2** (*law* 律) used at the beginning of a sentence in an official document to mean 'because of the fact that...'（用于正式文件中句子的开头）鉴于

where·by AW /weə'baɪ; *NAmE* wer-/ *adv.* (*formal*) by which; because of which 凭此；借以；由于：*They have introduced a new system whereby all employees must undergo regular training.* 他们采用了新的制度，所有的雇员都必须定期培训。

where·fore /'weəfɔː(r); *NAmE* 'werf-/ *noun* IDM SEE WHY *n.*

where·in /weər'ɪn; *NAmE* wer-/ *adv., conj.* (*formal*) in which place, situation or thing; in what way 其中；在那里；在那种情况下；以什么方式：*Wherein lies the difference between conservatism and liberalism?* 保守主义和自由主义的区别在哪里？

where·of /weər'ɒv; *NAmE* wer'ʌv/ *conj.* (*old use* or *humorous*) of what or which 关于什么；关于那个：*I know whereof I speak* (= I know a lot about what I am talking about). 我知道自己在说些什么。

where·upon /ˌweərə'pɒn; *NAmE* ˌwerə'pɑːn/ *conj.* (*formal*) and then; as a result of this 然后；于是；随之；据此；因此：*He told her she was a liar, whereupon she walked out.* 他对她说她在说谎，她便愤然而去。

wher·ever 🔑 /weər'evə(r); *NAmE* wer-/ *conj., adv.*
■*conj.* **1** 🔑 in any place 在任何地方：*Sit wherever you like.* 你爱坐在哪儿就坐哪儿。◇ *He comes from Boula,* ***wherever that may be*** (= I don't know where it is). 他的原籍是布拉，管它在什么地方呢。**2** 🔑 in all places that 在…的各个地方；各处；处处 SYN **everywhere**：*Wherever she goes, there are crowds of people waiting to see her.* 她所到之处都有成群的人等着见她。**3** 🔑 in all cases that 在所有…的情况下 SYN **whenever**：*Use wholegrain breakfast cereals* ***wherever possible.*** 只要有可能就用全谷物早餐食品。
IDM **or wher'ever** (*informal*) or any other place 或其他任何地方：*tourists from Spain, France or wherever* 来自西班牙、法国或任何别的地方的游客
■*adv.* used in questions to mean 'where', expressing surprise（用于问句，表示惊讶）究竟在哪里，究竟到哪儿：*Wherever can he have gone to?* 他究竟会到哪儿去了呢？

the where·withal /'weəwɪðɔːl; *NAmE* 'werw-/ *noun* [sing.] ~ (**to do sth**) the money, things or skill that you need in order to be able to do sth（做某事的）所需资金，必要的设备，所需技术：*They lacked the wherewithal to pay for the repairs.* 他们缺少维修费。

whet /wet/ *verb* (**-tt-**) ~ **sth** to increase your desire for or interest in sth 刺激…的欲望；增强…的兴趣：*The book will* ***whet your appetite*** *for more of her work.* 你看了这本书就会更想多读她的著作。

whether 🔑 /'weðə(r)/ *conj.* **1** 🔑 used to express a doubt or choice between two possibilities（表示迟疑或两个可能性之间的选择）是否：*He seemed undecided* ***whether*** *to go* ***or*** *stay.* 他似乎还没有决定去留。◇ *It remains to be seen* ***whether or not*** *this idea can be put into practice.* 这一想法能否付诸实践还有待于观察。◇ *I asked him* ***whether*** *he had done it all himself* ***or whether*** *someone had helped him.* 我问过他这都是他自己做的还是有人帮他做的。◇ *I'll see whether she's at home* (= or not at home). 我来看看她

在不在家。◇ *It's doubtful whether there'll be any seats left.* 看来未必还有座位。➲ NOTE AT IF **2** 🔑 used to show that sth is true in either of two cases（表示两种情况都真实）是…（还是），或者…（或者），不管…（还是）：*You are entitled to a free gift whether you accept our offer of insurance or not.* 无论你接不接受我们的保险提议，你都可以免费得到一份礼物。◇ *I'm going* **whether** *you like it* **or not**. 不管你愿意不愿意，我都要走了。◇ ***Whether or not*** *we're successful, we can be sure that we did our best.* 不管成功与否，我们确已尽了最大努力。

whet·stone /ˈwetstəʊn; *NAmE* -stoʊn/ *noun* a stone that is used to make tools, knives and weapons sharp 磨刀石

whew /hwjuː; fjuː/ *exclamation* a sound that people make to show that they are surprised or RELIEVED about sth or that they are very hot or tired（惊讶、宽慰或感到很热、疲劳时发出的声音）哟，噢：*Whew—and I thought it was serious!* 嚯，我原以为它有多么严重呢！◇ *Ten grand? Whew!* 一万英镑？哟！➲ COMPARE PHEW

whey /weɪ/ *noun* [U] the thin liquid that is left from sour milk after the solid part (called CURDS) has been removed 乳清，乳水（酸奶中的凝乳去掉后剩下的含水成分）

which 🔑 /wɪtʃ/ *pron., det.* **1** 🔑 used in questions to ask sb to be exact about one or more people or things from a limited number 哪一个；哪一些：*Which is better exercise—swimming or tennis?* 游泳和网球，哪种运动比较好？◇ *Which of the applicants has got the job?* 哪一位应聘者得到了这份工作？◇ *Which of the patients have recovered?* 哪些患者已经康复了？◇ *Which way is the wind blowing?* 风朝哪个方向刮？➲ COMPARE WHAT (1) **2** 🔑 used to be exact about the thing or things that you mean（明确所指的事物）…的那个，…的那些：*Houses which overlook the lake cost more.* 俯瞰湖泊的房子要价高些。◇ *It was a crisis for which she was totally unprepared.* 这是一场她完全没有防备的危机。**HELP** **That** can be used instead of **which** in this meaning, but it is not used immediately after a preposition. 此义中 that 可代替 which，但 that 不能紧跟在介词之后：*It was a crisis* ***that*** *she was totally unprepared* ***for***. 这是一场她完全没有防备的危机。**3** 🔑 used to give more information about sth（进一步提供有关某事物的信息）那个，那些：*His best movie, which won several awards, was about the life of Gandhi.* 他最优秀的电影，就是荣获几项大奖的那一部，是关于甘地生平的。◇ *Your claim ought to succeed,* ***in which case*** *the damages will be substantial.* 你的索赔应当能成功，假如这样的话，损害赔偿金将会相当可观。**HELP** **That** cannot be used instead of **which** in this meaning. * which 在此义中不能用 that 替代。

IDM ˌ**which is** ˈ**which** 🔑 used to talk about distinguishing one person or thing from another（区分人或事物）谁是谁，哪个是哪个：*The twins are so alike I can't tell which is which.* 这一对双胞胎长得一模一样，我分不清谁是谁。

which·ever /wɪtʃˈevə(r)/ *det., pron.* **1** used to say what feature or quality is important in deciding sth（表示什么特征或品质在作决定时重要）…的那个，…的那些：*Choose whichever brand you prefer.* 挑选你喜欢的那个品牌。◇ *Pensions should be increased annually in line with earnings or prices, whichever is the higher.* 养老金每年应该按照收入或物价中升幅较高的那一项增长。◇ *Whichever of you gets here first will get the prize.* 你们谁第一个到达这里谁就获奖。**2** used to say that it does not matter which, as the result will be the same 无论哪个；无论哪些：*It takes three hours, whichever route you take.* 无论你走哪一条路都需要三个小时。◇ *The situation is an awkward one,* ***whichever way you look at it***. 无论从哪一方面看，这个局面都很尴尬。◇ *Whichever they choose, we must accept their decision.* 无论他们如何选择，我们都必须接受他们的决定。

whiff /wɪf/ *noun, verb*

■ ***noun*** [usually sing.] **1** ~ (**of sth**) a smell, especially one that you only smell for a short time 一点儿气味；一股气味：*a whiff of cigar smoke* 一股雪茄烟味 ◇ *He caught a whiff of perfume as he leaned towards her.* 他探身靠近她时闻到一股香水味。**2** ~ (**of sth**) a slight sign or feeling of sth 轻微的迹象（或感觉）；一点点；些许：*a whiff of danger* 一点点危险 **3** (*NAmE*) (in GOLF or BASEBALL 高尔夫球或棒球) an unsuccessful attempt to hit the ball 挥空棒（击球未中）

■ ***verb*** **1** [I] (*BrE, informal*) to smell bad 有臭味；发臭 **2** [I] (*NAmE*) (in GOLF or BASEBALL 高尔夫球或棒球) to try without success to hit the ball 挥空棒（击球未中）

whiffy /ˈwɪfi/ *adj.* (*BrE, informal*) smelling bad 难闻的；发臭的

Whig /wɪɡ/ *noun* in Britain in the past, a member of a party that supported progress and reform and that later became the Liberal Party 辉格党党员（属于英国旧时的激进党派，自由党的前身）

while 🔑 /waɪl/ *conj., noun, verb*

■ ***conj.*** (*also formal* **whilst** /waɪlst/ *especially in BrE*) **1** 🔑 during the time that sth is happening 在…期间；当…的时候 **SYN** **when**：*We must have been burgled while we were asleep.* 我们肯定是在睡着时遭遇了入室盗窃。◇ *Her parents died while she was still at school.* 她还在读书时父母就去世了。◇ *While I was waiting at the bus stop, three buses went by in the opposite direction.* 我在公共汽车站等车时，路对面驶过了三辆公共汽车。**2** 🔑 at the same time as sth else is happening 与…同时：*You can go swimming while I'm having lunch.* 我吃午饭时你可以去游泳。◇ *shoes mended while you wait* 在你等候的时候修好的鞋 **3** 🔑 used to contrast two things（对比两件事物）…而，…然而：*While Tom's very good at science, his brother is absolutely hopeless.* 汤姆很擅长理科，而他的弟弟绝对是不可救药。➲ LANGUAGE BANK AT CONTRAST **4** 🔑 (used at the beginning of a sentence 用于句首) although; despite the fact that... 虽然；尽管：*While I am willing to help, I do not have much time available.* 尽管我愿意帮忙，但是没有多少时间。➲ LANGUAGE BANK AT NEVERTHELESS **5** (*NEngE*) until 到…时；直到…为止：*I waited while six o'clock.* 我一直等到了六点钟。

IDM ˌ**while you're/I'm etc.** ˈ**at it** used to suggest that sb could do sth while they are doing sth else 趁做某事的时候；顺便；顺带：*'I'm just going to buy some postcards.' 'Can you get me some stamps while you're at it?'* "我正想去买明信片。""你能顺便给我买些邮票吗？"

■ ***noun*** 🔑 [sing.] a period of time 一段时间；一会儿：*They chatted* ***for a while***. 他们聊了一会儿。◇ *I'll be back in* ***a little while*** (= a short time). 我一会儿就回来。◇ *I haven't seen him for* ***quite a while*** (= a fairly long time). 我有好一阵子没有见到他了。◇ *They walked back together, talking* ***all the while*** (= all the time). 他们一起边走边聊着回去的。

IDM SEE ONCE *adv.*, WORTH *adj.*

■ ***verb***

PHR V ˌ**while sth**↔**a**ˈ**way** to spend time in a pleasant lazy way 逍遥自在地度过，消磨（时间）：*We whiled away the time reading and playing cards.* 我们靠看书和玩纸牌消磨时间。

whim /wɪm/ *noun* [C, U] a sudden wish to do or have sth, especially when it is sth unusual or unnecessary 心血来潮；一时的兴致；突发的奇想：*He was forced to pander to* ***her every whim***. 她每次心血来潮他都不得不依随她。◇ *We bought the house* ***on a whim***. 我们一时冲动买了这所房子。◇ *My duties seem to change daily* ***at the whim of*** *the boss.* 我的职责似乎随着老板的兴致每天改变。◇ *the whims of fashion* 时尚的变化多端 ◇ *She hires and fires people* ***at whim***. 她随心所欲地雇用人和解雇人。

whim·per /ˈwɪmpə(r)/ *verb, noun*

■ ***verb*** [I, T] to make low, weak crying noises; to speak in this way 抽泣；呜咽；啜泣；泣诉；抽搭着说：*The child was lost and began to whimper.* 那孩子迷了路，抽抽搭搭地哭起来。◇ **+ speech** *'Don't leave me alone,' he whimpered.* "别丢下我不管。" 他呜咽着说。

■ ***noun*** a low weak cry that a person or an animal makes when they are hurt, frightened or sad 抽泣；呜咽声

whim·si·cal /ˈwɪmzɪkl/ *adj.* unusual and not serious in a way that is either amusing or annoying 异想天开的；想入非非的；心血来潮的；滑稽可笑的：*to have a whimsical sense of humour* 有离奇的幽默感 ◇ *Much of his writing has*

W

a whimsical quality. 他的大部分作品都很出奇。▶ **whim·si·cal·ly** /-kli/ *adv.*

whimsy /ˈwɪmzi/ *noun* [U] a way of thinking or behaving, or a style of doing sth that is unusual and not serious, in a way that is either amusing or annoying 怪念头；古怪可笑的举动；吊儿郎当；随心所欲

whine /waɪn/ *verb, noun*

■ ***verb*** **1** [I, T] (**+ speech**) | **~ that...** to complain in an annoying, crying voice 哭哭啼啼；哭嚷：*Stop whining!* 别哭哭啼啼的！◇ *'I want to go home,' whined Toby.* "我要回家。" 托比哭嚷道。➲ SYNONYMS AT COMPLAIN **2** [I] to make a long high unpleasant sound because you are in pain or unhappy 哀鸣；惨叫：*The dog whined and scratched at the door.* 那狗嗷嗷地叫着抓门。**3** [I] (of a machine 机器) to make a long high unpleasant sound 嘎嘎响；嗖嗖响；嘎吱嘎吱响 ▶ **whiny** /ˈwaɪni/ *adj.*: *a whiny voice/tone* 哭哭啼啼的声音 / 语气 ◇ *a whiny kid/brat* 哭哭啼啼的小孩 / 小子

■ ***noun*** [usually sing.] **1** a long high sound that is usually unpleasant or annoying 嘎吱声；吱吱声；嘎嘎声：*the steady whine of the engine* 发动机不停的嘎吱声 **2** a long high cry that a child or dog makes when it is hurt or wants sth（儿童发出的）哭喊声；（狗发出的）号叫声 **3** a high tone of voice that you use when you complain about sth 抱怨的语调

whinge /wɪndʒ/ *verb* (**whinge·ing**, **whing·ing**) [I] **~ (about sb/sth)** (*BrE, informal, disapproving*) to complain in an annoying way 絮絮叨叨地抱怨：*She's always whingeing about how unfair everything is.* 她总是嘟囔着说一切都太不公平了。▶ **whinge** *noun* **whin·ger** *noun*

whinny /ˈwɪni/ *verb* (**whin·nies**, **whinny·ing**, **whin·nied**, **whin·nied**) [I] (of a horse 马) to make a quiet NEIGH 轻声嘶鸣 ▶ **whinny** *noun* (*pl.* **-ies**)

whip /wɪp/ *noun, verb*

■ ***noun*** **1** [C] a long thin piece of rope or leather, attached to a handle, used for making animals move or punishing people 鞭子：*He cracked his whip and the horse leapt forward.* 他甩了个响鞭，马儿就奋蹄向前奔去。**2** [C] an official in a political party who is responsible for making sure that party members attend and vote in important government debates 党鞭（政党中负责督导党员参与重大问题辩论与投票的组织秘书）：*the chief whip* 首席党鞭 **3** [C] a written instruction telling members of a political party how to vote on a particular issue（政党发给党员的）投票通知书，投票指示 ➲ SEE ALSO THREE-LINE WHIP **4** [U, C] a sweet dish made from cream, eggs, sugar and fruit mixed together 搅打奶油甜食（用奶油、鸡蛋、糖和水果搅打而成）

IDM **have/hold, etc. the ˈwhip hand (over sb/sth)** to be in a position where you have power or control over sb/sth 执掌大权；执鞭在手 ➲ MORE AT CRACK *v.*, FAIR *adj.*

■ ***verb*** (**-pp-**) **1** [T] **~ sb/sth** to hit a person or an animal hard with a whip, as a punishment or to make them go faster or work harder 鞭打；鞭策；以鞭打责罚；鞭笞 **2** [I, T] to move, or make sth move, quickly and suddenly or violently in a particular direction（使朝某一方向）猛然移动：**+ adv./prep.** *A branch whipped across the car window.* 一条树枝突然划过车窗。◇ *Her hair whipped around her face in the wind.* 她的头发随风在脸际飘拂。◇ **~ sth** *The waves were being whipped by 50 mile an hour winds.* 时速 50 英里的大风卷起了波浪。**3** [T] **~ sth + adv./prep.** to remove or pull sth quickly and suddenly（突然迅速地）除去，拉动，抽出：*She whipped the mask off her face.* 她刷地一下子把脸上的面具摘掉了。◇ *The man whipped out a knife.* 那个人突然抽出一把刀来。**4** [T] to stir cream, etc. very quickly until it becomes stiff 搅打（奶油等）：**~ sth** *Serve the pie with* ***whipped cream.*** 馅饼得配搅打奶油。◇ **~ sth up** *Whip the egg whites up into stiff peaks.* 把蛋白打得起稠尖儿。➲ VISUAL VOCAB PAGE V30 **5** [T] **~ sb/sth** (*NAmE, informal*) to defeat sb very easily in a game（在比赛中）轻而易举地击败：*The team whipped its opponents by 35 points.* 这个队以 35 分的优势轻松击败对手。➲ COMPARE THRASH *v.* (3) **6** [T] **~ sth** (*BrE, informal*) to steal sth 偷；盗窃

PHR V **ˌwhip ˈthrough sth** (*informal*) to do or finish sth very quickly 匆匆做；迅速完成：*We whipped through customs in ten minutes.* 我们十分钟便办完了海关手续。**ˌwhip sb/sth↔ˈup 1** to deliberately try and make people excited or feel strongly about sth 激发；激励；煽动 SYN **rouse**：*The advertisements were designed to whip up public opinion.* 这些广告是为了激起公众的舆论。◇ *He was a speaker who could really* ***whip up a crowd.*** 他是个真正有感召力的演说者。**2** to quickly make a meal or sth to eat 匆匆做（饭等）：*She whipped up a delicious lunch for us in 15 minutes.* 她用了 15 分钟就给我们备好了一顿可口的午餐。

whip·lash /ˈwɪplæʃ/ *noun* **1** [C, usually sing.] a hit with a whip 鞭打 **2** [U] = WHIPLASH INJURY: *He was very bruised and suffering from whiplash.* 他满身青肿，而且颈部过度屈伸受伤。

ˈwhiplash injury *noun* [C, U] (*also* **whip·lash**) a neck injury caused when your head moves forward and back suddenly, especially in a car accident 挥鞭伤，鞭打损伤（尤指车祸造成的颈部过度屈伸损伤）

whip·per·snap·per /ˈwɪpəsnæpə(r); *NAmE* ˈwɪpərs-/ *noun* (*old-fashioned, informal*) a young and unimportant person who behaves in a way that others think is too confident and rude 狂妄小子

whip·pet /ˈwɪpɪt/ *noun* a small thin dog, similar to a GREYHOUND, that can run very fast and is often used for racing 小灵狗（类似灵猩，常用于赛狗）

whip·ping /ˈwɪpɪŋ/ *noun* [usually sing.] an act of hitting sb with a whip, as a punishment 鞭打，鞭笞（作为惩罚）

ˈwhipping boy *noun* a person who is often blamed or punished for things other people have done 代人受过者；替罪羊；出气筒

ˈwhipping cream *noun* [U] cream that becomes thicker when it is stirred quickly (= WHIPPED) 搅打奶油

whip·poor·will /ˈwɪpəwɪl; *NAmE* -pərw-/ *noun* a brown N American bird with a cry that sounds like its name 三声夜鹰

ˈwhip-round *noun* (*BrE, informal*) if a group of people have a **whip-round**, they all give money so they can buy sth for sb 凑份子

whir (*also* **whirr**) /wɜː(r)/ *verb, noun*

■ ***verb*** (**-rr-**) [I] to make a continuous low sound like the parts of a machine moving 嗡嗡地响；呼呼地响：*The clock began to whir before striking the hour.* 钟在敲响整点前先嘎啦嘎啦地响。

■ ***noun*** (*also* **whir·ring**) [usually sing.] a continuous low sound, for example the sound made by the regular movement of a machine or the wings of a bird 嗡嗡声；呼呼声：*the whir of a motor* 发动机的嗡嗡声 ◇ *There was a whirring of machinery.* 有机器发出的嗡嗡声。

whirl /wɜːl; *NAmE* wɜːrl/ *verb, noun*

■ ***verb*** **1** [I, T] to move, or make sb/sth move, around quickly in a circle or in a particular direction（使）旋转，回旋，打转 SYN **spin**：(**+ adv./prep.**) *Leaves whirled in the wind.* 落叶在风中旋转。◇ *She whirled around to face him.* 她猛地转过身子面对着他。◇ *the whirling blades of the helicopter* 直升机旋转着的桨叶 ◇ **~ sb/sth (+ adv./prep.)** *Tom whirled her across the dance floor.* 汤姆拥着她从舞池的一边旋转到另一边。**2** [I] if your mind, thoughts, etc. **whirl**, you feel confused and excited and cannot think clearly（头脑、思想等）混乱不清，激动，恍惚 SYN **reel**：*I couldn't sleep—my mind was whirling from all that had happened.* 我睡不着，所发生的一切一直在脑子里转来转去。◇ *So many thoughts whirled around in her mind.* 她思绪万千，脑子里乱作一团。

■ ***noun*** [sing.] **1** a movement of sth spinning round and round 旋转；回旋；急转：*a whirl of dust* 尘土飞扬 ◇ (*figurative*) *Her mind was* ***in a whirl*** (= in a state of confusion or excitement). 她脑子里乱糟糟的。**2** a number of activities or events happening one after the other 接连不断的活动；纷至沓来的事件：*Her life was one long whirl* *of parties.* 她的生活就是接连不断的聚会。◇ *It's easy to get caught up in the* ***social whirl.*** 很容易被纷繁的社交活动缠得脱不开身。

IDM **give sth a 'whirl** (*informal*) to try sth to see if you like it or can do it 试一试

whirli·gig /ˈwɜːlɪɡɪɡ; *NAmE* ˈwɜːrlɪɡɪɡ/ *noun* **1** something that is very active and always changing 活跃多变的事物；经常变换的东西；变迁：*the whirligig of fashion* 时尚的千变万化 **2** (*old-fashioned*) a MERRY-GO-ROUND at a FAIRGROUND for children to ride on 旋转木马

whirl·pool /ˈwɜːlpuːl; *NAmE* ˈwɜːrl-/ *noun* **1** a place in a river or the sea where currents of water spin round very fast（河水或海水的）旋涡 SYN **eddy**: (*figurative*) *She felt she was being dragged into a whirlpool of emotion.* 她觉得自己被卷入了感情的旋涡。**2** (*also* ˌ**whirlpool 'bath**) a special bath/BATHTUB or swimming pool for relaxing in, in which the water moves in circles 涡流浴缸；涡流游泳池 ➲ SEE ALSO JACUZZI™

whirl·wind /ˈwɜːlwɪnd; *NAmE* ˈwɜːrl-/ *noun, adj.*

▪ ***noun*** **1** a very strong wind that moves very fast in a spinning movement and causes a lot of damage 旋风；旋流 **2** a situation or series of events where a lot of things happen very quickly 一片忙乱：*To recover from the divorce, I threw myself into a whirlwind of activities.* 为了从离婚中恢复过来，我马不停蹄地投身于一系列的活动。

▪ ***adj.*** [only before noun] happening very fast 快速的；匆匆忙忙的；旋风似的：*a whirlwind romance* 旋风式恋爱 ◇ *a whirlwind tour of America* 旋风式的美国之行

whirr (*especially NAmE*) = WHIR

whisk /wɪsk/ *verb, noun*

▪ ***verb*** **1** ~ **sth** to mix liquids, eggs, etc. into a stiff light mass, using a fork or special tool 搅打，搅动（液体、鸡蛋等）SYN **beat**: *Whisk the egg whites until stiff.* 把蛋白搅打稠。**2** ~ **sb/sth + adv./prep.** to take sb/sth somewhere very quickly and suddenly 匆匆带走；迅速送走：*Jamie whisked her off to Paris for the weekend.* 杰米匆匆把她带到巴黎去度周末。◇ *The waiter whisked away the plates before we had finished.* 服务员没等我们吃完就匆忙把盘子收走了。

▪ ***noun*** a kitchen UTENSIL (= a tool) for stirring eggs, etc. very fast 打蛋器；搅拌器：*an electric whisk* 电动搅拌器 ➲ VISUAL VOCAB PAGES V26, V27, V30

whis·ker /ˈwɪskə(r)/ *noun* **1** [C] any of the long stiff hairs that grow near the mouth of a cat, mouse, etc.（猫、鼠等的）须 **2 whiskers** [pl.] (*old-fashioned* or *humorous*) the hair growing on a man's face, especially on his cheeks and chin 络腮胡子；连鬓胡子 ➲ VISUAL VOCAB PAGE V12

IDM **be, come, etc. within a whisker of sth/doing sth** to almost do sth 几乎要做；险些要做：*They came within a whisker of being killed.* 他们险些丢了性命。**by a 'whisker** by a very small amount 差一点儿 ➲ MORE AT CAT

whis·kered /ˈwɪskəd; *NAmE* -kərd/ (*also* **whis·kery** /ˈwɪskəri/) *adj.* having whiskers 有络腮胡子的；有须的

whisky (*BrE*) (*US, IrishE* **whis·key**) /ˈwɪski/ *noun* (*pl.* **whis·kies, whis·keys**) **1** [U, C] a strong alcoholic drink made from MALTED grain. It is sometimes drunk with water and/or ice. 威士忌：*a bottle of whisky* 一瓶威士忌 ◇ *Scotch whisky* 苏格兰威士忌 ◇ *highland whiskies* 高地威士忌 ➲ SEE ALSO BOURBON, SCOTCH *n.* **2** [C] a glass of whisky 一杯威士忌：*a whisky and soda* 一杯加苏打水的威士忌 ◇ *Two whiskies, please.* 请来两杯威士忌。➲ SEE ALSO SCOTCH *n.*

whis·per 🔑 /ˈwɪspə(r)/ *verb, noun*

▪ ***verb*** **1** 🔑 [I, T] to speak very quietly to sb so that other people cannot hear what you are saying 耳语；低语；私语；小声说 SYN **murmur**: *Don't you know it's rude to whisper?* 难道你不知道窃窃私语是不礼貌的吗？◇ ~ **about sth** *What are you two whispering about?* 你们两人在低声说些什么？◇ **+ speech** *'Can you meet me tonight?' he whispered.* "你今晚能和我见面吗？" 他小声问。◇ ~ **sth (to sb)** *She leaned over and whispered something in his ear.* 她探过身去附耳跟他说了些什么。◇ ~ **(to sb) that...** *He whispered to me that he was afraid.* 他低声对我说他害怕。**2** [T, often passive] ~ **that...** | **it is whispered that...** to say or suggest sth about sb/sth in a private or secret way 私下说；秘密告诉；悄声暗示：*It was whispered that he would soon die and he did.* 有人私下说他将不久于人世，他果然死了。**3** [I] (**+ adv./prep.**) (*literary*) (of leaves, the wind, etc. 叶子、风等) to make a soft, quiet sound 沙沙作响；发飒飒声

▪ ***noun*** **1** 🔑 a low quiet voice or the sound it makes 耳语（声）；低语（声）；私语（声）SYN **murmur**: *They spoke* ***in whispers.*** 他们在交头接耳。◇ *Her voice dropped to a whisper.* 她压低声音小声说话。➲ SEE ALSO STAGE WHISPER **2** (*also* **whis·per·ing**) (*literary*) a soft sound 轻柔的声音 SYN **murmur**: *I could hear the whispering of the sea.* 我听见大海在轻声诉说。**3** a piece of news that is spread by being talked about but may not be true 传言；谣传 SYN **rumour**: *I've heard whispers that he's leaving.* 我听到传言，说他要走。

'whispering campaign *noun* an attempt to damage sb's reputation by saying unpleasant things about them and passing this information from person to person 散布流言蜚语；造谣中伤

whist /wɪst/ *noun* [U] a card game for two pairs of players in which each pair tries to win the most cards 惠斯特（一种由两对游戏者玩的纸牌游戏）

whis·tle 🔑 /ˈwɪsl/ *noun, verb*

▪ ***noun*** **1** 🔑 a small metal or plastic tube that you blow to make a loud high sound, used to attract attention or as a signal 哨子：*The referee finally* ***blew the whistle*** *to stop the game.* 主裁判终于吹停了比赛。➲ SEE ALSO TIN WHISTLE **2** 🔑 the sound made by blowing a whistle 哨子声：*He scored the winning goal just seconds before the final whistle.* 他就在终场哨声前的几秒钟内打进了制胜的一球。**3** 🔑 the sound that you make by forcing your breath out when your lips are closed 口哨：*a shrill whistle* 尖厉的口哨声 ➲ SEE ALSO WOLF WHISTLE **4** 🔑 the high loud sound produced by air or steam being forced through a small opening, or by sth moving quickly through the air 汽笛声；警笛声；呼啸声 **5** a piece of equipment that makes a high loud sound when air or steam is forced through it 汽笛：*The train whistle blew as we left the station.* 我们离开车站时火车的汽笛响了。◇ *a factory whistle* 工厂的汽笛

IDM SEE BLOW *v.*, CLEAN *adj.*

▪ ***verb*** **1** 🔑 [T, I] to make a high sound or a musical tune by forcing your breath out when your lips are closed 吹口哨；打呼哨：~ **(sth)** *to whistle a tune* 用口哨吹曲子 ◇ *He whistled in amazement.* 他惊愕地吹了个口哨。◇ *The crowd booed and whistled as the player came onto the field.* 那队员上场时，人群又是发出嘘声又是吹口哨。◇ ~ **to sb/sth** *She whistled to the dog to come back.* 她打了个呼哨把狗唤回来。◇ ~ **at sb/sth** *Workmen whistled at her as she walked past.* 当她走过时工人向她吹口哨。**2** 🔑 [I] to make a high sound by blowing into a whistle 吹哨子：*The referee whistled for a foul.* 裁判吹哨子示意有人犯规。**3** 🔑 [I] (of a KETTLE or other machine 烧水壶或机器) to make a high sound 鸣叫；呼啸；发出笛声：*The kettle began to whistle.* 烧水壶呜呜地响了起来。◇ *The microphone was making a strange whistling sound.* 扩音器发出一种奇怪的哨音。**4** [I] **+ adv./prep.** to move quickly, making a high sound 呼啸而行；嗖嗖地移动：*The wind whistled down the chimney.* 风飕飕地灌进烟囱。◇ *A bullet whistled past his ear.* 子弹嗖的一声从他耳边飞过。**5** [I] (of a bird 鸟) to make a high sound 啭鸣；唧啾

IDM **sb can 'whistle for sth** (*BrE, informal*) used to say that you are not going to give sb sth that they have asked for（表示不给他人所要的东西）得不到，空指望

'whistle-blower *noun* (used especially in newspapers 尤用于报章) a person who informs people in authority or the public that the company they work for is doing sth wrong or illegal（公司等处）检举揭发舞弊内情的人

'whistle-stop *adj.* [only before noun] visiting a lot of different places in a very short time 走马观花的；浮光掠影的：*to go on a* ***whistle-stop tour*** *of Europe* 到欧洲各地作走马看花的观光 ◇ *politicians on a whistle-stop election campaign* 在各地进行蜻蜓点水式竞选宣传的政治人物

W

Whit /wɪt/ *adj.* connected with Whitsun 圣灵降临节的；圣神降临节的：*Whit Monday* 圣灵降临节后的第一个星期一

whit /wɪt/ *noun* [sing.] (*old-fashioned*) (usually in negative sentences 通常用于否定句) a very small amount 一点点；很少量；丝毫 SYN **jot**

IDM **not a 'whit | not one 'whit** not at all; not the smallest amount 丝毫不；一点不

white /waɪt/ *adj., noun*

■ ***adj.*** (**whiter**, **whit·est**) **1** having the colour of fresh snow or of milk 白的；白色的：*a crisp white shirt* 一件挺括的白衬衫 ◇ *white bread* 白面包 ◇ *a set of perfect white teeth* 一口洁白无瑕的牙齿 ◇ *His hair was **as white as snow**.* 他头发雪白。◇ *The horse was almost **pure white** in colour.* 那匹马几乎是纯白色。**2** belonging to or connected with a race of people who have pale skin 白种人的；白人的：*white middle-class families* 白人中产阶级家庭 ◇ *She writes about her experiences as a black girl in a predominantly white city.* 她写的是自己身为一个黑人姑娘在以白人为主的城市里的经历。**3** (of the skin 皮肤) pale because of emotion or illness 脸色苍白的：*white with shock* 震惊得脸色发白 ◇ *She went **white as a sheet** when she heard the news.* 她听到这消息时脸色变得煞白。**4** (*BrE*) (of tea or coffee 茶或咖啡) with milk added 加牛奶的：*Two white coffees, please.* 请来两杯加牛奶的咖啡。◇ *Do you take your coffee black or white?* 你喝咖啡加不加牛奶？ ➲ COMPARE BLACK *adj.* (4) ▶ **white·ness** *noun* [U, sing.]

■ ***noun*** **1** [U] the colour of fresh snow or of milk 白色；雪白；乳白：*the pure white of the newly painted walls* 新粉刷的墙壁的纯白色 ◇ *She was dressed all in white.* 她穿着一身白色的衣服。**2** [C, usually pl.] a member of a race or people who have pale skin 白种人；白人 **3** [U, C] white wine 白葡萄酒：*Would you like red or white?* 你喜欢喝红葡萄酒还是白葡萄酒？◇ *a very dry white* 特干白葡萄酒 **4** [C, U] the part of an egg that surrounds the YOLK (= the yellow part) 蛋白；蛋清：*Use the whites of two eggs.* 用两个鸡蛋的蛋清。**5** [C, usually pl.] the white part of the eye 眼白；白眼珠：*The whites of her eyes were bloodshot.* 她的白眼珠布满血丝。➲ VISUAL VOCAB PAGE V64 **6 whites** [pl.] white clothes, sheets, etc. when they are separated from coloured ones to be washed 要洗涤的白色衣服（或床单等）：(*BrE*) *Don't wash whites and coloureds together.* 别把白色衣服和带颜色的衣服一块洗。◇ (*NAmE*) *Don't wash whites and colors together.* 别把白色衣服和带颜色的衣服一起洗。**7 whites** [pl.] white clothes worn for playing some sports 白色运动服：***cricket/tennis whites*** 白色板球 / 网球运动服

IDM **,whiter than 'white** (of a person 人) completely honest and morally good 完全诚实清白；纯洁无瑕：*The government must be seen to be whiter than white.* 政府须让人觉得是清正廉洁的。➲ MORE AT BLACK *n.*

white·bait /'waɪtbeɪt/ *noun* [pl.] very small young fish of several types that are fried and eaten whole 小鲱鱼（可食用）

,white 'blood cell (*also* **'white cell**) (*also specialist* **leuco·cyte**) *noun* (*biology* 生) any of the clear cells in the blood that help to fight disease 白细胞；白血球

white·board /'waɪtbɔːd; *NAmE* -bɔːrd/ *noun* **1** a large board with a smooth white surface that teachers, etc. write on with special pens 白色书写板；白板 ➲ VISUAL VOCAB PAGE V72 ➲ COMPARE BLACKBOARD **2** = INTERACTIVE WHITEBOARD

,white 'bread *noun* [U] bread made with WHITE FLOUR 白面面包；精粉面包

'white-bread *adj.* [only before noun] (*NAmE, informal*) ordinary and traditional 普通的；一般传统的：*a white-bread town* 普普通通的老镇

white·caps /'waɪtkæps/ (*NAmE*) (*BrE* **,white 'horses**) *noun* [pl.] waves in the sea or ocean with white tops on them （海上的）白浪，白头浪

,white 'Christmas *noun* a Christmas during which there is snow on the ground 白色圣诞节（地面有雪）

,white-'collar *adj.* [usually before noun] working in an office, rather than in a factory, etc.; connected with work in offices 白领的；文职的；脑力劳动的：*white-collar workers* 白领工作者 ◇ *a white-collar job* 白领工作 ◇ *white-collar crime* (= in which office workers steal from their company, etc.) 白领犯罪 ➲ COMPARE BLUE-COLLAR, PINK-COLLAR

,white 'dwarf *noun* (*astronomy* 天) a small star that is near the end of its life and is very DENSE (= solid and heavy) 白矮星（密度大，处于演化末期的一类恒星）

,white 'elephant *noun* [usually sing.] a thing that is useless and no longer needed, although it may have cost a lot of money 昂贵而无用之物：*The new office block has become an expensive white elephant.* 这座新办公大楼成了昂贵的摆设。ORIGIN From the story that in Siam (now Thailand) the king would give a white elephant as a present to somebody that he did not like. That person would have to spend all their money on looking after the rare animal. 源自暹罗（今泰国）的一个故事。当时的国王会送白象给他讨厌的人，让这个人不得不花掉所有的钱来照顾这种稀有的动物。

,white 'fish *noun* [U, C] (*pl.* **white fish**) fish with pale flesh 白鱼

,white 'flag *noun* [usually sing.] a sign that you accept defeat and wish to stop fighting 白旗（承认失败并愿意停战的标志）：*to **raise/show/wave the white flag*** 举起 / 打出 / 摇动白旗

,white 'flight *noun* [U] (*US*) a situation where white people who can afford it go to live outside the cities because they are worried about crime in city centres 白人迁移（白人因担心市中心的治安而到郊区居住）

,white 'flour *noun* [U] flour made from WHEAT grains, from which most of the BRAN (= outer covering) and WHEATGERM (= centre part) have been removed 白面；精麦粉

'white goods *noun* [pl.] large pieces of electrical equipment in the house, such as WASHING MACHINES, etc. 白色家电；大件家用电器 ➲ COMPARE BROWN GOODS

White·hall /'waɪthɔːl/ *noun* **1** [U] a street in London where there are many government offices 怀特霍尔（伦敦的一条街，政府机关所在地）**2** [sing.+sing./pl. v.] a way of referring to the British Government 白厅（指英国政府）：*Whitehall are/is refusing to comment.* 白厅拒绝发表评论。➲ MORE LIKE THIS 19, page R27

,white 'heat *noun* [U] the very high temperature at which metal looks white 白热；白炽

,white 'hope *noun* [sing.] (*informal*) a person who is expected to bring success to a team, an organization, etc.（团队、组织等）被寄予厚望的人：*He was once the **great white hope** of British boxing.* 他一度曾是英国拳击的希望所在。

,white 'horses (*BrE*) (*NAmE* **white·caps**) *noun* [pl.] waves in the sea or ocean with white tops on them （大海中的）白浪

,white-'hot *adj.* **1** (of metal or sth burning 金属或燃烧物) so hot that it looks white 白热的；白炽的 **2** very strong and INTENSE 白热化的；极其激烈的

the 'White House *noun* [sing.] **1** the official home of the President of the US in Washington, DC 白宫（美国总统官邸，位于首都华盛顿）**2** the US President and his or her officials 白宫（指美国总统或美国政府）：*The White House has issued a statement.* 白宫已经发表了一项声明。◇ *White House aides* 总统助手 ➲ MORE LIKE THIS 19, page R27

,white 'knight *noun* a person or an organization that rescues a company from being bought by another company at too low a price 白武士，白衣骑士（把公司从不利的收购建议中挽救出来的个人或机构）

ˌwhite-ˈknuckle ride *noun* a ride at a FAIRGROUND that makes you feel very excited and frightened at the same time 令人既兴奋又紧张的游乐场乘行

ˌwhite ˈlie *noun* a harmless or small lie, especially one that you tell to avoid hurting sb（尤指为避免伤害他人感情的）善意的谎言，小谎

ˌwhite ˈlight *noun* [U] ordinary light that has no colour 白光

ˌwhite ˈmeat *noun* [U] **1** meat that is pale in colour when it has been cooked, such as chicken 白肉（烹煮后呈白色的肉，如鸡肉）➲ COMPARE RED MEAT **2** pale meat from the breast of a chicken or other bird that has been cooked（鸡或其他禽类的）熟胸脯肉

whiten /ˈwaɪtn/ *verb* [I, T] to become white or whiter; to make sth white or whiter（使）变白，变得更白：*He gripped the wheel until his knuckles whitened.* 他紧紧握住方向盘，握得指关节都变白了。◇ **~ sth** *Snow had whitened the tops of the trees.* 大雪把树冠变成了白色。

ˌwhite ˈnoise *noun* [U] unpleasant noise, like the noise that comes from a television or radio that is turned on but not TUNED IN 白噪声（整个频道范围内的噪声）

ˈwhite-out *noun* weather conditions in which there is so much snow or cloud that it is impossible to see anything 乳白天空（雪大或云重而看不见东西）➲ SEE ALSO WITEOUT™

the ˌwhite ˈpages *noun* [pl.] a telephone book (on white paper), or a section of a book, that lists the names, addresses and telephone numbers of people living in a particular area 白页（分区电话簿）

ˌWhite ˈPaper *noun* (in Britain) a government report that gives information about sth and explains government plans before a new law is introduced（英国）白皮书 ➲ COMPARE GREEN PAPER

ˌwhite ˈpepper *noun* [U] a greyish-brown powder made from dried BERRIES (called PEPPERCORNS), used to give flavour to food 白胡椒粉

ˌwhite ˈsauce *noun* [U] a thick sauce made from butter, flour and milk 白沙司，白酱，白汁（用黄油、面粉和牛奶调制而成）SYN **béchamel**

ˌwhite ˈspirit *noun* [U] (*BrE*) a clear liquid made from petrol/gas, used as a cleaning substance or to make paint thinner 白色溶剂油；石油溶剂油

ˌwhite ˈstick *noun* a long thin white stick carried by blind people to help them walk around without knocking things and to show others that they are blind 白色手杖（用以探索障碍物和表示用者为失明人）

ˌwhite ˈtie *noun* a man's white BOW TIE, also used to mean very formal evening dress for men（男用）白领结，正式晚礼服：*dressed in white tie and tails* 身穿燕尾服打着白领结

ˌwhite-ˈtie *adj.* (of social occasions 社交场合) very formal, when men are expected to wear white BOW TIES and jackets with TAILS 非常正式的；要求男士穿燕尾晚礼服打白领结的：*Is it a white-tie affair?* 这是个穿夜礼服的聚会吗？

ˌwhite-ˈvan man *noun* (*BrE, informal*) used to refer to the sort of man who drives a white van in an aggressive way, thought of as a symbol of the rude and sometimes violent way in which some men behave today 白色货车司机（借喻粗鲁疯狂的男子）

white·wall /ˈwaɪtwɔːl/ *noun* **1** (*BrE also* **ˌwhitewall ˈtyre**) (*NAmE also* **ˌwhitewall ˈtire**) a tyre with a white line going round it for decoration 白圈轮胎 **2 whitewalls** [pl.] (*especially US*) the shaved area at the sides of the head when the hair is cut in a very short style（锅盖短发侧面的）剃头圈

white·wash /ˈwaɪtwɒʃ; *NAmE* -wɑːʃ; -wɔːʃ/ *noun, verb*

■ ***noun*** **1** [U] a mixture of CHALK or LIME and water, used for painting houses and walls white（粉刷用的）石灰水，白涂料 **2** [U, sing.] (*disapproving*) an attempt to hide unpleasant facts about sb/sth 粉饰；掩盖 SYN **cover-up**: *The opposition claimed the report was a whitewash.* 反对派声称这份报告文过饰非。**3** [C, usually sing.] (*informal*) (in sport) a victory in every game in a series（在体育比赛中接连击败对手的）全胜，完胜：*a 7–0 whitewash* * 7:0 全胜 ◇ *a whitewash victory* 大获全胜

■ ***verb*** **1 ~ sth** to cover sth such as a wall with whitewash 粉刷（墙壁等）；刷石灰水 **2 ~ sb/sth** (*disapproving*) to try to hide unpleasant facts about sb/sth; to try to make sth seem better than it is 掩饰；粉饰：*His wife had wanted to whitewash his reputation after he died.* 他妻子在他死后本来想粉饰他的名声。**3 ~ sb/sth** (*especially BrE*) (in sport 体育运动) to defeat an opponent in every game in a series（在系列比赛中）完全击败，完胜

ˌwhite ˈwater *noun* [U] **1** a part of a river that looks white because the water is moving very fast over rocks（河水湍急流过岩石时呈现的）碎浪水花，白色水域：*a stretch of white water* 一段白色水域 ◇ *white-water rafting* 激流漂流运动 ➲ VISUAL VOCAB PAGE V54 **2** a part of the sea or ocean that looks white because it is very rough and the waves are high（海洋的）白色水域，惊涛骇浪的水域

ˌwhite ˈwedding *noun* a traditional wedding, especially in a church, at which the BRIDE wears a white dress（尤指在教堂举行的）新娘穿白色礼服的传统婚礼

ˌwhite ˈwine *noun* **1** [U, C] pale yellow wine 白葡萄酒；浅黄色果酒：*a bottle of dry white wine* 一瓶干白葡萄酒 ◇ *chilled white wine* 冰镇白葡萄酒 **2** [C] a glass of white wine 一杯白葡萄酒 ➲ COMPARE RED WINE, ROSÉ

ˌwhite ˈwitch *noun* a person who does magic that does not harm other people 行善女巫；行善巫师

whitey /ˈwaɪti/ *noun* (*slang*) an offensive word for a white person, used by black people（黑人用语，含冒犯意）白人，白鬼

whither /ˈwɪðə(r)/ *adv., conj.* **1** (*old use*) where; to which 哪里；何处；到何处：*Whither should they go?* 他们应往何处去？◇ *They did not know whither they should go.* 他们不知何去何从。◇ *the place whither they were sent* 他们被送往的地方 **2** (*formal*) used to ask what is likely to happen to sth in the future（询问将可能发生什么）怎样的情况，怎样的前途：*Whither modern architecture?* 现代建筑何去何从？

whit·ing /ˈwaɪtɪŋ/ *noun* [C, U] (*pl.* **whit·ing**) a small sea fish with white flesh that is used for food 牙鳕（一种肉为白色可食用的小海鱼）

whit·ish /ˈwaɪtɪʃ/ *adj.* fairly white in colour 发白的；稍白的：*a bird with a whitish throat* 白喉鸟

Whit·sun /ˈwɪtsn/ *noun* [U, C] the 7th Sunday after Easter and the days close to it 圣灵降临节，圣神降临节（复活节后的第 7 个星期日前后几天）

ˌWhit ˈSunday *noun* [U, C] (*BrE*) = PENTECOST (1)

Whit·sun·tide /ˈwɪtsntaɪd/ *noun* [U] the week or days close to Whit Sunday 圣神降临周；圣灵降临节周末

whit·tle /ˈwɪtl/ *verb* to form a piece of wood, etc. into a particular shape by cutting small pieces from it 把（木头等）削成…：**~ A (from B)** *He whittled a simple toy from the piece of wood.* 他把那块木头削成了一个简易的玩具。◇ **~ B (into A)** *He whittled the piece of wood into a simple toy.* 他把那块木头削成了一个简易的玩具。

PHR V **ˌwhittle sth↔aˈway** to make sth gradually decrease in value or amount 削减，减少，降低（…的价值或数量）**ˌwhittle sth↔ˈdown** to reduce the size or number of sth 减少，缩减（…的大小或数目）：*I finally managed to whittle down the names on the list to only five.* 我最后总算把名单上的名字减少到了只有五个。

whizz (*especially BrE*) (*also* **whiz** *especially in NAmE*) /wɪz/ *verb, noun*

■ ***verb*** (*informal*) **1** [I] **+ adv./prep.** to move very quickly, making a high continuous sound 嗖嗖地移动；飞速行驶：*A bullet whizzed past my ear.* 一颗子弹嗖的一声从我耳边飞

W

过。◇ *He whizzed down the road on his motorbike.* 他骑着摩托车呼啸着沿路绝尘而去。**2** [I] **+ adv./prep.** to do sth very quickly 快速地做；匆匆地干：*She whizzed through the work.* 她麻利地把活干完了。

■ ***noun*** (*informal*) a person who is very good at sth 能手；善于…的人：*She's a whizz at crosswords.* 她填纵横字谜很在行。

ˈwhizz-kid (*especially BrE*) (*NAmE usually* **ˈwhiz-kid**) *noun* (*informal*) a person who is very good and successful at sth, especially at a young age 神童；有为青年：*financial whizz-kids* 金融方面年轻有为的人物

whizzy /ˈwɪzi/ *adj.* (**whiz·zier**, **whiz·ziest**) (*informal*) having features that make use of advanced technology 采用先进技术的：*a whizzy new handheld computer* 技术先进的新型掌上电脑

WHO /ˌdʌbljuː eɪtʃ ˈəʊ; *NAmE* ˈoʊ/ *abbr.* World Health Organization (an international organization that aims to fight and control disease) 世界卫生组织

who /huː/ *pron.* **1** used in questions to ask about the name, identity or function of one or more people（询问姓名、身份或职务）谁，什么人：*Who is that woman?* 那个女的是谁？◇ *I wonder who that letter was from.* 我不知道是谁来的信。◇ *Who are you phoning?* 你在给谁打电话？◇ *Who's the money for?* 这是给谁的钱？**2** used to show which person or people you mean（表示所指的人）：*The people who called yesterday want to buy the house.* 昨天打电话来的人想买这座房子。◇ *The people (who) we met in France have sent us a card.* 我们在法国结识的人给我们寄来了一张贺卡。**3** used to give more information about sb（进一步提供有关某人的信息）：*Mrs Smith, who has a lot of teaching experience at junior level, will be joining the school in September.* 史密斯太太将在九月份加入这所学校，她在初级教育方面颇有经验。◇ *And then Mary, who we had been talking about earlier, walked in.* 随后玛丽走了进来，我们刚才还在谈论她呢。➲ COMPARE WHOM

IDM **who am ˈI, who are ˈyou, etc. to do sth?** used to ask what right or authority sb has to do sth …凭什么；…有什么资格：*Who are you to tell me I can't park here?* 你凭什么不让我在这儿停车？**who's ˈwho** people's names, jobs, status, etc. 谁是谁；人们的情况（姓名、工作、身份等）：*You'll soon find out who's who in the office.* 你很快就会了解办公室里每个人的情况。➲ SEE ALSO WHO'S WHO

whoa /wəʊ; *NAmE* woʊ/ *exclamation* used as a command to a horse, etc. to make it stop or stand still（吆喝马等停下或不动的口令）吁

who'd /huːd/ *short form* **1** who had **2** who would

who·dun·nit (*BrE*) (*also* **who·dun·it** *NAmE, BrE*) /ˌhuːˈdʌnɪt/ *noun* (*informal*) a story, play, etc. about a murder in which you do not know who did the murder until the end（到结尾才知道凶手的）侦探小说，侦探戏剧，侦探作品

who·ever /huːˈevə(r)/ *pron.* **1** the person or people who; any person who …的那个人（或那些人）；…的任何人：*Whoever says that is a liar.* 说那话的人都是骗子。◇ *Send it to whoever is in charge of sales.* 把这寄给负责销售的人。**2** used to say that it does not matter who, since the result will be the same 无论谁；不管什么人：*Come out of there, whoever you are.* 不管你是谁，从那里出来吧。◇ *I don't want to see them, whoever they are.* 无论他们是谁，我都不想见。**3** used in questions to mean 'who', expressing surprise（用于问句，表示惊讶）究竟是谁，到底是谁：*Whoever heard of such a thing!* 究竟有谁听说过这种事！

whole /həʊl; *NAmE* hoʊl/ *adj., noun, adv.*

■ ***adj.*** **1** [only before noun] full; complete 全部的；整体的；完全的；所有的：*He spent the whole day writing.* 他整整写了一天。◇ *We drank a whole bottle each.* 我们每人都喝了整整一瓶。◇ *The whole country (= all the people in it) mourned her death.* 举国都在为她的逝世哀悼。◇ *Let's forget the* **whole thing**. 咱们彻底忘掉这件事吧。◇ *She wasn't telling the* **whole truth**. 她没有把实情都讲出来。**2** [only before noun] used to emphasize how large or important sth is（强调大小或重要性）整个的，全部的：*We offer a whole variety of weekend breaks.* 我们提供的周末假日活动丰富多彩，一应俱全。◇ *I can't afford it—that's* **the whole point**. 我买不起，这就是全部的理由。**3** not broken or damaged 完整的；完好无损的 **SYN** **(all) in one piece**：*Owls usually swallow their prey whole* (= without chewing it). 猫头鹰通常把猎物囫囵吞下。➲ NOTE AT HALF ▸ **whole·ness** *noun* [U] ➲ SEE ALSO WHOLLY

IDM **HELP** Most idioms containing **whole** are at the entries for the nouns and verbs in the idioms, for example **go the whole hog** is at **hog**. 大多数含 whole 的习语，都可在该等习语中的名词及动词相关词条找到，如 go the whole hog 在词条 hog 下。**a ˈwhole lot** (*informal*) very much; a lot 非常；很多：*I'm feeling a whole lot better.* 我觉得好得多了。**a ˈwhole lot (of sth)** (*informal*) a large number or amount 许许多多；大量：*There were a whole lot of people I didn't know.* 有许多人我都不认识。◇ *I lost a whole lot of money.* 我丢了好多钱。**the ˌwhole ˈlot** everything; all of sth 一切；全部；所有：*I've sold the whole lot.* 我把所有的东西都卖了。

■ ***noun*** **1** [C] a thing that is complete in itself 整个；整体：*Four quarters make a whole.* 四个四分之一构成一个整体。◇ *The subjects of the curriculum form a coherent whole.* 课程中的科目构成了一个连贯的整体。**2** [sing.] **the ~ of sth** all that there is of sth 全部；全体；所有：*The effects will last for the whole of his life.* 这些将会持续影响他的一生。➲ NOTE AT HALF

IDM **as a ˈwhole** as one thing or piece and not as separate parts 作为一个整体；总体上：*The festival will be great for our city and for the country as a whole.* 这次会演对我们城市乃至整个国家都将是意义重大的。**on the whole** considering everything; in general 总的说来；大体上；基本上：*On the whole, I'm in favour of the idea.* 大体说来，我赞成这个想法。

■ ***adv.*** **~ new/different/other…** (*informal*) completely new/different 全新的；完全不同的：*It's a whole new world out here.* 这儿是一个全新的世界。◇ *That's a whole other story.* 那完全是另外一回事。

whole·food /ˈhəʊlfuːd; *NAmE* ˈhoʊl-/ *noun* [U] (*also* **whole·foods** [pl.]) food that is considered healthy because it is in a simple form, has not been REFINED, and does not contain artificial substances（未经加工且不含人造添加剂的）全营养食物；全天然食物

whole·grain /ˈhəʊlgreɪn; *NAmE* ˈhoʊl-/ *adj.* made with or containing whole grains, for example of WHEAT 含全谷物的；全谷物制作的

whole·heart·ed /ˌhəʊlˈhɑːtɪd; *NAmE* ˌhoʊlˈhɑːrtəd/ *adj.* (*approving*) complete and enthusiastic 全心全意的；赤诚的：*The plan was given wholehearted support.* 这项计划得到了全心全意的支持。▸ **whole·heart·ed·ly** *adv.*：*to agree wholeheartedly* 完全同意

whole·meal /ˈhəʊlmiːl; *NAmE* ˈhoʊl-/ (*BrE*) (*also* **whole·wheat** *NAmE, BrE*) *adj.* **wholemeal/wholewheat** bread or flour contains the whole grains of WHEAT, etc. including the HUSK 全麦的

ˈwhole note (*NAmE*) (*BrE* **semi·breve**) *noun* (*music* 音) a note that lasts as long as four CROTCHETS/QUARTER NOTES 全音符 ➲ PICTURE AT MUSIC

ˌwhole ˈnumber *noun* (*mathematics* 数) a number that consists of one or more units, with no FRACTIONS (= parts of a number less than one) 整数

whole·sale /ˈhəʊlseɪl; *NAmE* ˈhoʊl-/ *adj.* [only before noun] **1** connected with goods that are bought and sold in large quantities, especially so they can be sold again to make a profit 批发的；趸售的：*wholesale prices* 批发价格 ➲ COMPARE RETAIL[1] *n.* **2** (especially of sth bad 尤指负面的事物) happening or done to a very large number of people or things 大规模的：*the wholesale slaughter of innocent people* 对无辜人民的大屠杀 ▸ **whole·sale** *adv.*：*We buy the building materials wholesale.* 我们批量购买建

筑材料。◇ *These young people die wholesale from heroin overdoses.* 这些年轻人因过量吸食海洛因大批死亡。

whole·sal·ing /ˈhəʊlseɪlɪŋ; *NAmE* ˈhoʊl-/ *noun* [U] the business of buying and selling goods in large quantities, especially so they can be sold again to make a profit 批发业 ➲ COMPARE RETAILING ▶ **whole·saler** *noun*: *fruit and vegetable wholesalers* 水果和蔬菜批发商

whole·some /ˈhəʊlsəm; *NAmE* ˈhoʊl-/ *adj.* **1** good for your health 有益健康的: *fresh, wholesome food* 有益健康的新鲜食品 **2** morally good; having a good moral influence 有道德的；有良好道德影响的: *It was clean wholesome fun.* 这是健康有益的玩乐。**OPP** **unwholesome** ▶ **whole·some·ness** *noun* [U]

ˈ**whole step** (*US*) (*BrE* **tone**) *noun* (*music* 音) one of the five longer INTERVALS in a musical SCALE, for example the INTERVAL between C and D or between E and F♯ 全音

whole·wheat /ˈhəʊlwiːt; *NAmE* ˈhoʊl-/ (*BrE also* **whole·meal**) *adj.* **wholewheat** bread or flour contains the whole grains of WHEAT, etc. including the HUSK 全麦的

who'll /huːl/ *short form* who will

whol·ly /ˈhəʊlli; *NAmE* ˈhoʊlli/ *adv.* (*formal*) completely 完全；全面；整体地 **SYN** **totally**: *wholly inappropriate behaviour* 完全失当的行为 ◇ *The government is not wholly to blame for the recession.* 这次衰退不能完全怨政府。

whom 🔑 /huːm/ *pron.* (*formal*) used instead of 'who' as the object of a verb or preposition（代替 who，用作动词或介词的宾语）谁，什么人: *Whom did they invite?* 他们邀请谁了？◇ *To whom should I write?* 我应该把信写给谁？◇ *The author whom you criticized in your review has written a reply.* 你在评论中批评的那位作者已经回信答复了。◇ *Her mother, in whom she confided, said she would support her unconditionally.* 她向母亲坦露心扉，母亲说将无条件地支持她。

▼ **GRAMMAR POINT** 语法说明

whom

- **Whom** is not used very often in spoken English. **Who** is usually used as the object pronoun, especially in questions. 在口语中，whom 不常用，通常用 who 作宾格代词，尤其在疑问句中： *Who did you invite to the party?* 你邀请了哪些人来参加聚会？
- The use of **whom** as the pronoun after prepositions is very formal. * whom 作代词置于介词后的用法非常正式： *To whom should I address the letter?* 这封信我该写给谁呢？◇ *He asked me with whom I had discussed it.* 他问我和谁讨论过此事。 In spoken English it is much more natural to use **who** and put the preposition at the end of the sentence. 在口语中，疑问词用 who，将介词置于句末更自然： *Who should I address the letter to?* 这封信我该写给谁呢？◇ *He asked me who I had discussed it with.* 他问我和谁讨论过此事。
- In defining relative clauses the object pronoun **whom** is not often used. You can either use **who** or **that**, or leave out the pronoun completely. 在限定性关系从句中，宾格代词 whom 不常用，可用 who 或 that 或干脆省去代词: *The family (who/that/whom) I met at the airport were very kind.* 我在机场遇见的这家人非常友好。
- In non-defining relative clauses **who** or, more formally, **whom** (but not *that*) is used and the pronoun cannot be left out. 在非限定性关系从句中，要用 who 或更正式的 whom（但不能用 that），而且此代词不能省略： *Our doctor, who/whom we all liked very much, retired last week.* 我们的医生上周退休了，我们都很爱戴他。 This pattern is not used very much in spoken English. 此句型在英语口语中不很常用。

whom·ever /ˌhuːmˈevə(r)/, **whom·so·ever** /ˌhuːmsəʊˈevə(r); *NAmE* ˌhuːmsoʊˈevər/ *pron.* (*literary*) used instead of 'whoever' as the object of a verb or preposition（代替 whoever，用作动词或介词的宾语）谁，无论谁: *He was free to marry whomever he chose.* 他看上了谁就可以和谁结婚。

whoop /wuːp; huːp/ *noun, verb*

■ ***noun*** a loud cry expressing joy, excitement, etc.（高兴、激动等时的）高喊，大叫: *whoops of delight* 高兴的喊叫

■ ***verb*** [I] to shout loudly because you are happy or excited（因高兴或激动）高喊，喊叫

IDM ˌ**whoop it** ˈ**up** /ˌwuːp ɪt ˈʌp; *NAmE* ˌwʊp ɪt ˈʌp/ (*informal*) **1** to enjoy yourself very much with a noisy group of people 欢闹；狂欢作乐 **2** (*NAmE*) to make people excited or enthusiastic about sth 使群情振奋；使欢欣鼓舞

whoo·pee /wʊˈpiː/ *exclamation, noun*

■ ***exclamation*** used to express happiness（表示高兴）哈哈: *Whoopee, we've won!* 哈哈，我们赢了！➲ MORE LIKE THIS 2, page R25

■ ***noun*** [U]

IDM **make** ˈ**whoopee** (*old-fashioned, informal*) to celebrate in a noisy way 狂欢庆祝

ˈ**whoopee cushion** *noun* a rubber CUSHION that makes a noise like a FART when sb sits on it, used as a joke 放屁坐垫，屁袋（坐上去发出放屁声，开玩笑用）

whoop·ing cough /ˈhuːpɪŋ kɒf; *NAmE* kɔːf/ *noun* [U] an infectious disease, especially of children, that makes them cough and have difficulty breathing 百日咳

whoops /wʊps/ *exclamation* **1** used when sb has almost had an accident, broken sth, etc.（险些出事故或造成小失误时说）哎哟: *Whoops! Careful, you almost spilt coffee everywhere.* 哎哟！小心点，你差点把咖啡洒得到处都是。**2** used when you have done sth embarrassing, said sth rude by accident, told a secret, etc.（做了尴尬事或失言后说）唉: *Whoops, you weren't supposed to hear that.* 唉，你不该听到这事的。➲ MORE LIKE THIS 2, page R25

whoosh /wʊʃ; wuːʃ/ *noun, verb*

■ ***noun*** [usually sing.] (*informal*) the sudden movement and sound of air or water rushing past（风吹）呼呼；（水流）哗哗: *a whoosh of air* 呼的一口气 ◇ *There was a whoosh as everything went up in flames.* "呼"的一声，一切都毁于火海。

■ ***verb*** [I] + **adv./prep.** (*informal*) to move very quickly with the sound of air or water rushing（空气）呼呼地移动；（水）哗哗地流 ➲ MORE LIKE THIS 3, page R25

whop·per /ˈwɒpə(r); *NAmE* ˈwɑːp-/ *noun* (*informal*) **1** something that is very big for its type 特大的（或硕大的）东西: *Pete has caught a whopper* (= a large fish). 皮特捕到了一条特大的鱼。**2** a lie 谎言；瞎话: *She's told some whoppers about her past.* 关于她的过去，她说了些谎话。

whop·ping /ˈwɒpɪŋ; *NAmE* ˈwɑːp-/ (*also* ˈ**whopping great**) *adj.* [only before noun] (*informal*) very big 巨大的；很大的: *The company made a whopping 75 million dollar loss.* 公司遭受了 7 500 万美元的巨额损失。

whore /hɔː(r)/ *noun* **1** (*old-fashioned*) a female PROSTITUTE 娼妓；妓女 **2** (*taboo*) an offensive word used to refer to a woman who has sex with a lot of men 乱搞男女关系的女人；破鞋

who're /ˈhuːə(r)/ *short form* who are

whore·house /ˈhɔːhaʊs; *NAmE* ˈhɔːrh-/ *noun* (*old-fashioned*) a BROTHEL (= a place where people pay to have sex) 妓院

whor·ing /ˈhɔːrɪŋ/ *noun* [U] (*old-fashioned*) the activity of having sex with a PROSTITUTE 嫖妓；嫖娼；宿娼

whorl /wɜːl; *NAmE* wɜːrl/ *noun* **1** a pattern made by a curved line that forms a rough circle, with smaller circles inside bigger ones 螺旋状图案；螺纹: *the whorls on your fingertips* 指纹的涡 **2** (*specialist*) a ring of leaves, flowers, etc. around the STEM of a plant 轮，轮生体（环生于植物茎部的叶、花等）

who's /huːz/ *short form* **1** who is **2** who has

W

whose 🔑 /huːz/ *det., pron.* **1** 🔑 used in questions to ask who sth belongs to（用于问句）谁的：*Whose house is that?* 那是谁的房子？◇ *I wonder whose this is.* 我不知道这是谁的。**2** 🔑 used to say which person or thing you mean（特指）那个人的，那一个的，其：*He's a man whose opinion I respect.* 他是我尊重其意见的人。◇ *It's the house whose door is painted red.* 这就是那所门涂成红色的房子。**3** 🔑 used to give more information about a person or thing（进一步提供信息时用）：*Isobel, whose brother he was, had heard the joke before.* 伊索贝尔，就是他的弟弟，以前曾经听说过这个笑话。

who·so·ever /ˌhuːsəʊˈevə(r); *NAmE* -soʊ-/ *pron.* (*old use*) = WHOEVER

ˌwho's ˈwho *noun* a list or book of facts about famous people 名人一览表；名人录：*The list of delegates attending read like a who's who of the business world.* 与会代表名单读起来像个商界名人录。**ORIGIN** From the reference book *Who's Who*, which gives information about many well-known people and what they have done. 源自汇集众多名人及其事迹的参考书《名人录》。

who've /huːv/ *short form* who have

whup /wʌp/ *verb* (-pp-) **~ sb/sth** (*informal, especially US*) to defeat sb easily in a game, a fight, an election, etc.（在比赛、斗争、选举等中）轻易打败对方

why 🔑 /waɪ/ *adv., exclamation, noun*

■ ***adv.*** **1** 🔑 used in questions to ask the reason for or purpose of sth（用于问句）为什么，为何：*Why were you late?* 你为什么迟到？◇ *Tell me why you did it.* 告诉我你为什么这样做。◇ *'I would like you to go.' **'Why me?'*** "我希望你去。" "为什么要我去呢？" ◇ (*informal*) ***Why oh why*** *do people keep leaving the door open?* 人们到底为什么总不随手关门呢？**2** 🔑 used in questions to suggest that it is not necessary to do sth（反问，表示不必）何必：*Why get upset just because you got one bad grade?* 何必因为一次成绩不好就想不开呢？◇ *Why bother to write? We'll see him tomorrow.* 还费事写信干什么？我们明天就见到他了。**3** 🔑 used to give or talk about a reason（说明理由）为什么，…的原因：*That's why I left so early.* 这就是我早早离去的原因。◇ *I know you did it—I just want to know why.* 我知道这是你干的，我只是想知道为什么。◇ ***The reason why*** *the injection needs repeating every year is that the virus changes.* 每年需要重新注射的原因是这病毒经常变化。

IDM **why ˈever** used in questions to mean 'why', expressing surprise（用于问句，语带惊讶）究竟为什么：*Why ever didn't you tell us before?* 你为什么不早告诉我们呢？**ˌwhy ˈnot?** 🔑 used to make or agree to a suggestion（提出或赞同建议）为什么不呢，好哇：*Why not write to her?* 为什么不给她写信呢？◇ *'Let's eat out.' **'Why not?'*** "咱们到外边吃去吧。" "好哇。" ◇ ***Why don't*** *we go together?* 我们为什么不一起去呢？

■ ***exclamation*** (*old-fashioned* or *NAmE*) used to express surprise, lack of patience, etc.（表示惊讶、不耐烦等）哎呀，呦，哟，嗨：*Why Jane, it's you!* 呦，简，是你呀！◇ *Why, it's easy—a child could do it!* 嗨，这容易得很，连小孩子都干得了！

■ ***noun***

IDM **the ˌwhys and (the) ˈwherefores** the reasons for sth 理由；原因；缘故：*I had no intention of going into the whys and the wherefores of the situation.* 我无意深入调查这一情况的来龙去脉。

WI *abbr.* **1** West Indies 西印度群岛 **2** /ˌdʌbljuː ˈaɪ/ Women's Institute (a British women's organization in which groups of women meet regularly to take part in various activities)（英国）妇女协会

Wicca /ˈwɪkə/ *noun* [U] a modern form of WITCHCRAFT, practised as a religion（现代）巫术宗教 ▶ **Wic·can** /ˈwɪkən/ *adj.*

wick /wɪk/ *noun, verb*

■ ***noun*** **1** the piece of string in the centre of a CANDLE which you light so that the candle burns 烛芯 **2** the piece of material in an oil lamp which absorbs the oil and which you light so that the lamp burns 灯芯

IDM **get on sb's ˈwick** (*BrE, informal*) to annoy sb 激怒（某人）；招惹（某人）

■ ***verb*** **~ sth (away)** (of a material) to take small drops of liquid from an area and move them away（指材料）吸干，吸取，吸走：*Wool socks wick away sweat.* 羊毛袜吸汗。

wicked /ˈwɪkɪd/ *adj., noun*

■ ***adj.*** (**wick·ed·er**, **wick·ed·est**) **HELP** You can also use **more wicked** and **most wicked**. 亦可用 more wicked 和 most wicked。**1** morally bad 邪恶的；缺德的 **SYN** **evil**：*a wicked deed* 伤天害理的行为 ◇ *stories about a wicked witch* 关于邪恶女巫的故事 **2** (*informal*) slightly bad but in a way that is amusing and/or attractive 淘气的；调皮的；恶作剧的 **SYN** **mischievous**：*a wicked grin* 调皮的咧嘴一笑 ◇ *Jane has a wicked sense of humour.* 简有一种恶作剧的幽默感。**3** dangerous, harmful or powerful 危险的；有害的；强大的：*He has a wicked punch.* 他出拳凶猛。◇ *a wicked-looking knife* 寒光四射的刀 **4** (*slang*) very good 极好的；很棒的：*This song's wicked.* 这支歌太棒了。➲ MORE LIKE THIS 22, page R27 ▶ **wick·ed·ly** /ˈwɪkɪdli/ *adv.*：*Martin grinned wickedly.* 马丁顽皮地咧嘴笑了笑。◇ *a wickedly funny comedy* 恶作剧式的滑稽喜剧 ◇ *a wickedly sharp blade* 寒光四射的利刃 **wick·ed·ness** /ˈwɪkɪdnəs/ *noun* [U]

■ ***noun*** **the wicked** [pl.] people who are wicked 恶人；邪恶的人 ➲ MORE LIKE THIS 24, page R28

IDM **(there's) no peace/rest for the ˈwicked** (*usually humorous*) used when sb is complaining that they have a lot of work to do（有人抱怨工作太多时说）恶人绝无平安

wicker /ˈwɪkə(r)/ *noun* [U] thin sticks of wood twisted together to make BASKETS, furniture, etc.（编制筐篮、家具等用的）柳条，枝条：*a wicker chair* 柳条椅

wick·er·work /ˈwɪkəwɜːk; *NAmE* ˈwɪkərwɜːrk/ *noun* [U] BASKETS, furniture, etc. made from wicker 柳条编制品

wicket /ˈwɪkɪt/ *noun* (in CRICKET 板球) **1** either of the two sets of three vertical sticks (called STUMPS) with pieces of wood (called BAILS) lying across the top. The BOWLER tries to hit the wicket with the ball. 三柱门 ➲ VISUAL VOCAB PAGE V47 **2** the area of ground between the two wickets 两个三柱门之间的场地

IDM **keep ˈwicket** to act as a WICKETKEEPER 防守三柱门 ➲ MORE AT STICKY *adj.*

ˈwicket gate *noun* a small gate, especially one at the side of a larger one（尤指大门旁的）小门，便门，旁门

wicket·keep·er /ˈwɪkɪtkiːpə(r)/ (*also BrE, informal* **keep·er**) *noun* (in CRICKET 板球) a player who stands behind the

▼ **EXPRESS YOURSELF 情景表达**

Giving reasons, justifying a choice 对选择作出解释

In various exams, you are asked to make a choice and give reasons for it. In conversation or in a meeting, you need to explain and justify your decisions. 在各种考试中需要作出选择并给出理由，在谈话或会议上需要对决定加以解释，可用以下表达方式：

- ***There are two main reasons** why I think it's the best option: first, there's the cost and second, the quality.* 我认为这是最好的选择，主要原因有两个：第一是成本，第二是质量。
- ***I think/believe** it's the right thing to do **because** it gives everyone a fair chance.* 我认为这么做是正确的，因为这给予每个人公平的机会。
- ***I would choose** the newer one **on the grounds that** it will last longer.* 我会选择较新的那个，因为它更加耐用。
- *Of the three houses, the largest one **seems to me** to be the best, because they need the room.* 这三栋房子中，最大的那栋在我看来是最好的，因为他们需要这么大的空间。
- *My choice would be number 3, **simply because** it's the clearest design.* 我的选择是 3 号，原因就在于它的设计最清晰。

W

WICKET in order to stop or catch the ball 三柱门守门员；捕手 ➲ VISUAL VOCAB PAGE V47

wide 🔑 /waɪd/ *adj., adv., noun*

WORD FAMILY
wide *adj., adv.*
widely *adv.*
widen *verb*
width *noun*

■ ***adj.*** (**wider**, **wid·est**)

• **FROM ONE SIDE TO THE OTHER** 从一边到另一边 **1** 🔑 measuring a lot from one side to the other 宽的；宽阔的：*a wide river* 宽阔的河 ◇ *Sam has a wide mouth.* 萨姆有一张大嘴。◇ *a jacket with wide lapels* 宽翻领夹克衫 ◇ *Her face broke into a **wide grin**.* 她满脸堆笑。**OPP** **narrow** ➲ SEE ALSO WIDTH **2** 🔑 measuring a particular distance from one side to the other …宽的；宽度为…的：***How wide** is that stream?* 那条小溪有多宽？◇ *It's about 2 metres wide.* 它大约 2 米宽。◇ *The road was just wide enough for two vehicles to pass.* 这条路的宽度刚好能让两辆车开过。

• **LARGE NUMBER/AMOUNT** 大量 **3** 🔑 including a large number or variety of different people or things; covering a large area 大量的；广泛的；范围大的：*a **wide range/choice/variety** of goods* 一系列品种繁多的 / 大量可供选择的 / 各种各样的货品 ◇ *Her music appeals to a wide audience.* 她的音乐吸引了大批的听众。◇ *Jenny has a wide circle of friends.* 珍妮交友甚广。◇ *a manager with wide experience of industry* 在工业方面经验丰富的经理 ◇ *It's the best job in **the whole wide world**.* 这是整个大千世界中最好的工作。◇ *The incident has received wide coverage in the press.* 这个事件已被新闻界广泛报道。◇ *The festival attracts people from a wide area.* 这个艺术节吸引了四面八方的人。

• **DIFFERENCE/GAP** 差距；缺口 **4** 🔑 very big 很大的：*There are wide variations in prices.* 价格的变动很大。

• **GENERAL** 广泛 **5** (only used in the comparative and superlative 仅用于比较级和最高级) general; not only looking at details 一般的；广泛的：*the wider aims of the project* 该计划更广义的宗旨 ◇ *We are talking about education **in its widest sense**.* 我们在讨论最广义的教育。

• **EYES** 眼睛 **6** fully open 睁大的；全张开的：*She stared at him with wide eyes.* 她睁大了眼睛瞪着他。

▼ **WHICH WORD?** 词语辨析

wide / broad

These adjectives are frequently used with the following nouns. 以上形容词常与下列名词连用：

wide ~	broad ~
street	shoulders
river	back
area	smile
range	range
variety	agreement
choice	outline

• **Wide** is the word most commonly used to talk about something that measures a long distance from one side to the other. **Broad** is more often used to talk about parts of the body. (Although **wide** can be used with *mouth*.) It is used in more formal or written language to describe the features of the countryside, etc. * wide 为最普通用语，指宽阔。broad 较常用以指身体部位宽、阔。（不过 wide 可与 mouth 连用。）broad 在较正式的场合或书面语中指乡村景物辽阔、开阔：*a broad river* 宽阔的河流 ◇ *a broad stretch of meadowland* 一片辽阔的草原

• Both **wide** and **broad** can be used to describe something that includes a large variety of different people or things. * wide 和 broad 均可用以表示人或事物种类很多：*a wide/broad range of products* 各种各样的产品 **Broad**, but not **wide**, can be used to mean 'general' or 'not detailed'. * broad 可表示大概、粗略、不详细，wide 无此义：*All of us are in broad agreement on this matter.* 我们大家就此事基本达成一致意见。

• **NOT CLOSE** 距离远 **7** ~ (**of sth**) far from the point aimed at 远离目标：*Her shot was wide (of the target).* 她打的枪脱了靶。

• **-WIDE** 全…范围 **8** (in adjectives and adverbs 构成形容词和副词) happening or existing in the whole of a country, etc. 全（国等）范围的：*a nationwide search* 全国性的搜查 ◇ *We need to act on a Europe-wide scale.* 我们得在全欧洲范围内采取行动。

IDM **give sb/sth a wide 'berth** to not go too near sb/sth; to avoid sb/sth 对…避而远之；退避三舍：*He gave the dog a wide berth.* 他远远避开那条狗。**wide of the 'mark** not accurate 不准确；离谱：*Their predictions turned out to be wide of the mark.* 后来发现他们的预测结果太离谱了。

■ ***adv.*** (**wider**, **wid·est**) as far or fully as possible 尽可能远地；充分地：*The door was **wide open**.* 门四敞大开。◇ *The championship is still **wide open*** (= anyone could win). 谁将获得冠军还难以预料。◇ *She had a fear of **wide-open spaces**.* 身处开阔的空地中会使她感到害怕。◇ *He stood with his legs **wide apart**.* 他站在那里，两腿大张。◇ *In a few seconds she was **wide awake**.* 片刻之间她完全醒来。◇ ***Open** your mouth **wide**.* 把嘴张大。**IDM** SEE CAST *v.*, FAR *adv.*

■ ***noun*** (*sport* 体育) a ball that has been BOWLED (= thrown) where the BATSMAN or BATTER cannot reach it（板球或棒球）歪球，坏球

ˌwide-angle 'lens *noun* a camera LENS that can give a wider view than a normal lens 广角透镜

'wide boy *noun* (*BrE, informal, disapproving*) a man who makes money in dishonest ways 骗钱者

ˌwide-'eyed *adj.* **1** with your eyes fully open because of fear, surprise, etc.（因恐惧、惊讶等）睁大眼睛的：*She stared at him in wide-eyed amazement.* 她睁大眼睛惊讶地注视着他。**2** having little experience and therefore very willing to believe, trust or accept sb/sth 天真的 **SYN** **naive**

wide·ly 🔑 /'waɪdli/ *adv.* **1** 🔑 by a lot of people; in or to many places 普遍地；广泛地；范围广地：*a widely held belief* 普遍持有的信念 ◇ *The idea is now widely accepted.* 这个思想现在已获得普遍接受。◇ *He has travelled widely in Asia.* 他在亚洲许多地方旅游过。◇ *Her books are **widely read*** (= a lot of people read them). 她写的书有众多的读者。◇ *He's an educated, **widely-read** man* (= he has read a lot of books). 他这个人有教养，博览群书。**2** 🔑 to a large degree; a lot 很大程度上；大大地：*Standards vary widely.* 程度参差不齐。

widen /'waɪdn/ *verb* **1** [I, T] to become wider; to make sth wider（使）变宽；加宽；拓宽；放宽：*Her eyes widened in surprise.* 她惊讶地睁大了眼睛。◇ **~ into sth** *Here the stream widens into a river.* 溪水在这里变宽，成了一条河。◇ **~ sth** *They may have to widen the road to cope with the increase in traffic.* 他们可能得拓宽这条道路以适应车辆的增多。**2** [I, T] to become larger in degree or range; to make sth larger in degree or range（使）扩展，程度加深，范围扩大：*the widening gap between rich and poor* 贫富之间日益扩大的差距 ◇ **~ sth** *We plan to widen the scope of our existing activities by offering more language courses.* 我们计划通过开设更多的语言课程以扩大我们现有的活动范围。◇ *The legislation will be widened to include all firearms.* 这项法规的范围将扩大到包括所有的枪支。

ˌwide-'ranging *adj.* including or dealing with a large number of different subjects or areas 覆盖面广的；内容广泛的：*The commission has been given wide-ranging powers.* 委员会被授予的权限很广。◇ *a wide-ranging discussion* 广泛的讨论

wide·screen /'waɪdskriːn/ *noun* [U] a way of presenting images on television with the width a lot greater than the height（电视）宽屏幕模式，宽荧幕 **SYN** **letterbox**：*a widescreen TV* 宽屏电视

wide·spread **AW** /'waɪdspred/ *adj.* existing or happening over a large area or among many people 分布广的；普遍的；广泛的：*widespread damage* 大面积的损坏 ◇ *The plan* *received widespread support throughout the country.* 这项计划得到了全国的普遍支持。

widg·eon /ˈwɪdʒən/ = WIGEON

widget /ˈwɪdʒɪt/ *noun* **1** (*informal*) used to refer to any small device that you do not know the name of（不知名的）小器物，小装置，小玩意儿 **2** (*business* 商) a product that does not exist, used as an example of a typical product when making calculations 典型产品（并不真实存在，作计算之用）：*Company A produces two million widgets a year.* * A 公司年产 200 万件产品。**3** (*computing* 计) a small box on a computer screen that delivers changing information, such as news items or weather reports, while the rest of the page remains the same 微件，挂件（电脑屏幕上显示不时更新的信息的小窗口）

widow /ˈwɪdəʊ; *NAmE* ˈwɪdoʊ/ *noun, verb*
■*noun* a woman whose husband has died and who has not married again 寡妇；遗孀 ➲ WORDFINDER NOTE AT OLD
■*verb* **be widowed** if sb **is widowed**, their husband or wife has died 使丧偶；使成为寡妇（或鳏夫）：*She was widowed when she was 35.* 她 35 岁时就守了寡。
▸**widowed** *adj.*: *his widowed father* 他鳏居的父亲

wid·ow·er /ˈwɪdəʊə(r); *NAmE* ˈwɪdoʊər/ *noun* a man whose wife has died and who has not married again 鳏夫

widow·hood /ˈwɪdəʊhʊd; *NAmE* ˈwɪdoʊ-/ *noun* [U] the state or period of being a widow or widower 寡居（期）；鳏居（期）

ˌ**widow's ˈpeak** *noun* hair growing in the shape of a V on sb's FOREHEAD（额前的）V 形发尖 ➲ VISUAL VOCAB PAGE V65

width 🔑 /wɪdθ; wɪtθ/ *noun* **1** 🔑 [U, C] the measurement from one side of sth to the other; how wide sth is 宽度；广度：*It's about 10 metres **in width**.* 它宽约 10 米。◇ *The terrace runs **the full width of** the house.* 露台和房子一般宽。◇ *The carpet is available in different widths.* 这款地毯有各种宽度可供选择。**2** [C] a piece of material of a particular width 某一宽度的材料：*You'll need two widths of fabric for each curtain.* 每个窗帘你需要两块这样宽的布料。**3** [C] the distance between the two long sides of a swimming pool（游泳池两长边之间的）池宽：*How many widths can you swim?* 你在游泳池里横向能游几个来回？➲ COMPARE LENGTH (1)

width·ways /ˈwɪdθweɪz; ˈwɪtθ-/ *adv.* along the width and not the length 横向地；横着：*Cut the cake in half widthways.* 将这个蛋糕横着切成两半。➲ COMPARE LENGTHWAYS

wield /wiːld/ *verb* **1** ~ **sth** to have and use power, authority, etc. 拥有，运用，行使，支配（权力等）：*She wields enormous power within the party.* 她操纵着党内大权。**2** ~ **sth** to hold sth, ready to use it as a weapon or tool 挥，操，使用（武器、工具等）SYN **brandish**: *He was wielding a large knife.* 他挥舞着一把大刀。

wie·ner /ˈwiːnə(r)/ *noun* (*NAmE*) **1** = FRANKFURTER **2** (*slang*) a word for a PENIS, used especially by children 小鸡鸡（指阴茎，尤用于儿语）

wife 🔑 /waɪf/ *noun* (*pl.* **wives** /waɪvz/) the woman that sb is married to; a married woman 妻子：*the doctor's wife* 医生的太太 ◇ *She's his second wife.* 她是他的第二个妻子。◇ *an increase in the number of working wives* 已婚职业妇女人数的增加 ➲ COLLOCATIONS AT MARRIAGE ➲ SEE ALSO FISHWIFE, HOUSEWIFE, MIDWIFE, TROPHY WIFE
IDM SEE HUSBAND *n.*, OLD, WORLD

wife·ly /ˈwaɪfli/ *adj.* (*old-fashioned* or *humorous*) typical or expected of a wife 妻子特有（或应有）的；作为人妻的；已婚妇女的：*wifely duties* 妻子的责任

ˈ**wife-swapping** *noun* [U] (*informal*) the practice of exchanging sexual partners between a group of married couples 换妻（数对夫妻聚集交换性伴侣的活动）

Wi-Fi™ /ˈwaɪ faɪ/ *noun* [U] (*computing* 计) a system for sending data over computer networks using radio waves instead of wires * Wi-Fi，无线保真（利用无线电波而非网线在计算机网络传输数据的系统）

wig /wɪɡ/ *noun, verb*
■*noun* a piece of artificial hair that is worn on the head, for example to hide the fact that a person is BALD, to cover sb's own hair, or by a judge and some other lawyers in some courts of law 假发
■*verb* (-gg-)
PHR V ˌ**wig ˈout** (*NAmE, informal*) to become very excited, very anxious or angry about sth; to go crazy 变得激动（或焦虑、生气）；发狂

wig·eon (*also* **widg·eon**) /ˈwɪdʒən/ *noun* (*pl.* **wig·eon** or **widg·eon**) a type of wild DUCK 赤颈鸭

wig·gle /ˈwɪɡl/ *verb, noun*
■*verb* [I, T] (*informal*) ~ **sth** to move from side to side or up and down in short quick movements; to make sth move in this way（使）扭动，摆动，摇动，起伏 SYN **wriggle**: *He removed his shoes and wiggled his toes.* 他脱掉鞋子，扭动着脚趾。◇ *Her bottom wiggled as she walked past.* 她屁股一扭一扭地走了过去。
■*noun* a small movement from side to side or up and down（轻微的）摆动，扭动，摇动，起伏

ˈ**wiggle room** *noun* [U] (*informal*) the chance to change sth or to understand it in a different way 回旋余地；空子：*The buyer still has some wiggle room when the deal is under contract.* 根据合同，买方在交易时仍有一定的回旋余地。◇ *The amendment leaves no wiggle room for lawmakers.* 修正案没有给立法者留下漏洞。

wig·gly /ˈwɪɡli/ *adj.* (*informal*) (of a line 线) having many curves in it 弯弯曲曲的；波浪形的；起伏的 SYN **wavy**

wight /waɪt/ *noun* (*literary* or *old use*) **1** a GHOST or other spirit 鬼；幽灵 **2** (especially following an adjective 尤用于形容词之后) a person, considered in a particular way …的人：*a poor wight* 可怜鬼

wig·wam /ˈwɪɡwæm; *NAmE* -wɑːm/ *noun* a type of tent, shaped like a DOME or CONE, used by Native Americans in the past（旧时印第安人使用的圆顶或锥形的）棚屋 ➲ SEE ALSO TEPEE

wiki /ˈwɪki/ *noun* a website that allows any user to change or add to the information it contains 维基（允许用户修改或添加信息的网站）：*There's a wiki page hosted by the conference where you can share ideas and information.* 大会建立了维基网页，供大家交流想法和共享信息。

wilco /ˈwɪlkəʊ; *NAmE* -koʊ/ *exclamation* people say **Wilco!** in communication by radio to show that they agree to do sth（无线电用语）照办，遵办

wild 🔑 /waɪld/ *adj., noun*
■*adj.* (**wild·er**, **wild·est**)
• **ANIMALS/PLANTS** 动植物 **1** 🔑 living or growing in natural conditions; not kept in a house or on a farm 自然生长的；野的；野生的：***wild animals/flowers*** 野生动物；野花 ◇ *a wild rabbit* 野生兔 ◇ *wild strawberries* 野草莓 ◇ *The plants **grow wild** along the banks of rivers.* 沿河两岸生长着野生植物。
• **SCENERY/LAND** 风景；土地 **2** 🔑 in its natural state; not changed by people 天然的；荒凉的；荒芜的：*wild moorland* 荒凉的高沼地
• **OUT OF CONTROL** 失去控制 **3** 🔑 lacking discipline or control 缺乏管教的；无法无天的；放荡的：*The boy is wild and completely out of control.* 这男孩缺乏管教，简直是无法无天。◇ *He had a wild look in his eyes.* 他的眼神很不安分。
• **FEELINGS** 感情 **4** 🔑 full of very strong feeling 感情炽烈的：*wild laughter* 开怀大笑 ◇ *The crowd **went wild**.* 群情激昂。◇ *It makes me wild* (= very angry) *to see such waste.* 看到这种浪费现象让我非常生气。
• **NOT SENSIBLE** 不合情理 **5** 🔑 not carefully planned; not sensible or accurate 盲目的；瞎抓的：*He made a wild guess at the answer.* 他胡乱猜了个答案。◇ *wild accusations* 无端的指责

• **EXCITING** 激动 **6** (*informal*) very good, enjoyable or exciting 很棒的；高兴的；令人激动的：*We had a wild time in New York.* 我们在纽约玩得痛快极了。

• **ENTHUSIASTIC** 热情 **7 ~ about sb/sth** (*informal*) very enthusiastic about sb/sth 热衷于…；狂热：*She's totally wild about him.* 她对他简直是着了迷。◇ *I'm not wild about the idea.* 我对这个想法不太感兴趣。

• **WEATHER/SEA** 天气；海洋 **8** affected by storms and strong winds 狂暴的；暴风雨的 **SYN stormy**：*a wild night* 暴风雨之夜 ◇ *The sea was wild.* 大海波涛汹涌。

▸ **wild·ness** /ˈwaɪldnəs/ *noun* [U] ➲ SEE ALSO WILDLY

IDM **beyond sb's wildest 'dreams** far more, better, etc. than you could ever have imagined or hoped for 做梦都没想到；远远出乎所料；大大超出希望 **not/never in sb's wildest 'dreams** used to say that sth has happened in a way that sb did not expect at all（表示完全出乎意料）做梦都没有，从来没有想到：*Never in my wildest dreams did I think I'd meet him again.* 我连做梦都没想到会再见他。 **run 'wild 1** to grow or develop freely without any control 变得荒芜；自由生长；任其发展：*The ivy has run wild.* 常春藤长疯了。◇ *Let your* ***imagination run wild*** *and be creative.* 让你的想象力自由驰骋发挥创意吧。**2** if children or animals **run wild**, they behave as they like because nobody is controlling them 恣意妄为；变得狂野 **wild 'horses would not drag, make, etc. sb (do sth)** used to say that nothing would prevent sb from doing sth or make them do sth they do not want to do 任何事情都不能阻止（或促使某人做某事）；八匹马拉不了某人回头 ➲ MORE AT SOW[1]

■ ***noun* 1 the wild** [sing.] a natural environment that is not controlled by people 自然环境；野生状态：*The bird is too tame now to survive* ***in the wild.*** 这只鸟养得太温驯了，现在很难在野生环境中生存。**2 the wilds** [pl.] areas of a country far from towns or cities, where few people live 偏远地区；人烟稀少的地区：*the wilds of Alaska* 阿拉斯加人烟稀少的地区 ◇ (*humorous*) *They live on a farm somewhere out* ***in the wilds.*** 他们住在边远地区的一个农场里。

ˌwild 'boar *noun* = BOAR

'wild card *noun* **1** (in card games 纸牌游戏) a card that has no value of its own and takes the value of any card that the player chooses（由持牌人自由决定牌值的）百搭牌，变牌 **2** (*sport* 体育) an opportunity for sb to play in a competition when they have not qualified in the usual way; a player who enters a competition in this way "外卡"参赛，"外卡"选手（指没有正常参赛资格而参赛）**3** (*computing* 计) a symbol that can represent any letter or number 通配符 **4** a person or thing whose behaviour or effect is difficult to predict 难以预测的人（或事物）；未知因素；未知数

wild·cat /ˈwaɪldkæt/ *adj., verb, noun*

■ ***adj.*** [only before noun] **1** a **wildcat strike** happens suddenly and without the official support of a trade/labor union （罢工）未经工会同意的，突然自发进行的 **2** (of a business or project 企业或项目) that has not been carefully planned and that will probably not be successful; that does not follow normal standards and methods（计划不周密而）不稳妥的；不按正常标准的

■ ***verb*** (**-tt-**) [I] (*NAmE*) to look for oil in a place where nobody has found any yet 勘探石油 ▸ **wild·cat·ter** *noun*

■ ***noun*** a type of small wild cat that lives in mountains and forests 野猫（生活在山区或森林里）

wilde·beest /ˈwɪldəbiːst/ *noun* (*pl.* **wilde·beest**) (*also* **gnu**) a large ANTELOPE with curved horns 牛羚；角马：*a herd of wildebeest* 一群牛羚

wil·der·ness /ˈwɪldənəs; *NAmE* -dərn-/ *noun* [usually sing.] **1** a large area of land that has never been developed or used for growing crops because it is difficult to live there 未开发的地区；荒无人烟的地区；荒野：*The Antarctic is the world's last great wilderness.* 南极洲是世界上最后一个大荒原。◇ (*NAmE*) *a* ***wilderness area*** (= one where it is not permitted to build houses or roads)（政府划定的）保留自然环境面貌地区 ◇ (*figurative*) *the barren wilderness of modern life* 现代生活贫瘠的荒漠 **2** a place that people do not take care of or control 荒芜的地方；杂草丛生处：*Their garden is a wilderness of grass and weeds.* 他们的花园杂草丛生。

IDM **in the 'wilderness** no longer in an important position, especially in politics 在野；不再当政（或掌权）

wild·fire /ˈwaɪldfaɪə(r)/ *noun* [U] **IDM** SEE SPREAD *v.*

wild·fowl /ˈwaɪldfaʊl/ *noun* [pl.] birds that people hunt for sport or food, especially birds that live near water such as DUCKS and GEESE（尤指生活在水边被人猎食的）野禽，野鸭，野鹅

ˌwild 'goose chase *noun* a search for sth that is impossible for you to find or that does not exist, that makes you waste a lot of time 徒劳的寻找；白费力气的追逐

wild·life /ˈwaɪldlaɪf/ *noun* [U] animals, birds, insects, etc. that are wild and live in a natural environment 野生动物：*Development of the area would endanger wildlife.* 开发这一地区将会危及野生动物。◇ *a* ***wildlife habitat/sanctuary*** 野生动物栖息地 / 保护区

wild·ly 🔑 /ˈwaɪldli/ *adv.* **1** 🔑 in a way that is not controlled 失控地；紊乱地：*She looked wildly around for an escape.* 她环顾四周，拼命寻找逃路。◇ *His heart was beating wildly.* 他的心脏剧烈地跳着。**2** 🔑 extremely; very 极其；非常：*The story had been wildly exaggerated.* 这件事被过分地夸大了。◇ *It is not a wildly funny play.* 这并不是一出太滑稽的戏剧。

the ˌWild 'West *noun* [sing.] the western states of the US during the years when the first Europeans were settling there, used especially when you are referring to the fact that there was not much respect for the law there 荒野西部，西大荒（开拓时期，尤指尚无法制的美国西部）

wiles /waɪlz/ *noun* [pl.] clever tricks that sb uses in order to get what they want or to make sb behave in a particular way 花招；诡计；奸计

wil·ful (*especially BrE*) (*NAmE usually* **will·ful**) /ˈwɪlfl/ *adj.* (*disapproving*) **1** [usually before noun] (*formal, disapproving* or *law* 律) (of a bad or harmful action 不友好或有害行为) done deliberately, although the person doing it knows that it is wrong 故意的；有意的；成心的：*wilful damage* 蓄意破坏 **2** determined to do what you want; not caring about what other people want 任性的；固执的；倔强的 **SYN headstrong**：*a wilful child* 任性的孩子 ▸ **wil·ful·ly** /-fəli/ *adv.* **wil·ful·ness** *noun* [U]

will 🔑 /wɪl/ *modal verb, verb, noun*

■ ***modal verb*** (*short form* **'ll** /l/, *negative* **will not**, *short form* **won't** /wəʊnt; *NAmE* woʊnt/, *pt* **would** /*weak form* wəd; *strong form* wʊd/, *short form* **'d** /d/, *negative* **would not**, *short form* **wouldn't** /ˈwʊdnt/) **1** 🔑 used for talking about or predicting the future（谈及将来）：*You'll be in time if you hurry.* 你要是抓紧一点儿就会来得及。◇ *How long will you be staying in Paris?* 你将在巴黎待多久？◇ *Fred said he'd be leaving soon.* 弗雷德说他很快就要走了。◇ *By next year all the money will have been spent.* 到明年所有的钱都将花光了。**2** 🔑 used for showing that sb is willing to do sth（表示愿意）愿，要，会，定要：*I'll check this letter for you, if you want.* 你要是愿意，我会给你查查这封信的。◇ *They won't lend us any more money.* 他们不愿再借给我们钱了。◇ *He wouldn't come—he said he was too busy.* 他不愿来，他说他太忙。◇ *We said we would keep them.* 我们说过要保存它们的。**3** 🔑 used for asking sb to do sth（烦劳别人做事时用）：*Will you send this letter for me, please?* 请你替我把这封信寄出去行吗？◇ *You'll water the plants while I'm away, won't you?* 我外出的时候请你给花草浇浇水，行不行？◇ *I asked him if he wouldn't mind calling later.* 我问他能否过会儿再来电话。**4** 🔑 used for ordering sb to do sth（命令时用）：*You'll do it this minute!* 你现在就要做这事！◇ *Will you be quiet!* 安静点儿！**5** 🔑 used for stating what you think is probably true（含有肯定的意思）：*That'll be the doctor now.* 这会儿准是医生来了。◇ *You'll have had dinner already, I suppose.* 我想，到时候你大概已经吃过饭了。**6** 🔑 used for stating what is generally true（叙述一般真理）：*If it's made of wood it will float.* 这要是木材做的就能浮在水面上。◇ *Engines won't run without lubricants.* 没有润滑油发动机就不能运转。**7** 🔑 used for

W

stating what is true or possible in a particular case（叙述在某种情况下是真实或可能的事）: *This jar will hold a kilo.* 这个罐子能盛一千克。◇ *The door won't open!* 那扇门就是打不开！**8** 🔑 used for talking about habits（谈及习惯）: *She'll listen to music, alone in her room, for hours.* 她总是独自一个人在屋里听音乐，一听就是几个小时。◇ *He would spend hours on the telephone.* 他一打电话往往就是几个小时。**HELP** If you put extra stress on the word **will** or **would** in this meaning, it shows that the habit annoys you. 在此义中如果重读 will 或 would，即表示这一习惯令人恼火：*He will comb his hair at the table, even though he knows I don't like it.* 他喜欢在桌子旁梳头，即便他知道我讨厌他这个习惯。➲ NOTE AT MODAL, SHALL

■ ***verb*** (*third person sing. pres. t.* **will**) [I] (only used in the simple present tense 仅用于简单现在时) (*old-fashioned* or *formal*) to want or like 想要；希望；愿意；喜欢：*Call it what you will, it's still a problem.* 不管怎么说，这仍然是个问题。

■ ***verb*** **1** to use the power of your mind to do sth or to make sth happen 立定志向；决心；决意：**~ sth** *As a child he had thought he could fly, if he willed it enough.* 他小时候曾经以为，只要有足够决心，想要飞就能飞起来。◇ **~ sb/sth to do sth** *She willed her eyes to stay open.* 她使劲睁着眼睛。◇ *He willed himself not to panic.* 他竭力让自己不要恐慌。**2** **~ sth | ~ that...** (*old use*) to intend or want sth to happen 想要（某事发生）: *They thought they had been victorious in battle because God had willed it.* 他们以为自己打了胜仗是上帝的旨意。**3** to formally give your property or possessions to sb after you have died, by means of a WILL (3) 立遗嘱将（财产等）赠与（某人）；立遗嘱赠与：**~ sb sth** *Joe had willed them everything he possessed.* 乔把自己拥有的一切都遗赠给了他们。◇ **~ sth (to sb)** *Joe had willed everything he possessed to them.* 乔把自己拥有的一切都遗赠给了他们。

■ ***noun*** **1** 🔑 [C, U] the ability to control your thoughts and actions in order to achieve what you want to do; a feeling of strong determination to do sth that you want to do 意志；毅力；自制力：*to have a* ***strong will*** 有坚强的意志 ◇ *to have* ***an iron will/a will of iron*** 有钢铁般的意志 ◇ *Her decision to continue shows great strength of will.* 她决心坚持下去，显示出了很大的意志力。◇ *In spite of what happened, he never lost* ***the will to live.*** 尽管如此遭遇，他从未丧失活下去的意志。◇ *The meeting turned out to be a* ***clash of wills.*** 这次会议结果成了一次意志的角力。◇ *She always wants to impose her will on other people* (= to get what she wants). 她总是想把自己的意志强加于人。➲ SEE ALSO FREE WILL, WILLPOWER **2** 🔑 [sing.] what sb wants to happen in a particular situation 意愿；心愿：*I don't want to go against your will.* 我不想违背您的意愿。◇ (*formal*) *It is God's will.* 这是上帝的旨意。**3** 🔑 (*also* **tes·ta·ment**) [C] a legal document that says what is to happen to sb's money and property after they die 遗嘱：*I ought to* ***make a will.*** 我应该立份遗嘱。◇ *My father left me the house in his will.* 我父亲在遗嘱中把这所房子遗赠给了我。➲ SEE ALSO LIVING WILL **4** **-willed** (in adjectives 构成形容词) having the type of will mentioned 有…意志的；…毅力的：*a strong-willed young woman* 意志坚强的年轻女子 ◇ *weak-willed greedy people* 意志薄弱而贪婪的人

IDM **against your 'will** 🔑 when you do not want to 不情愿地；违心地：*I was forced to sign the agreement against my will.* 我被迫违心地签了这份协议。**at 'will** whenever or wherever you like 任意；随意：*They were able to come and go at will.* 他们能够来去自由。**where there's a ˌwill there's a 'way** (*saying*) if you really want to do sth then you will find a way of doing it 有志者事竟成 **with a 'will** in a willing and enthusiastic way 愿意地；热情地；乐意地 **with the ˌbest will in the 'world** used to say that you cannot do sth, even though you really want to 尽管已尽心竭力；尽管真心愿意：*With the best will in the world I could not describe him as a good father.* 尽管我心里极想美言几句，却怎么也不能说他是位好父亲。

'will-call *noun* [U] (*NAmE*) a service by which items, especially tickets, can be paid for and then collected later 预售寄存服务（为顾客保存已付款商品，待以后领取）: *Up to the day of the event, will-call is located at the main Ticket Office.* 到活动当天为止，在主售票处提供预订票领取服务。◇ *He was standing in the will-call line to collect two tickets.* 他在预售票队列排队领取两张票。

will·ful /ˈwɪlfl/ (*NAmE*) = WILFUL

wil·lie /ˈwɪli/ = WILLY

the wil·lies /ˈwɪliz/ *noun* [pl.] (*informal*) if sth **gives you the willies**, you are frightened by it or find it unpleasant 心里发毛；心惊肉跳

will·ing 🔑 /ˈwɪlɪŋ/ *adj.* **1** 🔑 [not usually before noun] **~ (to do sth)** not objecting to doing sth; having no reason for not doing sth 愿意；乐意：*They keep a list of people (who are) willing to work nights.* 他们有一份愿意夜间工作的人的名单。◇ *I'm* ***perfectly willing*** *to discuss the problem.* 我十分乐意讨论这个问题。**2** 🔑 [usually before noun] ready or pleased to help and not needing to be persuaded; done or given in an enthusiastic way 自愿的；乐于相助的；积极肯干的：***willing helpers/volunteers*** 主动帮忙的人；志愿工作者 ◇ *willing support* 自愿的支持 ◇ *She's very willing.* 她非常积极肯干。**OPP** **unwilling** ▶ **will·ing·ly** 🔑 *adv.*: *People would willingly pay more for better services.* 有好一些的服务，人们是愿意多花钱的。◇ *'Will you help me?' 'Willingly.'* "请帮帮我好吗？""当然可以。" **will·ing·ness** 🔑 *noun* [U, sing.] **IDM** SEE GOD, SHOW *v.*, SPIRIT *n.*

will-o'-the-wisp /ˌwɪl ə ðə ˈwɪsp/ *noun* [usually sing.] **1** a thing that is impossible to obtain; a person that you cannot depend on 难以捉摸的人（或事物）；镜花水月；虚无之物 **2** a blue light that is sometimes seen at night on soft wet ground and is caused by natural gases burning 磷火；鬼火

wil·low /ˈwɪləʊ; *NAmE* ˈwɪloʊ/ *noun* **1** [C] a tree with long thin branches and long thin leaves, that often grows near water 柳；柳树 ➲ **VISUAL VOCAB** PAGE V10 ➲ SEE ALSO PUSSY WILLOW **2** [U] the wood of the willow tree, used especially for making CRICKET BATS 柳木（常用以制作板球拍）

wil·lowy /ˈwɪləʊi; *NAmE* ˈwɪloʊi/ *adj.* (*approving*) (of a person, especially a woman 人，尤指女人) tall, thin and attractive 修长苗条的；婀娜多姿的

will·power /ˈwɪlpaʊə(r)/ *noun* [U] the ability to control your thoughts and actions in order to achieve what you want to do 意志力

willy (*also* **wil·lie**) /ˈwɪli/ *noun* (*pl.* **-ies**) (*BrE*, *informal*) a word for a PENIS, used especially by children or when speaking to children 小鸡鸡（尤作儿童用语）➲ SEE ALSO WILLIES

willy-nilly /ˌwɪli ˈnɪli/ *adv.* (*informal*) **1** whether you want to or not 不管愿意不愿意；无论想要不想要：*She was forced willy-nilly to accept the company's proposals.* 她被迫无奈接受了公司的提议。**2** in a careless way without planning 随意地；乱糟糟地：*Don't use your credit card willy-nilly.* 别拿着你的信用卡随便花。

wilt /wɪlt/ *verb* **1** [I, T] **~ (sth)** if a plant or flower **wilts**, or sth **wilts** it, it bends towards the ground because of the heat or a lack of water（使）枯萎，凋谢，蔫 **SYN** **droop** **2** [I] (*informal*) to become weak or tired or less confident 变得委靡不振；发蔫；变得又累又乏；失去自信 **SYN** **flag**: *The spectators were wilting visibly in the hot sun.* 看得出观众在炎热的阳光下快支撑不住了。◇ *He was wilting under the pressure of work.* 他被工作压得喘不过气来。**3** **thou wilt** (*old use*) used to mean 'you will', when talking to one person（同一个人谈话时用，即 you will）

wilt·ed /ˈwɪltɪd/ *adj.* **wilted** vegetable leaves, for example LETTUCE leaves, have been cooked for a short time and then used in a salad（菜叶）稍煮的，焯水的

wily /ˈwaɪli/ *adj.* (**wili·er**, **wili·est**) clever at getting what you want, and willing to trick people 狡猾的；诡计多端的；爱捉弄人的 **SYN** **cunning**: *The boss is a wily old fox.* 老板是个狡猾的老狐狸。

wimp /wɪmp/ *noun, verb*

■ ***noun*** (*informal, disapproving*) a person who is not strong, brave or confident 懦夫；窝囊废 **SYN** **weed** ▶ **wimp·ish**

W

(*also* **wimpy**) *adj.*: *wimpish behaviour* 懦弱的行为

■ ***verb***

PHR V **ˌwimp ˈout (of sth)** (*informal, disapproving*) to not do sth that you intended to do because you are too frightened or not confident enough to do it 畏缩而不敢做；怯而不做

wim·ple /ˈwɪmpl/ *noun* a head covering made of cloth folded around the head and neck, worn by women in the Middle Ages and now by some NUNS（中世纪妇女和当今某些修女戴的）温帕尔头巾

win /wɪn/ *verb, noun*

■ ***verb*** (**win·ning, won, won** /wʌn/) **1** [I, T] to be the most successful in a competition, race, battle, etc.（在比赛、赛跑、战斗等中）获胜，赢：*Which team won?* 哪个队赢了？◇ **~ at sth** *to* ***win at cards/chess, etc.*** 赢牌、赢棋等 ◇ **~ against sb/sth** *France won by six goals to two against Denmark.* 法国队以六比二战胜丹麦队。◇ **~ sth** *to* ***win an election/a game/a war, etc.*** 赢得选举、比赛、战争等 ◇ *She loves to win an argument.* 她喜欢在辩论中获胜。**2** [T] to get sth as the result of a competition, race, election, etc.（在比赛、赛跑、选举等中）赢得，夺取，获得，挣得：**~ sth** *Britain won five gold medals.* 英国夺取了五块金牌。◇ *He won £3 000 in the lottery.* 他中彩得了 3 000 英镑。◇ *How many states did the Republicans win?* 共和党在多少个州的选举中获胜？◇ **~ sth from sb** *The Conservatives won the seat from Labour in the last election.* 在上次选举中保守党从工党手中夺得了这个议席。◇ **~ yourself/sb sth** *You've won yourself a trip to New York.* 你赢得了一次纽约之旅。**3** [T] **~ sth** to achieve or get sth that you want, especially by your own efforts（尤指通过自己的努力）取得，获得：*They are trying to* ***win support for*** *their proposals.* 他们在努力争取人们支持他们的建议。◇ *The company has won a contract to supply books and materials to schools.* 这家公司得到了一份向学校供应图书资料的合同。◇ *She won the admiration of many people in her battle against cancer.* 她在与癌症的对抗中赢得了许多人的钦佩。➲ SEE ALSO NO-WIN, WINNER, WINNING, WIN-WIN

IDM **you, he, etc. ˌcan't ˈwin** (*informal*) used to say that there is no acceptable way of dealing with a particular situation 怎么做都不讨好；没有令人满意的方法 **you can't win them ˈall | you ˈwin some, you ˈlose some** (*informal*) used to express sympathy for sb who has been disappointed about sth（用于勉慰）一个人不可能事事都成功，有所得就有所失 **ˈyou win** (*informal*) used to agree to what sb wants after you have failed to persuade them to do or let you do sth else（被迫表示同意时说）你赢了，我服输了：*OK, you win, I'll admit I was wrong.* 行，你赢了。我承认我错了。**win (sth) ˌhands ˈdown** (*informal*) to win sth very easily 轻易取得；唾手可得 **win sb's ˈheart** to make sb love you 赢得（某人）的爱 **ˌwin or ˈlose** whether you succeed or fail 不论成败；不管输赢；无论胜负：*Win or lose, we'll know we've done our best.* 无论胜负，我们都知道自己已尽了最大努力。➲ MORE AT DAY, SPUR *n.*

PHR V **ˌwin sb↔aˈround/ˈover/ˈround (to sth)** to get sb's support or approval by persuading them that you are right 赢得…的支持；说服；把…争取过来：*She's against the idea but I'm sure I can win her over.* 她反对这一想法，但我相信我能把她争取过来。**ˌwin sth/sb↔ˈback** to get or have again sth/sb that you had before 重新获得；把…争取回来：*The party is struggling to win back voters who have been alienated by recent scandals.* 这个政党正尽力把最近因丑闻而疏远的选民争取回来。**ˌwin ˈout/ˈthrough** (*informal*) to be successful despite difficulties（克服困难）终获成功：*It won't be easy but we'll win through in the end.* 这并不容易，但我们最终会获得成功。

■ ***noun*** a victory in a game, contest, etc.（在比赛、竞赛等中的）胜利：*two wins and three defeats* 两胜三负 ◇ *They have not had a win so far this season.* 他们这一赛季迄今还没有赢过一场。◇ *France swept to a 6–2 win over Denmark.* 法国队以 6:2 狂胜丹麦队。

wince /wɪns/ *verb* [I] **~ (at sth)** to suddenly make an expression with your face that shows that you are feeling pain or embarrassment（因痛苦或尴尬）龇牙咧嘴，皱眉蹙额：*He winced as a sharp pain shot through his left leg.* 他左腿一阵剧痛疼得他直龇牙咧嘴。◇ *I still wince when I think about that stupid thing I said.* 我想到我说过的蠢话时仍懊悔不已。➲ WORDFINDER NOTE AT EXPRESSION

▸ **wince** *noun* [usually sing.]: *a wince of pain* 痛得龇牙咧嘴

winch /wɪntʃ/ *noun, verb*

■ ***noun*** a machine for lifting or pulling heavy objects using a rope or chain 绞车；卷扬机；牵引机

■ ***verb*** **~ sb/sth + adv./prep.** to lift sb/sth up into the air using a winch（用绞车）吊起，拉起

Win·ches·ter /ˈwɪntʃɪstə(r)/ (*also* **ˌWinchester ˈrifle**) *noun* a type of long gun that fires several bullets one after the other 温切斯特连发步枪

wind[1] /wɪnd/ *noun, verb* ➲ SEE ALSO WIND[2]

■ ***noun*** **1** [C, U] (*also* **the wind**) air that moves quickly as a result of natural forces 风；气流：***strong/high winds*** 强劲的风；大风 ◇ ***gale-force winds*** 七到十级的风 ◇ *a* ***light wind*** 微风 ◇ *a* ***north/south/east/west wind*** 北风；南风；东风；西风 ◇ *a* ***chill/cold/biting wind*** *from the north* 冷飕飕的 / 寒冷的 / 刺骨的北风 ◇ *The wind is blowing from the south.* 刮的是南风。◇ *The trees were swaying* ***in the wind.*** 树在风中摇晃。◇ ***A gust of wind*** *blew my hat off.* 一阵风把我的帽子刮掉了。◇ *The weather was hot, without a* ***breath of wind.*** 天气炎热，连一丝风都没有。◇ *The wall gives some protection from the* ***prevailing wind.*** 这堵墙挡着常刮的风，起到一些保护作用。◇ *The wind is getting up* (= starting to blow strongly). 风势越来越大。◇ *The wind has dropped* (= stopped blowing strongly). 风势已经减弱。◇ ***wind speed/direction*** 风速；风向 ➲ COLLOCATIONS AT WEATHER ➲ SEE ALSO CROSSWIND, DOWNWIND, HEADWIND, TAILWIND, TRADE WINDS, WINDY

> **WORDFINDER** 联想词：breeze, buffet, calm, force, gale, gust, hurricane, prevailing, tornado

2 (*BrE*) (*NAmE* **gas**) [U] air that you swallow with food or drink; gas that is produced in your stomach or INTESTINES that makes you feel uncomfortable（随食物或饮料）吞下的气；胃气；肠气：*I can't eat beans—they give me wind.* 我不能吃豆子，吃了肚子就胀气。◇ *Try to bring the baby's wind up.* 设法让婴儿嗳气。**3** [U] breath that you need when you do exercise or blow into a musical instrument（运动或吹奏乐器时的）呼吸：*I need time to get my wind back after that run.* 我跑过之后需要时间喘口气。◇ *He kicked Gomez in the stomach, knocking the wind out of him.* 他踢了戈麦斯的肚子，把他踢得喘不上气来。➲ SEE ALSO SECOND WIND **4** [U+sing./pl. v.] (*also* **winds** [pl.]) the group of musical instruments in an ORCHESTRA that produce sounds when you blow into them; the musicians who play those instruments（管弦乐团的）管乐器，管乐器组：*music for wind and strings* 管弦乐 ◇ *The wind section played beautifully.* 管乐组吹奏得很动听。➲ COMPARE WOODWIND

IDM **break ˈwind** to release gas from your BOWELS through your ANUS 放屁 **get ˈwind of sth** (*informal*) to hear about sth secret or private 听到…的风声；获悉…的秘密消息 **get/have the ˈwind up (about sth)** (*informal*) to become/be frightened about sth 因…害怕（或忧虑）**in the ˈwind** about to happen soon, although you do not know exactly how or when 即将发生；在酝酿中 **like the ˈwind** very quickly 一阵风似的；飞快地 **put the ˈwind up sb** (*BrE, informal*) to make sb frightened 使害怕；使惊吓 **take the ˈwind out of sb's sails** (*informal*) to make sb suddenly less confident or angry, especially when you do or say sth that they do not expect 出其不意地打击某人的信心；突然减轻某人的怒气 **a wind/the winds of ˈchange** (used especially by journalists 常作新闻用语) an event or a series of events that has started to happen and will cause important changes or results 改革之风；变化的趋向：*A wind of change was blowing through the banking world.* 银行界刮起了改革之风。➲ MORE AT CAUTION *n.*, FOLLOWING *adj.*, ILL *adj.*, SAIL *v.*, STRAW, WAY *n.*

■ ***verb*** **1** [usually passive] **~ sb** to make sb unable to breathe easily for a short time 使喘不过气来；使喘大气：*He was momentarily winded by the blow to his stomach.* 他的肚子上挨了一击，一时喘不过气来。**2** **~ sb** (*BrE*) to gently hit or rub a baby's back to make it BURP (= release gas from its stomach through its mouth)（轻拍婴儿后背）使嗳气 SYN burp ➲ SEE ALSO LONG-WINDED

wind² /waɪnd/ *verb* ➲ SEE ALSO WIND¹ (**wound**, **wound** /waʊnd/) **1** [I, T] (of a road, river, etc. 路、河等) to have many bends and twists 蜿蜒；曲折而行；迂回：**+ adv./prep.** *The path wound down to the beach.* 这条小路弯弯曲曲通向海滩。◇ **~ its way + adv./prep.** *The river winds its way between two meadows.* 这条河蜿蜒流经两个牧场之间。➲ SEE ALSO WINDING **2** [T] **~ sth + adv./prep.** to wrap or twist sth around itself or sth else 卷缠；缠绕；绕成团：*He wound the wool into a ball.* 他把毛线缠绕成一团。◇ *Wind the bandage around your finger.* 用绷带把你的手指包扎起来。**3** [T, I] to make a clock or other piece of machinery work by turning a KNOB, handle, etc. several times; to be able to be made to work in this way 给（钟表等）上发条；（通过转动把手等）操作；可上发条；可通过转动把手（等）操作：**~ sth (up)** *He had forgotten to wind his watch.* 他忘了给表上发条了。◇ **~ up** *It was one of those old-fashioned gramophones that winds up.* 那是一台上弦的老式留声机。➲ SEE ALSO WIND-UP *adj.* (1) **4** [T, I] to operate a tape, film, etc. so that it moves nearer to its ending or starting position 卷绕，倒（磁带、胶卷等）：**~ sth forward/back** *He wound the tape back to the beginning.* 他把磁带倒到了开头。◇ **~ forward/back** *Wind forward to the bit where they discover the body.* 向前快进，到他们发现尸体的那一段。**5** [T] **~ sth** to turn a handle several times 转动（把手）：*You operate the trapdoor by winding this handle.* 你要转动这个手柄来操纵活动天窗。IDM SEE LITTLE FINGER ▶ **wind** *noun*: *Give the handle another couple of winds.* 再转动两下手柄。

PHR V **ˌwind ˈdown** **1** (of a person 人) to rest or relax after a period of activity or excitement 喘口气；喘息一下 SYN **unwind** **2** (of a piece of machinery 机器) to go slowly and then stop 慢下来后停住 **ˌwind sth↔ˈdown** **1** to bring a business, an activity, etc. to an end gradually over a period of time 使（业务、活动等）逐步结束：*The government is winding down its nuclear programme.* 政府在逐步取消核计划。**2** to make sth such as the window of a car move downwards by turning a handle, pressing a button, etc. 把（汽车窗玻璃等）摇下：*Can I wind my window down?* 我可以把我这边的窗户摇下来吗？ **ˌwind ˈup** (*informal*) (of a person 人) to find yourself in a particular place or situation 以…告终（或终结）：*I always said he would wind up in prison.* 我以前一直说他终归要进班房。◇ **wind up doing sth** *We eventually wound up staying in a little hotel a few miles from town.* 我们最后在离城几英里的一家小旅馆里落脚。◇ **+ adj.** *If you take risks like that you'll wind up dead.* 你要是冒那种险就会把命赔上。**ˌwind ˈup | ˌwind sth↔ˈup** to bring sth such as a speech or meeting to an end 结束（讲话、会议等）：*The speaker was just winding up when the door was flung open.* 演讲者刚要结束讲话时门突然被推开了。◇ *If we all agree, let's wind up the discussion.* 如果我们大家都同意，咱们就结束讨论吧。**ˌwind sb↔ˈup** (*BrE, informal*) to deliberately say or do sth in order to annoy sb 惹…生气；戏弄：*Calm down! Can't you see he's only winding you up?* 别激动！难道你看不出他只是在故意气你吗？◇ *That can't be true! You're winding me up.* 那不会是真的！你在故意气我。➲ RELATED NOUN WIND-UP **ˌwind sth↔ˈup** **1** to stop running a company, business, etc. and close it completely 关闭（公司、企业等）；（完全）停止营业 **2** to make sth such as the window of a car move upwards by turning a handle, pressing a button, etc. 把（汽车窗玻璃等）摇上

wind·bag /ˈwɪndbæɡ/ *noun* (*informal, disapproving*) a person who talks too much, and does not say anything important or interesting 夸夸其谈的人；空话连篇的人；话匣子

wind-blown /ˈwɪnd bləʊn; *NAmE* bloʊn/ *adj.* **1** carried from one place to another by the wind 被风吹的；随风飘的 **2** made untidy by the wind 被风刮乱的；被风吹散的：*wind-blown hair* 被风吹乱的头发

wind·break /ˈwɪndbreɪk/ *noun* a row of trees, a fence, etc. that provides protection from the wind 防风林；挡风篱；挡风墙；风障

wind·cheat·er /ˈwɪndtʃiːtə(r)/ (*old-fashioned, BrE*) (*NAmE* **wind·break·er** /ˈwɪndbreɪkə(r)/) *noun* a jacket designed to protect you from the wind 防风夹克；风衣

wind chill /ˈwɪnd tʃɪl/ *noun* [U] the effect of low temperature combined with wind on sb/sth 风寒（与风速相关的冷却作用）：*Take the **wind-chill factor** into account.* 把风寒指数考虑进去。

wind chimes /ˈwɪnd tʃaɪmz/ *noun* [pl.] a set of hanging pieces of metal, etc. that make a pleasant ringing sound in the wind 风铃；风铎

wind-down /ˈwaɪnd daʊn/ (*also* **ˌwinding-ˈdown**) *noun* [sing.] a gradual reduction in activity as sth comes to an end 逐渐减少至终止；逐步结束：*The wind-down of the company was handled very efficiently.* 公司逐步关停，处理得很有效率。

wind·er /ˈwaɪndə(r)/ *noun* a device or piece of machinery that winds sth, for example sth that winds a watch or the film in a camera 缠绕器；卷簧器；卷线机

wind·fall /ˈwɪndfɔːl/ *noun* **1** an amount of money that sb/sth wins or receives unexpectedly 意外之财；意外获得的东西：*The hospital got a sudden windfall of £300 000.* 这家医院获得了一笔 30 万英镑的意外款项。◇ *windfall profits* 意外的利润 ◇ *The government imposed a **windfall tax*** (= a tax on profits to be paid once only, not every year) *on some industries.* 政府对某些行业征收暴利税。**2** a fruit, especially an apple, that the wind has blown down from a tree 风吹落的果子（尤指苹果）

wind farm /ˈwɪnd fɑːm; *NAmE* fɑːrm/ *noun* an area of land on which there are a lot of WINDMILLS or WIND TURBINES for producing electricity 风力发电场；风电场；风力田 ➲ **WORDFINDER NOTE** AT ENERGY ➲ **COLLOCATIONS** AT ENVIRONMENT

wind gauge /ˈwɪnd ɡeɪdʒ/ *noun* = ANEMOMETER

the Win·dies /ˈwɪndɪz; -diːz/ *noun* [pl.] (*informal*) the West Indian CRICKET team 西印度群岛板球队

wind·ing /ˈwaɪndɪŋ/ *adj.* having a curving and twisting shape 曲折的；弯曲的；蜿蜒的：*a long and winding road* 漫长而曲折的道路

winding-down /ˌwaɪndɪŋ ˈdaʊn/ *noun* = WIND-DOWN

winding sheet /ˈwaɪndɪŋ ʃiːt/ *noun* (especially in the past) a piece of cloth that a dead person's body was wrapped in before it was buried（尤指旧时的）裹尸布 SYN **shroud**

wind instrument /ˈwɪnd ɪnstrəmənt/ *noun* any musical instrument that you play by blowing 管乐器；吹奏乐器 ➲ COMPARE BRASS (2), WOODWIND

wind·lass /ˈwɪndləs/ *noun* a type of WINCH (= a machine for lifting or pulling heavy objects) 绞盘；卷扬机；辘轳

wind·less /ˈwɪndləs/ *adj.* (*formal*) without wind 无风的；平静的：*a windless day* 风平浪静的一天 OPP **windy**

wind machine /ˈwɪnd məʃiːn/ *noun* **1** a machine used in the theatre or in films/movies that blows air to give the effect of wind（剧院或电影用的）造风机，风力效果机 **2** a machine used in ORCHESTRAS to produce the sound of wind（管弦乐队的）风声器，风鸣器

wind·mill /ˈwɪndmɪl/ *noun* **1** a building with machinery for GRINDING grain into flour that is driven by the power of the wind turning long arms (called SAILS) 风车磨房 ➲ **VISUAL VOCAB** PAGE V3 **2** a tall thin structure with parts that turn round, used to change the power of the wind into electricity（通过转动将风能转化为电能的）风车 **3** (*BrE*) (*NAmE* **pin·wheel**) a toy with curved plastic parts that form the shape of a flower which turns round on the end of a stick when you blow on it 玩具风车 IDM SEE TILT *v.*

W

win·dow /ˈwɪndəʊ; *NAmE* ˈwɪndoʊ/ *noun* **1** an opening in the wall or roof of a building, car, etc., usually covered with glass, that allows light and air to come in and people to see out; the glass in a window 窗；窗户；窗口；窗玻璃：*She looked out of the window.* 她向窗外看去。◇ *to open/close the window* 打开 / 关上窗户 ◇ *the bedroom/car/kitchen, etc. window* 卧室、汽车、厨房等的窗户 ◇ *a broken window* 破碎的窗玻璃 ➲ VISUAL VOCAB PAGES V18, V56 ➲ SEE ALSO BAY WINDOW, DORMER WINDOW, FRENCH WINDOW, PICTURE WINDOW, ROSE WINDOW, SASH WINDOW **2** = SHOP WINDOW: *I saw the dress I wanted in the window.* 我在橱窗里看到了我想买的连衣裙。◇ *a window display* 橱窗陈列 **3** an area within a frame on a computer screen, in which a particular program is operating or in which information of a particular type is shown（计算机屏幕的）窗口，视窗：*to create/open a window* 新建 / 打开窗口 ➲ VISUAL VOCAB PAGE V74 **4** a small area of sth that you can see through, for example to talk to sb or read sth on the other side 墙上（或信封等上）开的窗形的口；透明窗口：*There was a long line of people at the box-office window.* 在售票处窗口外排了一长队人。◇ *The address must be clearly visible through the window of the envelope.* 从信封的透明窗必须能够看清楚地址。**5** [sing.] ~ **on/into sth** a way of seeing and learning about sth 了解信息的渠道；窗口：*Television is a sort of window on the world.* 电视是了解世界的窗口。◇ *It gave me an intriguing window into the way people live.* 这为我提供了一个了解人们的生活方式的有趣窗口。**6** a time when there is an opportunity to do sth, although it may not last long 一丝机会；短暂的时机：*We now have a small window of opportunity in which to make our views known.* 我们现在有一线机会使人了解我们的观点。

IDM **fly/go out (of) the ˈwindow** (*informal*) to stop existing; to disappear completely 化为乌有；消失殆尽：*As soon as the kids arrived, order went out of the window.* 孩子们一到，一切就都乱了套。

ˈwindow box *noun* a long narrow box outside a window, in which plants are grown 窗口花坛；窗栏花箱 ➲ VISUAL VOCAB PAGE V18

ˈwindow cleaner *noun* a person whose job is to clean windows 擦窗工

ˈwindow dressing *noun* [U] **1** the art of arranging goods in shop/store windows in an attractive way 橱窗装饰艺术；橱窗设计艺术 **2** (*disapproving*) the fact of doing or saying sth in a way that creates a good impression but does not show the real facts 装饰门面；弄虚作假：*The reforms are seen as window dressing.* 这些改革被视为是装饰门面。

ˈwindow ledge *noun* = WINDOWSILL

win·dow·less /ˈwɪndəʊləs; *NAmE* -doʊ-/ *adj.* without windows 无窗的：*a tiny, windowless cell* 一间没有窗户的斗室

win·dow·pane /ˈwɪndəʊpeɪn; *NAmE* -doʊ-/ *noun* a piece of glass in a window（一块）窗玻璃 ➲ VISUAL VOCAB PAGE V18

ˈwindow shade *noun* (*NAmE*) = BLIND (1)

ˈwindow-shopping *noun* [U] the activity of looking at the goods in shop/store windows, usually without intending to buy anything 浏览橱窗（通常无意购买）：*to go window-shopping* 去逛街浏览橱窗 ➲ COLLOCATIONS AT SHOPPING

win·dow·sill /ˈwɪndəʊsɪl; *NAmE* ˈwɪndoʊ-/ (*also* **sill**, **ˈwindow ledge**) *noun* a narrow shelf below a window, either inside or outside 窗沿；窗台：*Place the plants on a sunny windowsill.* 把这些植物放在阳光充足的窗台上。➲ VISUAL VOCAB PAGE V18

wind·pipe /ˈwɪndpaɪp/ *noun* the tube in the throat that carries air to the lungs 气管 SYN **trachea** ➲ VISUAL VOCAB PAGE V64

wind·screen /ˈwɪndskriːn/ (*BrE*) (*NAmE* **wind·shield**) *noun* the window across the front of a vehicle（机动车前面的）挡风玻璃，风挡 ➲ COLLOCATIONS AT DRIVING ➲ VISUAL VOCAB PAGE V56

ˈwindscreen wiper (*BrE*) (*NAmE* **ˈwindshield wiper**) (*also* **wiper** *BrE, NAmE*) *noun* a blade with a rubber edge that moves across a windscreen to make it clear of rain, snow, etc. 挡风玻璃刮水器；风挡雨雪刷；雨刮器 ➲ VISUAL VOCAB PAGE V56

wind·shield /ˈwɪndʃiːld/ *noun* **1** (*NAmE*) (*BrE* **wind·screen**) the window across the front of a vehicle（机动车前面的）挡风玻璃，风挡 ➲ VISUAL VOCAB PAGE V56 **2** a glass or plastic screen that provides protection from the wind, for example at the front of a motorcycle（摩托车等前面的）挡风玻璃，风挡

wind·sock /ˈwɪndsɒk; *NAmE* -sɑːk/ *noun* a tube made of soft material, open at both ends, that hangs at the top of a pole, to show the direction of the wind 风向袋

wind·storm /ˈwɪndstɔːm; *NAmE* -stɔːrm/ *noun* (*NAmE*) a storm where there is very strong wind but little rain or snow 风暴

wind·surf·er /ˈwɪndsɜːfə(r); *NAmE* -sɜːrf-/ *noun* **1** (*also* **sail·board** *BrE, NAmE*) a long narrow board with a sail, that you stand on and sail across water on 帆板 **2** a person on a windsurfer 帆板运动员

wind·surf·ing /ˈwɪndsɜːfɪŋ; *NAmE* -sɜːrf-/ (*also* **board·sail·ing**) *noun* [U] the sport of sailing on water standing on a windsurfer 帆板运动：*to go windsurfing* 去玩帆板 ➲ VISUAL VOCAB PAGE V54 ▶ **wind·surf** *verb* [I]: *Most visitors come to sail or windsurf.* 游客大多是来进行帆船或帆板运动的。

wind·swept /ˈwɪndswept/ *adj.* **1** (of a place 地方) having strong winds and little protection from them 受大风吹的；当风的：*the windswept Atlantic coast* 受大风侵袭的大西洋海岸 **2** looking as though you have been in a strong wind 似被风吹散的；乱蓬蓬的：*windswept hair* 凌乱的头发

wind tunnel /ˈwɪnd tʌnl/ *noun* a large tunnel where aircraft, etc. are tested by forcing air past them（试验飞机等用的）风洞

wind turbine /ˈwɪnd tɜːbaɪn; *NAmE* tɜːrb-/ *noun* a type of modern WINDMILL used for producing electricity 风力机；风力涡轮机；风力发电机 ➲ VISUAL VOCAB PAGE V9

wind-up /ˈwaɪnd ʌp/ *adj., noun*

■ *adj.* [only before noun] **1** that you operate by turning a key or handle 装有发条的；用手柄操作的：*an old-fashioned wind-up gramophone* 装有发条的老式留声机 **2** intended to bring sth to an end 意欲结束的；终了的；收场的：*a wind-up speech* 结束语

■ *noun* (*BrE, informal*) something that sb says or does in order to be deliberately annoying, especially as a joke 戏弄人或惹人气恼的言语（或行动）

wind·ward /ˈwɪndwəd; *NAmE* -wərd/ *adj., noun*

■ *adj.* on the side of sth from which the wind is blowing 向风的；迎风的；顶风的；上风的：*the windward side of the boat* 船向风的一侧 OPP **leeward** ➲ SEE ALSO LEE (1) ▶ **wind·ward** *adv.* OPP **leeward**

■ *noun* [U] the side or direction from which the wind is blowing 向风面；迎风面；上风面：*to sail to windward* 迎风航行 ➲ COMPARE LEEWARD *n.*

windy /ˈwɪndi/ *adj.* (**wind·ier**, **windi·est**) **1** (of weather, etc. 天气等) with a lot of wind 多风的；风大的：*a windy day* 大风天 OPP **windless** **2** (of a place 地方) getting a lot of wind 当风的；受大风吹的：*windy hills* 当风的丘陵 **3** (*informal, disapproving*) (of speech 讲话) involving speaking for longer than necessary and in a way that is complicated and not clear 夸夸其谈的；空话连篇的；空洞无物的

the ˌWindy ˈCity *noun* [sing.] a name for the US city of Chicago 风城（美国芝加哥市的别称）

wine /waɪn/ *noun, verb*

■ *noun* **1** [U, C] an alcoholic drink made from the juice of

GRAPES that has been left to FERMENT. There are many different kinds of wine. 葡萄酒：*a bottle of wine* 一瓶葡萄酒 ◇ *a glass of **dry/sweet wine*** 一杯干 / 甜葡萄酒 ◇ ***red/rosé/white wine*** 红 / 玫瑰红 / 白葡萄酒 ◇ ***sparkling wine*** 汽酒 ➲ SEE ALSO TABLE WINE **2** [U, C] an alcoholic drink made from plants or fruits other than GRAPES（用植物或除葡萄以外的水果酿制的）酒，果酒：*elderberry/rice wine* 接骨木果酒；米酒 **3** [U] (*also* **wine 'red**) a dark red colour 紫红色；深红色 ➲ **MORE LIKE THIS** 15, page R26

■ ***verb***

IDM **ˌwine and 'dine (sb)** to go to restaurants, etc. and enjoy good food and drink; to entertain sb by buying them good food and drink（去餐馆等）大吃大喝；用酒宴款待：*The firm spent thousands wining and dining potential clients.* 这家公司成千上万地花费在大摆酒宴款待潜在的客户上。 ➲ **MORE LIKE THIS** 12, page R26

'wine bar *noun* a bar or small restaurant where wine is the main drink available （主要供应葡萄酒的）酒吧，小酒馆

'wine cellar (*also* **cel·lar**) *noun* an underground room where wine is stored; the wine stored in this room 酒窖；贮藏在酒窖里的酒

ˌwine 'cooler *noun* **1** (*NAmE*) a drink made with wine, fruit juice, ice and SODA WATER（用葡萄酒、果汁、冰和苏打水制成的）冰镇果酒饮料 **2 'wine cooler** a container for putting a bottle of wine in to cool it 镇酒冰壶

'wine farm *noun* (*SAfrE*) a VINEYARD (= a place where GRAPES are grown for making wine)（种植酿酒用葡萄的）葡萄园

'wine glass *noun* a glass for drinking wine from（饮葡萄酒用的）葡萄酒杯 ➲ **VISUAL VOCAB** PAGE V23

wine·grow·er /ˈwaɪngrəʊə(r); *NAmE* -groʊ-/ *noun* a person who grows GRAPES for wine（酿酒）葡萄园主

'wine gum *noun* (*BrE*) a small fruit-flavoured sweet/candy 果味软糖块

'wine list *noun* a list of wines available in a restaurant （餐馆供应的）酒单 ➲ **COLLOCATIONS** AT RESTAURANT

wine·maker /ˈwaɪnmeɪkə(r)/ *noun* a person who produces wine 葡萄酒酿造者；葡萄酒生产者 ▸ **wine·mak·ing** /ˈwaɪnmeɪkɪŋ/ *noun* [U]

win·ery /ˈwaɪnəri/ *noun* (*pl.* **-ies**) (*especially NAmE*) a place where wine is made 葡萄酒厂；酿酒厂 ➲ COMPARE VINEYARD

ˌwine 'vinegar *noun* [U] VINEGAR which is made from wine rather than from grain or apples 葡萄酒醋

wing 🔑 /wɪŋ/ *noun, verb*

■ ***noun***

• **OF BIRD/INSECT** 鸟；昆虫 **1** 🔑 [C] one of the parts of the body of a bird, insect or BAT that it uses for flying （鸟、昆虫或蝙蝠）翅膀，翼：*The swan **flapped its wings** noisily.* 天鹅大声地拍打着翅膀。◇ *wing feathers* 翅膀上的羽毛 ➲ **VISUAL VOCAB** PAGES V12, V13

• **OF PLANE** 飞机 **2** 🔑 [C] one of the large flat parts that stick out from the side of a plane and help to keep it in the air when it is flying（飞行器的）翅膀；机翼 ➲ **VISUAL VOCAB** PAGE V57

• **OF BUILDING** 建筑物 **3** [C] one of the parts of a large building that sticks out from the main part 侧翼部分；侧厅；耳房；厢房：*the east wing* 东翼楼 ◇ *the new wing of the hospital* 与医院一侧相连的新楼房

• **OF CAR** 汽车 **4** (*BrE*) (*NAmE* **fend·er**) [C] a part of a car that is above a wheel 挡泥板；翼子板：*There was a dent in the nearside wing.* 左边挡泥板上有一个凹痕。 ➲ **VISUAL VOCAB** PAGE V56

• **OF ORGANIZATION** 组织 **5** [C] one section of an organization that has a particular function or whose members share the same opinions（起某种作用或持相同观点的）派，翼 **SYN** **arm**：*the radical wing of the party* 这个政党中的激进派 ◇ *the political wing of the National Resistance Army* 国民抵抗军的政治组织 ➲ SEE ALSO LEFT WING, RIGHT WING

• **IN FOOTBALL/HOCKEY** 足球；曲棍球 **6** [C] = WINGER ➲ SEE ALSO LEFT WING, RIGHT WING **7** [C] the far left or right side of the sports field（运动场地的左右）翼，侧翼：*He plays on the wing.* 他踢边锋。

• **IN THEATRE** 剧院 **8 the wings** [pl.] the area at either side of the stage that cannot be seen by the audience（舞台上观众看不到的）边厢，翼部，侧面 ➲ **WORDFINDER NOTE** AT STAGE

IDM **get your 'wings** to pass the exams that mean you are allowed to fly a plane 获得飞行资格；通过飞行考试 **(waiting) in the 'wings** ready to take over a particular job or be used in a particular situation when needed 准备接替某工作；准备就绪 **on a ˌwing and a 'prayer** with only a very slight chance of success 只有一线成功的可能 **on the 'wing** (*literary*) (of a bird, insect, etc. 鸟、昆虫等) flying 飞行中的；飞着的 **take sb under your 'wing** to take care of and help sb who has less experience of sth than you 呵护；庇护；把…置于卵翼之下 **take 'wing** (*literary*) (of a bird, insect, etc. 鸟、昆虫等) to fly away 展翅飞翔；飞走：(*figurative*) *Her imagination took wing.* 她发挥了海阔天空的想象。 ➲ **MORE AT** CLIP *v.*, SPREAD *v.*

■ ***verb***

• **FLY** 飞 **1** [T, I] **~ (its way) + adv./prep.** (*literary*) to fly somewhere 飞；飞行：*A solitary seagull winged its way across the bay.* 一只孤零零的海鸥飞过了海湾。

• **GO QUICKLY** 快走 **2** [T] **~ its way + adv./prep.** to be sent somewhere very quickly 被迅速送往：*An application form will be winging its way to you soon.* 申请表不久将送达你处。

IDM **'wing it** (*informal*) to do sth without planning or preparing it first 临时应付；即兴；匆匆拼凑 **SYN** **improvise**：*I didn't know I'd have to make a speech—I just had to wing it.* 我不知道还得讲话，只好临场即兴发挥。

'wing back *noun* (in football (SOCCER) 足球) a player who plays near the edge of the field and who both attacks and defends 边后卫

'wing chair *noun* a comfortable chair that has a high back with pieces pointing forwards at the sides 翼状靠背扶手椅

ˌwing 'collar *noun* a high stiff shirt COLLAR for men, worn with formal clothes（男子正式服装的）翼领，燕子领

'wing commander *noun* an officer of high rank in the British AIR FORCE（英国空军的）空军中校：*Wing Commander Brian Moore* 空军中校布赖恩•穆尔

wing·ding /ˈwɪŋdɪŋ/ *noun* (*old-fashioned, NAmE, informal*) a party 聚会

winged /wɪŋd/ *adj.* **1** having wings 有翅膀的；有翼的：*winged insects* 有翼昆虫 **OPP** **wingless** **2 -winged** (in adjectives 构成形容词) having the number or type of wings mentioned 有…只翅膀的；有…翅膀的：*a long-winged bird* 长翼鸟

wing·er /ˈwɪŋə(r)/ *noun* (*also* **wing**) (*sport* 体育) either of the attacking players who play towards the side of the playing area in sports such as football (SOCCER) or HOCKEY（足球、曲棍球等）边锋队员

wing·less /ˈwɪŋləs/ *adj.* (especially of insects 尤指昆虫) without wings 无翅的；无翼的 **OPP** **winged**

'wing mirror (*BrE*) (*NAmE* **'side-view mirror**) *noun* a mirror that sticks out from the side of a vehicle and allows the driver to see behind the vehicle（车辆）侧翼后视镜 ➲ **VISUAL VOCAB** PAGE V56

'wing nut *noun* a NUT (2) for holding things in place, which has parts that stick out at the sides so that you can turn it easily 翼形螺母

wing·span /ˈwɪŋspæn/ *noun* the distance between the end of one wing and the end of the other when the wings are fully stretched 翼展：*a bird with a two-foot wingspan* 翼展为两英尺的鸟

wing·tips /ˈwɪŋtɪps/ *noun* [pl.] (*NAmE*) strong leather shoes that fasten with LACES and have an extra piece of leather with small holes in it over the toe 翼形饰孔皮鞋（鞋头有带孔盖饰）

wink /wɪŋk/ *verb, noun*

■ *verb* **1** [I] ~ (**at sb**) to close one eye and open it again quickly, especially as a private signal to sb, or to show sth is a joke 眨一只眼，眨眼示意（尤指使眼色或表示开玩笑）：*He winked at her and she knew he was thinking the same thing that she was.* 他冲她眨了眨眼，她便知道他的想法和她一样。➲ COMPARE BLINK *v.* (1) **2** [I] to shine with an unsteady light; to flash on and off 闪烁；明灭 SYN **blink**: *We could see the lights of the ship winking in the distance.* 我们看见船在远方忽明忽暗地闪着灯光。

PHR V **'wink at sth** to pretend that you have not noticed sth, especially sth bad or illegal（尤指对坏事）视而不见；睁一只眼闭一只眼

■ *noun* an act of winking, especially as a signal to sb 眨一只眼；眨眼示意；眼色：*He gave her a knowing wink.* 他向她会意地眨了一下眼睛。➲ SEE ALSO FORTY WINKS

IDM **not get/have a 'wink of sleep | not sleep a 'wink** to not be able to sleep 没合一下眼；不能入睡：*I didn't get a wink of sleep last night.* 我昨天一夜都没合眼。◇ *I hardly slept a wink.* 我几乎连个盹儿都没打。➲ MORE AT NOD *n.*, NUDGE *n.*, TIP *v.*

win·kle /'wɪŋkl/ *noun, verb*

■ *noun* (*BrE*) (*also* **peri·win·kle** *NAmE, BrE*) a small SHELLFISH, like a SNAIL, that can be eaten 滨螺，蛾螺，玉黍螺（可食用）

■ *verb* (*BrE, informal*)

PHR V **ˌwinkle sth/sb↔'out** (**of sth**) to get sth/sb out of a place or position, especially when this is not easy to do（从…处）挖出，掏出；迫使…离开（某地方或位置）**ˌwinkle sth 'out of sb** to get information from sb, especially with difficulty 从…套出（实情等）SYN **extract**: *She always manages to winkle secrets out of people.* 她总是能从别人那里探听出秘密。

Win·ne·bago™ /ˌwɪnɪ'beɪɡəʊ; *NAmE* -ɡoʊ/ *noun* (*NAmE*) (*pl.* **Win·ne·bago** or **-os**) a large vehicle designed for people to live and sleep in when they are camping; a type of RV 温内巴戈露营车；探险野营车；房车

win·ner 🔑 /'wɪnə(r)/ *noun* **1** 🔑 a person, a team, an animal, etc. that wins sth 获胜的人（或队、动物等）；优胜者：*The winners of the competition will be announced next month.* 竞赛的获胜者将于下月公布。◇ *There are no winners in a divorce* (= everyone suffers). 离婚的人都是两败俱伤。➲ WORDFINDER NOTE AT COMPETITION **2** [usually sing.] (*informal*) a thing or person that is successful or likely to be successful 成功者；可能成功的人（或事物）：*I think your idea is a winner.* 我认为你的想法能够成功。◇ *The design is very good. We could be* **onto a winner** (= we may do or produce sth successful). 这设计很好。我们的产品可能会成功。**3** [sing.] (*sport* 体育) a goal or point that causes a team or a person to win a game 制胜的一记入球；赢得比赛的一分：*Rooney scored the winner after 20 minutes.* 鲁尼在 20 分钟后射入了制胜的一球。➲ COMPARE LOSER IDM SEE PICK *v.*

win·ning 🔑 /'wɪnɪŋ/ *adj.* **1** 🔑 [only before noun] that wins or has won sth, for example a race or competition 获胜的；赢的：*the winning horse* 获胜的马 ◇ *the winning goal* 制胜的一记入球 **2** [usually before noun] attractive in a way that makes other people like you 吸引人的；动人的；迷人的；可爱的：*a winning smile* 动人的微笑 ▶ **win·ning·ly** *adv.* IDM SEE CARD *n.*

win·ning·est /'wɪnɪŋɪst/ *adj.* (*NAmE, informal*) having won the most games, races or competitions 赢得最多比赛项目的：*the winningest coach in the history of the US national team* 美国国家队历史上赢得最多项比赛的教练

'winning post *noun* (*especially BrE*) a post that shows where the end of a race is 终点柱：*to be first past the winning post* 第一个跑过终点柱

win·nings /'wɪnɪŋz/ *noun* [pl.] money that sb wins in a competition or game or by gambling（比赛、赌博中）赢得的钱

win·now /'wɪnəʊ; *NAmE* -noʊ/ *verb* ~ **sth** to blow air through grain in order to remove its outer covering (called the CHAFF) 簸，扬，风选（以去掉谷壳）

PHR V **ˌwinnow sb/sth 'out** (**of sth**) (*formal*) to remove people or things from a group so that only the best ones are left 筛选；遴选；选拔 SYN **sift**

wino /'waɪnəʊ; *NAmE* -noʊ/ *noun* (*pl.* **-os**) (*informal*) a person who drinks a lot of cheap alcohol and who has no home（无家可归的）酒鬼

win·some /'wɪnsəm/ *adj.* (*especially literary*) (of people or their manner 人或其举止) pleasant and attractive 讨人喜欢的；惹人喜爱的；楚楚动人的 SYN **engaging**: *a winsome smile* 莞尔一笑 ▶ **win·some·ly** *adv.*

win·ter 🔑 /'wɪntə(r)/ *noun, verb*

■ *noun* 🔑 [U, C] the coldest season of the year, between autumn/fall and spring 冬天；冬季：*a* **mild/severe/hard** *winter* 暖冬；严冬；隆冬 ◇ *Our house can be very cold* **in (the) winter**. 我们的房子到了冬天有时会非常冷。◇ *They worked on the building all through the winter.* 他们整个冬天都在建这座大楼。◇ *We went to New Zealand last winter.* 我们去年冬天去了新西兰。◇ *the* **winter months** 冬季的月份 ◇ *a* **winter coat** 过冬的大衣 IDM SEE DEAD *n.*

■ *verb* [I] (+ **adv./prep.**) to spend the winter somewhere 过冬：*Many British birds winter in Africa.* 许多英国的鸟在非洲过冬。➲ COMPARE OVERWINTER

ˌwinter 'sports *noun* [pl.] sports that people do on snow or ice 冬季运动（指雪上和冰上的运动）➲ VISUAL VOCAB PAGE V52

win·ter·time /'wɪntətaɪm; *NAmE* -tərt-/ *noun* [U] the period of time when it is winter 冬季；冬天；冬令：*The days are shorter in (the) wintertime.* 冬季白天较短。

ˌwinter 'vomiting bug (*also* **ˌwinter 'vomiting virus**) *noun* (*BrE*) = NOROVIRUS

win·try /'wɪntri/ *adj.* **1** typical of winter; cold 冬天的；冬令的；寒冷的：*wintry weather* 冬季的天气 ◇ *a wintry landscape* 冬景 ◇ ***wintry showers*** (= of snow) 冬季的阵雪 **2** not friendly 冷漠的；冷冰冰的 SYN **frosty**: *a wintry smile* 冷冷一笑

ˌwin-'win *adj.* [only before noun] (of a situation 局面) in which there is a good result for each person or group involved 对各方都有益的；双赢的：*This is a* ***win-win situation*** *all around.* 这是一个各得其所的局面。

wipe /waɪp/ *verb, noun*

■ *verb* **1** to rub sth against a surface, in order to remove dirt or liquid from it; to rub a surface with a cloth, etc. in order to clean it 擦；拭；抹；揩；蹭：~ **sth** (**on sth**) *Please wipe your feet on the mat.* 请在垫子上蹭一蹭脚。◇ *He wiped his hands on a clean towel.* 他用一块干净的手巾擦了擦双手。◇ ~ **sth with sth** *She was sniffing and wiping her eyes with a tissue.* 她边抽泣边用手巾纸拭擦眼泪。◇ ~ **sth + adj.** *He wiped his plate clean with a piece of bread.* 他用一块面包把碟子擦干净。**2** to remove dirt, liquid, etc. from sth by using a cloth, your hand, etc.（用布、手等）擦干净，抹掉：~ **sth** (**from/off sth**) *He wiped the sweat from his forehead.* 他擦去额头上的汗。◇ (*figurative*) *Wipe that stupid smile off your face.* 别那么傻笑啦。◇ ~ **sth away/off/up** *She wiped off her make-up.* 她把化的妆擦掉了。◇ *Use that cloth to wipe up the mess.* 用那块布把脏东西擦掉。**3** to remove information, sound, images, etc. from a computer, video, etc. 消除，抹去（计算机、录像带等上的信息）SYN **erase**: ~ **sth off** (**sth**) *You must have wiped off that programme I recorded.* 你一定是把我录制的节目给抹掉了。◇ ~ **sth** *Somebody had wiped all the tapes.* 有人把所有磁带上录制的内容都抹掉了。**4** to deliberately forget an experience because it was unpleasant or embarrassing 抹去（旧事）SYN **erase**: ~ **sth from sth** *I tried to wipe the whole episode from my mind.* 我设法把这整个经历从心中抹掉。◇ ~ **sth out** *You can never wipe out the past.* 你永远不能把过去一笔勾销。

IDM **wipe sb/sth off the ˌface of the 'earth | wipe sth off the 'map** to destroy or remove sb/sth completely 使…从地球上消失；彻底消除 **wipe the slate 'clean** to

W

agree to forget about past mistakes or arguments and start again with a relationship 把以往过错一笔勾销；一消前愆；捐弃前嫌 ➲ MORE AT FLOOR *n.*

PHR V **ˌwipe sth↔ˈdown** to clean a surface completely, using a wet cloth（用湿布）彻底揩擦干净：*She took a cloth and wiped down the kitchen table.* 她拿了一块布把厨房桌面擦得干干净净。**wipe sth off sth** to remove sth from sth 从…除掉（或抹掉）：*Billions of pounds were wiped off share prices today.* 今天的股票价格下挫造成数十亿英镑的损失。**ˌwipe ˈout** (*informal*) to fall over, especially when you are doing a sport such as SKIING or SURFING（尤指做滑雪或冲浪等体育运动时）跌倒，翻跌下来 **ˌwipe sb↔ˈout** (*informal*) to make sb extremely tired 使疲惫不堪：*All that travelling has wiped her out.* 一路舟车劳顿让她疲惫不堪。➲ SEE ALSO WIPED OUT **ˌwipe sb/sth↔ˈout** [often passive] to destroy or remove sb/sth completely 彻底消灭；全部摧毁：*Whole villages were wiped out by the earthquake.* 地震把整座整座的村庄夷为平地。◇ *Last year's profits were virtually wiped out.* 去年的利润几乎全都赔光了。◇ *a campaign to wipe out malaria* 消灭疟疾的运动 ➲ RELATED NOUN WIPEOUT

■ ***noun* 1** an act of cleaning sth using a cloth 擦；揩；拭：*Can you give the table a quick wipe?* 你把桌子快速擦一下行吗？**2** a special piece of thin cloth or soft paper that has been treated with a liquid and that you use to clean away dirt and bacteria（湿）抹布，纸巾：*Remember to take nappies and **baby wipes**.* 记住带尿布和婴儿的湿纸巾。

ˌwiped ˈout *adj.* [not before noun] (*informal*) extremely tired 十分疲劳；筋疲力尽：*You look wiped out.* 你看上去疲惫不堪。

wipe·out /ˈwaɪpaʊt/ *noun* (*informal*) **1** [U, C] complete destruction, failure or defeat 全部摧毁；彻底失败：*The party faces virtual wipeout in the election.* 这个政党在选举中面临着近乎全军覆灭。◇ *a 5–0 wipeout* * 5 比 0 的大败 **2** [C] a fall from a SURFBOARD（从冲浪板上的）跌倒，翻跌

wiper /ˈwaɪpə(r)/ *noun* = WINDSCREEN WIPER

wire 🔑 /ˈwaɪə(r)/ *noun, verb*

■ ***noun* 1** 🔑 [U, C] metal in the form of thin thread; a piece of this 金属丝；金属线；一段金属丝（或线）：*a coil of copper wire* 一卷铜丝 ◇ *a wire basket* 金属丝编织篮 ◇ *The box was fastened with a rusty wire.* 那个箱子是用生锈的铁丝捆紧的。➲ PICTURE AT CORD ➲ SEE ALSO BARBED WIRE, HIGH WIRE, TRIPWIRE **2** 🔑 [C, U] a piece of wire that is used to carry an electric current or signal 电线；导线：*overhead wires* 架空电线 ◇ *fuse wire* 保险丝 ◇ *The telephone wires had been cut.* 电话线被割断了。➲ WORDFINDER NOTE AT ELECTRICITY ➲ SEE ALSO HOT-WIRE **3 the wire** [sing.] a wire fence 金属丝编制的栅栏；铁丝网：*Three prisoners escaped by crawling under the wire.* 三个囚犯从铁丝网栅栏下钻出去越狱了。**4** [C] (*informal, especially NAmE*) = TELEGRAM：*We sent a wire asking him to join us.* 我们给他发了一份电报请他加入我们的行列。➲ SEE ALSO WIRY

IDM **get your ˈwires crossed** (*informal*) to become confused about what sb has said to you so that you think they meant sth else 误会（别人的意思）**go, come, etc. (right) down to the ˈwire** (*informal*) if you say that a situation goes **down to the wire**, you mean that the result will not be decided or known until the very end 直到最后才见分晓 **under the ˈwire** (*informal, especially NAmE*) at the last possible opportunity; just in time 在最后期限前；勉强赶得及 ➲ MORE AT LIVE² *adj.*, PULL *v.*

■ ***verb* 1 ~ sth (up)** to connect a building, piece of equipment, etc. to an electricity supply using wires 用导线给（建筑物、设备等）接通电源：*Make sure the plug is wired up correctly.* 插头一定要接对。**2 ~ sb/sth up (to sth) | ~ sb/sth to sth** to connect sb/sth to a piece of equipment 将…连接到（某设备）：*In the test, volunteers were wired up to brain monitors.* 在测试中，志愿参与者被连接到脑监测器上。**3 ~ sth (for sth)** to put a special device somewhere in order to listen secretly to other people's conversations 给…安装窃听器 SYN **bug**：*The room had been wired for sound.* 这个房间已经装上了窃听器。**4** (*especially NAmE*) to send sb a message by TELEGRAM 给（某人）打电报：**~ sth (to sb)** *He wired the news to us.* 他打电报把这个消息通知了我们。◇ **~ sb (sth)** *He wired us the news.* 他打电报把这个消息通知了我们。**5** to send money from one bank to another using an electronic system 给（某人）电汇：**~ sth (to sb)** *The bank wired the money to her.* 银行将钱电汇给了她。◇ **~ sb sth** *The bank wired her the money.* 银行将钱电汇给了她。**6 ~ sth** to join things together using wire 用金属丝把…连在一起

ˈwire cutters *noun* [pl.] a tool for cutting wire 钢丝钳；铁丝钳：*a pair of wire cutters* 一把钢丝钳 ➲ VISUAL VOCAB PAGE V21

wired /ˈwaɪəd; *NAmE* ˈwaɪərd/ *adj.* **1** connected to a system of computers（与计算机系统）联网的，连线的：*Many colleges now have wired dormitories.* 现在许多大学的学生宿舍已经联网。**2** (of glass, material, etc. 玻璃、材料等) containing wires that make it strong or stiff（为使坚挺或坚固）内含金属丝的，夹丝的 **3** (*informal*) excited or nervous; not relaxed 兴奋的；紧张不安的 **4** (*informal, especially NAmE*) under the influence of alcohol or an illegal drug（受酒精或毒品影响而）迷醉的

ˈwire fraud *noun* [U, C] FRAUD (= dishonest ways of getting money) using computers and telephones（利用计算机或电话的）远程诈骗（罪）

wire·less /ˈwaɪələs; *NAmE* ˈwaɪərləs/ *noun, adj.*

■ ***noun* 1** [C] (*old-fashioned, especially BrE*) a radio 无线电收音机：*I heard it on the wireless.* 我是从无线电收音机里听到的。**2** [U] a system of sending and receiving signals 无线电发射和接收系统；无线电报：*a message sent by wireless* 用无线电报发出的信息

■ ***adj.*** not using wires 无线的：*wireless communications* 无线通信 ▶ **wire·less·ly** *adv.*

ˌwire ˈnetting *noun* [U] wire that is twisted into a net, used especially for fences 金属丝网（尤用作栅栏）

wire·pull·er /ˈwaɪəpʊlə(r); *NAmE* ˈwaɪər-/ *noun* (*NAmE*) a person who is able to control or influence events without people realizing it 幕后牵线者；背后操纵者

ˈwire service *noun* (*especially NAmE*) an organization that supplies news to newspapers and to radio and television stations 新闻通讯社；电讯社

ˈwire strippers *noun* [pl.] a tool for removing the plastic covering from electric wires（电线）剥皮钳

wire·tap·ping /ˈwaɪətæpɪŋ; *NAmE* ˈwaɪərt-/ *noun* [U] the act of secretly listening to other people's telephone conversations by attaching a device to the telephone line（用秘密连线方法）窃听电话 ▶ **wire·tap** *verb* (-pp-) **~ sth** **wire·tap** *noun*: *the use of illegal wiretaps* 非法窃听电话 ➲ SEE ALSO TAP *n.* (4)

ˌwire ˈwool *noun* [U] (*BrE*) = STEEL WOOL

wir·ing /ˈwaɪərɪŋ/ *noun* [U] the system of wires that is used for supplying electricity to a building or machine（给建筑物或机器供电的）线路：*to check the wiring* 检查线路 ◇ *a wiring diagram* 线路图

wiry /ˈwaɪəri/ *adj.* (**wiri·er**, **wiri·est**) **1** (of a person 人) thin but strong 瘦而结实的 SYN **sinewy**：*a wiry little man* 清瘦结实的小个男子 **2** (of hair, plants, etc. 头发、植物等) stiff and strong; like wire 硬而结实的；像金属丝的

wis·dom /ˈwɪzdəm/ *noun* [U] **1** the ability to make sensible decisions and give good advice because of the experience and knowledge that you have 智慧；才智；精明：*a woman of great wisdom* 才女 ◇ *words of wisdom* 至理名言 **2 ~ of sth/of doing sth** how sensible sth is 明智：*I question **the wisdom of** giving a child so much money.* 我对给孩子这么多钱是否明智怀有疑问。**3** the knowledge that a society or culture has gained over a long period of time（社会或文化长期积累的）知识，学问：*the collective wisdom of the Native American people* 美洲原住民的集体智慧

IDM **conventional/received ˈwisdom** the view or belief that most people hold 大多数人的看法；普遍信念：*Conventional wisdom has it that riots only ever happen in cities.* 人们普遍认为，只有城市里才发生暴乱。**in his/her/its, etc. (infinite) ˈwisdom** used when you are saying

W

that you do not understand why sb has done sth（表示不理解他人的无知）以其（无限的）智慧: *The government in its wisdom has decided to support the ban.* 政府竟愚蠢到决定支持这项禁令。 ➲ MORE AT PEARL

'wisdom tooth *noun* any of the four large teeth at the back of the mouth that do not grow until you are an adult 智牙；智齿

wise 🔑 /waɪz/ *adj., verb*

■ *adj.* (**wiser**, **wis·est**) **1** 🔑 (of people 人) able to make sensible decisions and give good advice because of the experience and knowledge that you have 充满智慧的；明智的；英明的；明察善断的: *a wise old man* 智叟 ◇ *I'm* ***older and wiser*** *after ten years in the business.* 在商界混了十年之后，我变得老成聪明了。**2** 🔑 (of actions and behaviour 行动和行为) sensible; based on good judgement 明智的；高明的；有判断力的 SYN **prudent**: *a wise decision* 明智的决定 ◇ ***It was very wise to*** *leave when you did.* 你那时离开非常明智。◇ *The wisest course of action is just to say nothing.* 最明智的做法就是缄默不言。◇ *I was grateful for her wise counsel.* 我感激她为我指点迷津。▶ **wise·ly** *adv.*: *She nodded wisely.* 她聪明地点了点头。◇ *He wisely decided to tell the truth.* 他明智地决定实话实说。

IDM **be none the 'wiser | not be any the 'wiser 1** to not understand sth, even after it has been explained to you（解释之后）依然不懂，仍不明白: *I've read the instructions, but I'm still none the wiser.* 我看了用法说明，但仍然弄不明白。**2** to not know or find out about sth bad that sb has done 不知道，发现不了（某人做的坏事）: *If you put the money back, no one will be any the wiser.* 只要你把钱放回去，谁都不会察觉。 **be ˌwise after the e'vent** (*often disapproving*) to understand sth, or realize what you should have done, only after sth has happened 事后聪明；马后炮 **be/get 'wise to sb/sth** (*informal*) to become aware that sb is being dishonest 明白，察觉（某人的不轨行为）: *He thought he could fool me but I got wise to him.* 他以为能耍得了我，其实我清楚他是怎么一号人。 **put sb 'wise (to sth)** (*informal*) to inform sb about sth 告诉…（内情）；使…知道

■ *verb*

PHR V **ˌwise 'up (to sth)** (*informal*) to become aware of the unpleasant truth about a situation 意识到，觉察（令人不愉快的实情）

-wise *suffix* (in adjectives and adverbs 构成形容词和副词) **1** in the manner or direction of 以…方式；朝…方向: *likewise* 同样 ◇ *clockwise* 顺时针方向 **2** (*informal*) concerning 关于；在…方面: *Things aren't too good businesswise.* 业务方面的情况不太好。

wise·acre /'waɪzeɪkə(r)/ *noun* (*old-fashioned, informal, especially NAmE*) a person who is annoying because they are very confident and think they know a lot 自以为无所不知的人；自以为是的人

wise·crack /'waɪzkræk/ *noun* (*informal*) a clever remark or joke 俏皮话；风凉话 ▶ **wise·crack** *verb* [I, T]: (**+ speech**) *He plays a wisecracking detective.* 他扮演一位满嘴俏皮话的侦探。

'wise guy *noun* **1** (*informal, disapproving, especially NAmE*) a person who speaks or behaves as if they know more than other people 自以为无所不知的人；万事通 SYN **know-all 2** (*US, slang*) a member of the Mafia 黑手党成员

'wise woman *noun* (*old use*) a woman with knowledge of traditional medicines and magic（深谙传统医术和幻术的）神婆，巫婆

wish 🔑 /wɪʃ/ *verb, noun*

■ *verb* **1** 🔑 [T] (not usually used in the present progressive tense 通常不用于现在进行时) to want sth to happen or to be true even though it is unlikely or impossible 希望（不大可能的事）发生；怀着（不可能实现的）愿望: **~ (that)...** *I wish I were taller.* 我要是个子高一些就好了。◇ (*BrE also*) *I wish I was taller.* 我要是个子高一些就好了。◇ *I wish I hadn't eaten so much.* 我倒希望我没有吃这么多。◇ *'Where is he now?' '****I only wish*** *I knew!'* "他现在在哪儿？" "我要是知道就好了！" ◇ *I wish you wouldn't leave your clothes all over the floor.* 我真希望你不把衣服丢得满地都是。◇ **~ sb/sth/yourself + adj.** *He's dead and it's no use wishing him alive again.* 他死了，希望他死而复生是无济于事的。◇ **~ sb/sth/yourself + adv./prep.** *She wished herself a million miles away.* 她恨不得自己远在百万英里之外。**2** 🔑 [I, T] (*especially BrE, formal*) to want to do sth; to want sth to happen 希望（做某事）；想要（某事发生）: *You may stay until morning,* ***if you wish.*** 如果你愿意，你可以一直待到早晨。◇ *'I'd rather not talk now.' '(****Just****)* ***as you wish.****'* "现在我最好还是不说话。" "悉听尊便。" ◇ **~ to do sth** *This course is designed for people wishing to update their computer skills.* 这门课程是为想要提高电脑技术的人而设的。◇ *I wish to speak to the manager.* 我想跟经理说话。◇ *I don't wish* (= I don't mean) *to be rude, but could you be a little quieter?* 我不想无礼，但请您安静一点儿好吗？ ◇ **~ sb sth** *She could not believe that he wished her harm.* 她不能相信他希望她受到伤害。◇ **~ sb/sth to do sth** *He was not sure whether he wished her to stay or go.* 他说不准他到底是希望她留下还是离开。 ➲ MORE LIKE THIS 26, page R28 **3** 🔑 [I] **~ (for sth)** to think very hard that you want sth, especially sth that can only be achieved by good luck or magic 盼望；企求；想要: *She shut her eyes and wished for him to get better.* 她闭上眼睛盼祷他好起来。◇ *If you wish really hard, maybe you'll get what you want.* 心诚则灵。◇ *It's no use wishing for the impossible.* 企求不可能的事情是徒劳无益的。◇ *He has everything he could possibly wish for.* 他可能想要的一切东西他都有了。**4** 🔑 [T] to say that you hope that sb will be happy, lucky, etc. 祝；祝愿: **~ sb sth** *I wished her a happy birthday.* 我祝她生日快乐。◇ *Wish me luck!* 祝我交好运吧！◇ **~ sb well** *We wish them both well in their retirement.* 我们祝愿他们两位退休后颐养天年。 ➲ MORE LIKE THIS 33, page R28

IDM **I 'wish!** (*informal*) used to say that sth is impossible or very unlikely, although you wish it were possible 但愿如此（但不可能或不大可能） SYN **if only**: *'You'll have finished by tomorrow.' 'I wish!'* "你到明天就完成了。" "但愿如此！"

PHR V **ˌwish sth a'way** to try to get rid of sth by wishing it did not exist 从心里竭力摆脱；希望…不再存在 **'wish sb/sth on sb** (*informal*) (used in negative sentences 用于否定句) to want sb to have sth unpleasant 想让…有（不愉快的事）: *I wouldn't wish something like that on my worst enemy.* 即使是我的死对头，我也不想他出那样的事。

▼ **GRAMMAR POINT** 语法说明

wish

- After the verb **wish** in sense 1, a past tense is always used in a *that* clause. 动词 wish 作第 1 义时，后面的 that 从句总是用过去时: *Do you wish (that) you had a better job?* 你希望有个更好的工作吗？ In more formal English, especially in *NAmE*, many people use *were* after *I, he, she, it* instead of *was.* 在更正式的英语，尤其是美式英语中，许多人在 I、he、she、it 之后用 were，而不用 was: *I wish he* ***were*** *here tonight.* 要是他今晚在这儿就好了。

■ *noun* **1** 🔑 [C] a desire or a feeling that you want to do sth or have sth 愿望；希望: **~ (to do sth)** *She expressed a wish to be alone.* 她表示希望一个人待着。◇ *He* ***had no wish to*** *start a fight.* 他无意挑衅。◇ *His dearest wish* (= what he wants most of all) *is to see his grandchildren again.* 他最大的愿望是能再次见到自己的孙子孙女。◇ **~ for sth** *I can understand her wish for secrecy.* 我可以理解她想保守秘密的愿望。◇ **~ that...** *It was her dying wish that I should have it.* 她的临终愿望是把这东西留给我。**2** 🔑 [C] a thing that you want to have or to happen 想要的东西；希望的事: *to carry out sb's wishes* 实现某人的愿望 ◇ *I'm sure that you will get your wish.* 我相信你会心想事成。◇ *She married* ***against*** *her parents'* ***wishes.*** 她违背父母的愿望嫁给了别的人。 ➲ SEE ALSO DEATH WISH **3** 🔑 [C] an attempt to make sth happen by thinking hard about it, especially in stories when it often happens by magic 愿；心愿: *Throw some money in the fountain and* ***make a wish.*** 往喷泉里扔

W

些钱，许个愿。◇ *The genie granted him three wishes.* 精灵答应满足他三个心愿。◇ *The prince's* **wish came true.** 王子的愿望实现了。**4** **wishes** [pl.] ~ (**for sth**) used especially in a letter or card to say that you hope that sb will be happy, well or successful（书信或贺卡等中的）祝愿，祝福：*We all send our* **best wishes** *for the future.* 我们都对未来致以最好的祝愿。◇ *Give my good wishes to the family.* 请替我向全家致意。◇ **With best wishes** (= for example, at the end of a letter) 祝好（如信中结尾语）

IDM **if wishes were ˌhorses, beggars would/might ˈride** (*saying*) wishing for sth does not make it happen 想有不见得就有；愿望不等于事实 **your wish is my comˈmand** (*humorous*) used to say that you are ready to do whatever sb asks you to do 悉听阁下吩咐 **the wish is father to the ˈthought** (*saying*) we believe a thing because we want it to be true 希望什么就相信什么

wish·bone /ˈwɪʃbəʊn; *NAmE* -boʊn/ *noun* a V-shaped bone between the neck and breast of a chicken, DUCK, etc. When the bird is eaten, this bone is sometimes pulled apart by two people, and the person who gets the larger part can make a wish. 叉骨，许愿骨（吃禽肉时两人将颈与胸之间的V形骨拉开，得较大块者可许愿）

ˌwishful ˈthinking *noun* [U] the belief that sth that you want to happen is happening or will happen, although this is actually not true or very unlikely 不实际的幻想；一厢情愿：*I've got a feeling that Alex likes me, but that might just be wishful thinking.* 我感觉亚历克斯喜欢上我了，但那可能只是我一厢情愿的想法。

ˈwishing well *noun* a WELL that people drop a coin into and make a wish（投币）许愿井

ˈwish list *noun* (*informal*) all the things that you would like to have, or that you would like to happen 希望一览表（指所有希望得到的东西或全部希望发生的事情）

wishy-washy /ˈwɪʃi wɒʃi; *NAmE* wɑːʃi; wɔːʃi/ *adj.* (*informal, disapproving*) **1** not having clear or firm ideas or beliefs（思想或信仰）稀里糊涂的，不清楚的，不坚定的：*a wishy-washy liberal* 不坚定的自由主义者 **2** not bright in colour（颜色）浅的，淡的：*a wishy-washy blue* 淡淡的蓝色 ➲ MORE LIKE THIS 11, page R26

wisp /wɪsp/ *noun* ~ (**of sth**) **1** a small, thin piece of hair, grass, etc.（头发、草等的）小绺，小绺，小把，小束 **2** a long thin line of smoke or cloud（烟、云等的）一缕

wispy /ˈwɪspi/ *adj.* consisting of small, thin pieces; not thick 一绺绺的；一缕缕的；成束的；纤细的：*wispy hair/clouds* 一缕缕头发 / 云彩 ◇ *a wispy beard* 一绺绺胡须

wis·teria /wɪˈstɪəriə; *NAmE* -ˈstɪr-/ (*also* **wis·taria** /wɪˈsteəriə; *NAmE* -ˈster-/) *noun* [U] a climbing plant with bunches of pale purple or white flowers that hang down 紫藤属植物

W

wist·ful /ˈwɪstfl/ *adj.* thinking sadly about sth that you would like to have, especially sth in the past that you can no longer have 伤感的；（对已不可能发生之事）徒然神往的：*a wistful smile* 伤感的微笑 ▸ **wist·ful·ly** /-fəli/ *adv.*: *She sighed wistfully.* 她伤感地叹息。◇ *'If only I had known you then,' he said wistfully.* "要是我那时认识你就好了。" 他向往地说道。**wist·ful·ness** *noun* [U]

wit /wɪt/ *noun* **1** [U, sing.] the ability to say or write things that are both clever and amusing 措辞巧妙的能力；风趣；才思：*to have a* **quick/sharp/dry/ready wit** 才思敏捷；敏锐机智；假装正经的诙谐；头脑机敏 ◇ *a woman of wit and intelligence* 才思敏捷、聪颖的女子 ◇ *a book full of the* **wit and wisdom** *of his 30 years in politics* 一本有关他 30 年政治生涯中才思与智慧的书 **2** [C] a person who has the ability to say or write things that are both clever and amusing 才思敏捷说话诙谐的人；机智幽默的人：*a well-known wit and raconteur* 一位闻名遐迩、妙语连珠的故事大王 **3** **wits** [pl.] your ability to think quickly and clearly and to make good decisions 理解力；颖悟力；头脑；智力：*He needed all his wits to find his way out.* 他需要绞尽脑汁找到出路。◇ *The game was a long* **battle of wits**. 这场游戏是长时间的斗智。◇ *Kate paused and* **gathered her wits**. 凯特停下来恢复一下理智。◇ *a chance to* **pit your wits against** (= compete with, using your intelligence) *our quiz champion* 用你的智慧同我们的知识竞赛冠军进行较量的机会 **4** **-witted** (in adjectives 构成形容词) having the type of intelligence mentioned 有…智慧的；头脑…的：*a quick-witted group of students* 一群头脑聪明的学生 **5** [U] ~ **to do sth** the intelligence or good sense to know what is the right thing to do（正确判断的）能力，智力；明智：*At least you had the wit to ask for help.* 你起码还能意识到要求救。◇ *It should not be* **beyond the wit of man** *to resolve this dispute.* 解决这一纠纷应当是人力所能及的事。➲ SEE ALSO WITLESS

> **WORD FAMILY**
> **wit** *noun*
> **witty** *adj.*
> **witticism** *noun*
> **outwit** *verb*

IDM **be at your wits' ˈend** to be so worried by a problem that you do not know what to do next 智穷计尽；全然不知所措 **be frightened/scared/terrified out of your ˈwits** to be very frightened 吓得魂不附体 **have/keep your ˈwits about you** to be aware of what is happening around you and ready to think and act quickly 时刻保持头脑冷静；随机应变 **to ˈwit** (*old-fashioned, formal*) you use **to wit** when you are about to be more exact about sth that you have just referred to 也就是说；即：*Pilot error, to wit failure to follow procedures, was the cause of the accident.* 飞行员的失误，即没有遵守操作程序，是事故的原因。➲ MORE AT LIVE[1]

witch /wɪtʃ/ *noun* **1** a woman who is believed to have magic powers, especially to do evil things. In stories, she usually wears a black pointed hat and flies on a BROOMSTICK. 女巫；巫婆 **2** (*disapproving*) an ugly unpleasant old woman 丑老太婆 IDM SEE BREW *n.*

witch·craft /ˈwɪtʃkrɑːft; *NAmE* -kræft/ *noun* [U] the use of magic powers, especially evil ones 巫术；（尤指）妖术，魔法

ˈwitch doctor *noun* (especially in Africa) a person who is believed to have special magic powers that can be used to heal people（尤指非洲的）巫医 ➲ COMPARE MEDICINE MAN

ˈwitch hazel *noun* [U] a liquid that is used for treating injuries on the skin 金缕梅酊剂（用于治疗皮肤创伤）

ˈwitch-hunt *noun* (*usually disapproving*) an attempt to find and punish people who hold opinions that are thought to be unacceptable or dangerous to society（对被认为持不为社会所接受或危及社会政见者的）搜捕，政治迫害

the ˈwitching hour *noun* [sing.] the time, late at night, when it is thought that magic things can happen 半夜三更；魔幻之事发生的时刻

Wite·out™ /ˈwaɪtaʊt/ *noun* [U] (*NAmE*) a white liquid that you use to cover mistakes that you make when you are writing or typing, and that you can write on top of; a type of CORRECTION FLUID 惠陶特修正液 ➲ SEE ALSO WHITE-OUT

with /wɪð; wɪθ/ *prep.* HELP For the special uses of **with** in phrasal verbs, look at the entries for the verbs. For example **bear with sb/sth** is in the phrasal verb section at **bear**. * with 在短语动词中的特殊用法见有关动词词条。如 bear with sb/sth 在词条 bear 的短语动词部分。**1** in the company or presence of sb/sth 和…在一起；和；同；跟：*She lives with her parents.* 她同父母住在一起。◇ *I have a client with me right now.* 我现在有个客户。◇ *a nice steak with a bottle of red wine* 一份美味牛排再加上一瓶红葡萄酒 **2** having or carrying sth 有；具有；带有：*a girl with* (= who has) *red hair* 一位红发女郎 ◇ *a jacket with a hood* 带风帽的短上衣 ◇ *He looked at her with a hurt expression.* 他带着受伤害的神情看着她。◇ *They're both in bed with flu.* 他们双双患流感卧病在床。◇ *a man with a suitcase* 提行李箱的男子 **3** using sth 用；使用；以；借：*Cut it with a knife.* 用刀把它切开。◇ *It is treated with acid before being analysed.* 对它先用酸处理再进行分析。**4** used to say what fills, covers, etc. sth（表示以某物填充、覆盖等）：*The bag was stuffed with dirty clothes.* 袋子里塞满了脏衣服。◇ *Sprinkle the dish with salt.* 在这盘菜上撒上盐。**5**

in opposition to sb/sth; against sb/sth 与…对立；反对：*to fight with sb* 与某人打架 ◇ *to play tennis with sb* 与某人打网球 ◇ *at war with a neighbouring country* 与邻国交战 ◇ *I had an argument with my boss.* 我跟老板吵了一架。**6** 🔑 concerning; in the case of 关于；对于；对…来说：*Be careful with the glasses.* 小心这些玻璃杯。◇ *Are you pleased with the result?* 你对结果满意吗？◇ *Don't be angry with her.* 别生她的气。◇ *With these students it's pronunciation that's the problem.* 对这些学生来说，成问题的是发音。**7** 🔑 used when considering one fact in relation to another（涉及一事与另一事的关系）：*She won't be able to help us with all the family commitments she has.* 她有这么多家务事，帮不了我们。◇ *It's much easier compared with last time.* 这与上次相比容易得多。**8** 🔑 including 包括；还有：*The meal with wine came to $20 each.* 包括酒这顿饭每人 20 美元。◇ *With all the lesson preparation I have to do I work 12 hours a day.* 加上必须的备课在内，我每天工作 12 个小时。**9** 🔑 used to show the way in which sb does sth（表示行为方式）：*He behaved with great dignity.* 他举止庄重威严。◇ *She sleeps with the window open.* 她爱开着窗户睡觉。◇ *Don't stand with your hands in your pockets.* 站着的时候别把双手插在口袋里。**10** 🔑 because of; as a result of 因为；由于；作为…的结果：*She blushed with embarrassment.* 她难为情得脸红了。◇ *His fingers were numb with cold.* 他的手指冻麻了。**11** 🔑 because of sth and as it happens 由于；随着：*The shadows lengthened with the approach of sunset.* 随着太阳西沉，影子越来越长。◇ *Skill comes with practice.* 熟能生巧。**12** in the same direction as sth 与…方向一致；顺着：*Marine mammals generally swim with the current.* 海洋哺乳动物一般顺水而游。**13** 🔑 used to show who has possession of or responsibility for sth 由…持有；由…负责：*The keys are with reception.* 钥匙在服务台。◇ *Leave it with me.* 把这交给我吧。**14** 🔑 employed by; using the services of 为…工作；受雇于；利用…的服务：*She acted with a touring company for three years.* 她在一巡回剧团里演出了三年。◇ *I bank with HSBC.* 我的钱存在汇丰银行里。**15** showing separation from sth/sb（表示分离）：*I could never part with this ring.* 我永远也不摘掉这枚戒指。◇ *Can we dispense with the formalities?* 我们可以免去这些客套吗？**16** despite sth 虽然；尽管：*With all her faults I still love her.* 尽管她有种种缺点，我依然爱着她。**17** used in exclamations（用于感叹）：*Off to bed with you!* 你给我睡觉去！◇ *Down with school!* 取缔学校！

IDM **be 'with me/you** (*informal*) to be able to understand what sb is talking about 能理解…讲的话：*Are you with me?* 你明白我说的话吗？◇ *I'm afraid I'm not quite with you.* 对不起，我不太懂你的意思。**be 'with sb (on sth)** to support sb and agree with what they say 支持；与…站在一起；同意…说的话：*We're all with you on this one.* 在这个问题上我们都支持你。**'with it** (*informal*) **1** knowing about current fashions and ideas 时新；时髦 **SYN** **trendy**: *Don't you have anything more with it to wear?* 难道你没有更时髦一点儿的衣服穿？**2** understanding what is happening around you 明白周围情况；敏感 **SYN** **alert**: *You don't seem very with it today.* 你今天脑瓜子似乎不太管用。**with 'that** straight after that; then 紧接着；随即；然后：*He muttered a few words of apology and with that he left.* 他低声叽咕了几句道歉的话，然后就走了。

with·draw 🔑 /wɪð'drɔː; wɪθ'd-/ *verb* (**with·drew** /-'druː/, **with·drawn** /-'drɔːn/) **1** 🔑 [I, T] to move back or away from a place or situation; to make sb/sth do this（使）撤回，撤离 **SYN** **pull out (of sth)**: *Government troops were forced to withdraw.* 政府部队被迫撤走了。◇ **~ (sb/sth) (from sth)** *Both powers withdrew their forces from the region.* 两个大国都把部队撤离了这个地区。◇ *She withdrew her hand from his.* 她把手从他的手里抽了回来。**2** 🔑 [T] to stop giving or offering sth to sb 停止提供；不再给予：**~ sth** *Workers have threatened to withdraw their labour* (= go on strike). 工人扬言要罢工。◇ *He withdrew his support for our campaign.* 他停止了对我们运动的支持。◇ **~ sth from sth** *The drug was* **withdrawn from sale** *after a number of people suffered serious side effects.* 这药因许多人服后产生严重副作用而被停止销售。**3** 🔑 [I, T] to stop taking part in an activity or being a member of an organization; to stop sb/sth from doing these things（使）退出：**~ (from sth)** *There have been calls for Britain to withdraw from the EU.* 一直有人呼吁英国退出欧盟。◇ **~ sb/sth (from sth)** *The horse had been withdrawn from the race.* 那匹马被停赛了。**4** 🔑 [T] **~ sth (from sth)** to take money out of a bank account 提，取（银行账户中的款）：*I'd like to withdraw £250 please.* 劳驾，我想提取 250 英镑。➲ COLLOCATIONS AT FINANCE **5** 🔑 [T] **~ sth** (*formal*) to say that you no longer believe that sth you previously said is true 收回，撤回，撤销（说过的话）**SYN** **retract**: *The newspaper withdrew the allegations the next day.* 这家报纸第二天收回了这些说法。**6** [I] **~ (from sth) (into sth/yourself)** to become quieter and spend less time with other people 脱离（社会）；不与人交往：*She's beginning to withdraw into herself.* 她开始变得不爱与人交往了。

with·draw·al /wɪð'drɔːəl; wɪθ'd-/ *noun* **1** [U, C] the act of moving or taking sth away or back 撤走；收回；取回：*the withdrawal of support* 不再支持 ◇ *the withdrawal of the UN troops from the region* 联合国部队从该地区的撤离 ◇ *the withdrawal of a product from the market* 从市场上召回一种产品 **2** [U] the act of no longer taking part in sth or being a member of an organization 不再参加；退出（组织）：*his withdrawal from the election* 他从选举中退出 ◇ *a campaign for Britain's withdrawal from the EU* 争取英国退出欧盟的运动 **3** [C] the act of taking an amount of money out of your bank account（从银行账户中）提款，取款：*You can* **make withdrawals** *of up to $250 a day.* 你一天可以从银行账户中提取最多不超过 250 美元。➲ WORDFINDER NOTE AT BANK ➲ COLLOCATIONS AT FINANCE **4** [U] the period of time when sb is getting used to not taking a drug that they have become ADDICTED to, and the unpleasant effects of doing this 戒毒过程；脱瘾期：*I got* **withdrawal symptoms** *after giving up smoking.* 我戒烟之后出现了脱瘾症状。➲ WORDFINDER NOTE AT DRUG **5** [C, usually sing., U] the act of saying that you no longer believe that sth you have previously said is true（对说过的话）收回，撤回 **SYN** **retraction**: *The newspaper published a withdrawal the next day.* 报纸第二天发表了撤销声明。**6** [U] (*psychology* 心) the behaviour of sb who wants to be alone and does not want to communicate with other people 退缩；孤僻

with·drawn /wɪð'drɔːn/ *adj.* not wanting to talk to other people; extremely quiet and shy 沉默寡言的；怕羞的；内向的

wither /'wɪðə(r)/ *verb* **1** [I, T] **~ (sth)** if a plant **withers** or sth **withers** it, it dries up and dies（使）枯萎，凋谢：*The grass had withered in the warm sun.* 这些草在温暖的阳光下枯死了。**2** [I] **~ (away)** to become less or weaker, especially before disappearing completely 萎缩；（尤指渐渐）破灭，消失：*All our hopes just withered away.* 我们所有的希望都渐渐破灭了。

withered /'wɪðəd; *NAmE* -ərd/ *adj.* [usually before noun] **1** (of plants 植物) dried up and dead 干枯的；枯萎的 **SYN** **shrivelled**: *withered leaves* 枯叶 **2** (of people 人) looking old because they are thin and weak and have very dry skin 衰老憔悴的；枯槁的；干瘪的 **3** (of parts of the body 身体部位) thin and weak and not fully developed because of disease 瘦弱的；发育不良的；病态的：*withered limbs* 干瘪的四肢

wither·ing /'wɪðərɪŋ/ *adj.* (of a look, remark, etc. 神情、话语等) intended to make sb feel silly or ashamed 尖刻的；使人难堪的；令人无地自容的：*withering scorn* 使人难堪的轻蔑 ◇ *She gave him a withering look.* 她极其蔑视地看了他一眼。▶ **wither·ing·ly** *adv.*

with·ers /'wɪðəz; *NAmE* -ərz/ *noun* [pl.] the highest part of a horse's back, between its shoulders 鬐甲（马肩胛骨间隆起部分）

with·hold /wɪð'həʊld; wɪθ'h-; *NAmE* -'hoʊld/ *verb* (**with·held**, **with·held** /-'held/) **~ sth (from sb/sth)** (*formal*) to refuse to give sth to sb 拒绝给；不给 **SYN** **keep back**: *She was accused of withholding information from the police.* 她被指控对警方知情不报。

W

with'holding tax *noun* [C, U] (in the US) an amount of money that an employer takes out of sb's income as tax and pays directly to the government（美国由雇主从员工收入中扣除并直接交给政府的）须扣税款 ➲ COMPARE PAY AS YOU EARN

with·in /wɪ'ðɪn/ *prep., adv.*

■ ***prep.*** **1** before a particular period of time has passed; during a particular period of time 不出（某段时间）；在（某段时间）之内：*You should receive a reply within seven days.* 你会在七天之内收到答复。◇ *The ambulance arrived* ***within minutes of*** *the call being made.* 打电话后几分钟内救护车就到了。◇ *Two elections were held* ***within the space of*** *a year.* 在一年的时间之内举行了两次选举。**2** not further than a particular distance from sth 不出（某段距离）；在（某段距离）之间：*a house within a mile of the station* 离车站不到一英里的一所房子 ◇ *Is it* ***within walking distance****?* 那里步行走得到吗？**3** inside the range or limits of sth 不出（某范围或限度）；在（某范围）之内：*That question is not within the scope of this talk.* 那个问题不在本次会谈范围之内。◇ *We are now within range of enemy fire.* 我们现在处于敌人的火力射程以内。◇ *He finds it hard to live within his income* (= without spending more than he earns). 他觉得靠自己的收入生活难以为继。**4** (*formal*) inside sth/sb 在…里；在…内部：*The noise seems to be coming from within the building.* 吵闹声像是从楼房里传出来的。◇ *There is discontent within the farming industry.* 农业界内部存在不满。

■ ***adv.*** (*formal*) inside 在里面；在内部：*Cleaner required. Apply within.* (= on a sign) 招聘清洁工。应聘者请进。

with·out /wɪ'ðaʊt/ *prep., adv.*

■ ***prep.*** **1** not having, experiencing or showing sth 没有；缺乏：*They had gone two days without food.* 他们两天没吃东西了。◇ *He found the place without difficulty.* 他毫不费力地找到了那地方。◇ *She spoke without much enthusiasm.* 她说话冷冰冰的。**2** not in the company of sb 不和…在一起；无…相伴：*Don't go without me.* 别甩下我就走。**3** not using or taking sth 不用；不拿；不带：*Can you see without your glasses?* 你不戴眼镜能看见吗？◇ *Don't go out without your coat.* 别不穿大衣就出去。**4** not doing the action mentioned 不（做某事）；无；没：**~ doing sth** *He left without saying goodbye.* 他不辞而别。◇ *You can't make an omelette without breaking eggs.* 你不可能不打破鸡蛋就做成煎蛋卷。◇ ***Without wanting to*** *criticize, I think you could have done better.* (= used before you make a critical comment) 我不是想要批评谁，只是认为你本可以做得更好一些。◇ **~ sb doing sth** *The party was organized without her knowing anything about it.* 聚会已操办妥当，她却一无所知。

■ ***adv.*** not having or showing sth 没有；缺乏：*Do you want a room with a bath or one without?* 你要不要带洗澡间的房间？◇ *If there's none left we'll have to* ***do without****.* 如果没有剩余的我们就只得将就了。◇ *I'm sure we'll* ***manage without****.* 我相信我们能凑合的。

W

ˌwith-'profit (*also* **ˌwith-'profits**) *adj.* (*BrE*) used to describe an insurance policy or an investment where the amount paid includes a share in the company's profits（保单或投资）分红的，共享利润的

with·stand /wɪð'stænd; wɪθ's-/ *verb* (**with·stood**, **with·stood** /-'stʊd/) **~ sth** (*formal*) to be strong enough not to be hurt or damaged by extreme conditions, the use of force, etc. 承受；抵住；顶住；经受住 SYN **resist**, **stand up to**：*The materials used have to be able to withstand high temperatures.* 所使用的材料必须能够耐高温。◇ *They had withstood siege, hunger and deprivation.* 他们经受了围困、饥饿和贫穷。

wit·less /'wɪtləs/ *adj.* silly or stupid; not sensible 愚蠢的；不明事理的 SYN **foolish**

IDM **be scared/bored 'witless** (*informal*) to be extremely frightened or bored 被吓破了胆；乏味得要命

wit·ness /'wɪtnəs/ *noun, verb*

■ ***noun***

• **PERSON WHO SEES STH** 目睹者 **1** (*also* **eye·wit·ness**) [C] a person who sees sth happen and is able to describe it to other people 目击者；见证人：*Police have appealed for witnesses to the accident.* 警方呼吁这起事故的目击者出来作证。◇ *a witness to the killing* 杀人案的目击证人 ➲ WORDFINDER NOTE AT ACCIDENT ➲ COLLOCATIONS AT CRIME, JUSTICE

• **IN COURT** 法庭上 **2** [C] a person who gives evidence in court 证人：*a* ***defence/prosecution witness*** 被告的 / 控方的证人 ◇ ***to appear as*** *(a)* ***witness for the defence/prosecution*** 出庭为被告 / 控方作证

• **OF SIGNATURE** 签名 **3** [C] a person who is present when an official document is signed and who also signs it to prove that they saw this happen 见证人；联署人：*He was one of the witnesses at our wedding.* 他是我们婚礼的证婚人之一。

• **OF RELIGIOUS BELIEFS** 宗教信仰 **4** [U] evidence of a person's strong religious beliefs, that they show by what they say and do in public 见证（以言行证实信仰）➲ SEE ALSO JEHOVAH'S WITNESS

IDM **be (a) 'witness to sth 1** (*formal*) to see sth take place 目击，看见（某事发生）：*He has been witness to a terrible murder.* 他目击了一起残忍的凶杀事件。**2** to show that sth is true; to provide evidence for sth 证明…真实；为…提供证据：*His good health is a witness to the success of the treatment.* 他身体健康证明这种疗法是成功的。**bear/give 'witness (to sth)** to provide evidence of the truth of sth 为…作证；证明

▼ SYNONYMS 同义词辨析

witness

observer • onlooker • passer-by • bystander • eyewitness

These are all words for a person who sees sth happen. 以上各词均指目睹事情发生的人。

witness a person who sees sth happen and is able to describe it to other people; a person who gives evidence in a court of law 指目击者、见证人、证人：*Police have appealed for* ***witnesses to*** *the accident.* 警方呼吁这起事故的目击者出来作证。

observer a person who sees sth happen 指观察者、目击者：*According to observers, the plane exploded shortly after take-off.* 据目击者说，飞机起飞后不久就爆炸了。

onlooker a person who watches sth that is happening but is not involved in it 指旁观者：*A crowd of onlookers gathered at the scene of the crash.* 在撞车地点聚集了一大群围观者。

passer-by a person who is going past sb/sth by chance, especially when sth unexpected happens 指路人、过路的人，尤指意想不到的事发生时碰巧路过的：*Police asked passers-by if they had witnessed the accident.* 警察询问过路的人是否目击了这次事故。

bystander a person who is near and can see what is happening when sth such as an accident or fight takes place 指现场目击者、旁观者：*Three innocent bystanders were killed in the crossfire.* 三名无辜的旁观者在交火中丧生。

eyewitness a person who has seen a crime or accident and can describe it afterwards 指犯罪或事故现场的目击者、见证人

PATTERNS

- a witness/an observer/an onlooker/a passer-by/a bystander/an eyewitness **sees** sth
- an observer/an onlooker/a passer-by/a bystander **witnesses** sth

■ ***verb***

• **SEE STH** 看到 **1** [T] **~ sth** to see sth happen (typically a crime or an accident) 当场看到，目击（尤指罪行或事故）：*She was shocked by the violent scenes she had witnessed.* 她被亲眼目睹的暴虐场面惊呆了。◇ *Police have* *appealed for anyone who witnessed the incident to contact them.* 警方呼吁凡是目击这一事件的人与他们联系。◇ *We are now witnessing an unprecedented increase in violent crime.* 我们现在亲眼看到暴力犯罪空前增多。➲ SYNONYMS AT NOTICE

• **OF TIME/PLACE** 时间；地点 **2** [T] **~ sth** to be the place, period, organization, etc. in which particular events take place 是发生…的地点（或时间、组织等）；见证：*Recent years have witnessed a growing social mobility.* 近年来人们的社会流动性越来越大。◇ *The retail trade is witnessing a sharp fall in sales.* 零售业的销售额在急剧下降。

• **SIGNATURE** 签署 **3** [T] **~ sth** to be present when an official document is signed and sign it yourself to prove that you saw this happen（为正式文件的签署）作证，联署：*to witness a signature* 联署作证 ➲ WORDFINDER NOTE AT DOCUMENT

• **BE SIGN/PROOF** 迹象；证据 **4** [T, I, usually passive] to be a sign or proof of sth 是…的迹象；为…的证据：**~ sth** *There has been increasing interest in her life and work, as* **witnessed by** *the publication of two new biographies.* 从两部新传记的出版可以看出，人们对她的生活和工作越来越感兴趣。◇ **~ to sth** *The huge attendance figures for the exhibition witness to a healthy interest in modern art.* 从展览会参观人数之多可以看出，人们对现代艺术具有浓厚兴趣。**5** [T] **~ sth** (*formal*) used when giving an example that proves sth you have just said（摆证据）…就是证据，看…就知道：*Authentic Italian cooking is very healthy—witness the low incidence of heart disease in Italy.* 正宗的意大利烹饪对健康非常有益，在意大利心脏病发病率低就是证据。

• **TO RELIGIOUS BELIEFS** 宗教信仰 **6** [I] **~ (to sth)** (*especially NAmE*) to speak to people about your strong religious beliefs（为宗教信仰）做见证 SYN **testify**

'witness box (*BrE*) (*NAmE* **'witness stand**) (*also* **stand** *BrE, NAmE*) *noun* the place in court where people stand to give evidence（法庭上的）证人席 ➲ COLLOCATIONS AT JUSTICE

wit·ter /ˈwɪtə(r)/ *verb* [I] **~ (on) (about sth)** (*BrE, informal, usually disapproving*) to talk about sth unimportant and boring for a long time 唠叨；夸夸其谈：*What's he wittering on about?* 他在唠叨什么？

wit·ti·cism /ˈwɪtɪsɪzəm/ *noun* a clever and amusing remark 妙语；俏皮话；诙谐语

wit·ting·ly /ˈwɪtɪŋli/ *adv.* (*formal*) in a way that shows that you are aware of what you are doing 有意地；故意地；明知地 SYN **intentionally**：*It was clear that, wittingly or unwittingly, he had offended her.* 很显然，不管是有意还是无意，他反正得罪了她。OPP **unwittingly**

witty /ˈwɪti/ *adj.* (**wit·tier, wit·ti·est**) able to say or write clever, amusing things 言辞诙谐的；巧妙的；妙趣横生的；机智的：*a witty speaker* 幽默的演讲人 ◇ *a witty remark* 机智的话 ➲ SYNONYMS AT FUNNY ▶ **wit·tily** *adv.* **wit·ti·ness** *noun* [U]

wives /waɪvz/ PL. OF WIFE

wiz·ard /ˈwɪzəd; *NAmE* -ərd/ *noun* **1** (in stories) a man with magic powers（传说中的）男巫，术士 **2** a person who is especially good at sth 行家；能手；奇才：*a* **computer/financial, etc. wizard** 计算机、金融等奇才 **3** (*computing* 计) a program that makes it easy to use another program or perform a task by giving you a series of simple choices 向导（程序）

wiz·ard·ry /ˈwɪzədri; *NAmE* -ərd-/ *noun* [U] a very impressive and clever achievement; great skill 杰出的成就；非凡的才能：*electronic wizardry* 电子方面的非凡才能 ◇ *The second goal was sheer wizardry.* 第二记入球真是神奇。

wiz·ened /ˈwɪznd/ *adj.* looking smaller and having many folds and lines in the skin, because of being old（由于年老）干瘪的，多皱的，干枯的 SYN **shrivelled**：*a wizened little man* 干瘪的小老头 ◇ *wizened apples* 皱瘪的苹果

WLAN /ˌdʌblju: ˈlæn/ *abbr.* (*computing* 计) wireless local area network (a system for communicating by computer within a large building or group of buildings, that does not use wires) 无线局域网（全写为 wireless local area network）➲ SEE ALSO LAN, WAN

WLTM *abbr.* would like to meet (used in personal advertisements)（用于个人广告）愿意见面，希望见面

WMD /ˌdʌblju: em ˈdi:/ *abbr.* WEAPON OF MASS DESTRUCTION 大规模杀伤性武器

woad /wəʊd; *NAmE* woʊd/ *noun* [U] a blue substance that people used to paint their bodies and faces with in ancient times 靛蓝（古时人们用来涂染身体和脸）

wob·ble /ˈwɒbl; *NAmE* ˈwɑ:bl/ *verb, noun*

■ ***verb*** **1** [I, T] to move from side to side in an unsteady way; to make sth do this（使）摇摆，摇晃：*This chair wobbles.* 这把椅子不稳。◇ (*figurative*) *Her voice wobbled with emotion.* 她激动得声音发颤。◇ **~ sth** *Don't wobble the table—I'm trying to write.* 别摇桌子，我在写字呢。**2** [I] + **adv./prep.** to go in a particular direction while moving from side to side in an unsteady way 一摇一摆地走：*He wobbled off on his bike.* 他摇摇晃晃地骑着自行车走了。**3** [I] to hesitate or lose confidence about doing sth 犹豫不决；信心动摇：*Yesterday the president showed the first signs of wobbling over the issue.* 昨天总统第一次在这个问题上表现得有些摇摆不定。

■ ***noun*** **1** [usually sing.] a slight unsteady movement from side to side 松动；摇晃：*The handlebars developed a wobble.* 这车把松动摇晃了。**2** a moment when you hesitate or lose confidence about sth 犹豫不决；信心动摇：*The team is experiencing a mid-season wobble.* 这支队正处于赛季中期的不稳定状态。

wobble·board /ˈwɒblbɔ:d; *NAmE* ˈwɑ:blbɔ:rd/ *noun* a musical instrument consisting of a piece of board which is shaken to produce low sounds, originally played by Australian Aborigines 晃动板（原澳大利亚土著乐器，晃动发低音）

wob·bly /ˈwɒbli; *NAmE* ˈwɑ:bli/ *adj., noun*

■ ***adj.*** (*informal*) **1** moving in an unsteady way from side to side 摇摆的；摇摇晃晃的：*a chair with a wobbly leg* 一条腿不稳的椅子 ◇ *a wobbly tooth* 松动的牙齿 ◇ *He's still a bit wobbly after the operation* (= not able to stand firmly). 他动了手术之后仍然有点儿站不稳。**2** not firm or confident 颤动的；不稳的；不自信的 SYN **shaky**：*the wobbly singing of the choir* 唱诗班发颤的歌声 ◇ *The evening got off to a wobbly start.* 这次晚会一开始就不顺当。

■ ***noun***

IDM **throw a 'wobbly** (*BrE, informal*) to suddenly become very angry or upset 勃然大怒；发脾气

wodge /wɒdʒ; *NAmE* wɑ:dʒ/ *noun* **~ (of sth)** (*BrE, informal*) a large piece or amount of sth 大块；大堆；大量：*a thick wodge of ten-pound notes* 厚厚一沓十英镑钞票

woe /wəʊ; *NAmE* woʊ/ *noun* (*old-fashioned* or *humorous*) **1 woes** [pl.] the troubles and problems that sb has 麻烦；问题；困难：*financial woes* 财政困难 ◇ *Thanks for listening to my woes.* 谢谢您听我诉说不幸的遭遇。**2** [U] great unhappiness 痛苦；苦恼；悲伤；悲哀 SYN **misery**：*a tale of woe* 悲惨的故事

IDM **ˌwoe be'tide sb | 'woe to sb** (*formal* or *humorous*) a phrase that is used to warn sb that there will be trouble for them if they do sth or do not do sth（用以警告某人会有麻烦）…就要倒霉，…将会遭殃：*Woe betide anyone who gets in her way!* 谁挡住她的路谁就会遭殃！**ˌwoe is 'me!** *exclamation* (*old use* or *humorous*) a phrase that is used to say that you are very unhappy 我好苦哇！

woe·be·gone /ˈwəʊbɪɡɒn; *NAmE* ˈwoʊbɪɡɔ:n; -ɡɑ:n/ *adj.* (*formal*) looking very sad（神情）悲伤的，忧伤的；愁眉苦脸的 SYN **miserable**：*a woebegone expression* 悲伤的表情

woe·ful /ˈwəʊfl; *NAmE* ˈwoʊfl/ *adj.* **1** [usually before noun] very bad or serious; that you disapprove of 糟糕的；严重的；不合意的 SYN **deplorable**：*She displayed a woeful ignorance of the rules.* 她对这些条例表现出可悲的无知。**2** (*literary* or *formal*) very sad 悲惨的；忧伤的：*a woeful face* 忧伤的面孔 ◇ *woeful tales of broken romances* 破裂爱情的悲惨故事 ▶ **woe·ful·ly** /ˈwəʊfəli; *NAmE* ˈwoʊfəli/ *adv.*

W

wog /wɒɡ; *NAmE* wɑːɡ/ *noun* **1** (*BrE, taboo, slang*) a very offensive word for a person who does not have white skin 外国佬（对有色人种的蔑称）**2** (*AustralE, taboo, slang*) an offensive word for a person from southern Europe or whose parents came from southern Europe 南蛮子（对南欧人或其后裔的蔑称）**3** (*AustralE, informal*) an illness, usually one that is not very serious 病；小病：*A flu wog struck.* 突患流感。

wok /wɒk; *NAmE* wɑːk/ *noun* (*from Chinese*) a large pan shaped like a bowl, used for cooking food, especially Chinese food 炒菜锅；镬子 ➲ VISUAL VOCAB PAGE V28

woke PAST TENSE OF WAKE

woken PAST PART. OF WAKE

wolds /wəʊldz; *NAmE* woʊldz/ *noun* [pl.] used in the names of places in Britain for an area of high open land（用于英国的地名）丘陵：*the Yorkshire Wolds* 约克郡丘陵

wolf /wʊlf/ *noun, verb*

■ *noun* (*pl.* **wolves** /wʊlvz/) a large wild animal of the dog family, that lives and hunts in groups 狼：*a pack of wolves* 一群狼

IDM **keep the 'wolf from the door** (*informal*) to have enough money to avoid going hungry; to stop sb feeling hungry 勉强度日；糊口 **throw sb to the 'wolves** to leave sb to be roughly treated or criticized without trying to help or defend them 弃…于险境而不顾；见死不救 **a wolf in sheep's 'clothing** a person who seems to be friendly or harmless but is really an enemy 披着羊皮的狼 ➲ MORE AT CRY *v.*, LONE

■ *verb* ~ sth (**down**) (*informal*) to eat food very quickly, especially by putting a lot of it in your mouth at once 大口地快吃；狼吞虎咽 SYN **gobble**

wolf·hound /ˈwʊlfhaʊnd/ *noun* a very large tall dog with long hair and long legs, originally used for hunting wolves 猎狼犬：*an Irish wolfhound* 爱尔兰猎狼犬

wolf·ish /ˈwʊlfɪʃ/ *adj.* (*especially literary*) like a wolf 似狼的：*wolfish yellow eyes* 狼一般的黄眼睛 ◇ (*figurative*) *a wolfish grin* (= showing sexual interest in sb) 淫荡的露齿笑 ▶ **wolf·ish·ly** *adv.*

'wolf whistle *noun* a whistle with a short rising note and a long falling note, used by sb, usually a man, to show that they find sb else attractive, especially sb passing in the street 挑逗呼哨（尤指男子在街上向美貌女子吹的）：*She was fed up with the builders' wolf whistles each morning.* 每天早上都有建筑工人冲她挑逗地吹口哨，她烦都烦死了。▶ **'wolf-whistle** *verb* [I, T] ~ (**sb**)

wol·ver·ine /ˈwʊlvəriːn/ *noun* a wild animal that looks similar to a small bear, with short legs, long brown hair and a long tail. Wolverines live in cold, northern areas of Europe and North America. 狼獾

wolves PL. OF WOLF

woman /ˈwʊmən/ *noun* (*pl.* **women** /ˈwɪmɪn/) **1** [C] an adult female human 成年女子；妇女：*men, women and children* 男人、女人和儿童 ◇ *a 24-year-old woman* * 24 岁的女子 ◇ *I prefer to see a woman doctor.* 我希望让女医生给我看病。**2** [U] female humans in general（泛指）女性：(*informal*) *She's all woman!* (= has qualities that are typical of women) 她是典型的女人！**3** [C] (in compounds 构成复合词) a woman who comes from the place mentioned or whose job or interest is connected with the thing mentioned 来自…（或做…、喜欢…等）的女子：*an Englishwoman* 英格兰女人 ◇ *a businesswoman* 女商人 ◇ *a Congresswoman* 女议员 ◇ *a horsewoman* 女骑师 ➲ NOTE AT GENDER **4** [C] a female worker, especially one who works with her hands（尤指做手工劳动的）女工：*We used to have a woman to do the cleaning.* 我们曾雇过一位女工打扫卫生。**5** [sing.] (*old-fashioned*) a rude way of addressing a female person in an angry or important way（对女人无礼的称呼）娘儿们：*Be quiet, woman!* 安静，你这个臭娘儿们！**6** [C] (*sometimes disapproving*) a wife or sexual partner 妻子；女朋友；女相好：*He's got a new woman in his life.* 他生命中又有了一个女人。➲ SEE ALSO FALLEN WOMAN, KEPT WOMAN, OTHER WOMAN

IDM **be your own 'man/'woman** to act or think independently, not following others or being ordered 独立自主：*Working for herself meant that she could be her own woman.* 独立工作意味着她能够自主。➲ MORE AT HEART, HELL, HONEST, MAN *n.*, PART *n.*, POSSESSED, SUBSTANCE, WORLD

woman·hood /ˈwʊmənhʊd/ *noun* [U] (*formal*) **1** the state of being a woman, rather than a girl 成年女子的状态：*He watched his daughters grow to womanhood.* 他看着自己的女儿们都长大成人了。**2** women in general（统称）妇女：*the womanhood of this country* 这个国家的妇女 ➲ COMPARE MANHOOD

woman·ish /ˈwʊmənɪʃ/ *adj.* (*disapproving*) (especially of a man 尤指男子) behaving in a way that is more suitable for a woman; more suitable for women than men 脂粉气的；娘娘腔的；更适合女性的：*He has a womanish manner.* 他举手投足像个女人。◇ *a womanish novel* 女性小说

woman·iz·ing (*BrE also* **-is·ing**) /ˈwʊmənaɪzɪŋ/ *noun* [U] (*disapproving*) the fact of having sexual relationships with many different women 玩弄女性；沉溺于女色 SYN **philandering** ▶ **woman·izer, -iser** *noun*

woman·kind /ˈwʊmənkaɪnd/ *noun* [U] (*old-fashioned, formal*) women in general（统称）女人，女性 ➲ COMPARE MANKIND

woman·ly /ˈwʊmənli/ *adj.* (*approving*) behaving, dressing, etc. in a way that people think is typical of or very suitable for a woman 女性特有的；女子般的；适合女人的 SYN **feminine**：*womanly qualities* 女子的特性 ◇ *a soft womanly figure* 婀娜多姿的体态 ▶ **woman·li·ness** *noun* [U]

womb /wuːm/ *noun* the organ in women and female animals in which babies develop before they are born 子宫 SYN **uterus** ➲ WORDFINDER NOTE AT PREGNANT

wom·bat /ˈwɒmbæt; *NAmE* ˈwɑːm-/ *noun* an Australian animal like a small BEAR, that carries its young in a POUCH (= a pocket of skin) on the front of the mother's body 毛鼻袋熊（体形像熊的澳大利亚有袋动物）

women·folk /ˈwɪmɪnfəʊk; *NAmE* -foʊk/ *noun* [pl.] (*formal* or *humorous*) all the women in a community or family, especially one that is led by men（一个集体或家庭的，尤指由男人领导的）女人们，妇女们：*The male hunters brought back the food for their womenfolk to cook.* 男猎手们带回食物让他们的女人烹调。➲ COMPARE MENFOLK

women's lib·ber /ˌwɪmɪnz ˈlɪbə(r)/ *noun* (*old-fashioned, informal, often disapproving*) a person who supports Women's Liberation (2) 妇解分子；支持妇女解放运动的人

,women's libe'ration *noun* [U] (*old-fashioned*) **1** (*informal* **women's lib** /ˌwɪmɪnz ˈlɪb/) the freedom of women to have the same social and economic rights as men 妇女解放 **2 Women's Liberation** (*also informal* **Women's Lib**) the movement that aimed to achieve equal social and economic rights for women 妇女解放运动

'women's studies *noun* [U+sing./pl. v.] the study of women and their role in history, literature and society 女性研究（研究女性及其在历史、文学和社会中的作用）：*to major in women's studies* 主修女性研究

womens·wear /ˈwɪmɪnzweə(r); *NAmE* -wer/ *noun* [U] (used especially in shops/stores) clothes for women（尤用于商店）女式服装，女装

won PAST TENSE, PAST PART. OF WIN

won·der /ˈwʌndə(r)/ *verb, noun*

■ *verb* **1** [T, I] to think about sth and try to decide what is true, what will happen, what you should do, etc. 想知道；想弄明白；琢磨：**~ who, where, etc....** *I wonder who she is.* 我在想她到底是谁。◇ *I was just beginning to wonder where you were.* 我刚才正琢磨你上哪儿了呢。◇ **~ (about sth)** *'Why do you want to know?' 'No particular reason. I was just wondering.'* "你为什么想要知道？" "没有特殊原因。我就是想搞清楚。" ◇ *We were wondering about* *next April for the wedding.* 我们寻思着下个四月举行婚礼可好。◇ **+ speech** *'What should I do now?' she wondered.* "我现在该怎么办呢？" 她自忖道。**2** [T] **~ if, whether...** used as a polite way of asking a question or asking sb to do sth（礼貌地提问或请人做事时说）：*I wonder if you can help me.* 不知您是否能帮我的忙？◇ *I was wondering whether you'd like to come to a party.* 不知您能否来参加聚会。**3** [I, T] to be very surprised by sth 感到诧异；非常惊讶：**~ (at sth)** *She wondered at her own stupidity.* 她没想到自己竟会这样愚蠢。◇ (*BrE, informal*) *He's gone and left us to do all the work, **I shouldn't wonder*** (= I wouldn't be surprised if he had). 他走了，把所有的活都留给我们干。我对此并不感到奇怪。◇ **~ (that)...** *I wonder (that) he didn't hurt himself jumping over that wall.* 我纳闷他怎么从那墙上跳过去竟没摔伤自己。◇ ***I don't wonder** you're tired. You've had a busy day.* 你累了，这我一点儿不奇怪。你已经忙了一整天。

■ ***noun*** **1** [U] a feeling of surprise and admiration that you have when you see or experience sth beautiful, unusual or unexpected 惊讶；惊奇；惊异；惊叹 **SYN awe**：*He retained a childlike sense of wonder.* 他仍然有一种孩子般的好奇感。◇ *She gazed down **in wonder** at the city spread below her.* 她俯视展现在眼前的城市，惊叹不已。**2** [C] something that fills you with surprise and admiration 奇迹；奇观；奇事；奇妙之处 **SYN marvel**：*The Grand Canyon is one of the natural wonders of the world.* 科罗拉多大峡谷是世界自然奇观之一。◇ *the wonders of modern technology* 现代技术的奇迹 ◇ *That's the wonder of poetry—you're always discovering something new.* 这就是诗的奇妙之处，你总有新的发现。◇ *the **Seven Wonders of the World*** (= the seven most impressive structures of the ancient world) 世界七大奇观 **3** [sing.] (*informal*) a person who is very clever at doing sth; a person or thing that seems very good or effective 能人；奇才；有特效的东西：*Dita, you're a wonder! I would never have thought of doing that.* 蒂塔，你真神了！我从来想不到那样做。◇ *Have you seen the **boy wonder** play yet?* 你看过那场神童表演没有？◇ *a new wonder drug* 一种新的特效药

IDM **do 'wonders (for sb/sth)** to have a very good effect on sb/sth（为某人或替某事）创造奇迹；产生神奇作用：*The news has done wonders for our morale.* 这消息大大振奋了我们的士气。**(it's) no/little/small 'wonder (that)...** it is not surprising 不足为奇；并不奇怪：*It is little wonder (that) she was so upset.* 她如此心烦意乱，并不奇怪。◇ (*informal*) *No wonder you're tired, you've been walking for hours.* 难怪你累了呢，你一直走了好几个小时。**it's a 'wonder (that)...** (*informal*) it is surprising or strange 令人惊奇的是；莫名其妙的是：*It's a wonder (that) more people weren't hurt.* 奇怪的是没有更多的人受到伤害。**wonders will never 'cease** (*informal, usually ironic*) a phrase used to express surprise and pleasure at sth（表示惊喜）真是无奇不有，怪事何其多：*'I've cleaned my room.' 'Wonders will never cease!'* "我把我的房间打扫干净了。" "怎么太阳从西边出来了！" **work 'wonders** to achieve very good results 创造奇迹；取得优良的成绩；产生良好的效果：*Her new diet and exercise programme has worked wonders for her.* 她新的饮食和锻炼计划对她产生了奇效。⊃ MORE AT CHINLESS, NINE

won·der·ful /ˈwʌndəfl; *NAmE* -dərfl/ *adj.* **1** very good, pleasant or enjoyable 精彩的；绝妙的；令人高兴的；使人愉快的：*a wonderful surprise* 惊喜 ◇ *We had a wonderful time last night.* 我们昨晚过得非常愉快。◇ *You've all been **absolutely wonderful**!* 你们真是都太好了！◇ ***It's wonderful** to see you!* 看到你真叫人高兴！**2** making you feel surprise or admiration 令人惊奇的；令人赞叹的 **SYN remarkable**：*It's wonderful what you can do when you have to.* 在迫不得已时，人的潜能令人惊叹。

won·der·ful·ly /ˈwʌndəfəli; *NAmE* -dərf-/ *adv.* (*formal*) **1** very; very well 非常；很好地：*The hotel is wonderfully comfortable.* 这家旅馆非常舒适。◇ *Things have worked out wonderfully (well).* 事情的结果很不错。**2** unusually; in a surprising way 异乎寻常地；令人惊奇地：*He's wonderfully fit for his age.* 他年纪那么大，可身体出奇地好。

won·der·ing·ly /ˈwʌndrɪŋli/ *adv.* (*formal*) in a way that shows surprise and/or admiration 显得惊奇地；惊讶地；惊叹地：*She gazed at him wonderingly.* 她惊奇地瞅着他。

won·der·land /ˈwʌndəlænd; *NAmE* -dərl-/ *noun* [usually sing.] **1** an imaginary place in children's stories（童话中的）仙境，奇境 **2** a place that is exciting and full of beautiful and interesting things 非常奇妙的地方；极为美丽的地方

won·der·ment /ˈwʌndəmənt; *NAmE* -dərm-/ *noun* [U] (*formal*) a feeling of pleasant surprise or WONDER 惊喜；惊叹

won·drous /ˈwʌndrəs/ *adj.* (*literary*) strange, beautiful and impressive 奇异的；美好的；了不起的 **SYN wonderful** ▸ **won·drous·ly** *adv.*

wonga /ˈwɒŋgə; *NAmE* ˈwɑːŋgə/ *noun* [U] (*BrE, slang*) money 钱

wonk /wɒŋk; *NAmE* wɑːŋk/ *noun* (*especially US, informal*) **1** (*disapproving*) a person who works too hard and is considered boring 一味苦干的人；书呆子 **2** a person who takes a great deal of interest in the details of political policy 死抠政策细枝末节的人：*the President's chief economic **policy wonk*** 总统的首席经济问题策士

wonky /ˈwɒŋki; *NAmE* ˈwɑːŋki/ *adj.* (*informal*) not steady; not straight 不稳的；摇晃的；歪斜的：*a wonky chair* 摇摇晃晃的椅子

wont /wəʊnt; *NAmE* wɔːnt/ *adj., noun*

■ ***adj.*** [not before noun] **~ (to do sth)** (*old-fashioned, formal*) in the habit of doing sth 习惯于 **SYN accustomed**：*He was wont to fall asleep after supper.* 他习惯吃完晚饭就打盹。

▼ **SYNONYMS 同义词辨析**

wonderful

lovely • delightful

These words all describe an experience, feeling or sight that gives you great pleasure. 以上各词均指经历、感觉或景象令人高兴、使人愉快。

wonderful that you enjoy very much; that gives you great pleasure; extremely good 指使人愉快的、令人高兴的、精彩的、绝妙的：*We had a wonderful time last night.* 我们昨天晚上过得非常愉快。◇ *The weather was absolutely wonderful.* 天气好极了。

lovely (*rather informal, especially BrE*) that you enjoy very much; that gives you great pleasure; very attractive 指令人愉快的、有吸引力的、迷人的：*What a lovely day!* (= the weather is very good) 多么好的天气啊！◇ *It's been lovely having you here.* 有你在这儿真是太好了。

delightful that gives you great pleasure; very attractive 指令人愉快的、宜人的：*a delightful little fishing village* 宜人的小渔村

WONDERFUL, LOVELY OR DELIGHTFUL? 用 wonderful、lovely 还是 delightful?

All these words can describe times, events, places, sights, feelings and the weather. **Wonderful** can also describe a chance or ability. **Lovely** is the most frequent in spoken British English, but in North American English **wonderful** is the most frequent, both spoken and written. **Delightful** is used especially to talk about times, events and places. 以上各词均可形容时光、活动、地方、景色、感觉和天气。wonderful 亦可形容机会或能力。lovely 在英式英语口语中最常用，但在美式英语中，无论是口语还是书面语 wonderful 最常用。delightful 尤用以形容时光、活动和地方。

PATTERNS

- wonderful/lovely/delightful **weather/views/scenery**
- It's wonderful/lovely **to be/feel/find/have/know/see**...
- **It would be** wonderful/lovely/delightful **if**...
- It's wonderful/lovely **that**...
- That **sounds** wonderful/lovely/delightful.
- **really/quite/absolutely** wonderful/lovely/delightful

W

■ *noun* [sing.] (*old-fashioned, formal*) something a person often does 惯常做法；习惯 SYN **habit**: *She got up early, as was her wont.* 她像惯常一样起得很早。

won't /wəʊnt; *NAmE* woʊnt/ *short form* will not

won·ton /ˌwɒnˈtɒn; *NAmE* ˈwɑːntɑːn/ *noun* (*from Chinese*) a small piece of food wrapped in DOUGH, often served in Chinese soup or as DIM SUM 馄饨

woo /wuː/ *verb* **1 ~ sb** to try to get the support of sb 争取…的支持；寻求…的赞同：*Voters are being wooed with promises of lower taxes.* 通过许诺减低税收争取选民。**2 ~ sb** (*old-fashioned*) (of a man 男子) to try to persuade a woman to love him and marry him 追求（异性）；求爱 SYN **court**

wood /wʊd/ *noun* **1** [U, C] the hard material that the TRUNK and branches of a tree are made of; this material when it is used to build or make things with, or as a fuel 木；木头；木料；木柴：*He chopped some wood for the fire.* 他劈了些柴烧火。◇ *a plank of wood* 一长条木板 ◇ *All the furniture was made **of wood**.* 这里所有的家具都是用木料制作的。◇ *a wood floor* 木地板 ◇ *furniture made of a variety of different woods* 用各种不同的木材制作的家具 ➲ VISUAL VOCAB PAGE V10 ➲ SEE ALSO DEAD WOOD, HARDWOOD, SOFTWOOD, WOODEN (1), WOODY **2** [C] (*also* **woods** [pl.]) an area of trees, smaller than a forest 树林；林地：*a large wood* 一大片树林 ◇ *a walk in the woods* 在树林中散步 ➲ VISUAL VOCAB PAGE V3 ➲ SEE ALSO WOODED **3** [C] a heavy wooden ball used in the game of BOWLS（保龄球戏的）木瓶 **4** [C] a GOLF CLUB with a large head, that was usually made of wood in the past 木头球杆（旧时通常有木制顶部的高尔夫球棒）➲ COMPARE IRON *n.* (5)

IDM **not ˌout of the ˈwoods** (*informal*) not yet free from difficulties or problems 尚未摆脱困境；尚未渡过难关 **not see the ˌwood for the ˈtrees** (*BrE*) (*NAmE* **not see the ˌforest for the ˈtrees**) to not see or understand the main point about sth, because you are paying too much attention to small details 见树不见林 ➲ MORE AT KNOCK *v.*, NECK *n.*, TOUCH *v.*

wood·block /ˈwʊdblɒk; *NAmE* -blɑːk/ *noun* **1** each of the small flat pieces of wood that are fitted together to cover a floor（铺地板用的）木条，木块：*a woodblock floor* 木条地板 ➲ COMPARE PARQUET **2** a piece of wood with a pattern cut into it, used for printing 木刻印版；版木

wood·carv·ing /ˈwʊdkɑːvɪŋ; *NAmE* -kɑːrv-/ *noun* [U, C] the process of shaping a piece of wood with a sharp tool; a decorative object made in this way 木雕；木雕品 ▸ **wood·carver** *noun*

wood·chuck /ˈwʊdtʃʌk/ (*also* **ground·hog**) *noun* a small N American animal of the SQUIRREL family 美洲旱獭，美洲土拨鼠（北美洲松鼠科动物）

W

wood·cock /ˈwʊdkɒk; *NAmE* -kɑːk/ *noun* (*pl.* **wood·cock** or **wood·cocks**) a brown bird with a long straight beak, short legs and a short tail, hunted for food or sport 丘鹬（长喙黄褐色猎禽）

wood·cut /ˈwʊdkʌt/ *noun* a print that is made from a pattern cut in a piece of wood 木版画；木刻

wood·cut·ter /ˈwʊdkʌtə(r)/ *noun* (*old-fashioned*) a person whose job is cutting down trees 伐木工

wood·ed /ˈwʊdɪd/ *adj.* (of land 土地) covered with trees 长满树木的；树木覆盖的 ➲ WORDFINDER NOTE AT LANDSCAPE

wood·en /ˈwʊdn/ *adj.* **1** [usually before noun] made of wood 木制的；木头的：*a wooden box* 木箱 **2** not showing enough natural expression, emotion or movement 木头似的；死板的；呆板的；木讷的 SYN **stiff**: *The actor playing the father was too wooden.* 饰演父亲的演员太呆板。▸ **wood·en·ly** *adv.*: *She speaks her lines very woodenly.* 她台词念得毫无表情。**wood·en·ness** *noun* [U]

ˌwooden ˈspoon *noun* a spoon made of wood, used in cooking for stirring and mixing 木匙；木勺 ➲ VISUAL VOCAB PAGE V27

IDM **get, win, take, etc. the ˌwooden ˈspoon** (*BrE, informal*) to come last in a race or competition（在赛跑或比赛中）获得最后一名，成为末名

wood·land /ˈwʊdlənd/ *noun* [U, C] (*also* **wood·lands** [pl.]) an area of land that is covered with trees 树林；林地；林区：*ancient woodland* 原始林区 ◇ *The house is fringed by fields and woodlands.* 这房子的周围是田地和树林。◇ *woodland walks* 林地小径

wood·louse /ˈwʊdlaʊs/ *noun* (*pl.* **wood·lice** /ˈwʊdlaɪs/) a small grey creature like an insect, with a hard shell, that lives in decaying wood or damp soil 潮虫 ➲ VISUAL VOCAB PAGE V13

wood·man /ˈwʊdmən/ *noun* (*pl.* **-men** /-mən/) (*also* **woods·man**) a person who works or lives in a forest, taking care of and sometimes cutting down trees, etc. 护林人；伐木工；樵夫

wood·peck·er /ˈwʊdpekə(r)/ *noun* a bird with a long beak that it uses to make holes in trees when it is looking for insects to eat 啄木鸟

ˈwood pigeon *noun* a bird of the PIGEON family, that lives in woods and fields rather than in cities 林鸽；斑尾鸽

wood·pile /ˈwʊdpaɪl/ *noun* a pile of wood that will be used for fuel 木柴堆

ˈwood pulp *noun* [U] wood that has been broken into small pieces and crushed until it is soft. It is used for making paper. 木浆（用于造纸）

wood·shed /ˈwʊdʃed/ *noun* a small building for storing wood in, especially for fuel 木料间；（尤指）柴房，柴棚

woods·man /ˈwʊdzmən/ *noun* (*pl.* **-men** /-mən/) = WOODMAN

woodsy /ˈwʊdzi/ *adj.* (*informal, especially NAmE*) covered with trees; connected with woods 树林覆盖的；树林的

wood·turn·ing /ˈwʊdtɜːnɪŋ; *NAmE* -tɜːrn-/ *noun* [U] the process of shaping a piece of wood by turning it against a sharp tool on a machine (called a LATHE) 木工车床加工 ▸ **wood·turn·er** *noun*

wood·wind /ˈwʊdwɪnd/ *noun* [U+sing./pl. v.] (*also* **wood·winds** [pl.]) the group of musical instruments in an ORCHESTRA that are mostly made of wood or metal and are played by blowing. FLUTES, CLARINETS and BASSOONS are all woodwind instruments.（管弦乐团的）木管乐器，木管乐器组：*the woodwind section of the orchestra* 管弦乐队的木管乐器组 ➲ VISUAL VOCAB PAGE V38 ➲ COMPARE BRASS (2), PERCUSSION (1), STRING *n.* (5), (6), WIND[1] *n.* (4), WIND INSTRUMENT

wood·work /ˈwʊdwɜːk; *NAmE* -wɜːrk/ *noun* [U] **1** things made of wood in a building or room, such as doors and stairs（建筑物或房间的）木建部分，木构件，木制品：*The woodwork needs painting.* 木建部分需要上油漆。◇ (*BrE*) ***He hit the woodwork*** (= the wooden frame of the goal in the game of football/SOCCER, etc.) *twice before scoring.* 他两次射门击中球门框之后，终得进球。**2** (*BrE*) (*also* **ˈwood·work·ing** *NAmE, BrE*) the activity or skill of making things from wood 木工活；木工手艺

IDM **blend/fade into the ˈwoodwork** to behave in a way that does not attract any attention; to disappear or hide 默默无闻；销声匿迹；蛰伏 **come/crawl out of the ˈwoodwork** (*informal, disapproving*) if you say that sb **comes/crawls out of the woodwork**, you mean that they have suddenly appeared in order to express an opinion or to take advantage of a situation 突然露面；纷纷出笼：*When he won the lottery, all sorts of distant relatives came out of the woodwork.* 他博彩中奖后，八杆子打不着的亲戚都突然来登门造访。

wood·worm /ˈwʊdwɜːm; *NAmE* -wɜːrm/ *noun* **1** [C] a small WORM that eats wood, making a lot of small holes in it 木蛀虫；木蠹 **2** [U] the damage caused by woodworms 木蛀虫害；木蠹虫害：*The beams are riddled with woodworm.* 这些木梁被蛀虫蛀得都是洞。

woody /ˈwʊdi/ *adj.* **1** (of plants 植物) having a thick, hard STEM like wood 木本的；木质的 **2** covered with trees 长满树木的；树木茂盛的：*a woody valley* 树木茂盛的山谷 **3** having a smell like wood 像木头味的

woof /wʊf/ *exclamation, noun*
■ ***exclamation*** (*informal*) a word used to describe the loud noise that a dog makes（狗叫声）汪汪：*'Woof! Woof!' he barked.* "汪！汪！" 它叫着。▶ **woof** *verb* [I] ➲ MORE LIKE THIS 4, page R25
■ ***noun*** = WEFT

woof·er /ˈwuːfə(r)/ *noun* a LOUDSPEAKER for reproducing the low notes in a SOUND SYSTEM（音响系统的）低音扬声器，低音喇叭 ➲ COMPARE TWEETER

woo hoo /ˌwuː ˈhuː/ *exclamation* (*informal*) used when you are glad because sth happens that you enjoy 哦呵（表示高兴）：*Woo hoo! The weekend is here.* 哇哈！到周末了。➲ MORE LIKE THIS 2, page R25

wool 🔑 /wʊl/ *noun* [U] **1** 🔑 the soft fine hair that covers the body of sheep, GOATS and some other animals（羊等的）绒，毛 **2** 🔑 long thick thread made from animal's wool, used for knitting 毛线；绒线：*a ball of wool* 一团毛线 ➲ VISUAL VOCAB PAGE V45 **3** 🔑 cloth made from animal's wool, used for making clothes, etc. 毛料；毛织物：*This scarf is 100% wool.* 这条披肩是纯毛的。◇ *pure new wool* 纯新毛料 ◇ *a wool blanket* 毛毯 ➲ SEE ALSO COTTON WOOL, DYED IN THE WOOL, LAMBSWOOL, STEEL WOOL, WIRE WOOL IDM SEE PULL *v.*

wool·len (*BrE*) (*also NAmE* **wool·en**) /ˈwʊlən/ *adj.* **1** [usually before noun] made of wool 毛纺的；羊毛的；毛料的；毛线的：*a woollen blanket* 毛毯 ◇ *woollen cloth* 毛料 **2** [only before noun] involved in making cloth from wool 毛纺的；毛纺织业的：*the woollen industry* 毛纺业

wool·lens (*BrE*) (*NAmE* **wool·ens**) /ˈwʊlənz/ *noun* [pl.] clothes made of wool, especially knitted clothes（尤指针织的）毛衣

wool·ly /ˈwʊli/ *adj., noun*
■ ***adj.*** (*NAmE also* **wooly**) (**wool·lier, wool·li·est**) **1** covered with wool or with hair like wool 有毛覆盖的；毛状物覆盖的：*woolly monkeys* 毛茸茸的猴子 **2** (*informal, especially BrE*) made of wool; like wool 毛制的；毛的；似毛的 SYN **woollen**：*a woolly hat* 毛质的帽子 **3** (of people or their ideas, etc. 人或思想等) not thinking clearly; not clearly expressed 糊涂的；混乱的；模糊的 SYN **confused**：*woolly arguments* 混乱的论点 ▶ **wool·li·ness** *noun* [U]
■ ***noun*** (*pl.* **-ies**) (*informal*) **1** (*BrE, becoming old-fashioned*) a piece of clothing made of wool, especially one that has been knitted 毛料衣服；（尤指针织的）毛线衣 **2** (*AustralE, NZE*) a sheep 羊

Woop Woop /ˈwʊp wʊp/ *noun* (*AustralE, informal*) a humorous name for a town or area that is a long way from a big city 偏远城镇（或地区）

woozy /ˈwuːzi/ *adj.* (*informal*) **1** feeling unsteady, confused and unable to think clearly 眩晕的；头昏的；晕头涨脑的 **2** (*especially NAmE*) feeling as though you might VOMIT 恶心的；要呕吐的

wop /wɒp; *NAmE* wɑːp/ *noun* (*taboo, slang*) a very offensive word for a person from southern Europe, especially an Italian 南欧人；南蛮子；（尤指）意大利佬

Wor·ces·ter sauce /ˌwʊstə ˈsɔːs; *NAmE* ˌwʊstər/ (*also* **Wor·ces·ter·shire sauce** /ˌwʊstəʃə; *NAmE* ˌwʊstərʃɪr/) *noun* [U] a dark thin sauce made of VINEGAR, SOY SAUCE and spices 伍斯特沙司（用醋、酱油和香料调制而成）

word 🔑 /wɜːd; *NAmE* wɜːrd/ *noun, verb, exclamation*
■ ***noun***
• **UNIT OF LANGUAGE** 语言单位 **1** 🔑 [C] a single unit of language which means sth and can be spoken or written 单词；词；字：*Do not write more than 200 words.* 写的东西不要超过 200 字。◇ *Do you know the words to this song?* 你知道这首歌的歌词吗？◇ *What's the Spanish word for 'table'?* * table 这个词西班牙语怎么说？◇ *He was a true friend* ***in all senses of the word.*** 从任何意义上来说他都是位真正的朋友。◇ *Tell me what happened* ***in your own words.*** 用你自己的话告诉我出了什么事。◇ *I could hear every word they were saying.* 我可以听到他们说的每一个字。◇ *He couldn't* ***find the words*** *to thank her enough.* 他找不出适当的话语来充分表达对她的感激之情。◇ ***Words fail me*** (= I cannot express how I feel). 我无法用语言来表达我的感受。◇ *There are no words to say how sorry we are.* 我们十分后悔，实在无以言喻。◇ *I can't remember her exact words.* 我记不清她的原话了。◇ *Angry* ***is not the word for it****—I was furious.* 用"生气"来形容并不够，我是怒不可遏。➲ WORDFINDER NOTE AT LANGUAGE ➲ SEE ALSO BUZZWORD, FOUR-LETTER WORD, HOUSEHOLD WORD, SWEAR WORD

WORDFINDER 联想词：connotation, definition, **dictionary**, homonym, meaning, pronunciation, spelling, synonym, vocabulary

• **STH YOU SAY** 说的话 **2** 🔑 [C] a thing that you say; a remark or statement 说的话；话语；言语：***Have a word with*** *Pat and see what she thinks.* 和帕特谈一谈，看看她是怎么想的。◇ *Could I have a quick word with you* (= speak to you quickly)? 我能跟你很快地说句话吗？◇ ***A word of warning:*** *read the instructions very carefully.* 警示：仔细阅读说明。◇ *words of love* 情话 ◇ *She left* ***without a word*** (= without saying anything). 她一句话也没说就走了。◇ *I don't believe a word of his story* (= I don't believe any of it). 他说的这件事我一句都不相信。◇ ***a man of few words*** (= who doesn't talk very much) 少言寡语的男子 ◇ *I'd like to say a few words about future plans.* 我想就今后的计划说几句。◇ *Remember—***not a word to** (= don't tell) *Peter about any of this.* 记住，对彼得可要只字不提这件事的任何情况。◇ *He* ***never breathed a word*** *of this to me.* 这事他从来没向我透露过一点风声。
• **PROMISE** 诺言 **3** 🔑 [sing.] a promise or guarantee that you will do sth or that sth will happen or is true 诺言；许诺；保证：***I give you my word*** *that this won't happen again.* 我向你保证这种事不会再次发生。◇ *I give you my* ***word of honour*** (= my sincere promise)… 我向你庄严承诺… ◇ *We never doubted her word.* 我们从不怀疑她的许诺。◇ *We only* ***have his word for it*** *that the cheque is in the post.* 他只是向我们保证支票在邮寄之中。◇ *to* ***keep your word*** (= do what you promised) 遵守诺言 ◇ *He promised to help and* ***was as good as his word*** (= did what he promised). 他答应帮忙，并且说话算数。◇ *He's a* ***man of his word*** (= he does what he promises). 他是个守信用的人。◇ *I trusted her not to* ***go back on her word*** (= break her promise). 我相信她不会食言。◇ *I can't prove it—you'll have to* ***take my word for it*** (= believe me). 我无法证明此事，你就相信我好了。
• **INFORMATION/NEWS** 信息；消息 **4** [sing.] a piece of information or news 信息；消息：*There's been no word from them since before Christmas.* 自圣诞节前就一直没有他们的消息。◇ *She* ***sent word*** *that she would be late.* 她捎信来说她要晚些来。◇ *If* ***word gets out*** *about the affair, he will have to resign.* 要是这一绯闻传出去，他就得辞职。◇ ***Word has it*** *that she's leaving.* 据说她要走了。◇ ***The word is*** *they've split up.* 据说他们分手了。◇ *He likes to* ***spread the word*** *about the importance of healthy eating.* 他喜欢宣传健康饮食的重要性。
• **BIBLE**《圣经》 **5 the Word** (*also* **the ˌWord of ˈGod**) [sing.] the Bible and its teachings《圣经》；福音

IDM **by ˌword of ˈmouth** because people tell each other and not because they read about it 口头上；经口述：*The news spread by word of mouth.* 这消息是口头传开的。**(right) from the word ˈgo** (*informal*) from the very beginning 从一开始 **(not) get a word in ˈedgeways** (*BrE*) (*NAmE* **(not) get a word in ˈedgewise**) (not) to be able to say anything because sb else is speaking too much（因别人说话太多）插（不上）嘴：*When Mary starts talking, no one else can get a word in edgeways.* 玛丽讲起话来，别人谁也插不上嘴。**have a word in sb's ˈear** (*BrE*) to speak to sb privately about sth 和…说私话；与…密谈 **have/exchange ˈwords (with sb) (about sth)** (*especially BrE*) to have an argument with sb（与某人）争论，争吵：*We've had words.* 我们吵过架。◇ *Words were exchanged.* 发生过

W

争吵了。**in 'other words** used to introduce an explanation of sth 换句话说；也就是说；换言之：*They asked him to leave—in other words he was fired.* 他们请他走人，也就是说，他被解雇了。➲ LANGUAGE BANK AT I.E. **(not) in so/as many 'words** (not) in exactly the same words as sb says were used（并非）一字不差地，原原本本地：*'Did she say she was sorry?' 'Not in so many words.'* "她道歉了没有？" "没有直截了当地说。" ◇ *He didn't approve of the plan and said so in as many words.* 他明确地说他不同意这计划。**in a 'word** (*informal*) used for giving a very short, usually negative, answer or comment 简言之；一句话；总之：*'Would you like to help us?' 'In a word, no.'* "你愿意帮助我们吗？" "一句话，不愿意。" **in words of one 'syllable** using very simple language 用极其简单的言语：*Could you say that again in words of one syllable?* 你能用很简单的言语把这再说一遍吗？ **the last/final word (on sth)** the last comment or decision about sth（对某事的）最后意见，最后决定：*He always has to have the last word in any argument.* 在任何争论中总是得他最后说了算。**(upon) my 'word** (*old-fashioned*) used to show that you are surprised about sth（表示惊奇）哎呀，咦 **not have a good word to 'say for sb/sth** (*informal*) to never say anything good about sb/sth 从不说…的好话：*Nobody had a good word to say about him.* 没有一个人说过他好。**put in a (good) 'word for sb** to praise sb to sb else in order to help them get a job, etc. 为某人说好话；替某人美言；推荐某人 **put 'words into sb's mouth** to suggest that sb has said sth when in fact they have not 硬说某人说过某些话 **say/give the 'word** to give an order; to make a request 下命令；吩咐一下；提请求：*Just say the word, and I'll go.* 只要发句话，我就走。**take sb at their 'word** to believe exactly what sb says or promises 完全相信…的话（或许诺）；深信不疑 **take the 'words right out of sb's mouth** to say what sb else was going to say 说出…想要讲的话 **too funny, silly, ridiculous, etc. for 'words** extremely funny, silly, ridiculous, etc. 有趣（或愚蠢、荒唐等）得难以言表；极其有趣（或愚蠢、荒唐等）**,word for 'word** in exactly the same words or (when translated) exactly equivalent words 一字不差地；（翻译时）逐字地：*She repeated their conversation word for word to me.* 她一字不差地把他们的谈话对我复述了一遍。◇ *a word-for-word translation* 逐字的翻译 **sb's word is their 'bond** somebody's promise can be relied on completely 一诺千金；言而有信 **words to that ef'fect** used to show that you are giving the general meaning of what sb has said rather than the exact words 诸如此类的话；大致是这个意思的话：*He told me to leave—or words to that effect.* 他叫我离开，或诸如此类的话。➲ MORE AT ACTION *n.*, BANDY *v.*, DIRTY *adj.*, EAT, FAMOUS, HANG *v.*, LAST[1] *det.*, LOST, MINCE *v.*, MUM *adj.*, OPERATIVE *adj.*, PLAY *n.*, PRINT *v.*, WAR, WEIGH, WRITTEN

■ ***verb*** [often passive] ~ **sth** to write or say sth using particular words 措辞；用词：*How was the letter worded (= what did it say exactly)?* 这封信到底写了些什么？ ▶ **word·ed** *adj.*: *a carefully worded speech* 措辞严谨的演讲 ◇ *a strongly worded letter of protest* 措辞强硬的抗议信

■ ***exclamation*** **word!** (*NAmE*) used to show that you accept or agree with what sb has just said（表示接受或同意别人刚说的话）就是，说得对

▼ SYNONYMS 同义词辨析

word

term • phrase • expression • idiom

These are all words for a unit of language used to express sth. 以上各词均为表达意思的语言单位。

word a single unit of language which means sth and can be spoken or written 指单词、词、字：*Do not write more than 200 words.* 写的东西不要超过 200 字。◇ *He uses a lot of long words.* 他使用了很多长词。

term (*rather formal*) a word or phrase used as the name of sth, especially one connected with a particular type of language 指词语、术语、措辞：*technical/legal/scientific terms* 专门/法律/科学用语 ◇ *'Old man' is a slang term for 'father'.* * old man 为俚语，指父亲。

phrase a group of words which have a particular meaning when used together 指短语、词组、惯用法：*Who coined the phrase 'desktop publishing'?* 谁创造了 desktop publishing（桌面出版）这个词组？ NOTE In grammar, a **phrase** is a group of words without a finite verb, especially one that forms part of a sentence: 'the green car' and 'on Friday morning' are phrases. 在语法上，phrase 指不含限定动词、构成句子一部分的短语、词组，如 the green car 和 on Friday morning 均为词组。

expression a word or phrase 指词语、措辞、表达方式：*He tends to use a lot of slang expressions that I've never heard before.* 他往往用许多我以前从未听说过的俚语。

idiom a group of words whose meaning is different from the meanings of the individual words 指习语、成语、惯用语：*'Let the cat out of the bag' is an idiom meaning to tell a secret by mistake.* * let the cat out of the bag（让猫从袋子里跑出来）为成语，意为无意中泄露秘密。

PATTERNS

- a word/term **for** sth
- a **new** word/term/phrase/expression
- a **technical/colloquial** word/term/phrase/expression
- a **slang** word/term/phrase
- an **idiomatic** phrase/expression
- to **use** a(n) word/term/phrase/expression/idiom
- to **coin** a(n) word/term/phrase/expression
- a(n) word/term/phrase/expression/idiom **means** sth

'word break (*also* **'word division**) *noun* (*specialist*) a point at which a word is split between two lines of text 断字（一个单词可在转行时断开的地方）

'word class *noun* (*grammar* 语法) one of the classes into which words are divided according to their grammar, such as noun, verb, adjective, etc. 词类；词性 SYN **part of speech**

word·ing /ˈwɜːdɪŋ; *NAmE* ˈwɜːrd-/ *noun* [U, C, usually sing.] the words that are used in a piece of writing or speech, especially when they have been carefully chosen 措辞；用词：*The wording was deliberately ambiguous.* 这里的措辞故意模棱两可。➲ SYNONYMS AT LANGUAGE

word·less /ˈwɜːdləs; *NAmE* ˈwɜːrd-/ *adj.* (*formal* or *literary*) **1** [usually before noun] without saying any words; silent 默默无言的；沉默的：*a wordless cry/prayer* 无言的痛哭；默默的祷告 **2** (of people 人) not saying anything 不语的；沉默寡言的 ▶ **word·less·ly** *adv.*

'word list (*also* **word·list**) *noun* a list of words or phrases that are useful or important, often on a particular topic or of a particular type（关于某主题或某类别的）词汇表：*the Academic Word List* 学术词汇表

,word-'perfect (*BrE*) (*NAmE* **,letter-'perfect**) *adj.* able to remember and repeat sth exactly without making any mistakes 能背得一字不差的；能背得滚瓜烂熟的

word·play /ˈwɜːdpleɪ; *NAmE* ˈwɜːrd-/ *noun* [U] making jokes by using words in a clever or amusing way, especially by using a word that has two meanings, or different words that sound the same 巧妙的应答；双关语 ➲ COMPARE PUN *n.*

'word processing *noun* [U] the use of a computer to create, store and print a piece of text, usually typed in from a keyboard（计算机）字处理

'word processor *noun* a computer that runs a word processing program and is usually used for writing letters, reports, etc. 文字处理机

'word search *noun* a game consisting of letters arranged in a square, containing several hidden words that you must find 文字搜索游戏（从字母方格中找出隐藏的词）➲ VISUAL VOCAB PAGE V43

word·smith /ˈwɜːdsmɪθ; *NAmE* ˈwɜːrd-/ *noun* a person who is skilful at using words 词语大师

wordy /ˈwɜːdi; *NAmE* ˈwɜːrdi/ *adj.* (*usually disapproving*) using too many words, especially formal ones 话多的；冗长的；啰嗦的 SYN **verbose**: *a wordy and repetitive essay* 一篇冗长繁复的文章 ▶ **wordi·ness** *noun* [U]

wore PAST TENSE OF WEAR

work /wɜːk; *NAmE* wɜːrk/ *verb, noun*

■ *verb*

• **DO JOB/TASK** 做工；执行任务 **1** [I] to do sth that involves physical or mental effort, especially as part of a job 做体力（或脑力）工作；劳动；干活：*I can't work if I'm cold.* 我要是觉得冷就干不了活。◇ **~ at sth** *I've been working at my assignment all day.* 我整天都在做作业。◇ **~ on sth** *He is working on a new novel.* 他正在写一部新小说。◇ *She's outside, working on the car.* 她在外面修理汽车。◇ **+ noun** *Doctors often work very long hours.* 医生经常长时间工作。**2** [I] to have a job 受雇于；从事…工作：*Both my parents work.* 我父母都工作。◇ **~ for sb/sth** *She works for an engineering company.* 她在一家工程公司工作。◇ **~ in sth** *I've always worked in education.* 我一直从事教育工作。◇ **~ with sb/sth** *Do you enjoy working with children?* 你喜欢做儿童工作吗？◇ **~ as sth** *My son is working as a teacher.* 我的儿子是当老师的。

• **MAKE EFFORT** 努力 **3** [T] **~ yourself/sb + adv./prep.** to make yourself/sb work, especially very hard 使工作；（尤指）使卖力干活：*She works herself too hard.* 她工作起来太不辞劳苦了。**4** [I] to make efforts to achieve sth 争取；力争；努力取得：**~ for sth** *She dedicated her life to working for peace.* 她为争取和平奉献了自己的一生。◇ **~ to do sth** *The committee is working to get the prisoners freed.* 委员会正在设法营救那些被监禁的人出狱。

• **MANAGE** 管理 **5** [T] **~ sth** to manage or operate sth to gain benefit from it 管理，经营（以获利）：*to work the land* (= grow crops on it, etc.) 耕种土地 ◇ *He works a large area* (= selling a company's goods, etc.). 他负责一个大地区的工作。◇ (*figurative*) *She was a skilful speaker who knew how to* **work a crowd** (= to excite them or make them feel sth strongly). 她是个很有技巧的演讲者，善于感召听众。

• **MACHINE/DEVICE** 机器；装置 **6** [I] to function; to operate 运转；运行：*The phone isn't working.* 这部电话坏了。◇ *It works by electricity.* 这是电动的。◇ *Are they any closer to understanding how the brain works?* 他们对大脑功能的了解有进展吗？**7** [T] **~ sth** to make a machine, device, etc. operate 开动，操作（机器、装置等）；使运作：*Do you know how to work the coffee machine?* 你会使用咖啡机吗？◇ *The machine is worked by wind power.* 这台机器是以风力推动的。

• **HAVE RESULT/EFFECT** 有结果 / 作用 **8** [I] to have the result or effect that you want 奏效；产生预期的结果（或作用）：*The pills the doctor gave me aren't working.* 医生给我的药片不管事。◇ *My plan worked, and I got them to agree.* 我的计划奏效了，我让他们同意了。◇ **~ on sb/sth** *His charm doesn't work on me* (= does not affect or impress me). 我不为他的魅力所动。**9** [I] to have a particular effect 产生…作用：**~ against sb** *Your age can work against you in this job.* 你的年纪会妨碍你干这个工作。◇ **~ in sb's favour** *Speaking Italian should work in his favour.* 会说意大利语应对他有好处。**10** [T] **~ sth** to cause or produce sth as a result of effort 使奏效；（由于努力）造成，产生：*You can work miracles with very little money if you follow our home decoration tips.* 你要是按照我们的家居装饰建议行事，可以用很少的钱就产生奇妙的效果。

• **USE MATERIAL** 使用材料 **11** [T] to make a material into a particular shape or form by pressing, stretching, hitting it, etc.（通过压挤、拉长、锤击等）使成形，使定形：**~ sth** *to work clay* 制陶 ◇ *to work gold* 打制金器 ◇ **~ sth into sth** *to work the mixture into a paste* 把混合物调成糊状 **12** [I] **~ in/with sth** (of an artist, etc. 艺术家等) to use a particular material to produce a picture or other item 用某种材料作画（或编制、编织等）：*an artist working in oils* 油画画家 ◇ *a craftsman working with wool* 毛织手工艺人

• **OF PART OF FACE/BODY** 脸 / 身体部位 **13** [I] (*formal*) to move violently 抽动；抽搐；颤动：*He stared at me in horror, his mouth working.* 他恐惧地盯着我，嘴在抽搐着。

• **MOVE GRADUALLY** 逐渐移动 **14** [I, T] to move or pass to a particular place or state, usually gradually（逐渐地）移动（到某位置）；（逐步）变成（某状态）：**+ adv./prep.** *It will take a while for the drug to work out of your system.* 这药需要一段时间才能从你体内排出。◇ **~ your way + adv./prep.** (*figurative*) *He worked his way to the top of his profession.* 他一步一步努力，终于成为行业内的翘楚。◇ **~ yourself/sth + adj.** *I was tied up, but managed to work myself free.* 我被捆绑起来，但设法挣脱了绳索。◇ **+ adj.** *The screw had* **worked loose**. 这螺丝钉松动了。

IDM HELP Most idioms containing **work** are at the entries for the nouns and adjectives in the idioms, for example **work your fingers to the bone** is at **finger**. 大多数含 work 的习语，都可在该等习语中的名词及形容词相关词条找到，如 work your fingers to the bone 在词条 finger 下。**ˈwork it/things** (*informal*) to arrange sth in a particular way, especially by being clever（尤指巧妙地）办成，办妥：*Can you work it so that we get free tickets?* 你能不能为我们搞到些免费票？

PHR V **ˌwork aˈround/ˈround to sth/sb** to gradually turn a conversation towards a particular topic, subject, etc. 渐渐转变（话题、主题等）：*It was some time before he worked around to what he really wanted to say.* 他东拉西扯了一会才绕到真正要说的事情上来。**ˈwork at sth** to make great efforts to achieve sth or do sth well 致力于；努力做：*He's working at losing weight.* 他正在努力减肥。◇ *Learning to play the piano isn't easy. You have to* **work at it**. 学弹钢琴不容易，你非得下功夫不可。**ˌwork sth ˈin | work sth into sth 1** to try to include sth 尽量包括；设法把…加进：*Can't you work a few more jokes into your speech?* 难道你就不能在讲话中再增加几句笑话吗？**2** to add one substance to another and mix them together 掺入；将…搅拌进：*Gradually work in the butter.* 逐渐掺进黄油。**ˌwork sth↔ˈoff 1** to get rid of sth, especially a strong feeling, by using physical effort（通过消耗体力）宣泄感情：*She worked off her anger by going for a walk.* 她散散步气就消了。**2** to earn money in order to be able to pay a debt 工作以偿债：*They had a large bank loan to work off.* 他们有一大笔银行贷款需要偿还。**ˈwork on sb** to try to persuade sb to agree to sth or to do sth 努力说服（使某人答应或做某事）：*He hasn't said he'll do it yet, but I'm working on him.* 他还没说他会做这事，不过我正在设法说服他。**ˈwork on sth** to try hard to improve or achieve sth 努力改善（或完成）：*You need to work on your pronunciation a bit more.* 你需要再加把劲改进发音。◇ *'Have you sorted out a babysitter yet?' 'No, but* **I'm working on it**.*'* "你找到临时看孩子的保姆了吗？" "还没有，我正在找呢。" **ˌwork ˈout 1** to train the body by physical exercise 锻炼身体；做运动：*I work out regularly to keep fit.* 我经常做运动以保持健康。➲ RELATED NOUN WORKOUT **2** to develop in a successful way 成功地发展：*My first job didn't work out.* 我的第一份工作干得不好。◇ *Things have worked out quite well for us.* 事情的结果对我们很不错。**ˌwork ˈout (at sth)** if sth **works out** at sth, you calculate that it will be a particular amount 计算；计算出：**+ adj.** *It'll work out cheaper to travel by bus.* 算来还是乘公共汽车便宜些。**ˌwork sb↔ˈout** (*BrE*) to understand sb's character 了解，理解（某人的性格）：*I've never been able to work her out.* 我从未能摸准她的秉性。**ˌwork sth↔ˈout 1** to calculate sth 计算；算出：*to work out the answer* 计算出答案 **2** (*especially BrE*) to find the answer to sth 找…的答案；解决 SYN **solve**: *to work out a problem* 解决问题 ◇ **work out what, where, etc.…** *Can you work out what these squiggles mean?* 你能辨认出这些潦草的字迹是什么意思吗？◇ *I couldn't work out where the music was coming from.* 我弄不清这音乐是从哪里传来的。**3** to plan or think of sth 计划；思考：*I've worked out a new way of doing it.* 我想出了做这事的一个新方法。**4** [usually passive] to remove all the coal, minerals, etc. from a mine over a period of time 挖尽，开采光（煤、矿产等）：*a worked-out silver mine* 开采光了的银矿 **ˌwork sb↔ˈover** (*slang*) to attack sb and hit them, for example to make them give you information 拷问；逼供 **ˈwork to sth** to follow a plan, schedule, etc. 按照（计划、时间表等）；根据…行事：*to work to a budget* 按照预算办事 ◇ *We're working*

W

to a very tight deadline (= we have little time in which to do the work). 我们的工期很紧。 **ˈwork towards sth** to try to reach or achieve a goal 努力达到，设法完成（目标） **ˌwork sth↔ˈup** to develop or improve sth with some effort 逐步发展；努力改进：*I can't work up any enthusiasm for his idea.* 我对他的想法怎么也热心不起来。◇ *She went for a long walk to work up an appetite.* 她为了增加食欲散步了很长时间。 **ˌwork sb/yourself ˈup (into sth)** to make sb/yourself reach a state of great excitement, anger, etc. 使激动；使发怒：*Don't work yourself up into a state about it. It isn't worth it.* 别为此大动肝火。这不值得。◇ *What are you so worked up about?* 什么事使得你这么激动？ **ˌwork sth ˈup into sth** to bring sth to a more complete or more acceptable state 使完整；使完好；修整：*I'm working my notes up into a dissertation.* 我正在把我的笔记整理成一篇论文。 **ˌwork ˈup to sth** to develop or move gradually towards sth, usually sth more exciting or extreme 逐步发展到，逐渐达到（更高或更深的程度）：*The music worked up to a rousing finale.* 乐曲渐变到一个激动人心的末乐章。◇ *I began by jogging in the park and worked up to running five miles a day.* 我开始在公园里慢跑，后来逐渐增加到一天跑五英里。

■ ***noun***

• **JOB/TASK** 工作；任务 **1** [U] the job that a person does especially in order to earn money 工作；职业 **SYN** **employment**：*She had been **out of work** (= without a job) for a year.* 她已经失业一年了。◇ (*BrE*) *They are **in work*** (= have a job). 他们有工作。◇ *He **started work** as a security guard.* 他开始工作时做保安员。◇ *It is difficult to find work in the present economic climate.* 在目前这种经济大气候下很难找到工作。◇ *I'm still looking for work.* 我仍在找工作。◇ *She's planning to **return to work** once the children start school.* 她正计划孩子一入学就恢复上班。◇ *What **line of work** are you in* (= what type of work do you do)? 你干哪种工作？◇ ***before/after work*** (= in the morning/evening each day) 上班前；下班后 ◇ ***full-time/part-time/unpaid/voluntary work*** 全日制 / 兼职 / 无报酬的 / 志愿工作 ➲ WORDFINDER NOTE AT EMPLOY ➲ COLLOCATIONS AT JOB, UNEMPLOYMENT

> **WORDFINDER** 联想词： administrative, freelance, managerial, manual, part-time, seasonal, skilled, temporary, voluntary

2 [U] the duties that you have and the activities that you do as part of your job 职责；工作内容：*Police work is mainly routine.* 警察的工作主要都是按常规的。◇ *The accountant described his work to the sales staff.* 会计师向销售部的职员介绍了自己的职责。➲ SEE ALSO PIECEWORK, SOCIAL WORK **3** [U] tasks that need to be done 工作；活计：*There is plenty of **work to be done** in the garden.* 花园里有很多活儿要干。◇ *Taking care of a baby is **hard work**.* 照看婴儿是件苦差。◇ *I have some work for you to do.* 我有些事要你做。◇ *Stop talking and get on with your work.* 别说话了，继续干你们的活儿吧。➲ SEE ALSO HOMEWORK, SCHOOLWORK **4** [U] materials needed or used for doing work, especially books, papers, etc. 工作所需的材料（或档案等）：*She often brings work* (= for example, files and documents) *home with her from the office.* 她经常把办公室里的工作带回家。◇ *His work was spread all over the floor.* 他工作的材料摊了一地。➲ SEE ALSO PAPERWORK

• **PLACE OF JOB** 工作地点 **5** [U] (used without *the* 不与 the 连用) the place where you do your job 工作地点；工作单位；工作场所：*I **go to work** at 8 o'clock.* 我 8 点钟去上班。◇ *When do you **leave for work**?* 你什么时候去上班？◇ *The new legislation concerns health and safety **at work**.* 这项新法规涉及工作场所的健康与安全。◇ *I have to **leave work** early today.* 我今天得早点儿下班。◇ *Her friends **from work** came to see her in the hospital.* 她工作单位的朋友来医院看望她。

• **EFFORT** 努力 **6** [U] the use of physical strength or mental power in order to do or make sth 工作；劳动：*She earned her grades through sheer **hard work**.* 她的学习成绩完全是靠刻苦用功得来的。◇ *We **started work on** the project in 2009.* 我们从 2009 年开始干这个项目。◇ *Work continues on renovating the hotel.* 修整这家旅馆的工作在继续。◇ *The work of building the bridge took six months.* 修建这座桥的工作用了六个月的时间。◇ *The art collection was his **life's work**.* 收集艺术品是他一生的工作。◇ *She **set them to work** painting the fence.* 她让他们粉刷围墙。➲ SEE ALSO DONKEY WORK, FIELDWORK

• **PRODUCT OF WORK** 工作成果 **7** [U] a thing or things that are produced as a result of work 工作成果；产品；作品：*She's an artist whose work I really admire.* 她这位艺术家的作品令我赞赏不已。◇ *Is this **all your own work*** (= did you do it without help from others)? 这件作品是你独立完成的吗？◇ *The book is a detailed and thorough **piece of work** covering all aspects of the subject.* 这本书包括了这一学科的方方面面，是一部缜密翔实的大作。

• **RESULT OF ACTION** 行动结果 **8** [U] the result of an action; what is done by sb 作为；行动结果：*The damage is clearly the work of vandals.* 这毁损显然是些恣意破坏公物的人所为。

• **BOOK/MUSIC/ART** 书；音乐；艺术 **9** [C] a book, piece of music, painting, etc. 著作；作品：*the **collected/complete works** of Tolstoy* 托尔斯泰选集 / 全集 ◇ ***works of fiction/literature*** 小说 / 文学作品 ◇ *Beethoven's piano works* 贝多芬的钢琴曲 ➲ COMPARE OPUS ➲ SEE ALSO WORK OF ART

> **▼SYNONYMS** 同义词辨析
>
> **work**
>
> **employment • career • profession • occupation • trade**
>
> These are all words for the work that sb does in return for payment, especially over a long period of time. 以上各词均指有报酬的工作，尤指长期从事的职业。
>
> **work** the job that sb does, especially in order to earn money 指工作、职业： *It's very difficult to find work at the moment.* 目前很难找到工作。
>
> **employment** (*rather formal*) work, especially when it is done to earn money; the state of being employed or the situation in which people have work 指工作、职业、受雇、就业： *Only half the people here are in paid employment.* 这儿只有一半的人有拿工资的工作。
>
> **career** the job or series of jobs that sb has in a particular area of work, usually involving more responsibility as time passes 指生涯、职业： *He had a very distinguished career in the Foreign Office.* 他在外交部有过一段光辉的事业。
>
> **profession** a type of job that needs special training or skill, especially one that needs a high level of education 指需要专门技能（尤其是较高教育水平）的职业、专业： *He hopes to enter the medical profession.* 他希望能从事医务工作。 **NOTE** **The profession** is all the people who work in a particular profession. * the profession 统称某专业的人、同行、同业： *the legal profession* 法律界 **The professions** are the traditional jobs that need a high level of education and training, such as being a doctor or lawyer. * the professions 统称需要较高教育水平的传统职业，如医生、律师等。
>
> **occupation** (*rather formal*) a job or profession 指工作、职业： *Please state your name, age, and occupation.* 请写明姓名、年龄和职业。
>
> **trade** a job, especially one that involves working with your hands and requires special training and skills 指行业，尤指手工职业、手艺、行当： *Carpentry is a highly skilled trade.* 木工是需要纯熟技巧的职业。
>
> **PATTERNS**
>
> - **in/out of** work/employment
> - (a) **full-time/part-time** work/employment/career/occupation
> - **permanent/temporary** work/employment
> - (a) **well-paid** work/employment/profession/occupation
> - (a) **low-paid** work/employment/occupation
> - to **look for/seek/find** work/employment/a career/an occupation
> - to **get/obtain/give sb/offer sb/create/generate/provide** work/employment

W

• BUILDING/REPAIRING 修造 **10 works** [pl.] (often in compounds 常构成复合词) activities involving building or repairing sth 建；修；修建：*roadworks* 道路施工 ◇ *They expanded the shipyards and started engineering works.* 他们扩建造船厂，开始了工程施工。➲ SEE ALSO PUBLIC WORKS

• FACTORY 工厂 **11 works** (*pl.* **works**) [C+sing./pl. v.] (often in compounds 常构成复合词) a place where things are made or industrial processes take place 工厂：*an engineering works* 机器制造厂 ◇ *a brickworks* 砖厂 ➲ SYNONYMS AT FACTORY

• PARTS OF MACHINE 机器部件 **12 the works** [pl.] the moving parts of a machine, etc.（机器等的）活动部件 SYN **mechanism**

• EVERYTHING 所有的事物 **13 the works** [pl.] (*informal*) everything 所有的事物；全套物品：*We went to the chip shop and had the works: fish, chips, gherkins, mushy peas.* 我们去薯条店吃了套餐：炸鱼、炸薯条、小黄瓜、豆泥。

• PHYSICS 物理 **14** [U] the use of force to produce movement 功；做功 ➲ SEE ALSO JOULE

IDM **all ˌwork and no ˈplay (makes ˌJack a dull ˈboy)** (*saying*) it is not healthy to spend all your time working; you need to relax too 只工作不玩耍，聪明的孩子也变傻 **at ˈwork 1** having an effect on sth 起作用：*She suspected that secret influences were at work.* 她怀疑有些秘密势力在作祟。**2** ⚷ ~ **(on sth)** busy doing sth 忙着（做某事）：*He is still at work on the painting.* 他仍在忙着画那幅画。◇ *Danger—men at work.* 危险——施工进行中。**get (down) to/set to ˈwork** ⚷ to begin; to make a start 开始，着手（工作）：*We set to work on the outside of the house* (= for example, painting it). 我们从屋子的外部开始干了起来。**give sb the ˈworks** (*informal*) to give or tell sb everything 给（或告诉）…一切 **good ˈworks** kind acts to help others 善行；善举 **go/set about your ˈwork** to do/start to do your work 做（或着手做）自己的工作：*She went cheerfully about her work.* 她高高兴兴地做自己的工作。**have your ˈwork cut out** (*informal*) to be likely to have difficulty doing sth（做某事）可能有困难：*You'll have your work cut out to get there by nine o'clock.* 你九点钟前赶到那里可不容易。**in the ˈworks** something that is **in the works** is being discussed, planned or prepared and will happen or exist soon 在讨论（或计划、筹备等）中；在酝酿中 SYN **in the pipeline** **the work of a ˈmoment, ˈsecond, etc.** (*formal*) a thing that takes a very short time to do 即刻做完的事 ➲ MORE AT DAY, DEVIL, DIRTY *adj.*, HAND *n.*, HARD *adj.*, JOB, LIGHT *adj.*, NASTY, NICE, SHORT *adj.*, SPANNER

work·able /ˈwɜːkəbl; *NAmE* ˈwɜːrk-/ *adj.* **1** (of a system, an idea, etc. 系统、想法等) that can be used successfully and effectively 可行的；行得通的 SYN **practical**：*a workable plan* 切实可行的计划 **2** that you can shape, spread, dig, etc. 可成形（或延长、挖掘等）的：*Add more water until the dough is workable.* 往面团里再加点儿水，直到能揉成形为止。**3** (of a mine, etc. 矿等) that can still be used and will make a profit 可开采的；可开发的

work·aday /ˈwɜːkədeɪ; *NAmE* ˈwɜːrk-/ *adj.* [usually before noun] (*formal*) ordinary; not very interesting 普通的；平凡的；平淡无奇的 SYN **everyday**

work·ahol·ic /ˌwɜːkəˈhɒlɪk; *NAmE* ˌwɜːrkəˈhɔːlɪk; -ˈhɑːl-/ *noun* (*informal, usually disapproving*) a person who works very hard and finds it difficult to stop working and do other things 工作狂；工作迷；醉心于工作的人 ➲ MORE LIKE THIS 1, page R25

work·around /ˈwɜːkəraʊnd; *NAmE* ˈwɜːrk-/ *noun* (*computing* 计) a way of working with a piece of software in order to avoid a particular problem even though you do not solve that problem（处理软件问题的）绕路，变通方法（虽不能解决问题，但能避开其不良影响）

ˈwork basket *noun* (*old-fashioned, BrE*) a container for the things you need for sewing 针线筐

work·bench /ˈwɜːkbentʃ; *NAmE* ˈwɜːrk-/ (*also* **bench**) *noun* a long heavy table used for doing practical jobs, working with tools, etc. 工作台

work·book /ˈwɜːkbʊk; *NAmE* ˈwɜːrk-/ (*NAmE also* **ˈexercise book**) *noun* a book with exercises in it, often with spaces for students to write answers in, to help them practise what they have learnt 练习册；作业本

work·day /ˈwɜːkdeɪ; *NAmE* ˈwɜːrk-/ *noun* **1** (*NAmE*) (*BrE* **ˌworking ˈday**) the part of a day during which you work 工作日（一天中的工作时间）：*an 8-hour workday* * 8 小时工作日 **2** = WORKING DAY (2)：*workday traffic* 平日的交通

ˌworked ˈup *adj.* [not before noun] ~ **(about sth)** (*informal*) very excited or upset about sth 异常兴奋；十分生气：*There's no point in **getting worked up** about it.* 为此大发脾气也无济于事。

work·er 🔑 /ˈwɜːkə(r); *NAmE* ˈwɜːrk-/ *noun* **1** ⚷ (often in compounds 常构成复合词) a person who works, especially one who does a particular kind of work 工作者；人员：*farm/factory/office workers* 农场 / 工厂工人；职员 ◇ *rescue/aid/research workers* 救援 / 援助 / 研究人员 ◇ ***temporary/part-time/casual workers*** 临时工；兼职工；零工 ◇ ***manual/skilled/unskilled workers*** 体力劳动者；熟练 / 非熟练工人 ➲ COLLOCATIONS AT JOB ➲ SEE ALSO GUEST WORKER, SEX WORKER, SOCIAL WORKER **2** ⚷ [usually pl.] a person who is employed in a company or industry, especially sb who does physical work rather than organizing things or managing people 雇员；（尤指）劳工，工人：*Conflict between employers and workers intensified and the number of strikes rose.* 劳资矛盾加剧，罢工次数增多。◇ *talks between workers and management* 劳资谈判 **3** ⚷ (usually after an adjective 通常置于形容词后) a person who works in a particular way 干活…的人：***a hard/fast/quick/slow worker*** 做事努力 / 快 / 麻利 / 慢的人 **4** a female BEE that helps do the work of the group of bees but does not reproduce 工蜂 ➲ COMPARE DRONE *n.* (3), QUEEN BEE (1) IDM SEE FAST *adj.*

ˈwork experience *noun* [U] **1** the work or jobs that you have done in your life so far 工作经历：*The opportunities available will depend on your previous work experience and qualifications.* 能否有机会要看你的工作经历和学历。**2** (*BrE*) a period of time that a young person, especially a student, spends working in a company as a form of training（学生）实习 ➲ COMPARE INTERNSHIP ➲ WORDFINDER NOTE AT TRAINING

work·fare /ˈwɜːkfeə(r); *NAmE* ˈwɜːrkfer/ *noun* [U] a system in which unemployed people have to work in order to get money for food, rent, etc. from the government 工作福利制（领取福利金的失业者须要参与公益工作等）

work·flow /ˈwɜːkfləʊ; *NAmE* ˈwɜːrkfloʊ/ *noun* [C, U] the series of stages that a particular piece or type of work passes through from the beginning until it is finished; the rate at which it passes through these stages 工作流程；工作流

work·force /ˈwɜːkfɔːs; *NAmE* ˈwɜːrkfɔːrs/ *noun* [C+sing./pl. v.] **1** all the people who work for a particular company, organization, etc. 全体员工 SYN **staff**：*The factory has a 1 000-strong workforce.* 这家工厂的职工多达千人。◇ *Two thirds of the workforce is/are women.* 职工中的三分之二是妇女。➲ WORDFINDER NOTE AT FACTORY ➲ COLLOCATIONS AT UNEMPLOYMENT **2** all the people in a country or an area who are available for work（国家或行业等的）劳动力，劳动大军，劳动人口：*A quarter of the local workforce is/are unemployed.* 本地四分之一的劳动力都失业了。➲ WORDFINDER NOTE AT EMPLOY

work·horse /ˈwɜːkhɔːs; *NAmE* ˈwɜːrkhɔːrs/ *noun* a person or machine that you can rely on to do hard and/or boring work 埋头苦干的人；老黄牛（指吃苦耐劳的人）；耐用的机器

work·house /ˈwɜːkhaʊs; *NAmE* ˈwɜːrk-/ (*BrE*) (*also* **poor·house** *NAmE, BrE*) *noun* (in Britain in the past) a building where very poor people were sent to live and given work to do（英国旧时的）济贫院，劳动救济所

work·ing 🔑 /ˈwɜːkɪŋ; *NAmE* ˈwɜːrk-/ *adj., noun*

■ *adj.* [only before noun] **1** ⚷ having a job for which you are

W

paid 有工作的；有职业的 SYN **employed**: *the working population* 劳动人口 ◇ *a **working mother*** 在职母亲 ➲ SEE ALSO HARD-WORKING **2** having a job that involves hard physical work rather than office work, studying, etc. 做工的；从事体力劳动的：*a **working man*** 工人 ◇ *a working men's club* 工人俱乐部 **3** connected with your job and the time you spend doing it 工作上的；工作时间的：*long **working hours*** 长的工作时间 ◇ *poor **working conditions*** 恶劣的工作环境 ◇ *I have a good **working relationship** with my boss.* 我和老板的工作关系很好。◇ *She spent most of her **working life** as a teacher.* 她一生中大部分工作时间都当教师。◇ *recent changes in **working practices*** 工作做法方面最近的变化 **4** a **working** breakfast or lunch is one at which you discuss business（早餐或午餐等）边吃边谈公事的 **5** used as a basis for work, discussion, etc. but likely to be changed or improved in the future 初步的；暂定的：*a working theory* 初步的理论 ◇ *Have you decided on a working title for your thesis yet?* 你选了论文的暂定题目吗？ **6** if you have a **working** knowledge of sth, you can use it at a basic level 尚可应付工作的；基本够用的 **7** the **working** parts of a machine are the parts that move in order to make it function（机械部件）操纵用的，用于启动的 **8** a **working** majority is a small majority that is enough to enable a government to win votes in parliament and make new laws（议会票数）足够多数的 IDM SEE ORDER *n.*

■ ***noun*** [usually pl.] **1** ~ **(of sth)** the way in which a machine, a system, an organization, etc. works（机器、系统、组织等的）运作，工作方法：*an introduction to the workings of Congress* 对国会运作方式的介绍 ◇ *the workings of the human mind* 人脑的活动方式 ◇ *the machine's inner workings* 这台机器的内部运转情况 **2** the parts of a mine or QUARRY where coal, metal, stone, etc. is or has been dug from the ground（矿山或采石场的）矿，巷道，作业区

ˌworking ˈcapital *noun* [U] (*business* 商) the money that is needed to run a business rather than the money that is used to buy buildings and equipment when starting the business 流动资本；运营资本；周转资金 ➲ COMPARE VENTURE CAPITAL

the ˌworking ˈclass *noun* [sing.+sing./pl. v.] (*also* **the ˌworking ˈclasses** [pl.]) the social class whose members do not have much money or power and are usually employed to do MANUAL work (= physical work using their hands) 工人阶级：*the political party of the working class* 工人阶级的政党 ◇ *The working class has/have rejected them in the elections.* 工人阶级在选举中没有投他们的票。➲ COMPARE MIDDLE CLASS, UPPER CLASS ▶ **ˌworking ˈclass** *adj.*: *a working-class background* 工人阶级出身

ˌworking ˈday *noun* (*BrE*) **1** (*NAmE also* **work·day**) the part of a day during which you work 一天中的工作时间：*I spend most of my working day sitting at a desk.* 我一天之中大部分工作时间都坐在办公桌旁。**2** (*also less frequent* **work·day**) a day on which you usually work or on which most people usually work 工作日：*Sunday is a normal working day for me.* 星期日是我的正常工作日。◇ *Thousands of working days were lost through strikes last year.* 去年因罢工损失了数以千计的工作日。◇ *Allow two working days* (= not Saturday or Sunday) *for delivery.* 发货需两个工作日。

ˈworking girl *noun* (*informal*) **1** (*becoming old-fashioned*) a PROSTITUTE. People say 'working girl' to avoid saying 'prostitute'. 上班女郎（婉指妓女）**2** (*sometimes offensive*) a woman who has a paid job 劳动女子；女工；职业妇女

ˈworking paper *noun* **1** [C] a report written by a group of people chosen to study an aspect of law, education, health, etc.（委员会等的）研究报告 **2 working papers** [pl.] (in the US) an official document that enables sb under 16 years old or born outside the US to have a job（美国 16 岁以下或侨居者的）工作证，雇佣证书

ˈworking party (*BrE*) (*also* **ˈworking group** *NAmE, BrE*) *noun* [C+sing./pl. v.] ~ **(on sth)** a group of people chosen to study a particular problem or situation in order to suggest ways of dealing with it（专题）调查委员会 ➲ MORE LIKE THIS 9, page R26

ˌworking ˈweek (*BrE*) (*NAmE* **work·week**) *noun* the total amount of time that you spend at work during the week 一周的工作时间；工作周：*a 40-hour working week* * 40 个小时的工作周

ˌwork-life ˈbalance *noun* [sing.] the number of hours per week you spend working, compared with the number of hours you spend with your family, relaxing, etc. 工作与生活的平衡；劳逸结合：*Part-time working is often the best way to improve your work-life balance.* 兼职工作往往是更好地平衡工作与生活的最佳方式。

work·load /ˈwɜːkləʊd; *NAmE* ˈwɜːrkloʊd/ *noun* the amount of work that has to be done by a particular person or organization（某人或某组织的）工作量：*a heavy workload* 沉重的工作负担 ◇ *We have taken on extra staff to cope with the increased workload.* 我们已经额外雇用员工来应付增加了的工作量。➲ COLLOCATIONS AT JOB

work·man /ˈwɜːkmən; *NAmE* ˈwɜːrk-/ *noun* (*pl.* **-men** /-mən/) **1** a man who is employed to do physical work 男工人；工匠 **2** (with an adjective 与形容词连用) a person who works in the way mentioned 工作…的人：*a good/bad workman* 工作好的 / 差的人

work·man·like /ˈwɜːkmənlaɪk; *NAmE* ˈwɜːrk-/ *adj.* done, made, etc. in a skilful and thorough way but not usually very original or exciting 技术娴熟（但无新意）的

work·man·ship /ˈwɜːkmənʃɪp; *NAmE* ˈwɜːrk-/ *noun* [U] the skill with which sb makes sth, especially when this affects the way it looks or works 手艺；技艺；工艺：*Our buyers insist on high standards of workmanship and materials.* 我们的买主对工艺和材料坚持要高标准。

work·mate /ˈwɜːkmeɪt; *NAmE* ˈwɜːrk-/ *noun* (*especially BrE*) a person that you work with, often doing the same job, in an office, a factory, etc. 一起工作的人；同事；工友 SYN **colleague**

ˌwork of ˈart *noun* (*pl.* **ˌworks of ˈart**) **1** a painting, statue, etc. 艺术品；（绘画、雕塑等）艺术作品：*A number of priceless works of art were stolen from the gallery.* 美术馆中许多价值连城的艺术品被盗。**2** something that is attractive and skilfully made 令人赏心悦目的东西；精致的物品：*The bride's dress was a work of art.* 新娘的礼服十分精美。

work·out /ˈwɜːkaʊt; *NAmE* ˈwɜːrk-/ *noun* a period of physical exercise that you do to keep fit 锻炼：*She does a 20-minute workout every morning.* 她每天早晨做运动 20 分钟。➲ WORDFINDER NOTE AT FIT

ˈwork permit *noun* an official document that sb needs in order to work in a particular foreign country（国外就业）工作许可证

work·place /ˈwɜːkpleɪs; *NAmE* ˈwɜːrk-/ *noun* (*often* **the workplace**) [sing.] the office, factory, etc. where people work 工作场所：*the introduction of new technology into the workplace* 把新技术引进工厂

ˈwork placement *noun* [U, C] (*BrE*) = PLACEMENT (2)

ˈwork release *noun* [U] (*US*) a system that allows prisoners to leave prison during the day to go to work 监外就业（允许囚犯日间离开监狱外出工作的制度）

work·room /ˈwɜːkruːm; -rʊm; *NAmE* ˈwɜːrk-/ *noun* a room in which work is done, especially work that involves making things 工作室；工场间；作坊：*The jeweller has a workroom at the back of his shop.* 珠宝商在他的店铺后面有一间作坊。

works *noun* ➲ WORK *n.*

ˌworks ˈcouncil *noun* (*especially BrE*) a group of employees who represent all the employees at a factory, etc. in discussions with their employers over conditions of work 职工委员会（负责和雇主协商工作条件等）

work·sheet /ˈwɜːkʃiːt; *NAmE* ˈwɜːrk-/ *noun* **1** a piece of paper on which there is a series of questions and exercises to be done by a student（学生做的）活页练习题 **2**

W

a piece of paper on which work that has been done or has to be done is recorded 工作记录（或进度）表

work·shop /ˈwɜːkʃɒp; *NAmE* ˈwɜːrkʃɑːp/ *noun* **1** a room or building in which things are made or repaired using tools or machinery 车间；工场；作坊 ➲ SYNONYMS AT FACTORY **2** a period of discussion and practical work on a particular subject, in which a group of people share their knowledge and experience 研讨会；讲习班：*a drama workshop* 戏剧研讨班 ◇ *a poetry workshop* 诗歌讲习班 ➲ WORDFINDER NOTE AT CONFERENCE ➲ COLLOCATIONS AT EDUCATION

ˈwork-shy *adj.* (*BrE, disapproving*) unwilling to work 不愿工作的；怕干活的；懒惰的 **SYN** lazy

work·space /ˈwɜːkspeɪs; *NAmE* ˈwɜːrk-/ *noun* **1** [U, C] a space in which to work, especially in an office（办公室等的）工作场所 **2** [C] (*computing* 计) a place where information that is being used by one person on a computer network is stored（计算机网络的）工作区

work·sta·tion /ˈwɜːksteɪʃn; *NAmE* ˈwɜːrk-/ *noun* the desk and computer at which a person works; one computer that is part of a computer network（计算机）工作站 ➲ VISUAL VOCAB PAGE V71

work·top /ˈwɜːktɒp; *NAmE* ˈwɜːrktɑːp/ (*also* **ˈwork surface** *both BrE*) (*NAmE* **counter**, **counter·top**) *noun* a flat surface in a kitchen for preparing food on（厨房的）操作台 ➲ VISUAL VOCAB PAGE V26

ˌwork-to-ˈrule *noun* [usually sing.] a situation in which workers refuse to do any work that is not in their contracts, in order to protest about sth 按章工作（为表示抗议而拒绝做超出合同规定的工作）➲ COMPARE GO-SLOW

work·week /ˈwɜːkwiːk; *NAmE* ˈwɜːrk-/ (*NAmE*) (*BrE* **ˌworking ˈweek**) *noun* the total amount of time that you spend at work during the week 一周的工作时间；工作周

world /wɜːld; *NAmE* wɜːrld/ *noun*

• **THE EARTH/ITS PEOPLE** 地球；地球人 **1** **the world** [sing.] the earth, with all its countries, peoples and natural features 世界；地球；天下：*to sail* ***around the world*** 环球航行 ◇ *travelling* (***all over***) ***the world*** 周游世界 ◇ *a map of the world* 世界地图 ◇ *French is spoken in many* ***parts of the world.*** 世界上许多地方都说法语。◇ *Which is the largest city* ***in the world?*** 世界上最大的城市是哪个？◇ *He's the world's highest paid entertainer.* 他是世界上薪酬最高的演艺人。◇ *a meeting of world leaders* 世界各国领导人大会 ◇ *campaigning for world peace* 发起世界和平运动 **2** [C, usually sing.] a particular part of the earth; a particular group of countries or people; a particular period of history and the people of that period 某地域（或民族、历史时期等）的人类社会；世界：*the Arab world* 阿拉伯世界 ◇ *the English-speaking world* 讲英语的地区 ◇ *the industrialized and developing worlds* 工业化国家和发展中国家 ◇ *the ancient/modern world* 古代/现代社会 ➲ SEE ALSO FIRST WORLD, NEW WORLD, OLD WORLD, THIRD WORLD

• **ANOTHER PLANET** 另一颗行星 **3** [C] a planet like the earth（像地球的）星球，天体：*There may be other worlds out there.* 那里可能有其他星球。

• **TYPE OF LIFE** 生命 **4** [C] the people or things belonging to a particular group or connected with a particular interest, job, etc. 按性质（或职业等）划分的类别；界；界别：*the* ***animal/plant/insect world*** 动物界；植物界；昆虫界 ◇ *the world of fashion* 时装界 ◇ *stars from the sporting and artistic worlds* 体育和艺术界的众明星 **5** [usually sing.] (usually used with an adjective 通常与形容词连用) everything that exists of a particular kind; a particular kind of life or existence 某领域的一切事物；自然界：***the natural world*** (= animals, plants, minerals, etc.) 自然界 ◇ *They are a couple in* ***the real world*** *as well as in the movie.* 他们在电影和现实生活中都是一对夫妇。◇ *The island is a world of brilliant colours and dramatic sunsets.* 这个岛是个绚丽多彩、晚霞娇妍的世界。◇ *They had little contact with the* ***outside world*** (= people and places that were not part of their normal life). 他们与外界没有什么联系。

• **PERSON'S LIFE** 人生 **6** [sing.] a person's environment, experiences, friends and family, etc. 生活环境；阅历；生活圈子：*Parents are the most important people in a child's world.* 父母在儿童的天地里是最重要的人。◇ *When his wife died, his entire world was turned upside down.* 他妻子死后，他的整个生活变得一塌糊涂。

• **SOCIETY** 社会 **7** [sing.] our society and the way people live and behave; the people in the world 社会；世情；世故；世人：*We live in a rapidly changing world.* 我们生活在瞬息万变的社会里。◇ *He's too young to understand* ***the ways of the world.*** 他还太年轻，不懂得处世之道。◇ ***The whole world*** *was waiting for news of the astronauts.* 全世界的人都在等待宇航员的消息。◇ *She felt that the world was against her.* 她觉得整个世界都在与她作对。◇ ***The eyes of the world*** *are on the President.* 世人的眼睛都在盯着总统。**8** **the world** [sing.] a way of life where possessions and physical pleasures are important, rather than spiritual values 尘世；世俗；世事；世情：*monks and nuns renouncing the world* 弃绝俗世享乐的修士和修女 ➲ SEE ALSO OLDE WORLDE, OLD-WORLD

• **HUMAN EXISTENCE** 人类的生存 **9** [sing.] the state of human existence 人世；今世；来世：*this world and the next* (= life on earth and existence after death) 今世和来世

IDM **be ˌall the ˈworld to sb** to be loved by and very important to sb 是…的最喜爱的人（或事物）；对…非常重要；是…的一切 **the best of ˈboth worlds/ˈall possible worlds** the benefits of two or more completely different situations that you can enjoy at the same time 两种（或多种）不同情况的优点；两全其美：*If you enjoy the coast and the country, you'll get the best of both worlds on this walk.* 你要是喜欢海滨和乡村，那么这次散步你会一举两得。**be ˈworlds apart** to be completely different in attitudes, opinions, etc.（在态度、看法等方面）有天壤之别，截然不同 **come/go ˈdown/ˈup in the world** to become less/more important or successful in society 落泊；衰落；倒运；飞黄腾达；发迹；兴盛 **come into the ˈworld** (*literary*) to be born 出生；降生人间 **do sb/sth the ˈworld of good** to make sb feel much better; to improve sth 使…感到好得多；对…大有好处；改善：*A change of job would do you the world of good.* 换一下工作会对你大有好处。**for all the world as if/though...** | **for all the world like sb/sth** (*formal*) exactly as if...; exactly like sb/sth 简直像是；恰似：*She behaved for all the world as if nothing unusual had happened.* 看她的表现就像根本没有发生过什么大事似的。◇ *He looked for all the world like a schoolboy caught stealing apples.* 他那个样子简直就像偷苹果时被当场抓住的小学生。**have the world at your ˈfeet** to be very successful and admired 功成名就；为世人仰慕 **how, why, etc. in the ˈworld** (*informal*) used to emphasize sth and to show that you are surprised or annoyed（用于强调，表示惊讶或不悦）到底，究竟：*What in the world did they think they were doing?* 他们到底认为自己在做什么？**in an ideal/a perfect ˈworld** used to say that sth is what you would like to happen or what should happen, but you know it cannot 在理想状态下：*In an ideal world we would be recycling and reusing everything.* 我们要是能回收并再利用所有的东西就再理想不过了。**in the ˈworld** used to emphasize what you are saying（加强语气）世界上，天下，根本，到底：*There's nothing in the world I'd like more than to visit New York.* 访问纽约是我最想做的事。◇ *Don't rush—we've got* ***all the time in the world.*** 别急急忙忙的，我们有的是时间。◇ *You look as if you haven't got* ***a care in the world!*** 你看上去好像一丝牵挂都没有！**(be/live) in a world of your ˈown** if you are **in a world of your own**, you are so concerned with your own thoughts that you do not notice what is happening around you（生活）在自己的小天地里 **a man/woman of the ˈworld** a person with a lot of experience of life, who is not easily surprised or shocked 生活阅历丰富的人；老成持重的人 **not for (all) the ˈworld** used to say that you would never do sth 绝不：*I wouldn't hurt you for the world.* 我绝不会伤害你。**the... of this world** (*informal*) used to refer to people of a particular type …这类人：*We all envy the Bill Gateses of this world* (= the people who are as rich and successful as Bill Gates). 我们大家都羡慕比尔·盖茨这样的人。**ˌout of this ˈworld** (*informal*) used to emphasize how good, beautiful, etc. sth is 好（或美等）得不得了；非凡；呱呱叫：*The meal was*

W

out of this world. 这顿饭简直是没治了。**see the 'world** to travel widely and gain wide experience 见多识广；见世面 **set/put the world to 'rights** to talk about how the world could be changed to be a better place 谈论如何使世界变得更好：*We stayed up all night, setting the world to rights.* 我们一夜没睡，谈论着如何拯救世界。 **set the 'world on fire** (*BrE also* **set the 'world alight**) (*informal*) (usually used in negative sentences 通常用于否定句) to be very successful and gain the admiration of other people 大获成功；引起轰动：*He's never going to set the world on fire with his paintings.* 他的绘画永远不会引起轰动。**what is the world 'coming to?** used to express disapproval, surprise or shock, especially at changes in people's attitudes or behaviour 这个世界要变成什么样子了；这世道是怎么了；太不像话：*When I listen to the news these days, I sometimes wonder what the world is coming to.* 我近来收听新闻时，有时纳闷这成了什么世道了。**(all) the ˌworld and his 'wife** (*BrE, informal, humorous*) everyone; a large number of people 人人；许多人 **a 'world away (from sth)** used to emphasize how different two things are （和…）截然不同，有天壤之别：*His new luxury mansion was a world away from the tiny house where he was born.* 他那座新的豪宅与他出生的小屋完全不能相比。**the ˌworld is your 'oyster** there is no limit to the opportunities open to you 世界是属于你的；你的前途无量 **a/the 'world of difference** (*informal*) used to emphasize how much difference there is between two things 完全不同；是两码事：*There's a world of difference between liking someone and loving them.* 喜欢一个人和爱一个人完全不是一回事。**the (whole) world 'over** everywhere in the world 世界各地；全世界：*People are basically the same the world over.* 世界各地的人基本上都一样。➲ MORE AT BRAVE *adj.*, DEAD *adj.*, END *n.*, LOST, PROMISE *v.*, SMALL *adj.*, TOP *n.*, WATCH *v.*, WAY *n.*, WILL *n.*, WORST *n.*

the ˌWorld 'Bank *noun* [sing.] an international organization that lends money to countries who are members at times when they are in difficulty and need more money 世界银行（向处于困境需要资助的成员国贷款的国际机构）

'world-beater *noun* a person or thing that is better than all others 天下无双的人（或事物） ▶ **'world-beating** *adj.*

ˌworld-'class *adj.* as good as the best in the world 世界级的；世界上一流的：*a world-class athlete* 世界一流的运动员

the ˌWorld 'Cup *noun* (in sports 体育运动) a competition between national teams from all over the world, usually held every few years 世界杯比赛（通常为几年一度）：*The next Rugby World Cup will take place in three years' time.* 下一届橄榄球世界杯赛将于三年后举行。

ˌworld 'English *noun* [U] the English language, used throughout the world for international communication, including all of its regional varieties, such as Australian, Indian and South African English 世界英语（通行于世界各地的国际交流英语，包括澳大利亚英语、印度英语、南非英语等地域变体）

ˌworld-'famous *adj.* known all over the world 举世闻名的；世界著名的：*a world-famous scientist* 世界著名的科学家 ◇ *His books are world-famous.* 他的著作举世闻名。

ˌWorld 'Heritage Site *noun* a natural or MAN-MADE place that is recognized as having great international importance and is therefore protected 世界遗产保护区

ˌworld 'language *noun* a language that is known or spoken in many countries 世界通用语；国际语言

world·ly /'wɜːldli; *NAmE* 'wɜːrld-/ *adj.* (*literary*) **1** [only before noun] connected with the world in which we live rather than with spiritual things 尘世的；世俗的；世事的：*worldly success* 世俗的成就 ◇ *your **worldly goods*** (= the things that you own) 你个人的物品 **OPP** **spiritual** **2** having a lot of experience of life and therefore not easily shocked 生活经验丰富的；老成持重的；世故的：*At 15, he was more worldly than his older cousins who lived in the country.* 他 15 岁时就比他那些居住在乡村的表兄们懂人情世故了。**OPP** **unworldly** ▶ **world·li·ness** *noun* [U]

ˌworldly-'wise *adj.* having a lot of experience of life and therefore not easily shocked 善于处世的；老于世故的

'world music *noun* [U] traditional music from non-Western countries; Western popular music that includes elements of traditional music from non-Western countries 世界音乐（非西方国家的传统音乐以及具有这些音乐元素的西方流行音乐）

ˌworld 'power *noun* a powerful country that has a lot of influence in international politics 世界强国

the ˌWorld 'Series™ *noun* a series of BASEBALL games played every year between the winners of the American League and the National League 世界系列赛（美国棒球联盟和全国棒球联盟优胜者之间的年度比赛）

ˌworld 'view *noun* a person's way of thinking about and understanding life, which depends on their beliefs and attitudes 世界观：*Your education is bound to shape your world view.* 一个人接受的教育必定会决定其世界观的形成。

ˌworld 'war *noun* [C, U] a war that involves many countries 世界大战

ˌWorld ˌWar 'One (*also* **ˌWorld ˌWar 'I**) *noun* = FIRST WORLD WAR

ˌWorld ˌWar 'Two (*also* **ˌWorld ˌWar 'II**) *noun* = SECOND WORLD WAR

'world-weary *adj.* no longer excited by life; showing this 厌世的；厌弃人生的 **SYN** **jaded** ▶ **'world-weariness** *noun* [U]

world·wide /'wɜːldwaɪd; *NAmE* 'wɜːrld-/ *adj.* [usually before noun] affecting all parts of the world 影响全世界的；世界各地的：*an increase in worldwide sales* 全球销售额的增长 ◇ *The story has attracted worldwide attention.* 这件事已经引起了全世界的关注。▶ **ˌworld·'wide** *adv.*: *We have 2 000 members worldwide.* 我们在全世界有 2 000 名成员。

the ˌWorld Wide 'Web (*also* **the Web**) *noun* (*abbr.* **WWW**) a system for finding information on the Internet, in which documents are connected to other documents using HYPERTEXT links 万维网：*to browse a site on the World Wide Web* 在万维网上浏览一个网站 ➲ VISUAL VOCAB PAGE V74

worm /wɜːm; *NAmE* wɜːrm/ *noun, verb*

■ ***noun*** **1** [C] a long thin creature with no bones or legs, that lives in soil 蠕虫：*birds looking for worms* 觅食蠕虫的鸟 ➲ SEE ALSO EARTHWORM, LUGWORM **2 worms** [pl.] long thin creatures that live inside the bodies of humans or animals and can cause illness （人或动物体内的）寄生虫；肠虫：*The dog has worms.* 这条狗体内有寄生虫。➲ SEE ALSO HOOKWORM, TAPEWORM **3** [C] the young form of an insect when it looks like a short worm （昆虫的）幼虫：*This apple is full of worms.* 这个苹果生满了虫子。➲ SEE ALSO GLOW-WORM, SILKWORM, WOODWORM **4** [C] (*computing* 计) a computer program that is a type of virus and that spreads across a network by copying itself 蠕虫；蠕虫程序；蠕虫病毒 **5** [C, usually sing.] (*informal, disapproving*) a person you do not like or respect, especially because they have a weak character and do not behave well towards other people 懦夫；可怜虫

IDM **the ˌworm will 'turn** (*saying*) a person who is normally quiet and does not complain will protest when the situation becomes too hard to bear 老实人被逼急了也要反抗；兔子急了也咬人 ➲ MORE AT CAN[2] *n.*, EARLY *adj.*

■ ***verb*** **1 ~ your way + adv./prep.** to use a twisting and turning movement, especially to move through a narrow or crowded place 蠕动，曲折行进（尤指通过狭窄或拥挤的地方）：*She wormed her way through the crowd to the reception desk.* 她在人群中左拐右绕走到服务台。**2 ~ sth** to give an animal medicine that makes worms pass out of its body in the FAECES 给（动物）驱肠虫

PHR V **ˌworm your way/yourself 'into sth** (*disapproving*) to make sb like you or trust you, in order to gain some advantage for yourself 赢得欢心，骗取信任（以获利） **SYN** **insinuate**: *He managed to worm his way into her life.* 他设法骗取信任进入了她的生活。**ˌworm sth 'out of**

sb (*informal*) to make sb tell you sth, by asking them questions in a clever way for a long period of time（慢慢地）从某人处套出话来；不断套问：*We eventually wormed the secret out of her.* 我们最后从她口里探听出了秘密。

ˈworm-eaten *adj.* full of holes made by WORMS or WOODWORMS 虫蛀的；虫咬的；被虫蛀成很多洞的

worm·ery /ˈwɜːməri; *NAmE* ˈwɜːrm-/ *noun* (*pl.* **-ies**) a container in which WORMS are kept, for example in order to produce COMPOST 饲虫箱

worm·hole /ˈwɜːmhəʊl; *NAmE* ˈwɜːrmhoʊl/ *noun* **1** a hole made by a worm or young insect 蛀洞；蛀孔；虫眼 **2** (*physics* 物) a possible connection between regions of SPACE-TIME that are far apart（蠕）虫洞（即相隔遥远的时空区之间的可能连接）

worm·wood /ˈwɜːmwʊd; *NAmE* ˈwɜːrm-/ *noun* [U] a plant with a bitter flavour, used in making alcoholic drinks and medicines 蒿，洋艾（有些具苦味，可入药或用来制苦艾酒等）

wormy /ˈwɜːmi; *NAmE* ˈwɜːrmi/ *adj.* containing WORMS 有虫子的；有蛀虫的：*a wormy apple* 生虫的苹果

worn /wɔːn; *NAmE* wɔːrn/ *adj.* **1** [usually before noun] (of a thing 物品) damaged or thinner than normal because it is old and has been used a lot 用坏的；用旧的；磨薄的：*an old pair of worn jeans* 一条破旧的牛仔裤 ◇ *The stone steps were worn and broken.* 这些石头台阶被磨平破裂了。➲ SEE ALSO WELL WORN **2** (of a person 人) looking very tired 疲惫的；筋疲力尽的 **SYN** **weary**：*She came out of the ordeal looking thin and worn.* 她经历过这场苦难后显得憔悴不堪。➲ SEE ALSO WEAR

ˌworn ˈout *adj.* **1** (of a thing 物品) badly damaged and/or no longer useful because it has been used a lot 破烂不堪的；废旧的：*These shoes are worn out.* 这双鞋破得不能再穿了。◇ *the gradual replacement of worn-out equipment* 破旧设备的逐渐更新 ◇ *a speech full of worn-out old clichés* 充满老掉牙的陈词滥调的演讲 **2** [not usually before noun] (of a person 人) looking or feeling very tired, especially as a result of hard work or physical exercise 疲惫不堪；精疲力竭：*Can we sit down? I'm worn out.* 我们能坐下吗？我都累坏了。➲ COMPARE OUTWORN

wor·ried 🔑 /ˈwʌrid; *NAmE* ˈwɜːr-/ *adj.* thinking about unpleasant things that have happened or that might happen and therefore feeling unhappy and afraid 担心的；担忧的；发愁的：*Don't look so worried!* 别这么愁眉苦脸的！◇ **~ about sb/sth** *I'm not worried about her—she can take care of herself.* 我不为她担心，她能照顾自己。◇ *Doctors are worried about the possible spread of the disease.* 医生担心这疾病可能会蔓延。◇ **~ by sth** *We're not too worried by these results.* 我们对这些结果并不太担心。◇ **~ (that…)** *The police are worried that the man may be armed.* 警方担心那个人可能携带着武器。◇ *I was worried you wouldn't come.* 我还担心你不来呢。◇ *Where have you been? I've been* ***worried sick*** (= extremely worried). 你到哪里去了？我都担心死了。◇ *Try not to* ***get worried.*** 尽量别担忧。◇ *She gave me a worried look.* 她心事重重地看了我一眼。▸ **wor·ried·ly** *adv.*: *He glanced worriedly at his father.* 他忧心忡忡地瞥了他父亲一眼。

IDM **you had me ˈworried** (*informal*) used to tell sb that you were worried because you had not understood what they had said correctly（误会所致）你让我虚惊一场：*You had me worried for a moment—I thought you were going to resign!* 你可让我担心了一阵子，我原以为你要辞职呢！

wor·rier /ˈwʌriə(r); *NAmE* ˈwɜːr-/ *noun* a person who worries a lot about unpleasant things that have happened or that might happen 爱担忧的人；常发愁的人

wor·ri·some /ˈwʌrisəm; *NAmE* ˈwɜːr-/ *adj.* (*especially NAmE*) that makes you worry 令人担心的；使人担忧的

worry 🔑 /ˈwʌri; *NAmE* ˈwɜːri/ *verb, noun*

■ *verb* (**wor·ries**, **worry·ing**, **wor·ried**, **wor·ried**) **1** 🔑 [I] to keep thinking about unpleasant things that might happen or about problems that you have 担心；担忧；发愁：***Don't worry.*** *We have plenty of time.* 不必担心。我们有很多时间。◇ **~ about sb/sth** *Don't worry about me. I'll be all right.* 别为我担忧。我会没事的。◇ *He's always worrying about his weight.* 他总是为自己的体重发愁。◇ **~ over sb/sth** *There's no point in worrying over things you can't change.* 对改变不了的事情担心也没用。◇ **~ (that)…** *I worry that I won't get into college.* 我担心自己进不了大学。**2** 🔑 [T] to make sb/yourself anxious about sb/sth 使担心；使担忧；使发愁：**~ sb/yourself** (**about sb/sth**) *What worries me is how I am going to get another job.* 使我发愁的是如何再找到工作。◇ **~ sb/yourself + adj.** (**about sb/sth**) *He's*

▼ **SYNONYMS 同义词辨析**

worried

concerned • nervous • anxious • uneasy

These words all describe feeling unhappy and afraid because you are thinking about unpleasant things that might happen or might have happened. 以上各词均指感到不安、担忧。

worried thinking about unpleasant things that might happen or might have happened and therefore feeling unhappy and afraid 指因想到令人不快的事而担心的、担忧的

concerned worried and feeling concern about sth 指担心的、忧虑的、关切的

WORRIED OR CONCERNED? 用 worried 还是 concerned?

Concerned is usually used when you are talking about a problem that affects another person, society, the world, etc, while **worried** can be used for this or for more personal matters. * concerned 通常指对影响他人、社会、世界等问题的担忧，而 worried 既可指对这类问题、也可指对个人问题的忧虑。

nervous feeling worried about sth or slightly afraid of sth 指焦虑的、担忧的、惶恐的

anxious feeling worried or nervous about sth 指焦虑的、忧虑的、担心的

WORRIED, NERVOUS OR ANXIOUS? 用 worried、nervous 还是 anxious?

Worried is the most frequent word to describe how you feel when you are thinking about a problem or something bad that might happen. **Anxious** can describe a stronger feeling and is more formal. **Nervous** is more often used to describe how you feel before you do something very important such as an exam or an interview, or something unpleasant or difficult. **Nervous** can describe sb's personality: *a very nervous girl* is often or usually nervous; *a worried girl* is worried on a particular occasion or about a particular thing. **Worried** describes her feelings, not her personality. **Anxious** may describe feelings or personality. * worried 最常用，表示对某个问题或可能发生的不幸有所担忧。anxious 可指较强烈的担忧和不安，且较正式。nervous 较常用以形容重要事情（如考试、面试）、令人不快或困难的事情发生前的紧张不安、战战兢兢。nervous 亦可指人的性格：a very nervous girl 指性格易紧张不安的女孩，而 a worried girl 指在某个时刻或对某事担忧的女孩。worried 形容感觉而非性格，anxious 既可形容感觉也可形容性格。

uneasy feeling worried or unhappy about a particular situation, especially because you think sth bad may happen or because you are not sure that what you are doing is right 指担心的、忧虑的、不安的，尤其想到不幸的事情可能发生或不确定自己是否做得对

PATTERNS

- worried/concerned/nervous/anxious/uneasy **about** (**doing**) sth
- worried/concerned/anxious **for** sb/sth
- worried/concerned/nervous/anxious **that…**
- a(n) worried/concerned/nervous/anxious/uneasy **expression/look/smile**
- to **get** worried/nervous/anxious

W

worried himself sick (= become extremely anxious) *about his daughter.* 他的女儿可把他愁坏了。◇ **it worries sb that…** *It worries me that he hasn't come home yet.* 他还没有回家，这叫我放心不下。◇ **it worries sb to do sth** *It worried me to think what might happen.* 想到可能会发生的事情我就发愁了。**3** [T] to annoy or disturb sb 骚扰；烦扰；使不安宁：**~ sb** *The noise never seems to worry her.* 这噪音似乎从不让她厌烦。◇ **~ sb with sth** *Don't keep worrying him with a lot of silly questions.* 别老用许多愚蠢的问题打扰他。**4** [T] **~ sth** (of a dog 狗) to attack animals, especially sheep, by chasing and/or biting them 攻击，撕咬（动物，尤指羊）

IDM **ˌnot to ˈworry** (*informal, especially BrE*) it is not important; it does not matter 别担心；不必发愁；没关系：*Not to worry—I can soon fix it.* 别着急，我很快就能把它修理好。◇ *Not to worry—no harm done.* 别担心，没伤着。

PHR V **ˈworry at sth** **1** to bite sth and shake or pull it 咬；撕扯；摇晃；拉扯：*Rebecca worried at her lip.* 丽贝卡咬着嘴唇。◇ *He began to worry at the knot in the cord.* 他开始解绳子上的结。**2** to think about a problem a lot and try and find a solution 思考，苦想（解决办法）

■ **noun** (*pl.* **-ies**) **1** [U] the state of worrying about sth 担心；忧虑；发愁 SYN **anxiety**: *The threat of losing their jobs is a constant source of worry to them.* 丢掉工作的威胁时常使他们忧心忡忡。◇ *to be frantic* **with worry** 愁得要命 **2** [C] something that worries you 令人担忧的事；让人发愁的事：*family/financial worries* 家庭中的 / 财务上的烦恼 ◇ **~ (about/over sth)** *worries about the future* 对未来的担忧 ◇ **~ (for/to sb)** *Mugging is a real worry for many old people.* 行凶抢劫确实令许多老人心神不安。◇ *My only worry is that…* 唯一令我担忧的是…

IDM **ˈno worries!** (*informal*) it's not a problem; it's all right (often used as a reply when sb thanks you for sth) 没什么，不客气，没关系（常用以回答别人的道谢）

ˈworry beads *noun* [pl.] small BEADS on a string that you move and turn in order to keep calm 排愁串珠，安神串珠（用手捻转使自己镇静）

worry·ing /ˈwʌriɪŋ; *NAmE* ˈwɜːr-/ *adj.* that makes you worry 令人担忧的；令人发愁的：*a worrying development* 令人担忧的发展 ◇ *It must be worrying for you not to know where he is.* 你不知道他的下落一定很着急。◇ *It is particularly worrying that nobody seems to be in charge.* 特别令人担忧的是，似乎没有任何人在负责。◇ *It's been a* **worrying time** *for us all.* 我们大家一直忧心忡忡。

▸ **worry·ing·ly** *adv.*: *worryingly high levels of radiation* 令人担忧的强辐射 ◇ *Worryingly, the plan contains few details on how spending will be cut.* 令人担忧的是，这项计划中有关如何削减开支的细则很少。

worry·wart /ˈwʌriwɔːt; *NAmE* ˈwɜːriwɔːrt/ *noun* (*NAmE, informal*) a person who worries about unimportant things 自寻烦恼的人；爱发愁的人

wors /vɔːs; *NAmE* vɔːrs/ *noun* [U] (*SAfrE*) SAUSAGE 香肠；腊肠

worse /wɜːs; *NAmE* wɜːrs/ *adj., adv., noun*

■ **adj.** (comparative of *bad* * bad 的比较级) **1** of poorer quality or lower standard; less good or more unpleasant 更差的；更糟的；更坏的：*The rooms were awful and the food was worse.* 房间很糟糕，吃的更差。◇ *The weather* **got worse** *during the day.* 日间天气变得更恶劣了。◇ *I've been to far worse places.* 我到过糟糕得多的地方。◇ **~ than sth** *The interview was* **much worse than** *he had expected.* 这次面试比他预计的要糟得多。◇ **~ than doing sth** *There's nothing worse than going out in the cold with wet hair.* 没有比在大冷天头发湿着外出更糟糕的了。**2** **~ (than sth/doing sth)** more serious or severe 更严重的；更严厉的：*They were trying to prevent an* **even worse** *tragedy.* 他们正在设法避免更大的悲剧发生。◇ *The crisis was getting* **worse and worse.** 危机越来越严重了。◇ *Don't tell her that—you'll only* **make things worse.** 别把这事告诉她，你只会火上浇油。◇ *Never mind—it* **could be worse** (= although the situation is bad, it is not as bad as it might have been). 没关系，原本可能还要更糟。**3** [not before noun] more ill/sick or unhappy 病情更重；健康恶化；更不愉快：*If he gets any worse we'll call the doctor.* 要是他的病情恶化，我们就请医生。◇ *He told her she'd let them down and she felt* **worse than ever.** 他对她说，她让他们失望了，于是她难过极了。

IDM **come off ˈworse** to lose a fight, competition, etc. or suffer more compared with others（战斗、比赛等）失败，输得更惨 **go from ˌbad to ˈworse** (of a bad condition, situation, etc. 不好的情况、局势等) to get even worse 每况愈下；越来越糟 **ˌworse ˈluck!** (*BrE, informal*) used to show that you are disappointed about sth（表示失望）倒霉，不幸，可惜：*I shall have to miss the party, worse luck!* 我参加不了这次聚会了，真倒霉！ ➲ MORE AT BARK *n.*, FATE

■ **adv.** (comparative of *badly* * badly 的比较级) **1** **~ (than sth)** less well 更坏；更差；更糟：*I didn't do it very well, but, if anything, he did it worse than I did.* 我干得不太好，但其实他干得比我还糟。**2** **~ (than sth)** more seriously or severely 更严重；更厉害：*It's raining worse than ever.* 雨下得比以往都大。**3** **~ (than sth)** used to introduce a statement about sth that is more serious or unpleasant than things already mentioned 更糟的是；更倒霉的是：*She'd lost her job. Even worse, she'd lost her house and her children, too.* 她丢了工作。更倒霉的是，她还失去了房子和孩子。

IDM **be ˌworse ˈoff (than sb/sth)** to be poorer, unhappier, etc. than before or than sb else（比以前或其他人）更穷，更不愉快，更差：*The increase in taxes means that we'll be £30 a month worse off than before.* 税收的增加意味着我们将比以前每月少挣 30 英镑。**you can/could do worse than do sth** used to say that you think sth is a good idea 倒不如试做某事；你做某事倒不失可取：*If you want a safe investment, you could do a lot worse than put your money in a building society.* 你要是想投资而不冒风险，倒不如把钱存到房屋互助协会。

■ **noun** [U] more problems or bad news 更多的问题；更坏的消息：*I'm afraid there is worse to come.* 恐怕更糟的还在后头呢。

IDM **be none the ˈworse (for sth)** to not be harmed by sth 没有受到（…的）不良影响：*The kids were none the worse for their adventure.* 孩子们没有因历险而受伤。**the ˌworse for ˈwear** (*informal*) **1** in a poor condition because of being used a lot 用旧的；用坏的 **2** drunk 喝醉的 ➲ MORE AT BETTER *n.*, CHANGE *n.*

worsen /ˈwɜːsn; *NAmE* ˈwɜːrsn/ *verb* [I, T] to become or make sth worse than it was before（使）变得更坏，变得更糟，恶化：*The political situation is steadily worsening.* 政治局势在持续恶化。◇ *Her health has worsened considerably since we last saw her.* 自从我们上次见到她以来，她的身体差多了。◇ **~ sth** *Staff shortages were worsened by the flu epidemic.* 由于流感，职员短缺的情况更加严重了。

▸ **worsen·ing** *noun* [sing.]: *a worsening of the international debt crisis* 国际债务危机的加剧 **worsen·ing** *adj.*: *worsening weather conditions* 正在变坏的天气

wor·ship /ˈwɜːʃɪp; *NAmE* ˈwɜːrʃɪp/ *noun, verb*

■ **noun** **1** [U] the practice of showing respect for God or a god, by saying prayers, singing with others, etc.; a ceremony for this（对上帝或神的）崇拜，敬仰，礼拜：**an act/a place of worship** 礼拜；礼拜场所 ◇ *ancestor worship* 对祖先的崇拜 ◇ *morning worship* (= a church service in the morning) 早晨的礼拜 **2** [U] a strong feeling of love and respect for sb/sth 崇拜；崇敬；爱慕 SYN **adoration** ➲ SEE ALSO HERO WORSHIP **3** **His, Your, etc. Worship** [C] (*BrE, formal*) a polite way of addressing or referring to a MAGISTRATE or MAYOR（对治安官或市长的尊称）阁下

■ **verb** (**-pp-**, *NAmE also* **-p-**) **1** [T] **~ sb/sth** to show respect for God or a god, especially by saying prayers, singing, etc. with other people in a religious building 崇敬，崇拜（上帝或神）；（尤指在宗教场所）做礼拜 ➲ COLLOCATIONS AT RELIGION **2** [I] to go to a service in a religious building 到宗教场所参加礼拜：*We worship at St Mary's.* 我们在圣马利教堂做礼拜。◇ *He worshipped at the local mosque.* 他在当地的清真寺做礼拜。**3** [T] **~ sb/sth** to love and admire sb very much, especially so much that you cannot see their faults 热爱；爱慕，崇拜（尤指达到看不到缺点的地步）：*She worships her children.* 她极度疼爱自己的儿

W

女。◇ *He worshipped her from afar* (= he loved her but did not tell her his feelings). 他暗恋着她。◇ *She **worships the ground he walks on**.* 她对他的爱达到痴迷的程度。

wor·ship·ful /ˈwɜːʃɪpfl; *NAmE* ˈwɜːrʃ-/ *adj.* [only before noun] **1** (*formal*) showing or feeling respect and admiration for sb/sth 崇敬的；敬重的；爱慕的 **2 Worshipful** used in Britain in the titles of some MAYORS and some groups of CRAFTSMEN 尊敬的（英国用于某些市长和工匠团体的称号中）: *the Worshipful Company of Goldsmiths*（伦敦）金匠公会

wor·ship·per (*NAmE also* **wor·ship·er**) /ˈwɜːʃɪpə(r); *NAmE* ˈwɜːrʃ-/ *noun* a person who worships God or a god 崇拜上帝（或神）的人；做礼拜的人；敬神者；拜神者: *regular worshippers at St Andrew's Church* 经常到圣安德烈教堂做礼拜的人 ◇ (*figurative*) *sun worshippers lying on the beach* 躺在海滩上晒太阳的人们

worst 🔑 /wɜːst; *NAmE* wɜːrst/ *adj., adv., noun, verb*

■ ***adj.*** 🔑 (superlative of *bad* * bad 的最高级) of the poorest quality or lowest standard; worse than any other person or thing of a similar kind 最差的；最坏的；最糟的: *It was **by far the worst** speech he had ever made.* 这是他迄今发表过的最差的演讲。◇ *What's the worst thing that could happen?* 情况最坏会怎么样？◇ *What she said confirmed my **worst fears*** (= proved they were right). 她的话证实了我最担心的事。

IDM **be your ˌown worst ˈenemy** to be the cause of your own problems 自讨苦吃；是自己问题的根源 **come off ˈworst** to lose a fight, competition, etc. or suffer more compared with others（在战斗、比赛等中）吃败仗，输得最惨

■ ***adv.*** 🔑 (superlative of *badly* * badly 的最高级) most badly or seriously 最坏；最糟；最严重: *He was voted the worst dressed celebrity.* 大家一致认为他是衣着最差的名人。◇ *Manufacturing industry was worst affected by the fuel shortage.* 制造业受燃料短缺的影响最为严重。◇ ***Worst of all**, I lost the watch my father had given me.* 最糟糕的是，我把父亲送给我的表丢了。

■ ***noun*** 🔑 **the worst** [sing.] the most serious or unpleasant thing that could happen; the part, situation, possibility, etc. that is worse than any other（可能发生的）最严重的事；最坏的部分（或情况、可能性等）: *The worst of the storm was over.* 最厉害的一阵风暴过去了。◇ *When they did not hear from her, they **feared the worst**.* 他们听不到她的消息时，唯恐发生了最坏的事。◇ ***The worst of it** is that I can't even be sure if they received my letter.* 最糟糕的是，我甚至不能确定他们是否收到了我的信。◇ *He was always optimistic, even when things were **at their worst**.* 他即使在情况最糟糕的时候也总是很乐观。

IDM **at (the) ˈworst** 🔑 used for saying what is the worst thing that can happen（指可能出现的最坏情况）往最坏处说，充其量: *At the very worst, he'll have to pay a fine.* 最坏的情况是，他得交罚款。**bring out the ˈworst in sb** to make sb show their worst qualities 使原形毕露；使表现出最坏的品质: *Pressure can bring out the worst in people.* 压力可以使人现出原形。**do your ˈworst** (of a person 人) to do as much damage or be as unpleasant as possible 进行最大破坏；使尽最坏的招数: *Let them do their worst—we'll fight them every inch of the way.* 随便他们干什么坏事吧，我们一定和他们拼到底。**get the ˈworst of it** to be defeated 遭遇失败；吃败仗: *He'd been in a fight and had obviously got the worst of it.* 他打架了，而且显然是大败而归。**if the ˌworst comes to the ˈworst** (*NAmE also* **if ˌworst comes to ˈworst**) if the situation becomes too difficult or dangerous 如果发生最坏的事情；如果情况变得过于艰难（或危险）: *If the worst comes to the worst, we'll just have to sell the house.* 如果最坏的事发生，我们就只好把房子卖掉。**the worst of ˈall (possible) worlds** all the disadvantages of every situation 各种情况的所有不利因素

■ ***verb*** **~ sb** (*old-fashioned* or *formal*) [usually passive] to defeat sb in a fight, a contest or an argument（在打斗、比赛或辩论中）打败，战胜 SYN **get the better of**

ˈworst-case *adj.* [only before noun] involving the worst situation that could happen 最坏情况的: *In the **worst-case scenario** more than ten thousand people might be affected.* 在最坏的情况下，有一万多人可能会受到影响。

worst·ed /ˈwʊstɪd/ *noun* [U] a type of cloth made of wool with a smooth surface, used for making clothes 精纺毛料: *a grey worsted suit* 一套灰色的精纺毛料西服

worth 🔑 /wɜːθ; *NAmE* wɜːrθ/ *adj., noun*

■ ***adj.*** [not before noun] (used like a preposition, followed by a noun, pronoun or number, or by the *-ing* form of a verb 用法同介词，后接名词、代词、数字或动词的 -ing 形式) **1** 🔑 **~ sth** having a value in money, etc. 有…价值；值…钱: *Our house is worth about £100 000.* 我们的房子大约值 10 万英镑。◇ *How much is this painting worth?* 这幅画值多少钱？◇ *to be **worth a bomb/packet/fortune*** (= a lot of money) 值一大笔钱 ◇ *It isn't worth much.* 这不值多少钱。◇ *If you answer this question correctly, it's worth five points.* 答对了这道题可以得五分。➲ SYNONYMS AT PRICE **2** 🔑 used to recommend the action mentioned because you think it may be useful, enjoyable, etc.（指行动）值得，有价值: **~ sth** *The museum is certainly worth a visit.* 这家博物馆的确值得参观。◇ **~ doing sth** *This idea is **well worth** considering.* 这个想法很值得考虑。◇ *It's worth making an appointment before you go.* 去之前预约一下是值得的。**3** 🔑 **~ sth/doing sth** important, good or enjoyable enough to make sb feel satisfied, especially when difficulty or effort is involved 值得（费周折）: *Was it worth the effort?* 这值得花费力气吗？◇ *The new house really wasn't worth all the expense involved.* 这座新房子确实不值这么多的花费。◇ *The job involves a lot of hard work but **it's worth it**.* 这工作需要花费很大力气，但是值得。◇ *The trip was expensive but it was **worth every penny**.* 这次旅行花费很大，但是花的每一分钱都不冤枉。➲ SEE ALSO WORTHWHILE **4** **~ sth** (of a person 人) having money and possessions of a particular value 拥有…价值的财产: *He's worth £10 million.* 他拥有 1 000 万英镑的财产。

IDM **for ˌall sb/it is ˈworth 1** with great energy, effort and determination 竭尽全力；拼命；十分坚定: *He was rowing for all he was worth.* 他在拼命地划船。**2** in order to get as much as you can from sb/sth 尽量（多得）；拼命（榨取）: *She is milking her success for all it's worth.* 她在利用自己的成功拼命捞好处。 **for ˌwhat it's ˈworth** (*informal*) used to emphasize that what you are saying is only your own opinion or suggestion and may not be very helpful（所说的只是个人意见）无论管不管用，不论好坏: *I prefer this colour, for what it's worth.* 无论好坏，我喜欢这个颜色。**(the game is) not worth the ˈcandle** (*old-fashioned, saying*) the advantages to be gained from doing sth are not great enough, considering the effort or cost involved 得不偿失；代价太高 **not worth the paper it's ˈwritten/ˈprinted on** (of an agreement or official document 协议或正式文件) having no value, especially legally, or because one of the people involved has no intention of doing what they said they would（尤指在法律上）毫无价值 **ˌworth your/its ˈsalt** deserving respect, especially because you do your job well 称职；胜任: *Any teacher worth her salt knows that.* 凡称职的教师都知道这一点。**ˌworth your/its ˌweight in ˈgold** very useful or valuable 非常有用；很有价值: *A good mechanic is worth his weight in gold.* 优秀的技工是不可多得的。**ˌworth sb's ˈwhile** interesting or useful for sb to do 对…有好处（或用处）；值得: *It will be worth your while to come to the meeting.* 你来参加会议对你会大有好处。◇ *He'll do the job if you **make it worth his while*** (= pay him well). 你要是给他的报酬丰厚，他会做这份工作的。 ➲ MORE AT BIRD *n.*, JOB

■ ***noun*** [U] **1 ten dollars', £40, etc. ~ of sth** an amount of sth that has the value mentioned 价值（十美元、40 英镑等）的东西: *The winner will receive fifty pounds' worth of books.* 获胜者将得到价值五十英镑的书。◇ *a dollar's worth of change* 一美元的零钱 **2 a week's, month's, etc. ~ of sth** an amount of sth that lasts a week, etc. 能用（一个星期、一个月等）的东西 **3** the financial, practical or moral value of sb/sth 价值；意义；作用: *Their contribution was of great worth.* 他们的贡献具有伟大的意义。◇ *The activities help children to develop a sense of their own worth.* 这些活动有助于儿童培养自身的价值感。◇ *A good interview enables candidates to prove their worth* (= show how

W

good they are). 好的面试可以让求职者证明他们的价值。◇ *a personal net worth of $10 million* 价值 1 000 万美元的个人净资产 ➲ SYNONYMS AT PRICE IDM SEE CENT, MONEY

worth·less /ˈwɜːθləs; *NAmE* ˈwɜːrθ-/ *adj.* **1** having no practical or financial value 没用的；无价值的：*Critics say his paintings are worthless.* 评论家说他的画毫无价值。OPP **valuable 2** (of a person 人) having no good qualities or useful skills 品质坏的；不中用的：*a worthless individual* 品质坏的人 ◇ *Constant rejections made him feel worthless.* 不断地遭到拒绝使他觉得一无是处。▸ **worth·less·ness** *noun* [U]：*a sense of worthlessness* 一无是处的感觉

worth·while /ˌwɜːθˈwaɪl; *NAmE* ˌwɜːrθ-/ *adj.* important, enjoyable, interesting, etc.; worth spending time, money or effort on 重要的；令人愉快的；有趣的；值得花时间（或花钱、努力等）：*It was in aid of a* ***worthwhile cause*** (= a charity, etc.) 这是在为高尚的事业尽一份力。◇ *The smile on her face made it all worthwhile.* 她脸上的笑容使得这一切都非常值得。◇ **~ for sb to do sth** *High prices in the UK* ***make it worthwhile*** *for buyers to look abroad.* 英国的高价足以使买主把视线转向国外。◇ **~ to do sth** ***It is worthwhile to*** *include really high-quality illustrations.* 把真正高质量的插图包括进去是值得的。◇ **~ doing sth** *It didn't seem worthwhile writing it all out again.* 把这再都写出来似乎不必要。HELP This word can be written **worth while**, except when it is used before a noun. 除非用在名词前，否则可写成 worth while。

worthy /ˈwɜːði; *NAmE* ˈwɜːrði/ *adj.*, *noun*

■ *adj.* (**wor·thier**, **wor·thi·est**) **1** ~(**of sb/sth**) (*formal*) having the qualities that deserve sb/sth 值得（或应得）…的：*to be worthy of attention* 值得注意 ◇ *A number of the report's findings are* ***worthy of note.*** 这份报告里有些调查结果值得注意。◇ *No composer was considered worthy of the name until he had written an opera.* 作曲家直到写出一部歌剧来才被认为是名副其实。◇ *a worthy champion* (= one who deserved to win) 当之无愧的冠军 ◇ *He felt he was not worthy of her.* 他觉得他配不上她。OPP **unworthy 2** [usually before noun] having qualities that deserve your respect, attention or admiration 值得尊敬的；值得注意的；值得敬仰的 SYN **deserving**：*The money we raise will be going to a very* ***worthy cause.*** 我们筹集的钱款将用于非常崇高的事业。◇ *a worthy member of the team* 一位优秀的队员 **3** having good qualities but not very interesting or exciting 值得尊敬的，有价值的（但不太令人感兴趣或激动的）：*her worthy but dull husband* 她那为人正派却呆板的丈夫 **4 ~ of sb/sth** typical of what a particular person or thing might do, give, etc. 有（某人或事物）的典型特征：*He gave a speech that was worthy of Martin Luther King.* 他作了一次典型的马丁•路德•金式的演讲。**5 -worthy** (in compounds 构成复合词) deserving, or suitable for, the thing mentioned 值得…的；适于…的：*trustworthy* 值得信任的 ◇ *roadworthy* 适于在公路上行驶的 ▸ **wor·thily** *adv.* **worthi·ness** *noun* [U]

■ *noun* (*pl.* **-ies**) (*often humorous*) an important person 要人；大人物；知名人士：*a meeting attended by local worthies* 当地知名人士参加的会议

W

wot (*BrE, non-standard, often humorous*) a way of writing 'what', used to show that sb is speaking very informal English （what 的一种写法，表示说话者用极不正规的英语）什么：*'Wot's going on?' he shouted.* "出了什么事？" 他喊道。

wotcha /ˈwɒtʃə; *NAmE* ˈwɑːtʃə/ *exclamation* (*BrE, informal*) used as a friendly way of saying hello to a person 你好；嗨：*Wotcha Dave—thanks for coming.* 你好，戴夫，谢谢光临。

would /*strong form* wʊd; *weak form* wəd; əd/ *modal verb* (*short form* **'d** /d/, *negative* **would not**, *short form* **wouldn't** /ˈwʊdnt/) **1** used as the past form of *will* when reporting what sb has said or thought（will 的过去式，用于转述）将，将会：*He said he would be here at eight o'clock* (= His words were: 'I will be there at eight o'clock.'). 他说他将在八点钟到达这里。◇ *She asked if I would help.* 她问我是否会帮忙。◇ *They told me that they probably wouldn't come.* 他们对我说他们多半不会来。**2** used for talking about the result of an event that you imagine（带出想象的结果）：*She'd look better with shorter hair.* 她留短发会显得好看些。◇ *If you went to see him, he would be delighted.* 倘若你去看望他，他会高兴的。◇ *Hurry up! It would be a shame to miss the beginning of the play.* 快点儿！要是错过这出戏的开场就太可惜了。◇ *She'd be a fool to accept it* (= if she accepted). 她倘若接受，那她就是个傻瓜。**3** used for describing a possible action or event that did not in fact happen, because sth else did not happen first（表示可能发生的事情没有发生，是因为之前另一件事没有发生）就会：*If I had seen the advertisement in time I would have applied for the job.* 我要是及时看到了这则广告，我就应聘那份工作了。◇ *They would never have met if she hadn't gone to Emma's party.* 她如果不去参加埃玛的聚会，他们就永远不会相会。**4** **so that/in order that sb/sth ~** used for saying why sb does sth（说明动机）：*She burned the letters so that her husband would never read them.* 她把那些信都烧了以便永远不让她丈夫看见。**5** **wish (that) sb/sth ~** used for saying what you want to happen（表达愿望）会，将会：*I wish you'd be quiet for a minute.* 我希望你会安静一会儿。**6** used to show that sb/sth was not willing or refused to do sth（表示不愿意）：*She wouldn't change it, even though she knew it was wrong.* 尽管她知道这错了，她也不肯改变。◇ *My car wouldn't start this morning.* 今天早晨我的汽车怎么也发动不起来。**7** used to ask sb politely to do sth（客气地请求）：***Would you mind*** *leaving us alone for a few minutes?* 你不介意让我们单独待一会儿吧？◇ *Would you open the door for me, please?* 请你给我开门好吗？**8** used in polite offers or invitations（客气地建议或邀请）：***Would you like*** *a sandwich?* 您来一个三明治好吗？◇ *Would you have dinner with me on Friday?* 请你星期五和我一起用餐好吗？**9** **~ like, love, hate, prefer, etc. sth/(sb) to do sth | ~ rather do sth/sb did sth** used to say what you like, love, hate, etc.（表示愿意、喜欢、不愿意等）：*I'd love a coffee.* 我想喝杯咖啡。◇ *I'd be only too glad to help.* 我非常愿意帮忙。◇ *I'd hate you to think I was criticizing you.* 我可不愿意让你认为我是在批评你。◇ *I'd rather come with you.* 我倒愿意和你一起去。◇ *I'd rather you came with us.* 我倒愿意你和我们一块儿去。**10** **~ imagine, say, think, etc. (that)...** used to give opinions that you are not certain about（提出拿不准的看法）：*I would imagine the job will take about two days.* 我猜想这工作大概需要两天左右的时间吧。◇ *I'd say he was about fifty.* 我猜他五十岁上下。**11** **I would...** used to give advice（提出忠告）：***I wouldn't*** *have any more to drink,* ***if I were you.*** 我要是你的话，我就不会再喝酒了。**12** used for talking about things that often happened in the past（带出过去常见的情况）总是，老是 SYN **used to**：*When my parents were away, my grandmother would take care of me.* 我父母外出的时候，总是祖母照看我。◇ *He'd always be the first to offer to help.* 他总是第一个主动提出帮忙。**13** (*usually disapproving*) used for talking about behaviour that you think is typical（带出一贯的行为）总是，爱，好，就：*'She said it was your fault.'* ***'Well, she would say that, wouldn't she?*** *She's never liked me.'* "她说这是你的错。" "唉，她总是这么说，不是吗？她从来就没有喜欢过我。" **14** **~ that...** (*literary*) used to express a strong wish（用以表示强烈的愿望）：*Would that he had lived to see it.* 他要是能活到看见这该多好哇。➲ NOTE AT MODAL, SHOULD

'would-be *adj.* [only before noun] used to describe sb who is hoping to become the type of person mentioned（形容想要成为…的人）未来的：*a would-be actor* 想要成为演员的人 ◇ *advice for would-be parents* 对即将成为父母的人的忠告

wound[1] /wuːnd/ *noun*, *verb* ➲ SEE ALSO WOUND[2]

■ *noun* **1** an injury to part of the body, especially one in which a hole is made in the skin using a weapon（身体上的）伤，伤口；（武器造成的）伤：***a leg/head, etc. wound*** 腿伤，头伤等 ◇ ***a bullet/knife/gunshot/stab wound*** 枪伤；刀伤；枪伤；刺伤 ◇ *an old* ***war wound*** 战争中的旧伤 ◇ *The nurse* ***cleaned the wound.*** 护士清洗了伤口。◇ *The* ***wound healed*** *slowly.* 伤口愈合得很慢。◇ *He died from the wounds he had received to his chest.* 他由于胸部受伤而死亡。➲ SYNONYMS AT INJURE ➲ WORDFINDER

NOTE AT HURT ➲ **COLLOCATIONS** AT INJURY ➲ SEE ALSO FLESH WOUND **2** mental or emotional pain caused by sth unpleasant that has been said or done to you（心灵上的）伤，创伤：*After a serious argument, it can take some time for the wounds to heal.* 激烈争吵之后的感情创伤需要一些时间才能愈合。◇ *Seeing him again* ***opened up old wounds.*** 再次见到他打开了旧的创伤。IDM SEE LICK *v.*, REOPEN, RUB *v.*

■*verb* [often passive] **1** ~ **sb/sth** to injure part of the body, especially by making a hole in the skin using a weapon 使（身体）受伤；（用武器）伤害：*He had been wounded in the arm.* 他的手臂受过伤。**2** ~ **sb** to hurt sb's feelings 使（心灵）受伤；伤感情：*She felt* ***deeply wounded*** *by his cruel remarks.* 他那刻薄的话语使她感到深受伤害。

wound² /waʊnd/ PAST TENSE, PAST PART. OF WIND² ➲ SEE ALSO WOUND¹

wound·ed /ˈwuːndɪd/ *adj.* **1** injured by a weapon, for example in a war（身体）受伤的；负伤的：*wounded soldiers* 伤兵 ◇ ***seriously wounded*** 伤势严重 ◇ *There were 79 killed and 230 wounded.* 有 79 人死亡，230 人受伤。**2** feeling emotional pain because of sth unpleasant that sb has said or done（感情）受损害的，受伤害的：*wounded pride* 受到伤害的自尊心 **3 the wounded** *noun* [pl.] people who are wounded, for example in a war 伤员；伤兵；伤号 ➲**MORE LIKE THIS** 24, page R28

wound·ing /ˈwuːndɪŋ/ *adj.* that hurts sb's feelings 伤感情的：*He found her remarks deeply wounding.* 他觉得她的话十分伤人。

wove PAST TENSE OF WEAVE

woven PAST PART. OF WEAVE

wow /waʊ/ *exclamation, verb, noun*

■***exclamation*** (*also* **wowee** /ˌwaʊˈiː/) (*informal*) used to express great surprise or admiration（表示极大的惊奇或钦佩）哇，呀：*Wow! You look terrific!* 哇！你的样子太酷了！➲**MORE LIKE THIS** 2, page R25

■*verb* ~ **sb** (**with sth**) (*informal*) to impress sb very much, especially with a performance（尤指以表演）博得…的称赞，使喝彩，使叫绝：*He wowed audiences around the country with his new show.* 他以他的新节目博得了全国各地观众的交口称赞。

■*noun* **1** [sing.] (*informal*) a great success 极大的成功；一鸣惊人之举：*Don't worry. You'll be a wow.* 别担心。你会一鸣惊人的。**2** [U] (*specialist*) gradual changes in the PITCH of sound played on a record or tape（唱片或录音磁带逐渐出现的）走调，失真，颤动 ➲COMPARE FLUTTER *n.* (6)

ˈwow factor *noun* [sing.] (*informal*) the quality sth has of being very impressive or surprising to people 令人叫好的性质；使人惊奇的因素：*If you want to sell your house quickly, it needs a wow factor.* 若想很快把房子卖掉，就得找个卖点。

wow·ser /ˈwaʊzə(r)/ *noun* (*AustralE, NZE, informal*) **1** a person who criticizes people who are enjoying themselves 批评别人玩乐者；扫别人兴的人 SYN **killjoy** **2** a person who does not drink alcohol 不喝酒的人 SYN **teetotaller**

WPC /ˌdʌbljuː piː ˈsiː/ *noun* (*BrE*) the abbreviation for 'woman police constable' (a woman police officer of the lowest rank) 女警察（全写为 woman police constable，警衔最低的女警察）：*WPC (Linda) Green* 女警（琳达•）格林

wpm *abbr.* words per minute 每分钟字数；字每分：*to type at 60 wpm* 每分钟打 60 个字

WRAC /ræk; ˌdʌbljuː ɑːr eɪ ˈsiː/ *abbr.* (in Britain) Women's Royal Army Corps（英国）皇家陆军妇女队

wrack /ræk/ = RACK *v.*

WRAF /ræf; ˌdʌbljuː ɑːr eɪ ˈef/ *abbr.* (in Britain) Women's Royal Air Force（英国）皇家空军妇女队

wraith /reɪθ/ *noun* the GHOST of a person that is seen a short time before or after that person dies（临终前后显现的）活人灵魂，鬼魂 SYN **spectre**：*a wraith-like figure* (= a very thin, pale person) 瘦削苍白、幽灵似的人

wran·gle /ˈræŋɡl/ *noun, verb*

■*noun* ~ (**with sb**)(**over sth**) | ~ (**between A and B**) an argument that is complicated and continues over a long period of time（长时间的）争论，争吵：*a legal wrangle between the company and their suppliers* 这家公司与各供货商之间长期的法律纠纷 ➲ **MORE LIKE THIS** 20, page R27
▸ **wran·gling** /ˈræŋɡlɪŋ/ *noun* [U, C]

■*verb* [I] ~ (**with sb**) (**over/about sth**) to argue angrily and usually for a long time about sth（通常为长时间地）争吵，争辩：*They're still wrangling over the financial details.* 他们仍在为财务细节争吵。

wran·gler /ˈræŋɡlə(r)/ *noun* (*NAmE, informal*) a COWBOY or a COWGIRL, especially one who takes care of horses（尤指放马的）牛仔，女牛仔

wrap /ræp/ *verb, noun*

■*verb* (**-pp-**) **1** [T] ~ **sth** (**up**) (**in sth**) to cover sth completely in paper or other material, for example when you are giving it as a present 包，裹（礼物等）：*He spent the evening wrapping up the Christmas presents.* 他花了一个晚上的时间把圣诞礼物都包了起来。◇ *individually wrapped chocolates* 单块包装的巧克力 ➲ SEE ALSO GIFT-WRAP **2** [T] to cover sth/sb in material, for example in order to protect it/them 用…包裹（或包扎、覆盖等）：~ **A** (**up**) **in B** *Wrap the meat in foil before you cook it.* 把肉用锡箔裹起来后再烹调。◇ *I wrapped the baby (up) in a blanket.* 我用毯子把婴儿裹了起来。◇ ~ **B round/around A** *I wrapped a blanket around the baby.* 我用毯子把婴儿裹了起来。➲ SEE ALSO SHRINK-WRAPPED **3** [T] ~ **sth around/round sth/sb** to put sth firmly around sth/sb 用…缠绕（或围紧）：*A scarf was wrapped around his neck.* 他的脖子上围着一条围巾。◇ *His arms were wrapped around her waist.* 他的双臂紧紧环抱她的腰。**4** [T, I] (*computing* 计) to cause text to be carried over to a new line automatically as you reach the end of the previous line; to be carried over in this way（使文字）换行：~ **sth** (**around/round**) *How can I wrap the text around?* 我怎么才能使文本换行呢？◇ ~ (**around/round**) *The text wraps around if it is too long to fit the screen.* 如果文本太长，在显示屏放不下的话，会自动换行。➲COMPARE UNWRAP ➲**MORE LIKE THIS** 20, page R27

IDM **be ˌwrapped ˈup in sb/sth** to be so involved with sb/sth that you do not pay enough attention to other people or things 专心致志于；全神贯注于；完全沉浸于 SYN **absorbed, engrossed** ➲MORE AT LITTLE FINGER

PHR V **ˌwrap ˈup** | **ˌwrap it ˈup** (*slang*) usually used as an order to tell sb to stop talking or causing trouble, etc. 住口；闭嘴；别再捣乱 **ˌwrap ˈup** | **ˌwrap sb/yourself ˈup** to put warm clothes on sb/yourself（使）穿得暖和：*She told them to* ***wrap up warm/warmly.*** 她叫他们穿暖和点。**ˌwrap sth↔ˈup** (*informal*) to complete sth such as an agreement or a meeting in an acceptable way 圆满完成，顺利结束（协议或会议等）：*That just about wraps it up for today.* 这就差不多给今天画了个圆满的句号。

■*noun* **1** [C] a piece of cloth that a woman wears around her shoulders for decoration or to keep warm, or a loose piece of clothing worn over sth else（女用）披肩，围巾，裹巾 **2** [U] paper, plastic, etc. that is used for wrapping things in 包裹（或包装）材料：*We stock a wide range of cards and* ***gift wrap.*** 我们备有各种各样的贺卡和礼品包装材料。➲ SEE ALSO PLASTIC WRAP **3** [sing.] used when making a film/movie to say that filming has finished（拍摄电影时）完成拍摄，停机：*Cut! That's a wrap.* 停！就拍摄到这儿。**4** [C] a type of SANDWICH made with a cold TORTILLA rolled around meat or vegetables 墨西哥卷（用冻玉米薄饼裹肉或蔬菜的三明治）

IDM **under ˈwraps** (*informal*) being kept secret until some time in the future 保密；隐藏：*Next year's collection is still being kept under wraps.* 明年的时装系列仍在保密之中。

ˈwrap-around *adj.* **1** curving or stretching round at the sides 弯曲（或伸展）至两边的：*wrap-around sunglasses* 面罩型太阳眼镜 **2** (of a piece of clothing 衣服) having one part that is pulled over to cover another part at the front and then loosely fastened 围裹式的：*a wrap-around skirt* 裹裙

W

wrap·arounds /ˈræpəraʊndz/ *noun* [pl.] a pair of SUNGLASSES that fit closely and curve round the sides of the head 面罩型太阳眼镜

wrapped /ræpt/ *adj.* (*AustralE, informal*) extremely pleased 极高兴的；十分满意的：*The minister declared that he was wrapped.* 部长公开表示他特别满意。

wrap·per /ˈræpə(r)/ *noun* **1** a piece of paper, plastic, etc. that is wrapped around sth, especially food, when you buy it in order to protect it and keep it clean（食品等的）包装材料，包装纸，包装塑料：(*BrE*) *sweet wrappers* 糖果包装纸 ◇ (*NAmE*) *candy wrappers* 糖果包装纸 **2** (*WAfrE*) a piece of cloth that is worn as an item of clothing around the waist and legs（腰际和腿部的）围裹式服装

wrap·ping /ˈræpɪŋ/ *noun* [U] (*also* **wrap·pings** [pl.]) paper, plastic, etc. used for covering sth in order to protect it 包装材料；包装纸；包装塑料：*She tore the cellophane wrapping off the box.* 她把包装盒子的玻璃纸撕了下来。◇ *shrink wrapping* (= plastic designed to SHRINK around objects so that it fits them tightly) 收缩塑料薄膜 ◇ *The painting was still in its wrappings.* 那幅画还没有拆除包装。

ˈwrapping paper *noun* [U] coloured paper used for wrapping presents（包装礼品的）彩色包装纸：*a* ***piece/sheet/roll of wrapping paper*** 一块 / 一张 / 一卷彩色包装纸

wrasse /ræs/ *noun* (*pl.* **wrasse** or **wrasses**) a sea fish with thick lips and strong teeth 隆头鱼

wrath /rɒθ; *NAmE* ræθ/ *noun* [U] (*old-fashioned* or *formal*) extreme anger 盛怒；震怒；怒火：*the wrath of God* 上帝的愤怒 ▶ **wrath·ful** /-fl/ *adj.* **wrath·ful·ly** *adv.*

wreak /riːk/ *verb* ~ **sth** (**on sb**) (*formal*) to do great damage or harm to sb/sth 造成（巨大的破坏或伤害）：*Their policies would* ***wreak havoc*** *on the economy.* 他们的政策将对经济造成巨大的破坏。◇ *He swore to* ***wreak vengeance*** *on those who had betrayed him.* 他发誓要对背叛他的人进行报复。

wreath /riːθ/ *noun* (*pl.* **wreaths** /riːðz/) **1** an arrangement of flowers and leaves, especially in the shape of a circle, placed on graves, etc. as a sign of respect for sb who has died 花圈（用于祭奠）：*The Queen* ***laid a wreath*** *at the war memorial.* 女王向阵亡将士纪念碑献了花圈。**2** an arrangement of flowers and/or leaves in the shape of a circle, traditionally hung on doors as a decoration at Christmas 花环（传统上圣诞节时挂在门上）：*a holly wreath* 圣诞冬青花环 **3** a circle of flowers or leaves worn on the head, and used in the past as a sign of honour 花冠（旧时用作荣誉的象征）：*a laurel wreath* 桂冠 **4** (*literary*) a circle of smoke, cloud, etc.（烟、云等的）圈，缭绕 ➲ MORE LIKE THIS 20, page R27

wreathe /riːð/ *verb* (*formal*) **1** [T, usually passive] ~ **sth** (**in/with sth**) to surround or cover sth 环绕；覆盖；笼罩：*The mountain tops were wreathed in mist.* 山顶笼罩在薄雾之中。◇ (*figurative*) *Her face was* ***wreathed in smiles*** (= she was smiling a lot). 她脸上乐开了花。**2** [I] + **adv./prep.** to move slowly and lightly, especially in circles 缓缓移动；盘绕；缠绕；萦绕 SYN **weave**：*smoke wreathing into the sky* 袅袅升空的烟

wreck /rek/ *noun, verb*

■ *noun* **1** a ship that has sunk or that has been very badly damaged 沉船；严重损毁的船 ➲ SEE ALSO SHIPWRECK *n.* **2** a car, plane, etc. that has been very badly damaged in an accident（事故中）遭严重毁坏的汽车（或飞机等）：*Two passengers are still trapped in the wreck.* 有两名乘客仍被困在失事的车辆里。➲ SYNONYMS AT CRASH **3** [usually sing.] (*informal*) a person who is in a bad physical or mental condition（身体或精神上）受到严重损伤的人：*Physically, I was a total wreck.* 从身体上说，我完全是一个废人。◇ *The interview reduced him to* ***a nervous wreck.*** 这次面试使得他的精神高度紧张。**4** (*informal*) a vehicle, building, etc. that is in very bad condition 状况非常糟糕的车辆（或建筑物等）：*The house was a wreck when we bought it.* 我们买下这座房子时，它破烂不堪。◇ (*figurative*) *They still hoped to salvage something from the wreck of their marriage.* 他们仍然希望从他们破碎的婚姻中挽回点什么。**5** (*NAmE*) = CRASH (1)：***a car/train wreck*** 汽车 / 火车失事 ➲ MORE LIKE THIS 20, page R27

■ *verb* **1** ~ **sth** to damage or destroy sth 破坏；损坏；毁坏：*The building had been wrecked by the explosion.* 那座楼房被炸毁了。◇ *The road was littered with wrecked cars.* 公路上到处都是被撞坏的汽车。**2** ~ **sth** (**for sb**) to spoil sth completely 毁灭；毁掉：*The weather wrecked all our plans.* 天气把我们的计划全都毁了。◇ *A serious injury nearly wrecked his career.* 一次重伤差点儿葬送了他的前程。**3** [usually passive] ~ **sth** to damage a ship so much that it sinks or can no longer sail 使（船舶）失事；使遇难；使下沉：*The ship was wrecked off the coast of France.* 那艘船在法国的沿岸失事。➲ SEE ALSO SHIPWRECK *v.*

wreck·age /ˈrekɪdʒ/ *noun* [U] the parts of a vehicle, building, etc. that remain after it has been badly damaged or destroyed（车辆等的）残骸；（建筑物等的）废墟：*A few survivors were pulled from the wreckage.* 从废墟中扒出了几个幸存者。◇ *Pieces of wreckage were found ten miles away from the scene of the explosion.* 在离爆炸现场十英里的地方发现了残骸碎片。◇ (*figurative*) *Could nothing be rescued from the wreckage of her dreams?* 难道从她那破灭的梦想中就找不出一丝希望了吗？

wrecked /rekt/ *adj.* **1** [only before noun] having been wrecked 失事的；遇难的；毁坏的：*a wrecked ship/marriage* 遇难的船只；破裂的婚姻 **2** [not before noun] (*BrE, slang*) very drunk 喝得烂醉

wreck·er /ˈrekə(r)/ *noun* **1** a person who ruins another person's plans, relationship, etc.（对他人计划、关系等的）破坏者 **2** (*NAmE*) a vehicle used for moving other vehicles that have been damaged in an accident 救援车

ˈwrecking ball *noun* a heavy metal ball that swings from a CRANE and is used to hit a building to make it fall down（悬挂于吊车供拆除建筑物用的）破碎球，落锤

wren /ren/ *noun* a very small brown bird 鹪鹩（形小，浅褐色）

wrench /rentʃ/ *verb, noun*

■ *verb* **1** [T, I] to pull or twist sth/sb/yourself suddenly and violently 猛拉；猛扭；猛拧 SYN **jerk**：~ (**sth/sb/yourself**) + **adv./prep.** *The bag was wrenched from her grasp.* 那个包从她紧握的手里被夺了出来。◇ *He grabbed Ben, wrenching him away from his mother.* 他抓住本，把他从他母亲那里一把抢走了。◇ (*figurative*) *Guy wrenched his mind back to the present.* 盖伊的思绪猛地回到现在。◇ ~ (**sth/sb/yourself**) + **adj.** *They wrenched the door open.* 他们猛地把门拉开了。◇ *She managed to wrench herself free.* 她终于设法挣脱出来。**2** [T] ~ **sth** to twist and injure a part of your body, especially your ankle or shoulder 扭伤（脚踝、肩膀等）SYN **twist**：*She wrenched her knee when she fell.* 她跌倒时把膝盖扭伤了。**3** [T, I] (*formal*) to make sb feel great pain or unhappiness, especially so that they make a sound or cry 使痛苦，使十分难过（尤指以致哭喊出声）：~ (**sth**) (**from sb**) *His words wrenched a sob from her.* 他的话使得她难过得抽泣起来。◇ *a wrenching experience* 苦难的经历 ◇ ~ **at sth** *Her words wrenched at my heart.* 她的话使得我心如刀绞。➲ SEE ALSO GUT-WRENCHING

■ *noun* **1** (*especially NAmE*) (*BrE usually* **span·ner**) [C] a metal tool with a specially shaped end for holding and turning things, including one which can be adjusted to fit objects of different sizes, also called a MONKEY WRENCH or an ADJUSTABLE SPANNER 扳钳；扳手 ➲ VISUAL VOCAB PAGE V21 **2** [sing.] pain or unhappiness that you feel when you have to leave a person or place that you love（离别的）痛苦，难受：*Leaving home was a terrible wrench for me.* 对我来说离开家是件十分痛苦的事。**3** [C, usually sing.] a sudden and violent twist or pull 猛扭；猛拉：*She stumbled and gave her ankle a painful wrench.* 她绊了一跤，把脚踝崴得很痛。➲ MORE LIKE THIS 20, page R27

IDM **throw a ˈwrench in/into sth** (*NAmE, informal*) = THROW A MONKEY WRENCH IN/INTO STH

wrest /rest/ *verb*

PHR V **ˈwrest sth from sb/sth** (*formal*) **1** to take sth such as power or control from sb/sth with great effort 攫取，抢夺（权力）：*They attempted to* **wrest control** *of the town from government forces.* 他们企图从政府军手中夺取对这个城镇的控制权。**2** to take sth from sb that they do not want to give, suddenly or violently 抢，夺（物品）**SYN** **wrench**：*He wrested the gun from my grasp.* 他把枪从我手里抢走了。

wres·tle /ˈresl/ *verb* **1** [I, T] to fight sb by holding them and trying to throw or force them to the ground, sometimes as a sport 摔跤：*As a boy he had boxed and wrestled.* 他小时候练过拳击和摔跤。◇ **~ with sb** *Armed guards wrestled with the intruder.* 武装警卫和闯入者扭打起来。◇ **~ sb (+ adv./prep.)** *Shoppers wrestled the raider to the ground.* 购物的人把抢劫者摔倒在地上。**2** [I, T] to struggle to deal with sth that is difficult 奋力对付；努力处理；全力解决 **SYN** **battle, grapple**：**~ (with) sth** *She had spent the whole weekend wrestling with the problem.* 她整个周末都在绞尽脑汁处理这个问题。◇ *He wrestled with the controls as the plane plunged.* 飞机向下冲时，他竭力控制住操纵装置。◇ **~ to do sth** *She has been wrestling to raise the money all year.* 她一年来一直在想方设法筹集这笔资金。➲ MORE LIKE THIS 20, page R27

wrest·ler /ˈreslə(r)/ *noun* a person who takes part in the sport of wrestling 摔跤运动员

wrest·ling /ˈreslɪŋ/ *noun* [U] a sport in which two people fight by holding each other and trying to throw or force the other one to the ground 摔跤运动

wretch /retʃ/ *noun* **1** a person that you feel sympathy or pity for 不幸的人；可怜的人：*a poor wretch* 可怜的人 **2** (*often humorous*) an evil, unpleasant or annoying person 恶棍；坏蛋；无赖；无耻之徒

wretch·ed /ˈretʃɪd/ *adj.* **1** (of a person 人) feeling ill/sick or unhappy 感到不适的；难受的；不愉快的：*You look wretched—what's wrong?* 你看起来愁眉苦脸的，怎么啦？◇ *I felt wretched about the way things had turned out.* 事情落了这么个结局，我感到很难受。**2** (*formal*) extremely bad or unpleasant 极坏的；恶劣的 **SYN** **awful**：*She had a wretched time of it at school.* 她上学时的日子十分难熬。◇ *The animals are kept in the most wretched conditions.* 这些动物的饲养条件极其恶劣。**3** (*formal*) making you feel sympathy or pity 可怜的；悲惨的 **SYN** **pitiful**：*She finally agreed to have the wretched animal put down.* 她最后同意用药结束这个可怜的动物的生命。**4** [only before noun] (*informal*) used to show that you think that sb/sth is extremely annoying（表示憎恶）该死的，无法容忍的：*Is it that wretched woman again?* 这又是那个该死的女人吗？
▶ **wretch·ed·ly** *adv.* **wretch·ed·ness** *noun* [U]

wrig·gle /ˈrɪɡl/ *verb, noun*

■ ***verb*** **1** [I, T] to twist and turn your body or part of it with quick short movements 扭动身体；扭来扭去 **SYN** **wiggle**：**~ (about/around)** *The baby was wriggling around on my lap.* 婴儿在我大腿上扭来扭去。◇ **~ sth** *She wriggled her toes.* 她扭动着脚趾。**2** [I, T] to move somewhere by twisting and turning your body or part of it 蠕动；甩动而行；蜿蜒行进 **SYN** **squirm**：(**+ adv./prep.**) *The fish wriggled out of my fingers.* 那条鱼从我指缝中一甩身溜走了。◇ **+ adj.** *She managed to wriggle free.* 她设法扭动着挣脱了。◇ **~ your way/yourself + adv./prep.** *They wriggled their way through the tunnel.* 他们在地道中蜿蜒行进。➲ MORE LIKE THIS 20, page R27

PHR V ˌ**wriggle ˈout of sth/out of doing sth** (*informal, disapproving*) to avoid doing sth that you should do, especially by thinking of clever excuses 耍滑不做，逃避（应做的事）：*He tried desperately to wriggle out of giving a clear answer.* 他竭力支支吾吾不给予明确的回答。

■ ***noun*** [usually sing.] an act of wriggling 扭动；蠕动；蜿蜒行进

wring /rɪŋ/ *verb* (**wrung, wrung** /rʌŋ/) **1 ~ sth (out)** to twist and squeeze clothes, etc. in order to get the water out of them 拧，绞，拧出，绞出（衣服等中的水）➲ PICTURE AT SQUEEZE **2 ~ sth** if you **wring** a bird's neck, you twist it in order to kill the bird 拧，扭（鸟的脖子，以将其杀死）➲ MORE LIKE THIS 20, page R27

IDM ˌ**wring sb's ˈhand** to squeeze sb's hand very tightly when you shake hands（握手时）攥紧…的手 ˌ**wring your ˈhands** to hold your hands together, and twist and squeeze them in a way that shows you are anxious or upset, especially when you cannot change the situation（尤指出于焦急或烦恼）扭绞双手 ˌ**wring sb's ˈneck** (*informal*) when you say that you will **wring sb's neck**, you mean that you are very angry or annoyed with them（表示愤怒或气恼）拧断…的脖子，非掐死…不可

PHR V ˈ**wring sth from/out of sb** to obtain sth from sb with difficulty, especially by putting pressure on them 从…处费力弄到；从…压榨出 **SYN** **extract**

wring·er /ˈrɪŋə(r)/ *noun* = MANGLE

IDM **go through the ˈwringer** (*informal*) to have a difficult or unpleasant experience, or a series of them 受尽磨难；历尽艰难

ˌ**wringing ˈwet** *adj.* (especially of clothes 尤指衣服) very wet 很湿的；湿得能拧出水的

wrin·kle /ˈrɪŋkl/ *noun, verb*

■ ***noun*** **1** a line or small fold in your skin, especially on your face, that forms as you get older（尤指脸上的）皱纹：*There were fine wrinkles around her eyes.* 她眼角上出现了鱼尾纹。➲ COLLOCATIONS AT PHYSICAL **2** [usually pl.] a small fold that you do not want in a piece of cloth or paper（布或纸上的）褶皱，皱痕 **SYN** **crease**

■ ***verb*** **1** [T, I] to make the skin on your face form into lines or folds; to form lines or folds in this way（使脸上）起皱纹；皱起：**~ sth (up)** *She wrinkled up her nose in distaste.* 她厌恶地皱起鼻子。◇ *He wrinkled his brow in concentration.* 他全神贯注地锁紧眉头。◇ **~ (up)** *His face wrinkled in a grin.* 他咧嘴一笑满脸都是皱纹。**2** [I, T] **~ (sth)** to form raised folds or lines in an untidy way; to make sth do this（使）起褶皱：*Her stockings were wrinkling at the knees.* 她长袜的膝盖处起了褶皱。

wrin·kled /ˈrɪŋkld/ *adj.* (of skin, clothing, etc. 皮肤、衣服等) having wrinkles 有皱纹的

wrink·ling /ˈrɪŋklɪŋ/ *noun* [U] the process by which WRINKLES form in the skin（皮肤）起皱纹

wrin·kly /ˈrɪŋkli/ *adj., noun*

■ ***adj.*** (*informal*) (of skin, clothing, etc. 皮肤、衣服等) having WRINKLES 皱的；有皱纹的

■ ***noun*** (*pl.* **-ies**) (*BrE, informal*) an offensive word for an old person, used by younger people（对老年人的冒犯称呼）老皱皮

wrist 🔑 /rɪst/ *noun* the joint between the hand and the arm 手腕；腕关节：*She's broken her wrist.* 她的腕关节骨折了。◇ *He wore a copper bracelet* **on his wrist**. 他腕上戴着只铜手镯。➲ VISUAL VOCAB PAGE V64 **IDM** SEE SLAP *n.*

wrist·band /ˈrɪstbænd/ *noun* a strip of material worn around the wrist, as a decoration, to absorb sweat during exercise, or to show support for sth 腕带；腕套；腕箍：*He was wearing an anti-racism wristband.* 他戴着一只反种族歧视的腕带。

wrist·watch /ˈrɪstwɒtʃ; *NAmE* -wɑːtʃ/ *noun* a watch that you wear on your wrist 手表

writ /rɪt/ *noun, verb*

■ ***noun*** **~ (for sth) (against sb)** a legal document from a court telling sb to do or not to do sth（法庭的）令状，书面命令：*The company has been* **served with a writ** *for breach of contract.* 这家公司因违约已接到法院令状。◇ *We fully intend to* **issue a writ** *against the newspaper.* 我们一心想传讯这家报纸。➲ SEE ALSO HOLY WRIT

■ ***verb*** (*old use*) PAST PART. OF WRITE

IDM ˌ**writ ˈlarge** (*literary*) **1** easy to see or understand 显而易见的；公然：*Mistrust was writ large on her face.* 她脸上明显流露出不信任的神情。**2** (used after a noun 用于名词后) being a large or obvious example of the thing mentioned 明摆着；典型：*This is deception writ large.* 这是明目张胆的欺骗。

write 🔑 /raɪt/ *verb* (**wrote** /rəʊt; *NAmE* roʊt/, **writ·ten** /ˈrɪtn/)

W

• **LETTERS/NUMBERS** 字母；数字 **1** [I, T] to make letters or numbers on a surface, especially using a pen or a pencil 书写；写字：*In some countries children don't start learning to* ***read and write*** *until they are six.* 有些国家的儿童到了六岁才开始学习读书写字。◇ **~ in/on/with sth** *Please write in pen on both sides of the paper.* 请用钢笔在纸的正反两面书写。◇ *I haven't got anything to write with.* 我没有笔可以写字。◇ **~ sth** *Write your name at the top of the paper.* 请把名字写在纸的顶端。◇ *The teacher wrote the answers on the board.* 老师把答案写在黑板上。◇ *The 'b' had been wrongly written as a 'd'.* * b 错写成 d 了。

• **BOOK/MUSIC/PROGRAM** 书籍；音乐；程序 **2** [T, I] to produce sth in written form so that people can read, perform or use it, etc. 写作；作曲；编写：**~ sth** *to write a novel/a song/an essay/a computer program, etc.* 写小说、写歌、写散文、编计算机程序等 ◇ *Who was 'The Grapes of Wrath' written by?* 《愤怒的葡萄》是谁写的？◇ *Which opera did Verdi write first?* 威尔第最早写的是哪一部歌剧？◇ **~ sth about/on sth** *He hopes to write a book about his experiences one day.* 他希望有一天写一部关于自己经历的书。◇ *She had to write a report on the project.* 她必须就这个项目写一份报告。◇ **~ (about sth)** *I wanted to travel and then write about it.* 我本想去旅行，然后把见闻写下来。◇ *He writes for the 'New Yorker'* (= works as a writer). 他为《纽约客》撰稿。◇ *No decision has been made* ***at the time of writing.*** 写这个的时候尚未作出决定。◇ **~ sb sth** *She wrote him several poems.* 她为他写了几首诗。

WORDFINDER 联想词：author, **book**, classic, critic, **drama**, fiction, genre, **literature**, **poetry**

• **A LETTER** 信 **3** [I, T] to put information, a message of good wishes, etc. in a letter and send it to sb 写信：*Bye! Don't forget to write.* 再见！别忘了写信。◇ *Can you write and confirm your booking?* 你能写信来确认你的预订项目吗？◇ *I'm writing to enquire about language courses.* 特此致函询问有关语言课程事宜。◇ **~ to sb** *She wrote to him in France.* 她给他往法国写信。◇ **~ sth (to sb)** *I wrote a letter to the Publicity Department.* 我给宣传部写了一封信。◇ **~ sb sth** *I wrote the Publicity Department a letter.* 我给宣传部写了一封信。◇ **~ that…** *She wrote that they were all fine.* 她信上说他们一切安好。◇ **~ sb** (*NAmE*) *Write me while you're away.* 你外出期间给我写信。◇ **~ sb that…** (*NAmE*) *He wrote me that he would be arriving Monday.* 他给我写信说他将于星期一到达。◇ **~ doing sth** *They wrote thanking us for the present.* 他们写信来感谢我们赠送的礼物。

• **STATE IN WRITING** 书面陈述 **4** [T, I] to state the information or the words mentioned 写道；（以文字）说：**~ that…** *In his latest book he writes that the theory has since been disproved.* 他在最近的一本书里写道，那个理论后来被证明不成立。◇ **~ of sth** *Ancient historians wrote of a lost continent beneath the ocean.* 古代史学家写过有关一个沉没海底的大陆的事迹。◇ **+ speech** *'Of all my books,' wrote Dickens, 'I like this the best.'* 狄更斯写道："在我所有的书中，我最喜欢这本。"

W

• **CHEQUE/FORM** 支票；表格 **5** [T] to put information in the appropriate places on a cheque or other form 开（支票等）；填写（表格等）：**~ sth (out)** *to write out a cheque* 开一张支票 ◇ **~ sb (out) sth** *I'll write you a receipt.* 我来给你开一张收据。

• **COMPUTING** 计算机技术 **6** [T, I] **~ (sth) to/onto sth** to record data in the memory of a computer 将（数据）写入（存储器）：*An error was reported when he tried to write data to the file for the first time.* 当他第一次尝试把数据写入文档时，报告说有错。

• **OF PEN/PENCIL** 笔 **7** [I] to work correctly or in the way mentioned 好使；能使用；以…方式写：*This pen won't write.* 这支钢笔不好使。➲ MORE LIKE THIS 20, page R27, ➲ MORE LIKE THIS 33, page R28

IDM **be written all over sb's 'face** (of a feeling 感情) to be very obvious to other people from the expression on sb's face 形之于色；表现得十分明显：*Guilt was written all over his face.* 他满脸愧疚。 **have sth/sb written all 'over it/sb** (*informal*) to show clearly the quality mentioned or the influence of the person mentioned 明显有（某性质）；显然受到（某人影响）：*It was a performance with star quality written all over it.* 这次演出显然明星气派十足。◇ *This essay has got Mike written all over it.* 这篇散文俨然是迈克的手笔。 **nothing (much) to write 'home about** (*informal*) not especially good; ordinary 不特别好；很普通；一般 **that's all she 'wrote** (*NAmE, informal*) used when you are stating that there is nothing more that can be said about sth or that sth is completely finished（表示没有其他要说或某事已彻底结束）就这么多，到此结束 ➲ MORE AT WORTH *adj.*

PHR V **ˌwrite aˈway** = WRITE OFF/AWAY (TO SB/STH) (FOR STH) **ˌwrite ˈback (to sb)** to write sb a letter replying to their letter（给某人）写回信，复信 SYN **reply**: *I'm afraid I never wrote back.* 我恐怕从未写过回信。◇ *She wrote back saying that she couldn't come.* 她回信说她来不了。 **ˌwrite sth↔ˈdown 1** to write sth on paper, especially in order to remember or record it 写下；记录下：*Write down the address before you forget it.* 把地址记下来，免得忘了。**2** (*business* 商) to reduce the value of ASSETS when stating it in a company's accounts 减记，划减（资产的账面价值）➲ RELATED NOUN WRITE-DOWN **ˌwrite ˈin (to sb/sth) (for sth)** to write a letter to an organization or a company, for example to ask about sth or to express an opinion 致函（某机构）（表达意见等）：*I'll write in for more information.* 我要写信索取更详细的材料。 **ˌwrite sb/sth↔ˈin** (*NAmE, politics* 政) to add an extra name to your voting paper in an election in order to be able to vote for them（在选票上）写上非候选人姓名 ➲ RELATED NOUN WRITE-IN **ˌwrite sth ˈinto sth** to include a rule or condition in a contract or an agreement when it is made 把…写入（合同或协议） **ˌwrite ˈoff/aˈway (to sb/sth) (for sth)** to write to an organization or a company, usually in order to ask them to send you sth 致函（某机构）（索取资料等）SYN **send off (for sth)**: *I've written off for the catalogue.* 我已去函索取商品目录。 **ˌwrite sth↔ˈoff 1** (*business* 商) to cancel a debt; to recognize that sth is a failure, has no value, etc. 注销，销记（账项、资产等）：*to write off a debt/an investment* 注销一笔债务 / 一项投资 **2** (*BrE*) to damage sth, especially a vehicle, so badly that it cannot be repaired 把（车辆等）毁坏，报废 ➲ RELATED NOUN WRITE-OFF (1) ➲ SEE ALSO TOTAL *v.* (3) **ˌwrite sb/sth↔ˈoff (as sth)** to decide that sb/sth is a failure or not worth paying any attention to 认定…失败（或没有价值、不可救药等）SYN **dismiss** **ˌwrite sth↔ˈout** to write sth on paper, including all the details, especially a piece of work or an account of sth 把…全部写出 ➲ SEE ALSO WRITE (5) **ˌwrite sb↔ˈout (of sth)** to remove a character from a regular series on television or radio 去掉（系列电视剧或广播剧中的角色） **ˌwrite sth↔ˈup** to record sth in writing in a full and complete form, often using notes that you made earlier（利用笔记等）详细写出：*to write up your notes/the minutes of a meeting* 把笔记 / 会议记录整理成文 ➲ RELATED NOUN WRITE-UP

ˈwrite-back *noun* [C, U] (*business* 商) a situation where an ASSET gets a value which it was thought to have lost; an amount of money entered in the financial records because of this（对呆账的）拨回；拨回资产的账面值

ˈwrite-down *noun* (*business* 商) a reduction in the value of ASSETS, etc.（资产等账面价值的）减记，划减

ˈwrite-in *noun* (*US*) a vote for sb who is not an official candidate in an election, in which you write their name on your BALLOT PAPER 投给非候选人的票

ˈwrite-off *noun* **1** (*BrE*) a vehicle that has been so badly damaged in an accident that it is not worth spending money to repair it 报废车辆 **2** [sing.] (*informal*) a period of time during which you do not achieve anything 无所作为的一段时间：*With meetings and phone calls, yesterday was a complete write-off.* 昨天都在开会和打电话，瞎忙了一天。**3 ~ (of sth)** (*business* 商) an act of cancelling a debt and accepting that it will never be paid（债项的）注销，销记

ˌwrite-proˈtect *verb* **~ sth** (*computing* 计) to protect the information on a computer disk from being changed or DELETED (= destroyed) 给（磁盘信息）写保护

writer 🔑 /ˈraɪtə(r)/ *noun* **1** 🔑 a person whose job is writing books, stories, articles, etc. 作家；作者；著者：*writers of poetry* 诗人 ◇ *a **travel/cookery, etc. writer*** 游记作家、写菜谱的人等 **2** 🔑 a person who has written a particular thing 写…的人；执笔者；撰写人：*the writer of this letter* 写这封信的人 **3** 🔑 (with an adjective 与形容词连用) a person who forms letters in a particular way when they are writing 写字…的人：*a messy writer* 书写潦草的人

ˌwriter's ˈblock *noun* [U] a problem that writers sometimes have when they cannot think of what to write and have no new ideas（写作人的）灵感障碍，神思枯竭，写作笔障

ˌwriter's ˈcramp *noun* [U] a pain or stiff feeling in the hand caused by writing for a long time 书写痉挛（长时间写字造成的手部疼痛或僵硬感）

ˈwrite-up *noun* an article in a newspaper or magazine in which sb writes what they think about a new book, play, product, etc.（报刊上的）评论，评述，评介

writhe /raɪð/ *verb* [I] ~ **(about/around)** **(in/with sth)** to twist or move your body without stopping, often because you are in great pain（常指因剧痛不停地）扭动，翻滚：*She was writhing around on the floor in agony.* 她痛得在地板上直打滚。◇ *The snake writhed and hissed.* 那蛇蠕动着，发出嘶嘶的声音。◇ (*figurative*) *He was writhing* (= suffering a lot) *with embarrassment.* 他难堪得无地自容。

writ·ing 🔑 /ˈraɪtɪŋ/ *noun* **1** 🔑 [U] the activity of writing, in contrast to reading, speaking, etc. 写；书写；写作：*Our son's having problems with his **reading and writing*** (= at school). 我们儿子在读写方面有困难。◇ *a **writing case*** (= containing paper, pens, etc.) 文具盒 **2** 🔑 [U] the activity of writing books, articles, etc., especially as a job（专职）写作；著书立说：*Only later did she discover a talent for writing.* 她后来才发现自己的写作天分。◇ *He is leaving the band to concentrate on his writing.* 他要离开乐队去专职写作。◇ ***creative writing*** 文学创作 ◇ ***feminist/travel, etc. writing*** 女权主义文章、游记等的写作 ➲ SEE ALSO SONGWRITING **3** 🔑 [U] books, articles, etc. in general 著作；文字作品；文章：*The review is a brilliant piece of writing.* 这篇评论很精彩。**4** 🔑 **writings** [pl.] a group of pieces of writing, especially by a particular person or on a particular subject（某作家或专题的）著作，作品：*His experiences in India influenced his later writings.* 他在印度的经历影响了他后来的著作。◇ *the writings of Hegel* 黑格尔的著作 **5** 🔑 [U] words that have been written or painted on sth（书写或涂画的）文字：*There was writing all over the desk.* 书桌上写满了字。**6** 🔑 [U] the particular way in which sb forms letters when they write 笔迹；字迹；书法 **SYN** **handwriting**：*Who's this from? I don't recognize the writing.* 这是谁写来的？我辨认不出笔迹。

IDM **in ˈwriting** 🔑 in the form of a letter, document, etc. (that gives proof of sth) 以书面形式（作为凭证）：*All telephone reservations must be confirmed in writing.* 所有的电话预订必须以书面形式确认。◇ *Could you **put** your complaint **in writing**?* 你能把投诉的内容写下来吗？◇ *You must **get it in writing**.* 你必须用书面的形式。 **the ˌwriting is on the ˈwall | see the ˌwriting on the ˈwall** (*NAmE also* **the ˌhandwriting on the ˈwall**) (*saying*) used when you are describing a situation in which there are signs that sth is going to have problems or that it is going to be a failure（看出）厄运临头的预兆，不祥之兆：*It is amazing that not one of them saw the writing on the wall.* 令人吃惊的是他们就没有一个人看出大难临头的预兆。**ORIGIN** From the Bible story in which strange writing appeared on a wall during a feast given by King Belshazzar, predicting Belshazzar's death and the fall of his city. 源自《圣经》故事，伯沙撒国王大摆宴席时，墙上出现了奇怪的字迹，预言伯沙撒的死亡及其王国的覆灭。

ˈwriting paper *noun* [U] = NOTEPAPER

writ·ten 🔑 /ˈrɪtn/ *adj.* **1** 🔑 [usually before noun] expressed in writing rather than in speech 书面的：*written instructions* 书面指示 **2** 🔑 [usually before noun] (of an exam, a piece of work, etc. 测验、工作等) involving writing rather than speaking or practical skills 书面的；笔头的：*a written test* 笔试 ◇ *written communication skills* 书面交流技巧 **3** 🔑 [only before noun] in the form of a letter, document, etc. and therefore official 以书信（或文件等）形式的；书面的；成文的；正式的：*a written apology* 书面道歉 ◇ *a written contract* 书面合同 ➲ SEE ALSO WRITE

IDM **the ˌwritten ˈword** language expressed in writing rather than in speech 书面语：*the permanence of the written word* 书面语传之久远的特性

wrong 🔑 /rɒŋ; *NAmE* rɔːŋ/ *adj., adv., noun, verb*

■ ***adj.***

• **NOT CORRECT** 不正确 **1** 🔑 not right or correct 错误的；不对的；不正确的：*I got all the answers wrong.* 我的答案全都错了。◇ *He was driving on the wrong side of the road.* 他开车行驶在道路逆行的一侧。◇ *Sorry, I must have dialled the wrong number.* 对不起，我一定是拨错电话号码了。◇ *You're holding the camera **the wrong way up**!* 你把照相机拿颠倒了！◇ *That picture is **the wrong way round**.* 那幅画挂反了。**OPP** **right** **2** 🔑 [not before noun] (of a person 人) not right about sth/sb 出错；搞错；有错误 **SYN** **mistaken**：*I think she lives at number 44, but I could be wrong.* 我想她是住在 44 号，不过我可能记错了。◇ ~ **(about sth/sb)** *You were wrong about Tom; he's not married after all.* 你把汤姆的情况搞错了，他根本没结婚。◇ ~ **(to do sth)** *We were wrong to assume that she'd agree.* 我们错误地以为她会同意。◇ *She would **prove him wrong*** (= prove that he was wrong) *whatever happened.* 不论发生的是什么事，她都会证明他是错的。◇ (*informal*) *You think you've beaten me but **that's where you're wrong**.* 你以为已经赢了我了，可你错就错在这里。◇ (*informal*) ***Correct me if I'm wrong*** (= I may be wrong) *but didn't you say you two knew each other?* 我若说错了请你纠正，你不是说过你们彼此认识吗？

• **CAUSING PROBLEMS** 造成问题 **3** 🔑 [not before noun] causing problems or difficulties; not as it should be 引起问题（或麻烦）；有毛病；不正常：*Is **anything wrong**? You look worried.* 出了什么事？看你愁眉苦脸的样子。◇ ***'What's wrong?'*** *'Oh, nothing.'* "哪儿不舒服？" "噢，没事。" ◇ ~ **with sb/sth** *There's **something wrong** with the printer.* 打印机出了故障。◇ *The doctor could find **nothing wrong** with him.* 医生查不出他有什么病。◇ *I **have something wrong with** my foot.* 我的脚有点儿不对劲。

• **NOT SUITABLE** 不适合 **4** 🔑 [usually before noun] not suitable, right or what you need 不合适的；不适当的；不合意的：~ **(sth)** **(for sth)** *He's the wrong person for the job.* 他不适合做这项工作。◇ ~ **(sth to do)** *I realized that it was the wrong thing to say.* 我意识到说这话不恰当。◇ *We don't want this document **falling into the wrong hands**.* 我们不想让这份文件落入不对路的人手里。◇ *It was his bad luck to be **in the wrong place at the wrong time*** (= so that he got involved in trouble without intending to). 算他倒霉，在错误的时间出现在错误的地方。

• **NOT MORALLY RIGHT** 不道德 **5** 🔑 [not usually before noun] not morally right or honest 不道德；不义；不诚实：*This man has **done nothing wrong**.* 这位男子没有做过不正当的事。◇ ~ **(of/for sb)** **(to do sth)** *It is wrong to tell lies.* 说谎是不道德的。◇ *It was wrong of me to get so angry.* 我不该发这么大脾气。◇ ~ **with sth/with doing sth** *What's wrong with eating meat?* 吃肉有什么不对？◇ ~ **that…** *It is wrong that he should not be punished for what he did.* 他的所作所为竟可不受惩罚，这太不公平了。➲ MORE LIKE THIS 20, page R27

▸ **wrong·ness** *noun* [U] (*formal*)

IDM **from/on the ˌwrong side of the ˈtracks** from or living in a poor area or part of town 来自（城里的）贫民区；住在贫穷的地区（或城区） **get (hold of) the ˌwrong end of the ˈstick** (*BrE, informal*) to understand sth in the wrong way 误解；误会 **on the ˌwrong side of the ˈlaw** in trouble with the police 违法 **take sth the wrong ˈway** to be offended by a remark that was not intended to be offensive 误会本意良好的话 ➲ MORE AT BACK *v.*, BARK *v.*, BED *n.*, FAR *adv.*, FOOT *n.*, NOTE *n.*, RUB *v.*, SIDE *n.*, TRACK *n.*

■ ***adv.*** 🔑 (used after verbs 用于动词之后) in a way that produces a result that is not correct or that you do not want 错误地；不正确；不对：*My name is spelt wrong.* 我

W

的名字给拼错了。◇ *The program won't load. What am I **doing wrong**?* 这程序载入不了。我哪里出错了？◇ *I was trying to apologize but it **came out wrong*** (= what I said sounded wrong). 我是想要道歉，可是话一出口却变了味儿。◇ *'I thought you were going out.' 'Well you must have **thought wrong**, then!'* "我原以为你要出去呢。" "啊，那你一定是想错了！" OPP **right**

IDM **get sb 'wrong** (*informal*) to not understand correctly what sb means 误会，误解，曲解（某人的意思）: ***Don't get me wrong*** (= do not be offended by what I am going to say), *I think he's doing a good job, but...* 别误解我，我认为他活儿干得不错，不过… **get sth 'wrong** (*informal*) **1** to not understand a situation correctly 误会，误解，曲解（某事）: *No, you've got it all wrong. She's his wife.* 不，你完全误会了。她是他的妻子。**2** to make a mistake

▼ **SYNONYMS 同义词辨析**

wrong

false • mistaken • incorrect • inaccurate • misguided • untrue

These words all describe sth that is not right or correct, or sb who is not right about sth. 以上各词均指错误的、不正确的、犯错的。

wrong not right or correct; (of a person) not right about sb/sth 指错误的、不正确的，（人）出错、搞错、有错误： *I got all the answers wrong.* 我的答案全都错了。◇ *We were wrong to assume she'd agree.* 我们错误地以为她会同意。

false not true or correct; wrong because it is based on sth that is not true or correct 指不正确的、不真实的、错误的： *A whale is a fish. **True or false?*** 鲸鱼是鱼，对还是错？◇ *She gave false information to the insurance company.* 她向保险公司提供了虚假信息。

mistaken wrong in your opinion or judgement; based on a wrong opinion or bad judgement 指意见或判断不正确的、以错误的意见或判断为基础的： *You're completely mistaken about Jane.* 你对简的看法完全错了。

incorrect (*rather formal*) wrong according to the facts; containing mistakes 指与事实不符的、不准确的、不正确的： *Many of the figures were incorrect.* 这些数字有许多是不准确的。

inaccurate wrong according to the facts; containing mistakes 指与事实不符的、不准确的、不正确的： *The report was badly researched and quite inaccurate.* 这报告没有经过认真调查，颇为失实。

INCORRECT OR INACCURATE? 用 incorrect 还是 inaccurate?

A fact, figure or spelling that is wrong is **incorrect**; information, a belief or a description based on incorrect facts can be **incorrect** or **inaccurate**; something that is produced, such as a film, report or map, that contains incorrect facts is **inaccurate**. 事实、数据或拼写错误用 incorrect；以错误事实为基础的信息、看法或描述可用 incorrect 或 inaccurate；影片、报告或地图等制品包含与事实不符的内容用 inaccurate。

misguided wrong because you have understood or judged a situation badly 指理解不当的、判断失误的： *In her misguided attempts to help, she only made the situation worse.* 她想帮忙，但做法不对头，反把事情弄得更糟。

untrue not based on facts, but invented or guessed 指无事实根据的、捏造的、凭空猜想的： *These accusations are totally untrue.* 这些指控纯属捏造。

PATTERNS

- to be wrong/mistaken **about** sth
- wrong/false/mistaken/incorrect/inaccurate/untrue **information**
- a(n) false/mistaken/incorrect/inaccurate/misguided **belief**
- a(n) wrong/incorrect **answer**

with sth 把…搞错；把…弄错：*I must have got the figures wrong.* 我一定是把数字给搞错了。**go 'wrong 1** to make a mistake 犯错误；做错事；搞错；弄错：*If you do what she tells you, you won't go far wrong.* 你要是按照她说的做，就不会出大差错。◇ *Where did we go wrong with those kids* (= what mistakes did we make for them to behave so badly)? 我们在什么地方把这些孩子惯坏了？**2** (of a machine 机器) to stop working correctly 发生故障；出毛病：*My watch keeps going wrong.* 我的表不断地出毛病。**3** to experience problems or difficulties 出现问题；遇到困难：*The relationship started to go wrong when they moved abroad.* 移居国外后，他们的关系开始出现问题了。◇ *What else can go wrong* (= what other problems are we going to have)? 还会出现什么问题？ **you can't go 'wrong (with sth)** (*informal*) used to say that sth will always be acceptable in a particular situation 绝对不会出错；绝不会有问题：*For a quick lunch you can't go wrong with pasta.* 想要吃一顿快捷的午餐，吃意大利面准错不了。 ➲ MORE AT FOOT *n.*

▼ **WHICH WORD? 词语辨析**

wrong / wrongly / wrongfully

- In informal language **wrong** can be used as an adverb instead of **wrongly**, when it means 'incorrectly' and comes after a verb or its object. 在非正式用法中，wrong 可作副词代替 wrongly，表示错误地，置于动词或动词宾语之后： *My name was spelled wrong.* 我的名字拼错了。◇ *I'm afraid you guessed wrong.* 恐怕你猜错了。 **Wrongly** is used before a past participle or a *that* clause. * wrongly 用于过去分词或 that 从句之前： *My name was wrongly spelt.* 我的名字拼错了。◇ *She guessed wrongly that he was a teacher.* 她误以为他是个教师。
- **Wrongfully** is usually used in a formal legal situation with words like *convicted, dismissed* and *imprisoned*. * wrongfully 通常用于正式的法律场合，与 convicted、dismissed、imprisoned 等词连用。

■ ***noun*** **1** [U] behaviour that is not honest or morally acceptable 不义行为；欺骗行径；恶行：*Children must be taught the difference between right and wrong.* 必须教儿童分清是非。◇ *Her son can **do no wrong** in her eyes.* 在她眼里，她的儿子不可能做坏事。**2** [C] (*formal*) an act that is not legal, honest or morally acceptable 犯罪；欺骗；罪恶：*It is time to forgive past wrongs if progress is to be made.* 如果想有进步，现在就该宽恕过去的罪过。OPP **right**

IDM **in the 'wrong** responsible for an accident, a mistake, an argument, etc.（在事故、错误、争论等中）有错，应承担责任：*The motorcyclist was clearly in the wrong.* 骑摩托车的人显然对事故负有责任。**two ˌwrongs don't make a 'right** (*saying*) used to say that if sb does sth bad to you, the situation will not be improved by doing sth bad to them 冤冤相报永无完了；以牙还牙行不通 ➲ MORE AT RIGHT *v.*

■ ***verb*** [usually passive] **~ sb** (*formal*) to treat sb badly or in an unfair way 不公正（或不诚实）对待：*He felt deeply wronged by the allegations.* 这些指控让他感到深受冤枉。

wrong·doer /ˈrɒŋduːə(r); *NAmE* ˈrɔːŋ-; ˈrɑːŋ-/ *noun* (*formal*) a person who does sth dishonest or illegal 做坏事的人；违法犯罪者；作恶者 SYN **criminal, offender**

wrong·doing /ˈrɒŋduːɪŋ; *NAmE* ˈrɔːŋ-/ *noun* [U, C] (*formal*) illegal or dishonest behaviour 不法行为；坏事；作恶；欺骗行径 SYN **crime, offence**

ˌwrong-'foot *verb* **~ sb** (*BrE*) to put sb in a difficult or embarrassing situation by doing sth that they do not expect 使措手不及；使窘态毕露：*It was an attempt to wrong-foot the opposition.* 这一举动为的是让对手措手不及。

wrong·ful /ˈrɒŋfl; *NAmE* ˈrɔːŋ-/ *adj.* [usually before noun] (*law* 律) not fair, morally right or legal 不公正的；不道德的；不合法的：*She decided to sue her employer for wrongful dismissal.* 她决定起诉雇主非法解雇她。▶ **wrong·ful·ly** /-fəli/ *adv.*: *to be wrongfully convicted/dismissed* 遭非法定罪 / 解雇 ➲ NOTE AT WRONG

W

ˌwrong-ˈheaded *adj.* having or showing bad judgement 判断错误的；执迷不悟的：*wrong-headed beliefs* 错误的信念

wrong·ly /ˈrɒŋli; *NAmE* ˈrɔːŋ-/ *adv.* in a way that is unfair, immoral or not correct 不公正地；不道德地；错误地：*She was wrongly accused of stealing.* 她被诬告犯了偷盗罪。◇ *He assumed, wrongly, that she did not care.* 他误以为她并不在乎。◇ *The sentence had been wrongly translated.* 这个句子翻译错了。◇ *They knew they had acted wrongly.* 他们知道他们做得不对。◇ ***Rightly or wrongly,*** *they felt they should have been better informed* (= I do not know whether they were right to feel this way). 不论对错，他们觉得本该让他们了解到更多的情况。➲ NOTE AT WRONG

wrote PAST TENSE OF WRITE

wrought /rɔːt/ *verb* **~ sth** (*formal* or *literary*) (used only in the past tense 仅用于过去时) caused sth to happen, especially a change 使发生了，造成了（尤指变化）：*This century wrought major changes in our society.* 本世纪给我们的社会带来了重大变革。◇ *The storm wrought havoc in the south.* 这场暴风雨在南方造成了巨大的灾害。**HELP** **Wrought** is an old form of the past tense of **work**. * wrought 是 work 过去式的旧式。

ˌwrought ˈiron *noun* [U] a form of iron used to make decorative fences, gates, etc. 锻铁；熟铁：*The gates were made of wrought iron.* 这些大门是用熟铁制成的。◇ *wrought-iron gates* 熟铁门 ➲ COMPARE CAST IRON

wrung PAST TENSE, PAST PART. OF WRING

wry /raɪ/ *adj.* [usually before noun] **1** showing that you are both amused and disappointed or annoyed 啼笑皆非的：*'At least we got one vote,' she said with a wry smile.* "我们起码还得了一票。" 她苦笑着解嘲道。◇ *He pulled a wry face when I asked him how it had gone.* 我问他近况如何，他有些哭笑不得。**2** amusing in a way that shows IRONY 挖苦的；讽刺的；揶揄的：*a wry comedy about family life* 关于家庭生活的讽刺喜剧 ◇ *a wry comment* 挖苦的评论 ◇ *wry humour* 冷嘲式的幽默 ▶ **wryly** *adv.*: *to smile wryly* 冷笑 **wry·ness** *noun* [U]

WTO /ˌdʌbljuː tiː ˈəʊ; *NAmE* ˈoʊ/ *abbr.* World Trade Organization (an international organization that encourages international trade and economic development, especially by reducing restrictions on trade) 世界贸易组织

Wu /wuː/ *noun* [U] a form of Chinese spoken in Jiangsu, Zhejiang and Shanghai 吴语（通行于江苏、浙江和上海的汉语方言）

wun·der·kind /ˈwʊndəkɪnd; *NAmE* -dərk-/ *noun* (*pl.* **wunder·kind·er** /ˈwʊndəkɪndə(r); *NAmE* -dərk-/) (*from German, sometimes disapproving*) a person who is very successful at a young age 神童；少年得志者

wuss /wʊs/ *noun* (*slang*) a person who is not strong or brave 懦夫；脓包：*Don't be such a wuss!* 别这么软弱！

WWW /ˌdʌbljuː dʌbljuː ˈdʌbljuː/ *abbr.* = WORLD WIDE WEB：*several useful WWW addresses* 几个有用的万维网网址

WYSIWYG /ˈwɪziwɪɡ/ *abbr.* (*computing* 计) what you see is what you get (what you see on the computer screen is exactly the same as will be printed or displayed) 所见即所得（全写为 what you see is what you get，表示在电脑屏幕上看到的效果与打印或呈现出来的一致）

W

X /eks/ (*also* **x**) *noun, symbol*

■***noun*** (*pl.* **Xs**, **X's**, **x's** /ˈeksɪz/) **1** [C, U] the 24th letter of the English alphabet 英语字母表的第 24 个字母：*'Xylophone' begins with (an) X/'X'.* * xylophone 一词以字母 x 开头。**2** [U] (*mathematics* 数) used to represent a number whose value is not mentioned（代表未知数）：*The equation is impossible for any value of x greater than 2.* 当 x 的值大于 2 时，这个等式不成立。**3** [U] a person, a number, an influence, etc. that is not known or not named 未知的人（或数、影响等）；未指明的人（或数、影响等）：*Let's suppose X knows what Y is doing.* 假设 X 知道 Y 正在干什么。➲SEE ALSO X CHROMOSOME, X-RATED, X-RAY *n.*

■***symbol*** **1** the number 10 in ROMAN NUMERALS（罗马数字）10 **2** used to represent a kiss at the end of a letter, etc.（置于书信等的结尾，表示亲吻）：*Love from Kathy XXX.* 爱你的凯西，吻你，吻你，吻你。 **3** used to show a vote for sb in an election（在选举中表示投给某人的一票）：*Write X beside the candidate of your choice.* 在你选择的候选人旁边标一个 X。**4** used to show that a written answer is wrong（表示书面答案是错的）➲ COMPARE TICK *n.* (1) **5** used to show position, for example on a map（用以标明方位，如在地图上）：*X marks the spot.* * X 标出了所说的地点。

ˈX chromosome *noun* (*biology* 生) a SEX CHROMOSOME. Two X chromosomes exist in the cells of human females. In human males each cell has one X chromosome and one Y chromosome. * X 染色体

xenon /ˈzenɒn; ˈziː-; *NAmE* -nɑːn/ *noun* [U] (*symb.* **Xe**) a chemical element. Xenon is a gas that is found in very small quantities in the air and is used in some special electric lamps. 氙；氙气

xeno·pho·bia /ˌzenəˈfəʊbiə; *NAmE* -ˈfoʊ-/ *noun* [U] (*disapproving*) a strong feeling of dislike or fear of people from other countries 仇外，惧外（对外国人的厌恶或惧怕）：*a campaign against racism and xenophobia* 反对种族主义和仇外情绪的运动 ▶ **xeno·pho·bic** /-ˈfəʊbɪk; *NAmE* -ˈfoʊ-/ *adj.*

xeno·trans·plan·ta·tion /ˌziːnəʊˌtrænsplɑːnˈteɪʃn; -ˌtrænz-; *NAmE* ˌziːnoʊ-; -plænˈt-/ *noun* [U] (*medical* 医) the process of taking organs from animals and putting them into humans for medical purposes（从动物到人体的）异种移植

X factor /ˈeks fæktə(r)/ *noun* [sing.] a special quality, especially one that is essential for success and is difficult to describe 特质，X 因素（尤指获得成功所必需又难以描述的素质）：*She certainly has the X factor that all great singers have.* 她确实具备所有伟大的歌唱家所拥有的特质。

Xhosa /ˈkɔːsə; ˈkəʊ-; *NAmE* ˈkoʊ-/ *noun* [U] a language spoken by the Xhosa people in South Africa（南非）科萨语

xi /saɪ; zaɪ; ksaɪ; gzaɪ/ *noun* the 14th letter of the Greek alphabet (Ξ, ξ) 希腊字母表的第 14 个字母

Xiang (*also* **Hsiang**) /ʃiːˈæŋ/ *noun* [U] a form of Chinese spoken mainly in Hunan 湘语；湘方言；湖南话

-xion ➲-ION

XL /ˌeks ˈel/ *abbr.* extra large (used for sizes of things, especially clothes)（尤指服装的尺码）特大号：*an XL T-shirt* 一件特大号 T 恤衫

Xmas /ˈkrɪsməs; ˈeksməs/ *noun* [C, U] (*informal*) used as a short form of 'Christmas', usually in writing 圣诞节（Christmas 的缩写）：*A merry Xmas to all our readers!* 祝广大读者圣诞快乐！

XML /ˌeks em ˈel/ *noun* (*computing* 计) Extensible Markup Language (a system used for marking the structure of text on a computer, for example when creating website pages) 可扩展置标语言，可扩展标记语言（制作网页等用的文本结构标记系统）

ˈX-rated *adj.* (especially of a film/movie 尤指电影) that people under 18 are not allowed to see because it contains sex and/or violence * X 级的，青少年不宜的（充斥性和 / 或暴力而禁止 18 岁以下的青少年观看）

X-ray /ˈeks reɪ/ *noun, verb*

■***noun*** **1** [usually pl.] a type of RADIATION that can pass through objects that are not transparent and make it possible to see inside or through them * X 射线；X 光：*an X-ray machine* (= one that produces X-rays) * X 光机 **2** a photograph made by X-rays, especially one showing bones or organs in the body * X 光照片：*a chest X-ray* 胸部 X 光照片 ◇ *The doctor studied the X-rays of her lungs.* 医生研究了她肺部的 X 光照片。◇ *to take an X-ray* 拍摄 X 光照片 ➲**WORDFINDER NOTE** AT EXAMINE **3** a medical examination using X-rays 用 X 射线进行的临床检查：*I had to go for an X-ray.* 我得去做 X 光检查。

■***verb*** **~ sth** to photograph and examine bones and organs inside the body, using X-rays 用 X 射线拍摄检查：*He had to have his chest X-rayed.* 他得做胸部 X 光检查。

xylem /ˈzaɪləm/ *noun* [U] (*biology* 生) the material in plants that carries water and minerals upwards from the root 木质部（植物中将水分和矿物质从根部向上输送的组织）➲ COMPARE PHLOEM

xylo·phone /ˈzaɪləfəʊn; *NAmE* -foʊn/ *noun* a musical instrument made of two rows of wooden bars of different lengths that you hit with two small sticks 木琴 ➲ COMPARE GLOCKENSPIEL ➲**VISUAL VOCAB** PAGE V37

Y /waɪ/ *noun, abbr., symbol*

▪ ***noun*** (*also* **y**) (*pl.* **Ys**, **Y's**, **y's** /waɪz/) **1** [C, U] the 25th letter of the English alphabet 英语字母表的第 25 个字母：*'Year' begins with (a) Y/'Y'.* * year 一词以字母 y 开头。**2** [U] (*mathematics* 数) used to represent a number whose value is not mentioned（代表未知数）：*Can the value of y be predicted from the value of x?* 能从 x 值推知 y 值吗？**3** [U] a person, a number, an influence, etc. that is not known or not named 未知的人（或数、影响等）；未指明的人（或数、影响等）：*Let's suppose X knows what Y is doing.* 假设 X 知道 Y 正在干什么。➲ SEE ALSO Y CHROMOSOME, Y-FRONTS™

▪ ***abbr.* the Y** (*NAmE, informal*) YMCA, YWCA 基督教青年会；基督教女青年会

▪ ***symbol*** the symbol for the chemical element YTTRIUM（化学元素）钇

-y *suffix* **1** (*also* **-ey**) (in adjectives 构成形容词) full of; having the quality of 充满…的；有…特性的：*dusty* 积满灰尘的 ◇ *clayey* 像黏土的 **2** (in adjectives 构成形容词) tending to 有…倾向的：*runny* 水分过多的 ◇ *sticky* 黏性的 **3** (in nouns 构成名词) the action or process of …的动作（或过程）：*inquiry* 询问 **4** (*also* **-ie**) (in nouns, showing affection 构成名词，表示喜爱)：*doggy* 小狗 ◇ *daddy* 爸爸

ya /jə/ *pron., det.* (*informal, non-standard*) used in writing as a way of showing the way people sometimes pronounce the word 'you' or 'your' 你，你的（书写时用，表示口语的 you 或 your）：*He said, 'I got something for ya.'* 他说："我有东西给你。" ➲ MORE LIKE THIS 5, page R25

yaar /jɑː; *NAmE* jɑːr/ *noun* (*IndE, informal*) (used as a friendly way of addressing sb) a friend（用作友好称呼）朋友，伙计：*Let's go for a drink, yaar!* 咱们去喝一杯吧，朋友！

yacht /jɒt; *NAmE* jɑːt/ (*NAmE also* **sail·boat**) *noun* a large sailing boat, often also with an engine and a place to sleep on board, used for pleasure trips and racing 帆船；游艇；快艇：*a yacht club/race* 帆船俱乐部 / 比赛 ◇ *a motor yacht* 摩托艇 ◇ *a luxury yacht* 豪华游艇 ➲ VISUAL VOCAB PAGE V61 ➲ COMPARE DINGHY ➲ MORE LIKE THIS 20, page R27

yacht·ing /ˈjɒtɪŋ; *NAmE* ˈjɑːt-/ *noun* [U] the sport or activity of sailing or racing yachts 快艇（或帆船）运动

yachts·man /ˈjɒtsmən; *NAmE* ˈjɑːt-/, **yachts·woman** /ˈjɒtswʊmən; *NAmE* ˈjɑːt-/ *noun* (*pl.* **-men** /-mən/, **-women** /-wɪmɪn/) a person who sails a yacht for pleasure or as a sport 游艇（或快艇）驾驶者；帆船比赛选手：*a round-the-world yachtsman* 驾驶帆船环球旅行的人

yack *verb* = YAK

yada yada yada (*also* **yadda yadda yadda**) /jædə jædə ˈjædə/ *exclamation* (*NAmE, informal*) used when you are talking about sth to show that some of the details are not worth saying because they are not important or are boring or obvious 等等；如此这般：*His new girlfriend is attractive, funny, smart, yada yada yada.* 他的新女友有魅力、有趣、聪明，等等等等。

yah /jɑː/ *exclamation* **1** a way of writing 'yes' to show that the speaker has an upper-class accent 是，好（书写时用，表示带上流社会口音的 yes）**2** used to show that you have a low opinion of sb/sth（表示评价低）啧，哎：*Yah, you missed!* 喂，你没打中！

yahoo /ˈjɑːhuː; jəˈhuː/ *noun, exclamation*

▪ ***noun*** (*pl.* **-oos**) (*disapproving*) a rude, noisy or violent person 粗人；野蛮人

▪ ***exclamation*** /jɑːˈhuː; jæˈhuː/ (*informal*) used to show that you are very happy（表示高兴）哈哈，哇哈：*Yahoo, we did it!* 啊哈，我们成功了！

Yah·weh /ˈjɑːweɪ/ *noun* = JEHOVAH

yak /jæk/ *noun, verb*

▪ ***noun*** an animal of the cow family, with long horns and long hair, that lives in central Asia 牦牛（生活于中亚）

▪ ***verb*** (**-kk-**) (*also* **yack**) [I] (*informal, often disapproving*) to talk continuously about things that are not very serious or important 没完没了地说些无聊的话：*She just kept yakking on.* 她只是一个劲地东拉西扯。

yakka /ˈjækə/ *noun* [U] (*AustralE, NZE, informal*) work, especially of a hard physical kind 工作；艰苦劳作：*hard yakka* 沉重的体力活

Yale lock™ /ˈjeɪl lɒk; *NAmE* lɑːk/ *noun* (*BrE*) a type of lock that is often fitted in the front door of a house and which opens by using a flat key with a series of pointed edges 耶鲁锁（常装于房屋大门，钥匙呈扁平锯齿状）

y'all /jɔːl/ *pron.* = YOU-ALL

yam /jæm/ *noun* [C, U] the large root of a tropical plant that is cooked as a vegetable 薯蓣；山药 ➲ VISUAL VOCAB PAGE V33

yang /jæŋ/ *noun* [U] (*from Chinese*) (in Chinese philosophy) the bright active male principle of the universe（中国哲学）阳 ➲ COMPARE YIN

Yank /jæŋk/ (*also* **Yan·kee**) *noun* (*BrE, informal*) an offensive word for a person from the US; an American（含冒犯意）美国佬；美国人

yank /jæŋk/ *verb* [T, I] (*informal*) to pull sth/sb hard, quickly and suddenly 猛拉；猛拽：**~ sth/sb (+ adv./prep.)** *He yanked her to her feet.* 他一下子把她拉起来。◇ **~ sth/sb + adj.** *I yanked the door open.* 我猛地把门拽开。◇ **(+ adv./prep.)** *Liz yanked at my arm.* 利兹猛地拉了一下我的胳膊。▸ **yank** *noun*: *She gave the rope a yank.* 她猛地拽了拽绳子。

Yan·kee /ˈjæŋki/ *noun* **1** (*NAmE*) a person who comes from or lives in any of the northern states of the US, especially New England 美国北方人；（尤指）新英格兰人 **2** a soldier who fought for the Union (= the northern states) in the American Civil War（美国南北战争时的）北军士兵 **3** (*BrE, informal*) = YANK

yap /jæp/ *verb* (**-pp-**) **1** [I] **~ (at sb/sth)** (especially of small dogs 尤指小狗) to BARK a lot, making a high, sharp and usually irritating sound（常指令人感到烦厌的高声）吠叫：*The dogs yapped at his heels.* 几只狗跟在他后面汪汪乱叫。◇ *yapping dogs* 吠叫的狗 **2** [I] (*informal*) to talk in a silly, noisy and usually irritating way 哇哩哇啦地胡扯 ▸ **yap** *noun*

yard /jɑːd; *NAmE* jɑːrd/ *noun* **1** (*BrE*) an area outside a building, usually with a hard surface and a surrounding wall 院子：*the prison yard* 监狱里的院子 ◇ *The children were playing in the yard at the front of the school.* 孩子们在学校前面的空地上玩耍。➲ SEE ALSO BACKYARD **2** (*NAmE*) (*BrE* **gar·den**) a piece of land next to or around your house where you can grow flowers, fruit, vegetables, etc., usually with a LAWN (= an area of grass)（住宅旁或周围的）园圃，花园，果园，菜园 ➲ VISUAL VOCAB PAGE V20 ➲ SEE ALSO BACKYARD **3** (usually in compounds 通常构成复合词) an area of land used for a special purpose or business（某种用途的）区域，场地：*a boat yard* 船坞 HELP You will find other compounds ending in **yard** at their place in the alphabet. 其他以 yard 结尾的复合词可在各字母中的适当位置查到。➲ SYNONYMS AT FACTORY **4** (*abbr.* **yd**) a unit for measuring length, equal to 3 feet (36 inches) or 0.9144 of a metre 码（长度单位，等于 3 英尺（36 英寸）或 0.9144 米）**5** (*specialist*) a long piece of wood fastened to a MAST that supports a sail on a boat or ship 桁；桅横杆 IDM SEE INCH *n.*, NINE

yard·age /ˈjɑːdɪdʒ; *NAmE* ˈjɑːrd-/ *noun* [C, U] (*specialist*) **1** size measured in yards or square yards 码数；平方码数 **2** (in AMERICAN FOOTBALL 美式足球) the number of yards that a team or player has moved forward（球队或球员向前推进的）码数

yard·arm /ˈjɑːdɑːm; *NAmE* ˈjɑːrdɑːrm/ *noun* (*specialist*) either end of the long piece of wood fastened to a ship's MAST that supports a sail 桁端

Yardie /ˈjɑːdi; *NAmE* ˈjɑːrdi/ *noun* (*BrE, informal*) (in the UK) a member of a group of criminals from Jamaica or the West Indies（英国）亚迪（牙买加或西印度群岛的犯罪组织成员）

ˈyard sale *noun* (*NAmE*) a sale of things from sb's house, held in their yard 庭院拍卖会（在自家庭院售卖二手家什）➲ SEE ALSO GARAGE SALE

yard·stick /ˈjɑːdstɪk; *NAmE* ˈjɑːrd-/ *noun* **1** (*especially NAmE*) a ruler for measuring one yard 码尺 **2** a standard used for judging how good or successful sth is（好坏或成败的）衡量标准；准绳：*a yardstick by which to measure sth* 衡量某事物的标准 ◇ *Exam results are not the only yardstick of a school's performance.* 考试结果不是衡量学校水平的唯一标准。

yar·mulke (*also* **yar·mulka**) /ˈjɑːmʊlkə; *NAmE* ˈjɑːrm-/ (*also* **kippa**) *noun* a small round cap worn on top of the head by Jewish men; a type of SKULLCAP（犹太男子戴的）圆顶小帽；无檐便帽

yarn /jɑːn; *NAmE* jɑːrn/ *noun* **1** [U, C] thread that has been spun, used for knitting, making cloth, etc. 纱；纱线 ➲ VISUAL VOCAB PAGE V45 **2** [C] (*informal*) a long story, especially one that is exaggerated or invented（尤指夸张的或编造的）故事：*He used to* ***spin yarns*** (= tell stories) *about his time in the Army.* 他过去经常编造一些有关他在部队时的离奇故事。 IDM SEE PITCH *v.*

ˈyarn bombing (*also* **ˈyarn storming**) *noun* [U] (*informal*) a type of art in which people decorate items in the streets with colourful pieces of knitting or other items made using wool, cotton, etc., often doing it secretly 针织涂鸦（用五彩缤纷的毛棉织品等装饰街头物品的艺术，常秘密进行）：*Yarn bombing is another recent form of graffiti.* 针织涂鸦是另一种新兴的涂鸦形式。▶ **ˈyarn bomb** (*also* **ˈyarn storm**) *verb* ~ **sth** **ˈyarn bomber** (*also* **ˈyarn stormer**) *noun*

yar·row /ˈjærəʊ; *NAmE* -roʊ/ *noun* [U, C] a plant with flat groups of many small white or pinkish flowers that have a strong smell 蓍草

yash·mak /ˈjæʃmæk/ *noun* a piece of cloth covering most of the face, worn by some Muslim women（穆斯林妇女戴的）面纱

yatra /ˈjɑːtrɑː/ *noun* (*IndE*) **1** a line of people or vehicles that move along slowly as part of a ceremony or a journey to a holy place, usually carried out for religious reasons 典礼中缓行的队伍；朝圣队伍 **2** a tour by an official or members of a movement, etc.（官员或运动成员等的）巡视，巡游：*Party leaders are planning on embarking on their campaign yatras later in the year.* 党的领导人正计划在今年晚些时候开始他们的竞选之旅。

yaw /jɔː/ *verb* [I] (*specialist*) (of a ship or plane 轮船或飞机) to turn to one side, away from a straight course, in an unsteady way 偏航 ▶ **yaw** *noun* [C, U]

Y

yawl /jɔːl/ *noun* **1** a type of boat with sails 双桅轻便帆船 **2** a ROWING BOAT carried on a ship 船载小划艇

yawn 🔑 /jɔːn/ *verb, noun*

■ ***verb*** **1** 🔑 [I] to open your mouth wide and breathe in deeply through it, usually because you are tired or bored 打哈欠：*He stood up, stretched and yawned.* 他站起身来，伸了个懒腰，打了个哈欠。**2** [I] (of a large hole or an empty space 大的洞穴或空间) to be very wide and often frightening and difficult to get across 非常宽；难以逾越 SYN **gape**: *A crevasse yawned at their feet.* 他们的脚下是一条张开大口的裂缝。◇ (*figurative*) *There's a* ***yawning gap*** *between rich and poor.* 贫富之间有一条鸿沟。

■ ***noun*** **1** 🔑 an act of yawning 哈欠：*She stifled another yawn and tried hard to look interested.* 她又忍住了哈欠，竭力显出感兴趣的样子。**2** [usually sing.] (*informal*) a boring event, idea, etc. 乏味的事情；无趣的想法：*The meeting was one big yawn from start to finish.* 这个会议自始至终都无聊透顶。

yaws /jɔːz/ *noun* [U] a tropical skin disease that causes large red swellings 雅司病（热带皮肤病，可导致皮肤严重肿胀）

yay /jeɪ/ *exclamation, adv.* (*informal, especially NAmE*)

■ ***exclamation*** used to show that you are very pleased about sth（表示高兴）吔：*I won! Yay!* 吔，我赢了！➲ MORE LIKE THIS 2, page R25

■ ***adv.*** **1** to this degree 这么；那么；多么 SYN **so**: *The fish I caught was yay big.* 我钓的鱼有这么大呢。**2** to a high degree 非常；极其 SYN **extremely**: *Yay good movie!* 非常棒的电影！

ˈY chromosome *noun* (*biology* 生) a SEX CHROMOSOME. In human males each cell has one X chromosome and one Y chromosome. In human females there is never a Y chromosome. * Y 染色体

yd *abbr.* (*pl.* **yds**) YARD 码：*12 yds of silk* * 12 码的丝绸

ye *pron., det.*

■ ***pron.*** /jiː; *weak form* ji/ (*old use or dialect*) a word meaning 'you', used when talking to more than one person 你们：*Gather ye rosebuds while ye may.* 花开堪折直须折。

■ ***det.*** /jiː/ a word meaning 'the', used in the names of pubs, shops, etc. to make them seem old（相当于 the，用于酒吧、商店等的名称，以使其显得古色古香）：*Ye Olde Starre Inn* 老斯塔尔酒店

yea /jeɪ/ *adv., noun* (*old use*) yes 是 ➲ COMPARE NAY (2)

yeah 🔑 /jeə/ *exclamation* (*informal*) yes 是的；对

IDM **ˌoh ˈyeah?** used when you are commenting on what sb has just said（回应时用）哦，是吗：*'We're off to France soon.' 'Oh yeah? When's that?'* "我们很快就要去法国了。" "哦，是吗？什么时候去呀？" ◇ *'I'm going to be rich one day.' 'Oh yeah?'* (= I don't believe you.) "总有一天我会发财的。" "哦，真的？" **ˌyeah, ˈright** used to say that you do not believe what sb has just said, disagree with it, or are not interested in it（表示不相信、不同意或不感兴趣）算了吧：*'You'll be fine.' 'Yeah, right.'* "你会没事的。" "得了吧。"

year 🔑 /jɪə(r); jɜː(r); *NAmE* jɪr/ *noun* (*abbr.* **yr**) **1** 🔑 (*also* **ˌcalendar ˈyear**) [C] the period from 1 January to 31 December, that is 365 or 366 days, divided into 12 months 年；日历年：*in the year 1865* 在 1865 年 ◇ *I lost my job earlier this year.* 今年早些时候，我失业了。◇ *Elections take place every year.* 每年都进行各项选举。◇ *The museum is open* ***all*** ***(the) year round*** (= during the whole year). 博物馆全年开放。➲ SEE ALSO LEAP YEAR, NEW YEAR **2** 🔑 [C] a period of 12 months, measured from any particular time 一年时间：*It's exactly a year since I started working here.* 我来这里工作已经整整一年了。◇ *She gave up teaching three years ago.* 三年前，她放弃了教学工作。◇ *in the first year of their marriage* 在他们婚后第一年里 ◇ *the pre-war/war/post-war years* (= the period before/during/after the war) 战前的 / 战争的 / 战后的年代 ◇ *I have happy memories of my years in Poland* (= the time I spent there). 在波兰的岁月给我留下了美好的回忆。➲ SEE ALSO GAP YEAR, LIGHT YEAR (2), OFF YEAR **3** 🔑 [C] a period of 12 months connected with a particular activity 与某事相关的一年；年度：*the* ***academic/school year*** 学年 ◇ *the* ***tax year*** 财政年度 ➲ SEE ALSO FINANCIAL YEAR **4** [C] (*especially BrE*) (at a school, etc. 学校等) a level that you stay in for one year; a student at a particular level 年级；某年级的学生：*We started German in year seven.* 我们在七年级开始学习德语。◇ *a year-seven pupil* 七年级学生 ◇ *The first years do French.* 一年级学生学习法语。◇ *She was in my year at school.* 她上学时跟我同级。**5** 🔑 [C, usually pl.] age; time of life 年岁；年纪；年龄：*He was* ***14 years old*** *when it happened.* 这件事情发生的时候，他 14 岁。◇ *She looks young for her years.* 她看上去比她的年龄小。◇ *They were both only* ***20 years of age****.* 他们两人都只有 20 岁。◇ *a twenty-year-old man* 一名二十岁的男子 ◇ *He died in his sixtieth year.* 他是六十岁时去世的。◇ *She's* ***getting on*** *in years* (= is no longer young). 她已经上年纪了。**6** 🔑 **years** [pl.] (*informal*) a long time 很久；好长时间：*It's years since we* *last met.* 我们多年没有见面了。◇ *They haven't seen each other* **for years**. 他们彼此多年没有见面了。◇ *That's the best movie I've seen* **in years**. 那是我多年来看过的最好的电影。◇ *We've had a lot of fun* **over the years**. 这些年来我们过得很开心。

IDM **man, woman, car, etc. of the 'year** a person or thing that people decide is the best in a particular field in a particular year 某年度最优秀人物（或事物） **not/never in a hundred, etc. 'years** (*informal*) used to emphasize that you will/would never do sth 永远不；绝对不：*I'd never have thought of that in a million years.* 我永远也想不出这个主意。 **put 'years on sb** to make sb feel or look older 使感到老迈；使显得年老 **take 'years off sb** to make sb feel or look younger 使觉得（或显得）年轻 **,year after 'year** every year for many years 年年；每年 **,year by 'year** as the years pass; each year 一年一年地；每年；年复一年：*Year by year their affection for each other grew stronger.* 年复一年，他们对彼此的爱愈加强烈。 **the year 'dot** (*BrE*) (*NAmE* **the year 'one**) (*informal*) a very long time ago 很久以前：*I've been going there every summer since the year dot.* 我从很久以前就每年夏天都去那里。 **year 'in, year 'out** every year 年复一年；年年 **,year of 'grace | ,year of our 'Lord** (*formal*) any particular year after the birth of Christ 纪元某年；公元某年 **,year on 'year** (used especially when talking about figures, prices, etc. 尤用于统计数字、价格等) each year, compared with the last year 与前一年同期比较：*Spending has increased year on year.* 与去年同期比较，开销增加了。◇ *a year-on-year increase in spending* 开销的年度增长 ➲ MORE AT ADVANCED, DECLINE *v.*, DONKEY, SEVEN, TURN *n.*

year·book /ˈjɪəbʊk; *NAmE* ˈjɪrbʊk/ *noun* **1** a book published once a year, giving details of events, etc. of the previous year, especially those connected with a particular area of activity 年鉴；年刊 **2** (*especially NAmE*) a book that is produced by the senior class in a school or college, containing photographs of students and details of school activities（每年出版的）校刊；学校年刊

year·ling /ˈjɪəlɪŋ; *NAmE* ˈjɪrlɪŋ/ *noun* an animal, especially a horse, between one and two years old 一至两岁的动物（尤指马）；一岁（或两岁）幼崽

,year-'long *adj.* [only before noun] continuing for a whole year 一整年的；持续一年的：*a year-long dispute* 持续一年的争端

year·ly /ˈjɪəli; ˈjɜːli; *NAmE* ˈjɪrli/ *adj.* **1** happening once a year or every year 每年的；一年一次的：*Pay is reviewed on a yearly basis.* 工资每年审查一次。**2** paid, valid or calculated for one year 年度的；一年的：***yearly income/interest*** 年度收入；年利率 ▸ **year·ly** *adv.*: *The magazine is issued twice yearly* (= twice every year). 这份杂志每年发行两期。

yearn /jɜːn; *NAmE* jɜːrn/ *verb* [I] (*literary*) to want sth very much, especially when it is very difficult to get 渴望；渴求 SYN **long**: ~ (**for sth/sb**) *The people yearned for peace.* 人民渴望和平。◇ *There was a yearning look in his eyes.* 他两眼流露出渴望的神情。◇ ~ **to do sth** *She yearned to escape from her office job.* 她一心想着躲避办公室里的工作。

yearn·ing /ˈjɜːnɪŋ; *NAmE* ˈjɜːrnɪŋ/ *noun* [C, U] (*formal*) a strong and emotional desire 渴望；向往 SYN **longing**: ~ (**for sb/sth**) *a yearning for a quiet life* 对宁静生活的向往 ◇ ~ (**to do sth**) *She had no great yearning to go back.* 她并不十分想回去。▸ **yearn·ing·ly** *adv.*

,year-'round *adj.* all through the year 全年的；整整一年的：*an island with year-round sunshine* 一年四季阳光灿烂的岛

yeast /jiːst/ *noun* [U, C] a FUNGUS used in making beer and wine, or to make bread rise 酵母；酵母菌 ▸ **yeasty** *adj.*: *a yeasty smell* 发酵的气味

'yeast extract *noun* [U] a black substance made from yeast, spread on bread, etc. 酵母膏，马麦酱（呈黑色，抹在面包等食物上食用） ➲ SEE ALSO MARMITE™

'yeast infection (*NAmE*) (*BrE* **thrush**) *noun* an infectious disease that affects the VAGINA 阴道炎

yebo /ˈjebɒ; *NAmE* -bɔː/ *exclamation* (*SAfrE, informal*) **1** yes 是；对 **2** hello 喂；你好：*Yebo Craig. Thanks for the email.* 你好，克雷格。谢谢你的电邮。

yell /jel/ *verb, noun*

■ ***verb*** [I, T] to shout loudly, for example because you are angry, excited, frightened or in pain 叫喊；大喊；吼叫：~ (**at sb/sth**) *He yelled at the other driver.* 他冲着另一位司机大叫。◇ ~ **at sb to do sth** *She yelled at the child to get down from the wall.* 她喊着让小孩从墙上下来。◇ ~ **with sth** *They yelled with excitement.* 他们兴奋得喊叫起来。◇ ~ **out** (**in sth**) *She yelled out in pain.* 她疼得大声喊叫。◇ + **speech** *'Be careful!' he yelled.* 他大叫道："当心！"◇ ~ **sth** (**at sb/sth**) *The crowd yelled encouragement at the players.* 人群大声叫喊着给运动员加油。◇ ~ **out sth** *He yelled out her name.* 他大声喊她的名字。➲ SYNONYMS AT SHOUT

■ ***noun*** **1** a loud cry of pain, excitement, etc. 喊叫；叫嚷；大喊：*to **let out/give a yell*** 大喊一声 ◇ *a yell of delight* 欢呼 **2** (*NAmE*) an organized shout of support for a team at a sports event（为运动队加油的）呐喊，欢呼

yel·low 🔑 /ˈjeləʊ; *NAmE* ˈjeloʊ/ *adj., noun, verb*

■ ***adj.*** (**yel·lower**, **yel·lowest**) **1** 🔑 having the colour of lemons or butter 黄的；黄色的：*pale yellow flowers* 淡黄色的花朵 ◇ *a bright yellow waterproof jacket* 明黄色的防水夹克 **2** (*taboo*) an offensive word used to describe the light brown skin of people from some E Asian countries（轻蔑语）黄皮肤的，黄色人种的 **3** (*informal, disapproving*) easily frightened 胆怯的 SYN **cowardly** ▸ **yel·low·ness** *noun* [U, sing.]

■ ***noun*** 🔑 [U, C] the colour of lemons or butter 黄；黄色：*She was dressed in yellow.* 她穿着黄衣服。◇ *the reds and yellows of the trees* 红色和黄色的树叶

■ ***verb*** [I, T] ~ (**sth**) to become yellow; to make sth become yellow（使）变黄

'yellow-belly *noun* (*old-fashioned, informal, disapproving*) a COWARD (= sb who is not brave) 胆小鬼；懦夫 ▸ **'yellow-bellied** *adj.* [usually before noun]

,yellow 'card *noun* (in football (SOCCER) 足球) a card shown by the REFEREE to a player as a warning about bad behaviour 黄牌（由裁判员出示，作为对犯规行为的警告） ➲ COMPARE RED CARD

,yellow 'fever *noun* [U] an infectious tropical disease that makes the skin turn yellow and often causes death 黄热病（热带疾病，可导致死亡）

,yellow 'flag *noun* **1** a type of yellow IRIS (= a flower) that grows near water 黄鸢尾；黄菖蒲 **2** a yellow flag on a ship showing that sb has or may have an infectious disease（表示船上有疫情而挂起的）检疫旗，黄旗

yel·low·ham·mer /ˈjeləʊhæmə(r); *NAmE* -loʊ-/ *noun* a small bird, the male of which has a yellow head, neck and breast 黄鹀（雄性的头、颈和胸黄色）

yel·low·ish /ˈjeləʊɪʃ; *NAmE* -loʊ-/ (*also less frequent* **yel·lowy** /ˈjeləʊi; *NAmE* -loʊ-/) *adj.* fairly yellow in colour 微黄色的；发黄的：*The paper had a yellowish tinge because it was so old.* 这份报纸很旧，已经有些发黄了。

,yellow 'journalism *noun* [U] (*US*) newspaper reports that are exaggerated and written to shock readers 黄色新闻（夸张或耸人听闻的报章报道） ORIGIN From a comic strip *The Yellow Kid* that was printed in yellow ink to attract readers' attention. 源自以黄色油墨印刷以吸引读者的连环画《黄色小子》。

,yellow 'line *noun* (in Britain) a yellow line painted at the side of a road to show that you can only park your car there at particular times or for a short time（英国路边限制停车的）黄线：***double yellow lines*** (= two lines that mean you cannot park there at all) 禁止停车的双黄线

,Yellow 'Pages™ (*BrE*) (*NAmE* **,yellow 'pages**) *noun* [pl.] a book with yellow pages that gives a list of companies and organizations and their telephone numbers, arranged according to the type of services they offer 黄页（分类商业电话号码簿）

ˌyellow ˈribbon *noun* (in the US) a piece of yellow material that sb ties around a tree as a sign that they are thinking about sb who has gone away, especially a soldier fighting in a war, or sb taken as a HOSTAGE or prisoner, and that they hope that the person will soon return safely 黄丝带（系在树上表示期盼亲友，尤指参战的士兵、人质或囚犯，能早日平安归来）

yelp /jelp/ *verb* [I, T] (**+ speech**) to give a sudden short cry, usually of pain（因疼痛等）突然尖叫 ▶ **yelp** *noun*

yen /jen/ *noun* **1** (*pl.* **yen**) [C] the unit of money in Japan 日元（日本货币单位） **2 the yen** [sing.] (*finance* 财) the value of the yen compared with the value of the money of other countries 日元比价 **3** [C, usually sing.] ~ (**for sth/to do sth**) a strong desire 强烈的欲望；渴望 SYN **longing**: *I've always had a yen to travel around the world.* 我一直非常渴望周游世界。

yeo·man /ˈjəʊmən; *NAmE* ˈjoʊ-/ *noun* (*pl.* **-men** /-mən/) **1** (in Britain in the past) a farmer who owned and worked on his land（英国旧时的）自耕农，自由民 **2** an officer in the US Navy who does mainly office work（美国海军的）文书军士

yeo·man·ry /ˈjəʊmənri; *NAmE* ˈjoʊ-/ *noun* [sing.+sing./pl. v.] **1** (in Britain in the past) the social class of farmers who owned their land（统称英国旧时的）自耕农 **2** (in Britain in the past) farmers who became soldiers and provided their own horses（英国旧时的）携马当兵的农民

yeow /jiːˈaʊ/ *exclamation* (*informal*) used to express sudden pain（突然感到疼痛时发出的声音）哎哟，啊唷

yep /jep/ *exclamation* (*informal*) used to say 'yes'（用以表示yes）是的，好了: *'Are you ready?' 'Yep.'* "准备好了吗？" "好了。"

yer /jə(r)/ *pron., det.* (*informal, non-standard*) used in writing as a way of showing the way people sometimes pronounce the word 'you' or 'your' 你，你的（书写时用，表示口语的 you 或 your）: *See yer when I get back.* 等我回来时再见吧。◇ *What's yer name?* 你叫什么名字？ ➲ MORE LIKE THIS 5, page R25

yes 🔑 /jes/ *exclamation, noun*

▪ ***exclamation*** **1** 🔑 used to answer a question and say that sth is correct or true（答话时表示正确或真实）: *'Is this your car?' 'Yes, it is.'* "这是你的车吗？" "对，是的。" ◇ *'Are you coming? Yes or no?'* "你来吗？来还是不来？" **2** 🔑 used to show that you agree with what has been said（表示同意所说的话）: *'I enjoyed her latest novel.' 'Yes, me too.'* "我喜欢她最新的小说。" "对，我也是。" ◇ *'It's an excellent hotel.'* ***'Yes, but*** (= I don't completely agree) *it's too expensive.'* "这家旅馆好极了。" "是啊，但就是太贵了。" **3** 🔑 used to disagree with sth negative that sb has just said（反驳否定的话）: *'I've never met her before.' 'Yes, you have.'* "我以前从没见过她。" "不，你见过。" **4** 🔑 used to agree to a request or to give permission（表示答应或许可）: *'Dad, can I borrow the car?' 'Yes, but be careful.'* "爸爸，我借车用一下好吗？" "可以，不过要小心。" ◇ *We're hoping that they will* ***say yes to*** *our proposals.* 我们希望他们会同意我们的提议。**5** 🔑 used to accept an offer or invitation（接受提议或邀请）: *'Would you like a drink?'* ***'Yes, please/thanks.'*** "喝一杯好吗？" "好吧，谢谢。" **6** 🔑 used for asking sb what they want（询问某人所需）: *Yes? How can I help you?* 有事吗？我能帮你什么忙？ **7** 🔑 used for replying politely when sb calls you（礼貌地应答呼唤）: *'Waiter!' 'Yes, sir?'* "服务员！" "什么事，先生？" **8** 🔑 used to show that you have just remembered sth（表示刚想起某事）哦，对了: *Where did I put the keys? Oh, yes—in my pocket!* 我把钥匙放在哪儿了？哦，对了，在我口袋里！ **9** 🔑 used to encourage sb to continue speaking（鼓励某人继续讲）往下说: *'I'm going to Paris this weekend.' 'Yes…'* "我这周末要去巴黎。" "接着说。" **10** 🔑 used to show that you do not believe what sb has said（表示不相信某人所言）真的: *'Sorry I'm late—the bus didn't come.' 'Oh yes?'* "对不起，我迟到了，公共汽车没来。" "哦，是吗？" **11** 🔑 used to emphasize what you have just said（强调所说的话）一点不假: *Mrs Smith has just won £2 million—yes!—£2 million!* 史密斯夫人刚刚赢了 200 万英镑！一点没假，整整 200 万英镑！ **12** 🔑 used to show that you are excited or extremely pleased about sth that you have done or sth that has happened（感到兴奋或高兴时说）好啊: *'They've scored another goal.' 'Yes!!'* "他们又进了一球。" "太棒了！" **13 yes, yes** used to show that you are impatient or irritated about sth（表示不耐烦或气恼）得，得: *'Hurry up—it's late.' 'Yes, yes—I'm coming.'* "快点儿，来不及了。" "行了，行了，我就来。"

IDM **ˌyes and ˈno** used when you cannot give a clear answer to a question 说不准；也是也不是: *'Are you enjoying it?' 'Yes and no.'* "你喜欢这个吗？" "不好说。"

▪ ***noun*** 🔑 (*pl.* **yes·ses** or **yeses** /ˈjesɪz/) an answer that shows that you agree with an idea, a statement, etc.; a person who says 'yes' 表示同意的答复；表示同意的人: *I need a simple yes or no to my questions.* 我的问题只需要简单地回答是或不是。◇ *There will be two ballot boxes—one for yesses and one for noes.* 将设两个投票箱：一个放赞成票，一个放反对票。◇ *I'll put you down as a yes.* 我就当你同意了。

yesh·iva /jəˈʃiːvə/ *noun* a college or school for Orthodox Jews 授业座（正统派犹太教育机构）

ˈyes-man *noun* (*pl.* **-men** /-men/) (*disapproving*) a person who always agrees with people in authority in order to gain their approval 应声虫；唯唯诺诺的人

yes·sir /ˈjesə(r); ˈjessɜː(r)/ *exclamation* (*informal, especially NAmE*) used to emphasize your opinion or say that you agree very strongly（表示强调）的确，完全同意: *Yessir, she was beautiful.* 的确，她很漂亮。

yes·ter·day 🔑 /ˈjestədeɪ; ˈjestədi; *NAmE* -tərd-/ *adv., noun, adj.*

▪ ***adv.*** on the day before today 在昨天: *They arrived yesterday.* 他们昨天到达。◇ *I can remember our wedding as if it were yesterday.* 我们的婚礼我记忆犹新，就像昨天一样。◇ *Where were you yesterday morning?* 你昨天上午在哪儿？◇ *To think I was lying on a beach only* ***the day before yesterday.*** 想想吧，就在前天，我还躺在海滩上呢。IDM SEE BORN *v.*

▪ ***noun*** [U] **1** 🔑 the day before today 昨天: *Yesterday was Sunday.* 昨天是星期天。◇ *What happened at yesterday's meeting?* 昨天的会上发生了什么事？ **2** 🔑 (*also* **yes·ter·days** [pl.]) the recent past 不久前；近日；往昔: *Yesterday's students are today's employees.* 昨天还是学生，今天成了雇员。◇ *All her yesterdays had vanished without a trace.* 她的过去已经完全烟消云散了。

▪ ***adj.*** [not before noun] (*informal, often humorous*) no longer fashionable or new 过时: *Email—that's* ***so yesterday!*** 电子邮件，那太过时了！

yes·ter·year /ˈjestəjɪə(r); *NAmE* ˈjestərjɪr/ *noun* [U] (*old-fashioned or literary*) the past, especially a time when attitudes and ideas were different（尤指思想观念有别于当今的）旧时，往昔，过去

yet 🔑 /jet/ *adv., conj.*

▪ ***adv.*** **1** 🔑 used in negative sentences and questions to talk about sth that has not happened but that you expect to happen（用于否定句和疑问句，谈论尚未发生但可能发生的事）: (*BrE*) *I haven't received a letter from him yet.* 我还没有收到他的信呢。◇ (*NAmE*) *I didn't receive a letter from him yet.* 我还没有收到过他的信。◇ *'Are you ready?' 'No, not yet.'* "你准备好了吗？" "还没有。" ◇ ***We have yet to*** *decide what action to take* (= We have not decided what action to take). 我们尚未决定采取何种行动。➲ NOTE AT ALREADY **2** 🔑 (used in negative sentences 用于否定句) now; as soon as this 现在；即刻；马上: *Don't go yet.* 先别走。◇ *We don't need to start yet.* 我们不必马上开始。**3** 🔑 from now until the period of time mentioned has passed 从现在起直至某一时间；还: *He'll be busy for ages yet.* 他还要忙很长一段时间。◇ *They won't arrive for at least two hours yet.* 他们至少要过两个小时才能到。**4 could, might, may, etc. do sth ~** used to say that sth could, might, etc. happen in the future, even though it seems unlikely（表

示将来可能发生，尽管现在似乎没有可能）早晚，总有一天：*We may win yet.* 我们迟早会赢的。◇ *(formal) She could yet surprise us all.* 总有一天，她会让我们都大吃一惊。**5** **the best, longest, etc. sth ~ (done)** the best, longest, etc. thing of its kind made, produced, written, etc. until now/then 迄今为止，到当时为止（最好或最长等的）：*the most comprehensive study yet of his music* 迄今为止对他的音乐最为全面的研究 ◇ *It was the highest building yet constructed.* 这是到当时为止所建的最高的建筑物。**6** **~ another/more | ~ again** used to emphasize an increase in number or amount or the number of times sth happens（强调次数或数量的增加）：*snow, snow and yet more snow* 下雪，下雪，还要下雪 ◇ *yet another diet book* 又是一本关于节食的书 ◇ *Prices were cut* ***yet again*** (= once more, after many other times). 物价再一次降低。**7** **~ worse, more importantly, etc.** used to emphasize an increase in the degree of sth (= how bad, important, etc. it is)（强调程度的增加）更 SYN **even, still**: *a recent and yet more improbable theory* 一个新近提出的但更加不切实际的理论

IDM **as 'yet** until now or until a particular time in the past 直到现在；直至过去某时：*an as yet unpublished report* 一篇尚未发表的报告 ◇ *As yet little was known of the causes of the disease.* 当时人们对这种疾病的起因几乎一无所知。

■ ***conj.*** despite what has just been said 但是；然而 SYN **nevertheless**: *It's a small car, yet it's surprisingly spacious.* 这辆汽车不大，然而却出奇地宽敞。◇ *He has a good job, and yet he never seems to have any money.* 他有份好工作，然而他却好像总也没有钱。

yeti /ˈjeti/ (*also* **A,bominable 'Snowman**) *noun* a large creature like a BEAR or a man covered with hair, that some people believe lives in the Himalayan mountains 雪人（似人或熊的巨大长毛动物，据传生活在喜马拉雅山脉）

yew /juː/ *noun* **1** [C, U] (*also* **'yew tree**) a small tree with dark green leaves and small red BERRIES 紫杉；红豆杉 ➲ VISUAL VOCAB PAGE V10 **2** [U] the wood of the yew tree 紫杉木

'Y-Fronts™ *noun* [pl.] (*BrE*) men's UNDERPANTS, with an opening in the front sewn in the shape of a Y upside-down（前缝呈倒 Y 形的）男内裤：*a pair of Y-Fronts* 一条前缝呈倒 Y 形的男内裤

YHA /ˌwaɪ eɪtʃ ˈeɪ/ *abbr.* Youth Hostels Association (an organization that exists in many countries and provides cheap simple accommodation) 青年旅舍协会

yid /jɪd/ *noun* (*taboo, slang*) a very offensive word for a Jewish person（蔑称）犹太人，犹太佬

Yid·dish /ˈjɪdɪʃ/ *noun* [U] a Jewish language, originally used in central and eastern Europe, based on a form of German with words from Hebrew and several modern languages 意第绪语，依地语（犹太人的语言，起源于欧洲中部和东部，以德语为基础，借用希伯来语和若干现代语言的词语）▶ **Yid·dish** *adj.*

yield /jiːld/ *verb, noun*

■ ***verb*** **1** [T] **~ sth** to produce or provide sth, for example a profit, result or crop 出产（作物）；产生（收益、效益等）；提供：*Higher-rate deposit accounts yield good returns.* 高利率的存款会产生丰厚的收益。◇ *The research has yielded useful information.* 这项研究提供了有用的资料。◇ *trees that no longer yield fruit* 不再结果实的树 **2** [I] (*formal*) to stop resisting sth/sb; to agree to do sth that you do not want to do 屈服；让步 SYN **give way**: *After a long siege, the town was forced to yield.* 经过长时间的包围，这座孤城被迫投降。◇ **~ to sth/sb** *He reluctantly yielded to their demands.* 他不情愿地同意了他们的要求。◇ *I yielded to temptation and had a chocolate bar.* 我经不住诱惑，吃了一大块巧克力。**3** [T] **~ sth/sb (up) (to sb)** (*formal*) to allow sb to win, have or take control of sth that has been yours until now 放弃；缴出 SYN **surrender**: *He refused to yield up his gun.* 他拒绝缴枪。◇ (*figurative*) *The universe is slowly yielding up its secrets.* 宇宙慢慢地展现出它的秘密。**4** [I] to move, bend or break because of pressure（受压）活动，变形，弯曲，折断：*Despite our attempts to break it, the lock would not yield.* 这把锁我们砸也砸不开。**5** [I] **~ (to sb/sth)** (*NAmE, IrishE*) to allow vehicles on a bigger road to go first 给（大路上的车辆）让路 SYN **give way**: *Yield to oncoming traffic.* 会车让行。◇ *a yield sign* 让行标志

PHR V **'yield to sth** (*formal*) to be replaced by sth 被…替代；为…所取代：*Barges yielded to road vehicles for transporting goods.* 在货物运输方面，驳船让位给了公路车辆。

■ ***noun*** [C, U] the total amount of crops, profits, etc. that are produced 产量；产出；利润：*a high crop yield* 作物丰收 ◇ *a reduction in milk yield* 牛奶产量的降低 ◇ *This will give a yield of 10% on your investment.* 这会给你的投资带来 10% 的利润。➲ WORDFINDER NOTE AT CROP

yield·ing /ˈjiːldɪŋ/ *adj.* (*formal*) **1** (of a substance 物质) soft and easy to bend or move when you press it 柔软的；易弯曲的；易变形的 **2** (of a person 人) willing to do what other people want 顺从的；百依百顺的 **3** (used with an adverb 与副词连用) giving the amount of crops, profits, etc. mentioned 带来…收成（或利润等）的：***high/low yielding*** *crops* 高产 / 低产作物

yikes /jaɪks/ *exclamation* (*informal*) used to show that you are surprised or suddenly afraid（惊讶或突然害怕时说）呀，啊

yin /jɪn/ *noun* [U] (*from Chinese*) (in Chinese philosophy) the dark, not active, female principle of the universe（中国哲学）阴 ➲ COMPARE YANG

yip·pee /jɪˈpiː; *NAmE* ˈjɪpi/ *exclamation* (*old-fashioned, informal*) used to show you are pleased or excited（高兴或兴奋时说）➲ MORE LIKE THIS 2, page R25

ylang-ylang (*also* **ilang-ilang**) /ˌiːlæŋ ˈiːlæŋ/ *noun* **1** [U] an oil from the flowers of a tropical tree, used in PERFUMES and AROMATHERAPY 伊兰油（从热带伊兰伊兰树的花中提取，用于香水和芳香疗法）**2** [U, C] a tree with yellow flowers from which this oil is obtained 伊兰伊兰；芳香树；香依兰

YMCA /ˌwaɪ em siː ˈeɪ/ (*also NAmE, informal* **the Y**) *noun* Young Men's Christian Association (an organization that exists in many countries and provides accommodation and social and sports activities) 基督教青年会：*We stayed at the YMCA.* 我们住在基督教青年会。

YMMV /ˌwaɪ em em ˈviː/ *abbr.* (*informal*) (used to say that people may experience a particular thing in different ways) your mileage may vary 实际情况因人而异（表示不同人对某事可能有不一样的感受，全写为 your mileage may vary）：*Highly recommend the company! Of course, YMMV.* 非常推荐这家公司！不过当然了，有些人可能并不认同。

yo /jəʊ; *NAmE* joʊ/ *exclamation* (*slang*) used by young people to say hello（年轻人的招呼语）喂，嘿

yob /jɒb; *NAmE* jɑːb/ (*also* **yobbo** /ˈjɒbəʊ; *NAmE* ˈjɑːboʊ/ *pl.* **-os**) *noun* (*BrE, informal*) a rude, noisy and sometimes aggressive and violent boy or young man 粗野的男孩；粗俗横蛮的青年男子 SYN **lout** ▶ **yob·bish** *adj.* [usually before noun]

yodel /ˈjəʊdl; *NAmE* ˈjoʊdl/ *verb, noun*

■ ***verb*** (**-ll-**, *especially US* **-l-**) [I, T] **~ (sth)** to sing or call in the traditional Swiss way, changing your voice frequently between its normal level and a very high level 用约德尔唱法歌唱（以瑞士传统的真假嗓音交替歌唱）

■ ***noun*** a song or musical call in which sb yodels 约德尔唱法，约德尔歌曲（用真假嗓音交替歌唱）

yoga /ˈjəʊɡə; *NAmE* ˈjoʊɡə/ *noun* [U] **1** a Hindu philosophy that teaches you how to control your body and mind in the belief that you can become united with the spirit of the universe in this way 瑜伽派（印度哲学派别）**2** a system of exercises for your body and for controlling your breathing, used by people who want to become fitter or to relax 瑜伽术（健体和控制呼吸的锻炼）➲ VISUAL VOCAB PAGE V46 ▶ **yogic** /ˈjəʊɡɪk; *NAmE* ˈjoʊ-/ *adj.*: *yogic techniques* 瑜伽技巧

Y

yogi /ˈjəʊgi; *NAmE* ˈjoʊgi/ *noun* (*pl.* **yogis**) an expert in, or teacher of, the philosophy of yoga 瑜伽士；瑜伽哲学专家（或导师）

yog·urt (*also* **yog·hurt**, **yog·hourt**) /ˈjɒgət; *NAmE* ˈjoʊgərt/ *noun* [U, C] a thick white liquid food, made by adding bacteria to milk, served cold and often flavoured with fruit; an amount of this sold in a small pot 酸奶；一份酸奶：*natural yogurt* 原味酸奶 ◇ *There's a yogurt left if you're still hungry.* 如果你还饿的话，还有一份酸奶。◇ *a lemon yogurt* 柠檬酸奶

yoke /jəʊk; *NAmE* joʊk/ *noun, verb*
■ ***noun*** **1** [C] a long piece of wood that is fastened across the necks of two animals, especially OXEN, so that they can pull heavy loads 轭；（尤指）牛轭 **2** [sing.] (*literary* or *formal*) rough treatment or sth that restricts your freedom and makes your life very difficult to bear 奴役；束缚；枷锁；羁绊：*the yoke of imperialism* 帝国主义的枷锁 **3** [C] a piece of wood that is shaped to fit across a person's shoulders so that they can carry two equal loads 轭形扁担 **4** [C] a part of a dress, skirt, etc. that fits around the shoulders or hips and from which the rest of the cloth hangs 上衣抵肩；裙（或裤）腰
■ ***verb*** **1** to join two animals together with a yoke; to attach an animal to sth with a yoke 用轭把（动物）套在一起；给（动物）上轭：**~ A and B together** *A pair of oxen, yoked together, was used.* 把两头牛用轭套在一起使唤。◇ **~ sth to sth** *an ox yoked to a plough* 用轭套在犁上的牛 **2** [usually passive] **~ A and B together | ~ sth to sth** (*formal*) to bring two people, countries, ideas, etc. together so that they are forced into a close relationship（强行）使结合，使联合：*The Hong Kong dollar was yoked to the American dollar for many years.* 港元多年来与美元挂钩。

yokel /ˈjəʊkl; *NAmE* ˈjoʊkl/ *noun* (*often humorous*) if you call a person a **yokel**, you are saying that they do not have much education or understanding of modern life, because they come from the countryside 乡巴佬；乡下人

yolk /jəʊk; *NAmE* joʊk/ *noun* [C, U] the round yellow part in the middle of an egg 蛋黄：*Separate the whites from the yolks.* 将蛋清和蛋黄分开。➲ MORE LIKE THIS 20, page R27

Yom Kip·pur /ˌjɒm ˈkɪpə(r); kɪˈpʊə(r); *NAmE* ˌjɑːm kɪˈpʊr; ˌjoːm/ *noun* [U] a Jewish religious holiday in September or October when people eat nothing all day and say prayers of PENITENCE in the SYNAGOGUE, also known as the Day of Atonement 赎罪日（犹太教的重大节日，在每年的九月或十月，人们于此日禁食并忏悔祈祷）

yomp /jɒmp; *NAmE* jɑːmp/ *verb* [I] **+ adv./prep.** (*BrE, informal*) (of a soldier 军人) to march with heavy equipment over rough ground 负重越野行军；全副武装跋涉 ▶ **yomp** *noun*: *a 30-mile yomp* * 30 英里的负重越野行军

yon /jɒn; *NAmE* jɑːn/ *det., adv.*
■ ***det.*** (*old use* or *dialect*) that 那；那个：*There's an old farm over yon hill.* 小山那边有一个旧农场。
■ ***adv.*** IDM SEE HITHER

yon·der /ˈjɒndə(r); *NAmE* ˈjɑːn-/ *det.* (*old use* or *dialect*) that is over there; that you can see over there 那里的；那边的：*Let's rest under yonder tree.* 我们在那边的树下休息吧。▶ **yon·der** *adv.*: *Whose is that farm over yonder?* 那边的农场是谁的？

yonks /jɒŋks; *NAmE* jɑːŋks/ *noun* [U] (*BrE, informal, becoming old-fashioned*) a long time 很长时间：*I haven't seen you for yonks!* 我很久没见你了！

yoof /juːf/ *noun* [U] (*BrE, informal, humorous*) a non-standard spelling of 'youth', used to refer to young people as a group, especially as the group that particular types of entertainment, magazines, etc. are designed for（youth 的不规范拼写，统称）年轻人；年轻人目标群体 ▶ **yoof** *adj.* [only before noun]

yoo-hoo /ˈjuː huː/ *exclamation* (*informal, becoming old-fashioned*) used to attract sb's attention, especially when they are some distance away（尤用以引起远处的人的注意）哟－嚯

yore /jɔː(r)/ *noun*
IDM **of 'yore** (*old use* or *literary*) long ago 很久以前：*in days of yore* 在很久以前

York·shire pud·ding /ˌjɔːkʃə ˈpʊdɪŋ; *NAmE* jɔːrkʃər/ *noun* [U, C] a type of British food made from BATTER that is baked until it rises, traditionally eaten with ROAST beef 约克夏布丁（在英国习惯上和烤牛肉同食）

York·shire ter·rier /ˌjɔːkʃə ˈteriə(r); *NAmE* jɔːrkʃər/ *noun* a very small dog with long brown and grey hair 约克夏㹴（棕灰两色的长毛小狗）

Yor·uba /ˈjɒrʊbə; *NAmE* ˈjɔːrəbə/ *noun* [U] a language spoken by the Yoruba people of W Africa, especially in SW Nigeria 约鲁巴语（非洲西部，尤其尼日利亚西南部的约鲁巴人的语言）

you 🔑 /ju; *NAmE* jə; *strong form* juː/ *pron.* **1** 🔑 used as the subject or object of a verb or after a preposition to refer to the person or people being spoken or written to 你；您；你们：*You said you knew the way.* 你说过你知道路的。◇ *I thought she told you.* 我以为她告诉你了。◇ *Can I sit next to you?* 我可以坐在你旁边吗？◇ *I don't think that hairstyle is you* (= it doesn't suit your appearance or personality). 我觉得那种发型不适合你。**2** 🔑 used with nouns and adjectives to speak to sb directly（与名词及形容词连用，直接称呼某人）：*You girls, stop talking!* 你们这些女孩子，别说话了！◇ *You stupid idiot!* 你这个白痴！**3** 🔑 used for referring to people in general（泛指任何人）：*You learn a language better if you visit the country where it is spoken.* 如果到说某种语言的国家去，就会把这种语言学得更好。◇ *It's a friendly place—people come up to you in the street and start talking.* 这个地方的人很友好，在街上走着就有人上来跟你攀谈。

you-all /ˈjuː ɔːl/ (*also* **y'all**) *pron.* (*informal*) used especially in the southern US to mean *you* when talking to more than one person（尤用于美国南部）你们：*Have you-all brought swimsuits?* 你们都带游泳衣了吗？

you'd /juːd/ *short form* **1** you had **2** you would

you'll /juːl/ *short form* you will

young 🔑 /jʌŋ/ *adj., noun*
■ ***adj.*** (**young·er** /ˈjʌŋgə(r)/, **young·est** /ˈjʌŋgɪst/) **1** 🔑 having lived or existed for only a short time; not fully developed 幼小的；未成熟的：*young babies* 幼婴 ◇ *a young country* 新成立的国家 ◇ *Caterpillars eat the young leaves of this plant.* 毛毛虫吃这种植物的嫩叶。◇ *a young wine* 新酿的葡萄酒 ◇ *The night is* ***still young*** (= it has only just started). 夜晚刚刚开始。OPP **old** **2** 🔑 not yet old; not as old as others 年轻的；岁数不大的；相对年轻的：*young people* 年轻人 ◇ *talented young football players* 天才的年轻足球运动员 ◇ *I am the youngest of four sisters.* 我是四姐妹当中最小的。◇ ***In his younger days*** *he played rugby for Wales.* 他年轻的时候在威尔士队踢橄榄球。◇ *I met the young Michelle Obama at Princeton.* 米歇尔·奥巴马年轻的时候，我在普林斯顿见过她。◇ *Her grandchildren keep her young.* 她的孙子孙女让她保持年轻。◇ *My son's thirteen but he's* ***young for his age*** (= not as developed as other boys of the same age). 我儿子十三岁了，但他比实际年龄显得小。◇ *They* ***married young*** (= at an early age). 他们结婚很早。◇ *My mother* ***died young***. 我母亲去世得早。OPP **old** ➲ WORDFINDER NOTE AT AGE

> **WORDFINDER** 联想词：adolescent, immature, mixed up, naive, puberty, rebellious, sulky, tearaway, teenager

3 🔑 consisting of young people or young children; with a low average age 由年轻人（或儿童）构成的；青少年的；平均年龄小的：*They have a young family.* 他们家的孩子还小。◇ *a young audience* 青少年观众 **4** suitable or appropriate for young people 年轻人的；青年的；适合青年人的 SYN **youthful**：*young fashion* 年轻人的时尚 ◇ *The clothes she wears are much too young for her.* 她穿的衣服显得过于年轻了。**5 ~ man/lady/woman** used to show that you are angry or annoyed with a particular young person (对年轻人表示生气或恼怒)：*I think you owe me an apology, young lady!* 小姐，我认为你应该向我道歉！**6 the younger** used before or after a person's name to distinguish them from an older relative (用于姓名之前或之后，以区别于年长的亲戚)：*the younger Kennedy* 年纪较轻的那位肯尼迪 ◇ (*BrE, formal*) *William Pitt the younger* 小威廉·皮特 ➲COMPARE ELDER *adj.*, JUNIOR *adj.*

IDM **be getting 'younger** (*informal*) used to say that people seem to be doing sth at a younger age than they used to, or that they seem younger because you are now older (表示做某事的人好像越来越年轻)：*The band's fans are getting younger.* 这支乐队的歌迷越来越年轻了。◇ *Why do police officers seem to be getting younger?* 为什么警察好像越来越年轻了？ **not be getting any 'younger** (*informal*) used when you are commenting that time is passing and that you are growing older 老了；岁月不饶人 **,young at 'heart** thinking and behaving like a young person even when you are old 人老心不老 ➲MORE AT OLD, ONLY *adv.*

■ *noun* [pl.] **1** **the young** young people considered as a group (统称) 年轻人，青年人：*It's a movie that will appeal to the young.* 这部电影年轻人会感兴趣。◇ *It's a book for* **young and old alike**. 这本书老少咸宜。➲MORE LIKE THIS 24, page R28 **2** young animals of a particular type or that belong to a particular mother 幼崽；幼兽；幼鸟：*a mother bird feeding her young* 喂养幼鸟的鸟妈妈

young·ish /'jʌŋɪʃ/ *adj.* fairly young 颇年轻的：*a youngish president* 相当年轻的总裁

,young of'fender *noun* (*BrE*) a criminal who, according to the law, is not yet an adult but no longer a child 少年犯：*a young offender institution* 少年犯管教所

,young 'person *noun* (*BrE, law* 律) a person between the ages of 14 and 17 (14 至 17 岁的) 青少年

young·ster /'jʌŋstə(r)/ *noun* (*informal*) a young person or a child 年轻人；少年；儿童：*The camp is for youngsters aged 8 to 14.* 这个度假营是针对 8 至 14 岁的少年儿童的。

,young 'thing *noun* (*informal*) a young adult 青年人：*bright young things working in the computer business* 在电脑行业工作的聪明的青年人

,young 'Turk *noun* (*old-fashioned*) a young person who wants great changes to take place in the established political system 少壮派激进分子

your /jə(r); *BrE strong form* jɔː(r); *NAmE strong form* jʊr/ *det.* (the possessive form of *you* * you 的所有格形式) **1** of or belonging to the person or people being spoken or written to 你的；您的；你们的：*I like your dress.* 我喜欢你的连衣裙。◇ *Excuse me, is this your seat?* 对不起，这是您的座位吗？◇ *The bank is on your right.* 银行在你的右边。**2** of or belonging to people in general (泛指) 大家的，人们的：*Dentists advise you to have your teeth checked every six months.* 牙医建议大家每六个月检查一次牙齿。◇ *In Japan you are taught great respect for your elders.* 在日本，人们要学会非常尊敬长辈。**3** (*informal*) used to show that sb/sth is well known or often talked about (指有名或经常被谈论的人或事物)：*This is your typical English pub.* 这就是典型的英格兰酒吧。◇ (*ironic, disapproving*) *You and your bright ideas!* 你的主意可真高明！**4** **Your** used in some titles, especially those of royal people (用于某些称呼，尤指王室成员)：*Your Majesty* 陛下 ◇ *Your Excellency* 阁下

you're /jʊə(r); jɔː(r); *NAmE* jʊr; *weak form* jər/ *short form* you are

yours /jɔːz; *NAmE* jərz; jɔːrz; jʊrz/ *pron.* **1** of or belonging to you 你的；您的；你们的：*Is that book yours?* 这是您的书吗？◇ *Is she a friend of yours?* 她是你的朋友吗？◇ *My hair is very fine. Yours is much thicker.* 我的头发很稀。你的头发密多了。**2** (*usually* **Yours**) used at the end of a letter before signing your name (用于书信结尾的签名前)：(*BrE*) *Yours sincerely/faithfully* 您的诚挚的 / 忠实的 ◇ (*NAmE*) *Sincerely Yours* 您的真挚的 ◇ (*NAmE*) *Yours Truly* 你的忠实的 **3** (*BrE, informal*) your home 你的住所：*Let's go back to yours after the show.* 演出结束后我们回你家。

your·self /jɔː'self; *NAmE* jɔːr-; jʊr-; *weak form* jə-; *NAmE weak form* jər-/ (*pl.* **your·selves** /-'selvz/) *pron.* **1** (the reflexive form of *you* * you 的反身形式) used when the person or people being spoken to both cause and are affected by an action 你自己；您自己；你们自己：*Have you hurt yourself?* 你伤着自己了吗？◇ *You don't seem quite yourself today* (= you do not seem well or do not seem as happy as usual). 你今天看上去好像不大舒服。◇ *Enjoy yourselves!* 祝你们玩得开心！**2** used to emphasize the fact that the person who is being spoken to is doing sth (强调说话对象做某事)：*Do it yourself—I don't have time.* 你自己做吧，我没时间。◇ *You can try it out for yourselves.* 你们可以亲自试一试。◇ *You yourself are one of the chief offenders.* 你本人就是主犯之一。**3** you 你；您：*We sell a lot of these to people like yourself.* 我们把许多这种东西卖给您这样的人。◇ *'And yourself,' he replied, 'How are you?'* "你呢，"他回应道，"你好吗？"

IDM **(all) by your'self/your'selves** **1** alone; without anyone else (你 / 你们) 独自，单独：*How long were you by yourself in the house?* 你自己一个人在屋里待了多长时间？**2** without help (你 / 你们) 独立地：*Are you sure you did this exercise by yourself?* 这个练习真是你自己做的吗？**(all) to your'self/your'selves** for only you to have, use, etc. 独有；专用：*I'm going to be away next week so you'll have the office to yourself.* 我下周要出差，所以这间办公室就归你一个人了。**be your'self** to act naturally 行为自然；不做作：*Don't act sophisticated—just be yourself.* 不要装得老成持重，表现出你平常的样子就行了。

youse (*also* **yous**) /juːz/ *pron.* (*non-standard, dialect*) a word meaning 'you', used when talking to more than one person 你们

youth /juːθ/ *noun* (*pl.* **youths** /juːðz/) **1** [U] the time of life when a person is young, especially the time before a child becomes an adult 青年时期 (尤指成年以前)：*He had been a talented musician in his youth.* 他年轻时很有音乐天才。**2** [U] the quality or state of being young 年轻；青春；朝气：*She brings to the job a rare combination of youth and experience.* 她很年轻，然而干这份工作已有经验，这是很难得的。**3** [C] (*often disapproving*) a young man 青年男子；小伙子：*The fight was started by a gang of youths.* 这场打斗是一帮小伙子挑起来的。**4** (*also* **the youth**) [pl.] young people considered as a group (统称) 青年，年轻人：*the nation's youth* 全国青年 ◇ *the youth of today* 当代青年 ◇ *youth culture* 年轻人的文化 ◇ *youth unemployment* 青年失业问题

'youth club *noun* (in Britain) a club where young people can meet each other and take part in various activities (英国) 青年俱乐部

,youth 'custody *noun* [U] (*BrE*) a period of time when a young criminal is kept in a type of prison as a punishment 青少年犯的拘禁期：*He was sentenced to two years' youth custody.* 他被判处在少年犯拘留所拘禁两年。◇ *a youth custody centre* 青少年犯拘留所

youth·ful /'juːθfl/ *adj.* **1** typical of young people 年轻人的；青年的；青春的：*youthful enthusiasm/energy/inexperience* 青春的激情 / 活力；年轻人的不谙世事 **2** young or seeming younger than you are 年轻的；显得年轻的：*She's a very youthful 65.* 她 65 岁了，但显得非常年轻。▸ **youth·ful·ly** /-fəli/ *adv.* **youth·ful·ness** *noun* [U]

'youth hostel *noun* a building that provides cheap and simple accommodation and meals, especially to young people who are travelling 青年招待所，青年旅舍 (为旅行的青年人提供廉价食宿) ➲COLLOCATIONS AT TRAVEL

'youth hostelling *noun* [U] (*BrE*) the activity of staying in different youth hostels and walking, etc. between them 在各地住青年招待所：*to go youth hostelling* 借助青年招待所到处去旅行

YouTube™ /'juːtjuːb; *NAmE* 'juːtuːb/ *noun* [U] a website where people can watch and share short videos 视频网站；影片分享网站

Y

you've /juːv/ *short form* you have

yowl /jaʊl/ *verb* [I] to make a long loud cry that sounds unhappy 哭叫；号哭；号啕大哭 **SYN wail** ▸ **yowl** *noun*

'yo-yo *noun, verb, adj.*

■ ***noun*** (*also* **Yo Yo™**) (*pl.* **yo-yos**, **Yo Yos**) a toy that consists of two round pieces of plastic or wood joined together, with a piece of string wound between them. You put one end of the string around your finger and make the yo-yo go up and down. 悠悠球，溜溜球，摇摇（拉线使圆盘旋转着沿线上下来回移动）：*He kept bouncing up and down **like a yo-yo**.* 他像个悠悠球似的不停地上窜下跳。

■ ***verb*** [I] (+ **adv./prep.**) to change repeatedly in size, amount, quality, etc. from one extreme to another 上下跳动；左右摇摆：*When I was young my weight yo-yoed between 140 and 190 pounds.* 我年轻时体重在 140 到 190 磅之间忽上忽下。

■ ***adj.*** [only before noun] changing repeatedly in size, amount, quality, etc. from one extreme to another 上下跳动的；左右摇摆的：*She worries about her pattern of yo-yo dieting.* 节食后体重反弹，再节食再反弹，她对这种模式很担心。

yr (*also* **yr.** *especially in NAmE*) *abbr.* **1** (*pl.* **yrs**) YEAR(S) 年；岁；年度：*children aged 4–11 yrs* * 4 至 11 岁的儿童 **2** YOUR 你的；你们的；人们的

yt·ter·bium /ɪˈtɜːbiəm; *NAmE* ɪˈtɜːrb-/ *noun* [U] (*symb.* **Yb**) a chemical element. Ytterbium is a silver-white metal used to make steel stronger and in some X-RAY machines. 镱

yt·trium /ˈɪtriəm/ *noun* [U] (*symb.* **Y**) a chemical element. Yttrium is a grey-white metal used in MAGNETS. 钇

yuan /juˈɑːn/ *noun* (*pl.* **yuan**) the unit of money in China 元（中国货币单位）➲ SEE ALSO RENMINBI

yucca /ˈjʌkə/ *noun* a tropical plant with long stiff pointed leaves on a thick straight STEM, often grown indoors 丝兰（叶剑形坚挺，常种于室内）

yuck (*also* **yuk**) /jʌk/ *exclamation* (*informal*) used to show that you think sth is disgusting or unpleasant（表示憎厌）讨厌，可恶：*It's filthy! Yuck!* 脏死了！真恶心！➲ MORE LIKE THIS 2, page R25

yucky (*also* **yukky**) /ˈjʌki/ *adj.* (*informal*) disgusting or very unpleasant 讨厌的；令人生厌的；令人厌恶的：*yucky food* 难以下咽的食物

Yue /jəˈweɪ; jʊˈeɪ/ *noun* = CANTONESE (1)

Yule /juːl/ *noun* [C, U] (*old use* or *literary*) the festival of Christmas 圣诞节

'yule log *noun* **1** a large LOG of wood traditionally burnt on Christmas Eve 圣诞节原木（传统上在圣诞夜烧的大原木）**2** a chocolate cake in the shape of a LOG, traditionally eaten at Christmas 圣诞节原木（巧克力）蛋糕

Yule·tide /ˈjuːltaɪd/ *noun* [U, C] (*old use* or *literary*) the period around Christmas Day 圣诞节期间：*Yuletide food and drink* 圣诞食物和饮料

yum /jʌm/ (*also* **ˌyum-ˈyum**) *exclamation* (*informal*) used to show that you think sth tastes or smells very nice（表示味道或气味非常好）➲ MORE LIKE THIS 2, page R25

yummy /ˈjʌmi/ *adj.* (*informal*) very good to eat 很好吃的 **SYN delicious**：*a yummy cake* 好吃的蛋糕

'yummy mummy *noun* (*pl.* **-ies**) (*BrE, informal*) an attractive young woman who is the mother of a young child or children 年轻漂亮的妈妈；辣妈：*celebrity yummy mummies* 年轻漂亮的名人妈妈

yup·pie (*also* **yuppy**) /ˈjʌpi/ *noun* (*pl.* **-ies**) (*informal, becoming old-fashioned, often disapproving*) a young professional person who lives in a city and earns a lot of money that they spend on expensive and fashionable things 雅皮士（城市中收入高、生活优裕的年轻专业人员）

ORIGIN Formed from the first letters of the words 'young urban professional'. 由 young urban professional 的首字母组成。

yurt /jɜːt; *NAmE* jɜːrt/ *noun* a type of traditional tent used in Central Asia and Siberia 蒙古包

YWCA /ˌwaɪ dʌbljuː siː ˈeɪ/ (*also NAmE, informal* **the Y**) *noun* Young Women's Christian Association (an organization that exists in many countries and provides accommodation and social and sports activities) 基督教女青年会：*members of the YWCA* 基督教女青年会的会员

Zz

Z (*also* **z**) /zed; *US* ziː/ *noun* (*pl.* **Zs**, **Z's**, **z's** /zedz; *US* ziːz/) **1** [C, U] the 26th and last letter of the English alphabet 英语字母表的第 26 个字母：*'Zebra' begins with (a) Z/'Z'.* * zebra 一词以字母 z 开头。 **2** **Z's** [pl.] (*NAmE, informal, humorous*) sleep 睡觉；睡眠：*I need to* ***catch some Z's.*** 我需要睡一会儿。 IDM SEE A *n.*

'Z angles *noun* = ALTERNATE ANGLES

zany /ˈzemi/ *adj.* (**zani·er**, **zani·est**) (*informal*) strange or unusual in an amusing way 古怪的；滑稽可笑的 SYN **wacky**: *zany humour* 古怪的幽默

zap /zæp/ *verb* (**-pp-**) (*informal*) **1** [T] to destroy, kill or hit sb/sth suddenly and with force（突然而猛烈地）毁坏，杀死，打击：**~ sb/sth** *The monster* ***got zapped*** *by a flying saucer* (= in a computer game). 怪兽被飞碟杀死了。◇ *It's vital to zap stress fast.* 快速消除压力非常重要。◇ **~ sb/sth with sth** *He jumped like a man who'd been zapped with 1 000 volts.* 他像受到 1 000 伏的电击似的猛跳起来。 **2** [I] **+ adv./prep.** to do sth very fast 很快地做；迅速做：*I'm zapping through* (= reading very fast) *some modern novels at the moment.* 我现在正在浏览一些现代小说。 **3** [I, T] **~ (sth)** to use the REMOTE CONTROL to change television channels quickly（用遥控器）快速变换频道 **4** [I, T] **~ (sb/sth) + adv./prep.** to move, or make sb/sth move, very fast in the direction mentioned（使沿某方向）快速移动 SYN **zip**: *The racing cars zapped past us.* 赛车从我们身边飞驰而过。

zap·per /ˈzæpə(r)/ *noun* (*informal*) **1** = REMOTE CONTROL (2) **2** a device or weapon that attacks or destroys sth quickly 灭杀器：*a bug zapper* 灭虫器

ZAR *abbr.* the written abbreviation for the South African RAND (= the national money of South Africa) 南非兰特（全写为 South African Rand，书面语，即南非货币）：*All prices listed are in ZAR.* 所有价格都是用南非兰特列出的。

zeal /ziːl/ *noun* [U, C] **~ (for/in sth)** (*formal*) great energy or enthusiasm connected with sth that you feel strongly about 热情；激情：*her* ***missionary/reforming/religious/political zeal*** 她的传教士般的 / 改革 / 宗教 / 政治热情

zealot /ˈzelət/ *noun* (*often disapproving*) a person who is extremely enthusiastic about sth, especially religion or politics （尤指宗教或政治的）狂热分子，狂热者 SYN **fanatic**

zeal·ot·ry /ˈzelətri/ *noun* [U] (*often disapproving*) the attitude or behaviour of a zealot 狂热分子的态度（或行为）：*religious zealotry* 宗教狂热行为

zeal·ous /ˈzeləs/ *adj.* (*formal*) showing great energy and enthusiasm for sth, especially because you feel strongly about it 热情的；热烈的；充满激情的：*a zealous reformer* 充满激情的改革者 ▶ **zeal·ous·ly** *adv.*

zebra /ˈzebrə; ˈziːbrə/ *noun* (*pl.* **zebra** or **zebras**) an African wild animal like a horse with black and white lines (= STRIPES) on its body 斑马

,zebra 'crossing *noun* (*BrE*) an area of road marked with broad black and white lines where vehicles must stop for people to walk across 斑马线；人行横道 ➲ SEE ALSO PEDESTRIAN CROSSING, PELICAN CROSSING ➲ WORDFINDER NOTE AT TRAFFIC

zebu /ˈziːbuː/ *noun* (*pl.* **zebus** or **zebu**) an animal of the cow family with long horns and a HUMP (= high part) on its back, kept on farms especially in hot climates 瘤牛：*Kenya's beef comes from the zebu cattle.* 肯尼亚的牛肉是瘤牛肉。

zeit·geist /ˈzaɪtgaɪst/ *noun* [sing.] (*from German, formal*) the general mood or quality of a particular period of history, as shown by the ideas, beliefs, etc. common at the time 时代精神；时代思潮 SYN **spirit**

Zen /zen/ *noun* [U] a Japanese form of Buddhism 日本禅宗

zen·ith /ˈzenɪθ/ *noun* **1** the highest point that the sun or moon reaches in the sky, directly above you 天顶（太阳或月亮在天空中的最高点） **2** (*formal*) the time when sth is strongest and most successful 鼎盛时期；顶峰 SYN **peak** OPP **nadir**

zephyr /ˈzefə(r)/ *noun* (*old-fashioned* or *literary*) a soft gentle wind 和风；微风

Zep·pelin /ˈzepəlɪn/ *noun* a German type of large AIRSHIP 齐柏林飞艇（源自德国的大型飞艇）

zero /ˈzɪərəʊ; *NAmE* ˈzɪroʊ; ˈziː-/ *number, verb*

■ ***number*** **1** (*pl.* **-os**) (*BrE also* **nought**) 0 零：*Five, four, three, two, one, zero… We have lift-off.* 五、四、三、二、一、零… 我们升空了。 **2** a temperature, pressure, etc. that is equal to zero on a scale（气温、压力等的）零度，零点：*It was ten degrees below zero last night* (= –10°C). 昨天夜里的气温是零下 10 摄氏度。◇ *The thermometer had fallen to zero.* 温度计显示温度降到了零度。 **3** the lowest possible amount or level; nothing at all 最少量；最低点；最低程度；毫无：*I rated my chances as zero.* 我觉得我根本没有机会。◇ *zero inflation* 零通胀

■ ***verb*** (**zer·oes**, **zero·ing**, **zer·oed**, **zer·oed**) **~ sth** to turn an instrument, control, etc. to zero 将（仪器、控制装置等）调到零

PHR V **,zero 'in on sb/sth** **1** to fix all your attention on the person or thing mentioned 集中全部注意力于：*They zeroed in on the key issues.* 他们集中讨论了关键问题。 **2** to aim guns, etc. at the person or thing mentioned（用枪炮等）瞄准

,zero-'carbon *adj.* in which the amount of CARBON DIOXIDE produced has been reduced to nothing or is balanced by actions that protect the environment 零碳的（指碳排放量减为零或通过环保行为抵消的） SYN **carbon neutral**: *a zero-carbon house that uses no energy from external sources* 不使用外部能源的零碳环保住宅

,zero 'gravity *noun* [U] (*abbr.* **,zero 'G**) a state in which there is no GRAVITY, or where gravity has no effect, for example in space（太空等的）零重力状态，失重状态

,zero 'grazing *noun* [U] a farming method that involves keeping cows inside and bringing them cut grass, rather than letting them feed in the fields 零放牧（刈割牧草饲牛的圈养方式）

'zero hour *noun* [U] the time when an important event, an attack, etc. is planned to start 零时；发动（进攻等的）时刻

,zero-'rated *adj.* (*BrE, specialist*) (of goods, services, etc. 货品、服务等) that you do not need to pay VAT (= value added tax) on 免付增值税的

,zero-'sum game *noun* a situation in which what is gained by one person or group is lost by another person or group 零和对策，零和博弈（一方得益一方受损、两者得失相抵的情形）

,zero 'tolerance *noun* [U] the policy of applying laws very strictly so that people are punished even for offences that are not very serious 零容忍政策（指对轻微过失都不予放过的严厉执法政策）

zest /zest/ *noun* **1** [sing., U] **~ (for sth)** enjoyment and enthusiasm 热情；狂热 SYN **appetite**: *He had a great zest for life.* 他对生命有着极大的热情。 **2** [U, sing.] the quality of being exciting, interesting and enjoyable 兴奋；激动；有趣；愉快：*The slight risk added zest to the experience.* 冒了一点儿险使得这次经历更加有趣。 **3** [U] the outer skin of an orange, a lemon, etc., when it is used to give flavour in cooking 柑橘外皮（包括柠檬或橙子等的外皮层，用于调味） ➲ COMPARE PEEL *n.* (1), RIND (1), SKIN *n.* (4) ▶ **zest·ful** /-fl/ *adj.* **zesty** /ˈzesti/ *adj.*

Z

zeta /'zi:tə/ *noun* the 6th letter of the Greek alphabet (Z, ζ) 希腊字母表的第 6 个字母

zeug·ma /'zju:gmə; *NAmE* 'zu:g-/ *noun* [C, U] (*specialist*) the use of a word which must be understood in two different ways at the same time in order to make sense, for example 'The bread was baking, and so was I.' 轭式搭配（一个词以不同的词义同时与两个词搭配使用）

zhoosh (*also* **zhush**) /ʒʊʃ; *BrE also* ʒu:ʃ/ (*also* **zhuzh** /ʒʊʒ/) *verb* (*BrE, informal*) **~ sth (up)** to make sth more exciting, lively or attractive 使更令人兴奋；使更有吸引力：*You can zhoosh up the basic pudding mix with all sorts of lovely things.* 可以往原味布丁粉里添加各种好东西，使它更加美味。

zig·gurat /'zɪgəræt/ *noun* in ancient Mesopotamia, a tower with steps going up the sides, sometimes with a TEMPLE at the top 塔庙，庙塔（古代美索不达米亚的阶梯式金字塔形建筑）

zig·zag /'zɪgzæg/ *noun, verb*
■ *noun* a line or pattern that looks like a series of letter W's as it bends to the left and then to the right again 锯齿形线条（或形状）；之字形：*The path descended the hill in a series of zigzags.* 小路顺着山坡蜿蜒而下。▶ **zig·zag** *adj.* [only before noun]：*a zigzag line/path/pattern* 弯弯曲曲的线条 / 小路 / 形状
■ *verb* (**-gg-**) [I] (**+ adv./prep.**) to move forward by making sharp sudden turns first to the left and then to the right 曲折前进：*The narrow path zigzags up the cliff.* 狭窄的小路曲曲折折通向悬崖。

zilch /zɪltʃ/ *noun* [U] (*informal*) nothing 没有；毫无：*I arrived in this country with zilch.* 我来到这个国家时一无所有。

zilla (*also* **zillah**) /'zɪlə/ *noun* (in S Asia) a district that has its own local government（南亚）行政专区

zil·lion /'zɪljən/ *noun* (*informal, especially NAmE*) a very large number 非常多：*There was a bunch of kids waiting and zillions of reporters.* 有一大批等待的孩子和不计其数的记者。

Zim·mer frame™ /'zɪmə freɪm; *NAmE* 'zɪmər/ (*also informal* **Zim·mer** /'zɪmə(r)/) (*both BrE*) (*NAmE* **walk·er**) *noun* a metal frame that people use to help them to walk, for example people who are old or who have sth wrong with their legs 齐默式助行架 ➲ PICTURE AT FRAME

zinc /zɪŋk/ *noun* **1** [U] (*symb.* **Zn**) a chemical element. Zinc is a bluish-white metal that is mixed with COPPER to produce BRASS and is often used to cover other metals to prevent them from RUSTING. 锌 **2** [C] (*informal*) (in some places in Africa) a sheet of CORRUGATED iron that is used to make a roof, shelter, etc.（非洲某些地方用于搭建屋顶、棚子等的）波纹铁板，瓦楞铁板：*They built a temporary home out of zincs.* 他们用瓦楞铁板搭建了一个临时住所。

ˌzinc ˈoxide *noun* [U] (*symb.* **ZnO**) a substance used in creams as a treatment for certain skin conditions 氧化锌（用于皮肤膏）

zin·da·bad /'zɪndɑ:bɑ:d/ *exclamation* (*IndE*) used to express approval or agreement, usually after the name of a leader, a political movement, an idea, etc. …万岁（通常用在领袖、政治运动、思想等的名称之后，表示拥护）

'zine (*also* **zine**) /zi:n/ *noun* (*informal*) a magazine, especially a FANZINE 杂志（尤指爱好者杂志）

zing /zɪŋ/ *verb, noun*
■ *verb* (*informal*) **1** [I, T] **~ (sth) + adv./prep.** to move or to make sth move very quickly, often with a high whistling sound（使）呼啸疾行：*electrical pulses zinging down a wire* 迅速通过电线的电脉冲 **2** [T] **~ sb/sth (for/on sth)** (*NAmE*) to criticize sb strongly 严厉批评；斥责
■ *noun* [U] (*informal*) interest or excitement 兴趣；激动；兴奋 ▶ **zingy** *adj.*

zing·er /'zɪŋə(r)/ *noun* (*informal, especially NAmE*) a clever or amusing remark 妙语；有趣的话：*She opened the speech with a real zinger.* 她的开场白十分风趣。

Zion·ism /'zaɪənɪzəm/ *noun* [U] a political movement that was originally concerned with establishing an independent state for Jewish people, and is now concerned with developing the state of Israel 犹太复国运动；犹太复国主义；锡安主义 ▶ **Zion·ist** /'zaɪənɪst/ *noun, adj.*

zip /zɪp/ *noun, verb*
■ *noun* **1** (*also* **'zip fastener**) (*both BrE*) (*also* **zip·per** *NAmE, BrE*) [C] a thing that you use to fasten clothes, bags, etc. It consists of two rows of metal or plastic teeth that you can pull together to close sth or pull apart to open it. 拉链；拉锁：*to* **do up/close/undo/open** *a zip* 拉上 / 拉开拉链 ◇ *My zip's stuck.* 我的拉链卡住了。➲ VISUAL VOCAB PAGE V68 **2** [U] (*informal*) energy or speed 能量；速度 **3** [sing.] (*informal, especially NAmE*) nothing 零；没有；毫无：*We won four zip* (= 4–0). 我们以四比零获胜。◇ *He said zip all evening.* 整个晚上他一声不吭。
■ *verb* (**-pp-**) **1** [T] to fasten clothes, bags, etc. with a zip/zipper 拉上拉链：**~ sth** *I zipped and buttoned my jacket.* 我把夹克的拉链拉上，系好扣子。◇ **~ sb/yourself into sth** *The children were safely zipped into their sleeping bags.* 孩子们都安安稳稳地躺在睡袋里，拉链也给他们拉好了。◇ **~ sth + adj.** *He zipped his case shut.* 他拉上了箱子的拉锁。➲ COMPARE UNZIP (1) **2** [I] **~ (up/together)** to be fastened with a ZIP/ZIPPER 用拉链锁上：*The sleeping bags can zip together.* 这些睡袋可用拉链连起来。**3** [I, T] **~ (sth) + adv./prep.** (*informal*) to move very quickly or to make sth move very quickly in the direction mentioned（使沿某方向）快速移动：*A sports car zipped past us.* 一辆跑车从我们身边呼啸而过。**4** [T] **~ sth** (*computing* 计) to COMPRESS a file (= make it smaller) 压缩（文件） OPP **unzip**
PHR V **ˌzip 'up | ˌzip sb/sth 'up** to be fastened with a ZIP/ZIPPER; to fasten sth with a ZIP/ZIPPER 拉上拉链；拉上…的拉链：*This jacket zips up right to the neck.* 这件夹克的拉链一直拉到脖子。◇ *Shall I zip you up* (= fasten your dress, etc.)? 要我给你拉上拉链吗？➲ COMPARE UNZIP (1)

'zip code (*also* **ZIP code**) (*US*) *noun* a group of numbers that are used as part of an address so that post/mail can be separated into groups and delivered more quickly 邮政编码；邮编 ➲ SEE ALSO POSTCODE

'zip file (*also* **'ZIP file**, **'zipped file**) *noun* a computer file that has been COMPRESSED (= made smaller) to make it easier to store and send 压缩文件

'zip gun *noun* (*NAmE, informal*) a simple gun that a person has made himself or herself 土手枪；自制手枪

Ziploc bag™ /ˌzɪplɒk 'bæg; *NAmE* -lɑ:k/ *noun* (*NAmE*) a small plastic bag for storing food, that has edges that seal when you press them together in order to keep the air out 密保诺保鲜袋；自封袋；夹链袋

zip·per /'zɪpə(r)/ (*especially NAmE*) (*BrE also* **zip**, **'zip fastener**) *noun* a thing that you use to fasten clothes, bags, etc. It consists of two rows of metal or plastic teeth that you can pull together to close sth or pull apart to open it. 拉链；拉锁 ➲ VISUAL VOCAB PAGE V68

zippy /'zɪpi/ *adj.* (**zip·pier**, **zip·pi·est**) (*informal*) **1** able to move very quickly 迅捷的；速度快的：*a zippy little car* 飞快的小汽车 **2** lively and exciting, especially in flavour 活泼的；（味道）清新浓郁的，提神的：*a wine with a zippy tang* 味道浓郁的葡萄酒

'zip-up *adj.* [only before noun] (*especially BrE*) (of clothing, a bag, etc. 衣服、袋子等) fastened with a ZIP/ZIPPER 用拉链的：*a zip-up top* 拉链上衣

zir·co·nium /zɜ:'kəʊniəm; *NAmE* zɜ:r'koʊ-/ *noun* [U] (*symb.* **Zr**) a chemical element. Zirconium is a hard silver-grey metal that does not CORRODE very easily. 锆

zit /zɪt/ *noun* (*informal, especially NAmE*) a spot on the skin, especially on the face（尤指脸上的）丘疹 SYN **pimple** ➲ COMPARE SPOT *n.* (3)

zith·er /ˈzɪðə(r)/ *noun* a musical instrument with a lot of metal strings stretched over a flat wooden box, that you play with your fingers or a PLECTRUM 齐特琴（匣式弦乐器，用手指或拨子演奏）

zo·diac /ˈzəʊdiæk; *NAmE* ˈzoʊ-/ *noun* **1 the zodiac** [sing.] the imaginary area in the sky in which the sun, moon and planets appear to lie, and which has been divided into twelve equal parts each with a special name and symbol 黄道带（天球上的十二个等份区，各有其名称和符号，日、月、行星分布其中）：*the signs of the zodiac* 黄道十二宫 **2** [C] a diagram of these twelve parts, and signs that some people believe can be used to predict how the planets will influence our lives 黄道十二宫图（用于占星术）▶ **zo·di·ac·al** /zəʊˈdaɪəkl; *NAmE* zoʊ-/ *adj.*

zom·bie /ˈzɒmbi; *NAmE* ˈzɑːmbi/ *noun* **1** (*informal*) a person who seems only partly alive, without any feeling or interest in what is happening 无生气的人；麻木迟钝的人 **2** (in some African and Caribbean religions and in horror stories) a dead body that has been made alive again by magic（某些非洲和加勒比地区的宗教及恐怖故事中靠巫术起死回生的）僵尸

zonal /ˈzəʊnl; *NAmE* ˈzoʊnl/ *adj.* (*specialist*) connected with zones; arranged in zones 地带的；区域的；分成区的

zone /zəʊn; *NAmE* zoʊn/ *noun, verb*

■ ***noun*** **1** an area or a region with a particular feature or use（有某特色或作用的）地区，地带：*a war/security/demilitarized, etc. zone* 交战区、安全区、非军事区等 ◇ *an earthquake/danger, etc. zone* 地震带、危险地带等 ◇ *a pedestrian zone* (= where vehicles may not go) 步行区 ➲ SEE ALSO NO-FLY ZONE, TIME ZONE, TWILIGHT *n.* **2** one of the areas that a larger area is divided into for the purpose of organization（规划的）区域，分区：*postal charges to countries in zone 2* 到位于第 2 邮区的国家的邮资 **3** an area or a part of an object, especially one that is different from its surroundings（尤指有别于周围的）区域，部分：*When the needle enters the red zone the engine is too hot.* 当指针进入红色区域时，发动机就过热了。◇ *the erogenous zones of the body* 身体的性敏感区 ➲ SEE ALSO CRUMPLE ZONE **4** one of the parts that the earth's surface is divided into by imaginary lines that are parallel to the EQUATOR（地球表面与赤道平行的）气候带：*the northern/southern temperate zone* 北温带；南温带 ➲ WORDFINDER NOTE AT CLIMATE

IDM **in the ˈzone** (*NAmE, informal*) in a state in which you feel confident and are performing at your best 处于最佳状态：*When I'm in the zone, writing is the most satisfying thing in the world.* 当我状态好的时候，写作是世界上最让我愉快的事。➲ SEE ALSO COMFORT ZONE

■ ***verb*** [usually passive] **1 ~ sth (for sth)** to keep an area of land to be used for a particular purpose 将…划作特殊区域；指定…为某项用途的区域：*The town centre was zoned for office development.* 镇中心被划定为写字楼开发区。**2 ~ sth** to divide an area of land into smaller areas 将…分成区（或划成带）▶ **zon·ing** *noun* [U]

PHR V **ˌzone ˈout** (*especially NAmE, informal*) to fall asleep, become unconscious or stop paying attention 入睡；失去知觉；走神：*I just zoned out for a moment.* 我刚睡着了一会儿。

zoned /zəʊnd; *NAmE* zoʊnd/ *adj.* **1** divided into areas designed for a particular use 划成（特殊）区域的：*zoned housing land* 划定为住宅区的土地 **2** (*also* **ˌzoned ˈout**) (*both NAmE, informal*) not behaving or thinking normally because of the effects of a drug such as MARIJUANA or alcohol（因毒品或酒精作用而）举止怪异的，精神恍惚的，神志不清的

zonked /zɒŋkt; *NAmE* zɑːŋkt; zɔːŋkt/ *adj.* [not before noun] **~ (out)** (*slang*) extremely tired or suffering from the effects of alcohol or drugs 极度疲惫；筋疲力尽；醉酒；麻醉

zoo /zuː/ *noun* (*pl.* **zoos**) (*also formal* **ˌzoological ˈgarden(s)**) a place where many kinds of wild animals are kept for the public to see and where they are studied, bred and protected 动物园

zoo·keep·er /ˈzuːkiːpə(r)/ *noun* a person who works in a zoo, taking care of the animals 动物园管理员

zoo·logic·al /ˌzuːəˈlɒdʒɪkl; ˌzəʊəˈl-; *NAmE* ˌzuːəˈlɑːdʒ-; ˌzoʊəˈlɑːdʒ-/ *adj.* connected with the science of ZOOLOGY 动物学的

ˌzoological ˈgarden *noun* (*also* **ˌzoological ˈgardens** [pl.]) (*formal*) = ZOO

zo·olo·gist /zuˈɒlədʒɪst; zəʊˈɒl-; *NAmE* zuˈɑːl-; zoʊˈɑːl-/ *noun* a scientist who studies zoology 动物学家

zo·ology /zuˈɒlədʒi; zəʊˈɒl-; *NAmE* zuˈɑːl-; zoʊˈɑːl-/ *noun* [U] the scientific study of animals and their behaviour 动物学 ➲ COMPARE BIOLOGY (1), BOTANY

zoom /zuːm/ *verb, noun*

■ ***verb*** **1** [I] **+ adv./prep.** (*informal*) to move or go somewhere very fast 快速移动；迅速前往 SYN **rush, whizz**：*Traffic zoomed past us.* 车辆从我们身边疾驰而过。◇ *For five weeks they zoomed around Europe.* 他们在欧洲各国马不停蹄地奔波了五个星期。**2** [I] **~ (up) (to…)** (*informal*) (of prices, costs, etc. 价格、费用等) to increase a lot quickly and suddenly 急剧增长；猛涨：*House prices have zoomed up this year.* 今年房屋价格飞涨。

PHR V **ˌzoom ˈin/ˈout** (of a camera 摄影机或摄像机) to show the object that is being photographed from closer/further away, with the use of a ZOOM LENS（用变焦距镜头）拉近，推远；使画面放大（或缩小）：*The camera zoomed in on the actor's face.* 摄影机将演员的脸拉近了。

■ ***noun*** **1** [C] = ZOOM LENS：*a zoom shot* 用变焦距镜头拍的照片 **2** [sing.] the sound of a vehicle moving very fast（车辆等）疾驰的声音 ➲ MORE LIKE THIS 3, page R25

ˈzoom lens (*also* **zoom**) *noun* a camera LENS that you use to make the thing that you are photographing appear nearer to you or further away from you than it really is 变焦镜头 ➲ VISUAL VOCAB PAGE V45

zoot suit /ˈzuːt suːt; *BrE also* sjuːt/ *noun* a man's suit with wide trousers/pants and a long loose jacket with wide shoulders that was popular in the 1940s 佐特套装（流行于 20 世纪 40 年代的男装，裤管宽大、上衣长而宽松、肩宽）

zorb·ing /ˈzɔːbɪŋ; *NAmE* ˈzɔːrb-/ *noun* [U] a sport in which sb is put inside a large transparent plastic ball which is then rolled along the ground or down hills 滚人球运动（人在大型透明塑料球中沿地面或山坡翻滚）

Zoro·ast·rian·ism /ˌzɒrəʊˈæstriənɪzəm; *NAmE* ˌzɔːroʊ-/ *noun* [U] a religion started in ancient Persia by Zoroaster, that teaches that there is one God and a continuing struggle in the world between forces of light and dark 琐罗亚斯德教，拜火教（始于古代波斯，由琐罗亚斯德创立，宣扬一神论，认为世界上存在光明与黑暗之间的永恒斗争）▶ **Zoro·ast·rian** *noun, adj.* ➲ SEE ALSO PARSEE

zuc·chini /zuˈkiːni/ *noun* (*pl.* **zuc·chini** or **zuc·chi·nis**) (*NAmE*) (*BrE* **cour·gette**) a long vegetable with dark green skin and white flesh 密生西葫芦，小胡瓜（深绿皮）➲ VISUAL VOCAB PAGE V34

Zulu /ˈzuːluː/ *noun* **1** [C] a member of a race of black people who live in South Africa 祖鲁人（南非的一个黑人种族）**2** [U] the language spoken by Zulus and many other black South Africans 祖鲁语 ▶ **Zulu** *adj.*

Zuni /ˈzuːni/ *noun* (*pl.* **Zuni** or **Zunis**) a member of a Native American people many of whom live in western New Mexico 祖尼人（美洲土著，多居于美国新墨西哥州西部）

zwie·back /ˈzwiːbæk/ *noun* [U] (*NAmE, from German*) slices of sweet bread that are cooked again until they are dry and hard 烤干面包片

Z

zy·deco /ˈzaɪdɪkəʊ; *NAmE* -koʊ/ *noun* [U] a type of dance music, originally played by black Americans in Louisiana 柴迪科舞曲（最早由美国路易斯安那州的黑人演奏）

zy·gote /ˈzaɪɡəʊt; *NAmE* -ɡoʊt/ *noun* (*biology* 生) a single cell that develops into a person or animal, formed by the joining together of a male and a female GAMETE (= a cell that is provided by each parent) 合子；受精卵

Z

Oxford Speaking Tutor 牛津口语指南

The dictionary can be just as helpful to you when you are preparing to speak as it is when you are writing. These pages show you how you can use it when you are getting ready for an oral exam, or when you have to give a talk, or when you are just interacting with other people in English. You will be able to listen to the model answers and to do a range of interactive activities with Oxford iSpeaker on the bundled DVD. 如同对写作一样，本词典对口语同样有所裨益。接下来的内容教你如何使用本词典准备口试、演讲或用英语与他人交流。利用本词典附赠的 iSpeaker 软件，还可以听到一些口语表达的范例，做各种互动练习。

Improving your conversational English 提高英语会话水平

In the main part of the dictionary, you will find 'Express yourself' boxes with language that will be useful in many situations. For example, if you want to ask somebody to do something for you, you can find polite ways of making requests. In meetings at work as well as simply in conversation with friends, you have to put forward your own opinions and discuss other people's suggestions. In the Speaking Tutor you will find examples of this kind of conversation. 本词典的正文部分有"情景表达"用法说明框，提供适用于各种场合的表达。比如，要请求别人为自己做某事，可以查到礼貌地提出要求的方式。在工作会议或与朋友的交谈中，要提出自己的意见或讨论他人的建议，可以在牛津口语指南里找到这类谈话的示例。

Working on pronunciation 改进发音

The main part of the dictionary gives you information on how to pronounce all the headwords, with a reminder of what the symbols stand for at the bottom of the page and an explanation on page R47. There is much more information and practice on pronunciation in Oxford iSpeaker on the bundled DVD. 本词典的正文部分给出了所有词目的读音信息，并在每一页的底部给出了音标符号及相应示例。另在 R47 页还有对读音和音标的说明。在 iSpeaker 里有更多关于语音的信息和练习。

Preparing for Speaking tests 准备口语考试

1 Revise the subject vocabulary 复习主题词汇

If you have an idea of the kind of topic that may come up in your oral exam, you can revise relevant vocabulary using the dictionary. For example, use the Collocations notes such as those at the following entries in the dictionary 如果了解口试中可能讨论的主题，可使用本词典复习相关词汇。比如，学习本词典下列词条中的"词语搭配"用法说明：**age**, **art**, **crime**, **diet**, **education**, **environment**, **job**, **life**, **literature**, **town**, and **travel**.

2 Practise the functional language 做功能语言练习

Besides looking at vocabulary to do with the topics you may have to talk about, you can revise the kind of language that is needed in discussions or for presenting information or preferences. In many exams you will be asked to put forward your opinions and to justify choices. Prepare this by looking at the 'Express yourself' notes, such as those at **why** or **think**. If your test is done with a partner, you may have to have a discussion, and the language in notes such as those at **agree** or **disagree** will be useful. You may be given a picture or a written cue as a starting point. The note at **speculate** suggests how you can present your ideas when you have to say what you think something might be about, or what might be happening. 除了查阅与可能出现的主题相关的词汇外，还可以复习在讨论、提供信息或表达偏好时需要用到的语言。许多考试都会要求考生提出自己的见解或对选择作出解释。做准备时可查看 why 或 think 等词条的"情景表达"用法说明。如果考试是与一位搭档一起完成，可能会要求考生互相讨论，这时 agree 或 disagree 等词条的"情景表达"用法说明所提供的信息会很有用。考试中或许会给考生看一幅图或提供一个书面提示，以此作为谈话的起点。如果需要谈谈某事物可能是什么，或可能发生了什么等，speculate 词条的"情景表达"用法说明就给出了如何表达自己想法的建议。

You will not be able to produce perfect English sentences all the time, but there are strategies that you can use to keep the presentation or conversation going. There is more information on this on pages ST15–16. 考生说出的英文句子不可能总是完美的，但要使陈述或谈话顺利进行，有一些策略可以运用。在 ST15–16 页有更多这方面的信息。

3 Practise your pronunciation
练习发音

Keep a note of words that you find difficult to pronounce and revise them before the exam. 把自己觉得难发音的词记下来，考试前复习。

Remember that words are often pronounced differently from the way they are spelt. For example, you don't pronounce the red letters in these words. 记住，单词的读音常常与其拼写方式并不一致。比如，下列单词中红色的字母不发音：
castle climber doubt folk honest

Remember that some pairs of words have exactly the same spelling but are pronounced differently, for example 记住，有些单词虽然拼写完全一样，但读音不同，比如：
read (present or past), **row**, **live** (verb or adjective), **object** (noun or verb) 单词 read 的现在式与过去式读音不同；单词 row 表达不同含义时读音不同；单词 live 作动词与作形容词时读音不同；单词 object 作名词与动词时读音不同。

Use the dictionary to check if you are unsure of the pronunciation. 如果对读音拿不准，可查词典核实。

During the speaking test
参加口语考试时

On the following pages you will find model answers for various types of oral exam, with advice on how to structure your answers and information on the Common European Framework scales. 接下来的内容是为各种类型的口语考试提供的范例，还有关于如何组织答案的建议，以及对"欧洲共同语言参考标准"能力分级的介绍。

Talking about a topic
谈论一个话题

IELTS | TOEIC | TOEFL | Cambridge English: Advanced, Proficiency, Business Certificates | Trinity GESE

In some exams, you are asked to talk for a short time about a topic which you are given during the test. You may have a few minutes to prepare it and to make a few notes. You could be asked to choose something that is the most important, best, most useful, etc. of its kind, and you have to describe it and explain why you have chosen it. 在一些考试中，考生会被要求在短时间内谈论一个规定话题。考生通常有几分钟时间做准备，可以做一些笔记。可能让考生在同类事物中选出一个最重要的、最好的或最有用的等等，对此加以描述，解释如此选择的原因。

Describe a place that you sometimes visit which is very important to you.
描述一个对你来说很重要、你间或会到访的地方。
You should say 你应该谈谈：

- where it is, how often and why you go there.
  它在什么地方，你多长时间去一次，以及为什么去。
- what it is like. 它是什么样子的。
- why it is so important to you. 它对你来说为什么如此重要。

explaining where, when and why 说明地点、时间和原因

One place that is very important in my life is my grandmother's house. She lives in a small village in the south of the country. I go there every summer, and any time when I can get away for a few days. I go there to visit my grandmother, get away from the city and relax.

describing the appearance and sounds of the place 描述这个地方的外观和声音

The village is just a group of white houses on a hillside with a couple of shops, and it's really peaceful. There's no traffic, just the sound of goat bells, birds and insects.

explaining why the place is important 解释这个地方为什么重要

One reason why I like it is because it's a beautiful place. My grandmother has a lovely garden and we always sit outside in the shade of her olive trees, drinking sweet tea and chatting. It's so peaceful. But the main reason why this place is so important to me is my grandmother. She is so kind to me, and wonderful to talk to. Whenever I have a problem in my life, she has some good advice for me. Also, she's a great cook and the meals she prepares are simple but so fresh and … – rich? No, no, I mean tasty. And she's always giving me eh … What do you call them? – small plates of food during the day, so I always return home feeling calm and refreshed – and fat!

justifying a choice 解释选择的理由

I wouldn't like to live there, though. I prefer living in the city, definitely. I'm a city person. I couldn't live in a small village where everybody knows each other and nothing happens. I'd rather live in a busy, exciting place. But I really love visiting the village for holidays.

Pink shows a variety of ways you can describe something. 粉色表示描述事物的各种方式。

Green shows ways of explaining and giving your reasons. 绿色表示解释和陈述理由的方式。

Yellow shows ways of correcting yourself or finding alternative ways of expressing something. 黄色表示纠正自己或尝试使用另一种表达方式。

Blue shows ways of expressing your preferences. 蓝色表示表达偏好的方式。

Speaking at CEFR level B2 欧洲共同语言参考标准 B2 级口语能力

- ✔ Can give clear, detailed descriptions on subjects related to his/her field of interest. B2
  能对自己感兴趣的相关领域话题进行清晰、详细的描述。
- ✔ Has a good range of vocabulary and can vary formulation to avoid frequent repetition. B2
  拥有丰富的词汇，能变换措辞以避免经常重复。
- ✔ Can use circumlocution and paraphrase to cover gaps in vocabulary and structure. B2
  能采用迂回说法和解释技巧来弥补用词和语法结构上的不足。
- ✔ Can correct slips and errors if he/she becomes conscious of them. B2
  意识到口误和错误，能自行纠正。

Before the exam 在考试前

Remind yourself of useful phrases by looking at the Express yourself notes in the dictionary for 阅读本词典的"情景表达"用法说明，提醒自己记住有用的短语，比如：

- expressing a preference (at **prefer**) 表达偏好（prefer 条）
- giving reasons, justifying a choice (at **why**) 对选择作出解释（why 条）
- correcting yourself (at **correct**) 纠正自己的话（correct 条）

During the exam 在考试中

Write brief notes to use as prompts, for example 写简短的笔记作为提示，比如：

place – grandmother's village
where – south-west coast
how often – summer, other holidays
why – visit, relax
what like – small, peaceful, quiet, goat bells, birds, insects, olive trees

Don't 不该做的事

- spend too much time trying to think of the ideal topic. 不要花太多时间去想一个最好的话题。
- use your note-making time to write full sentences. 做笔记时不要写完整句子。
- speak too quickly. 不要说得太快。
- just read out your notes to the examiner or give a prepared speech. 不要只是对着考官读笔记或背诵准备好的话。
- stop if you can't remember a word. 不要因想不起某个词而停下来。

Do 该做的事

- use a wide range of vocabulary. 使用丰富多样的词汇。
- try to use the full time allowed. 充分利用所给的时间。
- think of a different way of expressing your idea if you've forgotten a word. 如果忘记某个词，试着换一种说法表达意思。
- correct yourself if you make a mistake, and continue. 讲错了就纠正过来，继续说下去。
- make eye contact with the examiner. 跟考官要有眼神交流。

Express yourself 情景表达

Explaining and giving reasons 解释和说明理由

*We went there **to** see the sunset.*

*I couldn't sleep **because of** the heat.*

***One reason why** I like spring is the sound of birds singing.*

Expressing preferences 表达偏好

***I prefer** living in a city to living in the country.*

***I'd prefer to** arrive early rather than risk being late.*

***I'd rather** take the train than drive.*

***I like** olive oil **better** than butter.*

***I think** giving presents is **better than** receiving them.*

Correcting yourself 纠正自己的话

*Thanks, the soup was very rich – **no sorry, I mean** tasty.*

*I think he comes from England – **or rather**, the UK.*

*She's very thin – **or perhaps I should say** slim.*

Making your talk more interesting 使谈话更生动有趣

To give more emphasis to a point, you can use adverbs. 可以使用副词来强调某一点：

*I'd prefer to live in the city, **definitely**.*

*I **really** love visiting the village.*

You can also turn the sentence around. 还可以改变句子的结构：

I like it because it's simple. ➔ *One reason I like it is because it's simple.*

I like the price. ➔ *What I like about it is the price.*

It's special because it was a gift. ➔ *The reason it's special is that it was a gift.*

I particularly liked the food. ➔ *One thing I particularly liked was the food.*

Tip 提示

- Try to vary the vocabulary you use. For example, choose descriptive adjectives, not just 'nice', 'good' or 'interesting'. (Look at the pink highlights in the sample answer on p. ST3.) 尽量变换所用的词汇。比如，选择描述性形容词，不要只用 nice、good 或 interesting。（参见 ST3 页示例中以粉色突出显示的部分。）

Discussing opinions 讨论看法

Cambridge English: First, Advanced, Proficiency, Business Certificates | Trinity ISE, GESE | IELTS

You may be taking an exam where you and a partner have to discuss something, for example pictures that the examiner shows you. You may not have to describe the pictures in detail, but to interpret the situations that they show and express an opinion about them. You must make sure that you take part in the conversation, but also that you involve your partner. 考试中，考生会被要求和一位搭档就某事展开讨论，比如讨论考官展示的图片。不一定要详细描述图片，但需要诠释图片所展示的情境并发表看法。考生务必参与谈话，还要确保搭档参与其中。

Look at the pictures and discuss the questions. 看图片并讨论如下问题。

What are the good and bad points about cycling? 骑自行车的好处和坏处是什么？

Which situation in the pictures seems more dangerous for the cyclists? 下图中哪种情况看上去对骑车人更危险？

Well, **in my opinion**（在我看来）, the best thing about cycling is the exercise. You can go from A to B and keep fit at the same time. What do YOU think?（你觉得呢？）

I agree.（我同意。）And it's quiet and clean. I mean, bikes don't create pollution like cars, and they don't use oil.

Yes, bikes are better for the environment.

Uh huh, yeah, exactly. **But on the other hand**（但另一方面）**, there are bad points too**（也有不好的地方）. I mean, it can be quite dangerous, can't it?（是不是？）

Yes, that's true.（是的，的确。）Especially in a city, with all the traffic. **And another bad point is**（另一个不利之处是）the weather – cycling isn't pleasant when it's rainy and cold.

No. And it's really tiring if you have to go up a hill. I don't cycle because I live in the mountains. If I lived in a flat place like Holland, I might cycle more. What about you? Do you cycle?（你呢？你骑车吗？）

Sometimes, but only on holidays, not to go to work. I think the people in the photos are going to work.

So which place do you think looks more dangerous for the cyclists?（那你认为哪个地方看上去对骑车人更危险？）

Well, I would say（我觉得）it's OK in the first picture, because there is a special part of the road for cyclists（自行车专用道）, but not in the second picture – the cyclists are in the middle of the traffic, and it looks quite dangerous.

Yes, and I think（我认为）the man in the first picture is better prepared. He's wearing a bright coloured coat and a – what do you call it?（你管它叫什么？）A cycling hat?

A helmet, you mean?（你是指头盔？）

A helmet, yes. The people in the second picture haven't got helmets. But there again（不过）, it could be more dangerous in the first picture because the traffic is going much faster, isn't it?

Yes, I suppose so.（是的，我想是这样。）But there is plenty of space. On the whole（总体说来）, I think it's more dangerous in the second picture.

Yeah, yeah, I think you're probably right.（是的，我想你可能是对的。）

Ways of giving and responding to opinions. 发表和回应看法的方式。	Ways of involving the other person in the conversation. 引导别人参与谈话的方式。	Phrases for linking one idea to the next. 起承接作用的短语。	Ways of coping when you don't know the word. 不知道某个词怎么说时的应对方法。

Speaking at CEFR level B2/C1
欧洲共同语言参考标准 B2/C1 级口语能力

- ✔ Can take an active part in informal discussion in familiar contexts, commenting, putting point of view clearly, evaluating alternative proposals and making and responding to hypotheses. 能积极参与熟悉语境中的非正式讨论，发表评论，清晰地表达观点，对其他建议进行评估，提出自己的假设并回应别人的假设。 B2
- ✔ Can initiate, maintain and end discourse appropriately with effective turntaking. 能有效地遵守话轮顺序，以得体的方式开始讲话、延续话题和结束发言。 B2
- ✔ Can relate own contribution skilfully to those of other speakers. 能巧妙地让自己的发言与其他说话者的发言相呼应。 C1
- ✔ Has a good command of a broad lexical repertoire allowing gaps to be readily overcome with circumlocutions; little obvious searching for expressions or avoidance strategies. Good command of idiomatic expressions and colloquialisms. 熟练掌握丰富的词汇，能借助迂回说法轻松地弥补表达的不足；基本看不出需要寻找表达方式或采用回避策略。熟练掌握习语和俗语。 C1

Before the exam 在考试前

Look at the tips on pages ST1–2 about learning vocabulary for typical topics and the useful phrases in the Express yourself notes. 阅读 ST1–2 页上的建议，学习与典型话题相关的词汇和“情景表达”用法说明里有用的短语。

During the exam 在考试中

Do 该做的事

- listen to what the other person says and respond to it. 听搭档怎么说，并予以回应。
- use expressions like 'Let's see now', to buy thinking time. 使用 Let's see now 之类的说法，让自己有多一点思考时间。
- use questions or question tags like 'isn't it?' to involve the other person in the conversation. 使用问句或 isn't it? 之类的附加疑问成分，引导搭档加入谈话。
- talk about each of the questions. 逐一讨论每个问题。
- relate your comments to the photographs. 将评论跟照片联系起来。
- open out the discussion beyond the questions. 将讨论拓展到问题以外。
- indicate personal opinions and relate the topic to your own life. 表明个人观点并将话题与自己的生活联系起来。

Don't 不该做的事

- say things that you know the other person won't understand. 不要说你明知搭档不懂的东西。
- give one-word answers to a question. 不要只用一个词来回答问题。
- change to a completely different topic from the task. 不要转到完全不相关的话题。

Express yourself 情景表达

Giving opinions 发表看法

I think drivers should respect cyclists more.
In my opinion, public transport is too expensive.
I would say that Saturday is the busiest shopping day.

Responding to opinions 回应看法

Yes, I agree.
You're absolutely right.
Yes, you're probably right.
Yes, I suppose so.
Umm – I'm not so sure about that.
No, I don't think that's quite true.

Inviting a response 请他人回应

It's fantastic, isn't it?
They're very sweet, aren't they?
What about you?
What do you think?
It's rather strange, don't you think?

Pronunciation 语音

Intonation 语调

You're absolutely right.
(*sure* 确定的)

Yes, I suppose so.
(*tentative* 不确定的)

Sentence stress 句子重音

We could talk about pollution. What do you THINK? (*asking an opinion* 询问看法)

I think the traffic's worse in the second picture. What do YOU think? (*comparing an opinion* 比较看法)

Negotiating 协商

There are many occasions when you will have to discuss various possibilities with someone and try to come to an agreement. In some exams, you have to agree on a solution, for example the choice of a particular suggestion. 很多时候需要和某个人讨论各种可能性并努力达成一致。一些考试要求考生就某事商定一个解决办法，比如选出一个特定的建议。

Look at the pictures and think about which ones would best promote Scotland as a tourist destination for international visitors. Discuss and decide together which one image would be the best to place on the front cover of a travel brochure. 看图片，想一想哪些图片能最有效地将苏格兰推广为国际旅游胜地。一起讨论并决定在旅游手册封面上放哪张图片最合适。

OK, so we have to choose one picture to put on the front of a brochure. Shall we get started, then?（那我们就开始吧，好吗？）

Erm, let's see … It's really difficult. Personally（就我个人而言）, if I were choosing a holiday, I think I would pick up a brochure with the picture of the dancers on the front（如果要我来选择一个度假地，我想我会拿起一本封面印有舞者的旅游手册）, but that's because I enjoy folk dancing. Maybe that would not be so good for most people.

No, possibly not.（嗯，也许不太好。）To be honest（老实说）, that one looks boring. If you ask me（要我说的话）we should choose one which most people would find attractive. How about（…怎么样）the photo of the food? Everybody likes eating!

That's true（的确如此）, but I don't think Scotland is famous for food. My feeling is that if people wanted a food holiday, they would choose Italy（我觉得如果想要一个美食假期，人们会选择意大利）or France or somewhere like that.

OK, that's a good point.（嗯，这话说得很对。）It's the same with the picture of the beach – It's beautiful, but I've never heard of people going to Scotland for a beach holiday. From what I've heard（据我听闻）, it's always raining in Britain.

Yes, that's right.（是的，没错。）Everybody says the weather's terrible. Well … We could（我们可以）use the picture of the mountain climbers. It would give people the idea of things you can do in Scotland.

Hmm. Would that be very popular? I doubt it. Maybe we should（也许我们该）focus on history and culture. What's happening in the first picture, for example?

I've no idea. It looks like a carnival or something. But I think I would opt for（但我觉得我会选择）the castle. To me（对我来说）, that's a typical image of Scotland, and I can imagine it would look great on the cover of the brochure. What do you think?

Well, as far as I'm concerned（就我而言）, the carnival or the castle would be fine. So shall we use the castle then?

Yes, OK. That's fine by me.（我没意见。）Right, so I think we're agreed?（好，那么我们都同意了，是吗？）We'll use the photo of the castle.

Ways you can organize a discussion. 组织讨论的方式。	Ways you can express a personal view. 表达个人观点的方式。	Ways you can express alternative possibilities. 表达其他可能性的方式。	Ways you can agree or concede a point. 表示同意或承认对方有理的方式。	Ways you can make suggestions. 提建议的方式。

Speaking at CEFR level B2/C1
欧洲共同语言参考标准 B2/C1 级口语能力

- ✔ Can initiate discourse, take his/her turn when appropriate and end conversation when he/she needs to. 能在恰当的时候开始讲话、承接话轮，并能适时结束谈话。 B2
- ✔ Can use a limited number of cohesive devices to link his/her utterances into clear, coherent discourse. 能运用有限的衔接手段把自己的话语连接成清晰、连贯的语段。 B2
- ✔ Can select a suitable phrase from a readily available range of discourse functions to preface his/her remarks appropriately in order to get the floor, or to gain time and keep the floor whilst thinking. 能从现成的话语功能中选取合适的短语作为恰当的开场白，以便在讨论中取得发言权或者在思考的同时赢得时间并保有说话的权利。 C1
- ✔ Can qualify opinions and statements precisely in relation to degrees of, for example, certainty/uncertainty, belief/doubt, likelihood etc. 能根据确定／不确定、相信／怀疑、可能性等的程度对自己的观点或说法准确地加以限定。 C1

Before the exam 在考试前

Remind yourself of useful phrases by looking at the Express yourself notes in the dictionary at **recommend**, **suggest**, **think**, **disagree**, and **concede**. 阅读本词典 recommend、suggest、think、disagree 和 concede 条的“情景表达”用法说明里的提示，提醒自己记住有用的短语。

During the exam 在考试中

Don't 不该做的事

- move too far away from the task. 不要离题太远。
- agree on the first idea mentioned, without discussing the other options. 不要未讨论其他选择就同意第一个提到的观点。
- insist on your choice without carefully considering your partner's ideas. 不要不仔细考虑搭档的想法而一味坚持自己的选择。
- spend too long talking about one option, leaving no time to consider the others. 不要花太长时间讨论一个选项而不预留时间考虑其他的选项。
- take the outcome too seriously – you are here to show your English, not your decision-making skills! 不要把结果看得太重——在此要展示的是自己的英语水平而非决策能力！

Do 该做的事

- listen to what the other person says and respond to it. 听搭档怎么说，并予以回应。
- use expressions like 'personally' to show you are giving a personal opinion rather than a statement of fact. 使用 personally 之类的说法以表明所言为个人观点，而非陈述事实。
- show that you understand and appreciate the other person's suggestions. 表示理解并欣赏搭档的建议。
- try to reach a decision which is satisfactory for both or all participants in the discussion. 努力达成令参与讨论的双方或所有人都满意的决定。

Express yourself 情景表达

Expressing personal viewpoints 表达个人观点

***As far as I'm concerned**, e-books are as easy to read as paper books.*

***Personally, I think** the police were wrong in this case.*

***If you ask me**, they should abolish border controls.*

***My feeling** is that people should be allowed to take risks.*

***To be honest**, I don't care which party wins the election.*

Agreeing with or conceding a point 表示同意或承认对方有理

***OK**, that's a good point.*

***Yes**, I think you're probably right.*

***No**, possibly not.*

***Yes**, I see what you mean.*

*That's **true**!*

Oral presentations 口头报告

You may have to give an oral presentation or talk as part of your academic course, for an examination or at work. In many ways, preparing a talk is similar to preparing an essay. The guidelines below apply to most types of talk. 学一门课程、参加考试或在工作中都有可能被要求做口头报告。准备报告在很多方面与写文章类似。下面的指导原则适用于大多数类型的报告。

Preparing an oral presentation 准备口头报告

Good preparation is the most important factor for a successful presentation. 做好准备是报告成功最重要的因素。

First steps 前期准备

- Check the **time** allowed for your talk and any **guidelines** you have been given. 弄清楚你可以用多长时间来做报告以及应遵循的指导原则。
- Think about the **purpose** of your talk: is it to inform, to entertain or to persuade your audience? 考虑报告的目的：是向听众传达信息，娱乐听众，还是说服听众？
- Think about the **audience**. Who are they? How much do they already know? How much do you need to tell them? What will interest them? 考虑听众：对象是谁？他们对报告主题了解多少？你需要告诉他们多少？哪些内容是他们感兴趣的？
- Decide on the **topic** if you do not know this already. If you do, decide on the specific area that you will present. Be realistic about how much you can cover in the time allowed. 如果还不知道主题，就选定主题。如果知道的话，就选定你想谈的具体方面。要实事求是地估计在规定时间内能说多少内容。
- **Collect** your ideas and gather more information if you need to. 整理自己的想法；如有必要可再搜集资料。

Writing your talk 写讲稿

- Make notes on what you want to include. Think about what you must tell the audience, what you should tell them and what you would like to tell them if you have time. 将想说的东西记下来。考虑一下有什么必须告诉听众，有什么应该告诉听众，如果有时间，还有什么想要告诉他们。
- Produce an outline or a plan of your talk. 写报告的提纲。

Tip 提示

- **Structure** your talk as you would an essay: have an introduction, a middle and a conclusion. 像写文章那样组织好报告的结构，要有引言、中间部分和结论。
- Use **headings** to show the different sections of your talk. 用标题标示出报告的各个部分。

- Some people prefer to write out the whole talk like an essay. If you do this, it is better not to read this when you give your talk, but make notes as below and talk from those. 有些人喜欢把整篇报告像文章那样写出来。如果那么做，做报告时最好不要读稿子，而是做笔记（如下文所示），并根据笔记来讲。

Producing notes 做笔记

- Make notes in English on cards or the printout of your slides that you can refer to while you are speaking. 在卡片上或幻灯片的打印件上用英语做笔记，供做报告时参考。

- Open with an introduction to the title and an overview of what you want to say. 报告开场是对题目的介绍和对所讲内容的概述：

The benefits of learning a foreign language 1

Show Slide 1

Intro:
Good morning. My talk today examines the benefits of learning a foreign language.

Overview:
I intend to outline 3 imp. benefits of learning another lang.

The benefits of learning a foreign language 2

Show Slide 2

The first benefit I shall describe is practical – communicate with other nationalities

A further benefit is increased cultural understanding – breaks down barriers / bridges gap between cultures.

The final benefit that I shall describe is improved cognitive skills – research shows → brain power

Number note card. 给笔记卡片标号。

Note the number of the visual you will show. 记下要展示的视觉资料的序号。

Write out and highlight key words and phrases to guide your audience through your talk. 写出关键词和短语并做重点标记，用以在报告过程中引导听众。

- Try to get the attention of your audience at the beginning with e.g. a story, joke or surprising fact. 开头讲个故事、玩笑或令人惊奇的事实等，尽量吸引听众的注意力。
- Close with a summary and an invitation for people to ask questions. 结束时要有总结，并请听众提问。
- Some people find it helpful to write out the whole introduction and conclusion. 有些人觉得把引言和结论全部写出来很有帮助。

Preparing visual aids 准备视觉资料

Visual aids help you to communicate your talk to the audience, if they are prepared carefully and used well. For how to talk about graphs and charts, look at page WT25. 如果精心准备视觉资料并使用得当，有助于把报告的内容传达给听众。关于如何描述图表，请参阅 WT25 页。

Tip 提示

- If you use PowerPoint™ or similar programs, writing and diagrams must be large and clear. 如果使用 PPT 或类似的演示文稿程序，文字和图表必须大而清晰。
- Think about the colours you use and how visible they are. 考虑使用的颜色及其可见度。
- Do not put too much information on each slide. 每张幻灯片上不要放太多信息。
- If you use posters or pictures, check that the people at the back of the room will be able to see/read them. 如果使用海报或图片，要确保位于后排的人都能看到。

Examples of slides 幻灯片示例

The benefits of learning a foreign language 2

Three main benefits:
- Practical uses
- Increased cultural understanding
- Improved cognitive skills

Leave lots of white space. 多留些空白。

Use headings and bullets to show the relationship between ideas. 用标题和项目符号来显示要点之间的关系。

Use notes, not sentences. 用短语，不要用句子。

The benefits of learning a foreign language 3

1. Practical uses for:
   - Travel
   - Work
   - Study

Practising your talk 做报告前练习

The more you practise, the more confident you will feel and the better your talk will be. 练习越多就越有自信，报告也会做得越好。

- First, practise your talk alone several times until you can speak fluently and confidently from your notes and keep to the time allowed. 首先，独自练习做几次报告，直到能利用笔记流利而自信地讲话，并且不超出限定的时间。
- Then practise with one or more friends listening. Is the talk clear? Is your voice loud and clear? Are you looking at the audience? 然后找一两个朋友当听众，在他们面前做报告。你的表达是否清楚明白？你的声音是否响亮清晰？你讲话时是否看着听众？
- If you can, practise at least once with the equipment you will use. 可以的话，用所要使用的设备排练至少一次。
- Use your dictionary to check pronunciation, vocabulary and grammar. 使用词典核查读音、词汇和语法。

Preparing for questions 准备应对提问

- Try to predict some of the questions your audience may ask you and practise your answers. 试着预测听众可能会问的问题并练习回答。

Express yourself 情景表达

Introduction 引言

Good morning. My talk today examines …

The subject/title of my talk/paper is …

Hello. Today I'm going to talk about/discuss …

I am here today to present …

Explaining structure 讲解结构

In this talk I intend to outline …

In my talk I will discuss the main features of …

I am going to examine three benefits/advantages of …

Firstly I'll talk about … secondly/thirdly/then we'll look at … and finally I'll summarize …

Introducing each point 介绍各个要点

The first/second/next/last point/area … I would like to discuss is … Let's start by looking at … I'd now like to look at another/the second benefit of … Let's look at … in a bit more detail.

Clarifying 阐明

In other words, …

That is to say …

Changing the subject 转换话题

So, I have discussed …

Now I'd like to turn to …

This leads me on to …

Moving on to the next/second/last benefit …

Concluding 引出结论

So, I have talked about …

I'm now going to summarize …

To sum up/summarize: in my talk I have …

In conclusion, I believe it is clear that …

To conclude: the benefits I have described in my talk are important and therefore I consider that …

Answering difficult questions 回答疑难问题

I'm sorry, I don't quite understand your question. Could you repeat it?

Well, I'm not sure about that, but I think …

Successful communication 成功的交流

Having a conversation in English does not mean that you have to produce perfectly formed sentences all the time. You should not worry that you might not know the exact word for something, or that you might not understand the meaning of everything that the other person says. Even in an exam situation, you will be given credit for using strategies to keep the conversation running smoothly despite any gaps in your vocabulary or your understanding. Here are some useful ideas to help you in everyday conversations or in more formal situations. 用英语交谈并不意味着自始至终都要说出完美的句子。在交谈过程中你可能不知道表达某事物的确切用词，或者不一定能全部理解别人说的话，这都不必担心。即使在考试中，运用策略克服词汇或理解方面的不足，使谈话顺利进行，也会为你加分。下面的技巧对于日常交谈或更正式的场合中的交流会有帮助。

When you don't understand 没听懂时

When you are talking to someone in English, you may not understand everything they say, but you can practise focusing on what is important. If you are asking for information, think about the key words that you will expect to hear (for example, if you ask about prices or times, be prepared for numbers in the answer). Repeat it back to them to make sure you have understood correctly. 用英语与人交谈时，你或许不能完全听懂对方说的话，但可以练习把注意力集中在重要的点上。如果是询问信息，设想一下有望听到的关键词。比如，询问价格或时间，要注意听清楚回答里的数字。把听到的信息向对方重复一下，确保自己理解无误。

Here are some useful phrases. 下面是一些有用的表达方式。

Saying that you don't understand 表示没听懂

Sorry, I don't (quite) understand.

I beg your pardon?

Sorry, I'm not sure I understand what you're saying.

Asking for repetition 请对方再说一遍

Sorry, I wonder if you could repeat that, please?

Sorry, what did you say your name was again?

Sorry, I missed what you said about meal times – can you tell me again?

Asking someone to speak more slowly 请某人说慢一点

Can you speak more slowly, please?

Could you slow down a bit?

Sorry, that was too fast for me.

Checking that you understood correctly 核实自己的理解是否正确

Have I understood you correctly – did you say five-fifty?

Do you mean 'frozen', as in *very cold*?

Asking what something means 询问某个词的含义

Sorry, can you tell me what 'gasket' means?

What is Plasticine, exactly?

Asking how you spell something 询问拼写

Could you spell that for me, please?

I haven't heard that name before – how do you spell it?

When you don't know how to say something 不知道表示某事物的词时

Think about those words that are often used in dictionary definitions: a type of ..., a kind of ..., a device for ..., an organization that ... , a person who ... They will help you explain what you mean even when you don't know the exact word. 想一想常用于词典词条释义的那些短语，如 a type of ...、a kind of ...、a device for ...、an organization that ...、a person who ...。当你不知道某个词时，这些表达法可帮助你说明想表达的意思。

Saying it another way 以另一种方式表达

We saw a kind of animal with a long nose.

It's something you make with eggs.

Saying that you don't know 告诉对方你不知道

I don't know how to say this in English – in German, we say ...

I'm sorry, I can't think of the word in English.

Asking for a translation 请求翻译

What is the English equivalent of 'afiyet olsun'?

How do you say 'siesta' in English?

Explaining an idea from your language 解释母语中的一个概念

I don't think there's an exact equivalent in English.

Roughly speaking, 'saudade' means when you miss a person or a place.

In my country, we normally say 'Que aproveche' when somebody is eating.

Suggesting a change of topic 建议转换话题

Look, I really can't think how to explain it – perhaps we should move on?

This is too difficult for me to talk about in English.

When you make a mistake 说错了时

We all make mistakes when we speak, even in our own language, but it need not cause a problem if we can find a way to explain what we really meant. We also need time to think about what we are going to say, but there are expressions that we can use to gain time while we do so. 人们说话难免会出错，即便用母语也不例外。但如果能想办法解释我们真正的意思，就不会造成问题。我们也需要时间思考要说的话，这种情况下可以运用一些表达方式为自己赢得时间。

Words you can use while thinking 思考时可以使用的说法

... you know ...

Now let me think ...

... what's the word for it?

... how shall I put it? ...

Correcting yourself 纠正自己的话

No, I meant ...

... or rather ...

That's not exactly what I meant.

Sorry, I was trying to say *price*, not *prize*.

Oxford Writing Tutor 牛津写作指南

Using the *Oxford Advanced Learner's English-Chinese Dictionary* to improve your writing
利用《牛津高阶英汉双解词典》提高写作水平

Whether you are writing a business email or a long research essay, your dictionary can be a powerful tool to assist you in becoming a better writer in English. 无论撰写商务类电子邮件还是长篇研究论文，本词典都是提高英语写作水平的利器。

1. Using the main part of the dictionary 利用本词典的正文部分

You can use the main A–Z of the dictionary to help you 本词典的 A–Z 正文部分有助于：

- **Choose your words carefully.** Many words in English have similar or related meanings, but are used in different contexts or situations. **慎重选择词汇。**英语中有许多词语意思相近或相关，但所用的语境或场合不同。

> Look carefully at the example sentences provided in the entries for words you want to use. Also look at any **synonym notes, vocabulary notes** and **topic notes** to help you choose the most appropriate word. If you need academic vocabulary, look for the AW symbol. 仔细阅读拟用单词所在词条中提供的例句，也要阅读“同义词辨析”说明、“词汇辨析”说明和“主题”说明，以便选择最恰当的词。如果需要使用学术词汇，请查找 AW 标识。

- **Combine words naturally** and effectively. In English, certain pairs of words go together and sound natural to native speakers (for example, *heavy rain*) – and others do not (~~strong rain~~). This is called **collocation**. Information on which words collocate with one another can be found in the example sentences in the dictionary entries. **搭配道地自然。**在英语中，有些词必须搭配使用，母语为英语的人听上去才道地自然（如 heavy rain）——而与其他词搭配使用则听起来不自然（~~strong rain~~）。这称作词语搭配。有关词相互搭配的情况可在本词典词条的例句中找到。

> Look up the key nouns you have used in your writing to check which verbs or adjectives are usually used with them. 在词典中查阅写作时所使用的主要名词，弄清楚哪些动词或形容词通常与它们搭配。

- **Become more flexible.** Rather than repeating the same word or phrase many times in your work, try to find other ways to express your ideas. **表达方式更多样。**设法找到其他表达方式，而不是在文章中多次重复同一个词或短语。

> Look for the SYN symbol to find synonyms and also study the **synonyms notes**. Look for **word families** and try using words in the same family that are different parts of speech (e.g. *different*, adjective and *differ*, verb). For example, you could write: *French **is different from** English in this respect.* You could also express this: *French **differs from** English in this respect.* 找到 SYN 标识下所列同义词并研读

"同义词辨析"说明。找到"词族"，试着使用同一词族中不同词性的词汇（如形容词 different 和动词 differ）。例如，可以写：French **is different from** English in this respect.（在这方面法语有别于英语。）也可以写：French **differs from** English in this respect.

- **Edit and check your work.** You can use your dictionary to check any problem areas such as spelling, parts of speech, irregular forms, grammar, phrasal verbs and prepositions. **校订和检查作业。**利用本词典可检查任何有可能产生问题的地方，如拼写、词类、不规则形式、语法、短语动词和介词。

2. Using the Writing Tutor 利用牛津写作指南

In the following pages you will find examples of essays and practical types of writing that you can use as models for your own work. You will also find advice about planning, organizing and writing each type of text. 在本指南的余下部分会提供各类文章和实用文体的参考范文，还有关于各类文本谋篇布局和写作的建议。

- **Examples of written texts** 范文
  Look carefully at 仔细阅读以下几方面：
  - the structure and organization of the text 篇章结构和组织
  - the way ideas and paragraphs are linked 构思和段落衔接
  - the language and style 语言和文体
  - the notes on particular points 特别说明
- **Tips** 提示 These are quick reminders and advice to help when you are writing. 这部分提供写作的便捷提醒和建议。
- **Language banks** give you some useful phrases that you can use in each type of writing. 用语库提供各类写作的一些有用短语。

Check that you are familiar with these phrases and know how to use them correctly. 一定要熟悉这些短语并知道如何正确使用。

You can add other phrases when you meet them in your reading. In the main part of the dictionary there are more notes like this which give you further phrases and examples to show you how to use them. (*For example, look at the note at 'however'.*) 也可以加上自己在阅读过程中遇到的其他短语。在本词典的正文部分有更多类似的说明，提供更多的短语和例子说明它们的用法，如 however 条的说明。

Contents 目录

The writing process 写作过程	WT3
Answering the question 回答问题	WT8
Writing a comparison essay 写对比文	WT11
Writing an argument essay 写议论文	WT14
Writing a longer essay or dissertation 写长篇论文或学位论文	WT18
Writing a summary 写摘要	WT22
Reporting on data 报告数据	WT25
Writing a report 写报告	WT28
Writing a review of a book or film/movie 写书评或影评	WT31
Discussing pictures and cartoons 描述图片和漫画	WT34
Writing a formal letter 写正式信函	WT37
Writing emails 写电子邮件	WT40
Writing a CV/résumé and covering letter 写简历和附信	WT47

The writing process 写作过程

Each individual writer has their own aims and needs and their own way of approaching various parts of the writing process. However, whether you are writing a short essay, an article, a report or a research paper, the overall process is generally the same. 每个作者都有自己的目的、需要以及对写作过程各阶段的处理方式。不过，无论是写短文、文章、报告，还是写研究论文，总体过程大致相同。

1 Preliminary Phase 准备阶段

Ask yourself some planning questions that will help guide the rest of the process. 在构思时给自己提出一些问题，这将有助于指导余下过程。

What is the purpose of this piece of writing? 这篇文章的目的是什么？

For example 例如：

- To answer a specific essay, examination or research question 回答特定的论述题、考试题或研究课题
- To convince others of your point of view 说服他人相信你的观点
- To communicate your knowledge or understanding to others, such as a teacher or an examiner 将自己的知识或看法告诉他人，比如老师或主考人

Who is my audience? 我的读者是谁？

For example 例如：

- A teacher or professor 老师或教授
- Fellow students or colleagues 同学或同事
- An employer 雇主
- The general public 公众

The answers (you may have more than one purpose or type of audience) will help you to choose the appropriate level of formality. They will also help you make decisions about the amount of research required, as well as the kinds of examples and supporting evidence you will use. 这些答案（可能有不止一个目的或一类读者）有助于选择适当的正式程度，也有助于确定需要投入的研究工作量以及要引用何种例子和佐证。

2 Pre-Writing Phase 写作前阶段

Explore 探讨

Brainstorm ideas using whatever method suits you best 以最适合自己的方式开动脑筋找灵感：

- Mind maps 画思维导图
- Lists of interesting concepts, facts, questions, etc. 列出有趣的概念、事实、问题等
- Conversations with colleagues 与同事交谈讨论

Research 调查研究

Next, research your topic and gather information from a variety of sources 接下来，就论题进行调查研究并通过各种渠道收集信息：

- Books and journals 书籍和报刊
- The media 媒体
- Websites 网站
- Interviews or questionnaires 访谈或问卷调查
- Scientific studies 科学研究

When you read sources, take detailed notes and keep an accurate record of each source. (*Look at page WT19.*) 阅读原始资料时要做详细笔记并准确记录出处。（见 WT19 页。）

Organize 组织

After carrying out your research, you can draft a thesis (your main argument, statement or idea) to guide you. 完成调研之后可草拟论题（主要论点或想法）以引导写作。

Then, using your notes, make a detailed outline of the logical plan of your essay, article or report to support this thesis, giving a structure to your writing before you begin to write. 然后，利用笔记围绕这个论题对文章或报告的谋篇布局列出详细提纲，给文章设计好框架再动笔写。

- Decide roughly how many words you will give to each part of your essay/report. 确定文章/报告各个部分的大致字数。
- Collect or prepare any visual aids such as charts or diagrams that you might need. 收集或准备任何可能需要的视觉资料，如图表或简图。

3 Writing Phase 写作阶段

In this phase, you will draft and revise several times until you have what you consider to be a final draft. 在这一阶段，要起草并反复修改初稿，直到自己认为可以定稿。

Draft 初稿

Write your draft in formal sentences and paragraphs. 写正式的句子，组织段落，写出初稿。

- Remain focused on your thesis or main idea. If you do change this, go back and adapt your original plan to ensure that your essay/report continues to support the new thesis. 紧扣主要论点。如果一定要改变论点，那么就回头修改原提纲以确保文章/报告仍然支持新的论点。
- Follow your outline, modifying it if necessary. 按照提纲写作，如果有必要可边写边修改提纲。
- In early drafts, concentrate on structure rather than spelling and punctuation. 写前几稿时把注意力放在结构上，而不是放在拼写和标点符号上。

Review/Edit 检查/修订

In this step, you read your writing with a critical eye. 在这一步，用挑剔的眼光阅读自己的文章。

In early drafts, ask yourself 检查前几稿时问自己：

- Have you answered the question or achieved your original purpose? 回答了问题或达到了最初的目的吗？
- Have you introduced your subject, developed it logically and come to a conclusion? 介绍了主题、有逻辑地阐述主题并得出结论了吗？
- Is your supporting evidence appropriate and complete? Do you need more examples, statistics or quotes? 佐证恰当且充分吗？需要增加例子、统计数据或引文吗？
- Have you used headings to help the reader, if appropriate? 适当运用标题方便读者阅读了吗？
- Are the relationships between ideas clear and clearly signalled to the reader? 思路清楚吗？清晰地传达给读者了吗？
- Is each part the right length for the demands of the topic – with no part too long? 各部分长度符合题目要求吗？有没有哪里写得过于冗长？

In later drafts, ask yourself 检查后几稿时问自己：

- Have you used paragraph breaks well? 段落划分得当吗？

- Is the level of formality appropriate for your readers? 文体正式程度适合读者吗？
- Have you chosen your words carefully, using correct collocations? 选词是否谨慎？搭配是否正确？
- Have you avoided repeating the same words or phrases too often (except technical terms)? 避免过多地重复相同的词或短语（术语除外）了吗？
- Have you met any word count requirements? 符合字数的要求吗？

If possible, ask someone else to read your text. 可以的话，请人读一下你的文章。

After each review, return to the drafting step, revising and editing your writing as necessary. 每检查一次都要回到写初稿这一步，如果有必要就修改和校正。

Using sources in essays 在文章中使用原始资料

Ask yourself 问自己：

Have you quoted or mentioned sources to support your points? 引用或提及原始资料以支持自己的论点了吗？

Have you used the citation style recommended by your teachers or institution? 使用老师或学校所推荐的引文格式了吗？

Have you listed your references in the style recommended? 按推荐使用的格式列出参考文献了吗？

(*Look also at pages WT20–21.* 另见 WT20–21 页。)

4 Presentation Phase 提交前最后检查阶段

Proofread 校对

When you have a final draft of your writing, you will need to read it once more to find and correct surface errors. 终稿完成之后需要再读一遍，以便发现并改正字面错误。

Tip 提示

- Try to leave some time between your final draft and proofreading as you will find it easier to see your mistakes. 在完成终稿和校对之间尽量留出一段时间。这可以使你更容易看到自己的错误。

Check for 检查
- Spelling 拼写
- Punctuation 标点符号
- Grammatical mistakes 语法是否正确

You may find it helpful to ask someone else to proofread your final draft as a last step. 最后请人校对一下终稿会很有帮助。

Format 格式

Check with your teacher or tutor how you should present your work in terms of 跟老师或导师确认提交文章所要求的格式：
- Font size 字体大小
- Margins 边距
- Line spacing 行距
- Paper size 纸张大小

Examinations 考试

In an exam, you will not have time for all these stages, but your answers will be more successful if you 考试时不会有时间让你完成所有这些步骤，但采取以下步骤会让你答得更好：
- brainstorm ideas 开动脑筋找灵感
- organize and plan 组织和构思
- re-read, check and edit 重新阅读、检查和修订

What makes writing formal? 写正式作文的要素

Whatever type of text you are writing, your aim should always be to express your ideas clearly and in a way that your readers can easily understand. 无论写何种体裁的文章，目标始终应该是清楚地、用读者容易理解的方式阐述自己的思想。

When you read, notice the kind of language that is used in the type of writing you need to do. 阅读时留意自己需要使用的写作体裁的语言。

To make your writing more formal, consider 写较正式的文章需要考虑：

1. **Word choice 选词**
   - It is usually best to use standard English words and phrases, that is, those with no label in the dictionary. 通常最好使用标准的英语词汇和短语，即本词典中没有特别语体标识的词语。
   - Only use words and phrases marked *formal* if you are sure they are appropriate. 只有在十分肯定是合适的情况下，才用标示为 formal（正式）的词和短语。
   - Avoid anything marked *informal, slang, offensive*, etc. 避免使用在词条中标有 informal（非正式）、slang（俚语）或 offensive（冒犯）等的词和短语。
   - Use suitable synonyms for common words such as *do, put, get, make*. e.g. *Several operations* ***were carried out/performed*** (not *done*). 用适当的同义词替代如 do、put、get、make 等常用词。例如 Several operations **were carried out/performed**（不用 done）。
   - Words that are frequently used in academic writing are marked **AW** in the dictionary. 在本词典中，学术文章中的常用词标示为 **AW**。
2. **Short forms 简写形式**
   - Avoid contracted forms (e.g. *haven't, I'm*) and abbreviations (e.g. *ad – advertisement*). 避免使用缩写形式（如 haven't、I'm）和缩略语（如 ad – advertisement）。
3. **Sentence structure 句子结构**
   - In formal writing you are likely to be expressing complex ideas. To do this you will need to write sentences using relative pronouns (e.g. *which, that*), subordinating conjunctions (e.g. *although, because, if*) and coordinating conjunctions (e.g. *and, but, or*). 写正式文章往往要表达复杂的思想，因此，需要使用关系代词（如 which、that）、从属连词（如 although、because、if）和并列连词（如 and、but、or）组句。
   - Very long sentences with many clauses can be difficult to understand. Aim for **clarity**. 带许多从句的长句会很难理解。要力求清楚。

Academic writing 学术写作

This tends to be **impersonal** in style in order to be objective. This makes it sound formal. When you read in your subject, notice how the writers express themselves. The following points may help you in your writing. 学术写作在风格方面往往不涉及个人感情以示客观。这使它显得正式。阅读有关的专业文献时，留意作者如何表达思想。以下几点可能有助于写作：

- Limit the use of the **first person pronouns** (*I* and *we*). Rather than *In this study I aim to …*, write: *This study aims to …* or *The aim of this study is to …* Look at how *I* and *we* are used in your subject area. Avoid using *you*. 尽量不用第一人称代词（I 和 we）。应该写：This study aims to … 或 The aim of this study is to …，而不要写：In this study I aim to …。看一下所涉及的专业领域中 I 和 we 的用法。避免使用 you。
- **Passive forms** are often used as they focus attention on the verb, not the person. 被动形式强调动词而不是人，因此经常使用。e.g. 如 *A study was conducted to see …*; *It can be argued that …*
- Patterns with **it and an adjective** are often used. 经常使用“it + 形容词”的句式：*It is clear that …*; *It is necessary to …*
- **Nouns** are often used as subjects of active verbs. 名词常用作主动动词的主语：*The results show that …*
- **Complex noun phrases** with prepositions are very common. 带介词的复合名词短语很常见：*The advantages of X are …*; *the use of light treatment in 95 patients with …*

Answering the question 回答问题

At all times, you must ensure that you really understand an examination question or assignment title and address all the required parts. 任何时候都要确保真正理解试题或作业题目，并处理所有需要解答的部分。

Questions can be considered in terms of three main components 可根据三个主要因素来考虑问题：

- **Topic** 主题
- **Scope and focus** 范围和重点
- **Question type** 问题类型

Topic 主题

The topic(s) of the question will usually be clear from the question itself. 问题的主题通常看问题本身就一目了然。For example 例如：

Explain the process of photosynthesis. 解释光合作用的过程。

When you write your answer think about why the examiner has chosen to ask about this topic. 解答时考虑一下出题人为什么选择问这个主题。

Scope and focus 范围和重点

Often, the wording of the question will include a word or phrase that either limits or expands the topic in a very specific way. These phrases show you the focus of the question. 问题的措辞中往往包含明确的限定或详述主题的词或短语。这些短语显示出问题的重点。

Try to avoid common mistakes, such as 尽量避免犯常见的错误，如：

- **Covering too broad an area. 覆盖面过宽。** For example, if the question asks about textile mills in the American South in the 1930s, think very carefully about including information about the 1920s or 1940s, or about textile mills in other parts of the country. 例如，如果问题是关于美国南部20世纪30年代的纺织厂，那就要十分慎重地考虑是否包括20世纪20年代和40年代的或美国其他地区纺织厂的信息。
- **Writing with too narrow a focus. 写作重点过窄。** For example, if you are asked about the impact of climate change on South America, you should not write about its impact only on Brazil. 例如，如果问题是关于气候变化对南美洲的影响，就不能只写气候变化对巴西的影响。
- **Including irrelevant information. 包含无关信息。** For example, if you are asked about using nuclear power as an energy source, you should not write about wind or solar power. 例如，如果问题是关于使用核能做能源，就不要写风能或太阳能。
- **Only answering half of the question. 解答问题不全面。** For example, if the question asks *What other effects will a reduction in air travel have and will the advantages outweigh the disadvantages?* you need to discuss both questions. 例如，如果问题是"减少飞机旅行会产生什么影响？会利大于弊吗？"，那么就得对两个问题都作出回答。

Question types 问题类型

The depth and type of information that you provide in your answer depends on the kind of question being asked. The table on the next page shows the key words that might appear in different types of questions. 回答问题时所提供信息的深度和类型取决于问题的类型。下页的表格中显示不同类型问题可能包含的关键词语。

1. Knowledge Questions 知识型问题

These ask you to recall important facts and are the simplest question. 此类问题要求复述重要的事实，是最简单的问题。

2. Comprehension Questions 理解型问题

These ask you to demonstrate your understanding of concepts. You must clearly show that you understand the ideas and theories that underlie the facts. 此类问题要求说明自己对概念的理解。必须清楚地表现出自己理解事实背后的概念和理论。

3. Application Questions 应用型问题

Here you use your knowledge of facts and concepts to address a specific problem. These questions require you to move beyond simple recollection. 此处要利用自己所掌握的事实和概念去解决具体问题。回答此类问题不能局限于简单的复述。

4. Analysis Questions 分析型问题

These examine relationships between/among various facts and concepts. 此类问题探讨各种事实和概念之间的关系。

5. Synthesis Questions 综合型问题

These ask you to create a new product or structure in written form. 此类问题要求以书面形式创建新论点或新体系。

6. Evaluation Questions 评价型问题

These ask you to make value judgments and present your own opinions. This kind of question is very common in academic work. It is important to support your opinions by citing the work and views of experts in the field, if possible. 此类问题要求做出价值判断并表达自己的看法，这在学术作业中很常见。尽可能引用该领域专家的著作和观点来支持自己的看法，这很重要。

IELTS Academic Writing 雅思考试学术写作

- Task 1 任务1: This is usually a combination of comprehension and analysis questions. 通常结合了理解型与分析型的问题：*Summarize the information … and make comparisons where relevant.*
- Task 2 任务2: This is usually an evaluation question. 通常为评价型问题：*At what age should young people be considered adults? Explain your position.*

Question Types 问题类型

Level of Difficulty 难度

4. Analysis Questions 分析型问题

Key verbs 关键动词

- analyze 分析
- compare 比较
- contrast 对比
- distinguish 区分
- differentiate 辨别
- subdivide 细分
- classify 分类
- categorize 归类
- select 选择
- infer 推断
- prioritize 划分优先顺序

Example 例如：
Compare the merits of 'renting' and 'squatting' as solutions to housing problems for the poor in cities in the developing world. 比较"租房"和"偷住空房"作为发展中国家城市贫民住房问题解决办法的各自优点。

5. Synthesis Questions 综合型问题

Key verbs 关键动词

- design 设计
- plan 规划
- construct 构想
- create 建立
- compose 撰写
- produce 制作
- develop 开发
- invent 发明
- combine 组合

Example 例如：
Design an experiment to investigate whether listening to music improves students' performance in their studies. 设计一个实验以研究听音乐能否提高学生的学习效率。

6. Evaluation Questions 评价型问题

Key verbs 关键动词

- discuss 讨论
- evaluate 评价
- compare 比较
- consider 考虑
- examine 检查
- explore 探讨
- comment (on) 评论
- justify 证明…正确
- appraise 评价
- weigh 权衡
- support 支持
- recommend 建议

Example 例如：
Discuss the argument that the use of force in self-defence is justifiable. 就用武力进行自卫是正当的这一论点进行讨论。

3. Application Questions 应用型问题

Key verbs 关键动词

- apply 应用
- show 说明
- solve 解决
- choose 选择
- organize 组织
- generalize 概括
- prepare 准备
- relate (X to Y) 说明（X 和 Y 的）关系

Example 例如：
Show how a national minimum wage will affect levels of unemployment and total output. 说明国家最低工资将如何影响失业率和总产量。

2. Comprehension Questions 理解型问题

Key verbs 关键动词

- explain 解释
- summarize 概括
- illustrate 说明
- restate 重新表述
- paraphrase 释义
- give examples 举例
- express 表述
- distinguish (between) 区分（…和…）
- trace 描述过程
- match 配对

Example 例如：
Give three examples of human activities that have major effects on our climate. 举出三个例子说明人类活动对气候产生了重大影响。

1. Knowledge Questions 知识型问题

Key verbs 关键动词

- outline 概述
- define 界定
- describe 描述
- give 给出
- state 说明
- summarize 概括
- label 归类
- identify 识别
- name 说出名字
- list 列举

Example 例如：
Define the term 'muscle tone' and describe how it can help good posture. 请界定术语"肌张力"并描述它如何能有助于保持良好的姿势。

Writing a comparison essay 写对比文

Cambridge English: Advanced | IELTS | TOEFL

You may often need to **compare** and **contrast** things in exams, academic essays, work and everyday life. Here is an example of a comparison essay. 考试、学术写作、工作和日常生活中经常需要对两个事物进行比较和对比。以下是一篇对比文范文。

Which is the better test of students' ability: continuous assessment or exams? Discuss.

Children's achievement at school may affect the whole of their future lives, but how can it best be measured?[1] In some educational systems, achievement may be tested by an examination at the end of the course, when candidates are expected to prove that they have understood and remembered all the material that has been covered. Continuous assessment, on the other hand, is carried out throughout the course and may consist of assignments to be completed at home, or tests on shorter modules of learning at intervals during the year.[2] This essay examines the advantages and disadvantages of each method.[3]

Both types of assessment have similar aims. Like continuous assessment, exams seek to measure students' progress, compare students with one another, and in some cases assess students' suitability for further education.

Despite these similarities, there are a number of marked differences between the two approaches. The exam system ensures that all students are tested on exactly the same material under the same conditions. In contrast, students completing coursework outside the classroom may have had help from parents or others, and it is harder for assessors to know how long they spent on it. A growing concern is widespread plagiarism made easier by the use of the Internet.

However, not all students perform well under exam conditions. For those who suffer from 'exam nerves', or anyone who is perhaps not feeling well on the day, exam results may not be an accurate reflection of their ability. A great advantage of continuous assessment is that it spreads the testing over a much longer period, relieving students of this acute stress.

Paragraph 1 — Introduction
第1段——引言

[1] The first sentence catches the reader's interest. 第1句引发读者的兴趣。

[2] The second and third sentences give a definition of the two types of assessment. (Note: a definition is optional) 第2、第3句给出两种评估的定义。（注：定义并非必要）

[3] The 4th sentence indicates the scope of the essay and leads to the next paragraph. 第4句指出文章的范围并引出下一段。

Paragraph 2 — Similarities
第2段——相似点

The writer notes 1 similarity here before emphasizing 3 differences in paragraphs 3–5. 在第3至5段强调3处差别之前，作者首先指出1个相似点。

Paragraph 3 — Difference 1
第3段——差别之一

Controlled conditions 对照条件

Despite these similarities indicates that the writer is now going to list the differences. * Despite these similarities 表示作者即将列举不同点。

Paragraph 4 — Difference 2
第4段——差别之二

Exam stress 考试压力

Paragraph 5 — Difference 3
第5段——差别之三

Cramming vs spreading the load
临阵磨枪相比按部就班

Some students being tested at the end of a course are tempted to leave all their work until the last minute, cramming a lot of revision into a few weeks just before the exam. Teachers may find that assessment at regular intervals has a beneficial effect on work during the year.

Paragraph 6 — Conclusion
第6段——结论

[1] The first sentence summarizes the findings in paragraphs 2–5. 第1句归纳第2–5段的讨论结果。

[2] The second sentence gives the writer's personal opinion. 第2句提出作者本人的看法。

It is clear, therefore, that there are significant differences between the two systems of assessment, with strengths and drawbacks to each.[1] Continuous assessment may mirror the real-life situations that students will find in their working lives more closely than the final exam, but the benefits must be balanced against the criticism that only exam conditions can ensure fairness for all.[2]

Key 说明

Blue shows ways of introducing similarities 蓝色表示介绍相似点的方式

Yellow shows ways of introducing contrasts 黄色表示介绍对比的方式

Collocations: adjectives + nouns 搭配：形容词 + 名词

To find interesting and appropriate adjectives to use with nouns, look up the nouns in the dictionary, e.g. *difference*, *concern*, *reflection*, *advantage*. 要找到与名词连用的有趣且恰当的形容词，在本词典中查阅有关名词，如 difference、concern、reflection、advantage。

Collocations: prepositions 搭配：介词

To find the correct preposition to use after a verb or noun, look up the word in the dictionary, e.g. *difference*, *balance*. 要找到动词或名词后接的正确的介词，在本词典中查阅这个词，如 difference、balance。

Preparing to write 准备写作

- **Brainstorm ideas** about similarities and differences. For example, arrange points in a table. 开动脑筋找出相似点和不同点。例如，将要点用表列出：

Characteristics 特点	**Exams 考试**	**Cont assessment 持续性评估**	**Similar or different? 相似还是不同?**
Aims 目标	Compare sts work, uni entrance 比较学生的课业，入读大学	Compare sts work, uni entrance 比较学生的课业，入读大学	Same 相同
Test conditions 测试条件	Same conditions for all 所有人的测试条件相同	Can't control conditions 测试条件不可控	Different 不同

- **Highlight the similarities and the differences** and decide which are more important. For this essay the differences are more important. 突出显示相似点和不同点并决定哪方面更重要。在范文中，不同点更重要。
- **Choose which points to include** in the essay and which to leave out. 选择文章中哪些要点要包括在内、哪些要舍弃。
- Decide how to **define** the two things you are comparing. 决定如何定义所比较的两个事物。

- Choose the **organization structure** (*see below*). Here **Type A1** was used. 选择组织结构（见下）。范文使用了 A1 类。

Shorter essays 短文	
Type A1 * A1 类 : to emphasize the **differences** 强调不同点 Introduction 引言 **Similarities** of X and Y * X 和 Y 的相似点 **Differences** between X and Y * X 和 Y 的不同点 Conclusion 结论 OR 或 **Type A2** * A2 类 : To emphasize the **similarities**, reverse the second and third sections. 将以上第二、三部分颠倒次序以强调相似点。	or 或 **Type B1** * B1 类 : Introduction 引言 Characteristics of X * X 的特点 Characteristics of Y * Y 的特点 Show how Y is **similar** to or **different** from X * 说明 Y 与 X 如何相似或不同 Conclusion 结论
Longer essays 较长的文章	
Type C1 * C1 类 Introduction 引言 Aspect 1 第一个方面 : compare X and Y 比较 X 和 Y Aspect 2 第二个方面 : compare X and Y (and so on) 比较 X 和 Y（以此类推） Conclusion 结论	OR 或 **Type A1** or **A2** above. 上述 A1 或 A2 类。

Language bank 用语库

Similarities 相似	**Differences** 不同
X … Similarly, Y… *Both X and Y…* *X … Y also …* Both + plural noun 复数名词 … e.g. *Both types of assessment …* Like X, Y … e.g. *Like continuous assessment, exams …* *X and Y are similar in that they both …* *X is similar to Y in terms of / with regard to …* *X resembles Y in that they both …* *X is the same as Y.*	*X … On the other hand, Y … / Y, on the other hand, …* *Unlike X, Y …* *X … In contrast, Y … / While X … , Y …* *X … , while Y…* *X … However, Y … / X … Y, however,…* *X differs from Y in terms of / with regard to … (e.g. the conditions for testing)* *X is different from / contrasts with Y in that … X … , whereas Y … / Whereas X …, Y …*
Being more precise 更加准确地比较 :	
Similarities 相似	**Differences** 不同
X is almost / nearly / virtually / just / exactly / precisely *the same as Y.* *X and Y are* very / rather / quite *similar.*	*X is* slightly / a little / somewhat *smaller than Y.* *X is* much / considerably *smaller than Y.* *X and Y are* completely / totally / entirely / quite *different.* *X and Y are* not quite / exactly / entirely *the same.*

Writing an argument essay 写议论文

Cambridge English: First | IELTS | TOEIC | TOEFL

Many essays that you have to write, whether during your school or college course or in an examination, will require you to present a reasoned argument on a particular issue. This will often be based on your research into the topic, but some questions may ask you to give your opinion. In both cases your argument must be clearly organized and supported with information, evidence and reasons. The language tends to be formal and impersonal. 在学校课程或在考试中经常需要写议论文，这一类文章要求就某一问题进行合乎逻辑的论述。这往往基于专题调查研究，但有些问题可能要求陈述己见。这两种情况均要求论述有条理，并且要有资料、证据和理由为依据。语言风格往往要正式和客观。

'Manned space missions should now be replaced with unmanned missions.' Discuss.

Paragraph 1—Introduction 第 1 段——引言

[1] Introduces the topic. 引出主题。

[2] States the focus of the essay. 说明文章重点。

It is clear that the study of space and the planets is by nature expensive. Scientists and politicians must constantly attempt to balance costs with potential research benefits.[1] A major question to be considered is whether the benefits of manned space flight are worth the costs.[2]

Paragraph 2—Introduces the argument 第 2 段——引出论点

The first point (manned missions are not cost effective) with a quote from an expert to give authority. 第一点（载人航天计划成本效益不高）引用专家的话以增加权威性。

[1] This is a useful way to introduce a quotation. 这是很有用的引用方式。

For Nobel Prize-winning physicist Steven Weinberg the answer is clear. As he noted in 2007[1] in a lecture at the Space Telescope Science Institute in Baltimore, 'Human beings don't serve any useful function in space. They radiate heat, they're very expensive to keep alive, and unlike robotic missions, they have a natural desire to come back, so that anything involving human beings is enormously expensive.'

Paragraph 3—Development 第 3 段——展开论述

Reasons and data are given to support the writer's point of view. 给出理由和数据以支持作者的观点。

Unmanned missions are much less expensive than manned, having no requirement for airtight compartments, food or life support systems. They are also lighter and therefore require less fuel and launch equipment. According to NASA, the 1992 manned Space Shuttle Endeavor cost $1.7 billion to build and required approximately $450 million for each launch. In contrast, the entire unmanned Voyager mission from 1972 until 1989, when it observed Neptune, cost only $865 million.

Paragraph 4—Development
第4段——展开论述

Introduces the second point (unmanned projects are more scientifically productive). 介绍第二点（无人项目的科学效益更高）。

In addition to their relative cost effectiveness, unmanned projects generally yield a much greater volume of data. While manned flights have yet to extend beyond the orbit of Earth's moon, unmanned missions have explored almost our entire solar system, and have recently observed an Earth-like planet in a nearby solar system. Manned missions would neither be able to travel so far, be away so long, nor collect so much data while at the same time guaranteeing the astronauts' safe return.

Paragraph 5—Counterargument
第5段——反方论点

[1] Presents the argument: *Some may argue* suggests that the writer will go on to argue against this position. 给出论点：Some may argue 表明作者将反驳这种观点。

[2] Refutes it. *However* introduces the argument against [1]. 反驳。However 引出相反的论点。

Some may argue that only manned space flight possesses the ability to inspire and engage the general population, providing much-needed momentum for continued governmental funding and educational interest in mathematics and the sciences.[1] However, media coverage of recent projects such as the Mars Rover, the Titan moon lander, and the Hubble telescope's photographs of extrasolar planets demonstrates that unmanned missions clearly have the ability to attract and hold public interest.[2]

Paragraph 6—Conclusion
第6段——结论

Summarizes the writer's points and states his/her conclusion on the title. 归纳作者的论点并申明他/她关于这个主题的结论。

[1] *Thus* introduces the conclusion. * Thus 引出结论。

[2] *I would argue that* clearly shows the writer's position. * I would argue that 清楚地表明作者的立场。

Thus,[1] taking into account the lower cost, the greater quantity of data and widespread popular support, I would argue that[2] for now, at least, unmanned space missions undoubtedly yield the most value in terms of public spending.

Linking words and phrases guide the reader through the argument and show the writer's opinion. 衔接词和短语引导读者阅读论证过程并表明作者的看法。

Adverbs can be used to show your opinion. 副词可用来表达看法。

These phrases make the argument less personal and more objective. 这些短语使论述更加客观。

Experts are quoted to support the argument. 引用专家的话支持论点。

Preparing to write 准备写作

- Brainstorm your ideas on the question, read and research the topic (unless in an examination). Which do you think are the strongest arguments? Decide what your viewpoint will be. 开动脑筋思考问题，阅读这个主题的相关资料并展开研究（考试时除外）。你认为哪些论据最有力？决定好从哪个角度论述。
- Select 2 or 3 strong ideas on each side, with supporting examples, ideas or evidence. For some questions you can use evidence from your personal experience. 每个方面选2到3个有说服力的论点，加上作为依据的例证、观点或证据。有些问题可以用个人经历作为证据。

- Decide how to organize your essay to persuade readers of your case. 决定好如何组织文章以说服读者。
- Note down some useful vocabulary on the topic. 记下有关论题的一些有用词汇。

Structure 1 (used in the model essay) **结构一（范文所用的结构）**	**Structure 2 结构二**
Introduction 引言	Introduction 引言
Arguments **for** your case + supporting evidence, examples or reasons 正方论点 + 作为依据的证据、例证或理由	Argument 1: + supporting evidence, examples or reasons 论点一：+ 作为依据的证据、例证或理由
Arguments **against** + evidence 反方论点 + 证据	Counterargument 反方论点
Evaluation of arguments 对论点的评论	Argument 2: + supporting evidence, examples or reasons 论点二：+ 作为依据的证据、例证或理由
Summary and conclusion 归纳总结	Counterargument (and so on) 反方论点（以此类推）
It is possible to reverse arguments for and against. 可以把正方和反方论点的次序互换。	Evaluation of arguments 对论点的评论
	Summary and conclusion 归纳总结

Tip 提示

- Look carefully at the **title or question** and make sure you really answer it. 仔细阅读题目或问题，确保没有离题。
- Use **general statements** to convey the main ideas, and then provide **evidence, examples, details** and **reasons** to support these statements. 概要说明主题思想，然后提供证据、例证、细节和理由作为依据。
- Use **paragraph divisions** and **connecting words and phrases** to make the structure of your essay clear to your readers. 划分段落并使用衔接词和短语，以便读者对文章的结构一目了然。
- For **language** to help you structure your argument, look at the notes at 'addition', 'first'. 有关行文的语言，请查阅本词典 addition 和 first 词条的用法说明。

Showing your position 说明立场

When you write an argument essay, you can show what your opinion is on the issue or question without using personal phrases such as *I think* ... or *In my opinion*, ... You can do this by choosing words carefully as you write. Some examples are given below. Look out for more in your reading. 写议论文时，不使用 I think ... 或 In my opinion ... 之类涉及个人的短语也可以表明自己对问题的看法。可以边写边仔细选词。下面列出了一些例子，平常阅读时可再多找一些表达方式。

Adjectives 形容词

important, major, serious, significant

e.g. *An **important** point to consider is …; This was a **highly significant** discovery.*

Patterns with It + adjective
* It + 形容词句式

clear, likely, possible, surprising, evident

e.g. ***It is clear that** the study of space is expensive.*

important, difficult, necessary, possible, interesting

e.g. ***It is important to** consider the practical effects of these measures.*

Adverbs and phrases 副词和短语

clearly, indeed, in fact, of course

generally, usually, mainly, widely

perhaps, probably, certainly, possibly

rarely, sometimes, often

e.g. ***Clearly**, this is a serious issue that deserves further study.*

*This book is **generally** held to be her greatest novel.*

Verbs 动词

These help show how certain you are about a point or an argument. 以下动词有助于表明对某个观点或论点的确定性。

Modal verbs 情态动词：can, could; may, might; will, would (*The first of each pair is most certain.* 每对情态动词的第一个词表示确定程度最高。)

Compare 比较：*I **argue** that…* (very certain 很确定) / *I **would argue** that…* (not so certain 不太确定)

It + verb * It + 动词：It appears that, It seems that …

It + passive verb * It + 动词被动式：It can be seen that …; It should/must be noted/emphasized that …

Showing verbs 表明类动词：show, indicate, demonstrate, suggest, imply (*These have a non-human subject.* 这些动词以非人类名词作主语。)

Arguing verbs 论说类动词：argue, suggest, consider, conclude (*These can have a human subject* e.g. *I.* 这些动词可用人作主语，如 I。)

Linking words and phrases 衔接词和短语

Firstly (= *I have several points to make* 我有几个论点要提出)

Furthermore …; In addition, … Moreover, … (= *I have another important point* 我还有另一个要点)

However, … (*to introduce a counterargument* 引出反方论点)

Thus, … Therefore, … (*to introduce a conclusion* 引出结论)

Writing a longer essay or dissertation 写长篇论文或学位论文

When you have a longer essay or dissertation to write, you will go through the same process of preparing and writing as for shorter essays. (*Look at pages WT3–4.*) However, there are additional things to bear in mind. 写长篇论文或学位论文时，其准备阶段和写作过程与短文一样。（参见 WT3–4 页。）不过，还要注意另外一些事项。

The title 题目

If your title or a question has been given to you, check that you understand exactly what it means (*Pages WT8–10*). If you are writing the title yourself, choose a clear title with definite boundaries. 如果有指定的题目或问题，注意确切地弄懂其意思。（见 WT8–10 页。）如需自定题目，就定一个清楚的、界定明确的题目。

Ask yourself 问自己：
- How can I define my subject so that it is not too wide in scope? 我如何界定自己的题目使之不过于宽泛？

e.g. **Not** 不说 *How does Dickens reflect Victorian society in his novels?* **but** 而说 *How does Little Dorrit reflect Dickens's view of Victorian society?*

Reading and research 阅读和搜集资料：

evaluate your sources 评估原始资料

The quality of your research will play a vital part in the success of your writing. Keep the question or title in mind when you look for source material in books, journals or websites. 搜集资料的质量对于写作成功与否至关重要。搜集书籍、报刊或网站的原始资料时要始终记住所研究的问题或题目。

Ask yourself 问自己：
- Is the content relevant? 内容切题吗？
- Is it reliable? Is it written by someone who is an expert in the field? 资料可靠吗？是所在领域的专家写的吗？
- Is it biased in any way? 有没有任何偏见？
- Is there evidence to support information on anonymous websites? 匿名网站的信息有依据吗？

If you are using surveys, questionnaires, market research or other studies, look carefully at the statistics and consider if the results are valid and the conclusions justified. 如果采用民意调查、调查问卷、市场调查或其他研究方法，仔细审查统计数据并研判结果是否可信、结论是否合理。

Making notes 做笔记

When you are reading, make clear, accurate notes which summarize the key points and main information. Keep a note of the full reference for your source (title, author, date, publisher and page numbers). 阅读文献时要清楚、准确地做笔记，笔记应归纳要点和主要信息。记下原始资料参考书目的完整信息（即题目、作者、日期、出版社和页码）。

Ask yourself 问自己：
- Have I summarized the information accurately? 我对信息的归纳准确吗？
- Is this part particularly useful? If so, have I written down the exact words used and the page number, so that I can quote it? 这部分特别有用吗？如果是，那么我有没有一字不差地摘录了内容和页码以便引用？

Planning and organizing
谋篇布局

A long text is usually divided into sections with subheadings and it has a list of references or a bibliography at the end. 长篇文章通常划分为带小标题的章节，末尾列出参考书目。

When you plan your work, ask yourself 谋划篇章时要问自己：

- How long should my text and each part be? 我的文章以及各部分应该写多长？
- Have I organized my notes, grouping together writers who have made similar points? 我有没有整理笔记、将观点相似的作者归为一类？
- Do I agree with their opinions? 我同意他们的观点吗？
- What is the point I want to make to my readers? 我想对读者说明什么？
- What do I want my readers to know by the end? 我最终想让读者知道什么？
- Have I planned what to write in the introduction, body and conclusion? 我对引言、主体部分和结论的内容有规划吗？

Using other people's ideas
引用他人的观点

When you have finished writing, look carefully at how you have used other people's words and ideas. 文章完成之后，仔细看一下自己是如何引用他人的话和观点的。

Ask yourself 问自己：

- Have I considered and discussed other people's ideas adequately? 我充分考虑和论述了他人的观点吗？
- Have I paraphrased their ideas accurately? 我对他们的观点表述得准确吗？
- Have I made it clear which words/ideas are mine and whose words/ideas I have quoted? 我是否已清楚说明哪些话/观点是我本人的，哪些话/观点是引用的？
- Have I included in my list of references all the works I have used and referred to? 我的参考书目中已列出我所使用和参考过的所有文献吗？

Dissertations 学位论文

A dissertation may differ from a long essay in the way in which it is organized. Check with your tutor. A dissertation will usually have all or some of the following chapters or parts. 学位论文与长篇论文组织方式可能不同。可向导师确认。学位论文通常包括下列全部或部分章节：

- Title 标题
- Contents 目录
- Abstract 摘要（*a short text summarizing your dissertation* 摘写论文要点的短文）
- Introductory chapter 序篇 (broad to narrow focus 焦点由宽到窄：*to give the background, justify your research, explain your approach, give major arguments and current ideas on your topic and show the structure of your dissertation* 给出研究背景、解释研究理由、说明研究方法、提出主要论点和当前有关该论题的观点，并说明论文结构）
- Review of the literature 文献回顾
- Methodology 研究方法 (*how you carried out any empirical research* 你是如何进行实验研究的）
- Results/Findings 结果/发现
- Discussion 论述
- Conclusion 结论 (narrow to broad focus 焦点由窄到宽：*a summary of your arguments and an evaluation of your work; further research needed* 对自己论点的总结和研究的评价；所需的进一步研究）
- Bibliography or list of references 参考书目

Quoting and writing a bibliography 引述和列出参考书目

If you use the words or ideas of another person, you must always say where these have come from. If you do not, you might be accused of **plagiarism** (= copying another person's ideas or words and pretending that they are yours). 引用他人的话或观点必须始终说明出处。如果不这么做，会被视为剽窃。

Mention the author briefly in the essay and then at the end write a full reference in your **bibliography** or list of references. Different institutions have different styles for this, so check to see the method and punctuation to use, and be consistent. 在文中简要提及作者，然后在参考书目中给出完整的参考信息。不同机构有不同的参考书目格式，所以要弄清楚应采用的格式和标点，并做到统一。

1. Author-date (Harvard) system 作者一发表年份（哈佛）格式

Used especially in social and physical sciences. 尤用于社会科学和自然科学。

In the essay or dissertation 文章或学位论文中

In your text, give the family name of the author or editor of the book or article you are referring to and the year of publication in brackets after your quotation or statement. 在正文中，将参考文献的作者或编者的姓和发表年份以括号方式放在引文或表述之后。For example 例如：

Dialects are not inferior. Most linguists agree that 'a standard language is not linguistically better.' (Swan, 2005:52)

Mason (1995) describes the procedure for a teacher to evaluate each student quickly during an oral presentation.

Give both authors if there are two, but if there are more, cite the first author and add 'et al.' (= and others). 有两个作者时，两个均要列出，但超过两个时，则列出第一作者然后加 et al.（…等人）: (Mason and Wood 2008) or 或 (Mason *et al.*, 2008)

Give the full reference in your bibliography. 参考书目中列出完整的参考信息。

The bibliography 参考书目

In this system, it is often called **References** and is a list of the works that you have mentioned in your text. Give the full reference. 在本格式中，参考书目常称作 References，是论文中所提到的文献一览表。应在此处给出完整的参考信息。

Swan, Michael. (2005) *Grammar*. Oxford: Oxford University Press.

You need to write 需要写：

- The surname of the author or editor, followed by the initials or first name 作者或编者的姓，后接名字的首字母或名字
- The year of publication in brackets 发表年份，置于括号内
- The title of the book, in *italics* or underlined 书名，用斜体或加下画线
- The edition number if it is not the first edition 版本，如果不是第一版的话
- The place of publication (sometimes omitted) 出版地（有时省略）
- The publisher 出版社

2. Footnote/endnote system 脚注/尾注格式

This is a common style to use in writing on arts subjects. One version is described here. 这是文科专业写作中常用的格式。下面介绍其中一种。

In the essay or dissertation
文章或学位论文中

Give details of the source in a numbered **footnote** at the bottom of the page, or at the end of the essay in an **endnote**. Put the same number in your text after the reference. 页脚带编号的脚注（footnote）或论文结尾处的尾注（endnote）注明文献来源的详细信息。正文中的引文后标上同一编号：

Phillips suggests that "parts of the city have remained untouched by the influences of modern life"[1]. He goes on to say that "it is unlike any city in the world"[2].

Footnote 脚注

[1] Patrick Phillips, *A Brief Guide to Rome* (London: Spire Press, 2001) p.36.

If your next quote is from the same source you can just write **ibid**. and the page number. 如果下一引文出处相同，就只写 ibid. 和页码：

[2] ibid. p.38.

Later references can be shorter. 之后的参考信息可简短些：

[23] Phillips, *Guide to Rome*, pp.56–60.

The bibliography 参考书目

Give a full list of references at the end of your text, in alphabetical order by the authors' names. Use this order. 论文末列出完整参考书目，按作者姓氏的字母顺序排列。用以下顺序：

Phillips, Patrick, *A Brief Guide to Rome*. London: Spire Press, 2001.

Other examples 其他示例

These apply to both systems, but in the author-date system, the year will go after the author's name. 以下示例对于两种格式均适用，但在作者—发表年份格式中，发表年份置于作者名之后。

Books 书籍

If the book is **edited** 如果是编的书：

Wehmeier, S. ed. *Oxford Advanced Learner's Dictionary*. 7th ed. Oxford: Oxford University Press, 2005.

For an **article** in an edited book or journal 文集或期刊中的文章：Johns, A.M., and T. Dudley-Evans, 'English for Specific Purposes: International in Scope, Specific in Purpose', *TESOL Quarterly* 25 (2), 1991, 297–314.

Newspaper articles 报纸上的文章

Fennell, E. 'How is the recession hitting lawyers?' *The Times*, 31 July 2008, p.54.

Electronic resources 电子资源

Include as much detail as you can find. 尽量列出所有能找到的信息。

In your **text**, cite by author if known, otherwise by title or URL, and the year if possible. 在正文中，如果知道作者就按作者引用，否则就按标题或URL 地址引用，可以的话给出年份：(Directgov, 2008).

In your **bibliography** give the author, the title, volume/page, type of medium, date and publishing organization. Provide the URL and the date you last accessed the page. 在参考书目中列出作者、标题、卷/页码、媒体类型、年份和出版机构。提供 URL 地址和最后登录网页的日期：

Directgov. 2008.<http://www.direct.gov.uk/en/index.htm> accessed 27 October 2014.

Writing a summary 写摘要

A summary is a shortened version of a text containing only the key information. The aim is to present readers with a short, clear account of the ideas in the text. Summary writing is an important skill in both academic and business contexts. Follow the steps in order to write a successful summary. 摘要是仅包含文本主要信息的简本，其目的是提供有关文章大意的简短而清晰的报告。摘要写作在学术和商业领域中均是一项重要技能。按以下步骤写一份好的摘要。

Preparing to write 准备写作

Select the key information 选择主要信息

- Read the text carefully, looking up words you don't know. It is important to understand the whole sequence of the argument. Ask yourself what the text is about. Think about the purpose of your summary and what your readers need to know. 仔细阅读文章，查出不懂的词的含义。重要的是要理解论述的整体思路。想想文章写的是什么。考虑一下写摘要的目的和读者需要了解什么。
- Highlight the **key information** (the main ideas). Omit details such as examples, quotations, information in brackets, repetitions, figures of speech and most figures and statistics. 用彩笔标示主要信息（主题思想）。略去细节，如例子、引语、括号内的信息、重复的内容、修辞以及大部分数字和统计数据。
- Underline any information which you are not sure about. Only include it in your summary if you have space. 用下画线标示不确定如何处理的信息。只有当篇幅允许时才把这些信息写到摘要里。
- Make notes on the key information in your own words. 用自己的语言写下关于主要信息的笔记。

Are we living in a surveillance society?

The number of CCTV (or closed-circuit television) cameras in Britain has grown enormously in recent years. There are now more than 4 million, which makes an astonishing one camera for every 14 people.

CCTV has been used for many years for the surveillance of public areas associated with an obvious security risk, such as military installations, airports, casinos and banks. However, since the 1990s, there has been a huge increase in the surveillance of everyday locations such as city and town centres, car parks, shops and traffic. Added to this, more and more individuals are buying their own consumer CCTV systems for personal or commercial use. The most common function of these systems is to survey the area in front of a house or business and record any antisocial or criminal behaviour. People who buy these systems range from wealthy individuals who are afraid of being targeted by burglars, to people who are not wealthy at all but who live in high-crime areas, such as inner cities, and are trying to protect themselves.

For some people, the huge increase in public surveillance is a threat to the individual's civil liberties and is a sign that society is becoming increasingly authoritarian. They argue that the individual's right to privacy and right to live anonymously is an important aspect of being British. They also fear that present or future governments might abuse the information gathered by surveillance in order to manipulate, control or persecute the population, as happens in George Orwell's novel *1984*.

Individuals and groups in favour of CCTV, including the police, believe that it is a valuable weapon against crime. In fact, there is no strong evidence that CCTV reduces crime overall. It may act as a deterrent in certain locations, but the crime is displaced to another location. It is not even always a good deterrent. Many criminals aren't afraid of CCTV because they know that the cameras may not be running, or that no one is likely to be watching the screens. Few crimes are solved through CCTV. Sometimes CCTV footage is analysed retrospectively to identify criminals after a crime has taken place, but even this process is enormously time-consuming and expensive. One promising new development is the computer monitoring of CCTV, where computers are programmed to notice unusual movements, such as those of a car thief in a supermarket car park, and sound an alarm. Meanwhile we can expect the argument about the rights and wrongs of CCTV to continue.

Writing the summary 写摘要

Write a first draft of your summary using the information you have selected.
用选取的信息写摘要初稿。

Britain has a very high number of CCTV cameras. **Originally** used for locations with an obvious security risk, CCTV surveillance has **now** spread to ordinary public areas, **while** individuals are **also** buying private systems to protect themselves from crime.

Opponents of the growth in CCTV surveillance base their arguments on the threat to civil liberties and the danger of government misuse of the data acquired by surveillance.

Supporters of CCTV argue that it reduces crime, although there is no clear proof of this. If it acts as a deterrent, crime probably moves to another area. Often it is not a deterrent and it does not solve many crimes. However, the technology is developing in ways that may be effective.

Combine sentences in new ways to condense the argument, e.g. by linking the key ideas with different conjunctions and adverbs from those in the original text. 重新组合句子以简缩论述，如使用有别于原文的连词和副词连接主要观点。

Your own words: try using synonyms or rephrasing words and expressions such as adjective + noun phrases. Use the dictionary to help you. 自己的话：尽量用同义词，或将形容词 + 名词短语等的表达方式换个说法。可借助词典。

- *everyday* → ***ordinary***
- *their own consumer CCTV systems for personal ... use* → ***private systems***
- *no strong evidence* → ***no clear proof***
- *promising* → ***that may be effective***

Introduce **new terms** and concepts to condense and clarify the argument. For example, **opponents** and **supporters** can be used to refer to those against, and those in favour of, CCTV. 使用新的术语和概念以简缩和阐明论点。例如，可以用 opponents 和 supporters 指称反对和支持闭路电视的人。

Rephrase information to shorten it: try changing the verb form or the part of speech. Examples and word families in the dictionary can help. 改变措辞以精简内容：试着变换动词形式或词性。本词典的示例和词族会有助于这方面的改写。
e.g. **passive** 被动式 → **active verb** 主动式：*Few crimes **are solved** through CCTV* → ***it does not solve many crimes***
noun 名词 → **verb** 动词：*One promising new **development** is ...* → ***the technology is developing***

- **Organize** the ideas in your notes into a logical order. This need not be the same order as in the original text, but must show the same argument. 有条理地组织摘录的要点。不必按原文顺序排列，但必须体现原文论点。
- **Condense** the information where possible. 尽可能地简缩信息。
- **Express the ideas in your own words.** This will usually be shorter than the original. Rewrite phrases in the text, but keep any **key terms** from the subject area. 用自己的话表述要点，通常要比原文简短。重写原文，但要保留论题领域的关键术语。
- Do not give your own opinion on the topic. 不要发表自己对论题的看法。

Working on the draft 修改初稿

Ask yourself these questions 问自己以下问题：

- **Is it the right length?** 长度合适吗？
  If there is a word limit, try to stay as close to it as possible. If your summary is too long, you can usually reduce it further by 如有字数限制，尽量将字数控制在接近上限。如果摘要过长，通常可用下面的方法缩短：
  - cutting adjectives 删除形容词, e.g. *locations with an obvious security risk* → *locations with a security risk; no clear proof* → *no proof*
  - replacing phrases with shorter versions 用更简短的表达方式替换短语, e.g. *a lot of/not a lot of* → *many/few*

  If it is still too long, go back and reduce your key information. 如果仍然过长，就从头开始缩减主要内容。
- **Does it contain all the important points from the text?**
  摘要已包括原文的所有要点吗？
- **Does it read well?**
  读上去通顺吗？
- **Are the grammar and spelling correct?**
  语法和拼写正确吗？

Reporting on data 报告数据

The most common types of graphs and charts are **line graphs** (showing developments over a period of time), **bar charts** (comparing the proportions or amounts of different things) and **pie charts** (comparing percentages of parts of a whole piece of data). 图和图表中最常见的类型是线形图（line graph，显示一段时间内的变化）、条形图（bar chart，比较不同事物所占比例或量）和饼分图（pie chart，比较各部分占整体的百分比）。

Preparing to write 准备写作

Interpreting a line graph 读懂线形图

It is essential that you understand the information presented in the diagram before you begin writing. 动笔写之前先弄懂图表中显示的信息，这一点十分重要。

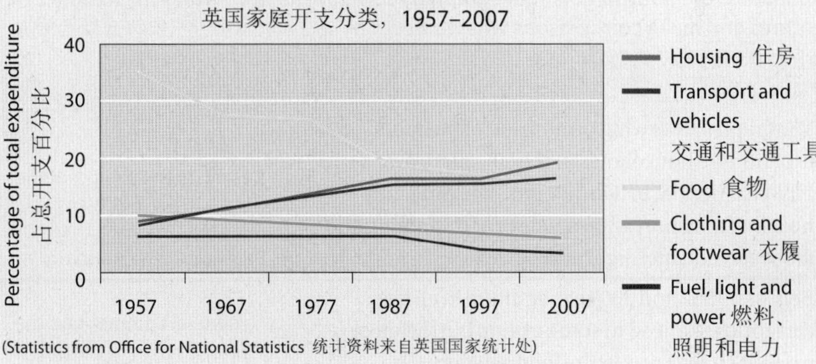

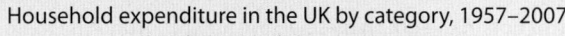

(Statistics from Office for National Statistics 统计资料来自英国国家统计处)

You should ask yourself these questions 应该问自己以下问题：

What is the information about? 这些信息是关于什么的？	*the proportion of their money that UK households spent on certain things, on average, over a period of 50 years*
What do the numbers on each axis represent? 每一条轴上的数字代表什么？	*horizontal axis: years; vertical axis: percentages*
What changes do the lines show? 这些线显示出什么变化？	*Two show an increase and three show a decrease.*
How do the lines stand in relation to each other? 这些线相互之间有什么关系？	*Two almost always remain below the rest; expenditure is always lower.*
Which feature of the lines stands out most? 这些线最明显的特征是什么？	*Expenditure on food shows a huge decrease.*
What conclusions can be drawn from the graph? 从图表中可以得出什么结论？	*Patterns of household expenditure have changed over 50 years; expenditure on food has changed the most.*

Writing the report 写报告

- **Language: accuracy** and **clarity** are the essential features of a good report. The language you use should be plain and simple, but academic in style. 语言：好的报告最重要的特点是准确和清晰。所使用的语言应该简单明了，但要有学术风格。
- **Vocabulary:** the range of language you need for describing data is small. (*See the Language Bank*) 词汇：描述数据的语言很有限。（见用语库）
- **Organization:** organize the information so that you highlight the **main trends** or features. There is usually more than one suitable way of doing this. For example, for the graph above, you could focus on the relationship between the various spending categories, **or** you could focus on the different directions each has taken over 50 years. (*Look at the structure of the report below*) 组织：组织内容时要突出主要趋势或特征。这通常有不止一种适用的方法。例如，关于上页的图表，可集中讨论各类开支之间的关系，或集中讨论50年间各类开支所呈现的不同趋势。（见下面的报告结构）

Summarize the information in the graph by selecting and reporting the main features and make comparisons where relevant. 通过选取和报告主要特征概括图表信息，如信息互相关联，可进行比较。

The graph shows what proportion of their total expenditure households in the UK spent, over a fifty-year period, in five different categories: housing; transport and vehicles; food; clothing and footwear; and fuel, light and power.

Between 1957 and 2007 expenditure in all five categories changed to some extent, but the most marked change was in the food category.[1] At the beginning of the period the proportion of expenditure on food was more than three times as high as that in all the other categories, representing more than thirty per cent of total household expenditure.[2] However, by 2007 this figure had more than halved to around fifteen per cent, and was slightly less than expenditure on both housing and transport.[3]

The two other areas where proportions of expenditure fell over the period are clothing and footwear, and fuel, light and power.[1] However, the changes here were much less dramatic.[2] Expenditure on the former dropped steadily from ten per cent to five per cent, and on the latter from six per cent to three per cent.[3] For most of the fifty-year period, these categories used up a significantly smaller proportion of the household budget than the others.[4]

Paragraph 1—Introduction
第1段——引言

Describes the subject of the data. 描述数据的主题。

Paragraph 2—Trends
第2段——趋势

[1] a general comment on the trends shown in the graph + main trend. 概要评论图表显示的各种趋势 + 主要趋势。

[2–3] provide supporting detail on the main trend. 提供可证实主要趋势的细节。

Paragraph 3—Trends
第3段——趋势

More detail on other trends where expenditure has fallen. 有关其他开支下降趋势的更多细节。

[1, 2] a general comment, explained in detail in[3]. 概括评论，在[3]中详细说明。

[4] compares these trends with other expenditure. 将这些趋势与其他开支进行比较。

In two categories, housing and transport, the proportions of expenditure almost doubled, rising from nine and eight per cent to nineteen and sixteen per cent respectively.[1] Thus, by the end of the period, the highest proportion of household expenditure went on housing, and the lowest on fuel, light and power.[2]

In conclusion, the graph shows that the patterns of spending in UK households changed to some extent over the period 1957 to 2007, the part of the budget spent on food showing the most marked change.

Paragraph 4—Trends
第4段——趋势

[1] more detail on trends where spending rose. 关于开支上升趋势的更多细节。

[2] summarizes the main contrast in the trends. 总结各种趋势的主要对比。

Paragraph 5—Conclusion
第5段——总结

This summarizes the report with a general conclusion. 概要总结报告。

Core language for describing graphs
描述图表的关键用语

Language bank 用语库

General 概述	**Pie charts: describing proportions of a whole 饼分图：描述整体中的比例**
The graph/chart shows/represents/indicates … *The figures show/indicate (that) …* draw conclusions from, e.g. 从…中得出结论，如：*The following conclusions can be drawn from the data.*	*More/Less* than half *of the total…* *Only* a third/a quarter … *Just/Well under/over* 50% … *The biggest/smallest proportion/sector …* *The vast majority of …* *As many (people were learning French) as (Spanish).*
Bar charts: describing differences between amounts 条形图：描述数量之间的差别	**Graphs: describing developments over time 线形图：描述一段时间内的变化**
There were almost *twice/three times/half as many … as* Far/Slightly/20% *fewer X … than Y …* Many/Far/A few/20% *more X … than Y …* *A greater proportion of … than of …* *20% of women …, while only 10% of men …* *80% of (adults send emails), compared to 34% (who prefer texts).*	a small/slight/gradual *increase/decrease* a significant/marked/dramatic *increase/decrease* a small/slight *rise/fall/dip* *steady growth* *to rise/increase/fall/decrease/decline/drop* *to rise/fall* steadily/dramatically/sharply/rapidly *Customer numbers have fluctuated.* *(Online sales) reached an all-time high/low.* *The graph shows a marked change in …*

Writing a report 写报告

A report describes a study, an investigation, or a project. Its purpose is to provide recommendations or updates, and sometimes to persuade the readers to accept an idea. It is written by a single person or a group who has investigated the issue. It is read by people who require the information. 报告是对研究、调查或专题研究的描述，其目的是提供建议或报告最新情况，有时是说服读者接受某观点。它是由研究过该课题的个人或小组撰写的，其读者是需要了解有关信息的人。

Tip 提示

- Reports can vary in length but a good rule to remember is that they should be as long as necessary and as short as possible. 报告的长度不尽相同，一条有用的原则是：有必要则长，但尽可能简短。

Think about the reader 考虑读者

You need to make the objective of the report clear so that the people who are reading the report know why they are reading. Thinking about the readers and what they need to know will help improve your report. 要清楚说明报告的目的，以便读者明白他们为什么读。考虑读者和他们需要知道什么会有助于改进报告。

- Is the purpose of the report clear throughout? 报告自始至终都目的明确吗？
- Can the readers find the information they need? 读者能找到他们想了解的信息吗？
- Will diagrams or tables make the information clearer? 图表或表格可以使信息更加清楚吗？
- Should I just present the facts or include recommendations as well? 应该只报告事实还是也要提出建议？

Organizing your report 组织报告

A typical report should follow the structure outlined below. Shorter reports might not need all the sections but they should at least include the highlighted sections. 一篇典型的报告应该遵从下面的结构。短篇报告可能不需要包括所有部分，但至少应包括以蓝色突出显示的部分。

1 Title 标题

Your title should tell the reader exactly what the report is about. 标题应准确说明报告主题。

2 Contents List 目录

If your report has a number of sections it is important to include a table of contents so that the readers can find the information they want. A good way to structure a report is to use numbered headings. 如果报告包括许多部分，那么列出目录以方便读者查找信息，这一点很重要。使用带编号的标题是一种很好的编排方式：

2.0 Research
2.1 Focus groups
2.2 Technology for accessing the Internet

3 Summary 摘要

This section is often called an **Executive Summary**. It tells the reader what the objectives of the report are as well as the main findings, conclusions and any recommendations. 这部分通常称作"报告摘要"（Executive Summary），其中说明报告的目的和主要调研结果、结论及建议。

4 Introduction 引言

This should give the reader the background to the report: why you are writing it. You should also include what the report will cover (and what it won't) and how you got the information you have based the report on. 这部分应该说明报告背景：为什么写这份报告。也应说明报告所涉及（和不涉及）的内容以及报告所依据的信息是如何收集的。

5 Body of the report 报告主体

The main body of the report will follow the structure in the Contents List. It will give precise information about the research you have carried out and what you have discovered from it. The information here should be mainly factual and not based on opinion. Tables, charts and bulleted lists can make the information clearer. Some of the more detailed information can go into Appendices and the Bibliography. 报告主体部分将依照目录所列的结构编排。这部分给出研究和调研结果的确切信息。这些信息应主要基于事实而非主观看法。表格、图表和项目符号列表可使内容更清楚。有些较详细的信息可放在附录和参考书目中。

6 Conclusions 结论

This is where you give your opinions on the facts that you have discovered. 此处给出对调研结果的看法。

7 Recommendations 建议

If you have been asked to give recommendations, they should be based on your conclusions. You should also let the reader know what you predict will happen if your recommendations are followed. 如要求提出建议，所提建议应以自己的结论为基础。亦应说明，如果建议被采纳，你预计会出现什么情况。

8 Appendices 附录

In a long report, you should put very detailed information in the Appendices with cross references to them in the body of the report. 长篇报告应把十分详细的信息放在附录中，并在报告主体部分设参见项。

9 Bibliography 参考书目

If your report refers to a number of other publications, you should list these in a Bibliography. 如果报告提及一些其他出版物，就应该在参考书目部分列出。

Executive summary 报告摘要

The summary below gives some useful language in context. In the Language bank are some other phrases that you can use in reports. Notice that the language used should be **clear**, **accurate** and **formal**. *We* and *I* are often used in internal reports, for example for describing research. 以下摘要就某个情景给出了一些有用的说法。用语库列出其他一些可用于报告的短语。注意所使用的语言应清晰、准确和正式。We 和 I 常用于内部报告，如用来描述研究。

Web Page Design

The purpose of this report is to compare two different web designs. The reason for this is to decide what kind of web page is most likely to attract new customers and to encourage existing customers to buy more products from us.

We asked two developers to produce alternative web pages for our company. We asked Developer A to produce a simple, easy-to-use design and we asked Developer B to produce a more sophisticated design with lots of eye-catching graphics. We conducted our research by asking a group of twenty existing customers and twenty non-customers to use the web page over a month. The group was made up of people with a range of ages, professions, incomes, and computer expertise. We divided the group in two and asked one sub-group to use Design A and the other to use Design B. We asked each sub-group to log on once a day and to use the web page to perform certain tasks, including: buying products, getting information, returning damaged products, and tracking deliveries. We also asked the sub-groups to assess how attractive they found their designs and whether they would be encouraged to return to the web page.

In addition, we researched the technology that people had available for accessing the Internet, including the devices people used and the connection speeds available.

We found that, on the whole, people preferred to be able to purchase products quickly and easily. In conclusion, users do not visit a site such as ours for entertainment. While they initially enjoyed some of the aspects of Design B these could take a long time to load and users eventually became bored.

We recommend that we adopt Design A with two or three of the more practical features from Design B.

Language bank 用语库

Stating objectives 说明目的

The purpose/aim/objective of this report is to …
This report aims to …
This reports presents/gives information on …

Outlining research 概述调查研究

We asked (*two developers*) *to …*
We conducted our research by … (e.g. *asking a group of …*)
We examined/looked at/researched … (e.g. *the problem/the cost/several companies*)
We surveyed … (e.g. *a total of 250 employees*)
We compared A and B.
The group was made up of …

Presenting findings 描述调研结果

We found that, on the whole, …
According to the majority of respondents …
Overall, people preferred …
50% of those surveyed said (*that*) *…*

Giving conclusions 做总结

In conclusion …
The research shows/demonstrates (*that*)*…*
The research shows/demonstrates + noun 名词 (e.g. *the effect of …*)
From the research/the evidence we conclude that …

Giving recommendations 提建议

We recommend that …
It is recommended that …
The best solution is/would be to … (e.g. *to adopt design A*)
The best solution is/would be + noun 名词 (e.g. *a reduction in office hours*)
If we do A, we will see B.
This will have an impact on + noun 名词 (e.g. *costs/productivity/the business*)

Writing a review of a book or film/movie 写书评或影评

Cambridge English: First

The main purpose of a book review is to give information to a potential reader so that they can decide whether or not they want to read the book. A review of a film/movie has the same purpose. You can approach it in the same way as a book review.
书评的主要目的是向潜在读者提供信息，以便他们决定是否想读这本书。影评的目的亦相同，可按书评的模式写影评。

Asking a question is one way to engage the reader. Or you could start with a personal opinion. **提问题**是吸引读者的一种方式，亦可先提出自己的看法。

Information about the setting and era can be useful. **背景**和**时代**信息会很有用。

Most nouns can be enhanced with an **adjective** – but make sure it is a natural collocation. 大多数名词可用**形容词**修饰，但要确保搭配得当。

Linking words aid organization and can also give your opinion. **衔接词**有助于篇章组织连贯，也可以用来提出看法。

Wuthering Heights by Emily Brontë

Is it a darkly passionate tale of love? Or should we call it a highly original gothic story? The classic novel *Wuthering Heights* by Emily Brontë is, in my opinion, a unique and gripping blend of these genres. Written in 1847, it is an epic family saga full of desire, hate, revenge and regret, focusing on the main characters of Heathcliff and Catherine. The atmospheric setting of the wild Yorkshire moors cleverly mirrors these violent emotions.

When Catherine's father adopts the starving orphan boy Heathcliff, Catherine's brother Hindley feels deeply hurt and resentful. She, on the other hand, develops an immensely strong bond with Heathcliff, which becomes an all-consuming love. Upon her father's death, Hindley becomes the head of the family and forces Heathcliff to assume the position of a servant. Despite loving Heathcliff, Catherine chooses to marry Edgar Linton, who is closer to her class and position in society. It is this decision which leads to heartbreak and tragedy, not only for them but for many others.

Heathcliff could be described as an anti-hero with his rough manners and lack of control. Likewise, Catherine displays many flaws, but the reader can still empathize with these characters. In fact, this is the main reason why I believe this novel is so brilliant. It rings with truth. The reader may be horrified at the way that Heathcliff and Catherine behave, and yet, at the same time, the writer ensures that we never hate them because the reasons for their actions are crystal clear.

The **title** and **author's name** should appear in the introductory paragraph. 应在引言段说明**作品的名称**和**作者姓名**。

This is one of many **synonyms** of 'interesting'. Look at the note at the dictionary entry 'interesting'. 这是 interesting 的多个**同义词**之一。查阅本词典 interesting 条的用法说明。

It is usual to use the present tense to describe the story. 用现在时讲述故事很常见。

Collocations of adverb + adjective show your vocabulary knowledge. Look up **hurt** adjective. 使用副词 + 形容词的搭配展示自己的词汇知识。查阅形容词 hurt。

Conclusion. Restate your opinion of the book as a recommendation to read it or not to read it. 总结。重申自己的看法，表明是否推荐阅读这本书。

The main part of the book relies on a narrator, Ellen Dean, who is a servant at Wuthering Heights and I think that this is a useful device which holds the complex plot together. However, *Wuthering Heights* is not what I would call an 'easy read'. There is dense description and some of the dialogue is written in dialect, which can be difficult to follow.

Nevertheless, I persevered and, all in all, I can highly recommend *Wuthering Heights*. I challenge you to remain unmoved after reading this exceptional book.

Including information on the **style of writing** can be helpful. 加入**写作风格**方面的信息会有帮助。

Writing your review 写书评

1. Read or re-read the book and make notes 阅读或重读这本书并做笔记

Your notes should try to answer the questions a reader might have. 做笔记时应尽量涵盖读者可能问的问题：

- What kind of book is it? 这是一本什么样的书？
- What is the main theme of the book? 书的主题是什么？
- What happens in the story? 故事情节是什么？
- Is it well written? 这本书写得好吗？
- Who are the main characters? 主要人物是谁？
- Would you recommend this book? 你会推荐阅读这本书吗？

2. Organize your notes 组织笔记

You can use the same plan as the model review (see below). A successful review will contain these elements, but the order can be changed. 可采用下列书评范文的提纲。好的书评都包括这些要素，但次序可以改变。

Paragraph 1—Introduction 第1段——引言

General comments about the book. 对这本书的概要评论。

Paragraph 2—Plot 第2段——情节

A brief summary of what happens. 简要说明故事梗概。

Paragraph 3—Characters 第3段——人物

Briefly describe and comment on the main characters. 简要描述和评论主要人物。

Paragraph 4—Other information 第4段——其他信息

Anything else important that you want to say about the book. 你想说的关于这本书的其他要点。

Paragraph 5—Conclusion 第5段——总结

Include your personal recommendation here. 本段写你个人的建议。

3. Write your review 写书评

Remember not to include too many details and don't give away the ending of the book. The reviewer recommends this book but the review also contains some criticisms. It is a good idea to try to write about both positive and negative aspects of the book. 记住不要加入太多细节，也不要透露书的结局。即便书评作者推荐阅读这本书，书评中也要有所批评。最好对书的优点和缺点均加以评论。

Tip 提示

- Remember at all times that the person who reads your review has NOT read the book! 始终记着书评读者没有读过这本书！
- Use your dictionary to help you find synonyms of words such as **book** or **story**. 在词典中查找 book 或 story 等词的同义词。
- Find a range of adjectives to use to describe the book, plot and characters. 找出一系列用于介绍书、情节和人物的形容词。

Reviews of non-fiction books 非小说类作品书评

The purpose of a non-fiction book review is basically the same as fiction but the potential reader will have different questions. 非小说类作品书评的目的与小说书评基本相同，但其潜在读者会有不同的问题：

- What is the author's reason for writing the book? 作者写这本书的原因是什么？
- Is it well organized? Can you follow the argument easily and find the important information? 篇章组织得好吗？你能轻松地读懂作者的论述并找到重要信息吗？
- Does the author support his/her findings well? 作者很好地证明了自己的研究结果吗？
- How does it compare to other books on the same subject? 这本书与其他同一题材的书相比如何？

Language bank 用语库

Beginnings 开头	**Giving your opinion 发表看法**
It is a fascinating tale of … (e.g. *rural life*) *This moving account of …* (e.g. *a young man's experiences*) *I found this story far-fetched and unconvincing.*	*The writer excels at …* (e.g. *describing …*) *I was impressed by …* *One aspect I found a little disappointing was …* *One possible flaw is that …*
Details/Plot 细节/情节 *Written in …, the story begins with …* *The events unfold in …* *The tale is set in …* **Characters 人物** *The writer introduces us to…* *The principal characters are…* *My favourite character is undoubtedly …* *The story focuses on …* *We experience all this through the eyes of …*	**Conclusions 总结** *I would highly recommend this rewarding book.* *I thoroughly enjoyed this book. In fact I couldn't put it down!* *By the end of this book, you feel …* *I was left unmoved by this story.* *I would strongly advise against reading this book.*

Discussing pictures and cartoons 描述图片和漫画

This task may occur in written or spoken examinations. Describing photographs or pictures can be similar to interpreting cartoons. There may not be a caption or any speech, but the photo can still have a message. You can also discuss the effect it has on you. 此任务可能出现在笔试或口试中。描述图片与解说漫画相似。图片中可能没有说明文字或显示任何人说的话，但仍然会有想要表达的信息。亦可谈论你看了之后有何感受。

Look at the cartoon and the interpretation below. 看下面的漫画和解说文字。

"It is good to see people doing their bit for the environment!"

The cartoon shows a bird's-eye view of part of a European city or town. There is a large factory, several rows of houses, two vehicles and some people.[1] In the foreground, there is a rubbish collection truck, with two men collecting household waste for recycling. On the left of the cartoon, a man is putting a bottle in a street recycling bin. Watching him are two other men who are obviously managers in the local factory.[2] The caption reads "It is good to see people doing their bit for the environment!"[3]

The caption is clearly the words that one of the factory managers is saying to his colleague, because the focus of attention is on them and also on the man with the bottle: all three of them are drawn in detail[1] and they also stand out because of the black clothing they are wearing.[2]

Another important element in the cartoon is the factory and the pollution from its chimneys. The cartoonist has exaggerated the size of the factory in relation to the surrounding houses and has also exaggerated the pollution by blackening a wide expanse of sky.[3] These aspects of the picture show the way that the pollution from the factory dominates the town and causes a serious environmental impact.

The factory itself is a symbol representing industry in general.[4] It seems that the man who is dropping off his one empty bottle in the recycling bin has driven there in his car, so he has probably damaged the environment more than if he had just thrown the bottle away. He represents ordinary people.[4]

The cartoon is about our attitude to the environment. It is clear that the cartoonist is suggesting that while people focus on small-scale activities, such as recycling household waste, they are ignoring much more serious environmental problems such as the pollution from industries and from cars.[1] He/She uses irony to show that we are becoming complacent about saving the environment. This is done by contrasting what the factory managers are saying with what is really happening all around them: serious pollution that they themselves are responsible for.

Personally, I believe that the cartoonist is right. Many people are now very good about recycling their household waste. But, because we do this, we have become complacent about pollution and feel we are doing enough to protect the environment. We need also to address other more important sources of environmental damage.

Paragraph 1—Description
第 1 段——描述
1 General description 概括描述
2 Detailed description 详细描述
3 Caption or speech bubble 说明文字或说话框

Paragraphs 2–4—Artistic techniques
第 2–4 段——艺术技巧
1 Technique 1–detail 技巧 1：细部
2 Technique 2–emphasis 技巧 2：突出
3 Technique 3–exaggeration 技巧 3：夸张
4 Technique 4–symbolism 技巧 4：象征

Paragraph 5—Message
第 5 段——信息
1 Use of irony 反讽手法的使用

Paragraph 6—Personal reaction 第 6 段——个人的反应

Key 颜色说明

shows the key language in each section. 黄色显示各部分的关键用语。

focuses on prepositions and phrasal verbs. 绿色提醒注意介词和短语动词。

Writing a description and interpretation 写描述和解说

Follow these steps when you prepare for this task. Think about the questions and make notes; then, when you write, use some of the phrases in the Language banks and take note of the tips. 按照以下步骤准备这项任务。思考下列问题并做笔记。然后，在写作过程中，使用用语库里的短语并留意提示里的建议。

Stage 1—Description
第 1 步——描述

The scene 情景：

- What is the scene in the cartoon/picture? 漫画/图片中的情景是什么？
- Where is it? 在哪里？
- What are the major features? 主要特点是什么？

Details 细部：

- Who/What is in the picture? 画面中有谁/什么？
- What are they doing? 他们在做什么？
- What is happening? 发生了什么事？

Language bank 用语库

The scene is of … (e.g. *a café in which two people …*)
The cartoon shows/depicts …
There is/are … (e.g. *two people who look angry.*)
In the centre of the cartoon is/are …, (who/which …)
At the top/bottom of the cartoon is/are …
On the left/right …
In the foreground/background …
The central feature of the cartoon is …
You can use prepositions 可使用介词，e.g. 例如 ***behind** the houses*
Avoid using 避免使用：~~I/You can see …~~; ~~In the picture …~~

Tip 提示

- Only describe the details that are important for the message. 只描述对于表达中心思想很重要的细部。
- Try to avoid using short simple sentences such as: ~~*In the centre is a man. He is shouting.*~~ **Relative sentences** are particularly useful: *In the centre is a man who is shouting.* 尽量避免使用很短的简单句，如：~~*In the centre is a man. He is shouting.*~~ 关系从句（relative sentence）特别有用，如：In the centre is a man who is shouting.

The caption or speech bubble 说明文字或说话框：

- What is written in the caption or in any speech bubbles? 说明文字或说话框中写的是什么？
- Who is talking and to whom? 谁在说话，对谁说？

Language bank 用语库

The caption reads "…"
One man is saying to the other "…"
The woman is asking whether …
He/She is commenting that …
He/She is wondering whether … (to go/he/she should go …)

Stage 2—Interpretation 第 2 步——解说

Tip 提示

- Start a new paragraph for this section. Give evidence and reasons for your interpretation. 这部分另开新段。为自己的解说提供依据或理由。

Artistic techniques 艺术技巧：

How does the artist draw attention to important parts of the cartoon/picture? 画家如何使读者注意到漫画/图片中的重点部分？ Does he/she use 他/她是否使用：

- detail? Where? 细部？ 在哪里？
- emphasis? What is emphasized? How? 突出？ 突出的是什么？ 如何突出的？
- exaggeration? What is exaggerated? 夸张？ 什么地方用了夸张？
- symbolism? Which objects or people are symbols? What do they mean? 象征？ 哪些东西或人是象征？ 有何含义？

Language bank 用语库

The focus of attention is on …
X is/are drawn in detail, (which shows/ to show …)
X stand(s) out because of the …
The most important element in the cartoon is …
This aspect of the cartoon indicates …
The X symbolize(s)/represent(s) …
The cartoonist has exaggerated X (in order to …/because …)
The reason for this is that …
Use your dictionary to find synonyms so that you use a wide range of vocabulary. 在词典中查找同义词以丰富写作的词汇，e.g. 例如 *clearly/obviously; indicate/show*

Message 中心思想：

- What is the cartoon/picture really about? 漫画/图画实际上是关于什么的？
- What is the artist trying to say? 画家想表达什么？
- How does he/she try to persuade you? Does he/she use **irony** (contrasting the way the cartoon shows things with the way they really are) or **analogy** (using a simple situation to make a more complex situation clear)? 画家如何设法说服你？ 他/她有没有使用反讽（irony，即将漫画中的情形与真实情况对比）或类比（analogy，即用简单的情况解释较复杂的情况）？

Language bank 用语库

The cartoon is about/refers to/deals with …
The cartoon has to do with …
The cartoonist is obviously trying to show …
What the cartoon is saying is that …
I take/understand the cartoon to mean that …

Stage 3—Personal reaction 第 3 步——个人的反应

- Do you agree or disagree with the message? 你是否认同这一中心思想？
- Why? 为什么？

Tip 提示

- Start a new paragraph for this section. 这部分另开新段。

Language bank 用语库

Personally, I believe that the cartoonist is right.
I only partly/partially agree with the artist's message because …
In my opinion/view, the artist is wrong, because …
Use phrases such as 使用此类短语，例如 *I think …; In my opinion …;* or 或 *It seems to me that …*
Do not use 不要用 ~~*According to me/my opinion …*~~

Writing a formal letter
写正式信函

Cambridge English: First, Advanced, Proficiency
Business Certificates | IELTS

Writing a letter of complaint 写投诉信

The important things to remember about writing formal letters are the layout, which follows particular conventions, and the language, which must be formal or semi-formal and polite, even when you are complaining. 写正式信函时需要记住的重点之一是格式，它有其惯用的格式；二是语言，用语必须是正式或半正式的，而且要有礼貌，即便是表达不满亦应如此。

6 Fore Street
Kensington
London W8 9NW

Customer Services Manager
FlyHigh Airways
PO Box 589
London W3 5NJ

1 August 2014

Dear Sir/Madam

Booking reference: Porter POR 1359AZ

My wife and I and our two children, aged 2 and 4, were passengers on flight LZ238 from London to Orlando, USA on July 23rd 2014. I am writing to complain about a number of aspects of the service we received.

Firstly, when the flight was delayed, the staff at the airline's information desk were very unhelpful. We were not even given a voucher for a drink or meal, when it was clear the delay would be at least seven hours. This meant that we had to spend a considerable amount of money in the restaurant.

Then, when we were finally able to board, families were not allowed to board first, although we had paid for this. As a result we were not able to sit together, making our children, already very tired, extremely distressed.

It is a legal requirement for airline operators to provide suitable refreshments in the event of a long delay. I would therefore expect some compensation for your failure both to comply with this regulation and to provide us with the priority boarding for which we had paid.

I enclose our boarding passes and look forward to hearing from you shortly.

Yours faithfully

S R Porter (Dr)

Paragraph 1 第1段

Explain clearly why you are writing. 清楚说明为什么写信。

Paragraph 2 第2段

Explain the problem and how you were affected. 说明问题和自己所受的影响。

Paragraph 3 第3段

Explain any further problem and the consequences. 说明其他问题和后果。

Paragraph 4 第4段

State clearly what action you wish the company to take. 清楚提出自己希望该公司采取的行动。

Ending 结束语

General comment. Say you would like a quick reply. 概要评论。表明你希望尽快得到答复。

Key 颜色说明

Yellow = key language
黄色 = 关键用语

Writing the letter 写信

Layout 格式

Look carefully at the layout of the model letter and note 仔细看范文的格式并注意：

- Your address, but not your name, goes at the top on the right. 右上角写上写信人的地址，不写姓名。
- The name and address of the person you are writing to goes on the left. 左边写收信人姓名和地址。
- If you do not know a name, use a position e.g. 'Customer Services Manager'. 如果不知道收信人姓名，就使用职衔，如 Customer Services Manager（客户服务部经理）。
- The date goes under either address. 日期放在左边或右边地址的下方均可。
- Give some kind of reference or use a heading (e.g. **Poor service levels**). 写出相关的事宜或使用标题，如 Poor service levels（服务质量差）。

Tip 提示

- **Tone:** be polite and formal, but keep your language simple and clear. 语气：有礼貌而且正式，但语言要简单明了。
- Use short sentences rather than long ones. 用短句，不要用长句。
- Try not to be emotional; avoid *you/you didn't* if possible. 尽量不要情绪激动；尽可能避免使用 you/you didn't。

If you are writing in **American English**, remember 如果用美式英语写信，记住：

- Use American spelling and punctuation e.g. Mrs., Dr., etc. 用美式拼写和标点符号，如 Mrs.、Dr. 等。
- End your letter **Sincerely, Sincerely yours,** or **Yours truly,**. 结尾使用 Sincerely、Sincerely yours 或 Yours truly。

Language bank 用语库

Openings and closings 开头和结尾套语

Dear Sir/Madam.........Yours faithfully

Dear Ms Walker.........Yours sincerely

Introducing the topic 引入话题

I am writing to complain about/to express my dissatisfaction with ...

The purpose of this letter is to express my disappointment with ...

Describing the problem 描述问题

Strong adjectives 语气强的形容词：*appalled, distressed, disgusted, shocked*

Less strong 较温和的形容词：*disappointed, dismayed, dissatisfied.*

What do you want? 你的诉求是什么？

Definite 明确的：*a full/partial refund, a replacement, an apology*

More flexible 有商讨余地的：*compensation, reimbursement, recompense*

Endings 结束语

I look forward to your swift reply.

I look forward to hearing from you at your earliest convenience.

I look forward to hearing from you without delay.

I very much hope to hear from you shortly.

I await your prompt reply.

Writing a letter to a newspaper 给报纸写信

This should still be a formal letter, but because it is for the public, it should show your opinion clearly or tell people something interesting or new. It can be direct and feel quite personal – you can use *I*, *we* and *you*. 这同样属于正式信件，但对象是公众，所以应清楚表明自己的观点，或向人介绍有趣或新鲜的事物。语气可以直截了当，带有个人色彩——可以使用 I、we 和 you。

A title attracts the readers' attention. 标题吸引读者的注意力。

Give information about you if relevant. 如有必要，写出关于自己的相关信息。

Use strong adjectives. 使用语气强烈的形容词。

Exclamation marks are acceptable to show how you feel. 为表达情感而使用感叹号是可以的。

A challenge to readers can be effective. 向读者发出倡议会是有效的做法。

Ending: No finishing phrase is needed. 结尾：不需要结尾套语。

Sir

The craze for reality TV

As a student in my early twenties I am part of a key audience for TV channels. Why then, do I find so little to interest or entertain me? One trend I find particularly appalling is the increase in 'reality' TV programmes such as Survivor, Big Brother and Fear Factor, to name but a few.

'Reality' TV shows involve 'real' people performing ridiculous and often dangerous acts and generally behaving horribly towards each other. These shows appeal to that part of us which takes pleasure in watching the humiliation of others and I believe that programme-makers are being irresponsible by promoting this. It is demeaning to both the participants and the viewers.

Even worse, these programmes are having a negative effect on society, particularly on young people, who no longer feel any shame at watching or taking part in this kind of disgraceful behaviour. A national survey recently stated that one in seven British teenagers hopes to become famous by going on a show like this! The average British adult watches 26 hours of television per week. Reality TV is not only a waste of time, but it is dangerous. I believe it can and will affect our society, dragging it down into the gutter.

It is time we made a stand against reality TV, in favour of quality TV. How can we do it? Start by changing the channel.

Maria Fedora
Madrid

Paragraph 1
第1段

Clear introduction of the topic and the writer's opinion. 清楚地介绍主题和作者的看法。

Paragraph 2
第2段

Main point, with reasons. 主要观点，同时提出理由。

Paragraph 3
第3段

Further point to support main one, with reasons and/or examples. 支持主要观点的进一步的观点，给出理由和/或例证。

Paragraph 4
第4段

Repeats the writer's opinion and offers a challenge. 重申作者的看法并发出倡议。

Writing emails 写电子邮件

Cambridge English: First, Advanced, Proficiency, Business Certificates | IELTS | TOEIC

- Emails **vary in formality** depending on how well you know the reader and what your status is in relation to them. 根据写信人和收信人关系密切程度和彼此的地位高低，电子邮件的正式程度亦不尽相同。
- All emails should be polite, but they **vary in level of politeness** depending on who you are writing to and what you are asking them. 所有电子邮件都应该有礼貌，但根据收信人的身份和写信人对他们所提的要求，其礼貌程度不尽相同。
- Writers use level of formality and politeness to achieve an appropriate **tone**. 写信人应根据情况采用相应的正式程度和礼貌程度，使邮件的语气恰当得体。
- Emails between colleagues of a similar status can be informal and personal, but should still be polite and friendly. 地位相近的同事之间的电邮可以是非正式的、个性化的，但依然应礼貌友好。

Email etiquette 电子邮件礼节

- Always use a short, informative **subject line**, not single general words e.g. *Urgent* or *Enquiry*. 在主题栏（subject line）中填入简短明确的标题，不要使用笼统的单个词语，如 Urgent 或 Enquiry。
- Mention **attachments** and say what they contain. Don't leave the body of the email empty. 提及附件（attachment）并说明其内容。电子邮件的正文部分不能空白。
- **Acknowledge** email attachments you receive. *Thanks* + your name is often enough. 复函告知收悉电邮附件。一般用 Thanks + 自己的名字就行了。
- **Re-read** your email before you send it to make sure it is understandable and not offensive. 发出电邮前重读一遍，确保行文易懂且没有冒犯性。

Writing business emails 写商务类电子邮件

Formal – An enquiry to a company – *formal, polite*
正式——向一家公司查询：正式，有礼貌

Tip 提示

Formal business emails are shorter and less formal than letters. 正式的商务电邮比信函短而且正式程度较低。

- You should **not** use very informal language, incomplete sentences, exclamation marks or emoticons. 不应使用很不正式的语言、不完整的句子、感叹号或表情符号。
- You **can** use contracted verb forms, except where first impressions are important. 可以使用动词的缩略形式，第一印象很重要的情况除外。
- You can become **less formal** as you establish a working relationship with somebody. 与某人建立了工作关系后，语气可以变得不那么正式。

Greeting: Title plus last name as this is the first contact with this company.
称呼：因为是首次与该公司联系，称呼时要用称谓加上对方姓氏。

Abbreviations: ***promo*** is acceptable in formal emails, as are ***asap*** (as soon as possible), ***ad*** (advertisement), ***re***: (regarding).
缩写：在正式电邮中可使用缩写，如 promo（promotion，促销）。其他常见缩写还有 asap（as soon as possible，尽快）、ad（advertisement，广告）和 re:（regarding，关于）。

To: office@trainersrus.com
Cc: Andrea.penn@fgt.com
Subject: Query about training DVDs

Dear Mr Baxter

I am the HR assistant at FeelGood Training plc. I am contacting you to say that we have received the promo material about your sales training DVDs and are interested in purchasing some.

Could you please send us some more information regarding their content as we are not sure which would be the most useful for our staff.

We would also require a price list and payment terms.

Looking forward to your reply

Regards
Renata Klein

Renata Klein, HR assistant
FeelGood Training plc
484 London Road,Uxbridge,UX3 6HO
www.fgt.com

Clear **subject line**
清楚的主题栏

Opening: introduce yourself (use your position, not your name) and explain why you are writing.
开头：自我介绍（写出你的职位，不用写姓名），说明写邮件的原因。

We rather than *I* makes the message less personal and more formal.
用 we 而不用 I 使内容更加客观正式。

Ending: formal and friendly **结束语**：正式而友好

Signature: give your position and contact details.
署名：写出职位和详细联系方式。

Close: Most writers use one before their name. Give your full name in the first email. The reader can use *Renata* or *Ms Klein* in a reply.
结尾：大多数人写电邮时会在自己的名字前加上结尾套语。第一次与对方通电邮应写上你的完整姓名，对方回复可使用名字（Renata）或称谓＋姓（Ms Klein）。

Language: formal vocabulary: ***purchase*** = *buy*, ***require*** = *need*. **语言**：使用正式词汇，如 purchase = buy（购买）、require = need（需要；要求）。

Modal verbs (**could, would**) make the request more formal and polite. 情态动词（could、would）使所提要求更加正式和有礼貌。

A reply – *Less formal (semi-formal), polite*
回复——不太正式（半正式），有礼貌

Greeting and close: Jim chooses to use first names – correspondence will now tend to be less formal. **开头称呼和结尾：** Jim 选择称呼对方的名字，意味着这封信不太正式。

Language sets a polite, semi-formal, friendly tone 以下**用语**使语气有礼貌、半正式、友好：

- ***We're happy to …*** OR 或 ***We're pleased to …***

NOT 不可说：~~*We're delighted to …*~~ – too formal for emails 对于电邮而言过于正式

- ***Please feel free to …***

NOT 不可说：~~*Please don't hesitate to …*~~ – too formal 太正式

- ***Should you need help***: more formal than *'If you …'* * Should you need help 比 If you … 的说法更正式

To: Renata.klein@fgt.com
Subject: Re: Query about training DVDs

Dear Renata

Thank you for your interest in our training material.

We're happy to provide you with more detailed information regarding the contents of the DVDs. Attached you'll find a PDF containing a brochure plus purchasing agreement where you'll find terms and conditions are clearly explained.

Should you need help choosing a product to suit your company's needs, please feel free to contact us again. Either email me or alternatively you can speak to one of our customer service team by calling 05 471 375 31.

Best regards

Jim

Jim Baxter, Marketing Manager
Trainers-R-Us
j.baxter@trainersrus.com

Opening: a formal, polite opening sentence is appropriate for the first reply. **开头：**正式、有礼貌的开首语适合第一次回复。

Contracted forms can be used as the language is less formal now. 可使用**缩略形式**，因为此处的语言不太正式。

Say what's in the **attachment**. 说明**附件**中有什么。

Language bank 用语库

Greetings 称呼

Formal 正式	**Semi-formal** 半正式	**Informal** 非正式
Dear Ms Klein/Dear Professor Smith/ Dear Chris White (if you don't know the gender 假如不清楚对方性别) Do **not** use title and first name 不要用称谓 + 名字：~~*Dear Ms Mary.*~~	*Dear Renata*	*Hi/Hi Renata/ Hello/ Hello Renata*
Dear All (to a group)	*Dear All*	*Hi everyone/Hello all*
FAO/For the attention of the Sales Manager	—	—

Closes 结尾

Best wishes/Best regards/Regards + your full name. * Best wishes/Best regards/ Regards + 写信人的全名 Add position and contact details. 附上职位和详细联系方式。	*All the best/Best/ Yours/Many thanks* + your first name or your full name. * All the best/Best/Yours/ Many thanks + 写信人的名字或全名 (or formal closes 或正式结尾)	*Thanks/Cheers/ Speak to you soon* + your first name. * Thanks/ Cheers/Speak to you soon + 写信人的名字

Requesting action 请求

Very polite 很有礼貌	**Polite** 有礼貌	**Informal request** 非正式请求
Would it be possible (for you) to send me…?/I would be grateful if you could send me…	*Could you (please) send me …?*	*Can you send me …?/Pls can you let me have …?*
I was wondering if you have had a chance to do it yet?	*Have you had a chance to [do it yet?] …?*	*Have you [done it yet]?*
Would it be possible for me to come…? *I would really appreciate your help./ I would be very grateful (indeed) for your help.*	*Could I come…?* *Thank you./Many thanks*	*Can I come …?* *Thanks*

Writing academic emails 写学术类电子邮件

- Academic emails are usually **personal**, not official. You are writing to a specific, named individual, not to somebody in their official role. 学术类电子邮件通常为私人而非公务性通信。收信人是特定的、有名有姓的个人，而不是处在某职位的人。
- The level of **politeness** you need will vary. If you are asking a favour of an academic outside your university, you need to express a higher level of politeness than if you are asking your own teacher for a meeting. Emails between colleagues can be very **informal.** 所需要的礼貌程度亦不尽相同。请其他大学的老师帮忙要比请自己的老师见面表现得更加礼貌。同事之间的电邮可以很不正式。
- Remember to use a level of formality and politeness to achieve an appropriate **tone.** 记得要采用恰当的正式程度和礼貌程度，使语气得体。

Formal – A request from a student to an academic from a different department 正式——学生向其他院系的老师提出请求

Lower status writer to higher status reader whom he does not know.
地位较低的人写信给地位较高的陌生读者。

Tone: *Personal, very formal, very polite*
语气：私人色彩、很正式、很有礼貌

Subject: Request for statistical help

Dear Dr Barr

I am a first year PhD student in the department of linguistics and my research topic is a quantitative study of verb forms in academic writing. As I need to use advanced statistical tools for processing the data, my supervisor, Dr John Pugh, suggested I contact you to ask for advice. Would it be possible for me to come and see you to discuss what I need? I attach a copy of my draft research proposal to give you an idea of the scope of my study.

I would be very grateful indeed for your help.

Best wishes

David Samuels

Greeting: use **Dear** + academic title and family name, or Mr, Ms, etc. and family name **称呼**：使用 Dear + 学术头衔和姓氏，或 Mr、Ms 等和姓氏

Clear **subject line** 清楚的**主题栏**

Introduce yourself by giving your position in the university. 通过说明自己在大学中的身份做**自我介绍**。

Say **why you are writing.** Mention any academic contact. 说明**为什么写信**。提一下学术圈的熟人。

Be specific about what you want the reader to do. **具体**说明想要读者做什么。

Give **supporting details.** 提供**细节予以证明**。

Would it be possible … Very polite. 很礼貌 OR 或 *Could I possibly …* (NOT 不可说 ~~*I kindly request*~~ – too official 公务语气太重)

Close 结尾：OR 或 Best regards, Regards. Give your full name. Add position and contact details if necessary. 写出全名。如果有必要应写上职位和详细联系方式。

Ending: very polite **结束语**：非常有礼貌 OR 或：*I would really appreciate your help.* (NOT 不可说：~~*Thank you for your time*~~ – official. 公务语气 NOT 不可说：~~*Thank you for your attention*~~ – very formal spoken 很正式的口语)

Less formal – request from a student to their own supervisor
不太正式——学生向自己的导师提出请求

Lower status writer to higher status reader whom she knows very well.
地位较低的人写信给地位较高的熟悉的读者。

Tone: *Personal, polite, less formal*
语气：私人色彩、有礼貌、不太正式

Subject: use ? to show a request
主题栏：用？表示请求

A polite indirect question. Use it to remind somebody of higher status about something. 有礼貌的间接问句。用于向地位较高的人提醒某事。

Subject: Meeting this week?

Dear Ruth

I was wondering if you've had a chance to look at my paper yet. If so, could we have a meeting some time this week?

The best day for me would be Tues. I start my fieldwork at the end of the week and it would be very useful to have some feedback before then.

Many thanks

Nicole

Greeting: first names can be used as they know each other well.
称呼：可用名字，因双方很熟悉。

***Could, would*:** Less abrupt/ direct forms. Use them to make a suggestion/ request to somebody of higher status.
* could、would：不太唐突/直率的形式。用于向地位较高的人提出建议/请求。

Abbreviations can be used as style is less formal. 可用缩写，因为文体风格不太正式。

Close: informal – Nicole has the right to ask for a meeting
结尾：非正式—— Nicole 有权要求会面

Using American style in emails 美式风格的电子邮件

- If you are writing emails in an American English environment, the points about formality, politeness and tone on pages WT40–43 still apply. The language you use will be very similar. However, there are one or two things that you should be aware of, as shown below. 如果在美式英语环境中写电子邮件，WT40–43 页上有关正式程度、礼貌和语气的要点仍然适用，所使用的语言会非常相似。不过，还应留意以下几点。

Formality 正式程度

The main difference between American and British style in emails is that US emails do not use the very formal language that British emails often do and can be more direct. 美式和英式电邮风格的主要区别在于美式电邮不使用英式电邮常用的很正式的语言，而会更直率。 Look at these examples 参看以下示例：

British (formal) 英式风格（正式）	**American** 美式风格
I would be grateful If you could send your payment to …	*Please send your payment to …*
A list of fees can be found on our website.	*You can find a list of fees on our website.*
Please don't hesitate to contact me …	*Please feel free to contact me.*

Business emails 商务类电子邮件

Notice how the date is written. 注意日期的写法。(*BrE* 英式英语写法为：19/8/2014)

Notice the use of full stops and commas in these emails. Use full stops after abbreviations. 注意这些电邮中句点和逗号的使用。缩写后加上句点。

Use US spellings (e.g. customize, flavor, center, etc.) consistently. 使用美式拼写（如 customize、flavor、center 等）要前后一致。

Direct but polite questions using "you" are fine when writing to Americans. 给美国人写电邮时，用 you 提出直接但有礼貌的问句是可以的。

Close: *Sincerely yours*, or *Sincerely*, are good ways to close a business email. **结尾**：用 Sincerely yours 或 Sincerely 作为商务类电邮的结尾是不错的做法。

To: kmiller@charitytrainers.org
From: risai@newgreenspaces.jp
Date: 08/19/2014
Subject: Request for customized training

Dear Ms. Miller,

I am writing to ask about the possibility of organizing a customized training program for a group of five of our mid-level managers. We would be interested in having them learn more about staff recruitment, project management, and fundraising practices in the American charity and nonprofit sector. Could you please let me know what scheduling and pricing options are available for a week-long course fulfilling these requirements?

Sincerely yours,
Risa Inyaka
New Green Spaces, Japan

Academic emails 学术类电子邮件

Short, clear subject line 简短明了的主题栏

Attachments should be no larger than 2MB, if possible. 附件尽量不要大于2兆。

Use full stops after short titles. 缩写形式的职衔后加上句点。

Close: courteous and fairly formal **结尾**：客气且较正式

To: jacobi@bussch.clemson.edu
From: rwagner@stud.clemson.edu
Date: 8/23/2014
Subject: Proposed meeting this week
Attachments: mif.doc

Dear Dr. Jacobi,

I'm planning to submit the attached paper to 'Markets in Focus' next week. I wonder if it might be possible for us to meet to discuss it before I send it off? I'd be very grateful for your comments and advice. I'm available every day after 3 p.m., or in the mornings on either Tuesday or Thursday.

Many thanks,
Ross Wagner

Writing a CV/résumé and covering letter 写简历和附信

A well-written, well-produced, appropriate CV (*British English*) or résumé (*American English*) is vital for getting you to the interview stage for a job. Use the examples and advice here to help you. On page WT51 you will find an example of a good covering (cover) letter. 一份写得好、制作得体、恰如其分的简历（英式英语称 CV，美式英语称 résumé）是求职者通向面试阶段至关重要的一环。以下示例和建议可以助你达成这一目的。WT51 页上有一份很好的附信范文。

Tip 提示

- Adapt your CV/résumé so that it is appropriate for the job you are applying for. 修改简历，使之适合所申请的工作。
- Keep your CV short – no more than 2 pages if possible. 简历不要过长，尽量不要超过 2 页。
- Present yourself positively and accurately. 如实地介绍自己的优点。
- Make your CV attractive and easy to read: use capitals, bold type, spacing and underlining. 将简历制作得有吸引力并一目了然：适当使用大写字母、粗体、间距和下画线。
- Choose a typeface such as Times New Roman, Arial or Verdana. Use at least 10 pt. 选择合适的字体，如 Times New Roman、Arial 或 Verdana。至少使用 10 磅的字号。

British style CV (curriculum vitae) – *new graduate*
英式简历（CV，即 curriculum vitae）——应届毕业大学生

Name	Emily Jane Wilson
Address	29 Greenlands Avenue, London, SW3 6RF
Telephone	01924 786512
Mobile	0779 9238182
e-mail	em_wilson@scapenet.com

Objective To find a role in a film or TV production company that will enable me to acquire and develop the skills required for a career in film or television.

Profile An outgoing and articulate graduate with work experience in both television and teaching

Personal information. 个人信息 You can omit the labels. There is no need to mention your age, gender, nationality, race, religion or marital status. Don't send a photo unless you are asked to. 这些标记可省略。不必提及自己的年龄、性别、国籍、种族、宗教或婚姻状况。如非招聘的公司要求，不要寄照片。

Profile and objective. 简介和目标 Some people do not include these, but they do give an employer an idea of who you are. 有些人不写这些部分，但这些部分的确会让雇主对自己有所了解。

Education and qualifications

2014– MA in Media Studies. Bristol University. Expected 2015

2010–2014 BA in Media Studies with French (2:1) Bristol University

2002–2009 Beacon School, London
3 A levels: Drama (A); French (A); German (B)
5 AS levels 9 GCSEs

Work experience

October 2012–June 2013: Language assistant in secondary school in France. Taught English to large classes and small groups. Ran a film club and a holiday dance and drama club. Assisted with school drama productions.

September 2009–August 2010: Production assistant at Oordman and Associates Filmmakers, London N16. Performed office and on-set duties.

June–September 2009: Tutor for Jacaranda Drama Workshops. Led groups of teenagers of different backgrounds in dance and drama activities.

July–August 2008: Host at Adventure Camping holiday campsite in France. Led the children's club for 4-10 year olds and performed various practical duties on the campsite.

Skills

Languages: French–near native-speaker fluency (CEFR C1); German (B2).

Good keyboard skills. Familiarity with Word, Excel and film editing packages.

Clean driving licence.

Interests

Drama, both acting and directing; singing (was member of university choral society). Regular volunteer at a local centre for the homeless.

References – attached

Education. 学历 Put the most recent first. Add prizes and awards. Omit primary school. Try to give British equivalents of your qualifications. 先列出最近的学历，附带列出获奖情况。不要列出小学。尽量提供与英国对应的学历。

Work experience. 工作经历 Put this in reverse order. Experienced candidates: put this before Education and write more about your most recent post. 按倒序排列。有工作经历的求职者应将这部分放在学历之前，着重写一下最近的工作。

Skills. 技能 Your practical abilities. Include exams passed. Write more here if you are experienced. 个人的实践能力。列出所通过的考试。如果有相关经验，此部分着力写一下。

Interests. 兴趣 Keep this short. Include a sport, a creative and a community activity, if you can. Avoid vague subjects such as *reading or travel*. 这部分要简短。可能的话，列出一项体育运动、一项有创意的活动和一项社区活动。避免过于笼统的主题，如阅读或旅行。

References. 推荐人 Give the names, titles, and addresses when you send your CV, either here or on a separate page. 寄简历时要提供推荐人的姓名、职衔和地址，列在此处或放在单独一页上均可。

American style résumé – *new graduate*
美式简历（résumé）——应届毕业大学生

These are similar to British style CVs. But notice 美式简历与英式简历相似。不过要注意：

- For new graduates your résumé should be only one page. 应届毕业大学生的简历不应超过一页。
- Describe your work experience in terms of self-motivation, teamwork, organization, problem-solving, and enthusiasm. 从主动性、团队合作、组织、解决问题和工作热情几方面描述工作经历。

Tip 提示

- The standard US paper size is not A4 (210 × 297 mm) but 216 × 279 mm. 标准美国纸张的大小不是 A4（210毫米 × 297毫米），而是216毫米 × 279毫米。

Jessica M. Brown
jmbrown@mba.nau.edu

Present Address:	Permanent Address:
508 Blackbird's Roost	50, rue de Vaugirard
Flagstaff, AZ, USA 86011	Saint-Sulpice, France 75006
Tel +1 929 555 1212	Tel +33 1234 567 890

Provide your college or temporary **address** if you have one. 提供大学住址或当前临时住址（如有）。

OBJECTIVE To obtain an entry-level management position within an international hospitality organization.

Objective. 目标
To summarize your goals and customize your résumé for specific positions. State a realistic short-term goal and/or a job for which you are currently qualified. 概述自己的目标并按特定职位写简历。说出一个现实的短期目标和/或目前能够胜任的工作。

EDUCATION **Masters in Business Administration** (M.B.A.), 2011–2013
Northern Arizona University, Flagstaff, Arizona, USA
B.A. in International Hospitality, 2007–2011
Université de Savoie, Chambéry, France

EXPERIENCE **Travel Agent**, Sep. 2011–Present
Kokopelli Extreme Tours, Sedona, Arizona, USA Organized adventure package tours for large student groups, trained and supervized new staff members, and maintained partner relationships.
Camp Counselor, Jun 2007–Aug 2011
Voyageurs Summer Camp, Voglans, France
Group leader for children aged 10–15. Developed curriculum for campers and led overnight hiking trips.

HONORS Agent of the Month, Kokopelli Extreme Tours, March 2013
Voted 'Most Popular Counselor,' Voyageurs, 2010 & 2011

SKILLS & INTERESTS Fluent in French and English; conversational Spanish. Enjoy web design in HTML and Flash.

Use **bold** to highlight key information. 用**粗体字**强调关键信息。

Use US **spelling** and **punctuation**. 用美式拼写和标点符号。

Language bank 用语库

Action verbs 动作动词

Use action verbs to describe your achievements and make them look more dynamic. 用动作动词描述所取得的成绩，这样看上去更有表现力。

Examples 例子：*achieved, administered, analyzed, advised, arranged, compiled, conducted, coordinated, created, designed, developed, devised, distributed, evaluated, examined, executed, implemented, increased, introduced, instructed, liaised, managed, mentored, monitored, negotiated, organized, oversaw, prepared, recommended, reduced, researched, represented, solved, supervised, trained.*

Positive adjectives 褒义形容词

Use positive adjectives to describe yourself. 用褒义形容词描述自己。

Examples 例子：*active, adaptable, committed, competent, dynamic, effective, efficient, enthusiastic, experienced, flexible, (highly) motivated, organized, professional, proficient, qualified, successful.*

Other useful phrases 其他有用的短语

Skills 技能

Native French speaker

Near-native command of English

Good spoken and written German

Computer literate

Familiar with HTML

Experienced trainer and facilitator

Education and experience 学历和经历

Baccalauréat, série C (equivalent of A levels in Maths and Physics)

The qualifications described below do not have exact equivalents in the British/American system.

Four weeks' work experience at …

Summer internship at a marketing firm.

Personal qualities 个人素质

Work well as part of a team

Work well under pressure

Able to meet deadlines

Welcome new challenges

Can-do attitude

Writing a covering letter 写附信

A covering letter (*NAmE* cover letter) accompanies a CV/résumé or an application form. In Britain and North America they are usually typed on a single page. A good letter uses formal language and presents some key arguments for why your application should be taken seriously. 简历或申请表须附上附信。在英国和北美，附信通常是一页长。好的附信使用正式语言，提出一些主要理由说明为什么自己的申请应受到重视。

Flat 3
19 Strangelands Road
London
NE23 6ZB
Tel: 0207 337 34589
20 January 2015

Mrs F Hunter
Human Resources Manager
Timson Office Supplies
Unit 5 Males Industrial Estate
Cambridge CB7 9HD

Dear Mrs Hunter

Senior Accounts Clerk

I am writing to apply for the post of senior accounts clerk advertised in the Cambridge Evening News of 17 January.

As you will see from my enclosed CV I am currently an accounts clerk in a medium-sized printing firm. In addition to my normal bookkeeping duties, I am responsible for invoicing and chasing up late payments. I also deal with credit checks on potential customers.

I am committed to pursuing a career in management accounting and am currently studying for further professional qualifications by distance learning. I am particularly interested in your post as it would enable me to gain experience of working in a larger company with the opportunities for professional training and development that this brings. In addition to my skills and experience as an accounts clerk, I would bring to the post a proven ability to deal successfully and tactfully with customers and clients.

I am available for interview for the next three weeks.

I look forward to hearing from you.

Yours sincerely

Adil Desai

Adil Desai
Enc. CV

For advice on layout see Formal letters pages. 有关格式方面的建议，参见“正式信函”页。

The date could also be January 20, 2015, 20/1/15 (*BrE*), or 1/20/15 (*NAmE*). 日期亦可写成 January 20, 2015、20/1/15（英式英语），或 1/20/15（美式英语）。

In a cover letter use the words **post**, **position** or **vacancy**, not *job*. 在附信中使用 post、position 或 vacancy，不用 job。

Avoid contracted forms such as *I'm*. 避免使用缩略形式，如 I'm。

Use **Yours faithfully** here if you have begun Dear Sir or Madam. 如果开头是 Dear Sir or Madam，此处用 Yours faithfully。

Sign your name and print it in full underneath. 签名并在下方打印全名。

Enc. or **encl.** shows you have enclosed something. * enc. 或 encl. 表示有附件。

Key phrases 关键短语

Paragraph 1 states your purpose for writing. Say which job you are applying for and how/where you heard about it. 第1段说明写信目的。说明要申请什么职位以及如何/从何处知悉。

Paragraph 2 outlines your current job and responsibilities. Make it relevant to the post you are applying for. 第2段概述目前的工作和职责。将它与所申请的工作联系起来。

Paragraph 3 says why you want the job and what you can bring to the company. It is very important to say what you can do for them. 第3段说明自己为什么需要这份工作以及能为雇主作出什么贡献。说明自己能为雇主做什么，这很重要。

Paragraph 4 gives other relevant information and when you are available for interview. 第4段给出其他相关信息和可参加面试的时间。

Language bank 用语库

Since graduating from …, I have …

I have considerable/extensive experience in (*the field of …*)

I consider/feel that my qualifications and work experience could/might be of interest to the company.

If called for (*an*) *interview, I would be available at any time convenient for you.*

Please find attached a copy of my curriculum vitae/résumé for your consideration.

I look forward to hearing from you in due course.

Visual Vocabulary Builder Contents
图解词汇扩充目录

V2 City and countryside 城市和乡村
V4 Mountains and coast 山和海滨
V6 The environment 环境
V10 Trees, plants and flowers 树、植物和花
V12 The animal kingdom 动物界
V14 Architecture 建筑设计
V15 Buildings 建筑物
V16 Homes 住宅
V18 House 房屋
V20 Garden / Yard 园圃
V21 DIY and cleaning 自己动手和清洁用具
V22 Living room 客厅
V23 Dining room 饭厅
V24 Bedroom 卧室
V25 Bathroom 浴室
V26 Kitchen 厨房
V28 Cooking 烹饪
V32 Fruit and vegetables 水果和蔬菜
V35 Herbs, spices, nuts and cereals 香草、香料、坚果和谷物
V36 Packaging 包装
V37 Musical instruments 乐器
V41 Toys and games 玩具和游戏
V44 Hobbies 业余爱好
V47 Sports 体育运动
V53 Extreme sports 极限运动
V55 Cycles 自行车；摩托车
V56 Cars 汽车
V57 Aircraft 航空器
V59 Boats and ships 船
V62 Vehicles 车辆
V64 The body 身体
V65 Hair and make-up 发型和化妆品
V66 Clothes 服装
V69 Accessories（服装）配饰
V71 Office 办公室
V72 Classroom 教室
V73 Computing 计算机信息处理技术

City and countryside 城市和乡村

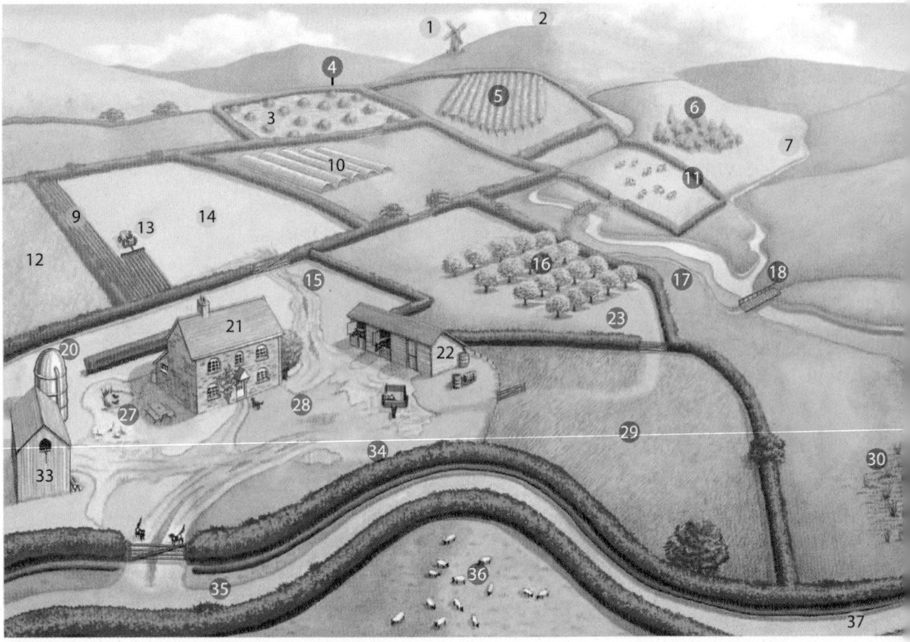

City 城市

1 skyscraper 摩天大楼
2 crane 起重机
3 office block (*BrE*) (*also* office building *especially NAmE*) 办公大楼
4 dome 穹顶
5 museum 博物馆
6 clock tower 钟楼
7 hoarding (*BrE*) (*also* billboard *especially NAmE*) 大幅广告牌
8 cinema (*BrE*) / movie theater (*NAmE*) 电影院
9 banner 旗幡
10 flag 旗
11 flagpole (*also* flagstaff) 旗杆
12 alley (*also* alleyway) 小巷
13 awning 遮阳篷；雨篷
14 fountain 喷泉
15 statue 塑像
16 shopping centre (*BrE*) / shopping center (*NAmE*) 购物中心
17 arcade 拱廊
18 street light 路灯
19 lamp post (*especially BrE*) 灯柱
20 market 集市
21 market stall 集市摊位
22 road sign 路标
23 theatre (*BrE*) / theater (*especially US*) 剧院
24 shop (*BrE*) / store (*NAmE*) 商店
25 cafe (*also* café) 咖啡馆
26 postbox / letter box (*both BrE*) / mailbox (*NAmE*) 邮筒
27 busker 街头艺人
28 traffic lights (*NAmE also* stoplights) 交通信号灯
29 bollard 路桩
30 litter bin (*BrE*) / trash can (*NAmE*) 垃圾箱
31 pedestrian precinct (*BrE*) / pedestrian mall (*NAmE*) 步行区
32 taxi rank (*BrE*) (*also* taxi stand *especially NAmE*) 出租汽车站
33 railings 栏杆
34 pavement (*BrE*) / sidewalk (*NAmE*) 人行道
35 kerb (*BrE*) / curb (*NAmE*) 路缘
36 parking meter (*also* meter) 停车计时器
37 pedestrian crossing (*BrE*) / crosswalk (*NAmE*) 人行横道
38 cycle lane (*BrE*) / bicycle lane (*NAmE*) 自行车道
39 bus stop 公交车站
40 high street (*BrE*) / main street (*NAmE*) 大街

Countryside 乡村

1 windmill 风车
2 hill 山丘
3 hay 干草
4 haystack 干草堆
5 vineyard 葡萄园
6 copse (*also* coppice) 矮林
7 stream 溪流
8 wood (*also* woods) 树林
9 furrow 犁沟
10 polytunnel 塑料大棚
11 pasture 牧场
12 crops 作物
13 tractor 拖拉机
14 field 农田
15 farmyard 农家庭院
16 orchard 果园
17 footpath 人行小道
18 footbridge 人行桥
19 stile 梯磴
20 silo 筒仓
21 farmhouse 农舍
22 stable 马厩
23 hedge 树篱
24 signpost 路标
25 village green (*BrE*) 村镇公用绿地
26 village 村庄
27 duck pond 养鸭池
28 farm 农场
29 meadow 草地
30 marsh 沼泽
31 reeds 芦苇
32 fence 篱笆
33 barn 谷仓
34 hedgerow 矮树篱
35 ditch 沟渠
36 livestock 家畜
37 lane 小路
38 bridge 桥
39 river 河
40 riverbank 河岸

Mountains and coast 山和海滨

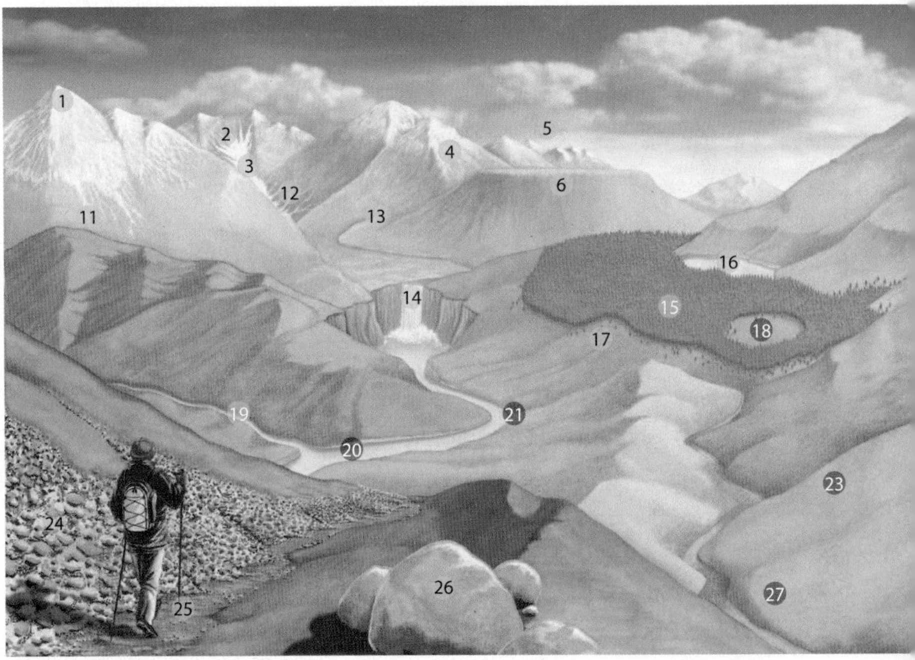

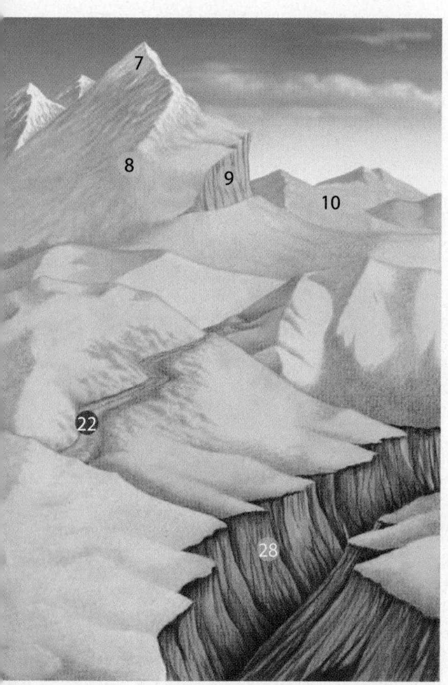

Mountains 山

1 summit 山顶
2 ridge 山脊
3 glacier 冰川
4 snow 雪
5 mountain range 山脉
6 plateau 高原
7 peak 山峰
8 mountain 山
9 precipice 峭壁
10 foothills 山麓小丘
11 snowline 雪线
12 ice 冰
13 source 源头
14 waterfall 瀑布
15 forest 森林
16 lake 湖泊
17 conifers 针叶林
18 clearing (*also* glade) 林中空地
19 tributary 支流
20 river 河
21 meander 河曲
22 pass 山口
23 slope 斜坡
24 scree 碎石坡
25 track 小路
26 boulder 巨石
27 valley 山谷
28 gorge (*also* canyon) 峡谷

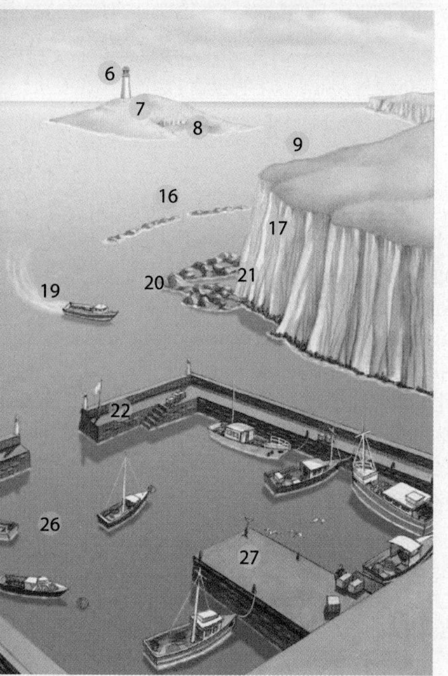

Coast 海滨

1 coastal path 海滨小道
2 cave 洞穴
3 headland (*also* promontory) 岬角
4 horizon 地平线
5 sea (*BrE*) / ocean (*NAmE*) 海
6 lighthouse 灯塔
7 island 岛
8 cove 小海湾
9 clifftop 悬崖顶
10 dune (*also* sand dune) 沙丘
11 estuary （入海的）河口
12 wave 海浪
13 spit 沙嘴
14 crest 波峰
15 foam 泡沫
16 reef 礁
17 cliff 悬崖
18 sandbank 沙洲
19 wake 尾流
20 rocks 岩石
21 rock pool (*BrE*) / tide pool (*NAmE*) 岩石区潮水潭
22 quay 码头
23 beach 海滩
24 bay 海湾
25 shingle 卵石滩
26 harbour (*BrE*) / harbor (*NAmE*) 港湾
27 jetty (*NAmE also* dock) 栈桥
28 sand 沙滩
29 seashore 海岸

The environment 环境

Causes of the greenhouse effect 温室效应的原因

- **Carbon dioxide** is produced by **vehicle exhaust fumes** (1) and by **burning fossil fuels** (2) from power plants (*BrE also* power stations), factories and homes. This causes temperatures to rise. Trees, which absorb carbon dioxide, are felled by logging, causing **deforestation** (3). 二氧化碳（carbon dioxide）是由车辆排放的废气（vehicle exhaust fumes）（图示1）和发电厂、工厂、住宅燃烧的化石燃料（burning fossil fuels）（图示2）产生的。这导致气温上升。吸收二氧化碳的树木遭到砍伐，森林被毁坏（deforestation）（图示3）。
- **Nitrogen oxide** comes from vehicles and power plants, and from agricultural fertilizers and pesticides used in **intensive farming** (4). 氮氧化合物（nitrogen oxide）来自车辆和发电厂，还来自用于集约耕作（intensive farming）（图示4）的农业化肥和杀虫剂。
- Many **household products**, such as **refrigerators and aerosols**, emit **CFCs (chlorofluorocarbons)** which damage the ozone layer. 许多家用

产品（household product），如冰箱（refrigerator）和喷雾器（aerosol），会排放破坏臭氧层的氯氟烃（CFC，或 chlorofluorocarbon）。

- **Methane gas** is released from household and industrial waste in **landfill sites** (5), and also from **cattle** (6). 处理生活垃圾和工业废物的填埋场（landfill site）（图示5），还有牛（cattle）（图示6），都会排放沼气（methane gas）。
- Sunlight causes these **greenhouse gases** to undergo **chemical change** and react with **water vapour** (*BrE*) (*especially US* **vapor**), creating **acid rain.** 这些温室气体（greenhouse gas）经阳光照射发生化学变化（chemical change）并与水蒸气（water vapour/vapor）发生反应，产生了酸雨（acid rain）。

Acid rain 酸雨

- **Acid rain** (7) falls on leaves and bark, damaging trees and plants in **forests. Nutrients** are **leached out** of the soil, and plants die. 酸雨（acid rain）（图示7）落到叶子和树皮上，毁坏森林（forest）里的树木和植物。土壤中的养分（nutrient）被淋失（leached out），造成植物死亡。
- **Acid levels** build up in **lakes** and **rivers** (8), poisoning and killing fish. 湖泊（lake）和河流（river）（图示8）中的含酸量（acid level）上升，使鱼中毒和死亡。
- **Acid corrosion** attacks buildings, eating away at metal, stone and wood. 酸腐蚀（acid corrosion）损坏建筑物，腐蚀金属、石料和木料。
- **Pollution** from **smog** (9) causes **respiratory diseases** such as **asthma** and **bronchitis.** 烟雾（smog）（图示9）污染（pollution）引发呼吸道疾病（respiratory disease），如哮喘（asthma）和支气管炎（bronchitis）。

Global warming 全球气候变暖

- **Global warming** can cause **climate change** and **environmental disaster.** Long-term changes in **temperature, wind, pressure, precipitation** (rain and snow) and **humidity** present challenges to our survival. 全球气候变暖（global warming）可导致气候变化（climate change）和环境灾难（environmental disaster）。气温（temperature）、风（wind）、气压（pressure）、降水（precipitation，即雨和雪）以及湿度（humidity）的长期变化对我们的生存构成挑战。
- **Environmental degradation**, such as **desertification** and **desiccation,** creates problems in many parts of the world. 沙漠化（desertification）和干燥（desiccation）等环境恶化（environmental degradation）给世界上许多地区带来了问题。
- **Rising temperatures** cause **ice caps** to **melt. Rising sea levels** lead to coastal and river **flooding** and **erosion.** 日益上升的气温（rising temperature）造成冰盖（ice cap）融化（melt），逐渐上升的海平面（rising sea level）导致沿海和河岸地区发生洪灾（flooding）与侵蚀（erosion）。
- **Extreme events** occur, such as **storms, drought, forest fires, soil erosion, landslides, avalanches, tsunamis** and the sudden appearance of **pests** and **diseases.** 极端恶劣的情况（extreme event）发生，例如风暴（storm）、干旱（drought）、森林大火（forest fire）、土壤侵蚀（soil erosion）、滑坡（landslide）、雪崩（avalanche）、海啸（tsunami）以及突然出现害虫（pest）和疾病（disease）。

SOME RECYCLABLE MATERIALS 一些可回收材料

- batteries 电池
- cans 金属罐
- cardboard 硬纸板
- engine oil 发动机油
- fluorescent tubes 荧光灯管
- glass 玻璃
- organic garden waste 园林有机废弃物
- paper 纸
- plastic bottles 塑料瓶
- scrap metal 废金属
- textiles 纺织品
- timber 木材

Solutions and sustainability 解决办法和可持续性

- **Wind turbines** (1), **solar power** and **hydroelectric power** (2) provide **alternative sources of energy** that are **renewable** and do not pollute the air. 风力发电机（wind turbine）（图示1）、太阳能（solar power）和水力发电（hydroelectric power）（图示2）提供可再生（renewable）且不污染空气的替代能源（alternative source of energy）。
- In the home, **solar panels** (3), **insulation, energy-efficient light bulbs** and **biodegradable products** are **environmentally friendly.** Rubbish can be sorted for **recycling in bins** (4) and **bottle banks** (5), and **biodegradable waste** becomes **compost** (6). 在家中，太阳能电池板（solar panel）（图示3）、隔热材料（insulation）、节能灯（energy-efficient light bulb）和可生物降解的产品（biodegradable product）均对环境无害（environmentally friendly）。垃圾可分类放进垃圾箱（bin）（图示4）和旧瓶回收箱（bottle bank）（图示5）供回收（recycle），可生物降解的废品（biodegradable waste）可变成堆肥（compost）（图示6）。
- Using a **bicycle** (7), an **electric car** (8) or **public transport** (9) helps to **reduce carbon emissions.** Avoiding long-distance travel and buying local, seasonal food with **low food miles** reduces your **carbon footprint.** 骑自行车（bicycle）（图示7）、开电动车（electric car）（图示8）或使用公共交通（public transport）（图示9）有助于减少碳排放（reduce carbon emission）。避免长距离旅行和购买食物里程短（low food mile）的本地时令食物可减少碳足迹（carbon footprint）。
- **Reforestation** (10) and **organic farming** (11) help to restore the earth's balance. Trees give off **oxygen,** absorb **carbon dioxide** and provide **habitats for wildlife. Organic farming is chemical-free.** 重新造林（reforestation）（图示10）和有机耕作（organic farming）（图示11）有助于恢复地球的平衡。树木释放氧气（oxygen）、吸收二氧化碳（carbon dioxide）并为野生动物提供栖息地（habitat for wildlife）。有机耕作不使用化学制品（chemical-free）。

Trees, plants and flowers 树、植物和花

Trees 树

foliage 枝叶
twig 细枝
blossom 花朵
bud 花蕾
leaf 叶
branch 树枝
limb 大枝
trunk 树干
twig 细枝
roots 根
tree 树
rings 年轮
wood 木
bark 树皮
log 原木

Evergreen trees 常青树

berry 浆果
palm 棕榈树
yew 紫杉
cone (BrE also fir cone) 球果
needles 针叶
fir 冷杉

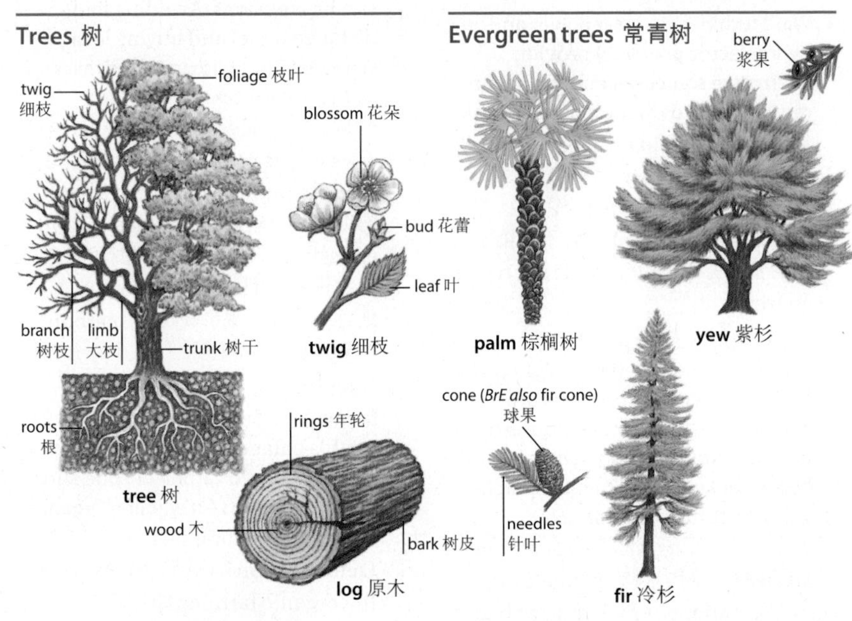

Deciduous trees 落叶树

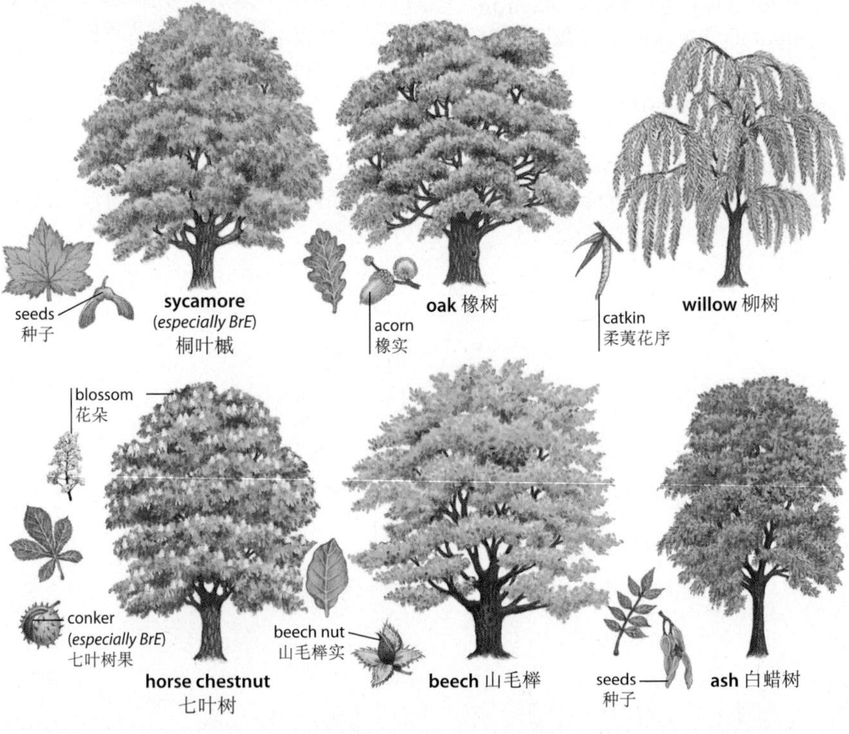

seeds 种子
sycamore (especially BrE) 桐叶槭
oak 橡树
acorn 橡实
catkin 柔荑花序
willow 柳树
blossom 花朵
conker (especially BrE) 七叶树果
horse chestnut 七叶树
beech nut 山毛榉实
beech 山毛榉
seeds 种子
ash 白蜡树

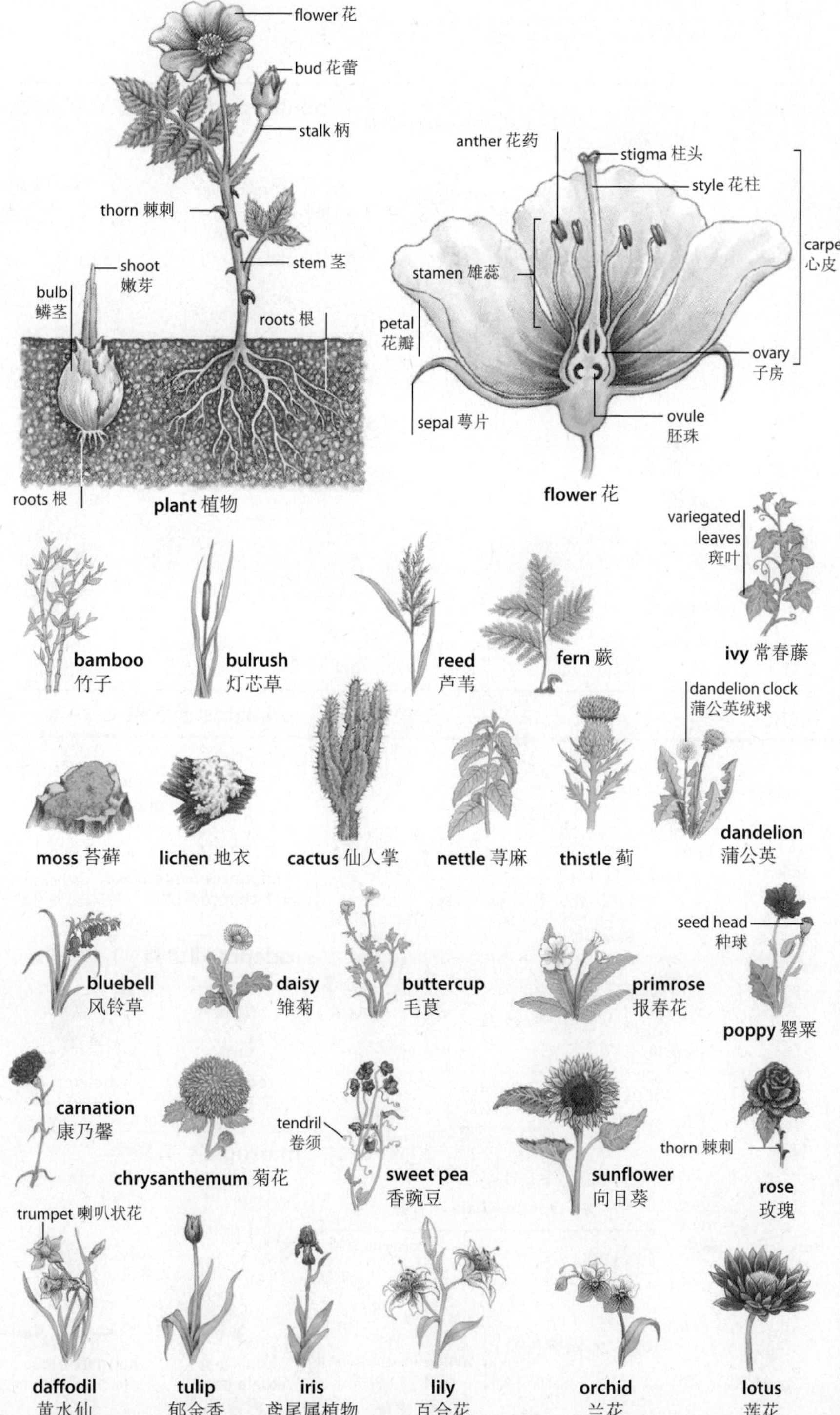
flower 花
bud 花蕾
stalk 柄
thorn 棘刺
stem 茎
shoot 嫩芽
bulb 鳞茎
roots 根
roots 根
plant 植物
anther 花药
stigma 柱头
style 花柱
carpel 心皮
stamen 雄蕊
petal 花瓣
ovary 子房
sepal 萼片
ovule 胚珠
flower 花
variegated leaves 斑叶
bamboo 竹子
bulrush 灯芯草
reed 芦苇
fern 蕨
ivy 常春藤
dandelion clock 蒲公英绒球
moss 苔藓
lichen 地衣
cactus 仙人掌
nettle 荨麻
thistle 蓟
dandelion 蒲公英
seed head 种球
bluebell 风铃草
daisy 雏菊
buttercup 毛茛
primrose 报春花
poppy 罂粟
carnation 康乃馨
chrysanthemum 菊花
tendril 卷须
sweet pea 香豌豆
sunflower 向日葵
thorn 棘刺
rose 玫瑰
trumpet 喇叭状花
daffodil 黄水仙
tulip 郁金香
iris 鸢尾属植物
lily 百合花
orchid 兰花
lotus 莲花

The animal kingdom 动物界

Birds 鸟类
webbed foot 蹼足
talons (猛禽的) 爪
toe 脚趾
claw 爪
beak / bill 喙
wing 翅膀
tail 尾巴
finch 雀
crest 羽冠
feather 羽毛
nest 鸟巢
egg 鸟蛋
poultry and game 家禽和野禽
pheasant 野鸡
duck 鸭
turkey 火鸡
chicken 鸡
birds of prey 猛禽
golden eagle 金雕
carrion 腐肉
vulture 秃鹫
barn owl 仓鸮
seabirds 海鸟
gull 海鸥
albatross 信天翁
puffin 海鹦
Mammals 哺乳类
coat 皮毛
mane 鬣毛
tail 尾
lion 狮子
paw 爪
claw 脚趾
muzzle (狗马等) 口鼻部
snout (猪等) 口鼻部
whisker 须
antlers 鹿角
horn 角
hooves 蹄
primates 灵长类
chimpanzee (also informal chimp) 黑猩猩
spider monkey 蜘蛛猴
prehensile tail 长卷尾
rodents 啮齿类
red squirrel 红松鼠
beaver 河狸
cetacean 鲸类
blowhole 呼吸孔
sperm whale 抹香鲸
tusk 长牙
trunk 象鼻
bat 蝙蝠
Fish 鱼类
tail 尾
dorsal fin 背鳍
gill 鳃
scales 鳞
anal fin 臀鳍
ventral fin 腹鳍
pectoral fin 胸鳍
trout 鳟鱼
marsupials 有袋类
eucalyptus tree 桉树
koala (also koala bear) 树袋熊
joey 幼袋鼠
pouch 育儿袋
kangaroo (also informal roo) 袋鼠

Amphibians 两栖类

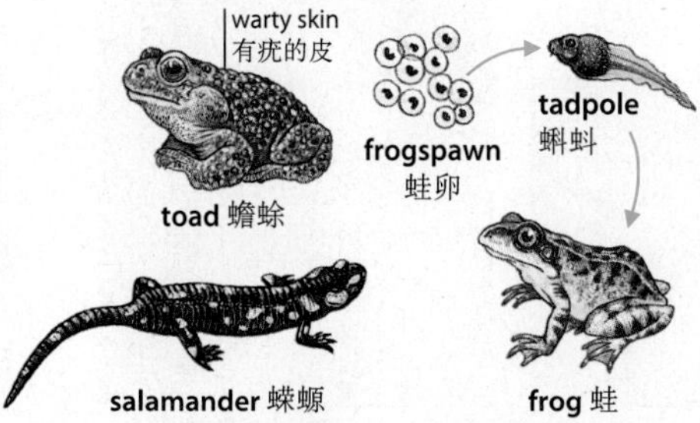

warty skin 有疣的皮

toad 蟾蜍

frogspawn 蛙卵

tadpole 蝌蚪

frog 蛙

salamander 蝾螈

Reptiles 爬行类

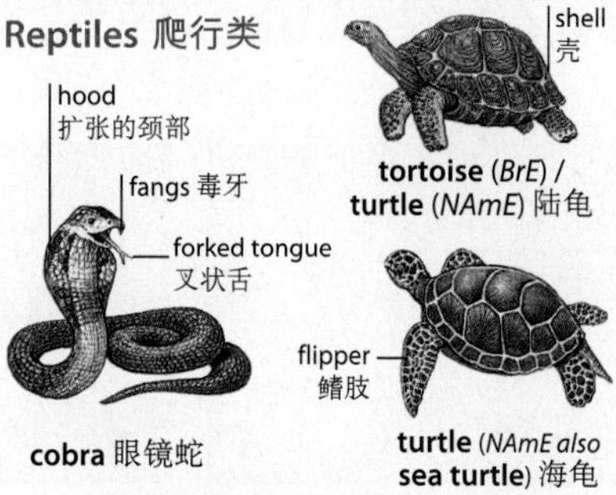

hood 扩张的颈部

fangs 毒牙

forked tongue 叉状舌

cobra 眼镜蛇

shell 壳

tortoise (*BrE*) / **turtle** (*NAmE*) 陆龟

flipper 鳍肢

turtle (*NAmE also* **sea turtle**) 海龟

Insects 昆虫类

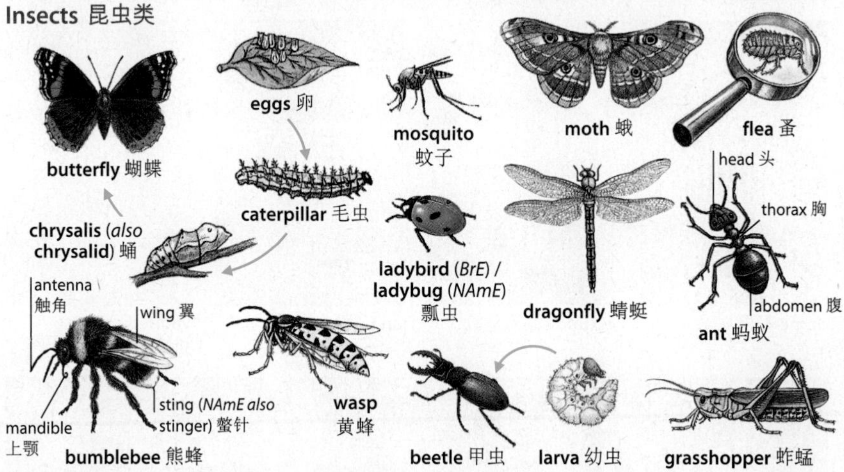

butterfly 蝴蝶

eggs 卵

mosquito 蚊子

moth 蛾

flea 蚤

caterpillar 毛虫

chrysalis (*also* **chrysalid**) 蛹

ladybird (*BrE*) / **ladybug** (*NAmE*) 瓢虫

dragonfly 蜻蜓

head 头

thorax 胸

abdomen 腹

ant 蚂蚁

antenna 触角

wing 翼

sting (*NAmE also* stinger) 螫针

mandible 上颚

bumblebee 熊蜂

wasp 黄蜂

beetle 甲虫

larva 幼虫

grasshopper 蚱蜢

Crustaceans 甲壳类

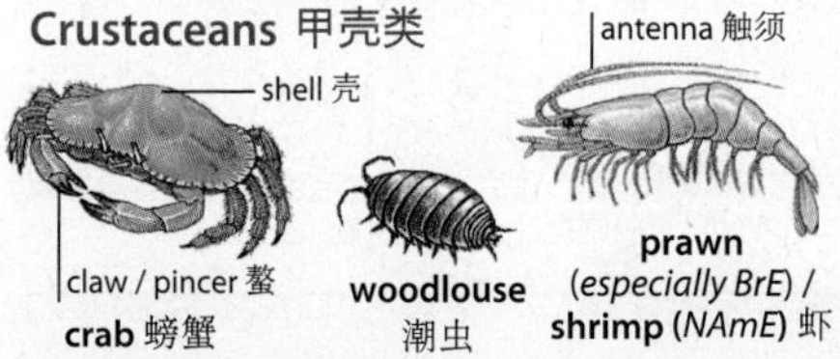

shell 壳

claw / pincer 螯

crab 螃蟹

woodlouse 潮虫

antenna 触须

prawn (*especially BrE*) / **shrimp** (*NAmE*) 虾

Arachnids 蛛形类

tick 蜱

sting (*NAmE also* stinger) 螫针

scorpion 蝎子

web 蜘蛛网

spider 蜘蛛

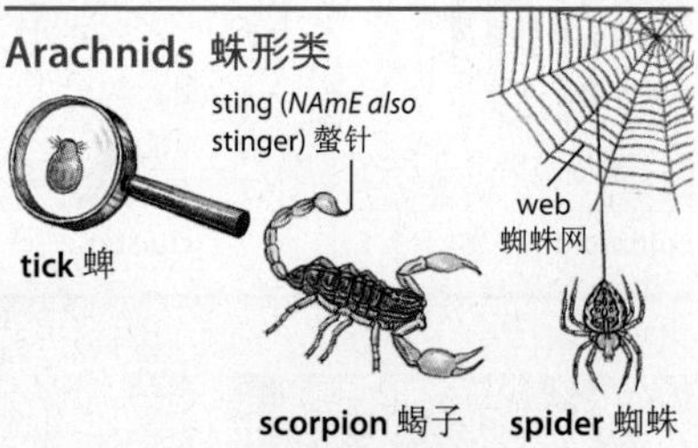

Taxonomy 分类学

Living things are grouped on the basis of their similarities and differences into smaller and smaller groups. This scientific process of classification is called **taxonomy**. The main groups, from the largest to the smallest, are 生物根据其异同逐级分类，这种科学的分类过程叫做分类学（taxonomy）。生物从大到小的主要类别有：

- **kingdom** (animal or plant) 界（动物或植物）
- **phylum** (*plural* **phyla**) (e.g. mollusc, arthropod) 门（例如：软体动物、节肢动物）
- **class** (e.g. mammal, gastropod, insect) 纲（例如：哺乳动物、腹足动物、昆虫）
- **order** (e.g. primate, marsupial) 目（例如：灵长目动物、有袋目动物）
- **family** 科
- **genus** (*plural* **genera**) 属
- **species** 种

Gastropods 腹足类

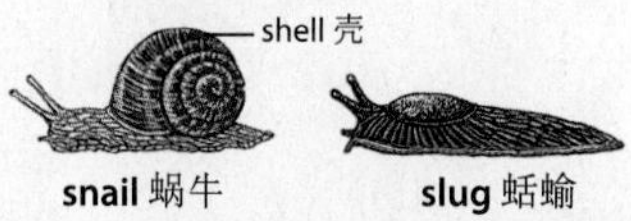

shell 壳

snail 蜗牛

slug 蛞蝓

Cephalopod 头足类

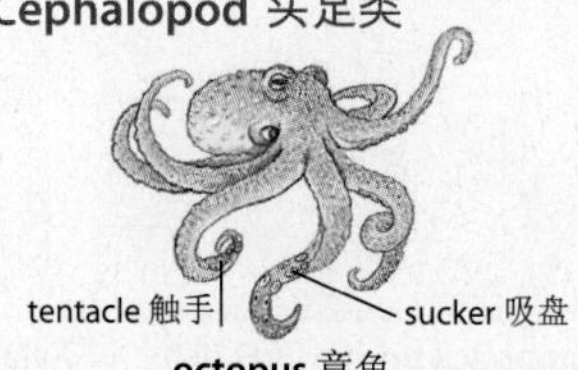

octopus 章鱼

Architecture 建筑设计

geodesic dome 短程线穹顶

gargoyle 滴水兽

obelisk 方尖碑 pedestal 基座

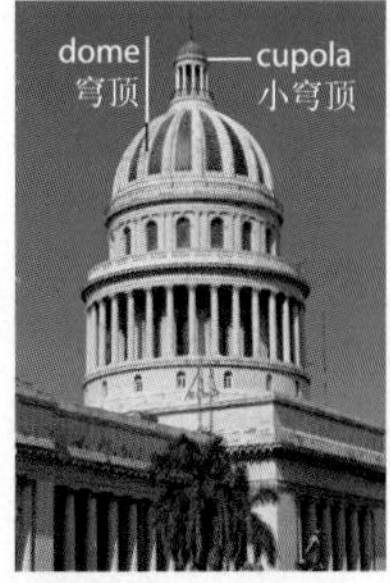

dome 穹顶

rotunda 圆形建筑

arch 拱

vaulted ceiling 拱形天花板

colonnade 柱廊

cloister 回廊

portico 门廊

Bridges 桥

humpback bridge (*BrE*) 拱桥

suspension bridge 悬索桥

cantilever bridge 悬臂桥

viaduct 高架桥

aqueduct 渡槽

Buildings
建筑物

amphitheatre 圆形露天剧场

fort 堡垒

palace 宫殿

castle 城堡

stately home 豪华大宅

glasshouse 温室

pyramid（古埃及）金字塔

log cabin 原木小屋

pub (*BrE*) 酒吧

warehouse 仓库

lighthouse 灯塔

oil rig / oil platform 钻油平台

hut 棚屋

barn 谷仓

pagoda 佛塔

Work connected with building 与建筑有关的工作

	person 人员	work – all [U] 工作（均为不可数名词）
building houses and other buildings 建房屋:	**builder** 建筑工人	**building** 建筑
designing buildings 设计房屋:	**architect** 建筑师	**architecture** 建筑设计
designing roads and bridges, etc. 设计公路、桥梁等:	**civil engineer** 土木工程师	**civil engineering** 土木工程
building walls, etc. with bricks 用砖砌墙等:	**bricklayer** 砌砖工	**bricklaying** 砌砖
repairing or building roofs 修或盖屋顶:	**roofer** 盖屋顶工人	**roofing** 盖屋顶
making doors and window frames from wood 用木材做门窗:	**joiner** 细木工人	**joinery** 细木工作
making and repairing wooden objects and structures 制作或修理木制品和木结构:	**carpenter** 木匠	**carpentry** 木工制作
fitting glass into the frames of windows, etc. 给窗户等安装玻璃:	**glazier** 镶玻璃工人	**glazing** 玻璃装配
putting plaster on walls 用灰泥抹墙:	**plasterer** 抹灰工人	**plastering** 抹灰泥
fitting and repairing water pipes, toilets, etc. 安装和修理水管、抽水马桶等:	**plumber** 管子工	**plumbing** 管道工程
connecting, repairing, etc. electrical equipment 接通、修理电器设备:	**electrician** 电工	**wiring** 布线工作

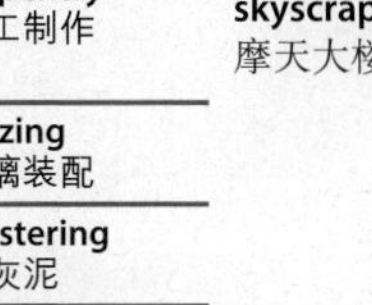
skyscraper 摩天大楼

Homes
住宅

semi-detached house (*BrE*)
半独立式住宅

duplex (*especially NAmE*)
二联式住宅

town house (*BrE*) 联排式住宅

row house (*NAmE*) 联排式住宅

terraced house (*BrE*) 联排式住宅

block of flats (*BrE*) 公寓大楼

fire escape 太平梯

apartment building (*NAmE*)
公寓大楼

bungalow (*BrE*) 平房

thatch
茅草屋顶

thatched cottage 茅屋

mobile home (*especially NAmE*)
活动住房

houseboat 水上住宅

Other types of home 其他类型的住宅

- **Duplex** (*especially NAmE*) has two meanings: it is a building divided into two separate homes, each with its own entrance, or it is a flat/an apartment with rooms on two floors, with a shared entrance from the street. * duplex（二联式住宅 / 复式住宅）有两种含义：一是指分隔为两个独立住宅的一栋房子，它们有各自的大门；二是指跨两层的单元房，它们共用一个临街入口。
- An apartment building or group of houses in which each flat/apartment/house is owned by the person living in it but the building and shared areas are owned by everyone together is a **condominium** (*especially NAmE*) (*also informal* **condo**). * condominium（非正式亦作 condo）指一种公寓大楼或一组住房，每套住房各有其主，但整个大楼及公用场地属业主共有。
- A flat/an apartment with rooms on two floors, and usually its own entrance from the street, is a **maisonette** (*BrE*). * maisonette（两层独立公寓）指房间分为两层，通常有自己的临街入口。
- A house built on one level, that is very wide but not very deep from front to back, and has a roof that is not very steep, is a **ranch house** (*NAmE*) – compare **bungalow.** * ranch house（平房住宅）指一种单层住房，正面很宽，但纵深并不大，屋顶较平缓。比较 bungalow。
- A very large house is a **mansion.** * mansion 指公馆、宅第。
- An expensive and comfortable flat/apartment at the top of a tall building is a **penthouse.** * penthouse 指高层建筑顶层的豪华公寓。
- A set of rooms for an old person, especially in a relative's house, is called a **granny flat** (*BrE*)/**in-law apartment/mother-in-law apartment** (*both NAmE*). * granny flat/in-law apartment/mother-in-law apartment 尤指亲戚家中留出的老人套间。

House 房屋

1 chimney pot 烟囱管帽
2 chimney 烟囱
3 aerial (*especially BrE*) / antenna (*NAmE, BrE*) 天线
4 ridge 屋脊
5 gable 山墙
6 roof 屋顶
7 skylight 天窗
8 dormer window 屋顶窗
9 eaves 屋檐
10 burglar alarm 防盗铃
11 gutter 檐沟
12 drainpipe (*NAmE also* downspout) 雨水管
13 shutter 活动护窗
14 windowpane 窗玻璃
15 sash window 垂直推拉窗
16 casement window 平开窗
17 balcony 阳台
18 window box 窗口花坛
19 windowsill 窗台
20 porch 门廊
21 tile 瓦
22 hanging basket 吊花篮
23 door knocker 门环
24 French window (*BrE*) / French door (*NAmE*) 落地窗
25 bay window 凸窗
26 letter box (*BrE*) / mail slot (*NAmE*) 信箱
27 front door 正门
28 wall 墙
29 garage 车库
30 brick 砖
31 doorstep 门阶
32 basement 地下室
33 step 台阶
34 drive (*also* driveway) 车道

Where you live 住处

- The area surrounding a house is the **neighbourhood** (*BrE*) / **neighborhood** (*NAmE*). * neighbourhood/neighborhood 指邻里。
- A person who lives next or near to you is your **neighbour** (*BrE*) / **neighbor** (*NAmE*). * neighbour/neighbor 指邻居。

  The next house, room or building is **next door.** * next door 指隔壁：
  ▸ *our next-door neighbours* 我们隔壁的邻居
- An area where people live that is outside the main part of a city or town is called a **suburb**, or **the suburbs**. The adjective is **suburban.** * suburb 或 the suburbs 指郊区、城外，形容词为 suburban：
  ▸ *suburban houses/streets* 郊区住宅/街道
- An area where a large number of houses are planned and built as a group is called an **estate** or a **development.** * estate 或 development 指住宅区、开发区：
  ▸ *a new housing estate/development* 新建住宅区
- If you go and live in another house, you **move**, or **move house.** You **move in/move into** a new house, then **move out/move out of** it when you stop living there. * move 或 move house 指搬家、搬迁；move in/move into 指搬入（新居）；move out/move out of 指搬出、迁出。

Buying or renting a house 买房或租房

- A house that is available to buy is **for sale** or **on the market.** * for sale 或 on the market 指待售、供出售：
  ▸ *This property has been on the market for about six weeks.* 这房产已在市场上放售约六周了。
- A person whose job is to buy and sell houses and land for other people is an **estate agent** (*BrE*) / **real estate agent** (*NAmE*). * estate agent/real estate agent 指房地产经纪人。
- When you borrow money from a bank or building society in order to buy a house, you **take out a mortgage.** * take out a mortgage 指取得按揭贷款，即从银行或房屋互助协会贷款购房。
- If you pay money for the use of a room, house, etc., you **rent** it (**from** sb). The money that you pay, probably each month, is **rent.** The person who rents a room, house, etc. is a **tenant** and the person who owns the property is a **landlord** (or **landlady** if it is a woman). * rent (from sb) 指（向某人）租用（房间、房屋等），房屋租金（有可能是一月一付）叫 rent，租用房屋等的房客或租户叫 tenant，拥有房地产的房东或地主叫 landlord 或 landlady（女）：
  ▸ *The landlord has put the rent up again.* 房东又把租金提高了。

Garden (*BrE*) / Yard (*NAmE*) 园圃

1 greenhouse 温室
2 shed 棚屋
3 hedge 树篱
4 bird table (*BrE*) / bird feeder (*NAmE*) 鸟食平台
5 parasol / sunshade 大遮阳伞
6 conservatory (*BrE*) 暖房
7 pergola 蔓藤架
8 climber 攀缘植物
9 gate 门
10 fence 篱笆
11 sunlounger (*BrE*) (*also* lounger *BrE, NAmE*) 日光浴椅
12 deckchair 帆布折叠椅
13 barbecue (*also* BBQ) （户外烧烤）烤架
14 water butt (*BrE*) / rain barrel (*NAmE*) 雨水桶
15 bench 长椅
16 trellis 攀缘架
17 stake 篱笆桩
18 deck 木制平台
19 flowerpot 花盆
20 patio 露台
21 planter 花盆
22 flower bed 花坛
23 compost bin 堆肥箱
24 border 狭长花坛
25 lawn 草坪
26 cane 茎
27 water feature 人工水景
28 pond 水池
29 cold frame (*also* frame) 冷床
30 seedling 幼苗
31 cloche 玻璃罩
32 vegetable patch / vegetable plot 小块菜地

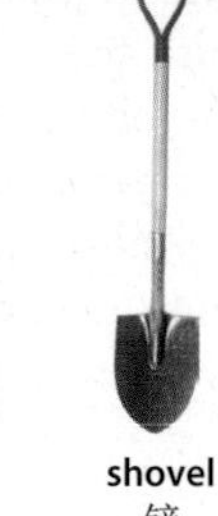

rakes 耙子
fork 叉
hoe 锄头
spade 锹
shovel 铲
trowel 小铲子
hand fork 小叉子

lawnmower (*also* **mower**) 割草机
wheelbarrow (*also* **barrow**) 独轮手推车
hose (*also* **hosepipe**) 橡皮管
watering can 洒水壶
Strimmer™ (*BrE*) 草坪修剪器
sprinkler 喷洒器

DIY and cleaning 自己动手和清洁用具

Tools 工具
claw 拔钉爪
hammer 锤子
bit 钻头
chuck 夹盘
plane 刨子
drill 电钻
handsaw 手锯
blade 刃
coping saw
手弓锯
mallet 木槌
screwdriver 螺丝刀
head 钉头
bradawl 锥钻
hacksaw 钢锯
bolt 螺栓
thread
螺纹
file 锉刀
nut 螺帽
chisel 凿子
nail
钉子
screw
螺丝钉
washer
垫圈
spanner (BrE) /
wrench (especially NAmE) 扳手
vice (especially BrE) /
vise (especially NAmE) 台钳
spirit level 气泡式水准仪
blade 刀片
scissors
剪刀
adjustable spanner (BrE) /
monkey wrench (especially
NAmE) 活动扳手
toolbox
工具箱
Cleaning
清洁用具
penknife 小折刀
wire cutters 钢丝钳
pliers 夹钳
Decorating 粉刷用具
rung 横档
mop
拖把
bucket
(NAmE also pail) 水桶
feather
duster
羽毛掸子
broom
扫把
squeegee mop
胶棉拖把
dustpan and brush
簸箕和刷子
duster
抹布
step
梯级
ladder
梯子
stepladder 折梯
squeegee
橡皮刮水刷
iron
熨斗
rubber gloves
橡胶手套
vacuum cleaner
(BrE also Hoover™)
真空吸尘器
ironing board 烫衣板
roller
滚筒式油漆刷
paintbrushes
漆刷

Living room 客厅

1 MP3 player * MP3 播放器
2 docking station 扩展坞
3 waste-paper basket (*BrE*) / wastebasket (*NAmE*) 废纸篓
4 mantelpiece (*also* mantel *especially NAmE*) 壁炉台
5 fire surround 壁炉框
6 fireplace 壁炉
7 grate 炉箅
8 hearth 炉前地面
9 houseplant (*BrE also* pot plant) 室内盆栽植物
10 plant pot 花盆
11 armchair 扶手椅
12 rug 地毯
13 shelf 搁板
14 bookcase 书柜
15 flat-screen TV 平板电视
16 vase 花瓶
17 coaster 玻璃杯垫
18 footstool 脚凳
19 coffee table 茶几
20 remote control 遥控器
21 radiator 暖气片
22 magazine rack 报刊架
23 recliner 躺椅
24 scatter cushion (*BrE*) / throw pillow (*NAmE*) 小靠垫
25 throw 沙发罩
26 sofa / couch 长沙发
27 occasional table 临时茶几
28 floorboards 木地板

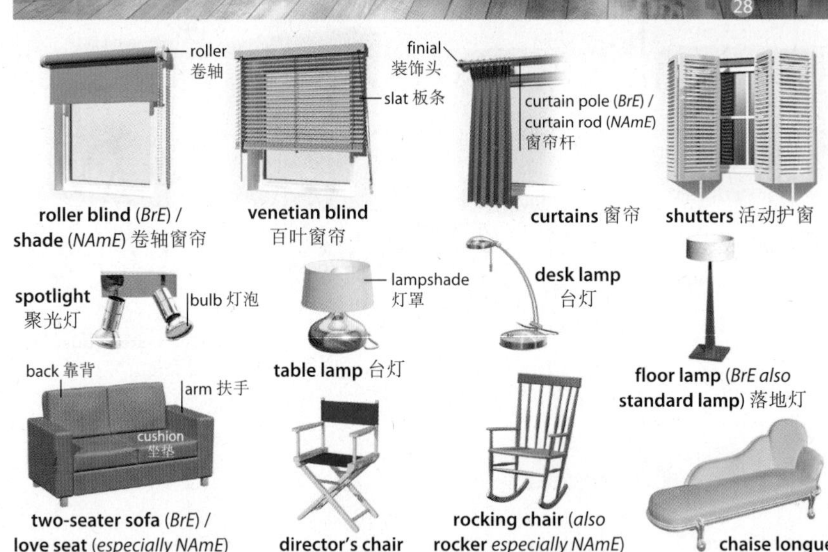

roller blind (*BrE*) / **shade** (*NAmE*) 卷轴窗帘

venetian blind 百叶窗帘

curtains 窗帘

shutters 活动护窗

spotlight 聚光灯

table lamp 台灯

desk lamp 台灯

floor lamp (*BrE also* **standard lamp**) 落地灯

two-seater sofa (*BrE*) / **love seat** (*especially NAmE*) 双人沙发

director's chair 轻便折叠椅

rocking chair (*also* **rocker** *especially NAmE*) 摇椅

chaise longue 躺椅

Dining room 饭厅

1 fruit bowl 水果盆
2 cheeseboard 干酪切板
3 cheese knife 干酪刀
4 sideboard 餐具柜
5 drawer 抽屉
6 cutlery (*especially BrE*) / flatware (*NAmE*) 餐具（刀、叉和匙）
7 napkin 餐巾
8 bowl 碗
9 plate 盘子
10 side plate 面包盘
11 glass 玻璃杯
12 pepper pot (*especially BrE*) / pepper shaker (*NAmE*) 胡椒瓶
13 salt cellar (*BrE*) / salt shaker (*NAmE*) 小盐瓶
14 serving dish 餐盘
15 lid 盖子
16 candlestick 蜡烛台
17 carafe （喇叭口）饮料瓶
18 dining chair 餐椅
19 high chair 高脚椅
20 dining table 餐桌
21 tablecloth 桌布

Bedroom 卧室

1 bedside table (*especially BrE*) (*NAmE usually* nightstand, night table) 床头柜
2 clock radio 收音机闹钟
3 headboard 床头板
4 pillow 枕头
5 pillowcase 枕头套
6 bottom sheet 床单
7 double bed 双人床
8 duvet 羽绒被
9 en-suite (*BrE, from French*) (卧室的) 配套浴室
10 built-in/fitted wardrobe (*BrE*) / closet (*especially NAmE*) 壁橱
11 rail 横杆
12 hanger 衣架
13 chest of drawers (*NAmE also* bureau, dresser) 五斗橱
14 drawer 抽屉
15 full-length mirror 全身镜
16 mirror 镜子
17 dressing table (*NAmE also* vanity) 梳妆台
18 stool 凳子
19 fitted carpet (*BrE*) / wall-to-wall carpet (*NAmE*) 满铺地毯
20 rug 小地毯

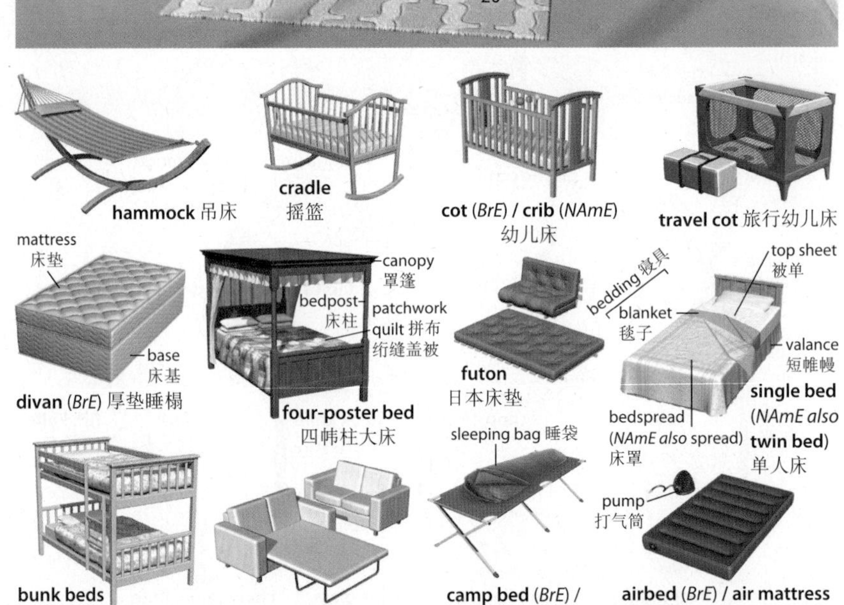

Bathroom 浴室

1 bathroom cabinet 浴室柜
2 beaker 塑料杯
3 mixer tap 冷热水混合龙头
4 washbasin 洗脸盆
5 soap dispenser 皂液瓶
6 flannel (*BrE*) / washcloth (*NAmE*) 毛巾
7 vanity unit (*BrE*) 组合式盥洗盆
8 shower cubicle 淋浴间
9 shower head 淋浴喷头
10 soap dish 肥皂盘
11 shower tray 淋浴间底盘
12 plughole (*BrE*) / drain (*US*) 排水孔
13 towel rail (*BrE*) / towel rack (*NAmE*) 毛巾架
14 hand towel 擦手巾
15 bath towel 浴巾
16 bathroom scales 浴室秤
17 bath (*BrE*) / bathtub (*especially NAmE*) 浴缸
18 bath mat 浴室脚垫
19 tiling 瓷砖面
20 bath panel 浴缸裙板
21 tap (*especially BrE*) / faucet (*NAmE*) 水龙头
22 bathrobe (*also* robe) 浴衣
23 bidet 坐浴盆
24 toilet 坐便器
25 cistern 水箱
26 toilet paper 卫生纸

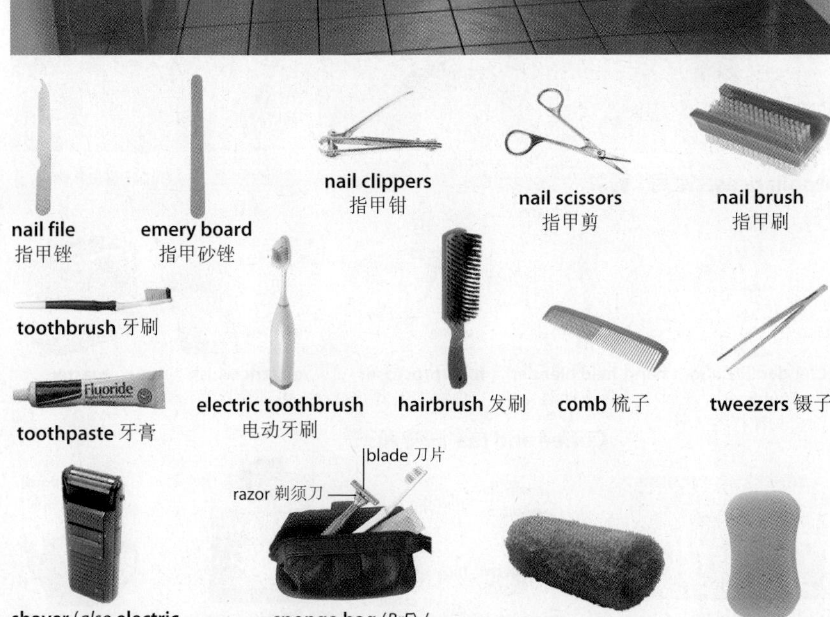

sponge 海绵块

Kitchen 厨房

1 worktop (*BrE*) / counter (*NAmE*) 操作台
2 knife block 刀架
3 kitchen units 厨房组合柜
4 cooker hood 排气罩
5 splashback 防溅挡板
6 gas ring (*especially BrE*) / burner (*NAmE*) 煤气灶火圈
7 drawer 抽屉
8 oven glove (*also* oven mitt) 烤箱手套
9 grill (*BrE*) 烤架
10 oven 烤箱
11 fridge (*BrE*) / refrigerator (*NAmE*) 冰箱
12 breakfast bar 早餐台
13 stool 高凳
14 door 门
15 shelf 搁板
16 kitchen roll holder 厨房卷纸架
17 kitchen paper (*BrE*) / paper towel (*NAmE*) 厨房卷纸
18 draining board (*BrE*) / drainboard (*NAmE*) 滴水板
19 dishcloth 洗碗布
20 sink 洗碗槽
21 tap (*especially BrE*) / faucet (*NAmE*) 水龙头
22 kettle 水壶
23 dishwasher 洗碗碟机
24 tea towel (*BrE*) / dishtowel (*US*) 茶巾

Appliances (家用) 器具

blender (*BrE also* **liquidizer**) 食物搅拌器

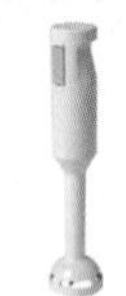

hand-held blender 手持搅拌器

food processor 食物加工器

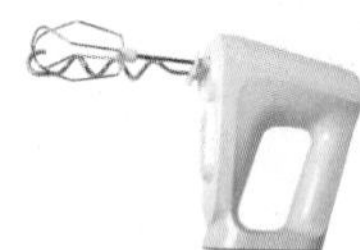

electric whisk 电动搅拌器

toaster 吐司炉

Coffee and tea 咖啡和茶

microwave 微波炉

cafetière (*BrE*) / **French press** (*NAmE*) 法式咖啡壶

coffee maker (*also* **coffee machine**) 煮咖啡机

teapot 茶壶

Kitchen utensils 厨房用具

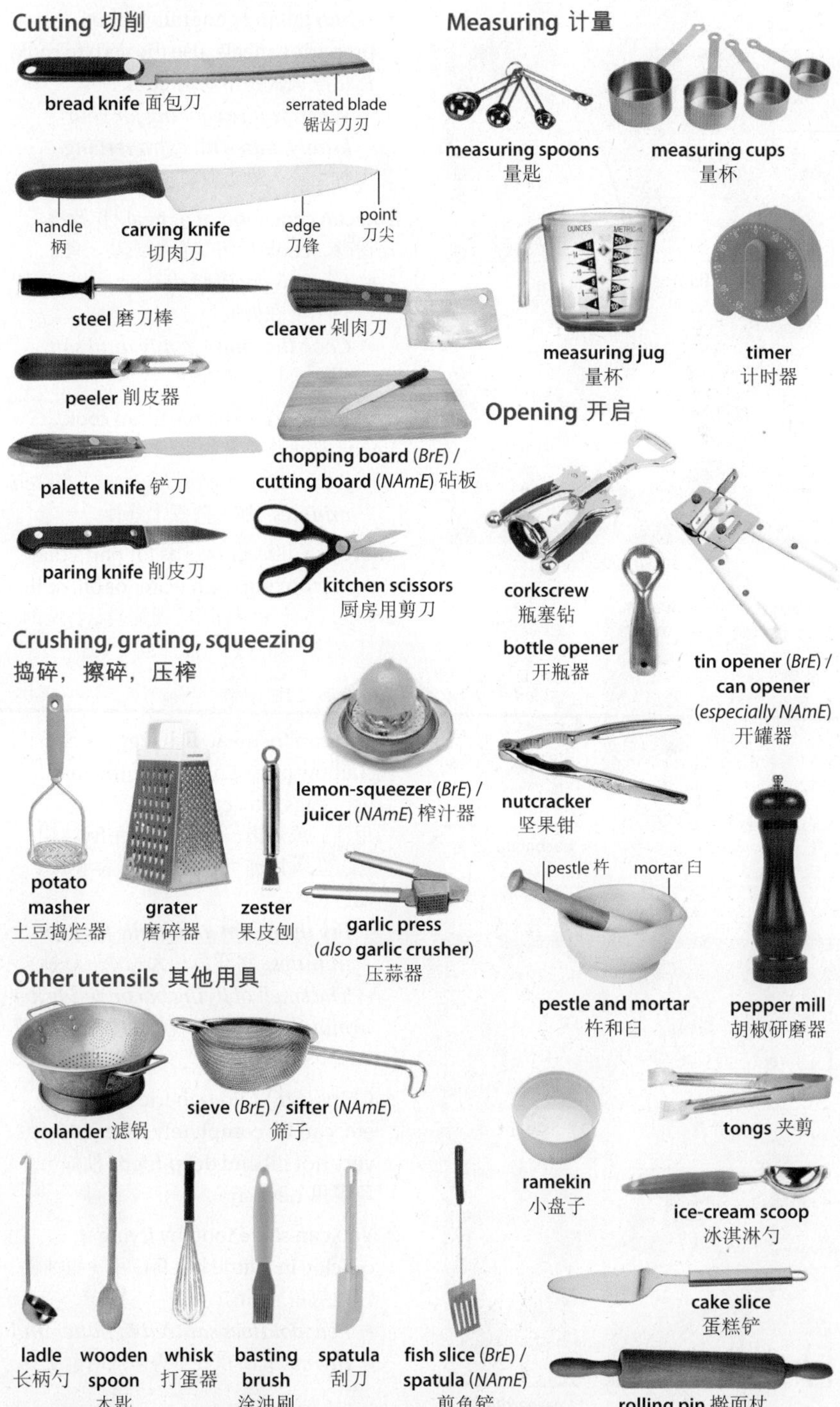
Cutting 切削
bread knife 面包刀
serrated blade
锯齿刀刃
handle
柄
carving knife
切肉刀
edge
刀锋
point
刀尖
steel 磨刀棒
cleaver 剁肉刀
peeler 削皮器
chopping board (BrE) /
cutting board (NAmE) 砧板
palette knife 铲刀
paring knife 削皮刀
kitchen scissors
厨房用剪刀
Crushing, grating, squeezing
捣碎，擦碎，压榨
lemon-squeezer (BrE) /
juicer (NAmE) 榨汁器
potato
masher
土豆捣烂器
grater
磨碎器
zester
果皮刨
garlic press
(also garlic crusher)
压蒜器
Other utensils 其他用具
colander 滤锅
sieve (BrE) / sifter (NAmE)
筛子
ladle
长柄勺
wooden
spoon
木匙
whisk
打蛋器
basting
brush
涂油刷
spatula
刮刀
fish slice (BrE) /
spatula (NAmE)
煎鱼铲
Measuring 计量
measuring spoons
量匙
measuring cups
量杯
measuring jug
量杯
timer
计时器
Opening 开启
corkscrew
瓶塞钻
bottle opener
开瓶器
tin opener (BrE) /
can opener
(especially NAmE)
开罐器
nutcracker
坚果钳
pestle 杵
mortar 臼
pestle and mortar
杵和臼
pepper mill
胡椒研磨器
tongs 夹剪
ramekin
小盘子
ice-cream scoop
冰淇淋勺
cake slice
蛋糕铲
rolling pin 擀面杖

Cooking 烹饪

flambé 火焰菜品

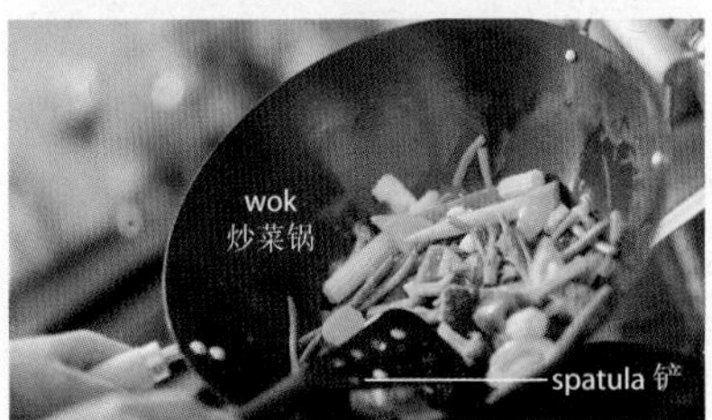

stir-fry 炒

fry 煎

barbecue 烧烤

boil 煮

steam 蒸

bake 烤

casserole 炖

Cook 烹煮食物

- When talking generally about preparing meals, use the verb **to cook**. 泛指烹调食物用动词 cook：
  - ▶ *When you're cooking for your family, make an extra serving.* 你给家人做饭时，多做一份。

You can **cook** food or a meal, 作及物动词时，cook 后可接食物或某一餐：

- ▶ *Lucas is cooking dinner.* 卢卡斯在做饭。
- ▶ *Cook the onion gently until soft.* 用文火把洋葱煮软。

... or the food or the meal can **cook**.
* cook 亦可作不及物动词：

- ▶ *Add the meat and let it cook for ten minutes.* 加上肉煮十分钟。

There are different verbs for particular ways of cooking: with water or oil, or in dry heat. 有各种不同的动词表示特定的烹饪方法，如水煮、油炸或干烘。

Fry 煎，炸，炒

- You can **fry** meat, fish, eggs, etc. in a shallow pan of hot oil, or the meat, fish, eggs, etc. can **fry**. 在平底浅锅中用油煎或炒肉、鱼、蛋等用 fry。肉、鱼、蛋等后亦可直接用 fry 表示煎炒的意思：
  - ▶ *Fry the onion and garlic for five minutes.* 将洋葱和大蒜炒五分钟。
  - ▶ *The smell of frying bacon made her mouth water.* 炒熏肉的香味馋得她流口水。
- Chips (*BrE*) / French fries (*NAmE*), etc. can be completely covered in very hot oil and **deep-fried**. 油炸土豆条等用 deep-fry。
- You can **sauté** food by frying it quickly in a little hot fat. 用少量油快速地煎用 sauté：
  - ▶ *new potatoes sautéed in butter and thyme* 黄油和百里香嫩煎时鲜土豆

Boil 煮

- You can **boil** vegetables, eggs, rice, etc. by covering them with water and heating to **boiling point** (=100°C). 用水煮的方式将菜、蛋、米饭等加热至沸点（boiling point）用 boil :
  - ▶ *Boil the potatoes until tender, then drain.* 将土豆煮软，然后沥掉水。
- You can also just **boil** the water, * boil 后可接 water，表示烧开水 :
  - ▶ *I'm boiling the water for the pasta now.* 我在烧水准备煮意大利面。

... or the container the water is in. * boil 的宾语也可以是装水的容器 :

  - ▶ *Boil a large pan of salted water.* 烧一大锅加了盐的水。
- The vegetables, the water, or (in British English) the container, can **boil**. 菜、水或（在英式英语中）容器均可后接 boil 表示烧煮 :
  - ▶ *The potatoes were boiling away merrily.* 土豆在咕嘟咕嘟地煮着。
  - ▶ *The kettle's boiled! Do you want some tea?* (*BrE*) 壶里的水烧开了！你想喝点茶吗？
- If you **bring something to the boil** (*BrE*) / **a boil** (*NAmE*) you heat it until it boils; you can then **simmer** it or let it **simmer** by letting it boil gently for a period of time. 把东西加热至沸点说 bring something to the boil/a boil，然后用文火煨或炖用 simmer :
  - ▶ *Simmer the carrots in a large pan of water.* 用一大锅水文火炖胡萝卜。
  - ▶ *Bring to the boil and let it simmer for five minutes.* 烧开后用文火煨五分钟。
- You can **poach** food by cooking it gently in a small amount of liquid. 在少量水中煨用 poach :
  - ▶ *Gently poach the salmon fillets for eight minutes.* 将鲑鱼片慢煨八分钟。

Steam 蒸

- You can **steam** fish, vegetables, etc. by placing the food above boiling water in a covered container with holes in the bottom so the steam reaches it. 蒸鱼、菜等用 steam :
  - ▶ *Chinese rice is always white and usually prepared by steaming.* 中国米饭一向是白的，通常是蒸熟的。

Roast 烘，烤，焙

- You can **roast** large pieces of meat, potatoes, etc. by covering the surface of the food with oil in the heat of an oven. 将大块肉、土豆等食物的表面抹上油在烤炉里烧烤用 roast。

Grill 炙烤

- You can **grill** (*BrE*) / **broil** (*NAmE*) food under direct heat on a **grill pan** (*BrE*) / **broiler pan** (*NAmE*). 在烤盘（英式英语用 grill pan，美式英语用 broiler pan）上烤制食物用 grill 或 broil。

Preparation 准备

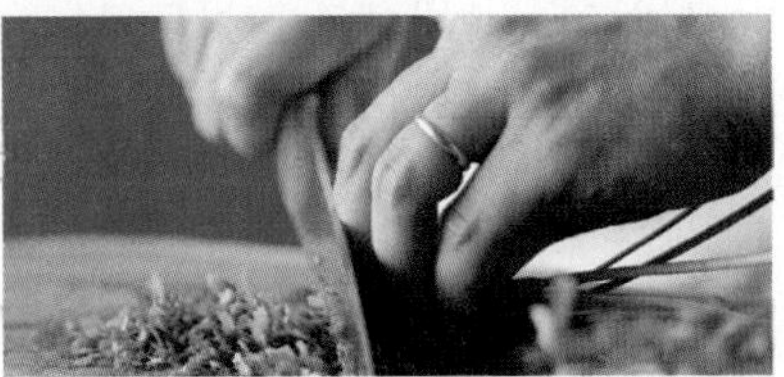
chop 切碎

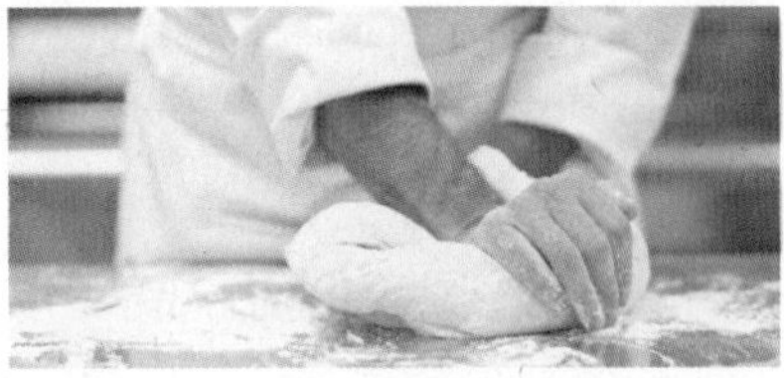
knead 揉面

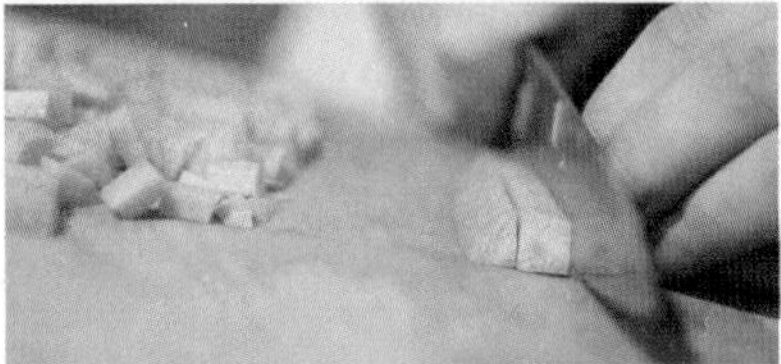
dice 切成丁

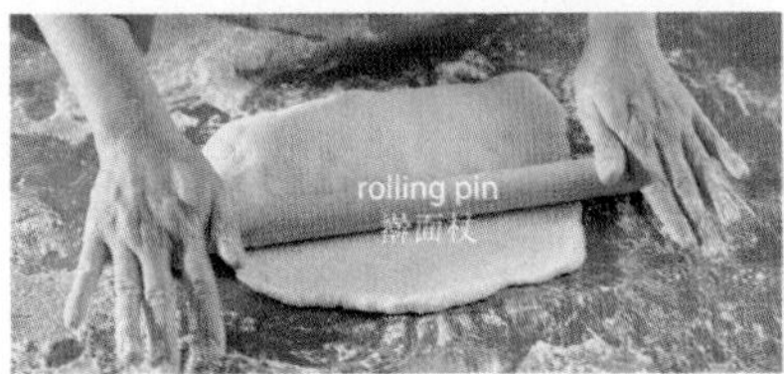

roll out 擀面

slice 切成片

grate 擦成细丝

whip 搅打

Bake 烘烤

- You can **bake** bread, cakes, potatoes, etc. in the dry heat of an oven or a fire, 在烤箱或火炉内烤面包、蛋糕、土豆等用 bake：
  - ▸ *He baked a cake for her birthday.* 他为她的生日烤了一个蛋糕。

  ... or the bread, cakes, etc. can **bake**. * bake 亦可作不及物动词：
  - ▸ *While the cake is baking, avoid opening the oven door.* 蛋糕在烘烤时不要打开烤箱门。

- **Baking** can be used for things that are baked, or for the activity of baking them. * baking 可指烘烤的食物或烘烤这种活动：
  - ▸ *A nice smell of baking came from the kitchen.* 厨房里飘来烘烤食物的香味。
  - ▸ *My grandmother always used to bake/do the baking on Saturdays.* 以前我的祖母总是在星期六烤制食物。

GRAMMAR POINT 语法说明

- The past participle (**-ed** form) of most cooking verbs can be used as an adjective before an item of food, meaning 'that has been cooked in this way'. 多数表示烹调的动词其过去分词形式（-ed）可用作形容词，置于食物名称前，表示是用这种方法烹调的：
  - *a cooked breakfast* (*BrE*)
    a warm breakfast (*NAmE*)
    煮熟的早餐
  - *a boiled egg* 煮熟的蛋
  - *sautéed potatoes* (*also sauté potatoes*) 嫩煎土豆
  - BUT 但 *roast chicken* 烤鸡
- The gerund (**-ing** form) of some cooking verbs can be used as an adjective before an item of food, meaning 'suitable to be cooked in this way', 有些表示烹调的动词其动名词形式（-ing）可用作形容词，置于食物名称前，表示宜用这种方法烹制：
  - *cooking apples* (= that must be cooked before they are eaten) 烹调用苹果
  - *stewing steak* 宜炖煮的牛排

  … or before a piece of equipment, meaning 'suitable to be used when cooking in this way'. 或置于炊具名称前，表示适用于这种烹调方法：
  - *a frying pan* 煎锅
  - *a baking tray* (*BrE*) / *baking sheet* (*NAmE*) 烘烤盘

Fruit and vegetables 水果和蔬菜

- Some fruit and vegetables are always countable. 有些水果和蔬菜总是可数名词：
  - ▸ *Do you like bananas?* 你喜欢香蕉吗？

  Some are always uncountable. 而有些总是不可数名词：
  - ▸ *Celery is usually eaten raw.* 芹菜通常生吃。
- Some may be countable or uncountable, depending on whether you are thinking of them as plants or as food and on how they are prepared as food. If you are thinking of a fruit or vegetable as a plant you are usually talking about the whole fruit or vegetable, so it will be countable. 还有些既可以是可数名词，也可以是不可数名词，取决于你把它视为植物还是食物，以及作为食物时如何烹制。如果把某种水果或蔬菜视为植物，通常指整个水果或整棵蔬菜，所以是可数名词：
  - ▸ *Plant the cabbages in rows.* 把卷心菜一行一行地栽种到土里。
- Larger fruit or vegetables, that you do not eat whole, are uncountable as food. 较大的不能整个吃的水果或整棵吃的蔬菜作为食物时为不可数名词：
  - ▸ *duck with spring cabbage* 春甘蓝煮鸭

  Others may be eaten whole (countable) ... 其他可以整个吃的水果或整棵吃的蔬菜为可数名词：
  - ▸ *baked apples* 烤苹果
  - ▸ *baby carrots* 小胡萝卜

  ... or prepared in such a way that they are not eaten whole (uncountable in British English but still countable in American English). 或以某种方式烹调而不是整个吃，在英式英语中为不可数名词，但在美式英语中仍为可数名词：
  - ▸ *stewed apple* (*BrE*) / *stewed apples* (*NAmE*) 炖苹果
  - ▸ *grated raw carrot* (*BrE*) / *grated raw carrots* (*NAmE*) 生胡萝卜细丝

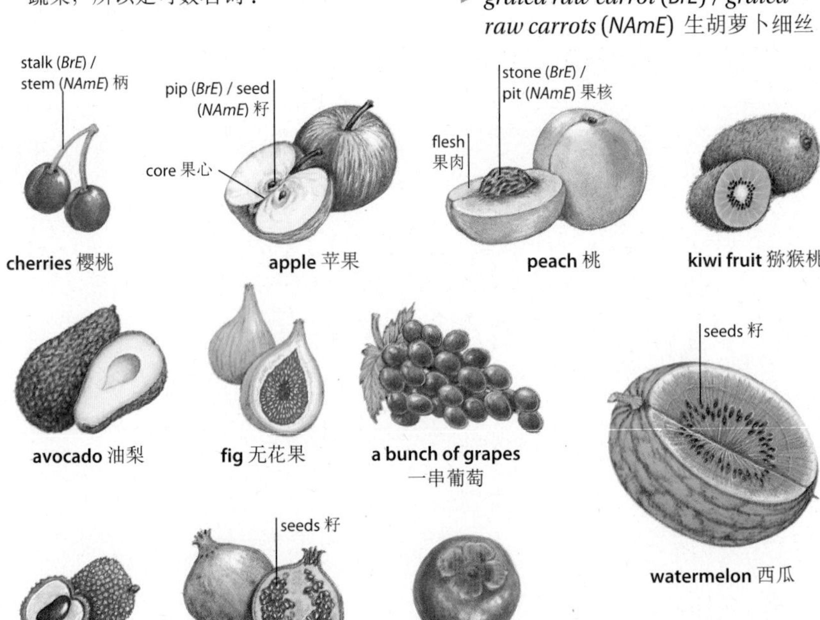

cherries 樱桃 **apple** 苹果 **peach** 桃 **kiwi fruit** 猕猴桃

avocado 油梨 **fig** 无花果 **a bunch of grapes** 一串葡萄 **watermelon** 西瓜

lychee 荔枝 **pomegranate** 石榴 **persimmon** 柿子

Berries 浆果

strawberries 草莓

raspberries 悬钩子

blackberries 黑莓

gooseberries 醋栗

Citrus fruits 柑橘类水果

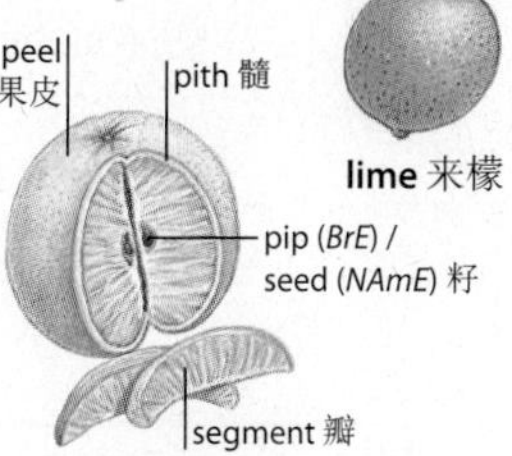

grapefruit 葡萄柚

lime 来檬

lemon
柠檬

orange 橙子

Tropical fruits 热带水果

pineapple
菠萝

passion fruit
百香果

mango 芒果

mangosteen 山竹

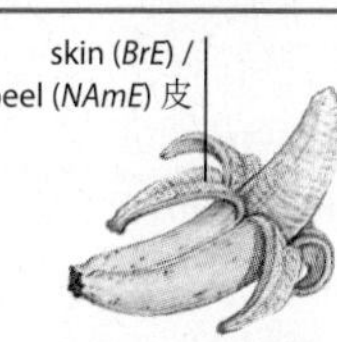

banana 香蕉

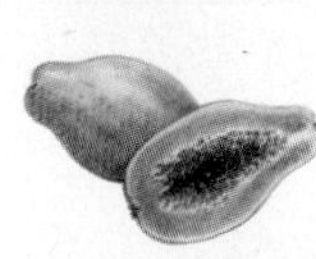

papaya 番木瓜

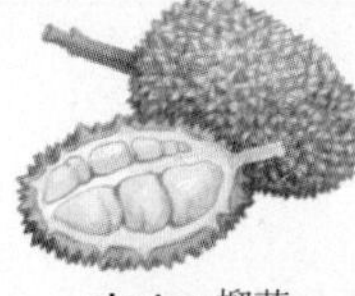

durian 榴莲

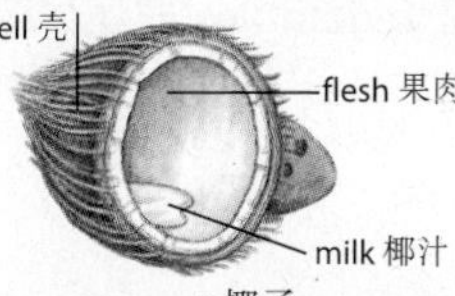

coconut 椰子

garlic 大蒜

onion 洋葱

shallots
红葱头

fennel 茴香

cabbage 卷心菜

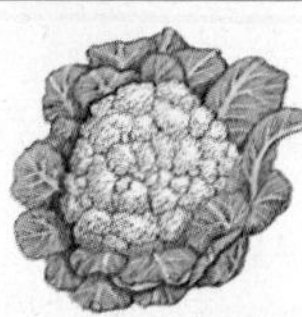

cauliflower 花椰菜

leek 韭葱

Brussels sprouts
汤菜

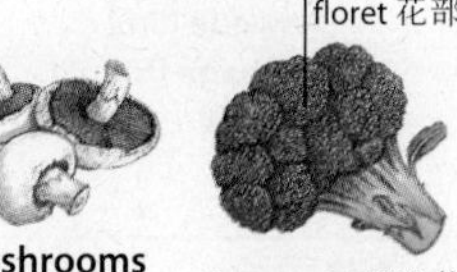

mushrooms
蘑菇

broccoli 西兰花

artichoke (*also* globe artichoke)
洋蓟

spring onions (*BrE*) /
green onions (*NAmE*) 小葱

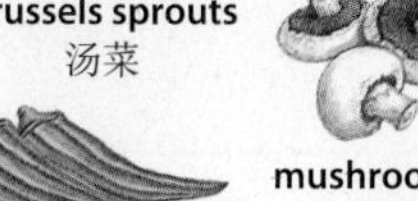

okra 秋葵

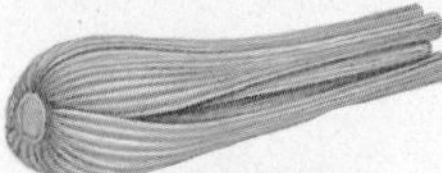

celery 芹菜

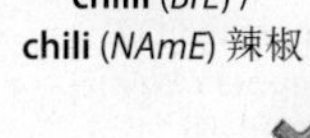

chilli (*BrE*) /
chili (*NAmE*) 辣椒

asparagus 芦笋

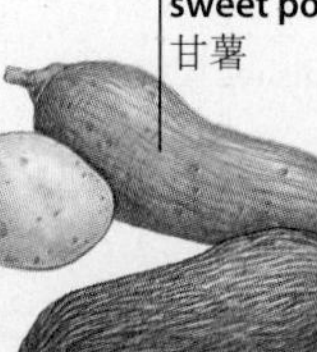

sweet potato
甘薯

potato
马铃薯

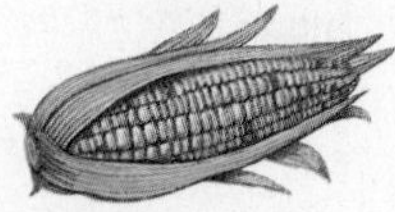

corn on the cob
玉米棒子

sweetcorn
(*NAmE also* corn)
（甜）玉米粒

aubergine (*BrE*) /
eggplant (*NAmE*)
茄子

yam 薯蓣

Squash 南瓜类

marrow (*BrE*) 西葫芦

courgette (*BrE*) / **zucchini** (*NAmE*) 小胡瓜

pumpkin 南瓜

Peas and beans 豆类

green beans 四季豆

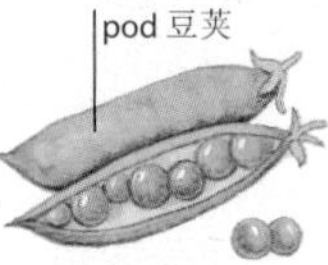

peas 豌豆

kidney beans 红腰豆

chickpeas (*especially BrE*) / **garbanzos** (*NAmE*) 鹰嘴豆

bean sprouts 豆芽

Root vegetables 根茎类蔬菜

carrot 胡萝卜

parsnip 欧洲萝卜

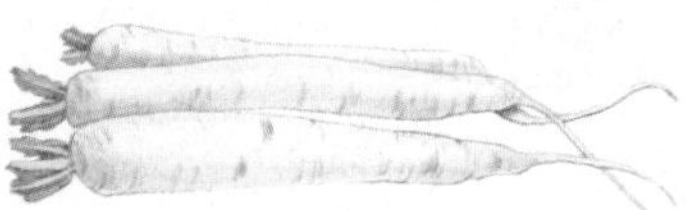
moolis / daikons 白萝卜

beetroot (*BrE*) / **beet** (*NAmE*) 甜菜根

swede (*BrE*) / **rutabaga** (*NAmE*) 芜菁甘蓝

turnip 芜菁

Salad vegetables 色拉蔬菜

radishes 樱桃萝卜

tomato 番茄

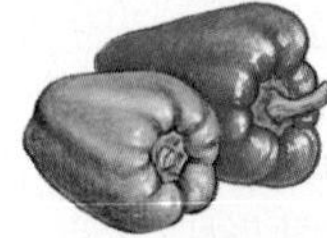
peppers (*BrE*) / **bell peppers** (*NAmE*) 灯笼椒

lettuce 生菜

cucumber 黄瓜

Herbs, spices, nuts and cereals
香草、香料、坚果和谷物

Herbs 香草
bay
月桂
sage
鼠尾草
basil
罗勒
oregano
牛至
mint
薄荷
parsley
欧芹
thyme
百里香
rosemary
迷迭香
dill
莳萝
tarragon
龙蒿
chives
细香葱
coriander (NAmE also cilantro) 芫荽
Spices 香料
pod 荚
seeds
籽
cloves
丁香
black peppercorns
黑胡椒粒
star anise
八角茴香
cinnamon
桂皮
cardamom
豆蔻干籽
nutmeg
肉豆蔻
ginger
姜
saffron
西红花
turmeric
姜黄根粉
paprika
红辣椒粉
cumin seeds
莳萝籽
coriander seeds
芫荽籽
Nuts 坚果
cashew
腰果
peanut
花生
macadamia
澳洲坚果
hazelnut
(also filbert
especially NAmE)
榛子
pecan
美国山核桃
almond
扁桃仁
pistachio
开心果
shell 壳
brazil
巴西坚果
walnut
核桃
chestnut
栗子
Cereals 谷物
grain
谷粒
wheat
小麦
ear of wheat
麦穗
barley
大麦
maize (BrE) /
corn (NAmE)
玉米
rye 黑麦
rice 稻米
oats 燕麦
millet 谷子

Packaging 包装

multipack
合装包

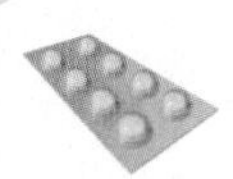
blister pack
吸塑包装

box 盒

box (*BrE also* **packet**) 盒

matchbox
火柴盒

packet (*BrE*) /
stick (*NAmE*) 条

stick 条
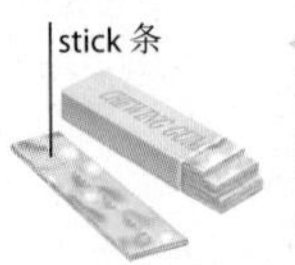
packet (*BrE*) /
pack (*NAmE*) 纸包

packet (*BrE*) /
package (*NAmE*) 包

packet (*BrE*) /
roll (*NAmE*)
包；管

cap / top 盖子
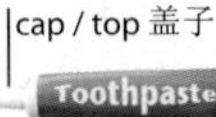

tube 软管；管

sachet (*BrE*) /
packet (*NAmE*) 小袋

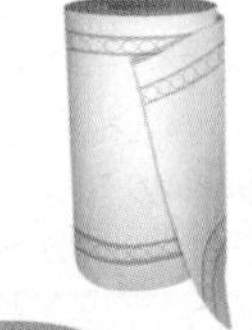
roll 卷

straw 吸管

carton (*BrE*) /
juice box (*NAmE*)
果汁纸盒

carton 硬纸盒

carton (*BrE also* **pot**)
纸盒；塑料盒

tub 食品盒

nozzle 喷嘴
top 盖子
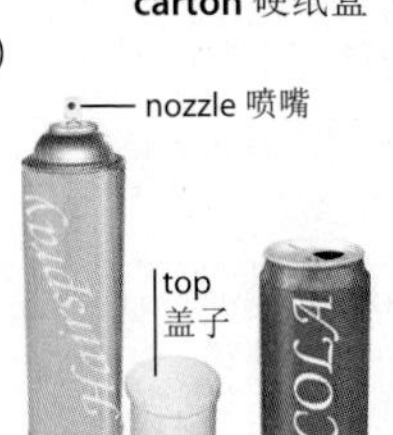

aerosol can
喷雾罐

can 罐

cork 软木塞
screw top 螺旋盖

bottle 瓶子

lid 盖子

tin
金属食品盒

lid 盖子
ring pull (*BrE*) /
pull tab (*NAmE*)
拉环
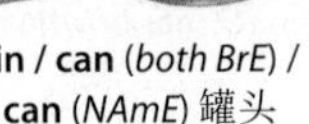

tin / can (*both BrE*) /
can (*NAmE*) 罐头

punnet (*BrE*)
小果盒

label
标签

tray 托盘

jar 广口瓶

bag (*BrE also*
packet) 袋

bag 袋

shopping bag
购物袋

carrier bag
(*BrE*) 购物袋

shopping basket
购物篮

shopping trolley (*BrE*) /
shopping cart (*NAmE*)
购物手推车

Musical instruments 乐器

Playing an instrument 演奏乐器

- When talking generally about playing musical instruments, **the** is usually used before the name of the instrument. 泛指演奏乐器时，通常在乐器名称前加定冠词 the :
  - ▸ *He played **the** trumpet in a jazz band.* 他在爵士乐队吹小号。
  - ▸ *She decided to take up* (= start learning to play) ***the** flute.* 她决定学习吹奏长笛。
- **The** is not usually used when two or more instruments are mentioned. 涉及两种或以上乐器时，一般不用定冠词 the :
  - ▸ *She teaches violin, cello and piano.* 她教小提琴、大提琴和钢琴。
- The preposition **on** is used to say who is playing which instrument. 指某人演奏某种乐器，用介词 on :
  - ▸ *The CD features James Galway **on** the flute.* 这张 CD 唱片主推詹姆斯•高尔韦的长笛演奏。
  - ▸ *She sang and he accompanied her **on** the piano.* 她演唱，他用钢琴伴奏。
- **The** is not usually used when you are talking about pop or jazz musicians. 指流行音乐家或爵士音乐家的演奏，通常不用定冠词 the :
  - ▸ *John Squire on guitar* 约翰•斯夸尔的吉他演奏
  - ▸ *Miles Davis played trumpet.* 迈尔斯•戴维斯吹小号。

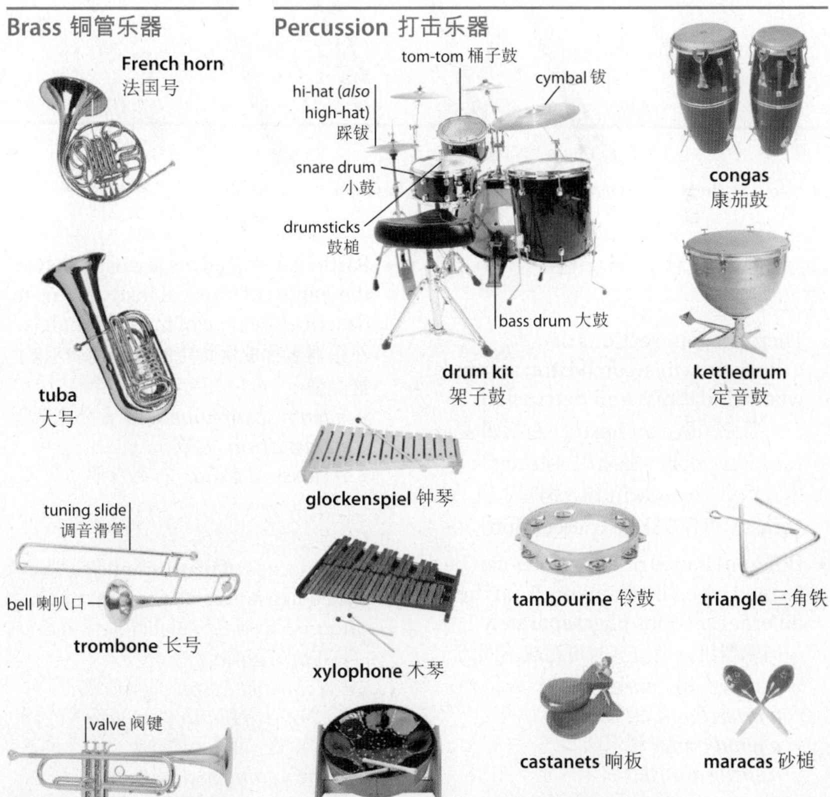

Strings 弦乐器

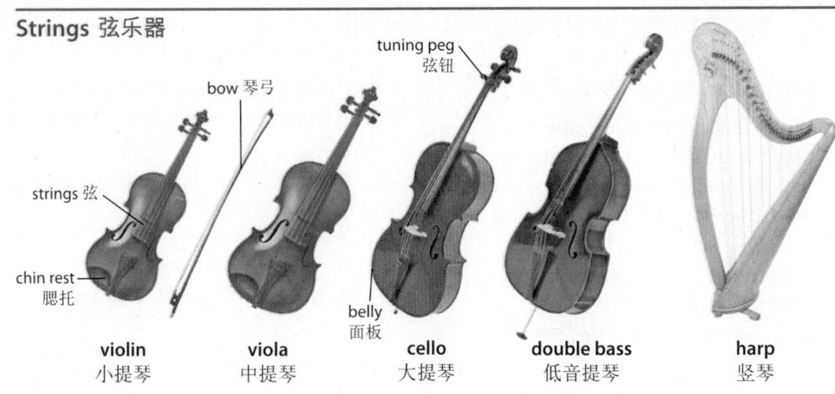

Woodwind 木管乐器

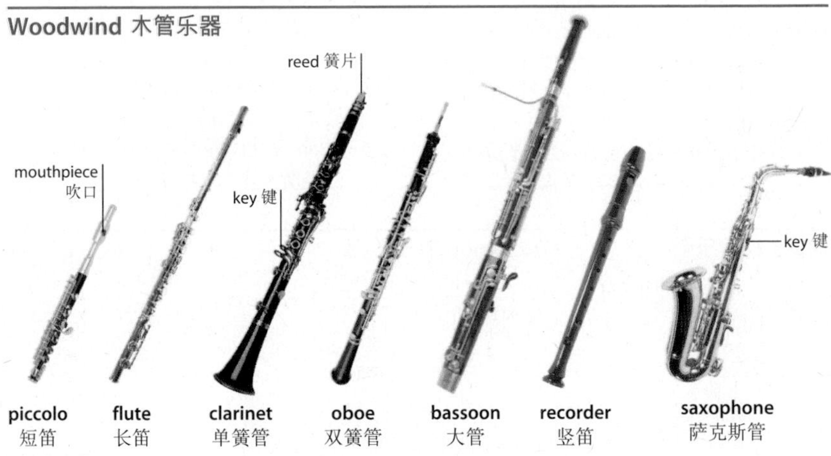

Describing instruments 描述乐器

- There are four **sections** of instruments in an **orchestra: strings, woodwind, brass** and **percussion.** 一个管弦乐队（orchestra）包括四组（section）乐器：弦乐组（strings）、木管乐组（woodwind）、铜管乐组（brass）和打击乐组（percussion）。
- Different bands or **ensembles** can be formed when instruments from the different sections play separately. 不同乐器组分别演奏时可组成不同的乐队或合奏组（ensemble）：
  - ▸ *a brass band* 铜管乐队
  - ▸ *a wind band* 管乐队
  - ▸ *a string quartet* 弦乐四重奏小组
  - ▸ *a jazz trio* 爵士乐三重奏小组
- Particular adjectives are used before the names of musical instruments to describe the type of instrument it is. 在乐器名称前用特定的形容词表示乐器类型：
  - ▸ *a tenor saxophone* 次中音萨克斯管
  - ▸ *a bass drum* 大鼓
  - ▸ *a classical guitar* 古典吉他

GRAMMAR POINT 语法说明

- The names of instruments can be used like adjectives before other nouns. 乐器名称可用作形容词置于其他名词前：
  - ▸ *a clarinet lesson* 单簧管课
  - ▸ *Chopin's Piano Concerto No. 1* 肖邦第一钢琴协奏曲
  - ▸ *She's going to do her cello practice.* 她要练习大提琴。

People who play instruments 乐器演奏者

- Some musical instruments have a special name, ending in **-ist** or **-er** for the people who play them. 有些乐器有特定的名称，词末加 -ist 或 -er 表示演奏这种乐器的人：
  - ▸ *The violinist lifted his bow.* 小提琴演奏者拿起琴弓。
  - ▸ *the South African drummer, Louis Moholo* 南非鼓手路易斯•莫霍洛
- Check near the entry for each instrument to find the correct word. If there is no special word, you use **player** after the name of the instrument. 表示某种乐器的演奏者的词可在相关的乐器词条附近查找，如果没有特定名称就在乐器名称后加 player：
  - ▸ *the quartet's viola player* 四重奏的中提琴演奏者
- When talking about pop or jazz, people often use **player** even when there is a word for the person like **saxophonist** or **bassist**. 谈及流行音乐或爵士乐时，虽然有萨克斯管吹奏者（saxophonist）或低音吉他手（bassist）等特定名称，人们仍常用 player：
  - ▸ *a brilliant young sax player* 才华横溢的青年萨克斯管吹奏者
  - ▸ *We're looking for a new bass player.* 我们在物色新的低音吉他手。
- In an orchestra playing classical music, **principal, deputy principal** (*BrE*), **associate principal** (*NAmE*) and **assistant principal** (*NAmE*) are used with the names of instruments to describe a player's position or importance. 在演奏古典音乐的管弦乐队中，首席演奏者（principle）、副首席演奏者（deputy principle 或 associate principle）和助理首席演奏者（assistant principle）与乐器名称连用表示演奏者的地位和重要性：
  - ▸ *He became principal cellist within a few years.* 他几年内就成为首席大提琴手。
- A person who directs (or **conducts**) an orchestra is a **conductor**. The principal violinist (who **leads** the orchestra) is the **leader** (*BrE*) or the **concertmaster** (*NAmE*). 指挥（conduct）管弦乐队的人称作 conductor。首席小提琴手（担当管弦乐队的领奏）称作 leader 或 concertmaster。

Music for instruments 器乐

- Music is **composed** or **written** for an instrument. In a piece of music written for a group of instruments, each has a different **part** to play. 乐曲是为某种乐器谱写（compose 或 write）的。合奏乐中的声部或分谱称为 part：
  - ▸ *There are parts for oboe and bassoon.* 有双簧管和大管声部。
- If there is more than one part for the same type of instrument, the terms **first** and **second**, and sometimes **third** and **fourth**, are used. 如果同种乐器有两个或以上声部就用第一、第二，有时还有第三、第四声部表示：
  - ▸ *She's a second violin* (= plays the second violin part). 她是第二声部小提琴手。
  - ▸ *the deep low notes of the third horn* 法国号第三声部的低音
- A **solo** is a part for one instrument playing alone. A **soloist** plays it.
  * solo 指独奏，soloist 指独奏者：
  - ▸ *She performs regularly as a soloist and in chamber music.* 她定期独奏表演并参与室内乐演奏。
  - ▸ *I love the saxophone solo in this song.* 我喜欢这首歌曲中的萨克斯管独奏。

More illustrations at ACCORDION and MUSIC. 更多插图见正文内 accordion 和 music 词条。

upright piano
立式钢琴

grand piano
三角钢琴

electric guitar
电吉他

acoustic guitar
原声吉他

banjo
班卓琴

mandolin
曼陀林

balalaika
巴拉莱卡琴

sitar
西塔尔

Toys and games 玩具和游戏

Frisbee™ 弗里斯比飞盘

kite 风筝

skipping rope (*BrE*) / **jump rope** (*NAmE*) 跳绳

sandpit (*BrE*) / **sandbox** (*NAmE*) 沙坑

swing 秋千

slide 滑梯

trampoline 蹦床

climbing frame (*BrE*) / **jungle gym** (*NAmE*) 攀爬架

teddy bear (*also* **teddy**) 泰迪熊

soft toy (*BrE*) / **stuffed animal** (*especially NAmE*) 布绒玩具

rag doll 布娃娃

glove puppet (*BrE*) / **hand puppet** (*NAmE*) 手偶

rocking horse 木马

building blocks 积木

doll's house (*BrE*) / **dollhouse** (*NAmE*) 玩具小屋

playing cards / cards 纸牌

pack of cards (*especially BrE*) / **deck of cards** (*especially NAmE*) 一副纸牌

Cards 纸牌

- To mix the playing cards is to **shuffle** them. 洗牌叫 shuffle：
  - ▸ *Shuffle the cards well.* 把牌彻底洗开。
  - ▸ *Shall I shuffle?* 我来洗牌好吗？
- To give cards to each individual person who is playing the game is to **deal** them (**out**). The person who does this is called the **dealer**. 给大家发牌用 deal ... (out)。发牌人称作 dealer：
  - ▸ *Whose turn is it to deal?* 轮到谁发牌了？
  - ▸ *Deal the cards.* 发牌。

suits 花色

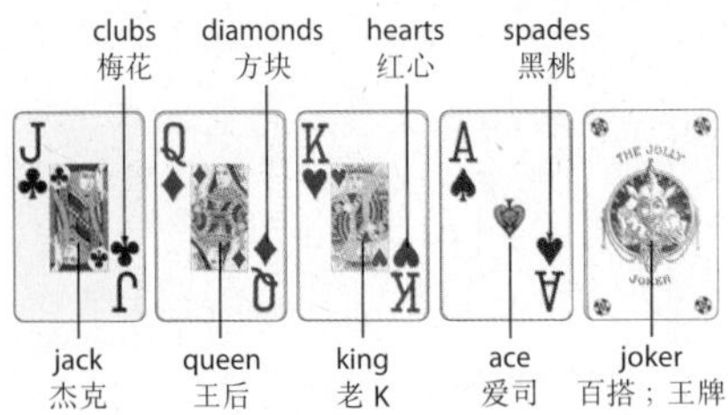

court cards (*BrE*) /
face cards (*especially NAmE*) 花牌

dominoes 多米诺骨牌

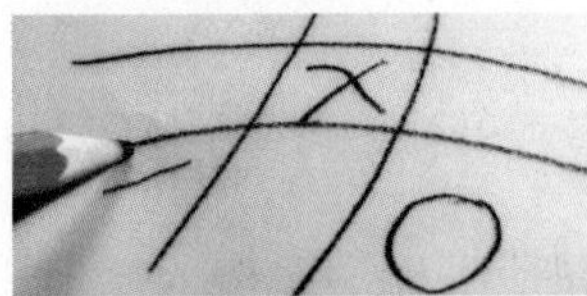

noughts and crosses (*BrE*) / **tic-tac-toe** (*NAmE*)
圈叉游戏

Chinese chequers (*BrE*) / **Chinese checkers** (*NAmE*)
（弹子）跳棋

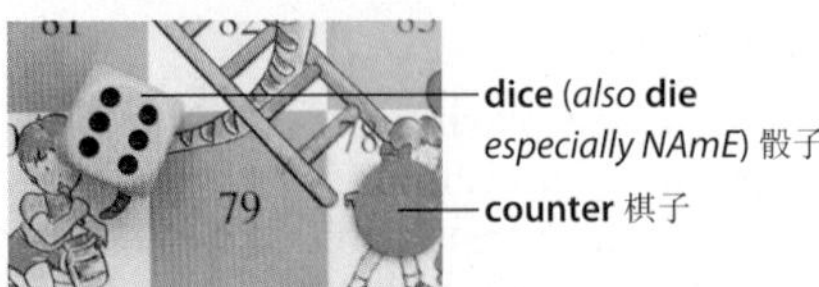

snakes and ladders (*BrE*)
蛇梯棋

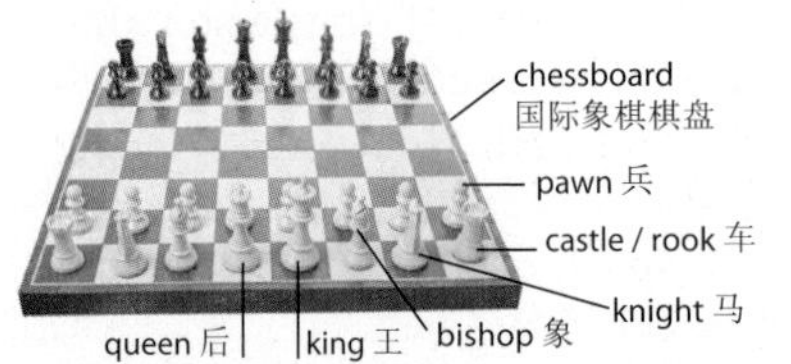

chess 国际象棋

- To divide the pack of cards into two or three parts is to **cut** them. 切牌用 cut :
  ▸ *Cut the cards to see who starts.* 切牌决定从谁开始。
- A card which is on the table showing the picture side is **face up**. A card which is on the table so that you cannot see the picture side is **face down.** 纸牌正面朝上放为 face up，正面朝下放为 face down。
- The cards that you have in your hand when you play cards is a **hand**. 一手牌称为 a hand。
  ▸ *I knew I'd win - I had a really good hand* (=I had good cards). 我就知道我会赢的，我拿了一手特好的牌。

Playing games 玩游戏

- The official statements that tell you what you can or cannot do in a game are the **rules**; something which is not allowed in a game is **against the rules.** 游戏规则称作 rules，违反游戏规则称作 against the rules。
- To play a game in a dishonest or unfair way: **cheat**; *noun* [U]: **cheating**; a person who cheats is **a cheat**. 玩游戏时作弊用动词 cheat，名词形式为 cheating（不可数）；作弊者称作 cheat :
  ▸ *You can't do that, it's cheating.* 你不能那么做，那是作弊。
  ▸ *He's such a cheat.* 他真能耍赖。

Board games 棋类游戏

- A game played on a flat hard piece of wood or cardboard is a **board game**. 棋类游戏称为 board game。
- A small cube with a different number of spots on each side, used in certain games, is called a **dice** (*also* **die** *especially NAmE*) (*plural* **dice**). 某些游戏中使用的骰子称作 dice 或 die，复数形式为 dice。

- A small round flat object that is used in some games to show where a player is on the board is a **counter**. 某些游戏中使用的棋子称作 counter。
- To take a piece or a counter and move it to another place on the board: **move** (something). 走棋用 move：
  - ▸ *You can only move your counter one square in any direction.* 棋子往任何方向只能走一格。
- The time in a game when one person must do something (for example move a piece) is called a **move, turn, go** (*plural* **goes**). 下棋时轮到的走棋机会称作 move、turn 或 go（复数形式为 goes）：
  - ▸ *It's your move/turn/go.* 该你走了。
  - ▸ *You've just had two goes.* 你刚才走了两步。

backgammon 十五子棋

sudoku 数独

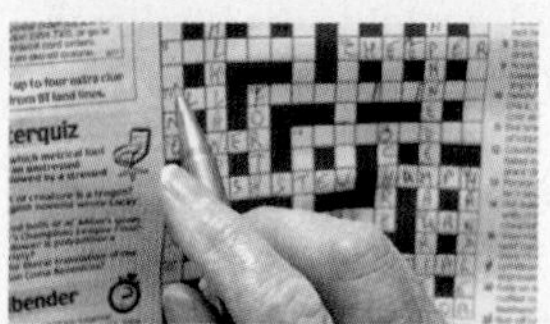
crossword (*also* **crossword puzzle**) 纵横字谜

word search 文字搜索游戏

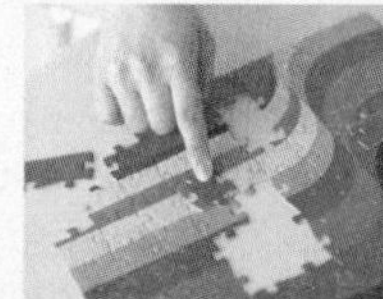
jigsaw (puzzle) (*BrE*) (*also* **puzzle** *especially NAmE*) 拼图

Chess 国际象棋

- A stage in the game of chess when a player's king could be taken by the other person is called **check** *noun* [U]. When you are in this position, you are **in check**. 将军的局面称作 check（不可数名词），被将军为 in check。
- When one player cannot move his or her king out of check and the game ends is called **checkmate** *noun* [U]. 被将死或输棋称作 checkmate（不可数名词）。
- The end of a game of chess when neither player can win is **stalemate** *noun* [U]. 和棋或僵局为 stalemate（不可数名词）。

Puzzles 智力游戏

- A game that tests your knowledge or intelligence is a **puzzle**. * puzzle 指测试知识或智力的游戏：
  - ▸ *to do a puzzle* 做智力游戏
  - ▸ *a mathematical puzzle* 数学智力游戏
- A picture on cardboard or wood that is cut into small pieces which you have to join together is a **jigsaw (puzzle)**. * jigsaw (puzzle) 指拼图。
- A word game with black and white squares where you write the word in the white squares is a **crossword (puzzle)**. To find the right word, you have to **solve a clue**. * crossword (puzzle) 指纵横字谜。根据提示填出一个词叫作 solve a clue：
  - ▸ *I can't do this crossword, the clues are too difficult.* 这个填字游戏我做不出来，给的提示太难了。
  - ▸ *to solve a crossword puzzle* 解答纵横字谜

Hobbies 业余爱好

orienteering
定向运动

caving 洞穴探察

archery 射箭运动

ice skating 滑冰

scuba-diving
戴水肺潜水

snorkelling (*also* snorkeling *especially US*) 浮潜

in-line skating
直排滚轴溜冰

skateboarding 滑板运动

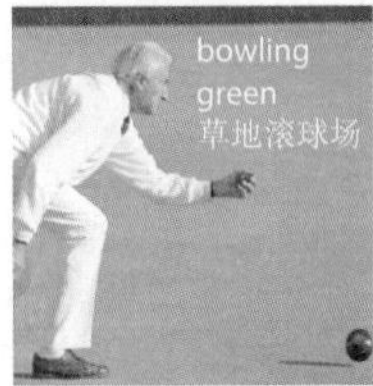

bowls 草地滚球运动

tenpin bowling
十柱保龄球

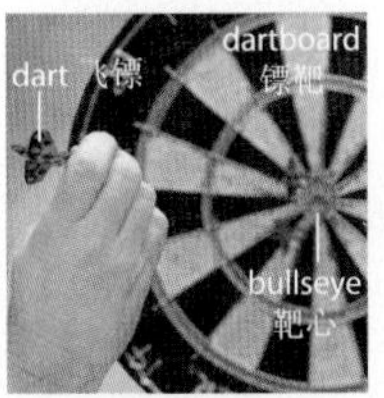

darts 掷镖游戏

pool 普尔

golf 高尔夫球运动

Golf 高尔夫球运动

- A game of golf is called a **round of golf** (nine or eighteen **holes**). 一轮高尔夫球称作 a round of golf，打九洞或十八洞（hole）。
- At the start of each hole a player **tees off** by hitting the ball from the **tee** (= an area of flat ground). 球员从发球区（tee）开球（tee off）。
- The act of hitting the ball is called a **shot**. The swinging movement players make with their arms and body when they hit the ball is called their **swing**. 击球的动作称作 shot。扭动身体挥杆击球称作 swing：
  - ▸ *My golf swing is in need of improvement.* 我需要提高我的高尔夫球挥杆技巧。
- Players attempt to hit their ball down the **fairway** (= a long strip of short grass), avoiding the **bunker** (*also* **sand trap**, **trap** *especially NAmE*) and **the rough** (= the part of the golf course with long grass making it difficult to hit the ball), to the **green**. 球员尽力避开沙坑（bunker、sand trap、trap）和长草区（rough），将球沿球道（fairway）击到果岭（green）上。
- The **green** is an area of short grass on which you **putt** your ball (= hit the ball gently so that it rolls across the ground a short distance into or towards the **hole**). 在果岭（green）推（putt）球入洞（hole）。

Snooker, pool and billiards 斯诺克、普尔和台球

- **Snooker** is a game for two people, played on a long table covered with green cloth (**baize**). Players use **cues** to hit the **cue ball** (white) against the other balls (fifteen red, and six of other colours) in order to **pot** the coloured balls (= hit them into **pockets** at the edge of the table), in a particular order. 斯诺克（snooker）是两人游戏，在铺有台面呢（baize）的长桌上进行。玩游戏者用球杆（cue）将白色母球（cue ball）击向其他球（十五个红球和六个其他颜色的球），按一定顺序将不同颜色的球击进（pot）球袋（pocket）。
- Snooker also refers to a position in the game of snooker in which one player has made it very difficult for the opponent to play a shot within the rules. * snooker 也指在斯诺克比赛中给对手设置障碍球。
- A game of snooker is called a **frame**. 一局斯诺克比赛称作 frame：
  ▶ *He won the frame easily.* 他轻松赢了这局斯诺克比赛。
- **Pool** is similar to snooker, but is played with a cue ball (white), a black ball, and two sets of coloured balls (seven solid colours and seven striped balls). 普尔（pool）与斯诺克相似，但使用一个母球（白色）、一个黑球和两组彩球（七个单色球和七个花球）。
- **Billiards** is played with three balls (one white, one white with a spot, and one red). Each player uses one of the white balls as the cue ball. Points are scored by pocketing a ball after contact with another ball, or by striking your cue ball against the other two balls. 台球（billiards）使用三个球（一个白球、一个带斑点的白球和一个红球）。球手使用两个白球之一作为母球，击球落袋或用母球撞击到其他两个球即得分。

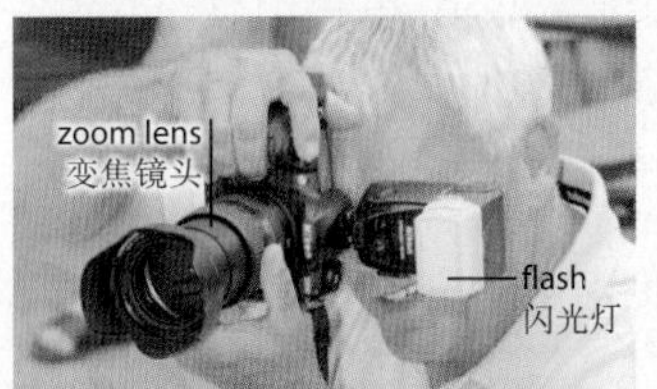

photography 摄影

painting 绘画

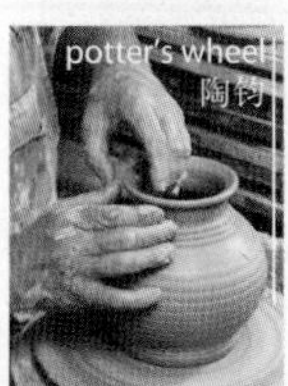

pottery 制陶

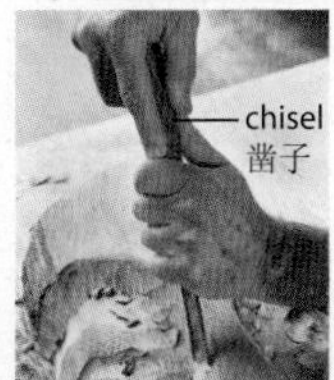

woodcarving 木雕

model making 制作模型

stamp collecting 集邮

gardening 园艺

knitting 编织

crochet 钩针编织

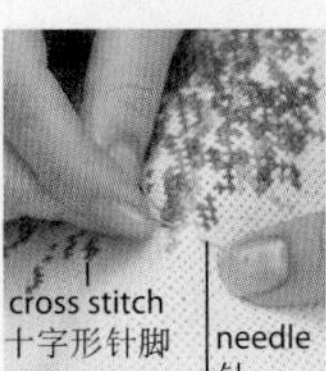

embroidery 绣花

sewing 缝纫

Keeping fit 健身

press-up (*BrE*) / **push-up** (*especially NAmE*)
俯卧撑

sit-up
仰卧起坐

jogging
慢跑锻炼

yoga
瑜伽

exercise bike
健身脚踏车

barbell 杠铃

dumb-bell 哑铃

rowing machine
划船练习架

treadmill
跑步机

Staying healthy 保持健康

- If you are **fit** (*BrE*), **physically fit**, or **in shape** (*especially NAmE*), you are healthy and strong, especially as a result of diet and exercise. * fit、physically fit 或 in shape 指身体健康，尤指通过均衡饮食和锻炼来达到：
  - *Top athletes have to be very fit.* 顶级运动员体格必须十分健壮。
  - *The doctor said I should get more **exercise*** (*BrE also* ***... take** more **exercise***). 医生说我应该加强锻炼。
  - *No cream for me – I'm **on a diet**.* 我不要奶油，我在节食。
  - *She cycles up to 90 miles a day to **keep fit**.* 她每天骑自行车90英里以保持健康。
  - *I still run every day to **stay in shape**.* (*especially NAmE*) 我仍然坚持每天跑步以保持健康。

Aerobics, step, and circuit training 有氧运动、踏板操和循环训练

- **Aerobics** involves physical exercises to make the heart and lungs stronger, often done in classes and to music. 有氧运动（aerobics）是能增强心肺功能的体育锻炼，常以上课形式伴随音乐进行：
  - *do an aerobics class* 上有氧运动课
- **Step** is a type of aerobics that you do by stepping on and off a raised piece of equipment called a **step**. 踏板操（step）是在踏板（step）上踏上踏下的健身操。
- **Circuit training** is a type of training in which different exercises are each done for a short time. 循环训练（circuit training）指轮番做不同的体育运动，每种只做很短的时间。

Sports 体育运动

Talking about a particular sport 谈论某项体育运动

- You can **play** a specific sport. 参加特定的体育运动用 play :
  - ▸ *Do you play tennis?* 你打网球吗？
- This is used particularly for competitive sports in which one team or person **plays** or **plays against** another. 这个词尤用于队与队或个人之间竞技性的体育运动（用 play 或 play against）:
  - ▸ *We played them in last year's final.* 在去年的决赛中我们与他们对垒。
  - ▸ *Who are you playing against this afternoon?* 你今天下午同谁比赛？
- Members of a sports team **play for** their team. 为某队效力用 play for :
  - ▸ *He used to play for the Dallas Cowboys.* 他以前效力于达拉斯牛仔队。
- If the name of a sport or an activity ends in **-ing** we often use it with the verb **to go**. 某项体育运动或活动的名称以 -ing 结尾时，常与动词 to go 连用：
  - ▸ *I go swimming twice a week.* 我一周游泳两次。
  - ▸ *Have you ever been rock climbing?* 你攀过岩吗？
- Typical sports and activities with this pattern include: **go skiing; go sailing; go riding** (*BrE*) or **go horseback riding** (*NAmE*); and **go dancing.** Check at the entry for each sport to see if it can be used in this way. 常用该句型的体育项目和活动有 go skiing（滑雪）、go sailing（乘帆船航行）、go riding 或 go horseback riding（骑马）以及 go dancing（跳舞）。可查阅词典内各项体育运动的词条以确定是否有这一用法。

Other sports and activities can take the verbs **to do** or **to go to.** 其他一些体育项目和活动可用动词 to do 或 to go to :

- *I do aerobics once or twice a week.* 我每周做一两次有氧运动。
- *I go to judo* (= to my judo class) *on Mondays.* 我每星期一去练习柔道。

Team sports 团队体育运动

cricket 板球

basketball 篮球

baseball 棒球

rugby 橄榄球

soccer (*BrE also* **football**) 足球

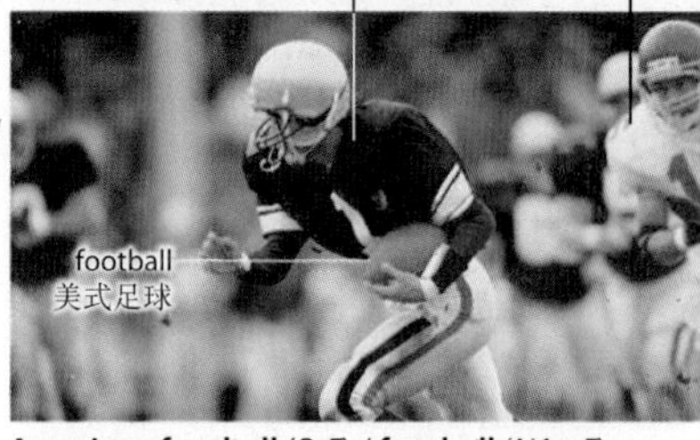

American football (*BrE*) / **football** (*NAmE*)
美式足球

hockey (*BrE*) / **field hockey** (*NAmE*)
曲棍球

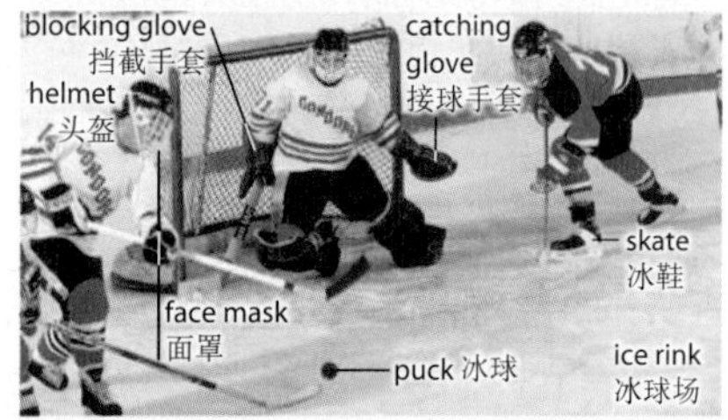

ice hockey (*BrE*) / **hockey** (*NAmE*) 冰球

Swimming 游泳

crawl 自由泳

butterfly 蝶泳

backstroke 仰泳

breaststroke 蛙泳

Racket sports 球拍运动

tennis 网球

badminton 羽毛球

squash 壁球

table tennis 乒乓球

Where sports are played 体育运动场地

- The area that is specially marked for playing a sports game is often called a **pitch** (*BrE*), **field** or **court**, depending on the sport being played. 体育运动场地常用 pitch、field 或 court 表示，依所进行的运动类型而定：
  - ▸ *a cricket/football/rugby/hockey pitch* (*BrE*) 板球场；足球场；橄榄球场；曲棍球场
  - ▸ *a soccer/baseball field* (*especially NAmE*) 足球场；棒球场
  - ▸ *a tennis/badminton/squash/basketball court* 网球场；羽毛球场；壁球场；篮球场
- A large sports ground surrounded by rows of seats for **spectators** is called a **stadium** (*plural* **stadiums** or **stadia**). 备有座位供观众观赏比赛的大型体育场称作 stadium（复数形式为 stadiums 或 stadia），观众称作 spectator：
  - ▸ *an all-seater stadium* 全座席体育场

GRAMMAR POINT 语法说明

- Names of American sports teams always start with 'the'; names of British sports teams almost never do. Names of sports teams may look either singular or plural but always take a plural verb. 美国体育运动队的名称总是以 the 开头，而英国的运动队名称几乎从不用 the。体育运动队的名称看上去可能是单数，也可能是复数，但总是用复数动词：
  - ▸ *The Jazz are playing the Chicago Bulls.* 爵士队在与芝加哥公牛队比赛。
  - ▸ *Aston Villa have started the season well.* 阿斯顿维拉队在本赛季旗开得胜。
- Teams are often referred to just by the name of the place they come from. In American English this means a singular verb is used, but in British English the verb is still plural. 运动队常以该队来自的地方名称指代。在美式英语中这就意味着要用单数动词，但在英式英语中谓语动词仍然用复数：
  - ▸ *Cincinnati is having a great season.* 辛辛那提队这一赛季成绩辉煌。
  - ▸ *Norwich were disappointed with the score.* 诺里奇队对比分感到失望。

People who take part in sports 参加体育运动的人

- A person who **plays** a particular sport is usually called a football/tennis/basketball **player**. 参加（play）某项体育运动，如足球、网球、篮球的人通常称作 player：
  - ▸ *Welsh rugby players could get £2000 each from a new sponsorship deal.* 威尔士橄榄球运动员每人可从一项新的赞助中得到 2000 英镑。
- Some sports have a special name for the players or people who do them. Some of these names end in **-er** but others do not follow a particular pattern. Check near the entry for each sport to find the correct word. 某些体育运动的运动员或参加这些运动的人有专门的名称，有的以 -er 结尾，有的并没有特定的构词模式。想知道正确的词，可在相关的体育运动词条附近查找：
  - ▸ *talented young footballers* (*BrE only*) 有才华的年轻足球运动员
  - ▸ *an Olympic boxer* 奥运拳击手
  - ▸ *top athletes from around the world* 来自世界各地的顶尖田径运动员
  - ▸ *cyclists competing in the Tour de France* 参加环法自行车赛的车手

Track events 径赛项目

hurdling 跨栏赛跑

starting blocks
起跑器

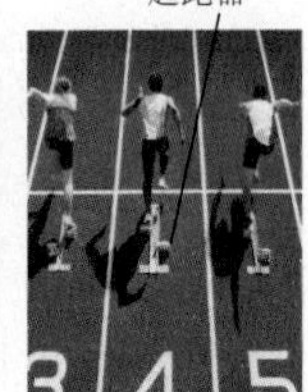

sprinting 短跑

Track events 径赛项目

- ***run** the 100 metres* 跑 100 米
- ***run** the relay* 跑接力赛

Field events 田赛项目

the high jump 跳高

the discus 掷铁饼

the pole vault 撑竿跳高

the hammer 掷链球

the javelin 掷标枪

Field events 田赛项目

- ***do** the long jump* 跳远
- ***do** the high jump* 跳高
- ***do** the pole vault* 撑竿跳高
- ***do** the triple jump* 三级跳远
- ***throw** the javelin* 掷标枪
- ***throw** the discus* 掷铁饼
- ***throw** the hammer* 掷链球
- ***put** the shot* 推铅球

Equestrian sports 马术运动

horse racing 赛马运动

showjumping
马术障碍赛

polo 马球

Talking about sports in general 一般地谈论体育运动

- You can **do sport** (*BrE*), 做体育运动可用 do sport :
  - ▸ *Do you do a lot of sport?* 你常做体育运动吗？

  ... or you can **play sports** (*especially NAmE*), 亦可用 play sports :
  - ▸ *We played sports together when we were kids.* 孩提时，我们曾一起做体育运动。

  ... but these verbs are not used very often. It is more usual to talk about liking sport/sports or **being good at** sport/sports. 不过上述动词并不很常用。较常用的有 like sport/sports（喜欢运动）或 be good at sport/sports（擅长运动）:
  - ▸ *Are you good at sport?* (*BrE*) 你擅长体育运动吗？
  - ▸ *Are you good at sports?* (*NAmE*) 你擅长体育运动吗？
  - ▸ *What sports do you like best?* 你最喜欢什么运动？
- Do **not** say that you 'practise' sport or a sport if you just mean that you do or play it. 如果只是笼统地表示做运动不要用 practise sport 或 a sport。Say 可说：
  - ▸ *I love sport.* (*BrE*) 我喜爱体育运动。
  - ▸ *I love sports.* (*NAmE*) 我喜爱体育运动。

    (No other verb is necessary. 不用加其他动词。)

    NOT 不可说 ~~*I love practising sport.*~~
- Say which sports you play. 应明确说出是何种体育运动：
  - ▸ *Every Sunday I play volleyball or badminton with my friends.* 我每个星期日都与朋友一起打排球或羽毛球。

    NOT 不可说 ~~*Every Sunday I practise sport with my friends.*~~
- However, you can use the verb 'practise', especially in American English (where it is spelt 'practice'), if it means 'to train'. 但表示练习时，可用动词 practise，尤其在美式英语中，注意美式英语的拼法为 practice :
  - ▸ *The team is practicing for its big game.* (*NAmE*) 这个队正在进行大赛前的训练。
  - ▸ *The team are in training for their big match.* (*BrE*) 这个队正在进行大赛前的训练。

GRAMMAR POINT 语法说明

- The names of sports can be used like adjectives before other nouns. 运动项目名称可用作形容词，置于其他名词前：
  - ▸ *a tennis match* 网球比赛
  - ▸ *cycling shorts* 自行车运动短裤
  - ▸ *a football team* 足球队
- The words **sports** and **sporting** (but not 'sport') can be used in the same way. * sports 和 sporting 两词均可用于上述用法（但 sport 不能）：
  - ▸ *a sports club* 体育俱乐部
  - ▸ *sports shoes* 运动鞋
  - ▸ *a sporting event* 体育比赛项目
  - ▸ *sporting goods* 体育用品

cycling 自行车运动

gymnastics 体操

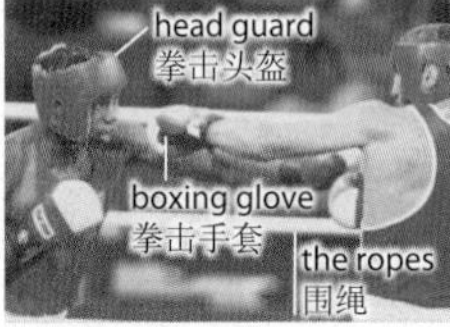

boxing 拳击运动

fencing 击剑运动

Winter sports 冬季运动

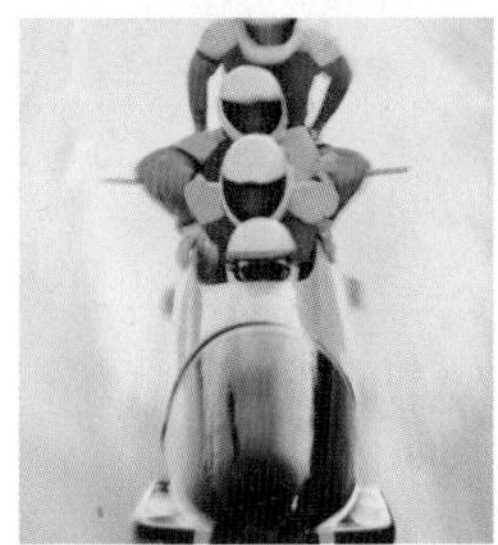
bobsleigh (*BrE*) / **bobsled** (*NAmE*) 大雪橇

the luge 无舵雪橇运动

downhill skiing 速降滑雪

cross-country skiing 越野滑雪

Extreme sports 极限运动

paragliding
滑翔伞运动

hang-gliding
悬挂式滑翔运动

snowboarding
单板滑雪运动

abseiling (*BrE*) / **rappelling** (*NAmE*)
绕绳下降运动

- Activities that involve danger or speed or both are often called **extreme sports.** Many extreme sports are done on or in water. 极限运动（extreme sports）常指危险性高、速度快或两者兼有的运动，许多极限运动是在水上或水下进行。
- **Surfing** and **bodyboarding** are similar, but a surfer stands on a surfboard to ride on the waves while a bodyboarder lies on their stomach on a bodyboard. **Kitesurfing** involves riding on a type of surfboard and being pulled along by a kite. 冲浪运动（surfing）和俯伏冲浪板运动（bodyboarding）相似，但冲浪运动员是站在冲浪板上踏浪而行，俯伏冲浪板运动员则是俯卧在冲浪板上。风筝冲浪运动（kitesurfing）是站在冲浪板上由风筝牵引行进。
- **Waterskiing** and **wakeboarding** both involve being pulled through the water by a fast boat: a waterskier wears one or two waterskis, while a wakeboarder stands sideways on a wakeboard. 水橇滑水运动（waterskiing）和尾浪滑水运动（wakeboarding）均由快艇牵引；水橇滑水运动员穿着一只或两只滑水橇，尾浪滑水运动员则是侧站在尾波板上滑行。
- Other extreme sports involve jumping from great heights. **Skydivers** jump from a plane and fall for as long as they safely can before opening their **parachutes.** You can jump from the side of a mountain, wearing a kind of parachute in **paragliding**, or a frame like a very large kite in **hang-gliding. Parasailing** and **base jumping** are both also done wearing parachutes. In parasailing you are pulled behind a fast boat and rise into the air. A base jumper jumps from the top of a tall building or bridge (BASE stands for building, antenna, span, earth). 其他一些极限运动是从高处往下跳。特技跳伞运动员（skydiver）是从飞机上往下跳，在安全的前提下尽可能延迟张伞（parachute）；做滑翔伞运动（paragliding）是系着降落伞从山崖上往下跳；做悬挂式滑翔运动（hang-gliding）则系着像风筝一样的支架往下跳。帆伞运动（parasailing）和高处跳伞运动（base jumping）也是系着降落伞进行的。做帆伞运动由快艇牵引在空中滑翔；高处跳伞运动员则从高楼顶或桥上往下跳（BASE 由 building、antenna、span 和 earth 的首字母组成）。
- In **rock climbing**, a rope is attached to the climber and the rock for safety – this is called **belaying.** The climber wears a **harness** to which the rope is attached with a metal ring called a **karabiner.** 在攀岩运动（rock climbing）中，攀岩者身上绑着绳索，另一头系在岩石上以保安全，叫作 belaying。攀岩者身系保护带（harness），用穿索铁锁（karabiner）将绳索扣在保护带上。

- **Skateboarders** and **snowboarders** may ride on a **half-pipe**: a U-shaped structure or a U-shaped channel cut into the snow. They do jumps and tricks, for example a **fakie**, an **ollie**, or a **kick-turn**. 滑板运动员（skateboarder）和滑雪板运动员（snowboarder）可在 U 形滑道（half-pipe）上做各种飞跃和技巧动作，如倒溜（fakie）、翱骊（ollie）或倒板调头（kick-turn）。

skydiving 特技跳伞运动

bungee jumping
蹦极跳

waterskiing
水橇滑水运动

wakeboarding
尾浪滑水运动

windsurfing
帆板运动

surfing 冲浪运动

jet-skiing
喷气式滑艇运动

bodyboarding
俯伏冲浪板运动

white-water rafting
激流漂流运动

kitesurfing / kiteboarding
风筝冲浪运动

parkour 跑酷

Cycles 自行车；摩托车

Other types of bicycle and motorcycle 其他类型的自行车和摩托车

- An early type of bicycle with a very large front wheel and a very small back wheel is a **penny-farthing.** 早期自行车（penny-farthing）前轮很大，后轮很小。
- A stationary bicycle that is used indoors to exercise is an **exercise bike.** 健身脚踏车（exercise bike）置于室内，供人进行锻炼。
- A motorcycle with a small engine and pedals is a **moped.** 机器脚踏车（moped）是使用小型发动机、带脚蹬的摩托车。

Cars 汽车

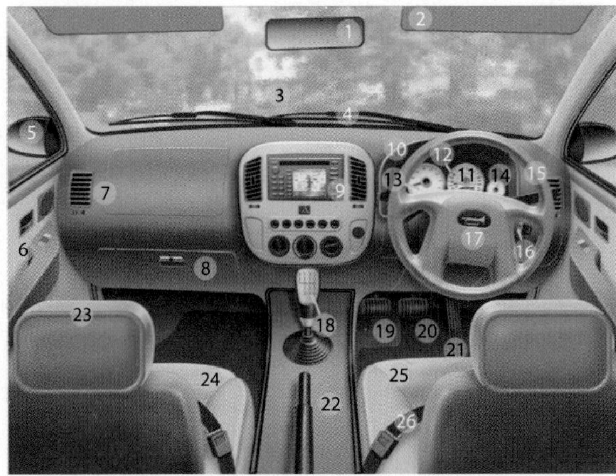

1 rear-view mirror 后视镜
2 visor 遮阳板
3 windscreen (*BrE*) / windshield (*NAmE*) 挡风玻璃
4 windscreen wiper (*BrE*) / windshield wiper (*NAmE*) 雨刮器
5 wing mirror (*BrE*) / side-view mirror (*NAmE*) 侧翼后视镜
6 door handle 门把手
7 air vent 通气孔
8 glove compartment / glove box 杂物箱
9 satnav (*also* sat nav) 卫星导航
10 dashboard 仪表板
11 milometer (*BrE*) / odometer (*NAmE*) 里程表
12 speedometer 车速计
13 rev counter 转速计
14 fuel gauge 燃料表
15 steering wheel 方向盘
16 ignition 点火装置
17 horn 喇叭
18 gear lever (*BrE*) / gearshift (*NAmE*) 变速杆
19 clutch 离合器踏板
20 brake 刹车
21 accelerator 油门
22 handbrake (*especially BrE*) / emergency brake (*NAmE*) 手闸
23 headrest 头枕
24 passenger seat 副驾驶座
25 driver's seat 驾驶座
26 seat belt 安全带

convertible 活动顶篷式汽车

aerial (*especially BrE*) / antenna (*especially NAmE*) 天线
side window 侧窗
wing (*BrE*) / fender (*NAmE*) 翼子板
rear window 后窗
door 车门
bumper 保险杠
hubcap 轮毂盖

hatchback 掀背式汽车

saloon (*BrE*) / **sedan** (*NAmE*) 小轿车

four-wheel drive 四轮驱动轿车

sports car (*US also* **sport car**) 跑车

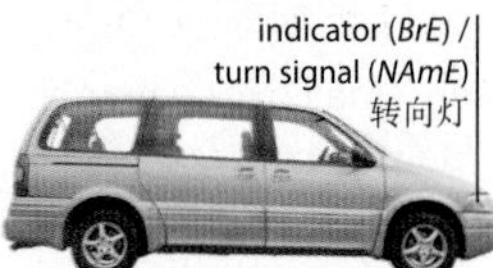

people carrier (*BrE*) / **minivan** (*especially NAmE*) 小型面包车

estate car (*BrE*) / **station wagon** (*NAmE*) 旅行轿车

Verbs to talk about driving 有关驾驶的动词

- to control the direction in which the car is going: **steer** 掌控方向盘
- to change direction suddenly: **swerve** 突然转向；急转弯
- to signal that your car is going to turn: **indicate** 打行车转向信号
- to make a car go faster: **speed up, accelerate, put your foot down** 加速行驶；踩油门
- to make a car go more slowly: **slow down, brake, put the brake on** 减缓车速；踩刹车
- to put the engine into a higher/lower gear as you get faster/slower: **change up/down** 换高/低挡；加/减速
- to allow another vehicle to go before you: **give way** (*BrE*) / **yield** (*NAmE*) 让路
- to pass another vehicle because you are moving faster: **overtake** 超车
- to turn round and go back along the same road: **do/make a U-turn** *U 形转弯；180度转弯
- to stop and leave the car: **park** 停车

Aircraft 航空器

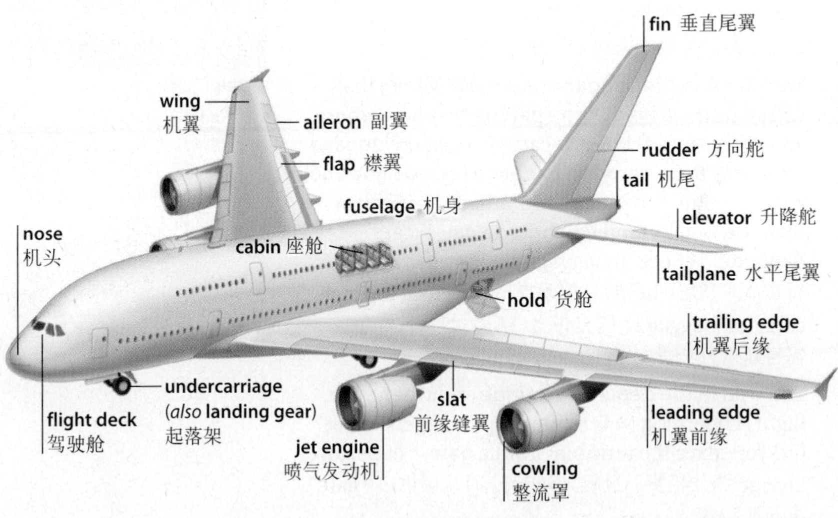

aerobatic display 特技飞行表演

light aircraft 轻型飞机

helicopter 直升机

ski-plane 滑橇起落架飞机

glider 滑翔机

microlight (*BrE*) 微型飞机

seaplane 水上飞机

fighter 战斗机

biplane 双翼飞机

At the airport 在机场

- An airport building where journeys begin and end is a **terminal.** You go to the **check-in desk** and say you have arrived (**check in**). * terminal 指航站楼，是旅程开始和结束的地方。在登机手续办理处（check-in desk）办理登机手续用 check in。

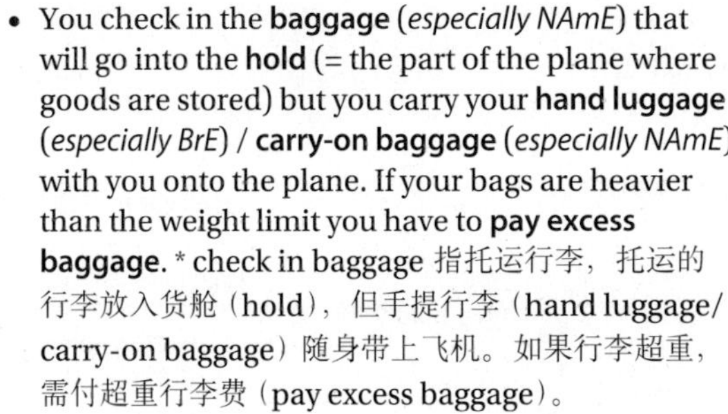

- You check in the **baggage** (*especially NAmE*) that will go into the **hold** (= the part of the plane where goods are stored) but you carry your **hand luggage** (*especially BrE*) / **carry-on baggage** (*especially NAmE*) with you onto the plane. If your bags are heavier than the weight limit you have to **pay excess baggage.** * check in baggage 指托运行李，托运的行李放入货舱（hold），但手提行李（hand luggage/ carry-on baggage）随身带上飞机。如果行李超重，需付超重行李费（pay excess baggage）。
- You wait in the **departure lounge** and when your flight **is boarding** (= is ready for passengers to get on) you leave the terminal from a **gate.** * departure lounge 指候机室，登机（board）时从登机口（gate）离开航站楼。
- When you arrive at your destination in a different country you **disembark** and go through **immigration**. Collect your **luggage** (*especially BrE*) from **baggage reclaim** (*BrE*) / **baggage claim** (*NAmE*) and exit through **customs.** 到达另一国家目的地下机（disembark）后要通过移民局检查站（immigration）。在行李提取处（baggage reclaim/ baggage claim）领取行李，然后通过海关（customs）离开。

airship 飞艇

hot-air balloon 热气球

Boats and ships 船

container ship 集装箱船

lifeboat 救生船

ferry 渡船

hovercraft 气垫船

hydrofoil 水翼船

catamaran 双体船

liner 邮轮

canal boat / narrowboat 运河船

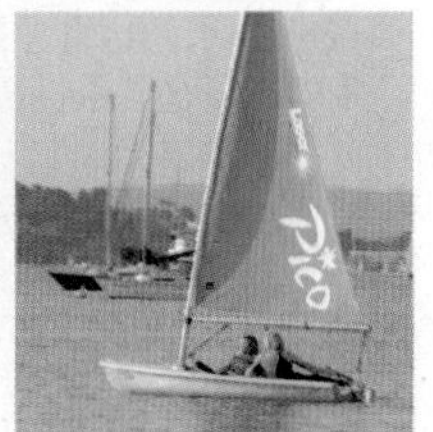

sailing dinghy (*NAmE also* **sailboat**) 帆船

paddle steamer (*BrE*) / **paddleboat** (*NAmE*) 桨轮蒸汽船

cruiser / cabin cruiser（可住宿的）舱式游艇

speedboat 快艇

rowing boat (*BrE*) / **rowboat** (*NAmE*) 划艇

More kinds of boat 其他种类的船

- Any large boat that is used for carrying passengers or goods by sea is a **ship**, or (*formal*) a **vessel**. * ship 或（正式用语）vessel 指轮船：
  - ▸ *In which country was this vessel registered?* 这艘船是在哪个国家注册的？
- A ship that carries goods from one place to another is a **freighter** or **cargo ship**, and one that is used for carrying large amounts of petrol, oil, etc. is an **(oil) tanker**. * freighter 或 cargo ship 指货船，(oil) tanker 指油轮。
- A boat that is used for catching fish is a **fishing boat**, and a special type of fishing boat which pulls a long net through the sea to catch fish is a **trawler**. * fishing boat 指渔船，trawler 指拖网渔船。

- **Lifeboat** has two meanings: it is a special boat that is used to rescue people who are in danger at sea, or it is a small boat that is kept on a ship and used by people to escape if the ship is going to sink.
  * lifeboat 有两个含义：一是指派往海上救援的救生船，二是指船上备用的救生艇。
- **Raft** also has two meanings: it is a small boat made of rubber or plastic that is filled with air, or it is a flat structure made of pieces of wood tied together and used as a boat. * raft 亦有两个含义：一是指橡皮艇、充气船，二是指木排、筏。

kayak (*BrE also* **canoe**)
皮划艇

canoe 划艇

punt 方头平底船

gondola 威尼斯小划船

Groups of boats 船队

- A group of boats that sail and work together is a **fleet.** * fleet 指一起航行和作业的船队：
  - ▸ *a fishing fleet* 捕鱼船队
- A group of boats travelling together is a **flotilla** or a **convoy.** * flotilla 或 convoy 指同行的船队：
  - ▸ *The boats travelled **in convoy**.* 这些船只结队航行。
  - ▸ *We were travelling in a flotilla of boats.* 我们随船队航行。

Travelling by boat 驾船/乘船旅行

- You **sail** a sailing boat or yacht, **row** a rowing boat, and **paddle** a canoe or kayak. * sail 指驾驶或乘坐（帆船或游船）；row 指划（划艇）；paddle 指用桨划（皮划艇）：
  - ▸ *My brother's planning to sail (his yacht) to Bermuda.* 我哥哥计划驾（帆）船去百慕大群岛。
  - ▸ *They rowed (the boat) back to shore.* 他们划船回到了岸上。
- You **go sailing, go yachting, go rowing** and **go canoeing.** * go sailing 指驾船运动；go yachting 指驾快艇或帆船运动；go rowing 指划船；go canoeing 指划/乘独木舟。
- When you get on a ship you **board** (it), or (*formal*) **embark.** * board 或（正式用语）embark 指上船：
  - ▸ *We boarded the ship at midday.* 我们正午上了船。
  - ▸ *One passenger had embarked at Alexandria.* 一名乘客在亚历山德里亚登船了。
- When you get off a ship you **go ashore**, or (*formal*) **disembark.** * go ashore 或（正式用语）disembark 指下船（离船上岸）。
- To begin a journey by sea is to **set sail (from/to/for** a place). * set sail 指（从某地）起航（前往某地）：
  - ▸ *Twenty competitors set sail from Rio on the round-the-world race.* 二十名参赛者从里约热内卢起航进行环球航行比赛。
- When you are on a ship you are **on board** or **aboard.** * on board 或 aboard 指在船上：
  - ▸ *There were a thousand passengers on board.* 船上有一千名乘客。
  - ▸ *All aboard please!* 请大家上船！

- When you are sailing on the sea in a ship, you are **at sea.** * at sea 指在海上航行。
- A holiday where you travel by boat and visit a number of places is a **cruise.** * cruise 指乘船游览：
  ▸ *They're going on a cruise.* 他们正在乘船游览。
- A long journey by sea is a **voyage.** * voyage 指航海：
  ▸ *Captain Cook made his first voyage to the South Pacific in 1768.* 库克船长于 1768 年第一次航行去南太平洋。
- If a boat moves backwards and forwards it **pitches;** if it moves from side to side it **rolls.** * pitch 指船颠簸、前后摇荡；roll 指船摇摆、左右摇晃：
  ▸ *The trawler was pitching and rolling violently in the storm.* 拖网渔船在暴风雨中剧烈地颠簸摇晃。
- To be carried along by wind or water in no particular direction is to **drift.** * drift 指随风或随水漂流（或漂浮）：
  ▸ *The boat drifted out to sea.* 船向海上漂去。

Parts of boats 船的各个部位

yacht (*NAmE also* **sailboat**) 帆船

- The side of a boat that is on the left when you are facing the front: **port** * port 指船的左舷
- The side of a boat that is on the right when you are facing the front: **starboard** * starboard 指船的右舷
- The top outside floor of a boat is called the **deck.** * deck 是甲板、舱面：
  ▸ *Let's go and sit **on deck**.* 我们去甲板上坐吧。
- The other floors are also called **decks.** * deck 亦指船的一层、（某一）层：
  ▸ *the lower deck of a ship* 船的下层
- A small room in a boat where you can sleep is a **cabin,** and a kind of bed in a cabin is a **bunk** or a **berth.** * cabin 指轮船上供休息睡觉的舱室；bunk 或 berth 指船上隔间里的卧铺/铺位：
  ▸ *a cabin with four berths* 有四个铺位的船舱
- The kitchen on a boat is the **galley** and a round window is called a **porthole.** * galley 指船上的厨房；porthole 指圆形的舷窗。

Steering a boat 驾驶船只

- A piece of wood or metal in the water at the back of a boat that is used for controlling its direction is a **rudder.** * rudder 指船尾控制方向的木制或金属舵。
- A bar that is used to turn the rudder of a small boat in order to steer it is a **tiller.** * tiller 指小船的舵柄。
- A handle or wheel used for steering a larger boat or ship is called the **helm.** * helm 指大船的舵柄或舵轮。
- The part of a ship where the captain and other officers stand when they are controlling the ship is **the bridge.** * bridge 指船的驾驶台、船桥。

Vehicles 车辆

Buses 公交车

double-decker 双层公交车

single-decker 单层公交车

minibus 小型公交车

school bus 校车

bus (*BrE also* **coach**) （长途）客车

Trucks, etc. 卡车等

articulated lorry (*BrE*) / **tractor-trailer** (*NAmE*) 铰接式卡车

lorry (*BrE*) / **truck** (*especially NAmE*) 卡车

transporter 大型载重运输车

tanker 罐车

van 厢式客货车

forklift truck 叉车

breakdown truck (*BrE*) / **tow truck** (*especially NAmE*) 救险车

pickup (*also* **pickup truck**) 轻型货车

Jeep™ 吉普车

Transporting goods 运输货物

- Items that are carried by lorries, trains, aeroplanes and ships are called **freight** [U]. * freight 指陆运、空运或海运的货物：
  ▸ *a freight train* 货运列车
- Items that are carried by road or rail are also called **goods** (*BrE*) (*pl.*). 陆运的货物又称 goods：
  ▸ *a goods vehicle* 运货车
- Items that are carried by air and sea are also called **cargo** [C, U]. 空运或海运的货物又称 cargo：
  ▸ *a cargo plane* 货机
- Something that is being carried, usually in large amounts, is a **load**. * load 指（通常量大的）负载：
  ▸ *A lorry shed its load* (= accidentally dropped its load) *on the motorway.* 一辆卡车在高速公路上掉下了货物。

- A load of goods that is sent from one place to another is a **shipment**. * shipment 指运输的大量货物。
- A large metal box in which goods are transported by sea, rail or road is a **container**. * container 指海运或陆运集装箱。

caravan (*BrE*) / **camper** (*NAmE*) 旅行拖车

camper (*BrE*) / **recreational vehicle (RV)** (*NAmE*) 野营车

tractor 拖拉机

taxi (*also* **cab, taxicab**) 出租车

Trains, etc. 火车等

high-speed train 高速列车

freight train (*BrE also* **goods train**) 货运列车

passenger train 客运列车

underground (*BrE*) / **subway** (*NAmE*) 地铁

steam train 蒸汽火车

funicular 缆索铁道

cable car （悬空的）缆车

tram (*BrE*) / **streetcar** (*US*) 有轨电车

Construction vehicles 建筑施工车辆

excavator 挖掘机

dumper truck (*NAmE also* **dump truck**) 翻斗车

cement mixer 混凝土搅拌机

bulldozer 推土机

The body 身体

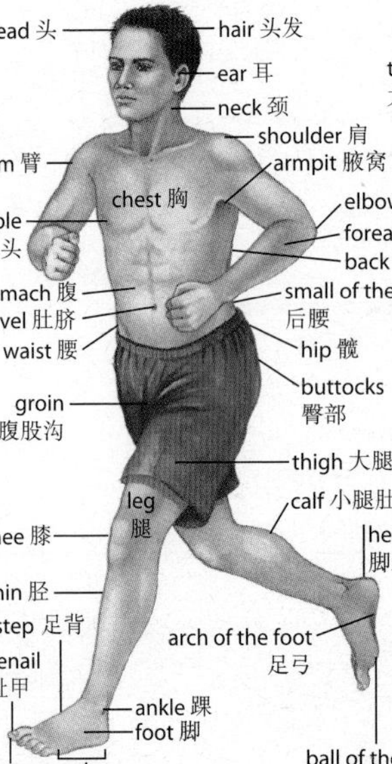

head 头
hair 头发
ear 耳
neck 颈
shoulder 肩
armpit 腋窝
arm 臂
chest 胸
nipple 乳头
elbow 肘
forearm 前臂
back 背
stomach 腹
small of the back 后腰
navel 肚脐
waist 腰
hip 髋
buttocks 臀部
groin 腹股沟
thigh 大腿
leg 腿
calf 小腿肚
knee 膝
heel 脚跟
shin 胫
instep 足背
arch of the foot 足弓
toenail 趾甲
ankle 踝
foot 脚
ball of the foot 跖球
big toe 大脚趾
sole 足底

the body 身体

crown of the head 头顶
temple 太阳穴
forehead 额
bridge of the nose 鼻梁
cheek 面颊
nose 鼻
nostril 鼻孔
mouth 嘴
lip 嘴唇
tooth 牙
nape of the neck 颈背
jaw 颌
chin 下巴

the face 脸

middle finger 中指
ring finger 无名指
index finger / first finger 食指
cuticle 甲小皮
thumb 拇指
knuckle 指关节
little finger 小指
palm 手掌
fingernail 指甲
wrist 手腕

the hand 手

eyebrow 眉
eyelid 眼睑
white 眼白
eyelash 睫毛
iris 虹膜
pupil 瞳孔
tear duct 鼻泪管
ciliary muscle 睫状肌
iris 虹膜
sclera 巩膜
cornea 角膜
retina 视网膜
lens 晶状体
optic nerve 视神经
eyeball 眼球

the eye 眼睛

skull / cranium 颅骨
cheekbone 颧骨
jawbone / mandible 下颌骨
breastbone / sternum 胸骨
collarbone / clavicle 锁骨
shoulder blade / scapula 肩胛骨
ribcage 胸廓
humerus 肱骨
rib 肋骨
vertebra 椎骨
backbone / spine 脊柱
ulna 尺骨
radius 桡骨
hip bone 髋骨
pelvis 骨盆
tailbone / coccyx 尾骨
thigh bone / femur 股骨
cartilage 软骨
shin bone / tibia 胫骨
fibula 腓骨

the skeleton 骨骼

brain 脑
spinal cord 脊髓
uvula 悬雍垂
tonsil 扁桃体
pharynx 咽
gullet / oesophagus (*BrE*) / esophagus (*NAmE*) 食道
larynx 喉
windpipe / trachea 气管
bronchial tube 支气管
lung 肺
heart 心脏
capillaries 毛细血管
liver 肝
bile duct 胆管
stomach 胃
kidney 肾
spleen 脾
gall bladder 胆囊
duodenum 十二指肠
pancreas 胰腺
colon 结肠
large intestine 大肠
small intestine 小肠
appendix 阑尾
rectum 直肠
bladder 膀胱
anus 肛门

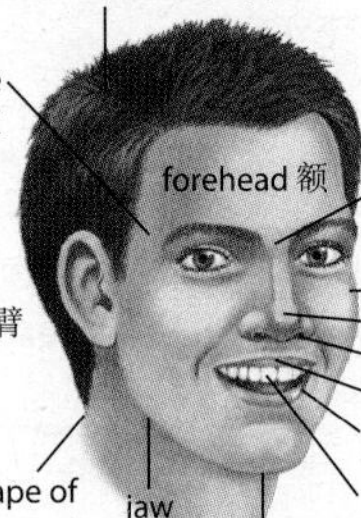

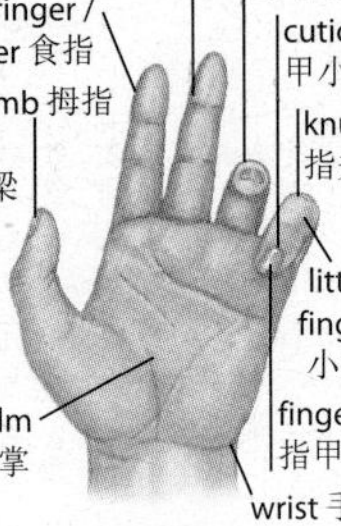

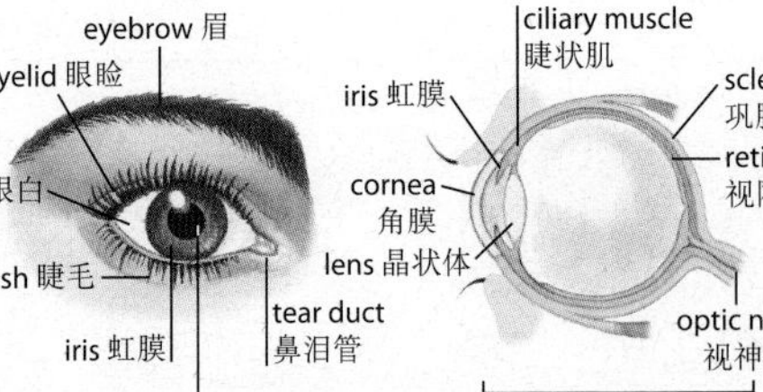

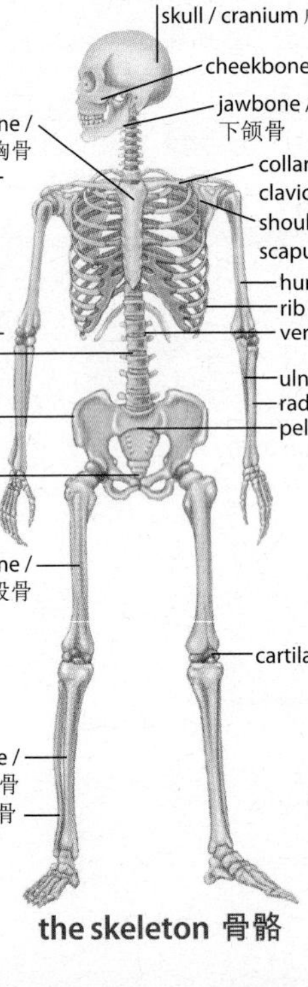

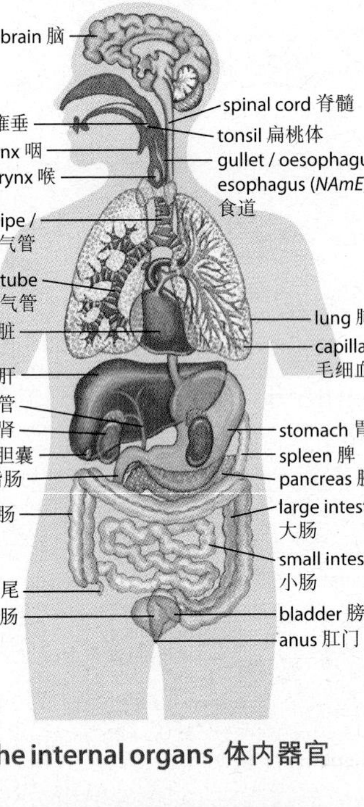

the internal organs 体内器官

Hair 发型

crew cut 平头 | **shaved head** 剃光的头 | **bald head** 秃头 | **receding hairline** 渐秃的头 | **long hair** 长发

flat-top 平顶头 | **spiky** 刺猬头 | **dreadlocks** 长发绺 | **cornrows** 玉米垄 | **bob** 女式齐短发 | **shoulder-length** 齐肩发

chignon 发髻 | **bun** 圆发髻 | **French pleat** (*BrE*) / **French twist** (*NAmE*) 法式盘发 | **long, wavy** 长波浪发 | **curly** 鬈发 | **perm** 烫发

plait (*BrE*) / **braid** (*NAmE*) （一根）发辫

French plait (*BrE*) / **French braid** (*NAmE*) 法式辫子

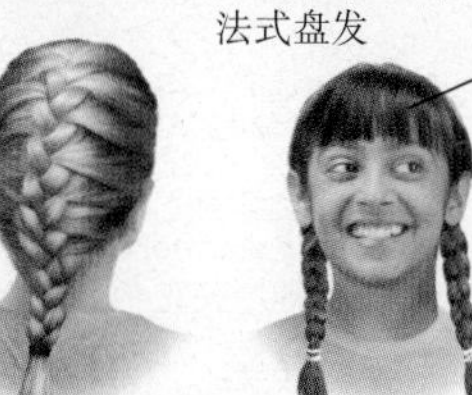

pigtails (*BrE*) / **braids** (*NAmE*) （两根）辫子

bunches (*BrE*) / **pigtails** (*NAmE*) 束发

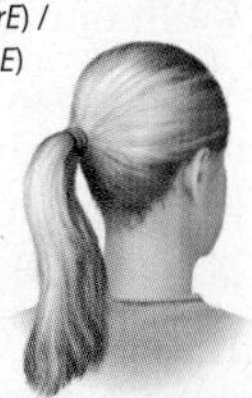

ponytail 马尾辫

Make-up 化妆品

foundation 粉底霜

concealer 遮瑕膏

blusher (*NAmE* *also* **blush**) 胭脂

powder 扑面粉

eyeliner (*also* **liner**) 眼线笔

eyeshadow 眼影

lip gloss 唇彩

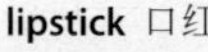

lip liner 唇线笔

lipstick 口红

mascara 睫毛膏

nail polish (*BrE* *also* **nail varnish**) 指甲油

Clothes 服装

patterned waistcoat (*BrE*) / **vest** (*NAmE*) 印花西服背心

striped 条纹

polka dots 圆点

tartan / plaid 花格

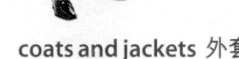

bow ties 蝶形领结

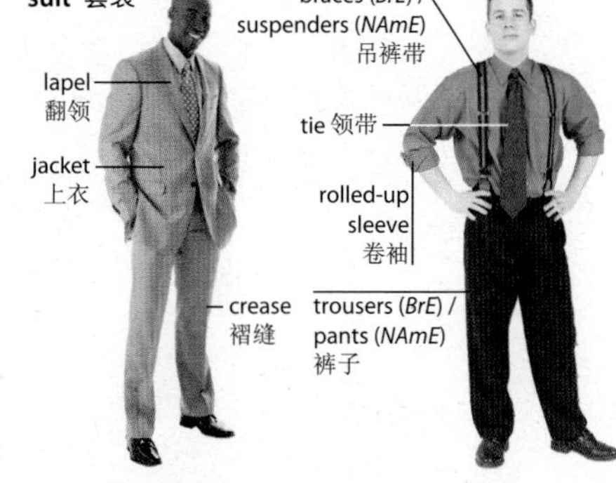

- The general word for what you wear is **clothes** (*plural*) or **clothing** [U] (*formal*). 泛指衣服用 clothes 或 clothing :
  - ▸ *She always wears such lovely clothes.* 她总是穿着这么漂亮的衣服。
  - ▸ *a piece of clothing* 一件衣服
- A set of clothes that you wear together, especially for a particular occasion or purpose, is an **outfit**. 全套服装（尤指为特定场合或目的而穿）用 outfit。
- Any piece of clothing worn on the top part of the body, especially by women, can be called a **top**. 上衣（尤指女人穿的）可叫作 top。
- The clothes which some children wear at school, or which some people wear at work, are called a **uniform** [C, U]. 校服或制服叫作 uniform。
- When police officers wear ordinary clothes instead of uniforms, they are in **plain clothes**. 警察穿的便衣是 plain clothes :
  - ▸ *a plain-clothes police sergeant* 一名便衣警长

Describing clothes and the way people look 描述衣服和衣着

Clothes can be 形容衣服可用 :

- attractive and designed well: **elegant** 漂亮雅致

coats and jackets 外套和上衣

overcoat 长大衣

raincoat 雨衣

body warmer 无袖厚夹克

denim jacket 牛仔布夹克

leather jacket 皮夹克

anorak 带帽防寒短上衣

sleeveless dress 无袖连衣裙

skirt 女裙

- untidy and dirty:
scruffy 不整洁、邋遢
- clean, tidy and rather formal:
smart (*especially BrE*) 光鲜、讲究、正式
- not formal: **casual** 随便
- fashionable and attractive:
stylish 时髦、高雅
- very fashionable:
trendy (*informal*) 很时髦
- fitting closely to your body:
tight, close-fitting, skintight 紧身
- not fitting closely:
loose, baggy 宽松
- If a piece of clothing is not too big and not too small, it **fits** you. 衣服合身用 fit :
  - ▸ *These jeans don't fit me any more.* 我这条牛仔裤不合身了。
- If a piece of clothing looks good on you, it **suits** you. 衣服与人相配用 suit :
  - ▸ *It's a nice coat, but it doesn't really suit you.* 这大衣很好，但不大适合你穿。

British and American differences 英美服装用语的区别

- a short piece of clothing with buttons down the front but no sleeves, usually worn over a shirt and under a jacket 西服背心：英式英语是 waistcoat，美式英语是 vest :

British English	**waistcoat**
American English	**vest**

- a piece of underwear worn under a shirt, etc. next to the skin 贴身穿的背心或汗衫：英式英语是 vest，美式英语是 undershirt :

British English	**vest**
American English	**undershirt**

- a piece of clothing that covers the body from the waist down, and is divided into two parts to cover each leg separately 裤子：英式英语是 trousers，美式英语是 pants :

British English	**trousers**
American English	**pants**

- a piece of men's underwear worn under their trousers/pants 男内裤：英式英语是 pants（或 underpants），美式英语是 underpants :

British English	**pants** (*or* **underpants**)
American English	**underpants**

- a loose dress with no sleeves, usually worn over a shirt or blouse 通常套在衬衫外面的无袖女装：英式英语是 pinafore，美式英语是 jumper :

British English	**pinafore**
American English	**jumper**

- a knitted woollen or cotton piece of clothing for the upper part of the body with long sleeves and no buttons 针织套衫：英式英语是 jumper，美式英语是 sweater :

British English	**jumper**
American English	**sweater**

- straps for holding trousers/pants up 吊裤带：英式英语是 braces，美式英语是 suspenders :

British English	**braces**
American English	**suspenders**

- short elastic fastenings for holding up socks or stockings 吊袜带：英式英语是 suspenders，美式英语是 garters :

British English	**suspenders**
American English	**garters**

Fastening clothes 扣/系衣服

- To talk about fastening a piece of clothing in general, use **do** sth **up**, **fasten** sth; *opposite*: **undo** sth. 扣好或系好用 do up、fasten，解开用 undo：
  - ▸ *Do your coat up.* 把你的外套扣上。
  - ▸ *Your shirt is undone.* 你的衬衫没扣好。
- There are some special verbs for particular types of fastener. 有一些动词适用于特定扣件：
  - ▸ buttons: **button** sth (**up**); *opposite*: **unbutton** sth 纽扣：button (up)（扣上…的纽扣），反义为 unbutton（解开…的纽扣）
  - ▸ a zip: **zip** sth **up**; *opposite*: **unzip** sth 拉链：zip up（拉上…的拉链），反义为 unzip（拉开…的拉链）

button-down collar 纽扣领
breast pocket 胸袋
shirt 男衬衫
sleeve 袖子
belt 腰带
cuff 袖口
fly （裤子的）前裆开口
jeans 牛仔裤

hoody 连帽运动衫
cargo pants （多口袋）工装裤
pocket 口袋

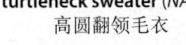

V-neck V形领
cardigan 开襟毛衣

hanger 衣架
polo shirt 马球衫

T-shirt * T恤衫

shorts 短裤

pyjamas / **pajamas** (*especially US*)（一套）睡衣裤

dressing gown (*BrE*) / **bathrobe** (*NAmE*) 晨衣

sweaters (*BrE also* jumpers) 针织套衫

polo neck (*BrE*) / **turtleneck sweater** (*NAmE*) 高圆翻领毛衣

crew-neck sweater 圆领套头毛衣

fasteners 扣件

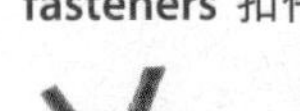

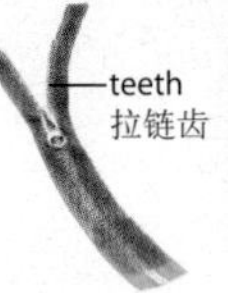

zip (*BrE*) / **zipper** (*especially NAmE*) 拉链

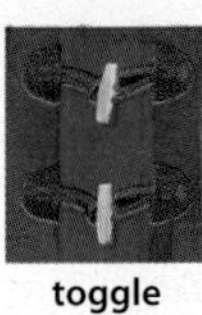
toggle 棒形纽扣

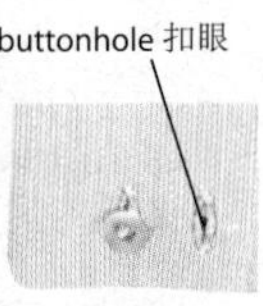

button 纽扣

Velcro™ 魔术贴

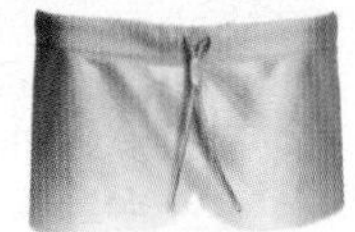
drawstring 拉绳

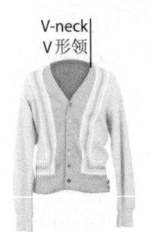

buckle 搭扣

safety pin 安全别针

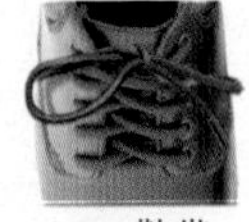
lace 鞋带

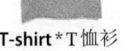

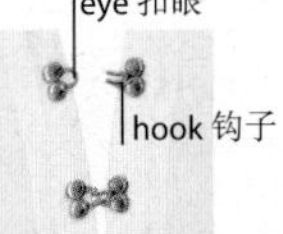

hook and eye 钩眼扣

press stud / **popper** (*both BrE*) / **snap** (*NAmE*) 摁扣

Accessories（服装）配饰

Shoes 鞋

slingback
露跟女鞋

mule 凉拖鞋

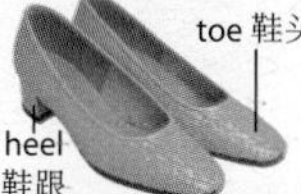

court shoes (*BrE*) / **pumps** (*NAmE*)
半高跟女鞋

flats (*BrE also* **pumps**)
休闲女鞋

clogs 木屐

stiletto
细高跟女鞋

wedge 坡跟鞋

platform
厚底鞋

kitten heels
弧状细矮跟鞋

slippers 便鞋

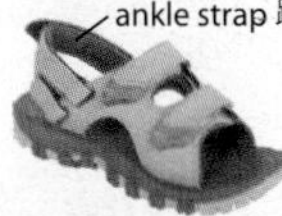

sandal 凉鞋

jelly shoe 轻便塑料鞋

flip-flops (*NAmE also* **thongs**) 人字拖鞋

moccasins
莫卡辛软皮鞋

lace-ups 系带鞋

brogues
（粗革）拷花皮鞋

loafer
平底便鞋

trainers (*BrE*) / **sneakers** (*NAmE*)
运动鞋

baseball boots
棒球鞋

boot 靴子

cowboy boot 牛仔靴

hiking boots (*also* **walking boots**) 远足旅行靴

wellingtons (*BrE*) / **rubber boots** (*NAmE*)
及膝胶靴

Bags 包

handbag
(*NAmE also* **purse**)
手提包

shoulder bag
（小）挎包

clutch bag
女式小手提包

bumbag (*BrE*) / **fanny pack** (*NAmE*) 腰包

backpack (*BrE also* **rucksack**) 背包

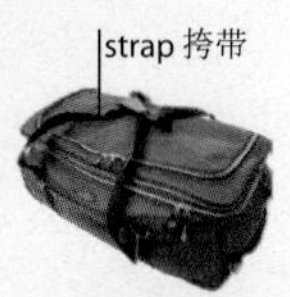

holdall (*BrE*) / **duffel bag** (*NAmE*)
旅行袋

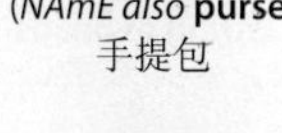
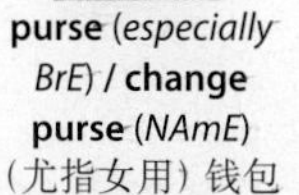
purse (*especially BrE*) / **change purse** (*NAmE*)
（尤指女用）钱包

wallet
(*NAmE also* **billfold**)
皮夹子

attaché case
(*also* **briefcase**)
公文包

briefcase
公文包

suitcase
手提箱

trunk
大箱子

Hats 帽子

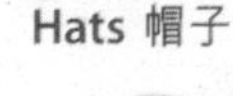

panama 巴拿马草帽

boater 平顶硬草帽

trilby 软毡帽

cowboy hat 牛仔帽

bowler (*BrE*) / **derby** (*NAmE*) 常礼帽

top hat 高顶礼帽

mortar board 学位帽

cap 制服帽

cloth cap / flat cap (*both BrE*) 布帽

baseball cap 棒球帽

beret 贝雷帽

hard hat 安全帽

crash helmet 防护头盔

beanie 无檐小便帽

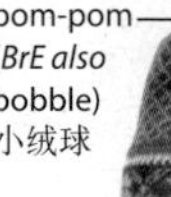

bobble hat 绒球帽

sou'wester 防雨帽

hood 风帽

sun hats 阔边遮阳帽

sombrero 墨西哥阔边帽

Gloves 手套

fingerless gloves 无指手套

mitten 连指手套

glove （分指）手套

Scarves 围巾

scarf 围巾

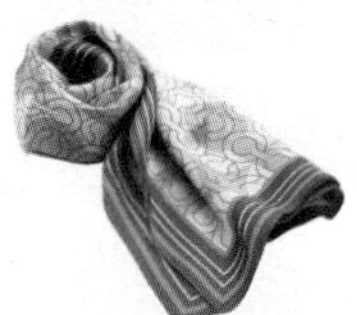
silk scarf 丝绸围巾

Jewellery 首饰

stud 耳钉

clip-on earring 夹式耳环

pendant 项链垂饰

medallion 纪念章式项链坠

locket 盒式项链坠

chain 项链

string of beads 一串珠子

hoop earring 圈状耳环

dangly earrings 耳坠

signet ring 图章戒指

wedding ring / wedding band 结婚戒指

cufflinks 袖扣

bangle 手镯

charm bracelet 吊饰手镯

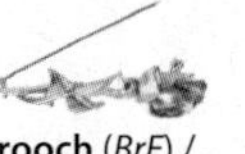
brooch (*BrE*) / **pin** (*NAmE*) 饰针

badge (*also* **button** *especially NAmE*) 徽章

pearl necklace 珍珠项链

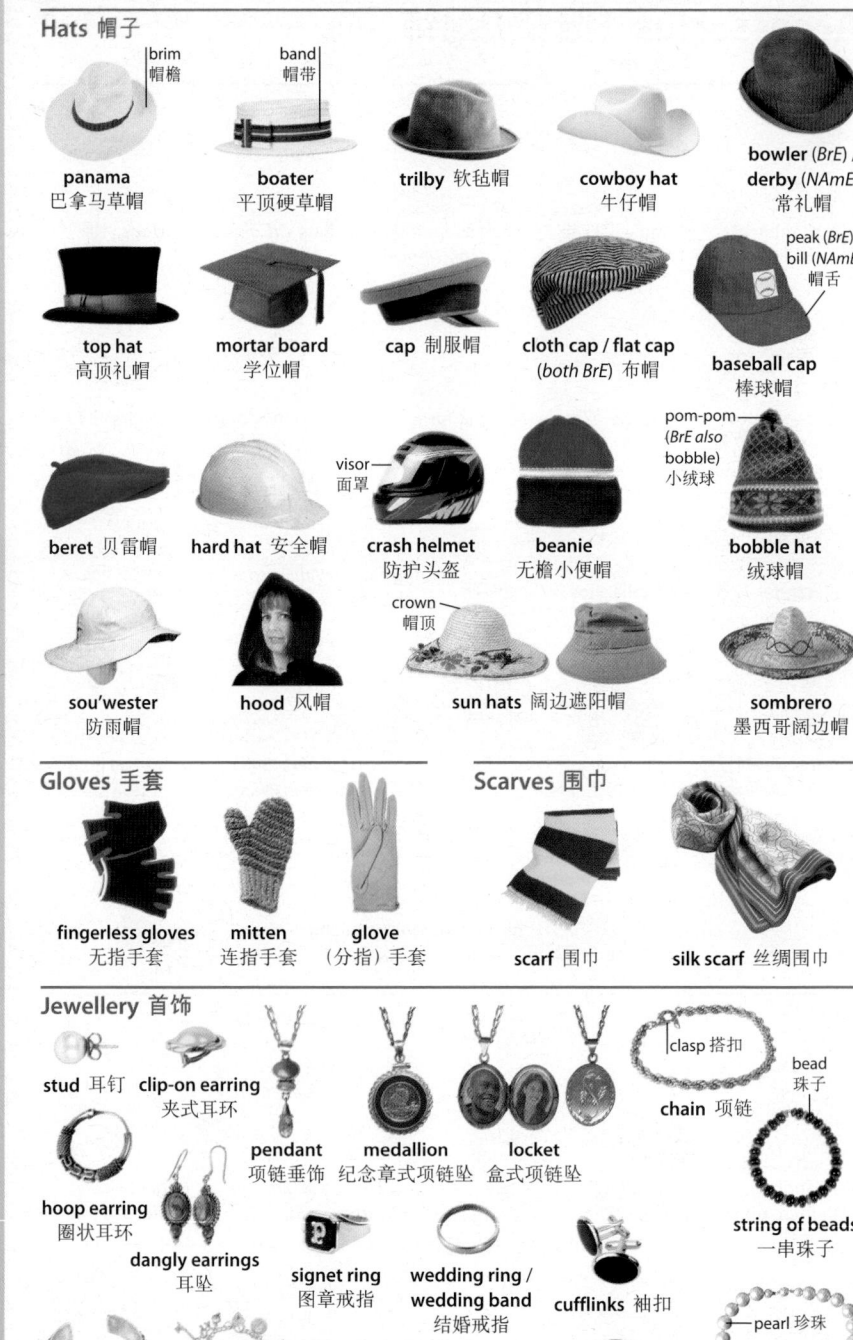

Office 办公室

1 wall planner 壁挂式规划表
2 noticeboard (*BrE*) / bulletin board (*NAmE*) 布告板
3 flip chart 活动挂图
4 data projector 数码投影仪
5 laptop 笔记本电脑
6 meeting/conference room 会议室
7 water cooler 饮水冷却机
8 desk lamp 台灯
9 workstation / PC 工作站/个人计算机
10 partition 隔板
11 in tray (*BrE*) / inbox (*NAmE*) 收件盘
12 out tray (*BrE*) / outbox (*NAmE*) 待发信件盘
13 calendar 日历
14 pen holder 笔筒
15 mouse mat (*BrE*) / mouse pad (*NAmE*) 鼠标垫
16 flatbed scanner 平板扫描仪
17 calculator 计算器
18 desk diary (*BrE*) / appointment book (*NAmE*) 台式记事簿
19 desk 办公桌
20 stationery tray 文具盘
21 waste-paper basket (*BrE*) / wastebasket (*NAmE*) 废纸篓
22 swivel chair 转椅
23 arm 扶手
24 printer 打印机
25 hard copy / printout 打印件
26 castor (*BrE*) / caster (*NAmE*) 小脚轮
27 filing cabinet (*BrE*) / file cabinet (*NAmE*) 文件柜
28 suspension file 悬挂式文件夹
29 photocopier 复印机

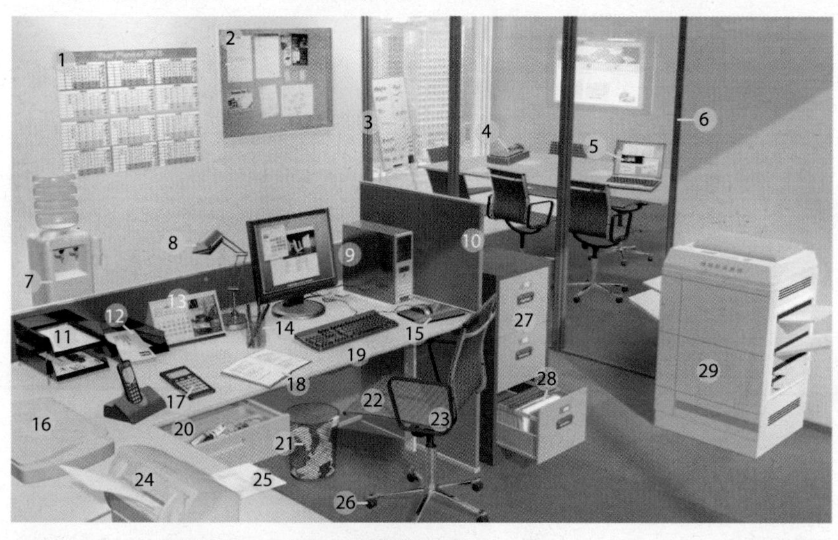

Stationery and office supplies 文具和办公用品

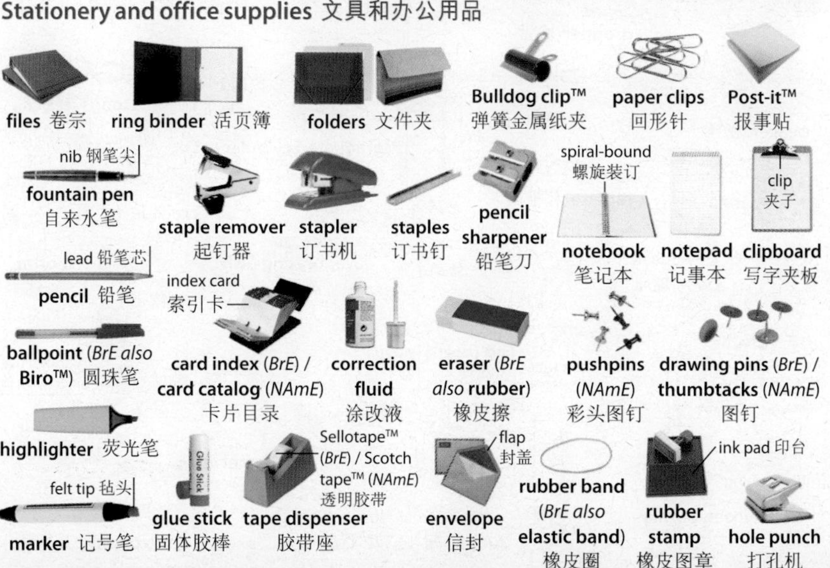

Classroom 教室

1 projector 投影仪
2 corridor (*NAmE also* hallway) 走廊
3 poster 装饰画
4 locker 寄存柜
5 interactive whiteboard 交互式电子白板
6 whiteboard 白板
7 board pen 白板笔
8 sports field 运动场
9 desk 书桌
10 textbook (*NAmE also* text) 课本
11 exercise book (*BrE*) / notebook (*NAmE*) 练习本
12 pencil case 铅笔盒
13 protractor 量角器
14 ruler 直尺
15 set square (*BrE*) / triangle (*NAmE*) 三角板

Laboratory equipment 实验室设备

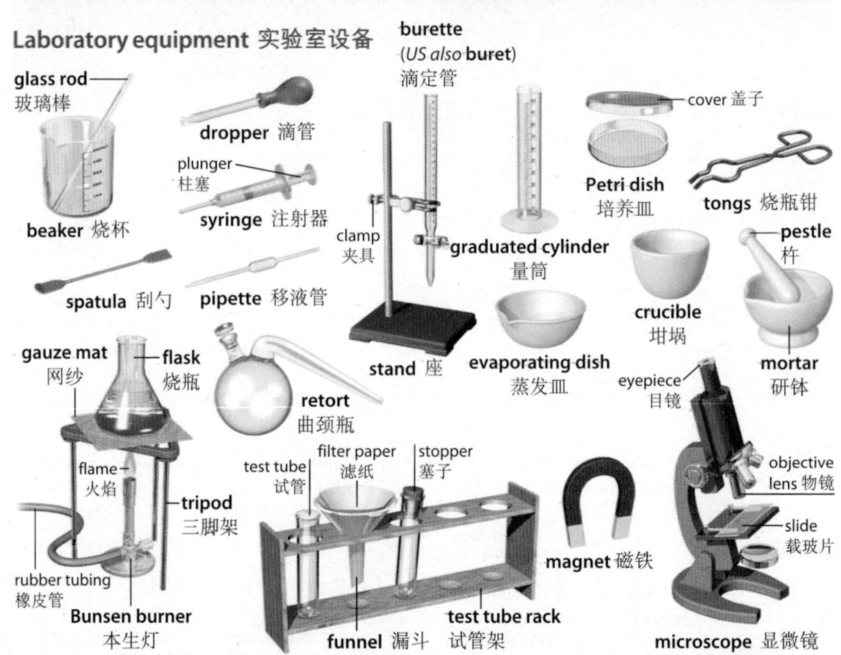

Computing 计算机信息处理技术

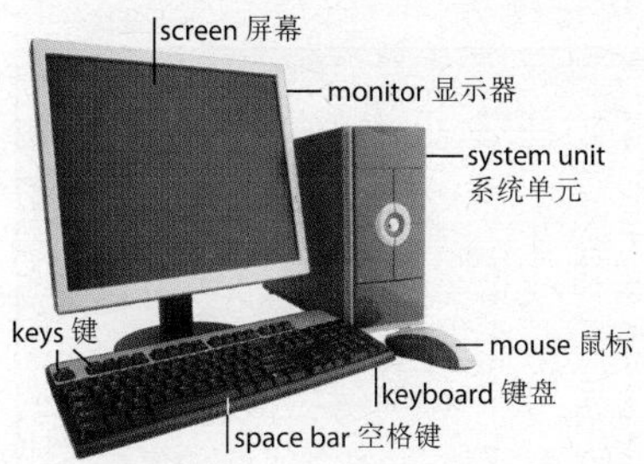

PC 个人计算机

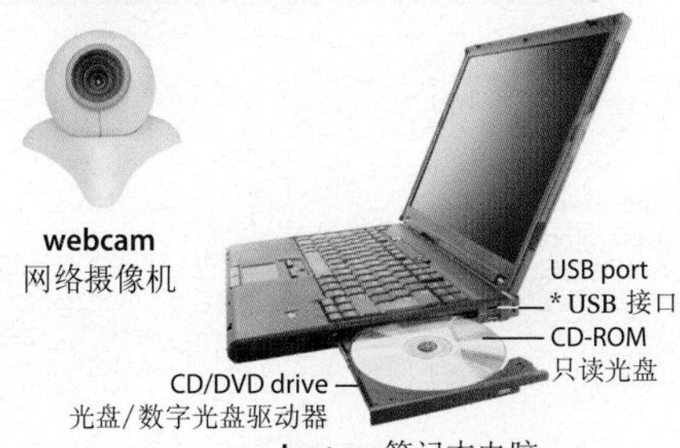

webcam
网络摄像机

laptop 笔记本电脑

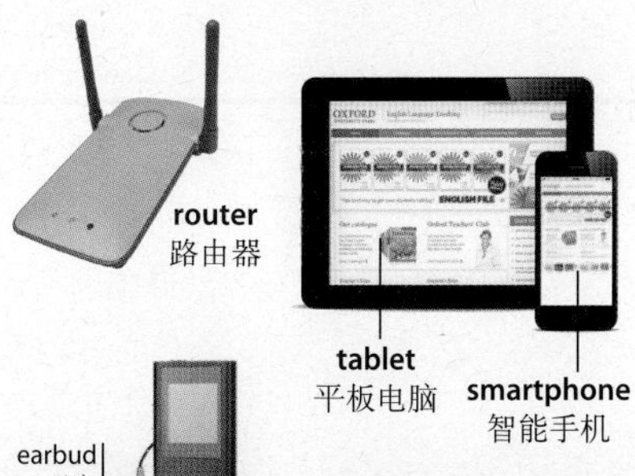

router
路由器

tablet
平板电脑

smartphone
智能手机

earbud
耳塞

MP3 player
* MP3 播放器

flash drive / USB drive
(*also* **memory stick**
especially BrE)
闪存盘；U 盘

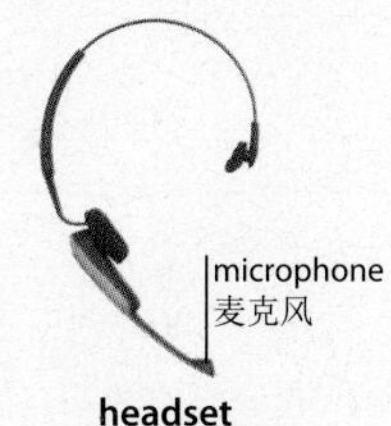

headset
头戴式受话器

Getting started 启动

- **PC users** should **log on** to the **network** by **entering** their **username** and **password.** 个人计算机用户（PC user）应输入（enter）用户名（username）和密码（password）登入（log on）计算机网络（network）。
- **Save** your **files** onto your **hard disk** and **back** them **up** onto **CDs** or **DVDs.** 将文件（file）存入（save）硬盘（hard disk），然后备份（back up）到光盘（CD）或数字光盘（DVD）。
- Important **data** is **archived** on the central **file server.** 重要数据（data）在中央文件服务器（file server）存档（archive）。

When things go wrong 计算机出毛病

- I can't **log in** – the **server** is **down.** 我无法登入（log in）系统，服务器（server）停机了（down）。
- The **system** keeps **crashing** – I've lost all my files. 系统（system）不断出故障（crash），我所有的文件都丢失了。
- You'll have to switch off and **reboot.** 必须关机，重新启动（reboot）。
- **Error.** Username contains **invalid characters.** 错误（error）。用户名含无效字符（invalid character）。
- My computer can't **read** this disk. 我的计算机不能读取（read）这张磁盘。
- The **virus** in the **software** was **programmed** to **corrupt** the hard disk. 软件（software）中的病毒（virus）编有（program）破坏（corrupt）硬盘的程序。
- A **firewall** provides essential security for your computer network. 防火墙（firewall）为计算机网络提供基本的安全保护。
- Download and install this **patch** to fix the fault. 下载并安装这个补丁程序（patch）修正错误。

Screen 屏幕

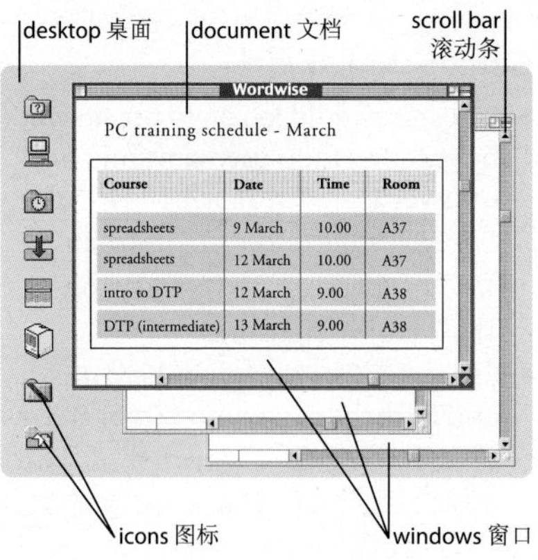

Home page 主页

Window 窗口

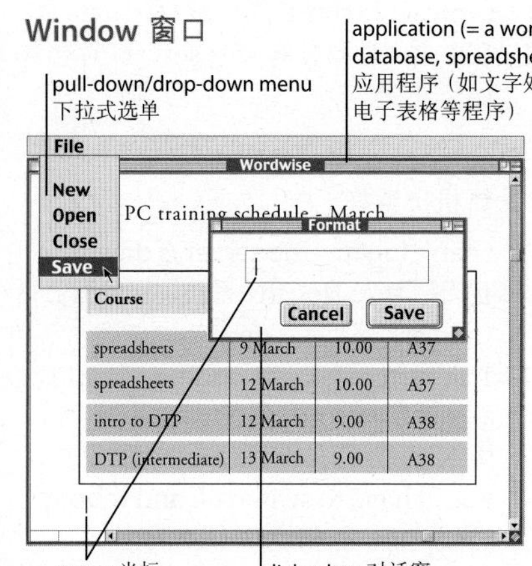

Irregular verbs 不规则动词

This appendix lists all the verbs with irregular forms that are included in the dictionary, except for those formed with a hyphenated prefix and the modal verbs (e.g. can, must). Irregular forms that are only used in certain senses are marked with an asterisk (e.g. *abode). Full information on usage, pronunciation, etc. is given at the entry.

本附录列出词典中收录的全部不规则动词，但由前缀带连字符构成的动词和情态动词（如 can、must）除外。只用于某些义项的不规则形式以星号标示（如 *abode）。有关用法、读音等细节在各词条内予以说明。

Infinitive 不定式	Past tense 过去式	Past participle 过去分词
abide	abided, *abode	abided, *abode
arise	arose	arisen
awake	awoke	awoken
babysit	babysat	babysat
bear	bore	borne
beat	beat	beaten
become	became	become
befall	befell	befallen
beget	begot, *begat	begot, *begotten
begin	began	begun
behold	beheld	beheld
bend	bent	bent
beseech	beseeched, besought	beseeched, besought
beset	beset	beset
bespeak	bespoke	bespoken
bet	bet	bet
betake	betook	betaken
bid¹	bid	bid
bid²	bade, bid	bidden, bid
bind	bound	bound
bite	bit	bitten
bleed	bled	bled
blow	blew	blown, *blowed
break	broke	broken
breastfeed	breastfed	breastfed
breed	bred	bred
bring	brought	brought
broadcast	broadcast	broadcast
browbeat	browbeat	browbeaten
build	built	built
burn	burnt, burned	burnt, burned
burst	burst	burst
bust	bust, busted	bust, busted
buy	bought	bought
cast	cast	cast
catch	caught	caught
choose	chose	chosen
cleave	cleaved, *cleft, *clove	cleaved, *cleft, *cloven
cling	clung	clung
come	came	come
cost	cost, *costed	cost, *costed
creep	crept	crept
cut	cut	cut
deal	dealt	dealt
dig	dug	dug
dive	dived (*NAmE also* dove)	dived
draw	drew	drawn
dream	dreamt, dreamed	dreamt, dreamed
drink	drank	drunk
drip-feed	drip-fed	drip-fed
drive	drove	driven
dwell	dwelt, dwelled	dwelt, dwelled
eat	ate	eaten
fall	fell	fallen
feed	fed	fed
feel	felt	felt
fight	fought	fought
find	found	found
fit	fitted (*NAmE usually* fit)	fitted (*NAmE usually* fit)
flee	fled	fled
fling	flung	flung
floodlight	floodlit	floodlit
fly	flew, *flied	flown, *flied
forbear	forbore	forborne
forbid	forbade	forbidden
forecast	forecast, forecasted	forecast, forecasted
foresee	foresaw	foreseen
foretell	foretold	foretold
forget	forgot	forgotten
forgive	forgave	forgiven
forgo	forwent	forgone
forsake	forsook	forsaken
forswear	forswore	forsworn
freeze	froze	frozen
gainsay	gainsaid	gainsaid
get	got	got (*NAmE, spoken* gotten)
give	gave	given
go	went	gone, *been
grind	ground	ground
grow	grew	grown
hamstring	hamstrung	hamstrung
hang	hung, *hanged	hung, *hanged
hear	heard	heard
heave	heaved, *hove	heaved, *hove
hew	hewed	hewed, hewn

Infinitive 不定式	Past tense 过去式	Past participle 过去分词
hide	hid	hidden
hit	hit	hit
hold	held	held
hurt	hurt	hurt
inlay	inlaid	inlaid
input	input, inputted	input, inputted
inset	inset	inset
intercut	intercut	intercut
interweave	interwove	interwoven
keep	kept	kept
kneel	knelt (*NAmE also* kneeled)	knelt (*NAmE also* kneeled)
knit	knitted, *knit	knitted, *knit
know	knew	known
lay	laid	laid
lead	led	led
lean	leaned (*BrE also* leant)	leaned (*BrE also* leant)
leap	leapt, leaped	leapt, leaped
learn	learnt, learned	learnt, learned
leave	left	left
lend	lent	lent
let	let	let
lie[1]	lay	lain
light	lit, *lighted	lit, *lighted
lose	lost	lost
make	made	made
mean	meant	meant
meet	met	met
miscast	miscast	miscast
mishear	misheard	misheard
mishit	mishit	mishit
mislay	mislaid	mislaid
mislead	misled	misled
misread	misread	misread
misspeak	misspoke	misspoken
misspell	misspelled, misspelt	misspelled, misspelt
misspend	misspent	misspent
mistake	mistook	mistaken
misunderstand	misunderstood	misunderstood
mow	mowed	mown, mowed
multicast	multicast	multicast
narrowcast	narrowcast, narrowcasted	narrowcast, narrowcasted
offset	offset	offset
outbid	outbid	outbid
outdo	outdid	outdone
outgrow	outgrew	outgrown
output	output	output
outrun	outran	outrun
outsell	outsold	outsold
outshine	outshone	outshone
overcome	overcame	overcome
overdo	overdid	overdone
overdraw	overdrew	overdrawn
overeat	overate	overeaten

Infinitive 不定式	Past tense 过去式	Past participle 过去分词
overfeed	overfed	overfed
overfly	overflew	overflown
overhang	overhung	overhung
overhear	overheard	overheard
overlay	overlaid	overlaid
overlie	overlay	overlain
overpay	overpaid	overpaid
override	overrode	overridden
overrun	overran	overrun
oversee	oversaw	overseen
oversell	oversold	oversold
overshoot	overshot	overshot
oversleep	overslept	overslept
overspend	overspent	overspent
overtake	overtook	overtaken
overthink	overthought	overthought
overthrow	overthrew	overthrown
overwrite	overwrote	overwritten
partake	partook	partaken
pay	paid	paid
plead	pleaded (*NAmE also* pled)	pleaded (*NAmE also* pled)
preset	preset	preset
proofread	proofread	proofread
prove	proved	proved (*also* proven *especially in NAmE*)
put	put	put
quit	quit (*BrE also* quitted)	quit (*BrE also* quitted)
read /riːd/	read /red/	read /red/
rebuild	rebuilt	rebuilt
recast	recast	recast
redo	redid	redone
redraw	redrew	redrawn
rehear	reheard	reheard
remake	remade	remade
rend	rent	rent
rerun	reran	rerun
resell	resold	resold
reset	reset	reset
resit	resat	resat
restring	restrung	restrung
retake	retook	retaken
retell	retold	retold
rethink	rethought	rethought
rewind	rewound	rewound
rewrite	rewrote	rewritten
rid	rid	rid
ride	rode	ridden
ring[2]	rang	rung
rise	rose	risen
run	ran	run
saw	sawed	sawn (*NAmE also* sawed)
say	said	said
see	saw	seen

Infinitive 不定式	Past tense 过去式	Past participle 过去分词
seek	sought	sought
sell	sold	sold
send	sent	sent
set	set	set
sew	sewed	sewn, sewed
shake	shook	shaken
shear	sheared	shorn, sheared
shed	shed	shed
shine	shone, *shined	shone, *shined
shit	shit, shat (*BrE* *also* shitted)	shit, shat (*BrE* *also* shitted)
shoe	shod	shod
shoot	shot	shot
show	showed	shown, *showed
shrink	shrank, shrunk	shrunk
shut	shut	shut
simulcast	simulcast	simulcast
sing	sang	sung
sink	sank, *sunk	sunk
sit	sat	sat
slay	slew	slain
sleep	slept	slept
slide	slid	slid
sling	slung	slung
slink	slunk	slunk
slit	slit	slit
smell	smelled (*BrE* *also* smelt)	smelled (*BrE* *also* smelt)
smite	smote	smitten
sow	sowed	sown, sowed
speak	spoke	spoken
speed	speeded, *sped	speeded, *sped
spell	spelt, spelled	spelt, spelled
spend	spent	spent
spill	spilled (*BrE* *also* spilt)	spilled (*BrE* *also* spilt)
spin	spun	spun
spit	spat (*also* spit *especially in NAmE*)	spat (*also* spit *especially in NAmE*)
split	split	split
spoil	spoiled (*BrE* *also* spoilt)	spoiled (*BrE* *also* spoilt)
spotlight	spotlit, *spotlighted	spotlit, *spotlighted
spread	spread	spread
spring	sprang (*NAmE* *also* sprung)	sprung
stand	stood	stood
stave	staved, *stove	staved, *stove
steal	stole	stolen
stick	stuck	stuck
sting	stung	stung
stink	stank, stunk	stunk
strew	strewed	strewed, strewn
stride	strode	—
strike	struck	struck (*NAmE also* stricken)
string	strung	strung
strive	strove, *strived	striven, *strived
sublet	sublet	sublet
swear	swore	sworn
sweep	swept	swept
swell	swelled	swollen, swelled
swim	swam	swum
swing	swung	swung
take	took	taken
teach	taught	taught
tear	tore	torn
telecast	telecast	telecast
tell	told	told
think	thought	thought
throw	threw	thrown
thrust	thrust	thrust
tread	trod	trodden, trod
typecast	typecast	typecast
typeset	typeset	typeset
unbend	unbent	unbent
underbid	underbid	underbid
undercut	undercut	undercut
undergo	underwent	undergone
underlie	underlay	underlain
underpay	underpaid	underpaid
undersell	undersold	undersold
understand	understood	understood
undertake	undertook	undertaken
underwrite	underwrote	underwritten
undo	undid	undone
unfreeze	unfroze	unfrozen
unwind	unwound	unwound
uphold	upheld	upheld
upset	upset	upset
wake	woke	woken
waylay	waylaid	waylaid
wear	wore	worn
weave	wove, *weaved	woven, *weaved
wed	wedded, wed	wedded, wed
weep	wept	wept
wet	wet, wetted	wet, wetted
win	won	won
wind² /waɪnd/	wound /waʊnd/	wound /waʊnd/
withdraw	withdrew	withdrawn
withhold	withheld	withheld
withstand	withstood	withstood
wring	wrung	wrung
write	wrote	written

Full forms 全写	Short forms 缩写	Negative short forms 缩写否定式
***be* present tense** 现在式		
I am	I'm	I'm not
you are	you're	you aren't/you're not
he is	he's	he isn't/he's not
she is	she's	she isn't/she's not
it is	it's	it isn't/it's not
we are	we're	we aren't/we're not
you are	you're	you aren't/you're not
they are	they're	they aren't/they're not
***be* past tense** 过去式		
I was	—	I wasn't
you were	—	you weren't
he was	—	he wasn't
she was	—	she wasn't
it was	—	it wasn't
we were	—	we weren't
you were	—	you weren't
they were	—	they weren't
***have* present tense** 现在式		
I have	I've	I haven't/I've not
you have	you've	you haven't/you've not
he has	he's	he hasn't/he's not
she has	she's	she hasn't/she's not
it has	it's	it hasn't/it's not
we have	we've	we haven't/we've not
you have	you've	you haven't/you've not
they have	they've	they haven't/they've not
***have* past tense** (all persons) 过去式(所有人称)		
had	I'd you'd etc.	hadn't
***do* present tense** 现在式		
I do	—	I don't
you do	—	you don't
he does	—	he doesn't
she does	—	she doesn't
it does	—	it doesn't
we do	—	we don't
you do	—	you don't
they do	—	they don't
***do* past tense** (all persons) 过去式(所有人称)		
did	—	didn't

	be	*do*	*have*
present participle 现在分词	being	doing	having
past participle 过去分词	been	done	had

be, do, have

- The negative full forms are formed by adding **not**. 全写否定式在上述动词后加 not 构成。
- Questions in the present and past are formed by placing the verb before the subject. 把动词置于主语前构成现在时和过去时的疑问式：
  - ▶ *am I?* *isn't he?* *was I?* *weren't we?* *do I?* *don't you?* *did I?* *didn't I?* *have I?* *hadn't they?* etc.
- Questions using the negative full form are more formal. 疑问句用全写否定式较为正式：
  - ▶ *has he not?* *do you not?* etc.
- The short negative question form for **I am** is **aren't**. * I am 的否定疑问式的缩写为 aren't：
  - ▶ *aren't I?*
- When **do** or **have** is used as a main verb, questions and negative statements can be formed with **do/does/don't/doesn't** and **did/didn't**. * do 或 have 用作主要动词时，疑问式和否定式可由 do/does/don't/doesn't 和 did/didn't 构成：
  - ▶ *How did you do it?*
  - ▶ *I don't do any teaching now.*
  - ▶ *Do you have any money on you?*
  - ▶ *We didn't have much time.*
- The short forms *'ve*, *'s* and *'d* are not usually used when **have** is a main verb. 当 have 为主要动词时，通常不用缩写 've、's 和 'd：
  - ▶ *I have a shower every morning.* NOT 不可说 ~~*I've a shower every morning.*~~
- The short form *'s* can be added to other subjects. * is 和 has 的缩写 's 可加在其他一些主语后：
  - ▶ *Sally's ill.* *The car's been damaged.*
- The **other tenses** of **be**, **do** and **have** are formed in the same way as those of other verbs. * be、do 和 have 的其他时态与其他动词的时态构成相同：
  - ▶ *will be* *would be* *has been* *will do* *would do* *has done* *will have* *would have* *have had;* etc.
- The **pronunciation** of each form of **be**, **do** and **have** is given at its entry in the dictionary. 关于 be、do 和 have 各种形式的读音，参见本词典中相关词条。

Verbs 动词

Transitive and intransitive 及物动词和不及物动词

- ▸ *He sighed.* 他叹了口气。
  ▸ *She cut her hand.* 她割伤了手。
  ▸ *The soup tastes salty.* 这汤咸咸的。

  Each of these sentences has a subject (**he, she, the soup**) and a verb (**sigh, cut, taste**). 以上各句均有主语（he、she、the soup）和动词（sigh、cut、taste）。

  In the first sentence, **sigh** stands alone. Verbs like this are called INTRANSITIVE. 在第一句，sigh 单独作谓语，这类动词称为不及物（intransitive）动词。

  In the second sentence, **cut** is TRANSITIVE because it is used with an object (**her hand**). 在第二句，cut 为及物（transitive）动词，其后接宾语（her hand）。

  In the third sentence, **taste** has no object but it cannot be used alone without an adjective. An adjective like **salty** that gives more information about the subject of a verb is called a COMPLEMENT. Verbs that take complements are called LINKING VERBS. 在第三句，taste 后无宾语，但不能无形容词而单独作谓语。像 salty 这类对动词的主语加以说明的形容词称为补语（complement），后接补语的动词称为连系动词（linking verb）。

Verb codes 动词代码

- In the dictionary, grammatical codes at the start of each meaning show you whether a verb is always transitive or always intransitive, or whether it can be sometimes transitive and sometimes intransitive. 在本词典中，义项开头的语法代码表明动词是否总是及物或不及物，或有时及物、有时不及物。

The code [I] shows you that in this meaning **change** is always intransitive. 代码 [I] 表示，在本义项中，change 总是不及物。

change ⚷ /tʃeɪndʒ/ *verb, noun*
■ *verb*
• BECOME/MAKE DIFFERENT（使）变化 **1** ⚷ [I] to become different 改变；变化：*Rick hasn't changed. He looks exactly the same as he did at school.* 里克一点儿没变，他和上学时一模一样。◇ *changing attitudes towards education* 不断变化的对教育的看法 ◇ *Her life changed completely when she won the lottery.* 买彩票中奖后她的生活完全变了。**2** ⚷ [T] ~ **sb/sth** to make sb/sth different 使不同：*Fame hasn't really changed him.* 名声并没有使他有丝毫改变。◇ *Computers have changed the way people work.* 计算机已改变了人的工作方式。**3** ⚷ [I, T] to pass or make sb/sth pass from one state or form into another（使）变换，改换，变成：*Wait for the traffic lights to change.* 等待交通灯变换颜色。◇ ~ **(from A) to/into B** *The lights changed from red to green.* 交通灯已由红变绿。◇ *Caterpillars change into butterflies.* 毛虫变成蝴蝶。◇ ~ **sb/sth (from A) to/into B** *With a wave of her magic wand, she changed the frog into a handsome prince.* 她魔杖一挥，把青蛙变成了英俊的王子。

The code [T] shows you that in this meaning **change** is always transitive. 代码 [T] 表示，在本义项中，change 总是及物。

The code [I, T] shows you that in this meaning **change** is sometimes intransitive and sometimes transitive. 代码 [I, T] 表示，在本义项中，change 有时不及物、有时及物。

Transitive verbs are the most common type of verb. A verb that is always transitive in all its meanings is just marked *verb*, and no other verb code is given. 及物动词是最常见的动词类型。所有义项均为及物用法的动词只标注 verb，不再标上其他代码。

Verb frames 动词框架

- Transitive verbs can take different types of object – a noun, phrase or clause. Both transitive and intransitive verbs can combine with different prepositions or adverbs. Different linking verbs can take either adjectives or nouns as complements. 及物动词可后接不同类型的宾语，包括名词、短语或从句。及物动词和不及物动词均可与不同的介词或副词组合。不同的连系动词可后接形容词或名词作补语。

pro·vide /prəˈvaɪd/ *verb* **1** to give sth to sb or make it available for them to use 提供；供应；给予 SYN **supply**: **~ sth** *The hospital has a commitment to provide the best possible medical care.* 这家医院承诺要提供最好的医疗服务。◇ *The report was not expected to provide any answers.* 人们没有指望这个报告会提供什么答案。◇ *Please answer questions in the space provided.* 请在留出的空白处答题。◇ **~ sth for sb** *We are here to provide a service for the public.* 我们来这里是为公众服务。◇ **~ sb with sth** *We are here to provide the public with a service.* 我们来这里是为公众服务。◇ **~ sth to sb** *The charity aims to provide assistance to people in need.* 这家慈善机构的宗旨是向贫困者提供帮助。 **2 ~ that...** (*formal*) (of a law or rule 法律或规则) to state that sth will or must happen 规定 SYN **stipulate**: *The final section provides that any work produced for the company is thereafter owned by the company.* 最后一节规定，此后为公司创作的一切作品均为该公司所有。 ➲ SEE ALSO PROVISION

In the dictionary, the different patterns (or 'verb frames') in which a verb can be used are shown in **bold type**, usually just before an example showing that pattern in context. 在本词典中，动词的各种用法模式（或"动词框架"）以**粗体**字表示，通常置于显示该模式的示例前。

If a particular verb, or one particular meaning of a verb, is always used in the same pattern, this pattern is shown in **bold type** before the definition. 如果某特定动词或动词的某特定义项总是使用同一模式，则将该模式以**粗体**字标示于释义前。

Intransitive verbs [I] 不及物动词

- Intransitive verbs do not take an object. When they are used alone after a subject, there is no verb frame. 不及物动词后无宾语。当它们单独用于主语后时，没有动词框架。

The example showing this use will usually appear first, before any other patterns and examples. 显示这一用法的示例通常出现于其他模式和示例之前。

shiver /ˈʃɪvə(r)/ *verb, noun*
▪ *verb* [I] (of a person 人) to shake slightly because you are cold, frightened, excited, etc. 颤抖，哆嗦（因寒冷、恐惧、激动等）: *Don't stand outside shivering—come inside and get warm!* 别站在外面冻得打哆嗦了，进来暖暖身子吧！◇ *He shivered at the thought of the cold, dark sea.* 那寒冷黑暗的大海，他想想都吓得发抖。◇ **~ with sth** *to shiver with cold/excitement/pleasure, etc.* 冷得发抖、激动得发抖、高兴得发抖等

Some intransitive verbs are often used with a particular preposition or adverb. This pattern will be shown in **bold type**, usually before an example. 有些不及物动词常与特定介词或副词连用。这种模式以**粗体**字表示，通常置于示例前。

- Some intransitive verbs are always or usually used with a preposition or an adverb, but not always the same one. These are often verbs showing movement in a particular direction. 有些不及物动词总是或通常与介词或副词连用，但不总是用同一介词或副词。这类动词常表示向特定方向运动。
  - *A runaway car came **hurtling towards** us.* 一辆失控的汽车朝我们飞驰而来。
  - *A group of swans **floated by**.* 一群天鹅缓缓游过。

In the dictionary this use will be shown by the frame + **adv./prep.** If a preposition or an adverb is often used, but not always, there will be brackets round the frame: (+ **adv./prep.**) 在本词典中，这一用法以框架 + adv./prep. 表示。如果常常但不总是使用介词或副词，该框架将置于括号内：(+ adv./prep.)

hur·tle /ˈhɜːtl; *NAmE* ˈhɜːrtl/ *verb* [I] **+ adv./prep.** to move very fast in a particular direction （向某个方向）飞驰，猛冲: *A runaway car **came hurtling** towards us.* 一辆失控的汽车朝我们飞驰而来。

Transitive verbs [T] 及物动词

- Transitive verbs must have an object. The object can be a noun or a pronoun, a noun phrase or a clause. 及物动词后一定接宾语，这个宾语可以是名词、代词、名词短语或从句。

For information on verbs that take a clause as the object, see page R8. 有关以从句作宾语的动词信息，另见 R8 页。

The frames used to show a transitive verb with a noun, pronoun or noun phrase as object are **~ sb**, **~ sth** and **~ sb/sth**. 以名词、代词或名词短语作宾语的及物动词用框架 ~ sb、~ sth 和 ~ sb/sth 表示。

ac·com·mo·date AW /əˈkɒmədeɪt; *NAmE* əˈkɑːm-/ *verb* **1** [T] **~ sb** to provide sb with a room or place to sleep, live or sit 提供住宿（或膳宿、座位等）: *The hotel can accommodate up to 500 guests.* 这家旅馆可供 500 位旅客住宿。 **2** [T] **~ sb/sth** to provide enough space for sb/sth 容纳；提供空间: *Over 70 minutes of music can be accommodated on one CD.* 一张激光唱片可以容纳 70 多分钟的音乐。 **3** [T] **~ sth** (*formal*) to consider sth, such as sb's opinion or a fact, and be influenced by it when you are deciding what to do or explaining sth 考虑到；顾及: *Our proposal tries to accommodate the special needs of minority groups.* 我们的提案尽量照顾到少数群体的特殊需要。 **4** [T] **~ sb (with sth)** (*formal*) to help sb by doing what they want 帮忙；给…提供方便 SYN **oblige**: *I have accommodated the press a great deal, giving numerous interviews.* 我多次接受采访，已给了报界许多方便。 **5** [I, T] **~ (sth/yourself) to sth** (*formal*) to change your behaviour so that you can deal with a new situation better 顺应，适应（新情况）: *I needed to accommodate to the new schedule.* 我需要适应新的时间表。

~ sb is used when the object is a person. 当宾语为人时，用框架 ~ sb。

~ sth is used when the object is a thing. 当宾语为事物时，用框架 ~ sth。

~ sb/sth is used when the object can be a person or a thing. 当宾语可以是人也可以是事物时，用框架 ~ sb/sth。

As with intransitive verbs, some transitive verbs are often used with a preposition or an adverb. 与不及物动词一样，某些及物动词常与介词或副词连用。

If there is a wide range of possible prepositions or adverbs a frame such as **~ sb/sth + adv./prep.** is used. 如果可以搭配的介词或副词有很多，则使用 ~ sb/sth + adv./prep. 之类的框架。

hack /hæk/ *verb, noun*
■ *verb* **1** [T, I] to cut sb/sth with rough, heavy blows 砍；劈: **~ sb/sth + adv./prep.** *I hacked the dead branches off.* 我把枯树枝砍掉了。◇ *They were hacked to death as they tried to escape.* 他们企图逃走时被砍死了。◇ *We had to hack our way through the jungle.* 我们不得不在丛林中辟路穿行。◇ **+ adv./prep.** *We hacked away at the bushes.* 我们劈开灌木丛。 **2** [T] **~ sb/sth + adv./prep.** to kick sth roughly or without control 猛踢: *He hacked the ball away.* 他把球一脚踢开。 **3** (*computing* 计) [I, T] to secretly find a way of looking at and/or changing information on sb else's computer system without permission 非法侵入（他人的计算机系统）: **~ into sth** *He hacked into the bank's computer.* 他侵入了这家银行的计算机。◇ **~ sth** *They had hacked secret data.* 他们窃取了保密数据。

If a particular preposition or adverb is used, then it is given in the frame. 如果使用特定的介词或副词，框架内会标明该介词或副词。

Transitive verbs with two objects 后接双宾语的及物动词

■ Some verbs, like **sell** and **buy**, can be used with two objects. This is shown by the frame **~ sb sth**. 有些动词，如 sell 和 buy，可接两个宾语。这种情况以框架 ~ sb sth 表示：

▸ *I sold Jim a car.*
我卖了一辆车给吉姆。

▸ *I bought Mary a book.*
我买了一本书给玛丽。

You can often express the same idea by using the verb as an ordinary transitive verb and adding a prepositional phrase starting with **to** or **for**. 要表达相同的意思，常常可将该动词作一般及物动词，后加一个以 to 或 for 开头的介词短语：

▸ *I sold a car **to** Jim.*
我卖了一辆车给吉姆。

▸ *I bought a book **for** Mary.*
我买了一本书给玛丽。

These will be shown by the frames **~ to sb** and **~ for sb**. 这些用法将以框架 ~ to sb 和 ~ for sb 表示。

bake /beɪk/ *verb, noun*
■ *verb* **1** [T, I] to cook food in an oven without extra fat or liquid; to be cooked in this way （在烤炉里）烘烤；焙: **~ (sth)** *baked apples* 烤苹果 ◇ *the delicious smell of baking bread* 烤制面包的香味 ◇ **~ sth for sb** *I'm baking a birthday cake for Alex.* 我在给亚历克斯烤生日蛋糕。◇ **~ sb sth** *I'm baking Alex a cake.* 我在给亚历克斯烤蛋糕。 ➲ COLLOCATIONS AT COOKING ➲ VISUAL VOCAB PAGE V28

A pair of examples, with different frames, shows the same idea expressed in two different ways. 两个一组的示例使用不同的框架，显示两种不同方法表达相同的意思。

Linking verbs 连系动词

■ ▸ *His voice sounds hoarse.*
他的声音听起来沙哑。

▸ *Elena became a doctor.*
埃琳娜成了医生。

In these sentences the linking verb (**sound, become**) is followed by a complement, an adjective (**hoarse**) or a noun phrase (**a doctor**) that tells you more about the subject. 在上述例句中，连系动词（sound、become）后跟补语，即对主语作补充说明的形容词（hoarse）或名词短语（a doctor）。

Verbs that have an adjective as the complement have the frame + **adj.**, and verbs with a noun phrase as the complement have the frame + **noun**. Verbs that can take either an adjective or a noun phrase as the complement may have the frame + **adj./noun**, or the two frames may be shown separately with an example for each. 以形容词为补语的动词用框架 + adj. 标示，以名词短语为补语的动词用框架 + noun 标示。 以形容词或名词短语为补语的动词用框架 + adj./noun 标示，或将这两个框架置于各自的示例前分别标示。

be·come /bɪ'kʌm/ *verb* (**be·came** /bɪ'keɪm/, **be·come**) **1** *linking verb* to start to be sth 开始变得；变成；成为：**+ adj.** *It was becoming more and more difficult to live on his salary.* 他越来越难以靠他的工资维持生计了。◇ *It soon became apparent that no one was going to come.* 很快就很清楚，没人会来。◇ *She was becoming confused.* 她开始糊涂了。◇ **+ noun** *She became queen in 1952.* 她于 1952 年成为女王。◇ *The bill will become law next year.* 该议案将于明年成为法律。 **2** [T, no passive] (not used in the progressive tenses 不用于进行时) ~ **sb**

The linking verb **become** can be used with either an adjective or a noun phrase. 连系动词 become 既可与形容词连用，也可与名词短语连用。

There are also verbs that take both an object and a complement. 也有一些动词同时接宾语加补语：

- *She considered herself lucky.*
  她觉得自己幸运。
- *They elected him president.*
  他们选了他当主席。

The complement (**lucky, president**) tells you more about the object (**herself, him**) of the verb. The frames for these verbs are ~ **sb/sth** + **adj.**, ~ **sb/sth** + **noun** or ~ **sb/sth** + **adj./noun**. 补语（lucky、president）是对动词宾语（herself、him）的补充说明。这些动词的框架为 ~ sb/sth + adj.、~ sb/sth + noun 或 ~ sb/sth + adj./noun。

Verbs used with 'that clauses'
后接 that 从句的动词

- The frame ~ **that** ... shows that a verb is followed by a clause beginning with **that**. 框架 ~ that ... 表示动词后接以 that 开头的从句：
  - *She **replied that** she would prefer to walk.* 她回答说她宁愿走路。

However, it is not always necessary to use the word **that** itself. 不过，有时 that 可以省略：

- *I **said that** he would come.*
  我说他会来。
- *I **said** he would come.*
  我说他会来。

These two sentences mean the same. In the dictionary they are shown by the frame ~ **(that)** ... and a single example is given, using brackets. 上面两个句子意思相同。在本词典中，用框架 ~ (that) ... 标示，并给出一个带括号的示例：

- ***I said (that)** he would come.*
  我说他会来。

Some verbs can be used with both a noun phrase and a 'that clause'. The frame for verbs used like this is ~ **sb that** ... or ~ **sb (that)** .... 有些动词可同时与名词短语和 that 从句连用，此类动词用框架 ~ sb that ... 或 ~ sb (that) ... 标示：

- *Can you **remind me that** I need to buy some milk?* 你提醒我买牛奶好吗？
- ***I told her (that)** I would be late.*
  我告诉她我会迟到。

Verbs used with 'wh- clauses'
后接 wh- 从句的动词

- A 'wh- clause' (or phrase) is a clause or phrase beginning with one of the following words: **which, what, whose, why, where, when, who, whom,** how, if, **whether.** * wh- 从句（或短语）指以下列词开头的从句或短语：which、what、whose、why、where、when、who、whom、how、if、whether：
  - *I **wonder what** the new job will be like.* 我想知道那份新工作会是什么样。
  - *He doesn't **care how** he looks.*
    他不介意自己的外表。
  - *Did you **see which** way they went?*
    你看到他们往哪边走了吗？

In the dictionary, verbs used like this have a frame such as ~ **how, what, etc.** ... or ~ **why, where, etc.** .... 在本词典中，此类动词用框架 ~ how, what, etc. ... 或 ~ why, where, etc. ... 标示。

The particular 'wh-words' given in each frame will be words that are typical for that verb, but the 'etc.' shows that other 'wh- clauses' are possible. 每个框架中特别给出的 wh- 词为该动词通常后接的词，而 etc. 表示也可以后接其他 wh- 从句。

won·der /'wʌndə(r)/ *verb, noun*
■ *verb* **1** [T, I] to think about sth and try to decide what is true, what will happen, what you should do, etc. 想知道；想弄明白；琢磨：**~ who, where, etc....** *I wonder who she is.* 我在想她到底是谁。◇ *I was just beginning to wonder where you were.* 我刚才正琢磨你上哪儿了呢。◇ **~ (about sth)** *'Why do you want to know?' 'No particular reason. I was just wondering.'* "你为什么想要知道？" "没有特殊原因。我就是想搞清楚。" ◇ *We were wondering about next April for the wedding.* 我们寻思着下个四月举行婚礼可好。◇ **+ speech** *'What should I do now?' she wondered.* "我现在该怎么办呢？" 她自忖道。**2** [T] **~ if, whether...** used as a polite way of asking a question or asking sb to do sth（礼貌地提问或请人做事时说）：*I wonder if you can help me.* 不知您是否能帮我的忙？

If there is no 'etc.' in the frame, then this verb or meaning can only take the particular 'wh-words' that are listed. 如果框架中没有 etc.，那么该动词或义项只能使用所列出的 wh- 词。

Some verbs can be used with both a noun phrase and a 'wh-clause'. Verbs used like this have a frame such as **~ sb where, when, etc. ...**. 有些动词可同时与名词短语和 wh- 从句连用，此类动词用框架 ~ sb where, when, etc. ... 标示：

- *I **asked him where** the library was.*
  我问他图书馆在哪儿。
- *I **told her when** the baby was due.*
  我告诉她宝宝预计什么时候出生。
- *He **teaches his students how** to research a subject thoroughly.*
  他教学生如何透彻地研究一个课题。

Verbs with infinitive phrases 后接不定式短语的动词

■ **Eat** and **to eat** are both the infinitive form of the verb. **Eat** is called a BARE INFINITIVE and TO EAT is called a TO-INFINITIVE. Most verbs that take an infinitive are used with the to-infinitive. The frame for these verbs is **~ to do sth**. * eat 和 to eat 均为动词不定式，eat 称作原形不定式（bare infinitive），to eat 称作带 to 不定式（to-infinitive）。大多数后接不定式的动词后都用带 to 不定式。此类动词用框架 ~ to do sth 标示：

- *The goldfish **need to be fed**.*
  金鱼需要喂饲。
- *She never **learned to read**.*
  她从未学会阅读。

Some verbs can be used with both a noun phrase and a to-infinitive. The frame for these is **~ sb to do sth, ~ sth to do sth** or **~ sb/sth to do sth**. The noun phrase can be the object of the main verb, 有些动词可同时与名词短语和带 to 不定式连用。此类动词用框架 ~ sb to do sth、~ sth to do sth 或 ~ sb/sth to do sth 标示。名词短语可作主要动词的宾语：

- *Can you **persuade Sheila to chair** the meeting?* 你可以说服希拉来主持这次会议吗？

or the noun phrase and the infinitive phrase together can be the object. 或名词短语加动词不定式短语作宾语：

- *I **expected her to pass** her driving test first time.* 我预计她第一次就能通过驾驶考试。
- *We'd **love you to come** and visit us.* 非常欢迎你来探访我们。

Only two groups of verbs are used with a bare infinitive (without **to**). One is the group of MODAL VERBS (or MODAL AUXILIARIES). These are the special verbs like **can**, **must** and **will** that go before a main verb and show that an action is possible, necessary, etc. These verbs have special treatment in the dictionary and are labelled *modal verb*. 只有两类动词与原形不定式（不带 to）连用。一类为情态动词（modal verb）或情态助动词（modal auxiliary）。这类动词（如 can、must 和 will）置于主要动词前，表示某一行动的可能、必要等。本词典将这类动词特别处理，并标示为 modal verb。

A small group of ordinary verbs, for example **see** and **hear**, can be used with a noun phrase and a bare infinitive. The frame for these is **~ sb do sth, ~ sth do sth** or **~ sb/sth do sth**. 一小类普通动词（如 see 和 hear）可同时与名词短语和原形不定式连用，此类动词用框架 ~ sb do sth、~ sth do sth 或 ~ sb/sth do sth 标示：

- *She **watched him eat** his lunch.*
  她看着他吃午餐。
- *Did you **hear the phone ring** just then?*
  那时你听到电话铃响了吗？

Verbs with '*-ing* phrases'
后接 -ing 短语的动词

- An '*-ing* phrase' is a phrase containing a PRESENT PARTICIPLE (or GERUND). The present participle is the form of the verb that ends in *-ing*, for example **doing**, **eating** or **catching**. Sometimes the '*-ing* phrase' consists of a present participle on its own. The frame for a verb that takes an '*-ing* phrase' is **~ doing sth**. * -ing 短语指含有现在分词（present participle）或动名词（gerund）的短语。现在分词是以 -ing 结尾的动词形式，如 doing、eating 或 catching。有时一个现在分词独立构成 -ing 短语。后接 -ing 短语的动词用框架 ~ doing sth 标示：
  - ▸ *She never stops talking!* 她总是喋喋不休！
  - ▸ *I started looking for a job two years ago.* 我两年前开始找工作。

  Some verbs can be used with both a noun phrase and an '*-ing* phrase'. The frame for this is **~ sb doing sth**, **~ sth doing sth** or **~ sb/sth doing sth**. The noun phrase can be the object of the main verb, 有些动词可同时与名词短语和 -ing 短语连用。此类动词用框架 ~ sb doing sth、~ sth doing sth 或 ~ sb/sth doing sth 标示。名词短语可作主要动词的宾语：
  - ▸ *His comments set **me** thinking.* 他的话让我开始思考。
  - ▸ *I can smell **something** nice cooking.* 我闻到烧菜的香味。

  or the noun phrase and the '*-ing* phrase' together can be the object. 或名词短语加 -ing 短语作宾语：
  - ▸ *I hate **him joking*** (= the fact that he jokes) *about serious things.* 我讨厌他拿正经事开玩笑。

  In this pattern, you can replace **him** with the possessive pronoun **his**. 在此句型中可用物主代词 his 取代 him：
  - ▸ *I hate **his joking** about serious things.* 我讨厌他拿正经事开玩笑。

  However, sentences with a possessive pronoun sound very formal and the object pronoun is more common, especially in American English. In cases where the verb itself is formal and the possessive pronoun may well be used, this is shown in the dictionary entry. 不过，用物主代词的句子听起来非常正式，用宾格代词更常见，尤其在美式英语中。如果动词本身为正式用语，使用物主代词是完全可以的，此用法见于本词典的词条中。

Verbs with direct speech
与直接引语连用的动词

- Verbs like **say**, **answer** and **demand** can be used either to report what somebody has said using a 'that clause' or to give their exact words in DIRECT SPEECH, using quotation marks (' '). Verbs that can be used with direct speech have the frame **+ speech**. * say、answer 和 demand 之类的动词既可用 that 从句转述某人的话，也可用直接引语（direct speech）加引号引用原话。可与直接引语连用的动词用框架 + speech 标示。Compare these two sentences. 比较下列句子：
  - ▸ **+ speech** *'It's snowing,' she said.* "下雪了。"她说。
  - ▸ **~ (that) …** *She said (that) it was snowing.* 她说下雪了。

  Some verbs can be used with both direct speech and a noun phrase, to show who is being spoken to. The frame for this is **~ sb + speech**. 有些动词可同时与直接引语和名词短语连用，引出说话的对象。此类动词用框架 ~ sb + speech 标示：
  - ▸ *'Tom's coming to lunch,' she **told him**.* 她对他说："汤姆会来吃午饭。"

Verbs in the passive
用于被动语态的动词

- Most transitive verbs can be used in the passive. 大多数及物动词可用于被动语态：

▸ *Jill's behaviour* **annoyed me.**
吉尔的行为令我恼火。

▸ **I was annoyed by** *Jill's behaviour.*
我被吉尔的行为惹恼了。

If a verb can be active or passive, the same verb frame is used. If the verb is often passive, there will be an example in the passive. 如果动词可用于主动语态或被动语态，则用同一框架标示。如果动词常用于被动语态，则给出被动语态的示例。

con·firm AW /kən'fɜːm; *NAmE* -'fɜːrm/ *verb* **1** to state or show that sth is definitely true or correct, especially by providing evidence（尤指提供证据来）证实，证明，确认：**~ sth** *Rumours of job losses were later confirmed.* 裁员的传言后来得到了证实。◇ *His guilty expression confirmed my suspicions.* 他内疚的表情证实了我的猜疑。◇ *Please write to confirm your reservation* (= say that it is definite). 预订后请来函确认。◇ **~ (that)...** *Has everyone confirmed (that) they're coming?* 他们是不是每个人都确定了一定会来？◇ **~ what/when, etc....** *Can you confirm what happened?* 你能证实一下发生了什么事吗？◇ **it is confirmed that...** *It has been confirmed that the meeting will take place next week.* 已经确定会议将于下个星期举行。**2** **~ sth | ~ sb (in sth)** to make sb feel or believe sth even more strongly 使感觉更强烈；使确信：*The walk in the mountains confirmed his fear of heights.* 在山里步行使他更加确信自己有恐高症。

If a pattern is *only* used in the passive, then the frame is put in the passive. This happens especially with verbs that take 'it' and a 'that clause'. 如果一个句型只能用于被动语态，那么该框架采用被动语态的形式。这种情况尤见于同 it 和 that 从句连用的动词。

If a transitive verb cannot be used in the passive, the label [no passive] appears before the definition. 如果某个及物动词不能用于被动语态，则在释义前标示 [no passive]。

Verbs in different patterns 不同句型的动词

■ Many verbs, for example **watch**, can be used in a number of different ways. 许多动词如 watch 可有不同的用法：

▸ **~ sb/sth do sth** *I watched him eat.* 我看着他吃了东西。

▸ **~ sb/sth doing sth** *I watched him eating.* 我看着他吃东西。

▸ **~ sb/sth** *I watched the pianist's left hand.* 我观察钢琴师的左手。

▸ **~ what, how, etc. ...** *I watched how the pianist used her left hand.* 我观察钢琴师如何用她的左手。

The dictionary entry for each verb shows the different ways in which it can be used by giving a range of example sentences. The frame before each example shows what type of grammatical pattern is being used. When an example follows another one illustrating the same pattern, the frame is not repeated. 本词典中每个动词词条均提供多个示例表明不同用法，每个示例前的框架表明语法模式。用法相同的示例不重复列出框架。

Sometimes patterns can combine with each other to form a longer pattern. This happens especially with patterns involving particular prepositions or adverbs; and sometimes there is a choice of two or three different prepositions or adverbs. 有时几个句型可相互结合构成较长的模式，这尤见于涉及特定的介词或副词的模式；有时有两三个不同的介词或副词供选用：

▸ **~ sth** *We shared the pizza.* 我们把那份比萨饼分着吃了。

▸ **~ sth out** *We shared out the pizza.* 我们把那份比萨饼分着吃了。

▸ **~ sth among sb** *We shared the pizza among the four of us.* 我们四个人把那份比萨饼分着吃了。

▸ **~ sth between sb** *We shared the pizza between the four of us.* 我们四个人把那份比萨饼分着吃了。

▸ **~ sth out among sb** *We shared the pizza out among the four of us.* 我们四个人把那份比萨饼分着吃了。

▸ **~ sth out between sb** *We shared the pizza out between the four of us.* 我们四个人把那份比萨饼分着吃了。

In cases like this the dictionary does not always give a separate frame and example for each different combination. It may use brackets to show where part of a long frame can be left out, and slashes to show where there is a choice between two or three different words in the frame. 这种情况下，本词典不总是为每个不同的组合单独给出框架和示例，而可能用括号标示长框架中可省略的部分，用斜线号标示框架中有两三个单词供选择：

• DIVIDE BETWEEN PEOPLE 分给若干人 **2** [T] **~ sth (out) (among/between sb)** to divide sth between two or more people 分配；分摊：*We shared the pizza between the four of us.* 我们四个人把那份比萨饼分着吃了。➲ SEE ALSO JOB-SHARING, POWER-SHARING

The frame **~ (sb)**, **~ (sth)** or **~ (sb/sth)** may also be used, where a verb can be used without an object (that is, it can be intransitive), but is more commonly used with a noun phrase as object. In these cases the more common, transitive use, is given in the first example(s), and any intransitive examples are placed after that. 有时也使用框架 ~ (sb)、~ (sth) 或 ~ (sb/sth)，表示动词后可不接宾语（即可以是不及物动词），但更常用名词短语作宾语。此类情况下，首先给出更常见的及物用法示例，不及物用法示例列在其后：

broad·cast /ˈbrɔːdkɑːst; *NAmE* -kæst/ *verb, noun* ■ *verb* (**broad·cast, broad·cast**) **1** [T, I] **~ (sth)** to send out programmes on television or radio 播送（电视或无线电节目）；广播：*The concert will be* ***broadcast live*** (= at the same time as it takes place) *tomorrow evening.* 明晚的音乐会将现场直播。◇ *They began broadcasting in 1922.* 他们于 1922 年开播。 ➲ COLLOCATIONS AT TELEVISION **2** [T] **~ sth** to tell a lot of people about sth 散布，传播（信息等）：*I don't like to* ***broadcast the fact*** *that my father owns the company.* 我不想宣扬这家公司为我父亲所有。

Sb and **sth** may also appear within brackets within longer frames, for example to show a verb that can take a preposition, an adverb or a 'that clause' either with or without a noun phrase as another object. * sb 和 sth 也可能以括号形式出现于较长框架中，如表示某个动词可与介词、副词或 that 从句连用，这动词后既可以接名词短语作另一个宾语，也可以不接：

warn /wɔːn; *NAmE* wɔːrn/ *verb* **1** [T, I] to tell sb about sth, especially sth dangerous or unpleasant that is likely to happen, so that they can avoid it 提醒注意（可能发生的事）；使警惕：**~ sb** *I tried to warn him, but he wouldn't listen.* 我设法提醒过他，可他就是不听。◇ *If you're thinking of getting a dog,* ***be warned****—they take a lot of time and money.* 如果你想养条狗，有话说在前头，那可既费时间又费钱。◇ **~ (sb) about/against sb/sth** *He warned us against pickpockets.* 他提醒我们要提防小偷。◇ **~ (sb) of sth** *Police have warned of possible delays.* 警方已经通知交通可能受阻。◇ **~ (sb) that…** *She was warned that if she did it again she would lose her job.* 她被警告说如果她再这样做就会丢掉工作。◇ **~ sb what, how, etc…** *I had been warned what to expect.* 有人事先告诉过我要出什么事。◇ **~ (sb) + speech** *'Beware of pickpockets,' she warned (him).* "当心扒手。" 她提醒（他）道。

Phrasal verbs 短语动词

What are phrasal verbs?
什么是短语动词？

- ▸ *Jan **turned down** the chance to work abroad.* 简回绝了到国外工作的机会。
  ▸ *Buying that new car has really **eaten into** my savings.* 买那辆新车的确耗掉我部分存款。
  ▸ *I don't think I can **put up with** his behaviour much longer.* 我想我再也不能容忍他的行为了。

  PHRASAL VERBS (sometimes called MULTI-WORD VERBS) are verbs that consist of two, or sometimes three, words. The first word is a verb and it is followed by an adverb (turn **down**) or a preposition (eat **into**) or both (put **up with**). These adverbs or prepositions are sometimes called PARTICLES. 短语动词（有时也叫多词动词 multi-word verb）指由两个、有时是三个词组成的动词。第一个词为动词，其后接副词（如 turn down）或介词（如 eat into）或副词加介词（如 put up with）。此类副词或介词有时称作小品词（particle）。

- In this dictionary, phrasal verbs are listed at the end of the entry for the main verb in a section marked **PHR V**. They are listed in alphabetical order of the particles following them. 在本词典中，短语动词列在主要动词词条后段标有 **PHR V** 的地方，按后接小品词的字母顺序排列：

> **PHR V** ˌ**fight** ˈ**back** (**against sb/sth**) to resist strongly or attack sb who has attacked you 奋力抵抗；还击：*Don't let them bully you. Fight back!* 别让他们欺侮你。要还击！◇ *It is time to fight back against street crime.* 现在是打击街头犯罪行为的时候了。ˌ**fight sth**↔**back**/ˈ**down** to try hard not to do or show sth, especially not to show your feelings 忍住，抑制住（尤指情感）：*I was fighting back the tears.* 我强忍住眼泪。◇ *He fought down his disgust.* 他强忍住心里的厌恶。ˌ**fight sb/sth**↔**off** to resist sb/sth by fighting against them/it 抵抗；击退：*The jeweller was stabbed as he tried to fight the robbers off.* 珠宝商在试图抵抗强盗时被刺伤了。ˌ**fight** ˈ**out sth** | ˌ**fight it** ˈ**out** to fight or argue until an argument has been settled 以斗争方式解决；辩论出结果：*The conflict is still being fought out.* 仍在通过战斗解决这次冲突。◇ *They hadn't reached any agreement so we left them to fight it out.* 他们未能取得一致意见，所以我们让他们争出个结果。

Meaning of phrasal verbs
短语动词的含义

- ▸ *He **sat down** on the bed.* 他坐到床上。

  The meaning of some phrasal verbs, such as **sit down**, is easy to guess because the verb and the particle keep their usual meaning. However, many phrasal verbs have idiomatic meanings that you need to learn. The separate meanings of **put**, **up** and **with**, for example, do not add up to the meaning of **put up with** (= tolerate). 有些短语动词的含义很容易推断，如 sit down，因为动词和小品词都保持通常的意思。但许多短语动词具有习语的意思，须通过学习才知道，如 put、up 和 with 各自的意思加起来并非 put up with（容忍；忍受）的意思。

- Some particles have particular meanings that are the same when they are used with a number of different verbs. 有些小品词具有特定的含义，与不同的动词连用时本身意思不变：
  ▸ *I didn't see the point of **hanging around** waiting for him, so I went home.* 我觉得没必要闲荡着等他，就回家去了。
  ▸ *I wish you wouldn't leave all those books **lying around**.* 我希望你不要再把那些书到处乱放。

  Around adds the meaning of 'with no particular purpose or aim' and is also used in a similar way with many other verbs, such as **play**, **sit** and **wait**.
  * around 增加了“无一定目的或目标”的含义，亦可用同样的方式与其他许多动词如 play、sit、wait 连用。

- The meaning of a phrasal verb can sometimes be explained with a one-word verb. However, phrasal verbs are frequently used in spoken English and, if there is a one-word equivalent, it is usually more formal in style. 短语动词的含义有时可用另一单个动词表达。不过，短语动词常用于口语中，而含义相同的单个动词通常较正式：

- ▸ *I wish my ears didn't* ***stick out*** *so much.* 真希望我的耳朵没那么招风。
- ▸ *The garage* ***projects*** *five metres beyond the front of the house.* 车库在房子的正面延伸出五米。

Both **stick out** and **project** have the same meaning – 'to extend beyond a surface' – but they are very different in style. **Stick out** is used in informal contexts, and **project** in formal or technical contexts. * stick out 和 project 含义相同，均有突出、伸出之义，但语体大不相同。stick out 用于非正式语境，project 则作正式用语或术语。

Grammar of phrasal verbs 短语动词的语法

- Phrasal verbs can be TRANSITIVE (they take an object) or INTRANSITIVE (they have no object). Some phrasal verbs can be used in both ways. 短语动词可以是及物（transitive），带有宾语，也可以是不及物（intransitive），不带宾语。有些短语动词用于及物或不及物均可：
  - ▸ *For heaven's sake* ***shut*** *her* ***up****. (transitive)* 行行好，让她住口吧。（及物）
  - ▸ *He told me to* ***shut up****. (intransitive)* 他叫我闭嘴。（不及物）
- INTRANSITIVE phrasal verbs are written in the dictionary without **sb** (somebody) or **sth** (something) after them. This shows that they do not have an object. 在本词典中，不及物短语动词后没有 sb（某人）或 sth（某物），表明其后不接宾语：

> ˌ**eat ˈout** to have a meal in a restaurant, etc. rather than at home 上馆子吃饭；在外用餐： *Do you feel like eating out tonight?* 你今晚想下馆子吗？

Eat out is intransitive, and the two parts of the verb cannot be separated by any other word. * eat out 为不及物短语动词，动词和小品词之间不能加入任何单词。You can say 可说：

- ▸ *Shall we eat out tonight?* 我们今晚下馆子好吗？

BUT NOT 不可说 ~~*Shall we eat tonight out?*~~

- In order to use TRANSITIVE phrasal verbs correctly, you need to know where to put the object. With some phrasal verbs (often called SEPARABLE verbs), the object can go either between the verb and the particle or after the particle. 要正确使用及物短语动词，必须知道宾语的位置。有些短语动词（常称作可分动词 separable verb）的宾语既可置于动词与小品词之间，也可置于小品词之后：
  - ▸ *She* ***tore*** *the letter* ***up****.* 她把信撕碎了。
  - ▸ *She* ***tore up*** *the letter.* 她把信撕碎了。
- When the object is a long phrase, it usually comes after the particle. 宾语为较长的短语时，通常置于小品词之后：
  - ▸ *She* ***tore up*** *all the letters he had sent her.* 她把他寄给她的信都撕碎了。
- When the object is a pronoun (for example **it** standing for 'the letter'), it must always go between the verb and the particle. 宾语为代词时（如 it 代表 the letter），必须置于动词与小品词之间：
  - ▸ *She read the letter and then* ***tore it up****.* 她看过信以后就把它撕毁了。
- In the dictionary, verbs that are separable are written like this. 在本词典中，可分的短语动词标示为：
  tear sth ↔ up
- The double arrow between the object and the particle shows that the object may come either before or after the particle. 宾语与小品词之间的双箭头表示宾语可置于小品词之前，也可置于小品词之后：

> ˌ**call sth↔ˈoff** to cancel sth; to decide that sth will not happen 取消；停止进行： *to call off a deal/trip/strike* 取消交易／旅行／罢工 ◇ *They have called off their engagement* (= decided not to get married). 他们已经解除婚约。◇ *The game was called off because of bad weather.* 比赛因天气恶劣被取消。

You can say 可说：

▸ *They **called** the deal **off**.*
他们取消了交易。
AND 和 *They **called off** the deal.*
他们取消了交易。

■ With other phrasal verbs (sometimes called INSEPARABLE verbs), the two parts of the verb cannot be separated by an object. 其他短语动词（有时也叫不可分动词 inseparable verb）的宾语不能置于动词和小品词之间：

▸ *I didn't really **take to** her husband.*
我对她的丈夫不是很有好感。
NOT 不可说 ~~*I didn't really **take** her husband **to**.*~~

▸ *I didn't really **take to** him.*
我对他不是很有好感。
NOT 不可说 ~~*I didn't really **take** him **to**.*~~

In the dictionary, verbs that are inseparable are written like this. 在本词典中，不可分的短语动词标示为：

take to sb

When you see **sb** or **sth** after the two parts of a phrasal verb, and there is no double arrow, you know that they cannot be separated by an object. 短语动词后有 sb 或 sth，而且无双箭头，说明宾语不能置于动词和小品词之间：

ˌrun ˈinto sb (*informal*) to meet sb by chance 偶然遇见，碰到（某人）： *Guess who I ran into today!* 猜猜我今天碰见谁了！

You can say 可说：

▸ *I **ran into** Joe yesterday.* 我昨天碰见乔。
BUT NOT 不可说 ~~*I **ran** Joe **into**.*~~

■ There are a few phrasal verbs in which the two parts of the verb must be separated by the object. 有少数短语动词的动词和小品词之间必须加入宾语。You can say 可说：

▸ *They changed the plans and **messed** everyone **around**.* 他们改变了计划，给大家添了麻烦。
BUT NOT 不可说 ~~*They changed the plans and **messed around** everyone.*~~

■ In the dictionary, these verbs are written like this. 在本词典中，这类短语动词标示为：

mess sb around

When you see **sb** or **sth** between the two parts of a phrasal verb and there is no double arrow, you know that they must be separated by the object. 短语动词的动词和小品词之间有 sb 或 sth，而且无双箭头，说明宾语必须要置于两者之间。

■ Some transitive phrasal verbs can be made passive. 有些及物短语动词可用于被动语态：

▸ *The deal **has been called off**.*
交易取消了。

When this is common, you will find an example at the dictionary entry. 如果此用法常见，在本词典的词条中有示例说明。

Phrasal verbs used with phrases and clauses 与短语和从句连用的短语动词

Like other verbs, some phrasal verbs can be used with another phrase or clause. The different types of clause and phrase are explained on pages R8–10. When a phrasal verb can be used with a particular type of clause or phrase, an example is given in the dictionary entry, labelled with a special frame. 与其他动词一样，有些短语动词可与另一短语或从句连用。不同类型的从句和短语见 R8–10 页的说明。如果短语动词可与某种类型的从句或短语连用，本词典相关词条中有示例予以说明，并以特别框架标示：

~ that	*We **found out** later **that** we had been at the same school.* 后来我们才弄清楚我们是校友。
~ how, what, etc. …	*I can't **figure out how** to do this.* 我弄不懂这事怎么做。
~ to do sth	*It didn't **occur to** her **to ask** for help.* 她没想到请人帮忙。

~ doing sth	***I didn't bargain on finding Matthew there as well.*** 我没想到马修也在那里。
+ speech	***'Help!' he cried out.*** "救命!"他喊道。

Related nouns 相关名词

A particular phrasal verb may have a noun related to it. This noun will be mentioned at the verb entry. 短语动词可能与某个名词相关，该名词将在动词词条内提及：

ˌbreak ˈin to enter a building by force 强行进入；破门而入： *Burglars had broken in while we were away.* 我们不在家时，窃贼闯进屋里了。 ➲ RELATED NOUN BREAK-IN
ˌbreak sb/sth ˈin 1 to train sb/sth in sth new that they must do 训练某人 / 某物；培训： *to break in new recruits* 训练新人 ◇ *The young horse was not yet broken in* (= trained to carry a rider). 那匹刚长成的马还没被驯服。 **2** to wear sth, especially new shoes, until they become comfortable 把…穿得合身，使舒适自如（尤指新鞋） **ˌbreak ˈin (on sth)** to interrupt or disturb sth 打断；搅扰： *She longed to break in on their conversation but didn't want to appear rude.* 她很想打断他们的谈话，但又不愿显得粗鲁。 ◇ **+ speech** *'I didn't do it!' she broke in.* "不是我干的！"她插嘴说。
ˌbreak ˈinto sth 1 to enter a building by force; to open a car, etc. by force 强行闯入；撬开（汽车等）： *We had our car broken into last week.* 我们的车上周被撬了。 ➲ RELATED NOUN BREAK-IN **2** to begin laughing, singing, etc. suddenly 突然开始（笑、唱等）： *As the President's car drew up, the crowd broke into loud applause.* 总统的座驾停下时，人群中爆发出热烈的掌声。

ˌbreak ˈout (of war, fighting or other unpleasant events 战争、打斗等不愉快事件) to start suddenly 突然开始；爆发： *They had escaped to America shortly before war broke out in 1939.* * 1939 年战争爆发前不久他们逃到了美国。 ◇ *Fighting had broken out between rival groups of fans.* 双方球迷发生了打斗。 ◇ *Fire broke out during the night.* 夜间突然发生了火灾。 ➲ RELATED NOUN OUTBREAK
ˌbreak ˈout (of sth) to escape from a place or situation 逃离（某地）；摆脱（某状况）： *Several prisoners broke out of the jail.* 几名囚犯越狱了。 ◇ *She needed to break out of her daily routine and do something exciting.* 她需要从日常事务中解脱出来，找点有意思的事做。 ➲ RELATED NOUN BREAKOUT

A noun is often related in meaning to only one or two of the phrasal verbs using a particle. **Break-in** is related to **break in** and the first meaning of **break into sth**, but not to **break sb/sth in** or **break in (on sth)**. **Breakout** is related to **break out (of sth)**, whereas the noun **outbreak** relates to **break out**. 一个名词在意义上通常只与一个或两个含小品词的短语动词相关。break-in 与 break in 以及 break into sth 的第一义相关，但与 break sb/sth in 或 break in (on sth) 不相关。breakout 与 break out (of sth) 相关，而名词 outbreak 与 break out 相关。

Nouns and adjectives 名词和形容词

Nouns 名词

Countable and uncountable 可数名词和不可数名词

The two biggest groups of nouns are COUNTABLE nouns (or COUNT nouns) and UNCOUNTABLE nouns (also called UNCOUNT nouns or MASS nouns). Most countable nouns are words for separate things that can be counted, like **apples**, **books** or **teachers**. Uncountable nouns are usually words for things that are thought of as a quantity or mass, like **water** or **time**. 最大的两类名词是可数名词（countable noun，或称具数名词 count noun）和不可数名词（uncountable noun，也称不具数名词 uncount noun 或整体名词 mass noun）。多数可数名词为可以数算的可分事物，如 apple（苹果）、book（书）或 teacher（教师）。不可数名词通常被视为一个量或一个整体，如 water（水）或 time（时间）。

However, there are some nouns in English that you might expect to be countable but which are not. For example, **furniture, information** and **equipment** are all uncountable nouns in English, although they are countable in some other languages. 不过，英语中一些名词可能会被认为是可数的，其实却不是。如 furniture（家具）、information（信息）和 equipment（设备）。虽然这些词在其他一些语言里是可数的，但是在英语中为不可数名词。

Countable nouns [C] 可数名词

A countable noun has a singular form and a plural form. When it is singular, it must always have a DETERMINER (a word such as **a, the, both, each**) in front of it. In the plural it can be used with or without a determiner. 可数名词有单、复数两种形式。作单数时，前面一定要有限定词（determiner），如 a、the、both、each 等；作复数时，前面有无限定词均可：

- *I'm having **a** driving **lesson** this afternoon.* 我今天下午要上驾驶课。
- *I've had **several lessons** already.* 我已经上了几节课。
- ***Lessons** cost £20 an hour.* 每小时的课学费是 20 英镑。

Countable nouns are the most common type of noun. If they have only one meaning, or if all the meanings are countable, they are just marked *noun*. For nouns that have a number of meanings, some of which are not countable, each meaning that is countable is marked [C]. 可数名词是最常见的一类名词。如果只有一个含义或所有含义均为可数，本词典只标注 noun；如果有几个含义，有些含义为不可数，则每个可数的含义都标注 [C]。

Uncountable nouns [U] 不可数名词

An uncountable noun has only one form, not a separate singular and plural. It can be used with or without a determiner. 不可数名词只有一种形式，无单、复数之分，前面有或没有限定词均可：

- *Can we make **space** for an extra chair?* 我们能不能腾个地方再放一把椅子？
- *There isn't **much space** in this room.* 这房间没有多大的空间。

If an uncountable noun is the subject of a verb, the verb is singular. 如果不可数名词是动词的主语，该动词用单数：

- *Extra money **has been found** for this project.* 已有额外的款项供这个项目之用。

With nouns such as **furniture, information** and **equipment**, as with many other uncountable nouns, you can talk about amounts of the thing or separate parts of the thing by using phrases like **a piece of, three items of, some bits of**. Nouns like **piece, item** and **bit** are called PARTITIVES when used in this way. 像 furniture、information、equipment 一类的名词与其他许多不可数名词一样，可用 a piece of、three items of、some bits of 等短语来表示量或件数；piece、item 和 bit 之类的名词作此用法时称为表量词（partitive）：

- *I picked up **some information** that might interest you.* 我得到一些信息，或许你会感兴趣。
- *I picked up **two pieces of information** that might interest you.* 我得到两则消息，或许你会感兴趣。

Plural nouns [pl.] 复数名词

Some nouns are always plural and have no singular form. Nouns that refer to things that have two parts joined together, for example **glasses, jeans** and **scissors**, are often plural nouns. You can usually also talk about **a pair of jeans, a pair of scissors**, etc. 有些名词总是复数，无单数形式。由两部分组成的东西，如 glasses（眼镜）、jeans（牛仔裤）和 scissors（剪刀）等均常为复数名词；通常亦可用 a pair of jeans、a pair of scissors 等表示：

- *I'm going to buy **some new jeans**.* 我要买新的牛仔裤。
- *I'm going to buy **a** new **pair of jeans**.* 我要买一条新牛仔裤。

An example is given in the entry for the noun to show that it can be used in this way. 在名词词条中有示例表明该名词可以这样用。

Some plural nouns, such as **police** and **cattle**, look as if they are singular. Nouns like this usually refer to a group of people or animals of a particular type, when they are considered together as one unit. They also take a plural verb. 有些复数名词，如 police（警方）和 cattle（牛），看上去似乎是单数。这类名词作为一个整体看待时，通常指特定的人或动物群体，谓语动词用复数：

- ***Police are searching** for a man who escaped from Pentonville prison today.* 警方正在搜捕一名今天下午从本顿维尔监狱逃跑的犯人。
- *The **cattle are fed** on barley and grass.* 这些牛喂大麦和草。

Singular nouns [sing.] 单数名词

Some nouns are always singular and have no plural form. Many nouns like this can be used in only a limited number of ways. For example, some singular nouns must be or are often used with a particular determiner in front of them or with a particular preposition after them. The correct determiner or preposition is shown before the definition. In the case of **fillip** the pattern given is **a ~ (to/for sth)**. 有些名词总是单数，无复数形式，许多这样的名词只有有限的几种用法。例如，有些单数名词必须或常常前接某个特定限定词或后接某个特定介词。适用的限定词或介词列于释义前。如 fillip 一词显示的模式为 a ~ (to/for sth)：

> **fil·lip** /ˈfɪlɪp/ *noun* [sing.] **a ~ (to/for sth)** *(formal)* a thing or person that causes sth to improve suddenly 起推动作用的人（或事物） **SYN** **boost**: *A drop in interest rates gave a welcome fillip to the housing market.* 降低利率给房屋市场带来利好刺激。

Nouns with singular or plural verbs 与单数或复数动词连用的名词

[sing.+sing./pl. v.] [C+sing./pl. v.] [U+sing./pl. v.]

In British English some singular nouns (or countable nouns in their singular form) can be used with a plural verb as well as a singular one. Nouns like this usually refer to a group of people, an organization, or a place, and can be thought of either as the organization, place or group (singular) or as many individual people (plural). In the dictionary an example is usually given to show agreement with a singular and a plural verb. 在英式英语中有些单数名词（或可数名词的单数形式）既可与单数动词连用，也可与复数动词连用。这类名词通常指人的集体、机构或地点等，既可视为一个整体（单数），也可视为许多个体（复数）。本词典中通常给出这类名词与单数动词和复数动词一致的示例：

- *The **Vatican has/have** issued a further statement this morning.* 梵蒂冈今早发表了进一步的声明。
- *The **committee has/have** decided to dismiss him.* 委员会已决定将他免职。

These nouns are marked [sing.+sing./pl. v.] if they are always singular in form, and [C+sing./pl. v.] if they also have a plural form. The plural form always agrees with a plural verb. 这些名词如果总是单数形式，则标示为 [sing.+sing./pl. v.]；如果亦有复数形式，则标示为 [C+sing./pl. v.]。复数形式用复数动词。

NOTE In American English the singular form of these nouns must take a singular verb. 在美式英语中，这些名词的单数形式必须用单数动词：

- *The government **says it is** committed to tax reform.* 政府承诺要进行税制改革。

Some uncountable nouns can be used with a plural verb as well as a singular one. These include some nouns that end in **-s** and therefore look as though they are plural, 有些不可数名词既可与单数动词连用，也可与复数动词连用，其中包括某些以 -s 结尾而看上去像是复数的名词：

- *His **whereabouts are/is** still unknown.* 他仍然下落不明。

and some nouns that refer to a group of people or things and can be thought of either as a group (singular) or as many individual people or things (plural). 另有一些名词，既可视为集体（单数），也可视为许多个体（复数）：

- ***Personnel is/are** currently reviewing pay scales.* 人事部正在审核工资标准。

Patterns with nouns 与名词连用的句型

- Many nouns are followed by a particular preposition, adverb or other pattern. 许多名词后接特定介词、副词或其他句型：
  - *My comments were taken as an allegation of negligence.* 我的评论被看成指称有人疏忽。

The correct pattern to use is shown in **bold type**, either before the definition or before an individual example. Where any part of a pattern is optional, it is given in brackets. 正确的句型在释义或单个示例前用**粗体**字显示，可省略的部分放在括号内。

> **al·le·ga·tion** /ˌæləˈɡeɪʃn/ *noun* a public statement that is made without giving proof, accusing sb of doing sth that is wrong or illegal（无证据的）说法，指控 SYN **accusation**: *to investigate/deny/withdraw an allegation* 调查 / 否认 / 撤回指控 ◇ **~ of sth** *Several newspapers made allegations of corruption in the city's police department.* 有几家报纸声称该市警察局腐败。◇ **~ (of sth) against sb** *allegations of dishonesty against him* 关于他不诚实的多种说法 ◇ **~ about sb/sth** *The committee has made serious allegations about interference in its work.* 委员会严厉谴责对其工作的干涉。◇ **~ that...** *an allegation that he had been dishonest* 一种关于他不诚实的说法 ➲ SYNONYMS AT CLAIM

The example sentences show the patterns in use. 例句表明句型的应用。

Adjectives 形容词

- Many adjectives can be used both before a noun, 许多形容词既可用于名词前：
  - *a serious expression* 严肃的表情
  - *grey hair* 灰白的头发

  and after a LINKING VERB. 也可用于连系动词之后：
  - *She looked serious.* 她一脸严肃。
  - *His hair had turned grey.* 他的头发已变得灰白。
- However, some adjectives, or particular meanings of adjectives, are always used before a noun, and cannot be used after a linking verb. They are called ATTRIBUTIVE adjectives. 但是，有些形容词或形容词的某些特定含义只用于名词前，不能用于连系动词后。这类形容词称作定语（attributive）形容词：
  - *the chief reason* 主要原因
- Others are only used after a linking verb. They are called PREDICATIVE adjectives. 另一些形容词只用于连系动词后，这类形容词称作表语（predicative）形容词：
  - *The baby is awake.* 婴儿醒着。

➔ For more information about LINKING VERBS, look at pages R7–8. 关于连系动词的详细说明，见 R7–8 页。

[only before noun] [usually before noun]

Attributive adjectives are labelled [only before noun]. The label [usually before noun] is used when it is rare but possible to use the adjective after a verb. 定语形容词标注为 [only before noun]；标注为 [usually before noun] 的形容词可用于连系动词后，但罕见。

Senses **1** and **3** can only be used before a noun. 第 1 义和第 3 义只能用于名词前。

con·tin·en·tal /ˌkɒntɪˈnentl; *NAmE* ˌkɑːn-/ *adj., noun*
■ *adj.* **1** (*also* **Continental**) [only before noun] (*BrE*) of or in the continent of Europe, not including Britain and Ireland 欧洲大陆的（不包括英国和爱尔兰）：*a popular continental holiday resort* 受欢迎的欧洲大陆度假胜地 ◇ *Britain's continental neighbours* 英国的欧洲大陆邻国 **2** (*BrE*) following the customs of countries in western and southern Europe 随（西、南欧国家）大陆风俗的：*a continental lifestyle* 西、南欧大陆的生活方式 ◇ *The shutters and the balconies make the street look almost continental.* 活动护窗和阳台使这条街看起来颇具欧洲大陆风格。 **3** [only before noun] connected with the main part of the N American continent 北美大陆的：*Prices are often higher in Hawaii than in the continental United States.* 夏威夷的物价常常比美国大陆高。

Sense **2** has no grammar label because it can be used both before a noun and after a linking verb. 第 2 义没有语法标注，因为既可用于名词前也可用于连系动词后。

[not before noun] [not usually before noun]

Predicative adjectives, labelled [not before noun], are used only after a linking verb, never before a noun. The label [not usually before noun] is used when it is rare but possible to use the adjective before a noun. 表语形容词标注为 [not before noun]，只能用于连系动词后，不能用于名词前；标注为 [not usually before noun] 的形容词可用于名词前，但罕见。

rife /raɪf/ *adj.* [not before noun] **1** if sth bad or unpleasant is **rife** in a place, it is very common there（坏事）盛行，普遍 **SYN** **widespread**：*It is a country where corruption is rife.* 这是个腐败成风的国家。◇ *Rumours are rife that he is going to resign.* 到处都在传，说他要辞职了。 **2** ~ (**with sth**) full of sth bad or unpleasant 充斥，充满（坏事）：*Los Angeles is rife with gossip about the stars' private lives.* 洛杉矶盛传明星私生活的流言蜚语。

The grammar label straight after the *adj.* label shows that both meanings must be used after a linking verb. 在 adj. 标记后的语法标识表示两个义项都必须用于连系动词后。

[after noun]

A few adjectives always follow the noun they describe. This is shown in the dictionary by the label [after noun]. 少数形容词总是置于所修饰的名词之后，此用法在本词典中用 [after noun] 标示：

gal·ore /ɡəˈlɔː(r)/ *adj.* [after noun] (*informal*) in large quantities 大量；很多：*There will be games and prizes galore.* 将有很多游戏和奖品。

Collocation 词语搭配

What is collocation?
什么是词语搭配？

COLLOCATION is the way in which particular words tend to occur or belong together. 词语搭配指比较典型或规范的词语组合。For example, you can say 比如，可说：

▸ *Meals will be served outside on the terrace, **weather permitting**.*
天气许可的话，可在餐馆露天座用餐。

BUT NOT 不可说 ~~*Meals will be served outside on the terrace, weather allowing.*~~

Both these sentences seem to mean the same thing: **allow** and **permit** have very similar meanings. But in this combination only **permitting** is correct. It COLLOCATES with **weather** and **allowing** does not. 上述两句含义似乎相同。allow 和 permit 意思非常相似，但在这一组合里只有 permitting 才是正确的，因为它可与 weather 搭配，allowing 却不能。

Types of collocation
词语搭配类型

In order to write and speak natural and correct English, you need to know, for example 要说写自然而正确的英语，需要知道：

- which adjectives are used with a particular noun 哪些形容词可与某个名词搭配
- which nouns a particular adjective is used with 某个形容词可与哪些名词搭配
- which verbs are used with a particular noun 哪些动词可与某个名词搭配
- which adverbs are used to intensify a particular adjective 哪些副词可用以加强某个形容词的词义

Collocation in this dictionary
本词典的词语搭配

To find out which adjectives to use with a particular noun, look at the examples at the entry for the noun. Typical adjectives used with the noun are separated by a slash (/). 查找哪些形容词可与某个名词搭配，见该名词词条的示例。与该名词搭配的典型形容词用斜线号 (/) 隔开：

Can you say 'pink wine'?
可以说 pink wine 吗？

wine /waɪn/ *noun, verb*
■ ***noun* 1** [U, C] an alcoholic drink made from the juice of GRAPES that has been left to FERMENT. There are many different kinds of wine. 葡萄酒：*a bottle of wine* 一瓶葡萄酒 ◇ *a glass of **dry/sweet** wine* 一杯干 / 甜葡萄酒 ◇ ***red/rosé/white wine*** 红 / 玫瑰红 / 白葡萄酒 ◇ ***sparkling wine*** 汽酒 ➲ SEE ALSO TABLE WINE

(No, **rosé**. 不能说 pink wine，该说 rosé wine。)

If you look up an adjective you will see what nouns are commonly used with it. 查看形容词词条便可知道通常有哪些名词可与之搭配：

Which words can be used with the adjective heady?
哪些词可与形容词 heady 搭配？

heady /ˈhedi/ *adj.* (**head·ier**, **headi·est**) **1** [usually before noun] having a strong effect on your senses; making you feel excited and confident 强烈作用于感官的；使兴奋的；使有信心的 SYN **intoxicating**: *the heady days of youth* 令人陶醉的年轻时代 ◇ *the heady scent of hot spices* 辣味香料的刺鼻气味 ◇ *a heady mixture of desire and fear* 既期待又害怕的复杂心情 ➲ SYNONYMS AT EXCITING

(**days, scent, mixture**)

Look at the examples in a noun entry to find out what verbs can be used with it. 查看名词词条中的示例便可知道哪些动词可与之搭配：

Which verbs are used with mortgage?
哪些动词可与 mortgage 搭配？

mort·gage /ˈmɔːɡɪdʒ; *NAmE* ˈmɔːrɡ-/ *noun, verb*
■ *noun* (*also informal* ˌ**home ˈloan**) a legal agreement by which a bank or similar organization lends you money to buy a house, etc., and you pay the money back over a particular number of years; the sum of money that you borrow 按揭（由银行等提供房产等的抵押借款）；按揭贷款：*to* ***apply for/take out/pay off*** *a mortgage* 申请 / 取得 / 还清抵押贷款 ◇ *mortgage rates* (= of interest) 按揭贷款利率 ◇ *a mortgage on the house* 一项房产按揭 ◇ *a mortgage of £60 000* * 6 万英镑的按揭贷款 ◇ *monthly mortgage payments* 月供

(apply for, take out, pay off)

If you look up an adjective, you will see which adverbs you can use to intensify it.
查看形容词词条便可知道哪些副词可用以加强其词义：

Strongly or bitterly disappointed?
用 strongly 还是 bitterly 修饰 disappointed？

dis·ap·point·ed /ˌdɪsəˈpɔɪntɪd/ *adj.* upset because sth you hoped for has not happened or been as good, successful, etc. as you expected 失望的；沮丧的；失意的： ~ (**at/by sth**) *They were* ***bitterly disappointed*** *at the result of the game.* 他们对比赛结果极为失望。◇ *I was disappointed by the quality of the wine.* 这酒的质量令我失望。◇ ~ (**in/with sb/sth**) *I'm disappointed in you—I really thought I could trust you!* 你真让我失望，我原以为可以相信你的！◇ *I was very disappointed with myself.* 我对自己感到非常失望。◇ ~ (**to see, hear, etc.**) *He was disappointed to see she wasn't at the party.* 看到她没来参加晚会，他感到很失望。◇ ~ (**that...**) *I'm disappointed (that) it was sold out.* 全都卖完了，我感到很失望。◇ ~ (**not**) **to be...** *She was disappointed not to be chosen.* 她没有被选中感到很沮丧。

(bitterly)

Important collocations are printed in **bold type** within the examples. If the meaning of the collocation is not obvious there is a short explanation after it in brackets.
重要的词语搭配在示例中用**粗体字**显示；如果搭配的含义并非简明易懂，会在后面用括号予以简短注释。

hoping you will be lucky 希望自己运气好

having unexpected luck 非常幸运，喜出望外

luck /lʌk/ *noun, verb*
■ *noun* [U] **1** good things that happen to you by chance, not because of your own efforts or abilities 好运；幸运；侥幸：*With (any) luck, we'll be home before dark.* 如果一切顺利的话，我们可在天黑前回到家。◇ (*BrE*) ***With a bit of luck,*** *we'll finish on time.* 如果我们运气好，就能够准时完成。◇ *So far I have had no luck with finding a job.* 我找工作一直不走运。◇ ***I could hardly believe my luck*** *when he said yes.* 听他说行，我几乎不敢相信自己会这么走运。◇ *It was* ***a stroke of luck*** *that we found you.* 真巧我们找到了你。◇ ***By sheer luck*** *nobody was hurt in the explosion.* 万幸的是，没有人在爆炸中受伤。◇ ***We wish her luck*** *in her new career.* 我们祝愿她在新的事业中一帆风顺。◇ *You're* ***in luck*** (= lucky)—*there's one ticket left.* 你运气不错，还剩一张票。◇ *You're* ***out of luck.*** *She's not here.* 真不巧，她不在。◇ *What a* ***piece of luck!*** 运气真好！ ➲ SEE ALSO BEGINNER'S LUCK **2** chance; the force that causes good or bad things to happen to people 机遇；命运；运

not being lucky 运气不好

being lucky 运气好

hoping someone else will be lucky
希望别人运气好

Idioms 习语

What are idioms? 什么是习语?

An idiom is a phrase whose meaning is difficult or sometimes impossible to guess by looking at the meanings of the individual words it contains. For example, the phrase **be in the same boat** has a literal meaning that is easy to understand, but it also has a common idiomatic meaning. 习语是一种短语，仅凭其中各个词的意思很难，有时甚至不可能推断出其含义。如短语 be in the same boat 既有一个容易理解的字面含义，也有一个常见的习语含义：

- *I found the job difficult at first. But we were all in the same boat; we were all learning.* 开始的时候我觉得这工作挺难的，但我们处境相同，大家都在学习。

Here, **be in the same boat** means 'to be in the same difficult or unfortunate situation'. 这里的 be in the same boat 指处于同样困境、境遇相同。

Some idioms are imaginative expressions such as proverbs and sayings. 有些习语是富有想象力的表达方式，如谚语和格言：

- *Too many cooks spoil the broth.* 厨师多了烧坏汤。
(= If too many people are involved in something, it will not be well done. 人多手杂反坏事；人多添乱)

If the expression is well known, part of it may be left out. 如果某个表达为人所熟悉，其中一部分可以省略：

- *Well, I knew everything would go wrong – it's the usual story of too many cooks!* 唉，我就知道事情会搞砸，常言道，人多手杂！

Other idioms are short expressions that are used for a particular purpose. 另外一些习语比较短，用以表达特定的意思：

- *Hang in there!* 坚持下去！(used to encourage somebody in a difficult situation 用以鼓励身陷困境的人)
- *Get lost!* 滚开！(a rude way of saying 'go away' 粗鲁地叫人离开)

Many idioms, however, are not vivid in this way. They are considered as idioms because their form is fixed. 但也有许多习语并非如此生动，它们被视为习语是因为形式固定：

- *for certain* 肯定地
- *in any case* 不管怎样

Idioms in the dictionary 本词典中的习语

Idioms are defined at the entry for the first 'full' word (a noun, a verb, an adjective or an adverb) that they contain. This means ignoring any grammatical words such as articles and prepositions. Idioms follow the main senses of a word, in a section marked IDM. 习语的释义在第一个实词（名词、动词、形容词或副词）所在的词条中，撇除冠词和介词等语法词。习语部分位于单词的主要义项之后标有 IDM 的地方：

> IDM **in the blink of an 'eye** very quickly; in a short time 眨眼的工夫；很快 **on the 'blink** (*informal*) (of a machine 机器) no longer working correctly 失灵；出毛病

The words **in**, **the** and **on** in these idioms do not count as 'full' words, and so the idioms are not listed at the entries for these words. 两个习语中的 in、the 和 on 不算实词，故习语不列入这几个单词所在的词条中。

Deciding where idioms start and stop is not always easy. 确定习语从何处开始到何处结束并不总是那么容易。If you hear the expression 如果你听到这样的表达：

- *They decided to bury the hatchet and try to be friends again.* 他们决定捐弃前嫌，重归于好。

you might think that **hatchet** is the only word you do not know and look that up. In fact, **bury the hatchet** is an idiomatic expression and it is defined at **bury**. At **hatchet** you will find a cross reference directing you to **bury**. 你可能会认为你不认识的单词只有 hatchet，并会去查找这个词。事实上，bury the hatchet 是一个

习语，其释义在 bury 词条。而在 hatchet 词条则有参见项指向 bury 词条：

> **hatchet** /ˈhætʃɪt/ *noun* a small AXE (= a tool with a heavy blade for chopping things) with a short handle 短柄小斧 ➲ PICTURE AT AXE IDM SEE BURY

Sometimes one 'full' word of an idiom can be replaced by another. For example, in the idiom **be a bag of nerves**, **bag** can be replaced by **bundle**. This is shown as **be a bag / bundle of nerves** and the idiom is defined at the first full fixed word, **nerve**. If you try to look the phrase up at either **bag** or **bundle** you will find a cross reference to **nerve** at the end of the idioms section. 有时习语的某个实词可用另一实词替换。如习语 be a bag of nerves 中的 bag 可换成 bundle。这种情况便用 be a bag/bundle of nerves 表示，其释义在第一个固定不变的实词 nerve 词条内。如果在 bag 或 bundle 词条中查找此短语，会在习语部分末看到参见项，指向 nerve 词条。

> IDM **not go a bundle on sb/sth** (*BrE, informal*) to not like sb/sth very much 不十分喜欢某人 / 某事物 ➲ MORE AT DROP *v.*, NERVE *n.*

A few very common verbs and the adjectives **bad** and **good** have so many idioms that they cannot all be listed in the entry. Instead, there is a note telling you to look at the entry for the next noun, verb, adjective, etc. in the idiom. 一些很常见的动词以及形容词 bad 和 good 的习语非常多，不可能全部列入该词条，所以有提示引导你去查阅习语中的下一个名词、动词、形容词等词条：

> IDM HELP Most idioms containing **go** are at the entries for the nouns and adjectives in the idioms, for example **go it alone** is at **alone**. 大多数含 go 的习语，都可在该等习语中的名词及形容词相关词条找到，如 go it alone 在词条 alone 下。

In some idioms, many alternatives are possible. In the expression **disappear into thin air**, you could replace **disappear** with **vanish**, **melt** or **evaporate**. In the dictionary this is shown as **disappear, vanish, etc. into thin air**, showing that you can use other words with a similar meaning to **disappear** in the idiom. Since the first 'full' word of the idiom is not fixed, the expression is defined at **thin** with a cross reference only at **air**. 有些习语中的某个词可以换成多个不同的词，比如 disappear into thin air 中的 disappear 可用 vanish、melt 或 evaporate 替换。在本词典中用 disappear, vanish, etc. into thin air 表示，表明在此习语中可用与 disappear 意思相近的其他词。由于此习语中的第一个实词并非固定不变，释义放在 thin 词条，只在 air 词条中提供参见项。

If you cannot find an idiom in the dictionary, look it up at the entry for one of the other main words in the expression. 查不到某个习语时，可在其包含的其他主要词的词条中查找。

Some idioms only contain grammatical words such as **one**, **it**, or **in**. These idioms are defined at the first word that appears in them. For example, the idiom **one up on sb** is defined at the entry for **one**. 有些习语只包含 one、it 或 in 等语法词，这类习语的释义放在第一个词的词条中。如习语 one up on sb 的释义放在 one 词条。

Idioms are given in alphabetical order within the idioms sections. Grammatical words such as **a/an** or **the**, **sb/sth** and the possessive forms **your**, **sb's**, **his**, **her**, etc., as well as words in brackets ( ) or after a slash (/), are ignored. 习语在词条的习语部分按字母顺序排列，语法词（如 a/an、the 或 sb/sth）、所有格形式（如 your、sb's、his、her 等）以及括号内或斜线号后的词不计。

More like this 同类词语学习

Besides learning groups of words that go together by meaning, for example all the vocabulary that belongs in a topic, it can be useful to know about words that behave in a similar way. For example, when you revise an uncountable word like **news**, it makes sense to think about others that are like it – **information**, **advice**, and so on. Or you may just be interested in a quirky expression such as *as fit as a fiddle*. What other idioms are there that follow this **as ~ as** pattern? In the main part of the dictionary you will find cross references that bring you to these pages where you can see groups of words that are similar in some way to the one you have looked up. 除了学习因词义相关联而归为同一类的词语，比如属于同一主题的词汇以外，了解一些表现形式相似的词语也很有用。比如，复习不可数名词 news 时，很容易会想与之相似的 information、advice 等词。或许你对 as fit as a fiddle（非常健康）这样奇特有趣的表达法感兴趣，那么还有其他遵循 as ~ as 这一模式的习语吗？在本词典的正文部分会有参见项引导至本部分的同类词语学习页，查看与所查单词具有类似表现形式的词汇。

1 Blended or portmanteau words 混成词或缩合词

alcopop, breathalyser, bromance, brunch, chillax, chugger, docusoap, edutainment, greenwash, guesstimate, infomercial, mechatronics, metrosexual, mockney, motel, multiplex, pleather, podcast, robocall, simulcast, sitcom, smog, staycation, telethon, televangelist, workaholic.

2 Exclamations 感叹词

aargh, ah, aha, ahem, atishoo, aw, bah, boo, coo, d'oh, eek, eh, er, eww, gee, ha, hey, ho ho, ho-hum, hooray, huh, mm, oh, oho, oi, ooh, oops, ouch, ow, pah, phew, psst, sh, tsk tsk, tut, ugh, uh, uh-huh, uh-oh, uh-uh, um, whoopee, whoops, woo hoo, wow, yay, yippee, yuck, yum.

3 Onomatopoeic words 拟声词

beep, bleep, boohoo, brrr, buzz, click, clip-clop, ding-dong, hiss, mwah, peep, ping, plop, pop, rat-tat, splat, splosh, squeak, squeal, squelch, swish, tee-hee, thud, thwack, tick-tock, toot, vroom, wham, whoosh, zoom.

4 Animal sounds 模拟动物叫声的词

baa, caw, coo, meow, moo, neigh, oink, quack, tu-whit, tu-whoo, tweet, woof.

5 Contractions in non-standard language 非标准用法的缩约词

ain't, doncha, dunno, 'em, gonna, gotcha, gotta, innit, 'nother, wanna, ya, yer.

6 Prefixes 前缀

a-, ante-, anti-, be-, co-, de-, demi-, dis-, en-, ex-, extra-, hyper-, hypo-, in-, infra-, inter-, intra-, mis-, non-, off-, oft-, out-, over-, para-, post-, pre-, pro-, re-, retro-, semi-, sub-, trans-, ultra-, un-, under-, up-.

7 Suffixes 后缀

-able, -age, -al, -ance, -ant, -arian, -ary, -dom, -ee, -er, -ese, -esque, -ess, -fold, -ful, -hood, -ify, -ion, -ish, -ism, -ist, -ista, -ite, -itis, -ize, -less, -let, -ling, -ly, -ment, -most, -ness, -oid, -or, -ous, -ship.

8 Compound adjectives for physical characteristics 描述身体特征的复合形容词

-beaked, -bellied, -billed, -blooded, -bodied, -cheeked, -chested, -eared, -eyed, -faced, -fingered, -footed, -haired, -handed, -headed, -hearted, -hipped, -lidded, -limbed, -mouthed, -necked, -nosed, -skinned, -tailed, -throated, -toothed.

9 Compound nouns with -ing forms 带 -ing 形式的复合名词

airing cupboard, answering machine, asking price, baking powder, betting shop, boarding school, booking office, bowling alley, breathing space, breeding ground, changing room, clotting factor, cutting room, draining board, drinking water, eating apple, housing estate, icing sugar, living room, meeting place, nursing home, punching bag, racing car, sleeping pill, starting point, tuning fork, waiting room, working party.

10 Descriptive compound adjectives with parts of the body 带身体部位的描述性复合形容词

back-breaking, ear-splitting, eye-popping, gut-wrenching, hair-raising, jaw-dropping, lung-busting, mind-boggling, nail-biting, rib-tickling, side-splitting, spine-chilling, stomach-churning, toe-curling.

11 Reduplicative words 叠声词

airy-fairy, argy-bargy, chit-chat, criss-cross, dilly-dally, fuddy-duddy, harum-scarum, helter-skelter, higgledy-piggledy, hocus-pocus, hoity-toity, hotchpotch, hurly-burly, itty-bitty, mishmash, mumbo jumbo, nitty-gritty, ping-pong, pitter-patter, riff-raff, shilly-shally, teeny-weeny, tittle-tattle, touchy-feely, wishy-washy.

12 Rhyming pairs in idioms 同韵对习语

doom and gloom, fair and square, high and dry, huff and puff, name and shame, slice and dice, thrills and spills, wear and tear, wheel and deal, wine and dine.

13 Alliteration in idioms 押头韵的习语

belt and braces, black and blue, born and bred, chalk and cheese, chop and change, done and dusted, down and dirty, in dribs and drabs, eat sb out of house and home, facts and figures, fast and furious, first and foremost, forgive and forget, hale and hearty, hem and haw, kith and kin, mix and match, part and parcel, puff and pant, go to rack and ruin, rant and rave, risk life and limb, short and sweet, signed and sealed, spick and span, through thick and thin, this and that, top and tail, tried and tested, wax and wane.

14 Similes in idioms 使用明喻的习语

as bald as a coot, as blind as a bat, as bold as brass, as bright as a button, as busy as a bee, as clean as a whistle, as dead as a dodo, as deaf as a post, as dull as ditchwater, as fit as a fiddle, as flat as a pancake, as good as gold, as mad as a hatter, as miserable/ugly as sin, as old as the hills, as pleased as Punch, as pretty as a picture, as quick as a flash, as regular as clockwork, as safe as houses, as sound as a bell, as steady as a rock, as thick as two short planks, as tough as old boots.

15 Colour compounds 颜色复合词

baby blue, china-blue, cobalt blue, electric blue, ice-blue, midnight blue, navy blue, peacock blue, petrol blue, powder blue, royal blue, sky-blue; blood-red, cherry red, pillar-box red, wine red; bottle-green, emerald green, jade green, lime green, olive-green, pea-green, sea-green; lemon yellow, primrose yellow; lily-white, snow-white; coal-black, jet black, pitch-black; charcoal grey, iron-grey, slate-grey; rose pink, salmon pink, shocking pink; nut-brown.

16 Expressions from history and legend 源自历史和传说的词语

Achilles heel, Cinderella, Herculean, Mephistophelian, Midas touch, narcissism, odyssey, Pandora's box, Prince Charming, Procrustean, Promethean, Pyrrhic victory, Robin Hood, Scylla and Charybdis, Sleeping Beauty, Stygian, Titan.

17 Expressions from literary sources 源自文学作品的词语

Alice in Wonderland, Casanova, Cassandra, Don Juan, Dorian Gray, Falstaffian, Frankenstein, Jekyll and Hyde, Lilliputian, Lothario, Orwellian, Peter Pan, Pied Piper, Pollyanna, Rip Van Winkle, Ruritanian, Scrooge, Shangri-La, Sherlock, Stepford wife, Svengali, Tweedledum and Tweedledee, Utopia, Walter Mitty.

18 Expressions with people's names 带人名的词语

Aunt Sally, Hobson's choice, Hooray Henry, Houdini, Jack Robinson, Jack the Lad, Jane Doe, Joe Bloggs, Joe Public, Joe Sixpack, John Bull, John Doe, John Hancock, Johnny Reb, PC Plod, Uncle Sam.

19 Place names representing activities 指代活动的地名

Downing Street, Grub Street, Holyrood, Madison Avenue, Main Street, Number Ten, the Oval Office, the Palace, Silicon Valley, the Vatican, Whitehall, the White House.

20 Silent letters 含不发音字母的词

gnarled, gnash, gnat, gnaw, gnome;

haute cuisine, heir, (*NAmE*) herb, honour, hors d'oeuvre, hour;

knack, knee, kneel, knife, knight, knit, knob, knock, knot, know, knuckle;

psalm, psephology, psychic, psychology, ptarmigan, pterodactyl;

wrangle, wrap, wreath, wreck, wrench, wrestle, wriggle, wring, write, wrong;

bomb, climb, crumb, doubt, lamb, limb;

ascent, fascinate, muscle, scene, scissors;

height, right, sleigh, weight;

align, campaign, design, foreign, malign, reign, unfeigned;

balmy, calf, calm, half, yolk;

autumn, column, condemn, damn, hymn, solemn;

bristle, fasten, listen, mortgage, soften, thistle, wrestle;

biscuit, build, circuit, disguise, guilty, league, rogue, vague;

yacht; answer, sword, two.

21 Pronunciation changes by part of speech 随词性改变而发音不同的词

abuse, advocate, alternate, approximate, articulate, contract, converse, convict, decrease, delegate, discount, duplicate, estimate, export, extract, graduate, import, increase, intimate, moderate, object, permit, present, protest, record, refund, refuse, subject, survey, suspect, torment, upgrade.

22 Adjectives ending in -ed pronounced /-ɪd/ 以 -ed（发音为/-ɪd/）结尾的形容词

aged, beloved, crooked, dogged, learned, naked, ragged, rugged, sacred, wicked.

23 Words that look like opposites, but aren't 形似而实非反义词的词语

different/indifferent, famous/infamous, flammable/inflammable, interested/disinterested, savoury/unsavoury, sensible/insensible, valuable/invaluable.

24 Plural adjectival nouns "the + 形容词"表复数的名词

the blind, the dead, the deaf, the destitute, the dying, the elderly, the faithful, the homeless, the injured, the insane, the jobless, the middle aged, the old, the poor, the rich, the sick, the squeamish, the wealthy, the wicked, the wounded, the young.

25 Masculine, feminine and ungendered form 阳性、阴性和无性名词

actor/actress, anchorman/anchorwoman/anchor, assemblyman/assemblywoman, businessman/businesswoman/business person, cameraman/camerawoman, chairman/chairwoman/chair/chairperson, congressman/congresswoman, nobleman/noblewoman, patrolman/patrolwoman, policeman/policewoman/police officer, salesman/saleswoman/salesperson, spokesman/spokeswoman/spokesperson, sportsman/sportswoman/sportsperson, stuntman/stuntwoman, waiter/waitress/waitperson, weatherman/weathergirl.

26 Verbs usually followed by infinitives 后面通常跟不定式的动词

afford, agree, appear, arrange, attempt, beg, choose, consent, decide, expect, fail, happen, hesitate, hope, intend, learn, manage, mean, neglect, offer, prepare, pretend, promise, refuse, swear, try, want, wish.

27 Verbs usually followed by -ing forms 后面通常跟 -ing 形式的动词

avoid, consider, delay, deny, enjoy, escape, finish, give up, imagine, involve, mention, mind, miss, postpone, practise, resist, risk, suggest.

28 Uncountable nouns often used wrongly 常用错的不可数名词

accommodation, advice, chewing gum, equipment, feedback, furniture, information, luggage, news, progress, software.

29 Uncountable nouns ending in -ics 以 -ics 结尾的不可数名词

athletics, ballistics, civics, cybernetics, genetics, geophysics, gymnastics, linguistics, optics, orthodontics, orthopaedics, phonetics, phonics, physics, semantics, semiotics, stylistics, thermodynamics.

30 Easily-confused plural/singular forms 易混淆的单复数形式

bacteria/bacterium, criteria/criterion, data/datum, media/medium, phenomena/phenomenon, strata/stratum.

31 Adjectives that do not come before a noun 不用于名词前的形容词

addicted, afloat, afraid, alike, alive, alone, ashamed, asleep, awake.

32 Adjectives that only come before a noun 只用于名词前的形容词

all-round, antenatal, aspiring, chief, dedicated, eventual, express, high-flying, live, lone, mere, mitigating, rogue, sheer, standout, ulterior, utter.

33 Verbs with two objects 带双宾语的动词

bet, bring, build, buy, cost, get, give, leave, lend, make, offer, owe, pass, pay, play, post, promise, read, refuse, sell, send, show, sing, take, teach, tell, throw, wish, write.

34 Shops, etc. with apostrophes 以所有格形式表示店铺等的词

baker's, barber's, butcher's, chemist's, dentist's, doctor's, fishmonger's, florist's, greengrocer's, grocer's, hairdresser's, ironmonger's, jeweller's, newsagent's, optician's, stationer's, tobacconist's, travel agent's.

35 Consonant-doubling adjectives 词形变化时词尾辅音字母须双写的形容词

big, drab, fat, fit, flat, hot, mad, red, sad, wet.

36 Consonant-doubling verbs 词形变化时词尾辅音字母须双写的动词

bob, club, dub, grab, rub, sob, throb;

kid, nod, pad, plod, prod, shred, skid, thud;

beg, blog, bug, drag, drug, flag, hug, jog, log, mug, nag, plug;

bar, confer, infer, occur, prefer, refer, star, stir, transfer;

acquit, admit, allot, chat, clot, commit, jut, knit, pat, regret, rot, spot, submit;

(in British English 英式英语) appal, cancel, channel, control, counsel, enrol, equal, excel, fuel, fulfil, label, level, marvel, model, pedal, quarrel, signal, travel.

Punctuation 标点符号用法

. full stop (*BrE*) period (*NAmE*) 句号

- at the end of a sentence that is not a question or an exclamation 用于除疑问句和感叹句以外的句子末尾：
  - ▸ *I knocked at the door. There was no reply.*
  - ▸ *I knocked again.*
- sometimes in abbreviations 有时用于缩写：
  - ▸ *Jan. e.g. a.m. etc.*
- in Internet and email addresses (said 'dot') 用于互联网和电邮地址中（读作 dot）
  - ▸ *http://www.oup.com*

, comma 逗号

- to separate words in a list, though they are often omitted before *and* 用以分隔列举的词语，但在 and 之前常常省略：
  - ▸ *a bouquet of red, pink and white roses*
  - ▸ *tea, coffee, milk or hot chocolate*
- to separate phrases or clauses 用以分隔短语或从句：
  - ▸ *If you keep calm, take your time, concentrate and think ahead, then you're likely to pass your test.*
  - ▸ *Worn out after all the excitement of the party, the children soon fell asleep.*
- before and after a clause or phrase that gives additional, but not essential, information about the noun it follows 用于给前面的名词作非必要补充的从句或短语前后：
  - ▸ *The Pennine Hills, which are very popular with walkers, are situated between Lancashire and Yorkshire.*

  (do not use commas before and after a clause that **defines** the noun it follows 在限定性名词从句前后不用逗号）
  - ▸ *The hills that separate Lancashire from Yorkshire are called the Pennines.*
- to separate main clauses, especially long ones, linked by a conjunction such as *and, as, but, for, or* 用以分隔由连词 and、as、but、for、or 等连接的主句，尤其是较长的主句：
  - ▸ *We had been looking forward to our holiday all year, but unfortunately it rained every day.*
- to separate an introductory word or phrase, or an adverb or adverbial phrase that applies to the whole sentence, from the rest of the sentence 用以将引导词或短语、修饰整个句子的副词或副词短语与句子的其余部分隔开：
  - ▸ *Oh, so that's where it was.*
  - ▸ *As it happens, however, I never saw her again.*
  - ▸ *By the way, did you hear about Sue's car?*
- to separate a tag question from the rest of the sentence 用以将附加疑问句与句子的其余部分隔开：
  - ▸ *It's quite expensive, isn't it?*
  - ▸ *You live in Bristol, right?*
- before or after 'he said', etc. when writing down conversation 书写对话时用于 he said 等词语前后：
  - ▸ *'Come back soon,' she said.*
- before a short quotation 用于短引语前：
  - ▸ *Disraeli said, 'Little things affect little minds'.*

: colon 冒号

- to introduce a list of items 用于引出下文各项：
  - ▸ *These are our options: we go by train and leave before the end of the show; or we take the car and see it all.*
- in formal writing, before a clause or phrase that gives more information about the main clause. (You can use a semicolon or a full stop, but not a comma, instead of a colon here.)

在正式书面语中，用于补充说明主句的从句或短语之前。（此处可用分号或句号代替冒号，但不可以用逗号。）

▸ *The garden had been neglected for a long time: it was overgrown and full of weeds.*

- to introduce a quotation, which may be indented 用于引出引语，引语可能缩进：

▸ *As Kenneth Morgan writes:*
The truth was, perhaps, that Britain in the years from 1914 to 1983 had not changed all that fundamentally.
Others, however, have challenged this view ...

; semicolon 分号

- instead of a comma to separate parts of a sentence that already contain commas 用以代替逗号，分隔句中已含逗号的部分：

▸ *She was determined to succeed whatever the cost; she would achieve her aim, whoever might suffer on the way.*

- in formal writing, to separate two main clauses, especially those not joined by a conjunction 在正式书面语中，用以分隔两个主句，尤其是无连词的两个主句：

▸ *The sun was already low in the sky; it would soon be dark.*

? question mark 问号

- at the end of a direct question 用于直接问句末尾：

▸ *Where's the car?*

▸ *You're leaving already?*

Do not use a question mark at the end of an indirect question. 转述问句末尾不用问号：

▸ *He asked if I was leaving.*

- especially with a date, to express doubt 尤与日期连用，表示存疑：

▸ *John Marston (?1575–1634)*

! exclamation mark (*BrE*) exclamation point (*NAmE*) 感叹号

- at the end of a sentence expressing surprise, joy, anger, shock or another strong emotion 用于表示惊讶、欣喜、愤怒、震惊或其他强烈感情的句子末尾：

▸ *That's marvellous!*

▸ *'Never!' she cried.*

- in informal written English, you can use more than one exclamation mark, or an exclamation mark and a question mark 在非正式书面语中，可以用一个以上的感叹号或一个感叹号加一个问号：

▸ *'Your wife's just given birth to triplets.' 'Triplets!?'*

’ apostrophe 撇号

- with *s* to indicate that a thing or person belongs to somebody 与 s 连用表示所有格：

▸ *my friend's brother*

▸ *the waitress's apron*

▸ *King James's crown / King James' crown*

▸ *the students' books*

▸ *the women's coats*

- in short forms, to indicate that letters or figures have been omitted 在缩写中表示字母或数字的省略：

▸ *I'm (I am)*

▸ *they'd (they had/they would)*

▸ *the summer of '89 (1989)*

- sometimes, with *s* to form the plural of a letter, a figure or an abbreviation 有时与 s 连用构成字母、数字或缩写的复数形式：

▸ *roll your r's*

▸ *during the 1990's*

- hyphen 连字符；连（字）号

- to form a compound from two or more other words 将两个或更多的词组成复合词：
  - ▸ *hard-hearted* ▸ *fork-lift truck*
  - ▸ *mother-to-be*
- to form a compound from a prefix and a proper name 将前缀和专有名词组成复合词：
  - ▸ *pre-Raphaelite* ▸ *pro-European*
- when writing compound numbers between 21 and 99 in words 用于书写21–99之间的复合数字：
  - ▸ *seventy-three* ▸ *thirty-one*
- sometimes, in British English, to separate a prefix ending in a vowel from a word beginning with the same vowel 有时在英式英语中用以将以元音结尾的前缀与以相同元音开始的词隔开：
  - ▸ *co-operate* ▸ *pre-eminent*
- after the first section of a word that is divided between one line and the next 转行时用于单词的前半部分后：
  - ▸ *decide what to do in order to avoid mis-takes of this kind in the future*

– dash 破折号

- in informal English, instead of a colon or semicolon, to indicate that what follows is a summary or conclusion of what has gone before 在非正式英语中，用以代替冒号或分号，表示后面所说是对前面的总结或结论：
  - ▸ *Men were shouting, women were screaming, children were crying – it was chaos.*
  - ▸ *You've admitted that you lied to me – how can I trust you again?*
- singly or in pairs to separate a comment or an afterthought from the rest of the sentence 单个或成对使用，用以将句中的评语或事后想到的补充说明与句子的其余部分隔开：
  - ▸ *He knew nothing at all about it – or so he said.*

... dots / ellipsis 省略号

- to indicate that words have been omitted, especially from a quotation or at the end of a conversation 表示词的省略，尤用于引语或对话末尾的省略：
  - ▸ *... challenging the view that Britain ... had not changed all that fundamentally.*

/ slash / oblique 斜线号

- to separate alternative words or phrases 用以分隔可供选择的词或短语：
  - ▸ *have a pudding and/or cheese*
  - ▸ *single/married/widowed/divorced*
- in Internet and email addresses to separate the different elements (often said 'forward slash') 在互联网和电邮地址中用以分隔各个不同的成分（通常叫作“正斜杠”）
  - ▸ *http: //www.oup.com/elt/*

' " quotation marks 引号

- to enclose words and punctuation in direct speech 用以标明引号内的词句和标点符号为直接引语：
  - ▸ *'Why on earth did you do that?' he asked.*
  - ▸ *'I'll fetch it,' she replied.*
- to draw attention to a word that is unusual for the context, for example a slang expression, or to a word that is being used for special effect, such as irony 用以提醒注意文中的特殊词（如俚语）或为特殊效果而使用的词（如反语）：
  - ▸ *He told me in no uncertain terms to 'get lost'.*
  - ▸ *Thousands were imprisoned in the name of 'national security'.*
- around the titles of articles, books, poems, plays, etc. 用以标明文章、书、诗歌、戏剧等的名称：
  - ▸ *Keats's 'Ode to Autumn'*
  - ▸ *I was watching 'Match of the Day'.*
- around short quotations or sayings 用以标明短引语或谚语：

- *Do you know the origin of the saying: 'A little learning is a dangerous thing'?*

- in American English, double quotation marks are used 美式英语用双引号：
  - *"Help! I'm drowning!"*

( ) brackets (*BrE*) parentheses (*NAmE or formal*) （圆）括号

- to separate extra information or a comment from the rest of a sentence 用以将句中的附加信息或评语与句子的其余部分隔开：
  - *Mount Robson (12972 feet) is the highest mountain in the Canadian Rockies.*
  - *He thinks that modern music (i.e. anything written after 1900) is rubbish.*
- to enclose cross references 用以标明参见项：
  - *This moral ambiguity is a feature of Shakespeare's later works (see Chapter Eight).*
- around numbers or letters in text 用以标明文中号码或字母编号：
  - *Our objectives are (1) to increase output,(2) to improve quality and (3) to maximize profits.*

[ ] square brackets (*BrE*) brackets (*NAmE*) 方括号

- around words inserted to make a quotation grammatically correct 用以标明使引语合乎语法的插入词：
  - *Britain in [these] years was without ...*

italics 斜体字

- to show emphasis 表示强调：
  - I'm not going to do it – *you* are.
  - ... proposals which we cannot accept *under any circumstances*
- to indicate the titles of books, plays, etc. 表示书、戏剧等的名称：
  - Joyce's *Ulysses*
  - the title role in Puccini's *Tosca*
  - a letter in *The Times*
- for foreign words or phrases 表示外来语：
  - the English oak (*Quercus robur*)
  - I had to renew my *permesso di soggiorno* (residence permit).

Quoting conversation 引述对话

When you write down a conversation, you normally begin a new paragraph for each new speaker. 书写对话时不同人说的话一般独立成段。

Quotation marks enclose the words spoken. 引号标明说话内容：

- *'You're sure of this?' I asked.*
  He nodded grimly.
  'I'm certain.'

Verbs used to indicate direct speech, for example *he said, she complained*, are separated by commas from the words spoken, unless a question mark or an exclamation mark is used. 用逗号将表示直接引语的动词（如 he said、she complained）与说话内容隔开，除非直接引语后为问号或感叹号：

- *'That's all I know,' said Nick.*
- *Nick said, 'That's all I know.'*
- *'Why?' asked Nick.*

When *he said* or *said Nick* follows the words spoken, the comma is placed inside the quotation marks, as in the first example above. If, however, the writer puts the words *said Nick* within the actual words Nick speaks, the comma is outside the quotation marks. * he said 或 said Nick 在直接引语之后，逗号置于引号里面，如上面第1例所示。若 said Nick 置于 Nick 所说内容的中间，则逗号置于引号外面：

- *'That', said Nick, 'is all I know.'*

Double quotation marks are used to indicate direct speech being quoted by somebody else within direct speech. 双引号用以表示直接引语被另一人引用于直接引语中：

- *'But you said you loved me! "I'll never leave you, Sue, as long as I live." That's what you said, isn't it?'*

Numbers 数字用法

Writing and saying numbers 数字的读和写

Numbers over 20 20 以上的数字

- are written with a hyphen 书写时用连字符：

  35 *thirty-five*
  67 *sixty-seven*
- When writing a cheque we often use words for the pounds or dollars and figures for the pence or cents. 填写支票时常用英语词表示英镑或美元，用阿拉伯数字表示便士或分：

  £22.45 *twenty-two pounds (and) 45 pence*
  $79.30 *seventy-nine dollars (and) 30 cents*

Numbers over 100 100 以上的数字

329 *three hundred and twenty-nine*

- The **and** is pronounced /n/ and the stress is on the final number. * and 的发音为 /n/，重音在最后一个数字。
- In American English the **and** is sometimes left out. 美式英语有时省略 and。

Numbers over 1 000 1 000 以上的数字

1 100 *one thousand one hundred* (*also informal* 非正式亦作 *eleven hundred*)
2 500 *two thousand five hundred* (*also informal, especially in NAmE* 非正式，美式英语尤作 *twenty-five hundred*)

- These informal forms are most common for whole hundreds between 1 100 and 1 900. 上述非正式形式最常用于 1 100 到 1 900 之间的整百数字。
- A comma or (*in BrE*) a space is often used to divide large numbers into groups of 3 figures. 常常用逗号或英式英语用空格将数额大的数字分成 3 个数字一组：
  - ▸ *33,423* or *33 423 (thirty-three thousand four hundred and twenty-three)*
  - ▸ *2,768,941* or *2 768 941 (two million seven hundred and sixty-eight thousand nine hundred and forty-one)*

A or one? 用 a 还是用 one?

130 *a / one hundred and thirty*
1 000 000 *a / one million*

- **one** is more formal and more precise and can be used for emphasis * one 更正式、更准确，可表示强调：
  - ▸ *The total cost was one hundred and sixty-three pounds exactly.*
  - ▸ *It cost about a hundred and fifty quid.*
- **a** can only be used at the beginning of a number * a 只能用于数字的开头：

  1 000 *a / one thousand*
  2 100 *two thousand one hundred*
  ~~*two thousand a hundred*~~
- **a** is not usually used between 1 100 and 1 999 * 1 100 到 1 999 之间的数字一般不用 a：

  1 099 *a / one thousand and ninety-nine*
  1 100 *one thousand one hundred*
  1 340 *one thousand three hundred and forty*
  ~~*a thousand three hundred and forty*~~

Ordinal numbers 序数词

1st	*first*	5th	*fifth*
2nd	*second*	9th	*ninth*
3rd	*third*	12th	*twelfth*
4th	*fourth*	21st	*twenty-first*
			etc.

Fractions 分数

$^1/_2$ *a / one half*
$^1/_3$ *a / one third*
$^1/_4$ *a / one quarter* (*NAmE also* 美式英语亦作 *a / one fourth*)

(for emphasis use **one** instead of **a** 表示强调用 one 不用 a)

$^1/_{12}$ *one twelfth*
$^1/_{16}$ *one sixteenth*
$^2/_3$ *two thirds*
$^3/_4$ *three quarters* (*NAmE also* 美式英语亦作 *three fourths*)
$^9/_{10}$ *nine tenths*

More complex fractions 较复杂的分数

- use **over** 用 over：
  $^{19}/_{56}$ *nineteen* ***over*** *fifty-six*
  $^{31}/_{144}$ *thirty-one* ***over*** *one four four*

Whole numbers and fractions 整数和分数

- link with **and** 用 and 连接：
  $2^1/_2$ *two* ***and*** *a half*
  $5^2/_3$ *five* ***and*** *two thirds*
- **one** plus a fraction is followed by a plural noun * one 加分数后用复数名词：
  $1^1/_2$ pts *one and a half* ***pints***

Fractions/percentages and noun phrases 分数 / 百分数和名词短语

- use **of** 用 of 连接：
  - ***a fifth of*** *the women questioned*
  - *three quarters* ***of*** *the population*
  - *75%* ***of*** *the population*
- with **half** do not use **a**, and **of** can sometimes be omitted 表示一半（half）时不用冠词 a，有时可省略 of：
  - *Half (of) the work is already finished.*
- do not use **of** in expressions of measurement or quantity 在表示量度或数量的短语中不用 of：
  - *How much is half a pint of milk?*
  - *It takes me half an hour by bus.*
- use **of** before pronouns 在代词前用 of：
  - *We can't start – only half* ***of*** *us are here.*

Fractions/percentages and verbs 分数 / 百分数和动词

- If a fraction/percentage is used with an uncountable or a singular noun the verb is generally singular. 分数 / 百分数与不可数名词或单数名词连用时，动词一般为单数：
  - *Fifty per cent of the land is cultivated.*
  - *Half (of) the land is cultivated.*
- If the noun is singular but represents a group of people, the verb is singular in American English but in British English it may be singular or plural. 单数集合名词的谓语动词在美式英语中用单数，但在英式英语中用单、复数均可：
  - *Three quarters/75% of the workforce is/are against the strike.*
- If the noun is plural, the verb is plural. 名词为复数，谓语动词亦为复数：
  - *Two thirds/65% of children play computer games.*

Decimals 小数

- write and say with a point (.) (not a comma) 读和写均用小数点（.）（不用逗号）表示
- say each figure after the point separately 小数点后的数字逐个读出：
  79.3 *seventy-nine point three*
  3.142 *three point one four two*
  0.67 *(zero) point six seven* (*BrE also* 英式英语亦读作 *nought point six seven*)

Mathematical expressions 数学表达式

+	plus
–	minus
×	times/multiplied by
÷	divided by
=	equals/is
%	per cent (*NAmE usually* 美式英语通常用 percent)
3^2	three squared
5^3	five cubed
6^{10}	six to the power of ten
$\sqrt{\ }$	square root of

The figure '0' 数字 0

The figure 0 has several different names in English, although in American English *zero* is commonly used in all cases. 数字 0 在英式英语中有几个不同的名称，而在美式英语中通常用 zero 表示：

Zero

- used in precise scientific, medical and economic contexts and to talk about temperature 用于精确的科学、医学和经济语境，亦用以表示温度：
  - ▸ *It was ten degrees below zero last night.*
  - ▸ *zero inflation/growth/profit*

Nought

- used in British English to talk about a number, age, etc. 在英式英语中用以表示数字、年龄等：
  - ▸ *A million is written with six noughts.*
  - ▸ *The car goes from nought to sixty in ten seconds.*
  - ▸ *clothes for children aged nought to six*

'o' /əʊ; *NAmE* oʊ/

- used when saying a bank account number, telephone number, etc. 用以读出银行账号、电话号码等

Nil

- used to talk about the score in a team game, for example in football 用以表示团队比赛（如足球赛）的比分：
  - ▸ *The final score was one nil. (1–0)*
- used to mean 'nothing at all' 用以表示完全没有：
  - ▸ *The doctors rated her chances as nil.*

Telephone numbers 电话号码

- All numbers are said separately. 0 is pronounced /əʊ/ (*BrE*) or /oʊ/ (*NAmE*). 每个数字逐一读出，0 读作 /əʊ/（英式英语）或 /oʊ/（美式英语）：
  - ▸ (01865) 556767
    o one eight six five, five five six seven six seven (or *double five six seven six seven*)

Temperature 温度

- The Celsius or Centigrade (°C) scale is officially used in Britain and for scientific purposes in the US. 摄氏温标（°C）在英国为官方用法，在美国用于科学语境：
  - ▸ *a high of thirty-five degrees Celsius*
  - ▸ *The normal temperature of the human body is 37°C.*
- The Fahrenheit (°F) scale is used in all other contexts in the US and is also still commonly used in Britain. The words 'degrees Fahrenheit/Centigrade/Celsius' are often omitted. 华氏温标（°F）在美国用于科学语境以外的所有场合，在英国亦普遍使用。degrees Fahrenheit/Centigrade/Celsius（华氏度 / 摄氏度）这些词常常省略：
  - ▸ *Temperatures soared to over a hundred. (100°F)*
  - ▸ *She's ill in bed with a temperature of a hundred and two. (102°F)*

Money 货币

In Britain 在英国

- ▸ *100 pence/p = 1 British pound (£1)*
- ▸ *It costs 90p/90 pence return on the bus.*

- when talking about an individual coin 表示单枚硬币：
  a twenty pence piece/a twenty p piece
- when talking about pounds and pence people often only say the numbers 表示英镑和便士通常只说数字：
  It only cost five ninety-nine. (£5.99)
- in informal British English 非正式英式英语：

£1	*a quid*
£5	*five quid* or *a fiver*
£10	*ten quid* or *a tenner*

In the US 在美国

1c	one cent	a penny 一分硬币
5c	five cents	a nickel 五分硬币
10c	ten cents	a dime 一角硬币
25c	twenty-five cents	a quarter 二角五分硬币
$1.00	one dollar	a dollar bill 一元纸币

- in informal American English dollars are called **bucks** 在非正式美式英语中美元叫 buck：
  - ▸ *This shirt cost fifty bucks.*

Writing and saying dates 日期的读和写

British English 英式英语

▸ *14 October 1998* or *14th October 1998 (14/10/98)*

▸ *Her birthday is on* **the** *ninth* **of** *December.*

▸ *Her birthday is on December* **the** *ninth.*

American English 美式英语

▸ *October 14, 1998 (10/14/98)*

▸ *Her birthday is December 9th.*

Years 年份

1999 *nineteen ninety-nine*
1608 *sixteen o eight* (or, less commonly 或不那么普遍地读作 *nineteen hundred and ninety-nine* and *sixteen hundred and eight*)
1700 *seventeen hundred*
2000 *(the year) two thousand*
2002 *two thousand and two*
2015 *twenty fifteen*

AD 76 / A.D. 76 *AD seventy-six*
76 CE / 76 C.E. *seventy-six CE*

(Both these expressions mean '76 years after the beginning of the Christian calendar'. 上述两种表达法均指公元76年。)

1000 BC / 1000 B.C. *one thousand BC*
1000 BCE / 1000 B.C.E. *one thousand BCE*

(Both these expressions mean '1000 years before the beginning of the Christian calendar'. 上述两种表达法均指公元前1000年。)

Age 年龄

- when saying a person's age use only numbers 表示人的年龄只用数字：
  - ▸ *Sue is ten and Tom is six.*
  - ▸ *She left home at sixteen.*
- a man/woman/boy/girl, etc. of ... 表示某个年龄的男子 / 女子 / 男孩 / 女孩等用 of:
  - ▸ *They've got a girl of three and a boy of five.*
  - ▸ *a young woman of nineteen*
- in writing, in descriptions or to emphasize sb's age use **... years old** 书写、描述或强调某人的年龄用 ... years old：
  - ▸ *She was thirty-one years old and a barrister by profession.*
  - ▸ *He is described as white, 5ft 10 ins tall and about 50 years old.*
  - ▸ *You're forty years old – stop behaving like a teenager!*
- **... years old** is also used for things. * ... years old 亦用以表示事物存在的时间：
  - ▸ *The monument is 120 years old.*
- You can also say **a ... year-old/ month-old/ week-old**, etc. 亦可用 a ... year-old/month-old/week-old 等表示：
  - ▸ *Youth training is available to all sixteen-year-olds.*
  - ▸ *a ten week-old baby*
  - ▸ *a remarkable 1 000 year-old tomb*
- Use **... years of age** in formal or written contexts. 正式用语或书面语用 ... years of age：
  - ▸ *Not applicable to persons under eighteen years of age*
- Use **the ... age group** to talk about people between certain ages. 表示某一年龄段的人用 the ... age group：
  - ▸ *He took first prize in the 10–16 age group.*
- To give the approximate age of a person. 表示一个人的大致年龄：

  13–19 *in his/her teens*
  21–29 *in his/her twenties*
  31–33 *in his/her early thirties*
  34–36 *in his/her mid thirties*
  37–39 *in his/her late thirties*
- To refer to a particular event you can use **at/by/before, etc. the age of ....** 特指某事情与某年龄有关可用 at/by/before etc. the age of ...：
  - ▸ *Most smokers start smoking cigarettes before the age of sixteen.*

Numbers in time 用于时间的数字

There is often more than one way of telling the time. 表示时间的方法通常不止一种：

Half hours 半小时

6:30 *six thirty*
half past six (*BrE*)
half six (*BrE informal*)

Other times 其他时刻

5:45 *five forty-five*
(a) quarter to six (*BrE*)
(a) quarter to/of six (*NAmE*)

2:15 *two fifteen*
(a) quarter past two (*BrE*)
(a) quarter after two (*NAmE*)

1:10 *one ten*
ten past one (*BrE*)
ten after one (*NAmE*)

3:05 *three o five*
five past three (*BrE*)
five after three (*NAmE*)

1:55 *one fifty-five*
five to two (*BrE*)
five to/of two (*NAmE*)

- with 5, 10, 20 and 25 the word **minutes** is not necessary, but it is used with other numbers 表示 5、10、20 和 25 分钟可以省略 minute，但表示其他分钟要用 minute：
  10:25 *twenty-five past/after ten*
  10:17 *seventeen* ***minutes*** *past/after ten*
- use **o'clock** only for whole hours 只有表示整点才用 o'clock：
  ▸ *It's three o'clock.*
- If it is necessary to specify the time of day use **in the morning**, **in the afternoon**, **in the evening** or **at night**. 有必要说明是上午、下午、傍晚或晚上就用 in the morning、in the afternoon、in the evening 或 at night。
- in more formal contexts use 在较正式的语境中用：
  a.m. = in the morning or after midnight
  早上或午夜以后
  p.m. = in the afternoon, in the evening or before midnight
  下午、晚上或午夜以前
  ▸ *He gets up at 4 a.m. to deliver the mail.*

Do not use **o'clock** with **a.m.** or **p.m.**
* o'clock 不与 a.m. 或 p.m. 同时用：
▸ ~~*He gets up at 4 o'clock a.m.*~~
▸ *He gets up at 4 o'clock in the morning.*
▸ ~~*I'll see you at 6 o'clock p.m.*~~
▸ *I'll see you at 6 o'clock this evening.*

Twenty-four hour clock 二十四小时制

- used for military purposes and in some other particular contexts, for example on train timetables in Britain 用于军事和其他特定场合，如英国的火车时刻表：
  13:52 *thirteen fifty-two* (1:52 p.m.)
  22:30 *twenty-two thirty* (10:30 p.m.)
- for military purposes whole hours are said as **hundred hours** 在军事上，整点读作 hundred hours：
  0400 *(o) four hundred hours* (4 a.m.)
  2400 *twenty four hundred hours* (midnight)

Expressing time 表示时间

When referring to days, weeks, etc. in the past, present and future the following expressions are used, speaking from a point of view in the present. 以现在为基点说过去、现在和将来的日期、星期等，用下列词语表示：

	past 过去	**present** 现在	**future** 将来
morning	yesterday morning	this morning	tomorrow morning
afternoon	yesterday afternoon	this afternoon	tomorrow afternoon
evening	yesterday evening	this evening	tomorrow evening
night	last night	tonight	tomorrow night
day	yesterday	today	tomorrow
week	last week	this week	next week
month	last month	this month	next month
year	last year	this year	next year

To talk about a time further back in the past or further forward in the future use 表示更远的过去或将来的时间可用下面的表达：

past 过去	**future** 将来
the day before yesterday	the day after tomorrow
the week/month/year before last	the week/month/year after next
two days/weeks, etc. ago	in two days/weeks, etc. time

To talk about sth that happens regularly use expressions with '**every**'. 定期发生的事用 every 表示：

▸ *He has to work* ***every third*** *weekend.*
▸ *I wash my hair* ***every other*** *day* (= every second day).

In British English a period of two weeks is a **fortnight**. 在英式英语中，fortnight 表示两周：

▸ *I've got a* ***fortnight's*** *holiday in Spain.*

Prepositions of time 表示时间的介词

in (the)

parts of the day (not night) 一天中（不包括夜间）的时段	*in the morning(s), in the evening(s), etc.*
months 月份	*in February*
seasons 季节	*in (the) summer*
years 年份	*in 1995*
decades 十年	*in the 1920s*
centuries 世纪	*in the 20th century*

at (the)

clock time 时间的某一点	*at 5 o'clock* *at 7:45 p.m.*
night 夜晚	*at night*
holiday periods 假期	*at Christmas* *at the weekend* (*BrE*)

on (the)

day of the week 星期…	*on Saturdays*
dates 日期	*on (the) 20th (of) May* (*NAmE also* 美式英语亦作 *on May 20th*)
particular days 特定的日期	*on Good Friday* *on New Year's Day* *on my birthday* *on the following day*

Geographical names 地名

These lists show the spelling and pronunciation of geographical names.
下表列出各地名的拼写和读音。

If a country has different words for the country, adjective and person, all are given, (e.g.**Denmark**; **Danish, a Dane**). To make the plural of a word for a person from a particular country, add **-s**, except for **Swiss** and for words ending in **-ese** (e.g. **Japanese**), which stay the same, and for words that end in **-man** or **-woman**, which change to **-men** or **-women.** 若某国的名称、形容词和该国的人用不同的词表示，此处均一并列出，如 Denmark（丹麦），Danish（丹麦的），Dane（丹麦人）。表示某国人的复数，在该词末尾加 s 构成，但 Swiss（瑞士人）和以 -ese 结尾的词（如 Japanese 日本人）复数同单数拼法一样；以 -man 和 -woman 结尾的词，复数分别作 -men 和 -women。

(Inclusion in this list does not imply status as a sovereign state. 本表所收录的不一定为主权国。)

Afghanistan /æf'gænɪstɑːn; -stæn/ 阿富汗
Afghan /'æfgæn/

Africa /'æfrɪkə/ 非洲 **African** /'æfrɪkən/

Albania /æl'beɪniə/ 阿尔巴尼亚
Albanian /æl'beɪniən/

Algeria /æl'dʒɪəriə; *NAmE* -'dʒɪr-/ 阿尔及利亚
Algerian /æl'dʒɪəriən; *NAmE* -'dʒɪr-/

America /ə'merɪkə/ 美洲；美国
American /ə'merɪkən/

Andorra /æn'dɔːrə/ 安道尔 **Andorran** /æn'dɔːrən/

Angola /æŋ'gəʊlə; *NAmE* -'goʊ-/ 安哥拉
Angolan /æŋ'gəʊlən; *NAmE* -'goʊ-/

Antarctica /æn'tɑːktɪkə; *NAmE* -'tɑːrk-/ 南极洲
Antarctic /æn'tɑːktɪk; *NAmE* -'tɑːrk-/

Antigua and Barbuda /æn,tiːgə ən bɑː'bjuːdə; *NAmE* bɑːr'b-/ 安提瓜和巴布达
Antiguan /æn'tiːgən/ **Barbudan** /bɑː'bjuːdən; *NAmE* bɑːr'b-/

(the) Arctic Ocean /,ɑːktɪk 'əʊʃn; *NAmE* ,ɑːrktɪk 'oʊʃn/ 北冰洋 **Arctic** /'ɑːktɪk; *NAmE* 'ɑːrk-/

Argentina /,ɑːdʒən'tiːnə; *NAmE* ,ɑːrdʒ-/ 阿根廷
Argentinian /,ɑːdʒən'tɪniən; *NAmE* ,ɑːrdʒ-/
Argentine /'ɑːdʒəntaɪn; *NAmE* 'ɑːrdʒ-/

Armenia /ɑː'miːniə; *NAmE* ɑːr'm-/ 亚美尼亚
Armenian /ɑː'miːniən; *NAmE* ɑːr'm-/

Asia /'eɪʒə; 'eɪʃə/ 亚洲 **Asian** /'eɪʒn; 'eɪʃn/

(the) Atlantic Ocean /ət,læntɪk 'əʊʃn; *NAmE* 'oʊʃn/ 大西洋

Australasia /,ɒstrə'leɪʒə; -'leɪʃə; *NAmE* ,ɔːstrə-/ 澳大拉西亚 **Australasian** /,ɒstrə'leɪʒn; -'leɪʃn; *NAmE* ,ɔːstrə-/

Australia /ɒ'streɪliə; *NAmE* ɔː's-/ 澳大利亚
Australian /ɒ'streɪliən; *NAmE* ɔː's-/

Austria /'ɒstriə; *NAmE* 'ɔːs-/ 奥地利
Austrian /'ɒstriən; *NAmE* 'ɔːs-/

Azerbaijan /,æzəbaɪ'dʒɑːn; *NAmE* -zərb-/ 阿塞拜疆
Azerbaijani /,æzəbaɪ'dʒɑːni; *NAmE* -zərb-/
Azeri /ə'zeəri; *NAmE* ə'zeri/

(the) Bahamas /bə'hɑːməz/ 巴哈马
Bahamian /bə'heɪmiən/

Bahrain /bɑː'reɪn/ 巴林 **Bahraini** /bɑː'reɪni/

Bangladesh /,bæŋglə'deʃ/ 孟加拉国
Bangladeshi /,bæŋglə'deʃi/

Barbados /bɑː'beɪdɒs; *NAmE* bɑːr'beɪdoʊs/ 巴巴多斯 **Barbadian** /bɑː'beɪdiən; *NAmE* bɑːr'b-/

Belarus /,belə'ruːs/ 白俄罗斯
Belarusian /,belə'ruːsiən/ **Belorussian** /,belə'rʌʃn/

Belgium /'beldʒəm/ 比利时 **Belgian** /'beldʒən/

Belize /bə'liːz; be'l-/ 伯利兹
Belizean /bə'liːziən; be'l-/

Benin /be'niːn/ 贝宁 **Beninese** /,benɪ'niːz/

Bhutan /buː'tɑːn/ 不丹 **Bhutanese** /,buːtə'niːz/

Bolivia /bə'lɪviə/ 玻利维亚 **Bolivian** /bə'lɪviən/

Bosnia and Herzegovina /,bɒzniə ən ,hɜːtsəgə'viːnə; *NAmE* ,bɑːzniə ən ,hɜːrts-; ,bɔːz-/ 波斯尼亚和黑塞哥维那
Bosnian /'bɒzniən; *NAmE* 'bɑːz-; 'bɔːz-/
Herzegovinian /,hɜːtsəgə'vɪniən; *NAmE* ,hɜːrts-/

Botswana /bɒt'swɑːnə; *NAmE* bɑːt-/ 博茨瓦纳
Botswanan /bɒt'swɑːnən; *NAmE* bɑːt-/
person a **Motswana** /mɒt'swɑːnə; *NAmE* mɑːt-/
people **Batswana** /bæt'swɑːnə/

Brazil /brə'zɪl/ 巴西 **Brazilian** /brə'zɪliən/

Brunei /bruː'naɪ/ 文莱 **Bruneian** /bruː'naɪən/

Bulgaria /bʌl'geəriə; *NAmE* -'ger-/ 保加利亚
Bulgarian /bʌl'geəriən; *NAmE* -'ger-/

Burkina /bɜː'kiːnə; *NAmE* bɜːr'k-/ 布基纳法索
Burkinan /,bɜː'kiːnən; *NAmE* ,bɜːr'k-/
Burkinabe /bɜː,kiːnə'beɪ; *NAmE* bɜːr,k-/

Burma /'bɜːmə; *NAmE* 'bɜːrmə/ 缅甸
Burmese /bɜː'miːz; *NAmE* bɜːr'm-/
➲ see also **Myanmar**

Burundi /bʊ'rʊndi/ 布隆迪 **Burundian** /bʊ'rʊndiən/

Cambodia /kæm'bəʊdiə; *NAmE* -'boʊ-/ 柬埔寨
Cambodian /kæm'bəʊdiən; *NAmE* -'boʊ-/

Cameroon /,kæmə'ruːn/ 喀麦隆
Cameroonian /,kæmə'ruːniən/

Canada /'kænədə/ 加拿大 **Canadian** /kə'neɪdiən/

Cape Verde /,keɪp 'vɜːd; *NAmE* 'vɜːrd/ 佛得角
Cape Verdean /,keɪp 'vɜːdiən; *NAmE* 'vɜːrd-/

(the) Caribbean Sea /,kærɪbiːən 'siː; kə,rɪbiən/ 加勒比海 **Caribbean** /,kærɪ'biːən; kə'rɪbiən/

(the) Central African Republic /ˌsentrəl ˌæfrɪkən rɪˈpʌblɪk/ 中非共和国
Central African /ˌsentrəl ˈæfrɪkən/
Chad /tʃæd/ 乍得 **Chadian** /ˈtʃædiən/
Chile /ˈtʃɪli/ 智利 **Chilean** /ˈtʃɪliən/
China /ˈtʃaɪnə/ 中国 **Chinese** /tʃaɪˈniːz/
Colombia /kəˈlɒmbiə; -ˈlʌm-; *NAmE* -ˈlʌm-/ 哥伦比亚
Colombian /kəˈlɒmbiən; -ˈlʌm-; *NAmE* -ˈlʌm-/
Comoros /ˈkɒmərəʊz; *NAmE* ˈkɑːməroʊz/ 科摩罗
Comoran /kəˈmɔːrən/
Congo /ˈkɒŋɡəʊ; *NAmE* ˈkɑːŋɡoʊ/ 刚果
Congolese /ˌkɒŋɡəˈliːz; *NAmE* ˌkɑːŋ-/
(the) Democratic Republic of the Congo (DR Congo) /ˌdeməˌkrætɪk rɪˌpʌblɪk əv ðə ˈkɒŋɡəʊ; *NAmE* ˈkɑːŋɡoʊ/ 刚果民主共和国
Congolese /ˌkɒŋɡəˈliːz; *NAmE* ˌkɑːŋ-/
Costa Rica /ˌkɒstə ˈriːkə; *NAmE* ˌkɑːstə; ˌkoʊstə/ 哥斯达黎加 **Costa Rican** /ˌkɒstə ˈriːkən; *NAmE* ˌkɑːstə; ˌkoʊstə/
Côte d'Ivoire /ˌkəʊt diːˈvwɑː; *NAmE* ˌkoʊt diːˈvwɑːr/ 科特迪瓦 **Ivorian** /aɪˈvɔːriən/ ➲ see also **Ivory Coast**
Croatia /krəʊˈeɪʃə; *NAmE* kroʊ-/ 克罗地亚
Croatian /krəʊˈeɪʃn; *NAmE* kroʊ-/
Cuba /ˈkjuːbə/ 古巴 **Cuban** /ˈkjuːbən/
Cyprus /ˈsaɪprəs/ 塞浦路斯 **Cypriot** /ˈsɪpriət/
(the) Czech Republic /ˌtʃek rɪˈpʌblɪk/ 捷克共和国
Czech /tʃek/
Denmark /ˈdenmɑːk; *NAmE* -mɑːrk/ 丹麦
Danish /ˈdeɪnɪʃ/ **a Dane** /deɪn/
Djibouti /dʒɪˈbuːti/ 吉布提 **Djiboutian** /dʒɪˈbuːtiən/
Dominica /ˌdɒmɪˈniːkə; *NAmE* ˌdɑːməˈn-/ 多米尼克
Dominican /ˌdɒmɪˈniːkən; *NAmE* ˌdɑːməˈn-/
(the) Dominican Republic /dəˌmɪnɪkən rɪˈpʌblɪk/ 多米尼加共和国 **Dominican** /dəˈmɪnɪkən/
East Timor /ˌiːst ˈtiːmɔː(r)/ 东帝汶
East Timorese /ˌiːst tɪməˈriːz/
Ecuador /ˈekwədɔː(r)/ 厄瓜多尔
Ecuadorian, Ecuadorean /ˌekwəˈdɔːriən/
Egypt /ˈiːdʒɪpt/ 埃及 **Egyptian** /iˈdʒɪpʃn/
El Salvador /ˌel ˈsælvədɔː(r)/ 萨尔瓦多
Salvadoran /ˌsælvəˈdɔːrən/
Salvadorean /ˌsælvəˈdɔːriən/
Equatorial Guinea /ˌekwətɔːriəl ˈɡɪni/ 赤道几内亚
Equatorial Guinean /ˌekwətɔːriəl ˈɡɪniən/
Eritrea /ˌerɪˈtreɪə; *NAmE* -ˈtriːə/ 厄立特里亚
Eritrean /ˌerɪˈtreɪən; *NAmE* -ˈtriːən/
Estonia /eˈstəʊniə; *NAmE* eˈstoʊ-/ 爱沙尼亚
Estonian /eˈstəʊniən; *NAmE* eˈstoʊ-/
Ethiopia /ˌiːθiˈəʊpiə; *NAmE* -ˈoʊ-/ 埃塞俄比亚
Ethiopian /ˌiːθiˈəʊpiən; *NAmE* -ˈoʊ-/
Europe /ˈjʊərəp; *NAmE* ˈjʊrəp/ 欧洲
European /ˌjʊərəˈpiːən; *NAmE* ˌjʊrə-/
Fiji /ˈfiːdʒiː/ 斐济
Fijian /fiːˈdʒiːən; *NAmE also* ˈfiːdʒiːən/
Finland /ˈfɪnlənd/ 芬兰 **Finnish** /ˈfɪnɪʃ/ **a Finn** /fɪn/
France /frɑːns; *NAmE* fræns/ 法国 **French** /frentʃ/
a Frenchman /ˈfrentʃmən/
a Frenchwoman /ˈfrentʃwʊmən/
FYROM /ˈfaɪrɒm; *NAmE* -rɑːm/ ➲ see also **(the) Former Yugoslav Republic of Macedonia**
Gabon /ɡæˈbɒn; *NAmE* ɡæˈboʊn/ 加蓬
Gabonese /ˌɡæbəˈniːz/
(the) Gambia /ˈɡæmbiə/ 冈比亚
Gambian /ˈɡæmbiən/
Georgia /ˈdʒɔːdʒə; *NAmE* ˈdʒɔːrdʒə/ 格鲁吉亚
Georgian /ˈdʒɔːdʒən; *NAmE* ˈdʒɔːrdʒən/
Germany /ˈdʒɜːməni; *NAmE* ˈdʒɜːrm-/ 德国
German /ˈdʒɜːmən; *NAmE* ˈdʒɜːrm-/
Ghana /ˈɡɑːnə/ 加纳 **Ghanaian** /ɡɑːˈneɪən/
Greece /ɡriːs/ 希腊 **Greek** /ɡriːk/
Grenada /ɡrəˈneɪdə/ 格林纳达
Grenadian /ɡrəˈneɪdiən/
Guatemala /ˌɡwɑːtəˈmɑːlə; *BrE also* ˌɡwæt-/ 危地马拉 **Guatemalan** /ˌɡwɑːtəˈmɑːlən; *BrE also* ˌɡwæt-/
Guinea /ˈɡɪni/ 几内亚 **Guinean** /ˈɡɪniən/
Guinea-Bissau /ˌɡɪni bɪˈsaʊ/ 几内亚比绍
Guinean /ˈɡɪniən/
Guyana /ɡaɪˈænə/ 圭亚那 **Guyanese** /ˌɡaɪəˈniːz/
Haiti /ˈheɪti/ 海地 **Haitian** /ˈheɪʃn/
Honduras /hɒnˈdjʊərəs; *NAmE* hɑːnˈdʊrəs/ 洪都拉斯 **Honduran** /hɒnˈdjʊərən; *NAmE* hɑːnˈdʊrən/
Hungary /ˈhʌŋɡəri/ 匈牙利
Hungarian /hʌŋˈɡeəriən; *NAmE* -ˈɡer-/
Iceland /ˈaɪslənd/ 冰岛 **Icelandic** /aɪsˈlændɪk/
an Icelander /ˈaɪsləndə(r)/
India /ˈɪndiə/ 印度 **Indian** /ˈɪndiən/
(the) Indian Ocean /ˌɪndiən ˈəʊʃn; *NAmE* ˈoʊʃn/ 印度洋
Indonesia /ˌɪndəˈniːʒə; *BrE also* -ˈniːziə/ 印度尼西亚
Indonesian /ˌɪndəˈniːʒn; *BrE also* -ˈniːziən/
Iran /ɪˈrɑːn; ɪˈræn/ 伊朗 **Iranian** /ɪˈreɪniən/
Iraq /ɪˈrɑːk; ɪˈræk/ 伊拉克 **Iraqi** /ɪˈrɑːki; ɪˈræki/
Israel /ˈɪzreɪl/ 以色列 **Israeli** /ɪzˈreɪli/
Italy /ˈɪtəli/ 意大利 **Italian** /ɪˈtæliən/
(the) Ivory Coast /ˌaɪvəri ˈkəʊst; *NAmE* ˈkoʊst/ 象牙海岸 **Ivorian** /aɪˈvɔːriən/ ➲ see also **Côte d'Ivoire**
Jamaica /dʒəˈmeɪkə/ 牙买加 **Jamaican** /dʒəˈmeɪkən/
Japan /dʒəˈpæn/ 日本 **Japanese** /ˌdʒæpəˈniːz/
Jordan /ˈdʒɔːdn; *NAmE* ˈdʒɔːrdn/ 约旦
Jordanian /dʒɔːˈdeɪniən; *NAmE* dʒɔːrˈd-/
Kazakhstan /ˌkæzəkˈstɑːn; -ˈstæn/ 哈萨克斯坦
Kazakh /kəˈzæk; ˈkæzæk/
Kenya /ˈkenjə; *NAmE also* ˈkiːnjə/ 肯尼亚
Kenyan /ˈkenjən; *NAmE also* ˈkiːnjən/
Kiribati /ˌkɪrɪˈbɑːti; -ˈbæs; *NAmE* ˈkɪrəbæs; ˌkɪrəˈbɑːti/ 基里巴斯 **Kiribati, i-Kiribati** /ˌi ˌkɪrɪˈbɑːti; -ˈbæs; *NAmE* ˌi ˈkɪrəbæs; ˌi ˌkɪrəˈbɑːti/
Korea /kəˈriə/ 朝鲜；韩国 **Korean** /kəˈriən/ ➲ see also **North Korea, South Korea**
Kuwait /kʊˈweɪt/ 科威特 **Kuwaiti** /kʊˈweɪti/
Kyrgyzstan /ˌkɜːɡɪˈstɑːn; ˌkɪəɡ-; -ˈstæn; *NAmE* ˌkɪrɡ-/ 吉尔吉斯斯坦 **Kyrgyz** /ˈkɜːɡɪz; ˈkɪəɡɪz; *NAmE* ˈkɪrɡɪz/ **Kyrgyzstani** /ˌkɜːɡɪˈstɑːni; ˌkɪəɡ-; -ˈstæni; *NAmE* ˌkɪrɡ-/
Laos /laʊs/ 老挝 **Laotian** /ˈlaʊʃn; *NAmE also* leɪˈoʊʃn/
Lao /laʊ/
Latvia /ˈlætviə/ 拉脱维亚 **Latvian** /ˈlætviən/
Lebanon /ˈlebənən; *NAmE also* -nɑːn/ 黎巴嫩
Lebanese /ˌlebəˈniːz/

Lesotho /lə'suːtuː/ 莱索托 person a **Mosotho** /mə'suːtuː/ people **Basotho** /bə'suːtuː/
Liberia /laɪ'bɪəriə; *NAmE* -'bɪr-/ 利比里亚 **Liberian** /laɪ'bɪəriən; *NAmE* -'bɪr-/
Libya /'lɪbiə/ 利比亚 **Libyan** /'lɪbiən/
Liechtenstein /'lɪktənstaɪn; 'lɪxt-/ 列支敦士登 **Liechtenstein** /'lɪktənstaɪn; 'lɪxt-/ a **Liechtensteiner** /'lɪktenstaɪnə(r); 'lɪxt-/
Lithuania /ˌlɪθju'eɪniə; *NAmE* ˌlɪθu-/ 立陶宛 **Lithuanian** /ˌlɪθju'eɪniən; *NAmE* ˌlɪθu-/
Luxembourg /'lʌksəmbɜːg; *NAmE* -bɜːrg/ 卢森堡 **Luxembourg** /'lʌksəmbɜːg; *NAmE* -bɜːrg/ a **Luxembourger** /'lʌksəmbɜːgə(r); *NAmE* -bɜːrgər/
(the) Former Yugoslav Republic of Macedonia /ˌfɔːmə ˌjuːgəslɑːv rɪˌpʌblɪk əv ˌmæsə'dəʊniə; *NAmE* ˌfɔːrmər ˌjuːgəslɑːv rɪˌpʌblɪk əv ˌmæsə'doʊniə; *NAmE also* -goʊ-/ 前南斯拉夫马其顿共和国 **Macedonian** /ˌmæsə'dəʊniən; *NAmE* -'doʊ-/
Madagascar /ˌmædə'gæskə(r)/ 马达加斯加 **Madagascan** /ˌmædə'gæskən/ **Malagasy** /ˌmælə'gæsi/
Malawi /mə'lɑːwi/ 马拉维 **Malawian** /mə'lɑːwiən/
Malaysia /mə'leɪʒə; *BrE also* -'leɪziə/ 马来西亚 **Malaysian** /mə'leɪʒn; *BrE also* -'leɪziən/
(the) Maldives /'mɔːldiːvz/ 马尔代夫 **Maldivian** /mɔːl'dɪviən/
Mali /'mɑːli/ 马里 **Malian** /'mɑːliən/
Malta /'mɔːltə/ 马耳他 **Maltese** /mɔːl'tiːz/
(the) Marshall Islands /'mɑːʃl aɪləndz; *NAmE* 'mɑːrʃl/ 马绍尔群岛 **Marshallese** /ˌmɑːʃə'liːz; *NAmE* ˌmɑːrʃ-/
Mauritania /ˌmɒrɪ'teɪniə; *NAmE* ˌmɔːr-/ 毛里塔尼亚 **Mauritanian** /ˌmɒrɪ'teɪniən; *NAmE* ˌmɔːr-/
Mauritius /mə'rɪʃəs; *NAmE* mɔː'r-/ 毛里求斯 **Mauritian** /mə'rɪʃn; *NAmE* mɔː'r-/
Mexico /'meksɪkəʊ; *NAmE* -koʊ/ 墨西哥 **Mexican** /'meksɪkən/
Micronesia /ˌmaɪkrə'niːziə; *NAmE* -'niːʒə/ 密克罗尼西亚 **Micronesian** /ˌmaɪkrə'niːziən; *NAmE* -'niːʒn/
Moldova /mɒl'dəʊvə; *NAmE* mɑːl'doʊvə; mɔːl-/ 摩尔多瓦 **Moldovan** /mɒl'dəʊvn; *NAmE* mɑːl'doʊvn; mɔːl-/
Monaco /'mɒnəkəʊ; *NAmE* 'mɑːnəkoʊ/ 摩纳哥 **Monégasque** /ˌmɒnɪ'gæsk; ˌmɒneɪ'g-; *NAmE* ˌmɑːn-/
Mongolia /mɒŋ'gəʊliə; *NAmE* mɑːŋ'goʊ-/ 蒙古 **Mongolian** /mɒŋ'gəʊliən; *NAmE* mɑːŋ'goʊ-/ **Mongol** /'mɒŋgl; *NAmE* 'mɑːŋgl/
Montenegro /ˌmɒntɪ'niːgrəʊ; *NAmE* ˌmɑːntə'neɪgroʊ; -'neg-/ 黑山 **Montenegrin** /ˌmɒntɪ'niːgrɪn; *NAmE* ˌmɑːntə'neɪgrɪn; -'neg-/
Morocco /mə'rɒkəʊ; *NAmE* mə'rɑːkoʊ/ 摩洛哥 **Moroccan** /mə'rɒkən; *NAmE* -'rɑːk-/
Mozambique /ˌməʊzæm'biːk; *NAmE* ˌmoʊ-/ 莫桑比克 **Mozambican** /ˌməʊzæm'biːkən; *NAmE* ˌmoʊ-/
Myanmar /miˌæn'mɑː(r)/ 缅甸 ➲ see also **Burma**
Namibia /nə'mɪbiə/ 纳米比亚 **Namibian** /nə'mɪbiən/
Nauru /'naʊruː/ 瑙鲁 **Nauruan** /naʊ'ruːən/
Nepal /nə'pɔːl/ 尼泊尔 **Nepalese** /ˌnepə'liːz/
(the) Netherlands /'neðələndz; *NAmE* -ðərl-/ 荷兰 **Dutch** /dʌtʃ/ a **Dutchman** /'dʌtʃmən/ a **Dutchwoman** /'dʌtʃwʊmən/
New Zealand (NZ) /ˌnjuː 'ziːlənd; *NAmE* ˌnuː/ 新西兰 **New Zealand, a New Zealander** /ˌnjuː 'ziːləndə(r); *NAmE* ˌnuː/
Nicaragua /ˌnɪkə'rægjuə; *NAmE* -gwə/ 尼加拉瓜 **Nicaraguan** /ˌnɪkə'rægjuən; *NAmE* -gwən/
Niger /niː'ʒeə(r); *NAmE* -'ʒer/ 尼日尔 **Nigerien** /niː'ʒeəriən; *NAmE* -'ʒeriən/
Nigeria /naɪ'dʒɪəriə; *NAmE* -'dʒɪr-/ 尼日利亚 **Nigerian** /naɪ'dʒɪəriən; *NAmE* -'dʒɪr-/
North Korea /ˌnɔːθ kə'riə; *NAmE* ˌnɔːrθ/ 朝鲜 **North Korean** /ˌnɔːθ kə'riən; *NAmE* ˌnɔːrθ/
Norway /'nɔːweɪ; *NAmE* 'nɔːrweɪ/ 挪威 **Norwegian** /nɔː'wiːdʒən; *NAmE* nɔːr'w-/
Oman /əʊ'mɑːn; *BrE also* -'mæn; *NAmE* oʊ'mɑːn/ 阿曼 **Omani** /əʊ'mɑːni; *BrE also* -'mæni; *NAmE* oʊ'mɑːni/
(the) Pacific Ocean /pəˌsɪfɪk 'əʊʃn; *NAmE* 'oʊʃn/ 太平洋
Pakistan /ˌpɑːkɪ'stɑːn; ˌpækɪ-; -'stæn/ 巴基斯坦 **Pakistani** /ˌpɑːkɪ'stɑːni; ˌpækɪ-; -'stæni/
Palau /pə'laʊ/ 帕劳 **Palauan** /pə'laʊən/
Panama /'pænəmɑː/ 巴拿马 **Panamanian** /ˌpænə'meɪniən/
Papua New Guinea (PNG) /ˌpæpjuə ˌnjuː 'gɪni; *BrE also* ˌpæpuə; *NAmE* ˌpæpuə ˌnuː 'gɪni/ 巴布亚新几内亚 **Papua New Guinean** /ˌpæpjuə ˌnjuː 'gɪniən; *BrE also* ˌpæpuə; *NAmE* ˌpæpuə ˌnuː 'gɪniən/
Paraguay /'pærəgwaɪ/ 巴拉圭 **Paraguayan** /ˌpærə'gwaɪən/
Peru /pə'ruː/ 秘鲁 **Peruvian** /pə'ruːviən/
(the) Philippines /'fɪlɪpiːnz/ 菲律宾 **Philippine** /'fɪlɪpiːn/ a **Filipino** /ˌfɪlɪ'piːnəʊ; *NAmE* -noʊ/ a **Filipina** /ˌfɪlɪ'piːnə/
Poland /'pəʊlənd; *NAmE* 'poʊ-/ 波兰 **Polish** /'pəʊlɪʃ; *NAmE* 'poʊ-/ a **Pole** /pəʊl; *NAmE* poʊl/
Portugal /'pɔːtʃʊgl; *NAmE* 'pɔːrtʃ-/ 葡萄牙 **Portuguese** /ˌpɔːtʃʊ'giːz; *NAmE* ˌpɔːrtʃ-/
Qatar /'kʌtɑː(r); 'kæt-; *NAmE* 'kɑːtɑːr; -tər/ 卡塔尔 **Qatari** /kʌ'tɑːri; kæ't-; *NAmE* kə'tɑːri/
Romania /ru'meɪniə/ 罗马尼亚 **Romanian** /ru'meɪniən/
Russia /'rʌʃə/ 俄罗斯 **Russian** /'rʌʃn/
Rwanda /ru'ændə/ 卢旺达 **Rwandan** /ru'ændən/
Samoa /sə'məʊə; *NAmE* sə'moʊə/ 萨摩亚 **Samoan** /sə'məʊən; *NAmE* sə'moʊən/
San Marino /ˌsæn mə'riːnəʊ; *NAmE* -noʊ/ 圣马力诺
São Tomé and Príncipe /ˌsaʊ təˌmeɪ ən 'prɪnsɪpeɪ/ 圣多美和普林西比
Saudi Arabia /ˌsaʊdi ə'reɪbiə/ 沙特阿拉伯 **Saudi** /'saʊdi/ **Saudi Arabian** /ˌsaʊdi ə'reɪbiən/
Senegal /ˌsenɪ'gɔːl/ 塞内加尔 **Senegalese** /ˌsenɪgə'liːz/
Serbia /'sɜːbiə; *NAmE* 'sɜːrb-/ 塞尔维亚 **Serbian** /'sɜːbiən; *NAmE* 'sɜːrb-/ **Serb** /sɜːb; *NAmE* sɜːrb/

(the) Seychelles /seɪ'ʃelz/ 塞舌尔
Seychellois /ˌseɪʃel'wɑː/
Sierra Leone /siˌerə li'əʊn; *NAmE* li'oʊn/ 塞拉利昂
Sierra Leonean / siˌerə li'əʊniən; *NAmE* li'oʊniən/
Singapore /ˌsɪŋə'pɔː(r)/ 新加坡
Singaporean /ˌsɪŋə'pɔːriən/
Slovakia /slə'vækiə; *NAmE* sloʊ'v-/ 斯洛伐克
Slovak /'sləʊvæk; *NAmE* 'sloʊ-/
Slovakian /slə'vækiən; *NAmE* sloʊ'v-/
Slovenia /slə'viːniə; *NAmE* sloʊ'v-/ 斯洛文尼亚
Slovene /'sləʊviːn; *NAmE* 'sloʊ-/
Slovenian /slə'viːniən; *NAmE* sloʊ'v-/
(the) Solomon Islands /'sɒləmən aɪləndz; *NAmE* 'sɑːl-/ 所罗门群岛 **a Solomon Islander** /'sɒləmən aɪləndə(r); *NAmE* 'sɑːl-/
Somalia /sə'mɑːliə/ 索马里 **Somali** /sə'mɑːli/
South Africa /ˌsaʊθ 'æfrɪkə/ 南非
South African /ˌsaʊθ 'æfrɪkən/
South Korea /ˌsaʊθ kə'riə/ 韩国
South Korean /ˌsaʊθ kə'riən/
South Sudan /ˌsaʊθ su'dɑːn; -'dæn/ 南苏丹
South Sudanese /ˌsaʊθ suːdə'niːz/
Spain /speɪn/ 西班牙 **Spanish** /'spænɪʃ/
a Spaniard /'spænjəd; *NAmE* -njərd/
Sri Lanka /ˌsri 'læŋkə; *NAmE also* 'lɑːŋkə/ 斯里兰卡
Sri Lankan /ˌsri 'læŋkən; *NAmE also* 'lɑːŋ-/
St Kitts and Nevis /snt ˌkɪts ən 'niːvɪs; *NAmE also* seɪnt/ 圣基茨和尼维斯 **Kittitian** /kɪ'tɪʃn/
Nevisian /niː'vɪsiən; *NAmE* nə'vɪʒn/
St Lucia /ˌsnt 'luːʃə; *NAmE also* ˌseɪnt/ 圣卢西亚
St Lucian /ˌsnt 'luːʃən; *NAmE also* ˌseɪnt/
St Vincent and the Grenadines /snt ˌvɪnsnt ən ðə 'grenədiːnz; *NAmE also* seɪnt/ 圣文森特和格林纳丁斯 **Vincentian** /vɪn'senʃn/
Sudan /su'dɑːn; -'dæn/ 苏丹 **Sudanese** /ˌsuːdə'niːz/
Suriname /ˌsʊərɪ'nɑːm; -'næm; *NAmE* ˌsʊr-/ 苏里南
Surinamese /ˌsʊərɪnə'miːz; *NAmE* ˌsʊr-/
Swaziland /'swɑːzilænd/ 斯威士兰 **Swazi** /'swɑːzi/
Sweden /'swiːdn/ 瑞典 **Swedish** /'swiːdɪʃ/
a Swede /swiːd/
Switzerland /'swɪtsələnd; *NAmE* -ərl-/ 瑞士
Swiss /swɪs/
Syria /'sɪriə/ 叙利亚 **Syrian** /'sɪriən/
Tajikistan /tæˌdʒiːkɪ'stɑːn; -'stæn/ 塔吉克斯坦
Tajik /tæ'dʒiːk/
Tanzania /ˌtænzə'niːə/ 坦桑尼亚
Tanzanian /ˌtænzə'niːən/
Thailand /'taɪlænd/ 泰国 **Thai** /taɪ/
Togo /'təʊgəʊ; *NAmE* 'toʊgoʊ/ 多哥
Togolese /ˌtəʊgə'liːz; *NAmE* ˌtoʊ-/
Tonga /'tɒŋə; 'tɒŋgə; *NAmE* 'tɑːŋgə/ 汤加
Tongan /'tɒŋən; 'tɒŋgən; *NAmE* 'tɑːŋgən/
Trinidad and Tobago /ˌtrɪnɪdæd ən tə'beɪgəʊ; *NAmE* -goʊ/ 特立尼达和多巴哥
Trinidadian /ˌtrɪnɪ'dædiən/ **Tobagan** /tə'beɪgən/
Tobagonian /ˌtəʊbə'gəʊniən; *NAmE* ˌtoʊbə'goʊ-/
Tunisia /tju'nɪziə; *NAmE usually* tu'niːʒə/ 突尼斯
Tunisian /tju'nɪziən; *NAmE usually* tu'niːʒən/
Turkey /'tɜːki; *NAmE* 'tɜːrki/ 土耳其
Turkish /'tɜːkɪʃ; *NAmE* 'tɜːrkɪʃ/ **a Turk** /tɜːk; *NAmE* tɜːrk/
Turkmenistan /tɜːkˌmenɪ'stɑːn; -'stæn; *NAmE* tɜːrk-/ 土库曼斯坦 **Turkmen** /'tɜːkmen; *NAmE* 'tɜːrk-/
Tuvalu /tuː'vɑːluː/ 图瓦卢 **Tuvaluan** /ˌtuːvɑː'luːən, ˌtuː'vɑːluːən/
Uganda /juː'gændə/ 乌干达 **Ugandan** /juː'gændən/
Ukraine /juː'kreɪn/ 乌克兰 **Ukrainian** /juː'kreɪniən/
(the) United Arab Emirates (UAE) /juˌnaɪtɪd ˌærəb 'emɪrəts/ 阿拉伯联合酋长国
Emirati /emɪ'rɑːti/
(the) United States of America (USA) /juˌnaɪtɪd ˌsteɪts əv ə'merɪkə/ 美利坚合众国；美国 **American** /ə'merɪkən/
Uruguay /'jʊərəgwaɪ; *NAmE* 'jʊr-/ 乌拉圭
Uruguayan /ˌjʊərə'gwaɪən; *NAmE* ˌjʊr-/
Uzbekistan /ʊzˌbekɪ'stɑːn; -'stæn/ 乌兹别克斯坦
Uzbek /'ʊzbek/ **Uzbekistani** /ʊzˌbekɪ'stɑːni; -'stæni/
Vanuatu /ˌvænuː'ɑːtuː; ˌvænwɑː'tuː; *NAmE also* ˌvɑːn-/ 瓦努阿图 **Vanuatuan** /ˌvænuː'ɑːtuən; ˌvænwɑː'tuən; *NAmE also* ˌvɑːn-/
ni-Vanuatu /ˌni ˌvænuː'ɑːtu; ˌni ˌvænwɑː'tu; *NAmE also* ˌvɑːn-/
(the) Vatican City /ˌvætɪkən 'sɪti/ 梵蒂冈城
Venezuela /ˌvenə'zweɪlə/ 委内瑞拉
Venezuelan /ˌvenə'zweɪlən/
Vietnam /ˌvjet'næm; ˌviːet-; -'nɑːm/ 越南
Vietnamese /ˌvjetnə'miːz; viːˌetnə-/
Yemen /'jemən/ 也门 **Yemeni** /'jeməni/
Zambia /'zæmbiə/ 赞比亚 **Zambian** /'zæmbiən/
Zimbabwe /zɪm'bɑːbwi; -weɪ/ 津巴布韦
Zimbabwean /zɪm'bɑːbwiən/

the British Isles /ðə ˌbrɪtɪʃ 'aɪlz/ 不列颠群岛

(the) United Kingdom (UK) /juˌnaɪtɪd 'kɪŋdəm/ 联合王国
Great Britain /ˌgreɪt 'brɪtn/ 大不列颠
England /'ɪŋglənd/ 英格兰
Scotland /'skɒtlənd; *NAmE* 'skɑːt-/ 苏格兰
Wales /weɪlz/ 威尔士
Northern Ireland /ˌnɔːðən 'aɪələnd; *NAmE* ˌnɔːrðərn 'aɪərlənd/ 北爱尔兰
(the Republic of) Ireland /rɪˌpʌblɪk əv 'aɪələnd; *NAmE* 'aɪərlənd/ 爱尔兰

British and American English
英式英语和美式英语

American English differs from British English not only in pronunciation but also in vocabulary, spelling and grammar. 美式英语与英式英语不仅在读音上有区别，在词汇、拼写和语法上也有所不同。

Pronunciation 读音

- When the American pronunciation is different from the British pronunciation it is given after the British pronunciation in the dictionary. 如果美式读音与英式读音有差异，本词典先给出英式读音，然后给出美式读音：
  tomato /təˈmɑːtəʊ; *NAmE* təˈmeɪtoʊ/
- Some important differences: Stressed vowels are usually longer in American English. In **packet**, for example, the /æ/ is longer. 在读音上的一些主要差异有：在美式英语中重读元音通常发音较长，如 packet 中的 /æ/。
- In British English the consonant /r/ is pronounced only before a vowel (for example in **red** and **bedroom**). In all other cases the /r/ is silent (for example in **car**, **learn**, **over**). In American English the /r/ is always pronounced. 在英式英语中，辅音 /r/ 只在元音前才发音（如 red 和 bedroom），其他情况下均不发音（如 car、learn、over）。在美式英语中，/r/ 在任何位置都发音。
- In American English the t between vowels is pronounced as a soft d /d/, so that **writer** and **rider** sound similar. British English speakers usually pronounce the t as /t/. 在美式英语中，元音之间的 t 读成弱化的 /d/，因此 writer 和 rider 听起来相似，而说英式英语者通常将 t 读成 /t/。

Vocabulary 词汇

The dictionary tells you which words are used only in American English or have different meanings in British and American English, for example **cookie**, **elevator**, **trunk**. 本词典对只用于美式英语或在英式英语和美式英语中含义不同的单词予以注明，如 cookie、elevator、trunk。

Spelling 拼写

- The dictionary shows different spellings in British and American English. The following differences are particularly common. 本词典标有英式英语和美式英语的不同拼法，常见区别如下：
- In verbs which end in *l* and are not stressed on the final syllable, the *l* is not doubled in the *-ing* form and the past participle: **cancelling**; (*NAmE*) **canceling**. 在美式英语中，以 l 结尾的动词，如果最后一个音节为非重读音节，该动词的 -ing 形式和过去分词均不双写 l，如 cancelling（英式拼法）；canceling（美式拼法）。
- Words which end in *-tre* are spelt *-ter* in American English: **centre**; (*NAmE*) **center**. 以 -tre 结尾的词，美式英语拼作 -ter，如 centre（英式拼法）；center（美式拼法）。
- Words which end in *-our* are usually spelt *-or* in American English: **colour**; (*NAmE*) **color**. 以 -our 结尾的词，美式英语通常拼作 -or，如 colour（英式拼法）；color（美式拼法）。
- Words which end in *-ogue* are usually spelt *-og* in American English: **dialogue**; (*NAmE*) **dialog**. 以 -ogue 结尾的词，美式英语中通常拼作 -og，如 dialogue（英式拼法）；dialog（美式拼法）。

- In British English many verbs can be spelt with either *-ize* or *-ise*. In American English only the spelling with *-ize* is possible: **realize, -ise**; (*NAmE*) **realize**. 在英式英语中，许多动词的结尾拼作 -ize 或 -ise 均可，但在美式英语中只能拼作 -ize，如 realize/realise（英式拼法）；realize（美式拼法）。

Grammar 语法

Present perfect/Simple past 现在完成时；一般过去时

In American English the simple past can be used with **already**, **just** and **yet**. In British English the present perfect is used. 在美式英语中，already、just 和 yet 可用于一般过去时；在英式英语中，这些词只能用于现在完成时：

- *I have already given her the present.* (*BrE*) 我已把礼物送给她了。
- *I already gave her the present.* (*NAmE*) 我已把礼物送给她了。
- *I've just seen her.* (*BrE*) 我刚见过她。
- *I just saw her.* (*NAmE*) 我刚见过她。
- *Have you heard the news yet?* (*BrE*) 你听说这消息了吗？
- *Did you hear the news yet?* (*NAmE*) 你听说这消息了吗？

Have/Have got

In British English it is possible to use **have got** or **have** to express the idea of possession. In American English only **have** can be used in questions and negative sentences. 在英式英语中，表示拥有用 have got 或 have 均可；而在美式英语的疑问句和否定句中，表达此义只能用 have：

- *They have/have got two computers.* (*BrE* and *NAmE*) 他们有两台计算机。
- *Have you got a computer? Yes, I have.* (*BrE*) 你有计算机吗？我有。
- *Do you have a computer? Yes, I do.* (*BrE* and *NAmE*) 你有计算机吗？我有。

Get/Gotten

In American English the past participle of **get** is **gotten**. 在美式英语中，get 的过去分词为 gotten：

- *Your English has got better.* (*BrE*) 你的英语进步了。
- *Your English has gotten better.* (*NAmE*) 你的英语进步了。

Prepositions and adverbs 介词和副词

Some prepositions and adverbs are used differently in British and American English, for example **stay at home** (*BrE*); **stay home** (*NAmE*). 有些介词和副词在英式英语和美式英语中用法不同，如 stay at home（英式英语）；stay home（美式英语）。

Form of the adverb 副词的形式

In informal American English the adverb form ending in *-ly* is often not used. 在非正式的美式英语中，副词经常用不以 -ly 结尾的形式：

- *He looked at me really strangely.* (*BrE*) 他用十分异样的目光看我。
- *He looked at me really strange.* (*NAmE*) 他用十分异样的目光看我。

Shall

Shall is not used instead of **will** in American English for the first person singular of the future. 在美式英语中，将来时的第一人称单数不用 shall，只用 will：

- *I shall/will be here tomorrow.* (*BrE*) 我明天在这里。
- *I will be here tomorrow.* (*NAmE*) 我明天在这里。

Nor is it used in polite offers. 表示礼貌的提议也不用 shall：

- *Shall I open the window?* (*BrE*) 我把窗户打开好吗？
- *Should I open the window?* (*NAmE*) 我把窗户打开好吗？

Irregular verbs 不规则动词

In British English the past simple and past participle of many verbs can be formed with *-ed* or *-t*, for example **burned/burnt**. In American English only the forms ending in *-ed* are used. 在英式英语中，许多动词的一般过去式和过去分词可以加 -ed 或 -t 构成，如 burned/burnt，美式英语只用 -ed 结尾的形式：

- *They burned/burnt the documents.* (BrE) 他们把文件烧了。
- *They burned the documents.* (NAmE) 他们把文件烧了。

When the past participle is used as an adjective, British English prefers the *-t* form, whereas in American English the *-ed* form is preferred, with the exception of **burnt**. 在英式英语中，过去分词用作形容词时常用 -t 结尾的形式，在美式英语中则更常用 -ed 结尾的形式，但 burnt 除外：

- *a spoilt child* (BrE) 娇惯坏了的孩子
- *a spoiled child* (NAmE) 娇惯坏了的孩子
- *burnt toast* (BrE and NAmE) 烤焦了的面包片

Go/Come and ...

In these expressions **and** is often omitted. 在下列表达方式中 and 通常省略：

- *Go and take a look outside.* (BrE) 到外面去看看吧。
- *Go take a look outside.* (NAmE) 到外面去看看吧。

On the telephone 打电话

- *Hello, is that David?* (BrE) 喂，是戴维吗？
- *Hello, is this David?* (NAmE) 喂，是戴维吗？

Pronunciation and phonetic symbols 读音和音标

The British pronunciations given are those of younger speakers of General British. This includes RP (Received Pronunciation) and a range of similar accents which are not strongly regional. The American pronunciations chosen are also as far as possible the most general (not associated with any particular region). If there is a difference between British and American pronunciations of a word, the British one is given first, with *NAmE* before the American pronunciation. 本词典标出的英式读音为较年轻的人使用的通用英语读音，其中包括标准读音和一些地方音不太重的类似口音。所选的美式读音也是尽可能通用的（不与任何特定地区的读音相关）。如果某个词的英式读音和美式读音有差异，则先给出英式读音，再给出美式读音，美式读音前用 *NAmE* 标示。

Consonants 辅音

p	pen	/pen/	s	see	/siː/
b	bad	/bæd/	z	zoo	/zuː/
t	tea	/tiː/	ʃ	shoe	/ʃuː/
d	did	/dɪd/	ʒ	vision	/ˈvɪʒn/
k	cat	/kæt/	h	hat	/hæt/
ɡ	get	/ɡet/	m	man	/mæn/
tʃ	chain	/tʃeɪn/	n	now	/naʊ/
dʒ	jam	/dʒæm/	ŋ	sing	/sɪŋ/
f	fall	/fɔːl/	l	leg	/leɡ/
v	van	/væn/	r	red	/red/
θ	thin	/θɪn/	j	yes	/jes/
ð	this	/ðɪs/	w	wet	/wet/

The symbol (r) indicates that British pronunciation will have /r/ only if a vowel sound follows directly at the beginning of the next word, as in **far away**; otherwise the /r/ is omitted. For American English, all the /r/ sounds should be pronounced. 符号 (r) 表示只有当后面紧跟一个以元音开头的词时，英式读音的 /r/ 才发音，如 far away，否则这个 /r/ 就省略不读。在美式英语中，所有的 /r/ 音都应读出。

/x/ represents a fricative sound as in /lɒx/ for Scottish **loch**, Irish **lough**. * /x/ 表示摩擦音，如苏格兰英语的 loch 以及爱尔兰英语的 lough 的发音 /lɒx/。

Vowels and diphthongs 元音和双元音

iː	see	/siː/	
i	happy	/ˈhæpi/	
ɪ	sit	/sɪt/	
e	ten	/ten/	
æ	cat	/kæt/	
ɑː	father	/ˈfɑːðə(r)/	
ɒ	got	/ɡɒt/	(*British English*)
ɔː	saw	/sɔː/	
ʊ	put	/pʊt/	
u	actual	/ˈæktʃuəl/	
uː	too	/tuː/	
ʌ	cup	/kʌp/	
ɜː	fur	/fɜː(r)/	
ə	about	/əˈbaʊt/	
eɪ	say	/seɪ/	
əʊ	go	/ɡəʊ/	(*British English*)
oʊ	go	/ɡoʊ/	(*American English*)
aɪ	my	/maɪ/	
ɔɪ	boy	/bɔɪ/	
aʊ	now	/naʊ/	
ɪə	near	/nɪə(r)/	(*British English*)
eə	hair	/heə(r)/	(*British English*)
ʊə	pure	/pjʊə(r)/	(*British English*)

Many British speakers use /ɔː/ instead of the diphthong /ʊə/, especially in common words, so that **sure** becomes /ʃɔː(r)/, etc. 英式发音常用 /ɔː/ 代替双元音 /ʊə/，尤其在一些常见词汇中，如 sure 的发音就成了 /ʃɔː(r)/。

The sound /ɒ/ does not occur in American English, and words which have this vowel in British pronunciation will instead have /ɑː/ or /ɔː/ in American English. For instance, **got** is /ɡɒt/ in British English, but /ɡɑːt/ in American English, while **dog** is British /dɒɡ/, American /dɔːɡ/. 在美式英语中没有 /ɒ/ 音，在英式读音中有这个元音的词汇在美式英语中发 /ɑː/ 或 /ɔː/ 音，如 got 在英式英语中为 /ɡɒt/，在美式英语中则为 /ɡɑːt/；而 dog 在英式英语中为 /dɒɡ/，在美式英语中则为 /dɔːɡ/。

The three diphthongs /ɪə eə ʊə/ are found only in British English. In corresponding places, American English has a simple vowel followed by /r/, so **near** is /nɪr/, **hair** is /her/, and **pure** is /pjʊr/. 只有在英式英语中才有 /ɪə eə ʊə/ 这三个双元音，美式英语则对应为一个单元音后跟一个 /r/，故 near 读作 /nɪr/，hair 读作 /her/，pure 读作 /pjʊr/。

Nasalized vowels, marked with /˜/, may be retained in certain words taken from French, as in **penchant** /ˈpɒ̃ʃɒ̃/, **coq au vin** /ˌkɒk əʊ ˈvæ̃/. 标有 /˜/ 的鼻元音在某些源自法语的词中可能保留下来，如 penchant /ˈpɒ̃ʃɒ̃/、coq au vin /ˌkɒk əʊ ˈvæ̃/。

Syllabic consonants 音节辅音

The sounds /l/ and /n/ can often be 'syllabic' – that is, they can form a syllable by themselves without a vowel. There is a syllabic /l/ in the usual pronunciation of **middle** /ˈmɪdl/, and a syllabic /n/ in **sudden** /ˈsʌdn/. * /l/ 和 /n/ 常可自成音节，即没有元音它们本身也可构成一个音节。在 middle /ˈmɪdl/ 的通常读音中有一个成音节 /l/，sudden /ˈsʌdn/ 的读音中也有一个成音节 /n/。

Weak vowels /i/ and /u/ 弱元音 /i/ 和 /u/

The sounds represented by /iː/ and /ɪ/ must always be made different, as in **heat** /hiːt/ compared with **hit** /hɪt/. The symbol /i/ represents a vowel that can be sounded as either /iː/ or /ɪ/, or as a sound which is a compromise between them. In a word such as **happy** /ˈhæpi/, younger speakers use a quality more like /iː/, but short in duration. When /i/ is followed by /ə/ the sequence can also be pronounced /jə/. So the word **dubious** can be /ˈdjuːbiəs/ or /ˈdjuːbjəs/. * /iː/ 和 /ɪ/ 这两个音一定要区分清楚，如 heat /hiːt/ 与 hit /hɪt/。音标 /i/ 是一个元音，它听起来像 /iː/ 或 /ɪ/，或介于两者之间，如在 happy /ˈhæpi/ 一词中，年轻人的读音更像 /iː/ 音，只是发得较短。/i/ 后接 /ə/ 时亦可读作 /jə/，因此 dubious 一词可读作 /ˈdjuːbiəs/ 或 /ˈdjuːbjəs/。

In the same way, the two vowels represented /uː/ and /ʊ/ must be kept distinct but /u/ represents a weak vowel that varies between them. If /u/ is followed directly by a consonant sound, it can also be pronounced as /ə/. So **stimulate** can be /ˈstɪmjuleɪt/ or /ˈstɪmjəleɪt/. 同样，/uː/ 和 /ʊ/ 这两个元音必须区分清楚，但是 /u/ 是一个弱元音，介于 /uː/ 和 /ʊ/ 之间。如果 /u/ 后紧跟一个辅音，亦可读作 /ə/，因此，stimulate 可读作 /ˈstɪmjʊleɪt/ 或 /ˈstɪmjəleɪt/。

Weak forms and strong forms 弱读式与强读式

Certain very common words, for example **at, and, for, can**, have two pronunciations. We give the usual (weak) pronunciation first. The second pronunciation (strong) must be used if the word is stressed, and also generally when the word is at the end of a sentence. 某些常用词（如 at、and、for、can）有两种读音，本词典先给出常用的弱读式，如要强调此词就必须用第二种读音，即强读式；如果位于句末，一般也用强读。For example 如：

- *Can* /kən/ *you help?*
- *I'll help if I can* /kæn/.

Stress 重音

The mark /ˈ/ shows the main stress in a word. Compare **able** /ˈeɪbl/, stressed on the first syllable, with **ability** /əˈbɪləti/, stressed on the second. A stressed syllable is relatively loud, long in duration, said clearly and distinctly, and made noticeable by the pitch of the voice. 符号 /ˈ/ 表示词的主重音。比较 able /ˈeɪbl/（重音在第一音节）和 ability /əˈbɪləti/（重音在第二音节）。重读音节相对而言声音较响，发音较长，读得清晰，音调较高，使音节明显。

Longer words may have one or more secondary stresses coming before the main stress. These are marked with /ˌ/ as in **abbreviation** /əˌbriːviˈeɪʃn/, **agricultural** /ˌæɡrɪˈkʌltʃərəl/. They feel like beats in a rhythm leading up to the main stress. 较长的词在主重音之前可能有一个或多个次重音，以 /ˌ/ 标示，如 abbreviation /əˌbriːvɪˈeɪʃn/，agricultural /ˌæɡrɪˈkʌltʃərəl/。它们就像节奏中的拍子一样带出主重音。

Weak stresses coming after the main stress in a word can sometimes be heard, but they are not marked in this dictionary. 有时在单词中的主重音后可听到一个弱重音，不过本词典不标弱重音。

When two words are put together in a phrase, the main stress in the first word may shift to the place of the secondary stress to avoid a clash between two stressed syllables next to each other. For instance, **ˌafterˈnoon** has the main stress on **noon**, but in the phrase **ˌafternoon ˈtea** the stress on **noon** is missing. **ˌWell ˈknown** has the main stress on **known**, but in the phrase **ˌwell-known ˈactor** the stress on **known** is missing. 两个单词同在一个短语中时，第一个单词的主重音可能转化为次重音，以避免两个相邻的重音音节相冲突。如 ˌafterˈnoon 的主重音在 noon，但在短语 ˌafternoon ˈtea 中，noon 的重音就消失了。ˌwell ˈknown 的主重音在 known，但在短语 ˌwell-known ˈactor 中，known 的重音消失了。

Stress in phrasal verbs 短语动词的重音

One type of phrasal verb has a single strong stress on the first word. Examples are **ˈcome to sth**, **ˈgo for sb**, **ˈlook at sth**. This stress pattern is kept in all situations, and the second word is never stressed. If the second word is one which normally appears in a weak form, remember that the strong form must be used at the end of a phrase. 有一种短语动词只在第一个单词上有一个强读重音，如 ˈcome to sth、ˈgo for sb、ˈlook at sth。这种重音模式适用于此类短语动词的所有情况，第二个单词永远不重读。如果第二个单词通常为弱读式，那么切记在短语的末尾必须强读。

Another type of phrasal verb is shown with two stresses. The pattern shown in the dictionary, with the main stress on the second word, is the one which is used when the verb is said on its own, or when the verb as a whole is the last important word in a phrase. 另一种短语动词标有两个重音。本词典中，如果短语动词的主重音在第二个单词上，则它只适用于两种情况，即该短语动词独立出现，或其作为一个整体是某个短语中最后出现的重要的词：

- *What time are you ˌcoming ˈback?*
- *He ˌmade it ˈup.*
- *ˌFill them ˈin.*

But the speaker will put a strong stress on any other important word if it comes later than the verb. The stress on the second word of the verb is then weakened or lost, especially if it would otherwise be next to the other strong stress. This happens whether the important word which receives the strong stress is between the two parts of the phrasal verb, or after both of them. 但说话人可能把强读重音放在动词后任何一个重要单词上。在这种情况下，短语动词的第二个单词的重音便弱化或消失，尤其当这个重音又靠近另一个强读重音时。无论具有强读重音的重要单词是在该短语动词的两部分之间还是之后，都可能发生这种情况。

- *We ˌcame back ˈearly.*
- *I ˌfilled in a ˈform.*

▸ ˌ*Fill this* ˈ*form in.*

If more than one stress pattern is possible, or the stress depends on the context, no stress is shown. 如果重音模式不止一种，或重音要依据上下文来确定，本词典就不标重音。

Stress in idioms 习语的重音

Idioms are shown in the dictionary with at least one main stress unless more than one stress pattern is possible or the stress depends on the context. The learner should not change the position of this stress when speaking or the special meaning of the idiom may be lost. 本词典中的习语至少标有一个主重音，除非重音模式不止一种或重音要依据上下文来确定。学习者在说话时不应改变此重音的位置，否则该习语就可能失去既定的含义。

Tapping of /t/ 轻触音 /t/

In American English, if a /t/ sound is between two vowels, and the second vowel is not stressed, the /t/ can be pronounced very quickly, and made voiced so that it is like a brief /d/ or the r-sound of certain languages. Technically, the sound is a 'tap', and can be symbolised by /t̬/. So Americans can pronounce **potato** as /pəˈteɪt̬oʊ/, tapping the second /t/ in the word (but not the first, because of the stress). British speakers don't generally do this. 在美式英语中，如果 /t/ 音在两个元音之间，而且第二个元音不重读，则 /t/ 可能读得很快，而且浊化，听起来就像一个短 /d/ 音或某些语言中的 r 音。术语称作轻触音（tap），可用 /t̬/ 表示。因此美国人可能将 potato 读作 /pəˈteɪt̬oʊ/，第二个 /t/ 轻轻一触（由于重音的缘故第一个 t 不读轻触音）。说英式英语的人一般不这样发音。

The conditions for tapping also arise very frequently when words are put together, as in **not only**, **what I**, etc. In this case it doesn't matter whether the following vowel is stressed or not, and even British speakers can use taps in this situation, though they sound rather casual. 几个单词连在一起时常常出现轻触音现象，如在 not only、what I 等中。这时，后面的元音是否重读无关紧要，在这种情况下，甚至说英式英语的人也可能使用轻触音，但听起来很不正式。

The glottal stop 声门闭塞音

In both British and American varieties of English, a /t/ which comes at the end of a word or syllable can often be pronounced as a glottal stop /ʔ/ (a silent gap produced by holding one's breath briefly) instead of a /t/. For this to happen, the next sound must not be a vowel or a syllabic /l/. So **football** can be /ˈfʊʔbɔːl/ instead of /ˈfʊtbɔːl/, and **button** can be /ˈbʌʔn/ instead of /ˈbʌtn/. But a glottal stop would not be used for the /t/ sounds in **bottle** or **better** because of the sounds which come afterwards. 在英式英语和美式英语中，单词或音节末的 /t/ 音常用声门闭塞音 /ʔ/（短暂的屏息产生的停顿）代替。但只有当下一个音不是元音或成音节 /l/ 时，才可能出现上述情况。因此，football 可能读作 /ˈfʊʔbɔːl/ 而不读 /ˈfʊtbɔːl/，button 可能读作 /ˈbʌʔn/ 而不读 /ˈbʌtn/。但 bottle 和 better 因为后接的音不符合这种条件，故不能用声门闭塞音代替 /t/ 音。

Using the dictionary — a detailed guide to the entries
本词典用法——词条使用详细说明

The **Key to dictionary entries** provided at the front of the dictionary is a general introduction designed to give information on how to use *Oxford Advanced Learner's English-Chinese Dictionary* (9th edition). The following pages are intended for the more advanced student and the teacher. They describe in detail all the major categories of information that the dictionary contains, by identifying problems that the dictionary is designed to solve and explaining how it deals with them. 本词典开头提供《本词典词条说明》，对如何使用《牛津高阶英汉双解词典》(第 9 版) 做概括性介绍。以下则为详细说明，供程度较高的学生和教师参考。其中详细介绍本词典包含的主要方面，提出本词典力求解决的问题并说明解决的办法。

Contents 目录

ENTRIES AND HEADWORDS 词条和词目

1 Types of headword 词目类型

2 Derivatives 派生词

3 Compounds 复合词

4 Variant forms and synonyms of the headword 词目的异体形式及同义词

5 Headword division 词目断字

6 Cross references 参见项

7 Style, region and field 风格、地域和领域

8 Pronunciation 读音

INFORMATION OUTSIDE THE MAIN ENTRIES 词条以外的资料

9 Illustrations 插图

10 Notes on usage 用法说明

11 Grammar 语法

12 Oxford Writing Tutor 牛津写作指南

13 Oxford Speaking Tutor 牛津口语指南

14 Visual Vocabulary Builder 图解词汇扩充

15 Reference Section 参考信息

16 Oxford iWriter 牛津 iWriter

17 Oxford iSpeaker 牛津 iSpeaker

ENTRIES AND HEADWORDS 词条和词目

The basic organizational unit of the dictionary is the entry. Each entry is a block of information introduced by a headword, which is made prominent by bold print and set out slightly from the printed column. 词条是本词典的基本组成单位。词条内容以词目开头。词目用较醒目的粗体印刷，排列稍向左侧突出：

dic·tion·ary /ˈdɪkʃənri; *NAmE* -neri/ *noun* (*pl.* **-ies**)
1 a book that gives a list of the words of a language in alphabetical order and explains what they mean, or gives a word for them in a foreign language 词典；字典；辞书：*a Spanish-English dictionary* 西班牙语－英语词典

WORDFINDER 联想词：alphabetical, definition, entry, example, headword, meaning, part of speech, **pronunciation**, register

2 a book that explains the words that are used in a particular subject 专业术语大全；专业词典：*a dictionary of mathematics* 数学词典 **3** a list of words in electronic form, for example stored in a computer's SPELLCHECKER 电子词典 ⊃WORDFINDER NOTE AT WORD

One of the aims of this dictionary is to help the learner understand how longer words (i.e. derivatives and compounds) are formed from shorter words (or parts of words). The various smaller elements involved are themselves listed as headwords, and the first section below explains the different types of headword and, where appropriate, how they can be combined. 本词典的宗旨之一是帮助读者了解较长的单词（即派生词和复合词）如何由较短小的单词（或词的组成部分）构成。较短小的成分本身亦列为词目。下面第一部分即说明词目的类型，适当时还介绍一些构词的方法。

1 TYPES OF HEADWORD 词目类型

1.1 Simple words. 单纯词

Most headwords in this dictionary are simple words, or 'roots'. A root is the smallest vocabulary item that can occur independently with a meaning of its own, so that *lady*, *child*, *talk* and *happy* are all roots. Roots can be contrasted with derivatives (e.g. *bravely*, *happiness*), formed by adding affixes (*-ly*, *-ness*) to roots, and with compounds (e.g. *childbirth*) in which two or more roots are joined together. In the dictionary, a number of derivatives and compounds are also listed as headwords. For details, look at 2.2 and 3. 本词典中大部分词目为单纯词或"词根"。词根是词汇中的最小单位，有本身的词义，可独立存在。因此，lady、child、talk、happy 都是词根。词根可与派生词（如 bravely、happiness）相对，派生词是在词根上加词缀（-ly、-ness）构成的；词根也可与复合词（如 childbirth）相对，复合词是由两个或两个以上的词根结合而成的。本词典中，很多派生词和复合词亦列为词目，详细介绍参见 2.2 和 3。

1.2 Homographs. 同形异义词

Homographs are separate roots which happen to share the same spelling. They differ completely in meaning, and they may differ in grammatical use as well. Examples of homographs are *bow* (a type of weapon) and *bow* (to bend the head or body), which apart from the differences of meaning and grammar are also pronounced differently. Homographs are given separate numbered entries, as follows. 同形异义词是拼法相同的独立词根。它们的含义完全不同，语法功能也可能不同。例如 bow（用作武器的弓）和 bow（低头或躬身），两个单词不仅含义和语法功能不同，读音也不同。同形异义词分别列为独立词条，用数字区别，如：

bow¹ /baʊ/ *verb, noun* ⊃SEE ALSO BOW²

bow² /bəʊ; *NAmE* boʊ/ *noun, verb* ⊃SEE ALSO BOW¹

1.3 Affixes. 词缀

Meaningful elements such *-ish*, *-ment* and *-ly* cannot be used independently. These are affixes, used to form derivatives such as *clownish*, *astonishment* and *bravely*. To help students understand how affixes (i.e. prefixes and suffixes) in their various meanings are used to form derivatives, the dictionary lists them as headwords, indicates the classes of words they can be attached to, supplies definitions, and gives examples of the derivatives formed.

有些有意义的成分，如 -ish、-ment、-ly 并不能独立使用。这些成分是词缀，用以构成派生词，如 clownish、astonishment、bravely 等。为帮助读者了解各种意义的词缀（即前缀和后缀）构成派生词的方法，本词典将词缀列为词目，注明可与哪类词结合，再提供释义，并举出构成的派生词的示例：

-ship *suffix* (in nouns 构成名词) **1** the state or quality of 状态；性质；品质：*ownership* 所有权 ◇ *friendship* 友谊 **2** the status or office of 地位；资格；职位：*citizenship* 公民资格 ◇ *professorship* 教授职位 **3** skill or ability as 技艺；技能：*musicianship* 音乐技艺 **4** the group of 集体：*membership* 全体成员 ➲ MORE LIKE THIS 7, page R25

re- /riː/ *prefix* (in verbs and related nouns, adjectives and adverbs 构成动词及相关的名词、形容词和副词) again 又；再；重新：*reapply* 再申请 ◇ *reincarnation* 转世化身 ◇ *reassuring* 使人放心的 ➲ MORE LIKE THIS 6, page R25

1.4 Combining forms. 构词成分

These are very important elements in the creation of technical or scientific words. They may occur at the beginning of a word (as *bio-* does in *biodegradable*) or at the end (as *-cide* does in *suicide*). Like a root (a simple word), a combining form can be made into a larger word by adding an affix (e.g. *neur-* + *-al*), or by joining it to another combining form (e.g. *biblio-* + *-phile*); but unlike a root, a combining form cannot occur alone. Entries for combining forms contain definitions and illustrate the types of word that can be formed. 构词成分是构成术语及科技词语的重要成分，或出现在词的开头（如 biodegradable 中的 bio-），或出现在词的末尾（如 suicide 中的 -cide）。构词成分和词根（单纯词）一样，也可以加词缀（如 neur- + -al），或与另一构词成分一起（如 biblio- + -phile）构成较长的单词。但它又不同于词根，不能单独存在。构词成分的词条包含释义，并注明可构成的词类：

elec·tro- /ɪˈlektrəʊ; *NAmE* -troʊ/ *combining form* (in nouns, adjectives, verbs and adverbs 构成名词、形容词、动词和副词) connected with electricity 电的：*electromagnetism* 电磁学

-mania *combining form* (in nouns 构成名词) mental illness of a particular type …狂；…癖：*kleptomania* 偷窃癖 ▸ **-maniac** (in nouns 构成名词): *a pyromaniac* 纵火狂

1.5 Abbreviations. 缩略式

The dictionary contains many common abbreviations of simple words (cf. *barbecue*, *BBQ*; *captain*, *Capt.*), compounds (cf. *postal order*, *PO*) and phrases (cf. *garbage in, garbage out*, *GIGO*). All abbreviations are entered as headwords in the dictionary, with alternative forms, pronunciations and examples as appropriate. 本词典包含许多常见的缩略式，有单纯词（参看 barbecue 和 BBQ；captain 和 Capt.）、复合词（参看 postal order 和 PO）、词组（参看 garbage in, garbage out 和 GIGO）等的缩略式。所有缩略式都列为词目，并附有关的异体形式、读音及示例：

ct (*also* **c.** *especially in NAmE*) *abbr.* **1** (in writing 书写形式) CARAT 开；克拉：*an 18ct gold ring* 一枚 18 开的金戒指 **2** (in writing 书写形式) CENT(S) 分（币）：*50 cts* * 50 分

TB *abbr.* **1** /ˌtiː ˈbiː/ TUBERCULOSIS 结核病 **2** (in writing 书写形式) TERABYTE 太字节（计算机内存或数据单位）

As well as being headwords in their own right, abbreviations appear in the entries for the full words which they represent. 缩略式不仅本身列为词目，而且还列入其代表的词条中：

volt /vəʊlt; vɒlt; *NAmE* voʊlt/ *noun* (*abbr.* **V**) a unit for measuring the force of an electric current 伏，伏特（电压单位）：*a high security fence with 5 000 volts passing through it* 通有 5 000 伏电流的森严铁丝网

post·script /ˈpəʊstskrɪpt; *NAmE* ˈpoʊst-/ *noun* **1** (*abbr.* **PS**) ~ (**to sth**) an extra message that you add at the end of a letter after your signature （加于信末的）附言，又及

1.6 Dummy entries. 假位词条

When an irregular past tense, plural, etc. is so different from the headword to which it relates that the dictionary user may not connect the two, a 'dummy' entry is provided for the irregular form. A dummy entry is one which contains no definitions or examples but is intended simply to refer the user to the main entry, thus 有些不规则的动词过去式、名词复数形式等与其原形迥异，本词典使用者未必能联想到原词，因而将不规则形式列为"假位词条"。假位词条不提供释义和示例，仅指示其出自的原词条，如：

took PAST TENSE OF TAKE

mice PL. OF MOUSE

For other uses of the dummy entry, look at 4.1 and 4.3. 假位词条的其他用法见 4.1 和 4.3。

2 DERIVATIVES 派生词

2.1 Position. 位置

A derivative is formed from a simple word (root) by the addition of a prefix (e.g. **assign** → **reassign**) or suffix (e.g. **resign** → **resignation**). Sometimes a word moves from one grammatical class to another without any such addition (e.g. **adolescent** (*noun*) → **adolescent** (*adj.*)). Derivatives formed with a change of grammatical class only are called 'zero-derivatives'. Many words that are derivatives of other words do not have their own entry in the dictionary because they can be easily understood from the meaning of the word from which they are derived (the root word). They are given in the same entry as the root word, preceded by the symbol ▶. 派生词由单纯词（词根）加上前缀（如 assign → reassign）或后缀（如 resign → resignation）构成。有时一个词从一个词类变成另一词类并不加词缀（如 adolescent (*noun*) → adolescent (*adj.*)）。这种词类发生变化而词形不变的派生词叫做"零位派生词"。许多派生词可以根据其源词（根词）轻松理解其含义，因而本词典未将其单独列条，而是在其根词词条中将其列出，前标符号 ▶：

adept /əˈdept/ *adj.* ~ (**at/in sth**) | ~ (**at/in doing sth**) good at doing sth that is quite difficult 内行的；熟练的；擅长的 **SYN** skilful ▶ **adept** /ˈædept/ *noun* **adept·ly** *adv.*

2.2 Derivatives as headwords. 作为词目的派生词

In some derivatives the spelling of the root word is changed so that the link between root and derivative is less clear. These derivatives are made headwords in the dictionary. The same is also true for derivatives which have developed distinct meanings from those of their roots. So *scarce* and its derivative *scarcely* are both separate headwords. 某些派生词的拼写与根词差异甚大，因而二者联系不明显。本词典将此类派生词列为词目。词义与根词不同的派生词也列为词目。因而 scarce 及其派生词 scarcely 都是独立的词目。

satisfy (*verb*)

satisfaction (*noun*)

example (*noun*)

exemplary (*adj.*)

2.3 Pronunciation. 发音

Many derivatives are formed by adding a suffix to the end of a word. These derivatives are pronounced by simply saying the suffix after the word. For example, the adverb *abruptly* is pronounced by joining the suffix *-ly* /li/ to the word *abrupt* /əˈbrʌpt/. Phonetic spelling for these derivatives with regular change in pronunciation is not given in the dictionary. 许多派生词由词尾加后缀构成，其读音就是在词根读音后加上后缀的读音。例如，副词 abruptly 的读音就是将 -ly /li/ 加在 abrupt /əˈbrʌpt/ 之后而成。对于读音变化规则的派生词，本词典不标出其音标。

However, whenever there may be doubt about how a suffix or a derivative is pronounced, the phonetic spelling is given. For example *flamboyance* /-ˈbɔɪəns/. Also, if a change of stress is caused by adding a suffix to a word, then the pronunciation of the derivative is given in full, e.g. *flexibility* /ˌfleksəˈbɪləti/. 但是，当后缀或派生词的读音难以推断或读音变化并不规则时，本词典会注明音标，例如 flamboyance /-ˈbɔɪəns/。再者，若一个词加上后缀后重音产生了变化，则给这个派生词标注完整音标，如 flexibility /ˌfleksəˈbɪləti/。

3 COMPOUNDS 复合词

Words or expressions which are formed from two or more words functioning as a single unit are called compounds. Compounds may be written as unbroken single words (e.g. *birthplace*) or with a hyphen (e.g. *bitter-sweet*) or as two or more separate words (e.g. *boarding card, bird of prey*). In this dictionary compounds are usually treated in entries of their own. 复合词是由两个或两个以上的单词组成的词或短语，但作为一个整体被视为单个词。复合词可以连写（如 birthplace），也可以用连字符连接（如 bitter-sweet），还可以是两个或两个以上单词组合（如 boarding card、bird of prey）。本词典中，复合词通常独立成条。

3.1 Pronunciation. 读音

The pronunciation of closed compounds (compounds written as unbroken single words) is given in the dictionary, e.g. *checklist* /ˈtʃeklɪst/. The pronunciation of open compounds (compounds with a space between the words) is not shown after the compound itself when the separate components are listed as headwords. This is because the pronunciation of the components appears elsewhere in the dictionary, e.g. *slow cooker*. However, if one or both of the separate components are not in the dictionary, then the pronunciation of the compound is shown in full, e.g. *Ebola fever* /iːˈbəʊlə fiːvə(r); əˈbəʊlə; *NAmE* -ˈboʊlə fiːvər/. The same is also true for hyphenated compounds. 本词典中，连写的复合词标注音标，如 checklist /ˈtʃeklɪst/。对于非连写复合词（词之间有空格），如每个成分词均为词目则不标注音标，因为在成分词的词目处已标注音标，如 slow cooker。但是，若复合词中的某个成分词没被列为本词典的词目，或者所有成分词都没有收录，则为该复合词标注音标，如 Ebola fever /iːˈbəʊlə fiːvə(r); əˈbəʊlə; *NAmE* -ˈboʊlə fiːvər/。带连字符的复合词注音规则与非连写复合词相同。

3.2 Stress in compounds. 复合词的重音

Compounds have their own stress patterns which may be different from the normal pattern of the separate parts. When an adjective modifies a noun, the noun usually has the primary stress, for example ˌ*gold* ˈ*medal*. When an adjective and a noun combine to form a compound noun, the compound may be spoken with the strong stress on the first word, for example ˈ*gold mine*. This second stress pattern is also especially common when two nouns form a two-word or hyphenated compound, for example ˈ*car pool*, ˈ*field sports*, ˈ*party-goer*. To help the dictionary user, the stress is explicitly marked on all compounds. 复合词有自己的重音模式，该模式与其成分词的正常读音不尽相同。若形容词修饰名词，主重音通常在名词上，如 ˌgold ˈmedal。若形容词与名词结合构成复合名词，发音时重音可能放在第一个词上，如 ˈgold mine。这后一种重音模式在两个名词构成双词复合词或带连字符的复合词时尤其常见，如 ˈcar pool、ˈfield sports、ˈparty-goer。为方便本词典使用者，所有复合词均标注重音。

4 VARIANT FORMS AND SYNONYMS OF THE HEADWORD 词目的异体形式及同义词

4.1 Alternative written forms. 词目的异体书写形式

When a word can be spelt in two or more different ways (e.g. *adaptor, adapter*) and there are no differences of pronunciation or grammar, the most usual spelling is given as the headword, and the variant form(s) is/are given immediately after the headword, thus 若一个单词有不止一种拼法（如 adaptor、adapter），而读音或语法上并无区别，则将最通用的拼法列为词目，其异体形式置于其后，例如：

adap·tor (*also* **adap·ter**) /əˈdæptə(r)/ *noun*

However, if the form chosen as the headword and its variant(s) is/are so different in spelling that the user is unlikely to trace the one from the other(s), dummy entries (see 1.6) are given for the variants. 但是有的词目形式与其异体形式在拼法上差别很大，使用者很难由一个推及另一个，则用假位词条（见 1.6）列出异体形式：

boat·swain /ˈbəʊsn; *NAmE* ˈboʊ-/ *noun* = BOSUN

4.2 US/NAmE equivalents. 美式英语对等词

Differences between British and American equivalents present special problems for the foreign learner. Sometimes the difference is one of spelling alone. In such cases, the US (or NAmE) form follows the British one (given as the headword) but precedes the pronunciation. 英美对等词之间的差异给学英语的人带来特别的困难。有时差异仅为拼法不同。对于这种情况，美式拼法列于英式拼法（作为词目）之后，读音之前：

hu·mour (*especially US* **hu·mor**) /ˈhjuːmə(r)/ *noun, verb*

breath·alyse (*BrE*) (*NAmE* **breath·alyze**) /ˈbreθəlaɪz/ *verb*

If the difference is one of pronunciation as well as spelling, each written form is followed by the appropriate phonetic transcription. 若拼法、读音均不同，则分别于每一书写形式后列出其音标：

alu·min·ium /ˌæljəˈmɪniəm; ˌæljə-/ (*BrE*) (*NAmE* **alu·mi·num** /əˈluːmɪnəm/)

4.3 US/NAmE synonyms of British words. 英式英语的美式英语同义词

A particular word (e.g. *nappy*) which is limited to British English may have a synonym (in this case *diaper*) which is restricted to US/NAmE English. In such cases, both the British word and the US/NAmE equivalent will be treated in a full entry, with the synonym placed near the beginning in brackets. 英式英语的某个词（如 nappy）可能在美式英语中有同义词（此例为 diaper）。这种情况下，英式英语用词及其美式英语的同义词均列为词条，同义词置于词条开头的括号内：

nappy /ˈnæpi/ *noun* (*pl.* **-ies**) (*BrE*) (*NAmE* **di·aper**)

di·aper /ˈdaɪəpə(r); *NAmE* ˈdaɪpər/ (*NAmE*) (*BrE* **nappy**)

Sometimes, the US/NAmE word is given a dummy entry at its own alphabetical place and the user is referred to the entry where the definition is to be found. 有时，美式英语同义词立为假位词条，使用者可根据指示查阅英式英语词条：

eˈstate tax *noun* [U] (*NAmE*) = INHERITANCE TAX

any·place /ˈenipleɪs/ *adv.* (*NAmE*) = ANYWHERE

If a word is used in both British and US/NAmE English, but has a synonym which is only British or only US/NAmE, the former is treated in a full entry, and the synonym is labelled '(*BrE also* ...)' or '(*US also* ...)/(*NAmE also* ...)'. 若英式、美式英语虽用同一词，但仅于英式或美式英语中另有一同义词，则前者列为词目，其同义词用 (*BrE also* ...) 或 (*US also* ...)/(*NAmE also* ...) 标明：

ˈdining car (*BrE also* **ˈrestaurant car**)

ˈdriving test (*NAmE also* **ˈroad test**)

If a word is British only, but its US/NAmE equivalent can be used by British as well as US/NAmE speakers, both words are indicated as appropriate. 若仅用于英式英语的词，其美式英语同义词不仅说美式英语的人使用，说英式英语的人也使用，则这两个词均予以适当标注：

ˈridge tent (*BrE*) (*also* **ˈA-frame tent** *BrE, NAmE*)

ˈA-frame tent *noun* = RIDGE TENT

Similarly, if a word is US/NAmE only, but its British equivalent can be used by US/NAmE as well as British speakers, both words are labelled. 同样，若仅用于美式英语的词，其英式英语同义词不仅说英式英语的人使用，说美式英语的人也使用，则这两个词均予以标注：

lay·over /ˈleɪəʊvə(r); *NAmE* -oʊ-/ (*NAmE*) (*BrE, NAmE* **stop·over**) *noun* a short stay somewhere between two parts of a journey 中途停留

stop·over /ˈstɒpəʊvə(r); *NAmE* ˈstɑːpoʊ-/ (*NAmE also* **lay·over**) *noun*

4.4 Other synonyms. 其他同义词

A number of words have quite widely used synonyms. (In some cases the synonym may be a compound.) One word is treated in a full entry and the equivalent(s) is/are entered prominently near the beginning in brackets. 有些词有广泛使用的同义词（有时同义词为复合词）。这种情况下，其中一个词列为词条，而对等词以显著形式列出，置于音标之后：

Cel·sius /ˈselsiəs/ (*also* **centi·grade**) *adj.* (*abbr.* **C**) of or using a scale of temperature in which water freezes at 0° and boils at 100° 摄氏的：*It will be a mild night, around nine degrees Celsius.* 晚间天气温和，温度约九摄氏度。◇ *the Celsius Scale* 摄氏温标 ▶ **Cel·sius** *noun* [U]: *temperatures in Celsius and Fahrenheit* 摄氏和华氏温度

ba·guette /bæˈget/ *noun* **1** (*also* ˌ**French** ˈ**loaf**, ˌ**French** ˈ**stick**) a LOAF of white bread in the shape of a long thick stick that is crisp on the outside and soft inside（法国）脆皮白面包棒 **2** a small baguette or part of one that is filled with food and eaten as a SANDWICH 脆皮夹馅面包棒；三明治小面包棒：*a cheese baguette* 奶酪夹心小面包棒

5 HEADWORD DIVISION 词目断字

When writing, it is sometimes necessary to divide a word at the end of a line because there is not enough space for the complete word. Recommended places of division are shown in the dictionary by means of a dot. The dot is used in all headwords which can be divided (e.g. **che·ster·field**, **dia·lect·ic**) and in derivatives and many variant forms. Headwords that are hyphenated compounds can only be divided (apart from at the hyphen) when there are at least six letters after the hyphen (e.g. **all-consum·ing**). Non-hyphenated compounds show wordbreaks according to the rules in the *New Oxford Spelling Dictionary*. If one or both of the separate components are not in the dictionary, the dots will be shown (e.g. **Fi·bo·nacci ser·ies**). 在书写时，有时在一行末尾写不下一个完整的单词，需要断字移行。本词典用小圆点标出了断字之处。这种圆点标于所有可断字的词目（如 che·ster·field、dia·lect·ic）、派生词和许多异体形式。带连字符的复合词词目除了可在连字符处断字之外，连字符后必须有六个或六个以上字母时才可有另一断字处（如 all-consum·ing）。不带连字符的复合词的断字依照《新牛津拼写词典》（*New Oxford Spelling Dictionary*）的规则处理。若复合词词目中的某个成分词没有收录进本词典，或者所有成分词都没有收录，则会在该复合词中标出断字点（如 Fi·bo·nacci ser·ies）。

6 CROSS REFERENCES 参见项

The dictionary gives extra help by regularly referring you elsewhere for more information about words. These references may be to other entries, or to pictures, or to notes on usage, or to one of the appendices at the back of the book. They are of various types, as follows. When a word in another entry is referred to, it is given in SMALL CAPITAL LETTERS. 本词典设置大量参见项，指引使用者参见相关条目以获取更多信息。参见指向的可能是词条、插图、用法说明，或者本词典末尾的附录。参见种类多样，如下方所示。指引参见的词条以小号大写字母显示。

6.1 '➲' in dummy entries refers you to the main entry.

*“➲”用于假位词条，指向主词条。

dri·est ➲ DRY *adj.*

6.2 '=' in dummy entries refers you to the main entry, indicating a word with exactly the same meaning.

*“=”用于假位词条，指向主词条，表明两词意思完全相同。

ˌ**compact** ˈ**disc** *noun* = CD

6.3 'COMPARE' refers you to another word with an opposite or contrasted meaning.

*“COMPARE”引导使用者查阅意义相反或相对的词。

filly /ˈfɪli/ *noun* (*pl.* **-ies**) a young female horse 小牝马 ➲ COMPARE COLT (1), MARE (1)

6.4 'SEE ALSO' refers you to another word with a similar or related meaning.

*"SEE ALSO"引导使用者查阅意义相近或相关的词。

the ˌFourth of Juˈly *noun* [sing.] a national holiday in the US when people celebrate the anniversary of the Declaration of Independence in 1776 独立日（7 月 4 日，美国节日，庆祝 1776 年美国宣告脱离英国独立）➲ SEE ALSO INDEPENDENCE DAY

6.5 'RELATED NOUN' shows the noun which comes from the phrasal verb.

*"RELATED NOUN"给出源自该短语动词的名词。

PHR V **ˌprint sth↔ˈoff/ˈout** to produce a document or information from a computer in printed form （从计算机中）打印出 ➲ RELATED NOUN PRINTOUT

6.6 'IDM SEE' shows an idiom containing the headword that is defined at another entry.

*"IDM SEE"表明包含该词目的习语及其释义可在另一词条中找到。

ice·berg /ˈaɪsbɜːg; *NAmE* -bɜːrg/ *noun* an extremely large mass of ice floating in the sea 冰山（浮在海上的巨大冰块） IDM SEE TIP *n.*

6.7 'MORE AT' at the end of idioms section shows another idiomatic expression containing the headword that is shown in the cross reference.

*"MORE AT"位于习语部分的末尾，表明包含该词目的另一习语出现在指引参见的词条中。

IDM **full of the joys of ˈspring** very cheerful 快活极了；非常愉快；活泼愉快 ➲ MORE AT PRIDE *n.*

6.8 'NOTE AT' directs you to a note on usage.

*"NOTE AT"引导使用者查阅用法说明。

bar·ris·ter /ˈbærɪstə(r)/ *noun* a lawyer in Britain who has the right to argue cases in the higher courts of law 出庭律师，大律师，辩护律师（在英国有资格出席高等法庭进行辩护） ➲ NOTE AT LAWYER

6.9 'PICTURE AT' directs you to an illustration.

*"PICTURE AT"引导使用者查阅插图。

cheque·book (*BrE*) (*US* **check·book**) /ˈtʃekbʊk/ *noun* a book of printed cheques 支票簿 ➲ PICTURE AT MONEY

6.10 'MORE LIKE THIS' refers you to the MORE LIKE THIS page at the back of the book that shows you other words that behave in a similar way.

*"MORE LIKE THIS"引导使用者查阅本词典末尾的"同类词语学习"页，该页列出了其他具有同一特点的词。

ˈchewing gum (*also* **gum**) *noun* [U] a sweet/candy that you chew but do not swallow 口香糖 ➲ MORE LIKE THIS 28 page R28

6.11 'VISUAL VOCAB' refers you to the VISUAL VOCABULARY BUILDER page at the back of the book that shows you a picture.

*"VISUAL VOCAB"引导使用者查阅本词典末尾的"图解词汇扩充"的彩图。

basil /ˈbæzl; *NAmE also* ˈbeɪzl/ *noun* [U] a plant with shiny green leaves that smell sweet and are used in cooking as a HERB 罗勒（叶子碧绿芳香，用于烹调） ➲ VISUAL VOCAB PAGE V35

6.12 'EXPRESS YOURSELF', 'SYNONYMS', 'COLLOCATIONS', 'LANGUAGE BANK' and 'WORDFINDER NOTE' refer you to the type of usage notes.

"情景表达"(EXPRESS YOURSELF)、"同义词辨析"(SYNONYMS)、"词语搭配"(COLLOCATIONS)、"用语库"(LANGUAGE BANK) 引导使用者查阅相应的用法说明。

apo·lo·gize (*BrE also* **-ise**) /ə'pɒlədʒaɪz; *NAmE* ə'pɑːl-/ *verb* [I] ~ (**to sb**) (**for sth**) to say that you are sorry for doing sth wrong or causing a problem 道歉；谢罪： *Why should I apologize?* 我为什么要道歉？ ◇ *Go and apologize to her.* 去给她赔不是。 ◇ *We apologize for the late departure of this flight.* 本航班起飞延误，谨致歉意。 ⇨ **WORDFINDER NOTE** AT SORRY ⇨**EXPRESS YOURSELF** AT SORRY

7 STYLE, REGION AND FIELD 风格、地域和领域

Words in this dictionary are given a special label if they are often used in a particular geographic region, academic subject or style of writing or speech. Below are the lists of the three main types of labels.

若某个词常用于特定地区、特定学科或带有特定的语体风格，本词典加注标识予以表明。下面列出三种主要的标识。

7.1 Geographic labels. 地区标识

AustralE – Australian English
BrE – British English
CanE – Canadian English
EAfrE – East African English
IndE – Indian English
IrishE – Irish English
NAmE – North American English
NEngE – English from Northern England
NZE – New Zealand English
SAfrE – South African English
ScotE – Scottish English
SEAsianE – South-East Asian English
US – English from the United States
WAfrE – West African English
WelshE – Welsh English
from Chinese
from French
from German
from Italian
from Japanese
from Latin
from Portuguese
from Russian
from Spanish
from Swedish
from Turkish

7.2 Subject labels. 学科标识

anatomy	*law*
architecture	*linguistics*
art	*mathematics*
astronomy	*medical*
biology	*music*
business	*philosophy*
chemistry	*phonetics*
computing	*physics*
economics	*politics*
finance	*psychology*
geology	*religion*
geometry	*sport*
grammar	*statistics*

7.3 Register labels. 语体标识

approving	*offensive*
dialect	*old-fashioned*
disapproving	*old use*
figurative	*saying*
formal	*slang*
humorous	*specialist*
informal	*spoken*
ironic	*taboo*
literary	*written*
non-standard	

8 PRONUNCIATION 读音

A comprehensive introduction to pronunciation and phonetic symbols used in the dictionary can be found at R47–50 at the back of the dictionary. 本词典使用的读音和音标的详尽介绍参见词典末尾R47–50页。

INFORMATION OUTSIDE THE MAIN ENTRIES 词条以外的资料

9 ILLUSTRATIONS 插图

At or near the words listed below, you will find pictures to help you to understand words and expand your vocabulary. Many of these pictures have different parts labelled, for example the picture at **money** includes the items *stub, cheque/check, chequebook/checkbook, credit card, coin, cash* and *note.* 下列单词所在位置或附近位置带有插图，有助于使用者理解单词，扩充词汇量。许多插图都会对不同的部分做出标记，如 money（钱）一词的插图包含 stub（存根）、cheque/check（支票）、chequebook/checkbook（支票簿）、credit card（信用卡）、coin（硬币）、cash（现金）和 note（纸币）。

accordion
ammonite
anchor
angle
ankh
axe
axis
ball-and-socket joint
ball bearing
bar
barbed wire
basket
bellows
bevelled
binoculars
blade
block and tackle
bolt
bonsai
boomerang
bow[1]
bow[2]
bridge
broken
catapult
cat's cradle
chart
chip
circle
clock
cogwheel
compass
concentric
conic section
convex
cord
corrugated
cracker
curved
dovetail
dreamcatcher
edge
elk
fan
filter
frame
froth
gazebo
handle
helix
hieroglyphics
hinge
hook
ideogram
jug
key
knot
label
letter
mask
matchstick figure
medal
megaphone
metronome
Möbius strip
money
music
neck
optical illusion
overall
oxbow
padlock
parallelogram
peg
penknife
pipe
piston
plug
polygon
pushchair
rabbit
rack
ratchet
rebus
ring[1]
roll
rope
roundabout
scale
shade
shellfish
sledge
solid
spring
sprocket
squeeze
staircase
stick
stile
sundial
sword
tassel
trapezium
triangle
trunk
Venn diagram
wavelength
weathercock

10 NOTES ON USAGE 用法说明

In this dictionary, you will find a lot of notes on various aspects of usage in English, which should help you expand your vocabulary and improve your knowledge of many words. Here is a list of the notes in this dictionary, listed according to the type of note. 本词典中有大量有关英语不同方面用法的说明，有助于使用者扩充词汇量，增进对许多单词的理解。下面列出了本词典包含的不同种类的说明。

10.1 BRITISH/AMERICAN 英式 / 美式英语

These notes explain differences between British and American usage. The word in **bold** shows you the entry where you can find the note. 解释英式英语和美式英语用法的区别。黑体词为该说明所在词条。

already / just / yet

bit – a bit / a little

college / university

course / program

different from / to / than

floor

have – have you got? / do you have?

holiday / vacation

hospital

inclusive / through

phone / call / ring

platform / track

post / mail

presently

rent / hire / let

rubbish / garbage / trash / refuse

school – at / in school

sea / ocean

toilet / bathroom

underground / subway / metro / tube

10.2 COLLOCATIONS 词语搭配

These notes show useful words and phrases connected with particular topics, and a selection of verbs to use with those words and phrases. The word in **bold** shows you the entry where you can find the note. 列出与某个主题有关的单词和短语，以及与这些单词和短语搭配的诸多动词。黑体词为该说明所在词条。

age – The ages of life

art – Fine arts

biotechnology – Biotechnology

business – Business

child – Children

cinema – Cinema / the movies

cooking – Cooking

crime – Crime

decorate – Decorating and home improvement

diet – Diet and exercise

driving – Driving

economy – The economy

education – Education

email – Email and the Internet

environment – The environment

farming – Farming

fashion – Clothes and fashion

finance – Finance

house – Moving house

ill – Illnesses

injury – Injuries

international – International relations

job – Jobs

justice – Criminal justice

life – The living world

literature – Literature

marriage – Marriage and divorce

music – Music

phone – Phones

physical – Physical appearance
politics – Politics
race – Race and immigration
religion – Religion
restaurant – Restaurants
scientific – Scientific research
shopping – Shopping
television – Television
town – Town and country
travel – Travel and tourism
unemployment – Unemployment
vote – Voting in elections
war – War and peace
weather – The weather

10.3 EXPRESS YOURSELF 情景表达

These notes help you to find the right thing to say in everyday situations. The word in **bold** shows you the entry where you can find the note. 提供日常生活情景中的正确表达法。黑体词为该说明所在词条。

advice – Giving somebody advice
agree – Agreeing
certain – Expressing certainty or uncertainty
complaint – Making a complaint
concede – Conceding a point
congratulate – Congratulating somebody on an achievement or a family event
correct – Correcting yourself
describe – Describing a picture
disagree – Disagreeing
end – Ending a conversation
explain – Asking for clarification
finish – Wrapping up a discussion
forbid – Forbidding somebody to do something
have to – Asking about obligation
help – Asking for help
information – Asking for information
interrupt – Interrupting
introduce – Making introductions
invite – Inviting somebody to something
know – Saying that you don't know something or giving yourself time to think
likely – Expressing likelihood
luck – Wishing somebody luck
message – Leaving a phone message
offer – Offering somebody something
open – Conversation openers
permission – Asking for permission/ a favour
please – Asking for something
prefer – Expressing a preference
question – Dealing with questions
recommend – Asking for and making a recommendation
shall – Offering to do something
sorry – Apologizing
speculate – Speculating
suggest – Making suggestions
sympathy – Expressing sympathy
tell – Telling somebody to do something
thank – Thanking somebody for something
think – Asking for somebody's opinion and involving others in a conversation
warn – Warning people of danger
why – Giving reasons, justifying a choice

10.4 GRAMMAR POINT 语法说明

These notes help explain points of grammar that often cause problems. The word in **bold** shows you the entry where you can find the note. 对经常造成困惑的语法点进行解释。黑体词为该说明所在词条。

avenge – avenge / revenge

can – can / could / be able to / manage

dare – dare

depend – depend on

each – each / every

enjoy – enjoy

fail – fail / failure

half – half / whole / quarter

hardly – hardly / scarcely / barely / no sooner

if – if / whether

kind – kind / sort

late – late / lately

likely – likely

many – many / a lot of / lots of

modal – modal verbs

much – much / a lot of / lots of

must – must / have (got) to / must not / don't have to

need – need

neither – neither / either

none – none of

one – one / ones

percentage – expressing percentages

proportion – proportion

school – school

shall – shall / will

should – should / ought / had better

should – should / would

sit – sit

staff – staff

used to – used to

very – very / very much

well – well

whom – whom

wish – wish

10.5 LANGUAGE BANK 用语库

These notes show you how to express similar ideas in a variety of ways, particularly in writing. The word in **bold** shows you the entry where you can find the note. 展示如何用不同的方式表达相同的意思，特别是在书面表达中。黑体词为该说明所在词条。

about – Saying what a text is about

according to – Reporting someone's opinion

addition – Adding another item

argue – Verbs for reporting an opinion

because – Explaining reasons

cause – X causes Y

conclusion – Summing up an argument

consequently – Describing the effect of something

contrast – Highlighting differences

define – Defining terms

e.g. – Giving examples

emphasis – Highlighting an important point

evidence – Giving proof

except – Making an exception

expect – Discussing predictions

fall – Describing a decrease

first – Ordering your points

generally – Ways of saying 'in general'

however – Ways of saying 'but'

i.e. – Explaining what you mean

illustrate – Referring to a chart, graph or table

impersonal – Giving opinions using impersonal language

increase – Describing an increase

nevertheless – Conceding a point and making a counter-argument

opinion – Giving your personal opinion

perhaps – Making an opinion sound less definite

process – Describing a process

proportion – Describing fractions and proportions

similarly – Making comparisons

surprising – Highlighting interesting data

therefore – Ways of saying 'For this reason ...'

vital – Saying that something is necessary

10.6 MORE ABOUT 补充说明

These notes give you more information about an aspect of life or language in Britain and America and show you the correct words to use. The word in **bold** shows you the entry where you can find the note. 提供英美生活或语言方面的补充说明，同时给出正确的用词。黑体词为该说明所在词条。

American

British – the British

course – of course

exam – exams

gender – ways of talking about men and women

hello – greetings

lawyer – lawyers

meal – meals

name – names and titles

road – roads

Scottish – describing things from Scotland

student – students

want – offers and invitations

10.7 SYNONYMS 同义词辨析

These notes show the differences between groups of words with similar meanings. The words in each group are given in order of frequency — from the most common to the least common. The word in **bold** shows you the entry where you can find the note. 解释意思相近的词之间的区别。每组词按使用频率排列——从最常见到最少见。黑体词为该说明所在词条。

action / measure / step / act / move

admit / acknowledge / recognize / concede / confess

advertisement / publicity / ad / commercial / promotion / trailer

afraid / frightened / scared / terrified / alarmed / paranoid

agree / accept / approve / go along with sb/sth / consent

angry / mad / indignant / cross / irate

artificial / synthetic / false / man-made / fake / imitation

ask / enquire / demand

basis / foundation / base

beat / batter / pound / lash / hammer

beautiful / pretty / handsome / attractive / lovely / good-looking / gorgeous

bill / account / invoice / check

bitter / pungent / sour / acrid / sharp / acid

border / boundary / frontier

boring / dull / tedious

bottom / base / foundation / foot

bright / brilliant / vivid / vibrant

build / construct / assemble / erect / put sth up

building / property / premises / complex / structure / block

burn / char / scald / scorch / singe

call / cry out / exclaim / blurt / burst out

campaign / battle / struggle / drive / war / fight

care / caution / prudence

certain / bound / sure / definite / guaranteed

cheap / competitive / budget / affordable / reasonable / inexpensive

cheat / fool / deceive / betray / take in / trick / con

check / examine / inspect / go over sth

choice / favourite / preference / selection / pick

choose / select / pick / decide / opt / go for

claim / allegation / assertion

clear / obvious / apparent / evident / plain

clothes / clothing / garment / dress / wear / gear

coast / beach / seaside / coastline / sand / seashore

cold / cool / freezing / chilly / lukewarm / tepid

collect / gather / accumulate / amass

colour / shade / hue / tint / tinge

comment / note / remark / observe

complain / protest / object / grumble / moan / whine

consist of sb/sth / comprise / make up sth / constitute / be composed of sb/sth

costs / spending / expenditure / expenses / overheads / outlay

country / landscape / countryside / terrain / land / scenery

crash / slam / collide / smash / wreck

cut / slash / cut sth back / scale sth back / rationalize / downsize

damage / hurt / harm / impair

declare / state / indicate / announce

demand / require / expect / insist / ask

difficult / hard / challenging / demanding / taxing

dirty / dusty / filthy / muddy / soiled / grubby / stained

discussion / conversation / dialogue / talk / debate / consultation / chat / gossip

disease / illness / disorder / infection / condition / ailment / bug

disgusting / foul / revolting / repulsive / offensive / gross

economic / financial / commercial / monetary / budgetary

election / vote / poll / referendum / ballot

entertainment / fun / recreation / relaxation / play / pleasure / amusement

environment / setting / surroundings / background

equipment / material / gear / kit / apparatus

essential / vital / crucial / critical / decisive / indispensable

examine / analyse / review / study / discuss

example / case / instance / specimen / illustration

excellent / outstanding / perfect / superb

excited / ecstatic / elated / euphoric / rapturous / exhilarated

exciting / dramatic / heady / thrilling / exhilarating

expensive / costly / overpriced / pricey / dear

explode / blow up / go off / burst / erupt / detonate

fabric / cloth / material / textile

factory / plant / mill / works / yard / workshop / foundry

fear / terror / panic / alarm / fright

fight / clash / brawl / struggle / scuffle

floor / ground / land / earth

frighten / scare / alarm / terrify

fun / pleasure / (a) good time / enjoyment / (a) great time

funny / amusing / entertaining / witty / humorous / comic / hilarious

glad / happy / pleased / delighted / proud / relieved / thrilled

great / cool / fantastic / fabulous / terrific / brilliant / awesome / epic

happy / satisfied / content / contented / joyful / blissful

hate / dislike / can't stand / despise / can't bear / loathe / detest

hide / conceal / cover / disguise / mask / camouflage

hit / knock / bang / strike / bump / bash

hold / hold on / cling / clutch / grip / grasp / clasp / hang on

honest / frank / direct / open / outspoken / straight / blunt

hurt / ache / burn / sting / tingle / itch / throb

identify / know / recognize / name / make sb/sth out

illness / sickness / ill health / trouble

imagine / think / see / envisage / envision

income / wage / wages / pay / salary / earnings

injure / wound / hurt / bruise / sprain / pull / strain

intelligent / smart / clever / brilliant / bright

interest / hobby / game / pastime

interesting / fascinating / compelling / stimulating / gripping / absorbing

interview / interrogation / audience / consultation

job / position / post / vacancy / appointment

label / tag / sticker

land / lot / ground / space / plot

language / vocabulary / terms / wording / terminology

lid / top / cork / cap / plug

like / love / be fond of / be keen on sth / adore

limit / restriction / control / constraint / restraint / limitation

look / watch / see / view / observe

look / glance / gaze / stare / glimpse / glare

love / like / be fond of sb / adore / be devoted to sb / care for sb / dote on sb

luck / chance / coincidence / accident / fate / destiny

mad / crazy / nuts / batty / out of your mind / (not) in your right mind

main / major / key / central / principal / chief / prime

make / do / create / develop / produce / generate / form

mark / stain / fingerprint / streak / speck / blot / smear / spot

mentally ill / insane / neurotic / psychotic / disturbed / unstable

mention / refer to sb/sth / speak / cite / quote

mistake / error / inaccuracy / slip / howler / misprint

mix / stir / mingle / blend

money / cash / change

nervous / neurotic / on edge / jittery

notice / note / detect / observe / witness

old / elderly / aged / long-lived / mature

option / choice / alternative / possibility

order / tell / instruct / direct / command

painful / sore / raw / inflamed / excruciating / burning / itchy

patch / dot / mark / spot

payment / premium / contribution / subscription / repayment / deposit / instalment

photograph / picture / photo / shot / snapshot / snap / print

picture / painting / drawing / portrait / print / sketch

place / site / area / position / point / location / scene / spot / venue

plain / simple / stark / bare / unequivocal

pleasure / delight / joy / privilege / treat / honour

poor / disadvantaged / needy / impoverished / deprived / penniless / hard up

pressure / stress / tension / strain

price / cost / value / expense / worth

product / goods / commodity / merchandise / produce

pull / drag / draw / haul / tow / tug

purpose / aim / intention / plan / point / idea

rate / charge / fee / rent / fine / fare / toll / rental

reason / explanation / grounds / basis / excuse / motive / justification / pretext

recommend / advise / advocate / urge

regard / call / find / consider / see / view

report / story / account / version

rest / break / respite / time out / breathing space

result / consequence / outcome / repercussion

return / come back / go back / get back / turn back

rich / wealthy / prosperous / affluent / well off / comfortable

right / correct

rude / cheeky / insolent / disrespectful / impolite / impertinent / discourteous

satisfaction / happiness / pride / contentment / fulfilment

satisfying / rewarding / pleasing / gratifying / fulfilling

save / budget / economize / tighten your belt

save / rescue / bail out / redeem

see / spot / catch / glimpse

serious / grave / earnest / solemn

shine / gleam / glow / sparkle / glisten / shimmer / glitter / twinkle / glint

shock / appal / horrify / disgust / sicken / repel

shout / yell / cry / scream / cheer / bellow / raise your voice

sight / view / vision

sign / indication / symptom / symbol / indicator / signal

sit / sit down / be seated / take a seat / perch

situation / circumstances / position / conditions / things / the case / state of affairs

sleep / doze / nap / snooze

soil / mud / dust / clay / land / earth / dirt / ground

speaker / communicator / gossip / talker

speech / lecture / address / talk / sermon

spoken / oral / vocal

stand / get up / stand up / rise / get to your feet / be on your feet

stare / gaze / peer / glare

start / begin / start off / kick off / commence / open

statement / comment / announcement / remark / declaration / observation

stress / emphasize

structure / framework / form / composition / construction / fabric

student / pupil / schoolboy /schoolchild / schoolgirl

successful / profitable / commercial / lucrative / economic

sure / confident / convinced / certain / positive / clear

surprise / startle / amaze / stun / astonish / take sb aback / astound

take / lead / escort / drive / show / walk / guide / usher / direct

talk / discuss / speak / communicate / debate / consult

target / objective / goal / object / end

task / duties / mission / job / chore

tax / duty / customs / tariff / rates

terrible / awful / horrible / dreadful / vile / horrendous

thing / stuff / property / possessions / junk / belongings / goods / valuables

think / believe / feel / reckon / be under the impression

throw / toss / hurl / fling / chuck / lob / bowl / pitch

trip / journey / tour / expedition / excursion / outing / day out

true / right / correct

trust / depend on sb/sth / rely on sb/sth / count on sb/sth / believe in sb

understand / see / get / follow / grasp / comprehend

valuable / precious / priceless / irreplaceable

view / sight / scene / panorama

wet / moist / damp / soaked / drenched / saturated

witness / observer / onlooker / passer-by / bystander / eyewitness

wonderful / lovely / delightful

word / term / phrase / expression / idiom

work / employment / career / profession / occupation / trade

worried / concerned / nervous / anxious / uneasy

wrong / false / mistaken / incorrect / inaccurate / misguided / untrue

10.8 VOCABULARY BUILDING 词汇扩充

These notes help you to choose more interesting and varied words to use and so increase your vocabulary. The word in **bold** shows you the entry where you can find the note. 帮助使用者选用更有趣而多样化的单词，从而增加词汇量。黑体词为该说明所在词条。

approximately – Ways of saying approximately

bad – Bad and very bad

bar – A bar of ...

body – Actions expressing emotions

break – Words that mean 'break'

cry – Cry

do – Household jobs: do or make?

face – Expressions on your face

fat – Saying that somebody is fat

good – Good and very good

hand – Using your hands

laugh – Different ways of laughing

learn – Learning

nice – Nice and very nice

object – Objects you can use

piece – Pieces

rain – Rain and storms

smell – Smells

teach – Teach and teachers

thin – Saying that somebody is thin

thing – Other words for thing

walk – Ways of walking

10.9 WHICH WORD? 词语辨析

These notes show the differences between words that are often confused. The word in **bold** shows you the entry where you can find the note. 解释易混淆单词之间的区别。黑体词为该说明所在词条。

above / over

actual / current / present

affect / effect

agenda / diary / schedule / timetable

almost / nearly / practically

alone / lonely / lone

also / as well / too

although / even though / though

altogether / all together

answer / reply

around / round / about

as / like

ashamed / embarrassed

awake / awaken / wake up / waken

back – at the back / at the rear / behind

baggage / luggage

bath / bathe / swim / sunbathe

become / get / go / turn

begin / start

beside / besides

besides / apart from / except

big / large / great

blind / blindly

borrow / lend

calm / calmness

can / may

care – take care of / look after / care for

cautious / careful

classic / classical

close / shut

compliment / complement

condition / state

continuous / continual

country / state

court / law court / court of law

deep / deeply

disabled / handicapped

distrust / mistrust

double / dual

economic / economical

electric / electrical

especially / specially

farther / further / farthest / furthest

fast / quick / rapid

firstly / first of all / at first

front – in front of / in the front of

good / goodness

hard / hardly

hate / hatred

high / tall

historic / historical

infer / imply

interested / interesting / uninterested / disinterested / uninteresting

last / take

lastly / at last

light / lighting

long – (for) long / (for) a long time

loud / loudly / aloud

naked / bare

narrow / thin

near / close

next / nearest

noise / sound

old – older / elder

partly / partially

peace / peacefulness

persuade / convince

quick / quickly / fast

quite / fairly / rather / pretty

regretfully / regrettably

right / rightly

rise / raise

say / tell

sensible / sensitive

shade / shadow

slow / slowly

storey / floor

surely / certainly

tight / tightly

used to / be used to

wide / broad

wrong / wrongly / wrongfully

10.10 WORD FAMILIES 词族

These notes show the different forms of words. For example at the entry for *able*, you can see a note containing different words belonging to this word family and their part of speech, such as *ability* and *disabled*. The word in **bold** shows you the entry where you can find the note. 列出单词的不同形式，以 able 条为例，其下列出了属于该词族的不同词汇，并给这些单词注明了词类，诸如 ability 和 disabled。黑体词为该说明所在词条。

able, ably, ability, disabled, disability

accuse, accusation, accusing, accusatory, accused

ally, allied, alliance

broad, broadly, broaden, breadth

care, careful, carefully, caring

clear, clearly, clarity, clarify

comfort, comfortable, comfortably, comforting

conceive, conceivable, conceivably, concept, conception, conceptual

deceive, deceit, deceitful, deception, deceptive

decide, decision, decisive, undecided

deep, deeply, deepen, depth

defy, defiance, defiant

deny, denial, undeniable, undeniably

destroy, destroyer, destruction, destructive, indestructible

discreet, discretion

divide, division, divisive

explain, explanation, explanatory, explicable

explode, explosion, explosive, unexploded

fat, fatty, fatten, fattening

force, forceful, forcefully, forced, forcible, forcibly, enforce

grateful, gratefully, gratitude

happy, happily, happiness

high, highly, height, heighten

inhabit, habitable, inhabited, inhabitant, habitation

intend, intended, intention, intentional, intentionally

long, length, lengthy, lengthen

marry, marriage, married

nature, natural, naturally

perceive, perception, perceptive, perceptible

pity, pitiful, pitiless, pitiable, piteous

produce, producer, production, productive, productively, product, produce

pronounce, pronunciation, unpronounceable, mispronounce

prove, proof, proven

rely, reliable, reliably, reliability, reliance

repeat, repeatable, repeated, repeatedly, repetition, repetitive, repetitious

satisfaction, satisfactory, satisfy, satisfying, satisfied

separate, separately, separable, separate, separated, separation

speak, speaker, speech, spoken

stable, stability, stabilize

strong, strongly, strength, strengthen

suspect, suspected, suspicion, suspicious, suspiciously, suspect

true, truth, truthful, truthfully, truly

understand, understandable, misunderstood, understanding

value, valuable, invaluable, valuables

vary, varied, variable, variation, various, variety

wide, widely, widen, width

wit, witty, witticism, outwit

10.11 WORDFINDER 联想词

These notes help you to find words that are related in meaning to the word you are looking up. For example at the entry for *adventure*, there is a note containing a group of related words. The word in **bold** shows you the entry where you can find the note. 提示与词目意义相关的词，例如 adventure 条中，联想词框中列出了一组相关的单词。黑体词为该说明所在词条。

accident – ambulance, casualty, first aid, hospital, injure, paramedic, stretcher, victim, witness

actor – audition, body double, cameo, cast, play, role, star, stuntman, understudy

adventure – adrenaline, attempt, challenge, enthusiasm, escapade, explore, excitement, kick, thrill

advertise – cold-calling, leaflet, mailing, mailshot, marketing, poster, product placement, prospectus, publicize

age – adolescent, elderly, generation, infant, juvenile, middle-aged, minor, teenage, young

aircraft – bomber, drone, fighter, helicopter, jet, jump jet, parachute, pilot, warplane

airport – baggage reclaim, board, check-in, gate, immigration, lounge, passport, security, terminal

ally – accord, bilateral, cross-border, diplomat, embassy, international, rapprochement, relationship, treaty

apply – appoint, candidate, CV, experience, interview, job description, qualification, reference, shortlist

army – artillery, battalion, command, defend, invade, officer, regiment, tactics, weapon

atom – antiparticle, electron, ion, neutron, nucleus, particle, positron, proton, valency

attack – alert, assassinate, campaign, execute, extremist, hijack, hostage, kidnap, terrorism

baby – birth, child, dummy, feed, incubator, nappy, pram, premature, teethe

bank – account, balance, credit, debit, deposit, interest, loan, statement, withdrawal

behaviour – action, approach, attitude, conform, eccentric, etiquette, habit, manner, morality

biology – biotechnology, breed, cell, chromosome, DNA, gene, mutation, organism, protein

birth – breech birth, caesarean, contraction, deliver, induce, labour, midwife, obstetrics, umbilical cord

blonde – auburn, dark, fair, ginger, grey, jet black, mousy, redhead, sandy

book – biography, blockbuster, character, editor, narrator, novel, plot, publish, title

breed – class, classification, genus, hybrid, kingdom, order, phylum, species, taxonomy

businessman – accountant, agent, auditor, CEO, chairman, consultant, entrepreneur, executive, manager

buy – discount, loyalty card, purchase, receipt, reduction, refund, short-change, store card, voucher

call – area code, dial, engaged, hold, line, message, phone, ring off, voicemail

car – accelerate, brake, commute, driving, licence, motorist, road, road tax, traffic

card – ace, cut, deal, gambling, hand, jack, shuffle, suit, trump

celebrate – anniversary, birthday, commemorate, festivity, jubilee, occasion, parade, party, reception

character – anti-hero, baddy, goody, hero, love interest, narrator, protagonist, trait, villain

charity – appeal, benefit, collection, donation, fundraiser, handout, telethon, volunteer, welfare

chemistry – acid, catalyst, compound, formula, molecule, pH, react, solution, valency

city – amenity, ghetto, high-rise, metropolitan, population, slum, suburb, town, urban

climate – arid, continental climate, equatorial, frigid, harsh, humidity, rainfall, tropical, zone

club – AGM, the chair, hobby, member, newsletter, secretary, society, subscription, treasurer

coast – beach, cliff, dune, headland, inlet, promontory, sea, shore, tide

comedy – caricature, funny, joke, parody, pun, sketch, slapstick, spoof, take-off

command – connect, desktop, drag, enter, insert, refresh, scroll, select, toggle

company – agent, business, competitor, customer, director, employ, franchise, manager, shareholder

competition – closing date, disqualify, judge, prize, round, runner-up, submit, tiebreaker, winner

computer – display, drive, keyboard, memory, platform, program, reboot, router, screen

concert – audience, auditorium, interval, microphone, perform, programme, soloist, support, venue

condition – anorexia, autism, bipolar disorder, dementia, depression, mentally, paranoia, psychosis, schizophrenia

conference – delegate, exhibition, name tag, plenary, register, speaker, talk, venue, workshop

conflict – aggression, arms, army, attack, casualty, defend, hostile, territory, war

congress – caucus, electoral college, House of Representatives, nomination, president, primary, running mate, senate, swing state

construction – cement, foundation, girder, joist, masonry, plaster, rubble, scaffolding, site

crisp – chewy, creamy, crunchy, greasy, juicy, mushy, rubbery, tender, tough

crop – blight, cereal, genetically modified, grain, harvest, monoculture, organic, staple, yield

cure – chemotherapy, disease, drug, injection, medication, osteopathy, palliative, physiotherapy, radiotherapy

cycling – back-pedal, dismount, handlebar, pedal, ride, saddle, speed, tandem, velodrome

dance – ballet, ballroom, band, choreograph, floor, folk dance, music, partner, step

deal – acquisition, bid, broker, contract, merger, negotiation, offer, proposal, takeover

debate – argument, ayes, chair, the floor, motion, propose, second, speak, vote

democracy – candidate, constituency, contest, election, majority, manifesto, poll, referendum, swing vote

dentist – anaesthetic, cavity, check-up, crown, dentures, drill, extract, filling, hygienist

dictionary – alphabetical, definition, entry, example, headword, meaning, part of speech, pronunciation, register

die – ashes, cemetery, coffin, cremation, funeral, grave, hearse, morgue, mourn

disaster – avalanche, cyclone, earthquake, eruption, flood, hurricane, landslide, tornado, tsunami

disease – bacteria, epidemic, fever, illness, immunity, infection, spread, vaccinate, virus

doctor – cure, examine, medicine, patient, practice, prescribe, receptionist, specialist, surgeon

document – agreement, binding, certificate, clause, deed, draft, draw up, subsection, witness

drama – comedy, denouement, dialogue, dramatic irony, play, scene, set, soliloquy, speech

drug – abuse, addict, deal, dependence, detoxification, hallucinate, overdose, rehab, withdrawal

earth – climate, equator, equinox, hemisphere, International Date Line, latitude, map, planet, tropic

eat – binge, calorie, diet, digest, fattening, food, meal, restaurant, taste

electricity – battery, charge, conduct, connect, generate, insulate, power, switch, wire

employ – apply, appoint, contract, dismiss, job, pay, retire, work, workforce

energy – fossil fuel, fracking, fuel, hydroelectric, nuclear, oil, power station, solar, wind farm

equal – bias, discriminate, feminism, homophobia, human right, marginalize, persecute, race, society

exam – candidate, grade, invigilate, mark, oral, paper, practical, resit, revise

examine – biopsy, diagnose, sample, scan, swab, symptom, test, ultrasound, X-ray

explore – colonize, discover, pioneer, reconnaissance, scout, settle, terrain, territory, voyage

expression – beam, frown, grimace, grin, leer, scowl, smirk, sneer, wince

factory – assembly line, capacity, foreman, plant, process, production, shift, shop floor, workforce

family – adopt, child, generation, heir, in-laws, parent, relation, stepfamily, surrogate mother

farm – arable, barn, crop, cultivate, dairy, fallow, graze, livestock, tractor

file – copy, data, delete, folder, icon, menu, open, password, print

film – actor, cameraman, cinema, dialogue, director, dub, location, scenario, sound effect

fishing – bait, bite, dragnet, fly, hook, line, net, rod, trawl

fit – diet, exercise, gym, health spa, nutrition, personal trainer, sport, stamina, workout

freedom – allow, independence, liberty, oppress, restriction, rule, slave

friend – acquaintance, bond, buddy, companion, comrade, mate, neighbour, platonic, playmate

gambling – bet, casino, chip, croupier, lottery, odds, roulette, stake, streak

government – cabinet, checks and balances, constitution, federal, minister, the Opposition, parliament, politics, system

grammar – case, conjugate, gender, inflect, noun, part of speech, singular, subject, tense

green – biodiversity, conservation, endanger, the environment, extinct, managed, species, sustainable, toxic

health – acute, condition, medicine, outbreak, pain, recover, relapse, terminal, treatment

holiday – break, camp, cruise, honeymoon, package tour, self-catering, tourist, travel, visa

home – accommodation, deed, house, lease, let, location, mortgage, squat, tenant

horse – bridle, gallop, harness, paddock, rein, stable, stirrup, tack, thoroughbred

hospital – A & E, admit, consultant, doctor, ICU, inpatient, nurse, operation, ward

hotel – accommodation, book, full board, holiday, reception, reservation, room service, suite, vacancy

hunt – chase, falconry, game, open season, pack, poach, prey, safari, trail

hurt – bandage, bleed, bruise, fracture, injury, plaster, sore, swell, wound

image – alliteration, euphemism, figure of speech, hyperbole, litotes, metaphor, metonymy, onomatopoeia, paradox

industry – capacity, just-in-time, labour, lead time, output, raw material, shipping, supply chain, warehouse

insurance – actuary, annuity, cover, excess, no-claims bonus, policy, premium, risk, underwrite

invest –asset, bond, capital, dividend, equity, fund, interest, portfolio, share

journalist – censorship, correspondent, coverage, editor, exclusive, news agency, newspaper, report, stringer

journey – commute, departure, destination, excursion, expedition, itinerary, pilgrimage, safari, travel

keyboard – backspace, click, control, cursor, escape, return, shift, slash, space bar

king – abdicate, accede, crown, government, monarch, throne, reign, royal, succession

landscape – barren, fertile, lush, mountainous, rolling, rugged, undulate, volcanic, wooded

language – accent, alphabet, dialect, grammar, literacy, literature, pronunciation, translate, word

law – abide by sth, court, crime, justice, legal, police, prosecute, punish, trial

liquid – absorb, condense, dilute, dissolve, evaporate, filter, immerse, rinse, saturated

loan – credit, debt, deposit, interest, lend, money, mortgage, overdraft, risk

location – isolated, neighbourhood, outskirts, provincial, residential, rough, rural, suburban, urban

love – affair, date, go out with sb, jealous, marriage, partner, passionate, relationship, romantic

luck – amulet, charm, coincidence, fate, fortune, jinx, mascot, superstition, talisman

make-up – blusher, cleanser, eyeliner, eyeshadow, foundation, lipstick, mascara, moisturizer, nail polish

map – compass, globe, GPS, grid, key, latitude, navigate, reference, scale

maths – algebra, arithmetic, calculus, equation, geometry, logarithm, numeracy, problem, trigonometry

medicine – administer, capsule, dispense, dose, ill, inhaler, medication, pharmacy, placebo

meeting – agenda, AGM, apology, brainstorming, breakout, chair, committee, convene, the minutes

message – address, attachment, compose, draft, email, emoticon, forward, inbox, re

money – afford, bank, bankrupt, capital, economy, expense, finance, invest, profit

mountain – altitude, foothill, peak, precipice, ridge, slope, summit, valley, volcano

navy – admiral, aircraft carrier, base, captain, command, fleet, submarine, torpedo, warship

newspaper – article, columnist, editorial, feature, headline, journalist, obituary, review, supplement

old – care home, dementia, frail, geriatric, mobility, pensioner, retire, sprightly, widow

opera – aria, chorus, coloratura, diva, libretto, orchestra pit, recitative, score, surtitles

operation – amputate, anaesthetic, graft, procedure, scalpel, scrubs, stitch, surgery, transplant

painting – art, background, canvas, exhibition, foreground, frame, fresco, portrait, watercolour

parliament – act, bill, Chamber, coalition, election, law, legislation, politician, vote

pattern – band, check, dot, fleck, speckle, splash, spot, streak, stripe

pay – bonus, commission, deduction, earn, overtime, rise, salary, tax, wage

peace – agreement, armistice, ceasefire, disengage, negotiate, reparations, surrender, treaty, truce

performance – cue, dresser, matinee, opening night, ovation, prompter, rehearsal, stage manager

physics – amplitude, atom, energy, fission, force, frequency, gravity, molecule, nuclear

plane – cabin crew, charter, flight path, in-flight, land, long-haul, refuel, take-off, travel

play – act, cast, drama, entrance, exit, line, role, scene, speech

plot – dialogue, ending, flashback, narrate, scenario, scene, storyline, tension, twist

poetry – couplet, image, lyric, recite, refrain, rhyme, scansion, stanza, verse

police – arrest, charge, cordon, detain, detective, interrogate, plain clothes, raid, undercover

poor – beg, benefit, charity, homeless, hostel, poverty, shanty town, sweatshop, unemployment

pregnant – antenatal, child, conception, fetus, maternity leave, miscarriage, morning sickness, scan, womb

prison – cell, death row, discharge, justice, parole, probation, remission, sentence, warder

program – code, data, functionality, input, interface, keyword, operating system, retrieve, software

programme – chat show, documentary, drama, game show, news, quiz, reality TV, sitcom, television

pronunciation – cluster, consonant, diphthong, elide, intonation, phonetics, stress, tone, voiced

protest – civil disobedience, demonstrate, hunger strike, march, occupy, placard, riot, sabotage, uprising

radio – air, announce, bulletin, jingle, phone-in, podcast, programme, public service broadcasting, station

rain – downpour, drought, flash flood, monsoon, precipitation, puddle, shelter, shower, squall

relation – ancestor, branch, descent, dynasty, family tree, genealogy, generation, inherit, trace

restaurant – à la carte, course, cuisine, menu, order, reservation, service charge, speciality, waiter

river – bend, course, current, dam, downstream, estuary, source, tributary, waterfall

road – bypass, carriageway, diversion, hard shoulder, lane, lay-by, motorway, roundabout, signpost

science – analysis, evaluate, evidence, experiment, hypothesis, laboratory, research, result, study

sea – beach, coast, harbour, pier, sandbank, shoreline, surf, tide, wave

sew – baste, bind, embroidery, hem, lining, seam, stitch, tack, thread

shop – assistant, buy, counter, display, fitting room, promotion, sale, store, till

sing – beat, harmony, melody, music, note, rhythm, tempo, tone, vocal

sleep – doze, dream, drowsy, insomnia, oversleep, REM, sedative, soporific, tired

snow – avalanche, blizzard, drift, flurry, hail, icicle, sleet, slush, thaw

society – civil rights, class, conform, convention, culture, custom, elite, equality, outsider

software – animation, application, authoring, beta version, configure, demo, install, interactive, spreadsheet

sorry – amends, apologize, ashamed, embarrassed, forgive, regret, remorse, repent, sympathy

space – astronaut, countdown, dock, launch, mission, orbit, rocket, satellite, weightless

specialist – cardiologist, dermatologist, gynaecologist, neurologist, obstetrician, ophthalmologist, paediatrician, psychiatrist, radiologist

sport – athlete, champion, compete, fixture, match, record, spectator, stadium, tournament

stage – backdrop, costume, curtain, footlights, prop, proscenium, scenery, set, the wings

store – appliances, cookware, fashion, furnishings, hardware, linen, lingerie, menswear, stationery

story – comic, far-fetched, gripping, historical, mannered, moving, rambling, readable, tragic

study – course, distance learning, education, exam, further education, graduate, higher education, qualification, tertiary

sun – daylight, eclipse, equinox, ray, rise, solar, solstice, twilight, the universe

swim – armband, dive, flipper, float, goggles, length, paddle, stroke, water wings

system – capitalism, communism, democracy, dictatorship, fascism, imperialism, liberal, radical, socialism

taste – bitter, bland, hot, pungent, savoury, sour, spicy, sweet, tart

theatre – artistic director, auditorium, balcony, box office, circle, director, foyer, stage, the stalls

tourist – abroad, backpack, border, guide, passport, resort, sightseeing, travel, visa

trade – boom, business, commerce, embargo, import, market, monopoly, sanction, tariff

traffic – clamp, cone, contraflow, pedestrian, roadworks, speed hump, tailback, toll, zebra crossing

train – aisle, buffet, carriage, connection, locomotive, luggage rack, platform, station, track

training – apprentice, certificate, coaching, college, course, intern, probation, qualify, work experience

treatment – acupuncture, chiropractor, complementary medicine, herbalism, holistic, homeopathy, hypnotist, massage, reflexology

trend – boom, decline, dip, fluctuate, level off/out, peak, plateau, plummet, slump

trial – accuse, appeal, counsel, defendant, evidence, justice, offence, plea, prosecution

union – ballot, closed shop, collective bargaining, industrial action, labour, picket, protest, representative, strike

universe – asteroid, astronomy, comet, constellation, cosmic, galaxy, meteorite, orbit, space

university – degree, dissertation, education, graduate, hall of residence, lecture, major, seminar, tutorial

waste – drain, dump, effluent, exhaust, fly-tip, incinerator, landfill, rubbish, sewage

web – access, blog, browse, chat, google, navigate, search engine, unsubscribe, visit

website – bookmark, cookie, domain, home page, hyperlink, landing page, online, social media, URL

wedding – best man, bride, ceremony, engaged, honeymoon, marriage, propose, reception, stag night

wind[1] – breeze, buffet, calm, force, gale, gust, hurricane, prevailing, tornado

word – connotation, definition, dictionary, homonym, meaning, pronunciation, spelling, synonym, vocabulary

work – administrative, freelance, managerial, manual, part-time, seasonal, skilled, temporary, voluntary

write – author, book, classic, critic, drama, fiction, genre, literature, poetry

young – adolescent, immature, mixed up, naive, puberty, rebellious, sulky, tearaway, teenager

11 GRAMMAR 语法

For a full explanation of topics in English grammar, please refer to the grammar reference pages at the back of the dictionary, where you can find information on verbs, nouns and adjectives, collocations, etc. 英语语法的详细介绍请参见本词典末尾语法参考部分，该部分有动词、名词、形容词和搭配等的相关信息。

12 OXFORD WRITING TUTOR 牛津写作指南

This is a section specially designed to improve your skills of writing. It can be found on pages WT1–52 in the dictionary. 专门为提高英语写作技巧而编写，见本词典 WT1–52。

13 OXFORD SPEAKING TUTOR 牛津口语指南

This is a section specially designed to improve your spoken English and practice for oral exams. It can be found on pages ST1–16 in the dictionary. 专门为提高英语口语水平而编写，提供英语口语应试技巧，见本词典 ST1–16。

14 VISUAL VOCABULARY BUILDER 图解词汇扩充

This is a section that allows users to build vocabulary for specific topics with the help of colour photos and illustrations. It can be found on pages V1–74 in the dictionary. 丰富的彩图搭配文字介绍，帮助使用者扩充主题词汇，见本词典 V1–74。

15 REFERENCE SECTION 参考信息

This is a collection of useful information on grammar, vocabulary, and other topics that learners of English may find beneficial. It is available at R1–80 in the dictionary. 包含一系列实用信息，如语法、词汇，以及英语学习者可能会用到的其他方面的信息。见本词典 R1–80。

16 Oxford iWriter 牛津 iWriter

The Oxford iWriter on the bundled DVD guides users through the stages of planning, writing and reviewing a range of different written tasks. Task types include essays, presentations, reports, letters, reviews, CVs and more. 配套光盘中的 iWriter 应用软件可全程辅助英语写作，包括如何构思、写作和检查文章。文章种类涵盖议论文、口头报告、报告、信件、评论、简历等。

17 Oxford iSpeaker 牛津 iSpeaker

The Oxford iSpeaker on the bundled DVD is an interactive tool designed for learners of English who want to speak more accurately and fluently in a variety of situations. It is divided into four sections, each with a focus on a different element of spoken English. 配套光盘中的 iSpeaker 应用软件旨在帮助使用者在不同情境中准确流利地开口说英语。它共分为四个部分，每个部分所针对的英语口语训练的侧重点都不同。

Alamy Ltd.: pp ST4 (P Tuson/cyclist and bus), V12 (V Abbey/gargoyle; B Boston/aqueduct; curved-light/viaduct; D R Frazier Photolibrary, Inc./humpback bridge; graficart.net/portico; J Kase/cantilever bridge; H Sadura/geodesic dome), V14 (P Evans/thatched cottage; Eye Candy Images 4/houseboat; M Frost/Adams Picture Library /block of flats; KAKIMAGE/apartment building; J Kase/terraced house; Philipus/duplex; M Richardson/bungalow, mobile home), V17 (D Hurst/ironing board; Image Farm Inc./bradawl), V21 (D Hurst/electric toothbrush; stockpix/nail scissors), V23 (D Amado/paring knife; D Hurst/measuring cups; J.F.T.L IMAGES/kitchen scissors), V24 (I MacDonald/steam; A Shalamov/stir-fry; Studio EYE/Photo Agency EYE/casserole; E Westmacott/boil), V32 (J Helgason/teddy bear; InspireStock Inc./Frisbee™; THINGX/slide), V33 (W Heidasch/dominoes; Ilanphoto/PhotoStock-Israel/Chinese chequers; G Kollidas/backgammon; S May/sudoku; reppans/crossword; L Ryder/snakes and ladders), V34 (C Hochachka/Design Pics Inc./caving; J Kase/ice skating; T Kraus/tenpin bowling; TongRo Image Stock/archery; J Warrington/scuba-diving), V35 (Images-USA/photography; VStock/Tetra Images LLC/model making; I Zhorov/embroidery), V40 (M Keith/hang-gliding; PHOVOIR/FCM Graphic/paragliding), V41 (S Sloan/scooter), V42 (i car/convertible, sports car; Luminis/estate car, hatchback, people carrier; I Montero/saloon), V43 (P Brogden/light aircraft, E Clendennen/aerobatic display; Thierry GRUN-Aero/biplane; A Scott/airship), V44 (D R Frazier Photolibrary, Inc./liner; Dacorum Gold/container ship; C George/canal boat; (Greece/hydrofoil); Images-USA/speedboat; J Kase/catamaran; I MacDonald/paddle steamer; R Naude/hovercraft; D Newham/ferry; I Patrick/lifeboat; A Stiop/cruiser; J Sullivan/sailing dinghy), V46 (M Dalton/single-decker bus; J Kase/articulated lorry, lorry, minibus, tanker, transporter, van; E Nguyen/school bus; Philipus/pickup; Pixoi Ltd./double-decker bus; A Schein/bus; A Stone/jeep), V47 (M Anderson/high-speed train, L Ashley/cab, A Bell/freight train, passenger train, I Blair/funicular, H Ibrahim/Photov.com/underground, J Kase/caravan, I MacDonald/bulldozer, Photolink Ltd./cablecar, R Rayworth/steam train, M Richardson/tractor, RMT/cement mixer, Steppenwolf/tram, C Young/dumper truck), V50 (P Hakimata/suit; S Lihodeev/dress), V52 (T Large/baseball boots; T Payne/jelly shoe; P Springett/platform; Sugarstock Ltd/clutch bag; H Threlfall/wedge; E Westmacott/flats), V53 (D Templeton/sou'wester), V54 (I Genkin/notepad; T Yumada/glue stick), V56 (A Buckin/flash drive; StockPhotosArt-Technology/mp3 player); Julian Baker & Janet Baker (JB Illustrations): basket, dreamcatcher, gazebo, oxbow, stile; pp V2–7, V15, V16 (garden), V29 (packet, sachet), V42 (dashboard), V43 (aircraft), V48; Corbis Corporation: pp V13 (R Kaestner/palace), V14 (PictureNet/row house), V21 (image100 /nail file; L Manning/toothpaste), V23 (L Manning/measuring spoons), V25 (image100/dice), V32 (L Manning/soft toy), V33 (BLOOMimage/jigsaw), V35 (T Grill/painting; R Gross/pottery, woodcarving), V36 (M Karrass/basketball), V37 (image100/butterfly; Floresco Productions/table tennis; Moodboard/Mike Watson Images Limited/breaststroke, tennis), V38 (Moodboard/Mike Watson Images Limited/polo), V39 (R Michael/gymnastics), V40 (B Blankenburg/jet-skiing, windsurfing; DLILLC/bungee jumping; D Madison/white-water rafting; Moodboard/Mike Watson Images Limited/wakeboarding), V41 (J Nazz/racing bike, unicycle), V43 (B Blankenburg/glider), V47 (A Levenson/excavator; Moodboard/Mike Watson Images Limited/camper); Corel: pp V12 (cloister), V13 (amphitheatre, castle, glasshouse, hut, lighthouse, log cabin, oil rig, pub, pyramid, skyscraper, stately home, warehouse), V39 (boxing), V45 (punt); M Dunn: chart; Getty Images, Inc.: V23 (lemon-squeezer); Hardlines: optical illusion; Hemera Technologies Inc.: accordion, ammonite, anchor, axe, axis (butterfly, globe), bellows, binoculars, bonsai, boomerang, clock (alarm clock, grandfather clock, watch), compass, cracker, fan, hinge, jug, key (flute), letter, mask, medal, megaphone, metronome, overall, padlock, penknife, roll, rope, shellfish, sledge, stick, sundial, sword, tassel, trunk (elephant, tree), weathercock; all A-Z photographs except clock (clock, digital watch), edge (glass), trunk (packing trunk, swimming trunks); pp V13 (barn), V16 (all except garden, sprinkler, strimmer), V17 (all except bradawl, ironing board, mop, squeegee mop, toolbox), V19 (all except dining room, fish knife and fork, steak knife), V21 (comb, emery board, hairbrush, nail brush, nail clippers, shaver, sponge bag, toothbrush, tweezers), V22 (blenders, cafetière, electric whisk, food processor, teapot), V23 (all except basting brush, cake slice, fish slice, garlic press, lemon-squeezer, measuring cups, measuring jug, measuring spoons, paring knife, potato masher, ramekin, scissors, timer), V30 (castanets, cello, clarinet, congas, drum kit, flute, French horn, glockenspiel, harp, maracas, recorder, saxophone, steel drum, tambourine, triangle, trombone, viola, violin), V31 (all except sitar, upright piano), V32 (glove puppet, pack of cards, suits), V41 (D-lock, helmet, light, motorcycle, pump), V50 (all except dress, suit), V51 (all except crew neck, fasteners, nightwear, polo neck), V52 (all except baseball boots, clutch bag, flats, handbag, jelly shoe, platform, shoulder bag, wedge), V53 (all except charm bracelet, locket, sombrero, sou'wester), V54 (all except correction fluid, envelopes, glue stick, highlighter, notepad, Post-it™); K Hiscock: pp V8–11, V26–28; Image Source Ltd.: pp V14 (A Jones/town house), V24 (bake, barbecue), V25 (chop), V33 (wordsearch), V34 (in-line skating, snorkelling), V35 (H Arden/press-up; rowing machine; R Lewine/barbell), V37 (squash), V39 (fencing), V40 (abseiling, parkour), V43 (P Mastrovito/hot-air balloon); M Jones: matchstick figure; KJA-artists.com: ball-and-socket joint, ball bearing, barbed wire, bevelled, blade, block and tackle, bolt, chip, cogwheel, cord, dovetail joint, elk, knot, label, money, piston, plug, rabbit, ratchet, sprocket wheel, staircase;

* 注：数字代表本词典英文原文版 (*Oxford Advanced Learner's Dictionary* 2015) 的页码。

pp V29 (all except packet, punnet, sachet), V51 (fasteners); Oxford University Press: axis (graph), bar (barcode, music), concentric, convex, ideogram, musical notation, rebus, wavelength; J Shaw/Venn diagram; pp V14 (semi-detached house), V19 (steak knife), V23 (basting brush, fish slice, garlic press, potato masher, timer), V32 (M Mason/rag doll), V51 (polo neck), V53 (charm bracelet, locket), V54 (correction fluid, drawing pins, highlighter), V56 (screen, screenshots, window),; Photolibrary Group Ltd./ Getty Images, Inc.: pp ST7 (Photodisc/castle) V12 (Alanie/Life File/PhotoDisc/rotunda; R Chapple Stock/Photolibrary RF/vaulted ceiling; FOTOG/ Tetra Images LLC/suspension bridge; D Fox/ Purestock/Superstock, Inc./colonnade; Ingram Publishing RF/Ingram Publishing Limited/arch; M Milbradt/Brand X Pictures/Jupiterimages (UK) Ltd./obelisk; S Nicolas/ICONOTEC/dome), V13 (M Fife/PhotoDisc/fort; Thinkstock Images/ Jupiterimages (UK) Ltd./pagoda), V16 (Comstock Images/Jupiterimages (UK) Ltd./strimmer; Tetra Images LLC/sprinkler), V17 (Lynx/ICONOTEC/ toolbox; Photolibrary RF/squeegee mop, Stockdisc/Stockbyte/mop), V19 (R McVay/ PhotoDisc/fish knife and fork), V21 (J Atlas/ Brand X Pictures/Jupiterimages (UK) Ltd./loofah, Stockbyte/sponge), V23 (T Northcut/PhotoDisc/ measuring jug; Photolibrary RF/ramekin; Stockbyte/cake slice), V24 (Glow Images RF/ Glow Images Inc./fry; Jetta Productions/Dana Neely/Tetra Images LLC/flambé), V25 (J Baigrie/ Digital Vision/grate; Ben Fink Photo Inc./Brand X Pictures/Jupiterimages (UK) Ltd./roll out; Fancy/ Veer Incorporated/whip;Jetta Productions/Dana Neely/Tetra Images LLC/knead; J Silva/Digital Vision/slice), V30 (C Squared Studios/PhotoDisc bassoon, double bass, kettledrum, oboe, piccolo, trumpet, xylophone; Stockbyte/tuba), V31 (C Squared Studios/PhotoDisc/sitar; Stockbyte/ upright piano), V32 (Buccina Studios/PhotoDisc/ doll's house; Comstock Images/Jupiterimages (UK) Ltd./building blocks; Dex Image/sandpit; G Doyle/Stockbyte/kite; O Drew/National Geographic/climbing frame; Dynamic Graphics/ Creatas Images/Jupiterimages (UK) Ltd./playing cards; D Laurens/PhotoAlto/swing; PhotoDisc/ trampoline; RubberBall Productions/skipping rope; Stockbyte/rocking horse), V33 (Medioimages/noughts and crosses), V34 (Digital Vision/bowls; Duomo TIPS RF/Tips Italia RF/ skateboarding;P Lee Harvey/Cultura Limited/ orienteering; PhotoLink/PhotoDisc/darts; PNC/ Brand X Pictures/ Jupiterimages (UK) Ltd./golf; Polka Dot Images/Jupiterimages (UK) Ltd./pool), V35 (S Baccon/Digital Vision/sewing; BananaStock/Jupiterimages (UK) Ltd./gardening; J Henley/Blend Images, LLC/stamp collecting;JGI/ Blend Images, LLC/treadmill;dumb-bell, yoga; D Madison/Digital Vision/jogging; S Mason/ PhotoDisc/crochet; Moodboard/Mike Watson Images Limited/exercise bike; Photolibrary RF/ sit-up; Polka Dot Images/Jupiterimages (UK) Ltd./ knitting), V36 (Duomo TIPS RF/Tips Italia RF/ice hockey; D Hammond/Design Pics Inc./baseball, rugby; Moodboard/Mike Watson Images Limited/soccer; PhotoLink/PhotoDisc/American football; A Somvanshi/India Picture RF/cricket), V37 (Glow Images RF/Glowimages Inc./ backstroke; Goodshoot/Jupiterimages (UK) Ltd./ badminton; R Michael/crawl), V38 (B Blankenburg/showjumping; E Calderoni/Score Royalty Free Images/Aflo Foto Agency Inc./ hammer; M Colomb/Digital Vision/horse racing; CS Productions/Brand X Pictures/Jupiterimages (UK) Ltd./javelin, pole vault; T Levine/zefa/discus; J Oliver/Digital Vision/sprinting; PhotoLink/ PhotoDisc/hurdling), V39 (K Aoki/Score Royalty Free Images/Aflo Foto Agency Inc./downhill skiing; Digital Vision/luge; D Madison/Digital Vision/bobsleigh, cross-country skiing; R McVay/ Digital Vision/cycling), V40 (Brand X Pictures/ Jupiterimages (UK) Ltd/bodyboarding; Buzz Pictures/Purestock/Superstock, Inc./surfing; Digital Vision/skydiving; D Leniuk/Radius Images/Masterfile Corporation/kitesurfing; Thinkstock Images/Jupiterimages (UK) Ltd./ snowboarding; K Weatherly/ PhotoDisc/ waterskiing), V41 (C Squared Studios/PhotoDisc/ bicycle, child's bicycle, tandem, tricycle; Glow Images RF/Glowimages Inc./dirt bike; Moodboard/Mike Watson Images Limited/quad bike; K Weatherly/PhotoDisc/mountain bike), V43 (Creatas Images/Jupiterimages (UK) Ltd./ seaplane; L Mayer/Creatas Images/Jupiterimages (UK) Ltd./ski-plane; Photolibrary RF/helicopter; StockTrek/Purestock/Superstock, Inc./fighter; P Tom/ICONOTEC/microlight), V44 (CAMP/ RelaXimages/rowing boat), V45 (Creatas Images/ Jupiter Images (UK) Ltd./canoe; Medioimages/ PhotoDisc/yacht; L Riß/Westend61 GmbH/ gondola; K Weatherly/PhotoDisc/kayak), V46 (A Berg/Digital Vision/forklift truck; Thinkstock Images/Jupiterimages (UK) Ltd./breakdown truck), V47 (Thinkstock Images/Jupiterimages (UK) Ltd./black cab), V51 (M Andersen/ RubberBall Productions/nightwear; T Northcut/ PhotoDisc/crew neck), V52 (Stockbyte/handbag, shoulder bag), V53 (S Cole/PhotoDisc/sombrero), V54 (C Squared Studios/PhotoDisc/envelope; Stockbyte/Post-it™), V56 (Y Arcurs/Tetra Images LLC/laptop; Brand X Pictures/Jupiterimages (UK) Ltd./headset; G Doyle & C Griffin/Stockbyte/ router, webcam; Tetra Images LLC/PC); Press Association Images: pST4 (L Whyld/PA Archive/ cycle path); Q2AMedia: angles, ankh, broken, cat's cradle, circles, conic sections, corrugated, edge (frame, table), filter, frame, handle, hieroglyphics, key (all except flute), Möbius strip, parallelograms, peg, pipe, polygons, pushchair, rack, roundabout, scale, solids, triangles; P Schramm/Meiklejohn Illustration: bar (all except barcode, music), bow[1], bow[2], bridge, catapult, curved, froth, hook, neck, ring, shade, spring, squeeze; pp V18, V19 (dining room), V20, V21 (bathroom), V22 (kitchen), V49, V54 (office), V55; Shutterstock.com: I Akinshin/ edge (glass), A Berenyi/clock (digital watch), M Garcia Saavedra/trunk (packing trunk), sagir/ trunk (swimming trunks), wormig/clock (clock); p ST7 (M Fleming/Military Tattoo; K Guan Toh/ salmon; P McKinnon/Highland dancers; Spumador/beach; Stewart Smith Photography/ walker); pp V22 (J Ivantsova/coffee maker; O Mark/microwave; WM_idea/toaster), V33 (ra3rn/chess), V36 (A Yahya/hockey), V53 (discpicture/silk scarf), V56 (d3images/ smartphone, tablet); G White: helix

* 注：数字代表本词典英文原文版（*Oxford Advanced Learner's Dictionary* 2015）的页码。

图书在版编目(CIP)数据

牛津高阶英汉双解词典:第9版/(英)霍恩比(A. S. Hornby)原著;李旭影等译. —北京:商务印书馆,2018(2019.4重印)

ISBN 978-7-100-15860-2

Ⅰ. ①牛… Ⅱ. ①霍… ②李… Ⅲ. ①英语—双解词典 ②双解词典—英、汉 Ⅳ. ①H316

中国版本图书馆CIP数据核字(2018)第028847号

NIÚJĪN GĀOJIĒ YĪNGHÀN SHUĀNGJIĚ CÍDIĂN

牛津高阶英汉双解词典(第九版)

出版:商务印书馆

(北京王府井大街36号 邮政编码100710)

牛津大学出版社(中国)有限公司

(香港九龙湾宏远街1号一号九龙39楼)

国内总发行:商务印书馆

中国香港、澳门、台湾地区以及世界其他地区总发行:

牛津大学出版社(中国)有限公司

南京爱德印刷有限公司印刷

ISBN 978-7-100-15860-2

1997年9月第1版	开本880×1230 1/32
2004年8月第2版	印张86¼
2009年4月第3版	印数100 000册
2014年6月第4版	
2018年3月第5版	
2019年4月第202次印刷	

定价:169.00元